Appendix

Budget of the U.S. Government

Fiscal Year 2023

OFFICE OF MANAGEMENT AND BUDGET

THE WHITE HOUSE
WASHINGTON

THE BUDGET DOCUMENTS

Budget of the United States Government, Fiscal Year 2023 contains the Budget Message of the President, information on the President's priorities, and summary tables.

Analytical Perspectives, Budget of the United States Government, Fiscal Year 2023 contains analyses that are designed to highlight specified subject areas or provide other significant presentations of budget data that place the budget in perspective. This volume includes economic and accounting analyses, information on Federal receipts and collections, analyses of Federal spending, information on Federal borrowing and debt, baseline or current services estimates, and other technical presentations.

Supplemental tables and other materials that are part of the Analytical Perspectives volume are available at https://whitehouse.gov/omb/analytical-perspectives/.

Appendix, Budget of the United States Government, Fiscal Year 2023 contains detailed information on the various appropriations and funds that constitute the budget and is designed primarily for the use of the Appropriations Committees. The Appendix contains more detailed financial information on individual programs and appropriation accounts than any of the other budget documents. It includes for each agency: the proposed text of appropriations language; budget schedules for each account; legislative proposals; narrative explanations of each budget account; and proposed general provisions applicable to the appropriations of entire agencies or group of agencies. Information is also provided on certain activities whose transactions are not part of the budget totals.

BUDGET INFORMATION AVAILABLE ONLINE

The President's Budget and supporting materials are available online at https://whitehouse.gov/omb/budget/. This link includes electronic versions of all the budget volumes, supplemental materials that are part of the Analytical Perspectives volume, spreadsheets of many of the budget tables, and a public use budget database. This link also includes Historical Tables that provide data on budget receipts, outlays, surpluses or deficits, Federal debt, and Federal employment over an extended time period, generally from 1940 or earlier to 2027. Also available are links to documents and materials from budgets of prior years.

For more information on access to electronic versions of the budget documents, call (202) 512-1530 in the D.C. area or toll-free (888) 293-6498. To purchase the printed documents call (202) 512-1800.

GENERAL NOTES

1. All years referenced for budget data are fiscal years unless otherwise noted. All years referenced for economic data are calendar years unless otherwise noted.
2. At the time the Budget was prepared, none of the full-year appropriations bills for 2022 have been enacted, therefore, the programs and activities normally provided for in the full-year appropriations bills were operating under a continuing resolution (Public Law 117-43, division A, as amended by Public Law 117-70, division A; Public Law 117-86, division A; and Public Law 117-95). References to 2022 spending in the text and tables reflect the levels provided by the continuing resolution and, if applicable, the following Public Laws which provided additional appropriations to certain accounts in 2022—
   - The Disaster Relief Supplemental Appropriations Act, 2022 (Public Law 117-43, division B);
   - The Afghanistan Supplemental Appropriations Act, 2022 (Public Law 117-43, division C);
   - The Infrastructure Investment and Jobs Appropriations Act (Public Law 117-58, division J); and
   - The Additional Afghanistan Supplemental Appropriations Act, 2022 (Public Law 117-70, division B).
3. The estimates in the 2023 Budget do not reflect the effects of the Ukraine Supplemental Appropriations Act, 2022 (included in Public Law 117-103) due to the late date of enactment.
4. Detail in this document may not add to the totals due to rounding.

U.S. GOVERNMENT PUBLISHING OFFICE, WASHINGTON 2022

For sale by the Superintendent of Documents, U.S. Government Publishing Office
Internet: bookstore.gpo.gov Phone: toll free (866) 512-1800; DC area (202) 512-1800
Fax: (202) 512-2104 Mail: Stop IDCC, Washington, DC 20402-0001

ISBN 978-0-16-095231-9

TABLE OF CONTENTS

Page

Detailed Budget Estimates by Agency:

Explanation of Estimates	1
General Provisions Government-Wide	7
Legislative Branch	11
Judicial Branch	49
Department of Agriculture	63
Department of Commerce	191
Department of Defense—Military Programs	231
Department of Education	327
Department of Energy	367
Department of Health and Human Services	423
Department of Homeland Security	497
Department of Housing and Urban Development	559
Department of the Interior	615
Department of Justice	715
Department of Labor	761
Department of State and Other International Programs	799
Department of Transportation	889
Department of the Treasury	977
Department of Veterans Affairs	1037
Corps of Engineers—Civil Works	1079
Other Defense—Civil Programs	1097
Environmental Protection Agency	1107
Executive Office of the President	1131
General Services Administration	1145
National Aeronautics and Space Administration	1163
National Science Foundation	1173
Office of Personnel Management	1179
Small Business Administration	1191
Social Security Administration	1205
Other Independent Agencies	1215

Other Materials:

Amendments to and Revisions in Budget Authority for 2022	1347
Advance Appropriations	1349
Financing Vehicles and the Board of Governors of the Federal Reserve	1351
Government-Sponsored Enterprises	1353
Index	1359

DETAILED BUDGET ESTIMATES

DETAILED BUDGET ESTIMATES

The Budget *Appendix* contains various tables and schedules in support of the Budget. It includes explanations of the work to be performed and the money needed. It includes the language proposed for enactment by the Congress on each item that requires congressional action in an appropriations bill. It also contains the language proposed for the general provisions of appropriations Acts that apply to entire agencies or groups of agencies. The "Budget Concepts" chapter in the *Analytical Perspectives* volume explains the terms and budget concepts used throughout the Budget.

ARRANGEMENT

The second chapter in the *Appendix* presents general provisions of law that apply to all Government activities (see explanation below). Chapters for the Legislative Branch and the Judiciary follow. These are succeeded by chapters for the Executive Branch. The cabinet departments appear first in alphabetical order and are followed by the larger non-departmental agencies, such as Other Defense—Civil Programs, and the Executive Office of the President. The remaining small agencies are listed under the heading Other Independent Agencies. If the amounts in the individual accounts for other independent agencies are below the million dollar reporting threshold applicable to data in the *Appendix*, the data are consolidated into a single set of schedules under "Other Commissions and Boards." Appropriations language for these agencies is presented individually under the same heading.

A section for a large agency is usually organized by major subordinate organizations within the agency (usually bureaus) or by major program area (such as military personnel in the Department of Defense).

Within each bureau or major program area, accounts usually appear in the following order:
—general fund accounts;
—special fund accounts;
—public enterprise revolving funds;
—intragovernmental revolving funds and management funds;
—credit reform accounts, in the following order: program account, financing account, and liquidating account;
—trust funds; and
—trust revolving funds.

By law, the Old-Age and Survivors Insurance and Disability Insurance trust funds (Social Security) are outside the budget totals. These accounts are presented in the Social Security Administration section. Also, by law, the Postal Service Fund is outside the budget totals. A presentation for the Fund is included in the Other Independent Agencies section.

General provisions are provisions in appropriations Acts that apply, or have the potential to apply, to more than one appropriation. The proposed language for general provisions of appropriations Acts that are applicable to one agency appear at the end of the section for that agency. When they apply only to the appropriations for two or more agencies covered by the Act, they will appear at the end of the section for one of those agencies. The Government-wide general provisions apply to all appropriations Government-wide.

The following table indicates the location of all general provisions. The first column of the table lists the most recently enacted appropriations and the major agencies responsible for programs funded by each Act. The second column provides the location of the general provisions that apply to the agencies listed in the first column. The general provisions that are Government-wide in scope (identified as "Departments, Agencies, and Corporations") contained in the Financial Services and General Government Appropriations Act, appear in a separate chapter following this one. At the time the President's 2023 Budget request was developed, none of the full-year appropriations bills for 2022 had been enacted. Therefore, the programs and activities normally provided for in the full-year appropriations bills were operating under a continuing resolution for 2022 (Division A of Public Law 117–43, as amended). The continuing resolution carried forward the Consolidated Appropriations Act, 2021 (Public Law 116–260).

Appropriations Act	Chapter in which general provisions appear
Agriculture, Rural Development, Food and Drug Administration, and Related Agencies Appropriations Act, P.L. 116–260.	
Department of Agriculture, excluding Forest Service.	Department of Agriculture
Department of Health and Human Services, Food and Drug Administration.	Department of Agriculture
Commerce, Justice, Science, and Related Agencies Appropriations Act, P.L. 116–260.	
Department of Commerce.	Department of Commerce
Department of Justice.	Department of Justice
National Aeronautics and Space Administration.	Department of Commerce
National Science Foundation.	Department of Commerce
Department of Defense Appropriations Act, P.L. 116–260.	Department of Defense
Energy and Water Development and Related Agencies Appropriations Act, P.L. 116–260.	
Department of Energy.	Department of Energy
Corps of Engineers.	Corps of Engineers—Civil Works
Department of the Interior, Bureau of Reclamation.	Department of the Interior
Financial Services and General Government Appropriations Act, P.L. 116–260.	
Department of the Treasury.	Department of the Treasury
District of Columbia.	Other Independent Agencies
Executive Office of the President.	Department of the Treasury
Department of Homeland Security Appropriations Act, P.L. 116–260.	Department of Homeland Security

Appropriations Act	Chapter in which general provisions appear
Department of the Interior, Environment, and Related Agencies Appropriations Act, P.L. 116–260.	
Department of the Interior, excluding Bureau of Reclamation........................	Department of the Interior
Department of Agriculture, Forest Service........................	Department of the Interior
Department of Health and Human Services, Indian Health Service............	Department of the Interior
Environmental Protection Agency........................	Department of the Interior
Departments of Labor, Health and Human Services, and Education, and Related Agencies Appropriations Act, P.L. 116–260.	
Department of Labor........................	Department of Labor
Department of Health and Human Services, excluding Food and Drug Administration, and the Indian Health Service........................	Department of Health and Human Services
Department of Education........................	Department of Education
Social Security Administration........................	Department of Labor
Legislative Branch Appropriations Act, P.L. 116–260........................	Legislative Branch
Military Construction and Veterans Affairs and Related Agencies Appropriations Act, P.L. 116–260.	
Department of Defense, Military Construction........................	Department of Defense
Department of Veterans Affairs........................	Department of Veterans Affairs
Department of State, Foreign Operations, and Related Programs Appropriations Act, P.L. 116–260.	
Department of State........................	Department of State and Other International Programs
Agency for International Development........................	Department of State and Other International Programs
Transportation, Housing and Urban Development, and Related Agencies Appropriations Act, P.L. 116–260.	
Department of Transportation........................	Department of Transportation
Department of Housing and Urban Development........................	Department of Housing and Urban Development

FORM OF DETAILED MATERIAL

APPROPRIATIONS LANGUAGE

The language proposed for inclusion in the 2023 appropriations Acts appears following the account title, and the amounts are stated in dollars. Accounts included in the enacted 2023 appropriations bills are printed in roman type as a base. Bolded brackets enclose material that is proposed for deletion; italic type indicates proposed new language. The citation to the specific appropriations Act from which the basic text of the 2022 language is taken appears at the end of the final language paragraph, printed in italic type within parentheses. If an appropriation is being proposed for the first time for an account assumed to be covered by these bills in 2023 all of the language is printed in italics. An illustration of proposed appropriations language for 2023 follows:

NATIONAL EYE INSTITUTE

For carrying out section 301 and title IV of the PHS Act with respect to eye diseases and visual disorders, $853,355,000.

Note.—A full-year 2022 appropriation for this account was not enacted at the time the budget was prepared; therefore, the budget assumes this account is operating under the Continuing Appropriations Act, 2022 (Division A of Public Law 117–43, as amended). The amounts included for 2022 reflect the annualized level provided by the continuing resolution.

BASIS FOR SCHEDULES

Dollar amounts in *Appendix* schedules are stated in millions, unless otherwise specified.

The 2021 column of the budget presents the actual transactions and balances for that year, as recorded in agency accounts.

For 2022, the regular schedules include the enacted appropriations. They may also include indefinite appropriations on the basis of amounts likely to be required.

The 2023 column of the regular schedules includes proposed appropriations for all programs.

Amounts for proposed new legislation are shown generally in separate schedules, following the regular schedules or in budget sequence in the respective bureau. These schedules are identified as "Legislative proposals, subject to PAYGO" or "Legislative proposals not subject to PAYGO." The term "PAYGO" refers to the "pay-as-you-go" requirements of the Statutory Pay-As-You-Go Act of 2010 (2 U.S.C. 931–39). Appropriations language is included with the regular schedule, but usually not with the separate schedules for proposed legislation. Usually the necessary appropriations language is transmitted later upon enactment of the proposed legislation.

PROGRAM AND FINANCING SCHEDULE

This schedule provides the following information:
—obligations by program activity;
—budgetary resources;
—change in obligated balance; and
—budget authority and outlays, net.

The "Obligations by program activity" section shows obligations for specific activities or projects. The activity structure is developed for each appropriation or fund account to provide a meaningful presentation of information for the program. Where the amounts are significant, this section distinguishes between operating expenses and capital investment and between direct and reimbursable programs. The last entry, "Total new obligations, unexpired accounts" indicates the amount of budgetary resources required to finance the activities of the account.

The "Budgetary resources" section shows the budgetary resources available or estimated to be available to finance the obligations. The resources available for obligation include the start-of-year unobligated balances of prior year's resources that have not expired, new budget authority, and adjusting entries, such as recoveries from prior year obligations. This section provides detailed information on the total new budget authority (gross) available to finance the program. It includes information on the type of budget authority that is available, reductions, and amounts precluded from obligation. It indicates whether the budget authority is discretionary (controlled by appropriations Acts) or mandatory (controlled by other laws).

The "Change in obligated balance" section shows components of the change in obligated balances from the start to the end of the year. The two components of the obligated balance—unpaid obligations and uncollected payments from Federal sources—are presented separately. New obligations are added to the obligations that were incurred in a previous year but not liquidated. Total disbursements to liquidate obligations (outlays, gross) are subtracted from these amounts. Adjusting entries, such as adjustments in expired accounts and recoveries of prior year unpaid obligations, are included as appropriate, resulting in the end-of-year obligated balance.

The "Budget authority and outlays, net" section bridges from gross budget authority and outlays to net budget authority and outlays. The section presents discretionary and mandatory amounts separately and indicates whether the outlays pertain to balances or new authority. It also indicates the amounts to be deducted from gross budget authority and outlays and the resulting net budget authority and outlay amounts. Offsetting collections (cash) and the change in uncollected payments from Federal sources are deducted from gross budget authority; only offsetting collections (cash) are deducted from gross outlays.

A schedule titled "Summary of Budget Authority and Outlays" immediately follows the first program and financing schedule for any account that has additional program and financing schedules for supplemental requests, legislative proposals, or current year cancellation proposals.

NARRATIVE STATEMENT OF PROGRAM AND PERFORMANCE

Narrative statements present briefly the objectives of the program and the work to be financed primarily for 2023. They may include measures of expected performance and describe a relationship to the financial estimates.

SCHEDULE OF OBJECT CLASSIFICATION AND EMPLOYMENT SUMMARY

Object classes reflect the nature of the things or services purchased, regardless of the purpose of the program for which they are used. Object class entry 11.9, "Total personnel compensation" sums the amounts in object classes 11.1 through 11.8. Except for revolving funds, reimbursable obligations are aggregated in a single line and not identified by object class. Amounts for any object class that are below the reporting threshold (i.e., amounts that are $500 thousand or less) are reported together as a single entry. If all of the obligations for an account are in a single object class, the schedule is omitted and the object class code is printed in the Program and Financing Schedule on the "Total new obligations, unexpired accounts" line.

When obligations for personnel compensation are shown in the object classification schedule, an employment summary generally follows the object classification schedule.

Federal civilian employment generally is stated on a full-time equivalent (FTE) basis. It is the total number of hours worked (or to be worked) divided by the number of compensable hours applicable to each fiscal year.

BALANCE SHEETS

Balance sheets are presented for all direct and guaranteed loan liquidating and financing accounts and most Government-sponsored enterprises.

The balance sheets show assets, liabilities, and equity for the fund at the close of each fiscal year. In addition to this information, which is similar to commercial balance sheet data, budget needs also require additional information, such as appropriated capital, which is shown in the equity section. The amounts in the 2020 column are audited.

FEDERAL CREDIT SCHEDULES

Federal credit programs provide benefits to the public in the form of direct loans and loan guarantees. The Federal Credit Reform Act of 1990 (2 U.S.C. 661–661f) requires that the costs of direct and guaranteed loans of a program be calculated on a net present value basis, excluding administrative costs. For most programs, direct loan obligations and loan guarantee commitments cannot be made unless appropriations for the cost have been provided in advance in annual appropriations Acts. Annual limitations on the amount of obligations and commitments may also be enacted in appropriations language. For additional information on Federal Credit Reform Act accounts, see below.

Appropriations for the costs of direct loans and loan guarantees are recorded as budget authority in credit program accounts. The administrative expenses associated with a credit program are also recorded in the program account, but on a cash basis. All cash flows to and from the public arising from direct loan obligations and loan guarantee commitments are recorded in separate financing accounts. The transactions of the financing accounts are not included in the budget totals. Program accounts make subsidy payments, recorded as budget outlays, to the financing accounts at the time of the disbursement of the direct or guaranteed loans.

The transactions associated with direct loan obligations and loan guarantee commitments made prior to 1992 continue to be accounted for on a cash flow basis and are recorded in liquidating accounts. In most cases, the liquidating account is the account that was used for the program prior to the enactment of the new requirements.

Program and Financing schedules (described above) are shown for program, financing, and liquidating accounts. In addition, a Summary of Loan Levels, Subsidy Budget Authority, and Outlays by Program schedule is shown for program accounts. This schedule displays credit program information at the risk category level. Status of Direct Loans and Status of Guaranteed Loans schedules (as applicable) are shown for financing accounts and liquidating accounts. Summary information on Federal credit programs is provided in the chapter titled "Credit and Insurance" in the *Analytical Perspectives* volume of the Budget.

SPECIAL AND TRUST FUND RECEIPTS SCHEDULE

This schedule is printed for special fund and trust fund accounts to show the amount of receipts that are credited to them. It also shows any balances of unappropriated receipts or receipts that are only available for investment or precluded from obligation because of a provision of law, such as a benefit formula or limitation on obligations. When present, it appears after the appropriation language, but before the Program and Financing schedule for the account.

STATUS OF FUNDS SCHEDULE

This schedule reports balances, cash income, and cash outgo for major trust funds and certain other accounts. It also includes outstanding debt for certain funds. When present, it appears after the narrative statement for the account.

GENERAL FUND RECEIPT ACCOUNTS SCHEDULE

This schedule shows the amount of receipts attributed to an agency that are credited to the general fund of the Treasury. It is printed at the end of the presentation for the agency, before any general provisions.

ALLOCATIONS BETWEEN AGENCIES

In some cases, funds appropriated to the President or to an agency are allocated to one or more agencies that help to carry out a program. Obligations incurred under such allocations are included in the data for the account to which the appropriation is made in the allocating agency. The object classification schedule for such accounts identifies the amount of such obligations by performing agency. A note at the end of a bureau or equivalent grouping identifies allocations received from other agencies.

FEDERAL CREDIT REFORM ACT ACCOUNTS

PROGRAM ACCOUNTS

As required by the Federal Credit Reform Act of 1990, this account records, for this program, the subsidy costs associated with the direct loans obligated and loan guarantees committed in 1992 and beyond (including modifications of direct loans or loan guarantees that resulted from obligations or commitments in any year), as well as administrative expenses of this program. The subsidy amounts are estimated on a present value basis; the administrative expenses are recorded on a cash basis.

DIRECT LOAN FINANCING ACCOUNTS

As required by the Federal Credit Reform Act of 1990, this non-budgetary account records all cash flows to and from the Government resulting from direct loans obligated in 1992 and beyond (including modifications of direct loans that resulted from obligations in any year). The amounts in this account are a means of financing and are not included in the budget totals.

GUARANTEED LOAN FINANCING ACCOUNTS

As required by the Federal Credit Reform Act of 1990, this non-budgetary account records all cash flows to and from the Government resulting from loan guarantees committed in 1992 and beyond (including modifications of loan guarantees that resulted from commitments in any year). The amounts in this account are a means of financing and are not included in the budget totals.

BUDGETS FOR OFFICES OF INSPECTOR GENERAL

The "separate statement of the budget estimate" for each Office of Inspector General, referenced in section 6(f)(3)(A) of the Inspector General Act of 1978 ("the Act"; 5 U.S.C. App.), is included in the respective congressional justification for that Office.

BUDGETS NOT SUBJECT TO REVIEW

In accordance with law or established practice, the presentations for the Legislative Branch, the Judiciary, the Milk Market Orders Assessment Fund of the Department of Agriculture, and the International Trade Commission have been included, without review, in the amounts submitted by the agencies.

The budgets of the privately owned Government-sponsored enterprises and the Board of Governors of the Federal Reserve System are not subject to review. Data for these entities are included for information purposes only.

GENERAL PROVISIONS GOVERNMENT-WIDE

GENERAL PROVISIONS GOVERNMENT-WIDE

DEPARTMENTS, AGENCIES, AND CORPORATIONS
(INCLUDING TRANSFER OF FUNDS)

SEC. 701. No department, agency, or instrumentality of the United States receiving appropriated funds under this or any other Act for fiscal year 2023 shall obligate or expend any such funds, unless such department, agency, or instrumentality has in place, and will continue to administer in good faith, a written policy designed to ensure that all of its workplaces are free from the illegal use, possession, or distribution of controlled substances (as defined in the Controlled Substances Act (21 U.S.C. 802)) by the officers and employees of such department, agency, or instrumentality.

SEC. 702. Unless otherwise specifically provided, the maximum amount allowable during the current fiscal year in accordance with subsection 1343(c) of title 31, United States Code, for the purchase of any passenger motor vehicle (exclusive of buses, ambulances, law enforcement vehicles, protective vehicles, and undercover surveillance vehicles), is hereby fixed at $24,934 except station wagons for which the maximum shall be $25,996: Provided, That these limits may be exceeded by not to exceed $7,250 for police-type vehicles: Provided further, That the limits set forth in this section may not be exceeded by more than 5 percent for electric or hybrid vehicles purchased for demonstration under the provisions of the Electric and Hybrid Vehicle Research, Development, and Demonstration Act of 1976: Provided further, That the limits set forth in this section may be exceeded by the incremental cost of clean alternative fuels vehicles acquired pursuant to Public Law 101-549 over the cost of comparable conventionally fueled vehicles: Provided further, That the limits set forth in this section shall not apply to any vehicle that is a commercial item and which operates on alternative fuel, including but not limited to electric, plug-in hybrid electric, and hydrogen fuel cell vehicles.

SEC. 703. Appropriations of the executive departments and independent establishments for the current fiscal year available for expenses of travel, or for the expenses of the activity concerned, are hereby made available for quarters allowances and cost-of-living allowances, in accordance with 5 U.S.C. 5922-5924.

SEC. 704. Unless otherwise specified in law during the current fiscal year, no part of any appropriation contained in this or any other Act shall be used to pay the compensation of any officer or employee of the Government of the United States (including any agency the majority of the stock of which is owned by the Government of the United States) whose post of duty is in the continental United States unless such person: (1) is a citizen of the United States; (2) is a person who is lawfully admitted for permanent residence and is seeking citizenship as outlined in 8 U.S.C. 1324b(a)(3)(B); (3) is a person who is admitted as a refugee under 8 U.S.C. 1157 or is granted asylum under 8 U.S.C. 1158 and has filed a declaration of intention to become a lawful permanent resident and then a citizen when eligible; or (4) is a person who owes allegiance to the United States: Provided, That for purposes of this section, affidavits signed by any such person shall be considered prima facie evidence that the requirements of this section with respect to his or her status are being complied with: Provided further, That for purposes of subsections (2) and (3) such affidavits shall be submitted prior to employment and updated thereafter as necessary: Provided further, That any person making a false affidavit shall be guilty of a felony, and upon conviction, shall be fined no more than $4,000 or imprisoned for not more than 1 year, or both: Provided further, That the above penal clause shall be in addition to, and not in substitution for, any other provisions of existing law: Provided further, That any payment made to any officer or employee contrary to the provisions of this section shall be recoverable in action by the Federal Government: Provided further, That this section shall not apply to any person who is an officer or employee of the Government of the United States on the date of enactment of this Act, or to international broadcasters employed by the Broadcasting Board of Governors, or to temporary employment of translators, or to temporary employment in the field service (not to exceed 60 days) as a result of emergencies: Provided further, That this section does not apply to the employment as Wildland firefighters for not more than 120 days of nonresident aliens employed by the Department of the Interior or the USDA Forest Service pursuant to an agreement with another country.

SEC. 705. Appropriations available to any department or agency during the current fiscal year for necessary expenses, including maintenance or operating expenses, shall also be available for payment to the General Services Administration for charges for space and services and those expenses of renovation and alteration of buildings and facilities which constitute public improvements performed in accordance with the Public Buildings Act of 1959 (73 Stat. 479), the Public Buildings Amendments of 1972 (86 Stat. 216), or other applicable law.

SEC. 706. In addition to funds provided in this or any other Act, all Federal agencies are authorized to receive and use funds resulting from the sale of materials, including Federal records disposed of pursuant to a records schedule recovered through recycling or waste prevention programs. Such funds shall be available until expended for the following purposes:

(1) Acquisition, waste reduction and prevention, and recycling programs as described in Executive Order No. 14057 (December 8, 2021), including any such programs adopted prior to the effective date of the Executive order.

(2) Other Federal agency environmental management programs, including, but not limited to, the development and implementation of hazardous waste management and pollution prevention programs.

(3) Other employee programs as authorized by law or as deemed appropriate by the head of the Federal agency.

SEC. 707. Funds made available by this or any other Act for administrative expenses in the current fiscal year of the corporations and agencies subject to chapter 91 of title 31, United States Code, shall be available, in addition to objects for which such funds are otherwise available, for rent in the District of Columbia; services in accordance with 5 U.S.C. 3109; and the objects specified under this head, all the provisions of which shall be applicable to the expenditure of such funds unless otherwise specified in the Act by which they are made available: Provided, That in the event any functions budgeted as administrative expenses are subsequently transferred to or paid from other funds, the limitations on administrative expenses shall be correspondingly reduced.

SEC. 708. No part of any appropriation contained in this or any other Act shall be available for interagency financing of boards (except Federal Executive Boards), commissions, councils, committees, or similar groups (whether or not they are interagency entities) which do not have a prior and specific statutory approval to receive financial support from more than one agency or instrumentality.

SEC. 709. None of the funds made available pursuant to the provisions of this or any other Act shall be used to implement, administer, or enforce any regulation which has been disapproved pursuant to a joint resolution duly adopted in accordance with the applicable law of the United States.

SEC. 710. During the period in which the head of any department or agency, or any other officer or civilian employee of the Federal Government appointed by the President of the United States, holds office, no funds may be obligated or expended in excess of $5,000 to furnish or redecorate the office of such department head, agency head, officer, or employee, or to purchase furniture or make improvements for any such office, unless advance notice of such furnishing or redecoration is transmitted to the Committees on Appropriations of the House of Representatives and the Senate. For the purposes of this section, the term "office" shall include the entire suite of offices assigned to the individual, as well as any other space used primarily by the individual or the use of which is directly controlled by the individual.

SEC. 711. Notwithstanding 31 U.S.C. 1346, or section 708 of this Act, funds made available for the current fiscal year by this or any other Act shall be available for the interagency funding of national security and emergency preparedness telecommunications initiatives which benefit multiple Federal departments, agencies, or entities, as provided by Executive Order No. 13618 (July 6, 2012).

SEC. 712. (a) None of the funds made available by this or any other Act may be obligated or expended by any department, agency, or other instrumentality of the Federal Government to pay the salaries or expenses of any individual appointed to a position of a confidential or policy-determining character that is excepted from the competitive service under section 3302 of title 5, United States Code, (pursuant to schedule C of subpart C of part 213 of title 5 of the Code of Federal Regulations) unless the head of the applicable department, agency, or other instrumentality employing such schedule C individual certifies to the Director of the Office of Personnel Management that the schedule C position occupied by the individual was not created solely or primarily in order to detail the individual to the White House.

(b) The provisions of this section shall not apply to Federal employees or members of the armed forces detailed to or from an element of the intelligence community (as that term is defined under section 3(4) of the National Security Act of 1947 (50 U.S.C. 3003(4))).

SEC. 713. Except where necessary to prevent unauthorized disclosure of classified or privileged information, no part of any appropriation contained in this or any other Act shall be available for the payment of the salary of any officer or employee of the Federal Government, who—

(1) prohibits or prevents, or attempts or threatens to prohibit or prevent, any other officer or employee of the Federal Government from having any direct oral or written communication or contact with any Member, committee, or subcommittee of the Congress in connection with any matter pertaining to the employment of such other officer or employee or pertaining to the department

or agency of such other officer or employee in any way, irrespective of whether such communication or contact is at the initiative of such other officer or employee or in response to the request or inquiry of such Member, committee, or subcommittee; or

(2) removes, suspends from duty without pay, demotes, reduces in rank, seniority, status, pay, or performance or efficiency rating, denies promotion to, relocates, reassigns, transfers, disciplines, or discriminates in regard to any employment right, entitlement, or benefit, or any term or condition of employment of, any other officer or employee of the Federal Government, or attempts or threatens to commit any of the foregoing actions with respect to such other officer or employee, by reason of any communication or contact of such other officer or employee with any Member, committee, or subcommittee of the Congress as described in paragraph (1).

SEC. 714. None of the funds appropriated by this or any other Act may be used by an agency to provide a Federal employee's home address to any labor organization except when the employee has authorized such disclosure or when such disclosure has been ordered by a court of competent jurisdiction.

SEC. 715. (a) In this section, the term "agency"—
(1) means an Executive agency, as defined under 5 U.S.C. 105; and
(2) includes a military department, as defined under section 102 of such title, the United States Postal Service, and the Postal Regulatory Commission.
(b) Unless authorized in accordance with law or regulations to use such time for other purposes, an employee of an agency shall use official time in an honest effort to perform official duties. An employee not under a leave system, including a Presidential appointee exempted under 5 U.S.C. 6301(2), has an obligation to expend an honest effort and a reasonable proportion of such employee's time in the performance of official duties.

SEC. 716. Notwithstanding 31 U.S.C. 1346 and section 708 of this Act, funds made available for the current fiscal year by this or any other Act to any department or agency, which is a member of the Federal Accounting Standards Advisory Board (FASAB), shall be available to finance an appropriate share of FASAB administrative costs.

SEC. 717. Notwithstanding 31 U.S.C. 1346 and section 708 of this Act, the head of each Executive department and agency is hereby authorized to transfer to or reimburse "General Services Administration, Government-wide Policy" with the approval of the Director of the Office of Management and Budget, funds made available for the current fiscal year by this or any other Act, including rebates from charge card and other contracts: Provided, That these funds shall be administered by the Administrator of General Services to support Government-wide and other multi-agency financial, information technology, procurement, and other management innovations, initiatives, and activities, including improving coordination and reducing duplication, as approved by the Director of the Office of Management and Budget, in consultation with the appropriate interagency and multi-agency groups designated by the Director (including the President's Management Council for overall management improvement initiatives, the Chief Financial Officers Council for financial management initiatives, the Chief Information Officers Council for information technology initiatives, the Chief Human Capital Officers Council for human capital initiatives, the Chief Acquisition Officers Council for procurement initiatives, and the Performance Improvement Council for performance improvement initiatives): Provided further, That the total funds transferred or reimbursed shall not exceed $15,000,000 to improve coordination, reduce duplication, and for other activities related to Federal Government Priority Goals established by 31 U.S.C. 1120, and not to exceed $17,000,000 for Government-Wide innovations, initiatives, and activities: Provided further, That the funds transferred to or for reimbursement of "General Services Administration, Government-wide Policy" during fiscal year 2023 shall remain available for obligation through September 30, 2024: Provided further, That such transfers or reimbursements may only be made after 15 days following notification of the Committees on Appropriations of the House of Representatives and the Senate by the Director of the Office of Management and Budget.

SEC. 718. Notwithstanding any other provision of law, a woman may breastfeed her child at any location in a Federal building or on Federal property, if the woman and her child are otherwise authorized to be present at the location.

SEC. 719. Notwithstanding 31 U.S.C. 1346, or section 708 of this Act, funds made available for the current fiscal year by this or any other Act shall be available for the interagency funding of specific projects, workshops, studies, and similar efforts to carry out the purposes of the National Science and Technology Council (authorized by Executive Order No. 12881), which benefit multiple Federal departments, agencies, or entities: Provided, That the Office of Management and Budget shall provide a report describing the budget of and resources connected with the National Science and Technology Council to the Committees on Appropriations, the House Committee on Science, Space, and Technology, and the Senate Committee on Commerce, Science, and Transportation 90 days after enactment of this Act.

SEC. 720. Any request for proposals, solicitation, grant application, form, notification, press release, or other publications involving the distribution of Federal funds shall comply with any relevant requirements in part 200 of title 2, Code of Federal Regulations: Provided, That this section shall apply to direct payments, formula funds, and grants received by a State receiving Federal funds.

SEC. 721. (a) PROHIBITION OF FEDERAL AGENCY MONITORING OF INDIVIDUALS' INTERNET USE.—None of the funds made available in this or any other Act may be used by any Federal agency—
(1) to collect, review, or create any aggregation of data, derived from any means, that includes any personally identifiable information relating to an individual's access to or use of any Federal Government Internet site of the agency; or
(2) to enter into any agreement with a third party (including another government agency) to collect, review, or obtain any aggregation of data, derived from any means, that includes any personally identifiable information relating to an individual's access to or use of any nongovernmental Internet site.
(b) EXCEPTIONS.—The limitations established in subsection (a) shall not apply to—
(1) any record of aggregate data that does not identify particular persons;
(2) any voluntary submission of personally identifiable information;
(3) any action taken for law enforcement, regulatory, or supervisory purposes, in accordance with applicable law; or
(4) any action described in subsection (a)(1) that is a system security action taken by the operator of an Internet site and is necessarily incident to providing the Internet site services or to protecting the rights or property of the provider of the Internet site.
(c) DEFINITIONS.—For the purposes of this section:
(1) The term "regulatory" means agency actions to implement, interpret or enforce authorities provided in law.
(2) The term "supervisory" means examinations of the agency's supervised institutions, including assessing safety and soundness, overall financial condition, management practices and policies and compliance with applicable standards as provided in law.

SEC. 722. (a) None of the funds appropriated by this Act may be used to enter into or renew a contract which includes a provision providing prescription drug coverage, except where the contract also includes a provision for contraceptive coverage.
(b) Nothing in this section shall apply to a contract with—
(1) any of the following religious plans:
(A) Personal Care's HMO; and
(B) OSF HealthPlans, Inc.; and
(2) any existing or future plan, if the carrier for the plan objects to such coverage on the basis of religious beliefs.
(c) In implementing this section, any plan that enters into or renews a contract under this section may not subject any individual to discrimination on the basis that the individual refuses to prescribe or otherwise provide for contraceptives because such activities would be contrary to the individual's religious beliefs or moral convictions.
(d) Nothing in this section shall be construed to require coverage of abortion or abortion-related services.

SEC. 723. The United States is committed to ensuring the health of its Olympic, Pan American, and Paralympic athletes, and supports the strict adherence to anti-doping in sport through testing, adjudication, education, and research as performed by nationally recognized oversight authorities.

SEC. 724. Notwithstanding any other provision of law, funds appropriated for official travel to Federal departments and agencies may be used by such departments and agencies, if consistent with Office of Management and Budget Circular A-126 regarding official travel for Government personnel, to participate in the fractional aircraft ownership pilot program.

SEC. 725. Notwithstanding any other provision of law, no executive branch agency shall purchase, construct, or lease any additional facilities, except within or contiguous to existing locations, to be used for the purpose of conducting Federal law enforcement training without the advance notification to the Committees on Appropriations of the House of Representatives and the Senate, except that the Federal Law Enforcement Training Center is authorized to obtain the temporary use of additional facilities by lease, contract, or other agreement for training which cannot be accommodated in existing Center facilities.

SEC. 726. Unless otherwise authorized by existing law, none of the funds provided in this or any other Act may be used by an executive branch agency to produce any prepackaged news story intended for broadcast or distribution in the United States, unless the story includes a clear notification within the text or audio of the prepackaged news story that the prepackaged news story was prepared or funded by that executive branch agency.

SEC. 727. (a) IN GENERAL.—None of the funds appropriated or otherwise made available by this or any other Act may be used for any Federal Government contract with any foreign incorporated entity which is treated as an inverted domestic corporation under section 835(b) of the Homeland Security Act of 2002 (6 U.S.C. 395(b)) or any subsidiary of such an entity.

(b) WAIVERS.—

(1) IN GENERAL.—Any Secretary shall waive subsection (a) with respect to any Federal Government contract under the authority of such Secretary if the Secretary determines that the waiver is required in the interest of national security.

(2) REPORT TO CONGRESS.—Any Secretary issuing a waiver under paragraph (1) shall report such issuance to Congress.

(c) EXCEPTION.—This section shall not apply to any Federal Government contract entered into before the date of the enactment of this Act, or to any task order issued pursuant to such contract.

SEC. 728. During fiscal year 2023, for each employee who—

(1) retires under section 8336(d)(2) or 8414(b)(1)(B) of title 5, United States Code; or

(2) retires under any other provision of subchapter III of chapter 83 or chapter 84 of such title 5 and receives a payment as an incentive to separate, the separating agency shall remit to the Civil Service Retirement and Disability Fund an amount equal to the Office of Personnel Management's average unit cost of processing a retirement claim for the preceding fiscal year. Such amounts shall be available until expended to the Office of Personnel Management and shall be deemed to be an administrative expense under section 8348(a)(1)(B) of title 5, United States Code.

SEC. 729. None of the funds made available in this or any other Act may be used to pay for the painting of a portrait of an officer or employee of the Federal Government, including the President, the Vice President, a member of Congress (including a Delegate or a Resident Commissioner to Congress), the head of an executive branch agency (as defined in section 133 of title 41, United States Code), or the head of an office of the legislative branch.

SEC. 730. (a)

(1) Notwithstanding any other provision of law, and except as otherwise provided in this section, no part of any of the funds appropriated for fiscal year 2023, by this or any other Act, may be used to pay any prevailing rate employee described in section 5342(a)(2)(A) of title 5, United States Code—

(A) during the period from the date of expiration of the limitation imposed by the comparable section for the previous fiscal years until the normal effective date of the applicable wage survey adjustment that is to take effect in fiscal year 2023, in an amount that exceeds the rate payable for the applicable grade and step of the applicable wage schedule in accordance with such section; and

(B) during the period consisting of the remainder of fiscal year 2023, in an amount that exceeds, as a result of a wage survey adjustment, the rate payable under subparagraph (A) by more than the sum of—

(i) the percentage adjustment taking effect in fiscal year 2023 under section 5303 of title 5, United States Code, in the rates of pay under the General Schedule; and

(ii) the difference between the overall average percentage of the locality-based comparability payments taking effect in fiscal year 2023 under section 5304 of such title (whether by adjustment or otherwise), and the overall average percentage of such payments which was effective in the previous fiscal year under such section.

(2) Notwithstanding any other provision of law, no prevailing rate employee described in subparagraph (B) or (C) of section 5342(a)(2) of title 5, United States Code, and no employee covered by section 5348 of such title, may be paid during the periods for which paragraph (1) is in effect at a rate that exceeds the rates that would be payable under paragraph (1) were paragraph (1) applicable to such employee.

(3) For the purposes of this subsection, the rates payable to an employee who is covered by this subsection and who is paid from a schedule not in existence on September 30, 2022, shall be determined under regulations prescribed by the Office of Personnel Management.

(4) Notwithstanding any other provision of law, rates of premium pay for employees subject to this subsection may not be changed from the rates in effect on September 30, 2022, except to the extent determined by the Office of Personnel Management to be consistent with the purpose of this subsection.

(5) This subsection shall apply with respect to pay for service performed after September 30, 2022.

(6) For the purpose of administering any provision of law (including any rule or regulation that provides premium pay, retirement, life insurance, or any other employee benefit) that requires any deduction or contribution, or that imposes any requirement or limitation on the basis of a rate of salary or basic pay, the rate of salary or basic pay payable after the application of this subsection shall be treated as the rate of salary or basic pay.

(7) Nothing in this subsection shall be considered to permit or require the payment to any employee covered by this subsection at a rate in excess of the rate that would be payable were this subsection not in effect.

(8) The Office of Personnel Management may provide for exceptions to the limitations imposed by this subsection if the Office determines that such exceptions are necessary to ensure the recruitment or retention of qualified employees.

(b) Notwithstanding subsection (a), the adjustment in rates of basic pay for the statutory pay systems that take place in fiscal year 2023 under sections 5344 and 5348 of title 5, United States Code, shall be—

(1) not less than the percentage received by employees in the same location whose rates of basic pay are adjusted pursuant to the statutory pay systems under sections 5303 and 5304 of title 5, United States Code: Provided, That prevailing rate employees at locations where there are no employees whose pay is increased pursuant to sections 5303 and 5304 of title 5, United States Code, and prevailing rate employees described in section 5343(a)(5) of title 5, United States Code, shall be considered to be located in the pay locality designated as "Rest of United States" pursuant to section 5304 of title 5, United States Code, for purposes of this subsection; and

(2) effective as of the first day of the first applicable pay period beginning after September 30, 2022.

SEC. 731. None of the funds made available by this or any other Act may be used to implement, administer, enforce, or apply the rule entitled "Competitive Area" published by the Office of Personnel Management in the Federal Register on April 15, 2008 (73 Fed. Reg. 20180 et seq.).

SEC. 732. None of the funds appropriated or otherwise made available by this or any other Act may be used to begin or announce a study or public-private competition regarding the conversion to contractor performance of any function performed by Federal employees pursuant to Office of Management and Budget Circular A-76 or any other administrative regulation, directive, or policy.

SEC. 733. (a) None of the funds appropriated or otherwise made available by this or any other Act may be available for a contract, grant, or cooperative agreement with an entity that requires employees or contractors of such entity seeking to report fraud, waste, or abuse to sign internal confidentiality agreements or statements prohibiting or otherwise restricting such employees or contractors from lawfully reporting such waste, fraud, or abuse to a designated investigative or law enforcement representative of a Federal department or agency authorized to receive such information.

(b) The limitation in subsection (a) shall not contravene requirements applicable to Standard Form 312, Form 4414, or any other form issued by a Federal department or agency governing the nondisclosure of classified information.

SEC. 734. (a) No funds appropriated in this or any other Act may be used to implement or enforce the agreements in Standard Forms 312 and 4414 of the Government or any other nondisclosure policy, form, or agreement if such policy, form, or agreement does not contain the following provisions: "These provisions are consistent with and do not supersede, conflict with, or otherwise alter the employee obligations, rights, or liabilities created by existing statute or Executive order relating to (1) classified information, (2) communications to Congress, (3) the reporting to an Inspector General of a violation of any law, rule, or regulation, or mismanagement, a gross waste of funds, an abuse of authority, or a substantial and specific danger to public health or safety, or (4) any other whistleblower protection. The definitions, requirements, obligations, rights, sanctions, and liabilities created by controlling Executive orders and statutory provisions are incorporated into this agreement and are controlling.": Provided, That notwithstanding the preceding provision of this section, a nondisclosure policy form or agreement that is to be executed by a person connected with the conduct of an intelligence or intelligence-related activity, other than an employee or officer of the United States Government, may contain provisions appropriate to the particular activity for which such document is to be used. Such form or agreement shall, at a minimum, require that the person will not disclose any classified information received in the course of such activity unless specifically authorized to do so by the United States Government. Such nondisclosure forms shall also make it clear that they do not bar disclosures to Congress, or to an authorized official of an executive agency or the Department of Justice, that are essential to reporting a substantial violation of law.

(b) A nondisclosure agreement may continue to be implemented and enforced notwithstanding subsection (a) if—

(1) it complies with the requirements for such agreement that were in effect when the agreement was entered into; or

(2) the failure to implement or enforce such agreement or any other nondisclosure policy, form, or agreement would result in the unauthorized disclosure of classified or privileged information.

(c) Except as provided in subsection (b), no funds appropriated in this or any other Act may be used to implement or enforce any agreement entered into during fiscal year 2014 which does not contain substantially similar language to that required in subsection (a).

SEC. 735. None of the funds made available by this or any other Act may be used to enter into a contract, memorandum of understanding, or cooperative agreement with, make a grant to, or provide a loan or loan guarantee to, any corporation that has any unpaid Federal tax liability that has been assessed, for which all judicial and administrative remedies have been exhausted or have lapsed, and that is not being paid in a timely manner pursuant to an agreement with the authority responsible for collecting the tax liability, where the awarding agency is aware of the unpaid tax liability, unless a Federal agency has considered suspension or debarment of the corporation and has made a determination that this further action is not necessary to protect the interests of the Government.

SEC. 736. None of the funds made available by this or any other Act may be used to enter into a contract, memorandum of understanding, or cooperative agreement with, make a grant to, or provide a loan or loan guarantee to, any corporation that was convicted of a felony criminal violation under any Federal law within the preceding 24 months, where the awarding agency is aware of the conviction, unless a Federal agency has considered suspension or debarment of the corporation and has made a determination that this further action is not necessary to protect the interests of the Government.

SEC. 737. (a) During fiscal year 2023, on the date on which a request is made for a transfer of funds in accordance with section 1017 of Public Law 111–203, the Bureau of Consumer Financial Protection shall notify the Committees on Appropriations of the House of Representatives and the Senate, the Committee on Financial Services of the House of Representatives, and the Committee on Banking, Housing, and Urban Affairs of the Senate of such request.

(b) Any notification required by this section shall be made available on the Bureau's public website.

SEC. 738. (a) Notwithstanding any official rate adjusted under section 104 of title 3, United States Code, the rate payable to the Vice President during calendar year 2023 shall be the rate payable to the Vice President on December 31, 2021, by operation of section 748 of division E of Public Law 116–260.

(b) Notwithstanding any official rate adjusted under section 5318 of title 5, United States Code, or any other provision of law, the payable rate during calendar year 2023 for an employee serving in an Executive Schedule position, or in a position for which the rate of pay is fixed by statute at an Executive Schedule rate, shall be the rate payable for the applicable Executive Schedule level on December 31, 2021, by operation of section 748 of division E of Public Law 116–260. Such an employee may not receive a rate increase during calendar year 2023, except as provided in subsection (i).

(c) Notwithstanding section 401 of the Foreign Service Act of 1980 (Public Law 96–465) or any other provision of law, a chief of mission or ambassador at large is subject to subsection (b) in the same manner as other employees who are paid at an Executive Schedule rate.

(d)(1) This subsection applies to—
(A) a noncareer appointee in the Senior Executive Service paid a rate of basic pay at or above the official rate for level IV of the Executive Schedule; or
(B) a limited term appointee or limited emergency appointee in the Senior Executive Service serving under a political appointment and paid a rate of basic pay at or above the official rate for level IV of the Executive Schedule.

(2) Notwithstanding sections 5382 and 5383 of title 5, United States Code, an employee described in paragraph (1) may not receive a pay rate increase during calendar year 2023, except as provided in subsection (i).

(e) Notwithstanding any other provision of law, any employee paid a rate of basic pay (including any locality-based payments under section 5304 of title 5, United States Code, or similar authority) at or above the official rate for level IV of the Executive Schedule who serves under a political appointment may not receive a pay rate increase during calendar year 2023, except as provided in subsection (i). This subsection does not apply to employees in the General Schedule pay system or the Foreign Service pay system, to employees appointed under section 3161 of title 5, United States Code, or to employees in another pay system whose position would be classified at GS-15 or below if chapter 51 of title 5, United States Code, applied to them.

(f) Nothing in subsections (b) through (e) shall prevent employees who do not serve under a political appointment from receiving pay increases as otherwise provided under applicable law.

(g) This section does not apply to an individual who makes an election to retain Senior Executive Service basic pay under section 3392(c) of title 5, United States Code, for such time as that election is in effect.

(h) This section does not apply to an individual who makes an election to retain Senior Foreign Service pay entitlements under section 302(b) of the Foreign Service Act of 1980 (Public Law 96–465) for such time as that election is in effect.

(i) Notwithstanding subsections (b) through (e), an employee in a covered position may receive a pay rate increase upon an authorized movement to a different covered position only if that new position has higher-level duties and a pre-established level or range of pay higher than the level or range for the position held immediately before the movement. Any such increase must be based on the rates of pay and applicable limitations on payable rates of pay in effect on December 31, 2021, by operation of section 748 of division E of Public Law 116–260.

(j) Notwithstanding any other provision of law, for an individual who is newly appointed to a covered position during the period of time subject to this section, the initial pay rate shall be based on the rates of pay and applicable limitations on payable rates of pay in effect on December 31, 2021, by operation of section 748 of division E of Public Law 116–260.

(k) If an employee affected by this section is subject to a biweekly pay period that begins in calendar year 2023 but ends in calendar year 2024, the bar on the employee's receipt of pay rate increases shall apply through the end of that pay period.

(l) For the purpose of this section, the term "covered position" means a position occupied by an employee whose pay is restricted under this section.

(m) This section takes effect on the first day of the first applicable pay period beginning on or after January 1, 2023.

LEGISLATIVE BRANCH

SENATE
Federal Funds

EXPENSE ALLOWANCES

For expense allowances of the Vice President, $20,000; the President Pro Tempore of the Senate, $40,000; Majority Leader of the Senate, $40,000; Minority Leader of the Senate, $40,000; Majority Whip of the Senate, $10,000; Minority Whip of the Senate, $10,000; President Pro Tempore Emeritus, $15,000; Chairmen of the Majority and Minority Conference Committees, $5,000 for each Chairman; and Chairmen of the Majority and Minority Policy Committees, $5,000 for each Chairman; in all, $195,000.

For representation allowances of the Majority and Minority Leaders of the Senate, $15,000 for each such Leader; in all, $30,000.

Note.—A full-year 2022 appropriation for this account was not enacted at the time the Budget was prepared; therefore, the Budget assumes this account is operating under the Continuing Appropriations Act, 2022 (Division A of Public Law 117–43, as amended). The amounts included for 2022 reflect the annualized level provided by the continuing resolution.

SALARIES, OFFICERS AND EMPLOYEES

For compensation of officers, employees, and others as authorized by law, including agency contributions, $257,893,100, which shall be paid from this appropriation as follows:

OFFICE OF THE VICE PRESIDENT

For the Office of the Vice President, $2,907,100.

OFFICE OF THE PRESIDENT PRO TEMPORE

For the Office of the President Pro Tempore, $832,000.

OFFICE OF THE PRESIDENT PRO TEMPORE EMERITUS

For the Office of the President Pro Tempore Emeritus, $359,000.

OFFICES OF THE MAJORITY AND MINORITY LEADERS

For Offices of the Majority and Minority Leaders, $5,996,000.

OFFICES OF THE MAJORITY AND MINORITY WHIPS

For Offices of the Majority and Minority Whips, $3,876,000.

COMMITTEE ON APPROPRIATIONS

For salaries of the Committee on Appropriations, $17,616,000.

CONFERENCE COMMITTEES

For the Conference of the Majority and the Conference of the Minority, at rates of compensation to be fixed by the Chairman of each such committee, $1,891,000 for each such committee; in all, $3,782,000.

OFFICES OF THE SECRETARIES OF THE CONFERENCE OF THE MAJORITY AND THE CONFERENCE OF THE MINORITY

For Offices of the Secretaries of the Conference of the Majority and the Conference of the Minority, $940,000.

POLICY COMMITTEES

For salaries of the Majority Policy Committee and the Minority Policy Committee, $1,931,000 for each such committee; in all, $3,862,000.

OFFICE OF THE CHAPLAIN

For Office of the Chaplain, $588,000.

OFFICE OF THE SECRETARY

For Office of the Secretary, $29,282,000.

OFFICE OF THE SERGEANT AT ARMS AND DOORKEEPER

For Office of the Sergeant at Arms and Doorkeeper, $108,639,000.

OFFICES OF THE SECRETARIES FOR THE MAJORITY AND MINORITY

For Offices of the Secretary for the Majority and the Secretary for the Minority, $2,126,000.

AGENCY CONTRIBUTIONS AND RELATED EXPENSES

For agency contributions for employee benefits, as authorized by law, and related expenses, $77,088,000.

Note.—A full-year 2022 appropriation for this account was not enacted at the time the Budget was prepared; therefore, the Budget assumes this account is operating under the Continuing Appropriations Act, 2022 (Division A of Public Law 117–43, as amended). The amounts included for 2022 reflect the annualized level provided by the continuing resolution.

OFFICE OF THE LEGISLATIVE COUNSEL OF THE SENATE

For salaries and expenses of the Office of the Legislative Counsel of the Senate, $7,781,000.

Note.—A full-year 2022 appropriation for this account was not enacted at the time the Budget was prepared; therefore, the Budget assumes this account is operating under the Continuing Appropriations Act, 2022 (Division A of Public Law 117–43, as amended). The amounts included for 2022 reflect the annualized level provided by the continuing resolution.

OFFICE OF SENATE LEGAL COUNSEL

For salaries and expenses of the Office of Senate Legal Counsel, $1,350,000.

Note.—A full-year 2022 appropriation for this account was not enacted at the time the Budget was prepared; therefore, the Budget assumes this account is operating under the Continuing Appropriations Act, 2022 (Division A of Public Law 117–43, as amended). The amounts included for 2022 reflect the annualized level provided by the continuing resolution.

EXPENSE ALLOWANCES OF THE SECRETARY OF THE SENATE, SERGEANT AT ARMS AND DOORKEEPER OF THE SENATE, AND SECRETARIES FOR THE MAJORITY AND MINORITY OF THE SENATE

For expense allowances of the Secretary of the Senate, $7,500; Sergeant at Arms and Doorkeeper of the Senate, $7,500; Secretary for the Majority of the Senate, $7,500; Secretary for the Minority of the Senate, $7,500; in all, $30,000.

Note.—A full-year 2022 appropriation for this account was not enacted at the time the Budget was prepared; therefore, the Budget assumes this account is operating under the Continuing Appropriations Act, 2022 (Division A of Public Law 117–43, as amended). The amounts included for 2022 reflect the annualized level provided by the continuing resolution.

CONTINGENT EXPENSES OF THE SENATE
INQUIRIES AND INVESTIGATIONS

For expenses of inquiries and investigations ordered by the Senate, or conducted under paragraph 1 of rule XXVI of the Standing Rules of the Senate, section 112 of the Supplemental Appropriations and Rescission Act, 1980 (Public Law 96–304), and Senate Resolution 281, 96th Congress, agreed to March 11, 1980, $145,615,000, of which $14,561,500 shall remain available until September 30, 2025.

Note.—A full-year 2022 appropriation for this account was not enacted at the time the Budget was prepared; therefore, the Budget assumes this account is operating under the Continuing Appropriations Act, 2022 (Division A of Public Law 117–43, as amended). The amounts included for 2022 reflect the annualized level provided by the continuing resolution.

U.S. SENATE CAUCUS ON INTERNATIONAL NARCOTICS CONTROL

For expenses of the United States Senate Caucus on International Narcotics Control, $552,000.

Note.—A full-year 2022 appropriation for this account was not enacted at the time the Budget was prepared; therefore, the Budget assumes this account is operating under the Continuing Appropriations Act, 2022 (Division A of Public Law 117–43, as amended). The amounts included for 2022 reflect the annualized level provided by the continuing resolution.

SECRETARY OF THE SENATE

For expenses of the Office of the Secretary of the Senate, $14,303,000 of which $10,553,000 shall remain available until September 30, 2027 and of which $3,750,000 shall remain available until expended.

Note.—A full-year 2022 appropriation for this account was not enacted at the time the Budget was prepared; therefore, the Budget assumes this account is operating under the Continuing Appropriations Act, 2022 (Division A of Public Law 117–43, as amended). The amounts included for 2022 reflect the annualized level provided by the continuing resolution.

SERGEANT AT ARMS AND DOORKEEPER OF THE SENATE

For expenses of the Office of the Sergeant at Arms and Doorkeeper of the Senate, $170,002,000, of which $165,002,000 shall remain available until September 30, 2027, and of which $5,000,000 shall remain available until expended.

Note.—A full-year 2022 appropriation for this account was not enacted at the time the Budget was prepared; therefore, the Budget assumes this account is operating under the Continuing Appropriations Act, 2022 (Division A of Public Law 117–43, as amended). The amounts included for 2022 reflect the annualized level provided by the continuing resolution.

MISCELLANEOUS ITEMS

For miscellaneous items, $26,213,500 which shall remain available until September 30, 2025.

Note.—A full-year 2022 appropriation for this account was not enacted at the time the Budget was prepared; therefore, the Budget assumes this account is operating under the Continuing Appropriations Act, 2022 (Division A of Public Law 117–43, as amended). The amounts included for 2022 reflect the annualized level provided by the continuing resolution.

SENATORS' OFFICIAL PERSONNEL AND OFFICE EXPENSE ACCOUNT

For Senators' Official Personnel and Office Expense Account, $522,315,000 of which $20,128,950 shall remain available until September 30, 2025 and of which $7,000,000 shall be allocated solely for the purpose of providing financial compensation to Senate interns.

Note.—A full-year 2022 appropriation for this account was not enacted at the time the Budget was prepared; therefore, the Budget assumes this account is operating under the Continuing Appropriations Act, 2022 (Division A of Public Law 117–43, as amended). The amounts included for 2022 reflect the annualized level provided by the continuing resolution.

OFFICIAL MAIL COSTS

For expenses necessary for official mail costs of the Senate, $300,000.

Note.—A full-year 2022 appropriation for this account was not enacted at the time the Budget was prepared; therefore, the Budget assumes this account is operating under the Continuing Appropriations Act, 2022 (Division A of Public Law 117–43, as amended). The amounts included for 2022 reflect the annualized level provided by the continuing resolution.

HOUSE OF REPRESENTATIVES

Federal Funds

SALARIES AND EXPENSES

For salaries and expenses of the House of Representatives, $1,829,474,384, as follows:

HOUSE LEADERSHIP OFFICES

For salaries and expenses, as authorized by law, $34,949,640, including: Office of the Speaker, $10,036,950, including $25,000 for official expenses of the Speaker; Office of the Majority Floor Leader, $3,565,870, including $10,000 for official expenses of the Majority Leader; Office of the Minority Floor Leader, $10,036,950, including $10,000 for official expenses of the Minority Leader; Office of the Majority Whip, including the Chief Deputy Majority Whip, $2,962,080, including $5,000 for official expenses of the Majority Whip; Office of the Minority Whip, including the Chief Deputy Minority Whip, $2,684,990, including $5,000 for official expenses of the Minority Whip; Democratic Caucus, $2,831,400; Republican Conference, $2,831,400: Provided, That such amount for salaries and expenses shall remain available from January 3, 2023 until January 2, 2024.

MEMBERS' REPRESENTATIONAL ALLOWANCES

INCLUDING MEMBERS' CLERK HIRE, OFFICIAL EXPENSES OF MEMBERS, AND OFFICIAL MAIL

For Members' representational allowances, including Members' clerk hire, official expenses, and official mail, $813,120,000.

ALLOWANCE FOR COMPENSATION OF INTERNS IN MEMBER OFFICES

For the allowance established under section 120 of the Legislative Branch Appropriations Act, 2019 (2 U.S.C. 5322a) for the compensation of interns who serve in the offices of Members of the House of Representatives, $15,435,000, to remain available through January 2, 2024: Provided, That notwithstanding section 120(b) of such Act, an office of a Member of the House of Representatives may use not more than $35,000 of the allowance available under this heading during legislative year 2023.

ALLOWANCE FOR COMPENSATION OF INTERNS IN HOUSE LEADERSHIP OFFICES

For the allowance established under section 113 of the Legislative Branch Appropriations Act, 2020 (2 U.S.C. 5106) for the compensation of interns who serve in House leadership offices, $438,000, to remain available through January 2, 2024: Provided, That of the amount provided under this heading, $240,500 shall be available for the compensation of interns who serve in House leadership offices of the majority, to be allocated among such offices by the Speaker of the House of Representatives, and $197,500 shall be available for the compensation of interns who serve in House leadership offices of the minority, to be allocated among such offices by the Minority Floor Leader.

ALLOWANCE FOR COMPENSATION OF INTERNS IN HOUSE STANDING COMMITTEES, SPECIAL AND SELECT OFFICES

For the allowance established under section 113(a)(1) of this Act, for the compensation of interns who serve in offices of standing, special, and select committees (other than the Committee on Appropriations), $1,943,910, to remain available through January 2, 2024: Provided, That of the amount provided under this heading, $971,955 shall be available for the compensation of interns who serve in offices of the majority, and $971,955 shall be available for the compensation of interns who serve in offices of the minority, to be allocated among such offices by the Chair, in consultation with the ranking minority member, of the Committee on House Administration.

ALLOWANCE FOR COMPENSATION OF INTERNS IN HOUSE APPROPRIATION COMMITTEE OFFICES

For the allowance established under section 113(a)(2) of this Act for the compensation of interns who serve in offices of the Committee on Appropriations, $345,584: Provided, That of the amount provided under this heading, $172,792 shall be available for the compensation of interns who serve in offices of the majority, and $172,792 shall be available for the compensation of interns who serve in offices of the minority, to be allocated among such offices by the Chair, in consultation with the ranking minority member, of the Committee on Appropriations.

COMMITTEE EMPLOYEES

STANDING COMMITTEES, SPECIAL AND SELECT

For salaries and expenses of standing committees, special and select, authorized by House resolutions, $182,003,000: Provided, That such amount shall remain available for such salaries and expenses until December 31, 2024, except that $5,800,000 of such amount shall remain available until expended for hearing room renovations.

COMMITTEE ON APPROPRIATIONS

For salaries and expenses of the Committee on Appropriations, $29,917,250, including studies and examinations of executive agencies and temporary personal services for such committee, to be expended in accordance with section 202(b) of the Legislative Reorganization Act of 1946 and to be available for reimbursement to agencies for services performed: Provided, That such amount shall remain available for such salaries and expenses until December 31, 2024.

SALARIES, OFFICERS AND EMPLOYEES

For compensation and expenses of officers and employees, as authorized by law, $322,707,000, including: for salaries and expenses of the Office of the Clerk, including the positions of the Chaplain and the Historian, and including not more than $39,000 for official representation and reception expenses, of which not more than $25,000 is for the Family Room and not more than $6,000 is for the Office of the Chaplain, $40,327,000, of which $9,000,000 shall remain available until expended; for salaries and expenses of the Office of the Sergeant at Arms, including the position of Superintendent of Garages and the Office of Emergency Management, and including not more than $3,000 for official representation and reception expenses, $38,793,000, of which $22,232,000 shall remain available until expended; for salaries and expenses of the Office of the Chief Administrative Officer including not more than $3,000 for official representation and reception expenses, $211,222,000, of which $25,977,000 shall remain available until expended; for salaries and expenses of the Office of Diversity and Inclusion, $3,000,000, of which $1,000,000 shall remain available until expended; for salaries and expenses of the Office of the Whistleblower Ombuds, $1,250,000; for salaries and expenses of the Office of the Inspector General, $5,138,000; for salaries and expenses of the Office of General Counsel, $1,912,000; for salaries and expenses of the Office of the Parliamentarian, including the Parliamentarian, $2,000 for preparing the Digest of Rules, and not more than $1,000 for official representation and reception expenses, $2,184,000; for salaries and expenses of the Office of the Law Revision Counsel of the House,

$3,746,000; for salaries and expenses of the Office of the Legislative Counsel of the House, $13,457,000, of which $2,000,000 shall remain available until expended; for salaries and expenses of the Office of Interparliamentary Affairs, $934,000; for other authorized employees, $744,000.

ALLOWANCES AND EXPENSES

For allowances and expenses as authorized by House resolution or law, $426,615,000, including: supplies, materials, administrative costs and Federal tort claims, $1,555,000; official mail for committees, leadership offices, and administrative offices of the House, $190,000; Government contributions for health, retirement, Social Security, contractor support for actuarial projections, and other applicable employee benefits, $372,368,000, to remain available until March 31, 2024, except that $25,000,000 of such amount shall remain available until expended; salaries and expenses for Business Continuity and Disaster Recovery, $20,841,000, of which $4,776,000 shall remain available until expended; transition activities for new members and staff, $19,225,000, to remain available until expended; Wounded Warrior Program and the Congressional Gold Star Family Fellowship Program, $9,674,000, to remain available until expended; Office of Congressional Ethics, $1,762,000; and miscellaneous items including purchase, exchange, maintenance, repair and operation of House motor vehicles, interparliamentary receptions, and gratuities to heirs of deceased employees of the House, $1,000,000.

HOUSE OF REPRESENTATIVES MODERNIZATION INITIATIVES ACCOUNT

(INCLUDING TRANSFER OF FUNDS)

For the House of Representatives Modernization Initiatives Account established under section 115 of the Legislative Branch Appropriations Act, 2021, $2,000,000, to remain available until expended: Provided, That disbursement from this account is subject to approval of the Committee on Appropriations of the House of Representatives: Provided further, That funds provided in this account shall only be used for initiatives recommended by the Select Committee on Modernization or approved by the Committee on House Administration.

Note.—A full-year 2022 appropriation for this account was not enacted at the time the Budget was prepared; therefore, the Budget assumes this account is operating under the Continuing Appropriations Act, 2022 (Division A of Public Law 117–43, as amended). The amounts included for 2022 reflect the annualized level provided by the continuing resolution.

ADMINISTRATIVE PROVISIONS

REQUIRING AMOUNTS REMAINING IN MEMBERS' REPRESENTATIONAL ALLOWANCES TO BE USED FOR DEFICIT REDUCTION OR TO REDUCE THE FEDERAL DEBT

SEC. 110. (a) Notwithstanding any other provision of law, any amounts appropriated under this Act for "HOUSE OF REPRESENTATIVES—Salaries and Expenses—members' representational allowances" shall be available only for fiscal year 2023. Any amount remaining after all payments are made under such allowances for fiscal year 2023 shall be deposited in the Treasury and used for deficit reduction (or, if there is no Federal budget deficit after all such payments have been made, for reducing the Federal debt, in such manner as the Secretary of the Treasury considers appropriate).

(b) The Committee on House Administration of the House of Representatives shall have authority to prescribe regulations to carry out this section.

(c) As used in this section, the term "Member of the House of Representatives" means a Representative in, or a Delegate or Resident Commissioner to, the Congress.

LIMITATION ON AMOUNT AVAILABLE TO LEASE VEHICLES

SEC. 111. None of the funds made available in this Act may be used by the Chief Administrative Officer of the House of Representatives to make any payments from any Members' Representational Allowance for the leasing of a vehicle, excluding mobile district offices, in an aggregate amount that exceeds $1,000 for the vehicle in any month.

CYBERSECURITY ASSISTANCE FOR HOUSE OF REPRESENTATIVES

SEC. 112. The head of any Federal entity that provides assistance to the House of Representatives in the House's efforts to deter, prevent, mitigate, or remediate cybersecurity risks to, and incidents involving, the information systems of the House shall take all necessary steps to ensure the constitutional integrity of the separate branches of the government at all stages of providing the assistance, including applying minimization procedures to limit the spread or sharing of privileged House and Member information.

ALLOWANCES FOR COMPENSATION OF INTERNS IN HOUSE COMMITTEE OFFICES

SEC. 113. (a) ESTABLISHMENT OF ALLOWANCES. There are established for the House of Representatives the following allowances: (1) An allowance which shall be available for the compensation of interns who serve in offices of a standing, special, or select committee of the House (other than the Committee on Appropriations). (2) An allowance which shall be available for the compensation of interns who serve in offices of the Committee on Appropriations. (b) BENEFIT EXCLUSION. Section 104(b) of the House of Representatives Administrative Reform Technical Corrections Act (2 U.S.C. 5321(b)) shall apply with respect to an intern who is compensated under an allowance under this section in the same manner as such section applies with respect to an intern who is compensated under the Members Representational Allowance. (c) DEFINITIONS. In this section, the term intern, with respect to a committee of the House, has the meaning given such term with respect to a Member of the House of Representatives in section 104(c)(2) of the House of Representatives Administrative Reform Technical Corrections Act (2 U.S.C. 5321(c)(2)). (d) CONFORMING AMENDMENT RELATING TO TRANSFER OF AMOUNTS. Section 101(c)(2) of the Legislative Branch Appropriations Act, 1993 (2 U.S.C. 5507(c)(2)) is amended by inserting after Allowance for Compensation of Interns in Member Offices, the following: Allowance for Compensation of Interns in House Appropriations Committee Offices, Allowance for Compensation of Interns in House Standing, Special and Select Committee Offices,. (e) AUTHORIZATION OF APPROPRIATIONS. There are authorized to be appropriated to carry out this section such sums as may be necessary for fiscal year 2023 and each succeeding fiscal year.

JOINT ITEMS

Federal Funds

JOINT ECONOMIC COMMITTEE

For salaries and expenses of the Joint Economic Committee, $4,283,000, to be disbursed by the Secretary of the Senate.

Note.—A full-year 2022 appropriation for this account was not enacted at the time the Budget was prepared; therefore, the Budget assumes this account is operating under the Continuing Appropriations Act, 2022 (Division A of Public Law 117–43, as amended). The amounts included for 2022 reflect the annualized level provided by the continuing resolution.

JOINT COMMITTEE ON TAXATION

For salaries and expenses of the Joint Committee on Taxation, $12,876,000, to be disbursed by the Chief Administrative Officer of the House of Representatives.

For other joint items, as follows:

Note.—A full-year 2022 appropriation for this account was not enacted at the time the Budget was prepared; therefore, the Budget assumes this account is operating under the Continuing Appropriations Act, 2022 (Division A of Public Law 117–43, as amended). The amounts included for 2022 reflect the annualized level provided by the continuing resolution.

OFFICE OF THE ATTENDING PHYSICIAN

For medical supplies, equipment, and contingent expenses of the emergency rooms, and for the Attending Physician and his assistants, including:

(1) an allowance of $3,500 per month to the Attending Physician;

(2) an allowance of $2,500 per month to the Senior Medical Officer;

(3) an allowance of $900 per month each to three medical officers while on duty in the Office of the Attending Physician;

(4) an allowance of $900 per month to 2 assistants and $900 per month each not to exceed 11 assistants on the basis heretofore provided for such assistants; and

(5) $2,880,000 for reimbursement to the Department of the Navy for expenses incurred for staff and equipment assigned to the Office of the Attending Physician, which shall be advanced and credited to the applicable appropriation or appropriations from which such salaries, allowances, and other expenses are payable and shall be available for all the purposes thereof, $4,181,000, to be disbursed by the Chief Administrative Officer of the House of Representatives.

Note.—A full-year 2022 appropriation for this account was not enacted at the time the Budget was prepared; therefore, the Budget assumes this account is operating under the Continuing Appropriations Act, 2022 (Division A of Public Law 117–43, as amended). The amounts included for 2022 reflect the annualized level provided by the continuing resolution.

OFFICE OF CONGRESSIONAL ACCESSIBILITY SERVICES

SALARIES AND EXPENSES

For salaries and expenses of the Office of Congressional Accessibility Services, $1,702,000, to be disbursed by the Secretary of the Senate.

OFFICE OF CONGRESSIONAL ACCESSIBILITY SERVICES—Continued

Note.—A full-year 2022 appropriation for this account was not enacted at the time the Budget was prepared; therefore, the Budget assumes this account is operating under the Continuing Appropriations Act, 2022 (Division A of Public Law 117–43, as amended). The amounts included for 2022 reflect the annualized level provided by the continuing resolution.

CAPITOL POLICE

Federal Funds

SALARIES

For salaries of employees of the Capitol Police, including overtime, hazardous duty pay, and Government contributions for health, retirement, social security, professional liability insurance, and other applicable employee benefits, $522,280,000 of which overtime shall not exceed $64,912,000 unless the Committee on Appropriations of the House and Senate are notified, to be disbursed by the Chief of the Capitol Police or his designee.

Note.—A full-year 2022 appropriation for this account was not enacted at the time the Budget was prepared; therefore, the Budget assumes this account is operating under the Continuing Appropriations Act, 2022 (Division A of Public Law 117–43, as amended). The amounts included for 2022 reflect the annualized level provided by the continuing resolution.

Program and Financing (in millions of dollars)

Identification code 002–0477–0–1–801		2021 actual	2022 est.	2023 est.
	Obligations by program activity:			
0001	Salaries (Direct)	433	455	522
	Budgetary resources:			
	Unobligated balance:			
1000	Unobligated balance brought forward, Oct 1	6	32	1
1010	Unobligated balance transfer to other accts [002–0476]	–3		
1070	Unobligated balance (total)	3	32	1
	Budget authority:			
	Appropriations, discretionary:			
1100	Appropriation	462	424	522
1930	Total budgetary resources available	465	456	523
	Memorandum (non-add) entries:			
1941	Unexpired unobligated balance, end of year	32	1	1
	Change in obligated balance:			
	Unpaid obligations:			
3000	Unpaid obligations, brought forward, Oct 1	23	40	37
3010	New obligations, unexpired accounts	433	455	522
3011	Obligations ("upward adjustments"), expired accounts	7		
3020	Outlays (gross)	–419	–458	–530
3041	Recoveries of prior year unpaid obligations, expired	–4		
3050	Unpaid obligations, end of year	40	37	29
	Memorandum (non-add) entries:			
3100	Obligated balance, start of year	23	40	37
3200	Obligated balance, end of year	40	37	29
	Budget authority and outlays, net:			
	Discretionary:			
4000	Budget authority, gross	462	424	522
	Outlays, gross:			
4010	Outlays from new discretionary authority	393	390	496
4011	Outlays from discretionary balances	26	68	34
4020	Outlays, gross (total)	419	458	530
4180	Budget authority, net (total)	462	424	522
4190	Outlays, net (total)	419	458	530

Object Classification (in millions of dollars)

Identification code 002–0477–0–1–801		2021 actual	2022 est.	2023 est.
	Direct obligations:			
11.1	Personnel compensation: Full-time permanent	305	319	353
12.1	Civilian personnel benefits	128	136	169
99.9	Total new obligations, unexpired accounts	433	455	522

Employment Summary

Identification code 002–0477–0–1–801		2021 actual	2022 est.	2023 est.
1001	Direct civilian full-time equivalent employment	2,232	2,514	2,693

GENERAL EXPENSES

For necessary expenses of the Capitol Police, including motor vehicles, communications and other equipment, security equipment and installation, uniforms, weapons, supplies, materials, training, medical services, forensic services, stenographic services, personal and professional services, the employee assistance program, the awards program, postage, communication services, travel advances, relocation of instructor and liaison personnel for the Federal Law Enforcement Training Center, and not more than $10,000 to be expended on the certification of the Chief of the Capitol Police in connection with official representation and reception expenses, $185,818,000, to be disbursed by the Chief of the Capitol Police or his designee: Provided, That, notwithstanding any other provision of law, the cost of basic training for the Capitol Police at the Federal Law Enforcement Training Center for fiscal year 2023 shall be paid by the Secretary of Homeland Security from funds available to the Department of Homeland Security.

Note.—A full-year 2022 appropriation for this account was not enacted at the time the Budget was prepared; therefore, the Budget assumes this account is operating under the Continuing Appropriations Act, 2022 (Division A of Public Law 117–43, as amended). The amounts included for 2022 reflect the annualized level provided by the continuing resolution.

Program and Financing (in millions of dollars)

Identification code 002–0476–0–1–801		2021 actual	2022 est.	2023 est.
	Obligations by program activity:			
0001	General Expenses (Direct)	97	106	186
0801	Reimbursable program activity	8	2	1
0900	Total new obligations, unexpired accounts	105	108	187
	Budgetary resources:			
	Unobligated balance:			
1000	Unobligated balance brought forward, Oct 1	19	39	27
1011	Unobligated balance transfer from other acct [002–0477]	3		
1070	Unobligated balance (total)	22	39	27
	Budget authority:			
	Appropriations, discretionary:			
1100	Appropriation	125	91	186
	Spending authority from offsetting collections, discretionary:			
1700	Collected	4	4	2
1701	Change in uncollected payments, Federal sources	1	1	1
1750	Spending auth from offsetting collections, disc (total)	5	5	3
1900	Budget authority (total)	130	96	189
1930	Total budgetary resources available	152	135	216
	Memorandum (non-add) entries:			
1940	Unobligated balance expiring	–8		–1
1941	Unexpired unobligated balance, end of year	39	27	28
	Change in obligated balance:			
	Unpaid obligations:			
3000	Unpaid obligations, brought forward, Oct 1	57	72	41
3010	New obligations, unexpired accounts	105	108	187
3011	Obligations ("upward adjustments"), expired accounts	1		
3020	Outlays (gross)	–85	–139	–152
3041	Recoveries of prior year unpaid obligations, expired	–6		
3050	Unpaid obligations, end of year	72	41	76
	Uncollected payments:			
3060	Uncollected pymts, Fed sources, brought forward, Oct 1		–1	–2
3070	Change in uncollected pymts, Fed sources, unexpired	–1	–1	–1
3090	Uncollected pymts, Fed sources, end of year	–1	–2	–3
	Memorandum (non-add) entries:			
3100	Obligated balance, start of year	57	71	39
3200	Obligated balance, end of year	71	39	73
	Budget authority and outlays, net:			
	Discretionary:			
4000	Budget authority, gross	130	96	189
	Outlays, gross:			
4010	Outlays from new discretionary authority	36	38	113
4011	Outlays from discretionary balances	49	101	39
4020	Outlays, gross (total)	85	139	152

	Offsets against gross budget authority and outlays: Offsetting collections (collected) from:			
4030	Federal sources	−4	−4	−2
	Additional offsets against gross budget authority only:			
4050	Change in uncollected pymts, Fed sources, unexpired	−1	−1	−1
4070	Budget authority, net (discretionary)	125	91	186
4080	Outlays, net (discretionary)	81	135	150
4180	Budget authority, net (total)	125	91	186
4190	Outlays, net (total)	81	135	150

Object Classification (in millions of dollars)

Identification code 002–0476–0–1–801	2021 actual	2022 est.	2023 est.
Direct obligations:			
21.0 Travel and transportation of persons	15	15	23
23.3 Communications, utilities, and miscellaneous charges	3	3	5
25.2 Other services from non-Federal sources	53	62	84
26.0 Supplies and materials	8	8	14
31.0 Equipment	18	18	60
99.0 Direct obligations	97	106	186
99.0 Reimbursable obligations	8	2	1
99.9 Total new obligations, unexpired accounts	105	108	187

SECURITY ENHANCEMENTS

Program and Financing (in millions of dollars)

Identification code 002–0461–0–1–801	2021 actual	2022 est.	2023 est.
Budgetary resources:			
Unobligated balance:			
1000 Unobligated balance brought forward, Oct 1	1	1	1
1930 Total budgetary resources available	1	1	1
Memorandum (non-add) entries:			
1941 Unexpired unobligated balance, end of year	1	1	1
4180 Budget authority, net (total)			
4190 Outlays, net (total)			

UNITED STATES CAPITOL POLICE MUTUAL AID REIMBURSEMENTS

Program and Financing (in millions of dollars)

Identification code 002–0478–0–1–801	2021 actual	2022 est.	2023 est.
Obligations by program activity:			
0001 Direct program activity	9	9	9
0900 Total new obligations, unexpired accounts (object class 25.2)	9	9	9
Budgetary resources:			
Unobligated balance:			
1000 Unobligated balance brought forward, Oct 1		26	17
Budget authority:			
Appropriations, discretionary:			
1100 Appropriation	35		
1930 Total budgetary resources available	35	26	17
Memorandum (non-add) entries:			
1941 Unexpired unobligated balance, end of year	26	17	8
Change in obligated balance:			
Unpaid obligations:			
3010 New obligations, unexpired accounts	9	9	9
3020 Outlays (gross)	−9	−9	−9
Budget authority and outlays, net:			
Discretionary:			
4000 Budget authority, gross	35		
Outlays, gross:			
4010 Outlays from new discretionary authority	9		
4011 Outlays from discretionary balances		9	9
4020 Outlays, gross (total)	9	9	9
4180 Budget authority, net (total)	35		
4190 Outlays, net (total)	9	9	9

ADMINISTRATIVE PROVISIONS

VOLUNTEER CHAPLAIN SERVICES

SEC. 120. (a) ESTABLISHMENT.—*In order to retain qualified personnel, the Chief of the Capitol Police shall have authority to accept unpaid chaplain services whereby volunteers may advise, administer, supervise, or perform professional work involved in a program of spiritual welfare and religious guidance for Capitol Police employees.*

(b) EFFECTIVE DATE.—*This section shall apply with respect to fiscal year 2023 and each succeeding fiscal year.*

OFFICE OF CONGRESSIONAL WORKPLACE RIGHTS

Federal Funds

SALARIES AND EXPENSES

For salaries and expenses necessary for the operation of the Office of Congressional Workplace Rights, $7,500,000, of which $2,000,000 shall remain available until September 30, 2024, and of which not more than $1,000 may be expended on the certification of the Executive Director in connection with official representation and reception expenses.

Note.—A full-year 2022 appropriation for this account was not enacted at the time the Budget was prepared; therefore, the Budget assumes this account is operating under the Continuing Appropriations Act, 2022 (Division A of Public Law 117–43, as amended). The amounts included for 2022 reflect the annualized level provided by the continuing resolution.

Program and Financing (in millions of dollars)

Identification code 009–1600–0–1–801	2021 actual	2022 est.	2023 est.
Obligations by program activity:			
0001 Salaries and Expenses (Direct)	7	8	8
Budgetary resources:			
Unobligated balance:			
1000 Unobligated balance brought forward, Oct 1	1	1	1
Budget authority:			
Appropriations, discretionary:			
1100 Appropriation	8	8	8
1930 Total budgetary resources available	9	9	9
Memorandum (non-add) entries:			
1940 Unobligated balance expiring	−1		
1941 Unexpired unobligated balance, end of year	1	1	1
Change in obligated balance:			
Unpaid obligations:			
3000 Unpaid obligations, brought forward, Oct 1	1	2	
3010 New obligations, unexpired accounts	7	8	8
3020 Outlays (gross)	−6	−10	−8
3050 Unpaid obligations, end of year	2		
Memorandum (non-add) entries:			
3100 Obligated balance, start of year	1	2	
3200 Obligated balance, end of year	2		
Budget authority and outlays, net:			
Discretionary:			
4000 Budget authority, gross	8	8	8
Outlays, gross:			
4010 Outlays from new discretionary authority	5	8	8
4011 Outlays from discretionary balances	1	2	
4020 Outlays, gross (total)	6	10	8
4180 Budget authority, net (total)	8	8	8
4190 Outlays, net (total)	6	10	8

The Congressional Accountability Act (CAA) established an independent Office of Congressional Workplace Rights (OCWR) to apply the rights and protections of the following labor and employment statutes to covered employees within the Legislative Branch: the Fair Labor Standards Act, Title VII of the Civil Rights Act, the Americans with Disabilities Act, the Age Discrimination in Employment Act, the Family and Medical Leave Act, the Occupational Safety and Health Act, the Federal Service Labor Management Relations Act, the Employee Polygraph Protection Act, the Worker Adjustment and Retraining Notification Act, the Rehabilitation

Office of Congressional Workplace Rights—Continued
Federal Funds—Continued

SALARIES AND EXPENSES—Continued

Act, and the Uniformed Services Employment and Reemployment Rights Act. This Act was amended in 1998 to apply the Veterans Employment Opportunities Act and in 2008 to apply the Genetic Information and Nondiscrimination Act. On December 21, 2018, the Congressional Accountability Act of 1995 Reform Act was signed into law expanding the Office's duties and responsibilities, as well as the number of employees covered by the CAA.

The Office of Congressional Workplace Rights administers and ensures the integrity of the neutral dispute resolution process concerning claims that arise under the CAA. The Office also carries out an education and training program for congressional Members, employing offices and congressional employees to assist them in understanding their rights and responsibilities under the CAA.

Object Classification (in millions of dollars)

Identification code 009–1600–0–1–801		2021 actual	2022 est.	2023 est.
	Direct obligations:			
11.1	Personnel compensation: Full-time permanent	5	4	4
12.1	Civilian personnel benefits		1	1
99.0	Direct obligations	5	5	5
99.5	Adjustment for rounding	2	3	3
99.9	Total new obligations, unexpired accounts	7	8	8

Employment Summary

Identification code 009–1600–0–1–801		2021 actual	2022 est.	2023 est.
1001	Direct civilian full-time equivalent employment	31	31	32

AWARDS AND SETTLEMENTS FUNDS

Program and Financing (in millions of dollars)

Identification code 009–1450–0–1–801		2021 actual	2022 est.	2023 est.
	Obligations by program activity:			
0001	Direct program activity	1	1	1
0900	Total new obligations, unexpired accounts (object class 41.0)	1	1	1
	Budgetary resources:			
	Budget authority:			
	Appropriations, discretionary:			
1100	Appropriation	1	1	1
1930	Total budgetary resources available	1	1	1
	Change in obligated balance:			
	Unpaid obligations:			
3010	New obligations, unexpired accounts	1	1	1
3020	Outlays (gross)	–1	–1	–1
	Budget authority and outlays, net:			
	Discretionary:			
4000	Budget authority, gross	1	1	1
	Outlays, gross:			
4010	Outlays from new discretionary authority	1	1	1
4180	Budget authority, net (total)	1	1	1
4190	Outlays, net (total)	1	1	1

Section 415 of the Congressional Accountability Act (CAA) established "an account of the Office in the Treasury of the United States for the payment of awards and settlements under this Act," and further authorized to be appropriated "such sums as may be necessary to pay such awards and settlements." Section 415 stipulated that awards and settlements under the CAA should only be paid from that account, which was to be kept separate from the operating expenses account of the Office of Compliance.

The Legislative Branch Appropriations Acts have appropriated funds for awards and settlements under the CAA by means of the following language:

Such sums as may be necessary are appropriated to the account described in subsection (a) of section 415 of Public Law 104–1 to pay awards and settlements as authorized under such subsection.

CONGRESSIONAL BUDGET OFFICE
Federal Funds

SALARIES AND EXPENSES

For salaries and expenses necessary for operation of the Congressional Budget Office, including not more than $6,000 to be expended on the certification of the Director of the Congressional Budget Office in connection with official representation and reception expenses, $64,637,000.

Note.—A full-year 2022 appropriation for this account was not enacted at the time the Budget was prepared; therefore, the Budget assumes this account is operating under the Continuing Appropriations Act, 2022 (Division A of Public Law 117–43, as amended). The amounts included for 2022 reflect the annualized level provided by the continuing resolution.

Program and Financing (in millions of dollars)

Identification code 008–0100–0–1–801		2021 actual	2022 est.	2023 est.
	Obligations by program activity:			
0001	Salaries and Expenses (Direct)	57	57	65
	Budgetary resources:			
	Budget authority:			
	Appropriations, discretionary:			
1100	Appropriation	57	57	65
1930	Total budgetary resources available	57	57	65
	Change in obligated balance:			
	Unpaid obligations:			
3000	Unpaid obligations, brought forward, Oct 1	5	5	5
3010	New obligations, unexpired accounts	57	57	65
3020	Outlays (gross)	–57	–57	–64
3050	Unpaid obligations, end of year	5	5	6
	Memorandum (non-add) entries:			
3100	Obligated balance, start of year	5	5	5
3200	Obligated balance, end of year	5	5	6
	Budget authority and outlays, net:			
	Discretionary:			
4000	Budget authority, gross	57	57	65
	Outlays, gross:			
4010	Outlays from new discretionary authority	52	51	58
4011	Outlays from discretionary balances	5	6	6
4020	Outlays, gross (total)	57	57	64
4180	Budget authority, net (total)	57	57	65
4190	Outlays, net (total)	57	57	64

The Congressional Budget Office (CBO) was established as a non-partisan office of Congress by Title II of the Congressional Budget and Impoundment Control Act of 1974 (2 U.S.C. 601 et seq.). CBO provides objective economic and budgetary analysis and information to assist the Congress in fulfilling its responsibilities. That information includes: 1) forecasts of the economy; 2) 10-year and long-term federal budget projections; 3) cost estimates, which are required by law for reported bills, showing how federal outlays and revenue would change if legislation was enacted, as well as providing the costs of state, local, tribal, or private sector mandates; and 4) upon request, studies covering every major area of federal policy, including spending programs, the tax code, and budgetary and economic challenges.

Object Classification (in millions of dollars)

Identification code 008–0100–0–1–801		2021 actual	2022 est.	2023 est.
	Direct obligations:			
	Personnel compensation:			
11.1	Full-time permanent	35	35	38
11.3	Other than full-time permanent	1	1	2
11.5	Other personnel compensation	1	1	1
11.9	Total personnel compensation	37	37	41
12.1	Civilian personnel benefits	15	15	17
23.3	Communications, utilities, and miscellaneous charges			1

LEGISLATIVE BRANCH

Architect of the Capitol
Federal Funds   17

		2021 actual	2022 est.	2023 est.
25.1	Advisory and assistance services	1	1	1
25.2	Other services from non-Federal sources	1	1	1
25.7	Operation and maintenance of equipment	2	2	3
26.0	Supplies and materials		1	1
31.0	Equipment	1		
99.0	Direct obligations	57	57	65
99.9	Total new obligations, unexpired accounts	57	57	65

Employment Summary

Identification code 008–0100–0–1–801	2021 actual	2022 est.	2023 est.
1001 Direct civilian full-time equivalent employment	267	275	279

ARCHITECT OF THE CAPITOL

Federal Funds

CAPITAL CONSTRUCTION AND OPERATIONS

For salaries for the Architect of the Capitol, and other personal services, at rates of pay provided by law; for all necessary expenses for surveys and studies, construction, operation, and general and administrative support in connection with facilities and activities under the care of the Architect of the Capitol including the Botanic Garden; electrical substations of the Capitol, Senate and House office buildings, and other facilities under the jurisdiction of the Architect of the Capitol; including furnishings and office equipment; including not more than $5,000 for official reception and representation expenses, to be expended as the Architect of the Capitol may approve; for purchase or exchange, maintenance, and operation of a passenger motor vehicle, $155,843,000, of which $5,000,000 shall remain available until September 30, 2027.

Note.—A full-year 2022 appropriation for this account was not enacted at the time the Budget was prepared; therefore, the Budget assumes this account is operating under the Continuing Appropriations Act, 2022 (Division A of Public Law 117–43, as amended). The amounts included for 2022 reflect the annualized level provided by the continuing resolution.

Program and Financing (in millions of dollars)

Identification code 001–0100–0–1–801		2021 actual	2022 est.	2023 est.
	Obligations by program activity:			
0001	General Administration (Direct)	136	145	154
	Budgetary resources:			
	Unobligated balance:			
1000	Unobligated balance brought forward, Oct 1	3	19	1
1011	Unobligated balance transfer from other acct [001–0123]	1		
1021	Recoveries of prior year unpaid obligations	2		
1070	Unobligated balance (total)	6	19	1
	Budget authority:			
	Appropriations, discretionary:			
1100	Appropriation	149	127	156
	Spending authority from offsetting collections, discretionary:			
1700	Collected	1		
1900	Budget authority (total)	150	127	156
1930	Total budgetary resources available	156	146	157
	Memorandum (non-add) entries:			
1940	Unobligated balance expiring	–1		
1941	Unexpired unobligated balance, end of year	19	1	3
	Change in obligated balance:			
	Unpaid obligations:			
3000	Unpaid obligations, brought forward, Oct 1	39	44	48
3010	New obligations, unexpired accounts	136	145	154
3011	Obligations ("upward adjustments"), expired accounts	6		
3020	Outlays (gross)	–130	–141	–175
3040	Recoveries of prior year unpaid obligations, unexpired	–2		
3041	Recoveries of prior year unpaid obligations, expired	–5		
3050	Unpaid obligations, end of year	44	48	27
	Memorandum (non-add) entries:			
3100	Obligated balance, start of year	39	44	48
3200	Obligated balance, end of year	44	48	27
	Budget authority and outlays, net:			
	Discretionary:			
4000	Budget authority, gross	150	127	156
	Outlays, gross:			
4010	Outlays from new discretionary authority	92	114	140
4011	Outlays from discretionary balances	38	27	35
4020	Outlays, gross (total)	130	141	175
	Offsets against gross budget authority and outlays:			
	Offsetting collections (collected) from:			
4030	Federal sources	–1		
4033	Non-Federal sources	–1		
4040	Offsets against gross budget authority and outlays (total)	–2		
	Additional offsets against gross budget authority only:			
4052	Offsetting collections credited to expired accounts	1		
4070	Budget authority, net (discretionary)	149	127	156
4080	Outlays, net (discretionary)	128	141	175
4180	Budget authority, net (total)	149	127	156
4190	Outlays, net (total)	128	141	175

Object Classification (in millions of dollars)

Identification code 001–0100–0–1–801		2021 actual	2022 est.	2023 est.
	Direct obligations:			
	Personnel compensation:			
11.1	Full-time permanent	48	50	59
11.5	Other personnel compensation	2	2	2
11.9	Total personnel compensation	50	52	61
12.1	Civilian personnel benefits	21	21	24
23.1	Rental payments to GSA	1	1	1
25.1	Advisory and assistance services	22	18	17
25.2	Other services from non-Federal sources		6	6
25.4	Operation and maintenance of facilities	36	41	39
26.0	Supplies and materials	2	2	2
31.0	Equipment	4	4	4
99.9	Total new obligations, unexpired accounts	136	145	154

Employment Summary

Identification code 001–0100–0–1–801	2021 actual	2022 est.	2023 est.
1001 Direct civilian full-time equivalent employment	394	417	458

CAPITOL BUILDING

For all necessary expenses for the maintenance, care and operation of the Capitol, $101,964,000, of which $29,999,000 shall remain available until September 30, 2027, and of which $40,200,000 shall remain available until expended.

Note.—A full-year 2022 appropriation for this account was not enacted at the time the Budget was prepared; therefore, the Budget assumes this account is operating under the Continuing Appropriations Act, 2022 (Division A of Public Law 117–43, as amended). The amounts included for 2022 reflect the annualized level provided by the continuing resolution.

Program and Financing (in millions of dollars)

Identification code 001–0105–0–1–801		2021 actual	2022 est.	2023 est.
	Obligations by program activity:			
0001	Capitol Building (Direct)	55	56	50
	Budgetary resources:			
	Unobligated balance:			
1000	Unobligated balance brought forward, Oct 1	56	37	16
1021	Recoveries of prior year unpaid obligations	1		
1070	Unobligated balance (total)	57	37	16
	Budget authority:			
	Appropriations, discretionary:			
1100	Appropriation	35	35	102
1900	Budget authority (total)	35	35	102
1930	Total budgetary resources available	92	72	118
	Memorandum (non-add) entries:			
1941	Unexpired unobligated balance, end of year	37	16	68
	Change in obligated balance:			
	Unpaid obligations:			
3000	Unpaid obligations, brought forward, Oct 1	18	30	44
3010	New obligations, unexpired accounts	55	56	50
3011	Obligations ("upward adjustments"), expired accounts	2		
3020	Outlays (gross)	–43	–42	–62
3040	Recoveries of prior year unpaid obligations, unexpired	–1		
3041	Recoveries of prior year unpaid obligations, expired	–1		
3050	Unpaid obligations, end of year	30	44	32

Architect of the Capitol—Continued
Federal Funds—Continued

CAPITOL BUILDING—Continued

Program and Financing—Continued

Identification code 001–0105–0–1–801	2021 actual	2022 est.	2023 est.
Memorandum (non-add) entries:			
3100 Obligated balance, start of year	18	30	44
3200 Obligated balance, end of year	30	44	32
Budget authority and outlays, net:			
Discretionary:			
4000 Budget authority, gross	35	35	102
Outlays, gross:			
4010 Outlays from new discretionary authority	25	14	41
4011 Outlays from discretionary balances	18	28	21
4020 Outlays, gross (total)	43	42	62
4180 Budget authority, net (total)	35	35	102
4190 Outlays, net (total)	43	42	62

This presentation includes the Flag Office Revolving fund.

Object Classification (in millions of dollars)

Identification code 001–0105–0–1–801	2021 actual	2022 est.	2023 est.
Direct obligations:			
Personnel compensation:			
11.1 Full-time permanent	17	18	19
11.3 Other than full-time permanent	1	1	1
11.5 Other personnel compensation	2	2	2
11.9 Total personnel compensation	20	21	22
12.1 Civilian personnel benefits	8	8	9
25.1 Advisory and assistance services	2	2	4
25.4 Operation and maintenance of facilities	3	3	3
26.0 Supplies and materials	3	3	3
32.0 Land and structures	19	19	9
99.9 Total new obligations, unexpired accounts	55	56	50

Employment Summary

Identification code 001–0105–0–1–801	2021 actual	2022 est.	2023 est.
1001 Direct civilian full-time equivalent employment	216	221	225

CAPITOL GROUNDS

For all necessary expenses for care and improvement of grounds surrounding the Capitol, the Senate and House office buildings, and the Capitol Power Plant, $16,465,000, of which $2,000,000 shall remain available until September 30, 2027.

Note.—A full-year 2022 appropriation for this account was not enacted at the time the Budget was prepared; therefore, the Budget assumes this account is operating under the Continuing Appropriations Act, 2022 (Division A of Public Law 117–43, as amended). The amounts included for 2022 reflect the annualized level provided by the continuing resolution.

Program and Financing (in millions of dollars)

Identification code 001–0108–0–1–801	2021 actual	2022 est.	2023 est.
Obligations by program activity:			
0001 Capitol Grounds (Direct)	17	20	25
Budgetary resources:			
Unobligated balance:			
1000 Unobligated balance brought forward, Oct 1	14	19	20
1021 Recoveries of prior year unpaid obligations	1		
1070 Unobligated balance (total)	15	19	20
Budget authority:			
Appropriations, discretionary:			
1100 Appropriation	21	21	16
1930 Total budgetary resources available	36	40	36
Memorandum (non-add) entries:			
1941 Unexpired unobligated balance, end of year	19	20	11
Change in obligated balance:			
Unpaid obligations:			
3000 Unpaid obligations, brought forward, Oct 1	5	6	5
3010 New obligations, unexpired accounts	17	20	25
3011 Obligations ("upward adjustments"), expired accounts	1		
3020 Outlays (gross)	–15	–21	–17
3040 Recoveries of prior year unpaid obligations, unexpired	–1		
3041 Recoveries of prior year unpaid obligations, expired	–1		
3050 Unpaid obligations, end of year	6	5	13
Memorandum (non-add) entries:			
3100 Obligated balance, start of year	5	6	5
3200 Obligated balance, end of year	6	5	13
Budget authority and outlays, net:			
Discretionary:			
4000 Budget authority, gross	21	21	16
Outlays, gross:			
4010 Outlays from new discretionary authority	10	15	11
4011 Outlays from discretionary balances	5	6	6
4020 Outlays, gross (total)	15	21	17
4180 Budget authority, net (total)	21	21	16
4190 Outlays, net (total)	15	21	17

Object Classification (in millions of dollars)

Identification code 001–0108–0–1–801	2021 actual	2022 est.	2023 est.
Direct obligations:			
Personnel compensation:			
11.1 Full-time permanent	6	6	6
11.5 Other personnel compensation	1	1	1
11.9 Total personnel compensation	7	7	7
12.1 Civilian personnel benefits	3	3	3
25.1 Advisory and assistance services	3	5	8
25.4 Operation and maintenance of facilities	2	2	2
26.0 Supplies and materials	1	1	1
31.0 Equipment	1	2	4
99.9 Total new obligations, unexpired accounts	17	20	25

Employment Summary

Identification code 001–0108–0–1–801	2021 actual	2022 est.	2023 est.
1001 Direct civilian full-time equivalent employment	72	71	86

SENATE OFFICE BUILDINGS

For all necessary expenses for the maintenance, care and operation of Senate office buildings; and furniture and furnishings to be expended under the control and supervision of the Architect of the Capitol, $150,681,000, of which $35,200,000 shall remain available until September 30, 2027, and of which $38,100,000 shall remain availabile until expended.

Note.—A full-year 2022 appropriation for this account was not enacted at the time the Budget was prepared; therefore, the Budget assumes this account is operating under the Continuing Appropriations Act, 2022 (Division A of Public Law 117–43, as amended). The amounts included for 2022 reflect the annualized level provided by the continuing resolution.

Program and Financing (in millions of dollars)

Identification code 001–0123–0–1–801	2021 actual	2022 est.	2023 est.
Obligations by program activity:			
0001 Senate Office Buildings (Direct)	95	97	104
Budgetary resources:			
Unobligated balance:			
1000 Unobligated balance brought forward, Oct 1	43	39	32
1010 Unobligated balance transfer to other accts [001–0100]	–1		
1021 Recoveries of prior year unpaid obligations	2		
1070 Unobligated balance (total)	44	39	32
Budget authority:			
Appropriations, discretionary:			
1100 Appropriation	90	90	151
1900 Budget authority (total)	90	90	151
1930 Total budgetary resources available	134	129	183
Memorandum (non-add) entries:			
1941 Unexpired unobligated balance, end of year	39	32	79
Change in obligated balance:			
Unpaid obligations:			
3000 Unpaid obligations, brought forward, Oct 1	68	37	42
3010 New obligations, unexpired accounts	95	97	104
3011 Obligations ("upward adjustments"), expired accounts	3		

LEGISLATIVE BRANCH

Architect of the Capitol—Continued
Federal Funds—Continued

19

		2021 actual	2022 est.	2023 est.
3020	Outlays (gross)	−123	−92	−144
3040	Recoveries of prior year unpaid obligations, unexpired	−2		
3041	Recoveries of prior year unpaid obligations, expired	−4		
3050	Unpaid obligations, end of year	37	42	2
	Memorandum (non-add) entries:			
3100	Obligated balance, start of year	68	37	42
3200	Obligated balance, end of year	37	42	2
	Budget authority and outlays, net:			
	Discretionary:			
4000	Budget authority, gross	90	90	151
	Outlays, gross:			
4010	Outlays from new discretionary authority	61	58	97
4011	Outlays from discretionary balances	62	34	47
4020	Outlays, gross (total)	123	92	144
	Offsets against gross budget authority and outlays:			
	Offsetting collections (collected) from:			
4033	Non-Federal sources	−1		
4040	Offsets against gross budget authority and outlays (total)	−1		
	Additional offsets against gross budget authority only:			
4052	Offsetting collections credited to expired accounts	1		
4070	Budget authority, net (discretionary)	90	90	151
4080	Outlays, net (discretionary)	122	92	144
4180	Budget authority, net (total)	90	90	151
4190	Outlays, net (total)	122	92	144

This presentation includes the Senate Restaurant Fund and Senate Wellness Center Fund.

Object Classification (in millions of dollars)

Identification code 001–0123–0–1–801		2021 actual	2022 est.	2023 est.
	Direct obligations:			
	Personnel compensation:			
11.1	Full-time permanent	33	34	35
11.3	Other than full-time permanent	2	2	2
11.5	Other personnel compensation	5	5	5
11.9	Total personnel compensation	40	41	42
12.1	Civilian personnel benefits	17	17	18
23.2	Rental payments to others	8	8	8
25.1	Advisory and assistance services	8	8	10
25.4	Operation and maintenance of facilities	13	14	14
26.0	Supplies and materials	4	4	4
31.0	Equipment	1	1	1
32.0	Land and structures	4	4	7
99.9	Total new obligations, unexpired accounts	95	97	104

Employment Summary

Identification code 001–0123–0–1–801		2021 actual	2022 est.	2023 est.
1001	Direct civilian full-time equivalent employment	479	483	494

HOUSE OFFICE BUILDINGS

(INCLUDING TRANSFER OF FUNDS)

For all necessary expenses for the maintenance, care and operation of the House office buildings, $144,029,000, of which $41,850,000 shall remain available until September 30, 2027, and of which $31,000,000 shall remain available until expended for the restoration and renovation of the Cannon House Office Building: Provided, That of the amount made available under this heading, $9,000,000 shall be derived by transfer from the House Office Building Fund established under section 176(d) of the Continuing Appropriations Act, 2017, as added by section 101(3) of the Further Continuing Appropriation Act, 2017 (Public Law 114–254; 2 U.S.C. 2001 note).

Note.—A full-year 2022 appropriation for this account was not enacted at the time the Budget was prepared; therefore, the Budget assumes this account is operating under the Continuing Appropriations Act, 2022 (Division A of Public Law 117-43, as amended). The amounts included for 2022 reflect the annualized level provided by the continuing resolution.

Program and Financing (in millions of dollars)

Identification code 001–0127–0–1–801		2021 actual	2022 est.	2023 est.
	Obligations by program activity:			
0001	House Office Buildings (Direct)	106	189	98
0801	House Office Buildings (Reimbursable)	9	9	9
0900	Total new obligations, unexpired accounts	115	198	107
	Budgetary resources:			
	Unobligated balance:			
1000	Unobligated balance brought forward, Oct 1	105	129	70
	Budget authority:			
	Appropriations, discretionary:			
1100	Appropriation	130	130	135
	Spending authority from offsetting collections, discretionary:			
1711	Spending authority from offsetting collections transferred from other accounts [001–0137]	9	9	9
1900	Budget authority (total)	139	139	144
1930	Total budgetary resources available	244	268	214
	Memorandum (non-add) entries:			
1941	Unexpired unobligated balance, end of year	129	70	107
	Change in obligated balance:			
	Unpaid obligations:			
3000	Unpaid obligations, brought forward, Oct 1	241	160	186
3010	New obligations, unexpired accounts	115	198	107
3011	Obligations ("upward adjustments"), expired accounts	4		
3020	Outlays (gross)	−196	−172	−144
3041	Recoveries of prior year unpaid obligations, expired	−4		
3050	Unpaid obligations, end of year	160	186	149
	Memorandum (non-add) entries:			
3100	Obligated balance, start of year	241	160	186
3200	Obligated balance, end of year	160	186	149
	Budget authority and outlays, net:			
	Discretionary:			
4000	Budget authority, gross	139	139	144
	Outlays, gross:			
4010	Outlays from new discretionary authority	73	77	79
4011	Outlays from discretionary balances	123	95	65
4020	Outlays, gross (total)	196	172	144
	Offsets against gross budget authority and outlays:			
	Offsetting collections (collected) from:			
4033	Non-Federal sources	−1		
4040	Offsets against gross budget authority and outlays (total)	−1		
	Additional offsets against gross budget authority only:			
4052	Offsetting collections credited to expired accounts	1		
4060	Additional offsets against budget authority only (total)	1		
4070	Budget authority, net (discretionary)	139	139	144
4080	Outlays, net (discretionary)	195	172	144
4180	Budget authority, net (total)	139	139	144
4190	Outlays, net (total)	195	172	144

This presentation includes the House of Representatives Wellness Center Fund.

Object Classification (in millions of dollars)

Identification code 001–0127–0–1–801		2021 actual	2022 est.	2023 est.
	Direct obligations:			
	Personnel compensation:			
11.1	Full-time permanent	29	30	35
11.3	Other than full-time permanent	2	2	2
11.5	Other personnel compensation	6	6	6
11.9	Total personnel compensation	37	38	43
12.1	Civilian personnel benefits	15	15	16
25.1	Advisory and assistance services	17	17	17
25.4	Operation and maintenance of facilities	4	4	4
26.0	Supplies and materials	6	6	6
31.0	Equipment	2	2	2
32.0	Land and structures	25	107	10
99.0	Direct obligations	106	189	98
99.0	Reimbursable obligations	9	9	9
99.9	Total new obligations, unexpired accounts	115	198	107

HOUSE OFFICE BUILDINGS—Continued

Employment Summary

Identification code 001–0127–0–1–801	2021 actual	2022 est.	2023 est.
1001 Direct civilian full-time equivalent employment	525	536	551

HOUSE HISTORIC BUILDINGS REVITALIZATION TRUST FUND

Program and Financing (in millions of dollars)

Identification code 001–1833–0–1–801	2021 actual	2022 est.	2023 est.
Obligations by program activity:			
0001 House Historic Buildings Revitalization Trust Fund (Direct)	1		
0900 Total new obligations, unexpired accounts (object class 32.0)	1		
Budgetary resources:			
Unobligated balance:			
1000 Unobligated balance brought forward, Oct 1	2	1	1
1930 Total budgetary resources available	2	1	1
Memorandum (non-add) entries:			
1941 Unexpired unobligated balance, end of year	1	1	1
Change in obligated balance:			
Unpaid obligations:			
3000 Unpaid obligations, brought forward, Oct 1			1
3010 New obligations, unexpired accounts	1		
3020 Outlays (gross)		–1	
3050 Unpaid obligations, end of year	1		
Memorandum (non-add) entries:			
3100 Obligated balance, start of year			1
3200 Obligated balance, end of year	1		
Budget authority and outlays, net:			
Discretionary:			
Outlays, gross:			
4011 Outlays from discretionary balances		1	
4180 Budget authority, net (total)			
4190 Outlays, net (total)		1	

HOUSE OFFICE BUILDINGS FUND

Program and Financing (in millions of dollars)

Identification code 001–0137–0–1–801	2021 actual	2022 est.	2023 est.
Budgetary resources:			
Budget authority:			
Spending authority from offsetting collections, discretionary:			
1700 Collected	10	8	2
1702 Offsetting collections (previously unavailable)	9	10	13
1710 Spending authority from offsetting collections transferred to other accounts [001–0127]	–9	–9	–9
1724 Spending authority from offsetting collections precluded from obligation (limitation on obligations)	–10	–9	–6
Budget authority and outlays, net:			
Discretionary:			
Offsets against gross budget authority and outlays:			
Offsetting collections (collected) from:			
4030 Federal sources	–10	–8	–2
4180 Budget authority, net (total)	–10	–8	–2
4190 Outlays, net (total)	–10	–8	–2
Memorandum (non-add) entries:			
5090 Unexpired unavailable balance, SOY: Offsetting collections	16	17	16
5092 Unexpired unavailable balance, EOY: Offsetting collections	17	16	9

CAPITOL POWER PLANT

For all necessary expenses for the maintenance, care and operation of the Capitol Power Plant; lighting, heating, power (including the purchase of electrical energy) and water and sewer services for the Capitol, Senate and House office buildings, Library of Congress buildings, and the grounds about the same, Botanic Garden, Senate garage, and air conditioning refrigeration not supplied from plants in any of such buildings; heating the Government Publishing Office and Washington City Post Office, and heating and chilled water for air conditioning for the Supreme Court Building, the Union Station complex, the Thurgood Marshall Federal Judiciary Building and the Folger Shakespeare Library, expenses for which shall be advanced or reimbursed upon request of the Architect of the Capitol and amounts so received shall be deposited into the Treasury to the credit of this appropriation, $170,211,000, of which $76,300,000 shall remain available until September 30, 2027: Provided, That not more than $10,000,000 of the funds credited or to be reimbursed to this appropriation as herein provided shall be available for obligation during fiscal year 2023.

Note.—A full-year 2022 appropriation for this account was not enacted at the time the Budget was prepared; therefore, the Budget assumes this account is operating under the Continuing Appropriations Act, 2022 (Division A of Public Law 117–43, as amended). The amounts included for 2022 reflect the annualized level provided by the continuing resolution.

Program and Financing (in millions of dollars)

Identification code 001–0133–0–1–801	2021 actual	2022 est.	2023 est.
Obligations by program activity:			
0001 Capitol Power Plant (Direct)	108	102	114
0801 Capitol Power Plant (Reimbursable)	9	10	10
0900 Total new obligations, unexpired accounts	117	112	124
Budgetary resources:			
Unobligated balance:			
1000 Unobligated balance brought forward, Oct 1	40	27	23
1010 Unobligated balance transfer to other accts [009–0200]	–3		
1070 Unobligated balance (total)	37	27	23
Budget authority:			
Appropriations, discretionary:			
1100 Appropriation	98	98	170
Spending authority from offsetting collections, discretionary:			
1700 Collected	8	10	10
1701 Change in uncollected payments, Federal sources	1		
1750 Spending auth from offsetting collections, disc (total)	9	10	10
1900 Budget authority (total)	107	108	180
1930 Total budgetary resources available	144	135	203
Memorandum (non-add) entries:			
1941 Unexpired unobligated balance, end of year	27	23	79
Change in obligated balance:			
Unpaid obligations:			
3000 Unpaid obligations, brought forward, Oct 1	53	51	8
3010 New obligations, unexpired accounts	117	112	124
3011 Obligations ("upward adjustments"), expired accounts	2		
3020 Outlays (gross)	–115	–155	–126
3041 Recoveries of prior year unpaid obligations, expired	–6		
3050 Unpaid obligations, end of year	51	8	6
Uncollected payments:			
3060 Uncollected pymts, Fed sources, brought forward, Oct 1	–1	–1	–1
3070 Change in uncollected pymts, Fed sources, unexpired	–1		
3071 Change in uncollected pymts, Fed sources, expired	1		
3090 Uncollected pymts, Fed sources, end of year	–1	–1	–1
Memorandum (non-add) entries:			
3100 Obligated balance, start of year	52	50	7
3200 Obligated balance, end of year	50	7	5
Budget authority and outlays, net:			
Discretionary:			
4000 Budget authority, gross	107	108	180
Outlays, gross:			
4010 Outlays from new discretionary authority	72	84	95
4011 Outlays from discretionary balances	43	71	31
4020 Outlays, gross (total)	115	155	126
Offsets against gross budget authority and outlays:			
Offsetting collections (collected) from:			
4030 Federal sources	–8	–8	–8
4033 Non-Federal sources	–1	–2	–2
4040 Offsets against gross budget authority and outlays (total)	–9	–10	–10
Additional offsets against gross budget authority only:			
4050 Change in uncollected pymts, Fed sources, unexpired	–1		
4052 Offsetting collections credited to expired accounts	1		
4070 Budget authority, net (discretionary)	98	98	170
4080 Outlays, net (discretionary)	106	145	116
4180 Budget authority, net (total)	98	98	170

		2021 actual	2022 est.	2023 est.
4190	Outlays, net (total)	106	145	116

Object Classification (in millions of dollars)

Identification code 001–0133–0–1–801		2021 actual	2022 est.	2023 est.
	Direct obligations:			
	Personnel compensation:			
11.1	Full-time permanent	9	9	11
11.5	Other personnel compensation	1	1	1
11.9	Total personnel compensation	10	10	12
12.1	Civilian personnel benefits	4	4	6
23.3	Communications, utilities, and miscellaneous charges	37	40	42
25.1	Advisory and assistance services	8	8	8
25.4	Operation and maintenance of facilities	32	29	32
26.0	Supplies and materials	1	1	1
32.0	Land and structures	16	10	13
99.0	Direct obligations	108	102	114
99.0	Reimbursable obligations	9	10	10
99.9	Total new obligations, unexpired accounts	117	112	124

Employment Summary

Identification code 001–0133–0–1–801		2021 actual	2022 est.	2023 est.
1001	Direct civilian full-time equivalent employment	82	112	115

LIBRARY BUILDINGS AND GROUNDS

For all necessary expenses for the mechanical and structural maintenance, care and operation of the Library buildings and grounds, $183,520,000, of which $147,300,000 shall remain available until September 30, 2027.

Note.—A full-year 2022 appropriation for this account was not enacted at the time the Budget was prepared; therefore, the Budget assumes this account is operating under the Continuing Appropriations Act, 2022 (Division A of Public Law 117–43, as amended). The amounts included for 2022 reflect the annualized level provided by the continuing resolution.

Program and Financing (in millions of dollars)

Identification code 001–0155–0–1–801		2021 actual	2022 est.	2023 est.
	Obligations by program activity:			
0001	Library Buildings and Grounds (Direct)	46	62	95
0801	Library Buildings and Grounds (Reimbursable)	2	2	2
0900	Total new obligations, unexpired accounts	48	64	97
	Budgetary resources:			
	Unobligated balance:			
1000	Unobligated balance brought forward, Oct 1	71	69	90
1021	Recoveries of prior year unpaid obligations	1		
1070	Unobligated balance (total)	72	69	90
	Budget authority:			
	Appropriations, discretionary:			
1100	Appropriation	83	83	184
1120	Appropriations transferred to other acct [001–0171]	–40		
1160	Appropriation, discretionary (total)	43	83	184
	Spending authority from offsetting collections, discretionary:			
1700	Collected	3	2	2
1900	Budget authority (total)	46	85	186
1930	Total budgetary resources available	118	154	276
	Memorandum (non-add) entries:			
1940	Unobligated balance expiring	–1		
1941	Unexpired unobligated balance, end of year	69	90	179
	Change in obligated balance:			
	Unpaid obligations:			
3000	Unpaid obligations, brought forward, Oct 1	50	32	19
3010	New obligations, unexpired accounts	48	64	97
3011	Obligations ("upward adjustments"), expired accounts	2		
3020	Outlays (gross)	–66	–77	–116
3040	Recoveries of prior year unpaid obligations, unexpired	–1		
3041	Recoveries of prior year unpaid obligations, expired	–1		
3050	Unpaid obligations, end of year	32	19	
	Memorandum (non-add) entries:			
3100	Obligated balance, start of year	50	32	19
3200	Obligated balance, end of year	32	19	
	Budget authority and outlays, net:			
	Discretionary:			
4000	Budget authority, gross	46	85	186
	Outlays, gross:			
4010	Outlays from new discretionary authority	25	34	72
4011	Outlays from discretionary balances	41	43	44
4020	Outlays, gross (total)	66	77	116
	Offsets against gross budget authority and outlays:			
	Offsetting collections (collected) from:			
4030	Federal sources	–3	–2	–2
4033	Non-Federal sources	–1		
4040	Offsets against gross budget authority and outlays (total)	–4	–2	–2
	Additional offsets against gross budget authority only:			
4052	Offsetting collections credited to expired accounts	1		
4070	Budget authority, net (discretionary)	43	83	184
4080	Outlays, net (discretionary)	62	75	114
4180	Budget authority, net (total)	43	83	184
4190	Outlays, net (total)	62	75	114

Object Classification (in millions of dollars)

Identification code 001–0155–0–1–801		2021 actual	2022 est.	2023 est.
	Direct obligations:			
	Personnel compensation:			
11.1	Full-time permanent	17	18	19
11.3	Other than full-time permanent	1	1	1
11.5	Other personnel compensation	2	2	1
11.9	Total personnel compensation	20	21	21
12.1	Civilian personnel benefits	8	8	8
25.1	Advisory and assistance services	5	10	29
25.4	Operation and maintenance of facilities	7	7	8
26.0	Supplies and materials	3	3	4
32.0	Land and structures	3	13	25
99.0	Direct obligations	46	62	95
99.0	Reimbursable obligations	2	2	2
99.9	Total new obligations, unexpired accounts	48	64	97

Employment Summary

Identification code 001–0155–0–1–801		2021 actual	2022 est.	2023 est.
1001	Direct civilian full-time equivalent employment	163	168	179

CAPITOL POLICE BUILDINGS, GROUNDS AND SECURITY

For all necessary expenses for the maintenance, care and operation of buildings, grounds and security enhancements of the United States Capitol Police, wherever located, the Alternate Computing Facility, and Architect of the Capitol security operations, $699,452,000, of which $37,800,000 shall remain available until September 30, 2027, and of which $605,000,000 shall remain available until expended.

Note.—A full-year 2022 appropriation for this account was not enacted at the time the Budget was prepared; therefore, the Budget assumes this account is operating under the Continuing Appropriations Act, 2022 (Division A of Public Law 117–43, as amended). The amounts included for 2022 reflect the annualized level provided by the continuing resolution.

Program and Financing (in millions of dollars)

Identification code 001–0171–0–1–801		2021 actual	2022 est.	2023 est.
	Obligations by program activity:			
0001	Capitol Police Buildings, Grounds, and Security (Direct)	60	350	280
	Budgetary resources:			
	Unobligated balance:			
1000	Unobligated balance brought forward, Oct 1	63	388	84
	Budget authority:			
	Appropriations, discretionary:			
1100	Appropriation	346	46	699
1121	Appropriations transferred from other acct [001–0155]	40		
1160	Appropriation, discretionary (total)	386	46	699
1930	Total budgetary resources available	449	434	783
	Memorandum (non-add) entries:			
1940	Unobligated balance expiring	–1		

CAPITOL POLICE BUILDINGS, GROUNDS AND SECURITY—Continued

Program and Financing—Continued

Identification code 001–0171–0–1–801		2021 actual	2022 est.	2023 est.
1941	Unexpired unobligated balance, end of year	388	84	503
	Change in obligated balance:			
	Unpaid obligations:			
3000	Unpaid obligations, brought forward, Oct 1	16	27	329
3010	New obligations, unexpired accounts	60	350	280
3020	Outlays (gross)	−49	−48	−297
3050	Unpaid obligations, end of year	27	329	312
	Memorandum (non-add) entries:			
3100	Obligated balance, start of year	16	27	329
3200	Obligated balance, end of year	27	329	312
	Budget authority and outlays, net:			
	Discretionary:			
4000	Budget authority, gross	386	46	699
	Outlays, gross:			
4010	Outlays from new discretionary authority	34	23	175
4011	Outlays from discretionary balances	15	25	122
4020	Outlays, gross (total)	49	48	297
4180	Budget authority, net (total)	386	46	699
4190	Outlays, net (total)	49	48	297

Object Classification (in millions of dollars)

Identification code 001–0171–0–1–801		2021 actual	2022 est.	2023 est.
	Direct obligations:			
11.1	Personnel compensation: Full-time permanent	3	3	6
12.1	Civilian personnel benefits	1	1	2
23.2	Rental payments to others	8	8	8
25.1	Advisory and assistance services	6	54	50
25.4	Operation and maintenance of facilities	40	42	50
32.0	Land and structures	2	242	164
99.9	Total new obligations, unexpired accounts	60	350	280

Employment Summary

Identification code 001–0171–0–1–801		2021 actual	2022 est.	2023 est.
1001	Direct civilian full-time equivalent employment	24	28	42

CAPITOL VISITOR CENTER

For all necessary expenses for the operation of the Capitol Visitor Center, $27,692,000.

Note.—A full-year 2022 appropriation for this account was not enacted at the time the Budget was prepared; therefore, the Budget assumes this account is operating under the Continuing Appropriations Act, 2022 (Division A of Public Law 117–43, as amended). The amounts included for 2022 reflect the annualized level provided by the continuing resolution.

Program and Financing (in millions of dollars)

Identification code 001–0161–0–1–801		2021 actual	2022 est.	2023 est.
	Obligations by program activity:			
0001	Capitol Visitor Center (Direct)	25	25	28
	Budgetary resources:			
	Unobligated balance:			
1000	Unobligated balance brought forward, Oct 1	2	2	2
	Budget authority:			
	Appropriations, discretionary:			
1100	Appropriation	25	25	28
1930	Total budgetary resources available	27	27	30
	Memorandum (non-add) entries:			
1941	Unexpired unobligated balance, end of year	2	2	2
	Change in obligated balance:			
	Unpaid obligations:			
3000	Unpaid obligations, brought forward, Oct 1	5	7	5
3010	New obligations, unexpired accounts	25	25	28
3011	Obligations ("upward adjustments"), expired accounts	1		
3020	Outlays (gross)	−23	−27	−27
3041	Recoveries of prior year unpaid obligations, expired	−1		
3050	Unpaid obligations, end of year	7	5	6
	Memorandum (non-add) entries:			
3100	Obligated balance, start of year	5	7	5
3200	Obligated balance, end of year	7	5	6
	Budget authority and outlays, net:			
	Discretionary:			
4000	Budget authority, gross	25	25	28
	Outlays, gross:			
4010	Outlays from new discretionary authority	19	20	22
4011	Outlays from discretionary balances	4	7	5
4020	Outlays, gross (total)	23	27	27
4180	Budget authority, net (total)	25	25	28
4190	Outlays, net (total)	23	27	27

Object Classification (in millions of dollars)

Identification code 001–0161–0–1–801		2021 actual	2022 est.	2023 est.
	Direct obligations:			
	Personnel compensation:			
11.1	Full-time permanent	13	13	15
11.3	Other than full-time permanent	1	1	2
11.9	Total personnel compensation	14	14	17
12.1	Civilian personnel benefits	6	6	7
25.1	Advisory and assistance services	4	4	3
31.0	Equipment	1	1	1
99.9	Total new obligations, unexpired accounts	25	25	28

Employment Summary

Identification code 001–0161–0–1–801		2021 actual	2022 est.	2023 est.
1001	Direct civilian full-time equivalent employment	190	223	229

CAPITOL VISITOR CENTER REVOLVING FUND

Program and Financing (in millions of dollars)

Identification code 001–4296–0–3–801		2021 actual	2022 est.	2023 est.
	Obligations by program activity:			
0801	Capitol Visitor Center Revolving Fund (Reimbursable)	1	2	4
	Budgetary resources:			
	Unobligated balance:			
1000	Unobligated balance brought forward, Oct 1	7	6	5
	Budget authority:			
	Spending authority from offsetting collections, discretionary:			
1700	Collected		1	5
1930	Total budgetary resources available	7	7	10
	Memorandum (non-add) entries:			
1941	Unexpired unobligated balance, end of year	6	5	6
	Change in obligated balance:			
	Unpaid obligations:			
3000	Unpaid obligations, brought forward, Oct 1	14	6	1
3010	New obligations, unexpired accounts	1	2	4
3020	Outlays (gross)	−9	−7	−4
3050	Unpaid obligations, end of year	6	1	1
	Memorandum (non-add) entries:			
3100	Obligated balance, start of year	14	6	1
3200	Obligated balance, end of year	6	1	1
	Budget authority and outlays, net:			
	Discretionary:			
4000	Budget authority, gross		1	5
	Outlays, gross:			
4010	Outlays from new discretionary authority		1	4
4011	Outlays from discretionary balances	9	6	
4020	Outlays, gross (total)	9	7	4
	Offsets against gross budget authority and outlays:			
	Offsetting collections (collected) from:			
4033	Non-Federal sources		−1	−5
4040	Offsets against gross budget authority and outlays (total)		−1	−5
4180	Budget authority, net (total)			

		2021 actual	2022 est.	2023 est.
4190	Outlays, net (total)	9	6	–1

Memorandum (non-add) entries:
| 5000 | Total investments, SOY: Federal securities: Par value | 20 | 12 | 10 |
| 5001 | Total investments, EOY: Federal securities: Par value | 12 | 10 | 8 |

Object Classification (in millions of dollars)

Identification code 001–4296–0–3–801	2021 actual	2022 est.	2023 est.
Reimbursable obligations:			
25.1 Advisory and assistance services	1	2	2
26.0 Supplies and materials	....	....	2
99.9 Total new obligations, unexpired accounts	1	2	4

RECYCLABLE MATERIALS REVOLVING FUND

Program and Financing (in millions of dollars)

Identification code 001–4297–0–3–801	2021 actual	2022 est.	2023 est.
Budgetary resources:			
Unobligated balance:			
1000 Unobligated balance brought forward, Oct 1	1	1	1
1001 Discretionary unobligated balance brought fwd, Oct 1	1	....	....
1930 Total budgetary resources available	1	1	1
Memorandum (non-add) entries:			
1941 Unexpired unobligated balance, end of year	1	1	1
4180 Budget authority, net (total)	....	....	....
4190 Outlays, net (total)	....	....	....

JUDICIARY OFFICE BUILDING DEVELOPMENT AND OPERATIONS FUND

Program and Financing (in millions of dollars)

Identification code 001–4518–0–4–801	2021 actual	2022 est.	2023 est.
Obligations by program activity:			
0801 Operations and Maintenance	24	32	32
Budgetary resources:			
Unobligated balance:			
1000 Unobligated balance brought forward, Oct 1	6	7	6
1021 Recoveries of prior year unpaid obligations	1	....	....
1070 Unobligated balance (total)	7	7	6
Budget authority:			
Borrowing authority, mandatory:			
1400 Borrowing authority	5	17	17
Spending authority from offsetting collections, mandatory:			
1800 Collected	36	31	31
1825 Spending authority from offsetting collections applied to repay debt	–17	–17	–17
1850 Spending auth from offsetting collections, mand (total)	19	14	14
1900 Budget authority (total)	24	31	31
1930 Total budgetary resources available	31	38	37
Memorandum (non-add) entries:			
1941 Unexpired unobligated balance, end of year	7	6	5
Change in obligated balance:			
Unpaid obligations:			
3000 Unpaid obligations, brought forward, Oct 1	29	18	1
3010 New obligations, unexpired accounts	24	32	32
3020 Outlays (gross)	–34	–49	–31
3040 Recoveries of prior year unpaid obligations, unexpired	–1	....	....
3050 Unpaid obligations, end of year	18	1	2
Memorandum (non-add) entries:			
3100 Obligated balance, start of year	29	18	1
3200 Obligated balance, end of year	18	1	2
Budget authority and outlays, net:			
Mandatory:			
4090 Budget authority, gross	24	31	31
Outlays, gross:			
4100 Outlays from new mandatory authority	13	31	31
4101 Outlays from mandatory balances	21	18	....
4110 Outlays, gross (total)	34	49	31
Offsets against gross budget authority and outlays:			
Offsetting collections (collected) from:			
4120 Federal sources	–36	–31	–31
4180 Budget authority, net (total)	–12	....	....
4190 Outlays, net (total)	–2	18	....

Memorandum (non-add) entries:
| 5010 Total investments, SOY: non-Fed securities: Market value | 11 | 11 | .... |
| 5011 Total investments, EOY: non-Fed securities: Market value | 11 | .... | .... |

The Judiciary Office Building Development Act, Public Law 100–480, among other purposes, authorized the Architect of the Capitol to contract for the design and construction of a building adjacent to Union Station in the District of Columbia to be leased to the Judicial Branch of the United States. This schedule reflects the costs associated with the construction and operations and maintenance of the building. Costs of construction were financed by an initial $125 million of Federal agency debt (sales price less unamortized discount) issued in 1989.

Estimates prepared by the Legislative Branch assumed the financial arrangements to be a lease-purchase, which would distribute outlays associated with acquisition of the building over a period of thirty years. However, the arrangements involve Federally guaranteed financing and other characteristics that make them substantively the same as direct Federal construction, financed by direct Federal borrowing.

Estimates shown are consistent with the requirements of the Budget Enforcement Act and are presented with the agreement of the Budget and Appropriations Committees.

Object Classification (in millions of dollars)

Identification code 001–4518–0–4–801	2021 actual	2022 est.	2023 est.
11.1 Reimbursable obligations: Personnel compensation: Full-time permanent	2	2	2
11.9 Total personnel compensation	2	2	2
12.1 Civilian personnel benefits	1	1	1
23.3 Communications, utilities, and miscellaneous charges	3	3	3
25.1 Advisory and assistance services	3	3	3
25.4 Operation and maintenance of facilities	8	14	14
26.0 Supplies and materials	1	1	1
32.0 Land and structures	6	8	8
99.9 Total new obligations, unexpired accounts	24	32	32

Employment Summary

Identification code 001–4518–0–4–801	2021 actual	2022 est.	2023 est.
1001 Direct civilian full-time equivalent employment	15	15	15

ADMINISTRATIVE PROVISIONS

ADMINISTRATIVE PROVISION

NO BONUSES FOR CONTRACTORS BEHIND SCHEDULE OR OVER BUDGET

SEC. 130. *None of the funds made available in this Act for the Architect of the Capitol may be used to make incentive or award payments to contractors for work on contracts or programs for which the contractor is behind schedule or over budget, unless the Architect of the Capitol, or agency-employed designee, determines that any such deviations are due to unforeseeable events, government-driven scope changes, or are not significant within the overall scope of the project and/or program.*

SENATE RESTAURANT EMPLOYEE RETIREMENT INCENTIVES

SEC. 131. *Notwithstanding 2 U.S.C. 4505 (limiting voluntary separation incentives payments to congressional employees), the Architect of the Capitol may make a voluntary separation incentive payment to certain covered individuals under 2 U.S.C. 2051 in an amount not to exceed $2,700,000, subject to the approval of the Senate Committee on Rules and Administration, but no later than September 30, 2022.*

BOTANIC GARDEN

Federal Funds

BOTANIC GARDEN

For all necessary expenses for the maintenance, care and operation of the Botanic Garden and the nurseries, buildings, grounds, and collections; and purchase and exchange, maintenance, repair, and operation of a passenger motor vehicle; all under the direction of the Joint Committee on the Library, $23,560,000, of which $8,200,000 shall remain available until September 30, 2027: Provided, That, of the amount made available under this heading, the Architect of the Capitol may obligate and expend such sums as may be necessary for the maintenance, care and operation of the National Garden established under section 307E of the Legislative Branch Appropriations Act, 1989 (2 U.S.C. 2146), upon vouchers approved by the Architect of the Capitol or a duly authorized designee.

Note.—A full-year 2022 appropriation for this account was not enacted at the time the Budget was prepared; therefore, the Budget assumes this account is operating under the Continuing Appropriations Act, 2022 (Division A of Public Law 117–43, as amended). The amounts included for 2022 reflect the annualized level provided by the continuing resolution.

Program and Financing (in millions of dollars)

Identification code 009–0200–0–1–801	2021 actual	2022 est.	2023 est.
Obligations by program activity:			
0001 Botanic Garden (Direct)	15	19	23
Budgetary resources:			
Unobligated balance:			
1000 Unobligated balance brought forward, Oct 1	8	15	17
1011 Unobligated balance transfer from other acct [001–0133]	3		
1070 Unobligated balance (total)	11	15	17
Budget authority:			
Appropriations, discretionary:			
1100 Appropriation	21	21	24
1930 Total budgetary resources available	32	36	41
Memorandum (non-add) entries:			
1940 Unobligated balance expiring	–2		
1941 Unexpired unobligated balance, end of year	15	17	18
Change in obligated balance:			
Unpaid obligations:			
3000 Unpaid obligations, brought forward, Oct 1	5	6	1
3010 New obligations, unexpired accounts	15	19	23
3011 Obligations ("upward adjustments"), expired accounts	1		
3020 Outlays (gross)	–14	–24	–23
3041 Recoveries of prior year unpaid obligations, expired	–1		
3050 Unpaid obligations, end of year	6	1	1
Memorandum (non-add) entries:			
3100 Obligated balance, start of year	5	6	1
3200 Obligated balance, end of year	6	1	1
Budget authority and outlays, net:			
Discretionary:			
4000 Budget authority, gross	21	21	24
Outlays, gross:			
4010 Outlays from new discretionary authority	10	17	19
4011 Outlays from discretionary balances	4	7	4
4020 Outlays, gross (total)	14	24	23
4180 Budget authority, net (total)	21	21	24
4190 Outlays, net (total)	14	24	23

Object Classification (in millions of dollars)

Identification code 009–0200–0–1–801	2021 actual	2022 est.	2023 est.
11.1 Direct obligations: Personnel compensation: Full-time permanent	6	6	7
11.9 Total personnel compensation	6	6	7
12.1 Civilian personnel benefits	2	2	3
25.1 Advisory and assistance services	1	3	5
25.4 Operation and maintenance of facilities	4	4	4
26.0 Supplies and materials	1	1	1
32.0 Land and structures	1	3	3
99.9 Total new obligations, unexpired accounts	15	19	23

Employment Summary

Identification code 009–0200–0–1–801	2021 actual	2022 est.	2023 est.
1001 Direct civilian full-time equivalent employment	66	76	77

Trust Funds

GIFTS AND DONATIONS

Pursuant to 2 U.S.C. 2146, as amended, the Architect of the Capitol, subject to the direction of the Joint Committee on the Library, is authorized to construct a National Garden and to solicit and accept certain gifts on behalf of the United States Botanic Garden for the purpose of constructing the National Garden, or for the general benefit of the Botanic Garden and the renovation of the Botanic Garden conservatory, to deposit such gift funds in the Treasury of the United States, and, subject to approval in appropriations Acts, to obligate and expend such sums.

LIBRARY OF CONGRESS

Federal Funds

SALARIES AND EXPENSES

For all necessary expenses of the Library of Congress not otherwise provided for, including development and maintenance of the Library's catalogs; custody and custodial care of the Library buildings; information technology services provided centrally; special clothing; cleaning, laundering and repair of uniforms; preservation of motion pictures in the custody of the Library; operation and maintenance of the American Folklife Center in the Library; preparation and distribution of catalog records and other publications of the Library; hire or purchase of one passenger motor vehicle; and expenses of the Library of Congress Trust Fund Board not properly chargeable to the income of any trust fund held by the Board, $586,589,000, and, in addition, amounts credited to this appropriation during fiscal year 2023 under the Act of June 28, 1902 (chapter 1301; 32 Stat. 480; 2 U.S.C. 150), shall remain available until expended: Provided, That of the total amount appropriated, not more than $18,000 may be expended, on the certification of the Librarian of Congress, in connection with official representation and reception expenses, including for the Overseas Field Offices: Provided further, That of the total amount appropriated, $9,945,000 shall remain available until expended for the Teaching with Primary Sources program: Provided further, That of the total amount appropriated, $1,458,000 shall remain available until expended for upgrade of the Legislative Branch Financial Management System: Provided further, That of the total amount appropriated, $250,000 shall remain available until expended for the Surplus Books Program to promote the program and facilitate a greater number of donations to eligible entities across the United States: Provided further, That of the total amount appropriated, $3,976,000 shall remain available until expended for the Veterans History Project to continue digitization efforts of already collected materials, reach a greater number of veterans to record their stories, and promote public access to the Project.

Note.—A full-year 2022 appropriation for this account was not enacted at the time the Budget was prepared; therefore, the Budget assumes this account is operating under the Continuing Appropriations Act, 2022 (Division A of Public Law 117–43, as amended). The amounts included for 2022 reflect the annualized level provided by the continuing resolution.

Program and Financing (in millions of dollars)

Identification code 003–0101–0–1–503	2021 actual	2022 est.	2023 est.
Obligations by program activity:			
0001 Office of the Librarian	45	52	45
0002 Office of the Chief Operating Officer	83	82	100
0003 Library Services	218		
0004 Law Library	16	21	18
0005 Office of the Inspector General	4	4	5
0006 Office of the Chief Information Officer	134	135	168
0007 Library Collections and Services Group	6	9	9
0008 Discovery and Preservation Services		135	150
0009 Researcher and Collections Services		86	92
0799 Total direct obligations	506	524	587
0801 Reimbursable program - Interagency/ Intra-agency	28	40	55
0900 Total new obligations, unexpired accounts	534	564	642

	Budgetary resources:			
	Unobligated balance:			
1000	Unobligated balance brought forward, Oct 1	24	43	43
	Budget authority:			
	Appropriations, discretionary:			
1100	Appropriation	524	524	587
	Spending authority from offsetting collections, discretionary:			
1700	Collected	33	40	55
1900	Budget authority (total)	557	564	642
1930	Total budgetary resources available	581	607	685
	Memorandum (non-add) entries:			
1940	Unobligated balance expiring	–4		
1941	Unexpired unobligated balance, end of year	43	43	43
	Change in obligated balance:			
	Unpaid obligations:			
3000	Unpaid obligations, brought forward, Oct 1	160	168	146
3010	New obligations, unexpired accounts	534	564	642
3011	Obligations ("upward adjustments"), expired accounts	3		
3020	Outlays (gross)	–522	–586	–595
3041	Recoveries of prior year unpaid obligations, expired	–7		
3050	Unpaid obligations, end of year	168	146	193
	Memorandum (non-add) entries:			
3100	Obligated balance, start of year	160	168	146
3200	Obligated balance, end of year	168	146	193
	Budget authority and outlays, net:			
	Discretionary:			
4000	Budget authority, gross	557	564	642
	Outlays, gross:			
4010	Outlays from new discretionary authority	395	428	487
4011	Outlays from discretionary balances	127	158	108
4020	Outlays, gross (total)	522	586	595
	Offsets against gross budget authority and outlays:			
	Offsetting collections (collected) from:			
4030	Federal sources	–30	–40	–55
4033	Non-Federal sources	–4		
4040	Offsets against gross budget authority and outlays (total)	–34	–40	–55
	Additional offsets against gross budget authority only:			
4052	Offsetting collections credited to expired accounts	1		
4070	Budget authority, net (discretionary)	524	524	587
4080	Outlays, net (discretionary)	488	546	540
4180	Budget authority, net (total)	524	524	587
4190	Outlays, net (total)	488	546	540

Office of the Librarian.—The Office of the Librarian provides leadership to the Library, overseeing the implementation and management of the Library's mission to support the Congress in fulfilling its constitutional duties and to further the progress of knowledge and creativity for the benefit of the American people. The Librarian of Congress and the Principal Deputy Librarian of Congress provide executive management to the subordinate Library units, which include the Center for Exhibits and Interpretation, Center for Learning, Literacy and Engagement, Chief Operating Officer, Congressional Research Service, the Library Collections and Services Group, Office of the Chief Information Officer, and the U.S. Copyright Office. The Librarian of Congress chairs the Library's Executive Committee (EC).

Library Collections and Services Group (LCSG).— Library Collections and Services provides oversight for activities of three service units: Discovery & Preservation Services (DPS), Researcher & Collections Services (RCS), the Law Library. LCSG also includes the National Library for the Blind and Print Disabled (NLS) and LCSG Operations. Under the direction of the Deputy Librarian for Library Collections and Services, the group identifies and implements a coordinated vision, leverages systems and expertise, creates economics of scale and improves administrative functions across the group.

In fiscal 2022, within LCSG, Library Services reorganized into two new service units:

Discovery & Preservation Services (DPS).—This new service unit brings together the Acquisitions & Bibliographic Access (ABA) Directorate, the Digital Services Directorate (DSD), and the Preservation Directorate (PRES). Its central charge is to improve user discovery and stewardship by leveraging new metadata, digitization, and preservation workflows as digital and physical collections expand. Among other programs, DPS is home to the Cooperative Acquisitions Program (managed through ABA's six Overseas Offices) and the Surplus Books Program.

Researcher & Collections Services (RCS).—This new service unit brings together in close alignment the Collections Development Office (CDO), Special Collections Directorate (SCD), General & International Collections Directorate (ICD), and the National Audio-Visual Conservation Center (NAVCC). As an organization of visiting scholars that uses the collections and creates new knowledge, the John W. Kluge Center also joins this unit. RCS's central charge is to build the national collection, share the collections, and provide services to all users. Among other programs, RCS is home to the National Audio Visual Conservation Center, the Veterans History Project, the National Digital Newspaper Program, and the Congressional-Cartography Program.

Law Library.—The Law Library of Congress (Law Library) is the world's largest law and legislative library. Its primary mission is to provide the United States Congress, Executive Branch agencies, federal courts, the legal community, and others with legal research and/or reference services in U.S., foreign, international, and comparative law. The Law Library's core research capacity includes foreign and U.S. trained attorneys and librarians. Reference staff and foreign legal specialists utilize the Law Library's unparalleled collection of domestic, foreign and international legal materials, from more than 240 foreign and international jurisdictions. The collection consists of authoritative legal sources in original languages, with nearly 3 million volumes and 3 million pieces of microfiche. The Law Library acquires, maintains, organizes, preserves, and provides access to a comprehensive legal collection in both print and digital formats, and draws on technology to make the collection accessible through various systems and online interfaces. The Law Library is a key player in developing and maintaining the currency of content in Congress.gov, the authoritative legislative information system for the Congress and the public. The Law Library also develops electronic information products that provide access to historical and contemporary legal legislative, administrative, and judicial documents. The Law Library creates research and collection guides focusing on legal research techniques, issues, and events. Ensuring accuracy, authenticity, authoritativeness, and comprehensiveness of legal documents is a challenge the Law Library manages on a daily basis, enabling the highest quality of objective research and maintaining a legal collection encompassing countries and regions of strategic importance to the Congress.

Office of the Inspector General.—The Office of the Inspector General (OIG) functions within the Library of Congress as an independent, objective office with authority to: conduct and supervise audits and investigations relating to the Library; provide leadership and coordination in recommending policies and operational changes that promote economy, efficiency, and effectiveness; and inform the Librarian of Congress and the Congress fully about problems and deficiencies related to the administration and operations of the Library. The OIG specializes in auditing and analyzing the design of and compliance with the Library's systems of internal control, with special emphasis on deterring waste, fraud, and abuse. In its investigative capacity, it performs administrative, civil, and criminal investigations conerning fraud, conflict of interest, and other misconduct involving Library employees, contractors, and grantees.

Office of the Chief Information Officer (OCIO).—The IT vision of the Library of Congress is to deliver continuous uninterrupted digital services and enable the Congress and the American people to make maximal use of the Library's resources and services. The Office of the Chief Information Officer (OCIO), via the IT domain, manages IT as a strategic resource across the Library by providing the IT strategic direction, leadership, services, and capabilities that deliver the IT vision of the Library of Congress. OCIO's goals are to provide strategic direction and leadership for IT, deliver business-driven capabilities, improve IT investment management, and strengthen protection for IT systems and information. OCIO will continue to optimize existing Information Technology (IT) resources and integrate

Library of Congress—Continued
Federal Funds—Continued

SALARIES AND EXPENSES—Continued

advanced technology to support the daily work for the Congress, the creative community, the Library's service units, and the public.

Office of the Chief Operating Officer (OCOO).— OCOO provides comprehensive services, manages institutional programs, and overseas regulatory compliance in the areas of financial administration; human capital; contracting; facilities, safety and health; asset management; personnel security and emergency preparedness; and programs that deliver fee-based services.

Object Classification (in millions of dollars)

Identification code 003–0101–0–1–503		2021 actual	2022 est.	2023 est.
	Direct obligations:			
	Personnel compensation:			
11.1	Full-time permanent	227	238	260
11.3	Other than full-time permanent	3	3	4
11.5	Other personnel compensation	3	3	3
11.8	Special personal services payments			1
11.9	Total personnel compensation	233	244	268
12.1	Civilian personnel benefits	81	82	93
22.0	Transportation of things		1	1
23.1	Rental payments to GSA	1	1	1
23.2	Rental payments to others	2	2	2
23.3	Communications, utilities, and miscellaneous charges	15	16	25
24.0	Printing and reproduction	2	6	3
25.1	Advisory and assistance services	51	53	69
25.2	Other services from non-Federal sources	20	23	24
25.3	Other goods and services from Federal sources	20	15	17
25.4	Operation and maintenance of facilities	10	11	12
25.7	Operation and maintenance of equipment	17	19	20
26.0	Supplies and materials	2	8	3
31.0	Equipment	40	35	38
41.0	Grants, subsidies, and contributions	9	8	8
99.0	Direct obligations	503	524	584
99.0	Reimbursable obligations	28	39	55
99.5	Adjustment for rounding	3	1	3
99.9	Total new obligations, unexpired accounts	534	564	642

Employment Summary

Identification code 003–0101–0–1–503	2021 actual	2022 est.	2023 est.
1001 Direct civilian full-time equivalent employment	2,073	2,206	2,272
2001 Reimbursable civilian full-time equivalent employment	20	12	61

LIBRARY OF CONGRESS NATIONAL COLLECTION STEWARDSHIP FUND

Program and Financing (in millions of dollars)

Identification code 003–0103–0–1–503		2021 actual	2022 est.	2023 est.
	Budgetary resources:			
	Unobligated balance:			
1000	Unobligated balance brought forward, Oct 1	4	7	7
1012	Unobligated balance transfers between expired and unexpired accounts	3		
1070	Unobligated balance (total)	7	7	7
1930	Total budgetary resources available	7	7	7
	Memorandum (non-add) entries:			
1941	Unexpired unobligated balance, end of year	7	7	7
4180	Budget authority, net (total)			
4190	Outlays, net (total)			

Congress established the Library of Congress National Collection Stewardship Fund (NCSF) in May 2017 as part of the Consolidated Appropriations Act of 2017. An account for the fund was established in the Treasury of the United States in May 2017, following enactment. The Library of Congress NCSF may be used directly for the purpose of preparing collection materials of the Library of Congress for long-term storage, and the Librarian may transfer amounts to the Architect of the Capitol (AOC) for the purpose of designing, constructing, altering, upgrading, and equipping collections preservation and storage facilities for the Library of Congress, or for the purpose of acquiring real property by lease for the preservation and storage of Library of Congress collections. The NCSF provides direct assistance in funding these projects not by replacing current appropriations streams of funding but by accumulating funding over several appropriations cycles supplementing specifically appropriated program expenses. The NCSF consists of such amounts as may be transferred by the Librarian from available amounts appropriated for any fiscal year (starting with fiscal year 2017 and each succeeding fiscal year) for the Library of Congress under the heading Salaries and Expenses. Any amounts in the NCSF shall remain available until expended for the stated purpose of the fund.

COPYRIGHT OFFICE
SALARIES AND EXPENSES

For all necessary expenses of the Copyright Office, $100,674,000, of which not more than $39,702,000, to remain available until expended, shall be derived from collections credited to this appropriation during fiscal year 2023 under sections 708(d) and 1316 of title 17, United States Code: Provided, That the Copyright Office may not obligate or expend any funds derived from collections under such section in excess of the amount authorized for obligation or expenditure in appropriations Acts: Provided further, That not more than $6,969,000$7,210,000 shall be derived from collections during fiscal year 2023 under sections 111(d)(2), 119(b)(3), 803(e), and 1005 of such title: Provided further, That the total amount available for obligation shall be reduced by the amount by which collections are less than $46,912,000: Provided further, That of the funds provided under this heading, not less than $17,100,000 is for modernization initiatives, of which $10,000,000 shall remain available until September 30, 2024: Provided further, That not more than $100,000 of the amount appropriated is available for the maintenance of an "International Copyright Institute" in the Copyright Office of the Library of Congress for the purpose of training nationals of developing countries in intellectual property laws and policies: Provided further, That not more than $6,500 may be expended, on the certification of the Librarian of Congress, in connection with official representation and reception expenses for activities of the International Copyright Institute and for copyright delegations, visitors, and seminars: Provided further, That, notwithstanding any provision of chapter 8 of title 17, United States Code, any amounts made available under this heading which are attributable to royalty fees and payments received by the Copyright Office pursuant to sections 111, 119, and chapter 10 of such title may be used for the costs incurred in the administration of the Copyright Royalty Judges program, with the exception of the costs of salaries and benefits for the Copyright Royalty Judges and staff under section 802(e).

Note.—A full-year 2022 appropriation for this account was not enacted at the time the Budget was prepared; therefore, the Budget assumes this account is operating under the Continuing Appropriations Act, 2022 (Division A of Public Law 117–43, as amended). The amounts included for 2022 reflect the annualized level provided by the continuing resolution.

Program and Financing (in millions of dollars)

Identification code 003–0102–0–1–376		2021 actual	2022 est.	2023 est.
	Obligations by program activity:			
0001	Registration, recordation, cataloging, acquisitions, & public reference (Basic)	47	46	52
0002	Determinations by Copyright Royalty Judges	2	2	2
0799	Total direct obligations	49	48	54
0801	Registration, recordation, cataloging, acquisitions, & public reference (Basic)	36	38	39
0802	Licensing	6	6	7
0803	Copyright Royalty Judges	1	1	1
0899	Total reimbursable obligations	43	45	47
0900	Total new obligations, unexpired accounts	92	93	101
	Budgetary resources:			
	Unobligated balance:			
1000	Unobligated balance brought forward, Oct 1	25	28	28
	Budget authority:			
	Appropriations, discretionary:			
1100	Appropriation	49	48	54
	Spending authority from offsetting collections, discretionary:			
1700	Collected	47	45	47
1900	Budget authority (total)	96	93	101
1930	Total budgetary resources available	121	121	129
	Memorandum (non-add) entries:			
1940	Unobligated balance expiring	–1		

LEGISLATIVE BRANCH

Library of Congress—Continued
Federal Funds—Continued

		2021 actual	2022 est.	2023 est.
1941	Unexpired unobligated balance, end of year	28	28	28
	Change in obligated balance:			
	Unpaid obligations:			
3000	Unpaid obligations, brought forward, Oct 1	15	16	12
3010	New obligations, unexpired accounts	92	93	101
3011	Obligations ("upward adjustments"), expired accounts	1		
3020	Outlays (gross)	−92	−97	−102
3050	Unpaid obligations, end of year	16	12	11
	Memorandum (non-add) entries:			
3100	Obligated balance, start of year	15	16	12
3200	Obligated balance, end of year	16	12	11
	Budget authority and outlays, net:			
	Discretionary:			
4000	Budget authority, gross	96	93	101
	Outlays, gross:			
4010	Outlays from new discretionary authority	82	79	87
4011	Outlays from discretionary balances	10	18	15
4020	Outlays, gross (total)	92	97	102
	Offsets against gross budget authority and outlays:			
	Offsetting collections (collected) from:			
4030	Federal sources	−1	−7	−8
4033	Non-Federal sources	−47	−38	−39
4040	Offsets against gross budget authority and outlays (total)	−48	−45	−47
	Additional offsets against gross budget authority only:			
4052	Offsetting collections credited to expired accounts	1		
4060	Additional offsets against budget authority only (total)	1		
4070	Budget authority, net (discretionary)	49	48	54
4080	Outlays, net (discretionary)	44	52	55
4180	Budget authority, net (total)	49	48	54
4190	Outlays, net (total)	44	52	55

The U.S. Copyright Office (USCO) administers the U.S. copyright laws (including by its services on registration, recordation and statutory licensing), provides expert advice to the Congress on matters relating to copyright law and poicy (both domestic and international), provides information and assistance to the executive branch and the courts, and provides information and education to the public. It also maintains the largest database of copyrighted works and copyright ownership information in the world. Through its work, the Office contributes significantly to the development of the copyright law, the national economy, and the cultural heritage of the United States. Approximately forty-five percent of the USCO's 2021 Basic operations are funded by fees paid by authors and other copyright owners for services rendered, and the remainder is funded by appropriations. The amount requested is more than offset by projected fee receipts plus the value of books and other materials deposited with the USCO in accordance with the Copyright Act (17 U.S.C. subsections 407 and 408) and transferred annually to the Library of Congress for its permanent collections.

Registration, recordation, acquisitions, copyright records, public information, and expert advice on copyright issues.—The USCO is responsible for administering the national copyright registration system, including by reviewing applications for copyright registration and recording assignments and other copyright-related documents. In 2021, the USCO registered over 403,000 to copyright, covering millions of copies of original works of authorship; it expects to register an estimated 500,000 copyright claims in 2022 and 2023, which would reflect pre-pandemic levels. Additional responsibilities of the USCO include: creating and providing access to public records of copyright ownership; administering the mandatory deposit provision of the Copyright Act, which provides books, films, sound recordings, and other works for possible inclusion in Library of Congress collections; providing expert advice to Congress, executive agencies, and the courts on domestic and international copyright law and policy; participating in international discussions and negotiations regarding copyright matters; and providing copyright information, education, and events to the public.

Licensing Program.—The Licensing Program handles administrative provisions of statutory licenses and obligations under the copyright law, including those involving secondary transmissions by cable television systems and satellite carriers and the importation, manufacture and distribution of digital audio recording devices and distribution media. The Program collects specified royalty fees for distribution to copyright owners upon determinations rendered by the Copyright Royalty Judges. Distribution occurs after deduction of administrative costs incurred by the Program and by the Copyright Royalty Judges, as specified by this appropriation. The Licensing Program is fully funded directly from the royalties and filing fees collected, making it self-supporting with no tax dollars used for this operation.

Copyright Royalty Judges (CRJ).—The Copyright Royalty Judges and their staff, who operate under the Librarian of Congress, determine royalty distributions and adjust the royalty rates and terms of copyright statutory licenses.

Object Classification (in millions of dollars)

Identification code 003–0102–0–1–376		2021 actual	2022 est.	2023 est.
	Direct obligations:			
11.1	Personnel compensation: Full-time permanent	21	21	24
12.1	Civilian personnel benefits	7	7	9
25.1	Advisory and assistance services	1		
25.2	Other services from non-Federal sources		2	2
25.3	Other goods and services from Federal sources	16	14	14
31.0	Equipment	1	4	4
99.0	Direct obligations	46	48	53
99.0	Reimbursable obligations	43	44	47
99.5	Adjustment for rounding	3	1	1
99.9	Total new obligations, unexpired accounts	92	93	101

Employment Summary

Identification code 003–0102–0–1–376		2021 actual	2022 est.	2023 est.
1001	Direct civilian full-time equivalent employment	322	242	446
2001	Reimbursable civilian full-time equivalent employment	123	222	32

CONGRESSIONAL RESEARCH SERVICE

SALARIES AND EXPENSES

For all necessary expenses to carry out the provisions of section 203 of the Legislative Reorganization Act of 1946 (2 U.S.C. 166) and to revise and extend the Annotated Constitution of the United States of America, $133,132,000: Provided, That no part of such amount may be used to pay any salary or expense in connection with any publication, or preparation of material therefor (except the Digest of Public General Bills), to be issued by the Library of Congress unless such publication has obtained prior approval of either the Committee on House Administration of the House of Representatives or the Committee on Rules and Administration of the Senate: Provided further, That this prohibition does not apply to publication of non-confidential Congressional Research Service (CRS) products: Provided further, That a non-confidential CRS product includes any written product containing research or analysis that is currently available for general congressional access on the CRS Congressional Intranet, or that would be made available on the CRS Congressional Intranet in the normal course of business and does not include material prepared in response to Congressional requests for confidential analysis or research.

Note.—A full-year 2022 appropriation for this account was not enacted at the time the Budget was prepared; therefore, the Budget assumes this account is operating under the Continuing Appropriations Act, 2022 (Division A of Public Law 117–43, as amended). The amounts included for 2022 reflect the annualized level provided by the continuing resolution.

Program and Financing (in millions of dollars)

Identification code 003–0127–0–1–801		2021 actual	2022 est.	2023 est.
	Obligations by program activity:			
0001	Congressional Research Service, Salaries and Expenses (Direct)	125	125	133
	Budgetary resources:			
	Budget authority:			
	Appropriations, discretionary:			
1100	Appropriation	125	125	133
1930	Total budgetary resources available	125	125	133

CONGRESSIONAL RESEARCH SERVICE—Continued
Program and Financing—Continued

Identification code 003–0127–0–1–801		2021 actual	2022 est.	2023 est.
	Change in obligated balance:			
	Unpaid obligations:			
3000	Unpaid obligations, brought forward, Oct 1	19	19	11
3010	New obligations, unexpired accounts	125	125	133
3020	Outlays (gross)	–120	–133	–131
3041	Recoveries of prior year unpaid obligations, expired	–5		
3050	Unpaid obligations, end of year	19	11	13
	Memorandum (non-add) entries:			
3100	Obligated balance, start of year	19	19	11
3200	Obligated balance, end of year	19	11	13
	Budget authority and outlays, net:			
	Discretionary:			
4000	Budget authority, gross	125	125	133
	Outlays, gross:			
4010	Outlays from new discretionary authority	107	115	122
4011	Outlays from discretionary balances	13	18	9
4020	Outlays, gross (total)	120	133	131
4180	Budget authority, net (total)	125	125	133
4190	Outlays, net (total)	120	133	131

The Congressional Research Service (CRS) assists all Members and committees of Congress with its deliberations and legislative decisions by providing objective, authoritative, non-partisan, and confidential research and analysis. As a shared resource, serving Congress exclusively, CRS experts support the Congress at all stages of the legislative process by providing integrated and interdisciplinary analysis and insights in all areas of legislative activity.

Object Classification (in millions of dollars)

Identification code 003–0127–0–1–801		2021 actual	2022 est.	2023 est.
	Direct obligations:			
	Personnel compensation:			
11.1	Full-time permanent	79	81	88
11.3	Other than full-time permanent	1	1	
11.5	Other personnel compensation	1	1	
11.9	Total personnel compensation	81	83	88
12.1	Civilian personnel benefits	26	28	31
23.3	Communications, utilities, and miscellaneous charges	1	1	1
25.1	Advisory and assistance services	9	6	7
25.2	Other services from non-Federal sources	1		
25.7	Operation and maintenance of equipment	1	1	1
26.0	Supplies and materials	5	5	5
31.0	Equipment	1	1	
99.0	Direct obligations	125	125	133
99.9	Total new obligations, unexpired accounts	125	125	133

Employment Summary

Identification code 003–0127–0–1–801	2021 actual	2022 est.	2023 est.
1001 Direct civilian full-time equivalent employment	627	633	641

NATIONAL LIBRARY SERVICE FOR THE BLIND AND PRINT DISABLED
SALARIES AND EXPENSES

For all necessary expenses to carry out the Act of March 3, 1931 (chapter 400; 46 Stat. 1487; 2 U.S.C. 135a), $58,657,000: Provided, That of the total amount appropriated, $650,000 shall be available to contract to provide newspapers to blind and print disabled residents at no cost to the individual.

Note.—A full-year 2022 appropriation for this account was not enacted at the time the Budget was prepared; therefore, the Budget assumes this account is operating under the Continuing Appropriations Act, 2022 (Division A of Public Law 117–43, as amended). The amounts included for 2022 reflect the annualized level provided by the continuing resolution.

Program and Financing (in millions of dollars)

Identification code 003–0141–0–1–503		2021 actual	2022 est.	2023 est.
	Obligations by program activity:			
0001	Direct service to users	60	60	59
0801	Reimbursable program activity	1	1	1
0900	Total new obligations, unexpired accounts	61	61	60
	Budgetary resources:			
	Unobligated balance:			
1000	Unobligated balance brought forward, Oct 1	1	1	1
	Budget authority:			
	Appropriations, discretionary:			
1100	Appropriation	60	60	59
	Spending authority from offsetting collections, discretionary:			
1700	Collected	1	1	1
1900	Budget authority (total)	61	61	60
1930	Total budgetary resources available	62	62	61
	Memorandum (non-add) entries:			
1941	Unexpired unobligated balance, end of year	1	1	1
	Change in obligated balance:			
	Unpaid obligations:			
3000	Unpaid obligations, brought forward, Oct 1	33	34	32
3010	New obligations, unexpired accounts	61	61	60
3020	Outlays (gross)	–57	–63	–60
3041	Recoveries of prior year unpaid obligations, expired	–3		
3050	Unpaid obligations, end of year	34	32	32
	Memorandum (non-add) entries:			
3100	Obligated balance, start of year	33	34	32
3200	Obligated balance, end of year	34	32	32
	Budget authority and outlays, net:			
	Discretionary:			
4000	Budget authority, gross	61	61	60
	Outlays, gross:			
4010	Outlays from new discretionary authority	32	32	31
4011	Outlays from discretionary balances	25	31	29
4020	Outlays, gross (total)	57	63	60
	Offsets against gross budget authority and outlays:			
	Offsetting collections (collected) from:			
4030	Federal sources	–1	–1	–1
4180	Budget authority, net (total)	60	60	59
4190	Outlays, net (total)	56	62	59

The National Library Service for the Blind and Print Disabled (NLS) is responsible for administering a national program to provide reading material for blind and print disabled residents of the United States, its outlying areas, and for U.S. citizens residing abroad.

Direct service to users.—During fiscal year 2021, NLS and its network of cooperating libraries circulated 21.6 million books and magazines in accessible media.

Support services.—A variety of professional, technical, and clerical functions are performed by the NLS. About 9,900 requests for information concerning library and related services available to the blind and other print disabled persons were received in 2021 and nearly 67,000 interlibrary loan items were circulated.

Object Classification (in millions of dollars)

Identification code 003–0141–0–1–503		2021 actual	2022 est.	2023 est.
	Direct obligations:			
11.1	Personnel compensation: Full-time permanent	10	11	11
12.1	Civilian personnel benefits	4	4	4
23.1	Rental payments to GSA	3	3	3
24.0	Printing and reproduction	1	1	1
25.1	Advisory and assistance services	10	7	4
25.2	Other services from non-Federal sources	6	5	6
25.3	Other goods and services from Federal sources	1	2	3
25.7	Operation and maintenance of equipment	2	2	2
31.0	Equipment	23	23	24
99.0	Direct obligations	60	58	58
99.0	Reimbursable obligations	1	1	1
99.5	Adjustment for rounding		2	1
99.9	Total new obligations, unexpired accounts	61	61	60

Employment Summary

Identification code 003–0141–0–1–503	2021 actual	2022 est.	2023 est.
1001 Direct civilian full-time equivalent employment	100	113	113
2001 Reimbursable civilian full-time equivalent employment	3		

PAYMENTS TO COPYRIGHT OWNERS

Special and Trust Fund Receipts (in millions of dollars)

Identification code 003–5175–0–2–376	2021 actual	2022 est.	2023 est.
0100 Balance, start of year			
Receipts:			
Current law:			
1110 Fees from Jukebox, Satellite and Cable Television for Operating Costs, Copyright Office	6	7	7
2000 Total: Balances and receipts	6	7	7
Appropriations:			
Current law:			
2101 Payments to Copyright Owners	–6	–7	–7
5099 Balance, end of year			

Program and Financing (in millions of dollars)

Identification code 003–5175–0–2–376	2021 actual	2022 est.	2023 est.
Obligations by program activity:			
0001 Licensing costs	6	7	7
Budgetary resources:			
Budget authority:			
Appropriations, mandatory:			
1201 Appropriation (special or trust fund)	6	7	7
1930 Total budgetary resources available	6	7	7
Change in obligated balance:			
Unpaid obligations:			
3010 New obligations, unexpired accounts	6	7	7
3020 Outlays (gross)	–6	–7	–7
Budget authority and outlays, net:			
Mandatory:			
4090 Budget authority, gross	6	7	7
Outlays, gross:			
4100 Outlays from new mandatory authority	6	7	7
4180 Budget authority, net (total)	6	7	7
4190 Outlays, net (total)	6	7	7

Object Classification (in millions of dollars)

Identification code 003–5175–0–2–376	2021 actual	2022 est.	2023 est.
Direct obligations:			
25.3 Other goods and services from Federal sources	5	6	6
44.0 Refunds	1	1	1
99.9 Total new obligations, unexpired accounts	6	7	7

COOPERATIVE ACQUISITIONS PROGRAM REVOLVING FUND

Program and Financing (in millions of dollars)

Identification code 003–4325–0–3–503	2021 actual	2022 est.	2023 est.
Obligations by program activity:			
0801 Cooperative Acquisitions Program	3	10	11
Budgetary resources:			
Unobligated balance:			
1000 Unobligated balance brought forward, Oct 1	7	8	9
1021 Recoveries of prior year unpaid obligations	1		
1070 Unobligated balance (total)	8	8	9
Budget authority:			
Spending authority from offsetting collections, discretionary:			
1700 Collected	2	11	11
1701 Change in uncollected payments, Federal sources	1		
1750 Spending auth from offsetting collections, disc (total)	3	11	11
1930 Total budgetary resources available	11	19	20
Memorandum (non-add) entries:			
1941 Unexpired unobligated balance, end of year	8	9	9
Change in obligated balance:			
Unpaid obligations:			
3000 Unpaid obligations, brought forward, Oct 1	1	1	1
3010 New obligations, unexpired accounts	3	10	11
3020 Outlays (gross)	–2	–10	–12
3040 Recoveries of prior year unpaid obligations, unexpired	–1		
3050 Unpaid obligations, end of year	1	1	
Uncollected payments:			
3060 Uncollected pymts, Fed sources, brought forward, Oct 1		–1	–1
3070 Change in uncollected pymts, Fed sources, unexpired	–1		
3090 Uncollected pymts, Fed sources, end of year	–1	–1	–1
Memorandum (non-add) entries:			
3100 Obligated balance, start of year	1		
3200 Obligated balance, end of year			–1
Budget authority and outlays, net:			
Discretionary:			
4000 Budget authority, gross	3	11	11
Outlays, gross:			
4010 Outlays from new discretionary authority	2	10	10
4011 Outlays from discretionary balances			2
4020 Outlays, gross (total)	2	10	12
Offsets against gross budget authority and outlays:			
Offsetting collections (collected) from:			
4030 Federal sources	–1	–1	
4033 Non-Federal sources	–1	–10	–11
4040 Offsets against gross budget authority and outlays (total)	–2	–11	–11
Additional offsets against gross budget authority only:			
4050 Change in uncollected pymts, Fed sources, unexpired	–1		
4080 Outlays, net (discretionary)		–1	1
4180 Budget authority, net (total)			
4190 Outlays, net (total)		–1	1

Under the authority of 2 U.S.C. 182, the Library of Congress operates a revolving fund for the acquisition of foreign research materials for participating institutions through the Library's overseas offices.

Object Classification (in millions of dollars)

Identification code 003–4325–0–3–503	2021 actual	2022 est.	2023 est.
Reimbursable obligations:			
11.1 Personnel compensation: Full-time permanent		1	1
22.0 Transportation of things		1	1
23.3 Communications, utilities, and miscellaneous charges		1	1
25.3 Other goods and services from Federal sources		1	1
31.0 Equipment	1	5	6
99.0 Reimbursable obligations	1	9	10
99.5 Adjustment for rounding	2	1	1
99.9 Total new obligations, unexpired accounts	3	10	11

Employment Summary

Identification code 003–4325–0–3–503	2021 actual	2022 est.	2023 est.
2001 Reimbursable civilian full-time equivalent employment	1	7	12

DUPLICATION SERVICES

Under the authority of 2 U.S.C. 182a, the Library of Congress operates a revolving fund to provide preservation and duplication and delivery services for the Library's audio-visual collections, including duplication services for motion pictures, videotapes, sound recordings, and radio and

Library of Congress—Continued
Federal Funds—Continued

DUPLICATION SERVICES—Continued

television broadcasts. Audio-visual preservation and duplication services are also available to other archives, libraries, and industry constituents.

GIFT SHOP, DECIMAL CLASSIFICATION, PHOTO DUPLICATION, AND RELATED SERVICES

Program and Financing (in millions of dollars)

Identification code 003–4346–0–3–503	2021 actual	2022 est.	2023 est.
Obligations by program activity:			
0801 National Library	1	14	13
Budgetary resources:			
Unobligated balance:			
1000 Unobligated balance brought forward, Oct 1	6	6	2
1001 Discretionary unobligated balance brought fwd, Oct 1	6		
Budget authority:			
Spending authority from offsetting collections, discretionary:			
1700 Collected	1	10	13
1930 Total budgetary resources available	7	16	15
Memorandum (non-add) entries:			
1941 Unexpired unobligated balance, end of year	6	2	2
Change in obligated balance:			
Unpaid obligations:			
3000 Unpaid obligations, brought forward, Oct 1	1	1	5
3010 New obligations, unexpired accounts	1	14	13
3020 Outlays (gross)	–1	–10	–12
3050 Unpaid obligations, end of year	1	5	6
Memorandum (non-add) entries:			
3100 Obligated balance, start of year	1	1	5
3200 Obligated balance, end of year	1	5	6
Budget authority and outlays, net:			
Discretionary:			
4000 Budget authority, gross	1	10	13
Outlays, gross:			
4010 Outlays from new discretionary authority	1	9	11
4011 Outlays from discretionary balances		1	1
4020 Outlays, gross (total)	1	10	12
Offsets against gross budget authority and outlays:			
Offsetting collections (collected) from:			
4030 Federal sources	–1	–10	–13
4040 Offsets against gross budget authority and outlays (total)	–1	–10	–13
4180 Budget authority, net (total)			
4190 Outlays, net (total)			–1

Under the authority of 2 U.S.C. 182b, the Library of Congress operates a revolving fund for the support of the Library's retail marketing sales shop activities; for providing preservation microfilming services for the Library's collections and photocopy, microfilm, photographic and digital services to other libraries, research institutions, government agencies, and individuals in the United States and abroad; and for operating special events and programs.

Object Classification (in millions of dollars)

Identification code 003–4346–0–3–503	2021 actual	2022 est.	2023 est.
Reimbursable obligations:			
11.1 Personnel compensation: Full-time permanent		3	3
12.1 Civilian personnel benefits		1	1
25.1 Advisory and assistance services		1	1
25.2 Other services from non-Federal sources		5	5
25.3 Other goods and services from Federal sources		1	1
26.0 Supplies and materials		2	1
99.0 Reimbursable obligations		13	12
99.5 Adjustment for rounding	1	1	1
99.9 Total new obligations, unexpired accounts	1	14	13

Employment Summary

Identification code 003–4346–0–3–503	2021 actual	2022 est.	2023 est.
2001 Reimbursable civilian full-time equivalent employment	1	58	43

FEDLINK PROGRAM AND FEDERAL RESEARCH PROGRAM

Program and Financing (in millions of dollars)

Identification code 003–4543–0–4–503	2021 actual	2022 est.	2023 est.
Obligations by program activity:			
0801 Fedlink and Federal Research	99	222	278
Budgetary resources:			
Unobligated balance:			
1000 Unobligated balance brought forward, Oct 1	34	23	23
1001 Discretionary unobligated balance brought fwd, Oct 1	34		
1021 Recoveries of prior year unpaid obligations	2		
1070 Unobligated balance (total)	36	23	23
Budget authority:			
Spending authority from offsetting collections, discretionary:			
1700 Collected	97	222	278
1701 Change in uncollected payments, Federal sources	–11		
1750 Spending auth from offsetting collections, disc (total)	86	222	278
1930 Total budgetary resources available	122	245	301
Memorandum (non-add) entries:			
1941 Unexpired unobligated balance, end of year	23	23	23
Change in obligated balance:			
Unpaid obligations:			
3000 Unpaid obligations, brought forward, Oct 1	34	47	66
3010 New obligations, unexpired accounts	99	222	278
3020 Outlays (gross)	–84	–203	–255
3040 Recoveries of prior year unpaid obligations, unexpired	–2		
3050 Unpaid obligations, end of year	47	66	89
Uncollected payments:			
3060 Uncollected pymts, Fed sources, brought forward, Oct 1	–16	–5	–5
3070 Change in uncollected pymts, Fed sources, unexpired	11		
3090 Uncollected pymts, Fed sources, end of year	–5	–5	–5
Memorandum (non-add) entries:			
3100 Obligated balance, start of year	18	42	61
3200 Obligated balance, end of year	42	61	84
Budget authority and outlays, net:			
Discretionary:			
4000 Budget authority, gross	86	222	278
Outlays, gross:			
4010 Outlays from new discretionary authority	38	140	175
4011 Outlays from discretionary balances	46	63	80
4020 Outlays, gross (total)	84	203	255
Offsets against gross budget authority and outlays:			
Offsetting collections (collected) from:			
4030 Federal sources	–97	–222	–278
4040 Offsets against gross budget authority and outlays (total)	–97	–222	–278
Additional offsets against gross budget authority only:			
4050 Change in uncollected pymts, Fed sources, unexpired	11		
4060 Additional offsets against budget authority only (total)	11		
4080 Outlays, net (discretionary)	–13	–19	–23
4180 Budget authority, net (total)			
4190 Outlays, net (total)	–13	–19	–23

Under the authority of 2 U.S.C. 182c, the Library of Congress operates a revolving fund for providing support to federal agencies through the procurement of commercial information services, publications in any format, any library support services; related accounting services; education, information, and support services; and customized research services.

Object Classification (in millions of dollars)

Identification code 003–4543–0–4–503	2021 actual	2022 est.	2023 est.
Reimbursable obligations:			
Personnel compensation:			
11.1 Full-time permanent	4	6	7

LEGISLATIVE BRANCH

Library of Congress—Continued
Trust Funds

		2021 actual	2022 est.	2023 est.
11.3	Other than full-time permanent	1	1	
11.9	Total personnel compensation	5	7	7
12.1	Civilian personnel benefits	1	2	2
25.2	Other services from non-Federal sources	60	180	227
25.3	Other goods and services from Federal sources	1	2	2
31.0	Equipment	29	30	38
44.0	Refunds	1		
99.0	Reimbursable obligations	97	221	276
99.5	Adjustment for rounding	2	1	2
99.9	Total new obligations, unexpired accounts	99	222	278

Employment Summary

Identification code 003-4543-0-4-503	2021 actual	2022 est.	2023 est.
2001 Reimbursable civilian full-time equivalent employment	33	60	77

Trust Funds
GIFT AND TRUST FUND ACCOUNTS

Special and Trust Fund Receipts (in millions of dollars)

Identification code 003-9971-0-7-503	2021 actual	2022 est.	2023 est.
0100 Balance, start of year	12	10	26
Receipts:			
Current law:			
1130 Contributions, Library of Congress Gift Fund	16	17	18
1130 Contributions, Library of Congress Permanent Loan Account	7	7	7
1130 Income from Donated Securities, Library of Congress	11	5	5
1140 Interest, Library of Congress Permanent Loan Account		2	2
1140 Foreign Service National Separation Liability Trust Fund		1	1
1199 Total current law receipts	34	32	33
1999 Total receipts	34	32	33
2000 Total: Balances and receipts	46	42	59
Appropriations:			
Current law:			
2101 Gift and Trust Fund Accounts	-37	-16	-19
5098 Reconciliation adjustment	1		
5099 Balance, end of year	10	26	40

Program and Financing (in millions of dollars)

Identification code 003-9971-0-7-503	2021 actual	2022 est.	2023 est.
Obligations by program activity:			
0001 Office of the Librarian	26	8	8
0002 Office of the Chief Information Officer		1	1
0003 Office of the Chief Operating Officer		1	1
0004 Library Collections and Services Group		17	17
0900 Total new obligations, unexpired accounts	26	27	27
Budgetary resources:			
Unobligated balance:			
1000 Unobligated balance brought forward, Oct 1	26	37	26
Budget authority:			
Appropriations, mandatory:			
1201 Appropriation (special or trust fund)	37	16	19
1930 Total budgetary resources available	63	53	45
Memorandum (non-add) entries:			
1941 Unexpired unobligated balance, end of year	37	26	18
Change in obligated balance:			
Unpaid obligations:			
3000 Unpaid obligations, brought forward, Oct 1	5	10	18
3010 New obligations, unexpired accounts	26	27	27
3020 Outlays (gross)	-21	-19	-19
3050 Unpaid obligations, end of year	10	18	26
Memorandum (non-add) entries:			
3100 Obligated balance, start of year	5	10	18
3200 Obligated balance, end of year	10	18	26
Budget authority and outlays, net:			
Mandatory:			
4090 Budget authority, gross	37	16	19
Outlays, gross:			
4100 Outlays from new mandatory authority	19	13	15
4101 Outlays from mandatory balances	2	6	4
4110 Outlays, gross (total)	21	19	19
4180 Budget authority, net (total)	37	16	19
4190 Outlays, net (total)	21	19	19
Memorandum (non-add) entries:			
5000 Total investments, SOY: Federal securities: Par value	25	36	36
5001 Total investments, EOY: Federal securities: Par value	36	36	36
5010 Total investments, SOY: non-Fed securities: Market value	153	185	185
5011 Total investments, EOY: non-Fed securities: Market value	185	185	185

This schedule covers: (1) funds received as gifts for immediate expenditure, funds received as trust funds for expenditure, and receipts from the sale of recordings, publications, and other materials financed from capital originally received as gifts; (2) income from investments held by or for the Library of Congress Trust Fund Board; and (3) interest paid by the Treasury on the principal funds deposited therewith as described under "Library of Congress Trust Fund, Principal Accounts." The Library has seven program areas related to Gift and Trust funds:

The Library of Congress' collections document the history and further the creativity of the American people, as well as record and contribute to the advancement of civilization and knowledge throughout the world. Service units within the Library's Library Collections and Services Group (LCSG) perform most of the Library's conventional library functions, providing acquisitions, description, preservation, reference, and access services for the national collection. These service units also support government agencies, cultural institutions, and other libraries through its catalog records, standards work, and professional and collaborative programs. In fiscal 2022, within LCSG, Library Services reorganized into two new service units:

Discovery & Preservation Services (DPS).—This new service unit brings together the Acquisitions & Bibliographic Access (ABA) Directorate, the Digital Services Directorate (DSD), and the Preservation Directorate (PRES). Its central charge is to improve user discovery and stewardship by leveraging new metadata, digitization, and preservation workflows as digital and physical collections expand. Among other programs, DPS is home to the Cooperative Acquisitions Program (managed through ABA's six Overseas Offices) and the Surplus Books Program.

Researcher & Collections Services (RCS).—This new service unit brings together in close alignment the Collections Development Office (CDO), Special Collections Directorate (SCD), General & International Collections Directorate (GICD), and the National Audio-Visual Conservation Center (NAVCC). As an organization of visiting scholars that uses the collections and creates new knowledge, the John W. Kluge Center also joins this unit. RCS's central charge is to build the national collection, share the collections, and provide services to all users. Among other programs, RCS is home to the National Audio Visual ConservationCenter, the Veterans History Project, the National Digital Newspaper Program, and the Congressional Cartography Program.

Law Library.—The Law Library of Congress maintains a global law collection of U.S. legal materials, and collections from more than 240 foreign jurisdictions. The collection consists of nearly 3 million volumes and 3 million pieces of microfiche. Reference specialists and foreign legal staff provide legal research reference products and services, to all three branches of the government and the entire nation.

Copyright Office.—The Copyright Office administers the U.S. Copyright Laws (including by its services on registration, recordation and statutory licensing), provides expert advice to the Congress on matters relating to copyright law and policy (both domestic and international), provides information and assistance to the executive branch and the courts, and provides information and education to the public.

GIFT AND TRUST FUND ACCOUNTS—Continued

Congressional Research Service.—The Congressional Research Service (CRS) serves all Members and committees of Congress. CRS experts provide Congress with authoritative, confidential, non-partisan, and objective expertise across the full range of legislative policy issues.

Office of the Chief Operating Officer.—The Office of the Chief Operating Officer (OCOO) organization provides comprehensive services, manages institutional programs, and oversees regulatory compliance in the areas of financial management; human capital; contracting; facilities, safety and health services; asset management; personnel security and emergency preparedness; and programs that deliver fee-based services. OCOO oversees gift and trust fund activities that provide assistance to the Library of Congress staff with emergencies that exceed their financial capacity, supports leadership development at the Library with a focus on enabling minorities to ascend to leadership positions, supports workshops, seminars and training for professional development programs. For the purpose of supporting the Junior Fellows Summer Intern Program or, in the event that the Library ceases to maintain the Program, other programs consistent with bringing students to the Library for internships and fellowships that serve its mission and bring outstanding talent to the Library of Congress to benefit from first-hand interactions with its unparalleled collections, curators, and programs, and to train future leaders for the information age.

Object Classification (in millions of dollars)

Identification code 003–9971–0–7–503		2021 actual	2022 est.	2023 est.
	Direct obligations:			
11.1	Personnel compensation: Full-time permanent	2	2	2
12.1	Civilian personnel benefits	1	1	1
25.1	Advisory and assistance services	2	2	2
25.2	Other services from non-Federal sources	4	4	4
25.3	Other goods and services from Federal sources	1	1	1
31.0	Equipment	1	1	1
33.0	Investments and loans	13	14	14
41.0	Grants, subsidies, and contributions	2	3	3
99.0	Direct obligations	26	28	28
99.5	Adjustment for rounding		–1	–1
99.9	Total new obligations, unexpired accounts	26	27	27

Employment Summary

Identification code 003–9971–0–7–503	2021 actual	2022 est.	2023 est.
1001 Direct civilian full-time equivalent employment	13	16	17

ADMINISTRATIVE PROVISION

REIMBURSABLE AND REVOLVING FUND ACTIVITIES

SEC. 140. (a) IN GENERAL.—For fiscal year 2023, the obligational authority of the Library of Congress for the activities described in subsection (b) may not exceed $308,554,000.

(b) ACTIVITIES.—The activities referred to in subsection (a) are reimbursable and revolving fund activities that are funded from sources other than appropriations to the Library in appropriations Acts for the legislative branch.

LIBRARIAN ACCEPTANCE OF PERSONAL PROPERTY

SEC. 141. The first undesignated paragraph of section 4 of Act entitled "An Act to create a Library of Congress Trust Fund Board, and for other purposes", approved March 3, 1925 (2 U.S.C. 160), is amended—

(a) in the first sentence,

(1) by striking "and" before "(3) gifts or bequests of money for immediate disbursement"; and

(2) by striking the period at the end and inserting "; and (4) gifts or bequests of securities and other personal property.";

(b) in the second sentence, by inserting "of money" after "bequests";

(c) in the third sentence, by striking "enter them" and inserting "enter the gift, bequest or proceeds"; and

(d) by inserting after the second sentence the following new sentence: "In the case of a gift of securities, the Librarian shall sell the gift and provide the donor with such acknowledgment as needed for the donor to substantiate the gift."

(e) EFFECTIVE DATE.—The amendments made by this section shall apply with respect to fiscal year 2023 and each succeeding fiscal year.

LIBRARY OF CONGRESS ORDERS UNDER TASK AND DELIVERY ORDER CONTRACTS

SEC. 142. (a) SCOPE.—This section applies to task orders and delivery orders issued by the Library of Congress under task or delivery order contracts (as defined in section 4101 of title 41) established by the Library or other legislative branch agencies and to such contracts established by executive agencies under section 4103.

(b) CONTRACT MODIFICATIONS.—A task or delivery order may not increase the scope, period, or maximum value of the task or delivery order contract under which the order is issued. The scope, period, or maximum value of the contract may be increased only by modification of the contract.

(c) ACTION NOT REQUIRED FOR ISSUANCE OF ORDERS.—The Library of Congress may issue an order under task or delivery order contract without advertising for proposals for the order under section 6101.

(d) PROTESTS.—

(1) Protest not authorized.—A protest is not authorized in connection with the issuance or proposed issuance by the Library of Congress of an order under a task or delivery order contract except for—

(A) a protest on the ground that the order increases the scope, period, or maximum value of the contract under which the order is issued; or

(B) a protest of an order valued in excess of $10,000,000.

(2) Jurisdiction over protests.—Notwithstanding section 3556 of title 31, the Comptroller General shall have exclusive jurisdiction of a protest authorized under paragraph (1)(B).

(3) EFFECTIVE DATE.—This section and the amendment made by this section shall apply with respect to fiscal year 2023 and each succeeding fiscal year.

GOVERNMENT PUBLISHING OFFICE

Federal Funds

CONGRESSIONAL PUBLISHING

(INCLUDING TRANSFER OF FUNDS)

For authorized publishing of congressional information and the distribution of congressional information in any format; publishing of Government publications authorized by law to be distributed to Members of Congress; and publishing, and distribution of Government publications authorized by law to be distributed without charge to the recipient, $82,992,000: Provided, That this appropriation shall not be available for paper copies of the permanent edition of the Congressional Record for individual Representatives, Resident Commissioners or Delegates authorized under section 906 of title 44, United States Code: Provided further, That this appropriation shall be available for the payment of obligations incurred under the appropriations for similar purposes for preceding fiscal years: Provided further, That notwithstanding the 2-year limitation under section 718 of title 44, United States Code, none of the funds appropriated or made available under this Act or any other Act for printing and binding and related services provided to Congress under chapter 7 of title 44, United States Code, may be expended to print a document, report, or publication after the 27-month period beginning on the date that such document, report, or publication is authorized by Congress to be printed, unless Congress reauthorizes such printing in accordance with section 718 of title 44, United States Code: Provided further, That unobligated or unexpended balances of expired discretionary funds made available under this heading in this Act for this fiscal year may be transferred to, and merged with, funds under the heading "Government Publishing Office Business Operations Revolving Fund" no later than the end of the fifth fiscal year after the last fiscal year for which such funds are available for the purposes for which appropriated, to be available for carrying out the purposes of this heading, subject to the approval of the Committees on Appropriations of the House of Representatives and the Senate: Provided further, That notwithstanding sections 901, 902, and 906 of title 44, United States Code, this appropriation may be used to prepare indexes to the Congressional Record on only a monthly and session basis.

Note.—A full-year 2022 appropriation for this account was not enacted at the time the Budget was prepared; therefore, the Budget assumes this account is operating under the Continuing Appropriations Act, 2022 (Division A of Public Law 117–43, as amended). The amounts included for 2022 reflect the annualized level provided by the continuing resolution.

LEGISLATIVE BRANCH

Program and Financing (in millions of dollars)

Identification code 004–0203–0–1–801	2021 actual	2022 est.	2023 est.
Obligations by program activity:			
0001 Congressional Publishing	78	78	83
0900 Total new obligations, unexpired accounts (object class 24.0)	78	78	83
Budgetary resources:			
Budget authority:			
Appropriations, discretionary:			
1100 Appropriation	78	78	83
1930 Total budgetary resources available	78	78	83
Change in obligated balance:			
Unpaid obligations:			
3000 Unpaid obligations, brought forward, Oct 1	48	61	61
3010 New obligations, unexpired accounts	78	78	83
3020 Outlays (gross)	–64	–78	–83
3041 Recoveries of prior year unpaid obligations, expired	–1		
3050 Unpaid obligations, end of year	61	61	61
Memorandum (non-add) entries:			
3100 Obligated balance, start of year	48	61	61
3200 Obligated balance, end of year	61	61	61
Budget authority and outlays, net:			
Discretionary:			
4000 Budget authority, gross	78	78	83
Outlays, gross:			
4010 Outlays from new discretionary authority	47	55	59
4011 Outlays from discretionary balances	17	23	24
4020 Outlays, gross (total)	64	78	83
4180 Budget authority, net (total)	78	78	83
4190 Outlays, net (total)	64	78	83

This appropriation covers publishing for the Congress, content management, and the publishing of Government publications authorized by law to be distributed to Members of Congress. Also, this appropriation includes funding for the publishing and distribution of Government publications authorized by law to be distributed without charge to the recipients.

PUBLIC INFORMATION PROGRAMS OF THE SUPERINTENDENT OF DOCUMENTS

SALARIES AND EXPENSES

(INCLUDING TRANSFER OF FUNDS)

For expenses of the public information programs of the Office of Superintendent of Documents necessary to provide for the cataloging and indexing of Government publications in any format, and their distribution to the public, Members of Congress, other Government agencies, and designated depository and international exchange libraries as authorized by law, $35,257,000: Provided, That amounts of not more than $2,000,000 from current year appropriations are authorized for producing and disseminating Congressional serial sets and other related publications for the preceding two fiscal years to depository and other designated libraries: Provided further, That unobligated or unexpended balances of expired discretionary funds made available under this heading in this Act for this fiscal year may be transferred to, and merged with, funds under the heading "Government Publishing Office Business Operations Revolving Fund" no later than the end of the fifth fiscal year after the last fiscal year for which such funds are available for the purposes for which appropriated, to be available for carrying out the purposes of this heading, subject to the approval of the Committees on Appropriations of the House of Representatives and the Senate.

Note.—A full-year 2022 appropriation for this account was not enacted at the time the Budget was prepared; therefore, the Budget assumes this account is operating under the Continuing Appropriations Act, 2022 (Division A of Public Law 117–43, as amended). The amounts included for 2022 reflect the annualized level provided by the continuing resolution.

Program and Financing (in millions of dollars)

Identification code 004–0201–0–1–808	2021 actual	2022 est.	2023 est.
Obligations by program activity:			
0001 Depository Library Distribution	21	21	23
0002 Cataloging and Indexing	10	10	11
0003 International Exchange	1	1	1
0900 Total new obligations, unexpired accounts	32	32	35
Budgetary resources:			
Budget authority:			
Appropriations, discretionary:			
1100 Appropriation	32	32	35
1930 Total budgetary resources available	32	32	35
Change in obligated balance:			
Unpaid obligations:			
3000 Unpaid obligations, brought forward, Oct 1	16	17	16
3010 New obligations, unexpired accounts	32	32	35
3020 Outlays (gross)	–31	–33	–35
3050 Unpaid obligations, end of year	17	16	16
Memorandum (non-add) entries:			
3100 Obligated balance, start of year	16	17	16
3200 Obligated balance, end of year	17	16	16
Budget authority and outlays, net:			
Discretionary:			
4000 Budget authority, gross	32	32	35
Outlays, gross:			
4010 Outlays from new discretionary authority	26	26	28
4011 Outlays from discretionary balances	5	7	7
4020 Outlays, gross (total)	31	33	35
4180 Budget authority, net (total)	32	32	35
4190 Outlays, net (total)	31	33	35

The Public Information Programs of the Superintendent of Documents operate under a separate appropriation that provides funds (salaries and expenses) for: (1) the distribution of certain tangible publications to Members of Congress and other Government agencies, as authorized by law; (2) the distribution of Government publications to designated Federal depository libraries, as authorized by law, including tangible Government information products and online access via GPO's govinfo (https://www.govinfo.gov/); (3) the compilation of catalogs and indexes of Government publications, as authorized by law via the "Catalog of U.S. Government Publications (CGP)" (https://catalog.gpo.gov/); and (4) the distribution of Federal Government publications to foreign governments via the International Exchange Service. These four functions are related to the publication activity of Federal agencies and the demands of the public, Members of Congress, and depository libraries. Following is a description of these four functions:

Distribution for other Government agencies and Members of Congress (By-Law Distribution).—The Public Information Programs of the Superintendent of Documents maintain mailing lists and distribute, at the request of Government agencies and Members of Congress, certain publications specified by public law.

Federal Depository Library Program.—Established by Congress to ensure the American public has access to its Government's information, the Federal Depository Library Program (FDLP) involves the acquisition and dissemination of Government information in all formats to Federal depository libraries across the country.

The mission of the FDLP is to coordinate with depository libraries, 1,113 nationwide, to disseminate information products from all three branches of the Government. Libraries that have been designated as Federal depositories maintain these information products (as provided by GPO) as part of their existing collections and are responsible for assuring that the public has free access to the material provided by the FDLP.

Included in this program is the maintenance and expansion of free, electronic access to information products produced by the Federal Government via govinfo. Electronic information dissemination and access have greatly expanded the number of publications offered to the Federal depository libraries as well as increasing public use of the FDLP content. As the FDLP continues its transition to a primarily electronic program, the costs of the program are increasingly related to identifying, acquiring, cataloging, linking to, authenticating, modernizing, and providing permanent public access to digital Government information.

Cataloging and indexing.—The Public Information Programs of the Superintendent of Documents are charged with preparing catalogs and indexes

PUBLIC INFORMATION PROGRAMS OF THE SUPERINTENDENT OF DOCUMENTS—Continued

of all publications issued by the Federal Government that are not confidential in character. The principal publication is the web-based "Catalog of U.S. Government Publications (CGP)" (https://catalog.gpo.gov/). GPO's goal is to expand the CGP to a more comprehensive title listing of public documents, both historic and electronic, to increase the visibility and use of Government information products.

International Exchange Service (IES).—Under the direction of the Library of Congress (LC), the Public Information Programs of the Superintendent of Documents distributes tangible Government publications to foreign governments that agree to send the United States similar publications of their governments for LC collections.

Object Classification (in millions of dollars)

Identification code 004–0201–0–1–808		2021 actual	2022 est.	2023 est.
	Direct obligations:			
11.1	Personnel compensation: Full-time permanent	10	10	11
12.1	Civilian personnel benefits	4	5	4
22.0	Transportation of things	2	2	1
24.0	Printing and reproduction	7	7	5
25.2	Other services from non-Federal sources	9	8	14
99.9	Total new obligations, unexpired accounts	32	32	35

Employment Summary

Identification code 004–0201–0–1–808		2021 actual	2022 est.	2023 est.
1001	Direct civilian full-time equivalent employment	84	100	105

GOVERNMENT PUBLISHING OFFICE BUSINESS OPERATIONS REVOLVING FUND

For payment to the Government Publishing Office Business Operations Revolving Fund, $12,655,000, to remain available until expended, for information technology development and facilities repair: Provided, That the Government Publishing Office is hereby authorized to make such expenditures, within the limits of funds available and in accordance with law, and to make such contracts and commitments without regard to fiscal year limitations as provided by section 9104 of title 31, United States Code, as may be necessary in carrying out the programs and purposes set forth in the budget for the current fiscal year for the Government Publishing Office Business Operations Revolving Fund: Provided further, That not more than $7,500 may be expended on the certification of the Director of the Government Publishing Office in connection with official representation and reception expenses: Provided further, That the Business Operations Revolving Fund shall be available for the hire or purchase of not more than 12 passenger motor vehicles: Provided further, That expenditures in connection with travel expenses of the advisory councils to the Director of the Government Publishing Office shall be deemed necessary to carry out the provisions of title 44, United States Code: Provided further, That the Business Operations Revolving Fund shall be available for temporary or intermittent services under section 3109(b) of title 5, United States Code, but at rates for individuals not more than the daily equivalent of the annual rate of basic pay for level V of the Executive Schedule under section 5316 of such title: Provided further, That activities financed through the Business Operations Revolving Fund may provide information in any format: Provided further, That the Business Operations Revolving Fund and the funds provided under the heading "Public Information Programs of the Superintendent of Documents" may not be used for contracted security services at Government Publishing Office's passport facility in the District of Columbia.

Note.—A full-year 2022 appropriation for this account was not enacted at the time the Budget was prepared; therefore, the Budget assumes this account is operating under the Continuing Appropriations Act, 2022 (Division A of Public Law 117–43, as amended). The amounts included for 2022 reflect the annualized level provided by the continuing resolution.

Program and Financing (in millions of dollars)

Identification code 004–4505–0–4–808		2021 actual	2022 est.	2023 est.
	Obligations by program activity:			
0801	Business Operations	727	953	934
0811	Capital investment	47	21	15
0900	Total new obligations, unexpired accounts	774	974	949
	Budgetary resources:			
	Unobligated balance:			
1000	Unobligated balance brought forward, Oct 1	255	411	379
1012	Unobligated balance transfers between expired and unexpired accounts	1		
1070	Unobligated balance (total)	256	411	379
	Budget authority:			
	Appropriations, discretionary:			
1100	Appropriation	7	7	13
	Spending authority from offsetting collections, mandatory:			
1800	Collected	937	935	908
1801	Change in uncollected payments, Federal sources	–15		
1850	Spending auth from offsetting collections, mand (total)	922	935	908
1900	Budget authority (total)	929	942	921
1930	Total budgetary resources available	1,185	1,353	1,300
	Memorandum (non-add) entries:			
1941	Unexpired unobligated balance, end of year	411	379	351
	Change in obligated balance:			
	Unpaid obligations:			
3000	Unpaid obligations, brought forward, Oct 1	564	490	505
3010	New obligations, unexpired accounts	774	974	949
3020	Outlays (gross)	–848	–959	–944
3050	Unpaid obligations, end of year	490	505	510
	Uncollected payments:			
3060	Uncollected pymts, Fed sources, brought forward, Oct 1	–222	–207	–207
3070	Change in uncollected pymts, Fed sources, unexpired	15		
3090	Uncollected pymts, Fed sources, end of year	–207	–207	–207
	Memorandum (non-add) entries:			
3100	Obligated balance, start of year	342	283	298
3200	Obligated balance, end of year	283	298	303
	Budget authority and outlays, net:			
	Discretionary:			
4000	Budget authority, gross	7	7	13
	Outlays, gross:			
4010	Outlays from new discretionary authority		4	6
4011	Outlays from discretionary balances	16	10	10
4020	Outlays, gross (total)	16	14	16
	Mandatory:			
4090	Budget authority, gross	922	935	908
	Outlays, gross:			
4100	Outlays from new mandatory authority	577	748	726
4101	Outlays from mandatory balances	255	197	202
4110	Outlays, gross (total)	832	945	928
	Offsets against gross budget authority and outlays:			
	Offsetting collections (collected) from:			
4120	Federal sources	–934	–915	–884
4123	Non-Federal sources	–3	–20	–24
4130	Offsets against gross budget authority and outlays (total)	–937	–935	–908
	Additional offsets against gross budget authority only:			
4140	Change in uncollected pymts, Fed sources, unexpired	15		
4170	Outlays, net (mandatory)	–105	10	20
4180	Budget authority, net (total)	7	7	13
4190	Outlays, net (total)	–89	24	36

All GPO activities are financed through the agency's Business Operations Revolving Fund, established by section 309 of Title 44, U.S.C. This business-like fund is used to pay all GPO costs in performing congressional and agency publishing, printing and information product procurement, publications dissemination and space sharing activities. It is reimbursed from payments from customer agencies, sales to the public, and transfers from GPO's two annual appropriations: the Congressional Publishing Appropriation and the Public Information Programs of the Superintendent of Documents Appropriation. GPO pays its expenses from the Fund and the Fund is reimbursed when the Treasury Department transfers money from customer agency accounts to the Fund when they pay GPO's invoices. This procedure also applies to the payment of transfers from the Congressional Publishing and Public Information Programs appropriations, and to deposits of funds collected from sales to the public. GPO maintains a cash balance in the Business Operations Revolving Fund that is used to pay all expenses. The cash balance fluctuates daily as payments are received from agency reimbursements, customer payments, and transfers from GPO appropriations. Under GPO's system of accrual accounting, annual earnings generated since the inception of the Fund have been accumulated as retained earnings. Retained earnings make it possible for GPO to fund a significant amount of technology modernization. However, appropriations for essential investments in technology and facilities upgrades are requested when necessary. GPO is accountable for its finances. Each year, the agency's finances and financial controls are audited by an independent outside audit firm working under contract with GPO's Office of Inspector General. For FY 2021, the audit concluded with GPO earning an unmodified, or clean, opinion on its finances, the 25th consecutive year GPO has earned such an audit result.

Object Classification (in millions of dollars)

Identification code 004–4505–0–4–808		2021 actual	2022 est.	2023 est.
	Reimbursable obligations:			
	Personnel compensation:			
11.1	Full-time permanent	160	181	182
11.5	Other personnel compensation	3		
11.9	Total personnel compensation	163	181	182
12.1	Civilian personnel benefits	40	68	72
21.0	Travel and transportation of persons		1	1
22.0	Transportation of things	6	12	11
23.2	Rental payments to others		9	4
23.3	Communications, utilities, and miscellaneous charges	15	13	18
24.0	Printing and reproduction	343	395	341
25.2	Other services from non-Federal sources	30	75	83
26.0	Supplies and materials	130	174	222
31.0	Equipment	47	46	15
99.9	Total new obligations, unexpired accounts	774	974	949

Employment Summary

Identification code 004–4505–0–4–808		2021 actual	2022 est.	2023 est.
2001	Reimbursable civilian full-time equivalent employment	1,483	1,496	1,496

GOVERNMENT ACCOUNTABILITY OFFICE

Federal Funds

SALARIES AND EXPENSES

For necessary expenses of the Government Accountability Office, including not more than $12,500 to be expended on the certification of the Comptroller General of the United States in connection with official representation and reception expenses; temporary or intermittent services under section 3109(b) of title 5, United States Code, but at rates for individuals not more than the daily equivalent of the annual rate of basic pay for level IV of the Executive Schedule under section 5315 of such title; hire of one passenger motor vehicle; advance payments in foreign countries in accordance with section 3324 of title 31, United States Code; benefits comparable to those payable under sections 901(5), (6), and (8) of the Foreign Service Act of 1980 (22 U.S.C. 4081(5), (6), and (8)); and under regulations prescribed by the Comptroller General of the United States, rental of living quarters in foreign countries, $785,319,000: Provided, That, in addition, $55,865,000 of payments received under sections 782, 791, 3521, and 9105 of title 31, United States Code, shall be available without fiscal year limitation: Provided further, for oversight, including audits and investigations, in support of the Infrastructure Investment and Jobs Act, Pub. L. No. 117–58, an additional $25,000,000 to remain available until expended: Provided further, that not later than 90 days after the date of enactment of this Act, the Comptroller General shall submit to the Committees on Appropriations of the House of Representatives and the Senate a spend plan for such oversight: Provided further, That this appropriation and appropriations for administrative expenses of any other department or agency which is a member of the National Intergovernmental Audit Forum or a Regional Intergovernmental Audit Forum shall be available to finance an appropriate share of either Forums costs as determined by the respective Forum, including necessary travel expenses of non-Federal participants: Provided further, That payments hereunder to the Forum may be credited as reimbursements to any appropriation from which costs involved are initially financed.

Note.—A full-year 2022 appropriation for this account was not enacted at the time the Budget was prepared; therefore, the Budget assumes this account is operating under the Continuing Appropriations Act, 2022 (Division A of Public Law 117–43, as amended). The amounts included for 2022 reflect the annualized level provided by the continuing resolution.

Program and Financing (in millions of dollars)

Identification code 005–0107–0–1–801		2021 actual	2022 est.	2023 est.
	Obligations by program activity:			
0001	GOAL 1-Address Current and Emerging Challenges to the Well-being and Financial Security of the American People	253	253	301
0002	GOAL 2-Respond to Changing Security Threats and the Challenges of Global Interdependence	133	133	158
0003	GOAL 3-Help Transform the Federal Government to Address National Challenges	184	184	219
0004	GOAL 4-Maximize the Value of GAO by Enabling Quality, Timely Service to the Congress, and by Being a Leading Practices Federal Agency	24	24	28
0005	GOAL 8-Other Costs in Support of the Congress	67	67	79
0799	Total direct obligations	661	661	785
0801	Reimbursable program activity goal 1	33	39	39
0802	Reimbursable program activity goal 2	7	8	8
0803	Reimbursable program activity goal 3	12	14	14
0809	Reimbursable program activities, subtotal	52	61	61
0899	Total reimbursable obligations	52	61	61
0900	Total new obligations, unexpired accounts	713	722	846
	Budgetary resources:			
	Unobligated balance:			
1000	Unobligated balance brought forward, Oct 1	84	161	137
1001	Discretionary unobligated balance brought fwd, Oct 1	84		
1033	Recoveries of prior year paid obligations	8		
1070	Unobligated balance (total)	92	161	137
	Budget authority:			
	Appropriations, discretionary:			
1100	Appropriation	671	661	785
	Appropriations, mandatory:			
1200	Appropriation	77		
	Spending authority from offsetting collections, discretionary:			
1700	Collected	35	37	27
1701	Change in uncollected payments, Federal sources	–1		
1750	Spending auth from offsetting collections, disc (total)	34	37	27
1900	Budget authority (total)	782	698	812
1930	Total budgetary resources available	874	859	949
	Memorandum (non-add) entries:			
1941	Unexpired unobligated balance, end of year	161	137	103
	Change in obligated balance:			
	Unpaid obligations:			
3000	Unpaid obligations, brought forward, Oct 1	95	131	60
3010	New obligations, unexpired accounts	713	722	846
3011	Obligations ("upward adjustments"), expired accounts	9		
3020	Outlays (gross)	–682	–793	–814
3041	Recoveries of prior year unpaid obligations, expired	–4		
3050	Unpaid obligations, end of year	131	60	92
	Uncollected payments:			
3060	Uncollected pymts, Fed sources, brought forward, Oct 1	–16	–15	–15
3070	Change in uncollected pymts, Fed sources, unexpired	1		
3090	Uncollected pymts, Fed sources, end of year	–15	–15	–15
	Memorandum (non-add) entries:			
3100	Obligated balance, start of year	79	116	45
3200	Obligated balance, end of year	116	45	77
	Budget authority and outlays, net:			
	Discretionary:			
4000	Budget authority, gross	705	698	812
	Outlays, gross:			
4010	Outlays from new discretionary authority	582	691	803
4011	Outlays from discretionary balances	79	65	8
4020	Outlays, gross (total)	661	756	811
	Offsets against gross budget authority and outlays:			
	Offsetting collections (collected) from:			
4030	Federal sources	–35	–37	–27
4033	Non-Federal sources	–15		
4040	Offsets against gross budget authority and outlays (total)	–50	–37	–27
	Additional offsets against gross budget authority only:			
4050	Change in uncollected pymts, Fed sources, unexpired	1		
4052	Offsetting collections credited to expired accounts	7		
4053	Recoveries of prior year paid obligations, unexpired accounts	8		
4060	Additional offsets against budget authority only (total)	16		
4070	Budget authority, net (discretionary)	671	661	785

Government Accountability Office—Continued
Federal Funds—Continued

SALARIES AND EXPENSES—Continued

Program and Financing—Continued

Identification code 005–0107–0–1–801	2021 actual	2022 est.	2023 est.
4080 Outlays, net (discretionary)	611	719	784
Mandatory:			
4090 Budget authority, gross	77		
Outlays, gross:			
4100 Outlays from new mandatory authority	21		
4101 Outlays from mandatory balances		37	3
4110 Outlays, gross (total)	21	37	3
4180 Budget authority, net (total)	748	661	785
4190 Outlays, net (total)	632	756	787

GAO exists to support the Congress in meeting its constitutional responsibilities and to help improve the performance and ensure the accountability of the Federal Government for the benefit of the American people.

Object Classification (in millions of dollars)

Identification code 005–0107–0–1–801	2021 actual	2022 est.	2023 est.
Direct obligations:			
Personnel compensation:			
11.1 Full-time permanent	374	388	421
11.3 Other than full-time permanent	14	14	13
11.5 Other personnel compensation	6	5	9
11.9 Total personnel compensation	394	407	443
12.1 Civilian personnel benefits	135	146	164
21.0 Travel and transportation of persons			6
23.1 Rental payments to GSA	6	6	6
23.3 Communications, utilities, and miscellaneous charges	6	5	27
25.1 Advisory and assistance services	4	3	8
25.2 Other services from non-Federal sources	17	12	39
25.3 Other goods and services from Federal sources	3	2	2
25.4 Operation and maintenance of facilities	11	10	18
25.6 Medical care	1		1
25.7 Operation and maintenance of equipment	57	45	61
31.0 Equipment	7	6	3
32.0 Land and structures	20	19	7
99.0 Direct obligations	661	661	785
99.0 Reimbursable obligations	52	61	61
99.9 Total new obligations, unexpired accounts	713	722	846

Employment Summary

Identification code 005–0107–0–1–801	2021 actual	2022 est.	2023 est.
1001 Direct civilian full-time equivalent employment	2,944	3,033	3,227
2001 Reimbursable civilian full-time equivalent employment	265	284	273

ADMINISTRATIVE PROVISION

SEC. 1001. RECLASSIFICATION OF COMPTROLLER GENERAL OF THE UNITED STATES—

(a) Section 703(f)(1) of title 31, United States Code, is amended by striking "II" and inserting "I".

(b) Notwithstanding any other provision of law, upon the effective date of this act and through the last pay period of calendar year 2023, the payable rate of pay of the Comptroller General of the United States shall be the rate payable for Executive Schedule level I in effect on December 31, 2019.

UNITED STATES TAX COURT

Federal Funds

SALARIES AND EXPENSES

(INCLUDING TRANSFER OF FUNDS)

For necessary expenses, including contract reporting and other services as authorized by 5 U.S.C. 3109, and not to exceed $3,000 for official reception and representation expenses, $57,300,000, of which $1,000,000 shall remain available until expended: Provided, That the amount made available under 26 U.S.C. 7475 shall be transferred and added to any amounts available under 26 U.S.C. 7473, to remain available until expended, for the operation and maintenance of the United States Tax Court: Provided further, That travel expenses of the judges shall be paid upon the written certificate of the judge.

Note.—A full-year 2022 appropriation for this account was not enacted at the time the Budget was prepared; therefore, the Budget assumes this account is operating under the Continuing Appropriations Act, 2022 (Division A of Public Law 117–43, as amended). The amounts included for 2022 reflect the annualized level provided by the continuing resolution.

Program and Financing (in millions of dollars)

Identification code 023–0100–0–1–752	2021 actual	2022 est.	2023 est.
Obligations by program activity:			
0001 Salaries and Expenses (Direct)	56	56	57
Budgetary resources:			
Unobligated balance:			
1000 Unobligated balance brought forward, Oct 1	1	1	1
Budget authority:			
Appropriations, discretionary:			
1100 Appropriation	56	56	57
1930 Total budgetary resources available	57	57	58
Memorandum (non-add) entries:			
1941 Unexpired unobligated balance, end of year	1	1	1
Change in obligated balance:			
Unpaid obligations:			
3000 Unpaid obligations, brought forward, Oct 1	6	7	8
3010 New obligations, unexpired accounts	56	56	57
3020 Outlays (gross)	–54	–55	–56
3041 Recoveries of prior year unpaid obligations, expired	–1		
3050 Unpaid obligations, end of year	7	8	9
Memorandum (non-add) entries:			
3100 Obligated balance, start of year	6	7	8
3200 Obligated balance, end of year	7	8	9
Budget authority and outlays, net:			
Discretionary:			
4000 Budget authority, gross	56	56	57
Outlays, gross:			
4010 Outlays from new discretionary authority	49	50	51
4011 Outlays from discretionary balances	5	5	5
4020 Outlays, gross (total)	54	55	56
4180 Budget authority, net (total)	56	56	57
4190 Outlays, net (total)	54	55	56

The U.S. Tax Court is an independent judicial body established under Article I of the Constitution of the United States. The Tax Court's jurisdiction is established by various sections of U.S. Code Title 26. The Tax Court's jurisdiction includes income, estate, gift, and certain excise tax deficiencies, declaratory judgments, review of awards under the IRS whistleblower program, and review of certain certifications by the Commissioner of Internal Revenue.

The Tax Court provides a national forum for the resolution of disputes between taxpayers and the IRS, and it is the primary court in which taxpayers can seek resolution without prepaying any portion of the disputed taxes. The Tax Court resolves cases expeditiously while giving careful consideration to the merits of each matter, and ensures uniform interpretation of the Internal Revenue Code. Decisions by the Court are reviewable by the U.S. Courts of Appeals and, if certiorari is granted, by the Supreme Court.

The Court is composed of 19 judges who are appointed to 15-year terms by the President with the advice and consent of the Senate. Senior judges may be recalled by the chief judge to participate in case adjudication. The chief judge may also assign small tax cases and certain regular cases to special trial judges, who are appointed by the chief judge. The Court is headquartered in Washington, D.C. The Court conducts trial sessions in 74 cities throughout the United States.

Object Classification (in millions of dollars)

Identification code 023–0100–0–1–752	2021 actual	2022 est.	2023 est.
Direct obligations:			
11.1 Personnel compensation: Full-time permanent	27	27	29
12.1 Civilian personnel benefits	8	8	9
21.0 Travel and transportation of persons			1

LEGISLATIVE BRANCH

		2021 actual	2022 est.	2023 est.
23.1	Rental payments to GSA	10	10	11
23.3	Communications, utilities, and miscellaneous charges	1	1	1
25.1	Advisory and assistance services	3	3	
25.3	Other goods and services from Federal sources	5	5	4
26.0	Supplies and materials	1	1	1
31.0	Equipment	1	1	1
99.9	Total new obligations, unexpired accounts	56	56	57

Employment Summary

Identification code 023–0100–0–1–752	2021 actual	2022 est.	2023 est.
1001 Direct civilian full-time equivalent employment	209	224	234

U. S. TAX COURT FEES

Special and Trust Fund Receipts (in millions of dollars)

Identification code 023–5633–0–2–752	2021 actual	2022 est.	2023 est.
0100 Balance, start of year			
Receipts:			
Current law:			
1110 U. S. Tax Court Fees	1	1	1
2000 Total: Balances and receipts	1	1	1
Appropriations:			
Current law:			
2101 U. S. Tax Court Fees	–1	–1	–1
5099 Balance, end of year			

Program and Financing (in millions of dollars)

Identification code 023–5633–0–2–752	2021 actual	2022 est.	2023 est.
Obligations by program activity:			
0001 Salaries and Expenses			4
Budgetary resources:			
Unobligated balance:			
1000 Unobligated balance brought forward, Oct 1	3	4	5
Budget authority:			
Appropriations, mandatory:			
1201 Appropriation (special or trust fund)	1	1	1
1900 Budget authority (total)	1	1	1
1930 Total budgetary resources available	4	5	6
Memorandum (non-add) entries:			
1941 Unexpired unobligated balance, end of year	4	5	2
Change in obligated balance:			
Unpaid obligations:			
3000 Unpaid obligations, brought forward, Oct 1	2		
3010 New obligations, unexpired accounts			4
3020 Outlays (gross)	–2		–1
3050 Unpaid obligations, end of year			3
Memorandum (non-add) entries:			
3100 Obligated balance, start of year	2		
3200 Obligated balance, end of year			3
Budget authority and outlays, net:			
Mandatory:			
4090 Budget authority, gross	1	1	1
Outlays, gross:			
4100 Outlays from new mandatory authority			1
4101 Outlays from mandatory balances	2		
4110 Outlays, gross (total)	2		1
4180 Budget authority, net (total)	1	1	1
4190 Outlays, net (total)	2		1

Object Classification (in millions of dollars)

Identification code 023–5633–0–2–752	2021 actual	2022 est.	2023 est.
Direct obligations:			
25.1 Advisory and assistance services			1
31.0 Equipment			3

United States Tax Court—Continued
Trust Funds

37

		2021 actual	2022 est.	2023 est.
99.9	Total new obligations, unexpired accounts			4

Trust Funds

TAX COURT JUDGES SURVIVORS ANNUITY FUND

Special and Trust Fund Receipts (in millions of dollars)

Identification code 023–8115–0–7–602	2021 actual	2022 est.	2023 est.
0100 Balance, start of year	12	13	15
Receipts:			
Current law:			
1110 Tax Court Judges Survivors Annuity, Deductions from Employees Salaries		1	1
1140 Tax Court Judges Survivors Annuity, Interest and Profits on Investments		2	1
1199 Total current law receipts		3	2
1999 Total receipts		3	2
2000 Total: Balances and receipts	12	16	17
Appropriations:			
Current law:			
2101 Tax Court Judges Survivors Annuity Fund		–1	–1
5098 Reconciliation adjustment	1		
5099 Balance, end of year	13	15	16

Program and Financing (in millions of dollars)

Identification code 023–8115–0–7–602	2021 actual	2022 est.	2023 est.
Obligations by program activity:			
0001 Tax Court Judges Survivors Annuity Fund (Direct)		1	1
0900 Total new obligations, unexpired accounts (object class 11.5)		1	1
Budgetary resources:			
Budget authority:			
Appropriations, mandatory:			
1201 Appropriation (special or trust fund)		1	1
1930 Total budgetary resources available		1	1
Change in obligated balance:			
Unpaid obligations:			
3000 Unpaid obligations, brought forward, Oct 1			1
3010 New obligations, unexpired accounts		1	1
3050 Unpaid obligations, end of year		1	2
Memorandum (non-add) entries:			
3100 Obligated balance, start of year			1
3200 Obligated balance, end of year		1	2
Budget authority and outlays, net:			
Mandatory:			
4090 Budget authority, gross		1	1
4180 Budget authority, net (total)		1	1
4190 Outlays, net (total)			
Memorandum (non-add) entries:			
5000 Total investments, SOY: Federal securities: Par value	13	13	13
5001 Total investments, EOY: Federal securities: Par value	13	13	13

The Tax Court Judges' Survivors Annuity Fund provides survivorship benefits to eligible surviving spouses and dependent children of deceased Tax Court judges. Participating judges pay 3.5 percent of their salaries or retired pay into the fund to cover creditable service for which payment is required. Additional funds, as needed, are provided through the Court's annual appropriation.

LEGISLATIVE BRANCH BOARDS AND COMMISSIONS
Federal Funds

MEDICARE PAYMENT ADVISORY COMMISSION
SALARIES AND EXPENSES

For expenses necessary to carry out section 1805 of the Social Security Act, $13,440,075, to be transferred to this appropriation from the Federal Hospital Insurance and the Federal Supplementary Medical Insurance Trust Funds.

Note.—A full-year 2022 appropriation for this account was not enacted at the time the Budget was prepared; therefore, the Budget assumes this account is operating under the Continuing Appropriations Act, 2022 (Division A of Public Law 117–43, as amended). The amounts included for 2022 reflect the annualized level provided by the continuing resolution.

Program and Financing (in millions of dollars)

Identification code 235–1550–0–1–571		2021 actual	2022 est.	2023 est.
	Obligations by program activity:			
0801	Medicare Payment Advisory Commission (Reimbursable)	13	13	13
0809	Reimbursable program activities, subtotal	13	13	13
	Budgetary resources:			
	Budget authority:			
	Spending authority from offsetting collections, discretionary:			
1700	Collected	13	13	13
1930	Total budgetary resources available	13	13	13
	Change in obligated balance:			
	Unpaid obligations:			
3000	Unpaid obligations, brought forward, Oct 1	2	3	3
3010	New obligations, unexpired accounts	13	13	13
3020	Outlays (gross)	–12	–13	–13
3050	Unpaid obligations, end of year	3	3	3
	Memorandum (non-add) entries:			
3100	Obligated balance, start of year	2	3	3
3200	Obligated balance, end of year	3	3	3
	Budget authority and outlays, net:			
	Discretionary:			
4000	Budget authority, gross	13	13	13
	Outlays, gross:			
4010	Outlays from new discretionary authority	10	10	10
4011	Outlays from discretionary balances	2	3	3
4020	Outlays, gross (total)	12	13	13
	Offsets against gross budget authority and outlays:			
	Offsetting collections (collected) from:			
4030	Federal sources	–13	–13	–13
4040	Offsets against gross budget authority and outlays (total)	–13	–13	–13
4180	Budget authority, net (total)			
4190	Outlays, net (total)	–1		

The Medicare Payment Advisory Commission, established under section 1805 of the Social Security Act (42 U.S.C. 1395(b)(6) as amended by section 4022 of the Balanced Budget Act of 1997 (P.L. 105–33), is an independent legislative agency charged with advising the Congress on payment and other policy issues affecting the Medicare program, as well as on the implications of changes in health care delivery in the United States and in the market for health care services on the Medicare program.

The Commission's 17 members represent diverse points of view including providers, payers, consumers, employers, and individuals with expertise in biomedical, health services, and health economics research. It maintains a full time staff of 34 in Washington, D.C.

The Commission is required by law to report to the Congress on March 15 and June 15 of each year, and to comment on Congressionally mandated reports of the Secretary of Health and Human Services.

Object Classification (in millions of dollars)

Identification code 235–1550–0–1–571		2021 actual	2022 est.	2023 est.
	Reimbursable obligations:			
11.1	Personnel compensation: Full-time permanent	5	5	5
12.1	Civilian personnel benefits	2	2	2
23.3	Communications, utilities, and miscellaneous charges	1	1	1
25.1	Advisory and assistance services	5	5	5
99.9	Total new obligations, unexpired accounts	13	13	13

Employment Summary

Identification code 235–1550–0–1–571		2021 actual	2022 est.	2023 est.
2001	Reimbursable civilian full-time equivalent employment	32	33	34

MEDICAID AND CHIP PAYMENT AND ACCESS COMMISSION
SALARIES AND EXPENSES

For expenses necessary to carry out section 1900 of the Social Security Act, $9,727,000.

Note.—A full-year 2022 appropriation for this account was not enacted at the time the Budget was prepared; therefore, the Budget assumes this account is operating under the Continuing Appropriations Act, 2022 (Division A of Public Law 117–43, as amended). The amounts included for 2022 reflect the annualized level provided by the continuing resolution.

Program and Financing (in millions of dollars)

Identification code 009–1801–0–1–551		2021 actual	2022 est.	2023 est.
	Obligations by program activity:			
0123	Medicaid and CHIP Payment and Access Commission (Direct)	9	9	10
	Budgetary resources:			
	Unobligated balance:			
1000	Unobligated balance brought forward, Oct 1	1	1	1
	Budget authority:			
	Appropriations, discretionary:			
1100	Appropriation	9	9	10
1900	Budget authority (total)	9	9	10
1930	Total budgetary resources available	10	10	11
	Memorandum (non-add) entries:			
1941	Unexpired unobligated balance, end of year	1	1	1
	Change in obligated balance:			
	Unpaid obligations:			
3000	Unpaid obligations, brought forward, Oct 1	2	2	
3010	New obligations, unexpired accounts	9	9	10
3020	Outlays (gross)	–9	–11	–10
3050	Unpaid obligations, end of year	2		
	Memorandum (non-add) entries:			
3100	Obligated balance, start of year	2	2	
3200	Obligated balance, end of year	2		
	Budget authority and outlays, net:			
	Discretionary:			
4000	Budget authority, gross	9	9	10
	Outlays, gross:			
4010	Outlays from new discretionary authority	7	9	10
4011	Outlays from discretionary balances	2	2	
4020	Outlays, gross (total)	9	11	10
4180	Budget authority, net (total)	9	9	10
4190	Outlays, net (total)	9	11	10

The Medicaid and CHIP Payment and Access Commission (MACPAC) is a non-partisan legislative branch agency that provides policy and data analysis and makes recommendations to Congress, the Secretary of the U.S. Department of Health and Human Services, and the states on a wide array of issues affecting Medicaid and the State Children's Health Insurance Program (CHIP). The U.S. Comptroller General appoints MACPAC's 17 commissioners, who come from diverse regions across the United States and bring broad expertise and a wide range of perspectives on Medicaid and CHIP.

MACPAC serves as an independent source of information on Medicaid and CHIP, publishing issue briefs and data reports throughout the year to support policy analysis and program accountability. The Commission's authorizing statute, 42 U.S.C. 1396, outlines a number of areas for analysis, including: payment; eligibility; enrollment and retention; coverage; access to care; quality of care; and the programs' interaction with Medicare and the health care system generally.

MACPAC's authorizing statute also requires the Commission to submit reports to Congress by March 15 and June 15 of each year. In carrying out its work, the Commission holds public meetings and regularly consults with state officials, congressional and executive branch staff, beneficiaries, health care providers, researchers, and policy experts.

Object Classification (in millions of dollars)

Identification code 009–1801–0–1–551		2021 actual	2022 est.	2023 est.
	Direct obligations:			
11.1	Personnel compensation: Full-time permanent	4	4	5
12.1	Civilian personnel benefits	1	1	1
25.1	Advisory and assistance services	3	3	3
99.0	Direct obligations	8	8	9
99.5	Adjustment for rounding	1	1	1
99.9	Total new obligations, unexpired accounts	9	9	10

Employment Summary

Identification code 009–1801–0–1–551	2021 actual	2022 est.	2023 est.
1001 Direct civilian full-time equivalent employment	30	33	33

UNITED STATES-CHINA ECONOMIC AND SECURITY REVIEW COMMISSION

SALARIES AND EXPENSES

For necessary expenses of the United States-China Economic and Security Review Commission, as authorized by section 1238 of the Floyd D. Spence National Defense Authorization Act for Fiscal Year 2001 (22 U.S.C. 7002), $4,000,000, including not more than $4,000 for representation expenses, to remain available until September 30, 2024: Provided, That the authorities, requirements, limitations, and conditions contained in the second through fifth provisos under this heading in the Department of State, Foreign Operations, and Related Programs Appropriations Act, 2010 (division F of Public Law 111–117) shall continue in effect during fiscal year 2023 and shall apply to funds appropriated under this heading.

Note.—A full-year 2022 appropriation for this account was not enacted at the time the Budget was prepared; therefore, the Budget assumes this account is operating under the Continuing Appropriations Act, 2022 (Division A of Public Law 117–43, as amended). The amounts included for 2022 reflect the annualized level provided by the continuing resolution.

Program and Financing (in millions of dollars)

Identification code 292–2973–0–1–801		2021 actual	2022 est.	2023 est.
	Obligations by program activity:			
0001	United States-China Economic and Security Review Commission (Direct)	4	4	4
0900	Total new obligations, unexpired accounts	4	4	4
	Budgetary resources:			
	Unobligated balance:			
1000	Unobligated balance brought forward, Oct 1	1	1	1
	Budget authority:			
	Appropriations, discretionary:			
1100	Appropriation	4	4	4
1930	Total budgetary resources available	5	5	5
	Memorandum (non-add) entries:			
1941	Unexpired unobligated balance, end of year	1	1	1
	Change in obligated balance:			
	Unpaid obligations:			
3010	New obligations, unexpired accounts	4	4	4
3020	Outlays (gross)	–4	–4	–4
	Budget authority and outlays, net:			
	Discretionary:			
4000	Budget authority, gross	4	4	4
	Outlays, gross:			
4010	Outlays from new discretionary authority	3	3	3
4011	Outlays from discretionary balances	1	1	1
4020	Outlays, gross (total)	4	4	4
4180	Budget authority, net (total)	4	4	4
4190	Outlays, net (total)	4	4	4

U.S.-China Economic and Security Review Commission.—Congress created the U.S.-China Economic and Security Review Commission in 2000 in the National Defense Authorization Act (Public Law 106–398) as amended by Division P of the Consolidated Appropriations Resolution, 2003 (Public Law 108–7), as amended by Public Law 109–108 (November 10, 2005), as amended by Public Law 113–291 (December 19, 2014). The statute gives the Commission the mandate to monitor, investigate, and assess the "national security implications of the bilateral trade and economic relationship between the United States and the People's Republic of China." Its members are appointed by Congressional leaders, and its statutory mandate is to report to Congress on Chinese proliferation practices; the qualitative and quantitative effects of transfers of U.S. economic production activities to China; the effects of the need for energy on China's foreign and military policies and the impact of China's growing economy on world energy resources; foreign investment by the U.S. in China, and China's foreign investment in the U.S.; the military plans, strategy, doctrine and structure of China's military; strategic economic and security implications of China's cyber capabilities and operations; China's national budget, fiscal policy, monetary policy, and currency management practices; the drivers, nature, and implications of China's growing economic, technological, political, cultural, people-to-people, and security relations of China with other countries and international organizations; China's compliance with its commitments to the World Trade Organization and other bilateral and multilateral agreements; the implications of China's restrictions on freedom of expression; and the safety of food, drug, and other products imported from China. The Commission reports annually on these issues to the Congress, making recommendations for policy action and legislation when appropriate. In order to obtain new information and perspectives on these issues, the Commission conducts hearings throughout the year and maintains a website containing the records of these proceedings as well as original research on economic and security matters related to the Commission's statutory mandate.

The Commission is comprised of 12 Commissioners, 3 Commissioners appointed by each leader in the House and Senate, supported by a professional staff numbering approximately 20. The chairmanship of the Commission rotates between a Republican and a Democratic Commissioner upon issuance of each annual report to Congress.

Object Classification (in millions of dollars)

Identification code 292–2973–0–1–801		2021 actual	2022 est.	2023 est.
11.1	Direct obligations: Personnel compensation: Full-time permanent	2	2	2
99.5	Adjustment for rounding	2	2	2
99.9	Total new obligations, unexpired accounts	4	4	4

Employment Summary

Identification code 292–2973–0–1–801	2021 actual	2022 est.	2023 est.
1001 Direct civilian full-time equivalent employment	19	20	20
1001 Direct civilian full-time equivalent employment	12	12	12

UNITED STATES COMMISSION ON INTERNATIONAL RELIGIOUS FREEDOM

SALARIES AND EXPENSES

For necessary expenses for the United States Commission on International Religious Freedom, as authorized by title II of the International Religious Freedom Act of 1998 (22 U.S.C. 6431 et seq.), $4,500,000, including not more than $4,000 for representation expenses: Provided, That if the United States Commission on International Religious Freedom is authorized beyond September 30, 2022, this amount will remain available until September 30, 2024.

Note.—A full-year 2022 appropriation for this account was not enacted at the time the Budget was prepared; therefore, the Budget assumes this account is operating under the Continuing Appropriations Act, 2022 (Division A of Public Law 117–43, as amended). The amounts included for 2022 reflect the annualized level provided by the continuing resolution.

UNITED STATES COMMISSION ON INTERNATIONAL RELIGIOUS FREEDOM—Continued

Program and Financing (in millions of dollars)

Identification code 295–2975–0–1–801	2021 actual	2022 est.	2023 est.
Obligations by program activity:			
0001 United States Commission on International Religious Freedom (Direct)	4	4	4
Budgetary resources:			
Unobligated balance:			
1000 Unobligated balance brought forward, Oct 1	3	3	4
Budget authority:			
Appropriations, discretionary:			
1100 Appropriation	5	5	5
1930 Total budgetary resources available	8	8	9
Memorandum (non-add) entries:			
1940 Unobligated balance expiring	–1		
1941 Unexpired unobligated balance, end of year	3	4	5
Change in obligated balance:			
Unpaid obligations:			
3000 Unpaid obligations, brought forward, Oct 1	1	1	1
3010 New obligations, unexpired accounts	4	4	4
3020 Outlays (gross)	–4	–4	–4
3050 Unpaid obligations, end of year	1	1	1
Memorandum (non-add) entries:			
3100 Obligated balance, start of year	1	1	1
3200 Obligated balance, end of year	1	1	1
Budget authority and outlays, net:			
Discretionary:			
4000 Budget authority, gross	5	5	5
Outlays, gross:			
4010 Outlays from new discretionary authority	2	2	2
4011 Outlays from discretionary balances	2	2	2
4020 Outlays, gross (total)	4	4	4
4180 Budget authority, net (total)	5	5	5
4190 Outlays, net (total)	4	4	4

The United States Commission on International Religious Freedom is an independent, bipartisan U.S. Government agency that was created by the International Religious Freedom Act of 1998, as amended by the Frank R. Wolf International Religious Freedom Act, to monitor the status of the freedom of thought, conscience, and religion or belief abroad, as defined in the Universal Declaration of Human Rights and related international instruments, and to give independent policy recommendations to the President, the Secretary of State and the Congress.

Object Classification (in millions of dollars)

Identification code 295–2975–0–1–801	2021 actual	2022 est.	2023 est.
Direct obligations:			
11.1 Personnel compensation: Full-time permanent	2	2	2
21.0 Travel and transportation of persons	1	1	1
25.2 Other services from non-Federal sources	1	1	1
99.0 Direct obligations	4	4	4
99.9 Total new obligations, unexpired accounts	4	4	4

Employment Summary

Identification code 295–2975–0–1–801	2021 actual	2022 est.	2023 est.
1001 Direct civilian full-time equivalent employment	21	21	21

WORLD WAR I CENTENNIAL COMMISSION

SALARIES AND EXPENSES

Notwithstanding Section 9 of the World War I Centennial Commission Act, $1,000,000 is hereby appropriated to the World War I Centennial Commission to remain available for obligation until expended, for activities of the Commission including construction of the National WWI Memorial. It is the intent of the Congress that executive branch agencies, including specifically the Department of Defense and the uniformed services, in addition to this appropriation, shall support activities of the World War I Centennial Commission with in-kind personnel or other appropriate support; contractual support; and/or additional funding. Notwithstanding other applicable statutes or regulations, the World War I Centennial Commission shall continue in existence for not more than 180 days following the Dedication of the National World War I Memorial.

Note.—A full-year 2022 appropriation for this account was not enacted at the time the Budget was prepared; therefore, the Budget assumes this account is operating under the Continuing Appropriations Act, 2022 (Division A of Public Law 117–43, as amended). The amounts included for 2022 reflect the annualized level provided by the continuing resolution.

Program and Financing (in millions of dollars)

Identification code 480–5589–0–2–801	2021 actual	2022 est.	2023 est.
Obligations by program activity:			
0001 WWI Centennial Commission	7	7	1
Budgetary resources:			
Budget authority:			
Appropriations, discretionary:			
1100 Appropriation	7	7	1
1900 Budget authority (total)	7	7	1
1930 Total budgetary resources available	7	7	1
Change in obligated balance:			
Unpaid obligations:			
3000 Unpaid obligations, brought forward, Oct 1	1	2	1
3010 New obligations, unexpired accounts	7	7	1
3020 Outlays (gross)	–6	–8	–2
3050 Unpaid obligations, end of year	2	1	
Memorandum (non-add) entries:			
3100 Obligated balance, start of year	1	2	1
3200 Obligated balance, end of year	2	1	
Budget authority and outlays, net:			
Discretionary:			
4000 Budget authority, gross	7	7	1
Outlays, gross:			
4010 Outlays from new discretionary authority	6	7	1
4011 Outlays from discretionary balances		1	1
4020 Outlays, gross (total)	6	8	2
4180 Budget authority, net (total)	7	7	1
4190 Outlays, net (total)	6	8	2

The World War I Centennial Commission was created by Congress in 2013 by P.L. 112–272, and amended in 2014 by P.L. 113–291 to ensure a suitable observance of the centennial of World War I, which ushered in the 'American Century'. It began the advance of the rights of women and minorities in the U.S., and sowed the seeds for international conflicts for a century, many of which are ongoing today. America's support of Great Britain, France, Belgium, and its other allies in World War I marked the first time in United States history that American soldiers went abroad in defense of liberty against foreign aggression. 4.7 million men and women from the United States served in uniform during World War I, among them 2 future presidents, Harry S. Truman and Dwight D. Eisenhower. Two million individuals from the United States served overseas during World War I, including 200,000 naval personnel who served on the seas. The United States suffered 375,000 casualties during World War I, including 116,516 deaths, more than in the Korean War and Vietnam War combined. The centennial of World War I offers an opportunity for people in the United States to learn about and commemorate the sacrifices of their predecessors. Commemorative programs, activities, and sites allow them to learn about the history of World War I, the United States involvement in that war, and the war's effects on the remainder of the 20th and into the 21st century, and to commemorate and honor the participation of the United States and its citizens in the war effort. Congress also redesignated Pershing Park in the District of Columbia as a 'World War I Memorial', and authorized The Commission to plan, develop, and execute ceremonies for that redesignation, and for the enhancement of the General Pershing Commemorative Work by constructing an World War I Memorial containing appropriate sculptural and other commemorative elements, including landscaping, to further honor the service of members of the United States Armed Forces in World War I. Although the Commission is scheduled to sunset in July of 2019, P.L. 113–291 provides for continuation of the Commission to enable completion of the World War I Memorial under section 3091(b) of the National Defense Authorization Act for Fiscal Year 2015. The Commission is bipartisan and consists of 12 private citizens; 6 are appointed by the Congress, 3 are appointed by the President, 1 each is appointed by the National World War I Museum in Kansas City, MO, the VFW, and the American Legion. The Commission is augmented by ex-officio members and advisors: The Archivist of the United States, The Librarian of Congress, The Secretary of the Smithsonian Institution, The Secretary of Education, The Secretary of State, The Secretary of Veterans Affairs, The Administrator of General Services, The Department of Defense, The Department of Homeland Security, and the Secretary of the Interior.

Object Classification (in millions of dollars)

Identification code 480–5589–0–2–801		2021 actual	2022 est.	2023 est.
11.3	Direct obligations: Personnel compensation: Other than full-time permanent		1	1	
11.9	Total personnel compensation		1	1	
25.1	Advisory and assistance services		6	6	1
99.9	Total new obligations, unexpired accounts		7	7	1

Employment Summary

Identification code 480–5589–0–2–801	2021 actual	2022 est.	2023 est.
1001 Direct civilian full-time equivalent employment	4	4	4

CAPITAL CONSTRUCTION, DWIGHT D. EISENHOWER MEMORIAL COMMISSION

Program and Financing (in millions of dollars)

Identification code 283–2990–0–1–801		2021 actual	2022 est.	2023 est.
	Obligations by program activity:			
0001	Capital Construction, Dwight D. Eisenhower Memorial Commission (Direct)		2		
0293	Direct program activities, subtotal		2		
0900	Total new obligations, unexpired accounts (object class 25.1)		2		
	Budgetary resources:				
	Unobligated balance:				
1021	Recoveries of prior year unpaid obligations		2		
1930	Total budgetary resources available		2		
	Change in obligated balance:				
	Unpaid obligations:				
3000	Unpaid obligations, brought forward, Oct 1		5		
3010	New obligations, unexpired accounts		2		
3020	Outlays (gross)		–5		
3040	Recoveries of prior year unpaid obligations, unexpired		–2		
	Memorandum (non-add) entries:				
3100	Obligated balance, start of year		5		
	Budget authority and outlays, net:				
	Discretionary:				
	Outlays, gross:				
4011	Outlays from discretionary balances		5		
4180	Budget authority, net (total)				
4190	Outlays, net (total)		5		

DWIGHT D. EISENHOWER MEMORIAL COMMISSION

Program and Financing (in millions of dollars)

Identification code 283–2989–0–1–801		2021 actual	2022 est.	2023 est.
	Obligations by program activity:				
0001	Dwight D. Eisenhower Memorial Commission		1		
0900	Total new obligations, unexpired accounts (object class 25.2)		1		
	Budgetary resources:				
	Budget authority:				
	Appropriations, discretionary:				
1100	Appropriation		1		
1930	Total budgetary resources available		1		
	Change in obligated balance:				
	Unpaid obligations:				
3010	New obligations, unexpired accounts		1		
3020	Outlays (gross)		–1		
	Budget authority and outlays, net:				
	Discretionary:				
4000	Budget authority, gross		1		
	Outlays, gross:				
4010	Outlays from new discretionary authority		1		
4180	Budget authority, net (total)		1		
4190	Outlays, net (total)		1		

The Dwight D. Eisenhower Memorial Commission was created by Congress in 1999 by Public Law 106–79. The Commission's congressional mandate is to establish an appropriate, permanent national memorial to Dwight D. Eisenhower, who served as Supreme Commander of the Allied forces in Europe in World War II and subsequently as 34th President of the United States. The Commission's enabling legislation dictates that a memorial should be created in the nation's capital to perpetuate his memory and his contributions to the United States.

UNITED STATES SEMIQUINCENTENNIAL COMMISSION

SALARIES AND EXPENSES

For necessary expenses of the United States Semiquincentennial Commission to plan and coordinate observances and activities associated with the 250th anniversary of the founding of the United States, as authorized by Public Law 116–282, the technical amendments to Public Law 114–196, $15,000,000, to remain available until September 30, 2024.

Note.—A full-year 2022 appropriation for this account was not enacted at the time the Budget was prepared; therefore, the Budget assumes this account is operating under the Continuing Appropriations Act, 2022 (Division A of Public Law 117–43, as amended). The amounts included for 2022 reflect the annualized level provided by the continuing resolution.

Program and Financing (in millions of dollars)

Identification code 239–2780–0–1–801		2021 actual	2022 est.	2023 est.
	Obligations by program activity:				
0001	Direct program activity		8	8	15
	Budgetary resources:				
	Budget authority:				
	Appropriations, discretionary:				
1100	Appropriation				15
1121	Appropriations transferred from other acct [014–1036]		8	8	
1160	Appropriation, discretionary (total)		8	8	15
1930	Total budgetary resources available		8	8	15
	Change in obligated balance:				
	Unpaid obligations:				
3000	Unpaid obligations, brought forward, Oct 1		1	1	
3010	New obligations, unexpired accounts		8	8	15
3020	Outlays (gross)		–8	–9	–8
3050	Unpaid obligations, end of year		1		7
	Memorandum (non-add) entries:				
3100	Obligated balance, start of year		1	1	
3200	Obligated balance, end of year		1		7

UNITED STATES SEMIQUINCENTENNIAL COMMISSION—Continued

Program and Financing—Continued

Identification code 239–2780–0–1–801	2021 actual	2022 est.	2023 est.
Budget authority and outlays, net:			
Discretionary:			
4000 Budget authority, gross	8	8	15
Outlays, gross:			
4010 Outlays from new discretionary authority	7	8	8
4011 Outlays from discretionary balances	1	1	....
4020 Outlays, gross (total)	8	9	8
4180 Budget authority, net (total)	8	8	15
4190 Outlays, net (total)	8	9	8

The U.S. Semiquincentennial Commission was established by Congress in 2016 by Public Law 114–196. Technical amendments to Public Law 114–196 were authorized by enactment of Public Law 116–282. The Commission's congressional mandate is to provide for the observance and commemoration of the 250th anniversary of the founding of the United States and related events through local, State, national and international activities planned, encouraged, developed, and coordinated by the national commission representative of appropriate public and private authorities and organizations. The Commission's enabling legislation dictates that the Commission shall prepare an overall program for commemorating the 250th anniversary of the founding of the United States and the historic events preceding that anniversary, and plan, encourage, develop, and coordinate observances and activities commemorating the historic events that preceded, and associated with, the United States Semiquincentennial. The Commission is bipartisan and consists of 24 members. Four members are members of the U.S. Senate appointed by the majority leader and minority leader of the Senate equally divided, four members of the U.S. House of Representatives appointed by the Speaker and minority leader of the House of Representatives equally divided, and sixteen are private citizens. The majority leader and minority leader of the Senate, the Speaker and minority leader of the House of Representatives will each appoint four private citizens. The Commission has identified six primary activities to execute including operations, communications and marketing, external affairs, development, nationwide planning and programming, and budget (compliance, governance and stewardship).

As the Commission approaches 2026, increased activities will require escalating funding levels from the public and private sector to fulfill its mission. The Commission will be reviewing, approving and adopting a number of Commemorative National Signature Programs and National Partner Programs during calendar year 2022. The ability to execute these programs during the primary years from July 4, 2024, through July 4, 2026, will require initial operational funding. This early operational program funding will be used to mobilize 10–15 national programs. This funding will be critical to begin the implementation and execution phases of these America250 signature programs. The Commission envisions needing a minimum of one year or longer to build out the initial infrastructure and operational plan for each program to include but not be limited to; staffing, contracting, operational, and fundraising support. For FY 2023, the Commission requests $15,000,000 to continue necessary expenses and to initiate the execution of national programs and operational plans.

Object Classification (in millions of dollars)

Identification code 239–2780–0–1–801	2021 actual	2022 est.	2023 est.
Direct obligations:			
11.1 Personnel compensation: Full-time permanent	1	1	2
25.2 Other services from non-Federal sources	7	7	13
99.9 Total new obligations, unexpired accounts	8	8	15

Employment Summary

Identification code 239–2780–0–1–801	2021 actual	2022 est.	2023 est.
1001 Direct civilian full-time equivalent employment	7	7	8

DWIGHT D. EISENHOWER MEMORIAL FUND

Program and Financing (in millions of dollars)

Identification code 283–5549–0–2–801	2021 actual	2022 est.	2023 est.
Obligations by program activity:			
0001 Dwight D. Eisenhower Memorial	4	....	....
0900 Total new obligations, unexpired accounts (object class 41.0)	4	....	....
Budgetary resources:			
Unobligated balance:			
1000 Unobligated balance brought forward, Oct 1	4	....	....
1930 Total budgetary resources available	4	....	....
Change in obligated balance:			
Unpaid obligations:			
3000 Unpaid obligations, brought forward, Oct 1	....	1	....
3010 New obligations, unexpired accounts	4	....	....
3020 Outlays (gross)	–3	–1	....
3050 Unpaid obligations, end of year	1	....	....
Memorandum (non-add) entries:			
3100 Obligated balance, start of year	....	1	....
3200 Obligated balance, end of year	1	....	....
Budget authority and outlays, net:			
Mandatory:			
Outlays, gross:			
4101 Outlays from mandatory balances	3	1	....
4180 Budget authority, net (total)	....	....	....
4190 Outlays, net (total)	3	1	....

OPEN WORLD LEADERSHIP CENTER TRUST FUND

For a payment to the Open World Leadership Center Trust Fund for financing activities of the Open World Leadership Center under section 313 of the Legislative Branch Appropriations Act, 2001 (2 U.S.C. 1151), $6,000,000: Provided, That funds made available to support Russian participants shall only be used for those engaging in free market development, humanitarian activities, and civic engagement, and shall not be used for officials of the central government of Russia.

Note.—A full-year 2022 appropriation for this account was not enacted at the time the Budget was prepared; therefore, the Budget assumes this account is operating under the Continuing Appropriations Act, 2022 (Division A of Public Law 117–43, as amended). The amounts included for 2022 reflect the annualized level provided by the continuing resolution.

Program and Financing (in millions of dollars)

Identification code 009–0145–0–1–154	2021 actual	2022 est.	2023 est.
Obligations by program activity:			
0001 Open World Leadership Center Trust Fund (Direct)	6	6	6
0900 Total new obligations, unexpired accounts (object class 94.0)	6	6	6
Budgetary resources:			
Budget authority:			
Appropriations, discretionary:			
1100 Appropriation	6	6	6
1900 Budget authority (total)	6	6	6
1930 Total budgetary resources available	6	6	6
Change in obligated balance:			
Unpaid obligations:			
3000 Unpaid obligations, brought forward, Oct 1	2	1	....
3010 New obligations, unexpired accounts	6	6	6
3020 Outlays (gross)	–7	–7	–6
3050 Unpaid obligations, end of year	1	....	....
Memorandum (non-add) entries:			
3100 Obligated balance, start of year	2	1	....

		2021 actual	2022 est.	2023 est.
3200	Obligated balance, end of year	1		
	Budget authority and outlays, net:			
	Discretionary:			
4000	Budget authority, gross	6	6	6
	Outlays, gross:			
4010	Outlays from new discretionary authority	6	6	6
4011	Outlays from discretionary balances	1	1	
4020	Outlays, gross (total)	7	7	6
4180	Budget authority, net (total)	6	6	6
4190	Outlays, net (total)	7	7	6

The Open World Leadership Center, under the direction of its Board of Trustees, supports the identification of emerging leaders from foreign countries selected by the Board of Trustees and oversees the development of an intensive program in the United States to link up to 3,000 participants each year with U.S. counterparts. The Center's mission entails enhancing the understanding and capabilities for cooperation between the United States and participating countries by developing a network of leaders who have gained significant, first-hand exposure to America's democratic and accountable government. The Center has also administered a program to enable cultural leaders from the Russian Federation to gain exposure to the operations of American cultural institutions.

The Center is authorized to solicit and accept federal and private funds, in addition to receipt of this appropriation, and to invest appropriated funds in par value securities at the U.S. Treasury. The Center is governed by an eleven-member board of trustees, composed of the Librarian of Congress, members of the U.S. Senate and House of Representatives and representatives of the private sector. The Center is authorized to obtain a wide range of administrative support, including space, from the Library of Congress.

Fiscal 2023 funding supports U.S. grants and logistical services for hosting in communities throughout the United States as well as other operating expenses of the Center.

OTHER LEGISLATIVE BRANCH BOARDS AND COMMISSIONS

COMMISSION ON SECURITY AND COOPERATION IN EUROPE

SALARIES AND EXPENSES

For necessary expenses of the Commission on Security and Cooperation in Europe, as authorized by Public Law 94–304 (22 U.S.C. 3001 et seq.), $2,908,000, including not more than $6,000 for representation expenses, to remain available until September 30, 2023.

CONGRESSIONAL-EXECUTIVE COMMISSION ON THE PEOPLE'S REPUBLIC OF CHINA

SALARIES AND EXPENSES

For necessary expenses of the Congressional-Executive Commission on the People's Republic of China, as authorized by title III of the U.S.-China Relations Act of 2000 (22 U.S.C. 6911 et seq.), $2,300,000, including not more than $3,000 for representation expenses, to remain available until September 30, 2023.

Note.—A full-year 2022 appropriation for this account was not enacted at the time the Budget was prepared; therefore, the Budget assumes this account is operating under the Continuing Appropriations Act, 2022 (Division A of Public Law 117–43, as amended). The amounts included for 2022 reflect the annualized level provided by the continuing resolution.

Program and Financing (in millions of dollars)

Identification code 009–9911–0–1–999		2021 actual	2022 est.	2023 est.
	Obligations by program activity:			
0002	Women's Suffrage Centennial Commission	1		
0006	Commission on Security and Cooperation in Europe	3	3	3
0008	Congressional Executive Commission on the People's Republic of China	3	2	2
0900	Total new obligations, unexpired accounts	7	5	5
	Budgetary resources:			
	Unobligated balance:			
1000	Unobligated balance brought forward, Oct 1	7	5	5
	Budget authority:			
	Appropriations, discretionary:			
1100	Appropriation 09–0110 Comm. on Security and Cooperation in Europe	3	3	3
1100	Appropriation 272–2930 Congressional Executive Comm. on the PRC	2	2	2
1160	Appropriation, discretionary (total)	5	5	5
1930	Total budgetary resources available	12	10	10
	Memorandum (non-add) entries:			
1941	Unexpired unobligated balance, end of year	5	5	5
	Change in obligated balance:			
	Unpaid obligations:			
3000	Unpaid obligations, brought forward, Oct 1	1	1	1
3010	New obligations, unexpired accounts	7	5	5
3020	Outlays (gross)	–7	–5	–6
3050	Unpaid obligations, end of year	1	1	
	Memorandum (non-add) entries:			
3100	Obligated balance, start of year	1	1	1
3200	Obligated balance, end of year	1	1	
	Budget authority and outlays, net:			
	Discretionary:			
4000	Budget authority, gross	5	5	5
	Outlays, gross:			
4010	Outlays from new discretionary authority	2	2	3
4011	Outlays from discretionary balances	5	3	3
4020	Outlays, gross (total)	7	5	6
4180	Budget authority, net (total)	5	5	5
4190	Outlays, net (total)	7	5	6
	Memorandum (non-add) entries:			
5000	Total investments, SOY: Federal securities: Par value	1	1	
5001	Total investments, EOY: Federal securities: Par value	1		

This presentation includes the following:

Commission on Security and Cooperation in Europe.—The Commission on Security and Cooperation in Europe is authorized and directed to monitor the acts of the signatories which reflect compliance with or violation of the articles of the Final Act of the Conference on Security and Cooperation in Europe, with particular regard to the provisions relating to Cooperation in Humanitarian Fields. The law establishing the Commission on Security and Cooperation in Europe also mandated it to monitor and encourage U.S. Government and private activities designed to expand East-West trade and the exchange of people and ideas. The Commission will receive an annual report from the Secretary of State discussing the overall United States policy objectives that are advanced through meetings of decision-making bodies of the Organization for Security and Cooperation in Europe (OSCE), the OSCE implementation review process, and other activities of the OSCE.

Congressional-Executive Commission on the People's Republic of China.—Congress created the Congressional-Executive Commission on the People's Republic of China (CECC) in 2000 by passing Title III of P.L. 106–286, the China Relations Act of 2000. The statute gives the Commission the mandate to monitor the Chinese government's compliance with international human rights standards and to track the development of the rule of law in China. The Commission reports annually on these issues to the President and the Congressional leadership, making recommendations for policy action and legislation when appropriate. The CECC was also charged with creating and maintaining a registry of victims of human rights abuses in China, including prisoners of conscience. The CECC conducts hearings and staff-led issues roundtables throughout the year and maintains a website containing the records of these proceedings, as well as other information about human rights and rule of law issues in China. The CECC seeks to be a resource on these issues for Capitol Hill, the NGO community, the academic world, and the general public.

The Commission comprises nine Senators, nine Members of the House of Representatives, and five Executive Branch officials, supported by a professional staff numbering about 15 people. The chairmanship of the CECC rotates from the Senate to the House in even-numbered Congresses.

OTHER LEGISLATIVE BRANCH BOARDS AND COMMISSIONS—Continued

Women's Suffrage Centennial Commission.—The mission of the Women's Suffrage Centennial Commission is to commemorate and coordinate the nationwide celebration of the 100th anniversary of the 19th Amendment and to educate the American people about the history and leaders of the women's suffrage movement in the United States in a nonpartisan fashion.

Object Classification (in millions of dollars)

Identification code 009–9911–0–1–999		2021 actual	2022 est.	2023 est.
11.1	Direct obligations: Personnel compensation: Full-time permanent	4	4	4
11.9	Total personnel compensation	4	4	4
12.1	Civilian personnel benefits	1	1	1
25.1	Advisory and assistance services	2		
99.0	Direct obligations	7	5	5
99.9	Total new obligations, unexpired accounts	7	5	5

Employment Summary

Identification code 009–9911–0–1–999		2021 actual	2022 est.	2023 est.
1001	Direct civilian full-time equivalent employment	25	34	34

Trust Funds

JOHN C. STENNIS CENTER FOR PUBLIC SERVICE TRAINING AND DEVELOPMENT

For payment to the John C. Stennis Center for Public Service Development Trust Fund established under section 116 of the John C. Stennis Center for Public Service Training and Development Act (2 U.S.C. 1105), $430,000.

Note.—A full-year 2022 appropriation for this account was not enacted at the time the Budget was prepared; therefore, the Budget assumes this account is operating under the Continuing Appropriations Act, 2022 (Division A of Public Law 117–43, as amended). The amounts included for 2022 reflect the annualized level provided by the continuing resolution.

Special and Trust Fund Receipts (in millions of dollars)

Identification code 009–8275–0–7–801		2021 actual	2022 est.	2023 est.
0100	Balance, start of year	8	8	8
	Receipts:			
	Current law:			
1140	Payments, John C. Stennis Center for Public Service Training and Development	1	1	1
2000	Total: Balances and receipts	9	9	9
	Appropriations:			
	Current law:			
2101	John C. Stennis Center for Public Service Training and Development	–1	–1	–1
5099	Balance, end of year	8	8	8

Program and Financing (in millions of dollars)

Identification code 009–8275–0–7–801		2021 actual	2022 est.	2023 est.
	Obligations by program activity:			
0001	John C. Stennis Center for Public Service Training and Developme (Direct)	1	1	1
0900	Total new obligations, unexpired accounts (object class 25.2)	1	1	1
	Budgetary resources:			
	Unobligated balance:			
1000	Unobligated balance brought forward, Oct 1	10	10	10
	Budget authority:			
	Appropriations, mandatory:			
1201	Appropriation (special or trust fund)	1	1	1
1930	Total budgetary resources available	11	11	11
	Memorandum (non-add) entries:			
1941	Unexpired unobligated balance, end of year	10	10	10
	Change in obligated balance:			
	Unpaid obligations:			
3010	New obligations, unexpired accounts	1	1	1
3020	Outlays (gross)	–1	–1	–1
	Budget authority and outlays, net:			
	Mandatory:			
4090	Budget authority, gross	1	1	1
	Outlays, gross:			
4100	Outlays from new mandatory authority	1	1	1
4180	Budget authority, net (total)	1	1	1
4190	Outlays, net (total)	1	1	1
	Memorandum (non-add) entries:			
5000	Total investments, SOY: Federal securities: Par value	17	17	17
5001	Total investments, EOY: Federal securities: Par value	17	17	17

The principal for this fund was established by the transfer of $7,500,000 from the appropriation "Payment to the John C. Stennis Center". The principal for the Stennis Center Fund is a non-expendable corpus invested in Special Issue Certificates of Indebtedness with the U.S. Treasury. The Center's operations are funded by the interest on these Treasury investments as well as by other funds and contributions provided by outside sources.

U.S. CAPITOL PRESERVATION COMMISSION

Program and Financing (in millions of dollars)

Identification code 009–8300–0–7–801		2021 actual	2022 est.	2023 est.
	Budgetary resources:			
	Unobligated balance:			
1000	Unobligated balance brought forward, Oct 1	11	11	11
1930	Total budgetary resources available	11	11	11
	Memorandum (non-add) entries:			
1941	Unexpired unobligated balance, end of year	11	11	11
4180	Budget authority, net (total)			
4190	Outlays, net (total)			
	Memorandum (non-add) entries:			
5000	Total investments, SOY: Federal securities: Par value	11	11	11
5001	Total investments, EOY: Federal securities: Par value	11	11	11

OPEN WORLD LEADERSHIP CENTER TRUST FUND

Special and Trust Fund Receipts (in millions of dollars)

Identification code 009–8148–0–7–154		2021 actual	2022 est.	2023 est.
0100	Balance, start of year			2
	Receipts:			
	Current law:			
1130	Gifts and Donations, Open World Leadership Center Trust Fund		1	1
1140	Payment from the General Fund, Open World Leadership Center Trust Fund	6	7	6
1199	Total current law receipts	6	8	7
1999	Total receipts	6	8	7
2000	Total: Balances and receipts	6	8	9
	Appropriations:			
	Current law:			
2101	Open World Leadership Center Trust Fund	–6	–6	–6
5099	Balance, end of year		2	3

Program and Financing (in millions of dollars)

Identification code 009–8148–0–7–154		2021 actual	2022 est.	2023 est.
	Obligations by program activity:			
0001	Open World Leadership Center Trust Fund (Direct)	4	6	6
	Budgetary resources:			
	Unobligated balance:			
1000	Unobligated balance brought forward, Oct 1	1	3	4

		2021 actual	2022 est.	2023 est.
1021	Recoveries of prior year unpaid obligations		1	1
1070	Unobligated balance (total)	1	4	5
	Budget authority:			
	Appropriations, discretionary:			
1101	Appropriation (special or trust)	6	6	6
1930	Total budgetary resources available	7	10	11
	Memorandum (non-add) entries:			
1941	Unexpired unobligated balance, end of year	3	4	5
	Change in obligated balance:			
	Unpaid obligations:			
3000	Unpaid obligations, brought forward, Oct 1	3	4	2
3010	New obligations, unexpired accounts	4	6	6
3020	Outlays (gross)	–3	–7	–6
3040	Recoveries of prior year unpaid obligations, unexpired		–1	–1
3050	Unpaid obligations, end of year	4	2	1
	Memorandum (non-add) entries:			
3100	Obligated balance, start of year	3	4	2
3200	Obligated balance, end of year	4	2	1
	Budget authority and outlays, net:			
	Discretionary:			
4000	Budget authority, gross	6	6	6
	Outlays, gross:			
4010	Outlays from new discretionary authority	2	5	5
4011	Outlays from discretionary balances	1	2	1
4020	Outlays, gross (total)	3	7	6
4180	Budget authority, net (total)	6	6	6
4190	Outlays, net (total)	3	7	6
	Memorandum (non-add) entries:			
5000	Total investments, SOY: Federal securities: Par value	3	6	6
5001	Total investments, EOY: Federal securities: Par value	6	6	6

Object Classification (in millions of dollars)

Identification code 009–8148–0–7–154		2021 actual	2022 est.	2023 est.
	Direct obligations:			
11.1	Personnel compensation: Full-time permanent	1	1	1
25.1	Advisory and assistance services		2	1
25.3	Other goods and services from Federal sources	2		1
41.0	Grants, subsidies, and contributions		3	2
99.0	Direct obligations	3	6	5
99.5	Adjustment for rounding	1		1
99.9	Total new obligations, unexpired accounts	4	6	6

Employment Summary

Identification code 009–8148–0–7–154	2021 actual	2022 est.	2023 est.
1001 Direct civilian full-time equivalent employment	7	9	9

ADMINISTRATIVE PROVISIONS

SEC. 1. CONVERSION OF OPEN WORLD LEADERSHIP CENTER TO CONGRESSIONAL OFFICE FOR INTERNATIONAL LEADERSHIP —

(a) CONVERSION

(1) ESTABLISHMENT OF OFFICE.—Section 313 of the Legislative Branch Appropriations Act, 2001 (2 U.S.C. 1151) is amended—

(A) in the heading by striking "OPEN WORLD LEADERSHIP CENTER" and inserting "CONGRESSIONAL OFFICE FOR INTERNATIONAL LEADERSHIP";

(B) by amending paragraph (1) of subsection (a)(1) to read as follows:

"(1) In general.—There is established in the legislative branch of the Government an office to be known as the Congressional Office for International Leadership (the Office)."; and

(C) in paragraph (2) of subsection (a), by striking "The Center" and inserting "The Office".

(2) PURPOSE: GRANT PROGRAM: APPLICATION.—Section 313(b) of such Act (2 U.S.C. 1151(b)) is amended—

(A) in paragraph (1), by striking "the Center" and inserting "the Office";

(B) in paragraph (2), by striking "the Center" each place it appears and inserting "the Office";

(C) in paragraph (4)(A), by striking "the Center" each place it appears and inserting "the Office"; and

(D) in paragraph (4)(B)(iv), by striking "the Center" and inserting "the Office".

(3) TRUST FUND.— Section 313(c) of such Act (2 U.S.C. 1151(c)) is amended—

(A) by amending paragraph (1) to read as follows:

"(1) In general.—There is established in the Treasury of the United States a trust fund to be known as the 'Congressional Office for International Leadership Fund' (the 'Fund'), which shall consist of amounts which may be appropriated, credited, or transferred to it under this section."; and

(B) by striking "the Center" each place it appears in paragraphs (2) and (3)(B) and inserting "the Office".

(b) PARTICIPATION OF EMERGING CIVIC LEADERS OF ELIGIBLE FOREIGN STATES.—Section 313(b) of such Act (2 U.S.C. 1151(b)) is amended by striking "political leaders" each place it appears in paragraphs (1) and (2) and inserting "political and civic leaders".

(c) REFERENCES IN LAW.—Any reference in any law, rule, or regulation

(1) to the Open World Leadership Center shall be deemed to refer to the Congressional Office for International Leadership; and

(2) to the Open World Leadership Center Trust Fund shall be deemed to refer to the Congressional Office for International Leadership Fund.

(d) EFFECTIVE DATE: TRANSITION.—

(1) EFFECTIVE DATE.—This section and the amendments made by this section shall take effect on or after the later of October 1, 2021, or the date of enactment of this Act.

(2) SERVICE OF CURRENT EXECUTIVE DIRECTOR.—The individual serving as the Executive Director of the Open World Leadership Center as of the day before the date of the enactment of this Act will continue to serve as the Executive Director of the Congressional Office for International Leadership.

GENERAL FUND RECEIPT ACCOUNTS

(in millions of dollars)

	2021 actual	2022 est.	2023 est.
Offsetting receipts from the public:			
001–322000 All Other General Fund Proprietary Receipts Including Budget Clearing Accounts		2	2
General Fund Offsetting receipts from the public		2	2

GENERAL PROVISIONS

MAINTENANCE AND CARE OF PRIVATE VEHICLES

SEC. 201. No part of the funds appropriated in this Act shall be used for the maintenance or care of private vehicles, except for emergency assistance and cleaning as may be provided under regulations relating to parking facilities for the House of Representatives issued by the Committee on House Administration and for the Senate issued by the Committee on Rules and Administration.

FISCAL YEAR LIMITATION

SEC. 202. No part of the funds appropriated in this Act shall remain available for obligation beyond fiscal year 2023 unless expressly so provided in this Act.

RATES OF COMPENSATION AND DESIGNATION

SEC. 203. Whenever in this Act any office or position not specifically established by the Legislative Pay Act of 1929 (46 Stat. 32 et seq.) is appropriated for or the rate of compensation or designation of any office or position appropriated for is different from that specifically established by such Act, the rate of compensation and the designation in this Act shall be the permanent law with respect thereto: Provided, That the provisions in this Act for the various items of official expenses of Members, officers, and committees of the Senate and House of Representatives, and clerk hire for Senators and Members of the House of Representatives shall be the permanent law with respect thereto.

CONSULTING SERVICES

SEC. 204. The expenditure of any appropriation under this Act for any consulting service through procurement contract, under section 3109 of title 5, United States Code, shall be limited to those contracts where such expenditures are a matter of public record and available for public inspection, except where otherwise provided under existing law, or under existing Executive order issued under existing law.

COSTS OF LBFMC

SEC. 205. Amounts available for administrative expenses of any legislative branch entity which participates in the Legislative Branch Financial Managers Council

(LBFMC) established by charter on March 26, 1996, shall be available to finance an appropriate share of LBFMC costs as determined by the LBFMC, except that the total LBFMC costs to be shared among all participating legislative branch entities (in such allocations among the entities as the entities may determine) may not exceed $2,000.

LIMITATION ON TRANSFERS

SEC. 206. None of the funds made available in this Act may be transferred to any department, agency, or instrumentality of the United States Government, except pursuant to a transfer made by, or transfer authority provided in, this Act or any other appropriation Act.

GUIDED TOURS OF THE CAPITOL

SEC. 207. (a) Except as provided in subsection (b), none of the funds made available to the Architect of the Capitol in this Act may be used to eliminate or restrict guided tours of the United States Capitol which are led by employees and interns of offices of Members of Congress and other offices of the House of Representatives and Senate, unless through regulations as authorized by section 402(b)(8) of the Capitol Visitor Center Act of 2008 (2 U.S.C. 2242(b)(8)).

(b) At the direction of the Capitol Police Board, or at the direction of the Architect of the Capitol with the approval of the Capitol Police Board, guided tours of the United States Capitol which are led by employees and interns described in subsection (a) may be suspended temporarily or otherwise subject to restriction for security or related reasons to the same extent as guided tours of the United States Capitol which are led by the Architect of the Capitol.

LIMITATION ON TELECOMMUNICATIONS EQUIPMENT PROCUREMENT

SEC. 208. (a) None of the funds appropriated or otherwise made available under this Act may be used to acquire telecommunications equipment produced by Huawei Technologies Company or ZTE Corporation for a high or moderate impact information system, as defined for security categorization in the National Institute of Standards and Technology's (NIST) Federal Information Processing Standard Publication 199, "Standards for Security Categorization of Federal Information and Information Systems" unless the agency, office, or other entity acquiring the equipment or system has—

(1) reviewed the supply chain risk for the information systems against criteria developed by NIST to inform acquisition decisions for high or moderate impact information systems within the Federal Government;

(2) reviewed the supply chain risk from the presumptive awardee against available and relevant threat information provided by the Federal Bureau of Investigation and other appropriate agencies; and

(3) in consultation with the Federal Bureau of Investigation or other appropriate Federal entity, conducted an assessment of any risk of cyber-espionage or sabotage associated with the acquisition of such telecommunications equipment for inclusion in a high or moderate impact system, including any risk associated with such system being produced, manufactured, or assembled by one or more entities identified by the United States Government as posing a cyber threat, including but not limited to, those that may be owned, directed, or subsidized by the People's Republic of China, the Islamic Republic of Iran, the Democratic People's Republic of Korea, or the Russian Federation.

(b) None of the funds appropriated or otherwise made available under this Act may be used to acquire a high or moderate impact information system reviewed and assessed under subsection (a) unless the head of the assessing entity described in subsection (a) has—

(1) developed, in consultation with NIST and supply chain risk management experts, a mitigation strategy for any identified risks;

(2) determined, in consultation with NIST and the Federal Bureau of Investigation, that the acquisition of such telecommunications equipment for inclusion in a high or moderate impact system is in the vital national security interest of the United States; and

(3) reported that determination to the Committees on Appropriations of the House of Representatives and the Senate in a manner that identifies the telecommunications equipment for inclusion in a high or moderate impact system intended for acquisition and a detailed description of the mitigation strategies identified in paragraph (1), provided that such report may include a classified annex as necessary.

PROHIBITION ON CERTAIN OPERATIONAL EXPENSES

SEC. 209. (a) None of the funds made available in this Act may be used to maintain or establish a computer network unless such network blocks the viewing, downloading, and exchanging of pornography.

(b) Nothing in subsection (a) shall limit the use of funds necessary for any Federal, State, tribal, or local law enforcement agency or any other entity carrying out criminal investigations, prosecution, or adjudication activities or other official government activities.

PLASTIC WASTE REDUCTION

SEC. 210. All agencies and offices funded by this division that contract with a food service provider or providers shall confer and coordinate with such food service provider or providers, in consultation with disability advocacy groups, to eliminate or reduce plastic waste, including waste from plastic straws, explore the use of biodegradable items, and increase recycling and composting opportunities.

LIMITATION ON COST OF LIVING ADJUSTMENTS FOR MEMBERS

SEC. 211. Notwithstanding any other provision of law, no adjustment shall be made under section 601(a) of the Legislative Reorganization Act of 1946 (2 U.S.C. 4501) (relating to cost of living adjustments for Members of Congress) during fiscal year 2023.

AUTHORITY TO HIRE INDIVIDUALS COVERED BY THE DEFERRED ACTION FOR CHILDHOOD ARRIVALS PROGRAM

SEC. 212. Notwithstanding any other provision of law, an entity may use amounts appropriated or otherwise made available under this Act to pay the compensation of an officer or employee without regard to the officers or employees immigration status if the officer or employee has been issued an employment authorization document under the Deferred Action for Childhood Arrivals Program of the Secretary of Homeland Security, established pursuant to the memorandum from the Secretary of Homeland Security entitled Exercising Prosecutorial Discretion with Respect to Individuals Who Came to the United States as Children, dated June 15, 2012.

ANNUAL RATE OF PAY FOR PERSONNEL OF CERTAIN LEGISLATIVE BRANCH OFFICES

SEC. 213. (a) OFFICE OF THE ARCHITECT OF THE CAPITOL.—

(1) ARCHITECT OF THE CAPITOL.—The first section of the Act entitled "An Act to fix the annual rates of pay for the Architect of the Capitol and the Assistant Architect of the Capitol" (2 U.S.C. 1802) is amended to read as follows: "SECTION 1. COMPENSATION.

The compensation of the Architect of the Capitol shall be at an annual rate equal to the annual rate of basic pay for level II of the Executive Schedule.".

(2) DEPUTY ARCHITECT OF THE CAPITOL.—Section 1203(b) of the Legislative Branch Appropriations Act, 2003 (2 U.S.C. 1805(b)), as redesignated by section 701(b) of Public Law 116260 (134 Stat. 2154), is amended to read as follows:

(3) "(b) COMPENSATION.—The Deputy Architect of the Capitol shall be paid at an annual rate of pay equal to the highest total rate of pay for the Senior Executive Service under subchapter VIII of chapter 53 of title 5, United States Code, for the locality involved.".

(3) CHIEF EXECUTIVE OFFICE FOR VISITOR SERVICES.—Section 202(d) the Capitol Visitor Center Act of 2008 (2 U.S.C. 2212(d)) is amended by striking "the annual rate of pay of the Deputy Architect of the Capitol" and inserting "an annual rate of pay equal to the highest total rate of pay for the Senior Executive Service under subchapter VIII of chapter 53 of title 5, United States Code, for the locality involved".

(b) CHIEF OF THE CAPITOL POLICE.—Subsection (c) of the first section of the Act entitled An Act to establish by law the position of Chief of the Capitol Police, and for other purposes (2 U.S.C. 1902) is amended to read as follows:

"(c) The annual rate of pay for the Chief of the Capitol Police shall be equal to the annual rate of basic pay for level II of the Executive Schedule.".

(c) EFFECTIVE DATE.—This section and the amendments made by this section shall apply with respect to pay periods beginning on or after the later of October 1, 2022, or the date of enactment of this Act.

REMOVAL OF OFFENSIVE UNITED STATES CAPITOL STATUARY

SEC. 214. (a) REMOVAL AND STORAGE.—Not later than 45 days after the date of the enactment of this Act, the Architect of the Capitol—

(1) shall remove all Confederate statues and Confederate busts from any area of the United States Capitol which is accessible to the public; and shall remove all Confederate statues and Confederate busts from any area of the United States Capitol which is accessible to the public; and

(2) shall remove all Confederate statues and Confederate busts from any area of the United States Capitol which is accessible to the public; and(2) shall remove the bust of Roger Brooke Taney; the statue of Charles Brantley Aycock; the statue of John Caldwell Calhoun; and the statue of James Paul Clarke from any area of the United States Capitol, which is accessible to the public.

(b) STORAGE OF STATUES.—In the case of any statue removed under subsection (a), the Architect of the Capitol shall keep such statue in storage until the Architect and the State which provided the statue arrange for the return of the statue to the State.

(c) DEFINITIONS.—

(1) CONFEDERATE STATUE.—In this section, the term "Confederate statue" means a statue which was provided by a State for display in the United States Capitol under section 1814 of the Revised Statutes (2 U.S.C. 2131), including

a replacement statue provided by a State under section 311 of the Legislative Branch Appropriations Act, 2001 (2 U.S.C. 2132), which depicts—

(A) any individual who served voluntarily at any time as a member of the armed forces of the Confederate States of America or of the military forces of a State while the State was in rebellion against the United States; or

(B) any individual who served as an official in the government of the Confederate States of America or of a State while the State was in rebellion against the United States.

(2) CONFEDERATE BUST.—In this section, the term "Confederate bust" means a bust which depicts an individual described in subparagraph (A) or (B) of paragraph (1).

CAPITOL COMPLEX HEALTH AND SAFETY

SEC. 215. *In addition to the amounts appropriated under this Act under the heading Office of the Attending Physician, there is hereby appropriated to the Office of the Attending Physician $5,000,000, to remain available until expended, for response to COVID-19, including testing, subject to the same terms and conditions as the amounts appropriated under such heading.*

JUDICIAL BRANCH

SUPREME COURT OF THE UNITED STATES

Federal Funds

SALARIES AND EXPENSES

For expenses necessary for the operation of the Supreme Court, as required by law, excluding care of the building and grounds, including hire of passenger motor vehicles as authorized by 31 U.S.C. 1343 and 1344; not to exceed $10,000 for official reception and representation expenses; and for miscellaneous expenses, to be expended as the Chief Justice may approve, $107,153,000, of which $1,500,000 shall remain available until expended.

In addition, there are appropriated such sums as may be necessary under current law for the salaries of the chief justice and associate justices of the court.

Note.—A full-year 2022 appropriation for this account was not enacted at the time the Budget was prepared; therefore, the Budget assumes this account is operating under the Continuing Appropriations Act, 2022 (Division A of Public Law 117–43, as amended). The amounts included for 2022 reflect the annualized level provided by the continuing resolution.

Program and Financing (in millions of dollars)

Identification code 010–0100–0–1–752		2021 actual	2022 est.	2023 est.
	Obligations by program activity:			
0001	Salaries and Expenses (Direct)	96	98	110
	Budgetary resources:			
	Unobligated balance:			
1000	Unobligated balance brought forward, Oct 1		2	2
	Budget authority:			
	Appropriations, discretionary:			
1100	Appropriation	95	95	107
	Appropriations, mandatory:			
1200	Appropriation	3	3	3
1900	Budget authority (total)	98	98	110
1930	Total budgetary resources available	98	100	112
	Memorandum (non-add) entries:			
1941	Unexpired unobligated balance, end of year	2	2	2
	Change in obligated balance:			
	Unpaid obligations:			
3000	Unpaid obligations, brought forward, Oct 1		4	
3010	New obligations, unexpired accounts	96	98	110
3020	Outlays (gross)	–92	–102	–110
3050	Unpaid obligations, end of year	4		
	Memorandum (non-add) entries:			
3100	Obligated balance, start of year		4	
3200	Obligated balance, end of year	4		
	Budget authority and outlays, net:			
	Discretionary:			
4000	Budget authority, gross	95	95	107
	Outlays, gross:			
4010	Outlays from new discretionary authority	89	95	107
4011	Outlays from discretionary balances		4	
4020	Outlays, gross (total)	89	99	107
	Mandatory:			
4090	Budget authority, gross	3	3	3
	Outlays, gross:			
4100	Outlays from new mandatory authority	3	3	3
4180	Budget authority, net (total)	98	98	110
4190	Outlays, net (total)	92	102	110

The Supreme Court of the United States is the highest court of our country and stands at the apex of the judicial branch of our constitutional form of government. The U.S. Supreme Court is the only constitutionally indispensable court in the Federal court system of the United States. The jurisdiction of the Supreme Court is spelled out in the Constitution and allotted by the Congress. The funds herein requested are required to enable the U.S. Supreme Court to carry out its constitutional and congressionally allotted responsibilities.

Object Classification (in millions of dollars)

Identification code 010–0100–0–1–752		2021 actual	2022 est.	2023 est.
	Direct obligations:			
	Personnel compensation:			
11.1	Full-time permanent	49	50	54
11.3	Other than full-time permanent	3	3	3
11.9	Total personnel compensation	52	53	57
12.1	Civilian personnel benefits	20	21	25
21.0	Travel and transportation of persons	1	1	1
23.3	Communications, utilities, and miscellaneous charges	2	2	2
25.2	Other services from non-Federal sources	11	12	13
26.0	Supplies and materials	2	3	3
31.0	Equipment	8	6	9
99.9	Total new obligations, unexpired accounts	96	98	110

Employment Summary

Identification code 010–0100–0–1–752		2021 actual	2022 est.	2023 est.
1001	Direct civilian full-time equivalent employment	503	535	536

CARE OF THE BUILDING AND GROUNDS

For such expenditures as may be necessary to enable the Architect of the Capitol to carry out the duties imposed upon the Architect by 40 U.S.C. 6111 and 6112, $33,512,000, to remain available until expended.

Note.—A full-year 2022 appropriation for this account was not enacted at the time the Budget was prepared; therefore, the Budget assumes this account is operating under the Continuing Appropriations Act, 2022 (Division A of Public Law 117–43, as amended). The amounts included for 2022 reflect the annualized level provided by the continuing resolution.

Program and Financing (in millions of dollars)

Identification code 010–0103–0–1–752		2021 actual	2022 est.	2023 est.
	Obligations by program activity:			
0001	Care of the Building and Grounds (Direct)	16	24	31
	Budgetary resources:			
	Unobligated balance:			
1000	Unobligated balance brought forward, Oct 1	21	16	3
	Budget authority:			
	Appropriations, discretionary:			
1100	Appropriation	11	11	34
1930	Total budgetary resources available	32	27	37
	Memorandum (non-add) entries:			
1941	Unexpired unobligated balance, end of year	16	3	6
	Change in obligated balance:			
	Unpaid obligations:			
3000	Unpaid obligations, brought forward, Oct 1		2	6
3010	New obligations, unexpired accounts	16	24	31
3020	Outlays (gross)	–14	–20	–31
3050	Unpaid obligations, end of year	2	6	6
	Memorandum (non-add) entries:			
3100	Obligated balance, start of year		2	6
3200	Obligated balance, end of year	2	6	6
	Budget authority and outlays, net:			
	Discretionary:			
4000	Budget authority, gross	11	11	34
	Outlays, gross:			
4010	Outlays from new discretionary authority	11	8	26
4011	Outlays from discretionary balances	3	12	5
4020	Outlays, gross (total)	14	20	31
4180	Budget authority, net (total)	11	11	34
4190	Outlays, net (total)	14	20	31

Supreme Court of the United States—Continued
Federal Funds—Continued

CARE OF THE BUILDING AND GROUNDS—Continued

Object Classification (in millions of dollars)

Identification code 010–0103–0–1–752	2021 actual	2022 est.	2023 est.
Direct obligations:			
11.1 Personnel compensation: Full-time permanent	4	5	5
12.1 Civilian personnel benefits	2	2	2
23.3 Communications, utilities, and miscellaneous charges	2	3	3
25.1 Advisory and assistance services	3	3	3
25.4 Operation and maintenance of facilities	2	4	4
26.0 Supplies and materials	1	1	1
32.0 Land and structures	2	6	13
99.9 Total new obligations, unexpired accounts	16	24	31

Employment Summary

Identification code 010–0103–0–1–752	2021 actual	2022 est.	2023 est.
1001 Direct civilian full-time equivalent employment	43	50	50

UNITED STATES COURT OF APPEALS FOR THE FEDERAL CIRCUIT

Federal Funds

SALARIES AND EXPENSES

For salaries of officers and employees, and for necessary expenses of the court, as authorized by law, $36,448,000.

In addition, there are appropriated such sums as may be necessary under current law for the salaries of the chief judge and judges of the court.

Note.—A full-year 2022 appropriation for this account was not enacted at the time the Budget was prepared; therefore, the Budget assumes this account is operating under the Continuing Appropriations Act, 2022 (Division A of Public Law 117–43, as amended). The amounts included for 2022 reflect the annualized level provided by the continuing resolution.

Program and Financing (in millions of dollars)

Identification code 010–0510–0–1–752	2021 actual	2022 est.	2023 est.
Obligations by program activity:			
0001 Salaries and Expenses (Direct)	36	37	40
Budgetary resources:			
Budget authority:			
Appropriations, discretionary:			
1100 Appropriation	34	34	37
Appropriations, mandatory:			
1200 Appropriation	3	3	3
1900 Budget authority (total)	37	37	40
1930 Total budgetary resources available	37	37	40
Memorandum (non-add) entries:			
1940 Unobligated balance expiring	–1		
Change in obligated balance:			
Unpaid obligations:			
3000 Unpaid obligations, brought forward, Oct 1	5	6	6
3010 New obligations, unexpired accounts	36	37	40
3020 Outlays (gross)	–35	–37	–40
3050 Unpaid obligations, end of year	6	6	6
Memorandum (non-add) entries:			
3100 Obligated balance, start of year	5	6	6
3200 Obligated balance, end of year	6	6	6
Budget authority and outlays, net:			
Discretionary:			
4000 Budget authority, gross	34	34	37
Outlays, gross:			
4010 Outlays from new discretionary authority	29	27	30
4011 Outlays from discretionary balances	3	7	7
4020 Outlays, gross (total)	32	34	37
Mandatory:			
4090 Budget authority, gross	3	3	3
Outlays, gross:			
4100 Outlays from new mandatory authority	3	3	3
4180 Budget authority, net (total)	37	37	40
4190 Outlays, net (total)	35	37	40

The United States Court of Appeals for the Federal Circuit, located in Washington, D.C., has exclusive nationwide jurisdiction over a large number of diverse subject areas, such as appeals in all patent cases, all government contract cases, all international trade cases, all government contract cases, all government personnel cases, all cases involving monetary claims against the United States under the Tucker Acts, veterans cases, and many others. Additional subject areas have been added to this court's jurisdiction almost yearly. To keep abreast of its varied and growing jurisdiction, the court is requesting necessary increases.

The following is a more complete listing of the Federal Circuit's exclusive jurisdiction. It hears appeals from: (A) final decisions of all Federal district courts in cases arising under 28 U.S.C. 1338(a), relating to patent laws generally, 35 U.S.C. 145–146, relating to review of decisions of the Patent and Trademark Office, Board of Patent Appeals and Interferences, 28 U.S.C. 1346(a)(2), relating to Little Tucker Act claims against the United States, and section 211 of the Economic Stabilization Act of 1970, section 5 of the Emergency Petroleum Allocation Act of 1973, section 506(c) of the Natural Gas Policy Act of 1978, and section 523 of the Energy Policy and Conservation Act relating to all statutes formerly under the jurisdiction of the Temporary Emergency Court of Appeals; (B) final decisions of the United States Court of International Trade, 28 U.S.C. 2645(c); (C) final decisions of the United States Court of Appeals for Veterans Claims, 38 U.S.C. 7292; (D) final decisions of the United States Court of Federal Claims, 28 U.S.C. 2522 and 42 U.S.C. 300aa–12(f); (E) final decisions of the High Court of the Trust Territory of the Pacific Islands, 48 U.S.C. 1681 note (1988) (Compact of Free Association; Federated States of Micronesia, Republic of Marshall Islands, Title II, Title One, Article VII, 174(c)); (F) final determinations of the United States International Trade Commission relating to unfair practices in import trade made under 19 U.S.C. 1337; (G) findings of the Secretary of Commerce under U.S. note 6 to subchapter X of chapter 98 of the Harmonized Tariff Schedule of the United States relating to importation of educational or scientific instruments and apparatus; (H) final orders or decisions of the Merit Systems Protection Board and certain arbitrators, 5 U.S.C. 7703; (I) final decisions of the General Accounting Office Personnel Appeals Board, 31 U.S.C. 755; (J) final decisions of all agency Boards of Contract Appeals, 41 U.S.C. 607(g); (K) final decisions of the Patent and Trademark Office tribunals on patent applications and interferences, trademark applications and interferences, cancellations, concurrent use proceedings, and oppositions, 35 U.S.C. 142, 15 U.S.C. 1071, 37 CFR 1.304, 2.145; (L) appeals under section 71 of the Plant Variety Protection Act of 1970, 7 U.S.C. 2461; (M) certain actions of the Secretary of Veterans Affairs, 38 U.S.C. 502; (N) certain final orders of the Equal Employment Opportunity Commission relating to certain Presidential appointees, 2 U.S.C. 1219(a)(3) and 28 U.S.C. 2344; (O) final decisions of the Office of Personnel Management under 5 U.S.C. 8902a(g)(2); (P) certain actions of the Board of Directors of the Office of Compliance of the U.S. Congress under 2 U.S.C. 1407(a); and (Q) final decisions of certain agencies pursuant to 28 U.S.C. 1296.

The Federal Circuit also has exclusive jurisdiction pursuant to 28 U.S.C. 1292(c) of: (1) appealable interlocutory orders or decrees in cases where the court would otherwise have jurisdiction over an appeal; and (2) appeals from judgments in civil actions for patent infringement otherwise appealable to the court and final except for accounting. Under the provisions of 28 U.S.C. 1292(d), the court has: (1) exclusive jurisdiction of appeals from interlocutory orders granting or denying, in whole or in part, a motion to transfer an action to the Court of Federal Claims; and (2) may, in its discretion, permit an appeal from an interlocutory order of a judge who certifies that there is a controlling question of law and a substantial ground for difference of opinion thereon, and that an immediate appeal may materially advance the ultimate termination of the litigation. Pursuant to 38 U.S.C. 7292(b)(1), the court has exclusive jurisdiction of certain interlocutory orders of the Court of Appeals for Veterans Claims.

Legislation having an impact on the Federal Circuit is contained in P.L. 105–339 (51021) October 31, 1998, Veterans Employment Opportunities

Act of 1998, which provides a remedy through the Merit Systems Protection Board for those seeking review of the application of veterans preference rules to applicants for Federal employment.

Object Classification (in millions of dollars)

Identification code 010–0510–0–1–752	2021 actual	2022 est.	2023 est.
Direct obligations:			
11.1 Personnel compensation: Full-time permanent	17	19	20
12.1 Civilian personnel benefits	4	5	5
23.1 Rental payments to GSA	7	7	7
25.2 Other services from non-Federal sources	6	6	6
31.0 Equipment	2	....	2
99.9 Total new obligations, unexpired accounts	36	37	40

Employment Summary

Identification code 010–0510–0–1–752	2021 actual	2022 est.	2023 est.
1001 Direct civilian full-time equivalent employment	144	152	152

UNITED STATES COURT OF INTERNATIONAL TRADE

Federal Funds

SALARIES AND EXPENSES

For salaries of officers and employees of the court, services, and necessary expenses of the court, as authorized by law, $21,405,000.

In addition, there are appropriated such sums as may be necessary under current law for the salaries of the chief judge and judges of the court.

Note.—A full-year 2022 appropriation for this account was not enacted at the time the Budget was prepared; therefore, the Budget assumes this account is operating under the Continuing Appropriations Act, 2022 (Division A of Public Law 117–43, as amended). The amounts included for 2022 reflect the annualized level provided by the continuing resolution.

Program and Financing (in millions of dollars)

Identification code 010–0400–0–1–752	2021 actual	2022 est.	2023 est.
Obligations by program activity:			
0001 Salaries and Expenses (Direct)	22	22	24
Budgetary resources:			
Budget authority:			
Appropriations, discretionary:			
1100 Appropriation	20	20	22
Appropriations, mandatory:			
1200 Appropriation	2	2	2
1900 Budget authority (total)	22	22	24
1930 Total budgetary resources available	22	22	24
Change in obligated balance:			
Unpaid obligations:			
3000 Unpaid obligations, brought forward, Oct 1	4	5	1
3010 New obligations, unexpired accounts	22	22	24
3020 Outlays (gross)	–21	–26	–24
3050 Unpaid obligations, end of year	5	1	1
Memorandum (non-add) entries:			
3100 Obligated balance, start of year	4	5	1
3200 Obligated balance, end of year	5	1	1
Budget authority and outlays, net:			
Discretionary:			
4000 Budget authority, gross	20	20	22
Outlays, gross:			
4010 Outlays from new discretionary authority	18	19	21
4011 Outlays from discretionary balances	1	5	1
4020 Outlays, gross (total)	19	24	22
Mandatory:			
4090 Budget authority, gross	2	2	2
Outlays, gross:			
4100 Outlays from new mandatory authority	2	2	2
4180 Budget authority, net (total)	22	22	24
4190 Outlays, net (total)	21	26	24

The United States Court of International Trade, established under Article III of the Constitution of the United States, was created by the Act of October 10, 1980 (94 Stat. 1727), effective November 1, 1980, as successor to the former United States Customs Court. The court has original and exclusive jurisdiction of civil actions against the United States, its agencies and officers, and certain civil actions brought by the United States, arising out of import transactions and Federal statutes affecting customs and international trade. The court possesses all the powers in law and equity of, or as conferred by statute upon, a district court of the United States, and is authorized to conduct jury trials. The geographical jurisdiction of the court is nationwide and trials before the court or hearings may be held at any place within the jurisdiction of the United States. The court also is authorized to hold hearings in foreign countries. The principal statutory provisions pertaining to the court are contained in the following sections of Title 28 of the United States Code: Organization, sections 251–258; Jurisdiction, sections 1581–1585; and Procedures, sections 2631–2646.

Object Classification (in millions of dollars)

Identification code 010–0400–0–1–752	2021 actual	2022 est.	2023 est.
Direct obligations:			
11.1 Personnel compensation: Full-time permanent	8	8	10
12.1 Civilian personnel benefits	2	2	2
23.1 Rental payments to GSA	9	9	9
25.2 Other services from non-Federal sources	3	3	3
99.9 Total new obligations, unexpired accounts	22	22	24

Employment Summary

Identification code 010–0400–0–1–752	2021 actual	2022 est.	2023 est.
1001 Direct civilian full-time equivalent employment	65	77	77

COURTS OF APPEALS, DISTRICT COURTS, AND OTHER JUDICIAL SERVICES

Federal Funds

SALARIES AND EXPENSES

For the salaries of judges of the United States Court of Federal Claims, magistrate judges, and all other officers and employees of the Federal Judiciary not otherwise specifically provided for, necessary expenses of the courts, and the purchase, rental, repair, and cleaning of uniforms for Probation and Pretrial Services Office staff, as authorized by law, $5,973,325,000 (including the purchase of firearms and ammunition); of which not to exceed $27,817,000 shall remain available until expended for space alteration projects and for furniture and furnishings related to new space alteration and construction projects.

In addition, there are appropriated such sums as may be necessary under current law for the salaries of circuit and district judges (including judges of the territorial courts of the United States), bankruptcy judges, and justices and judges retired from office or from regular active service.

In addition, for expenses of the United States Court of Federal Claims associated with processing cases under the National Childhood Vaccine Injury Act of 1986 (Public Law 99–660), not to exceed $10,450,000, to be appropriated from the Vaccine Injury Compensation Trust Fund.

Note.—A full-year 2022 appropriation for this account was not enacted at the time the Budget was prepared; therefore, the Budget assumes this account is operating under the Continuing Appropriations Act, 2022 (Division A of Public Law 117–43, as amended). The amounts included for 2022 reflect the annualized level provided by the continuing resolution.

Program and Financing (in millions of dollars)

Identification code 010–0920–0–1–752	2021 actual	2022 est.	2023 est.
Obligations by program activity:			
0001 Courts of appeals	706	710	808
0002 District courts	2,770	2,875	3,091
0003 Bankruptcy courts	797	807	849
0004 Probation/Pretrial	1,601	1,647	1,883
0799 Total direct obligations	5,874	6,039	6,631
0801 Salaries and Expenses (Reimbursable)	10	10	10

SALARIES AND EXPENSES—Continued
Program and Financing—Continued

Identification code 010–0920–0–1–752	2021 actual	2022 est.	2023 est.
0803 Offsetting Collections	148	164	215
0899 Total reimbursable obligations	158	174	225
0900 Total new obligations, unexpired accounts	6,032	6,213	6,856
Budgetary resources:			
Unobligated balance:			
1000 Unobligated balance brought forward, Oct 1	38	34	231
1011 Unobligated balance transfer from other acct [010–0923]		32	
1021 Recoveries of prior year unpaid obligations	2		
1070 Unobligated balance (total)	40	66	231
Budget authority:			
Appropriations, discretionary:			
1100 Appropriation	5,394	5,394	5,973
1121 Appropriations transferred from other acct [010–0925]	2		
1121 Appropriations transferred from other acct [010–0928]	1		
1160 Appropriation, discretionary (total)	5,397	5,394	5,973
Appropriations, mandatory:			
1200 Appropriation	445	481	507
Spending authority from offsetting collections, discretionary:			
1700 Collected	14	33	33
1701 Change in uncollected payments, Federal sources	170	470	376
1750 Spending auth from offsetting collections, disc (total)	184	503	409
1900 Budget authority (total)	6,026	6,378	6,889
1930 Total budgetary resources available	6,066	6,444	7,120
Memorandum (non-add) entries:			
1941 Unexpired unobligated balance, end of year	34	231	264
Change in obligated balance:			
Unpaid obligations:			
3000 Unpaid obligations, brought forward, Oct 1	590	631	349
3010 New obligations, unexpired accounts	6,032	6,213	6,856
3011 Obligations ("upward adjustments"), expired accounts	21		
3020 Outlays (gross)	–5,958	–6,495	–6,865
3040 Recoveries of prior year unpaid obligations, unexpired	–2		
3041 Recoveries of prior year unpaid obligations, expired	–52		
3050 Unpaid obligations, end of year	631	349	340
Uncollected payments:			
3060 Uncollected pymts, Fed sources, brought forward, Oct 1	–412	–320	–790
3070 Change in uncollected pymts, Fed sources, unexpired	–170	–470	–376
3071 Change in uncollected pymts, Fed sources, expired	262		
3090 Uncollected pymts, Fed sources, end of year	–320	–790	–1,166
Memorandum (non-add) entries:			
3100 Obligated balance, start of year	178	311	–441
3200 Obligated balance, end of year	311	–441	–826
Budget authority and outlays, net:			
Discretionary:			
4000 Budget authority, gross	5,581	5,897	6,382
Outlays, gross:			
4010 Outlays from new discretionary authority	5,154	5,408	5,870
4011 Outlays from discretionary balances	395	606	488
4020 Outlays, gross (total)	5,549	6,014	6,358
Offsets against gross budget authority and outlays:			
Offsetting collections (collected) from:			
4030 Federal sources	–243	–288	–194
4033 Non-Federal sources	–1		
4040 Offsets against gross budget authority and outlays (total)	–244	–288	–194
Additional offsets against gross budget authority only:			
4050 Change in uncollected pymts, Fed sources, unexpired	–170	–470	–376
4052 Offsetting collections credited to expired accounts	230	255	161
4060 Additional offsets against budget authority only (total)	60	–215	–215
4070 Budget authority, net (discretionary)	5,397	5,394	5,973
4080 Outlays, net (discretionary)	5,305	5,726	6,164
Mandatory:			
4090 Budget authority, gross	445	481	507
Outlays, gross:			
4100 Outlays from new mandatory authority	409	481	507
4180 Budget authority, net (total)	5,842	5,875	6,480
4190 Outlays, net (total)	5,714	6,207	6,671

Funds appropriated under this heading are for the salaries and benefits of judges and supporting personnel, and all operating expenses of the United States courts of appeals, district courts, bankruptcy courts, United States Court of Federal Claims, and United States Probation and Pretrial Services offices are shown by activity:

Courts of Appeals.—This activity includes the salaries and benefits of all active United States circuit judges, and all such judges who have retired from office or from regular active service in pursuance of law. In addition, it provides for the salaries and expenses of the Courts of Appeals supporting personnel such as the administrative and legal aides required to assist the judges in the hearing and decision of appeals, and other judicial functions including all expenses of operation and maintenance such as travel expenses incurred by judges and supporting personnel in attending sessions of court or transacting other official business, and for relocation expenses, communications, printing, contractual services, supplies, equipment, and lawbooks and for rental of space, alterations, and related services for United States court facilities.

District Courts.—This activity includes the salaries and benefits of all active United States district judges, magistrate judges, and all such judges who have retired from office or from regular active service in pursuance of law. In addition, it provides for the salaries and expenses of the District Court supporting personnel such as the administrative and legal aides required to assist the judges in conduct of hearings, trials, and other judicial functions including all expenses of operation and maintenance such as travel expenses incurred by judges and supporting personnel in attending sessions of court or transacting other official business, and for relocation expenses, communications, printing, contractual services, supplies, equipment, and lawbooks, and for rental of space, alterations, and related services for United States court facilities.

Bankruptcy Courts.—This activity includes the salaries and benefits of all active United States bankruptcy judges. In addition, it provides for the salaries and expenses of the Bankruptcy Court supporting personnel, including all expenses of operation and maintenance such as travel expenses incurred by judges and supporting personnel in attending sessions of court or transacting other official business, and for relocation expenses, communications, printing, contractual services, supplies, equipment, and lawbooks, and for rental of space, alterations, and related services for United States court facilities.

Probation/Pretrial.—This activity includes the salaries and benefits of all probation and pretrial services officers, officer assistants and supporting personnel in attending sessions of court or transacting other official business, and for relocation expenses, communications, printing, contractual services, supplies, and equipment, and for rental of space, alterations, and related services for United States court facilities. It also provides for all expenses of law-enforcement related activities, which includes substance abuse and mental health treatment, Global Position Monitoring, purchase, rental, repair, and cleaning of uniforms for Probation and Pretrial Services Office staff, and operation and maintenance such as travel expenses incurred by probation officers, including travel costs related to the supervision of defendants and offenders in the community, and officer training expenses.

Object Classification (in millions of dollars)

Identification code 010–0920–0–1–752	2021 actual	2022 est.	2023 est.
Direct obligations:			
Personnel compensation:			
11.1 Full-time permanent	1,795	1,938	2,360
11.3 Other than full-time permanent	1,015	1,017	1,151
11.9 Total personnel compensation	2,810	2,955	3,511
12.1 Civilian personnel benefits	1,018	1,019	1,023
13.0 Benefits for former personnel	9	9	10
21.0 Travel and transportation of persons	22	23	25
22.0 Transportation of things	4	4	5
23.1 Rental payments to GSA	1,017	1,027	1,037
23.2 Rental payments to others	35	36	37
23.3 Communications, utilities, and miscellaneous charges	39	40	42
24.0 Printing and reproduction	7	7	8
25.1 Advisory and assistance services	329	330	335
25.2 Other services from non-Federal sources	18	19	21
25.7 Operation and maintenance of equipment	21	21	22
26.0 Supplies and materials	10	11	12

JUDICIAL BRANCH

		2021 actual	2022 est.	2023 est.
31.0	Equipment	45	46	48
94.0	Financial transfers	490	492	495
99.0	Direct obligations	5,874	6,039	6,631
99.0	Reimbursable obligations	158	174	225
99.9	Total new obligations, unexpired accounts	6,032	6,213	6,856

Employment Summary

Identification code 010–0920–0–1–752	2021 actual	2022 est.	2023 est.
1001 Direct civilian full-time equivalent employment	27,648	27,951	28,452
2001 Reimbursable civilian full-time equivalent employment	44	48	48

DEFENDER SERVICES

For the operation of Federal Defender organizations; the compensation and reimbursement of expenses of attorneys appointed to represent persons under 18 U.S.C. 3006A and 3599, and for the compensation and reimbursement of expenses of persons furnishing investigative, expert, and other services for such representations as authorized by law; the compensation (in accordance with the maximums under 18 U.S.C. 3006A) and reimbursement of expenses of attorneys appointed to assist the court in criminal cases where the defendant has waived representation by counsel; the compensation and reimbursement of expenses of attorneys appointed to represent jurors in civil actions for the protection of their employment, as authorized by 28 U.S.C. 1875(d)(1); the compensation and reimbursement of expenses of attorneys appointed under 18 U.S.C. 983(b)(1) in connection with certain judicial civil forfeiture proceedings; the compensation and reimbursement of travel expenses of guardians ad litem appointed under 18 U.S.C. 4100(b); and for necessary training and general administrative expenses, $1,461,711,000, to remain available until expended.

Note.—A full-year 2022 appropriation for this account was not enacted at the time the Budget was prepared; therefore, the Budget assumes this account is operating under the Continuing Appropriations Act, 2022 (Division A of Public Law 117–43, as amended). The amounts included for 2022 reflect the annualized level provided by the continuing resolution.

Program and Financing (in millions of dollars)

Identification code 010–0923–0–1–752	2021 actual	2022 est.	2023 est.
Obligations by program activity:			
0001 Defender Services (Direct)	1,219	1,412	1,492
Budgetary resources:			
Unobligated balance:			
1000 Unobligated balance brought forward, Oct 1	21	126	13
1010 Unobligated balance transfer to other accts [010–0920]		–32	
1021 Recoveries of prior year unpaid obligations	7	10	12
1033 Recoveries of prior year paid obligations	1	5	5
1070 Unobligated balance (total)	29	109	30
Budget authority:			
Appropriations, discretionary:			
1100 Appropriation	1,316	1,316	1,462
1900 Budget authority (total)	1,316	1,316	1,462
1930 Total budgetary resources available	1,345	1,425	1,492
Memorandum (non-add) entries:			
1941 Unexpired unobligated balance, end of year	126	13	
Change in obligated balance:			
Unpaid obligations:			
3000 Unpaid obligations, brought forward, Oct 1	75	99	127
3010 New obligations, unexpired accounts	1,219	1,412	1,492
3020 Outlays (gross)	–1,188	–1,374	–1,553
3040 Recoveries of prior year unpaid obligations, unexpired	–7	–10	–12
3050 Unpaid obligations, end of year	99	127	54
Memorandum (non-add) entries:			
3100 Obligated balance, start of year	75	99	127
3200 Obligated balance, end of year	99	127	54
Budget authority and outlays, net:			
Discretionary:			
4000 Budget authority, gross	1,316	1,316	1,462
Outlays, gross:			
4010 Outlays from new discretionary authority	1,132	1,277	1,418
4011 Outlays from discretionary balances	56	97	135
4020 Outlays, gross (total)	1,188	1,374	1,553
Offsets against gross budget authority and outlays:			
Offsetting collections (collected) from:			
4033 Non-Federal sources	–1	–5	–5
4040 Offsets against gross budget authority and outlays (total)	–1	–5	–5
Additional offsets against gross budget authority only:			
4053 Recoveries of prior year paid obligations, unexpired accounts	1	5	5
4070 Budget authority, net (discretionary)	1,316	1,316	1,462
4080 Outlays, net (discretionary)	1,187	1,369	1,548
4180 Budget authority, net (total)	1,316	1,316	1,462
4190 Outlays, net (total)	1,187	1,369	1,548

Funds appropriated under this heading provide for the administration and operation of the Criminal Justice Act of 1964 (18 U.S.C. 3006A), as amended, which provides for furnishing representation for any person financially unable to obtain adequate representation who: (1) is charged with a felony or Class A, B, or C misdemeanor, or infraction for which a sentence to confinement is authorized, or with committing an act of juvenile delinquency, or with a violation of probation; (2) is under arrest, when such representation is required by law; (3) is entitled to appointment of counsel in parole proceedings (18 U.S.C. 4201–18); (4) is charged with a violation of supervised release or faces modification, reduction, or enlargement of a condition, or extension or revocation of a term of supervised release; (5) is subject to a mental condition or other hearing (18 U.S.C. 4241–48); (6) is in custody as a material witness; (7) is entitled to appointment of counsel under the sixth amendment to the Constitution; (8) faces loss of liberty in a case, and Federal law requires the appointment of counsel; (9) is entitled to the appointment of counsel under 18 U.S.C. 4109; or (10) is seeking relief under 28 U.S.C. 2241, 2254, or 2255. Representation includes counsel and investigative, expert, and other necessary services. The appropriation includes funding for the compensation and expenses of court-appointed counsel and persons providing investigative, expert and other services under the Act, and also under 18 U.S.C. 3599 in capital representations; for the operation of the Federal Defender Organizations; for the compensation and reimbursement of travel expenses of guardians ad litem, appointed under 18 U.S.C. 4100(b), acting on behalf of financially eligible minors or incompetent offenders in connection with transfers from the United States to foreign countries with which the United States has a treaty for the execution of penal sentences (18 U.S.C. 4109(b)); and for the continuing education and training of persons providing representational services under the Act. In addition, this appropriation is available for the compensation and reimbursement of expenses of counsel: (1) appointed pursuant to 5 U.S.C. 3109 to assist the court in criminal cases where the defendant has waived representation by counsel; (2) appointed pursuant to 28 U.S.C. 1875(d)(1) to represent jurors in civil actions for the protection of their employment; and (3) appointed under 18 U.S.C. 983(b)(1) in connection with certain judicial civil forfeiture proceedings.

Object Classification (in millions of dollars)

Identification code 010–0923–0–1–752	2021 actual	2022 est.	2023 est.
Direct obligations:			
Personnel compensation:			
11.1 Full-time permanent	377	410	452
11.3 Other than full-time permanent	8	9	9
11.5 Other personnel compensation		1	1
11.9 Total personnel compensation	385	420	462
12.1 Civilian personnel benefits	141	152	163
13.0 Benefits for former personnel	1	1	1
21.0 Travel and transportation of persons	5	16	16
23.1 Rental payments to GSA	46	49	51
23.2 Rental payments to others	1	1	1
23.3 Communications, utilities, and miscellaneous charges	11	12	16
25.1 Advisory and assistance services	368	463	466
25.2 Other services	48	60	60
25.3 Other goods and services from Federal sources	6	8	8
25.4 Operation and maintenance of facilities	7	8	8
25.7 Operation and maintenance of equipment	1	2	2
26.0 Supplies and materials	2	2	2
31.0 Equipment	24	20	30
41.0 Grants, subsidies, and contributions	173	197	205

Courts of Appeals, District Courts, and Other Judicial Services—Continued
Federal Funds—Continued

DEFENDER SERVICES—Continued

Object Classification—Continued

Identification code 010–0923–0–1–752	2021 actual	2022 est.	2023 est.
99.0 Direct obligations	1,219	1,411	1,491
99.5 Adjustment for rounding	....	1	1
99.9 Total new obligations, unexpired accounts	1,219	1,412	1,492

Employment Summary

Identification code 010–0923–0–1–752	2021 actual	2022 est.	2023 est.
1001 Direct civilian full-time equivalent employment	3,102	3,383	3,459

FEES OF JURORS AND COMMISSIONERS

For fees and expenses of jurors as authorized by 28 U.S.C. 1871 and 1876; compensation of jury commissioners as authorized by 28 U.S.C. 1863; and compensation of commissioners appointed in condemnation cases pursuant to rule 71.1(h) of the Federal Rules of Civil Procedure (28 U.S.C. Appendix Rule 71.1(h)), $45,677,000, to remain available until expended: Provided, That the compensation of land commissioners shall not exceed the daily equivalent of the highest rate payable under 5 U.S.C. 5332.

Note.—A full-year 2022 appropriation for this account was not enacted at the time the Budget was prepared; therefore, the Budget assumes this account is operating under the Continuing Appropriations Act, 2022 (Division A of Public Law 117–43, as amended). The amounts included for 2022 reflect the annualized level provided by the continuing resolution.

Program and Financing (in millions of dollars)

Identification code 010–0925–0–1–752	2021 actual	2022 est.	2023 est.
Obligations by program activity:			
0003 Grand jurors	12	18	20
0004 Petit jurors	21	34	29
0900 Total new obligations, unexpired accounts	33	52	49
Budgetary resources:			
Unobligated balance:			
1000 Unobligated balance brought forward, Oct 1	20	19	2
1021 Recoveries of prior year unpaid obligations	1	2	1
1070 Unobligated balance (total)	21	21	3
Budget authority:			
Appropriations, discretionary:			
1100 Appropriation	33	33	46
1120 Appropriations transferred to other acct [010–0920]	–2	....	....
1160 Appropriation, discretionary (total)	31	33	46
1900 Budget authority (total)	31	33	46
1930 Total budgetary resources available	52	54	49
Memorandum (non-add) entries:			
1941 Unexpired unobligated balance, end of year	19	2	....
Change in obligated balance:			
Unpaid obligations:			
3000 Unpaid obligations, brought forward, Oct 1	2	2	....
3010 New obligations, unexpired accounts	33	52	49
3020 Outlays (gross)	–32	–52	–46
3040 Recoveries of prior year unpaid obligations, unexpired	–1	–2	–1
3050 Unpaid obligations, end of year	2	....	2
Memorandum (non-add) entries:			
3100 Obligated balance, start of year	2	2	....
3200 Obligated balance, end of year	2	....	2
Budget authority and outlays, net:			
Discretionary:			
4000 Budget authority, gross	31	33	46
Outlays, gross:			
4010 Outlays from new discretionary authority	30	33	46
4011 Outlays from discretionary balances	2	19	....
4020 Outlays, gross (total)	32	52	46
4180 Budget authority, net (total)	31	33	46
4190 Outlays, net (total)	32	52	46

This appropriation provides for the statutory fees and allowances of jurors, refreshments of jurors, and compensation of land commissioners appointed in condemnation cases pursuant to rule 71.1(h) of the Federal Rules of Civil Procedure. Budgetary requirements depend largely upon the volume and length of jury trials demanded by the parties to both civil and criminal actions and the number of grand juries being convened by the courts at the request of United States Attorneys.

Object Classification (in millions of dollars)

Identification code 010–0925–0–1–752	2021 actual	2022 est.	2023 est.
Direct obligations:			
11.8 Personnel compensation: Special personal services payments	15	25	23
21.0 Travel and transportation of persons (jurors)	14	22	20
23.3 Communications, utilities, and miscellaneous charges	2	3	3
25.2 Other services (meals and lodging furnished sequestered juror	1	1	2
26.0 Supplies and materials (Provisions for Juror Food/Beverages)	1	1	1
99.9 Total new obligations, unexpired accounts	33	52	49

COURT SECURITY

(INCLUDING TRANSFER OF FUNDS)

For necessary expenses, not otherwise provided for, incident to the provision of protective guard services for United States courthouses and other facilities housing Federal court operations or Administrative Office of the U.S. Courts operations, the procurement, installation, and maintenance of security systems and equipment for United States courthouses and other facilities housing Federal court operations or Administrative Office of the U.S. Courts, building ingress-egress control, inspection of mail and packages, directed security patrols, perimeter security, basic security services provided by the Federal Protective Service, and other similar activities as authorized by section 1010 of the Judicial Improvement and Access to Justice Act (Public Law 100–702), $785,589,000, of which not to exceed $20,000,000 shall remain available until expended, to be expended directly or transferred to the United States Marshals Service, which shall be responsible for administering the Judicial Facility Security Program consistent with standards or guidelines agreed to by the Director of the Administrative Office of the United States Courts and the Attorney General: Provided, That notwithstanding any other provision of law, funds may be used for identifying, redacting, and reducing personally identifiable information on the internet of judges and other persons who live at the judge's domicile; and managing a Judiciary-wide program to facilitate security and emergency management services among the Judiciary, United States Marshals Service, Federal Protective Service, General Services Administration, other federal agencies, state and local governments, and the public.

Note.—A full-year 2022 appropriation for this account was not enacted at the time the Budget was prepared; therefore, the Budget assumes this account is operating under the Continuing Appropriations Act, 2022 (Division A of Public Law 117–43, as amended). The amounts included for 2022 reflect the annualized level provided by the continuing resolution.

Program and Financing (in millions of dollars)

Identification code 010–0930–0–1–752	2021 actual	2022 est.	2023 est.
Obligations by program activity:			
0001 Court Security (Direct)	661	714	801
Budgetary resources:			
Unobligated balance:			
1000 Unobligated balance brought forward, Oct 1	24	35	....
1012 Unobligated balance transfers between expired and unexpired accounts	25	15	15
1021 Recoveries of prior year unpaid obligations	1	....	....
1033 Recoveries of prior year paid obligations	1	....	....
1070 Unobligated balance (total)	51	50	15
Budget authority:			
Appropriations, discretionary:			
1100 Appropriation	664	664	786
1930 Total budgetary resources available	715	714	801
Memorandum (non-add) entries:			
1940 Unobligated balance expiring	–19	....	....
1941 Unexpired unobligated balance, end of year	35	....	....

Change in obligated balance:

Unpaid obligations:

		2021 actual	2022 est.	2023 est.
3000	Unpaid obligations, brought forward, Oct 1	263	243	314
3010	New obligations, unexpired accounts	661	714	801
3011	Obligations ("upward adjustments"), expired accounts	8		
3020	Outlays (gross)	–664	–643	–709
3040	Recoveries of prior year unpaid obligations, unexpired	–1		
3041	Recoveries of prior year unpaid obligations, expired	–24		
3050	Unpaid obligations, end of year	243	314	406

Memorandum (non-add) entries:

| 3100 | Obligated balance, start of year | 263 | 243 | 314 |
| 3200 | Obligated balance, end of year | 243 | 314 | 406 |

Budget authority and outlays, net:

Discretionary:

| 4000 | Budget authority, gross | 664 | 664 | 786 |

Outlays, gross:

4010	Outlays from new discretionary authority	505	432	511
4011	Outlays from discretionary balances	159	211	198
4020	Outlays, gross (total)	664	643	709

Offsets against gross budget authority and outlays:

Offsetting collections (collected) from:

| 4030 | Federal sources | –1 | | |

Additional offsets against gross budget authority only:

4053	Recoveries of prior year paid obligations, unexpired accounts	1		
4070	Budget authority, net (discretionary)	664	664	786
4080	Outlays, net (discretionary)	663	643	709
4180	Budget authority, net (total)	664	664	786
4190	Outlays, net (total)	663	643	709

This appropriation provides for the necessary expenses not otherwise provided for, incident to providing protective guard services for the United States courthouses and other facilities housing Federal court operations and the procurement, installation, and maintenance of security equipment for United States courthouses and other facilities housing federal court operations, including building ingress-egress control, inspection of mail and packages, directed security patrols, perimeter security, basic security services provided by the Federal Protective Service, the Judiciary Vulnerability Management Program, and other similar activities, to be expended directly or transferred to the United States Marshals Service which shall be responsible for administering the Judicial Facility Security Program or to the Federal Protective Service for costs associated with building security.

Object Classification (in millions of dollars)

Identification code 010–0930–0–1–752		2021 actual	2022 est.	2023 est.
	Direct obligations:			
11.1	Personnel compensation: Full-time permanent	8	9	14
12.1	Civilian personnel benefits	3	3	4
21.0	Travel and transportation of persons	1	1	1
23.1	Rental payments to GSA	7	8	8
23.3	Communications, utilities, and miscellaneous charges	1	2	2
25.1	Advisory and assistance services	1		
25.2	Other services from non-Federal sources	5	7	8
25.3	Other goods and services from Federal sources	93	87	94
25.4	Operation and maintenance of facilities	427	454	491
25.7	Operation and maintenance of equipment	23	32	32
26.0	Supplies and materials	2		
31.0	Equipment	16	19	27
32.0	Land and structures	74	92	120
99.9	Total new obligations, unexpired accounts	661	714	801

Employment Summary

Identification code 010–0930–0–1–752	2021 actual	2022 est.	2023 est.
1001 Direct civilian full-time equivalent employment	65	79	96

JUDICIARY FILING FEES

Special and Trust Fund Receipts (in millions of dollars)

Identification code 010–5100–0–2–752	2021 actual	2022 est.	2023 est.
0100 Balance, start of year			
Receipts:			
Current law:			
1110 Filing Fees, U.S. Courts, Judiciary	154	166	203
2000 Total: Balances and receipts	154	166	203
Appropriations:			
Current law:			
2101 Judiciary Filing Fees	–154	–166	–203
5099 Balance, end of year			

Program and Financing (in millions of dollars)

Identification code 010–5100–0–2–752	2021 actual	2022 est.	2023 est.
Obligations by program activity:			
0001 Judiciary Filing Fees (Direct)	148	166	203
0900 Total new obligations, unexpired accounts (object class 25.2)	148	166	203
Budgetary resources:			
Unobligated balance:			
1000 Unobligated balance brought forward, Oct 1	259	265	255
Budget authority:			
Appropriations, mandatory:			
1201 Appropriation (special or trust fund)	154	166	203
1230 Appropriations and/or unobligated balance of appropriations permanently reduced		–10	–12
1260 Appropriations, mandatory (total)	154	156	191
1930 Total budgetary resources available	413	421	446
Memorandum (non-add) entries:			
1941 Unexpired unobligated balance, end of year	265	255	243

Change in obligated balance:

Unpaid obligations:

3000	Unpaid obligations, brought forward, Oct 1	410	322	300
3010	New obligations, unexpired accounts	148	166	203
3020	Outlays (gross)	–236	–188	–223
3050	Unpaid obligations, end of year	322	300	280

Memorandum (non-add) entries:

| 3100 | Obligated balance, start of year | 410 | 322 | 300 |
| 3200 | Obligated balance, end of year | 322 | 300 | 280 |

Budget authority and outlays, net:

Mandatory:

| 4090 | Budget authority, gross | 154 | 156 | 191 |

Outlays, gross:

4100	Outlays from new mandatory authority	10	156	191
4101	Outlays from mandatory balances	226	32	32
4110	Outlays, gross (total)	236	188	223
4180	Budget authority, net (total)	154	156	191
4190	Outlays, net (total)	236	188	223

REGISTRY ADMINISTRATION

Special and Trust Fund Receipts (in millions of dollars)

Identification code 010–5101–0–2–752	2021 actual	2022 est.	2023 est.
0100 Balance, start of year			
Receipts:			
Current law:			
1110 Fees, Registry Administration, Judiciary		1	1
2000 Total: Balances and receipts		1	1
Appropriations:			
Current law:			
2101 Registry Administration		–1	–1
5099 Balance, end of year			

REGISTRY ADMINISTRATION—Continued
Program and Financing (in millions of dollars)

Identification code 010–5101–0–2–752		2021 actual	2022 est.	2023 est.
	Obligations by program activity:			
0001	Registry Administration (Direct)	....	1	1
0900	Total new obligations, unexpired accounts (object class 25.2)	....	1	1
	Budgetary resources:			
	Budget authority:			
	Appropriations, mandatory:			
1201	Appropriation (special or trust fund)	....	1	1
1930	Total budgetary resources available	....	1	1
	Change in obligated balance:			
	Unpaid obligations:			
3010	New obligations, unexpired accounts	....	–1	1
3020	Outlays (gross)	....	–1	–1
	Budget authority and outlays, net:			
	Mandatory:			
4090	Budget authority, gross	....	1	1
	Outlays, gross:			
4100	Outlays from new mandatory authority	....	1	1
4180	Budget authority, net (total)	....	1	1
4190	Outlays, net (total)	....	1	1

This schedule reflects funds available to the Federal Judiciary, pursuant to Public Law 100–459, which provides that any funds collected by the Judiciary as a charge for services rendered in administering accounts kept in a court's registry shall be deposited into this account.

JUDICIARY INFORMATION TECHNOLOGY FUND
Special and Trust Fund Receipts (in millions of dollars)

Identification code 010–5114–0–2–752		2021 actual	2022 est.	2023 est.
0100	Balance, start of year	....	....	145
	Receipts:			
	Current law:			
1130	Proceeds from Sale of Property, Judiciary Information Technology Fund	143	145	145
1140	Advances and Reimbursements, Judiciary Information Technology Fund	508	591	633
1199	Total current law receipts	651	736	778
1999	Total receipts	651	736	778
2000	Total: Balances and receipts	651	736	923
	Appropriations:			
	Current law:			
2101	Judiciary Information Technology Fund	–651	–591	–778
5099	Balance, end of year	....	145	145

Program and Financing (in millions of dollars)

Identification code 010–5114–0–2–752		2021 actual	2022 est.	2023 est.
	Obligations by program activity:			
0001	Information Technology	648	736	837
	Budgetary resources:			
	Unobligated balance:			
1000	Unobligated balance brought forward, Oct 1	212	227	82
1021	Recoveries of prior year unpaid obligations	12	....	....
1070	Unobligated balance (total)	224	227	82
	Budget authority:			
	Appropriations, mandatory:			
1201	Appropriation (special or trust fund)	651	591	778
1930	Total budgetary resources available	875	818	860
	Memorandum (non-add) entries:			
1941	Unexpired unobligated balance, end of year	227	82	23
	Change in obligated balance:			
	Unpaid obligations:			
3000	Unpaid obligations, brought forward, Oct 1	365	348	547
3010	New obligations, unexpired accounts	648	736	837
3020	Outlays (gross)	–653	–537	–708
3040	Recoveries of prior year unpaid obligations, unexpired	–12	....	....
3050	Unpaid obligations, end of year	348	547	676
	Memorandum (non-add) entries:			
3100	Obligated balance, start of year	365	348	547
3200	Obligated balance, end of year	348	547	676
	Budget authority and outlays, net:			
	Mandatory:			
4090	Budget authority, gross	651	591	778
	Outlays, gross:			
4100	Outlays from new mandatory authority	355	272	358
4101	Outlays from mandatory balances	298	265	350
4110	Outlays, gross (total)	653	537	708
4180	Budget authority, net (total)	651	591	778
4190	Outlays, net (total)	653	537	708

The Judiciary Information Technology Fund provides the judiciary with a funds management tool which allows more effective and efficient planning, budgeting, and use of funds for information technology activities. The Fund was authorized "without fiscal year limitation," which allows the judiciary to carry forward funds for projects that incur obligations over multiple years. The Fund makes it possible to implement the *Long Range Plan for Information Technology in the Federal Judiciary* and to manage the information technology program over a multi-year planning cycle while maximizing efficiencies and benefits. The Fund is financed through deposits and transfers from appropriations, reimbursements, user fees, and the sale of surplus equipment.

Object Classification (in millions of dollars)

Identification code 010–5114–0–2–752		2021 actual	2022 est.	2023 est.
	Direct obligations:			
21.0	Travel and transportation of persons	1	4	7
23.3	Communications, utilities, and miscellaneous charges	76	79	98
24.0	Printing and reproduction	5	5	6
25.1	Advisory and assistance services	281	345	369
25.3	Other goods and services from Federal sources	88	25	40
25.7	Operation and maintenance of equipment	29	82	100
26.0	Supplies and materials	8	....	10
31.0	Equipment	160	196	207
99.9	Total new obligations, unexpired accounts	648	736	837

ADMINISTRATIVE OFFICE OF THE UNITED STATES COURTS

Federal Funds

SALARIES AND EXPENSES

For necessary expenses of the Administrative Office of the United States Courts as authorized by law, including travel as authorized by 31 U.S.C. 1345, hire of a passenger motor vehicle as authorized by 31 U.S.C. 1343(b), advertising and rent in the District of Columbia and elsewhere, $111,261,000, of which not to exceed $8,500 is authorized for official reception and representation expenses.

Note.—A full-year 2022 appropriation for this account was not enacted at the time the Budget was prepared; therefore, the Budget assumes this account is operating under the Continuing Appropriations Act, 2022 (Division A of Public Law 117–43, as amended). The amounts included for 2022 reflect the annualized level provided by the continuing resolution.

Program and Financing (in millions of dollars)

Identification code 010–0927–0–1–752		2021 actual	2022 est.	2023 est.
	Obligations by program activity:			
0002	Program direction and policy formulation	52	53	61
0012	Program Services	25	24	26
0013	Administrative Services	35	34	38
0014	Technology Services	3	2	2
0799	Total direct obligations	115	113	127
0801	Offsetting Collections	115	125	151
0900	Total new obligations, unexpired accounts	230	238	278

JUDICIAL BRANCH — Federal Judicial Center / Federal Funds — 57

		2021 actual	2022 est.	2023 est.
	Budgetary resources:			
	Budget authority:			
	Appropriations, discretionary:			
1100	Appropriation	96	96	111
	Spending authority from offsetting collections, discretionary:			
1700	Collected	119	142	167
1701	Change in uncollected payments, Federal sources	15		
1750	Spending auth from offsetting collections, disc (total)	134	142	167
1900	Budget authority (total)	230	238	278
1930	Total budgetary resources available	230	238	278
	Change in obligated balance:			
	Unpaid obligations:			
3000	Unpaid obligations, brought forward, Oct 1	14	15	15
3010	New obligations, unexpired accounts	230	238	278
3020	Outlays (gross)	−228	−238	−282
3041	Recoveries of prior year unpaid obligations, expired	−1		
3050	Unpaid obligations, end of year	15	15	11
	Uncollected payments:			
3060	Uncollected pymts, Fed sources, brought forward, Oct 1	−14	−16	−16
3070	Change in uncollected pymts, Fed sources, unexpired	−15		
3071	Change in uncollected pymts, Fed sources, expired	13		
3090	Uncollected pymts, Fed sources, end of year	−16	−16	−16
	Memorandum (non-add) entries:			
3100	Obligated balance, start of year		−1	−1
3200	Obligated balance, end of year	−1	−1	−5
	Budget authority and outlays, net:			
	Discretionary:			
4000	Budget authority, gross	230	238	278
	Outlays, gross:			
4010	Outlays from new discretionary authority	215	232	271
4011	Outlays from discretionary balances	13	6	11
4020	Outlays, gross (total)	228	238	282
	Offsets against gross budget authority and outlays:			
	Offsetting collections (collected) from:			
4030	Federal sources	−132	−142	−167
	Additional offsets against gross budget authority only:			
4050	Change in uncollected pymts, Fed sources, unexpired	−15		
4052	Offsetting collections credited to expired accounts	13		
4060	Additional offsets against budget authority only (total)	−2		
4070	Budget authority, net (discretionary)	96	96	111
4080	Outlays, net (discretionary)	96	96	115
4180	Budget authority, net (total)	96	96	111
4190	Outlays, net (total)	96	96	115

The Administrative Office, pursuant to section 604 of Title 28, United States Code, under the supervision and direction of the Judicial Conference of the United States, is responsible for the administration of the U.S. courts, including the probation and bankruptcy systems. The principal functions consist of providing staff and services for the courts; conducting a continuous study of the rules of practice and procedure in the Federal courts; examining the state of dockets of the various courts; compiling and publishing statistical data concerning the business transacted by the courts; and administering the judicial retirement and survivors annuities systems under Title 28, United States Code, sections 178, 376, and 377. The Administrative Office also is responsible for: the preparation and submission of the annual budget estimates as well as supplemental and deficiency estimates; the disbursement of and accounting for moneys appropriated for the operation of the courts, and the Federal Judicial Center; the audit and examination of accounts; the purchase and distribution of supplies and equipment; providing automated data processing services; securing adequate space for occupancy by the courts; and such other matters as may be assigned by the Supreme Court and Judicial Conference of the United States.

Object Classification (in millions of dollars)

Identification code 010–0927–0–1–752	2021 actual	2022 est.	2023 est.
Direct obligations:			
Personnel compensation:			
11.1 Full-time permanent	83	80	93
11.3 Other than full-time permanent	1	1	1
11.9 Total personnel compensation	84	81	94
12.1 Civilian personnel benefits	29	28	31
21.0 Travel and transportation of persons		1	1
25.2 Other services from non-Federal sources	1	3	1
31.0 Equipment	1		
99.0 Direct obligations	115	113	127
99.0 Reimbursable obligations	115	125	151
99.9 Total new obligations, unexpired accounts	230	238	278

Employment Summary

Identification code 010–0927–0–1–752	2021 actual	2022 est.	2023 est.
1001 Direct civilian full-time equivalent employment	602	595	648
2001 Reimbursable civilian full-time equivalent employment	605	682	815

Chapter 7 Trustee Fund

Program and Financing (in millions of dollars)

Identification code 010–5116–0–2–752	2021 actual	2022 est.	2023 est.
Obligations by program activity:			
0001 Direct program activity		14	14
0801 Reimbursable program activity		1	3
0900 Total new obligations, unexpired accounts (object class 25.2)		15	17
Budgetary resources:			
Unobligated balance:			
1011 Unobligated balance transfer from other acct [015–5073]		15	
Budget authority:			
Appropriations, mandatory:			
1221 Appropriations transferred from other acct [015–5073]			17
1900 Budget authority (total)			17
1930 Total budgetary resources available		15	17
Change in obligated balance:			
Unpaid obligations:			
3010 New obligations, unexpired accounts		15	17
3020 Outlays (gross)		−15	−15
3050 Unpaid obligations, end of year			2
Memorandum (non-add) entries:			
3200 Obligated balance, end of year			2
Budget authority and outlays, net:			
Mandatory:			
4090 Budget authority, gross			17
Outlays, gross:			
4100 Outlays from new mandatory authority			15
4101 Outlays from mandatory balances		15	
4110 Outlays, gross (total)		15	15
4180 Budget authority, net (total)			17
4190 Outlays, net (total)		15	15

The Chapter 7 Trustee Fund was established to pay the trustee serving in Chapter 7 cases or cases converted to Chapter 7 a fee in addition to the fee already authorized by 11 U.S.C. 330(b). The proceeds of the fund are derived from quarterly fees receipts from bankruptcy filings under chapter 11 of the title 11 of the United States Code. The supplemental compensation is funded only from eligible receipts tranferred into the Chapter 7 Trustee Fund.

FEDERAL JUDICIAL CENTER

Federal Funds

Salaries and Expenses

For necessary expenses of the Federal Judicial Center, as authorized by Public Law 90–219, $33,455,000; of which $1,800,000 shall remain available through September 30, 2022, to provide education and training to Federal court personnel; and of which not to exceed $1,500 is authorized for official reception and representation expenses.

Note.—A full-year 2022 appropriation for this account was not enacted at the time the Budget was prepared; therefore, the Budget assumes this account is operating under the Continuing

Federal Judicial Center—Continued
Federal Funds—Continued

SALARIES AND EXPENSES—Continued

Appropriations Act, 2022 (Division A of Public Law 117–43, as amended). The amounts included for 2022 reflect the annualized level provided by the continuing resolution.

Program and Financing (in millions of dollars)

Identification code 010–0928–0–1–752	2021 actual	2022 est.	2023 est.
Obligations by program activity:			
0001 Education and training	17	21	24
0002 Research	5	6	6
0003 Program support	4	4	4
0900 Total new obligations, unexpired accounts	26	31	34
Budgetary resources:			
Unobligated balance:			
1000 Unobligated balance brought forward, Oct 1	2	2	
Budget authority:			
Appropriations, discretionary:			
1100 Appropriation	29	29	34
1120 Appropriations transferred to other acct [010–0920]	–1		
1160 Appropriation, discretionary (total)	28	29	34
1900 Budget authority (total)	28	29	34
1930 Total budgetary resources available	30	31	34
Memorandum (non-add) entries:			
1940 Unobligated balance expiring	–2		
1941 Unexpired unobligated balance, end of year	2		
Change in obligated balance:			
Unpaid obligations:			
3000 Unpaid obligations, brought forward, Oct 1	3	2	3
3010 New obligations, unexpired accounts	26	31	34
3020 Outlays (gross)	–27	–30	–33
3050 Unpaid obligations, end of year	2	3	4
Memorandum (non-add) entries:			
3100 Obligated balance, start of year	3	2	3
3200 Obligated balance, end of year	2	3	4
Budget authority and outlays, net:			
Discretionary:			
4000 Budget authority, gross	28	29	34
Outlays, gross:			
4010 Outlays from new discretionary authority	24	28	32
4011 Outlays from discretionary balances	3	2	1
4020 Outlays, gross (total)	27	30	33
4180 Budget authority, net (total)	28	29	34
4190 Outlays, net (total)	27	30	33

This appropriation provides for the operation of the Federal Judicial Center pursuant to 28 U.S.C. 620 et seq. The Center is charged with the responsibility for furthering the development and adoption of improved judicial administration in the courts of the United States.

Object Classification (in millions of dollars)

Identification code 010–0928–0–1–752	2021 actual	2022 est.	2023 est.
Direct obligations:			
11.1 Personnel compensation: Full-time permanent	17	17	19
12.1 Civilian personnel benefits	6	6	6
21.0 Travel and transportation of persons		5	6
25.2 Other services from non-Federal sources	1	1	1
26.0 Supplies and materials	1	1	1
31.0 Equipment	1	1	1
99.9 Total new obligations, unexpired accounts	26	31	34

Employment Summary

Identification code 010–0928–0–1–752	2021 actual	2022 est.	2023 est.
1001 Direct civilian full-time equivalent employment	125	128	128

JUDICIAL RETIREMENT FUNDS

Federal Funds

PAYMENT TO JUDICIARY TRUST FUNDS

Program and Financing (in millions of dollars)

Identification code 010–0941–0–1–752	2021 actual	2022 est.	2023 est.
Obligations by program activity:			
0001 Payment to Judicial Officers' Retirement Fund	229	238	223
0002 Payment to Court of Federal Claims Judges Retirement Fund	4	4	3
0003 Payment to Judicial Survivors' Annuities Fund	29	31	26
0900 Total new obligations, unexpired accounts (object class 42.0)	262	273	252
Budgetary resources:			
Budget authority:			
Appropriations, mandatory:			
1200 Appropriation	262	273	252
1930 Total budgetary resources available	262	273	252
Change in obligated balance:			
Unpaid obligations:			
3010 New obligations, unexpired accounts	262	273	252
3020 Outlays (gross)	–262	–273	–252
Budget authority and outlays, net:			
Mandatory:			
4090 Budget authority, gross	262	273	252
Outlays, gross:			
4100 Outlays from new mandatory authority	262	273	252
4180 Budget authority, net (total)	262	273	252
4190 Outlays, net (total)	262	273	252

This appropriation request would provide funds necessary to pay the retirement annuities of bankruptcy judges and magistrate judges, pursuant to 28 U.S.C. 377, the retirement annuities of the United States Court of Federal Claims judges, pursuant to 28 U.S.C. 178, and annuities to participants' surviving widows, widowers, and dependent children, pursuant to 28 U.S.C. 376.

Trust Funds

JUDICIAL OFFICERS' RETIREMENT FUND

Special and Trust Fund Receipts (in millions of dollars)

Identification code 010–8122–0–7–602	2021 actual	2022 est.	2023 est.
0100 Balance, start of year			11
Receipts:			
Current law:			
1110 Deductions from Employee Salaries and Voluntary Contributions, Judicial Officers' Annuity	4	4	4
1140 Interest and Profits on Investments, Judicial Officers' Annuity	36	27	24
1140 Federal Payment to Judicial Officers Retirement Fund	229	238	223
1199 Total current law receipts	269	269	251
1999 Total receipts	269	269	251
2000 Total: Balances and receipts	269	269	262
Appropriations:			
Current law:			
2101 Judicial Officers' Retirement Fund	–269	–258	–251
5099 Balance, end of year		11	11

Program and Financing (in millions of dollars)

Identification code 010–8122–0–7–602	2021 actual	2022 est.	2023 est.
Obligations by program activity:			
0010 Judicial Officers Retirement Fund	128	130	140
0900 Total new obligations, unexpired accounts (object class 42.0)	128	130	140
Budgetary resources:			
Unobligated balance:			
1000 Unobligated balance brought forward, Oct 1	848	989	1,117

JUDICIAL BRANCH

		2021 actual	2022 est.	2023 est.
	Budget authority:			
	Appropriations, mandatory:			
1201	Appropriation (special or trust fund)	269	258	251
1930	Total budgetary resources available	1,117	1,247	1,368
	Memorandum (non-add) entries:			
1941	Unexpired unobligated balance, end of year	989	1,117	1,228
	Change in obligated balance:			
	Unpaid obligations:			
3000	Unpaid obligations, brought forward, Oct 1	10	11	5
3010	New obligations, unexpired accounts	128	130	140
3020	Outlays (gross)	–127	–136	–144
3050	Unpaid obligations, end of year	11	5	1
	Memorandum (non-add) entries:			
3100	Obligated balance, start of year	10	11	5
3200	Obligated balance, end of year	11	5	1
	Budget authority and outlays, net:			
	Mandatory:			
4090	Budget authority, gross	269	258	251
	Outlays, gross:			
4100	Outlays from new mandatory authority	117	130	140
4101	Outlays from mandatory balances	10	6	4
4110	Outlays, gross (total)	127	136	144
4180	Budget authority, net (total)	269	258	251
4190	Outlays, net (total)	127	136	144
	Memorandum (non-add) entries:			
5000	Total investments, SOY: Federal securities: Par value	854	991	1,118
5001	Total investments, EOY: Federal securities: Par value	991	1,118	1,229

This fund provides the retirement annuities of bankruptcy judges and magistrate judges pursuant to 28 U.S.C. 377.

JUDICIAL SURVIVORS' ANNUITIES FUND

Special and Trust Fund Receipts (in millions of dollars)

Identification code 010–8110–0–7–602		2021 actual	2022 est.	2023 est.
0100	Balance, start of year	....	....	5
	Receipts:			
	Current law:			
1110	Judicial Survivors Annuity, Deductions from Employees Salaries	9	6	8
1140	Judicial Survivors Annuity, Interest and Profits on Investments	25	17	16
1140	Federal Payment to Judicial Survivors Annuities Fund	29	31	26
1199	Total current law receipts	63	54	50
1999	Total receipts	63	54	50
2000	Total: Balances and receipts	63	54	55
	Appropriations:			
	Current law:			
2101	Judicial Survivors' Annuities Fund	–63	–49	–50
5099	Balance, end of year	....	5	5

Program and Financing (in millions of dollars)

Identification code 010–8110–0–7–602		2021 actual	2022 est.	2023 est.
	Obligations by program activity:			
0010	Judicial Survivor's Annuity Fund	34	35	34
0900	Total new obligations, unexpired accounts (object class 42.0)	34	35	34
	Budgetary resources:			
	Unobligated balance:			
1000	Unobligated balance brought forward, Oct 1	547	576	590
	Budget authority:			
	Appropriations, mandatory:			
1201	Appropriation (special or trust fund)	63	49	50
1930	Total budgetary resources available	610	625	640
	Memorandum (non-add) entries:			
1941	Unexpired unobligated balance, end of year	576	590	606
	Change in obligated balance:			
	Unpaid obligations:			
3000	Unpaid obligations, brought forward, Oct 1	3	3	....

Judicial Retirement Funds—Continued
Trust Funds—Continued

		2021 actual	2022 est.	2023 est.
3010	New obligations, unexpired accounts	34	35	34
3020	Outlays (gross)	–34	–38	–34
3050	Unpaid obligations, end of year	3	....	....
	Memorandum (non-add) entries:			
3100	Obligated balance, start of year	3	3	....
3200	Obligated balance, end of year	3	....	....
	Budget authority and outlays, net:			
	Mandatory:			
4090	Budget authority, gross	63	49	50
	Outlays, gross:			
4100	Outlays from new mandatory authority	31	35	34
4101	Outlays from mandatory balances	3	3	
4110	Outlays, gross (total)	34	38	34
4180	Budget authority, net (total)	63	49	50
4190	Outlays, net (total)	34	38	34
	Memorandum (non-add) entries:			
5000	Total investments, SOY: Federal securities: Par value	550	580	594
5001	Total investments, EOY: Federal securities: Par value	580	594	610

The Judicial Survivors' Annuities Fund (section 376 of title 28, United States Code) was established to receive sums deducted and withheld from salaries of justices, judges, the Director of the Federal Judicial Center, the Director of the Administrative Office of the U.S. Courts, and the Administrative Assistant to the Chief Justice who have elected to bring themselves within the purview of the above section, as well as amounts received from said judicial officers covering Federal civilian service prior to date of election.

This fund provides annuities for participants' surviving widows, widowers, and dependent children.

UNITED STATES COURT OF FEDERAL CLAIMS JUDGES' RETIREMENT FUND

Special and Trust Fund Receipts (in millions of dollars)

Identification code 010–8124–0–7–602		2021 actual	2022 est.	2023 est.
0100	Balance, start of year	....	....	....
	Receipts:			
	Current law:			
1140	Federal Payment to Claims Court Judges' Retirement Fund	4	4	3
1140	Interest, Claims Court Judges' Retirement Fund	2	1	1
1199	Total current law receipts	6	5	4
1999	Total receipts	6	5	4
2000	Total: Balances and receipts	6	5	4
	Appropriations:			
	Current law:			
2101	United States Court of Federal Claims Judges' Retirement Fund	–6	–5	–4
5099	Balance, end of year	....	....	....

Program and Financing (in millions of dollars)

Identification code 010–8124–0–7–602		2021 actual	2022 est.	2023 est.
	Obligations by program activity:			
0001	Court of Federal Claims Judges Retirement Fund	5	5	5
0900	Total new obligations, unexpired accounts (object class 42.0)	5	5	5
	Budgetary resources:			
	Unobligated balance:			
1000	Unobligated balance brought forward, Oct 1	38	39	39
	Budget authority:			
	Appropriations, mandatory:			
1201	Appropriation (special or trust fund)	6	5	4
1930	Total budgetary resources available	44	44	43
	Memorandum (non-add) entries:			
1941	Unexpired unobligated balance, end of year	39	39	38
	Change in obligated balance:			
	Unpaid obligations:			
3010	New obligations, unexpired accounts	5	5	5

UNITED STATES COURT OF FEDERAL CLAIMS JUDGES' RETIREMENT FUND—Continued

Program and Financing—Continued

Identification code 010–8124–0–7–602		2021 actual	2022 est.	2023 est.
3020	Outlays (gross)	–5	–5	–4
3050	Unpaid obligations, end of year			1
	Memorandum (non-add) entries:			
3200	Obligated balance, end of year			1
	Budget authority and outlays, net:			
	Mandatory:			
4090	Budget authority, gross	6	5	4
	Outlays, gross:			
4100	Outlays from new mandatory authority	5	5	4
4180	Budget authority, net (total)	6	5	4
4190	Outlays, net (total)	5	5	4
	Memorandum (non-add) entries:			
5000	Total investments, SOY: Federal securities: Par value	39	39	40
5001	Total investments, EOY: Federal securities: Par value	39	40	40

This fund provides the retirement annuities of United States Court of Federal Claims judges pursuant to 28 U.S.C. 178.

UNITED STATES SENTENCING COMMISSION

Federal Funds

SALARIES AND EXPENSES

For the salaries and expenses necessary to carry out the provisions of chapter 58 of title 28, United States Code, $21,892,000, of which not to exceed $1,000 is authorized for official reception and representation expenses.

Note.—A full-year 2022 appropriation for this account was not enacted at the time the Budget was prepared; therefore, the Budget assumes this account is operating under the Continuing Appropriations Act, 2022 (Division A of Public Law 117–43, as amended). The amounts included for 2022 reflect the annualized level provided by the continuing resolution.

Program and Financing (in millions of dollars)

Identification code 010–0938–0–1–752		2021 actual	2022 est.	2023 est.
	Obligations by program activity:			
0001	Salaries and Expenses (Direct)	20	20	22
	Budgetary resources:			
	Budget authority:			
	Appropriations, discretionary:			
1100	Appropriation	20	20	22
1930	Total budgetary resources available	20	20	22
	Change in obligated balance:			
	Unpaid obligations:			
3000	Unpaid obligations, brought forward, Oct 1	5	5	3
3010	New obligations, unexpired accounts	20	20	22
3020	Outlays (gross)	–20	–22	–22
3050	Unpaid obligations, end of year	5	3	3
	Memorandum (non-add) entries:			
3100	Obligated balance, start of year	5	5	3
3200	Obligated balance, end of year	5	3	3
	Budget authority and outlays, net:			
	Discretionary:			
4000	Budget authority, gross	20	20	22
	Outlays, gross:			
4010	Outlays from new discretionary authority	16	17	19
4011	Outlays from discretionary balances	4	5	3
4020	Outlays, gross (total)	20	22	22
4180	Budget authority, net (total)	20	20	22
4190	Outlays, net (total)	20	22	22

The United States Sentencing Commission, an independent agency within the judicial branch, was established pursuant to provisions of the Comprehensive Crime Control Act of 1984 (Public Law 98–473, Title II), as amended. The Commission's principal purposes are to: (1) collect, analyze, and distribute a broad array of information on Federal crime and sentencing issues, serving as an information resource for the Congress, the executive branch, the courts, criminal justice practitioners, the academic community, and the public; (2) establish sentencing policies and practices for the Federal courts, including guidelines prescribing the appropriate form and severity of punishment for offenders convicted of Federal crimes; (3) advise and assist the Congress and the executive branch in the development of effective and efficient crime policy; and (4) provide training to judges, prosecutors, probation officers, the defense bar, and other members of the criminal justice community on the application of the guidelines.

Object Classification (in millions of dollars)

Identification code 010–0938–0–1–752		2021 actual	2022 est.	2023 est.
	Direct obligations:			
11.1	Personnel compensation: Full-time permanent	11	12	14
12.1	Civilian personnel benefits	4	4	5
25.2	Other services from non-Federal sources	3	2	1
31.0	Equipment	2	2	2
99.9	Total new obligations, unexpired accounts	20	20	22

Employment Summary

Identification code 010–0938–0–1–752		2021 actual	2022 est.	2023 est.
1001	Direct civilian full-time equivalent employment	95	95	95

GENERAL FUND RECEIPT ACCOUNTS

(in millions of dollars)

	2021 actual	2022 est.	2023 est.
Offsetting receipts from the public:			
010–322000 All Other General Fund Proprietary Receipts Including Budget Clearing Accounts	–10		
General Fund Offsetting receipts from the public	–10		
Intragovernmental payments:			
010–388500 Undistributed intragovernmental payments and receivables from cancelled accounts	3		
General Fund Intragovernmental payments	3		

ADMINISTRATIVE PROVISIONS—THE JUDICIARY

(INCLUDING TRANSFER OF FUNDS)

SEC. 301. *Appropriations and authorizations made in this title which are available for salaries and expenses shall be available for services as authorized by 5 U.S.C. 3109.*

SEC. 302. *Not to exceed 5 percent of any appropriation made available for the current fiscal year for the Judiciary in this Act may be transferred between such appropriations, but no such appropriation, except "Courts of Appeals, District Courts, and Other Judicial Services, Defender Services" and "Courts of Appeals, District Courts, and Other Judicial Services, Fees of Jurors and Commissioners", shall be increased by more than 10 percent by any such transfers: Provided, That any transfer pursuant to this section shall be treated as a reprogramming of funds under sections 604 and 608 of this Act and shall not be available for obligation or expenditure except in compliance with the procedures set forth in section 608.*

SEC. 303. *Notwithstanding any other provision of law, the salaries and expenses appropriation for "Courts of Appeals, District Courts, and Other Judicial Services" shall be available for official reception and representation expenses of the Judicial Conference of the United States: Provided, That such available funds shall not exceed $11,000 and shall be administered by the Director of the Administrative Office of the United States Courts in the capacity as Secretary of the Judicial Conference.*

SEC. 304. *Section 3315(a) of title 40, United States Code, shall be applied by substituting "Federal" for "executive" each place it appears.*

SEC. 305. *In accordance with 28 U.S.C. 561–569, and notwithstanding any other provision of law, the United States Marshals Service shall provide, for such courthouses as its Director may designate in consultation with the Director of the Administrative Office of the United States Courts, for purposes of a pilot program, the security services that 40 U.S.C. 1315 authorizes the Department of Homeland Security to provide, except for the services specified in 40 U.S.C. 1315(b)(2)(E). For building-*

specific security services at these courthouses, the Director of the Administrative Office of the United States Courts shall reimburse the United States Marshals Service rather than the Department of Homeland Security.

SEC. 306. (a) Section 203(c) of the Judicial Improvements Act of 1990 (Public Law 101–650; 28 U.S.C. 133 note), is amended in the second sentence (relating to the District of Kansas) following paragraph (12), by striking "30 years and 6 months" and inserting "32 years and 6 months".

(b) Section 406 of the Transportation, Treasury, Housing and Urban Development, the Judiciary, the District of Columbia, and Independent Agencies Appropriations Act, 2006 (Public Law 109–115; 119 Stat. 2470; 28 U.S.C. 133 note) is amended in the second sentence (relating to the eastern District of Missouri) by striking "28 years and 6 months" and inserting "30 years and 6 months".

(c) Section 312(c)(2) of the 21st Century Department of Justice Appropriations Authorization Act (Public Law 107–273; 28 U.S.C. 133 note), is amended—

(1) in the first sentence by striking "19 years" and inserting "21 years";

(2) in the second sentence (relating to the central District of California), by striking "18 years and 6 months" and inserting "20 years and 6 months"; and

(3) in the third sentence (relating to the western district of North Carolina), by striking "17 years" and inserting "19 years".

DEPARTMENT OF AGRICULTURE

OFFICE OF THE SECRETARY
Federal Funds

PROCESSING, RESEARCH, AND MARKETING

OFFICE OF THE SECRETARY

(INCLUDING TRANSFERS OF FUNDS)

For necessary expenses of the Office of the Secretary, $81,010,000 of which not to exceed $10,623,000 shall be available for the Immediate Office of the Secretary; not to exceed $2,306,000 shall be available for the Office of Homeland Security; not to exceed $10,525,000 shall be available for the Office of Partnerships and Public Engagement; not to exceed $6,450,000 shall be available for the Office of Tribal Relations; not to exceed $35,047,000 shall be available for the Office of the Assistant Secretary for Administration, of which $33,300,000 shall be available for Departmental Administration to provide for necessary expenses for management support services to offices of the Department and for general administration, security, repairs and alterations, and other miscellaneous supplies and expenses not otherwise provided for and necessary for the practical and efficient work of the Department: *Provided*, That funds made available by this Act to an agency in the Administration mission area for salaries and expenses are available to fund up to one administrative support staff for the Office; not to exceed $4,671,000 shall be available for the Office of Assistant Secretary for Congressional Relations and Intergovernmental Affairs to carry out the programs funded by this Act, including programs involving intergovernmental affairs and liaison within the executive branch; and not to exceed $11,388,000 shall be available for the Office of Communications: *Provided further*, That the Secretary of Agriculture is authorized to transfer funds appropriated for any office of the Office of the Secretary to any other office of the Office of the Secretary: *Provided further*, That no appropriation for any office shall be increased or decreased by more than 5 percent: *Provided further*, That not to exceed $22,000 of the amount made available under this paragraph for the immediate Office of the Secretary shall be available for official reception and representation expenses, not otherwise provided for, as determined by the Secretary: *Provided further*, That the amount made available under this heading for Departmental Administration shall be reimbursed from applicable appropriations in this Act for travel expenses incident to the holding of hearings as required by 5 U.S.C. 551–558: *Provided further*, That funds made available under this heading for the Office of the Assistant Secretary for Congressional Relations and Intergovernmental Affairs may be transferred to agencies of the Department of Agriculture funded by this Act to maintain personnel at the agency level.

OFFICE OF THE ASSISTANT SECRETARY FOR CIVIL RIGHTS

For necessary expenses of the Office of the Assistant Secretary for Civil Rights, $1,530,000: *Provided*, That funds made available by this Act to an agency in the Civil Rights mission area for salaries and expenses are available to fund up to one administrative support staff for the Office.

OFFICE OF THE UNDER SECRETARY FOR RESEARCH, EDUCATION, AND ECONOMICS

For necessary expenses of the Office of the Under Secretary for Research, Education, and Economics, $6,376,000: *Provided*, That funds made available by this Act to an agency in the Research, Education, and Economics mission area for salaries and expenses are available to fund up to one administrative support staff for the Office: *Provided further*, That of the amounts made available under this heading, $4,950,000 shall be made available for the Office of the Chief Scientist.

OFFICE OF THE UNDER SECRETARY FOR MARKETING AND REGULATORY PROGRAMS

For necessary expenses of the Office of the Under Secretary for Marketing and Regulatory Programs, $1,676,000: *Provided*, That funds made available by this Act to an agency in the Marketing and Regulatory Programs mission area for salaries and expenses are available to fund up to one administrative support staff for the Office.

OFFICE OF THE UNDER SECRETARY FOR FOOD SAFETY

For necessary expenses of the Office of the Under Secretary for Food Safety, $1,176,000: *Provided*, That funds made available by this Act to an agency in the Food Safety mission area for salaries and expenses are available to fund up to one administrative support staff for the Office.

OFFICE OF THE UNDER SECRETARY FOR FARM PRODUCTION AND CONSERVATION

For necessary expenses of the Office of the Under Secretary for Farm Production and Conservation, $1,792,000: *Provided*, That funds made available by this Act to an agency in the Farm Production and Conservation mission area for salaries and expenses are available to fund up to one administrative support staff for the Office.

OFFICE OF THE UNDER SECRETARY FOR RURAL DEVELOPMENT

For necessary expenses of the Office of the Under Secretary for Rural Development, $1,679,000: *Provided*, That funds made available by this Act to an agency in the Rural Development mission area for salaries and expenses are available to fund up to one administrative support staff for the Office.

OFFICE OF THE UNDER SECRETARY FOR FOOD, NUTRITION, AND CONSUMER SERVICES

For necessary expenses of the Office of the Under Secretary for Food, Nutrition, and Consumer Services, $1,426,000: *Provided*, That funds made available by this Act to an agency in the Food, Nutrition and Consumer Services mission area for salaries and expenses are available to fund up to one administrative support staff for the Office.

OFFICE OF THE UNDER SECRETARY FOR TRADE AND FOREIGN AGRICULTURAL AFFAIRS

For necessary expenses of the Office of the Under Secretary for Trade and Foreign Agricultural Affairs, $1,018,000: *Provided*, That funds made available by this Act to any agency in the Trade and Foreign Agricultural Affairs mission area for salaries and expenses are available to fund up to one administrative support staff for the Office.

OFFICE OF CODEX ALIMENTARIUS

For necessary expenses of the Office of Codex Alimentarius, $4,978,000, including not to exceed $40,000 for official reception and representation expenses.

OFFICE OF THE UNDER SECRETARY FOR NATURAL RESOURCES AND ENVIRONMENT

For necessary expenses of the Office of the Under Secretary for Natural Resources and Environment, $1,429,000: *Provided*, That funds made available by this Act to any agency in the Natural Resources and Environment mission area for salaries and expenses are available to fund up to one administrative support staff for the office.

Note.—A full-year 2022 appropriation for this account was not enacted at the time the Budget was prepared; therefore, the Budget assumes this account is operating under the Continuing Appropriations Act, 2022 (Division A of Public Law 117–43, as amended). The amounts included for 2022 reflect the annualized level provided by the continuing resolution.

PROCESSING, RESEARCH AND MARKETING

AGRICULTURAL PROGRAMS

OFFICE OF THE SECRETARY

[For an additional amount for the "Office of the Secretary", $10,000,000,000, which shall remain available until December 31, 2023, for necessary expenses related to losses of crops (including milk, on-farm stored commodities, crops prevented from planting in 2020 and 2021, and harvested adulterated wine grapes), trees, bushes, and vines, as a consequence of droughts, wildfires, hurricanes, floods, derechos, excessive heat, winter storms, freeze, including a polar vortex, smoke exposure, quality losses of crops, and excessive moisture occurring in calendar years 2020 and 2021 under such terms and conditions as determined by the Secretary: *Provided*, That, with respect to smoke tainted wine grapes, the loss (including a quality loss) of such crop during the coverage period due to wildfire, as determined by the Secretary, is considered a qualified loss: *Provided further*, That losses due to drought shall only be eligible under this heading in this Act if any area within the county in which the loss occurs was rated by the U.S. Drought Monitor as having a D2 (Severe Drought) for eight consecutive weeks or a D3 (Extreme Drought) or higher level of drought intensity during the applicable calendar years: *Provided further*, That of the amounts provided under this heading in this Act, the Secretary shall use $750,000,000 to provide assistance to producers of livestock, as determined by the Secretary of Agriculture, for losses incurred during calendar year 2021 due to drought or wildfires: *Provided further*, That at the election of a processor eligible for a loan under section 156 of the Federal Agriculture Improvement and Reform Act of 1996 (7 U.S.C. 7272) or a cooperative processor of dairy, the Secretary shall make payments for losses in 2021 to such processors (to be paid to producer members, as determined by such processors) in lieu of payments to producers and under

Office of the Secretary—Continued
Federal Funds—Continued

OFFICE OF THE SECRETARY—Continued

the same terms and conditions as payments made to processors pursuant to title I of the Additional Supplemental Appropriations for Disaster Relief Act, 2019 (Public Law 116–20) under the heading "Department of Agriculture—Agricultural Programs—Processing, Research and Marketing—Office of the Secretary", as last amended by section 791(c) of title VII of division B of the Further Consolidated Appropriations Act, 2020 (Public Law 116–94): *Provided further*, That notwithstanding section 760.1503(j) of title 7 of the Code of Federal Regulations, in the event that a processor described in the preceding proviso does not elect to receive payments under such clause, the Secretary shall make direct payments to producers under this heading in this Act: *Provided further*, That of the amounts provided under this heading in this Act, not more than one percent of the funds provided herein may be used for administrative costs, including for streamlining the application process and easing the burden on county office employees, to carry out the matter under this heading in this Act: *Provided further*, That, except as otherwise provided under this heading in this Act, the Secretary shall impose payment limitations consistent with section 760.1507 of title 7, Code of Federal Regulations (as in effect on the date of enactment of this Act): *Provided further*, That, in the case of specialty crops or high value crops, as determined by the Secretary, the Secretary shall impose payment limitations consistent with section 760.1507(a)(2) of title 7, Code of Federal Regulations (as in effect on January 1, 2019): *Provided further*, That, with respect to the payment limitations described under this heading in this Act, the Secretary shall apply separate payment limits for each of 2020 and 2021: *Provided further*, That the total amount of payments received under this heading in this Act and applicable policies of crop insurance under the Federal Crop Insurance Act (7 U.S.C. 1501 et seq.) or the Noninsured Crop Disaster Assistance Program (NAP) under section 196 of the Federal Agriculture Improvement and Reform Act of 1996 (7 U.S.C. 7333) (minus any premiums or fees paid for such coverages) shall not exceed 90 percent of the loss as determined by the Secretary: *Provided further*, That the total amount of payments received under this heading in this Act for producers who did not obtain a policy or plan of insurance for an insurable commodity for the applicable crop year under the Federal Crop Insurance Act (7 U.S.C. 1501 et seq.) for the crop incurring the losses or did not file the required paperwork and pay the service fee by the applicable State filing deadline for a noninsurable commodity for the applicable crop year under NAP for the crop incurring the losses shall not exceed 70 percent of the loss as determined by the Secretary: *Provided further*, That producers receiving payments under this heading in this Act, as determined by the Secretary, shall be required to purchase crop insurance where crop insurance is available for the next two available crop years and producers receiving payments under this heading in this Act shall be required to purchase coverage under NAP where crop insurance is not available in the next two available crop years, as determined by the Secretary: *Provided further*, That not later than 120 days after the end of fiscal year 2021, the Secretary shall submit a report to the Congress specifying the type, amount, and method of such assistance by state and territory.] *(Disaster Relief Supplemental Appropriations Act, 2022.)*

Program and Financing (in millions of dollars)

Identification code 012–9913–0–1–999	2021 actual	2022 est.	2023 est.
Obligations by program activity:			
0001 Office of the Secretary	4	5	11
0002 Under/Assistant Secretaries	13	17	36
0004 Departmental Administration	22	21	33
0005 Office of Communications	7	7	11
0007 Office of Homeland Security and Emergency Coordination	1	1	2
0008 Outreach & Assistance for Socially Disadvantaged Farmers & Ranchers & Veteran Farmers & Ranchers	16	16	19
0010 Office of Partnerships and Public Engagement	5	7	11
0011 Disaster Relief Supplemental	2,411	643	
0012 COVID-19 CARES CFAP	339	1,619	
0013 COVID-19 CCC CFAP	11,979	1,210	
0014 General Provision: Farming Opportunities Training and Outreach	2	2	2
0015 ARP: Dairy Margin Coverage		412	163
0017 ARP: Socially Disadvantaged Producers		1,010	
0018 ARP: Pandemic Program Administration	1	47	
0019 Consolidated Approp Div N: Food Box Distribution Program - No Year	1,920	80	
0020 Consolidated Approp Div N: Covid-19 CFAP Payments	6,482	3,206	
0021 Consolidated Approp Div N: Farming Opportunities Training and Outreach			36
0022 Consolidated Approp Div N: Farming Opportunities Training and Outreach Admin		2	
0023 Disaster Assistance Payments FY 2022		9,000	1,000
0024 Bio Energy Grants COVID-19		700	
0025 Market Disruption Assistance Relief		500	
0026 Drought Relief		500	
0799 Total direct obligations	23,202	19,041	1,288
0802 Office of the Secretary (Reimbursable)	69	65	59
0900 Total new obligations, unexpired accounts	23,271	19,106	1,347
Budgetary resources:			
Unobligated balance:			
1000 Unobligated balance brought forward, Oct 1	18,183	13,154	1,005
1001 Discretionary unobligated balance brought fwd, Oct 1	4,977		
1020 Adjustment of unobligated bal brought forward, Oct 1		–3,600	
1021 Recoveries of prior year unpaid obligations	1,169	1	1
1033 Recoveries of prior year paid obligations	222		
1070 Unobligated balance (total)	19,574	9,555	1,006
Budget authority:			
Appropriations, discretionary:			
1100 Appropriation	1,132	106	104
1100 Appropriations P.L. 117–43 Supplemental		10,000	
1120 Appropriations transferred to other acct [012–4609]	–2		
1120 Appropriations transferred to other acct [012–3700]	–16	–16	
1120 Appropriations transferred to other acct [012–0403]	–10	–10	
1120 Appropriations transferred to other acct [012–0013]	–20	–20	
1131 Unobligated balance of appropriations permanently reduced	–1,024		
1160 Appropriation, discretionary (total)	60	10,060	104
Appropriations, mandatory:			
1200 Appropriation	15,883	437	178
1222 Exercised borrowing authority transferred from other accounts [012–4336]	1,000		
1222 Exercised borrowing authority transferred from other accounts [012–4336]	18	20	20
1230 Appropriations and/or unobligated balance of appropriations permanently reduced	–1	–26	–11
1260 Appropriations, mandatory (total)	16,900	431	187
Spending authority from offsetting collections, discretionary:			
1700 Collected	41	65	60
1701 Change in uncollected payments, Federal sources	32		
1750 Spending auth from offsetting collections, disc (total)	73	65	60
1900 Budget authority (total)	17,033	10,556	351
1930 Total budgetary resources available	36,607	20,111	1,357
Memorandum (non-add) entries:			
1940 Unobligated balance expiring	–182		
1941 Unexpired unobligated balance, end of year	13,154	1,005	10
Change in obligated balance:			
Unpaid obligations:			
3000 Unpaid obligations, brought forward, Oct 1	4,570	1,010	14,062
3010 New obligations, unexpired accounts	23,271	19,106	1,347
3011 Obligations ("upward adjustments"), expired accounts	34		
3020 Outlays (gross)	–25,657	–6,053	–7,584
3040 Recoveries of prior year unpaid obligations, unexpired	–1,169	–1	–1
3041 Recoveries of prior year unpaid obligations, expired	–39		
3050 Unpaid obligations, end of year	1,010	14,062	7,824
Uncollected payments:			
3060 Uncollected pymts, Fed sources, brought forward, Oct 1	–40	–56	–56
3070 Change in uncollected pymts, Fed sources, unexpired	–32		
3071 Change in uncollected pymts, Fed sources, expired	16		
3090 Uncollected pymts, Fed sources, end of year	–56	–56	–56
Memorandum (non-add) entries:			
3100 Obligated balance, start of year	4,530	954	14,006
3200 Obligated balance, end of year	954	14,006	7,768
Budget authority and outlays, net:			
Discretionary:			
4000 Budget authority, gross	133	10,125	164
Outlays, gross:			
4010 Outlays from new discretionary authority	92	1,119	156
4011 Outlays from discretionary balances	4,467	859	6,009
4020 Outlays, gross (total)	4,559	1,978	6,165
Offsets against gross budget authority and outlays:			
Offsetting collections (collected) from:			
4030 Federal sources	–53	–65	–60
4033 Non-Federal sources	–204		
4040 Offsets against gross budget authority and outlays (total)	–257	–65	–60
Additional offsets against gross budget authority only:			
4050 Change in uncollected pymts, Fed sources, unexpired	–32		
4052 Offsetting collections credited to expired accounts	13		
4053 Recoveries of prior year paid obligations, unexpired accounts	203		
4060 Additional offsets against budget authority only (total)	184		

DEPARTMENT OF AGRICULTURE

Office of the Secretary—Continued
Federal Funds—Continued

		2021 actual	2022 est.	2023 est.
4070	Budget authority, net (discretionary)	60	10,060	104
4080	Outlays, net (discretionary)	4,302	1,913	6,105
	Mandatory:			
4090	Budget authority, gross	16,900	431	187
	Outlays, gross:			
4100	Outlays from new mandatory authority	1,547	140	69
4101	Outlays from mandatory balances	19,551	3,935	1,350
4110	Outlays, gross (total)	21,098	4,075	1,419
	Offsets against gross budget authority and outlays:			
	Offsetting collections (collected) from:			
4123	Non-Federal sources	−19		
	Additional offsets against gross budget authority only:			
4143	Recoveries of prior year paid obligations, unexpired accounts	19		
4160	Budget authority, net (mandatory)	16,900	431	187
4170	Outlays, net (mandatory)	21,079	4,075	1,419
4180	Budget authority, net (total)	16,960	10,491	291
4190	Outlays, net (total)	25,381	5,988	7,524

The Office of the Secretary is responsible for the overall planning, coordination and administration of the Department's programs. This includes the Secretary, Deputy Secretary, Under Secretaries, Assistant Secretaries, and other related offices, who provide policy guidance for the Department; and provide liaison with the Executive Office of the President and Members of Congress.

In 2023, the Office of the Secretary will continue to administer unobligated balances from supplemental funding appropriated by Congress in 2018, 2019, 2020, and 2021 for prior disasters. In addition, unobligated balances are projected for the supplemental funding Congress provided to the Office of the Secretary through the Coronavirus Aid, Relief, and Economic and Security Act, and the American Rescue Plan.

In line with the President's environmental justice goals, the Budget increases targeting of benefits to disadvantaged communities to help achieve the Justice40 goals.

Object Classification (in millions of dollars)

Identification code 012–9913–0–1–999 | 2021 actual | 2022 est. | 2023 est.

		2021 actual	2022 est.	2023 est.
	Direct obligations:			
11.1	Personnel compensation: Full-time permanent	23	28	48
12.1	Civilian personnel benefits	8	9	16
21.0	Travel and transportation of persons		1	1
23.1	Rental payments to GSA	1	1	1
23.3	Communications, utilities, and miscellaneous charges	2	2	2
25.2	Other services from non-Federal sources	21,112	16,428	1,202
25.3	Other goods and services from Federal sources	9	10	15
26.0	Supplies and materials	1,902	81	
31.0	Equipment	1		
41.0	Grants, subsidies, and contributions	85	2,481	3
42.0	Insurance claims and indemnities	59		
99.0	Direct obligations	23,202	19,041	1,288
99.0	Reimbursable obligations	69	65	59
99.9	Total new obligations, unexpired accounts	23,271	19,106	1,347

Employment Summary

Identification code 012–9913–0–1–999 | 2021 actual | 2022 est. | 2023 est.

		2021 actual	2022 est.	2023 est.
1001	Direct civilian full-time equivalent employment	176	198	305
2001	Reimbursable civilian full-time equivalent employment	143	153	138

FOOD SUPPLY CHAIN AND AGRICULTURE PANDEMIC RESPONSE PROGRAM ACCOUNT

Program and Financing (in millions of dollars)

Identification code 012–0408–0–1–351 | 2021 actual | 2022 est. | 2023 est.

		2021 actual	2022 est.	2023 est.
	Obligations by program activity:			
0001	American Rescue Plan		845	1,384
0002	Food Bank Network		350	50
0003	The Emergency Food Assistance Program Grants		100	
0004	Healthy Food Financing Initiative		20	
0005	Meat and Poultry Processing Expansion Program		120	30
0006	Meat and Poultry Processing Expansion Program TA		10	
0007	Local Food Promotion Program and Regional Food Systems Partnership		65	65
0008	Dairy Business Innovation Program		80	
0091	Direct program activities, subtotal		1,590	1,529
	Credit program obligations:			
0702	Loan guarantee subsidy		60	28
0709	Administrative expenses		2	1
0791	Direct program activities, subtotal		62	29
0900	Total new obligations, unexpired accounts		1,652	1,558
	Budgetary resources:			
	Unobligated balance:			
1000	Unobligated balance brought forward, Oct 1			1,948
1020	Adjustment of unobligated bal brought forward, Oct 1		3,600	
1070	Unobligated balance (total)		3,600	1,948
1930	Total budgetary resources available		3,600	1,948
	Memorandum (non-add) entries:			
1941	Unexpired unobligated balance, end of year		1,948	390
	Change in obligated balance:			
	Unpaid obligations:			
3000	Unpaid obligations, brought forward, Oct 1			234
3010	New obligations, unexpired accounts		1,652	1,558
3020	Outlays (gross)		−1,418	−1,759
3050	Unpaid obligations, end of year		234	33
	Memorandum (non-add) entries:			
3100	Obligated balance, start of year			234
3200	Obligated balance, end of year		234	33
	Budget authority and outlays, net:			
	Mandatory:			
	Outlays, gross:			
4101	Outlays from mandatory balances		1,418	1,759
4180	Budget authority, net (total)			
4190	Outlays, net (total)		1,418	1,759

Summary of Loan Levels, Subsidy Budget Authority and Outlays by Program (in millions of dollars)

Identification code 012–0408–0–1–351 | 2021 actual | 2022 est. | 2023 est.

		2021 actual	2022 est.	2023 est.
	Guaranteed loan levels supportable by subsidy budget authority:			
215001	Food Processing Supply Chain Loan Guarantees		828	400
	Guaranteed loan subsidy (in percent):			
232001	Food Processing Supply Chain Loan Guarantees		7.30	6.91
232999	Weighted average subsidy rate	0.00	7.30	6.91
	Guaranteed loan subsidy budget authority:			
233001	Food Processing Supply Chain Loan Guarantees		60	28
	Guaranteed loan subsidy outlays:			
234001	Food Processing Supply Chain Loan Guarantees		36	35
	Administrative expense data:			
3510	Budget authority		1	1
3580	Outlays from balances		1	

The American Rescue Plan provided funding to the Office of the Secretary. Funds are disbursed to support the following programs:

The Food Bank Network.—This program supports Local, Regional and Socially Disadvantaged Farmers through cooperative agreements with state and Tribal governments or other local entities to purchase food from local and regional producers and from socially disadvantaged producers. Innovative approaches ensure these agreements facilitate relationships between farmers, ranchers and producers and local and regional food systems.

The Emergency Food Assistance Program (TEFAP).—Reach and Resiliency grants through this program provide State agencies with an opportunity to re-envision how they can work with currently participating organizations, including food banks, and/or new partner organizations, to reach underserved populations. Activities undertaken with grant funds may look vastly different among States/Territories; however, in all cases, activities should be informed by relevant data and/or the expert advice of program stakeholders. All activities must focus on expansion into remote, rural, Tribal, and/or low-income areas that are currently underserved by the program. Underserved areas are defined as those in which TEFAP foods are not easily accessible to all eligible populations as determined by the State agency.

Food Supply Chain and Agriculture Pandemic Response Program Account—Continued

The Healthy Food Financing Initiative (7 U.S.C. 6953).—This program improves access to healthy foods in underserved areas, to create and preserve quality jobs, and to revitalize low-income communities by providing loans and grants to eligible fresh, healthy food retailers and enterprises to overcome the higher costs and initial barriers to entry in underserved areas.

The Meat and Poultry Processing Expansion Program.—This funding provides better options to producers and consumers by providing grants to meat and poultry processors to start and expand processing operations to maintain and improve food and agricultural supply chain resiliency. The funds aligns with the programs goal of increasing competition in a sector that is highly consolidated and vulnerable to disruption.

The Meat and Poultry Processing Capacity Technical Assistance.—This funding provides technical support by awarding cooperative agreements with external cooperators, this program makes available a broad range of pre-award and post-award technical assistance to grant applicants and grant-funded projects under USDA Meat and Poultry Supply Chain initiatives.

The Local Food Promotion Program (LFPP) and the Regional Food Systems Partnership Program (RFSP).—This program provides grant funds to build local farm and agricultural market networks and capacity to supply institutional markets by emphasizing that farm-to-institution projects are an eligible project type. Through these two interrelated programs, grants support the development, coordination, and expansion of local and regional food systems; additional funds will be utilized to emphasize farm-to-institution projects under each program.

Dairy Business Innovation (DBI) Initiatives.—Through four existing funds this program supports dairy businesses in the development, production, marketing, and distribution of dairy products. DBI Initiatives provide direct technical assistance and grants to dairy businesses, including niche dairy products, such as specialty cheese, or dairy products derived from the milk of a dairy animal, including cow, sheep, and goat milk.

Food Processing Supply Chain Loan Guarantee.—This funding is provided for the following uses (1) to purchase food and agricultural commodities; (2) to purchase and distribute agricultural commodities (including fresh produce, dairy, eggs, and meat) to individuals in need, including through delivery to nonprofit organizations and through restaurants and other food related entities, as determined by the Secretary, that may receive, store, process, and distribute food items; (3) to make grants and loans for small or midsized food processors or distributors, farmers markets, producers, or other organizations to respond to COVID19, including for measures to protect workers against COVID19; and (4) to make loans and grants and provide other assistance to maintain and improve food and agricultural supply chain resiliency.

Object Classification (in millions of dollars)

Identification code 012–0408–0–1–351		2021 actual	2022 est.	2023 est.
	Direct obligations:			
25.3	Other goods and services from Federal sources		2	1
41.0	Grants, subsidies, and contributions		1,650	1,557
99.9	Total new obligations, unexpired accounts		1,652	1,558

Food Supply Chain and Agriculture Pandemic Response Guaranteed Loans Financing Account

Program and Financing (in millions of dollars)

Identification code 012–4391–0–3–351		2021 actual	2022 est.	2023 est.
	Obligations by program activity:			
	Credit program obligations:			
0711	Default claim payments on principal			7
0713	Payment of interest to Treasury			2
0900	Total new obligations, unexpired accounts			9

		2021 actual	2022 est.	2023 est.
	Budgetary resources:			
	Unobligated balance:			
1000	Unobligated balance brought forward, Oct 1			60
	Financing authority:			
	Spending authority from offsetting collections, mandatory:			
1800	Collected		36	37
1801	Change in uncollected payments, Federal sources		24	–7
1850	Spending auth from offsetting collections, mand (total)		60	30
1900	Budget authority (total)		60	30
1930	Total budgetary resources available		60	90
	Memorandum (non-add) entries:			
1941	Unexpired unobligated balance, end of year		60	81
	Change in obligated balance:			
	Unpaid obligations:			
3010	New obligations, unexpired accounts			9
3020	Outlays (gross)			–9
	Uncollected payments:			
3060	Uncollected pymts, Fed sources, brought forward, Oct 1			–24
3070	Change in uncollected pymts, Fed sources, unexpired		–24	7
3090	Uncollected pymts, Fed sources, end of year		–24	–17
	Memorandum (non-add) entries:			
3100	Obligated balance, start of year			–24
3200	Obligated balance, end of year		–24	–17
	Financing authority and disbursements, net:			
	Mandatory:			
4090	Budget authority, gross		60	30
	Financing disbursements:			
4110	Outlays, gross (total)			9
	Offsets against gross financing authority and disbursements:			
	Offsetting collections (collected) from:			
4120	Federal sources		–36	–35
4122	Interest on uninvested funds			–2
4130	Offsets against gross budget authority and outlays (total)		–36	–37
	Additional offsets against financing authority only (total):			
4140	Change in uncollected pymts, Fed sources, unexpired		–24	7
4170	Outlays, net (mandatory)		–36	–28
4180	Budget authority, net (total)			
4190	Outlays, net (total)		–36	–28

Status of Guaranteed Loans (in millions of dollars)

Identification code 012–4391–0–3–351		2021 actual	2022 est.	2023 est.
	Position with respect to appropriations act limitation on commitments:			
2111	Guaranteed loan commitments from current-year authority		1,370	
2121	Limitation available from carry-forward			573
2143	Uncommitted limitation carried forward		–542	–173
2150	Total guaranteed loan commitments		828	400
2199	Guaranteed amount of guaranteed loan commitments		672	323
	Cumulative balance of guaranteed loans outstanding:			
2210	Outstanding, start of year			475
2231	Disbursements of new guaranteed loans		497	488
2251	Repayments and prepayments		–22	–72
2263	Adjustments: Terminations for default that result in claim payments			–7
2290	Outstanding, end of year		475	884
	Memorandum:			
2299	Guaranteed amount of guaranteed loans outstanding, end of year		386	718
	Addendum:			
	Cumulative balance of defaulted guaranteed loans that result in loans receivable:			
2310	Outstanding, start of year			
2331	Disbursements for guaranteed loan claims			7
2390	Outstanding, end of year			7

As required by the Federal Credit Reform Act of 1990, this non-budgetary account records all cash flows to and from the Government resulting from loan guarantees committed in 1992 and beyond. The amounts in this account are a means of financing and are not included in budget totals.

This account finances loan guarantee commitments for business development in rural areas. The subsidy cost of this program is funded through the Food Supply Chain and Agriculture Pandemic Response Program Account.

Trust Funds
GIFTS AND BEQUESTS

Special and Trust Fund Receipts (in millions of dollars)

Identification code 012–8203–0–7–352		2021 actual	2022 est.	2023 est.
0100	Balance, start of year			
	Receipts:			
	Current law:			
1130	Gifts and Bequests, Departmental Administration	1	1	1
2000	Total: Balances and receipts	1	1	1
	Appropriations:			
	Current law:			
2101	Gifts and Bequests	–1	–1	–1
5099	Balance, end of year			

Program and Financing (in millions of dollars)

Identification code 012–8203–0–7–352		2021 actual	2022 est.	2023 est.
	Obligations by program activity:			
0001	Gifts and bequests	1	1	1
0900	Total new obligations, unexpired accounts (object class 99.5)	1	1	1
	Budgetary resources:			
	Unobligated balance:			
1000	Unobligated balance brought forward, Oct 1	5	5	5
	Budget authority:			
	Appropriations, mandatory:			
1201	Appropriation (special or trust fund)	1	1	1
1930	Total budgetary resources available	6	6	6
	Memorandum (non-add) entries:			
1941	Unexpired unobligated balance, end of year	5	5	5
	Change in obligated balance:			
	Unpaid obligations:			
3000	Unpaid obligations, brought forward, Oct 1	1	1	
3010	New obligations, unexpired accounts	1	1	1
3020	Outlays (gross)	–1	–2	–1
3050	Unpaid obligations, end of year	1		
	Memorandum (non-add) entries:			
3100	Obligated balance, start of year	1	1	
3200	Obligated balance, end of year	1		
	Budget authority and outlays, net:			
	Mandatory:			
4090	Budget authority, gross	1	1	1
	Outlays, gross:			
4100	Outlays from new mandatory authority		1	1
4101	Outlays from mandatory balances	1	1	
4110	Outlays, gross (total)	1	2	1
4180	Budget authority, net (total)	1	1	1
4190	Outlays, net (total)	1	2	1

The Secretary is authorized to accept and administer gifts and bequests of real and personal property to facilitate the work of the Department. Property and the proceeds thereof are used in accordance with the terms of the gift or bequest (7 U.S.C. 2269).

EXECUTIVE OPERATIONS
Federal Funds
EXECUTIVE OPERATIONS
OFFICE OF THE CHIEF ECONOMIST

For necessary expenses of the Office of the Chief Economist, $32,012,000, of which not more than $8,000,000 shall be for grants or cooperative agreements for policy research under 7 U.S.C. 3155 and $6,500,000 shall remain available until expended for activities relating to climate change, including coordinating such activities across the Department.

OFFICE OF HEARINGS AND APPEALS

For necessary expenses of the Office of Hearings and Appeals, $16,743,000.

OFFICE OF BUDGET AND PROGRAM ANALYSIS

For necessary expenses of the Office of Budget and Program Analysis, $25,738,000.

OFFICE OF THE CHIEF INFORMATION OFFICER

For necessary expenses of the Office of the Chief Information Officer, $97,547,000.

OFFICE OF THE CHIEF FINANCIAL OFFICER

For necessary expenses of the Office of the Chief Financial Officer, $7,374,000.

OFFICE OF CIVIL RIGHTS

For necessary expenses of the Office of Civil Rights, $31,696,000.

OFFICE OF SAFETY, SECURITY, AND PROTECTION

For necessary expenses of the Office of Safety, Security, and Protection, $25,528,000.

HAZARDOUS MATERIALS MANAGEMENT
(INCLUDING TRANSFERS OF FUNDS)

For necessary expenses of the Department of Agriculture, to comply with the Comprehensive Environmental Response, Compensation, and Liability Act (42 U.S.C. 9601 et seq.) and the Solid Waste Disposal Act (42 U.S.C. 6901 et seq.), $6,586,000, to remain available until expended: Provided, That appropriations and funds available herein to the Department for Hazardous Materials Management may be transferred to any agency of the Department for its use in meeting all requirements pursuant to the above Acts on Federal and non-Federal lands.

OFFICE OF THE GENERAL COUNSEL

For necessary expenses of the Office of the General Counsel, $57,645,000.

OFFICE OF ETHICS

For necessary expenses of the Office of Ethics, $5,544,000.

OFFICE OF INFORMATION AFFAIRS

For necessary expenses of the Office of Information Affairs, $15,939,000.

Note.—A full-year 2022 appropriation for this account was not enacted at the time the Budget was prepared; therefore, the Budget assumes this account is operating under the Continuing Appropriations Act, 2022 (Division A of Public Law 117–43, as amended). The amounts included for 2022 reflect the annualized level provided by the continuing resolution.

Program and Financing (in millions of dollars)

Identification code 012–9914–0–1–999		2021 actual	2022 est.	2023 est.
	Obligations by program activity:			
0001	Office of the Chief Financial Officer	6	6	7
0002	Office of Budget and Program Analysis	10	10	21
0003	Office of the Chief Economist	24	25	32
0004	Office of the Chief Information Officer	68	67	97
0005	Office of Civil Rights	23	23	32
0006	Office of the General Counsel	45	45	58
0007	Office of Ethics	4	4	5
0008	Office of Hearings and Appeals	15	15	17
0009	Hazardous Materials Management	6	7	7
0010	Office of Safety, Security, and Protection	20	23	25
0011	Office of Information Affairs			16
0799	Total direct obligations	221	225	317
0801	Office of Civil Rights Reimb	6	6	
0802	Office of the Chief Information Officer Reimb	53	37	37
0803	Office of the Chief Economist Reimb	3	2	1
0804	Office of the General Counsel Reimb	6	6	4
0805	Office of Safety, Security and Protection	4	8	4
0807	Office of Ethics	1		
0809	Reimbursable program activities, subtotal	73	59	46
0899	Total reimbursable obligations	73	59	46
0900	Total new obligations, unexpired accounts	294	284	363
	Budgetary resources:			
	Unobligated balance:			
1000	Unobligated balance brought forward, Oct 1	4	24	16
1001	Discretionary unobligated balance brought fwd, Oct 1	3		
1021	Recoveries of prior year unpaid obligations	1	6	6
1070	Unobligated balance (total)	5	30	22

EXECUTIVE OPERATIONS—Continued
Program and Financing—Continued

Identification code 012–9914–0–1–999	2021 actual	2022 est.	2023 est.
Budget authority:			
Appropriations, discretionary:			
1100 Appropriation	225	225	317
1121 Appropriations transferred from other acct [012–0115]	20	20	
1160 Appropriation, discretionary (total)	245	245	317
Appropriations, mandatory:			
1222 Exercised borrowing authority transferred from other accounts [012–4336]		1	1
Spending authority from offsetting collections, discretionary:			
1700 Collected	47	15	15
1701 Change in uncollected payments, Federal sources	28	15	15
1750 Spending auth from offsetting collections, disc (total)	75	30	30
1900 Budget authority (total)	320	276	348
1930 Total budgetary resources available	325	306	370
Memorandum (non-add) entries:			
1940 Unobligated balance expiring	–7	–6	–6
1941 Unexpired unobligated balance, end of year	24	16	1
Change in obligated balance:			
Unpaid obligations:			
3000 Unpaid obligations, brought forward, Oct 1	100	105	10
3010 New obligations, unexpired accounts	294	284	363
3011 Obligations ("upward adjustments"), expired accounts	1	4	4
3020 Outlays (gross)	–284	–373	–341
3040 Recoveries of prior year unpaid obligations, unexpired	–1	–6	–6
3041 Recoveries of prior year unpaid obligations, expired	–5	–4	–4
3050 Unpaid obligations, end of year	105	10	26
Uncollected payments:			
3060 Uncollected pymts, Fed sources, brought forward, Oct 1	–39	–33	–37
3070 Change in uncollected pymts, Fed sources, unexpired	–28	–15	–15
3071 Change in uncollected pymts, Fed sources, expired	34	11	11
3090 Uncollected pymts, Fed sources, end of year	–33	–37	–41
Memorandum (non-add) entries:			
3100 Obligated balance, start of year	61	72	–27
3200 Obligated balance, end of year	72	–27	–15
Budget authority and outlays, net:			
Discretionary:			
4000 Budget authority, gross	320	275	347
Outlays, gross:			
4010 Outlays from new discretionary authority	214	251	316
4011 Outlays from discretionary balances	70	120	24
4020 Outlays, gross (total)	284	371	340
Offsets against gross budget authority and outlays:			
Offsetting collections (collected) from:			
4030 Federal sources	–78	–26	–26
4040 Offsets against gross budget authority and outlays (total)	–78	–26	–26
Additional offsets against gross budget authority only:			
4050 Change in uncollected pymts, Fed sources, unexpired	–28	–15	–15
4052 Offsetting collections credited to expired accounts	31	11	11
4060 Additional offsets against budget authority only (total)	3	–4	–4
4070 Budget authority, net (discretionary)	245	245	317
4080 Outlays, net (discretionary)	206	345	314
Mandatory:			
4090 Budget authority, gross		1	1
Outlays, gross:			
4100 Outlays from new mandatory authority		1	1
4101 Outlays from mandatory balances		1	
4110 Outlays, gross (total)		2	1
4180 Budget authority, net (total)	245	246	318
4190 Outlays, net (total)	206	347	315

The Office of the Chief Economist advises the Secretary of Agriculture on the economic implications of Department policies, programs and proposed legislation. The Office is a focal point for USDA's economic intelligence and analysis; projections related to agricultural commodity markets; risk assessment and cost-benefit analysis related to domestic and international food and agriculture; policy direction for renewable energy development; coordination, analysis and advice on climate adaptation and environmental market activities; and coordination and review of all commodity and aggregate agricultural and food-related data used to develop outlook and situation material within the Department. The 2023 Budget requests $32 million for the office of which $6 million is dedicated to climate change, including coordinating climate change activities across the Department.

The Office of Hearings and Appeals (OHA) is responsible for conducting first and second-level administrative adjudications at USDA through fair, transparent, and consistent processes. Activities are carried out by three offices, the National Appeals Division (NAD), the Office of Administrative Law Judges (OALJ), and the Office of the Judicial Officer (OJO). NAD is responsible for listening to farmers and other rural program participants concerning their disputes with certain agencies within USDA through fair and impartial administrative hearings and appeals. OALJ and OJO (previously housed in Departmental Administration) are responsible for regulatory hearings and administrative proceedings. OHA was established in 2016 with the consolidation of the three offices. The 2023 Budget requests $16.7 million and reflects this realignment.

The Office of Budget and Program Analysis (OBPA) coordinates the preparation of Departmental budget estimates, regulations, and legislative reports; administers systems for the allotment and apportionment of funds; provides analysis of USDA program issues, draft regulations, and budget proposals; participates in strategic planning; and provides assistance to USDA policy makers in the development and execution of desired policies and programs. The 2023 Budget requests $25.7 million.

The Clinger-Cohen Act of 1996 required the establishment of a Chief Information Officer (CIO) for all major Federal agencies. The Act requires USDA to maximize the value of information technology acquisitions to improve the efficiency and effectiveness of USDA programs. To meet the intent of the law and to provide a Departmental focus for information resources management issues, Secretary's Memorandum 1030–30, dated August 8, 1996, established the Office of the Chief Information Office (OCIO). The CIO serves as the primary advisor to the Secretary on Information Technology (IT) issues. OCIO provides leadership for the Department's information and IT management activities in support of USDA program delivery. The 2023 Budget requests $97.5 million.

The Office of the Chief Financial Officer (OCFO) was established in 1995 under authority provided in Reorganization Plan Number 2 of 1953 (7 U.S.C. 2201) to comply with the Chief Financial Officers Act of 1990. The OCFO focuses on the Department's financial management activities to improve program delivery and assure maximum contribution to the Secretary's Strategic Goals. The 2023 Budget requests $7.4 million.

The Office of Civil Rights provides overall leadership for all Departmentwide civil rights activities, including employment opportunity and program non-discrimination policy development, analysis, coordination, and compliance. The Office provides leadership to implement best practices that will create an environment where a diverse workforce is valued as a source of strength. The Office monitors program activities to ensure that all USDA programs are delivered in a non-discriminatory manner. The 2023 Budget requests $31.7 million.

The Office of the General Counsel of the Department of Agriculture provides legal advice, counsel, and services to the Secretary and to all agencies, offices, and corporations of the Department on all aspects of their operations and programs. It represents the Department in administrative proceedings; non-litigation debt collection proceedings; State water rights adjudications; proceedings before the Civilian Board of Contract Appeal, the Merit System Protection Board, the Equal Employment Opportunity Commission, the USDA Office of Administrative Law Judges, and other Federal agencies; and, in conjunction with the Department of Justice, in judicial proceedings and litigation in the Federal and State courts. All attorneys and support personnel devoted to those efforts are supervised by the General Counsel. The 2023 Budget requests $57.6 million.

The Office of Ethics provides ethics advice, counsel and training to all USDA officials and employees, and conducts annual financial disclosure reviews. The work of the Office of Ethics promotes employee compliance

DEPARTMENT OF AGRICULTURE

with the Federal conflict of interest laws and regulations. The 2023 Budget requests $5.5 million.

The Office of Safety, Security and Protection (OSSP) is responsible for facility security, emergency management and response. OSSP provides Department-wide leadership, policy, and management in the safeguarding of property and personnel. OSSP is committed to identifying and addressing all security risks that may affect USDA personnel, infrastructure, and facilities. The 2023 Budget requests $25.5 million.

Under the Comprehensive Environmental Response, Compensation, and Liability Act and the Resource Conservation and Recovery Act, the Department must meet the same standards for environmental cleanup and regulatory compliance regarding hazardous wastes and hazardous substances as private businesses. With substantial commitments under these Acts, the Hazardous Materials Management account was established as a central fund so the Department's agencies may be reimbursed for their cleanup efforts. The Department determines what projects to fund by using objective criteria to identify what sites pose the greatest threats to public health, safety, and the environment. The 2023 Budget requests $6.6 million.

The Office of Information Affairs (OIA) requests $15.9 million to establish a new stand-alone office within the Office of the General Counsel, which aids USDA in providing day-to-day oversight over USDA's Freedom of Information Act (FOIA) program, responding to the increasing number of complex records requests for those FOIA functions, creating FOIA policy and training directives, and preparing all statutorily required reports. OIA will also perform the Department's Records Management functions as the Department seeks to regain control of its intellectual property and move towards a fully digital infrastructure that is in line with an OMB/National Archives mandate M-19-21.

Object Classification (in millions of dollars)

Identification code 012–9914–0–1–999		2021 actual	2022 est.	2023 est.
	Direct obligations:			
11.1	Personnel compensation: Full-time permanent	80	80	111
12.1	Civilian personnel benefits	29	29	39
21.0	Travel and transportation of persons			1
23.1	Rental payments to GSA	2	2	3
23.3	Communications, utilities, and miscellaneous charges	2	2	3
25.2	Other services from non-Federal sources	33	33	75
25.3	Other goods and services from Federal sources	54	55	52
25.7	Operation and maintenance of equipment	14	17	26
26.0	Supplies and materials	2	2	2
31.0	Equipment	5	5	5
99.0	Direct obligations	221	225	317
99.0	Reimbursable obligations	73	59	46
99.9	Total new obligations, unexpired accounts	294	284	363

Employment Summary

Identification code 012–9914–0–1–999	2021 actual	2022 est.	2023 est.
1001 Direct civilian full-time equivalent employment	629	677	824
2001 Reimbursable civilian full-time equivalent employment	140	155	131

NONRECURRING EXPENSES FUND

Program and Financing (in millions of dollars)

Identification code 012–0133–0–1–352		2021 actual	2022 est.	2023 est.
	Obligations by program activity:			
0001	Direct program activity	17	75	
0900	Total new obligations, unexpired accounts (object class 25.3)	17	75	
	Budgetary resources:			
	Unobligated balance:			
1000	Unobligated balance brought forward, Oct 1	32	75	
1012	Unobligated balance transfers between expired and unexpired accounts	59		
1021	Recoveries of prior year unpaid obligations	1		

Executive Operations—Continued
Federal Funds—Continued

		2021	2022	2023
1070	Unobligated balance (total)	92	75	
1930	Total budgetary resources available	92	75	
	Memorandum (non-add) entries:			
1941	Unexpired unobligated balance, end of year	75		
	Change in obligated balance:			
	Unpaid obligations:			
3000	Unpaid obligations, brought forward, Oct 1	75	39	70
3010	New obligations, unexpired accounts	17	75	
3020	Outlays (gross)	–52	–44	–70
3040	Recoveries of prior year unpaid obligations, unexpired	–1		
3050	Unpaid obligations, end of year	39	70	
	Memorandum (non-add) entries:			
3100	Obligated balance, start of year	75	39	70
3200	Obligated balance, end of year	39	70	
	Budget authority and outlays, net:			
	Discretionary:			
	Outlays, gross:			
4011	Outlays from discretionary balances	52	44	70
4180	Budget authority, net (total)			
4190	Outlays, net (total)	52	44	70

WORKING CAPITAL FUND

Program and Financing (in millions of dollars)

Identification code 012–4609–0–4–352		2021 actual	2022 est.	2023 est.
	Obligations by program activity:			
0801	Administration	49	50	50
0802	Communications	7	5	6
0803	Finance and Management	319	324	332
0804	Information Technology	858	851	851
0805	Executive Secretariat	3	4	4
0809	Reimbursable program activities, subtotal	1,236	1,234	1,243
0815	Capital Funding Availability	16	46	52
0816	Proceeds from Purchase Card Rebate Programs		25	10
0817	Proceeds from Transfers of Discretionary Unobligated Balances	4	17	
0818	Technology Modernization	1		
0819	Reimbursable program activities, subtotal	21	88	62
0900	Total new obligations, unexpired accounts	1,257	1,322	1,305
	Budgetary resources:			
	Unobligated balance:			
1000	Unobligated balance brought forward, Oct 1	342	389	389
1011	Unobligated balance transfer from other acct [047–0616]	1		
1070	Unobligated balance (total)	343	389	389
	Budget authority:			
	Appropriations, discretionary:			
1121	Appropriations transferred from other acct [012–0115]	2		
1121	Appropriations transferred from other acct [012–2081]	1		
1121	Appropriations transferred from other acct [012–2500]	3		
1121	Appropriations transferred from other acct [012–2707]	1		
1121	Appropriations transferred from other acct [012–2900]	2		
1121	Appropriations transferred from other acct [012–3508]	1		
1121	Appropriations transferred from other acct [012–3700]	1		
1121	Appropriations transferred from other acct [012–1955]	2		
1121	Appropriations transferred from other acct [012–2069]	1		
1160	Appropriation, discretionary (total)	14		
	Spending authority from offsetting collections, discretionary:			
1700	Collected	1,263	939	1,327
1701	Change in uncollected payments, Federal sources	26	383	
1750	Spending auth from offsetting collections, disc (total)	1,289	1,322	1,327
1900	Budget authority (total)	1,303	1,322	1,327
1930	Total budgetary resources available	1,646	1,711	1,716
	Memorandum (non-add) entries:			
1941	Unexpired unobligated balance, end of year	389	389	411
	Change in obligated balance:			
	Unpaid obligations:			
3000	Unpaid obligations, brought forward, Oct 1	370	452	249
3010	New obligations, unexpired accounts	1,257	1,322	1,305
3020	Outlays (gross)	–1,175	–1,525	–1,346
3050	Unpaid obligations, end of year	452	249	208
	Uncollected payments:			
3060	Uncollected pymts, Fed sources, brought forward, Oct 1	–243	–269	–652

Executive Operations—Continued
Federal Funds—Continued

WORKING CAPITAL FUND—Continued

Program and Financing—Continued

Identification code 012–4609–0–4–352		2021 actual	2022 est.	2023 est.
3070	Change in uncollected pymts, Fed sources, unexpired	–26	–383	....
3090	Uncollected pymts, Fed sources, end of year	–269	–652	–652
	Memorandum (non-add) entries:			
3100	Obligated balance, start of year	127	183	–403
3200	Obligated balance, end of year	183	–403	–444
	Budget authority and outlays, net:			
	Discretionary:			
4000	Budget authority, gross	1,303	1,322	1,327
	Outlays, gross:			
4010	Outlays from new discretionary authority	797	1,144	1,148
4011	Outlays from discretionary balances	378	381	198
4020	Outlays, gross (total)	1,175	1,525	1,346
	Offsets against gross budget authority and outlays:			
	Offsetting collections (collected) from:			
4030	Federal sources	–1,251	–939	–1,327
4033	Non-Federal sources	–12	....	....
4040	Offsets against gross budget authority and outlays (total)	–1,263	–939	–1,327
	Additional offsets against gross budget authority only:			
4050	Change in uncollected pymts, Fed sources, unexpired	–26	–383	....
4070	Budget authority, net (discretionary)	14	....	....
4080	Outlays, net (discretionary)	–88	586	19
4180	Budget authority, net (total)	14	....	....
4190	Outlays, net (total)	–88	586	19

This fund finances, by advances or reimbursements, certain central services in the Department of Agriculture, including supply, mail, and reproduction services; financial, procurement, and other administrative systems; telecommunications and network services; mainframe computer processing and hosting services; correspondence management services; payroll, financial management, and human resources services; and video production, conferencing, design, and Web support services.

Object Classification (in millions of dollars)

Identification code 012–4609–0–4–352		2021 actual	2022 est.	2023 est.
	Reimbursable obligations:			
	Personnel compensation:			
11.1	Full-time permanent - OCFO	99	113	116
11.1	Full-time permanent - OCIO	128	156	155
11.1	Full-time permanent - DA SE OC	16	21	22
11.3	Other than full-time permanent	1	....	....
11.5	Other personnel compensation - OCFO	6	....	....
11.5	Other personnel compensation - OCIO	10	....	....
11.5	Other personnel compensation - DA SE OC	1	....	....
11.9	Total personnel compensation	261	290	293
12.1	Civilian personnel benefits OCFO	39	43	44
12.1	Civilian personnel benefits OCIO	50	57	59
12.1	Civilian personnel benefits - DA SE OC	6	8	8
21.0	Travel and transportation of persons OCFO	....	1	1
21.0	Travel and transportation of persons - OCIO	1	3	3
22.0	Transportation of things - DA SE OC	1	1	1
23.1	Rental payments to GSA - OCFO	2	2	2
23.1	Rental payments to GSA - OCIO	3	4	4
23.1	Rental payments to GSA - DA SE OC	1	1	1
23.2	Rental payments to others - OCFO	3	3	3
23.2	Rental payments to others - OCIO	59	....	....
23.3	Communications, utilities, and miscellaneous charges - OCFO	3	4	4
23.3	Communications, utilities, and miscellaneous charges - OCIO	100	180	170
23.3	Communications, utilities, and miscellaneous charges - DA SE OC	3	2	2
25.1	Advisory and assistance services - OCFO	1	....	....
25.1	Advisory and assistance services - DA SE OC	1	....	1
25.2	Other services from non-Federal sources - OCFO	70	67	68
25.2	Other services from non-Federal sources - OCIO	216	180	176
25.2	Other services from non-Federal sources - DA SE OC	17	13	13
25.3	Other goods and services from Federal sources - OCFO	72	71	72
25.3	Other goods and services from Federal sources - OCIO	100	61	66
25.3	Other goods and services from Federal sources - DA SE OC	8	8	8
25.4	Operation and maintenance of facilities	2	2	2
25.7	Operation and maintenance of equipment - OCFO	23	20	20
25.7	Operation and maintenance of equipment - OCIO	182	187	204
25.7	Operation and maintenance of equipment - DA SE OC	2	1	1
26.0	Supplies and materials - OCFO	....	1	1
26.0	Supplies and materials - OCIO	2	3	3
26.0	Supplies and materials - DA SE OC	3	1	2
31.0	Equipment - OCFO	3	....	....
31.0	Equipment - OCIO	21	20	11
31.0	Equipment - Availability	....	88	62
32.0	Land and structures	2	....	....
99.9	Total new obligations, unexpired accounts	1,257	1,322	1,305

Employment Summary

Identification code 012–4609–0–4–352	2021 actual	2022 est.	2023 est.
2001 Reimbursable civilian full-time equivalent employment	2,582	2,930	2,948

BUILDINGS AND FACILITIES

Federal Funds

AGRICULTURE BUILDINGS AND FACILITIES

(INCLUDING TRANSFERS OF FUNDS)

For payment of space rental and related costs pursuant to Public Law 92–313, including authorities pursuant to the 1984 delegation of authority from the Administrator of General Services to the Department of Agriculture under 40 U.S.C. 121, for programs and activities of the Department which are included in this Act, and for alterations and other actions needed for the Department and its agencies to consolidate unneeded space into configurations suitable for release to the Administrator of General Services, and for the operation, maintenance, improvement, and repair of Agriculture buildings and facilities, and for related costs, $134,827,000, to remain available until expended, of which $25,000,000 shall be available for the hire and purchase of zero emission passenger motor vehicles and supporting charging or fueling infrastructure.

Note.—A full-year 2022 appropriation for this account was not enacted at the time the Budget was prepared; therefore, the Budget assumes this account is operating under the Continuing Appropriations Act, 2022 (Division A of Public Law 117–43, as amended). The amounts included for 2022 reflect the annualized level provided by the continuing resolution.

Program and Financing (in millions of dollars)

Identification code 012–0117–0–1–352		2021 actual	2022 est.	2023 est.
	Obligations by program activity:			
0002	Building Operations and Maintenance	48	108	135
0799	Total direct obligations	48	108	135
0802	Agriculture Buildings and Facilities and Rental Payments (Reimbursable)	11	6	6
0900	Total new obligations, unexpired accounts	59	114	141
	Budgetary resources:			
	Unobligated balance:			
1000	Unobligated balance brought forward, Oct 1	101	162	164
1021	Recoveries of prior year unpaid obligations	2	....	....
1070	Unobligated balance (total)	103	162	164
	Budget authority:			
	Appropriations, discretionary:			
1100	Appropriation	108	108	135
	Spending authority from offsetting collections, discretionary:			
1700	Collected	11	8	8
1701	Change in uncollected payments, Federal sources	–1	....	....
1750	Spending auth from offsetting collections, disc (total)	10	8	8
1900	Budget authority (total)	118	116	143
1930	Total budgetary resources available	221	278	307
	Memorandum (non-add) entries:			
1941	Unexpired unobligated balance, end of year	162	164	166
	Change in obligated balance:			
	Unpaid obligations:			
3000	Unpaid obligations, brought forward, Oct 1	39	27	15
3010	New obligations, unexpired accounts	59	114	141
3020	Outlays (gross)	–69	–126	–156
3040	Recoveries of prior year unpaid obligations, unexpired	–2	....	....
3050	Unpaid obligations, end of year	27	15	....
	Uncollected payments:			
3060	Uncollected pymts, Fed sources, brought forward, Oct 1	–15	–14	–14
3070	Change in uncollected pymts, Fed sources, unexpired	1	....	....

DEPARTMENT OF AGRICULTURE

Office of Inspector General
Federal Funds

		2021 actual	2022 est.	2023 est.
3090	Uncollected pymts, Fed sources, end of year	−14	−14	−14
	Memorandum (non-add) entries:			
3100	Obligated balance, start of year	24	13	1
3200	Obligated balance, end of year	13	1	−14
	Budget authority and outlays, net:			
	Discretionary:			
4000	Budget authority, gross	118	116	143
	Outlays, gross:			
4010	Outlays from new discretionary authority	32	100	123
4011	Outlays from discretionary balances	37	26	33
4020	Outlays, gross (total)	69	126	156
	Offsets against gross budget authority and outlays:			
	Offsetting collections (collected) from:			
4030	Federal sources	−11	−8	−8
	Additional offsets against gross budget authority only:			
4050	Change in uncollected pymts, Fed sources, unexpired	1		
4070	Budget authority, net (discretionary)	108	108	135
4080	Outlays, net (discretionary)	58	118	148
4180	Budget authority, net (total)	108	108	135
4190	Outlays, net (total)	58	118	148

This account finances the operations, repair, improvement and maintenance activities of two headquarters buildings in Washington, DC and the George Washington Carver Center in Beltsville, MD. The 2023 Budget requests $134.8 million for operations and maintenance, of which $25.0 million is to be used for the hire and purchase of zero emission passenger motor vehicles and supporting charging or fueling infrastructure.

Object Classification (in millions of dollars)

Identification code 012–0117–0–1–352		2021 actual	2022 est.	2023 est.
	Direct obligations:			
11.1	Personnel compensation: Full-time permanent	7	8	8
12.1	Civilian personnel benefits	3	3	3
23.1	Rental payments to GSA		5	6
23.3	Communications, utilities, and miscellaneous charges	6	8	1
25.2	Other services from non-Federal sources	19	23	21
25.3	Other goods and services from Federal sources		4	2
25.4	Operation and maintenance of facilities	13	57	94
99.0	Direct obligations	48	108	135
99.0	Reimbursable obligations	11	6	6
99.9	Total new obligations, unexpired accounts	59	114	141

Employment Summary

Identification code 012–0117–0–1–352	2021 actual	2022 est.	2023 est.
1001 Direct civilian full-time equivalent employment	62	63	63

OFFICE OF INSPECTOR GENERAL

Federal Funds

OFFICE OF INSPECTOR GENERAL

For necessary expenses of the Office of Inspector General, including employment pursuant to the Inspector General Act of 1978 (Public Law 95–452; 5 U.S.C. App.), $112,061,000, including such sums as may be necessary for contracting and other arrangements with public agencies and private persons pursuant to section 6(a)(9) of the Inspector General Act of 1978 (Public Law 95–452; 5 U.S.C. App.), and including not to exceed $125,000 for certain confidential operational expenses, including the payment of informants, to be expended under the direction of the Inspector General pursuant to the Inspector General Act of 1978 (Public Law 95–452; 5 U.S.C. App.) and section 1337 of the Agriculture and Food Act of 1981 (Public Law 97–98).

Note.—A full-year 2022 appropriation for this account was not enacted at the time the Budget was prepared; therefore, the Budget assumes this account is operating under the Continuing Appropriations Act, 2022 (Division A of Public Law 117–43, as amended). The amounts included for 2022 reflect the annualized level provided by the continuing resolution.

Program and Financing (in millions of dollars)

Identification code 012–0900–0–1–352		2021 actual	2022 est.	2023 est.
	Obligations by program activity:			
0001	Office of the Inspector General	102	100	112
0002	Office of Inspector (IIJA)		9	
0799	Total direct obligations	102	109	112
0801	Office of Inspector General (Reimbursable)	3	3	3
0900	Total new obligations, unexpired accounts	105	112	115
	Budgetary resources:			
	Unobligated balance:			
1000	Unobligated balance brought forward, Oct 1	17	14	15
	Budget authority:			
	Appropriations, discretionary:			
1100	Appropriation	100	100	112
1121	Appropriations transferred from other acct [012–1105]		2	
1121	Appropriations transferred from other acct [012–1106]		4	
1121	Appropriations transferred from other acct [012–1115]		3	
1160	Appropriation, discretionary (total)	100	109	112
	Advance appropriations, discretionary:			
1173	Advance appropriations transferred from other accounts [012–1105]			2
1173	Advance appropriations transferred from other accounts [012–1106]			3
1180	Advanced appropriation, discretionary (total)			5
	Appropriations, mandatory:			
1200	Appropriation	3		
	Spending authority from offsetting collections, discretionary:			
1700	Collected	3	4	4
1701	Change in uncollected payments, Federal sources	2		
1750	Spending auth from offsetting collections, disc (total)	5	4	4
1900	Budget authority (total)	108	113	121
1930	Total budgetary resources available	125	127	136
	Memorandum (non-add) entries:			
1940	Unobligated balance expiring	−6		
1941	Unexpired unobligated balance, end of year	14	15	21
	Change in obligated balance:			
	Unpaid obligations:			
3000	Unpaid obligations, brought forward, Oct 1	23	26	19
3010	New obligations, unexpired accounts	105	112	115
3011	Obligations ("upward adjustments"), expired accounts	1	1	1
3020	Outlays (gross)	−102	−120	−118
3041	Recoveries of prior year unpaid obligations, expired	−1		
3050	Unpaid obligations, end of year	26	19	17
	Uncollected payments:			
3060	Uncollected pymts, Fed sources, brought forward, Oct 1	−6	−7	−7
3070	Change in uncollected pymts, Fed sources, unexpired	−2		
3071	Change in uncollected pymts, Fed sources, expired	1		
3090	Uncollected pymts, Fed sources, end of year	−7	−7	−7
	Memorandum (non-add) entries:			
3100	Obligated balance, start of year	17	19	12
3200	Obligated balance, end of year	19	12	10
	Budget authority and outlays, net:			
	Discretionary:			
4000	Budget authority, gross	105	113	121
	Outlays, gross:			
4010	Outlays from new discretionary authority	82	95	105
4011	Outlays from discretionary balances	18	25	13
4020	Outlays, gross (total)	100	120	118
	Offsets against gross budget authority and outlays:			
	Offsetting collections (collected) from:			
4030	Federal sources	−4	−4	−4
	Additional offsets against gross budget authority only:			
4050	Change in uncollected pymts, Fed sources, unexpired	−2		
4052	Offsetting collections credited to expired accounts	1		
4060	Additional offsets against budget authority only (total)	−1		
4070	Budget authority, net (discretionary)	100	109	117
4080	Outlays, net (discretionary)	96	116	114
	Mandatory:			
4090	Budget authority, gross	3		
	Outlays, gross:			
4100	Outlays from new mandatory authority	2		
4180	Budget authority, net (total)	103	109	117
4190	Outlays, net (total)	98	116	114

OFFICE OF INSPECTOR GENERAL—Continued

The Office of Inspector General provides the Secretary and Congress with information or intelligence about fraud, other serious problems, mismanagement, and deficiencies in Department programs and operations, recommends corrective action, and reports on the progress made in correcting the problems. The Office reviews existing and proposed legislation and regulations and makes recommendations to the Secretary and Congress regarding the impact these laws have on the Department's programs and the prevention and detection of fraud and mismanagement in such programs. The Office provides policy direction and conducts, supervises, and coordinates all audits and investigations. The Office supervises and coordinates other activities in the Department and between the Department and other Federal, State and local government agencies whose purposes are to: (a) promote economy and efficiency; (b) prevent and detect fraud and mismanagement; and (c) identify and prosecute people involved in fraud or mismanagement. The 2023 Budget requests $112.1 million.

Object Classification (in millions of dollars)

Identification code 012–0900–0–1–352		2021 actual	2022 est.	2023 est.
	Direct obligations:			
11.1	Personnel compensation: Full-time permanent	54	60	62
12.1	Civilian personnel benefits	26	27	28
21.0	Travel and transportation of persons	1	2	2
23.3	Communications, utilities, and miscellaneous charges	8	7	7
25.2	Other services from non-Federal sources	5	5	4
25.3	Other goods and services from Federal sources	5	4	5
26.0	Supplies and materials	1	1	1
31.0	Equipment	2	3	3
99.0	Direct obligations	102	109	112
99.0	Reimbursable obligations	3	3	3
99.9	Total new obligations, unexpired accounts	105	112	115

Employment Summary

Identification code 012–0900–0–1–352	2021 actual	2022 est.	2023 est.
1001 Direct civilian full-time equivalent employment	431	450	450

ECONOMIC RESEARCH SERVICE

Federal Funds

ECONOMIC RESEARCH SERVICE

For necessary expenses of the Economic Research Service, $99,552,000.

Note.—A full-year 2022 appropriation for this account was not enacted at the time the Budget was prepared; therefore, the Budget assumes this account is operating under the Continuing Appropriations Act, 2022 (Division A of Public Law 117–43, as amended). The amounts included for 2022 reflect the annualized level provided by the continuing resolution.

Program and Financing (in millions of dollars)

Identification code 012–1701–0–1–352		2021 actual	2022 est.	2023 est.
	Obligations by program activity:			
0001	Economic Research Service	86	85	100
0002	Economic Research Service (Supplemental)	2		
0799	Total direct obligations	88	85	100
0801	Economic Research Service (Reimbursable)		2	2
0900	Total new obligations, unexpired accounts	88	87	102
	Budgetary resources:			
	Unobligated balance:			
1000	Unobligated balance brought forward, Oct 1	1		
	Budget authority:			
	Appropriations, discretionary:			
1100	Appropriation	85	85	100
	Appropriations, mandatory:			
1200	Appropriation	2		
	Spending authority from offsetting collections, discretionary:			
1701	Change in uncollected payments, Federal sources	1	2	2
1900	Budget authority (total)	88	87	102
1930	Total budgetary resources available	89	87	102
	Memorandum (non-add) entries:			
1940	Unobligated balance expiring	–1		
	Change in obligated balance:			
	Unpaid obligations:			
3000	Unpaid obligations, brought forward, Oct 1	51	54	41
3010	New obligations, unexpired accounts	88	87	102
3011	Obligations ("upward adjustments"), expired accounts	5		
3020	Outlays (gross)	–85	–100	–114
3041	Recoveries of prior year unpaid obligations, expired	–5		
3050	Unpaid obligations, end of year	54	41	29
	Uncollected payments:			
3060	Uncollected pymts, Fed sources, brought forward, Oct 1	–8	–4	–2
3070	Change in uncollected pymts, Fed sources, unexpired	–1	–2	–2
3071	Change in uncollected pymts, Fed sources, expired	5	4	2
3090	Uncollected pymts, Fed sources, end of year	–4	–2	–2
	Memorandum (non-add) entries:			
3100	Obligated balance, start of year	43	50	39
3200	Obligated balance, end of year	50	39	27
	Budget authority and outlays, net:			
	Discretionary:			
4000	Budget authority, gross	86	87	102
	Outlays, gross:			
4010	Outlays from new discretionary authority	57	70	82
4011	Outlays from discretionary balances	28	28	32
4020	Outlays, gross (total)	85	98	114
	Offsets against gross budget authority and outlays:			
	Offsetting collections (collected) from:			
4030	Federal sources	–5	–2	–2
	Additional offsets against gross budget authority only:			
4050	Change in uncollected pymts, Fed sources, unexpired	–1	–2	–2
4052	Offsetting collections credited to expired accounts	5	2	2
4060	Additional offsets against budget authority only (total)	4		
4070	Budget authority, net (discretionary)	85	85	100
4080	Outlays, net (discretionary)	80	96	112
	Mandatory:			
4090	Budget authority, gross	2		
	Outlays, gross:			
4101	Outlays from mandatory balances		2	
4180	Budget authority, net (total)	87	85	100
4190	Outlays, net (total)	80	98	112

The Economic Research Service (ERS) will use its 2023 funding for core programs of research, analysis, market outlook, and data development. Proposals for ERS budget priorities include research that: (1) builds on unique or confidential data sources or investments at the Federal level (2) provides coordination for a national perspective or framework; (3) requires sustained investment and large teams; (4) directly serves the U.S. Government's or USDA's long-term national goals; and (5) addresses questions with short-run payoff or that have immediate policy implications. ERS also seeks to cover the breadth of USDA programs (except forestry) and requests funding to ensure sustained expertise and to support the department through analysis of farming, commodity markets and trade, conservation, productivity growth, rural communities, food safety, food markets, and nutrition. ERS strength in data linking, and in developing, modeling and monitoring outcome measures, including program performance and agricultural productivity growth, will contribute substantively to USDA's implementation of the Evidence Act as well as to USDA's top priority goals for climate change, open and competitive markets, racial and social equity, tackling the pandemic, nutritional food security, rural economic growth and development, and more.

The 2023 Budget request is $99.5 million, an increase of $14 million from 2022.

Object Classification (in millions of dollars)

Identification code 012–1701–0–1–352		2021 actual	2022 est.	2023 est.
	Direct obligations:			
	Personnel compensation:			
11.1	Full-time permanent	25	32	36
11.3	Other than full-time permanent	1	1	1
11.5	Other personnel compensation	1	1	1
11.9	Total personnel compensation	27	34	38

DEPARTMENT OF AGRICULTURE

		2021 actual	2022 est.	2023 est.
12.1	Civilian personnel benefits	12	13	15
23.1	Rental payments to GSA			5
23.3	Communications, utilities, and miscellaneous charges	1	1	1
25.2	Other services from non-Federal sources	1	2	2
25.3	Other goods and services from Federal sources	14	18	16
25.5	Research and development contracts	13	15	21
26.0	Supplies and materials	19	2	2
99.0	Direct obligations	87	85	100
99.0	Reimbursable obligations	1	2	2
99.9	Total new obligations, unexpired accounts	88	87	102

Employment Summary

Identification code 012–1701–0–1–352	2021 actual	2022 est.	2023 est.
1001 Direct civilian full-time equivalent employment	288	329	329

NATIONAL AGRICULTURAL STATISTICS SERVICE

Federal Funds

NATIONAL AGRICULTURAL STATISTICS SERVICE

For necessary expenses of the National Agricultural Statistics Service, $217,474,000, of which up to $66,413,000 shall be available until expended for the Census of Agriculture: Provided, That amounts made available for the Census of Agriculture may be used to conduct Current Industrial Report surveys subject to 7 U.S.C. 2204g(d) and (f).

Note.—A full-year 2022 appropriation for this account was not enacted at the time the Budget was prepared; therefore, the Budget assumes this account is operating under the Continuing Appropriations Act, 2022 (Division A of Public Law 117–43, as amended). The amounts included for 2022 reflect the annualized level provided by the continuing resolution.

Program and Financing (in millions of dollars)

Identification code 012–1801–0–1–352	2021 actual	2022 est.	2023 est.
Obligations by program activity:			
0001 Agricultural estimates	129	127	140
0002 Statistical research and service	9	11	11
0003 Census of agriculture	58	46	66
0799 Total direct obligations	196	184	217
0801 National Agricultural Statistics Service (Reimbursable)	26	24	24
0900 Total new obligations, unexpired accounts	222	208	241
Budgetary resources:			
Unobligated balance:			
1021 Recoveries of prior year unpaid obligations	12		
Budget authority:			
Appropriations, discretionary:			
1100 Appropriation	184	184	217
Spending authority from offsetting collections, discretionary:			
1700 Collected	19		
1701 Change in uncollected payments, Federal sources	7	24	24
1750 Spending auth from offsetting collections, disc (total)	26	24	24
1900 Budget authority (total)	210	208	241
1930 Total budgetary resources available	222	208	241
Change in obligated balance:			
Unpaid obligations:			
3000 Unpaid obligations, brought forward, Oct 1	58	66	25
3010 New obligations, unexpired accounts	222	208	241
3011 Obligations ("upward adjustments"), expired accounts	12		
3020 Outlays (gross)	–202	–249	–237
3040 Recoveries of prior year unpaid obligations, unexpired	–12		
3041 Recoveries of prior year unpaid obligations, expired	–12		
3050 Unpaid obligations, end of year	66	25	29
Uncollected payments:			
3060 Uncollected pymts, Fed sources, brought forward, Oct 1	–3	–7	–31
3070 Change in uncollected pymts, Fed sources, unexpired	–7	–24	–24
3071 Change in uncollected pymts, Fed sources, expired	3		
3090 Uncollected pymts, Fed sources, end of year	–7	–31	–55
Memorandum (non-add) entries:			
3100 Obligated balance, start of year	55	59	–6
3200 Obligated balance, end of year	59	–6	–26
Budget authority and outlays, net:			
Discretionary:			
4000 Budget authority, gross	210	208	241
Outlays, gross:			
4010 Outlays from new discretionary authority	164	188	217
4011 Outlays from discretionary balances	38	61	20
4020 Outlays, gross (total)	202	249	237
Offsets against gross budget authority and outlays:			
Offsetting collections (collected) from:			
4030 Federal sources	–19	–21	–23
4033 Non-Federal sources	–3	–2	–2
4040 Offsets against gross budget authority and outlays (total)	–22	–23	–25
Additional offsets against gross budget authority only:			
4050 Change in uncollected pymts, Fed sources, unexpired	–7	–24	–24
4052 Offsetting collections credited to expired accounts	3	23	25
4060 Additional offsets against budget authority only (total)	–4	–1	1
4070 Budget authority, net (discretionary)	184	184	217
4080 Outlays, net (discretionary)	180	226	212
4180 Budget authority, net (total)	184	184	217
4190 Outlays, net (total)	180	226	212

The National Agricultural Statistics Service (NASS) mission is to provide timely, accurate, and useful statistics in service to U.S. agriculture. The statistical data provided by NASS is essential to the public and private sectors for making effective policy, production, and marketing decisions on a wide range of agricultural commodities. In addition, every 5 years the Census of Agriculture (COA) provides comprehensive national, State and county data as well as selected data for Puerto Rico, Guam, Virgin Islands, Northern Mariana Islands and American Samoa Islands. NASS responsibilities are authorized under the Agricultural Marketing Act of 1946 (7 U.S.C. 1621 1627), and the Census of Agriculture Act of 1997, Public Law 105–113 (Title 7 U.S. Code 2204g).

The 2023 total request is $217 million for NASS, including $151 million for Agricultural Estimates to 1) produce the essential Federal Principal Economic Indicator reports; and 2) conduct other Core Integrated Surveys and Estimates to support USDA programs. The 2023 NASS request includes $66 million for the Census of Agriculture. NASS will: 1) use the largest portion of the funding for outsourcing all necessary functions associated with mailing and processing the Census of Agriculture; 2) focus on outreach and research activities to improve response rates.

Agricultural Estimates.— NASS provides the official National and State estimates of acreage, yield, and production of crops, grain stocks, value and expenditures associated with farm commodities and inventory, values and expenditures of livestock items. Data on approximately 120 crops and 45 livestock products are covered in more than 450 reports issued each year. Staff in 12 Regional offices and 33 State offices serving all 50 States conduct the work to produce the Agricultural Estimates statistical reports. Cooperative arrangements with State agencies provide additional State and county data.

An increase of $8 million will be used to support enhancements to our existing geospatial program, which provides critical information on the impact of extreme weather events.

Census of Agriculture.—The Census of Agriculture provides the only source of comparable and consistent detailed data about agriculture and helps to measure trends and new development in the agricultural sector of our Nation's economy. The Census of Agriculture provides comprehensive data on the agriculture economy, land use, production expenses, value of land and buildings, farm size and characteristics of farm operators, market value of agricultural production sold, acreage of major crops, inventory of livestock and poultry, and farm irrigation practices. Miscellaneous funds received from local organizations, commodity groups, and others are available for dissemination of reports and for survey work conducted under cooperative agreements (7 U.S.C. 450b, 450h, 3318b). NASS also provides technical consultation, support, and assistance for international programs under participating agency service agreements.

National Agricultural Statistics Service—Continued
Federal Funds—Continued

Object Classification (in millions of dollars)

Identification code 012–1801–0–1–352	2021 actual	2022 est.	2023 est.
Direct obligations:			
Personnel compensation:			
11.1 Full-time permanent	82	82	85
11.3 Other than full-time permanent	1	1	1
11.5 Other personnel compensation	1	1	1
11.9 Total personnel compensation	84	84	87
12.1 Civilian personnel benefits	32	29	30
21.0 Travel and transportation of persons	1	2	2
22.0 Transportation of things	1	1	2
23.1 Rental payments to GSA	6	7	7
23.3 Communications, utilities, and miscellaneous charges	7	8	10
25.2 Other services from non-Federal sources	40	21	40
25.3 Other goods and services from Federal sources	20	28	36
25.7 Operation and maintenance of equipment	3	1	1
26.0 Supplies and materials	1	1	1
31.0 Equipment	1	2	1
99.0 Direct obligations	196	184	217
99.0 Reimbursable obligations	26	24	24
99.9 Total new obligations, unexpired accounts	222	208	241

Employment Summary

Identification code 012–1801–0–1–352	2021 actual	2022 est.	2023 est.
1001 Direct civilian full-time equivalent employment	715	744	784
2001 Reimbursable civilian full-time equivalent employment	106	106	106

AGRICULTURAL RESEARCH SERVICE
Federal Funds

SALARIES AND EXPENSES

For necessary expenses of the Agricultural Research Service and for acquisition of lands by donation, exchange, or purchase at a nominal cost not to exceed $100, and for land exchanges where the lands exchanged shall be of equal value or shall be equalized by a payment of money to the grantor which shall not exceed 25 percent of the total value of the land or interests transferred out of Federal ownership, $1,858,719,000: Provided, That appropriations hereunder shall be available for the operation and maintenance of aircraft and the purchase of not to exceed one for replacement only: Provided further, That appropriations hereunder shall be available pursuant to 7 U.S.C. 2250 for the construction, alteration, and repair of buildings and improvements, but unless otherwise provided, the cost of constructing any one building shall not exceed $500,000, except for headhouses or greenhouses which shall each be limited to $1,800,000, except for 10 buildings to be constructed or improved at a cost not to exceed $1,100,000 each, and except for four buildings to be constructed at a cost not to exceed $5,000,000 each, and the cost of altering any one building during the fiscal year shall not exceed 10 percent of the current replacement value of the building or $500,000, whichever is greater: Provided further, That appropriations hereunder shall be available for entering into lease agreements at any Agricultural Research Service location for the construction of a research facility by a non-Federal entity for use by the Agricultural Research Service and a condition of the lease shall be that any facility shall be owned, operated, and maintained by the non-Federal entity and shall be removed upon the expiration or termination of the lease agreement: Provided further, That the limitations on alterations contained in this Act shall not apply to modernization or replacement of existing facilities at Beltsville, Maryland: Provided further, That appropriations hereunder shall be available for granting easements at the Beltsville Agricultural Research Center: Provided further, That the foregoing limitations shall not apply to replacement of buildings needed to carry out the Act of April 24, 1948 (21 U.S.C. 113a): Provided further, That appropriations hereunder shall be available for granting easements at any Agricultural Research Service location for the construction of a research facility by a non-Federal entity for use by, and acceptable to, the Agricultural Research Service and a condition of the easements shall be that upon completion the facility shall be accepted by the Secretary, subject to the availability of funds herein, if the Secretary finds that acceptance of the facility is in the interest of the United States: Provided further, That funds may be received from any State, other political subdivision, organization, or individual for the purpose of establishing or operating any research facility or research project of the Agricultural Research Service, as authorized by law.

Note.—A full-year 2022 appropriation for this account was not enacted at the time the Budget was prepared; therefore, the Budget assumes this account is operating under the Continuing Appropriations Act, 2022 (Division A of Public Law 117–43, as amended). The amounts included for 2022 reflect the annualized level provided by the continuing resolution.

Special and Trust Fund Receipts (in millions of dollars)

Identification code 012–1400–0–1–352	2021 actual	2022 est.	2023 est.
0100 Balance, start of year	6	6	6
2000 Total: Balances and receipts	6	6	6
5099 Balance, end of year	6	6	6

Program and Financing (in millions of dollars)

Identification code 012–1400–0–1–352	2021 actual	2022 est.	2023 est.
Obligations by program activity:			
0001 Product quality/value added	120	121	205
0002 Livestock production	124	124	144
0003 Crop production	300	300	347
0004 Food safety	116	116	130
0005 Livestock protection	127	127	160
0006 Crop protection	223	223	249
0007 Human nutrition research	99	99	102
0008 Environmental stewardship	251	251	355
0009 National Agricultural Library	29	29	35
0010 Repair and maintenance of facilities	20	20	20
0013 National Bio-Agro Defense Facility	81	81	112
0014 Miscellaneous Fees/Supplementals	20	108	20
0799 Total direct obligations	1,510	1,599	1,879
0881 Salaries and Expenses (Reimbursable)	149	149	149
0889 Reimbursable program activities, subtotal	149	149	149
0900 Total new obligations, unexpired accounts	1,659	1,748	2,028
Budgetary resources:			
Unobligated balance:			
1000 Unobligated balance brought forward, Oct 1	75	88	101
1021 Recoveries of prior year unpaid obligations	1	96	96
1070 Unobligated balance (total)	76	184	197
Budget authority:			
Appropriations, discretionary:			
1100 Appropriation	1,493	1,492	1,859
Appropriations, mandatory:			
1200 Appropriation	20	20	20
1230 Appropriations and/or unobligated balance of appropriations permanently reduced		–1	–1
1260 Appropriations, mandatory (total)	20	19	19
Spending authority from offsetting collections, discretionary:			
1700 Collected	108	154	154
1701 Change in uncollected payments, Federal sources	54		
1750 Spending auth from offsetting collections, disc (total)	162	154	154
1900 Budget authority (total)	1,675	1,665	2,032
1930 Total budgetary resources available	1,751	1,849	2,229
Memorandum (non-add) entries:			
1940 Unobligated balance expiring	–4		
1941 Unexpired unobligated balance, end of year	88	101	201
Change in obligated balance:			
Unpaid obligations:			
3000 Unpaid obligations, brought forward, Oct 1	827	964	757
3010 New obligations, unexpired accounts	1,659	1,748	2,028
3011 Obligations ("upward adjustments"), expired accounts	15		
3020 Outlays (gross)	–1,510	–1,859	–2,152
3040 Recoveries of prior year unpaid obligations, unexpired	–1	–96	–96
3041 Recoveries of prior year unpaid obligations, expired	–26		
3050 Unpaid obligations, end of year	964	757	537
Uncollected payments:			
3060 Uncollected pymts, Fed sources, brought forward, Oct 1	–155	–185	–185
3070 Change in uncollected pymts, Fed sources, unexpired	–54		
3071 Change in uncollected pymts, Fed sources, expired	24		
3090 Uncollected pymts, Fed sources, end of year	–185	–185	–185
Memorandum (non-add) entries:			
3100 Obligated balance, start of year	672	779	572
3200 Obligated balance, end of year	779	572	352
Budget authority and outlays, net:			
Discretionary:			
4000 Budget authority, gross	1,655	1,646	2,013

DEPARTMENT OF AGRICULTURE

		2021 actual	2022 est.	2023 est.
	Outlays, gross:			
4010	Outlays from new discretionary authority	1,001	1,256	1,549
4011	Outlays from discretionary balances	507	584	584
4020	Outlays, gross (total)	1,508	1,840	2,133
	Offsets against gross budget authority and outlays:			
	Offsetting collections (collected) from:			
4030	Federal sources	–96	–92	–92
4033	Non-Federal sources	–35	–62	–62
4040	Offsets against gross budget authority and outlays (total)	–131	–154	–154
	Additional offsets against gross budget authority only:			
4050	Change in uncollected pymts, Fed sources, unexpired	–54		
4052	Offsetting collections credited to expired accounts	23		
4060	Additional offsets against budget authority only (total)	–31		
4070	Budget authority, net (discretionary)	1,493	1,492	1,859
4080	Outlays, net (discretionary)	1,377	1,686	1,979
	Mandatory:			
4090	Budget authority, gross	20	19	19
	Outlays, gross:			
4100	Outlays from new mandatory authority	2	19	19
4180	Budget authority, net (total)	1,513	1,511	1,878
4190	Outlays, net (total)	1,379	1,705	1,998

The Agricultural Research Service (ARS) is the principal in-house research agency of the U.S. Department of Agriculture (USDA). ARS conducts scientific research to develop and transfer solutions to agricultural problems of high national priority and to provide information access and dissemination to: ensure high-quality, safe food, and other agricultural products; assess the nutritional needs of Americans; sustain a competitive agricultural economy; enhance the natural resource base and the environment; and provide economic opportunities for rural citizens, communities, and society as a whole. This mission is carried out through ARS' major research program areas: New Products/Product Quality/Value Added; Livestock/Crop Production; Livestock/Crop Protection; Food Safety; Human Nutrition; and Environmental Stewardship.

The 2023 Salaries and Expenses Budget for ARS requests $1.9 billion, which supports ongoing intramural research conducted by ARS. The Budget also requests $112 million within this account for costs to operate and maintain the new National Bio and Agro-Defense Facility (NBAF), which replaces the outdated and inadequate Plum Island Animal Disease Center (PIADC). NBAF will be a state-of-the-art biocontainment facility for the study of foreign, emerging, and zoonotic animal diseases that pose a threat to both U.S. animal agriculture and public health.

Specific increases for research proposed in 2023 include: $15 million for improving specialty crop and animal production for small farm profitability; $14 million for mitigating extreme events to ensure production system sustainability; $16 million for biotechnology innovation centers; and $10 million for sustainable and resilient small farm production systems.

Object Classification (in millions of dollars)

Identification code 012–1400–0–1–352		2021 actual	2022 est.	2023 est.
	Direct obligations:			
	Personnel compensation:			
11.1	Full-time permanent	471	471	521
11.3	Other than full-time permanent	16	16	17
11.5	Other personnel compensation	16	16	16
11.9	Total personnel compensation	503	503	554
12.1	Civilian personnel benefits	196	196	204
21.0	Travel and transportation of persons	1	1	1
22.0	Transportation of things	1	1	1
23.1	Rental payments to GSA	5	5	5
23.2	Rental payments to others	2	2	3
23.3	Communications, utilities, and miscellaneous charges	42	47	60
24.0	Printing and reproduction	4	4	5
25.1	Advisory and assistance services	1	1	2
25.2	Other services from non-Federal sources	24	27	33
25.3	Other goods and services from Federal sources	6	7	9
25.4	Operation and maintenance of facilities	51	56	70
25.5	Research and development contracts	391	435	540
25.7	Operation and maintenance of equipment	31	34	43
26.0	Supplies and materials	85	95	118
31.0	Equipment	85	94	117
32.0	Land and structures	37	41	52
41.0	Grants, subsidies, and contributions	45	50	62

		2021 actual	2022 est.	2023 est.
99.0	Direct obligations	1,510	1,599	1,879
99.0	Reimbursable obligations	149	149	149
99.9	Total new obligations, unexpired accounts	1,659	1,748	2,028

Employment Summary

Identification code 012–1400–0–1–352	2021 actual	2022 est.	2023 est.
1001 Direct civilian full-time equivalent employment	5,462	5,855	6,908
2001 Reimbursable civilian full-time equivalent employment	533	496	533

BUILDINGS AND FACILITIES

For the acquisition of land, construction, repair, improvement, extension, alteration, and purchase of fixed equipment or facilities as necessary to carry out the agricultural research programs of the Department of Agriculture, where not otherwise provided, $45,405,000, to remain available until expended.

Note.—A full-year 2022 appropriation for this account was not enacted at the time the Budget was prepared; therefore, the Budget assumes this account is operating under the Continuing Appropriations Act, 2022 (Division A of Public Law 117–43, as amended). The amounts included for 2022 reflect the annualized level provided by the continuing resolution.

Program and Financing (in millions of dollars)

Identification code 012–1401–0–1–352		2021 actual	2022 est.	2023 est.
	Obligations by program activity:			
0001	Building and facilities projects	46	9	4
0900	Total new obligations, unexpired accounts (object class 32.0)	46	9	4
	Budgetary resources:			
	Unobligated balance:			
1000	Unobligated balance brought forward, Oct 1	109	100	127
1021	Recoveries of prior year unpaid obligations	1		
1070	Unobligated balance (total)	110	100	127
	Budget authority:			
	Appropriations, discretionary:			
1100	Appropriation	36	36	45
1930	Total budgetary resources available	146	136	172
	Memorandum (non-add) entries:			
1941	Unexpired unobligated balance, end of year	100	127	168
	Change in obligated balance:			
	Unpaid obligations:			
3000	Unpaid obligations, brought forward, Oct 1	845	790	556
3010	New obligations, unexpired accounts	46	9	4
3020	Outlays (gross)	–100	–243	–280
3040	Recoveries of prior year unpaid obligations, unexpired	–1		
3050	Unpaid obligations, end of year	790	556	280
	Memorandum (non-add) entries:			
3100	Obligated balance, start of year	845	790	556
3200	Obligated balance, end of year	790	556	280
	Budget authority and outlays, net:			
	Discretionary:			
4000	Budget authority, gross	36	36	45
	Outlays, gross:			
4010	Outlays from new discretionary authority		7	4
4011	Outlays from discretionary balances	100	236	276
4020	Outlays, gross (total)	100	243	280
4180	Budget authority, net (total)	36	36	45
4190	Outlays, net (total)	100	243	280

The Buildings and Facilities account provides funds for the acquisition of land, construction, repair, improvement, extension, alteration, and purchase of fixed equipment or facilities of or used by the Agricultural Research Service (ARS).

The Agency operates an extensive network of federally-owned research facilities strategically located throughout the United States, reflective of the wide geographic diversity and site specificity of agricultural production and distinct climatic and agroecosystem zones. Its laboratories and facilities have a capitalization value of nearly $4 billion. Many of these laboratories/facilities have outlived their functional lifespan, and are badly in need of major repairs, renovation or replacement. In 2012, ARS completed an

Agricultural Research Service—Continued
Federal Funds—Continued

BUILDINGS AND FACILITIES—Continued

extensive review of its laboratory portfolio and developed a plan for future capital investments. The report, known as the "Capital Investment Strategy" (CIS), highlighted ARS' aging infrastructure. ARS has updated its 2012 CIS to identify its highest priority facilities in need of modernization or replacement. The 2023 Budget includes $45.4 million for the design/construction of selected high priority ARS laboratories.

Trust Funds

MISCELLANEOUS CONTRIBUTED FUNDS

Special and Trust Fund Receipts (in millions of dollars)

Identification code 012–8214–0–7–352	2021 actual	2022 est.	2023 est.
0100 Balance, start of year	....	....	1
Receipts:			
Current law:			
1130 Deposits of Miscellaneous Contributed Funds, Science and Education Administration	17	18	18
2000 Total: Balances and receipts	17	18	19
Appropriations:			
Current law:			
2101 Miscellaneous Contributed Funds	–17	–17	–17
5099 Balance, end of year	....	1	2

Program and Financing (in millions of dollars)

Identification code 012–8214–0–7–352	2021 actual	2022 est.	2023 est.
Obligations by program activity:			
0001 Miscellaneous contributed funds	18	18	18
Budgetary resources:			
Unobligated balance:			
1000 Unobligated balance brought forward, Oct 1	29	29	28
1021 Recoveries of prior year unpaid obligations	1	....	....
1070 Unobligated balance (total)	30	29	28
Budget authority:			
Appropriations, mandatory:			
1201 Appropriation (special or trust fund)	17	17	17
1930 Total budgetary resources available	47	46	45
Memorandum (non-add) entries:			
1941 Unexpired unobligated balance, end of year	29	28	27
Change in obligated balance:			
Unpaid obligations:			
3000 Unpaid obligations, brought forward, Oct 1	5	5	6
3010 New obligations, unexpired accounts	18	18	18
3020 Outlays (gross)	–17	–17	–17
3040 Recoveries of prior year unpaid obligations, unexpired	–1	....	....
3050 Unpaid obligations, end of year	5	6	7
Memorandum (non-add) entries:			
3100 Obligated balance, start of year	5	5	6
3200 Obligated balance, end of year	5	6	7
Budget authority and outlays, net:			
Mandatory:			
4090 Budget authority, gross	17	17	17
Outlays, gross:			
4100 Outlays from new mandatory authority	4	17	17
4101 Outlays from mandatory balances	13	....	....
4110 Outlays, gross (total)	17	17	17
4180 Budget authority, net (total)	17	17	17
4190 Outlays, net (total)	17	17	17

Miscellaneous contributed funds received from States, local organizations, individuals, and others are available for work under cooperative agreements on research activities.

Object Classification (in millions of dollars)

Identification code 012–8214–0–7–352	2021 actual	2022 est.	2023 est.
Direct obligations:			
Personnel compensation:			
11.1 Full-time permanent	2	2	2
11.3 Other than full-time permanent	2	2	2
11.5 Other personnel compensation	1	1	1
11.9 Total personnel compensation	5	5	5
12.1 Civilian personnel benefits	1	1	1
25.2 Other services from non-Federal sources	1	1	1
25.5 Research and development contracts	4	4	4
26.0 Supplies and materials	3	3	3
31.0 Equipment	1	1	1
41.0 Grants, subsidies, and contributions	3	3	3
99.9 Total new obligations, unexpired accounts	18	18	18

Employment Summary

Identification code 012–8214–0–7–352	2021 actual	2022 est.	2023 est.
1001 Direct civilian full-time equivalent employment	50	54	50

NATIONAL INSTITUTE OF FOOD AND AGRICULTURE

Federal Funds

NATIONAL INSTITUTE OF FOOD AND AGRICULTURE

For payments to agricultural experiment stations, for cooperative forestry and other research, for facilities, for payments to States, the District of Columbia, Puerto Rico, Guam, the Virgin Islands, Micronesia, the Northern Marianas, and American Samoa for cooperative extension activities, for integrated activities, for research, education, and extension grant programs, including necessary administrative expenses, and for other expenses, $1,820,882,000: Provided, That of the amount provided under this heading, $695,424,000, to remain available until expended, shall be for research grants for 1994 institutions, education grants for 1890 institutions, the agriculture and food research initiative, veterinary medicine loan repayment, grants management systems, Hispanic serving institutions education grants, tribal colleges education equity grants, scholarships at 1890 institutions, extension services at 1994 institutions, New Beginning for Tribal Students, 1890s Centers of Excellence, and facility improvements at 1890 institutions: Provided further, That each institution eligible to receive funds under the Evans-Allen program shall receive no less than $1,000,000: Provided further, That $3,194,000, to remain available until September 30, 2024, shall be for providing grants for food and agricultural sciences for Alaska Native- and Native Hawaiian-Serving Institutions: Provided further, That $2,000,000, to remain available until September 30, 2024, shall be for providing grants for food and agricultural sciences for Insular Areas: Provided further, That funds for education grants for 1890 institutions shall be made available to institutions eligible to receive funds under 7 U.S.C. 3221 and 3222: Provided further, That institutions eligible to receive funds under 7 U.S.C. 3221 for cooperative extension shall each receive not less than $1,000,000: Provided further, That funds for cooperative extension under sections 3(b) and (c) of the Smith-Lever Act (7 U.S.C. 343(b) and (c)) and section 208(c) of Public Law 93–471 shall be available for retirement and employees' compensation costs for extension agents: Provided further, That $5,000,000, to remain available until September 30, 2024, shall be for Enhancing Agriculture Opportunities for Military Veterans: Provided further, That $2,000,000, to remain available until expended, shall be for Business Innovation Centers at Historically Black Colleges and Universities: Provided further, That $1,000,000, to remain available until September 30, 2024, shall be for the Open Data Standards Repository: Provided further, That $3,000,000 is available for the Farm of the Future and shall remain available until September 30, 2024: Provided further, That $8,000,000 shall be available for the Food and Agriculture Defense Initiative, to remain available until September 30, 2024: Provided further: That notwithstanding any other provision of law, indirect costs shall not be charged against any Extension Implementation Program Area grant awarded under the Crop Protection/Pest Management Program (7 U.S.C. 7626).

Note.—A full-year 2022 appropriation for this account was not enacted at the time the Budget was prepared; therefore, the Budget assumes this account is operating under the Continuing Appropriations Act, 2022 (Division A of Public Law 117–43, as amended). The amounts included for 2022 reflect the annualized level provided by the continuing resolution.

DEPARTMENT OF AGRICULTURE

Program and Financing (in millions of dollars)

Identification code 012–0520–0–1–999	2021 actual	2022 est.	2023 est.
Obligations by program activity:			
0001 Hatch Act			265
0002 Cooperative Forestry Research			43
0003 Payments to 1890 Colleges and Tuskegee University and West Virginia			93
0004 Special and Other Research Grants			52
0005 Agriculture Food and Research Initiative			564
0006 Veterinary Services Grant Program			3
0007 Federal Administration			30
0008 Higher Education			88
0009 Continuing Animal Health and Disease Research Program			4
0010 Veterinary Medical Loan Repayment			9
0011 Sustainable Agriculture Research and Education			60
0012 Research Grants for 1994 Institutions			5
0013 Farm Business Management and Benchmarking			2
0014 Food Animal Residue Avoidance Database (FARAD) Program			2
0017 Smith-Lever Act 3(b) and 3(c)			320
0018 Youth at Risk			9
0019 Expanded Food and Nutrition Education Program (EFNEP)			70
0020 Farm Safety			5
0021 Federally Recognized Tribes Extension Program			8
0022 1890's Extension			65
0023 Renewable Resources Extension Act			4
0025 1890 Facilities (section 1447)			22
0026 Extension Services to 1994 Institutions			19
0027 Rural Health and Safety Education			4
0028 Risk Management Education			9
0029 New Technologies for Ag. Extension			3
0031 Beginning Farmers and Ranchers Program			27
0032 Food Safety Outreach Program			10
0033 Gus Schumacher Nutrition Incentive Program			53
0035 Farmer Stress Assistance Network			10
0036 Crop Protection/Pest Management			20
0037 Methyl Bromide Transition Program			2
0038 Homeland Security			8
0039 Scholarships for Students at 1890 Institutions			10
0041 Specialty Crop Research Initiative			75
0042 Regional Rural Development Centers			2
0043 Organic Transition			7
0044 Organic Research and Extension Initiative			47
0045 Women and Minorities in STEM Fields			2
0046 Ag in the Classroom			1
0799 Total direct obligations			2,032
0801 Reimbursable program activity			37
0809 Reimbursable program activities, subtotal			37
0900 Total new obligations, unexpired accounts			2,069
Budgetary resources:			
Budget authority:			
Appropriations, discretionary:			
1100 Appropriation			1,824
Appropriations, mandatory:			
1221 Appropriations transferred from other acct [012–4085]			10
1222 Exercised borrowing authority transferred from other accounts [012–4336]			211
1230 Appropriations and/or unobligated balance of appropriations permanently reduced			–13
1260 Appropriations, mandatory (total)			208
Spending authority from offsetting collections, discretionary:			
1700 Collected			37
1900 Budget authority (total)			2,069
1930 Total budgetary resources available			2,069
Change in obligated balance:			
Unpaid obligations:			
3010 New obligations, unexpired accounts			2,069
3020 Outlays (gross)			–1,048
3050 Unpaid obligations, end of year			1,021
Memorandum (non-add) entries:			
3200 Obligated balance, end of year			1,021
Budget authority and outlays, net:			
Discretionary:			
4000 Budget authority, gross			1,861
Outlays, gross:			
4010 Outlays from new discretionary authority			1,041
Offsets against gross budget authority and outlays:			
Offsetting collections (collected) from:			
4030 Federal sources			–37
Mandatory:			
4090 Budget authority, gross			208
Outlays, gross:			
4100 Outlays from new mandatory authority			7
4180 Budget authority, net (total)			2,032
4190 Outlays, net (total)			1,011

The National Institute of Food and Agriculture (NIFA) participates in a nationwide system of agricultural research, education, and extension program planning and coordination between State and Tribal institutions and the U.S. Department of Agriculture. It assists in maintaining cooperation among the State and Tribal institutions, and between the State and Tribal institutions and their federal research partners. The agency administers grants and payments to State and Tribal institutions to leverage State and local funding for agricultural research, extension, and higher education.

The Cooperative Extension System, a national educational network, is a dynamic organization pledged to meeting the country's needs for research-based educational programs that will enable people to make practical decisions to improve their lives. To accomplish its mission, the Cooperative Extension System adjusts programs to meet the shifting needs and priorities of the people it serves. The non-formal educational network combines the expertise and resources of Federal, State, and local partners. The partners in this unique System are, a) The National Institute of Food and Agriculture at the U.S. Department of Agriculture; b) Extension professionals at land-grant universities throughout the United States and its territories; and c) Extension professionals in nearly all of the Nation's 3,144 counties and county equivalents. Thousands of paraprofessionals and nearly 3 million volunteers support this partnership and magnify its impact. Strong linkages with both public and private external groups are also crucial to the Cooperative Extension System's strength and vitality.

NIFA funds activities under the Hatch Act, cooperative forestry research, payments to 1890 institutions for research and Extension, Agriculture and Food Research Initiative (AFRI) Competitive Grants, Competitive Grants at land-grant universities (1862, 1890, and 1994) and other institutions, Sustainable Agriculture Research and Education (SARE) program funds and grants, the Cooperative Extension System, Smith-Lever 3(b) and 3(c) formula funds and 3(d) program funds, and other extension programs. Integrated research, education and/or extension grants are awarded for competitive and non-competitive programs.

In 2023, NIFA will invest $265 million for Hatch Act programs, to support continuing agricultural research at 1862 Land-grant Universities (LGUs) and State Agricultural Experiment Stations (SAES). Funding addresses local, regional, and national challenges in agriculture. This program serves LGUs, which in turn serve the producers and consumers in their states. Hatch Act funded scientists undertake research on the problems of agriculture in its broadest aspects, which serve to develop and improve rural communities. The innovations supported by Hatch funds have demonstrably helped increase farm incomes, improved nutrition security, and enhanced the quality of life in America. This funding provides critical support for data-driven, long-term research on local and regional agricultural systems that are carbon-neutral, climate-smart and maintain profitability and productivity for U.S. farmers and ranchers.

An increase of $7.3 million will be invested into the McIntire-Stennis Research Program in 2023, which is the only formula fund that is directed exclusively to support forestry, range, and the forest products industry, and supports programs in the 1890s and 1862s LGUs and non-land-grant colleges of forestry. These funds, totaling $43.3 million, will be used to support research in some of the following topic areas: understanding the impacts of new stressors and developing management solutions; adaptation to climate change environmental factors and utilization of forest ecosystems to mitigate climate change; utilization of wood and new applications for forest products; and increasing the use of agroforestry by landowners and communities, with a priority on underserved and minority audiences.

An increase of $18.5 million are provided to Extension capacity programs for increasing services and ensuring equity in access and opportunities to minority, historically underserved, or Tribal communities with special

NATIONAL INSTITUTE OF FOOD AND AGRICULTURE—Continued

emphasis on climate change, workforce, nutrition and health promotion education, and support for youth climate corps through 4-H programming. The Cooperative Extension Service provides non-formal education and learning activities for people throughout the country for farmers and other residents of rural communities as well as to people living in urban areas. Extension emphasizes taking research and education discoveries and knowledge and delivering it directly to the people to create positive change and solutions to contemporary problems. All universities conduct research and teaching, but the nation's more than 100 land-grant colleges and universities have a third, critical mission extension outreach. Through Extension, land-grant colleges and universities bring vital, practical information to agricultural producers, small business owners, consumers, families, and young people. In 2023, NIFA will invest $315 million into minority-serving institutions. These include research, Extension, teaching, and facilities programs at the 1890 Land-grant Institutions; research, education and Extension grants for Tribal colleges (including the Federally Recognized Tribes Extension Program) and Hispanic-serving institutions; education grants for Alaska Native-serving, Native Hawaiian-serving institutions; New Beginning for Tribal Students; Centers of Excellence at 1890 Institutions; Institution Challenge, Multicultural Scholars, and Graduate Fellowships; Agriculture Business Innovation Centers at Historically Black Colleges and Universities; and grants for Insular Areas. Evans-Allen capacity funds support agricultural research activities at the 1890 LGUs. The 2023 funding totaling $93 million is distributed to Historically Black LGUs and is leveraged with matching funding from non-federal sources. Currently, the program is supporting over 200 active research projects that will enhance innovation, support training of the next generation of Black workers and researchers and address various issues in limited-resourced communities such as food security and nutrition, climate change and workforce development. This program supports many of the Administration's budget priorities, including ensuring the benefits accrue to underserved communities.

In 2023, NIFA will invest an additional $129 million across all AFRI programs, including interagency investments, for a total of $564 million for America's flagship competitive grants program for food and agricultural sciences. NIFA proposes to include broad emphasis throughout the AFRI program on climate-smart agriculture and application of clean energy. Focused investments in these topics will be made in the three major complementary components of AFRI: 1) Sustainable Agricultural Systems, 2) Foundational and Applied Science, and 3) Education and Workforce Development. Transformative innovations in U.S. agriculture are needed to address climate change, promote innovations in nutrition security, and enhance economic growth and agricultural education, especially in socially disadvantaged and under-served communities. Through this investment, NIFA will contribute to a whole-of-government approach to climate change by supporting research, Extension and education projects that advance the achievement of economy-wide, net-zero emissions, by 2050. These investments in AFRI also support the President's priorities of addressing climate-smart agriculture and forestry practices, mitigation of agricultural greenhouse gas emissions, nutrition security, and promoting prosperity in Americas historically underserved communities. NIFA will continue to promote equity and inclusion through increased awarding of Food and Agricultural Science Enhancement (FASE) grants to minority-serving institutions, especially for grants that serve underserved communities, and grants that promote healthy foods and nutritional security. SARE will receive an increase of $20 million in 2023, which will enable development of climate-smart research and delivery of climate-smart education programs to help farmers and ranchers adapt to a changing climate and mitigate effects of climate change in their food production systems. An $8 million increase in funding for Minor Crop Pest Management (IR-4) will affect the number of funded pesticide data projects per year as well as additional biopesticide and organic projects. Increased funding will also allow the IR-4 programs harmonization activities with America's key trading allies.

Native American Institutions Endowment Fund.— The 2023 Budget includes $11.9 million, for an endowment for the 1994 Land-grant Institutions (the legislatively eligible Tribally controlled colleges) to strengthen the infrastructure of these institutions and develop Indian expertise for the food and agricultural sciences and businesses and their own communities. At the termination of each fiscal year, the Secretary withdraws the income from the endowment fund for the fiscal year, and after adjusting for the cost of administering the fund, distributes the adjusted income on a formula basis to the 1994 Land-grant Institutions. An estimated $5 million in interest earned in 2022 will be available to the program in 2023.

Reimbursable Program.— Funds support basic and applied agriculture research and activities performed for other USDA, Federal, and non-Federal agencies.

Object Classification (in millions of dollars)

Identification code 012–0520–0–1–999		2021 actual	2022 est.	2023 est.
	Direct obligations:			
11.1	Personnel compensation: Full-time permanent			39
12.1	Civilian personnel benefits			15
21.0	Travel and transportation of persons			1
22.0	Transportation of things			1
23.1	Rental payments to GSA			1
25.2	Other services from non-Federal sources			10
25.3	Other goods and services from Federal sources			2
25.4	Operation and maintenance of facilities			3
25.5	Research and development contracts			33
41.0	Grants, subsidies, and contributions			1,927
99.0	Direct obligations			2,032
99.0	Reimbursable obligations			37
99.9	Total new obligations, unexpired accounts			2,069

Employment Summary

Identification code 012–0520–0–1–999	2021 actual	2022 est.	2023 est.
1001 Direct civilian full-time equivalent employment			406

INTEGRATED ACTIVITIES

Note.—A full-year 2022 appropriation for this account was not enacted at the time the Budget was prepared; therefore, the Budget assumes this account is operating under the Continuing Appropriations Act, 2022 (Division A of Public Law 117–43, as amended). The amounts included for 2022 reflect the annualized level provided by the continuing resolution.

Program and Financing (in millions of dollars)

Identification code 012–1502–0–1–352		2021 actual	2022 est.	2023 est.
	Obligations by program activity:			
0050	Crop Protection/Pest Management	20	20	
0070	Methyl bromide transition program	2	2	
0071	Homeland Security (Food and Agriculture Defense Initiative)	8	8	
0080	Urban, Indoor, and Other Emerging Agricultural Production Research, Education, and Extension Initiative		10	
0085	Emergency Citrus Research and Extension Program		4	
0086	Specialty Crop Research Initiative	77	77	
0087	Regional Rural development centers	2	2	
0088	Organic transition	7	7	
0089	Organic Research and Extension Initiative	24	29	
0900	Total new obligations, unexpired accounts	140	159	
	Budgetary resources:			
	Unobligated balance:			
1000	Unobligated balance brought forward, Oct 1	17	16	
1001	Discretionary unobligated balance brought fwd, Oct 1	1	1	
1021	Recoveries of prior year unpaid obligations	1		
1070	Unobligated balance (total)	18	16	
	Budget authority:			
	Appropriations, discretionary:			
1100	Appropriation	39	39	
	Appropriations, mandatory:			
1222	Exercised borrowing authority transferred from other accounts [012–4336]	105	110	

DEPARTMENT OF AGRICULTURE

National Institute of Food and Agriculture—Continued
Federal Funds—Continued 79

		2021 actual	2022 est.	2023 est.
1230	Appropriations and/or unobligated balance of appropriations permanently reduced	-6	-6	
1260	Appropriations, mandatory (total)	99	104	
1900	Budget authority (total)	138	143	
1930	Total budgetary resources available	156	159	
	Memorandum (non-add) entries:			
1941	Unexpired unobligated balance, end of year	16		
	Change in obligated balance:			
	Unpaid obligations:			
3000	Unpaid obligations, brought forward, Oct 1	355	382	491
3010	New obligations, unexpired accounts	140	159	
3011	Obligations ("upward adjustments"), expired accounts	4		
3020	Outlays (gross)	-110	-50	-105
3040	Recoveries of prior year unpaid obligations, unexpired	-1		
3041	Recoveries of prior year unpaid obligations, expired	-6		
3050	Unpaid obligations, end of year	382	491	386
	Memorandum (non-add) entries:			
3100	Obligated balance, start of year	355	382	491
3200	Obligated balance, end of year	382	491	386
	Budget authority and outlays, net:			
	Discretionary:			
4000	Budget authority, gross	39	39	
	Outlays, gross:			
4010	Outlays from new discretionary authority		1	
4011	Outlays from discretionary balances	35	37	39
4020	Outlays, gross (total)	35	38	39
	Mandatory:			
4090	Budget authority, gross	99	104	
	Outlays, gross:			
4100	Outlays from new mandatory authority	1	2	
4101	Outlays from mandatory balances	74	10	66
4110	Outlays, gross (total)	75	12	66
4180	Budget authority, net (total)	138	143	
4190	Outlays, net (total)	110	50	105

Programs previously funded under this account are proposed under a consolidated National Institute of Food and Agriculture account.

Organic Agriculture Research and Extension Initiative.— The purpose of this mandatory program is to make competitive grants to support research, education, and extension activities regarding organically grown and processed agricultural commodities and their economic impact on producers, processors, and rural communities. Section 7210 of the 2018 Farm Bill (Pub. L. 115–334) amended section 1672B of the FACT Act (7 U.S.C. 5925b) to provide mandatory funding in the enacted amount of $20 million for FYs 2019 and 2020, $25 million for FY 2021, $30 million for FY 2022, and $50 million for FY 2023 and each year thereafter.

Specialty Crop Research Initiative.— This purpose of this program is to make competitive grants to solve critical industry issues through research and extension activities. Specialty crops are defined as fruits and vegetables, tree nuts, dried fruits, and horticulture and nursery crops including floriculture. SCRI will give priority to projects that are multistate, multi-institutional, or trans-disciplinary; and include explicit mechanisms to communicate results to producers and the public. Section 7305 of the 2018 Farm Bill (Pub L. 115–334) reauthorized and amended Section 412 of AREERA of 1998 (7 U.S.C. 7632) and provides $80 million each year in mandatory funding for the program.

Emergency Citrus Disease Research and Extension Program.— The purpose of this program is to provide funding for a competitive research and extension grant program to combat diseases of citrus by conducting scientific research and extension activities, technical assistance, and development activities to combat citrus diseases and pests, both domestic and invasive, which pose imminent harm to the U.S. citrus production and threaten industry viability. The ECDRE program also combats citrus diseases by supporting the dissemination and commercialization of relevant information, techniques, and technologies. Section 12605 of the 2018 Farm Bill (Pub. L. 115–334) also established the Citrus Trust Fund and provides $25 million for each of the FYs 2019 through 2023, to carry out the Emergency Citrus Disease Research and Extension (ECDRE) Program in section 412 of AREERA (7 U.S.C. 7632).

Object Classification (in millions of dollars)

Identification code 012–1502–0–1–352	2021 actual	2022 est.	2023 est.
Direct obligations:			
12.1 Civilian personnel benefits	1	1	
41.0 Grants, subsidies, and contributions	139	158	
99.9 Total new obligations, unexpired accounts	140	159	

Employment Summary

Identification code 012–1502–0–1–352	2021 actual	2022 est.	2023 est.
1001 Direct civilian full-time equivalent employment	5	6	

BIOMASS RESEARCH AND DEVELOPMENT

Program and Financing (in millions of dollars)

Identification code 012–1003–0–1–271	2021 actual	2022 est.	2023 est.
Obligations by program activity:			
0001 Biomass research and development		4	
0900 Total new obligations, unexpired accounts (object class 41.0)		4	
Budgetary resources:			
Unobligated balance:			
1000 Unobligated balance brought forward, Oct 1	3	4	
1021 Recoveries of prior year unpaid obligations	1		
1070 Unobligated balance (total)	4	4	
1930 Total budgetary resources available	4	4	
Memorandum (non-add) entries:			
1941 Unexpired unobligated balance, end of year	4		
Change in obligated balance:			
Unpaid obligations:			
3000 Unpaid obligations, brought forward, Oct 1	4	1	4
3010 New obligations, unexpired accounts		4	
3020 Outlays (gross)	-2	-1	-3
3040 Recoveries of prior year unpaid obligations, unexpired	-1		
3050 Unpaid obligations, end of year	1	4	1
Memorandum (non-add) entries:			
3100 Obligated balance, start of year	4	1	4
3200 Obligated balance, end of year	1	4	1
Budget authority and outlays, net:			
Mandatory:			
Outlays, gross:			
4101 Outlays from mandatory balances	2	1	3
4180 Budget authority, net (total)			
4190 Outlays, net (total)	2	1	3

Biomass Research and Development is authorized by the Biomass Research and Development Act of 2000. The program provides competitive grants for research, development, and demonstration to encourage innovation and development related to biomass, and improved commercialization of biobased products and energy. USDA and the Department of Energy jointly administer the program. In 2023, there is no mandatory funding for the program.

RESEARCH AND EDUCATION ACTIVITIES

NATIVE AMERICAN INSTITUTIONS ENDOWMENT FUND

For the Native American Institutions Endowment Fund authorized by Public Law 103–382 (7 U.S.C. 301 note), $11,880,000, to remain available until expended.

Note.—A full-year 2022 appropriation for this account was not enacted at the time the Budget was prepared; therefore, the Budget assumes this account is operating under the Continuing Appropriations Act, 2022 (Division A of Public Law 117–43, as amended). The amounts included for 2022 reflect the annualized level provided by the continuing resolution.

RESEARCH AND EDUCATION ACTIVITIES—Continued

Special and Trust Fund Receipts (in millions of dollars)

Identification code 012–1500–0–1–352		2021 actual	2022 est.	2023 est.
0100	Balance, start of year	249	260	272
	Receipts:			
	Current law:			
1140	Earnings on Investments, Native American Institutions Endowment Fund	5	5	5
2000	Total: Balances and receipts	254	265	277
	Appropriations:			
	Current law:			
2101	Research and Education Activities	–5	–5	–5
2135	Research and Education Activities	12	12	12
2199	Total current law appropriations	7	7	7
2999	Total appropriations	7	7	7
5098	Reconciliation adjustment	–1		
5099	Balance, end of year	260	272	284

Program and Financing (in millions of dollars)

Identification code 012–1500–0–1–352		2021 actual	2022 est.	2023 est.
	Obligations by program activity:			
0001	Payments under the Hatch Act	259	259	
0002	Cooperative forestry research	36	36	
0003	Payments to 1890 colleges and Tuskegee Univ. and West Virginia State University	73	73	
0004	Special Grants	76	93	
0005	Agriculture and Food Research Initiative	524	926	
0006	Animal health and disease research	4	4	
0007	Federal Administration	19	19	
0008	Higher education	102	140	10
0009	Native American Institutions Endowment Fund	6	7	5
0012	Veterinary Medical Services Act	7	24	
0013	Veterinary Services Grant Program	3	3	
0015	Sun Grant Program	3	3	
0016	Farm Business Management and Benchmarking	2	2	
0021	Alfalfa Seed and Alfalfa Forage Systems	3	3	
0022	Capacity Building for Non-Land Grant Colleges of Agriculture	7	8	
0023	Agricultural Genome to Phenome Initiative	1	1	
0024	Bioproducts Pilot Program		5	5
0799	Total direct obligations	1,125	1,606	20
0801	Research and Education Activities (Reimbursable)	10	10	
0900	Total new obligations, unexpired accounts	1,135	1,616	20
	Budgetary resources:			
	Unobligated balance:			
1000	Unobligated balance brought forward, Oct 1	606	540	10
1001	Discretionary unobligated balance brought fwd, Oct 1	575	532	
1021	Recoveries of prior year unpaid obligations	39	49	
1033	Recoveries of prior year paid obligations	1	1	
1070	Unobligated balance (total)	646	590	10
	Budget authority:			
	Appropriations, discretionary:			
1100	Appropriation	1,027	1,027	12
1100	Appropriation [IIJA Bioproduct Pilot Program]		5	
1101	Appropriation (Native American Endowment Interest)	5	5	5
1135	Appropriations precluded from obligation (special or trust)	–12	–12	–12
1160	Appropriation, discretionary (total)	1,020	1,025	5
	Advance appropriations, discretionary:			
1170	Advance appropriation			5
	Spending authority from offsetting collections, discretionary:			
1700	Collected	1	1	
1701	Change in uncollected payments, Federal sources	8	10	
1750	Spending auth from offsetting collections, disc (total)	9	11	
1900	Budget authority (total)	1,029	1,036	10
1930	Total budgetary resources available	1,675	1,626	20
	Memorandum (non-add) entries:			
1941	Unexpired unobligated balance, end of year	540	10	
	Change in obligated balance:			
	Unpaid obligations:			
3000	Unpaid obligations, brought forward, Oct 1	1,576	1,885	2,457
3010	New obligations, unexpired accounts	1,135	1,616	20
3011	Obligations ("upward adjustments"), expired accounts	2		
3020	Outlays (gross)	–780	–995	–889
3040	Recoveries of prior year unpaid obligations, unexpired	–39	–49	
3041	Recoveries of prior year unpaid obligations, expired	–9		
3050	Unpaid obligations, end of year	1,885	2,457	1,588
	Uncollected payments:			
3060	Uncollected pymts, Fed sources, brought forward, Oct 1	–17	–16	–26
3070	Change in uncollected pymts, Fed sources, unexpired	–8	–10	
3071	Change in uncollected pymts, Fed sources, expired	9		
3090	Uncollected pymts, Fed sources, end of year	–16	–26	–26
	Memorandum (non-add) entries:			
3100	Obligated balance, start of year	1,559	1,869	2,431
3200	Obligated balance, end of year	1,869	2,431	1,562
	Budget authority and outlays, net:			
	Discretionary:			
4000	Budget authority, gross	1,029	1,036	10
	Outlays, gross:			
4010	Outlays from new discretionary authority	127	174	1
4011	Outlays from discretionary balances	649	818	880
4020	Outlays, gross (total)	776	992	881
	Offsets against gross budget authority and outlays:			
	Offsetting collections (collected) from:			
4030	Federal sources	–10	–10	
4033	Non-Federal sources	–1	–1	
4040	Offsets against gross budget authority and outlays (total)	–11	–11	
	Additional offsets against gross budget authority only:			
4050	Change in uncollected pymts, Fed sources, unexpired	–8	–10	
4052	Offsetting collections credited to expired accounts	9	9	
4053	Recoveries of prior year paid obligations, unexpired accounts	1	1	
4060	Additional offsets against budget authority only (total)	2		
4070	Budget authority, net (discretionary)	1,020	1,025	10
4080	Outlays, net (discretionary)	765	981	881
	Mandatory:			
	Outlays, gross:			
4101	Outlays from mandatory balances	4	3	8
4180	Budget authority, net (total)	1,020	1,025	10
4190	Outlays, net (total)	769	984	889
	Memorandum (non-add) entries:			
5000	Total investments, SOY: Federal securities: Par value	238	250	262
5001	Total investments, EOY: Federal securities: Par value	250	262	274
5096	Unexpired unavailable balance, SOY: Appropriations		46	46
5098	Unexpired unavailable balance, EOY: Appropriations		68	68

Programs previously funded under this account are proposed under a consolidated National Institute of Food and Agriculture account.

Bioproducts Pilot Program.—The Infrastructure Investment and Jobs Act (IIJA), 2022 (P.L. 117–58, Title V, Section 70501) provides $10,000,000 to remain available until expended, of which $5,000,000 to remain available until expended, shall be made available for fiscal year 2022 and $5,000,000 to remain available until expended, shall be made available for fiscal year 2023. Title V, Section 70501 establishes the Bioproducts Pilot Program on use of agricultural commodities in construction and consumer products. Covered agricultural commodities will be used as bioproduct feedstocks and will mean any agricultural commodity, food, feed, fiber, livestock, oil, or a derivative thereof, that the Secretary determines to have been used in the production of materials that have demonstrated market viability and benefits.

Scholarships for Students at 1890 Institutions.—The purpose of this program is to provide scholarships to support recruiting, engaging, retaining, mentoring, and training of undergraduate students at the 1890 land-grant institutions, resulting in baccalaureate degrees in the food and agricultural sciences and related fields. The scholarships are intended to encourage outstanding students at 1890 institutions to pursue and complete baccalaureate degrees in the food and agricultural sciences and related fields that would add to a highly skilled food and agricultural systems workforce. Section 7117 of the Agriculture Improvement Act of 2018 (P.L. 115–334) provided $40,000,000. Up to $10,000,000 may be used for each year for four years.

Native American Institutions Endowment Fund.—The 2023 Budget includes $11.9 million, for an endowment for the 1994 Land-grant Institutions (the legislatively eligible Tribally controlled colleges) to strengthen the

DEPARTMENT OF AGRICULTURE

infrastructure of these institutions and develop Native American expertise for the food and agricultural sciences and businesses and their own communities. At the termination of each fiscal year, the Secretary withdraws the income from the endowment fund for the fiscal year, and after adjusting for the cost of administering the fund, distributes the adjusted income on a formula basis to the 1994 Land-grant Institutions. An estimated $5 million in interest earned in 2022 will be available to the program in 2023.

Object Classification (in millions of dollars)

Identification code 012–1500–0–1–352		2021 actual	2022 est.	2023 est.
	Direct obligations:			
11.1	Personnel compensation: Full-time permanent	17	21	
12.1	Civilian personnel benefits	6	6	
23.1	Rental payments to GSA		1	
23.3	Communications, utilities, and miscellaneous charges	1		
25.2	Other services from non-Federal sources	7	10	
25.3	Other goods and services from Federal sources	2	3	
25.4	Operation and maintenance of facilities	2	3	
25.5	Research and development contracts	19	26	
41.0	Grants, subsidies, and contributions	1,070	1,536	20
99.0	Direct obligations	1,124	1,606	20
99.0	Reimbursable obligations	11	10	
99.9	Total new obligations, unexpired accounts	1,135	1,616	20

Employment Summary

Identification code 012–1500–0–1–352		2021 actual	2022 est.	2023 est.
1001	Direct civilian full-time equivalent employment	178	242	

BUILDINGS AND FACILITIES

Program and Financing (in millions of dollars)

Identification code 012–1501–0–1–352		2021 actual	2022 est.	2023 est.
	Obligations by program activity:			
0001	Buildings and Facilities		1	
0900	Total new obligations, unexpired accounts (object class 41.0)		1	
	Budgetary resources:			
	Unobligated balance:			
1000	Unobligated balance brought forward, Oct 1	1	1	
1930	Total budgetary resources available	1	1	
	Memorandum (non-add) entries:			
1941	Unexpired unobligated balance, end of year	1		
	Change in obligated balance:			
	Unpaid obligations:			
3000	Unpaid obligations, brought forward, Oct 1			1
3010	New obligations, unexpired accounts		1	
3050	Unpaid obligations, end of year		1	1
	Memorandum (non-add) entries:			
3100	Obligated balance, start of year			1
3200	Obligated balance, end of year		1	1
4180	Budget authority, net (total)			
4190	Outlays, net (total)			

Funds provide grants to States and other eligible recipients for the acquisition of land, construction, repair, improvement, extension, alteration and purchase of fixed equipment or facilities to carry out agricultural research, extension, and teaching programs. No funding has been appropriated to this account since 1997.

EXTENSION ACTIVITIES

Note.—A full-year 2022 appropriation for this account was not enacted at the time the Budget was prepared; therefore, the Budget assumes this account is operating under the Continuing Appropriations Act, 2022 (Division A of Public Law 117–43, as amended). The amounts included for 2022 reflect the annualized level provided by the continuing resolution.

Program and Financing (in millions of dollars)

Identification code 012–0502–0–1–352		2021 actual	2022 est.	2023 est.
	Obligations by program activity:			
0001	Smith-Lever Act, 3(b) and 3(c)	315	315	
0002	Youth at risk	8	8	
0004	Expanded food and nutrition education program (EFNEP)	70	70	
0006	Farm Safety and Youth Farm Safety	5	5	
0009	Federally Recognized Tribes Extension Program	3	3	
0013	Payments to 1890 colleges and Tuskegee Univ. and West Virginia State University	62	62	
0015	Renewable resources extension act	4	4	
0016	Federal administration	8	8	
0019	1890 facilities (section 1447)	25	46	
0022	1994 institutions activities	8	9	
0024	Rural health and safety education	4	4	
0026	Risk management education	10	10	
0027	New technologies for ag. extension	4	4	
0030	Food Animal Residue Avoidance Database	3	3	
0031	Beginning Farmers and Ranchers Program	51	31	
0032	Food Safety Outreach Program	10	10	
0034	Enhancing Agricultural Opportunities for Military Veterans	5	5	
0035	Food and Ag Service Learning	2	2	
0036	Farm Stress Assistance Network	36	13	
0037	The Gus Schumacher Nutrition Incentive Program	117	56	
0799	Total direct obligations	750	668	
0801	Extension Activities (Reimbursable)	29	28	
0900	Total new obligations, unexpired accounts	779	696	
	Budgetary resources:			
	Unobligated balance:			
1000	Unobligated balance brought forward, Oct 1	30	43	
1001	Discretionary unobligated balance brought fwd, Oct 1	28		
1021	Recoveries of prior year unpaid obligations	2		
1033	Recoveries of prior year paid obligations	4		
1070	Unobligated balance (total)	36	43	
	Budget authority:			
	Appropriations, discretionary:			
1100	Appropriation	546	546	
	Appropriations, mandatory:			
1200	Appropriation [DIV N COVID ALL]	141		
1221	Appropriations transferred from other acct [012–4085]	10	10	
1222	Exercised borrowing authority transferred from other accounts [012–4336]	66	73	
1230	Appropriations and/or unobligated balance of appropriations permanently reduced	–5	–5	
1260	Appropriations, mandatory (total)	212	78	
	Spending authority from offsetting collections, discretionary:			
1700	Collected	9		
1701	Change in uncollected payments, Federal sources	19	29	
1750	Spending auth from offsetting collections, disc (total)	28	29	
1900	Budget authority (total)	786	653	
1930	Total budgetary resources available	822	696	
	Memorandum (non-add) entries:			
1941	Unexpired unobligated balance, end of year	43		
	Change in obligated balance:			
	Unpaid obligations:			
3000	Unpaid obligations, brought forward, Oct 1	887	1,113	1,172
3010	New obligations, unexpired accounts	779	696	
3011	Obligations ("upward adjustments"), expired accounts	1		
3020	Outlays (gross)	–547	–637	–667
3040	Recoveries of prior year unpaid obligations, unexpired	–2		
3041	Recoveries of prior year unpaid obligations, expired	–5		
3050	Unpaid obligations, end of year	1,113	1,172	505
	Uncollected payments:			
3060	Uncollected pymts, Fed sources, brought forward, Oct 1	–24	–30	–59
3070	Change in uncollected pymts, Fed sources, unexpired	–19	–29	
3071	Change in uncollected pymts, Fed sources, expired	13		
3090	Uncollected pymts, Fed sources, end of year	–30	–59	–59
	Memorandum (non-add) entries:			
3100	Obligated balance, start of year	863	1,083	1,113
3200	Obligated balance, end of year	1,083	1,113	446
	Budget authority and outlays, net:			
	Discretionary:			
4000	Budget authority, gross	574	575	
	Outlays, gross:			
4010	Outlays from new discretionary authority	128	160	
4011	Outlays from discretionary balances	363	418	525

National Institute of Food and Agriculture—Continued
Federal Funds—Continued

EXTENSION ACTIVITIES—Continued
Program and Financing—Continued

Identification code 012–0502–0–1–352		2021 actual	2022 est.	2023 est.
4020	Outlays, gross (total)	491	578	525
	Offsets against gross budget authority and outlays:			
	Offsetting collections (collected) from:			
4030	Federal sources	−21	−29	....
4033	Non-Federal sources	−2	....	....
4040	Offsets against gross budget authority and outlays (total)	−23	−29	....
	Additional offsets against gross budget authority only:			
4050	Change in uncollected pymts, Fed sources, unexpired	−19	−29	....
4052	Offsetting collections credited to expired accounts	14	29	....
4060	Additional offsets against budget authority only (total)	−5	....	....
4070	Budget authority, net (discretionary)	546	546	....
4080	Outlays, net (discretionary)	468	549	525
	Mandatory:			
4090	Budget authority, gross	212	78	....
	Outlays, gross:			
4100	Outlays from new mandatory authority	5	....	....
4101	Outlays from mandatory balances	51	59	142
4110	Outlays, gross (total)	56	59	142
	Offsets against gross budget authority and outlays:			
	Offsetting collections (collected) from:			
4123	Non-Federal sources	−4	....	....
	Additional offsets against gross budget authority only:			
4143	Recoveries of prior year paid obligations, unexpired accounts	4	....	....
4160	Budget authority, net (mandatory)	212	78	....
4170	Outlays, net (mandatory)	52	59	142
4180	Budget authority, net (total)	758	624	....
4190	Outlays, net (total)	520	608	667

Programs previously funded under this account are proposed under a consolidated National Institute of Food and Agriculture account.

Beginning Farmer and Rancher Development Program.—This mandatory program provides funding to support the nations beginning farmers and ranchers by making competitive grants to new and established local and regional training, education, outreach, and technical assistance initiatives that address the needs of beginning farmers and ranchers. Section 12301 of the 2018 Farm Bill (Pub. L. 115–334) amended Section 2501 of the Food, Agriculture, Conservation, and Trade Act of 1990 (7 U.S.C. 2279) and made available the enacted amount of $15 million for FYs 2019 and 2020, $17.5 million for FY 2021, $20 million for FY 2022, and $25 million for FY 2023 and each year thereafter to carry out the program. In addition to the mandatory funds provided under the 2018 Farm Bill, Section 756 of the Further Consolidated Appropriations Act, 2021, provided $2.5 million for the program.

Extension Risk Management Education Program.—This mandatory program provides funding for educating agricultural producers and providing technical assistance to agricultural producers on a full range of farm viability and risk management activities. These activities include futures, options, agricultural trade options, crop insurance, business planning, enterprise analysis, transfer and succession planning, management coaching, market assessment, cash flow analysis, cash forward contracting, debt reduction, production diversification, farm resources risk reduction, farm financial benchmarking, conservation activities, and other appropriate risk management strategies. Mandatory funding in the enacted amount of $10 million is to be made available annually for competitive awards.

Gus Schumacher Nutrition Incentive Program.—Section 4205 of the 2018 Farm Bill (Pub. L. 115–334), which amended section 4405 of the Food, Conservation, and Energy Act of 2008 (7 U.S.C. 7517), authorizes the Gus Schumacher Nutrition Incentive Program to support projects to increase the purchase of fruits and vegetables among low-income consumers participating in the Supplemental Nutrition Assistance Program (SNAP) by providing incentives at the point of purchase. Mandatory funding was made available in the enacted amount of $45 million for FY 2019, $48 million for FYs 2020 and 2021, $53 million for FY 2022, and $56 million for FY 2023 and each year thereafter to carry out the program. Section 755

(Division M) of the Consolidated Appropriation Act, 2021 (P.L. 116–260) provided $75 million for additional coronavirus response and relief.

Object Classification (in millions of dollars)

Identification code 012–0502–0–1–352		2021 actual	2022 est.	2023 est.
	Direct obligations:			
11.1	Personnel compensation: Full-time permanent	9	11	....
12.1	Civilian personnel benefits	5	5	....
25.2	Other services from non-Federal sources	4	4	....
25.4	Operation and maintenance of facilities	1	1	....
25.5	Research and development contracts	13	11	....
41.0	Grants, subsidies, and contributions	721	636	....
99.0	Direct obligations	753	668	....
99.0	Reimbursable obligations	26	28	....
99.9	Total new obligations, unexpired accounts	779	696	....

Employment Summary

Identification code 012–0502–0–1–352	2021 actual	2022 est.	2023 est.
1001 Direct civilian full-time equivalent employment	97	133	....

Trust Funds

EMERGENCY CITRUS DISEASE RESEARCH AND DEVELOPMENT TRUST FUND

Special and Trust Fund Receipts (in millions of dollars)

Identification code 012–8559–0–7–352		2021 actual	2022 est.	2023 est.
0100	Balance, start of year	....	1	2
	Receipts:			
	Current law:			
1140	Payment from Commodity Credit Corporation Fund, Emergency Citrus Disease Research and Development Trust Fund	25	25	25
2000	Total: Balances and receipts	25	26	27
	Appropriations:			
	Current law:			
2101	Emergency Citrus Disease Research and Development Trust Fund	−25	−25	−25
2132	Emergency Citrus Disease Research and Development Trust Fund	1	1	1
2199	Total current law appropriations	−24	−24	−24
2999	Total appropriations	−24	−24	−24
5099	Balance, end of year	1	2	3

Program and Financing (in millions of dollars)

Identification code 012–8559–0–7–352		2021 actual	2022 est.	2023 est.
	Obligations by program activity:			
0001	Emergency Citrus Disease Research and Extension	25	29	24
0900	Total new obligations, unexpired accounts (object class 41.0)	25	29	24
	Budgetary resources:			
	Unobligated balance:			
1000	Unobligated balance brought forward, Oct 1	5	5	....
1021	Recoveries of prior year unpaid obligations	1	....	....
1070	Unobligated balance (total)	6	5	....
	Budget authority:			
	Appropriations, mandatory:			
1201	Appropriation (special or trust fund)	25	25	25
1232	Appropriations and/or unobligated balance of appropriations temporarily reduced	−1	−1	−1
1260	Appropriations, mandatory (total)	24	24	24
1930	Total budgetary resources available	30	29	24
	Memorandum (non-add) entries:			
1941	Unexpired unobligated balance, end of year	5	....	....
	Change in obligated balance:			
	Unpaid obligations:			
3000	Unpaid obligations, brought forward, Oct 1	45	60	79
3010	New obligations, unexpired accounts	25	29	24
3020	Outlays (gross)	−9	−10	−28

3040	Recoveries of prior year unpaid obligations, unexpired	–1		
3050	Unpaid obligations, end of year	60	79	75
	Memorandum (non-add) entries:			
3100	Obligated balance, start of year	45	60	79
3200	Obligated balance, end of year	60	79	75
	Budget authority and outlays, net:			
	Mandatory:			
4090	Budget authority, gross	24	24	24
	Outlays, gross:			
4100	Outlays from new mandatory authority		1	1
4101	Outlays from mandatory balances	9	9	27
4110	Outlays, gross (total)	9	10	28
4180	Budget authority, net (total)	24	24	24
4190	Outlays, net (total)	9	10	28

ANIMAL AND PLANT HEALTH INSPECTION SERVICE

Federal Funds

SALARIES AND EXPENSES

(INCLUDING TRANSFERS OF FUNDS)

For necessary expenses of the Animal and Plant Health Inspection Service, including up to $30,000 for representation allowances and for expenses pursuant to the Foreign Service Act of 1980 (22 U.S.C. 4085), $1,149,286,000, of which $514,000, to remain available until expended, shall be available for the control of outbreaks of insects, plant diseases, animal diseases and for control of pest animals and birds ("contingency fund") to the extent necessary to meet emergency conditions; of which $13,980,000, to remain available until expended, shall be used for the cotton pests program, including for cost share purposes or for debt retirement for active eradication zones; of which $39,268,000, to remain available until expended, shall be for Animal Health Technical Services; of which $2,100,000, shall be for activities under the authority of the Horse Protection Act of 1970, as amended (15 U.S.C. 1831); of which $65,071,000, to remain available until expended, shall be used to support avian health; of which $7,451,000, to remain available until expended, shall be for information technology infrastructure; of which $219,533,000, to remain available until expended, shall be for specialty crop pests; of which, $14,672,000, to remain available until expended, shall be for field crop and rangeland ecosystem pests; of which $24,111,000, to remain available until expended, shall be for zoonotic disease management; of which $44,242,000, to remain available until expended, shall be for emergency preparedness and response; of which $62,854,000, to remain available until expended, shall be for tree and wood pests; of which $5,791,000, to remain available until expended, shall be for the National Veterinary Stockpile; of which $6,038,000, to remain available until expended, shall be for invasive species control in coordination with other Federal agencies and the Civilian Climate Corps; of which up to $1,500,000, to remain available until expended, shall be for the scrapie program for indemnities; of which $2,500,000, to remain available until expended, shall be for the wildlife damage management program for aviation safety: Provided, That of amounts available under this heading for wildlife services methods development, $1,000,000 shall remain available until expended: Provided further, That of amounts available under this heading for the screwworm program, $4,990,000 shall remain available until expended; of which $24,619,000, to remain available until expended, shall be used to carry out the science program and transition activities for the National Bio and Agro-defense Facility located in Manhattan, Kansas: Provided further, That no funds shall be used to formulate or administer a brucellosis eradication program for the current fiscal year that does not require minimum matching by the States of at least 40 percent: Provided further, That this appropriation shall be available for the purchase, replacement, operation, and maintenance of aircraft: Provided further, That in addition, in emergencies which threaten any segment of the agricultural production industry of the United States, the Secretary may transfer from other appropriations or funds available to the agencies or corporations of the Department such sums as may be deemed necessary, to be available only in such emergencies for the arrest and eradication of contagious or infectious disease or pests of animals, poultry, or plants, and for expenses in accordance with sections 10411 and 10417 of the Animal Health Protection Act (7 U.S.C. 8310 and 8316) and sections 431 and 442 of the Plant Protection Act (7 U.S.C. 7751 and 7772), and any unexpended balances of funds transferred for such emergency purposes in the preceding fiscal year shall be merged with such transferred amounts: Provided further, That appropriations hereunder shall be available pursuant to law (7 U.S.C. 2250) for the repair and alteration of leased buildings and improvements,

but unless otherwise provided the cost of altering any one building during the fiscal year shall not exceed 10 percent of the current replacement value of the building.

In fiscal year 2023, the agency is authorized to collect fees to cover the total costs of providing technical assistance, goods, or services requested by States, other political subdivisions, domestic and international organizations, foreign governments, or individuals, provided that such fees are structured such that any entity's liability for such fees is reasonably based on the technical assistance, goods, or services provided to the entity by the agency, and such fees shall be reimbursed to this account, to remain available until expended, without further appropriation, for providing such assistance, goods, or services.

Note.—A full-year 2022 appropriation for this account was not enacted at the time the Budget was prepared; therefore, the Budget assumes this account is operating under the Continuing Appropriations Act, 2022 (Division A of Public Law 117–43, as amended). The amounts included for 2022 reflect the annualized level provided by the continuing resolution.

Special and Trust Fund Receipts (in millions of dollars)

Identification code 012–1600–0–1–352	2021 actual	2022 est.	2023 est.
0100 Balance, start of year	33	15	33
Receipts:			
Current law:			
1110 1990 Food, Agricultural Quarantine Inspection Fees	320	460	596
2000 Total: Balances and receipts	353	475	629
Appropriations:			
Current law:			
2101 Salaries and Expenses	–320	–460	–596
2103 Salaries and Expenses	–33	–15	–33
2132 Salaries and Expenses	15	33	36
2199 Total current law appropriations	–338	–442	–593
2999 Total appropriations	–338	–442	–593
5099 Balance, end of year	15	33	36

Program and Financing (in millions of dollars)

Identification code 012–1600–0–1–352	2021 actual	2022 est.	2023 est.
Obligations by program activity:			
0001 Animal Health	357	361	392
0002 Plant Health	364	362	392
0003 Wildlife Services	132	133	141
0004 Regulatory Management	36	35	39
0005 Emergency Management	39	41	48
0006 Safe Trade and International Technical Assistance	40	40	43
0007 Animal Welfare	34	34	36
0008 Agency-Wide Programs	52	52	58
0009 Emergency Program Funding	2	41	55
0010 Agricultural Quarantine Inspection User Fees	234	234	234
0013 H1N1 Transfer From HHS	1		
0014 2018 Farm Bill, Section 7721	70	71	71
0015 2018 Farm Bill, Section 12101	39	35	35
0016 2018 Farm Bill, Section 2408	7	7	5
0018 Refunds for Equipment Sold	2		
0020 USMCA Lacey Act		2	
0021 Citrus Greening - GP 739	8	8	
0022 Cogongrass - GP 797	4	5	
0024 American Rescue Plan Act		63	69
0100 Total direct program	1,421	1,524	1,618
0799 Total direct obligations	1,421	1,524	1,618
0801 Salaries and Expenses (Reimbursable)	259	259	261
0900 Total new obligations, unexpired accounts	1,680	1,783	1,879
Budgetary resources:			
Unobligated balance:			
1000 Unobligated balance brought forward, Oct 1	487	1,511	1,388
1001 Discretionary unobligated balance brought fwd, Oct 1	307		
1021 Recoveries of prior year unpaid obligations	35		
1070 Unobligated balance (total)	522	1,511	1,388
Budget authority:			
Appropriations, discretionary:			
1100 Appropriation	1,078	1,076	1,149
1122 Exercised borrowing authority transferred from other accounts [012–4336]	500		
1131 Unobligated balance of appropriations permanently reduced	–2		
1160 Appropriation, discretionary (total)	1,576	1,076	1,149
Appropriations, mandatory:			
1200 Appropriation (GP 799D AQI User Fees)	635		

Animal and Plant Health Inspection Service—Continued
Federal Funds—Continued

SALARIES AND EXPENSES—Continued

Program and Financing—Continued

Identification code 012–1600–0–1–352		2021 actual	2022 est.	2023 est.
1200	Appropriation (American Rescue Plan Act)	300		
1201	Appropriation (AQI User Fees)	320	460	596
1203	Appropriation (previously unavailable)(special or trust)	33	15	33
1220	Appropriations transferred to other accts [070–0530]	–533	–189	–417
1222	Exercised borrowing authority transferred from other accounts [012–4336]	75	75	105
1230	Appropriations and/or unobligated balance of appropriations permanently reduced	–4	–4	–4
1232	Appropriations and/or unobligated balance of appropriations temporarily reduced	–15	–33	–36
1260	Appropriations, mandatory (total)	811	324	277
	Spending authority from offsetting collections, discretionary:			
1700	Collected	224	260	260
1701	Change in uncollected payments, Federal sources	66		
1750	Spending auth from offsetting collections, disc (total)	290	260	260
1900	Budget authority (total)	2,677	1,660	1,686
1930	Total budgetary resources available	3,199	3,171	3,074
	Memorandum (non-add) entries:			
1940	Unobligated balance expiring	–8		
1941	Unexpired unobligated balance, end of year	1,511	1,388	1,195
	Change in obligated balance:			
	Unpaid obligations:			
3000	Unpaid obligations, brought forward, Oct 1	668	643	604
3010	New obligations, unexpired accounts	1,680	1,783	1,879
3011	Obligations ("upward adjustments"), expired accounts	17		
3020	Outlays (gross)	–1,676	–1,822	–1,780
3040	Recoveries of prior year unpaid obligations, unexpired	–35		
3041	Recoveries of prior year unpaid obligations, expired	–11		
3050	Unpaid obligations, end of year	643	604	703
	Uncollected payments:			
3060	Uncollected pymts, Fed sources, brought forward, Oct 1	–187	–184	–184
3070	Change in uncollected pymts, Fed sources, unexpired	–66		
3071	Change in uncollected pymts, Fed sources, expired	69		
3090	Uncollected pymts, Fed sources, end of year	–184	–184	–184
	Memorandum (non-add) entries:			
3100	Obligated balance, start of year	481	459	420
3200	Obligated balance, end of year	459	420	519
	Budget authority and outlays, net:			
	Discretionary:			
4000	Budget authority, gross	1,866	1,336	1,409
	Outlays, gross:			
4010	Outlays from new discretionary authority	928	1,175	1,237
4011	Outlays from discretionary balances	399	296	261
4020	Outlays, gross (total)	1,327	1,471	1,498
	Offsets against gross budget authority and outlays:			
	Offsetting collections (collected) from:			
4030	Federal sources	–113	–103	–103
4033	Non-Federal sources	–148	–157	–157
4040	Offsets against gross budget authority and outlays (total)	–261	–260	–260
	Additional offsets against gross budget authority only:			
4050	Change in uncollected pymts, Fed sources, unexpired	–66		
4052	Offsetting collections credited to expired accounts	37		
4060	Additional offsets against budget authority only (total)	–29		
4070	Budget authority, net (discretionary)	1,576	1,076	1,149
4080	Outlays, net (discretionary)	1,066	1,211	1,238
	Mandatory:			
4090	Budget authority, gross	811	324	277
	Outlays, gross:			
4100	Outlays from new mandatory authority	204	246	165
4101	Outlays from mandatory balances	145	105	117
4110	Outlays, gross (total)	349	351	282
4180	Budget authority, net (total)	2,387	1,400	1,426
4190	Outlays, net (total)	1,415	1,562	1,520

The Secretary of Agriculture established the Animal and Plant Health Inspection Service (APHIS) on April 2, 1972, under the authority of Reorganization Plan No. 2 of 1953 and other authorities. The Agency has a broad mission area that includes protecting the health and value of American agricultural and natural resources that are vulnerable to pests and diseases as well as natural disasters; developing and advancing science-based standards with trading partners to ensure U.S. agricultural exports are protected from unjustified restrictions; regulating genetically engineered organisms; administering the Animal Welfare and Horse Protection Acts; and, carrying out wildlife damage management activities. APHIS performs this important work using three major areas of activity, as follows:

Safeguarding and Emergency Preparedness/Response.—APHIS monitors animal and plant health throughout the world and uses the information to set effective agricultural import policies to prevent the introduction of foreign animal and plant pests and diseases. Should a pest or disease enter the United States, APHIS works cooperatively with Federal, State, Tribal, industry, and other partners to rapidly diagnose them and determine if there is a need to establish new pest or disease management programs. APHIS, in conjunction with partners and stakeholders, protects American agriculture by eradicating harmful pests and diseases or, where eradication is not feasible, by minimizing their economic impact. The Agency monitors endemic pests and diseases through surveys and sampling to detect their locations and works with partners to implement controls and conduct outreach to prevent the spread of pests and diseases into non-infested parts of the country. The Agency maintains a cadre of trained professionals prepared to respond immediately to potential animal and plant health emergencies. Program personnel investigate reports of suspected presence of foreign and exotic pests and diseases and work with partners to determine an appropriate course of action, including emergency action if necessary. APHIS conducts diagnostic laboratory activities that support the Agency's animal disease and plant pest prevention, detection, control, and eradication programs. The Agency also provides and directs technology development to support animal and plant protection programs of the Agency and its cooperators at the State, Tribal, national, and international levels. APHIS provides technical and some operational assistance to States, Tribes, and local entities to reduce wildlife damage to natural and agricultural resources. Finally, the Agency protects plant health by optimizing its oversight of genetically engineered organisms.

Safe Trade and International Technical Assistance.—Sanitary (animal) and phytosanitary (plant) (SPS) regulations can have a significant impact on market access for the United States as an exporter of agricultural products. The Agency participates in the development of international standards. APHIS also plays a central role in resolving technical trade issues to ensure the smooth and safe movement of agricultural commodities into and out of the United States. APHIS helps protect the United States from emerging animal and plant pests and diseases while meeting obligations under the World Trade Organization's SPS agreement by assisting developing countries in improving their protection systems. Finally, APHIS develops and implements programs designed to identify and reduce agricultural pest and disease threats, while they are still outside of U.S. borders, to enhance safe agricultural trade, and to strengthen emergency response preparedness.

Animal Welfare.—The Agency conducts regulatory activities to ensure the humane care and treatment of animals, including horses, as required by the Animal Welfare Act of 1966 as amended (7 U.S.C. 2131–2159), and the Horse Protection Act of 1970 as amended (15 U.S.C. 1821–1831). These activities include inspecting certain establishments that handle animals intended for research, exhibition, and sale as pets, and monitoring of certain horse shows.

APHIS' 2023 Budget request is $1.149 billion. The Budget includes an increase of $6.038 million to support APHIS as the lead coordination agency between Federal agencies and the Civilian Climate Corps on issues related to invasive species control and climate change, funding increases to support our ongoing efforts to combat antimicrobial resistance, chronic wasting disease, and exotic fruit flies. The Budget includes increases to support domestic and international programs in the face of rising operating costs, and reflects the shift of funds to combat citrus greening and cogongrass from General Provisions to baseline programs under the agency's appropriated line items. In addition, the Budget continues the transition of the Agency's foreign animal disease laboratory operations from Plum Island,

DEPARTMENT OF AGRICULTURE

New York, to the new-state-of-the-art National Bio and Agro-Defense Facility in Manhattan, Kansas.

Object Classification (in millions of dollars)

Identification code 012–1600–0–1–352		2021 actual	2022 est.	2023 est.
	Direct obligations:			
	Personnel compensation:			
11.1	Full-time permanent	482	498	537
11.3	Other than full-time permanent	3	3	3
11.5	Other personnel compensation	8	8	8
11.9	Total personnel compensation	493	509	548
12.1	Civilian personnel benefits	195	195	203
13.0	Benefits for former personnel	1	1	1
21.0	Travel and transportation of persons	17	20	22
22.0	Transportation of things	3	5	6
23.1	Rent, Communications, and Utilities	78	80	84
24.0	Printing and reproduction	1	1	1
25.2	Other services from non-Federal sources	555	583	623
26.0	Supplies and materials	53	82	84
31.0	Equipment	21	39	39
42.0	Other insurance claims and indemnities	5	9	7
99.0	Direct obligations	1,422	1,524	1,618
99.0	Reimbursable obligations	258	259	261
99.9	Total new obligations, unexpired accounts	1,680	1,783	1,879

Employment Summary

Identification code 012–1600–0–1–352	2021 actual	2022 est.	2023 est.
1001 Direct civilian full-time equivalent employment	5,831	6,416	6,496
2001 Reimbursable civilian full-time equivalent employment	1,740	1,785	1,785

BUILDINGS AND FACILITIES

For plans, construction, repair, preventive maintenance, environmental support, improvement, extension, alteration, and purchase of fixed equipment or facilities, as authorized by 7 U.S.C. 2250, and acquisition of land as authorized by 7 U.S.C. 2268a, $3,175,000, to remain available until expended.

Note.—A full-year 2022 appropriation for this account was not enacted at the time the Budget was prepared; therefore, the Budget assumes this account is operating under the Continuing Appropriations Act, 2022 (Division A of Public Law 117–43, as amended). The amounts included for 2022 reflect the annualized level provided by the continuing resolution.

Program and Financing (in millions of dollars)

Identification code 012–1601–0–1–352		2021 actual	2022 est.	2023 est.
	Obligations by program activity:			
0001	Buildings and facilities	5	4	4
	Budgetary resources:			
	Unobligated balance:			
1000	Unobligated balance brought forward, Oct 1	44	44	43
1021	Recoveries of prior year unpaid obligations	2		
1070	Unobligated balance (total)	46	44	43
	Budget authority:			
	Appropriations, discretionary:			
1100	Appropriation	3	3	3
1930	Total budgetary resources available	49	47	46
	Memorandum (non-add) entries:			
1941	Unexpired unobligated balance, end of year	44	43	42
	Change in obligated balance:			
	Unpaid obligations:			
3000	Unpaid obligations, brought forward, Oct 1	6	3	1
3010	New obligations, unexpired accounts	5	4	4
3020	Outlays (gross)	–6	–6	–3
3040	Recoveries of prior year unpaid obligations, unexpired	–2		
3050	Unpaid obligations, end of year	3	1	2
	Memorandum (non-add) entries:			
3100	Obligated balance, start of year	6	3	1
3200	Obligated balance, end of year	3	1	2
	Budget authority and outlays, net:			
	Discretionary:			
4000	Budget authority, gross	3	3	3
	Outlays, gross:			
4010	Outlays from new discretionary authority		1	1
4011	Outlays from discretionary balances	6	5	2
4020	Outlays, gross (total)	6	6	3
4180	Budget authority, net (total)	3	3	3
4190	Outlays, net (total)	6	6	3

This account provides for plans, construction, repair, preventive maintenance, environmental support, improvement, extension, alteration, purchase of fixed equipment or facilities, and acquisition of land, as needed, for Animal and Plant Health Inspection Service (APHIS) operated facilities, which include animal quarantine stations, plant inspection stations, sterile insect rearing facilities, and laboratories.

The 2023 Budget request proposes $3.2 million which would maintain funding for this account and allow the agency to address the needs of several facilities.

Object Classification (in millions of dollars)

Identification code 012–1601–0–1–352		2021 actual	2022 est.	2023 est.
	Direct obligations:			
25.1	Advisory and assistance services	2		
25.4	Operation and maintenance of facilities	3	4	4
99.9	Total new obligations, unexpired accounts	5	4	4

Trust Funds

MISCELLANEOUS TRUST FUNDS

Special and Trust Fund Receipts (in millions of dollars)

Identification code 012–9971–0–7–999		2021 actual	2022 est.	2023 est.
0100	Balance, start of year			
	Receipts:			
	Current law:			
1130	Deposits of Miscellaneous Contributed Funds, APHIS	8	9	9
2000	Total: Balances and receipts	8	9	9
	Appropriations:			
	Current law:			
2101	Miscellaneous Trust Funds	–8	–9	–9
5099	Balance, end of year			

Program and Financing (in millions of dollars)

Identification code 012–9971–0–7–999		2021 actual	2022 est.	2023 est.
	Obligations by program activity:			
0001	Miscellaneous trust funds	8	9	9
	Budgetary resources:			
	Unobligated balance:			
1000	Unobligated balance brought forward, Oct 1	9	9	9
	Budget authority:			
	Appropriations, mandatory:			
1201	Appropriation (special or trust fund)	8	9	9
1930	Total budgetary resources available	17	18	18
	Memorandum (non-add) entries:			
1941	Unexpired unobligated balance, end of year	9	9	9
	Change in obligated balance:			
	Unpaid obligations:			
3000	Unpaid obligations, brought forward, Oct 1	3	3	1
3010	New obligations, unexpired accounts	8	9	9
3020	Outlays (gross)	–8	–11	–10
3050	Unpaid obligations, end of year	3	1	
	Memorandum (non-add) entries:			
3100	Obligated balance, start of year	3	3	1
3200	Obligated balance, end of year	3	1	
	Budget authority and outlays, net:			
	Mandatory:			
4090	Budget authority, gross	8	9	9
	Outlays, gross:			
4100	Outlays from new mandatory authority	3	8	8

MISCELLANEOUS TRUST FUNDS—Continued
Program and Financing—Continued

Identification code 012–9971–0–7–999	2021 actual	2022 est.	2023 est.
4101 Outlays from mandatory balances	5	3	2
4110 Outlays, gross (total)	8	11	10
4180 Budget authority, net (total)	8	9	9
4190 Outlays, net (total)	8	11	10

APHIS provides inspection and preclearance activities for growers, exporting associations and foreign government entities. Those benefiting from the service must deposit funds into this account in advance of the service. The Agency uses the funds to cover the costs associated with inspecting and preclearing certain fruits, vegetables, flower bulbs, and other products in foreign countries before they are shipped to the United States.

Object Classification (in millions of dollars)

Identification code 012–9971–0–7–999	2021 actual	2022 est.	2023 est.
Direct obligations:			
11.1 Personnel compensation: Full-time permanent	5	5	5
12.1 Civilian personnel benefits	2	2	2
21.0 Travel and transportation of persons	1	1	1
25.2 Other services from non-Federal sources	.....	1	1
99.9 Total new obligations, unexpired accounts	8	9	9

Employment Summary

Identification code 012–9971–0–7–999	2021 actual	2022 est.	2023 est.
1001 Direct civilian full-time equivalent employment	34	50	50

FOOD SAFETY AND INSPECTION SERVICE

Federal Funds

FOOD SAFETY AND INSPECTION SERVICE

For necessary expenses to carry out services authorized by the Federal Meat Inspection Act, the Poultry Products Inspection Act, and the Egg Products Inspection Act, including not to exceed $10,000 for representation allowances and for expenses pursuant to section 8 of the Act approved August 3, 1956 (7 U.S.C. 1766), $1,226,148,000; and in addition, $1,000,000 may be credited to this account from fees collected for the cost of laboratory accreditation as authorized by section 1327 of the Food, Agriculture, Conservation and Trade Act of 1990 (7 U.S.C. 138f): Provided, That funds provided for the Public Health Data Communication Infrastructure system shall remain available until expended: Provided further, That funds provided for the relocation of the Mid-Western Laboratory shall remain available until expended: Provided further, That no fewer than 148 full-time equivalent positions shall be employed during fiscal year 2023 for purposes dedicated solely to inspections and enforcement related to the Humane Methods of Slaughter Act (7 U.S.C. 1901 et seq.): Provided further, That this appropriation shall be available pursuant to law (7 U.S.C. 2250) for the alteration and repair of buildings and improvements, but the cost of altering any one building during the fiscal year shall not exceed 10 percent of the current replacement value of the building.

Note.—A full-year 2022 appropriation for this account was not enacted at the time the Budget was prepared; therefore, the Budget assumes this account is operating under the Continuing Appropriations Act, 2022 (Division A of Public Law 117–43, as amended). The amounts included for 2022 reflect the annualized level provided by the continuing resolution.

Program and Financing (in millions of dollars)

Identification code 012–3700–0–1–554	2021 actual	2022 est.	2023 est.
Obligations by program activity:			
0001 Salaries and expenses	1,108	1,133	1,236
0801 Salaries and Expenses (Reimbursable)	238	215	205
0900 Total new obligations, unexpired accounts	1,346	1,348	1,441
Budgetary resources:			
Unobligated balance:			
1000 Unobligated balance brought forward, Oct 1	101	200	169
1001 Discretionary unobligated balance brought fwd, Oct 1	101	.....	.....
1021 Recoveries of prior year unpaid obligations	9	.....	.....
1070 Unobligated balance (total)	110	200	169
Budget authority:			
Appropriations, discretionary:			
1100 Appropriation	1,076	1,076	1,226
1120 Appropriations transferred to other acct [012–4609]	–1	.....	.....
1121 Appropriations transferred from other acct [012–0115]	16	16	.....
1160 Appropriation, discretionary (total)	1,091	1,092	1,226
Appropriations, mandatory:			
1200 Appropriation (American Rescue Plan)	100	.....	.....
Spending authority from offsetting collections, discretionary:			
1700 Collected	253	225	205
1701 Change in uncollected payments, Federal sources	–8	.....	.....
1750 Spending auth from offsetting collections, disc (total)	245	225	205
1900 Budget authority (total)	1,436	1,317	1,431
1930 Total budgetary resources available	1,546	1,517	1,600
Memorandum (non-add) entries:			
1941 Unexpired unobligated balance, end of year	200	169	159
Change in obligated balance:			
Unpaid obligations:			
3000 Unpaid obligations, brought forward, Oct 1	163	159	154
3010 New obligations, unexpired accounts	1,346	1,348	1,441
3011 Obligations ("upward adjustments"), expired accounts	2	.....	.....
3020 Outlays (gross)	–1,330	–1,353	–1,422
3040 Recoveries of prior year unpaid obligations, unexpired	–9	.....	.....
3041 Recoveries of prior year unpaid obligations, expired	–13	.....	.....
3050 Unpaid obligations, end of year	159	154	173
Uncollected payments:			
3060 Uncollected pymts, Fed sources, brought forward, Oct 1	–53	–39	–39
3070 Change in uncollected pymts, Fed sources, unexpired	8	.....	.....
3071 Change in uncollected pymts, Fed sources, expired	6	.....	.....
3090 Uncollected pymts, Fed sources, end of year	–39	–39	–39
Memorandum (non-add) entries:			
3100 Obligated balance, start of year	110	120	115
3200 Obligated balance, end of year	120	115	134
Budget authority and outlays, net:			
Discretionary:			
4000 Budget authority, gross	1,336	1,317	1,431
Outlays, gross:			
4010 Outlays from new discretionary authority	1,100	1,126	1,221
4011 Outlays from discretionary balances	219	202	191
4020 Outlays, gross (total)	1,319	1,328	1,412
Offsets against gross budget authority and outlays:			
Offsetting collections (collected) from:			
4030 Federal sources	–9	.....	.....
4033 Non-Federal sources	–250	–225	–205
4040 Offsets against gross budget authority and outlays (total)	–259	–225	–205
Additional offsets against gross budget authority only:			
4050 Change in uncollected pymts, Fed sources, unexpired	8	.....	.....
4052 Offsetting collections credited to expired accounts	6	.....	.....
4060 Additional offsets against budget authority only (total)	14	.....	.....
4070 Budget authority, net (discretionary)	1,091	1,092	1,226
4080 Outlays, net (discretionary)	1,060	1,103	1,207
Mandatory:			
4090 Budget authority, gross	100	.....	.....
Outlays, gross:			
4100 Outlays from new mandatory authority	11	.....	.....
4101 Outlays from mandatory balances	.....	25	10
4110 Outlays, gross (total)	11	25	10
4180 Budget authority, net (total)	1,191	1,092	1,226
4190 Outlays, net (total)	1,071	1,128	1,217
Memorandum (non-add) entries:			
5090 Unexpired unavailable balance, SOY: Offsetting collections	2	2	2
5092 Unexpired unavailable balance, EOY: Offsetting collections	2	2	2

The primary objective of the Food Safety and Inspection Service (FSIS) is to ensure that meat, poultry, and egg products are safe, wholesome, unadulterated, and accurately labeled and packaged, as required by the Federal Meat Inspection Act, the Poultry Products Inspection Act, and the Egg Products Inspection Act. In carrying out this mission, FSIS oversight responsibility covers a significant percentage of American spending on food. Providing adequate resources for Federal Food Safety agencies is a priority of the Administration. The 2023 Budget proposes $1.266 billion for inspection of meat, poultry and egg products. With these funds, FSIS will fully support all Federal, in-plant and other frontline personnel; the Federal share of State inspection programs; and continue to improve its data infrastructure and modernize its scientific approach to food safety.

FEDERALLY FUNDED INSPECTION ACTIVITIES

	2021 actual	2022 est.	2023 est.
FEDERALLY INSPECTED ESTABLISHMENTS:			
Slaughter only Establishments	14	14	14
Processing only Establishments	4224	4300	4300
Combination Slaughter and Processing Establishments	1143	1150	1150
Import Establishments	164	170	170
Egg Plants	77	80	80
Other Establishments	1,008	1,100	1,100
FEDERALLY INSPECTED and PASSED PRODUCTION (millions of pounds):			
Meat Slaughter	66,230	67,000	67,000
Poultry Slaughter	67,024	69,000	69,000
Egg Products	2,743	2,800	2,800
IMPORT/EXPORT ACTIVITY (millions of pounds):			
Meat and Poultry Imported	4,510	4,600	4,600
Meat and Poultry Exported	19,069	20,000	20,000
STATES AND TERRITORIES with COOPERATIVE PROGRAMS:			
Intrastate Inspection[1] (number of states)	27	27	27
Number of Slaughter and/or Processing Plants (excludes exempt plants)	1,246	1,200	1,200
Talmadge-Aiken Inspection (number of states)	9	9	9
Number of Talmadge-Aiken establishments[2]	363	370	370
COMPLIANCE ACTIVITIES:			
Investigations and Surveillance Activities	14,217	14,200	14,200
Enforcement Actions Completed	1,220	1,256	1,295
LABORATORY SAMPLING:			
Microbiology (Samples Analyzed)	129,449	130,000	130,000
Microbiology (Tests Performed)	344,368	346,000	346,000
Microbiology (Analytes Analyzed)	828,913	830,000	830,000
Chemistry (Samples Analyzed)	14,141	15,000	15,000
Chemistry (Tests Performed)	26,809	27,000	27,000
Chemistry (Analytes Analyzed)	2,074,282	2,100,000	2,100,000
Pathology Samples (Samples Analyzed)	3,821	4,000	4,000
CONSUMER EDUCATION and PUBLIC OUTREACH:			
Meat and Poultry Hotline Calls Received	8,531	8,958	9,405
Website Visits	15,589,441	16,057,124	16,538,837
Electronic Messages Received	6,434	6,756	7,093
Publications Distributed	129,080	132,952	136,941
E-mail Alert Service Subscribers	3,308,299	3,407,548	3,509,774
EPIDEMIOLOGICAL INVESTIGATIONS:			
Cooperative Efforts with State and Public Health Offices	11	11	11
Illnesses Reported and Treated[3]	209	531	531

[1] States with cooperative agreements which are operating programs.
[2] These establishments are included in the counts of Federally inspected establishments.
[3] Data must be collected over a number of years to chart national trends and estimate the incidence of foodborne illness and treatment.

Object Classification (in millions of dollars)

Identification code 012–3700–0–1–554		2021 actual	2022 est.	2023 est.
	Direct obligations:			
	Personnel compensation:			
11.1	Full-time permanent	513	479	547
11.3	Other than full-time permanent	3	3	3
11.5	Other personnel compensation	102	102	121
11.9	Total personnel compensation	618	584	671
12.1	Civilian personnel benefits	265	289	301
13.0	Benefits for former personnel	1	1	1
21.0	Travel and transportation of persons	32	32	33
22.0	Transportation of things	4	4	4
23.1	Rental payments to GSA	8	7	8
23.3	Communications, utilities, and miscellaneous charges	14	14	14
24.0	Printing and reproduction	1	1	1
25.1	Advisory and assistance services	4	5	3
25.2	Other services from non-Federal sources	35	35	42
25.3	Other goods and services from Federal sources	51	88	84
25.4	Operation and maintenance of facilities	1	1	1
26.0	Supplies and materials	9	9	9
31.0	Equipment	6	5	5
41.0	Grants, subsidies, and contributions	59	58	59
99.0	Direct obligations	1,108	1,133	1,236
99.0	Reimbursable obligations	238	215	205
99.9	Total new obligations, unexpired accounts	1,346	1,348	1,441

Employment Summary

Identification code 012–3700–0–1–554	2021 actual	2022 est.	2023 est.
1001 Direct civilian full-time equivalent employment	8,297	8,666	8,666
2001 Reimbursable civilian full-time equivalent employment	21	21	21

Trust Funds

EXPENSES AND REFUNDS, INSPECTION AND GRADING OF FARM PRODUCTS

Special and Trust Fund Receipts (in millions of dollars)

Identification code 012–8137–0–7–352		2021 actual	2022 est.	2023 est.
0100	Balance, start of year	1	2	1
	Receipts:			
	Current law:			
1130	Deposits of Fees, Inspection and Grading of Farm Products, Food Safety and Quality Service	18	16	16
2000	Total: Balances and receipts	19	18	17
	Appropriations:			
	Current law:			
2101	Expenses and Refunds, Inspection and Grading of Farm Products	−17	−17	−17
5099	Balance, end of year	2	1	

Program and Financing (in millions of dollars)

Identification code 012–8137–0–7–352		2021 actual	2022 est.	2023 est.
	Obligations by program activity:			
0001	Expenses and refunds, inspection and grading of farm products	17	17	17
	Budgetary resources:			
	Unobligated balance:			
1000	Unobligated balance brought forward, Oct 1	4	4	4
	Budget authority:			
	Appropriations, mandatory:			
1201	Appropriation (special or trust fund)	17	17	17
1930	Total budgetary resources available	21	21	21
	Memorandum (non-add) entries:			
1941	Unexpired unobligated balance, end of year	4	4	4
	Change in obligated balance:			
	Unpaid obligations:			
3000	Unpaid obligations, brought forward, Oct 1	1	1	
3010	New obligations, unexpired accounts	17	17	17
3020	Outlays (gross)	−17	−18	−17
3050	Unpaid obligations, end of year	1		
	Memorandum (non-add) entries:			
3100	Obligated balance, start of year	1	1	
3200	Obligated balance, end of year	1		
	Budget authority and outlays, net:			
	Mandatory:			
4090	Budget authority, gross	17	17	17
	Outlays, gross:			
4100	Outlays from new mandatory authority	13	17	17
4101	Outlays from mandatory balances	4	1	
4110	Outlays, gross (total)	17	18	17
4180	Budget authority, net (total)	17	17	17
4190	Outlays, net (total)	17	18	17

Under authority of the Agricultural Marketing Act of 1946, Federal meat and poultry inspection services are provided upon request and for a fee in cases where inspection is not mandated by statute. This service includes: certifying products for export beyond the requirements of export certificates; inspecting certain animals and poultry intended for human food where inspection is not required by statute, such as buffalo, rabbit, deer, and quail; and inspecting products intended for animal consumption.

EXPENSES AND REFUNDS, INSPECTION AND GRADING OF FARM PRODUCTS—Continued

Object Classification (in millions of dollars)

Identification code 012–8137–0–7–352	2021 actual	2022 est.	2023 est.
Direct obligations:			
Personnel compensation:			
11.1 Full-time permanent	8	8	8
11.5 Other personnel compensation	4	4	4
11.9 Total personnel compensation	12	12	12
12.1 Civilian personnel benefits	3	3	3
21.0 Travel and transportation of persons	1	1	1
25.2 Other services from non-Federal sources	1	1	1
99.9 Total new obligations, unexpired accounts	17	17	17

Employment Summary

Identification code 012–8137–0–7–352	2021 actual	2022 est.	2023 est.
1001 Direct civilian full-time equivalent employment	90	90	90

AGRICULTURAL MARKETING SERVICE

Federal Funds

MARKETING SERVICES

For necessary expenses of the Agricultural Marketing Service, $232,960,000, of which $6,000,000 shall be available for the purposes of section 12306 of Public Law 113–79: Provided, That this appropriation shall be available pursuant to law (7 U.S.C. 2250) for the alteration and repair of buildings and improvements, but the cost of altering any one building during the fiscal year shall not exceed 10 percent of the current replacement value of the building.

Fees may be collected for the cost of standardization activities, as established by regulation pursuant to law (31 U.S.C. 9701), except for the cost of activities relating to the development or maintenance of grain standards under the United States Grain Standards Act, 7 U.S.C. 71 et seq.

LIMITATION ON ADMINISTRATIVE EXPENSES

Not to exceed $62,596,000 (from fees collected) shall be obligated during the current fiscal year for administrative expenses: Provided, That if crop size is understated and/or other uncontrollable events occur, the agency may exceed this limitation by up to 10 percent with notification to the Committees on Appropriations of both Houses of Congress.

Note.—A full-year 2022 appropriation for this account was not enacted at the time the Budget was prepared; therefore, the Budget assumes this account is operating under the Continuing Appropriations Act, 2022 (Division A of Public Law 117–43, as amended). The amounts included for 2022 reflect the annualized level provided by the continuing resolution.

Program and Financing (in millions of dollars)

Identification code 012–2500–0–1–352	2021 actual	2022 est.	2023 est.
Obligations by program activity:			
0001 Market news service	34	35	37
0002 Inspection and standardization	8	8	8
0003 Market protection and promotion	49	41	43
0004 Transportation and market development	10	9	10
0005 National Bioengineered Food Disclosure Standard	2	2	2
0006 Packers and Stockyards	21	24	36
0007 Grain Regulatory	17	19	20
0008 U.S. Warehouse Act	10	10	11
0009 International Food Procurement	9	9	9
0010 Dairy Business Innovation Centers	2	22	22
0011 ACER Access and Development	6	6	6
0012 GSA Rent & DHS Security	5	4	6
0013 Hemp Production	12	14	16
0014 Farmers Market and Local Program	34	7	7
0091 Direct program activities, subtotal	219	210	233
0687 Emergency Funding	....	500	....
0688 Supplemental Funding	7	200	....
0689 CARES ACT	32	....	....
0691 Direct program activities, subtotal	39	700	....
0799 Total direct obligations	258	910	233
0801 Marketing Services (Reimbursable)	154	166	166
0900 Total new obligations, unexpired accounts	412	1,076	399
Budgetary resources:			
Unobligated balance:			
1000 Unobligated balance brought forward, Oct 1	128	1,120	454
1001 Discretionary unobligated balance brought fwd, Oct 1	78		
1021 Recoveries of prior year unpaid obligations	3	....	....
1070 Unobligated balance (total)	131	1,120	454
Budget authority:			
Appropriations, discretionary:			
1100 Appropriation	210	210	233
1120 Appropriations transferred to other acct [012–4609]	–3	....	....
1160 Appropriation, discretionary (total)	207	210	233
Appropriations, mandatory:			
1200 Appropriation	522	....	....
1222 Exercised borrowing authority transferred from other accounts [012–4336]	536	36	36
1230 Appropriations and/or unobligated balance of appropriations permanently reduced	–2	–2	–2
1260 Appropriations, mandatory (total)	1,056	34	34
Spending authority from offsetting collections, discretionary:			
1700 Collected	110	166	166
1701 Change in uncollected payments, Federal sources	35	....	....
1750 Spending auth from offsetting collections, disc (total)	145	166	166
1900 Budget authority (total)	1,408	410	433
1930 Total budgetary resources available	1,539	1,530	887
Memorandum (non-add) entries:			
1940 Unobligated balance expiring	–7	....	....
1941 Unexpired unobligated balance, end of year	1,120	454	488
Change in obligated balance:			
Unpaid obligations:			
3000 Unpaid obligations, brought forward, Oct 1	186	203	452
3010 New obligations, unexpired accounts	412	1,076	399
3011 Obligations ("upward adjustments"), expired accounts	3	26	26
3020 Outlays (gross)	–389	–853	–700
3040 Recoveries of prior year unpaid obligations, unexpired	–3	....	....
3041 Recoveries of prior year unpaid obligations, expired	–6	....	....
3050 Unpaid obligations, end of year	203	452	177
Uncollected payments:			
3060 Uncollected pymts, Fed sources, brought forward, Oct 1	–52	–66	–66
3070 Change in uncollected pymts, Fed sources, unexpired	–35	....	....
3071 Change in uncollected pymts, Fed sources, expired	21	....	....
3090 Uncollected pymts, Fed sources, end of year	–66	–66	–66
Memorandum (non-add) entries:			
3100 Obligated balance, start of year	134	137	386
3200 Obligated balance, end of year	137	386	111
Budget authority and outlays, net:			
Discretionary:			
4000 Budget authority, gross	352	376	399
Outlays, gross:			
4010 Outlays from new discretionary authority	211	263	279
4011 Outlays from discretionary balances	152	135	111
4020 Outlays, gross (total)	363	398	390
Offsets against gross budget authority and outlays:			
Offsetting collections (collected) from:			
4030 Federal sources	–83	–79	–79
4033 Non-Federal sources	–45	–87	–87
4040 Offsets against gross budget authority and outlays (total)	–128	–166	–166
Additional offsets against gross budget authority only:			
4050 Change in uncollected pymts, Fed sources, unexpired	–35	....	....
4052 Offsetting collections credited to expired accounts	18	....	....
4060 Additional offsets against budget authority only (total)	–17	....	....
4070 Budget authority, net (discretionary)	207	210	233
4080 Outlays, net (discretionary)	235	232	224
Mandatory:			
4090 Budget authority, gross	1,056	34	34
Outlays, gross:			
4100 Outlays from new mandatory authority	2	8	8
4101 Outlays from mandatory balances	24	447	302
4110 Outlays, gross (total)	26	455	310
4180 Budget authority, net (total)	1,263	244	267
4190 Outlays, net (total)	261	687	534

The 2023 Budget requests about $233 million for the Agricultural Marketing Service (AMS) Marketing Services account. The following Marketing Services activities assist producers and handlers of agricultural commodities by providing a variety of marketing-related services. These services continue to become more complex as the volume of agricultural commodities increases, as greater numbers of new processed commodities are developed, and as the agricultural market structure undergoes extensive changes. Marketing changes include increased concentration in food retailing, direct buying, decentralization of processing, growth of interregional competition, vertical integration, and contract farming. The activities include:

Market News Service.—The market news program provides the agricultural community with information pertaining to the movement of agricultural products. This nationwide service provides daily reports on the supply, demand, and price of nearly 1,000 commodities on domestic and foreign markets.

Grain Regulatory Program.—This program promotes and enforces the accurate and uniform application of the U.S. Grain Standards Act; identifies, evaluates, and implements new or improved techniques for measuring grain quality; and establishes and updates testing and grading standards to facilitate the marketing of U.S. grain, oilseeds, and related products.

Hemp Production Program.—This program provides a national regulatory framework for commercial production of industrial hemp in the U.S. through regulations and guidance. In addition to those regulated under USDA plans, USDA approves state and Tribal nation plans to provide licensing services, technical assistance, compliance, and program management support.

National Bioengineered Food Disclosure Standard.—Public Law 114–216 charges AMS with developing a national mandatory system for disclosing the presence of bioengineered material. This will increase consumers' confidence and understanding of the foods they buy, and avoid uncertainty for food companies and farmers.

Inspection, Grading and Standardization.—Nationally uniform standards of quality for agricultural products are established and applied to specific lots of products to: promote confidence between buyers and sellers; reduce hazards in marketing due to misunderstandings and disputes arising from the use of nonstandard descriptions; and encourage better preparation of uniform quality products for market. Grading services are provided on request for cotton and tobacco. The program inspections of egg handlers quarterly and hatcheries annually to ensure the proper disposition of shell eggs unfit for human consumption.

MARKET NEWS PROGRAM

	2021 actual	2022 est.	2023 est.
Percentage of reports released on time	96%	96%	96%

COTTON AND TOBACCO USER FEE PROGRAM

	2021 actual	2022 est.	2023 est.
Cotton classed (bales in millions)	13.9	17.4	17.4
Domestic tobacco graded (million lbs)	7.0	15.0	15.0
Imported tobacco inspected (million kilograms)	4.5	4.5	4.5
Insurance Grading (for USDA Risk Management Agency) (millions of lbs)	23.6	23.5	23

FEDERALLY FUNDED INSPECTION AND MARKETING ACTIVITIES

	2021 actual	2022 est.	2023 est.
Percent of firms complying with EPIA and the Shell Egg Surveillance program	97%	97%	97%

STANDARDIZATION ACTIVITIES

	2021 actual	2022 est.	2023 est.
U.S. and international standards revised, eliminated, or approved	625	742	742

Market Protection and Promotion.—This program consists of: 1) the industry-funded research and promotion programs which are designed to improve the competitive position and expand markets for a variety of agricultural commodities; 2) the Federal Seed Act; 3) the Pesticide Data Program; 4) Country of Origin Labeling; and 5) the National Organic Program. The Pesticide Data program develops comprehensive, statistically defensible information on pesticide residues in food to improve government dietary risk procedures. Federal seed inspectors conduct tests on seed samples to help ensure truthful labeling of agricultural and vegetable seeds sold in interstate commerce. Currently, 22 research and promotion programs (also referred to as "check-off" programs), are operated by commodity groups to pool resources for advertising campaigns, market research, new product development, and consumer education. Country of Origin Labeling reviews and verifies that retailers are notifying their customers of the country of origin of certain foods as specified in the law. The National Organic Program develops national standards for organically-produced agricultural products, assuring consumers that products with the USDA organic seal meet consistent, uniform standards.

MARKET PROTECTION AND PROMOTION ACTIVITIES

	2021 actual	2022 est.	2023 est.
Pesticide data program (PDP):			
Number of foreign countries PDP contacts to share program information	42	4	4
Seed Act:			
Percentage of seed shipped that is accurately labeled	96%	97%	97%
Plant Variety Protection Act:			
Number of applications received	500	475	475
Percentage of Research and Promotion Board budgets and marketing plans approved within time frame goal	100%	100%	100%
Country of Origin Labeling:			
Percent of retailers in compliance	36%	36%	36%
State and Commonwealths with cooperative agreements	46	46	46

Transportation and Market Development.—This program is designed to enhance the marketing of domestic agricultural commodities by conducting research into more efficient marketing methods and by providing technical assistance to areas interested in improving their food distribution facilities, and by helping to ensure that the Nation's transportation systems will adequately serve the needs of agriculture and rural areas of the United States.

WHOLESALE MARKET DEVELOPMENT ACTIVITIES

	2021 actual	2022 est.	2023 est.
New markets established or expanded	272	343	314

TRANSPORTATION SERVICES ACTIVITIES

	2021 actual	2022 est.	2023 est.
Number of projects completed	117	119	113

The Packers and Stockyards Program.—This program promotes fair business practices, financial integrity, and competitive environments to market livestock, meat, and poultry. Through its oversight activities, including monitoring programs, reviews, and investigations, the Program fosters fair competition, provides payment protection, and guards against deceptive and fraudulent trade practices that affect the movement and price of meat animals and their products. The Program's work protects consumers and members of the livestock, meat, and poultry industries. The Program enforces the Packers and Stockyards (P&S) Act, which prohibits unfair, deceptive, and unjust discriminatory practices by market agencies, dealers, stockyards, packers, swine contractors, and live poultry dealers in the livestock, meat packing, and poultry industries. The P&S Act provides an important safety net for livestock producers and poultry growers in rural America. The Program issues licenses and conducts routine and ongoing regulatory inspections and audits to assess whether subject entities are operating in compliance with the Act, and conducts investigations of potential P&S Act violations identified by either industry complaints or previous regulatory inspections.

The U.S. Warehouse Act Program.—USDA supports the efficient use of commercial facilities in the storage of Commodity Credit Corporation-owned commodities, and administers the U.S. Warehouse Act (USWA) and certain provisions of the Commodity Credit Corporation (CCC) Charter Act. Its mission is to oversee the formulation of national policies and procedures to administer a nationwide warehousing system, establish posted county prices for major farm program commodities, and manage CCC commodity inventories and cotton economic assistance programs.

Agricultural Marketing Service—Continued
Federal Funds—Continued

MARKETING SERVICES—Continued

The International Food Procurement Program.—AMS purchases, through reimburseable agreements, and delivers U.S. commodities for international food aid programs for overseas use to meet USDA and USAID program requirements, assisting vulnerable population around the world.

The Acer Access and Development Program.—As authorized under section 12306 of the 2014 Farm Bill (P.L. 113–79), AMS awards grants to support the efforts of states, tribal governments, and research institutions to promote the domestic maple syrup industry.

Dairy Business Innovation Centers.—Dairy Business Innovation Initiatives provide valuable technical assistance and sub-grants to dairy farmers and businesses across their regions, assisting them with business plan development, marketing and branding, as well as increasing access to innovative production and processing techniques to support the development of value-added products.

Object Classification (in millions of dollars)

Identification code 012–2500–0–1–352		2021 actual	2022 est.	2023 est.
	Direct obligations:			
	Personnel compensation:			
11.1	Full-time permanent	62	62	75
11.3	Other than full-time permanent	1	1	1
11.5	Other personnel compensation	27	1	22
11.9	Total personnel compensation	90	64	98
12.1	Civilian personnel benefits	26	23	35
21.0	Travel and transportation of persons	1	1	2
22.0	Transportation of things	1	....	....
23.1	Rental payments to GSA	5	5	5
23.2	Rental payments to others	1	1	1
23.3	Communications, utilities, and miscellaneous charges	3	2	2
24.0	Printing and reproduction	2	....	....
25.2	Other services from non-Federal sources	54	50	41
25.3	Other goods and services from Federal sources	13	30	28
25.4	Operation and maintenance of facilities	13	1	....
25.7	Operation and maintenance of equipment	1	1	1
26.0	Supplies and materials	1	501	1
31.0	Equipment	3	3	3
41.0	Grants, subsidies, and contributions	44	228	16
99.0	Direct obligations	258	910	233
99.0	Reimbursable obligations	154	166	166
99.9	Total new obligations, unexpired accounts	412	1,076	399

Employment Summary

Identification code 012–2500–0–1–352	2021 actual	2022 est.	2023 est.
1001 Direct civilian full-time equivalent employment	665	732	762
2001 Reimbursable civilian full-time equivalent employment	382	517	517

PAYMENTS TO STATES AND POSSESSIONS

For payments to departments of agriculture, bureaus and departments of markets, and similar agencies for marketing activities under section 204(b) of the Agricultural Marketing Act of 1946 (7 U.S.C. 1623(b)), $1,235,000.

Note.—A full-year 2022 appropriation for this account was not enacted at the time the Budget was prepared; therefore, the Budget assumes this account is operating under the Continuing Appropriations Act, 2022 (Division A of Public Law 117–43, as amended). The amounts included for 2022 reflect the annualized level provided by the continuing resolution.

Program and Financing (in millions of dollars)

Identification code 012–2501–0–1–352		2021 actual	2022 est.	2023 est.
	Obligations by program activity:			
0001	Payments to states and possessions	1	1	1
0002	Specialty crop block grants	83	83	83
0004	Micro Grants for Food Security	5	5	....
0900	Total new obligations, unexpired accounts	89	89	84
	Budgetary resources:			
	Unobligated balance:			
1000	Unobligated balance brought forward, Oct 1	14	111	108
1001	Discretionary unobligated balance brought fwd, Oct 1	5	....	....
	Budget authority:			
	Appropriations, discretionary:			
1100	Appropriation	6	6	1
	Appropriations, mandatory:			
1200	Appropriation	100	....	....
1222	Exercised borrowing authority transferred from other accounts [012–4336]	85	85	85
1230	Appropriations and/or unobligated balance of appropriations permanently reduced	−5	−5	−5
1260	Appropriations, mandatory (total)	180	80	80
1900	Budget authority (total)	186	86	81
1930	Total budgetary resources available	200	197	189
	Memorandum (non-add) entries:			
1941	Unexpired unobligated balance, end of year	111	108	105
	Change in obligated balance:			
	Unpaid obligations:			
3000	Unpaid obligations, brought forward, Oct 1	203	220	186
3010	New obligations, unexpired accounts	89	89	84
3011	Obligations ("upward adjustments"), expired accounts	....	....	12
3020	Outlays (gross)	−69	−123	−113
3041	Recoveries of prior year unpaid obligations, expired	−3	....	....
3050	Unpaid obligations, end of year	220	186	169
	Memorandum (non-add) entries:			
3100	Obligated balance, start of year	203	220	186
3200	Obligated balance, end of year	220	186	169
	Budget authority and outlays, net:			
	Discretionary:			
4000	Budget authority, gross	6	6	1
	Outlays, gross:			
4010	Outlays from new discretionary authority	....	2	....
4011	Outlays from discretionary balances	2	4	4
4020	Outlays, gross (total)	2	6	4
	Mandatory:			
4090	Budget authority, gross	180	80	80
	Outlays, gross:			
4100	Outlays from new mandatory authority	2	....	−5
4101	Outlays from mandatory balances	65	117	114
4110	Outlays, gross (total)	67	117	109
4180	Budget authority, net (total)	186	86	81
4190	Outlays, net (total)	69	123	113

The discretionary funds in this account are for Federal-State Marketing Improvement Program grants, which are made on a matching fund basis to State departments of agriculture to carry out specifically approved value-added programs designed to the spotlight local marketing initiatives and enhance marketing efficiency. Under this activity, specialists work with farmers, marketing firms, and other agencies in solving marketing problems and in using research results. The mandatory funds in this account are for Specialty Crop Block Grant-Farm Bill grants, which are block grants made to State departments of agriculture to enhance the competitiveness of specialty crops.

Object Classification (in millions of dollars)

Identification code 012–2501–0–1–352		2021 actual	2022 est.	2023 est.
	Direct obligations:			
11.1	Personnel compensation: Full-time permanent	1	1	1
12.1	Civilian personnel benefits	1	1	1
25.3	Other goods and services from Federal sources	2	2	2
41.0	Grants, subsidies, and contributions	85	85	80
99.9	Total new obligations, unexpired accounts	89	89	84

Employment Summary

Identification code 012–2501–0–1–352	2021 actual	2022 est.	2023 est.
1001 Direct civilian full-time equivalent employment	11	12	13

FEE FUNDED INSPECTION, WEIGHING, AND EXAMINATION SERVICES

LIMITATION ON INSPECTION AND WEIGHING SERVICES EXPENSES

Not to exceed $55,000,000 (from fees collected) shall be obligated during the current fiscal year for inspection and weighing services: Provided, That if grain export activities require additional supervision and oversight, or other uncontrollable factors occur, this limitation may be exceeded by up to 10 percent with notification to the Committees on Appropriations of both Houses of Congress.

Note.—A full-year 2022 appropriation for this account was not enacted at the time the Budget was prepared; therefore, the Budget assumes this account is operating under the Continuing Appropriations Act, 2022 (Division A of Public Law 117–43, as amended). The amounts included for 2022 reflect the annualized level provided by the continuing resolution.

Program and Financing (in millions of dollars)

Identification code 012–4050–0–3–352		2021 actual	2022 est.	2023 est.
	Obligations by program activity:			
0801	Limitation on inspection and weighing services	46	55	55
	Budgetary resources:			
	Unobligated balance:			
1000	Unobligated balance brought forward, Oct 1	18	15	15
1021	Recoveries of prior year unpaid obligations	1		
1070	Unobligated balance (total)	19	15	15
	Budget authority:			
	Spending authority from offsetting collections, mandatory:			
1800	Collected [Inspection and Weighing Services]	43	55	55
1801	Change in uncollected payments, Federal sources	–1		
1802	Offsetting collections (previously unavailable)	3	2	2
1823	New and/or unobligated balance of spending authority from offsetting collections temporarily reduced	–3	–2	–2
1850	Spending auth from offsetting collections, mand (total)	42	55	55
1930	Total budgetary resources available	61	70	70
	Memorandum (non-add) entries:			
1941	Unexpired unobligated balance, end of year	15	15	15
	Change in obligated balance:			
	Unpaid obligations:			
3000	Unpaid obligations, brought forward, Oct 1	6	6	2
3010	New obligations, unexpired accounts	46	55	55
3020	Outlays (gross)	–45	–59	–53
3040	Recoveries of prior year unpaid obligations, unexpired	–1		
3050	Unpaid obligations, end of year	6	2	4
	Uncollected payments:			
3060	Uncollected pymts, Fed sources, brought forward, Oct 1	–7	–6	–6
3070	Change in uncollected pymts, Fed sources, unexpired	1		
3090	Uncollected pymts, Fed sources, end of year	–6	–6	–6
	Memorandum (non-add) entries:			
3100	Obligated balance, start of year	–1		–4
3200	Obligated balance, end of year		–4	–2
	Budget authority and outlays, net:			
	Mandatory:			
4090	Budget authority, gross	42	55	55
	Outlays, gross:			
4100	Outlays from new mandatory authority	34	53	53
4101	Outlays from mandatory balances	11	6	
4110	Outlays, gross (total)	45	59	53
	Offsets against gross budget authority and outlays:			
	Offsetting collections (collected) from:			
4123	Non-Federal sources	–43	–55	–55
	Additional offsets against gross budget authority only:			
4140	Change in uncollected pymts, Fed sources, unexpired	1		
4170	Outlays, net (mandatory)	2	4	–2
4180	Budget authority, net (total)			
4190	Outlays, net (total)	2	4	–2
	Memorandum (non-add) entries:			
5090	Unexpired unavailable balance, SOY: Offsetting collections	3	3	3
5092	Unexpired unavailable balance, EOY: Offsetting collections	3	3	3

AMS provides a uniform system for the inspection and weighing of grain and related products for marketing and trade purposes. Services provided under this system accurately and consistently describe the quality and quantity of grain and are partially financed through a fee-supported revolving fund. Fee-supported programs include direct services, supervision activities and administrative functions. Direct services include official grain inspection and weighing by AMS employees at certain export ports as well as the inspection of U.S. grain shipped through Canada. AMS supervises the inspection and weighing activities performed by its own employees. AMS also supervises 42 official private and state agencies: 32 official private agencies and six official state agencies that are designated to provide official inspection and/or weighing services in domestic and export (international containers and land based carriers to Canada and Mexico) markets; three official state agencies that are delegated to provide mandatory official export inspection and weighing services and designated to provide official domestic inspection and weighing services within the state; and one official state agency that is delegated to provide mandatory official export inspection and weighing services within the state. AMS provides an appeal service of original grain inspections and a registration system for the grain exporting firms. Through support from user fees, AMS conducts a railroad track scale testing program. In addition, AMS provides grading services, on request, for rice, graded commodities, and processed products under the authority of the Agricultural Marketing Act of 1946.

	2021 actual	2022 est.	2023 est.
Export standardized grain inspected and/or weighed (million metric tons):			
By Federal personnel	90.8	85.7	85.7
By delegated states/official agencies	60.4	65.4	65.4
Quantity of standardized grain inspected (official inspections) domestically (million metric tons)	198	195.3	195.3
Number of official grain inspections and reinspections:			
By Federal personnel	109,436	99,834	99,834
By delegated states/official agencies	3,176,284	2,710,280	2,710,280
Number of appeals (Grain, Rice, and Pulses)	2,012	2,100	2,100
Number of appeals to the Board of Appeals and Review (Grain, Rice, and Pulses)	176	200	200

Object Classification (in millions of dollars)

Identification code 012–4050–0–3–352		2021 actual	2022 est.	2023 est.
	Reimbursable obligations:			
	Personnel compensation:			
11.1	Full-time permanent	19	20	20
11.3	Other than full-time permanent	1	1	1
11.5	Other personnel compensation	7	8	8
11.9	Total personnel compensation	27	29	29
12.1	Civilian personnel benefits	9	10	10
21.0	Travel and transportation of persons	1	1	1
23.2	Rental payments to others	1	1	1
23.3	Communications, utilities, and miscellaneous charges	1	1	1
25.2	Other services from non-Federal sources	1	5	5
25.3	Other goods and services from Federal sources	4	6	6
26.0	Supplies and materials	1	1	1
31.0	Equipment	1	1	1
99.9	Total new obligations, unexpired accounts	46	55	55

Employment Summary

Identification code 012–4050–0–3–352	2021 actual	2022 est.	2023 est.
2001 Reimbursable civilian full-time equivalent employment	360	421	421

PERISHABLE AGRICULTURAL COMMODITIES ACT FUND

Special and Trust Fund Receipts (in millions of dollars)

Identification code 012–5070–0–2–352		2021 actual	2022 est.	2023 est.
0100	Balance, start of year	1	1	1
	Receipts:			
	Current law:			
1110	License Fees and Defaults, Perishable Agricultural Commodities Act Fund	11	11	12
2000	Total: Balances and receipts	12	12	13
	Appropriations:			
	Current law:			
2101	Perishable Agricultural Commodities Act Fund	–11	–11	–11
2103	Perishable Agricultural Commodities Act Fund	–1	–1	–1
2132	Perishable Agricultural Commodities Act Fund	1	1	1
2199	Total current law appropriations	–11	–11	–11

Agricultural Marketing Service—Continued
Federal Funds—Continued

PERISHABLE AGRICULTURAL COMMODITIES ACT FUND—Continued

Special and Trust Fund Receipts—Continued

Identification code 012–5070–0–2–352		2021 actual	2022 est.	2023 est.
2999	Total appropriations	–11	–11	–11
5099	Balance, end of year	1	1	2

Program and Financing (in millions of dollars)

Identification code 012–5070–0–2–352		2021 actual	2022 est.	2023 est.
	Obligations by program activity:			
0001	Perishable Agricultural Commodities Act	11	11	11
	Budgetary resources:			
	Unobligated balance:			
1000	Unobligated balance brought forward, Oct 1	18	18	18
	Budget authority:			
	Appropriations, mandatory:			
1201	Appropriation (special or trust fund)	11	11	11
1203	Appropriation (previously unavailable)(special or trust)	1	1	1
1232	Appropriations and/or unobligated balance of appropriations temporarily reduced	–1	–1	–1
1260	Appropriations, mandatory (total)	11	11	11
1930	Total budgetary resources available	29	29	29
	Memorandum (non-add) entries:			
1941	Unexpired unobligated balance, end of year	18	18	18
	Change in obligated balance:			
	Unpaid obligations:			
3000	Unpaid obligations, brought forward, Oct 1	1	1	1
3010	New obligations, unexpired accounts	11	11	11
3020	Outlays (gross)	–11	–11	–11
3050	Unpaid obligations, end of year	1	1	1
	Memorandum (non-add) entries:			
3100	Obligated balance, start of year	1	1	1
3200	Obligated balance, end of year	1	1	1
	Budget authority and outlays, net:			
	Mandatory:			
4090	Budget authority, gross	11	11	11
	Outlays, gross:			
4100	Outlays from new mandatory authority		10	10
4101	Outlays from mandatory balances	11	1	1
4110	Outlays, gross (total)	11	11	11
4180	Budget authority, net (total)	11	11	11
4190	Outlays, net (total)	11	11	11

License fees are deposited in this special fund and are used to meet the costs of administering the Perishable Agricultural Commodities and the Produce Agency Acts (7 U.S.C. 491–497, 499a–499s).

The Perishable Agricultural Commodities Act (PACA) establishes a code of fair trading practices covering the marketing of fresh and frozen fruits and vegetables in interstate and foreign commerce. The PACA protects growers, shippers, distributors, retailers, and others who deal in those commodities by prohibiting unfair and fraudulent practices. In general, individuals and companies operating in the produce industry who meet certain requirements must be licensed under the PACA. PACA investigates complaints of violations of the Act through: a) informal agreements between the two publication of the facts; b) formal decisions involving payment of reparation awards; c) suspension or revocation of license and/or publication of the facts; or d) monetary penalty in lieu of license suspension or revocation.

The Perishable Agricultural Commodities Act requires that purchasers maintain trust assets on hand to meet their obligations to fruit and vegetable suppliers. The trust automatically goes into effect when the buyer receives the goods but produce sellers must notify their customers in writing of their intent to preserve their trust rights. The Act provides permanent authority to the Secretary of Agriculture to set license and reparation complaint filing fees.

PERISHABLE AGRICULTURAL COMMODITIES ACT ACTIVITIES

	2021 actual	2022 est.	2023 est.
Percentage of informal reparation complaints completed within time frame goal	86%	87%	87%

Object Classification (in millions of dollars)

Identification code 012–5070–0–2–352		2021 actual	2022 est.	2023 est.
	Direct obligations:			
11.1	Personnel compensation: Full-time permanent	6	6	6
12.1	Civilian personnel benefits	2	2	2
23.2	Rental payments to others	1	1	1
25.3	Other goods and services from Federal sources	2	2	2
99.9	Total new obligations, unexpired accounts	11	11	11

Employment Summary

Identification code 012–5070–0–2–352		2021 actual	2022 est.	2023 est.
1001	Direct civilian full-time equivalent employment	61	69	69

FUNDS FOR STRENGTHENING MARKETS, INCOME, AND SUPPLY (SECTION 32)

(INCLUDING TRANSFERS OF FUNDS)

Funds available under section 32 of the Act of August 24, 1935 (7 U.S.C. 612c), shall be used only for commodity program expenses as authorized therein, and other related operating expenses, except for: (1) transfers to the Department of Commerce as authorized by the Fish and Wildlife Act of 1956 (16 U.S.C. 742a et seq.); (2) transfers otherwise provided in this Act; and (3) not more than $21,501,000 for formulation and administration of marketing agreements and orders pursuant to the Agricultural Marketing Agreement Act of 1937 and the Agricultural Act of 1961 (Public Law 87–128).

Note.—A full-year 2022 appropriation for this account was not enacted at the time the Budget was prepared; therefore, the Budget assumes this account is operating under the Continuing Appropriations Act, 2022 (Division A of Public Law 117–43, as amended). The amounts included for 2022 reflect the annualized level provided by the continuing resolution.

Special and Trust Fund Receipts (in millions of dollars)

Identification code 012–5209–0–2–605		2021 actual	2022 est.	2023 est.
0100	Balance, start of year	41,019	44,071	50,257
	Receipts:			
	Current law:			
1110	30 Percent of Customs Duties, Funds for Strengthening Markets, Income and Supply (section 32)	25,672	27,791	16,183
1140	General Fund Payment, Funds for Strengthening Markets, Income, and Supply (section 32)		1	1
1199	Total current law receipts	25,672	27,792	16,184
1999	Total receipts	25,672	27,792	16,184
2000	Total: Balances and receipts	66,691	71,863	66,441
	Appropriations:			
	Current law:			
2101	Funds for Strengthening Markets, Income, and Supply (section 32)	–22,697	–21,679	–27,123
2132	Funds for Strengthening Markets, Income, and Supply (section 32)	71	73	78
2135	Funds for Strengthening Markets, Income, and Supply (section 32)	6		
2199	Total current law appropriations	–22,620	–21,606	–27,045
2999	Total appropriations	–22,620	–21,606	–27,045
5099	Balance, end of year	44,071	50,257	39,396

Program and Financing (in millions of dollars)

Identification code 012–5209–0–2–605		2021 actual	2022 est.	2023 est.
	Obligations by program activity:			
0001	Child nutrition program purchases	495	485	485
0002	Emergency surplus removal	710	411	521
0004	State option contract		5	5
0005	Removal of defective commodities		3	3
0006	Disaster Relief		5	5
0007	2008 Farm Bill Specialty Crop Purchases		206	206

DEPARTMENT OF AGRICULTURE

Agricultural Marketing Service—Continued
Trust Funds

		2021 actual	2022 est.	2023 est.
0091	Subtotal, Commodity program payments	1,205	1,115	1,225
0101	Administrative expenses	54	57	59
0192	Total direct program	1,259	1,172	1,284
0799	Total direct obligations	1,259	1,172	1,284
0811	Funds for Strengthening Markets, Income, and Supply (section 32) (Reimbursable)	7	5	5
0900	Total new obligations, unexpired accounts	1,266	1,177	1,289
	Budgetary resources:			
	Unobligated balance:			
1000	Unobligated balance brought forward, Oct 1	428	378	378
1021	Recoveries of prior year unpaid obligations	74		
1070	Unobligated balance (total)	502	378	378
	Budget authority:			
	Appropriations, discretionary:			
1130	Appropriations permanently reduced		–31	
	Appropriations, mandatory:			
1201	Appropriation (special or trust fund)	22,697	21,679	27,123
1220	Transferred to Food and Nutrition Service [012–3539]	–21,223	–20,149	–25,398
1220	Transferred to Department of Commerce [013–5139]	–262	–254	–363
1232	Appropriations and/or unobligated balance of appropriations temporarily reduced	–71	–73	–78
1235	Appropriations precluded from obligation (special or trust)	–6		
1260	Appropriations, mandatory (total)	1,135	1,203	1,284
	Spending authority from offsetting collections, mandatory:			
1800	Collected	7	5	5
1900	Budget authority (total)	1,142	1,177	1,289
1930	Total budgetary resources available	1,644	1,555	1,667
	Memorandum (non-add) entries:			
1941	Unexpired unobligated balance, end of year	378	378	378
	Change in obligated balance:			
	Unpaid obligations:			
3000	Unpaid obligations, brought forward, Oct 1	859	561	577
3010	New obligations, unexpired accounts	1,266	1,177	1,289
3020	Outlays (gross)	–1,490	–1,161	–1,239
3040	Recoveries of prior year unpaid obligations, unexpired	–74		
3050	Unpaid obligations, end of year	561	577	627
	Uncollected payments:			
3060	Uncollected pymts, Fed sources, brought forward, Oct 1	–2	–2	–2
3090	Uncollected pymts, Fed sources, end of year	–2	–2	–2
	Memorandum (non-add) entries:			
3100	Obligated balance, start of year	857	559	575
3200	Obligated balance, end of year	559	575	625
	Budget authority and outlays, net:			
	Discretionary:			
4000	Budget authority, gross		–31	
	Mandatory:			
4090	Budget authority, gross	1,142	1,208	1,289
	Outlays, gross:			
4100	Outlays from new mandatory authority	701	842	898
4101	Outlays from mandatory balances	789	319	341
4110	Outlays, gross (total)	1,490	1,161	1,239
	Offsets against gross budget authority and outlays:			
	Offsetting collections (collected) from:			
4120	Federal sources	–7	–5	–5
4180	Budget authority, net (total)	1,135	1,172	1,284
4190	Outlays, net (total)	1,483	1,156	1,234

Funds for Strengthening Markets, Income, and Supply (Section 32) Program.—The Agriculture Appropriations Act of 1935 (7 U.S.C. 612c) established the Section 32 program, which provides that 30 percent of U.S. Customs receipts for each calendar year are transferred to this account within the Department of Agriculture. The purpose of the Section 32 program is three-fold: to encourage the exportation of agricultural commodities and products, to encourage domestic consumption of agricultural products by diverting them, and to reestablish farmers' purchasing power by making payments in connection with the normal production of any agricultural commodity for domestic consumption. There is also a requirement that the funds available under Section 32 shall be principally devoted to perishable agricultural commodities (e.g., fruits and vegetables). Program funds are used for a variety of purposes in support of the three primary purposes specified in the program's authorizing legislation. Funds may be used to stabilize market conditions through purchasing surplus commodities which are in turn, distributed to nutrition assistance programs. A General Provision in this Budget proposes that carryover funds, with certain limitations, may be used to make direct payments under clause 3 of the authorizing legislation. Program funds are also used to purchase commodities that are distributed to schools as part of Child Nutrition Programs entitlements. Furthermore, the majority of these funds are transferred to the Food and Nutrition Service for commodity purchases under section 6 of the National School Lunch Act and other authorities specified in the Child Nutrition Programs statutes.

Marketing Agreements & Orders Program (MA&O).— MA&O programs are authorized by the Agricultural Marketing Agreement Act of 1937 ("AMAA"), as amended, 7 U.S.C. 60127; 67174. MA&O are binding on industry segments and regulate the marketing and handling of detain dairy and specialty crops. The Orders are administered locally by marketing order committees and market administrators whose costs are funded through assessments on regulated handlers. Funds from Section 32 pay for the Federal costs of overseeing the MA&O program. Some costs are funded through assessments on regulated handlers.

Object Classification (in millions of dollars)

Identification code 012–5209–0–2–605		2021 actual	2022 est.	2023 est.
	Direct obligations:			
11.1	Personnel compensation: Full-time permanent	15	16	18
12.1	Civilian personnel benefits	5	6	7
21.0	Travel and transportation of persons		1	1
22.0	Transportation of things	1	1	1
23.3	Communications, utilities, and miscellaneous charges	1	1	1
24.0	Printing and reproduction		1	1
25.2	Other services from non-Federal sources	14	9	9
25.3	Other goods and services from Federal sources	21	21	21
26.0	Supplies and materials: Grants of commodities to States	1,201	1,115	1,224
31.0	Equipment	1	1	1
99.0	Direct obligations	1,259	1,172	1,284
99.0	Reimbursable obligations	7	5	5
99.9	Total new obligations, unexpired accounts	1,266	1,177	1,289

Employment Summary

Identification code 012–5209–0–2–605	2021 actual	2022 est.	2023 est.
1001 Direct civilian full-time equivalent employment	134	154	154
2001 Reimbursable civilian full-time equivalent employment	36	32	36

Trust Funds

EXPENSES AND REFUNDS, INSPECTION AND GRADING OF FARM PRODUCTS

Special and Trust Fund Receipts (in millions of dollars)

Identification code 012–8015–0–7–352		2021 actual	2022 est.	2023 est.
0100	Balance, start of year			2
	Receipts:			
	Current law:			
1130	Deposits of Fees, Inspection and Grading of Farm Products, AMS	197	169	174
1140	Interest on Investments in Public Debt Securities, AMS		1	1
1140	Payments from General Fund, Wool Research, Development, and Promotion Trust Fund	2	2	2
1199	Total current law receipts	199	172	177
1999	Total receipts	199	172	177
2000	Total: Balances and receipts	199	172	179
	Appropriations:			
	Current law:			
2101	Expenses and Refunds, Inspection and Grading of Farm Products	–199	–170	–175
5099	Balance, end of year		2	4

Agricultural Marketing Service—Continued
Trust Funds—Continued

EXPENSES AND REFUNDS, INSPECTION AND GRADING OF FARM PRODUCTS—Continued

Program and Financing (in millions of dollars)

Identification code 012–8015–0–7–352	2021 actual	2022 est.	2023 est.
Obligations by program activity:			
0001 Dairy products	10	7	8
0002 Specialty Crops	65	65	65
0003 Meat grading	25	23	23
0004 Poultry products	61	47	51
0005 Miscellaneous agricultural commodities	14	26	26
0006 Ware Houses	4	4	4
0900 Total new obligations, unexpired accounts	179	172	177
Budgetary resources:			
Unobligated balance:			
1000 Unobligated balance brought forward, Oct 1	75	100	100
1021 Recoveries of prior year unpaid obligations	3		
1070 Unobligated balance (total)	78	100	100
Budget authority:			
Appropriations, mandatory:			
1201 Appropriation (special or trust fund)	199	170	175
1222 Exercised borrowing authority transferred from other accounts [012–4336]	2	2	2
1260 Appropriations, mandatory (total)	201	172	177
1930 Total budgetary resources available	279	272	277
Memorandum (non-add) entries:			
1941 Unexpired unobligated balance, end of year	100	100	100
Change in obligated balance:			
Unpaid obligations:			
3000 Unpaid obligations, brought forward, Oct 1	30	28	29
3010 New obligations, unexpired accounts	179	172	177
3020 Outlays (gross)	–178	–171	–176
3040 Recoveries of prior year unpaid obligations, unexpired	–3		
3050 Unpaid obligations, end of year	28	29	30
Memorandum (non-add) entries:			
3100 Obligated balance, start of year	30	28	29
3200 Obligated balance, end of year	28	29	30
Budget authority and outlays, net:			
Mandatory:			
4090 Budget authority, gross	201	172	177
Outlays, gross:			
4100 Outlays from new mandatory authority	100	120	124
4101 Outlays from mandatory balances	78	51	52
4110 Outlays, gross (total)	178	171	176
4180 Budget authority, net (total)	201	172	177
4190 Outlays, net (total)	178	171	176

Expenses and refunds, inspection and grading of farm products.—The Agricultural Marketing Service's commodity grading programs provide grading, examination, and certification services for a wide variety of fresh and processed food commodities using Federally approved grade standards and purchase specifications. Commodities graded include poultry, livestock, meat, dairy products, and fresh and processed fruits and vegetables. These programs use official grade standards which reflect the relative quality of a particular food commodity based on laboratory testing and characteristics such as taste, color, weight, and physical condition. Producers voluntarily request grading and certification services which are provided on a fee for service basis.

Object Classification (in millions of dollars)

Identification code 012–8015–0–7–352	2021 actual	2022 est.	2023 est.
Direct obligations:			
Personnel compensation:			
11.1 Full-time permanent	80	80	82
11.3 Other than full-time permanent	5	6	6
11.5 Other personnel compensation	1	1	1
11.9 Total personnel compensation	86	87	89
12.1 Civilian personnel benefits	38	38	39
13.0 Benefits for former personnel	1	1	1
21.0 Travel and transportation of persons	8	8	8
23.1 Rental payments to GSA	1	1	1
23.2 Rental payments to others	4	4	4
23.3 Communications, utilities, and miscellaneous charges	4	4	4
25.2 Other services from non-Federal sources	6	5	6
25.3 Other goods and services from Federal sources	26	20	21
25.7 Operation and maintenance of equipment	1	1	1
26.0 Supplies and materials	1	1	1
31.0 Equipment	1	1	1
41.0 Grants, subsidies, and contributions	2	1	1
99.9 Total new obligations, unexpired accounts	179	172	177

Employment Summary

Identification code 012–8015–0–7–352	2021 actual	2022 est.	2023 est.
1001 Direct civilian full-time equivalent employment	1,324	1,376	1,376

MILK MARKET ORDERS ASSESSMENT FUND

Program and Financing (in millions of dollars)

Identification code 012–8412–0–8–351	2021 actual	2022 est.	2023 est.
Obligations by program activity:			
0801 Administration	69	81	86
0802 Marketing service	6	10	10
0900 Total new obligations, unexpired accounts	75	91	96
Budgetary resources:			
Budget authority:			
Spending authority from offsetting collections, mandatory:			
1800 Collected	75	91	96
1802 Offsetting collections (previously unavailable)		4	4
1823 New and/or unobligated balance of spending authority from offsetting collections temporarily reduced		–4	–4
1850 Spending auth from offsetting collections, mand (total)	75	91	96
1930 Total budgetary resources available	75	91	96
Change in obligated balance:			
Unpaid obligations:			
3010 New obligations, unexpired accounts	75	91	96
3020 Outlays (gross)	–75	–91	–96
Budget authority and outlays, net:			
Mandatory:			
4090 Budget authority, gross	75	91	96
Outlays, gross:			
4100 Outlays from new mandatory authority	75	91	96
Offsets against gross budget authority and outlays:			
Offsetting collections (collected) from:			
4123 Non-Federal sources	–75	–91	–96
4180 Budget authority, net (total)			
4190 Outlays, net (total)			

The Milk Market Orders Assessment Fund displays the non-Federal costs of administrating Federal milk marketing orders, and includes salaries and expenses, travel, and rent for office space.

The Secretary of Agriculture is authorized by the Agricultural Marketing Agreement Act of 1937, to issue Federal Milk Marketing Orders (FMMO) establishing minimum prices which handlers are required to pay for milk purchased from producers. Section 1403 of the 2018 Farm Bill requires AMS to implement changes to these milk price formulas through the FMMOs. There are currently 11 Federally-sanctioned milk market orders in operation. Market administrators are appointed by the Secretary and are responsible for carrying out the terms of specific marketing orders. Their operating expenses are financed by assessments on regulated handlers and partly by deductions from producers, which are reported to the Agricultural Marketing Service.

Object Classification (in millions of dollars)

Identification code 012–8412–0–8–351	2021 actual	2022 est.	2023 est.
Reimbursable obligations:			
Personnel compensation:			
11.1 Full-time permanent	34	40	46
11.3 Other than full-time permanent	1	2	1
11.5 Other personnel compensation	1	2	2

		2021 actual	2022 est.	2023 est.
11.9	Total personnel compensation	36	44	49
12.1	Civilian personnel benefits	13	11	15
21.0	Travel and transportation of persons	1	1	1
23.2	Rental payments to others	5	10	14
23.3	Communications, utilities, and miscellaneous charges	15	15	13
25.2	Other services from non-Federal sources	1	1	1
26.0	Supplies and materials	2	6	1
31.0	Equipment	2	3	2
99.9	Total new obligations, unexpired accounts	75	91	96

Employment Summary

Identification code 012–8412–0–8–351	2021 actual	2022 est.	2023 est.
2001 Reimbursable civilian full-time equivalent employment	344	404	404

FARM PRODUCTION AND CONSERVATION

Federal Funds

SALARIES AND EXPENSES

(INCLUDING TRANSFERS OF FUNDS)

For necessary expenses of the Farm Production and Conservation Business Center, $261,783,000: Provided, That $60,228,000 of amounts appropriated for the current fiscal year pursuant to section 1241(a) of the Farm Security and Rural Investment Act of 1985 (16 U.S.C. 3841(a)) shall be transferred to and merged with this account.

Note.—A full-year 2022 appropriation for this account was not enacted at the time the Budget was prepared; therefore, the Budget assumes this account is operating under the Continuing Appropriations Act, 2022 (Division A of Public Law 117–43, as amended). The amounts included for 2022 reflect the annualized level provided by the continuing resolution.

Program and Financing (in millions of dollars)

Identification code 012–0180–0–1–351		2021 actual	2022 est.	2023 est.
	Obligations by program activity:			
0001	Direct program activity	286	292	322
0801	Reimbursable program activity	10		
0900	Total new obligations, unexpired accounts	296	292	322
	Budgetary resources:			
	Unobligated balance:			
1000	Unobligated balance brought forward, Oct 1			1
	Budget authority:			
	Appropriations, discretionary:			
1100	Appropriation	231	231	262
1121	Appropriations transferred from other acct [012–1004]		60	60
1160	Appropriation, discretionary (total)	231	291	322
	Appropriations, mandatory:			
1221	Appropriations transferred from other acct [012–1004]	60		
	Spending authority from offsetting collections, discretionary:			
1700	Collected	1	2	
1701	Change in uncollected payments, Federal sources	12		
1750	Spending auth from offsetting collections, disc (total)	13	2	
1900	Budget authority (total)	304	293	322
1930	Total budgetary resources available	304	293	323
	Memorandum (non-add) entries:			
1940	Unobligated balance expiring	–8		
1941	Unexpired unobligated balance, end of year		1	1
	Change in obligated balance:			
	Unpaid obligations:			
3000	Unpaid obligations, brought forward, Oct 1	80	69	60
3010	New obligations, unexpired accounts	296	292	322
3011	Obligations ("upward adjustments"), expired accounts	13		
3020	Outlays (gross)	–316	–301	–302
3041	Recoveries of prior year unpaid obligations, expired	–4		
3050	Unpaid obligations, end of year	69	60	80
	Uncollected payments:			
3060	Uncollected pymts, Fed sources, brought forward, Oct 1	–10	–12	–12
3070	Change in uncollected pymts, Fed sources, unexpired	–12		
3071	Change in uncollected pymts, Fed sources, expired	10		
3090	Uncollected pymts, Fed sources, end of year	–12	–12	–12
	Memorandum (non-add) entries:			
3100	Obligated balance, start of year	70	57	48
3200	Obligated balance, end of year	57	48	68
	Budget authority and outlays, net:			
	Discretionary:			
4000	Budget authority, gross	244	293	322
	Outlays, gross:			
4010	Outlays from new discretionary authority	195	235	258
4011	Outlays from discretionary balances	61	66	44
4020	Outlays, gross (total)	256	301	302
	Offsets against gross budget authority and outlays:			
	Offsetting collections (collected) from:			
4030	Federal sources	–8	–2	
	Additional offsets against gross budget authority only:			
4050	Change in uncollected pymts, Fed sources, unexpired	–12		
4052	Offsetting collections credited to expired accounts	7		
4060	Additional offsets against budget authority only (total)	–5		
4070	Budget authority, net (discretionary)	231	291	322
4080	Outlays, net (discretionary)	248	299	302
	Mandatory:			
4090	Budget authority, gross	60		
	Outlays, gross:			
4100	Outlays from new mandatory authority	60		
4180	Budget authority, net (total)	291	291	322
4190	Outlays, net (total)	308	299	302

The Farm Production and Conservation (FPAC) Business Center (FBC) is a centralized operations office within the FPAC Mission Area and headed by the Chief Operating Officer (COO), who is also the Executive Vice President, Commodity Credit Corporation (CCC). The FBC is responsible for financial management, budgeting, human resources, information technology, acquisitions/procurement, customer experience, internal controls, risk management, strategic and annual planning, and other similar activities for the FPAC Mission area and component agencies, including the Farm Service Agency (FSA), the Natural Resources Conservation Service (NRCS), and Risk Management Agency (RMA). The FBC ensures that systems, policies, procedures, and practices are developed that provide a consistent enterprise-wide view that encompasses FSA, NRCS, and RMA and the services they require from those functions to effectively and efficiently deliver programs to FPAC customers. The COO has the responsibility to ensure that FPAC administrative services are provided efficiently, effectively, and professionally and with a commitment to excellent customer service for FPAC, its customers, including farmers, ranchers, and forest landowners. The 2023 Budget requests $261.8 million in discretionary appropriations and $60.2 million in a transfer from the mandatory funding within NRCS, for a total funding amount of $322 million.

Object Classification (in millions of dollars)

Identification code 012–0180–0–1–351		2021 actual	2022 est.	2023 est.
	Direct obligations:			
	Personnel compensation:			
11.1	Full-time permanent	166	178	198
11.3	Other than full-time permanent	4		
11.9	Total personnel compensation	170	178	198
12.1	Civilian personnel benefits	61	58	64
23.1	Rental payments to GSA	7	3	2
23.2	Rental payments to others		3	3
25.1	Advisory and assistance services	43	50	55
25.2	Other services from non-Federal sources	2		
31.0	Equipment	3		
99.0	Direct obligations	286	292	322
99.0	Reimbursable obligations	10		
99.9	Total new obligations, unexpired accounts	296	292	322

Employment Summary

Identification code 012–0180–0–1–351	2021 actual	2022 est.	2023 est.
1001 Direct civilian full-time equivalent employment	1,561	1,606	1,677

RISK MANAGEMENT AGENCY

Federal Funds

SALARIES AND EXPENSES

For necessary expenses of the Risk Management Agency, $75,443,000; of which $2,000,000 shall be available to research, review, and ensure actuarial soundness of new products addressing climate change; and of which $4,500,000 shall be available to conduct research and development and carry out contracting and partnerships as described under subsections 522(c) and (d) of the Federal Crop Insurance Act, as amended (7 U.S.C. 1522(c) and (d)), in addition to amounts otherwise provided for such purposes: Provided, That $1,000,000 of the amount appropriated under this heading shall be available for compliance and integrity activities required under section 516(b)(2)(C) of the Federal Crop Insurance Act of 1938 (7 U.S.C. 1516(b)(2)(C)), and shall be in addition to amounts otherwise provided for such purpose: Provided further, That not to exceed $1,000 shall be available for official reception and representation expenses, as authorized by 7 U.S.C. 1506(i).

Note.—A full-year 2022 appropriation for this account was not enacted at the time the Budget was prepared; therefore, the Budget assumes this account is operating under the Continuing Appropriations Act, 2022 (Division A of Public Law 117–43, as amended). The amounts included for 2022 reflect the annualized level provided by the continuing resolution.

Program and Financing (in millions of dollars)

Identification code 012–2707–0–1–351	2021 actual	2022 est.	2023 est.
Obligations by program activity:			
0001 Salaries and Expenses	65	67	82
0799 Total direct obligations	65	67	82
Budgetary resources:			
Budget authority:			
Appropriations, discretionary:			
1100 Appropriation	60	60	75
1120 Appropriations transferred to other acct [012–4609]	–1		
1121 Appropriations transferred from other acct [012–4085]	7		
1160 Appropriation, discretionary (total)	66	60	75
Appropriations, mandatory:			
1221 Appropriations transferred from other acct [012–4085]		7	7
1900 Budget authority (total)	66	67	82
1930 Total budgetary resources available	66	67	82
Memorandum (non-add) entries:			
1940 Unobligated balance expiring	–1		
Change in obligated balance:			
Unpaid obligations:			
3000 Unpaid obligations, brought forward, Oct 1	13	11	13
3010 New obligations, unexpired accounts	65	67	82
3020 Outlays (gross)	–65	–65	–79
3041 Recoveries of prior year unpaid obligations, expired	–2		
3050 Unpaid obligations, end of year	11	13	16
Memorandum (non-add) entries:			
3100 Obligated balance, start of year	13	11	13
3200 Obligated balance, end of year	11	13	16
Budget authority and outlays, net:			
Discretionary:			
4000 Budget authority, gross	66	60	75
Outlays, gross:			
4010 Outlays from new discretionary authority	57	48	60
4011 Outlays from discretionary balances	8	11	12
4020 Outlays, gross (total)	65	59	72
Mandatory:			
4090 Budget authority, gross		7	7
Outlays, gross:			
4100 Outlays from new mandatory authority		6	6
4101 Outlays from mandatory balances			1
4110 Outlays, gross (total)		6	7
4180 Budget authority, net (total)	66	67	82
4190 Outlays, net (total)	65	65	79

The Risk Management Agency (RMA) was established under provisions of the Federal Agriculture Improvement and Reform Act of 1996 (1996 Act), P.L. 104–127, approved April 4, 1996. RMA is responsible for administration and oversight of the crop insurance program as authorized under the Federal Crop Insurance Act (7 U.S.C. 1501 et seq.). This account includes resources to maintain ongoing operations of the Federal crop insurance program and other functions assigned to RMA. The 2023 Budget requests $75 million in discretionary funds. RMA also plans to transfer $7 million from mandatory FCIC funding for reviews, compliance and integrity under section 516(b)(2)(C) to the S&E account in 2023. By transferring these additional mandatory funds into the S&E account, RMA will be able to use these funds more efficiently and flexibly to maintain operations.

The funding level for the direct appropriation for RMA S&E reflects the shifting of activities to the Farm Production and Conservation (FPAC) Business Center, which has centralized a number of administrative and information technology operations for RMA, NRCS and FSA that were formerly performed within each of those individual agencies.

The Federal crop insurance program is delivered through private insurance companies. Certain administrative expenses incurred by the companies are reimbursed through mandatory funding that is reflected in the FCIC Fund account. RMA is provided approximately $15 million in additional mandatory funding that is authorized in the Farm Bill for specific administrative and IT related costs, and spent directly out of the FCIC fund. The funding is further enhanced by the availability of $41 million in mandatory funding from the fees collected from the sale of insurance policies, which can be for administrative and IT related costs, and spent directly out of the FCIC fund.

Object Classification (in millions of dollars)

Identification code 012–2707–0–1–351	2021 actual	2022 est.	2023 est.
11.1 Direct obligations: Personnel compensation: Full-time permanent	40	42	48
11.9 Total personnel compensation	40	42	48
12.1 Civilian personnel benefits	15	16	18
21.0 Travel and transportation of persons		1	1
23.1 Rental payments to GSA	4	4	4
25.1 Advisory and assistance services			5
25.2 Other services from non-Federal sources	1	1	3
25.3 Other goods and services from Federal sources	4	2	2
25.4 Operation and maintenance of facilities		1	1
32.0 Land and structures	1		
99.0 Direct obligations	65	67	82
99.9 Total new obligations, unexpired accounts	65	67	82

Employment Summary

Identification code 012–2707–0–1–351	2021 actual	2022 est.	2023 est.
1001 Direct civilian full-time equivalent employment	385	385	426

CORPORATIONS

The following corporations and agencies are hereby authorized to make expenditures, within the limits of funds and borrowing authority available to each such corporation or agency and in accord with law, and to make contracts and commitments without regard to fiscal year limitations as provided by section 104 of the Government Corporation Control Act as may be necessary in carrying out the programs set forth in the budget for the current fiscal year for such corporation or agency, except as hereinafter provided.

Note.—A full-year 2022 appropriation for this account was not enacted at the time the Budget was prepared; therefore, the Budget assumes this account is operating under the Continuing Appropriations Act, 2022 (Division A of Public Law 117–43, as amended). The amounts included for 2022 reflect the annualized level provided by the continuing resolution.

FEDERAL CROP INSURANCE CORPORATION FUND

For payments as authorized by section 516 of the Federal Crop Insurance Act (7 U.S.C. 1516), such sums as may be necessary, to remain available until expended.

Note.—A full-year 2022 appropriation for this account was not enacted at the time the Budget was prepared; therefore, the Budget assumes this account is operating under the Continuing Appropriations Act, 2022 (Division A of Public Law 117–43, as amended). The amounts included for 2022 reflect the annualized level provided by the continuing resolution.

Program and Financing (in millions of dollars)

Identification code 012–4085–0–3–351	2021 actual	2022 est.	2023 est.
Obligations by program activity:			
0001 Indemnities	4,264	8,884	9,630
0002 Delivery Expenses	1,907	1,719	1,736
0003 Underwriting Gains	1,517	1,638	1,837
0004 All Others	19	21	21
0005 AMA	4	4	4
0799 Total direct obligations	7,711	12,266	13,228
0801 Reimbursable program - indemnities	4,249	5,580	5,338
0802 Reimbursable program - programs and activities	37	39	39
0899 Total reimbursable obligations	4,286	5,619	5,377
0900 Total new obligations, unexpired accounts	11,997	17,885	18,605
Budgetary resources:			
Unobligated balance:			
1000 Unobligated balance brought forward, Oct 1	595	591	591
1021 Recoveries of prior year unpaid obligations	1	1	1
1070 Unobligated balance (total)	596	592	592
Budget authority:			
Appropriations, mandatory:			
1200 Appropriation	7,720	12,281	13,243
1220 Appropriations transferred to other acct [012–0502]	–10	–10	
1220 Appropriations transferred to other acct [012–2707]	–7	–7	–7
1220 Appropriations transferred to other acct [012–0520]			–10
1222 Appropriations transferred from other acct [012–4336]	4	4	4
1232 Appropriations and/or unobligated balance of appropriations temporarily reduced	–2	–2	–2
1260 Appropriations, mandatory (total)	7,705	12,266	13,228
Spending authority from offsetting collections, mandatory:			
1800 Collected	4,289	5,619	5,377
1823 New and/or unobligated balance of spending authority from offsetting collections temporarily reduced	–2	–1	–1
1850 Spending auth from offsetting collections, mand (total)	4,287	5,618	5,376
1900 Budget authority (total)	11,992	17,884	18,604
1930 Total budgetary resources available	12,588	18,476	19,196
Memorandum (non-add) entries:			
1941 Unexpired unobligated balance, end of year	591	591	591
Change in obligated balance:			
Unpaid obligations:			
3000 Unpaid obligations, brought forward, Oct 1	2,500	3,529	2,953
3010 New obligations, unexpired accounts	11,997	17,885	18,605
3020 Outlays (gross)	–10,967	–18,460	–18,411
3040 Recoveries of prior year unpaid obligations, unexpired	–1	–1	–1
3050 Unpaid obligations, end of year	3,529	2,953	3,146
Memorandum (non-add) entries:			
3100 Obligated balance, start of year	2,500	3,529	2,953
3200 Obligated balance, end of year	3,529	2,953	3,146
Budget authority and outlays, net:			
Mandatory:			
4090 Budget authority, gross	11,992	17,884	18,604
Outlays, gross:			
4100 Outlays from new mandatory authority	8,613	14,376	14,867
4101 Outlays from mandatory balances	2,354	4,084	3,544
4110 Outlays, gross (total)	10,967	18,460	18,411
Offsets against gross budget authority and outlays:			
Offsetting collections (collected) from:			
4123 Non-Federal sources	–4,289	–5,619	–5,377
4180 Budget authority, net (total)	7,703	12,265	13,227
4190 Outlays, net (total)	6,678	12,841	13,034
Memorandum (non-add) entries:			
5090 Unexpired unavailable balance, SOY: Offsetting collections	10	12	13
5092 Unexpired unavailable balance, EOY: Offsetting collections	12	13	14
5096 Unexpired unavailable balance, SOY: Appropriations	26	28	30
5098 Unexpired unavailable balance, EOY: Appropriations	28	30	32

The Federal Crop Insurance Corporation (FCIC) is administered by the Risk Management Agency (RMA), and provides economic stability to agriculture through crop insurance. The Federal crop insurance program includes products providing crop yield and revenue insurance, pasture, rangeland forage, and livestock insurance, as well as other educational and risk mitigation initiatives/tools. The Federal crop insurance program provides farmers with a risk management program that protects against agricultural production losses due to natural disasters such as drought, excessive moisture, hail, wind, lightning, and insects. In addition to these causes, revenue insurance programs are available to protect against loss of revenue. Federal crop insurance is available for more than 350 different commodities in over 3,066 counties covering all 50 states, and Puerto Rico. For the 2021 Crop Year, there were 1.17 million policies written for crops with $13.7 billion in premiums.

Federal crop insurance policies are sold and serviced by 13 private crop insurance companies that share in the risk on the policies they sell under terms set out by USDA's Standard Reinsurance Agreement. Currently, the government provides companies, on average, $1.47 billion a year in underwriting gains. In addition, the government pays the companies an Administrative and Operating (A&O) subsidy to offset the costs incurred to carry out the program. They are reimbursed on average for about 13.8 percent of the premiums sold. The government currently pays, on average, $1.48 billion annually for A&O. For the 2023 Budget, the payments to the companies are projected to be $3.573 billion in combined subsidies.

The 2023 Budget requests funding to support $13.2 billion in obligations. Funding estimates for 2022 and 2023 as well as the outyears are based on a 1.0 loss ratio, which is the statutory target loss ratio used for estimating future crop insurance costs.

The minimum level of coverage is Catastrophic (CAT) crop insurance, which compensates the farmer for losses exceeding 50 percent of the individual's average yield at 55 percent of the expected market price; the premium is entirely subsidized. The cost to the producer for CAT coverage is an annual administrative fee of $655 per crop per county.

Additional coverage is available to producers and is commonly referred to as "buy-up" coverage. Policyholders can elect to be paid up to 100 percent of the market price established by FCIC for each unit of production their actual yield is less than the individual yield guarantee. Premium rates for additional coverage depend on the level of protection selected and vary from crop to crop and county to county. They also depend on the producer's average production history (APH). Producers are assessed a fee of $30 per crop, per county, in addition to a share of the premium. The additional levels of insurance coverage are more attractive to farmers due to availability of optional units, other policy provisions not available with CAT coverage, and the ability to obtain a level of protection that permits them to use crop insurance as loan collateral and to achieve greater financial security.

Revenue protection for specified products is provided by extending traditional crop insurance protection, based on actual production history, to include price variability based on futures market prices. Producers have a choice of revenue protection (protection against loss of revenue caused by low prices, low yields, or a combination of both) or yield protection (protection for production losses only) within one Basic Provision and the applicable Crop Provision.

Currently for revenue protection, the farmer can opt to cover the projected or the harvest price. Traditional revenue insurance only protects against a projected price, where the farmer is guaranteed a price at the time of planting. Revenue coverage that protects the price at the time of harvest guarantees the price to the farmer for the higher of the projected price or the harvest price. This additional revenue protection allows farmers to hedge against low prices at harvest. The harvest price protection policies are more costly than traditional revenue coverage and therefore more heavily subsidized by the government. Almost all farmers choose the harvest price option because taxpayers pay such a large portion of the extra premium.

A crop insurance policy also contains coverage for when a producer is prevented from planting their crop due to weather and other perils. When an insured producer is unable to plant their crop within the planting time period because of excessive drought or moisture, they may file a prevented planting claim, which pays a portion of their full coverage level. It is optional for the producer to plant a second crop on the acres. If the producer

Risk Management Agency—Continued
Federal Funds—Continued

FEDERAL CROP INSURANCE CORPORATION FUND—Continued

does, the prevented planting claim on the first crop is reduced and the producer's APH is updated to incorporate that year. If the producer does not plant a second crop, they get their full prevented planting claim, and their APH is not affected in subsequent years for premium calculation purposes.

he following table illustrates Crop Year statistics used to prepare the 2023 Budget. Crop Year (CY) is generally all activity for crops from July 1 - June 30 of a given year.

	CY 2020 est.	CY 2021 est.	CY 2022 est.
Number of States	50	50	50
Number of Counties	3,066	3,066	3,066
Insurance in Force (millions)	113,961	136,427	142,416
Insured Acreage (millions)	398	444	446
Producer Premium (millions)	3,748	5,109	5,418
Premium Subsidy (millions)	6,319	8,592	9,115
Total Premium (millions)	10,067	13,701	14,533
Indemnities (millions)	8,591	12,057	14,533
Loss Ratio	0.85	0.88	1.00

Financing.—The Corporation is authorized under the Federal Crop Insurance Act, as amended, to use funds from the issuance of capital stock which provides working capital for the Corporation.

Receipts, which are for deposit to this fund, mainly come from premiums paid by farmers. The principal payments from this fund are for indemnities to insured farmers, and administrative expenses for approved insurance providers.

Premium subsidies are authorized by section 508(b) of the Federal Crop Insurance Act, as amended, and are received through appropriations.

Object Classification (in millions of dollars)

Identification code 012–4085–0–3–351		2021 actual	2022 est.	2023 est.
	Direct obligations:			
25.2	Other services-Agriculture Risk Protection Act of 2000 Initiative	23	25	25
25.2	Other services from non-Federal sources	3,425	3,357	3,573
42.0	Insurance claims and indemnities	4,263	8,884	9,630
99.0	Direct obligations	7,711	12,266	13,228
	Reimbursable obligations:			
42.0	Insurance claims and indemnities	4,249	5,580	5,338
42.0	Programs and Activities	37	39	39
99.0	Reimbursable obligations	4,286	5,619	5,377
99.9	Total new obligations, unexpired accounts	11,997	17,885	18,605

FARM SERVICE AGENCY

Federal Funds

SALARIES AND EXPENSES

(INCLUDING TRANSFERS OF FUNDS)

For necessary expenses of the Farm Service Agency, $1,231,697,000: Provided, That the Secretary is authorized to use the services, facilities, and authorities (but not the funds) of the Commodity Credit Corporation to make program payments for all programs administered by the Agency: Provided further, That other funds made available to the Agency for authorized activities may be advanced to and merged with this account: Provided further, That of the amount appropriated under this heading, $696,594,000 shall be made available to county committees, to remain available until expended: Provided further, That, notwithstanding the preceding proviso, any funds made available to county committees in the current fiscal year that the Administrator of the Farm Service Agency deems to exceed or not meet the amount needed for the county committees may be transferred to or from the Farm Service Agency for necessary expenses.

Note.—A full-year 2022 appropriation for this account was not enacted at the time the Budget was prepared; therefore, the Budget assumes this account is operating under the Continuing Appropriations Act, 2022 (Division A of Public Law 117–43, as amended). The amounts included for 2022 reflect the annualized level provided by the continuing resolution.

Program and Financing (in millions of dollars)

Identification code 012–0600–0–1–351		2021 actual	2022 est.	2023 est.
	Obligations by program activity:			
0001	Agricultural Sector Support	1,142	1,190	1,232
0300	Subtotal, direct program	1,142	1,190	1,232
0801	Farm loans	288	294	306
0802	Other programs	10		
0899	Total reimbursable obligations	298	294	306
0900	Total new obligations, unexpired accounts	1,440	1,484	1,538
	Budgetary resources:			
	Unobligated balance:			
1000	Unobligated balance brought forward, Oct 1	45	38	
1012	Unobligated balance transfers between expired and unexpired accounts	16	9	
1070	Unobligated balance (total)	61	47	
	Budget authority:			
	Appropriations, discretionary:			
1100	Appropriation	1,143	1,143	1,232
	Spending authority from offsetting collections, discretionary:			
1700	Collected	303	294	306
1900	Budget authority (total)	1,446	1,437	1,538
1930	Total budgetary resources available	1,507	1,484	1,538
	Memorandum (non-add) entries:			
1940	Unobligated balance expiring	–29		
1941	Unexpired unobligated balance, end of year	38		
	Change in obligated balance:			
	Unpaid obligations:			
3000	Unpaid obligations, brought forward, Oct 1	265	276	276
3010	New obligations, unexpired accounts	1,440	1,484	1,538
3011	Obligations ("upward adjustments"), expired accounts	10		
3020	Outlays (gross)	–1,426	–1,484	–1,521
3041	Recoveries of prior year unpaid obligations, expired	–13		
3050	Unpaid obligations, end of year	276	276	293
	Uncollected payments:			
3060	Uncollected pymts, Fed sources, brought forward, Oct 1	–34	–27	–27
3071	Change in uncollected pymts, Fed sources, expired	7		
3090	Uncollected pymts, Fed sources, end of year	–27	–27	–27
	Memorandum (non-add) entries:			
3100	Obligated balance, start of year	231	249	249
3200	Obligated balance, end of year	249	249	266
	Budget authority and outlays, net:			
	Discretionary:			
4000	Budget authority, gross	1,446	1,437	1,538
	Outlays, gross:			
4010	Outlays from new discretionary authority	1,181	1,208	1,292
4011	Outlays from discretionary balances	245	276	229
4020	Outlays, gross (total)	1,426	1,484	1,521
	Offsets against gross budget authority and outlays:			
	Offsetting collections (collected) from:			
4030	Federal sources	–307	–294	–306
4033	Non-Federal sources	–17		
4040	Offsets against gross budget authority and outlays (total)	–324	–294	–306
	Additional offsets against gross budget authority only:			
4052	Offsetting collections credited to expired accounts	21		
4060	Additional offsets against budget authority only (total)	21		
4070	Budget authority, net (discretionary)	1,143	1,143	1,232
4080	Outlays, net (discretionary)	1,102	1,190	1,215
4180	Budget authority, net (total)	1,143	1,143	1,232
4190	Outlays, net (total)	1,102	1,190	1,215

The Farm Service Agency (FSA) was established October 13, 1994, pursuant to the Federal Crop Insurance Reform and Department of Agriculture Reorganization Act of 1994, P.L. 103–354. The Department of Agriculture Reorganization Act of 1994 was amended on April 4, 1996, by the Federal Agriculture Improvement and Reform Act of 1996 (1996 Act), Public Law 104–127. FSA administers a variety of activities, such as farm income support programs through various loans and payments; the Conservation Reserve Program (CRP); the Emergency Conservation Program; the Hazardous Waste Management Program; farm ownership, farm operating, emergency disaster, and other loan programs; and the Noninsured Crop

Disaster Assistance Program, which provides crop loss protection for growers of many crops for which crop insurance is not available.

This consolidated administrative expenses account includes funds to cover expenses of programs administered by, and functions assigned to, FSA. The funds consist of a direct appropriation, transfers from program loan accounts under credit reform procedures, user fees, and advances and reimbursements from other sources. This is a consolidated account for administrative expenses of national, regional, State, and county offices. The 2023 Budget requests a total of $1.54 billion for administrative expenses.

USDA's Service Center Agencies comprise FSA, Natural Resources Conservation Service, and Rural Development offices that act as separate franchises, with offices often located adjacent to each other. Prior efforts to improve the efficiency of USDA's county-based offices have resulted in significant co-location and introduction of new information technology to simplify customer transactions.

Farm programs.—These programs provide an economic safety net through farm income support to eligible producers, cooperatives, and associations to help improve the economic stability and viability of the agricultural sector and to ensure the production of an adequate and reasonably priced supply of food and fiber. Activities of the Agency include providing price loss coverage and agriculture risk coverage, providing marketing assistance loans and loan deficiency payments enabling recipients to continue farming operations without marketing their product immediately after harvest, and providing a financial safety net to eligible producers when natural disasters adversely affect their farming operation. These programs range from covering losses of grazing under the Livestock Forage Disaster Program; orchard trees and nursery to help replant or rehabilitate trees under the Tree Assistance Program; production under the Noninsured Crop Disaster Assistance Program; livestock under the Livestock Indemnity Program; and livestock, honeybees and farm raised fish for losses that are not covered under the previously listed programs under the Emergency Assistance for Livestock, Honeybees, and Farm Raised Fish.

Farm program activities include the following functions dealing with the administration of programs carried out through the farmer committee system of the FSA: (a) developing program regulations and procedures; (b) collecting and compiling basic data for individual farms; (c) establishing individual farm base acres for farm planting history; (d) notifying producers of established base acres and farm planting histories; (e) conducting referendums and certifying results; (f) accepting farmer certifications and checking compliance for specific purposes; (g) processing commodity loan documents and issuing checks; (h) processing Price Loss Coverage and Agriculture Risk Coverage payments and issuing checks; (i) certifying payment eligibility and monitoring payment limitations; and (j) processing farm storage facility loans and issuing checks.

Conservation and environment.—These programs assist agricultural producers and landowners in implementing practices to conserve soil, water, air, and wildlife resources on America's farmland and ranches to help protect the human and natural environment. Objectives of the Agency include improving environmental quality, protecting natural resources, and enhancing habitat for fish and wildlife, including threatened and endangered species; providing Emergency Conservation Program funding for farmers and ranchers to rehabilitate damaged farmland and for carrying out emergency conservation measures during periods of severe drought or flooding; protecting the public health of communities through implementation of the Hazardous Waste Management Program; and implementing contracting, financial reporting, and other administrative operations processes. These activities include: (a) processing producer requests for conservation cost-sharing and issuing conservation reserve rental payments; and (b) transferring funds to the Natural Resources Conservation Service and other agencies for other conservation programs.

Farm loans (reimbursable).—Provides for administering the direct and guaranteed loan programs covered under the Agricultural Credit Insurance Fund (ACIF). Objectives of the Agency include improving the economic viability of farmers and ranchers, reducing losses in direct loan programs, responding to loan making and servicing requests, and maximizing financial and technical assistance to underserved groups. Activities include reviewing applications, servicing the loan portfolio, and providing technical assistance and guidance to borrowers. Funding for farm loan administrative expenses is transferred to this consolidated account from the ACIF. Appropriations representing subsidy amounts necessary to support the individual program loan levels under Federal Credit Reform are made to the ACIF account.

Other reimbursable activities.—FSA collects a fee or is reimbursed for performing a variety of services for other Federal agencies, CCC, industry, and others, including certain administrative support services for county office services provided to Federal and non-Federal entities, including a variety of services to producers.

Object Classification (in millions of dollars)

Identification code 012–0600–0–1–351		2021 actual	2022 est.	2023 est.
	Direct obligations:			
11.1	Personnel compensation: Full-time permanent	121	115	119
12.1	Civilian personnel benefits	47	58	62
21.0	Travel and transportation of persons	2	5	3
22.0	Transportation of things	2	2	2
23.1	Rental payments to GSA	12		
23.2	Rental payments to others	3		
23.3	Communications, utilities, and miscellaneous charges	7	7	1
24.0	Printing and reproduction	1	1	5
25.1	Advisory and assistance services	60	27	18
25.2	Other services from non-Federal sources	1		
25.3	Other goods and services from Federal sources	190	237	223
25.7	Operation and maintenance of equipment	4		
26.0	Supplies and materials	2	2	1
31.0	Equipment	9	1	1
32.0	Land and structures	1		
41.0	Grants, subsidies, and contributions	680	735	797
99.0	Direct obligations	1,142	1,190	1,232
99.0	Reimbursable obligations	298	294	306
99.9	Total new obligations, unexpired accounts	1,440	1,484	1,538

Employment Summary

Identification code 012–0600–0–1–351	2021 actual	2022 est.	2023 est.
1001 Direct civilian full-time equivalent employment	3,008	3,038	3,117
2001 Reimbursable civilian full-time equivalent employment	37	40	40

STATE MEDIATION GRANTS

For grants pursuant to section 502(b) of the Agricultural Credit Act of 1987, as amended (7 U.S.C. 5101–5106), $6,914,000.

Note.—A full-year 2022 appropriation for this account was not enacted at the time the Budget was prepared; therefore, the Budget assumes this account is operating under the Continuing Appropriations Act, 2022 (Division A of Public Law 117–43, as amended). The amounts included for 2022 reflect the annualized level provided by the continuing resolution.

Program and Financing (in millions of dollars)

Identification code 012–0170–0–1–351		2021 actual	2022 est.	2023 est.
	Obligations by program activity:			
0001	State mediation grants	5	7	7
0900	Total new obligations, unexpired accounts (object class 41.0)	5	7	7
	Budgetary resources:			
	Budget authority:			
	Appropriations, discretionary:			
1100	Appropriation	7	7	7
1930	Total budgetary resources available	7	7	7
	Memorandum (non-add) entries:			
1940	Unobligated balance expiring	–2		
	Change in obligated balance:			
	Unpaid obligations:			
3000	Unpaid obligations, brought forward, Oct 1	2	2	2
3010	New obligations, unexpired accounts	5	7	7
3020	Outlays (gross)	–5	–7	–7
3050	Unpaid obligations, end of year	2	2	2

STATE MEDIATION GRANTS—Continued

Program and Financing—Continued

Identification code 012–0170–0–1–351		2021 actual	2022 est.	2023 est.
	Memorandum (non-add) entries:			
3100	Obligated balance, start of year	2	2	2
3200	Obligated balance, end of year	2	2	2
	Budget authority and outlays, net:			
	Discretionary:			
4000	Budget authority, gross	7	7	7
	Outlays, gross:			
4010	Outlays from new discretionary authority	3	3	3
4011	Outlays from discretionary balances	2	4	4
4020	Outlays, gross (total)	5	7	7
4180	Budget authority, net (total)	7	7	7
4190	Outlays, net (total)	5	7	7

This grant program is authorized by Title V of the Agricultural Credit Act of 1987, P.L. 100–233, as amended. Originally designed to address agricultural credit disputes, the program was expanded by the Federal Crop Insurance Reform and Department of Agriculture Reorganization Act of 1994 (P.L. 103–354) to include other agricultural issues such as wetland determinations, conservation compliance, rural water loan programs, grazing on National Forest System lands, and pesticide use. Grants are made to States whose agricultural mediation programs have been certified by the Farm Service Agency. A grant will not exceed 79 percent of the total fiscal year funds that a qualifying State requires to operate and administer its agricultural mediation program. In no case will the total amount of a grant exceed $500,000 annually. Current authority for the program under P.L. 115–334 expires September 30, 2023 as the program was extended by the Agriculture Improvement Act of 2018. The 2023 Budget requests $6.9 million for the program.

GRANT OBLIGATIONS

	2021 Actual	2022 Est.	2023 Est.
Number of States receiving grants	42	42	42
Amount of grants (in millions of dollars)	6.2	6.9	6.9

DISCRIMINATION CLAIMS SETTLEMENT

Program and Financing (in millions of dollars)

Identification code 012–1144–0–1–351		2021 actual	2022 est.	2023 est.
	Budgetary resources:			
	Unobligated balance:			
1000	Unobligated balance brought forward, Oct 1	28	28	28
1930	Total budgetary resources available	28	28	28
	Memorandum (non-add) entries:			
1941	Unexpired unobligated balance, end of year	28	28	28
4180	Budget authority, net (total)			
4190	Outlays, net (total)			

The Claims Resolution Act of 2010, Public Law 111–291 that was signed into law on December 8, 2010, provides funding to settle claims of prior discrimination brought by black farmers against the Department of Agriculture. These funds supplement funding previously provided to USDA for this purpose by section 14012 of Public Law 110–246. Claimants that suffered discrimination between 1989 and 1997 and submitted a late-filing request can seek fast-track payments of up to $50,000 plus debt relief, or choose a longer, more rigorous review and documentation process for damages of up to $250,000. The actual value of awards may be reduced based on the total amount of funds made available and the number of successful claims.

USDA SUPPLEMENTAL ASSISTANCE

Program and Financing (in millions of dollars)

Identification code 012–2701–0–1–351		2021 actual	2022 est.	2023 est.
	Obligations by program activity:			
0001	Geographically disadvantaged farmers and ranchers program	2	2	2
0900	Total new obligations, unexpired accounts (object class 41.0)	2	2	2
	Budgetary resources:			
	Unobligated balance:			
1000	Unobligated balance brought forward, Oct 1	4	4	4
	Budget authority:			
	Appropriations, discretionary:			
1100	Appropriation	2	2	
1930	Total budgetary resources available	6	6	4
	Memorandum (non-add) entries:			
1941	Unexpired unobligated balance, end of year	4	4	2
	Change in obligated balance:			
	Unpaid obligations:			
3000	Unpaid obligations, brought forward, Oct 1	2	2	2
3010	New obligations, unexpired accounts	2	2	2
3020	Outlays (gross)	–2	–2	–2
3050	Unpaid obligations, end of year	2	2	2
	Memorandum (non-add) entries:			
3100	Obligated balance, start of year	2	2	2
3200	Obligated balance, end of year	2	2	2
	Budget authority and outlays, net:			
	Discretionary:			
4000	Budget authority, gross	2	2	
	Outlays, gross:			
4011	Outlays from discretionary balances	2	2	2
4180	Budget authority, net (total)	2	2	
4190	Outlays, net (total)	2	2	2

The Reimbursement Transportation Cost Payment Program for Geographically Disadvantaged Farmers and Ranchers (RTCP) was established in the Food, Conservation, and Energy Act of 2008. The Agricultural Act of 2014 permanently re-authorized RTCP for FY 2012 and each succeeding fiscal year subject to appropriated funding. The purpose of RTCP is to offset a portion of the higher cost of transporting agricultural inputs and commodities over long distances. This program assists farmers and ranchers residing outside the 48 contiguous states that are at a competitive disadvantage when transporting agriculture products to the market. RTCP benefits are calculated based on the costs incurred by the producer for transportation of the agricultural commodity or inputs during a fiscal year, subject to an $8,000 per producer cap per fiscal year. The Reimbursement Transportation Cost Payment Program for Geographically Disadvantaged Farmers and Ranchers received appropriations in FY20 P.L. 116–94, Sec. 755 and in FY21 P.L. 116–260, Sec. 747 for $2 million in each act. The 2023 Budget does not request funding for this program.

EMERGENCY CONSERVATION PROGRAM

Program and Financing (in millions of dollars)

Identification code 012–3316–0–1–453		2021 actual	2022 est.	2023 est.
	Obligations by program activity:			
0001	Emergency conservation program	124	200	100
0900	Total new obligations, unexpired accounts (object class 41.0)	124	200	100
	Budgetary resources:			
	Unobligated balance:			
1000	Unobligated balance brought forward, Oct 1	776	722	522
1021	Recoveries of prior year unpaid obligations	70		
1070	Unobligated balance (total)	846	722	522
1930	Total budgetary resources available	846	722	522
	Memorandum (non-add) entries:			
1941	Unexpired unobligated balance, end of year	722	522	422

		2021 actual	2022 est.	2023 est.
	Change in obligated balance:			
	Unpaid obligations:			
3000	Unpaid obligations, brought forward, Oct 1	204	164	226
3010	New obligations, unexpired accounts	124	200	100
3020	Outlays (gross)	–94	–138	–103
3040	Recoveries of prior year unpaid obligations, unexpired	–70		
3050	Unpaid obligations, end of year	164	226	223
	Memorandum (non-add) entries:			
3100	Obligated balance, start of year	204	164	226
3200	Obligated balance, end of year	164	226	223
	Budget authority and outlays, net:			
	Discretionary:			
	Outlays, gross:			
4011	Outlays from discretionary balances	94	138	103
4180	Budget authority, net (total)			
4190	Outlays, net (total)	94	138	103

The Emergency Conservation Program (ECP) was authorized by the Agricultural Credit Act of 1978 (16 U.S.C. 2201–05). It provides funds for sharing the cost of emergency measures to deal with cases of severe damage to farmlands and rangelands resulting from natural disasters. During 2021, 37 States and 1 territory participated in ECP, with new or continued activity from the previous year, involving approximately $94 million in cost-share and technical assistance fund allocations. The 2023 Budget reflects the carryover balances for this program.

EMERGENCY FOREST RESTORATION PROGRAM

Program and Financing (in millions of dollars)

Identification code 012–0171–0–1–453	2021 actual	2022 est.	2023 est.
Obligations by program activity:			
0001 EFRP	61	100	100
0900 Total new obligations, unexpired accounts (object class 41.0)	61	100	100
Budgetary resources:			
Unobligated balance:			
1000 Unobligated balance brought forward, Oct 1	470	417	317
1021 Recoveries of prior year unpaid obligations	8		
1070 Unobligated balance (total)	478	417	317
1930 Total budgetary resources available	478	417	317
Memorandum (non-add) entries:			
1941 Unexpired unobligated balance, end of year	417	317	217
Change in obligated balance:			
Unpaid obligations:			
3000 Unpaid obligations, brought forward, Oct 1	74	121	100
3010 New obligations, unexpired accounts	61	100	100
3020 Outlays (gross)	–6	–121	
3040 Recoveries of prior year unpaid obligations, unexpired	–8		
3050 Unpaid obligations, end of year	121	100	200
Memorandum (non-add) entries:			
3100 Obligated balance, start of year	74	121	100
3200 Obligated balance, end of year	121	100	200
Budget authority and outlays, net:			
Discretionary:			
Outlays, gross:			
4011 Outlays from discretionary balances	6	121	
4180 Budget authority, net (total)			
4190 Outlays, net (total)	6	121	

The Emergency Forest Restoration Program (EFRP) provides payments to eligible owners of non-industrial private forest for implementation of emergency measures to restore land damaged by a natural disaster. During 2021, 10 States participated in EFRP with new or continued activity from the previous year, involving approximately $5.7 million in cost-share and technical assistance fund outlays. The 2023 Budget does not include funding for EFRP.

GRASSROOTS SOURCE WATER PROTECTION PROGRAM

For necessary expenses to carry out wellhead or groundwater protection activities under section 1240O of the Food Security Act of 1985 (16 U.S.C. 3839bb–2), $6,500,000, to remain available until expended.

Note.—A full-year 2022 appropriation for this account was not enacted at the time the Budget was prepared; therefore, the Budget assumes this account is operating under the Continuing Appropriations Act, 2022 (Division A of Public Law 117–43, as amended). The amounts included for 2022 reflect the annualized level provided by the continuing resolution.

Program and Financing (in millions of dollars)

Identification code 012–3304–0–1–302	2021 actual	2022 est.	2023 est.
Obligations by program activity:			
0001 Grassroots source water payments	7	7	7
0900 Total new obligations, unexpired accounts (object class 41.0)	7	7	7
Budgetary resources:			
Budget authority:			
Appropriations, discretionary:			
1100 Appropriation	7	7	7
1900 Budget authority (total)	7	7	7
1930 Total budgetary resources available	7	7	7
Change in obligated balance:			
Unpaid obligations:			
3010 New obligations, unexpired accounts	7	7	7
3020 Outlays (gross)	–7	–7	–7
Budget authority and outlays, net:			
Discretionary:			
4000 Budget authority, gross	7	7	7
Outlays, gross:			
4010 Outlays from new discretionary authority	7	7	7
4180 Budget authority, net (total)	7	7	7
4190 Outlays, net (total)	7	7	7

The Grassroots Source Water Protection Program (GSWPP) is a joint project by USDA's Farm Service Agency and the nonprofit National Rural Water Association. It is designed to help prevent source water pollution in States through voluntary practices installed by producers at the local level. GSWPP uses onsite technical assistance capabilities of each State rural water association that operates a wellhead or groundwater protection program in the State. State rural water associations can deliver assistance in developing source water protection plans within priority watersheds for the common goal of preventing the contamination of drinking water supplies. The Agriculture Improvement Act of 2018, the 2018 Farm Bill, continues the authority for this program through fiscal year 2023. The 2023 Budget requests $6.5 million for this program.

AGRICULTURAL CREDIT INSURANCE FUND PROGRAM ACCOUNT

(INCLUDING TRANSFERS OF FUNDS)

For gross obligations for the principal amount of direct and guaranteed farm ownership (7 U.S.C. 1922 et seq.) and operating (7 U.S.C. 1941 et seq.) loans, emergency loans (7 U.S.C. 1961 et seq.), Indian tribe land acquisition loans (25 U.S.C. 5136), boll weevil loans (7 U.S.C. 1989), guaranteed conservation loans (7 U.S.C. 1924 et seq.), relending program (7 U.S.C. 1936c), and Indian highly fractionated land loans (25 U.S.C. 5136) to be available from funds in the Agricultural Credit Insurance Fund, as follows: $3,500,000,000 for guaranteed farm ownership loans and $3,100,000,000 for farm ownership direct loans; $2,118,491,000 for unsubsidized guaranteed operating loans and $1,633,333,000 for direct operating loans; emergency loans, $4,062,000; Indian tribe land acquisition loans, $20,000,000; guaranteed conservation loans, $150,000,000; relending program, $61,426,000; Indian highly fractionated land loans, $5,000,000; and for boll weevil eradication program loans, $60,000,000: Provided, That the Secretary shall deem the pink bollworm to be a boll weevil for the purpose of boll weevil eradication program loans.

For the cost of direct and guaranteed loans and grants, including the cost of modifying loans as defined in section 502 of the Congressional Budget Act of 1974, as follows: $249,000 for emergency loans, to remain available until expended; and $23,520,000 for direct farm operating loans, $11,228,000 for unsubsidized guaran-

AGRICULTURAL CREDIT INSURANCE FUND PROGRAM ACCOUNT—Continued

teed farm operating loans, $10,983,000 for the relending program, and $894,000 for Indian highly fractionated land loans.

In addition, for administrative expenses necessary to carry out the direct and guaranteed loan programs, $326,461,000: Provided, That of this amount, $305,803,000 shall be transferred to and merged with the appropriation for "Farm Service Agency, Salaries and Expenses".

Funds appropriated by this Act to the Agricultural Credit Insurance Program Account for farm ownership, operating and conservation direct loans and guaranteed loans may be transferred among these programs: Provided, That the Committees on Appropriations of both Houses of Congress are notified at least 15 days in advance of any transfer.

DAIRY INDEMNITY PROGRAM

(INCLUDING TRANSFER OF FUNDS)

For necessary expenses involved in making indemnity payments to dairy farmers and manufacturers of dairy products under a dairy indemnity program, such sums as may be necessary, to remain available until expended: Provided, That such program is carried out by the Secretary in the same manner as the dairy indemnity program described in the Agriculture, Rural Development, Food and Drug Administration, and Related Agencies Appropriations Act, 2001 (Public Law 106–387, 114 Stat. 1549A-12).

Note.—A full-year 2022 appropriation for this account was not enacted at the time the Budget was prepared; therefore, the Budget assumes this account is operating under the Continuing Appropriations Act, 2022 (Division A of Public Law 117–43, as amended). The amounts included for 2022 reflect the annualized level provided by the continuing resolution.

Program and Financing (in millions of dollars)

Identification code 012–1140–0–1–351		2021 actual	2022 est.	2023 est.
	Obligations by program activity:			
0010	Administrative expenses - PLCE	11	13	20
0012	Dairy Indemnity	2	9	1
0091	Direct program activities, subtotal	13	22	21
	Credit program obligations:			
0701	Direct loan subsidy	24	58	54
0702	Loan guarantee subsidy	9	25	15
0703	Subsidy for modifications of direct loans	56		
0705	Reestimates of direct loan subsidy	261	140	
0706	Interest on reestimates of direct loan subsidy	28	63	
0707	Reestimates of loan guarantee subsidy	4	26	
0708	Interest on reestimates of loan guarantee subsidy	1	3	
0709	Administrative expenses	294	294	306
0791	Direct program activities, subtotal	677	609	375
0900	Total new obligations, unexpired accounts	690	631	396
	Budgetary resources:			
	Unobligated balance:			
1000	Unobligated balance brought forward, Oct 1	91	133	119
1021	Recoveries of prior year unpaid obligations	5		
1070	Unobligated balance (total)	96	133	119
	Budget authority:			
	Appropriations, discretionary:			
1100	Appropriation	376	376	373
1131	Unobligated balance of appropriations permanently reduced			−95
1160	Appropriation, discretionary (total)	376	376	278
	Appropriations, mandatory:			
1200	Appropriation	353	241	1
1900	Budget authority (total)	729	617	279
1930	Total budgetary resources available	825	750	398
	Memorandum (non-add) entries:			
1940	Unobligated balance expiring	−2		
1941	Unexpired unobligated balance, end of year	133	119	2
	Change in obligated balance:			
	Unpaid obligations:			
3000	Unpaid obligations, brought forward, Oct 1	18	14	18
3010	New obligations, unexpired accounts	690	631	396
3020	Outlays (gross)	−689	−627	−393
3040	Recoveries of prior year unpaid obligations, unexpired	−5		
3050	Unpaid obligations, end of year	14	18	21
	Memorandum (non-add) entries:			
3100	Obligated balance, start of year	18	14	18
3200	Obligated balance, end of year	14	18	21

	Budget authority and outlays, net:			
	Discretionary:			
4000	Budget authority, gross	376	376	278
	Outlays, gross:			
4010	Outlays from new discretionary authority	330	367	366
4011	Outlays from discretionary balances	7	19	26
4020	Outlays, gross (total)	337	386	392
	Mandatory:			
4090	Budget authority, gross	353	241	1
	Outlays, gross:			
4100	Outlays from new mandatory authority	352	241	1
4180	Budget authority, net (total)	729	617	279
4190	Outlays, net (total)	689	627	393

Summary of Loan Levels, Subsidy Budget Authority and Outlays by Program (in millions of dollars)

Identification code 012–1140–0–1–351		2021 actual	2022 est.	2023 est.
	Direct loan levels supportable by subsidy budget authority:			
115001	Farm Ownership	2,134	2,500	3,100
115002	Farm Operating	1,022	2,092	1,730
115003	Emergency Disaster	1	38	112
115004	Indian Tribe Land Acquisition		20	20
115005	Boll Weevil Eradication		60	60
115010	Indian Highly Fractionated Land		20	5
115013	Heirs Property Relending Program		61	117
115999	Total direct loan levels	3,157	4,791	5,144
	Direct loan subsidy (in percent):			
132001	Farm Ownership	−5.81	−12.27	−6.69
132002	Farm Operating	2.37	2.45	1.44
132003	Emergency Disaster	0.55	0.71	6.13
132004	Indian Tribe Land Acquisition		−56.22	−37.74
132005	Boll Weevil Eradication		−.49	−.62
132010	Indian Highly Fractionated Land		8.14	17.88
132013	Heirs Property Relending Program		8.14	17.88
132999	Weighted average subsidy rate	−3.16	−5.43	−3.14
	Direct loan subsidy budget authority:			
133001	Farm Ownership	−124	−307	−207
133002	Farm Operating	24	51	25
133003	Emergency Disaster			7
133004	Indian Tribe Land Acquisition		−11	−8
133010	Indian Highly Fractionated Land		2	1
133013	Heirs Property Relending Program		5	21
133999	Total subsidy budget authority	−100	−260	−161
	Direct loan subsidy outlays:			
134001	Farm Ownership	−74	−99	−99
134002	Farm Operating	−9	39	39
134003	Emergency Disaster	−15		
134010	Indian Highly Fractionated Land		1	2
134013	Heirs Property Relending Program		5	4
134999	Total subsidy outlays	−98	−54	−54
	Direct loan reestimates:			
135001	Farm Ownership	165	−278	
135002	Farm Operating	−39	26	
135003	Emergency Disaster	9	2	
135012	Farm Operating—ARRA	−1		
135999	Total direct loan reestimates	134	−250	
	Guaranteed loan levels supportable by subsidy budget authority:			
215001	Farm Ownership—Unsubsidized	2,733	3,300	3,500
215002	Farm Operating—Unsubsidized	781	3,268	2,750
215005	Conservation—Guaranteed		150	150
215999	Total loan guarantee levels	3,514	6,718	6,400
	Guaranteed loan subsidy (in percent):			
232001	Farm Ownership—Unsubsidized	−.24	−.38	−.43
232002	Farm Operating—Unsubsidized	1.12	0.78	0.53
232005	Conservation—Guaranteed		−.50	−.54
232999	Weighted average subsidy rate	0.06	0.18	−.02
	Guaranteed loan subsidy budget authority:			
233001	Farm Ownership—Unsubsidized	−7	−13	−15
233002	Farm Operating—Unsubsidized	9	25	15
233005	Conservation—Guaranteed		−1	−1
233999	Total subsidy budget authority	2	11	−1
	Guaranteed loan subsidy outlays:			
234001	Farm Ownership—Unsubsidized	−12	−7	−7
234002	Farm Operating—Unsubsidized	7	22	22
234999	Total subsidy outlays	−5	15	15
	Guaranteed loan reestimates:			
235001	Farm Ownership—Unsubsidized	−11	1	
235002	Farm Operating—Unsubsidized	−54	13	

		2021 actual	2022 est.	2023 est.
235999	Total guaranteed loan reestimates	−65	14	....
	Administrative expense data:			
3510	Budget authority	317	307	326
3590	Outlays from new authority	303	307	326

The Agricultural Credit Insurance Fund program account's loans are authorized by Title III of the Consolidated Farm and Rural Development Act, as amended.

This program account includes subsidies to provide direct and guaranteed loans for farm ownership, farm operating, conservation, and emergency loans to individuals. Indian tribes and tribal corporations are eligible for Indian land acquisition loans, while individual Native Americans are eligible for loans for the purchase of highly fractionated Indian lands. Boll weevil eradication loans are available to eliminate the cotton boll weevil pest from infested areas. The 2018 Farm Bill authorized a new loan type, the heirs relending program, to resolve ownership and succession on farm land that has multiple owners. The 2023 Budget requests $47 million for loan subsidies, and a collective program level of $10,652 billion for all loan and loan guarantees combined. Per the Federal Credit Reform Act of 1990, this account records for this program the subsidy costs associated with the direct loans obligated and loan guarantees committed in 1992 and beyond (including credit sales of acquired property), as well as administrative expenses of this program. The subsidy amounts are estimated on a present value basis; the administrative expenses are estimated on a cash basis. For administrative costs, the 2023 Budget requests $326.5 million.

Under the Dairy Indemnity Program, payments are made to farmers and manufacturers of dairy products who are directed to remove their milk or milk products from commercial markets because they contain residues of chemicals that have been registered and approved by the Federal Government, other chemicals, nuclear radiation, or nuclear fallout. Indemnification may also be paid for cows producing such milk. In 2020, 5.7 million was paid to producers who filed claims under the program. The 2023 Budget requests such sums as may be necessary, which are estimated to be $500,000 for this program in 2023.

Object Classification (in millions of dollars)

Identification code 012–1140–0–1–351		2021 actual	2022 est.	2023 est.
	Direct obligations:			
25.3	Other goods and services from Federal sources	305	307	326
41.0	Grants, subsidies, and contributions	385	324	70
99.9	Total new obligations, unexpired accounts	690	631	396

AGRICULTURAL CREDIT INSURANCE FUND DIRECT LOAN FINANCING ACCOUNT

Program and Financing (in millions of dollars)

Identification code 012–4212–0–3–351		2021 actual	2022 est.	2023 est.
	Obligations by program activity:			
0003	Capitalized costs	5	10	10
0005	Civil rights settlements	....	1	1
0091	Direct program by activities - subtotal (1 level)	5	11	11
	Credit program obligations:			
0710	Direct loan obligations	3,156	4,791	5,144
0713	Payment of interest to Treasury	415	358	358
0740	Negative subsidy obligations	124	318	215
0741	Modification savings	45	....	....
0742	Downward reestimates paid to receipt accounts	141	450	....
0743	Interest on downward reestimates	14	3	....
0791	Direct program activities, subtotal	3,895	5,920	5,717
0900	Total new obligations, unexpired accounts	3,900	5,931	5,728
	Budgetary resources:			
	Unobligated balance:			
1000	Unobligated balance brought forward, Oct 1	2,034	2,504	1,313
1021	Recoveries of prior year unpaid obligations	176	....	....
1023	Unobligated balances applied to repay debt	−1,935	−2,504	....
1024	Unobligated balance of borrowing authority withdrawn	−171	....	....
1070	Unobligated balance (total)	104	....	1,313
	Financing authority:			
	Appropriations, mandatory:			
1200	Appropriation	6	....	....
	Borrowing authority, mandatory:			
1400	Borrowing authority	3,516	5,000	5,000
1422	Borrowing authority applied to repay debt	−5	....	....
1440	Borrowing authority, mandatory (total)	3,511	5,000	5,000
	Spending authority from offsetting collections, mandatory:			
1800	Collected	2,866	2,244	2,428
1801	Change in uncollected payments, Federal sources	−4	....	....
1820	Capital transfer of spending authority from offsetting collections to general fund	−77	....	....
1825	Spending authority from offsetting collections applied to repay debt	−2	....	−1,500
1850	Spending auth from offsetting collections, mand (total)	2,783	2,244	928
1900	Budget authority (total)	6,300	7,244	5,928
1930	Total budgetary resources available	6,404	7,244	7,241
	Memorandum (non-add) entries:			
1941	Unexpired unobligated balance, end of year	2,504	1,313	1,513
	Change in obligated balance:			
	Unpaid obligations:			
3000	Unpaid obligations, brought forward, Oct 1	786	706	1,190
3010	New obligations, unexpired accounts	3,900	5,931	5,728
3020	Outlays (gross)	−3,804	−5,447	−5,552
3040	Recoveries of prior year unpaid obligations, unexpired	−176	....	....
3050	Unpaid obligations, end of year	706	1,190	1,366
	Uncollected payments:			
3060	Uncollected pymts, Fed sources, brought forward, Oct 1	−15	−11	−11
3070	Change in uncollected pymts, Fed sources, unexpired	4	....	....
3090	Uncollected pymts, Fed sources, end of year	−11	−11	−11
	Memorandum (non-add) entries:			
3100	Obligated balance, start of year	771	695	1,179
3200	Obligated balance, end of year	695	1,179	1,355
	Financing authority and disbursements, net:			
	Mandatory:			
4090	Budget authority, gross	6,300	7,244	5,928
	Financing disbursements:			
4110	Outlays, gross (total)	3,804	5,447	5,552
	Offsets against gross financing authority and disbursements:			
	Offsetting collections (collected) from:			
4120	Federal Sources: Reestimate payment from program account	−289	−203	....
4120	Federal Sources: Subsidy payment from program account	−24	−45	−45
4120	Federal sources: Modification Payment from Program Account	−55	....	....
4120	Federal sources: Payment from liquidating account	−33	....	....
4122	Federal Sources: Interest on uninvested funds	−90	−82	−82
4123	Repayments of principal	−2,037	−1,408	−1,486
4123	Repayments of interest	−332	−500	−809
4123	Sale of Foreclosed Property/Other	−6	−6	−6
4130	Offsets against gross budget authority and outlays (total)	−2,866	−2,244	−2,428
	Additional offsets against financing authority only (total):			
4140	Change in uncollected pymts, Fed sources, unexpired	4	....	....
4160	Budget authority, net (mandatory)	3,438	5,000	3,500
4170	Outlays, net (mandatory)	938	3,203	3,124
4180	Budget authority, net (total)	3,438	5,000	3,500
4190	Outlays, net (total)	938	3,203	3,124

Status of Direct Loans (in millions of dollars)

Identification code 012–4212–0–3–351		2021 actual	2022 est.	2023 est.
	Position with respect to appropriations act limitation on obligations:			
1111	Direct loan obligations from current-year authority	4,290	4,260	4,884
1121	Limitation available from carry-forward	3,263	3,862	260
1142	Unobligated direct loan limitation (-)	−4,397	−3,331	....
1150	Total direct loan obligations	3,156	4,791	5,144
	Cumulative balance of direct loans outstanding:			
1210	Outstanding, start of year	13,111	14,107	17,586
1231	Disbursements: Direct loan disbursements	3,056	4,949	4,949
1251	Repayments: Repayments and prepayments	−2,039	−1,408	−1,486
1261	Adjustments: Capitalized interest	9	....	....
1263	Write-offs for default: Direct loans	−26	−61	−61
1264	Other adjustments, net (+ or -)	−4	−1	−1

AGRICULTURAL CREDIT INSURANCE FUND DIRECT LOAN FINANCING ACCOUNT—Continued

Status of Direct Loans—Continued

Identification code 012–4212–0–3–351		2021 actual	2022 est.	2023 est.
1290	Outstanding, end of year	14,107	17,586	20,987

As required by the Federal Credit Reform Act of 1990, this non-budgetary account records all cash flows to and from the Government resulting from direct loans obligated in 1992 and beyond (including credit sales of acquired property that resulted from obligations in any year). The amounts in this account are a means of financing and are not included in the budget totals.

This account finances direct loans for farm ownership, farm operating, emergency disaster, Indian land acquisition, Indian highly fractionated land, boll weevil eradication, conservation, the heirs relending program authorized in the 2018 Farm Bill, and credit sales of acquired property.

Balance Sheet (in millions of dollars)

Identification code 012–4212–0–3–351		2020 actual	2021 actual
	ASSETS:		
	Federal assets:		
1101	Fund balances with Treasury	1,698	2,504
	Investments in U.S. securities:		
1106	Receivables, net	294	197
	Net value of assets related to post-1991 direct loans receivable:		
1401	Direct loans receivable, gross	13,111	14,107
1402	Interest receivable	300	319
1403	Accounts receivable from foreclosed property		
1404	Foreclosed property	10	10
1405	Allowance for subsidy cost (-)	–554	–168
1405	Allowance for Interest Receivable (-)		
1499	Net present value of assets related to direct loans	12,867	14,268
1999	Total assets	14,859	16,969
	LIABILITIES:		
	Federal liabilities:		
2103	Debt	14,700	16,514
2105	Other	159	454
2201	Non-Federal liabilities: Accounts payable		1
2999	Total liabilities	14,859	16,969
	NET POSITION:		
3300	Cumulative results of operations		
4999	Total liabilities and net position	14,859	16,969

AGRICULTURAL CREDIT INSURANCE FUND GUARANTEED LOAN FINANCING ACCOUNT

Program and Financing (in millions of dollars)

Identification code 012–4213–0–3–351		2021 actual	2022 est.	2023 est.
	Obligations by program activity:			
0003	Purchase of guaranteed loans		1	1
0091	Direct program by activities - subtotal (1 level)		1	1
	Credit program obligations:			
0711	Default claim payments on principal	43	48	48
0713	Payment of interest to Treasury	1	1	1
0740	Negative subsidy obligations	7	14	16
0741	Modification savings	8		
0742	Downward reestimates paid to receipt accounts	66	14	
0743	Interest on downward reestimates	4	1	
0791	Direct program activities, subtotal	129	78	65
0900	Total new obligations, unexpired accounts	129	79	66
	Budgetary resources:			
	Unobligated balance:			
1000	Unobligated balance brought forward, Oct 1	230	167	224
1021	Recoveries of prior year unpaid obligations	2		
1022	Capital transfer of unobligated balances to general fund	–5		
1023	Unobligated balances applied to repay debt		–16	–16
1033	Recoveries of prior year paid obligations	1		
1070	Unobligated balance (total)	228	151	208
	Financing authority:			
	Borrowing authority, mandatory:			
1400	Borrowing authority	3	30	30
	Spending authority from offsetting collections, mandatory:			
1800	Collected	65	122	97
1900	Budget authority (total)	68	152	127
1930	Total budgetary resources available	296	303	335
	Memorandum (non-add) entries:			
1941	Unexpired unobligated balance, end of year	167	224	269
	Change in obligated balance:			
	Unpaid obligations:			
3000	Unpaid obligations, brought forward, Oct 1	2	2	11
3010	New obligations, unexpired accounts	129	79	66
3020	Outlays (gross)	–127	–70	–63
3040	Recoveries of prior year unpaid obligations, unexpired	–2		
3050	Unpaid obligations, end of year	2	11	14
	Uncollected payments:			
3060	Uncollected pymts, Fed sources, brought forward, Oct 1	–1	–1	–1
3090	Uncollected pymts, Fed sources, end of year	–1	–1	–1
	Memorandum (non-add) entries:			
3100	Obligated balance, start of year	1	1	10
3200	Obligated balance, end of year	1	10	13
	Financing authority and disbursements, net:			
	Mandatory:			
4090	Budget authority, gross	68	152	127
	Financing disbursements:			
4110	Outlays, gross (total)	127	70	63
	Offsets against gross financing authority and disbursements:			
	Offsetting collections (collected) from:			
4120	Payments from program account upward reestimate	–15	–29	
4120	Payments from program account subsidy		–23	–23
4122	Interest on uninvested funds	–3	–4	–4
4123	Fees and premiums	–48	–65	–67
4123	Loss recoveries and repayments		–1	–3
4130	Offsets against gross budget authority and outlays (total)	–66	–122	–97
	Additional offsets against financing authority only (total):			
4143	Recoveries of prior year paid obligations, unexpired accounts	1		
4160	Budget authority, net (mandatory)	3	30	30
4170	Outlays, net (mandatory)	61	–52	–34
4180	Budget authority, net (total)	3	30	30
4190	Outlays, net (total)	61	–52	–34

Status of Guaranteed Loans (in millions of dollars)

Identification code 012–4213–0–3–351		2021 actual	2022 est.	2023 est.
	Position with respect to appropriations act limitation on commitments:			
2111	Guaranteed loan commitments from current-year authority	5,568	6,492	5,768
2121	Limitation available from carry-forward	2,414	5,403	632
2143	Uncommitted limitation carried forward	–4,468	–5,177	
2150	Total guaranteed loan commitments	3,514	6,718	6,400
2199	Guaranteed amount of guaranteed loan commitments	3,163	4,109	5,778
	Cumulative balance of guaranteed loans outstanding:			
2210	Outstanding, start of year	18,736	18,957	21,998
2231	Disbursements of new guaranteed loans	3,577	6,335	6,335
2251	Repayments and prepayments	–3,284	–3,200	–3,200
	Adjustments:			
2261	Terminations for default that result in loans receivable	–33	–13	–13
2263	Terminations for default that result in claim payments	–38	–81	–81
2264	Other adjustments, net	–1		
2290	Outstanding, end of year	18,957	21,998	25,039
	Memorandum:			
2299	Guaranteed amount of guaranteed loans outstanding, end of year	17,169	21,937	21,937
	Addendum:			
	Cumulative balance of defaulted guaranteed loans that result in loans receivable:			
2310	Outstanding, start of year	225	253	266
2331	Disbursements for guaranteed loan claims	46	24	24
2351	Repayments of loans receivable	–1	–1	–1
2361	Write-offs of loans receivable	–17	–10	–10
2390	Outstanding, end of year	253	266	279

DEPARTMENT OF AGRICULTURE

As required by the Federal Credit Reform Act of 1990, this non-budgetary account records all cash flows to and from the Government resulting from loan guarantees committed in 1992 and beyond. The amounts in this account are a means of financing and are not included in budget totals.

This account finances commitments made for farm ownership, operating and conservation guaranteed loan programs.

Balance Sheet (in millions of dollars)

Identification code 012–4213–0–3–351		2020 actual	2021 actual
	ASSETS:		
	Federal assets:		
1101	Fund balances with Treasury	229	167
	Investments in U.S. securities:		
1106	Receivables, net	25	29
1206	Non-Federal assets: Receivables, net		
	Net value of assets related to post-1991 acquired defaulted guaranteed loans receivable:		
1501	Defaulted guaranteed loans receivable, gross	225	253
1502	Interest receivable	76	90
1505	Allowance for subsidy cost (-)	–277	–323
1599	Net present value of assets related to defaulted guaranteed loans	24	20
1999	Total assets	278	216
	LIABILITIES:		
	Federal liabilities:		
2103	Debt	21	24
2104	Resources payable to Treasury		
2105	Other	53	15
	Non-Federal liabilities:		
2201	Accounts payable		1
2204	Liabilities for loan guarantees	204	176
2999	Total liabilities	278	216
	NET POSITION:		
3300	Cumulative results of operations		
4999	Total liabilities and net position	278	216

ASSISTANCE FOR SOCIALLY DISADVANTAGED FARMERS AND RANCHERS

Program and Financing (in millions of dollars)

Identification code 012–0172–0–1–351		2021 actual	2022 est.	2023 est.
	Obligations by program activity:			
0001	ARP Payments to SDA Borrowers Direct Farm Loans	1,960	1,565	
0002	ARP Payments to SDA Borrowers Guaranteed Farm Loans		2,750	
0003	ARP Payments to SDA Borrowers Farm Storage Facility Loans		26	
0900	Total new obligations, unexpired accounts (object class 41.0)	1,960	4,341	
	Budgetary resources:			
	Budget authority:			
	Appropriations, mandatory:			
1200	Appropriation	1,960	4,341	
1930	Total budgetary resources available	1,960	4,341	
	Change in obligated balance:			
	Unpaid obligations:			
3000	Unpaid obligations, brought forward, Oct 1		1,959	6,300
3010	New obligations, unexpired accounts	1,960	4,341	
3020	Outlays (gross)	–1		
3050	Unpaid obligations, end of year	1,959	6,300	6,300
	Memorandum (non-add) entries:			
3100	Obligated balance, start of year		1,959	6,300
3200	Obligated balance, end of year	1,959	6,300	6,300
	Budget authority and outlays, net:			
	Mandatory:			
4090	Budget authority, gross	1,960	4,341	
	Outlays, gross:			
4100	Outlays from new mandatory authority	1		
4180	Budget authority, net (total)	1,960	4,341	
4190	Outlays, net (total)	1		

The American Rescue Plan Act of 2021 authorized loan assistance and relief for socially disadvantaged farmers and ranchers. The purpose of the loan assistance is to cover up to 120 percent of the outstanding indebtedness of socially disadvantaged farmers or ranchers with Farm Service Agency direct or guaranteed farm loans.

AGRICULTURAL CREDIT INSURANCE FUND LIQUIDATING ACCOUNT

Program and Financing (in millions of dollars)

Identification code 012–4140–0–3–351		2021 actual	2022 est.	2023 est.
	Obligations by program activity:			
0008	Loan recoverable costs	1	1	1
0109	Costs incidental to acquisition of real property		1	1
0118	Civil rights settlements		1	1
0191	Total operating expenses		2	2
	Credit program obligations:			
0741	Modification savings	33		
0900	Total new obligations, unexpired accounts (object class 25.2)	34	3	3
	Budgetary resources:			
	Unobligated balance:			
1000	Unobligated balance brought forward, Oct 1	4	4	
1021	Recoveries of prior year unpaid obligations	1		
1022	Capital transfer of unobligated balances to general fund	–4	–4	
1070	Unobligated balance (total)	1		
	Budget authority:			
	Appropriations, mandatory:			
1200	Appropriation	33		
	Spending authority from offsetting collections, mandatory:			
1800	Collected	31	27	27
1820	Capital transfer of spending authority from offsetting collections to general fund	–27	–24	–24
1850	Spending auth from offsetting collections, mand (total)	4	3	3
1900	Budget authority (total)	37	3	3
1930	Total budgetary resources available	38	3	3
	Memorandum (non-add) entries:			
1941	Unexpired unobligated balance, end of year	4		
	Change in obligated balance:			
	Unpaid obligations:			
3000	Unpaid obligations, brought forward, Oct 1	1		
3010	New obligations, unexpired accounts	34	3	3
3020	Outlays (gross)	–34	–3	–3
3040	Recoveries of prior year unpaid obligations, unexpired	–1		
	Memorandum (non-add) entries:			
3100	Obligated balance, start of year	1		
	Budget authority and outlays, net:			
	Mandatory:			
4090	Budget authority, gross	37	3	3
	Outlays, gross:			
4100	Outlays from new mandatory authority	1	2	2
4101	Outlays from mandatory balances	33	1	1
4110	Outlays, gross (total)	34	3	3
	Offsets against gross budget authority and outlays:			
	Offsetting collections (collected) from:			
4123	Non-Federal sources Principal Repayments	–31	–20	–20
4123	Non-Federal sources Interest Repayments		–7	–7
4130	Offsets against gross budget authority and outlays (total)	–31	–27	–27
4160	Budget authority, net (mandatory)	6	–24	–24
4170	Outlays, net (mandatory)	3	–24	–24
4180	Budget authority, net (total)	6	–24	–24
4190	Outlays, net (total)	3	–24	–24

Status of Direct Loans (in millions of dollars)

Identification code 012–4140–0–3–351		2021 actual	2022 est.	2023 est.
	Cumulative balance of direct loans outstanding:			
1210	Outstanding, start of year	161	133	112
1251	Repayments: Repayments and prepayments	–23	–20	–20
1261	Adjustments: Capitalized interest	1	1	1
1263	Write-offs for default: Direct loans	–2	–2	–2
1264	Other adjustments, net (+ or -)	–4		
1290	Outstanding, end of year	133	112	91

Farm Service Agency—Continued
Federal Funds—Continued

AGRICULTURAL CREDIT INSURANCE FUND LIQUIDATING ACCOUNT—Continued

Status of Guaranteed Loans (in millions of dollars)

Identification code 012–4140–0–3–351		2021 actual	2022 est.	2023 est.
	Cumulative balance of guaranteed loans outstanding:			
2210	Outstanding, start of year	1	1	1
2251	Repayments and prepayments			
2290	Outstanding, end of year	1	1	1
	Memorandum:			
2299	Guaranteed amount of guaranteed loans outstanding, end of year	1	1	1

Balance Sheet (in millions of dollars)

Identification code 012–4140–0–3–351		2020 actual	2021 actual
	ASSETS:		
1101	Federal assets: Fund balances with Treasury	4	4
1601	Loans Receivable	161	133
1602	Interest receivable	97	96
1603	Allowance for estimated uncollectible loans and interest (–)	–96	–97
1604	Direct loans and interest receivable, net	162	132
1606	Foreclosed property	7	7
1699	Value of assets related to direct loans	169	139
1999	Total assets	173	143
	LIABILITIES:		
2104	Federal liabilities: Resources payable to Treasury	173	143
2201	Non-Federal liabilities: Accounts payable		
2999	Total liabilities	173	143
	NET POSITION:		
3300	Cumulative results of operations		
4999	Total liabilities and net position	173	143

COMMODITY CREDIT CORPORATION FUND

REIMBURSEMENT FOR NET REALIZED LOSSES

(INCLUDING TRANSFERS OF FUNDS)

For the current fiscal year, such sums as may be necessary to reimburse the Commodity Credit Corporation for net realized losses sustained, but not previously reimbursed, pursuant to section 2 of the Act of August 17, 1961 (15 U.S.C. 713a–11): Provided, That of the funds available to the Commodity Credit Corporation under section 11 of the Commodity Credit Corporation Charter Act (15 U.S.C. 714i) for the conduct of its business with the Foreign Agricultural Service, up to $5,000,000 may be transferred to and used by the Foreign Agricultural Service for information resource management activities of the Foreign Agricultural Service that are not related to Commodity Credit Corporation business.

HAZARDOUS WASTE MANAGEMENT

(LIMITATION ON EXPENSES)

For the current fiscal year, the Commodity Credit Corporation shall not expend more than $15,000,000 for site investigation and cleanup expenses, and operations and maintenance expenses to comply with the requirement of section 107(g) of the Comprehensive Environmental Response, Compensation, and Liability Act (42 U.S.C. 9607(g)), and section 6001 of the Solid Waste Disposal Act (42 U.S.C. 6961).

Note.—A full-year 2022 appropriation for this account was not enacted at the time the Budget was prepared; therefore, the Budget assumes this account is operating under the Continuing Appropriations Act, 2022 (Division A of Public Law 117–43, as amended). The amounts included for 2022 reflect the annualized level provided by the continuing resolution.

Program and Financing (in millions of dollars)

Identification code 012–4336–0–3–999		2021 actual	2022 est.	2023 est.
	Obligations by program activity:			
0001	Price Loss Coverage	615	563	618
0002	Agriculture Risk Coverage	191	196	99
0004	Marketing Loans — Recourse	17	16	16
0006	Marketing Loans — Non-Recourse	6,446	6,283	7,360
0007	Loan Deficiency Payments	10	2	
0008	Eco. Adjust. Assist. for Textile Mills (Upland Cotton)	34	34	35
0009	Livestock Indemnity Program	18	33	33
0010	Livestock Forage Program	558	1,558	364
0011	ELAP	77	199	127
0012	Tree Assistance Program	15	7	7
0015	Price Support Load In Charges	1	1	1
0016	Market Access Program	181	189	189
0018	Technical Assistance for Specialty Crops	7	8	9
0019	Emerging Markets Program	4	8	8
0021	Foreign Market Development Program	33	33	35
0022	Quality Samples Program	2	2	3
0023	Non-Insured Assistance Program	175	165	165
0024	Emergency Citrus Trust Fund		25	25
0026	Conservation Reserve Program Financial Assistance	3,264	2,102	2,436
0027	Conservation Reserve Program Technical Assistance	15	41	38
0029	Treasury Interest on Notes	9	19	16
0030	Capital Stock Interest	2	2	2
0031	Section 11 Reimbursable Agreements with State and Federal Agencies	51	53	53
0032	Food for Progress	175	165	175
0034	Section 4 Contracts	10	16	16
0035	Farm Bill Implementation		4	
0038	Electronic Warehouse Receipts	1	1	1
0040	Noninsured Assistance Program Loss Adjuster	2	2	2
0041	Margin Protection Program and Dairy Margin Coverage	1,124	1,562	1,003
0043	Organic Certification Cost Share	7	19	18
0044	Priority Trade		3	4
0048	Agricultural Trade Promotion Program	14	3	3
0049	Administrative Expenses for Implementation of Farm Bill Title I	9	14	14
0050	Oriental Fruit Fly		9	
0051	Seafood Trade Relief Program	308		
0052	All Other	58		
0053	UCC filing Fees	1	1	1
0054	Food for Progress Ocean Transport		38	38
0192	Total support and related programs	13,434	13,376	12,914
0799	Total direct obligations	13,434	13,376	12,914
0801	Reimbursable Obligations Incurred	1		
0809	Reimbursable program activities, subtotal	1		
0899	Total reimbursable obligations	1		
0900	Total new obligations, unexpired accounts	13,435	13,376	12,914
	Budgetary resources:			
	Unobligated balance:			
1000	Unobligated balance brought forward, Oct 1	352	352	1,315
1001	Discretionary unobligated balance brought fwd, Oct 1	8		
1021	Recoveries of prior year unpaid obligations	5,514		
1024	Unobligated balance of borrowing authority withdrawn	–5,483		
1033	Recoveries of prior year paid obligations	197		
1070	Unobligated balance (total)	580	352	1,315
	Budget authority:			
	Appropriations, mandatory:			
1200	Appropriation	31,831	14,402	14,402
1236	Appropriations applied to repay debt	–31,831	–14,402	–14,402
	Borrowing authority, mandatory:			
1400	Borrowing authority	2,970,878	20,231	17,205
1410	Exercised borrowing authority transferred to other accounts [012–9913]	–1,018	–20	–20
1410	Exercised borrowing authority transferred to other accounts [012–8015]	–2	–2	–2
1410	Exercised borrowing authority transferred to other accounts [012–0403]	–3	–3	–3
1410	Exercised borrowing authority transferred to other accounts [012–0502]	–66	–73	
1410	Exercised borrowing authority transferred to other accounts [012–1004]	–3,539	–3,639	–4,014
1410	Exercised borrowing authority transferred to other accounts [012–1072]	–50	–50	–50
1410	Exercised borrowing authority transferred to other accounts [012–1502]	–105	–110	
1410	Exercised borrowing authority transferred to other accounts [012–1600]	–575	–75	–105
1410	Exercised borrowing authority transferred to other accounts [012–1900]	–19	–19	–19
1410	Exercised borrowing authority transferred to other accounts [012–1908]	–50	–50	–50
1410	Exercised borrowing authority transferred to other accounts [012–2073]	–7	–107	–7
1410	Exercised borrowing authority transferred to other accounts [012–2500]	–536	–36	–36
1410	Exercised borrowing authority transferred to other accounts [012–2501]	–85	–85	–85
1410	Exercised borrowing authority transferred to other accounts [012–3507]	–20	–21	–21
1410	Exercised borrowing authority transferred to other accounts [012–3539]	–1,000		

DEPARTMENT OF AGRICULTURE

1410	Exercised borrowing authority transferred to other accounts [012–4085]	–4	–4	–4
1410	Exercised borrowing authority transferred to other accounts [012–5635]	–16	–16	–16
1410	Exercised borrowing authority transferred to other accounts [012–5636]	–30	–30	–30
1410	Exercised borrowing authority transferred to other accounts [012–3105]		–5	–5
1410	Exercised borrowing authority transferred to other accounts [012–9914]		–1	–1
1410	Exercised borrowing authority transferred to other accounts [012–0520]			–211
1410	Exercised borrowing authority transferred to other accounts [012–1000]		–1,000	
1421	Borrowing authority temporarily reduced	–2,131	–546	–144
1422	Borrowing authority applied to repay debt	–2,948,415		
1440	Borrowing authority, mandatory (total)	13,207	14,339	12,382
	Spending authority from offsetting collections, mandatory:			
1800	Collected	6,974	6,313	7,362
1801	Change in uncollected payments, Federal sources	–8		
1825	Spending authority from offsetting collections applied to repay debt	–6,966	–6,313	–7,362
1900	Budget authority (total)	13,207	14,339	12,382
1930	Total budgetary resources available	13,787	14,691	13,697
	Memorandum (non-add) entries:			
1941	Unexpired unobligated balance, end of year	352	1,315	783
	Change in obligated balance:			
	Unpaid obligations:			
3000	Unpaid obligations, brought forward, Oct 1	27,639	17,868	16,706
3010	New obligations, unexpired accounts	13,435	13,376	12,914
3020	Outlays (gross)	–17,692	–14,538	–13,076
3040	Recoveries of prior year unpaid obligations, unexpired	–5,514		
3050	Unpaid obligations, end of year	17,868	16,706	16,544
	Uncollected payments:			
3060	Uncollected pymts, Fed sources, brought forward, Oct 1	–92	–84	–84
3070	Change in uncollected pymts, Fed sources, unexpired	8		
3090	Uncollected pymts, Fed sources, end of year	–84	–84	–84
	Memorandum (non-add) entries:			
3100	Obligated balance, start of year	27,547	17,784	16,622
3200	Obligated balance, end of year	17,784	16,622	16,460
	Budget authority and outlays, net:			
	Discretionary:			
	Outlays, gross:			
4011	Outlays from discretionary balances	3	9	
	Mandatory:			
4090	Budget authority, gross	13,207	14,339	12,382
	Outlays, gross:			
4100	Outlays from new mandatory authority	8,787	7,940	4,802
4101	Outlays from mandatory balances	8,902	6,589	8,274
4110	Outlays, gross (total)	17,689	14,529	13,076
	Offsets against gross budget authority and outlays:			
	Offsetting collections (collected) from:			
4120	Federal sources	–10	–77	–74
4123	Commodity Loans Repaid	–7,161	–6,236	–7,288
4130	Offsets against gross budget authority and outlays (total)	–7,171	–6,313	–7,362
	Additional offsets against gross budget authority only:			
4140	Change in uncollected pymts, Fed sources, unexpired	8		
4143	Recoveries of prior year paid obligations, unexpired accounts	197		
4150	Additional offsets against budget authority only (total)	205		
4160	Budget authority, net (mandatory)	6,241	8,026	5,020
4170	Outlays, net (mandatory)	10,518	8,216	5,714
4180	Budget authority, net (total)	6,241	8,026	5,020
4190	Outlays, net (total)	10,521	8,225	5,714
	Memorandum (non-add) entries:			
5101	Unexpired unavailable balance, SOY: Borrowing authority	2,163	2,172	
5102	Unexpired unavailable balance, EOY: Borrowing authority	2,172		

Status of Direct Loans (in millions of dollars)

Identification code 012–4336–0–3–999		2021 actual	2022 est.	2023 est.
	Cumulative balance of direct loans outstanding:			
1210	Outstanding, start of year	902	591	2,360
1231	Disbursements: Direct loan disbursements	8,968	8,005	8,497
1251	Repayments: Repayments and prepayments	–9,279	–6,236	–7,288
1290	Outstanding, end of year	591	2,360	3,569

The Commodity Credit Corporation (CCC) was created to stabilize, support, and protect farm income and prices; help maintain balanced and adequate supplies of agricultural commodities, their products, foods, feeds, and fibers; and help in their orderly distribution.

The Agriculture Improvement Act of 2018 (2018 Farm Bill), Public Law 115–334, was signed by the President on December 20, 2018. The 2018 Farm Bill repealed certain programs, continued some programs with modifications, and authorized several new programs. In addition, the Bipartisan Budget Act of 2018 (BBA), Public Law 115–123 made changes to the CCC commodity and disaster programs.

BUDGET ASSUMPTIONS

The estimates for CCC spending in 2022 and 2023 reflect expenditures primarily related to commodity and conservation programs authorized under the 2018 Farm Bill. Outlay projections are subject to complex and unpredictable factors such as weather; U.S. and world consumer income growth; factors which affect the volume of production of crops not yet planted; demands for feed, food, and bio-energy here and overseas; and foreign currency exchange rates and the value of the U.S. dollar overall.

PROGRAMS FOR COMMODITY CROPS

Price Support, Marketing Assistance Loans, and Related Stabilization Programs.—As authorized in the 2018 Farm Bill, the Corporation conducts programs to support farm income and prices and stabilize the market for agricultural commodities. Price support is provided to producers of agricultural commodities through loans, purchases, payments, and other means.

Price support is mandatory for sugar. Marketing assistance loans are mandatory for wheat, feed grains, oilseeds, upland cotton, peanuts, rice, pulse crops, sugar, honey, wool, mohair, and extra-long staple cotton.

One method of providing support is loans to and purchases from producers. With limited exceptions, loans made on commodities are nonrecourse. The commodities serve as collateral for the loan and on maturity the producer may deliver or forfeit such collateral to satisfy the loan obligation without further payment.

Direct purchases may be made from processors as well as producers, depending on the commodity involved. Also, purchases are made under various laws; for example, the Act of August 19, 1958, as amended, and section 416 of the Agricultural Act of 1949, as amended.

Commodity Payment Programs.—Agriculture Risk Coverage (ARC) and Price Loss Coverage (PLC) payments are available for a wide variety of commodity crops. The BBA added seed cotton as a covered commodity eligible for ARC and PLC. The BBA also removed generic base acres beginning with the 2018 crop year, and allowed producers to reallocate generic base acres to seed cotton, or other covered commodities eligible for ARC/PLC payments.

Price Loss Coverage (PLC).—Payments are issued when the effective price of a covered commodity is less than the respective reference price for that commodity established in the statute. PLC payments are not dependent upon the planting of a covered commodity or planting of the applicable base crop on the farm. The payment is equal to 85 percent of the base acres of the covered commodity times the difference between the effective reference price and the effective price times the program payment yield for the covered commodity. The 2018 Farm Bill authorized a nationwide PLC yield update for the 2020 crop year.

Agriculture Risk Coverage (ARC).—There are two types: ARC-County (CO) and ARC-Individual (IC).

ARC-CO: Payments are issued when the actual county crop revenue of a covered commodity is less than the ARC county guarantee for the covered commodity and are based on county data, not farm data. The ARC county guarantee equals 86 percent of the previous 5-year average national farm price, excluding the years with the highest and lowest price (the ARC guarantee price), times the 5-year average county yield, excluding the years with the highest and lowest yield (the ARC county guarantee yield). Both the guarantee and actual revenue are computed using base acres, not planted acres. The payment is equal to 85 percent of the base acres of the covered

COMMODITY CREDIT CORPORATION FUND—Continued

commodity times the difference between the county guarantee and the actual county crop revenue for the covered commodity. Payments may not exceed 10 percent of the benchmark county revenue (the ARC guarantee price times the ARC county guarantee yield).

ARC-IC: Payments are issued when the actual individual crop revenues, for all covered commodities planted on the ARC-IC farm, are less than ARC-IC guarantee for those covered commodities on the farm. The farm for ARC-IC purposes is the sum of the producer's interest in all ARC-IC enrolled farms in the State. The farm's ARC individual guarantee equals 86 percent of the farm's individual benchmark guarantee, which is defined as the ARC guarantee price times the 5-year average individual yield, excluding the years with the highest and lowest yields, and summing across all crops on the farm. The actual revenue is computed in a similar fashion, with both the guarantee and actual revenue computed using planted acreage on the farm. The individual ARC payment equals: a) 65 percent of the sum of the base acres of all covered commodities on the farm, times b) the difference between the individual guarantee revenue and the actual individual crop revenue across all covered commodities planted on the farm. Payments may not exceed 10 percent of the individual benchmark revenue.

Yield Update.—Owners had a 1-time opportunity in 2020 to update PLC yields of covered commodity base crops on their farm, regardless of program election. The updated yield will be equal to 90 percent of the producers average yield per planted acre in crop years 2013–2017, subject to the ratio obtained by dividing the 2008–2012 average national yield by the 2013–2017 average national yield for the covered commodity. If the reported yield in any year is less than 75 percent of the 2013–2017 average county yield, then the yield will be substituted with 75 percent of the county average yield.

Election Required.—All farm producers with interest in the cropland were required to make a unanimous election in 2019 of either ARC-CO or PLC on a crop-by-crop basis; or ARC-IC for all covered commodity base acres on a farm. This election will apply to the farm for 2019 through 2023. Program election changes are permitted in crop years 2021, 2022 and 2023.

Adjusted Gross Income.—Adjusted gross income (AGI) provisions have been simplified and modified. Producers whose average AGI exceeds $900,000 during a crop, fiscal, or program year are not eligible to participate in most programs administered by FSA and the Natural Resources Conservation Service (NRCS). Previous AGI provisions distinguished between farm and nonfarm AGI.

Payment Limitations.—The total amount of payments received, directly and indirectly, by a person or legal entity (except joint ventures or general partnerships) for Price Loss Coverage and Agriculture Risk Coverage (other than for peanuts), may not exceed $125,000 per crop year. A person or legal entity that receives payments for peanuts has a separate $125,000 payment limitation. For the Supplemental Disaster Programs, a payment limit of $125,000 applies to payments under the Livestock Forage Disaster Program (LFP). The 2018 Farm Bill eliminated the payment limit for Emergency Assistance for Livestock, Honeybees and Farm-Raised Fish Program (ELAP), and the Bipartisan Budget Act of 2018 eliminated the payment limits for Livestock Indemnity Program (LIP) and the Tree Assistance Program (TAP).

Marketing Assistance Loans (MALs) and Sugar Loans.—The 2018 Farm Bill extends the authority for sugar loans for the 2019 through 2023 crop years and nonrecourse marketing assistance loans (MALs) and loan deficiency payment (LDPs) for the 2019–2023 crops of wheat, corn, grain sorghum, barley, oats, upland cotton, extra-long staple cotton (eligible for loans only), long grain rice, medium grain rice, soybeans, other oilseeds (including sunflower seed, rapeseed, canola, safflower, flaxseed, mustard seed, crambe and sesame seed), dry peas, lentils, small chickpeas, large chickpeas, graded and nongraded wool, mohair, honey, unshorn pelts, and peanuts. Availability of loans for some commodities may be affected by appropriations language. The Consolidated Appropriations Act, 2016 (Public Law 114–113) amended the Federal Agriculture Improvement and Reform Act of 1996, allowing producers to receive certificates in lieu of marketing loan gains or loan deficiency payments starting with the 2015 crop marketing year.

DAIRY PROGRAMS

Dairy Margin Coverage.—The 2018 Farm Bill authorized the Dairy Margin Coverage (DMC) program, which is a voluntary risk management program for dairy producers. The program provides payments to dairy producers when the difference between the all milk price and the average feed price (the margin) falls below a margin selected by the producer. Catastrophic coverage is available at no cost to the producers, other than an annual $100 administrative fee; and various levels of buy-up coverage that farmers may choose by paying premiums covering the dairy operation's production history, ranging from 5 percent to 95 percent of production.

Dairy Indemnity Payment Program (DIPP).—The program provides payments to dairy producers when a public regulatory agency directs them to remove their raw milk from the commercial market because it has been contaminated by pesticides and other residues. In 2021, the DIPP regulations were amended to add provisions for the indemnification of cows that are likely to be not marketable for longer durations, as a result, for example, of per- and polyfluoroalkyl substances.

PROGRAMS FOR BIOENEGY AND NON-COMMODITY CROPS

Noninsured Crop Disaster Assistance Program (NAP).—NAP provides coverage, similar to buy-up provisions offered under the Federal crop insurance program. Producers may elect coverage for each individual crop between 50 and 65 percent of production, in 5 percent increments, at 100 percent of the average market price. Producers also pay a fixed premium equal to 5.25 percent of the liability. The waiver of service fees has been expanded from just limited resource farmers to also include beginning farmers and socially disadvantaged farmers. The premiums for buy-up coverage are reduced by 50 percent for those same farmers.

Biomass Crop Assistance Program (BCAP).—BCAP provides incentives to farmers, ranchers and forest landowners to establish, cultivate and harvest eligible biomass for heat, power, bio-based products, research and advanced biofuels. Crop producers and bioenergy facilities can team together to submit proposals to USDA for selection as a BCAP project area. The 2018 Farm Bill did provide an authorization to spend up to $25 million annually through FY 2023 but changed the funding source from CCC mandatory funds to discretionary funds subject to annual appropriation.

Feedstock Flexibility Program (FFP).—FFP is continued through fiscal year 2023. Congress authorized the FFP in the 2008 Farm Bill, allowing for the purchase of sugar to be sold for the production of bioenergy in order to avoid forfeitures of sugar loan collateral under the Sugar Program.

DISASTER PROGRAMS

The following four disaster programs were authorized by the 2008 Farm Bill under the USDA Supplemental Disaster Assistance Program. These programs were permanently re-authorized under CCC in the 2014 Farm Bill and modified in the 2018 Farm Bill.

Livestock Forage Disaster Program (LFP).—LFP provides compensation to eligible livestock producers that have suffered grazing losses due to drought or fire on land that is native or improved pastureland with permanent vegetative cover or that is planted specifically for grazing. LFP payments for drought are equal to 60 percent of the monthly feed cost for up to 5 months, depending upon the severity of the drought. LFP payments for fire on federally managed rangeland are equal to 50 percent of the monthly feed cost for the number of days the producer is prohibited from grazing the managed rangeland, not to exceed 180 calendar days.

Livestock Indemnity Program (LIP).—LIP provides benefits to livestock producers for livestock deaths in excess of normal mortality caused by adverse weather or by attacks by animals reintroduced into the wild by the Federal Government. LIP payments are equal to 75 percent of the average fair market value of the livestock. The BBA removed the payment limit for LIP and added provisions to provide benefits for the sale of animals at a reduced price if the sale occurred due to injury that was a direct result of an eligible adverse weather event or due to an attack by an animal reintroduced into the wild.

Emergency Assistance for Livestock, Honey Bees, and Farm-Raised Fish (ELAP).—ELAP provides emergency assistance to eligible producers of livestock, honeybees and farm-raised fish for losses due to disease (including cattle tick fever), adverse weather, or other conditions, such as blizzards and wildfires, not covered by LFP and LIP. The BBA removed the annual funding limitation of $20 million per program year and clarified which losses are eligible for assistance. The 2018 Farm Bill eliminated the payment limit for ELAP.

Tree Assistance Program (TAP).—TAP provides financial assistance to qualifying orchardists and nursery tree growers to replant or rehabilitate eligible trees, bushes, and vines damaged by natural disasters. The BBA removed the payment limitation for TAP and increased the number of acres for which a producer can receive payment from 500 to 1,000 acres per year.

Foreign Assistance Programs

Market Access Program (MAP).—Under the MAP, CCC Funds are used to reimburse participating organizations for a portion of the costs of carrying out overseas marketing and promotional activities. The 2018 Farm Bill continues the authority for the MAP program with annual funding of $200 million for 2018–2023.

Foreign Market Development Cooperator Program (FMD) and Quality Samples Program.—Under the FMD program, cost-share assistance is provided to nonprofit commodity and agricultural trade associations to support overseas market development activities that are designed to remove long-term impediments to increased U.S. trade. CCC will fund the Quality Samples Program at an authorized annual level of $2.5 million. Under this initiative, samples of U.S. agricultural products will be provided to foreign importers to promote a better understanding and appreciation for the high quality of U.S. products.

Technical Assistance for Specialty Crops and Emerging Markets.—Technical Assistance for Specialty Crops and Emerging Markets were both extended through 2023 in the 2018 Farm Bill.

The Bill Emerson Humanitarian Trust.—The Bill Emerson Humanitarian Trust (BEHT) is a commodity and/or monetary reserve designed to ensure that the United States can meet its international food aid commitments. Assets of the Trust can be released any time the Administrator of the U.S. Agency for International Development determines that PL 480 Title II is inadequate to meet those needs in any fiscal year. When a release from the Trust is authorized, the Trust's assets cover all commodity costs associated with the release. All non-commodity costs, including ocean freight charges; internal transportation, handling, and storage overseas; and certain administrative costs are paid by CCC. The 2018 Farm Bill extends the authorization to replenish the BEHT through 2023.

Conservation Programs

Conservation Reserve Program (CRP).—The 2018 Farm Bill extended and modified the authorization of CRP through FY 2023. It limits the practice incentive payments to the actual cost of practice implementation and lowers the CRP soil rental payments to 85 percent of the rental rate for general program enrollment and 90 percent for continuous program enrollment. The acreage cap is increased from 24 million acres to 27 million acres by FY 2023. The 2018 Farm Bill also authorized up to $12 million in incentive payments for tree thinning and related activities. In 2021, the Secretary announced a number of administrative incentives to increase enrollment in CRP. These incentives are designed to further adoption of 'climate-smart" conservation practices with carbon sequestration-related benefits, including a number of tree-related practices. Additionally, the Farm Service Agency will study the climate benefits of CRP through a comprehensive CRP Monitoring, Assessment, and Evaluation program. Over the coming two years, USDA will work with research partners to study the carbon sequestration and reduced nitrous oxide emissions from enrolling acres into the program. Monitoring and assessment activities will be done in partnership with land grant universities and other research institutions and may also include technical service providers or other cooperators. As part of the effort, USDA will also conduct outreach to 1890s, Hispanic Serving Institutions, Tribal Colleges and other potential technical service providers from socially disadvantaged communities.

Transition Incentive Program (TIP).—The 2018 Farm Bill extended TIP through FY 2023. It authorized up to $50 million to encourage the transition of expiring CRP land to a beginning, socially disadvantaged, or veteran farmer or rancher so land can be returned to sustainable grazing or crop production.

Operating Expenses

The Corporation carries out its functions through utilization of employees and facilities of other Government agencies. Administrative expenses are incurred by: the Farm Service Agency (FSA); the Foreign Agricultural Service; the Natural Resources Conservation Service; other agencies of the Department engaged in the Corporation's activities; and the Office of Inspector General for audit functions. The table below summarizes some of the administrative expenses funded through the Corporation. These funds are in addition to discretionary appropriations for these agencies.

CCC Funding Used for Administrative Expenses

(Funding in thousands of dollars)

Program or Funding Category	2021 Actual	2022 Estimate	2023 Estimate
Emerging Markets Program (transferred for FAS)	746	970	970
Technical Assistance for Specialty Crops (transferred to AMS)	803	1,086	1,086
Foreign Market Development Cooperator Program (transferred to FAS)	1,160	1,321	1,321
Food for Progress (transferred to FAS)	2,331	6,020	6,020
Market Access Program (transferred to FAS)	4,788	5,604	5,604
Pima Cotton Trust (transferred to FSA)	135	135	135
Wool Apparel Manufacturers Trust (transferred to FSA)	135	135	135
CCC Section 4 authority (transferred to multiple agencies)	10,462	17,300	17,640
CCC Section 11 authority (transferred to multiple agencies)	56,102	56,102	56,102

Expenses are incurred for acquisition, operation, maintenance, improvement, or disposition of existing property that the Corporation owns or in which it has an interest. These expenses are treated as program expenses. Such program expenses include inspection, classing, and grading work performed on a fee basis by Federal employees or Federal- or State-licensed inspectors; and special services performed by Federal agencies within and outside this Department. Most of these general expenses, including storage and handling, transportation, inspection, classing and grading, and producer storage payments, are included in program costs. They are shown in the program and financing schedule in the entries entitled "Storage, transportation, and other obligations not included above."

Section 161 of the 1996 Act amended Section 11 of the CCC Charter Act to limit the use of CCC funds for the transfer and allotment of funds to State and Federal agencies. The Section 11 cap of $56 million remains in 2022 and 2023.

The Corporation receives reimbursement for grain requisitioned pursuant to Public Law 87–152 by the States from Corporation stocks to feed resident wildlife threatened with starvation through the appropriation reimbursement for net realized losses. There have been no requisitions in recent years, however. The Corporation receives reimbursement for the commodity costs and other costs, including administrative costs, for commodities supplied to domestic nutrition programs and international food aid programs.

Financing

Appropriations.—Reimbursement for Net Realized Losses. Under Section 2 of Public Law 87–155, the Act of August 17 1961 (15 U.S.C. 713a 11), annual appropriations are authorized for each fiscal year, commencing with 1961, to reimburse the Corporation for net realized losses. The Omnibus Budget Reconciliation Act of 1987 amended Public Law 87–155 to authorize that the Corporation is reimbursed for its net realized losses by means of a current, indefinite appropriation as provided in annual appropriations acts. Appropriations to the Corporation for net realized losses have no effect on budget authority, as they are used to repay debt directly with the Treasury.

COMMODITY CREDIT CORPORATION FUND—Continued

Borrowing Authority.—The Corporation has an authorized capital stock of $100 million held by the U.S. Treasury and, effective in 1988, authority to have outstanding borrowings up to $30 billion at any one time. Funds are borrowed from the Treasury and may also be borrowed from private lending agencies and others. The Corporation reserves a sufficient amount of its borrowing authority to purchase at any time all notes and other obligations evidencing loans made to the Corporation by such agencies and others. All bonds, notes, debentures, and similar obligations issued by the Corporation are subject to approval by the Secretary of the Treasury as required by the Act of March 8, 1938.

Interest on borrowings from the Treasury (and on capital stock) is paid at a rate based upon the average interest rate of all outstanding marketable obligations (of comparable maturity date) of the United States as of the preceding month. Interest is also paid on other notes and obligations at a rate prescribed by the Corporation and approved by the Secretary of the Treasury. The Department of Agriculture and Related Agencies Appropriation Act, 1966, made provision for terminating interest after June 30, 1964 on the portion of the Corporation's borrowings from the Treasury equal to the unreimbursed realized losses recorded on the books of the Corporation after the end of the fiscal year in which such losses are realized.

Non-Expenditure Transfers.—The Commodity Credit Corporation transfers CCC funds to several agencies responsible for administering Farm Bill and other Corporation programs. Once transferred, the expenses are recorded in the receiving agencies accounts. One-time supplemental non-expenditure transfers occurred in 2021 and 2022. In 2021, $3 billion was transferred out of CCC with $500 million transferred to the Office of the Secretary to support drought recovery and encourage the adoption of water-smart management practices, $500 million transferred to the Office of the Secretary to provide relief from agricultural market disruptions, $500 million transferred to the Animal and Plant Health Inspection Service to prevent the spread of African Swine Fever, and a total of $1.5 billion transferred to the Agricultural Marketing Service and Food and Nutrition Service to provide assistance to help schools respond to supply chain disruptions. In 2022, $1 billion was transferred out of CCC to the Natural Resources Conservation Service for the "Partnerships for Climate-Smart Commodities" initiative.

Object Classification (in millions of dollars)

Identification code 012–4336–0–3–999		2021 actual	2022 est.	2023 est.
	Direct obligations:			
33.0	Investments and loans	6,446	8,979	9,349
41.0	Grants, subsidies, and contributions	6,988	4,397	3,565
99.0	Direct obligations	13,434	13,376	12,914
25.3	Reimbursable obligations: Other goods and services from Federal sources	1		
99.0	Reimbursable obligations	1		
99.9	Total new obligations, unexpired accounts	13,435	13,376	12,914

COMMODITY CREDIT CORPORATION EXPORT (LOANS) CREDIT GUARANTEE PROGRAM ACCOUNT

(INCLUDING TRANSFERS OF FUNDS)

For administrative expenses to carry out the Commodity Credit Corporation's Export Guarantee Program, GSM 102 and GSM 103, $6,063,000, to cover common overhead expenses as permitted by section 11 of the Commodity Credit Corporation Charter Act and in conformity with the Federal Credit Reform Act of 1990, which shall be transferred to and merged with the appropriation for "Foreign Agricultural Service, Salaries and Expenses".

Note.—A full-year 2022 appropriation for this account was not enacted at the time the Budget was prepared; therefore, the Budget assumes this account is operating under the Continuing Appropriations Act, 2022 (Division A of Public Law 117–43, as amended). The amounts included for 2022 reflect the annualized level provided by the continuing resolution.

Program and Financing (in millions of dollars)

Identification code 012–1336–0–1–351		2021 actual	2022 est.	2023 est.
	Obligations by program activity:			
	Credit program obligations:			
0702	Loan guarantee subsidy	1	3	2
0707	Reestimates of loan guarantee subsidy	7		
0708	Interest on reestimates of loan guarantee subsidy	13	1	
0709	Administrative expenses	6	6	6
0900	Total new obligations, unexpired accounts	27	10	8
	Budgetary resources:			
	Unobligated balance:			
1000	Unobligated balance brought forward, Oct 1			2
	Budget authority:			
	Appropriations, discretionary:			
1100	Appropriation	6	6	6
	Appropriations, mandatory:			
1200	Appropriation	21	6	2
1900	Budget authority (total)	27	12	8
1930	Total budgetary resources available	27	12	10
	Memorandum (non-add) entries:			
1941	Unexpired unobligated balance, end of year		2	2
	Change in obligated balance:			
	Unpaid obligations:			
3000	Unpaid obligations, brought forward, Oct 1	6	4	1
3010	New obligations, unexpired accounts	27	10	8
3020	Outlays (gross)	–28	–13	–8
3041	Recoveries of prior year unpaid obligations, expired	–1		
3050	Unpaid obligations, end of year	4	1	1
	Memorandum (non-add) entries:			
3100	Obligated balance, start of year	6	4	1
3200	Obligated balance, end of year	4	1	1
	Budget authority and outlays, net:			
	Discretionary:			
4000	Budget authority, gross	6	6	6
	Outlays, gross:			
4010	Outlays from new discretionary authority	4	3	3
4011	Outlays from discretionary balances	3	3	3
4020	Outlays, gross (total)	7	6	6
	Mandatory:			
4090	Budget authority, gross	21	6	2
	Outlays, gross:			
4100	Outlays from new mandatory authority	21	6	2
4101	Outlays from mandatory balances		1	
4110	Outlays, gross (total)	21	7	2
4180	Budget authority, net (total)	27	12	8
4190	Outlays, net (total)	28	13	8

Summary of Loan Levels, Subsidy Budget Authority and Outlays by Program (in millions of dollars)

Identification code 012–1336–0–1–351	2021 actual	2022 est.	2023 est.
Guaranteed loan levels supportable by subsidy budget authority:			
215001 GSM 102	2,130	5,000	5,000
215003 Export Guarantee Program—Facilities		500	500
215999 Total loan guarantee levels	2,130	5,500	5,500
Guaranteed loan subsidy (in percent):			
232001 GSM 102	–.24	–.25	–.26
232003 Export Guarantee Program—Facilities		–2.49	–1.77
232999 Weighted average subsidy rate	–.24	–.45	–.40
Guaranteed loan subsidy budget authority:			
233001 GSM 102	–5	–12	–13
233003 Export Guarantee Program—Facilities		–12	–9
233999 Total subsidy budget authority	–5	–24	–22
Guaranteed loan subsidy outlays:			
234001 GSM 102	–4	–4	–4
234999 Total subsidy outlays	–4	–4	–4
Guaranteed loan reestimates:			
235001 GSM 102	16	–7	
235002 Supplier Credit	–2	–6	
235999 Total guaranteed loan reestimates	14	–13	
Administrative expense data:			
3510 Budget authority	6	6	6
3590 Outlays from new authority	6	6	6

DEPARTMENT OF AGRICULTURE

This is the program account for the GSM-102 CCC Export Credit Guarantee Program. The GSM-102 Export Credit Guarantee Program covers credit terms of up to 18 months. Under this program, CCC does not provide financing, but guarantees payments due from foreign banks and buyers. Because payment is guaranteed, financial institutions in the United States can offer competitive credit terms to foreign banks, usually with interest rates based on the London Inter-Bank Offered Rate (LIBOR). If the foreign bank fails to make any payment as agreed, the exporter or assignee must submit a notice of default to the CCC. A claim for loss must be filed, and the CCC will promptly pay claims found to be in good order. CCC usually guarantees 98 percent of the principal payment due and interest based on a percentage of the one-year Treasury rate.

A portion of the GSM-102 guarantees is also made available as Facilities Guarantees. Under this activity, CCC guarantees export financing for capital goods and services to improve handling, marketing, processing, storage, or distribution of imported agricultural commodities and products.

The subsidy estimates for the GSM-102 program are determined in large part by the obligor's sovereign or non-sovereign country risk grade. These grades are developed annually by the International Credit Risk Assessment System Committee (ICRAS). In unusual circumstances, an ICRAS grade for a country may change during the fiscal year. The default estimates for GSM-102 guarantees still use the ICRAS grades, but are now based on programmatic experience and country-specific assumptions rather than the government-wide risk premia used previously.

As required by the Federal Credit Reform Act of 1990, this account records, for this program, the subsidy costs associated with the credit guarantees committed in 1992 and beyond (including modifications of credit guarantees that resulted from obligations or commitments in any year), as well as administrative expenses of this program. The subsidy amounts are estimated on a present value basis; the administrative expenses are estimated on a cash basis. The 2023 Budget displays the GSM loan guarantee volume, the subsidy level that can be justified by forecast economic conditions, and the expected supply/demand conditions of countries requesting GSM loan guarantees. The 2023 Budget includes $6.1 million for administrative expenses.

Object Classification (in millions of dollars)

Identification code 012–1336–0–1–351		2021 actual	2022 est.	2023 est.
	Direct obligations:			
25.3	Other goods and services from Federal sources	6	6	6
41.0	Grants, subsidies, and contributions	21	4	2
99.9	Total new obligations, unexpired accounts	27	10	8

COMMODITY CREDIT CORPORATION EXPORT GUARANTEE FINANCING ACCOUNT

Program and Financing (in millions of dollars)

Identification code 012–4337–0–3–351		2021 actual	2022 est.	2023 est.
	Obligations by program activity:			
	Credit program obligations:			
0711	Default claim payments on principal		4	13
0713	Payment of interest to Treasury	13	13	13
0715	Pro Rata Share of Claims paid to banks	1	2	3
0740	Negative subsidy obligations	6	25	22
0742	Downward reestimates paid to receipt accounts	4	13	
0743	Interest on downward reestimates	2	2	
0900	Total new obligations, unexpired accounts	26	59	51
	Budgetary resources:			
	Unobligated balance:			
1000	Unobligated balance brought forward, Oct 1	15	19	120
1023	Unobligated balances applied to repay debt	–5		
1070	Unobligated balance (total)	10	19	120
	Financing authority:			
	Borrowing authority, mandatory:			
1400	Borrowing authority	106	66	67
1422	Borrowing authority applied to repay debt	–101		
1440	Borrowing authority, mandatory (total)	5	66	67
	Spending authority from offsetting collections, mandatory:			
1800	Collected	39	94	103
1825	Spending authority from offsetting collections applied to repay debt	–9		
1850	Spending auth from offsetting collections, mand (total)	30	94	103
1900	Budget authority (total)	35	160	170
1930	Total budgetary resources available	45	179	290
	Memorandum (non-add) entries:			
1941	Unexpired unobligated balance, end of year	19	120	239
	Change in obligated balance:			
	Unpaid obligations:			
3000	Unpaid obligations, brought forward, Oct 1	1	1	1
3010	New obligations, unexpired accounts	26	59	51
3020	Outlays (gross)	–26	–59	–52
3050	Unpaid obligations, end of year	1	1	
	Memorandum (non-add) entries:			
3100	Obligated balance, start of year	1	1	1
3200	Obligated balance, end of year	1	1	
	Financing authority and disbursements, net:			
	Mandatory:			
4090	Budget authority, gross	35	160	170
	Financing disbursements:			
4110	Outlays, gross (total)	26	59	52
	Offsets against gross financing authority and disbursements:			
	Offsetting collections (collected) from:			
4120	Payments from Program Account Upward Reestimate	–19	–2	
4120	Payments from Program Account Positive Subsidy	–2	–2	–3
4122	Interest on uninvested funds	–4	–2	–2
4123	Loan origination fee	–9	–43	–42
4123	Recoveries of Principal	–2	–38	–47
4123	Recoveries of Interest	–1	–7	–9
4123	Other Collections - Non-Federal sources	–2		
4130	Offsets against gross budget authority and outlays (total)	–39	–94	–103
4160	Budget authority, net (mandatory)	–4	66	67
4170	Outlays, net (mandatory)	–13	–35	–51
4180	Budget authority, net (total)	–4	66	67
4190	Outlays, net (total)	–13	–35	–51

Status of Guaranteed Loans (in millions of dollars)

Identification code 012–4337–0–3–351		2021 actual	2022 est.	2023 est.
	Position with respect to appropriations act limitation on commitments:			
2111	Guaranteed loan commitments from current-year authority	2,130	5,500	5,500
2150	Total guaranteed loan commitments	2,130	5,500	5,500
2199	Guaranteed amount of guaranteed loan commitments	2,045	5,400	5,400
	Cumulative balance of guaranteed loans outstanding:			
2210	Outstanding, start of year	2,178	1,981	2,275
2231	Disbursements of new guaranteed loans	1,960	5,500	5,500
2251	Repayments and prepayments	–2,157	–5,202	–5,202
2263	Adjustments: Terminations for default that result in claim payments		–4	–13
2290	Outstanding, end of year	1,981	2,275	2,560
	Memorandum:			
2299	Guaranteed amount of guaranteed loans outstanding, end of year	1,938	2,220	2,495
	Addendum:			
	Cumulative balance of defaulted guaranteed loans that result in loans receivable:			
2310	Outstanding, start of year	386	396	351
2331	Disbursements for guaranteed loan claims			
2351	Repayments of loans receivable	–2	–45	–52
2364	Other adjustments, net	12		
2390	Outstanding, end of year	396	351	299

Balance Sheet (in millions of dollars)

Identification code 012–4337–0–3–351		2020 actual	2021 actual
	ASSETS:		
	Federal assets:		
1101	Fund balances with Treasury	15	19

COMMODITY CREDIT CORPORATION EXPORT GUARANTEE FINANCING ACCOUNT—Continued
Balance Sheet—Continued

Identification code 012–4337–0–3–351	2020 actual	2021 actual
1101 Accounts Receivable, net		
Investments in U.S. securities:		
1106 Receivables, net	20	2
Net value of assets related to post-1991 acquired defaulted guaranteed loans receivable:		
1501 Defaulted guaranteed loans receivable, gross	386	396
1502 Interest receivable	17	18
1505 Allowance for subsidy cost (–)	–238	–246
1599 Net present value of assets related to defaulted guaranteed loans	165	168
1999 Total assets	200	189
LIABILITIES:		
Federal liabilities:		
2101 Accounts payable		
2103 Debt	179	169
2104 Resources payable to Treasury		
2105 Other	11	12
Non-Federal liabilities:		
2201 Accounts payable	1	1
2204 Liabilities for loan guarantees	7	3
2207 Other	2	4
2999 Total liabilities	200	189
NET POSITION:		
3300 Cumulative results of operations		
4999 Total liabilities and net position	200	189

COMMODITY CREDIT CORPORATION GUARANTEED LOANS LIQUIDATING ACCOUNT
Program and Financing (in millions of dollars)

Identification code 012–4338–0–3–351	2021 actual	2022 est.	2023 est.
Change in obligated balance:			
Unpaid obligations:			
3000 Unpaid obligations, brought forward, Oct 1	9	9	5
3020 Outlays (gross)		–4	–4
3050 Unpaid obligations, end of year	9	5	1
Memorandum (non-add) entries:			
3100 Obligated balance, start of year	9	9	5
3200 Obligated balance, end of year	9	5	1
Budget authority and outlays, net:			
Mandatory:			
Outlays, gross:			
4101 Outlays from mandatory balances		4	4
4180 Budget authority, net (total)			
4190 Outlays, net (total)		4	4

Balance Sheet (in millions of dollars)

Identification code 012–4338–0–3–351	2020 actual	2021 actual
ASSETS:		
1101 Federal assets: Fund balances with Treasury	9	9
1701 Defaulted guaranteed loans, gross		
1702 Interest receivable		
1703 Allowance for estimated uncollectible loans and interest (–)		
1799 Value of assets related to loan guarantees		
1999 Total assets	9	9
LIABILITIES:		
Federal liabilities:		
2101 Accounts payable		
2104 Resources payable to Treasury		
Non-Federal liabilities:		
2201 Accounts payable	9	9
2207 Other		
2999 Total liabilities	9	9

4999 Total liabilities and net position	9	9

FARM STORAGE FACILITY LOANS PROGRAM ACCOUNT
Program and Financing (in millions of dollars)

Identification code 012–3301–0–1–351	2021 actual	2022 est.	2023 est.
Obligations by program activity:			
Credit program obligations:			
0705 Reestimates of direct loan subsidy	7	3	
0706 Interest on reestimates of direct loan subsidy		1	
0900 Total new obligations, unexpired accounts (object class 41.0)	7	4	
Budgetary resources:			
Budget authority:			
Appropriations, mandatory:			
1200 Appropriation	7	4	
1930 Total budgetary resources available	7	4	
Change in obligated balance:			
Unpaid obligations:			
3010 New obligations, unexpired accounts	7	4	
3020 Outlays (gross)	–7	–4	
Budget authority and outlays, net:			
Mandatory:			
4090 Budget authority, gross	7	4	
Outlays, gross:			
4100 Outlays from new mandatory authority	7	4	
4180 Budget authority, net (total)	7	4	
4190 Outlays, net (total)	7	4	

Summary of Loan Levels, Subsidy Budget Authority and Outlays by Program (in millions of dollars)

Identification code 012–3301–0–1–351	2021 actual	2022 est.	2023 est.
Direct loan levels supportable by subsidy budget authority:			
115001 Farm Storage Facility Loans	429	500	500
115002 Sugar Storage Facility Loans	24	69	69
115999 Total direct loan levels	453	569	569
Direct loan subsidy (in percent):			
132001 Farm Storage Facility Loans	–.85	–1.45	–1.31
132002 Sugar Storage Facility Loans	–2.05	–4.11	–2.87
132999 Weighted average subsidy rate	–.91	–1.77	–1.50
Direct loan subsidy budget authority:			
133001 Farm Storage Facility Loans	–4	–7	–7
133002 Sugar Storage Facility Loans		–3	–2
133999 Total subsidy budget authority	–4	–10	–9
Direct loan subsidy outlays:			
134001 Farm Storage Facility Loans	–1	–4	–4
134999 Total subsidy outlays	–1	–4	–4
Direct loan reestimates:			
135001 Farm Storage Facility Loans	–42	–20	
135999 Total direct loan reestimates	–42	–20	

Farm Storage Facility Loan (FSFL) Program.—The FSFL program was established by the Commodity Credit Corporation (CCC) in 1949 to offer low-cost financing to producers for the construction or upgrade of on-farm storage facilities—the program was discontinued in the early 1980s when studies showed sufficient storage space was available. The FSFL was re-established in 2000 due to a severe shortage of available storage. The program was implemented in 2000 by CCC under Section 504(c) of the Federal Credit Reform Act of 1990. The Agriculture Improvement Act of 2018 (the 2018 Farm Bill) continues the authority for this program. The program now provides producers financing with seven, ten, or twelve-year repayment terms and low interest rates. The program also offers a micro-loan option for loans under $50,000 with three, five, or seven year repayment terms. The program gives producers greater marketing flexibility when farm storage is limited and/or transportation difficulties cause storage problems, allows farmers to benefit from new marketing and technological advances, and maximizes their returns through identity-preserved marketing.

DEPARTMENT OF AGRICULTURE

Sugar Storage Facility Loans.—The 2002 Farm Bill, as amended by the 2008 Farm Bill and extended through the 2018 Farm Bill, directs that CCC establish a sugar storage facility loan program to provide financing for processors of domestically produced sugarcane and sugar beets to construct or upgrade storage and handling facilities for raw sugars and refined sugars. The loan term is a minimum of seven years with the amount and terms being determined as any other commercial loan.

As required by the Federal Credit Reform Act of 1990, this account records the subsidy costs associated with the direct loans obligated in 1992 and beyond, as well as administrative expenses of this program. The subsidy amounts are estimated on a present value basis, and the administrative expenses are estimated on a cash basis.

FARM STORAGE FACILITY DIRECT LOAN FINANCING ACCOUNT

Program and Financing (in millions of dollars)

Identification code 012–4158–0–3–351	2021 actual	2022 est.	2023 est.
Obligations by program activity:			
Credit program obligations:			
0710 Direct loan obligations	453	569	569
0713 Payment of interest to Treasury	27	26	26
0740 Negative subsidy obligations	4	10	10
0742 Downward reestimates paid to receipt accounts	44	22	
0743 Interest on downward reestimates	5	2	
0900 Total new obligations, unexpired accounts	533	629	605
Budgetary resources:			
Unobligated balance:			
1000 Unobligated balance brought forward, Oct 1	109	62	
1021 Recoveries of prior year unpaid obligations	18		
1023 Unobligated balances applied to repay debt	–92	–62	
1070 Unobligated balance (total)	35		
Financing authority:			
Borrowing authority, mandatory:			
1400 Borrowing authority	542	629	605
1422 Borrowing authority applied to repay debt	–24		
1440 Borrowing authority, mandatory (total)	518	629	605
Spending authority from offsetting collections, mandatory:			
1800 Payments from program account (Upward Reestimate)	7	4	
1800 Principal repayments	210	221	239
1800 Interest repayments	21	21	22
1800 Interest on Uninvested Funds	11	11	11
1800 Fees and Other Collections		1	1
1825 Spending authority from offsetting collections applied to repay debt	–207	–258	–273
1850 Spending auth from offsetting collections, mand (total)	42		
1900 Budget authority (total)	560	629	605
1930 Total budgetary resources available	595	629	605
Memorandum (non-add) entries:			
1941 Unexpired unobligated balance, end of year	62		
Change in obligated balance:			
Unpaid obligations:			
3000 Unpaid obligations, brought forward, Oct 1	266	366	460
3010 New obligations, unexpired accounts	533	629	605
3020 Outlays (gross)	–415	–535	–605
3040 Recoveries of prior year unpaid obligations, unexpired	–18		
3050 Unpaid obligations, end of year	366	460	460
Memorandum (non-add) entries:			
3100 Obligated balance, start of year	266	366	460
3200 Obligated balance, end of year	366	460	460
Financing authority and disbursements, net:			
Mandatory:			
4090 Budget authority, gross	560	629	605
Financing disbursements:			
4110 Outlays, gross (total)	415	535	605
Offsets against gross financing authority and disbursements:			
Offsetting collections (collected) from:			
4120 Payment from program account Upward Reestimate	–7	–4	
4122 Interest on uninvested funds	–11	–11	–11
4123 Principal collections	–210	–221	–239
4123 Interest collections	–21	–21	–22
4123 Fees and Other Collections		–1	–1
4130 Offsets against gross budget authority and outlays (total)	–249	–258	–273
4160 Budget authority, net (mandatory)	311	371	332
4170 Outlays, net (mandatory)	166	277	332
4180 Budget authority, net (total)	311	371	332
4190 Outlays, net (total)	166	277	332

Status of Direct Loans (in millions of dollars)

Identification code 012–4158–0–3–351	2021 actual	2022 est.	2023 est.
Position with respect to appropriations act limitation on obligations:			
1111 Direct loan obligations from current-year authority	453	569	569
1150 Total direct loan obligations	453	569	569
Cumulative balance of direct loans outstanding:			
1210 Outstanding, start of year	913	1,047	1,307
1231 Disbursements: Direct loan disbursements	343	481	569
1251 Repayments: Repayments and prepayments	–210	–221	–239
1264 Other adjustments, net (+ or –)	1		
1290 Outstanding, end of year	1,047	1,307	1,637

Balance Sheet (in millions of dollars)

Identification code 012–4158–0–3–351	2020 actual	2021 actual
ASSETS:		
Federal assets:		
1101 Fund balances with Treasury	376	428
Investments in U.S. securities:		
1106 Receivables, net	7	4
1206 Non-Federal assets: Receivables, net	11	7
Net value of assets related to post-1991 direct loans receivable:		
1401 Direct loans receivable, gross	913	1,047
1402 Interest receivable	10	11
1405 Allowance for subsidy cost (-)	–20	–6
1499 Net present value of assets related to direct loans	903	1,052
1801 Other Federal assets: Cash and other monetary assets	1	1
1999 Total assets	1,298	1,492
LIABILITIES:		
Federal liabilities:		
2103 Debt payable to Treasury	1,242	1,460
2105 Other Federal Liabilities	49	8
2201 Non-Federal liabilities: Accounts payable	7	24
2999 Total liabilities	1,298	1,492
NET POSITION:		
3300 Cumulative results of operations		
4999 Total liabilities and net position	1,298	1,492

APPLE LOANS PROGRAM ACCOUNT

The Agricultural Risk Protection Act of 2000 authorized up to $5 million for the cost to provide loans to producers of apples for economic losses as the result of low prices. Although the program is funded through the Commodity Credit Corporation, program management is performed through farm loan programs. No further funding is requested for this program.

As required by the Federal Credit Reform Act of 1990, this account records, for this program, the subsidy costs associated with the direct loans obligated in 1992 and beyond (including modifications of direct loans or loan guarantees that resulted from obligations or commitments in any year), as well as administrative expenses of this program. The subsidy amounts are estimated on a present value basis.

EMERGENCY BOLL WEEVIL DIRECT LOAN FINANCING ACCOUNT

Program and Financing (in millions of dollars)

Identification code 012–4221–0–3–351	2021 actual	2022 est.	2023 est.
Budgetary resources:			
Unobligated balance:			
1000 Unobligated balance brought forward, Oct 1	1		
1023 Unobligated balances applied to repay debt	–1		

114 Farm Service Agency—Continued
Federal Funds—Continued

THE BUDGET FOR FISCAL YEAR 2023

EMERGENCY BOLL WEEVIL DIRECT LOAN FINANCING ACCOUNT—Continued

Program and Financing—Continued

Identification code 012–4221–0–3–351	2021 actual	2022 est.	2023 est.
Financing authority:			
Spending authority from offsetting collections, mandatory:			
1800 Principal repayments	2	....	....
1825 Spending authority from offsetting collections applied to repay debt	–2	....	....
Financing authority and disbursements, net:			
Mandatory:			
Offsets against gross financing authority and disbursements:			
Offsetting collections (collected) from:			
4123 Principal repayments	–2	....	....
4180 Budget authority, net (total)	–2	....	....
4190 Outlays, net (total)	–2	....	....

Status of Direct Loans (in millions of dollars)

Identification code 012–4221–0–3–351	2021 actual	2022 est.	2023 est.
Cumulative balance of direct loans outstanding:			
1210 Outstanding, start of year	2	....	....
1251 Repayments: Repayments and prepayments	–2	....	....

Balance Sheet (in millions of dollars)

Identification code 012–4221–0–3–351	2020 actual	2021 actual
ASSETS:		
Federal assets:		
Investments in U.S. securities:		
1106 Receivables, net	1	....
Net value of assets related to post-1991 direct loans receivable:		
1401 Direct loans receivable, gross	2	....
1405 Allowance for subsidy cost (–)	....	....
1499 Net present value of assets related to direct loans	2	....
1999 Total assets	3	....
LIABILITIES:		
Federal liabilities:		
2101 Accounts payable	....	....
2103 Debt	3	....
2999 Total liabilities	3	....
4999 Total liabilities and net position	3	....

AGRICULTURAL DISASTER RELIEF FUND

Program and Financing (in millions of dollars)

Identification code 012–5531–0–2–351	2021 actual	2022 est.	2023 est.
Budgetary resources:			
Unobligated balance:			
1000 Unobligated balance brought forward, Oct 1	15	....	....
1023 Unobligated balances applied to repay debt	–15	....	....
4180 Budget authority, net (total)	....	....	....
4190 Outlays, net (total)	....	....	....
Memorandum (non-add) entries:			
5080 Outstanding debt, SOY	–2,610	–2,610	–2,610
5081 Outstanding debt, EOY	–2,610	–2,610	–2,610

The Agricultural Disaster Relief Trust Fund, established under Section 902 of the Food, Conservation, and Energy Act of 2008, administered by USDA Farm Service Agency, used to execute payments to farmers and ranchers under the following five disaster assistance programs: Supplemental Revenue Assistance Payments (SURE) Program, Livestock Forage Disaster Program (LFP), Livestock Indemnity Program (LIP), Tree Assistance Program (TAP), and Emergency Assistance for Livestock, Honey Bees, and Farm-Raised Fish (ELAP) Program. The Agricultural Act of 2014, the 2014 Farm Bill, extended all but SURE and shifted the funding authority for these disaster programs from the Agriculture Disaster Relief Trust Fund to the Commodity Credit Corporation. In FY 2021, the outlays are due to residual payments, corrections and/or appeals to obligations incurred during prior crop years. Obligations in 2022 and 2023 may be still be required to make residual payments for disaster programs under the Disaster Trust authority.

PIMA AGRICULTURE COTTON TRUST FUND

Program and Financing (in millions of dollars)

Identification code 012–5635–0–2–351	2021 actual	2022 est.	2023 est.
Obligations by program activity:			
0001 Pima Cotton Agreements	15	15	15
0900 Total new obligations, unexpired accounts (object class 41.0)	15	15	15
Budgetary resources:			
Budget authority:			
Appropriations, mandatory:			
1222 Exercised borrowing authority transferred from other accounts [012–4336]	16	16	16
1232 Appropriations and/or unobligated balance of appropriations temporarily reduced	–1	–1	–1
1260 Appropriations, mandatory (total)	15	15	15
1930 Total budgetary resources available	15	15	15
Change in obligated balance:			
Unpaid obligations:			
3010 New obligations, unexpired accounts	15	15	15
3020 Outlays (gross)	–15	–15	–15
Budget authority and outlays, net:			
Mandatory:			
4090 Budget authority, gross	15	15	15
Outlays, gross:			
4100 Outlays from new mandatory authority	15	15	15
4180 Budget authority, net (total)	15	15	15
4190 Outlays, net (total)	15	15	15

The Pima Agriculture Cotton Trust Fund was authorized under Section 12314 of the Agricultural Act of 2014, the 2014 Farm Bill, to reduce the economic injury to domestic manufacturers resulting from tariffs on cotton fabric that are higher than tariffs on certain apparel articles made of cotton fabric. Mandatory funding as established in the Farm Bill is $16 million annually, to be transferred from funds of the Commodity Credit Corporation. Through the Agriculture Improvement Act of 2018, the 2018 Farm Bill, this program is extended through calendar year 2023.

AGRICULTURE WOOL APPAREL MANUFACTURERS TRUST FUND

Program and Financing (in millions of dollars)

Identification code 012–5636–0–2–351	2021 actual	2022 est.	2023 est.
Obligations by program activity:			
0001 Wool Manufacturers Payments	20	37	37
0900 Total new obligations, unexpired accounts (object class 41.0)	20	37	37
Budgetary resources:			
Unobligated balance:			
1000 Unobligated balance brought forward, Oct 1	18	26	17
Budget authority:			
Appropriations, mandatory:			
1222 Exercised borrowing authority transferred from other accounts [012–4336]	30	30	30
1232 Appropriations and/or unobligated balance of appropriations temporarily reduced	–2	–2	–2
1260 Appropriations, mandatory (total)	28	28	28
1930 Total budgetary resources available	46	54	45
Memorandum (non-add) entries:			
1941 Unexpired unobligated balance, end of year	26	17	8
Change in obligated balance:			
Unpaid obligations:			
3000 Unpaid obligations, brought forward, Oct 1	....	....	4

DEPARTMENT OF AGRICULTURE

Natural Resources Conservation Service
Federal Funds   115

		2021 actual	2022 est.	2023 est.
3010	New obligations, unexpired accounts	20	37	37
3020	Outlays (gross)	−20	−33	−33
3050	Unpaid obligations, end of year		4	8
	Memorandum (non-add) entries:			
3100	Obligated balance, start of year			4
3200	Obligated balance, end of year		4	8
	Budget authority and outlays, net:			
	Mandatory:			
4090	Budget authority, gross	28	28	28
	Outlays, gross:			
4100	Outlays from new mandatory authority	20	28	28
4101	Outlays from mandatory balances		5	5
4110	Outlays, gross (total)	20	33	33
4180	Budget authority, net (total)	28	28	28
4190	Outlays, net (total)	20	33	33

The Agriculture Wool Apparel Manufacturers Trust Fund was authorized under Section 12315 of the Agricultural Act of 2014, the 2014 Farm Bill, to reduce the economic injury to domestic manufacturers resulting from tariffs on wool fabric that are higher than tariffs on certain apparel articles made of wool fabric. Mandatory funding as established in the Farm Bill is the lesser of the amount the Secretary determines to be necessary to make payments in that year or $30 million each year, to be transferred from funds of the Commodity Credit Corporation. Per the Agriculture Improvement Act of 2018, the 2018 Farm Bill, this program is extended through calendar year 2023.

Trust Funds

TOBACCO TRUST FUND

Special and Trust Fund Receipts (in millions of dollars)

Identification code 012–8161–0–7–351		2021 actual	2022 est.	2023 est.
0100	Balance, start of year			
	Receipts:			
	Current law:			
1110	Excise Taxes for Tobacco Assessments, Tobacco Trust Fund	2		
2000	Total: Balances and receipts	2		
	Appropriations:			
	Current law:			
2101	Tobacco Trust Fund	−2		
5099	Balance, end of year			

Program and Financing (in millions of dollars)

Identification code 012–8161–0–7–351		2021 actual	2022 est.	2023 est.
	Obligations by program activity:			
0001	Tobacco Buyout Cost Reimbursement to CCC	2	1	1
0900	Total new obligations, unexpired accounts (object class 41.0)	2	1	1
	Budgetary resources:			
	Budget authority:			
	Appropriations, mandatory:			
1201	Appropriation (special or trust fund)	2		
	Spending authority from offsetting collections, mandatory:			
1800	Collected		1	1
1900	Budget authority (total)	2	1	1
1930	Total budgetary resources available	2	1	1
	Change in obligated balance:			
	Unpaid obligations:			
3010	New obligations, unexpired accounts	2	1	1
3020	Outlays (gross)	−2	−1	
3050	Unpaid obligations, end of year			1
	Memorandum (non-add) entries:			
3200	Obligated balance, end of year			1
	Budget authority and outlays, net:			
	Mandatory:			
4090	Budget authority, gross	2	1	1

		2021 actual	2022 est.	2023 est.
	Outlays, gross:			
4100	Outlays from new mandatory authority			1
4101	Outlays from mandatory balances	2		
4110	Outlays, gross (total)	2	1	
	Offsets against gross budget authority and outlays:			
	Offsetting collections (collected) from:			
4123	Non-Federal sources		−1	−1
4180	Budget authority, net (total)	2		
4190	Outlays, net (total)	2		−1

NATURAL RESOURCES CONSERVATION SERVICE

Federal Funds

CONSERVATION OPERATIONS

For necessary expenses for carrying out the provisions of the Act of April 27, 1935 (16 U.S.C. 590a-f), including preparation of conservation plans and establishment of measures to conserve soil and water (including farm irrigation and land drainage and such special measures for soil and water management as may be necessary to prevent floods and the siltation of reservoirs and to control agricultural related pollutants); operation of conservation plant materials centers; classification and mapping of soil; dissemination of information; acquisition of lands, water, and interests therein for use in the plant materials program by donation, exchange, or purchase at a nominal cost not to exceed $100 pursuant to the Act of August 3, 1956 (7 U.S.C. 2268a); purchase and erection or alteration or improvement of permanent and temporary buildings; and operation and maintenance of aircraft, $1,001,101,000, to remain available until September 30, 2024: Provided, That appropriations hereunder shall be available pursuant to 7 U.S.C. 2250 for construction and improvement of buildings and public improvements at plant materials centers, except that the cost of alterations and improvements to other buildings and other public improvements shall not exceed $250,000: Provided further, That when buildings or other structures are erected on non-Federal land, that the right to use such land is obtained as provided in 7 U.S.C. 2250a.

Note.—A full-year 2022 appropriation for this account was not enacted at the time the Budget was prepared; therefore, the Budget assumes this account is operating under the Continuing Appropriations Act, 2022 (Division A of Public Law 117–43, as amended). The amounts included for 2022 reflect the annualized level provided by the continuing resolution.

Program and Financing (in millions of dollars)

Identification code 012–1000–0–1–302		2021 actual	2022 est.	2023 est.
	Obligations by program activity:			
0001	Conservation Technical Assistance	736	791	885
0002	Soil surveys	76	88	87
0003	Snow survey and water forecasting	11	10	17
0004	Plant materials centers	10	11	14
0005	Watershed Projects	3	3	
0006	Partnerships for Climate-Smart Commodities		800	200
0799	Total direct obligations	836	1,703	1,203
0801	EPA Great Lakes - Reimbursable	3	5	5
0802	Reimbursable Agency Activity	10	8	8
0899	Total reimbursable obligations	13	13	13
0900	Total new obligations, unexpired accounts	849	1,716	1,216
	Budgetary resources:			
	Unobligated balance:			
1000	Unobligated balance brought forward, Oct 1	144	138	268
1021	Recoveries of prior year unpaid obligations	11		
1070	Unobligated balance (total)	155	138	268
	Budget authority:			
	Appropriations, discretionary:			
1100	Appropriation	833	833	1,001
	Appropriations, mandatory:			
1222	Exercised borrowing authority transferred from other accounts [012–4336]		1,000	
	Spending authority from offsetting collections, discretionary:			
1700	Collected	13	13	13
1701	Change in uncollected payments, Federal sources	7		
1750	Spending auth from offsetting collections, disc (total)	20	13	13
1900	Budget authority (total)	853	1,846	1,014
1930	Total budgetary resources available	1,008	1,984	1,282
	Memorandum (non-add) entries:			
1940	Unobligated balance expiring	−21		
1941	Unexpired unobligated balance, end of year	138	268	66

CONSERVATION OPERATIONS—Continued
Program and Financing—Continued

Identification code 012–1000–0–1–302	2021 actual	2022 est.	2023 est.
Change in obligated balance:			
Unpaid obligations:			
3000 Unpaid obligations, brought forward, Oct 1	535	538	1,077
3010 New obligations, unexpired accounts	849	1,716	1,216
3011 Obligations ("upward adjustments"), expired accounts	17		
3020 Outlays (gross)	–836	–1,177	–1,218
3040 Recoveries of prior year unpaid obligations, unexpired	–11		
3041 Recoveries of prior year unpaid obligations, expired	–16		
3050 Unpaid obligations, end of year	538	1,077	1,075
Uncollected payments:			
3060 Uncollected pymts, Fed sources, brought forward, Oct 1	–107	–102	–102
3070 Change in uncollected pymts, Fed sources, unexpired	–7		
3071 Change in uncollected pymts, Fed sources, expired	12		
3090 Uncollected pymts, Fed sources, end of year	–102	–102	–102
Memorandum (non-add) entries:			
3100 Obligated balance, start of year	428	436	975
3200 Obligated balance, end of year	436	975	973
Budget authority and outlays, net:			
Discretionary:			
4000 Budget authority, gross	853	846	1,014
Outlays, gross:			
4010 Outlays from new discretionary authority	532	610	731
4011 Outlays from discretionary balances	304	217	187
4020 Outlays, gross (total)	836	827	918
Offsets against gross budget authority and outlays:			
Offsetting collections (collected) from:			
4030 Federal sources	–12	–13	–13
4033 Non-Federal sources	–8		
4040 Offsets against gross budget authority and outlays (total)	–20	–13	–13
Additional offsets against gross budget authority only:			
4050 Change in uncollected pymts, Fed sources, unexpired	–7		
4052 Offsetting collections credited to expired accounts	7		
4070 Budget authority, net (discretionary)	833	833	1,001
4080 Outlays, net (discretionary)	816	814	905
Mandatory:			
4090 Budget authority, gross		1,000	
Outlays, gross:			
4100 Outlays from new mandatory authority		350	
4101 Outlays from mandatory balances			300
4110 Outlays, gross (total)		350	300
4180 Budget authority, net (total)	833	1,833	1,001
4190 Outlays, net (total)	816	1,164	1,205

The Natural Resources Conservation Service (NRCS) supports the rural economy and helps private landowners and producers protect the natural resource base on private lands. NRCS provides technical assistance to farmers, ranchers and other private landowners to support the development of conservation plans that are designed to safeguard natural resources and improve wildlife habitat. These plans are often used as a springboard toward receiving financial assistance through mandatory Farm Bill conservation programs. NRCS provides additional science-based support for conservation efforts through soil surveys, snow survey and water supply forecasting, and plant materials centers. These activities are supported by appropriated funding, including funding requested in the Private Lands Conservation Operations account, and by mandatory funding through Farm Bill programs. NRCS comprises over 11,000 employees with a wide range of natural resource backgrounds, including soil and rangeland conservation, plant science, wildlife biology, forestry and engineering. Through this collective conservationist workforce, the Administration strives to protect the natural resource base on private lands. The 2023 Budget proposes a total of $1.001 billion for the Private Lands Conservation Operations (PLCO) account.

Within the amounts provided for PLCO, the Budget includes $4 million for NRCS to support USDA efforts to develop and implement a program to measure, monitor, report, and verify the carbon sequestration, greenhouse gas reduction, and other environmental benefits of agricultural practices at the farm level and to increase the adoption of climate-smart agricultural practices.

Technical assistance.—Through the Conservation Technical Assistance (CTA) Program, NRCS provides its customers and partners—agricultural producers, private landowners, conservation districts, Tribes, and other organizations—the knowledge and conservation tools they need to conserve, maintain, and improve our private-land natural resources. This assistance centers around individual and landscape-scale conservation plans that contain optimal strategies tailored to protect the resources on the land they manage. Actions described in the plans help land managers reduce erosion; protect water quality and quantity; improve air quality; enhance the quality of fish and wildlife habitat; improve long-term sustainability of all lands; and facilitate land use changes while protecting and sustaining our natural resources. The CTA Program also provides the science-based tools that support conservation planning.

MAIN WORKLOAD FACTORS

	2021 Actual	2022 Estimate	2023 Estimate
Customers receiving technical assistance for planning & application, number	135,000	135,000	135,000
Conservation assessment completed, million acres	59	60	60
Conservation systems planned, million acres	23.9	24	24

In addition to technical assistance for conservation planning provided through the CTA Program, NRCS also offers technical assistance for the design, implementation, and management of conservation practices through mandatory Farm Bill conservation programs under the Farm Security and Rural Investment Programs. This combined technical assistance funding provides for the salaries and expenses of conservation professionals, including NRCS's extensive field staff and a growing number of technical service providers and other cooperators who work with land managers in assessing and applying conservation strategies.

NRCS Technical Assistance[1]

	2021 Actual	2022 Enacted	2023 Budget[2]
Discretionary			
Conservation Technical Assistance	731	731	885
Soil Surveys	79	79	87
Snow Surveys	9	9	17
Plant Materials	10	10	12
Watershed Projects	3	3	0
Total, Discretionary Programs	832	832	1,001
Mandatory			
Farm Bill Programs			
Environmental Quality Incentives Program	617	625	593
Agricultural Conservation Easement Program	192	219	162
Regional Conservation Partnership Program	289	370	287
Conservation Stewardship Program	659	504	423
Agricultural Management Assistance Program[3]	1	1	1
Conservation Reserve Program Technical Assistance	236	328	256
Voluntary Public Access and Habitat Incentive Program	1	2	0
Feral Swine Eradication and Control Pilot	3	1	1
Agriculture Water Enhancement Program	5	6	1
Farm and Ranchland Protection Program	47	40	14
Grassland Reserve Program	20	15	3
Wetland Reserve Program	17	11	1
Wildlife Habitat Incentives Program	5	5	1
Chesapeake Bay Watershed Program	4	4	0
Healthy Forests Reserve Program	1	1	0
Total, Mandatory Programs	2,097	2,132	1,743
Total, Private Lands Conservation Operations	2,929	2,964	2,744

[1] This table reflects the total staff resources necessary to implement private lands conservation programs administered by the Natural Resources Conservation Service. This table includes the total for discretionary technical assistance and associated science and technology programs provided through the Private Lands Conservation Operations account in addition to the total technical assistance necessary to implement Farm Bill programs.

[2] The 2023 Budget assumes estimated carryover of $504 million.

[3] NRCS is authorized to receive 50 percent of total AMA funding. The balance of the funds are allocated to the Risk Management Agency and the Agricultural Marketing Service.

Soil surveys.—The primary focus of the Soil Survey Program is to provide current and consistent map interpretations and data sets of the soil resources of the United States. Managing soil as a strategic natural resource is key to the vitality of the Nation's economy. Scientists and policy makers use soil survey information to help evaluate the sustainability and environmental effects of land use and management practices. Soil surveys are used by planners, engineers, farmers, ranchers, developers, and home owners to

DEPARTMENT OF AGRICULTURE

evaluate soil suitability and make management decisions for farms, home sites, subdivisions, commercial and industrial sites, and wildlife and recreational areas. NRCS is the lead Federal agency for the National Cooperative Soil Survey (NCSS), a partnership of Federal land management agencies, State agricultural experiment stations, private consultants, and State and local governments that works to cooperatively investigate, inventory, document, classify, interpret, disseminate, and publish information about soils. NRCS provides the scientific expertise to enable the NCSS to develop and maintain a uniform system for mapping and assessing soil resources.

MAIN WORKLOAD FACTORS

	2021 Actual	2022 Estimate	2023 Estimate
Acres mapped annually (millions)	55	60	65

Snow survey and water supply forecasting.—The purpose of the program is to provide western States and Alaska with information on annual water supplies for decisions relating to agricultural production, fish and wildlife management, municipal and industrial water supply, urban development, flood control, recreation, hydroelectric power generation, and water quantity management. NRCS field staff and cooperators collect and analyze data on snow depth, snow water equivalent, and other climate parameters at approximately 2,000 remote, high elevation data collection sites. Snow Survey data and water supply forecasts are used by individual farmers and ranchers; water resource managers; Federal, State, and local government agencies; municipal and industrial water providers; hydroelectric power generation utilities; irrigation districts; fish and wildlife management agencies; reservoir project managers; recreationists; Tribal Nations; and the countries of Canada and Mexico.

Plant Material Centers (PMCs).—NRCS's network of 25 PMCs identify, evaluate, and demonstrate the performance of plants and plant technologies to help solve natural resource problems and improve the utilization of our nation's natural resources. PMCs continue to build on their long and successful history of releasing plants for resource conservation that have been instrumental at increasing the commercial availability of appropriate plant materials to the public. PMC activities contribute to reducing soil erosion; increasing cropland soil health and productivity; restoring wetlands, improving water quality, improving wildlife habitat (including pollinators); protecting streambank and riparian areas; stabilizing coastal dunes; producing forage; improving air quality; and addressing other conservation treatment needs.

The results of studies conducted by PMCs provide much of the basis for NRCS vegetative recommendations and conservation practices. The work ensures that NRCS conservation practices are scientifically-based, improves the knowledge of NRCS field staff through PMC-led training sessions and demonstrations, and develops recommendations to meet new and emerging natural resource issues. PMCs carry out their work cooperatively with State and Federal agencies, universities, Tribes, commercial businesses, and seed and nursery associations. PMC activities directly benefit private landowners as well as Federal and State land managing agencies.

Object Classification (in millions of dollars)

Identification code 012–1000–0–1–302		2021 actual	2022 est.	2023 est.
	Direct obligations:			
	Personnel compensation:			
11.1	Full-time permanent	277	277	332
11.3	Other than full-time permanent	2	2	2
11.5	Other personnel compensation	11	11	13
11.9	Total personnel compensation	290	290	347
12.1	Civilian personnel benefits	120	120	144
21.0	Travel and transportation of persons		2	3
22.0	Transportation of things	3	4	4
23.1	Rental payments to GSA	16	20	16
23.2	Rental payments to others	32	36	37
25.2	Other services from non-Federal sources	162	196	249
25.3	Other goods and services from Federal sources	2	2	1
25.4	Operation and maintenance of facilities	153	167	153
25.7	Operation and maintenance of equipment	1	2	2
26.0	Supplies and materials	8	9	11
31.0	Equipment	42	48	34
32.0	Land and structures	7	7	2
41.0	Grants, subsidies, and contributions		800	200
99.0	Direct obligations	836	1,703	1,203
99.0	Reimbursable obligations	12	13	13
99.5	Adjustment for rounding	1		
99.9	Total new obligations, unexpired accounts	849	1,716	1,216

Employment Summary

Identification code 012–1000–0–1–302	2021 actual	2022 est.	2023 est.
1001 Direct civilian full-time equivalent employment	3,585	3,519	4,054
2001 Reimbursable civilian full-time equivalent employment	41	46	46

FARM SECURITY AND RURAL INVESTMENT PROGRAMS

Program and Financing (in millions of dollars)

Identification code 012–1004–0–1–302		2021 actual	2022 est.	2023 est.
	Obligations by program activity:			
0001	Wetlands Reserve Program	13	10	1
0002	Environmental Quality Incentives Program	1,887	1,926	1,884
0004	Agricultural Water Enhancement Program		5	1
0005	Wildlife Habitat Incentives Program		6	1
0006	Farm and Ranch Lands Protection Program	18	36	24
0008	Grassland Reserve Program	7	19	4
0009	Conservation Stewardship Program 2014	217	229	68
0010	Agricultural Management Assistance Program	5	5	5
0011	Chesapeake Bay Watershed Initiative		3	2
0012	Healthy Forests Reserve Program	3	4	
0013	Conservation Reserve Program - Direct	131	293	228
0014	Agricultural Conservation Easement Program	442	571	439
0015	Regional Conservation Partnership Program	80	351	331
0016	Voluntary Public Access and Habitat Incentive Program		2	
0017	Wetlands Mitigation Banking Program - Mandatory		1	
0018	Feral Swine Eradication and Control Pilot Program	18		1
0019	Conservation Stewardship Program - 2018	646	765	889
0020	Urban Agriculture and Innovative Production Program	7	7	
0021	Wetlands Mitigation Banking Program - Discretionary	5	10	
0799	Total direct obligations	3,479	4,243	3,878
0801	Reimbursable program activities	4	4	4
0802	Reimbursable EPA Great Lakes Environmental Quality Incentives Program	16	31	31
0899	Total reimbursable obligations	20	35	35
0900	Total new obligations, unexpired accounts	3,499	4,278	3,913
	Budgetary resources:			
	Unobligated balance:			
1000	Unobligated balance brought forward, Oct 1	2,334	2,514	1,654
1001	Discretionary unobligated balance brought fwd, Oct 1	5	5	
1021	Recoveries of prior year unpaid obligations	366		
1070	Unobligated balance (total)	2,700	2,514	1,654
	Budget authority:			
	Appropriations, discretionary:			
1100	Appropriation	12	12	
1120	Appropriations transferred to other acct [012–0180]		–60	–60
1160	Appropriation, discretionary (total)	12	–48	–60
	Appropriations, mandatory:			
1220	Appropriations transferred to other acct [012–0180]	–60		
1222	Exercised borrowing authority transferred from other accounts [012–4336]	3,539	3,639	4,014
1230	Appropriations and/or unobligated balance of appropriations permanently reduced	–202	–208	–229
1260	Appropriations, mandatory (total)	3,277	3,431	3,785
	Spending authority from offsetting collections, mandatory:			
1800	Offsetting Collections	15	35	35
1801	Change in uncollected payments, Federal sources	9		
1850	Spending auth from offsetting collections, mand (total)	24	35	35
1900	Budget authority (total)	3,313	3,418	3,760
1930	Total budgetary resources available	6,013	5,932	5,414
	Memorandum (non-add) entries:			
1941	Unexpired unobligated balance, end of year	2,514	1,654	1,501
	Change in obligated balance:			
	Unpaid obligations:			
3000	Unpaid obligations, brought forward, Oct 1	6,487	6,448	7,065

FARM SECURITY AND RURAL INVESTMENT PROGRAMS—Continued

Program and Financing—Continued

Identification code 012–1004–0–1–302	2021 actual	2022 est.	2023 est.
3010 New obligations, unexpired accounts	3,499	4,278	3,913
3011 Obligations ("upward adjustments"), expired accounts	4		
3020 Outlays (gross)	–3,169	–3,661	–3,997
3040 Recoveries of prior year unpaid obligations, unexpired	–366		
3041 Recoveries of prior year unpaid obligations, expired	–7		
3050 Unpaid obligations, end of year	6,448	7,065	6,981
Uncollected payments:			
3060 Uncollected pymts, Fed sources, brought forward, Oct 1	–64	–72	–72
3070 Change in uncollected pymts, Fed sources, unexpired	–9		
3071 Change in uncollected pymts, Fed sources, expired	1		
3090 Uncollected pymts, Fed sources, end of year	–72	–72	–72
Memorandum (non-add) entries:			
3100 Obligated balance, start of year	6,423	6,376	6,993
3200 Obligated balance, end of year	6,376	6,993	6,909
Budget authority and outlays, net:			
Discretionary:			
4000 Budget authority, gross	12	–48	–60
Outlays, gross:			
4010 Outlays from new discretionary authority		–35	–38
4011 Outlays from discretionary balances	1	3	–5
4020 Outlays, gross (total)	1	–32	–43
Mandatory:			
4090 Budget authority, gross	3,301	3,466	3,820
Outlays, gross:			
4100 Outlays from new mandatory authority	711	1,160	1,291
4101 Outlays from mandatory balances	2,457	2,533	2,749
4110 Outlays, gross (total)	3,168	3,693	4,040
Offsets against gross budget authority and outlays:			
Offsetting collections (collected) from:			
4120 Federal sources	–15	–35	–35
4123 Non-Federal sources	–4		
4130 Offsets against gross budget authority and outlays (total)	–19	–35	–35
Additional offsets against gross budget authority only:			
4140 Change in uncollected pymts, Fed sources, unexpired	–9		
4142 Offsetting collections credited to expired accounts	4		
4150 Additional offsets against budget authority only (total)	–5		
4160 Budget authority, net (mandatory)	3,277	3,431	3,785
4170 Outlays, net (mandatory)	3,149	3,658	4,005
4180 Budget authority, net (total)	3,289	3,383	3,725
4190 Outlays, net (total)	3,150	3,626	3,962

Title XII of the Food Security Act of 1985 provides mandatory funding for critical conservation efforts on private lands, including critical wetlands, grasslands, forests, and farm and ranch lands. For conservation programs where NRCS is the lead implementation agency, funds are transferred from the Commodity Credit Corporation (CCC) to the Farm Security and Rural Investment Programs account. This mandatory funding supports NRCS's efforts to protect the natural resource base on private lands by providing technical assistance to farmers, ranchers and other private landowners to support the development of conservation plans, and by providing financial assistance to partially offset the cost to implement conservation measures necessary to safeguard natural resources and improve wildlife habitat and provide funding to acquire easements either directly, or through third parties.

The Agriculture Improvement Act of 2018 amended Title XII of the Food Security Act of 1985, reauthorizing some programs, and creating one new conservation program that is administered by NRCS. Several conservation programs were extended in the 2023 Budget's baseline beyond 2023 based upon scorekeeping conventions.

Environmental Quality Incentives Program (EQIP).—This program is authorized under Subchapter A of Chapter 4 of Subtitle D of Title XII of the Food Security Act of 1985, as amended. The Agriculture Improvement Act of 2018 reauthorizes the program through 2023, and the 2023 Budget assumes that the program extends beyond that date in the baseline for scorekeeping purposes. The purpose of the program is to promote agricultural production and environmental quality as compatible national goals.

EQIP promotes the voluntary application of land-based conservation practices and activities that maintain or improve the condition of the soil, water, plants, and air; conserve energy; and address other natural resource concerns. Eligible land includes cropland, rangeland, pastureland, private non-industrial forestland, tribal land, and other farm or ranch lands. In 2023, the Budget proposes $2.025 billion for this program.

Conservation Stewardship Program (CSP).—This program is authorized by Subchapter B of Chapter 4 of Subtitle D of title XII of the Food Security Act of 1985, as amended. The Agriculture Improvement Act of 2018 reauthorized the program through 2023, and the 2023 Budget assumes that the program extends beyond that date in the baseline for scorekeeping purposes. The program encourages producers to address resource concerns in a comprehensive manner by undertaking additional conservation activities and improving, maintaining, and managing existing conservation activities. The 2023 Budget estimates $1.0 billion in 2023 for this program for new contracts, existing contracts, and reenrollments.

Conservation Reserve Program (CRP) Technical Assistance.—CRP is authorized by Sections 1231–1235A of the Food Security Act of 1985, as amended, and is administered by the Farm Service Agency. NRCS supports the program by providing technical assistance to producers to implement conservation practices on CRP land. The Agriculture Improvement Act of 2018 reauthorized the program, and the 2023 Budget assumes $236 million in technical assistance for NRCS support of CRP. Beginning in 2021, NRCS received an additional $139 million in technical assistance (for a total of $236 million in CRP-related technical assistance) to begin a nationwide soil sampling program to determine the level of soil carbon on land enrolled in CRP.

Agricultural Conservation Easement Program (ACEP).—ACEP consists of two components: 1) an agricultural land easement component under which NRCS assists eligible entities to protect agricultural land by limiting non-agricultural uses of that land through the purchase of agricultural land easements; and 2) a wetland reserve easement component under which NRCS provides financial and technical assistance directly to landowners to restore, protect and enhance wetlands through the purchase of wetlands reserve easements. The program is reauthorized through 2023 by the Agriculture Improvement Act of 2018 under Subtitle H of Title XII of the Food Security Act of 1985. The 2023 Budget assumes that the program extends beyond 2023 in the baseline for scorekeeping purposes. For 2023, the Budget proposes $450 million for ACEP.

Regional Conservation Partnership Program (RCPP).—RCPP promotes the implementation of conservation activities through agreements between NRCS and partners and through conservation program contracts and easements with producers and landowners. The program is reauthorized through 2023 by the Agriculture Improvement Act of 2018 under Subtitle I of Title XII of the Food Security Act of 1985. Through agreements between partners and conservation program contracts or easements directly with producers and landowners, RCPP helps implement conservation projects that may focus on water quality and quantity, soil erosion, wildlife habitat, drought mitigation, flood control, or other regional priorities. The 2023 Budget assumes that the program extends beyond 2023 in the baseline for scorekeeping purposes. For 2023, the Budget proposes $300 million for RCPP.

Voluntary Public Access and Habitat Incentive Program (VPA-HIP).—The program is authorized by Section 1240R of the Food Security Act of 1985, as amended by Section 2406 of the Agriculture Improvement Act of 2018. VPA-HIP provides $50 million for obligations between 2019 through 2023. VPA-HIP is a competitive grant program. Funding is limited to State and Tribal governments establishing new public access programs, expanding existing public access programs, and/or enhancing wildlife habitat on lands enrolled in public access programs.

Feral Swine Eradication and Control Pilot Program.—The program is authorized by Sections 2408 of the Agriculture Improvement Act of 2018. The program provides $75 million for obligations between 2019 and 2023, of which NRCS is to receive 50 percent. The program was implemented by NRCS and the Animal Plant Health Inspection Service. The program is used to respond to the threat feral swine pose to agriculture, native ecosystems, and human and animal health.

In addition to the programs authorized under the Food Security Act of 1985, NRCS implements the following conservation programs:

Agricultural Management Assistance Program (AMA).—This program is authorized by Section 524(b) of the Federal Crop Insurance Act (7 U.S.C. 1524(b)), as amended. It authorizes $10 million annually for the program, of which NRCS is to receive 50 percent. This program is implemented by NRCS, the Agricultural Marketing Service, and the Risk Management Agency. AMA activities are carried out in 16 States in which participation in the Federal Crop Insurance Program is historically low. The program provides assistance to producers to mitigate financial risk by using conservation to reduce soil erosion and improve water quality. The 2023 Budget proposes $5 million for the program.

NRCS works to deliver conservation programs using its technical field staff and by partnering with public and private entities through the Technical Service Provider (TSP) system. NRCS can contract with TSPs to help deliver the Farm Bill programs, or agricultural producers may select TSPs to help plan and implement conservation practices on their operations.

The U.S. has made great strides in improving water quality; however, nonpoint source pollution remains a significant challenge that requires policy attention and thoughtful new approaches. In 2023, the Budget continues the agency's efforts to better coordinate conservation efforts among key Federal partners, along with agricultural producer organizations, conservation districts, States, Tribes, non-governmental organizations, and other local leaders to identify areas where a focused and coordinated approach can achieve substantial improvements in water quality. The Budget builds upon the collaborative process already underway among Federal partners to demonstrate substantial improvements in water quality from conservation programs by ensuring that USDA's key investments through Farm Bill conservation programs and related efforts are appropriately leveraged by other Federal programs.

The Farm Production and Conservation (FPAC) Business Center is a centralized operations office within the FPAC Mission Area responsible for financial management, budgeting, human resources, information technology, acquisitions/procurement, customer experience, internal controls, risk management, strategic and annual planning, and other similar activities for the FPAC Mission area and its component agencies, including NRCS, the Farm Service Agency (FSA), and the Risk Management Agency (RMA). This account includes a transfer of $60,228,000 to offset funds associated with administration and oversight of mandatory conservation programs. The funding requested for the FPAC Business Center is an estimate based on current staffing in the FPAC agencies, including NRCS, FSA, and RMA, and the estimated costs in support of the Business Center.

Object Classification (in millions of dollars)

Identification code 012–1004–0–1–302		2021 actual	2022 est.	2023 est.
	Direct obligations:			
	Personnel compensation:			
11.1	Full-time permanent	412	528	560
11.3	Other than full-time permanent	1	2	2
11.5	Other personnel compensation	10	13	14
11.9	Total personnel compensation	423	543	576
12.1	Civilian personnel benefits	190	243	258
21.0	Travel and transportation of persons	3	5	5
22.0	Transportation of things	1	2	1
23.1	Rental payments to GSA	18	22	21
23.2	Rental payments to others	43	44	50
23.3	Communications, utilities, and miscellaneous charges	3	4	2
25.2	Other services from non-Federal sources	280	435	225
25.3	Other goods and services from Federal sources	2	2	2
25.4	Operation and maintenance of facilities	139	218	116
26.0	Supplies and materials	5	8	4
31.0	Equipment	69	109	58
32.0	Land and structures	223	254	250
41.0	Grants, subsidies, and contributions	2,080	2,354	2,310
99.0	Direct obligations	3,479	4,243	3,878
99.0	Reimbursable obligations	20	35	35
99.9	Total new obligations, unexpired accounts	3,499	4,278	3,913

Employment Summary

Identification code 012–1004–0–1–302		2021 actual	2022 est.	2023 est.
1001	Direct civilian full-time equivalent employment	5,806	7,255	7,353
2001	Reimbursable civilian full-time equivalent employment	20	33	33

WATERSHED AND FLOOD PREVENTION OPERATIONS

For necessary expenses to carry out preventive measures, including but not limited to surveys and investigations, engineering operations, works of improvement, and changes in use of land, in accordance with the Watershed Protection and Flood Prevention Act (16 U.S.C. 1001–1005 and 1007–1009) and in accordance with the provisions of laws relating to the activities of the Department, $125,000,000, to remain available until expended: Provided, That for funds provided by this Act or any other prior Act, the limitation regarding the size of the watershed or subwatershed exceeding two hundred and fifty thousand acres in which such activities can be undertaken shall only apply for activities undertaken for the primary purpose of flood prevention (including structural and land treatment measures): Provided further, That of the amounts made available under this heading, $25,000,000 shall be allocated to projects and activities that can commence promptly following enactment; that address regional priorities for flood prevention, agricultural water management, inefficient irrigation systems, fish and wildlife habitat, or watershed protection; or that address authorized ongoing projects under the authorities of section 13 of the Flood Control Act of December 22, 1944 (Public Law 78–534) with a primary purpose of watershed protection by preventing floodwater damage and stabilizing stream channels, tributaries, and banks to reduce erosion and sediment transport.

Note.—A full-year 2022 appropriation for this account was not enacted at the time the Budget was prepared; therefore, the Budget assumes this account is operating under the Continuing Appropriations Act, 2022 (Division A of Public Law 117–43, as amended). The amounts included for 2022 reflect the annualized level provided by the continuing resolution.

WATERSHED AND FLOOD PREVENTION OPERATIONS

[For an additional amount for "Watershed and Flood Prevention Operations" for necessary expenses for the Emergency Watershed Protection Program, $275,000,000, to remain available until expended, which shall be in addition to amounts otherwise available for such purposes.] *(Disaster Relief Supplemental Appropriations Act, 2022.)*

WATERSHED AND FLOOD PREVENTION OPERATIONS

[For an additional amount for "Watershed and Flood Prevention Operations", $500,000,000, to remain available until expended: *Provided*, That not later than 90 days after the date of enactment of this Act, the Secretary of Agriculture shall submit to the House and Senate Committees on Appropriations a detailed spend plan, including a list of project locations and project cost: *Provided further*, That such amount is designated by the Congress as being for an emergency requirement pursuant to section 4112(a) of H. Con. Res. 71 (115th Congress), the concurrent resolution on the budget for fiscal year 2018, and to section 251(b) of the Balanced Budget and Emergency Deficit Control Act of 1985.] *(Infrastructure Investments and Jobs Appropriations Act.)*

EMERGENCY WATERSHED PROTECTION PROGRAM

[For an additional amount for "Emergency Watershed Protection Program" to repair damages to the waterways and watersheds resulting from natural disasters, $300,000,000, to remain available until expended: *Provided*, That such amount is designated by the Congress as being for an emergency requirement pursuant to section 4112(a) of H. Con. Res. 71 (115th Congress), the concurrent resolution on the budget for fiscal year 2018, and to section 251(b) of the Balanced Budget and Emergency Deficit Control Act of 1985.] *(Infrastructure Investments and Jobs Appropriations Act.)*

Program and Financing (in millions of dollars)

Identification code 012–1072–0–1–301		2021 actual	2022 est.	2023 est.
	Obligations by program activity:			
0003	Emergency watershed protection operations	235	302	281
0004	Small watershed operations (P.L. 566)	85	521	352
0005	Flood Prevention Operations P.L. 78–534	27	97	116
0006	EWP (SANDY)	4	28	68
0007	Watershed Flood and Prevention Operations	47	47	47

WATERSHED AND FLOOD PREVENTION OPERATIONS—Continued
Program and Financing—Continued

Identification code 012–1072–0–1–301		2021 actual	2022 est.	2023 est.
0008	Rural Water Operations Program	....	10	10
0799	Total direct obligations	398	1,005	874
0802	Watershed and Flood Prevention Operations (Reimbursable)	21	3	3
0900	Total new obligations, unexpired accounts	419	1,008	877
	Budgetary resources:			
	Unobligated balance:			
1000	Unobligated balance brought forward, Oct 1	925	815	818
1021	Recoveries of prior year unpaid obligations	63	....	....
1070	Unobligated balance (total)	988	815	818
	Budget authority:			
	Appropriations, discretionary:			
1100	Appropriation	175	450	125
1100	Appropriation	....	500	....
1160	Appropriation, discretionary (total)	175	950	125
	Appropriations, mandatory:			
1222	Exercised borrowing authority transferred from other accounts [012–4336]	50	50	50
1230	Appropriations and/or unobligated balance of appropriations permanently reduced	–3	–3	–3
1260	Appropriations, mandatory (total)	47	47	47
	Spending authority from offsetting collections, discretionary:			
1700	Collected	10	14	14
1701	Change in uncollected payments, Federal sources	14	....	....
1750	Spending auth from offsetting collections, disc (total)	24	14	14
1900	Budget authority (total)	246	1,011	186
1930	Total budgetary resources available	1,234	1,826	1,004
	Memorandum (non-add) entries:			
1941	Unexpired unobligated balance, end of year	815	818	127
	Change in obligated balance:			
	Unpaid obligations:			
3000	Unpaid obligations, brought forward, Oct 1	826	855	1,418
3010	New obligations, unexpired accounts	419	1,008	877
3020	Outlays (gross)	–324	–445	–783
3040	Recoveries of prior year unpaid obligations, unexpired	–63	....	....
3041	Recoveries of prior year unpaid obligations, expired	–3	....	....
3050	Unpaid obligations, end of year	855	1,418	1,512
	Uncollected payments:			
3060	Uncollected pymts, Fed sources, brought forward, Oct 1	–73	–87	–87
3070	Change in uncollected pymts, Fed sources, unexpired	–14	....	....
3090	Uncollected pymts, Fed sources, end of year	–87	–87	–87
	Memorandum (non-add) entries:			
3100	Obligated balance, start of year	753	768	1,331
3200	Obligated balance, end of year	768	1,331	1,425
	Budget authority and outlays, net:			
	Discretionary:			
4000	Budget authority, gross	199	964	139
	Outlays, gross:			
4010	Outlays from new discretionary authority	2	184	33
4011	Outlays from discretionary balances	308	233	681
4020	Outlays, gross (total)	310	417	714
	Offsets against gross budget authority and outlays:			
	Offsetting collections (collected) from:			
4030	Federal sources	–9	–14	–14
4033	Non-Federal sources	–1	....	....
4040	Offsets against gross budget authority and outlays (total)	–10	–14	–14
	Additional offsets against gross budget authority only:			
4050	Change in uncollected pymts, Fed sources, unexpired	–14	....	....
4060	Additional offsets against budget authority only (total)	–14	....	....
4070	Budget authority, net (discretionary)	175	950	125
4080	Outlays, net (discretionary)	300	403	700
	Mandatory:			
4090	Budget authority, gross	47	47	47
	Outlays, gross:			
4100	Outlays from new mandatory authority	1	2	2
4101	Outlays from mandatory balances	13	26	67
4110	Outlays, gross (total)	14	28	69
4180	Budget authority, net (total)	222	997	172
4190	Outlays, net (total)	314	431	769

NRCS watershed programs provide for cooperative actions between the Federal Government and States and their political subdivisions to reduce damage from floodwater, sediment, and erosion; for the conservation, development, utilization, and disposal of water; and for the conservation and proper utilization of land. Funds in Watershed and Flood Prevention Operations can be used to implement authorized watershed project plans for the purpose of watershed flood protection; flood mitigation; water quality improvements; soil erosion reduction; rural, municipal and industrial water supply; irrigation water management; sediment control; fish and wildlife habitat enhancement; and wetland creation and restoration, depending upon the needs and opportunities.

Emergency Watershed Program.—NRCS undertakes such emergency measures for runoff retardation and soil erosion prevention as may be needed to safeguard life and property from floods and the products of erosion on any watershed whenever natural elements or forces cause a sudden impairment of that watershed. NRCS may acquire Floodplain Easements on lands impacted by frequent flooding. Funding for the Emergency Watershed Program is typically provided through emergency supplemental appropriations.

Watershed operations authorized by Public Law 78–534.—NRCS cooperates with soil conservation districts and other local organizations in planning and installing flood prevention improvements in 11 watersheds authorized by the Flood Control Act of 1944. The Federal Government shares the cost of improvements for flood prevention, agricultural water management, recreation, and fish and wildlife development. The 2023 Budget proposes $25 million for this program.

Small watershed operations authorized by Public Law 83–566.—NRCS provides technical and financial assistance to local organizations to install measures for watershed protection, flood prevention, agricultural water management, recreation, and fish and wildlife enhancement. NRCS is using unobligated balances from prior years to support watershed operations projects. The 2023 Budget proposes $100 million for this program.

Watershed Protection and Flood Program.—Authorized by Section 2401 of the Agriculture Improvement Act of 2018, Public Law 115–334. NRCS provides technical and financial assistance to local organizations to install measures for watershed protection, and flood prevention. The Agriculture Improvement Act of 2018 authorizes $50 million per year for fiscal year 2019 to 2023.

Loans through the Agricultural Credit Insurance Fund have been made in previous years to the local sponsors in order to fund the local cost of Public Law 83–566 or 78–534 projects. No funding for these loans is assumed in 2023.

Object Classification (in millions of dollars)

Identification code 012–1072–0–1–301		2021 actual	2022 est.	2023 est.
	Direct obligations:			
	Personnel compensation:			
11.1	Full-time permanent	15	15	13
11.5	Other personnel compensation	1	1	1
11.9	Total personnel compensation	16	16	14
12.1	Civilian personnel benefits	6	6	5
21.0	Travel and transportation of persons	....	1	1
25.1	Advisory and assistance services	14	10	11
25.2	Other services from non-Federal sources	58	175	123
25.4	Operation and maintenance of facilities	11	27	18
26.0	Supplies and materials	....	1	2
31.0	Equipment	1	5	7
32.0	Land and structures	57	114	143
41.0	Grants, subsidies, and contributions	235	650	549
99.0	Direct obligations	398	1,005	873
99.0	Reimbursable obligations	21	3	3
99.5	Adjustment for rounding	....	....	1
99.9	Total new obligations, unexpired accounts	419	1,008	877

DEPARTMENT OF AGRICULTURE

Employment Summary

Identification code 012–1072–0–1–301	2021 actual	2022 est.	2023 est.
1001 Direct civilian full-time equivalent employment	166	139	165
2001 Reimbursable civilian full-time equivalent employment	22	17	17

EMERGENCY WATERSHED PROTECTION

Program and Financing (in millions of dollars)

Identification code 012–0017–0–1–301	2021 actual	2022 est.	2023 est.
Obligations by program activity:			
0001 EWP Infrastructure 2022	....	216	64
Budgetary resources:			
Unobligated balance:			
1000 Unobligated balance brought forward, Oct 1	....	....	84
Budget authority:			
Appropriations, discretionary:			
1100 Appropriation	....	300	....
1930 Total budgetary resources available	....	300	84
Memorandum (non-add) entries:			
1941 Unexpired unobligated balance, end of year	....	84	20
Change in obligated balance:			
Unpaid obligations:			
3000 Unpaid obligations, brought forward, Oct 1	....	....	141
3010 New obligations, unexpired accounts	....	216	64
3020 Outlays (gross)	....	–75	–135
3050 Unpaid obligations, end of year	....	141	70
Memorandum (non-add) entries:			
3100 Obligated balance, start of year	....	....	141
3200 Obligated balance, end of year	....	141	70
Budget authority and outlays, net:			
Discretionary:			
4000 Budget authority, gross	....	300	....
Outlays, gross:			
4010 Outlays from new discretionary authority	....	75	....
4011 Outlays from discretionary balances	....	....	135
4020 Outlays, gross (total)	....	75	135
4180 Budget authority, net (total)	....	300	....
4190 Outlays, net (total)	....	75	135

NRCS undertakes such emergency measures for runoff retardation and soil erosion prevention as may be needed to safeguard life and property from floods and the products of erosion on any watershed whenever natural elements or forces cause a sudden impairment of that watershed. Funding for the Emergency Watershed Program is typically provided through emergency supplemental appropriations.

Object Classification (in millions of dollars)

Identification code 012–0017–0–1–301	2021 actual	2022 est.	2023 est.
Direct obligations:			
11.1 Personnel compensation: Full-time permanent	....	4	4
12.1 Civilian personnel benefits	....	2	1
25.1 Advisory and assistance services	....	2	1
25.2 Other services from non-Federal sources	....	30	8
25.4 Operation and maintenance of facilities	....	3	2
31.0 Equipment	....	1	1
32.0 Land and structures	....	104	29
41.0 Grants, subsidies, and contributions	....	70	18
99.9 Total new obligations, unexpired accounts	....	216	64

Employment Summary

Identification code 012–0017–0–1–301	2021 actual	2022 est.	2023 est.
1001 Direct civilian full-time equivalent employment	....	37	30

Natural Resources Conservation Service—Continued
Federal Funds—Continued

WATERSHED REHABILITATION PROGRAM

Under the authorities of section 14 of the Watershed Protection and Flood Prevention Act, $10,000,000 is provided.

Note.—A full-year 2022 appropriation for this account was not enacted at the time the Budget was prepared; therefore, the Budget assumes this account is operating under the Continuing Appropriations Act, 2022 (Division A of Public Law 117–43, as amended). The amounts included for 2022 reflect the annualized level provided by the continuing resolution.

WATERSHED REHABILITATION PROGRAM

[For an additional amount for "Watershed Rehabilitation Program", $118,000,000, to remain available until expended: *Provided*, That not later than 90 days after the date of enactment of this Act, the Secretary of Agriculture shall submit to the House and Senate Committees on Appropriations a detailed spend plan, including a list of project locations and project cost: *Provided further*, That such amount is designated by the Congress as being for an emergency requirement pursuant to section 4112(a) of H. Con. Res. 71 (115th Congress), the concurrent resolution on the budget for fiscal year 2018, and to section 251(b) of the Balanced Budget and Emergency Deficit Control Act of 1985.] *(Infrastructure Investments and Jobs Appropriations Act.)*

Program and Financing (in millions of dollars)

Identification code 012–1002–0–1–301	2021 actual	2022 est.	2023 est.
Obligations by program activity:			
0001 Watershed Rehabilitation Program	12	96	43
0002 Small Watershed Rehabilitation Program	30	19	13
0799 Total direct obligations	42	115	56
0801 Reimbursable program activity	3	18	18
0900 Total new obligations, unexpired accounts	45	133	74
Budgetary resources:			
Unobligated balance:			
1000 Unobligated balance brought forward, Oct 1	64	45	58
1001 Discretionary unobligated balance brought fwd, Oct 1	16	3	....
1021 Recoveries of prior year unpaid obligations	14	....	....
1070 Unobligated balance (total)	78	45	58
Budget authority:			
Appropriations, discretionary:			
1100 Appropriation	10	10	10
1100 Appropriation	....	118	....
1160 Appropriation, discretionary (total)	10	128	10
Spending authority from offsetting collections, discretionary:			
1700 Collected	2	18	18
1900 Budget authority (total)	12	146	28
1930 Total budgetary resources available	90	191	86
Memorandum (non-add) entries:			
1941 Unexpired unobligated balance, end of year	45	58	12
Change in obligated balance:			
Unpaid obligations:			
3000 Unpaid obligations, brought forward, Oct 1	163	151	259
3010 New obligations, unexpired accounts	45	133	74
3020 Outlays (gross)	–41	–25	–41
3040 Recoveries of prior year unpaid obligations, unexpired	–14	....	....
3041 Recoveries of prior year unpaid obligations, expired	–2	....	....
3050 Unpaid obligations, end of year	151	259	292
Memorandum (non-add) entries:			
3100 Obligated balance, start of year	163	151	259
3200 Obligated balance, end of year	151	259	292
Budget authority and outlays, net:			
Discretionary:			
4000 Budget authority, gross	12	146	28
Outlays, gross:			
4010 Outlays from new discretionary authority	1	22	4
4011 Outlays from discretionary balances	14	1	36
4020 Outlays, gross (total)	15	23	40
Offsets against gross budget authority and outlays:			
Offsetting collections (collected) from:			
4033 Non-Federal sources	–2	–18	–18
Mandatory:			
Outlays, gross:			
4101 Outlays from mandatory balances	26	2	1
4180 Budget authority, net (total)	10	128	10
4190 Outlays, net (total)	39	7	23

WATERSHED REHABILITATION PROGRAM—Continued

Under the authorities of Section 14 of the Watershed Protection and Flood Prevention Act (16 U.S.C. 1012), assistance is provided to communities to support the rehabilitation of local dams originally constructed with Federal assistance and near or past their evaluated life expectancy. The 2023 Budget proposes $10 million for this program.

Object Classification (in millions of dollars)

Identification code 012–1002–0–1–301		2021 actual	2022 est.	2023 est.
	Direct obligations:			
11.1	Personnel compensation: Full-time permanent	2	4	3
12.1	Civilian personnel benefits	1	1	1
25.2	Other services from non-Federal sources	7	8	9
25.4	Operation and maintenance of facilities	3	23	7
41.0	Grants, subsidies, and contributions	29	79	36
99.0	Direct obligations	42	115	56
99.0	Reimbursable obligations	3	18	18
99.9	Total new obligations, unexpired accounts	45	133	74

Employment Summary

Identification code 012–1002–0–1–301	2021 actual	2022 est.	2023 est.
1001 Direct civilian full-time equivalent employment	17	25	24
2001 Reimbursable civilian full-time equivalent employment	5	17	17

HEALTHY FORESTS RESERVE PROGRAM

For necessary expenses to carry out the Healthy Forests Reserve Program under the Healthy Forests Restoration Act of 2003 (16 U.S.C. 6571–6578), $20,000,000, to remain available until expended.

Note.—A full-year 2022 appropriation for this account was not enacted at the time the Budget was prepared; therefore, the Budget assumes this account is operating under the Continuing Appropriations Act, 2022 (Division A of Public Law 117–43, as amended). The amounts included for 2022 reflect the annualized level provided by the continuing resolution.

Program and Financing (in millions of dollars)

Identification code 012–1090–0–1–302		2021 actual	2022 est.	2023 est.
	Obligations by program activity:			
0001	Healthy Forests Reserve Program			20
	Budgetary resources:			
	Budget authority:			
	Appropriations, discretionary:			
1100	Appropriation			20
1930	Total budgetary resources available			20
	Change in obligated balance:			
	Unpaid obligations:			
3010	New obligations, unexpired accounts			20
3020	Outlays (gross)			–4
3050	Unpaid obligations, end of year			16
	Memorandum (non-add) entries:			
3200	Obligated balance, end of year			16
	Budget authority and outlays, net:			
	Discretionary:			
4000	Budget authority, gross			20
	Outlays, gross:			
4010	Outlays from new discretionary authority			4
4180	Budget authority, net (total)			20
4190	Outlays, net (total)			4

The Healthy Forests Reserve Program (HFRP), which is authorized by Title V of the Healthy Forests Restoration Act of 2003 (Public Law 108–148), helps landowners restore, enhance, and protect forest resources on private lands through easements and financial assistance. HFRP focuses on forest ecosystems to: 1) promote the recovery of threatened and endangered species; 2) improve biodiversity; and 3) enhance carbon sequestration.

Administered by NRCS, HFRP is a voluntary program with enrollment limited to land that is privately held or owned by a Tribe. Land enrolled in HFRP must have a restoration plan that includes practices necessary to restore and enhance habitat for species listed as threatened or endangered or are candidates for the threatened or endangered species list. Technical assistance is provided by USDA to assist owners in complying with the terms of restoration plans under HFRP. The 2023 Budget proposes $20,000,000 for the Healthy Forests Reserve Program.

Object Classification (in millions of dollars)

Identification code 012–1090–0–1–302		2021 actual	2022 est.	2023 est.
	Direct obligations:			
25.2	Other services from non-Federal sources			7
32.0	Land and structures			8
41.0	Grants, subsidies, and contributions			5
99.9	Total new obligations, unexpired accounts			20

Employment Summary

Identification code 012–1090–0–1–302	2021 actual	2022 est.	2023 est.
1001 Direct civilian full-time equivalent employment			1

URBAN AGRICULTURE PROGRAM

For necessary expenses to carry out the Urban Agriculture and Innovative Production Program under section 222 of subtitle A of the Department of Agriculture Reorganization Act of 1994 (7 U.S.C. 6923), as added by section 12302 of Public Law 115–334, $13,469,000.

Note.—A full-year 2022 appropriation for this account was not enacted at the time the Budget was prepared; therefore, the Budget assumes this account is operating under the Continuing Appropriations Act, 2022 (Division A of Public Law 117–43, as amended). The amounts included for 2022 reflect the annualized level provided by the continuing resolution.

Program and Financing (in millions of dollars)

Identification code 012–1005–0–1–302		2021 actual	2022 est.	2023 est.
	Obligations by program activity:			
0001	Urban Agriculture Program			13
0900	Total new obligations, unexpired accounts (object class 25.2)			13
	Budgetary resources:			
	Budget authority:			
	Appropriations, discretionary:			
1100	Appropriation			13
1930	Total budgetary resources available			13
	Change in obligated balance:			
	Unpaid obligations:			
3010	New obligations, unexpired accounts			13
3020	Outlays (gross)			–3
3050	Unpaid obligations, end of year			10
	Memorandum (non-add) entries:			
3200	Obligated balance, end of year			10
	Budget authority and outlays, net:			
	Discretionary:			
4000	Budget authority, gross			13
	Outlays, gross:			
4010	Outlays from new discretionary authority			3
4180	Budget authority, net (total)			13
4190	Outlays, net (total)			3

The Office of Urban Agriculture and Innovative Production is led by the Natural Resources Conservation Service (NRCS), working in partnership with numerous USDA agencies that support urban agriculture. The 2023 Budget proposes $13,469,000 for this program.

In 2023, NRCS will continue critical activities to support urban agriculture, including expanding grant opportunities to Historically Underserved and Socially Disadvantaged communities, leveraging existing authorities within USDA agencies to amplify ongoing programs, managing the needs of the Federal Advisory Committee, and supporting pilot Farm Service Agency Urban / Sub-Urban County Office Committees. The Office will also establish a communication and partnership framework across the Federal government to promote a coordinated approach to delivering assistance in communities.

The Office activities advance the Administrations priorities of establishing racial and economic equity and combatting climate change. Grant and agreement opportunities support innovative approaches to reclaiming distressed urban land, creating local jobs, and providing reliable and resilient food sources.

Employment Summary

Identification code 012–1005–0–1–302	2021 actual	2022 est.	2023 est.
1001 Direct civilian full-time equivalent employment			4

WATER BANK PROGRAM

Program and Financing (in millions of dollars)

Identification code 012–3320–0–1–302	2021 actual	2022 est.	2023 est.
Obligations by program activity:			
0001 Water Bank Program	4	4	....
0900 Total new obligations, unexpired accounts (object class 41.0)	4	4	....
Budgetary resources:			
Budget authority:			
Appropriations, discretionary:			
1100 Appropriation	4	4	....
1930 Total budgetary resources available	4	4	....
Change in obligated balance:			
Unpaid obligations:			
3000 Unpaid obligations, brought forward, Oct 1	19	19	19
3010 New obligations, unexpired accounts	4	4	....
3020 Outlays (gross)	–4	–4	–5
3050 Unpaid obligations, end of year	19	19	14
Memorandum (non-add) entries:			
3100 Obligated balance, start of year	19	19	19
3200 Obligated balance, end of year	19	19	14
Budget authority and outlays, net:			
Discretionary:			
4000 Budget authority, gross	4	4	....
Outlays, gross:			
4010 Outlays from new discretionary authority	....	4	....
4011 Outlays from discretionary balances	4	....	5
4020 Outlays, gross (total)	4	4	5
4180 Budget authority, net (total)	4	4	....
4190 Outlays, net (total)	4	4	5

The Water Bank Program, which is authorized by the Water Bank Act of 1970 (16 U.S.C. 1301–1311), is designed to preserve, restore, and improve wetlands, to conserve surface waters, to preserve and improve habitat for migratory waterfowl and other wildlife resources, and to promote comprehensive and total water management planning. Through the Water Bank Program, NRCS enters into ten-year agreements with landowners and operators to conserve water; to preserve, maintain, and improve the Nation's wetlands; to increase waterfowl habitat in migratory waterfowl nesting, breeding, and feeding areas in the United States; and to secure recreational and environmental benefits for the Nation. Given the short-term and temporary nature of contracts funded through the Water Bank Program, the Budget prioritizes fully funding wetland restoration and habitat preservation efforts through the Agricultural Conservation Easement Program.

Employment Summary

Identification code 012–3320–0–1–302	2021 actual	2022 est.	2023 est.
1001 Direct civilian full-time equivalent employment	1	1	....

DAMAGE ASSESSMENT AND RESTORATION REVOLVING FUND

Program and Financing (in millions of dollars)

Identification code 012–4368–0–3–306	2021 actual	2022 est.	2023 est.
Obligations by program activity:			
0001 Damage Assessment & Restoration Revolving	12	9	6
Budgetary resources:			
Unobligated balance:			
1000 Unobligated balance brought forward, Oct 1	6	8	3
1011 Unobligated balance transfer from other acct [014–5198]	13	4	4
1021 Recoveries of prior year unpaid obligations	1	....	....
1070 Unobligated balance (total)	20	12	7
1930 Total budgetary resources available	20	12	7
Memorandum (non-add) entries:			
1941 Unexpired unobligated balance, end of year	8	3	1
Change in obligated balance:			
Unpaid obligations:			
3000 Unpaid obligations, brought forward, Oct 1	5	14	22
3010 New obligations, unexpired accounts	12	9	6
3020 Outlays (gross)	–2	–1	–2
3040 Recoveries of prior year unpaid obligations, unexpired	–1	....	....
3050 Unpaid obligations, end of year	14	22	26
Memorandum (non-add) entries:			
3100 Obligated balance, start of year	5	14	22
3200 Obligated balance, end of year	14	22	26
Budget authority and outlays, net:			
Discretionary:			
Outlays, gross:			
4011 Outlays from discretionary balances	2	....	....
Mandatory:			
Outlays, gross:			
4101 Outlays from mandatory balances	....	1	2
4180 Budget authority, net (total)			
4190 Outlays, net (total)	2	1	2

Object Classification (in millions of dollars)

Identification code 012–4368–0–3–306	2021 actual	2022 est.	2023 est.
Direct obligations:			
11.1 Personnel compensation: Full-time permanent	1	....	....
25.1 Advisory and assistance services	4	3	....
25.2 Other services from non-Federal sources	2	3	3
41.0 Grants, subsidies, and contributions	5	3	3
99.9 Total new obligations, unexpired accounts	12	9	6

Employment Summary

Identification code 012–4368–0–3–306	2021 actual	2022 est.	2023 est.
1001 Direct civilian full-time equivalent employment	8	2	2

Trust Funds

MISCELLANEOUS CONTRIBUTED FUNDS

Funds received in this account from State, local, and other organizations are available for work under cooperative agreements for soil survey, watershed protection, and resource conservation and development activities.

RURAL DEVELOPMENT

Federal Funds

SALARIES AND EXPENSES

(INCLUDING TRANSFERS OF FUNDS)

For necessary expenses for carrying out the administration and implementation of Rural Development programs, including activities with institutions concerning the development and operation of agricultural cooperatives; and for cooperative agreements; $504,066,000: Provided, That of the amount made available under this heading, $39,000,000, to remain available until September 30, 2024, shall be for the Rural Partners Network activities of the Department of Agriculture, and may be transferred to other agencies of the Department of Agriculture or to other Federal agencies for such purpose, consistent with the missions and authorities of such agencies: Provided further, That of the amount made available under this heading, $3,000,000 shall be for Rural Placemaking Innovation Challenge Grants: Provided further, That notwithstanding any other provision of law, funds appropriated under this heading may be used for advertising and promotional activities that support Rural Development programs: Provided further, That in addition to any other funds appropriated for purposes authorized by section 502(i) of the Housing Act of 1949 (42 U.S.C. 1472(i)), any amounts collected under such section, as amended by this Act, will immediately be credited to this account and will remain available until expended for such purposes.

Note.—A full-year 2022 appropriation for this account was not enacted at the time the Budget was prepared; therefore, the Budget assumes this account is operating under the Continuing Appropriations Act, 2022 (Division A of Public Law 117–43, as amended). The amounts included for 2022 reflect the annualized level provided by the continuing resolution.

Program and Financing (in millions of dollars)

Identification code 012–0403–0–1–452		2021 actual	2022 est.	2023 est.
	Obligations by program activity:			
0001	Salaries and expenses	264	264	504
0002	Biobased		3	3
0799	Total direct obligations	264	267	507
0801	Reimbursable program - Program Transfers and Reimbursable Obligations	490	450	450
0811	LAMP and LAMP COVID		7	2
0812	Infrastructure transfer-Administration and Technical Assistance		33	
0814	RED Grants transfer-Administration and Technical Assistance		30	
0815	Electric Pilot Program			15
0816	Reconnect transfer for Administration and Technical Support		34	16
0817	American Rescue Plan		12	12
0818	Transfer for Information Technology		8	
0899	Total reimbursable obligations	490	574	495
0900	Total new obligations, unexpired accounts	754	841	1,002
	Budgetary resources:			
	Unobligated balance:			
1000	Unobligated balance brought forward, Oct 1	17	52	50
1001	Discretionary unobligated balance brought fwd, Oct 1	12	27	
1012	Unobligated balance transfers between expired and unexpired accounts	12	8	
1070	Unobligated balance (total)	29	60	50
	Budget authority:			
	Appropriations, discretionary:			
1100	Appropriation	264	264	504
1121	Appropriations transferred from other acct [012–9913]	10	10	
1160	Appropriation, discretionary (total)	274	274	504
	Appropriations, mandatory:			
1222	Exercised borrowing authority transferred from other accounts [012–4336]	3	3	3
	Spending authority from offsetting collections, discretionary:			
1700	Collected	474	550	528
	Spending authority from offsetting collections, mandatory:			
1800	Collected	34	4	
1900	Budget authority (total)	785	831	1,035
1930	Total budgetary resources available	814	891	1,085
	Memorandum (non-add) entries:			
1940	Unobligated balance expiring	–8		
1941	Unexpired unobligated balance, end of year	52	50	83
	Change in obligated balance:			
	Unpaid obligations:			
3000	Unpaid obligations, brought forward, Oct 1	131	142	105
3010	New obligations, unexpired accounts	754	841	1,002
3011	Obligations ("upward adjustments"), expired accounts	3		
3020	Outlays (gross)	–736	–878	–1,034
3041	Recoveries of prior year unpaid obligations, expired	–10		
3050	Unpaid obligations, end of year	142	105	73
	Uncollected payments:			
3060	Uncollected pymts, Fed sources, brought forward, Oct 1	–3	–2	–2
3071	Change in uncollected pymts, Fed sources, expired	1		
3090	Uncollected pymts, Fed sources, end of year	–2	–2	–2
	Memorandum (non-add) entries:			
3100	Obligated balance, start of year	128	140	103
3200	Obligated balance, end of year	140	103	71
	Budget authority and outlays, net:			
	Discretionary:			
4000	Budget authority, gross	748	824	1,032
	Outlays, gross:			
4010	Outlays from new discretionary authority	625	748	924
4011	Outlays from discretionary balances	105	125	95
4020	Outlays, gross (total)	730	873	1,019
	Offsets against gross budget authority and outlays:			
	Offsetting collections (collected) from:			
4030	Federal sources	–475	–550	–528
4040	Offsets against gross budget authority and outlays (total)	–475	–550	–528
	Additional offsets against gross budget authority only:			
4052	Offsetting collections credited to expired accounts	1		
4060	Additional offsets against budget authority only (total)	1		
4070	Budget authority, net (discretionary)	274	274	504
4080	Outlays, net (discretionary)	255	323	491
	Mandatory:			
4090	Budget authority, gross	37	7	3
	Outlays, gross:			
4100	Outlays from new mandatory authority	1	1	1
4101	Outlays from mandatory balances	5	4	14
4110	Outlays, gross (total)	6	5	15
	Offsets against gross budget authority and outlays:			
	Offsetting collections (collected) from:			
4120	Federal sources	–31	–4	
4123	Non-Federal sources	–3		
4130	Offsets against gross budget authority and outlays (total)	–34	–4	
4160	Budget authority, net (mandatory)	3	3	3
4170	Outlays, net (mandatory)	–28	1	15
4180	Budget authority, net (total)	277	277	507
4190	Outlays, net (total)	227	324	506

The Rural Development Salaries and Expenses (S&E) account is a consolidated account to administer all Rural Development programs, including programs administered by the Rural Utilities Service (RUS), the Rural Housing Service (RHS), and the Rural Business-Cooperative Service (RBS). The 2023 Budget includes a set aside of $39 million to support Rural Partners Network (formerly StrikeForce) activities across the Department of Agriculture and other Federal agencies. Rural Partners Network activities funding will support targeted training, technical assistance, and outreach to distressed communities in rural America, and to socially-disadvantaged farmers, ranchers, and forest stewards. Rural Development will be the primary agency and will share funding and coordinate with other USDA agencies and other Federal agencies in an all of government effort. There is also a set aside of $3 million in discretionary funding for the Rural Placemaking Innovation Challenge to provide planning support, technical assistance, and training to foster placemaking activities in rural communities. In addition, the account reflects $3 million in mandatory funding for the Biobased Markets Program. For more information about the Rural Development mission area go to www.rd.usda.gov.

Object Classification (in millions of dollars)

Identification code 012–0403–0–1–452		2021 actual	2022 est.	2023 est.
	Direct obligations:			
	Personnel compensation:			
11.1	Full-time permanent	135	124	244

DEPARTMENT OF AGRICULTURE

Rural Housing Service—Federal Funds—125

		2021 actual	2022 est.	2023 est.
11.3	Other than full-time permanent	1	1	1
11.9	Total personnel compensation	136	125	245
12.1	Civilian personnel benefits	51	54	85
21.0	Travel and transportation of persons	1	2	4
23.1	Rental payments to GSA	6	6	10
23.2	Rental payments to others	5	6	9
23.3	Communications, utilities, and miscellaneous charges	1	1	1
25.1	Advisory and assistance services	21	35	57
25.2	Other services from non-Federal sources			1
25.3	Other goods and services from Federal sources	9	9	19
25.5	Research and development contracts	6	8	40
25.7	Operation and maintenance of equipment	26	20	34
26.0	Supplies and materials			1
31.0	Equipment	2	1	1
99.0	Direct obligations	264	267	507
99.0	Reimbursable obligations	490	574	495
99.9	Total new obligations, unexpired accounts	754	841	1,002

Employment Summary

Identification code 012–0403–0–1–452	2021 actual	2022 est.	2023 est.
1001 Direct civilian full-time equivalent employment	4,405	4,736	5,329
2001 Reimbursable civilian full-time equivalent employment	29	30	30

RURAL DEVELOPMENT DISASTER ASSISTANCE FUND

Program and Financing (in millions of dollars)

Identification code 012–0405–0–1–453	2021 actual	2022 est.	2023 est.
Budgetary resources:			
Unobligated balance:			
1000 Unobligated balance brought forward, Oct 1	11	11	11
1001 Discretionary unobligated balance brought fwd, Oct 1		11	
1930 Total budgetary resources available	11	11	11
Memorandum (non-add) entries:			
1941 Unexpired unobligated balance, end of year	11	11	11
4180 Budget authority, net (total)			
4190 Outlays, net (total)			

The Disaster Assistance Fund account consolidates disaster supplemental funding for specific disasters that are no longer needed for the initial purpose. The funding in the account can be transferred to specific programs for other Presidential and Secretarial Declared disasters.

RURAL HOUSING SERVICE

Federal Funds

RURAL HOUSING ASSISTANCE GRANTS

For grants for very low-income housing repair and rural housing preservation made by the Rural Housing Service, as authorized by 42 U.S.C. 1474, and 1490m, $75,000,000, to remain available until expended.

Note.—A full-year 2022 appropriation for this account was not enacted at the time the Budget was prepared; therefore, the Budget assumes this account is operating under the Continuing Appropriations Act, 2022 (Division A of Public Law 117–43, as amended). The amounts included for 2022 reflect the annualized level provided by the continuing resolution.

Program and Financing (in millions of dollars)

Identification code 012–1953–0–1–604	2021 actual	2022 est.	2023 est.
Obligations by program activity:			
0012 Very Low-Income Housing Repair Grants	24	30	45
0016 Rural Housing Preservation Grants	14	15	30
0017 Domestic Violence Shelters with Pets	3	3	
0900 Total new obligations, unexpired accounts (object class 41.0)	41	48	75
Budgetary resources:			
Unobligated balance:			
1000 Unobligated balance brought forward, Oct 1	14	23	24
1001 Discretionary unobligated balance brought fwd, Oct 1		23	
1021 Recoveries of prior year unpaid obligations	2	1	1
1070 Unobligated balance (total)	16	24	25
Budget authority:			
Appropriations, discretionary:			
1100 Appropriation	48	48	75
1930 Total budgetary resources available	64	72	100
Memorandum (non-add) entries:			
1941 Unexpired unobligated balance, end of year	23	24	25
Change in obligated balance:			
Unpaid obligations:			
3000 Unpaid obligations, brought forward, Oct 1	37	43	49
3010 New obligations, unexpired accounts	41	48	75
3020 Outlays (gross)	–33	–41	–61
3040 Recoveries of prior year unpaid obligations, unexpired	–2	–1	–1
3050 Unpaid obligations, end of year	43	49	62
Memorandum (non-add) entries:			
3100 Obligated balance, start of year	37	43	49
3200 Obligated balance, end of year	43	49	62
Budget authority and outlays, net:			
Discretionary:			
4000 Budget authority, gross	48	48	75
Outlays, gross:			
4010 Outlays from new discretionary authority	8	31	42
4011 Outlays from discretionary balances	25	10	19
4020 Outlays, gross (total)	33	41	61
4180 Budget authority, net (total)	48	48	75
4190 Outlays, net (total)	33	41	61

The very low-income housing repair grant program is authorized under section 504 of the Housing Act of 1949, as amended. This grant program enables very low-income elderly residents in rural areas to improve or modernize their dwellings, to make the dwelling safer or more sanitary, or to remove health and safety hazards. The 2023 Budget requests $45 million for this account.

For other housing assistance grants authorized for funding in this account such as housing preservation grants and supervisory and technical assistance grants as authorized by section 509(f) and 525 of the Housing Act of 1949, as amended, the 2023 Budget requests $30 million for the housing preservation grants.

The Budget also includes a requirement that funding for construction, preservation or rehabilitation, including grant funding, should be targeted to projects that improve energy or water efficiency, implement green features, and addresses climate resilience.

RENTAL ASSISTANCE PROGRAM

(INCLUDING TRANSFER OF FUNDS)

For rental assistance agreements entered into or renewed pursuant to the authority under section 521(a)(2) of the Housing Act of 1949 or agreements entered into in lieu of debt forgiveness or payments for eligible households as authorized by section 502(c)(5)(D) of the Housing Act of 1949, and for the rural housing voucher program as authorized under section 542 of the Housing Act of 1949, notwithstanding subsection (b) of such section, $1,601,926,000, of which $40,000,000 shall be available until September 30, 2024; and in addition such sums as may be necessary, as authorized by section 521(c) of the Act, to liquidate debt incurred prior to fiscal year 1992 to carry out the rental assistance program under section 521(a)(2) of the Act: Provided, That of the amounts made available under this heading, $1,563,926,000 shall be available for renewal of rental assistance agreements, including agreements where the Secretary determines that a maturing loan for a project cannot reasonably be restructured with another USDA loan or modification and the project was operating with rental assistance under section 521 of the Housing Act of 1949: Provided further, That the Secretary may renew the rental assistance agreements in maturing properties, notwithstanding any provision of section 521 of the Housing Act of 1949, for a term of at least 10 years but not more than 20 years: Provided further, That any agreement to extend the term of the rental assistance contract under section 521 of the Housing Act of 1949 for a project shall obligate the owner to continue to maintain the project as decent, safe, and sanitary housing and to operate the development in accordance with the Housing Act of 1949, except that rents shall be based on the lesser of (a) the budget-based needs of the project; or (b) the operating cost adjustment factor as a payment standard as provided under section 524 of the Multifamily Assisted Housing Reform and Affordability Act of 1997 (42 U.S.C. 1437f note): Provided further, That of the amounts made available under this heading,

RENTAL ASSISTANCE PROGRAM—Continued

not less than $6,000,000 shall be available for newly constructed units financed under section 514 and 516 of the Housing Act of 1949: Provided further, That rental assistance agreements entered into or renewed during the current fiscal year shall be funded for a one-year period: Provided further, That notwithstanding any other provision of the Act, the Secretary may recapture rental assistance provided under agreements entered into prior to fiscal year 2023 for a project that the Secretary determines no longer needs rental assistance and use such recaptured funds for current needs: Provided further, That notwithstanding any other provision of this Act, the Secretary may recapture funds provided for rental assistance under agreements entered into prior to fiscal year 2023 for a project that the Secretary determines no longer needs rental assistance: Provided further, That such recaptured funds shall remain available for obligation in fiscal year 2023 for the purposes specified under this heading: Provided further, That of the amounts made available under this heading, $38,000,000 shall be available for rural housing vouchers to any low-income household, including a household that does not receive rental assistance, residing in a property financed with a section 515 loan that has been prepaid or otherwise paid off after September 30, 2005: Provided further, That the amount of such vouchers shall be equal to the difference between comparable market rent for the section 515 unit and the tenant paid rent for such unit: Provided further, That such vouchers shall be subject to the availability of annual appropriations: Provided further, That the Secretary shall, to the maximum extent practicable, administer such vouchers with current regulations and administrative guidance applicable to section 8 housing vouchers administered by the Secretary of the Department of Housing and Urban Development: Provided further, That any balances available for the rural housing voucher program in the "Multi-Family Housing Revitalization Program Account" shall be transferred to and merged with this account and available for the rural housing voucher program: Provided further, That if the Secretary determines that the amount made available for vouchers or rental assistance in this Act is not needed for vouchers or rental assistance, the Secretary may use such funds for any of the programs described under this heading.

Note.—A full-year 2022 appropriation for this account was not enacted at the time the Budget was prepared; therefore, the Budget assumes this account is operating under the Continuing Appropriations Act, 2022 (Division A of Public Law 117–43, as amended). The amounts included for 2022 reflect the annualized level provided by the continuing resolution.

Program and Financing (in millions of dollars)

Identification code 012–0137–0–1–604		2021 actual	2022 est.	2023 est.
	Obligations by program activity:			
0001	Rental assistance program	1,410	1,410	1,558
0003	Multi-Family Housing Revitalization Voucher			38
0004	American Rescue Act	100		
0005	Rental Assistance New Construction			6
0900	Total new obligations, unexpired accounts (object class 41.0)	1,510	1,410	1,602
	Budgetary resources:			
	Unobligated balance:			
1000	Unobligated balance brought forward, Oct 1	40	40	40
1001	Discretionary unobligated balance brought fwd, Oct 1		40	
1011	Unobligated balance transfer from other acct [012–2002]			7
1070	Unobligated balance (total)	40	40	47
	Budget authority:			
	Appropriations, discretionary:			
1100	Appropriation	1,410	1,410	1,602
1100	Appropriation	4	5	5
1139	Appropriations substituted for borrowing authority	–4	–5	–5
1160	Appropriation, discretionary (total)	1,410	1,410	1,602
	Appropriations, mandatory:			
1200	Appropriation	100		
1900	Budget authority (total)	1,510	1,410	1,602
1930	Total budgetary resources available	1,550	1,450	1,649
	Memorandum (non-add) entries:			
1941	Unexpired unobligated balance, end of year	40	40	47
	Change in obligated balance:			
	Unpaid obligations:			
3000	Unpaid obligations, brought forward, Oct 1	1,495	1,658	1,699
3010	New obligations, unexpired accounts	1,510	1,410	1,602
3020	Outlays (gross)	–1,347	–1,369	–1,525
3050	Unpaid obligations, end of year	1,658	1,699	1,776
	Memorandum (non-add) entries:			
3100	Obligated balance, start of year	1,495	1,658	1,699
3200	Obligated balance, end of year	1,658	1,699	1,776
	Budget authority and outlays, net:			
	Discretionary:			
4000	Budget authority, gross	1,410	1,410	1,602
	Outlays, gross:			
4010	Outlays from new discretionary authority	162	493	562
4011	Outlays from discretionary balances	1,168	821	935
4020	Outlays, gross (total)	1,330	1,314	1,497
	Offsets against gross budget authority and outlays:			
	Offsetting collections (collected) from:			
4033	Non-Federal sources	–1		
	Additional offsets against gross budget authority only:			
4052	Offsetting collections credited to expired accounts	1		
4070	Budget authority, net (discretionary)	1,410	1,410	1,602
4080	Outlays, net (discretionary)	1,329	1,314	1,497
	Mandatory:			
4090	Budget authority, gross	100		
	Outlays, gross:			
4100	Outlays from new mandatory authority	17		
4101	Outlays from mandatory balances		55	28
4110	Outlays, gross (total)	17	55	28
4180	Budget authority, net (total)	1,510	1,410	1,602
4190	Outlays, net (total)	1,346	1,369	1,525

The rental assistance program is authorized under section 521(a)(2) of the Housing Act of 1949, as amended, and is designed to reduce rent expenses for very low-income and low-income families living in RHS-financed rural rental and farm labor housing projects. The rural housing voucher program is authorized under section 542 of the Housing Act of 1949 and may be used to assist families who may face hardship when the mortgage on RHS-financed rural rental housing projects is prepaid or paid in full. A voucher can be used in lieu of rental assistance, which is no longer available once the property is paid-off in full. The 2023 request combines the appropriations for rental assistance and vouchers to facilitate funding flexibilities with like programs. A total of $1.602 billion is being requested, of which $1.564 billion is limited to renewals of existing rental assistance contracts for maintaining a sustainable rental assistance program. Of the total amount provided, the Budget requests $38 million for housing vouchers, which can be for prepayments and pay-offs. The Budget also requests authority to decouple Rental Assistance from the Multi-family Housing Direct Loan program, allowing RHS to continue offering Rental Assistance to certain properties that no longer have an RHS-financed loan. Decoupling these two programs will help ensure low-income rural tenants in USDA financed properties continue to have access to affordable rents when projects reach loan maturity and leave the portfolio. Decoupling will also lead to the preservation of the majority of USDA's project-based assistance, and, thus, decrease the number of tenant-based vouchers needed for USDA financed properties going forward. The Budget request for vouchers reflects just the funding needed for the legacy vouchers that will still be renewed by USDA. To assist the remaining displaced tenants going forward, this proposal is being done in tandem with a HUD tenant protection voucher (TPV) proposal, that will provide $20 million in TPVs for tenants in USDA properties that are unable to refinance, participate in the multi-family preservation and rehabilitation options, or decouple. Collectively, these proposals allow USDA to focus on preservation of low-income tenant based housing, while maintaining the protections for its tenant beneficiaries.

From 1978 through 1991, the rental assistance program was funded under the Rural Housing Insurance Fund (RHIF). Beginning in 1992, pursuant to Credit Reform, a separate grant account was established for this program. Prior year obligations are funded with "such sums" amounts to cover those pre-credit reform contracts in RHIF.

MULTI-FAMILY HOUSING REVITALIZATION PROGRAM ACCOUNT

Note.—A full-year 2022 appropriation for this account was not enacted at the time the Budget was prepared; therefore, the Budget assumes this account is operating under the Continuing Appropriations Act, 2022 (Division A of Public Law 117–43, as amended). The amounts included for 2022 reflect the annualized level provided by the continuing resolution.

DEPARTMENT OF AGRICULTURE

Rural Housing Service—Continued
Federal Funds—Continued

127

Program and Financing (in millions of dollars)

Identification code 012–2002–0–1–604	2021 actual	2022 est.	2023 est.
Obligations by program activity:			
0010 Vouchers & MPR Grants	35	50	....
Credit program obligations:			
0701 Direct loan subsidy	22	16	....
0703 Subsidy for modifications of direct loans	2	....	....
0705 Reestimates of direct loan subsidy	1	1	....
0706 Interest on reestimates of direct loan subsidy	....	1	....
0791 Direct program activities, subtotal	25	18	....
0900 Total new obligations, unexpired accounts (object class 41.0)	60	68	....
Budgetary resources:			
Unobligated balance:			
1000 Unobligated balance brought forward, Oct 1	8	22	26
1001 Discretionary unobligated balance brought fwd, Oct 1	....	22	....
1010 Unobligated balance transfer to other accts [012–2081]	....	....	–19
1010 Unobligated balance transfer to other accts [012–0137]	....	....	–7
1021 Recoveries of prior year unpaid obligations	3	....	....
1070 Unobligated balance (total)	11	22	....
Budget authority:			
Appropriations, discretionary:			
1100 Appropriation	70	70	....
Appropriations, mandatory:			
1200 Appropriation	1	2	....
1900 Budget authority (total)	71	72	....
1930 Total budgetary resources available	82	94	....
Memorandum (non-add) entries:			
1941 Unexpired unobligated balance, end of year	22	26	....
Change in obligated balance:			
Unpaid obligations:			
3000 Unpaid obligations, brought forward, Oct 1	91	106	137
3010 New obligations, unexpired accounts	60	68	....
3020 Outlays (gross)	–42	–37	–54
3040 Recoveries of prior year unpaid obligations, unexpired	–3	....	....
3050 Unpaid obligations, end of year	106	137	83
Memorandum (non-add) entries:			
3100 Obligated balance, start of year	91	106	137
3200 Obligated balance, end of year	106	137	83
Budget authority and outlays, net:			
Discretionary:			
4000 Budget authority, gross	70	70	....
Outlays, gross:			
4010 Outlays from new discretionary authority	8	14	....
4011 Outlays from discretionary balances	33	21	54
4020 Outlays, gross (total)	41	35	54
Mandatory:			
4090 Budget authority, gross	1	2	....
Outlays, gross:			
4100 Outlays from new mandatory authority	1	2	....
4180 Budget authority, net (total)	71	72	....
4190 Outlays, net (total)	42	37	54
Memorandum (non-add) entries:			
5103 Unexpired unavailable balance, SOY: Fulfilled purpose	1	1	....
5104 Unexpired unavailable balance, EOY: Fulfilled purpose	1	....	....

Summary of Loan Levels, Subsidy Budget Authority and Outlays by Program (in millions of dollars)

Identification code 012–2002–0–1–604	2021 actual	2022 est.	2023 est.
Direct loan levels supportable by subsidy budget authority:			
115002 Multifamily Housing Revitalization Seconds	37	38	....
115003 Multifamily Revitalization Zero	10	10	....
115006 Section 515 Multifamily Housing Revitalization Deferrals	42	43	....
115999 Total direct loan levels	89	91	....
Direct loan subsidy (in percent):			
132002 Multifamily Housing Revitalization Seconds	46.28	35.51	....
132003 Multifamily Revitalization Zero	41.26	34.09	....
132006 Section 515 Multifamily Housing Revitalization Deferrals	0.00	0.00	....
132999 Weighted average subsidy rate	23.88	18.57	....
Direct loan subsidy budget authority:			
133002 Multifamily Housing Revitalization Seconds	17	13	....
133003 Multifamily Revitalization Zero	4	3	....
133999 Total subsidy budget authority	21	16	....
Direct loan subsidy outlays:			
134001 Multifamily Housing Relending Demo	1	....	....
134002 Multifamily Housing Revitalization Seconds	3	10	....
134003 Multifamily Revitalization Zero	8	4	....
134006 Section 515 Multifamily Housing Revitalization Deferrals	3	1	....
134007 Section 514 Multifamily Housing Revitalization Modifications	6	1	....
134999 Total subsidy outlays	21	16	....
Direct loan reestimates:			
135001 Multifamily Housing Relending Demo	1	1	....
135002 Multifamily Housing Revitalization Seconds	–7	–3	....
135006 Section 515 Multifamily Housing Revitalization Deferrals	–13	–4	....
135999 Total direct loan reestimates	–19	–6	....

This account includes funding for vouchers as authorized in section 542 of the Housing Act of 1949 to be used to assist families who may face hardship when the mortgage on the RHS-financed rural rental housing projects is prepaid or paid in full. A voucher can be used in lieu of rental assistance, which is no longer available once the property is paid-off. This account also reflects the funding for pilot programs to repair and rehabilitate multi-family housing projects financed under USDA's section 514 and 515 direct loan programs. These have included grants and direct loans (zero percent, soft-second, modifications, and the relending demonstration program) since 2006. The 2023 Budget requests $38 million in funding for the rural housing voucher program in the Rental Assistance Program Account to facilitate funding flexibilities with like programs. The 2023 Budget requests $75 million in funding for the multi-family housing revitalization pilot program in the Rural Housing Insurance Fund account.

MULTIFAMILY HOUSING REVITALIZATION DIRECT LOAN FINANCING ACCOUNT

Program and Financing (in millions of dollars)

Identification code 012–4269–0–3–604	2021 actual	2022 est.	2023 est.
Obligations by program activity:			
Credit program obligations:			
0710 Direct loan obligations	89	91	....
0713 Payment of interest to Treasury	19	16	....
0739 Other	2	2	....
0742 Downward reestimates paid to receipt accounts	18	7	....
0743 Interest on downward reestimates	2	1	....
0900 Total new obligations, unexpired accounts	130	117	....
Budgetary resources:			
Unobligated balance:			
1000 Unobligated balance brought forward, Oct 1	71	8	25
1021 Recoveries of prior year unpaid obligations	3	2	....
1023 Unobligated balances applied to repay debt	–72	–8	....
1024 Unobligated balance of borrowing authority withdrawn	–1	–1	....
1070 Unobligated balance (total)	1	1	25
Financing authority:			
Borrowing authority, mandatory:			
1400 Borrowing authority	94	96	....
Spending authority from offsetting collections, mandatory:			
1800 Collected	29	30	....
1801 Change in uncollected payments, Federal sources	14	15	....
1850 Spending auth from offsetting collections, mand (total)	43	45	....
1900 Budget authority (total)	137	141	....
1930 Total budgetary resources available	138	142	25
Memorandum (non-add) entries:			
1941 Unexpired unobligated balance, end of year	8	25	25
Change in obligated balance:			
Unpaid obligations:			
3000 Unpaid obligations, brought forward, Oct 1	184	236	274
3010 New obligations, unexpired accounts	130	117	....
3020 Outlays (gross)	–75	–77	....
3040 Recoveries of prior year unpaid obligations, unexpired	–3	–2	....
3050 Unpaid obligations, end of year	236	274	274
Uncollected payments:			
3060 Uncollected pymts, Fed sources, brought forward, Oct 1	–65	–79	–94
3070 Change in uncollected pymts, Fed sources, unexpired	–14	–15	....
3090 Uncollected pymts, Fed sources, end of year	–79	–94	–94

MULTIFAMILY HOUSING REVITALIZATION DIRECT LOAN FINANCING ACCOUNT—Continued

Program and Financing—Continued

Identification code 012–4269–0–3–604	2021 actual	2022 est.	2023 est.
Memorandum (non-add) entries:			
3100 Obligated balance, start of year	119	157	180
3200 Obligated balance, end of year	157	180	180
Financing authority and disbursements, net:			
Mandatory:			
4090 Budget authority, gross	137	141	
Financing disbursements:			
4110 Outlays, gross (total)	75	77	
Offsets against gross financing authority and disbursements:			
Offsetting collections (collected) from:			
4120 Federal sources - subsidy outlays from program account	−21	−18	
4122 Interest on uninvested funds	−2	−2	
4123 Repayments of Principal	−6	−10	
4130 Offsets against gross budget authority and outlays (total)	−29	−30	
Additional offsets against financing authority only (total):			
4140 Change in uncollected pymts, Fed sources, unexpired	−14	−15	
4160 Budget authority, net (mandatory)	94	96	
4170 Outlays, net (mandatory)	46	47	
4180 Budget authority, net (total)	94	96	
4190 Outlays, net (total)	46	47	

Status of Direct Loans (in millions of dollars)

Identification code 012–4269–0–3–604	2021 actual	2022 est.	2023 est.
Position with respect to appropriations act limitation on obligations:			
1111 Direct loan obligations from current-year authority	89	91	
1150 Total direct loan obligations	89	91	
Cumulative balance of direct loans outstanding:			
1210 Outstanding, start of year	912	943	980
1231 Disbursements: Direct loan disbursements	33	37	
1251 Repayments: Repayments and prepayments	−2		
1264 Other adjustments, net (+ or -)			−980
1290 Outstanding, end of year	943	980	

This account reflects the financing for the direct pilot program loans (zero percent, soft-second, modifications, and the relending demonstration program) authorized in the Multi-family Housing Revitalization Program Account. Beginning in 2023 this activity will be reflected in the Rural Housing Insurance Fund Direct Loan Financing Account. This transition will facilitate the modification of post credit reform section 515 multifamily housing direct loans going forward.

Balance Sheet (in millions of dollars)

Identification code 012–4269–0–3–604	2020 actual	2021 actual
ASSETS:		
1101 Federal assets: Fund balances with Treasury	71	9
Net value of assets related to post-1991 direct loans receivable:		
1401 Direct loans receivable, gross	912	943
1402 Interest receivable	102	109
1405 Allowance for subsidy cost (-)	−545	−530
1499 Net present value of assets related to direct loans	469	522
1999 Total assets	540	531
LIABILITIES:		
Federal liabilities:		
2103 Debt	540	531
2104 Resources payable to Treasury		
2999 Total liabilities	540	531
NET POSITION:		
3300 Cumulative results of operations		
4999 Total liabilities and net position	540	531

MUTUAL AND SELF-HELP HOUSING GRANTS

For grants and contracts pursuant to section 523(b)(1)(A) of the Housing Act of 1949 (42 U.S.C. 1490c), $40,000,000, to remain available until expended.

Note.—A full-year 2022 appropriation for this account was not enacted at the time the Budget was prepared; therefore, the Budget assumes this account is operating under the Continuing Appropriations Act, 2022 (Division A of Public Law 117–43, as amended). The amounts included for 2022 reflect the annualized level provided by the continuing resolution.

Program and Financing (in millions of dollars)

Identification code 012–2006–0–1–604	2021 actual	2022 est.	2023 est.
Obligations by program activity:			
0001 Mutual and self-help housing grants	32	32	42
0900 Total new obligations, unexpired accounts (object class 41.0)	32	32	42
Budgetary resources:			
Unobligated balance:			
1000 Unobligated balance brought forward, Oct 1	3	2	2
1001 Discretionary unobligated balance brought fwd, Oct 1		2	
1021 Recoveries of prior year unpaid obligations		1	
1070 Unobligated balance (total)	3	3	2
Budget authority:			
Appropriations, discretionary:			
1100 Appropriation	31	31	40
1930 Total budgetary resources available	34	34	42
Memorandum (non-add) entries:			
1941 Unexpired unobligated balance, end of year	2	2	
Change in obligated balance:			
Unpaid obligations:			
3000 Unpaid obligations, brought forward, Oct 1	59	58	55
3010 New obligations, unexpired accounts	32	32	42
3020 Outlays (gross)	−33	−34	−40
3040 Recoveries of prior year unpaid obligations, unexpired		−1	
3050 Unpaid obligations, end of year	58	55	57
Memorandum (non-add) entries:			
3100 Obligated balance, start of year	59	58	55
3200 Obligated balance, end of year	58	55	57
Budget authority and outlays, net:			
Discretionary:			
4000 Budget authority, gross	31	31	40
Outlays, gross:			
4010 Outlays from new discretionary authority	1	5	6
4011 Outlays from discretionary balances	32	29	34
4020 Outlays, gross (total)	33	34	40
4180 Budget authority, net (total)	31	31	40
4190 Outlays, net (total)	33	34	40

This program is authorized under section 523 of the Housing Act of 1949, as amended. Grants and contracts are made for the purpose of providing technical and supervisory assistance to groups of families to enable them to build their own homes through the mutual exchange of labor. The 2023 Budget requests $40 million for this program.

RURAL COMMUNITY FACILITIES PROGRAM ACCOUNT

(INCLUDING TRANSFERS OF FUNDS)

For gross obligations for the principal amount of direct and guaranteed loans as authorized by section 306 and described in section 381E(d)(1) of the Consolidated Farm and Rural Development Act, $2,800,000,000 for direct loans and $500,000,000 for guaranteed loans.

For the cost of direct loans, loan guarantees and grants, including the cost of modifying loans, as defined in section 502 of the Congressional Budget Act of 1974, for rural community facilities programs as authorized by section 306 and described in section 381E(d)(1) of the Consolidated Farm and Rural Development Act, $74,000,000, to remain available until expended: Provided, That $12,000,000 of the amount appropriated under this heading shall be available for a Rural Community Development Initiative: Provided further, That such funds shall be used solely to develop the capacity and ability of private, nonprofit community-based housing and community development organizations, low-income rural communities, and Federally Recognized Native American Tribes to undertake projects to improve housing, community facilities, community and economic development projects in

DEPARTMENT OF AGRICULTURE

Rural Housing Service—Continued
Federal Funds—Continued

rural areas: Provided further, That such funds shall be made available to qualified private, nonprofit and public intermediary organizations proposing to carry out a program of financial and technical assistance: Provided further, That such intermediary organizations shall provide matching funds from other sources, including Federal funds for related activities, in an amount not less than funds provided: Provided further, That any unobligated balances from prior year appropriations under this heading for the cost of direct loans, loan guarantees and grants, including amounts deobligated or cancelled, may be made available to cover the subsidy costs for direct loans and or loan guarantees under this heading in this fiscal year: Provided further, That no amounts may be made available pursuant to the preceding proviso from amounts that were designated by the Congress as an emergency requirement pursuant to a Concurrent Resolution on the Budget or the Balanced Budget and Emergency Deficit Control Act of 1985: Provided further, That $10,000,000 of the amount appropriated under this heading shall be available for community facilities grants to tribal colleges, as authorized by section 306(a)(19) of such Act: Provided further, That sections 381E–H and 381N of the Consolidated Farm and Rural Development Act are not applicable to the funds made available under this heading.

Note.—A full-year 2022 appropriation for this account was not enacted at the time the Budget was prepared; therefore, the Budget assumes this account is operating under the Continuing Appropriations Act, 2022 (Division A of Public Law 117–43, as amended). The amounts included for 2022 reflect the annualized level provided by the continuing resolution.

Program and Financing (in millions of dollars)

Identification code 012–1951–0–1–452	2021 actual	2022 est.	2023 est.
Obligations by program activity:			
0010 CF Grants	100	32	52
0012 Rural Community Development Initiative Grants	6	6	12
0013 Economic Impact Initiative Grants	6	6	
0014 Tribal College Grants	5	5	10
0015 Grant Reserve/Subsidy BA		25	
0016 Rural Hospital Technical Assistance	2	2	
0017 American Rescue Plan Technical Assistance Grants	10		
0018 American Rescue Plan Administrative Expenses	15		
0019 CF Grants - American Rescue Act		175	300
0091 Direct program activities, subtotal	144	251	374
Credit program obligations:			
0701 Direct loan subsidy	22		
0705 Reestimates of direct loan subsidy	40	133	
0706 Interest on reestimates of direct loan subsidy	7	43	
0707 Reestimates of loan guarantee subsidy	1	3	
0708 Interest on reestimates of loan guarantee subsidy		1	
0791 Direct program activities, subtotal	70	180	
0900 Total new obligations, unexpired accounts	214	431	374
Budgetary resources:			
Unobligated balance:			
1000 Unobligated balance brought forward, Oct 1	135	548	376
1001 Discretionary unobligated balance brought fwd, Oct 1	135	33	
1021 Recoveries of prior year unpaid obligations	4	3	3
1070 Unobligated balance (total)	139	551	379
Budget authority:			
Appropriations, discretionary:			
1100 Appropriation	76	76	74
Appropriations, mandatory:			
1200 Appropriation	547	180	
1900 Budget authority (total)	623	256	74
1930 Total budgetary resources available	762	807	453
Memorandum (non-add) entries:			
1941 Unexpired unobligated balance, end of year	548	376	79
Change in obligated balance:			
Unpaid obligations:			
3000 Unpaid obligations, brought forward, Oct 1	137	202	96
3010 New obligations, unexpired accounts	214	431	374
3011 Obligations ("upward adjustments"), expired accounts	1		
3020 Outlays (gross)	–146	–534	–252
3040 Recoveries of prior year unpaid obligations, unexpired	–4	–3	–3
3050 Unpaid obligations, end of year	202	96	215
Memorandum (non-add) entries:			
3100 Obligated balance, start of year	137	202	96
3200 Obligated balance, end of year	202	96	215
Budget authority and outlays, net:			
Discretionary:			
4000 Budget authority, gross	76	76	74
Outlays, gross:			
4010 Outlays from new discretionary authority		15	9
4011 Outlays from discretionary balances	74	39	68
4020 Outlays, gross (total)	74	54	77
Mandatory:			
4090 Budget authority, gross	547	180	
Outlays, gross:			
4100 Outlays from new mandatory authority	72	180	
4101 Outlays from mandatory balances		300	175
4110 Outlays, gross (total)	72	480	175
4180 Budget authority, net (total)	623	256	74
4190 Outlays, net (total)	146	534	252

Summary of Loan Levels, Subsidy Budget Authority and Outlays by Program (in millions of dollars)

Identification code 012–1951–0–1–452	2021 actual	2022 est.	2023 est.
Direct loan levels supportable by subsidy budget authority:			
115002 Community Facility Loans	1,159	1,684	1,648
115006 Community Facility Loan-by-Loan	309		
115999 Total direct loan levels	1,468	1,684	1,648
Direct loan subsidy (in percent):			
132002 Community Facility Loans	–6.56	–5.81	–7.46
132006 Community Facility Loan-by-Loan	7.19		
132999 Weighted average subsidy rate	–3.67	–5.81	–7.46
Direct loan subsidy budget authority:			
133002 Community Facility Loans	–76	–98	–122
133006 Community Facility Loan-by-Loan	22		
133999 Total subsidy budget authority	–54	–98	–122
Direct loan subsidy outlays:			
134002 Community Facility Loans	–79	–79	–80
134999 Total subsidy outlays	–79	–79	–80
Direct loan reestimates:			
135002 Community Facility Loans	–129	115	
135005 Community Facility Relending	9	11	
135999 Total direct loan reestimates	–120	126	
Guaranteed loan levels supportable by subsidy budget authority:			
215002 Community Facility Loan Guarantees	242	153	155
215999 Total loan guarantee levels	242	153	155
Guaranteed loan subsidy (in percent):			
232002 Community Facility Loan Guarantees	–.36	–.29	–.66
232999 Weighted average subsidy rate	–.36	–.29	–.66
Guaranteed loan subsidy budget authority:			
233002 Community Facility Loan Guarantees	–1		–1
233999 Total subsidy budget authority	–1		–1
Guaranteed loan subsidy outlays:			
234002 Community Facility Loan Guarantees		6	6
234003 Community Facility Emergency Supplemental Loan Guarantees	2		
234999 Total subsidy outlays	2	6	6
Guaranteed loan reestimates:			
235002 Community Facility Loan Guarantees	–11	–5	
235999 Total guaranteed loan reestimates	–11	–5	

This account funds the direct and guaranteed community facility loans and community facility grants, which are authorized under sections 306(a)(1) and 306(a)(19) of the Consolidated Farm and Rural Development Act, as amended. Loans are provided to local governments and nonprofit organizations for the construction and improvement of community facilities providing essential services in rural areas of not more than 20,000 in population for direct loans, and not more than 50,000 for loan guarantees. Total program level in the 2023 Budget is projected to be $2.8 billion for direct loans, $500 million for guaranteed loans, and $74 million for grant purposes, of which $52 million is for regular community facilities grants, and $10 million for Tribal College Grants and $12 million is for the place-based Rural Community Development Initiative.

As required by the Federal Credit Reform Act of 1990, this account records, for this program, the subsidy costs associated with the direct loans obligated and loan guarantees committed in 1992 and beyond (including credit sales of acquired property). The subsidy amounts are estimated on a present value basis.

RURAL COMMUNITY FACILITIES PROGRAM ACCOUNT—Continued

Object Classification (in millions of dollars)

Identification code 012–1951–0–1–452	2021 actual	2022 est.	2023 est.
Direct obligations:			
25.3 Other goods and services from Federal sources	25		
41.0 Grants, subsidies, and contributions	189	431	374
99.9 Total new obligations, unexpired accounts	214	431	374

RURAL COMMUNITY FACILITY DIRECT LOANS FINANCING ACCOUNT

Program and Financing (in millions of dollars)

Identification code 012–4225–0–3–452	2021 actual	2022 est.	2023 est.
Obligations by program activity:			
Credit program obligations:			
0710 Direct loan obligations	1,159	1,684	1,648
0710 Direct loan obligations	309		
0713 Payment of interest to Treasury	336	342	370
0740 Negative subsidy obligations	76	98	123
0742 Downward reestimates paid to receipt accounts	136	48	
0743 Interest on downward reestimates	30	2	
0900 Total new obligations, unexpired accounts	2,046	2,174	2,141
Budgetary resources:			
Unobligated balance:			
1000 Unobligated balance brought forward, Oct 1	736	607	574
1021 Recoveries of prior year unpaid obligations	166	170	172
1023 Unobligated balances applied to repay debt	–730	–600	–568
1024 Unobligated balance of borrowing authority withdrawn	–166	–170	–172
1070 Unobligated balance (total)	6	7	6
Financing authority:			
Borrowing authority, mandatory:			
1400 Borrowing authority	1,565	1,652	1,569
Spending authority from offsetting collections, mandatory:			
1800 Collected	1,014	1,089	1,121
1801 Change in uncollected payments, Federal sources	68		
1850 Spending auth from offsetting collections, mand (total)	1,082	1,089	1,121
1900 Budget authority (total)	2,647	2,741	2,690
1930 Total budgetary resources available	2,653	2,748	2,696
Memorandum (non-add) entries:			
1941 Unexpired unobligated balance, end of year	607	574	555
Change in obligated balance:			
Unpaid obligations:			
3000 Unpaid obligations, brought forward, Oct 1	4,676	4,717	4,865
3010 New obligations, unexpired accounts	2,046	2,174	2,141
3020 Outlays (gross)	–1,839	–1,856	–1,873
3040 Recoveries of prior year unpaid obligations, unexpired	–166	–170	–172
3050 Unpaid obligations, end of year	4,717	4,865	4,961
Uncollected payments:			
3060 Uncollected pymts, Fed sources, brought forward, Oct 1		–68	–68
3070 Change in uncollected pymts, Fed sources, unexpired	–68		
3090 Uncollected pymts, Fed sources, end of year	–68	–68	–68
Memorandum (non-add) entries:			
3100 Obligated balance, start of year	4,676	4,649	4,797
3200 Obligated balance, end of year	4,649	4,797	4,893
Financing authority and disbursements, net:			
Mandatory:			
4090 Budget authority, gross	2,647	2,741	2,690
Financing disbursements:			
4110 Outlays, gross (total)	1,839	1,856	1,873
Offsets against gross financing authority and disbursements:			
Offsetting collections (collected) from:			
4120 Federal sources	–46	–176	
4122 Interest on uninvested funds	–37	–131	–131
4123 Repayment of principal	–931	–612	–651
4123 Interest received on loans		–170	–339
4130 Offsets against gross budget authority and outlays (total)	–1,014	–1,089	–1,121
Additional offsets against financing authority only (total):			
4140 Change in uncollected pymts, Fed sources, unexpired	–68		
4160 Budget authority, net (mandatory)	1,565	1,652	1,569
4170 Outlays, net (mandatory)	825	767	752
4180 Budget authority, net (total)	1,565	1,652	1,569
4190 Outlays, net (total)	825	767	752

Status of Direct Loans (in millions of dollars)

Identification code 012–4225–0–3–452	2021 actual	2022 est.	2023 est.
Position with respect to appropriations act limitation on obligations:			
1111 Direct loan obligations from current-year authority	1,468	1,684	1,648
1150 Total direct loan obligations	1,468	1,684	1,648
Cumulative balance of direct loans outstanding:			
1210 Outstanding, start of year	10,536	11,151	12,212
1231 Disbursements: Direct loan disbursements	1,259	1,684	1,648
1251 Repayments: Repayments and prepayments	–638	–612	–651
1263 Write-offs for default: Direct loans	–6	–11	–11
1290 Outstanding, end of year	11,151	12,212	13,198

This account reflects the financing for direct community facility loans to non-profit organizations and local governments for the construction and improvement of community facilities providing essential services in rural areas, such as hospitals, libraries, and fire/police stations. Loans made prior to 1992 are recorded in the Rural Development Insurance Fund Liquidating Account.

Balance Sheet (in millions of dollars)

Identification code 012–4225–0–3–452	2020 actual	2021 actual
ASSETS:		
Federal assets:		
1101 Fund balances with Treasury	736	608
Investments in U.S. securities:		
1106 Receivables, net	36	165
Net value of assets related to post-1991 direct loans receivable:		
1401 Direct loans receivable, gross	10,536	11,151
1402 Interest receivable	72	106
1405 Allowance for subsidy cost (-)	–119	–188
1499 Net present value of assets related to direct loans	10,489	11,069
1999 Total assets	11,261	11,842
LIABILITIES:		
Federal liabilities:		
2101 Accounts payable		
2103 Debt	11,095	11,792
2105 Other	166	50
2999 Total liabilities	11,261	11,842
4999 Total liabilities and net position	11,261	11,842

RURAL COMMUNITY FACILITY GUARANTEED LOANS FINANCING ACCOUNT

Program and Financing (in millions of dollars)

Identification code 012–4228–0–3–452	2021 actual	2022 est.	2023 est.
Obligations by program activity:			
Credit program obligations:			
0711 Default claim payments on principal	6	9	8
0713 Payment of interest to Treasury		1	1
0742 Downward reestimates paid to receipt accounts	9	9	
0743 Interest on downward reestimates	3	2	
0900 Total new obligations, unexpired accounts	18	21	9
Budgetary resources:			
Unobligated balance:			
1000 Unobligated balance brought forward, Oct 1	45	33	26
1023 Unobligated balances applied to repay debt	–1		
1070 Unobligated balance (total)	44	33	26
Financing authority:			
Borrowing authority, mandatory:			
1400 Borrowing authority	4	4	
Spending authority from offsetting collections, mandatory:			
1800 Collected	4	11	10
1801 Change in uncollected payments, Federal sources	–1	–1	
1850 Spending auth from offsetting collections, mand (total)	3	10	10
1900 Budget authority (total)	7	14	10
1930 Total budgetary resources available	51	47	36

DEPARTMENT OF AGRICULTURE

1941	Memorandum (non-add) entries: Unexpired unobligated balance, end of year	33	26	27
	Change in obligated balance: Unpaid obligations:			
3000	Unpaid obligations, brought forward, Oct 1	....	1	1
3010	New obligations, unexpired accounts	18	21	9
3020	Outlays (gross)	−17	−21	−9
3050	Unpaid obligations, end of year	1	1	1
	Uncollected payments:			
3060	Uncollected pymts, Fed sources, brought forward, Oct 1	−8	−7	−6
3070	Change in uncollected pymts, Fed sources, unexpired	1	1	....
3090	Uncollected pymts, Fed sources, end of year	−7	−6	−6
	Memorandum (non-add) entries:			
3100	Obligated balance, start of year	−8	−6	−5
3200	Obligated balance, end of year	−6	−5	−5
	Financing authority and disbursements, net: Mandatory:			
4090	Budget authority, gross	7	14	10
	Financing disbursements:			
4110	Outlays, gross (total)	17	21	9
	Offsets against gross financing authority and disbursements: Offsetting collections (collected) from:			
4120	Federal sources	−2	−11	−6
4122	Interest on uninvested funds	−1	....	−2
4123	Guarantee Fees	−1	....	−2
4130	Offsets against gross budget authority and outlays (total)	−4	−11	−10
	Additional offsets against financing authority only (total):			
4140	Change in uncollected pymts, Fed sources, unexpired	1	1	....
4160	Budget authority, net (mandatory)	4	4	....
4170	Outlays, net (mandatory)	13	10	−1
4180	Budget authority, net (total)	4	4	....
4190	Outlays, net (total)	13	10	−1

Status of Guaranteed Loans (in millions of dollars)

Identification code 012–4228–0–3–452		2021 actual	2022 est.	2023 est.
	Position with respect to appropriations act limitation on commitments:			
2111	Guaranteed loan commitments from current-year authority	242	153	155
2150	Total guaranteed loan commitments	242	153	155
2199	Guaranteed amount of guaranteed loan commitments	242	153	155
	Cumulative balance of guaranteed loans outstanding:			
2210	Outstanding, start of year	1,345	1,522	1,697
2231	Disbursements of new guaranteed loans	269	271	279
2251	Repayments and prepayments	−84	−87	−93
2263	Adjustments: Terminations for default that result in claim payments	−8	−9	−7
2290	Outstanding, end of year	1,522	1,697	1,876
	Memorandum:			
2299	Guaranteed amount of guaranteed loans outstanding, end of year	1,482	1,486	1,497
	Addendum: Cumulative balance of defaulted guaranteed loans that result in loans receivable:			
2310	Outstanding, start of year	8	8	10
2331	Disbursements for guaranteed loan claims	1	3	2
2351	Repayments of loans receivable	−1	−1	−1
2361	Write-offs of loans receivable	....	....	....
2390	Outstanding, end of year	8	10	11

This account finances loan guarantee commitments for essential community facilities in rural areas. Loans made prior to 1992 are recorded in the Rural Development Insurance Fund Liquidating Account.

Balance Sheet (in millions of dollars)

Identification code 012–4228–0–3–452		2020 actual	2021 actual
	ASSETS:		
1101	Federal assets: Fund balances with Treasury	37	27
	Net value of assets related to post-1991 acquired defaulted guaranteed loans receivable:		
1501	Defaulted guaranteed loans receivable, gross	8	8
1505	Allowance for subsidy cost (−)	....	....
1599	Net present value of assets related to defaulted guaranteed loans	8	8
1999	Total assets	45	35
	LIABILITIES: Federal liabilities:		
2103	Debt	2	5
2104	Resources payable to Treasury	....	....
2204	Non-Federal liabilities: Liabilities for loan guarantees	43	30
2999	Total liabilities	45	35
4999	Total liabilities and net position	45	35

RURAL HOUSING INSURANCE FUND PROGRAM ACCOUNT

(INCLUDING TRANSFERS OF FUNDS)

For gross obligations for the principal amount of direct and guaranteed loans as authorized by title V of the Housing Act of 1949, to be available from funds in the rural housing insurance fund, as follows: $1,500,000,000 shall be for direct loans, $20,842,000 shall be for a Single Family Housing Relending demonstration program for Native American Tribes, and $30,000,000,000 shall be for unsubsidized guaranteed loans; $50,000,000 for section 504 housing repair loans; $200,000,000 for section 515 rental housing; $400,000,000 for section 538 guaranteed multi-family housing loans; $10,000,000 for credit sales of single family housing acquired property; $5,000,000 for section 523 self-help housing land development loans; and $5,000,000 for section 524 site development loans.

For the cost of direct and guaranteed loans, including the cost of modifying loans, as defined in section 502 of the Congressional Budget Act of 1974, as follows: section 502 loans, $55,650,000 shall be for direct loans; $6,857,000 shall be for a Single Family Housing Relending demonstration program for Native American Tribes; section 504 housing repair loans, $4,150,000; section 523 self-help housing land development loans, $267,000; section 524 site development loans, $208,000; and repair, rehabilitation, and new construction of section 515 rental housing, $38,220,000: Provided, That to support the loan program level for section 538 guaranteed loans made available under this heading the Secretary may charge or adjust any fees to cover the projected cost of such loan guarantees pursuant to the provisions of the Credit Reform Act of 1990 (2 U.S.C. 661 et seq.), and the interest on such loans may not be subsidized: Provided further, That applicants in communities that have a current rural area waiver under section 541 of the Housing Act of 1949 (42 U.S.C. 1490q) shall be treated as living in a rural area for purposes of section 502 guaranteed loans provided under this heading.

In addition, for the cost of direct loans and grants, including the cost of modifying loans, as defined in section 502 of the Congressional Budget Act of 1974, $75,000,000, to remain available until expended, for a demonstration program for the preservation and revitalization of sections 514, 515, and 516 multi-family rental housing properties, including the restructuring of existing USDA multi-family housing loans, as the Secretary deems appropriate, expressly for the purposes of ensuring the project has sufficient resources to preserve the project for the purpose of providing safe and affordable housing for low-income residents and farm laborers including reducing or eliminating interest; deferring loan payments, subordinating, reducing or re-amortizing loan debt; and other financial assistance including advances, payments, and incentives (including the ability of owners to obtain reasonable returns on investment) required by the Secretary: Provided further, That the Secretary shall as part of the preservation and revitalization agreement obtain a restrictive use agreement consistent with the terms of the restructuring: Provided further, That any balances, including obligated balances, available for all demonstration programs for the preservation and revitalization of sections 514, 515, and 516 multi-family rental housing properties in the "Multi-Family Housing Revitalization Program Account" shall be transferred to and merged with this account, and shall be available for the preservation and revitalization of sections 514, 515, and 516 multi-family rental housing properties, including the restructuring of existing USDA multi-family housing loans: Provided further, That following the transfer of balances described in the preceding proviso, any adjustments to obligations for demonstration programs for the preservation and revitalization of sections 514, 515, and 516 multi-family rental housing properties incurred in the "Multi-Family Housing Revitalization Program Account" shall be made in this account.

In addition, for the cost of direct loans, grants, and contracts, as authorized by sections 514 and 516 of the Housing Act of 1949 (42 U.S.C. 1484, 1486), $28,210,000, to remain available until expended, for direct farm labor housing loans and domestic farm labor housing grants and contracts: Provided, That any balances available for the Farm Labor Program Account shall be transferred to and merged with this account.

Rural Housing Service—Continued
Federal Funds—Continued

RURAL HOUSING INSURANCE FUND PROGRAM ACCOUNT—Continued

In addition, for administrative expenses necessary to carry out the direct and guaranteed loan programs, $412,254,000 shall be paid to the appropriation for "Rural Development, Salaries and Expenses".

Note.—A full-year 2022 appropriation for this account was not enacted at the time the Budget was prepared; therefore, the Budget assumes this account is operating under the Continuing Appropriations Act, 2022 (Division A of Public Law 117–43, as amended). The amounts included for 2022 reflect the annualized level provided by the continuing resolution.

Program and Financing (in millions of dollars)

Identification code 012–2081–0–1–371		2021 actual	2022 est.	2023 est.
	Obligations by program activity:			
0010	MPR Grants			11
0011	Farm labor housing grants	2	6	18
0091	Direct program activities, subtotal	2	6	29
	Credit program obligations:			
0701	Direct loan subsidy	64	24	192
0701	Direct loan subsidy		5	3
0705	Reestimates of direct loan subsidy	30	20	
0706	Interest on reestimates of direct loan subsidy	38	12	
0707	Reestimates of loan guarantee subsidy	29	1	
0708	Interest on reestimates of loan guarantee subsidy	3		
0709	Administrative expenses	413	412	412
0791	Direct program activities, subtotal	577	474	607
0900	Total new obligations, unexpired accounts	579	480	636
	Budgetary resources:			
	Unobligated balance:			
1000	Unobligated balance brought forward, Oct 1	24	77	122
1001	Discretionary unobligated balance brought fwd, Oct 1	24	40	
1011	Unobligated balance transfer from other acct [012–2002]			19
1021	Recoveries of prior year unpaid obligations	2		
1070	Unobligated balance (total)	26	77	141
	Budget authority:			
	Appropriations, discretionary:			
1100	Appropriation	492	492	621
1120	Appropriations transferred to other acct [012–4609]	–1		
1160	Appropriation, discretionary (total)	491	492	621
	Appropriations, mandatory:			
1200	Appropriation	139	33	
1900	Budget authority (total)	630	525	621
1930	Total budgetary resources available	656	602	762
	Memorandum (non-add) entries:			
1941	Unexpired unobligated balance, end of year	77	122	126
	Change in obligated balance:			
	Unpaid obligations:			
3000	Unpaid obligations, brought forward, Oct 1	116	100	74
3010	New obligations, unexpired accounts	579	480	636
3020	Outlays (gross)	–589	–506	–504
3040	Recoveries of prior year unpaid obligations, unexpired	–2		
3041	Recoveries of prior year unpaid obligations, expired	–4		
3050	Unpaid obligations, end of year	100	74	206
	Memorandum (non-add) entries:			
3100	Obligated balance, start of year	116	100	74
3200	Obligated balance, end of year	100	74	206
	Budget authority and outlays, net:			
	Discretionary:			
4000	Budget authority, gross	491	492	621
	Outlays, gross:			
4010	Outlays from new discretionary authority	451	427	477
4011	Outlays from discretionary balances	37	45	25
4020	Outlays, gross (total)	488	472	502
	Mandatory:			
4090	Budget authority, gross	139	33	
	Outlays, gross:			
4100	Outlays from new mandatory authority	101	33	
4101	Outlays from mandatory balances		1	2
4110	Outlays, gross (total)	101	34	2
4180	Budget authority, net (total)	630	525	621
4190	Outlays, net (total)	589	506	504

Summary of Loan Levels, Subsidy Budget Authority and Outlays by Program (in millions of dollars)

Identification code 012–2081–0–1–371		2021 actual	2022 est.	2023 est.
	Direct loan levels supportable by subsidy budget authority:			
115001	Section 502 Single Family Housing	1,001	1,254	1,585
115004	Section 515 Multifamily Housing	38	40	200
115007	Section 504 Housing Repair	15	16	50
115011	Section 514 Farm Labor Housing	3	16	50
115012	Section 524 Site Development		1	5
115013	Section 523 Self-Help Housing		1	5
115014	Single Family Housing Credit Sales		1	10
115017	Multifamily Housing Revitalization Seconds			74
115020	Multifamily Housing Revitalization Zero			93
115021	Native American Single Family Relending Pilot			21
115999	Total direct loan levels	1,057	1,329	2,093
	Direct loan subsidy (in percent):			
132001	Section 502 Single Family Housing	5.54	1.86	3.71
132004	Section 515 Multifamily Housing	16.72	8.94	19.11
132007	Section 504 Housing Repair	7.91	1.73	8.30
132011	Section 514 Farm Labor Housing	18.19	10.11	20.42
132012	Section 524 Site Development		4.11	4.16
132013	Section 523 Self-Help Housing		1.10	5.33
132014	Single Family Housing Credit Sales		–2.78	–3.56
132017	Multifamily Housing Revitalization Seconds			48.89
132020	Multifamily Housing Revitalization Zero			43.56
132021	Native American Single Family Relending Pilot			32.90
132999	Weighted average subsidy rate	6.01	2.17	9.32
	Direct loan subsidy budget authority:			
133001	Section 502 Single Family Housing	55	23	59
133004	Section 515 Multifamily Housing	6	4	38
133007	Section 504 Housing Repair	1		4
133011	Section 514 Farm Labor Housing	1	2	10
133017	Multifamily Housing Revitalization Seconds			36
133020	Multifamily Housing Revitalization Zero			41
133021	Native American Single Family Relending Pilot			7
133999	Total subsidy budget authority	63	29	195
	Direct loan subsidy outlays:			
134001	Section 502 Single Family Housing	58	30	51
134004	Section 515 Multifamily Housing	11	17	8
134007	Section 504 Housing Repair	1	1	4
134011	Section 514 Farm Labor Housing	2	5	6
134017	Multifamily Housing Revitalization Seconds			2
134020	Multifamily Housing Revitalization Zero			4
134021	Native American Single Family Relending Pilot			5
134999	Total subsidy outlays	72	53	80
	Direct loan reestimates:			
135001	Section 502 Single Family Housing	–125	–177	
135004	Section 515 Multifamily Housing	–7	–9	
135007	Section 504 Housing Repair	2	–2	
135011	Section 514 Farm Labor Housing	1	–3	
135012	Section 524 Site Development		–1	
135014	Single Family Housing Credit Sales		–1	
135015	Multifamily Housing Credit Sales	1		
135999	Total direct loan reestimates	–128	–193	
	Guaranteed loan levels supportable by subsidy budget authority:			
215003	Guaranteed 538 Multifamily Housing	230	230	400
215011	Guaranteed 502 Single Family Housing	22,726	24,000	30,000
215999	Total loan guarantee levels	22,956	24,230	30,400
	Guaranteed loan subsidy (in percent):			
232003	Guaranteed 538 Multifamily Housing	–4.95	–3.08	–2.97
232011	Guaranteed 502 Single Family Housing	–.70	–1.41	–.76
232999	Weighted average subsidy rate	–.74	–1.43	–.79
	Guaranteed loan subsidy budget authority:			
233003	Guaranteed 538 Multifamily Housing	–11	–7	–12
233011	Guaranteed 502 Single Family Housing	–159	–338	–228
233999	Total subsidy budget authority	–170	–345	–240
	Guaranteed loan subsidy outlays:			
234003	Guaranteed 538 Multifamily Housing	–8	–9	–9
234011	Guaranteed 502 Single Family Housing	–162	–162	–162
234999	Total subsidy outlays	–170	–171	–171
	Guaranteed loan reestimates:			
235001	Guaranteed 502 Single Family Housing, Purchase	–213	–165	
235002	Guaranteed 502, Refinance	–2	–3	
235003	Guaranteed 538 Multifamily Housing	–12	–10	
235011	Guaranteed 502 Single Family Housing	–409	–1,703	
235999	Total guaranteed loan reestimates	–636	–1,881	
	Administrative expense data:			
3510	Budget authority	412	412	412

3590	Outlays from new authority	412	412	412

Rural Housing Insurance Fund.—This fund was established in 1965 (Public Law 89–117) pursuant to section 517 of title V of the Housing Act of 1949, as amended. Loan programs are limited to rural areas that include towns, villages, and other places which are not part of an urban area. These areas have a population not in excess of 2,500 inhabitants, or in excess of 2,500, but not in excess of 10,000 if rural in character, or a population in excess of 10,000 but not more than 20,000. Areas are within a standard metropolitan statistical area and have a serious lack of mortgage credit for low- and moderate-income borrowers.

For 2023, the Section 502 single family housing guarantees are requested at a $30 billion loan level. The subsidy rate for 2023 continues to be negative with the combination annual and up-front fee structure.

The Budget requests a loan level of $10 million for credit sales of acquired property for single family housing loans. For Section 502 single family housing direct loans the 2023 Budget requests $1.5 billion; for Section 515 multi-family housing direct loans, $200 million; for Section 504 very low-income housing repair loans, $50 million for Section 524 site development loans, $5 million, for Section 523 self-help housing land development loans, $5 million. The Budget also requests $75 million for the multi-family housing preservation and revitalization pilot program which is included in this account to facilitate preservation loan modifications on post-credit reform multi-family housing loans. This program was moved to this account from the Multi-family Housing Revitalization Program account for that reason. The Budget request includes $20.8 million for a Single Family Housing Direct Native American Tribal Relending program. The budget also includes a requirement that funding for construction, preservation or rehabilitation should be targeted to projects that improve energy or water efficiency, implement green features, and addresses climate resilience.

The 2023 Budget also requests a $400 million loan level for the multi-family housing guaranteed loan program and continues to include appropriations language that will allow the program to operate without interest subsidy and with a fee.

The 2023 Budget requests $50 million for farm labor housing loans and $18 million for grants. For administrative costs, the 2023 Budget requests $412.3 million.

As required by the Federal Credit Reform Act of 1990, this account records, for this program, the subsidy costs associated with the direct loans obligated and loan guarantees committed in 1992 and beyond (including credit sales of acquired property), as well as administrative expenses of this program. The subsidy amounts are estimated on a present value basis; the administrative expenses are estimated on a cash basis. Consistent with facilitating funding flexibilities and to be able to modify post credit reform section 515 multi-family housing loans in the future, all the balances associated with the multi-family housing demonstration programs in this account will be transferred and merged with the Rural Housing Insurance Fund Program Account.

Object Classification (in millions of dollars)

Identification code 012–2081–0–1–371		2021 actual	2022 est.	2023 est.
	Direct obligations:			
25.3	Other goods and services from Federal sources	412	412	412
41.0	Grants, subsidies, and contributions	167	68	224
99.9	Total new obligations, unexpired accounts	579	480	636

RURAL HOUSING INSURANCE FUND DIRECT LOAN FINANCING ACCOUNT

Program and Financing (in millions of dollars)

Identification code 012–4215–0–3–371		2021 actual	2022 est.	2023 est.
	Obligations by program activity:			
0005	Capitalized Costs	176	175	175
	Credit program obligations:			
0710	Direct loan obligations	1,058	1,074	2,008
0710	Direct loan obligations		254	85
0713	Payment of interest to Treasury	638	670	675
0742	Downward reestimates paid to receipt accounts	177	177	
0743	Interest on downward reestimates	20	48	
0791	Direct program activities, subtotal	1,893	2,223	2,768
0900	Total new obligations, unexpired accounts	2,069	2,398	2,943
	Budgetary resources:			
	Unobligated balance:			
1000	Unobligated balance brought forward, Oct 1	1,465	1,433	26
1021	Recoveries of prior year unpaid obligations	102		
1023	Unobligated balances applied to repay debt	–1,395	–1,433	
1024	Unobligated balance of borrowing authority withdrawn	–92		
1070	Unobligated balance (total)	80		26
	Financing authority:			
	Borrowing authority, mandatory:			
1400	Borrowing authority	1,412	1,998	2,400
	Spending authority from offsetting collections, mandatory:			
1800	Collected	2,025	1,768	1,758
1801	Change in uncollected payments, Federal sources	–15		
1825	Spending authority from offsetting collections applied to repay debt		–1,342	
1850	Spending auth from offsetting collections, mand (total)	2,010	426	1,758
1900	Budget authority (total)	3,422	2,424	4,158
1930	Total budgetary resources available	3,502	2,424	4,184
	Memorandum (non-add) entries:			
1941	Unexpired unobligated balance, end of year	1,433	26	1,241
	Change in obligated balance:			
	Unpaid obligations:			
3000	Unpaid obligations, brought forward, Oct 1	632	679	937
3010	New obligations, unexpired accounts	2,069	2,398	2,943
3020	Outlays (gross)	–1,920	–2,140	–2,467
3040	Recoveries of prior year unpaid obligations, unexpired	–102		
3050	Unpaid obligations, end of year	679	937	1,413
	Uncollected payments:			
3060	Uncollected pymts, Fed sources, brought forward, Oct 1	–84	–69	–69
3070	Change in uncollected pymts, Fed sources, unexpired	15		
3090	Uncollected pymts, Fed sources, end of year	–69	–69	–69
	Memorandum (non-add) entries:			
3100	Obligated balance, start of year	548	610	868
3200	Obligated balance, end of year	610	868	1,344
	Financing authority and disbursements, net:			
	Mandatory:			
4090	Budget authority, gross	3,422	2,424	4,158
	Financing disbursements:			
4110	Outlays, gross (total)	1,920	2,140	2,467
	Offsets against gross financing authority and disbursements:			
	Offsetting collections (collected) from:			
4120	Federal sources: payment from program account subsidy	–72	–53	–80
4120	Federal sources: payment from program account upward reestimate	–70	–33	
4122	Interest on uninvested funds	–78	–74	–74
4123	Non-Federal sources: Repayments of principal	–1,270	–1,015	–1,011
4123	Interest received on loans	–502	–510	–508
4123	Proceeds on sale of acquired property	–27	–83	–85
4123	Fees	–5		
4123	Other non-federal collections	–1		
4130	Offsets against gross budget authority and outlays (total)	–2,025	–1,768	–1,758
	Additional offsets against financing authority only (total):			
4140	Change in uncollected pymts, Fed sources, unexpired	15		
4160	Budget authority, net (mandatory)	1,412	656	2,400
4170	Outlays, net (mandatory)	–105	372	709
4180	Budget authority, net (total)	1,412	656	2,400
4190	Outlays, net (total)	–105	372	709

Status of Direct Loans (in millions of dollars)

Identification code 012–4215–0–3–371		2021 actual	2022 est.	2023 est.
	Position with respect to appropriations act limitation on obligations:			
1111	Direct loan obligations from current-year authority	1,791	3,275	1,991
1121	Limitation available from carry-forward	40	2,230	997
1142	Unobligated direct loan limitation (-)	–98	–2,201	
1143	Unobligated limitation carried forward (P.L. 117–2) (-)	–675	–1,976	–895

RURAL HOUSING INSURANCE FUND DIRECT LOAN FINANCING ACCOUNT—Continued

Status of Direct Loans—Continued

Identification code 012–4215–0–3–371		2021 actual	2022 est.	2023 est.
1150	Total direct loan obligations	1,058	1,328	2,093
	Cumulative balance of direct loans outstanding:			
1210	Outstanding, start of year	16,891	16,565	16,529
1231	Disbursements: Direct loan disbursements	1,220	1,071	1,152
	Repayments:			
1251	Repayments and prepayments	–1,268	–1,015	–1,055
1252	Proceeds from loan asset sales to the public or discounted	–63	–70	–70
	Adjustments:			
1261	Capitalized interest	....	8	8
1262	Discount on loan asset sales to the public or discounted	....	–4	–4
1263	Write-offs for default: Direct loans	....	–26	–26
1264	Other adjustments, net (+ or -)	–215	....	....
1290	Outstanding, end of year	16,565	16,529	16,534

This account reflects the financing for direct rural housing loans for section the 502 very low- and low-to-moderate-income home ownership loan program; section 504 very low-income housing repair loan program; section 514 domestic farm labor housing loan program; section 515 rural rental housing loan program; sections 523 self-help housing loans, and 524 site development loans; and single family and multi-family housing credit sales of acquired property. Beginning in FY 2023 the financing for the Multi-family Housing Preservation demonstration loan programs (zero percent, soft-seconds, bullet loans and 515 loan modifications) will be reflected in this account as well.

Balance Sheet (in millions of dollars)

Identification code 012–4215–0–3–371		2020 actual	2021 actual
	ASSETS:		
	Federal assets:		
1101	Fund balances with Treasury	1,465	1,433
	Investments in U.S. securities:		
1106	Receivables, net	62	30
1206	Non-Federal assets: Receivables, net	....	....
	Net value of assets related to post-1991 direct loans receivable:		
1401	Direct loans receivable, gross	16,891	16,565
1402	Interest receivable	363	324
1404	Foreclosed property	76	63
1405	Allowance for subsidy cost (-)	–1,755	–1,225
1499	Net present value of assets related to direct loans	15,575	15,727
1999	Total assets	17,102	17,190
	LIABILITIES:		
	Federal liabilities:		
2103	Debt	17,052	16,915
2105	Other	8	216
	Non-Federal liabilities:		
2201	Accounts payable	34	55
2207	Other	8	4
2999	Total liabilities	17,102	17,190
	NET POSITION:		
3300	Cumulative results of operations	....	....
4999	Total liabilities and net position	17,102	17,190

RURAL HOUSING INSURANCE FUND GUARANTEED LOAN FINANCING ACCOUNT

Program and Financing (in millions of dollars)

Identification code 012–4216–0–3–371		2021 actual	2022 est.	2023 est.
	Obligations by program activity:			
0003	Interest assistance paid to lenders	8	8	8
	Credit program obligations:			
0711	Default claim payments on principal	197	500	500
0713	Payment of interest to Treasury	36	42	42
0740	Negative subsidy obligations	170	345	240
0742	Downward reestimates paid to receipt accounts	565	1,711	....
0743	Interest on downward reestimates	103	171	....
0791	Direct program activities, subtotal	1,071	2,769	782
0799	Total direct obligations	1,079	2,777	790
0900	Total new obligations, unexpired accounts	1,079	2,777	790
	Budgetary resources:			
	Unobligated balance:			
1000	Unobligated balance brought forward, Oct 1	1,918	821	253
1021	Recoveries of prior year unpaid obligations	9	....	....
1023	Unobligated balances applied to repay debt	–904	–30	–30
1024	Unobligated balance of borrowing authority withdrawn	–1	....	....
1033	Recoveries of prior year paid obligations	6	....	....
1070	Unobligated balance (total)	1,028	791	223
	Financing authority:			
	Borrowing authority, mandatory:			
1400	Borrowing authority	159	1,500	500
	Spending authority from offsetting collections, mandatory:			
1800	Collected	713	739	793
1900	Budget authority (total)	872	2,239	1,293
1930	Total budgetary resources available	1,900	3,030	1,516
	Memorandum (non-add) entries:			
1941	Unexpired unobligated balance, end of year	821	253	726
	Change in obligated balance:			
	Unpaid obligations:			
3000	Unpaid obligations, brought forward, Oct 1	29	25	1,904
3010	New obligations, unexpired accounts	1,079	2,777	790
3020	Outlays (gross)	–1,074	–898	–975
3040	Recoveries of prior year unpaid obligations, unexpired	–9	....	....
3050	Unpaid obligations, end of year	25	1,904	1,719
	Memorandum (non-add) entries:			
3100	Obligated balance, start of year	29	25	1,904
3200	Obligated balance, end of year	25	1,904	1,719
	Financing authority and disbursements, net:			
	Mandatory:			
4090	Budget authority, gross	872	2,239	1,293
	Financing disbursements:			
4110	Outlays, gross (total)	1,074	898	975
	Offsets against gross financing authority and disbursements:			
	Offsetting collections (collected) from:			
4120	Federal sources	–32	....	....
4120	Federal sources Upward Reestimate	....	–1	....
4122	Interest on uninvested funds	–30	–37	–37
4123	Non-Federal sources: guarantee fees	–657	–695	–750
4123	Repayments of Principal	....	–5	–5
4123	Interest Received on Loans	....	–1	–1
4130	Offsets against gross budget authority and outlays (total)	–719	–739	–793
	Additional offsets against financing authority only (total):			
4143	Recoveries of prior year paid obligations, unexpired accounts	6	....	....
4160	Budget authority, net (mandatory)	159	1,500	500
4170	Outlays, net (mandatory)	355	159	182
4180	Budget authority, net (total)	159	1,500	500
4190	Outlays, net (total)	355	159	182

Status of Guaranteed Loans (in millions of dollars)

Identification code 012–4216–0–3–371		2021 actual	2022 est.	2023 est.
	Position with respect to appropriations act limitation on commitments:			
2111	Guaranteed loan commitments from current-year authority	30,230	24,230	30,400
2142	Uncommitted loan guarantee limitation	–7,274	....	....
2150	Total guaranteed loan commitments	22,956	24,230	30,400
2199	Guaranteed amount of guaranteed loan commitments	20,660	21,600	27,360
	Cumulative balance of guaranteed loans outstanding:			
2210	Outstanding, start of year	127,890	133,366	142,178
2231	Disbursements of new guaranteed loans	18,325	29,066	37,899
2251	Repayments and prepayments	–12,176	–19,678	–20,978
	Adjustments:			
2263	Terminations for default that result in claim payments	–673	–641	–683
2264	Other adjustments, net	....	....	....
2265	Capitalized interest	....	65	69
2290	Outstanding, end of year	133,366	142,178	158,485
	Memorandum:			
2299	Guaranteed amount of guaranteed loans outstanding, end of year	120,288	127,960	142,636

DEPARTMENT OF AGRICULTURE

Rural Housing Service—Continued
Federal Funds—Continued

	Addendum: Cumulative balance of defaulted guaranteed loans that result in loans receivable:			
2310	Outstanding, start of year	126	174	201
2331	Disbursements for guaranteed loan claims	41	31	31
2351	Repayments of loans receivable	−8	−2	−2
2361	Write-offs of loans receivable		−2	−2
2364	Other adjustments, net	15		
2390	Outstanding, end of year	174	201	228

This account finances the guaranteed section 502 low-to-moderate-income home ownership loan program as well as the re-financings of those loans and the section 538 guaranteed multi-family housing loan program. The guaranteed programs enable the Rural Housing Service to utilize private sector resources for the making and servicing of loans while the Agency provides a financial guarantee to encourage private sector activity.

Balance Sheet (in millions of dollars)

Identification code 012–4216–0–3–371		2020 actual	2021 actual
	ASSETS: Federal assets:		
1101	Fund balances with Treasury	1,918	820
	Investments in U.S. securities:		
1106	Receivables, net	796	15
	Net value of assets related to post-1991 acquired defaulted guaranteed loans receivable:		
1501	Defaulted guaranteed loans receivable, gross	126	174
1502	Interest receivable		
1505	Allowance for subsidy cost (−)	−93	−137
1505	Currently not collectible (−)		
1599	Net present value of assets related to defaulted guaranteed loans	33	37
1999	Total assets	2,747	872
	LIABILITIES: Federal liabilities:		
2103	Debt	1,786	1,042
2104	Resources payable to Treasury		
2105	Other	279	972
	Non-Federal liabilities:		
2201	Accounts payable	4	2
2204	Liabilities for loan guarantees	678	−1,144
2999	Total liabilities	2,747	872
	NET POSITION:		
3300	Cumulative results of operations		
4999	Total liabilities and net position	2,747	872

RURAL HOUSING INSURANCE FUND LIQUIDATING ACCOUNT

Program and Financing (in millions of dollars)

Identification code 012–4141–0–3–371		2021 actual	2022 est.	2023 est.
	Obligations by program activity:			
0107	Other costs incident to loans	30	23	20
0900	Total new obligations, unexpired accounts (object class 25.2)	30	23	20
	Budgetary resources: Unobligated balance:			
1000	Unobligated balance brought forward, Oct 1	91	66	
1021	Recoveries of prior year unpaid obligations	24		
1022	Capital transfer of unobligated balances to general fund	−91	−66	
1070	Unobligated balance (total)	24		
	Budget authority: Spending authority from offsetting collections, mandatory:			
1800	Collected	372	353	334
1820	Capital transfer of spending authority from offsetting collections to general fund	−300	−330	−314
1850	Spending auth from offsetting collections, mand (total)	72	23	20
1930	Total budgetary resources available	96	23	20
	Memorandum (non-add) entries:			
1941	Unexpired unobligated balance, end of year	66		
	Change in obligated balance: Unpaid obligations:			
3000	Unpaid obligations, brought forward, Oct 1	37	29	18
3010	New obligations, unexpired accounts	30	23	20
3020	Outlays (gross)	−14	−34	−30
3040	Recoveries of prior year unpaid obligations, unexpired	−24		
3050	Unpaid obligations, end of year	29	18	8
	Memorandum (non-add) entries:			
3100	Obligated balance, start of year	37	29	18
3200	Obligated balance, end of year	29	18	8
	Budget authority and outlays, net: Mandatory:			
4090	Budget authority, gross	72	23	20
	Outlays, gross:			
4100	Outlays from new mandatory authority	14	20	17
4101	Outlays from mandatory balances		14	13
4110	Outlays, gross (total)	14	34	30
	Offsets against gross budget authority and outlays: Offsetting collections (collected) from:			
4120	Federal sources	−12		
4123	Non-Federal sources	−360	−353	−334
4130	Offsets against gross budget authority and outlays (total)	−372	−353	−334
4160	Budget authority, net (mandatory)	−300	−330	−314
4170	Outlays, net (mandatory)	−358	−319	−304
4180	Budget authority, net (total)	−300	−330	−314
4190	Outlays, net (total)	−358	−319	−304

Status of Direct Loans (in millions of dollars)

Identification code 012–4141–0–3–371		2021 actual	2022 est.	2023 est.
	Cumulative balance of direct loans outstanding:			
1210	Outstanding, start of year	5,610	5,332	5,101
1251	Repayments: Repayments and prepayments	−239	−219	−209
1261	Adjustments: Capitalized interest	1	1	
1263	Write-offs for default: Direct loans	−10	−13	−13
1264	Other adjustments, net (+ or −)	−30		
1290	Outstanding, end of year	5,332	5,101	4,879

Status of Guaranteed Loans (in millions of dollars)

Identification code 012–4141–0–3–371		2021 actual	2022 est.	2023 est.
	Cumulative balance of guaranteed loans outstanding:			
2210	Outstanding, start of year	1	1	1
2251	Repayments and prepayments			
2290	Outstanding, end of year	1	1	1
	Memorandum:			
2299	Guaranteed amount of guaranteed loans outstanding, end of year	1	1	1

Balance Sheet (in millions of dollars)

Identification code 012–4141–0–3–371		2020 actual	2021 actual
	ASSETS:		
1101	Federal assets: Fund balances with Treasury	129	95
1601	Direct loans, gross	5,610	5,332
1602	Interest receivable	763	695
1603	Allowance for estimated uncollectible loans and interest (−)	−613	−628
1604	Direct loans and interest receivable, net	5,760	5,399
1606	Foreclosed property	6	8
1699	Value of assets related to direct loans	5,766	5,407
	Other Federal assets:		
1801	Cash and other monetary assets	46	51
1901	Other assets		
1999	Total assets	5,941	5,553
	LIABILITIES:		
2104	Federal liabilities: Resources payable to Treasury	5,869	5,480
	Non-Federal liabilities:		
2201	Accounts payable	9	11
2206	Total Other Liabilities Not Cross-walked (299X)		
2207	Other	63	62
2999	Total liabilities	5,941	5,553
	NET POSITION:		
3300	Cumulative results of operations		

RURAL HOUSING INSURANCE FUND LIQUIDATING ACCOUNT—Continued

Balance Sheet—Continued

Identification code 012–4141–0–3–371	2020 actual	2021 actual
4999 Total liabilities and net position	5,941	5,553

RURAL BUSINESS-COOPERATIVE SERVICE

Federal Funds

ENERGY ASSISTANCE PAYMENTS

Program and Financing (in millions of dollars)

Identification code 012–2073–0–1–452	2021 actual	2022 est.	2023 est.
Obligations by program activity:			
0010 Bioenergy Program for Advanced Biofuels Payments	7	7	7
0012 Higher Blends Infrastructure Incentive Program (Mandatory)	46	52	42
0900 Total new obligations, unexpired accounts (object class 41.0)	53	59	49
Budgetary resources:			
Unobligated balance:			
1000 Unobligated balance brought forward, Oct 1	85	39	87
Budget authority:			
Appropriations, mandatory:			
1222 Exercised borrowing authority transferred from other accounts [012–4336]	7	107	7
1930 Total budgetary resources available	92	146	94
Memorandum (non-add) entries:			
1941 Unexpired unobligated balance, end of year	39	87	45
Change in obligated balance:			
Unpaid obligations:			
3000 Unpaid obligations, brought forward, Oct 1	23	62	73
3010 New obligations, unexpired accounts	53	59	49
3020 Outlays (gross)	–14	–48	–101
3050 Unpaid obligations, end of year	62	73	21
Memorandum (non-add) entries:			
3100 Obligated balance, start of year	23	62	73
3200 Obligated balance, end of year	62	73	21
Budget authority and outlays, net:			
Mandatory:			
4090 Budget authority, gross	7	107	7
Outlays, gross:			
4100 Outlays from new mandatory authority	5	4	3
4101 Outlays from mandatory balances	9	44	98
4110 Outlays, gross (total)	14	48	101
4180 Budget authority, net (total)	7	107	7
4190 Outlays, net (total)	14	48	101

The purpose of the Bioenergy Program for Advanced Biofuels is to provide payments to eligible agricultural producers to support and ensure an expanding production of advanced biofuels. This program is authorized pursuant to section 9005 of the Farm Security and Rural Investment Act of 2002, as amended by the Farm, Conservation, and Energy Act of 2008, the Agricultural Act of 2014, and the Agriculture Improvement Act of 2018.

RURAL COOPERATIVE DEVELOPMENT GRANTS

For rural cooperative development grants authorized under section 310B(e) of the Consolidated Farm and Rural Development Act (7 U.S.C. 1932), $30,700,000, of which $2,800,000 shall be for cooperative agreements for the appropriate technology transfer for rural areas program: Provided, That not to exceed $4,100,000 shall be for grants for cooperative development centers, individual cooperatives, or groups of cooperatives that serve socially disadvantaged groups and a majority of the boards of directors or governing boards of which are comprised of individuals who are members of socially disadvantaged groups; and of which $18,000,000, to remain available until expended, shall be for value-added agricultural product market development grants, as authorized by section 210A of the Agricultural Marketing Act of 1946, of which $3,000,000, to remain available until expended, shall be for Agriculture Innovation Centers authorized pursuant to section 6402 of Public Law 107–171.

Note.—A full-year 2022 appropriation for this account was not enacted at the time the Budget was prepared; therefore, the Budget assumes this account is operating under the Continuing Appropriations Act, 2022 (Division A of Public Law 117–43, as amended). The amounts included for 2022 reflect the annualized level provided by the continuing resolution.

Program and Financing (in millions of dollars)

Identification code 012–1900–0–1–452	2021 actual	2022 est.	2023 est.
Obligations by program activity:			
0001 Rural Cooperative Development Grants	8	9	10
0011 Value Added Agricultural Producer Grants (discretionary)	14	21	20
0012 Appropriate Technology Transfer for Rural Areas	3	3	3
0013 Value Added Agricultural Product Marketing (mandatory)	2	2	1
0014 LAMP Value Added (mandatory)	24	18	18
0015 LAMP Administrative Expenses (mandatory)	2	2	2
0016 Additional Coronavirus Response and Relief LAMP (Mand)	32	2	....
0017 Additional Coronavirus Response and Relief LAMP Admin (Mand)	3	....	....
0900 Total new obligations, unexpired accounts	88	57	54
Budgetary resources:			
Unobligated balance:			
1000 Unobligated balance brought forward, Oct 1	19	17	7
1001 Discretionary unobligated balance brought fwd, Oct 1	5	9	....
1021 Recoveries of prior year unpaid obligations	3	2	2
1070 Unobligated balance (total)	22	19	9
Budget authority:			
Appropriations, discretionary:			
1100 Appropriation	27	27	31
Appropriations, mandatory:			
1200 Appropriation	38	....	....
1222 Exercised borrowing authority transferred from other accounts [012–4336]	19	19	19
1230 Appropriations and/or unobligated balance of appropriations permanently reduced	–1	–1	–1
1260 Appropriations, mandatory (total)	56	18	18
1900 Budget authority (total)	83	45	49
1930 Total budgetary resources available	105	64	58
Memorandum (non-add) entries:			
1941 Unexpired unobligated balance, end of year	17	7	4
Change in obligated balance:			
Unpaid obligations:			
3000 Unpaid obligations, brought forward, Oct 1	93	139	114
3010 New obligations, unexpired accounts	88	57	54
3020 Outlays (gross)	–39	–80	–78
3040 Recoveries of prior year unpaid obligations, unexpired	–3	–2	–2
3050 Unpaid obligations, end of year	139	114	88
Memorandum (non-add) entries:			
3100 Obligated balance, start of year	93	139	114
3200 Obligated balance, end of year	139	114	88
Budget authority and outlays, net:			
Discretionary:			
4000 Budget authority, gross	27	27	31
Outlays, gross:			
4010 Outlays from new discretionary authority	....	4	5
4011 Outlays from discretionary balances	25	32	34
4020 Outlays, gross (total)	25	36	39
Mandatory:			
4090 Budget authority, gross	56	18	18
Outlays, gross:			
4100 Outlays from new mandatory authority	2	1	1
4101 Outlays from mandatory balances	12	43	38
4110 Outlays, gross (total)	14	44	39
4180 Budget authority, net (total)	83	45	49
4190 Outlays, net (total)	39	80	78

Grants for rural cooperative development were authorized under section 310B(e) of the Consolidated Farm and Rural Development Act by Public Law 104–127, April 4, 1996. These grants are made available to nonprofit corporations and institutions of higher education to fund the establishment and operation of centers for rural cooperative development. The Appropriate Technology Transfer to Rural Areas (ATTRA) program was first authorized by the Food Security Act of 1985. The program provides information and

DEPARTMENT OF AGRICULTURE

technical assistance to agricultural producers to adopt sustainable agricultural practices that are environmentally friendly and lower production costs. These grants provide assistance to small minority producers through cooperatives and associations of cooperatives.

Additionally, USDA provides Value-Added Marketing Grants for producers of agricultural commodities. These grants can be used for planning activities and for working capital for marketing value-added agricultural products. The 2023 Budget requests $30.7 million for this program, including $15 million for Value-Added Marketing Grants, $3 million for the Agriculture Innovation Centers, $4.1 million for the Grants to Assist Minority Producers program, $5.8 million for Cooperative Development Grants, and $2.8 million for the Appropriate Technology Transfer to Rural Areas (ATTRA) program.

Object Classification (in millions of dollars)

Identification code 012–1900–0–1–452		2021 actual	2022 est.	2023 est.
	Direct obligations:			
25.3	Other goods and services from Federal sources	2	2	2
41.0	Grants, subsidies, and contributions	86	55	52
99.9	Total new obligations, unexpired accounts	88	57	54

HEALTHY FOODS FINANCING INITIATIVE

For the cost of loans and grants consistent with section 243 of subtitle D of title II of the Department of Agriculture Reorganization Act of 1994, as added by section 4206 of the Agricultural Act of 2014, for necessary expenses of the Secretary to support projects that provide access to healthy food in underserved areas, to create and preserve quality jobs, and to revitalize low-income communities, $5,000,000, to remain available until expended: Provided, That the cost of such loans, including the cost of modifying such loans, shall be as defined in section 502 of the Congressional Budget Act of 1974.

Note.—A full-year 2022 appropriation for this account was not enacted at the time the Budget was prepared; therefore, the Budget assumes this account is operating under the Continuing Appropriations Act, 2022 (Division A of Public Law 117–43, as amended). The amounts included for 2022 reflect the annualized level provided by the continuing resolution.

Program and Financing (in millions of dollars)

Identification code 012–0015–0–1–451		2021 actual	2022 est.	2023 est.
	Obligations by program activity:			
0011	Direct program activity	5	5	5
0900	Total new obligations, unexpired accounts (object class 41.0)	5	5	5
	Budgetary resources:			
	Unobligated balance:			
1000	Unobligated balance brought forward, Oct 1	3		
	Budget authority:			
	Appropriations, discretionary:			
1100	Appropriation	5	5	5
1930	Total budgetary resources available	8	5	5
	Memorandum (non-add) entries:			
1940	Unobligated balance expiring	–3		
	Change in obligated balance:			
	Unpaid obligations:			
3000	Unpaid obligations, brought forward, Oct 1	5	8	3
3010	New obligations, unexpired accounts	5	5	5
3020	Outlays (gross)	–2	–10	–8
3050	Unpaid obligations, end of year	8	3	
	Memorandum (non-add) entries:			
3100	Obligated balance, start of year	5	8	3
3200	Obligated balance, end of year	8	3	
	Budget authority and outlays, net:			
	Discretionary:			
4000	Budget authority, gross	5	5	5
	Outlays, gross:			
4010	Outlays from new discretionary authority		5	5
4011	Outlays from discretionary balances	2	5	3
4020	Outlays, gross (total)	2	10	8
4180	Budget authority, net (total)	5	5	5

4190	Outlays, net (total)	2	10	8

RURAL ECONOMIC DEVELOPMENT GRANTS

Program and Financing (in millions of dollars)

Identification code 012–3105–0–1–452		2021 actual	2022 est.	2023 est.
	Obligations by program activity:			
0001	Rural economic development grants	7	3	15
0002	Subsidy	5	2	7
0003	ReConnect funding	279	154	162
0004	ReConnect Admin	13	10	2
0005	ReConnect Technical Assistance		20	2
0900	Total new obligations, unexpired accounts	304	189	188
	Budgetary resources:			
	Unobligated balance:			
1000	Unobligated balance brought forward, Oct 1	358	242	156
1021	Recoveries of prior year unpaid obligations	122	80	37
1070	Unobligated balance (total)	480	322	193
	Budget authority:			
	Appropriations, mandatory:			
1222	Exercised borrowing authority transferred from other accounts [012–4336]		5	5
	Spending authority from offsetting collections, mandatory:			
1800	Collected	71	19	19
1801	Change in uncollected payments, Federal sources	–4		
1821	Spending authority from offsetting collections permanently reduced	–1	–1	–1
1850	Spending auth from offsetting collections, mand (total)	66	18	18
1900	Budget authority (total)	66	23	23
1930	Total budgetary resources available	546	345	216
	Memorandum (non-add) entries:			
1941	Unexpired unobligated balance, end of year	242	156	28
	Change in obligated balance:			
	Unpaid obligations:			
3000	Unpaid obligations, brought forward, Oct 1	433	589	265
3010	New obligations, unexpired accounts	304	189	188
3020	Outlays (gross)	–26	–433	–273
3040	Recoveries of prior year unpaid obligations, unexpired	–122	–80	–37
3050	Unpaid obligations, end of year	589	265	143
	Uncollected payments:			
3060	Uncollected pymts, Fed sources, brought forward, Oct 1	–4		
3070	Change in uncollected pymts, Fed sources, unexpired	4		
	Memorandum (non-add) entries:			
3100	Obligated balance, start of year	429	589	265
3200	Obligated balance, end of year	589	265	143
	Budget authority and outlays, net:			
	Mandatory:			
4090	Budget authority, gross	66	23	23
	Outlays, gross:			
4100	Outlays from new mandatory authority		12	14
4101	Outlays from mandatory balances	26	421	259
4110	Outlays, gross (total)	26	433	273
	Offsets against gross budget authority and outlays:			
	Offsetting collections (collected) from:			
4120	Cushion of Credit Payments	–51		
4123	Guaranteed Underwiter Fees	–20	–19	–19
4130	Offsets against gross budget authority and outlays (total)	–71	–19	–19
	Additional offsets against gross budget authority only:			
4140	Change in uncollected pymts, Fed sources, unexpired	4		
4160	Budget authority, net (mandatory)	–1	4	4
4170	Outlays, net (mandatory)	–45	414	254
4180	Budget authority, net (total)	–1	4	4
4190	Outlays, net (total)	–45	414	254

This grant program is authorized under section 313 of the Rural Electrification Act, as amended, and provides funds for the purpose of promoting rural economic development and job creation projects, including funding for project feasibility studies, start-up costs, incubator projects and other expenses for the purpose of fostering rural development. The 2023 Budget requests authority to provide $15 million in grants. This program also re-

138 | Rural Business–Cooperative Service—Continued
Federal Funds—Continued | THE BUDGET FOR FISCAL YEAR 2023

RURAL ECONOMIC DEVELOPMENT GRANTS—Continued

ceives mandatory funding through the Agriculture Improvement Act of 2018, which provided $5 million in 2022 and provides $5 million in 2023.

Object Classification (in millions of dollars)

Identification code 012–3105–0–1–452	2021 actual	2022 est.	2023 est.
Direct obligations:			
25.3 Other goods and services from Federal sources		10	2
41.0 Grants, subsidies, and contributions	304	179	186
99.9 Total new obligations, unexpired accounts	304	189	188

RURAL MICROENTREPRENEUR ASSISTANCE PROGRAM

For the principal amount of direct loans authorized by section 379E of the Consolidated Farm and Rural Development Act (7 U.S.C. 2008s), $25,000,000.

For the cost of loans and grants, $6,000,000 under the same terms and conditions as authorized by section 379E of the Consolidated Farm and Rural Development Act (7 U.S.C. 2008s).

Note.—A full-year 2022 appropriation for this account was not enacted at the time the Budget was prepared; therefore, the Budget assumes this account is operating under the Continuing Appropriations Act, 2022 (Division A of Public Law 117–43, as amended). The amounts included for 2022 reflect the annualized level provided by the continuing resolution.

Program and Financing (in millions of dollars)

Identification code 012–1955–0–1–452	2021 actual	2022 est.	2023 est.
Obligations by program activity:			
0011 Grants	4	4	5
Credit program obligations:			
0701 Direct loan subsidy			1
0900 Total new obligations, unexpired accounts (object class 41.0)	4	4	6
Budgetary resources:			
Unobligated balance:			
1000 Unobligated balance brought forward, Oct 1	1	1	3
Budget authority:			
Appropriations, discretionary:			
1100 Appropriation	6	6	6
1120 Appropriations transferred to other acct [012–4609]	–2		
1160 Appropriation, discretionary (total)	4	6	6
1900 Budget authority (total)	4	6	6
1930 Total budgetary resources available	5	7	9
Memorandum (non-add) entries:			
1941 Unexpired unobligated balance, end of year	1	3	3
Change in obligated balance:			
Unpaid obligations:			
3000 Unpaid obligations, brought forward, Oct 1	7	8	8
3010 New obligations, unexpired accounts	4	4	6
3020 Outlays (gross)	–3	–4	–5
3050 Unpaid obligations, end of year	8	8	9
Memorandum (non-add) entries:			
3100 Obligated balance, start of year	7	8	8
3200 Obligated balance, end of year	8	8	9
Budget authority and outlays, net:			
Discretionary:			
4000 Budget authority, gross	4	6	6
Outlays, gross:			
4011 Outlays from discretionary balances	2	4	5
Mandatory:			
Outlays, gross:			
4101 Outlays from mandatory balances	1		
4180 Budget authority, net (total)	4	6	6
4190 Outlays, net (total)	3	4	5

Summary of Loan Levels, Subsidy Budget Authority and Outlays by Program (in millions of dollars)

Identification code 012–1955–0–1–452	2021 actual	2022 est.	2023 est.
Direct loan levels supportable by subsidy budget authority:			
115001 Rural Microenterprise Direct Loans	4	25	10
Direct loan subsidy (in percent):			
132001 Rural Microenterprise Direct Loans	3.14	–4.10	5.34
132999 Weighted average subsidy rate	3.14	–4.10	5.34
Direct loan subsidy budget authority:			
133001 Rural Microenterprise Direct Loans		–1	1
Direct loan subsidy outlays:			
134001 Rural Microenterprise Direct Loans		–1	1

This program provides microentrepreneurs with the skills necessary to establish new rural microenterprises, and to support these types of businesses with technical and financial assistance. The program provides loans and grants to intermediaries that assist microentrepreneurs. The program is authorized pursuant to section 379E(d) of the Consolidated Farm and Rural Development Act, and as amended by the Agricultural Act of 2014, and as amended by the Agriculture Improvement Act of Act of 2018. The 2023 Budget includes $4.7 million for grants and requests $1.3 million in budget authority to support a program level of $25 million.

RURAL MICROENTERPRISE INVESTMENT DIRECT LOAN FINANCING ACCOUNT

Program and Financing (in millions of dollars)

Identification code 012–4354–0–3–452	2021 actual	2022 est.	2023 est.
Obligations by program activity:			
Credit program obligations:			
0710 Direct loan obligations	4	25	10
0713 Payment of interest to Treasury	1	1	1
0900 Total new obligations, unexpired accounts	5	26	11
Budgetary resources:			
Unobligated balance:			
1000 Unobligated balance brought forward, Oct 1	5	4	3
1021 Recoveries of prior year unpaid obligations	2		
1023 Unobligated balances applied to repay debt	–5	–4	–3
1024 Unobligated balance of borrowing authority withdrawn	–2		
Financing authority:			
Borrowing authority, mandatory:			
1400 Borrowing authority	4	25	10
Spending authority from offsetting collections, mandatory:			
1800 Collected	5	5	5
1801 Change in uncollected payments, Federal sources		–1	
1850 Spending auth from offsetting collections, mand (total)	5	4	5
1900 Budget authority (total)	9	29	15
1930 Total budgetary resources available	9	29	15
Memorandum (non-add) entries:			
1941 Unexpired unobligated balance, end of year	4	3	4
Change in obligated balance:			
Unpaid obligations:			
3000 Unpaid obligations, brought forward, Oct 1	8	7	28
3010 New obligations, unexpired accounts	5	26	11
3020 Outlays (gross)	–4	–5	–10
3040 Recoveries of prior year unpaid obligations, unexpired	–2		
3050 Unpaid obligations, end of year	7	28	29
Uncollected payments:			
3060 Uncollected pymts, Fed sources, brought forward, Oct 1	–1	–1	
3070 Change in uncollected pymts, Fed sources, unexpired		1	
3090 Uncollected pymts, Fed sources, end of year	–1		
Memorandum (non-add) entries:			
3100 Obligated balance, start of year	7	6	28
3200 Obligated balance, end of year	6	28	29
Financing authority and disbursements, net:			
Mandatory:			
4090 Budget authority, gross	9	29	15
Financing disbursements:			
4110 Outlays, gross (total)	4	5	10
Offsets against gross financing authority and disbursements:			
Offsetting collections (collected) from:			
4120 Federal sources	–1	–1	–1
4123 Repayments of Loan Principal	–3	–3	–3
4123 Interest received on loans	–1	–1	–1
4130 Offsets against gross budget authority and outlays (total)	–5	–5	–5
Additional offsets against financing authority only (total):			
4140 Change in uncollected pymts, Fed sources, unexpired		1	
4160 Budget authority, net (mandatory)	4	25	10
4170 Outlays, net (mandatory)	–1		5
4180 Budget authority, net (total)	4	25	10

		2021 actual	2022 est.	2023 est.
4190	Outlays, net (total)	-1		5

Status of Direct Loans (in millions of dollars)

Identification code 012–4354–0–3–452		2021 actual	2022 est.	2023 est.
	Position with respect to appropriations act limitation on obligations:			
1111	Direct loan obligations from current-year authority	13	25	25
1121	Limitation available from carry-forward	11	6	9
1143	Unobligated limitation carried forward (P.L. xx) (-)	-20	-6	-24
1150	Total direct loan obligations	4	25	10
	Cumulative balance of direct loans outstanding:			
1210	Outstanding, start of year	42	41	43
1231	Disbursements: Direct loan disbursements	3	5	10
1251	Repayments: Repayments and prepayments	-4	-3	-3
1290	Outstanding, end of year	41	43	50

This account finances direct loan commitments for micro-business development in rural areas. The subsidy cost of this program is funded through the Rural Microenterprise Investment Program Account.

Balance Sheet (in millions of dollars)

Identification code 012–4354–0–3–452		2020 actual	2021 actual
	ASSETS:		
1101	Federal assets: Fund balances with Treasury	5	4
	Net value of assets related to post-1991 direct loans receivable:		
1401	Direct loans receivable, gross	42	41
1405	Allowance for subsidy cost (-)	-3	-3
1499	Net present value of assets related to direct loans	39	38
1999	Total assets	44	42
	LIABILITIES:		
2103	Federal liabilities: Debt	44	42
	NET POSITION:		
3300	Cumulative results of operations		
4999	Total liabilities and net position	44	42

RURAL BUSINESS PROGRAM ACCOUNT

(INCLUDING TRANSFERS OF FUNDS)

For the cost of loan guarantees and grants, for the rural business development programs authorized by section 310B and described in subsections (a), (c), (f) and (g) of section 310B of the Consolidated Farm and Rural Development Act, $83,100,000, to remain available until expended: Provided, That of the amount appropriated under this heading, not to exceed $500,000 shall be made available for one grant to a qualified national organization to provide technical assistance for rural transportation in order to promote economic development and $9,000,000 shall be for grants to the Delta Regional Authority (7 U.S.C. 2009aa et seq.), the Northern Border Regional Commission (40 U.S.C. 15101 et seq.), and the Appalachian Regional Commission (40 U.S.C. 14101 et seq.) for any Rural Community Advancement Program purpose as described in section 381E(d) of the Consolidated Farm and Rural Development Act, of which not more than 5 percent may be used for administrative expenses: Provided further, That $4,000,000 of the amount appropriated under this heading shall be for business grants to benefit Federally Recognized Native American Tribes, including $250,000 for a grant to a qualified national organization to provide technical assistance for rural transportation in order to promote economic development: Provided further, That of the amount appropriated under this heading, $5,000,000 shall be for the Rural Innovation Stronger Economy Grant Program (7 U.S.C. 2008w): Provided further, That sections 381E-H and 381N of the Consolidated Farm and Rural Development Act are not applicable to funds made available under this heading.

Note.—A full-year 2022 appropriation for this account was not enacted at the time the Budget was prepared; therefore, the Budget assumes this account is operating under the Continuing Appropriations Act, 2022 (Division A of Public Law 117–43, as amended). The amounts included for 2022 reflect the annualized level provided by the continuing resolution.

Program and Financing (in millions of dollars)

Identification code 012–1902–0–1–452		2021 actual	2022 est.	2023 est.
	Obligations by program activity:			
0013	Rural Business Development Grants	39	40	39
0015	DRA and ARC Grants	9	9	9
0016	RISE Grants	10	5	5
0091	Direct program activities, subtotal	58	54	53
	Credit program obligations:			
0702	Loan guarantee subsidy	36	10	38
0707	Reestimates of loan guarantee subsidy	13	41	
0708	Interest on reestimates of loan guarantee subsidy	2	6	
0791	Direct program activities, subtotal	51	57	38
0900	Total new obligations, unexpired accounts (object class 41.0)	109	111	91
	Budgetary resources:			
	Unobligated balance:			
1000	Unobligated balance brought forward, Oct 1	28	4	8
1001	Discretionary unobligated balance brought fwd, Oct 1		4	
1021	Recoveries of prior year unpaid obligations	8	7	7
1070	Unobligated balance (total)	36	11	15
	Budget authority:			
	Appropriations, discretionary:			
1100	Appropriation	61	61	83
	Appropriations, mandatory:			
1200	Appropriation	16	47	
1900	Budget authority (total)	77	108	83
1930	Total budgetary resources available	113	119	98
	Memorandum (non-add) entries:			
1941	Unexpired unobligated balance, end of year	4	8	7
	Change in obligated balance:			
	Unpaid obligations:			
3000	Unpaid obligations, brought forward, Oct 1	128	140	132
3010	New obligations, unexpired accounts	109	111	91
3020	Outlays (gross)	-89	-112	-72
3040	Recoveries of prior year unpaid obligations, unexpired	-8	-7	-7
3050	Unpaid obligations, end of year	140	132	144
	Memorandum (non-add) entries:			
3100	Obligated balance, start of year	128	140	132
3200	Obligated balance, end of year	140	132	144
	Budget authority and outlays, net:			
	Discretionary:			
4000	Budget authority, gross	61	61	83
	Outlays, gross:			
4010	Outlays from new discretionary authority	5	5	15
4011	Outlays from discretionary balances	68	60	57
4020	Outlays, gross (total)	73	65	72
	Mandatory:			
4090	Budget authority, gross	16	47	
	Outlays, gross:			
4100	Outlays from new mandatory authority	16	47	
4180	Budget authority, net (total)	77	108	83
4190	Outlays, net (total)	89	112	72

Summary of Loan Levels, Subsidy Budget Authority and Outlays by Program (in millions of dollars)

Identification code 012–1902–0–1–452		2021 actual	2022 est.	2023 est.
	Direct loan reestimates:			
135004	Business and Industry Loans		-1	
	Guaranteed loan levels supportable by subsidy budget authority:			
215007	Business and Industry Loan Guarantees	2,022	521	1,758
215012	Business and Industry CARES Act	521		
215999	Total loan guarantee levels	2,543	521	1,758
	Guaranteed loan subsidy (in percent):			
232007	Business and Industry Loan Guarantees	1.14	2.01	2.14
232012	Business and Industry CARES Act	2.50		
232999	Weighted average subsidy rate	1.42	2.01	2.14
	Guaranteed loan subsidy budget authority:			
233007	Business and Industry Loan Guarantees	23	10	38
233012	Business and Industry CARES Act	13		
233999	Total subsidy budget authority	36	10	38
	Guaranteed loan subsidy outlays:			
234007	Business and Industry Loan Guarantees	22	19	22
234012	Business and Industry CARES Act	16	3	1
234999	Total subsidy outlays	38	22	23
	Guaranteed loan reestimates:			
235006	Guaranteed Business and Industry Loans - ARRA	-4	-3	
235007	Business and Industry Loan Guarantees	-62	-32	
235008	Business and Industry Emergency Supplemental Loan Guarantees	1	3	

RURAL BUSINESS PROGRAM ACCOUNT—Continued

Summary of Loan Levels, Subsidy Budget Authority and Outlays by Program—Continued

Identification code 012–1902–0–1–452	2021 actual	2022 est.	2023 est.
235012 Business and Industry CARES Act	....	8	....
235999 Total guaranteed loan reestimates	–65	–24	....

This account funds direct and guaranteed business and industry loans, and rural business development grants. Business and industry guaranteed loans are authorized under section 310B(a)(1) of the Consolidated Farm and Rural Development Act, as amended. These loans are made to public, private or cooperative organizations, Indian tribes or tribal groups, corporate entities, or individuals for the purpose of improving the economic climate in rural areas. The 2023 Budget request for loan guarantees is $1.5 billion. The 2023 Budget requests $37 million for the Rural Business Development grant program; $5 million for the Rural Innovation Stronger Economy (RISE) grant program; and $9 million for the Appalachia and Northern Border Regional Commissions and Delta Regional Authority.

RURAL BUSINESS AND INDUSTRY DIRECT LOANS FINANCING ACCOUNT

Program and Financing (in millions of dollars)

Identification code 012–4223–0–3–452	2021 actual	2022 est.	2023 est.
Obligations by program activity:			
Credit program obligations:			
0743 Interest on downward reestimates	....	1	....
0900 Total new obligations, unexpired accounts	....	1	....
Budgetary resources:			
Unobligated balance:			
1000 Unobligated balance brought forward, Oct 1	....	1	....
1023 Unobligated balances applied to repay debt	....	–1	....
Financing authority:			
Spending authority from offsetting collections, mandatory:			
1800 Collected	1	1	1
1900 Budget authority (total)	1	1	1
1930 Total budgetary resources available	1	1	1
Memorandum (non-add) entries:			
1941 Unexpired unobligated balance, end of year	1	....	1
Change in obligated balance:			
Unpaid obligations:			
3010 New obligations, unexpired accounts	....	1	....
3020 Outlays (gross)	....	–1	....
Financing authority and disbursements, net:			
Mandatory:			
4090 Budget authority, gross	1	1	1
Financing disbursements:			
4110 Outlays, gross (total)	....	1	....
Offsets against gross financing authority and disbursements:			
Offsetting collections (collected) from:			
4123 Repayments of principal	–1	–1	–1
4180 Budget authority, net (total)	....	....	....
4190 Outlays, net (total)	–1	....	–1

Status of Direct Loans (in millions of dollars)

Identification code 012–4223–0–3–452	2021 actual	2022 est.	2023 est.
Cumulative balance of direct loans outstanding:			
1210 Outstanding, start of year	4	3	2
1251 Repayments: Repayments and prepayments	–1	–1	–1
1290 Outstanding, end of year	3	2	1

The account finances direct loans for business development in rural areas. The subsidy cost of this program is funded through the Rural Business Program Account. Loans made prior to 1992 are recorded in the Rural Development Insurance Fund Liquidating Account.

Balance Sheet (in millions of dollars)

Identification code 012–4223–0–3–452	2020 actual	2021 actual
ASSETS:		
1101 Federal assets: Fund balances with Treasury	....	....
Net value of assets related to post-1991 direct loans receivable:		
1401 Direct loans receivable, gross	4	3
1405 Allowance for subsidy cost (-)	–4	–3
1499 Net present value of assets related to direct loans	....	....
1502 Net value of assets related to post-1991 acquired defaulted guaranteed loans receivable: Interest receivable	....	....
1999 Total assets	....	....
LIABILITIES:		
Federal liabilities:		
2103 Debt	....	....
2104 Resources payable to Treasury	....	....
2999 Total liabilities	....	....
NET POSITION:		
3300 Cumulative results of operations	....	....
4999 Total liabilities and net position	....	....

RURAL BUSINESS AND INDUSTRY GUARANTEED LOANS FINANCING ACCOUNT

Program and Financing (in millions of dollars)

Identification code 012–4227–0–3–452	2021 actual	2022 est.	2023 est.
Obligations by program activity:			
Credit program obligations:			
0711 Default claim payments on principal	57	153	164
0712 Default claim payments on interest	....	3	3
0713 Payment of interest to Treasury	2	2	2
0742 Downward reestimates paid to receipt accounts	72	62	....
0743 Interest on downward reestimates	9	8	....
0900 Total new obligations, unexpired accounts	140	228	169
Budgetary resources:			
Unobligated balance:			
1000 Unobligated balance brought forward, Oct 1	214	259	214
1021 Recoveries of prior year unpaid obligations	2	....	....
1023 Unobligated balances applied to repay debt	–33	–30	–30
1033 Recoveries of prior year paid obligations	2	....	....
1070 Unobligated balance (total)	185	229	184
Financing authority:			
Borrowing authority, mandatory:			
1400 Borrowing authority	57	30	30
Spending authority from offsetting collections, mandatory:			
1800 Collected	165	195	160
1801 Change in uncollected payments, Federal sources	–8	–12	2
1850 Spending auth from offsetting collections, mand (total)	157	183	162
1900 Budget authority (total)	214	213	192
1930 Total budgetary resources available	399	442	376
Memorandum (non-add) entries:			
1941 Unexpired unobligated balance, end of year	259	214	207
Change in obligated balance:			
Unpaid obligations:			
3010 New obligations, unexpired accounts	140	228	169
3020 Outlays (gross)	–138	–228	–169
3040 Recoveries of prior year unpaid obligations, unexpired	–2	....	....
Uncollected payments:			
3060 Uncollected pymts, Fed sources, brought forward, Oct 1	–28	–20	–8
3070 Change in uncollected pymts, Fed sources, unexpired	8	12	–2
3090 Uncollected pymts, Fed sources, end of year	–20	–8	–10
Memorandum (non-add) entries:			
3100 Obligated balance, start of year	–28	–20	–8
3200 Obligated balance, end of year	–20	–8	–10
Financing authority and disbursements, net:			
Mandatory:			
4090 Budget authority, gross	214	213	192
Financing disbursements:			
4110 Outlays, gross (total)	138	228	169
Offsets against gross financing authority and disbursements:			
Offsetting collections (collected) from:			
4120 Federal sources	–54	–69	–24
4122 Interest on uninvested funds	–5	–10	–11
4123 Repayments of principal	–40	–44	–47

DEPARTMENT OF AGRICULTURE

Identification code 012–4227–0–3–452		2021 actual	2022 est.	2023 est.
4123	Guarantee Fees	−65	−72	−78
4123	Repayments of interest	−3		
4130	Offsets against gross budget authority and outlays (total)	−167	−195	−160
	Additional offsets against financing authority only (total):			
4140	Change in uncollected pymts, Fed sources, unexpired	8	12	−2
4143	Recoveries of prior year paid obligations, unexpired accounts	2		
4150	Additional offsets against budget authority only (total)	10	12	−2
4160	Budget authority, net (mandatory)	57	30	30
4170	Outlays, net (mandatory)	−29	33	9
4180	Budget authority, net (total)	57	30	30
4190	Outlays, net (total)	−29	33	9

Status of Guaranteed Loans (in millions of dollars)

Identification code 012–4227–0–3–452		2021 actual	2022 est.	2023 est.
	Position with respect to appropriations act limitation on commitments:			
2111	Guaranteed loan commitments from current-year authority	912	517	1,500
2121	Limitation available from carry-forward	1,792	4	258
2143	Uncommitted limitation carried forward	−161		
2150	Total guaranteed loan commitments	2,543	521	1,758
	Cumulative balance of guaranteed loans outstanding:			
2210	Outstanding, start of year	6,614	7,749	7,949
2231	Disbursements of new guaranteed loans	2,208	1,482	1,151
2251	Repayments and prepayments	−981	−1,005	−1,031
	Adjustments:			
2261	Terminations for default that result in loans receivable	−41	−157	−165
2263	Terminations for default that result in claim payments	−51	−120	−126
2264	Other adjustments, net			
2290	Outstanding, end of year	7,749	7,949	7,778
	Memorandum:			
2299	Guaranteed amount of guaranteed loans outstanding, end of year	5,735	5,883	5,756
	Addendum:			
	Cumulative balance of defaulted guaranteed loans that result in loans receivable:			
2310	Outstanding, start of year	214	204	188
2331	Disbursements for guaranteed loan claims	69	93	95
2351	Repayments of loans receivable	−40	−26	−24
2361	Write-offs of loans receivable	−40	−83	−77
2364	Other adjustments, net	1		
2390	Outstanding, end of year	204	188	182

The account finances loan guarantee commitments for business development in rural areas. The subsidy cost of this program is funded through the Rural Business Program Account. Loans made prior to 1992 are recorded in the Rural Development Insurance Fund Liquidating Account.

Balance Sheet (in millions of dollars)

Identification code 012–4227–0–3–452		2020 actual	2021 actual
	ASSETS:		
	Federal assets:		
1101	Fund balances with Treasury	186	239
	Investments in U.S. securities:		
1106	Receivables, net	41	23
	Net value of assets related to post-1991 acquired defaulted guaranteed loans receivable:		
1501	Defaulted guaranteed loans receivable, gross	214	204
1502	Interest receivable		
1505	Allowance for subsidy cost (-)	−33	−43
1599	Net present value of assets related to defaulted guaranteed loans	181	161
1999	Total assets	408	423
	LIABILITIES:		
	Federal liabilities:		
2103	Debt	60	85
2105	Other	29	113
2204	Non-Federal liabilities: Liabilities for loan guarantees	319	225
2999	Total liabilities	408	423
	NET POSITION:		
3300	Cumulative results of operations		

4999	Total liabilities and net position	408	423

INTERMEDIARY RELENDING PROGRAM FUND ACCOUNT

(INCLUDING TRANSFER OF FUNDS)

For the principal amount of direct loans, as authorized by the Intermediary Relending Program Fund Account (7 U.S.C. 1936b), $18,889,000.

For the cost of direct loans, $3,313,000, as authorized by the Intermediary Relending Program Fund Account (7 U.S.C. 1936b), of which $331,000 shall be available through June 30, 2023, for Federally Recognized Native American Tribes; and of which $663,000 shall be available through June 30, 2023, for Mississippi Delta Region counties (as determined in accordance with Public Law 100–460): Provided, That such costs, including the cost of modifying such loans, shall be as defined in section 502 of the Congressional Budget Act of 1974.

In addition, for administrative expenses to carry out the direct loan programs, $4,468,000 shall be paid to the appropriation for "Rural Development, Salaries and Expenses".

Note.—A full-year 2022 appropriation for this account was not enacted at the time the Budget was prepared; therefore, the Budget assumes this account is operating under the Continuing Appropriations Act, 2022 (Division A of Public Law 117–43, as amended). The amounts included for 2022 reflect the annualized level provided by the continuing resolution.

Program and Financing (in millions of dollars)

Identification code 012–2069–0–1–452		2021 actual	2022 est.	2023 est.
	Obligations by program activity:			
	Credit program obligations:			
0701	Direct loan subsidy	3	2	4
0705	Reestimates of direct loan subsidy	1	1	
0706	Interest on reestimates of direct loan subsidy		1	
0709	Administrative expenses	4	4	4
0900	Total new obligations, unexpired accounts	8	8	8
	Budgetary resources:			
	Budget authority:			
	Appropriations, discretionary:			
1100	Appropriation	8	7	8
1120	Appropriations transferred to other acct [012–4609]	−1		
1160	Appropriation, discretionary (total)	7	7	8
	Appropriations, mandatory:			
1200	Appropriation	1	2	
1900	Budget authority (total)	8	9	8
1930	Total budgetary resources available	8	9	8
	Memorandum (non-add) entries:			
1940	Unobligated balance expiring		−1	
	Change in obligated balance:			
	Unpaid obligations:			
3000	Unpaid obligations, brought forward, Oct 1	11	10	8
3010	New obligations, unexpired accounts	8	8	8
3020	Outlays (gross)	−8	−10	−7
3041	Recoveries of prior year unpaid obligations, expired	−1		
3050	Unpaid obligations, end of year	10	8	9
	Memorandum (non-add) entries:			
3100	Obligated balance, start of year	11	10	8
3200	Obligated balance, end of year	10	8	9
	Budget authority and outlays, net:			
	Discretionary:			
4000	Budget authority, gross	7	7	8
	Outlays, gross:			
4010	Outlays from new discretionary authority	4	4	4
4011	Outlays from discretionary balances	3	4	3
4020	Outlays, gross (total)	7	8	7
	Mandatory:			
4090	Budget authority, gross	1	2	
	Outlays, gross:			
4100	Outlays from new mandatory authority	1	2	
4180	Budget authority, net (total)	8	9	8
4190	Outlays, net (total)	8	10	7

Rural Business-Cooperative Service—Continued
Federal Funds—Continued

INTERMEDIARY RELENDING PROGRAM FUND ACCOUNT—Continued

Summary of Loan Levels, Subsidy Budget Authority and Outlays by Program (in millions of dollars)

Identification code 012–2069–0–1–452		2021 actual	2022 est.	2023 est.
	Direct loan levels supportable by subsidy budget authority:			
115001	Intermediary Relending Program	14	19	19
	Direct loan subsidy (in percent):			
132001	Intermediary Relending Program	15.56	8.07	17.54
132999	Weighted average subsidy rate	15.56	8.07	17.54
	Direct loan subsidy budget authority:			
133001	Intermediary Relending Program	3	2	3
	Direct loan subsidy outlays:			
134001	Intermediary Relending Program	3	4	2
	Direct loan reestimates:			
135001	Intermediary Relending Program	–2		
	Administrative expense data:			
3510	Budget authority	4	4	4
3590	Outlays from new authority	4	4	4

This account finances loans to intermediary borrowers, who, in turn, relend the funds to small rural businesses, community development corporations, and other organizations for the purpose of improving economic opportunities in rural areas. Through the use of local intermediaries, this program serves small-scale enterprises and gives preference to those communities with the greatest need. The 2023 Budget requests $18.9 million in program level.

As required by the Federal Credit Reform Act of 1990, this account records for this program the subsidy costs associated with the direct loans obligated in 1992 and beyond, as well as administrative expenses of this program. The subsidy amounts are estimated on a present value basis; the administrative expenses are estimated on a cash basis.

Object Classification (in millions of dollars)

Identification code 012–2069–0–1–452		2021 actual	2022 est.	2023 est.
	Direct obligations:			
25.3	Other goods and services from Federal sources	4	4	4
41.0	Grants, subsidies, and contributions	4	4	4
99.9	Total new obligations, unexpired accounts	8	8	8

RURAL DEVELOPMENT LOAN FUND DIRECT LOAN FINANCING ACCOUNT

Program and Financing (in millions of dollars)

Identification code 012–4219–0–3–452		2021 actual	2022 est.	2023 est.
	Obligations by program activity:			
	Credit program obligations:			
0710	Direct loan obligations	14	19	19
0713	Payment of interest to Treasury	13	14	14
0742	Downward reestimates paid to receipt accounts	3	1	
0743	Interest on downward reestimates		1	
0900	Total new obligations, unexpired accounts	30	35	33
	Budgetary resources:			
	Unobligated balance:			
1000	Unobligated balance brought forward, Oct 1	23	31	15
1021	Recoveries of prior year unpaid obligations	3		
1023	Unobligated balances applied to repay debt	–24	–31	–15
1024	Unobligated balance of borrowing authority withdrawn	–2		
	Financing authority:			
	Borrowing authority, mandatory:			
1400	Borrowing authority	23	19	3
	Spending authority from offsetting collections, mandatory:			
1800	Collected	42	31	30
1801	Change in uncollected payments, Federal sources	–2		
1825	Spending authority from offsetting collections applied to repay debt	–2		
1850	Spending auth from offsetting collections, mand (total)	38	31	30
1900	Budget authority (total)	61	50	33
1930	Total budgetary resources available	61	50	33
	Memorandum (non-add) entries:			
1941	Unexpired unobligated balance, end of year	31	15	
	Change in obligated balance:			
	Unpaid obligations:			
3000	Unpaid obligations, brought forward, Oct 1	44	44	48
3010	New obligations, unexpired accounts	30	35	33
3020	Outlays (gross)	–27	–31	–31
3040	Recoveries of prior year unpaid obligations, unexpired	–3		
3050	Unpaid obligations, end of year	44	48	50
	Uncollected payments:			
3060	Uncollected pymts, Fed sources, brought forward, Oct 1	–12	–10	–10
3070	Change in uncollected pymts, Fed sources, unexpired	2		
3090	Uncollected pymts, Fed sources, end of year	–10	–10	–10
	Memorandum (non-add) entries:			
3100	Obligated balance, start of year	32	34	38
3200	Obligated balance, end of year	34	38	40
	Financing authority and disbursements, net:			
	Mandatory:			
4090	Budget authority, gross	61	50	33
	Financing disbursements:			
4110	Outlays, gross (total)	27	31	31
	Offsets against gross financing authority and disbursements:			
	Offsetting collections (collected) from:			
4120	Payments from program account	–4	–7	–3
4122	Interest on uninvested funds	–2	–1	–1
4123	Non-Federal sources - repayment of principal	–36	–23	–23
4123	Non-Federal sources - repayments of interest			–3
4130	Offsets against gross budget authority and outlays (total)	–42	–31	–30
	Additional offsets against financing authority only (total):			
4140	Change in uncollected pymts, Fed sources, unexpired	2		
4160	Budget authority, net (mandatory)	21	19	3
4170	Outlays, net (mandatory)	–15		1
4180	Budget authority, net (total)	21	19	3
4190	Outlays, net (total)	–15		1

Status of Direct Loans (in millions of dollars)

Identification code 012–4219–0–3–452		2021 actual	2022 est.	2023 est.
	Position with respect to appropriations act limitation on obligations:			
1111	Direct loan obligations from current-year authority	14	19	19
1150	Total direct loan obligations	14	19	19
	Cumulative balance of direct loans outstanding:			
1210	Outstanding, start of year	342	321	316
1231	Disbursements: Direct loan disbursements	14	18	23
1251	Repayments: Repayments and prepayments	–35	–23	–23
1290	Outstanding, end of year	321	316	316

Balance Sheet (in millions of dollars)

Identification code 012–4219–0–3–452		2020 actual	2021 actual
	ASSETS:		
1101	Federal assets: Fund balances with Treasury	26	31
	Net value of assets related to post-1991 direct loans receivable:		
1401	Direct loans receivable, gross	336	321
1402	Interest receivable	2	2
1405	Allowance for subsidy cost (-)	–70	–63
1499	Net present value of assets related to direct loans	268	260
1999	Total assets	294	291
	LIABILITIES:		
	Federal liabilities:		
2103	Debt	294	291
2104	Resources payable to Treasury		
2999	Total liabilities	294	291
	NET POSITION:		
3300	Cumulative results of operations		
4999	Total liabilities and net position	294	291

DEPARTMENT OF AGRICULTURE

RURAL DEVELOPMENT LOAN FUND LIQUIDATING ACCOUNT

Program and Financing (in millions of dollars)

Identification code 012–4233–0–3–452		2021 actual	2022 est.	2023 est.
	Budgetary resources:			
	Unobligated balance:			
1000	Unobligated balance brought forward, Oct 1	1		
1022	Capital transfer of unobligated balances to general fund	–1		
	Budget authority:			
	Spending authority from offsetting collections, mandatory:			
1800	Collected	1	1	1
1820	Capital transfer of spending authority from offsetting collections to general fund	–1	–1	–1
	Budget authority and outlays, net:			
	Mandatory:			
	Offsets against gross budget authority and outlays:			
	Offsetting collections (collected) from:			
4123	Non-Federal sources	–1	–1	–1
4180	Budget authority, net (total)	–1	–1	–1
4190	Outlays, net (total)	–1	–1	–1

Status of Direct Loans (in millions of dollars)

Identification code 012–4233–0–3–452		2021 actual	2022 est.	2023 est.
	Cumulative balance of direct loans outstanding:			
1210	Outstanding, start of year	2	1	1
1251	Repayments: Repayments and prepayments	–1	–1	–1
1264	Other adjustments, net (+ or -)		1	
1290	Outstanding, end of year	1	1	

Balance Sheet (in millions of dollars)

Identification code 012–4233–0–3–452		2020 actual	2021 actual
	ASSETS:		
1101	Federal assets: Fund balances with Treasury	1	
1601	Direct loans, gross	2	1
1999	Total assets	3	1
	LIABILITIES:		
2104	Federal liabilities: Resources payable to Treasury	3	1
4999	Total liabilities and net position	3	1

RURAL ECONOMIC DEVELOPMENT LOANS PROGRAM ACCOUNT

For the principal amount of direct loans, as authorized under section 313B(a) of the Rural Electrification Act, for the purpose of promoting rural economic development and job creation projects, $75,000,000.

The cost of grants authorized under section 313B(a) of the Rural Electrification Act, for the purpose of promoting rural economic development and job creation projects shall not exceed $15,000,000.

Note.—A full-year 2022 appropriation for this account was not enacted at the time the Budget was prepared; therefore, the Budget assumes this account is operating under the Continuing Appropriations Act, 2022 (Division A of Public Law 117–43, as amended). The amounts included for 2022 reflect the annualized level provided by the continuing resolution.

Program and Financing (in millions of dollars)

Identification code 012–3108–0–1–452		2021 actual	2022 est.	2023 est.
	Obligations by program activity:			
	Credit program obligations:			
0701	Direct loan subsidy	2	2	7
0900	Total new obligations, unexpired accounts (object class 41.0)	2	2	7
	Budgetary resources:			
	Unobligated balance:			
1000	Unobligated balance brought forward, Oct 1	1	5	6
1021	Recoveries of prior year unpaid obligations	1	1	1
1070	Unobligated balance (total)	2	6	7
	Budget authority:			
	Spending authority from offsetting collections, mandatory:			
1800	Collected	5	2	7
1900	Budget authority (total)	5	2	7

Rural Business-Cooperative Service—Continued
Federal Funds—Continued   143

1930	Total budgetary resources available	7	8	14
	Memorandum (non-add) entries:			
1941	Unexpired unobligated balance, end of year	5	6	7
	Change in obligated balance:			
	Unpaid obligations:			
3000	Unpaid obligations, brought forward, Oct 1	10	5	2
3010	New obligations, unexpired accounts	2	2	7
3020	Outlays (gross)	–6	–4	–6
3040	Recoveries of prior year unpaid obligations, unexpired	–1	–1	–1
3050	Unpaid obligations, end of year	5	2	2
	Memorandum (non-add) entries:			
3100	Obligated balance, start of year	10	5	2
3200	Obligated balance, end of year	5	2	2
	Budget authority and outlays, net:			
	Mandatory:			
4090	Budget authority, gross	5	2	7
	Outlays, gross:			
4100	Outlays from new mandatory authority			2
4101	Outlays from mandatory balances	6	4	4
4110	Outlays, gross (total)	6	4	6
	Offsets against gross budget authority and outlays:			
	Offsetting collections (collected) from:			
4120	Federal sources	–5	–2	–7
4180	Budget authority, net (total)			
4190	Outlays, net (total)	1	2	–1

Summary of Loan Levels, Subsidy Budget Authority and Outlays by Program (in millions of dollars)

Identification code 012–3108–0–1–452		2021 actual	2022 est.	2023 est.
	Direct loan levels supportable by subsidy budget authority:			
115001	Rural Economic Development Loans	22	51	75
	Direct loan subsidy (in percent):			
132001	Rural Economic Development Loans	9.55	4.68	9.87
132999	Weighted average subsidy rate	9.55	4.68	9.87
	Direct loan subsidy budget authority:			
133001	Rural Economic Development Loans	2	3	7
	Direct loan subsidy outlays:			
134001	Rural Economic Development Loans	6	4	6
	Direct loan reestimates:			
135001	Rural Economic Development Loans	–2	–4	

Rural economic development loans are made for the purpose of promoting rural economic development and job creation projects. Loans are made to electric and telecommunication borrowers, who, in turn, finance rural development projects in their service areas. The 2023 Budget assumes the continuation of this program and requests an increase to $75 million.

As required by the Federal Credit Reform Act of 1990, this account records for this program the subsidy costs associated with the direct loans obligated in 1992 and beyond. The subsidy amounts are estimated on a present value basis.

RURAL ECONOMIC DEVELOPMENT DIRECT LOAN FINANCING ACCOUNT

Program and Financing (in millions of dollars)

Identification code 012–4176–0–3–452		2021 actual	2022 est.	2023 est.
	Obligations by program activity:			
	Credit program obligations:			
0710	Direct loan obligations	22	51	75
0713	Payment of interest to Treasury	5	5	6
0742	Downward reestimates paid to receipt accounts	1	4	
0900	Total new obligations, unexpired accounts	28	60	81
	Budgetary resources:			
	Unobligated balance:			
1000	Unobligated balance brought forward, Oct 1	34	46	22
1021	Recoveries of prior year unpaid obligations	6	5	6
1023	Unobligated balances applied to repay debt	–34	–46	–22
1024	Unobligated balance of borrowing authority withdrawn	–5		–5
1070	Unobligated balance (total)	1		1
	Financing authority:			
	Borrowing authority, mandatory:			
1400	Borrowing authority	32	32	76

Rural Business-Cooperative Service—Continued
Federal Funds—Continued

RURAL ECONOMIC DEVELOPMENT DIRECT LOAN FINANCING ACCOUNT—Continued

Program and Financing—Continued

Identification code 012–4176–0–3–452	2021 actual	2022 est.	2023 est.
Spending authority from offsetting collections, mandatory:			
1800 Collected	46	44	43
1801 Change in uncollected payments, Federal sources	–5	6	–3
1850 Spending auth from offsetting collections, mand (total)	41	50	40
1900 Budget authority (total)	73	82	116
1930 Total budgetary resources available	74	82	117
Memorandum (non-add) entries:			
1941 Unexpired unobligated balance, end of year	46	22	36
Change in obligated balance:			
Unpaid obligations:			
3000 Unpaid obligations, brought forward, Oct 1	65	40	56
3010 New obligations, unexpired accounts	28	60	81
3020 Outlays (gross)	–47	–39	–54
3040 Recoveries of prior year unpaid obligations, unexpired	–6	–5	–6
3050 Unpaid obligations, end of year	40	56	77
Uncollected payments:			
3060 Uncollected pymts, Fed sources, brought forward, Oct 1	–10	–5	–11
3070 Change in uncollected pymts, Fed sources, unexpired	5	–6	3
3090 Uncollected pymts, Fed sources, end of year	–5	–11	–8
Memorandum (non-add) entries:			
3100 Obligated balance, start of year	55	35	45
3200 Obligated balance, end of year	35	45	69
Financing authority and disbursements, net:			
Mandatory:			
4090 Budget authority, gross	73	82	116
Financing disbursements:			
4110 Outlays, gross (total)	47	39	54
Offsets against gross financing authority and disbursements:			
Offsetting collections (collected) from:			
4120 Federal Funds: Program Account	–6	–4	–5
4122 Interest on uninvested funds	–1	–1	–1
4123 Non-Federal sources: Repayment of Principal	–39	–39	–37
4130 Offsets against gross budget authority and outlays (total)	–46	–44	–43
Additional offsets against financing authority only (total):			
4140 Change in uncollected pymts, Fed sources, unexpired	5	–6	3
4160 Budget authority, net (mandatory)	32	32	76
4170 Outlays, net (mandatory)	1	–5	11
4180 Budget authority, net (total)	32	32	76
4190 Outlays, net (total)	1	–5	11

Status of Direct Loans (in millions of dollars)

Identification code 012–4176–0–3–452	2021 actual	2022 est.	2023 est.
Position with respect to appropriations act limitation on obligations:			
1121 Limitation available from carry-forward	22	51	75
1150 Total direct loan obligations	22	51	75
Cumulative balance of direct loans outstanding:			
1210 Outstanding, start of year	200	201	195
1231 Disbursements: Direct loan disbursements	40	33	53
1251 Repayments: Repayments and prepayments	–39	–39	–37
1290 Outstanding, end of year	201	195	211

Balance Sheet (in millions of dollars)

Identification code 012–4176–0–3–452	2020 actual	2021 actual
ASSETS:		
1101 Federal assets: Fund balances with Treasury	34	47
Net value of assets related to post-1991 direct loans receivable:		
1401 Direct loans receivable, gross	200	201
1405 Allowance for subsidy cost (–)	–16	–17
1499 Net present value of assets related to direct loans	184	184
1999 Total assets	218	231
LIABILITIES:		
Federal liabilities:		
2103 Debt	218	231
2104 Resources payable to Treasury		
2999 Total liabilities	218	231
NET POSITION:		
3300 Cumulative results of operations		
4999 Total upward reestimate subsidy BA [12–3108]	218	231

RURAL BUSINESS INVESTMENT PROGRAM ACCOUNT

Program and Financing (in millions of dollars)

Identification code 012–1907–0–1–452	2021 actual	2022 est.	2023 est.
Budgetary resources:			
Unobligated balance:			
1000 Unobligated balance brought forward, Oct 1	3	3	3
1930 Total budgetary resources available	3	3	3
Memorandum (non-add) entries:			
1941 Unexpired unobligated balance, end of year	3	3	3
4180 Budget authority, net (total)			
4190 Outlays, net (total)			

The Rural Business Investment Program was authorized by section 6029 of the Farm Security and Rural Investment Act of 2002, Public Law 107–171. As required by the Federal Credit Reform Act of 1990, this account records for this program the subsidy costs associated with the loan guarantees committed in 1992 and beyond. The subsidy amounts are estimated on a present value basis. The 2023 Budget is not requesting funding for the loan program, however the Administration is committed to increasing the number of rural business investment companies through the licensing program.

RURAL BUSINESS INVESTMENT PROGRAM GUARANTEE FINANCING ACCOUNT

Program and Financing (in millions of dollars)

Identification code 012–4033–0–3–452	2021 actual	2022 est.	2023 est.
Budgetary resources:			
Unobligated balance:			
1000 Unobligated balance brought forward, Oct 1	2	2	2
1930 Total budgetary resources available	2	2	2
Memorandum (non-add) entries:			
1941 Unexpired unobligated balance, end of year	2	2	2
4180 Budget authority, net (total)			
4190 Outlays, net (total)			

Status of Guaranteed Loans (in millions of dollars)

Identification code 012–4033–0–3–452	2021 actual	2022 est.	2023 est.
Position with respect to appropriations act limitation on commitments:			
2111 Guaranteed loan commitments from current-year authority			
2150 Total guaranteed loan commitments			
Cumulative balance of guaranteed loans outstanding:			
2210 Outstanding, start of year	8	8	8
2231 Disbursements of new guaranteed loans			
2251 Repayments and prepayments			
Adjustments:			
2261 Terminations for default that result in loans receivable			
2264 Other adjustments, net			
2290 Outstanding, end of year	8	8	8
Memorandum:			
2299 Guaranteed amount of guaranteed loans outstanding, end of year			
Addendum:			
Cumulative balance of defaulted guaranteed loans that result in loans receivable:			
2310 Outstanding, start of year	8	8	8
2331 Disbursements for guaranteed loan claims			
2351 Repayments of loans receivable			
2390 Outstanding, end of year	8	8	8

Balance Sheet (in millions of dollars)

Identification code 012–4033–0–3–452		2020 actual	2021 actual
	ASSETS:		
1101	Federal assets: Fund balances with Treasury	2	2
	Net value of assets related to post-1991 acquired defaulted guaranteed loans receivable:		
1501	Defaulted guaranteed loans receivable, gross	8	8
1505	Allowance for subsidy cost (-)	–8	–8
1599	Net present value of assets related to defaulted guaranteed loans		
1999	Total assets	2	2
	LIABILITIES:		
2103	Federal liabilities: Debt	2	2
2204	Non-Federal liabilities: Liabilities for loan guarantees		
2999	Total liabilities	2	2
	NET POSITION:		
3300	Cumulative results of operations		
4999	Total liabilities and net position	2	2

RURAL ENERGY FOR AMERICA PROGRAM

For the cost of a program of loan guarantees and grants, under the same terms and conditions as authorized by section 9007 of the Farm Security and Rural Investment Act of 2002 (7 U.S.C. 8107), $30,018,000: Provided, That the cost of loan guarantees, including the cost of modifying such loans, shall be as defined in section 502 of the Congressional Budget Act of 1974.

For the principal amount of loan guarantees, under the same terms and conditions as authorized by section 9007 of the Farm Security and Rural Investment Act of 2002 (7 U.S.C. 8107), $20,000,000.

Note.—A full-year 2022 appropriation for this account was not enacted at the time the Budget was prepared; therefore, the Budget assumes this account is operating under the Continuing Appropriations Act, 2022 (Division A of Public Law 117–43, as amended). The amounts included for 2022 reflect the annualized level provided by the continuing resolution.

Program and Financing (in millions of dollars)

Identification code 012–1908–0–1–451		2021 actual	2022 est.	2023 est.
	Obligations by program activity:			
0011	Grants	46	52	63
	Credit program obligations:			
0702	Loan guarantee subsidy	12	5	1
0900	Total new obligations, unexpired accounts (object class 41.0)	58	57	64
	Budgetary resources:			
	Unobligated balance:			
1000	Unobligated balance brought forward, Oct 1	8	14	20
1021	Recoveries of prior year unpaid obligations	7	6	6
1070	Unobligated balance (total)	15	20	26
	Budget authority:			
	Appropriations, discretionary:			
1100	Appropriation	10	10	30
	Appropriations, mandatory:			
1222	Exercised borrowing authority transferred from other accounts [012–4336]	50	50	50
1230	Appropriations and/or unobligated balance of appropriations permanently reduced	–3	–3	–3
1260	Appropriations, mandatory (total)	47	47	47
1900	Budget authority (total)	57	57	77
1930	Total budgetary resources available	72	77	103
	Memorandum (non-add) entries:			
1941	Unexpired unobligated balance, end of year	14	20	39
	Change in obligated balance:			
	Unpaid obligations:			
3000	Unpaid obligations, brought forward, Oct 1	77	85	69
3010	New obligations, unexpired accounts	58	57	64
3020	Outlays (gross)	–43	–67	–63
3040	Recoveries of prior year unpaid obligations, unexpired	–7	–6	–6
3050	Unpaid obligations, end of year	85	69	64
	Memorandum (non-add) entries:			
3100	Obligated balance, start of year	77	85	69
3200	Obligated balance, end of year	85	69	64
	Budget authority and outlays, net:			
	Discretionary:			
4000	Budget authority, gross	10	10	30
	Outlays, gross:			
4011	Outlays from discretionary balances		10	11
	Mandatory:			
4090	Budget authority, gross	47	47	47
	Outlays, gross:			
4100	Outlays from new mandatory authority	7	2	2
4101	Outlays from mandatory balances	36	55	50
4110	Outlays, gross (total)	43	57	52
4180	Budget authority, net (total)	57	57	77
4190	Outlays, net (total)	43	67	63

Summary of Loan Levels, Subsidy Budget Authority and Outlays by Program (in millions of dollars)

Identification code 012–1908–0–1–451		2021 actual	2022 est.	2023 est.
	Guaranteed loan levels supportable by subsidy budget authority:			
215001	Renewable Energy Loan Guarantees	635	635	635
	Guaranteed loan subsidy (in percent):			
232001	Renewable Energy Loan Guarantees	1.96	0.84	0.09
232999	Weighted average subsidy rate	1.96	0.84	0.09
	Guaranteed loan subsidy budget authority:			
233001	Renewable Energy Loan Guarantees	12	5	1
	Guaranteed loan subsidy outlays:			
234001	Renewable Energy Loan Guarantees	7	9	7
	Guaranteed loan reestimates:			
235001	Renewable Energy Loan Guarantees	–19	–20	

The Rural Energy for America Program was formerly the Renewable Energy Systems and Energy Efficiency Improvements Program. This program provides loan guarantees and grants to farmers, ranchers, and small rural businesses to purchase renewable energy systems and make energy efficiency improvements. This program is authorized pursuant to Section 9007 of the Farm Security and Rural Investment Act of 2002, as amended by the Food, Conservation and Energy Act of 2008, as amended by the American Taxpayer Relief Act of 2012; as amended by the Agricultural Act of 2014; and as amended by the Agriculture Improvement Act of 2018, 7 U.S.C. 8107.

The 2023 Budget requests $30 million to support grants and $18,000 to support loans for this program.

RURAL ENERGY FOR AMERICA GUARANTEED LOAN FINANCING ACCOUNT

Program and Financing (in millions of dollars)

Identification code 012–4267–0–3–451		2021 actual	2022 est.	2023 est.
	Obligations by program activity:			
	Credit program obligations:			
0742	Downward reestimates paid to receipt accounts	17	18	
0743	Interest on downward reestimates	2	2	
0900	Total new obligations, unexpired accounts	19	20	
	Budgetary resources:			
	Unobligated balance:			
1000	Unobligated balance brought forward, Oct 1	53	51	53
	Financing authority:			
	Spending authority from offsetting collections, mandatory:			
1800	Collected	12	21	21
1801	Change in uncollected payments, Federal sources	5	1	1
1850	Spending auth from offsetting collections, mand (total)	17	22	22
1930	Total budgetary resources available	70	73	75
	Memorandum (non-add) entries:			
1941	Unexpired unobligated balance, end of year	51	53	75
	Change in obligated balance:			
	Unpaid obligations:			
3000	Unpaid obligations, brought forward, Oct 1			18
3010	New obligations, unexpired accounts	19	20	
3020	Outlays (gross)	–19	–2	–2
3050	Unpaid obligations, end of year		18	16
	Uncollected payments:			
3060	Uncollected pymts, Fed sources, brought forward, Oct 1	–13	–18	–19

Rural Business-Cooperative Service—Continued
Federal Funds—Continued

RURAL ENERGY FOR AMERICA GUARANTEED LOAN FINANCING ACCOUNT—Continued

Program and Financing—Continued

Identification code 012–4267–0–3–451	2021 actual	2022 est.	2023 est.
3070 .... Change in uncollected pymts, Fed sources, unexpired	−5	−1	−1
3090 .... Uncollected pymts, Fed sources, end of year	−18	−19	−20
Memorandum (non-add) entries:			
3100 .... Obligated balance, start of year	−13	−18	−1
3200 .... Obligated balance, end of year	−18	−1	−4
Financing authority and disbursements, net:			
Mandatory:			
4090 .... Budget authority, gross	17	22	22
Financing disbursements:			
4110 .... Outlays, gross (total)	19	2	2
Offsets against gross financing authority and disbursements:			
Offsetting collections (collected) from:			
4120 .... Federal sources	−7	−9	−7
4122 .... Interest on uninvested funds	−1	−5	−6
4123 .... Guarantee fees	−4	−7	−8
4130 .... Offsets against gross budget authority and outlays (total)	−12	−21	−21
Additional offsets against financing authority only (total):			
4140 .... Change in uncollected pymts, Fed sources, unexpired	−5	−1	−1
4170 .... Outlays, net (mandatory)	7	−19	−19
4180 Budget authority, net (total)	....	....	....
4190 Outlays, net (total)	7	−19	−19

Status of Guaranteed Loans (in millions of dollars)

Identification code 012–4267–0–3–451	2021 actual	2022 est.	2023 est.
Position with respect to appropriations act limitation on commitments:			
2111 .... Guaranteed loan commitments from current-year authority	635	635	635
2150 .... Total guaranteed loan commitments	635	635	635
2199 Guaranteed amount of guaranteed loan commitments	513	513	513
Cumulative balance of guaranteed loans outstanding:			
2210 .... Outstanding, start of year	1,181	1,200	1,486
2231 .... Disbursements of new guaranteed loans	185	375	523
2251 .... Repayments and prepayments	−165	−87	−28
2261 .... Adjustments: Terminations for default that result in loans receivable	−1	−2	−2
2290 .... Outstanding, end of year	1,200	1,486	1,979
Memorandum:			
2299 .... Guaranteed amount of guaranteed loans outstanding, end of year	969	1,149	1,149
Addendum:			
Cumulative balance of defaulted guaranteed loans that result in loans receivable:			
2310 .... Outstanding, start of year	5	5	7
2331 .... Disbursements for guaranteed loan claims	....	2	2
2351 .... Loss Settlement	....	....	....
2390 .... Outstanding, end of year	5	7	9

This account finances loan guarantee commitments to farmers, ranchers, and small businesses to purchase renewable energy systems and make energy efficiency improvements in rural areas. The subsidy cost of this program is funded through the Rural Energy for American Program Account.

Balance Sheet (in millions of dollars)

Identification code 012–4267–0–3–451	2020 actual	2021 actual
ASSETS:		
1101 .... Federal assets: Fund balances with Treasury	35	28
Net value of assets related to post-1991 acquired defaulted guaranteed loans receivable:		
1501 .... Defaulted guaranteed loans receivable, gross	5	5
1505 .... Allowance for subsidy cost (-)	−1	−1
1599 .... Net present value of assets related to defaulted guaranteed loans	4	4
1999 Total assets	39	32
LIABILITIES:		
2103 .... Federal liabilities: Debt	1	1
2204 .... Non-Federal liabilities: Liability for loan guarnatees	38	31
2999 Total liabilities	39	32
NET POSITION:		
3300 .... Cumulative results of operations	....	....
4999 Total liabilities and net position	39	32

BIOREFINERY ASSISTANCE PROGRAM ACCOUNT

Program and Financing (in millions of dollars)

Identification code 012–3106–0–1–452	2021 actual	2022 est.	2023 est.
Obligations by program activity:			
Credit program obligations:			
0702 .... Loan guarantee subsidy	35	47	49
0707 .... Reestimates of loan guarantee subsidy	4	....	....
0708 .... Interest on reestimates of loan guarantee subsidy	1	....	....
0900 Total new obligations, unexpired accounts (object class 41.0)	40	47	49
Budgetary resources:			
Unobligated balance:			
1000 .... Unobligated balance brought forward, Oct 1	291	256	209
Budget authority:			
Appropriations, mandatory:			
1200 .... Appropriation	5	....	....
1900 .... Budget authority (total)	5	....	....
1930 Total budgetary resources available	296	256	209
Memorandum (non-add) entries:			
1941 .... Unexpired unobligated balance, end of year	256	209	160
Change in obligated balance:			
Unpaid obligations:			
3000 .... Unpaid obligations, brought forward, Oct 1	121	121	21
3010 .... New obligations, unexpired accounts	40	47	49
3020 .... Outlays (gross)	−40	−147	−70
3050 .... Unpaid obligations, end of year	121	21	....
Memorandum (non-add) entries:			
3100 .... Obligated balance, start of year	121	121	21
3200 .... Obligated balance, end of year	121	21	....
Budget authority and outlays, net:			
Mandatory:			
4090 .... Budget authority, gross	5	....	....
Outlays, gross:			
4100 .... Outlays from new mandatory authority	5	....	....
4101 .... Outlays from mandatory balances	35	147	70
4110 .... Outlays, gross (total)	40	147	70
4180 Budget authority, net (total)	5	....	....
4190 Outlays, net (total)	40	147	70

Summary of Loan Levels, Subsidy Budget Authority and Outlays by Program (in millions of dollars)

Identification code 012–3106–0–1–452	2021 actual	2022 est.	2023 est.
Guaranteed loan levels supportable by subsidy budget authority:			
215001 Section 9003 Loan Guarantees	105	144	150
Guaranteed loan subsidy (in percent):			
232001 Section 9003 Loan Guarantees	32.96	32.96	32.96
232999 Weighted average subsidy rate	32.96	32.96	32.96
Guaranteed loan subsidy budget authority:			
233001 Section 9003 Loan Guarantees	35	47	49
Guaranteed loan subsidy outlays:			
234001 Section 9003 Loan Guarantees	35	147	70
Guaranteed loan reestimates:			
235001 Section 9003 Loan Guarantees	−1	−8	....

The Biorefinery, Renewable Chemical, and Biobased Product Manufacturing Assistance Program, also known as the "Section 9003 Program", provides loan guarantees to assist in the development of advanced biofuels, renewable chemicals, and biobased products manufacturing facilities. The 2023 Budget does not request discretionary funding for this program because mandatory funding is provided through the 2018 Farm Bill. The Section 9003 Program is authorized under section 9003 of the Farm Security and Rural Investment Act of 2002; as amended by the Food, Conservation, and Energy Act of 2008, the American Taxpayers Relief Act of 2012, the Agricultural Act of 2014, and the Agriculture Improvement Act of 2018.

DEPARTMENT OF AGRICULTURE

Rural Utilities Service
Federal Funds   147

Loan assumptions reflect an illustrative example for informational purposes only. The assumptions will be determined at the time of execution and will reflect the actual terms and conditions of the loan guarantee contracts.

BIOREFINERY ASSISTANCE GUARANTEED LOAN FINANCING ACCOUNT

Program and Financing (in millions of dollars)

Identification code 012–4355–0–3–452	2021 actual	2022 est.	2023 est.
Obligations by program activity:			
Credit program obligations:			
0742 Downward reestimates paid to receipt accounts	5	8	
0743 Interest on downward reestimates	1		
0900 Total new obligations, unexpired accounts	6	8	
Budgetary resources:			
Unobligated balance:			
1000 Unobligated balance brought forward, Oct 1	165	203	258
Financing authority:			
Spending authority from offsetting collections, mandatory:			
1800 Collected	44	162	75
1801 Change in uncollected payments, Federal sources		–99	–21
1850 Spending auth from offsetting collections, mand (total)	44	63	54
1900 Budget authority (total)	44	63	54
1930 Total budgetary resources available	209	266	312
Memorandum (non-add) entries:			
1941 Unexpired unobligated balance, end of year	203	258	312
Change in obligated balance:			
Unpaid obligations:			
3000 Unpaid obligations, brought forward, Oct 1			8
3010 New obligations, unexpired accounts	6	8	
3020 Outlays (gross)	–6		
3050 Unpaid obligations, end of year		8	8
Uncollected payments:			
3060 Uncollected pymts, Fed sources, brought forward, Oct 1	–121	–121	–22
3070 Change in uncollected pymts, Fed sources, unexpired		99	21
3090 Uncollected pymts, Fed sources, end of year	–121	–22	–1
Memorandum (non-add) entries:			
3100 Obligated balance, start of year	–121	–121	–14
3200 Obligated balance, end of year	–121	–14	7
Financing authority and disbursements, net:			
Mandatory:			
4090 Budget authority, gross	44	63	54
Financing disbursements:			
4110 Outlays, gross (total)	6		
Offsets against gross financing authority and disbursements:			
Offsetting collections (collected) from:			
4120 Federal sources	–40	–147	–70
4122 Interest on uninvested funds	–2	–4	–1
4123 Guaranteed Fees	–2	–11	–4
4130 Offsets against gross budget authority and outlays (total)	–44	–162	–75
Additional offsets against financing authority only (total):			
4140 Change in uncollected pymts, Fed sources, unexpired		99	21
4170 Outlays, net (mandatory)	–38	–162	–75
4180 Budget authority, net (total)			
4190 Outlays, net (total)	–38	–162	–75

Status of Guaranteed Loans (in millions of dollars)

Identification code 012–4355–0–3–452	2021 actual	2022 est.	2023 est.
Position with respect to appropriations act limitation on commitments:			
2111 Guaranteed loan commitments from current-year authority			
2121 Limitation available from carry-forward	105	144	150
2150 Total guaranteed loan commitments	105	144	150
2199 Guaranteed amount of guaranteed loan commitments	94	130	135
Cumulative balance of guaranteed loans outstanding:			
2210 Outstanding, start of year	311	311	892
2231 Disbursements of new guaranteed loans	105	581	211
2251 Repayments and prepayments	–105		
Adjustments:			
2263 Terminations for default that result in claim payments			–1
2264 Other adjustments, net			
2290 Outstanding, end of year	311	892	1,102
Memorandum:			
2299 Guaranteed amount of guaranteed loans outstanding, end of year	248	713	882
Addendum:			
Cumulative balance of defaulted guaranteed loans that result in loans receivable:			
2310 Outstanding, start of year			
2331 Disbursements for guaranteed loan claims			
2351 Repayments of loans receivable			
2364 Other adjustments, net			
2390 Outstanding, end of year			

The account finances loan guarantee commitments for bioenergy, renewable chemical, and biobased product manufacturing development. The subsidy cost of this program is funded through the Biorefinery Assistance Program Account.

Balance Sheet (in millions of dollars)

Identification code 012–4355–0–3–452	2020 actual	2021 actual
ASSETS:		
1101 Federal assets: Fund balances with Treasury	43	82
Net value of assets related to post-1991 acquired defaulted guaranteed loans receivable:		
1501 Defaulted guaranteed loans receivable, gross		
1502 Interest receivable		
1505 Allowance for subsidy cost (–)		
1599 Net present value of assets related to defaulted guaranteed loans		
1999 Total assets	43	82
LIABILITIES:		
2103 Federal liabilities: Debt	5	5
Non-Federal liabilities:		
2203 Debt		
2204 Liabilities for loan guarantees	38	77
2999 Total liabilities	43	82
NET POSITION:		
3300 Cumulative results of operations		
4999 Total liabilities and net position	43	82

ALTERNATIVE AGRICULTURAL RESEARCH AND COMMERCIALIZATION CORPORATION REVOLVING FUND

Program and Financing (in millions of dollars)

Identification code 012–4144–0–3–352	2021 actual	2022 est.	2023 est.
Budgetary resources:			
Unobligated balance:			
1000 Unobligated balance brought forward, Oct 1	1	1	1
1001 Discretionary unobligated balance brought fwd, Oct 1		1	
1930 Total budgetary resources available	1	1	1
Memorandum (non-add) entries:			
1941 Unexpired unobligated balance, end of year	1	1	1
4180 Budget authority, net (total)			
4190 Outlays, net (total)			

RURAL UTILITIES SERVICE

Federal Funds

HIGH ENERGY COST GRANTS

Program and Financing (in millions of dollars)

Identification code 012–2042–0–1–452	2021 actual	2022 est.	2023 est.
Obligations by program activity:			
0001 High energy cost grants	3	19	11
0900 Total new obligations, unexpired accounts (object class 41.0)	3	19	11

High Energy Cost Grants—Continued
Program and Financing—Continued

Identification code 012–2042–0–1–452	2021 actual	2022 est.	2023 est.
Budgetary resources:			
Unobligated balance:			
1000 Unobligated balance brought forward, Oct 1	2	9	1
1001 Discretionary unobligated balance brought fwd, Oct 1		9	
1021 Recoveries of prior year unpaid obligations		1	1
1070 Unobligated balance (total)	2	10	2
Budget authority:			
Appropriations, discretionary:			
1121 Appropriations transferred from other acct [012–1980]	10	10	10
1930 Total budgetary resources available	12	20	12
Memorandum (non-add) entries:			
1941 Unexpired unobligated balance, end of year	9	1	1
Change in obligated balance:			
Unpaid obligations:			
3000 Unpaid obligations, brought forward, Oct 1	31	19	14
3010 New obligations, unexpired accounts	3	19	11
3020 Outlays (gross)	–15	–23	–15
3040 Recoveries of prior year unpaid obligations, unexpired		–1	–1
3050 Unpaid obligations, end of year	19	14	9
Memorandum (non-add) entries:			
3100 Obligated balance, start of year	31	19	14
3200 Obligated balance, end of year	19	14	9
Budget authority and outlays, net:			
Discretionary:			
4000 Budget authority, gross	10	10	10
Outlays, gross:			
4010 Outlays from new discretionary authority		6	6
4011 Outlays from discretionary balances	15	17	9
4020 Outlays, gross (total)	15	23	15
4180 Budget authority, net (total)	10	10	10
4190 Outlays, net (total)	15	23	15

High energy costs grants can be made to eligible entities or the Denali Commission to construct, extend, upgrade, and otherwise improve energy generation, transmission, or distribution facilities serving communities in which the average residential expenditure for home energy is at least 275 percent of the national average residential expenditure for home energy (as determined by the Energy Information Agency using the most recent data available). Grants are also available to establish and support a revolving fund to provide a more cost-effective means of purchasing fuel where the fuel cannot be shipped by means of surface transportation. The Budget proposes $10 million in 2023 for these grants. Funding will be targeted to encourage recipients to purchase technologies that reduce greenhouse gases.

RURAL WATER AND WASTE DISPOSAL PROGRAM ACCOUNT
(INCLUDING TRANSFERS OF FUNDS)

For gross obligations for the principal amount of direct and guaranteed loans as authorized by section 306 and described in section 381E(d)(2) of the Consolidated Farm and Rural Development Act, as follows: $1,540,000,000 for direct loans; and $50,000,000 for guaranteed loans.

For the cost of loan guarantees and grants, including the cost of modifying loans, as defined in section 502 of the Congressional Budget Act of 1974, for rural water, waste water, waste disposal, and solid waste management programs authorized by sections 306, 306A, 306C, 306D, 306E, and 310B and described in sections 306C(a)(2), 306D, 306E, and 381E(d)(2) of the Consolidated Farm and Rural Development Act, $726,557,000, to remain available until expended, of which not to exceed $1,000,000 shall be available for the rural utilities program described in section 306(a)(2)(B) of such Act, and of which not to exceed $5,000,000 shall be available for the rural utilities program described in section 306E of such Act: Provided, That not to exceed $15,000,000 of the amount appropriated under this heading shall be for grants authorized by section 306A(i)(2) of the Consolidated Farm and Rural Development Act in addition to funding authorized by section 306A(i)(1) of such Act: Provided further, That $93,000,000 of the amount appropriated under this heading shall be for loans and grants including water and waste disposal systems grants authorized by section 306C(a)(2)(B) and section 306D of the Consolidated Farm and Rural Development Act, and Federally Recognized Native American Tribes authorized by 306C(a)(1) of such Act, and the Department of Hawaiian Home Lands (of the State of Hawaii): Provided further, That funding provided for section 306D of the Consolidated Farm and Rural Development Act may be provided to a consortium formed pursuant to section 325 of Public Law 105–83: Provided further, That not more than 2 percent of the funding provided for section 306D of the Consolidated Farm and Rural Development Act may be used by the State of Alaska for training and technical assistance programs and not more than 2 percent of the funding provided for section 306D of the Consolidated Farm and Rural Development Act may be used by a consortium formed pursuant to section 325 of Public Law 105–83 for training and technical assistance programs: Provided further, That not to exceed $40,000,000 of the amount appropriated under this heading shall be for technical assistance grants for rural water and waste systems pursuant to section 306(a)(14) of such Act, unless the Secretary makes a determination of extreme need, of which $8,000,000 shall be made available for a grant to a qualified nonprofit multi-State regional technical assistance organization, with experience in working with small communities on water and waste water problems, the principal purpose of such grant shall be to assist rural communities with populations of 3,300 or less, in improving the planning, financing, development, operation, and management of water and waste water systems, and of which not less than $800,000 shall be for a qualified national Native American organization to provide technical assistance for rural water systems for tribal communities: Provided further, That not to exceed $20,157,000 of the amount appropriated under this heading shall be for contracting with qualified national organizations for a circuit rider program to provide technical assistance for rural water systems: Provided further, That not to exceed $4,000,000 of the amounts made available under this heading shall be for solid waste management grants: Provided further, That, notwithstanding any other provision of law, not to exceed $100,000,000 of the amount appropriated under this heading shall be available as the Secretary deems appropriate for grants authorized by section 306C(a)(1)(A) of the Consolidated Farm and Rural Development Act for the purpose of replacement of lead service lines: Provided further, That if any funds made available pursuant to the previous proviso remain unobligated after July 31, 2023, such unobligated balances may be used for grant programs funded under this heading: Provided further, That not to exceed $26,499,000 of the amounts appropriated under this heading shall be available as the Secretary deems appropriate for water and waste direct one percent and zero percent loans for distressed communities: Provided further, That if the Secretary determines that any portion of the amount made available for one percent and zero percent loans is not needed for such loans, the Secretary may use such amounts for grants authorized by section 306(a)(2) of the Consolidated Farm and Rural Development Act: Provided further, That if any funds made available for the direct loan subsidy costs remain unobligated after July 31, 2023, such unobligated balances may be used for grant programs funded under this heading: Provided further, That $10,000,000 of the amount appropriated under this heading shall be transferred to, and merged with, the Rural Utilities Service, High Energy Cost Grants Account to provide grants authorized under section 19 of the Rural Electrification Act of 1936 (7 U.S.C. 918a): Provided further, That any prior year balances for high-energy cost grants authorized by section 19 of the Rural Electrification Act of 1936 (7 U.S.C. 918a) shall be transferred to and merged with the Rural Utilities Service, High Energy Cost Grants Account: Provided further, That sections 381E-H and 381N of the Consolidated Farm and Rural Development Act are not applicable to the funds made available under this heading.

Note.—A full-year 2022 appropriation for this account was not enacted at the time the Budget was prepared; therefore, the Budget assumes this account is operating under the Continuing Appropriations Act, 2022 (Division A of Public Law 117-43, as amended). The amounts included for 2022 reflect the annualized level provided by the continuing resolution.

Program and Financing (in millions of dollars)

Identification code 012–1980–0–1–452	2021 actual	2022 est.	2023 est.
Obligations by program activity:			
0010 Water and waste disposal systems grants	667	613	726
0011 Water and waste disposal systems grants supplemental	64	65	30
0012 Solid waste management grants	4	4	4
0015 Emergency Community Water Assistance Grants	14	16	15
0017 771 Water and Waste Pilot Program Grants		9	1
0091 Direct program activities, subtotal	749	707	776
Credit program obligations:			
0701 Direct loan subsidy			27
0705 Reestimates of direct loan subsidy	7	168	
0706 Interest on reestimates of direct loan subsidy	1	137	
0791 Direct program activities, subtotal	8	305	27
0900 Total new obligations, unexpired accounts (object class 41.0)	757	1,012	803

DEPARTMENT OF AGRICULTURE

Rural Utilities Service—Continued
Federal Funds—Continued   149

		2021 actual	2022 est.	2023 est.
	Budgetary resources:			
	Unobligated balance:			
1000	Unobligated balance brought forward, Oct 1	197	144	111
1021	Recoveries of prior year unpaid obligations	79	56	49
1070	Unobligated balance (total)	276	200	160
	Budget authority:			
	Appropriations, discretionary:			
1100	Appropriation	627	627	727
1120	Appropriations transferred to other accts [012–2042]	–10	–10	–10
1160	Appropriation, discretionary (total)	617	617	717
	Appropriations, mandatory:			
1200	Appropriation	8	306	....
1900	Budget authority (total)	625	923	717
1930	Total budgetary resources available	901	1,123	877
	Memorandum (non-add) entries:			
1941	Unexpired unobligated balance, end of year	144	111	74
	Change in obligated balance:			
	Unpaid obligations:			
3000	Unpaid obligations, brought forward, Oct 1	2,755	2,872	2,714
3010	New obligations, unexpired accounts	757	1,012	803
3020	Outlays (gross)	–561	–1,114	–800
3040	Recoveries of prior year unpaid obligations, unexpired	–79	–56	–49
3050	Unpaid obligations, end of year	2,872	2,714	2,668
	Memorandum (non-add) entries:			
3100	Obligated balance, start of year	2,755	2,872	2,714
3200	Obligated balance, end of year	2,872	2,714	2,668
	Budget authority and outlays, net:			
	Discretionary:			
4000	Budget authority, gross	617	617	717
	Outlays, gross:			
4010	Outlays from new discretionary authority	13	24	22
4011	Outlays from discretionary balances	540	783	776
4020	Outlays, gross (total)	553	807	798
	Mandatory:			
4090	Budget authority, gross	8	306	....
	Outlays, gross:			
4100	Outlays from new mandatory authority	8	306	....
4101	Outlays from mandatory balances	....	1	2
4110	Outlays, gross (total)	8	307	2
4180	Budget authority, net (total)	625	923	717
4190	Outlays, net (total)	561	1,114	800

Summary of Loan Levels, Subsidy Budget Authority and Outlays by Program (in millions of dollars)

Identification code 012–1980–0–1–452	2021 actual	2022 est.	2023 est.
Direct loan levels supportable by subsidy budget authority:			
115001 Water and Waste Disposal Loans	1,400	1,400	1,400
115005 Water and Waste Zero	....	....	70
115006 Water and Waste 1%	....	....	70
115999 Total direct loan levels	1,400	1,400	1,540
Direct loan subsidy (in percent):			
132001 Water and Waste Disposal Loans	–1.53	–5.16	–2.19
132005 Water and Waste Zero			24.23
132006 Water and Waste 1%			13.62
132999 Weighted average subsidy rate	–1.53	–5.16	–.27
Direct loan subsidy budget authority:			
133001 Water and Waste Disposal Loans	–21	–72	–31
133005 Water and Waste Zero			17
133006 Water and Waste 1%			10
133999 Total subsidy budget authority	–21	–72	–4
Direct loan subsidy outlays:			
134001 Water and Waste Disposal Loans	17	28	21
134006 Water and Waste 1%			1
134999 Total subsidy outlays	17	28	22
Direct loan reestimates:			
135001 Water and Waste Disposal Loans	–867	226	....
135999 Total direct loan reestimates	–867	226	....
Guaranteed loan levels supportable by subsidy budget authority:			
215001 Water and Waste Disposal Loan Guarantees	35	35	50
Guaranteed loan subsidy (in percent):			
232001 Water and Waste Disposal Loan Guarantees	0.12	0.09	–.02
232999 Weighted average subsidy rate	0.12	0.09	–.02

This account funds the direct and guaranteed water and waste disposal loans, water and waste disposal grants, emergency community water assistance grants, and solid waste management grants.

Water and waste disposal loans are authorized under 7 U.S.C. 1926. The program provides direct loans to municipalities, counties, special purpose districts, certain Indian Tribes, and non-profit corporations to develop water and waste disposal systems in rural areas and towns with populations of less than 20,000. The program also guarantees water and waste disposal loans made by banks and other eligible lenders.

Water and waste disposal grants are authorized under Section 306(a)(2) of the Consolidated Farm and Rural Development Act, as amended. Grants are authorized to be made to associations, including nonprofit corporations, municipalities, counties, public and quasi-public agencies, and certain Indian tribes. The grants can be used to finance development, storage, treatment, purification, or distribution of water or the collection, treatment, or disposal of waste in rural areas and cities or towns with populations of less than 10,000. The amount of any development grant may not exceed 75 percent of the eligible development cost of the project.

Emergency community water assistance grants are authorized under Section 306A of the Consolidated Farm and Rural Development Act, as amended. Grants are made to public bodies and nonprofit organizations for construction or extension of water lines, repair or maintenance of existing systems, replacement of equipment, and payment of costs to correct emergency situations. These grants are funded on an as needed basis using flexibility of funds authority.

Solid waste management grants are authorized under Section 310B(b) of the Consolidated Farm and Rural Development Act, as amended. Grants are made to non-profit organizations to provide regional technical assistance to local and regional governments and related agencies for the purpose of reducing or eliminating pollution of water resources, and for improving the planning and management of solid waste disposal facilities.

The 2023 Budget requests $1.54 billion in direct loans, $50 million in guaranteed loans, and $700 million in grants, which is $78.5 million over the 2021 enacted level. The increase will add $20 million to grants targeted to Colonias, Native Americans and Alaskan Native Villages and $48.5 million for regular grants targeted to rural, poor communities. The budget proposes to authorize one percent and zero percent borrower's interest rate direct loans for distressed communities. To support this effort, the budget allocates up to $26.5 million of the funding for this program. This is expected to fund $140 million in loans, $70 million for each risk category. The budget also authorizes up to $100 million of water and waste grant funds be to support replacing lead piping in rural areas. These two new funding options will be available until July 31, 2023, at which time any unused BA will revert back to the regular grant program.

As required by the Federal Credit Reform Act of 1990, this account records for this program the subsidy costs associated with the direct loans obligated and loan guarantees committed in 1992 and beyond (including credit sales of acquired property). The subsidy amounts are estimated on a present value basis.

RURAL WATER AND WASTE DISPOSAL DIRECT LOANS FINANCING ACCOUNT

Program and Financing (in millions of dollars)

Identification code 012–4226–0–3–452	2021 actual	2022 est.	2023 est.
Obligations by program activity:			
Credit program obligations:			
0710 Direct loan obligations	1,400	1,400	1,540
0713 Payment of interest to Treasury	498	553	553
0740 Negative subsidy obligations	21	72	31
0742 Downward reestimates paid to receipt accounts	528	78	....
0743 Interest on downward reestimates	347	2	....
0900 Total new obligations, unexpired accounts	2,794	2,105	2,124

Rural Utilities Service—Continued
Federal Funds—Continued

RURAL WATER AND WASTE DISPOSAL DIRECT LOANS FINANCING ACCOUNT—Continued

Program and Financing—Continued

Identification code 012–4226–0–3–452	2021 actual	2022 est.	2023 est.
Budgetary resources:			
Unobligated balance:			
1000 Unobligated balance brought forward, Oct 1	987	871	1,668
1021 Recoveries of prior year unpaid obligations	222		
1023 Unobligated balances applied to repay debt	–977	–871	–1,668
1024 Unobligated balance of borrowing authority withdrawn	–218		
1070 Unobligated balance (total)	14		
Financing authority:			
Borrowing authority, mandatory:			
1400 Borrowing authority	1,902	1,953	1,953
Spending authority from offsetting collections, mandatory:			
1800 Collected	1,771	1,845	1,536
1801 Change in uncollected payments, Federal sources	–22	–25	–25
1850 Spending auth from offsetting collections, mand (total)	1,749	1,820	1,511
1900 Budget authority (total)	3,651	3,773	3,464
1930 Total budgetary resources available	3,665	3,773	3,464
Memorandum (non-add) entries:			
1941 Unexpired unobligated balance, end of year	871	1,668	1,340
Change in obligated balance:			
Unpaid obligations:			
3000 Unpaid obligations, brought forward, Oct 1	4,790	4,967	4,960
3010 New obligations, unexpired accounts	2,794	2,105	2,124
3020 Outlays (gross)	–2,395	–2,112	–1,660
3040 Recoveries of prior year unpaid obligations, unexpired	–222		
3050 Unpaid obligations, end of year	4,967	4,960	5,424
Uncollected payments:			
3060 Uncollected pymts, Fed sources, brought forward, Oct 1	–101	–79	–54
3070 Change in uncollected pymts, Fed sources, unexpired	22	25	25
3090 Uncollected pymts, Fed sources, end of year	–79	–54	–29
Memorandum (non-add) entries:			
3100 Obligated balance, start of year	4,689	4,888	4,906
3200 Obligated balance, end of year	4,888	4,906	5,395
Financing authority and disbursements, net:			
Mandatory:			
4090 Budget authority, gross	3,651	3,773	3,464
Financing disbursements:			
4110 Outlays, gross (total)	2,395	2,112	1,660
Offsets against gross financing authority and disbursements:			
Offsetting collections (collected) from:			
4120 Federal sources	–26	–335	–22
4122 Interest on uninvested funds	–40	–69	–71
4123 Repayment of principal	–1,705	–915	–917
4123 Interest Received on Loans		–526	–526
4130 Offsets against gross budget authority and outlays (total)	–1,771	–1,845	–1,536
Additional offsets against financing authority only (total):			
4140 Change in uncollected pymts, Fed sources, unexpired	22	25	25
4160 Budget authority, net (mandatory)	1,902	1,953	1,953
4170 Outlays, net (mandatory)	624	267	124
4180 Budget authority, net (total)	1,902	1,953	1,953
4190 Outlays, net (total)	624	267	124

Status of Direct Loans (in millions of dollars)

Identification code 012–4226–0–3–452	2021 actual	2022 est.	2023 est.
Position with respect to appropriations act limitation on obligations:			
1111 Direct loan obligations from current-year authority	1,400	1,400	1,540
1150 Total direct loan obligations	1,400	1,400	1,540
Cumulative balance of direct loans outstanding:			
1210 Outstanding, start of year	13,204	12,897	13,830
1231 Disbursements: Direct loan disbursements	1,022	1,740	1,650
1251 Repayments: Repayments and prepayments	–1,342	–809	–868
1261 Adjustments: Capitalized interest		5	5
1263 Write-offs for default: Direct loans		–3	–3
1264 Other adjustments, net (+ or -)	13		
1290 Outstanding, end of year	12,897	13,830	14,614

The subsidy cost of these loans is provided through the Rural Water and Waste Disposal Program Account. Loans made prior to 1992 are recorded in the Rural Development Insurance Fund Liquidating Account.

Balance Sheet (in millions of dollars)

Identification code 012–4226–0–3–452	2020 actual	2021 actual
ASSETS:		
Federal assets:		
1101 Fund balances with Treasury	987	871
Investments in U.S. securities:		
1106 Receivables, net	8	306
Net value of assets related to post-1991 direct loans receivable:		
1401 Direct loans receivable, gross	13,204	12,897
1402 Interest receivable	88	87
1404 Foreclosed property	1	
1405 Allowance for subsidy cost (-)	589	429
1499 Net present value of assets related to direct loans	13,882	13,413
1999 Total assets	14,877	14,590
LIABILITIES:		
Federal liabilities:		
2103 Debt	14,002	14,510
2105 Other	875	80
2999 Total liabilities	14,877	14,590
NET POSITION:		
3300 Cumulative results of operations		
4999 Total liabilities and net position	14,877	14,590

RURAL WATER AND WASTE WATER DISPOSAL GUARANTEED LOANS FINANCING ACCOUNT

Program and Financing (in millions of dollars)

Identification code 012–4218–0–3–452	2021 actual	2022 est.	2023 est.
Budgetary resources:			
Unobligated balance:			
1000 Unobligated balance brought forward, Oct 1	5	5	5
1930 Total budgetary resources available	5	5	5
Memorandum (non-add) entries:			
1941 Unexpired unobligated balance, end of year	5	5	5
4180 Budget authority, net (total)			
4190 Outlays, net (total)			

Status of Guaranteed Loans (in millions of dollars)

Identification code 012–4218–0–3–452	2021 actual	2022 est.	2023 est.
Position with respect to appropriations act limitation on commitments:			
2111 Guaranteed loan commitments from current-year authority	35	35	50
2121 Limitation available from carry-forward			
2150 Total guaranteed loan commitments	35	35	50
2199 Guaranteed amount of guaranteed loan commitments	31	31	45
Cumulative balance of guaranteed loans outstanding:			
2210 Outstanding, start of year	94	108	131
2231 Disbursements of new guaranteed loans	20	32	32
2251 Repayments and prepayments	–6	–9	–9
2290 Outstanding, end of year	108	131	154
Memorandum:			
2299 Guaranteed amount of guaranteed loans outstanding, end of year	95	116	116

This account finances loan guarantee commitments for water systems and waste disposal facilities in rural areas.

Loans made prior to 1992 are recorded in the Rural Development Insurance Fund Liquidating Account.

Balance Sheet (in millions of dollars)

Identification code 012–4218–0–3–452	2020 actual	2021 actual
ASSETS:		
1101 Federal assets: Fund balances with Treasury	1	1
1999 Total assets	1	1
LIABILITIES:		
2105 Federal liabilities: Other		
2204 Non-Federal liabilities: Liabilities for loan guarantees	1	1

2999	Total liabilities	1	1
4999	Total liabilities and net position	1	1

Rural Electrification and Telecommunications Loans Program Account

(INCLUDING TRANSFER OF FUNDS)

The principal amount of loans as authorized by sections 4, 305, 306 and 317 of the Rural Electrification Act of 1936 (7 U.S.C. 904, 935, 936, and 940g) shall be made as follows: loans made pursuant to section 306, guaranteed rural electric loans, $2,167,000,000; loans made pursuant to sections 4, notwithstanding 4(c)(2), of that Act, and 317, notwithstanding 317(c), of that Act, cost-of-money direct loans, $4,333,000,000; and for loans made pursuant to section 305(d)(2) of that Act, cost of money rural telecommunications loans, $690,000,000.

For the cost of direct loans as authorized by section 305(d)(2) of the Rural Electrification Act of 1936 (7 U.S.C. 935(d)(2)), including the cost of modifying loans, as defined in section 502 of the Congressional Budget Act of 1974, cost of money rural telecommunications loans, $3,726,000.

For the cost of grants and loan modifications, as defined in section 502 of the Congressional Budget Act of 1974, including any associated penalties, for transitioning to pollution free electricity, $300,000,000, of which up to five percent can be used for administrative costs to carry out the program.

For the cost of modifications, as defined in section 502 of the Congressional Budget Act of 1974, for the direct rural telecommunication loans, $25,000,000.

In addition, $26,340,000, to remain available until expended, to carry out section 6407 of the Farm Security and Rural Investment Act of 2002 (7 U.S.C. 8107a): Provided, That the energy efficiency measures supported by the funding in this paragraph shall contribute in a demonstrable way to the reduction of greenhouse gases.

In addition, $15,000,000, to remain available until expended, for technical assistance to support the effective implementation of clean energy funding in rural areas, including coordination with the Department of Energy and the Department of the Interior.

In addition, for administrative expenses necessary to carry out the direct and guaranteed loan programs, $33,270,000, which shall be paid to the appropriation for "Rural Development, Salaries and Expenses".

Note.—A full-year 2022 appropriation for this account was not enacted at the time the Budget was prepared; therefore, the Budget assumes this account is operating under the Continuing Appropriations Act, 2022 (Division A of Public Law 117–43, as amended). The amounts included for 2022 reflect the annualized level provided by the continuing resolution.

Program and Financing (in millions of dollars)

Identification code 012–1230–0–1–271		2021 actual	2022 est.	2023 est.
	Obligations by program activity:			
0010	Clean Energy Technical Assistance Grants			9
	Credit program obligations:			
0701	Direct loan subsidy	4	2	22
0703	Subsidy for modifications of direct loans			285
0703	Subsidy for modifications of direct loans			25
0705	Reestimates of direct loan subsidy	813	486	
0706	Interest on reestimates of direct loan subsidy	560	95	
0709	Administrative expenses	33	33	33
0709	Administrative expenses			15
0791	Direct program activities, subtotal	1,410	616	380
0900	Total new obligations, unexpired accounts	1,410	616	389
	Budgetary resources:			
	Unobligated balance:			
1000	Unobligated balance brought forward, Oct 1	14	22	33
1001	Discretionary unobligated balance brought fwd, Oct 1	14	22	
	Budget authority:			
	Appropriations, discretionary:			
1100	Appropriation	47	46	403
	Appropriations, mandatory:			
1200	Appropriation	1,373	581	
1900	Budget authority (total)	1,420	627	403
1930	Total budgetary resources available	1,434	649	436
	Memorandum (non-add) entries:			
1940	Unobligated balance expiring	–2		
1941	Unexpired unobligated balance, end of year	22	33	47
	Change in obligated balance:			
	Unpaid obligations:			
3000	Unpaid obligations, brought forward, Oct 1	31	34	14
3010	New obligations, unexpired accounts	1,410	616	389
3020	Outlays (gross)	–1,407	–636	–378
3050	Unpaid obligations, end of year	34	14	25
	Memorandum (non-add) entries:			
3100	Obligated balance, start of year	31	34	14
3200	Obligated balance, end of year	34	14	25
	Budget authority and outlays, net:			
	Discretionary:			
4000	Budget authority, gross	47	46	403
	Outlays, gross:			
4010	Outlays from new discretionary authority	33	34	366
4011	Outlays from discretionary balances	1	21	12
4020	Outlays, gross (total)	34	55	378
	Mandatory:			
4090	Budget authority, gross	1,373	581	
	Outlays, gross:			
4100	Outlays from new mandatory authority	1,373	581	
4180	Budget authority, net (total)	1,420	627	403
4190	Outlays, net (total)	1,407	636	378

Summary of Loan Levels, Subsidy Budget Authority and Outlays by Program (in millions of dollars)

Identification code 012–1230–0–1–271		2021 actual	2022 est.	2023 est.
	Direct loan levels supportable by subsidy budget authority:			
115003	Treasury Electric Loans			3,800
115004	FFB Electric Loans	4,311	4,800	2,167
115006	Treasury Telecommunications Loans	69	69	194
115007	FFB Telecommunications Loans	2	18	
115008	FFB Guaranteed Underwriting	750	750	
115012	Rural Energy Savings Program	32	32	203
115014	Consumer Oriented Operating Loans	101		
115999	Total direct loan levels	5,265	5,669	6,364
	Direct loan subsidy (in percent):			
132003	Treasury Electric Loans			–2.96
132004	FFB Electric Loans	–4.97	–7.20	–5.87
132006	Treasury Telecommunications Loans	0.66	0.30	0.54
132007	FFB Telecommunications Loans	–3.19	–4.04	
132008	FFB Guaranteed Underwriting	–.57	–.64	
132012	Rural Energy Savings Program	10.25	5.52	10.37
132014	Consumer Oriented Operating Loans	–2.21		
132999	Weighted average subsidy rate	–4.12	–6.16	–3.42
	Direct loan subsidy budget authority:			
133003	Treasury Electric Loans			–112
133004	FFB Electric Loans	–214	–346	–127
133006	Treasury Telecommunications Loans			1
133007	FFB Telecommunications Loans		–1	
133008	FFB Guaranteed Underwriting	–4	–5	
133012	Rural Energy Savings Program	3	2	21
133014	Consumer Oriented Operating Loans	–2		
133999	Total subsidy budget authority	–217	–350	–217
	Direct loan subsidy outlays:			
134003	Treasury Electric Loans			–82
134004	FFB Electric Loans	–163	–170	–87
134006	Treasury Telecommunications Loans		1	1
134007	FFB Telecommunications Loans		–1	–1
134008	FFB Guaranteed Underwriting	–12	–6	–7
134011	Electric Loan Modifications			285
134012	Rural Energy Savings Program		2	10
134013	Electric Loan Modifications Pilot			25
134014	Consumer Oriented Operating Loans	–2		
134999	Total subsidy outlays	–177	–174	144
	Direct loan reestimates:			
135002	Municipal Electric Loans	4	14	
135003	Treasury Electric Loans	2	8	
135004	FFB Electric Loans	816	–255	
135005	Telecommunication Hardship Loans	3	12	
135006	Treasury Telecommunications Loans	53	16	
135007	FFB Telecommunications Loans	14	6	
135008	FFB Guaranteed Underwriting	127	–378	
135011	Electric Loan Modifications	67	40	
135013	Electric Loan Modifications Pilot	–4		
135999	Total direct loan reestimates	1,082	–537	
	Administrative expense data:			
3510	Budget authority	33	33	33
3590	Outlays from new authority	33	33	33

RURAL ELECTRIFICATION AND TELECOMMUNICATIONS LOANS PROGRAM ACCOUNT—Continued

The Rural Utilities Service (RUS) conducts the rural electrification and the rural telecommunications loan programs. The rural electrification loan program finances the construction and operation of generating facilities, electric transmission and distribution lines, or system improvements. The rural telecommunications loan program provides funding for construction, expansion, and operation of telecommunications lines and facilities or systems. The Budget requests $4.3 billion for rural electric cost-of-money direct loans and $2.2 billion for guaranteed rural electric loans. Together, these investments will support $6.5 billion, $1 billion above the 2021 enacted level for additional clean energy, energy storage, and transmission projects. The 2023 Budget also includes $300 million for grants and rural electric loan modifications to help rural electric borrowers accelerate the transition to carbon pollution free electricity by 2035 and support good jobs. The Budget includes $15 million in technical assistance for the Rural Clean Energy Initiative, which will support the effective implementation of clean energy alternatives in rural areas, including coordination with the Department of Energy and the Department of Interior regarding their programs and permitting rules.

For telecommunications cost-of-money direct loans, the Budget requests $690 million to support the expanded deployment of broadband in rural areas. The Budget also includes $25 million to refinance high interest telecommunications debt and support rural providers that want to upgrade to their systems.

For administrative costs, the 2023 Budget requests $33.3 million.

Funding provided by this account for coal-fueled electricity generating plants shall only be used for construction, acquisition, design, engineering, or improvement of plants that contribute in a demonstrable way to the reduction of carbon and greenhouse gases, consistent with achieving a carbon pollution free power sector by 2035 and creating good paying jobs.

As required by the Federal Credit Reform Act of 1990, this account records for the rural electrification and telecommunications programs the subsidy costs associated with the direct and guaranteed loans obligated in 1992 and beyond (including modifications of direct loans or loan guarantees that resulted from obligations or commitments in any year), and the administrative expenses of this program. The subsidy amounts are estimated on a present value basis; the administrative expenses are estimated on a cash basis.

Object Classification (in millions of dollars)

Identification code 012–1230–0–1–271		2021 actual	2022 est.	2023 est.
	Direct obligations:			
25.3	Other goods and services from Federal sources	33	33	33
41.0	Grants, subsidies, and contributions	1,377	583	356
99.9	Total new obligations, unexpired accounts	1,410	616	389

RURAL ELECTRIFICATION AND TELECOMMUNICATIONS DIRECT LOAN FINANCING ACCOUNT

Program and Financing (in millions of dollars)

Identification code 012–4208–0–3–271		2021 actual	2022 est.	2023 est.
	Obligations by program activity:			
0003	Interest on FFB Loans	1,391	1,735	1,735
	Credit program obligations:			
0710	Direct loan obligations	5,164	5,669	6,364
0710	Direct loan obligations	101		
0713	Payment of interest to Treasury	239	653	653
0740	Negative subsidy obligations	221	352	240
0741	Modification savings	4		
0742	Downward reestimates paid to receipt accounts	255	565	
0743	Interest on downward reestimates	36	554	
0791	Direct program activities, subtotal	6,020	7,793	7,257
0900	Total new obligations, unexpired accounts	7,411	9,528	8,992
	Budgetary resources:			
	Unobligated balance:			
1000	Unobligated balance brought forward, Oct 1	3,571	4,084	
1021	Recoveries of prior year unpaid obligations	140		
1023	Unobligated balances applied to repay debt	–903	–4,084	
1024	Unobligated balance of borrowing authority withdrawn	–140		
1070	Unobligated balance (total)	2,668		
	Financing authority:			
	Appropriations, mandatory:			
1200	Appropriation		3	
1236	Appropriations applied to repay debt		–3	
	Borrowing authority, mandatory:			
1400	Borrowing authority	5,501	4,799	4,526
	Spending authority from offsetting collections, mandatory:			
1800	Collected	5,180	4,722	4,459
1801	Change in uncollected payments, Federal sources		7	7
1825	Spending authority from offsetting collections applied to repay debt	–1,854		
1850	Spending auth from offsetting collections, mand (total)	3,326	4,729	4,466
1900	Budget authority (total)	8,827	9,528	8,992
1930	Total budgetary resources available	11,495	9,528	8,992
	Memorandum (non-add) entries:			
1941	Unexpired unobligated balance, end of year	4,084		
	Change in obligated balance:			
	Unpaid obligations:			
3000	Unpaid obligations, brought forward, Oct 1	14,814	15,743	15,249
3010	New obligations, unexpired accounts	7,411	9,528	8,992
3020	Outlays (gross)	–6,342	–10,022	–10,022
3040	Recoveries of prior year unpaid obligations, unexpired	–140		
3050	Unpaid obligations, end of year	15,743	15,249	14,219
	Uncollected payments:			
3060	Uncollected pymts, Fed sources, brought forward, Oct 1	–34	–34	–41
3070	Change in uncollected pymts, Fed sources, unexpired		–7	–7
3090	Uncollected pymts, Fed sources, end of year	–34	–41	–48
	Memorandum (non-add) entries:			
3100	Obligated balance, start of year	14,780	15,709	15,208
3200	Obligated balance, end of year	15,709	15,208	14,171
	Financing authority and disbursements, net:			
	Mandatory:			
4090	Budget authority, gross	8,827	9,528	8,992
	Financing disbursements:			
4110	Outlays, gross (total)	6,342	10,022	10,022
	Offsets against gross financing authority and disbursements:			
	Offsetting collections (collected) from:			
4120	Payment from program account	–1,374	–584	–321
4122	Interest on uninvested funds	–242	–259	–259
4123	Repayment of principal	–2,153	–2,514	–2,514
4123	Interest received on loans	–1,341	–1,106	–1,106
4123	Repayment of principal Cushion of Credit		–111	–111
4123	Repayment of interest Cushion of Credit		–148	–148
4123	Other Actual Business Type Collections Non-Federal sources	–70		
4130	Offsets against gross budget authority and outlays (total)	–5,180	–4,722	–4,459
	Additional offsets against financing authority only (total):			
4140	Change in uncollected pymts, Fed sources, unexpired		–7	–7
4160	Budget authority, net (mandatory)	3,647	4,799	4,526
4170	Outlays, net (mandatory)	1,162	5,300	5,563
4180	Budget authority, net (total)	3,647	4,799	4,526
4190	Outlays, net (total)	1,162	5,300	5,563

Status of Direct Loans (in millions of dollars)

Identification code 012–4208–0–3–271		2021 actual	2022 est.	2023 est.
	Position with respect to appropriations act limitation on obligations:			
1111	Direct loan obligations from current-year authority	5,265	5,669	6,364
1150	Total direct loan obligations	5,265	5,669	6,364
	Cumulative balance of direct loans outstanding:			
1210	Outstanding, start of year	49,204	51,310	54,118
1231	Disbursements: Direct loan disbursements	4,244	6,184	6,754
	Repayments:			
1251	Repayments and prepayments - Cash	–1,793	–2,706	–2,827
1251	Repayments and prepayments - CoC	–359	–676	–819
1261	Adjustments: Capitalized interest	11	7	
1263	Write-offs for default: Direct loans	–7	–1	
1264	Other adjustments, Reclassified, net	10		

DEPARTMENT OF AGRICULTURE

1290	Outstanding, end of year	51,310	54,118	57,226

Balance Sheet (in millions of dollars)

Identification code 012–4208–0–3–271		2020 actual	2021 actual
	ASSETS:		
	Federal assets:		
1101	Fund balances with Treasury	3,173	3,809
	Investments in U.S. securities:		
1106	Receivables, net	1,674	971
	Net value of assets related to post-1991 direct loans receivable:		
1401	Direct loans receivable, gross	47,011	49,235
1402	Interest receivable	27	30
1405	Allowance for subsidy cost (–)	–1,169	–1,171
1499	Net present value of assets related to direct loans	45,869	48,094
1999	Total assets	50,716	52,874
	LIABILITIES:		
	Federal liabilities:		
2102	Interest payable	26	30
2103	Debt	4,831	4,493
2103	FFB	45,582	47,899
2105	Other	255	452
2207	Non-Federal liabilities: Other		
2999	Total liabilities	50,694	52,874
	NET POSITION:		
3300	Cumulative results of operations	22	
4999	Total liabilities and net position	50,716	52,874
	ASSETS:		
	Federal assets:		
1101	Fund balances with Treasury	398	290
	Investments in U.S. securities:		
1106	Receivables, net	65	20
	Net value of assets related to post-1991 direct loans receivable:		
1401	Direct loans receivable, gross	2,193	2,075
1402	Interest receivable		1
1405	Allowance for subsidy cost (–)	20	–9
1499	Net present value of assets related to direct loans	2,213	2,067
1999	Total assets	2,676	2,377
	LIABILITIES:		
	Federal liabilities:		
2102	Interest payable		
2103	Debt	1,848	1,608
2103	FFB	816	766
2105	Other	12	3
2207	Non-Federal liabilities: Other		
2999	Total liabilities	2,676	2,377
4999	Total liabilities and net position	2,676	2,377

RURAL ELECTRIFICATION AND TELECOMMUNICATIONS GUARANTEED LOANS FINANCING ACCOUNT

Status of Guaranteed Loans (in millions of dollars)

Identification code 012–4209–0–3–271		2021 actual	2022 est.	2023 est.
	Cumulative balance of guaranteed loans outstanding:			
2210	Outstanding, start of year	147	139	135
2251	Repayments and prepayments	–8	–4	–4
2290	Outstanding, end of year	139	135	131
	Memorandum:			
2299	Guaranteed amount of guaranteed loans outstanding, end of year	139	135	131

RURAL ELECTRIFICATION AND TELECOMMUNICATIONS LIQUIDATING ACCOUNT

Program and Financing (in millions of dollars)

Identification code 012–4230–0–3–999		2021 actual	2022 est.	2023 est.
	Obligations by program activity:			
0002	Interest Expense, FFB direct	7	5	5
0005	Other: cushion of credit	46		
0091	Direct program activities, subtotal	53	5	5
	Credit program obligations:			
0739	CoC for Financing	599	259	259
0791	Direct program activities, subtotal	599	259	259
0900	Total new obligations, unexpired accounts	652	264	264
	Budgetary resources:			
	Unobligated balance:			
1000	Unobligated balance brought forward, Oct 1	1,853	1,161	1,037
1022	Capital transfer of unobligated balances to general fund	–51	–15	–15
1023	Unobligated balances applied to repay debt	–135		
1070	Unobligated balance (total)	1,667	1,146	1,022
	Budget authority:			
	Appropriations, mandatory:			
1200	Appropriation for CoC Borrower Interest	67	140	15
1200	Appropriation for RED Grants	48		
1260	Appropriations, mandatory (total)	115	140	15
	Spending authority from offsetting collections, mandatory:			
1800	Collected	74	40	25
1825	Spending authority from offsetting collections applied to repay debt	–43	–25	
1850	Spending auth from offsetting collections, mand (total)	31	15	25
1900	Budget authority (total)	146	155	40
1930	Total budgetary resources available	1,813	1,301	1,062
	Memorandum (non-add) entries:			
1941	Unexpired unobligated balance, end of year	1,161	1,037	798
	Change in obligated balance:			
	Unpaid obligations:			
3000	Unpaid obligations, brought forward, Oct 1	4		109
3010	New obligations, unexpired accounts	652	264	264
3020	Outlays (gross)	–656	–155	–40
3050	Unpaid obligations, end of year		109	333
	Memorandum (non-add) entries:			
3100	Obligated balance, start of year	4		109
3200	Obligated balance, end of year		109	333
	Budget authority and outlays, net:			
	Mandatory:			
4090	Budget authority, gross	146	155	40
	Outlays, gross:			
4100	Outlays from new mandatory authority	139	155	40
4101	Outlays from mandatory balances	517		
4110	Outlays, gross (total)	656	155	40
	Offsets against gross budget authority and outlays:			
	Offsetting collections (collected) from:			
4123	Loans Repaid - Cash	–27	–16	–11
4123	Interest Repaid - Cash	–6	–10	–8
4123	Loans Repaid - CoC	–35	–9	–5
4123	Interest Repaid - CoC	–6	–5	–1
4130	Offsets against gross budget authority and outlays (total)	–74	–40	–25
4160	Budget authority, net (mandatory)	72	115	15
4170	Outlays, net (mandatory)	582	115	15
4180	Budget authority, net (total)	72	115	15
4190	Outlays, net (total)	582	115	15

Status of Direct Loans (in millions of dollars)

Identification code 012–4230–0–3–999		2021 actual	2022 est.	2023 est.
	Cumulative balance of direct loans outstanding:			
1210	Outstanding, start of year	96	564	566
	Repayments:			
1251	Repayments and prepayments - Cash	–27	–19	–19
1251	Repayments and prepayments - CoC	–35	–6	–6
1261	Adjustments: Capitalized interest	530	27	27
1290	Outstanding, end of year	564	566	568

STATUS OF AGENCY DEBT

dollars in millions

	2021 actual	2022 est.	2023 est.
Agency debt held by FFB:			
Outstanding FFB direct, start of year	120	77	55
Outstanding Certificate of Beneficial Ownership (CBO's), start of year	135	0	0
New agency borrowing, FFB direct	0	0	0

RURAL ELECTRIFICATION AND TELECOMMUNICATIONS LIQUIDATING ACCOUNT—Continued

STATUS OF AGENCY DEBT—Continued

	2021 actual	2022 est.	2023 est.
Repayments and prepayments, FFB Direct	−43	−22	−16
Repayments, CBO's-344	−135	0	0
Outstanding FFB direct, end of year	77	55	39
Outstanding CBO's, end of year	0	0	0

The Rural Telephone Bank was dissolved in 2006. To accomplish this, the Rural Telephone Bank liquidating account loans were used to redeem a portion of the Government's stock. The Rural Telephone Bank liquidating account loans were transferred to the Rural Electrification and Telecommunications liquidating account in 2006.

The Rural Utilities Service (RUS) continues to service all loans in this account, providing business management and technical assistance to the borrowers on a regular basis over the life of the loans.

Rural electric loans.—This program is financed through RUS direct loans for the construction and operation of generating facilities, electric transmission and distribution lines or system improvements.

As required by the Federal Credit Reform Act of 1990, this account records, for rural electrification and telecommunications programs, all cash flows to and from the Government resulting from direct loans obligated and loan guarantees committed prior to 1992. All new activity in Rural Electrification and Telecommunications Revolving Fund in 1992 and beyond is recorded in corresponding program and financing accounts.

The following tables reflect statistics on loans made through the liquidating account only. Since 1992 new electric and telephone loans have been made through a separate program account.

ELECTRIC PROGRAM STATISTICS

dollars in millions

	2021 actual	2022 est.	2023 est.
Cumulative RUS financed direct loans	21,879	21,879	21,879
Cumulative FFB financed direct loans	26,598	26,598	26,598
Cumulative RUS funds advanced	21,879	21,879	21,879
Unadvanced RUS funds, end of year	0	0	0
Cumulative RUS principal repaid	21,875	21,878	21,878
Cumulative RUS interest paid	13,678	13,680	13,681
Cumulative loan guarantee commitments	0	0	0
Number of borrowers	25	17	10

Rural telecommunications.—This loan program is financed through RUS direct loans for the construction, expansion, and operation of telecommunications lines and facilities or systems.

TELECOMMUNICATIONS PROGRAM STATISTICS

dollars in millions

	2021 actual	2022 est.	2023 est.
Cumulative RUS financed direct loans	5,916	5,916	5,916
Cumulative FFB financed direct loans	562	562	562
Cumulative RUS funds advanced	5,916	5,916	5,916
Unadvanced RUS funds, end of period	0	0	0
Cumulative RUS principal repaid	5,888	5,906	5,910
Cumulative RUS interest paid	3,557	3,561	3,565
Cumulative loan guarantee commitments	0	0	0
Number of borrowers	57	34	20

RURAL TELEPHONE BANK PROGRAM STATISTICS

dollars in millions

	2021 actual	2022 est.	2023 est.
Cumulative net loans	2,471	2,471	2,471
Cumulative loan funds, advanced	2,471	2,471	2,471
Unadvanced loan funds, end of year	0	0	0
Cumulative principal repaid	2,471	2,471	2,471
Cumulative interest paid	2,463	2,463	2,463
Number of borrowers	5	3	3

Balance Sheet (in millions of dollars)

Identification code 012–4230–0–3–999		2020 actual	2021 actual
	ASSETS:		
1101	Federal assets: Fund balances with Treasury	1,858	1,162
1601	Direct loans, gross	96	564
1602	Interest receivable	2	2
1603	Allowance for estimated uncollectible loans and interest (−)	....	....
1699	Value of assets related to direct loans	98	566
1901	Other Federal assets: Other assets	−1,427	−1,427
1999	Total assets	529	301
	LIABILITIES:		
	Federal liabilities:		
2102	Interest payable	....	....
2103	Debt	255	76
2104	Resources payable to Treasury	389	225
2105	Other	4	....
2999	Total liabilities	648	301
	NET POSITION:		
3300	Cumulative results of operations	−119	....
4999	Total liabilities and net position	529	301

Object Classification (in millions of dollars)

Identification code 012–4230–0–3–999	2021 actual	2022 est.	2023 est.
Direct obligations:			
25.2 Other services from non-Federal sources	46	....	....
43.0 Interest and dividends	7	5	5
94.0 Financial transfers	599	259	259
99.9 Total new obligations, unexpired accounts	652	264	264

RURAL TELEPHONE BANK PROGRAM ACCOUNT

Program and Financing (in millions of dollars)

Identification code 012–1231–0–1–452	2021 actual	2022 est.	2023 est.
Obligations by program activity:			
Credit program obligations:			
0705 Reestimates of direct loan subsidy	1	1	....
0706 Interest on reestimates of direct loan subsidy	1	2	....
0900 Total new obligations, unexpired accounts (object class 41.0)	2	3	....
Budgetary resources:			
Budget authority:			
Appropriations, mandatory:			
1200 Appropriation	2	3	....
1930 Total budgetary resources available	2	3	....
Change in obligated balance:			
Unpaid obligations:			
3010 New obligations, unexpired accounts	2	3	....
3020 Outlays (gross)	−2	−3	....
Budget authority and outlays, net:			
Mandatory:			
4090 Budget authority, gross	2	3	....
Outlays, gross:			
4100 Outlays from new mandatory authority	2	3	....
4180 Budget authority, net (total)	2	3	....
4190 Outlays, net (total)	2	3	....

Summary of Loan Levels, Subsidy Budget Authority and Outlays by Program (in millions of dollars)

Identification code 012–1231–0–1–452	2021 actual	2022 est.	2023 est.
Direct loan reestimates:			
135001 Rural Telephone Bank	1	3	....

The Rural Telephone Bank (RTB) completed dissolution in 2006, therefore no federally funded RTB loans are proposed.

As required by the Federal Credit Reform Act of 1990, this account records, for the RTB, the subsidy costs associated with the direct loans obligated in 1992 and beyond. The subsidy amounts are estimated on a present value basis.

RURAL TELEPHONE BANK DIRECT LOAN FINANCING ACCOUNT

Program and Financing (in millions of dollars)

Identification code 012–4210–0–3–452	2021 actual	2022 est.	2023 est.
Obligations by program activity:			
Credit program obligations:			
0713 Payment of interest to Treasury	4	4	3
0743 Interest on downward reestimates	1	....	....
0900 Total new obligations, unexpired accounts	5	4	3
Budgetary resources:			
Unobligated balance:			
1000 Unobligated balance brought forward, Oct 1	15	11	4
1023 Unobligated balances applied to repay debt	–15	–11	....
1070 Unobligated balance (total)	....	....	4
Financing authority:			
Borrowing authority, mandatory:			
1400 Borrowing authority	18	....	....
1422 Borrowing authority applied to repay debt	–2	....	....
1440 Borrowing authority, mandatory (total)	16	....	....
Spending authority from offsetting collections, mandatory:			
1800 Collected	17	8	4
1825 Spending authority from offsetting collections applied to repay debt	–17	....	....
1850 Spending auth from offsetting collections, mand (total)	....	8	4
1900 Budget authority (total)	16	8	4
1930 Total budgetary resources available	16	8	8
Memorandum (non-add) entries:			
1941 Unexpired unobligated balance, end of year	11	4	5
Change in obligated balance:			
Unpaid obligations:			
3010 New obligations, unexpired accounts	5	4	3
3020 Outlays (gross)	–5	–4	–3
Financing authority and disbursements, net:			
Mandatory:			
4090 Budget authority, gross	16	8	4
Financing disbursements:			
4110 Outlays, gross (total)	5	4	3
Offsets against gross financing authority and disbursements:			
Offsetting collections (collected) from:			
4120 Federal sources	–2	–3	....
4122 Interest on uninvested funds	–1	....	....
4123 Principal received on loans	–14	–4	–3
4123 Interest received on loans	....	–1	–1
4130 Offsets against gross budget authority and outlays (total)	–17	–8	–4
4160 Budget authority, net (mandatory)	–1	....	....
4170 Outlays, net (mandatory)	–12	–4	–1
4180 Budget authority, net (total)	–1	....	....
4190 Outlays, net (total)	–12	–4	–1

Status of Direct Loans (in millions of dollars)

Identification code 012–4210–0–3–452	2021 actual	2022 est.	2023 est.
Cumulative balance of direct loans outstanding:			
1210 Outstanding, start of year	27	15	11
1251 Repayments: Repayments and prepayments	–12	–4	–3
1290 Outstanding, end of year	15	11	8

Balance Sheet (in millions of dollars)

Identification code 012–4210–0–3–452	2020 actual	2021 actual
ASSETS:		
1101 Federal assets: Fund balances with Treasury	15	11
Net value of assets related to post-1991 direct loans receivable:		
1401 Direct loans receivable, gross	27	15
1405 Allowance for subsidy cost (-)	46	46
1499 Net present value of assets related to direct loans	73	61
1999 Total assets	88	72
LIABILITIES:		
2103 Federal liabilities: Debt	88	72
2207 Non-Federal liabilities: Other	....	....
2999 Total liabilities	88	72
NET POSITION:		
3300 Cumulative results of operations	....	....
4999 Total liabilities and net position	88	72

DISTANCE LEARNING, TELEMEDICINE, AND BROADBAND PROGRAM

For the principal amount of broadband telecommunication loans, $14,674,000.

For grants for telemedicine and distance learning services in rural areas, as authorized by 7 U.S.C. 950aaa et seq., $60,000,000, to remain available until expended: Provided, That $3,000,000 shall be made available for grants authorized by section 379G of the Consolidated Farm and Rural Development Act: Provided further, That funding provided under this heading for grants under section 379G of the Consolidated Farm and Rural Development Act may only be provided to entities that meet all of the eligibility criteria for a consortium as established by this section.

For the cost of broadband loans, as authorized by section 601 of the Rural Electrification Act, $2,000,000, to remain available until expended: Provided, That the cost of direct loans shall be as defined in section 502 of the Congressional Budget Act of 1974.

For the cost to continue a broadband loan and grant pilot program established by section 779 of division A of the Consolidated Appropriations Act, 2018 (Public Law 115–141) under the Rural Electrification Act of 1936, as amended (7 U.S.C 901 et seq.), $600,000,000, to remain available until expended: Provided, That an entity to which a loan or grant is made under the pilot program shall not use the loan or grant to overbuild or duplicate broadband service in a service area by any entity that has received a broadband loan from the Rural Utilities Service unless such service is not provided sufficient access to broadband at the minimum service.

In addition, $35,000,000, to remain available until expended, for the Community Connect Grant Program authorized by 7 U.S.C. 950bb–3.

Note.—A full-year 2022 appropriation for this account was not enacted at the time the Budget was prepared; therefore, the Budget assumes this account is operating under the Continuing Appropriations Act, 2022 (Division A of Public Law 117–43, as amended). The amounts included for 2022 reflect the annualized level provided by the continuing resolution.

RURAL UTILITIES SERVICE—DISTANCE LEARNING, TELEMEDICINE, AND BROADBAND PROGRAM

[For an additional amount for "Rural Utilities Service—Distance Learning, Telemedicine, and Broadband Program", $2,000,000,000, to remain available until expended: *Provided*, That of the funds made available under this heading in this Act, $74,000,000 shall be for the cost of broadband loans, as authorized by section 601 of the Rural Electrification Act: *Provided further*, That, of the funds made available under this heading in this Act, $1,926,000,000 shall be for the broadband loan and grant pilot program established by section 779 of Public Law 115–141 under the Rural Electrification Act of 1936, as amended (7 U.S.C. 901 et seq.): *Provided further*, That at least 50 percent of the households to be served by a project receiving a loan or grant from funds provided under the preceding proviso shall be in a rural area, as defined in section 601(b)(3) of the Rural Electrification Act, without sufficient access to broadband defined for such funds as having speeds of not less than 25 megabits per second downloads and 3 megabits per second uploads: *Provided further*, That 10 percent of the amounts made available under this heading in this Act for the pilot program shall be set aside for service areas where at least 90 percent of households to be served by a project receiving a loan or grant are in a rural area without sufficient access to broadband, as defined in the preceding proviso: *Provided further*, That, to the extent possible, projects receiving funds provided under this heading in this Act for the pilot program must build out service to at least 100 megabits per second downloads and 20 megabits per second uploads: *Provided further*, That, in administering the pilot program under this heading in this Act, the Secretary of Agriculture may, for purposes of determining entities eligible to receive assistance, consider those communities which are "Areas Rural in Character", as defined in section 343(a)(13)(D) of the Consolidated Farm and Rural Development Act: *Provided further*, That not more than $50,000,000 of the funds made available under this heading in this Act for the pilot program may be used for the purpose of the preceding proviso: *Provided further*, That pole attachment fees and replacements charged by electric cooperatives for the shared use of their utility poles shall be an eligible use of funds provided under this heading in this Act for the pilot program to enable the deployment of broadband in rural areas: *Provided further*, That the Secretary shall waive any matching funds required for pilot program projects funded from amounts provided under this heading in this Act for Alaska Native Corporations for federally-recognized Tribes, on substantially underserved Trust areas, as defined in 7 U.S.C. 936f(a)(2), and residents of a rural area that was recognized as a colonia as of October 1, 1989, and for projects in which 75 percent of the service area is a persistent poverty county or counties: *Provided further*, That for purposes of the

DISTANCE LEARNING, TELEMEDICINE, AND BROADBAND PROGRAM—Continued

preceding proviso, the term "persistent poverty counties" means any county that has had 20 percent or more of its population living in poverty over the past 30 years, as measured by the 1990 and 2000 decennial censuses, and 2007–2011 American Community Survey 5–6 year average, or any territory or possession of the United States: *Provided further*, That, in addition to other funds available for such purpose, not more than four percent of the amounts provided under this heading in this Act shall be for administrative costs to carry out the pilot program and broadband loans: *Provided further*, That up to three percent of the amounts provided under this heading in this Act shall be for technical assistance and predevelopment planning activities to support rural communities, of which $5,000,000 shall have a priority for the establishment and growth of cooperatives to offer broadband, which shall be transferred to and merged with the appropriation for "Rural Development, Salaries and Expenses": *Provided further*, That the Secretary of Agriculture shall collaborate, to the extent practicable, with the Commissioner of the Federal Communications Commission and the Assistant Secretary for Communications and Information at the National Telecommunications and Information Administration to carry out the amounts provided under this heading in this Act for the pilot program: *Provided further*, That the Secretary may transfer funds provided under this heading in this Act between broadband loans, as authorized by section 601 of the Rural Electrification Act, and the pilot program to accommodate demand: *Provided further*, That no funds shall be transferred pursuant to the preceding proviso until the Secretary notifies in writing and receives approval from the Committees on Appropriations and Agriculture of both Houses of Congress at least 30 days in advance of the transfer of such funds or the use of such authority: *Provided further*, That for purposes of the amounts provided under this heading in this Act for the pilot program, the Secretary shall adhere to the notice, reporting, and service area assessment requirements set forth in section 701(a)–(d) of the Rural Electrification Act (7 U.S.C. 950cc(a)–(d)): *Provided further*, That such amount is designated by the Congress as being for an emergency requirement pursuant to section 4112(a) of H. Con. Res. 71 (115th Congress), the concurrent resolution on the budget for fiscal year 2018, and to section 251(b) of the Balanced Budget and Emergency Deficit Control Act of 1985.] *(Infrastructure Investments and Jobs Appropriations Act.)*

Program and Financing (in millions of dollars)

Identification code 012–1232–0–1–452		2021 actual	2022 est.	2023 est.
	Obligations by program activity:			
0010	Grants	191	840	825
0011	Grants IIJA		89	1,507
0091	Direct program activities, subtotal	191	929	2,332
	Credit program obligations:			
0701	Direct loan subsidy	18	178	370
0705	Reestimates of direct loan subsidy	1	15	
0706	Interest on reestimates of direct loan subsidy		5	
0709	Administrative expenses		64	63
0709	Administrative expenses		33	107
0791	Direct program activities, subtotal	19	295	540
0900	Total new obligations, unexpired accounts	210	1,224	2,872
	Budgetary resources:			
	Unobligated balance:			
1000	Unobligated balance brought forward, Oct 1	527	995	2,463
1001	Discretionary unobligated balance brought fwd, Oct 1		995	
1021	Recoveries of prior year unpaid obligations	66	48	39
1070	Unobligated balance (total)	593	1,043	2,502
	Budget authority:			
	Appropriations, discretionary:			
1100	Appropriation	628	628	697
1100	Appropriation from Infrastructure Investment and Jobs Act		2,000	
1131	Unobligated balance of appropriations permanently reduced	–12	–4	
1160	Appropriation, discretionary (total)	616	2,624	697
	Appropriations, mandatory:			
1200	Appropriation	1	20	
1900	Budget authority (total)	617	2,644	697
1930	Total budgetary resources available	1,210	3,687	3,199
	Memorandum (non-add) entries:			
1940	Unobligated balance expiring	–5		
1941	Unexpired unobligated balance, end of year	995	2,463	327
	Change in obligated balance:			
	Unpaid obligations:			
3000	Unpaid obligations, brought forward, Oct 1	881	948	1,588
3010	New obligations, unexpired accounts	210	1,224	2,872
3020	Outlays (gross)	–77	–536	–1,620
3040	Recoveries of prior year unpaid obligations, unexpired	–66	–48	–39
3050	Unpaid obligations, end of year	948	1,588	2,801
	Memorandum (non-add) entries:			
3100	Obligated balance, start of year	881	948	1,588
3200	Obligated balance, end of year	948	1,588	2,801
	Budget authority and outlays, net:			
	Discretionary:			
4000	Budget authority, gross	616	2,624	697
	Outlays, gross:			
4010	Outlays from new discretionary authority		76	47
4011	Outlays from discretionary balances	76	440	1,573
4020	Outlays, gross (total)	76	516	1,620
	Mandatory:			
4090	Budget authority, gross	1	20	
	Outlays, gross:			
4100	Outlays from new mandatory authority	1	20	
4180	Budget authority, net (total)	617	2,644	697
4190	Outlays, net (total)	77	536	1,620

Summary of Loan Levels, Subsidy Budget Authority and Outlays by Program (in millions of dollars)

Identification code 012–1232–0–1–452		2021 actual	2022 est.	2023 est.
	Direct loan levels supportable by subsidy budget authority:			
115003	Broadband Treasury Rate Loans		18	521
115005	ReConnect Direct Loans		658	953
115006	ReConnect Grant Assisted Loans	74	118	1,676
115999	Total direct loan levels	74	794	3,150
	Direct loan subsidy (in percent):			
132003	Broadband Treasury Rate Loans		14.93	13.63
132005	ReConnect Direct Loans		22.02	13.64
132006	ReConnect Grant Assisted Loans	24.63	25.84	10.10
132999	Weighted average subsidy rate	24.63	22.43	11.75
	Direct loan subsidy budget authority:			
133003	Broadband Treasury Rate Loans		3	71
133005	ReConnect Direct Loans		145	130
133006	ReConnect Grant Assisted Loans	18	30	169
133999	Total subsidy budget authority	18	178	370
	Direct loan subsidy outlays:			
134003	Broadband Treasury Rate Loans	2	4	7
134005	ReConnect Direct Loans	1	8	44
134006	ReConnect Grant Assisted Loans	6	37	66
134999	Total subsidy outlays	9	49	117
	Direct loan reestimates:			
135003	Broadband Treasury Rate Loans	–69	14	
135999	Total direct loan reestimates	–69	14	
	Administrative expense data:			
3510	Budget authority	21	101	24
3580	Outlays from balances		3	72
3590	Outlays from new authority	26	43	24

The loan and grant program provides access to advanced telecommunications services for improved education and health care in rural areas throughout the country. The loans and grants help education and health care providers bring the most modern technology, level of care, and education to rural America so its citizens can compete regionally, nationally, and globally.

The 2023 Budget proposes $60 million for Distance Learning and Telemedicine grants, including $3 million for grants for health care services in Mississippi. The Budget also provides $35 million for Broadband grants, supports the broadband Treasury rate loan program at $14.7 million in program level, and provides $600 million for the rural e-Connectivity pilot program to support loans and grants consistent with the authority in the 2018 Appropriations Act.

As required by the Federal Credit Reform Act of 1990, this account records for this program the subsidy costs associated with the direct loans obligated and loan guarantees committed in 1992 and beyond (including credit sales of acquired property), and administrative expenses of this program. The subsidy amounts are estimated on a present value basis; the administrative expenses are estimated on a cash basis.

DEPARTMENT OF AGRICULTURE

Rural Utilities Service—Continued
Federal Funds—Continued

157

Object Classification (in millions of dollars)

Identification code 012–1232–0–1–452	2021 actual	2022 est.	2023 est.
Direct obligations:			
25.3 Other goods and services from Federal sources	....	64	63
25.3 Other goods and services from Federal sources	....	33	107
41.0 Grants, subsidies, and contributions	210	1,127	2,702
99.9 Total new obligations, unexpired accounts	210	1,224	2,872

DISTANCE LEARNING, TELEMEDICINE, AND BROADBAND DIRECT LOAN FINANCING ACCOUNT

Program and Financing (in millions of dollars)

Identification code 012–4146–0–3–452	2021 actual	2022 est.	2023 est.
Obligations by program activity:			
Credit program obligations:			
0710 Direct loan obligations	74	794	3,150
0713 Payment of interest to Treasury	13	19	16
0742 Downward reestimates paid to receipt accounts	55	5	....
0743 Interest on downward reestimates	16	2	....
0900 Total new obligations, unexpired accounts	158	820	3,166
Budgetary resources:			
Unobligated balance:			
1000 Unobligated balance brought forward, Oct 1	150	36	....
1021 Recoveries of prior year unpaid obligations	111	....	....
1023 Unobligated balances applied to repay debt	–155	–36	....
1024 Unobligated balance of borrowing authority withdrawn	–82	....	....
1070 Unobligated balance (total)	24	....	....
Financing authority:			
Borrowing authority, mandatory:			
1400 Borrowing authority	83	532	2,681
1800 Collected	107	159	236
1801 Change in uncollected payments, Federal sources	–20	129	249
1850 Spending auth from offsetting collections, mand (total)	87	288	485
1900 Budget authority (total)	170	820	3,166
1930 Total budgetary resources available	194	820	3,166
Memorandum (non-add) entries:			
1941 Unexpired unobligated balance, end of year	36	....	....
Change in obligated balance:			
Unpaid obligations:			
3000 Unpaid obligations, brought forward, Oct 1	451	372	970
3010 New obligations, unexpired accounts	158	820	3,166
3020 Outlays (gross)	–126	–222	–502
3040 Recoveries of prior year unpaid obligations, unexpired	–111	....	....
3050 Unpaid obligations, end of year	372	970	3,634
Uncollected payments:			
3060 Uncollected pymts, Fed sources, brought forward, Oct 1	–115	–95	–224
3070 Change in uncollected pymts, Fed sources, unexpired	20	–129	–249
3090 Uncollected pymts, Fed sources, end of year	–95	–224	–473
Memorandum (non-add) entries:			
3100 Obligated balance, start of year	336	277	746
3200 Obligated balance, end of year	277	746	3,161
Financing authority and disbursements, net:			
Mandatory:			
4090 Budget authority, gross	170	820	3,166
Financing disbursements:			
4110 Outlays, gross (total)	126	222	502
Offsets against gross financing authority and disbursements:			
Offsetting collections (collected) from:			
4120 Federal sources	–10	–69	–117
4122 Interest on uninvested funds	–3	–2	–4
4123 Repayment of principal	–80	–76	–98
4123 Interest received on loans	–14	–12	–17
4130 Offsets against gross budget authority and outlays (total)	–107	–159	–236
Additional offsets against financing authority only (total):			
4140 Change in uncollected pymts, Fed sources, unexpired	20	–129	–249
4160 Budget authority, net (mandatory)	83	532	2,681
4170 Outlays, net (mandatory)	19	63	266
4180 Budget authority, net (total)	83	532	2,681
4190 Outlays, net (total)	19	63	266

Status of Direct Loans (in millions of dollars)

Identification code 012–4146–0–3–452	2021 actual	2022 est.	2023 est.
Position with respect to appropriations act limitation on obligations:			
1111 Direct loan obligations from current-year authority	74	794	3,150
1150 Total direct loan obligations	74	794	3,150
Cumulative balance of direct loans outstanding:			
1210 Outstanding, start of year	514	476	597
1231 Disbursements: Direct loan disbursements	42	197	486
1251 Repayments: Repayments and prepayments	–80	–76	–96
1290 Outstanding, end of year	476	597	987

Balance Sheet (in millions of dollars)

Identification code 012–4146–0–3–452	2020 actual	2021 actual
ASSETS:		
1101 Federal assets: Fund balances with Treasury	167	36
Net value of assets related to post-1991 direct loans receivable:		
1401 Direct loans receivable, gross	514	476
1402 Interest receivable	1	1
1405 Allowance for subsidy cost (–)	–56	1
1499 Net present value of assets related to direct loans	459	478
1999 Total assets	626	514
LIABILITIES:		
2103 Federal liabilities: Debt	626	514
2207 Non-Federal liabilities: Other	....	....
2999 Total liabilities	626	514
NET POSITION:		
3300 Cumulative results of operations	....	....
4999 Total liabilities and net position	626	514

RURAL DEVELOPMENT INSURANCE FUND LIQUIDATING ACCOUNT

Program and Financing (in millions of dollars)

Identification code 012–4155–0–3–452	2021 actual	2022 est.	2023 est.
Budgetary resources:			
Unobligated balance:			
1000 Unobligated balance brought forward, Oct 1	15	10	....
1022 Capital transfer of unobligated balances to general fund	–15	–10	....
Budget authority:			
Spending authority from offsetting collections, mandatory:			
1800 Collected	50	38	38
1820 Capital transfer of spending authority from offsetting collections to general fund	–40	–38	–38
1850 Spending auth from offsetting collections, mand (total)	10	....	....
1930 Total budgetary resources available	10	....	....
Memorandum (non-add) entries:			
1941 Unexpired unobligated balance, end of year	10	....	....
Budget authority and outlays, net:			
Mandatory:			
4090 Budget authority, gross	10	....	....
Offsets against gross budget authority and outlays:			
Offsetting collections (collected) from:			
4123 Non-Federal sources	–50	–38	–38
4180 Budget authority, net (total)	–40	–38	–38
4190 Outlays, net (total)	–50	–38	–38

Status of Direct Loans (in millions of dollars)

Identification code 012–4155–0–3–452	2021 actual	2022 est.	2023 est.
Cumulative balance of direct loans outstanding:			
1210 Outstanding, start of year	211	173	141
1251 Repayments: Repayments and prepayments	–38	–32	–32
1290 Outstanding, end of year	173	141	109

RURAL DEVELOPMENT INSURANCE FUND LIQUIDATING ACCOUNT—Continued

Status of Guaranteed Loans (in millions of dollars)

Identification code 012–4155–0–3–452	2021 actual	2022 est.	2023 est.
Cumulative balance of guaranteed loans outstanding:			
2210 Outstanding, start of year	2	2	2
2251 Repayments and prepayments			
2290 Outstanding, end of year	2	2	2
Memorandum:			
2299 Guaranteed amount of guaranteed loans outstanding, end of year	2	2	2

The Rural Development Insurance Fund (RDIF) was established on October 1, 1972, pursuant to section 116 of the Rural Development Act of 1972 (Public Law 92–419). Loans are no longer made through this account.

Balance Sheet (in millions of dollars)

Identification code 012–4155–0–3–452	2020 actual	2021 actual
ASSETS:		
1101 Federal assets: Fund balances with Treasury	14	10
1201 Non-Federal assets: Investments in non-Federal securities, net		
1601 Direct loans, gross	211	173
1602 Interest receivable	2	2
1603 Allowance for estimated uncollectible loans and interest (-)		
1699 Value of assets related to direct loans	213	175
1901 Other Federal assets: Other assets		
1999 Total assets	227	185
LIABILITIES:		
2104 Federal liabilities: Resources payable to Treasury	227	185
NET POSITION:		
3300 Cumulative results of operations		
4999 Total liabilities and net position	227	185

FOREIGN AGRICULTURAL SERVICE

Federal Funds

SALARIES AND EXPENSES

(INCLUDING TRANSFERS OF FUNDS)

For necessary expenses of the Foreign Agricultural Service, including not to exceed $250,000 for representation allowances and for expenses pursuant to section 8 of the Act approved August 3, 1956 (7 U.S.C. 1766), $240,663,000, of which no more than 6 percent shall remain available until September 30, 2024, for overseas operations to include the payment of locally employed staff: Provided, That the Service may utilize advances of funds, or reimburse this appropriation for expenditures made on behalf of Federal agencies, public and private organizations and institutions under agreements executed pursuant to the agricultural food production assistance programs (7 U.S.C. 1737) and the foreign assistance programs of the United States Agency for International Development: Provided further, That funds made available for middle-income country training programs, funds made available for the Borlaug International Agricultural Science and Technology Fellowship program, and up to $2,000,000 of the Foreign Agricultural Service appropriation solely for the purpose of offsetting fluctuations in international currency exchange rates, subject to documentation by the Foreign Agricultural Service, shall remain available until expended.

Note.—A full-year 2022 appropriation for this account was not enacted at the time the Budget was prepared; therefore, the Budget assumes this account is operating under the Continuing Appropriations Act, 2022 (Division A of Public Law 117–43, as amended). The amounts included for 2022 reflect the annualized level provided by the continuing resolution.

Program and Financing (in millions of dollars)

Identification code 012–2900–0–1–352	2021 actual	2022 est.	2023 est.
Obligations by program activity:			
0002 Trade Policy	76	77	84
0004 Trade Supporting Initiatives	68	70	75
0005 Market Analysis and Advice	50	51	56
0006 Efficient Operations	24	25	27
0799 Total direct obligations	218	223	242
0801 Salaries and Expenses (Reimbursable)	70	93	78
0900 Total new obligations, unexpired accounts	288	316	320
Budgetary resources:			
Unobligated balance:			
1000 Unobligated balance brought forward, Oct 1	38	36	87
1001 Discretionary unobligated balance brought fwd, Oct 1	36		
1021 Recoveries of prior year unpaid obligations	1		
1070 Unobligated balance (total)	39	36	87
Budget authority:			
Appropriations, discretionary:			
1100 Appropriation	223	223	241
1120 Appropriations transferred to other acct [012–4609]	–2		
1160 Appropriation, discretionary (total)	221	223	241
Spending authority from offsetting collections, discretionary:			
1700 Collected	38	55	48
1701 Change in uncollected payments, Federal sources	62	89	80
1750 Spending auth from offsetting collections, disc (total)	100	144	128
1900 Budget authority (total)	321	367	369
1930 Total budgetary resources available	360	403	456
Memorandum (non-add) entries:			
1940 Unobligated balance expiring	–36		
1941 Unexpired unobligated balance, end of year	36	87	136
Change in obligated balance:			
Unpaid obligations:			
3000 Unpaid obligations, brought forward, Oct 1	110	116	73
3010 New obligations, unexpired accounts	288	316	320
3011 Obligations ("upward adjustments"), expired accounts	5		
3020 Outlays (gross)	–274	–359	–366
3040 Recoveries of prior year unpaid obligations, unexpired	–1		
3041 Recoveries of prior year unpaid obligations, expired	–12		
3050 Unpaid obligations, end of year	116	73	27
Uncollected payments:			
3060 Uncollected pymts, Fed sources, brought forward, Oct 1	–147	–134	–223
3070 Change in uncollected pymts, Fed sources, unexpired	–62	–89	–80
3071 Change in uncollected pymts, Fed sources, expired	75		
3090 Uncollected pymts, Fed sources, end of year	–134	–223	–303
Memorandum (non-add) entries:			
3100 Obligated balance, start of year	–37	–18	–150
3200 Obligated balance, end of year	–18	–150	–276
Budget authority and outlays, net:			
Discretionary:			
4000 Budget authority, gross	321	367	369
Outlays, gross:			
4010 Outlays from new discretionary authority	194	257	257
4011 Outlays from discretionary balances	80	102	109
4020 Outlays, gross (total)	274	359	366
Offsets against gross budget authority and outlays:			
Offsetting collections (collected) from:			
4030 Federal sources	–84	–71	–48
4033 Non-Federal sources	–2		
4040 Offsets against gross budget authority and outlays (total)	–86	–71	–48
Additional offsets against gross budget authority only:			
4050 Change in uncollected pymts, Fed sources, unexpired	–62	–89	–80
4052 Offsetting collections credited to expired accounts	48	16	
4060 Additional offsets against budget authority only (total)	–14	–73	–80
4070 Budget authority, net (discretionary)	221	223	241
4080 Outlays, net (discretionary)	188	288	318
4180 Budget authority, net (total)	221	223	241
4190 Outlays, net (total)	188	288	318

The Foreign Agricultural Service's (FAS) mission is linking U.S. agriculture to the world to enhance export opportunities and global food security. FAS helps to provide outlets for the wide variety of U.S. agricultural products, thereby enhancing economic activity for U.S. workers. FAS serves U.S. agriculture's interests by expanding and maintaining international export opportunities, supporting international economic development and trade and capacity building, and global food security. The outcomes envisioned are exports that help U.S. agriculture prosper, the expansion of U.S. exports of organics and crops produced using new technologies and food that are globally available, accessible, and appropriately used. In addition to its Washington-based staff, the agency maintains a network of overseas offices that serve as first responders in cases of market disruption. The overseas offices also provide the Department with critical market and

DEPARTMENT OF AGRICULTURE

policy intelligence, and they represent U.S. agriculture in consultations with foreign governments. The 2023 Budget includes $240.7 million for FAS, an increase of $18.8 million over the 2022 annualized Continuing Resolution level. For more information on FAS's mission and program topic areas, please visit http://www.fas.usda.gov/topics.

Object Classification (in millions of dollars)

Identification code 012–2900–0–1–352		2021 actual	2022 est.	2023 est.
	Direct obligations:			
	Personnel compensation:			
11.1	Full-time permanent	71	60	65
11.3	Other than full-time permanent	23	36	39
11.5	Other personnel compensation	2		
11.9	Total personnel compensation	96	96	104
12.1	Civilian personnel benefits	34	37	41
21.0	Travel and transportation of persons	4	4	4
22.0	Transportation of things	1	2	2
23.2	Rental payments to others	5	6	7
23.3	Communications, utilities, and miscellaneous charges	2	2	2
25.1	Advisory and assistance services	22	18	20
25.2	Other services from non-Federal sources	42	39	43
25.3	Other goods and services from Federal sources	8	13	15
25.4	Operation and maintenance of facilities	2	2	2
26.0	Supplies and materials	1	2	1
31.0	Equipment	1	1	1
99.0	Direct obligations	218	222	242
99.0	Reimbursable obligations	70	94	78
99.9	Total new obligations, unexpired accounts	288	316	320

Employment Summary

Identification code 012–2900–0–1–352		2021 actual	2022 est.	2023 est.
1001	Direct civilian full-time equivalent employment	584	681	681
2001	Reimbursable civilian full-time equivalent employment	128	128	128

FOREIGN ASSISTANCE PROGRAMS

Multiple food aid programs are appropriated to USDA and administered by USDA or the U.S. Agency for International Development (USAID) to provide U.S. commodities, technical and financial assistance to address hunger and malnutrition needs worldwide. These programs address emergency needs and foster economic development activities to alleviate global food insecurity.

SUMMARY OF FOOD ASSISTANCE PROGRAMMING
In millions of dollars

	2021 actual	2022 est.	2023 est.
McGovern-Dole International Food for Education and Child Nutrition (budget authority)	230	230	230
P.L. 480:			
Title II Grants (budget authority)	1,740	1,740	1,740
Food for Progress:			
CCC Funded	175	165	175
Bill Emerson Humanitarian Trust	0[1]	0[1]	0[1]

[1] Assets of the trust can be released any time the Administrator of the U.S. Agency for International Development determines that P.L. 480 Title II funding for emergency needs are inadequate to meet these needs in an fiscal year.

Included in this category are the following activities carried out under Public Law 480 (P.L. 480):

Financing sales of agricultural commodities to developing countries for dollars on credit terms, or for local currencies (including for local currencies on credit terms) for use under sec. 104; and for furnishing commodities to carry out the Food for Progress Act of 1985, as amended (Title I).—Funds appropriated for P.L. 480 Title I since FY 2006 are used to finance all sales made pursuant to agreements concluded under the authority of Title I.

Commodities supplied in connection with dispositions abroad (Title II).—Title II of the Food for Peace Act (P.L. 83–480), as amended, formerly the Agricultural Trade Development and Assistance Act of 1954) authorizes the provision of U.S. food assistance to meet emergency food needs around the world, and funds development-oriented programs to help address the underlying causes of food insecurity. P.L. 480 Title II is appropriated to the U.S. Department of Agriculture and is administered by the U.S. Agency for International Development (USAID).

The Commodity Credit Corporation (the Corporation) is authorized to pay the costs of acquisition, packaging, processing, enrichment, preservation, fortification, transportation, handling, and other incidental costs incurred up to the time of delivery at U.S. ports. The Corporation also pays ocean freight charges, and pays transportation costs to points of entry other than ports in the case of landlocked countries, where carriers to a specific country are not available, where ports cannot be used effectively, or where a substantial savings in costs or time can be effected, and pays general average contributions arising from ocean transport. In addition, transportation costs from designated points of entry or ports of entry abroad to storage and distribution sites and associated storage and distribution costs may be paid for commodities made available to meet urgent and extraordinary relief requirements. P.L. 480 funds reimburse the Corporation for all of the cost items authorized above.

McGovern-Dole International Food for Education and Child Nutrition Program Grants

For necessary expenses to carry out the provisions of section 3107 of the Farm Security and Rural Investment Act of 2002 (7 U.S.C. 1736o–1), $230,112,000, to remain available until expended: Provided, That the Commodity Credit Corporation is authorized to provide the services, facilities, and authorities for the purpose of implementing such section, subject to reimbursement from amounts provided herein: Provided further, That of the amount made available under this heading, not more than 10 percent, but not less than $22,000,000, shall remain available until expended to purchase agricultural commodities as described in subsection 3107(a)(2) of the Farm Security and Rural Investment Act of 2002 (7 U.S.C. 1736o–1(a)(2)).

Note.—A full-year 2022 appropriation for this account was not enacted at the time the Budget was prepared; therefore, the Budget assumes this account is operating under the Continuing Appropriations Act, 2022 (Division A of Public Law 117–43, as amended). The amounts included for 2022 reflect the annualized level provided by the continuing resolution.

Program and Financing (in millions of dollars)

Identification code 012–2903–0–1–151		2021 actual	2022 est.	2023 est.
	Obligations by program activity:			
0001	McGovern-Dole International Food for Education & Child Nutrition Program	479	230	230
	Budgetary resources:			
	Unobligated balance:			
1000	Unobligated balance brought forward, Oct 1	260	30	30
1021	Recoveries of prior year unpaid obligations	19		
1070	Unobligated balance (total)	279	30	30
	Budget authority:			
	Appropriations, discretionary:			
1100	Appropriation	230	230	230
1900	Budget authority (total)	230	230	230
1930	Total budgetary resources available	509	260	260
	Memorandum (non-add) entries:			
1941	Unexpired unobligated balance, end of year	30	30	30
	Change in obligated balance:			
	Unpaid obligations:			
3000	Unpaid obligations, brought forward, Oct 1	576	822	490
3010	New obligations, unexpired accounts	479	230	230
3020	Outlays (gross)	–214	–562	–193
3040	Recoveries of prior year unpaid obligations, unexpired	–19		
3050	Unpaid obligations, end of year	822	490	527
	Memorandum (non-add) entries:			
3100	Obligated balance, start of year	576	822	490
3200	Obligated balance, end of year	822	490	527
	Budget authority and outlays, net:			
	Discretionary:			
4000	Budget authority, gross	230	230	230
	Outlays, gross:			
4010	Outlays from new discretionary authority	3	46	46
4011	Outlays from discretionary balances	211	516	147

McGovern-Dole International Food for Education and Child Nutrition Program Grants—Continued

Program and Financing—Continued

Identification code 012–2903–0–1–151	2021 actual	2022 est.	2023 est.
4020 Outlays, gross (total)	214	562	193
4180 Budget authority, net (total)	230	230	230
4190 Outlays, net (total)	214	562	193

The McGovern-Dole International Food for Education and Child Nutrition Program, as amended, is authorized under the Farm Security and Rural Investment Act of 2002 (Public Law 107–171). The program provides for the donation of U.S. agricultural commodities and associated technical and financial assistance to carry out preschool and school feeding programs in foreign countries. Maternal, infant, and child nutrition programs also are authorized. The 2023 Budget includes $230.1 million, an increase of $0.1 million over the 2022 annualized Continuing Resolution level.

Object Classification (in millions of dollars)

Identification code 012–2903–0–1–151	2021 actual	2022 est.	2023 est.
Direct obligations:			
11.1 Personnel compensation: Full-time permanent	2	2	2
12.1 Civilian personnel benefits	1	1	1
41.0 Grants, subsidies, and contributions	476	227	227
99.0 Direct obligations	479	230	230
99.9 Total new obligations, unexpired accounts	479	230	230

Employment Summary

Identification code 012–2903–0–1–151	2021 actual	2022 est.	2023 est.
1001 Direct civilian full-time equivalent employment	16	16	16

Food for Peace Title II Grants

For expenses during the current fiscal year, not otherwise recoverable, and unrecovered prior years' costs, including interest thereon, under the Food for Peace Act (Public Law 83–480), for commodities supplied in connection with dispositions abroad under title II of said Act, $1,740,000,000, to remain available until expended.

Note.—A full-year 2022 appropriation for this account was not enacted at the time the Budget was prepared; therefore, the Budget assumes this account is operating under the Continuing Appropriations Act, 2022 (Division A of Public Law 117–43, as amended). The amounts included for 2022 reflect the annualized level provided by the continuing resolution.

Program and Financing (in millions of dollars)

Identification code 012–2278–0–1–151	2021 actual	2022 est.	2023 est.
Obligations by program activity:			
0002 Title II Grants	1,680	1,898	1,840
0003 American Rescue Plan	648	152	....
0900 Total new obligations, unexpired accounts (object class 41.0)	2,328	2,050	1,840
Budgetary resources:			
Unobligated balance:			
1000 Unobligated balance brought forward, Oct 1	120	410	100
1001 Discretionary unobligated balance brought fwd, Oct 1	120	....	....
1021 Recoveries of prior year unpaid obligations	78	....	....
1070 Unobligated balance (total)	198	410	100
Budget authority:			
Appropriations, discretionary:			
1100 Appropriation	1,740	1,740	1,740
Appropriations, mandatory:			
1200 Appropriation	800	....	....
1900 Budget authority (total)	2,540	1,740	1,740
1930 Total budgetary resources available	2,738	2,150	1,840
Memorandum (non-add) entries:			
1941 Unexpired unobligated balance, end of year	410	100	....
Change in obligated balance:			
Unpaid obligations:			
3000 Unpaid obligations, brought forward, Oct 1	1,608	1,839	2,297
3010 New obligations, unexpired accounts	2,328	2,050	1,840
3020 Outlays (gross)	–2,019	–1,592	–1,635
3040 Recoveries of prior year unpaid obligations, unexpired	–78	....	....
3050 Unpaid obligations, end of year	1,839	2,297	2,502
Memorandum (non-add) entries:			
3100 Obligated balance, start of year	1,608	1,839	2,297
3200 Obligated balance, end of year	1,839	2,297	2,502
Budget authority and outlays, net:			
Discretionary:			
4000 Budget authority, gross	1,740	1,740	1,740
Outlays, gross:			
4010 Outlays from new discretionary authority	244	522	522
4011 Outlays from discretionary balances	1,566	750	873
4020 Outlays, gross (total)	1,810	1,272	1,395
Mandatory:			
4090 Budget authority, gross	800	....	....
Outlays, gross:			
4100 Outlays from new mandatory authority	209	....	....
4101 Outlays from mandatory balances	....	320	240
4110 Outlays, gross (total)	209	320	240
4180 Budget authority, net (total)	2,540	1,740	1,740
4190 Outlays, net (total)	2,019	1,592	1,635

Title II of the Food for Peace Act (P.L. 83–480), as amended, authorizes the provision of U.S. food assistance to meet emergency food needs around the world and funds development-oriented programs to help address the underlying causes of food insecurity. Funding for Title II is appropriated to the U.S. Department of Agriculture and is administered by the U.S. Agency for International Development (USAID). The 2023 request of $1.74 billion includes funding to be used for development programs in combination with additional funding requested in the Development Assistance account under USAID's Community Development Fund. Together, these resources support development food assistance efforts to address chronic food insecurity in areas of recurrent crises using a multi-sectoral approach to reduce poverty and build resilience. The balance of the request will be used to provide emergency food assistance in response to natural disasters and complex emergencies.

Food for Peace Title I Direct Credit and Food for Progress Program Account

Note.—A full-year 2022 appropriation for this account was not enacted at the time the Budget was prepared; therefore, the Budget assumes this account is operating under the Continuing Appropriations Act, 2022 (Division A of Public Law 117–43, as amended). The amounts included for 2022 reflect the annualized level provided by the continuing resolution.

Program and Financing (in millions of dollars)

Identification code 012–2277–0–1–351	2021 actual	2022 est.	2023 est.
Obligations by program activity:			
Credit program obligations:			
0705 Reestimates of direct loan subsidy	1	2	....
0706 Interest on reestimates of direct loan subsidy	3	8	....
0900 Total new obligations, unexpired accounts (object class 41.0)	4	10	....
Budgetary resources:			
Unobligated balance:			
1000 Unobligated balance brought forward, Oct 1	1	1	1
Budget authority:			
Appropriations, mandatory:			
1200 Appropriation	4	10	....
1900 Budget authority (total)	4	10	....
1930 Total budgetary resources available	5	11	1
Memorandum (non-add) entries:			
1941 Unexpired unobligated balance, end of year	1	1	1
Change in obligated balance:			
Unpaid obligations:			
3010 New obligations, unexpired accounts	4	10	....
3020 Outlays (gross)	–4	–10	....
Budget authority and outlays, net:			
Mandatory:			
4090 Budget authority, gross	4	10	....

DEPARTMENT OF AGRICULTURE

Foreign Agricultural Service—Continued
Federal Funds—Continued

		2021 actual	2022 est.	2023 est.
	Outlays, gross:			
4100	Outlays from new mandatory authority	4	10	
4180	Budget authority, net (total)	4	10	
4190	Outlays, net (total)	4	10	

Summary of Loan Levels, Subsidy Budget Authority and Outlays by Program (in millions of dollars)

Identification code 012–2277–0–1–351		2021 actual	2022 est.	2023 est.
	Direct loan reestimates:			
135001	P.L. 480 Title I Loans	2	10	

As required by the Federal Credit Reform Act of 1990, this account records, for the P.L. 480 Program, the subsidy costs associated with the direct credit obligated in 1992 and beyond (including modifications of direct credit agreements that resulted from obligation in any year), as well as administrative expenses of this program. The subsidy amounts are estimated on a present value basis; and the administrative expenses and grants are estimated on a cash basis. The current balance of Title I debt owed to USDA is $1.2 billion. No additional funding is requested for new Title I credit financing in 2023. Administrative expenses for this program have been moved to the Farm Production and Conservation Salaries and Expenses account.

P.L. 480 DIRECT CREDIT FINANCING ACCOUNT

Program and Financing (in millions of dollars)

Identification code 012–4049–0–3–351		2021 actual	2022 est.	2023 est.
	Obligations by program activity:			
	Credit program obligations:			
0713	Payment of interest to Treasury	21	28	28
0743	Interest on downward reestimates	1		
0900	Total new obligations, unexpired accounts	22	28	28
	Budgetary resources:			
	Unobligated balance:			
1000	Unobligated balance brought forward, Oct 1	28	28	
1023	Unobligated balances applied to repay debt	–26	–28	
1070	Unobligated balance (total)	2		
	Financing authority:			
	Borrowing authority, mandatory:			
1400	Borrowing authority	15	28	28
	Spending authority from offsetting collections, mandatory:			
1800	Collected	68	72	56
1825	Spending authority from offsetting collections applied to repay debt	–35	–72	–56
1850	Spending auth from offsetting collections, mand (total)	33		
1900	Budget authority (total)	48	28	28
1930	Total budgetary resources available	50	28	28
	Memorandum (non-add) entries:			
1941	Unexpired unobligated balance, end of year	28		
	Change in obligated balance:			
	Unpaid obligations:			
3010	New obligations, unexpired accounts	22	28	28
3020	Outlays (gross)	–22	–28	–28
	Financing authority and disbursements, net:			
	Mandatory:			
4090	Budget authority, gross	48	28	28
	Financing disbursements:			
4110	Outlays, gross (total)	22	28	28
	Offsets against gross financing authority and disbursements:			
	Offsetting collections (collected) from:			
4120	Payments from program account - Upward Reestimate	–4	–10	
4122	Interest on uninvested funds	–3	–4	–4
4123	Interest received on loans	–7	–6	–5
4123	Principal received on loans	–54	–52	–47
4130	Offsets against gross budget authority and outlays (total)	–68	–72	–56
4160	Budget authority, net (mandatory)	–20	–44	–28
4170	Outlays, net (mandatory)	–46	–44	–28
4180	Budget authority, net (total)	–20	–44	–28
4190	Outlays, net (total)	–46	–44	–28

Status of Direct Loans (in millions of dollars)

Identification code 012–4049–0–3–351		2021 actual	2022 est.	2023 est.
	Cumulative balance of direct loans outstanding:			
1210	Outstanding, start of year	388	328	276
1251	Repayments: Repayments and prepayments	–54	–52	–47
1264	Other adjustments, net (+ or -)	–6		
1290	Outstanding, end of year	328	276	229

Balance Sheet (in millions of dollars)

Identification code 012–4049–0–3–351		2020 actual	2021 actual
	ASSETS:		
	Federal assets:		
1101	Fund balances with Treasury	28	27
	Investments in U.S. securities:		
1106	Receivables, net	4	10
	Net value of assets related to post-1991 direct loans receivable:		
1401	Direct loans receivable, gross	388	328
1402	Interest receivable	7	6
1405	Allowance for subsidy cost (-)	–61	–54
1499	Net present value of assets related to direct loans	334	280
1901	Other Federal assets: Accounts Receivable		
1999	Total assets	366	317
	LIABILITIES:		
	Federal liabilities:		
2103	Debt	363	317
2105	Other	2	
2999	Total liabilities	365	317
	NET POSITION:		
3300	Cumulative results of operations	1	
4999	Total liabilities and net position	366	317

DEBT REDUCTION FINANCING ACCOUNT

Program and Financing (in millions of dollars)

Identification code 012–4143–0–3–351		2021 actual	2022 est.	2023 est.
	Budgetary resources:			
	Unobligated balance:			
1000	Unobligated balance brought forward, Oct 1	72	84	106
	Financing authority:			
	Spending authority from offsetting collections, mandatory:			
1800	Collected	12	22	6
1900	Budget authority (total)	12	22	6
1930	Total budgetary resources available	84	106	112
	Memorandum (non-add) entries:			
1941	Unexpired unobligated balance, end of year	84	106	112
	Financing authority and disbursements, net:			
	Mandatory:			
4090	Budget authority, gross	12	22	6
	Offsets against gross financing authority and disbursements:			
	Offsetting collections (collected) from:			
4120	Federal sources	–5	–15	
4122	Interest on uninvested funds	–4	–4	–3
4123	Loan Repayments - Principal	–3	–3	–3
4130	Offsets against gross budget authority and outlays (total)	–12	–22	–6
4170	Outlays, net (mandatory)	–12	–22	–6
4180	Budget authority, net (total)			
4190	Outlays, net (total)	–12	–22	–6

Status of Direct Loans (in millions of dollars)

Identification code 012–4143–0–3–351		2021 actual	2022 est.	2023 est.
	Cumulative balance of direct loans outstanding:			
1210	Outstanding, start of year	92	92	89
1251	Repayments: Repayments and prepayments		–3	–3
1290	Outstanding, end of year	92	89	86

Foreign Agricultural Service—Continued
Federal Funds—Continued

DEBT REDUCTION FINANCING ACCOUNT—Continued

Balance Sheet (in millions of dollars)

Identification code 012–4143–0–3–351	2020 actual	2021 actual
ASSETS:		
1101 Federal assets: Fund balances with Treasury	72	84
Net value of assets related to post-1991 direct loans receivable:		
1401 Direct loans receivable, gross	92	92
1402 Interest receivable	2	2
1405 Allowance for subsidy cost (-)	–19	–20
1499 Net present value of assets related to direct loans	75	74
1901 Other Federal assets: Accounts Receivable		
1999 Total assets	147	158
LIABILITIES:		
2104 Federal liabilities: Resources payable to Treasury		
Non-Federal liabilities:		
2201 Accounts payable		
2207 Total other liabilities not crosswalked	143	158
2999 Total liabilities	143	158
NET POSITION:		
3300 Cumulative results of operations	4	
4999 Total liabilities and net position	147	158

EXPENSES, PUBLIC LAW 480, FOREIGN ASSISTANCE PROGRAMS, AGRICULTURE LIQUIDATING ACCOUNT

Program and Financing (in millions of dollars)

Identification code 012–2274–0–1–151	2021 actual	2022 est.	2023 est.
Budgetary resources:			
Unobligated balance:			
1000 Unobligated balance brought forward, Oct 1	17	77	
1022 Capital transfer of unobligated balances to general fund	–17	–77	
Budget authority:			
Spending authority from offsetting collections, mandatory:			
1800 Offsetting collections (cash) (Principal and interest)	197	36	30
1820 Capital transfer of spending authority from offsetting collections to general fund	–120	–36	–30
1850 Spending auth from offsetting collections, mand (total)	77		
1930 Total budgetary resources available	77		
Memorandum (non-add) entries:			
1941 Unexpired unobligated balance, end of year	77		
Budget authority and outlays, net:			
Mandatory:			
4090 Budget authority, gross	77		
Offsets against gross budget authority and outlays:			
Offsetting collections (collected) from:			
4123 Principal repayments	–197	–30	–25
4123 Interest repayments		–6	–5
4130 Offsets against gross budget authority and outlays (total)	–197	–36	–30
4160 Budget authority, net (mandatory)	–120	–36	–30
4170 Outlays, net (mandatory)	–197	–36	–30
4180 Budget authority, net (total)	–120	–36	–30
4190 Outlays, net (total)	–197	–36	–30

Status of Direct Loans (in millions of dollars)

Identification code 012–2274–0–1–151	2021 actual	2022 est.	2023 est.
Cumulative balance of direct loans outstanding:			
1210 Outstanding, start of year	451	254	224
1251 Repayments: Repayments and prepayments	–197	–30	–25
1290 Outstanding, end of year	254	224	199

Balance Sheet (in millions of dollars)

Identification code 012–2274–0–1–151	2020 actual	2021 actual
ASSETS:		
1101 Federal assets: Fund balances with Treasury	17	77
1601 Direct loans, gross	451	254
1602 Interest receivable	7	5
1603 Allowance for estimated uncollectible loans and interest (-)	–72	–53
1604 Direct loans and interest receivable, net	386	206
1605 Accounts receivable		
1699 Value of assets related to direct loans	386	206
1999 Total assets	403	283
LIABILITIES:		
2104 Federal liabilities: Resources payable to Treasury	390	271
2207 Non-Federal liabilities: Other	13	12
2999 Total liabilities	403	283
NET POSITION:		
3300 Cumulative results of operations		
4999 Total liabilities and net position	403	283

Trust Funds

FOREIGN SERVICE NATIONAL SEPARATION LIABILITY TRUST FUND

Program and Financing (in millions of dollars)

Identification code 012–8505–0–7–602	2021 actual	2022 est.	2023 est.
Change in obligated balance:			
Unpaid obligations:			
3000 Unpaid obligations, brought forward, Oct 1	18	16	
3020 Outlays (gross)	–2	–16	
3050 Unpaid obligations, end of year	16		
Memorandum (non-add) entries:			
3100 Obligated balance, start of year	18	16	
3200 Obligated balance, end of year	16		
Budget authority and outlays, net:			
Mandatory:			
Outlays, gross:			
4101 Outlays from mandatory balances	2	16	
4180 Budget authority, net (total)			
4190 Outlays, net (total)	2	16	

This fund is maintained to pay separation costs for locally-employed staff in those countries in which such pay is legally authorized. The fund will be maintained by annual government contributions which are appropriated to the Foreign Agricultural Service Salaries and Expenses account.

FOOD AND NUTRITION SERVICE

Federal Funds

NUTRITION PROGRAMS ADMINISTRATION

For necessary administrative expenses of the Food and Nutrition Service for carrying out any domestic nutrition assistance program, $238,670,000: Provided, That of the funds provided herein, $2,000,000 shall be used for the purposes of section 4404 of Public Law 107–171, as amended by section 4401 of Public Law 110–246.

Note.—A full-year 2022 appropriation for this account was not enacted at the time the Budget was prepared; therefore, the Budget assumes this account is operating under the Continuing Appropriations Act, 2022 (Division A of Public Law 117–43, as amended). The amounts included for 2022 reflect the annualized level provided by the continuing resolution.

Program and Financing (in millions of dollars)

Identification code 012–3508–0–1–605	2021 actual	2022 est.	2023 est.
Obligations by program activity:			
0001 Nutrition programs administration	147	159	201
0002 Review of National Academy of Sciences Report for DGA's	1		
0003 Congressional hunger center fellowship	2	2	2
0005 Ensuring Scientific Integrity of Dietary Guidelines and Food Plans			15
0006 Nutrition Security, Education and Racial Equity			23
0007 Cross-Program Technical Assistance for Tribal Communities			2
0008 Dietary Guidelines for Americans (3-Year)	1		
0900 Total new obligations, unexpired accounts	151	161	243
Budgetary resources:			
Unobligated balance:			
1000 Unobligated balance brought forward, Oct 1	9	8	4

DEPARTMENT OF AGRICULTURE

Food and Nutrition Service—Continued
Federal Funds—Continued

163

		2021 actual	2022 est.	2023 est.
	Budget authority:			
	Appropriations, discretionary:			
1100	Appropriation	157	157	239
1120	Appropriations transferred to other acct [012–4609]	–1		
1160	Appropriation, discretionary (total)	156	157	239
	Spending authority from offsetting collections, discretionary:			
1701	Change in uncollected payments, Federal sources	1		
1900	Budget authority (total)	157	157	239
1930	Total budgetary resources available	166	165	243
	Memorandum (non-add) entries:			
1940	Unobligated balance expiring	–7		
1941	Unexpired unobligated balance, end of year	8	4	
	Change in obligated balance:			
	Unpaid obligations:			
3000	Unpaid obligations, brought forward, Oct 1	38	31	30
3010	New obligations, unexpired accounts	151	161	243
3011	Obligations ("upward adjustments"), expired accounts	1		
3020	Outlays (gross)	–152	–162	–226
3041	Recoveries of prior year unpaid obligations, expired	–7		
3050	Unpaid obligations, end of year	31	30	47
	Uncollected payments:			
3060	Uncollected pymts, Fed sources, brought forward, Oct 1		–1	–1
3070	Change in uncollected pymts, Fed sources, unexpired	–1		
3090	Uncollected pymts, Fed sources, end of year	–1	–1	–1
	Memorandum (non-add) entries:			
3100	Obligated balance, start of year	38	30	29
3200	Obligated balance, end of year	30	29	46
	Budget authority and outlays, net:			
	Discretionary:			
4000	Budget authority, gross	157	157	239
	Outlays, gross:			
4010	Outlays from new discretionary authority	125	133	202
4011	Outlays from discretionary balances	27	29	24
4020	Outlays, gross (total)	152	162	226
	Offsets against gross budget authority and outlays:			
	Offsetting collections (collected) from:			
4033	Non-Federal sources	–1		
4040	Offsets against gross budget authority and outlays (total)	–1		
	Additional offsets against gross budget authority only:			
4050	Change in uncollected pymts, Fed sources, unexpired	–1		
4052	Offsetting collections credited to expired accounts	1		
4070	Budget authority, net (discretionary)	156	157	239
4080	Outlays, net (discretionary)	151	162	226
4180	Budget authority, net (total)	156	157	239
4190	Outlays, net (total)	151	162	226

This account funds about half of the Federal operating expenses of the Food and Nutrition Service, including the Center for Nutrition Policy and Promotion (CNPP). CNPP is a non-regulatory organization, with several initiatives that serve as the foundation for many Federal departments' and agencies' policies and programs. CNPP's work includes the *Dietary Guidelines for Americans*, the Healthy Eating Index, USDA food plans such as the Thrifty Food Plan, and MyPlate.

Object Classification (in millions of dollars)

Identification code 012–3508–0–1–605		2021 actual	2022 est.	2023 est.
	Direct obligations:			
	Personnel compensation:			
11.1	Full-time permanent	77	80	104
11.5	Other personnel compensation	5	5	5
11.9	Total personnel compensation	82	85	109
12.1	Civilian personnel benefits	30	36	47
21.0	Travel and transportation of persons	1		
23.1	Rental payments to GSA	13	14	14
25.2	Other services from non-Federal sources	18	14	62
25.3	Other goods and services from Federal sources	3	4	4
26.0	Supplies and materials	1	1	
31.0	Equipment	1	1	1
32.0	Land and structures		4	4
41.0	Grants, subsidies, and contributions	2	2	2
99.9	Total new obligations, unexpired accounts	151	161	243

Employment Summary

Identification code 012–3508–0–1–605	2021 actual	2022 est.	2023 est.
1001 Direct civilian full-time equivalent employment	709	819	927

SUPPLEMENTAL NUTRITION ASSISTANCE PROGRAM

For necessary expenses to carry out the Food and Nutrition Act of 2008 (7 U.S.C. 2011 et seq.), $111,181,895,000, of which $3,000,000,000, to remain available through September 30, 2025, shall be placed in reserve for use only in such amounts and at such times as may become necessary to carry out program operations: Provided, That funds provided herein shall be expended in accordance with section 16 of the Food and Nutrition Act of 2008: Provided further, That of the funds made available under this heading, $998,000 may be used to provide nutrition education services to State agencies and Federally Recognized Tribes participating in the Food Distribution Program on Indian Reservations: Provided further, That of the funds made available under this heading, $1,000,000, to remain available until September 30, 2024, shall be used to carry out section 4208 of Public Law 115–334: Provided further, That of the funds made available under this heading, $3,000,000, to remain available until September 30, 2024, shall be used to carry out section 4003(b) of Public Law 115–334 relating to demonstration projects for tribal organizations: Provided further, That this appropriation shall be subject to any work registration or workfare requirements as may be required by law: Provided further, That funds made available for Employment and Training under this heading shall remain available through September 30, 2024: Provided further, That funds made available under this heading for section 28(d)(1), section 4(b), and section 27(a) of the Food and Nutrition Act of 2008 shall remain available through September 30, 2024: Provided further, That none of the funds made available under this heading may be obligated or expended in contravention of section 213A of the Immigration and Nationality Act (8 U.S.C. 1183A): Provided further, That funds made available under this heading may be used to enter into contracts and employ staff to conduct studies, evaluations, or to conduct activities related to program integrity provided that such activities are authorized by the Food and Nutrition Act of 2008.

For making, after June 30 of the current fiscal year, benefit payments to individuals and payments to States or other non-Federal entities pursuant to the Food and Nutrition Act of 2008 (7 U.S.C. 2011 et seq.) for unanticipated costs incurred for the last three months of the fiscal year, such sums as may be necessary.

For necessary expenses to carry out the Food and Nutrition Act of 2008 (7 U.S.C. 2011 et seq.) for the first quarter of fiscal year 2024, $27,795,473,800, to remain available through September 30, 2024.

Note.—A full-year 2022 appropriation for this account was not enacted at the time the Budget was prepared; therefore, the Budget assumes this account is operating under the Continuing Appropriations Act, 2022 (Division A of Public Law 117–43, as amended). The amounts included for 2022 reflect the annualized level provided by the continuing resolution.

Program and Financing (in millions of dollars)

Identification code 012–3505–0–1–605		2021 actual	2022 est.	2023 est.
	Obligations by program activity:			
0001	Benefits issued	89,664	121,379	97,694
0002	State administration	4,651	5,536	5,707
0003	Employment and training program	550	636	650
0004	Other program costs	236	269	381
0005	Nutrition Assistance for Puerto Rico	2,037	2,502	2,633
0006	Food Distribution Program on Indian Reservations (Commodities in lieu of food stamps)	30	63	82
0007	Food Distribution Program on Indian Reservations (Cooperator administrative expense)	57	63	63
0008	The Emergency Food Assistance Program (commodities)	404	400	419
0009	American Samoa	8	10	11
0010	Community Food Projects	5	5	5
0011	Commonwealth of the Northern Mariana Islands	12	12	31
0012	Nutrition Education Grant Program	434	464	486
0013	Program access	5	5	5
0015	Nutrition Assistance for Puerto Rico-COVID Funding (Division N and ARP)	1,564		
0016	American Samoa-COVID Funding (Division N and ARP)	2		
0017	Commonwealth of Northern Mariana Islands-COVID Funding (Division N and ARP)	14		
0018	FDPIR-COVID Funding	54		
0020	Benefits & Admin-PEBT	31,812	25,300	
0021	Waivers	3,582	3,600	
0022	SAE-Mass Change (Division N and ARP)	341		
0023	COVID relief benefits 15% addition (Division N and ARP)	11,452		

Food and Nutrition Service—Continued
Federal Funds—Continued

SUPPLEMENTAL NUTRITION ASSISTANCE PROGRAM—Continued
Program and Financing—Continued

Identification code 012–3505–0–1–605	2021 actual	2022 est.	2023 est.
0091 Direct program activities, subtotal	146,914	160,244	108,167
0799 Total direct obligations	146,914	160,244	108,167
0801 Supplemental Nutrition Assistance Program (Reimbursable)	69	90	95
0900 Total new obligations, unexpired accounts	146,983	160,334	108,262
Budgetary resources:			
Unobligated balance:			
1000 Unobligated balance brought forward, Oct 1	5,328	7,221	13,227
1001 Discretionary unobligated balance brought fwd, Oct 1	3		
1021 Recoveries of prior year unpaid obligations	22		
1070 Unobligated balance (total)	5,350	7,221	13,227
Budget authority:			
Appropriations, discretionary:			
1100 Appropriation	5	5	5
Appropriations, mandatory:			
1200 Appropriation	177,073	169,255	111,177
1230 Appropriations and/or unobligated balance of appropriations permanently reduced	−10	−10	−15
1260 Appropriations, mandatory (total)	177,063	169,245	111,162
Spending authority from offsetting collections, mandatory:			
1800 Collected	69	90	95
1900 Budget authority (total)	177,137	169,340	111,262
1930 Total budgetary resources available	182,487	176,561	124,489
Memorandum (non-add) entries:			
1940 Unobligated balance expiring	−28,283	−3,000	−3,000
1941 Unexpired unobligated balance, end of year	7,221	13,227	13,227
Change in obligated balance:			
Unpaid obligations:			
3000 Unpaid obligations, brought forward, Oct 1	13,086	21,883	22,713
3010 New obligations, unexpired accounts	146,983	160,334	108,262
3011 Obligations ("upward adjustments"), expired accounts	4,069	6,010	
3020 Outlays (gross)	−134,615	−165,514	−110,677
3040 Recoveries of prior year unpaid obligations, unexpired	−22		
3041 Recoveries of prior year unpaid obligations, expired	−7,618		
3050 Unpaid obligations, end of year	21,883	22,713	20,298
Uncollected payments:			
3060 Uncollected pymts, Fed sources, brought forward, Oct 1	−1		
3071 Change in uncollected pymts, Fed sources, expired	1		
Memorandum (non-add) entries:			
3100 Obligated balance, start of year	13,085	21,883	22,713
3200 Obligated balance, end of year	21,883	22,713	20,298
Budget authority and outlays, net:			
Discretionary:			
4000 Budget authority, gross	5	5	5
Outlays, gross:			
4010 Outlays from new discretionary authority	1	2	2
4011 Outlays from discretionary balances	1	6	3
4020 Outlays, gross (total)	2	8	5
Mandatory:			
4090 Budget authority, gross	177,132	169,335	111,257
Outlays, gross:			
4100 Outlays from new mandatory authority	125,333	159,171	103,180
4101 Outlays from mandatory balances	9,280	6,335	7,492
4110 Outlays, gross (total)	134,613	165,506	110,672
Offsets against gross budget authority and outlays:			
Offsetting collections (collected) from:			
4120 Federal sources	−1		
4123 State Option Plans	−88	−90	−95
4130 Offsets against gross budget authority and outlays (total)	−89	−90	−95
Additional offsets against gross budget authority only:			
4142 Offsetting collections credited to expired accounts	20		
4160 Budget authority, net (mandatory)	177,063	169,245	111,162
4170 Outlays, net (mandatory)	134,524	165,416	110,577
4180 Budget authority, net (total)	177,068	169,250	111,167
4190 Outlays, net (total)	134,526	165,424	110,582

Summary of Budget Authority and Outlays (in millions of dollars)

	2021 actual	2022 est.	2023 est.
Enacted/requested:			
Budget Authority	177,068	169,250	111,167
Outlays	134,526	165,424	110,582
Legislative proposal, subject to PAYGO:			
Budget Authority			63
Outlays			63
Total:			
Budget Authority	177,068	169,250	111,230
Outlays	134,526	165,424	110,645

Authorized by the Food and Nutrition Act of 2008, as amended, the Supplemental Nutrition Assistance Program (SNAP) is the cornerstone of the Nation's nutrition assistance safety net, touching the lives of approximately 42 million Americans each month in FY 2022. The program provides benefits that can be redeemed at authorized food retailers across the country, helping participants put food on the table. The majority of SNAP participants are children, the elderly, or people with disabilities. This account also includes funds for grants to Puerto Rico, American Samoa, and the Commonwealth of the Northern Marianas Islands (CNMI) to administer low-income nutrition assistance programs, in lieu of SNAP; funds to carry out the Emergency Food Assistance Act of 1983; and funds for food distribution and administrative expenses for Native Americans under section 4(b) of the Food and Nutrition Act.

The SNAP contingency fund holds benefits in reserve to cover unforeseen events, such as natural disasters and fluctuations in food prices.

Object Classification (in millions of dollars)

Identification code 012–3505–0–1–605	2021 actual	2022 est.	2023 est.
Direct obligations:			
11.1 Personnel compensation: Full-time permanent	42	43	54
12.1 Civilian personnel benefits	13	18	24
21.0 Travel and transportation of persons	2	2	2
24.0 Printing and reproduction	81	81	81
25.2 Other services from non-Federal sources	82	82	82
26.0 Supplies and materials	476	476	502
31.0 Equipment	1	1	1
41.0 Grants, subsidies, and contributions	146,217	159,541	107,421
99.0 Direct obligations	146,914	160,244	108,167
99.0 Reimbursable obligations	69	90	95
99.9 Total new obligations, unexpired accounts	146,983	160,334	108,262

Employment Summary

Identification code 012–3505–0–1–605	2021 actual	2022 est.	2023 est.
1001 Direct civilian full-time equivalent employment	374	376	462

SUPPLEMENTAL NUTRITION ASSISTANCE PROGRAM
(Legislative proposal, subject to PAYGO)

Program and Financing (in millions of dollars)

Identification code 012–3505–4–1–605	2021 actual	2022 est.	2023 est.
Obligations by program activity:			
0025 Immigrant eligibility for SNAP			36
0026 Special Immigrant Visas			27
0799 Total direct obligations			63
0900 Total new obligations, unexpired accounts (object class 41.0)			63
Budgetary resources:			
Budget authority:			
Appropriations, mandatory:			
1200 Appropriation			63
1900 Budget authority (total)			63
1930 Total budgetary resources available			63
Change in obligated balance:			
Unpaid obligations:			
3010 New obligations, unexpired accounts			63
3020 Outlays (gross)			−63
Budget authority and outlays, net:			
Mandatory:			
4090 Budget authority, gross			63

DEPARTMENT OF AGRICULTURE

Food and Nutrition Service—Continued
Federal Funds—Continued

	Outlays, gross:			
4100	Outlays from new mandatory authority	....	....	63
4180	Budget authority, net (total)	....	....	63
4190	Outlays, net (total)	....	....	63

The Budget proposes several immigration reforms related to Special Immigrant Visas, certain Special Immigrant Juveniles, and reunified families that have effects on SNAP.

CHILD NUTRITION PROGRAMS

(INCLUDING TRANSFERS OF FUNDS)

For necessary expenses to carry out the Richard B. Russell National School Lunch Act (42 U.S.C. 1751 et seq.), except section 21, and the Child Nutrition Act of 1966 (42 U.S.C. 1771 et seq.), except sections 17 and 21; $28,587,957,000, to remain available through September 30, 2024, of which such sums as are made available under section 14222(b)(1) of the Food, Conservation, and Energy Act of 2008 (Public Law 110–246), as amended by this Act, shall be merged with and available for the same time period and purposes as provided herein: Provided, That of the total amount available, $20,162,000 shall be available to carry out section 19 of the Child Nutrition Act of 1966 (42 U.S.C. 1788): Provided further, That of the total amount available, $21,005,000 shall be available to carry out studies and evaluations and shall remain available until expended: Provided further, That of the total amount available, $35,000,000 shall be available to provide competitive grants to State agencies for subgrants to local educational agencies and schools to purchase the equipment, with a value of greater than $1,000, needed to serve healthier meals, improve food safety, and to help support the establishment, maintenance, or expansion of the school breakfast program: Provided further, That of the total amount available, $45,000,000 shall remain available until expended to carry out section 749(g) of the Agriculture Appropriations Act of 2010 (Public Law 111–80): Provided further, That section 26(d) of the Richard B. Russell National School Lunch Act (42 U.S.C. 1769g(d)) is amended in the first sentence by striking "2010 through 2022" and inserting "2010 through 2024": Provided further, That section 9(h)(3) of the Richard B. Russell National School Lunch Act (42 U.S.C. 1758(h)(3)) is amended in the first sentence by striking "For fiscal year 2021" and inserting "For fiscal year 2023": Provided further, That section 9(h)(4) of the Richard B. Russell National School Lunch Act (42 U.S.C. 1758(h)(4)) is amended in the first sentence by striking "For fiscal year 2021" and inserting "For fiscal year 2023": Provided further, That notwithstanding section 18(g)(3)(C) of the Richard B. Russell National School Lunch Act (42 U.S.C. 1769(g)(3)(C)), the total grant amount provided to a farm to school grant recipient in fiscal year 2023 shall not exceed $500,000.

Note.—A full-year 2022 appropriation for this account was not enacted at the time the Budget was prepared; therefore, the Budget assumes this account is operating under the Continuing Appropriations Act, 2022 (Division A of Public Law 117–43, as amended). The amounts included for 2022 reflect the annualized level provided by the continuing resolution.

Program and Financing (in millions of dollars)

Identification code 012–3539–0–1–605	2021 actual	2022 est.	2023 est.
Obligations by program activity:			
0001 Above 185 of poverty	44	5,250	549
0002 130–185 of poverty	15	1,123	970
0003 Below 130 of poverty	5,786	15,731	13,524
0091 Subtotal, National School Lunch Program	5,845	22,104	15,043
0101 Above 185 of poverty	23	900	147
0102 130–185 of poverty	3	339	329
0103 Below 130 of poverty	2,495	5,131	5,569
0191 Subtotal, School Breakfast Program	2,521	6,370	6,045
0201 Above 185 of poverty	734	235	245
0202 130–185 of poverty	164	198	207
0203 Below 130 of poverty	3,092	3,918	4,079
0291 Subtotal, Child and Adult Care Feeding Program	3,990	4,351	4,531
0301 Summer Food Service Program	10,925	581	605
0302 Special Milk Program	3	6	8
0303 State Administrative Expenses	328	332	339
0304 Commodity Procurement	1,518	1,568	1,788
0310 Coordinated Review Effort	10	10	10
0315 Food Safety Education	3	3	4
0320 CN Studies and Evaluations	14	15	21
0325 Computer Support and Processing	18	19	28
0326 CNP CARES Act	2,317	....	....
0327 CNP Covid Third Supplemental	1,477	....	....
0328 School Food / CN Support for Local Food Procurement & Mgt	....	1,000	....
0340 Other Mandatory Program Costs	58	49	65
0391 Subtotal, Other mandatory activities	16,671	3,583	2,868
0401 Team Nutrition and HealthierUS Schools Challenge	18	18	20
0402 Child Nutrition Training/ICN	1	1	1
0405 Summer EBT Demonstration	16	42	45
0415 School Meals Equipment Grants 2 year	28	30	35
0416 School Breakfast Expansion Grants	8	6	....
0417 Farm to School CHIMP	12	12	12
0491 Subtotal, discretionary activities	83	109	113
0501 Fresh Fruit and Vegetable Program	203	187	198
0502 Tech. Assist. Program Integrity/Administrative Reviews	4	8	8
0504 National Food Service Management Inst./Information Clearinghouse	6	5	5
0520 Other Permanent Programs	1	6	6
0591 Subtotal, Permanent Programs	214	206	217
0799 Total direct obligations	29,324	36,723	28,817
0900 Total new obligations, unexpired accounts	29,324	36,723	28,817
Budgetary resources:			
Unobligated balance:			
1000 Unobligated balance brought forward, Oct 1	7,576	11,413	1,755
1001 Discretionary unobligated balance brought fwd, Oct 1	55	....	....
1021 Recoveries of prior year unpaid obligations	5,512	....	....
1033 Recoveries of prior year paid obligations	3	....	....
1070 Unobligated balance (total)	13,091	11,413	1,755
Budget authority:			
Appropriations, discretionary:			
1100 Appropriation	96	96	100
1100 Appropriation - CHIMPS	....	13	13
1160 Appropriation, discretionary (total)	96	109	113
Appropriations, mandatory:			
1200 Appropriation	5,802	6,792	3,287
1200 Appropriation- Permanent Appropriation	19	19	19
1221 Appropriations transferred from other acct [012–5209]	21,223	20,149	25,398
1222 Exercised borrowing authority transferred from other accounts [012–4336]	1,000	....	....
1230 Appropriations and/or unobligated balance of appropriations permanently reduced	–4	–4	–4
1260 Appropriations, mandatory (total)	28,040	26,956	28,700
1900 Budget authority (total)	28,136	27,065	28,813
1930 Total budgetary resources available	41,227	38,478	30,568
Memorandum (non-add) entries:			
1940 Unobligated balance expiring	–490	....	....
1941 Unexpired unobligated balance, end of year	11,413	1,755	1,751
Change in obligated balance:			
Unpaid obligations:			
3000 Unpaid obligations, brought forward, Oct 1	8,493	6,444	12,286
3010 New obligations, unexpired accounts	29,324	36,723	28,817
3011 Obligations ("upward adjustments"), expired accounts	5	....	....
3020 Outlays (gross)	–25,805	–30,881	–28,375
3040 Recoveries of prior year unpaid obligations, unexpired	–5,512	....	....
3041 Recoveries of prior year unpaid obligations, expired	–61	....	....
3050 Unpaid obligations, end of year	6,444	12,286	12,728
Memorandum (non-add) entries:			
3100 Obligated balance, start of year	8,493	6,444	12,286
3200 Obligated balance, end of year	6,444	12,286	12,728
Budget authority and outlays, net:			
Discretionary:			
4000 Budget authority, gross	96	109	113
Outlays, gross:			
4010 Outlays from new discretionary authority	5	24	25
4011 Outlays from discretionary balances	49	86	85
4020 Outlays, gross (total)	54	110	110
Mandatory:			
4090 Budget authority, gross	28,040	26,956	28,700
Outlays, gross:			
4100 Outlays from new mandatory authority	10,595	20,832	22,136
4101 Outlays from mandatory balances	15,156	9,939	6,129
4110 Outlays, gross (total)	25,751	30,771	28,265
Offsets against gross budget authority and outlays:			
Offsetting collections (collected) from:			
4123 Policy Program [Prior Year Collections]	–7	....	....
Additional offsets against gross budget authority only:			
4142 Offsetting collections credited to expired accounts	4	....	....
4143 Recoveries of prior year paid obligations, unexpired accounts	3	....	....
4150 Additional offsets against budget authority only (total)	7	....	....
4160 Budget authority, net (mandatory)	28,040	26,956	28,700

CHILD NUTRITION PROGRAMS—Continued
Program and Financing—Continued

Identification code 012–3539–0–1–605	2021 actual	2022 est.	2023 est.
4170 Outlays, net (mandatory)	25,744	30,771	28,265
4180 Budget authority, net (total)	28,136	27,065	28,813
4190 Outlays, net (total)	25,798	30,881	28,375

The Child Nutrition Programs provide reimbursement to State agencies for cash and commodity meal subsidies through the National School Lunch Program (NSLP), School Breakfast Program (SBP), Special Milk Program, Summer Food Service Program (SFSP), and Child and Adult Care Food Program (CACFP). These programs provide nutritionally balanced, low-cost or free breakfasts and lunches to children every school day; nutrition assistance to children when school is not in session during summer months; and reimbursement to child care providers for nutritious meals and snacks. In addition, the Fresh Fruit and Vegetable Program, targeted to low-income elementary schools, provides fresh fruits and vegetables at no charge to children during the school day. The Budget will support approximately 5.4 billion lunches and snacks served to about 30 million children in school as well as over 2.7 billion breakfasts, and almost 2.2 billion meals through the CACFP.

Object Classification (in millions of dollars)

Identification code 012–3539–0–1–605	2021 actual	2022 est.	2023 est.
Direct obligations:			
11.1 Personnel compensation: Full-time permanent	34	34	32
12.1 Civilian personnel benefits	11	11	14
21.0 Travel and transportation of persons	1	1	1
24.0 Printing and reproduction	1	1	1
25.2 Other services from non-Federal sources	60	60	24
26.0 Supplies and materials (Commodities)	1,461	1,568	2,061
41.0 Grants, subsidies, and contributions	27,756	35,048	26,684
99.0 Direct obligations	29,324	36,723	28,817
99.9 Total new obligations, unexpired accounts	29,324	36,723	28,817

Employment Summary

Identification code 012–3539–0–1–605	2021 actual	2022 est.	2023 est.
1001 Direct civilian full-time equivalent employment	264	297	359

SPECIAL SUPPLEMENTAL NUTRITION PROGRAM FOR WOMEN, INFANTS, AND CHILDREN (WIC)

For necessary expenses to carry out the special supplemental nutrition program as authorized by section 17 of the Child Nutrition Act of 1966 (42 U.S.C. 1786), $6,000,000,000, to remain available through September 30, 2024: Provided, That notwithstanding section 17(h)(10) of the Child Nutrition Act of 1966 (42 U.S.C. 1786(h)(10)), not less than $90,000,000 shall be used for breastfeeding peer counselors and other related activities, and $14,000,000 shall be used for infrastructure: Provided further, That the Secretary shall use funds made available under this heading to increase the amount of a cash-value voucher for women and children participants to an amount recommended by the National Academies of Science, Engineering and Medicine and adjusted for inflation: Provided further, That none of the funds provided in this account shall be available for the purchase of infant formula except in accordance with the cost containment and competitive bidding requirements specified in section 17 of such Act: Provided further, That none of the funds provided shall be available for activities that are not fully reimbursed by other Federal Government departments or agencies unless authorized by section 17 of such Act: Provided further, That upon termination of a federally mandated vendor moratorium and subject to terms and conditions established by the Secretary, the Secretary may waive the requirement at 7 CFR 246.12(g)(6) at the request of a State agency.

Note.—A full-year 2022 appropriation for this account was not enacted at the time the Budget was prepared; therefore, the Budget assumes this account is operating under the Continuing Appropriations Act, 2022 (Division A of Public Law 117–43, as amended). The amounts included for 2022 reflect the annualized level provided by the continuing resolution.

Program and Financing (in millions of dollars)

Identification code 012–3510–0–1–605	2021 actual	2022 est.	2023 est.
Obligations by program activity:			
0001 Grants to States	5,543	5,880	5,842
0004 WIC EBT/MIS	7	8	9
0010 Infrastructure Grants and Technical Assistance	12	14	14
0020 Breastfeeding Peer Counselors and Bonuses	90	90	90
0030 Program Evaluation & Monitoring	18	5	22
0031 WIC FFCRA	330		
0032 WIC Innovation Fund		90	
0034 WIC Cash Value Benefit (CVB)	490		
0035 Federal Oversight	12	11	32
0091 Direct program activities (discretionary), subtotal	6,502	6,098	6,009
0101 UPC Database (mandatory)	1	1	1
0900 Total new obligations, unexpired accounts	6,503	6,099	6,010
Budgetary resources:			
Unobligated balance:			
1000 Unobligated balance brought forward, Oct 1	1,221	1,280	828
1001 Discretionary unobligated balance brought fwd, Oct 1	1,216		
1021 Recoveries of prior year unpaid obligations	912	896	896
1033 Recoveries of prior year paid obligations	20		
1070 Unobligated balance (total)	2,153	2,176	1,724
Budget authority:			
Appropriations, discretionary:			
1100 Appropriation	6,000	6,000	6,000
1130 Appropriations permanently reduced	–1,250		
1131 Unobligated balance of appropriations permanently reduced		–1,250	–250
1160 Appropriation, discretionary (total)	4,750	4,750	5,750
Appropriations, mandatory:			
1200 Appropriation - Permanent Appropriation	881	1	1
1900 Budget authority (total)	5,631	4,751	5,751
1930 Total budgetary resources available	7,784	6,927	7,475
Memorandum (non-add) entries:			
1940 Unobligated balance expiring	–1		
1941 Unexpired unobligated balance, end of year	1,280	828	1,465
Change in obligated balance:			
Unpaid obligations:			
3000 Unpaid obligations, brought forward, Oct 1	1,871	2,411	2,860
3010 New obligations, unexpired accounts	6,503	6,099	6,010
3011 Obligations ("upward adjustments"), expired accounts	1	40	40
3020 Outlays (gross)	–5,049	–4,794	–5,872
3040 Recoveries of prior year unpaid obligations, unexpired	–912	–896	–896
3041 Recoveries of prior year unpaid obligations, expired	–3		
3050 Unpaid obligations, end of year	2,411	2,860	2,142
Memorandum (non-add) entries:			
3100 Obligated balance, start of year	1,871	2,411	2,860
3200 Obligated balance, end of year	2,411	2,860	2,142
Budget authority and outlays, net:			
Discretionary:			
4000 Budget authority, gross	4,750	4,750	5,750
Outlays, gross:			
4010 Outlays from new discretionary authority	2,289	3,162	4,205
4011 Outlays from discretionary balances	2,645	1,455	1,588
4020 Outlays, gross (total)	4,934	4,617	5,793
Offsets against gross budget authority and outlays:			
Offsetting collections (collected) from:			
4033 Non-Federal sources	–23		
Additional offsets against gross budget authority only:			
4052 Offsetting collections credited to expired accounts	3		
4053 Recoveries of prior year paid obligations, unexpired accounts	20		
4060 Additional offsets against budget authority only (total)	23		
4070 Budget authority, net (discretionary)	4,750	4,750	5,750
4080 Outlays, net (discretionary)	4,911	4,617	5,793
Mandatory:			
4090 Budget authority, gross	881	1	1
Outlays, gross:			
4100 Outlays from new mandatory authority	115		
4101 Outlays from mandatory balances		177	79
4110 Outlays, gross (total)	115	177	79
4180 Budget authority, net (total)	5,631	4,751	5,751
4190 Outlays, net (total)	5,026	4,794	5,872

DEPARTMENT OF AGRICULTURE

Food and Nutrition Service—Continued
Federal Funds—Continued

167

The Special Supplemental Nutrition Program for Women, Infants, and Children (WIC) provides low-income at-risk pregnant and postpartum women, infants, and children nutritious supplemental food packages, nutrition education and counseling, and health and immunization referrals. The budget request will support benefits for all women, infants, and children who seek to participate. The budget will also seek to update the food package consistent with recommendations such as those in the *Dietary Guidelines for Americans 2020–2025*.

Object Classification (in millions of dollars)

Identification code 012–3510–0–1–605		2021 actual	2022 est.	2023 est.
	Direct obligations:			
11.1	Personnel compensation: Full-time permanent	4	7	7
12.1	Civilian personnel benefits	5	5	5
25.2	Other services from non-Federal sources	9	9	9
26.0	Supplies and materials	1	1	1
41.0	Grants, subsidies, and contributions	6,484	6,077	5,988
99.9	Total new obligations, unexpired accounts	6,503	6,099	6,010

Employment Summary

Identification code 012–3510–0–1–605		2021 actual	2022 est.	2023 est.
1001	Direct civilian full-time equivalent employment	41	44	70

COMMODITY ASSISTANCE PROGRAM

For necessary expenses to carry out disaster assistance and the Commodity Supplemental Food Program as authorized by section 4(a) of the Agriculture and Consumer Protection Act of 1973 (7 U.S.C. 612c note); the Emergency Food Assistance Act of 1983; special assistance for the nuclear affected islands, as authorized by section 103(f)(2) of the Compact of Free Association Amendments Act of 2003 (Public Law 108–188); and the Farmers' Market Nutrition Program, as authorized by section 17(m) of the Child Nutrition Act of 1966, $464,210,000, to remain available through September 30, 2024: Provided, That none of these funds shall be available to reimburse the Commodity Credit Corporation for commodities donated to the program: Provided further, That notwithstanding any other provision of law, effective with funds made available in fiscal year 2023 to support the Seniors Farmers' Market Nutrition Program, as authorized by section 4402 of the Farm Security and Rural Investment Act of 2002, such funds shall remain available through September 30, 2024: Provided further, That of the funds made available under section 27(a) of the Food and Nutrition Act of 2008 (7 U.S.C. 2036(a)), the Secretary may use up to 20 percent for costs associated with the distribution of commodities.

Note.—A full-year 2022 appropriation for this account was not enacted at the time the Budget was prepared; therefore, the Budget assumes this account is operating under the Continuing Appropriations Act, 2022 (Division A of Public Law 117–43, as amended). The amounts included for 2022 reflect the annualized level provided by the continuing resolution.

Program and Financing (in millions of dollars)

Identification code 012–3507–0–1–605		2021 actual	2022 est.	2023 est.
	Obligations by program activity:			
0001	Commodity procurement	270	270	274
0002	Administrative costs	61	61	64
0091	Subtotal, commodity supplemental food program	331	331	338
0105	TEFAP Administrative	88	80	100
0110	Senior farmers' market	24	21	20
0115	Farmers' market nutrition program	30	24	24
0120	Pacific island and disaster assistance	1	1	1
0130	NSIP (Transfer Funds)	1	1	1
0131	TEFAP Supplemental FFCRA Food	196		
0132	TEFAP Farm Bill	4	4	4
0134	TEFAP Supplemental Food CARES Act	44		
0135	TEFAP Admin Supplemental CARES Act	1		
0136	TEFAP COVID Supplemental (Division N)	399		
0137	CSFP COVID Supplemental (Division N)	13		
0138	CSFP ARP Supplemental	37		
0191	Direct program activities, subtotal	838	131	150
0900	Total new obligations, unexpired accounts	1,169	462	488

	Budgetary resources:			
	Unobligated balance:			
1000	Unobligated balance brought forward, Oct 1	257	42	32
1001	Discretionary unobligated balance brought fwd, Oct 1	252		
1021	Recoveries of prior year unpaid obligations	60		
1070	Unobligated balance (total)	317	42	32
	Budget authority:			
	Appropriations, discretionary:			
1100	Appropriation	840	427	464
1121	Appropriations transferred from other acct [075–0142]	1	1	
1160	Appropriation, discretionary (total)	841	428	464
	Appropriations, mandatory:			
1200	Appropriation	41	4	4
1222	Exercised borrowing authority transferred from other accounts [012–4336]	20	21	21
1230	Appropriations and/or unobligated balance of appropriations permanently reduced	–1	–1	–1
1260	Appropriations, mandatory (total)	60	24	24
1900	Budget authority (total)	901	452	488
1930	Total budgetary resources available	1,218	494	520
	Memorandum (non-add) entries:			
1940	Unobligated balance expiring	–7		
1941	Unexpired unobligated balance, end of year	42	32	32
	Change in obligated balance:			
	Unpaid obligations:			
3000	Unpaid obligations, brought forward, Oct 1	467	505	95
3010	New obligations, unexpired accounts	1,169	462	488
3020	Outlays (gross)	–1,069	–872	–482
3040	Recoveries of prior year unpaid obligations, unexpired	–60		
3041	Recoveries of prior year unpaid obligations, expired	–2		
3050	Unpaid obligations, end of year	505	95	101
	Uncollected payments:			
3060	Uncollected pymts, Fed sources, brought forward, Oct 1	–5	–2	–2
3071	Change in uncollected pymts, Fed sources, expired	3		
3090	Uncollected pymts, Fed sources, end of year	–2	–2	–2
	Memorandum (non-add) entries:			
3100	Obligated balance, start of year	462	503	93
3200	Obligated balance, end of year	503	93	99
	Budget authority and outlays, net:			
	Discretionary:			
4000	Budget authority, gross	841	428	464
	Outlays, gross:			
4010	Outlays from new discretionary authority	409	349	379
4011	Outlays from discretionary balances	622	431	79
4020	Outlays, gross (total)	1,031	780	458
	Mandatory:			
4090	Budget authority, gross	60	24	24
	Outlays, gross:			
4100	Outlays from new mandatory authority	20	18	18
4101	Outlays from mandatory balances	18	74	6
4110	Outlays, gross (total)	38	92	24
	Offsets against gross budget authority and outlays:			
	Offsetting collections (collected) from:			
4120	Federal sources	–3		
	Additional offsets against gross budget authority only:			
4142	Offsetting collections credited to expired accounts	3		
4160	Budget authority, net (mandatory)	60	24	24
4170	Outlays, net (mandatory)	35	92	24
4180	Budget authority, net (total)	901	452	488
4190	Outlays, net (total)	1,066	872	482

This account funds the Commodity Supplemental Food Program (CSFP), administrative expenses of The Emergency Food Assistance Program (TEFAP), The WIC Farmers' Market Nutrition Program (FMNP), The Senior Farmers' Market Nutrition Program (SFMNP), assistance for the nuclear-affected islands, and disaster relief.

CSFP works to improve the health of low-income elderly persons at least 60 years of age by supplementing their diets with nutritious USDA foods. Participants receive a monthly food package and State and local administrative costs are provided to cover expenses such as warehousing, food delivery, participant certification, and nutrition education.

The TEFAP Administrative funding provides cash to support State administrative activities and to maintain the storage and distribution pipeline for USDA and privately-donated commodities (TEFAP commodities are

COMMODITY ASSISTANCE PROGRAM—Continued

separately funded through the Supplemental Nutrition Assistance Program (SNAP) account).

The account also includes funds for the SFMNP and FMNP, which provide low-income elderly and WIC-eligible participants, respectively, with vouchers to purchase produce directly from farmers, at farmers' markets, and roadside stands. The Senior Farmers' Market Nutrition Program is funded by a transfer from the Commodity Credit Corporation.

Object Classification (in millions of dollars)

Identification code 012–3507–0–1–605		2021 actual	2022 est.	2023 est.
	Direct obligations:			
25.3	Other goods and services from Federal sources	3	3	3
26.0	Supplies and materials (commodities)	1,008	304	316
41.0	Grants, subsidies, and contributions	158	155	169
99.9	Total new obligations, unexpired accounts	1,169	462	488

Employment Summary

Identification code 012–3507–0–1–605		2021 actual	2022 est.	2023 est.
1001	Direct civilian full-time equivalent employment	3	3	3

FOREST SERVICE

Federal Funds

CAPITAL IMPROVEMENT AND MAINTENANCE

(INCLUDING TRANSFER OF FUNDS)

For necessary expenses of the Forest Service, not otherwise provided for, $140,371,000, to remain available through September 30, 2026, for construction, capital improvement, maintenance, and acquisition of buildings and other facilities and infrastructure; and for construction, reconstruction, and decommissioning of roads that are no longer needed, including unauthorized roads that are not part of the transportation system; and for maintenance of forest roads and trails by the Forest Service as authorized by 16 U.S.C. 532–538 and 23 U.S.C. 101 and 205.

Note.—A full-year 2022 appropriation for this account was not enacted at the time the Budget was prepared; therefore, the Budget assumes this account is operating under the Continuing Appropriations Act, 2022 (Division A of Public Law 117–43, as amended). The amounts included for 2022 reflect the annualized level provided by the continuing resolution.

CAPITAL IMPROVEMENT AND MAINTENANCE

[For an additional amount for "Capital Improvement and Maintenance", $470,000,000, to remain available until expended, for necessary expenses related to the consequences of calendar year 2019, 2020, and 2021 wildfires, hurricanes and other natural disasters.] *(Disaster Relief Supplemental Appropriations Act, 2022.)*

CAPITAL IMPROVEMENT AND MAINTENANCE

[(INCLUDING TRANSFERS OF FUNDS)]

[For an additional amount for "Capital Improvement and Maintenance", $360,000,000, to remain available until September 30, 2029: *Provided*, That $72,000,000, to remain available until September 30, 2025, shall be made available for fiscal year 2022, $72,000,000, to remain available until September 30, 2026, shall be made available for fiscal year 2023, $72,000,000, to remain available until September 30, 2027, shall be made available for fiscal year 2024, $72,000,000, to remain available until September 30, 2028, shall be made available for fiscal year 2025, and $72,000,000, to remain available until September 30, 2029, shall be made available for fiscal year 2026: *Provided further*, That of the funds made available under this heading in this Act, the following amounts shall be for the following purposes in equal amounts for each of fiscal years 2022 through 2026—]

[(1) $250,000,000 to carry out activities of the Legacy Road and Trail Remediation Program, as authorized in Public Law 88–657 (16 U.S.C. 532 et seq.) (commonly known as the "Forest Roads and Trails Act"), as amended by section 40801 of division D of this Act;]

[(2) $100,000,000 for construction of temporary roads or reconstruction and maintenance of roads to facilitate forest restoration and management projects that reduce wildfire risk; and]

[(3) $10,000,000 for the removal of non-hydropower Federal dams and for providing dam removal technical assistance:]

[*Provided further*, That funds appropriated under this heading in this Act may be transferred to the United States Fish and Wildlife Service and the National Marine Fisheries Service for the costs of carrying out their responsibilities under the Endangered Species Act of 1973 (16 U.S.C. 1531 et seq.) to consult and conference, as required by section 7 of such Act, in connection with wildland fire management activities: *Provided further*, That amounts made available under this heading in this Act for each of fiscal years 2022 through 2026 may be transferred between accounts affected by the Forest Service budget restructure outlined in section 435 of division D of the Further Consolidated Appropriations Act, 2020 (Public Law 116–94) to carry out the activities in support of this heading: *Provided further*, That one-half of one percent of the amounts made available under this heading in this Act in each of fiscal years 2022 through 2026 shall be transferred to the Office of Inspector General of the Department of Agriculture for oversight of funding provided to the Forest Service in this title in this Act: *Provided further*, That such amount is designated by the Congress as being for an emergency requirement pursuant to section 4112(a) of H. Con. Res. 71 (115th Congress), the concurrent resolution on the budget for fiscal year 2018, and to section 251(b) of the Balanced Budget and Emergency Deficit Control Act of 1985.] *(Infrastructure Investments and Jobs Appropriations Act.)*

Program and Financing (in millions of dollars)

Identification code 012–1103–0–1–302		2021 actual	2022 est.	2023 est.
	Obligations by program activity:			
0001	Capital improvement and maintenance	188	341	436
0801	Capital Improvement and Maintenance (Reimbursable)	22	22	22
0900	Total new obligations, unexpired accounts	210	363	458
	Budgetary resources:			
	Unobligated balance:			
1000	Unobligated balance brought forward, Oct 1	138	112	448
1021	Recoveries of prior year unpaid obligations	17	17	17
1070	Unobligated balance (total)	155	129	465
	Budget authority:			
	Appropriations, discretionary:			
1100	Appropriation - Capital Impro and Maint [P.L. 116–260]	140	140	140
1100	Appropriation (Disaster Supplemental)		470	
1100	Appropriation (IIJA)		72	
1120	Appropriations transferred to other acct [012–1122]		–12	
1120	Appropriations transferred to other acct [012–1106]		–21	
1160	Appropriation, discretionary (total)	140	649	140
	Advance appropriations, discretionary:			
1170	Advance appropriation			72
1172	Advance appropriations transferred to other accounts [012–1106]			–22
1172	Advance appropriations transferred to other accounts [012–1122]			–9
1180	Advanced appropriation, discretionary (total)			41
	Spending authority from offsetting collections, discretionary:			
1700	Collected	24	33	
1701	Change in uncollected payments, Federal sources	6		
1750	Spending auth from offsetting collections, disc (total)	30	33	
1900	Budget authority (total)	170	682	181
1930	Total budgetary resources available	325	811	646
	Memorandum (non-add) entries:			
1940	Unobligated balance expiring	–3		
1941	Unexpired unobligated balance, end of year	112	448	188
	Change in obligated balance:			
	Unpaid obligations:			
3000	Unpaid obligations, brought forward, Oct 1	271	209	3
3010	New obligations, unexpired accounts	210	363	458
3020	Outlays (gross)	–255	–552	–277
3040	Recoveries of prior year unpaid obligations, unexpired	–17	–17	–17
3050	Unpaid obligations, end of year	209	3	167
	Uncollected payments:			
3060	Uncollected pymts, Fed sources, brought forward, Oct 1	–64	–67	–67
3070	Change in uncollected pymts, Fed sources, unexpired	–6		
3071	Change in uncollected pymts, Fed sources, expired	3		
3090	Uncollected pymts, Fed sources, end of year	–67	–67	–67
	Memorandum (non-add) entries:			
3100	Obligated balance, start of year	207	142	–64
3200	Obligated balance, end of year	142	–64	100

DEPARTMENT OF AGRICULTURE

Forest Service—Continued
Federal Funds—Continued

169

		2021 actual	2022 est.	2023 est.
	Budget authority and outlays, net:			
	Discretionary:			
4000	Budget authority, gross	170	682	181
	Outlays, gross:			
4010	Outlays from new discretionary authority	55	281	72
4011	Outlays from discretionary balances	200	271	205
4020	Outlays, gross (total)	255	552	277
	Offsets against gross budget authority and outlays:			
	Offsetting collections (collected) from:			
4030	Federal sources	–3	–3	
4033	Non-Federal sources	–22	–30	
4040	Offsets against gross budget authority and outlays (total)	–25	–33	
	Additional offsets against gross budget authority only:			
4050	Change in uncollected pymts, Fed sources, unexpired	–6		
4052	Offsetting collections credited to expired accounts	1		
4060	Additional offsets against budget authority only (total)	–5		
4070	Budget authority, net (discretionary)	140	649	181
4080	Outlays, net (discretionary)	230	519	277
4180	Budget authority, net (total)	140	649	181
4190	Outlays, net (total)	230	519	277

The 2023 Budget requests $140.3 million for Capital Improvement and Maintenance. Funding provides for capital improvement and maintenance of Forest Service assets, including facilities, roads, trails, and legacy roads and trails remediation. The program emphasizes efficient and effective re-investment and maintenance of National Forest System (NFS) infrastructure that supports public and administrative uses, and quality recreation experiences with minimal impact to ecosystem stability and conditions.

Facilities.—Provides for capital improvement and maintenance of recreation sites; visitor centers; fire, research, administrative, and other facilities; telecommunication sites and towers, dams, and the acquisition of buildings and other facilities necessary to carry out the mission of the Forest Service.

Roads.—Provides for capital improvement and maintenance of the NFS road system, including bridges and terminal facilities such as parking lots, trailhead parking, camping spurs, and truck turnarounds. Funding priorities include driver safety and resource protection, ecosystem health including clean water and aquatic passage.

Trails.—Provides for capital improvement and maintenance of NFS trails. Funding is used to keep trails open for access and to protect vegetation, soil, and water quality.

Object Classification (in millions of dollars)

Identification code 012–1103–0–1–302		2021 actual	2022 est.	2023 est.
	Direct obligations:			
	Personnel compensation:			
11.1	Full-time permanent	1		
11.3	Other than full-time permanent	1		
11.5	Other personnel compensation	1		
11.9	Total personnel compensation	3		
12.1	Civilian personnel benefits	1		
21.0	Travel and transportation of persons		1	1
22.0	Transportation of things	1	2	3
23.3	Communications, utilities, and miscellaneous charges	1	1	1
25.2	Other services from non-Federal sources	69	128	169
25.3	Other goods and services from Federal sources	60	111	140
25.4	Operation and maintenance of facilities	1	2	2
25.7	Operation and maintenance of equipment	1	2	3
26.0	Supplies and materials	11	20	26
31.0	Equipment	1	3	3
32.0	Land and structures	21	38	48
41.0	Grants, subsidies, and contributions	17	32	40
99.0	Direct obligations	187	340	436
99.0	Reimbursable obligations	22	22	22
99.5	Adjustment for rounding	1	1	
99.9	Total new obligations, unexpired accounts	210	363	458

Employment Summary

Identification code 012–1103–0–1–302	2021 actual	2022 est.	2023 est.
1001 Direct civilian full-time equivalent employment	110	8	2
2001 Reimbursable civilian full-time equivalent employment	185	185	185

	2021 actual	2022 est.	2023 est.
3001 Allocation account civilian full-time equivalent employment	15	15	15

FOREST AND RANGELAND RESEARCH

For necessary expenses of forest and rangeland research as authorized by law, $317,773,000, to remain available through September 30, 2026: Provided, That of the funds provided, $22,197,000 is for the forest inventory and analysis program: Provided further, That of the funds provided, $4,000,000 is for the Joint Fire Science Program: Provided further, That all authorities for the use of funds, including the use of contracts, grants, and cooperative agreements, available to execute the Forest and Rangeland Research appropriation, are also available in the utilization of these funds for Fire Science Research.

GIFTS, DONATIONS AND BEQUESTS FOR FOREST AND RANGELAND RESEARCH

For expenses authorized by 16 U.S.C. 1643(b), $45,000, to remain available through September 30, 2026, to be derived from the fund established pursuant to the above Act.

Note.—A full-year 2022 appropriation for this account was not enacted at the time the Budget was prepared; therefore, the Budget assumes this account is operating under the Continuing Appropriations Act, 2022 (Division A of Public Law 117–43, as amended). The amounts included for 2022 reflect the annualized level provided by the continuing resolution.

FOREST AND RANGELAND RESEARCH

[*For an additional amount for "Forest and Rangeland Research", $25,000,000, to remain available until expended, for necessary expenses related to the consequences of calendar year 2019, 2020, and 2021 wildfires, hurricanes and other natural disasters for the forest inventory and analysis program.*] *(Disaster Relief Supplemental Appropriations Act, 2022.)*

FOREST AND RANGELAND RESEARCH

[*For an additional amount for "Forest and Rangeland Research", $10,000,000, to remain available until September 30, 2029, for the Secretary of Agriculture, acting through the Chief of the Forest Service, to carry out activities of the Joint Fire Science Program, as authorized in section 40803 of division D of this Act: Provided, That $2,000,000, to remain available until September 30, 2025, shall be made available for fiscal year 2022, $2,000,000, to remain available until September 30, 2026, shall be made available for fiscal year 2023, $2,000,000, to remain available until September 30, 2027, shall be made available for fiscal year 2024, $2,000,000, to remain available until September 30, 2028, shall be made available for fiscal year 2025, and $2,000,000, to remain available until September 30, 2029, shall be made available for fiscal year 2026: Provided further, That such amount is designated by the Congress as being for an emergency requirement pursuant to section 4112(a) of H. Con. Res. 71 (115th Congress), the concurrent resolution on the budget for fiscal year 2018, and to section 251(b) of the Balanced Budget and Emergency Deficit Control Act of 1985.*] *(Infrastructure Investments and Jobs Appropriations Act.)*

Program and Financing (in millions of dollars)

Identification code 012–1104–0–1–302	2021 actual	2022 est.	2023 est.
Obligations by program activity:			
0006 Forest and rangeland research	267	345	383
0801 Forest and Rangeland Research (Reimbursable)	27	28	28
0900 Total new obligations, unexpired accounts	294	373	411
Budgetary resources:			
Unobligated balance:			
1000 Unobligated balance brought forward, Oct 1	39	36	51
1021 Recoveries of prior year unpaid obligations	4	4	4
1070 Unobligated balance (total)	43	40	55
Budget authority:			
Appropriations, discretionary:			
1100 Appropriation - Forest and Rangeland [P.L. 116–260]	59	58	102
1100 Appropriation - Forest and Rangeland [P.L. 116–260] (Salaries and Exp)	200	200	216
1100 Appropriation (Disaster Supplemental)		25	
1100 Appropriation (IIJA)		2	
1120 Appropriations transferred to other acct [012–1122]			–2
1121 Appropriations transferred from other acct [012–1105]		4	
1121 Appropriations transferred from other acct [012–1106]		55	
1121 Appropriations transferred from other acct [012–1115]		7	
1160 Appropriation, discretionary (total)	259	351	316
Advance appropriations, discretionary:			
1170 Advance appropriation			2

FOREST AND RANGELAND RESEARCH—Continued
Program and Financing—Continued

Identification code 012–1104–0–1–302	2021 actual	2022 est.	2023 est.
1173 Advance appropriations transferred from other accounts [012–1105]	....	....	4
1173 Advance appropriations transferred from other accounts [012–1106]	....	....	43
1173 Advance appropriations transferred from other accounts [012–1115]	....	....	4
1180 Advanced appropriation, discretionary (total)	....	....	53
Spending authority from offsetting collections, discretionary:			
1700 Collected	25	33	....
1701 Change in uncollected payments, Federal sources	3	....	....
1750 Spending auth from offsetting collections, disc (total)	28	33	....
1900 Budget authority (total)	287	384	369
1930 Total budgetary resources available	330	424	424
Memorandum (non-add) entries:			
1941 Unexpired unobligated balance, end of year	36	51	13
Change in obligated balance:			
Unpaid obligations:			
3000 Unpaid obligations, brought forward, Oct 1	161	161	107
3010 New obligations, unexpired accounts	294	373	411
3020 Outlays (gross)	–290	–423	–336
3040 Recoveries of prior year unpaid obligations, unexpired	–4	–4	–4
3050 Unpaid obligations, end of year	161	107	178
Uncollected payments:			
3060 Uncollected pymts, Fed sources, brought forward, Oct 1	–45	–48	–48
3070 Change in uncollected pymts, Fed sources, unexpired	–3	....	....
3090 Uncollected pymts, Fed sources, end of year	–48	–48	–48
Memorandum (non-add) entries:			
3100 Obligated balance, start of year	116	113	59
3200 Obligated balance, end of year	113	59	130
Budget authority and outlays, net:			
Discretionary:			
4000 Budget authority, gross	287	384	369
Outlays, gross:			
4010 Outlays from new discretionary authority	194	260	257
4011 Outlays from discretionary balances	96	163	79
4020 Outlays, gross (total)	290	423	336
Offsets against gross budget authority and outlays:			
Offsetting collections (collected) from:			
4030 Federal sources	–18	–22	....
4033 Non-Federal sources	–7	–11	....
4040 Offsets against gross budget authority and outlays (total)	–25	–33	....
Additional offsets against gross budget authority only:			
4050 Change in uncollected pymts, Fed sources, unexpired	–3	....	....
4070 Budget authority, net (discretionary)	259	351	369
4080 Outlays, net (discretionary)	265	390	336
4180 Budget authority, net (total)	259	351	369
4190 Outlays, net (total)	265	390	336

The 2023 Budget requests $317.7 million for Forest and Rangeland Research (Forest Service R&D). Within this funding level, $216 million is requested for workforce Salary and Expenses, $22 million is requested for Forest Inventory and Analysis to continue to implement the inventory program in all 50 States (including interior Alaska), the affiliated Pacific Islands, Puerto Rico, and the U.S. Virgin Islands, and $4 million for the Joint Fire Science Program to address important science needs associated with wildland fire that take into consideration climate and climate change, fire risk assessment and management through the Fire Risk Assessment framework, fuels management, and post-fire rehabilitation to promote resilience of forest and rangeland ecosystems. This request is an increase of $59 million to allow the Forest Service to restore scientific research to address the Administration's priorities, including climate change, environmental justice, and economic prosperity in the forest sector.

The Forest Service will apply $25 million of this increase to research and science delivery related to climate mitigation, adaptation, and resilience. This increase will allow Forest and Rangeland Research to increase its scientific contributions in support of the Administration's science-based approach to improving the climate resilience of forest and rangeland ecosystems. Relative to 2022, Forest and Rangeland Research will expand the scope and scale of research and science delivery programs related to reforestation, carbon sequestration, and carbon accounting, all of which are essential to informing climate adaptation and mitigation. The request also includes $6 million to contribute to scientific understanding of climate change through the Department of Agriculture's Climate Hubs. These hubs accelerate science production and technology transfer to aid land management agencies, private landowners, and agricultural producers, including foresters, with scientifically sound climate adaptation.

Object Classification (in millions of dollars)

Identification code 012–1104–0–1–302	2021 actual	2022 est.	2023 est.
Direct obligations:			
Personnel compensation:			
11.1 Full-time permanent	132	132	136
11.3 Other than full-time permanent	3	3	3
11.5 Other personnel compensation	4	4	4
11.9 Total personnel compensation	139	139	143
12.1 Civilian personnel benefits	53	53	54
21.0 Travel and transportation of persons	2	4	5
22.0 Transportation of things	2	2	3
23.2 Rental payments to others	....	....	1
25.2 Other services from non-Federal sources	9	18	22
25.3 Other goods and services from Federal sources	14	30	36
25.5 Research and development contracts	28	58	70
25.7 Operation and maintenance of equipment	....	1	1
26.0 Supplies and materials	3	7	8
31.0 Equipment	2	5	6
41.0 Grants, subsidies, and contributions	14	28	34
99.0 Direct obligations	266	345	383
99.0 Reimbursable obligations	27	27	27
99.5 Adjustment for rounding	1	1	1
99.9 Total new obligations, unexpired accounts	294	373	411

Employment Summary

Identification code 012–1104–0–1–302	2021 actual	2022 est.	2023 est.
1001 Direct civilian full-time equivalent employment	1,446	1,442	1,442
2001 Reimbursable civilian full-time equivalent employment	57	57	57

NATIONAL FOREST SYSTEM

(INCLUDING TRANSFERS OF FUNDS)

For necessary expenses of the Forest Service, not otherwise provided for, for management, protection, improvement, and utilization of the National Forest System, $2,180,915,000, to remain available through September 30, 2026: Provided, That of the funds provided, $80,000,000 shall be deposited in the Collaborative Forest Landscape Restoration Fund for ecological restoration treatments as authorized by 16 U.S.C. 7303(f): Provided further, That of the funds provided, $37,645,000 shall be for forest products: Provided further, That any unobligated funds appropriated in a previous fiscal year for hazardous fuels management may be transferred to the Wildland Fire Management account: Provided further, That notwithstanding section 33 of the Bankhead Jones Farm Tenant Act (7 U.S.C. 1012), the Secretary of Agriculture, in calculating a fee for grazing on a National Grassland, may provide a credit of up to 50 percent of the calculated fee to a Grazing Association or direct permittee for a conservation practice approved by the Secretary in advance of the fiscal year in which the cost of the conservation practice is incurred, and that the amount credited shall remain available to the Grazing Association or the direct permittee, as appropriate, in the fiscal year in which the credit is made and each fiscal year thereafter for use on the project for conservation practices approved by the Secretary: Provided further, That funds appropriated to this account shall be available for the base salary and expenses of employees that carry out the functions funded by the "Capital Improvement and Maintenance" account, the "Range Betterment Fund" account, and the "Management of National Forests for Subsistence Uses" account.

Note.—A full-year 2022 appropriation for this account was not enacted at the time the Budget was prepared; therefore, the Budget assumes this account is operating under the Continuing Appropriations Act, 2022 (Division A of Public Law 117–43, as amended). The amounts included for 2022 reflect the annualized level provided by the continuing resolution.

DEPARTMENT OF AGRICULTURE

NATIONAL FOREST SYSTEM

⟦For an additional amount for "National Forest System", $710,000,000, to remain available until expended: *Provided*, That of the amounts provided under this heading in this Act, $535,000,000 shall be for necessary expenses related to the consequences of calendar year 2019, 2020, and 2021 wildfires, hurricanes and other natural disasters, including no less than $175,000,000 for high priority post-wildfire restoration for watershed protection, critical habitat, and burned area recovery: *Provided further*, That of the amounts provided under this heading in this Act, $175,000,000 shall be for hazardous fuels mitigation.⟧ *(Disaster Relief Supplemental Appropriations Act, 2022.)*

NATIONAL FOREST SYSTEM

⟦(INCLUDING TRANSFERS OF FUNDS)⟧

⟦For an additional amount for "National Forest System", $2,854,000,000, to remain available until expended: *Provided*, That $734,800,000, to remain available until expended, shall be made available for fiscal year 2022, $529,800,000, to remain available until expended, shall be made available for fiscal year 2023, $529,800,000, to remain available until expended, shall be made available for fiscal year 2024, $529,800,000, to remain available until expended, shall be made available for fiscal year 2025, and $529,800,000, to remain available until expended, shall be made available for fiscal year 2026: *Provided further*, That of the funds made available under this heading in this Act, the following amounts shall be for the following purposes—⟧

⟦(1) $2,115,000,000 for the Secretary of Agriculture, acting through the Chief of the Forest Service, to carry out activities for the Department of Agriculture as authorized in sections 40803 and 40804 of division D of this Act, of which $587,000,000, to remain available until expended, shall be made available for fiscal year 2022 and $382,000,000, to remain available until expended, shall be made available for each of fiscal years 2023 through 2026;⟧

⟦(2) In addition to amounts made available in paragraph (1) for hazardous fuels management activities, $102,800,000 for each of fiscal years 2022 through 2026 for such purposes; and⟧

⟦(3) In addition to amounts made available in paragraph (1) for burned area recovery, $45,000,000 for each of fiscal years 2022 through 2026 for such purposes:⟧

⟦*Provided further*, That up to $12,000,000 for each of fiscal years 2022 through 2026 from funds made available in paragraph (2) of the preceding proviso may be used to make grants, using any authorities available for the Forest Service under the "State and Private Forestry" appropriation for the purposes of creating incentives for increased use of biomass from National Forest System lands, including the Community Wood Energy Program and the Wood Innovation Grants Program: *Provided further*, That up to $8,000,000 for each of fiscal years 2022 through 2026 from funds made available in paragraph (2) of the preceding proviso shall be for implementation of the Tribal Forestry Protection Act, as amended (Public Law 108–278): *Provided further*, That funds appropriated under this heading in this Act may be transferred to the United States Fish and Wildlife Service and the National Marine Fisheries Service for the costs of carrying out their responsibilities under the Endangered Species Act of 1973 (16 U.S.C. 1531 et seq.) to consult and conference, as required by section 7 of such Act, in connection with wildland fire management activities: *Provided further*, That the Secretary of the Interior and the Secretary of Agriculture, acting through the Chief of the Forest Service, may authorize the transfer of funds provided under this heading in this Act between the Departments for the purpose of carrying out activities as authorized in section 40804(b)(1) of division D of this Act: *Provided further*, That amounts made available under this heading in this Act for each of fiscal years 2022 through 2026 may be transferred between accounts affected by the Forest Service budget restructure outlined in section 435 of division D of the Further Consolidated Appropriations Act, 2020 (Public Law 116–94) to carry out the activities in support of this heading: *Provided further*, That amounts made available under this heading in this Act in each of fiscal years 2022 through 2026 shall be available for salaries and expenses: *Provided further*, That one-half of one percent of the amounts made available under this heading in this Act in each of fiscal years 2022 through 2026 shall be transferred to the Office of Inspector General of the Department of Agriculture for oversight of funding provided to the Forest Service in this title in this Act: *Provided further*, That such amount is designated by the Congress as being for an emergency requirement pursuant to section 4112(a) of H. Con. Res. 71 (115th Congress), the concurrent resolution on the budget for fiscal year 2018, and to section 251(b) of the Balanced Budget and Emergency Deficit Control Act of 1985.⟧ *(Infrastructure Investments and Jobs Appropriations Act.)*

Program and Financing (in millions of dollars)

Identification code 012–1106–0–1–302		2021 actual	2022 est.	2023 est.
	Obligations by program activity:			
0001	National forest system	1,844	2,245	2,726
0801	National Forest System (Reimbursable)	79	79	79
0900	Total new obligations, unexpired accounts	1,923	2,324	2,805
	Budgetary resources:			
	Unobligated balance:			
1000	Unobligated balance brought forward, Oct 1	282	244	1,107
1010	Unobligated balance transfer to other accts [012–1122]	–7		
1021	Recoveries of prior year unpaid obligations	54	52	52
1033	Recoveries of prior year paid obligations	1		
1070	Unobligated balance (total)	330	296	1,159
	Budget authority:			
	Appropriations, discretionary:			
1100	Appropriation National Forest Systems [P.L. 116–260]	378	378	500
1100	Appropriation Salaries and Expenses [P.L. 116–260]	1,409	1,409	1,681
1100	Appropriation (Disaster Supplemental)		710	
1100	Appropriation (IIJA)		735	
1120	Appropriations transferred to other acct [014–1125]	–1		
1120	Appropriations transferred to other acct [012–1122]	–9	–118	
1120	Appropriations transferred to other acct [012–1115]		–47	
1120	Appropriations transferred to other acct [012–0900]		–4	
1120	Appropriations transferred to other acct [012–1104]		–55	
1121	Appropriations transferred from other acct [012–5634]		5	
1121	Appropriations transferred from other acct [012–1103]		21	
1160	Appropriation, discretionary (total)	1,777	3,034	2,181
	Advance appropriations, discretionary:			
1170	Advance appropriation			530
1172	Advance appropriations transferred to other accounts [012–1104]			–43
1172	Advance appropriations transferred to other accounts [012–1115]			–28
1172	Advance appropriations transferred to other accounts [012–1122]			–63
1172	Advance appropriations transferred to other accounts [012–0900]			–3
1173	Advance appropriations transferred from other accounts [012–1103]			22
1180	Advanced appropriation, discretionary (total)			415
	Spending authority from offsetting collections, discretionary:			
1700	Collected	76	101	
1701	Change in uncollected payments, Federal sources	–10		
1750	Spending auth from offsetting collections, disc (total)	66	101	
1900	Budget authority (total)	1,843	3,135	2,596
1930	Total budgetary resources available	2,173	3,431	3,755
	Memorandum (non-add) entries:			
1940	Unobligated balance expiring	–6		
1941	Unexpired unobligated balance, end of year	244	1,107	950
	Change in obligated balance:			
	Unpaid obligations:			
3000	Unpaid obligations, brought forward, Oct 1	772	711	52
3010	New obligations, unexpired accounts	1,923	2,324	2,805
3020	Outlays (gross)	–1,928	–2,931	–2,614
3040	Recoveries of prior year unpaid obligations, unexpired	–54	–52	–52
3041	Recoveries of prior year unpaid obligations, expired	–2		
3050	Unpaid obligations, end of year	711	52	191
	Uncollected payments:			
3060	Uncollected pymts, Fed sources, brought forward, Oct 1	–190	–176	–176
3070	Change in uncollected pymts, Fed sources, unexpired	10		
3071	Change in uncollected pymts, Fed sources, expired	4		
3090	Uncollected pymts, Fed sources, end of year	–176	–176	–176
	Memorandum (non-add) entries:			
3100	Obligated balance, start of year	582	535	–124
3200	Obligated balance, end of year	535	–124	15
	Budget authority and outlays, net:			
	Discretionary:			
4000	Budget authority, gross	1,843	3,135	2,596
	Outlays, gross:			
4010	Outlays from new discretionary authority	1,472	2,159	1,975
4011	Outlays from discretionary balances	456	772	639
4020	Outlays, gross (total)	1,928	2,931	2,614
	Offsets against gross budget authority and outlays:			
	Offsetting collections (collected) from:			
4030	Federal sources	–40	–61	

NATIONAL FOREST SYSTEM—Continued
Program and Financing—Continued

Identification code 012–1106–0–1–302	2021 actual	2022 est.	2023 est.
4033 Non-Federal sources	–39	–40	
4040 Offsets against gross budget authority and outlays (total)	–79	–101	
Additional offsets against gross budget authority only:			
4050 Change in uncollected pymts, Fed sources, unexpired	10		
4052 Offsetting collections credited to expired accounts	2		
4053 Recoveries of prior year paid obligations, unexpired accounts	1		
4060 Additional offsets against budget authority only (total)	13		
4070 Budget authority, net (discretionary)	1,777	3,034	2,596
4080 Outlays, net (discretionary)	1,849	2,830	2,614
4180 Budget authority, net (total)	1,777	3,034	2,596
4190 Outlays, net (total)	1,849	2,830	2,614

The National Forest System (NFS) comprises 193 million acres, with 154 national forests and 20 national grasslands located in 44 States and Puerto Rico and managed under multiple-use and sustained-yield principles. The natural resources of timber, minerals, range, wildlife, outdoor recreation, watershed, and soil are used in a planned combination that best meets the needs of the Nation without impairing productivity of the land or damaging the environment. The Budget requests $2.18 billion for the stewardship and management of the NFS. Within this funding level, $1.681 billion is requested for workforce salaries and expenses.

Maintaining climate-resilient landscapes is central to Forest Service activities and goals. In line with Executive Order 14008, *Tackling Climate Crisis at Home and Abroad* and Executive Order 13990, *Protecting Public Health and the Environment and Restoring Science to Tackle the Climate Crisis*, the 2023 Budget prioritizes funding of programs designed to increase the health and resilience of the national forests and grasslands, while also meeting the multiple use requirements for the resources these lands provide.

The 2023 Budget requests $110 million for Recreation, Heritage and Wilderness, a $74 million increase above the 2022 annualized CR. Funds for this program will be used to provide public recreational access to over 193 million acres of scenic lands, with almost 159,000 miles of trails, 27,000 developed recreation sites, 220,000 miles of fishable streams, 122 ski areas, and over 450,000 heritage sites. The Forest Service will prioritize permitting for outfitters and guides, maintaining and growing strong collaborations with partners and volunteer groups, and working to address the recreational needs of today's public, who want year-round activities on National Forest System lands.

The 2023 Budget requests $38 million for Forest Products. Funds for this program will be used support of the 2023 performance target of 3.4 billion board feet of timber sold.

The overall objective of all NFS program activities is to reestablish and retain the resilience of NFS lands, to achieve sustainable management and use, and to provide a broad range of ecosystem services. A priority component in the Budget request is continuing support for Law Enforcement Operations to clean up and reclaim illegal marijuana grow sites on NFS lands.

The 2023 Budget continues the emphasis on Forest Service program performance and accountability agency-wide, as well as delivering critical services more efficiently. The Forest Service business rules for accomplishment reporting incorporate not only directly funded work, but also accomplishments achieved through integration between program areas or partnerships with external groups. This effort improves performance and accountability by shifting focus to accomplishments that naturally align with other programs and partner organizations to achieve multiple goals.

Object Classification (in millions of dollars)

Identification code 012–1106–0–1–302	2021 actual	2022 est.	2023 est.
Direct obligations:			
Personnel compensation:			
11.1 Full-time permanent	889	974	1,225
11.3 Other than full-time permanent	45	47	55
11.5 Other personnel compensation	46	48	56
11.9 Total personnel compensation	980	1,069	1,336
12.1 Civilian personnel benefits	407	443	554
21.0 Travel and transportation of persons	13	21	21
22.0 Transportation of things	8	14	14
23.2 Rental payments to others	1	1	1
23.3 Communications, utilities, and miscellaneous charges	1	2	2
24.0 Printing and reproduction	1		
25.2 Other services from non-Federal sources	124	200	200
25.3 Other goods and services from Federal sources	94	151	151
25.4 Operation and maintenance of facilities	1	1	1
25.5 Research and development contracts	1	1	1
25.7 Operation and maintenance of equipment	3	5	5
26.0 Supplies and materials	36	58	58
31.0 Equipment	7	12	12
32.0 Land and structures	1	1	1
41.0 Grants, subsidies, and contributions	164	263	366
42.0 Insurance claims and indemnities	2	3	3
99.0 Direct obligations	1,844	2,245	2,726
99.0 Reimbursable obligations	79	79	79
99.9 Total new obligations, unexpired accounts	1,923	2,324	2,805

Employment Summary

Identification code 012–1106–0–1–302	2021 actual	2022 est.	2023 est.
1001 Direct civilian full-time equivalent employment	13,236	14,435	18,021
2001 Reimbursable civilian full-time equivalent employment	255	259	259
3001 Allocation account civilian full-time equivalent employment	1,076	1,075	1,075

STATE AND PRIVATE FORESTRY

For necessary expenses of cooperating with and providing technical and financial assistance to States, territories, possessions, and others, and for forest health management, including for invasive plants, and conducting an international program and trade compliance activities as authorized, $306,963,000, to remain available through September 30, 2026, as authorized by law.

. Note.—A full-year 2022 appropriation for this account was not enacted at the time the Budget was prepared; therefore, the Budget assumes this account is operating under the Continuing Appropriations Act, 2022 (Division A of Public Law 117–43, as amended). The amounts included for 2022 reflect the annualized level provided by the continuing resolution.

STATE AND PRIVATE FORESTRY

[For an additional amount for "State and Private Forestry", $50,000,000, to remain available until expended, for necessary expenses related to the consequences of calendar year 2019, 2020, and 2021 wildfires, hurricanes and other natural disasters.]
(Disaster Relief Supplemental Appropriations Act, 2022.)

STATE AND PRIVATE FORESTRY

[(INCLUDING TRANSFERS OF FUNDS)]

[For an additional amount for "State and Private Forestry", $1,526,800,000, to remain available until September 30, 2029: *Provided*, That $305,360,000, to remain available until September 30, 2025, shall be made available for fiscal year 2022, $305,360,000, to remain available until September 30, 2026, shall be made available for fiscal year 2023, $305,360,000, to remain available until September 30, 2027, shall be made available for fiscal year 2024, $305,360,000, to remain available until September 30, 2028, shall be made available for fiscal year 2025, and $305,360,000, to remain available until September 30, 2029, shall be made available for fiscal year 2026: *Provided further*, That of the funds made available under this heading in this Act, the following amounts shall be for the following purposes in equal amounts for each of fiscal years 2022 through 2026—]

[(1) $718,000,000 for the Secretary of Agriculture, acting through the Chief of the Forest Service, to carry out activities for the Department of Agriculture, as authorized in sections 40803 and 40804 of division D of this Act;]

[(2) In addition to amounts made available in paragraph (1) for grants to at-risk communities for wildfire mitigation activities, not less than $500,000,000 for such purposes;]

[(3) Not less than $88,000,000 for State Fire Assistance; and]

[(4) Not less than $20,000,000 for Volunteer Fire Assistance:]

[*Provided further*, That amounts made available under this heading in this Act for each of fiscal years 2022 through 2026 may be transferred between accounts affected by the Forest Service budget restructure outlined in section 435 of division D of the Further Consolidated Appropriations Act, 2020 (Public Law 116–94) to carry out the activities in support of this heading: *Provided further*, That up to 3 percent of the amounts made available under this heading in this Act in each of fiscal years 2022 through 2026 shall be for salaries, expenses, and administration: *Provided further*, That one-half of one percent of the amounts made available under this heading in this Act in each of fiscal years 2022 through 2026 shall be transferred to the Office of Inspector General of the Department of Agriculture for oversight of funding provided to the Forest Service in this title in this Act: *Provided further*, That such amount is designated by the Congress as being for an emergency requirement pursuant to section 4112(a) of H. Con. Res. 71 (115th Congress), the concurrent resolution on the budget for fiscal year 2018, and to section 251(b) of the Balanced Budget and Emergency Deficit Control Act of 1985.] *(Infrastructure Investments and Jobs Appropriations Act.)*

Program and Financing (in millions of dollars)

Identification code 012–1105–0–1–302		2021 actual	2022 est.	2023 est.
	Obligations by program activity:			
0001	State and private forestry	274	502	634
0002	Forest Legacy	90	80	109
0799	Total direct obligations	364	582	743
0801	State and Private Forestry (Reimbursable)	72	71	71
0900	Total new obligations, unexpired accounts	436	653	814
	Budgetary resources:			
	Unobligated balance:			
1000	Unobligated balance brought forward, Oct 1	227	228	345
1001	Discretionary unobligated balance brought fwd, Oct 1	227		
1010	Unobligated balance transfer to other accts [012–1122]	–1		
1021	Recoveries of prior year unpaid obligations	26		
1070	Unobligated balance (total)	252	228	345
	Budget authority:			
	Appropriations, discretionary:			
1100	Appropriation - State and Private [PL 116–260]	216	216	242
1100	Appropriation - State and Private [P.L. 116–260] (Salaries and Exp)	51	51	65
1100	Appropriation (Disaster Supplemental)		50	
1100	Appropriation (IIJA)		305	
1120	Appropriations transferred to other acct [012–1122]	–5	–49	
1120	Appropriations transferred to other acct [012–1104]		–4	
1120	Appropriations transferred to other acct [012–0900]		–2	
1131	Unobligated balance of appropriations permanently reduced	–6	–6	
1160	Appropriation, discretionary (total)	256	561	307
	Advance appropriations, discretionary:			
1170	Advance appropriation			305
1172	Advance appropriations transferred to other accounts [012–1104]			–4
1172	Advance appropriations transferred to other accounts [012–1122]			–37
1172	Advance appropriations transferred to other accounts [012–0900]			–2
1180	Advanced appropriation, discretionary (total)			262
	Appropriations, mandatory:			
1201	Appropriation (special or trust fund) (LWCF-GAOA)	94	94	94
1203	Appropriation (previously unavailable)(special or trust)			5
1232	Appropriations and/or unobligated balance of appropriations temporarily reduced		–5	–5
1260	Appropriations, mandatory (total)	94	89	94
	Spending authority from offsetting collections, discretionary:			
1700	Collected	53	120	
1701	Change in uncollected payments, Federal sources	10		
1750	Spending auth from offsetting collections, disc (total)	63	120	
1900	Budget authority (total)	413	770	663
1930	Total budgetary resources available	665	998	1,008
	Memorandum (non-add) entries:			
1940	Unobligated balance expiring	–1		
1941	Unexpired unobligated balance, end of year	228	345	194
	Change in obligated balance:			
	Unpaid obligations:			
3000	Unpaid obligations, brought forward, Oct 1	681	755	279
3010	New obligations, unexpired accounts	436	653	814
3020	Outlays (gross)	–335	–1,129	–529
3040	Recoveries of prior year unpaid obligations, unexpired	–26		
3041	Recoveries of prior year unpaid obligations, expired	–1		
3050	Unpaid obligations, end of year	755	279	564
	Uncollected payments:			
3060	Uncollected pymts, Fed sources, brought forward, Oct 1	–211	–216	–216
3070	Change in uncollected pymts, Fed sources, unexpired	–10		
3071	Change in uncollected pymts, Fed sources, expired	5		
3090	Uncollected pymts, Fed sources, end of year	–216	–216	–216
	Memorandum (non-add) entries:			
3100	Obligated balance, start of year	470	539	63
3200	Obligated balance, end of year	539	63	348
	Budget authority and outlays, net:			
	Discretionary:			
4000	Budget authority, gross	319	681	569
	Outlays, gross:			
4010	Outlays from new discretionary authority	56	338	254
4011	Outlays from discretionary balances	267	755	211
4020	Outlays, gross (total)	323	1,093	465
	Offsets against gross budget authority and outlays:			
	Offsetting collections (collected) from:			
4030	Federal sources	–56	–120	
4040	Offsets against gross budget authority and outlays (total)	–56	–120	
	Additional offsets against gross budget authority only:			
4050	Change in uncollected pymts, Fed sources, unexpired	–10		
4052	Offsetting collections credited to expired accounts	3		
4060	Additional offsets against budget authority only (total)	–7		
4070	Budget authority, net (discretionary)	256	561	569
4080	Outlays, net (discretionary)	267	973	465
	Mandatory:			
4090	Budget authority, gross	94	89	94
	Outlays, gross:			
4100	Outlays from new mandatory authority	12	36	38
4101	Outlays from mandatory balances			26
4110	Outlays, gross (total)	12	36	64
4180	Budget authority, net (total)	350	650	663
4190	Outlays, net (total)	279	1,009	529

The 2023 Budget requests $306.9 million for State and Private Forestry programs, of which, $65 million is for workforce Salary and Expenses. These funds will be used to address climate resilience and help sustain forests on State and private lands in both rural and urban areas, and to protect communities and the natural environment from wildland fires, tree pests and diseases, and invasive plants through restoration and reforestation.

Technical assistance and grants help facilitate sound resource stewardship by providing tools to address forest health threats on a landscape scale, while maintaining the flexibility for individual forest landowners and resource managers to pursue their objectives. These funds will also continue to support the Forest Service's shared stewardship approach, which aims to increase emphasis on work across boundaries with States and other partners to prioritize investments in mutually defined projects that can make a difference in conditions across an entire landscape that restore healthy forests, protect watersheds, and create jobs. This collaboration between Federal, state, tribal, and local governments, as well as private landowners, will accelerate gains in reducing the incidence and spread of catastrophic wildfires by improving resilient forest conditions. Specific areas of emphasis are:

Landscape Scale Restoration.—$21 million is requested for competitive grants that carry out science-based restoration of priority forest landscapes by reducing the risk of catastrophic wildfire; improving fish and wildlife habitat; maintaining or improving water quality and watershed function; mitigating invasive species, insect infestation, and disease; improving important forest ecosystems; and measuring economic and ecological benefits, including air quality and soil quality and productivity.

Forest Health Management.—$59.2 million is requested for activities on Federal and cooperative lands to maintain healthy, productive ecosystems by preventing, detecting, and suppressing damaging native and invasive insect infestations and tree diseases across all land ownership jurisdictions, and invasive plants on cooperative lands. Based on a science-based forest health risk map, the 2023 Budget allocates funding to address national priorities and reduce risk for landscape damage in the most effective and efficient manner. The agency will document changes in insect, disease, and invasive plant geographic range, population dynamics of host preferences of pests, and other changes in pest activity, and will explore gene

STATE AND PRIVATE FORESTRY—Continued

conservation efforts. Funding of this program is a critical part of the Forest Service's capacity to continue to reduce the risk of catastrophic wildfires, improve water quality and quantity, and increase carbon sequestration.

Cooperative Forestry.—$17.9 million is requested for the Forest Stewardship Program, which provides professional forestry assistance to landowners to encourage sound environmental management of non-industrial private forest lands. Cooperative forestry activities help maintain the integrity of our Nation's valuable privately-owned forest landscapes, and support the Federal interest in obtaining and preserving for the public an array of social, economic, and environmental benefits from these forests. The Forest Service will track how cooperative funds are targeted to priority areas and themes identified in State Forest Action Plans.

Community Forest and Open Space Conservation.—$4 million is requested to provide financial assistance grants for acquiring and establishing working community forests that provide environmental, economic, and recreational benefits from sustainable forest management. Environmental and educational benefits provided by this program include the protection of vital water supplies and wildlife habitat and conservation education programs to diverse communities.

Urban and Community Forestry.—$31.9 million is requested to provide funding and technical assistance for communities to conserve, protect, and enhance forests across jurisdictional boundaries. In support of Executive Order 13985, *Advancing Racial Equity and Support for Underserved Communities*, this program helps improve the health and resilience of urban forests, remove hazardous trees, improve resident safety, and provide critical access to green spaces and urban canopy for underserved communities across the Nation.

International Programs and Trade Compliance.—$15.4 million is requested to promote sustainable forest management globally by providing technical assistance to other countries to combat illegal logging. This program also improves the management of forest invasive species, which cause $4.2 billion in loss and damage annually in the forest products industry by supporting collaborative work to control and prevent spread of invasives.

Cooperative Fire Programs.—Funds for the National Fire Capacity and Rural Fire Capacity programs are requested at $73.4 million and $19 million; respectively, to provide grants to States to: (1) increase their initial attack capabilities, and (2) purchase and maintain firefighting equipment. Funding also supports technical assistance to States through training, planning, and fire prevention and education programs to deal with the threat of more frequent and increasingly severe wildfire.

Object Classification (in millions of dollars)

Identification code 012–1105–0–1–302		2021 actual	2022 est.	2023 est.
	Direct obligations:			
	Personnel compensation:			
11.1	Full-time permanent	39	44	56
11.3	Other than full-time permanent	1	1	2
11.5	Other personnel compensation	2	2	4
11.9	Total personnel compensation	42	47	62
12.1	Civilian personnel benefits	15	17	23
21.0	Travel and transportation of persons	1	1	1
22.0	Transportation of things		1	1
23.1	Rental payments to GSA	1	1	1
25.2	Other services from non-Federal sources	17	28	36
25.3	Other goods and services from Federal sources	4	7	9
26.0	Supplies and materials	1	2	3
31.0	Equipment	1	2	2
41.0	Grants, subsidies, and contributions	283	476	605
99.0	Direct obligations	365	582	743
99.0	Reimbursable obligations	71	71	71
99.9	Total new obligations, unexpired accounts	436	653	814

Employment Summary

Identification code 012–1105–0–1–302		2021 actual	2022 est.	2023 est.
1001	Direct civilian full-time equivalent employment	393	450	591
2001	Reimbursable civilian full-time equivalent employment	90	90	90
3001	Allocation account civilian full-time equivalent employment	1	1	1

MANAGEMENT OF NATIONAL FOREST LANDS FOR SUBSISTENCE USES

For necessary expenses of the Forest Service to manage Federal lands in Alaska for subsistence uses under title VIII of the Alaska National Interest Lands Conservation Act (16 U.S.C. 3111 et seq.), $1,099,000, to remain available through September 30, 2026.

Note.—A full-year 2022 appropriation for this account was not enacted at the time the Budget was prepared; therefore, the Budget assumes this account is operating under the Continuing Appropriations Act, 2022 (Division A of Public Law 117–43, as amended). The amounts included for 2022 reflect the annualized level provided by the continuing resolution.

Program and Financing (in millions of dollars)

Identification code 012–1119–0–1–302		2021 actual	2022 est.	2023 est.
	Obligations by program activity:			
0001	Management of national forest lands for subsistence uses	1	1	1
0900	Total new obligations, unexpired accounts (object class 25.2)	1	1	1
	Budgetary resources:			
	Unobligated balance:			
1000	Unobligated balance brought forward, Oct 1	1	1	1
	Budget authority:			
	Appropriations, discretionary:			
1100	Appropriation	1	1	1
1930	Total budgetary resources available	2	2	2
	Memorandum (non-add) entries:			
1941	Unexpired unobligated balance, end of year	1	1	1
	Change in obligated balance:			
	Unpaid obligations:			
3000	Unpaid obligations, brought forward, Oct 1	1		
3010	New obligations, unexpired accounts	1	1	1
3020	Outlays (gross)	–2	–1	–1
	Memorandum (non-add) entries:			
3100	Obligated balance, start of year	1		
	Budget authority and outlays, net:			
	Discretionary:			
4000	Budget authority, gross	1	1	1
	Outlays, gross:			
4010	Outlays from new discretionary authority	1	1	1
4011	Outlays from discretionary balances	1		
4020	Outlays, gross (total)	2	1	1
4180	Budget authority, net (total)	1	1	1
4190	Outlays, net (total)	2	1	1

The 2023 Budget requests $1,099,000 for Management of National Forest Lands for Subsistence Uses. Funding under this program primarily supports fisheries and wildlife population assessments and forecasts, and the enforcement of harvest laws and regulations, to ensure that the subsistence needs of qualified rural Alaskans are met under the Alaska National Interest Lands Conservation Act (Public Law 96–487).

Employment Summary

Identification code 012–1119–0–1–302		2021 actual	2022 est.	2023 est.
1001	Direct civilian full-time equivalent employment	1	1	1

WILDLAND FIRE MANAGEMENT

(INCLUDING TRANSFERS OF FUNDS)

For necessary expenses for forest fire presuppression activities on National Forest System lands, for emergency wildland fire suppression on or adjacent to such lands or other lands under fire protection agreement, and for emergency rehabilitation of burned-over National Forest System lands and water, $2,678,659,000, to remain available until expended: Provided, That such funds including unobligated balances under this heading, are available for repayment of advances from other appropriations accounts previously transferred for such purposes: Provided further, That

DEPARTMENT OF AGRICULTURE

such funds shall be available to reimburse State and other cooperating entities for services provided in response to wildfire and other emergencies or disasters to the extent such reimbursements by the Forest Service for non-fire emergencies are fully repaid by the responsible emergency management agency: Provided further, That funds provided shall be available for support to Federal emergency response: Provided further, That the costs of implementing any cooperative agreement between the Federal Government and any non-Federal entity may be shared, as mutually agreed on by the affected parties: Provided further, That of the funds provided under this heading, $321,388,000 shall be for hazardous fuels management activities, of which not to exceed $15,000,000 may be used to make grants, using any authorities available to the Forest Service under the "State and Private Forestry" appropriation, for the purpose of creating incentives for increased use of biomass from National Forest System lands: Provided further, That funds made available in the previous proviso to implement the Community Forest Restoration Act, Public Law 106–393, title VI, shall be available for use on non-Federal lands in accordance with authorities made available to the Forest Service under the "State and Private Forestry" appropriation: Provided further, That of the funds provided under this heading, $20,000,000 may be used by the Secretary of Agriculture to enter into procurement contracts or cooperative agreements; to issue grants for hazardous fuels management activities; for training or monitoring associated with such hazardous fuels management activities on Federal land; or for training or monitoring associated with such hazardous fuels management activities on non-Federal land if the Secretary determines such activities benefit resources on Federal land: Provided further, That of the funds provided under this heading, $1,011,000,000 shall be available for wildfire suppression operations, and is provided as the average costs of wildfire suppression operations to the meet the terms of a concurrent resolution on the budget.

Note.—A full-year 2022 appropriation for this account was not enacted at the time the Budget was prepared; therefore, the Budget assumes this account is operating under the Continuing Appropriations Act, 2022 (Division A of Public Law 117-43, as amended). The amounts included for 2022 reflect the annualized level provided by the continuing resolution.

WILDLAND FIRE MANAGEMENT

[(INCLUDING TRANSFERS OF FUNDS)]

[For an additional amount for "Wildland Fire Management", $696,200,000 to remain available until expended, for the Secretary of Agriculture, acting through the Chief of the Forest Service, to carry out activities for the Department of Agriculture as authorized in section 40803 of division D of this Act: *Provided*, That $552,200,000, to remain available until expended, shall be made available for fiscal year 2022, $36,000,000, to remain available until expended, shall be made available for fiscal year 2023, $36,000,000, to remain available until expended, shall be made available for fiscal year 2024, $36,000,000, to remain available until expended, shall be made available for fiscal year 2025, and $36,000,000, to remain available until expended, shall be made available for fiscal year 2026: *Provided further*, That funds appropriated under this heading in this Act may be transferred to the United States Fish and Wildlife Service and the National Marine Fisheries Service for the costs of carrying out their responsibilities under the Endangered Species Act of 1973 (16 U.S.C. 1531 et seq.) to consult and conference, as required by section 7 of such Act, in connection with wildland fire management activities: *Provided further*, That amounts made available under this heading in this Act for each of fiscal years 2022 through 2026 may be transferred between accounts affected by the Forest Service budget restructure outlined in section 435 of division D of the Further Consolidated Appropriations Act, 2020 (Public Law 116-94) to carry out the activities in support of this heading: *Provided further*, That amounts made available under this heading in this Act in each of fiscal years 2022 through 2026, shall be available for salaries and expenses to carry out such purposes: *Provided further*, That one-half of one percent of the amounts made available under this heading in this Act in each of fiscal years 2022 through 2026 shall be transferred to the Office of Inspector General of the Department of Agriculture for oversight of funding provided to the Forest Service in this title in this Act: *Provided further*, That such amount is designated by the Congress as being for an emergency requirement pursuant to section 4112(a) of H. Con. Res. 71 (115th Congress), the concurrent resolution on the budget for fiscal year 2018, and to section 251(b) of the Balanced Budget and Emergency Deficit Control Act of 1985.] *(Infrastructure Investments and Jobs Appropriations Act.)*

Program and Financing (in millions of dollars)

Identification code 012–1115–0–1–302	2021 actual	2022 est.	2023 est.
Obligations by program activity:			
0001 Wildland fire management	4,798	4,337	4,677
0801 Wildland Fire Management (Reimbursable)	53	53	53
0900 Total new obligations, unexpired accounts	4,851	4,390	4,730

	Budgetary resources:			
	Unobligated balance:			
1000	Unobligated balance brought forward, Oct 1	311	392	366
1011	Unobligated balance transfer from other acct [012–1121]	1,000	1,220	1,490
1021	Recoveries of prior year unpaid obligations	180		
1033	Recoveries of prior year paid obligations	1		
1070	Unobligated balance (total)	1,492	1,612	1,856
	Budget authority:			
	Appropriations, discretionary:			
1100	Appropriation - Preparedness (WFWF)	1,927	152	192
1100	Appropriation - Suppression Operations (WFSU)		1,011	1,011
1100	Appropriation - Salaries & Expenses (WFSE)		764	1,154
1100	Appropriation - Hazardous Fuels			322
1100	Appropriation (IIJA)		552	
1120	Appropriations transferred to other acct [014–1125]	–2		
1120	Appropriations transferred to other acct [012–1122]	–4	–22	
1120	Appropriations transferred to other acct [012–0900]		–3	
1120	Appropriations transferred to other acct [012–1104]		–7	
1121	Appropriations transferred from Fire Reserve [012–1121]	1,770	550	280
1121	Appropriations transferred from other acct [012–1106]		47	
1160	Appropriation, discretionary (total)	3,691	3,044	2,959
	Advance appropriations, discretionary:			
1170	Advance appropriation			36
1172	Advance appropriations transferred to other accounts [012–1104]			–4
1172	Advance appropriations transferred to other accounts [012–1122]			–4
1173	Advance appropriations transferred from other accounts [012–1106]			28
1180	Advanced appropriation, discretionary (total)			56
	Spending authority from offsetting collections, discretionary:			
1700	Collected	54	100	
1701	Change in uncollected payments, Federal sources	45		
1750	Spending auth from offsetting collections, disc (total)	99	100	
1900	Budget authority (total)	3,790	3,144	3,015
1930	Total budgetary resources available	5,282	4,756	4,871
	Memorandum (non-add) entries:			
1940	Unobligated balance expiring	–39		
1941	Unexpired unobligated balance, end of year	392	366	141
	Change in obligated balance:			
	Unpaid obligations:			
3000	Unpaid obligations, brought forward, Oct 1	847	863	2,782
3010	New obligations, unexpired accounts	4,851	4,390	4,730
3020	Outlays (gross)	–4,652	–2,471	–2,436
3040	Recoveries of prior year unpaid obligations, unexpired	–180		
3041	Recoveries of prior year unpaid obligations, expired	–3		
3050	Unpaid obligations, end of year	863	2,782	5,076
	Uncollected payments:			
3060	Uncollected pymts, Fed sources, brought forward, Oct 1	–13	–58	–58
3070	Change in uncollected pymts, Fed sources, unexpired	–45		
3090	Uncollected pymts, Fed sources, end of year	–58	–58	–58
	Memorandum (non-add) entries:			
3100	Obligated balance, start of year	834	805	2,724
3200	Obligated balance, end of year	805	2,724	5,018
	Budget authority and outlays, net:			
	Discretionary:			
4000	Budget authority, gross	3,790	3,144	3,015
	Outlays, gross:			
4010	Outlays from new discretionary authority	3,790	1,608	1,508
4011	Outlays from discretionary balances	862	863	928
4020	Outlays, gross (total)	4,652	2,471	2,436
	Offsets against gross budget authority and outlays:			
	Offsetting collections (collected) from:			
4030	Federal sources	–53	–100	
4033	Non-Federal sources	–2		
4040	Offsets against gross budget authority and outlays (total)	–55	–100	
	Additional offsets against gross budget authority only:			
4050	Change in uncollected pymts, Fed sources, unexpired	–45		
4053	Recoveries of prior year paid obligations, unexpired accounts	1		
4060	Additional offsets against budget authority only (total)	–44		
4070	Budget authority, net (discretionary)	3,691	3,044	3,015
4080	Outlays, net (discretionary)	4,597	2,371	2,436
4180	Budget authority, net (total)	3,691	3,044	3,015
4190	Outlays, net (total)	4,597	2,371	2,436

WILDLAND FIRE MANAGEMENT—Continued

The 2023 Budget requests $2.678 billion for Wildland Fire Management (WFM), including Forest Service fire preparedness; fire suppression operations on National Forest System (NFS) lands, adjacent State and private lands, and other lands under fire protection agreements, and hazardous fuels. This program supports over 11,000 firefighters, 900 fire engines, and a robust aviation program (up to 18 exclusive use airtankers and up to 108 exclusive use helicopters) to ensure safe, timely, appropriate, and effective wildfire response. This requires a workforce that is fairly compensated, available year-round to respond to wildland fire, cared for both physically and mentally, and given the necessary tools to accomplish their mission safely, effectively, and efficiently. The 2023 Budget request for workforce salaries and expenses is $1.15 billion, a $390 million increase above the 2022 annualized CR level to support the Wildland Fire Management workforce framework.

The Wildland Fire Management workforce framework will be deployed starting in 2022 in four phases: in phase 1, a wildland fire workforce assessment will be conducted; in phase 2, a workforce analysis will be completed; in phase 3, recruitment and retention strategies will be identified and an implementation action plan will be developed; and phase 4 will consist of monitoring, evaluation, and revision of the action plan based on best practices identified.

Preparedness.—Preparedness provides for a base level of fire management assets to protect NFS lands, and other Federal, State, and private lands from damaging wildfires, thus reducing threats to life, property, infrastructure and natural resource values commensurate with land management objectives in the National Cohesive Wildland Fire Management Strategy. Key components of wildland fire response mission delivery are fire season readiness, year-round capability and program leadership necessary to ensure appropriate, risk informed, and effective operations. Preparedness also supports other vital elements of a comprehensive wildland fire management program, including modernization of the large airtanker fleet, planning, prevention, development of information technology and decision support systems, training and education, development and advancement of firefighting technology, and organizational learning through program analysis and review.

Through this program, the Forest Service also assists other Federal agencies and States with planning assistance, sharing joint equipment use contracts and interagency fire coordination centers. Readiness levels reflect improvements in efficiencies and management controls to strategically deploy firefighting resources, including predictive services analysis of fire season potential, web-based wildfire decision support tools, centralized management of aviation assets, ongoing analysis to optimize dispatch, and investment in information technology.

Suppression Operations.—Provides for risk-informed extended attack suppression and large fire support at wildland fires on or threatening National Forest System (NFS) lands, other Federal lands, and 20 million acres of non-Federal lands under fire protection agreements. The 2023 Budget requests funding at $1.011 billion, the amount stipulated by the Stephen Sepp Wildfire Suppression Funding and Forest Management Activities Act (division O of Public Law 115–141).

Wildfires continue to be larger and more difficult to suppress due to the effects of persistent drought, hazardous fuel conditions, and the ongoing growth of residential and commercial development adjacent to fire-prone areas in the wildland-urban interface (WUI). The Forest Service recognizes the costs of WUI suppression activities, and will continue to aggressively pursue management improvements, including:

—using risk-informed, performance-based suppression strategies,
—clarifying roles and responsibilities in the WUI,
—using appropriate cost-share agreements and pursuing 100 percent cost recovery from Federal, State, and local entities, and
—deploying decision support tools.

The Suppression program also funds Burned Area Emergency Response (BAER) activities, which address situations where life, property, water quality, and deteriorated ecosystems may be further threatened from post-fire flooding and other damage. The BAER program provides for immediate emergency post-fire response to manage unacceptable risks to people and resources triggered by the changed conditions to the landscape in the aftermath of a fire.

Development of necessary governance and risk management protocols to guide program management and incident response, with the application of resources to reduce unnecessary risk to firefighter safety in the short-term, and increase the long-term resilience of fire-adapted ecosystems, will continue to be a focus. The Forest Service will also continue efforts to allow fire to return to the landscape when it will improve the health of the forest, and when risks to community safety make it appropriate to do so.

Hazardous Fuels.—The 2023 Budget requests $321 million, an increase of $141 million above the 2022 annualized CR level, for Hazardous Fuels program funding to provide for treatment of hazardous fuels within the wildland-urban interface and highest priority areas of NFS lands and adjacent State and private lands through prescribed burning, mechanical treatments, and other methods in order to restore forest health and reduce wildfire risks. In 2023, the Forest Service will treat 3.8 million acres of hazardous fuels reduction projects.

Object Classification (in millions of dollars)

Identification code 012–1115–0–1–302		2021 actual	2022 est.	2023 est.
	Direct obligations:			
	Personnel compensation:			
11.1	Full-time permanent	468	503	829
11.3	Other than full-time permanent	67	67	67
11.5	Other personnel compensation	513	513	513
11.8	Special personal services payments	97	75	75
11.9	Total personnel compensation	1,145	1,158	1,484
12.1	Civilian personnel benefits	359	364	466
21.0	Travel and transportation of persons	120	103	100
22.0	Transportation of things	11	10	10
23.2	Rental payments to others	7	6	6
23.3	Communications, utilities, and miscellaneous charges	11	9	9
25.2	Other services from non-Federal sources	2,254	1,923	1,862
25.3	Other goods and services from Federal sources	215	183	178
25.4	Operation and maintenance of facilities	3	2	2
25.7	Operation and maintenance of equipment	3	3	3
26.0	Supplies and materials	214	182	177
31.0	Equipment	10	8	8
32.0	Land and structures	2	2	1
41.0	Grants, subsidies, and contributions	443	383	371
42.0	Insurance claims and indemnities	1	1	
99.0	Direct obligations	4,798	4,337	4,677
99.0	Reimbursable obligations	53	53	53
99.9	Total new obligations, unexpired accounts	4,851	4,390	4,730

Employment Summary

Identification code 012–1115–0–1–302		2021 actual	2022 est.	2023 est.
1001	Direct civilian full-time equivalent employment	10,283	10,085	13,338
2001	Reimbursable civilian full-time equivalent employment	29	29	29

FOREST SERVICE OPERATIONS

(INCLUDING TRANSFERS OF FUNDS)

For necessary expenses of the Forest Service, not otherwise provided for, $1,112,652,000, to remain available through September 30, 2026: Provided, That a portion of the funds made available under this heading shall be for the base salary and expenses of employees in the Chief's Office, the Work Environment and Performance Office, the Business Operations Deputy Area, and the Chief Financial Officer's Office to carry out administrative and general management support functions: Provided further, That funds provided under this heading shall be available for the costs of facility maintenance, repairs, and leases for buildings and sites where these administrative, general management and other Forest Service support functions take place; the costs of all utility and telecommunication expenses of the Forest Service, as well as business services and information technology, including cyber security requirements: Provided further, That funds provided under this heading

DEPARTMENT OF AGRICULTURE

may be used for necessary expenses to carry out administrative and general management support functions of the Forest Service not otherwise provided for and necessary for its operation.

Note.—A full-year 2022 appropriation for this account was not enacted at the time the Budget was prepared; therefore, the Budget assumes this account is operating under the Continuing Appropriations Act, 2022 (Division A of Public Law 117–43, as amended). The amounts included for 2022 reflect the annualized level provided by the continuing resolution.

FOREST SERVICE OPERATIONS

[For an additional amount for "Forest Service Operations", $105,000,000, to remain available until expended, for necessary expenses related to the consequences of calendar year 2019, 2020, and 2021 wildfires, hurricanes and other natural disasters.] *(Disaster Relief Supplemental Appropriations Act, 2022.)*

Program and Financing (in millions of dollars)

Identification code 012–1122–0–1–302		2021 actual	2022 est.	2023 est.
	Obligations by program activity:			
0001	FS Operations Direct	1,021	1,244	1,307
	Budgetary resources:			
	Unobligated balance:			
1000	Unobligated balance brought forward, Oct 1		30	118
1011	Unobligated balance transfer from other acct [012–1106]	7		
1011	Unobligated balance transfer from other acct [012–1105]	1		
1070	Unobligated balance (total)	8	30	118
	Budget authority:			
	Appropriations, discretionary:			
1100	Appropriation FS Operations [P.L. 116–260]	666	666	723
1100	Appropriation FS Operations [P.L. 116–260] (Salaries and Exp.)	360	360	390
1100	Appropriation (Disaster Supplemental)		105	
1120	Appropriations transferred to other acct [014–1125]	–1		
1121	Appropriations transferred from other acct [012–1103]		12	
1121	Appropriations transferred from other acct [012–1105]	5	49	
1121	Appropriations transferred from other acct [012–1106]	9	118	
1121	Appropriations transferred from other acct [012–1115]	4	22	
1121	Appropriations transferred from other acct [012–1104]			2
1160	Appropriation, discretionary (total)	1,043	1,332	1,115
	Advance appropriations, discretionary:			
1173	Advance appropriations transferred from other accounts [012–1103]			9
1173	Advance appropriations transferred from other accounts [012–1105]			37
1173	Advance appropriations transferred from other accounts [012–1106]			63
1173	Advance appropriations transferred from other accounts [012–1115]			4
1180	Advanced appropriation, discretionary (total)			113
1900	Budget authority (total)	1,043	1,332	1,228
1930	Total budgetary resources available	1,051	1,362	1,346
	Memorandum (non-add) entries:			
1941	Unexpired unobligated balance, end of year	30	118	39
	Change in obligated balance:			
	Unpaid obligations:			
3000	Unpaid obligations, brought forward, Oct 1		280	76
3010	New obligations, unexpired accounts	1,021	1,244	1,307
3020	Outlays (gross)	–741	–1,448	–1,262
3050	Unpaid obligations, end of year	280	76	121
	Memorandum (non-add) entries:			
3100	Obligated balance, start of year		280	76
3200	Obligated balance, end of year	280	76	121
	Budget authority and outlays, net:			
	Discretionary:			
4000	Budget authority, gross	1,043	1,332	1,228
	Outlays, gross:			
4010	Outlays from new discretionary authority	741	1,168	1,160
4011	Outlays from discretionary balances		280	102
4020	Outlays, gross (total)	741	1,448	1,262
4180	Budget authority, net (total)	1,043	1,332	1,228
4190	Outlays, net (total)	741	1,448	1,262

Forest Service Operations.—The 2023 Budget requests $1.112 billion for Forest Service Operations to support staff salaries and expenses, facilities maintenance and leases, information technology, and administrative support for the agency, including work related to diversity, equity, and inclusion.

The Budget requests $389 million for salaries and expenses for the following administrative organizations previously funded by cost pools: the Chief's Office, Work Environment and Performance, the Chief Financial Officer, and the Business Operations Deputy Area (including Chief Information Office, Strategic Planning and Budget Accountability, Procurement and Property Services, and Human Resources Management).

For Forest Service Operational Facilities Maintenance and Leases, the 2023 Budget requests $170 million; for Information Technology and Centralized Processing, the 2023 Budget requests $410 million; and for Organizational Services, such as utility expenses, business services and other administrative support functions, the 2023 Budget requests $143 million. These expenses were also previously funded by cost pools.

Object Classification (in millions of dollars)

Identification code 012–1122–0–1–302		2021 actual	2022 est.	2023 est.
	Direct obligations:			
	Personnel compensation:			
11.1	Full-time permanent	207	243	244
11.3	Other than full-time permanent	1	3	3
11.5	Other personnel compensation	7	10	10
11.9	Total personnel compensation	215	256	257
12.1	Civilian personnel benefits	80	94	95
13.0	Benefits for former personnel	39	46	46
21.0	Travel and transportation of persons		1	1
22.0	Transportation of things	2	2	2
23.1	Rental payments to GSA	33	41	43
23.2	Rental payments to others	59	73	78
23.3	Communications, utilities, and miscellaneous charges	84	103	111
25.1	Advisory and assistance services	3	3	3
25.2	Other services from non-Federal sources	86	106	114
25.3	Other goods and services from Federal sources	344	425	455
25.4	Operation and maintenance of facilities	3	3	4
25.5	Research and development contracts	1	2	2
25.7	Operation and maintenance of equipment	4	5	6
26.0	Supplies and materials	17	21	23
31.0	Equipment	42	52	56
32.0	Land and structures	3	3	3
41.0	Grants, subsidies, and contributions	6	8	8
99.9	Total new obligations, unexpired accounts	1,021	1,244	1,307

Employment Summary

Identification code 012–1122–0–1–302	2021 actual	2022 est.	2023 est.
1001 Direct civilian full-time equivalent employment	2,359	2,797	2,814

WILDFIRE SUPPRESSION OPERATIONS RESERVE FUND

(INCLUDING TRANSFERS OF FUNDS)

In addition to the amounts provided under the heading "Department of Agriculture—Forest Service—Wildland Fire Management" for wildfire suppression operations, $2,210,000,000, to remain available until transferred, is additional new budget authority in excess of the average costs for wildfire suppression operations for purposes of a concurrent resolution on the budget: Provided, That such amounts may be transferred to and merged with amounts made available under the headings "Department of the Interior—Department-Wide Programs—Wildland Fire Management" and "Department of Agriculture—Forest Service—Wildland Fire Management" for wildfire suppression operations in the fiscal year in which such amounts are transferred: Provided further: Provided further, That amounts may be transferred to the "Wildland Fire Management" accounts in the Department of the Interior or the Department of Agriculture only upon the notification of the House and Senate Committees on Appropriations that all wildfire suppression operations funds appropriated under that heading in this and prior appropriations Acts to the agency to which the funds will be transferred will be obligated within 30 days: Provided further, That the transfer authority provided under this heading is in addition to any other transfer authority provided by law.

Note.—A full-year 2022 appropriation for this account was not enacted at the time the Budget was prepared; therefore, the Budget assumes this account is operating under the Continuing

WILDFIRE SUPPRESSION OPERATIONS RESERVE FUND—Continued

Appropriations Act, 2022 (Division A of Public Law 117–43, as amended). The amounts included for 2022 reflect the annualized level provided by the continuing resolution.

Program and Financing (in millions of dollars)

Identification code 012–1121–0–1–302		2021 actual	2022 est.	2023 est.
	Budgetary resources:			
	Unobligated balance:			
1000	Unobligated balance brought forward, Oct 1	1,950	1,220	1,490
1010	Unobligated balance transfer to other accts [012–1115]	–1,000	–1,220	–1,490
1070	Unobligated balance (total)	950		
	Budget authority:			
	Appropriations, discretionary:			
1100	Appropriation	2,040	2,040	2,210
1120	Appropriations transferred to other acct [012–1115]	–1,770	–550	–280
1160	Appropriation, discretionary (total)	270	1,490	1,930
1930	Total budgetary resources available	1,220	1,490	1,930
	Memorandum (non-add) entries:			
1941	Unexpired unobligated balance, end of year	1,220	1,490	1,930
	Budget authority and outlays, net:			
	Discretionary:			
4000	Budget authority, gross	270	1,490	1,930
4180	Budget authority, net (total)	270	1,490	1,930
4190	Outlays, net (total)			

The Consolidated Appropriations Act, 2018 (P.L. 115–141) amended the Balanced Budget and Emergency Deficit Control Act to provide additional budget authority for fiscal years 2020 through 2027. This budget authority is available for fire suppression requirements when severe wildfire activity depletes annual appropriations. The 2023 Budget requests $2.21 billion of the $2.55 billion cap adjustment authorized for 2023 for wildfire suppression operations. The remaining $340 million will be requested by the Department of the Interior. This budget authority will help ensure that adequate resources are available to the Departments of Agriculture and the Interior to fight wildland fires, protect communities, and safeguard human life during the most severe wildland fire seasons.

RANGE BETTERMENT FUND

For necessary expenses of range rehabilitation, protection, and improvement, 50 percent of all moneys received during the prior fiscal year as fees for grazing domestic livestock on lands in National Forests in the 16 Western States, pursuant to section 401(b)(1) of Public Law 94–579, to remain available through September 30, 2026, of which not to exceed 6 percent shall be available for administrative expenses associated with on-the-ground range rehabilitation, protection, and improvements.

Note.—A full-year 2022 appropriation for this account was not enacted at the time the Budget was prepared; therefore, the Budget assumes this account is operating under the Continuing Appropriations Act, 2022 (Division A of Public Law 117–43, as amended). The amounts included for 2022 reflect the annualized level provided by the continuing resolution.

Special and Trust Fund Receipts (in millions of dollars)

Identification code 012–5207–0–2–302		2021 actual	2022 est.	2023 est.
0100	Balance, start of year			1
	Receipts:			
	Current law:			
1130	Receipts, Cooperative Range Improvements	3	3	3
2000	Total: Balances and receipts	3	3	4
	Appropriations:			
	Current law:			
2101	Range Betterment Fund		–2	–2
2103	Range Betterment Fund	–3		
2199	Total current law appropriations	–3	–2	–2
2999	Total appropriations	–3	–2	–2
5099	Balance, end of year		1	2

Program and Financing (in millions of dollars)

Identification code 012–5207–0–2–302		2021 actual	2022 est.	2023 est.
	Obligations by program activity:			
0001	Range betterment fund	2	2	2
0900	Total new obligations, unexpired accounts (object class 26.0)	2	2	2
	Budgetary resources:			
	Unobligated balance:			
1000	Unobligated balance brought forward, Oct 1	2	3	3
	Budget authority:			
	Appropriations, discretionary:			
1101	Appropriation (special or trust)		2	2
1103	Appropriation (previously unavailable)(special or trust)	3		
1160	Appropriation, discretionary (total)	3	2	2
1930	Total budgetary resources available	5	5	5
	Memorandum (non-add) entries:			
1941	Unexpired unobligated balance, end of year	3	3	3
	Change in obligated balance:			
	Unpaid obligations:			
3000	Unpaid obligations, brought forward, Oct 1	1	1	1
3010	New obligations, unexpired accounts	2	2	2
3020	Outlays (gross)	–2	–2	–2
3050	Unpaid obligations, end of year	1	1	1
	Memorandum (non-add) entries:			
3100	Obligated balance, start of year	1	1	1
3200	Obligated balance, end of year	1	1	1
	Budget authority and outlays, net:			
	Discretionary:			
4000	Budget authority, gross	3	2	2
	Outlays, gross:			
4010	Outlays from new discretionary authority	1	1	1
4011	Outlays from discretionary balances	1	1	1
4020	Outlays, gross (total)	2	2	2
4180	Budget authority, net (total)	3	2	2
4190	Outlays, net (total)	2	2	2

The 2023 Budget requests $1,719,000 for the Range Betterment Fund for range rehabilitation, protection, and improvement of lands on national forests in western States. Under the authority of the Federal Land Policy and Management Act of 1976 (43 U.S.C. 1751), as amended, appropriations of fifty percent of fees received for grazing domestic livestock on National Forest System lands are used to protect and improve rangeland productivity through revegetation, and construction, reconstruction, and maintenance of rangeland improvements. This program emphasizes essential structural and non-structural improvements prescribed in grazing allotment management plans and other project plans as developed in accordance with the National Environmental Policy Act. Treatment of invasive plant species related to permitted livestock use continues to be a priority for non-structural rangeland improvement work.

Employment Summary

Identification code 012–5207–0–2–302		2021 actual	2022 est.	2023 est.
1001	Direct civilian full-time equivalent employment	3	3	3

COMMUNICATIONS SITE ADMINISTRATION

(INCLUDING TRANSFER OF FUNDS)

Amounts collected in this fiscal year pursuant to section 8705(f)(2) of the Agriculture Improvement Act of 2018 (Public Law 115–334), shall be deposited in the special account established by section 8705(f)(1) of such Act, shall be available to cover the costs described in subsection (c)(3) of such section of such Act, and shall remain available until expended: Provided, That such amounts shall be transferred to the "National Forest System" account.

Note.—A full-year 2022 appropriation for this account was not enacted at the time the Budget was prepared; therefore, the Budget assumes this account is operating under the Continuing Appropriations Act, 2022 (Division A of Public Law 117–43, as amended). The amounts included for 2022 reflect the annualized level provided by the continuing resolution.

Special and Trust Fund Receipts (in millions of dollars)

Identification code 012–5634–0–2–302		2021 actual	2022 est.	2023 est.
0100	Balance, start of year			
	Receipts:			
	Current law:			
1130	Fees, Communications Site Administration		5	5
2000	Total: Balances and receipts		5	5
	Appropriations:			
	Current law:			
2101	Communications Site Administration		–5	
5099	Balance, end of year			5

Program and Financing (in millions of dollars)

Identification code 012–5634–0–2–302		2021 actual	2022 est.	2023 est.
	Budgetary resources:			
	Budget authority:			
	Appropriations, discretionary:			
1101	Appropriation (special or trust)		5	
1120	Appropriations transferred to other acct [012–1106]		–5	
4180	Budget authority, net (total)			
4190	Outlays, net (total)			

The Agriculture Improvement Act, 2018 authorizes the Forest Service to establish, collect, and retain a new administrative fee to cover costs incurred to manage communication site uses on National Forest System (NFS) lands. These funds will support improvement to the administration of Forest Service permits for infrastructure to provide more reliable wireless and wired communication networks, provide broadband access to unserved and underserved communities and rural areas, enable better coordination in emergency response, and increase overall safety for visitors, agency staff, and first responders.

STEWARDSHIP CONTRACTING PRODUCT SALES

Program and Financing (in millions of dollars)

Identification code 012–5540–0–2–302		2021 actual	2022 est.	2023 est.
	Obligations by program activity:			
0001	Stewardship contracting	21	21	21
	Budgetary resources:			
	Unobligated balance:			
1000	Unobligated balance brought forward, Oct 1	46	53	62
1021	Recoveries of prior year unpaid obligations	1	1	1
1070	Unobligated balance (total)	47	54	63
	Budget authority:			
	Appropriations, mandatory:			
1201	Appropriation (special or trust fund)	29	29	29
1203	Appropriation (previously unavailable)(special or trust)		2	2
1232	Appropriations and/or unobligated balance of appropriations temporarily reduced	–2	–2	–2
1260	Appropriations, mandatory (total)	27	29	29
1900	Budget authority (total)	27	29	29
1930	Total budgetary resources available	74	83	92
	Memorandum (non-add) entries:			
1941	Unexpired unobligated balance, end of year	53	62	71
	Change in obligated balance:			
	Unpaid obligations:			
3000	Unpaid obligations, brought forward, Oct 1	20	22	9
3010	New obligations, unexpired accounts	21	21	21
3020	Outlays (gross)	–18	–33	–23
3040	Recoveries of prior year unpaid obligations, unexpired	–1	–1	–1
3050	Unpaid obligations, end of year	22	9	6
	Memorandum (non-add) entries:			
3100	Obligated balance, start of year	20	22	9
3200	Obligated balance, end of year	22	9	6
	Budget authority and outlays, net:			
	Mandatory:			
4090	Budget authority, gross	27	29	29
	Outlays, gross:			
4100	Outlays from new mandatory authority		13	13
4101	Outlays from mandatory balances	18	20	10
4110	Outlays, gross (total)	18	33	23
4180	Budget authority, net (total)	27	29	29
4190	Outlays, net (total)	18	33	23

Stewardship Contracting.—Stewardship contracting enables the Forest Service to apply the value of timber or other forest products as an offset against project costs to accomplish land and resource management objectives. If the offset value of timber or other forest products exceeds the value of the resource improvement treatments, those receipts are retained in the Stewardship Contracting Fund, and are available until expended for other stewardship projects. This authority was reauthorized permanently, pursuant to P.L. 113–79, Agricultural Act of 2014. The Consolidated Appropriation Act of 2018 extended the maximum duration of stewardship contracts in areas of high risk for catastrophic fire from 10 years to 20 years, and allows for the obligation of funds to cover contract cancellation or termination costs in stages over multiple years rather than in the first year of the contract. Longer contract periods may create an incentive for industry to expand milling capacity and to invest in areas where mills are scarce. Spreading the cancellation ceiling cost over more than one year can make it more financially viable for forest supervisors to use stewardship contracts to actively manage and restore forests.

Object Classification (in millions of dollars)

Identification code 012–5540–0–2–302		2021 actual	2022 est.	2023 est.
	Direct obligations:			
11.1	Personnel compensation: Full-time permanent	2	2	2
12.1	Civilian personnel benefits	1	1	1
25.2	Other services from non-Federal sources	11	11	11
25.3	Other goods and services from Federal sources	1	1	1
26.0	Supplies and materials	2	2	2
41.0	Grants, subsidies, and contributions	4	4	4
99.0	Direct obligations	21	21	21
99.9	Total new obligations, unexpired accounts	21	21	21

Employment Summary

Identification code 012–5540–0–2–302		2021 actual	2022 est.	2023 est.
1001	Direct civilian full-time equivalent employment	31	31	31

NATIONAL PARKS AND PUBLIC LAND LEGACY RESTORATION FUND

Special and Trust Fund Receipts (in millions of dollars)

Identification code 012–5716–0–2–302		2021 actual	2022 est.	2023 est.
0100	Balance, start of year			16
2000	Total: Balances and receipts			16
	Appropriations:			
	Current law:			
2103	National Parks and Public Land Legacy Restoration Fund			–16
2132	National Parks and Public Land Legacy Restoration Fund		16	16
2199	Total current law appropriations		16	
2999	Total appropriations		16	
5099	Balance, end of year		16	16

Program and Financing (in millions of dollars)

Identification code 012–5716–0–2–302		2021 actual	2022 est.	2023 est.
	Obligations by program activity:			
0001	National Parks and Public Land Legacy Restoration	115	173	346
	Budgetary resources:			
	Unobligated balance:			
1000	Unobligated balance brought forward, Oct 1		170	266

NATIONAL PARKS AND PUBLIC LAND LEGACY RESTORATION FUND—Continued

Program and Financing—Continued

Identification code 012–5716–0–2–302	2021 actual	2022 est.	2023 est.
Budget authority:			
Appropriations, mandatory:			
1203 Appropriation (previously unavailable)(special or trust)			16
1221 Appropriations transferred from other acct [014–5715]	285	285	285
1232 Appropriations and/or unobligated balance of appropriations temporarily reduced		–16	–16
1260 Appropriations, mandatory (total)	285	269	285
1930 Total budgetary resources available	285	439	551
Memorandum (non-add) entries:			
1941 Unexpired unobligated balance, end of year	170	266	205
Change in obligated balance:			
Unpaid obligations:			
3000 Unpaid obligations, brought forward, Oct 1		97	48
3010 New obligations, unexpired accounts	115	173	346
3020 Outlays (gross)	–18	–222	–227
3050 Unpaid obligations, end of year	97	48	167
Memorandum (non-add) entries:			
3100 Obligated balance, start of year		97	48
3200 Obligated balance, end of year	97	48	167
Budget authority and outlays, net:			
Mandatory:			
4090 Budget authority, gross	285	269	285
Outlays, gross:			
4100 Outlays from new mandatory authority	18	134	142
4101 Outlays from mandatory balances		88	85
4110 Outlays, gross (total)	18	222	227
4180 Budget authority, net (total)	285	269	285
4190 Outlays, net (total)	18	222	227

National Parks and Public Land Legacy Restoration Fund.—On August 4, 2020, the Great American Outdoors Act established the National Parks and Public Lands Legacy Restoration Fund to address the backlog of deferred maintenance on public lands. Up to $285 million is authorized for Forest Service deferred maintenance projects each year through 2025.

Object Classification (in millions of dollars)

Identification code 012–5716–0–2–302	2021 actual	2022 est.	2023 est.
Direct obligations:			
Personnel compensation:			
11.1 Full-time permanent	2	2	2
11.3 Other than full-time permanent	1	1	1
11.9 Total personnel compensation	3	3	3
12.1 Civilian personnel benefits	1	1	1
25.2 Other services from non-Federal sources	62	100	150
25.3 Other goods and services from Federal sources	12	15	20
26.0 Supplies and materials	3	5	10
31.0 Equipment	1	1	1
32.0 Land and structures	3	3	3
41.0 Grants, subsidies, and contributions	30	45	158
99.9 Total new obligations, unexpired accounts	115	173	346

Employment Summary

Identification code 012–5716–0–2–302	2021 actual	2022 est.	2023 est.
1001 Direct civilian full-time equivalent employment	43	43	43

LAND ACQUISITION

ACQUISITION OF LANDS FOR NATIONAL FORESTS SPECIAL ACTS

For acquisition of lands within the exterior boundaries of the Cache, Uinta, and Wasatch National Forests, Utah; the Toiyabe National Forest, Nevada; and the Angeles, San Bernardino, Sequoia, and Cleveland National Forests, California; and the Ozark-St. Francis and Ouachita National Forests, Arkansas; as authorized by law, $664,000, to be derived from forest receipts.

ACQUISITION OF LANDS TO COMPLETE LAND EXCHANGES

For acquisition of lands, such sums, to be derived from funds deposited by State, county, or municipal governments, public school districts, or other public school authorities, and for authorized expenditures from funds deposited by non-Federal parties pursuant to Land Sale and Exchange Acts, pursuant to the Act of December 4, 1967 (16 U.S.C. 484a), to remain available through September 30, 2026, (16 U.S.C. 516–617a, 555a; Public Law 96–586; Public Law 76–589, 76–591; and Public Law 78–310).

Note.—A full-year 2022 appropriation for this account was not enacted at the time the Budget was prepared; therefore, the Budget assumes this account is operating under the Continuing Appropriations Act, 2022 (Division A of Public Law 117–43, as amended). The amounts included for 2022 reflect the annualized level provided by the continuing resolution.

Special and Trust Fund Receipts (in millions of dollars)

Identification code 012–9923–0–2–302	2021 actual	2022 est.	2023 est.
0100 Balance, start of year	4	14	29
Receipts:			
Current law:			
1130 Deposits, Acquisitions of Lands for National Forests, Special Acts	1	1	1
1130 Land Acquisition Proceeds for Exchanges, Acquisition of Lands to Complete Land Exchanges		2	2
1130 Land Acquisition Proceeds for Exchanges, Acquisition of Lands to Complete Land Exchanges	9	8	8
1199 Total current law receipts	10	11	11
1999 Total receipts	10	11	11
2000 Total: Balances and receipts	14	25	40
Appropriations:			
Current law:			
2101 Land Acquisition	–1		
2101 Land Acquisition	–3	–3	–3
2103 Land Acquisition			–7
2132 Land Acquisition		7	7
2199 Total current law appropriations	–4	4	–3
2999 Total appropriations	–4	4	–3
5098 Reconciliation adjustment	4		
5099 Balance, end of year	14	29	37

Program and Financing (in millions of dollars)

Identification code 012–9923–0–2–302	2021 actual	2022 est.	2023 est.
Obligations by program activity:			
0001 Land Acquisition (12X5004 LALW) Discretionary		57	70
0002 Land Facilities Enhancement (12X5216 EXSC/SL) Mandatory	2	2	2
0003 Land Acquisition - Special Acts (12Y5208) Discretionary	1	1	2
0004 Land Acquisition (12X5004 LALW) Mandatory	63	86	89
0005 Land Acquisition (12Y5216 EXEX)	1	2	2
0900 Total new obligations, unexpired accounts	67	148	165
Budgetary resources:			
Unobligated balance:			
1000 Unobligated balance brought forward, Oct 1	144	203	173
1001 Discretionary unobligated balance brought fwd, Oct 1	114	85	
1021 Recoveries of prior year unpaid obligations	3	3	3
1070 Unobligated balance (total)	147	206	176
Budget authority:			
Appropriations, discretionary:			
1101 Appropriation: Land for Natl Forests Special Acts (5208 ACAC)	1	1	1
1101 Appropriation: Land to Complete Land Exchanges (5216 EXEX)	1		
1131 Unobligated balance of appropriations permanently reduced	–6	–6	
1160 Appropriation, discretionary (total)	–4	–5	1
Appropriations, mandatory:			
1201 Appropriation: Acquisition of Lands to Complete Land Exchanges (5216 EXSC EXSL)	3	3	3
1201 Appropriation: Land Acquisition (5004 GAOA)	124	124	124
1203 Appropriation (previously unavailable)(special or trust)			7
1232 Appropriations and/or unobligated balance of appropriations temporarily reduced		–7	–7
1260 Appropriations, mandatory (total)	127	120	127
1900 Budget authority (total)	123	115	128
1930 Total budgetary resources available	270	321	304

DEPARTMENT OF AGRICULTURE

Forest Service—Continued
Federal Funds—Continued

181

		2021 actual	2022 est.	2023 est.
	Memorandum (non-add) entries:			
1941	Unexpired unobligated balance, end of year	203	173	139
	Special and non-revolving trust funds:			
1950	Other balances withdrawn and returned to unappropriated receipts		1	
1952	Expired unobligated balance, start of year	1		
1954	Unobligated balance canceling	1		
	Change in obligated balance:			
	Unpaid obligations:			
3000	Unpaid obligations, brought forward, Oct 1	23	16	59
3010	New obligations, unexpired accounts	67	148	165
3020	Outlays (gross)	−71	−102	−178
3040	Recoveries of prior year unpaid obligations, unexpired	−3	−3	−3
3050	Unpaid obligations, end of year	16	59	43
	Memorandum (non-add) entries:			
3100	Obligated balance, start of year	23	16	59
3200	Obligated balance, end of year	16	59	43
	Budget authority and outlays, net:			
	Discretionary:			
4000	Budget authority, gross	−4	−5	1
	Outlays, gross:			
4010	Outlays from new discretionary authority		1	1
4011	Outlays from discretionary balances	38	6	
4020	Outlays, gross (total)	38	7	1
	Mandatory:			
4090	Budget authority, gross	127	120	127
	Outlays, gross:			
4100	Outlays from new mandatory authority	33	51	54
4101	Outlays from mandatory balances		44	123
4110	Outlays, gross (total)	33	95	177
4180	Budget authority, net (total)	123	115	128
4190	Outlays, net (total)	71	102	178

Acquisition of Lands for National Forests, Special Acts.—To acquire lands within critical watersheds to provide soil stabilization and restoration of vegetation. Public Laws 76–589, 76–591 and 78–310 (54 Stat. 297, 298, 299, and 402; and 58 Stat. 227–228) authorize appropriations for the purchase of lands within the following national forests: the Cache, Uinta, and Wasatch, in Utah; the Toiyabe, in Nevada; the Angeles, Cleveland, San Bernardino, and Sequoia, in California; and the Ozark and Ouachita, in Arkansas. Appropriations are made from receipts on these national forests. The 2023 Budget requests $664,000 in funding for Special Acts with funds derived from forest receipts.

Acquisition of Lands to Complete Land Exchanges.—Deposits are made by State, county, or municipal governments, public school authorities, or non-Federal parties, and are used to acquire lands for the National Forest System or other authorized purposes. The 2023 Budget requests $150,000 in funding for Acquisition of Lands to complete land exchanges with funds derived from these deposits.

Object Classification (in millions of dollars)

Identification code 012–9923–0–2–302		2021 actual	2022 est.	2023 est.
	Direct obligations:			
11.1	Personnel compensation: Full-time permanent	4	3	3
12.1	Civilian personnel benefits	1	1	1
25.2	Other services from non-Federal sources	2	4	4
32.0	Land and structures	59	139	155
41.0	Grants, subsidies, and contributions	1	1	1
99.0	Direct obligations	67	148	164
99.5	Adjustment for rounding			1
99.9	Total new obligations, unexpired accounts	67	148	165

Employment Summary

Identification code 012–9923–0–2–302	2021 actual	2022 est.	2023 est.
1001 Direct civilian full-time equivalent employment	37	25	25
3001 Allocation account civilian full-time equivalent employment	23	23	23

FOREST SERVICE PERMANENT APPROPRIATIONS

Special and Trust Fund Receipts (in millions of dollars)

Identification code 012–9921–0–2–999		2021 actual	2022 est.	2023 est.
0100	Balance, start of year	219	387	546
	Receipts:			
	Current law:			
1130	National Forests Fund	55	55	55
1130	National Forests Fund, Payments to States	105	126	126
1130	Timber Roads, Purchaser Elections	2	2	2
1130	National Forests Fund, Roads and Trails for States	13	16	16
1130	Timber Salvage Sales	35	35	35
1130	Deposits, Brush Disposal	7	7	7
1130	Rents and Charges for Quarters, Forest Service	10	10	10
1130	Timber Sales Pipeline Restoration Fund	6	6	6
1130	Recreational Fee Demonstration Program, Forest Service	118	118	118
1130	Midewin National Tallgrass Prairie Rental Fees	1	1	1
1130	Charges, User Fees, and Natural Resource Utilization, Land between the Lakes, Forest Service	6	6	6
1130	Administration of Rights-of-way and Other Land Uses		5	5
1130	Administration of Rights-of-way and Other Land Uses	1	2	2
1130	Funds Retained, Stewardship Contracting Product Sales	29	30	30
1130	National Grasslands	117	117	117
1130	Miscellaneous Special Funds, Forest Service	2	2	2
1199	Total current law receipts	507	538	538
1999	Total receipts	507	538	538
2000	Total: Balances and receipts	726	925	1,084
	Appropriations:			
	Current law:			
2101	Stewardship Contracting Product Sales	−29	−29	−29
2101	Forest Service Permanent Appropriations	−99	−110	−110
2101	Forest Service Permanent Appropriations	−2	−2	−2
2101	Forest Service Permanent Appropriations	−13	−16	−16
2101	Forest Service Permanent Appropriations	−35	−35	−35
2101	Forest Service Permanent Appropriations	−7	−7	−7
2101	Forest Service Permanent Appropriations	−6	−6	−6
2101	Forest Service Permanent Appropriations	−1	−1	−1
2101	Forest Service Permanent Appropriations	−1	−1	−1
2101	Forest Service Permanent Appropriations	−10	−10	−10
2101	Forest Service Permanent Appropriations	−6	−6	−6
2101	Forest Service Permanent Appropriations	−118	−118	−118
2101	Forest Service Permanent Appropriations	−1	−1	−1
2101	Forest Service Permanent Appropriations	−7	−6	−6
2101	Forest Service Permanent Appropriations	−2	−7	−7
2101	Forest Service Permanent Appropriations	−22	−40	−40
2103	Stewardship Contracting Product Sales		−2	−2
2103	Forest Service Permanent Appropriations	−9	−10	−10
2132	Stewardship Contracting Product Sales	2	2	2
2132	Forest Service Permanent Appropriations	3	3	3
2132	Forest Service Permanent Appropriations	14	16	16
2132	Forest Service Permanent Appropriations	7	7	7
2199	Total current law appropriations	−342	−379	−379
2999	Total appropriations	−342	−379	−379
5098	Reconciliation adjustment	3		
5099	Balance, end of year	387	546	705

Program and Financing (in millions of dollars)

Identification code 012–9921–0–2–999		2021 actual	2022 est.	2023 est.
	Obligations by program activity:			
0001	Brush disposal (5206)	7	7	7
0002	Restoration of Forest Lands and Improvements (5215)	12	12	12
0003	Recreation fee demonstration / enhancement programs (5268)	99	99	99
0005	Timber Salvage Sale program (5204)	25	25	25
0006	Timber Pipeline Restoration fund (includes forest botanical products) (5264)	5	5	5
0008	Midewin Tallgrass Prairie funds (5277)	1	1	1
0009	Operation and maintenance of quarters (5219)	8	8	8
0010	Land between the lakes management fund (5360)	7	7	7
0012	Administration of rights-of-way and other land uses (5361 - URRF, URMN)	1	1	1
0013	Secure Rural Schools - National Forest Fund (5201)	77	109	109
0014	Secure Rural Schools - transfers from Treasury (1117)	128	116	116
0015	Payments to Minnesota (5213)	6	6	6
0016	Payments to Counties - National Grasslands (5896)	21	21	21
0018	Licensee Program (5214)	1	1	1
0799	Total direct obligations	398	418	418
0801	Admin rights of way - Reimbursable program (5361 - URMJ)	4	5	5

Forest Service—Continued
Federal Funds—Continued

FOREST SERVICE PERMANENT APPROPRIATIONS—Continued

Program and Financing—Continued

Identification code 012–9921–0–2–999	2021 actual	2022 est.	2023 est.
0900 Total new obligations, unexpired accounts	402	423	423
Budgetary resources:			
Unobligated balance:			
1000 Unobligated balance brought forward, Oct 1	578	621	657
1021 Recoveries of prior year unpaid obligations	9	9	9
1070 Unobligated balance (total)	587	630	666
Budget authority:			
Appropriations, discretionary:			
1140 Capital transfer of appropriations to general fund		–16	
Appropriations, mandatory:			
1200 Appropriation: Payments to States Northern Spotted Owl Guarantee (1117)	128	116	116
1201 Appropriation: Payment to States, National Forest Fund (5201)	99	110	110
1201 Appropriation: Timber Roads, Purchaser Elections (5202)	2	2	2
1201 Appropriation: Roads and Trails for States, National Forests Fund (5203)	13	16	16
1201 Appropriation: Timber Salvage Sales (5204)	35	35	35
1201 Appropriation: Expenses, Brush Disposal (5206)	7	7	7
1201 Appropriation: Payment to Minnesota (5213)	6	6	6
1201 Appropriation: Licensee Programs (5214)	1	1	1
1201 Appropriation: Restoration of Forest Lands and Improvements (5215)	1	1	1
1201 Appropriation: Operations and Maintenance of Quarters (5219)	10	10	10
1201 Appropriation: Timber Sales Pipeline Restoration Fund (5264)	6	6	6
1201 Appropriation: Recreation Fees (5268)	118	118	118
1201 Appropriation: Midewin National Tallgrass Prairie Rental Fees (5277)	1	1	1
1201 Appropriation: Land Between the Lakes Management Fund (5360)	7	6	6
1201 Appropriation: Administration of Rights of Way and Other Land Uses (5361)	2	7	7
1201 Appropriation: Payments to Counties, National Grasslands (5896)	22	40	40
1203 Appropriation (previously unavailable)(special or trust)	9	10	10
1232 Sequestration - Subfunction 302 (All Remaining Accts)	–3	–3	–3
1232 Sequestration - Subfunction 806 Pmts to States: 5201, 5213, 5896, 1117	–14	–16	–16
1232 Sequestration - Subfunction 303 Rec Fees: 5268	–7	–7	–7
1240 Capital transfer of appropriations to general fund	–13		
1260 Appropriations, mandatory (total)	430	466	466
Spending authority from offsetting collections, mandatory:			
1800 Collected	6		
1900 Budget authority (total)	436	450	466
1930 Total budgetary resources available	1,023	1,080	1,132
Memorandum (non-add) entries:			
1941 Unexpired unobligated balance, end of year	621	657	709
Change in obligated balance:			
Unpaid obligations:			
3000 Unpaid obligations, brought forward, Oct 1	139	119	140
3010 New obligations, unexpired accounts	402	423	423
3020 Outlays (gross)	–413	–393	–369
3040 Recoveries of prior year unpaid obligations, unexpired	–9	–9	–9
3050 Unpaid obligations, end of year	119	140	185
Memorandum (non-add) entries:			
3100 Obligated balance, start of year	139	119	140
3200 Obligated balance, end of year	119	140	185
Budget authority and outlays, net:			
Discretionary:			
4000 Budget authority, gross		–16	
Mandatory:			
4090 Budget authority, gross	436	466	466
Outlays, gross:			
4100 Outlays from new mandatory authority	164	274	274
4101 Outlays from mandatory balances	249	119	95
4110 Outlays, gross (total)	413	393	369
Offsets against gross budget authority and outlays:			
Offsetting collections (collected) from:			
4123 Non-Federal sources	–6		
4180 Budget authority, net (total)	430	450	466
4190 Outlays, net (total)	407	393	369

Brush Disposal.—Funds from payments made by purchasers of National Forest timber are used to dispose of or treat slash and other debris resulting from timber cutting operations (16 U.S.C. 490).

Restoration of Forest Lands and Improvements.—Funds from (1) forfeiture of deposits and bonds posted by permittees or purchasers of National Forest timber for failure to complete performance of improvement, protection, or rehabilitation work required under the permit or timber sale contract; or (2) the result of a judgment, compromise, or settlement of any claim, involving present or potential damage to lands or improvements, are used for the improvement, protection, or rehabilitation of lands under the administration of the Forest Service (16 U.S.C. 579c).

Recreation Fees, Forest Service (also referred to as the Federal Lands Recreation Enhancement Fund).—Fees collected from users of recreation facilities are used to pay for operation, maintenance, and improvement of recreation sites and services to maintain and enhance recreation opportunities, visitor experiences, and related fish and wildlife habitat. (16 U.S.C. 6806 et seq.). Section 423 of Division G of the Consolidated Appropriations Act, 2021 (P.L. 116–260) extended FLREA through 2022. The 2023 budget includes appropriations language to extend FLREA through October 1, 2024.

Timber Purchaser Election Roads Construction.—Funds from timber receipts are used to construct or reconstruct roads for purchasers of timber who qualify as small businesses and elect to have the Forest Service construct the roads designated under the timber sale contract (16 U.S.C. 472a(i)).

Timber Salvage Sales.—Funds are used for salvage logging of dead, damaged, insect-infested, or down timber, and to remove such trees for stand improvement (16 U.S.C. 472a(h)).

Timber Sales Pipeline Restoration Fund.—Funds are used for the preparation of timber sales and funding the backlog of recreation projects on National Forest System lands (16 U.S.C 1611 note).

Forest Botanical Products.—Permitting fees are based on the fair market value of forest botanical products to cover the costs of analyzing, granting, modifying, or administering permits for harvest, including the costs for environmental analyses (16 U.S.C. 528 note). The Budget proposes reauthorizing this program for one year, to September 30, 2023.

Midewin National Tallgrass Prairie Funds.—Funds collected through user and rental fees (Public Law 104–106, Div. B, (Title XXIX, sec. 2915 (b) through (f)), Feb. 10, 1996, 110 Stat. 601) can be used as follows:

Midewin National Tallgrass Prairie Rental Fees.—Available receipts from rental fees may be used to cover the cost of ecosystem restoration, prairie improvements, and directly related administrative activities at the Midewin National Tallgrass Prairie.

Midewin National Tallgrass Prairie Restoration Fund.—Receipts from grazing fees, agricultural leases for row crops, sales of surplus equipment, and proceeds from the sale of any facilities and improvements; are available to cover the cost of restoration of ecosystems; construction of a visitor center, recreational facilities, trails, an administrative office; prairie improvement; and operations and maintenance.

Operation and Maintenance of Quarters.—Rents collected from employees occupying Forest Service housing facilities for operation and maintenance of employee-occupied quarters (5 U.S.C. 5911).

Land Between the Lakes Management Fund.—Amounts received from charges, user fees and natural resource use on the Land Between the Lakes National Recreation Area (LBLNRA) are deposited into this fund and are available for the management of the LBLNRA, including salaries, and expenses (16 U.S.C. 460lll–24) (P.L. 105–277, div. A, Sec. 101(e) [title V, Sec. 524], Oct. 21, 1998, 112 Stat. 2681–315).

Cost Recovery (Lands Minor Projects, Administrative Rights-of-Way Program), and Cost Recovery (Lands Major Projects, including the Reimbursable Program).—Fees collected from applicants and holders of special use authorizations are available to pay for processing applications and monitoring compliance with special use authorizations. (31 U.S.C. 9701; 43 U.S.C. 1764(g); 30 U.S.C. 815(1); P.L. 82–137; P.L. 66–146; P.L.

94–579; 113 Stat. 1501A-196197 as amended by 118 Stat. 3105; 119 Stat. 555 and P.L. 110–161; 16 U.S.C. 46016d; 117 Stat. 294–297). This fund also includes:

Commercial Filming.—Collection of fees from commercial filming and still photography permits for maintenance of the filming site. (16 U.S.C. 460l–6d) (P.L. 106–206).

Organizational Camps.—Collection of land use fees from organizational camps located on National Forest System lands. (16 U.S.C. 6231 et seq.) (P.L. 108–7).

Secure Rural Schools and Community Self-Determination Act.—The Secure Rural Schools Act (SRS) as reauthorized by Public Law 117–58 directs that SRS Title I funds be used to fund county schools and roads. SRS Title II authorizes conservation projects on Federal lands. Any SRS Title II project funds not obligated by September 30, 2026, will be returned to the U.S. Treasury. Title III funds may be used on county projects, (1) to carry out activities under the Firewise Communities program, (2) to reimburse participating counties for search and rescue and other emergency services, including firefighting and law enforcement controls, (3) to cover training costs and equipment purchases directly related to emergency services, (4) to develop and carry out community wildfire protection plans, and (5) to provide or expand broadband telecommunications or other digital learning technology at local schools. The Agriculture Improvement Act of 2018 established a pilot program to allow for regional appointment of members of SRS Resource Advisory Committees (RACs) for the states of Arizona and Montana through October 1, 2023.

Payment to Minnesota.—The State of Minnesota is paid 0.75 percent of the appraised value of certain Superior National Forest lands in the counties of Cook, Lake, and St. Louis for distribution to those counties (16 U.S.C. 577g).

Payments to Counties, National Grasslands.—25 percent of net revenues from the use of lands acquired under Title III of the Bankhead-Jones Act is provided to counties in which Title III-Bankhead-Jones Acquired Lands are located for funding public schools and roads. (7 U.S.C. 1012).

Roads and Trails (10 Percent) Fund.—10 percent of all National Forest Fund receipts received by the Forest Service are used to repair or reconstruct roads, bridges, and trails on NFS lands, or to correct road and trail deficiencies that adversely affect ecosystems.

Licensee Program.—Fees for the private commercial use of intellectual property are collected under regulations promulgated by the Secretary. The licensee program includes Smokey Bear to further the nationwide forest fire prevention campaign (16 U.S.C. 580p(2)) and Woodsy Owl to promote wise use of the environment (16 U.S.C. 580p(1)).

Quinault Special Management Area.—The Forest Service manages the natural resources and distributes proceeds from the sale of forest products in the Quinault Special Management Area of the Olympic National Forest. Receipts are divided between the State of Washington (45 percent), the Quinault Tribe (45 percent) and the Quinault Special Management Area fund (10 percent) for use by the Olympic National Forest to administer future timber sales. (P.L. 100–638) (102 Stat. 3327).

Hardwood Technology Transfer and Applied Research Fund.—Funds collected from leasing the Wood Education and Research Center (WERC) wood shop and rough mill under a special use permit are available for the management and operation of the WERC and the payment of salaries and expenses (P.L. 106–113, div. B, 1000(a)(3) [Title III, 332], Nov. 29, 1999, 113 Stat. 1535, 1501A197).

Site-specific Lands Acts.—Proceeds from the sale of National Forest System land pursuant to special acts passed by Congress are used for specific improvements to lands and facilities within the same national forest or State. (16 U.S.C. 484a; P.L. 90–171).

Land and Water Conservation Fund Act.—The Forest Service uses Federal land acquisition funding from the Land and Water Conservation Fund (LWCF) Act of 1965 to acquire land within or adjacent to the boundaries of national forests and within wilderness areas, and to acquire inholdings. Land acquisitions improve recreational access and create efficiencies for priority stewardship activities, such as hazardous fuels treatments and watershed protection. LWCF also funds the State and Private Forestry Forest Legacy Program which provides grants to states for the protection of privately owned forest lands through conservation easements or land purchases. On August 4, 2020, the LWCF Act was amended by the Great American Outdoors Act (GAOA) to permanently fund the LWCF for investment in conservation and recreation opportunities in public and private lands. In 2023, the Forest Service requests $124 million for proposed Federal Land Acquisition projects and program administration and $94.3 million for proposed Forest Legacy Projects and program administration.

Object Classification (in millions of dollars)

Identification code 012–9921–0–2–999		2021 actual	2022 est.	2023 est.
	Direct obligations:			
	Personnel compensation:			
11.1	Full-time permanent	35	35	36
11.3	Other than full-time permanent	10	10	11
11.5	Other personnel compensation	3	3	3
11.9	Total personnel compensation	48	48	50
12.1	Civilian personnel benefits	17	16	17
21.0	Travel and transportation of persons	1	2	2
22.0	Transportation of things	1	1	1
23.3	Communications, utilities, and miscellaneous charges	1	1	1
24.0	Printing and reproduction	1	1	1
25.2	Other services from non-Federal sources	70	55	58
25.3	Other goods and services from Federal sources	9	9	12
25.4	Operation and maintenance of facilities		1	1
25.7	Operation and maintenance of equipment	1	1	2
26.0	Supplies and materials	10	11	12
31.0	Equipment	1	1	2
32.0	Land and structures		2	3
41.0	Grants, subsidies, and contributions	238	269	256
99.0	Direct obligations	398	418	418
99.0	Reimbursable obligations	4	5	5
99.9	Total new obligations, unexpired accounts	402	423	423

Employment Summary

Identification code 012–9921–0–2–999		2021 actual	2022 est.	2023 est.
1001	Direct civilian full-time equivalent employment	818	819	819
2001	Reimbursable civilian full-time equivalent employment	23	23	23

WORKING CAPITAL FUND

Program and Financing (in millions of dollars)

Identification code 012–4605–0–4–302		2021 actual	2022 est.	2023 est.
	Obligations by program activity:			
0801	Working capital fund	272	272	272
	Budgetary resources:			
	Unobligated balance:			
1000	Unobligated balance brought forward, Oct 1	230	247	227
1021	Recoveries of prior year unpaid obligations	7	7	7
1070	Unobligated balance (total)	237	254	234
	Budget authority:			
	Spending authority from offsetting collections, discretionary:			
1700	Collected	281	245	251
1701	Change in uncollected payments, Federal sources	1		
1750	Spending auth from offsetting collections, disc (total)	282	245	251
1930	Total budgetary resources available	519	499	485
	Memorandum (non-add) entries:			
1941	Unexpired unobligated balance, end of year	247	227	213
	Change in obligated balance:			
	Unpaid obligations:			
3000	Unpaid obligations, brought forward, Oct 1	107	114	51
3010	New obligations, unexpired accounts	272	272	272
3020	Outlays (gross)	–258	–328	–250
3040	Recoveries of prior year unpaid obligations, unexpired	–7	–7	–7
3050	Unpaid obligations, end of year	114	51	66

WORKING CAPITAL FUND—Continued
Program and Financing—Continued

Identification code 012–4605–0–4–302	2021 actual	2022 est.	2023 est.
Uncollected payments:			
3060 Uncollected pymts, Fed sources, brought forward, Oct 1	....	–1	–1
3070 Change in uncollected pymts, Fed sources, unexpired	–1	....	....
3090 Uncollected pymts, Fed sources, end of year	–1	–1	–1
Memorandum (non-add) entries:			
3100 Obligated balance, start of year	107	113	50
3200 Obligated balance, end of year	113	50	65
Budget authority and outlays, net:			
Discretionary:			
4000 Budget authority, gross	282	245	251
Outlays, gross:			
4010 Outlays from new discretionary authority	68	208	213
4011 Outlays from discretionary balances	190	120	37
4020 Outlays, gross (total)	258	328	250
Offsets against gross budget authority and outlays:			
Offsetting collections (collected) from:			
4030 Federal sources	–53	–38	–39
4033 Non-Federal sources	–228	–207	–212
4040 Offsets against gross budget authority and outlays (total)	–281	–245	–251
Additional offsets against gross budget authority only:			
4050 Change in uncollected pymts, Fed sources, unexpired	–1	....	....
4080 Outlays, net (discretionary)	–23	83	–1
4180 Budget authority, net (total)	....	....	....
4190 Outlays, net (total)	–23	83	–1

The Working Capital Fund is a self-sustaining revolving fund that provides services to national forests, research experiment stations, other Federal agencies when necessary, State and private agencies as provided by law, and to persons who cooperate with the Forest Service in fire control and other authorized programs. Forestry-related supply and support services include:

Equipment Services.—The Fund owns, operates, maintains, replaces, and repairs common-use, motor-driven, and similar equipment. This equipment is rented to administrative units including national forests, research experiment stations, other Forest Service units, and to other federal and non-federal agencies. Rental rates include an incremental charge which, when added to depreciation and residual value, provide funds to finance equipment replacement costs.

Aircraft Services.—The Fund operates, maintains, and repairs Forest Service-owned aircraft used in fire surveillance and suppression, and in other Forest Service programs. Aircraft replacement costs are financed from either appropriated funds or the Forest Service Working Capital Fund, or a combination of both.

Supply Services.—The Fund operates common services and provides for cost-recovery of Working Capital Fund Program Management. Common services include photo reproduction laboratories that store, reproduce, and supply aerial photographs, aerial maps, and other photographs of national forest lands. Photographic reproductions are sold to national forests, research experiment stations, and others at cost. Common services also include sign shops to manufacture special signs for regulating traffic and posting information for visitors to the national forests. These signs are sold to national forests and research experiment stations at cost.

Nurseries.—The Fund operates seed supply services that provide tree seeds for direct seeding or sowing in nurseries for the production of trees. Activities include purchase or collection of cones, extraction of seeds, cleaning and testing, and storage and delivery. The fund operates in conjunction with forest tree nurseries and cold storage facilities for storage of tree seedlings. Tree seedlings are sold to national forests, State foresters, and other cooperators at cost.

Object Classification (in millions of dollars)

Identification code 012–4605–0–4–302	2021 actual	2022 est.	2023 est.
Reimbursable obligations:			
Personnel compensation:			
11.1 Full-time permanent	20	20	20
11.3 Other than full-time permanent	1	1	1
11.5 Other personnel compensation	1	1	1
11.9 Total personnel compensation	22	22	22
12.1 Civilian personnel benefits	8	8	8
21.0 Travel and transportation of persons	1	1	1
22.0 Transportation of things	10	10	10
23.2 Rental payments to others	1	1	1
25.2 Other services from non-Federal sources	27	27	27
25.3 Other goods and services from Federal sources	5	5	5
25.7 Operation and maintenance of equipment	37	37	37
26.0 Supplies and materials	45	45	45
31.0 Equipment	116	116	116
99.9 Total new obligations, unexpired accounts	272	272	272

Employment Summary

Identification code 012–4605–0–4–302	2021 actual	2022 est.	2023 est.
2001 Reimbursable civilian full-time equivalent employment	551	551	551

Trust Funds
FOREST SERVICE TRUST FUNDS

Special and Trust Fund Receipts (in millions of dollars)

Identification code 012–9974–0–7–302	2021 actual	2022 est.	2023 est.
0100 Balance, start of year	4	5	4
Receipts:			
Current law:			
1110 Transfers from General Fund of Amounts Equal to Certain Customs Duties, Reforestation Trust Fund	30	150	150
1130 Forest Service Cooperative Fund	86	85	85
1199 Total current law receipts	116	235	235
1999 Total receipts	116	235	235
2000 Total: Balances and receipts	120	240	239
Appropriations:			
Current law:			
2101 Forest Service Trust Funds	–86	–86	–86
2101 Forest Service Trust Funds	–30	–150	–150
2103 Forest Service Trust Funds	–4	–5	–5
2132 Forest Service Trust Funds	5	5	5
2199 Total current law appropriations	–115	–236	–236
2999 Total appropriations	–115	–236	–236
5099 Balance, end of year	5	4	3

Program and Financing (in millions of dollars)

Identification code 012–9974–0–7–302	2021 actual	2022 est.	2023 est.
Obligations by program activity:			
0001 Cooperative work trust fund (8028 - CWKV CWF2)	73	98	90
0002 Cooperative work advance payments (8028 - CWF2)	....	32	25
0003 Reforestation trust fund (8046 - RTRT)	28	140	140
0799 Total direct obligations	101	270	255
0801 Reimbursable program-coop work other (8028 - CWFS)	23	25	25
0900 Total new obligations, unexpired accounts	124	295	280
Budgetary resources:			
Unobligated balance:			
1000 Unobligated balance brought forward, Oct 1	309	329	299
1021 Recoveries of prior year unpaid obligations	4	4	4
1070 Unobligated balance (total)	313	333	303
Budget authority:			
Appropriations, mandatory:			
1201 Appropriation: Cooperative Work Trust Fund (8028 CWKV CWF2)	86	86	86
1201 Appropriation: Reforestation Trust Fund (8046 RTRT)	30	150	150

		2021 actual	2022 est.	2023 est.
1203	Appropriation (previously unavailable)(special or trust)	4	5	5
1232	Appropriations and/or unobligated balance of appropriations temporarily reduced	−5	−5	−5
1260	Appropriations, mandatory (total)	115	236	236
	Spending authority from offsetting collections, mandatory:			
1800	Collected (CWFS)	25	25	25
1900	Budget authority (total)	140	261	261
1930	Total budgetary resources available	453	594	564
	Memorandum (non-add) entries:			
1941	Unexpired unobligated balance, end of year	329	299	284
	Change in obligated balance:			
	Unpaid obligations:			
3000	Unpaid obligations, brought forward, Oct 1	84	85	155
3010	New obligations, unexpired accounts	124	295	280
3020	Outlays (gross)	−119	−221	−196
3040	Recoveries of prior year unpaid obligations, unexpired	−4	−4	−4
3050	Unpaid obligations, end of year	85	155	235
	Memorandum (non-add) entries:			
3100	Obligated balance, start of year	84	85	155
3200	Obligated balance, end of year	85	155	235
	Budget authority and outlays, net:			
	Mandatory:			
4090	Budget authority, gross	140	261	261
	Outlays, gross:			
4100	Outlays from new mandatory authority	17	139	139
4101	Outlays from mandatory balances	102	82	57
4110	Outlays, gross (total)	119	221	196
	Offsets against gross budget authority and outlays:			
	Offsetting collections (collected) from:			
4123	Non-Federal sources	−25	−25	−25
4180	Budget authority, net (total)	115	236	236
4190	Outlays, net (total)	94	196	171
	Memorandum (non-add) entries:			
5000	Total investments, SOY: Federal securities: Par value	6	6	6
5001	Total investments, EOY: Federal securities: Par value	6	6	6

Cooperative Work Trust Fund-Knutson Vandenberg.—This fund receives deposits from purchasers of timber to accomplish improvement work within the timber sale area. Specified work includes reforestation of harvested areas, stand improvement, and other actions to protect National Forest System lands. Funds are also used for protection, reforestation, and timber stand improvement on private lands adjacent to National Forest System lands (7 U.S.C. 2269; 16 U.S.C. 498, 535, 572, 572a, 576b, 1643; and 31 U.S.C. 1321).

Cooperative Work Trust Fund-Advanced Payments (Non-Agreement Based).—This fund receives deposits from partners and cooperators for protecting and improving resources of the National Forest System as authorized by permits or sale contracts. Deposits from multiple contributors can be pooled to support a wide variety of activities that benefit Forest and Rangeland Research, National Forest System lands, and for other agency activities. There are multiple statutes that authorize this fund including 16 U.S.C. 572 and 31 U.S.C. 1321.

Cooperative Work Trust Fund-Reimbursable Program (Agreement Based).—This fund receives deposits from partners and cooperators to protect and improve resources of the National Forest System as authorized by cooperative agreements. These funds support a wide variety of activities that benefit and support Forest and Rangeland Research, National Forest System lands, and for other agency activities. There are multiple statutes that authorize this fund including 16 U.S.C. 498, 16 U.S.C. 532–537, and 31 U.S.C. 1321.

Reforestation Trust Fund.—Congress created this fund to fund reforestation and timber stand improvement (16 U.S.C. 1606a(d)). Funds are generated from import tariffs on wood products. The Infrastructure Investment and Jobs Act (P.L. 117–58) removed the $30 million annual cap on available funds.

Land Between the Lakes Trust Fund.—Interest earned from funds transferred by the Tennessee Valley Authority is available for public education, grants, recreation internships, conservation and multiple-use management of the Land Between the Lakes National Recreation Area in Kentucky and Tennessee. Annual trust fund earnings and program expenditures are less than $1 million (16 U.S.C. 460lll–31).

Object Classification (in millions of dollars)

Identification code 012–9974–0–7–302	2021 actual	2022 est.	2023 est.
Direct obligations:			
Personnel compensation:			
11.1 Full-time permanent	19	21	21
11.3 Other than full-time permanent	4	5	5
11.5 Other personnel compensation	2	2	2
11.9 Total personnel compensation	25	28	28
12.1 Civilian personnel benefits	9	10	10
21.0 Travel and transportation of persons	1	2	1
22.0 Transportation of things		1	1
23.3 Communications, utilities, and miscellaneous charges		1	1
25.2 Other services from non-Federal sources	41	138	129
25.3 Other goods and services from Federal sources	4	14	13
25.4 Operation and maintenance of facilities		1	1
25.7 Operation and maintenance of equipment		1	1
26.0 Supplies and materials	9	34	32
31.0 Equipment	1	4	3
32.0 Land and structures		1	1
41.0 Grants, subsidies, and contributions	11	36	35
99.0 Direct obligations	101	271	256
99.0 Reimbursable obligations	23	24	24
99.9 Total new obligations, unexpired accounts	124	295	280

Employment Summary

Identification code 012–9974–0–7–302	2021 actual	2022 est.	2023 est.
1001 Direct civilian full-time equivalent employment	368	438	438
2001 Reimbursable civilian full-time equivalent employment	106	106	106

ADMINISTRATIVE PROVISIONS—FOREST SERVICE

(INCLUDING TRANSFERS OF FUNDS)

Appropriations to the Forest Service for the current fiscal year shall be available for: (1) purchase of passenger motor vehicles; acquisition of passenger motor vehicles from excess sources, and hire of such vehicles; purchase, lease, operation, maintenance, and acquisition of aircraft to maintain the operable fleet for use in Forest Service wildland fire programs and other Forest Service programs; notwithstanding other provisions of law, existing aircraft being replaced may be sold, with proceeds derived or trade-in value used to offset the purchase price for the replacement aircraft; (2) services pursuant to 7 U.S.C. 2225, and not to exceed $100,000 for employment under 5 U.S.C. 3109; (3) purchase, erection, and alteration of buildings and other public improvements (7 U.S.C. 2250); (4) acquisition of land, waters, and interests therein pursuant to 7 U.S.C. 428a; (5) expenses pursuant to the Volunteers in the National Forest Act of 1972 (16 U.S.C. 558a, 558d, and 558a note); (6) the cost of uniforms as authorized by 5 U.S.C. 5901–5902; and (7) for debt collection contracts in accordance with 31 U.S.C. 3718(c).

Funds made available to the Forest Service in this Act may be transferred between accounts affected by the Forest Service budget restructure outlined in section 435 of division D of the Further Consolidated Appropriations Act, 2020 (Public Law 116–94): Provided, That any transfer of funds pursuant to this paragraph shall not increase or decrease the funds appropriated to any account in this fiscal year by more than ten percent: Provided further, That such transfer authority is in addition to any other transfer authority provided by law.

Any appropriations or funds available to the Forest Service may be transferred to the Wildland Fire Management appropriation for forest firefighting, emergency rehabilitation of burned-over or damaged lands or waters under its jurisdiction, and fire preparedness due to severe burning conditions upon the Secretary of Agriculture's notification of the House and Senate Committees on Appropriations that all fire suppression funds appropriated under the heading "Wildland Fire Management" will be obligated within 30 days: Provided, That all funds used pursuant to this paragraph must be replenished by a supplemental appropriation which must be requested as promptly as possible.

Not more than $50,000,000 of funds appropriated to the Forest Service shall be available for expenditure or transfer to the Department of the Interior for wildland fire management, hazardous fuels management, and State fire assistance when such

ADMINISTRATIVE PROVISIONS, FOREST SERVICE—Continued

transfers would facilitate and expedite wildland fire management programs and projects.

Notwithstanding any other provision of this Act, the Forest Service may transfer unobligated balances of discretionary funds appropriated to the Forest Service by this Act to or within the Wildland Fire Management Account for hazardous fuels management and urgent rehabilitation of burned-over National Forest System lands and water: Provided, That such transferred funds shall remain available through September 30, 2026: Provided further, That none of the funds transferred pursuant to this paragraph shall be available for obligation without written notification to the Committees on Appropriations of both Houses of Congress.

Funds appropriated to the Forest Service shall be available for assistance to or through the Agency for International Development in connection with forest and rangeland research, technical information, and assistance in foreign countries, and shall be available to support forestry and related natural resource activities outside the United States and its territories and possessions, including technical assistance, education and training, and cooperation with U.S. government, private sector, and international organizations. The Forest Service, acting for the International Program, may sign direct funding agreements with foreign governments and institutions as well as other domestic agencies (including the U.S. Agency for International Development, the Department of State, and the Millennium Challenge Corporation), U.S. private sector firms, institutions and organizations to provide technical assistance and training programs overseas on forestry and rangeland management.

Funds appropriated to the Forest Service shall be available for expenditure or transfer to the Department of the Interior, Bureau of Land Management, for removal, preparation, and adoption of excess wild horses and burros from National Forest System lands, and for the performance of cadastral surveys to designate the boundaries of such lands.

None of the funds made available to the Forest Service in this Act or any other Act with respect to any fiscal year shall be subject to transfer under the provisions of section 702(b) of the Department of Agriculture Organic Act of 1944 (7 U.S.C. 2257), section 442 of Public Law 106–224 (7 U.S.C. 7772), or section 10417(b) of Public Law 107–171 (7 U.S.C. 8316(b)).

Not more than $82,000,000 of funds available to the Forest Service shall be transferred to the Working Capital Fund of the Department of Agriculture and not more than $14,500,000 of funds available to the Forest Service shall be transferred to the Department of Agriculture for Department Reimbursable Programs, commonly referred to as Greenbook charges. Nothing in this paragraph shall prohibit or limit the use of reimbursable agreements requested by the Forest Service in order to obtain information technology services, including telecommunications and system modifications or enhancements, from the Working Capital Fund of the Department of Agriculture.

Of the funds available to the Forest Service, up to $5,000,000 shall be available for priority projects within the scope of the approved budget, which shall be carried out by the Youth Conservation Corps and shall be carried out under the authority of the Public Lands Corps Act of 1993 (16 U.S.C. 1721 et seq.).

Of the funds available to the Forest Service, $4,000 is available to the Chief of the Forest Service for official reception and representation expenses.

Pursuant to sections 405(b) and 410(b) of Public Law 101–593, of the funds available to the Forest Service, up to $3,000,000 may be advanced in a lump sum to the National Forest Foundation to aid conservation partnership projects in support of the Forest Service mission, without regard to when the Foundation incurs expenses, for projects on or benefitting National Forest System lands or related to Forest Service programs: Provided, That of the Federal funds made available to the Foundation, no more than $300,000 shall be available for administrative expenses: Provided further, That the Foundation shall obtain, by the end of the period of Federal financial assistance, private contributions to match funds made available by the Forest Service on at least a one-for-one basis: Provided further, That the Foundation may transfer Federal funds to a Federal or a non-Federal recipient for a project at the same rate that the recipient has obtained the non-Federal matching funds.

Pursuant to section 2(b)(2) of Public Law 98–244, up to $3,000,000 of the funds available to the Forest Service may be advanced to the National Fish and Wildlife Foundation in a lump sum to aid cost-share conservation projects, without regard to when expenses are incurred, on or benefitting National Forest System lands or related to Forest Service programs: Provided, That such funds shall be matched on at least a one-for-one basis by the Foundation or its sub-recipients: Provided further, That the Foundation may transfer Federal funds to a Federal or non-Federal recipient for a project at the same rate that the recipient has obtained the non-Federal matching funds.

Funds appropriated to the Forest Service shall be available for interactions with and providing technical assistance to rural communities and natural resource-based businesses for sustainable rural development purposes.

Funds appropriated to the Forest Service shall be available for payments to counties within the Columbia River Gorge National Scenic Area, pursuant to section 14(c)(1) and (2), and section 16(a)(2) of Public Law 99–663.

Any funds appropriated to the Forest Service may be used to meet the non-Federal share requirement in section 502(c) of the Older Americans Act of 1965 (42 U.S.C. 3056(c)(2)).

Notwithstanding any other provision of law, of any appropriations or funds available to the Forest Service, not to exceed $500,000 may be used to reimburse the Office of the General Counsel (OGC), Department of Agriculture, for travel and related expenses incurred as a result of OGC assistance or participation requested by the Forest Service at meetings, training sessions, management reviews, land purchase negotiations, and similar matters unrelated to civil litigation. Future budget justifications for both the Forest Service and the Department of Agriculture should clearly display the sums previously transferred and the sums requested for transfer.

An eligible individual who is employed in any project funded under title V of the Older Americans Act of 1965 (42 U.S.C. 3056 et seq.) and administered by the Forest Service shall be considered to be a Federal employee for purposes of chapter 171 of title 28, United States Code.

Funds appropriated to the Forest Service shall be available to pay, from a single account, the base salary and expenses of employees who carry out functions funded by other accounts for Enterprise Program, Geospatial Technology and Applications Center, remnant Natural Resource Manager, Job Corps, and National Technology and Development Program.

ADMINISTRATIVE PROVISION—FOREST SERVICE

[Not later than 90 days after the date of enactment of this Act, the Secretary of Agriculture, acting through the Chief of the Forest Service, shall submit to the House and Senate Committees on Appropriations a detailed spend plan for the funds provided to the Forest Service in this title in this Act for fiscal year 2022, and for each fiscal year through 2026, as part of the annual budget submission of the President under section 1105(a) of title 31, United States Code, the Secretary shall submit a detailed spend plan for the funds provided to the Forest Service in this title in this Act for that fiscal year.] *(Infrastructure Investments and Jobs Appropriations Act.)*

GENERAL FUND RECEIPT ACCOUNTS

(in millions of dollars)

	2021 actual	2022 est.	2023 est.
Governmental receipts:			
012–249700 Full Cost Recovery Fees Pursuant to OMB Circular A-25	5		
General Fund Governmental receipts	5		
Offsetting receipts from the public:			
012–181100 National Grasslands	67	90	90
012–222100 National Forest Fund	1	1	1
012–267530 Biorefinery Assistance, Downward Reestimates of Subsidies	6	8	
012–270110 Agriculture Credit Insurance, Negative Subsidies	192	106	106
012–270130 Agriculture Credit Insurance, Downward Reestimates of Subsidies	226	468	
012–270210 Rural Electrification and Telephone Loans, Negative Subsidies	177	177	177
012–270230 Rural Electrification and Telephone Loans, Downward Reestimates of Subsidies	291	1,118	
012–270310 Rural Water and Waste Disposal, Negative Subsidies	1	1	1
012–270330 Rural Water and Waste Disposal, Downward Reestimates of Subsidies	875	81	
012–270510 Rural Community Facility, Negative Subsidies	79	79	79
012–270530 Rural Community Facility, Downward Reestimates of Subsidies	178	61	
012–270610 Rural Housing Insurance, Negative Subsidies	171	171	171
012–270630 Rural Housing Insurance, Downward Reestimates of Subsidies	865	2,108	
012–270730 Rural Business and Industry, Downward Reestimates of Subsidies	81	72	
012–270830 P.L. 480 Loan Program, Downward Reestimates of Subsidies	2		
012–271030 Rural Development Loans, Downward Reestimates of Subsidies	3	2	
012–271130 Rural Telephone Bank Loans, Downward Reestimates of Subsidies	1		
012–271330 Economic Development Loans, Downward Reestimates of Subsidies	2	4	

012–274630	Downward Reestimates, Distance Learning, Telemedicine, and Broadband Program	70	7	
012–275610	Negative Subsidies, Farm Storage Facility Loans	1	4	4
012–275630	Farm Storage Facility Loans, Downward Reestimate of Subsidies	49	24	
012–275730	Commodity Credit Corporation Export Guarantee Financing, Downward Reestimate of Subsidies	5	15	
012–277930	Multifamily Housing Revitalization Fund, Downward Reestimates of Subsidies	20	8	
012–278630	Rural Energy for America Program, Downward Reestimates of Subsidies	19	20	
012–279310	Commodity Credit Corporation Export Guarantee Financing, Negative Subsidies	6	6	6
012–322000	All Other General Fund Proprietary Receipts Including Budget Clearing Accounts	20	20	20
General Fund Offsetting receipts from the public		3,408	4,651	655
Intragovernmental payments:				
012–388500	Undistributed Intragovernmental Payments and Receivables from Cancelled Accounts	–14		
General Fund Intragovernmental payments		–14		

TITLE VII—GENERAL PROVISIONS

(INCLUDING CANCELLATIONS AND TRANSFERS OF FUNDS)

SEC. 701. The Secretary may use any appropriations made available to the Department of Agriculture in this Act to purchase new passenger motor vehicles, in addition to specific appropriations for this purpose, so long as the total number of vehicles purchased in fiscal year 2023 does not exceed the number of vehicles owned or leased in fiscal year 2018: Provided, That, prior to purchasing additional motor vehicles, the Secretary must determine that such vehicles are necessary for transportation safety, to reduce operational costs, and for the protection of life, property, and public safety: Provided further, That the Secretary may not increase the Department of Agriculture's fleet until the Secretary has provided prior notification to the Committees on Appropriations of both Houses of Congress.

SEC. 702. Notwithstanding any other provision of this Act, the Secretary of Agriculture may transfer unobligated balances of discretionary funds appropriated by this Act or any other available unobligated discretionary balances that are remaining available of the Department of Agriculture to the Working Capital Fund for the acquisition of property, plant, and equipment and for the improvement, delivery, and implementation of Department financial, administrative, and information technology services, and other support systems necessary for the delivery of financial, administrative, and information technology services, including cloud adoption and migration, of primary benefit to the agencies of the Department of Agriculture, such transferred funds to remain available until expended: Provided, That none of the funds made available by this Act or any other Act shall be transferred to the Working Capital Fund without the prior approval of the agency administrator: Provided further, That none of the funds transferred to the Working Capital Fund pursuant to this section shall be available for obligation without prior notification to the Committees on Appropriations of both Houses of Congress: Provided further, That none of the funds appropriated by this Act or made available to the Department's Working Capital Fund shall be available for obligation or expenditure to make any changes to the Department's National Finance Center without prior notification to the Committees on Appropriations of both Houses of Congress: Provided further, That none of the funds appropriated by this Act or made available to the Department's Working Capital Fund shall be available for obligation or expenditure to initiate, plan, develop, implement, or make any changes to remove or relocate any systems, missions, personnel, or functions of the offices of the Chief Financial Officer and the Chief Information Officer, co-located with or from the National Finance Center prior to written notification to the Committee on Appropriations of both Houses of Congress: Provided further, That the National Finance Center Information Technology Services Division personnel and data center management responsibilities, and control of any functions, missions, and systems for current and future human resources management and integrated personnel and payroll systems (PPS) and functions provided by the Chief Financial Officer and the Chief Information Officer shall remain in the National Finance Center and under the management responsibility and administrative control of the National Finance Center: Provided further, That the Secretary of Agriculture and the offices of the Chief Financial Officer shall actively market to existing and new Departments and other government agencies National Finance Center shared services including, but not limited to, payroll, financial management, and human capital shared services and allow the National Finance Center to perform technology upgrades: Provided further, That an amount not to exceed 4 percent of the total annual income to Working Capital Fund Activity Centers may be retained in the Working Capital Fund, to remain available until expended, for the acquisition of property, plant, and equipment and for the improvement, delivery, and implementation of Department financial, administrative, and information technology services, including cloud adoption and migration, or to pay any unforeseen, extraordinary costs of the Working Capital Fund Activity Centers of primary benefit to the agencies of the Department of Agriculture: Provided further, That none of the amounts reserved shall be available for obligation unless the Secretary submits written notification of the obligation to the Committees on Appropriations of both Houses of Congress: Provided further, That the limitations on the obligation of funds pending notification to Congressional Committees shall not apply to any obligation that, as determined by the Secretary, is necessary to respond to a declared state of emergency that significantly impacts the operations of the National Finance Center; or to evacuate employees of the National Finance Center to a safe haven to continue operations of the National Finance Center.

SEC. 703. No part of any appropriation contained in this Act shall remain available for obligation beyond the current fiscal year unless expressly so provided herein.

SEC. 704. No funds appropriated by this Act may be used to pay negotiated indirect cost rates on cooperative agreements or similar arrangements between the United States Department of Agriculture and nonprofit institutions in excess of 10 percent of the total direct cost of the agreement when the purpose of such cooperative arrangements is to carry out programs of mutual interest between the two parties. This does not preclude appropriate payment of indirect costs on grants and contracts with such institutions when such indirect costs are computed on a similar basis for all agencies for which appropriations are provided in this Act.

SEC. 705. Appropriations to the Department of Agriculture for the cost of direct and guaranteed loans made available in the current fiscal year shall remain available until expended to disburse obligations made in the current fiscal year for the following accounts: the Rural Development Loan Fund program account, the Rural Electrification and Telecommunication Loans program account, and the Rural Housing Insurance Fund program account.

SEC. 706. None of the funds made available to the Department of Agriculture by this Act may be used to acquire new information technology systems or significant upgrades, as determined by the Office of the Chief Information Officer, without the approval of the Chief Information Officer and the concurrence of the Executive Information Technology Investment Review Board: Provided, That notwithstanding any other provision of law, none of the funds appropriated or otherwise made available by this Act may be transferred to the Office of the Chief Information Officer without written notification to the Committees on Appropriations of both Houses of Congress: Provided further, That, notwithstanding section 11319 of title 40, United States Code, none of the funds available to the Department of Agriculture for information technology shall be obligated for projects, contracts, or other agreements over $25,000 prior to receipt of written approval by the Chief Information Officer: Provided further, That the Chief Information Officer may authorize an agency to obligate funds without written approval from the Chief Information Officer for projects, contracts, or other agreements up to $250,000 based upon the performance of an agency measured against the performance plan requirements .

SEC. 707. Funds made available under section 524(b) of the Federal Crop Insurance Act (7 U.S.C. 1524(b)) in the current fiscal year shall remain available until expended to disburse obligations made in the current fiscal year.

SEC. 708. Notwithstanding any other provision of law, any former Rural Utilities Service borrower that has repaid or prepaid an insured, direct or guaranteed loan under the Rural Electrification Act of 1936, or any not-for-profit utility that is eligible to receive an insured or direct loan under such Act, shall be eligible for assistance under section 313B(a) of such Act in the same manner as a borrower under such Act.

SEC. 709. None of the funds appropriated or otherwise made available by this Act may be used for first-class travel by the employees of agencies funded by this Act in contravention of sections 301–10.122 through 301–10.124 of title 41, Code of Federal Regulations.

SEC. 710. In the case of each program established or amended by the Agricultural Act of 2014 (Public Law 113–79) or by a successor to that Act, other than by title I or subtitle A of title III of such Act, or programs for which indefinite amounts were provided in that Act, that is authorized or required to be carried out using funds of the Commodity Credit Corporation—

(1) such funds shall be available for salaries and related administrative expenses, including technical assistance, associated with the implementation of the program, without regard to the limitation on the total amount of allotments and fund transfers contained in section 11 of the Commodity Credit Corporation Charter Act (15 U.S.C. 714i); and

(2) the use of such funds for such purpose shall not be considered to be a fund transfer or allotment for purposes of applying the limitation on the total amount of allotments and fund transfers contained in such section.

SEC. 711. Of the funds made available by this Act, not more than $2,900,000 shall be used to cover necessary expenses of activities related to all Federal Advisory Committee Act committees of the Department of Agriculture.

SEC. 712. Notwithstanding subsection (b) of section 14222 of Public Law 110–246 (7 U.S.C. 612c–6; in this section referred to as "section 14222"), none of the funds appropriated or otherwise made available by this or any other Act shall be used to pay the salaries and expenses of personnel to carry out a program under section 32 of the Act of August 24, 1935 (7 U.S.C. 612c; in this section referred to as "section 32") in excess of $1,483,309,000 (exclusive of carryover appropriations from prior fiscal years), as follows: Child Nutrition Programs Entitlement Commodities—$485,000,000; State Option Contracts—$5,000,000; Removal of Defective Commodities—$2,500,000; Administration of Section 32 Commodity Purchases—$37,178,000: Provided, That of the total funds made available in the matter preceding this proviso that remain unobligated on October 1, 2023, such unobligated balances shall carryover into fiscal year 2024 and shall remain available until expended for any of the purposes of section 32, except that any such carryover funds used in accordance with clause (3) of section 32 may not exceed $350,000,000 and may not be obligated until the Secretary of Agriculture provides written notification of the expenditures to the Committees on Appropriations of both Houses of Congress at least two weeks in advance: Provided further, That, with the exception of any available carryover funds authorized in any prior appropriations Act to be used for the purposes of clause (3) of section 32, none of the funds appropriated or otherwise made available by this or any other Act shall be used to pay the salaries or expenses of any employee of the Department of Agriculture to carry out clause (3) of section 32.

SEC. 713. Notwithstanding section 310B(g)(5) of the Consolidated Farm and Rural Development Act (7 U.S.C. 1932(g)(5)), the Secretary may assess a one-time fee for any guaranteed business and industry loan in an amount that does not exceed 3 percent of the guaranteed principal portion of the loan.

SEC. 714. For loans and loan guarantees that do not require budget authority and the program level has been established in this Act, the Secretary of Agriculture may increase the program level for such loans and loan guarantees by not more than 25 percent: Provided, That prior to the Secretary implementing such an increase, the Secretary notifies, in writing, the Committees on Appropriations of both Houses of Congress at least 15 days in advance.

SEC. 715. None of the credit card refunds or rebates transferred to the Working Capital Fund pursuant to section 729 of the Agriculture, Rural Development, Food and Drug Administration, and Related Agencies Appropriations Act, 2002 (7 U.S.C. 2235a; Public Law 107–76) shall be available for obligation without prior notification to the Committees on Appropriations of both Houses of Congress: Provided, That the refunds or rebates so transferred shall be available for obligation only for the acquisition of property, plant and equipment, including equipment for the improvement, delivery, and implementation of Departmental financial management, information technology, and other support systems necessary for the delivery of financial, administrative, and information technology services, including cloud adoption and migration, of primary benefit to the agencies of the Department of Agriculture, and such transferred funds shall remain available until expended.

SEC. 716. None of the funds made available by this Act may be used to implement section 3.7(f) of the Farm Credit Act of 1971 in a manner inconsistent with section 343(a)(13) of the Consolidated Farm and Rural Development Act.

SEC. 717. None of the funds made available by this or any other Act may be used to enforce the final rule promulgated by the Food and Drug Administration entitled "Standards for the Growing, Harvesting, Packing, and Holding of Produce for Human Consumption," and published on November 27, 2015, with respect to the regulation of entities that grow, harvest, pack, or hold wine grapes, hops, pulse crops, or almonds.

SEC. 718. None of the funds made available by this Act or any other Act may be used—

(1) in contravention of section 7606 of the Agricultural Act of 2014 (7 U.S.C. 5940), subtitle G of the Agricultural Marketing Act of 1946, or section 10114 of the Agriculture Improvement Act of 2018; or

(2) to prohibit the transportation, processing, sale, or use of hemp, or seeds of such plant, that is grown or cultivated in accordance with section 7606 of the Agricultural Act of 2014 (7 U.S.C. 5940) within or outside the State in which the industrial hemp is grown or cultivated.

SEC. 719. The Secretary of Agriculture may waive the matching funds requirement under Section 412(g) of the Agricultural Research, Extension, and Education Reform Act of 1998 (7 U.S.C. 7632(g)).

SEC. 720. In response to an eligible community where the drinking water supplies are inadequate due to a natural disaster, as determined by the Secretary, including drought or severe weather, the Secretary may provide potable water through the Emergency Community Water Assistance Grant Program for an additional period of time not to exceed 120 days beyond the established period provided under the Program in order to protect public health.

SEC. 721. Notwithstanding any other provision of law, ARS facilities as described in the "Memorandum of Understanding Between the U.S. Department of Agriculture Animal and Plant Health Inspection Service (APHIS) and the U.S. Department of Agriculture Agricultural Research Service (ARS) Concerning Laboratory Animal Welfare" (16–6100–0103-MU Revision 16–1) shall be inspected by APHIS for compliance with the Animal Welfare Act and its regulations and standards.

SEC. 722. For school year 2023–2024, only a school food authority that had a negative balance in the nonprofit school food service account as of December 31, 2022, shall be required to establish a price for paid lunches in accordance with section 12(p) of the Richard B. Russell National School Lunch Act (42 U.S.C. 1760(p)).

SEC. 723. Any funds made available by this or any other Act that the Secretary withholds pursuant to section 1668(g)(2) of the Food, Agriculture, Conservation, and Trade Act of 1990 (7 U.S.C. 5921(g)(2)), as amended, shall be available for grants for biotechnology risk assessment research: Provided, That the Secretary may transfer such funds among appropriations of the Department of Agriculture for purposes of making such grants.

SEC. 724. The Secretary, acting through the Chief of the Natural Resources Conservation Service, may use funds appropriated under this Act or any other Act for the Watershed and Flood Prevention Operations Program and the Watershed Rehabilitation Program carried out pursuant to the Watershed Protection and Flood Prevention Act (16 U.S.C. 1001 et seq.), and for the Emergency Watershed Protection Program carried out pursuant to section 403 of the Agricultural Credit Act of 1978 (16 U.S.C. 2203) to provide technical services for such programs pursuant to section 1252(a)(1) of the Food Security Act of 1985 (16 U.S.C. 3851(a)(1)), notwithstanding subsection (c) of such section.

SEC. 725. None of the funds made available by this Act may be used to pay the salaries or expenses of personnel—

(1) to inspect horses under section 3 of the Federal Meat Inspection Act (21 U.S.C. 603);

(2) to inspect horses under section 903 of the Federal Agriculture Improvement and Reform Act of 1996 (7 U.S.C. 1901 note; Public Law 104–127); or

(3) to implement or enforce section 352.19 of title 9, Code of Federal Regulations (or a successor regulation).

SEC. 726. In addition to any other funds made available in this Act or any other Act, there is appropriated $12,000,000 to carry out section 18(g) of the Richard B. Russell National School Lunch Act, as amended (42 U.S.C. 1769(g)), to remain available until expended.

SEC. 727. Notwithstanding any other provision of law, unobligated balances from appropriations made available for salaries and expenses in this Act for the Farm Service Agency, the Farm Production and Conservation Business Center, and the Rural Development mission area shall remain available through September 30, 2024, for information technology expenses.

SEC. 728. The cost of inspection rendered under the requirements of laws relating to Federal inspection of meat and meat food productions, Federal Meat Inspection Act (21 U.S.C. 695); poultry and poultry products, Poultry Products Inspection Act (21 U.S.C. 468); and egg products, Egg Products Inspection Act (21 U.S.C. 1053(a)), shall be borne by the United States, except for the cost of inspection services provided outside of an establishment's approved inspection shift(s), and that provided on Federal holidays, which shall be borne by the establishment: Provided, That sums received by the Secretary shall remain available until expended without further appropriation and without fiscal year limitation.

SEC. 729. The National Bio and Agro-Defense Facility shall be transferred in this or any future fiscal year without reimbursement from the Secretary of Homeland Security to the Secretary of Agriculture.

SEC. 730. Section 801(e)(4) of the Federal Food, Drug, and Cosmetic Act (21 U.S.C. 381(e)(4)) is amended—

(a) in subparagraph (B) by striking "but shall not exceed $175 for each certification" and inserting "in an amount specified in subparagraph (E)"; and

(b) by adding at the end the following new subparagraphs:

"(E) The fee for each written export certification issued by the Secretary under this paragraph shall not exceed—

(i) $600 for fiscal year 2022; and

(ii) for each subsequent fiscal year, the prior fiscal year maximum amount multiplied by the inflation adjustment under section 738(c)(2)(C), applied without regard to the limitation in clause (ii)(II) of such subparagraph."; and

"(F) The Secretary shall, for each fiscal year, publish in the Federal Register a notice of the export certification fee under this paragraph for such year, not later than 60 days before such fee takes effect.".

SEC. 731. Funds appropriated in this or any prior Act that are available for salaries and expenses of employees of the Food and Drug Administration shall also be available for the primary and secondary schooling of eligible dependents of Department of Health and Human Services personnel stationed in the Commonwealth of Puerto Rico, the Commonwealth of the Northern Mariana Islands, and the possessions of the United States at costs not in excess of those paid for or reimbursed by the Department of Defense.

SEC. 732. None of the funds made available under this Act to carry out sections 504, 514, 515, 516, 523, 533 and 538 of the Housing Act of 1949 (42 U.S.C. 1474, 1484–1486, 1490c, 1490m, 1490p–2) may be used to award loans or grants for new construction or improvements projects unless such projects improve energy or water efficiency, indoor air quality, or sustainability improvements, implement low-emission technologies, materials, or processes, including zero-emission electricity generation, energy storage, building electrification, or electric car charging station installations; or address climate resilience of multifamily properties.

SEC. 733. Of the unobligated discretionary balances from amounts made available for the supplemental nutrition program as authorized by section 17 of the Child Nutrition Act of 1966 (42 U.S.C. 1786), $250,000,000 is hereby permanently cancelled.

SEC. 734. Section 4402 of the Farm Security and Rural Investment Act of 2002 (7 U.S.C. 3007, as amended) is amended by inserting after subsection (f) the following new subsection: (g) ADMINISTRATIVE WAIVER AUTHORITY FOR PROGRAM INNOVATION AND MODERNIZATION.—Notwithstanding any other provision of law, the Secretary of Agriculture may, upon request by a seniors farmers' market nutrition program State agency, modify or waive any administrative requirement to allow State agencies to test and implement new and innovative models to modernize operations, including transitioning from paper-based processes to electronic solutions in accordance with a plan approved by the Secretary. Waiver authority does not extend to the minimum value of federal benefits set forth in section 249.8(b) of Title 7, Code of Federal Regulations, or the nondiscrimination requirements set forth in section 249.7 of Title 7, Code of Federal Regulations, both in effect on the date of enactment of this Act.

SEC. 735. In addition to amounts otherwise provided, there is hereby appropriated $1,000,000, to remain available until expended, to carry out activities authorized under subsections (a)(2) and (e)(2) of Section 21 of the Richard B. Russell National School Lunch Act (42 U.S.C. 1769b1(a)(2) and (e)(2)).

SEC. 736. Section 346(b)(2) of the Consolidated Farm and Rural Development Act (7 U.S.C. 1994(b)(2)) is amended—

(a) In subparagraph (A)(i)(II) by inserting "to the extent practicable" after "April 1 of the fiscal year";

(b) In subparagraph (A)(iii) by inserting "to the extent practicable" after "September 1 of the fiscal year"; and

(c) In subparagraph (B)(iii) by inserting "to the extent practicable" after "April 1 of the fiscal year".

SEC. 737. Section 322 of the Consolidated Farm and Rural Development Act (7 U.S.C. 1962) is hereby repealed.

SEC. 738. Section 329 of the Consolidated Farm and Rural Development Act (7 U.S.C. 1970) is amended in the first sentence by striking "at least a 30 per centum" and all that follows through "in effect for the previous year", and inserting in lieu thereof the following: "a qualifying production loss, as determined by the Secretary, as a result of the disaster,".

SEC. 739. Of the unobligated carryover balances available to the Farm Service Agency in 12X1140, Agricultural Credit Insurance Fund Program Account, $94,959,000 is hereby permanently cancelled.

SEC. 740. There is hereby appropriated $5,000,000 to carry out section 2501 of the Food, Agriculture, Conservation, and Trade Act of 1990 (7 U.S.C. 2279).

GENERAL PROVISION—THIS TITLE

[SEC. 101. In addition to amounts otherwise made available for such purpose, there is hereby appropriated $10,000,000, to remain available until expended, to carry out section 70501 of division G of this Act: *Provided*, That $5,000,000, to remain available until expended, shall be made available for fiscal year 2022 and $5,000,000, to remain available until expended, shall be made available for fiscal year 2023: *Provided further*, That such amount is designated by the Congress as being for an emergency requirement pursuant to section 4112(a) of H. Con. Res. 71 (115th Congress), the concurrent resolution on the budget for fiscal year 2018, and to section 251(b) of the Balanced Budget and Emergency Deficit Control Act of 1985.] *(Infrastructure Investments and Jobs Appropriations Act.)*

DEPARTMENT OF COMMERCE

DEPARTMENTAL MANAGEMENT
Federal Funds

SALARIES AND EXPENSES

For necessary expenses for the management of the Department of Commerce provided for by law, including not to exceed $4,500 for official reception and representation, $104,004,000.

Note.—A full-year 2022 appropriation for this account was not enacted at the time the Budget was prepared; therefore, the Budget assumes this account is operating under the Continuing Appropriations Act, 2022 (Division A of Public Law 117–43, as amended). The amounts included for 2022 reflect the annualized level provided by the continuing resolution.

Program and Financing (in millions of dollars)

Identification code 013–0120–0–1–376	2021 actual	2022 est.	2023 est.
Obligations by program activity:			
0003 Operations and Administration	73	73	104
0801 Salaries and Expenses (Reimbursable)	117	127	139
0900 Total new obligations, unexpired accounts	190	200	243
Budgetary resources:			
Unobligated balance:			
1000 Unobligated balance brought forward, Oct 1	....	1	1
Budget authority:			
Appropriations, discretionary:			
1100 Appropriation	73	73	104
1121 Appropriations transferred from other acct [013–0450]	1	....	....
1160 Appropriation, discretionary (total)	74	73	104
Spending authority from offsetting collections, discretionary:			
1700 Collected	93	127	139
1701 Change in uncollected payments, Federal sources	24	....	....
1750 Spending auth from offsetting collections, disc (total)	117	127	139
1900 Budget authority (total)	191	200	243
1930 Total budgetary resources available	191	201	244
Memorandum (non-add) entries:			
1941 Unexpired unobligated balance, end of year	1	1	1
Change in obligated balance:			
Unpaid obligations:			
3000 Unpaid obligations, brought forward, Oct 1	36	37	11
3010 New obligations, unexpired accounts	190	200	243
3011 Obligations ("upward adjustments"), expired accounts	6	....	....
3020 Outlays (gross)	–182	–226	–240
3041 Recoveries of prior year unpaid obligations, expired	–13	....	....
3050 Unpaid obligations, end of year	37	11	14
Uncollected payments:			
3060 Uncollected pymts, Fed sources, brought forward, Oct 1	–26	–31	–31
3070 Change in uncollected pymts, Fed sources, unexpired	–24	....	....
3071 Change in uncollected pymts, Fed sources, expired	19	....	....
3090 Uncollected pymts, Fed sources, end of year	–31	–31	–31
Memorandum (non-add) entries:			
3100 Obligated balance, start of year	10	6	–20
3200 Obligated balance, end of year	6	–20	–17
Budget authority and outlays, net:			
Discretionary:			
4000 Budget authority, gross	191	200	243
Outlays, gross:			
4010 Outlays from new discretionary authority	163	191	231
4011 Outlays from discretionary balances	19	35	9
4020 Outlays, gross (total)	182	226	240
Offsets against gross budget authority and outlays:			
Offsetting collections (collected) from:			
4030 Federal sources	–106	–127	–139
4040 Offsets against gross budget authority and outlays (total)	–106	–127	–139
Additional offsets against gross budget authority only:			
4050 Change in uncollected pymts, Fed sources, unexpired	–24	....	....
4052 Offsetting collections credited to expired accounts	13	....	....
4060 Additional offsets against budget authority only (total)	–11	....	....
4070 Budget authority, net (discretionary)	74	73	104
4080 Outlays, net (discretionary)	76	99	101
4180 Budget authority, net (total)	74	73	104
4190 Outlays, net (total)	76	99	101

The Salaries and Expenses account funds Operations and Administration, which provides policy oversight and oversees day-to-day operations of the Department.

Reimbursable program.—Provides a centralized collection source for special tasks or costs and their billing to users.

Object Classification (in millions of dollars)

Identification code 013–0120–0–1–376	2021 actual	2022 est.	2023 est.
Direct obligations:			
11.1 Personnel compensation: Full-time permanent	31	32	45
12.1 Civilian personnel benefits	11	12	14
21.0 Travel and transportation of persons	1	1	1
23.1 Rental payments to GSA	5	5	6
23.3 Communications, utilities, and miscellaneous charges	1	1	1
25.1 Advisory and assistance services	....	....	1
25.2 Other services from non-Federal sources	6	6	8
25.3 Other goods and services from Federal sources	17	15	26
31.0 Equipment	1	1	2
99.0 Direct obligations	73	73	104
99.0 Reimbursable obligations	117	127	139
99.9 Total new obligations, unexpired accounts	190	200	243

Employment Summary

Identification code 013–0120–0–1–376	2021 actual	2022 est.	2023 est.
1001 Direct civilian full-time equivalent employment	200	272	299
2001 Reimbursable civilian full-time equivalent employment	72	64	66

NONRECURRING EXPENSES FUND
(INCLUDING TRANSFER OF FUNDS)

For necessary expenses for technology modernization projects of the Department of Commerce, including for cybersecurity risk mitigation, $50,000,000, to remain available until expended: Provided, That amounts in the Fund may be transferred to appropriation accounts of the Department as may be necessary to carry out modernization projects for which such funds are otherwise available: Provided further, That the Secretary of Commerce shall notify the Committees on Appropriations of both Houses of Congress at least 15 days in advance of any such transfer: Provided further, That any unobligated balances of expired discretionary funds transferred to the Department of Commerce Nonrecurring Expenses Fund, as authorized by section 111 of title I of division B of Public Law 116–93, may be obligated only after the Committees on Appropriations of the House of Representatives and the Senate are notified at least 15 days in advance of the planned use of funds.

Note.—A full-year 2022 appropriation for this account was not enacted at the time the Budget was prepared; therefore, the Budget assumes this account is operating under the Continuing Appropriations Act, 2022 (Division A of Public Law 117–43, as amended). The amounts included for 2022 reflect the annualized level provided by the continuing resolution.

Program and Financing (in millions of dollars)

Identification code 013–0133–0–1–376	2021 actual	2022 est.	2023 est.
Obligations by program activity:			
0001 Direct program activity	22	38	50
Budgetary resources:			
Unobligated balance:			
1000 Unobligated balance brought forward, Oct 1	3	1	1
1012 Unobligated balance transfers between expired and unexpired accounts	....	18	....
1070 Unobligated balance (total)	3	19	1
Budget authority:			
Appropriations, discretionary:			
1100 Appropriation	20	20	50
1930 Total budgetary resources available	23	39	51
Memorandum (non-add) entries:			
1941 Unexpired unobligated balance, end of year	1	1	1

Departmental Management—Continued
Federal Funds—Continued

NONRECURRING EXPENSES FUND—Continued

Program and Financing—Continued

Identification code 013–0133–0–1–376	2021 actual	2022 est.	2023 est.
Change in obligated balance:			
Unpaid obligations:			
3000 Unpaid obligations, brought forward, Oct 1	14	11	22
3010 New obligations, unexpired accounts	22	38	50
3020 Outlays (gross)	–25	–27	–44
3050 Unpaid obligations, end of year	11	22	28
Memorandum (non-add) entries:			
3100 Obligated balance, start of year	14	11	22
3200 Obligated balance, end of year	11	22	28
Budget authority and outlays, net:			
Discretionary:			
4000 Budget authority, gross	20	20	50
Outlays, gross:			
4010 Outlays from new discretionary authority	10	16	40
4011 Outlays from discretionary balances	15	11	4
4020 Outlays, gross (total)	25	27	44
4180 Budget authority, net (total)	20	20	50
4190 Outlays, net (total)	25	27	44

This account funds information and business technology system modernization and facilities infrastructure improvements, including cybersecurity risk mitigation and the Business Application Solutions, which is the planned successor to Commerce Business Systems.

Object Classification (in millions of dollars)

Identification code 013–0133–0–1–376	2021 actual	2022 est.	2023 est.
Direct obligations:			
11.1 Personnel compensation: Full-time permanent	2	3	
12.1 Civilian personnel benefits	1	1	
23.1 Rental payments to GSA		1	
25.2 Other services from non-Federal sources	15	30	50
25.3 Other goods and services from Federal sources	4	3	
99.9 Total new obligations, unexpired accounts	22	38	50

Employment Summary

Identification code 013–0133–0–1–376	2021 actual	2022 est.	2023 est.
1001 Direct civilian full-time equivalent employment	14	56	

OFFICE OF INSPECTOR GENERAL

For necessary expenses of the Office of Inspector General in carrying out the provisions of the Inspector General Act of 1978 (5 U.S.C. App.), $49,771,000.

Note.—A full-year 2022 appropriation for this account was not enacted at the time the Budget was prepared; therefore, the Budget assumes this account is operating under the Continuing Appropriations Act, 2022 (Division A of Public Law 117–43, as amended). The amounts included for 2022 reflect the annualized level provided by the continuing resolution.

Program and Financing (in millions of dollars)

Identification code 013–0126–0–1–376	2021 actual	2022 est.	2023 est.
Obligations by program activity:			
0001 Office of the Inspector General (Direct)	41	47	55
0002 Office of the Inspector General (Mandatory)		3	
0799 Total direct obligations	41	50	55
0801 Office of the Inspector General (Reimbursable)	7	7	5
0809 Reimbursable program activities, subtotal	7	7	5
0900 Total new obligations, unexpired accounts	48	57	60
Budgetary resources:			
Unobligated balance:			
1000 Unobligated balance brought forward, Oct 1	11	12	16
Budget authority:			
Appropriations, discretionary:			
1100 Appropriation	34	34	50
1121 Appropriations transferred NOAA PAC [013–1460]	2	2	
1121 Appropriations transferred Census [013–0450]	4	4	
1121 Appropriations transferred NTIA Broadband Equity, Access, and Deployment [013–0562]		12	
1121 Appropriations transferred NTIA Digital Equity [013–0563]		1	
1121 Appropriations transferred NTIA Middle Mile Deployment [013–0564]		1	
1160 Appropriation, discretionary (total)	40	54	50
Advance appropriations, discretionary:			
1173 Advance appropriations transferred from other accounts [013–0563]			1
Appropriations, mandatory:			
1200 Appropriation [American Rescue Plan Act 2021]	3		
Spending authority from offsetting collections, discretionary:			
1700 Collected (DOC Financial Audit)	2	3	3
1700 Collected (PSTF Transfer)	2	2	
1701 Change in uncollected payments, Federal sources	1		
1711 Offsetting collections transferred from PTO [013–1006]	2	2	2
1750 Spending auth from offsetting collections, disc (total)	7	7	5
1900 Budget authority (total)	50	61	56
1930 Total budgetary resources available	61	73	72
Memorandum (non-add) entries:			
1940 Unobligated balance expiring	–1		
1941 Unexpired unobligated balance, end of year	12	16	12
Change in obligated balance:			
Unpaid obligations:			
3000 Unpaid obligations, brought forward, Oct 1	12	9	
3010 New obligations, unexpired accounts	48	57	60
3011 Obligations ("upward adjustments"), expired accounts	1		
3020 Outlays (gross)	–51	–66	–57
3041 Recoveries of prior year unpaid obligations, expired	–1		
3050 Unpaid obligations, end of year	9		3
Uncollected payments:			
3060 Uncollected pymts, Fed sources, brought forward, Oct 1	–2	–2	–2
3070 Change in uncollected pymts, Fed sources, unexpired	–1		
3071 Change in uncollected pymts, Fed sources, expired	1		
3090 Uncollected pymts, Fed sources, end of year	–2	–2	–2
Memorandum (non-add) entries:			
3100 Obligated balance, start of year	10	7	–2
3200 Obligated balance, end of year	7	–2	1
Budget authority and outlays, net:			
Discretionary:			
4000 Budget authority, gross	47	61	56
Outlays, gross:			
4010 Outlays from new discretionary authority	32	54	50
4011 Outlays from discretionary balances	19	11	7
4020 Outlays, gross (total)	51	65	57
Offsets against gross budget authority and outlays:			
Offsetting collections (collected) from:			
4030 Federal sources (Financial Statement Audit)	–2	–3	–3
4030 Federal sources (PSTF Transfer)	–2	–2	
4040 Offsets against gross budget authority and outlays (total)	–4	–5	–3
Additional offsets against gross budget authority only:			
4050 Change in uncollected pymts, Fed sources, unexpired	–1		
4070 Budget authority, net (discretionary)	42	56	53
4080 Outlays, net (discretionary)	47	60	54
Mandatory:			
4090 Budget authority, gross	3		
Outlays, gross:			
4101 Outlays from mandatory balances		1	
4180 Budget authority, net (total)	45	56	53
4190 Outlays, net (total)	47	61	54

The Office of Inspector General promotes efficient and effective programs across the Department of Commerce through various analyses of bureau and Departmental programs and activities. It also endeavors to prevent waste, fraud, and abuse through audits, inspections, and investigations related to Department of Commerce programs.

Object Classification (in millions of dollars)

Identification code 013–0126–0–1–376	2021 actual	2022 est.	2023 est.
Direct obligations:			
Personnel compensation:			
11.1 Full-time permanent	20	22	28

DEPARTMENT OF COMMERCE

		2021 actual	2022 est.	2023 est.
11.5	Other personnel compensation	1	1	2
11.9	Total personnel compensation	21	23	30
12.1	Civilian personnel benefits	8	9	11
21.0	Travel and transportation of persons		1	1
23.1	Rental payments to GSA	2	2	2
23.3	Communications, utilities, and miscellaneous charges	1	1	1
25.2	Other services from non-Federal sources	2	6	2
25.3	Other goods and services from Federal sources	5	6	6
31.0	Equipment	2	2	2
99.0	Direct obligations	41	50	55
99.0	Reimbursable obligations	7	7	5
99.9	Total new obligations, unexpired accounts	48	57	60

Employment Summary

Identification code 013–0126–0–1–376	2021 actual	2022 est.	2023 est.
1001 Direct civilian full-time equivalent employment	160	177	198
2001 Reimbursable civilian full-time equivalent employment	20	21	13

HCHB RENOVATION AND MODERNIZATION

For necessary expenses for the renovation and modernization of the Herbert C. Hoover Building, $1,142,000, to remain available until expended.

Note.—A full-year 2022 appropriation for this account was not enacted at the time the Budget was prepared; therefore, the Budget assumes this account is operating under the Continuing Appropriations Act, 2022 (Division A of Public Law 117–43, as amended). The amounts included for 2022 reflect the annualized level provided by the continuing resolution.

Program and Financing (in millions of dollars)

Identification code 013–0123–0–1–376	2021 actual	2022 est.	2023 est.
Obligations by program activity:			
0001 HCHB Renovation and Modernization (Direct)	4	8	5
Budgetary resources:			
Unobligated balance:			
1000 Unobligated balance brought forward, Oct 1	26	24	17
1021 Recoveries of prior year unpaid obligations	1		
1070 Unobligated balance (total)	27	24	17
Budget authority:			
Appropriations, discretionary:			
1100 Appropriation	1	1	1
1930 Total budgetary resources available	28	25	18
Memorandum (non-add) entries:			
1941 Unexpired unobligated balance, end of year	24	17	13
Change in obligated balance:			
Unpaid obligations:			
3000 Unpaid obligations, brought forward, Oct 1	11	8	7
3010 New obligations, unexpired accounts	4	8	5
3020 Outlays (gross)	–6	–9	–1
3040 Recoveries of prior year unpaid obligations, unexpired	–1		
3050 Unpaid obligations, end of year	8	7	11
Memorandum (non-add) entries:			
3100 Obligated balance, start of year	11	8	7
3200 Obligated balance, end of year	8	7	11
Budget authority and outlays, net:			
Discretionary:			
4000 Budget authority, gross	1	1	1
Outlays, gross:			
4010 Outlays from new discretionary authority	1	1	1
4011 Outlays from discretionary balances	5	8	
4020 Outlays, gross (total)	6	9	1
4180 Budget authority, net (total)	1	1	1
4190 Outlays, net (total)	6	9	1

This account funds the Commerce Department's portion of expenses associated with renovating and modernizing the Herbert C. Hoover Building (HCHB). The renovation and modernization will upgrade infrastructure, modernize tenant spaces, remove safety hazards, and improve energy efficiency as Commerce optimizes utilization of HCHB space. The General Services Administration and Commerce are each responsible for certain aspects of the project's costs.

Object Classification (in millions of dollars)

Identification code 013–0123–0–1–376	2021 actual	2022 est.	2023 est.
Direct obligations:			
11.1 Personnel compensation: Full-time permanent	1	1	1
25.2 Other services from non-Federal sources	3	7	4
99.9 Total new obligations, unexpired accounts	4	8	5

Employment Summary

Identification code 013–0123–0–1–376	2021 actual	2022 est.	2023 est.
1001 Direct civilian full-time equivalent employment	5	5	5

WORKING CAPITAL FUND

Program and Financing (in millions of dollars)

Identification code 013–4511–0–4–376	2021 actual	2022 est.	2023 est.
Obligations by program activity:			
0803 Operations and Administration	269	264	302
Budgetary resources:			
Unobligated balance:			
1000 Unobligated balance brought forward, Oct 1	7	9	9
1021 Recoveries of prior year unpaid obligations	11		
1070 Unobligated balance (total)	18	9	9
Budget authority:			
Spending authority from offsetting collections, discretionary:			
1700 Collected	259	264	302
1701 Change in uncollected payments, Federal sources	1		
1750 Spending auth from offsetting collections, disc (total)	260	264	302
1930 Total budgetary resources available	278	273	311
Memorandum (non-add) entries:			
1941 Unexpired unobligated balance, end of year	9	9	9
Change in obligated balance:			
Unpaid obligations:			
3000 Unpaid obligations, brought forward, Oct 1	116	116	3
3010 New obligations, unexpired accounts	269	264	302
3020 Outlays (gross)	–258	–377	–302
3040 Recoveries of prior year unpaid obligations, unexpired	–11		
3050 Unpaid obligations, end of year	116	3	3
Uncollected payments:			
3060 Uncollected pymts, Fed sources, brought forward, Oct 1	–1	–2	–2
3070 Change in uncollected pymts, Fed sources, unexpired	–1		
3090 Uncollected pymts, Fed sources, end of year	–2	–2	–2
Memorandum (non-add) entries:			
3100 Obligated balance, start of year	115	114	1
3200 Obligated balance, end of year	114	1	1
Budget authority and outlays, net:			
Discretionary:			
4000 Budget authority, gross	260	264	302
Outlays, gross:			
4010 Outlays from new discretionary authority	166	264	302
4011 Outlays from discretionary balances	92	113	
4020 Outlays, gross (total)	258	377	302
Offsets against gross budget authority and outlays:			
Offsetting collections (collected) from:			
4030 Federal sources	–259	–264	–302
4040 Offsets against gross budget authority and outlays (total)	–259	–264	–302
Additional offsets against gross budget authority only:			
4050 Change in uncollected pymts, Fed sources, unexpired	–1		
4060 Additional offsets against budget authority only (total)	–1		
4080 Outlays, net (discretionary)	–1	113	
4180 Budget authority, net (total)			
4190 Outlays, net (total)	–1	113	

194   Departmental Management—Continued
Federal Funds—Continued

THE BUDGET FOR FISCAL YEAR 2023

WORKING CAPITAL FUND—Continued

This fund finances, on a reimbursable basis, Department-wide administrative functions that are more efficiently performed on a centralized basis, including general counsel, information technology, enterprise services, privacy and open government, civil rights, facilities and environmental quality, human resources, financial, procurement, and intelligence and security services.

Object Classification (in millions of dollars)

Identification code 013–4511–0–4–376		2021 actual	2022 est.	2023 est.
	Reimbursable obligations:			
11.1	Personnel compensation: Full-time permanent	82	90	105
12.1	Civilian personnel benefits	28	30	35
21.0	Travel and transportation of persons	....	1	1
23.1	Rental payments to GSA	8	8	10
23.3	Communications, utilities, and miscellaneous charges	4	4	5
24.0	Printing and reproduction	1	1	1
25.2	Other services from non-Federal sources	101	88	100
25.3	Other goods and services from Federal sources	39	39	40
26.0	Supplies and materials	1	2	2
31.0	Equipment	5	1	3
99.9	Total new obligations, unexpired accounts	269	264	302

Employment Summary

Identification code 013–4511–0–4–376	2021 actual	2022 est.	2023 est.
2001 Reimbursable civilian full-time equivalent employment	638	646	681

CONCRETE MASONRY PRODUCTS BOARD

Special and Trust Fund Receipts (in millions of dollars)

Identification code 013–5603–0–2–376		2021 actual	2022 est.	2023 est.
0100	Balance, start of year			6
	Receipts:			
	Current law:			
1110	Concrete Masonry Products Assessments, Available		6	7
2000	Total: Balances and receipts		6	13
	Appropriations:			
	Current law:			
2101	Concrete Masonry Products Board			–6
2135	Concrete Masonry Products Board			2
2199	Total current law appropriations			–4
2999	Total appropriations			–4
5099	Balance, end of year		6	9

Program and Financing (in millions of dollars)

Identification code 013–5603–0–2–376		2021 actual	2022 est.	2023 est.
	Obligations by program activity:			
0001	Direct program activity			4
0900	Total new obligations, unexpired accounts (object class 25.2)			4
	Budgetary resources:			
	Budget authority:			
	Appropriations, mandatory:			
1201	Appropriation (special or trust fund)			6
1235	Appropriations precluded from obligation (special or trust)			–2
1260	Appropriations, mandatory (total)			4
1930	Total budgetary resources available			4
	Change in obligated balance:			
	Unpaid obligations:			
3010	New obligations, unexpired accounts			4
3020	Outlays (gross)			–4
	Budget authority and outlays, net:			
	Mandatory:			
4090	Budget authority, gross			4

	Outlays, gross:			
4100	Outlays from new mandatory authority			4
4180	Budget authority, net (total)			4
4190	Outlays, net (total)			4

The Concrete Masonry Products Research, Education, and Promotion Act of 2018 (the Act) authorized the establishment of a program, including funds for marketing and market research activities, that is designed to: (1) strengthen the position of the concrete masonry products industry in the domestic marketplace; (2) maintain, develop, and expand markets and uses for concrete masonry products in the domestic marketplace; and (3) promote the use of concrete masonry products in construction and building.

The Act requires the Secretary of Commerce to issue an order that provides for the establishment of a Concrete Masonry Product Board to carry out a program of generic promotion, research, and education regarding concrete masonry products. Further, the Act provides that funding for the Board's activities shall be derived from an assessment on manufacturers of concrete masonry products.

Employment Summary

Identification code 013–5603–0–2–376	2021 actual	2022 est.	2023 est.
1001 Direct civilian full-time equivalent employment			1

Trust Funds

GIFTS AND BEQUESTS

Special and Trust Fund Receipts (in millions of dollars)

Identification code 013–8501–0–7–376		2021 actual	2022 est.	2023 est.
0100	Balance, start of year			
	Receipts:			
	Current law:			
1130	Gifts and Bequests		1	1
2000	Total: Balances and receipts		1	1
	Appropriations:			
	Current law:			
2101	Gifts and Bequests		–1	–1
5099	Balance, end of year			

Program and Financing (in millions of dollars)

Identification code 013–8501–0–7–376		2021 actual	2022 est.	2023 est.
	Obligations by program activity:			
0001	Gifts and Bequests (Direct)		1	1
0900	Total new obligations, unexpired accounts (object class 25.2)		1	1
	Budgetary resources:			
	Unobligated balance:			
1000	Unobligated balance brought forward, Oct 1	1	1	1
	Budget authority:			
	Appropriations, mandatory:			
1201	Appropriation (special or trust fund)		1	1
1930	Total budgetary resources available	1	2	2
	Memorandum (non-add) entries:			
1941	Unexpired unobligated balance, end of year	1	1	1
	Change in obligated balance:			
	Unpaid obligations:			
3010	New obligations, unexpired accounts		1	1
3020	Outlays (gross)		–1	–1
	Budget authority and outlays, net:			
	Mandatory:			
4090	Budget authority, gross		1	1
	Outlays, gross:			
4100	Outlays from new mandatory authority		1	1
4180	Budget authority, net (total)		1	1
4190	Outlays, net (total)		1	1

DEPARTMENT OF COMMERCE

The Secretary of Commerce is authorized to accept, hold, administer, and utilize gifts and bequests of property, both real and personal, for the purpose of aiding or facilitating the work of the Department of Commerce. Property and the proceeds thereof are used in accordance with the terms of the gift or bequest.

ECONOMIC DEVELOPMENT ADMINISTRATION
Federal Funds

SALARIES AND EXPENSES

For necessary expenses of administering the economic development assistance programs as provided for by law, $70,018,000: Provided, That funds provided under this heading may be used to monitor projects approved pursuant to title I of the Public Works Employment Act of 1976; title II of the Trade Act of 1974; sections 27 and 28 of the Stevenson-Wydler Technology Innovation Act of 1980 (15 U.S.C. 3722 and 3723), as amended; and the Community Emergency Drought Relief Act of 1977.

Note.—A full-year 2022 appropriation for this account was not enacted at the time the Budget was prepared; therefore, the Budget assumes this account is operating under the Continuing Appropriations Act, 2022 (Division A of Public Law 117–43, as amended). The amounts included for 2022 reflect the annualized level provided by the continuing resolution.

Program and Financing (in millions of dollars)

Identification code 013–0125–0–1–452	2021 actual	2022 est.	2023 est.
Obligations by program activity:			
0001 Salaries and Expenses (Direct)	66	49	70
0801 Salaries and Expenses (Reimbursable)	3	4	4
0900 Total new obligations, unexpired accounts	69	53	74
Budgetary resources:			
Unobligated balance:			
1000 Unobligated balance brought forward, Oct 1	10	10	
1011 Unobligated balance transfer from other acct [013–2050]	27	2	
1070 Unobligated balance (total)	37	12	
Budget authority:			
Appropriations, discretionary:			
1100 Appropriation	41	41	70
1121 Appropriations transferred from other acct [013–2050]	2		
1160 Appropriation, discretionary (total)	43	41	70
Spending authority from offsetting collections, discretionary:			
1700 Collected	3	4	4
1701 Change in uncollected payments, Federal sources	–3	–4	
1750 Spending auth from offsetting collections, disc (total)			4
1900 Budget authority (total)	43	41	74
1930 Total budgetary resources available	80	53	74
Memorandum (non-add) entries:			
1940 Unobligated balance expiring	–1		
1941 Unexpired unobligated balance, end of year	10		
Change in obligated balance:			
Unpaid obligations:			
3000 Unpaid obligations, brought forward, Oct 1	16	13	16
3010 New obligations, unexpired accounts	69	53	74
3011 Obligations ("upward adjustments"), expired accounts	1		
3020 Outlays (gross)	–72	–50	–74
3041 Recoveries of prior year unpaid obligations, expired	–1		
3050 Unpaid obligations, end of year	13	16	16
Uncollected payments:			
3060 Uncollected pymts, Fed sources, brought forward, Oct 1	–7	–4	
3070 Change in uncollected pymts, Fed sources, unexpired	3	4	
3090 Uncollected pymts, Fed sources, end of year	–4		
Memorandum (non-add) entries:			
3100 Obligated balance, start of year	9	9	16
3200 Obligated balance, end of year	9	16	16
Budget authority and outlays, net:			
Discretionary:			
4000 Budget authority, gross	43	41	74
Outlays, gross:			
4010 Outlays from new discretionary authority	37	33	64
4011 Outlays from discretionary balances	35	17	10
4020 Outlays, gross (total)	72	50	74
Offsets against gross budget authority and outlays:			
Offsetting collections (collected) from:			
4030 Federal sources	–3	–4	–4
Additional offsets against gross budget authority only:			
4050 Change in uncollected pymts, Fed sources, unexpired	3	4	
4070 Budget authority, net (discretionary)	43	41	70
4080 Outlays, net (discretionary)	69	46	70
4180 Budget authority, net (total)	43	41	70
4190 Outlays, net (total)	69	46	70

As the only Federal government agency with a mission and programs focused exclusively on economic development, the Economic Development Administration (EDA) plays a critical role in communities across the Nation. Through the agency's diverse and flexible programs, EDA provides a broad portfolio of activities including pre-application assistance and development, application processing, and project monitoring, as well as general support functions such as economic development research, technical assistance, information dissemination, legal and environmental compliance, financial management, budgeting, and debt management.

The administration and oversight of the EDA's programs are carried out utilizing a network of headquarters and regional personnel who work with local organizations and leaders to identify and invest in projects that demonstrate potential for the greatest economic impact in distressed communities.

Reimbursable program.—EDA provides grant review and processing services to other Federal agencies on a reimbursable basis. Funds received cover the cost of performing this work.

Object Classification (in millions of dollars)

Identification code 013–0125–0–1–452	2021 actual	2022 est.	2023 est.
Direct obligations:			
Personnel compensation:			
11.1 Full-time permanent	22	22	30
11.3 Other than full-time permanent	8		
11.5 Other personnel compensation	1	1	1
11.9 Total personnel compensation	31	23	31
12.1 Civilian personnel benefits	11	7	9
21.0 Travel and transportation of persons		1	1
23.1 Rental payments to GSA	2	2	3
25.1 Advisory and assistance services	5	5	2
25.2 Other services from non-Federal sources	5	5	10
25.3 Other goods and services from Federal sources	12	6	14
99.0 Direct obligations	66	49	70
99.0 Reimbursable obligations	3	4	4
99.9 Total new obligations, unexpired accounts	69	53	74

Employment Summary

Identification code 013–0125–0–1–452	2021 actual	2022 est.	2023 est.
1001 Direct civilian full-time equivalent employment	279	187	228

ECONOMIC DEVELOPMENT ASSISTANCE PROGRAMS

For economic development assistance as provided by the Public Works and Economic Development Act of 1965, for trade adjustment assistance, and for grants authorized by sections 27 and 28 of the Stevenson-Wydler Technology Innovation Act of 1980 (15 U.S.C. 3722 and 3723), as amended, $432,500,000, to remain available until expended: Provided, That of the amounts provided under this heading, $50,000,000 shall be for grants to support local labor markets and local communities experiencing high prime-age employment gaps: Provided further, That sections 204 and 301 of the Public Works and Economic Development Act of 1965 (42 U.S.C. 3144 and 3161) shall be inapplicable to grants awarded from amounts made available in the preceding proviso: Provided further, That of the amounts made available in the first proviso under this heading, up to 3 percent may be used for Federal costs to administer such assistance: Provided further, That any deviation from the amounts designated for specific activities in the explanatory statement described in section 4 (in the matter preceding division A of this consolidated Act), or any use of deobligated balances of funds provided under this heading in previous years, shall be subject to the procedures set forth in section 504 of this Act.

196 Economic Development Administration—Continued
Federal Funds—Continued

ECONOMIC DEVELOPMENT ASSISTANCE PROGRAMS—Continued

Note.—A full-year 2022 appropriation for this account was not enacted at the time the Budget was prepared; therefore, the Budget assumes this account is operating under the Continuing Appropriations Act, 2022 (Division A of Public Law 117–43, as amended). The amounts included for 2022 reflect the annualized level provided by the continuing resolution.

Program and Financing (in millions of dollars)

Identification code 013–2050–0–1–452		2021 actual	2022 est.	2023 est.
	Obligations by program activity:			
0001	Planning grants	31	33	37
0002	Technical assistance grants	11	10	14
0003	Public works grants	125	124	134
0004	Economic adjustment grants	44	38	53
0005	Research Grants	2	2	2
0009	Trade Adjustment Assistance	13	13	13
0018	Disaster Supplementals Prior to FY 2018	1		
0021	Regional Innovation Strategies and Sec. 27 Science Parks Loan Guarantees	37	38	51
0022	Assistance to Coal Communities	34	34	82
0024	Assistance to Nuclear Closure Communities	12	16	10
0025	STEM Apprenticeship Program	2	2	10
0026	CARES Act	581	96	
0027	2018 Disaster Supplemental (P.L. 115–123)	47	8	
0028	2019 Disaster Supplemental (P.L. 116–020)	237	57	
0029	American Rescue Plan (P.L. 117–002)	9	2,965	20
0030	Recompete Pilot Program			50
0091	Direct program activities, subtotal	1,186	3,436	476
0900	Total new obligations, unexpired accounts	1,186	3,436	476
	Budgetary resources:			
	Unobligated balance:			
1000	Unobligated balance brought forward, Oct 1	1,035	3,191	71
1001	Discretionary unobligated balance brought fwd, Oct 1	1,035		
1010	Unobligated balance transfer to other accts [013–0125]	–27	–2	
1021	Recoveries of prior year unpaid obligations	72	20	38
1033	Recoveries of prior year paid obligations	1		
1070	Unobligated balance (total)	1,081	3,209	109
	Budget authority:			
	Appropriations, discretionary:			
1100	Appropriation	306	306	433
1120	Appropriations transferred to other acct [013–0125]	–2		
1131	Unobligated balance of appropriations permanently reduced	–10	–10	–10
1160	Appropriation, discretionary (total)	294	296	423
	Appropriations, mandatory:			
1200	Appropriation [American Rescue Plan]	3,000		
	Spending authority from offsetting collections, discretionary:			
1700	Collected		2	
1701	Change in uncollected payments, Federal sources	2		
1750	Spending auth from offsetting collections, disc (total)	2	2	
1900	Budget authority (total)	3,296	298	423
1930	Total budgetary resources available	4,377	3,507	532
	Memorandum (non-add) entries:			
1941	Unexpired unobligated balance, end of year	3,191	71	56
	Change in obligated balance:			
	Unpaid obligations:			
3000	Unpaid obligations, brought forward, Oct 1	2,453	2,844	4,838
3010	New obligations, unexpired accounts	1,186	3,436	476
3020	Outlays (gross)	–723	–1,422	–1,662
3040	Recoveries of prior year unpaid obligations, unexpired	–72	–20	–38
3050	Unpaid obligations, end of year	2,844	4,838	3,614
	Uncollected payments:			
3060	Uncollected pymts, Fed sources, brought forward, Oct 1	–3	–5	–5
3070	Change in uncollected pymts, Fed sources, unexpired	–2		
3090	Uncollected pymts, Fed sources, end of year	–5	–5	–5
	Memorandum (non-add) entries:			
3100	Obligated balance, start of year	2,450	2,839	4,833
3200	Obligated balance, end of year	2,839	4,833	3,609
	Budget authority and outlays, net:			
	Discretionary:			
4000	Budget authority, gross	296	298	423
	Outlays, gross:			
4010	Outlays from new discretionary authority	4	45	64
4011	Outlays from discretionary balances	718	865	1,059
4020	Outlays, gross (total)	722	910	1,123
	Offsets against gross budget authority and outlays:			
	Offsetting collections (collected) from:			
4030	Federal sources			–2
4033	Non-Federal sources	–1		
4040	Offsets against gross budget authority and outlays (total)	–1	–2	
	Additional offsets against gross budget authority only:			
4050	Change in uncollected pymts, Fed sources, unexpired	–2		
4053	Recoveries of prior year paid obligations, unexpired accounts	1		
4060	Additional offsets against budget authority only (total)	–1		
4070	Budget authority, net (discretionary)	294	296	423
4080	Outlays, net (discretionary)	721	908	1,123
	Mandatory:			
4090	Budget authority, gross	3,000		
	Outlays, gross:			
4100	Outlays from new mandatory authority	1		
4101	Outlays from mandatory balances		512	539
4110	Outlays, gross (total)	1	512	539
4180	Budget authority, net (total)	3,294	296	423
4190	Outlays, net (total)	722	1,420	1,662

The Economic Development Administration Assistance Programs (EDAP).—The Economic Development Administration's (EDA) investments are administered through broad development assistance programs, which include: Build to Scale, Economic Adjustment Assistance, Local Technical Assistance, Planning, Public Works, Research and National Technical Assistance, STEM Apprenticeship Program, Trade Adjustment Assistance for Firms, and University Centers. For 2023, EDA is requesting $50 million to establish a new program that will act as a pilot for grants to communities experiencing high prime-age employment gaps. EDA provides grants within each of these areas to generate or retain jobs, attract new industry and private sector investment, encourage business expansion, and serve as a backstop to sudden and severe economic impacts.

The Budget also proposes a cancellation of $10 million of unobligated and deobligated EDAP balances made available in prior years.

Object Classification (in millions of dollars)

Identification code 013–2050–0–1–452		2021 actual	2022 est.	2023 est.
11.3	Direct obligations: Personnel compensation: Other than full-time permanent		12	9
11.9	Total personnel compensation		12	9
12.1	Civilian personnel benefits		4	4
21.0	Travel and transportation of persons			1
25.2	Other services from non-Federal sources	2	9	4
25.3	Other goods and services from Federal sources		5	2
41.0	Grants, subsidies, and contributions	1,184	3,406	456
99.9	Total new obligations, unexpired accounts	1,186	3,436	476

Employment Summary

Identification code 013–2050–0–1–452	2021 actual	2022 est.	2023 est.
1001 Direct civilian full-time equivalent employment	1	127	84

BUREAU OF THE CENSUS

Federal Funds

SUPPLEMENTAL SURVEYS

Note.—A full-year 2022 appropriation for this account was not enacted at the time the Budget was prepared; therefore, the Budget assumes this account is operating under the Continuing Appropriations Act, 2022 (Division A of Public Law 117–43, as amended). The amounts included for 2022 reflect the annualized level provided by the continuing resolution.

Program and Financing (in millions of dollars)

Identification code 013–0401–0–1–376		2021 actual	2022 est.	2023 est.
	Obligations by program activity:			
0001	Current economic statistics	197	196	
0002	Current demographic statistics	88	92	

DEPARTMENT OF COMMERCE

Bureau of the Census—Continued
Federal Funds—Continued

		2021 actual	2022 est.	2023 est.
0003	State Children's Health Insurance Program	19	19	19
0900	Total new obligations, unexpired accounts	304	307	19
	Budgetary resources:			
	Budget authority:			
	Appropriations, discretionary:			
1100	Appropriation	288	288	
	Appropriations, mandatory:			
1200	Appropriation	20	20	20
1230	Appropriations and/or unobligated balance of appropriations permanently reduced	–1	–1	–1
1260	Appropriations, mandatory (total)	19	19	19
1900	Budget authority (total)	307	307	19
1930	Total budgetary resources available	307	307	19
	Memorandum (non-add) entries:			
1940	Unobligated balance expiring	–3		
	Change in obligated balance:			
	Unpaid obligations:			
3000	Unpaid obligations, brought forward, Oct 1	24	25	29
3010	New obligations, unexpired accounts	304	307	19
3011	Obligations ("upward adjustments"), expired accounts	2		
3020	Outlays (gross)	–303	–303	–45
3041	Recoveries of prior year unpaid obligations, expired	–2		
3050	Unpaid obligations, end of year	25	29	3
	Memorandum (non-add) entries:			
3100	Obligated balance, start of year	24	25	29
3200	Obligated balance, end of year	25	29	3
	Budget authority and outlays, net:			
	Discretionary:			
4000	Budget authority, gross	288	288	
	Outlays, gross:			
4010	Outlays from new discretionary authority	266	262	
4011	Outlays from discretionary balances	18	22	26
4020	Outlays, gross (total)	284	284	26
	Mandatory:			
4090	Budget authority, gross	19	19	19
	Outlays, gross:			
4100	Outlays from new mandatory authority	19	19	19
4180	Budget authority, net (total)	307	307	19
4190	Outlays, net (total)	303	303	45

The activities of this appropriation produce statistically reliable annual data for each state on the number of low-income children who do not have health insurance coverage.

State Children's Health Insurance Program (SCHIP).—Mandatory appropriations are provided by the Medicare, Medicaid, and State Children's Health Insurance Program Balanced Budget Refinement Act of 1999. The program is designed to support data collection by the Current Population Survey (CPS) on the number of low-income children who do not have health insurance coverage. Data from this enhanced survey are used in the formula to allocate funds to States under the SCHIP program.

Object Classification (in millions of dollars)

Identification code 013–0401–0–1–376		2021 actual	2022 est.	2023 est.
	Direct obligations:			
	Personnel compensation:			
11.1	Full-time permanent	129	146	6
11.3	Other than full-time permanent	17	14	4
11.5	Other personnel compensation	8	5	1
11.9	Total personnel compensation	154	165	11
12.1	Civilian personnel benefits	53	56	4
13.0	Benefits for former personnel	2	1	
21.0	Travel and transportation of persons	3	5	1
22.0	Transportation of things	1		
23.1	Rental payments to GSA	11	11	1
23.3	Communications, utilities, and miscellaneous charges	10	9	
25.1	Advisory and assistance services	15	13	
25.2	Other services from non-Federal sources	9	8	
25.3	Other goods and services from Federal sources	7	12	1
25.4	Operation and maintenance of facilities	11	3	
25.5	Research and development contracts		1	
25.7	Operation and maintenance of equipment	25	21	1
26.0	Supplies and materials	1		
31.0	Equipment	2	2	

| 99.9 | Total new obligations, unexpired accounts | 304 | 307 | 19 |

Employment Summary

Identification code 013–0401–0–1–376	2021 actual	2022 est.	2023 est.
1001 Direct civilian full-time equivalent employment	1,639	1,841	183

CENSUSES AND SURVEY PROGRAMS

(INCLUDING TRANSFER OF FUNDS)

For necessary expenses for collecting, compiling, analyzing, preparing, and publishing statistics for censuses and survey programs provided for by law, $1,505,470,000, to remain available until September 30, 2024: Provided, That, from amounts provided herein, funds may be used for promotion, outreach, and marketing activities.

Note.—A full-year 2022 appropriation for this account was not enacted at the time the Budget was prepared; therefore, the Budget assumes this account is operating under the Continuing Appropriations Act, 2022 (Division A of Public Law 117–43, as amended). The amounts included for 2022 reflect the annualized level provided by the continuing resolution.

Program and Financing (in millions of dollars)

Identification code 013–0450–0–1–376		2021 actual	2022 est.	2023 est.
	Obligations by program activity:			
0003	Economic Statistics Programs	148	152	412
0008	Decennial Census	1,690	632	412
0013	Geographic support	76	80	
0015	Enterprise Data Collection and Dissemination Systems	171	160	
0016	Demographic Statistics Programs			357
0018	Enterprise Enabling Programs			324
0100	Total direct program	2,085	1,024	1,505
0900	Total new obligations, unexpired accounts	2,085	1,024	1,505
	Budgetary resources:			
	Unobligated balance:			
1000	Unobligated balance brought forward, Oct 1	1,916	210	
1021	Recoveries of prior year unpaid obligations	246		
1033	Recoveries of prior year paid obligations	16		
1070	Unobligated balance (total)	2,178	210	
	Budget authority:			
	Appropriations, discretionary:			
1100	Appropriation	818	818	1,505
1120	Appropriations transferred to other accts [013–0126]	–4	–4	
1120	Appropriations transferred to other acct [013–4512]	–208		
1120	Appropriations transferred to other acct [013–0120]	–1		
1160	Appropriation, discretionary (total)	605	814	1,505
1930	Total budgetary resources available	2,783	1,024	1,505
	Memorandum (non-add) entries:			
1940	Unobligated balance expiring	–488		
1941	Unexpired unobligated balance, end of year	210		
	Change in obligated balance:			
	Unpaid obligations:			
3000	Unpaid obligations, brought forward, Oct 1	1,616	629	382
3010	New obligations, unexpired accounts	2,085	1,024	1,505
3020	Outlays (gross)	–2,809	–1,271	–1,512
3040	Recoveries of prior year unpaid obligations, unexpired	–246		
3041	Recoveries of prior year unpaid obligations, expired	–17		
3050	Unpaid obligations, end of year	629	382	375
	Memorandum (non-add) entries:			
3100	Obligated balance, start of year	1,616	629	382
3200	Obligated balance, end of year	629	382	375
	Budget authority and outlays, net:			
	Discretionary:			
4000	Budget authority, gross	605	814	1,505
	Outlays, gross:			
4010	Outlays from new discretionary authority	497	627	1,264
4011	Outlays from discretionary balances	2,312	644	248
4020	Outlays, gross (total)	2,809	1,271	1,512
	Offsets against gross budget authority and outlays:			
	Offsetting collections (collected) from:			
4030	Federal sources	–4		
4033	Non-Federal sources	–12		

CENSUSES AND SURVEY PROGRAMS—Continued
Program and Financing—Continued

Identification code 013–0450–0–1–376	2021 actual	2022 est.	2023 est.
4040 Offsets against gross budget authority and outlays (total)	–16		
Additional offsets against gross budget authority only:			
4053 Recoveries of prior year paid obligations, unexpired accounts	16		
4070 Budget authority, net (discretionary)	605	814	1,505
4080 Outlays, net (discretionary)	2,793	1,271	1,512
4180 Budget authority, net (total)	605	814	1,505
4190 Outlays, net (total)	2,793	1,271	1,512

The Census Bureau has begun a multi-year process of transforming its organization and operations from a 20th century survey-centric model to a 21st century data-centric model that blends survey data with administrative and alternative digital data sources. To support this transformation, the Budget proposes a change to the Census Bureau's discretionary appropriations structure. The proposed structure combines the Current Surveys and Programs and the Periodic Censuses and Programs appropriations into a new, two-year appropriation entitled Censuses and Survey Programs.

This appropriation funds legislatively mandated economic and demographic surveys and censuses, and enterprise enabling programs that provide bureau-wide geographic information and data collection and dissemination systems and other authorized activities. Major programs include the current and periodic economic programs (including the monthly, quarterly, and annual economic surveys, and five-year economic census and census of governments), current demographic statistics programs, the American Community Survey, the decennial censuses, and enterprise enabling programs.

Economic Statistics Programs.—The Current Economic Statistics programs provide public and private sector data users with relevant, accurate, and timely national statistical profiles of every sector of the U.S. economy to enable governments and businesses to make informed decisions. The Economic Census and the Census of Governments programs are integral to the Bureau of Economic Analysis' estimates of gross domestic product, industry inputs and outputs, and the economic activities of more than 90,000 state and local governments. Together, these programs measure the structure and functioning of the U.S. economy. In 2023, the Census Bureau will expand its capacity to measure the economic and societal impacts of significant events or public policy challenges, advance measures of manufacturing activity, improve measures of state and local tax revenues, and modernize measures of the construction sector. The request for current economics sustains and expands new business formation statistics and measures new entrepreneurial activity, including production of more detailed, sub-national data. The Bureau will also conduct the major data collection, check-in, and data capture operations for the 2022 Economic Census, including agricultural services and following-up with non-responding business establishments. The Census Bureau will collect data for the Finance Component of the Census of Governments and continue to implement system improvements for more effective data editing strategies to increase efficiencies in data processing.

Demographic Statistics Programs.—The Current Demographic Statistics programs conduct surveys and data analyses to provide social and economic information on monthly, quarterly, and annual bases that policymakers and others need to make effective policy and program decisions. The American Community Survey (ACS) provides current demographic, social, economic, and housing information about America's communities, from the largest cities to the smallest rural communities. In 2023, the Census Bureau will research and test new content on Sexual Orientation and Gender Identity. Additionally, the Census Bureau will formalize the Community Resilience Estimates program that began during the pandemic, moving from a purely pandemic focused program toward other disasters. The request also supports an increase reflecting the rising costs of collecting data for the Current Population Survey (CPS) and, in coorindation with the Bureau of Labor Statistics, researching innovative approaches to generating estimates about smaller population groups. The request will also support improved global demographic and economic statistics. Finally, the Census Bureau will develop and test an internet self-response instrument for CPS.

Decennial Census.—In 2023, the Census Bureau will release its final data products, evaluations, and assessments for the 2020 Census. The Census Bureau will continue building off successful innovations and management practices developed for the 2020 Census, developing a 2030 Census design through its program of research and testing, capitalizing on innovations, such as the way that the address list is developed and maintained, using administrative records as a source of data for enumeration, and making field operations more efficient.

Enterprise Enabling Programs.—The Enterprise Enabling Programs support Census Bureau surveys and censuses with data collection, management, processing, and dissemination systems and capabilities as well as the geographic data that underpin the Census Bureau's programs. In 2023, these programs will enhance data collection capabilities; support expanding use of administrative records to improve sample survey operations, data quality, and data products; provide the Federal government with increased capacity to make data-driven decisions, deliver all data products for the 2020 Census, American Community Survey, Economic Census, and other major programs, and expand efforts to provide disclosure protection and modernize data storage and data analysis capabilities across all of the Census Bureau's programs. Additionally, the Geographic Support program provides the geographic data integral to censuses, surveys, and data products. These include address lists, geospatial data products and systems, and full-count data on persons, places, and the economy. The Budget includes an increase to maintain the geographic innovations made possible by the 2020 Census as a suite of evergreen products and services and transitions the Boundary and Annexation Survey and In-Office Address Canvassing from 2020 Census to provide these capabilities on a continuing basis for all Census Bureau programs. The Budget also supports expanded research on racial and ethnic inequality and creation of an enterprise partnership program that leverages 2020 Census partnerships and benefits all Census Bureau programs.

Object Classification (in millions of dollars)

Identification code 013–0450–0–1–376		2021 actual	2022 est.	2023 est.
	Direct obligations:			
	Personnel compensation:			
11.1	Full-time permanent	389	299	531
11.3	Other than full-time permanent	293	60	70
11.5	Other personnel compensation	125	16	23
11.9	Total personnel compensation	807	375	624
12.1	Civilian personnel benefits	202	123	210
13.0	Benefits for former personnel	7	1	1
21.0	Travel and transportation of persons	74	20	27
22.0	Transportation of things	9	1	1
23.1	Rental payments to GSA	72	29	30
23.2	Rental payments to others	4		
23.3	Communications, utilities, and miscellaneous charges	52	31	47
24.0	Printing and reproduction	3	5	5
25.1	Advisory and assistance services	376	186	225
25.2	Other services from non-Federal sources	145	59	72
25.3	Other goods and services from Federal sources	54	30	73
25.4	Operation and maintenance of facilities	48	9	11
25.5	Research and development contracts	3	1	1
25.7	Operation and maintenance of equipment	148	145	165
25.8	Subsistence and support of persons	21		
26.0	Supplies and materials	3	2	2
31.0	Equipment	55	7	11
42.0	Insurance claims and indemnities	2		
99.9	Total new obligations, unexpired accounts	2,085	1,024	1,505

Employment Summary

Identification code 013–0450–0–1–376	2021 actual	2022 est.	2023 est.
1001 Direct civilian full-time equivalent employment	9,638	4,366	6,379

DEPARTMENT OF COMMERCE

CENSUS WORKING CAPITAL FUND

Program and Financing (in millions of dollars)

Identification code 013–4512–0–4–376	2021 actual	2022 est.	2023 est.
Obligations by program activity:			
0810 Economic programs	50	55	49
0811 Demographic programs	297	276	334
0812 Decennial programs & special censuses	1	1	1
0813 Other programs	18	21	28
0819 Reimbursable program activities, subtotal	366	353	412
0820 Management, administration, & IT infrastructure	515	495	525
0821 IT Modernization & Facilities Infrastructure Improvement	208		
0828 Cost collection	83	100	87
0829 Reimbursable program activities, subtotal	806	595	612
0900 Total new obligations, unexpired accounts	1,172	948	1,024
Budgetary resources:			
Unobligated balance:			
1000 Unobligated balance brought forward, Oct 1	393	442	369
1021 Recoveries of prior year unpaid obligations	12	25	25
1033 Recoveries of prior year paid obligations	3		
1070 Unobligated balance (total)	408	467	394
Budget authority:			
Appropriations, discretionary:			
1121 Appropriations transferred from other acct [013–0450]	208		
Spending authority from offsetting collections, discretionary:			
1700 Collected	1,014	850	996
1701 Change in uncollected payments, Federal sources	–16		
1750 Spending auth from offsetting collections, disc (total)	998	850	996
1900 Budget authority (total)	1,206	850	996
1930 Total budgetary resources available	1,614	1,317	1,390
Memorandum (non-add) entries:			
1941 Unexpired unobligated balance, end of year	442	369	366
Change in obligated balance:			
Unpaid obligations:			
3000 Unpaid obligations, brought forward, Oct 1	212	426	201
3010 New obligations, unexpired accounts	1,172	948	1,024
3020 Outlays (gross)	–946	–1,148	–1,024
3040 Recoveries of prior year unpaid obligations, unexpired	–12	–25	–25
3050 Unpaid obligations, end of year	426	201	176
Uncollected payments:			
3060 Uncollected pymts, Fed sources, brought forward, Oct 1	–67	–51	–51
3070 Change in uncollected pymts, Fed sources, unexpired	16		
3090 Uncollected pymts, Fed sources, end of year	–51	–51	–51
Memorandum (non-add) entries:			
3100 Obligated balance, start of year	145	375	150
3200 Obligated balance, end of year	375	150	125
Budget authority and outlays, net:			
Discretionary:			
4000 Budget authority, gross	1,206	850	996
Outlays, gross:			
4010 Outlays from new discretionary authority		765	896
4011 Outlays from discretionary balances	946	383	128
4020 Outlays, gross (total)	946	1,148	1,024
Offsets against gross budget authority and outlays:			
Offsetting collections (collected) from:			
4030 Federal sources	–983	–834	–977
4033 Non-Federal sources	–34	–16	–19
4040 Offsets against gross budget authority and outlays (total)	–1,017	–850	–996
Additional offsets against gross budget authority only:			
4050 Change in uncollected pymts, Fed sources, unexpired	16		
4053 Recoveries of prior year paid obligations, unexpired accounts	3		
4060 Additional offsets against budget authority only (total)	19		
4070 Budget authority, net (discretionary)	208		
4080 Outlays, net (discretionary)	–71	298	28
4180 Budget authority, net (total)	208		
4190 Outlays, net (total)	–71	298	28

The Working Capital Fund finances, on a reimbursable basis, functions within the Census Bureau that are more efficiently and economically performed on a centralized basis. The Fund also finances reimbursable work that the Census Bureau performs for other public, including Federal, and private entities.

Object Classification (in millions of dollars)

Identification code 013–4512–0–4–376	2021 actual	2022 est.	2023 est.
Reimbursable obligations:			
Personnel compensation:			
11.1 Full-time permanent	299	349	372
11.3 Other than full-time permanent	106	76	101
11.5 Other personnel compensation	28	14	14
11.9 Total personnel compensation	433	439	487
12.1 Civilian personnel benefits	146	158	155
13.0 Benefits for former personnel	10	2	
21.0 Travel and transportation of persons	19	21	32
22.0 Transportation of things	6	3	3
23.1 Rental payments to GSA	39	36	47
23.2 Rental payments to others	1	1	1
23.3 Communications, utilities, and miscellaneous charges	28	32	12
24.0 Printing and reproduction	4	7	3
25.1 Advisory and assistance services	51	39	24
25.2 Other services from non-Federal sources	36	36	41
25.3 Other goods and services from Federal sources	113	61	74
25.4 Operation and maintenance of facilities	142	10	12
25.5 Research and development contracts		1	
25.7 Operation and maintenance of equipment	101	90	125
25.8 Subsistence and support of persons	1	1	1
26.0 Supplies and materials	5	3	3
31.0 Equipment	37	8	4
99.9 Total new obligations, unexpired accounts	1,172	948	1,024

Employment Summary

Identification code 013–4512–0–4–376	2021 actual	2022 est.	2023 est.
2001 Reimbursable civilian full-time equivalent employment	2,997	2,649	3,065

BUREAU OF ECONOMIC ANALYSIS

Federal Funds

SALARIES AND EXPENSES

For necessary expenses, as authorized by law, of economic and statistical analysis programs of the Department of Commerce, $140,878,000, to remain available until September 30, 2024.

Note.—A full-year 2022 appropriation for this account was not enacted at the time the Budget was prepared; therefore, the Budget assumes this account is operating under the Continuing Appropriations Act, 2022 (Division A of Public Law 117–43, as amended). The amounts included for 2022 reflect the annualized level provided by the continuing resolution.

Program and Financing (in millions of dollars)

Identification code 013–1500–0–1–376	2021 actual	2022 est.	2023 est.
Obligations by program activity:			
0001 Bureau of Economic Analysis	109	109	127
0002 Policy support	3	3	13
0799 Total direct obligations	112	112	140
0801 Reimbursable	5	3	3
0900 Total new obligations, unexpired accounts	117	115	143
Budgetary resources:			
Unobligated balance:			
1000 Unobligated balance brought forward, Oct 1	1	2	3
1021 Recoveries of prior year unpaid obligations	1	1	1
1070 Unobligated balance (total)	2	3	4
Budget authority:			
Appropriations, discretionary:			
1100 Appropriation	112	112	141
Spending authority from offsetting collections, discretionary:			
1700 Collected	5	3	3
1900 Budget authority (total)	117	115	144
1930 Total budgetary resources available	119	118	148
Memorandum (non-add) entries:			
1941 Unexpired unobligated balance, end of year	2	3	5

Bureau of Economic Analysis—Continued
Federal Funds—Continued

SALARIES AND EXPENSES—Continued

Program and Financing—Continued

Identification code 013–1500–0–1–376	2021 actual	2022 est.	2023 est.
Change in obligated balance:			
Unpaid obligations:			
3000 Unpaid obligations, brought forward, Oct 1	13	15	14
3010 New obligations, unexpired accounts	117	115	143
3020 Outlays (gross)	–112	–115	–140
3040 Recoveries of prior year unpaid obligations, unexpired	–1	–1	–1
3041 Recoveries of prior year unpaid obligations, expired	–2		
3050 Unpaid obligations, end of year	15	14	16
Uncollected payments:			
3060 Uncollected pymts, Fed sources, brought forward, Oct 1	–3	–2	–2
3071 Change in uncollected pymts, Fed sources, expired	1		
3090 Uncollected pymts, Fed sources, end of year	–2	–2	–2
Memorandum (non-add) entries:			
3100 Obligated balance, start of year	10	13	12
3200 Obligated balance, end of year	13	12	14
Budget authority and outlays, net:			
Discretionary:			
4000 Budget authority, gross	117	115	144
Outlays, gross:			
4010 Outlays from new discretionary authority	101	102	127
4011 Outlays from discretionary balances	11	13	13
4020 Outlays, gross (total)	112	115	140
Offsets against gross budget authority and outlays:			
Offsetting collections (collected) from:			
4030 Federal sources	–4	–3	–3
4033 Non-Federal sources	–1		
4040 Offsets against gross budget authority and outlays (total)	–5	–3	–3
4070 Budget authority, net (discretionary)	112	112	141
4080 Outlays, net (discretionary)	107	112	137
4180 Budget authority, net (total)	112	112	141
4190 Outlays, net (total)	107	112	137

Bureau of Economic Analysis (BEA).—BEA, a principal Federal statistical agency, promotes a better understanding of the U.S. economy by providing timely, relevant, and accurate economic data in an objective and cost-effective manner. BEA's national, regional, and international economic statistics present crucial information on key issues such as U.S. economic growth, regional economic development, inter-industry relationships, and the Nation's position in the world economy. These key statistics provide a comprehensive picture of the U.S. economy and affect decisions related to interest and exchange rates, tax and budget projections, and business investment plans. The statistics are used by Federal, State, and local governments for budget development and projections and to support the allocation of over $500 billion in Federal funds. The statistics are also used by the American public to follow and understand the performance of the Nation's economy. Some of the Bureau's widely used statistical measures include national measures of gross domestic product (GDP), personal income and outlays, corporate profits, balance of payments, GDP by county, state, and industry. BEA also publishes sector specific statistics on areas such as healthcare, outdoor recreation and arts and culture. BEA's strategic vision is to remain the world's most respected producer of economic accounts.

Object Classification (in millions of dollars)

Identification code 013–1500–0–1–376	2021 actual	2022 est.	2023 est.
Direct obligations:			
Personnel compensation:			
11.1 Full-time permanent	63	63	73
11.3 Other than full-time permanent	1	1	1
11.9 Total personnel compensation	64	64	74
12.1 Civilian personnel benefits	19	19	22
23.1 Rental payments to GSA	5	5	4
23.2 Rental payments to others	1	1	1
23.3 Communications, utilities, and miscellaneous charges	1	1	1
25.1 Advisory and assistance services	1	1	1
25.2 Other services from non-Federal sources	12	12	21
25.3 Other goods and services from Federal sources	6	6	13
25.4 Operation and maintenance of facilities	1	1	1
26.0 Supplies and materials	1	1	1
31.0 Equipment	1	1	1
99.0 Direct obligations	112	112	140
99.0 Reimbursable obligations	5	3	3
99.9 Total new obligations, unexpired accounts	117	115	143

Employment Summary

Identification code 013–1500–0–1–376	2021 actual	2022 est.	2023 est.
1001 Direct civilian full-time equivalent employment	481	481	514
2001 Reimbursable civilian full-time equivalent employment	14	14	17

INTERNATIONAL TRADE ADMINISTRATION
Federal Funds

OPERATIONS AND ADMINISTRATION

For necessary expenses for international trade activities of the Department of Commerce provided for by law, to carry out activities associated with facilitating, attracting, and retaining business investment in the United States, and for engaging in trade promotional activities abroad, including expenses of grants and cooperative agreements for the purpose of promoting exports of United States firms, without regard to sections 3702 and 3703 of title 44, United States Code; full medical coverage for dependent members of immediate families of employees stationed overseas and employees temporarily posted overseas; travel and transportation of employees of the International Trade Administration between two points abroad, without regard to section 40118 of title 49, United States Code; employment of citizens of the United States and aliens by contract for services; rental of space abroad for periods not exceeding 10 years, and expenses of alteration, repair, or improvement; purchase or construction of temporary demountable exhibition structures for use abroad; payment of tort claims, in the manner authorized in the first paragraph of section 2672 of title 28, United States Code, when such claims arise in foreign countries; not to exceed $294,300 for official representation expenses abroad; purchase of passenger motor vehicles for official use abroad, not to exceed $45,000 per vehicle; not to exceed $325,000 for purchase of armored vehicles without regard to the general purchase price limitations; purchase of insurance on official motor vehicles; and rental of tie lines, $642,831,000, of which $80,000,000 shall remain available until September 30, 2024: Provided, That $12,000,000 is to be derived from fees to be retained and used by the International Trade Administration, notwithstanding section 3302 of title 31, United States Code: Provided further, That, of amounts provided under this heading, not less than $16,400,000 shall be for China antidumping and countervailing duty enforcement and compliance activities: Provided further, That the provisions of the first sentence of section 105(f) and all of section 108(c) of the Mutual Educational and Cultural Exchange Act of 1961 (22 U.S.C. 2455(f) and 2458(c)) shall apply in carrying out these activities; and that for the purpose of this Act, contributions under the provisions of the Mutual Educational and Cultural Exchange Act of 1961 shall include payment for assessments for services provided as part of these activities.

Note.—A full-year 2022 appropriation for this account was not enacted at the time the Budget was prepared; therefore, the Budget assumes this account is operating under the Continuing Appropriations Act, 2022 (Division A of Public Law 117–43, as amended). The amounts included for 2022 reflect the annualized level provided by the continuing resolution.

Program and Financing (in millions of dollars)

Identification code 013–1250–0–1–376	2021 actual	2022 est.	2023 est.
Obligations by program activity:			
0006 Industry and Analysis	66	69	87
0007 Enforcement and Compliance	100	99	125
0008 Global Markets	349	342	392
0009 Executive Direction and Administration	24	24	27
0100 Total direct program	539	534	631
0799 Total direct obligations	539	534	631
0801 Operations and Administration (Reimbursable)	33	33	33
0900 Total new obligations, unexpired accounts	572	567	664
Budgetary resources:			
Unobligated balance:			
1000 Unobligated balance brought forward, Oct 1	15	21	29

DEPARTMENT OF COMMERCE

Bureau of Industry and Security
Federal Funds — 201

		2021 actual	2022 est.	2023 est.
1021	Recoveries of prior year unpaid obligations	10	7	7
1070	Unobligated balance (total)	25	28	36
	Budget authority:			
	Appropriations, discretionary:			
1100	Appropriation	530	530	631
	Spending authority from offsetting collections, discretionary:			
1700	Collected	31	38	38
1701	Change in uncollected payments, Federal sources	10		
1750	Spending auth from offsetting collections, disc (total)	41	38	38
1900	Budget authority (total)	571	568	669
1930	Total budgetary resources available	596	596	705
	Memorandum (non-add) entries:			
1940	Unobligated balance expiring	−3		
1941	Unexpired unobligated balance, end of year	21	29	41
	Change in obligated balance:			
	Unpaid obligations:			
3000	Unpaid obligations, brought forward, Oct 1	107	107	103
3010	New obligations, unexpired accounts	572	567	664
3011	Obligations ("upward adjustments"), expired accounts	2	2	3
3020	Outlays (gross)	−558	−560	−614
3040	Recoveries of prior year unpaid obligations, unexpired	−10	−7	−7
3041	Recoveries of prior year unpaid obligations, expired	−6	−6	−6
3050	Unpaid obligations, end of year	107	103	143
	Uncollected payments:			
3060	Uncollected pymts, Fed sources, brought forward, Oct 1	−21	−29	−28
3070	Change in uncollected pymts, Fed sources, unexpired	−10		
3071	Change in uncollected pymts, Fed sources, expired	2	1	1
3090	Uncollected pymts, Fed sources, end of year	−29	−28	−27
	Memorandum (non-add) entries:			
3100	Obligated balance, start of year	86	78	75
3200	Obligated balance, end of year	78	75	116
	Budget authority and outlays, net:			
	Discretionary:			
4000	Budget authority, gross	571	568	669
	Outlays, gross:			
4010	Outlays from new discretionary authority	460	462	543
4011	Outlays from discretionary balances	98	98	71
4020	Outlays, gross (total)	558	560	614
	Offsets against gross budget authority and outlays:			
	Offsetting collections (collected) from:			
4030	Federal sources	−26	−26	−26
4033	Non-Federal sources	−7	−12	−12
4040	Offsets against gross budget authority and outlays (total)	−33	−38	−38
	Additional offsets against gross budget authority only:			
4050	Change in uncollected pymts, Fed sources, unexpired	−10		
4052	Offsetting collections credited to expired accounts	2		
4060	Additional offsets against budget authority only (total)	−8		
4070	Budget authority, net (discretionary)	530	530	631
4080	Outlays, net (discretionary)	525	522	576
4180	Budget authority, net (total)	530	530	631
4190	Outlays, net (total)	525	522	576

The mission of the International Trade Administration (ITA) is to create prosperity by strengthening the international competitiveness of U.S. industry, promoting trade and investment, and ensuring fair trade and compliance with trade laws and agreements. ITA leads the Department's export and investment platform, working with several other bureaus both within and outside the Department to achieve this goal.

ITA, through its programs, services, and workforce, leverages its relationships with an understanding of industry and its domestic and overseas field presence to serve a range of customers and stakeholders. The organization consists of four business units that work together to achieve ITA's mission effectively and efficiently: (1) Industry and Analysis; (2) Enforcement and Compliance; (3) Global Markets; and (4) Executive Direction and Administration. The combination of industry sector, regional, and trade expertise, alongside export promotion, enforcement and compliance, and policy responsibilities, enables ITA to analyze customer issues and needs holistically, and support trade enforcement and export promotion efforts in key, growing markets abroad.

Object Classification (in millions of dollars)

Identification code 013–1250–0–1–376		2021 actual	2022 est.	2023 est.
	Direct obligations:			
	Personnel compensation:			
11.1	Full-time permanent	170	180	207
11.3	Other than full-time permanent	34	38	38
11.5	Other personnel compensation	10	1	2
11.9	Total personnel compensation	214	219	247
12.1	Civilian personnel benefits	80	82	96
13.0	Benefits for former personnel	2	3	2
21.0	Travel and transportation of persons	5	6	7
22.0	Transportation of things	6	5	7
23.1	Rental payments to GSA	17	19	27
23.2	Rental payments to others	12	10	12
23.3	Communications, utilities, and miscellaneous charges	7	12	13
24.0	Printing and reproduction	2		
25.1	Advisory and assistance services	34	5	11
25.2	Other services from non-Federal sources	23	47	64
25.3	Other goods and services from Federal sources	108	105	122
25.4	Operation and maintenance of facilities	7		
25.7	Operation and maintenance of equipment	1		
25.8	Subsistence and support of persons		1	1
26.0	Supplies and materials	3	13	13
31.0	Equipment	15	7	8
41.0	Grants, subsidies, and contributions	1		1
43.0	Interest and dividends	2		
99.0	Direct obligations	539	534	631
99.0	Reimbursable obligations	33	33	33
99.9	Total new obligations, unexpired accounts	572	567	664

Employment Summary

Identification code 013–1250–0–1–376	2021 actual	2022 est.	2023 est.
1001 Direct civilian full-time equivalent employment	1,304	1,531	1,634
2001 Reimbursable civilian full-time equivalent employment	34	34	34

BUREAU OF INDUSTRY AND SECURITY

Federal Funds

OPERATIONS AND ADMINISTRATION

For necessary expenses for export administration and national security activities of the Department of Commerce, including costs associated with the performance of export administration field activities both domestically and abroad; full medical coverage for dependent members of immediate families of employees stationed overseas; employment of citizens of the United States and aliens by contract for services abroad; payment of tort claims, in the manner authorized in the first paragraph of section 2672 of title 28, United States Code, when such claims arise in foreign countries; not to exceed $13,500 for official representation expenses abroad; awards of compensation to informers under the Export Control Reform Act of 2018 (subtitle B of title XVII of the John S. McCain National Defense Authorization Act for Fiscal Year 2019; Public Law 115–232; 132 Stat. 2208; 50 U.S.C. 4801 et seq.), and as authorized by section 1(b) of the Act of June 15, 1917 (40 Stat. 223; 22 U.S.C. 401(b)); and purchase of passenger motor vehicles for official use and motor vehicles for law enforcement use with special requirement vehicles eligible for purchase without regard to any price limitation otherwise established by law, $199,547,000, to remain available until expended: Provided, That the provisions of the first sentence of section 105(f) and all of section 108(c) of the Mutual Educational and Cultural Exchange Act of 1961 (22 U.S.C. 2455(f) and 2458(c)) shall apply in carrying out these activities: Provided further, That payments and contributions collected and accepted for materials or services provided as part of such activities may be retained for use in covering the cost of such activities, and for providing information to the public with respect to the export administration and national security activities of the Department of Commerce and other export control programs of the United States and other governments.

Note.—A full-year 2022 appropriation for this account was not enacted at the time the Budget was prepared; therefore, the Budget assumes this account is operating under the Continuing Appropriations Act, 2022 (Division A of Public Law 117–43, as amended). The amounts included for 2022 reflect the annualized level provided by the continuing resolution.

202 Bureau of Industry and Security—Continued
Federal Funds—Continued

THE BUDGET FOR FISCAL YEAR 2023

OPERATIONS AND ADMINISTRATION—Continued

Program and Financing (in millions of dollars)

Identification code 013–0300–0–1–999	2021 actual	2022 est.	2023 est.
Obligations by program activity:			
0001 Management and policy coordination	4	4	41
0002 Export administration	61	61	73
0003 Export enforcement	78	73	85
0091 Direct program activities, subtotal	143	138	199
0100 Total direct program	143	138	199
0799 Total direct obligations	143	138	199
0801 Operations and Administration (Reimbursable)	3	4	4
0900 Total new obligations, unexpired accounts	146	142	203
Budgetary resources:			
Unobligated balance:			
1000 Unobligated balance brought forward, Oct 1	5	5	5
1021 Recoveries of prior year unpaid obligations	9	5	
1070 Unobligated balance (total)	14	10	5
Budget authority:			
Appropriations, discretionary:			
1100 Appropriation	133	133	200
Spending authority from offsetting collections, discretionary:			
1700 Collected	1	1	1
1701 Change in uncollected payments, Federal sources	3	3	1
1750 Spending auth from offsetting collections, disc (total)	4	4	2
1900 Budget authority (total)	137	137	202
1930 Total budgetary resources available	151	147	207
Memorandum (non-add) entries:			
1941 Unexpired unobligated balance, end of year	5	5	4
Change in obligated balance:			
Unpaid obligations:			
3000 Unpaid obligations, brought forward, Oct 1	50	48	50
3010 New obligations, unexpired accounts	146	142	203
3020 Outlays (gross)	–139	–135	–195
3040 Recoveries of prior year unpaid obligations, unexpired	–9	–5	
3050 Unpaid obligations, end of year	48	50	58
Uncollected payments:			
3060 Uncollected pymts, Fed sources, brought forward, Oct 1	–2	–5	–8
3070 Change in uncollected pymts, Fed sources, unexpired	–3	–3	–1
3090 Uncollected pymts, Fed sources, end of year	–5	–8	–9
Memorandum (non-add) entries:			
3100 Obligated balance, start of year	48	43	42
3200 Obligated balance, end of year	43	42	49
Budget authority and outlays, net:			
Discretionary:			
4000 Budget authority, gross	137	137	202
Outlays, gross:			
4010 Outlays from new discretionary authority	109	117	172
4011 Outlays from discretionary balances	30	18	23
4020 Outlays, gross (total)	139	135	195
Offsets against gross budget authority and outlays:			
Offsetting collections (collected) from:			
4030 Federal sources	–1	–1	–1
4040 Offsets against gross budget authority and outlays (total)	–1	–1	–1
Additional offsets against gross budget authority only:			
4050 Change in uncollected pymts, Fed sources, unexpired	–3	–3	–1
4070 Budget authority, net (discretionary)	133	133	200
4080 Outlays, net (discretionary)	138	134	194
4180 Budget authority, net (total)	133	133	200
4190 Outlays, net (total)	138	134	194

The Bureau of Industry and Security (BIS) advances U.S. national security, foreign policy, and economic objectives, by administering and enforcing controls on the export of sensitive goods and technologies. BIS also enforces antiboycott laws, monitors the economic viability of the U.S. defense industry, and assists U.S. companies in complying with certain international arms agreements. The Budget enhances BIS's ability to strengthen, streamline, and manage the U.S. export control system, while increasing BIS's capability to complete effective investigations and assessments that identify the impacts that imports of industry-specific products have on U.S. national security.

Object Classification (in millions of dollars)

Identification code 013–0300–0–1–999	2021 actual	2022 est.	2023 est.
Direct obligations:			
Personnel compensation:			
11.1 Full-time permanent	47	57	76
11.5 Other personnel compensation	4	5	6
11.9 Total personnel compensation	51	62	82
12.1 Civilian personnel benefits	21	24	33
21.0 Travel and transportation of persons	1	1	2
23.1 Rental payments to GSA	7	6	14
23.3 Communications, utilities, and miscellaneous charges	3	3	4
24.0 Printing and reproduction			1
25.1 Advisory and assistance services	9	4	4
25.2 Other services from non-Federal sources	12	7	24
25.3 Other goods and services from Federal sources	35	26	28
26.0 Supplies and materials	2	2	3
31.0 Equipment	2	3	4
99.0 Direct obligations	143	138	199
99.0 Reimbursable obligations	3	4	4
99.9 Total new obligations, unexpired accounts	146	142	203

Employment Summary

Identification code 013–0300–0–1–999	2021 actual	2022 est.	2023 est.
1001 Direct civilian full-time equivalent employment	366	448	556
2001 Reimbursable civilian full-time equivalent employment	2	5	5

MINORITY BUSINESS DEVELOPMENT AGENCY

Federal Funds

MINORITY BUSINESS DEVELOPMENT

For necessary expenses of the Department of Commerce in fostering, promoting, and developing minority business enterprises, as authorized by the Minority Business Development Act of 2021 (Division K of Public Law 117–58), $110,000,000.

Note.—A full-year 2022 appropriation for this account was not enacted at the time the Budget was prepared; therefore, the Budget assumes this account is operating under the Continuing Appropriations Act, 2022 (Division A of Public Law 117–43, as amended). The amounts included for 2022 reflect the annualized level provided by the continuing resolution.

Program and Financing (in millions of dollars)

Identification code 013–0201–0–1–376	2021 actual	2022 est.	2023 est.
Obligations by program activity:			
0001 Business Development	47	48	110
0003 Direct program activity Additional Coronavirus Response and Relief, Title III	18		
0900 Total new obligations, unexpired accounts	65	48	110
Budgetary resources:			
Unobligated balance:			
1000 Unobligated balance brought forward, Oct 1		7	7
Budget authority:			
Appropriations, discretionary:			
1100 Appropriation	73	48	110
1930 Total budgetary resources available	73	55	117
Memorandum (non-add) entries:			
1940 Unobligated balance expiring	–1		
1941 Unexpired unobligated balance, end of year	7	7	7
Change in obligated balance:			
Unpaid obligations:			
3000 Unpaid obligations, brought forward, Oct 1	35	51	51
3010 New obligations, unexpired accounts	65	48	110
3011 Obligations ("upward adjustments"), expired accounts	1		
3020 Outlays (gross)	–49	–48	–81
3041 Recoveries of prior year unpaid obligations, expired	–1		
3050 Unpaid obligations, end of year	51	51	80
Memorandum (non-add) entries:			
3100 Obligated balance, start of year	35	51	51

DEPARTMENT OF COMMERCE

National Oceanic and Atmospheric Administration
Federal Funds
203

		2021 actual	2022 est.	2023 est.
3200	Obligated balance, end of year	51	51	80
	Budget authority and outlays, net:			
	Discretionary:			
4000	Budget authority, gross	73	48	110
	Outlays, gross:			
4010	Outlays from new discretionary authority	21	24	55
4011	Outlays from discretionary balances	28	24	26
4020	Outlays, gross (total)	49	48	81
4180	Budget authority, net (total)	73	48	110
4190	Outlays, net (total)	49	48	81

The Minority Business Development Agency (MBDA) is the only Federal agency solely dedicated to the growth and global competitiveness of minority business enterprises (MBEs). MBDA supports a national network of Business Centers, Speciality Centers, and Grantees. These programs offer customized business development and industry-focused services to provide greater access to capital, contracts, and markets. Additionally, MBDA supports MBEs through policy, advocacy, research, and public-private partnerships. Consistent with the Minority Business Development Act of 2021, MBDA will implement new efforts including a Rural Business Center program, initiatives to promote economic resiliency, and opening regional offices.

Object Classification (in millions of dollars)

Identification code 013–0201–0–1–376		2021 actual	2022 est.	2023 est.
	Direct obligations:			
11.1	Personnel compensation: Full-time permanent	5	5	13
12.1	Civilian personnel benefits	2	2	5
23.1	Rental payments to GSA	1	1	3
25.1	Advisory and assistance services	1	1	2
25.2	Other services from non-Federal sources	2	2	5
25.3	Other goods and services from Federal sources	5	5	19
41.0	Grants, subsidies, and contributions	49	32	63
99.9	Total new obligations, unexpired accounts	65	48	110

Employment Summary

Identification code 013–0201–0–1–376	2021 actual	2022 est.	2023 est.
1001 Direct civilian full-time equivalent employment	38	50	134

NATIONAL OCEANIC AND ATMOSPHERIC ADMINISTRATION

Federal Funds

OPERATIONS, RESEARCH, AND FACILITIES

(INCLUDING TRANSFER OF FUNDS)

For necessary expenses of activities authorized by law for the National Oceanic and Atmospheric Administration, including maintenance, operation, and hire of aircraft and vessels; pilot programs for State-led fisheries management, notwithstanding any other provision of law; grants, contracts, or other payments to nonprofit organizations for the purposes of conducting activities pursuant to cooperative agreements; and relocation of facilities, $4,484,209,000, to remain available until September 30, 2024: Provided, That fees and donations received by the National Ocean Service for the management of national marine sanctuaries may be retained and used for the salaries and expenses associated with those activities, notwithstanding section 3302 of title 31, United States Code: Provided further, That in addition, $348,871,000 shall be derived by transfer from the fund entitled "Promote and Develop Fishery Products and Research Pertaining to American Fisheries", which shall only be used for fishery activities related to the Saltonstall-Kennedy Grant Program; Fisheries Data Collections, Surveys, and Assessments; Fisheries Management Programs and Services; and Interjurisdictional Fisheries Grants: Provided further, That not to exceed $71,299,000 shall be for payment to the "Department of Commerce Working Capital Fund": Provided further, That of the $4,850,580,000 provided for in direct obligations under this heading, $4,484,209,000 is appropriated from the general fund, $348,871,000 is provided by transfer, and $17,500,000 is derived from recoveries of prior year obligations: Provided further, That in addition, for necessary retired pay expenses under the Retired Serviceman's Family Protection and Survivor Benefits Plan, and for payments for the medical care of retired personnel and their dependents under the Dependents' Medical Care Act (10 U.S.C. ch. 55), such sums as may be necessary.

Note.—A full-year 2022 appropriation for this account was not enacted at the time the Budget was prepared; therefore, the Budget assumes this account is operating under the Continuing Appropriations Act, 2022 (Division A of Public Law 117-43, as amended). The amounts included for 2022 reflect the annualized level provided by the continuing resolution.

OPERATIONS, RESEARCH, AND FACILITIES

[For an additional amount for "Operations, Research, and Facilities" for necessary expenses related to the consequences of hurricanes and of wildfires in calendar years 2020 and 2021, $92,834,000, to remain available until September 30, 2023, as follows:]

[(1) $4,709,000 for repair and replacement of observing assets, real property, and equipment;]

[(2) $3,425,000 for marine debris assessment and removal;]

[(3) $4,700,000 for mapping, charting, and geodesy services;]

[(4) $35,000,000 to improve:]

[(A) hurricane intensity and track forecasting, including through deployment of unmanned ocean observing platforms and enhanced data assimilation; and(B) precipitation and flood prediction, forecasting, and mitigation capabilities;]

[(5) $20,000,000 to improve wildfire research, prediction, detection, forecasting, monitoring, data management, and communication and engagement; and]

[(6) $25,000,000 for Title IX Fund grants as authorized under section 906(c) of division O of Public Law 114–113: *Provided*, That the National Oceanic and Atmospheric Administration shall submit a spending plan to the Committees on Appropriations of the House of Representatives and the Senate within 45 days after the date of enactment of this Act.] *(Disaster Relief Supplemental Appropriations Act, 2022.)*

OPERATIONS, RESEARCH, AND FACILITIES

[For an additional amount for "Operations, Research, and Facilities", $2,611,000,000, to remain available until September 30, 2027: *Provided*, That $557,250,000, to remain available until September 30, 2023, shall be made available for fiscal year 2022, $515,584,000, to remain available until September 30, 2024, shall be made available for fiscal year 2023, $515,583,000, to remain available until September 30, 2025, shall be made available for fiscal year 2024, $515,583,000, to remain available until September 30, 2026, shall be made available for fiscal year 2025, and $507,000,000, to remain available until September 30, 2027, shall be made available for fiscal year 2026: *Provided further*, That of the funds made available under this heading in this Act, the following amounts shall be for the following purposes in equal amounts for each of fiscal years 2022 through 2026, including for administrative costs, technical support, and oversight, unless stated otherwise—]

[(1)$492,000,000 shall be for National Oceans and Coastal Security Fund grants, as authorized under section 906(c) of division O of Public Law 114–113;]

[(2) $491,000,000 shall be for contracts, grants, and cooperative agreements to provide funding and technical assistance for purposes of restoring marine, estuarine, coastal, or Great Lakes ecosystem habitat, or constructing or protecting ecological features that protect coastal communities from flooding or coastal storms;]

[(3) $492,000,000 shall be for coastal and inland flood and inundation mapping and forecasting, and next-generation water modeling activities, including modernized precipitation frequency and probable maximum studies;]

[(4) $25,000,000 shall be for data acquisition activities pursuant to section 511(b) of the Water Resources Development Act of 2020 (division AA of Public Law 116–260), of which $8,334,000 shall be available in fiscal year 2023 and $8,333,000 shall be available in each of fiscal years 2024 and 2025;]

[(5) $50,000,000 shall be for wildfire prediction, detection, observation, modeling, and forecasting, for fiscal year 2022;]

[(6) $1,000,000 shall be for the study of soil moisture and snowpack monitoring network in the Upper Missouri River Basin pursuant to section 511(b)(3) of the Water Resources Development Act of 2020 (division AA of Public Law 116–260), in equal amounts for each of fiscal years 2022 through 2025;]

[(7) $150,000,000 shall be for marine debris assessment, prevention, mitigation, and removal;]

[(8) $50,000,000 shall be for marine debris prevention and removal through the National Sea Grant College Program (33 U.S.C. 1121 et seq.);]

[(9) $207,000,000 shall be for habitat restoration projects pursuant to section 310 of the Coastal Zone Management Act (16 U.S.C. 1456c), including ecosystem conservation pursuant to section 12502 of the Omnibus Public Land Management Act of 2009 (16 U.S.C. 1456–1), notwithstanding subsection (g) of that section;]

[(10) $77,000,000 shall be for habitat restoration projects through the National Estuarine Research Reserve System (16 U.S.C. 1456c), including ecosystem

OPERATIONS, RESEARCH, AND FACILITIES—Continued

conservation pursuant to section 12502 of the Omnibus Public Land Management Act of 2009 (16 U.S.C. 1456–1);]

[(11) $100,000,000 shall be for supporting improved and enhanced coastal, ocean, and Great Lakes observing systems;]

[(12) $56,000,000 shall be for established Regional Ocean Partnerships (ROPs) to coordinate the interstate and intertribal management of ocean and coastal resources and to implement their priority actions, including to enhance associated sharing and integration of Federal and non-Federal data by ROPs, or their equivalent;]

[(13) $20,000,000 shall be for consultations and permitting related to the Endangered Species Act, the Marine Mammal Protection Act, and Essential Fish Habitat; and(14) $400,000,000 shall be for restoring fish passage by removing instream barriers and providing technical assistance pursuant to section 117 of the Magnuson-Stevens Fishery Conservation and Management Reauthorization Act of 2006 (16 U.S.C. 1891a), of which up to 15 percent shall be reserved for Indian Tribes or partnerships of Indian Tribes in conjunction with an institution of higher education, non-profit, commercial (for profit) organizations, U.S. territories, and state or local governments, and of which the remaining amount shall be for all eligible entities, including Indian Tribes and such partnerships of Indian Tribes:] [*Provided further*, That under this heading the term Indian Tribe shall have the meaning given to the term in section 4 of the Indian Self-Determination and Education Act (25 U.S.C. 5304): *Provided further*, That nothing under this heading in this Act shall be construed as providing any new authority to remove, breach, or otherwise alter the operations of a Federal hydropower dam and dam removal projects shall include written consent of the dam owner, if ownership is established: *Provided further*, That amounts made available under this heading in this Act may be used for consultations and permitting related to the Endangered Species Act and the Marine Mammal Protection Act for projects funded under this heading in this Act: *Provided further*, That not later than 90 days after the date of enactment of this Act, the National Oceanic and Atmospheric Administration shall submit to the Committees on Appropriations of the House of Representatives and the Senate a detailed spend plan for fiscal year 2022: *Provided further*, That for each of fiscal years 2023 through 2026, as part of the annual budget submission of the President under section 1105(a) of title 31, United States Code, the Secretary of Commerce shall submit a detailed spend plan for that fiscal year: *Provided further*, That the Secretary may waive or reduce the required non-Federal share for amounts made available under this heading in this Act: *Provided further*, That such amount is designated by the Congress as being for an emergency requirement pursuant to section 4112(a) of H. Con. Res. 71 (115th Congress), the concurrent resolution on the budget for fiscal year 2018, and to section 251(b) of the Balanced Budget and Emergency Deficit Control Act of 1985.] (*Infrastructure Investments and Jobs Appropriations Act.*)

Program and Financing (in millions of dollars)

Identification code 013–1450–0–1–306		2021 actual	2022 est.	2023 est.
	Obligations by program activity:			
0001	National Ocean Service	620	620	687
0002	National Marine Fisheries Service	993	965	1,107
0003	Oceanic and Atmospheric Research	579	571	666
0004	National Weather Service	1,089	1,101	1,219
0005	National Environmental Satellite Service	295	292	409
0007	Mission Support	311	303	450
0008	Office of Marine and Aviation Operations	261	254	313
0009	Retired pay for NOAA Corps Officers	30	31	31
0010	Spectrum Relocation Fund	12	22	4
0012	Spectrum Pipeline			2
0014	CARES	9		
0016	USMCA	6		
0017	2022 Supplemental		93	
0018	IIJA		557	516
0100	Total direct program	4,205	4,809	5,404
0799	Total direct obligations	4,205	4,809	5,404
0801	National Ocean Service	19	34	24
0802	National Marine Fisheries Service	54	85	95
0803	Oceanic and Atmospheric Research	51	129	50
0804	National Weather Service	74	77	44
0805	National Environmental Satellite Service	45	39	15
0806	Mission Support	29	23	12
0810	OMAO	6	1	2
0815	NWSS	2		
0899	Total reimbursable obligations	280	388	242
0900	Total new obligations, unexpired accounts	4,485	5,197	5,646

	Budgetary resources:			
	Unobligated balance:			
1000	Unobligated balance brought forward, Oct 1	347	239	216
1001	Discretionary unobligated balance brought fwd, Oct 1	308	144	
1021	Recoveries of prior year unpaid obligations	67	18	18
1033	Recoveries of prior year paid obligations	1		
1070	Unobligated balance (total)	415	257	234
	Budget authority:			
	Appropriations, discretionary:			
1100	Operations, research & facilities	3,840	4,490	4,484
1120	Appropriations transferred to other accts [013–1460]	–33		
1121	Appropriations transferred from other acct [013–5139]	246	246	349
1121	Appropriations transferred from other acct [013–1460]	3		
1160	Appropriation, discretionary (total)	4,056	4,736	4,833
	Advance appropriations, discretionary:			
1170	Advance appropriation			516
	Appropriations, mandatory:			
1200	Appropriation	33	32	32
	Spending authority from offsetting collections, discretionary:			
1700	Collected	268	388	242
1701	Change in uncollected payments, Federal sources	–42		
1750	Spending auth from offsetting collections, disc (total)	226	388	242
1900	Budget authority (total)	4,315	5,156	5,623
1930	Total budgetary resources available	4,730	5,413	5,857
	Memorandum (non-add) entries:			
1940	Unobligated balance expiring	–6		
1941	Unexpired unobligated balance, end of year	239	216	211

	Change in obligated balance:			
	Unpaid obligations:			
3000	Unpaid obligations, brought forward, Oct 1	2,862	3,002	3,476
3010	New obligations, unexpired accounts	4,485	5,197	5,646
3011	Obligations ("upward adjustments"), expired accounts	6		
3020	Outlays (gross)	–4,253	–4,705	–5,085
3040	Recoveries of prior year unpaid obligations, unexpired	–67	–18	–18
3041	Recoveries of prior year unpaid obligations, expired	–31		
3050	Unpaid obligations, end of year	3,002	3,476	4,019
	Uncollected payments:			
3060	Uncollected pymts, Fed sources, brought forward, Oct 1	–479	–437	–437
3070	Change in uncollected pymts, Fed sources, unexpired	42		
3090	Uncollected pymts, Fed sources, end of year	–437	–437	–437
	Memorandum (non-add) entries:			
3100	Obligated balance, start of year	2,383	2,565	3,039
3200	Obligated balance, end of year	2,565	3,039	3,582

	Budget authority and outlays, net:			
	Discretionary:			
4000	Budget authority, gross	4,282	5,124	5,591
	Outlays, gross:			
4010	Outlays from new discretionary authority	2,485	2,506	2,831
4011	Outlays from discretionary balances	1,732	2,147	2,213
4020	Outlays, gross (total)	4,217	4,653	5,044
	Offsets against gross budget authority and outlays:			
	Offsetting collections (collected) from:			
4030	Federal sources	–234	–344	–208
4033	Non-Federal sources	–39	–44	–34
4040	Offsets against gross budget authority and outlays (total)	–273	–388	–242
	Additional offsets against gross budget authority only:			
4050	Change in uncollected pymts, Fed sources, unexpired	42		
4052	Offsetting collections credited to expired accounts	4		
4053	Recoveries of prior year paid obligations, unexpired accounts	1		
4060	Additional offsets against budget authority only (total)	47		
4070	Budget authority, net (discretionary)	4,056	4,736	5,349
4080	Outlays, net (discretionary)	3,944	4,265	4,802
	Mandatory:			
4090	Budget authority, gross	33	32	32
	Outlays, gross:			
4100	Outlays from new mandatory authority	30	32	32
4101	Outlays from mandatory balances	6	20	9
4110	Outlays, gross (total)	36	52	41
4180	Budget authority, net (total)	4,089	4,768	5,381
4190	Outlays, net (total)	3,980	4,317	4,843

The mission of the National Oceanic and Atmospheric Administration (NOAA) is to understand and predict changes in the Earth's environment and to conserve and manage coastal and marine resources to meet our Nation's economic, social, and environmental needs.

NOAA executes programs and activities to achieve its mission through seven line activities:

National Ocean Service (NOS).—NOS programs work to promote safe navigation; assess and restore the health of coastal and marine resources; improve coastal communities' resilience to extreme weather events, climate hazards, and changing ocean conditions and uses; and conserve the coastal and ocean environment.

National Marine Fisheries Service (NMFS).—NMFS programs provide for the management and conservation of the Nation's living marine resources including fish stocks, marine mammals, and endangered species and their habitats within the United States Exclusive Economic Zone (EEZ).

Office of Oceanic and Atmospheric Research (OAR).—OAR programs provide climate, weather, air chemistry, ocean and coastal research and technology with applications across NOAA's mission. To accomplish these goals, OAR supports a network of scientists in its Federal research laboratories, universities, and cooperative institutes and partnership programs.

National Weather Service (NWS).—NWS programs provide timely and accurate meteorological, hydrologic, and oceanographic warnings and forecasts to ensure the safety of the population, minimize property losses, and improve the economic productivity of the Nation.

National Environmental Satellite, Data, and Information Service (NESDIS).—NESDIS operates polar orbiting and geostationary satellites, and collects and archives global environmental data and information for distribution to private and public sector users.

Mission Support.—Mission Support provides management and administrative support for NOAA, including acquisition and grant administration, budget, accounting functions, and human resources.

Office of Marine and Aviation Operations (OMAO).—OMAO provides aircraft and marine data acquisition, fleet repair and maintenance, and operations that provide technical and management support for NOAA-wide activities.

Object Classification (in millions of dollars)

Identification code 013–1450–0–1–306		2021 actual	2022 est.	2023 est.
	Direct obligations:			
	Personnel compensation:			
11.1	Full-time permanent	1,206	1,251	1,350
11.3	Other than full-time permanent	6	13	13
11.5	Other personnel compensation	75	68	69
11.7	Military personnel	39	38	39
11.9	Total personnel compensation	1,326	1,370	1,471
12.1	Civilian personnel benefits	473	476	510
12.2	Military personnel benefits	9	9	9
13.0	Benefits for former personnel	28	29	29
21.0	Travel and transportation of persons	10	22	22
22.0	Transportation of things	13	14	14
23.1	Rental payments to GSA	91	95	97
23.2	Rental payments to others	30	30	30
23.3	Communications, utilities, and miscellaneous charges	90	80	81
24.0	Printing and reproduction	3	4	4
25.1	Advisory and assistance services	307	309	314
25.2	Other services from non-Federal sources	670	772	939
25.3	Other goods and services from Federal sources	137	142	144
25.5	Research and development contracts	13	10	10
26.0	Supplies and materials	107	102	104
31.0	Equipment	37	47	48
32.0	Land and structures	2		
41.0	Grants, subsidies, and contributions	859	1,298	1,578
99.0	Direct obligations	4,205	4,809	5,404
99.0	Reimbursable obligations	280	388	242
99.9	Total new obligations, unexpired accounts	4,485	5,197	5,646

Employment Summary

Identification code 013–1450–0–1–306		2021 actual	2022 est.	2023 est.
1001	Direct civilian full-time equivalent employment	10,767	10,979	11,344
1101	Direct military average strength employment	323	330	338
2001	Reimbursable civilian full-time equivalent employment	465	469	469

GULF COAST ECOSYSTEM RESTORATION SCIENCE, OBSERVATION, MONITORING, AND TECHNOLOGY

Program and Financing (in millions of dollars)

Identification code 013–1455–0–1–304		2021 actual	2022 est.	2023 est.
	Obligations by program activity:			
0801	Gulf Coast Restoration	7	7	8
	Budgetary resources:			
	Unobligated balance:			
1000	Unobligated balance brought forward, Oct 1	2	1	
	Budget authority:			
	Spending authority from offsetting collections, mandatory:			
1800	Collected	6	6	8
1930	Total budgetary resources available	8	7	8
	Memorandum (non-add) entries:			
1941	Unexpired unobligated balance, end of year	1		
	Change in obligated balance:			
	Unpaid obligations:			
3000	Unpaid obligations, brought forward, Oct 1	9	10	11
3010	New obligations, unexpired accounts	7	7	8
3020	Outlays (gross)	–6	–6	–7
3050	Unpaid obligations, end of year	10	11	12
	Memorandum (non-add) entries:			
3100	Obligated balance, start of year	9	10	11
3200	Obligated balance, end of year	10	11	12
	Budget authority and outlays, net:			
	Mandatory:			
4090	Budget authority, gross	6	6	8
	Outlays, gross:			
4100	Outlays from new mandatory authority	1	2	2
4101	Outlays from mandatory balances	5	4	5
4110	Outlays, gross (total)	6	6	7
	Offsets against gross budget authority and outlays:			
	Offsetting collections (collected) from:			
4120	Federal sources	–6	–6	–8
4180	Budget authority, net (total)			
4190	Outlays, net (total)			–1

The Gulf Coast Ecosystem Restoration Science, Observation, Monitoring and Technology Fund provides funding for the NOAA RESTORE Act Science Program. The purpose of this program is to initiate and sustain an integrative, holistic understanding of the Gulf of Mexico ecosystem and support, to the maximum extent practicable, restoration efforts and the long-term sustainability of the ecosystem, including its fish stocks, fishing industries, habitat, and wildlife through ecosystem research, observation, monitoring, and technology development. To ensure the best use of resources the Program will coordinate with existing federal and state science and technology programs, including other activities funded under the RESTORE Act. Section 1604 of the RESTORE Act authorized funding for the Program by providing 2.5 percent of the funds made available through the Gulf Coast Restoration Trust Fund.

Object Classification (in millions of dollars)

Identification code 013–1455–0–1–304		2021 actual	2022 est.	2023 est.
	Reimbursable obligations:			
25.2	Other services from non-Federal sources	1	1	1
41.0	Grants, subsidies, and contributions	5	5	6
99.0	Reimbursable obligations	6	6	7
99.5	Adjustment for rounding	1	1	1
99.9	Total new obligations, unexpired accounts	7	7	8

GULF COAST ECOSYSTEM RESTORATION SCIENCE, OBSERVATION, MONITORING, AND TECHNOLOGY—Continued

Employment Summary

Identification code 013–1455–0–1–304	2021 actual	2022 est.	2023 est.
1001 Direct civilian full-time equivalent employment	3	2	2

PROCUREMENT, ACQUISITION AND CONSTRUCTION

(INCLUDING TRANSFER OF FUNDS)

For procurement, acquisition and construction of capital assets, including alteration and modification costs, of the National Oceanic and Atmospheric Administration, $2,332,662,000, to remain available until September 30, 2025, except that funds provided for acquisition and construction of vessels and aircraft, and construction of facilities shall remain available until expended: Provided, That of the $2,345,662,000 provided for in direct obligations under this heading, $2,332,662,000 is appropriated from the general fund and $13,000,000 is provided from recoveries of prior year obligations: Provided further, That the Secretary of Commerce shall include in budget justification materials for fiscal year 2024 that the Secretary submits to Congress in support of the Department of Commerce budget (as submitted with the budget of the President under section 1105(a) of title 31, United States Code) an estimate for each National Oceanic and Atmospheric Administration procurement, acquisition or construction project having a total of more than $5,000,000 and simultaneously the budget justification shall include an estimate of the budgetary requirements for each such project for each of the 5 subsequent fiscal years.

Note.—A full-year 2022 appropriation for this account was not enacted at the time the Budget was prepared; therefore, the Budget assumes this account is operating under the Continuing Appropriations Act, 2022 (Division A of Public Law 117–43, as amended). The amounts included for 2022 reflect the annualized level provided by the continuing resolution.

PROCUREMENT, ACQUISITION AND CONSTRUCTION

[For an additional amount for "Procurement, Acquisition and Construction" for necessary expenses related to the consequences of hurricanes and of wildfires in calendar years 2020 and 2021, $52,205,000, to remain available until September 30, 2024, as follows:]

[(1) $2,205,000 for repair and replacement of observing assets, real property, and equipment; and]

[(2) $50,000,000 for improvements to operational and research weather and climate supercomputing and dissemination infrastructure, observing assets, and satellites, along with associated ground systems, used for hurricane intensity and track prediction; precipitation and flood prediction, forecasting, and mitigation; and wildfire research, prediction, detection, forecasting, and monitoring: *Provided*, That the National Oceanic and Atmospheric Administration shall submit a spending plan to the Committees on Appropriations of the House of Representatives and the Senate within 45 days after the date of enactment of this Act.] *(Disaster Relief Supplemental Appropriations Act, 2022.)*

PROCUREMENT, ACQUISITION AND CONSTRUCTION

[For an additional amount for "Procurement, Acquisition and Construction", $180,000,000, to remain available until September 30, 2024, as follows:]

[(1) $50,000,000 shall be for observation and dissemination infrastructure used for wildfire prediction, detection, and forecasting;]

[(2) $80,000,000 shall be for research supercomputing infrastructure used for weather and climate model development to improve drought, flood, and wildfire prediction, detection, and forecasting; and]

[(3) $50,000,000 shall be for coastal, ocean, and Great Lakes observing systems:]

[*Provided*, That not later than 90 days after the date of enactment of this Act, the National Oceanic and Atmospheric Administration shall submit to the Committees on Appropriations of the House of Representatives and the Senate a detailed spend plan: *Provided further*, That such amount is designated by the Congress as being for an emergency requirement pursuant to section 4112(a) of H. Con. Res. 71 (115th Congress), the concurrent resolution on the budget for fiscal year 2018, and to section 251(b) of the Balanced Budget and Emergency Deficit Control Act of 1985.] *(Infrastructure Investments and Jobs Appropriations Act.)*

Program and Financing (in millions of dollars)

Identification code 013–1460–0–1–306	2021 actual	2022 est.	2023 est.
Obligations by program activity:			
0001 National Ocean Service	8	9	9
0003 Office of Oceanic and Atmospheric Research	43	44	108
0004 National Weather Service	133	104	104
0005 National Environmental Satellite Service	1,224	1,225	1,874
0007 Spectrum Relocation Fund	21	30	10
0008 Mission Support	28	43	146
0009 Office of Marine and Aviation Operations	68	120	105
0010 2022 Supplemental	....	52	....
0011 IIJA	....	180	....
0900 Total new obligations, unexpired accounts	1,525	1,807	2,356
Budgetary resources:			
Unobligated balance:			
1000 Unobligated balance brought forward, Oct 1	273	328	297
1001 Discretionary unobligated balance brought fwd, Oct 1	215	288	....
1021 Recoveries of prior year unpaid obligations	18	13	13
1033 Recoveries of prior year paid obligations	1	....	....
1070 Unobligated balance (total)	292	341	310
Budget authority:			
Appropriations, discretionary:			
1100 Appropriation	1,533	1,765	2,333
1120 Appropriations transferred to other accts [013–1450]	–3	....	....
1120 Appropriations transferred to other accts [013–0126]	–2	–2	....
1121 Appropriations transferred from other acct [013–1450]	33	....	....
1160 Appropriation, discretionary (total)	1,561	1,763	2,333
1900 Budget authority (total)	1,561	1,763	2,333
1930 Total budgetary resources available	1,853	2,104	2,643
Memorandum (non-add) entries:			
1941 Unexpired unobligated balance, end of year	328	297	287
Change in obligated balance:			
Unpaid obligations:			
3000 Unpaid obligations, brought forward, Oct 1	2,510	2,538	1,981
3010 New obligations, unexpired accounts	1,525	1,807	2,356
3020 Outlays (gross)	–1,474	–2,351	–1,933
3040 Recoveries of prior year unpaid obligations, unexpired	–18	–13	–13
3041 Recoveries of prior year unpaid obligations, expired	–5	....	....
3050 Unpaid obligations, end of year	2,538	1,981	2,391
Memorandum (non-add) entries:			
3100 Obligated balance, start of year	2,510	2,538	1,981
3200 Obligated balance, end of year	2,538	1,981	2,391
Budget authority and outlays, net:			
Discretionary:			
4000 Budget authority, gross	1,561	1,763	2,333
Outlays, gross:			
4010 Outlays from new discretionary authority	255	520	793
4011 Outlays from discretionary balances	1,195	1,803	1,126
4020 Outlays, gross (total)	1,450	2,323	1,919
Offsets against gross budget authority and outlays:			
Offsetting collections (collected) from:			
4030 Federal sources	–1	....	....
4040 Offsets against gross budget authority and outlays (total)	–1	....	....
Additional offsets against gross budget authority only:			
4053 Recoveries of prior year paid obligations, unexpired accounts	1	....	....
4060 Additional offsets against budget authority only (total)	1	....	....
4070 Budget authority, net (discretionary)	1,561	1,763	2,333
4080 Outlays, net (discretionary)	1,449	2,323	1,919
Mandatory:			
Outlays, gross:			
4101 Outlays from mandatory balances	24	28	14
4180 Budget authority, net (total)	1,561	1,763	2,333
4190 Outlays, net (total)	1,473	2,351	1,933

This account funds capital acquisition, construction, and fleet and aircraft replacement projects that support NOAA's operational mission across all line offices. The Budget maintains continuity of major systems needed for weather forecasting and continues implementation of NOAA's fleet recapitalization plan.

DEPARTMENT OF COMMERCE

Object Classification (in millions of dollars)

Identification code 013–1460–0–1–306	2021 actual	2022 est.	2023 est.
Direct obligations:			
Personnel compensation:			
11.1 Full-time permanent	45	41	52
11.5 Other personnel compensation	1	1	1
11.9 Total personnel compensation	46	42	53
12.1 Civilian personnel benefits	19	18	23
21.0 Travel and transportation of persons	....	1	1
23.1 Rental payments to GSA	5	5	7
23.3 Communications, utilities, and miscellaneous charges	4	3	4
25.1 Advisory and assistance services	263	231	301
25.2 Other services from non-Federal sources	186	404	527
25.3 Other goods and services from Federal sources	697	917	1,198
25.5 Research and development contracts	52	20	26
26.0 Supplies and materials	14	20	26
31.0 Equipment	187	90	117
32.0 Land and structures	....	3	4
41.0 Grants, subsidies, and contributions	52	53	69
99.9 Total new obligations, unexpired accounts	1,525	1,807	2,356

Employment Summary

Identification code 013–1460–0–1–306	2021 actual	2022 est.	2023 est.
1001 Direct civilian full-time equivalent employment	309	287	323

LIMITED ACCESS SYSTEM ADMINISTRATION FUND

Special and Trust Fund Receipts (in millions of dollars)

Identification code 013–5284–0–2–306	2021 actual	2022 est.	2023 est.
0100 Balance, start of year	1	2	2
Receipts:			
Current law:			
1110 Permit Title Registration Fees, Limited Access System Administration Fund	12	15	15
2000 Total: Balances and receipts	13	17	17
Appropriations:			
Current law:			
2101 Limited Access System Administration Fund	–12	–15	–15
2103 Limited Access System Administration Fund	....	–1	–1
2132 Limited Access System Administration Fund	1	1	1
2199 Total current law appropriations	–11	–15	–15
2999 Total appropriations	–11	–15	–15
5099 Balance, end of year	2	2	2

Program and Financing (in millions of dollars)

Identification code 013–5284–0–2–306	2021 actual	2022 est.	2023 est.
Obligations by program activity:			
0001 Limited Access System Administration Fund (Direct)	13	14	15
Budgetary resources:			
Unobligated balance:			
1000 Unobligated balance brought forward, Oct 1	20	20	21
1021 Recoveries of prior year unpaid obligations	2	....	....
1070 Unobligated balance (total)	22	20	21
Budget authority:			
Appropriations, mandatory:			
1201 Appropriation (special or trust fund)	12	15	15
1203 Appropriation (Mandatory, Sequestration pop-up, Authorizing Committee)	....	1	1
1232 Appropriations and/or unobligated balance of appropriations temporarily reduced	–1	–1	–1
1260 Appropriations, mandatory (total)	11	15	15
1930 Total budgetary resources available	33	35	36
Memorandum (non-add) entries:			
1941 Unexpired unobligated balance, end of year	20	21	21
Change in obligated balance:			
Unpaid obligations:			
3000 Unpaid obligations, brought forward, Oct 1	11	10	6
3010 New obligations, unexpired accounts	13	14	15
3020 Outlays (gross)	–12	–18	–20
3040 Recoveries of prior year unpaid obligations, unexpired	–2	....	....
3050 Unpaid obligations, end of year	10	6	1
Memorandum (non-add) entries:			
3100 Obligated balance, start of year	11	10	6
3200 Obligated balance, end of year	10	6	1
Budget authority and outlays, net:			
Mandatory:			
4090 Budget authority, gross	11	15	15
Outlays, gross:			
4100 Outlays from new mandatory authority	5	8	8
4101 Outlays from mandatory balances	7	10	12
4110 Outlays, gross (total)	12	18	20
4180 Budget authority, net (total)	11	15	15
4190 Outlays, net (total)	12	18	20

Under the authority of the Magnuson-Stevens Act Section 304(d)(2)(A), NMFS must collect a fee to recover the incremental costs of management, data collection, and enforcement of Limited Access Privilege (LAP) Programs. Funds collected under this authority are deposited into the Limited Access System Administrative Fund. Fees shall not exceed three percent of the ex-vessel value of fish harvested under any such program, and shall be collected at either the time of the landing, filing of a landing report, or sale of such fish during a fishing season or in the last quarter of the calendar year in which the fish is harvested. The Limited Access Administration Fund shall be available, without appropriation or fiscal year limitation, only for the purposes of administering the central registry system and administering and implementing the Magnuson-Stevens Act in the fishery in which the fees were collected. Sums in the fund that are not currently needed for these purposes shall be kept on deposit or invested in obligations of, or guaranteed by the U.S. Also, in establishing a LAP program, a Regional Council can consider, and may provide, if appropriate, an auction system or other program to collect royalties for the initial or any subsequent distribution of allocations. If an auction system is developed, revenues from these royalties are deposited in the Limited Access System Administration Fund.

Object Classification (in millions of dollars)

Identification code 013–5284–0–2–306	2021 actual	2022 est.	2023 est.
11.1 Direct obligations: Personnel compensation: Full-time permanent	4	4	4
11.9 Total personnel compensation	4	4	4
12.1 Civilian personnel benefits	1	2	1
25.2 Other services from non-Federal sources	5	4	6
41.0 Grants, subsidies, and contributions	3	4	4
99.0 Direct obligations	13	14	15
99.9 Total new obligations, unexpired accounts	13	14	15

Employment Summary

Identification code 013–5284–0–2–306	2021 actual	2022 est.	2023 est.
1001 Direct civilian full-time equivalent employment	28	28	28

PACIFIC COASTAL SALMON RECOVERY

For necessary expenses associated with the restoration of Pacific salmon populations, $65,000,000, to remain available until September 30, 2024: Provided, That, of the funds provided herein, the Secretary of Commerce may issue grants to the States of Washington, Oregon, Idaho, Nevada, California, and Alaska, and to the federally recognized Tribes of the Columbia River and Pacific Coast (including Alaska), for projects necessary for conservation of salmon and steelhead populations that are listed as threatened or endangered, or that are identified by a State as at-risk to be so listed, for maintaining populations necessary for exercise of Tribal treaty fishing rights or native subsistence fishing, or for conservation of Pacific coastal salmon and steelhead habitat, based on guidelines to be developed by the Secretary of Commerce: Provided further, That all funds shall be allocated based

PACIFIC COASTAL SALMON RECOVERY—Continued

on scientific and other merit principles and shall not be available for marketing activities: Provided further, That funds disbursed to States shall be subject to a matching requirement of funds or documented in-kind contributions of at least 33 percent of the Federal funds.

Note.—A full-year 2022 appropriation for this account was not enacted at the time the Budget was prepared; therefore, the Budget assumes this account is operating under the Continuing Appropriations Act, 2022 (Division A of Public Law 117–43, as amended). The amounts included for 2022 reflect the annualized level provided by the continuing resolution.

PACIFIC COASTAL SALMON RECOVERY

[For an additional amount for "Pacific Coastal Salmon Recovery", $172,000,000, to remain available until September 30, 2027: *Provided*, That $34,400,000, to remain available until September 30, 2023, shall be made available for fiscal year 2022, $34,400,000, to remain available until September 30, 2024, shall be made available for fiscal year 2023, $34,400,000, to remain available until September 30, 2025, shall be made available for fiscal year 2024, $34,400,000, to remain available until September 30, 2026, shall be made available for fiscal year 2025, and $34,400,000, to remain available until September 30, 2027, shall be made available for fiscal year 2026: *Provided*, That not later than 90 days after the date of enactment of this Act, the National Oceanic and Atmospheric Administration shall submit to the Committees on Appropriations of the House of Representatives and the Senate a spend plan for fiscal year 2022: *Provided further*, That for each of fiscal years 2023 through 2026, as part of the annual budget submission of the President under section 1105(a) of title 31, United States Code, the Secretary of Commerce shall submit a detailed spend plan for that fiscal year: *Provided further*, That the Secretary may waive or reduce the required non-Federal share for amounts made available under this heading in this Act: *Provided further*, That such amount is designated by the Congress as being for an emergency requirement pursuant to section 4112(a) of H. Con. Res. 71 (115th Congress), the concurrent resolution on the budget for fiscal year 2018, and to section 251(b) of the Balanced Budget and Emergency Deficit Control Act of 1985.] *(Infrastructure Investments and Jobs Appropriations Act.)*

Program and Financing (in millions of dollars)

Identification code 013–1451–0–1–306	2021 actual	2022 est.	2023 est.
Obligations by program activity:			
0008 Grants to States and Tribes	65	99	99
0900 Total new obligations, unexpired accounts (object class 41.0)	65	99	99
Budgetary resources:			
Budget authority:			
Appropriations, discretionary:			
1100 Appropriation	65	99	65
Advance appropriations, discretionary:			
1170 Advance appropriation			34
1900 Budget authority (total)	65	99	99
1930 Total budgetary resources available	65	99	99
Change in obligated balance:			
Unpaid obligations:			
3000 Unpaid obligations, brought forward, Oct 1	200	207	208
3010 New obligations, unexpired accounts	65	99	99
3020 Outlays (gross)	−58	−98	−107
3050 Unpaid obligations, end of year	207	208	200
Memorandum (non-add) entries:			
3100 Obligated balance, start of year	200	207	208
3200 Obligated balance, end of year	207	208	200
Budget authority and outlays, net:			
Discretionary:			
4000 Budget authority, gross	65	99	99
Outlays, gross:			
4010 Outlays from new discretionary authority		24	24
4011 Outlays from discretionary balances	58	74	83
4020 Outlays, gross (total)	58	98	107
4180 Budget authority, net (total)	65	99	99
4190 Outlays, net (total)	58	98	107

The Pacific Coastal Salmon Recovery Fund account was established in 2000 to augment State, tribal, and local programs to conserve and restore sustainable Pacific salmon populations and their habitats. Through 2021, over $1.6 billion has been provided to the States of California, Oregon, Washington, Alaska, and Idaho and to the Pacific Coastal and Columbia River Tribes to conserve salmon.

Employment Summary

Identification code 013–1451–0–1–306	2021 actual	2022 est.	2023 est.
1001 Direct civilian full-time equivalent employment	2	2	2

MEDICARE-ELIGIBLE RETIREE HEALTH FUND CONTRIBUTION, NOAA

Program and Financing (in millions of dollars)

Identification code 013–1465–0–1–306	2021 actual	2022 est.	2023 est.
Obligations by program activity:			
0001 Medicare-eligible Retiree Health Fund Contribution, NOAA (Direct)	2	2	2
0900 Total new obligations, unexpired accounts (object class 25.3)	2	2	2
Budgetary resources:			
Budget authority:			
Appropriations, discretionary:			
1100 Appropriation	2	2	2
1930 Total budgetary resources available	2	2	2
Change in obligated balance:			
Unpaid obligations:			
3010 New obligations, unexpired accounts	2	2	2
3020 Outlays (gross)	−2	−2	−2
Budget authority and outlays, net:			
Discretionary:			
4000 Budget authority, gross	2	2	2
Outlays, gross:			
4010 Outlays from new discretionary authority	2	2	2
4180 Budget authority, net (total)	2	2	2
4190 Outlays, net (total)	2	2	2

This account includes amounts necessary to finance the cost of Tricare retirement health care benefits accrued by the active duty members of the NOAA Commissioned Corps. The Ronald W. Reagan National Defense Authorization Act for 2005 (P.L. 108–375) provided permanent, indefinite appropriations to finance these costs for all uniformed service members. As these costs are borne in support of NOAA's mission, they are shown as part of the NOAA discretionary total. Total obligations on behalf of active NOAA Commissioned Corps personnel include both the wages and related amounts requested for appropriation and amounts paid from the permanent, indefinite authority.

FISHERIES ENFORCEMENT ASSET FORFEITURE FUND

Special and Trust Fund Receipts (in millions of dollars)

Identification code 013–5583–0–2–376	2021 actual	2022 est.	2023 est.
0100 Balance, start of year	5		
Receipts:			
Current law:			
1120 Fisheries Enforcement Asset Forfeiture Fund, Deposits (PDF Account)	2	3	3
2000 Total: Balances and receipts	7	3	3
Appropriations:			
Current law:			
2101 Fisheries Enforcement Asset Forfeiture Fund	−2	−3	−3
2103 Fisheries Enforcement Asset Forfeiture Fund	−5		
2199 Total current law appropriations	−7	−3	−3
2999 Total appropriations	−7	−3	−3
5099 Balance, end of year			

DEPARTMENT OF COMMERCE

Program and Financing (in millions of dollars)

Identification code 013–5583–0–2–376	2021 actual	2022 est.	2023 est.
Obligations by program activity:			
0001 Fisheries Enforcement Asset Forfeiture Fund (Direct)	5	5	3
Budgetary resources:			
Unobligated balance:			
1000 Unobligated balance brought forward, Oct 1	10	7	....
Budget authority:			
Appropriations, discretionary:			
1131 Unobligated balance of appropriations permanently reduced	....	–5	....
Appropriations, mandatory:			
1201 Appropriation (special or trust fund)	2	3	3
1203 Appropriation (previously unavailable)(special or trust)	5	....	....
1230 Appropriations and/or unobligated balance of appropriations permanently reduced	–5	....	....
1260 Appropriations, mandatory (total)	2	3	3
1900 Budget authority (total)	2	–2	3
1930 Total budgetary resources available	12	5	3
Memorandum (non-add) entries:			
1941 Unexpired unobligated balance, end of year	7	....	....
Change in obligated balance:			
Unpaid obligations:			
3000 Unpaid obligations, brought forward, Oct 1	4	6	7
3010 New obligations, unexpired accounts	5	5	3
3020 Outlays (gross)	–3	–4	–5
3050 Unpaid obligations, end of year	6	7	5
Memorandum (non-add) entries:			
3100 Obligated balance, start of year	4	6	7
3200 Obligated balance, end of year	6	7	5
Budget authority and outlays, net:			
Discretionary:			
4000 Budget authority, gross	....	–5	....
Outlays, gross:			
4010 Outlays from new discretionary authority	....	–5	....
Mandatory:			
4090 Budget authority, gross	2	3	3
Outlays, gross:			
4100 Outlays from new mandatory authority	2	2	2
4101 Outlays from mandatory balances	1	7	3
4110 Outlays, gross (total)	3	9	5
4180 Budget authority, net (total)	2	–2	3
4190 Outlays, net (total)	3	4	5

Section 311(e)(1) of the Magnuson-Stevens Fishery Conservation and Management Act (MSA) authorizes the Secretary of Commerce (Secretary) to pay certain enforcement-related expenses from fines, penalties and forfeiture proceeds received for violations of the Magnuson-Stevens Act, or of any other marine resource law enforced by the Secretary. Pursuant to this authority, NOAA has established a Civil Monetary Penalty/Asset Forfeiture Fund (AFF) where proceeds are deposited. When Congress authorized the AFF, it was deemed appropriate to use these proceeds to offset in part the costs of administering the enforcement program. Expenses funded through this source include: costs directly related to the storage, maintenance, and care of seized fish, vessels, or other property during a civil or criminal proceeding; expenditures related directly to specific investigations and enforcement proceedings such as travel for interviewing witnesses; enforcement-unique information technology infrastructure; and annual interagency agreement costs for the administration, adjudication process, including Administrative Law Judges.

Object Classification (in millions of dollars)

Identification code 013–5583–0–2–376	2021 actual	2022 est.	2023 est.
Direct obligations:			
21.0 Travel and transportation of persons	1	1	1
25.3 Other goods and services from Federal sources	3	4	2
99.0 Direct obligations	4	5	3
99.5 Adjustment for rounding	1	....	....
99.9 Total new obligations, unexpired accounts	5	5	3

PROMOTE AND DEVELOP FISHERY PRODUCTS AND RESEARCH PERTAINING TO AMERICAN FISHERIES

Special and Trust Fund Receipts (in millions of dollars)

Identification code 013–5139–0–2–376	2021 actual	2022 est.	2023 est.
0100 Balance, start of year	11	15	14
Receipts:			
Current law:			
1110 Access Fees, Western Pacific Sustainable Fisheries Fund	1	1	1
2000 Total: Balances and receipts	12	16	15
Appropriations:			
Current law:			
2101 Promote and Develop Fishery Products and Research Pertaining to American Fisheries	–1	–1	–1
2103 Promote and Develop Fishery Products and Research Pertaining to American Fisheries	–11	–15	–14
2132 Promote and Develop Fishery Products and Research Pertaining to American Fisheries	15	14	21
2199 Total current law appropriations	3	–2	6
2999 Total appropriations	3	–2	6
5099 Balance, end of year	15	14	21

Program and Financing (in millions of dollars)

Identification code 013–5139–0–2–376	2021 actual	2022 est.	2023 est.
Obligations by program activity:			
0001 Promote and Develop Fishery Products and Research	11	8	7
0002 Western Pacific Sustainability Fisheries Fund	1	1	1
0900 Total new obligations, unexpired accounts	12	9	8
Budgetary resources:			
Unobligated balance:			
1000 Unobligated balance brought forward, Oct 1	1	2	3
Budget authority:			
Appropriations, discretionary:			
1120 Appropriations transferred to other accts [013–1450]	....	–246	–349
Appropriations, mandatory:			
1201 Appropriation (special or trust fund)	1	1	1
1203 Appropriation (Sequestration pop-up, Authorizing Committee)	11	15	14
1220 Appropriations transferred to other accts [013–1450]	–246	....	....
1221 Appropriations transferred from other acct [012–5209]	262	254	363
1232 Appropriations and/or unobligated balance of appropriations temporarily reduced	–15	–14	–21
1260 Appropriations, mandatory (total)	13	256	357
1900 Budget authority (total)	13	10	8
1930 Total budgetary resources available	14	12	11
Memorandum (non-add) entries:			
1941 Unexpired unobligated balance, end of year	2	3	3
Change in obligated balance:			
Unpaid obligations:			
3000 Unpaid obligations, brought forward, Oct 1	17	23	21
3010 New obligations, unexpired accounts	12	9	8
3020 Outlays (gross)	–6	–11	–10
3050 Unpaid obligations, end of year	23	21	19
Memorandum (non-add) entries:			
3100 Obligated balance, start of year	17	23	21
3200 Obligated balance, end of year	23	21	19
Budget authority and outlays, net:			
Discretionary:			
4000 Budget authority, gross	....	–246	–349
Outlays, gross:			
4010 Outlays from new discretionary authority	....	–246	–349
Mandatory:			
4090 Budget authority, gross	13	256	357
Outlays, gross:			
4100 Outlays from new mandatory authority	....	240	342
4101 Outlays from mandatory balances	6	17	17
4110 Outlays, gross (total)	6	257	359
4180 Budget authority, net (total)	13	10	8

PROMOTE AND DEVELOP FISHERY PRODUCTS AND RESEARCH PERTAINING TO AMERICAN FISHERIES—Continued

Program and Financing—Continued

Identification code 013–5139–0–2–376	2021 actual	2022 est.	2023 est.
4190 Outlays, net (total)	6	11	10

An amount equal to 30 percent of the gross receipts from customs duties on imported fishery products is transferred to the Department of Commerce annually from the Department of Agriculture. NOAA transfers a portion of these funds to offset the appropriations for fisheries research and management in the Operations, Research, and Facilities account. Remaining funds will support the Saltonstall-Kennedy grants program for fisheries research and development projects to enhance to productivity and improve the sustainable yield of domestic marine fisheries resouces.

Object Classification (in millions of dollars)

Identification code 013–5139–0–2–376	2021 actual	2022 est.	2023 est.
Direct obligations:			
25.2 Other services from non-Federal sources	1	1	1
41.0 Grants, subsidies, and contributions	11	8	7
99.0 Direct obligations	12	9	8
99.9 Total new obligations, unexpired accounts	12	9	8

FISHERMEN'S CONTINGENCY FUND

For carrying out the provisions of title IV of Public Law 95–372, not to exceed $349,000, to be derived from receipts collected pursuant to that Act, to remain available until expended.

Note.—A full-year 2022 appropriation for this account was not enacted at the time the Budget was prepared; therefore, the Budget assumes this account is operating under the Continuing Appropriations Act, 2022 (Division A of Public Law 117–43, as amended). The amounts included for 2022 reflect the annualized level provided by the continuing resolution.

Program and Financing (in millions of dollars)

Identification code 013–5120–0–2–376	2021 actual	2022 est.	2023 est.
Budgetary resources:			
Unobligated balance:			
1000 Unobligated balance brought forward, Oct 1	1	1	1
1930 Total budgetary resources available	1	1	1
Memorandum (non-add) entries:			
1941 Unexpired unobligated balance, end of year	1	1	1
4180 Budget authority, net (total)			
4190 Outlays, net (total)			

The Fishermen's Contingency Fund is authorized under Section 402 of Title IV of the Outer Continental Shelf Lands Act Amendments of 1978. NOAA compensates U.S. commercial fishermen for damage or loss of fishing gear, vessels, and resulting economic loss caused by obstructions related to oil and gas exploration, development, and production in any area of the Outer Continental Shelf. The funds used to provide this compensation are derived from fees collected by the Secretary of the Interior from the holders of leases, exploration permits, easements, or rights-of-way in areas of the Outer Continental Shelf. This activity is funded entirely through user fees. Disbursements can be made only to the extent authorized in appropriation acts.

FISHERIES DISASTER ASSISTANCE

For necessary expenses of administering the fishery disaster assistance programs authorized by the Magnuson-Stevens Fishery Conservation and Management Act (Public Law 94–265) and the Interjurisdictional Fisheries Act (title III of Public Law 99–659), $300,000, to remain available until September 30, 2023.

Note.—A full-year 2022 appropriation for this account was not enacted at the time the Budget was prepared; therefore, the Budget assumes this account is operating under the Continuing Appropriations Act, 2022 (Division A of Public Law 117–43, as amended). The amounts included for 2022 reflect the annualized level provided by the continuing resolution.

FISHERIES DISASTER ASSISTANCE

[*For an additional amount for "Fisheries Disaster Assistance" for necessary expenses associated with the mitigation of fishery disasters, $200,000,000, to remain available until expended: Provided, That such funds shall be used for mitigating the effects of commercial fishery failures and fishery resource disasters declared by the Secretary of Commerce, including those declared by the Secretary to be a direct result of hurricanes in calendar years 2020 and 2021.*] *(Disaster Relief Supplemental Appropriations Act, 2022.)*

Program and Financing (in millions of dollars)

Identification code 013–2055–0–1–376	2021 actual	2022 est.	2023 est.
Obligations by program activity:			
0001 Declared Fishery Disaster - (State TBD)	354	315	
Budgetary resources:			
Unobligated balance:			
1000 Unobligated balance brought forward, Oct 1	169	115	
Budget authority:			
Appropriations, discretionary:			
1100 Appropriation	300	200	
1930 Total budgetary resources available	469	315	
Memorandum (non-add) entries:			
1941 Unexpired unobligated balance, end of year	115		
Change in obligated balance:			
Unpaid obligations:			
3000 Unpaid obligations, brought forward, Oct 1	402	493	410
3010 New obligations, unexpired accounts	354	315	
3020 Outlays (gross)	–263	–398	–240
3050 Unpaid obligations, end of year	493	410	170
Memorandum (non-add) entries:			
3100 Obligated balance, start of year	402	493	410
3200 Obligated balance, end of year	493	410	170
Budget authority and outlays, net:			
Discretionary:			
4000 Budget authority, gross	300	200	
Outlays, gross:			
4010 Outlays from new discretionary authority	16		
4011 Outlays from discretionary balances	247	398	240
4020 Outlays, gross (total)	263	398	240
4180 Budget authority, net (total)	300	200	
4190 Outlays, net (total)	263	398	240

Fishery disaster assistance is administered by NOAA's National Marine Fisheries Service within the Department of Commerce. Two statutes, the Magnuson-Stevens Fishery Conservation and Management Act and the Interjurisdictional Fisheries Act, provide the authority for fishery disaster assistance. Under both statutes, a request for a fishery disaster determination is generally made by the Governor of a State, or an elected leader of a fishing community, although the Secretary of Commerce may also initiate a review at his or her own discretion. The Secretary determines whether the circumstances are consistent with relevant statutes and warrant a fishery disaster determination. If the Secretary determines that a fishery disaster has occurred, the fishery is eligible for disaster assistance subject to appropriation of funds by Congress.

Object Classification (in millions of dollars)

Identification code 013–2055–0–1–376	2021 actual	2022 est.	2023 est.
Direct obligations:			
25.1 Advisory and assistance services	3	3	
41.0 Grants, subsidies, and contributions	351	311	
99.0 Direct obligations	354	314	
99.5 Adjustment for rounding		1	
99.9 Total new obligations, unexpired accounts	354	315	

DEPARTMENT OF COMMERCE

National Oceanic and Atmospheric Administration—Continued
Federal Funds—Continued
211

Employment Summary

Identification code 013–2055–0–1–376	2021 actual	2022 est.	2023 est.
1001 Direct civilian full-time equivalent employment	....	....	1

NORTH PACIFIC FISHERY OBSERVER FUND

Special and Trust Fund Receipts (in millions of dollars)

Identification code 013–5598–0–2–306	2021 actual	2022 est.	2023 est.
0100 Balance, start of year	....	....	....
Receipts:			
Current law:			
1110 Fees, North Pacific Fishery Observer Fund	2	3	4
2000 Total: Balances and receipts	2	3	4
Appropriations:			
Current law:			
2101 North Pacific Fishery Observer Fund	–2	–3	–4
5099 Balance, end of year	....	....	....

Program and Financing (in millions of dollars)

Identification code 013–5598–0–2–306	2021 actual	2022 est.	2023 est.
Obligations by program activity:			
0001 North Pacific Fishery Observer Fund	3	3	4
0900 Total new obligations, unexpired accounts (object class 25.2)	3	3	4
Budgetary resources:			
Unobligated balance:			
1000 Unobligated balance brought forward, Oct 1	1	....	....
Budget authority:			
Appropriations, mandatory:			
1201 Appropriation (special or trust fund)	2	3	4
1930 Total budgetary resources available	3	3	4
Change in obligated balance:			
Unpaid obligations:			
3000 Unpaid obligations, brought forward, Oct 1	5	6	6
3010 New obligations, unexpired accounts	3	3	4
3020 Outlays (gross)	–2	–3	–3
3050 Unpaid obligations, end of year	6	6	7
Memorandum (non-add) entries:			
3100 Obligated balance, start of year	5	6	6
3200 Obligated balance, end of year	6	6	7
Budget authority and outlays, net:			
Mandatory:			
4090 Budget authority, gross	2	3	4
Outlays, gross:			
4101 Outlays from mandatory balances	2	3	3
4180 Budget authority, net (total)	2	3	4
4190 Outlays, net (total)	2	3	3

In 2013, the North Pacific Observer Fund was established to support the restructured North Pacific Groundfish Observer Program (NPGOP). The observer program places all vessels and processors in the groundfish and halibut fisheries off Alaska into one of two observer coverage categories: (1) a full coverage category, and (2) a partial coverage category. Vessels and processors in the full coverage category (100% observer coverage) will obtain observers by contracting directly with observer providers. Vessels and processors in the partial coverage category (less than 100% observer coverage) will no longer contract independently with an observer provider, and will be required to carry an observer when they are selected through the Observer Declare and Deploy System (ODDS). Additionally, landings from all vessels in the partial coverage category will be assessed a 1.25 percent fee on standard ex-vessel prices of the landed catch weight of groundfish and halibut to be deposited in the North Pacific Observer Fund. The fee percentage is set in regulation and will be reviewed periodically by the North Pacific Fishery Management Council. The money generated by this fee will be used to pay for observer coverage on the vessels and processors in the partial coverage category in the following year.

ENVIRONMENTAL IMPROVEMENT AND RESTORATION FUND

Special and Trust Fund Receipts (in millions of dollars)

Identification code 013–5362–0–2–302	2021 actual	2022 est.	2023 est.
0100 Balance, start of year	3	3	8
Receipts:			
Current law:			
1140 Interest Earned, Environmental Improvement and Restoration Fund	....	5	2
2000 Total: Balances and receipts	3	8	10
5099 Balance, end of year	3	8	10

Program and Financing (in millions of dollars)

Identification code 013–5362–0–2–302	2021 actual	2022 est.	2023 est.
Obligations by program activity:			
0001 North Pacific Research Board	7	5	2
0900 Total new obligations, unexpired accounts (object class 41.0)	7	5	2
Budgetary resources:			
Budget authority:			
Appropriations, mandatory:			
1201 Appropriation (special or trust fund)	7	5	2
1930 Total budgetary resources available	7	5	2
Change in obligated balance:			
Unpaid obligations:			
3000 Unpaid obligations, brought forward, Oct 1	23	24	18
3010 New obligations, unexpired accounts	7	5	2
3020 Outlays (gross)	–6	–11	–11
3050 Unpaid obligations, end of year	24	18	9
Memorandum (non-add) entries:			
3100 Obligated balance, start of year	23	24	18
3200 Obligated balance, end of year	24	18	9
Budget authority and outlays, net:			
Mandatory:			
4090 Budget authority, gross	7	5	2
Outlays, gross:			
4101 Outlays from mandatory balances	6	11	11
4180 Budget authority, net (total)	7	5	2
4190 Outlays, net (total)	6	11	11

This fund was established by Title IV of P.L. 105–83. Twenty percent of the interest earned from this fund is made available to the Department of Commerce. Funds are to be used by Federal, State, private or foreign organizations or individuals to conduct research activities on or relating to the fisheries or marine ecosystems in the North Pacific Ocean, Bering Sea, and Arctic Ocean. Research priorities and grant requests are reviewed and approved by the North Pacific Research Board with emphasis placed on cooperative research efforts designed to address pressing fishery management or marine ecosystem information needs.

COASTAL ZONE MANAGEMENT FUND

Program and Financing (in millions of dollars)

Identification code 013–4313–0–3–306	2021 actual	2022 est.	2023 est.
Budgetary resources:			
Budget authority:			
Spending authority from offsetting collections, mandatory:			
1800 Collected	1	1	....
1820 Capital transfer of spending authority from offsetting collections to general fund	–1	–1	....

COASTAL ZONE MANAGEMENT FUND—Continued
Program and Financing—Continued

Identification code 013–4313–0–3–306	2021 actual	2022 est.	2023 est.
Budget authority and outlays, net:			
Mandatory:			
Offsets against gross budget authority and outlays:			
Offsetting collections (collected) from:			
4123 Non-Federal sources	....	–1	–1
4180 Budget authority, net (total)	....	–1	–1
4190 Outlays, net (total)	–1	–1	....

Status of Direct Loans (in millions of dollars)

Identification code 013–4313–0–3–306	2021 actual	2022 est.	2023 est.
Cumulative balance of direct loans outstanding:			
1210 Outstanding, start of year	17	16	15
1251 Repayments: Repayments and prepayments	–1	–1	....
1290 Outstanding, end of year	16	15	15

This fund consists of loan repayments from the former Coastal Energy Impact Program. The Department of Commerce Appropriations Act, 2012, cancelled all balances in the Coastal Zone Management Fund, made future payments to the Fund subject to the Federal Credit Reform Act of 1990, and eliminated the annual transfer from this account to the Operations, Research, and Facilities account. The display below includes reporting information consistent with all other credit liquidating accounts.

Balance Sheet (in millions of dollars)

Identification code 013–4313–0–3–306	2020 actual	2021 actual
ASSETS:		
1601 Direct loans, gross	17	16
1602 Interest receivable	5	5
1603 Allowance for estimated uncollectible loans and interest (-)	–19	–18
1699 Value of assets related to direct loans	3	3
1999 Total assets	3	3
LIABILITIES:		
2104 Federal liabilities: Resources payable to Treasury	....	....
NET POSITION:		
3300 Cumulative results of operations	3	3
4999 Total liabilities and net position	3	3

DAMAGE ASSESSMENT AND RESTORATION REVOLVING FUND

Program and Financing (in millions of dollars)

Identification code 013–4316–0–3–306	2021 actual	2022 est.	2023 est.
Obligations by program activity:			
0801 Damage Assessment and Restoration Revolving Fund (Reimbursable)	145	82	83
Budgetary resources:			
Unobligated balance:			
1000 Unobligated balance brought forward, Oct 1	165	238	272
1011 Unobligated balance transfer from other acct [014–1618]	193	50	50
1021 Recoveries of prior year unpaid obligations	2	20	20
1070 Unobligated balance (total)	360	308	342
Budget authority:			
Appropriations, mandatory:			
1221 Appropriations transferred from other acct [014–1618]	4	6	6
Spending authority from offsetting collections, mandatory:			
1800 Collected	19	40	10
1900 Budget authority (total)	23	46	16
1930 Total budgetary resources available	383	354	358
Memorandum (non-add) entries:			
1941 Unexpired unobligated balance, end of year	238	272	275
Change in obligated balance:			
Unpaid obligations:			
3000 Unpaid obligations, brought forward, Oct 1	38	144	60
3010 New obligations, unexpired accounts	145	82	83
3020 Outlays (gross)	–37	–146	–81
3040 Recoveries of prior year unpaid obligations, unexpired	–2	–20	–20
3050 Unpaid obligations, end of year	144	60	42
Memorandum (non-add) entries:			
3100 Obligated balance, start of year	38	144	60
3200 Obligated balance, end of year	144	60	42
Budget authority and outlays, net:			
Mandatory:			
4090 Budget authority, gross	23	46	16
Outlays, gross:			
4100 Outlays from new mandatory authority	15	23	8
4101 Outlays from mandatory balances	22	123	73
4110 Outlays, gross (total)	37	146	81
Offsets against gross budget authority and outlays:			
Offsetting collections (collected) from:			
4120 Federal sources	–16	–40	–10
4124 Offsetting governmental collections	–3	....	....
4130 Offsets against gross budget authority and outlays (total)	–19	–40	–10
4160 Budget authority, net (mandatory)	4	6	6
4170 Outlays, net (mandatory)	18	106	71
4180 Budget authority, net (total)	4	6	6
4190 Outlays, net (total)	18	106	71

The Damage Assessment and Restoration Revolving Fund is authorized under Section 1012(a) of the Oil Pollution Act of 1990, for the deposit of sums provided by any party or governmental entity to respond to the environmental effects of discharges of oil and other hazardous substances. Through the Revolving Fund, NOAA retains funds that are recovered through settlement or awarded by a court for the assessment and restoration of injured natural resources. NOAA also ensures deposited funds shall remain available to the trustee, without further appropriation, until expended to pay costs associated with the response, damage assessment, and restoration of natural resources.

These program functions are conducted jointly within NOAA by the Office of General Counsel, the National Ocean Service, and the National Marine Fisheries Service.

Object Classification (in millions of dollars)

Identification code 013–4316–0–3–306	2021 actual	2022 est.	2023 est.
11.1 Reimbursable obligations: Personnel compensation: Full-time permanent	5	2	2
11.9 Total personnel compensation	5	2	2
12.1 Civilian personnel benefits	2	1	1
25.1 Advisory and assistance services	2	1	1
25.2 Other services from non-Federal sources	106	55	56
41.0 Grants, subsidies, and contributions	25	18	18
44.0 Refunds	4	4	4
99.0 Reimbursable obligations	144	81	82
99.5 Adjustment for rounding	1	1	1
99.9 Total new obligations, unexpired accounts	145	82	83

Employment Summary

Identification code 013–4316–0–3–306	2021 actual	2022 est.	2023 est.
2001 Reimbursable civilian full-time equivalent employment	43	30	30

FISHERIES FINANCE PROGRAM ACCOUNT

Subject to section 502 of the Congressional Budget Act of 1974, during fiscal year 2023, obligations of direct loans may not exceed $24,000,000 for Individual Fishing Quota loans and not to exceed $100,000,000 for traditional direct loans as authorized by the Merchant Marine Act of 1936.

Note.—A full-year 2022 appropriation for this account was not enacted at the time the Budget was prepared; therefore, the Budget assumes this account is operating under the Continuing Appropriations Act, 2022 (Division A of Public Law 117–43, as amended). The amounts included for 2022 reflect the annualized level provided by the continuing resolution.

DEPARTMENT OF COMMERCE

Program and Financing (in millions of dollars)

Identification code 013–1456–0–1–376	2021 actual	2022 est.	2023 est.
Obligations by program activity:			
Credit program obligations:			
0705 Reestimates of direct loan subsidy		3	9
0706 Interest on reestimates of direct loan subsidy		1	8
0791 Direct program activities, subtotal		4	17
0900 Total new obligations, unexpired accounts (object class 41.0)		4	17
Budgetary resources:			
Unobligated balance:			
1000 Unobligated balance brought forward, Oct 1	3	3	3
Budget authority:			
Appropriations, mandatory:			
1200 Appropriation		4	17
1930 Total budgetary resources available	7	20	3
Memorandum (non-add) entries:			
1941 Unexpired unobligated balance, end of year	3	3	3
Change in obligated balance:			
Unpaid obligations:			
3010 New obligations, unexpired accounts		4	17
3020 Outlays (gross)		–4	–17
Budget authority and outlays, net:			
Mandatory:			
4090 Budget authority, gross		4	17
Outlays, gross:			
4100 Outlays from new mandatory authority		4	17
4180 Budget authority, net (total)		4	17
4190 Outlays, net (total)		4	17

Summary of Loan Levels, Subsidy Budget Authority and Outlays by Program (in millions of dollars)

Identification code 013–1456–0–1–376	2021 actual	2022 est.	2023 est.
Direct loan levels supportable by subsidy budget authority:			
115001 Individual Fishing Quota Loans	4	24	24
115002 Traditional Direct Loans	83	100	100
115013 Community Development Quota		120	77
115999 Total direct loan levels	87	244	201
Direct loan subsidy (in percent):			
132001 Individual Fishing Quota Loans	–13.17	–15.27	–13.69
132002 Traditional Direct Loans	–8.81	–10.37	–7.76
132013 Community Development Quota		–12.14	–10.00
132999 Weighted average subsidy rate	–9.01	–11.72	–9.33
Direct loan subsidy budget authority:			
133001 Individual Fishing Quota Loans	–1	–4	–3
133002 Traditional Direct Loans	–8	–10	–8
133013 Community Development Quota		–15	–8
133999 Total subsidy budget authority	–9	–29	–19
Direct loan subsidy outlays:			
134001 Individual Fishing Quota Loans		–2	–2
134002 Traditional Direct Loans	–7	–8	–8
134013 Community Development Quota		–3	–9
134999 Total subsidy outlays	–7	–13	–19
Direct loan reestimates:			
135001 Individual Fishing Quota Loans	1		
135002 Traditional Direct Loans	–4	13	
135008 Crab Buyback loans		2	
135999 Total direct loan reestimates	–3	15	

The Fisheries Finance Program (FFP) is a national loan program that makes long-term fixed-rate financing available to U.S. citizens who otherwise qualify for financing or refinancing of the reconstruction, reconditioning, and, in some cases, the purchasing of fishing vessels, shoreside processing, aquaculture, and mariculture facilities. The FFP also provides fishery-wide financing to ease the transition to sustainable fisheries through its fishing capacity reduction programs and provides financial assistance in the form of loans to fishermen who fish from small vessels and entry-level fishermen to promote stability and reduce consolidation in already rationalized fisheries. Additionally, FFP can provide loans for fisheries investments of Native American Community Development Quota groups.

The FFP operates under the authority of Title XI of the Merchant Marine Act of 1936, as amended; Section 303(a) of the Sustainable Fisheries Act amendments to the Magnuson-Stevens Act; and, from time to time FFP-specific legislation. The overriding guideline for all FFP financings is that they cannot contribute or be construed to contribute to an increase in existing fish harvesting.

FISHERIES FINANCE DIRECT LOAN FINANCING ACCOUNT

Program and Financing (in millions of dollars)

Identification code 013–4324–0–3–376	2021 actual	2022 est.	2023 est.
Obligations by program activity:			
Credit program obligations:			
0710 Direct loan obligations	87	244	201
0713 Payment of interest to Treasury	13	14	14
0740 Negative subsidy obligations	8	29	19
0742 Downward reestimates paid to receipt accounts	5	2	
0743 Interest on downward reestimates	1		
0900 Total new obligations, unexpired accounts	114	289	234
Budgetary resources:			
Unobligated balance:			
1000 Unobligated balance brought forward, Oct 1		1	
1021 Recoveries of prior year unpaid obligations	3	2	2
1024 Unobligated balance of borrowing authority withdrawn	–3	–2	–2
1070 Unobligated balance (total)		1	
Financing authority:			
Borrowing authority, mandatory:			
1400 Borrowing authority	96	260	224
Spending authority from offsetting collections, mandatory:			
1800 Collected	114	103	85
1825 Spending authority from offsetting collections applied to repay debt	–95	–75	–75
1850 Spending auth from offsetting collections, mand (total)	19	28	10
1900 Budget authority (total)	115	288	234
1930 Total budgetary resources available	115	289	234
Memorandum (non-add) entries:			
1941 Unexpired unobligated balance, end of year	1		
Change in obligated balance:			
Unpaid obligations:			
3000 Unpaid obligations, brought forward, Oct 1	125	124	286
3010 New obligations, unexpired accounts	114	289	234
3020 Outlays (gross)	–112	–125	–195
3040 Recoveries of prior year unpaid obligations, unexpired	–3	–2	–2
3050 Unpaid obligations, end of year	124	286	323
Memorandum (non-add) entries:			
3100 Obligated balance, start of year	125	124	286
3200 Obligated balance, end of year	124	286	323
Financing authority and disbursements, net:			
Mandatory:			
4090 Budget authority, gross	115	288	234
Financing disbursements:			
4110 Outlays, gross (total)	112	125	195
Offsets against gross financing authority and disbursements:			
Offsetting collections (collected) from:			
4120 Payments from program account	–4	–17	
4122 Interest on uninvested funds	–2	–1	–1
4123 Repayments of principal, net	–85	–63	–63
4123 Interest Received on loans	–23	–21	–21
4123 Other income		–1	
4130 Offsets against gross budget authority and outlays (total)	–114	–103	–85
4160 Budget authority, net (mandatory)	1	185	149
4170 Outlays, net (mandatory)	–2	22	110
4180 Budget authority, net (total)	1	185	149
4190 Outlays, net (total)	–2	22	110

Status of Direct Loans (in millions of dollars)

Identification code 013–4324–0–3–376	2021 actual	2022 est.	2023 est.
Position with respect to appropriations act limitation on obligations:			
1111 Direct loan obligations from current-year authority	87	244	201

FISHERIES FINANCE DIRECT LOAN FINANCING ACCOUNT—Continued

Status of Direct Loans—Continued

Identification code 013–4324–0–3–376		2021 actual	2022 est.	2023 est.
1150	Total direct loan obligations	87	244	201
	Cumulative balance of direct loans outstanding:			
1210	Outstanding, start of year	353	339	375
1231	Disbursements: Direct loan disbursements	86	99	168
1251	Repayments: Repayments and prepayments	–85	–63	–63
1263	Write-offs for default: Direct loans	–15		
1290	Outstanding, end of year	339	375	480

This account covers the financing of direct loans as authorized by the Magnuson-Stevens Fishery Conservation and Management Act to promote market-based approaches to sustainable fisheries management. Funds are not used for purposes that would contribute to the overcapitalization of the fishing industry. The amounts in this account are a means of financing and are not included in the budget totals.

Balance Sheet (in millions of dollars)

Identification code 013–4324–0–3–376		2020 actual	2021 actual
	ASSETS:		
	Federal assets:		
1101	Fund balances with Treasury		1
	Investments in U.S. securities:		
1106	Federal Receivables, net	4	17
	Net value of assets related to post-1991 direct loans receivable:		
1401	Direct loans receivable, gross	353	339
1402	Interest receivable	3	1
1404	Foreclosed property		
1405	Allowance for subsidy cost (-)	34	31
1499	Net present value of assets related to direct loans	390	371
1999	Total assets	394	389
	LIABILITIES:		
	Federal liabilities:		
2101	Accounts payable		
2103	Federal liabilities, debt	388	387
2105	Other	6	2
2999	Total liabilities	394	389
	NET POSITION:		
3300	Cumulative results of operations		
4999	Total liabilities and net position	394	389

FEDERAL SHIP FINANCING FUND FISHING VESSELS LIQUIDATING ACCOUNT

Status of Guaranteed Loans (in millions of dollars)

Identification code 013–4417–0–3–376		2021 actual	2022 est.	2023 est.
	Cumulative balance of guaranteed loans outstanding:			
2210	Outstanding, start of year			
2290	Outstanding, end of year			
	Memorandum:			
2299	Guaranteed amount of guaranteed loans outstanding, end of year			
	Addendum:			
	Cumulative balance of defaulted guaranteed loans that result in loans receivable:			
2310	Outstanding, start of year	7	7	7
2351	Repayments of loans receivable			
2390	Outstanding, end of year	7	7	7

Balance Sheet (in millions of dollars)

Identification code 013–4417–0–3–376		2020 actual	2021 actual
	ASSETS:		
1601	Direct loans, gross		
1603	Allowance for estimated uncollectible loans and interest (-)		
1699	Value of assets related to direct loans		
1701	Defaulted guaranteed loans, gross	7	7
1703	Allowance for estimated uncollectible loans and interest (-)	–7	–7
1799	Value of assets related to loan guarantees		
1999	Total assets		
	LIABILITIES:		
2104	Federal liabilities: Resources payable to Treasury		
4999	Total liabilities and net position		

U.S. PATENT AND TRADEMARK OFFICE

Federal Funds

SALARIES AND EXPENSES

(INCLUDING TRANSFERS OF FUNDS)

For necessary expenses of the United States Patent and Trademark Office (USPTO) provided for by law, including defense of suits instituted against the Under Secretary of Commerce for Intellectual Property and Director of the USPTO, $4,253,404,000, to remain available until expended: Provided, That the sum herein appropriated from the general fund shall be reduced as offsetting collections of fees and surcharges assessed and collected by the USPTO under any law are received during fiscal year 2023, so as to result in a fiscal year 2023 appropriation from the general fund estimated at $0: Provided further, That during fiscal year 2023, should the total amount of such offsetting collections be less than $4,253,404,000, this amount shall be reduced accordingly: Provided further, That any amount received in excess of $4,253,404,000 in fiscal year 2023 and deposited in the Patent and Trademark Fee Reserve Fund shall remain available until expended: Provided further, That the Director of USPTO shall submit a notification to reprogram funds to the Committees on Appropriations of the House of Representatives and the Senate for any amounts made available by the preceding proviso and such notification to reprogram funds shall be treated as a reprogramming under section 504 of this Act and shall not be available for obligation or expenditure except in compliance with the procedures set forth in that section: Provided further, That any amounts reprogrammed in accordance with the preceding proviso shall be transferred to the United States Patent and Trademark Office "Salaries and Expenses" account: Provided further, That the budget of the President submitted for fiscal year 2024 under section 1105 of title 31, United States Code, shall include within amounts provided under this heading for necessary expenses of the USPTO any increases that are expected to result from an increase promulgated through rule or regulation in offsetting collections of fees and surcharges assessed and collected by the USPTO under any law in either fiscal year 2023 or fiscal year 2024: Provided further, That from amounts provided herein, not to exceed $13,500 shall be made available in fiscal year 2023 for official reception and representation expenses: Provided further, That in fiscal year 2023 from the amounts made available for "Salaries and Expenses" for the USPTO, the amounts necessary to pay (1) the difference between the percentage of basic pay contributed by the USPTO and employees under section 8334(a) of title 5, United States Code, and the normal cost percentage (as defined by section 8331(17) of that title) as provided by the Office of Personnel Management (OPM) for USPTO's specific use, of basic pay, of employees subject to subchapter III of chapter 83 of that title, and (2) the present value of the otherwise unfunded accruing costs, as determined by OPM for USPTO's specific use of post-retirement life insurance and post-retirement health benefits coverage for all USPTO employees who are enrolled in Federal Employees Health Benefits (FEHB) and Federal Employees Group Life Insurance (FEGLI), shall be transferred to the Civil Service Retirement and Disability Fund, the FEGLI Fund, and the Employees FEHB Fund, as appropriate, and shall be available for the authorized purposes of those accounts: Provided further, That any differences between the present value factors published in OPM's yearly 300 series benefit letters and the factors that OPM provides for USPTO's specific use shall be recognized as an imputed cost on USPTO's financial statements, where applicable: Provided further, That, notwithstanding any other provision of law, all fees and surcharges assessed and collected by USPTO are available for USPTO only pursuant to section 42(c) of title 35, United States Code, as amended by section 22 of the Leahy-Smith America Invents Act (Public Law 112–29): Provided further, That within the amounts appropriated, $2,450,000 shall be transferred to the "Office of Inspector General" account for activities associated with carrying out investigations and audits related to the USPTO.

Note.—A full-year 2022 appropriation for this account was not enacted at the time the Budget was prepared; therefore, the Budget assumes this account is operating under the Continuing Appropriations Act, 2022 (Division A of Public Law 117–43, as amended). The amounts included for 2022 reflect the annualized level provided by the continuing resolution.

Program and Financing (in millions of dollars)

Identification code 013–1006–0–1–376		2021 actual	2022 est.	2023 est.
	Obligations by program activity:			
0801	Patents	3,319	3,550	3,646
0802	Trademarks	403	464	504
0809	Reimbursable program activities, subtotal	3,722	4,014	4,150
0900	Total new obligations, unexpired accounts	3,722	4,014	4,150
	Budgetary resources:			
	Unobligated balance:			
1000	Unobligated balance brought forward, Oct 1	513	684	417
1011	Unobligated balance transfer from other acct [013–1008]	232		431
1021	Recoveries of prior year unpaid obligations	34	47	47
1070	Unobligated balance (total)	779	731	895
	Budget authority:			
	Spending authority from offsetting collections, discretionary:			
1700	Base Fee Collections	3,625	4,126	4,253
1700	Other Income	4	7	7
1710	Spending authority from offsetting collections transferred to other accounts [013–0126]	–2	–2	–2
1710	Spending authority from offsetting collections transferred to other accounts [013–1008]		–431	
1750	Spending auth from offsetting collections, disc (total)	3,627	3,700	4,258
1930	Total budgetary resources available	4,406	4,431	5,153
	Memorandum (non-add) entries:			
1941	Unexpired unobligated balance, end of year	684	417	1,003
	Change in obligated balance:			
	Unpaid obligations:			
3000	Unpaid obligations, brought forward, Oct 1	668	802	881
3010	New obligations, unexpired accounts	3,722	4,014	4,150
3020	Outlays (gross)	–3,554	–3,888	–4,154
3040	Recoveries of prior year unpaid obligations, unexpired	–34	–47	–47
3050	Unpaid obligations, end of year	802	881	830
	Memorandum (non-add) entries:			
3100	Obligated balance, start of year	668	802	881
3200	Obligated balance, end of year	802	881	830
	Budget authority and outlays, net:			
	Discretionary:			
4000	Budget authority, gross	3,627	3,700	4,258
	Outlays, gross:			
4010	Outlays from new discretionary authority	3,010	3,097	3,564
4011	Outlays from discretionary balances	544	791	590
4020	Outlays, gross (total)	3,554	3,888	4,154
	Offsets against gross budget authority and outlays:			
	Offsetting collections (collected) from:			
4030	Federal sources	–13	–11	–11
4033	Non-Federal sources	–3,616	–4,122	–4,249
4040	Offsets against gross budget authority and outlays (total)	–3,629	–4,133	–4,260
4070	Budget authority, net (discretionary)	–2	–433	–2
4080	Outlays, net (discretionary)	–75	–245	–106
4180	Budget authority, net (total)	–2	–433	–2
4190	Outlays, net (total)	–75	–245	–106
	Memorandum (non-add) entries:			
5090	Unexpired unavailable balance, SOY: Offsetting collections	938	938	938
5092	Unexpired unavailable balance, EOY: Offsetting collections	938	938	938

The United States Patent and Trademark Office (USPTO) issues patents and registers trademarks, which provide protection to inventors and businesses for their inventions and corporate and product identifications. USPTO also advises other U.S. Government agencies on intellectual property (IP) issues and promotes stronger IP protections in other countries. USPTO is funded through fees that are paid to obtain and renew patents and trademarks.

Patent program.—The 2023 Budget requests spending authority for examining patent applications and granting patents. USPTO will continue its priorities to issue reliable and predictable IP rights; enhance patent quality; shorten patent application pendency; ensure optimal information technology service delivery to all users; improve appeal and post-grant processes; and promote the enforcement of IP protections worldwide.

Trademark program.—The 2023 Budget requests spending authority for examining trademark applications; registering trademarks; maintaining high trademark quality; ensuring optimal information technology service delivery to all users; and improving trademark practices worldwide.

Object Classification (in millions of dollars)

Identification code 013–1006–0–1–376		2021 actual	2022 est.	2023 est.
	Reimbursable obligations:			
	Personnel compensation:			
11.1	Full-time permanent	1,677	1,753	1,894
11.5	Other personnel compensation	154	169	184
11.9	Total personnel compensation	1,831	1,922	2,078
12.1	Civilian personnel benefits	707	767	828
13.0	Benefits for former personnel	1		
21.0	Travel and transportation of persons		7	7
23.1	Rental payments to GSA	90	93	94
23.2	Rental payments to others	13	15	16
23.3	Communications, utilities, and miscellaneous charges	11	19	21
24.0	Printing and reproduction	154	171	183
25.1	Advisory and assistance services	58	79	57
25.2	Other services from non-Federal sources	191	186	160
25.3	Other goods and services from Federal sources	42	63	61
25.4	Operation and maintenance of facilities	19	25	27
25.7	Operation and maintenance of equipment	313	420	390
26.0	Supplies and materials	46	51	53
31.0	Equipment	240	194	173
32.0	Land and structures	2		
42.0	Insurance claims and indemnities	1		
44.0	Refunds	3	2	2
99.9	Total new obligations, unexpired accounts	3,722	4,014	4,150

Employment Summary

Identification code 013–1006–0–1–376		2021 actual	2022 est.	2023 est.
2001	Reimbursable civilian full-time equivalent employment	13,125	13,091	13,794

PATENT AND TRADEMARK FEE RESERVE FUND

Program and Financing (in millions of dollars)

Identification code 013–1008–0–1–376		2021 actual	2022 est.	2023 est.
	Budgetary resources:			
	Unobligated balance:			
1000	Unobligated balance brought forward, Oct 1	232		431
1010	Unobligated balance transfer to other accts [013–1006]	–232		–431
	Budget authority:			
	Spending authority from offsetting collections, discretionary:			
1711	Spending authority from offsetting collections transferred from other accounts [013–1006]		431	
1930	Total budgetary resources available		431	
	Memorandum (non-add) entries:			
1941	Unexpired unobligated balance, end of year		431	
	Budget authority and outlays, net:			
	Discretionary:			
4000	Budget authority, gross		431	
4180	Budget authority, net (total)		431	
4190	Outlays, net (total)			

NATIONAL TECHNICAL INFORMATION SERVICE

Federal Funds

NTIS REVOLVING FUND

Program and Financing (in millions of dollars)

Identification code 013–4295–0–3–376		2021 actual	2022 est.	2023 est.
	Obligations by program activity:			
0801	NTIS Revolving Fund (Reimbursable)	58	100	100

NTIS REVOLVING FUND—Continued
Program and Financing—Continued

Identification code 013–4295–0–3–376	2021 actual	2022 est.	2023 est.
Budgetary resources:			
Unobligated balance:			
1000 Unobligated balance brought forward, Oct 1	25	24	24
Budget authority:			
Spending authority from offsetting collections, discretionary:			
1700 Collected	63	100	100
1701 Change in uncollected payments, Federal sources	–6		
1750 Spending auth from offsetting collections, disc (total)	57	100	100
1930 Total budgetary resources available	82	124	124
Memorandum (non-add) entries:			
1941 Unexpired unobligated balance, end of year	24	24	24
Change in obligated balance:			
Unpaid obligations:			
3000 Unpaid obligations, brought forward, Oct 1	29	27	22
3010 New obligations, unexpired accounts	58	100	100
3020 Outlays (gross)	–60	–105	–100
3050 Unpaid obligations, end of year	27	22	22
Uncollected payments:			
3060 Uncollected pymts, Fed sources, brought forward, Oct 1	–37	–31	–31
3070 Change in uncollected pymts, Fed sources, unexpired	6		
3090 Uncollected pymts, Fed sources, end of year	–31	–31	–31
Memorandum (non-add) entries:			
3100 Obligated balance, start of year	–8	–4	–9
3200 Obligated balance, end of year	–4	–9	–9
Budget authority and outlays, net:			
Discretionary:			
4000 Budget authority, gross	57	100	100
Outlays, gross:			
4010 Outlays from new discretionary authority	40	77	77
4011 Outlays from discretionary balances	20	28	23
4020 Outlays, gross (total)	60	105	100
Offsets against gross budget authority and outlays:			
Offsetting collections (collected) from:			
4030 Federal sources	–62	–95	–95
4033 Non-Federal sources	–1	–5	–5
4040 Offsets against gross budget authority and outlays (total)	–63	–100	–100
Additional offsets against gross budget authority only:			
4050 Change in uncollected pymts, Fed sources, unexpired	6		
4080 Outlays, net (discretionary)	–3	5	
4180 Budget authority, net (total)			
4190 Outlays, net (total)	–3	5	

The National Technical Information Service (NTIS) provides data science innovations, leveraging its unique authorities under Title 15, U.S.C. NTIS also collects and disseminates government scientific, technical, and business-related information, as well as provides secure access to select government databases. NTIS operates a revolving fund for the payment of all expenses incurred in fulfilling its mission.

Object Classification (in millions of dollars)

Identification code 013–4295–0–3–376	2021 actual	2022 est.	2023 est.
Reimbursable obligations:			
11.1 Personnel compensation: Full-time permanent	5	6	6
12.1 Civilian personnel benefits	1	2	2
23.1 Rental payments to GSA	1	2	2
23.3 Communications, utilities, and miscellaneous charges		2	2
25.2 Other services from non-Federal sources	48	82	82
25.3 Other goods and services from Federal sources	2	4	4
25.7 Operation and maintenance of equipment	1	1	1
31.0 Equipment		1	1
99.9 Total new obligations, unexpired accounts	58	100	100

Employment Summary

Identification code 013–4295–0–3–376	2021 actual	2022 est.	2023 est.
2001 Reimbursable civilian full-time equivalent employment	40	43	43

NATIONAL INSTITUTE OF STANDARDS AND TECHNOLOGY

Federal Funds

SCIENTIFIC AND TECHNICAL RESEARCH AND SERVICES

(INCLUDING TRANSFER OF FUNDS)

For necessary expenses of the National Institute of Standards and Technology (NIST), $974,946,000, to remain available until expended, of which not to exceed $9,000,000 may be transferred to the "Working Capital Fund": Provided, That not to exceed $5,000 shall be for official reception and representation expenses: Provided further, That NIST may provide local transportation for summer undergraduate research fellowship program participants.

Note.—A full-year 2022 appropriation for this account was not enacted at the time the Budget was prepared; therefore, the Budget assumes this account is operating under the Continuing Appropriations Act, 2022 (Division A of Public Law 117–43, as amended). The amounts included for 2022 reflect the annualized level provided by the continuing resolution.

SCIENTIFIC AND TECHNICAL RESEARCH AND SERVICES

[*For an additional amount for "Scientific and Technical Research and Services" for necessary expenses to carry out investigations of building failures pursuant to the National Construction Safety Team Act of 2002 (15 U.S.C. 7301), $22,000,000, to remain available until September 30, 2023.*] *(Disaster Relief Supplemental Appropriations Act, 2022.)*

Program and Financing (in millions of dollars)

Identification code 013–0500–0–1–376	2021 actual	2022 est.	2023 est.
Obligations by program activity:			
0001 Laboratory programs	694	729	855
0201 Corporate services	18	17	19
0301 Standards coordination and special programs	90	93	103
0401 CARES Act	2		
0900 Total new obligations, unexpired accounts	804	839	977
Budgetary resources:			
Unobligated balance:			
1000 Unobligated balance brought forward, Oct 1	34	26	
1021 Recoveries of prior year unpaid obligations	5		
1070 Unobligated balance (total)	39	26	
Budget authority:			
Appropriations, discretionary:			
1100 New budget authority (gross), detail	788	810	975
1121 Transferred from State and Local Law Enforcement Assistance, DoJ [015–0404]	2	2	2
1121 Transferred from EAC [525–1650]	1	1	
1160 Appropriation, discretionary (total)	791	813	977
1930 Total budgetary resources available	830	839	977
Memorandum (non-add) entries:			
1941 Unexpired unobligated balance, end of year	26		
Change in obligated balance:			
Unpaid obligations:			
3000 Unpaid obligations, brought forward, Oct 1	187	217	256
3010 New obligations, unexpired accounts	804	839	977
3020 Outlays (gross)	–769	–800	–931
3040 Recoveries of prior year unpaid obligations, unexpired	–5		
3050 Unpaid obligations, end of year	217	256	302
Memorandum (non-add) entries:			
3100 Obligated balance, start of year	187	217	256
3200 Obligated balance, end of year	217	256	302
Budget authority and outlays, net:			
Discretionary:			
4000 Budget authority, gross	791	813	977
Outlays, gross:			
4010 Outlays from new discretionary authority	581	626	752
4011 Outlays from discretionary balances	188	174	179
4020 Outlays, gross (total)	769	800	931

DEPARTMENT OF COMMERCE

4180	Budget authority, net (total)	791	813	977
4190	Outlays, net (total)	769	800	931

The National Institute of Standards and Technology (NIST) mission is to promote U.S. innovation and industrial competitiveness by advancing measurement science, standards, and technology in ways that enhance economic security and improve our quality of life. NIST is authorized by the NIST Organic Act (15 U.S.C. 271), which outlines major roles for NIST in promoting national competitiveness and innovation. For more than 110 years, NIST has maintained the national standards of measurement, a role that the U.S. Constitution assigns to the Federal Government to ensure fairness in the marketplace. NIST was founded in 1901 and is one of the nation's oldest physical science laboratories. Today, the NIST Laboratory Programs, which is funded by the Scientific and Technical Research and Services (STRS) appropriation, work at the frontiers of measurement science to ensure that the U.S. system of measurements is firmly grounded on sound scientific and technical principles. The NIST Laboratories address increasingly complex measurement challenges, ranging from the very small (quantum devices for sensing and advanced computing) to the very large (vehicles and buildings), and from the physical infrastructure to the virtual (cybersecurity and the internet of things). As new technologies develop and evolve, NIST's measurement research and services remain critical to national defense, homeland security, trade, and innovation. The 2023 request includes program increases for measurement research and services for the following areas: Advanced Communications Research and Standards; Climate and Energy Measurements, Tools, and Testbeds; Measurements for the Circular Economy; Artificial Intelligence (AI)-Centric Challenges; Quantum Information Science, Engineering, and Metrology; Strengthening Equity and Diversity in the Standards Workforce; Supporting the American Bioeconomy, Cybersecurity (Supply Chain, 5G and Beyond, Identify Management); NIST Center for Neutron Research (NCNR) Controls and Corrective Actions; Public Safety Communications Research Accelerator; Measurement Services Modernization; Standards for Critical and Emerging Technologies; and iEdison. The 2023 total Budget request for STRS is $975.0 million.

Object Classification (in millions of dollars)

Identification code 013–0500–0–1–376		2021 actual	2022 est.	2023 est.
	Direct obligations:			
	Personnel compensation:			
11.1	Full-time permanent	278	290	327
11.3	Other than full-time permanent	22	22	24
11.5	Other personnel compensation	8	8	11
11.9	Total personnel compensation	308	320	362
12.1	Civilian personnel benefits	108	112	125
21.0	Travel and transportation of persons	1	5	5
22.0	Transportation of things	1	1	2
23.2	Rental payments to others	2	2	2
23.3	Communications, utilities, and miscellaneous charges	17	19	32
24.0	Printing and reproduction	1	1	1
25.1	Advisory and assistance services	4	3	2
25.2	Other services from non-Federal sources	66	68	56
25.3	Other goods and services from Federal sources	51	55	72
25.5	Research and development contracts	42	48	49
25.7	Operation and maintenance of equipment	15	15	20
26.0	Supplies and materials	26	26	31
31.0	Equipment	50	52	79
41.0	Grants, subsidies, and contributions	112	112	139
99.9	Total new obligations, unexpired accounts	804	839	977

Employment Summary

Identification code 013–0500–0–1–376	2021 actual	2022 est.	2023 est.
1001 Direct civilian full-time equivalent employment	2,382	2,520	2,711

INDUSTRIAL TECHNOLOGY SERVICES

For necessary expenses for industrial technology services, $372,318,000, to remain available until expended, of which $275,266,000 shall be for the Hollings Manufacturing Extension Partnership, and of which $97,052,000 shall be for the Manufacturing USA Program (formerly known as the National Network for Manufacturing Innovation).

Note.—A full-year 2022 appropriation for this account was not enacted at the time the Budget was prepared; therefore, the Budget assumes this account is operating under the Continuing Appropriations Act, 2022 (Division A of Public Law 117–43, as amended). The amounts included for 2022 reflect the annualized level provided by the continuing resolution.

Program and Financing (in millions of dollars)

Identification code 013–0525–0–1–376		2021 actual	2022 est.	2023 est.
	Obligations by program activity:			
0002	Hollings Manufacturing Extension Partnership	157	153	275
0003	Manufacturing USA	14	20	97
0005	American Rescue Plan Act	90	60	
0100	Total direct program	261	233	372
0900	Total new obligations, unexpired accounts	261	233	372
	Budgetary resources:			
	Unobligated balance:			
1000	Unobligated balance brought forward, Oct 1	9	66	
1001	Discretionary unobligated balance brought fwd, Oct 1	9	66	
1021	Recoveries of prior year unpaid obligations	2		
1070	Unobligated balance (total)	11	66	
	Budget authority:			
	Appropriations, discretionary:			
1100	Appropriation	166	167	372
	Appropriations, mandatory:			
1200	Appropriation	150		
1900	Budget authority (total)	316	167	372
1930	Total budgetary resources available	327	233	372
	Memorandum (non-add) entries:			
1941	Unexpired unobligated balance, end of year	66		
	Change in obligated balance:			
	Unpaid obligations:			
3000	Unpaid obligations, brought forward, Oct 1	242	261	248
3010	New obligations, unexpired accounts	261	233	372
3020	Outlays (gross)	–240	–246	–268
3040	Recoveries of prior year unpaid obligations, unexpired	–2		
3050	Unpaid obligations, end of year	261	248	352
	Memorandum (non-add) entries:			
3100	Obligated balance, start of year	242	261	248
3200	Obligated balance, end of year	261	248	352
	Budget authority and outlays, net:			
	Discretionary:			
4000	Budget authority, gross	166	167	372
	Outlays, gross:			
4010	Outlays from new discretionary authority	41	57	118
4011	Outlays from discretionary balances	192	144	113
4020	Outlays, gross (total)	233	201	231
	Mandatory:			
4090	Budget authority, gross	150		
	Outlays, gross:			
4100	Outlays from new mandatory authority	7		
4101	Outlays from mandatory balances		45	37
4110	Outlays, gross (total)	7	45	37
4180	Budget authority, net (total)	316	167	372
4190	Outlays, net (total)	240	246	268

NIST's Industrial Technology Services (ITS) appropriations account consists of two extramural programs:

1. Manufacturing USA: Manufacturing USA, previously referred to as the National Network for Manufacturing Innovation, serves to create effective robust manufacturing research infrastructure for U.S. industry and academia to solve industry-relevant problems. The Manufacturing USA consists of linked Institutes for Manufacturing Innovation with common goals, but unique concentrations. In an institute, industry, academia, and government partners leverage existing resources, collaborate, and co-invest to nurture manufacturing innovation and accelerate commercialization.

National Institute of Standards and Technology—Continued
Federal Funds—Continued

INDUSTRIAL TECHNOLOGY SERVICES—Continued

The request funds existing institutes and funds an additional two Department of Commerce Manufacturing USA Institutes.

2. Hollings Manufacturing Extension Partnership (MEP): The Hollings Manufacturing Extension Partnership Program is a national network of Federal, State, and Industry partnerships that provide U.S. manufacturers with access to technology, resources, and industry experts. The MEP consists of Manufacturing Extension Partnership centers located across the coutry that work directly with their local manufacturing communities to strengthen the competitiveness of the U.S. manufacturing base. Funding for the MEP centers is a cost-sharing arrangement consisting of support from the federal government, non-federal sources including state and local government/entities, and fees charged to the manufacturing clients for services provided by the MEP centers. The request includes program increases and reflects MEP's plan for increased capabilities to be able to assist all growth oriented small- and medium-sized enterprises (SMEs) to respond to critical national needs. The plan is based on adherence to a comprehensive strategic plan, a focus on operational excellence, system-wide refresh through a formal, multiyear organizational competition, and progressive growth in funding to serve all innovative manufacturing firms. The 2023 request provides additional services to an increased number of companies with critical supply chains and workforce development.

Object Classification (in millions of dollars)

Identification code 013–0525–0–1–376		2021 actual	2022 est.	2023 est.
	Direct obligations:			
	Personnel compensation:			
11.1	Full-time permanent	17	17	21
11.3	Other than full-time permanent	1	1	1
11.9	Total personnel compensation	18	18	22
12.1	Civilian personnel benefits	6	6	8
21.0	Travel and transportation of persons			1
23.3	Communications, utilities, and miscellaneous charges	1	1	7
25.2	Other services from non-Federal sources	9	9	18
25.3	Other goods and services from Federal sources	2	2	4
25.5	Research and development contracts			1
25.7	Operation and maintenance of equipment	1	1	2
26.0	Supplies and materials	1	1	1
31.0	Equipment		1	1
41.0	Grants, subsidies, and contributions	223	194	307
99.0	Direct obligations	261	233	372
99.9	Total new obligations, unexpired accounts	261	233	372

Employment Summary

Identification code 013–0525–0–1–376	2021 actual	2022 est.	2023 est.
1001 Direct civilian full-time equivalent employment	118	120	147

CONSTRUCTION OF RESEARCH FACILITIES

For construction of new research facilities, including architectural and engineering design, and for renovation and maintenance of existing facilities, not otherwise provided for the National Institute of Standards and Technology, as authorized by sections 13 through 15 of the National Institute of Standards and Technology Act (15 U.S.C. 278c–278e), $120,285,000, to remain available until expended: Provided, That the Secretary of Commerce shall include in the budget justification materials for fiscal year 2023 that the Secretary submits to Congress in support of the Department of Commerce budget (as submitted with the budget of the President under section 1105(a) of title 31, United States Code) an estimate for each National Institute of Standards and Technology construction project having a total multi-year program cost of more than $5,000,000, and simultaneously the budget justification materials shall include an estimate of the budgetary requirements for each such project for each of the 5 subsequent fiscal years.

Note.—A full-year 2022 appropriation for this account was not enacted at the time the Budget was prepared; therefore, the Budget assumes this account is operating under the Continuing Appropriations Act, 2022 (Division A of Public Law 117–43, as amended). The amounts included for 2022 reflect the annualized level provided by the continuing resolution.

Program and Financing (in millions of dollars)

Identification code 013–0515–0–1–376		2021 actual	2022 est.	2023 est.
	Obligations by program activity:			
0001	Construction of Research Facilities (Direct)	250	144	120
0801	Construction of Research Facilities (Reimbursable)	1	1	
0900	Total new obligations, unexpired accounts	251	145	120
	Budgetary resources:			
	Unobligated balance:			
1000	Unobligated balance brought forward, Oct 1	231	65	
1021	Recoveries of prior year unpaid obligations	4		
1070	Unobligated balance (total)	235	65	
	Budget authority:			
	Appropriations, discretionary:			
1100	Appropriation	80	80	120
	Spending authority from offsetting collections, discretionary:			
1700	Collected	1		
1900	Budget authority (total)	81	80	120
1930	Total budgetary resources available	316	145	120
	Memorandum (non-add) entries:			
1941	Unexpired unobligated balance, end of year	65		
	Change in obligated balance:			
	Unpaid obligations:			
3000	Unpaid obligations, brought forward, Oct 1	195	320	269
3010	New obligations, unexpired accounts	251	145	120
3020	Outlays (gross)	–122	–196	–170
3040	Recoveries of prior year unpaid obligations, unexpired	–4		
3050	Unpaid obligations, end of year	320	269	219
	Memorandum (non-add) entries:			
3100	Obligated balance, start of year	195	320	269
3200	Obligated balance, end of year	320	269	219
	Budget authority and outlays, net:			
	Discretionary:			
4000	Budget authority, gross	81	80	120
	Outlays, gross:			
4010	Outlays from new discretionary authority		16	24
4011	Outlays from discretionary balances	122	180	146
4020	Outlays, gross (total)	122	196	170
	Offsets against gross budget authority and outlays:			
	Offsetting collections (collected) from:			
4034	Offsetting governmental collections	–1		
4040	Offsets against gross budget authority and outlays (total)	–1		
4180	Budget authority, net (total)	80	80	120
4190	Outlays, net (total)	121	196	170

The Construction of Research Facilities appropriation funds construction activities, including maintenance, repairs, and major improvements, and major renovations of facilities occupied or used by NIST in Gaithersburg, Maryland; Boulder and Fort Collins, Colorado; and Kauai, Hawaii with the intent to meet current and future advancements in measurements science, standards, and technology to promote innovation and industrial competitiveness for the Nation. The 2023 total Budget request for CRF is $120.3 million for the repair and revitalization of NIST facilities.

Object Classification (in millions of dollars)

Identification code 013–0515–0–1–376		2021 actual	2022 est.	2023 est.
	Direct obligations:			
	Personnel compensation:			
11.1	Full-time permanent	15	14	15
11.5	Other personnel compensation		1	1
11.9	Total personnel compensation	15	15	16
12.1	Civilian personnel benefits	5	5	5
23.3	Communications, utilities, and miscellaneous charges			
25.2	Other services from non-Federal sources	104	83	86
25.3	Other goods and services from Federal sources		1	1
25.7	Operation and maintenance of equipment	5	5	5
26.0	Supplies and materials	1	1	1
31.0	Equipment	4	6	5
32.0	Land and structures	116	27	
41.0	Grants, subsidies, and contributions		1	
99.0	Direct obligations	250	144	120
99.0	Reimbursable obligations	1	1	

DEPARTMENT OF COMMERCE

National Institute of Standards and Technology—Continued
Federal Funds—Continued

| 99.9 | Total new obligations, unexpired accounts | 251 | 145 | 120 |

Employment Summary

Identification code 013–0515–0–1–376	2021 actual	2022 est.	2023 est.
1001 Direct civilian full-time equivalent employment	143	145	145

WORKING CAPITAL FUND

Program and Financing (in millions of dollars)

Identification code 013–4650–0–4–376	2021 actual	2022 est.	2023 est.
Obligations by program activity:			
0801 Laboratory programs	139	163	134
0802 Corporate services	5	6	6
0803 Standards coordination and special programs	8	10	9
0805 Hollings manufacturing extension partnership	....	2	2
0900 Total new obligations, unexpired accounts	152	181	151
Budgetary resources:			
Unobligated balance:			
1000 Unobligated balance brought forward, Oct 1	150	189	189
Budget authority:			
Spending authority from offsetting collections, discretionary:			
1700 Collected	194	181	151
1701 Change in uncollected payments, Federal sources	–3	....	....
1750 Spending auth from offsetting collections, disc (total)	191	181	151
1900 Budget authority (total)	191	181	151
1930 Total budgetary resources available	341	370	340
Memorandum (non-add) entries:			
1941 Unexpired unobligated balance, end of year	189	189	189
Change in obligated balance:			
Unpaid obligations:			
3000 Unpaid obligations, brought forward, Oct 1	206	227	127
3010 New obligations, unexpired accounts	152	181	151
3020 Outlays (gross)	–131	–281	–164
3050 Unpaid obligations, end of year	227	127	114
Uncollected payments:			
3060 Uncollected pymts, Fed sources, brought forward, Oct 1	–45	–42	–42
3070 Change in uncollected pymts, Fed sources, unexpired	3	....	....
3090 Uncollected pymts, Fed sources, end of year	–42	–42	–42
Memorandum (non-add) entries:			
3100 Obligated balance, start of year	161	185	85
3200 Obligated balance, end of year	185	85	72
Budget authority and outlays, net:			
Discretionary:			
4000 Budget authority, gross	191	181	151
Outlays, gross:			
4010 Outlays from new discretionary authority	....	139	116
4011 Outlays from discretionary balances	131	142	48
4020 Outlays, gross (total)	131	281	164
Offsets against gross budget authority and outlays:			
Offsetting collections (collected) from:			
4030 Federal sources	–134	–103	–91
4033 Non-Federal sources	–60	–78	–60
4040 Offsets against gross budget authority and outlays (total)	–194	–181	–151
Additional offsets against gross budget authority only:			
4050 Change in uncollected pymts, Fed sources, unexpired	3	....	....
4080 Outlays, net (discretionary)	–63	100	13
4180 Budget authority, net (total)	....	....	....
4190 Outlays, net (total)	–63	100	13

The Working Capital Fund finances research and technical services performed for other Government agencies and the public. These activities are funded through advances and reimbursements. The Fund also finances the acquisition of equipment, standard reference materials, and storeroom inventories until issued or sold.

Object Classification (in millions of dollars)

Identification code 013–4650–0–4–376	2021 actual	2022 est.	2023 est.
Reimbursable obligations:			
Personnel compensation:			
11.1 Full-time permanent	64	66	68
11.3 Other than full-time permanent	5	5	5
11.5 Other personnel compensation	1	1	1
11.9 Total personnel compensation	70	72	74
12.1 Civilian personnel benefits	25	25	25
21.0 Travel and transportation of persons	....	1	....
22.0 Transportation of things	....	1	....
23.3 Communications, utilities, and miscellaneous charges	3	4	3
25.2 Other services from non-Federal sources	12	16	9
25.3 Other goods and services from Federal sources	8	8	6
25.5 Research and development contracts	11	19	11
25.7 Operation and maintenance of equipment	3	6	3
26.0 Supplies and materials	6	11	7
31.0 Equipment	2	2	3
41.0 Grants, subsidies, and contributions	12	16	10
99.9 Total new obligations, unexpired accounts	152	181	151

Employment Summary

Identification code 013–4650–0–4–376	2021 actual	2022 est.	2023 est.
2001 Reimbursable civilian full-time equivalent employment	558	618	674

PUBLIC SAFETY COMMUNICATIONS RESEARCH FUND

Program and Financing (in millions of dollars)

Identification code 013–0513–0–1–376	2021 actual	2022 est.	2023 est.
Obligations by program activity:			
0801 Public Safety Communications Research Fund (Reimbursable)	64	47	....
Budgetary resources:			
Unobligated balance:			
1000 Unobligated balance brought forward, Oct 1	109	47	....
1021 Recoveries of prior year unpaid obligations	2	....	....
1070 Unobligated balance (total)	111	47	....
1930 Total budgetary resources available	111	47	....
Memorandum (non-add) entries:			
1941 Unexpired unobligated balance, end of year	47	....	....
Change in obligated balance:			
Unpaid obligations:			
3000 Unpaid obligations, brought forward, Oct 1	31	44	35
3010 New obligations, unexpired accounts	64	47	....
3020 Outlays (gross)	–49	–56	–31
3040 Recoveries of prior year unpaid obligations, unexpired	–2	....	....
3050 Unpaid obligations, end of year	44	35	4
Memorandum (non-add) entries:			
3100 Obligated balance, start of year	31	44	35
3200 Obligated balance, end of year	44	35	4
Budget authority and outlays, net:			
Mandatory:			
Outlays, gross:			
4101 Outlays from mandatory balances	49	56	31
4180 Budget authority, net (total)	....	....	....
4190 Outlays, net (total)	49	56	31

Object Classification (in millions of dollars)

Identification code 013–0513–0–1–376	2021 actual	2022 est.	2023 est.
Reimbursable obligations:			
Personnel compensation:			
11.1 Full-time permanent	13	11	....
11.3 Other than full-time permanent	3	3	....
11.9 Total personnel compensation	16	14	....
12.1 Civilian personnel benefits	5	5	....
23.3 Communications, utilities, and miscellaneous charges	1	2	....
25.1 Advisory and assistance services	1	4	....
25.2 Other services from non-Federal sources	7	2	....

PUBLIC SAFETY COMMUNICATIONS RESEARCH FUND—Continued

Object Classification—Continued

Identification code 013–0513–0–1–376		2021 actual	2022 est.	2023 est.
25.3	Other goods and services from Federal sources	5		
25.5	Research and development contracts	5		
26.0	Supplies and materials	1	1	
31.0	Equipment	7	1	
41.0	Grants, subsidies, and contributions	16	18	
99.0	Reimbursable obligations	64	47	
99.9	Total new obligations, unexpired accounts	64	47	

Employment Summary

Identification code 013–0513–0–1–376		2021 actual	2022 est.	2023 est.
2001	Reimbursable civilian full-time equivalent employment	111	111	

NATIONAL TELECOMMUNICATIONS AND INFORMATION ADMINISTRATION

Federal Funds

SALARIES AND EXPENSES

For necessary expenses, as provided for by law, of the National Telecommunications and Information Administration (NTIA), $67,605,000, to remain available until September 30, 2024: Provided, That, notwithstanding 31 U.S.C. 1535(d), the Secretary of Commerce shall recover from Federal agencies the costs incurred in spectrum management, analysis, and operations, and such sums shall be collected from the agencies through non-expenditure transfers, to be retained and used for such purposes until expended: Provided further, That the Secretary of Commerce is authorized to retain and use as offsetting collections all funds transferred, or previously transferred, from other Government agencies for all costs incurred in telecommunications research, engineering, and related activities by the Institute for Telecommunication Sciences of NTIA, in furtherance of its assigned functions under this paragraph, and such funds received from other Government agencies shall remain available until expended.

Note.—A full-year 2022 appropriation for this account was not enacted at the time the Budget was prepared; therefore, the Budget assumes this account is operating under the Continuing Appropriations Act, 2022 (Division A of Public Law 117–43, as amended). The amounts included for 2022 reflect the annualized level provided by the continuing resolution.

Program and Financing (in millions of dollars)

Identification code 013–0550–0–1–376		2021 actual	2022 est.	2023 est.
	Obligations by program activity:			
0001	Domestic and international policy	11	13	15
0002	Spectrum management	7	7	9
0004	Broadband programs	18	23	27
0007	Advanced Communication Research	11	12	13
0008	Public Safety Communications		1	4
0100	Total, direct program	47	56	68
0799	Total direct obligations	47	56	68
0801	Spectrum management	37	60	45
0802	Telecommunication sciences research	13	47	12
0803	Other		1	1
0899	Total reimbursable obligations	50	108	58
0900	Total new obligations, unexpired accounts	97	164	126
	Budgetary resources:			
	Unobligated balance:			
1000	Unobligated balance brought forward, Oct 1	33	63	2
1021	Recoveries of prior year unpaid obligations	1		
1070	Unobligated balance (total)	34	63	2
	Budget authority:			
	Appropriations, discretionary:			
1100	Appropriation	46	46	68
	Spending authority from offsetting collections, discretionary:			
1700	Collected	83	57	58
1701	Change in uncollected payments, Federal sources	–3		
1750	Spending auth from offsetting collections, disc (total)	80	57	58
1900	Budget authority (total)	126	103	126
1930	Total budgetary resources available	160	166	128
	Memorandum (non-add) entries:			
1941	Unexpired unobligated balance, end of year	63	2	2
	Change in obligated balance:			
	Unpaid obligations:			
3000	Unpaid obligations, brought forward, Oct 1	38	48	88
3010	New obligations, unexpired accounts	97	164	126
3020	Outlays (gross)	–85	–124	–121
3040	Recoveries of prior year unpaid obligations, unexpired	–1		
3041	Recoveries of prior year unpaid obligations, expired	–1		
3050	Unpaid obligations, end of year	48	88	93
	Uncollected payments:			
3060	Uncollected pymts, Fed sources, brought forward, Oct 1	–4	–1	–1
3070	Change in uncollected pymts, Fed sources, unexpired	3		
3090	Uncollected pymts, Fed sources, end of year	–1	–1	–1
	Memorandum (non-add) entries:			
3100	Obligated balance, start of year	34	47	87
3200	Obligated balance, end of year	47	87	92
	Budget authority and outlays, net:			
	Discretionary:			
4000	Budget authority, gross	126	103	126
	Outlays, gross:			
4010	Outlays from new discretionary authority	54	83	100
4011	Outlays from discretionary balances	31	41	21
4020	Outlays, gross (total)	85	124	121
	Offsets against gross budget authority and outlays:			
	Offsetting collections (collected) from:			
4030	Federal sources	–83	–57	–58
4040	Offsets against gross budget authority and outlays (total)	–83	–57	–58
	Additional offsets against gross budget authority only:			
4050	Change in uncollected pymts, Fed sources, unexpired	3		
4060	Additional offsets against budget authority only (total)	3		
4070	Budget authority, net (discretionary)	46	46	68
4080	Outlays, net (discretionary)	2	67	63
4180	Budget authority, net (total)	46	46	68
4190	Outlays, net (total)	2	67	63

The National Telecommunications and Information Administration (NTIA) is the principal Executive Branch adviser on domestic and international telecommunications and Internet policy. NTIA also manages the Federal Government's use of the radio frequency spectrum and performs extensive research in telecommunication sciences. The Budget: (1) continues to provide spectrum assignment and analysis support to Federal agencies; (2) supports NTIA's responsibilities under the Spectrum Pipeline Act of 2015 and MOBILE NOW Act (2018) to help identify additional federal spectrum to be shared or reallocated for commercial use.

The Budget proposes to increase the Public Safety Communications program by $4 million to transition statutory, delegated, and other key public safety communications activities from mandatory accounts (which expire on September 30, 2022) to annual appropriations within NTIA's Salaries and Expenses. NTIA is faced with sunsetting resources, but the requirements to perform these functions remain.

NTIA plays a critical role within the federal government in developing and driving adoption of market-based, risk-based cybersecurity guidelines to improve the private sectors cyber-security resilience. In support of this, the Budget proposes an increase to the Domestic and International Policies program by $2 million to build additional program capacity and bolster expertise.

Object Classification (in millions of dollars)

Identification code 013–0550–0–1–376		2021 actual	2022 est.	2023 est.
	Direct obligations:			
11.1	Personnel compensation: Full-time permanent	15	18	23
12.1	Civilian personnel benefits	5	6	8
21.0	Travel and transportation of persons		1	2
23.1	Rental payments to GSA	2	2	3
25.2	Other services from non-Federal sources	12	19	24
25.3	Other goods and services from Federal sources	6	6	8
31.0	Equipment	7	4	

		2021 actual	2022 est.	2023 est.
99.0	Direct obligations	47	56	68
99.0	Reimbursable obligations	49	108	58
99.5	Adjustment for rounding	1		
99.9	Total new obligations, unexpired accounts	97	164	126

Employment Summary

Identification code 013–0550–0–1–376	2021 actual	2022 est.	2023 est.
1001 Direct civilian full-time equivalent employment	118	157	188
2001 Reimbursable civilian full-time equivalent employment	121	159	159

BROADBAND CONNECTIVITY FUND

[For an additional amount for "Broadband Connectivity Fund", $2,000,000,000, to remain available until expended, for grants for the Tribal Broadband Connectivity Program, as authorized under section 905(c) of division N of the Consolidated Appropriations Act, 2021 (Public Law 116–260), as amended by section 60201 of division F this Act: *Provided*, That such amount is designated by the Congress as being for an emergency requirement pursuant to section 4112(a) of H. Con. Res. 71 (115th Congress), the concurrent resolution on the budget for fiscal year 2018, and to section 251(b) of the Balanced Budget and Emergency Deficit Control Act of 1985.] *(Infrastructure Investments and Jobs Appropriations Act.)*

Program and Financing (in millions of dollars)

Identification code 013–0560–0–1–376	2021 actual	2022 est.	2023 est.
Obligations by program activity:			
0001 Tribal Broadband Connectivity Program	9	1,986	1,005
0002 Broadband Infrastructure Program	2	291	7
0900 Total new obligations, unexpired accounts	11	2,277	1,012
Budgetary resources:			
Unobligated balance:			
1000 Unobligated balance brought forward, Oct 1		1,289	1,012
Budget authority:			
Appropriations, discretionary:			
1100 Appropriation		2,000	
Appropriations, mandatory:			
1200 Appropriation	1,300		
1900 Budget authority (total)	1,300	2,000	
1930 Total budgetary resources available	1,300	3,289	1,012
Memorandum (non-add) entries:			
1941 Unexpired unobligated balance, end of year	1,289	1,012	
Change in obligated balance:			
Unpaid obligations:			
3000 Unpaid obligations, brought forward, Oct 1		7	2,049
3010 New obligations, unexpired accounts	11	2,277	1,012
3020 Outlays (gross)	–4	–235	–749
3050 Unpaid obligations, end of year	7	2,049	2,312
Memorandum (non-add) entries:			
3100 Obligated balance, start of year		7	2,049
3200 Obligated balance, end of year	7	2,049	2,312
Budget authority and outlays, net:			
Discretionary:			
4000 Budget authority, gross		2,000	
Outlays, gross:			
4011 Outlays from discretionary balances			200
Mandatory:			
4090 Budget authority, gross	1,300		
Outlays, gross:			
4100 Outlays from new mandatory authority	4		
4101 Outlays from mandatory balances		235	549
4110 Outlays, gross (total)	4	235	549
4180 Budget authority, net (total)	1,300	2,000	
4190 Outlays, net (total)	4	235	749

The Consolidated Appropriations Act, 2021, provided $1 billion to NTIA for the Tribal Broadband Connectivity Program (TBCP) and $300 million for the Broadband Infrastructure Program. The TBCP directs funds to Tribal governments to deploy broadband on Tribal lands, as well as for telehealth, distance learning, broadband affordability, and digital inclusion. The Broadband Infrastructure Program directs funds to partnerships between a state, or one or more political subdivisions of a state, and providers of fixed broadband service to support broadband infrastructure deployment to areas lacking broadband, especially rural areas.

The Infrastructure Investment and Jobs Act directs NTIA to award $2 billion in Tribal Broadband Connectivity grants to Tribal governments for broadband deployment on tribal lands, as well as for telehealth, distance learning, broadband affordability, and digital inclusion.

Object Classification (in millions of dollars)

Identification code 013–0560–0–1–376	2021 actual	2022 est.	2023 est.
Direct obligations:			
11.1 Personnel compensation: Full-time permanent	1	3	3
12.1 Civilian personnel benefits		1	1
25.2 Other services from non-Federal sources	8		2
25.3 Other goods and services from Federal sources	2	4	5
41.0 Grants, subsidies, and contributions		2,268	1,000
99.0 Direct obligations	11	2,276	1,011
99.5 Adjustment for rounding		1	1
99.9 Total new obligations, unexpired accounts	11	2,277	1,012

Employment Summary

Identification code 013–0560–0–1–376	2021 actual	2022 est.	2023 est.
1001 Direct civilian full-time equivalent employment	5	20	20

CONNECTING MINORITY COMMUNITIES FUND

Program and Financing (in millions of dollars)

Identification code 013–0561–0–1–376	2021 actual	2022 est.	2023 est.
Obligations by program activity:			
0001 Connecting Minority Communities	6	272	7
Budgetary resources:			
Unobligated balance:			
1000 Unobligated balance brought forward, Oct 1		279	7
Budget authority:			
Appropriations, mandatory:			
1200 Appropriation	285		
1930 Total budgetary resources available	285	279	7
Memorandum (non-add) entries:			
1941 Unexpired unobligated balance, end of year	279	7	
Change in obligated balance:			
Unpaid obligations:			
3000 Unpaid obligations, brought forward, Oct 1		4	174
3010 New obligations, unexpired accounts	6	272	7
3020 Outlays (gross)	–2	–102	–138
3050 Unpaid obligations, end of year	4	174	43
Memorandum (non-add) entries:			
3100 Obligated balance, start of year		4	174
3200 Obligated balance, end of year	4	174	43
Budget authority and outlays, net:			
Mandatory:			
4090 Budget authority, gross	285		
Outlays, gross:			
4100 Outlays from new mandatory authority	2		
4101 Outlays from mandatory balances		102	138
4110 Outlays, gross (total)	2	102	138
4180 Budget authority, net (total)	285		
4190 Outlays, net (total)	2	102	138

The Consolidated Appropriations Act, 2021, provided $285 million to NTIA for the Connecting Minority Communities pilot program. This grant program targets Historically Black Colleges and Universities, Tribal Colleges and Universities, and Minority-Serving Institutions, as well as their surrounding communities to support the purchase of broadband internet access services, eligible equipment, or to hire and train information technology personnel.

National Telecommunications and Information Administration—Continued
Federal Funds—Continued

CONNECTING MINORITY COMMUNITIES FUND—Continued

Object Classification (in millions of dollars)

Identification code 013–0561–0–1–376	2021 actual	2022 est.	2023 est.
Direct obligations:			
11.1 Personnel compensation: Full-time permanent		1	1
25.2 Other services from non-Federal sources	5	1	2
25.3 Other goods and services from Federal sources	1	1	3
41.0 Grants, subsidies, and contributions		268	
99.0 Direct obligations	6	271	6
99.5 Adjustment for rounding		1	1
99.9 Total new obligations, unexpired accounts	6	272	7

Employment Summary

Identification code 013–0561–0–1–376	2021 actual	2022 est.	2023 est.
1001 Direct civilian full-time equivalent employment	2	7	7

MIDDLE MILE DEPLOYMENT

[(INCLUDING TRANSFER OF FUNDS)]

[For an additional amount for "Middle Mile Deployment", $1,000,000,000, to remain available September 30, 2026, for competitive grants as authorized under section 60401 of division F of this Act: *Provided*, That the Secretary of Commerce shall issue notices of funding opportunity not later than 180 days after the date of enactment of this Act: *Provided further*, That the Secretary of Commerce shall make awards not later than 270 days after issuing the notices of funding opportunity required under the preceding proviso: *Provided further*, That up to 2 percent of the amounts made available under this heading in this Act shall be for salaries and expenses, administration, and oversight, during fiscal years 2022 through 2026 of which $1,000,000 shall be transferred to the Office of Inspector General of the Department of Commerce for oversight of funding provided to the National Telecommunications and Information Administration in this title in this Act: *Provided further*, That such amount is designated by the Congress as being for an emergency requirement pursuant to section 4112(a) of H. Con. Res. 71 (115th Congress), the concurrent resolution on the budget for fiscal year 2018, and to section 251(b) of the Balanced Budget and Emergency Deficit Control Act of 1985.] *(Infrastructure Investments and Jobs Appropriations Act.)*

Program and Financing (in millions of dollars)

Identification code 013–0564–0–1–376	2021 actual	2022 est.	2023 est.
Obligations by program activity:			
0001 Middle Mile Program Admin		9	10
0002 Middle Mile Grants			980
0900 Total new obligations, unexpired accounts		9	990
Budgetary resources:			
Unobligated balance:			
1000 Unobligated balance brought forward, Oct 1			990
Budget authority:			
Appropriations, discretionary:			
1100 Appropriation		1,000	
1120 Appropriations transferred to other acct [013–0126]		–1	
1160 Appropriation, discretionary (total)		999	
1930 Total budgetary resources available		999	990
Memorandum (non-add) entries:			
1941 Unexpired unobligated balance, end of year		990	
Change in obligated balance:			
Unpaid obligations:			
3000 Unpaid obligations, brought forward, Oct 1			9
3010 New obligations, unexpired accounts		9	990
3020 Outlays (gross)			–250
3050 Unpaid obligations, end of year		9	749
Memorandum (non-add) entries:			
3100 Obligated balance, start of year			9
3200 Obligated balance, end of year		9	749
Budget authority and outlays, net:			
Discretionary:			
4000 Budget authority, gross		999	
Outlays, gross:			
4011 Outlays from discretionary balances			250
4180 Budget authority, net (total)		999	
4190 Outlays, net (total)			250

The Infrastructure Investment and Jobs Act provides $1 billion to NTIA for competitive grants, including program administration and oversight, to expand and extend middle mile infrastructure to reduce costs and establish connection resiliency for broadband networks to unserved and underserved areas.

Object Classification (in millions of dollars)

Identification code 013–0564–0–1–376	2021 actual	2022 est.	2023 est.
Direct obligations:			
11.1 Personnel compensation: Full-time permanent		2	3
12.1 Civilian personnel benefits		1	1
25.2 Other services from non-Federal sources		3	3
25.3 Other goods and services from Federal sources		3	3
41.0 Grants, subsidies, and contributions			980
99.0 Direct obligations		9	990
99.9 Total new obligations, unexpired accounts		9	990

Employment Summary

Identification code 013–0564–0–1–376	2021 actual	2022 est.	2023 est.
1001 Direct civilian full-time equivalent employment		19	19

DIGITAL EQUITY

[(INCLUDING TRANSFER OF FUNDS)]

[For an additional amount for "Digital Equity", $2,750,000,000, to remain available until expended, for competitive grants as authorized under sections 60304 and 60305 of division F of this Act: *Provided*, That of the amount provided under this heading in this Act—]

[(1) $550,000,000, to remain available until expended, shall be made available for fiscal year 2022, of which $60,000,000 is for the award of grants under section 60304 (c)(3) of division F of this Act, $240,000,000 is for the award of grants under section 60304(d) of division F of this Act, and $250,000,000 is for the award of grants under section 60305 of division F of this Act;]

[(2) $550,000,000, to remain available until expended, shall be made available for fiscal year 2023, of which $300,000,000 is for the award of grants under section 60304(d) of division F of this Act and $250,000,000 is for the award of grants under section 60305 of division F of this Act;]

[(3) $550,000,000, to remain available until expended, shall be made available for fiscal year 2024, of which $300,000,000 is for the award of grants under section 60304(d) of division F of this Act and $250,000,000 is for the award of grants under section 60305 of division F of this Act;]

[(4) $550,000,000, to remain available until expended, shall be made available for fiscal year 2025, of which $300,000,000 is for the award of grants under section 60304(d) of division F of this Act and $250,000,000 is for the award of grants under section 60305 of division F of this Act; and]

[(5) $550,000,000, to remain available until expended, shall be made available for fiscal year 2026, of which $300,000,000 is for the award of grants under section 60304(d) of division F of this Act and $250,000,000 is for the award of grants under section 60305 of division F of this Act:]

[Provided further, That the Secretary shall issue notices of funding opportunity not later than 180 days after each date upon which funds are made available under the preceding proviso: Provided further, That the Secretary shall make awards not later than 270 days after issuing the notices of funding opportunity required under the preceding proviso: Provided further, That up to 2 percent of the amounts made available in each fiscal year shall be for salaries and expenses, administration, and oversight, of which $1,000,000 in each of fiscal years 2022 through 2026 shall be transferred to the Office of Inspector General of the Department of Commerce for oversight of funding provided to the National Telecommunications and Information Administration in this title in this Act: Provided further, That such amount is designated by the Congress as being for an emergency requirement pursuant to section 4112(a) of H. Con. Res. 71 (115th Congress), the concurrent resolution on the budget for fiscal year 2018, and to section 251(b) of the Balanced Budget

DEPARTMENT OF COMMERCE

and Emergency Deficit Control Act of 1985.】 *(Infrastructure Investments and Jobs Appropriations Act.)*

Program and Financing (in millions of dollars)

Identification code 013–0563–0–1–376	2021 actual	2022 est.	2023 est.
Obligations by program activity:			
0001 Digital Equity Admin		5	6
0002 Digital Equity Grants		59	
0900 Total new obligations, unexpired accounts		64	6
Budgetary resources:			
Unobligated balance:			
1000 Unobligated balance brought forward, Oct 1			485
Budget authority:			
Appropriations, discretionary:			
1100 Appropriation		550	
1120 Appropriations transferred to other acct [013–0126]		–1	
1160 Appropriation, discretionary (total)		549	
Advance appropriations, discretionary:			
1170 Advance appropriation			550
1172 Advance appropriations transferred to other accounts [013–0126]			–1
1180 Advanced appropriation, discretionary (total)			549
1900 Budget authority (total)		549	549
1930 Total budgetary resources available		549	1,034
Memorandum (non-add) entries:			
1941 Unexpired unobligated balance, end of year		485	1,028
Change in obligated balance:			
Unpaid obligations:			
3000 Unpaid obligations, brought forward, Oct 1			59
3010 New obligations, unexpired accounts		64	6
3020 Outlays (gross)		–5	–10
3050 Unpaid obligations, end of year		59	55
Memorandum (non-add) entries:			
3100 Obligated balance, start of year			59
3200 Obligated balance, end of year		59	55
Budget authority and outlays, net:			
Discretionary:			
4000 Budget authority, gross		549	549
Outlays, gross:			
4010 Outlays from new discretionary authority		5	5
4011 Outlays from discretionary balances			5
4020 Outlays, gross (total)		5	10
4180 Budget authority, net (total)		549	549
4190 Outlays, net (total)		5	10

The Infrastructure Investment and Jobs Act provides $2.75 billion to NITA to implement two digital equity programs: the State Digital Equity Capacity Program and the Digital Equity Competitive Grant Program.

The State Digital Equity Capacity Grant Program will provide formula grants to ensure States and territories have the capacity to promote digital equity and support digital inclusion activities. The grants will fund the development and implementation of State Digital Equity Plans.

The Digital Equity Competitive Grant Program will provide competitive grants to support digital equity, promote digital inclusion activities, and spur greater adoption of broadband.

Object Classification (in millions of dollars)

Identification code 013–0563–0–1–376	2021 actual	2022 est.	2023 est.
Direct obligations:			
11.1 Personnel compensation: Full-time permanent		1	1
25.2 Other services from non-Federal sources		2	3
25.3 Other goods and services from Federal sources		2	2
41.0 Grants, subsidies, and contributions		59	
99.9 Total new obligations, unexpired accounts		64	6

Employment Summary

Identification code 013–0563–0–1–376	2021 actual	2022 est.	2023 est.
1001 Direct civilian full-time equivalent employment		8	8

BROADBAND EQUITY, ACCESS, AND DEPLOYMENT PROGRAM

【(INCLUDING TRANSFER OF FUNDS)】

【For an additional amount for "Broadband Equity, Access, and Deployment Program", $42,450,000,000, to remain available until expended, for grants as authorized under section 60102 of division F of this Act: *Provided*, That not later than 90 days after the date of enactment of this Act, the Secretary of Commerce shall submit to the House and Senate Committees on Appropriations a detailed spend plan for fiscal year 2022: *Provided further*, That up to 2 percent of the amounts made available under this heading in this Act in fiscal year 2022 shall be for salaries and expenses, administration, and oversight, of which $12,000,000 shall be transferred to the Office of Inspector General of the Department of Commerce for oversight of funding provided to the National Telecommunications and Information Administration in this title in this Act: *Provided further*, That such amount is designated by the Congress as being for an emergency requirement pursuant to section 4112(a) of H. Con. Res. 71 (115th Congress), the concurrent resolution on the budget for fiscal year 2018, and to section 251(b) of the Balanced Budget and Emergency Deficit Control Act of 1985.】 *(Infrastructure Investments and Jobs Appropriations Act.)*

Program and Financing (in millions of dollars)

Identification code 013–0562–0–1–376	2021 actual	2022 est.	2023 est.
Obligations by program activity:			
0001 Broadband Equity, Access, and Deployment Admin		118	94
0002 Broadband Equity, Access, and Deployment Grants		5,300	
0900 Total new obligations, unexpired accounts		5,418	94
Budgetary resources:			
Unobligated balance:			
1000 Unobligated balance brought forward, Oct 1			37,020
Budget authority:			
Appropriations, discretionary:			
1100 Appropriation		42,450	
1120 Appropriations transferred to other acct [013–0126]		–12	
1160 Appropriation, discretionary (total)		42,438	
1930 Total budgetary resources available		42,438	37,020
Memorandum (non-add) entries:			
1941 Unexpired unobligated balance, end of year		37,020	36,926
Change in obligated balance:			
Unpaid obligations:			
3000 Unpaid obligations, brought forward, Oct 1			3,720
3010 New obligations, unexpired accounts		5,418	94
3020 Outlays (gross)		–1,698	–2,546
3050 Unpaid obligations, end of year		3,720	1,268
Memorandum (non-add) entries:			
3100 Obligated balance, start of year			3,720
3200 Obligated balance, end of year		3,720	1,268
Budget authority and outlays, net:			
Discretionary:			
4000 Budget authority, gross		42,438	
Outlays, gross:			
4010 Outlays from new discretionary authority		1,698	
4011 Outlays from discretionary balances			2,546
4020 Outlays, gross (total)		1,698	2,546
4180 Budget authority, net (total)		42,438	
4190 Outlays, net (total)		1,698	2,546

The Infrastructure Investment and Jobs Act provides $42.45 billion to NTIA for the Broadband Equity, Access, and Deployment program grants, administration, and oversight authorized under section 60102 of the Act. This grants program makes formula grants to States for broadband equity, access, and deployment projects to bridge the digital divide.

BROADBAND EQUITY, ACCESS, AND DEPLOYMENT PROGRAM—Continued

Object Classification (in millions of dollars)

Identification code 013–0562–0–1–376		2021 actual	2022 est.	2023 est.
11.1	Direct obligations: Personnel compensation: Full-time permanent	....	8	11
11.9	Total personnel compensation	....	8	11
12.1	Civilian personnel benefits	....	3	4
21.0	Travel and transportation of persons	....	1	1
23.1	Rental payments to GSA	....	1	1
25.2	Other services from non-Federal sources	....	86	66
25.3	Other goods and services from Federal sources	....	18	11
41.0	Grants, subsidies, and contributions	....	5,300	....
99.0	Direct obligations	....	5,417	94
99.5	Adjustment for rounding	....	1	....
99.9	Total new obligations, unexpired accounts	....	5,418	94

Employment Summary

Identification code 013–0562–0–1–376	2021 actual	2022 est.	2023 est.
1001 Direct civilian full-time equivalent employment	....	68	91

PUBLIC TELECOMMUNICATIONS FACILITIES, PLANNING AND CONSTRUCTION

For the administration of prior-year grants, recoveries and unobligated balances of funds previously appropriated are available for the administration of all open grants until their expiration.

Note.—A full-year 2022 appropriation for this account was not enacted at the time the Budget was prepared; therefore, the Budget assumes this account is operating under the Continuing Appropriations Act, 2022 (Division A of Public Law 117–43, as amended). The amounts included for 2022 reflect the annualized level provided by the continuing resolution.

Program and Financing (in millions of dollars)

Identification code 013–0551–0–1–503		2021 actual	2022 est.	2023 est.
	Budgetary resources: Unobligated balance:			
1000	Unobligated balance brought forward, Oct 1	1	1	1
1930	Total budgetary resources available	1	1	1
	Memorandum (non-add) entries:			
1941	Unexpired unobligated balance, end of year	1	1	1
4180	Budget authority, net (total)	....	....	....
4190	Outlays, net (total)	....	....	....

This program was terminated in 2011; however, the 2023 Budget proposes to continue to use grant recoveries and unobligated balances of funds previously appropriated to administer prior-year grants until their expiration.

DIGITAL TELEVISION TRANSITION AND PUBLIC SAFETY FUND

Program and Financing (in millions of dollars)

Identification code 013–5396–0–2–376		2021 actual	2022 est.	2023 est.
	Change in obligated balance: Unpaid obligations:			
3000	Unpaid obligations, brought forward, Oct 1	5	2	....
3020	Outlays (gross)	–3	–2	....
3050	Unpaid obligations, end of year	2	....	....
	Memorandum (non-add) entries:			
3100	Obligated balance, start of year	5	2	....
3200	Obligated balance, end of year	2	....	....
	Budget authority and outlays, net: Mandatory: Outlays, gross:			
4101	Outlays from mandatory balances	3	2	....
4180	Budget authority, net (total)	....	....	....
4190	Outlays, net (total)	3	2	....
	Memorandum (non-add) entries:			
5103	Unexpired unavailable balance, SOY: Fulfilled purpose	8,810	8,810	8,807
5104	Unexpired unavailable balance, EOY: Fulfilled purpose	8,810	8,807	8,807

The Digital Television Transition and Public Safety Fund, created by the Deficit Reduction Act of 2005, as amended by the Digital Television Delay Act (DTV Delay Act) of 2009, received offsetting receipts from the auction of licenses to use electromagnetic spectrum formerly assigned to broadcast television service, and provided funding for several one-time programs from these receipts. Authority for all programs funded under the Act has expired.

STATE AND LOCAL IMPLEMENTATION FUND

Program and Financing (in millions of dollars)

Identification code 013–0516–0–1–376		2021 actual	2022 est.	2023 est.
	Obligations by program activity:			
0801	State and Local Implementation Fund (Reimbursable)	2	1	....
	Budgetary resources: Unobligated balance:			
1000	Unobligated balance brought forward, Oct 1	8	13	....
1021	Recoveries of prior year unpaid obligations	7	....	....
1070	Unobligated balance (total)	15	13	....
1930	Total budgetary resources available	15	13	....
	Memorandum (non-add) entries:			
1940	Unobligated balance expiring	....	–12	....
1941	Unexpired unobligated balance, end of year	13	....	....
	Change in obligated balance: Unpaid obligations:			
3000	Unpaid obligations, brought forward, Oct 1	16	7	3
3010	New obligations, unexpired accounts	2	1	....
3020	Outlays (gross)	–4	–5	–2
3040	Recoveries of prior year unpaid obligations, unexpired	–7	....	....
3050	Unpaid obligations, end of year	7	3	1
	Memorandum (non-add) entries:			
3100	Obligated balance, start of year	16	7	3
3200	Obligated balance, end of year	7	3	1
	Budget authority and outlays, net: Mandatory: Outlays, gross:			
4101	Outlays from mandatory balances	4	5	2
4180	Budget authority, net (total)	....	....	....
4190	Outlays, net (total)	4	5	2

The Middle Class Tax Relief and Job Creation Act of 2012 provided $135 million for grants to States and territories to plan for the build-out of a nationwide broadband network for first responders. In 2022, NTIA will close out all outstanding grant activities, which were used for the purpose to support state and local governments to maximize the benefits of the nationwide public safety broadband network. This program will expire September 30, 2022.

Object Classification (in millions of dollars)

Identification code 013–0516–0–1–376		2021 actual	2022 est.	2023 est.
	Reimbursable obligations:			
11.1	Personnel compensation: Full-time permanent	1	....	....
25.2	Other services from non-Federal sources	1	1	....
99.0	Reimbursable obligations	2	1	....
99.9	Total new obligations, unexpired accounts	2	1	....

Employment Summary

Identification code 013–0516–0–1–376	2021 actual	2022 est.	2023 est.
1001 Direct civilian full-time equivalent employment	4	....	....

NETWORK CONSTRUCTION FUND

Program and Financing (in millions of dollars)

Identification code 013–4358–0–3–376	2021 actual	2022 est.	2023 est.
Obligations by program activity:			
0801 FirstNet	7		
Budgetary resources:			
Unobligated balance:			
1000 Unobligated balance brought forward, Oct 1	5		
1021 Recoveries of prior year unpaid obligations	1		
1070 Unobligated balance (total)	6		
Budget authority:			
Spending authority from offsetting collections, mandatory:			
1800 Collected	1		
1930 Total budgetary resources available	7		
Change in obligated balance:			
Unpaid obligations:			
3000 Unpaid obligations, brought forward, Oct 1	2,919	1,433	20
3010 New obligations, unexpired accounts	7		
3020 Outlays (gross)	–1,492	–1,413	–20
3040 Recoveries of prior year unpaid obligations, unexpired	–1		
3050 Unpaid obligations, end of year	1,433	20	
Memorandum (non-add) entries:			
3100 Obligated balance, start of year	2,919	1,433	20
3200 Obligated balance, end of year	1,433	20	
Budget authority and outlays, net:			
Mandatory:			
4090 Budget authority, gross	1		
Outlays, gross:			
4101 Outlays from mandatory balances	1,492	1,413	20
Offsets against gross budget authority and outlays:			
Offsetting collections (collected) from:			
4120 Federal sources	–1		
4180 Budget authority, net (total)			
4190 Outlays, net (total)	1,491	1,413	20

The Middle Class Tax Relief and Job Creation Act of 2012 created the Network Construction Fund (NCF) to receive transfers from the Public Safety Trust Fund in support of the construction and deployment of FirstNet's nationwide broadband network. In 2017, FirstNet awarded a contract to build the nationwide network, and activities in the NCF are largely related to disbursement of contract payments. FirstNet's activities are now primarily reflected in the First Responder Network Authority account. The obligation authority for this account expires September 30, 2022.

Object Classification (in millions of dollars)

Identification code 013–4358–0–3–376	2021 actual	2022 est.	2023 est.
Reimbursable obligations:			
11.1 Personnel compensation: Full-time permanent	1		
23.1 Rental payments to GSA	1		
25.2 Other services from non-Federal sources	4		
99.0 Reimbursable obligations	6		
99.5 Adjustment for rounding	1		
99.9 Total new obligations, unexpired accounts	7		

Employment Summary

Identification code 013–4358–0–3–376	2021 actual	2022 est.	2023 est.
1001 Direct civilian full-time equivalent employment	4		

FIRST RESPONDER NETWORK AUTHORITY

Program and Financing (in millions of dollars)

Identification code 013–4421–0–3–376	2021 actual	2022 est.	2023 est.
Obligations by program activity:			
0801 First Responder Network Authority	71	195	195
Budgetary resources:			
Unobligated balance:			
1000 Unobligated balance brought forward, Oct 1	204	253	253
Budget authority:			
Spending authority from offsetting collections, mandatory:			
1800 Collected	120	195	195
1802 Offsetting collections (previously unavailable)	1	1	1
1823 New and/or unobligated balance of spending authority from offsetting collections temporarily reduced	–1	–1	–1
1850 Spending auth from offsetting collections, mand (total)	120	195	195
1930 Total budgetary resources available	324	448	448
Memorandum (non-add) entries:			
1941 Unexpired unobligated balance, end of year	253	253	253
Change in obligated balance:			
Unpaid obligations:			
3000 Unpaid obligations, brought forward, Oct 1	223	180	87
3010 New obligations, unexpired accounts	71	195	195
3020 Outlays (gross)	–114	–288	–174
3050 Unpaid obligations, end of year	180	87	108
Memorandum (non-add) entries:			
3100 Obligated balance, start of year	223	180	87
3200 Obligated balance, end of year	180	87	108
Budget authority and outlays, net:			
Mandatory:			
4090 Budget authority, gross	120	195	195
Outlays, gross:			
4100 Outlays from new mandatory authority		108	108
4101 Outlays from mandatory balances	114	180	66
4110 Outlays, gross (total)	114	288	174
Offsets against gross budget authority and outlays:			
Offsetting collections (collected) from:			
4123 Non-Federal sources	–120	–195	–195
4180 Budget authority, net (total)			
4190 Outlays, net (total)	–6	93	–21
Memorandum (non-add) entries:			
5090 Unexpired unavailable balance, SOY: Offsetting collections	1	1	1
5092 Unexpired unavailable balance, EOY: Offsetting collections	1	1	1

The Middle Class Tax Relief and Job Creation Act of 2012 created the First Responder Network Authority (FirstNet) to ensure the building, deployment, and operation of the nationwide public safety broadband network. FirstNet is an independent authority within the Department of Commerce's National Telecommunications and Information Administration and is overseen by a 15-member Board comprised of the Secretary of Homeland Security, the Attorney General of the United States, the Director of the Office of Management and Budget, as well as 12 members that have public safety expertise, represent the interests of states, localities, tribes, and territories and/or have technical, network or financial expertise. The First Responder Network Authority account reflects funds that FirstNet is authorized to collect to reinvest into the network, enhance public safety communications, and manage FirstNet operations. Incoming funds that are shown in the budget schedule represent funds that FirstNet will collect for use of spectrum licensed to FirstNet.

Object Classification (in millions of dollars)

Identification code 013–4421–0–3–376	2021 actual	2022 est.	2023 est.
Reimbursable obligations:			
11.1 Personnel compensation: Full-time permanent	31	33	33
12.1 Civilian personnel benefits	10	11	11
21.0 Travel and transportation of persons	1	2	2
23.1 Rental payments to GSA	1	2	2
25.1 Advisory and assistance services	7	7	7
25.2 Other services from non-Federal sources	18	136	136
25.3 Other goods and services from Federal sources		2	2

National Telecommunications and Information Administration—Continued
Federal Funds—Continued

FIRST RESPONDER NETWORK AUTHORITY—Continued
Object Classification—Continued

Identification code 013–4421–0–3–376		2021 actual	2022 est.	2023 est.
31.0	Equipment	2	2	2
99.0	Reimbursable obligations	70	195	195
99.5	Adjustment for rounding	1		
99.9	Total new obligations, unexpired accounts	71	195	195

Employment Summary

Identification code 013–4421–0–3–376	2021 actual	2022 est.	2023 est.
2001 Reimbursable civilian full-time equivalent employment	212	212	212

Trust Funds
PUBLIC SAFETY TRUST FUND

Special and Trust Fund Receipts (in millions of dollars)

Identification code 013–8233–0–7–376		2021 actual	2022 est.	2023 est.
0100	Balance, start of year	7,657	12,155	12,195
	Receipts:			
	Current law:			
1120	Spectrum Auction Receipts, Public Safety Trust Fund	4,476		
1140	Earnings on Federal Investments, Public Safety Trust Fund	22	40	50
1199	Total current law receipts	4,498	40	50
1999	Total receipts	4,498	40	50
2000	Total: Balances and receipts	12,155	12,195	12,245
	Appropriations:			
	Current law:			
2101	Public Safety Trust Fund	–4,498		
2135	Public Safety Trust Fund	4,498		
2199	Total current law appropriations			
2999	Total appropriations			
5099	Balance, end of year	12,155	12,195	12,245

Program and Financing (in millions of dollars)

Identification code 013–8233–0–7–376		2021 actual	2022 est.	2023 est.
	Obligations by program activity:			
0002	NTIA Programmatic and Oversight	3	3	
0006	Office of Inspector General (transfer)	2	2	
0007	NTIA Next Generation 9–1–1	1	1	
0900	Total new obligations, unexpired accounts	6	6	
	Budgetary resources:			
	Unobligated balance:			
1000	Unobligated balance brought forward, Oct 1	18	12	
	Budget authority:			
	Appropriations, mandatory:			
1201	Appropriation (special or trust fund)	4,498		
1235	Appropriations precluded from obligation (special or trust)	–4,498		
1930	Total budgetary resources available	18	12	
	Memorandum (non-add) entries:			
1940	Unobligated balance expiring		–6	
1941	Unexpired unobligated balance, end of year	12		
	Special and non-revolving trust funds:			
1951	Unobligated balance expiring		6	
1952	Expired unobligated balance, start of year			6
1953	Expired unobligated balance, end of year			6
	Change in obligated balance:			
	Unpaid obligations:			
3000	Unpaid obligations, brought forward, Oct 1	1	1	1
3010	New obligations, unexpired accounts	6	6	
3020	Outlays (gross)	–6	–6	
3050	Unpaid obligations, end of year	1	1	1
	Memorandum (non-add) entries:			
3100	Obligated balance, start of year	1	1	1
3200	Obligated balance, end of year	1	1	1
	Budget authority and outlays, net:			
	Mandatory:			
	Outlays, gross:			
4101	Outlays from mandatory balances	6	6	
4180	Budget authority, net (total)			
4190	Outlays, net (total)	6	6	
	Memorandum (non-add) entries:			
5000	Total investments, SOY: Federal securities: Par value	7,666	12,159	12,209
5001	Total investments, EOY: Federal securities: Par value	12,159	12,209	12,259

The Middle Class Tax Relief and Job Creation Act of 2012 created the First Responder Network Authority (FirstNet) within the National Telecommunications and Information Administration (NTIA) and directed that up to $7 billion of auction proceeds be used to support the establishment of a nationwide, interoperable public safety broadband network. Resources in this account have primarily funded FirstNet's and NTIA's public safety activities with some support for public safety communications research and Next Generation 911 activities. This account will expire September 30, 2022.

Object Classification (in millions of dollars)

Identification code 013–8233–0–7–376		2021 actual	2022 est.	2023 est.
	Direct obligations:			
11.1	Personnel compensation: Full-time permanent	1	1	
25.2	Other services from non-Federal sources	1	1	
25.3	Other goods and services from Federal sources	2	2	
94.0	Financial transfers	2	2	
99.0	Direct obligations	6	6	
99.9	Total new obligations, unexpired accounts	6	6	

Employment Summary

Identification code 013–8233–0–7–376	2021 actual	2022 est.	2023 est.
1001 Direct civilian full-time equivalent employment	10	10	

GENERAL FUND RECEIPT ACCOUNTS
(in millions of dollars)

	2021 actual	2022 est.	2023 est.
Offsetting receipts from the public:			
013–271710 Fisheries Finance, Negative Subsidies	7	13	19
013–271730 Fisheries Finance, Downward Reestimates of Subsidies	6	2	
013–322000 All Other General Fund Proprietary Receipts Including Budget Clearing Accounts	4		
General Fund Offsetting receipts from the public	17	15	19
Intragovernmental payments:			
013–388500 Undistributed Intragovernmental Payments and Receivables from Cancelled Accounts	4		
General Fund Intragovernmental payments	4		

GENERAL PROVISIONS—DEPARTMENT OF COMMERCE

(INCLUDING TRANSFER OF FUNDS)

SEC. 101. During the current fiscal year, applicable appropriations and funds made available to the Department of Commerce by this Act shall be available for the activities specified in the Act of October 26, 1949 (15 U.S.C. 1514), to the extent and in the manner prescribed by the Act, and, notwithstanding 31 U.S.C. 3324, may be used for advanced payments not otherwise authorized only upon the certification of officials designated by the Secretary of Commerce that such payments are in the public interest.

SEC. 102. During the current fiscal year, appropriations made available to the Department of Commerce by this Act for salaries and expenses shall be available for hire of passenger motor vehicles as authorized by 31 U.S.C. 1343 and 1344, including zero emission passenger motor vehicles and supporting charging or fueling infrastructure; services as authorized by 5 U.S.C. 3109; and uniforms or allowances therefor, as authorized by law (5 U.S.C. 5901–5902).

SEC. 103. Not to exceed 5 percent of any appropriation made available for the current fiscal year for the Department of Commerce in this Act may be transferred between such appropriations, but no such appropriation shall be increased by more than 10 percent by any such transfers: Provided, That any transfer pursuant to this section shall be treated as a reprogramming of funds under section 504 of this Act and shall not be available for obligation or expenditure except in compliance with the procedures set forth in that section: Provided further, That the Secretary of Commerce shall notify the Committees on Appropriations at least 15 days in advance of the acquisition or disposal of any capital asset (including land, structures, and equipment) not specifically provided for in this Act or any other law appropriating funds for the Department of Commerce.

SEC. 104. Notwithstanding any other provision of law, the Secretary of Commerce may furnish services (including but not limited to utilities, telecommunications, and security services) necessary to support the operation, maintenance, and improvement of space that persons, firms, or organizations are authorized, pursuant to the Public Buildings Cooperative Use Act of 1976 or other authority, to use or occupy in the Herbert C. Hoover Building, Washington, DC, or other buildings, the maintenance, operation, and protection of which has been delegated to the Secretary from the Administrator of General Services pursuant to the Federal Property and Administrative Services Act of 1949 on a reimbursable or non-reimbursable basis. Amounts received as reimbursement for services provided under this section or the authority under which the use or occupancy of the space is authorized, up to $200,000, shall be credited to the appropriation or fund which initially bears the costs of such services.

SEC. 105. Nothing in this title shall be construed to prevent a grant recipient from deterring child pornography, copyright infringement, or any other unlawful activity over its networks.

SEC. 106. The Administrator of the National Oceanic and Atmospheric Administration is authorized to use, with their consent, with reimbursement and subject to the limits of available appropriations, the land, services, equipment, personnel, and facilities of any department, agency, or instrumentality of the United States, or of any State, local government, Indian Tribal government, Territory, or possession, or of any political subdivision thereof, or of any foreign government or international organization, for purposes related to carrying out the responsibilities of any statute administered by the National Oceanic and Atmospheric Administration.

SEC. 107. The National Technical Information Service shall not charge any customer for a copy of any report or document generated by the Legislative Branch unless the Service has provided information to the customer on how an electronic copy of such report or document may be accessed and downloaded for free online. Should a customer still require the Service to provide a printed or digital copy of the report or document, the charge shall be limited to recovering the Service's cost of processing, reproducing, and delivering such report or document.

SEC. 108. To carry out the responsibilities of the National Oceanic and Atmospheric Administration (NOAA), the Administrator of NOAA is authorized to: (1) enter into grants and cooperative agreements with; (2) use on a non-reimbursable basis land, services, equipment, personnel, and facilities provided by; and (3) receive and expend funds made available on a consensual basis from: a Federal agency, State or subdivision thereof, local government, Tribal government, Territory, or possession or any subdivisions thereof, foreign government, international or intergovernmental organization, public or private organization, or individual: Provided, That funds received pursuant to this section shall be deposited under the heading "National Oceanic and Atmospheric Administration—Operations, Research, and Facilities" and shall remain available until expended for such purposes: Provided further, That all funds within this section and their corresponding uses are subject to section 504 of this Act.

SEC. 109. Amounts provided by this Act or by any prior appropriations Act that remain available for obligation, for necessary expenses of the programs of the Economics and Statistics Administration of the Department of Commerce, including amounts provided for programs of the Bureau of Economic Analysis and the Bureau of the Census, shall be available for expenses of cooperative agreements with appropriate entities, including any Federal, State, or local governmental unit, or institution of higher education, to aid and promote statistical, research, and methodology activities which further the purposes for which such amounts have been made available.

SEC. 110. Amounts provided by this Act for the Hollings Manufacturing Extension Partnership under the heading "National Institute of Standards and Technology—Industrial Technology Services" shall not be subject to cost share requirements under 15 U.S.C. 278k(e)(2): Provided, That the authority made available pursuant to this section shall be elective, in whole or in part, for any Manufacturing Extension Partnership Center that also receives funding from a State that is conditioned upon the application of a Federal cost sharing requirement.

SEC. 111. The Secretary of Commerce, or the designee of the Secretary, may waive, in whole or in part, the matching requirements under sections 306 and 306A, and the cost sharing requirements under section 315, of the Coastal Zone Management Act of 1972 (16 U.S.C. 1455, 1455a, and 1461) as necessary at the request of the grant applicant, for amounts made available under this Act under the heading "Operations, Research, and Facilities" under the heading "National Oceanic and Atmospheric Administration".

GENERAL PROVISIONS
(INCLUDING CANCELLATIONS)
(INCLUDING TRANSFER OF FUNDS)

SEC. 501. No part of any appropriation contained in this Act shall remain available for obligation beyond the current fiscal year unless expressly so provided herein.

SEC. 502. The expenditure of any appropriation under this Act for any consulting service through procurement contract, pursuant to section 3109 of title 5, United States Code, shall be limited to those contracts where such expenditures are a matter of public record and available for public inspection, except where otherwise provided under existing law, or under existing Executive order issued pursuant to existing law.

SEC. 503. If any provision of this Act or the application of such provision to any person or circumstances shall be held invalid, the remainder of the Act and the application of each provision to persons or circumstances other than those as to which it is held invalid shall not be affected thereby.

SEC. 504. None of the funds provided under this Act, or provided under previous appropriations Acts to the agencies funded by this Act that remain available for obligation or expenditure in fiscal year 2023, or provided from any accounts in the Treasury of the United States derived by the collection of fees available to the agencies funded by this Act, shall be available for obligation or expenditure through a reprogramming of funds that: (1) creates or initiates a new program, project, or activity; (2) eliminates a program, project, or activity; (3) increases funds or personnel by any means for any project or activity for which funds have been denied or restricted; (4) relocates an office or employees; (5) reorganizes or renames offices, programs, or activities; (6) contracts out or privatizes any functions or activities presently performed by Federal employees; (7) augments existing programs, projects, or activities in excess of $1,000,000 or 10 percent, whichever is less, or reduces by 10 percent funding for any program, project, or activity, or numbers of personnel by 10 percent; or (8) results from any general savings, including savings from a reduction in personnel, which would result in a change in existing programs, projects, or activities as approved by Congress; unless the House and Senate Committees on Appropriations are notified 15 days in advance of such reprogramming of funds.

SEC. 505. (a) If it has been finally determined by a court or Federal agency that any person intentionally affixed a label bearing a "Made in America" inscription, or any inscription with the same meaning, to any product sold in or shipped to the United States that is not made in the United States, the person shall be ineligible to receive any contract or subcontract made with funds made available in this Act, pursuant to the debarment, suspension, and ineligibility procedures described in sections 9.400 through 9.409 of title 48, Code of Federal Regulations.

(b)

(1) To the extent practicable, with respect to authorized purchases of promotional items, funds made available by this Act shall be used to purchase items that are manufactured, produced, or assembled in the United States, its territories or possessions.

(2) The term "promotional items" has the meaning given the term in OMB Circular A-87, Attachment B, Item (1)(f)(3).

SEC. 506. (a) The Departments of Commerce and Justice, the National Science Foundation, and the National Aeronautics and Space Administration shall provide to the Committees on Appropriations of the House of Representatives and the Senate a quarterly report on the status of balances of appropriations at the account level. For unobligated, uncommitted balances and unobligated, committed balances the quarterly reports shall separately identify the amounts attributable to each source year of appropriation from which the balances were derived. For balances that are obligated, but unexpended, the quarterly reports shall separately identify amounts by the year of obligation.

(b) The report described in subsection (a) shall be submitted within 30 days of the end of each quarter.

(c) If a department or agency is unable to fulfill any aspect of a reporting requirement described in subsection (a) due to a limitation of a current accounting system, the department or agency shall fulfill such aspect to the maximum extent practicable under such accounting system and shall identify and describe in each quarterly report the extent to which such aspect is not fulfilled.

SEC. 507. Any costs incurred by a department or agency funded under this Act resulting from, or to prevent, personnel actions taken in response to funding reductions included in this Act shall be absorbed within the total budgetary resources available to such department or agency: Provided, That the authority to transfer funds between appropriations accounts as may be necessary to carry out this section is provided in addition to authorities included elsewhere in this Act: Provided further, That use of funds to carry out this section shall be treated as a reprogramming of funds under section 504 of this Act and shall not be available for obligation or expenditure except in compliance with the procedures set forth in that section: Provided further, That for the Department of Commerce, this section shall also apply to actions taken for the care and protection of loan collateral or grant property.

SEC. 508. None of the funds provided by this Act shall be available to promote the sale or export of tobacco or tobacco products.

SEC. 509. None of the funds made available to the Department of Justice in this Act may be used to discriminate against or denigrate the religious or moral beliefs of students who participate in programs for which financial assistance is provided from those funds, or of the parents or legal guardians of such students.

SEC. 510. None of the funds made available in this Act may be transferred to any department, agency, or instrumentality of the United States Government, except pursuant to a transfer made by, or transfer authority provided in, this Act or any other appropriations Act.

SEC. 511. (a) The Inspectors General of the Department of Commerce, the Department of Justice, the National Aeronautics and Space Administration, the National Science Foundation, and the Legal Services Corporation shall conduct audits, pursuant to the Inspector General Act (5 U.S.C. App.), of grants or contracts for which funds are appropriated by this Act, and shall submit reports to Congress on the progress of such audits, which may include preliminary findings and a description of areas of particular interest, within 180 days after initiating such an audit and every 180 days thereafter until any such audit is completed.

(b) Within 60 days after the date on which an audit described in subsection (a) by an Inspector General is completed, the Secretary, Attorney General, Administrator, Director, or President, as appropriate, shall make the results of the audit available to the public on the Internet website maintained by the Department, Administration, Foundation, or Corporation, respectively. The results shall be made available in redacted form to exclude—

(1) any matter described in section 552(b) of title 5, United States Code; and
(2) sensitive personal information for any individual, the public access to which could be used to commit identity theft or for other inappropriate or unlawful purposes.

(c) Any person awarded a grant or contract funded by amounts appropriated by this Act shall submit a statement to the Secretary of Commerce, the Attorney General, the Administrator, Director, or President, as appropriate, certifying that no funds derived from the grant or contract will be made available through a subcontract or in any other manner to another person who has a financial interest in the person awarded the grant or contract.

(d) The provisions of the preceding subsections of this section shall take effect 30 days after the date on which the Director of the Office of Management and Budget, in consultation with the Director of the Office of Government Ethics, determines that a uniform set of rules and requirements, substantially similar to the requirements in such subsections, consistently apply under the executive branch ethics program to all Federal departments, agencies, and entities.

SEC. 512. (a) None of the funds appropriated or otherwise made available under this Act may be used by the Departments of Commerce and Justice, the National Aeronautics and Space Administration, or the National Science Foundation to acquire a high-impact or moderate-impact information system, as defined for security categorization in the National Institute of Standards and Technology's (NIST) Federal Information Processing Standard Publication 199, "Standards for Security Categorization of Federal Information and Information Systems" unless the agency has—

(1) reviewed the supply chain risk for the information systems against criteria developed by NIST and the Federal Bureau of Investigation (FBI) to inform acquisition decisions for high-impact and moderate-impact information systems within the Federal Government;
(2) reviewed the supply chain risk from the presumptive awardee against available and relevant threat information provided by the FBI and other appropriate agencies; and
(3) in consultation with the FBI or other appropriate Federal entity, conducted an assessment of any risk of cyber-espionage or sabotage associated with the acquisition of such system, including any risk associated with such system being produced, manufactured, or assembled by one or more entities identified by the United States Government as posing a cyber threat, including but not limited to, those that may be owned, directed, or subsidized by the People's Republic of China, the Islamic Republic of Iran, the Democratic People's Republic of Korea, or the Russian Federation.

(b) None of the funds appropriated or otherwise made available under this Act may be used to acquire a high-impact or moderate-impact information system reviewed and assessed under subsection (a) unless the head of the assessing entity described in subsection (a) has—

(1) developed, in consultation with NIST, the FBI, and supply chain risk management experts, a mitigation strategy for any identified risks;
(2) determined, in consultation with NIST and the FBI, that the acquisition of such system is in the national interest of the United States; and
(3) reported that determination to the Committees on Appropriations of the House of Representatives and the Senate and the agency Inspector General.

SEC. 513. None of the funds made available in this Act shall be used in any way whatsoever to support or justify the use of torture by any official or contract employee of the United States Government.

SEC. 514. None of the funds made available in this Act may be used to authorize or issue a national security letter in contravention of any of the following laws authorizing the Federal Bureau of Investigation to issue national security letters: The Right to Financial Privacy Act of 1978; The Electronic Communications Privacy Act of 1986; The Fair Credit Reporting Act; The National Security Act of 1947; USA PATRIOT Act; USA FREEDOM Act of 2015; and the laws amended by these Acts.

SEC. 515. If at any time during any quarter, the program manager of a project within the jurisdiction of the Departments of Commerce or Justice, the National Aeronautics and Space Administration, or the National Science Foundation totaling more than $75,000,000 has reasonable cause to believe that the total program cost has increased by 10 percent or more, the program manager shall immediately inform the respective Secretary, Administrator, or Director. The Secretary, Administrator, or Director shall notify the House and Senate Committees on Appropriations within 30 days in writing of such increase, and shall include in such notice: the date on which such determination was made; a statement of the reasons for such increases; the action taken and proposed to be taken to control future cost growth of the project; changes made in the performance or schedule milestones and the degree to which such changes have contributed to the increase in total program costs or procurement costs; new estimates of the total project or procurement costs; and a statement validating that the project's management structure is adequate to control total project or procurement costs.

SEC. 516. Funds appropriated by this Act, or made available by the transfer of funds in this Act, for intelligence or intelligence related activities are deemed to be specifically authorized by the Congress for purposes of section 504 of the National Security Act of 1947 (50 U.S.C. 3094) during fiscal year 2023 until the enactment of the Intelligence Authorization Act for fiscal year 2023.

SEC. 517. None of the funds appropriated or otherwise made available by this Act may be used to enter into a contract in an amount greater than $5,000,000 or to award a grant in excess of such amount unless the prospective contractor or grantee certifies in writing to the agency awarding the contract or grant that, to the best of its knowledge and belief, the contractor or grantee has filed all Federal tax returns required during the three years preceding the certification, has not been convicted of a criminal offense under the Internal Revenue Code of 1986, and has not, more than 90 days prior to certification, been notified of any unpaid Federal tax assessment for which the liability remains unsatisfied, unless the assessment is the subject of an installment agreement or offer in compromise that has been approved by the Internal Revenue Service and is not in default, or the assessment is the subject of a non-frivolous administrative or judicial proceeding.

(CANCELLATIONS)

SEC. 518. (a) Of the unobligated balances from prior year appropriations available to the Department of Commerce under the heading "Economic Development Administration—Economic Development Assistance Programs", $10,000,000 are hereby permanently cancelled, not later than September 30, 2023.

(b) The Department of Commerce shall submit to the Committees on Appropriations of the House of Representatives and the Senate a report no later than September 1, 2022, specifying the amount of the cancellation made pursuant to subsection (a).

(c) The amount cancelled in subsection (a) shall not be from amounts that were designated by the Congress as an emergency or disaster relief requirement pursuant to the concurrent resolution on the budget or the Balanced Budget and Emergency Deficit Control Act of 1985.

SEC. 519. None of the funds made available in this Act may be used to purchase first class or premium airline travel in contravention of sections 301–10.122 through 301–10.124 of title 41 of the Code of Federal Regulations.

SEC. 520. None of the funds made available in this Act may be used to send or otherwise pay for the attendance of more than 50 employees from a Federal department or agency, who are stationed in the United States, at any single conference occurring outside the United States unless—

(1) such conference is a law enforcement training or operational conference for law enforcement personnel and the majority of Federal employees in attendance are law enforcement personnel stationed outside the United States;

(2) such conference is a scientific conference and the department or agency head determines that such attendance is in the national interest and notifies the Committees on Appropriations of the House of Representatives and the Senate within at least 15 days of that determination and the basis for that determination;

(3) the department or agency head determines that such attendance is in the national interest and notifies the Committees on Appropriations of the House of Representatives and the Senate within at least 10 days of that determination and basis for that determination; or

(4) such conference pertains to diplomatic relations.

SEC. 521. The Director of the Office of Management and Budget shall instruct any department, agency, or instrumentality of the United States receiving funds appropriated under this Act to track undisbursed balances in expired grant accounts and include in its annual performance plan and performance and accountability reports the following:

(1) Details on future action the department, agency, or instrumentality will take to resolve undisbursed balances in expired grant accounts.

(2) The method that the department, agency, or instrumentality uses to track undisbursed balances in expired grant accounts.

(3) Identification of undisbursed balances in expired grant accounts that may be returned to the Treasury of the United States.

(4) In the preceding 3 fiscal years, details on the total number of expired grant accounts with undisbursed balances (on the first day of each fiscal year) for the department, agency, or instrumentality and the total finances that have not been obligated to a specific project remaining in the accounts.

SEC. 522. To the extent practicable, funds made available in this Act should be used to purchase light bulbs that are "Energy Star" qualified or have the "Federal Energy Management Program" designation.

SEC. 523. (a) None of the funds made available in this Act may be used to maintain or establish a computer network unless such network blocks the viewing, downloading, and exchanging of pornography.

(b) Nothing in subsection (a) shall limit the use of funds necessary for any Federal, State, Tribal, or local law enforcement agency or any other entity carrying out criminal investigations, prosecution, adjudication, or other law enforcement- or victim assistance-related activity.

SEC. 524. The Departments of Commerce and Justice, the National Aeronautics and Space Administration, the National Science Foundation, the Commission on Civil Rights, the Equal Employment Opportunity Commission, the International Trade Commission, the Legal Services Corporation, the Marine Mammal Commission, the Offices of Science and Technology Policy and the United States Trade Representative, the National Space Council, and the State Justice Institute shall submit spending plans, signed by the respective department or agency head, to the Committees on Appropriations of the House of Representatives and the Senate not later than 60 days after the date of enactment of this Act.

SEC. 525. Notwithstanding any other provision of this Act, none of the funds appropriated or otherwise made available by this Act may be used to pay award or incentive fees for contractor performance that has been judged to be below satisfactory performance or for performance that does not meet the basic requirements of a contract.

SEC. 526. None of the funds made available by this Act may be used in contravention of section 7606 ("Legitimacy of Industrial Hemp Research") of the Agricultural Act of 2014 (Public Law 113–79) by the Department of Justice or the Drug Enforcement Administration.

SEC. 527. None of the funds made available under this Act to the Department of Justice may be used, with respect to any of the States of Alabama, Alaska, Arizona, Arkansas, California, Colorado, Connecticut, Delaware, Florida, Georgia, Hawaii, Illinois, Indiana, Iowa, Kentucky, Louisiana, Maine, Maryland, Massachusetts, Michigan, Minnesota, Mississippi, Missouri, Montana, Nevada, New Hampshire, New Jersey, New Mexico, New York, North Carolina, North Dakota, Ohio, Oklahoma, Oregon, Pennsylvania, Rhode Island, South Carolina, South Dakota, Tennessee, Texas, Utah, Vermont, Virginia, Washington, West Virginia, Wisconsin, and Wyoming, or with respect to the District of Columbia, the Commonwealth of the Northern Mariana Islands, the United States Virgin Islands, Guam, or Puerto Rico, to prevent any of them from implementing their own laws that authorize the use, distribution, possession, or cultivation of medical marijuana.

SEC. 528. The Department of Commerce, the National Aeronautics and Space Administration, and the National Science Foundation shall provide a quarterly report to the Committees on Appropriations of the House of Representatives and the Senate on any official travel to China by any employee of such Department or agency, including the purpose of such travel.

SEC. 529. Of the amounts made available by this Act, not less than 10 percent of the total amount provided for Public Works grants authorized by the Public Works and Economic Development Act of 1965 shall be allocated for assistance in persistent poverty counties: Provided, That for purposes of this section, the term "persistent poverty counties" means any county that has had 20 percent or more of its population living in poverty over the past 30 years, as measured by the 1990 and 2000 decennial censuses and the most recent Small Area Income and Poverty Estimates, or any Territory or possession of the United States.

SEC. 530. Section 514 of the Commerce, Justice, Science, and Related Agencies Appropriations Act, 2013 (division B of Public Law 113–6) is repealed.

DEPARTMENT OF DEFENSE—MILITARY PROGRAMS

MILITARY PERSONNEL
ACTIVE AND RESERVE FORCES

These appropriations finance the personnel costs of the Active, Reserve, and Guard forces of the Army, Navy, Marine Corps, Air Force, and Space Force. They include pay and allowances of officers, enlisted personnel, cadets and midshipmen, permanent change of station travel, inactive duty and active duty training, accruing retirement and health benefits, enlistment, reenlistment and affiliation bonuses, special and incentive pays, and other personnel costs.

Included in these accounts is funding for a 4.6 percent across-the-board pay raise for all pay grades, effective January 1, 2023. This pay raise is equal to the increase in the Employment Cost Index (ECI) for wages and salaries, for private industry workers as called for in law. Even with this modest increase, military salaries, as defined by Regular Military Compensation, which includes basic pay, a tax-free allowance for housing or the value of in-kind housing, a tax-free allowance for subsistence (food), and the tax savings because these allowances are tax free, will continue to grow and will average more than $70,200 for enlisted personnel and more than $127,100 for officers in FY 2023. Many military personnel also receive one-time or yearly bonuses, monthly special pays, other allowances, and significant non-cash benefits, including comprehensive health care.

The Ronald W. Reagan National Defense Authorization Act for Fiscal Year 2005 (P.L. 108–375) provided permanent, indefinite appropriations to finance the cost of accruing TRICARE benefits of uniformed servicemembers. These costs are included in the DOD discretionary total.

The following summary table reflects the FY 2022 annualized Continuing Resolution amounts, and, where appropriate, enacted amounts and the base FY 2023 military personnel appropriation request (includes amounts for Overseas Operations) and the additional amounts for TRICARE accrual funded from permanent, indefinite authority. Total base FY 2023 military personnel requirements are $173,883 million.

MILITARY PERSONNEL TOTALS WITH TRICARE ACCRUAL AMOUNTS[1]

	2022 Appropriation Enacted[2] ($ mil) With Accrual	2023 Appropriation Request ($ mil) With Accrual
Military Personnel, Army	47,736	50,305
Tricare accrual (permanent, indefinite authority)	2,623	2,694
Total, Military Personnel, Army	50,359	52,999
Military Personnel, Navy	34,211	36,629
Tricare accrual (permanent, indefinite authority)	1,884	1,986
Total, Military Personnel, Navy	36,095	38,615
Military Personnel, Marine Corps	14,713	15,330
Tricare accrual (permanent, indefinite authority)	993	1,027
Total, Military Personnel, Marine Corps	15,706	16,357
Military Personnel, Air Force[3]	33,969	35,140
Tricare accrual (permanent, indefinite authority)[3]	1,824	1,855
Total, Military Personnel, Air Force	35,793	36,995
Military Personnel, Space Force	—	1,117
Tricare accrual (permanent, indefinite authority)	—	49
Total, Military Personnel, Space Force	—	1,166
Reserve Personnel, Army	5,071	5,385
Tricare accrual (permanent, indefinite authority)	460	490
Total, Reserve Personnel, Army	5,531	5,875
Reserve Personnel, Navy	2,212	2,411
Tricare accrual (permanent, indefinite authority)	160	168
Total, Reserve Personnel, Navy	2,372	2,579
Reserve Personnel, Marine Corps	846	850
Tricare accrual (permanent, indefinite authority)	86	83
Total, Reserve Personnel, Marine Corps	931	933
Reserve Personnel, Air Force	2,210	2,520
Tricare accrual (permanent, indefinite authority)	169	181
Total, Reserve Personnel, Air Force	2,379	2,701
National Guard Personnel, Army	8,859	9,325
Tricare accrual (permanent, indefinite authority)	822	874
Total, National Guard Personnel, Army	9,681	10,199
National Guard Personnel, Air Force	4,536	5,127
Tricare accrual (permanent, indefinite authority)	314	336
Total, National Guard Personnel, Air Force	4,850	5,463
Total, Appropriated Military Personnel Accounts	154,363	164,140
Total, Permanent, Indefinite Authority	9,336	9,744
Total, Military Personnel	163,699	173,883

[1] Totals may not add due to rounding.
[2] A full-year FY 2022 appropriation for this account was not enacted at the time the budget was prepared; therefore, the budget assumes this account is operating under the Extending Government Funding and Delivering Emergency Assistance Act (Public Law 117–43), Further Extending Government Funding Act (Public Law 117–70), and Further Additional Extending Government Funding Act (Public Law 117–86). The amounts included for FY 2022 reflect the annualized level provided by the continuing resolution adjusted by any full year enactments in the above mentioned legislation.
[3] 2022 Includes funding for Space Force.

ACTIVE FORCES
YEAR-END NUMBER

	2021 actual	2022 est.[1]	2023 est.
Defense total	1,348,479	1,332,439	1,328,300
Officers	236,061	236,611	236,100
Enlisted	1,099,378	1,082,825	1,079,354
Academy cadets and midshipmen	13,040	13,003	12,846
Army	486,490	476,000	473,000
Officers	93,443	93,329	92,647
Enlisted	388,564	378,201	375,857
Military Academy cadets	4,483	4,470	4,496
Navy	347,677	347,484	346,300
Officers	56,044	56,657	55,845
Enlisted	287,179	286,434	286,105
Naval Academy midshipmen	4,454	4,393	4,350
Marine Corps	179,678	177,249	177,000
Officers	21,701	21,668	21,750
Enlisted	157,977	155,581	155,250
Air Force	328,071	323,305	323,400
Officers	61,217	60,623	61,544
Enlisted	262,751	258,542	257,856
Air Force Academy cadets	4,103	4,140	4,000
Space Force	6,563	8,401	8,600
Officer	3,656	4,334	4,314
Enlisted	2,907	4,067	4,286

[1] The 2022 column reflects the projected end strength levels.

RESERVE FORCES

The number of National Guard and Reserve personnel estimated to participate in the Selected Reserve training programs and the number of full-time active duty military personnel provided for are summarized in the following table.

YEAR-END NUMBER

	2021 actual	2022 est.[1]	2023 est.
Defense total	793,808	795,108	794,600
Trained inactive duty	647,446	648,853	648,744
Training pipeline	56,232	54,882	53,119
Full-time active duty	90,130	91,373	92,737
Army Reserve	184,358	189,500	189,500
Trained inactive duty	154,808	160,791	162,372
Training pipeline	12,890	12,198	10,617
Full-time active duty	16,660	16,511	16,511
Navy Reserve	57,632	58,651	57,700
Trained inactive duty	45,883	46,821	46,383
Training pipeline	1,608	1,537	1,240

231

Military Personnel—Continued
Bureau Introduction—Continued

YEAR-END NUMBER—Continued

	2021 actual	2022 est.[1]	2023 est.
Full-time active duty	10,141	10,293	10,077
Marine Corps Reserve	35,240	32,357	33,000
Trained inactive duty	29,677	26,388	27,170
Training pipeline	3,174	3,581	3,442
Full-time active duty	2,389	2,388	2,388
Air Force Reserve	70,570	70,300	70,000
Trained inactive duty	62,194	61,150	60,027
Training pipeline	3,173	3,147	3,687
Full-time active duty	5,203	6,003	6,286
Army National Guard	337,525	336,000	336,000
Trained inactive duty	276,530	274,184	274,795
Training pipeline	30,256	30,971	30,360
Full-time active duty	30,739	30,845	30,845
Air National Guard	108,483	108,300	108,400
Trained inactive duty	78,354	79,519	77,997
Training pipeline	5,131	3,448	3,773
Full-time active duty	24,998	25,333	26,630

[1] The 2022 column reflects the FY 2022 projected end strength levels.

The Reserve Officers' Training Corps (ROTC) program provides training for reserve and regular officer candidates who have enrolled in the course while attending a college at which an ROTC unit has been established. College graduates who satisfactorily complete the advanced course of the program are commissioned and may be ordered to active duty for a minimum of three years.

The Reserve Officers' Training Corps Vitalization Act of 1964, as amended, authorizes a limited number of scholarships for ROTC students on a competitive basis. Successful candidates for the scholarships generally serve a minimum period of four years on active duty upon graduation and appointment as a commissioned officer. A number of scholarship recipients will fulfill their entire obligation in the Reserve components.

The Armed Forces Health Professions Scholarship Program provides a source of active duty commissioned officers for the various health professions.

The numbers of commissioned officers graduated from these programs are summarized below:

	2021 actual	2022 est.	2023 est.
ROTC:			
Army	6,258	6,330	5,400
Navy	1,031	1,065	1,050
Air Force	2,188	2,473	2,220
Total	9,477	9,868	8,670
Marine Corps officer candidates	393	340	400
Total	393	340	400
Health Professions scholarship:			
Army	410	410	410
Navy	342	316	308
Air Force	446	426	421
Total	1,198	1,152	1,139

Federal Funds

MILITARY PERSONNEL, ARMY

For pay, allowances, individual clothing, subsistence, interest on deposits, gratuities, permanent change of station travel (including all expenses thereof for organizational movements), and expenses of temporary duty travel between permanent duty stations, for members of the Army on active duty (except members of reserve components provided for elsewhere), cadets, and aviation cadets; for members of the Reserve Officers' Training Corps; and for payments pursuant to section 156 of Public Law 97–377, as amended (42 U.S.C. 402 note), and to the Department of Defense Military Retirement Fund, $50,305,255,000, of which not to exceed $1,732,515,000 shall remain available until September 30, 2024, for permanent change of station travel.

Note.—A full-year 2022 appropriation for this account was not enacted at the time the Budget was prepared; therefore, the Budget assumes this account is operating under the Continuing Appropriations Act, 2022 (Division A of Public Law 117–43, as amended). The amounts included for 2022 reflect the annualized level provided by the continuing resolution.

MILITARY PERSONNEL, ARMY

[*For an additional amount for "Military Personnel, Army", $128,000,000, to remain available until September 30, 2022, for support of Operation Allies Welcome by the Department of Defense.*] *(Additional Afghanistan Supplemental Appropriations Act, 2022.)*

Program and Financing (in millions of dollars)

Identification code 021–2010–0–1–051		2021 actual	2022 est.	2023 est.
	Obligations by program activity:			
0001	Pay and Allowances of Officers	15,062	15,036	15,938
0002	Pay and Allowances of Enlisted	28,741	28,860	30,096
0003	Pay and Allowances of Cadets	94	94	102
0004	Subsistence of Enlisted Personnel	2,153	2,221	2,157
0005	Permanent change of station travel	1,592	1,644	1,733
0006	Other military personnel costs	298	280	279
0020	Undistributed	....	–399	....
0799	Total direct obligations	47,940	47,736	50,305
0801	Reimbursable program activity	321	338	342
0900	Total new obligations, unexpired accounts	48,261	48,074	50,647
	Budgetary resources:			
	Unobligated balance:			
1000	Unobligated balance brought forward, Oct 1	....	1	1
1011	Unobligated balance transfer from other acct [097–0801]	113	....	....
1070	Unobligated balance (total)	113	1	1
	Budget authority:			
	Appropriations, discretionary:			
1100	Appropriation	47,575	47,736	50,305
1120	Appropriations transferred to other acct [021–2060]	–30	....	....
1121	Appropriations transferred from other acct [057–3620]	32	....	....
1121	Appropriations transferred from other acct [017–1506]	10	....	....
1121	Appropriations transferred from other acct [057–3600]	72	....	....
1121	Appropriations transferred from other acct [021–2020]	43	....	....
1121	Appropriations transferred from other acct [017–1105]	126	....	....
1160	Appropriation, discretionary (total)	47,828	47,736	50,305
	Spending authority from offsetting collections, discretionary:			
1700	Collected	....	338	342
1701	Change in uncollected payments, Federal sources	153	....	....
1750	Spending auth from offsetting collections, disc (total)	153	338	342
	Spending authority from offsetting collections, mandatory:			
1800	Collected	168	....	....
1900	Budget authority (total)	48,149	48,074	50,647
1930	Total budgetary resources available	48,262	48,075	50,648
	Memorandum (non-add) entries:			
1941	Unexpired unobligated balance, end of year	1	1	1
	Change in obligated balance:			
	Unpaid obligations:			
3000	Unpaid obligations, brought forward, Oct 1	4,113	3,757	2,639
3010	New obligations, unexpired accounts	48,261	48,074	50,647
3011	Obligations ("upward adjustments"), expired accounts	1,338	....	....
3020	Outlays (gross)	–48,395	–49,192	–50,280
3041	Recoveries of prior year unpaid obligations, expired	–1,560	....	....
3050	Unpaid obligations, end of year	3,757	2,639	3,006
	Uncollected payments:			
3060	Uncollected pymts, Fed sources, brought forward, Oct 1	–255	–346	–346
3070	Change in uncollected pymts, Fed sources, unexpired	–153	....	....
3071	Change in uncollected pymts, Fed sources, expired	62	....	....
3090	Uncollected pymts, Fed sources, end of year	–346	–346	–346
	Memorandum (non-add) entries:			
3100	Obligated balance, start of year	3,858	3,411	2,293
3200	Obligated balance, end of year	3,411	2,293	2,660
	Budget authority and outlays, net:			
	Discretionary:			
4000	Budget authority, gross	47,981	48,074	50,647
	Outlays, gross:			
4010	Outlays from new discretionary authority	45,482	45,435	47,880
4011	Outlays from discretionary balances	2,745	3,757	2,400
4020	Outlays, gross (total)	48,227	49,192	50,280
	Offsets against gross budget authority and outlays:			
	Offsetting collections (collected) from:			
4030	Federal sources	–20	–338	–342
4033	Non-Federal sources	–2	....	....
4040	Offsets against gross budget authority and outlays (total)	–22	–338	–342
	Additional offsets against gross budget authority only:			
4050	Change in uncollected pymts, Fed sources, unexpired	–153	....	....
4052	Offsetting collections credited to expired accounts	22	....	....
4060	Additional offsets against budget authority only (total)	–131	....	....

DEPARTMENT OF DEFENSE—MILITARY PROGRAMS

		2021 actual	2022 est.	2023 est.
4070	Budget authority, net (discretionary)	47,828	47,736	50,305
4080	Outlays, net (discretionary)	48,205	48,854	49,938
	Mandatory:			
4090	Budget authority, gross	168		
	Outlays, gross:			
4100	Outlays from new mandatory authority	168		
	Offsets against gross budget authority and outlays:			
	Offsetting collections (collected) from:			
4120	Federal sources	−168		
4180	Budget authority, net (total)	47,828	47,736	50,305
4190	Outlays, net (total)	48,205	48,854	49,938

Object Classification (in millions of dollars)

Identification code 021–2010–0–1–051		2021 actual	2022 est.	2023 est.
	Direct obligations:			
	Personnel compensation:			
11.6	Military personnel - basic allowance for housing	7,420	7,356	7,847
11.7	Military personnel	26,775	26,711	27,742
11.9	Total personnel compensation	34,195	34,067	35,589
12.2	Military personnel benefits	7,936	8,088	8,778
12.2	Military personnel benefits	4,161	4,315	4,199
13.0	Benefits for former personnel	115	69	85
21.0	Travel and transportation of persons	291	340	308
22.0	Transportation of things	1,039	1,038	1,134
25.7	Operation and maintenance of equipment	8	9	9
26.0	Supplies and materials	135	150	148
42.0	Insurance claims and indemnities	57	56	53
43.0	Interest and dividends	3	3	2
92.0	Undistributed		−399	
99.0	Direct obligations	47,940	47,736	50,305
99.0	Reimbursable obligations	321	338	342
99.9	Total new obligations, unexpired accounts	48,261	48,074	50,647

MEDICARE-ELIGIBLE RETIREE HEALTH FUND CONTRIBUTION, ARMY

Program and Financing (in millions of dollars)

Identification code 021–1004–0–1–051		2021 actual	2022 est.	2023 est.
	Obligations by program activity:			
0001	Health care contribution - Officers	457	517	536
0002	Health care contribution - Enlisted	1,894	2,106	2,158
0900	Total new obligations, unexpired accounts (object class 12.2)	2,351	2,623	2,694
	Budgetary resources:			
	Budget authority:			
	Appropriations, discretionary:			
1100	Appropriation	2,351	2,623	2,694
1930	Total budgetary resources available	2,351	2,623	2,694
	Change in obligated balance:			
	Unpaid obligations:			
3010	New obligations, unexpired accounts	2,351	2,623	2,694
3020	Outlays (gross)	−2,351	−2,623	−2,694
	Budget authority and outlays, net:			
	Discretionary:			
4000	Budget authority, gross	2,351	2,623	2,694
	Outlays, gross:			
4010	Outlays from new discretionary authority	2,351	2,623	2,694
4180	Budget authority, net (total)	2,351	2,623	2,694
4190	Outlays, net (total)	2,351	2,623	2,694

MILITARY PERSONNEL, NAVY

For pay, allowances, individual clothing, subsistence, interest on deposits, gratuities, permanent change of station travel (including all expenses thereof for organizational movements), and expenses of temporary duty travel between permanent duty stations, for members of the Navy on active duty (except members of the Reserve provided for elsewhere), midshipmen, and aviation cadets; for members of the Reserve Officers' Training Corps; and for payments pursuant to section 156 of Public Law 97–377, as amended (42 U.S.C. 402 note), and to the Department of Defense Military Retirement Fund, $36,629,226,000, of which not to exceed $916,500,000 shall remain available until September 30, 2024, for permanent change of station travel.

Note.—A full-year 2022 appropriation for this account was not enacted at the time the Budget was prepared; therefore, the Budget assumes this account is operating under the Continuing Appropriations Act, 2022 (Division A of Public Law 117–43, as amended). The amounts included for 2022 reflect the annualized level provided by the continuing resolution.

MILITARY PERSONNEL, NAVY

〖For an additional amount for "Military Personnel, Navy", $7,000,000, to remain available until September 30, 2022, for support of Operation Allies Welcome by the Department of Defense.〗 *(Additional Afghanistan Supplemental Appropriations Act, 2022.)*

Program and Financing (in millions of dollars)

Identification code 017–1453–0–1–051		2021 actual	2022 est.	2023 est.
	Obligations by program activity:			
0001	Pay and allowances of officers	9,230	9,586	9,974
0002	Pay and allowances of enlisted personnel	22,454	23,439	24,091
0003	Pay and Allowances of Cadets	99	96	103
0004	Subsistence of enlisted personnel	1,333	1,362	1,439
0005	Permanent change of station travel	946	996	916
0006	Other Military Personnel Costs	123	117	107
0020	Undistributed		−1,384	
0799	Total direct obligations	34,185	34,212	36,630
0801	Reimbursable program activity	426	448	456
0900	Total new obligations, unexpired accounts	34,611	34,660	37,086
	Budgetary resources:			
	Unobligated balance:			
1000	Unobligated balance brought forward, Oct 1	1	1	
1011	Unobligated balance transfer from other acct [097–0801]	74		
1070	Unobligated balance (total)	75	1	
	Budget authority:			
	Appropriations, discretionary:			
1100	Appropriation	34,113	34,211	36,629
1120	Appropriations transferred to other acct [017–1804]	−22		
1121	Appropriations transferred from other acct [017–1506]	27		
1121	Appropriations transferred from other acct [017–1405]	12		
1121	Appropriations transferred from other acct [017–1105]	20		
1160	Appropriation, discretionary (total)	34,150	34,211	36,629
	Spending authority from offsetting collections, discretionary:			
1700	Collected	218	448	459
1701	Change in uncollected payments, Federal sources	20		
1750	Spending auth from offsetting collections, disc (total)	238	448	459
	Spending authority from offsetting collections, mandatory:			
1800	Collected	196		
1900	Budget authority (total)	34,584	34,659	37,088
1930	Total budgetary resources available	34,659	34,660	37,088
	Memorandum (non-add) entries:			
1940	Unobligated balance expiring	−47		
1941	Unexpired unobligated balance, end of year	1		2
	Change in obligated balance:			
	Unpaid obligations:			
3000	Unpaid obligations, brought forward, Oct 1	1,917	1,992	1,711
3010	New obligations, unexpired accounts	34,611	34,660	37,086
3011	Obligations ("upward adjustments"), expired accounts	329		
3020	Outlays (gross)	−34,546	−34,941	−36,796
3041	Recoveries of prior year unpaid obligations, expired	−319		
3050	Unpaid obligations, end of year	1,992	1,711	2,001
	Uncollected payments:			
3060	Uncollected pymts, Fed sources, brought forward, Oct 1	−9	−20	−20
3070	Change in uncollected pymts, Fed sources, unexpired	−20		
3071	Change in uncollected pymts, Fed sources, expired	9		
3090	Uncollected pymts, Fed sources, end of year	−20	−20	−20
	Memorandum (non-add) entries:			
3100	Obligated balance, start of year	1,908	1,972	1,691
3200	Obligated balance, end of year	1,972	1,691	1,981
	Budget authority and outlays, net:			
	Discretionary:			
4000	Budget authority, gross	34,388	34,659	37,088
	Outlays, gross:			
4010	Outlays from new discretionary authority	32,706	32,949	35,257
4011	Outlays from discretionary balances	1,644	1,992	1,539
4020	Outlays, gross (total)	34,350	34,941	36,796

MILITARY PERSONNEL, NAVY—Continued
Program and Financing—Continued

Identification code 017–1453–0–1–051		2021 actual	2022 est.	2023 est.
	Offsets against gross budget authority and outlays:			
	Offsetting collections (collected) from:			
4030	Federal sources	–225	–448	–459
4040	Offsets against gross budget authority and outlays (total)	–225	–448	–459
	Additional offsets against gross budget authority only:			
4050	Change in uncollected pymts, Fed sources, unexpired	–20		
4052	Offsetting collections credited to expired accounts	7		
4060	Additional offsets against budget authority only (total)	–13		
4070	Budget authority, net (discretionary)	34,150	34,211	36,629
4080	Outlays, net (discretionary)	34,125	34,493	36,337
	Mandatory:			
4090	Budget authority, gross	196		
	Outlays, gross:			
4100	Outlays from new mandatory authority	196		
	Offsets against gross budget authority and outlays:			
	Offsetting collections (collected) from:			
4120	Federal sources	–196		
4180	Budget authority, net (total)	34,150	34,211	36,629
4190	Outlays, net (total)	34,125	34,493	36,337

Object Classification (in millions of dollars)

Identification code 017–1453–0–1–051		2021 actual	2022 est.	2023 est.
	Direct obligations:			
	Personnel compensation:			
11.6	Military personnel - basic allowance for housing	6,658	7,136	7,044
11.7	Military personnel	18,182	18,609	19,379
11.9	Total personnel compensation	24,840	25,745	26,423
12.2	Military personnel benefits	5,411	5,609	6,093
12.2	Military personnel benefits	2,903	3,188	3,141
13.0	Benefits for former personnel	52	49	39
21.0	Travel and transportation of persons	231	248	238
22.0	Transportation of things	611	626	563
25.3	Other goods and services from Federal sources	1		
25.7	Operation and maintenance of equipment	18	16	16
26.0	Supplies and materials	90	91	92
42.0	Insurance claims and indemnities	27	23	25
43.0	Interest and dividends	1	1	1
92.0	Undistributed		–1,384	
99.0	Direct obligations	34,185	34,212	36,631
99.0	Reimbursable obligations	426	448	455
99.9	Total new obligations, unexpired accounts	34,611	34,660	37,086

MEDICARE-ELIGIBLE RETIREE HEALTH FUND CONTRIBUTION, NAVY

Program and Financing (in millions of dollars)

Identification code 017–1000–0–1–051		2021 actual	2022 est.	2023 est.
	Obligations by program activity:			
0001	Health care contribution - Officers	274	308	329
0002	Health care contribution - Enlisted	1,399	1,576	1,657
0900	Total new obligations, unexpired accounts (object class 12.2)	1,673	1,884	1,986
	Budgetary resources:			
	Budget authority:			
	Appropriations, discretionary:			
1100	Appropriation	1,673	1,884	1,986
1930	Total budgetary resources available	1,673	1,884	1,986
	Change in obligated balance:			
	Unpaid obligations:			
3010	New obligations, unexpired accounts	1,673	1,884	1,986
3020	Outlays (gross)	–1,673	–1,884	–1,986
	Budget authority and outlays, net:			
	Discretionary:			
4000	Budget authority, gross	1,673	1,884	1,986
	Outlays, gross:			
4010	Outlays from new discretionary authority	1,673	1,884	1,986
4180	Budget authority, net (total)	1,673	1,884	1,986
4190	Outlays, net (total)	1,673	1,884	1,986

MILITARY PERSONNEL, MARINE CORPS

For pay, allowances, individual clothing, subsistence, interest on deposits, gratuities, permanent change of station travel (including all expenses thereof for organizational movements), and expenses of temporary duty travel between permanent duty stations, for members of the Marine Corps on active duty (except members of the Reserve provided for elsewhere); and for payments pursuant to section 156 of Public Law 97–377, as amended (42 U.S.C. 402 note), and to the Department of Defense Military Retirement Fund, $15,330,068,000, of which not to exceed $419,491,000 shall remain available until September 30, 2024, for permanent change of station travel.

Note.—A full-year 2022 appropriation for this account was not enacted at the time the Budget was prepared; therefore, the Budget assumes this account is operating under the Continuing Appropriations Act, 2022 (Division A of Public Law 117–43, as amended). The amounts included for 2022 reflect the annualized level provided by the continuing resolution.

MILITARY PERSONNEL, MARINE CORPS

⟦For an additional amount for "Military Personnel, Marine Corps", $32,000,000, to remain available until September 30, 2022, for support of Operation Allies Welcome by the Department of Defense.⟧ *(Additional Afghanistan Supplemental Appropriations Act, 2022.)*

Program and Financing (in millions of dollars)

Identification code 017–1105–0–1–051		2021 actual	2022 est.	2023 est.
	Obligations by program activity:			
0001	Pay and allowances of officers	3,307	3,385	3,570
0002	Pay and allowances of enlisted personnel	9,873	10,120	10,504
0004	Subsistence of enlisted personnel	744	771	784
0005	Permanent change of station travel	457	449	419
0006	Other military personnel costs	60	60	53
0020	Undistributed		–72	
0799	Total direct obligations	14,441	14,713	15,330
0801	Reimbursable program activity	28	29	30
0900	Total new obligations, unexpired accounts	14,469	14,742	15,360
	Budgetary resources:			
	Unobligated balance:			
1011	Unobligated balance transfer from other acct [097–0801]	22		
	Budget authority:			
	Appropriations, discretionary:			
1100	Appropriation	14,676	14,713	15,330
1120	Appropriations transferred to other acct [017–1106]	–18		
1120	Appropriations transferred to other acct [057–3500]	–29		
1120	Appropriations transferred to other acct [017–1804]	–24		
1120	Appropriations transferred to other acct [017–1453]	–20		
1120	Appropriations transferred to other acct [021–2010]	–126		
1120	Appropriations transferred to other acct [017–1108]	–8		
1121	Appropriations transferred from other acct [097–0105]	2		
1160	Appropriation, discretionary (total)	14,453	14,713	15,330
	Spending authority from offsetting collections, discretionary:			
1700	Collected	24	29	30
1701	Change in uncollected payments, Federal sources	4		
1750	Spending auth from offsetting collections, disc (total)	28	29	30
1900	Budget authority (total)	14,481	14,742	15,360
1930	Total budgetary resources available	14,503	14,742	15,360
	Memorandum (non-add) entries:			
1940	Unobligated balance expiring	–34		
	Change in obligated balance:			
	Unpaid obligations:			
3000	Unpaid obligations, brought forward, Oct 1	931	939	1,030
3010	New obligations, unexpired accounts	14,469	14,742	15,360
3011	Obligations ("upward adjustments"), expired accounts	126		
3020	Outlays (gross)	–14,424	–14,651	–15,243
3041	Recoveries of prior year unpaid obligations, expired	–163		
3050	Unpaid obligations, end of year	939	1,030	1,147
	Uncollected payments:			
3060	Uncollected pymts, Fed sources, brought forward, Oct 1	–5	–4	–4
3070	Change in uncollected pymts, Fed sources, unexpired	–4		
3071	Change in uncollected pymts, Fed sources, expired	5		
3090	Uncollected pymts, Fed sources, end of year	–4	–4	–4
	Memorandum (non-add) entries:			
3100	Obligated balance, start of year	926	935	1,026

DEPARTMENT OF DEFENSE—MILITARY PROGRAMS

Military Personnel—Continued
Federal Funds—Continued

		2021 actual	2022 est.	2023 est.
3200	Obligated balance, end of year	935	1,026	1,143
	Budget authority and outlays, net:			
	Discretionary:			
4000	Budget authority, gross	14,481	14,742	15,360
	Outlays, gross:			
4010	Outlays from new discretionary authority	13,597	13,712	14,287
4011	Outlays from discretionary balances	827	939	956
4020	Outlays, gross (total)	14,424	14,651	15,243
	Offsets against gross budget authority and outlays:			
	Offsetting collections (collected) from:			
4030	Federal sources	–19	–29	–30
4033	Non-Federal sources	–10		
4040	Offsets against gross budget authority and outlays (total)	–29	–29	–30
	Additional offsets against gross budget authority only:			
4050	Change in uncollected pymts, Fed sources, unexpired	–4		
4052	Offsetting collections credited to expired accounts	5		
4060	Additional offsets against budget authority only (total)	1		
4070	Budget authority, net (discretionary)	14,453	14,713	15,330
4080	Outlays, net (discretionary)	14,395	14,622	15,213
4180	Budget authority, net (total)	14,453	14,713	15,330
4190	Outlays, net (total)	14,395	14,622	15,213

Object Classification (in millions of dollars)

Identification code 017–1105–0–1–051	2021 actual	2022 est.	2023 est.
Direct obligations:			
Personnel compensation:			
11.6 Military personnel - basic allowance for housing	2,143	2,202	2,320
11.7 Military personnel	8,280	8,277	8,496
11.9 Total personnel compensation	10,423	10,479	10,816
12.2 Military personnel benefits	2,475	2,534	2,736
12.2 Military personnel benefits	1,054	1,179	1,321
13.0 Benefits for former personnel	40	40	31
21.0 Travel and transportation of persons	225	225	209
22.0 Transportation of things	208	209	199
25.7 Operation and maintenance of equipment	1	16	3
26.0 Supplies and materials		88	
42.0 Insurance claims and indemnities	15	15	15
92.0 Undistributed		–72	
99.0 Direct obligations	14,441	14,713	15,330
99.0 Reimbursable obligations	28	29	30
99.9 Total new obligations, unexpired accounts	14,469	14,742	15,360

MEDICARE-ELIGIBLE RETIREE HEALTH FUND CONTRIBUTION, MARINE CORPS

Program and Financing (in millions of dollars)

Identification code 017–1001–0–1–051	2021 actual	2022 est.	2023 est.
Obligations by program activity:			
0001 Health care contribution - Officers	107	121	127
0002 Health care contribution - Enlisted	798	873	900
0900 Total new obligations, unexpired accounts (object class 12.2)	905	994	1,027
Budgetary resources:			
Budget authority:			
Appropriations, discretionary:			
1100 Appropriation	905	994	1,027
1930 Total budgetary resources available	905	994	1,027
Change in obligated balance:			
Unpaid obligations:			
3010 New obligations, unexpired accounts	905	994	1,027
3020 Outlays (gross)	–905	–994	–1,027
Budget authority and outlays, net:			
Discretionary:			
4000 Budget authority, gross	905	994	1,027
Outlays, gross:			
4010 Outlays from new discretionary authority	905	994	1,027
4180 Budget authority, net (total)	905	994	1,027
4190 Outlays, net (total)	905	994	1,027

MILITARY PERSONNEL, AIR FORCE

For pay, allowances, individual clothing, subsistence, interest on deposits, gratuities, permanent change of station travel (including all expenses thereof for organizational movements), and expenses of temporary duty travel between permanent duty stations, for members of the Air Force on active duty (except members of reserve components provided for elsewhere), cadets, and aviation cadets; for members of the Reserve Officers' Training Corps; and for payments pursuant to section 156 of Public Law 97–377, as amended (42 U.S.C. 402 note), and to the Department of Defense Military Retirement Fund, $35,140,287,000, of which not to exceed $1,114,452,000 shall remain available until September 30, 2024, for permanent change of station travel.

Note.—A full-year 2022 appropriation for this account was not enacted at the time the Budget was prepared; therefore, the Budget assumes this account is operating under the Continuing Appropriations Act, 2022 (Division A of Public Law 117–43, as amended). The amounts included for 2022 reflect the annualized level provided by the continuing resolution.

MILITARY PERSONNEL, AIR FORCE

[For an additional amount for "Military Personnel, Air Force", $145,000,000, to remain available until September 30, 2022, for support of Operation Allies Welcome by the Department of Defense.] *(Additional Afghanistan Supplemental Appropriations Act, 2022.)*

Program and Financing (in millions of dollars)

Identification code 057–3500–0–1–051	2021 actual	2022 est.	2023 est.
Obligations by program activity:			
0001 Pay and allowances of officers	10,763	11,203	11,111
0002 Pay and allowances of enlisted	20,470	21,158	21,227
0003 Pay and allowances of cadets	91	88	90
0004 Subsistence of enlisted personnel	1,386	1,447	1,477
0005 Permanent Change of Station Travel	1,185	1,206	1,114
0006 Other Military Personnel Costs	130	118	121
0020 Undistributed		–1,252	
0799 Total direct obligations	34,025	33,968	35,140
0801 Reimbursable program activity	443	457	481
0900 Total new obligations, unexpired accounts	34,468	34,425	35,621
Budgetary resources:			
Unobligated balance:			
1000 Unobligated balance brought forward, Oct 1			1
1011 Unobligated balance transfer from other acct [097–0801]	162		
1070 Unobligated balance (total)	162		1
Budget authority:			
Appropriations, discretionary:			
1100 Appropriation	33,796	33,969	35,140
1121 Appropriations transferred from other acct [057–3020]	107		
1121 Appropriations transferred from other acct [057–3010]	27		
1121 Appropriations transferred from other acct [017–1105]	29		
1160 Appropriation, discretionary (total)	33,959	33,969	35,140
Spending authority from offsetting collections, discretionary:			
1700 Collected	143	457	480
1701 Change in uncollected payments, Federal sources	100		
1750 Spending auth from offsetting collections, disc (total)	243	457	480
Spending authority from offsetting collections, mandatory:			
1800 Collected	200		
1900 Budget authority (total)	34,402	34,426	35,620
1930 Total budgetary resources available	34,564	34,426	35,621
Memorandum (non-add) entries:			
1940 Unobligated balance expiring	–96		
1941 Unexpired unobligated balance, end of year		1	
Change in obligated balance:			
Unpaid obligations:			
3000 Unpaid obligations, brought forward, Oct 1	2,715	3,237	2,371
3010 New obligations, unexpired accounts	34,468	34,425	35,621
3011 Obligations ("upward adjustments"), expired accounts	9		
3020 Outlays (gross)	–33,805	–35,291	–35,363
3041 Recoveries of prior year unpaid obligations, expired	–150		
3050 Unpaid obligations, end of year	3,237	2,371	2,629
Uncollected payments:			
3060 Uncollected pymts, Fed sources, brought forward, Oct 1	–280	–184	–184
3070 Change in uncollected pymts, Fed sources, unexpired	–100		

MILITARY PERSONNEL, AIR FORCE—Continued
Program and Financing—Continued

Identification code 057–3500–0–1–051	2021 actual	2022 est.	2023 est.
3071 Change in uncollected pymts, Fed sources, expired	196	....	....
3090 Uncollected pymts, Fed sources, end of year	–184	–184	–184
Memorandum (non-add) entries:			
3100 Obligated balance, start of year	2,435	3,053	2,187
3200 Obligated balance, end of year	3,053	2,187	2,445
Budget authority and outlays, net:			
Discretionary:			
4000 Budget authority, gross	34,202	34,426	35,620
Outlays, gross:			
4010 Outlays from new discretionary authority	31,978	32,054	33,160
4011 Outlays from discretionary balances	1,627	3,237	2,203
4020 Outlays, gross (total)	33,605	35,291	35,363
Offsets against gross budget authority and outlays:			
Offsetting collections (collected) from:			
4030 Federal sources	–284	–457	–480
4033 Non-Federal sources	–14	....	....
4040 Offsets against gross budget authority and outlays (total)	–298	–457	–480
Additional offsets against gross budget authority only:			
4050 Change in uncollected pymts, Fed sources, unexpired	–100	....	....
4052 Offsetting collections credited to expired accounts	155	....	....
4060 Additional offsets against budget authority only (total)	55	....	....
4070 Budget authority, net (discretionary)	33,959	33,969	35,140
4080 Outlays, net (discretionary)	33,307	34,834	34,883
Mandatory:			
4090 Budget authority, gross	200	....	....
Outlays, gross:			
4100 Outlays from new mandatory authority	200	....	....
Offsets against gross budget authority and outlays:			
Offsetting collections (collected) from:			
4120 Federal sources	–200	....	....
4180 Budget authority, net (total)	33,959	33,969	35,140
4190 Outlays, net (total)	33,307	34,834	34,883

Object Classification (in millions of dollars)

Identification code 057–3500–0–1–051	2021 actual	2022 est.	2023 est.
Direct obligations:			
Personnel compensation:			
11.6 Military personnel - basic allowance for housing	5,901	6,153	6,155
11.7 Military personnel	18,777	18,934	19,314
11.9 Total personnel compensation	24,678	25,087	25,469
12.2 Military personnel benefits	5,558	5,778	5,962
12.2 Military personnel benefits	2,602	3,203	2,555
13.0 Benefits for former personnel	40	26	28
21.0 Travel and transportation of persons	165	254	197
22.0 Transportation of things	844	748	788
25.7 Operation and maintenance of equipment	41	27	42
26.0 Supplies and materials	72	73	75
42.0 Insurance claims and indemnities	23	22	23
43.0 Interest and dividends	2	2	2
92.0 Undistributed	....	–1,252	....
99.0 Direct obligations	34,025	33,968	35,141
99.0 Reimbursable obligations	443	457	480
99.9 Total new obligations, unexpired accounts	34,468	34,425	35,621

MEDICARE-ELIGIBLE RETIREE HEALTH FUND CONTRIBUTION, AIR FORCE
Program and Financing (in millions of dollars)

Identification code 057–1007–0–1–051	2021 actual	2022 est.	2023 est.
Obligations by program activity:			
0001 Health care contribution - Officers	319	356	354
0002 Health care contribution - Enlisted	1,304	1,468	1,501
0900 Total new obligations, unexpired accounts (object class 12.2)	1,623	1,824	1,855

	2021 actual	2022 est.	2023 est.
Budgetary resources:			
Budget authority:			
Appropriations, discretionary:			
1100 Appropriation	1,623	1,824	1,855
1930 Total budgetary resources available	1,623	1,824	1,855
Change in obligated balance:			
Unpaid obligations:			
3010 New obligations, unexpired accounts	1,623	1,824	1,855
3020 Outlays (gross)	–1,623	–1,824	–1,855
Budget authority and outlays, net:			
Discretionary:			
4000 Budget authority, gross	1,623	1,824	1,855
Outlays, gross:			
4010 Outlays from new discretionary authority	1,623	1,824	1,855
4180 Budget authority, net (total)	1,623	1,824	1,855
4190 Outlays, net (total)	1,623	1,824	1,855

MILITARY PERSONNEL, SPACE FORCE

For pay, allowances, individual clothing, subsistence, interest on deposits, gratuities, permanent change of station travel (including all expenses thereof for organizational movements), and expenses of temporary duty travel between permanent duty stations, for members of the Space Force on active duty, cadets; for members of the Reserve Officers Training Corps; and for payments pursuant to section 156 of Public Law 97–377, as amended (42 U.S.C. 402 note), and to the Department of Defense Military Retirement Fund, $1,117,361,000, of which not to exceed $32,976,000 shall remain available until September 30, 2024, for permanent change of station travel.

Program and Financing (in millions of dollars)

Identification code 057–3510–0–1–051	2021 actual	2022 est.	2023 est.
Obligations by program activity:			
0001 Pay and Allowances of Officers	....	....	715
0002 Pay and Allowances of Enlisted	....	....	348
0004 Subsistence of Enlisted Personnel	....	....	20
0005 Permanent Change of Station Travel	....	....	33
0006 Other Military Personnel Costs	....	....	1
0900 Total new obligations, unexpired accounts	....	....	1,117
Budgetary resources:			
Budget authority:			
Appropriations, discretionary:			
1100 Appropriation	....	....	1,117
1930 Total budgetary resources available	....	....	1,117
Change in obligated balance:			
Unpaid obligations:			
3010 New obligations, unexpired accounts	....	....	1,117
3020 Outlays (gross)	....	....	–1,039
3050 Unpaid obligations, end of year	....	....	78
Memorandum (non-add) entries:			
3200 Obligated balance, end of year	....	....	78
Budget authority and outlays, net:			
Discretionary:			
4000 Budget authority, gross	....	....	1,117
Outlays, gross:			
4010 Outlays from new discretionary authority	....	....	1,039
4180 Budget authority, net (total)	....	....	1,117
4190 Outlays, net (total)	....	....	1,039

Object Classification (in millions of dollars)

Identification code 057–3510–0–1–051	2021 actual	2022 est.	2023 est.
Direct obligations:			
Personnel compensation:			
11.6 Military personnel - basic allowance for housing	....	....	212
11.7 Military personnel	....	....	604
11.9 Total personnel compensation	....	....	816
12.2 Military personnel benefits	....	....	208
12.2 Military personnel benefits	....	....	62
21.0 Travel and transportation of persons	....	....	5
22.0 Transportation of things	....	....	23

DEPARTMENT OF DEFENSE—MILITARY PROGRAMS

25.7	Operation and maintenance of equipment			1
26.0	Supplies and materials			1
42.0	Insurance claims and indemnities			1
99.9	Total new obligations, unexpired accounts			1,117

MEDICARE-ELIGIBLE RETIREE HEALTH FUND CONTRIBUTION, SPACE FORCE

Program and Financing (in millions of dollars)

Identification code 057–1010–0–1–051	2021 actual	2022 est.	2023 est.
Obligations by program activity:			
0001 Healthcare Contributions - Officers			25
0002 Heathcare Contributions - Enlisted			24
0900 Total new obligations, unexpired accounts (object class 12.2)			49
Budgetary resources:			
Budget authority:			
Appropriations, discretionary:			
1100 Appropriation			49
1930 Total budgetary resources available			49
Change in obligated balance:			
Unpaid obligations:			
3010 New obligations, unexpired accounts			49
3020 Outlays (gross)			–49
Budget authority and outlays, net:			
Discretionary:			
4000 Budget authority, gross			49
Outlays, gross:			
4010 Outlays from new discretionary authority			49
4180 Budget authority, net (total)			49
4190 Outlays, net (total)			49

RESERVE PERSONNEL, ARMY

For pay, allowances, clothing, subsistence, gratuities, travel, and related expenses for personnel of the Army Reserve on active duty under sections 10211, 10302, and 7038 of title 10, United States Code, or while serving on active duty under section 12301(d) of title 10, United States Code, in connection with performing duty specified in section 12310(a) of title 10, United States Code, or while undergoing reserve training, or while performing drills or equivalent duty or other duty, and expenses authorized by section 16131 of title 10, United States Code; and for payments to the Department of Defense Military Retirement Fund, $5,384,686,000.

Note.—A full-year 2022 appropriation for this account was not enacted at the time the Budget was prepared; therefore, the Budget assumes this account is operating under the Continuing Appropriations Act, 2022 (Division A of Public Law 117–43, as amended). The amounts included for 2022 reflect the annualized level provided by the continuing resolution.

Program and Financing (in millions of dollars)

Identification code 021–2070–0–1–051	2021 actual	2022 est.	2023 est.
Obligations by program activity:			
0001 Reserve component training and support	5,066	5,230	5,385
0020 Undistributed		–159	
0799 Total direct obligations	5,066	5,071	5,385
0801 Reimbursable program activity	32	43	43
0900 Total new obligations, unexpired accounts	5,098	5,114	5,428
Budgetary resources:			
Budget authority:			
Appropriations, discretionary:			
1100 Appropriation	5,071	5,230	5,385
1100 Appropriation		–159	
1120 Appropriations transferred to other acct [097–0105]	–2		
1120 Appropriations transferred to other acct [057–3400]	–6		
1121 Appropriations transferred from other acct [097–0100]	2		
1121 Appropriations transferred from other acct [097–0105]	6		
1160 Appropriation, discretionary (total)	5,071	5,071	5,385
Spending authority from offsetting collections, discretionary:			
1700 Collected	24	43	43
1701 Change in uncollected payments, Federal sources	8		
1750 Spending auth from offsetting collections, disc (total)	32	43	43
1900 Budget authority (total)	5,103	5,114	5,428
1930 Total budgetary resources available	5,103	5,114	5,428
Memorandum (non-add) entries:			
1940 Unobligated balance expiring	–5		
Change in obligated balance:			
Unpaid obligations:			
3000 Unpaid obligations, brought forward, Oct 1	508	418	381
3010 New obligations, unexpired accounts	5,098	5,114	5,428
3011 Obligations ("upward adjustments"), expired accounts	283		
3020 Outlays (gross)	–5,100	–5,151	–5,379
3041 Recoveries of prior year unpaid obligations, expired	–371		
3050 Unpaid obligations, end of year	418	381	430
Uncollected payments:			
3060 Uncollected pymts, Fed sources, brought forward, Oct 1	–22	–18	–18
3070 Change in uncollected pymts, Fed sources, unexpired	–8		
3071 Change in uncollected pymts, Fed sources, expired	12		
3090 Uncollected pymts, Fed sources, end of year	–18	–18	–18
Memorandum (non-add) entries:			
3100 Obligated balance, start of year	486	400	363
3200 Obligated balance, end of year	400	363	412
Budget authority and outlays, net:			
Discretionary:			
4000 Budget authority, gross	5,103	5,114	5,428
Outlays, gross:			
4010 Outlays from new discretionary authority	4,885	4,733	5,024
4011 Outlays from discretionary balances	215	418	355
4020 Outlays, gross (total)	5,100	5,151	5,379
Offsets against gross budget authority and outlays:			
Offsetting collections (collected) from:			
4030 Federal sources	–30	–43	–43
4040 Offsets against gross budget authority and outlays (total)	–30	–43	–43
Additional offsets against gross budget authority only:			
4050 Change in uncollected pymts, Fed sources, unexpired	–8		
4052 Offsetting collections credited to expired accounts	6		
4060 Additional offsets against budget authority only (total)	–2		
4070 Budget authority, net (discretionary)	5,071	5,071	5,385
4080 Outlays, net (discretionary)	5,070	5,108	5,336
4180 Budget authority, net (total)	5,071	5,071	5,385
4190 Outlays, net (total)	5,070	5,108	5,336

Object Classification (in millions of dollars)

Identification code 021–2070–0–1–051	2021 actual	2022 est.	2023 est.
Direct obligations:			
Personnel compensation:			
11.6 Military personnel - basic allowance for housing	533	585	577
11.7 Military personnel	2,855	2,988	3,029
11.9 Total personnel compensation	3,388	3,573	3,606
12.2 Military personnel benefits	840	824	894
12.2 Military personnel benefits	515	518	580
21.0 Travel and transportation of persons	271	274	264
26.0 Supplies and materials	39	40	41
42.0 Insurance claims and indemnities	13	1	
92.0 Undistributed		–159	
99.0 Direct obligations	5,066	5,071	5,385
99.0 Reimbursable obligations	32	43	43
99.9 Total new obligations, unexpired accounts	5,098	5,114	5,428

MEDICARE-ELIGIBLE RETIREE HEALTH FUND CONTRIBUTION, RESERVE PERSONNEL, ARMY

Program and Financing (in millions of dollars)

Identification code 021–1005–0–1–051	2021 actual	2022 est.	2023 est.
Obligations by program activity:			
0001 Health care contribution - Reserve component	418	460	490
0900 Total new obligations, unexpired accounts (object class 12.2)	418	460	490

MEDICARE-ELIGIBLE RETIREE HEALTH FUND CONTRIBUTION, RESERVE PERSONNEL, ARMY—Continued

Program and Financing—Continued

Identification code 021–1005–0–1–051	2021 actual	2022 est.	2023 est.
Budgetary resources:			
Budget authority:			
Appropriations, discretionary:			
1100 Appropriation	418	460	490
1930 Total budgetary resources available	418	460	490
Change in obligated balance:			
Unpaid obligations:			
3010 New obligations, unexpired accounts	418	460	490
3020 Outlays (gross)	–418	–460	–490
Budget authority and outlays, net:			
Discretionary:			
4000 Budget authority, gross	418	460	490
Outlays, gross:			
4010 Outlays from new discretionary authority	418	460	490
4180 Budget authority, net (total)	418	460	490
4190 Outlays, net (total)	418	460	490

RESERVE PERSONNEL, NAVY

For pay, allowances, clothing, subsistence, gratuities, travel, and related expenses for personnel of the Navy Reserve on active duty under section 10211 of title 10, United States Code, or while serving on active duty under section 12301(d) of title 10, United States Code, in connection with performing duty specified in section 12310(a) of title 10, United States Code, or while undergoing reserve training, or while performing drills or equivalent duty, and expenses authorized by section 16131 of title 10, United States Code; and for payments to the Department of Defense Military Retirement Fund, $2,410,777,000.

Note.—A full-year 2022 appropriation for this account was not enacted at the time the Budget was prepared; therefore, the Budget assumes this account is operating under the Continuing Appropriations Act, 2022 (Division A of Public Law 117–43, as amended). The amounts included for 2022 reflect the annualized level provided by the continuing resolution.

Program and Financing (in millions of dollars)

Identification code 017–1405–0–1–051	2021 actual	2022 est.	2023 est.
Obligations by program activity:			
0001 Reserve Component Training and Support	2,184	2,317	2,411
0020 Undistributed	....	–105	....
0799 Total direct obligations	2,184	2,212	2,411
0801 Reimbursable program activity	28	39	40
0900 Total new obligations, unexpired accounts	2,212	2,251	2,451
Budgetary resources:			
Budget authority:			
Appropriations, discretionary:			
1100 Appropriation	2,212	2,317	2,411
1100 Appropriation	....	–105	....
1120 Appropriations transferred to other acct [017–1804]	–15	....	....
1120 Appropriations transferred to other acct [017–1453]	–12	....	....
1121 Appropriations transferred from other acct [097–0105]	4	....	....
1121 Appropriations transferred from other acct [097–0100]	2	....	....
1160 Appropriation, discretionary (total)	2,191	2,212	2,411
Spending authority from offsetting collections, discretionary:			
1700 Collected	16	39	40
1701 Change in uncollected payments, Federal sources	15	....	....
1750 Spending auth from offsetting collections, disc (total)	31	39	40
1900 Budget authority (total)	2,222	2,251	2,451
1930 Total budgetary resources available	2,222	2,251	2,451
Memorandum (non-add) entries:			
1940 Unobligated balance expiring	–10	....	....
Change in obligated balance:			
Unpaid obligations:			
3000 Unpaid obligations, brought forward, Oct 1	137	145	142
3010 New obligations, unexpired accounts	2,212	2,251	2,451
3011 Obligations ("upward adjustments"), expired accounts	46	....	....
3020 Outlays (gross)	–2,202	–2,254	–2,428
3041 Recoveries of prior year unpaid obligations, expired	–48	....	....
3050 Unpaid obligations, end of year	145	142	165
Uncollected payments:			
3060 Uncollected pymts, Fed sources, brought forward, Oct 1	–26	–22	–22
3070 Change in uncollected pymts, Fed sources, unexpired	–15	....	....
3071 Change in uncollected pymts, Fed sources, expired	19	....	....
3090 Uncollected pymts, Fed sources, end of year	–22	–22	–22
Memorandum (non-add) entries:			
3100 Obligated balance, start of year	111	123	120
3200 Obligated balance, end of year	123	120	143
Budget authority and outlays, net:			
Discretionary:			
4000 Budget authority, gross	2,222	2,251	2,451
Outlays, gross:			
4010 Outlays from new discretionary authority	2,081	2,116	2,304
4011 Outlays from discretionary balances	121	138	124
4020 Outlays, gross (total)	2,202	2,254	2,428
Offsets against gross budget authority and outlays:			
Offsetting collections (collected) from:			
4030 Federal sources	–34	–39	–40
4033 Non-Federal sources	–7	....	....
4040 Offsets against gross budget authority and outlays (total)	–41	–39	–40
Additional offsets against gross budget authority only:			
4050 Change in uncollected pymts, Fed sources, unexpired	–15	....	....
4052 Offsetting collections credited to expired accounts	25	....	....
4060 Additional offsets against budget authority only (total)	10	....	....
4070 Budget authority, net (discretionary)	2,191	2,212	2,411
4080 Outlays, net (discretionary)	2,161	2,215	2,388
4180 Budget authority, net (total)	2,191	2,212	2,411
4190 Outlays, net (total)	2,161	2,215	2,388

Object Classification (in millions of dollars)

Identification code 017–1405–0–1–051	2021 actual	2022 est.	2023 est.
Direct obligations:			
Personnel compensation:			
11.6 Military personnel - basic allowance for housing	299	302	327
11.7 Military personnel	1,207	1,297	1,339
11.9 Total personnel compensation	1,506	1,599	1,666
12.2 Military personnel benefits	336	342	357
12.2 Military personnel benefits	172	140	144
21.0 Travel and transportation of persons	145	208	215
22.0 Transportation of things	19	19	20
26.0 Supplies and materials	6	9	9
92.0 Undistributed	....	–105	....
99.0 Direct obligations	2,184	2,212	2,411
99.0 Reimbursable obligations	28	39	40
99.9 Total new obligations, unexpired accounts	2,212	2,251	2,451

MEDICARE-ELIGIBLE RETIREE HEALTH FUND CONTRIBUTION, RESERVE PERSONNEL, NAVY

Program and Financing (in millions of dollars)

Identification code 017–1002–0–1–051	2021 actual	2022 est.	2023 est.
Obligations by program activity:			
0001 Health care contribution - Reserve component	146	160	168
0900 Total new obligations, unexpired accounts (object class 12.2)	146	160	168
Budgetary resources:			
Budget authority:			
Appropriations, discretionary:			
1100 Appropriation	146	160	168
1930 Total budgetary resources available	146	160	168
Change in obligated balance:			
Unpaid obligations:			
3010 New obligations, unexpired accounts	146	160	168
3020 Outlays (gross)	–146	–160	–168

RESERVE PERSONNEL, MARINE CORPS

For pay, allowances, clothing, subsistence, gratuities, travel, and related expenses for personnel of the Marine Corps Reserve on active duty under section 10211 of title 10, United States Code, or while serving on active duty under section 12301(d) of title 10, United States Code, in connection with performing duty specified in section 12310(a) of title 10, United States Code, or while undergoing reserve training, or while performing drills or equivalent duty, and for members of the Marine Corps platoon leaders class, and expenses authorized by section 16131 of title 10, United States Code; and for payments to the Department of Defense Military Retirement Fund, $849,942,000.

Note.—A full-year 2022 appropriation for this account was not enacted at the time the Budget was prepared; therefore, the Budget assumes this account is operating under the Continuing Appropriations Act, 2022 (Division A of Public Law 117–43, as amended). The amounts included for 2022 reflect the annualized level provided by the continuing resolution.

Program and Financing (in millions of dollars)

Identification code 017–1108–0–1–051	2021 actual	2022 est.	2023 est.
Obligations by program activity:			
0001 Reserve component training and support	786	882	850
0020 Undistributed		–36	
0799 Total direct obligations	786	846	850
0801 Reimbursable program activity	10	11	16
0900 Total new obligations, unexpired accounts	796	857	866
Budgetary resources:			
Budget authority:			
Appropriations, discretionary:			
1100 Appropriation	846	846	850
1120 Appropriations transferred to other acct [017–1106]	–10		
1120 Appropriations transferred to other acct [017–1804]	–8		
1120 Appropriations transferred to other acct [097–0130]	–31		
1120 Appropriations transferred to other acct [021–2020]	–19		
1121 Appropriations transferred from other acct [097–0100]	1		
1121 Appropriations transferred from other acct [017–1105]	8		
1160 Appropriation, discretionary (total)	787	846	850
Spending authority from offsetting collections, discretionary:			
1700 Collected	10	11	16
1900 Budget authority (total)	797	857	866
1930 Total budgetary resources available	797	857	866
Memorandum (non-add) entries:			
1940 Unobligated balance expiring	–1		
Change in obligated balance:			
Unpaid obligations:			
3000 Unpaid obligations, brought forward, Oct 1	53	44	49
3010 New obligations, unexpired accounts	796	857	866
3011 Obligations ("upward adjustments"), expired accounts	15		
3020 Outlays (gross)	–794	–852	–861
3041 Recoveries of prior year unpaid obligations, expired	–26		
3050 Unpaid obligations, end of year	44	49	54
Uncollected payments:			
3060 Uncollected pymts, Fed sources, brought forward, Oct 1	–2		
3071 Change in uncollected pymts, Fed sources, expired	2		
Memorandum (non-add) entries:			
3100 Obligated balance, start of year	51	44	49
3200 Obligated balance, end of year	44	49	54
Budget authority and outlays, net:			
Discretionary:			
4000 Budget authority, gross	797	857	866
Outlays, gross:			
4010 Outlays from new discretionary authority	758	806	815
4011 Outlays from discretionary balances	36	46	46
4020 Outlays, gross (total)	794	852	861
Offsets against gross budget authority and outlays:			
Offsetting collections (collected) from:			
4030 Federal sources	–12	–11	–16
4040 Offsets against gross budget authority and outlays (total)	–12	–11	–16
Additional offsets against gross budget authority only:			
4052 Offsetting collections credited to expired accounts	2		
4060 Additional offsets against budget authority only (total)	2		
4070 Budget authority, net (discretionary)	787	846	850
4080 Outlays, net (discretionary)	782	841	845
4180 Budget authority, net (total)	787	846	850
4190 Outlays, net (total)	782	841	845

Object Classification (in millions of dollars)

Identification code 017–1108–0–1–051	2021 actual	2022 est.	2023 est.
Direct obligations:			
Personnel compensation:			
11.6 Military personnel - basic allowance for housing	85	91	93
11.7 Military personnel	458	506	485
11.9 Total personnel compensation	543	597	578
12.2 Military personnel benefits	122	127	125
12.2 Military personnel benefits	50	63	71
21.0 Travel and transportation of persons	52	75	53
22.0 Transportation of things	7	7	7
26.0 Supplies and materials	11	12	15
41.0 Grants, subsidies, and contributions	1	1	1
92.0 Undistributed		–36	
99.0 Direct obligations	786	846	850
99.0 Reimbursable obligations	10	11	16
99.9 Total new obligations, unexpired accounts	796	857	866

MEDICARE-ELIGIBLE RETIREE HEALTH FUND CONTRIBUTION, RESERVE PERSONNEL, MARINE CORPS

Program and Financing (in millions of dollars)

Identification code 017–1003–0–1–051	2021 actual	2022 est.	2023 est.
Obligations by program activity:			
0001 Health care contribution - Reserve component	82	86	83
0900 Total new obligations, unexpired accounts (object class 12.2)	82	86	83
Budgetary resources:			
Budget authority:			
Appropriations, discretionary:			
1100 Appropriation	82	86	83
1930 Total budgetary resources available	82	86	83
Change in obligated balance:			
Unpaid obligations:			
3010 New obligations, unexpired accounts	82	86	83
3020 Outlays (gross)	–82	–86	–83
Budget authority and outlays, net:			
Discretionary:			
4000 Budget authority, gross	82	86	83
Outlays, gross:			
4010 Outlays from new discretionary authority	82	86	83
4180 Budget authority, net (total)	82	86	83
4190 Outlays, net (total)	82	86	83

RESERVE PERSONNEL, AIR FORCE

For pay, allowances, clothing, subsistence, gratuities, travel, and related expenses for personnel of the Air Force Reserve on active duty under sections 10211, 10305, and 9038 of title 10, United States Code, or while serving on active duty under section 12301(d) of title 10, United States Code, in connection with performing duty specified in section 12310(a) of title 10, United States Code, or while undergoing reserve training, or while performing drills or equivalent duty or other duty, and expenses authorized by section 16131 of title 10, United States Code; and for payments to the Department of Defense Military Retirement Fund, $2,519,878,000.

(Preceding table, top portion:)

	2021 actual	2022 est.	2023 est.
Budget authority and outlays, net:			
Discretionary:			
4000 Budget authority, gross	146	160	168
Outlays, gross:			
4010 Outlays from new discretionary authority	146	160	168
4180 Budget authority, net (total)	146	160	168
4190 Outlays, net (total)	146	160	168

240　Military Personnel—Continued
Federal Funds—Continued

THE BUDGET FOR FISCAL YEAR 2023

RESERVE PERSONNEL, AIR FORCE—Continued

Note.—A full-year 2022 appropriation for this account was not enacted at the time the Budget was prepared; therefore, the Budget assumes this account is operating under the Continuing Appropriations Act, 2022 (Division A of Public Law 117–43, as amended). The amounts included for 2022 reflect the annualized level provided by the continuing resolution.

Program and Financing (in millions of dollars)

Identification code 057–3700–0–1–051	2021 actual	2022 est.	2023 est.
Obligations by program activity:			
0001　Reserve component training and support	2,198	2,386	2,520
0020　Undistributed	....	–176	....
0799　Total direct obligations	2,198	2,210	2,520
0801　Reimbursable program activity	10	12	12
0900　Total new obligations, unexpired accounts	2,208	2,222	2,532
Budgetary resources:			
Budget authority:			
Appropriations, discretionary:			
1100　Appropriation	2,210	2,386	2,520
1100　Appropriation	....	–176	....
1121　Appropriations transferred from other acct [097–0100]	2	....	....
1121　Appropriations transferred from other acct [097–0105]	3	....	....
1160　Appropriation, discretionary (total)	2,215	2,210	2,520
Spending authority from offsetting collections, discretionary:			
1700　Collected	11	12	12
1900　Budget authority (total)	2,226	2,222	2,532
1930　Total budgetary resources available	2,226	2,222	2,532
Memorandum (non-add) entries:			
1940　Unobligated balance expiring	–18	....	....
Change in obligated balance:			
Unpaid obligations:			
3000　Unpaid obligations, brought forward, Oct 1	311	308	175
3010　New obligations, unexpired accounts	2,208	2,222	2,532
3011　Obligations ("upward adjustments"), expired accounts	59	....	....
3020　Outlays (gross)	–2,176	–2,355	–2,494
3041　Recoveries of prior year unpaid obligations, expired	–94	....	....
3050　Unpaid obligations, end of year	308	175	213
Uncollected payments:			
3060　Uncollected pymts, Fed sources, brought forward, Oct 1	–1	–1	–1
3090　Uncollected pymts, Fed sources, end of year	–1	–1	–1
Memorandum (non-add) entries:			
3100　Obligated balance, start of year	310	307	174
3200　Obligated balance, end of year	307	174	212
Budget authority and outlays, net:			
Discretionary:			
4000　Budget authority, gross	2,226	2,222	2,532
Outlays, gross:			
4010　Outlays from new discretionary authority	1,998	2,047	2,330
4011　Outlays from discretionary balances	178	308	164
4020　Outlays, gross (total)	2,176	2,355	2,494
Offsets against gross budget authority and outlays:			
Offsetting collections (collected) from:			
4030　Federal sources	–11	–12	–12
4033　Non-Federal sources	–6	....	....
4040　Offsets against gross budget authority and outlays (total)	–17	–12	–12
Additional offsets against gross budget authority only:			
4052　Offsetting collections credited to expired accounts	6	....	....
4060　Additional offsets against budget authority only (total)	6	....	....
4070　Budget authority, net (discretionary)	2,215	2,210	2,520
4080　Outlays, net (discretionary)	2,159	2,343	2,482
4180　Budget authority, net (total)	2,215	2,210	2,520
4190　Outlays, net (total)	2,159	2,343	2,482

Object Classification (in millions of dollars)

Identification code 057–3700–0–1–051	2021 actual	2022 est.	2023 est.
Direct obligations:			
Personnel compensation:			
11.6　Military personnel - basic allowance for housing	229	269	282
11.7　Military personnel	1,301	1,388	1,497
11.9　Total personnel compensation	1,530	1,657	1,779
12.2　Military personnel benefits	....	308	328	339
12.2　Military personnel benefits	139	165	167
21.0　Travel and transportation of persons	192	203	204
22.0　Transportation of things	10	15	8
26.0　Supplies and materials	17	16	16
41.0　Grants, subsidies, and contributions	1	2	1
42.0　Insurance claims and indemnities	....	....	6
92.0　Undistributed	....	–176	....
99.0　Direct obligations	2,197	2,210	2,520
99.0　Reimbursable obligations	11	12	12
99.9　Total new obligations, unexpired accounts	2,208	2,222	2,532

MEDICARE-ELIGIBLE RETIREE HEALTH FUND CONTRIBUTION, RESERVE PERSONNEL, AIR FORCE

Program and Financing (in millions of dollars)

Identification code 057–1008–0–1–051	2021 actual	2022 est.	2023 est.
Obligations by program activity:			
0001　Health care contribution - Reserve component	150	169	181
0900　Total new obligations, unexpired accounts (object class 12.2)	150	169	181
Budgetary resources:			
Budget authority:			
Appropriations, discretionary:			
1100　Appropriation	150	169	181
1930　Total budgetary resources available	150	169	181
Change in obligated balance:			
Unpaid obligations:			
3010　New obligations, unexpired accounts	150	169	181
3020　Outlays (gross)	–150	–169	–181
Budget authority and outlays, net:			
Discretionary:			
4000　Budget authority, gross	150	169	181
Outlays, gross:			
4010　Outlays from new discretionary authority	150	169	181
4180　Budget authority, net (total)	150	169	181
4190　Outlays, net (total)	150	169	181

NATIONAL GUARD PERSONNEL, ARMY

For pay, allowances, clothing, subsistence, gratuities, travel, and related expenses for personnel of the Army National Guard while on duty under sections 10211, 10302, or 12402 of title 10 or section 708 of title 32, United States Code, or while serving on duty under section 12301(d) of title 10 or section 502(f) of title 32, United States Code, in connection with performing duty specified in section 12310(a) of title 10, United States Code, or while undergoing training, or while performing drills or equivalent duty or other duty, and expenses authorized by section 16131 of title 10, United States Code; and for payments to the Department of Defense Military Retirement Fund, $9,324,813,000.

Note.—A full-year 2022 appropriation for this account was not enacted at the time the Budget was prepared; therefore, the Budget assumes this account is operating under the Continuing Appropriations Act, 2022 (Division A of Public Law 117–43, as amended). The amounts included for 2022 reflect the annualized level provided by the continuing resolution.

Program and Financing (in millions of dollars)

Identification code 021–2060–0–1–051	2021 actual	2022 est.	2023 est.
Obligations by program activity:			
0001　Reserve Component Training and Support	9,329	9,051	9,325
0020　Undistributed	....	–192	....
0799　Total direct obligations	9,329	8,859	9,325
0801　Reimbursable program activity	2,654	51	1,550
0900　Total new obligations, unexpired accounts	11,983	8,910	10,875
Budgetary resources:			
Budget authority:			
Appropriations, discretionary:			
1100　Appropriation	9,090	9,051	9,325
1100　Appropriation	....	–192	....
1120　Appropriations transferred to other acct [097–0105]	–4	....	....
1121　Appropriations transferred from other acct [097–0105]	191	....	....

DEPARTMENT OF DEFENSE—MILITARY PROGRAMS

		2021 actual	2022 est.	2023 est.
1121	Appropriations transferred from other acct [097–0100]	6	....	....
1121	Appropriations transferred from other acct [021–2065]	50	....	....
1121	Appropriations transferred from other acct [021–2010]	30	....	....
1160	Appropriation, discretionary (total)	9,363	8,859	9,325
	Spending authority from offsetting collections, discretionary:			
1700	Collected	948	51	1,550
1701	Change in uncollected payments, Federal sources	1,705	....	....
1750	Spending auth from offsetting collections, disc (total)	2,653	51	1,550
1900	Budget authority (total)	12,016	8,910	10,875
1930	Total budgetary resources available	12,016	8,910	10,875
	Memorandum (non-add) entries:			
1940	Unobligated balance expiring	–33	....	....
	Change in obligated balance:			
	Unpaid obligations:			
3000	Unpaid obligations, brought forward, Oct 1	706	1,452	532
3010	New obligations, unexpired accounts	11,983	8,910	10,875
3011	Obligations ("upward adjustments"), expired accounts	1,139	....	....
3020	Outlays (gross)	–11,278	–9,830	–10,804
3041	Recoveries of prior year unpaid obligations, expired	–1,098	....	....
3050	Unpaid obligations, end of year	1,452	532	603
	Uncollected payments:			
3060	Uncollected pymts, Fed sources, brought forward, Oct 1 ..	–407	–1,738	–1,738
3070	Change in uncollected pymts, Fed sources, unexpired	–1,705	....	....
3071	Change in uncollected pymts, Fed sources, expired	374	....	....
3090	Uncollected pymts, Fed sources, end of year	–1,738	–1,738	–1,738
	Memorandum (non-add) entries:			
3100	Obligated balance, start of year	299	–286	–1,206
3200	Obligated balance, end of year	–286	–1,206	–1,135
	Budget authority and outlays, net:			
	Discretionary:			
4000	Budget authority, gross	12,016	8,910	10,875
	Outlays, gross:			
4010	Outlays from new discretionary authority	10,540	8,378	10,316
4011	Outlays from discretionary balances	738	1,452	488
4020	Outlays, gross (total)	11,278	9,830	10,804
	Offsets against gross budget authority and outlays:			
	Offsetting collections (collected) from:			
4030	Federal sources	–1,424	–51	–1,550
4040	Offsets against gross budget authority and outlays (total)	–1,424	–51	–1,550
	Additional offsets against gross budget authority only:			
4050	Change in uncollected pymts, Fed sources, unexpired	–1,705	....	....
4052	Offsetting collections credited to expired accounts	476	....	....
4060	Additional offsets against budget authority only (total)	–1,229	....	....
4070	Budget authority, net (discretionary)	9,363	8,859	9,325
4080	Outlays, net (discretionary)	9,854	9,779	9,254
4180	Budget authority, net (total)	9,363	8,859	9,325
4190	Outlays, net (total)	9,854	9,779	9,254

Object Classification (in millions of dollars)

Identification code 021–2060–0–1–051		2021 actual	2022 est.	2023 est.
	Direct obligations:			
	Personnel compensation:			
11.6	Military personnel - basic allowance for housing	1,108	1,121	1,104
11.7	Military personnel	5,725	5,352	5,737
11.9	Total personnel compensation	6,833	6,473	6,841
12.2	Military personnel benefits	1,483	1,348	1,409
12.2	Military personnel benefits	749	797	727
21.0	Travel and transportation of persons	184	320	241
26.0	Supplies and materials	72	112	106
42.0	Insurance claims and indemnities	8	1	1
92.0	Undistributed	....	–192	....
99.0	Direct obligations	9,329	8,859	9,325
99.0	Reimbursable obligations	2,654	51	1,550
99.9	Total new obligations, unexpired accounts	11,983	8,910	10,875

MEDICARE-ELIGIBLE RETIREE HEALTH FUND CONTRIBUTION, NATIONAL GUARD PERSONNEL, ARMY

Program and Financing (in millions of dollars)

Identification code 021–1006–0–1–051		2021 actual	2022 est.	2023 est.
	Obligations by program activity:			
0001	Health care contribution - Reserve component	747	822	874
0900	Total new obligations, unexpired accounts (object class 12.2)	747	822	874
	Budgetary resources:			
	Budget authority:			
	Appropriations, discretionary:			
1100	Appropriation	747	822	874
1930	Total budgetary resources available	747	822	874
	Change in obligated balance:			
	Unpaid obligations:			
3010	New obligations, unexpired accounts	747	822	874
3020	Outlays (gross)	–747	–822	–874
	Budget authority and outlays, net:			
	Discretionary:			
4000	Budget authority, gross	747	822	874
	Outlays, gross:			
4010	Outlays from new discretionary authority	747	822	874
4180	Budget authority, net (total)	747	822	874
4190	Outlays, net (total)	747	822	874

NATIONAL GUARD PERSONNEL, AIR FORCE

For pay, allowances, clothing, subsistence, gratuities, travel, and related expenses for personnel of the Air National Guard on duty under sections 10211, 10305, or 12402 of title 10 or section 708 of title 32, United States Code, or while serving on duty under section 12301(d) of title 10 or section 502(f) of title 32, United States Code, in connection with performing duty specified in section 12310(a) of title 10, United States Code, or while undergoing training, or while performing drills or equivalent duty or other duty, and expenses authorized by section 16131 of title 10, United States Code; and for payments to the Department of Defense Military Retirement Fund, $5,127,335,000.

Note.—A full-year 2022 appropriation for this account was not enacted at the time the Budget was prepared; therefore, the Budget assumes this account is operating under the Continuing Appropriations Act, 2022 (Division A of Public Law 117–43, as amended). The amounts included for 2022 reflect the annualized level provided by the continuing resolution.

Program and Financing (in millions of dollars)

Identification code 057–3850–0–1–051		2021 actual	2022 est.	2023 est.
	Obligations by program activity:			
0001	Reserve component training and support	4,624	4,815	5,127
0020	Undistributed	....	–279	....
0799	Total direct obligations	4,624	4,536	5,127
0801	Reimbursable program activity	616	54	54
0900	Total new obligations, unexpired accounts	5,240	4,590	5,181
	Budgetary resources:			
	Unobligated balance:			
1000	Unobligated balance brought forward, Oct 1	....	....	357
	Budget authority:			
	Appropriations, discretionary:			
1100	Appropriation	4,565	4,815	5,127
1100	Appropriation	....	–279	....
1120	Appropriations transferred to other acct [097–0105]	–2	....	....
1121	Appropriations transferred from other acct [097–0100]	6	....	....
1121	Appropriations transferred from other acct [097–0105]	61	....	....
1160	Appropriation, discretionary (total)	4,630	4,536	5,127
	Spending authority from offsetting collections, discretionary:			
1700	Collected	419	411	54
1701	Change in uncollected payments, Federal sources	197	....	....
1750	Spending auth from offsetting collections, disc (total)	616	411	54
1900	Budget authority (total)	5,246	4,947	5,181
1930	Total budgetary resources available	5,246	4,947	5,538
	Memorandum (non-add) entries:			
1940	Unobligated balance expiring	–6	....	....

NATIONAL GUARD PERSONNEL, AIR FORCE—Continued
Program and Financing—Continued

Identification code 057–3850–0–1–051	2021 actual	2022 est.	2023 est.
1941 Unexpired unobligated balance, end of year		357	357
Change in obligated balance:			
Unpaid obligations:			
3000 Unpaid obligations, brought forward, Oct 1	369	725	128
3010 New obligations, unexpired accounts	5,240	4,590	5,181
3011 Obligations ("upward adjustments"), expired accounts	138		
3020 Outlays (gross)	−4,861	−5,187	−5,274
3041 Recoveries of prior year unpaid obligations, expired	−161		
3050 Unpaid obligations, end of year	725	128	35
Uncollected payments:			
3060 Uncollected pymts, Fed sources, brought forward, Oct 1	−158	−232	−232
3070 Change in uncollected pymts, Fed sources, unexpired	−197		
3071 Change in uncollected pymts, Fed sources, expired	123		
3090 Uncollected pymts, Fed sources, end of year	−232	−232	−232
Memorandum (non-add) entries:			
3100 Obligated balance, start of year	211	493	−104
3200 Obligated balance, end of year	493	−104	−197
Budget authority and outlays, net:			
Discretionary:			
4000 Budget authority, gross	5,246	4,947	5,181
Outlays, gross:			
4010 Outlays from new discretionary authority	4,670	4,552	4,857
4011 Outlays from discretionary balances	191	635	417
4020 Outlays, gross (total)	4,861	5,187	5,274
Offsets against gross budget authority and outlays:			
Offsetting collections (collected) from:			
4030 Federal sources	−546	−411	−54
4033 Non-Federal sources	−12		
4040 Offsets against gross budget authority and outlays (total)	−558	−411	−54
Additional offsets against gross budget authority only:			
4050 Change in uncollected pymts, Fed sources, unexpired	−197		
4052 Offsetting collections credited to expired accounts	139		
4060 Additional offsets against budget authority only (total)	−58		
4070 Budget authority, net (discretionary)	4,630	4,536	5,127
4080 Outlays, net (discretionary)	4,303	4,776	5,220
4180 Budget authority, net (total)	4,630	4,536	5,127
4190 Outlays, net (total)	4,303	4,776	5,220

Object Classification (in millions of dollars)

Identification code 057–3850–0–1–051	2021 actual	2022 est.	2023 est.
Direct obligations:			
Personnel compensation:			
11.6 Military personnel - basic allowance for housing	659	733	771
11.7 Military personnel	2,741	2,822	2,996
11.9 Total personnel compensation	3,400	3,555	3,767
12.2 Military personnel benefits	763	785	848
12.2 Military personnel benefits	278	304	326
21.0 Travel and transportation of persons	175	160	176
22.0 Transportation of things	4	7	6
42.0 Insurance claims and indemnities	4	4	4
92.0 Undistributed		−279	
99.0 Direct obligations	4,624	4,536	5,127
99.0 Reimbursable obligations	616	54	54
99.9 Total new obligations, unexpired accounts	5,240	4,590	5,181

MEDICARE-ELIGIBLE RETIREE HEALTH FUND CONTRIBUTION, NATIONAL GUARD PERSONNEL, AIR FORCE

Program and Financing (in millions of dollars)

Identification code 057–1009–0–1–051	2021 actual	2022 est.	2023 est.
Obligations by program activity:			
0001 Health care contribution - Reserve component	279	314	336
0900 Total new obligations, unexpired accounts (object class 12.2)	279	314	336
Budgetary resources:			
Budget authority:			
Appropriations, discretionary:			
1100 Appropriation	279	314	336
1930 Total budgetary resources available	279	314	336
Change in obligated balance:			
Unpaid obligations:			
3010 New obligations, unexpired accounts	279	314	336
3020 Outlays (gross)	−279	−314	−336
Budget authority and outlays, net:			
Discretionary:			
4000 Budget authority, gross	279	314	336
Outlays, gross:			
4010 Outlays from new discretionary authority	279	314	336
4180 Budget authority, net (total)	279	314	336
4190 Outlays, net (total)	279	314	336

CONCURRENT RECEIPT ACCRUAL PAYMENTS TO THE MILITARY RETIREMENT FUND

Program and Financing (in millions of dollars)

Identification code 097–0041–0–1–051	2021 actual	2022 est.	2023 est.
Obligations by program activity:			
0010 Direct program activity	9,845	10,569	10,897
0900 Total new obligations, unexpired accounts (object class 12.2)	9,845	10,569	10,897
Budgetary resources:			
Budget authority:			
Appropriations, mandatory:			
1200 Appropriation	10,736	11,526	11,883
1230 Appropriations and/or unobligated balance of appropriations permanently reduced	−891	−957	−986
1260 Appropriations, mandatory (total)	9,845	10,569	10,897
1930 Total budgetary resources available	9,845	10,569	10,897
Change in obligated balance:			
Unpaid obligations:			
3010 New obligations, unexpired accounts	9,845	10,569	10,897
3020 Outlays (gross)	−9,845	−10,569	−10,897
Budget authority and outlays, net:			
Mandatory:			
4090 Budget authority, gross	9,845	10,569	10,897
Outlays, gross:			
4100 Outlays from new mandatory authority	9,845	10,569	10,897
4180 Budget authority, net (total)	9,845	10,569	10,897
4190 Outlays, net (total)	9,845	10,569	10,897

OPERATION AND MAINTENANCE

These appropriations finance the cost of operating and maintaining the Armed Forces, including the Reserve components and related support activities of the Department of Defense, except military personnel pay and allowances. Included are amounts for training and operation costs, pay of civilians, contract services for maintenance of equipment and facilities, fuel, supplies, and repair parts for weapons and equipment. Financial requirements are influenced by many factors, including the number of aircraft squadrons, Army brigades and Marine Corps regiments, installations, military strength and deployments, rates of operational activity, and the quantity and complexity of major equipment (aircraft, ships, missiles, tanks, et cetera) in operation.

Federal Funds

OPERATION AND MAINTENANCE, ARMY

For expenses, not otherwise provided for, necessary for the operation and maintenance of the Army, as authorized by law, $58,117,556,000: Provided, That not to exceed $12,478,000 may be used for emergencies and extraordinary expenses, to

DEPARTMENT OF DEFENSE—MILITARY PROGRAMS

Operation and Maintenance—Continued
Federal Funds—Continued

be expended upon the approval or authority of the Secretary of the Army, and payments may be made upon the Secretary's certificate of necessity for confidential military purposes.

Note.—A full-year 2022 appropriation for this account was not enacted at the time the Budget was prepared; therefore, the Budget assumes this account is operating under the Continuing Appropriations Act, 2022 (Division A of Public Law 117–43, as amended). The amounts included for 2022 reflect the annualized level provided by the continuing resolution.

Program and Financing (in millions of dollars)

Identification code 021–2020–0–1–051		2021 actual	2022 est.	2023 est.
	Obligations by program activity:			
0001	Operating Forces	38,129	36,869	39,181
0002	Mobilization	816	739	817
0003	Training and Recruiting	5,336	5,461	5,953
0004	Administration and Service-wide Activities	11,808	11,571	12,167
0020	Undistributed		998	
0799	Total direct obligations	56,089	55,638	58,118
0801	Reimbursable program activity	8,801	11,699	9,195
0900	Total new obligations, unexpired accounts	64,890	67,337	67,313
	Budgetary resources:			
	Unobligated balance:			
1000	Unobligated balance brought forward, Oct 1	82	124	132
1001	Discretionary unobligated balance brought fwd, Oct 1	72		
1011	Unobligated balance transfer from other acct [097–0801]	125		
1012	Unobligated balance transfers between expired and unexpired accounts	47		
1070	Unobligated balance (total)	254	124	132
	Budget authority:			
	Appropriations, discretionary:			
1100	Appropriation	55,615	55,638	58,118
1120	Appropriations transferred to other acct [097–0105]	–29		
1120	Appropriations transferred to other acct [057–3400]	–115		
1120	Appropriations transferred to other acct [097–0130]	–148		
1120	Appropriations transferred to other acct [021–2010]	–43		
1120	Appropriations transferred to other acct [097–4930.001]	–48		
1120	Appropriations transferred to other acct [097–0300]	–1		
1120	Appropriations transferred to other acct [017–1804]	–1		
1120	Appropriations transferred to other acct [097–0811]	–5		
1120	Appropriations transferred to other acct [097–0819]	–289		
1121	Appropriations transferred from other acct [097–0105]	254		
1121	Appropriations transferred from other acct [017–1506]	17		
1121	Appropriations transferred from other acct [097–0130]	2		
1121	Appropriations transferred from other acct [021–2034]	8		
1121	Appropriations transferred from other acct [021–2040]	2		
1121	Appropriations transferred from other acct [017–1319]	38		
1121	Appropriations transferred from other acct [057–3620]	17		
1121	Appropriations transferred from other acct [017–1810]	3		
1121	Appropriations transferred from other acct [017–1108]	19		
1121	Appropriations transferred from other acct [021–0810]	264		
1121	Appropriations transferred from other acct [097–0100]	97		
1121	Appropriations transferred from other acct [097–0811]	289		
1121	Appropriations transferred from other acct [021–2035]	9		
1121	Appropriations transferred from other acct [021–2033]	6		
1121	Appropriations transferred from other acct [057–3080]	4		
1160	Appropriation, discretionary (total)	55,965	55,638	58,118
	Appropriations, mandatory:			
1221	Appropriations transferred from other acct [011–5512]	9	8	16
	Spending authority from offsetting collections, discretionary:			
1700	Collected	3,802	11,699	9,195
1701	Change in uncollected payments, Federal sources	5,001		
1750	Spending auth from offsetting collections, disc (total)	8,803	11,699	9,195
1900	Budget authority (total)	64,777	67,345	67,329
1930	Total budgetary resources available	65,031	67,469	67,461
	Memorandum (non-add) entries:			
1940	Unobligated balance expiring	–17		
1941	Unexpired unobligated balance, end of year	124	132	148
	Change in obligated balance:			
	Unpaid obligations:			
3000	Unpaid obligations, brought forward, Oct 1	46,666	41,572	35,349
3010	New obligations, unexpired accounts	64,890	67,337	67,313
3011	Obligations ("upward adjustments"), expired accounts	3,725		
3020	Outlays (gross)	–67,728	–73,560	–69,010
3041	Recoveries of prior year unpaid obligations, expired	–5,981		
3050	Unpaid obligations, end of year	41,572	35,349	33,652
	Uncollected payments:			
3060	Uncollected pymts, Fed sources, brought forward, Oct 1	–9,032	–8,790	–8,790
3070	Change in uncollected pymts, Fed sources, unexpired	–5,001		
3071	Change in uncollected pymts, Fed sources, expired	5,243		
3090	Uncollected pymts, Fed sources, end of year	–8,790	–8,790	–8,790
	Memorandum (non-add) entries:			
3100	Obligated balance, start of year	37,634	32,782	26,559
3200	Obligated balance, end of year	32,782	26,559	24,862
	Budget authority and outlays, net:			
	Discretionary:			
4000	Budget authority, gross	64,768	67,337	67,313
	Outlays, gross:			
4010	Outlays from new discretionary authority	38,714	43,969	42,903
4011	Outlays from discretionary balances	29,013	29,583	26,095
4020	Outlays, gross (total)	67,727	73,552	68,998
	Offsets against gross budget authority and outlays:			
	Offsetting collections (collected) from:			
4030	Federal sources	–7,825	–11,699	–9,195
4033	Non-Federal sources	–897		
4040	Offsets against gross budget authority and outlays (total)	–8,722	–11,699	–9,195
	Additional offsets against gross budget authority only:			
4050	Change in uncollected pymts, Fed sources, unexpired	–5,001		
4052	Offsetting collections credited to expired accounts	4,920		
4060	Additional offsets against budget authority only (total)	–81		
4070	Budget authority, net (discretionary)	55,965	55,638	58,118
4080	Outlays, net (discretionary)	59,005	61,853	59,803
	Mandatory:			
4090	Budget authority, gross	9	8	16
	Outlays, gross:			
4100	Outlays from new mandatory authority		5	9
4101	Outlays from mandatory balances	1	3	3
4110	Outlays, gross (total)	1	8	12
4180	Budget authority, net (total)	55,974	55,646	58,134
4190	Outlays, net (total)	59,006	61,861	59,815

Object Classification (in millions of dollars)

Identification code 021–2020–0–1–051		2021 actual	2022 est.	2023 est.
	Direct obligations:			
	Personnel compensation:			
11.1	Full-time permanent	8,018	8,137	8,614
11.3	Other than full-time permanent	120	131	141
11.5	Other personnel compensation	458	326	346
11.9	Total personnel compensation	8,596	8,594	9,101
12.1	Civilian personnel benefits	3,363	3,424	3,611
13.0	Benefits for former personnel	20	16	17
21.0	Travel and transportation of persons	1,402	1,226	1,243
22.0	Transportation of things	2,105	1,363	1,239
23.1	Rental payments to GSA	59	161	189
23.2	Rental payments to others	218	439	409
23.3	Communications, utilities, and miscellaneous charges	1,837	1,591	2,036
24.0	Printing and reproduction	173	254	241
25.1	Advisory and assistance services	4,550	3,297	3,139
25.2	Other services from non-Federal sources	4,974	3,762	3,980
25.3	Other goods and services from Federal sources	4,560	2,990	3,282
25.3	Other goods and services from Federal sources	452	420	454
25.3	Other goods and services from Federal sources	2,639	2,631	4,636
25.4	Operation and maintenance of facilities	5,682	6,004	6,619
25.6	Medical care	45	146	45
25.7	Operation and maintenance of equipment	5,475	6,858	6,008
25.8	Subsistence and support of persons	206	119	114
26.0	Supplies and materials	6,915	8,130	8,548
31.0	Equipment	1,426	2,144	1,998
32.0	Land and structures	929	576	671
33.0	Investments and loans	35		
41.0	Grants, subsidies, and contributions	405	442	484
42.0	Insurance claims and indemnities	21	25	26
43.0	Interest and dividends	2	27	27
44.0	Refunds		1	1
92.0	Undistributed		998	
99.0	Direct obligations	56,089	55,638	58,118
99.0	Reimbursable obligations	8,801	11,699	9,195
99.9	Total new obligations, unexpired accounts	64,890	67,337	67,313

Employment Summary

Identification code 021–2020–0–1–051		2021 actual	2022 est.	2023 est.
1001	Direct civilian full-time equivalent employment	99,994	98,631	100,179

OPERATION AND MAINTENANCE, ARMY—Continued

Employment Summary—Continued

Identification code 021–2020–0–1–051	2021 actual	2022 est.	2023 est.
2001 Reimbursable civilian full-time equivalent employment	9,495	8,644	9,054

OPERATION AND MAINTENANCE, NAVY

For expenses, not otherwise provided for, necessary for the operation and maintenance of the Navy and the Marine Corps, as authorized by law, $66,151,951,000: Provided, That not to exceed $15,055,000 may be used for emergencies and extraordinary expenses, to be expended upon the approval or authority of the Secretary of the Navy, and payments may be made upon the Secretary's certificate of necessity for confidential military purposes.

Note.—A full-year 2022 appropriation for this account was not enacted at the time the Budget was prepared; therefore, the Budget assumes this account is operating under the Continuing Appropriations Act, 2022 (Division A of Public Law 117–43, as amended). The amounts included for 2022 reflect the annualized level provided by the continuing resolution.

OPERATION AND MAINTENANCE, NAVY

[For an additional amount for "Operation and Maintenance, Navy", $565,000,000, to remain available until September 30, 2022, for necessary expenses related to the consequences of severe storms, straight-line winds, flooding, tornadoes, earthquakes, wildfires, and hurricanes occurring in calendar years 2020 and 2021.] *(Disaster Relief Supplemental Appropriations Act, 2022.)*

Program and Financing (in millions of dollars)

Identification code 017–1804–0–1–051		2021 actual	2022 est.	2023 est.
	Obligations by program activity:			
0001	Operating forces	50,043	51,859	56,287
0002	Mobilization	1,292	1,626	1,671
0003	Training and recruiting	2,294	2,476	2,621
0004	Administration and servicewide activities	5,367	5,114	5,573
0020	Undistributed	....	–1,775	....
0799	Total direct obligations	58,996	59,300	66,152
0801	Reimbursable program activity	5,078	4,921	5,056
0900	Total new obligations, unexpired accounts	64,074	64,221	71,208
	Budgetary resources:			
	Unobligated balance:			
1000	Unobligated balance brought forward, Oct 1	82	136	155
1001	Discretionary unobligated balance brought fwd, Oct 1	45		
1011	Unobligated balance transfer from other acct [097–0801]	25	....	....
1012	Unobligated balance transfers between expired and unexpired accounts	70	....	....
1021	Recoveries of prior year unpaid obligations	1	....	....
1070	Unobligated balance (total)	178	136	155
	Budget authority:			
	Appropriations, discretionary:			
1100	Appropriation	58,666	59,300	66,152
1120	Appropriations transferred to other acct [017–0810]	–42		
1120	Appropriations transferred to other acct [017–4557]	–342	....	....
1120	Appropriations transferred to other acct [021–2040]	–27	....	....
1120	Appropriations transferred to other acct [017–1810]	–33	....	....
1120	Appropriations transferred to other acct [097–0105]	–9	....	....
1121	Appropriations transferred from other acct [017–0810]	421	....	....
1121	Appropriations transferred from other acct [057–3080]	3	....	....
1121	Appropriations transferred from other acct [017–1108]	8	....	....
1121	Appropriations transferred from other acct [021–2020]	1	....	....
1121	Appropriations transferred from other acct [017–1405]	15	....	....
1121	Appropriations transferred from other acct [017–1105]	24	....	....
1121	Appropriations transferred from other acct [057–3022]	16	....	....
1121	Appropriations transferred from other acct [017–1453]	22	....	....
1121	Appropriations transferred from other acct [017–1319]	11	....	....
1121	Appropriations transferred from other acct [097–0100]	95	....	....
1121	Appropriations transferred from other acct [017–1507]	3	....	....
1121	Appropriations transferred from other acct [097–0130]	2	....	....
1121	Appropriations transferred from other acct [057–3600]	11	....	....
1121	Appropriations transferred from other acct [097–0105]	138	....	....
1121	Appropriations transferred from other acct [017–1810]	5	....	....
1160	Appropriation, discretionary (total)	58,988	59,300	66,152
	Appropriations, mandatory:			
1221	Appropriations transferred from other acct [011–5512]	16	16	35
1230	Appropriations and/or unobligated balance of appropriations permanently reduced	–1	....	....
1260	Appropriations, mandatory (total)	15	16	35
	Spending authority from offsetting collections, discretionary:			
1700	Collected	4,226	4,921	5,056
1701	Change in uncollected payments, Federal sources	1,847	....	....
1750	Spending auth from offsetting collections, disc (total)	6,073	4,921	5,056
	Spending authority from offsetting collections, mandatory:			
1800	Collected	5	3	3
1801	Change in uncollected payments, Federal sources	3	....	....
1850	Spending auth from offsetting collections, mand (total)	8	3	3
1900	Budget authority (total)	65,084	64,240	71,246
1930	Total budgetary resources available	65,262	64,376	71,401
	Memorandum (non-add) entries:			
1940	Unobligated balance expiring	–1,052		
1941	Unexpired unobligated balance, end of year	136	155	193
	Change in obligated balance:			
	Unpaid obligations:			
3000	Unpaid obligations, brought forward, Oct 1	26,501	27,094	23,884
3010	New obligations, unexpired accounts	64,074	64,221	71,208
3011	Obligations ("upward adjustments"), expired accounts	2,435		
3020	Outlays (gross)	–62,673	–67,431	–68,061
3040	Recoveries of prior year unpaid obligations, unexpired	–1	....	....
3041	Recoveries of prior year unpaid obligations, expired	–3,242	....	....
3050	Unpaid obligations, end of year	27,094	23,884	27,031
	Uncollected payments:			
3060	Uncollected pymts, Fed sources, brought forward, Oct 1	–4,031	–3,327	–3,327
3070	Change in uncollected pymts, Fed sources, unexpired	–1,850	....	....
3071	Change in uncollected pymts, Fed sources, expired	2,554	....	....
3090	Uncollected pymts, Fed sources, end of year	–3,327	–3,327	–3,327
	Memorandum (non-add) entries:			
3100	Obligated balance, start of year	22,470	23,767	20,557
3200	Obligated balance, end of year	23,767	20,557	23,704
	Budget authority and outlays, net:			
	Discretionary:			
4000	Budget authority, gross	65,061	64,221	71,208
	Outlays, gross:			
4010	Outlays from new discretionary authority	45,569	46,014	50,701
4011	Outlays from discretionary balances	17,096	21,399	17,328
4020	Outlays, gross (total)	62,665	67,413	68,029
	Offsets against gross budget authority and outlays:			
	Offsetting collections (collected) from:			
4030	Federal sources	–4,894	–4,921	–5,056
4033	Non-Federal sources	–699	....	....
4040	Offsets against gross budget authority and outlays (total)	–5,593	–4,921	–5,056
	Additional offsets against gross budget authority only:			
4050	Change in uncollected pymts, Fed sources, unexpired	–1,847	....	....
4052	Offsetting collections credited to expired accounts	1,367	....	....
4060	Additional offsets against budget authority only (total)	–480	....	....
4070	Budget authority, net (discretionary)	58,988	59,300	66,152
4080	Outlays, net (discretionary)	57,072	62,492	62,973
	Mandatory:			
4090	Budget authority, gross	23	19	38
	Outlays, gross:			
4100	Outlays from new mandatory authority	5	14	27
4101	Outlays from mandatory balances	3	4	5
4110	Outlays, gross (total)	8	18	32
	Offsets against gross budget authority and outlays:			
	Offsetting collections (collected) from:			
4120	Federal sources	....	–3	–3
4123	Non-Federal sources	–5	....	....
4130	Offsets against gross budget authority and outlays (total)	–5	–3	–3
	Additional offsets against gross budget authority only:			
4140	Change in uncollected pymts, Fed sources, unexpired	–3	....	....
4160	Budget authority, net (mandatory)	15	16	35
4170	Outlays, net (mandatory)	3	15	29
4180	Budget authority, net (total)	59,003	59,316	66,187
4190	Outlays, net (total)	57,075	62,507	63,002

Object Classification (in millions of dollars)

Identification code 017–1804–0–1–051	2021 actual	2022 est.	2023 est.
Direct obligations:			
Personnel compensation:			
11.1 Full-time permanent	8,521	8,208	8,767

DEPARTMENT OF DEFENSE—MILITARY PROGRAMS

Operation and Maintenance—Continued
Federal Funds—Continued

		2021 actual	2022 est.	2023 est.
11.3	Other than full-time permanent	64	112	96
11.5	Other personnel compensation	695	669	741
11.8	Special personal services payments	46	50	51
11.9	Total personnel compensation	9,326	9,039	9,655
12.1	Civilian personnel benefits	3,336	3,461	3,731
13.0	Benefits for former personnel	15	15	11
21.0	Travel and transportation of persons	1,001	765	849
22.0	Transportation of things	450	556	584
23.1	Rental payments to GSA	37	32	34
23.2	Rental payments to others	312	270	284
23.3	Communications, utilities, and miscellaneous charges	1,209	1,275	1,423
24.0	Printing and reproduction	76	66	68
25.1	Advisory and assistance services	2,222	1,123	1,344
25.2	Other services from non-Federal sources	1,482	1,468	1,682
25.3	Other goods and services from Federal sources	3,586	4,116	4,219
25.3	Other goods and services from Federal sources	61	79	79
25.3	Other goods and services from Federal sources	9,302	10,321	11,007
25.4	Operation and maintenance of facilities	3,271	2,655	3,156
25.5	Research and development contracts	63	20	24
25.6	Medical care	84	161	80
25.7	Operation and maintenance of equipment	10,544	11,924	12,977
25.8	Subsistence and support of persons	132	120	145
26.0	Supplies and materials	6,637	7,234	7,603
31.0	Equipment	5,076	5,698	6,399
32.0	Land and structures	703	605	724
41.0	Grants, subsidies, and contributions	56	57	58
42.0	Insurance claims and indemnities	12	14	15
43.0	Interest and dividends	3	1	1
92.0	Undistributed	....	–1,775	....
99.0	Direct obligations	58,996	59,300	66,152
99.0	Reimbursable obligations	5,078	4,921	5,056
99.9	Total new obligations, unexpired accounts	64,074	64,221	71,208

Employment Summary

Identification code 017–1804–0–1–051	2021 actual	2022 est.	2023 est.
1001 Direct civilian full-time equivalent employment	97,632	93,786	98,409
2001 Reimbursable civilian full-time equivalent employment	12,649	15,751	13,889

OPERATION AND MAINTENANCE, MARINE CORPS

For expenses, not otherwise provided for, necessary for the operation and maintenance of the Marine Corps, as authorized by law, $9,660,944,000.

Note.—A full-year 2022 appropriation for this account was not enacted at the time the Budget was prepared; therefore, the Budget assumes this account is operating under the Continuing Appropriations Act, 2022 (Division A of Public Law 117–43, as amended). The amounts included for 2022 reflect the annualized level provided by the continuing resolution.

Program and Financing (in millions of dollars)

Identification code 017–1106–0–1–051	2021 actual	2022 est.	2023 est.
Obligations by program activity:			
0001 Operating forces	6,928	7,462	8,082
0003 Training and recruiting	925	988	1,037
0004 Administration and Service-wide Activities	561	575	542
0020 Undistributed	....	–654	....
0799 Total direct obligations	8,414	8,371	9,661
0801 Reimbursable program activity	282	252	258
0900 Total new obligations, unexpired accounts	8,696	8,623	9,919
Budgetary resources:			
Unobligated balance:			
1000 Unobligated balance brought forward, Oct 1	32	51	54
1001 Discretionary unobligated balance brought fwd, Oct 1	3		
1011 Unobligated balance transfer from other acct [097–0801]	5	....	....
1012 Unobligated balance transfers between expired and unexpired accounts	17	....	....
1070 Unobligated balance (total)	54	51	54
Budget authority:			
Appropriations, discretionary:			
1100 Appropriation	8,371	8,371	9,661
1121 Appropriations transferred from other acct [097–0105]	7	....	....
1121 Appropriations transferred from other acct [017–1108]	10	....	....
1121 Appropriations transferred from other acct [017–1105]	18	....	....
1121 Appropriations transferred from other acct [097–0100]	15	....	....
1160 Appropriation, discretionary (total)	8,421	8,371	9,661
Appropriations, mandatory:			
1221 Appropriations transferred from other acct [011–5512]	3	3	11
Spending authority from offsetting collections, discretionary:			
1700 Collected	258	252	258
1701 Change in uncollected payments, Federal sources	16	....	....
1750 Spending auth from offsetting collections, disc (total)	274	252	258
Spending authority from offsetting collections, mandatory:			
1800 Collected	10		
1900 Budget authority (total)	8,708	8,626	9,930
1930 Total budgetary resources available	8,762	8,677	9,984
Memorandum (non-add) entries:			
1940 Unobligated balance expiring	–15	....	....
1941 Unexpired unobligated balance, end of year	51	54	65
Change in obligated balance:			
Unpaid obligations:			
3000 Unpaid obligations, brought forward, Oct 1	5,466	4,867	4,146
3010 New obligations, unexpired accounts	8,696	8,623	9,919
3011 Obligations ("upward adjustments"), expired accounts	199	....	....
3020 Outlays (gross)	–9,155	–9,344	–9,337
3041 Recoveries of prior year unpaid obligations, expired	–339	....	....
3050 Unpaid obligations, end of year	4,867	4,146	4,728
Uncollected payments:			
3060 Uncollected pymts, Fed sources, brought forward, Oct 1	–34	–22	–22
3070 Change in uncollected pymts, Fed sources, unexpired	–16	....	....
3071 Change in uncollected pymts, Fed sources, expired	28	....	....
3090 Uncollected pymts, Fed sources, end of year	–22	–22	–22
Memorandum (non-add) entries:			
3100 Obligated balance, start of year	5,432	4,845	4,124
3200 Obligated balance, end of year	4,845	4,124	4,706
Budget authority and outlays, net:			
Discretionary:			
4000 Budget authority, gross	8,695	8,623	9,919
Outlays, gross:			
4010 Outlays from new discretionary authority	5,399	5,274	6,055
4011 Outlays from discretionary balances	3,747	4,068	3,274
4020 Outlays, gross (total)	9,146	9,342	9,329
Offsets against gross budget authority and outlays:			
Offsetting collections (collected) from:			
4030 Federal sources	–217	–252	–258
4033 Non-Federal sources	–66	....	....
4040 Offsets against gross budget authority and outlays (total)	–283	–252	–258
Additional offsets against gross budget authority only:			
4050 Change in uncollected pymts, Fed sources, unexpired	–16	....	....
4052 Offsetting collections credited to expired accounts	25	....	....
4060 Additional offsets against budget authority only (total)	9	....	....
4070 Budget authority, net (discretionary)	8,421	8,371	9,661
4080 Outlays, net (discretionary)	8,863	9,090	9,071
Mandatory:			
4090 Budget authority, gross	13	3	11
Outlays, gross:			
4100 Outlays from new mandatory authority	2	2	7
4101 Outlays from mandatory balances	7	....	1
4110 Outlays, gross (total)	9	2	8
Offsets against gross budget authority and outlays:			
Offsetting collections (collected) from:			
4123 Non-Federal sources	–10		
4180 Budget authority, net (total)	8,424	8,374	9,672
4190 Outlays, net (total)	8,862	9,092	9,079

Object Classification (in millions of dollars)

Identification code 017–1106–0–1–051	2021 actual	2022 est.	2023 est.
Direct obligations:			
Personnel compensation:			
11.1 Full-time permanent	1,374	1,486	1,590
11.3 Other than full-time permanent	18	6	....
11.5 Other personnel compensation	63	37	40
11.8 Special personal services payments	1	7	7
11.9 Total personnel compensation	1,456	1,536	1,637
12.1 Civilian personnel benefits	550	573	568
21.0 Travel and transportation of persons	404	433	366
22.0 Transportation of things	133	125	117
23.1 Rental payments to GSA	8	8	9
23.2 Rental payments to others	43	45	46
23.3 Communications, utilities, and miscellaneous charges	346	345	415
24.0 Printing and reproduction	127	115	116
25.1 Advisory and assistance services	1,013	1,057	1,076
25.2 Other services from non-Federal sources	434	486	486

OPERATION AND MAINTENANCE, MARINE CORPS—Continued

Object Classification—Continued

Identification code 017–1106–0–1–051		2021 actual	2022 est.	2023 est.
25.3	Other goods and services from Federal sources	514	484	498
25.3	Other goods and services from Federal sources	17	25	25
25.3	Other goods and services from Federal sources	729	862	835
25.4	Operation and maintenance of facilities	846	1,019	1,119
25.5	Research and development contracts	4	2	2
25.6	Medical care	2	2	2
25.7	Operation and maintenance of equipment	470	518	584
25.8	Subsistence and support of persons	35	41	44
26.0	Supplies and materials	768	753	935
31.0	Equipment	406	452	652
32.0	Land and structures	102	138	123
41.0	Grants, subsidies, and contributions	6	6	6
92.0	Undistributed	....	–654	....
99.0	Direct obligations	8,413	8,371	9,661
99.0	Reimbursable obligations	283	252	258
99.9	Total new obligations, unexpired accounts	8,696	8,623	9,919

Employment Summary

Identification code 017–1106–0–1–051		2021 actual	2022 est.	2023 est.
1001	Direct civilian full-time equivalent employment	16,171	16,466	16,606
2001	Reimbursable civilian full-time equivalent employment	695	735	735

OPERATION AND MAINTENANCE, AIR FORCE

For expenses, not otherwise provided for, necessary for the operation and maintenance of the Air Force, as authorized by law, $58,281,242,000: Provided, That not to exceed $7,699,000 may be used for emergencies and extraordinary expenses, to be expended upon the approval or authority of the Secretary of the Air Force, and payments may be made upon the Secretary's certificate of necessity for confidential military purposes.

Note.—A full-year 2022 appropriation for this account was not enacted at the time the Budget was prepared; therefore, the Budget assumes this account is operating under the Continuing Appropriations Act, 2022 (Division A of Public Law 117–43, as amended). The amounts included for 2022 reflect the annualized level provided by the continuing resolution.

OPERATION AND MAINTENANCE, AIR FORCE

[For an additional amount for "Operation and Maintenance, Air Force", $330,000,000, to remain available until September 30, 2022, for necessary expenses related to the consequences of Winter Storm Uri occurring in calendar year 2021.] *(Disaster Relief Supplemental Appropriations Act, 2022.)*

Program and Financing (in millions of dollars)

Identification code 057–3400–0–1–051		2021 actual	2022 est.	2023 est.
	Obligations by program activity:			
0001	Operating forces	41,495	43,101	45,829
0002	Mobilization	3,376	3,091	3,502
0003	Training and recruiting	2,546	2,773	3,044
0004	Administration and servicewide activities	5,310	5,242	5,906
0020	Undistributed	....	–2,702	....
0799	Total direct obligations	52,727	51,505	58,281
0801	Reimbursable program activity	2,730	1,493	3,830
0900	Total new obligations, unexpired accounts	55,457	52,998	62,111
	Budgetary resources:			
	Unobligated balance:			
1000	Unobligated balance brought forward, Oct 1	77	123	127
1001	Discretionary unobligated balance brought fwd, Oct 1	31		
1011	Unobligated balance transfer from other acct [097–0801]	88		
1012	Unobligated balance transfers between expired and unexpired accounts	38		
1033	Recoveries of prior year paid obligations	5		
1070	Unobligated balance (total)	208	123	127
	Budget authority:			
	Appropriations, discretionary:			
1100	Appropriation	51,174	53,876	58,281
1100	Appropriation	....	–2,702	....
1100	Appropriation	....	330	....
1120	Appropriations transferred to other acct [057–0810]	–43		
1120	Appropriations transferred to other acct [097–0105]	–7		
1121	Appropriations transferred from other acct [097–0100]	126		
1121	Appropriations transferred from other acct [097–0400]	33		
1121	Appropriations transferred from other acct [097–0111]	12		
1121	Appropriations transferred from other acct [021–2080]	15		
1121	Appropriations transferred from other acct [057–3010]	431		
1121	Appropriations transferred from other acct [057–3020]	7		
1121	Appropriations transferred from other acct [057–3620]	1		
1121	Appropriations transferred from other acct [057–3600]	92		
1121	Appropriations transferred from other acct [097–0130]	2		
1121	Appropriations transferred from other acct [021–2020]	115		
1121	Appropriations transferred from other acct [057–0810]	509		
1121	Appropriations transferred from other acct [021–2070]	6		
1121	Appropriations transferred from other acct [097–0105]	183		
1121	Appropriations transferred from other acct [057–3011]	113		
1160	Appropriation, discretionary (total)	52,769	51,504	58,281
	Appropriations, mandatory:			
1221	Appropriations transferred from other acct [011–5512]	14	5	17
1230	Appropriations and/or unobligated balance of appropriations permanently reduced	–1		
1260	Appropriations, mandatory (total)	13	5	17
	Spending authority from offsetting collections, discretionary:			
1700	Collected	1,977	1,493	3,762
1701	Change in uncollected payments, Federal sources	755		
1750	Spending auth from offsetting collections, disc (total)	2,732	1,493	3,762
	Spending authority from offsetting collections, mandatory:			
1800	Collected	8		
1900	Budget authority (total)	55,522	53,002	62,060
1930	Total budgetary resources available	55,730	53,125	62,187
	Memorandum (non-add) entries:			
1940	Unobligated balance expiring	–150		
1941	Unexpired unobligated balance, end of year	123	127	76
	Change in obligated balance:			
	Unpaid obligations:			
3000	Unpaid obligations, brought forward, Oct 1	33,395	32,008	29,099
3010	New obligations, unexpired accounts	55,457	52,998	62,111
3011	Obligations ("upward adjustments"), expired accounts	1,766		
3020	Outlays (gross)	–55,886	–55,907	–58,275
3041	Recoveries of prior year unpaid obligations, expired	–2,724		
3050	Unpaid obligations, end of year	32,008	29,099	32,935
	Uncollected payments:			
3060	Uncollected pymts, Fed sources, brought forward, Oct 1	–1,175	–1,333	–1,333
3070	Change in uncollected pymts, Fed sources, unexpired	–755		
3071	Change in uncollected pymts, Fed sources, expired	597		
3090	Uncollected pymts, Fed sources, end of year	–1,333	–1,333	–1,333
	Memorandum (non-add) entries:			
3100	Obligated balance, start of year	32,220	30,675	27,766
3200	Obligated balance, end of year	30,675	27,766	31,602
	Budget authority and outlays, net:			
	Discretionary:			
4000	Budget authority, gross	55,501	52,997	62,043
	Outlays, gross:			
4010	Outlays from new discretionary authority	34,308	33,040	39,313
4011	Outlays from discretionary balances	21,563	22,862	18,950
4020	Outlays, gross (total)	55,871	55,902	58,263
	Offsets against gross budget authority and outlays:			
	Offsetting collections (collected) from:			
4030	Federal sources	–2,388	–1,493	–3,762
4033	Non-Federal sources	–424		
4040	Offsets against gross budget authority and outlays (total)	–2,812	–1,493	–3,762
	Additional offsets against gross budget authority only:			
4050	Change in uncollected pymts, Fed sources, unexpired	–755		
4052	Offsetting collections credited to expired accounts	835		
4060	Additional offsets against budget authority only (total)	80		
4070	Budget authority, net (discretionary)	52,769	51,504	58,281
4080	Outlays, net (discretionary)	53,059	54,409	54,501
	Mandatory:			
4090	Budget authority, gross	21	5	17
	Outlays, gross:			
4100	Outlays from new mandatory authority	8	3	10
4101	Outlays from mandatory balances	7	2	2
4110	Outlays, gross (total)	15	5	12
	Offsets against gross budget authority and outlays:			
	Offsetting collections (collected) from:			
4123	Non-Federal sources	–13		
	Additional offsets against gross budget authority only:			
4143	Recoveries of prior year paid obligations, unexpired accounts	5		

DEPARTMENT OF DEFENSE—MILITARY PROGRAMS

Operation and Maintenance—Continued
Federal Funds—Continued

		2021 actual	2022 est.	2023 est.
4160	Budget authority, net (mandatory)	13	5	17
4170	Outlays, net (mandatory)	2	5	12
4180	Budget authority, net (total)	52,782	51,509	58,298
4190	Outlays, net (total)	53,061	54,414	54,513

Object Classification (in millions of dollars)

Identification code 057–3400–0–1–051		2021 actual	2022 est.	2023 est.
	Direct obligations:			
	Personnel compensation:			
11.1	Full-time permanent	6,053	6,707	7,564
11.3	Other than full-time permanent	23	68	27
11.5	Other personnel compensation	266	258	117
11.9	Total personnel compensation	6,342	7,033	7,708
12.1	Civilian personnel benefits	2,500	2,355	2,239
13.0	Benefits for former personnel	9	43	54
21.0	Travel and transportation of persons	1,161	1,212	1,407
22.0	Transportation of things	231	410	356
23.1	Rental payments to GSA	8	4	4
23.2	Rental payments to others	151	224	238
23.3	Communications, utilities, and miscellaneous charges	3,501	4,228	4,672
24.0	Printing and reproduction	98	104	124
25.1	Advisory and assistance services	2,115	1,470	1,510
25.2	Other services from non-Federal sources	2,288	2,196	2,345
25.3	Other goods and services from Federal sources	993	638	739
25.3	Other goods and services from Federal sources	107	3	70
25.3	Other goods and services from Federal sources	5,259	5,385	6,434
25.4	Operation and maintenance of facilities	1,606	2,008	2,234
25.5	Research and development contracts	21	24	25
25.6	Medical care	113	34	27
25.7	Operation and maintenance of equipment	12,693	13,384	14,007
25.8	Subsistence and support of persons	344	231	243
26.0	Supplies and materials	7,747	7,700	8,165
31.0	Equipment	2,501	2,387	2,739
32.0	Land and structures	2,875	3,063	2,869
41.0	Grants, subsidies, and contributions	54	37	38
42.0	Insurance claims and indemnities	9	33	33
43.0	Interest and dividends	1	1	1
92.0	Undistributed		–2,702	
99.0	Direct obligations	52,727	51,505	58,281
99.0	Reimbursable obligations	2,730	1,493	3,830
99.9	Total new obligations, unexpired accounts	55,457	52,998	62,111

Employment Summary

Identification code 057–3400–0–1–051		2021 actual	2022 est.	2023 est.
1001	Direct civilian full-time equivalent employment	75,138	78,696	79,876
2001	Reimbursable civilian full-time equivalent employment	10,218	8,116	7,838

OPERATION AND MAINTENANCE, SPACE FORCE

For expenses, not otherwise provided for, necessary for the operation and maintenance of the Space Force, as authorized by law, $4,034,658,000: Provided, That not to exceed $7,699,000 may be used for emergencies and extraordinary expenses, to be expended upon the approval or authority of the Secretary of the Air Force, and payments may be made upon the Secretary's certificate of necessity for confidential military purposes.

Note.—A full-year 2022 appropriation for this account was not enacted at the time the Budget was prepared; therefore, the Budget assumes this account is operating under the Continuing Appropriations Act, 2022 (Division A of Public Law 117–43, as amended). The amounts included for 2022 reflect the annualized level provided by the continuing resolution.

Program and Financing (in millions of dollars)

Identification code 057–3410–0–1–051		2021 actual	2022 est.	2023 est.
	Obligations by program activity:			
0001	Operating forces	2,439	3,284	3,806
0004	Administration and service-wide activities	116	157	228
0020	Undistributed		–871	
0799	Total direct obligations	2,555	2,570	4,034
0801	Reimbursable program activity	30	34	185
0900	Total new obligations, unexpired accounts	2,585	2,604	4,219
	Budgetary resources:			
	Budget authority:			
	Appropriations, discretionary:			
1100	Appropriation	2,570	3,441	4,035
1100	Appropriation		–871	
1121	Appropriations transferred from other acct [057–3600]	5		
1121	Appropriations transferred from other acct [097–0100]	4		
1160	Appropriation, discretionary (total)	2,579	2,570	4,035
	Spending authority from offsetting collections, discretionary:			
1700	Collected	26	34	185
1701	Change in uncollected payments, Federal sources	8		
1750	Spending auth from offsetting collections, disc (total)	34	34	185
1900	Budget authority (total)	2,613	2,604	4,220
1930	Total budgetary resources available	2,613	2,604	4,220
	Memorandum (non-add) entries:			
1940	Unobligated balance expiring	–28		
1941	Unexpired unobligated balance, end of year			1
	Change in obligated balance:			
	Unpaid obligations:			
3000	Unpaid obligations, brought forward, Oct 1	26	1,291	1,643
3010	New obligations, unexpired accounts	2,585	2,604	4,219
3020	Outlays (gross)	–1,320	–2,252	–3,735
3050	Unpaid obligations, end of year	1,291	1,643	2,127
	Uncollected payments:			
3060	Uncollected pymts, Fed sources, brought forward, Oct 1		–8	–8
3070	Change in uncollected pymts, Fed sources, unexpired	–8		
3090	Uncollected pymts, Fed sources, end of year	–8	–8	–8
	Memorandum (non-add) entries:			
3100	Obligated balance, start of year	26	1,283	1,635
3200	Obligated balance, end of year	1,283	1,635	2,119
	Budget authority and outlays, net:			
	Discretionary:			
4000	Budget authority, gross	2,613	2,604	4,220
	Outlays, gross:			
4010	Outlays from new discretionary authority	1,296	1,602	2,646
4011	Outlays from discretionary balances	24	650	1,089
4020	Outlays, gross (total)	1,320	2,252	3,735
	Offsets against gross budget authority and outlays:			
	Offsetting collections (collected) from:			
4030	Federal sources	–2	–34	–185
4033	Non-Federal sources	–24		
4040	Offsets against gross budget authority and outlays (total)	–26	–34	–185
	Additional offsets against gross budget authority only:			
4050	Change in uncollected pymts, Fed sources, unexpired	–8		
4060	Additional offsets against budget authority only (total)	–8		
4070	Budget authority, net (discretionary)	2,579	2,570	4,035
4080	Outlays, net (discretionary)	1,294	2,218	3,550
4180	Budget authority, net (total)	2,579	2,570	4,035
4190	Outlays, net (total)	1,294	2,218	3,550

Object Classification (in millions of dollars)

Identification code 057–3410–0–1–051		2021 actual	2022 est.	2023 est.
	Direct obligations:			
	Personnel compensation:			
11.1	Full-time permanent	122	191	218
11.3	Other than full-time permanent	3	4	4
11.5	Other personnel compensation	3	9	9
11.9	Total personnel compensation	128	204	231
12.1	Civilian personnel benefits	43	91	95
13.0	Benefits for former personnel		1	1
21.0	Travel and transportation of persons	16	21	40
22.0	Transportation of things	1	2	36
23.2	Rental payments to others		6	20
23.3	Communications, utilities, and miscellaneous charges	19	113	109
24.0	Printing and reproduction	1	1	1
25.1	Advisory and assistance services	142	61	95
25.2	Other services from non-Federal sources	44	69	142
25.3	Other goods and services from Federal sources	2	1	1
25.3	Other goods and services from Federal sources	50	59	41
25.4	Operation and maintenance of facilities	37	55	93
25.5	Research and development contracts	2		
25.6	Medical care	4	1	1
25.7	Operation and maintenance of equipment	1,873	2,269	2,598
26.0	Supplies and materials	39	123	95
31.0	Equipment	145	151	187
32.0	Land and structures	9	213	248

OPERATION AND MAINTENANCE, SPACE FORCE—Continued

Object Classification—Continued

Identification code 057–3410–0–1–051		2021 actual	2022 est.	2023 est.
92.0	Undistributed	......	−871	......
99.0	Direct obligations	2,555	2,570	4,034
99.0	Reimbursable obligations	30	34	185
99.9	Total new obligations, unexpired accounts	2,585	2,604	4,219

Employment Summary

Identification code 057–3410–0–1–051		2021 actual	2022 est.	2023 est.
1001	Direct civilian full-time equivalent employment	1,412	2,302	2,595

OPERATION AND MAINTENANCE, DEFENSE-WIDE

(INCLUDING TRANSFER OF FUNDS)

For expenses, not otherwise provided for, necessary for the operation and maintenance of activities and agencies of the Department of Defense (other than the military departments), as authorized by law, $48,406,516,000: Provided, That not more than $2,981,000 may be used for the Combatant Commander Initiative Fund authorized under section 166a of title 10, United States Code: Provided further, That not to exceed $36,000,000 may be used for emergencies and extraordinary expenses, to be expended upon the approval or authority of the Secretary of Defense, and payments may be made upon the Secretary's certificate of necessity for confidential military purposes: Provided further, That $29,071,000 to remain available until expended, is available only for expenses relating to certain classified activities, and may be transferred as necessary by the Secretary of Defense to operation and maintenance appropriations or research, development, test and evaluation appropriations, to be merged with and to be available for the same time period as the appropriations to which transferred: Provided further, That any ceiling on the investment item unit cost of items that may be purchased with operation and maintenance funds shall not apply to the funds described in the preceding proviso: Provided further, That the transfer authority provided under this heading is in addition to any other transfer authority provided elsewhere in this Act.

Note.—A full-year 2022 appropriation for this account was not enacted at the time the Budget was prepared; therefore, the Budget assumes this account is operating under the Continuing Appropriations Act, 2022 (Division A of Public Law 117–43, as amended). The amounts included for 2022 reflect the annualized level provided by the continuing resolution.

Program and Financing (in millions of dollars)

Identification code 097–0100–0–1–051		2021 actual	2022 est.	2023 est.
	Obligations by program activity:			
0001	Operating forces	10,353	10,315	11,008
0003	Training and recruiting	291	296	313
0004	Administration and servicewide activities	33,849	34,407	37,086
0020	Undistributed	......	746	......
0799	Total direct obligations	44,493	45,764	48,407
0801	Reimbursable program activity	2,057	3,220	3,274
0900	Total new obligations, unexpired accounts	46,550	48,984	51,681
	Budgetary resources:			
	Unobligated balance:			
1000	Unobligated balance brought forward, Oct 1	1,288	1,852	1,866
1001	Discretionary unobligated balance brought fwd, Oct 1	1,278		
1010	Unobligated balance transfer to other accts [097–0819]	−32		
1011	Unobligated balance transfer from other acct [097–0801]	14		
1021	Recoveries of prior year unpaid obligations	1		
1033	Recoveries of prior year paid obligations	7		
1070	Unobligated balance (total)	1,278	1,852	1,866
	Budget authority:			
	Appropriations, discretionary:			
1100	Appropriation	45,664	45,764	48,407
1120	Appropriations transferred to other acct [021–2080]	−4		
1120	Appropriations transferred to other acct [097–0105]	−7		
1120	Appropriations transferred to other acct [021–2065]	−11		
1120	Appropriations transferred to other acct [017–1804]	−95		
1120	Appropriations transferred to other acct [097–0130]	−3		
1120	Appropriations transferred to other acct [057–3410]	−4		
1120	Appropriations transferred to other acct [057–3840]	−12		
1120	Appropriations transferred to other acct [017–1106]	−15		
1120	Appropriations transferred to other acct [017–1108]	−1		
1120	Appropriations transferred to other acct [021–2060]	−6		
1120	Appropriations transferred to other acct [021–2020]	−97		
1120	Appropriations transferred to other acct [072–1037]	−15		
1120	Appropriations transferred to other acct [021–2070]	−2		
1120	Appropriations transferred to other acct [097–0300]	−6		
1120	Appropriations transferred to other acct [075–0944]	−15		
1120	Appropriations transferred to other acct [017–1405]	−2		
1120	Appropriations transferred to other acct [057–3850]	−6		
1120	Appropriations transferred to other acct [017–1806]	−2		
1120	Appropriations transferred to other acct [057–3400]	−126		
1120	Appropriations transferred to other acct [057–3740]	−5		
1120	Appropriations transferred to other acct [097–0819]	−10		
1120	Appropriations transferred to other acct [057–3700]	−2		
1121	Appropriations transferred from other acct [057–3010]	27		
1121	Appropriations transferred from other acct [097–0105]	73		
1121	Appropriations transferred from other acct [097–0810]	9		
1121	Appropriations transferred from other acct [017–1507]	5		
1121	Appropriations transferred from other acct [467–0401]	29		
1121	Appropriations transferred from other acct [097–0400]	9		
1131	Unobligated balance of appropriations permanently reduced	−120		
1160	Appropriation, discretionary (total)	45,250	45,764	48,407
	Appropriations, mandatory:			
1221	Appropriations transferred from other acct [011–5512]	15	14	25
	Spending authority from offsetting collections, discretionary:			
1700	Collected	1,018	3,220	3,274
1701	Change in uncollected payments, Federal sources	1,093		
1750	Spending auth from offsetting collections, disc (total)	2,111	3,220	3,274
1900	Budget authority (total)	47,376	48,998	51,706
1930	Total budgetary resources available	48,654	50,850	53,572
	Memorandum (non-add) entries:			
1940	Unobligated balance expiring	−252		
1941	Unexpired unobligated balance, end of year	1,852	1,866	1,891
	Change in obligated balance:			
	Unpaid obligations:			
3000	Unpaid obligations, brought forward, Oct 1	22,586	21,971	20,008
3010	New obligations, unexpired accounts	46,550	48,984	51,681
3011	Obligations ("upward adjustments"), expired accounts	2,021		
3020	Outlays (gross)	−46,699	−50,947	−51,029
3040	Recoveries of prior year unpaid obligations, unexpired	−1		
3041	Recoveries of prior year unpaid obligations, expired	−2,486		
3050	Unpaid obligations, end of year	21,971	20,008	20,660
	Uncollected payments:			
3060	Uncollected pymts, Fed sources, brought forward, Oct 1	−1,609	−1,570	−1,570
3070	Change in uncollected pymts, Fed sources, unexpired	−1,093		
3071	Change in uncollected pymts, Fed sources, expired	1,132		
3090	Uncollected pymts, Fed sources, end of year	−1,570	−1,570	−1,570
	Memorandum (non-add) entries:			
3100	Obligated balance, start of year	20,977	20,401	18,438
3200	Obligated balance, end of year	20,401	18,438	19,090
	Budget authority and outlays, net:			
	Discretionary:			
4000	Budget authority, gross	47,361	48,984	51,681
	Outlays, gross:			
4010	Outlays from new discretionary authority	29,953	31,228	32,899
4011	Outlays from discretionary balances	16,738	19,706	18,111
4020	Outlays, gross (total)	46,691	50,934	51,010
	Offsets against gross budget authority and outlays:			
	Offsetting collections (collected) from:			
4030	Federal sources	−2,040	−3,220	−3,274
4033	Non-Federal sources	−124		
4040	Offsets against gross budget authority and outlays (total)	−2,164	−3,220	−3,274
	Additional offsets against gross budget authority only:			
4050	Change in uncollected pymts, Fed sources, unexpired	−1,093		
4052	Offsetting collections credited to expired accounts	1,139		
4053	Recoveries of prior year paid obligations, unexpired accounts	7		
4060	Additional offsets against budget authority only (total)	53		
4070	Budget authority, net (discretionary)	45,250	45,764	48,407
4080	Outlays, net (discretionary)	44,527	47,714	47,736
	Mandatory:			
4090	Budget authority, gross	15	14	25
	Outlays, gross:			
4100	Outlays from new mandatory authority	2	9	15
4101	Outlays from mandatory balances	6	4	4
4110	Outlays, gross (total)	8	13	19
4180	Budget authority, net (total)	45,265	45,778	48,432

		2021 actual	2022 est.	2023 est.
4190	Outlays, net (total)	44,535	47,727	47,755

Summary of Budget Authority and Outlays (in millions of dollars)

	2021 actual	2022 est.	2023 est.
Enacted/requested:			
Budget Authority	45,265	45,778	48,432
Outlays	44,535	47,727	47,755
Legislative proposal, subject to PAYGO:			
Budget Authority			1
Outlays			1
Total:			
Budget Authority	45,265	45,778	48,433
Outlays	44,535	47,727	47,756

Object Classification (in millions of dollars)

Identification code 097–0100–0–1–051		2021 actual	2022 est.	2023 est.
	Direct obligations:			
	Personnel compensation:			
11.1	Full-time permanent	9,145	9,746	11,539
11.3	Other than full-time permanent	209	191	230
11.5	Other personnel compensation	530	497	388
11.8	Special personal services payments	104	102	95
11.9	Total personnel compensation	9,988	10,536	12,252
12.1	Civilian personnel benefits	3,762	3,836	2,873
13.0	Benefits for former personnel	10	10	10
21.0	Travel and transportation of persons	773	1,021	1,022
22.0	Transportation of things	324	205	267
23.1	Rental payments to GSA	160	135	135
23.2	Rental payments to others	325	568	569
23.3	Communications, utilities, and miscellaneous charges	1,666	1,467	1,590
24.0	Printing and reproduction	34	47	42
25.1	Advisory and assistance services	5,945	5,554	6,069
25.2	Other services from non-Federal sources	3,670	4,193	4,603
25.3	Other goods and services from Federal sources	3,184	3,639	4,078
25.3	Other goods and services from Federal sources	9	10	9
25.3	Other goods and services from Federal sources	1,181	939	1,105
25.4	Operation and maintenance of facilities	792	817	940
25.5	Research and development contracts	25	6	9
25.6	Medical care	73	71	89
25.7	Operation and maintenance of equipment	7,724	7,688	8,630
25.8	Subsistence and support of persons	35	25	27
26.0	Supplies and materials	1,545	1,465	1,355
31.0	Equipment	2,142	2,153	2,181
32.0	Land and structures	363	325	244
41.0	Grants, subsidies, and contributions	762	308	308
42.0	Insurance claims and indemnities	1		
92.0	Undistributed		746	
99.0	Direct obligations	44,493	45,764	48,407
99.0	Reimbursable obligations	2,057	3,220	3,274
99.9	Total new obligations, unexpired accounts	46,550	48,984	51,681

Employment Summary

Identification code 097–0100–0–1–051	2021 actual	2022 est.	2023 est.
1001 Direct civilian full-time equivalent employment	86,310	88,641	89,341
2001 Reimbursable civilian full-time equivalent employment	2,641	2,843	2,863
3001 Allocation account civilian full-time equivalent employment	3,868	3,868	3,868

OPERATION AND MAINTENANCE, DEFENSE-WIDE

(Legislative proposal, subject to PAYGO)

Program and Financing (in millions of dollars)

Identification code 097–0100–4–1–051	2021 actual	2022 est.	2023 est.
Obligations by program activity:			
0004 Administration and servicewide activities			1
0799 Total direct obligations			1
0900 Total new obligations, unexpired accounts (object class 11.5)			1
Budgetary resources:			
Budget authority:			
Appropriations, mandatory:			
1200 Appropriation			1
1930 Total budgetary resources available			1

Change in obligated balance:				
Unpaid obligations:				
3010	New obligations, unexpired accounts			1
3020	Outlays (gross)			−1
Budget authority and outlays, net:				
Mandatory:				
4090	Budget authority, gross			1
Outlays, gross:				
4100	Outlays from new mandatory authority			1
4180	Budget authority, net (total)			1
4190	Outlays, net (total)			1

OFFICE OF THE INSPECTOR GENERAL

For expenses and activities of the Office of the Inspector General in carrying out the provisions of the Inspector General Act of 1978, as amended, $479,359,000, of which $475,971,000 shall be for operation and maintenance, of which not to exceed $700,000 is available for emergencies and extraordinary expenses to be expended upon the approval or authority of the Inspector General, and payments may be made upon the Inspector General's certificate of necessity for confidential military purposes; of which $1,524,000, to remain available for obligation until September 30, 2025, shall be for procurement; and of which $1,864,000, to remain available until September 30, 2024, shall be for research, development, test and evaluation.

Note.—A full-year 2022 appropriation for this account was not enacted at the time the Budget was prepared; therefore, the Budget assumes this account is operating under the Continuing Appropriations Act, 2022 (Division A of Public Law 117–43, as amended). The amounts included for 2022 reflect the annualized level provided by the continuing resolution.

Program and Financing (in millions of dollars)

Identification code 097–0107–0–1–051	2021 actual	2022 est.	2023 est.
Obligations by program activity:			
0001 Operation and maintenance	392	435	476
0002 Research, Development, Test, and Evaluation	16	5	2
0003 Procurement			1
0020 Undistributed		−40	
0799 Total direct obligations	408	400	479
0801 Reimbursable program activity	6	10	10
0900 Total new obligations, unexpired accounts	414	410	489
Budgetary resources:			
Unobligated balance:			
1000 Unobligated balance brought forward, Oct 1	9	1	
1021 Recoveries of prior year unpaid obligations	3		
1033 Recoveries of prior year paid obligations	4		
1070 Unobligated balance (total)	16	1	
Budget authority:			
Appropriations, discretionary:			
1100 Appropriation	400	399	479
Spending authority from offsetting collections, discretionary:			
1700 Collected	3	10	10
1701 Change in uncollected payments, Federal sources	2		
1750 Spending auth from offsetting collections, disc (total)	5	10	10
1900 Budget authority (total)	405	409	489
1930 Total budgetary resources available	421	410	489
Memorandum (non-add) entries:			
1940 Unobligated balance expiring	−6		
1941 Unexpired unobligated balance, end of year	1		
Change in obligated balance:			
Unpaid obligations:			
3000 Unpaid obligations, brought forward, Oct 1	82	72	120
3010 New obligations, unexpired accounts	414	410	489
3011 Obligations ("upward adjustments"), expired accounts	22		
3020 Outlays (gross)	−420	−362	−463
3040 Recoveries of prior year unpaid obligations, unexpired	−3		
3041 Recoveries of prior year unpaid obligations, expired	−23		
3050 Unpaid obligations, end of year	72	120	146
Uncollected payments:			
3060 Uncollected pymts, Fed sources, brought forward, Oct 1	−3	−4	−4
3070 Change in uncollected pymts, Fed sources, unexpired	−2		
3071 Change in uncollected pymts, Fed sources, expired	1		
3090 Uncollected pymts, Fed sources, end of year	−4	−4	−4
Memorandum (non-add) entries:			
3100 Obligated balance, start of year	79	68	116

OFFICE OF THE INSPECTOR GENERAL—Continued
Program and Financing—Continued

Identification code 097–0107–0–1–051	2021 actual	2022 est.	2023 est.
3200 Obligated balance, end of year	68	116	142
Budget authority and outlays, net:			
Discretionary:			
4000 Budget authority, gross	405	409	489
Outlays, gross:			
4010 Outlays from new discretionary authority	348	309	369
4011 Outlays from discretionary balances	72	53	94
4020 Outlays, gross (total)	420	362	463
Offsets against gross budget authority and outlays:			
Offsetting collections (collected) from:			
4030 Federal sources	–10	–10	–10
4033 Non-Federal sources	–1		
4040 Offsets against gross budget authority and outlays (total)	–11	–10	–10
Additional offsets against gross budget authority only:			
4050 Change in uncollected pymts, Fed sources, unexpired	–2		
4052 Offsetting collections credited to expired accounts	4		
4053 Recoveries of prior year paid obligations, unexpired accounts	4		
4060 Additional offsets against budget authority only (total)	6		
4070 Budget authority, net (discretionary)	400	399	479
4080 Outlays, net (discretionary)	409	352	453
4180 Budget authority, net (total)	400	399	479
4190 Outlays, net (total)	409	352	453

Object Classification (in millions of dollars)

Identification code 097–0107–0–1–051	2021 actual	2022 est.	2023 est.
Direct obligations:			
Personnel compensation:			
11.1 Full-time permanent	196	209	218
11.3 Other than full-time permanent	13	7	12
11.5 Other personnel compensation	18	17	22
11.9 Total personnel compensation	227	233	252
12.1 Civilian personnel benefits	89	94	98
21.0 Travel and transportation of persons	4	11	9
23.1 Rental payments to GSA	7	7	7
23.2 Rental payments to others	11	12	11
23.3 Communications, utilities, and miscellaneous charges	4	4	4
25.1 Advisory and assistance services	11	8	8
25.2 Other services from non-Federal sources	3	2	2
25.3 Other goods and services from Federal sources	11	20	22
25.4 Operation and maintenance of facilities	4	2	11
25.5 Research and development contracts	3	2	2
25.7 Operation and maintenance of equipment	27	31	45
26.0 Supplies and materials	1	2	2
31.0 Equipment	6	12	6
92.0 Undistributed		–40	
99.0 Direct obligations	408	400	479
99.0 Reimbursable obligations	6	10	10
99.9 Total new obligations, unexpired accounts	414	410	489

Employment Summary

Identification code 097–0107–0–1–051	2021 actual	2022 est.	2023 est.
1001 Direct civilian full-time equivalent employment	1,734	1,823	1,845
2001 Reimbursable civilian full-time equivalent employment		4	4

OPERATION AND MAINTENANCE, ARMY RESERVE

For expenses, not otherwise provided for, necessary for the operation and maintenance, including training, organization, and administration, of the Army Reserve; repair of facilities and equipment; hire of passenger motor vehicles; travel and transportation; care of the dead; recruiting; procurement of services, supplies, and equipment; and communications, $3,228,504,000.

Note.—A full-year 2022 appropriation for this account was not enacted at the time the Budget was prepared; therefore, the Budget assumes this account is operating under the Continuing Appropriations Act, 2022 (Division A of Public Law 117–43, as amended). The amounts included for 2022 reflect the annualized level provided by the continuing resolution.

Program and Financing (in millions of dollars)

Identification code 021–2080–0–1–051	2021 actual	2022 est.	2023 est.
Obligations by program activity:			
0001 Operating forces	2,799	2,873	3,089
0004 Administration and servicewide activities	108	128	140
0020 Undistributed		–85	
0799 Total direct obligations	2,907	2,916	3,229
0801 Reimbursable program activity	13	18	18
0900 Total new obligations, unexpired accounts	2,920	2,934	3,247
Budgetary resources:			
Unobligated balance:			
1000 Unobligated balance brought forward, Oct 1	3	7	7
1012 Unobligated balance transfers between expired and unexpired accounts	5		
1070 Unobligated balance (total)	8	7	7
Budget authority:			
Appropriations, discretionary:			
1100 Appropriation	2,915	3,001	3,229
1100 Appropriation		–85	
1120 Appropriations transferred to other acct [057–3400]	–15		
1121 Appropriations transferred from other acct [097–0100]	4		
1121 Appropriations transferred from other acct [097–0105]	3		
1160 Appropriation, discretionary (total)	2,907	2,916	3,229
Spending authority from offsetting collections, discretionary:			
1700 Collected	8	18	18
1701 Change in uncollected payments, Federal sources	5		
1750 Spending auth from offsetting collections, disc (total)	13	18	18
1900 Budget authority (total)	2,920	2,934	3,247
1930 Total budgetary resources available	2,928	2,941	3,254
Memorandum (non-add) entries:			
1940 Unobligated balance expiring	–1		
1941 Unexpired unobligated balance, end of year	7	7	7
Change in obligated balance:			
Unpaid obligations:			
3000 Unpaid obligations, brought forward, Oct 1	1,631	1,492	1,417
3010 New obligations, unexpired accounts	2,920	2,934	3,247
3011 Obligations ("upward adjustments"), expired accounts	113		
3020 Outlays (gross)	–2,984	–3,009	–3,116
3041 Recoveries of prior year unpaid obligations, expired	–188		
3050 Unpaid obligations, end of year	1,492	1,417	1,548
Uncollected payments:			
3060 Uncollected pymts, Fed sources, brought forward, Oct 1	–18	–12	–12
3070 Change in uncollected pymts, Fed sources, unexpired	–5		
3071 Change in uncollected pymts, Fed sources, expired	11		
3090 Uncollected pymts, Fed sources, end of year	–12	–12	–12
Memorandum (non-add) entries:			
3100 Obligated balance, start of year	1,613	1,480	1,405
3200 Obligated balance, end of year	1,480	1,405	1,536
Budget authority and outlays, net:			
Discretionary:			
4000 Budget authority, gross	2,920	2,934	3,247
Outlays, gross:			
4010 Outlays from new discretionary authority	1,954	1,855	2,052
4011 Outlays from discretionary balances	1,030	1,154	1,064
4020 Outlays, gross (total)	2,984	3,009	3,116
Offsets against gross budget authority and outlays:			
Offsetting collections (collected) from:			
4030 Federal sources	–15	–18	–18
4033 Non-Federal sources	–2		
4040 Offsets against gross budget authority and outlays (total)	–17	–18	–18
Additional offsets against gross budget authority only:			
4050 Change in uncollected pymts, Fed sources, unexpired	–5		
4052 Offsetting collections credited to expired accounts	9		
4060 Additional offsets against budget authority only (total)	4		
4070 Budget authority, net (discretionary)	2,907	2,916	3,229
4080 Outlays, net (discretionary)	2,967	2,991	3,098
4180 Budget authority, net (total)	2,907	2,916	3,229
4190 Outlays, net (total)	2,967	2,991	3,098

DEPARTMENT OF DEFENSE—MILITARY PROGRAMS

Operation and Maintenance—Continued
Federal Funds—Continued

251

Object Classification (in millions of dollars)

Identification code 021–2080–0–1–051		2021 actual	2022 est.	2023 est.
	Direct obligations:			
	Personnel compensation:			
11.1	Full-time permanent	725	721	763
11.5	Other personnel compensation	32	23	24
11.9	Total personnel compensation	757	744	787
12.1	Civilian personnel benefits	312	317	336
21.0	Travel and transportation of persons	113	105	144
22.0	Transportation of things	80	40	88
23.1	Rental payments to GSA	2	4	5
23.2	Rental payments to others	29	28	31
23.3	Communications, utilities, and miscellaneous charges	176	185	153
24.0	Printing and reproduction	2	2	3
25.1	Advisory and assistance services	17	37	26
25.2	Other services from non-Federal sources	90	186	200
25.3	Other goods and services from Federal sources	200	62	71
25.3	Other goods and services from Federal sources	17	15	108
25.4	Operation and maintenance of facilities	365	387	410
25.6	Medical care	106	117	128
25.7	Operation and maintenance of equipment	131	158	110
25.8	Subsistence and support of persons	30	28	34
26.0	Supplies and materials	347	418	540
31.0	Equipment	81	168	55
32.0	Land and structures	52	....	....
92.0	Undistributed	....	–85	....
99.0	Direct obligations	2,907	2,916	3,229
99.0	Reimbursable obligations	13	18	18
99.9	Total new obligations, unexpired accounts	2,920	2,934	3,247

Employment Summary

Identification code 021–2080–0–1–051	2021 actual	2022 est.	2023 est.
1001 Direct civilian full-time equivalent employment	10,590	10,400	10,568
2001 Reimbursable civilian full-time equivalent employment	17	21	21

OPERATION AND MAINTENANCE, NAVY RESERVE

For expenses, not otherwise provided for, necessary for the operation and maintenance, including training, organization, and administration, of the Navy Reserve; repair of facilities and equipment; hire of passenger motor vehicles; travel and transportation; care of the dead; recruiting; procurement of services, supplies, and equipment; and communications, $1,228,300,000.

Note.—A full-year 2022 appropriation for this account was not enacted at the time the Budget was prepared; therefore, the Budget assumes this account is operating under the Continuing Appropriations Act, 2022 (Division A of Public Law 117–43, as amended). The amounts included for 2022 reflect the annualized level provided by the continuing resolution.

Program and Financing (in millions of dollars)

Identification code 017–1806–0–1–051		2021 actual	2022 est.	2023 est.
	Obligations by program activity:			
0001	Operating Forces	1,098	1,132	1,212
0004	Administration and Service-wide Activities	15	17	16
0020	Undistributed	....	–35	....
0799	Total direct obligations	1,113	1,114	1,228
0801	Reimbursable program activity	12	17	27
0900	Total new obligations, unexpired accounts	1,125	1,131	1,255
	Budgetary resources:			
	Budget authority:			
	Appropriations, discretionary:			
1100	Appropriation	1,114	1,114	1,228
1121	Appropriations transferred from other acct [097–0100]	2	....	....
1160	Appropriation, discretionary (total)	1,116	1,114	1,228
	Spending authority from offsetting collections, discretionary:			
1700	Collected	9	17	27
1701	Change in uncollected payments, Federal sources	3	....	....
1750	Spending auth from offsetting collections, disc (total)	12	17	27
1900	Budget authority (total)	1,128	1,131	1,255
1930	Total budgetary resources available	1,128	1,131	1,255
	Memorandum (non-add) entries:			
1940	Unobligated balance expiring	–3	....	....
	Change in obligated balance:			
	Unpaid obligations:			
3000	Unpaid obligations, brought forward, Oct 1	622	615	582
3010	New obligations, unexpired accounts	1,125	1,131	1,255
3011	Obligations ("upward adjustments"), expired accounts	43	....	....
3020	Outlays (gross)	–1,095	–1,164	–1,209
3041	Recoveries of prior year unpaid obligations, expired	–80	....	....
3050	Unpaid obligations, end of year	615	582	628
	Uncollected payments:			
3060	Uncollected pymts, Fed sources, brought forward, Oct 1	–6	–5	–5
3070	Change in uncollected pymts, Fed sources, unexpired	–3	....	....
3071	Change in uncollected pymts, Fed sources, expired	4	....	....
3090	Uncollected pymts, Fed sources, end of year	–5	–5	–5
	Memorandum (non-add) entries:			
3100	Obligated balance, start of year	616	610	577
3200	Obligated balance, end of year	610	577	623
	Budget authority and outlays, net:			
	Discretionary:			
4000	Budget authority, gross	1,128	1,131	1,255
	Outlays, gross:			
4010	Outlays from new discretionary authority	752	719	801
4011	Outlays from discretionary balances	343	445	408
4020	Outlays, gross (total)	1,095	1,164	1,209
	Offsets against gross budget authority and outlays:			
	Offsetting collections (collected) from:			
4030	Federal sources	–11	–17	–27
4033	Non-Federal sources	–2	....	....
4040	Offsets against gross budget authority and outlays (total)	–13	–17	–27
	Additional offsets against gross budget authority only:			
4050	Change in uncollected pymts, Fed sources, unexpired	–3	....	....
4052	Offsetting collections credited to expired accounts	4	....	....
4060	Additional offsets against budget authority only (total)	1	....	....
4070	Budget authority, net (discretionary)	1,116	1,114	1,228
4080	Outlays, net (discretionary)	1,082	1,147	1,182
4180	Budget authority, net (total)	1,116	1,114	1,228
4190	Outlays, net (total)	1,082	1,147	1,182

Object Classification (in millions of dollars)

Identification code 017–1806–0–1–051		2021 actual	2022 est.	2023 est.
	Direct obligations:			
	Personnel compensation:			
11.1	Full-time permanent	73	66	73
11.5	Other personnel compensation	2	2	2
11.8	Special personal services payments	1	....	1
11.9	Total personnel compensation	76	68	76
12.1	Civilian personnel benefits	22	25	26
21.0	Travel and transportation of persons	36	42	45
22.0	Transportation of things	5	10	11
23.2	Rental payments to others	1	1	1
23.3	Communications, utilities, and miscellaneous charges	33	23	34
24.0	Printing and reproduction	1	....	1
25.1	Advisory and assistance services	16	4	5
25.2	Other services from non-Federal sources	20	23	21
25.3	Other goods and services from Federal sources	44	57	54
25.3	Other goods and services from Federal sources	201	136	276
25.4	Operation and maintenance of facilities	58	34	41
25.6	Medical care	2	4	4
25.7	Operation and maintenance of equipment	241	233	244
25.8	Subsistence and support of persons	10	18	16
26.0	Supplies and materials	238	244	249
31.0	Equipment	89	212	109
32.0	Land and structures	20	15	15
92.0	Undistributed	....	–35	....
99.0	Direct obligations	1,113	1,114	1,228
99.0	Reimbursable obligations	12	17	27
99.9	Total new obligations, unexpired accounts	1,125	1,131	1,255

Employment Summary

Identification code 017–1806–0–1–051	2021 actual	2022 est.	2023 est.
1001 Direct civilian full-time equivalent employment	925	890	924

OPERATION AND MAINTENANCE, NAVY RESERVE—Continued

Employment Summary—Continued

Identification code 017–1806–0–1–051	2021 actual	2022 est.	2023 est.
2001 Reimbursable civilian full-time equivalent employment	7	11	11

OPERATION AND MAINTENANCE, MARINE CORPS RESERVE

For expenses, not otherwise provided for, necessary for the operation and maintenance, including training, organization, and administration, of the Marine Corps Reserve; repair of facilities and equipment; hire of passenger motor vehicles; travel and transportation; care of the dead; recruiting; procurement of services, supplies, and equipment; and communications, $304,233,000.

Note.—A full-year 2022 appropriation for this account was not enacted at the time the Budget was prepared; therefore, the Budget assumes this account is operating under the Continuing Appropriations Act, 2022 (Division A of Public Law 117–43, as amended). The amounts included for 2022 reflect the annualized level provided by the continuing resolution.

Program and Financing (in millions of dollars)

Identification code 017–1107–0–1–051	2021 actual	2022 est.	2023 est.
Obligations by program activity:			
0001 Operating forces	279	271	292
0004 Administration and servicewide activities	11	14	12
0020 Undistributed	....	7	....
0799 Total direct obligations	290	292	304
0801 Reimbursable program activity	....	2	2
0900 Total new obligations, unexpired accounts	290	294	306
Budgetary resources:			
Unobligated balance:			
1000 Unobligated balance brought forward, Oct 1	....	1	1
Budget authority:			
Appropriations, discretionary:			
1100 Appropriation	292	285	304
1100 Appropriation	....	7	....
1160 Appropriation, discretionary (total)	292	292	304
Spending authority from offsetting collections, discretionary:			
1700 Collected	1	2	2
1900 Budget authority (total)	293	294	306
1930 Total budgetary resources available	293	295	307
Memorandum (non-add) entries:			
1940 Unobligated balance expiring	–2	....	....
1941 Unexpired unobligated balance, end of year	1	1	1
Change in obligated balance:			
Unpaid obligations:			
3000 Unpaid obligations, brought forward, Oct 1	207	202	177
3010 New obligations, unexpired accounts	290	294	306
3011 Obligations ("upward adjustments"), expired accounts	15	....	....
3020 Outlays (gross)	–281	–319	–299
3041 Recoveries of prior year unpaid obligations, expired	–29	....	....
3050 Unpaid obligations, end of year	202	177	184
Memorandum (non-add) entries:			
3100 Obligated balance, start of year	207	202	177
3200 Obligated balance, end of year	202	177	184
Budget authority and outlays, net:			
Discretionary:			
4000 Budget authority, gross	293	294	306
Outlays, gross:			
4010 Outlays from new discretionary authority	162	171	178
4011 Outlays from discretionary balances	119	148	121
4020 Outlays, gross (total)	281	319	299
Offsets against gross budget authority and outlays:			
Offsetting collections (collected) from:			
4030 Federal sources	–1	–2	–2
4180 Budget authority, net (total)	292	292	304
4190 Outlays, net (total)	280	317	297

Object Classification (in millions of dollars)

Identification code 017–1107–0–1–051	2021 actual	2022 est.	2023 est.
Direct obligations:			
Personnel compensation:			
11.1 Full-time permanent	18	21	24
11.5 Other personnel compensation	1	1	1
11.9 Total personnel compensation	19	22	25
12.1 Civilian personnel benefits	6	8	8
21.0 Travel and transportation of persons	23	18	19
22.0 Transportation of things	9	9	9
23.3 Communications, utilities, and miscellaneous charges	22	12	12
25.1 Advisory and assistance services	13	30	31
25.2 Other services from non-Federal sources	2	3	4
25.3 Other goods and services from Federal sources	10	11	12
25.3 Other goods and services from Federal sources	19	21	20
25.4 Operation and maintenance of facilities	53	59	63
25.7 Operation and maintenance of equipment	17	6	6
25.8 Subsistence and support of persons	12	13	14
26.0 Supplies and materials	50	44	50
31.0 Equipment	11	8	8
32.0 Land and structures	24	21	23
92.0 Undistributed	....	7	....
99.0 Direct obligations	290	292	304
99.0 Reimbursable obligations	....	2	2
99.9 Total new obligations, unexpired accounts	290	294	306

Employment Summary

Identification code 017–1107–0–1–051	2021 actual	2022 est.	2023 est.
1001 Direct civilian full-time equivalent employment	233	266	282
2001 Reimbursable civilian full-time equivalent employment	....	2	2

OPERATION AND MAINTENANCE, AIR FORCE RESERVE

For expenses, not otherwise provided for, necessary for the operation and maintenance, including training, organization, and administration, of the Air Force Reserve; repair of facilities and equipment; hire of passenger motor vehicles; travel and transportation; care of the dead; recruiting; procurement of services, supplies, and equipment; and communications, $3,564,544,000.

Note.—A full-year 2022 appropriation for this account was not enacted at the time the Budget was prepared; therefore, the Budget assumes this account is operating under the Continuing Appropriations Act, 2022 (Division A of Public Law 117–43, as amended). The amounts included for 2022 reflect the annualized level provided by the continuing resolution.

Program and Financing (in millions of dollars)

Identification code 057–3740–0–1–051	2021 actual	2022 est.	2023 est.
Obligations by program activity:			
0001 Operating forces	3,096	3,217	3,431
0004 Administration and servicewide activities	126	135	134
0020 Undistributed	....	–110	....
0799 Total direct obligations	3,222	3,242	3,565
0801 Reimbursable program activity	206	284	289
0900 Total new obligations, unexpired accounts	3,428	3,526	3,854
Budgetary resources:			
Unobligated balance:			
1000 Unobligated balance brought forward, Oct 1	2	2	2
Budget authority:			
Appropriations, discretionary:			
1100 Appropriation	3,242	3,352	3,565
1100 Appropriation	....	–110	....
1120 Appropriations transferred to other acct [097–0130]	–72	....	....
1121 Appropriations transferred from other acct [057–3020]	11	....	....
1121 Appropriations transferred from other acct [057–3010]	12	....	....
1121 Appropriations transferred from other acct [097–0105]	2	....	....
1121 Appropriations transferred from other acct [057–3011]	14	....	....
1121 Appropriations transferred from other acct [057–3600]	16	....	....
1121 Appropriations transferred from other acct [057–3080]	19	....	....
1121 Appropriations transferred from other acct [097–0100]	5	....	....
1160 Appropriation, discretionary (total)	3,249	3,242	3,565
Spending authority from offsetting collections, discretionary:			
1700 Collected	172	284	289

		2021 actual	2022 est.	2023 est.
1701	Change in uncollected payments, Federal sources	34		
1750	Spending auth from offsetting collections, disc (total)	206	284	289
1900	Budget authority (total)	3,455	3,526	3,854
1930	Total budgetary resources available	3,457	3,528	3,856
	Memorandum (non-add) entries:			
1940	Unobligated balance expiring	−27		
1941	Unexpired unobligated balance, end of year	2	2	2
	Change in obligated balance:			
	Unpaid obligations:			
3000	Unpaid obligations, brought forward, Oct 1	1,263	1,088	1,018
3010	New obligations, unexpired accounts	3,428	3,526	3,854
3011	Obligations ("upward adjustments"), expired accounts	102		
3020	Outlays (gross)	−3,593	−3,596	−3,737
3041	Recoveries of prior year unpaid obligations, expired	−112		
3050	Unpaid obligations, end of year	1,088	1,018	1,135
	Uncollected payments:			
3060	Uncollected pymts, Fed sources, brought forward, Oct 1	−45	−43	−43
3070	Change in uncollected pymts, Fed sources, unexpired	−34		
3071	Change in uncollected pymts, Fed sources, expired	36		
3090	Uncollected pymts, Fed sources, end of year	−43	−43	−43
	Memorandum (non-add) entries:			
3100	Obligated balance, start of year	1,218	1,045	975
3200	Obligated balance, end of year	1,045	975	1,092
	Budget authority and outlays, net:			
	Discretionary:			
4000	Budget authority, gross	3,455	3,526	3,854
	Outlays, gross:			
4010	Outlays from new discretionary authority	2,650	2,651	2,891
4011	Outlays from discretionary balances	943	945	846
4020	Outlays, gross (total)	3,593	3,596	3,737
	Offsets against gross budget authority and outlays:			
	Offsetting collections (collected) from:			
4030	Federal sources	−209	−284	−289
4033	Non-Federal sources	−32		
4040	Offsets against gross budget authority and outlays (total)	−241	−284	−289
	Additional offsets against gross budget authority only:			
4050	Change in uncollected pymts, Fed sources, unexpired	−34		
4052	Offsetting collections credited to expired accounts	69		
4060	Additional offsets against budget authority only (total)	35		
4070	Budget authority, net (discretionary)	3,249	3,242	3,565
4080	Outlays, net (discretionary)	3,352	3,312	3,448
4180	Budget authority, net (total)	3,249	3,242	3,565
4190	Outlays, net (total)	3,352	3,312	3,448

Object Classification (in millions of dollars)

Identification code 057–3740–0–1–051		2021 actual	2022 est.	2023 est.
	Direct obligations:			
	Personnel compensation:			
11.1	Full-time permanent	930	928	953
11.5	Other personnel compensation	46	37	37
11.9	Total personnel compensation	976	965	990
12.1	Civilian personnel benefits	414	368	356
21.0	Travel and transportation of persons	21	20	24
22.0	Transportation of things	5	6	7
23.2	Rental payments to others	3		
23.3	Communications, utilities, and miscellaneous charges	37	39	47
24.0	Printing and reproduction	16	15	
25.1	Advisory and assistance services	5	5	7
25.2	Other services from non-Federal sources	9	5	6
25.3	Other goods and services from Federal sources	11	7	10
25.3	Other goods and services from Federal sources	586	720	678
25.4	Operation and maintenance of facilities	75	72	92
25.6	Medical care	2	3	4
25.7	Operation and maintenance of equipment	310	301	405
25.8	Subsistence and support of persons	43	39	49
26.0	Supplies and materials	545	654	730
31.0	Equipment	82	45	61
32.0	Land and structures	76	83	91
42.0	Insurance claims and indemnities	6	6	8
92.0	Undistributed		−110	
99.0	Direct obligations	3,222	3,243	3,565
99.0	Reimbursable obligations	206	283	289
99.9	Total new obligations, unexpired accounts	3,428	3,526	3,854

Employment Summary

Identification code 057–3740–0–1–051	2021 actual	2022 est.	2023 est.
1001 Direct civilian full-time equivalent employment	12,184	11,489	11,206
2001 Reimbursable civilian full-time equivalent employment		12	12

OPERATION AND MAINTENANCE, ARMY NATIONAL GUARD

For expenses of training, organizing, and administering the Army National Guard, including medical and hospital treatment and related expenses in non-Federal hospitals; maintenance, operation, and repairs to structures and facilities; hire of passenger motor vehicles; personnel services in the National Guard Bureau; travel expenses (other than mileage), as authorized by law for Army personnel on active duty, for Army National Guard division, regimental, and battalion commanders while inspecting units in compliance with National Guard Bureau regulations when specifically authorized by the Chief, National Guard Bureau; supplying and equipping the Army National Guard as authorized by law; and expenses of repair, modification, maintenance, and issue of supplies and equipment (including aircraft), $8,157,237,000.

Note.—A full-year 2022 appropriation for this account was not enacted at the time the Budget was prepared; therefore, the Budget assumes this account is operating under the Continuing Appropriations Act, 2022 (Division A of Public Law 117–43, as amended). The amounts included for 2022 reflect the annualized level provided by the continuing resolution.

Program and Financing (in millions of dollars)

Identification code 021–2065–0–1–051		2021 actual	2022 est.	2023 est.
	Obligations by program activity:			
0001	Operating forces	7,186	7,209	7,720
0004	Administration and servicewide activities	394	438	437
0020	Undistributed		−246	
0799	Total direct obligations	7,580	7,401	8,157
0801	Reimbursable program activity	163	263	263
0900	Total new obligations, unexpired accounts	7,743	7,664	8,420
	Budgetary resources:			
	Unobligated balance:			
1000	Unobligated balance brought forward, Oct 1	14	25	25
1012	Unobligated balance transfers between expired and unexpired accounts	12		
1070	Unobligated balance (total)	26	25	25
	Budget authority:			
	Appropriations, discretionary:			
1100	Appropriation	7,619	7,401	8,157
1120	Appropriations transferred to other acct [097–0105]	−1		
1120	Appropriations transferred to other acct [021–2060]	−50		
1121	Appropriations transferred from other acct [097–0100]	11		
1121	Appropriations transferred from other acct [097–0105]	20		
1160	Appropriation, discretionary (total)	7,599	7,401	8,157
	Spending authority from offsetting collections, discretionary:			
1700	Collected	67	263	263
1701	Change in uncollected payments, Federal sources	96		
1750	Spending auth from offsetting collections, disc (total)	163	263	263
1900	Budget authority (total)	7,762	7,664	8,420
1930	Total budgetary resources available	7,788	7,689	8,445
	Memorandum (non-add) entries:			
1940	Unobligated balance expiring	−20		
1941	Unexpired unobligated balance, end of year	25	25	25
	Change in obligated balance:			
	Unpaid obligations:			
3000	Unpaid obligations, brought forward, Oct 1	3,766	3,602	3,571
3010	New obligations, unexpired accounts	7,743	7,664	8,420
3011	Obligations ("upward adjustments"), expired accounts	865		
3020	Outlays (gross)	−7,794	−7,695	−7,962
3041	Recoveries of prior year unpaid obligations, expired	−978		
3050	Unpaid obligations, end of year	3,602	3,571	4,029
	Uncollected payments:			
3060	Uncollected pymts, Fed sources, brought forward, Oct 1	−157	−137	−137
3070	Change in uncollected pymts, Fed sources, unexpired	−96		
3071	Change in uncollected pymts, Fed sources, expired	116		
3090	Uncollected pymts, Fed sources, end of year	−137	−137	−137
	Memorandum (non-add) entries:			
3100	Obligated balance, start of year	3,609	3,465	3,434

OPERATION AND MAINTENANCE, ARMY NATIONAL GUARD—Continued

Program and Financing—Continued

Identification code 021–2065–0–1–051	2021 actual	2022 est.	2023 est.
3200 Obligated balance, end of year	3,465	3,434	3,892
Budget authority and outlays, net:			
Discretionary:			
4000 Budget authority, gross	7,762	7,664	8,420
Outlays, gross:			
4010 Outlays from new discretionary authority	5,276	4,999	5,483
4011 Outlays from discretionary balances	2,518	2,696	2,479
4020 Outlays, gross (total)	7,794	7,695	7,962
Offsets against gross budget authority and outlays:			
Offsetting collections (collected) from:			
4030 Federal sources	–164	–263	–263
4033 Non-Federal sources	–16	....	....
4040 Offsets against gross budget authority and outlays (total)	–180	–263	–263
Additional offsets against gross budget authority only:			
4050 Change in uncollected pymts, Fed sources, unexpired	–96	....	....
4052 Offsetting collections credited to expired accounts	113	....	....
4060 Additional offsets against budget authority only (total)	17	....	....
4070 Budget authority, net (discretionary)	7,599	7,401	8,157
4080 Outlays, net (discretionary)	7,614	7,432	7,699
4180 Budget authority, net (total)	7,599	7,401	8,157
4190 Outlays, net (total)	7,614	7,432	7,699

Object Classification (in millions of dollars)

Identification code 021–2065–0–1–051	2021 actual	2022 est.	2023 est.
Direct obligations:			
Personnel compensation:			
11.1 Full-time permanent	1,850	1,870	1,965
11.5 Other personnel compensation	28	56	59
11.9 Total personnel compensation	1,878	1,926	2,024
12.1 Civilian personnel benefits	819	851	889
13.0 Benefits for former personnel	2	....	....
21.0 Travel and transportation of persons	99	125	111
22.0 Transportation of things	78	126	143
23.1 Rental payments to GSA	37	35	37
23.2 Rental payments to others	56	49	52
23.3 Communications, utilities, and miscellaneous charges	374	223	386
24.0 Printing and reproduction	55	....	....
25.1 Advisory and assistance services	214	324	335
25.2 Other services from non-Federal sources	358	259	272
25.3 Other goods and services from Federal sources	118	132	166
25.3 Other goods and services from Federal sources	156	171	267
25.4 Operation and maintenance of facilities	581	911	645
25.6 Medical care	62	67	131
25.7 Operation and maintenance of equipment	201	230	125
25.8 Subsistence and support of persons	27	41	47
26.0 Supplies and materials	1,202	1,347	1,359
31.0 Equipment	203	288	314
32.0 Land and structures	850	340	639
41.0 Grants, subsidies, and contributions	210	202	215
92.0 Undistributed	....	–246	....
99.0 Direct obligations	7,580	7,401	8,157
99.0 Reimbursable obligations	163	263	263
99.9 Total new obligations, unexpired accounts	7,743	7,664	8,420

Employment Summary

Identification code 021–2065–0–1–051	2021 actual	2022 est.	2023 est.
1001 Direct civilian full-time equivalent employment	26,908	26,690	26,900
2001 Reimbursable civilian full-time equivalent employment	74	....	....

OPERATION AND MAINTENANCE, AIR NATIONAL GUARD

For expenses of training, organizing, and administering the Air National Guard, including medical and hospital treatment and related expenses in non-Federal hospitals; maintenance, operation, and repairs to structures and facilities; transportation of things, hire of passenger motor vehicles; supplying and equipping the Air National Guard, as authorized by law; expenses for repair, modification, maintenance, and issue of supplies and equipment, including those furnished from stocks under the control of agencies of the Department of Defense; travel expenses (other than mileage) on the same basis as authorized by law for Air National Guard personnel on active Federal duty, for Air National Guard commanders while inspecting units in compliance with National Guard Bureau regulations when specifically authorized by the Chief, National Guard Bureau, $6,900,679,000.

Note.—A full-year 2022 appropriation for this account was not enacted at the time the Budget was prepared; therefore, the Budget assumes this account is operating under the Continuing Appropriations Act, 2022 (Division A of Public Law 117–43, as amended). The amounts included for 2022 reflect the annualized level provided by the continuing resolution.

Program and Financing (in millions of dollars)

Identification code 057–3840–0–1–051	2021 actual	2022 est.	2023 est.
Obligations by program activity:			
0001 Operating Forces	6,808	6,486	6,800
0004 Administration and Service-wide Activities	94	88	100
0020 Undistributed	....	291	....
0799 Total direct obligations	6,902	6,865	6,900
0801 Reimbursable program activity	504	524	530
0900 Total new obligations, unexpired accounts	7,406	7,389	7,430
Budgetary resources:			
Unobligated balance:			
1000 Unobligated balance brought forward, Oct 1	2	8	8
1012 Unobligated balance transfers between expired and unexpired accounts	5	....	....
1070 Unobligated balance (total)	7	8	8
Budget authority:			
Appropriations, discretionary:			
1100 Appropriation	6,907	6,574	6,901
1100 Appropriation	....	291	....
1120 Appropriations transferred to other acct [097–0300]	–2	....	....
1121 Appropriations transferred from other acct [097–0100]	12	....	....
1121 Appropriations transferred from other acct [097–0105]	2	....	....
1160 Appropriation, discretionary (total)	6,919	6,865	6,901
Spending authority from offsetting collections, discretionary:			
1700 Collected	424	524	530
1701 Change in uncollected payments, Federal sources	80	....	....
1750 Spending auth from offsetting collections, disc (total)	504	524	530
Spending authority from offsetting collections, mandatory:			
1800 Collected	1	....	....
1900 Budget authority (total)	7,424	7,389	7,431
1930 Total budgetary resources available	7,431	7,397	7,439
Memorandum (non-add) entries:			
1940 Unobligated balance expiring	–17	....	....
1941 Unexpired unobligated balance, end of year	8	8	9
Change in obligated balance:			
Unpaid obligations:			
3000 Unpaid obligations, brought forward, Oct 1	3,380	3,568	3,328
3010 New obligations, unexpired accounts	7,406	7,389	7,430
3011 Obligations ("upward adjustments"), expired accounts	282	....	....
3020 Outlays (gross)	–7,216	–7,629	–7,599
3041 Recoveries of prior year unpaid obligations, expired	–284	....	....
3050 Unpaid obligations, end of year	3,568	3,328	3,159
Uncollected payments:			
3060 Uncollected pymts, Fed sources, brought forward, Oct 1	–174	–161	–161
3070 Change in uncollected pymts, Fed sources, unexpired	–80	....	....
3071 Change in uncollected pymts, Fed sources, expired	93	....	....
3090 Uncollected pymts, Fed sources, end of year	–161	–161	–161
Memorandum (non-add) entries:			
3100 Obligated balance, start of year	3,206	3,407	3,167
3200 Obligated balance, end of year	3,407	3,167	2,998
Budget authority and outlays, net:			
Discretionary:			
4000 Budget authority, gross	7,423	7,389	7,431
Outlays, gross:			
4010 Outlays from new discretionary authority	5,049	5,193	5,223
4011 Outlays from discretionary balances	2,167	2,436	2,376
4020 Outlays, gross (total)	7,216	7,629	7,599
Offsets against gross budget authority and outlays:			
Offsetting collections (collected) from:			
4030 Federal sources	–513	–524	–530
4033 Non-Federal sources	–59	....	....
4040 Offsets against gross budget authority and outlays (total)	–572	–524	–530
Additional offsets against gross budget authority only:			
4050 Change in uncollected pymts, Fed sources, unexpired	–80	....	....

DEPARTMENT OF DEFENSE—MILITARY PROGRAMS

		2021 actual	2022 est.	2023 est.
4052	Offsetting collections credited to expired accounts	148		
4060	Additional offsets against budget authority only (total)	68		
4070	Budget authority, net (discretionary)	6,919	6,865	6,901
4080	Outlays, net (discretionary)	6,644	7,105	7,069
	Mandatory:			
4090	Budget authority, gross	1		
	Offsets against gross budget authority and outlays:			
	Offsetting collections (collected) from:			
4123	Non-Federal sources	–1		
4180	Budget authority, net (total)	6,919	6,865	6,901
4190	Outlays, net (total)	6,643	7,105	7,069

Object Classification (in millions of dollars)

Identification code 057–3840–0–1–051		2021 actual	2022 est.	2023 est.
	Direct obligations:			
	Personnel compensation:			
11.1	Full-time permanent	1,278	1,054	998
11.5	Other personnel compensation	33	131	152
11.9	Total personnel compensation	1,311	1,185	1,150
12.1	Civilian personnel benefits	529	429	429
13.0	Benefits for former personnel	1	1	1
21.0	Travel and transportation of persons	73	56	62
22.0	Transportation of things	11	10	8
23.2	Rental payments to others	8	4	4
23.3	Communications, utilities, and miscellaneous charges	106	114	115
24.0	Printing and reproduction	30	29	35
25.1	Advisory and assistance services	13	2	2
25.2	Other services from non-Federal sources	187	53	53
25.3	Other goods and services from Federal sources	11	1	1
25.3	Other goods and services from Federal sources	949	1,176	1,090
25.4	Operation and maintenance of facilities	354	365	385
25.6	Medical care	23	9	4
25.7	Operation and maintenance of equipment	1,522	1,277	1,510
25.8	Subsistence and support of persons	27	16	15
26.0	Supplies and materials	1,373	1,490	1,590
31.0	Equipment	38	63	68
32.0	Land and structures	337	282	365
42.0	Insurance claims and indemnities		12	13
92.0	Undistributed		291	
99.0	Direct obligations	6,903	6,865	6,900
99.0	Reimbursable obligations	503	524	530
99.9	Total new obligations, unexpired accounts	7,406	7,389	7,430

Employment Summary

Identification code 057–3840–0–1–051		2021 actual	2022 est.	2023 est.
1001	Direct civilian full-time equivalent employment	16,751	14,553	14,389
2001	Reimbursable civilian full-time equivalent employment	290	241	241

OVERSEAS CONTINGENCY OPERATIONS TRANSFER FUND

Program and Financing (in millions of dollars)

Identification code 097–0118–0–1–051		2021 actual	2022 est.	2023 est.
	Budgetary resources:			
	Unobligated balance:			
1000	Unobligated balance brought forward, Oct 1	10	10	10
1930	Total budgetary resources available	10	10	10
	Memorandum (non-add) entries:			
1941	Unexpired unobligated balance, end of year	10	10	10
4180	Budget authority, net (total)			
4190	Outlays, net (total)			

RED HILL RECOVERY FUND

(INCLUDING TRANSFER OF FUNDS)

For the "Red Hill Recovery Fund", $1,000,000,000, to remain available until expended, for transfer only to other appropriations or funds available to the Department of Defense (including military construction): *Provided*, That such funds shall be available to the Secretary of Defense for the purpose of conducting activities taken to comply with State of Hawaii Department of Health laws or otherwise determined to be appropriate, including activities relating to improvements of infrastructure and defueling, at the Red Hill Bulk Fuel Storage Facility: *Provided further,* That amounts transferred pursuant to the authority herein shall be merged with, and be available for the same purposes and time period as the appropriations or funds to which transferred: *Provided further,* That upon a determination that all or part of the funds transferred from this appropriation are not necessary for the purposes provided herein, such amounts may be transferred back to this appropriation: *Provided further,* That the transfer authority provided herein is in addition to any other transfer authority available to the Department of Defense: *Provided further,* That not less than 30 days prior to any transfer of funds under this heading, the Secretary of Defense shall notify the congressional defense committees of the details of any such transfer.

Program and Financing (in millions of dollars)

Identification code 097–0043–0–1–051		2021 actual	2022 est.	2023 est.
	Obligations by program activity:			
0001	Red Hill Recovery Fund			400
0900	Total new obligations, unexpired accounts (object class 32.0)			400
	Budgetary resources:			
	Budget authority:			
	Appropriations, discretionary:			
1100	Appropriation			1,000
1930	Total budgetary resources available			1,000
	Memorandum (non-add) entries:			
1941	Unexpired unobligated balance, end of year			600
	Change in obligated balance:			
	Unpaid obligations:			
3010	New obligations, unexpired accounts			400
3020	Outlays (gross)			–200
3050	Unpaid obligations, end of year			200
	Memorandum (non-add) entries:			
3200	Obligated balance, end of year			200
	Budget authority and outlays, net:			
	Discretionary:			
4000	Budget authority, gross			1,000
	Outlays, gross:			
4010	Outlays from new discretionary authority			200
4180	Budget authority, net (total)			1,000
4190	Outlays, net (total)			200

The Red Hill Recovery Fund provides funding for transfer to other appropriations or funds available to the Department of Defense (including Military Construction) for the purpose of conducting activities taken to comply with the State of Hawaii Department of Health laws or otherwise determined to be appropriate, including activities relating to improvements of infrastructure and defueling, at the Red Hill Bulk Fuel Storage Facility.

UNITED STATES COURT OF APPEALS FOR THE ARMED FORCES

For salaries and expenses necessary for the United States Court of Appeals for the Armed Forces, $16,003,000, of which not to exceed $15,000 may be used for official representation purposes.

Note.—A full-year 2022 appropriation for this account was not enacted at the time the Budget was prepared; therefore, the Budget assumes this account is operating under the Continuing Appropriations Act, 2022 (Division A of Public Law 117–43, as amended). The amounts included for 2022 reflect the annualized level provided by the continuing resolution.

Program and Financing (in millions of dollars)

Identification code 097–0104–0–1–051		2021 actual	2022 est.	2023 est.
	Obligations by program activity:			
0004	Administration and associated activities	15	16	16
0020	Undistributed		–1	
0900	Total new obligations, unexpired accounts	15	15	16
	Budgetary resources:			
	Budget authority:			
	Appropriations, discretionary:			
1100	Appropriation	15	15	16

UNITED STATES COURT OF APPEALS FOR THE ARMED FORCES—Continued

Program and Financing—Continued

Identification code 097–0104–0–1–051	2021 actual	2022 est.	2023 est.
1930 Total budgetary resources available	15	15	16
Change in obligated balance:			
Unpaid obligations:			
3000 Unpaid obligations, brought forward, Oct 1	8	5	4
3010 New obligations, unexpired accounts	15	15	16
3011 Obligations ("upward adjustments"), expired accounts	1		
3020 Outlays (gross)	–18	–16	–16
3041 Recoveries of prior year unpaid obligations, expired	–1		
3050 Unpaid obligations, end of year	5	4	4
Memorandum (non-add) entries:			
3100 Obligated balance, start of year	8	5	4
3200 Obligated balance, end of year	5	4	4
Budget authority and outlays, net:			
Discretionary:			
4000 Budget authority, gross	15	15	16
Outlays, gross:			
4010 Outlays from new discretionary authority	13	12	13
4011 Outlays from discretionary balances	5	4	3
4020 Outlays, gross (total)	18	16	16
4180 Budget authority, net (total)	15	15	16
4190 Outlays, net (total)	18	16	16

Object Classification (in millions of dollars)

Identification code 097–0104–0–1–051	2021 actual	2022 est.	2023 est.
Direct obligations:			
Personnel compensation:			
11.1 Full-time permanent	4	7	8
11.3 Other than full-time permanent	3		
11.9 Total personnel compensation	7	7	8
12.1 Civilian personnel benefits	2	2	2
23.1 Rental payments to GSA	2	1	1
23.3 Communications, utilities, and miscellaneous charges	1	1	1
25.1 Advisory and assistance services	2	4	3
25.7 Operation and maintenance of equipment	1	1	1
92.0 Undistributed		–1	
99.9 Total new obligations, unexpired accounts	15	15	16

Employment Summary

Identification code 097–0104–0–1–051	2021 actual	2022 est.	2023 est.
1001 Direct civilian full-time equivalent employment	48	59	59

DRUG INTERDICTION AND COUNTER-DRUG ACTIVITIES, DEFENSE

(INCLUDING TRANSFER OF FUNDS)

For drug interdiction and counter-drug activities of the Department of Defense, for transfer to appropriations available to the Department of Defense for military personnel of the reserve components serving under the provisions of title 10 and title 32, United States Code; for operation and maintenance; for procurement; and for research, development, test and evaluation, $855,728,000: Provided, That the funds appropriated under this heading shall be available for obligation for the same time period and for the same purpose as the appropriation to which transferred: Provided further, That upon a determination that all or part of the funds transferred from this appropriation are not necessary for the purposes provided herein, such amounts may be transferred back to this appropriation: Provided further, That the transfer authority provided under this heading is in addition to any other transfer authority contained elsewhere in this Act.

Note.—A full-year 2022 appropriation for this account was not enacted at the time the Budget was prepared; therefore, the Budget assumes this account is operating under the Continuing Appropriations Act, 2022 (Division A of Public Law 117–43, as amended). The amounts included for 2022 reflect the annualized level provided by the continuing resolution.

Program and Financing (in millions of dollars)

Identification code 097–0105–0–1–051	2021 actual	2022 est.	2023 est.
Obligations by program activity:			
0001 Counter-narcotics support		593	620
0002 Drug demand reduction program		126	130
0003 National Guard counter-drug program		97	100
0004 National Guard counter-drug schools		6	6
0020 Undistributed		93	
0900 Total new obligations, unexpired accounts		915	856
Budgetary resources:			
Budget authority:			
Appropriations, discretionary:			
1100 Appropriation	914	822	856
1100 Appropriation		93	
1120 Appropriations transferred to other acct [057–3740]	–2		
1120 Appropriations transferred to other acct [057–3840]	–2		
1120 Appropriations transferred to other acct [097–0130]	–4		
1120 Appropriations transferred to other acct [021–2040]	–1		
1120 Appropriations transferred to other acct [017–1105]	–2		
1120 Appropriations transferred to other acct [017–1106]	–7		
1120 Appropriations transferred to other acct [097–0100]	–73		
1120 Appropriations transferred to other acct [021–2060]	–191		
1120 Appropriations transferred to other acct [017–1405]	–4		
1120 Appropriations transferred to other acct [057–3850]	–61		
1120 Appropriations transferred to other acct [057–3700]	–3		
1120 Appropriations transferred to other acct [021–2080]	–3		
1120 Appropriations transferred to other acct [057–3080]	–3		
1120 Appropriations transferred to other acct [021–2065]	–20		
1120 Appropriations transferred to other acct [057–3600]	–3		
1120 Appropriations transferred to other acct [021–2035]	–6		
1120 Appropriations transferred to other acct [017–1810]	–9		
1120 Appropriations transferred to other acct [021–2020]	–254		
1120 Appropriations transferred to other acct [017–1804]	–138		
1120 Appropriations transferred to other acct [017–1319]	–2		
1120 Appropriations transferred to other acct [057–3400]	–183		
1120 Appropriations transferred to other acct [021–2070]	–6		
1121 Appropriations transferred from other acct [021–2060]	4		
1121 Appropriations transferred from other acct [097–0100]	7		
1121 Appropriations transferred from other acct [057–3850]	2		
1121 Appropriations transferred from other acct [021–2065]	1		
1121 Appropriations transferred from other acct [021–2020]	29		
1121 Appropriations transferred from other acct [017–1804]	9		
1121 Appropriations transferred from other acct [057–3400]	7		
1121 Appropriations transferred from other acct [021–2070]	2		
1121 Appropriations transferred from other acct [017–1319]	2		
1160 Appropriation, discretionary (total)		915	856
1930 Total budgetary resources available		915	856
Change in obligated balance:			
Unpaid obligations:			
3000 Unpaid obligations, brought forward, Oct 1			320
3010 New obligations, unexpired accounts		915	856
3020 Outlays (gross)		–595	–739
3050 Unpaid obligations, end of year		320	437
Memorandum (non-add) entries:			
3100 Obligated balance, start of year			320
3200 Obligated balance, end of year		320	437
Budget authority and outlays, net:			
Discretionary:			
4000 Budget authority, gross		915	856
Outlays, gross:			
4010 Outlays from new discretionary authority		595	556
4011 Outlays from discretionary balances			183
4020 Outlays, gross (total)		595	739
4180 Budget authority, net (total)		915	856
4190 Outlays, net (total)		595	739

Object Classification (in millions of dollars)

Identification code 097–0105–0–1–051	2021 actual	2022 est.	2023 est.
Direct obligations:			
21.0 Travel and transportation of persons		10	10
22.0 Transportation of things		7	8
23.2 Rental payments to others		5	5
23.3 Communications, utilities, and miscellaneous charges		31	31
25.1 Advisory and assistance services		35	36
25.2 Other services from non-Federal sources		22	22
25.3 Other goods and services from Federal sources		208	214

DEPARTMENT OF DEFENSE—MILITARY PROGRAMS

Operation and Maintenance—Continued
Federal Funds—Continued

257

		2021 actual	2022 est.	2023 est.
25.3	Other goods and services from Federal sources		2	2
25.4	Operation and maintenance of facilities		37	38
25.7	Operation and maintenance of equipment		132	135
26.0	Supplies and materials		316	338
31.0	Equipment		17	17
92.0	Undistributed		93	
99.9	Total new obligations, unexpired accounts		915	856

SUPPORT FOR INTERNATIONAL SPORTING COMPETITIONS

Program and Financing (in millions of dollars)

Identification code 097–0838–0–1–051		2021 actual	2022 est.	2023 est.
	Obligations by program activity:			
0001	Direct program activity	1		10
	Budgetary resources:			
	Unobligated balance:			
1000	Unobligated balance brought forward, Oct 1	5	4	4
	Budget authority:			
	Appropriations, discretionary:			
1100	Appropriation			10
1900	Budget authority (total)			10
1930	Total budgetary resources available	5	4	14
	Memorandum (non-add) entries:			
1941	Unexpired unobligated balance, end of year	4	4	4
	Change in obligated balance:			
	Unpaid obligations:			
3000	Unpaid obligations, brought forward, Oct 1	1	1	
3010	New obligations, unexpired accounts	1		10
3020	Outlays (gross)	–1	–1	–2
3050	Unpaid obligations, end of year	1	1	8
	Memorandum (non-add) entries:			
3100	Obligated balance, start of year	1	1	
3200	Obligated balance, end of year	1	1	8
	Budget authority and outlays, net:			
	Discretionary:			
4000	Budget authority, gross			10
	Outlays, gross:			
4010	Outlays from new discretionary authority			2
4011	Outlays from discretionary balances	1	1	
4020	Outlays, gross (total)	1	1	2
4180	Budget authority, net (total)			10
4190	Outlays, net (total)	1	1	2

Object Classification (in millions of dollars)

Identification code 097–0838–0–1–051		2021 actual	2022 est.	2023 est.
	Direct obligations:			
21.0	Travel and transportation of persons	1		4
23.2	Rental payments to others			2
25.2	Other services from non-Federal sources			1
31.0	Equipment			3
99.9	Total new obligations, unexpired accounts	1		10

FOREIGN CURRENCY FLUCTUATIONS

Program and Financing (in millions of dollars)

Identification code 097–0801–0–1–051		2021 actual	2022 est.	2023 est.
	Budgetary resources:			
	Unobligated balance:			
1000	Unobligated balance brought forward, Oct 1	970	970	970
1010	Unobligated balance transfer to other accts [017–1105]	–22		
1010	Unobligated balance transfer to other accts [021–2010]	–113		
1010	Unobligated balance transfer to other accts [017–1804]	–25		
1010	Unobligated balance transfer to other accts [017–1106]	–5		
1010	Unobligated balance transfer to other accts [097–0100]	–14		
1010	Unobligated balance transfer to other accts [057–3400]	–88		
1010	Unobligated balance transfer to other accts [017–1453]	–74		
1010	Unobligated balance transfer to other accts [021–2020]	–125		
1010	Unobligated balance transfer to other accts [097–0130]	–7		
1010	Unobligated balance transfer to other accts [057–3500]	–162		
1010	Unobligated balance transfer to other accts [097–4930]	–600		
1012	Unobligated balance transfers between expired and unexpired accounts	1,235		
1070	Unobligated balance (total)	970	970	970
1930	Total budgetary resources available	970	970	970
	Memorandum (non-add) entries:			
1941	Unexpired unobligated balance, end of year	970	970	970
4180	Budget authority, net (total)			
4190	Outlays, net (total)			

This account transfers funds to operation and maintenance and military personnel appropriations, for Defense activities that purchase foreign currencies, to finance upward adjustments of recorded obligations due to foreign currency fluctuations above the budget rate. Transfers are made as needed to meet disbursement requirements in excess of funds otherwise available for obligation adjustment. Net gains resulting from favorable exchange rates are returned to this appropriation and are available for subsequent transfer when needed. The account is replenished through the utilization of a special transfer authority that allows the Department to withdraw unobligated balances from operation and maintenance and military personnel appropriations from prior years. By statute (10 U.S.C. 2779(d)(3)), the total amount of discretionary budget authority in this transfer account may not exceed $970,000,000.

DEFENSE HEALTH PROGRAM

For expenses, not otherwise provided for, for medical and health care programs of the Department of Defense as authorized by law, $36,932,174,000; of which $35,314,750,000 shall be for operation and maintenance, of which not to exceed two percent shall remain available for obligation until September 30, 2024; of which $570,074,000, to remain available for obligation until September 30, 2025, shall be for procurement; and of which $1,047,350,000, to remain available for obligation until September 30, 2024, shall be for research, development, test and evaluation.

Note.—A full-year 2022 appropriation for this account was not enacted at the time the Budget was prepared; therefore, the Budget assumes this account is operating under the Continuing Appropriations Act, 2022 (Division A of Public Law 117–43, as amended). The amounts included for 2022 reflect the annualized level provided by the continuing resolution.

Program and Financing (in millions of dollars)

Identification code 097–0130–0–1–051		2021 actual	2022 est.	2023 est.
	Obligations by program activity:			
0001	Operation and maintenance	34,269	34,023	35,132
0002	Research, Development, Test, & Evaluation	799	2,960	882
0003	Procurement	560	502	501
0020	Undistributed		–1,693	
0799	Total direct obligations	35,628	35,792	36,515
0801	Reimbursable program activity	4,184	5,320	5,374
0900	Total new obligations, unexpired accounts	39,812	41,112	41,889
	Budgetary resources:			
	Unobligated balance:			
1000	Unobligated balance brought forward, Oct 1	2,680	2,134	164
1011	Unobligated balance transfer from other acct [097–0801]	7		
1012	Unobligated balance transfers between expired and unexpired accounts	313		
1021	Recoveries of prior year unpaid obligations	335		
1070	Unobligated balance (total)	3,335	2,134	164
	Budget authority:			
	Appropriations, discretionary:			
1100	Appropriation	34,051	35,744	36,932
1100	Appropriation		–1,693	
1120	Appropriations transferred to other acct [057–3400]	–2		
1120	Appropriations transferred to other acct [017–1804]	–2		
1120	Appropriations transferred to other acct [021–2020]	–2		
1120	Appropriations transferred to other acct [036–0165]	–15	–15	–15
1120	Appropriations transferred to other acct [036–0169]	–137	–137	–168
1121	Appropriations transferred from other acct [017–1506]	17		
1121	Appropriations transferred from other acct [017–1508]	4		
1121	Appropriations transferred from other acct [057–3080]	21		
1121	Appropriations transferred from other acct [097–0100]	3		
1121	Appropriations transferred from other acct [017–1810]	45		
1121	Appropriations transferred from other acct [057–3600]	161		
1121	Appropriations transferred from other acct [021–2020]	148		

DEFENSE HEALTH PROGRAM—Continued
Program and Financing—Continued

Identification code 097–0130–0–1–051		2021 actual	2022 est.	2023 est.
1121	Appropriations transferred from other acct [057–3740]	72		
1121	Appropriations transferred from other acct [017–1108]	31		
1121	Appropriations transferred from other acct [097–0105]	4		
1121	Appropriations transferred from other acct [017–1109]	6		
1121	Appropriations transferred from other acct [017–1507]	9		
1121	Appropriations transferred from other acct [017–1319]	49		
1160	Appropriation, discretionary (total)	34,463	33,899	36,749
	Spending authority from offsetting collections, discretionary:			
1700	Collected	1,962	5,243	5,374
1701	Change in uncollected payments, Federal sources	245		
1750	Spending auth from offsetting collections, disc (total)	2,207	5,243	5,374
	Spending authority from offsetting collections, mandatory:			
1800	Collected	1,996		
1900	Budget authority (total)	38,666	39,142	42,123
1930	Total budgetary resources available	42,001	41,276	42,287
	Memorandum (non-add) entries:			
1940	Unobligated balance expiring	–55		
1941	Unexpired unobligated balance, end of year	2,134	164	398
	Change in obligated balance:			
	Unpaid obligations:			
3000	Unpaid obligations, brought forward, Oct 1	15,932	15,423	16,122
3010	New obligations, unexpired accounts	39,812	41,112	41,889
3011	Obligations ("upward adjustments"), expired accounts	762		
3020	Outlays (gross)	–39,207	–40,413	–41,558
3040	Recoveries of prior year unpaid obligations, unexpired	–335		
3041	Recoveries of prior year unpaid obligations, expired	–1,541		
3050	Unpaid obligations, end of year	15,423	16,122	16,453
	Uncollected payments:			
3060	Uncollected pymts, Fed sources, brought forward, Oct 1	–549	–448	–448
3070	Change in uncollected pymts, Fed sources, unexpired	–245		
3071	Change in uncollected pymts, Fed sources, expired	346		
3090	Uncollected pymts, Fed sources, end of year	–448	–448	–448
	Memorandum (non-add) entries:			
3100	Obligated balance, start of year	15,383	14,975	15,674
3200	Obligated balance, end of year	14,975	15,674	16,005
	Budget authority and outlays, net:			
	Discretionary:			
4000	Budget authority, gross	36,670	39,142	42,123
	Outlays, gross:			
4010	Outlays from new discretionary authority	27,803	29,311	31,466
4011	Outlays from discretionary balances	9,408	11,102	10,092
4020	Outlays, gross (total)	37,211	40,413	41,558
	Offsets against gross budget authority and outlays:			
	Offsetting collections (collected) from:			
4030	Federal sources	–1,125	–3,007	–3,092
4033	Non-Federal sources	–1,175	–2,236	–2,282
4040	Offsets against gross budget authority and outlays (total)	–2,300	–5,243	–5,374
	Additional offsets against gross budget authority only:			
4050	Change in uncollected pymts, Fed sources, unexpired	–245		
4052	Offsetting collections credited to expired accounts	338		
4060	Additional offsets against budget authority only (total)	93		
4070	Budget authority, net (discretionary)	34,463	33,899	36,749
4080	Outlays, net (discretionary)	34,911	35,170	36,184
	Mandatory:			
4090	Budget authority, gross	1,996		
	Outlays, gross:			
4100	Outlays from new mandatory authority	1,996		
	Offsets against gross budget authority and outlays:			
	Offsetting collections (collected) from:			
4120	Federal sources	–1,996		
4180	Budget authority, net (total)	34,463	33,899	36,749
4190	Outlays, net (total)	34,911	35,170	36,184

The Defense Health Program (DHP) provides care to current and retired members of the Armed Forces, their family members, and other eligible beneficiaries. Beneficiaries may obtain care from the Military Department medical and dental facilities or through the civilian health care network under the TRICARE program.

Accrual accounting for Medicare-eligible beneficiaries began in 2003 and the health care for these beneficiaries is funded from the Department of Defense Medicare-Eligible Retiree Health Care Fund. The DHP also manages Research and Development funds appropriated by Congress, which support medical research and health information management systems development.

The DHP and Department of Veterans Affairs (VA) share the goal of improving the access, quality, and cost effectiveness of health care provided by VA and DOD. To this end, each Department contributes a minimum of $15 million per year for joint health care incentives.

The requested appropriation for the Defense Health Program is $37.0 billion.

Health care is provided in military facilities as follows:

	2021	2022	2023
Inpatient Facilities	49	47	47
Outpatient Clinics	465	535	535
Dental Clinics	192	138	138

The DHP is staffed by:

	2021	2022	2023
Civilian work years (thousands)	56	57	57
Military personnel (thousands)	71	72	70

The number of eligible beneficiaries of the Defense Health Program is estimated as follows:

Eligible Beneficiary Categories	2021	2022	2023
Active Duty (AD) Personnel	1,629,824	1,630,622	1,609,734
Active Duty Family Members	1,936,875	1,941,603	1,919,303
(Medicare Eligible AD Family Members)	(4,650)	(4,652)	(4,597)
Retirees	1,038,187	1,035,771	1,033,859
(Medicare Eligible Retirees)	(1,210,777)	(1,225,743)	(1,238,969)
Retiree Family Members and Survivors	2,494,809	2,491,545	2,488,864
(Medicare Eligible Retiree Family Members and Survivors)	(1,282,869)	(1,292,176)	(1,301,293)
(Medicare Eligible Other)	(3,692)	(3,713)	(3,716)
Total	9,601,683	9,625,825	9,600,335
(Total Medicare Eligible)	(2,501,988)	(2,526,284)	(2,548,575)

Object Classification (in millions of dollars)

Identification code 097–0130–0–1–051		2021 actual	2022 est.	2023 est.
	Direct obligations:			
	Personnel compensation:			
11.1	Full-time permanent	4,009	4,217	4,313
11.3	Other than full-time permanent	75	103	29
11.5	Other personnel compensation	447	553	702
11.9	Total personnel compensation	4,531	4,873	5,044
12.1	Civilian personnel benefits	1,446	1,453	1,522
13.0	Benefits for former personnel	1	3	1
21.0	Travel and transportation of persons	130	130	121
22.0	Transportation of things	14	13	14
23.1	Rental payments to GSA	21	22	23
23.2	Rental payments to others	40	41	42
23.3	Communications, utilities, and miscellaneous charges	312	332	354
24.0	Printing and reproduction	15	16	19
25.1	Advisory and assistance services	459	348	353
25.2	Other services from non-Federal sources	700	267	330
25.3	Other goods and services from Federal sources	524	433	464
25.3	Other goods and services from Federal sources	33	44	55
25.3	Other goods and services from Federal sources	266	266	243
25.4	Operation and maintenance of facilities	570	472	533
25.5	Research and development contracts	2,054	260	541
25.6	Medical care	16,164	20,278	18,264
25.7	Operation and maintenance of equipment	2,260	1,771	1,939
25.8	Subsistence and support of persons	3	4	4
26.0	Supplies and materials	4,541	4,391	4,577
31.0	Equipment	807	1,386	1,245
32.0	Land and structures	395	374	410
41.0	Grants, subsidies, and contributions	329	305	415
42.0	Insurance claims and indemnities	11		
43.0	Interest and dividends	2	2	2
92.0	Undistributed		–1,693	
99.0	Direct obligations	35,628	35,791	36,515
99.0	Reimbursable obligations	4,184	5,321	5,374
99.9	Total new obligations, unexpired accounts	39,812	41,112	41,889

Employment Summary

Identification code 097–0130–0–1–051	2021 actual	2022 est.	2023 est.
1001 Direct civilian full-time equivalent employment	54,799	55,885	55,917

DEPARTMENT OF DEFENSE—MILITARY PROGRAMS

Operation and Maintenance—Continued
Federal Funds—Continued

2001	Reimbursable civilian full-time equivalent employment	46	92	402

THE DEPARTMENT OF DEFENSE ENVIRONMENTAL RESTORATION ACCOUNTS

ENVIRONMENTAL RESTORATION, ARMY

(INCLUDING TRANSFER OF FUNDS)

For the Department of the Army, $196,244,000, to remain available until transferred: Provided, That the Secretary of the Army shall, upon determining that such funds are required for environmental restoration, reduction and recycling of hazardous waste, removal of unsafe buildings and debris of the Department of the Army, or for similar purposes, transfer the funds made available by this appropriation to other appropriations made available to the Department of the Army, to be merged with and to be available for the same purposes and for the same time period as the appropriations to which transferred: Provided further, That upon a determination that all or part of the funds transferred from this appropriation are not necessary for the purposes provided herein, such amounts may be transferred back to this appropriation: Provided further, That the transfer authority provided under this heading is in addition to any other transfer authority provided elsewhere in this Act.

ENVIRONMENTAL RESTORATION, NAVY

(INCLUDING TRANSFER OF FUNDS)

For the Department of the Navy, $359,348,000, to remain available until transferred: Provided, That the Secretary of the Navy shall, upon determining that such funds are required for environmental restoration, reduction and recycling of hazardous waste, removal of unsafe buildings and debris of the Department of the Navy, or for similar purposes, transfer the funds made available by this appropriation to other appropriations made available to the Department of the Navy, to be merged with and to be available for the same purposes and for the same time period as the appropriations to which transferred: Provided further, That upon a determination that all or part of the funds transferred from this appropriation are not necessary for the purposes provided herein, such amounts may be transferred back to this appropriation: Provided further, That the transfer authority provided under this heading is in addition to any other transfer authority provided elsewhere in this Act.

ENVIRONMENTAL RESTORATION, AIR FORCE

(INCLUDING TRANSFER OF FUNDS)

For the Department of the Air Force, $314,474,000, to remain available until transferred: Provided, That the Secretary of the Air Force shall, upon determining that such funds are required for environmental restoration, reduction and recycling of hazardous waste, removal of unsafe buildings and debris of the Department of the Air Force, or for similar purposes, transfer the funds made available by this appropriation to other appropriations made available to the Department of the Air Force, to be merged with and to be available for the same purposes and for the same time period as the appropriations to which transferred: Provided further, That upon a determination that all or part of the funds transferred from this appropriation are not necessary for the purposes provided herein, such amounts may be transferred back to this appropriation: Provided further, That the transfer authority provided under this heading is in addition to any other transfer authority provided elsewhere in this Act.

ENVIRONMENTAL RESTORATION, DEFENSE-WIDE

(INCLUDING TRANSFER OF FUNDS)

For the Department of Defense, $8,924,000, to remain available until transferred: Provided, That the Secretary of Defense shall, upon determining that such funds are required for environmental restoration, reduction and recycling of hazardous waste, removal of unsafe buildings and debris of the Department of Defense, or for similar purposes, transfer the funds made available by this appropriation to other appropriations made available to the Department of Defense, to be merged with and to be available for the same purposes and for the same time period as the appropriations to which transferred: Provided further, That upon a determination that all or part of the funds transferred from this appropriation are not necessary for the purposes provided herein, such amounts may be transferred back to this appropriation: Provided further, That the transfer authority provided under this heading is in addition to any other transfer authority provided elsewhere in this Act.

Note.—A full-year 2022 appropriation for this account was not enacted at the time the Budget was prepared; therefore, the Budget assumes this account is operating under the Continuing Appropriations Act, 2022 (Division A of Public Law 117–43, as amended). The amounts included for 2022 reflect the annualized level provided by the continuing resolution.

Program and Financing (in millions of dollars)

Identification code 097–0810–0–1–051		2021 actual	2022 est.	2023 est.
	Obligations by program activity:			
0001	Department of the Army		201	196
0002	Department of the Navy		298	359
0003	Department of the Air Force		302	315
0004	Defense-wide		9	9
0020	Undistributed		405	
0900	Total new obligations, unexpired accounts		1,215	879
	Budgetary resources:			
	Unobligated balance:			
1000	Unobligated balance brought forward, Oct 1	38	136	136
1010	Unobligated balance transfer to other accts [097–9999]	–1		
1033	Recoveries of prior year paid obligations	2		
1070	Unobligated balance (total)	39	136	136
	Budget authority:			
	Appropriations, discretionary:			
1100	Appropriation	1,215	810	879
1100	Appropriation		405	
1120	Appropriations transferred to other acct [097–0100]	–9		
1120	Appropriations transferred to other acct [057–3400]	–509		
1120	Appropriations transferred to other acct [017–1804]	–421		
1120	Appropriations transferred to other acct [021–2020]	–264		
1121	Appropriations transferred from other acct [057–3400]	43		
1121	Appropriations transferred from other acct [017–1804]	42		
1160	Appropriation, discretionary (total)	97	1,215	879
1900	Budget authority (total)	97	1,215	879
1930	Total budgetary resources available	136	1,351	1,015
	Memorandum (non-add) entries:			
1941	Unexpired unobligated balance, end of year	136	136	136
	Change in obligated balance:			
	Unpaid obligations:			
3000	Unpaid obligations, brought forward, Oct 1			517
3010	New obligations, unexpired accounts		1,215	879
3020	Outlays (gross)		–698	–790
3050	Unpaid obligations, end of year		517	606
	Memorandum (non-add) entries:			
3100	Obligated balance, start of year			517
3200	Obligated balance, end of year		517	606
	Budget authority and outlays, net:			
	Discretionary:			
4000	Budget authority, gross	97	1,215	879
	Outlays, gross:			
4010	Outlays from new discretionary authority		608	440
4011	Outlays from discretionary balances		90	350
4020	Outlays, gross (total)		698	790
	Offsets against gross budget authority and outlays:			
	Offsetting collections (collected) from:			
4033	Non-Federal sources	–2		
4040	Offsets against gross budget authority and outlays (total)	–2		
	Additional offsets against gross budget authority only:			
4053	Recoveries of prior year paid obligations, unexpired accounts	2		
4060	Additional offsets against budget authority only (total)	2		
4070	Budget authority, net (discretionary)	97	1,215	879
4080	Outlays, net (discretionary)	–2	698	790
4180	Budget authority, net (total)	97	1,215	879
4190	Outlays, net (total)	–2	698	790

Object Classification (in millions of dollars)

Identification code 097–0810–0–1–051		2021 actual	2022 est.	2023 est.
	Direct obligations:			
25.2	Other services from non-Federal sources		4	4
32.0	Land and structures		807	875
92.0	Undistributed		404	
99.9	Total new obligations, unexpired accounts		1,215	879

ENVIRONMENTAL RESTORATION, FORMERLY USED DEFENSE SITES

(INCLUDING TRANSFER OF FUNDS)

For the Department of the Army, $227,262,000, to remain available until transferred: Provided, That the Secretary of the Army shall, upon determining that such funds are required for environmental restoration, reduction and recycling of hazardous waste, removal of unsafe buildings and debris at sites formerly used by the Department of Defense, transfer the funds made available by this appropriation to other appropriations made available to the Department of the Army, to be merged with and to be available for the same purposes and for the same time period as the appropriations to which transferred: Provided further, That upon a determination that all or part of the funds transferred from this appropriation are not necessary for the purposes provided herein, such amounts may be transferred back to this appropriation: Provided further, That the transfer authority provided under this heading is in addition to any other transfer authority provided elsewhere in this Act.

Note.—A full-year 2022 appropriation for this account was not enacted at the time the Budget was prepared; therefore, the Budget assumes this account is operating under the Continuing Appropriations Act, 2022 (Division A of Public Law 117–43, as amended). The amounts included for 2022 reflect the annualized level provided by the continuing resolution.

Program and Financing (in millions of dollars)

Identification code 097–0811–0–1–051		2021 actual	2022 est.	2023 est.
	Obligations by program activity:			
0005	DEFENSE-WIDE	....	219	219
0020	Undistributed	....	70	....
0900	Total new obligations, unexpired accounts	....	289	219
	Budgetary resources:			
	Unobligated balance:			
1000	Unobligated balance brought forward, Oct 1	....	5	5
	Budget authority:			
	Appropriations, discretionary:			
1100	Appropriation	289	219	227
1100	Appropriation	....	70	....
1120	Appropriations transferred to other acct [021–2020]	–289	....	....
1121	Appropriations transferred from other acct [021–2020]	5	....	....
1160	Appropriation, discretionary (total)	5	289	227
1930	Total budgetary resources available	5	294	232
	Memorandum (non-add) entries:			
1941	Unexpired unobligated balance, end of year	5	5	13
	Change in obligated balance:			
	Unpaid obligations:			
3000	Unpaid obligations, brought forward, Oct 1	....	....	140
3010	New obligations, unexpired accounts	....	289	219
3020	Outlays (gross)	....	–149	–186
3050	Unpaid obligations, end of year	....	140	173
	Memorandum (non-add) entries:			
3100	Obligated balance, start of year	....	....	140
3200	Obligated balance, end of year	....	140	173
	Budget authority and outlays, net:			
	Discretionary:			
4000	Budget authority, gross	5	289	227
	Outlays, gross:			
4010	Outlays from new discretionary authority	....	144	114
4011	Outlays from discretionary balances	....	5	72
4020	Outlays, gross (total)	....	149	186
4180	Budget authority, net (total)	5	289	227
4190	Outlays, net (total)	....	149	186

The Defense Environmental Restoration Program provides for the identification, investigation, and cleanup of contamination resulting from past DOD activities. The Department has 35,353 sites that have a remedy in place or a response completed, leaving 3,192 open sites at active and Base Realignment and Closure (BRAC) military installations and 1,614 open sites at Formerly Used Defense Sites (FUDS). For these remaining open sites, DOD is engaged in the cleanup process, including investigation to determine the extent of the contamination and the actual clean-up of the contamination, as appropriate.

The Department's environmental restoration program is funded by five separate environmental restoration accounts, one for each military department, one for defense agencies and one for FUDS. The first four accounts, Army, Navy, Air Force and defense-wide environmental restoration accounts cover funding for active installations, and are shown separately from the FUDS program environmental restoration account, which funds environmental cleanup on properties no longer owned and/or used by DOD. These five accounts include restoration activities ranging from inventory to preliminary assessment, then to investigation and cleanup of contamination, and finally to closeout of a site. BRAC sites are funded separately under the BRAC account.

Object Classification (in millions of dollars)

Identification code 097–0811–0–1–051		2021 actual	2022 est.	2023 est.
	Direct obligations:			
32.0	Land and structures	....	219	219
92.0	Undistributed	....	70	....
99.9	Total new obligations, unexpired accounts	....	289	219

OVERSEAS HUMANITARIAN, DISASTER, AND CIVIC AID

For expenses relating to the Overseas Humanitarian, Disaster, and Civic Aid programs of the Department of Defense (consisting of the programs provided under sections 401, 402, 404, 407, 2557, and 2561 of title 10, United States Code), $112,800,000, to remain available until September 30, 2024: Provided, That such amounts shall not be subject to the limitation in section 407(c)(3) of title 10, United States Code.

Note.—A full-year 2022 appropriation for this account was not enacted at the time the Budget was prepared; therefore, the Budget assumes this account is operating under the Continuing Appropriations Act, 2022 (Division A of Public Law 117–43, as amended). The amounts included for 2022 reflect the annualized level provided by the continuing resolution.

OVERSEAS HUMANITARIAN, DISASTER, AND CIVIC AID

[For an additional amount for "Overseas Humanitarian, Disaster, and Civic Aid", $2,200,000,000, to remain available until September 30, 2023, for support of Operation Allies Welcome by the Department of Defense.] *(Afghanistan Supplemental Appropriations Act, 2022.)*

OVERSEAS HUMANITARIAN, DISASTER, AND CIVIC AID

[For an additional amount for "Overseas Humanitarian, Disaster, and Civic Aid", $4,000,000,000, to remain available until September 30, 2023, for support of Operation Allies Welcome by the Department of Defense.] *(Additional Afghanistan Supplemental Appropriations Act, 2022.)*

Program and Financing (in millions of dollars)

Identification code 097–0819–0–1–051		2021 actual	2022 est.	2023 est.
	Obligations by program activity:			
0001	Humanitarian assistance	1,796	6,310	113
0020	Undistributed	....	37	....
0900	Total new obligations, unexpired accounts	1,796	6,347	113
	Budgetary resources:			
	Unobligated balance:			
1000	Unobligated balance brought forward, Oct 1	216	524	524
1011	Unobligated balance transfer from other acct [097–0100]	32	....	....
1011	Unobligated balance transfer from other acct [021–2091]	66	....	....
1011	Unobligated balance transfer from other acct [021–2099]	60	....	....
1011	Unobligated balance transfer from other acct [097–0400]	3	....	....
1070	Unobligated balance (total)	377	524	524
	Budget authority:			
	Appropriations, discretionary:			
1100	Appropriation	648	110	113
1100	Appropriation	....	37	....
1100	Appropriation	....	2,200	....
1100	Appropriation	....	4,000	....
1121	Appropriations transferred from other acct [021–2020]	289	....	....
1121	Appropriations transferred from other acct [097–0100]	10	....	....
1121	Appropriations transferred from other acct [021–2091]	1,000	....	....
1121	Appropriations transferred from other acct [097–0390]	2	....	....
1160	Appropriation, discretionary (total)	1,949	6,347	113
1900	Budget authority (total)	1,949	6,347	113
1930	Total budgetary resources available	2,326	6,871	637
	Memorandum (non-add) entries:			
1940	Unobligated balance expiring	–6	....	....

DEPARTMENT OF DEFENSE—MILITARY PROGRAMS

Operation and Maintenance—Continued
Federal Funds—Continued

Line	Description	2021 actual	2022 est.	2023 est.
1941	Unexpired unobligated balance, end of year	524	524	524
	Change in obligated balance:			
	Unpaid obligations:			
3000	Unpaid obligations, brought forward, Oct 1	208	1,772	6,722
3010	New obligations, unexpired accounts	1,796	6,347	113
3011	Obligations ("upward adjustments"), expired accounts	9		
3020	Outlays (gross)	–231	–1,397	–2,405
3041	Recoveries of prior year unpaid obligations, expired	–10		
3050	Unpaid obligations, end of year	1,772	6,722	4,430
	Memorandum (non-add) entries:			
3100	Obligated balance, start of year	208	1,772	6,722
3200	Obligated balance, end of year	1,772	6,722	4,430
	Budget authority and outlays, net:			
	Discretionary:			
4000	Budget authority, gross	1,949	6,347	113
	Outlays, gross:			
4010	Outlays from new discretionary authority	43	571	10
4011	Outlays from discretionary balances	188	826	2,395
4020	Outlays, gross (total)	231	1,397	2,405
	Offsets against gross budget authority and outlays:			
	Offsetting collections (collected) from:			
4033	Non-Federal sources	–2		
4040	Offsets against gross budget authority and outlays (total)	–2		
	Additional offsets against gross budget authority only:			
4052	Offsetting collections credited to expired accounts	2		
4060	Additional offsets against budget authority only (total)	2		
4070	Budget authority, net (discretionary)	1,949	6,347	113
4080	Outlays, net (discretionary)	229	1,397	2,405
4180	Budget authority, net (total)	1,949	6,347	113
4190	Outlays, net (total)	229	1,397	2,405

Object Classification (in millions of dollars)

Identification code 097–0819–0–1–051		2021 actual	2022 est.	2023 est.
	Direct obligations:			
21.0	Travel and transportation of persons	7	72	
22.0	Transportation of things	17	7	
23.2	Rental payments to others	3		
25.1	Advisory and assistance services	20	14	
25.2	Other services from non-Federal sources	44	5,952	113
25.3	Other goods and services from Federal sources	8	5	
25.4	Operation and maintenance of facilities	846		
25.6	Medical care	126	22	
25.7	Operation and maintenance of equipment		1	
25.8	Subsistence and support of persons	334		
26.0	Supplies and materials	181	195	
31.0	Equipment	168	23	
32.0	Land and structures	42	19	
92.0	Undistributed		37	
99.9	Total new obligations, unexpired accounts	1,796	6,347	113

COOPERATIVE THREAT REDUCTION ACCOUNT

For assistance, including assistance provided by contract or by grants, under programs and activities of the Department of Defense Cooperative Threat Reduction Program authorized under the Department of Defense Cooperative Threat Reduction Act, $341,598,000, to remain available until September 30, 2025.

Note.—A full-year 2022 appropriation for this account was not enacted at the time the Budget was prepared; therefore, the Budget assumes this account is operating under the Continuing Appropriations Act, 2022 (Division A of Public Law 117–43, as amended). The amounts included for 2022 reflect the annualized level provided by the continuing resolution.

Special and Trust Fund Receipts (in millions of dollars)

Identification code 097–0134–0–1–051		2021 actual	2022 est.	2023 est.
0100	Balance, start of year			6
	Receipts:			
	Current law:			
1130	Collections, Contributions to the Cooperative Threat Reduction Program		6	6
2000	Total: Balances and receipts		6	12
5099	Balance, end of year		6	12

Program and Financing (in millions of dollars)

Identification code 097–0134–0–1–051		2021 actual	2022 est.	2023 est.
	Obligations by program activity:			
0001	FSU Threat Reduction	322	283	342
0020	Undistributed		120	
0799	Total direct obligations	322	403	342
0801	Reimbursable program activity	2	3	3
0900	Total new obligations, unexpired accounts	324	406	345
	Budgetary resources:			
	Unobligated balance:			
1000	Unobligated balance brought forward, Oct 1	95	200	157
1001	Discretionary unobligated balance brought fwd, Oct 1	95		
1021	Recoveries of prior year unpaid obligations	65		
1033	Recoveries of prior year paid obligations	1		
1070	Unobligated balance (total)	161	200	157
	Budget authority:			
	Appropriations, discretionary:			
1100	Appropriation	360	240	342
1100	Appropriation		120	
1160	Appropriation, discretionary (total)	360	360	342
	Spending authority from offsetting collections, discretionary:			
1700	Collected		3	3
1701	Change in uncollected payments, Federal sources	3		
1750	Spending auth from offsetting collections, disc (total)	3	3	3
1900	Budget authority (total)	363	363	345
1930	Total budgetary resources available	524	563	502
	Memorandum (non-add) entries:			
1941	Unexpired unobligated balance, end of year	200	157	157
	Change in obligated balance:			
	Unpaid obligations:			
3000	Unpaid obligations, brought forward, Oct 1	508	450	500
3010	New obligations, unexpired accounts	324	406	345
3011	Obligations ("upward adjustments"), expired accounts	2		
3020	Outlays (gross)	–304	–356	–359
3040	Recoveries of prior year unpaid obligations, unexpired	–65		
3041	Recoveries of prior year unpaid obligations, expired	–15		
3050	Unpaid obligations, end of year	450	500	486
	Uncollected payments:			
3060	Uncollected pymts, Fed sources, brought forward, Oct 1	–7	–10	–10
3070	Change in uncollected pymts, Fed sources, unexpired	–3		
3090	Uncollected pymts, Fed sources, end of year	–10	–10	–10
	Memorandum (non-add) entries:			
3100	Obligated balance, start of year	501	440	490
3200	Obligated balance, end of year	440	490	476
	Budget authority and outlays, net:			
	Discretionary:			
4000	Budget authority, gross	363	363	345
	Outlays, gross:			
4010	Outlays from new discretionary authority	18	43	41
4011	Outlays from discretionary balances	281	313	318
4020	Outlays, gross (total)	299	356	359
	Offsets against gross budget authority and outlays:			
	Offsetting collections (collected) from:			
4030	Federal sources	–1	–3	–3
4033	Non-Federal sources	–1		
4040	Offsets against gross budget authority and outlays (total)	–2	–3	–3
	Additional offsets against gross budget authority only:			
4050	Change in uncollected pymts, Fed sources, unexpired	–3		
4052	Offsetting collections credited to expired accounts	1		
4053	Recoveries of prior year paid obligations, unexpired accounts	1		
4060	Additional offsets against budget authority only (total)	–1		
4070	Budget authority, net (discretionary)	360	360	342
4080	Outlays, net (discretionary)	297	353	356
	Mandatory:			
	Outlays, gross:			
4101	Outlays from mandatory balances	5		
4180	Budget authority, net (total)	360	360	342
4190	Outlays, net (total)	302	353	356

COOPERATIVE THREAT REDUCTION ACCOUNT—Continued

Object Classification (in millions of dollars)

Identification code 097–0134–0–1–051		2021 actual	2022 est.	2023 est.
	Direct obligations:			
21.0	Travel and transportation of persons	1	3	3
25.1	Advisory and assistance services	172	92	197
25.2	Other services from non-Federal sources	23	28	21
25.3	Other goods and services from Federal sources	26	55	60
25.4	Operation and maintenance of facilities	22	6	3
25.5	Research and development contracts	2	1	
25.7	Operation and maintenance of equipment	12	6	3
26.0	Supplies and materials	15	64	19
31.0	Equipment	1	2	2
32.0	Land and structures	12	12	22
41.0	Grants, subsidies, and contributions	36	14	12
92.0	Undistributed		120	
99.0	Direct obligations	322	403	342
99.0	Reimbursable obligations	2	3	3
99.9	Total new obligations, unexpired accounts	324	406	345

AFGHANISTAN SECURITY FORCES FUND

Note.—A full-year 2022 appropriation for this account was not enacted at the time the Budget was prepared; therefore, the Budget assumes this account is operating under the Continuing Appropriations Act, 2022 (Division A of Public Law 117–43, as amended). The amounts included for 2022 reflect the annualized level provided by the continuing resolution.

Program and Financing (in millions of dollars)

Identification code 021–2091–0–1–051		2021 actual	2022 est.	2023 est.
	Obligations by program activity:			
0005	Contributions	178		
0006	Afghan National Army	1,096	1,078	
0007	Afghan National Police	252	496	
0008	Afghan Air Force	889	777	
0009	Afghan Special Security Forces	431	891	
0020	Undistributed		–280	
0799	Total direct obligations	2,846	2,962	
0801	Reimbursable program activity	187		
0900	Total new obligations, unexpired accounts	3,033	2,962	
	Budgetary resources:			
	Unobligated balance:			
1000	Unobligated balance brought forward, Oct 1	3,390	641	727
1010	Unobligated balance transfer to other accts [097–0819]	–66		
1010	Unobligated balance transfer to other accts [097–4930.003]	–80		
1021	Recoveries of prior year unpaid obligations	163		
1033	Recoveries of prior year paid obligations	9		
1070	Unobligated balance (total)	3,416	641	727
	Budget authority:			
	Appropriations, discretionary:			
1100	Appropriation	3,048	3,328	
1100	Appropriation		–280	
1120	Appropriations transferred to other acct [097–0819]	–1,000		
1120	Appropriations transferred to other acct [097–4930.003]	–309		
1131	Unobligated balance of appropriations permanently reduced	–1,100		
1160	Appropriation, discretionary (total)	639	3,048	
	Spending authority from offsetting collections, discretionary:			
1700	Collected	1		
1900	Budget authority (total)	640	3,048	
1930	Total budgetary resources available	4,056	3,689	727
	Memorandum (non-add) entries:			
1940	Unobligated balance expiring	–382		
1941	Unexpired unobligated balance, end of year	641	727	727
	Change in obligated balance:			
	Unpaid obligations:			
3000	Unpaid obligations, brought forward, Oct 1	1,046	977	1,686
3010	New obligations, unexpired accounts	3,033	2,962	
3011	Obligations ("upward adjustments"), expired accounts	226		
3020	Outlays (gross)	–2,825	–2,253	–1,345
3040	Recoveries of prior year unpaid obligations, unexpired	–163		
3041	Recoveries of prior year unpaid obligations, expired	–340		
3050	Unpaid obligations, end of year	977	1,686	341
	Memorandum (non-add) entries:			
3100	Obligated balance, start of year	1,046	977	1,686
3200	Obligated balance, end of year	977	1,686	341
	Budget authority and outlays, net:			
	Discretionary:			
4000	Budget authority, gross	640	3,048	
	Outlays, gross:			
4010	Outlays from new discretionary authority	742	1,158	
4011	Outlays from discretionary balances	2,083	1,095	1,345
4020	Outlays, gross (total)	2,825	2,253	1,345
	Offsets against gross budget authority and outlays:			
	Offsetting collections (collected) from:			
4030	Federal sources	–115		
4033	Non-Federal sources	–1		
4040	Offsets against gross budget authority and outlays (total)	–116		
	Additional offsets against gross budget authority only:			
4052	Offsetting collections credited to expired accounts	106		
4053	Recoveries of prior year paid obligations, unexpired accounts	9		
4060	Additional offsets against budget authority only (total)	115		
4070	Budget authority, net (discretionary)	639	3,048	
4080	Outlays, net (discretionary)	2,709	2,253	1,345
4180	Budget authority, net (total)	639	3,048	
4190	Outlays, net (total)	2,709	2,253	1,345

Object Classification (in millions of dollars)

Identification code 021–2091–0–1–051		2021 actual	2022 est.	2023 est.
	Direct obligations:			
25.3	Other goods and services from Federal sources	2,846	3,242	
92.0	Undistributed		–280	
99.0	Direct obligations	2,846	2,962	
99.0	Reimbursable obligations	187		
99.9	Total new obligations, unexpired accounts	3,033	2,962	

COUNTER-ISIS TRAIN AND EQUIP FUND

For the "Counter-Islamic State of Iraq and Syria Train and Equip Fund", $541,692,000, to remain available until September 30, 2024: Provided, That such funds shall be available to the Secretary of Defense in coordination with the Secretary of State, to provide assistance, including training; equipment; logistics support, supplies, and services; stipends; infrastructure repair and renovation; construction for facility fortification and humane treatment; and sustainment, to foreign security forces, irregular forces, groups, or individuals participating, or preparing to participate in activities to counter, or prevent the re-emergence of, the Islamic State of Iraq and Syria, and their affiliated or associated groups: Provided further, That amounts made available under this heading shall be available to provide assistance only for activities in a country designated by the Secretary of Defense, in coordination with the Secretary of State, as having a security mission to counter the Islamic State of Iraq and Syria, and following written notification to the congressional defense committees of such designation: Provided further, That the Secretary of Defense shall ensure that prior to providing assistance to elements of any forces or individuals, such elements or individuals are appropriately vetted, including at a minimum, assessing such elements for associations with terrorist groups or groups associated with the Government of Iran; and receiving commitments from such elements to promote respect for human rights and the rule of law: Provided further, That the Secretary of Defense shall, not fewer than 15 days prior to obligating from this appropriation account, notify the congressional defense committees in writing of the details of any such obligation: Provided further, That the Secretary of Defense may accept and retain contributions, including assistance in-kind, from foreign governments, including the Government of Iraq and other entities, to carry out assistance authorized under this heading: Provided further, That contributions of funds for the purposes provided herein from any foreign government or other entity may be credited to this Fund, to remain available until expended, and used for such purposes: Provided further, That the Secretary of Defense shall prioritize such contributions when providing any assistance for construction for facility fortification: Provided further, That the Secretary of Defense may waive a provision of law relating to the acquisition of items and support services or sections 40 and 40A of the Arms Export

Control Act (22 U.S.C. 2780 and 2785) if the Secretary determines that such provision of law would prohibit, restrict, delay or otherwise limit the provision of such assistance and a notice of and justification for such waiver is submitted to the congressional defense committees, the Committees on Appropriations and Foreign Relations of the Senate and the Committees on Appropriations and Foreign Affairs of the House of Representatives: Provided further, That the United States may accept equipment procured using funds provided under this heading, or under the heading, "Iraq Train and Equip Fund" in prior Acts, that was transferred to security forces, irregular forces, or groups participating, or preparing to participate in activities to counter, or prevent the re-emergence of, the Islamic State of Iraq and Syria and returned by such forces or groups to the United States, and such equipment may be treated as stocks of the Department of Defense upon written notification to the congressional defense committees: Provided further, That equipment procured using funds provided under this heading, or under the heading, "Iraq Train and Equip Fund" in prior Acts, and not yet transferred to security forces, irregular forces, or groups participating, or preparing to participate in activities to counter, or prevent the re-emergence of, the Islamic State of Iraq and Syria may be treated as stocks of the Department of Defense when determined by the Secretary to no longer be required for transfer to such forces or groups and upon written notification to the congressional defense committees: Provided further, That the Secretary of Defense shall provide quarterly reports to the congressional defense committees on the use of funds provided under this heading, including, but not limited to, the number of individuals trained, the nature and scope of support and sustainment provided to each group or individual, the area of operations for each group, and the contributions of other countries, groups, or individuals.

Note.—A full-year 2022 appropriation for this account was not enacted at the time the Budget was prepared; therefore, the Budget assumes this account is operating under the Continuing Appropriations Act, 2022 (Division A of Public Law 117–43, as amended). The amounts included for 2022 reflect the annualized level provided by the continuing resolution.

Program and Financing (in millions of dollars)

Identification code 021–2099–0–1–051		2021 actual	2022 est.	2023 est.
	Obligations by program activity:			
0001	Counter-Islamic State of Iraq and Syria Train and Equip	792	635	530
0020	Undistributed		188	
0799	Total direct obligations	792	823	530
0900	Total new obligations, unexpired accounts	792	823	530
	Budgetary resources:			
	Unobligated balance:			
1000	Unobligated balance brought forward, Oct 1	1,090	448	335
1010	Unobligated balance transfer to other accts [097–0819]	–60		
1021	Recoveries of prior year unpaid obligations	10		
1070	Unobligated balance (total)	1,040	448	335
	Budget authority:			
	Appropriations, discretionary:			
1100	Appropriation	710	522	542
1100	Appropriation		188	
1131	Unobligated balance of appropriations permanently reduced	–400		
1160	Appropriation, discretionary (total)	310	710	542
1900	Budget authority (total)	310	710	542
1930	Total budgetary resources available	1,350	1,158	877
	Memorandum (non-add) entries:			
1940	Unobligated balance expiring	–110		
1941	Unexpired unobligated balance, end of year	448	335	347
	Change in obligated balance:			
	Unpaid obligations:			
3000	Unpaid obligations, brought forward, Oct 1	110	521	892
3010	New obligations, unexpired accounts	792	823	530
3011	Obligations ("upward adjustments"), expired accounts	73		
3020	Outlays (gross)	–386	–452	–545
3040	Recoveries of prior year unpaid obligations, unexpired	–10		
3041	Recoveries of prior year unpaid obligations, expired	–58		
3050	Unpaid obligations, end of year	521	892	877
	Memorandum (non-add) entries:			
3100	Obligated balance, start of year	110	521	892
3200	Obligated balance, end of year	521	892	877
	Budget authority and outlays, net:			
	Discretionary:			
4000	Budget authority, gross	310	710	542
	Outlays, gross:			
4010	Outlays from new discretionary authority	57	142	108
4011	Outlays from discretionary balances	329	310	437
4020	Outlays, gross (total)	386	452	545
	Offsets against gross budget authority and outlays:			
	Offsetting collections (collected) from:			
4030	Federal sources	–10		
4040	Offsets against gross budget authority and outlays (total)	–10		
	Additional offsets against gross budget authority only:			
4052	Offsetting collections credited to expired accounts	10		
4070	Budget authority, net (discretionary)	310	710	542
4080	Outlays, net (discretionary)	376	452	545
4180	Budget authority, net (total)	310	710	542
4190	Outlays, net (total)	376	452	545

Object Classification (in millions of dollars)

Identification code 021–2099–0–1–051		2021 actual	2022 est.	2023 est.
	Direct obligations:			
25.2	Other services from non-Federal sources	792	635	530
92.0	Undistributed		188	
99.0	Direct obligations	792	823	530
99.9	Total new obligations, unexpired accounts	792	823	530

IRAQ TRAIN AND EQUIP FUND

Program and Financing (in millions of dollars)

Identification code 021–2097–0–1–051		2021 actual	2022 est.	2023 est.
	Change in obligated balance:			
	Unpaid obligations:			
3000	Unpaid obligations, brought forward, Oct 1	19	1	
3011	Obligations ("upward adjustments"), expired accounts	81		
3020	Outlays (gross)		–1	
3041	Recoveries of prior year unpaid obligations, expired	–99		
3050	Unpaid obligations, end of year	1		
	Memorandum (non-add) entries:			
3100	Obligated balance, start of year	19	1	
3200	Obligated balance, end of year	1		
	Budget authority and outlays, net:			
	Discretionary:			
	Outlays, gross:			
4011	Outlays from discretionary balances		1	
	Offsets against gross budget authority and outlays:			
	Offsetting collections (collected) from:			
4030	Federal sources	–45		
4040	Offsets against gross budget authority and outlays (total)	–45		
	Additional offsets against gross budget authority only:			
4052	Offsetting collections credited to expired accounts	45		
4080	Outlays, net (discretionary)	–45	1	
4180	Budget authority, net (total)			
4190	Outlays, net (total)	–45	1	

DEPARTMENT OF DEFENSE ACQUISITION WORKFORCE DEVELOPMENT ACCOUNT

For the Department of Defense Acquisition Workforce Development Account, $53,791,000.

Note.—A full-year 2022 appropriation for this account was not enacted at the time the Budget was prepared; therefore, the Budget assumes this account is operating under the Continuing Appropriations Act, 2022 (Division A of Public Law 117–43, as amended). The amounts included for 2022 reflect the annualized level provided by the continuing resolution.

Program and Financing (in millions of dollars)

Identification code 097–0111–0–1–051		2021 actual	2022 est.	2023 est.
	Obligations by program activity:			
0001	Department of Defense Acquisition Workforce Development	190	55	54
0020	Undistributed		33	
0900	Total new obligations, unexpired accounts	190	88	54

DEPARTMENT OF DEFENSE ACQUISITION WORKFORCE DEVELOPMENT ACCOUNT—Continued

Program and Financing—Continued

Identification code 097–0111–0–1–051	2021 actual	2022 est.	2023 est.
Budgetary resources:			
Unobligated balance:			
1000 Unobligated balance brought forward, Oct 1	133		
1001 Discretionary unobligated balance brought fwd, Oct 1	133		
1021 Recoveries of prior year unpaid obligations	18		
1033 Recoveries of prior year paid obligations	3		
1070 Unobligated balance (total)	154		
Budget authority:			
Appropriations, discretionary:			
1100 Appropriation	88	88	54
1120 Appropriations transferred to other acct [057–3400]	–12		
1160 Appropriation, discretionary (total)	76	88	54
1900 Budget authority (total)	76	88	54
1930 Total budgetary resources available	230	88	54
Memorandum (non-add) entries:			
1940 Unobligated balance expiring	–40		
Change in obligated balance:			
Unpaid obligations:			
3000 Unpaid obligations, brought forward, Oct 1	211	161	74
3010 New obligations, unexpired accounts	190	88	54
3011 Obligations ("upward adjustments"), expired accounts	3		
3020 Outlays (gross)	–202	–175	–71
3040 Recoveries of prior year unpaid obligations, unexpired	–18		
3041 Recoveries of prior year unpaid obligations, expired	–23		
3050 Unpaid obligations, end of year	161	74	57
Memorandum (non-add) entries:			
3100 Obligated balance, start of year	211	161	74
3200 Obligated balance, end of year	161	74	57
Budget authority and outlays, net:			
Discretionary:			
4000 Budget authority, gross	76	88	54
Outlays, gross:			
4010 Outlays from new discretionary authority	15	44	27
4011 Outlays from discretionary balances	187	131	44
4020 Outlays, gross (total)	202	175	71
Offsets against gross budget authority and outlays:			
Offsetting collections (collected) from:			
4033 Non-Federal sources	–3		
4040 Offsets against gross budget authority and outlays (total)	–3		
Additional offsets against gross budget authority only:			
4053 Recoveries of prior year paid obligations, unexpired accounts	3		
4060 Additional offsets against budget authority only (total)	3		
4070 Budget authority, net (discretionary)	76	88	54
4080 Outlays, net (discretionary)	199	175	71
4180 Budget authority, net (total)	76	88	54
4190 Outlays, net (total)	199	175	71

The Defense Acquisition Workforce Development Account provides funding for the Department of Defense acquisition workforce to ensure it has the capacity, in both personnel and skills, needed to properly perform its mission, provide appropriate oversight of contractor performance, and ensure the Department receives the best value for the expenditure of public resources.

Object Classification (in millions of dollars)

Identification code 097–0111–0–1–051	2021 actual	2022 est.	2023 est.
Direct obligations:			
Personnel compensation:			
11.1 Full-time permanent	13		
11.5 Other personnel compensation	1	1	1
11.9 Total personnel compensation	14	1	1
12.1 Civilian personnel benefits	4		
21.0 Travel and transportation of persons	2	7	8
23.3 Communications, utilities, and miscellaneous charges	1	1	
25.1 Advisory and assistance services	119	24	22
25.2 Other services from non-Federal sources	24	5	8
25.3 Other goods and services from Federal sources	13	13	11
25.7 Operation and maintenance of equipment	4	2	2
26.0 Supplies and materials	4	1	1
31.0 Equipment	3	1	1
32.0 Land and structures	2		
92.0 Undistributed		33	
99.9 Total new obligations, unexpired accounts	190	88	54

Employment Summary

Identification code 097–0111–0–1–051	2021 actual	2022 est.	2023 est.
1001 Direct civilian full-time equivalent employment	158		

EMERGENCY RESPONSE FUND

Program and Financing (in millions of dollars)

Identification code 097–0833–0–1–051	2021 actual	2022 est.	2023 est.
Budgetary resources:			
Unobligated balance:			
1000 Unobligated balance brought forward, Oct 1	225	227	227
1021 Recoveries of prior year unpaid obligations	2		
1070 Unobligated balance (total)	227	227	227
1930 Total budgetary resources available	227	227	227
Memorandum (non-add) entries:			
1941 Unexpired unobligated balance, end of year	227	227	227
Change in obligated balance:			
Unpaid obligations:			
3000 Unpaid obligations, brought forward, Oct 1	17	15	5
3020 Outlays (gross)		–10	–4
3040 Recoveries of prior year unpaid obligations, unexpired	–2		
3050 Unpaid obligations, end of year	15	5	1
Memorandum (non-add) entries:			
3100 Obligated balance, start of year	17	15	5
3200 Obligated balance, end of year	15	5	1
Budget authority and outlays, net:			
Discretionary:			
Outlays, gross:			
4011 Outlays from discretionary balances		10	4
4180 Budget authority, net (total)			
4190 Outlays, net (total)		10	4

EMERGENCY RESPONSE

Program and Financing (in millions of dollars)

Identification code 097–4965–0–4–051	2021 actual	2022 est.	2023 est.
Budgetary resources:			
Unobligated balance:			
1000 Unobligated balance brought forward, Oct 1	11	11	11
1930 Total budgetary resources available	11	11	11
Memorandum (non-add) entries:			
1941 Unexpired unobligated balance, end of year	11	11	11
Change in obligated balance:			
Unpaid obligations:			
3000 Unpaid obligations, brought forward, Oct 1	3	3	
3020 Outlays (gross)		–3	
3050 Unpaid obligations, end of year	3		
Memorandum (non-add) entries:			
3100 Obligated balance, start of year	3	3	
3200 Obligated balance, end of year	3		
Budget authority and outlays, net:			
Discretionary:			
Outlays, gross:			
4011 Outlays from discretionary balances		3	
4180 Budget authority, net (total)			

DEPARTMENT OF DEFENSE—MILITARY PROGRAMS

Operation and Maintenance—Continued
Federal Funds—Continued

		2021 actual	2022 est.	2023 est.
4190	Outlays, net (total)		3	

ALLIED CONTRIBUTIONS AND COOPERATION ACCOUNT

Special and Trust Fund Receipts (in millions of dollars)

Identification code 097–9927–0–2–051		2021 actual	2022 est.	2023 est.
0100	Balance, start of year	8	8	8
	Receipts:			
	Current law:			
1130	Contributions for Burdensharing and Other Cooperative Activities (Kuwait)	38	38	39
1130	Contributions for Burdensharing and Other Cooperative Activities (Japan)	228	233	237
1130	Contributions for Burdensharing and Other Cooperative Activities (So. Korea)	886	486	496
1199	Total current law receipts	1,152	757	772
1999	Total receipts	1,152	757	772
2000	Total: Balances and receipts	1,160	765	780
	Appropriations:			
	Current law:			
2101	Allied Contributions and Cooperation Account	–1,152	–757	–772
5099	Balance, end of year	8	8	8

Program and Financing (in millions of dollars)

Identification code 097–9927–0–2–051		2021 actual	2022 est.	2023 est.
	Obligations by program activity:			
0010	Defense burdensharing	1,288	803	819
0900	Total new obligations, unexpired accounts (object class 26.0)	1,288	803	819
	Budgetary resources:			
	Unobligated balance:			
1000	Unobligated balance brought forward, Oct 1	1,119	1,014	968
1033	Recoveries of prior year paid obligations	31		
1070	Unobligated balance (total)	1,150	1,014	968
	Budget authority:			
	Appropriations, mandatory:			
1201	Appropriation (special or trust fund)	1,152	757	772
1930	Total budgetary resources available	2,302	1,771	1,740
	Memorandum (non-add) entries:			
1941	Unexpired unobligated balance, end of year	1,014	968	921
	Change in obligated balance:			
	Unpaid obligations:			
3000	Unpaid obligations, brought forward, Oct 1	1	2	73
3010	New obligations, unexpired accounts	1,288	803	819
3020	Outlays (gross)	–1,287	–732	–769
3050	Unpaid obligations, end of year	2	73	123
	Memorandum (non-add) entries:			
3100	Obligated balance, start of year	1	2	73
3200	Obligated balance, end of year	2	73	123
	Budget authority and outlays, net:			
	Mandatory:			
4090	Budget authority, gross	1,152	757	772
	Outlays, gross:			
4100	Outlays from new mandatory authority	918	613	625
4101	Outlays from mandatory balances	369	119	144
4110	Outlays, gross (total)	1,287	732	769
	Offsets against gross budget authority and outlays:			
	Offsetting collections (collected) from:			
4123	Non-Federal sources	–31		
	Additional offsets against gross budget authority only:			
4143	Recoveries of prior year paid obligations, unexpired accounts	31		
4160	Budget authority, net (mandatory)	1,152	757	772
4170	Outlays, net (mandatory)	1,256	732	769
4180	Budget authority, net (total)	1,152	757	772
4190	Outlays, net (total)	1,256	732	769
	Memorandum (non-add) entries:			
5000	Total investments, SOY: Federal securities: Par value	8	8	8
5001	Total investments, EOY: Federal securities: Par value	8	8	8

Cash contributions from foreign countries, international organizations, and individuals are deposited into this account for DOD costs such as compensation of local national employees, military construction, and supplies and services. Contributions are used to offset costs of DOD's overseas presence.

MISCELLANEOUS SPECIAL FUNDS

Special and Trust Fund Receipts (in millions of dollars)

Identification code 097–9922–0–2–051		2021 actual	2022 est.	2023 est.
0100	Balance, start of year	1	2	9
	Receipts:			
	Current law:			
1120	Restoration of the Rocky Mountain Arsenal, Army	1	7	7
1130	Proceeds from the Transfer or Disposition of Commissary Facilities		1	1
1199	Total current law receipts	1	8	8
1999	Total receipts	1	8	8
2000	Total: Balances and receipts	2	10	17
	Appropriations:			
	Current law:			
2101	Miscellaneous Special Funds	–1	–1	–1
2103	Miscellaneous Special Funds	–1	–1	–1
2132	Miscellaneous Special Funds	2	1	1
2199	Total current law appropriations		–1	–1
2999	Total appropriations		–1	–1
5099	Balance, end of year	2	9	16

Program and Financing (in millions of dollars)

Identification code 097–9922–0–2–051		2021 actual	2022 est.	2023 est.
	Obligations by program activity:			
0010	Miscellaneous special funds	3	1	1
	Budgetary resources:			
	Unobligated balance:			
1000	Unobligated balance brought forward, Oct 1	19	16	16
	Budget authority:			
	Appropriations, mandatory:			
1201	Appropriation (special or trust fund)	1	1	1
1203	Appropriation (previously unavailable)(special or trust)	1	1	1
1232	Appropriations and/or unobligated balance of appropriations temporarily reduced	–2	–1	–1
1260	Appropriations, mandatory (total)		1	1
1900	Budget authority (total)		1	1
1930	Total budgetary resources available	19	17	17
	Memorandum (non-add) entries:			
1941	Unexpired unobligated balance, end of year	16	16	16
	Change in obligated balance:			
	Unpaid obligations:			
3000	Unpaid obligations, brought forward, Oct 1	1	4	
3010	New obligations, unexpired accounts	3	1	1
3020	Outlays (gross)		–5	–1
3050	Unpaid obligations, end of year	4		
	Memorandum (non-add) entries:			
3100	Obligated balance, start of year	1	4	
3200	Obligated balance, end of year	4		
	Budget authority and outlays, net:			
	Mandatory:			
4090	Budget authority, gross		1	1
	Outlays, gross:			
4100	Outlays from new mandatory authority		1	1
4101	Outlays from mandatory balances		4	
4110	Outlays, gross (total)		5	1
4180	Budget authority, net (total)		1	1
4190	Outlays, net (total)		5	1

265

MISCELLANEOUS SPECIAL FUNDS—Continued

Object Classification (in millions of dollars)

Identification code 097–9922–0–2–051		2021 actual	2022 est.	2023 est.
	Direct obligations:			
25.3	Other goods and services from Federal sources	2	1	1
25.4	Operation and maintenance of facilities	1		
99.9	Total new obligations, unexpired accounts	3	1	1

DISPOSAL OF DEPARTMENT OF DEFENSE REAL PROPERTY

Special and Trust Fund Receipts (in millions of dollars)

Identification code 097–5188–0–2–051		2021 actual	2022 est.	2023 est.
0100	Balance, start of year			
	Receipts:			
	Current law:			
1130	Disposal of Department of Defense Real Property	11	6	8
2000	Total: Balances and receipts	11	6	8
	Appropriations:			
	Current law:			
2101	Disposal of Department of Defense Real Property	–11	–6	–8
5099	Balance, end of year			

Program and Financing (in millions of dollars)

Identification code 097–5188–0–2–051		2021 actual	2022 est.	2023 est.
	Obligations by program activity:			
0010	Concept Obligations	9	7	8
	Budgetary resources:			
	Unobligated balance:			
1000	Unobligated balance brought forward, Oct 1	70	73	72
1033	Recoveries of prior year paid obligations	1		
1070	Unobligated balance (total)	71	73	72
	Budget authority:			
	Appropriations, discretionary:			
1101	Appropriation (special or trust)	11	6	8
1900	Budget authority (total)	11	6	8
1930	Total budgetary resources available	82	79	80
	Memorandum (non-add) entries:			
1941	Unexpired unobligated balance, end of year	73	72	72
	Change in obligated balance:			
	Unpaid obligations:			
3000	Unpaid obligations, brought forward, Oct 1	20	11	2
3010	New obligations, unexpired accounts	9	7	8
3020	Outlays (gross)	–18	–16	–8
3050	Unpaid obligations, end of year	11	2	2
	Uncollected payments:			
3060	Uncollected pymts, Fed sources, brought forward, Oct 1	–3	–3	–3
3090	Uncollected pymts, Fed sources, end of year	–3	–3	–3
	Memorandum (non-add) entries:			
3100	Obligated balance, start of year	17	8	–1
3200	Obligated balance, end of year	8	–1	–1
	Budget authority and outlays, net:			
	Discretionary:			
4000	Budget authority, gross	11	6	8
	Outlays, gross:			
4010	Outlays from new discretionary authority	9	4	6
4011	Outlays from discretionary balances	9	12	2
4020	Outlays, gross (total)	18	16	8
	Offsets against gross budget authority and outlays:			
	Offsetting collections (collected) from:			
4033	Non-Federal sources	–1		
4040	Offsets against gross budget authority and outlays (total)	–1		
	Additional offsets against gross budget authority only:			
4053	Recoveries of prior year paid obligations, unexpired accounts	1		
4060	Additional offsets against budget authority only (total)	1		
4070	Budget authority, net (discretionary)	11	6	8
4080	Outlays, net (discretionary)	17	16	8
4180	Budget authority, net (total)	11	6	8
4190	Outlays, net (total)	17	16	8

Receipts from the disposal of DOD real property are applied to real property maintenance and environmental efforts at DOD installations.

Object Classification (in millions of dollars)

Identification code 097–5188–0–2–051		2021 actual	2022 est.	2023 est.
	Direct obligations:			
25.3	Other goods and services from Federal sources	2		
25.4	Operation and maintenance of facilities	7	7	8
99.9	Total new obligations, unexpired accounts	9	7	8

LEASE OF DEPARTMENT OF DEFENSE REAL PROPERTY

Special and Trust Fund Receipts (in millions of dollars)

Identification code 097–5189–0–2–051		2021 actual	2022 est.	2023 est.
0100	Balance, start of year			
	Receipts:			
	Current law:			
1130	Lease of Department of Defense Real Property	33	31	32
2000	Total: Balances and receipts	33	31	32
	Appropriations:			
	Current law:			
2101	Lease of Department of Defense Real Property	–33	–31	–32
5099	Balance, end of year			

Program and Financing (in millions of dollars)

Identification code 097–5189–0–2–051		2021 actual	2022 est.	2023 est.
	Obligations by program activity:			
0010	Concept Obligations	26	26	26
	Budgetary resources:			
	Unobligated balance:			
1000	Unobligated balance brought forward, Oct 1	196	205	210
1021	Recoveries of prior year unpaid obligations	1		
1033	Recoveries of prior year paid obligations	1		
1070	Unobligated balance (total)	198	205	210
	Budget authority:			
	Appropriations, discretionary:			
1101	Appropriation (special or trust)	33	31	32
1900	Budget authority (total)	33	31	32
1930	Total budgetary resources available	231	236	242
	Memorandum (non-add) entries:			
1941	Unexpired unobligated balance, end of year	205	210	216
	Change in obligated balance:			
	Unpaid obligations:			
3000	Unpaid obligations, brought forward, Oct 1	33	34	24
3010	New obligations, unexpired accounts	26	26	26
3020	Outlays (gross)	–24	–36	–39
3040	Recoveries of prior year unpaid obligations, unexpired	–1		
3050	Unpaid obligations, end of year	34	24	11
	Memorandum (non-add) entries:			
3100	Obligated balance, start of year	33	34	24
3200	Obligated balance, end of year	34	24	11
	Budget authority and outlays, net:			
	Discretionary:			
4000	Budget authority, gross	33	31	32
	Outlays, gross:			
4010	Outlays from new discretionary authority	1	19	19
4011	Outlays from discretionary balances	23	17	20
4020	Outlays, gross (total)	24	36	39
	Offsets against gross budget authority and outlays:			
	Offsetting collections (collected) from:			
4033	Non-Federal sources	–1		
4040	Offsets against gross budget authority and outlays (total)	–1		

DEPARTMENT OF DEFENSE—MILITARY PROGRAMS

Operation and Maintenance—Continued
Federal Funds—Continued

		2021 actual	2022 est.	2023 est.
	Additional offsets against gross budget authority only:			
4053	Recoveries of prior year paid obligations, unexpired accounts	1	....	....
4060	Additional offsets against budget authority only (total)	1	....	....
4070	Budget authority, net (discretionary)	33	31	32
4080	Outlays, net (discretionary)	23	36	39
4180	Budget authority, net (total)	33	31	32
4190	Outlays, net (total)	23	36	39

Receipts from the lease of DOD real property are applied to real property maintenance and environmental efforts at DOD installations. Receipts are available for maintenance, protection, alteration, repair, improvement, restoration of property or facilities, construction or acquisition of new facilities, lease of facilities, and facilities operation support.

Object Classification (in millions of dollars)

Identification code 097–5189–0–2–051		2021 actual	2022 est.	2023 est.
	Direct obligations:			
23.3	Communications, utilities, and miscellaneous charges	10	10	10
25.4	Operation and maintenance of facilities	12	12	12
26.0	Supplies and materials	1	1	1
32.0	Land and structures	3	3	3
99.9	Total new obligations, unexpired accounts	26	26	26

OVERSEAS MILITARY FACILITY INVESTMENT RECOVERY

Special and Trust Fund Receipts (in millions of dollars)

Identification code 097–5193–0–2–051		2021 actual	2022 est.	2023 est.
0100	Balance, start of year	2	2	2
2000	Total: Balances and receipts	2	2	2
5099	Balance, end of year	2	2	2

Program and Financing (in millions of dollars)

Identification code 097–5193–0–2–051		2021 actual	2022 est.	2023 est.
	Change in obligated balance:			
	Unpaid obligations:			
3000	Unpaid obligations, brought forward, Oct 1	2	2	1
3020	Outlays (gross)	....	–1	–1
3050	Unpaid obligations, end of year	2	1	....
	Memorandum (non-add) entries:			
3100	Obligated balance, start of year	2	2	1
3200	Obligated balance, end of year	2	1	....
	Budget authority and outlays, net:			
	Discretionary:			
	Outlays, gross:			
4011	Outlays from discretionary balances	....	1	1
4180	Budget authority, net (total)	....	....	....
4190	Outlays, net (total)	....	1	1

MUTUALLY BENEFICIAL ACTIVITIES

Special and Trust Fund Receipts (in millions of dollars)

Identification code 097–5613–0–2–051		2021 actual	2022 est.	2023 est.
0100	Balance, start of year	....	....	....
	Receipts:			
	Current law:			
1130	Contributions for Mutually Beneficial Activities (Kuwait)	....	116	116
2000	Total: Balances and receipts	....	116	116
	Appropriations:			
	Current law:			
2101	Mutually Beneficial Activities	....	–116	–116
5099	Balance, end of year	....	....	....

Program and Financing (in millions of dollars)

Identification code 097–5613–0–2–051		2021 actual	2022 est.	2023 est.
	Obligations by program activity:			
0010	Direct program activity	7	130	120
0900	Total new obligations, unexpired accounts (object class 32.0)	7	130	120
	Budgetary resources:			
	Unobligated balance:			
1000	Unobligated balance brought forward, Oct 1	46	39	25
	Budget authority:			
	Appropriations, mandatory:			
1201	Appropriation (special or trust fund)	....	116	116
1930	Total budgetary resources available	46	155	141
	Memorandum (non-add) entries:			
1941	Unexpired unobligated balance, end of year	39	25	21
	Change in obligated balance:			
	Unpaid obligations:			
3000	Unpaid obligations, brought forward, Oct 1	....	....	115
3010	New obligations, unexpired accounts	7	130	120
3020	Outlays (gross)	–7	–15	–40
3050	Unpaid obligations, end of year	....	115	195
	Memorandum (non-add) entries:			
3100	Obligated balance, start of year	....	....	115
3200	Obligated balance, end of year	....	115	195
	Budget authority and outlays, net:			
	Mandatory:			
4090	Budget authority, gross	....	116	116
	Outlays, gross:			
4100	Outlays from new mandatory authority	....	7	7
4101	Outlays from mandatory balances	7	8	33
4110	Outlays, gross (total)	7	15	40
4180	Budget authority, net (total)	....	116	116
4190	Outlays, net (total)	7	15	40

Section 2807 of Public Law 114–92 (National Defense Authorization Act for Fiscal Year 2017) extended temporary authority for acceptance and use of contributions for certain construction, maintenance, and repair projects mutually beneficial to the Department of Defense and Kuwait military forces.

DEPARTMENT OF DEFENSE WORLD WAR II COMMEMORATION FUND

Program and Financing (in millions of dollars)

Identification code 017–5630–0–2–051		2021 actual	2022 est.	2023 est.
	Budgetary resources:			
	Unobligated balance:			
1000	Unobligated balance brought forward, Oct 1	3	3	3
1001	Discretionary unobligated balance brought fwd, Oct 1	3	....	....
1930	Total budgetary resources available	3	3	3
	Memorandum (non-add) entries:			
1941	Unexpired unobligated balance, end of year	3	3	3
4180	Budget authority, net (total)	....	....	....
4190	Outlays, net (total)	....	....	....

DEPARTMENT OF DEFENSE VIETNAM WAR COMMEMORATION FUND

Program and Financing (in millions of dollars)

Identification code 097–5750–0–2–051		2021 actual	2022 est.	2023 est.
	Obligations by program activity:			
0010	Direct program activity	1	....	....
0900	Total new obligations, unexpired accounts (object class 25.1)	1	....	....
	Budgetary resources:			
	Unobligated balance:			
1000	Unobligated balance brought forward, Oct 1	9	8	8
1930	Total budgetary resources available	9	8	8

DEPARTMENT OF DEFENSE VIETNAM WAR COMMEMORATION FUND—Continued

Program and Financing—Continued

Identification code 097–5750–0–2–051	2021 actual	2022 est.	2023 est.
Memorandum (non-add) entries:			
1941 Unexpired unobligated balance, end of year	8	8	8
Change in obligated balance:			
Unpaid obligations:			
3000 Unpaid obligations, brought forward, Oct 1	1	2	
3010 New obligations, unexpired accounts	1		
3020 Outlays (gross)		–2	
3050 Unpaid obligations, end of year	2		
Memorandum (non-add) entries:			
3100 Obligated balance, start of year	1	2	
3200 Obligated balance, end of year	2		
Budget authority and outlays, net:			
Mandatory:			
Outlays, gross:			
4101 Outlays from mandatory balances			2
4180 Budget authority, net (total)			
4190 Outlays, net (total)			2

SUPPORT OF ATHLETIC PROGRAMS

Special and Trust Fund Receipts (in millions of dollars)

Identification code 057–5616–0–2–051	2021 actual	2022 est.	2023 est.
0100 Balance, start of year			3
Receipts:			
Current law:			
1130 Proceeds, Support of Athletic Programs	4	3	3
2000 Total: Balances and receipts	4	3	6
Appropriations:			
Current law:			
2101 Support of Athletic Programs	–4		
5099 Balance, end of year		3	6

Program and Financing (in millions of dollars)

Identification code 057–5616–0–2–051	2021 actual	2022 est.	2023 est.
Obligations by program activity:			
0010 Direct program activity		2	2
0900 Total new obligations, unexpired accounts (object class 25.3)		2	2
Budgetary resources:			
Unobligated balance:			
1000 Unobligated balance brought forward, Oct 1	12	16	14
Budget authority:			
Appropriations, mandatory:			
1201 Appropriation (special or trust fund)	4		
1930 Total budgetary resources available	16	16	14
Memorandum (non-add) entries:			
1941 Unexpired unobligated balance, end of year	16	14	12
Change in obligated balance:			
Unpaid obligations:			
3010 New obligations, unexpired accounts		2	2
3020 Outlays (gross)		–2	–2
Budget authority and outlays, net:			
Mandatory:			
4090 Budget authority, gross	4		
Outlays, gross:			
4101 Outlays from mandatory balances		2	2
4180 Budget authority, net (total)	4		
4190 Outlays, net (total)		2	2

INTERNATIONAL RECONSTRUCTION AND OTHER ASSISTANCE

Federal Funds

IRAQ RELIEF AND RECONSTRUCTION FUND, ARMY

Program and Financing (in millions of dollars)

Identification code 021–2089–0–1–151	2021 actual	2022 est.	2023 est.
Budgetary resources:			
Unobligated balance:			
1000 Unobligated balance brought forward, Oct 1	3	3	3
1930 Total budgetary resources available	3	3	3
Memorandum (non-add) entries:			
1941 Unexpired unobligated balance, end of year	3	3	3
Change in obligated balance:			
Unpaid obligations:			
3000 Unpaid obligations, brought forward, Oct 1	1		
3020 Outlays (gross)	–1		
Memorandum (non-add) entries:			
3100 Obligated balance, start of year	1		
Budget authority and outlays, net:			
Discretionary:			
Outlays, gross:			
4011 Outlays from discretionary balances	1		
4180 Budget authority, net (total)			
4190 Outlays, net (total)	1		

PROCUREMENT

Appropriations in this title support the acquisition of aircraft, ships, combat and support vehicles, satellites and their launch vehicles, weapons, munitions, and all capital equipment. Major systems in production typically are budgeted annually to maintain production continuity through the life of the acquisition program, and in several instances multiyear contracts are used to ensure stability of production and economies of scale. Initial spares and support as well as the modification of existing equipment are also funded. Resources presented under the Procurement title contribute primarily to achieving the Department's annual goals of assuring readiness and sustainability, transforming the force for new missions, and reforming processes and organizations. Performance targets in support of these goals contribute to the Department's efforts to mitigate force management and operational risk, future challenges risk, and institutional risk.

Procurement in support of the ground forces encompasses wheeled and tracked vehicles, aircraft, ammunition, and equipment to meet inventory requirements dictated by the force size and anticipated mission requirements. Similarly, procurement in support of naval forces includes ships, equipment for the ships, aircraft, munitions, tactical and ballistic missile weapons, the Marine Corps air and ground elements, and other equipment to sustain future naval operations. The Air Force programs support a broad range of missions and include aircraft, munitions, tactical and ballistic missile weapons, surveillance assets, U.S. Space Force space assets, and other mission support equipment. Procurement is also in support of missile defense and cyberspace missions.

Funds for each fiscal year are available for obligation for a three-year period beginning on the first day of that fiscal year.

Federal Funds

AIRCRAFT PROCUREMENT, ARMY

For construction, procurement, production, modification, and modernization of aircraft, equipment, including ordnance, ground handling equipment, spare parts, and accessories therefor; specialized equipment and training devices; expansion of public and private plants, including the land necessary therefor, for the foregoing purposes, and such lands and interests therein, may be acquired, and construction prosecuted thereon prior to approval of title; and procurement and installation of equipment, appliances, and machine tools in public and private plants; reserve plant

DEPARTMENT OF DEFENSE—MILITARY PROGRAMS

Procurement—Continued
Federal Funds—Continued

269

and Government and contractor-owned equipment layaway; and other expenses necessary for the foregoing purposes, $2,849,655,000, to remain available for obligation until September 30, 2025, of which $1,474,732,000 shall be available for the Army National Guard and Army Reserve.

Note.—A full-year 2022 appropriation for this account was not enacted at the time the Budget was prepared; therefore, the Budget assumes this account is operating under the Continuing Appropriations Act, 2022 (Division A of Public Law 117–43, as amended). The amounts included for 2022 reflect the annualized level provided by the continuing resolution.

Program and Financing (in millions of dollars)

Identification code 021–2031–0–1–051		2021 actual	2022 est.	2023 est.
	Obligations by program activity:			
0001	Aircraft	2,998	1,982	1,829
0002	Modification of aircraft	724	503	441
0004	Support equipment and facilities	522	489	568
0020	Undistributed		1,219	
0799	Total direct obligations	4,244	4,193	2,838
0801	Reimbursable program activity	63	500	500
0900	Total new obligations, unexpired accounts	4,307	4,693	3,338
	Budgetary resources:			
	Unobligated balance:			
1000	Unobligated balance brought forward, Oct 1	1,220	1,413	1,263
1001	Discretionary unobligated balance brought fwd, Oct 1	1,011		
1010	Unobligated balance transfer to other accts [097–4930.001]	–19		
1021	Recoveries of prior year unpaid obligations	305		
1070	Unobligated balance (total)	1,506	1,413	1,263
	Budget authority:			
	Appropriations, discretionary:			
1100	Appropriation	4,052	2,806	2,850
1100	Appropriation		1,246	
1131	Unobligated balance of appropriations permanently reduced	–27	–27	
1160	Appropriation, discretionary (total)	4,025	4,025	2,850
	Appropriations, mandatory:			
1221	Appropriations transferred from other acct [011–5512]	70	18	6
1230	Appropriations and/or unobligated balance of appropriations permanently reduced	–5		
1260	Appropriations, mandatory (total)	65	18	6
	Spending authority from offsetting collections, discretionary:			
1700	Collected	129	500	500
1701	Change in uncollected payments, Federal sources	–4		
1750	Spending auth from offsetting collections, disc (total)	125	500	500
1900	Budget authority (total)	4,215	4,543	3,356
1930	Total budgetary resources available	5,721	5,956	4,619
	Memorandum (non-add) entries:			
1940	Unobligated balance expiring	–1		
1941	Unexpired unobligated balance, end of year	1,413	1,263	1,281
	Change in obligated balance:			
	Unpaid obligations:			
3000	Unpaid obligations, brought forward, Oct 1	8,006	6,698	5,975
3010	New obligations, unexpired accounts	4,307	4,693	3,338
3011	Obligations ("upward adjustments"), expired accounts	85		
3020	Outlays (gross)	–5,197	–5,416	–3,995
3040	Recoveries of prior year unpaid obligations, unexpired	–305		
3041	Recoveries of prior year unpaid obligations, expired	–198		
3050	Unpaid obligations, end of year	6,698	5,975	5,318
	Uncollected payments:			
3060	Uncollected pymts, Fed sources, brought forward, Oct 1	–264	–247	–247
3070	Change in uncollected pymts, Fed sources, unexpired	4		
3071	Change in uncollected pymts, Fed sources, expired	13		
3090	Uncollected pymts, Fed sources, end of year	–247	–247	–247
	Memorandum (non-add) entries:			
3100	Obligated balance, start of year	7,742	6,451	5,728
3200	Obligated balance, end of year	6,451	5,728	5,071
	Budget authority and outlays, net:			
	Discretionary:			
4000	Budget authority, gross	4,150	4,525	3,350
	Outlays, gross:			
4010	Outlays from new discretionary authority	585	942	814
4011	Outlays from discretionary balances	4,464	4,460	3,173
4020	Outlays, gross (total)	5,049	5,402	3,987
	Offsets against gross budget authority and outlays:			
	Offsetting collections (collected) from:			
4030	Federal sources	–141	–500	–500
4040	Offsets against gross budget authority and outlays (total)	–141	–500	–500
	Additional offsets against gross budget authority only:			
4050	Change in uncollected pymts, Fed sources, unexpired	4		
4052	Offsetting collections credited to expired accounts	12		
4060	Additional offsets against budget authority only (total)	16		
4070	Budget authority, net (discretionary)	4,025	4,025	2,850
4080	Outlays, net (discretionary)	4,908	4,902	3,487
	Mandatory:			
4090	Budget authority, gross	65	18	6
	Outlays, gross:			
4100	Outlays from new mandatory authority		14	4
4101	Outlays from mandatory balances	148		4
4110	Outlays, gross (total)	148	14	8
4180	Budget authority, net (total)	4,090	4,043	2,856
4190	Outlays, net (total)	5,056	4,916	3,495

Object Classification (in millions of dollars)

Identification code 021–2031–0–1–051		2021 actual	2022 est.	2023 est.
	Direct obligations:			
21.0	Travel and transportation of persons	5	2	1
22.0	Transportation of things	2	1	
25.1	Advisory and assistance services	85	85	85
25.2	Other services from non-Federal sources		199	134
25.3	Other goods and services from Federal sources	1,324	240	
25.3	Other goods and services from Federal sources			66
25.4	Operation and maintenance of facilities	1	1	1
25.7	Operation and maintenance of equipment	180	82	82
26.0	Supplies and materials	69	59	95
31.0	Equipment	2,578	2,305	2,374
92.0	Undistributed		1,219	
99.0	Direct obligations	4,244	4,193	2,838
99.0	Reimbursable obligations	63	500	500
99.9	Total new obligations, unexpired accounts	4,307	4,693	3,338

MISSILE PROCUREMENT, ARMY

For construction, procurement, production, modification, and modernization of missiles, equipment, including ordnance, ground handling equipment, spare parts, and accessories therefor; specialized equipment and training devices; expansion of public and private plants, including the land necessary therefor, for the foregoing purposes, and such lands and interests therein, may be acquired, and construction prosecuted thereon prior to approval of title; and procurement and installation of equipment, appliances, and machine tools in public and private plants; reserve plant and Government and contractor-owned equipment layaway; and other expenses necessary for the foregoing purposes, $3,761,915,000, to remain available for obligation until September 30, 2025, of which $23,212,000 shall be available for the Army National Guard and Army Reserve.

Note.—A full-year 2022 appropriation for this account was not enacted at the time the Budget was prepared; therefore, the Budget assumes this account is operating under the Continuing Appropriations Act, 2022 (Division A of Public Law 117–43, as amended). The amounts included for 2022 reflect the annualized level provided by the continuing resolution.

Program and Financing (in millions of dollars)

Identification code 021–2032–0–1–051		2021 actual	2022 est.	2023 est.
	Obligations by program activity:			
0002	Other missiles	3,405	3,310	3,207
0003	Modification of missiles	951	647	506
0004	Spares and repair parts	12	8	6
0005	Support equipment and facilities	8	11	11
0020	Undistributed		459	
0799	Total direct obligations	4,376	4,435	3,730
0801	Reimbursable program activity	254	550	550
0900	Total new obligations, unexpired accounts	4,630	4,985	4,280
	Budgetary resources:			
	Unobligated balance:			
1000	Unobligated balance brought forward, Oct 1	1,330	1,050	630
1010	Unobligated balance transfer to other accts [097–4930.001]	–10		

MISSILE PROCUREMENT, ARMY—Continued
Program and Financing—Continued

Identification code 021–2032–0–1–051	2021 actual	2022 est.	2023 est.
1010 Unobligated balance transfer to other accts [021–2040]	–35		
1021 Recoveries of prior year unpaid obligations	43		
1070 Unobligated balance (total)	1,328	1,050	630
Budget authority:			
Appropriations, discretionary:			
1100 Appropriation	4,017	3,556	3,762
1100 Appropriation		461	
1131 Unobligated balance of appropriations permanently reduced	–2	–2	
1160 Appropriation, discretionary (total)	4,015	4,015	3,762
Spending authority from offsetting collections, discretionary:			
1700 Collected	63	550	550
1701 Change in uncollected payments, Federal sources	298		
1750 Spending auth from offsetting collections, disc (total)	361	550	550
1900 Budget authority (total)	4,376	4,565	4,312
1930 Total budgetary resources available	5,704	5,615	4,942
Memorandum (non-add) entries:			
1940 Unobligated balance expiring	–24		
1941 Unexpired unobligated balance, end of year	1,050	630	662
Change in obligated balance:			
Unpaid obligations:			
3000 Unpaid obligations, brought forward, Oct 1	9,389	9,135	8,639
3010 New obligations, unexpired accounts	4,630	4,985	4,280
3011 Obligations ("upward adjustments"), expired accounts	277		
3020 Outlays (gross)	–4,924	–5,481	–4,829
3040 Recoveries of prior year unpaid obligations, unexpired	–43		
3041 Recoveries of prior year unpaid obligations, expired	–194		
3050 Unpaid obligations, end of year	9,135	8,639	8,090
Uncollected payments:			
3060 Uncollected pymts, Fed sources, brought forward, Oct 1	–249	–520	–520
3070 Change in uncollected pymts, Fed sources, unexpired	–298		
3071 Change in uncollected pymts, Fed sources, expired	27		
3090 Uncollected pymts, Fed sources, end of year	–520	–520	–520
Memorandum (non-add) entries:			
3100 Obligated balance, start of year	9,140	8,615	8,119
3200 Obligated balance, end of year	8,615	8,119	7,570
Budget authority and outlays, net:			
Discretionary:			
4000 Budget authority, gross	4,376	4,565	4,312
Outlays, gross:			
4010 Outlays from new discretionary authority	394	791	776
4011 Outlays from discretionary balances	4,530	4,690	4,053
4020 Outlays, gross (total)	4,924	5,481	4,829
Offsets against gross budget authority and outlays:			
Offsetting collections (collected) from:			
4030 Federal sources	–65	–550	–550
4033 Non-Federal sources	–79		
4040 Offsets against gross budget authority and outlays (total)	–144	–550	–550
Additional offsets against gross budget authority only:			
4050 Change in uncollected pymts, Fed sources, unexpired	–298		
4052 Offsetting collections credited to expired accounts	81		
4060 Additional offsets against budget authority only (total)	–217		
4070 Budget authority, net (discretionary)	4,015	4,015	3,762
4080 Outlays, net (discretionary)	4,780	4,931	4,279
4180 Budget authority, net (total)	4,015	4,015	3,762
4190 Outlays, net (total)	4,780	4,931	4,279

Object Classification (in millions of dollars)

Identification code 021–2032–0–1–051	2021 actual	2022 est.	2023 est.
Direct obligations:			
21.0 Travel and transportation of persons	1	69	
22.0 Transportation of things	5		
23.3 Communications, utilities, and miscellaneous charges	1		
25.1 Advisory and assistance services	39	39	39
25.2 Other services from non-Federal sources	39		
25.3 Other goods and services from Federal sources	313		
25.3 Other goods and services from Federal sources	19		18
26.0 Supplies and materials	20	310	3
31.0 Equipment	3,939	3,558	3,670
92.0 Undistributed		459	
99.0 Direct obligations	4,376	4,435	3,730
99.0 Reimbursable obligations	254	550	550
99.9 Total new obligations, unexpired accounts	4,630	4,985	4,280

PROCUREMENT OF WEAPONS AND TRACKED COMBAT VEHICLES, ARMY

For construction, procurement, production, and modification of weapons and tracked combat vehicles, equipment, including ordnance, spare parts, and accessories therefor; specialized equipment and training devices; expansion of public and private plants, including the land necessary therefor, for the foregoing purposes, and such lands and interests therein, may be acquired, and construction prosecuted thereon prior to approval of title; and procurement and installation of equipment, appliances, and machine tools in public and private plants; reserve plant and Government and contractor-owned equipment layaway; and other expenses necessary for the foregoing purposes, $3,576,030,000, to remain available for obligation until September 30, 2025, of which $642,756,000 shall be available for the Army National Guard and Army Reserve.

Note.—A full-year 2022 appropriation for this account was not enacted at the time the Budget was prepared; therefore, the Budget assumes this account is operating under the Continuing Appropriations Act, 2022 (Division A of Public Law 117–43, as amended). The amounts included for 2022 reflect the annualized level provided by the continuing resolution.

Program and Financing (in millions of dollars)

Identification code 021–2033–0–1–051	2021 actual	2022 est.	2023 est.
Obligations by program activity:			
0001 Tracked combat vehicles	4,329	3,456	3,058
0002 Weapons and other combat vehicles	186	258	418
0020 Undistributed		–497	
0799 Total direct obligations	4,515	3,217	3,476
0801 Reimbursable program activity	2	15	15
0900 Total new obligations, unexpired accounts	4,517	3,232	3,491
Budgetary resources:			
Unobligated balance:			
1000 Unobligated balance brought forward, Oct 1	2,102	1,473	1,635
1010 Unobligated balance transfer to other accts [097–4930.001]	–36		
1010 Unobligated balance transfer to other accts [021–2035]	–7		
1010 Unobligated balance transfer to other accts [021–2040]	–3		
1021 Recoveries of prior year unpaid obligations	731		
1070 Unobligated balance (total)	2,787	1,473	1,635
Budget authority:			
Appropriations, discretionary:			
1100 Appropriation	3,627	3,627	3,576
1120 Appropriations transferred to other acct [097–4930.001]	–1		
1120 Appropriations transferred to other acct [021–2020]	–6		
1131 Unobligated balance of appropriations permanently reduced	–362	–248	
1160 Appropriation, discretionary (total)	3,258	3,379	3,576
Spending authority from offsetting collections, discretionary:			
1700 Collected	4	15	15
1701 Change in uncollected payments, Federal sources	–1		
1750 Spending auth from offsetting collections, disc (total)	3	15	15
1900 Budget authority (total)	3,261	3,394	3,591
1930 Total budgetary resources available	6,048	4,867	5,226
Memorandum (non-add) entries:			
1940 Unobligated balance expiring	–58		
1941 Unexpired unobligated balance, end of year	1,473	1,635	1,735
Change in obligated balance:			
Unpaid obligations:			
3000 Unpaid obligations, brought forward, Oct 1	8,482	7,418	6,191
3010 New obligations, unexpired accounts	4,517	3,232	3,491
3011 Obligations ("upward adjustments"), expired accounts	38		
3020 Outlays (gross)	–4,766	–4,459	–3,902
3040 Recoveries of prior year unpaid obligations, unexpired	–731		
3041 Recoveries of prior year unpaid obligations, expired	–122		
3050 Unpaid obligations, end of year	7,418	6,191	5,780
Uncollected payments:			
3060 Uncollected pymts, Fed sources, brought forward, Oct 1	–1		
3070 Change in uncollected pymts, Fed sources, unexpired	1		
Memorandum (non-add) entries:			
3100 Obligated balance, start of year	8,481	7,418	6,191

DEPARTMENT OF DEFENSE—MILITARY PROGRAMS

		2021 actual	2022 est.	2023 est.
3200	Obligated balance, end of year	7,418	6,191	5,780
	Budget authority and outlays, net:			
	Discretionary:			
4000	Budget authority, gross	3,261	3,394	3,591
	Outlays, gross:			
4010	Outlays from new discretionary authority	285	251	265
4011	Outlays from discretionary balances	4,481	4,208	3,637
4020	Outlays, gross (total)	4,766	4,459	3,902
	Offsets against gross budget authority and outlays:			
	Offsetting collections (collected) from:			
4030	Federal sources	–4	–15	–15
4040	Offsets against gross budget authority and outlays (total)	–4	–15	–15
	Additional offsets against gross budget authority only:			
4050	Change in uncollected pymts, Fed sources, unexpired	1		
4060	Additional offsets against budget authority only (total)	1		
4070	Budget authority, net (discretionary)	3,258	3,379	3,576
4080	Outlays, net (discretionary)	4,762	4,444	3,887
4180	Budget authority, net (total)	3,258	3,379	3,576
4190	Outlays, net (total)	4,762	4,444	3,887

Object Classification (in millions of dollars)

Identification code 021–2033–0–1–051		2021 actual	2022 est.	2023 est.
	Direct obligations:			
21.0	Travel and transportation of persons	5	1	1
22.0	Transportation of things	29	12	
23.1	Rental payments to GSA	1		
23.2	Rental payments to others	1		
23.3	Communications, utilities, and miscellaneous charges	5		
25.1	Advisory and assistance services	33	33	33
25.2	Other services from non-Federal sources	11	25	25
25.3	Other goods and services from Federal sources		182	182
25.3	Other goods and services from Federal sources	875	315	15
25.7	Operation and maintenance of equipment	2	7	7
26.0	Supplies and materials	175	75	62
31.0	Equipment	3,377	3,064	3,151
92.0	Undistributed		–497	
99.0	Direct obligations	4,514	3,217	3,476
99.0	Reimbursable obligations	3	15	15
99.9	Total new obligations, unexpired accounts	4,517	3,232	3,491

PROCUREMENT OF AMMUNITION, ARMY

For construction, procurement, production, and modification of ammunition, and accessories therefor; specialized equipment and training devices; expansion of public and private plants, including ammunition facilities, authorized by section 2854 of title 10, United States Code, and the land necessary therefor, for the foregoing purposes, and such lands and interests therein, may be acquired, and construction prosecuted thereon prior to approval of title; and procurement and installation of equipment, appliances, and machine tools in public and private plants; reserve plant and Government and contractor-owned equipment layaway; and other expenses necessary for the foregoing purposes, $2,639,051,000, to remain available for obligation until September 30, 2025, of which $163,476,000 shall be available for the Army National Guard and Army Reserve.

Note.—A full-year 2022 appropriation for this account was not enacted at the time the Budget was prepared; therefore, the Budget assumes this account is operating under the Continuing Appropriations Act, 2022 (Division A of Public Law 117–43, as amended). The amounts included for 2022 reflect the annualized level provided by the continuing resolution.

Program and Financing (in millions of dollars)

Identification code 021–2034–0–1–051		2021 actual	2022 est.	2023 est.
	Obligations by program activity:			
0001	Ammunition	2,217	1,950	1,592
0002	Ammunition production base support	764	912	621
0020	Undistributed		728	
0799	Total direct obligations	2,981	3,590	2,213
0801	Reimbursable program activity	1,170	1,900	2,319
0900	Total new obligations, unexpired accounts	4,151	5,490	4,532
	Budgetary resources:			
	Unobligated balance:			
1000	Unobligated balance brought forward, Oct 1	1,869	1,704	1,376
1010	Unobligated balance transfer to other accts [021–2040]	–10		
1010	Unobligated balance transfer to other accts [097–4930.001]	–25		
1021	Recoveries of prior year unpaid obligations	298		
1070	Unobligated balance (total)	2,132	1,704	1,376
	Budget authority:			
	Appropriations, discretionary:			
1100	Appropriation	2,894	2,158	2,639
1100	Appropriation		736	
1120	Appropriations transferred to other acct [021–2020]	–8		
1120	Appropriations transferred to other acct [021–2035]	–18		
1120	Appropriations transferred to other acct [097–4930.001]	–25		
1120	Appropriations transferred to other acct [021–2040]	–15		
1131	Unobligated balance of appropriations permanently reduced	–8	–8	
1160	Appropriation, discretionary (total)	2,820	2,886	2,639
	Spending authority from offsetting collections, discretionary:			
1700	Collected	716	2,276	1,900
1701	Change in uncollected payments, Federal sources	195		
1750	Spending auth from offsetting collections, disc (total)	911	2,276	1,900
1900	Budget authority (total)	3,731	5,162	4,539
1930	Total budgetary resources available	5,863	6,866	5,915
	Memorandum (non-add) entries:			
1940	Unobligated balance expiring	–8		
1941	Unexpired unobligated balance, end of year	1,704	1,376	1,383
	Change in obligated balance:			
	Unpaid obligations:			
3000	Unpaid obligations, brought forward, Oct 1	6,822	7,230	6,508
3010	New obligations, unexpired accounts	4,151	5,490	4,532
3011	Obligations ("upward adjustments"), expired accounts	68		
3020	Outlays (gross)	–3,413	–6,212	–5,213
3040	Recoveries of prior year unpaid obligations, unexpired	–298		
3041	Recoveries of prior year unpaid obligations, expired	–100		
3050	Unpaid obligations, end of year	7,230	6,508	5,827
	Uncollected payments:			
3060	Uncollected pymts, Fed sources, brought forward, Oct 1	–2,735	–2,620	–2,620
3070	Change in uncollected pymts, Fed sources, unexpired	–195		
3071	Change in uncollected pymts, Fed sources, expired	310		
3090	Uncollected pymts, Fed sources, end of year	–2,620	–2,620	–2,620
	Memorandum (non-add) entries:			
3100	Obligated balance, start of year	4,087	4,610	3,888
3200	Obligated balance, end of year	4,610	3,888	3,207
	Budget authority and outlays, net:			
	Discretionary:			
4000	Budget authority, gross	3,731	5,162	4,539
	Outlays, gross:			
4010	Outlays from new discretionary authority	183	2,507	2,111
4011	Outlays from discretionary balances	3,230	3,705	3,102
4020	Outlays, gross (total)	3,413	6,212	5,213
	Offsets against gross budget authority and outlays:			
	Offsetting collections (collected) from:			
4030	Federal sources	–1,047	–2,276	–1,900
4033	Non-Federal sources	–19		
4040	Offsets against gross budget authority and outlays (total)	–1,066	–2,276	–1,900
	Additional offsets against gross budget authority only:			
4050	Change in uncollected pymts, Fed sources, unexpired	–195		
4052	Offsetting collections credited to expired accounts	350		
4060	Additional offsets against budget authority only (total)	155		
4070	Budget authority, net (discretionary)	2,820	2,886	2,639
4080	Outlays, net (discretionary)	2,347	3,936	3,313
4180	Budget authority, net (total)	2,820	2,886	2,639
4190	Outlays, net (total)	2,347	3,936	3,313

Object Classification (in millions of dollars)

Identification code 021–2034–0–1–051		2021 actual	2022 est.	2023 est.
	Direct obligations:			
22.0	Transportation of things	20	23	
25.1	Advisory and assistance services	6	6	6
25.2	Other services from non-Federal sources	83	4	4
25.3	Other goods and services from Federal sources	86	161	161
25.3	Other goods and services from Federal sources	116	170	90
25.4	Operation and maintenance of facilities	44	10	10

PROCUREMENT OF AMMUNITION, ARMY—Continued
Object Classification—Continued

Identification code 021–2034–0–1–051		2021 actual	2022 est.	2023 est.
25.7	Operation and maintenance of equipment	1		
26.0	Supplies and materials	2,286	2,386	1
31.0	Equipment	5		1,839
32.0	Land and structures	334	102	102
92.0	Undistributed		728	
99.0	Direct obligations	2,981	3,590	2,213
99.0	Reimbursable obligations	1,170	1,900	2,319
99.9	Total new obligations, unexpired accounts	4,151	5,490	4,532

OTHER PROCUREMENT, ARMY

For construction, procurement, production, and modification of vehicles, including tactical, support, and non-tracked combat vehicles; the purchase of passenger motor vehicles for replacement only; communications and electronic equipment; other support equipment; spare parts, ordnance, and accessories therefor; specialized equipment and training devices; expansion of public and private plants, including the land necessary therefor, for the foregoing purposes, and such lands and interests therein, may be acquired, and construction prosecuted thereon prior to approval of title; and procurement and installation of equipment, appliances, and machine tools in public and private plants; reserve plant and Government and contractor-owned equipment layaway; and other expenses necessary for the foregoing purposes, $8,457,509,000, to remain available for obligation until September 30, 2025, of which $705,861,000 shall be available for the Army National Guard and Army Reserve.

Note.—A full-year 2022 appropriation for this account was not enacted at the time the Budget was prepared; therefore, the Budget assumes this account is operating under the Continuing Appropriations Act, 2022 (Division A of Public Law 117–43, as amended). The amounts included for 2022 reflect the annualized level provided by the continuing resolution.

Program and Financing (in millions of dollars)

Identification code 021–2035–0–1–051		2021 actual	2022 est.	2023 est.
	Obligations by program activity:			
0001	Tactical and support vehicles	1,820	1,200	1,003
0002	Communications and electronics equipment	5,538	5,164	5,358
0003	Other support equipment	2,350	2,161	1,762
0004	Spare and repair parts	11	9	9
0020	Undistributed		641	
0799	Total direct obligations	9,719	9,175	8,132
0801	Reimbursable program activity	23	158	161
0900	Total new obligations, unexpired accounts	9,742	9,333	8,293
	Budgetary resources:			
	Unobligated balance:			
1000	Unobligated balance brought forward, Oct 1	2,067	2,306	2,652
1001	Discretionary unobligated balance brought fwd, Oct 1	2,002		
1010	Unobligated balance transfer to other accts [097–9999]	–2		
1010	Unobligated balance transfer to other accts [097–4930.001]	–94		
1011	Unobligated balance transfer from other acct [021–2033]	7		
1021	Recoveries of prior year unpaid obligations	558		
1070	Unobligated balance (total)	2,536	2,306	2,652
	Budget authority:			
	Appropriations, discretionary:			
1100	Appropriation	9,528	8,874	8,458
1100	Appropriation		654	
1120	Appropriations transferred to other acct [021–2020]	–9		
1120	Appropriations transferred to other acct [097–4930.001]	–35		
1121	Appropriations transferred from other acct [097–0105]	6		
1121	Appropriations transferred from other acct [021–2034]	18		
1131	Unobligated balance of appropriations permanently reduced	–13	–13	
1160	Appropriation, discretionary (total)	9,495	9,515	8,458
	Appropriations, mandatory:			
1221	Appropriations transferred from other acct [011–5512]	18	6	5
1230	Appropriations and/or unobligated balance of appropriations permanently reduced	–2		
1260	Appropriations, mandatory (total)	16	6	5
	Spending authority from offsetting collections, discretionary:			
1700	Collected	23	158	161
1701	Change in uncollected payments, Federal sources	–4		
1750	Spending auth from offsetting collections, disc (total)	19	158	161
1900	Budget authority (total)	9,530	9,679	8,624
1930	Total budgetary resources available	12,066	11,985	11,276
	Memorandum (non-add) entries:			
1940	Unobligated balance expiring	–18		
1941	Unexpired unobligated balance, end of year	2,306	2,652	2,983
	Change in obligated balance:			
	Unpaid obligations:			
3000	Unpaid obligations, brought forward, Oct 1	10,394	10,333	11,723
3010	New obligations, unexpired accounts	9,742	9,333	8,293
3011	Obligations ("upward adjustments"), expired accounts	88		
3020	Outlays (gross)	–9,127	–7,943	–8,622
3040	Recoveries of prior year unpaid obligations, unexpired	–558		
3041	Recoveries of prior year unpaid obligations, expired	–206		
3050	Unpaid obligations, end of year	10,333	11,723	11,394
	Uncollected payments:			
3060	Uncollected pymts, Fed sources, brought forward, Oct 1	–53	–30	–30
3070	Change in uncollected pymts, Fed sources, unexpired	4		
3071	Change in uncollected pymts, Fed sources, expired	19		
3090	Uncollected pymts, Fed sources, end of year	–30	–30	–30
	Memorandum (non-add) entries:			
3100	Obligated balance, start of year	10,341	10,303	11,693
3200	Obligated balance, end of year	10,303	11,693	11,364
	Budget authority and outlays, net:			
	Discretionary:			
4000	Budget authority, gross	9,514	9,673	8,619
	Outlays, gross:			
4010	Outlays from new discretionary authority	1,554	1,680	1,514
4011	Outlays from discretionary balances	7,572	6,248	7,098
4020	Outlays, gross (total)	9,126	7,928	8,612
	Offsets against gross budget authority and outlays:			
	Offsetting collections (collected) from:			
4030	Federal sources	–29	–158	–161
4033	Non-Federal sources	–12		
4040	Offsets against gross budget authority and outlays (total)	–41	–158	–161
	Additional offsets against gross budget authority only:			
4050	Change in uncollected pymts, Fed sources, unexpired	4		
4052	Offsetting collections credited to expired accounts	18		
4060	Additional offsets against budget authority only (total)	22		
4070	Budget authority, net (discretionary)	9,495	9,515	8,458
4080	Outlays, net (discretionary)	9,085	7,770	8,451
	Mandatory:			
4090	Budget authority, gross	16	6	5
	Outlays, gross:			
4100	Outlays from new mandatory authority		1	1
4101	Outlays from mandatory balances	1	14	9
4110	Outlays, gross (total)	1	15	10
4180	Budget authority, net (total)	9,511	9,521	8,463
4190	Outlays, net (total)	9,086	7,785	8,461

Object Classification (in millions of dollars)

Identification code 021–2035–0–1–051		2021 actual	2022 est.	2023 est.
	Direct obligations:			
21.0	Travel and transportation of persons	20	24	24
22.0	Transportation of things	49	112	111
23.1	Rental payments to GSA		1	1
23.3	Communications, utilities, and miscellaneous charges	2	13	12
25.1	Advisory and assistance services	499	506	506
25.2	Other services from non-Federal sources	1,612	586	578
25.3	Other goods and services from Federal sources	778	830	818
25.3	Other goods and services from Federal sources	904	1,029	679
25.4	Operation and maintenance of facilities	26	71	70
25.7	Operation and maintenance of equipment	276	548	540
26.0	Supplies and materials	103	242	1,061
31.0	Equipment	5,444	4,563	3,723
32.0	Land and structures	6	9	9
92.0	Undistributed		641	
99.0	Direct obligations	9,719	9,175	8,132
99.0	Reimbursable obligations	23	158	161

DEPARTMENT OF DEFENSE—MILITARY PROGRAMS

Procurement—Continued
Federal Funds—Continued

		2021 actual	2022 est.	2023 est.
99.9	Total new obligations, unexpired accounts	9,742	9,333	8,293

JOINT IMPROVISED-THREAT DEFEAT FUND

Program and Financing (in millions of dollars)

Identification code 097–2093–0–1–051		2021 actual	2022 est.	2023 est.
	Change in obligated balance:			
	Unpaid obligations:			
3000	Unpaid obligations, brought forward, Oct 1	85	78	34
3011	Obligations ("upward adjustments"), expired accounts	17		
3020	Outlays (gross)		–44	–30
3041	Recoveries of prior year unpaid obligations, expired	–24		
3050	Unpaid obligations, end of year	78	34	4
	Uncollected payments:			
3060	Uncollected pymts, Fed sources, brought forward, Oct 1	–24	–31	–31
3071	Change in uncollected pymts, Fed sources, expired	–7		
3090	Uncollected pymts, Fed sources, end of year	–31	–31	–31
	Memorandum (non-add) entries:			
3100	Obligated balance, start of year	61	47	3
3200	Obligated balance, end of year	47	3	–27
	Budget authority and outlays, net:			
	Discretionary:			
	Outlays, gross:			
4011	Outlays from discretionary balances		44	30
	Offsets against gross budget authority and outlays:			
	Offsetting collections (collected) from:			
4033	Non-Federal sources	–3		
4040	Offsets against gross budget authority and outlays (total)	–3		
	Additional offsets against gross budget authority only:			
4052	Offsetting collections credited to expired accounts	3		
4060	Additional offsets against budget authority only (total)	3		
4080	Outlays, net (discretionary)	–3	44	30
4180	Budget authority, net (total)			
4190	Outlays, net (total)	–3	44	30

AIRCRAFT PROCUREMENT, NAVY

For construction, procurement, production, modification, and modernization of aircraft, equipment, including ordnance, spare parts, and accessories therefor; specialized equipment; expansion of public and private plants, including the land necessary therefor, and such lands and interests therein, may be acquired, and construction prosecuted thereon prior to approval of title; and procurement and installation of equipment, appliances, and machine tools in public and private plants; reserve plant and Government and contractor-owned equipment layaway, $16,848,428,000, to remain available for obligation until September 30, 2025, of which $634,879,000 shall be available for the Navy Reserve and Marine Corps Reserve.

Note.—A full-year 2022 appropriation for this account was not enacted at the time the Budget was prepared; therefore, the Budget assumes this account is operating under the Continuing Appropriations Act, 2022 (Division A of Public Law 117–43, as amended). The amounts included for 2022 reflect the annualized level provided by the continuing resolution.

Program and Financing (in millions of dollars)

Identification code 017–1506–0–1–051		2021 actual	2022 est.	2023 est.
	Obligations by program activity:			
0001	Combat aircraft	9,663	8,590	8,013
0003	Trainer aircraft	170	174	211
0004	Other aircraft	1,357	1,115	1,669
0005	Modification of aircraft	3,484	3,690	4,112
0006	Aircraft spares and repair parts	2,237	2,120	1,793
0007	Aircraft support equipment and facilities	742	838	1,034
0020	Undistributed		2,619	
0799	Total direct obligations	17,653	19,146	16,832
0801	Reimbursable program activity	136	6	6
0900	Total new obligations, unexpired accounts	17,789	19,152	16,838
	Budgetary resources:			
	Unobligated balance:			
1000	Unobligated balance brought forward, Oct 1	4,418	6,348	6,349
1001	Discretionary unobligated balance brought fwd, Oct 1	4,416		
1021	Recoveries of prior year unpaid obligations	618		17,099
1070	Unobligated balance (total)	5,036	6,348	23,448
	Budget authority:			
	Appropriations, discretionary:			
1100	Appropriation	19,513	16,477	16,848
1100	Appropriation		3,036	
1120	Appropriations transferred to other acct [021–2020]	–17		
1120	Appropriations transferred to other acct [017–1611]	–16		
1120	Appropriations transferred to other acct [017–1319]	–29		
1120	Appropriations transferred to other acct [097–0130]	–17		
1120	Appropriations transferred to other acct [017–1453]	–27		
1120	Appropriations transferred to other acct [021–2010]	–10		
1131	Unobligated balance of appropriations permanently reduced	–440	–417	
1160	Appropriation, discretionary (total)	18,957	19,096	16,848
	Appropriations, mandatory:			
1221	Appropriations transferred from other acct [011–5512]	40	51	108
	Spending authority from offsetting collections, discretionary:			
1700	Collected	137	6	6
1900	Budget authority (total)	19,134	19,153	16,962
1930	Total budgetary resources available	24,170	25,501	40,410
	Memorandum (non-add) entries:			
1940	Unobligated balance expiring	–33		
1941	Unexpired unobligated balance, end of year	6,348	6,349	23,572
	Change in obligated balance:			
	Unpaid obligations:			
3000	Unpaid obligations, brought forward, Oct 1	33,217	31,128	31,888
3010	New obligations, unexpired accounts	17,789	19,152	16,838
3011	Obligations ("upward adjustments"), expired accounts	63		
3020	Outlays (gross)	–18,942	–18,392	–20,340
3040	Recoveries of prior year unpaid obligations, unexpired	–618		–17,099
3041	Recoveries of prior year unpaid obligations, expired	–381		
3050	Unpaid obligations, end of year	31,128	31,888	11,287
	Memorandum (non-add) entries:			
3100	Obligated balance, start of year	33,217	31,128	31,888
3200	Obligated balance, end of year	31,128	31,888	11,287
	Budget authority and outlays, net:			
	Discretionary:			
4000	Budget authority, gross	19,094	19,102	16,854
	Outlays, gross:			
4010	Outlays from new discretionary authority	3,834	3,253	2,870
4011	Outlays from discretionary balances	15,086	15,101	17,417
4020	Outlays, gross (total)	18,920	18,354	20,287
	Offsets against gross budget authority and outlays:			
	Offsetting collections (collected) from:			
4030	Federal sources	–2	–6	–6
4033	Non-Federal sources	–137		
4040	Offsets against gross budget authority and outlays (total)	–139	–6	–6
	Additional offsets against gross budget authority only:			
4052	Offsetting collections credited to expired accounts	2		
4060	Additional offsets against budget authority only (total)	2		
4070	Budget authority, net (discretionary)	18,957	19,096	16,848
4080	Outlays, net (discretionary)	18,781	18,348	20,281
	Mandatory:			
4090	Budget authority, gross	40	51	108
	Outlays, gross:			
4100	Outlays from new mandatory authority		9	18
4101	Outlays from mandatory balances	22	29	35
4110	Outlays, gross (total)	22	38	53
4180	Budget authority, net (total)	18,997	19,147	16,956
4190	Outlays, net (total)	18,803	18,386	20,334

Object Classification (in millions of dollars)

Identification code 017–1506–0–1–051		2021 actual	2022 est.	2023 est.
	Direct obligations:			
22.0	Transportation of things	7	4	12
23.3	Communications, utilities, and miscellaneous charges	1		
25.1	Advisory and assistance services	316	242	206
25.2	Other services from non-Federal sources	12	5	
25.3	Other goods and services from Federal sources	1,179	102	132
25.3	Other goods and services from Federal sources	873	1,602	1,448
25.4	Operation and maintenance of facilities	1		
25.5	Research and development contracts	43	5	
25.7	Operation and maintenance of equipment	92	1	
26.0	Supplies and materials	3,317	1,868	1,448
31.0	Equipment	11,811	12,695	13,586

273

AIRCRAFT PROCUREMENT, NAVY—Continued
Object Classification—Continued

Identification code 017–1506–0–1–051	2021 actual	2022 est.	2023 est.
32.0 Land and structures	....	3	....
92.0 Undistributed	....	2,619	....
99.0 Direct obligations	17,652	19,146	16,832
99.0 Reimbursable obligations	137	6	6
99.9 Total new obligations, unexpired accounts	17,789	19,152	16,838

WEAPONS PROCUREMENT, NAVY

For construction, procurement, production, modification, and modernization of missiles, torpedoes, other weapons, and related support equipment including spare parts, and accessories therefor; expansion of public and private plants, including the land necessary therefor, and such lands and interests therein, may be acquired, and construction prosecuted thereon prior to approval of title; and procurement and installation of equipment, appliances, and machine tools in public and private plants; reserve plant and Government and contractor-owned equipment layaway, $4,738,705,000, to remain available for obligation until September 30, 2025.

Note.—A full-year 2022 appropriation for this account was not enacted at the time the Budget was prepared; therefore, the Budget assumes this account is operating under the Continuing Appropriations Act, 2022 (Division A of Public Law 117–43, as amended). The amounts included for 2022 reflect the annualized level provided by the continuing resolution.

Program and Financing (in millions of dollars)

Identification code 017–1507–0–1–051	2021 actual	2022 est.	2023 est.
Obligations by program activity:			
0001 Ballistic missiles	1,195	1,134	1,059
0002 Other missiles	2,622	2,710	2,772
0003 Torpedoes and related equipment	266	463	534
0004 Other weapons	190	179	168
0006 Spares and repair parts	119	158	167
0020 Undistributed	....	255	....
0799 Total direct obligations	4,392	4,899	4,700
0801 Reimbursable program activity	16	40	31
0900 Total new obligations, unexpired accounts	4,408	4,939	4,731
Budgetary resources:			
Unobligated balance:			
1000 Unobligated balance brought forward, Oct 1	956	1,104	672
1021 Recoveries of prior year unpaid obligations	95	....	....
1033 Recoveries of prior year paid obligations	1	....	....
1070 Unobligated balance (total)	1,052	1,104	672
Budget authority:			
Appropriations, discretionary:			
1100 Appropriation	4,483	4,221	4,739
1100 Appropriation	....	263	....
1120 Appropriations transferred to other acct [097–0130]	–9	....	....
1120 Appropriations transferred to other acct [017–1804]	–3	....	....
1120 Appropriations transferred to other acct [097–0100]	–5	....	....
1131 Unobligated balance of appropriations permanently reduced	–8	–8	....
1160 Appropriation, discretionary (total)	4,458	4,476	4,739
Spending authority from offsetting collections, discretionary:			
1700 Collected	23	31	31
1701 Change in uncollected payments, Federal sources	2	....	....
1750 Spending auth from offsetting collections, disc (total)	25	31	31
1900 Budget authority (total)	4,483	4,507	4,770
1930 Total budgetary resources available	5,535	5,611	5,442
Memorandum (non-add) entries:			
1940 Unobligated balance expiring	–23	....	....
1941 Unexpired unobligated balance, end of year	1,104	672	711
Change in obligated balance:			
Unpaid obligations:			
3000 Unpaid obligations, brought forward, Oct 1	6,819	7,215	8,151
3010 New obligations, unexpired accounts	4,408	4,939	4,731
3011 Obligations ("upward adjustments"), expired accounts	51	....	....
3020 Outlays (gross)	–3,900	–4,003	–4,539
3040 Recoveries of prior year unpaid obligations, unexpired	–95	....	....
3041 Recoveries of prior year unpaid obligations, expired	–68	....	....
3050 Unpaid obligations, end of year	7,215	8,151	8,343
Uncollected payments:			
3060 Uncollected pymts, Fed sources, brought forward, Oct 1	....	–2	–2
3070 Change in uncollected pymts, Fed sources, unexpired	–2	....	....
3090 Uncollected pymts, Fed sources, end of year	–2	–2	–2
Memorandum (non-add) entries:			
3100 Obligated balance, start of year	6,819	7,213	8,149
3200 Obligated balance, end of year	7,213	8,149	8,341
Budget authority and outlays, net:			
Discretionary:			
4000 Budget authority, gross	4,483	4,507	4,770
Outlays, gross:			
4010 Outlays from new discretionary authority	556	568	600
4011 Outlays from discretionary balances	3,344	3,433	3,937
4020 Outlays, gross (total)	3,900	4,001	4,537
Offsets against gross budget authority and outlays:			
Offsetting collections (collected) from:			
4030 Federal sources	–19	–31	–31
4033 Non-Federal sources	–5	....	....
4040 Offsets against gross budget authority and outlays (total)	–24	–31	–31
Additional offsets against gross budget authority only:			
4050 Change in uncollected pymts, Fed sources, unexpired	–2	....	....
4053 Recoveries of prior year paid obligations, unexpired accounts	1	....	....
4060 Additional offsets against budget authority only (total)	–1	....	....
4070 Budget authority, net (discretionary)	4,458	4,476	4,739
4080 Outlays, net (discretionary)	3,876	3,970	4,506
Mandatory:			
Outlays, gross:			
4101 Outlays from mandatory balances	....	2	2
4180 Budget authority, net (total)	4,458	4,476	4,739
4190 Outlays, net (total)	3,876	3,972	4,508

Object Classification (in millions of dollars)

Identification code 017–1507–0–1–051	2021 actual	2022 est.	2023 est.
Direct obligations:			
22.0 Transportation of things	8	....	3
25.1 Advisory and assistance services	49	22	81
25.2 Other services from non-Federal sources	11	....	....
25.3 Other goods and services from Federal sources	212	189	139
25.3 Other goods and services from Federal sources	233	416	218
25.4 Operation and maintenance of facilities	7	7	7
25.5 Research and development contracts	16	169	11
25.7 Operation and maintenance of equipment	161	87	76
26.0 Supplies and materials	2,101	1,633	2,152
31.0 Equipment	1,594	2,121	2,013
92.0 Undistributed	....	255	....
99.0 Direct obligations	4,392	4,899	4,700
99.0 Reimbursable obligations	16	40	31
99.9 Total new obligations, unexpired accounts	4,408	4,939	4,731

PROCUREMENT OF AMMUNITION, NAVY AND MARINE CORPS

For construction, procurement, production, and modification of ammunition, and accessories therefor; specialized equipment and training devices; expansion of public and private plants, including ammunition facilities, authorized by section 2854 of title 10, United States Code, and the land necessary therefor, for the foregoing purposes, and such lands and interests therein, may be acquired, and construction prosecuted thereon prior to approval of title; and procurement and installation of equipment, appliances, and machine tools in public and private plants; reserve plant and Government and contractor-owned equipment layaway; and other expenses necessary for the foregoing purposes, $1,052,292,000, to remain available for obligation until September 30, 2025, of which $427,000 shall be available for the Navy Reserve and Marine Corps Reserve.

Note.—A full-year 2022 appropriation for this account was not enacted at the time the Budget was prepared; therefore, the Budget assumes this account is operating under the Continuing Appropriations Act, 2022 (Division A of Public Law 117–43, as amended). The amounts included for 2022 reflect the annualized level provided by the continuing resolution.

DEPARTMENT OF DEFENSE—MILITARY PROGRAMS

Procurement—Continued
Federal Funds—Continued

Program and Financing (in millions of dollars)

Identification code 017–1508–0–1–051		2021 actual	2022 est.	2023 est.
	Obligations by program activity:			
0001	Procurement of Ammunition, Navy	558	535	595
0002	Ammunition, Marine Corps	298	379	380
0020	Undistributed		–128	
0799	Total direct obligations	856	786	975
0801	Reimbursable program activity	13	29	27
0900	Total new obligations, unexpired accounts	869	815	1,002
	Budgetary resources:			
	Unobligated balance:			
1000	Unobligated balance brought forward, Oct 1	63	89	163
1021	Recoveries of prior year unpaid obligations	19		
1070	Unobligated balance (total)	82	89	163
	Budget authority:			
	Appropriations, discretionary:			
1100	Appropriation	869	988	1,052
1100	Appropriation transferred to other acct [097–0130]		–119	
1120	Appropriations transferred to other acct [097–0130]	–4		
1131	Unobligated balance of appropriations permanently reduced	–9	–9	
1160	Appropriation, discretionary (total)	856	860	1,052
	Spending authority from offsetting collections, discretionary:			
1700	Collected	18	29	27
1701	Change in uncollected payments, Federal sources	3		
1750	Spending auth from offsetting collections, disc (total)	21	29	27
1900	Budget authority (total)	877	889	1,079
1930	Total budgetary resources available	959	978	1,242
	Memorandum (non-add) entries:			
1940	Unobligated balance expiring	–1		
1941	Unexpired unobligated balance, end of year	89	163	240
	Change in obligated balance:			
	Unpaid obligations:			
3000	Unpaid obligations, brought forward, Oct 1	2,057	1,880	1,717
3010	New obligations, unexpired accounts	869	815	1,002
3011	Obligations ("upward adjustments"), expired accounts	19		
3020	Outlays (gross)	–1,017	–978	–951
3040	Recoveries of prior year unpaid obligations, unexpired	–19		
3041	Recoveries of prior year unpaid obligations, expired	–29		
3050	Unpaid obligations, end of year	1,880	1,717	1,768
	Uncollected payments:			
3060	Uncollected pymts, Fed sources, brought forward, Oct 1		–3	–3
3070	Change in uncollected pymts, Fed sources, unexpired	–3		
3090	Uncollected pymts, Fed sources, end of year	–3	–3	–3
	Memorandum (non-add) entries:			
3100	Obligated balance, start of year	2,057	1,877	1,714
3200	Obligated balance, end of year	1,877	1,714	1,765
	Budget authority and outlays, net:			
	Discretionary:			
4000	Budget authority, gross	877	889	1,079
	Outlays, gross:			
4010	Outlays from new discretionary authority	91	106	122
4011	Outlays from discretionary balances	926	872	829
4020	Outlays, gross (total)	1,017	978	951
	Offsets against gross budget authority and outlays:			
	Offsetting collections (collected) from:			
4030	Federal sources	–17	–29	–27
4033	Non-Federal sources	–1		
4040	Offsets against gross budget authority and outlays (total)	–18	–29	–27
	Additional offsets against gross budget authority only:			
4050	Change in uncollected pymts, Fed sources, unexpired	–3		
4060	Additional offsets against budget authority only (total)	–3		
4070	Budget authority, net (discretionary)	856	860	1,052
4080	Outlays, net (discretionary)	999	949	924
4180	Budget authority, net (total)	856	860	1,052
4190	Outlays, net (total)	999	949	924

Object Classification (in millions of dollars)

Identification code 017–1508–0–1–051		2021 actual	2022 est.	2023 est.
	Direct obligations:			
22.0	Transportation of things	6	4	2
25.1	Advisory and assistance services	5	4	4
25.2	Other services from non-Federal sources	1		
25.3	Other goods and services from Federal sources	67	12	25
25.3	Other goods and services from Federal sources	74	94	116
26.0	Supplies and materials	611	734	769
31.0	Equipment	91	66	59
92.0	Undistributed		–128	
99.0	Direct obligations	855	786	975
99.0	Reimbursable obligations	14	29	27
99.9	Total new obligations, unexpired accounts	869	815	1,002

SHIPBUILDING AND CONVERSION, NAVY

For expenses necessary for the construction, acquisition, or conversion of vessels as authorized by law, including armor and armament thereof, plant equipment, appliances, and machine tools and installation thereof in public and private plants; reserve plant and Government and contractor-owned equipment layaway; procurement of critical, long lead time components and designs for vessels to be constructed or converted in the future; and expansion of public and private plants, including land necessary therefor, and such lands and interests therein, may be acquired, and construction prosecuted thereon prior to approval of title, $27,917,854,000, to remain available for obligation until September 30, 2027: Provided, That additional obligations may be incurred after September 30, 2027, for engineering services, tests, evaluations, and other such budgeted work that must be performed in the final stage of ship construction: Provided further, That none of the funds provided under this heading for the construction or conversion of any naval vessel to be constructed in shipyards in the United States shall be expended in foreign facilities for the construction of major components of such vessel: Provided further, That none of the funds provided under this heading shall be used for the construction of any naval vessel in foreign shipyards.

Note.—A full-year 2022 appropriation for this account was not enacted at the time the Budget was prepared; therefore, the Budget assumes this account is operating under the Continuing Appropriations Act, 2022 (Division A of Public Law 117–43, as amended). The amounts included for 2022 reflect the annualized level provided by the continuing resolution.

Program and Financing (in millions of dollars)

Identification code 017–1611–0–1–051		2021 actual	2022 est.	2023 est.
	Obligations by program activity:			
0001	Fleet ballistic missile ships		3,845	4,737
0002	Other warships	18,458	14,521	15,373
0003	Amphibious ships	1,636	1,111	2,104
0005	Auxiliaries, craft, and prior-year program costs	1,403	2,747	3,018
0020	Undistributed		612	
0799	Total direct obligations	21,497	22,836	25,232
0900	Total new obligations, unexpired accounts	21,497	22,836	25,232
	Budgetary resources:			
	Unobligated balance:			
1000	Unobligated balance brought forward, Oct 1	12,468	12,561	12,908
1011	Unobligated balance transfer from other acct [017–1810]	6		
1012	Unobligated balance transfers between expired and unexpired accounts	1,279		
1021	Recoveries of prior year unpaid obligations	2,338		
1070	Unobligated balance (total)	16,091	12,561	12,908
	Budget authority:			
	Appropriations, discretionary:			
1100	Appropriation	23,269	22,571	27,918
1100	Appropriation		698	
1120	Appropriations transferred to other acct [017–1612]	–4,122		
1121	Appropriations transferred from other acct [017–1506]	16		
1131	Unobligated balance of appropriations permanently reduced	–153	–86	
1160	Appropriation, discretionary (total)	19,010	23,183	27,918
1900	Budget authority (total)	19,010	23,183	27,918
1930	Total budgetary resources available	35,101	35,744	40,826
	Memorandum (non-add) entries:			
1940	Unobligated balance expiring	–1,043		
1941	Unexpired unobligated balance, end of year	12,561	12,908	15,594
	Change in obligated balance:			
	Unpaid obligations:			
3000	Unpaid obligations, brought forward, Oct 1	51,938	51,891	55,522
3010	New obligations, unexpired accounts	21,497	22,836	25,232
3011	Obligations ("upward adjustments"), expired accounts	6		

275

SHIPBUILDING AND CONVERSION, NAVY—Continued
Program and Financing—Continued

Identification code 017–1611–0–1–051	2021 actual	2022 est.	2023 est.
3020 Outlays (gross)	−19,187	−19,205	−19,784
3030 Unpaid obligations transferred to other accts [097–9999]	−3,344		
3031 Unpaid obligations transferred from other accts [097–9999]	3,344		
3040 Recoveries of prior year unpaid obligations, unexpired	−2,338		
3041 Recoveries of prior year unpaid obligations, expired	−25		
3050 Unpaid obligations, end of year	51,891	55,522	60,970
Memorandum (non-add) entries:			
3100 Obligated balance, start of year	51,938	51,891	55,522
3200 Obligated balance, end of year	51,891	55,522	60,970
Budget authority and outlays, net:			
Discretionary:			
4000 Budget authority, gross	19,010	23,183	27,918
Outlays, gross:			
4010 Outlays from new discretionary authority	1,109	1,275	1,535
4011 Outlays from discretionary balances	18,078	17,930	18,249
4020 Outlays, gross (total)	19,187	19,205	19,784
4180 Budget authority, net (total)	19,010	23,183	27,918
4190 Outlays, net (total)	19,187	19,205	19,784

Object Classification (in millions of dollars)

Identification code 017–1611–0–1–051	2021 actual	2022 est.	2023 est.
Direct obligations:			
25.1 Advisory and assistance services	326	308	178
25.2 Other services from non-Federal sources	18		
25.3 Other goods and services from Federal sources	203	110	9
25.3 Other goods and services from Federal sources	917	771	776
25.5 Research and development contracts	12	12	113
25.7 Operation and maintenance of equipment	27	27	30
26.0 Supplies and materials	60	57	58
31.0 Equipment	19,934	20,939	24,068
92.0 Undistributed		612	
99.9 Total new obligations, unexpired accounts	21,497	22,836	25,232

NATIONAL SEA-BASED DETERRENCE FUND
Program and Financing (in millions of dollars)

Identification code 017–1612–0–1–051	2021 actual	2022 est.	2023 est.
Obligations by program activity:			
0001 Direct program activity	3,972		
Budgetary resources:			
Unobligated balance:			
1000 Unobligated balance brought forward, Oct 1	36	224	224
1021 Recoveries of prior year unpaid obligations	38		
1070 Unobligated balance (total)	74	224	224
Budget authority:			
Appropriations, discretionary:			
1121 Appropriations transferred from other acct [017–1611]	4,122		
1930 Total budgetary resources available	4,196	224	224
Memorandum (non-add) entries:			
1941 Unexpired unobligated balance, end of year	224	224	224
Change in obligated balance:			
Unpaid obligations:			
3000 Unpaid obligations, brought forward, Oct 1	2,970	4,401	2,783
3010 New obligations, unexpired accounts	3,972		
3020 Outlays (gross)	−2,503	−1,618	−1,185
3040 Recoveries of prior year unpaid obligations, unexpired	−38		
3050 Unpaid obligations, end of year	4,401	2,783	1,598
Memorandum (non-add) entries:			
3100 Obligated balance, start of year	2,970	4,401	2,783
3200 Obligated balance, end of year	4,401	2,783	1,598
Budget authority and outlays, net:			
Discretionary:			
4000 Budget authority, gross	4,122		
Outlays, gross:			
4010 Outlays from new discretionary authority	1,384		
4011 Outlays from discretionary balances	1,119	1,618	1,185
4020 Outlays, gross (total)	2,503	1,618	1,185
4180 Budget authority, net (total)	4,122		
4190 Outlays, net (total)	2,503	1,618	1,185

Object Classification (in millions of dollars)

Identification code 017–1612–0–1–051	2021 actual	2022 est.	2023 est.
Direct obligations:			
25.1 Advisory and assistance services	28		
25.3 Other goods and services from Federal sources	129		
31.0 Equipment	3,815		
99.9 Total new obligations, unexpired accounts	3,972		

OTHER PROCUREMENT, NAVY

For procurement, production, and modernization of support equipment and materials not otherwise provided for, Navy ordnance (except ordnance for new aircraft, new ships, and ships authorized for conversion); the purchase of passenger motor vehicles for replacement only; expansion of public and private plants, including the land necessary therefor, and such lands and interests therein, may be acquired, and construction prosecuted thereon prior to approval of title; and procurement and installation of equipment, appliances, and machine tools in public and private plants; reserve plant and Government and contractor-owned equipment layaway, $11,746,503,000, to remain available for obligation until September 30, 2025, of which $1,024,000 shall be available for the Navy Reserve and Marine Corps Reserve: Provided, That such funds are also available for the maintenance, repair, and modernization of ships under a pilot program established for such purposes.

Note.—A full-year 2022 appropriation for this account was not enacted at the time the Budget was prepared; therefore, the Budget assumes this account is operating under the Continuing Appropriations Act, 2022 (Division A of Public Law 117–43, as amended). The amounts included for 2022 reflect the annualized level provided by the continuing resolution.

Program and Financing (in millions of dollars)

Identification code 017–1810–0–1–051	2021 actual	2022 est.	2023 est.
Obligations by program activity:			
0001 Ships support equipment	3,603	3,884	4,144
0002 Communications and electronics equipment	3,991	3,369	3,349
0003 Aviation support equipment	720	708	909
0004 Ordnance support equipment	1,086	1,028	1,143
0005 Civil engineering support equipment	149	150	159
0006 Supply support equipment	661	662	650
0007 Personnel and command support equipment	660	373	527
0008 Spares and repair parts	361	397	476
0020 Undistributed		−109	
0799 Total direct obligations	11,231	10,462	11,357
0801 Reimbursable program activity	207	143	20
0900 Total new obligations, unexpired accounts	11,438	10,605	11,377
Budgetary resources:			
Unobligated balance:			
1000 Unobligated balance brought forward, Oct 1	2,011	2,154	2,496
1001 Discretionary unobligated balance brought fwd, Oct 1	1,979		
1010 Unobligated balance transfer to other accts [017–1611]	−6		
1021 Recoveries of prior year unpaid obligations	642		
1070 Unobligated balance (total)	2,647	2,154	2,496
Budget authority:			
Appropriations, discretionary:			
1100 Appropriation	10,854	10,854	11,747
1120 Appropriations transferred to other acct [017–1804]	−5		
1120 Appropriations transferred to other acct [097–0130]	−45		
1120 Appropriations transferred to other acct [021–2020]	−3		
1120 Appropriations transferred to other acct [097–0300]	−5		
1121 Appropriations transferred from other acct [017–1804]	33		
1121 Appropriations transferred from other acct [097–0105]	9		
1121 Appropriations transferred from other acct [017–1319]	18		
1131 Unobligated balance of appropriations permanently reduced	−87	−87	
1160 Appropriation, discretionary (total)	10,769	10,767	11,747
Appropriations, mandatory:			
1221 Appropriations transferred from other acct [011–5512]	30	37	84

DEPARTMENT OF DEFENSE—MILITARY PROGRAMS

		2021 actual	2022 est.	2023 est.
1230	Appropriations and/or unobligated balance of appropriations permanently reduced	−2		
1260	Appropriations, mandatory (total)	28	37	84
	Spending authority from offsetting collections, discretionary:			
1700	Collected	239	143	20
1701	Change in uncollected payments, Federal sources	−63		
1750	Spending auth from offsetting collections, disc (total)	176	143	20
1900	Budget authority (total)	10,973	10,947	11,851
1930	Total budgetary resources available	13,620	13,101	14,347
	Memorandum (non-add) entries:			
1940	Unobligated balance expiring	−28		
1941	Unexpired unobligated balance, end of year	2,154	2,496	2,970
	Change in obligated balance:			
	Unpaid obligations:			
3000	Unpaid obligations, brought forward, Oct 1	12,800	13,364	14,850
3010	New obligations, unexpired accounts	11,438	10,605	11,377
3011	Obligations ("upward adjustments"), expired accounts	40		
3020	Outlays (gross)	−10,130	−9,119	−10,335
3040	Recoveries of prior year unpaid obligations, unexpired	−642		
3041	Recoveries of prior year unpaid obligations, expired	−142		
3050	Unpaid obligations, end of year	13,364	14,850	15,892
	Uncollected payments:			
3060	Uncollected pymts, Fed sources, brought forward, Oct 1	−163	−104	−104
3070	Change in uncollected pymts, Fed sources, unexpired	63		
3071	Change in uncollected pymts, Fed sources, expired	−4		
3090	Uncollected pymts, Fed sources, end of year	−104	−104	−104
	Memorandum (non-add) entries:			
3100	Obligated balance, start of year	12,637	13,260	14,746
3200	Obligated balance, end of year	13,260	14,746	15,788
	Budget authority and outlays, net:			
	Discretionary:			
4000	Budget authority, gross	10,945	10,910	11,767
	Outlays, gross:			
4010	Outlays from new discretionary authority	2,449	2,296	2,369
4011	Outlays from discretionary balances	7,663	6,798	7,925
4020	Outlays, gross (total)	10,112	9,094	10,294
	Offsets against gross budget authority and outlays:			
	Offsetting collections (collected) from:			
4030	Federal sources	−245	−143	−20
4040	Offsets against gross budget authority and outlays (total)	−245	−143	−20
	Additional offsets against gross budget authority only:			
4050	Change in uncollected pymts, Fed sources, unexpired	63		
4052	Offsetting collections credited to expired accounts	6		
4060	Additional offsets against budget authority only (total)	69		
4070	Budget authority, net (discretionary)	10,769	10,767	11,747
4080	Outlays, net (discretionary)	9,867	8,951	10,274
	Mandatory:			
4090	Budget authority, gross	28	37	84
	Outlays, gross:			
4100	Outlays from new mandatory authority	1	7	17
4101	Outlays from mandatory balances	17	18	24
4110	Outlays, gross (total)	18	25	41
4180	Budget authority, net (total)	10,797	10,804	11,831
4190	Outlays, net (total)	9,885	8,976	10,315

Object Classification (in millions of dollars)

Identification code 017–1810–0–1–051	2021 actual	2022 est.	2023 est.
Direct obligations:			
21.0 Travel and transportation of persons	1	3	
22.0 Transportation of things	7		6
23.3 Communications, utilities, and miscellaneous charges	7	1	1
25.1 Advisory and assistance services	385	536	157
25.2 Other services from non-Federal sources	168	38	34
25.3 Other goods and services from Federal sources	909	664	306
25.3 Other goods and services from Federal sources	2,023	2,105	1,948
25.4 Operation and maintenance of facilities	26	8	8
25.5 Research and development contracts	51	6	16
25.7 Operation and maintenance of equipment	1,062	875	975
26.0 Supplies and materials	848	435	513
31.0 Equipment	5,735	5,900	7,393
32.0 Land and structures	8		
92.0 Undistributed		−109	
99.0 Direct obligations	11,230	10,462	11,357
99.0 Reimbursable obligations	208	143	20
99.9 Total new obligations, unexpired accounts	11,438	10,605	11,377

COASTAL DEFENSE AUGMENTATION

Program and Financing (in millions of dollars)

Identification code 017–0380–0–1–051	2021 actual	2022 est.	2023 est.
Budgetary resources:			
Unobligated balance:			
1000 Unobligated balance brought forward, Oct 1	4	4	4
1930 Total budgetary resources available	4	4	4
Memorandum (non-add) entries:			
1941 Unexpired unobligated balance, end of year	4	4	4
Change in obligated balance:			
Unpaid obligations:			
3000 Unpaid obligations, brought forward, Oct 1	52	52	26
3020 Outlays (gross)		−26	−23
3050 Unpaid obligations, end of year	52	26	3
Memorandum (non-add) entries:			
3100 Obligated balance, start of year	52	52	26
3200 Obligated balance, end of year	52	26	3
Budget authority and outlays, net:			
Discretionary:			
Outlays, gross:			
4011 Outlays from discretionary balances		26	23
4180 Budget authority, net (total)			
4190 Outlays, net (total)		26	23

PROCUREMENT, MARINE CORPS

For expenses necessary for the procurement, manufacture, and modification of missiles, armament, military equipment, spare parts, and accessories therefor; plant equipment, appliances, and machine tools, and installation thereof in public and private plants; reserve plant and Government and contractor-owned equipment layaway; vehicles for the Marine Corps, including the purchase of passenger motor vehicles for replacement only; and expansion of public and private plants, including land necessary therefor, and such lands and interests therein, may be acquired, and construction prosecuted thereon prior to approval of title, $3,681,506,000, to remain available for obligation until September 30, 2025, of which $16,233,000 shall be available for the Marine Corps Reserve.

Note.—A full-year 2022 appropriation for this account was not enacted at the time the Budget was prepared; therefore, the Budget assumes this account is operating under the Continuing Appropriations Act, 2022 (Division A of Public Law 117–43, as amended). The amounts included for 2022 reflect the annualized level provided by the continuing resolution.

Program and Financing (in millions of dollars)

Identification code 017–1109–0–1–051	2021 actual	2022 est.	2023 est.
Obligations by program activity:			
0002 Weapons and combat vehicles	702	707	658
0003 Guided missiles and equipment	306	221	294
0004 Communications and electronics equipment	1,099	1,436	1,510
0005 Support vehicles	398	481	296
0006 Engineer and other equipment	280	34	406
0007 Spares and repair parts	25	27	31
0020 Undistributed		−402	
0799 Total direct obligations	2,810	2,504	3,195
0801 Reimbursable program activity	8	53	54
0900 Total new obligations, unexpired accounts	2,818	2,557	3,249
Budgetary resources:			
Unobligated balance:			
1000 Unobligated balance brought forward, Oct 1	674	623	771
1001 Discretionary unobligated balance brought fwd, Oct 1	667		
1021 Recoveries of prior year unpaid obligations	102		
1070 Unobligated balance (total)	776	623	771
Budget authority:			
Appropriations, discretionary:			
1100 Appropriation	2,696	3,043	3,682
1100 Appropriation		−347	
1120 Appropriations transferred to other acct [097–0130]	−6		

PROCUREMENT, MARINE CORPS—Continued
Program and Financing—Continued

Identification code 017–1109–0–1–051	2021 actual	2022 est.	2023 est.
1131 Unobligated balance of appropriations permanently reduced	–55	–55	....
1160 Appropriation, discretionary (total)	2,635	2,641	3,682
Appropriations, mandatory:			
1221 Appropriations transferred from other acct [011–5512]	35	11	12
1230 Appropriations and/or unobligated balance of appropriations permanently reduced	–1	....	....
1260 Appropriations, mandatory (total)	34	11	12
Spending authority from offsetting collections, discretionary:			
1700 Collected	....	53	54
1701 Change in uncollected payments, Federal sources	8	....	....
1750 Spending auth from offsetting collections, disc (total)	8	53	54
1900 Budget authority (total)	2,677	2,705	3,748
1930 Total budgetary resources available	3,453	3,328	4,519
Memorandum (non-add) entries:			
1940 Unobligated balance expiring	–12	....	....
1941 Unexpired unobligated balance, end of year	623	771	1,270
Change in obligated balance:			
Unpaid obligations:			
3000 Unpaid obligations, brought forward, Oct 1	3,109	3,247	3,374
3010 New obligations, unexpired accounts	2,818	2,557	3,249
3011 Obligations ("upward adjustments"), expired accounts	9	....	....
3020 Outlays (gross)	–2,567	–2,430	–2,852
3040 Recoveries of prior year unpaid obligations, unexpired	–102	....	....
3041 Recoveries of prior year unpaid obligations, expired	–20	....	....
3050 Unpaid obligations, end of year	3,247	3,374	3,771
Uncollected payments:			
3060 Uncollected pymts, Fed sources, brought forward, Oct 1	....	–8	–8
3070 Change in uncollected pymts, Fed sources, unexpired	–8	....	....
3090 Uncollected pymts, Fed sources, end of year	–8	–8	–8
Memorandum (non-add) entries:			
3100 Obligated balance, start of year	3,109	3,239	3,366
3200 Obligated balance, end of year	3,239	3,366	3,763
Budget authority and outlays, net:			
Discretionary:			
4000 Budget authority, gross	2,643	2,694	3,736
Outlays, gross:			
4010 Outlays from new discretionary authority	400	449	606
4011 Outlays from discretionary balances	2,158	1,961	2,228
4020 Outlays, gross (total)	2,558	2,410	2,834
Offsets against gross budget authority and outlays:			
Offsetting collections (collected) from:			
4030 Federal sources	....	–53	–54
4040 Offsets against gross budget authority and outlays (total)	....	–53	–54
Additional offsets against gross budget authority only:			
4050 Change in uncollected pymts, Fed sources, unexpired	–8	....	....
4060 Additional offsets against budget authority only (total)	–8	....	....
4070 Budget authority, net (discretionary)	2,635	2,641	3,682
4080 Outlays, net (discretionary)	2,558	2,357	2,780
Mandatory:			
4090 Budget authority, gross	34	11	12
Outlays, gross:			
4100 Outlays from new mandatory authority	1	2	2
4101 Outlays from mandatory balances	8	18	16
4110 Outlays, gross (total)	9	20	18
4180 Budget authority, net (total)	2,669	2,652	3,694
4190 Outlays, net (total)	2,567	2,377	2,798

Object Classification (in millions of dollars)

Identification code 017–1109–0–1–051	2021 actual	2022 est.	2023 est.
Direct obligations:			
21.0 Travel and transportation of persons	1	1	1
22.0 Transportation of things	3	3	....
23.2 Rental payments to others	9	....	....
23.3 Communications, utilities, and miscellaneous charges	2	1	1
25.1 Advisory and assistance services	126	92	77
25.2 Other services from non-Federal sources	10	15	16
25.3 Other goods and services from Federal sources	159	35	24
25.3 Other goods and services from Federal sources	....	51	154
25.4 Operation and maintenance of facilities	2	....	....
25.5 Research and development contracts	10	11	10
25.7 Operation and maintenance of equipment	60	....	....
26.0 Supplies and materials	404	240	122
31.0 Equipment	2,023	2,457	2,790
32.0 Land and structures	1	....	....
92.0 Undistributed	....	–402	....
99.0 Direct obligations	2,810	2,504	3,195
99.0 Reimbursable obligations	8	53	54
99.9 Total new obligations, unexpired accounts	2,818	2,557	3,249

AIRCRAFT PROCUREMENT, AIR FORCE

For construction, procurement, and modification of aircraft and equipment, including armor and armament, specialized ground handling equipment, and training devices, spare parts, and accessories therefor; specialized equipment; expansion of public and private plants, Government-owned equipment and installation thereof in such plants, erection of structures, and acquisition of land, for the foregoing purposes, and such lands and interests therein, may be acquired, and construction prosecuted thereon prior to approval of title; reserve plant and Government and contractor-owned equipment layaway; and other expenses necessary for the foregoing purposes including rents and transportation of things, $18,517,428,000, to remain available for obligation until September 30, 2025, of which $356,825,000 shall be available for the Air National Guard and Air Force Reserve.

Note.—A full-year 2022 appropriation for this account was not enacted at the time the Budget was prepared; therefore, the Budget assumes this account is operating under the Continuing Appropriations Act, 2022 (Division A of Public Law 117–43, as amended). The amounts included for 2022 reflect the annualized level provided by the continuing resolution.

Program and Financing (in millions of dollars)

Identification code 057–3010–0–1–051	2021 actual	2022 est.	2023 est.
Obligations by program activity:			
0001 Combat aircraft	1,744	5,291	8,569
0002 Airlift aircraft	5,489	3,386	2,438
0003 Trainer aircraft	....	4	8
0004 Other aircraft	1,416	1,290	1,234
0005 Modification of inservice aircraft	3,822	3,368	3,753
0006 Aircraft spares and repair parts	579	782	788
0007 Aircraft support equipment and facilities	1,545	1,180	1,170
0020 Undistributed	....	3,715	....
0799 Total direct obligations	14,595	19,016	17,960
0801 Reimbursable program activity	238	340	340
0900 Total new obligations, unexpired accounts	14,833	19,356	18,300
Budgetary resources:			
Unobligated balance:			
1000 Unobligated balance brought forward, Oct 1	9,230	13,103	13,430
1001 Discretionary unobligated balance brought fwd, Oct 1	9,222	....	....
1010 Unobligated balance transfer to other accts [057–3080]	–29	....	....
1010 Unobligated balance transfer to other accts [097–0300]	–10	....	....
1021 Recoveries of prior year unpaid obligations	235	....	....
1070 Unobligated balance (total)	9,426	13,103	13,430
Budget authority:			
Appropriations, discretionary:			
1100 Appropriation	19,985	15,728	18,517
1100 Appropriation	....	4,258	....
1120 Appropriations transferred to other acct [057–3400]	–431	....	....
1120 Appropriations transferred to other acct [057–3740]	–12	....	....
1120 Appropriations transferred to other acct [057–3500]	–27	....	....
1120 Appropriations transferred to other acct [097–0100]	–27	....	....
1120 Appropriations transferred to other acct [097–0300]	–19	....	....
1131 Unobligated balance of appropriations permanently reduced	–1,025	–543	....
1160 Appropriation, discretionary (total)	18,444	19,443	18,517
Appropriations, mandatory:			
1221 Appropriations transferred from other acct [011–5512]	3	....	....
Spending authority from offsetting collections, discretionary:			
1700 Collected	258	240	340
1701 Change in uncollected payments, Federal sources	–1	....	....
1750 Spending auth from offsetting collections, disc (total)	257	240	340
1900 Budget authority (total)	18,704	19,683	18,857
1930 Total budgetary resources available	28,130	32,786	32,287
Memorandum (non-add) entries:			
1940 Unobligated balance expiring	–194	....	....
1941 Unexpired unobligated balance, end of year	13,103	13,430	13,987

DEPARTMENT OF DEFENSE—MILITARY PROGRAMS

Change in obligated balance:

		2021 actual	2022 est.	2023 est.
	Unpaid obligations:			
3000	Unpaid obligations, brought forward, Oct 1	28,703	25,917	27,287
3010	New obligations, unexpired accounts	14,833	19,356	18,300
3011	Obligations ("upward adjustments"), expired accounts	132		
3020	Outlays (gross)	−17,173	−17,986	−16,282
3040	Recoveries of prior year unpaid obligations, unexpired	−235		
3041	Recoveries of prior year unpaid obligations, expired	−343		
3050	Unpaid obligations, end of year	25,917	27,287	29,305
	Uncollected payments:			
3060	Uncollected pymts, Fed sources, brought forward, Oct 1	−31	−30	−30
3070	Change in uncollected pymts, Fed sources, unexpired	1		
3090	Uncollected pymts, Fed sources, end of year	−30	−30	−30
	Memorandum (non-add) entries:			
3100	Obligated balance, start of year	28,672	25,887	27,257
3200	Obligated balance, end of year	25,887	27,257	29,275

Budget authority and outlays, net:

	Discretionary:			
4000	Budget authority, gross	18,701	19,683	18,857
	Outlays, gross:			
4010	Outlays from new discretionary authority	1,786	1,601	1,636
4011	Outlays from discretionary balances	15,387	16,385	14,646
4020	Outlays, gross (total)	17,173	17,986	16,282
	Offsets against gross budget authority and outlays:			
	Offsetting collections (collected) from:			
4030	Federal sources	−162	−240	−340
4033	Non-Federal sources	−107		
4040	Offsets against gross budget authority and outlays (total)	−269	−240	−340
	Additional offsets against gross budget authority only:			
4050	Change in uncollected pymts, Fed sources, unexpired	1		
4052	Offsetting collections credited to expired accounts	11		
4060	Additional offsets against budget authority only (total)	12		
4070	Budget authority, net (discretionary)	18,444	19,443	18,517
4080	Outlays, net (discretionary)	16,904	17,746	15,942
	Mandatory:			
4090	Budget authority, gross	3		
4180	Budget authority, net (total)	18,447	19,443	18,517
4190	Outlays, net (total)	16,904	17,746	15,942

Object Classification (in millions of dollars)

Identification code 057–3010–0–1–051		2021 actual	2022 est.	2023 est.
	Direct obligations:			
25.1	Advisory and assistance services	74	128	90
25.3	Other goods and services from Federal sources			364
26.0	Supplies and materials			442
31.0	Equipment	14,521	15,173	17,064
92.0	Undistributed		3,715	
99.0	Direct obligations	14,595	19,016	17,960
99.0	Reimbursable obligations	238	340	340
99.9	Total new obligations, unexpired accounts	14,833	19,356	18,300

MISSILE PROCUREMENT, AIR FORCE

For construction, procurement, and modification of missiles, rockets, and related equipment, including spare parts and accessories therefor; ground handling equipment, and training devices; expansion of public and private plants, Government-owned equipment and installation thereof in such plants, erection of structures, and acquisition of land, for the foregoing purposes, and such lands and interests therein, may be acquired, and construction prosecuted thereon prior to approval of title; reserve plant and Government and contractor-owned equipment layaway; and other expenses necessary for the foregoing purposes including rents and transportation of things, $2,962,417,000, to remain available for obligation until September 30, 2025.

Note.—A full-year 2022 appropriation for this account was not enacted at the time the Budget was prepared; therefore, the Budget assumes this account is operating under the Continuing Appropriations Act, 2022 (Division A of Public Law 117–43, as amended). The amounts included for 2022 reflect the annualized level provided by the continuing resolution.

Procurement—Continued
Federal Funds—Continued   279

Program and Financing (in millions of dollars)

Identification code 057–3020–0–1–051		2021 actual	2022 est.	2023 est.
	Obligations by program activity:			
0001	Ballistic missiles	70	71	59
0002	Other missiles	2,045	1,909	1,692
0003	Modification of inservice missiles	166	226	227
0004	Spares and repair parts	90	90	79
0005	Other support	556	573	656
0020	Undistributed		−328	
0799	Total direct obligations	2,927	2,541	2,713
0801	Reimbursable program activity	18	130	130
0900	Total new obligations, unexpired accounts	2,945	2,671	2,843
	Budgetary resources:			
	Unobligated balance:			
1000	Unobligated balance brought forward, Oct 1	1,133	468	269
1010	Unobligated balance transfer to other accts [057–3600]	−90		
1021	Recoveries of prior year unpaid obligations	6		
1033	Recoveries of prior year paid obligations	147		
1070	Unobligated balance (total)	1,196	468	269
	Budget authority:			
	Appropriations, discretionary:			
1100	Appropriation	2,366	2,670	2,962
1100	Appropriation		−304	
1120	Appropriations transferred to other acct [057–3500]	−107		
1120	Appropriations transferred to other acct [057–3400]	−7		
1120	Appropriations transferred to other acct [057–3740]	−11		
1131	Unobligated balance of appropriations permanently reduced	−25	−24	
1160	Appropriation, discretionary (total)	2,216	2,342	2,962
	Spending authority from offsetting collections, discretionary:			
1700	Collected	13	130	130
1900	Budget authority (total)	2,229	2,472	3,092
1930	Total budgetary resources available	3,425	2,940	3,361
	Memorandum (non-add) entries:			
1940	Unobligated balance expiring	−12		
1941	Unexpired unobligated balance, end of year	468	269	518
	Change in obligated balance:			
	Unpaid obligations:			
3000	Unpaid obligations, brought forward, Oct 1	4,887	4,918	4,963
3010	New obligations, unexpired accounts	2,945	2,671	2,843
3011	Obligations ("upward adjustments"), expired accounts	15		
3020	Outlays (gross)	−2,899	−2,626	−2,596
3040	Recoveries of prior year unpaid obligations, unexpired	−6		
3041	Recoveries of prior year unpaid obligations, expired	−24		
3050	Unpaid obligations, end of year	4,918	4,963	5,210
	Memorandum (non-add) entries:			
3100	Obligated balance, start of year	4,887	4,918	4,963
3200	Obligated balance, end of year	4,918	4,963	5,210
	Budget authority and outlays, net:			
	Discretionary:			
4000	Budget authority, gross	2,229	2,472	3,092
	Outlays, gross:			
4010	Outlays from new discretionary authority	316	434	515
4011	Outlays from discretionary balances	2,583	2,192	2,081
4020	Outlays, gross (total)	2,899	2,626	2,596
	Offsets against gross budget authority and outlays:			
	Offsetting collections (collected) from:			
4030	Federal sources	−13	−130	−130
4033	Non-Federal sources	−148		
4040	Offsets against gross budget authority and outlays (total)	−161	−130	−130
	Additional offsets against gross budget authority only:			
4052	Offsetting collections credited to expired accounts	1		
4053	Recoveries of prior year paid obligations, unexpired accounts	147		
4060	Additional offsets against budget authority only (total)	148		
4070	Budget authority, net (discretionary)	2,216	2,342	2,962
4080	Outlays, net (discretionary)	2,738	2,496	2,466
4180	Budget authority, net (total)	2,216	2,342	2,962
4190	Outlays, net (total)	2,738	2,496	2,466

MISSILE PROCUREMENT, AIR FORCE—Continued

Object Classification (in millions of dollars)

Identification code 057–3020–0–1–051		2021 actual	2022 est.	2023 est.
	Direct obligations:			
25.1	Advisory and assistance services	46	16	43
31.0	Equipment	2,881	2,853	2,670
92.0	Undistributed		–328	
99.0	Direct obligations	2,927	2,541	2,713
99.0	Reimbursable obligations	18	130	130
99.9	Total new obligations, unexpired accounts	2,945	2,671	2,843

SPACE PROCUREMENT, AIR FORCE

Program and Financing (in millions of dollars)

Identification code 057–3021–0–1–051		2021 actual	2022 est.	2023 est.
	Obligations by program activity:			
0001	Space procurement, Air Force	812	192	
0020	Undistributed		–64	
0799	Total direct obligations	812	128	
0900	Total new obligations, unexpired accounts	812	128	
	Budgetary resources:			
	Unobligated balance:			
1000	Unobligated balance brought forward, Oct 1	1,079	219	27
1021	Recoveries of prior year unpaid obligations	45		
1070	Unobligated balance (total)	1,124	219	27
	Budget authority:			
	Appropriations, discretionary:			
1131	Unobligated balance of appropriations permanently reduced	–64	–64	
1900	Budget authority (total)	–64	–64	
1930	Total budgetary resources available	1,060	155	27
	Memorandum (non-add) entries:			
1940	Unobligated balance expiring	–29		
1941	Unexpired unobligated balance, end of year	219	27	27
	Change in obligated balance:			
	Unpaid obligations:			
3000	Unpaid obligations, brought forward, Oct 1	3,588	2,345	1,355
3010	New obligations, unexpired accounts	812	128	
3011	Obligations ("upward adjustments"), expired accounts	17		
3020	Outlays (gross)	–2,017	–1,118	–580
3040	Recoveries of prior year unpaid obligations, unexpired	–45		
3041	Recoveries of prior year unpaid obligations, expired	–10		
3050	Unpaid obligations, end of year	2,345	1,355	775
	Memorandum (non-add) entries:			
3100	Obligated balance, start of year	3,588	2,345	1,355
3200	Obligated balance, end of year	2,345	1,355	775
	Budget authority and outlays, net:			
	Discretionary:			
4000	Budget authority, gross	–64	–64	
	Outlays, gross:			
4010	Outlays from new discretionary authority		–64	
4011	Outlays from discretionary balances	2,017	1,182	580
4020	Outlays, gross (total)	2,017	1,118	580
4180	Budget authority, net (total)	–64	–64	
4190	Outlays, net (total)	2,017	1,118	580

Object Classification (in millions of dollars)

Identification code 057–3021–0–1–051		2021 actual	2022 est.	2023 est.
	Direct obligations:			
25.1	Advisory and assistance services	35		
31.0	Equipment	777	192	
92.0	Undistributed		–64	
99.0	Direct obligations	812	128	

| 99.9 | Total new obligations, unexpired accounts | 812 | 128 | |

PROCUREMENT, SPACE FORCE

For construction, procurement, and modification of spacecraft, rockets, and related equipment, including spare parts and accessories therefor; ground handling equipment, and training devices; expansion of public and private plants, Government-owned equipment and installation thereof in such plants, erection of structures, and acquisition of land, for the foregoing purposes, and such lands and interests therein, may be acquired, and construction prosecuted thereon prior to approval of title; reserve plant and Government and contractor-owned equipment layaway; and other expenses necessary for the foregoing purposes including rents and transportation of things, $3,629,669,000, to remain available for obligation until September 30, 2027.

Note.—A full-year 2022 appropriation for this account was not enacted at the time the Budget was prepared; therefore, the Budget assumes this account is operating under the Continuing Appropriations Act, 2022 (Division A of Public Law 117–43, as amended). The amounts included for 2022 reflect the annualized level provided by the continuing resolution.

Program and Financing (in millions of dollars)

Identification code 057–3022–0–1–051		2021 actual	2022 est.	2023 est.
	Obligations by program activity:			
0001	Space procurement, Space Force	1,636	2,363	3,237
0002	Spares	1	1	1
0020	Undistributed		–456	
0799	Total direct obligations	1,637	1,908	3,238
0801	Reimbursable program activity	1	45	54
0900	Total new obligations, unexpired accounts	1,638	1,953	3,292
	Budgetary resources:			
	Unobligated balance:			
1000	Unobligated balance brought forward, Oct 1		674	1,047
	Budget authority:			
	Appropriations, discretionary:			
1100	Appropriation	2,311	2,767	3,630
1100	Appropriation		–456	
1120	Appropriations transferred to other acct [017–1804]	–16		
1121	Appropriations transferred from other acct [057–3600]	5		
1160	Appropriation, discretionary (total)	2,300	2,311	3,630
	Spending authority from offsetting collections, discretionary:			
1700	Collected	12	15	54
1900	Budget authority (total)	2,312	2,326	3,684
1930	Total budgetary resources available	2,312	3,000	4,731
	Memorandum (non-add) entries:			
1941	Unexpired unobligated balance, end of year	674	1,047	1,439
	Change in obligated balance:			
	Unpaid obligations:			
3000	Unpaid obligations, brought forward, Oct 1		1,264	2,162
3010	New obligations, unexpired accounts	1,638	1,953	3,292
3020	Outlays (gross)	–374	–1,055	–1,839
3050	Unpaid obligations, end of year	1,264	2,162	3,615
	Memorandum (non-add) entries:			
3100	Obligated balance, start of year		1,264	2,162
3200	Obligated balance, end of year	1,264	2,162	3,615
	Budget authority and outlays, net:			
	Discretionary:			
4000	Budget authority, gross	2,312	2,326	3,684
	Outlays, gross:			
4010	Outlays from new discretionary authority	374	431	707
4011	Outlays from discretionary balances		624	1,132
4020	Outlays, gross (total)	374	1,055	1,839
	Offsets against gross budget authority and outlays:			
	Offsetting collections (collected) from:			
4030	Federal sources	–12	–15	–54
4180	Budget authority, net (total)	2,300	2,311	3,630
4190	Outlays, net (total)	362	1,040	1,785

Object Classification (in millions of dollars)

Identification code 057–3022–0–1–051		2021 actual	2022 est.	2023 est.
	Direct obligations:			
25.1	Advisory and assistance services	72	147	144

DEPARTMENT OF DEFENSE—MILITARY PROGRAMS

Procurement—Continued
Federal Funds—Continued

		2021 actual	2022 est.	2023 est.
31.0	Equipment	1,565	2,217	3,094
92.0	Undistributed		−456	
99.0	Direct obligations	1,637	1,908	3,238
99.0	Reimbursable obligations	1	45	54
99.9	Total new obligations, unexpired accounts	1,638	1,953	3,292

PROCUREMENT OF AMMUNITION, AIR FORCE

For construction, procurement, production, and modification of ammunition, and accessories therefor; specialized equipment and training devices; expansion of public and private plants, including ammunition facilities, authorized by section 2854 of title 10, United States Code, and the land necessary therefor, for the foregoing purposes, and such lands and interests therein, may be acquired, and construction prosecuted thereon prior to approval of title; and procurement and installation of equipment, appliances, and machine tools in public and private plants; reserve plant and Government and contractor-owned equipment layaway; and other expenses necessary for the foregoing purposes, $903,630,000, to remain available for obligation until September 30, 2025, of which $26,555,000 shall be available for the Air National Guard and Air Force Reserve.

Note.—A full-year 2022 appropriation for this account was not enacted at the time the Budget was prepared; therefore, the Budget assumes this account is operating under the Continuing Appropriations Act, 2022 (Division A of Public Law 117–43, as amended). The amounts included for 2022 reflect the annualized level provided by the continuing resolution.

Program and Financing (in millions of dollars)

Identification code 057–3011–0–1–051		2021 actual	2022 est.	2023 est.
	Obligations by program activity:			
0001	Ammunition	1,207	1,386	1,136
0002	Weapons	65		
0020	Undistributed		492	
0799	Total direct obligations	1,272	1,878	1,136
0801	Reimbursable program activity	31	110	220
0900	Total new obligations, unexpired accounts	1,303	1,988	1,356
	Budgetary resources:			
	Unobligated balance:			
1000	Unobligated balance brought forward, Oct 1	1,122	1,063	472
1021	Recoveries of prior year unpaid obligations	77		
1070	Unobligated balance (total)	1,199	1,063	472
	Budget authority:			
	Appropriations, discretionary:			
1100	Appropriation	1,336	795	904
1100	Appropriation		542	
1120	Appropriations transferred to other acct [057–3400]	−113		
1120	Appropriations transferred to other acct [057–3740]	−14		
1131	Unobligated balance of appropriations permanently reduced	−50	−50	
1160	Appropriation, discretionary (total)	1,159	1,287	904
	Spending authority from offsetting collections, discretionary:			
1700	Collected	7	110	220
1701	Change in uncollected payments, Federal sources	2		
1750	Spending auth from offsetting collections, disc (total)	9	110	220
1900	Budget authority (total)	1,168	1,397	1,124
1930	Total budgetary resources available	2,367	2,460	1,596
	Memorandum (non-add) entries:			
1940	Unobligated balance expiring	−1		
1941	Unexpired unobligated balance, end of year	1,063	472	240
	Change in obligated balance:			
	Unpaid obligations:			
3000	Unpaid obligations, brought forward, Oct 1	4,180	3,307	3,209
3010	New obligations, unexpired accounts	1,303	1,988	1,356
3011	Obligations ("upward adjustments"), expired accounts	18		
3020	Outlays (gross)	−2,096	−2,086	−1,792
3040	Recoveries of prior year unpaid obligations, unexpired	−77		
3041	Recoveries of prior year unpaid obligations, expired	−21		
3050	Unpaid obligations, end of year	3,307	3,209	2,773
	Uncollected payments:			
3060	Uncollected pymts, Fed sources, brought forward, Oct 1	−7	−8	−8
3070	Change in uncollected pymts, Fed sources, unexpired	−2		
3071	Change in uncollected pymts, Fed sources, expired	1		
3090	Uncollected pymts, Fed sources, end of year	−8	−8	−8

	Memorandum (non-add) entries:			
3100	Obligated balance, start of year	4,173	3,299	3,201
3200	Obligated balance, end of year	3,299	3,201	2,765
	Budget authority and outlays, net:			
	Discretionary:			
4000	Budget authority, gross	1,168	1,397	1,124
	Outlays, gross:			
4010	Outlays from new discretionary authority	28	136	238
4011	Outlays from discretionary balances	2,068	1,950	1,554
4020	Outlays, gross (total)	2,096	2,086	1,792
	Offsets against gross budget authority and outlays:			
	Offsetting collections (collected) from:			
4030	Federal sources	−7	−110	−220
4040	Offsets against gross budget authority and outlays (total)	−7	−110	−220
	Additional offsets against gross budget authority only:			
4050	Change in uncollected pymts, Fed sources, unexpired	−2		
4060	Additional offsets against budget authority only (total)	−2		
4070	Budget authority, net (discretionary)	1,159	1,287	904
4080	Outlays, net (discretionary)	2,089	1,976	1,572
4180	Budget authority, net (total)	1,159	1,287	904
4190	Outlays, net (total)	2,089	1,976	1,572

Object Classification (in millions of dollars)

Identification code 057–3011–0–1–051		2021 actual	2022 est.	2023 est.
	Direct obligations:			
25.1	Advisory and assistance services	31	63	27
31.0	Equipment	1,241	1,323	1,109
92.0	Undistributed		492	
99.0	Direct obligations	1,272	1,878	1,136
99.0	Reimbursable obligations	31	110	220
99.9	Total new obligations, unexpired accounts	1,303	1,988	1,356

OTHER PROCUREMENT, AIR FORCE

For procurement and modification of equipment (including ground guidance and electronic control equipment, and ground electronic and communication equipment), and supplies, materials, and spare parts therefor, not otherwise provided for; the purchase of passenger motor vehicles for replacement only; lease of passenger motor vehicles; and expansion of public and private plants, Government-owned equipment and installation thereof in such plants, erection of structures, and acquisition of land, for the foregoing purposes, and such lands and interests therein, may be acquired, and construction prosecuted thereon, prior to approval of title; reserve plant and Government and contractor-owned equipment layaway, $25,691,113,000, to remain available for obligation until September 30, 2025, of which $126,543,000 shall be available for the Air National Guard and Air Force Reserve.

Note.—A full-year 2022 appropriation for this account was not enacted at the time the Budget was prepared; therefore, the Budget assumes this account is operating under the Continuing Appropriations Act, 2022 (Division A of Public Law 117–43, as amended). The amounts included for 2022 reflect the annualized level provided by the continuing resolution.

Program and Financing (in millions of dollars)

Identification code 057–3080–0–1–051		2021 actual	2022 est.	2023 est.
	Obligations by program activity:			
0002	Vehicular equipment	350	414	285
0003	Electronics and telecommunications equipment	1,371	2,326	2,126
0004	Other base maintenance and support equipment	22,746	22,582	23,122
0005	Spare and repair parts	54	16	21
0020	Undistributed		−636	
0799	Total direct obligations	24,521	24,702	25,554
0801	Reimbursable program activity	2,087	400	645
0900	Total new obligations, unexpired accounts	26,608	25,102	26,199
	Budgetary resources:			
	Unobligated balance:			
1000	Unobligated balance brought forward, Oct 1	4,481	4,419	4,332
1001	Discretionary unobligated balance brought fwd, Oct 1	4,470		
1011	Unobligated balance transfer from other acct [057–3010]	29		
1021	Recoveries of prior year unpaid obligations	102		
1033	Recoveries of prior year paid obligations	6		

281

OTHER PROCUREMENT, AIR FORCE—Continued
Program and Financing—Continued

Identification code 057–3080–0–1–051	2021 actual	2022 est.	2023 est.
1070 Unobligated balance (total)	4,618	4,419	4,332
Budget authority:			
Appropriations, discretionary:			
1100 Appropriation	23,797	25,251	25,691
1100 Appropriation	....	–1,454	....
1100 Appropriation	....	885	....
1120 Appropriations transferred to other acct [021–2020]	–4		
1120 Appropriations transferred to other acct [057–3740]	–19		
1120 Appropriations transferred to other acct [097–0130]	–21		
1120 Appropriations transferred to other acct [017–1804]	–3		
1121 Appropriations transferred from other acct [097–0105]	3		
1121 Appropriations transferred from other acct [097–0400]	35		
1121 Appropriations transferred from other acct [057–3600]	7		
1131 Unobligated balance of appropriations permanently reduced	–79	–67	....
1160 Appropriation, discretionary (total)	23,716	24,615	25,691
Appropriations, mandatory:			
1221 Appropriations transferred from other acct [011–5512]	1	....	1
1230 Appropriations and/or unobligated balance of appropriations permanently reduced	–1	....	....
1260 Appropriations, mandatory (total)	....	....	1
Spending authority from offsetting collections, discretionary:			
1700 Collected	987	400	645
1701 Change in uncollected payments, Federal sources	1,765	....	....
1750 Spending auth from offsetting collections, disc (total)	2,752	400	645
1900 Budget authority (total)	26,468	25,015	26,337
1930 Total budgetary resources available	31,086	29,434	30,669
Memorandum (non-add) entries:			
1940 Unobligated balance expiring	–59	....	....
1941 Unexpired unobligated balance, end of year	4,419	4,332	4,470
Change in obligated balance:			
Unpaid obligations:			
3000 Unpaid obligations, brought forward, Oct 1	7,541	8,959	11,226
3010 New obligations, unexpired accounts	26,608	25,102	26,199
3011 Obligations ("upward adjustments"), expired accounts	178	....	....
3020 Outlays (gross)	–25,077	–22,835	–24,888
3040 Recoveries of prior year unpaid obligations, unexpired	–102	....	....
3041 Recoveries of prior year unpaid obligations, expired	–189	....	....
3050 Unpaid obligations, end of year	8,959	11,226	12,537
Uncollected payments:			
3060 Uncollected pymts, Fed sources, brought forward, Oct 1	–504	–2,268	–2,268
3070 Change in uncollected pymts, Fed sources, unexpired	–1,765	....	....
3071 Change in uncollected pymts, Fed sources, expired	1	....	....
3090 Uncollected pymts, Fed sources, end of year	–2,268	–2,268	–2,268
Memorandum (non-add) entries:			
3100 Obligated balance, start of year	7,037	6,691	8,958
3200 Obligated balance, end of year	6,691	8,958	10,269
Budget authority and outlays, net:			
Discretionary:			
4000 Budget authority, gross	26,468	25,015	26,336
Outlays, gross:			
4010 Outlays from new discretionary authority	18,251	17,630	18,629
4011 Outlays from discretionary balances	6,823	5,205	6,258
4020 Outlays, gross (total)	25,074	22,835	24,887
Offsets against gross budget authority and outlays:			
Offsetting collections (collected) from:			
4030 Federal sources	–989	–400	–645
4033 Non-Federal sources	–153	....	....
4040 Offsets against gross budget authority and outlays (total)	–1,142	–400	–645
Additional offsets against gross budget authority only:			
4050 Change in uncollected pymts, Fed sources, unexpired	–1,765	....	....
4052 Offsetting collections credited to expired accounts	152	....	....
4053 Recoveries of prior year paid obligations, unexpired accounts	3	....	....
4060 Additional offsets against budget authority only (total)	–1,610	....	....
4070 Budget authority, net (discretionary)	23,716	24,615	25,691
4080 Outlays, net (discretionary)	23,932	22,435	24,242
Mandatory:			
4090 Budget authority, gross	....	....	1
Outlays, gross:			
4100 Outlays from new mandatory authority	....	....	1
4101 Outlays from mandatory balances	3	....	....
4110 Outlays, gross (total)	3	....	1
Offsets against gross budget authority and outlays:			
Offsetting collections (collected) from:			
4123 Non-Federal sources	–3	....	....
Additional offsets against gross budget authority only:			
4143 Recoveries of prior year paid obligations, unexpired accounts	3	....	....
4160 Budget authority, net (mandatory)	....	....	1
4170 Outlays, net (mandatory)	....	....	1
4180 Budget authority, net (total)	23,716	24,615	25,692
4190 Outlays, net (total)	23,932	22,435	24,243

Object Classification (in millions of dollars)

Identification code 057–3080–0–1–051	2021 actual	2022 est.	2023 est.
Direct obligations:			
25.1 Advisory and assistance services	649	77	2
25.3 Other goods and services from Federal sources	....	....	181
26.0 Supplies and materials	....	....	95
31.0 Equipment	23,872	25,261	25,276
92.0 Undistributed	....	–636	....
99.0 Direct obligations	24,521	24,702	25,554
99.0 Reimbursable obligations	2,087	400	645
99.9 Total new obligations, unexpired accounts	26,608	25,102	26,199

PROCUREMENT, DEFENSE-WIDE

For expenses of activities and agencies of the Department of Defense (other than the military departments) necessary for procurement, production, and modification of equipment, supplies, materials, and spare parts therefor, not otherwise provided for; the purchase of passenger motor vehicles for replacement only; expansion of public and private plants, equipment, and installation thereof in such plants, erection of structures, and acquisition of land for the foregoing purposes, and such lands and interests therein, may be acquired, and construction prosecuted thereon prior to approval of title; reserve plant and Government and contractor-owned equipment layaway, $5,245,500,000, to remain available for obligation until September 30, 2025.

Note.—A full-year 2022 appropriation for this account was not enacted at the time the Budget was prepared; therefore, the Budget assumes this account is operating under the Continuing Appropriations Act, 2022 (Division A of Public Law 117–43, as amended). The amounts included for 2022 reflect the annualized level provided by the continuing resolution.

Program and Financing (in millions of dollars)

Identification code 097–0300–0–1–051	2021 actual	2022 est.	2023 est.
Obligations by program activity:			
0001 Major equipment	2,923	2,215	2,777
0002 Special Operations Command	2,304	2,554	2,216
0003 Chemical/Biological Defense	279	375	347
0020 Undistributed	....	756	....
0799 Total direct obligations	5,506	5,900	5,340
0801 Reimbursable program activity	551	465	453
0900 Total new obligations, unexpired accounts	6,057	6,365	5,793
Budgetary resources:			
Unobligated balance:			
1000 Unobligated balance brought forward, Oct 1	1,718	2,616	3,078
1010 Unobligated balance transfer to other accts [097–0400]	–2	....	....
1011 Unobligated balance transfer from other acct [057–3010]	10	....	....
1021 Recoveries of prior year unpaid obligations	75	....	....
1033 Recoveries of prior year paid obligations	4	....	....
1070 Unobligated balance (total)	1,805	2,616	3,078
Budget authority:			
Appropriations, discretionary:			
1100 Appropriation	6,304	5,548	5,246
1100 Appropriation	....	756	....
1120 Appropriations transferred to other acct [097–0400]	–1	....	....
1121 Appropriations transferred from other acct [097–0100]	6	....	....
1121 Appropriations transferred from other acct [017–1810]	5	....	....
1121 Appropriations transferred from other acct [057–3840]	2	....	....
1121 Appropriations transferred from other acct [057–3010]	19	....	....
1121 Appropriations transferred from other acct [021–2020]	1	....	....
1160 Appropriation, discretionary (total)	6,336	6,304	5,246
Spending authority from offsetting collections, discretionary:			
1700 Collected	495	523	511

DEPARTMENT OF DEFENSE—MILITARY PROGRAMS

		2021 actual	2022 est.	2023 est.
1701	Change in uncollected payments, Federal sources	130		
1750	Spending auth from offsetting collections, disc (total)	625	523	511
1900	Budget authority (total)	6,961	6,827	5,757
1930	Total budgetary resources available	8,766	9,443	8,835
	Memorandum (non-add) entries:			
1940	Unobligated balance expiring	−93		
1941	Unexpired unobligated balance, end of year	2,616	3,078	3,042
	Change in obligated balance:			
	Unpaid obligations:			
3000	Unpaid obligations, brought forward, Oct 1	9,578	8,016	9,318
3010	New obligations, unexpired accounts	6,057	6,365	5,793
3011	Obligations ("upward adjustments"), expired accounts	54		
3020	Outlays (gross)	−7,465	−5,063	−6,496
3040	Recoveries of prior year unpaid obligations, unexpired	−75		
3041	Recoveries of prior year unpaid obligations, expired	−133		
3050	Unpaid obligations, end of year	8,016	9,318	8,615
	Uncollected payments:			
3060	Uncollected pymts, Fed sources, brought forward, Oct 1	−204	−313	−313
3070	Change in uncollected pymts, Fed sources, unexpired	−130		
3071	Change in uncollected pymts, Fed sources, expired	21		
3090	Uncollected pymts, Fed sources, end of year	−313	−313	−313
	Memorandum (non-add) entries:			
3100	Obligated balance, start of year	9,374	7,703	9,005
3200	Obligated balance, end of year	7,703	9,005	8,302
	Budget authority and outlays, net:			
	Discretionary:			
4000	Budget authority, gross	6,961	6,827	5,757
	Outlays, gross:			
4010	Outlays from new discretionary authority	1,472	1,595	1,403
4011	Outlays from discretionary balances	5,993	3,468	5,093
4020	Outlays, gross (total)	7,465	5,063	6,496
	Offsets against gross budget authority and outlays:			
	Offsetting collections (collected) from:			
4030	Federal sources	−206	−523	−511
4033	Non-Federal sources	−330		
4040	Offsets against gross budget authority and outlays (total)	−536	−523	−511
	Additional offsets against gross budget authority only:			
4050	Change in uncollected pymts, Fed sources, unexpired	−130		
4052	Offsetting collections credited to expired accounts	37		
4053	Recoveries of prior year paid obligations, unexpired accounts	4		
4060	Additional offsets against budget authority only (total)	−89		
4070	Budget authority, net (discretionary)	6,336	6,304	5,246
4080	Outlays, net (discretionary)	6,929	4,540	5,985
4180	Budget authority, net (total)	6,336	6,304	5,246
4190	Outlays, net (total)	6,929	4,540	5,985

Object Classification (in millions of dollars)

Identification code 097–0300–0–1–051		2021 actual	2022 est.	2023 est.
	Direct obligations:			
21.0	Travel and transportation of persons	2	2	2
22.0	Transportation of things	4	2	3
23.2	Rental payments to others	2		1
23.3	Communications, utilities, and miscellaneous charges	17	1	1
25.1	Advisory and assistance services	74	126	102
25.2	Other services from non-Federal sources	79	63	48
25.3	Other goods and services from Federal sources	137	187	121
25.5	Research and development contracts	2	6	
25.7	Operation and maintenance of equipment	304	25	30
26.0	Supplies and materials	622	849	1,050
31.0	Equipment	4,259	3,882	3,982
32.0	Land and structures	3		
44.0	Refunds	1		
92.0	Undistributed		756	
99.0	Direct obligations	5,506	5,899	5,340
99.0	Reimbursable obligations	551	466	453
99.9	Total new obligations, unexpired accounts	6,057	6,365	5,793

◄

NATIONAL GUARD AND RESERVE EQUIPMENT

Note.—A full-year 2022 appropriation for this account was not enacted at the time the Budget was prepared; therefore, the Budget assumes this account is operating under the Continuing Appropriations Act, 2022 (Division A of Public Law 117–43, as amended). The amounts included for 2022 reflect the annualized level provided by the continuing resolution.

Program and Financing (in millions of dollars)

Identification code 097–0350–0–1–051		2021 actual	2022 est.	2023 est.
	Obligations by program activity:			
0001	Reserve equipment	219	427	133
0002	National Guard equipment	547		
0020	Undistributed		950	
0900	Total new obligations, unexpired accounts	766	1,377	133
	Budgetary resources:			
	Unobligated balance:			
1000	Unobligated balance brought forward, Oct 1	508	732	305
1021	Recoveries of prior year unpaid obligations	45		
1033	Recoveries of prior year paid obligations	1		
1070	Unobligated balance (total)	554	732	305
	Budget authority:			
	Appropriations, discretionary:			
1100	Appropriation	950		
1100	Appropriation		950	
1160	Appropriation, discretionary (total)	950	950	
1900	Budget authority (total)	950	950	
1930	Total budgetary resources available	1,504	1,682	305
	Memorandum (non-add) entries:			
1940	Unobligated balance expiring	−6		
1941	Unexpired unobligated balance, end of year	732	305	172
	Change in obligated balance:			
	Unpaid obligations:			
3000	Unpaid obligations, brought forward, Oct 1	1,556	1,128	2,007
3010	New obligations, unexpired accounts	766	1,377	133
3011	Obligations ("upward adjustments"), expired accounts	92		
3020	Outlays (gross)	−1,155	−498	−702
3040	Recoveries of prior year unpaid obligations, unexpired	−45		
3041	Recoveries of prior year unpaid obligations, expired	−86		
3050	Unpaid obligations, end of year	1,128	2,007	1,438
	Memorandum (non-add) entries:			
3100	Obligated balance, start of year	1,556	1,128	2,007
3200	Obligated balance, end of year	1,128	2,007	1,438
	Budget authority and outlays, net:			
	Discretionary:			
4000	Budget authority, gross	950	950	
	Outlays, gross:			
4010	Outlays from new discretionary authority	7	12	
4011	Outlays from discretionary balances	1,148	486	702
4020	Outlays, gross (total)	1,155	498	702
	Offsets against gross budget authority and outlays:			
	Offsetting collections (collected) from:			
4033	Non-Federal sources	−1		
4040	Offsets against gross budget authority and outlays (total)	−1		
	Additional offsets against gross budget authority only:			
4053	Recoveries of prior year paid obligations, unexpired accounts	1		
4060	Additional offsets against budget authority only (total)	1		
4070	Budget authority, net (discretionary)	950	950	
4080	Outlays, net (discretionary)	1,154	498	702
4180	Budget authority, net (total)	950	950	
4190	Outlays, net (total)	1,154	498	702

Object Classification (in millions of dollars)

Identification code 097–0350–0–1–051		2021 actual	2022 est.	2023 est.
	Direct obligations:			
22.0	Transportation of things	12		
25.1	Advisory and assistance services	3		
25.2	Other services from non-Federal sources	24		
25.3	Other goods and services from Federal sources	5		
25.7	Operation and maintenance of equipment	2		
26.0	Supplies and materials	155		
31.0	Equipment	564	427	133
32.0	Land and structures	1		
92.0	Undistributed		950	

NATIONAL GUARD AND RESERVE EQUIPMENT—Continued
Object Classification—Continued

Identification code 097–0350–0–1–051	2021 actual	2022 est.	2023 est.
99.9 Total new obligations, unexpired accounts	766	1,377	133

DEFENSE PRODUCTION ACT PURCHASES

For activities by the Department of Defense pursuant to sections 108, 301, 302, and 303 of the Defense Production Act of 1950 (50 U.S.C. 4518, 4531, 4532, and 4533), $659,906,000, to remain available until expended.

Note.—A full-year 2022 appropriation for this account was not enacted at the time the Budget was prepared; therefore, the Budget assumes this account is operating under the Continuing Appropriations Act, 2022 (Division A of Public Law 117–43, as amended). The amounts included for 2022 reflect the annualized level provided by the continuing resolution.

Program and Financing (in millions of dollars)

Identification code 097–0360–0–1–051		2021 actual	2022 est.	2023 est.
	Obligations by program activity:			
0001	Defense Production Act Purchases	336	341	660
0020	Undistributed		–166	
0900	Total new obligations, unexpired accounts	336	175	660
	Budgetary resources:			
	Unobligated balance:			
1000	Unobligated balance brought forward, Oct 1	283	152	152
1021	Recoveries of prior year unpaid obligations	30		
1070	Unobligated balance (total)	313	152	152
	Budget authority:			
	Appropriations, discretionary:			
1100	Appropriation	175	175	660
1900	Budget authority (total)	175	175	660
1930	Total budgetary resources available	488	327	812
	Memorandum (non-add) entries:			
1941	Unexpired unobligated balance, end of year	152	152	152
	Change in obligated balance:			
	Unpaid obligations:			
3000	Unpaid obligations, brought forward, Oct 1	668	491	343
3010	New obligations, unexpired accounts	336	175	660
3020	Outlays (gross)	–483	–323	–562
3040	Recoveries of prior year unpaid obligations, unexpired	–30		
3050	Unpaid obligations, end of year	491	343	441
	Memorandum (non-add) entries:			
3100	Obligated balance, start of year	668	491	343
3200	Obligated balance, end of year	491	343	441
	Budget authority and outlays, net:			
	Discretionary:			
4000	Budget authority, gross	175	175	660
	Outlays, gross:			
4010	Outlays from new discretionary authority	40	96	363
4011	Outlays from discretionary balances	443	227	199
4020	Outlays, gross (total)	483	323	562
4180	Budget authority, net (total)	175	175	660
4190	Outlays, net (total)	483	323	562

The Defense Production Act (50 U.S.C. App. 2061, et seq.) authorizes the use of Federal funds to expedite and expand the supply of critical resources and services from the U.S. industrial base to support national defense and homeland security.

Object Classification (in millions of dollars)

Identification code 097–0360–0–1–051		2021 actual	2022 est.	2023 est.
	Direct obligations:			
11.8	Personnel compensation: Special personal services payments	18		
25.1	Advisory and assistance services	313	316	406
25.3	Other goods and services from Federal sources	1		
26.0	Supplies and materials	4		
31.0	Equipment		5	254
32.0	Land and structures		20	
92.0	Undistributed		–166	
99.9	Total new obligations, unexpired accounts	336	175	660

DEFENSE PRODUCTION ACT PROGRAM ACCOUNT

Program and Financing (in millions of dollars)

Identification code 097–0361–0–1–051		2021 actual	2022 est.	2023 est.
	Obligations by program activity:			
	Credit program obligations:			
0709	Administrative expenses	13	6	4
0900	Total new obligations, unexpired accounts (object class 25.3)	13	6	4
	Budgetary resources:			
	Unobligated balance:			
1000	Unobligated balance brought forward, Oct 1	100	87	81
1930	Total budgetary resources available	100	87	81
	Memorandum (non-add) entries:			
1941	Unexpired unobligated balance, end of year	87	81	77
	Change in obligated balance:			
	Unpaid obligations:			
3000	Unpaid obligations, brought forward, Oct 1		7	7
3010	New obligations, unexpired accounts	13	6	4
3020	Outlays (gross)	–6	–6	–4
3050	Unpaid obligations, end of year	7	7	7
	Memorandum (non-add) entries:			
3100	Obligated balance, start of year		7	7
3200	Obligated balance, end of year	7	7	7
	Budget authority and outlays, net:			
	Discretionary:			
	Outlays, gross:			
4011	Outlays from discretionary balances	6	6	4
4180	Budget authority, net (total)			
4190	Outlays, net (total)	6	6	4

Summary of Loan Levels, Subsidy Budget Authority and Outlays by Program (in millions of dollars)

Identification code 097–0361–0–1–051		2021 actual	2022 est.	2023 est.
	Direct loan levels supportable by subsidy budget authority:			
115001	Defense Production Act Loans	590	906	
	Direct loan subsidy (in percent):			
132001	Defense Production Act Loans	–2.12	0.00	
132999	Weighted average subsidy rate	–2.12	0.00	0.00
	Direct loan subsidy budget authority:			
133001	Defense Production Act Loans	–13		
	Administrative expense data:			
3510	Budget authority	13	6	4

CHEMICAL AGENTS AND MUNITIONS DESTRUCTION, DEFENSE

For expenses, not otherwise provided for, necessary for the destruction of the United States stockpile of lethal chemical agents and munitions in accordance with the provisions of section 1412 of the Department of Defense Authorization Act, 1986 (50 U.S.C. 1521), and for the destruction of other chemical warfare materials that are not in the chemical weapon stockpile, $1,059,818,000, of which $84,612,000 shall be for operation and maintenance, of which no less than $22,778,000 shall be for the Chemical Stockpile Emergency Preparedness Program, consisting of $31,426,000 for activities on military installations and $30,408,000 to remain available until September 30, 2024, to assist State and local governments; and $975,206,000, to remain available until September 30, 2024, shall be for research, development, test and evaluation, of which $971,742,000 shall only be for the Assembled Chemical Weapons Alternatives program.

Note.—A full-year 2022 appropriation for this account was not enacted at the time the Budget was prepared; therefore, the Budget assumes this account is operating under the Continuing Appropriations Act, 2022 (Division A of Public Law 117–43, as amended). The amounts included for 2022 reflect the annualized level provided by the continuing resolution.

DEPARTMENT OF DEFENSE—MILITARY PROGRAMS

Procurement—Continued
Federal Funds—Continued

Program and Financing (in millions of dollars)

Identification code 097–0390–0–1–051	2021 actual	2022 est.	2023 est.
Obligations by program activity:			
0001 Operation and maintenance	76	90	57
0002 Research, Development, Test, and Evaluation	975	1,030	825
0003 Procurement	1	....	....
0020 Undistributed	....	–63	....
0799 Total direct obligations	1,052	1,057	882
0801 Reimbursable program activity	....	10	10
0900 Total new obligations, unexpired accounts	1,052	1,067	892
Budgetary resources:			
Unobligated balance:			
1000 Unobligated balance brought forward, Oct 1	8	7	....
1021 Recoveries of prior year unpaid obligations	3	....	....
1070 Unobligated balance (total)	11	7	....
Budget authority:			
Appropriations, discretionary:			
1100 Appropriation	1,050	1,050	1,060
1120 Appropriations transferred to other acct [097–0819]	–2	....	....
1160 Appropriation, discretionary (total)	1,048	1,050	1,060
Spending authority from offsetting collections, discretionary:			
1700 Collected	....	10	10
1900 Budget authority (total)	1,048	1,060	1,070
1930 Total budgetary resources available	1,059	1,067	1,070
Memorandum (non-add) entries:			
1941 Unexpired unobligated balance, end of year	7	....	178
Change in obligated balance:			
Unpaid obligations:			
3000 Unpaid obligations, brought forward, Oct 1	344	414	834
3010 New obligations, unexpired accounts	1,052	1,067	892
3011 Obligations ("upward adjustments"), expired accounts	2	....	....
3020 Outlays (gross)	–978	–647	–859
3040 Recoveries of prior year unpaid obligations, unexpired	–3	....	....
3041 Recoveries of prior year unpaid obligations, expired	–3	....	....
3050 Unpaid obligations, end of year	414	834	867
Uncollected payments:			
3060 Uncollected pymts, Fed sources, brought forward, Oct 1	–6	....	....
3071 Change in uncollected pymts, Fed sources, expired	6	....	....
Memorandum (non-add) entries:			
3100 Obligated balance, start of year	338	414	834
3200 Obligated balance, end of year	414	834	867
Budget authority and outlays, net:			
Discretionary:			
4000 Budget authority, gross	1,048	1,060	1,070
Outlays, gross:			
4010 Outlays from new discretionary authority	644	398	402
4011 Outlays from discretionary balances	334	249	457
4020 Outlays, gross (total)	978	647	859
Offsets against gross budget authority and outlays:			
Offsetting collections (collected) from:			
4030 Federal sources	....	–10	–10
4040 Offsets against gross budget authority and outlays (total)	....	–10	–10
4180 Budget authority, net (total)	1,048	1,050	1,060
4190 Outlays, net (total)	978	637	849

The Chemical Agents and Munitions Destruction, Defense account supports the Chemical Demilitarization Program, which supports the safe and secure disposal of the U.S. inventory of lethal chemical agents, munitions and related (non-stockpile) material, thus avoiding future risks and costs associated with the continued storage of chemical warfare materials. The program supports the Chemical Weapons Convention initiative of eliminating chemical weapons.

Object Classification (in millions of dollars)

Identification code 097–0390–0–1–051	2021 actual	2022 est.	2023 est.
Direct obligations:			
Personnel compensation:			
11.1 Full-time permanent	17	31	32
11.5 Other personnel compensation	2	2	2
11.9 Total personnel compensation	19	33	34
12.1 Civilian personnel benefits	6	12	13
21.0 Travel and transportation of persons	1	....	....
23.2 Rental payments to others	5	....	....
25.1 Advisory and assistance services	17	35	35
25.2 Other services from non-Federal sources	125	121	97
25.3 Other goods and services from Federal sources	....	2	2
25.4 Operation and maintenance of facilities	....	10	10
25.5 Research and development contracts	878	905	689
25.7 Operation and maintenance of equipment	....	1	1
31.0 Equipment	1	1	1
92.0 Undistributed	....	–63	....
99.0 Direct obligations	1,052	1,057	882
99.0 Reimbursable obligations	....	10	10
99.9 Total new obligations, unexpired accounts	1,052	1,067	892

Employment Summary

Identification code 097–0390–0–1–051	2021 actual	2022 est.	2023 est.
1001 Direct civilian full-time equivalent employment	148	355	355
2001 Reimbursable civilian full-time equivalent employment	....	43	43

DEFENSE PRODUCTION ACT, DIRECT LOAN FINANCING ACCOUNT

Program and Financing (in millions of dollars)

Identification code 097–4387–0–3–051	2021 actual	2022 est.	2023 est.
Obligations by program activity:			
Credit program obligations:			
0710 Direct loan obligations	590	906	....
0740 Negative subsidy obligations	13	....	....
0900 Total new obligations, unexpired accounts	603	906	....
Budgetary resources:			
Unobligated balance:			
1021 Recoveries of prior year unpaid obligations	....	603	....
1024 Unobligated balance of borrowing authority withdrawn	....	–603	....
Financing authority:			
Borrowing authority, mandatory:			
1400 Borrowing authority	603	906	....
1900 Budget authority (total)	603	906	....
1930 Total budgetary resources available	603	906	....
Change in obligated balance:			
Unpaid obligations:			
3000 Unpaid obligations, brought forward, Oct 1	....	603	453
3010 New obligations, unexpired accounts	603	906	....
3020 Outlays (gross)	....	–453	–453
3040 Recoveries of prior year unpaid obligations, unexpired	....	–603	....
3050 Unpaid obligations, end of year	603	453	....
Memorandum (non-add) entries:			
3100 Obligated balance, start of year	....	603	453
3200 Obligated balance, end of year	603	453	....
Financing authority and disbursements, net:			
Mandatory:			
4090 Budget authority, gross	603	906	....
Financing disbursements:			
4110 Outlays, gross (total)	....	453	453
4180 Budget authority, net (total)	603	906	....
4190 Outlays, net (total)	....	453	453

Status of Direct Loans (in millions of dollars)

Identification code 097–4387–0–3–051	2021 actual	2022 est.	2023 est.
Position with respect to appropriations act limitation on obligations:			
1111 Direct loan obligations from current-year authority	590	906	....
1150 Total direct loan obligations	590	906	....
Cumulative balance of direct loans outstanding:			
1210 Outstanding, start of year	....	....	453
1231 Disbursements: Direct loan disbursements	....	453	453
1290 Outstanding, end of year	....	453	906

RESEARCH, DEVELOPMENT, TEST, AND EVALUATION

Appropriations in this title support basic and applied research, as well as development, demonstration, testing, prototyping, and evaluation activities. For select Software & Digital Technology Pilot Programs, appropriations may be used for expenses for the agile research, development, test and evaluation, procurement, production, modification, and operation and maintenance. This work is performed by government employees and contractors, in government and corporate laboratories and facilities, at universities, and by nonprofit organizations. Research and development programs are funded to cover annual needs. Resources presented under the RDT&E title contribute primarily to maintaining military technical superiority.

Funds for each fiscal year are available for obligation for a two-year period beginning on the first day of that fiscal year.

Federal Funds

RESEARCH, DEVELOPMENT, TEST AND EVALUATION, ARMY

For expenses necessary for basic and applied scientific research, development, test and evaluation, including maintenance, rehabilitation, lease, and operation of facilities and equipment, $13,710,273,000, to remain available for obligation until September 30, 2024.

Note.—A full-year 2022 appropriation for this account was not enacted at the time the Budget was prepared; therefore, the Budget assumes this account is operating under the Continuing Appropriations Act, 2022 (Division A of Public Law 117–43, as amended). The amounts included for 2022 reflect the annualized level provided by the continuing resolution.

Program and Financing (in millions of dollars)

Identification code 021–2040–0–1–051		2021 actual	2022 est.	2023 est.
	Obligations by program activity:			
0001	Basic research	544	543	468
0002	Applied Research	1,385	1,191	914
0003	Advanced technology development	1,846	1,622	1,298
0004	Advanced Component Development and Prototypes	3,497	4,089	2,623
0005	System development and demonstration	2,879	3,568	3,392
0006	Management support	2,189	1,681	1,417
0007	Operational system development	1,754	1,616	1,380
0008	Software and digital technology pilot programs	56	110	119
0020	Undistributed		1,345	
0799	Total direct obligations	14,150	15,765	11,611
0801	Reimbursable program activity	42,266	30,641	39,440
0900	Total new obligations, unexpired accounts	56,416	46,406	51,051
	Budgetary resources:			
	Unobligated balance:			
1000	Unobligated balance brought forward, Oct 1	5,052	7,457	14,679
1001	Discretionary unobligated balance brought fwd, Oct 1	5,044		
1010	Unobligated balance transfer to other accts [097–4930.001]	–6		
1011	Unobligated balance transfer from other acct [021–2032]	35		
1011	Unobligated balance transfer from other acct [021–2033]	3		
1011	Unobligated balance transfer from other acct [021–2034]	10		
1012	Unobligated balance transfers between expired and unexpired accounts	1		
1021	Recoveries of prior year unpaid obligations	706		
1070	Unobligated balance (total)	5,801	7,457	14,679
	Budget authority:			
	Appropriations, discretionary:			
1100	Appropriation	14,145	12,800	13,710
1100	Appropriation		1,345	
1120	Appropriations transferred to other acct [021–2020]	–2		
1121	Appropriations transferred from other acct [021–2034]	15		
1121	Appropriations transferred from other acct [017–1804]	27		
1121	Appropriations transferred from other acct [097–0105]	1		
1131	Unobligated balance of appropriations permanently reduced	–287		
1160	Appropriation, discretionary (total)	13,899	14,145	13,710
	Appropriations, mandatory:			
1221	Appropriations transferred from other acct [011–5512]	11	39	30
	Spending authority from offsetting collections, discretionary:			
1700	Collected	24,328	39,440	37,000
1701	Change in uncollected payments, Federal sources	19,839		
1750	Spending auth from offsetting collections, disc (total)	44,167	39,440	37,000
	Spending authority from offsetting collections, mandatory:			
1800	Collected	1	2	2
1801	Change in uncollected payments, Federal sources		2	
1850	Spending auth from offsetting collections, mand (total)	1	4	2
1900	Budget authority (total)	58,078	53,628	50,742
1930	Total budgetary resources available	63,879	61,085	65,421
	Memorandum (non-add) entries:			
1940	Unobligated balance expiring	–6		
1941	Unexpired unobligated balance, end of year	7,457	14,679	14,370
	Change in obligated balance:			
	Unpaid obligations:			
3000	Unpaid obligations, brought forward, Oct 1	20,329	37,155	24,388
3010	New obligations, unexpired accounts	56,416	46,406	51,051
3011	Obligations ("upward adjustments"), expired accounts	80		
3020	Outlays (gross)	–38,670	–59,173	–57,594
3040	Recoveries of prior year unpaid obligations, unexpired	–706		
3041	Recoveries of prior year unpaid obligations, expired	–294		
3050	Unpaid obligations, end of year	37,155	24,388	17,845
	Uncollected payments:			
3060	Uncollected pymts, Fed sources, brought forward, Oct 1	–13,981	–33,135	–33,137
3070	Change in uncollected pymts, Fed sources, unexpired	–19,839	–2	
3071	Change in uncollected pymts, Fed sources, expired	685		
3090	Uncollected pymts, Fed sources, end of year	–33,135	–33,137	–33,137
	Memorandum (non-add) entries:			
3100	Obligated balance, start of year	6,348	4,020	–8,749
3200	Obligated balance, end of year	4,020	–8,749	–15,292
	Budget authority and outlays, net:			
	Discretionary:			
4000	Budget authority, gross	58,066	53,585	50,710
	Outlays, gross:			
4010	Outlays from new discretionary authority	20,562	45,381	42,758
4011	Outlays from discretionary balances	18,085	13,771	14,806
4020	Outlays, gross (total)	38,647	59,152	57,564
	Offsets against gross budget authority and outlays:			
	Offsetting collections (collected) from:			
4030	Federal sources	–24,799	–39,440	–37,000
4033	Non-Federal sources	–99		
4040	Offsets against gross budget authority and outlays (total)	–24,898	–39,440	–37,000
	Additional offsets against gross budget authority only:			
4050	Change in uncollected pymts, Fed sources, unexpired	–19,839		
4052	Offsetting collections credited to expired accounts	570		
4060	Additional offsets against budget authority only (total)	–19,269		
4070	Budget authority, net (discretionary)	13,899	14,145	13,710
4080	Outlays, net (discretionary)	13,749	19,712	20,564
	Mandatory:			
4090	Budget authority, gross	12	43	32
	Outlays, gross:			
4100	Outlays from new mandatory authority	1	20	15
4101	Outlays from mandatory balances	22	1	15
4110	Outlays, gross (total)	23	21	30
	Offsets against gross budget authority and outlays:			
	Offsetting collections (collected) from:			
4120	Federal sources		–2	–2
4123	Non-Federal sources	–1		
4130	Offsets against gross budget authority and outlays (total)	–1	–2	–2
	Additional offsets against gross budget authority only:			
4140	Change in uncollected pymts, Fed sources, unexpired		–2	
4160	Budget authority, net (mandatory)	11	39	30
4170	Outlays, net (mandatory)	22	19	28
4180	Budget authority, net (total)	13,910	14,184	13,740
4190	Outlays, net (total)	13,771	19,731	20,592

Object Classification (in millions of dollars)

Identification code 021–2040–0–1–051		2021 actual	2022 est.	2023 est.
	Direct obligations:			
	Personnel compensation:			
11.1	Full-time permanent	290	413	371
11.3	Other than full-time permanent		4	
11.5	Other personnel compensation	16	14	13
11.9	Total personnel compensation	306	431	384
12.1	Civilian personnel benefits	109	157	140
21.0	Travel and transportation of persons	32	62	31
22.0	Transportation of things	27	31	15
23.1	Rental payments to GSA	10	5	2
23.2	Rental payments to others	7	5	3

DEPARTMENT OF DEFENSE—MILITARY PROGRAMS

Research, Development, Test, and Evaluation—Continued
Federal Funds—Continued

287

		2021 actual	2022 est.	2023 est.
23.3	Communications, utilities, and miscellaneous charges	12	14	7
24.0	Printing and reproduction		5	3
25.1	Advisory and assistance services	735	750	750
25.2	Other services from non-Federal sources	489	310	156
25.3	Other goods and services from Federal sources	3,181	1,939	977
25.3	Other goods and services from Federal sources	26		86
25.4	Operation and maintenance of facilities	216	151	76
25.5	Research and development contracts	7,931	9,156	8,266
25.6	Medical care	3		
25.7	Operation and maintenance of equipment	206	196	99
26.0	Supplies and materials	134	312	164
31.0	Equipment	648	806	406
32.0	Land and structures	14	35	18
41.0	Grants, subsidies, and contributions	64	56	28
92.0	Undistributed		1,345	
99.0	Direct obligations	14,150	15,766	11,611
99.0	Reimbursable obligations	42,266	30,640	39,440
99.9	Total new obligations, unexpired accounts	56,416	46,406	51,051

Employment Summary

Identification code 021–2040–0–1–051	2021 actual	2022 est.	2023 est.
1001 Direct civilian full-time equivalent employment	2,687	3,747	3,210
2001 Reimbursable civilian full-time equivalent employment	16,601	14,298	13,903

RESEARCH, DEVELOPMENT, TEST AND EVALUATION, NAVY

For expenses necessary for basic and applied scientific research, development, test and evaluation, including maintenance, rehabilitation, lease, and operation of facilities and equipment, $24,078,718,000, to remain available for obligation until September 30, 2024: Provided, That funds appropriated in this paragraph which are available for the V-22 may be used to meet unique operational requirements of the Special Operations Forces.

Note.—A full-year 2022 appropriation for this account was not enacted at the time the Budget was prepared; therefore, the Budget assumes this account is operating under the Continuing Appropriations Act, 2022 (Division A of Public Law 117–43, as amended). The amounts included for 2022 reflect the annualized level provided by the continuing resolution.

Program and Financing (in millions of dollars)

Identification code 017–1319–0–1–051	2021 actual	2022 est.	2023 est.
Obligations by program activity:			
0001 Basic research	614	608	590
0002 Applied Research	1,086	998	972
0003 Advanced technology development	832	785	856
0004 Advanced Component Development and Prototypes	5,350	6,928	8,263
0005 System development and demonstration	6,056	5,915	6,531
0006 Management support	1,391	998	1,118
0007 Operational system development	5,004	5,295	5,462
0008 Software and digital technology pilot programs	24	886	122
0020 Undistributed		−2,501	
0799 Total direct obligations	20,357	19,912	23,914
0801 Reimbursable program activity	486	487	685
0900 Total new obligations, unexpired accounts	20,843	20,399	24,599
Budgetary resources:			
Unobligated balance:			
1000 Unobligated balance brought forward, Oct 1	2,162	2,307	2,588
1001 Discretionary unobligated balance brought fwd, Oct 1	2,118		
1011 Unobligated balance transfer from other acct [057–3600]	5		
1021 Recoveries of prior year unpaid obligations	391		
1070 Unobligated balance (total)	2,558	2,307	2,588
Budget authority:			
Appropriations, discretionary:			
1100 Appropriation	20,138	20,138	24,079
1120 Appropriations transferred to other acct [097–0105]	−2		
1120 Appropriations transferred to other acct [097–0130]	−49		
1120 Appropriations transferred to other acct [017–1810]	−18		
1120 Appropriations transferred to other acct [021–2020]	−38		
1120 Appropriations transferred to other acct [017–1804]	−11		
1121 Appropriations transferred from other acct [017–1506]	29		
1121 Appropriations transferred from other acct [097–0105]	2		
1131 Unobligated balance of appropriations permanently reduced	−84		
1160 Appropriation, discretionary (total)	19,967	20,138	24,079
Appropriations, mandatory:			
1221 Appropriations transferred from other acct [011–5512]	100	63	208
1230 Appropriations and/or unobligated balance of appropriations permanently reduced	−3		
1260 Appropriations, mandatory (total)	97	63	208
Spending authority from offsetting collections, discretionary:			
1700 Collected	326	479	685
1701 Change in uncollected payments, Federal sources	212		
1750 Spending auth from offsetting collections, disc (total)	538	479	685
Spending authority from offsetting collections, mandatory:			
1800 Collected	6		
1900 Budget authority (total)	20,608	20,680	24,972
1930 Total budgetary resources available	23,166	22,987	27,560
Memorandum (non-add) entries:			
1940 Unobligated balance expiring	−16		
1941 Unexpired unobligated balance, end of year	2,307	2,588	2,961
Change in obligated balance:			
Unpaid obligations:			
3000 Unpaid obligations, brought forward, Oct 1	12,168	12,568	12,452
3010 New obligations, unexpired accounts	20,843	20,399	24,599
3011 Obligations ("upward adjustments"), expired accounts	198		
3020 Outlays (gross)	−19,976	−20,515	−23,299
3040 Recoveries of prior year unpaid obligations, unexpired	−391		
3041 Recoveries of prior year unpaid obligations, expired	−274		
3050 Unpaid obligations, end of year	12,568	12,452	13,752
Uncollected payments:			
3060 Uncollected pymts, Fed sources, brought forward, Oct 1	−8	−367	−367
3070 Change in uncollected pymts, Fed sources, unexpired	−212		
3071 Change in uncollected pymts, Fed sources, expired	−147		
3090 Uncollected pymts, Fed sources, end of year	−367	−367	−367
Memorandum (non-add) entries:			
3100 Obligated balance, start of year	12,160	12,201	12,085
3200 Obligated balance, end of year	12,201	12,085	13,385
Budget authority and outlays, net:			
Discretionary:			
4000 Budget authority, gross	20,505	20,617	24,764
Outlays, gross:			
4010 Outlays from new discretionary authority	10,466	10,548	12,725
4011 Outlays from discretionary balances	9,430	9,895	10,436
4020 Outlays, gross (total)	19,896	20,443	23,161
Offsets against gross budget authority and outlays:			
Offsetting collections (collected) from:			
4030 Federal sources	−319	−479	−685
4033 Non-Federal sources	−7		
4040 Offsets against gross budget authority and outlays (total)	−326	−479	−685
Additional offsets against gross budget authority only:			
4050 Change in uncollected pymts, Fed sources, unexpired	−212		
4060 Additional offsets against budget authority only (total)	−212		
4070 Budget authority, net (discretionary)	19,967	20,138	24,079
4080 Outlays, net (discretionary)	19,570	19,964	22,476
Mandatory:			
4090 Budget authority, gross	103	63	208
Outlays, gross:			
4100 Outlays from new mandatory authority		32	104
4101 Outlays from mandatory balances	80	40	34
4110 Outlays, gross (total)	80	72	138
Offsets against gross budget authority and outlays:			
Offsetting collections (collected) from:			
4120 Federal sources	−3		
4123 Non-Federal sources	−3		
4130 Offsets against gross budget authority and outlays (total)	−6		
4160 Budget authority, net (mandatory)	97	63	208
4170 Outlays, net (mandatory)	74	72	138
4180 Budget authority, net (total)	20,064	20,201	24,287
4190 Outlays, net (total)	19,644	20,036	22,614

Object Classification (in millions of dollars)

Identification code 017–1319–0–1–051	2021 actual	2022 est.	2023 est.
Direct obligations:			
Personnel compensation:			
11.1 Full-time permanent	97	93	97
11.3 Other than full-time permanent	1	2	4
11.5 Other personnel compensation	3	3	3
11.9 Total personnel compensation	101	98	104

RESEARCH, DEVELOPMENT, TEST AND EVALUATION, NAVY—Continued
Object Classification—Continued

Identification code 017–1319–0–1–051		2021 actual	2022 est.	2023 est.
12.1	Civilian personnel benefits	34	39	39
21.0	Travel and transportation of persons	18	24	33
22.0	Transportation of things	7	4	3
23.1	Rental payments to GSA	6	2	2
23.2	Rental payments to others	18	21	17
23.3	Communications, utilities, and miscellaneous charges	40	20	29
25.1	Advisory and assistance services	1,280	843	990
25.2	Other services from non-Federal sources	84	124	132
25.3	Other goods and services from Federal sources	2,063	1,038	1,221
25.3	Other goods and services from Federal sources	3,512	4,970	6,019
25.4	Operation and maintenance of facilities	90	4	29
25.5	Research and development contracts	9,620	12,207	12,440
25.7	Operation and maintenance of equipment	1,110	982	989
26.0	Supplies and materials	207	158	101
31.0	Equipment	1,517	1,433	1,427
32.0	Land and structures	14	....	1
41.0	Grants, subsidies, and contributions	636	446	338
92.0	Undistributed	....	–2,501	....
99.0	Direct obligations	20,357	19,912	23,914
99.0	Reimbursable obligations	486	487	685
99.9	Total new obligations, unexpired accounts	20,843	20,399	24,599

Employment Summary

Identification code 017–1319–0–1–051		2021 actual	2022 est.	2023 est.
1001	Direct civilian full-time equivalent employment	742	693	687
2001	Reimbursable civilian full-time equivalent employment	313	87	87

RESEARCH, DEVELOPMENT, TEST AND EVALUATION, AIR FORCE

For expenses necessary for basic and applied scientific research, development, test and evaluation, including maintenance, rehabilitation, lease, and operation of facilities and equipment, $44,134,301,000, to remain available for obligation until September 30, 2024.

Note.—A full-year 2022 appropriation for this account was not enacted at the time the Budget was prepared; therefore, the Budget assumes this account is operating under the Continuing Appropriations Act, 2022 (Division A of Public Law 117–43, as amended). The amounts included for 2022 reflect the annualized level provided by the continuing resolution.

Program and Financing (in millions of dollars)

Identification code 057–3600–0–1–051		2021 actual	2022 est.	2023 est.
	Obligations by program activity:			
0001	Basic research	481	495	539
0002	Applied Research	1,591	1,343	1,310
0003	Advanced technology development	879	771	814
0004	Advanced component development and prototypes	7,456	8,654	8,122
0005	System development and demonstration	2,615	2,537	5,834
0006	Management support	3,612	2,978	3,038
0007	Operational system development	21,306	21,398	22,920
0008	Software and digital technology pilot programs	....	351	864
0020	Undistributed	....	–2,823	....
0799	Total direct obligations	37,940	35,704	43,441
0801	Reimbursable program activity	3,692	5,608	5,608
0900	Total new obligations, unexpired accounts	41,632	41,312	49,049
	Budgetary resources:			
	Unobligated balance:			
1000	Unobligated balance brought forward, Oct 1	7,343	5,570	6,257
1001	Discretionary unobligated balance brought fwd, Oct 1	7,312		
1010	Unobligated balance transfer to other accts [017–1319]	–5		
1011	Unobligated balance transfer from other acct [057–3020]	90		
1021	Recoveries of prior year unpaid obligations	430		
1033	Recoveries of prior year paid obligations	40		
1070	Unobligated balance (total)	7,898	5,570	6,257
	Budget authority:			
	Appropriations, discretionary:			
1100	Appropriation	36,361	36,361	44,134
1120	Appropriations transferred to other acct [057–3620]	–17		
1120	Appropriations transferred to other acct [057–3400]	–92		
1120	Appropriations transferred to other acct [017–1804]	–11		
1120	Appropriations transferred to other acct [057–3740]	–16		
1120	Appropriations transferred to other acct [057–3022]	–5		
1120	Appropriations transferred to other acct [057–3080]	–7		
1120	Appropriations transferred to other acct [057–3410]	–5		
1120	Appropriations transferred to other acct [097–0130]	–161		
1120	Appropriations transferred to other acct [021–2010]	–72		
1121	Appropriations transferred from other acct [097–0105]	3		
1131	Unobligated balance of appropriations permanently reduced	–252		
1160	Appropriation, discretionary (total)	35,726	36,361	44,134
	Appropriations, mandatory:			
1221	Appropriations transferred from other acct [011–5512]	46	30	48
1240	Capital transfer of appropriations to general fund	–2		
1260	Appropriations, mandatory (total)	44	30	48
	Spending authority from offsetting collections, discretionary:			
1700	Collected	3,744	5,608	5,608
1701	Change in uncollected payments, Federal sources	–34		
1750	Spending auth from offsetting collections, disc (total)	3,710	5,608	5,608
1900	Budget authority (total)	39,480	41,999	49,790
1930	Total budgetary resources available	47,378	47,569	56,047
	Memorandum (non-add) entries:			
1940	Unobligated balance expiring	–176		
1941	Unexpired unobligated balance, end of year	5,570	6,257	6,998
	Change in obligated balance:			
	Unpaid obligations:			
3000	Unpaid obligations, brought forward, Oct 1	24,621	20,485	19,830
3010	New obligations, unexpired accounts	41,632	41,312	49,049
3011	Obligations ("upward adjustments"), expired accounts	260		
3020	Outlays (gross)	–45,220	–41,967	–46,477
3040	Recoveries of prior year unpaid obligations, unexpired	–430		
3041	Recoveries of prior year unpaid obligations, expired	–378		
3050	Unpaid obligations, end of year	20,485	19,830	22,402
	Uncollected payments:			
3060	Uncollected pymts, Fed sources, brought forward, Oct 1	–1,590	–1,442	–1,442
3070	Change in uncollected pymts, Fed sources, unexpired	34		
3071	Change in uncollected pymts, Fed sources, expired	114		
3090	Uncollected pymts, Fed sources, end of year	–1,442	–1,442	–1,442
	Memorandum (non-add) entries:			
3100	Obligated balance, start of year	23,031	19,043	18,388
3200	Obligated balance, end of year	19,043	18,388	20,960
	Budget authority and outlays, net:			
	Discretionary:			
4000	Budget authority, gross	39,436	41,969	49,742
	Outlays, gross:			
4010	Outlays from new discretionary authority	22,950	23,788	27,675
4011	Outlays from discretionary balances	22,233	18,144	18,763
4020	Outlays, gross (total)	45,183	41,932	46,438
	Offsets against gross budget authority and outlays:			
	Offsetting collections (collected) from:			
4030	Federal sources	–3,754	–5,608	–5,608
4033	Non-Federal sources	–218		
4040	Offsets against gross budget authority and outlays (total)	–3,972	–5,608	–5,608
	Additional offsets against gross budget authority only:			
4050	Change in uncollected pymts, Fed sources, unexpired	34		
4052	Offsetting collections credited to expired accounts	188		
4053	Recoveries of prior year paid obligations, unexpired accounts	40		
4060	Additional offsets against budget authority only (total)	262		
4070	Budget authority, net (discretionary)	35,726	36,361	44,134
4080	Outlays, net (discretionary)	41,211	36,324	40,830
	Mandatory:			
4090	Budget authority, gross	44	30	48
	Outlays, gross:			
4100	Outlays from new mandatory authority		15	24
4101	Outlays from mandatory balances	37	20	15
4110	Outlays, gross (total)	37	35	39
4180	Budget authority, net (total)	35,770	36,391	44,182
4190	Outlays, net (total)	41,248	36,359	40,869

Object Classification (in millions of dollars)

Identification code 057–3600–0–1–051		2021 actual	2022 est.	2023 est.
	Direct obligations:			
	Personnel compensation:			
11.1	Full-time permanent	2,767	1,951	2,572
11.3	Other than full-time permanent	33		

Code	Description	2021 actual	2022 est.	2023 est.
11.5	Other personnel compensation	4	62	62
11.9	Total personnel compensation	2,804	2,013	2,634
12.1	Civilian personnel benefits	37	577	
25.1	Advisory and assistance services	2,454	1,172	2,182
25.3	Other goods and services from Federal sources			432
25.5	Research and development contracts	32,645	34,765	38,148
26.0	Supplies and materials			45
92.0	Undistributed		−2,823	
99.0	Direct obligations	37,940	35,704	43,441
99.0	Reimbursable obligations	3,692	5,608	5,608
99.9	Total new obligations, unexpired accounts	41,632	41,312	49,049

Employment Summary

Identification code 057–3600–0–1–051	2021 actual	2022 est.	2023 est.
1001 Direct civilian full-time equivalent employment	19,352	18,323	18,942
2001 Reimbursable civilian full-time equivalent employment	2,449	4,096	4,091

RESEARCH, DEVELOPMENT, TEST AND EVALUATION, SPACE FORCE

For expenses necessary for basic and applied scientific research, development, test and evaluation, including maintenance, rehabilitation, lease, and operation of facilities and equipment, $15,819,372,000, to remain available until September 30, 2024.

Note.—A full-year 2022 appropriation for this account was not enacted at the time the Budget was prepared; therefore, the Budget assumes this account is operating under the Continuing Appropriations Act, 2022 (Division A of Public Law 117–43, as amended). The amounts included for 2022 reflect the annualized level provided by the continuing resolution.

Program and Financing (in millions of dollars)

Identification code 057–3620–0–1–051	2021 actual	2022 est.	2023 est.
Obligations by program activity:			
0002 Applied research	131	182	233
0003 Advanced technology development		63	482
0004 Advanced component development and prototypes	1,229	1,535	2,763
0005 System development and demonstration	3,232	3,389	5,016
0006 Management support	294	340	415
0007 Operational system development	4,361	5,419	6,045
0008 Software and digital technology pilot programs	139	153	156
0020 Undistributed		−726	
0799 Total direct obligations	9,386	10,355	15,110
0801 Reimbursable program activity	1,141	1,722	1,880
0900 Total new obligations, unexpired accounts	10,527	12,077	16,990
Budgetary resources:			
Unobligated balance:			
1000 Unobligated balance brought forward, Oct 1		1,183	1,368
Budget authority:			
Appropriations, discretionary:			
1100 Appropriation	10,540	11,266	15,819
1100 Appropriation		−726	
1120 Appropriations transferred to other acct [021–2010]	−32		
1120 Appropriations transferred to other acct [057–3400]	−1		
1120 Appropriations transferred to other acct [021–2020]	−17		
1121 Appropriations transferred from other acct [057–3600]	17		
1160 Appropriation, discretionary (total)	10,507	10,540	15,819
Spending authority from offsetting collections, discretionary:			
1700 Collected	681	1,722	1,880
1701 Change in uncollected payments, Federal sources	522		
1750 Spending auth from offsetting collections, disc (total)	1,203	1,722	1,880
1900 Budget authority (total)	11,710	12,262	17,699
1930 Total budgetary resources available	11,710	13,445	19,067
Memorandum (non-add) entries:			
1941 Unexpired unobligated balance, end of year	1,183	1,368	2,077
Change in obligated balance:			
Unpaid obligations:			
3000 Unpaid obligations, brought forward, Oct 1		4,350	5,493
3010 New obligations, unexpired accounts	10,527	12,077	16,990
3020 Outlays (gross)	−6,177	−10,934	−14,575
3050 Unpaid obligations, end of year	4,350	5,493	7,908
Uncollected payments:			
3060 Uncollected pymts, Fed sources, brought forward, Oct 1		−522	−522
3070 Change in uncollected pymts, Fed sources, unexpired	−522		
3090 Uncollected pymts, Fed sources, end of year	−522	−522	−522
Memorandum (non-add) entries:			
3100 Obligated balance, start of year		3,828	4,971
3200 Obligated balance, end of year	3,828	4,971	7,386
Budget authority and outlays, net:			
Discretionary:			
4000 Budget authority, gross	11,710	12,262	17,699
Outlays, gross:			
4010 Outlays from new discretionary authority	6,177	6,992	9,790
4011 Outlays from discretionary balances		3,942	4,785
4020 Outlays, gross (total)	6,177	10,934	14,575
Offsets against gross budget authority and outlays:			
Offsetting collections (collected) from:			
4030 Federal sources	−679	−1,722	−1,880
4033 Non-Federal sources	−2		
4040 Offsets against gross budget authority and outlays (total)	−681	−1,722	−1,880
Additional offsets against gross budget authority only:			
4050 Change in uncollected pymts, Fed sources, unexpired	−522		
4070 Budget authority, net (discretionary)	10,507	10,540	15,819
4080 Outlays, net (discretionary)	5,496	9,212	12,695
4180 Budget authority, net (total)	10,507	10,540	15,819
4190 Outlays, net (total)	5,496	9,212	12,695

Object Classification (in millions of dollars)

Identification code 057–3620–0–1–051	2021 actual	2022 est.	2023 est.
Direct obligations:			
Personnel compensation:			
11.1 Full-time permanent	277	232	340
11.3 Other than full-time permanent	1		
11.5 Other personnel compensation		6	6
11.9 Total personnel compensation	278	238	346
12.1 Civilian personnel benefits		68	
25.1 Advisory and assistance services	1,704	337	3,142
25.5 Research and development contracts	7,404	10,438	11,622
92.0 Undistributed		−726	
99.0 Direct obligations	9,386	10,355	15,110
99.0 Reimbursable obligations	1,141	1,722	1,880
99.9 Total new obligations, unexpired accounts	10,527	12,077	16,990

Employment Summary

Identification code 057–3620–0–1–051	2021 actual	2022 est.	2023 est.
1001 Direct civilian full-time equivalent employment	1,972	2,138	2,230
2001 Reimbursable civilian full-time equivalent employment	48	46	41

RESEARCH, DEVELOPMENT, TEST AND EVALUATION, DEFENSE-WIDE

For expenses of activities and agencies of the Department of Defense (other than the military departments), necessary for basic and applied scientific research, development, test and evaluation; advanced research projects as may be designated and determined by the Secretary of Defense, pursuant to law; maintenance, rehabilitation, lease, and operation of facilities and equipment, $32,077,552,000, to remain available for obligation until September 30, 2024, of which $100,000,000, to remain available until expended, shall be available for a pilot program to accelerate the procurement and fielding of innovative technologies pursuant to section 834 of the National Defense Authorization Act for Fiscal Year 2022 (Public Law 117–81): Provided, That amounts available for such pilot program may be transferred to appropriations available to the Department of Defense for research, development, test and evaluation and for procurement, to be merged with, and to be available for the same purposes and time period as the appropriations to which transferred, to be used for the conduct of pilot program activities pursuant to section 834: Provided further, That not later than 30 days prior to exercising the transfer authority in the preceding proviso, the Secretary of Defense shall notify the congressional defense committees of such transfer: Provided further, That upon a determination that all or part of the funds transferred from this appropriation are not necessary for the purposes provided herein, such amounts may be transferred back to this appropriation's pilot program subdivision: Provided further, That the transfer authority provided under this heading is in addition to any other transfer authority provided by law.

RESEARCH, DEVELOPMENT, TEST AND EVALUATION, DEFENSE-WIDE—Continued

Note.—A full-year 2022 appropriation for this account was not enacted at the time the Budget was prepared; therefore, the Budget assumes this account is operating under the Continuing Appropriations Act, 2022 (Division A of Public Law 117–43, as amended). The amounts included for 2022 reflect the annualized level provided by the continuing resolution.

Program and Financing (in millions of dollars)

Identification code 097–0400–0–1–051		2021 actual	2022 est.	2023 est.
	Obligations by program activity:			
0001	Basic research	1,117	743	765
0002	Applied Research	1,914	2,102	2,130
0003	Advanced technology development	4,071	4,000	4,008
0004	Advanced Component Development and Prototypes	10,538	9,892	15,064
0005	System development and demonstration	939	575	549
0006	Management support	1,719	1,389	1,384
0007	Operational system development	6,630	6,607	6,608
0008	Software and digital technology pilot programs		575	608
0020	Undistributed		156	
0799	Total direct obligations	26,928	26,039	31,116
0801	Reimbursable program activity	1,358	2,173	2,206
0900	Total new obligations, unexpired accounts	28,286	28,212	33,322
	Budgetary resources:			
	Unobligated balance:			
1000	Unobligated balance brought forward, Oct 1	5,330	4,110	4,184
1001	Discretionary unobligated balance brought fwd, Oct 1	5,244		
1010	Unobligated balance transfer to other accts [097–4930]	–21		
1010	Unobligated balance transfer to other accts [097–0819]	–3		
1011	Unobligated balance transfer from other acct [097–0300]	2		
1021	Recoveries of prior year unpaid obligations	266		
1033	Recoveries of prior year paid obligations	17		
1070	Unobligated balance (total)	5,591	4,110	4,184
	Budget authority:			
	Appropriations, discretionary:			
1100	Appropriation	26,013	25,858	32,078
1100	Appropriation		156	
1120	Appropriations transferred to other acct [057–3080]	–35		
1120	Appropriations transferred to other acct [097–0100]	–9		
1120	Appropriations transferred to other acct [057–3400]	–33		
1121	Appropriations transferred from other acct [097–0300]	1		
1131	Unobligated balance of appropriations permanently reduced	–385		
1160	Appropriation, discretionary (total)	25,552	26,014	32,078
	Appropriations, mandatory:			
1221	Appropriations transferred from other acct [011–5512]	61	99	71
1230	Appropriations and/or unobligated balance of appropriations permanently reduced	–4		
1260	Appropriations, mandatory (total)	57	99	71
	Spending authority from offsetting collections, discretionary:			
1700	Collected	928	2,173	2,072
1701	Change in uncollected payments, Federal sources	303		
1750	Spending auth from offsetting collections, disc (total)	1,231	2,173	2,072
1900	Budget authority (total)	26,840	28,286	34,221
1930	Total budgetary resources available	32,431	32,396	38,405
	Memorandum (non-add) entries:			
1940	Unobligated balance expiring	–35		
1941	Unexpired unobligated balance, end of year	4,110	4,184	5,083
	Change in obligated balance:			
	Unpaid obligations:			
3000	Unpaid obligations, brought forward, Oct 1	19,547	20,738	20,859
3010	New obligations, unexpired accounts	28,286	28,212	33,322
3011	Obligations ("upward adjustments"), expired accounts	466		
3020	Outlays (gross)	–26,547	–28,091	–31,530
3040	Recoveries of prior year unpaid obligations, unexpired	–266		
3041	Recoveries of prior year unpaid obligations, expired	–748		
3050	Unpaid obligations, end of year	20,738	20,859	22,651
	Uncollected payments:			
3060	Uncollected pymts, Fed sources, brought forward, Oct 1	–1,398	–1,236	–1,236
3070	Change in uncollected pymts, Fed sources, unexpired	–303		
3071	Change in uncollected pymts, Fed sources, expired	465		
3090	Uncollected pymts, Fed sources, end of year	–1,236	–1,236	–1,236
	Memorandum (non-add) entries:			
3100	Obligated balance, start of year	18,149	19,502	19,623
3200	Obligated balance, end of year	19,502	19,623	21,415
	Budget authority and outlays, net:			
	Discretionary:			
4000	Budget authority, gross	26,783	28,187	34,150
	Outlays, gross:			
4010	Outlays from new discretionary authority	9,972	12,579	14,903
4011	Outlays from discretionary balances	16,559	15,457	16,554
4020	Outlays, gross (total)	26,531	28,036	31,457
	Offsets against gross budget authority and outlays:			
	Offsetting collections (collected) from:			
4030	Federal sources	–1,268	–2,173	–2,072
4033	Non-Federal sources	–124		
4040	Offsets against gross budget authority and outlays (total)	–1,392	–2,173	–2,072
	Additional offsets against gross budget authority only:			
4050	Change in uncollected pymts, Fed sources, unexpired	–303		
4052	Offsetting collections credited to expired accounts	447		
4053	Recoveries of prior year paid obligations, unexpired accounts	17		
4060	Additional offsets against budget authority only (total)	161		
4070	Budget authority, net (discretionary)	25,552	26,014	32,078
4080	Outlays, net (discretionary)	25,139	25,863	29,385
	Mandatory:			
4090	Budget authority, gross	57	99	71
	Outlays, gross:			
4100	Outlays from new mandatory authority		40	28
4101	Outlays from mandatory balances	16	15	45
4110	Outlays, gross (total)	16	55	73
4180	Budget authority, net (total)	25,609	26,113	32,149
4190	Outlays, net (total)	25,155	25,918	29,458

Object Classification (in millions of dollars)

Identification code 097–0400–0–1–051		2021 actual	2022 est.	2023 est.
	Direct obligations:			
	Personnel compensation:			
11.1	Full-time permanent	391	363	371
11.3	Other than full-time permanent	19	19	22
11.5	Other personnel compensation	32	26	30
11.8	Special personal services payments	33	32	25
11.9	Total personnel compensation	475	440	448
12.1	Civilian personnel benefits	154	135	148
21.0	Travel and transportation of persons	21	29	68
22.0	Transportation of things	17	12	16
23.1	Rental payments to GSA	12	6	5
23.2	Rental payments to others	45	35	46
23.3	Communications, utilities, and miscellaneous charges	199	109	324
24.0	Printing and reproduction	4	1	1
25.1	Advisory and assistance services	3,904	3,006	3,070
25.2	Other services from non-Federal sources	806	75	103
25.3	Other goods and services from Federal sources	3,663	2,521	2,438
25.4	Operation and maintenance of facilities	133	137	99
25.5	Research and development contracts	9,918	15,594	21,264
25.7	Operation and maintenance of equipment	1,434	393	626
26.0	Supplies and materials	683	1,495	547
31.0	Equipment	5,051	1,676	1,718
32.0	Land and structures	57	1	2
41.0	Grants, subsidies, and contributions	347	218	193
44.0	Refunds	5		
92.0	Undistributed		156	
99.0	Direct obligations	26,928	26,039	31,116
99.0	Reimbursable obligations	1,358	2,173	2,206
99.9	Total new obligations, unexpired accounts	28,286	28,212	33,322

Employment Summary

Identification code 097–0400–0–1–051	2021 actual	2022 est.	2023 est.
1001 Direct civilian full-time equivalent employment	3,199	2,998	2,972
2001 Reimbursable civilian full-time equivalent employment	171	191	191

DEPARTMENT OF DEFENSE—MILITARY PROGRAMS

DEPARTMENT OF DEFENSE RAPID PROTOTYPING FUND

Program and Financing (in millions of dollars)

Identification code 097–0402–0–1–051	2021 actual	2022 est.	2023 est.
Obligations by program activity:			
0001 Direct program activity	54	....	....
0900 Total new obligations, unexpired accounts (object class 25.5)	54	....	....
Budgetary resources:			
Unobligated balance:			
1000 Unobligated balance brought forward, Oct 1	32		
1021 Recoveries of prior year unpaid obligations	22		
1070 Unobligated balance (total)	54		
1930 Total budgetary resources available	54		
Change in obligated balance:			
Unpaid obligations:			
3000 Unpaid obligations, brought forward, Oct 1	155	97	33
3010 New obligations, unexpired accounts	54		
3020 Outlays (gross)	–90	–64	–28
3040 Recoveries of prior year unpaid obligations, unexpired	–22		
3050 Unpaid obligations, end of year	97	33	5
Memorandum (non-add) entries:			
3100 Obligated balance, start of year	155	97	33
3200 Obligated balance, end of year	97	33	5
Budget authority and outlays, net:			
Discretionary:			
Outlays, gross:			
4011 Outlays from discretionary balances	90	64	28
4180 Budget authority, net (total)	....	....	....
4190 Outlays, net (total)	90	64	28

OPERATIONAL TEST AND EVALUATION, DEFENSE

For expenses, not otherwise provided for, necessary for the independent activities of the Director, Operational Test and Evaluation, in the direction and supervision of operational test and evaluation, including initial operational test and evaluation which is conducted prior to, and in support of, production decisions; joint operational testing and evaluation; and administrative expenses in connection therewith, $277,194,000, to remain available for obligation until September 30, 2024.

Note.—A full-year 2022 appropriation for this account was not enacted at the time the Budget was prepared; therefore, the Budget assumes this account is operating under the Continuing Appropriations Act, 2022 (Division A of Public Law 117–43, as amended). The amounts included for 2022 reflect the annualized level provided by the continuing resolution.

Program and Financing (in millions of dollars)

Identification code 097–0460–0–1–051	2021 actual	2022 est.	2023 est.
Obligations by program activity:			
0006 Management Support	243	222	217
0020 Undistributed	....	41	....
0900 Total new obligations, unexpired accounts	243	263	217
Budgetary resources:			
Unobligated balance:			
1000 Unobligated balance brought forward, Oct 1	33	47	42
Budget authority:			
Appropriations, discretionary:			
1100 Appropriation	257	217	277
1100 Appropriation	....	41	....
1160 Appropriation, discretionary (total)	257	258	277
1900 Budget authority (total)	257	258	277
1930 Total budgetary resources available	290	305	319
Memorandum (non-add) entries:			
1941 Unexpired unobligated balance, end of year	47	42	102
Change in obligated balance:			
Unpaid obligations:			
3000 Unpaid obligations, brought forward, Oct 1	196	178	195
3010 New obligations, unexpired accounts	243	263	217
3011 Obligations ("upward adjustments"), expired accounts	6		
3020 Outlays (gross)	–260	–246	–265
3041 Recoveries of prior year unpaid obligations, expired	–7		
3050 Unpaid obligations, end of year	178	195	147
Memorandum (non-add) entries:			
3100 Obligated balance, start of year	196	178	195
3200 Obligated balance, end of year	178	195	147
Budget authority and outlays, net:			
Discretionary:			
4000 Budget authority, gross	257	258	277
Outlays, gross:			
4010 Outlays from new discretionary authority	105	103	111
4011 Outlays from discretionary balances	155	143	154
4020 Outlays, gross (total)	260	246	265
Offsets against gross budget authority and outlays:			
Offsetting collections (collected) from:			
4033 Non-Federal sources	–1		
4040 Offsets against gross budget authority and outlays (total)	–1		
Additional offsets against gross budget authority only:			
4052 Offsetting collections credited to expired accounts	1		
4060 Additional offsets against budget authority only (total)	1		
4070 Budget authority, net (discretionary)	257	258	277
4080 Outlays, net (discretionary)	259	246	265
4180 Budget authority, net (total)	257	258	277
4190 Outlays, net (total)	259	246	265

Object Classification (in millions of dollars)

Identification code 097–0460–0–1–051	2021 actual	2022 est.	2023 est.
Direct obligations:			
21.0 Travel and transportation of persons	1	4	3
22.0 Transportation of things	....	1	1
23.3 Communications, utilities, and miscellaneous charges	2		
25.1 Advisory and assistance services	165	126	111
25.2 Other services from non-Federal sources	....	2	2
25.3 Other goods and services from Federal sources	74	79	91
25.4 Operation and maintenance of facilities	....	3	3
25.5 Research and development contracts	1		
25.7 Operation and maintenance of equipment	....	2	2
26.0 Supplies and materials	....	3	2
31.0 Equipment	....	2	2
92.0 Undistributed	....	41	....
99.9 Total new obligations, unexpired accounts	243	263	217

CONTRIBUTIONS FOR RENEWABLE ENERGY IMPACT ASSESSMENTS AND MITIGATION, DEFENSE

Special and Trust Fund Receipts (in millions of dollars)

Identification code 097–5753–0–2–051	2021 actual	2022 est.	2023 est.
0100 Balance, start of year	....	1	1
Receipts:			
Current law:			
1130 Contributions from Applicants, Renewable Energy Impact Assessments and Mitigation, Defense	1	1	1
2000 Total: Balances and receipts	1	2	2
Appropriations:			
Current law:			
2101 Contributions for Renewable Energy Impact Assessments and Mitigation, Defense	....	–1	–1
5099 Balance, end of year	1	1	1

Program and Financing (in millions of dollars)

Identification code 097–5753–0–2–051	2021 actual	2022 est.	2023 est.
Obligations by program activity:			
0010 Direct program activity	....	2	2
0900 Total new obligations, unexpired accounts (object class 25.3)	....	2	2
Budgetary resources:			
Unobligated balance:			
1000 Unobligated balance brought forward, Oct 1	2	2	1

CONTRIBUTIONS FOR RENEWABLE ENERGY IMPACT ASSESSMENTS AND MITIGATION, DEFENSE—Continued

Program and Financing—Continued

Identification code 097–5753–0–2–051	2021 actual	2022 est.	2023 est.
Budget authority:			
Appropriations, mandatory:			
1201 Appropriation (special or trust fund)		1	1
1900 Budget authority (total)		1	1
1930 Total budgetary resources available	2	3	2
Memorandum (non-add) entries:			
1941 Unexpired unobligated balance, end of year	2	1	
Change in obligated balance:			
Unpaid obligations:			
3000 Unpaid obligations, brought forward, Oct 1	1	1	1
3010 New obligations, unexpired accounts		2	2
3020 Outlays (gross)		–2	–2
3050 Unpaid obligations, end of year	1	1	1
Memorandum (non-add) entries:			
3100 Obligated balance, start of year	1	1	1
3200 Obligated balance, end of year	1	1	1
Budget authority and outlays, net:			
Mandatory:			
4090 Budget authority, gross		1	1
Outlays, gross:			
4100 Outlays from new mandatory authority		1	1
4101 Outlays from mandatory balances		1	1
4110 Outlays, gross (total)		2	2
4180 Budget authority, net (total)		1	1
4190 Outlays, net (total)		2	2

Contributions of funds from applicants for renewable energy projects filed with the Secretary of Transportation pursuant to section 44718 of title 49, United States Code. Voluntary contributions received by the Department of Defense are used to conduct studies of potential measures to mitigate the adverse impacts of energy projects on military operations and readiness, or to offset the cost of actual measures undertaken by the Department of Defense to mitigate adverse impacts of approved energy projects on military operations and readiness.

MILITARY CONSTRUCTION

The Military Construction Program provides facilities required for new weapon systems entering the Department's inventory, including aircraft and naval vessels, and other high priority initiatives. The Program continues to invest in global defense posture initiatives, improve living and working conditions, reduce operating costs, and increase productivity. Further, the Program supports energy resiliency and adaptation by replacing or upgrading facilities which are functionally obsolete or can be made more efficient through economical improvements and that enhance mission resiliency and operational capabilities through innovation and investments to increase the Department's contingency preparedness while reducing climate impacts. Also, included in this request are resources required to clean up and dispose of property consistent with the five closure rounds required by the prior Base Realignment and Closure Acts.

Resources presented under the Military Construction title contribute primarily to achieving the Department's annual performance goals of assuring readiness and sustainability.

Federal Funds

MILITARY CONSTRUCTION, ARMY

For acquisition, construction, installation, and equipment of temporary or permanent public works, military installations, facilities, and real property for the Army as currently authorized by law, including personnel in the Army Corps of Engineers and other personal services necessary for the purposes of this appropriation, and for construction and operation of facilities in support of the functions of the Commander in Chief, $845,565,000, to remain available until September 30, 2027: Provided, That, of this amount, not to exceed $193,151,000 shall be available for study, planning, design, architect and engineer services, and host nation support, as authorized by law, unless the Secretary of the Army determines that additional obligations are necessary for such purposes and notifies the Committees on Appropriations of both Houses of Congress of the determination and the reasons therefor.

Note.—A full-year 2022 appropriation for this account was not enacted at the time the Budget was prepared; therefore, the Budget assumes this account is operating under the Continuing Appropriations Act, 2022 (Division A of Public Law 117–43, as amended). The amounts included for 2022 reflect the annualized level provided by the continuing resolution.

Program and Financing (in millions of dollars)

Identification code 021–2050–0–1–051	2021 actual	2022 est.	2023 est.
Obligations by program activity:			
0001 Major construction	1,103	770	558
0002 Minor construction	12	43	73
0003 Planning	106	170	174
0004 Supporting activities	1		
0020 Undistributed		95	
0799 Total direct obligations	1,222	1,078	805
0801 Reimbursable program activity	4,514	7,071	6,861
0900 Total new obligations, unexpired accounts	5,736	8,149	7,666
Budgetary resources:			
Unobligated balance:			
1000 Unobligated balance brought forward, Oct 1	3,930	4,169	2,540
1010 Unobligated balance transfer to other accts [097–0803]	–35		
1011 Unobligated balance transfer from other acct [057–3300]	14		
1011 Unobligated balance transfer from other acct [097–0803]	36		
1021 Recoveries of prior year unpaid obligations	180		
1033 Recoveries of prior year paid obligations	12		
1070 Unobligated balance (total)	4,137	4,169	2,540
Budget authority:			
Appropriations, discretionary:			
1100 Appropriation	930	835	846
1100 Appropriation		95	
1160 Appropriation, discretionary (total)	930	930	846
Spending authority from offsetting collections, discretionary:			
1700 Collected	4,929	5,590	7,071
1701 Change in uncollected payments, Federal sources	–66		
1750 Spending auth from offsetting collections, disc (total)	4,863	5,590	7,071
1900 Budget authority (total)	5,793	6,520	7,917
1930 Total budgetary resources available	9,930	10,689	10,457
Memorandum (non-add) entries:			
1940 Unobligated balance expiring	–25		
1941 Unexpired unobligated balance, end of year	4,169	2,540	2,791
Change in obligated balance:			
Unpaid obligations:			
3000 Unpaid obligations, brought forward, Oct 1	10,716	10,029	10,116
3010 New obligations, unexpired accounts	5,736	8,149	7,666
3011 Obligations ("upward adjustments"), expired accounts	155		
3020 Outlays (gross)	–6,229	–8,062	–9,453
3040 Recoveries of prior year unpaid obligations, unexpired	–180		
3041 Recoveries of prior year unpaid obligations, expired	–169		
3050 Unpaid obligations, end of year	10,029	10,116	8,329
Uncollected payments:			
3060 Uncollected pymts, Fed sources, brought forward, Oct 1	–10,929	–10,611	–10,611
3070 Change in uncollected pymts, Fed sources, unexpired	66		
3071 Change in uncollected pymts, Fed sources, expired	252		
3090 Uncollected pymts, Fed sources, end of year	–10,611	–10,611	–10,611
Memorandum (non-add) entries:			
3100 Obligated balance, start of year	–213	–582	–495
3200 Obligated balance, end of year	–582	–495	–2,282
Budget authority and outlays, net:			
Discretionary:			
4000 Budget authority, gross	5,793	6,520	7,917
Outlays, gross:			
4010 Outlays from new discretionary authority	601	5,599	7,079
4011 Outlays from discretionary balances	5,628	2,463	2,374
4020 Outlays, gross (total)	6,229	8,062	9,453
Offsets against gross budget authority and outlays:			
Offsetting collections (collected) from:			
4030 Federal sources	–5,100	–5,590	–7,071
4033 Non-Federal sources	–74		
4040 Offsets against gross budget authority and outlays (total)	–5,174	–5,590	–7,071

DEPARTMENT OF DEFENSE—MILITARY PROGRAMS

		2021 actual	2022 est.	2023 est.
	Additional offsets against gross budget authority only:			
4050	Change in uncollected pymts, Fed sources, unexpired	66		
4052	Offsetting collections credited to expired accounts	233		
4053	Recoveries of prior year paid obligations, unexpired accounts	12		
4060	Additional offsets against budget authority only (total)	311		
4070	Budget authority, net (discretionary)	930	930	846
4080	Outlays, net (discretionary)	1,055	2,472	2,382
4180	Budget authority, net (total)	930	930	846
4190	Outlays, net (total)	1,055	2,472	2,382

Object Classification (in millions of dollars)

Identification code 021–2050–0–1–051		2021 actual	2022 est.	2023 est.
	Direct obligations:			
32.0	Land and structures	1,222	983	805
92.0	Undistributed		95	
99.0	Direct obligations	1,222	1,078	805
99.0	Reimbursable obligations	4,514	7,071	6,861
99.9	Total new obligations, unexpired accounts	5,736	8,149	7,666

Employment Summary

Identification code 021–2050–0–1–051	2021 actual	2022 est.	2023 est.
2001 Reimbursable civilian full-time equivalent employment	502	1,415	1,415

MILITARY CONSTRUCTION, NAVY AND MARINE CORPS

For acquisition, construction, installation, and equipment of temporary or permanent public works, naval installations, facilities, and real property for the Navy and Marine Corps as currently authorized by law, including personnel in the Naval Facilities Engineering Command and other personal services necessary for the purposes of this appropriation, $3,752,391,000, to remain available until September 30, 2027: Provided, That, of this amount, not to exceed $397,124,000 shall be available for study, planning, design, and architect and engineer services, as authorized by law, unless the Secretary of the Navy determines that additional obligations are necessary for such purposes and notifies the Committees on Appropriations of both Houses of Congress of the determination and the reasons therefor.

Note.—A full-year 2022 appropriation for this account was not enacted at the time the Budget was prepared; therefore, the Budget assumes this account is operating under the Continuing Appropriations Act, 2022 (Division A of Public Law 117–43, as amended). The amounts included for 2022 reflect the annualized level provided by the continuing resolution.

Program and Financing (in millions of dollars)

Identification code 017–1205–0–1–051		2021 actual	2022 est.	2023 est.
	Obligations by program activity:			
0001	Major construction	2,765	2,668	3,327
0002	Minor construction	39	67	124
0003	Planning	250	319	367
0020	Undistributed		–480	
0799	Total direct obligations	3,054	2,574	3,818
0801	Reimbursable program activity	383	180	184
0900	Total new obligations, unexpired accounts	3,437	2,754	4,002
	Budgetary resources:			
	Unobligated balance:			
1000	Unobligated balance brought forward, Oct 1	4,778	3,916	3,230
1010	Unobligated balance transfer to other accts [097–9999]	–1		
1011	Unobligated balance transfer from other acct [097–9999]	1		
1021	Recoveries of prior year unpaid obligations	485		
1070	Unobligated balance (total)	5,263	3,916	3,230
	Budget authority:			
	Appropriations, discretionary:			
1100	Appropriation	1,936	2,368	3,752
1100	Appropriation		–432	
1131	Unobligated balance of appropriations permanently reduced	–48	–48	
1160	Appropriation, discretionary (total)	1,888	1,888	3,752
	Spending authority from offsetting collections, discretionary:			
1700	Collected	561	180	184
1701	Change in uncollected payments, Federal sources	–171		
1750	Spending auth from offsetting collections, disc (total)	390	180	184
1900	Budget authority (total)	2,278	2,068	3,936
1930	Total budgetary resources available	7,541	5,984	7,166
	Memorandum (non-add) entries:			
1940	Unobligated balance expiring	–188		
1941	Unexpired unobligated balance, end of year	3,916	3,230	3,164
	Change in obligated balance:			
	Unpaid obligations:			
3000	Unpaid obligations, brought forward, Oct 1	6,544	6,274	6,184
3010	New obligations, unexpired accounts	3,437	2,754	4,002
3011	Obligations ("upward adjustments"), expired accounts	352		
3020	Outlays (gross)	–3,310	–2,844	–2,759
3040	Recoveries of prior year unpaid obligations, unexpired	–485		
3041	Recoveries of prior year unpaid obligations, expired	–264		
3050	Unpaid obligations, end of year	6,274	6,184	7,427
	Uncollected payments:			
3060	Uncollected pymts, Fed sources, brought forward, Oct 1	–363	–89	–89
3070	Change in uncollected pymts, Fed sources, unexpired	171		
3071	Change in uncollected pymts, Fed sources, expired	103		
3090	Uncollected pymts, Fed sources, end of year	–89	–89	–89
	Memorandum (non-add) entries:			
3100	Obligated balance, start of year	6,181	6,185	6,095
3200	Obligated balance, end of year	6,185	6,095	7,338
	Budget authority and outlays, net:			
	Discretionary:			
4000	Budget authority, gross	2,278	2,068	3,936
	Outlays, gross:			
4010	Outlays from new discretionary authority	134	269	222
4011	Outlays from discretionary balances	3,176	2,575	2,537
4020	Outlays, gross (total)	3,310	2,844	2,759
	Offsets against gross budget authority and outlays:			
	Offsetting collections (collected) from:			
4030	Federal sources	–439	–180	–184
4033	Non-Federal sources	–195		
4040	Offsets against gross budget authority and outlays (total)	–634	–180	–184
	Additional offsets against gross budget authority only:			
4050	Change in uncollected pymts, Fed sources, unexpired	171		
4052	Offsetting collections credited to expired accounts	73		
4060	Additional offsets against budget authority only (total)	244		
4070	Budget authority, net (discretionary)	1,888	1,888	3,752
4080	Outlays, net (discretionary)	2,676	2,664	2,575
4180	Budget authority, net (total)	1,888	1,888	3,752
4190	Outlays, net (total)	2,676	2,664	2,575

Object Classification (in millions of dollars)

Identification code 017–1205–0–1–051		2021 actual	2022 est.	2023 est.
	Direct obligations:			
32.0	Land and structures	3,054	3,054	3,818
92.0	Undistributed		–480	
99.0	Direct obligations	3,054	2,574	3,818
99.0	Reimbursable obligations	383	180	184
99.9	Total new obligations, unexpired accounts	3,437	2,754	4,002

MILITARY CONSTRUCTION, AIR FORCE

For acquisition, construction, installation, and equipment of temporary or permanent public works, military installations, facilities, and real property for the Air Force as currently authorized by law, $2,055,456,000, to remain available until September 30, 2027: Provided, That, of this amount, not to exceed $135,794,000 shall be available for study, planning, design, and architect and engineer services, as authorized by law, unless the Secretary of the Air Force determines that additional obligations are necessary for such purposes and notifies the Committees on Appropriations of both Houses of Congress of the determination and the reasons therefor.

Note.—A full-year 2022 appropriation for this account was not enacted at the time the Budget was prepared; therefore, the Budget assumes this account is operating under the Continuing Appropriations Act, 2022 (Division A of Public Law 117–43, as amended). The amounts included for 2022 reflect the annualized level provided by the continuing resolution.

MILITARY CONSTRUCTION, AIR FORCE—Continued

Program and Financing (in millions of dollars)

Identification code 057–3300–0–1–051		2021 actual	2022 est.	2023 est.
	Obligations by program activity:			
0001	Major construction	1,416	1,469	1,868
0002	Minor construction	55	67	64
0003	Planning	220	242	164
0020	Undistributed		–1,093	
0799	Total direct obligations	1,691	685	2,096
0900	Total new obligations, unexpired accounts	1,691	685	2,096
	Budgetary resources:			
	Unobligated balance:			
1000	Unobligated balance brought forward, Oct 1	7,024	6,324	6,649
1010	Unobligated balance transfer to other accts [021–2050]	–14		
1011	Unobligated balance transfer from other acct [097–0803]	11		
1021	Recoveries of prior year unpaid obligations	26		
1070	Unobligated balance (total)	7,047	6,324	6,649
	Budget authority:			
	Appropriations, discretionary:			
1100	Appropriation	1,020	2,103	2,055
1100	Appropriation		–1,083	
1131	Unobligated balance of appropriations permanently reduced	–10	–10	
1160	Appropriation, discretionary (total)	1,010	1,010	2,055
1900	Budget authority (total)	1,010	1,010	2,055
1930	Total budgetary resources available	8,057	7,334	8,704
	Memorandum (non-add) entries:			
1940	Unobligated balance expiring	–42		
1941	Unexpired unobligated balance, end of year	6,324	6,649	6,608
	Change in obligated balance:			
	Unpaid obligations:			
3000	Unpaid obligations, brought forward, Oct 1	3,292	3,289	1,046
3010	New obligations, unexpired accounts	1,691	685	2,096
3011	Obligations ("upward adjustments"), expired accounts	32		
3020	Outlays (gross)	–1,693	–2,928	–2,039
3040	Recoveries of prior year unpaid obligations, unexpired	–26		
3041	Recoveries of prior year unpaid obligations, expired	–7		
3050	Unpaid obligations, end of year	3,289	1,046	1,103
	Memorandum (non-add) entries:			
3100	Obligated balance, start of year	3,292	3,289	1,046
3200	Obligated balance, end of year	3,289	1,046	1,103
	Budget authority and outlays, net:			
	Discretionary:			
4000	Budget authority, gross	1,010	1,010	2,055
	Outlays, gross:			
4010	Outlays from new discretionary authority	18	279	41
4011	Outlays from discretionary balances	1,675	2,649	1,998
4020	Outlays, gross (total)	1,693	2,928	2,039
	Offsets against gross budget authority and outlays:			
	Offsetting collections (collected) from:			
4030	Federal sources	–6		
4040	Offsets against gross budget authority and outlays (total)	–6		
	Additional offsets against gross budget authority only:			
4052	Offsetting collections credited to expired accounts	6		
4060	Additional offsets against budget authority only (total)	6		
4070	Budget authority, net (discretionary)	1,010	1,010	2,055
4080	Outlays, net (discretionary)	1,687	2,928	2,039
4180	Budget authority, net (total)	1,010	1,010	2,055
4190	Outlays, net (total)	1,687	2,928	2,039

Object Classification (in millions of dollars)

Identification code 057–3300–0–1–051		2021 actual	2022 est.	2023 est.
	Direct obligations:			
32.0	Land and structures	1,691	1,778	2,096
92.0	Undistributed		–1,093	
99.0	Direct obligations	1,691	685	2,096
99.9	Total new obligations, unexpired accounts	1,691	685	2,096

MILITARY CONSTRUCTION, DEFENSE-WIDE

(INCLUDING TRANSFER OF FUNDS)

For acquisition, construction, installation, and equipment of temporary or permanent public works, installations, facilities, and real property for activities and agencies of the Department of Defense (other than the military departments), as currently authorized by law, $2,416,398,000, to remain available until September 30, 2027: Provided, That such amounts of this appropriation as may be determined by the Secretary of Defense may be transferred to such appropriations of the Department of Defense available for military construction or family housing as the Secretary may designate, to be merged with and to be available for the same purposes, and for the same time period, as the appropriation or fund to which transferred: Provided further, That, of the amount, not to exceed $422,377,000 shall be available for study, planning, design, and architect and engineer services, as authorized by law, unless the Secretary of Defense determines that additional obligations are necessary for such purposes and notifies the Committees on Appropriations of both Houses of Congress of the determination and the reasons therefor.

Note.—A full-year 2022 appropriation for this account was not enacted at the time the Budget was prepared; therefore, the Budget assumes this account is operating under the Continuing Appropriations Act, 2022 (Division A of Public Law 117–43, as amended). The amounts included for 2022 reflect the annualized level provided by the continuing resolution.

Program and Financing (in millions of dollars)

Identification code 097–0500–0–1–051		2021 actual	2022 est.	2023 est.
	Obligations by program activity:			
0001	Major construction	2,037	1,963	1,961
0002	Minor construction	65	78	106
0003	Planning	176	273	406
0020	Undistributed		55	
0900	Total new obligations, unexpired accounts	2,278	2,369	2,473
	Budgetary resources:			
	Unobligated balance:			
1000	Unobligated balance brought forward, Oct 1	3,286	2,999	2,642
1010	Unobligated balance transfer to other accts [097–0803]	–10		
1011	Unobligated balance transfer from other acct [097–0803]	47		
1021	Recoveries of prior year unpaid obligations	49		
1033	Recoveries of prior year paid obligations	1		
1070	Unobligated balance (total)	3,373	2,999	2,642
	Budget authority:			
	Appropriations, discretionary:			
1100	Appropriation	2,173	1,957	2,416
1100	Appropriation		216	
1131	Unobligated balance of appropriations permanently reduced	–161	–161	
1160	Appropriation, discretionary (total)	2,012	2,012	2,416
1900	Budget authority (total)	2,012	2,012	2,416
1930	Total budgetary resources available	5,385	5,011	5,058
	Memorandum (non-add) entries:			
1940	Unobligated balance expiring	–108		
1941	Unexpired unobligated balance, end of year	2,999	2,642	2,585
	Change in obligated balance:			
	Unpaid obligations:			
3000	Unpaid obligations, brought forward, Oct 1	5,448	5,356	6,282
3010	New obligations, unexpired accounts	2,278	2,369	2,473
3011	Obligations ("upward adjustments"), expired accounts	289		
3020	Outlays (gross)	–2,502	–1,443	–2,267
3040	Recoveries of prior year unpaid obligations, unexpired	–49		
3041	Recoveries of prior year unpaid obligations, expired	–108		
3050	Unpaid obligations, end of year	5,356	6,282	6,488
	Uncollected payments:			
3060	Uncollected pymts, Fed sources, brought forward, Oct 1	–1	–1	–1
3090	Uncollected pymts, Fed sources, end of year	–1	–1	–1
	Memorandum (non-add) entries:			
3100	Obligated balance, start of year	5,447	5,355	6,281
3200	Obligated balance, end of year	5,355	6,281	6,487
	Budget authority and outlays, net:			
	Discretionary:			
4000	Budget authority, gross	2,012	2,012	2,416
	Outlays, gross:			
4010	Outlays from new discretionary authority	32	50	60
4011	Outlays from discretionary balances	2,470	1,393	2,207
4020	Outlays, gross (total)	2,502	1,443	2,267

DEPARTMENT OF DEFENSE—MILITARY PROGRAMS

Military Construction—Continued
Federal Funds—Continued

		2021 actual	2022 est.	2023 est.
	Offsets against gross budget authority and outlays:			
	Offsetting collections (collected) from:			
4030	Federal sources	–2		
4033	Non-Federal sources	–12		
4040	Offsets against gross budget authority and outlays (total)	–14		
	Additional offsets against gross budget authority only:			
4052	Offsetting collections credited to expired accounts	13		
4053	Recoveries of prior year paid obligations, unexpired accounts	1		
4060	Additional offsets against budget authority only (total)	14		
4070	Budget authority, net (discretionary)	2,012	2,012	2,416
4080	Outlays, net (discretionary)	2,488	1,443	2,267
4180	Budget authority, net (total)	2,012	2,012	2,416
4190	Outlays, net (total)	2,488	1,443	2,267

Object Classification (in millions of dollars)

Identification code 097–0500–0–1–051		2021 actual	2022 est.	2023 est.
	Direct obligations:			
32.0	Land and structures	2,278	2,314	2,473
92.0	Undistributed		55	
99.9	Total new obligations, unexpired accounts	2,278	2,369	2,473

NORTH ATLANTIC TREATY ORGANIZATION SECURITY INVESTMENT PROGRAM

For the United States share of the cost of the North Atlantic Treaty Organization Security Investment Program for the acquisition and construction of military facilities and installations (including international military headquarters) and for related expenses for the collective defense of the North Atlantic Treaty Area as authorized by section 2806 of title 10, United States Code, and Military Construction Authorization Acts, $210,139,000, to remain available until expended.

Note.—A full-year 2022 appropriation for this account was not enacted at the time the Budget was prepared; therefore, the Budget assumes this account is operating under the Continuing Appropriations Act, 2022 (Division A of Public Law 117–43, as amended). The amounts included for 2022 reflect the annualized level provided by the continuing resolution.

Program and Financing (in millions of dollars)

Identification code 097–0804–0–1–051		2021 actual	2022 est.	2023 est.
	Obligations by program activity:			
0001	NATO infrastructure	214	206	210
0020	Undistributed		–33	
0799	Total direct obligations	214	173	210
0801	Reimbursable program activity	23		
0900	Total new obligations, unexpired accounts	237	173	210
	Budgetary resources:			
	Unobligated balance:			
1000	Unobligated balance brought forward, Oct 1	101	108	108
1021	Recoveries of prior year unpaid obligations	71		
1070	Unobligated balance (total)	172	108	108
	Budget authority:			
	Appropriations, discretionary:			
1100	Appropriation	173	206	210
1100	Appropriation		–33	
1160	Appropriation, discretionary (total)	173	173	210
	Spending authority from offsetting collections, discretionary:			
1700	Collected	23		
1701	Change in uncollected payments, Federal sources	–23		
1900	Budget authority (total)	173	173	210
1930	Total budgetary resources available	345	281	318
	Memorandum (non-add) entries:			
1941	Unexpired unobligated balance, end of year	108	108	108
	Change in obligated balance:			
	Unpaid obligations:			
3000	Unpaid obligations, brought forward, Oct 1	935	869	692
3010	New obligations, unexpired accounts	237	173	210
3020	Outlays (gross)	–232	–350	–359
3040	Recoveries of prior year unpaid obligations, unexpired	–71		
3050	Unpaid obligations, end of year	869	692	543
	Uncollected payments:			
3060	Uncollected pymts, Fed sources, brought forward, Oct 1	–23		
3070	Change in uncollected pymts, Fed sources, unexpired	23		
	Memorandum (non-add) entries:			
3100	Obligated balance, start of year	912	869	692
3200	Obligated balance, end of year	869	692	543
	Budget authority and outlays, net:			
	Discretionary:			
4000	Budget authority, gross	173	173	210
	Outlays, gross:			
4010	Outlays from new discretionary authority		78	94
4011	Outlays from discretionary balances	232	272	265
4020	Outlays, gross (total)	232	350	359
	Offsets against gross budget authority and outlays:			
	Offsetting collections (collected) from:			
4030	Federal sources	–23		
4040	Offsets against gross budget authority and outlays (total)	–23		
	Additional offsets against gross budget authority only:			
4050	Change in uncollected pymts, Fed sources, unexpired	23		
4070	Budget authority, net (discretionary)	173	173	210
4080	Outlays, net (discretionary)	209	350	359
4180	Budget authority, net (total)	173	173	210
4190	Outlays, net (total)	209	350	359

Object Classification (in millions of dollars)

Identification code 097–0804–0–1–051		2021 actual	2022 est.	2023 est.
	Direct obligations:			
25.3	Other goods and services from Federal sources	1		
32.0	Land and structures	213	206	210
92.0	Undistributed		–33	
99.0	Direct obligations	214	173	210
99.0	Reimbursable obligations	23		
99.9	Total new obligations, unexpired accounts	237	173	210

MILITARY CONSTRUCTION, ARMY NATIONAL GUARD

For construction, acquisition, expansion, rehabilitation, and conversion of facilities for the training and administration of the Army National Guard, and contributions therefor, as authorized by chapter 1803 of title 10, United States Code, and Military Construction Authorization Acts, $297,278,000, to remain available until September 30, 2027: Provided, That, of the amount, not to exceed $28,245,000 shall be available for study, planning, design, and architect and engineer services, as authorized by law, unless the Director of the Army National Guard determines that additional obligations are necessary for such purposes and notifies the Committees on Appropriations of both Houses of Congress of the determination and the reasons therefor.

Note.—A full-year 2022 appropriation for this account was not enacted at the time the Budget was prepared; therefore, the Budget assumes this account is operating under the Continuing Appropriations Act, 2022 (Division A of Public Law 117–43, as amended). The amounts included for 2022 reflect the annualized level provided by the continuing resolution.

Program and Financing (in millions of dollars)

Identification code 021–2085–0–1–051		2021 actual	2022 est.	2023 est.
	Obligations by program activity:			
0001	Major construction	600	235	220
0002	Minor construction	22	42	37
0003	Planning	32	30	26
0020	Undistributed		142	
0900	Total new obligations, unexpired accounts	654	449	283
	Budgetary resources:			
	Unobligated balance:			
1000	Unobligated balance brought forward, Oct 1	884	870	820
1021	Recoveries of prior year unpaid obligations	244		
1070	Unobligated balance (total)	1,128	870	820
	Budget authority:			
	Appropriations, discretionary:			
1100	Appropriation	399	257	297
1100	Appropriation		142	
1160	Appropriation, discretionary (total)	399	399	297
1900	Budget authority (total)	399	399	297
1930	Total budgetary resources available	1,527	1,269	1,117

295

MILITARY CONSTRUCTION, ARMY NATIONAL GUARD—Continued

Program and Financing—Continued

Identification code 021–2085–0–1–051	2021 actual	2022 est.	2023 est.
Memorandum (non-add) entries:			
1940 Unobligated balance expiring	–3		
1941 Unexpired unobligated balance, end of year	870	820	834
Change in obligated balance:			
Unpaid obligations:			
3000 Unpaid obligations, brought forward, Oct 1	444	613	566
3010 New obligations, unexpired accounts	654	449	283
3011 Obligations ("upward adjustments"), expired accounts	46		
3020 Outlays (gross)	–238	–496	–494
3040 Recoveries of prior year unpaid obligations, unexpired	–244		
3041 Recoveries of prior year unpaid obligations, expired	–49		
3050 Unpaid obligations, end of year	613	566	355
Memorandum (non-add) entries:			
3100 Obligated balance, start of year	444	613	566
3200 Obligated balance, end of year	613	566	355
Budget authority and outlays, net:			
Discretionary:			
4000 Budget authority, gross	399	399	297
Outlays, gross:			
4010 Outlays from new discretionary authority	1	8	6
4011 Outlays from discretionary balances	237	488	488
4020 Outlays, gross (total)	238	496	494
4180 Budget authority, net (total)	399	399	297
4190 Outlays, net (total)	238	496	494

Object Classification (in millions of dollars)

Identification code 021–2085–0–1–051	2021 actual	2022 est.	2023 est.
Direct obligations:			
32.0 Land and structures	654	307	283
92.0 Undistributed		142	
99.9 Total new obligations, unexpired accounts	654	449	283

MILITARY CONSTRUCTION, AIR NATIONAL GUARD

For construction, acquisition, expansion, rehabilitation, and conversion of facilities for the training and administration of the Air National Guard, and contributions therefor, as authorized by chapter 1803 of title 10, United States Code, and Military Construction Authorization Acts, $148,883,000, to remain available until September 30, 2027: Provided, That, of the amount, not to exceed $28,412,000 shall be available for study, planning, design, and architect and engineer services, as authorized by law, unless the Director of the Air National Guard determines that additional obligations are necessary for such purposes and notifies the Committees on Appropriations of both Houses of Congress of the determination and the reasons therefor.

Note.—A full-year 2022 appropriation for this account was not enacted at the time the Budget was prepared; therefore, the Budget assumes this account is operating under the Continuing Appropriations Act, 2022 (Division A of Public Law 117–43, as amended). The amounts included for 2022 reflect the annualized level provided by the continuing resolution.

Program and Financing (in millions of dollars)

Identification code 057–3830–0–1–051	2021 actual	2022 est.	2023 est.
Obligations by program activity:			
0001 Major construction	170	130	99
0002 Minor construction	20	23	40
0003 Planning	13	14	25
0020 Undistributed		–104	
0900 Total new obligations, unexpired accounts	203	63	164
Budgetary resources:			
Unobligated balance:			
1000 Unobligated balance brought forward, Oct 1	374	271	302
1021 Recoveries of prior year unpaid obligations	12		
1070 Unobligated balance (total)	386	271	302
Budget authority:			
Appropriations, discretionary:			
1100 Appropriation	94	198	149
1100 Appropriation		–104	
1160 Appropriation, discretionary (total)	94	94	149
1900 Budget authority (total)	94	94	149
1930 Total budgetary resources available	480	365	451
Memorandum (non-add) entries:			
1940 Unobligated balance expiring	–6		
1941 Unexpired unobligated balance, end of year	271	302	287
Change in obligated balance:			
Unpaid obligations:			
3000 Unpaid obligations, brought forward, Oct 1	225	287	176
3010 New obligations, unexpired accounts	203	63	164
3011 Obligations ("upward adjustments"), expired accounts	1		
3020 Outlays (gross)	–130	–174	–128
3040 Recoveries of prior year unpaid obligations, unexpired	–12		
3050 Unpaid obligations, end of year	287	176	212
Memorandum (non-add) entries:			
3100 Obligated balance, start of year	225	287	176
3200 Obligated balance, end of year	287	176	212
Budget authority and outlays, net:			
Discretionary:			
4000 Budget authority, gross	94	94	149
Outlays, gross:			
4010 Outlays from new discretionary authority		2	3
4011 Outlays from discretionary balances	130	172	125
4020 Outlays, gross (total)	130	174	128
4180 Budget authority, net (total)	94	94	149
4190 Outlays, net (total)	130	174	128

Object Classification (in millions of dollars)

Identification code 057–3830–0–1–051	2021 actual	2022 est.	2023 est.
Direct obligations:			
32.0 Land and structures	203	167	164
92.0 Undistributed		–104	
99.9 Total new obligations, unexpired accounts	203	63	164

MILITARY CONSTRUCTION, ARMY RESERVE

For construction, acquisition, expansion, rehabilitation, and conversion of facilities for the training and administration of the Army Reserve as authorized by chapter 1803 of title 10, United States Code, and Military Construction Authorization Acts, $99,878,000, to remain available until September 30, 2027: Provided, That, of the amount, not to exceed $9,829,000 shall be available for study, planning, design, and architect and engineer services, as authorized by law, unless the Chief of the Army Reserve determines that additional obligations are necessary for such purposes and notifies the Committees on Appropriations of both Houses of Congress of the determination and the reasons therefor.

Note.—A full-year 2022 appropriation for this account was not enacted at the time the Budget was prepared; therefore, the Budget assumes this account is operating under the Continuing Appropriations Act, 2022 (Division A of Public Law 117–43, as amended). The amounts included for 2022 reflect the annualized level provided by the continuing resolution.

Program and Financing (in millions of dollars)

Identification code 021–2086–0–1–051	2021 actual	2022 est.	2023 est.
Obligations by program activity:			
0001 Major construction	59	60	60
0002 Minor construction	7	9	18
0003 Planning	8	5	8
0020 Undistributed		23	
0900 Total new obligations, unexpired accounts	74	97	86
Budgetary resources:			
Unobligated balance:			
1000 Unobligated balance brought forward, Oct 1	54	67	58
Budget authority:			
Appropriations, discretionary:			
1100 Appropriation	88	65	100
1100 Appropriation		23	
1160 Appropriation, discretionary (total)	88	88	100
1900 Budget authority (total)	88	88	100
1930 Total budgetary resources available	142	155	158

		2021 actual	2022 est.	2023 est.
	Memorandum (non-add) entries:			
1940	Unobligated balance expiring	−1		
1941	Unexpired unobligated balance, end of year	67	58	72
	Change in obligated balance:			
	Unpaid obligations:			
3000	Unpaid obligations, brought forward, Oct 1	178	126	154
3010	New obligations, unexpired accounts	74	97	86
3011	Obligations ("upward adjustments"), expired accounts	4		
3020	Outlays (gross)	−129	−69	−89
3041	Recoveries of prior year unpaid obligations, expired	−1		
3050	Unpaid obligations, end of year	126	154	151
	Memorandum (non-add) entries:			
3100	Obligated balance, start of year	178	126	154
3200	Obligated balance, end of year	126	154	151
	Budget authority and outlays, net:			
	Discretionary:			
4000	Budget authority, gross	88	88	100
	Outlays, gross:			
4010	Outlays from new discretionary authority		3	3
4011	Outlays from discretionary balances	129	66	86
4020	Outlays, gross (total)	129	69	89
4180	Budget authority, net (total)	88	88	100
4190	Outlays, net (total)	129	69	89

Object Classification (in millions of dollars)

Identification code 021–2086–0–1–051	2021 actual	2022 est.	2023 est.
Direct obligations:			
32.0 Land and structures	74	74	86
92.0 Undistributed		23	
99.9 Total new obligations, unexpired accounts	74	97	86

MILITARY CONSTRUCTION, NAVY RESERVE

For construction, acquisition, expansion, rehabilitation, and conversion of facilities for the training and administration of the reserve components of the Navy and Marine Corps as authorized by chapter 1803 of title 10, United States Code, and Military Construction Authorization Acts, $30,337,000, to remain available until September 30, 2027: Provided, That, of the amount, not to exceed $2,590,000 shall be available for study, planning, design, and architect and engineer services, as authorized by law, unless the Secretary of the Navy determines that additional obligations are necessary for such purposes and notifies the Committees on Appropriations of both Houses of Congress of the determination and the reasons therefor.

Note.—A full-year 2022 appropriation for this account was not enacted at the time the Budget was prepared; therefore, the Budget assumes this account is operating under the Continuing Appropriations Act, 2022 (Division A of Public Law 117–43, as amended). The amounts included for 2022 reflect the annualized level provided by the continuing resolution.

Program and Financing (in millions of dollars)

Identification code 017–1235–0–1–051	2021 actual	2022 est.	2023 est.
Obligations by program activity:			
0001 Major construction	52	60	26
0002 Minor construction		13	24
0003 Planning	2	13	7
0020 Undistributed		−1	
0900 Total new obligations, unexpired accounts	54	85	57
Budgetary resources:			
Unobligated balance:			
1000 Unobligated balance brought forward, Oct 1	87	111	97
1021 Recoveries of prior year unpaid obligations	15		
1070 Unobligated balance (total)	102	111	97
Budget authority:			
Appropriations, discretionary:			
1100 Appropriation	71	71	30
1930 Total budgetary resources available	173	182	127
Memorandum (non-add) entries:			
1940 Unobligated balance expiring	−8		
1941 Unexpired unobligated balance, end of year	111	97	70

Military Construction—Continued
Federal Funds—Continued

		2021 actual	2022 est.	2023 est.
	Change in obligated balance:			
	Unpaid obligations:			
3000	Unpaid obligations, brought forward, Oct 1	109	79	97
3010	New obligations, unexpired accounts	54	85	57
3011	Obligations ("upward adjustments"), expired accounts	7		
3020	Outlays (gross)	−70	−67	−65
3040	Recoveries of prior year unpaid obligations, unexpired	−15		
3041	Recoveries of prior year unpaid obligations, expired	−6		
3050	Unpaid obligations, end of year	79	97	89
	Memorandum (non-add) entries:			
3100	Obligated balance, start of year	109	79	97
3200	Obligated balance, end of year	79	97	89
	Budget authority and outlays, net:			
	Discretionary:			
4000	Budget authority, gross	71	71	30
	Outlays, gross:			
4010	Outlays from new discretionary authority		1	1
4011	Outlays from discretionary balances	70	66	64
4020	Outlays, gross (total)	70	67	65
4180	Budget authority, net (total)	71	71	30
4190	Outlays, net (total)	70	67	65

Object Classification (in millions of dollars)

Identification code 017–1235–0–1–051	2021 actual	2022 est.	2023 est.
Direct obligations:			
32.0 Land and structures	54	86	57
92.0 Undistributed		−1	
99.9 Total new obligations, unexpired accounts	54	85	57

MILITARY CONSTRUCTION, AIR FORCE RESERVE

For construction, acquisition, expansion, rehabilitation, and conversion of facilities for the training and administration of the Air Force Reserve as authorized by chapter 1803 of title 10, United States Code, and Military Construction Authorization Acts, $56,623,000, to remain available until September 30, 2027: Provided, That, of the amount, not to exceed $11,773,000 shall be available for study, planning, design, and architect and engineer services, as authorized by law, unless the Chief of the Air Force Reserve determines that additional obligations are necessary for such purposes and notifies the Committees on Appropriations of both Houses of Congress of the determination and the reasons therefor.

Note.—A full-year 2022 appropriation for this account was not enacted at the time the Budget was prepared; therefore, the Budget assumes this account is operating under the Continuing Appropriations Act, 2022 (Division A of Public Law 117–43, as amended). The amounts included for 2022 reflect the annualized level provided by the continuing resolution.

Program and Financing (in millions of dollars)

Identification code 057–3730–0–1–051	2021 actual	2022 est.	2023 est.
Obligations by program activity:			
0001 Major construction	113	72	40
0002 Minor construction		17	13
0003 Planning	4	6	10
0020 Undistributed		−30	
0900 Total new obligations, unexpired accounts	117	65	63
Budgetary resources:			
Unobligated balance:			
1000 Unobligated balance brought forward, Oct 1	184	113	96
Budget authority:			
Appropriations, discretionary:			
1100 Appropriation	48	78	57
1100 Appropriation		−30	
1160 Appropriation, discretionary (total)	48	48	57
1900 Budget authority (total)	48	48	57
1930 Total budgetary resources available	232	161	153
Memorandum (non-add) entries:			
1940 Unobligated balance expiring	−2		
1941 Unexpired unobligated balance, end of year	113	96	90
Change in obligated balance:			
Unpaid obligations:			
3000 Unpaid obligations, brought forward, Oct 1	133	171	137
3010 New obligations, unexpired accounts	117	65	63

MILITARY CONSTRUCTION, AIR FORCE RESERVE—Continued
Program and Financing—Continued

Identification code 057–3730–0–1–051		2021 actual	2022 est.	2023 est.
3011	Obligations ("upward adjustments"), expired accounts	3		
3020	Outlays (gross)	−81	−99	−77
3041	Recoveries of prior year unpaid obligations, expired	−1		
3050	Unpaid obligations, end of year	171	137	123
	Memorandum (non-add) entries:			
3100	Obligated balance, start of year	133	171	137
3200	Obligated balance, end of year	171	137	123
	Budget authority and outlays, net:			
	Discretionary:			
4000	Budget authority, gross	48	48	57
	Outlays, gross:			
4010	Outlays from new discretionary authority		1	1
4011	Outlays from discretionary balances	81	98	76
4020	Outlays, gross (total)	81	99	77
4180	Budget authority, net (total)	48	48	57
4190	Outlays, net (total)	81	99	77

Object Classification (in millions of dollars)

Identification code 057–3730–0–1–051		2021 actual	2022 est.	2023 est.
	Direct obligations:			
32.0	Land and structures	117	95	63
92.0	Undistributed		−30	
99.9	Total new obligations, unexpired accounts	117	65	63

CHEMICAL DEMILITARIZATION CONSTRUCTION, DEFENSE-WIDE
Program and Financing (in millions of dollars)

Identification code 097–0391–0–1–051		2021 actual	2022 est.	2023 est.
	Change in obligated balance:			
	Unpaid obligations:			
3000	Unpaid obligations, brought forward, Oct 1	15	1	
3011	Obligations ("upward adjustments"), expired accounts	3		
3020	Outlays (gross)	−14	−1	
3041	Recoveries of prior year unpaid obligations, expired	−3		
3050	Unpaid obligations, end of year	1		
	Memorandum (non-add) entries:			
3100	Obligated balance, start of year	15	1	
3200	Obligated balance, end of year	1		
	Budget authority and outlays, net:			
	Discretionary:			
	Outlays, gross:			
4011	Outlays from discretionary balances	14	1	
4180	Budget authority, net (total)			
4190	Outlays, net (total)	14	1	

DEPARTMENT OF DEFENSE BASE CLOSURE ACCOUNT

For deposit into the Department of Defense Base Closure Account, established by section 2906(a) of the Defense Base Closure and Realignment Act of 1990 (10 U.S.C. 2687 note), $284,687,000, to remain available until expended.

Note.—A full-year 2022 appropriation for this account was not enacted at the time the Budget was prepared; therefore, the Budget assumes this account is operating under the Continuing Appropriations Act, 2022 (Division A of Public Law 117–43, as amended). The amounts included for 2022 reflect the annualized level provided by the continuing resolution.

Program and Financing (in millions of dollars)

Identification code 097–0516–0–1–051		2021 actual	2022 est.	2023 est.
	Obligations by program activity:			
0001	DoD Base realignment and closure	519	285	285
0020	Undistributed		145	
0900	Total new obligations, unexpired accounts	519	430	285
	Budgetary resources:			
	Unobligated balance:			
1000	Unobligated balance brought forward, Oct 1	429	405	405
1021	Recoveries of prior year unpaid obligations	51		
1033	Recoveries of prior year paid obligations	1		
1070	Unobligated balance (total)	481	405	405
	Budget authority:			
	Appropriations, discretionary:			
1100	Appropriation	480	480	285
1131	Unobligated balance of appropriations permanently reduced	−50	−50	
1160	Appropriation, discretionary (total)	430	430	285
	Spending authority from offsetting collections, discretionary:			
1700	Collected	13		
1900	Budget authority (total)	443	430	285
1930	Total budgetary resources available	924	835	690
	Memorandum (non-add) entries:			
1941	Unexpired unobligated balance, end of year	405	405	405
	Change in obligated balance:			
	Unpaid obligations:			
3000	Unpaid obligations, brought forward, Oct 1	802	899	793
3010	New obligations, unexpired accounts	519	430	285
3020	Outlays (gross)	−371	−536	−435
3040	Recoveries of prior year unpaid obligations, unexpired	−51		
3050	Unpaid obligations, end of year	899	793	643
	Memorandum (non-add) entries:			
3100	Obligated balance, start of year	802	899	793
3200	Obligated balance, end of year	899	793	643
	Budget authority and outlays, net:			
	Discretionary:			
4000	Budget authority, gross	443	430	285
	Outlays, gross:			
4010	Outlays from new discretionary authority	274	171	113
4011	Outlays from discretionary balances	97	365	322
4020	Outlays, gross (total)	371	536	435
	Offsets against gross budget authority and outlays:			
	Offsetting collections (collected) from:			
4033	Non-Federal sources	−14		
4040	Offsets against gross budget authority and outlays (total)	−14		
	Additional offsets against gross budget authority only:			
4053	Recoveries of prior year paid obligations, unexpired accounts	1		
4060	Additional offsets against budget authority only (total)	1		
4070	Budget authority, net (discretionary)	430	430	285
4080	Outlays, net (discretionary)	357	536	435
4180	Budget authority, net (total)	430	430	285
4190	Outlays, net (total)	357	536	435

Object Classification (in millions of dollars)

Identification code 097–0516–0–1–051		2021 actual	2022 est.	2023 est.
11.1	Direct obligations: Personnel compensation: Full-time permanent	7	7	7
11.9	Total personnel compensation	7	7	7
12.1	Civilian personnel benefits	2	2	3
21.0	Travel and transportation of persons	3		2
23.3	Communications, utilities, and miscellaneous charges	1		
25.1	Advisory and assistance services	7	3	3
25.2	Other services from non-Federal sources	7	4	4
25.3	Other goods and services from Federal sources	90	28	30
25.3	Other goods and services from Federal sources	6	3	3
25.4	Operation and maintenance of facilities	161	92	70
25.7	Operation and maintenance of equipment	1		
31.0	Equipment	3	1	1
32.0	Land and structures	230	144	162
41.0	Grants, subsidies, and contributions	1	1	
92.0	Undistributed		145	
99.9	Total new obligations, unexpired accounts	519	430	285

DEPARTMENT OF DEFENSE—MILITARY PROGRAMS

Employment Summary

Identification code 097–0516–0–1–051	2021 actual	2022 est.	2023 est.
1001 Direct civilian full-time equivalent employment	55	52	54

DEPARTMENT OF DEFENSE BASE CLOSURE ACCOUNT 1990

Program and Financing (in millions of dollars)

Identification code 097–0510–0–1–051	2021 actual	2022 est.	2023 est.
Obligations by program activity:			
0004 Base Closure (IV)	9		
0900 Total new obligations, unexpired accounts (object class 32.0)	9		
Budgetary resources:			
Unobligated balance:			
1000 Unobligated balance brought forward, Oct 1	73	82	82
1021 Recoveries of prior year unpaid obligations	18		
1070 Unobligated balance (total)	91	82	82
1930 Total budgetary resources available	91	82	82
Memorandum (non-add) entries:			
1941 Unexpired unobligated balance, end of year	82	82	82
Change in obligated balance:			
Unpaid obligations:			
3000 Unpaid obligations, brought forward, Oct 1	28	10	
3010 New obligations, unexpired accounts	9		
3020 Outlays (gross)	–9	–10	
3040 Recoveries of prior year unpaid obligations, unexpired	–18		
3050 Unpaid obligations, end of year	10		
Uncollected payments:			
3060 Uncollected pymts, Fed sources, brought forward, Oct 1	–14	–14	–14
3090 Uncollected pymts, Fed sources, end of year	–14	–14	–14
Memorandum (non-add) entries:			
3100 Obligated balance, start of year	14	–4	–14
3200 Obligated balance, end of year	–4	–14	–14
Budget authority and outlays, net:			
Discretionary:			
Outlays, gross:			
4011 Outlays from discretionary balances	9	10	
4180 Budget authority, net (total)			
4190 Outlays, net (total)	9	10	

DEPARTMENT OF DEFENSE BASE CLOSURE ACCOUNT 2005

Program and Financing (in millions of dollars)

Identification code 097–0512–0–1–051	2021 actual	2022 est.	2023 est.
Obligations by program activity:			
0001 BRAC 2005	11		
0900 Total new obligations, unexpired accounts (object class 32.0)	11		
Budgetary resources:			
Unobligated balance:			
1000 Unobligated balance brought forward, Oct 1	437	450	450
1021 Recoveries of prior year unpaid obligations	24		
1070 Unobligated balance (total)	461	450	450
1930 Total budgetary resources available	461	450	450
Memorandum (non-add) entries:			
1941 Unexpired unobligated balance, end of year	450	450	450
Change in obligated balance:			
Unpaid obligations:			
3000 Unpaid obligations, brought forward, Oct 1	147	131	81
3010 New obligations, unexpired accounts	11		
3020 Outlays (gross)	–3	–50	–40
3040 Recoveries of prior year unpaid obligations, unexpired	–24		
3050 Unpaid obligations, end of year	131	81	41

Family Housing
Federal Funds 299

	2021 actual	2022 est.	2023 est.
Uncollected payments:			
3060 Uncollected pymts, Fed sources, brought forward, Oct 1	–1	–1	–1
3090 Uncollected pymts, Fed sources, end of year	–1	–1	–1
Memorandum (non-add) entries:			
3100 Obligated balance, start of year	146	130	80
3200 Obligated balance, end of year	130	80	40
Budget authority and outlays, net:			
Discretionary:			
Outlays, gross:			
4011 Outlays from discretionary balances	3	50	40
4180 Budget authority, net (total)			
4190 Outlays, net (total)	3	50	40

FOREIGN CURRENCY FLUCTUATIONS, CONSTRUCTION

Program and Financing (in millions of dollars)

Identification code 097–0803–0–1–051	2021 actual	2022 est.	2023 est.
Budgetary resources:			
Unobligated balance:			
1000 Unobligated balance brought forward, Oct 1	56	125	125
1010 Unobligated balance transfer to other accts [057–3300]	–11		
1010 Unobligated balance transfer to other accts [057–0745]	–30		
1010 Unobligated balance transfer to other accts [021–2050]	–36		
1010 Unobligated balance transfer to other accts [097–0500]	–47		
1010 Unobligated balance transfer to other accts [017–0735]	–2		
1010 Unobligated balance transfer to other accts [057–0740]	–42		
1010 Unobligated balance transfer to other accts [021–0720]	–25		
1010 Unobligated balance transfer to other accts [021–0725]	–14		
1011 Unobligated balance transfer from other acct [057–0740]	19		
1011 Unobligated balance transfer from other acct [021–2050]	35		
1011 Unobligated balance transfer from other acct [097–0500]	10		
1012 Unobligated balance transfers between expired and unexpired accounts	212		
1070 Unobligated balance (total)	125	125	125
1930 Total budgetary resources available	125	125	125
Memorandum (non-add) entries:			
1941 Unexpired unobligated balance, end of year	125	125	125
4180 Budget authority, net (total)			
4190 Outlays, net (total)			

FAMILY HOUSING

The Family Housing Program funds construction, improvements, operations, maintenance, utilities, privatization, and leasing of all military family housing. The Program supports quality of life enhancements and initiatives to reduce operating costs and conserve energy by upgrading or replacing facilities.

The Family Housing Improvement Fund (FHIF) and the Military Unaccompanied Housing Improvement Fund (MUHIF) finance the use of authorities authorized in the National Defense Authorization Act for Fiscal Year 1996 (Public Law 104–106) to support of the Military Housing Privatization Initiative (MHPI). Funds which are required to support the MHPI are transferred from the military departments' family housing construction accounts into the FHIF and from the military departments' construction accounts into the MUHIF.

Resources presented under the Family Housing title contribute primarily to achieving the Department's annual performance goals of assuring readiness and sustainability.

Federal Funds

FAMILY HOUSING CONSTRUCTION, ARMY

For expenses of family housing for the Army for construction, including acquisition, replacement, addition, expansion, extension, and alteration, as authorized by law, $169,339,000, to remain available until September 30, 2027.

Note.—A full-year 2022 appropriation for this account was not enacted at the time the Budget was prepared; therefore, the Budget assumes this account is operating under the Continuing

FAMILY HOUSING CONSTRUCTION, ARMY—Continued

Appropriations Act, 2022 (Division A of Public Law 117–43, as amended). The amounts included for 2022 reflect the annualized level provided by the continuing resolution.

Program and Financing (in millions of dollars)

Identification code 021–0720–0–1–051		2021 actual	2022 est.	2023 est.
	Obligations by program activity:			
0001	New Construction	149	96	145
0004	Planning and design	11	7	16
0020	Undistributed	....	24	....
0900	Total new obligations, unexpired accounts	160	127	161
	Budgetary resources:			
	Unobligated balance:			
1000	Unobligated balance brought forward, Oct 1	346	329	326
1011	Unobligated balance transfer from other acct [097–0803]	25	....	....
1021	Recoveries of prior year unpaid obligations	1	....	....
1070	Unobligated balance (total)	372	329	326
	Budget authority:			
	Appropriations, discretionary:			
1100	Appropriation	124	100	169
1100	Appropriation	....	24	....
1160	Appropriation, discretionary (total)	124	124	169
1900	Budget authority (total)	124	124	169
1930	Total budgetary resources available	496	453	495
	Memorandum (non-add) entries:			
1940	Unobligated balance expiring	–7	....	....
1941	Unexpired unobligated balance, end of year	329	326	334
	Change in obligated balance:			
	Unpaid obligations:			
3000	Unpaid obligations, brought forward, Oct 1	319	292	223
3010	New obligations, unexpired accounts	160	127	161
3020	Outlays (gross)	–181	–196	–179
3040	Recoveries of prior year unpaid obligations, unexpired	–1	....	....
3041	Recoveries of prior year unpaid obligations, expired	–5	....	....
3050	Unpaid obligations, end of year	292	223	205
	Memorandum (non-add) entries:			
3100	Obligated balance, start of year	319	292	223
3200	Obligated balance, end of year	292	223	205
	Budget authority and outlays, net:			
	Discretionary:			
4000	Budget authority, gross	124	124	169
	Outlays, gross:			
4010	Outlays from new discretionary authority	2	2	3
4011	Outlays from discretionary balances	179	194	176
4020	Outlays, gross (total)	181	196	179
4180	Budget authority, net (total)	124	124	169
4190	Outlays, net (total)	181	196	179

Object Classification (in millions of dollars)

Identification code 021–0720–0–1–051		2021 actual	2022 est.	2023 est.
	Direct obligations:			
32.0	Land and structures	160	103	161
92.0	Undistributed	....	24	....
99.9	Total new obligations, unexpired accounts	160	127	161

FAMILY HOUSING OPERATION AND MAINTENANCE, ARMY

For expenses of family housing for the Army for operation and maintenance, including debt payment, leasing, minor construction, principal and interest charges, and insurance premiums, as authorized by law, $436,411,000.

Note.—A full-year 2022 appropriation for this account was not enacted at the time the Budget was prepared; therefore, the Budget assumes this account is operating under the Continuing Appropriations Act, 2022 (Division A of Public Law 117–43, as amended). The amounts included for 2022 reflect the annualized level provided by the continuing resolution.

Program and Financing (in millions of dollars)

Identification code 021–0725–0–1–051		2021 actual	2022 est.	2023 est.
	Obligations by program activity:			
0005	Utilities	46	44	47
0006	Operation	75	70	79
0007	Leasing	109	128	127
0008	Maintenance	102	111	118
0012	Housing Privatization Support	37	38	65
0020	Undistributed	....	–19	....
0799	Total direct obligations	369	372	436
0801	Reimbursable program activity	3	15	10
0900	Total new obligations, unexpired accounts	372	387	446
	Budgetary resources:			
	Unobligated balance:			
1000	Unobligated balance brought forward, Oct 1	13	21	21
1011	Unobligated balance transfer from other acct [097–0803]	14	....	....
1021	Recoveries of prior year unpaid obligations	1	....	....
1033	Recoveries of prior year paid obligations	1	....	....
1070	Unobligated balance (total)	29	21	21
	Budget authority:			
	Appropriations, discretionary:			
1100	Appropriation	372	391	436
1100	Appropriation	....	–19	....
1160	Appropriation, discretionary (total)	372	372	436
	Spending authority from offsetting collections, discretionary:			
1700	Collected	2	15	10
1701	Change in uncollected payments, Federal sources	1	....	....
1750	Spending auth from offsetting collections, disc (total)	3	15	10
1900	Budget authority (total)	375	387	446
1930	Total budgetary resources available	404	408	467
	Memorandum (non-add) entries:			
1940	Unobligated balance expiring	–11	....	....
1941	Unexpired unobligated balance, end of year	21	21	21
	Change in obligated balance:			
	Unpaid obligations:			
3000	Unpaid obligations, brought forward, Oct 1	334	302	286
3010	New obligations, unexpired accounts	372	387	446
3011	Obligations ("upward adjustments"), expired accounts	6	....	....
3020	Outlays (gross)	–378	–403	–422
3040	Recoveries of prior year unpaid obligations, unexpired	–1	....	....
3041	Recoveries of prior year unpaid obligations, expired	–31	....	....
3050	Unpaid obligations, end of year	302	286	310
	Uncollected payments:			
3060	Uncollected pymts, Fed sources, brought forward, Oct 1	–5	–4	–4
3070	Change in uncollected pymts, Fed sources, unexpired	–1	....	....
3071	Change in uncollected pymts, Fed sources, expired	2	....	....
3090	Uncollected pymts, Fed sources, end of year	–4	–4	–4
	Memorandum (non-add) entries:			
3100	Obligated balance, start of year	329	298	282
3200	Obligated balance, end of year	298	282	306
	Budget authority and outlays, net:			
	Discretionary:			
4000	Budget authority, gross	375	387	446
	Outlays, gross:			
4010	Outlays from new discretionary authority	235	232	268
4011	Outlays from discretionary balances	143	171	154
4020	Outlays, gross (total)	378	403	422
	Offsets against gross budget authority and outlays:			
	Offsetting collections (collected) from:			
4030	Federal sources	....	–15	–10
4033	Non-Federal sources	–4	....	....
4040	Offsets against gross budget authority and outlays (total)	–4	–15	–10
	Additional offsets against gross budget authority only:			
4050	Change in uncollected pymts, Fed sources, unexpired	–1	....	....
4052	Offsetting collections credited to expired accounts	1	....	....
4053	Recoveries of prior year paid obligations, unexpired accounts	1	....	....
4060	Additional offsets against budget authority only (total)	1	....	....
4070	Budget authority, net (discretionary)	372	372	436
4080	Outlays, net (discretionary)	374	388	412
4180	Budget authority, net (total)	372	372	436
4190	Outlays, net (total)	374	388	412

Object Classification (in millions of dollars)

Identification code 021–0725–0–1–051		2021 actual	2022 est.	2023 est.
	Direct obligations:			
	Personnel compensation:			
11.1	Full-time permanent	30	31	32
11.3	Other than full-time permanent	2	2	2
11.5	Other personnel compensation	1	1	1
11.9	Total personnel compensation	33	34	35
12.1	Civilian personnel benefits	13	13	14
21.0	Travel and transportation of persons	2	2	2
22.0	Transportation of things	3	3	3
23.1	Rental payments to GSA	1	1	1
23.2	Rental payments to others	97	95	95
23.3	Communications, utilities, and miscellaneous charges	35	39	39
25.1	Advisory and assistance services	5	5	5
25.2	Other services from non-Federal sources	19	21	21
25.3	Other goods and services from Federal sources	14	14	15
25.3	Other goods and services from Federal sources	58	64	64
25.4	Operation and maintenance of facilities	82	92	134
25.7	Operation and maintenance of equipment	6	7	7
31.0	Equipment	1	1	1
92.0	Undistributed		–19	
99.0	Direct obligations	369	372	436
99.0	Reimbursable obligations	3	15	10
99.9	Total new obligations, unexpired accounts	372	387	446

Employment Summary

Identification code 021–0725–0–1–051	2021 actual	2022 est.	2023 est.
1001 Direct civilian full-time equivalent employment	474	474	471

FAMILY HOUSING CONSTRUCTION, NAVY AND MARINE CORPS

For expenses of family housing for the Navy and Marine Corps for construction, including acquisition, replacement, addition, expansion, extension, and alteration, as authorized by law, $337,297,000, to remain available until September 30, 2027.

Note.—A full-year 2022 appropriation for this account was not enacted at the time the Budget was prepared; therefore, the Budget assumes this account is operating under the Continuing Appropriations Act, 2022 (Division A of Public Law 117–43, as amended). The amounts included for 2022 reflect the annualized level provided by the continuing resolution.

Program and Financing (in millions of dollars)

Identification code 017–0730–0–1–051		2021 actual	2022 est.	2023 est.
	Obligations by program activity:			
0001	New Construction	4	10	161
0003	Construction Improvements	75	64	75
0004	Planning and design	2	5	12
0020	Undistributed		–35	
0900	Total new obligations, unexpired accounts	81	44	248
	Budgetary resources:			
	Unobligated balance:			
1000	Unobligated balance brought forward, Oct 1	105	69	68
1021	Recoveries of prior year unpaid obligations	5		
1070	Unobligated balance (total)	110	69	68
	Budget authority:			
	Appropriations, discretionary:			
1100	Appropriation	43	78	337
1100	Appropriation		–35	
1160	Appropriation, discretionary (total)	43	43	337
1930	Total budgetary resources available	153	112	405
	Memorandum (non-add) entries:			
1940	Unobligated balance expiring	–3		
1941	Unexpired unobligated balance, end of year	69	68	157
	Change in obligated balance:			
	Unpaid obligations:			
3000	Unpaid obligations, brought forward, Oct 1	203	197	166
3010	New obligations, unexpired accounts	81	44	248
3011	Obligations ("upward adjustments"), expired accounts	6		
3020	Outlays (gross)	–82	–75	–67
3040	Recoveries of prior year unpaid obligations, unexpired	–5		
3041	Recoveries of prior year unpaid obligations, expired	–6		
3050	Unpaid obligations, end of year	197	166	347
	Memorandum (non-add) entries:			
3100	Obligated balance, start of year	203	197	166
3200	Obligated balance, end of year	197	166	347
	Budget authority and outlays, net:			
	Discretionary:			
4000	Budget authority, gross	43	43	337
	Outlays, gross:			
4010	Outlays from new discretionary authority		1	7
4011	Outlays from discretionary balances	82	74	60
4020	Outlays, gross (total)	82	75	67
4180	Budget authority, net (total)	43	43	337
4190	Outlays, net (total)	82	75	67

Object Classification (in millions of dollars)

Identification code 017–0730–0–1–051		2021 actual	2022 est.	2023 est.
	Direct obligations:			
32.0	Land and structures	81	80	248
92.0	Undistributed		–36	
99.9	Total new obligations, unexpired accounts	81	44	248

FAMILY HOUSING OPERATION AND MAINTENANCE, NAVY AND MARINE CORPS

For expenses of family housing for the Navy and Marine Corps for operation and maintenance, including debt payment, leasing, minor construction, principal and interest charges, and insurance premiums, as authorized by law, $368,224,000.

Note.—A full-year 2022 appropriation for this account was not enacted at the time the Budget was prepared; therefore, the Budget assumes this account is operating under the Continuing Appropriations Act, 2022 (Division A of Public Law 117–43, as amended). The amounts included for 2022 reflect the annualized level provided by the continuing resolution.

Program and Financing (in millions of dollars)

Identification code 017–0735–0–1–051		2021 actual	2022 est.	2023 est.
	Obligations by program activity:			
0005	Utilities	43	56	43
0006	Operation	82	89	92
0007	Leasing	57	63	66
0008	Maintenance	108	95	105
0012	Housing Privatization Support	114	55	62
0020	Undistributed		9	
0799	Total direct obligations	404	367	368
0801	Reimbursable program activity	7	19	19
0900	Total new obligations, unexpired accounts	411	386	387
	Budgetary resources:			
	Unobligated balance:			
1000	Unobligated balance brought forward, Oct 1	43	1	
1011	Unobligated balance transfer from other acct [097–0803]	2		
1021	Recoveries of prior year unpaid obligations	1		
1070	Unobligated balance (total)	46	1	
	Budget authority:			
	Appropriations, discretionary:			
1100	Appropriation	366	357	368
1100	Appropriation		9	
1160	Appropriation, discretionary (total)	366	366	368
	Spending authority from offsetting collections, discretionary:			
1700	Collected	7	19	19
1701	Change in uncollected payments, Federal sources	1		
1750	Spending auth from offsetting collections, disc (total)	8	19	19
1900	Budget authority (total)	374	385	387
1930	Total budgetary resources available	420	386	387
	Memorandum (non-add) entries:			
1940	Unobligated balance expiring	–8		
1941	Unexpired unobligated balance, end of year	1		
	Change in obligated balance:			
	Unpaid obligations:			
3000	Unpaid obligations, brought forward, Oct 1	242	278	235
3010	New obligations, unexpired accounts	411	386	387
3011	Obligations ("upward adjustments"), expired accounts	42		

Family Housing—Continued
Federal Funds—Continued

FAMILY HOUSING OPERATION AND MAINTENANCE, NAVY AND MARINE CORPS—Continued

Program and Financing—Continued

Identification code 017–0735–0–1–051	2021 actual	2022 est.	2023 est.
3020 Outlays (gross)	–367	–429	–397
3040 Recoveries of prior year unpaid obligations, unexpired	–1		
3041 Recoveries of prior year unpaid obligations, expired	–49		
3050 Unpaid obligations, end of year	278	235	225
Uncollected payments:			
3060 Uncollected pymts, Fed sources, brought forward, Oct 1	–3	–2	–2
3070 Change in uncollected pymts, Fed sources, unexpired	–1		
3071 Change in uncollected pymts, Fed sources, expired	2		
3090 Uncollected pymts, Fed sources, end of year	–2	–2	–2
Memorandum (non-add) entries:			
3100 Obligated balance, start of year	239	276	233
3200 Obligated balance, end of year	276	233	223
Budget authority and outlays, net:			
Discretionary:			
4000 Budget authority, gross	374	385	387
Outlays, gross:			
4010 Outlays from new discretionary authority	192	242	243
4011 Outlays from discretionary balances	175	187	154
4020 Outlays, gross (total)	367	429	397
Offsets against gross budget authority and outlays:			
Offsetting collections (collected) from:			
4030 Federal sources	–1	–19	–19
4033 Non-Federal sources	–10		
4040 Offsets against gross budget authority and outlays (total)	–11	–19	–19
Additional offsets against gross budget authority only:			
4050 Change in uncollected pymts, Fed sources, unexpired	–1		
4052 Offsetting collections credited to expired accounts	4		
4060 Additional offsets against budget authority only (total)	3		
4070 Budget authority, net (discretionary)	366	366	368
4080 Outlays, net (discretionary)	356	410	378
4180 Budget authority, net (total)	366	366	368
4190 Outlays, net (total)	356	410	378

Object Classification (in millions of dollars)

Identification code 017–0735–0–1–051	2021 actual	2022 est.	2023 est.
Direct obligations:			
Personnel compensation:			
11.1 Full-time permanent	52	52	60
11.3 Other than full-time permanent		4	
11.5 Other personnel compensation	1	1	1
11.9 Total personnel compensation	53	57	61
12.1 Civilian personnel benefits	15	20	23
21.0 Travel and transportation of persons		1	
22.0 Transportation of things	1	1	
23.2 Rental payments to others	40	37	1
23.3 Communications, utilities, and miscellaneous charges	9	14	70
25.1 Advisory and assistance services	19	17	15
25.2 Other services from non-Federal sources	5		
25.3 Other goods and services from Federal sources	57	76	75
25.3 Other goods and services from Federal sources	2	3	3
25.4 Operation and maintenance of facilities	125	114	115
25.7 Operation and maintenance of equipment	2	1	
26.0 Supplies and materials	4	3	
31.0 Equipment	11	10	5
32.0 Land and structures	61	4	
92.0 Undistributed		9	
99.0 Direct obligations	404	367	368
99.0 Reimbursable obligations	7	19	19
99.9 Total new obligations, unexpired accounts	411	386	387

Employment Summary

Identification code 017–0735–0–1–051	2021 actual	2022 est.	2023 est.
1001 Direct civilian full-time equivalent employment	723	796	826

FAMILY HOUSING CONSTRUCTION, AIR FORCE

For expenses of family housing for the Air Force for construction, including acquisition, replacement, addition, expansion, extension, and alteration, as authorized by law, $232,788,000, to remain available until September 30, 2027.

Note.—A full-year 2022 appropriation for this account was not enacted at the time the Budget was prepared; therefore, the Budget assumes this account is operating under the Continuing Appropriations Act, 2022 (Division A of Public Law 117–43, as amended). The amounts included for 2022 reflect the annualized level provided by the continuing resolution.

Program and Financing (in millions of dollars)

Identification code 057–0740–0–1–051	2021 actual	2022 est.	2023 est.
Obligations by program activity:			
0001 New Construction		44	
0003 Construction Improvements	84	141	269
0004 Planning and design	2	9	7
0020 Undistributed		–19	
0900 Total new obligations, unexpired accounts	86	175	276
Budgetary resources:			
Unobligated balance:			
1000 Unobligated balance brought forward, Oct 1	339	345	267
1010 Unobligated balance transfer to other accts [097–0803]	–19		
1011 Unobligated balance transfer from other acct [097–0803]	42		
1021 Recoveries of prior year unpaid obligations	2		
1070 Unobligated balance (total)	364	345	267
Budget authority:			
Appropriations, discretionary:			
1100 Appropriation	97	116	233
1100 Appropriation		–19	
1160 Appropriation, discretionary (total)	97	97	233
1900 Budget authority (total)	97	97	233
1930 Total budgetary resources available	461	442	500
Memorandum (non-add) entries:			
1940 Unobligated balance expiring	–30		
1941 Unexpired unobligated balance, end of year	345	267	224
Change in obligated balance:			
Unpaid obligations:			
3000 Unpaid obligations, brought forward, Oct 1	109	153	221
3010 New obligations, unexpired accounts	86	175	276
3011 Obligations ("upward adjustments"), expired accounts	4		
3020 Outlays (gross)	–43	–107	–112
3040 Recoveries of prior year unpaid obligations, unexpired	–2		
3041 Recoveries of prior year unpaid obligations, expired	–1		
3050 Unpaid obligations, end of year	153	221	385
Memorandum (non-add) entries:			
3100 Obligated balance, start of year	109	153	221
3200 Obligated balance, end of year	153	221	385
Budget authority and outlays, net:			
Discretionary:			
4000 Budget authority, gross	97	97	233
Outlays, gross:			
4010 Outlays from new discretionary authority		2	5
4011 Outlays from discretionary balances	43	105	107
4020 Outlays, gross (total)	43	107	112
Offsets against gross budget authority and outlays:			
Offsetting collections (collected) from:			
4033 Non-Federal sources	–1		
4040 Offsets against gross budget authority and outlays (total)	–1		
Additional offsets against gross budget authority only:			
4052 Offsetting collections credited to expired accounts	1		
4060 Additional offsets against budget authority only (total)	1		
4070 Budget authority, net (discretionary)	97	97	233
4080 Outlays, net (discretionary)	42	107	112
4180 Budget authority, net (total)	97	97	233
4190 Outlays, net (total)	42	107	112

Object Classification (in millions of dollars)

Identification code 057–0740–0–1–051	2021 actual	2022 est.	2023 est.
Direct obligations:			
32.0 Land and structures	86	194	276
92.0 Undistributed		–19	

DEPARTMENT OF DEFENSE—MILITARY PROGRAMS

		2021 actual	2022 est.	2023 est.
99.9	Total new obligations, unexpired accounts	86	175	276

FAMILY HOUSING OPERATION AND MAINTENANCE, AIR FORCE

For expenses of family housing for the Air Force for operation and maintenance, including debt payment, leasing, minor construction, principal and interest charges, and insurance premiums, as authorized by law, $355,222,000.

Note.—A full-year 2022 appropriation for this account was not enacted at the time the Budget was prepared; therefore, the Budget assumes this account is operating under the Continuing Appropriations Act, 2022 (Division A of Public Law 117–43, as amended). The amounts included for 2022 reflect the annualized level provided by the continuing resolution.

Program and Financing (in millions of dollars)

Identification code 057–0745–0–1–051		2021 actual	2022 est.	2023 est.
	Obligations by program activity:			
0005	Utilities	45	44	46
0006	Operation	104	107	117
0007	Leasing	10	10	8
0008	Maintenance	151	142	150
0012	Housing Privatization support	20	23	34
0020	Undistributed		12	
0799	Total direct obligations	330	338	355
0801	Reimbursable program activity	3	6	3
0900	Total new obligations, unexpired accounts	333	344	358
	Budgetary resources:			
	Unobligated balance:			
1000	Unobligated balance brought forward, Oct 1	26	19	18
1011	Unobligated balance transfer from other acct [097–0803]	30		
1021	Recoveries of prior year unpaid obligations	1		
1070	Unobligated balance (total)	57	19	18
	Budget authority:			
	Appropriations, discretionary:			
1100	Appropriation	337	325	355
1100	Appropriation		12	
1160	Appropriation, discretionary (total)	337	337	355
	Spending authority from offsetting collections, discretionary:			
1700	Collected	2	6	3
1701	Change in uncollected payments, Federal sources	1		
1750	Spending auth from offsetting collections, disc (total)	3	6	3
1900	Budget authority (total)	340	343	358
1930	Total budgetary resources available	397	362	376
	Memorandum (non-add) entries:			
1940	Unobligated balance expiring	–45		
1941	Unexpired unobligated balance, end of year	19	18	18
	Change in obligated balance:			
	Unpaid obligations:			
3000	Unpaid obligations, brought forward, Oct 1	351	390	400
3010	New obligations, unexpired accounts	333	344	358
3011	Obligations ("upward adjustments"), expired accounts	26		
3020	Outlays (gross)	–290	–334	–362
3040	Recoveries of prior year unpaid obligations, unexpired	–1		
3041	Recoveries of prior year unpaid obligations, expired	–29		
3050	Unpaid obligations, end of year	390	400	396
	Uncollected payments:			
3060	Uncollected pymts, Fed sources, brought forward, Oct 1		–1	–1
3070	Change in uncollected pymts, Fed sources, unexpired	–1		
3090	Uncollected pymts, Fed sources, end of year	–1	–1	–1
	Memorandum (non-add) entries:			
3100	Obligated balance, start of year	351	389	399
3200	Obligated balance, end of year	389	399	395
	Budget authority and outlays, net:			
	Discretionary:			
4000	Budget authority, gross	340	343	358
	Outlays, gross:			
4010	Outlays from new discretionary authority	141	137	143
4011	Outlays from discretionary balances	149	197	219
4020	Outlays, gross (total)	290	334	362
	Offsets against gross budget authority and outlays:			
	Offsetting collections (collected) from:			
4030	Federal sources	–1	–6	–3
4033	Non-Federal sources	–4		
4040	Offsets against gross budget authority and outlays (total)	–5	–6	–3
	Additional offsets against gross budget authority only:			
4050	Change in uncollected pymts, Fed sources, unexpired	–1		
4052	Offsetting collections credited to expired accounts	3		
4060	Additional offsets against budget authority only (total)	2		
4070	Budget authority, net (discretionary)	337	337	355
4080	Outlays, net (discretionary)	285	328	359
4180	Budget authority, net (total)	337	337	355
4190	Outlays, net (total)	285	328	359

Object Classification (in millions of dollars)

Identification code 057–0745–0–1–051		2021 actual	2022 est.	2023 est.
	Direct obligations:			
	Personnel compensation:			
11.1	Full-time permanent	58	53	74
11.3	Other than full-time permanent		2	
11.5	Other personnel compensation	1	4	3
11.9	Total personnel compensation	59	59	77
12.1	Civilian personnel benefits	16	10	10
21.0	Travel and transportation of persons		1	1
22.0	Transportation of things	2	1	1
23.2	Rental payments to others	7	9	7
23.3	Communications, utilities, and miscellaneous charges	20	43	45
25.1	Advisory and assistance services	7	19	11
25.2	Other services from non-Federal sources	10	5	4
25.3	Other goods and services from Federal sources	4		
25.3	Other goods and services from Federal sources		3	3
25.3	Other goods and services from Federal sources			1
25.4	Operation and maintenance of facilities	129	131	149
25.7	Operation and maintenance of equipment	5	3	6
26.0	Supplies and materials	22	8	7
31.0	Equipment	2	1	1
32.0	Land and structures	47	33	33
92.0	Undistributed		12	
99.0	Direct obligations	330	338	356
99.0	Reimbursable obligations	3	6	2
99.9	Total new obligations, unexpired accounts	333	344	358

Employment Summary

Identification code 057–0745–0–1–051		2021 actual	2022 est.	2023 est.
1001	Direct civilian full-time equivalent employment	826	921	921

FAMILY HOUSING OPERATION AND MAINTENANCE, DEFENSE-WIDE

For expenses of family housing for the activities and agencies of the Department of Defense (other than the military departments) for operation and maintenance, leasing, and minor construction, as authorized by law, $50,113,000.

Note.—A full-year 2022 appropriation for this account was not enacted at the time the Budget was prepared; therefore, the Budget assumes this account is operating under the Continuing Appropriations Act, 2022 (Division A of Public Law 117–43, as amended). The amounts included for 2022 reflect the annualized level provided by the continuing resolution.

Program and Financing (in millions of dollars)

Identification code 097–0765–0–1–051		2021 actual	2022 est.	2023 est.
	Obligations by program activity:			
0005	Utilities	4	4	4
0006	Operation	1	1	1
0007	Leasing	49	45	45
0020	Undistributed		5	
0900	Total new obligations, unexpired accounts	54	55	50
	Budgetary resources:			
	Budget authority:			
	Appropriations, discretionary:			
1100	Appropriation	55	50	50
1100	Appropriation		5	
1160	Appropriation, discretionary (total)	55	55	50
1900	Budget authority (total)	55	55	50
1930	Total budgetary resources available	55	55	50

304 Family Housing—Continued
Federal Funds—Continued

THE BUDGET FOR FISCAL YEAR 2023

FAMILY HOUSING OPERATION AND MAINTENANCE, DEFENSE-WIDE—Continued

Program and Financing—Continued

Identification code 097–0765–0–1–051	2021 actual	2022 est.	2023 est.
Memorandum (non-add) entries:			
1940 Unobligated balance expiring	–1		
Change in obligated balance:			
Unpaid obligations:			
3000 Unpaid obligations, brought forward, Oct 1	8	14	22
3010 New obligations, unexpired accounts	54	55	50
3011 Obligations ("upward adjustments"), expired accounts	4		
3020 Outlays (gross)	–47	–47	–49
3041 Recoveries of prior year unpaid obligations, expired	–5		
3050 Unpaid obligations, end of year	14	22	23
Memorandum (non-add) entries:			
3100 Obligated balance, start of year	8	14	22
3200 Obligated balance, end of year	14	22	23
Budget authority and outlays, net:			
Discretionary:			
4000 Budget authority, gross	55	55	50
Outlays, gross:			
4010 Outlays from new discretionary authority	44	39	36
4011 Outlays from discretionary balances	3	8	13
4020 Outlays, gross (total)	47	47	49
4180 Budget authority, net (total)	55	55	50
4190 Outlays, net (total)	47	47	49

Object Classification (in millions of dollars)

Identification code 097–0765–0–1–051	2021 actual	2022 est.	2023 est.
Direct obligations:			
23.2 Rental payments to others	38	40	44
23.3 Communications, utilities, and miscellaneous charges	5	4	4
25.3 Other goods and services from Federal sources	9	6	2
25.4 Operation and maintenance of facilities	2		
92.0 Undistributed		5	
99.9 Total new obligations, unexpired accounts	54	55	50

HOMEOWNERS ASSISTANCE FUND

Program and Financing (in millions of dollars)

Identification code 097–4090–0–3–051	2021 actual	2022 est.	2023 est.
Obligations by program activity:			
0801 Payment to homeowners (private sale and foreclosure assistance)	1		
0900 Total new obligations, unexpired accounts (object class 25.3)	1		
Budgetary resources:			
Unobligated balance:			
1000 Unobligated balance brought forward, Oct 1	50	49	49
1930 Total budgetary resources available	50	49	49
Memorandum (non-add) entries:			
1941 Unexpired unobligated balance, end of year	49	49	49
Change in obligated balance:			
Unpaid obligations:			
3010 New obligations, unexpired accounts	1		
3020 Outlays (gross)	–1		
Budget authority and outlays, net:			
Discretionary:			
Outlays, gross:			
4011 Outlays from discretionary balances	1		
4180 Budget authority, net (total)			
4190 Outlays, net (total)	1		
Memorandum (non-add) entries:			
5090 Unexpired unavailable balance, SOY: Offsetting collections	19	19	19
5092 Unexpired unavailable balance, EOY: Offsetting collections	19	19	19

The Homeowners Assistance Fund finances a program which provides assistance to eligible homeowners by mitigating losses incident to the disposal of a primary residence.

DEPARTMENT OF DEFENSE FAMILY HOUSING IMPROVEMENT FUND

For the Department of Defense Family Housing Improvement Fund, $6,442,000, to remain available until expended, for family housing initiatives undertaken pursuant to section 2883 of title 10, United States Code, providing alternative means of acquiring and improving military family housing and supporting facilities.

Note.—A full-year 2022 appropriation for this account was not enacted at the time the Budget was prepared; therefore, the Budget assumes this account is operating under the Continuing Appropriations Act, 2022 (Division A of Public Law 117–43, as amended). The amounts included for 2022 reflect the annualized level provided by the continuing resolution.

Program and Financing (in millions of dollars)

Identification code 097–0834–0–1–051	2021 actual	2022 est.	2023 est.
Obligations by program activity:			
Credit program obligations:			
0703 Subsidy for modifications of direct loans		4	
0705 Reestimates of direct loan subsidy	49	18	
0706 Interest on reestimates of direct loan subsidy	21	11	
0709 Administrative expenses	6	6	6
0900 Total new obligations, unexpired accounts	76	39	6
Budgetary resources:			
Unobligated balance:			
1000 Unobligated balance brought forward, Oct 1	19	19	15
1001 Discretionary unobligated balance brought fwd, Oct 1	19		
Budget authority:			
Appropriations, discretionary:			
1100 Appropriation	6	6	6
Appropriations, mandatory:			
1200 Appropriation	70	29	
1900 Budget authority (total)	76	35	6
1930 Total budgetary resources available	95	54	21
Memorandum (non-add) entries:			
1941 Unexpired unobligated balance, end of year	19	15	15
Change in obligated balance:			
Unpaid obligations:			
3000 Unpaid obligations, brought forward, Oct 1	34	29	3
3010 New obligations, unexpired accounts	76	39	6
3020 Outlays (gross)	–81	–65	–9
3050 Unpaid obligations, end of year	29	3	
Memorandum (non-add) entries:			
3100 Obligated balance, start of year	34	29	3
3200 Obligated balance, end of year	29	3	
Budget authority and outlays, net:			
Discretionary:			
4000 Budget authority, gross	6	6	6
Outlays, gross:			
4010 Outlays from new discretionary authority		4	4
4011 Outlays from discretionary balances	11	32	5
4020 Outlays, gross (total)	11	36	9
Mandatory:			
4090 Budget authority, gross	70	29	
Outlays, gross:			
4100 Outlays from new mandatory authority	70	29	
4180 Budget authority, net (total)	76	35	6
4190 Outlays, net (total)	81	65	9
Memorandum (non-add) entries:			
5090 Unexpired unavailable balance, SOY: Offsetting collections	22	22	22
5092 Unexpired unavailable balance, EOY: Offsetting collections	22	22	22

Summary of Loan Levels, Subsidy Budget Authority and Outlays by Program (in millions of dollars)

Identification code 097–0834–0–1–051	2021 actual	2022 est.	2023 est.
Direct loan subsidy outlays:			
134001 Family Housing Improvement Fund Direct Loans	8	21	
Direct loan reestimates:			
135001 Family Housing Improvement Fund Direct Loans	60	6	
Guaranteed loan reestimates:			
235001 Family Housing Improvement Fund Guaranteed Loans	–8	–8	

DEPARTMENT OF DEFENSE—MILITARY PROGRAMS

Family Housing—Continued
Federal Funds—Continued

305

	Administrative expense data:	2021 actual	2022 est.	2023 est.
3510	Budget authority	6	6	5
3590	Outlays from new authority	2	6	5

Object Classification (in millions of dollars)

Identification code 097–0834–0–1–051	2021 actual	2022 est.	2023 est.
Direct obligations:			
25.1 Advisory and assistance services	5	6	6
41.0 Grants, subsidies, and contributions	71	33	....
99.9 Total new obligations, unexpired accounts	76	39	6

FAMILY HOUSING IMPROVEMENT DIRECT LOAN FINANCING ACCOUNT

Program and Financing (in millions of dollars)

Identification code 097–4166–0–3–051	2021 actual	2022 est.	2023 est.
Obligations by program activity:			
Credit program obligations:			
0713 Payment of interest to Treasury	63	69	65
0742 Downward reestimates paid to receipt accounts	7	15	....
0743 Interest on downward reestimates	4	8	....
0791 Direct program activities, subtotal	74	92	65
0900 Total new obligations, unexpired accounts	74	92	65
Budgetary resources:			
Financing authority:			
Borrowing authority, mandatory:			
1400 Borrowing authority	22	46	....
Spending authority from offsetting collections, mandatory:			
1800 Collected	168	134	91
1801 Change in uncollected payments, Federal sources	–8	–17	....
1820 Capital transfer of spending authority from offsetting collections to general fund	....	–2	....
1825 Spending authority from offsetting collections applied to repay debt	–108	–69	–26
1850 Spending auth from offsetting collections, mand (total)	52	46	65
1900 Budget authority (total)	74	92	65
1930 Total budgetary resources available	74	92	65
Change in obligated balance:			
Unpaid obligations:			
3000 Unpaid obligations, brought forward, Oct 1	106	74	....
3010 New obligations, unexpired accounts	74	92	65
3020 Outlays (gross)	–106	–166	–65
3050 Unpaid obligations, end of year	74	....	....
Uncollected payments:			
3060 Uncollected pymts, Fed sources, brought forward, Oct 1	–26	–18	–1
3070 Change in uncollected pymts, Fed sources, unexpired	8	17	....
3090 Uncollected pymts, Fed sources, end of year	–18	–1	–1
Memorandum (non-add) entries:			
3100 Obligated balance, start of year	80	56	–1
3200 Obligated balance, end of year	56	–1	–1
Financing authority and disbursements, net:			
Mandatory:			
4090 Budget authority, gross	74	92	65
Financing disbursements:			
4110 Outlays, gross (total)	106	166	65
Offsets against gross financing authority and disbursements:			
Offsetting collections (collected) from:			
4120 Federal sources	–49	–18	....
4120 Federal sources	–21	–11	....
4120 Federal sources	–9	–21	....
4122 Interest on uninvested funds	–3	....	....
4123 Non-Federal sources	–30	–34	–35
4123 Non-Federal sources	–56	–50	–56
4130 Offsets against gross budget authority and outlays (total)	–168	–134	–91
Additional offsets against financing authority only (total):			
4140 Change in uncollected pymts, Fed sources, unexpired	8	17	....
4160 Budget authority, net (mandatory)	–86	–25	–26
4170 Outlays, net (mandatory)	–62	32	–26
4180 Budget authority, net (total)	–86	–25	–26
4190 Outlays, net (total)	–62	32	–26

Status of Direct Loans (in millions of dollars)

Identification code 097–4166–0–3–051	2021 actual	2022 est.	2023 est.
Cumulative balance of direct loans outstanding:			
1210 Outstanding, start of year	1,755	1,757	1,777
1231 Disbursements: Direct loan disbursements	32	67	....
1251 Repayments: Repayments and prepayments	–30	–34	–34
1263 Write-offs for default: Direct loans	....	–6	–10
1264 Other adjustments, net (+ or -)	....	–7	....
1290 Outstanding, end of year	1,757	1,777	1,733

Balance Sheet (in millions of dollars)

Identification code 097–4166–0–3–051	2020 actual	2021 actual
ASSETS:		
Federal assets:		
Investments in U.S. securities:		
1106 Federal Assets: Receivables, net	75	47
Net value of assets related to post-1991 direct loans receivable:		
1401 Direct loans receivable, gross	1,751	1,757
1405 Allowance for subsidy cost (-)	–152	–159
1499 Net present value of assets related to direct loans	1,599	1,598
1999 Total assets	1,674	1,645
LIABILITIES:		
Federal liabilities:		
2103 Debt	1,659	1,600
2105 Other-Downward reestimate payables	15	45
2999 Total liabilities	1,674	1,645
NET POSITION:		
3300 Cumulative results of operations	....	....
4999 Total liabilities and net position	1,674	1,645

FAMILY HOUSING IMPROVEMENT GUARANTEED LOAN FINANCING ACCOUNT

Program and Financing (in millions of dollars)

Identification code 097–4167–0–3–051	2021 actual	2022 est.	2023 est.
Obligations by program activity:			
Credit program obligations:			
0711 Default claim payments on principal	....	15	9
0742 Downward reestimates paid to receipt accounts	6	6	....
0743 Interest on downward reestimates	2	2	....
0791 Direct program activities, subtotal	8	23	9
0900 Total new obligations, unexpired accounts	8	23	9
Budgetary resources:			
Unobligated balance:			
1000 Unobligated balance brought forward, Oct 1	52	45	23
Financing authority:			
Spending authority from offsetting collections, mandatory:			
1800 Collected	1	1	9
1930 Total budgetary resources available	53	46	32
Memorandum (non-add) entries:			
1941 Unexpired unobligated balance, end of year	45	23	23
Change in obligated balance:			
Unpaid obligations:			
3000 Unpaid obligations, brought forward, Oct 1	....	....	7
3010 New obligations, unexpired accounts	8	23	9
3020 Outlays (gross)	–8	–16	–16
3050 Unpaid obligations, end of year	....	7	....
Memorandum (non-add) entries:			
3100 Obligated balance, start of year	....	....	7
3200 Obligated balance, end of year	....	7	....
Financing authority and disbursements, net:			
Mandatory:			
4090 Budget authority, gross	1	1	9
Financing disbursements:			
4110 Outlays, gross (total)	8	16	16
Offsets against gross financing authority and disbursements:			
Offsetting collections (collected) from:			
4122 Interest on uninvested funds	–1	–1	–1

Family Housing—Continued
Federal Funds—Continued

FAMILY HOUSING IMPROVEMENT GUARANTEED LOAN FINANCING ACCOUNT—Continued

Program and Financing—Continued

Identification code 097–4167–0–3–051	2021 actual	2022 est.	2023 est.
4123 Non-Federal sources	....	....	–8
4130 Offsets against gross budget authority and outlays (total)	–1	–1	–9
4170 Outlays, net (mandatory)	7	15	7
4180 Budget authority, net (total)	....	....	....
4190 Outlays, net (total)	7	15	7

Status of Guaranteed Loans (in millions of dollars)

Identification code 097–4167–0–3–051	2021 actual	2022 est.	2023 est.
Position with respect to appropriations act limitation on commitments:			
2111 Guaranteed loan commitments from current-year authority	....	....	....
2150 Total guaranteed loan commitments	....	....	....
2199 Guaranteed amount of guaranteed loan commitments	....	....	....
Cumulative balance of guaranteed loans outstanding:			
2210 Outstanding, start of year	924	906	875
2231 Disbursements of new guaranteed loans	....	....	....
2251 Repayments and prepayments	–18	–35	–20
Adjustments:			
2263 Terminations for default that result in claim payments	....	–15	–8
2264 Other adjustments, net	....	19	....
2290 Outstanding, end of year	906	875	847
Memorandum:			
2299 Guaranteed amount of guaranteed loans outstanding, end of year	891	875	847

Balance Sheet (in millions of dollars)

Identification code 097–4167–0–3–051	2020 actual	2021 actual
ASSETS:		
Federal assets:		
1101 Fund balances with Treasury	45	52
Investments in U.S. securities:		
1106 Receivables, net	....	....
1999 Total assets	45	52
LIABILITIES:		
2105 Federal liabilities: Other: Downward reestimate payables	7	8
2204 Non-Federal liabilities: Liabilities for loan guarantees	38	44
2999 Total liabilities	45	52
NET POSITION:		
3300 Cumulative results of operations	....	....
4999 Total liabilities and net position	45	52

DEPARTMENT OF DEFENSE MILITARY UNACCOMPANIED HOUSING IMPROVEMENT FUND

For the Department of Defense Military Unaccompanied Housing Improvement Fund, $494,000, to remain available until expended, for unaccompanied housing initiatives undertaken pursuant to section 2883 of title 10, United States Code, providing alternative means of acquiring and improving military unaccompanied housing and supporting facilities.

Note.—A full-year 2022 appropriation for this account was not enacted at the time the Budget was prepared; therefore, the Budget assumes this account is operating under the Continuing Appropriations Act, 2022 (Division A of Public Law 117–43, as amended). The amounts included for 2022 reflect the annualized level provided by the continuing resolution.

Program and Financing (in millions of dollars)

Identification code 097–0836–0–1–051	2021 actual	2022 est.	2023 est.
Obligations by program activity:			
Credit program obligations:			
0709 Administrative expenses	1	1	1
0900 Total new obligations, unexpired accounts (object class 25.1)	1	1	1
Budgetary resources:			
Unobligated balance:			
1000 Unobligated balance brought forward, Oct 1	1	1	1
Budget authority:			
Appropriations, discretionary:			
1100 Appropriation	1	1	....
1930 Total budgetary resources available	2	2	1
Memorandum (non-add) entries:			
1941 Unexpired unobligated balance, end of year	1	1	....
Change in obligated balance:			
Unpaid obligations:			
3000 Unpaid obligations, brought forward, Oct 1	....	....	1
3010 New obligations, unexpired accounts	1	1	1
3020 Outlays (gross)	–1	....	....
3050 Unpaid obligations, end of year	....	1	2
Memorandum (non-add) entries:			
3100 Obligated balance, start of year	....	....	1
3200 Obligated balance, end of year	....	1	2
Budget authority and outlays, net:			
Discretionary:			
4000 Budget authority, gross	1	1	....
Outlays, gross:			
4011 Outlays from discretionary balances	1	....	....
4180 Budget authority, net (total)	1	1	....
4190 Outlays, net (total)	1	....	....

Summary of Loan Levels, Subsidy Budget Authority and Outlays by Program (in millions of dollars)

Identification code 097–0836–0–1–051	2021 actual	2022 est.	2023 est.
Administrative expense data:			
3510 Budget authority	1	1	1

REVOLVING AND MANAGEMENT FUNDS

Resources presented under the Revolving and Management Funds title support logistics and other infrastructure activities under the authority of 10 U.S.C. 2208 and other sections to accept customer reimbursable orders to meet customer needs. The activities include depot maintenance, supply management, distribution depots, transportation services, Navy research and development, finance and accounting services, information systems and telecommunications services, commissaries, and security background investigation services among others.

Federal Funds

NATIONAL DEFENSE STOCKPILE TRANSACTION FUND

For the National Defense Stockpile Transaction Fund, $253,500,000, for activities pursuant to the Strategic and Critical Materials Stock Piling Act (50 U.S.C. 98 et. seq.), to remain available until expended.

Program and Financing (in millions of dollars)

Identification code 097–4555–0–3–051	2021 actual	2022 est.	2023 est.
Obligations by program activity:			
0001 Acquisition, upgrade and relocation	....	....	94
0700 Direct program activities, subtotal	....	....	94
0801 Acquisition, upgrade and relocation	49	86	79
0804 Civilian pay and benefits	....	10	11
0899 Total reimbursable obligations	49	96	90
0900 Total new obligations, unexpired accounts	49	96	184
Budgetary resources:			
Unobligated balance:			
1000 Unobligated balance brought forward, Oct 1	211	262	316
1021 Recoveries of prior year unpaid obligations	15	....	....
1070 Unobligated balance (total)	226	262	316
Budget authority:			
Appropriations, discretionary:			
1100 Appropriation	....	....	254

DEPARTMENT OF DEFENSE—MILITARY PROGRAMS

Revolving and Management Funds—Continued
Federal Funds—Continued

		2021 actual	2022 est.	2023 est.
	Spending authority from offsetting collections, mandatory:			
1800	Collected	83	150	71
1802	Offsetting collections (previously unavailable)	24	4	4
1823	New and/or unobligated balance of spending authority from offsetting collections temporarily reduced	−22	−4	−4
1850	Spending auth from offsetting collections, mand (total)	85	150	71
1900	Budget authority (total)	85	150	325
1930	Total budgetary resources available	311	412	641
	Memorandum (non-add) entries:			
1941	Unexpired unobligated balance, end of year	262	316	457
	Change in obligated balance:			
	Unpaid obligations:			
3000	Unpaid obligations, brought forward, Oct 1	42	30	24
3010	New obligations, unexpired accounts	49	96	184
3020	Outlays (gross)	−46	−102	−128
3040	Recoveries of prior year unpaid obligations, unexpired	−15		
3050	Unpaid obligations, end of year	30	24	80
	Memorandum (non-add) entries:			
3100	Obligated balance, start of year	42	30	24
3200	Obligated balance, end of year	30	24	80
	Budget authority and outlays, net:			
	Discretionary:			
4000	Budget authority, gross			254
	Outlays, gross:			
4010	Outlays from new discretionary authority			38
	Mandatory:			
4090	Budget authority, gross	85	150	71
	Outlays, gross:			
4100	Outlays from new mandatory authority		85	40
4101	Outlays from mandatory balances	46	17	50
4110	Outlays, gross (total)	46	102	90
	Offsets against gross budget authority and outlays:			
	Offsetting collections (collected) from:			
4123	Non-Federal sources	−83	−150	−71
4180	Budget authority, net (total)	2		254
4190	Outlays, net (total)	−37	−48	57
	Memorandum (non-add) entries:			
5090	Unexpired unavailable balance, SOY: Offsetting collections	24	22	22
5092	Unexpired unavailable balance, EOY: Offsetting collections	22	22	22

The National Defense Stockpile program is managed under the authority of the Strategic and Critical Materials Stockpiling Act. The purpose of the Stockpile is to decrease or preclude U.S. dependence on foreign sources for supplies of strategic and critical materials in times of national emergency.

Revenues from the sales of excess commodities are either deposited into the National Defense Stockpile Transaction Fund to finance the National Defense Stockpile program or are transferred to the Treasury for specific congressionally-mandated programs or to reduce the deficit.

Object Classification (in millions of dollars)

Identification code 097–4555–0–3–051		2021 actual	2022 est.	2023 est.
26.0	Direct obligations: Supplies and materials			94
99.0	Direct obligations			94
	Reimbursable obligations:			
	Personnel compensation:			
11.1	Full-time permanent	5	6	7
11.5	Other personnel compensation	1	1	1
11.9	Total personnel compensation	6	7	8
12.1	Civilian personnel benefits	2	2	3
22.0	Transportation of things		1	1
23.1	Rental payments to GSA	1	1	1
25.1	Advisory and assistance services	9	12	14
25.2	Other services from non-Federal sources	22	27	29
25.3	Other goods and services from Federal sources		1	1
25.4	Operation and maintenance of facilities		1	2
26.0	Supplies and materials	9	44	31
99.0	Reimbursable obligations	49	96	90
99.9	Total new obligations, unexpired accounts	49	96	184

Employment Summary

Identification code 097–4555–0–3–051	2021 actual	2022 est.	2023 est.
2001 Reimbursable civilian full-time equivalent employment	57	72	62

PENTAGON RESERVATION MAINTENANCE REVOLVING FUND

Program and Financing (in millions of dollars)

Identification code 097–4950–0–4–051		2021 actual	2022 est.	2023 est.
	Obligations by program activity:			
0801	Operations	418	399	403
0803	PFPA	251	255	256
0805	Operations - Capital Program	5	5	7
0807	PFPA - Capital Program	6	7	7
0900	Total new obligations, unexpired accounts	680	666	673
	Budgetary resources:			
	Unobligated balance:			
1000	Unobligated balance brought forward, Oct 1	57	62	35
1021	Recoveries of prior year unpaid obligations	39		
1070	Unobligated balance (total)	96	62	35
	Budget authority:			
	Spending authority from offsetting collections, mandatory:			
1800	Collected	874	639	638
1801	Change in uncollected payments, Federal sources	−228		
1850	Spending auth from offsetting collections, mand (total)	646	639	638
1900	Budget authority (total)	646	639	638
1930	Total budgetary resources available	742	701	673
	Memorandum (non-add) entries:			
1941	Unexpired unobligated balance, end of year	62	35	
	Change in obligated balance:			
	Unpaid obligations:			
3000	Unpaid obligations, brought forward, Oct 1	483	475	384
3010	New obligations, unexpired accounts	680	666	673
3020	Outlays (gross)	−649	−757	−733
3040	Recoveries of prior year unpaid obligations, unexpired	−39		
3050	Unpaid obligations, end of year	475	384	324
	Uncollected payments:			
3060	Uncollected pymts, Fed sources, brought forward, Oct 1	−285	−57	−57
3070	Change in uncollected pymts, Fed sources, unexpired	228		
3090	Uncollected pymts, Fed sources, end of year	−57	−57	−57
	Memorandum (non-add) entries:			
3100	Obligated balance, start of year	198	418	327
3200	Obligated balance, end of year	418	327	267
	Budget authority and outlays, net:			
	Mandatory:			
4090	Budget authority, gross	646	639	638
	Outlays, gross:			
4100	Outlays from new mandatory authority	394	441	440
4101	Outlays from mandatory balances	255	316	293
4110	Outlays, gross (total)	649	757	733
	Offsets against gross budget authority and outlays:			
	Offsetting collections (collected) from:			
4120	Federal sources	−872	−639	−638
4123	Non-Federal sources	−2		
4130	Offsets against gross budget authority and outlays (total)	−874	−639	−638
	Additional offsets against gross budget authority only:			
4140	Change in uncollected pymts, Fed sources, unexpired	228		
4170	Outlays, net (mandatory)	−225	118	95
4180	Budget authority, net (total)			
4190	Outlays, net (total)	−225	118	95

The Pentagon Reservation Maintenance Revolving Fund was established by the 1991 National Defense Authorization Act and is codified in 10 U.S.C. 2674. The fund finances the maintenance, sustainment, protection, repair, and renovation of the Pentagon Reservation, which includes the Pentagon and its adjacent facilities, the Mark Center, and the Raven Rock Mountain Complex. Services provided are for space, building services, deep underground relocation capability, and force protection for Department

PENTAGON RESERVATION MAINTENANCE REVOLVING FUND—Continued

of Defense Components, including Military Departments and other activities located within the Reservation.

Object Classification (in millions of dollars)

Identification code 097–4950–0–4–051		2021 actual	2022 est.	2023 est.
	Reimbursable obligations:			
	Personnel compensation:			
11.1	Full-time permanent	166	203	205
11.5	Other personnel compensation	21	3	3
11.9	Total personnel compensation	187	206	208
12.1	Civilian personnel benefits	66	63	64
21.0	Travel and transportation of persons	2	1	1
22.0	Transportation of things		4	4
23.1	Rental payments to GSA	5		
23.2	Rental payments to others	2		
23.3	Communications, utilities, and miscellaneous charges	42	45	41
25.1	Advisory and assistance services	93	79	79
25.2	Other services from non-Federal sources	33	40	42
25.3	Other goods and services from Federal sources	5	10	11
25.3	Other goods and services from Federal sources	1		
25.4	Operation and maintenance of facilities	176	159	162
25.7	Operation and maintenance of equipment	35	29	31
26.0	Supplies and materials	13	19	20
31.0	Equipment	19	11	10
32.0	Land and structures	1		
99.0	Reimbursable obligations	680	666	673
99.9	Total new obligations, unexpired accounts	680	666	673

Employment Summary

Identification code 097–4950–0–4–051	2021 actual	2022 est.	2023 est.
2001 Reimbursable civilian full-time equivalent employment	1,624	1,786	1,786

NATIONAL DEFENSE SEALIFT FUND

Program and Financing (in millions of dollars)

Identification code 017–4557–0–4–051		2021 actual	2022 est.	2023 est.
	Obligations by program activity:			
0001	Construction and Conversion	1		
0002	Operations, Maintenance and Lease	360		
0799	Total direct obligations	361		
0801	Reimbursable program activity	36		
0900	Total new obligations, unexpired accounts	397		
	Budgetary resources:			
	Unobligated balance:			
1000	Unobligated balance brought forward, Oct 1	110	106	106
1021	Recoveries of prior year unpaid obligations	51		
1070	Unobligated balance (total)	161	106	106
	Budget authority:			
	Appropriations, discretionary:			
1121	Appropriations transferred from other acct [017–1804]	342		
1900	Budget authority (total)	342		
1930	Total budgetary resources available	503	106	106
	Memorandum (non-add) entries:			
1941	Unexpired unobligated balance, end of year	106	106	106
	Change in obligated balance:			
	Unpaid obligations:			
3000	Unpaid obligations, brought forward, Oct 1	88	103	35
3010	New obligations, unexpired accounts	397		
3020	Outlays (gross)	–331	–68	–35
3040	Recoveries of prior year unpaid obligations, unexpired	–51		
3050	Unpaid obligations, end of year	103	35	
	Uncollected payments:			
3060	Uncollected pymts, Fed sources, brought forward, Oct 1	–105	–105	–105
3090	Uncollected pymts, Fed sources, end of year	–105	–105	–105
	Memorandum (non-add) entries:			
3100	Obligated balance, start of year	–17	–2	–70
3200	Obligated balance, end of year	–2	–70	–105

	Budget authority and outlays, net:			
	Discretionary:			
4000	Budget authority, gross	342		
	Outlays, gross:			
4010	Outlays from new discretionary authority	309		
4011	Outlays from discretionary balances	22	68	35
4020	Outlays, gross (total)	331	68	35
4180	Budget authority, net (total)	342		
4190	Outlays, net (total)	331	68	35

Object Classification (in millions of dollars)

Identification code 017–4557–0–4–051		2021 actual	2022 est.	2023 est.
	Direct obligations:			
25.1	Advisory and assistance services	18		
25.3	Other goods and services from Federal sources	343		
99.0	Direct obligations	361		
	Reimbursable obligations:			
25.2	Other services from non-Federal sources	4		
25.3	Other goods and services from Federal sources	28		
26.0	Supplies and materials	1		
44.0	Refunds	3		
99.0	Reimbursable obligations	36		
99.9	Total new obligations, unexpired accounts	397		

DEFENSE WORKING CAPITAL FUNDS

For the Defense Working Capital Funds, $1,329,895,000.

Note.—A full-year 2022 appropriation for this account was not enacted at the time the Budget was prepared; therefore, the Budget assumes this account is operating under the Continuing Appropriations Act, 2022 (Division A of Public Law 117–43, as amended). The amounts included for 2022 reflect the annualized level provided by the continuing resolution.

WORKING CAPITAL FUND, ARMY

Program and Financing (in millions of dollars)

Identification code 097–493001–0–4–051		2021 actual	2022 est.	2023 est.
	Obligations by program activity:			
0001	Industrial operations	159	27	28
0004	Supply management - Army	966	358	2
0020	Undistributed		–183	
0799	Total direct obligations	1,125	202	30
0801	Industrial operations	4,891	4,563	4,135
0804	Supply management - Army	4,138	4,861	5,583
0809	Reimbursable program activities, subtotal	9,029	9,424	9,718
0811	Capital - industrial operations	57	55	126
0814	Capital - supply management - Army	25	18	17
0819	Reimbursable program activities, subtotal	82	73	143
0899	Total reimbursable obligations	9,111	9,497	9,861
0900	Total new obligations, unexpired accounts	10,236	9,699	9,891
	Budgetary resources:			
	Unobligated balance:			
1000	Unobligated balance brought forward, Oct 1	4,255	3,937	6,221
1001	Discretionary unobligated balance brought fwd, Oct 1	4,255		
1011	Unobligated balance transfer from other acct [021–2035]	94		
1011	Unobligated balance transfer from other acct [097–0801]	600		
1011	Unobligated balance transfer from other acct [021–2040]	6		
1011	Unobligated balance transfer from other acct [021–2033]	36		
1011	Unobligated balance transfer from other acct [021–2034]	25		
1011	Unobligated balance transfer from other acct [021–2031]	19		
1011	Unobligated balance transfer from other acct [097–0400]	21		
1011	Unobligated balance transfer from other acct [021–2032]	10		
1021	Recoveries of prior year unpaid obligations	1,027		
1025	Unobligated balance of contract authority withdrawn	–544		
1070	Unobligated balance (total)	5,549	3,937	6,221
	Budget authority:			
	Appropriations, discretionary:			
1100	Appropriation	1,494	1,494	1,330
1120	Appropriations transferred to other acct [097–4930.003]	–96	–96	–81

DEPARTMENT OF DEFENSE—MILITARY PROGRAMS

Revolving and Management Funds—Continued
Federal Funds—Continued

		2021 actual	2022 est.	2023 est.
1120	Appropriations transferred to other acct [097–4930.004]	–1,147	–1,146	–1,211
1120	Appropriations transferred to other acct [097–4930.005]	–50	–50	–8
1121	Appropriations transferred from other acct [021–2020]	48		
1121	Appropriations transferred from other acct [021–2033]	1		
1121	Appropriations transferred from other acct [021–2034]	25		
1121	Appropriations transferred from other acct [021–2035]	35		
1160	Appropriation, discretionary (total)	310	202	30
	Contract authority, mandatory:			
1600	Contract authority	4,220		
	Spending authority from offsetting collections, discretionary:			
1700	Collected	11,325	11,781	10,396
1701	Change in uncollected payments, Federal sources	–564		
1750	Spending auth from offsetting collections, disc (total)	10,761	11,781	10,396
	Spending authority from offsetting collections, mandatory:			
1826	Spending authority from offsetting collections applied to liquidate contract authority	–6,667		
1900	Budget authority (total)	8,624	11,983	10,426
1930	Total budgetary resources available	14,173	15,920	16,647
	Memorandum (non-add) entries:			
1941	Unexpired unobligated balance, end of year	3,937	6,221	6,756
	Change in obligated balance:			
	Unpaid obligations:			
3000	Unpaid obligations, brought forward, Oct 1	9,507	6,741	4,191
3010	New obligations, unexpired accounts	10,236	9,699	9,891
3020	Outlays (gross)	–11,975	–12,249	–11,206
3040	Recoveries of prior year unpaid obligations, unexpired	–1,027		
3050	Unpaid obligations, end of year	6,741	4,191	2,876
	Uncollected payments:			
3060	Uncollected pymts, Fed sources, brought forward, Oct 1	–6,288	–5,724	–5,724
3070	Change in uncollected pymts, Fed sources, unexpired	564		
3090	Uncollected pymts, Fed sources, end of year	–5,724	–5,724	–5,724
	Memorandum (non-add) entries:			
3100	Obligated balance, start of year	3,219	1,017	–1,533
3200	Obligated balance, end of year	1,017	–1,533	–2,848
	Budget authority and outlays, net:			
	Discretionary:			
4000	Budget authority, gross	11,071	11,983	10,426
	Outlays, gross:			
4010	Outlays from new discretionary authority	10,061	4,295	5,744
4011	Outlays from discretionary balances	1,914	7,954	5,462
4020	Outlays, gross (total)	11,975	12,249	11,206
	Offsets against gross budget authority and outlays:			
	Offsetting collections (collected) from:			
4030	Federal sources	–11,200	–11,049	–9,645
4033	Non-Federal sources	–125	–732	–751
4040	Offsets against gross budget authority and outlays (total)	–11,325	–11,781	–10,396
	Additional offsets against gross budget authority only:			
4050	Change in uncollected pymts, Fed sources, unexpired	564		
4070	Budget authority, net (discretionary)	310	202	30
4080	Outlays, net (discretionary)	650	468	810
	Mandatory:			
4090	Budget authority, gross	–2,447		
4180	Budget authority, net (total)	–2,137	202	30
4190	Outlays, net (total)	650	468	810
	Memorandum (non-add) entries:			
5051	Unobligated balance, EOY: Contract authority			306
5052	Obligated balance, SOY: Contract authority	6,173	3,182	3,182
5053	Obligated balance, EOY: Contract authority	3,182	3,182	2,876

The Army Working Capital Fund (AWCF) finances industrial and supply operations of the Army. The AWCF finances operating and capital costs (excluding Military Construction) through receipt of funded customer reimbursable orders from appropriated accounts in accordance with 10 U.S.C. 2208. The AWCF uses cost accounting and business management techniques to provide DOD Managers with information that can be used to monitor, control, and minimize the cost of operations.

Object Classification (in millions of dollars)

Identification code 097–493001–0–4–051	2021 actual	2022 est.	2023 est.
Direct obligations:			
26.0 Supplies and materials	1,125	385	30
92.0 Undistributed		–183	
99.0 Direct obligations	1,125	202	30
Reimbursable obligations:			
Personnel compensation:			
11.1 Full-time permanent	1,475	1,521	1,476
11.3 Other than full-time permanent	31	33	32
11.5 Other personnel compensation	133	178	136
11.8 Special personal services payments	4	4	4
11.9 Total personnel compensation	1,643	1,736	1,648
12.1 Civilian personnel benefits	558	646	596
13.0 Benefits for former personnel	5	2	4
21.0 Travel and transportation of persons	21	33	27
22.0 Transportation of things	89	117	106
23.1 Rental payments to GSA	14	13	13
23.2 Rental payments to others	3	5	5
23.3 Communications, utilities, and miscellaneous charges	67	70	67
24.0 Printing and reproduction	1	1	1
25.1 Advisory and assistance services	137	117	131
25.2 Other services from non-Federal sources	393	337	326
25.3 Other goods and services from Federal sources	271	259	217
25.3 Other goods and services from Federal sources	418	423	947
25.4 Operation and maintenance of facilities	148	185	170
25.7 Operation and maintenance of equipment	327	99	108
26.0 Supplies and materials	4,840	5,302	5,259
31.0 Equipment	176	152	236
99.0 Reimbursable obligations	9,111	9,497	9,861
99.9 Total new obligations, unexpired accounts	10,236	9,699	9,891

Employment Summary

Identification code 097–493001–0–4–051	2021 actual	2022 est.	2023 est.
2001 Reimbursable civilian full-time equivalent employment	21,409	22,272	20,998

WORKING CAPITAL FUND, NAVY

Program and Financing (in millions of dollars)

Identification code 097–493002–0–4–051	2021 actual	2022 est.	2023 est.
Obligations by program activity:			
0006 Base support	647		
0007 Transportation	7		
0799 Total direct obligations	654		
0801 Supply management - Navy	8,812	7,697	7,964
0802 Supply management - Marine Corps	113	111	85
0803 Depot maintenance - aviation	2,644	2,791	2,997
0805 Depot maintenance - Marine Corps		312	270
0806 Base support		9	
0807 Transportation	3,224	3,404	3,474
0808 Research and development activities	17,389	16,970	18,019
0809 Reimbursable program activities, subtotal	32,182	31,294	32,809
0820 Capital - supply management - Navy	13	16	13
0822 Capital - depot maintenance - aviation	35	46	45
0824 Capital - depot maintenance	2	5	6
0827 Capital - research and development activities	203	191	194
0829 Reimbursable program activities, subtotal	253	258	258
0899 Total reimbursable obligations	32,435	31,552	33,067
0900 Total new obligations, unexpired accounts	33,089	31,552	33,067
Budgetary resources:			
Unobligated balance:			
1000 Unobligated balance brought forward, Oct 1	4,075	6,247	8,360
1001 Discretionary unobligated balance brought fwd, Oct 1	4,075		
1020 Adjustment of unobligated bal brought forward, Oct 1	68		
1021 Recoveries of prior year unpaid obligations	3,044		
1025 Unobligated balance of contract authority withdrawn	–596		
1033 Recoveries of prior year paid obligations	2		
1070 Unobligated balance (total)	6,593	6,247	8,360
Budget authority:			
Contract authority, mandatory:			
1600 Contract authority	8,298		
Spending authority from offsetting collections, discretionary:			
1700 Collected	31,691	33,665	34,240
1701 Change in uncollected payments, Federal sources	765		
1750 Spending auth from offsetting collections, disc (total)	32,456	33,665	34,240

WORKING CAPITAL FUND, NAVY—Continued
Program and Financing—Continued

Identification code 097–493002–0–4–051	2021 actual	2022 est.	2023 est.
Spending authority from offsetting collections, mandatory:			
1826 Spending authority from offsetting collections applied to liquidate contract authority	−8,011		
1900 Budget authority (total)	32,743	33,665	34,240
1930 Total budgetary resources available	39,336	39,912	42,600
Memorandum (non-add) entries:			
1941 Unexpired unobligated balance, end of year	6,247	8,360	9,533
Change in obligated balance:			
Unpaid obligations:			
3000 Unpaid obligations, brought forward, Oct 1	19,409	18,043	15,798
3010 New obligations, unexpired accounts	33,089	31,552	33,067
3020 Outlays (gross)	−31,411	−33,797	−34,240
3040 Recoveries of prior year unpaid obligations, unexpired	−3,044		
3050 Unpaid obligations, end of year	18,043	15,798	14,625
Uncollected payments:			
3060 Uncollected pymts, Fed sources, brought forward, Oct 1	−13,215	−13,980	−13,980
3070 Change in uncollected pymts, Fed sources, unexpired	−765		
3090 Uncollected pymts, Fed sources, end of year	−13,980	−13,980	−13,980
Memorandum (non-add) entries:			
3100 Obligated balance, start of year	6,194	4,063	1,818
3200 Obligated balance, end of year	4,063	1,818	645
Budget authority and outlays, net:			
Discretionary:			
4000 Budget authority, gross	32,456	33,665	34,240
Outlays, gross:			
4010 Outlays from new discretionary authority	30,771	16,832	21,229
4011 Outlays from discretionary balances	640	16,965	13,011
4020 Outlays, gross (total)	31,411	33,797	34,240
Offsets against gross budget authority and outlays:			
Offsetting collections (collected) from:			
4030 Federal sources	−31,379	−33,248	−33,815
4033 Non-Federal sources	−314	−417	−425
4040 Offsets against gross budget authority and outlays (total)	−31,693	−33,665	−34,240
Additional offsets against gross budget authority only:			
4050 Change in uncollected pymts, Fed sources, unexpired	−765		
4053 Recoveries of prior year paid obligations, unexpired accounts	2		
4060 Additional offsets against budget authority only (total)	−763		
4080 Outlays, net (discretionary)	−282	132	
Mandatory:			
4090 Budget authority, gross	287		
4180 Budget authority, net (total)	287		
4190 Outlays, net (total)	−282	132	
Memorandum (non-add) entries:			
5052 Obligated balance, SOY: Contract authority	8,093	7,853	7,853
5053 Obligated balance, EOY: Contract authority	7,853	7,853	7,853

The Navy Working Capital Fund (NWCF) finances the operations of Navy industrial, logistical, commercial and support-type activities. These activities include Marine Corps Depot Maintenance, Marine Corps Supply, Navy Supply, Fleet Readiness Centers (Aviation Depots), Research and Development and Military Sealift Command. The NWCF finances operating and capital costs (excluding Military Construction) through the receipt of funded customer reimbursable orders from appropriated accounts in accordance with 10 U.S.C. 2208. The NWCF uses cost accounting and business management techniques to provide DOD managers with information that can be used to monitor, control, and minimize the cost of operations.

Object Classification (in millions of dollars)

Identification code 097–493002–0–4–051	2021 actual	2022 est.	2023 est.
Direct obligations:			
25.4 Operation and maintenance of facilities	647		
25.7 Operation and maintenance of equipment	7		
99.0 Direct obligations	654		
Reimbursable obligations:			
Personnel compensation:			
11.1 Full-time permanent	8,286	8,126	8,503
11.3 Other than full-time permanent	54	87	81
11.5 Other personnel compensation	649	726	713
11.8 Special personal services payments	110	76	76
11.9 Total personnel compensation	9,099	9,015	9,373
12.1 Civilian personnel benefits	3,058	3,140	3,319
13.0 Benefits for former personnel	10	3	3
21.0 Travel and transportation of persons	235	393	379
22.0 Transportation of things	127	67	73
23.1 Rental payments to GSA	2	2	8
23.2 Rental payments to others	412	459	401
23.3 Communications, utilities, and miscellaneous charges	470	426	486
24.0 Printing and reproduction	3	9	9
25.1 Advisory and assistance services	226	78	145
25.2 Other services from non-Federal sources	599	1,025	830
25.3 Other goods and services from Federal sources	659	713	688
25.3 Other goods and services from Federal sources	3	2	2
25.3 Other goods and services from Federal sources	421	760	758
25.4 Operation and maintenance of facilities		407	462
25.5 Research and development contracts	3,223	3,304	3,415
25.7 Operation and maintenance of equipment	1,871	1,661	1,818
26.0 Supplies and materials	10,689	8,960	9,666
31.0 Equipment	1,266	1,016	1,116
32.0 Land and structures	62	112	116
99.0 Reimbursable obligations	32,435	31,552	33,067
99.9 Total new obligations, unexpired accounts	33,089	31,552	33,067

Employment Summary

Identification code 097–493002–0–4–051	2021 actual	2022 est.	2023 est.
2001 Reimbursable civilian full-time equivalent employment	82,856	81,531	81,565

WORKING CAPITAL FUND, AIR FORCE
Program and Financing (in millions of dollars)

Identification code 097–493003–0–4–051	2021 actual	2022 est.	2023 est.
Obligations by program activity:			
0001 Transportation	175		
0003 Supply management	96	78	81
0004 Consolidated sustainment activity group maintenance	2		
0020 Undistributed		18	
0799 Total direct obligations	273	96	81
0801 Transportation	7,559	8,333	8,047
0802 Consolidated sustainment activity group supply	5,813	6,078	6,286
0803 Supply management - Air Force	4,109	4,747	4,818
0804 Consolidated sustainment activity group maintenance	6,968	7,380	7,461
0809 Reimbursable program activities, subtotal	24,449	26,538	26,612
0810 Capital - consolidated sustainment activity group maintenance	189	172	213
0811 Capital - transportation		66	64
0819 Reimbursable program activities, subtotal	189	238	277
0899 Total reimbursable obligations	24,638	26,776	26,889
0900 Total new obligations, unexpired accounts	24,911	26,872	26,970
Budgetary resources:			
Unobligated balance:			
1000 Unobligated balance brought forward, Oct 1	2,094	2,220	11,200
1001 Discretionary unobligated balance brought fwd, Oct 1	2,094		
1011 Unobligated balance transfer from other acct [021–2091]	80		
1021 Recoveries of prior year unpaid obligations	61		
1025 Unobligated balance of contract authority withdrawn	−17		
1070 Unobligated balance (total)	2,218	2,220	11,200
Budget authority:			
Appropriations, discretionary:			
1121 Appropriations transferred from other acct [097–4930.001]	96	96	81
1121 Appropriations transferred from other acct [021–2091]	309		
1160 Appropriation, discretionary (total)	405	96	81
Contract authority, mandatory:			
1600 Contract authority	10,176		
Spending authority from offsetting collections, discretionary:			
1700 Collected	24,542	35,756	27,383
1701 Change in uncollected payments, Federal sources	375		
1750 Spending auth from offsetting collections, disc (total)	24,917	35,756	27,383

DEPARTMENT OF DEFENSE—MILITARY PROGRAMS

Revolving and Management Funds—Continued
Federal Funds—Continued

		2021 actual	2022 est.	2023 est.
	Spending authority from offsetting collections, mandatory:			
1826	Spending authority from offsetting collections applied to liquidate contract authority	−10,585	....	....
1900	Budget authority (total)	24,913	35,852	27,464
1930	Total budgetary resources available	27,131	38,072	38,664
	Memorandum (non-add) entries:			
1941	Unexpired unobligated balance, end of year	2,220	11,200	11,694
	Change in obligated balance:			
	Unpaid obligations:			
3000	Unpaid obligations, brought forward, Oct 1	12,514	12,853	4,001
3010	New obligations, unexpired accounts	24,911	26,872	26,970
3020	Outlays (gross)	−24,511	−35,724	−27,444
3040	Recoveries of prior year unpaid obligations, unexpired	−61	....	....
3050	Unpaid obligations, end of year	12,853	4,001	3,527
	Uncollected payments:			
3060	Uncollected pymts, Fed sources, brought forward, Oct 1	−8,510	−8,885	−8,885
3070	Change in uncollected pymts, Fed sources, unexpired	−375	....	....
3090	Uncollected pymts, Fed sources, end of year	−8,885	−8,885	−8,885
	Memorandum (non-add) entries:			
3100	Obligated balance, start of year	4,004	3,968	−4,884
3200	Obligated balance, end of year	3,968	−4,884	−5,358
	Budget authority and outlays, net:			
	Discretionary:			
4000	Budget authority, gross	25,322	35,852	27,464
	Outlays, gross:			
4010	Outlays from new discretionary authority	23,632	23,323	18,689
4011	Outlays from discretionary balances	879	12,401	8,755
4020	Outlays, gross (total)	24,511	35,724	27,444
	Offsets against gross budget authority and outlays:			
	Offsetting collections (collected) from:			
4030	Federal sources	−24,173	−34,806	−26,721
4033	Non-Federal sources	−369	−950	−662
4040	Offsets against gross budget authority and outlays (total)	−24,542	−35,756	−27,383
	Additional offsets against gross budget authority only:			
4050	Change in uncollected pymts, Fed sources, unexpired	−375	....	....
4070	Budget authority, net (discretionary)	405	96	81
4080	Outlays, net (discretionary)	−31	−32	61
	Mandatory:			
4090	Budget authority, gross	−409	....	....
4180	Budget authority, net (total)	−4	96	81
4190	Outlays, net (total)	−31	−32	61
	Memorandum (non-add) entries:			
5050	Unobligated balance, SOY: Contract authority	....	....	264
5051	Unobligated balance, EOY: Contract authority	....	264	738
5052	Obligated balance, SOY: Contract authority	4,691	4,265	4,001
5053	Obligated balance, EOY: Contract authority	4,265	4,001	3,527

The Air Force Working Capital Fund (AFWCF) finances the operations of the Air Force and the United States Transportation Command's industrial, logistical, and commercial activities. Activities performed include depot maintenance, supply support, and the transport of cargo and personnel. The AFWCF finances operating and capital costs (excluding Military Construction) through receipt of funded customer reimbursable orders from appropriated accounts in accordance with 10 U.S.C. 2208. The AFWCF uses cost accounting and business management techniques to provide DOD managers with information that can be used to monitor, control, and minimize the cost of operations.

Object Classification (in millions of dollars)

Identification code 097–493003–0–4–051		2021 actual	2022 est.	2023 est.
	Direct obligations:			
26.0	Supplies and materials	273	77	81
92.0	Undistributed	....	18	....
99.0	Direct obligations	273	95	81
	Reimbursable obligations:			
	Personnel compensation:			
11.1	Full-time permanent	2,083	2,125	2,150
11.5	Other personnel compensation	381	364	413
11.8	Special personal services payments	62	63	68
11.9	Total personnel compensation	2,526	2,552	2,631
12.1	Civilian personnel benefits	1,170	1,208	1,268
13.0	Benefits for former personnel	1	1	1
21.0	Travel and transportation of persons	91	110	110
22.0	Transportation of things	3,863	4,390	3,649
23.2	Rental payments to others	8	13	14
23.3	Communications, utilities, and miscellaneous charges	162	193	193
25.1	Advisory and assistance services	316	368	366
25.2	Other services from non-Federal sources	798	688	759
25.3	Other goods and services from Federal sources	301	309	344
25.3	Other goods and services from Federal sources	9	9	10
25.3	Other goods and services from Federal sources	478	560	589
25.4	Operation and maintenance of facilities	305	316	358
25.7	Operation and maintenance of equipment	1,544	1,481	1,599
26.0	Supplies and materials	12,854	14,350	14,728
31.0	Equipment	212	229	270
99.0	Reimbursable obligations	24,638	26,777	26,889
99.9	Total new obligations, unexpired accounts	24,911	26,872	26,970

Employment Summary

Identification code 097–493003–0–4–051		2021 actual	2022 est.	2023 est.
2001	Reimbursable civilian full-time equivalent employment	33,174	35,009	33,649

WORKING CAPITAL FUND, DEFENSE-WIDE

Program and Financing (in millions of dollars)

Identification code 097–493005–0–4–051		2021 actual	2022 est.	2023 est.
	Obligations by program activity:			
0006	Energy management - Defense	92	40	8
0008	Supply chain management - Defense	130	88	....
0020	Undistributed	....	−78	....
0799	Total direct obligations	222	50	8
0803	Defense automation and production services	288	311	313
0804	Defense finance operations	1,410	1,455	1,517
0805	Information services	6,860	8,735	9,293
0806	Energy management - Defense	13,644	10,853	10,141
0808	Supply chain management - Defense	33,395	29,959	31,561
0809	Reimbursable program activities, subtotal	55,597	51,313	52,825
0812	Capital - Defense automation and production services	....	6	....
0813	Capital - Defense finance operations	....	61	9
0814	Capital - information services	....	220	221
0817	Capital - energy management - Defense	37	61	59
0818	Capital - supply chain management - Defense	138	132	248
0819	Reimbursable program activities, subtotal	175	480	537
0899	Total reimbursable obligations	55,772	51,793	53,362
0900	Total new obligations, unexpired accounts	55,994	51,843	53,370
	Budgetary resources:			
	Unobligated balance:			
1000	Unobligated balance brought forward, Oct 1	1,039	589	2,308
1001	Discretionary unobligated balance brought fwd, Oct 1	1,039	....	....
1021	Recoveries of prior year unpaid obligations	5,790	....	....
1025	Unobligated balance of contract authority withdrawn	−5,773	....	....
1070	Unobligated balance (total)	1,056	589	2,308
	Budget authority:			
	Appropriations, discretionary:			
1121	Appropriations transferred from other acct [097–4930.001]	50	50	8
	Contract authority, mandatory:			
1600	Contract authority	47,348	....	....
	Spending authority from offsetting collections, discretionary:			
1700	Collected	50,193	53,512	54,860
1701	Change in uncollected payments, Federal sources	−1,988	....	....
1750	Spending auth from offsetting collections, disc (total)	48,205	53,512	54,860
	Spending authority from offsetting collections, mandatory:			
1826	Spending authority from offsetting collections applied to liquidate contract authority	−40,076	....	....
1900	Budget authority (total)	55,527	53,562	54,868
1930	Total budgetary resources available	56,583	54,151	57,176
	Memorandum (non-add) entries:			
1941	Unexpired unobligated balance, end of year	589	2,308	3,806
	Change in obligated balance:			
	Unpaid obligations:			
3000	Unpaid obligations, brought forward, Oct 1	29,760	28,548	25,714
3010	New obligations, unexpired accounts	55,994	51,843	53,370
3020	Outlays (gross)	−51,416	−54,677	−55,973

WORKING CAPITAL FUND, DEFENSE-WIDE—Continued
Program and Financing—Continued

Identification code 097–493005–0–4–051		2021 actual	2022 est.	2023 est.
3040	Recoveries of prior year unpaid obligations, unexpired	–5,790	....	....
3050	Unpaid obligations, end of year	28,548	25,714	23,111
	Uncollected payments:			
3060	Uncollected pymts, Fed sources, brought forward, Oct 1	–17,614	–15,626	–15,626
3070	Change in uncollected pymts, Fed sources, unexpired	1,988	....	....
3090	Uncollected pymts, Fed sources, end of year	–15,626	–15,626	–15,626
	Memorandum (non-add) entries:			
3100	Obligated balance, start of year	12,146	12,922	10,088
3200	Obligated balance, end of year	12,922	10,088	7,485
	Budget authority and outlays, net:			
	Discretionary:			
4000	Budget authority, gross	48,255	53,562	54,868
	Outlays, gross:			
4010	Outlays from new discretionary authority	44,049	32,149	39,232
4011	Outlays from discretionary balances	7,218	22,528	16,741
4020	Outlays, gross (total)	51,267	54,677	55,973
	Offsets against gross budget authority and outlays:			
	Offsetting collections (collected) from:			
4030	Federal sources	–48,881	–52,698	–52,087
4033	Non-Federal sources	–1,312	–814	–2,773
4040	Offsets against gross budget authority and outlays (total)	–50,193	–53,512	–54,860
	Additional offsets against gross budget authority only:			
4050	Change in uncollected pymts, Fed sources, unexpired	1,988	....	....
4060	Additional offsets against budget authority only (total)	1,988	....	....
4070	Budget authority, net (discretionary)	50	50	8
4080	Outlays, net (discretionary)	1,074	1,165	1,113
	Mandatory:			
4090	Budget authority, gross	7,272		
	Outlays, gross:			
4100	Outlays from new mandatory authority	6		
4101	Outlays from mandatory balances	143		
4110	Outlays, gross (total)	149		
4180	Budget authority, net (total)	7,322	50	8
4190	Outlays, net (total)	1,223	1,165	1,113
	Memorandum (non-add) entries:			
5052	Obligated balance, SOY: Contract authority	8,815	10,314	10,314
5053	Obligated balance, EOY: Contract authority	10,314	10,314	10,314

The Defense-Wide Working Capital Fund finances the commercial and support-type operations of the Defense Logistics Agency, the Defense Finance and Accounting Service, and the Defense Information Systems Agency. The Fund supports activities such as the Department's finance and accounting operations, information systems to include command and control systems and enterprise infrastructure, global acquisition and delivery of fuel and repair parts, and document printing and distribution services. The Fund finances operating and capital expenses (excluding Military Construction) through the receipt of funded customer reimbursable orders from appropriated accounts in accordance with 10 U.S.C. 2208. The Fund uses cost accounting and business management techniques to provide DOD managers with information that can be used to monitor, control, and minimize its cost of operations.

Object Classification (in millions of dollars)

Identification code 097–493005–0–4–051		2021 actual	2022 est.	2023 est.
	Direct obligations:			
26.0	Supplies and materials	222	128	8
92.0	Undistributed	....	–78	....
99.0	Direct obligations	222	50	8
	Reimbursable obligations:			
	Personnel compensation:			
11.1	Full-time permanent	2,922	3,097	3,292
11.3	Other than full-time permanent	113	121	127
11.5	Other personnel compensation	184	208	215
11.8	Special personal services payments	72	78	79
11.9	Total personnel compensation	3,291	3,504	3,713
12.1	Civilian personnel benefits	1,176	1,146	1,269
13.0	Benefits for former personnel	12	15	14
21.0	Travel and transportation of persons	10	81	73
22.0	Transportation of things	846	1,052	1,084
23.1	Rental payments to GSA	33	46	39
23.2	Rental payments to others	88	115	111
23.3	Communications, utilities, and miscellaneous charges	2,182	2,359	2,327
24.0	Printing and reproduction	111	89	92
25.1	Advisory and assistance services	83	79	93
25.2	Other services from non-Federal sources	823	795	1,391
25.3	Other goods and services from Federal sources	4,733	2,328	2,550
25.3	Other goods and services from Federal sources	18	25	26
25.3	Other goods and services from Federal sources	691	729	691
25.4	Operation and maintenance of facilities	1,628	1,875	1,940
25.5	Research and development contracts	155		
25.6	Medical care	2	2	2
25.7	Operation and maintenance of equipment	2,473	4,989	4,908
26.0	Supplies and materials	36,037	31,240	31,799
31.0	Equipment	1,279	1,211	1,134
32.0	Land and structures	101	111	104
43.0	Interest and dividends	....	2	2
99.0	Reimbursable obligations	55,772	51,793	53,362
99.9	Total new obligations, unexpired accounts	55,994	51,843	53,370

Employment Summary

Identification code 097–493005–0–4–051	2021 actual	2022 est.	2023 est.
1001 Direct civilian full-time equivalent employment	....	....	7
2001 Reimbursable civilian full-time equivalent employment	37,827	38,753	39,327

WORKING CAPITAL FUND, DEFENSE COMMISSARY AGENCY
Program and Financing (in millions of dollars)

Identification code 097–493004–0–4–051		2021 actual	2022 est.	2023 est.
	Obligations by program activity:			
0002	Commissary operations	1,225	1,162	1,211
0020	Undistributed	....	–15	....
0700	Direct program activities, subtotal	1,225	1,147	1,211
0799	Total direct obligations	1,225	1,147	1,211
0801	Commissary resale stock	3,970	4,510	4,430
0802	Commissary operations	73	198	291
0810	Capital program	5	3	13
0899	Total reimbursable obligations	4,048	4,711	4,734
0900	Total new obligations, unexpired accounts	5,273	5,858	5,945
	Budgetary resources:			
	Unobligated balance:			
1000	Unobligated balance brought forward, Oct 1	123	79	40
1001	Discretionary unobligated balance brought fwd, Oct 1	8		
1021	Recoveries of prior year unpaid obligations	1		
1070	Unobligated balance (total)	124	79	40
	Budget authority:			
	Appropriations, discretionary:			
1121	Appropriations transferred from other acct [097–4930.001]	1,147	1,146	1,211
	Contract authority, mandatory:			
1600	Contract authority	3,976	....	....
	Spending authority from offsetting collections, discretionary:			
1700	Collected	4,109	4,673	4,763
1701	Change in uncollected payments, Federal sources	4		
1710	Spending authority from offsetting collections transferred to other accounts [097–9999]	–108		
1711	Spending authority from offsetting collections transferred from other accounts [097–9999]	108		
1750	Spending auth from offsetting collections, disc (total)	4,113	4,673	4,763
	Spending authority from offsetting collections, mandatory:			
1826	Spending authority from offsetting collections applied to liquidate contract authority	–4,008	....	....
1900	Budget authority (total)	5,228	5,819	5,974
1930	Total budgetary resources available	5,352	5,898	6,014
	Memorandum (non-add) entries:			
1941	Unexpired unobligated balance, end of year	79	40	69
	Change in obligated balance:			
	Unpaid obligations:			
3000	Unpaid obligations, brought forward, Oct 1	508	496	647

DEPARTMENT OF DEFENSE—MILITARY PROGRAMS

		2021 actual	2022 est.	2023 est.
3010	New obligations, unexpired accounts	5,273	5,858	5,945
3020	Outlays (gross)	−5,284	−5,707	−5,855
3040	Recoveries of prior year unpaid obligations, unexpired	−1		
3050	Unpaid obligations, end of year	496	647	737
	Uncollected payments:			
3060	Uncollected pymts, Fed sources, brought forward, Oct 1		−4	−4
3070	Change in uncollected pymts, Fed sources, unexpired	−4		
3090	Uncollected pymts, Fed sources, end of year	−4	−4	−4
	Memorandum (non-add) entries:			
3100	Obligated balance, start of year	508	492	643
3200	Obligated balance, end of year	492	643	733
	Budget authority and outlays, net:			
	Discretionary:			
4000	Budget authority, gross	5,260	5,819	5,974
	Outlays, gross:			
4010	Outlays from new discretionary authority	4,845	5,260	5,401
4011	Outlays from discretionary balances	439	447	454
4020	Outlays, gross (total)	5,284	5,707	5,855
	Offsets against gross budget authority and outlays:			
	Offsetting collections (collected) from:			
4030	Federal sources	−3	−12	−4
4033	Non-Federal sources	−4,106	−4,661	−4,759
4040	Offsets against gross budget authority and outlays (total)	−4,109	−4,673	−4,763
	Additional offsets against gross budget authority only:			
4050	Change in uncollected pymts, Fed sources, unexpired	−4		
4060	Additional offsets against budget authority only (total)	−4		
4070	Budget authority, net (discretionary)	1,147	1,146	1,211
4080	Outlays, net (discretionary)	1,175	1,034	1,092
	Mandatory:			
4090	Budget authority, gross	−32		
4180	Budget authority, net (total)	1,115	1,146	1,211
4190	Outlays, net (total)	1,175	1,034	1,092
	Memorandum (non-add) entries:			
5052	Obligated balance, SOY: Contract authority	97	65	65
5053	Obligated balance, EOY: Contract authority	65	65	65

The Defense Commissary Agency Working Capital Fund finances the cost of Commissary Operations and Resale Stocks activities. Commissary Operations pays the operating costs of 236 commissaries worldwide, agency headquarters, area offices and support services. Costs include civilian pay, transportation of commissary goods overseas, rewarehousing, shelf stocking, janitorial services in each commissary, and base support as a tenant organization. Resale Stocks pays for the purchase of inventory for resale to commissary patrons.

Object Classification (in millions of dollars)

Identification code 097–493004–0–4–051		2021 actual	2022 est.	2023 est.
	Direct obligations:			
	Personnel compensation:			
11.1	Full-time permanent	356	344	359
11.3	Other than full-time permanent	199	199	207
11.5	Other personnel compensation	44	56	58
11.8	Special personal services payments		1	1
11.9	Total personnel compensation	599	600	625
12.1	Civilian personnel benefits	192	182	189
13.0	Benefits for former personnel		1	1
21.0	Travel and transportation of persons	3	6	12
22.0	Transportation of things	24	18	17
23.1	Rental payments to GSA	1	1	1
23.3	Communications, utilities, and miscellaneous charges	84	68	45
25.2	Other services from non-Federal sources	37	40	48
25.3	Other goods and services from Federal sources	26	7	6
25.3	Other goods and services from Federal sources	32	40	40
25.3	Other goods and services from Federal sources	50	41	16
25.4	Operation and maintenance of facilities	128	109	147
25.7	Operation and maintenance of equipment	8	20	21
26.0	Supplies and materials	40	26	30
31.0	Equipment	1	3	13
92.0	Undistributed		−15	
99.0	Direct obligations	1,225	1,147	1,211
	Reimbursable obligations:			
12.1	Civilian personnel benefits		75	
22.0	Transportation of things	70		78
23.3	Communications, utilities, and miscellaneous charges			29
25.2	Other services from non-Federal sources	2	36	37

Revolving and Management Funds—Continued
Federal Funds—Continued

313

		2021 actual	2022 est.	2023 est.
25.3	Other goods and services from Federal sources	1	21	22
25.3	Other goods and services from Federal sources			24
25.4	Operation and maintenance of facilities		10	69
25.7	Operation and maintenance of equipment		16	17
26.0	Supplies and materials	3,975	4,550	4,455
31.0	Equipment		3	3
99.0	Reimbursable obligations	4,048	4,711	4,734
99.9	Total new obligations, unexpired accounts	5,273	5,858	5,945

Employment Summary

Identification code 097–493004–0–4–051	2021 actual	2022 est.	2023 est.
1001 Direct civilian full-time equivalent employment	11,598	11,488	11,488

BUILDINGS MAINTENANCE FUND

Program and Financing (in millions of dollars)

Identification code 097–4931–0–4–051		2021 actual	2022 est.	2023 est.
	Obligations by program activity:			
0801	Operations and maintenance	253	267	268
0802	Pentagon force protection agency	38	37	38
0900	Total new obligations, unexpired accounts	291	304	306
	Budgetary resources:			
	Unobligated balance:			
1000	Unobligated balance brought forward, Oct 1	31	39	130
1021	Recoveries of prior year unpaid obligations	5		
1070	Unobligated balance (total)	36	39	130
	Budget authority:			
	Spending authority from offsetting collections, mandatory:			
1800	Collected	332	395	395
1801	Change in uncollected payments, Federal sources	−38		
1850	Spending auth from offsetting collections, mand (total)	294	395	395
1900	Budget authority (total)	294	395	395
1930	Total budgetary resources available	330	434	525
	Memorandum (non-add) entries:			
1941	Unexpired unobligated balance, end of year	39	130	219
	Change in obligated balance:			
	Unpaid obligations:			
3000	Unpaid obligations, brought forward, Oct 1	75	62	60
3010	New obligations, unexpired accounts	291	304	306
3020	Outlays (gross)	−299	−306	−366
3040	Recoveries of prior year unpaid obligations, unexpired	−5		
3050	Unpaid obligations, end of year	62	60	
	Uncollected payments:			
3060	Uncollected pymts, Fed sources, brought forward, Oct 1	−93	−55	−55
3070	Change in uncollected pymts, Fed sources, unexpired	38		
3090	Uncollected pymts, Fed sources, end of year	−55	−55	−55
	Memorandum (non-add) entries:			
3100	Obligated balance, start of year	−18	7	5
3200	Obligated balance, end of year	7	5	−55
	Budget authority and outlays, net:			
	Mandatory:			
4090	Budget authority, gross	294	395	395
	Outlays, gross:			
4100	Outlays from new mandatory authority	240	237	237
4101	Outlays from mandatory balances	59	69	129
4110	Outlays, gross (total)	299	306	366
	Offsets against gross budget authority and outlays:			
	Offsetting collections (collected) from:			
4120	Federal sources	−332	−395	−395
	Additional offsets against gross budget authority only:			
4140	Change in uncollected pymts, Fed sources, unexpired	38		
4170	Outlays, net (mandatory)	−33	−89	−29
4180	Budget authority, net (total)			
4190	Outlays, net (total)	−33	−89	−29

The Buildings Maintenance Fund was established in accordance with enactment of the 1994 Appropriations Conference Report for the General Services Administration and operates under the authority provided in 10

Revolving and Management Funds—Continued
Federal Funds—Continued

BUILDINGS MAINTENANCE FUND—Continued

U.S.C. 2208. It provides for the operation, maintenance, protection and repair of 11 federally owned facilities, 25 delegated leased, and 33 non-delegated leased facilities occupied by the Department of Defense in the National Capital Region.

Object Classification (in millions of dollars)

Identification code 097–4931–0–4–051		2021 actual	2022 est.	2023 est.
	Reimbursable obligations:			
	Personnel compensation:			
11.1	Full-time permanent	14	15	15
11.5	Other personnel compensation	1	....	....
11.9	Total personnel compensation	15	15	15
12.1	Civilian personnel benefits	6	5	5
23.1	Rental payments to GSA	214	232	232
23.2	Rental payments to others	7	....	....
23.3	Communications, utilities, and miscellaneous charges	4	....	....
25.1	Advisory and assistance services	4	7	7
25.2	Other services from non-Federal sources	19	15	17
25.4	Operation and maintenance of facilities	17	24	24
25.7	Operation and maintenance of equipment	2	2	2
26.0	Supplies and materials	2	1	1
31.0	Equipment	1	3	3
99.0	Reimbursable obligations	291	304	306
99.9	Total new obligations, unexpired accounts	291	304	306

Employment Summary

Identification code 097–4931–0–4–051	2021 actual	2022 est.	2023 est.
2001 Reimbursable civilian full-time equivalent employment	116	136	136

DEFENSE COUNTERINTELLIGENCE AND SECURITY AGENCY WORKING CAPITAL FUND

Program and Financing (in millions of dollars)

Identification code 097–4932–0–4–051		2021 actual	2022 est.	2023 est.
	Obligations by program activity:			
0810	Defense counterintelligence and security agency	1,264	1,302	1,217
0819	Reimbursable program activities, subtotal	1,264	1,302	1,217
	Budgetary resources:			
	Unobligated balance:			
1000	Unobligated balance brought forward, Oct 1	984	917	823
1011	Unobligated balance transfer from other acct [024–4571]	58		
1021	Recoveries of prior year unpaid obligations	3		
1070	Unobligated balance (total)	1,045	917	823
	Budget authority:			
	Appropriations, discretionary:			
1131	Unobligated balance of appropriations permanently reduced	–100	–100	
	Spending authority from offsetting collections, discretionary:			
1700	Collected	1,209	1,308	1,485
1701	Change in uncollected payments, Federal sources	27		
1750	Spending auth from offsetting collections, disc (total)	1,236	1,308	1,485
1900	Budget authority (total)	1,136	1,208	1,485
1930	Total budgetary resources available	2,181	2,125	2,308
	Memorandum (non-add) entries:			
1941	Unexpired unobligated balance, end of year	917	823	1,091
	Change in obligated balance:			
	Unpaid obligations:			
3000	Unpaid obligations, brought forward, Oct 1	558	684	658
3010	New obligations, unexpired accounts	1,264	1,302	1,217
3020	Outlays (gross)	–1,135	–1,328	–1,539
3040	Recoveries of prior year unpaid obligations, unexpired	–3		
3050	Unpaid obligations, end of year	684	658	336
	Uncollected payments:			
3060	Uncollected pymts, Fed sources, brought forward, Oct 1	–2	–29	–29
3070	Change in uncollected pymts, Fed sources, unexpired	–27		
3090	Uncollected pymts, Fed sources, end of year	–29	–29	–29
	Memorandum (non-add) entries:			
3100	Obligated balance, start of year	556	655	629
3200	Obligated balance, end of year	655	629	307
	Budget authority and outlays, net:			
	Discretionary:			
4000	Budget authority, gross	1,136	1,208	1,485
	Outlays, gross:			
4010	Outlays from new discretionary authority		816	1,040
4011	Outlays from discretionary balances	1,135	512	499
4020	Outlays, gross (total)	1,135	1,328	1,539
	Offsets against gross budget authority and outlays:			
	Offsetting collections (collected) from:			
4030	Federal sources	–1,209	–1,308	–1,485
4040	Offsets against gross budget authority and outlays (total)	–1,209	–1,308	–1,485
	Additional offsets against gross budget authority only:			
4050	Change in uncollected pymts, Fed sources, unexpired	–27		
4060	Additional offsets against budget authority only (total)	–27		
4070	Budget authority, net (discretionary)	–100	–100	
4080	Outlays, net (discretionary)	–74	20	54
4180	Budget authority, net (total)	–100	–100	
4190	Outlays, net (total)	–74	20	54

The Defense Counterintelligence and Security Agency Working Capital Fund finances the operations of the Defense Counterintelligence and Security Agency (DCSA). The Fund operates under the authority provided in 10 U.S.C. 2208. The Fund supports DCSA's mission to conduct security background investigations for the Department of Defense and other Federal agencies.

Object Classification (in millions of dollars)

Identification code 097–4932–0–4–051		2021 actual	2022 est.	2023 est.
	Reimbursable obligations:			
	Personnel compensation:			
11.1	Full-time permanent	265	336	350
11.5	Other personnel compensation	8	28	1
11.9	Total personnel compensation	273	364	351
12.1	Civilian personnel benefits	88	61	65
21.0	Travel and transportation of persons	20	20	17
22.0	Transportation of things	2	2	2
23.1	Rental payments to GSA	14	14	15
23.2	Rental payments to others	2	2	2
23.3	Communications, utilities, and miscellaneous charges	3	31	32
24.0	Printing and reproduction	1	1	1
25.1	Advisory and assistance services	847	769	692
25.3	Other goods and services from Federal sources		4	4
25.4	Operation and maintenance of facilities	3	4	4
25.7	Operation and maintenance of equipment	2	21	21
26.0	Supplies and materials	2	3	2
31.0	Equipment	7	6	9
99.0	Reimbursable obligations	1,264	1,302	1,217
99.9	Total new obligations, unexpired accounts	1,264	1,302	1,217

Employment Summary

Identification code 097–4932–0–4–051	2021 actual	2022 est.	2023 est.
2001 Reimbursable civilian full-time equivalent employment	3,315	3,315	3,315

TRUST FUNDS

Trust Funds

VOLUNTARY SEPARATION INCENTIVE FUND

Special and Trust Fund Receipts (in millions of dollars)

Identification code 097–8335–0–7–051		2021 actual	2022 est.	2023 est.
0100	Balance, start of year	76	62	48
	Receipts:			
	Current law:			
1140	Payment to Voluntary Separation Incentive Fund	21	16	13
1140	Earnings on Investments	2	1	1
1199	Total current law receipts	23	17	14

DEPARTMENT OF DEFENSE—MILITARY PROGRAMS

		2021 actual	2022 est.	2023 est.
1999	Total receipts	23	17	14
2000	Total: Balances and receipts	99	79	62
	Appropriations:			
	Current law:			
2101	Voluntary Separation Incentive Fund	-24	-17	-14
2103	Voluntary Separation Incentive Fund	-16	-14	-12
2135	Voluntary Separation Incentive Fund	3		
2199	Total current law appropriations	-37	-31	-26
2999	Total appropriations	-37	-31	-26
5099	Balance, end of year	62	48	36

Program and Financing (in millions of dollars)

Identification code 097–8335–0–7–051		2021 actual	2022 est.	2023 est.
	Obligations by program activity:			
0010	Direct program activity	37	31	26
0900	Total new obligations, unexpired accounts (object class 41.0)	37	31	26
	Budgetary resources:			
	Budget authority:			
	Appropriations, mandatory:			
1201	Appropriation (special or trust fund)	24	17	14
1203	Appropriation (previously unavailable)(special or trust)	16	14	12
1235	Appropriations precluded from obligation (special or trust)	-3		
1260	Appropriations, mandatory (total)	37	31	26
1930	Total budgetary resources available	37	31	26
	Change in obligated balance:			
	Unpaid obligations:			
3000	Unpaid obligations, brought forward, Oct 1	2	2	
3010	New obligations, unexpired accounts	37	31	26
3020	Outlays (gross)	-37	-33	-26
3050	Unpaid obligations, end of year	2		
	Memorandum (non-add) entries:			
3100	Obligated balance, start of year	2	2	
3200	Obligated balance, end of year	2		
	Budget authority and outlays, net:			
	Mandatory:			
4090	Budget authority, gross	37	31	26
	Outlays, gross:			
4100	Outlays from new mandatory authority		31	26
4101	Outlays from mandatory balances	37	2	
4110	Outlays, gross (total)	37	33	26
4180	Budget authority, net (total)	37	31	26
4190	Outlays, net (total)	37	33	26
	Memorandum (non-add) entries:			
5000	Total investments, SOY: Federal securities: Par value	75	62	49
5001	Total investments, EOY: Federal securities: Par value	62	49	37

Section 662 of the National Defense Authorization Act for 1992 and 1993, Public Law 102–190, established the Voluntary Separation Incentive (VSI) Fund to more effectively manage and account for the costs of the Voluntary Separation Incentive program. The VSI program provides annual payments to former active-duty servicemembers who voluntarily left service after serving more than six but less than 20 years. For all members who left service after December 31, 1992, the Department of Defense was required to deposit the total present value of their future VSI benefits into the VSI fund by the time authority to approve VSI benefits ended on December 31, 2001. DOD was also required to cover the unfunded benefits of former members who separated before January 1, 1993 through yearly, actuarially-determined Government contributions from the DOD military personnel appropriations. Permanent authority to make these payments is contained in section 8044 of the 1997 Defense Appropriations Act. The fund also receives interest on its investments.

HOST NATION SUPPORT FUND FOR RELOCATION

Special and Trust Fund Receipts (in millions of dollars)

Identification code 097–8337–0–7–051		2021 actual	2022 est.	2023 est.
0100	Balance, start of year			34
	Receipts:			
	Current law:			
1110	Contributions, Host National Support for U.S. Relocation Activities	170	174	177
1110	Contributions from Japan, Support for U.S. Relocation to Guam Activities	402	164	262
1140	Earnings on Investments, Support for U.S. Relocation to Guam Activities	18	34	20
1198	Rounding adjustment	1		
1199	Total current law receipts	591	372	459
1999	Total receipts	591	372	459
2000	Total: Balances and receipts	591	372	493
	Appropriations:			
	Current law:			
2101	Host Nation Support Fund for Relocation	-591	-338	-439
5099	Balance, end of year		34	54

Program and Financing (in millions of dollars)

Identification code 097–8337–0–7–051		2021 actual	2022 est.	2023 est.
	Obligations by program activity:			
0010	Concept Obligations Undistributed	1,086	892	624
	Budgetary resources:			
	Unobligated balance:			
1000	Unobligated balance brought forward, Oct 1	1,812	1,333	779
	Budget authority:			
	Appropriations, mandatory:			
1201	Appropriation (special or trust fund)	591	338	439
	Spending authority from offsetting collections, mandatory:			
1800	Collected	19		
1801	Change in uncollected payments, Federal sources	-3		
1850	Spending auth from offsetting collections, mand (total)	16		
1900	Budget authority (total)	607	338	439
1930	Total budgetary resources available	2,419	1,671	1,218
	Memorandum (non-add) entries:			
1941	Unexpired unobligated balance, end of year	1,333	779	594
	Change in obligated balance:			
	Unpaid obligations:			
3000	Unpaid obligations, brought forward, Oct 1	522	1,177	1,416
3010	New obligations, unexpired accounts	1,086	892	624
3020	Outlays (gross)	-431	-653	-783
3050	Unpaid obligations, end of year	1,177	1,416	1,257
	Uncollected payments:			
3060	Uncollected pymts, Fed sources, brought forward, Oct 1	-9	-6	-6
3070	Change in uncollected pymts, Fed sources, unexpired	3		
3090	Uncollected pymts, Fed sources, end of year	-6	-6	-6
	Memorandum (non-add) entries:			
3100	Obligated balance, start of year	513	1,171	1,410
3200	Obligated balance, end of year	1,171	1,410	1,251
	Budget authority and outlays, net:			
	Mandatory:			
4090	Budget authority, gross	607	338	439
	Outlays, gross:			
4100	Outlays from new mandatory authority	146	159	181
4101	Outlays from mandatory balances	285	494	602
4110	Outlays, gross (total)	431	653	783
	Offsets against gross budget authority and outlays:			
	Offsetting collections (collected) from:			
4120	Federal sources	-1		
4123	Non-Federal sources	-18		
4130	Offsets against gross budget authority and outlays (total)	-19		
	Additional offsets against gross budget authority only:			
4140	Change in uncollected pymts, Fed sources, unexpired	3		
4160	Budget authority, net (mandatory)	591	338	439
4170	Outlays, net (mandatory)	412	653	783
4180	Budget authority, net (total)	591	338	439
4190	Outlays, net (total)	412	653	783

Trust Funds—Continued
Trust Funds—Continued

HOST NATION SUPPORT FUND FOR RELOCATION—Continued

Program and Financing—Continued

Identification code 097–8337–0–7–051	2021 actual	2022 est.	2023 est.
Memorandum (non-add) entries:			
5000 Total investments, SOY: Federal securities: Par value	1,788	1,797	1,136
5001 Total investments, EOY: Federal securities: Par value	1,797	1,136	1,190

Section 2350k of U.S.C. Title 10 established a trust fund for cash contributions from any nation in support of relocation of elements of the Armed Forces from or to any location within that nation. The Host Nation Support for Relocation account is financed through these cash contributions and interest accrued on the cash balances. Funds may be used to defray costs incurred in connection with the relocation for which the contribution was made.

Object Classification (in millions of dollars)

Identification code 097–8337–0–7–051	2021 actual	2022 est.	2023 est.
41.0 Direct obligations: Grants, subsidies, and contributions	1,085	892	624
99.0 Direct obligations	1,085	892	624
99.0 Reimbursable obligations	1	....	....
99.9 Total new obligations, unexpired accounts	1,086	892	624

DEPARTMENT OF DEFENSE GENERAL GIFT FUND

Special and Trust Fund Receipts (in millions of dollars)

Identification code 097–8163–0–7–051	2021 actual	2022 est.	2023 est.
0100 Balance, start of year	....	....	....
Receipts:			
Current law:			
1130 Contributions, Department of Defense General Gift Fund Deposits, Department	....	7	7
2000 Total: Balances and receipts	....	7	7
Appropriations:			
Current law:			
2101 Department of Defense General Gift Fund	....	–7	–7
5099 Balance, end of year	....	....	....

Program and Financing (in millions of dollars)

Identification code 097–8163–0–7–051	2021 actual	2022 est.	2023 est.
Obligations by program activity:			
0010 Direct program activity	....	7	7
0900 Total new obligations, unexpired accounts (object class 25.3)	....	7	7
Budgetary resources:			
Unobligated balance:			
1000 Unobligated balance brought forward, Oct 1	8	8	8
Budget authority:			
Appropriations, mandatory:			
1201 Appropriation (special or trust fund)	....	7	7
1930 Total budgetary resources available	8	15	15
Memorandum (non-add) entries:			
1941 Unexpired unobligated balance, end of year	8	8	8
Change in obligated balance:			
Unpaid obligations:			
3010 New obligations, unexpired accounts	....	7	7
3020 Outlays (gross)	....	–7	–7
Budget authority and outlays, net:			
Mandatory:			
4090 Budget authority, gross	....	7	7
Outlays, gross:			
4100 Outlays from new mandatory authority	....	7	7
4180 Budget authority, net (total)	....	7	7

4190 Outlays, net (total)	....	7	7

OTHER DOD TRUST FUNDS

Special and Trust Fund Receipts (in millions of dollars)

Identification code 021–9971–0–7–051	2021 actual	2022 est.	2023 est.
0100 Balance, start of year	1	....	5
Receipts:			
Current law:			
1130 Deposits, Other DOD Trust Funds	43	5	5
1140 Interest, Other DOD Trust Funds	....	1	1
1140 Proceeds, Ships' Stores Profit, Navy	11	20	20
1199 Total current law receipts	54	26	26
1999 Total receipts	54	26	26
2000 Total: Balances and receipts	55	26	31
Appropriations:			
Current law:			
2101 Other DOD Trust Funds	–55	–21	–21
2103 Other DOD Trust Funds	....	–1	–1
2132 Other DOD Trust Funds	....	1	1
2199 Total current law appropriations	–55	–21	–21
2999 Total appropriations	–55	–21	–21
5099 Balance, end of year	....	5	10

Program and Financing (in millions of dollars)

Identification code 021–9971–0–7–051	2021 actual	2022 est.	2023 est.
Obligations by program activity:			
0010 Other DoD trust funds	69	48	22
Budgetary resources:			
Unobligated balance:			
1000 Unobligated balance brought forward, Oct 1	99	91	64
1021 Recoveries of prior year unpaid obligations	1	....	....
1033 Recoveries of prior year paid obligations	5	....	....
1070 Unobligated balance (total)	105	91	64
Budget authority:			
Appropriations, mandatory:			
1201 Appropriation (special or trust fund)	55	21	21
1203 Appropriation (previously unavailable)(special or trust)	....	1	1
1232 Appropriations and/or unobligated balance of appropriations temporarily reduced	....	–1	–1
1260 Appropriations, mandatory (total)	55	21	21
1900 Budget authority (total)	55	21	21
1930 Total budgetary resources available	160	112	85
Memorandum (non-add) entries:			
1941 Unexpired unobligated balance, end of year	91	64	63
Change in obligated balance:			
Unpaid obligations:			
3000 Unpaid obligations, brought forward, Oct 1	27	19	33
3010 New obligations, unexpired accounts	69	48	22
3020 Outlays (gross)	–76	–34	–25
3040 Recoveries of prior year unpaid obligations, unexpired	–1	....	....
3050 Unpaid obligations, end of year	19	33	30
Memorandum (non-add) entries:			
3100 Obligated balance, start of year	27	19	33
3200 Obligated balance, end of year	19	33	30
Budget authority and outlays, net:			
Mandatory:			
4090 Budget authority, gross	55	21	21
Outlays, gross:			
4100 Outlays from new mandatory authority	14	20	20
4101 Outlays from mandatory balances	62	14	5
4110 Outlays, gross (total)	76	34	25
Offsets against gross budget authority and outlays:			
Offsetting collections (collected) from:			
4120 Federal sources	–5	....	....
Additional offsets against gross budget authority only:			
4143 Recoveries of prior year paid obligations, unexpired accounts	5	....	....

DEPARTMENT OF DEFENSE—MILITARY PROGRAMS

		2021 actual	2022 est.	2023 est.
4160	Budget authority, net (mandatory)	55	21	21
4170	Outlays, net (mandatory)	71	34	25
4180	Budget authority, net (total)	55	21	21
4190	Outlays, net (total)	71	34	25
	Memorandum (non-add) entries:			
5000	Total investments, SOY: Federal securities: Par value	5	7	7
5001	Total investments, EOY: Federal securities: Par value	7	7	7

This fund includes gifts and bequests limited to specific purposes by the donors. In addition, it accounts for gifts and bequests, not limited to specific use by the donors, which may be used for purposes as determined by the Secretaries of the Army, Navy, and Air Force.

Object Classification (in millions of dollars)

Identification code 021–9971–0–7–051		2021 actual	2022 est.	2023 est.
	Direct obligations:			
21.0	Travel and transportation of persons	1		
25.1	Advisory and assistance services	1		
25.2	Other services from non-Federal sources	22	22	22
25.3	Other goods and services from Federal sources	8		
26.0	Supplies and materials	11	10	
31.0	Equipment	15	6	
41.0	Grants, subsidies, and contributions	11	10	
99.9	Total new obligations, unexpired accounts	69	48	22

NATIONAL SECURITY EDUCATION TRUST FUND

Special and Trust Fund Receipts (in millions of dollars)

Identification code 097–8168–0–7–051	2021 actual	2022 est.	2023 est.
0100 Balance, start of year	1	1	1
2000 Total: Balances and receipts	1	1	1
5099 Balance, end of year	1	1	1

Program and Financing (in millions of dollars)

Identification code 097–8168–0–7–051	2021 actual	2022 est.	2023 est.
4180 Budget authority, net (total)			
4190 Outlays, net (total)			
Memorandum (non-add) entries:			
5000 Total investments, SOY: Federal securities: Par value	2	2	2
5001 Total investments, EOY: Federal securities: Par value	2	2	2

FOREIGN NATIONAL EMPLOYEES SEPARATION PAY

Special and Trust Fund Receipts (in millions of dollars)

Identification code 097–8165–0–7–051	2021 actual	2022 est.	2023 est.
0100 Balance, start of year			
Receipts:			
Current law:			
1140 Foreign National Employees Separation Pay Trust Fund	7	8	8
2000 Total: Balances and receipts	7	8	8
Appropriations:			
Current law:			
2101 Foreign National Employees Separation Pay	–7	–8	–8
5099 Balance, end of year			

Program and Financing (in millions of dollars)

Identification code 097–8165–0–7–051	2021 actual	2022 est.	2023 est.
Obligations by program activity:			
0010 Direct program activity	7	8	8
0900 Total new obligations, unexpired accounts (object class 13.0)	7	8	8

		2021 actual	2022 est.	2023 est.
	Budgetary resources:			
	Unobligated balance:			
1000	Unobligated balance brought forward, Oct 1	4	4	4
	Budget authority:			
	Appropriations, mandatory:			
1201	Appropriation (special or trust fund)	7	8	8
1900	Budget authority (total)	7	8	8
1930	Total budgetary resources available	11	12	12
	Memorandum (non-add) entries:			
1941	Unexpired unobligated balance, end of year	4	4	4
	Change in obligated balance:			
	Unpaid obligations:			
3000	Unpaid obligations, brought forward, Oct 1	653	654	494
3010	New obligations, unexpired accounts	7	8	8
3020	Outlays (gross)	–6	–168	–151
3050	Unpaid obligations, end of year	654	494	351
	Memorandum (non-add) entries:			
3100	Obligated balance, start of year	653	654	494
3200	Obligated balance, end of year	654	494	351
	Budget authority and outlays, net:			
	Mandatory:			
4090	Budget authority, gross	7	8	8
	Outlays, gross:			
4100	Outlays from new mandatory authority		2	2
4101	Outlays from mandatory balances	6	166	149
4110	Outlays, gross (total)	6	168	151
4180	Budget authority, net (total)	7	8	8
4190	Outlays, net (total)	6	168	151

This account funds separation payments for foreign nationals who are either employed by the Department of Defense or by a foreign government for the benefit of the Department of Defense. The payments are determined according to the applicable labor laws of the various countries.

COMMISSARY STORES SURCHARGE PROGRAM

Program and Financing (in millions of dollars)

Identification code 097–8164–0–8–051		2021 actual	2022 est.	2023 est.
	Obligations by program activity:			
0801	Reimbursable program activity	245	236	231
	Budgetary resources:			
	Unobligated balance:			
1000	Unobligated balance brought forward, Oct 1	59	17	93
	Budget authority:			
	Spending authority from offsetting collections, mandatory:			
1800	Collected	202	292	315
1802	Offsetting collections (previously unavailable)	21	20	
1823	New and/or unobligated balance of spending authority from offsetting collections temporarily reduced	–20		
1850	Spending auth from offsetting collections, mand (total)	203	312	315
1900	Budget authority (total)	203	312	315
1930	Total budgetary resources available	262	329	408
	Memorandum (non-add) entries:			
1941	Unexpired unobligated balance, end of year	17	93	177
	Change in obligated balance:			
	Unpaid obligations:			
3000	Unpaid obligations, brought forward, Oct 1	266	290	294
3010	New obligations, unexpired accounts	245	236	231
3020	Outlays (gross)	–221	–232	–268
3050	Unpaid obligations, end of year	290	294	257
	Memorandum (non-add) entries:			
3100	Obligated balance, start of year	266	290	294
3200	Obligated balance, end of year	290	294	257
	Budget authority and outlays, net:			
	Mandatory:			
4090	Budget authority, gross	203	312	315
	Outlays, gross:			
4100	Outlays from new mandatory authority		38	19
4101	Outlays from mandatory balances	221	194	249
4110	Outlays, gross (total)	221	232	268

COMMISSARY STORES SURCHARGE PROGRAM—Continued

Program and Financing—Continued

Identification code 097–8164–0–8–051	2021 actual	2022 est.	2023 est.
Offsets against gross budget authority and outlays:			
Offsetting collections (collected) from:			
4123 Non-Federal sources	−202	−292	−315
4180 Budget authority, net (total)	1	20	....
4190 Outlays, net (total)	19	−60	−47
Memorandum (non-add) entries:			
5090 Unexpired unavailable balance, SOY: Offsetting collections	21	20	....
5092 Unexpired unavailable balance, EOY: Offsetting collections	20	....	....

The Commissary Surcharge Collections Trust Fund was established in 1992 as a result of the consolidation of Defense Commissaries. The fund pays commissary costs to acquire (including leases), construct, convert, expand, improve, repair, maintain, and equip the physical infrastructure of commissary stores and central processing facilities of the Defense Commissary system. Surcharge funds are also utilized for real property, environmental evaluation, and construction costs including costs for surveys, administration, overhead, planning, and design. Per 10 U.S.C. 2484 the fund may be supplemented with Commissary profit margins resulting from improved management practices and the variable pricing program. The statute (10 U.S.C. 2484) also prescribes costs which may be financed by the fund.

Object Classification (in millions of dollars)

Identification code 097–8164–0–8–051	2021 actual	2022 est.	2023 est.
Reimbursable obligations:			
23.2 Rental payments to others	2	....	....
23.3 Communications, utilities, and miscellaneous charges	....	5	5
25.2 Other services from non-Federal sources	12	....	....
25.4 Operation and maintenance of facilities	87	82	80
25.7 Operation and maintenance of equipment	58	87	86
26.0 Supplies and materials	2	....	....
31.0 Equipment	59	53	52
32.0 Land and structures	25	9	8
99.0 Reimbursable obligations	245	236	231
99.9 Total new obligations, unexpired accounts	245	236	231

GENERAL FUND RECEIPT ACCOUNTS

(in millions of dollars)

	2021 actual	2022 est.	2023 est.
Offsetting receipts from the public:			
017–143517 General Fund Proprietary Interest Receipts, not Otherwise Classified, Navy	....	1	1
017–304117 Recoveries under the Foreign Military Sales Program, Navy	16	22	22
017–321017 General Fund Proprietary Receipts, not Otherwise Classified, Navy	145	146	146
021–301900 Recoveries for Government Property Lost or Damaged	28	12	12
021–304121 Recoveries under the Foreign Military Sales Program, Army	4	22	22
021–321021 General Fund Proprietary Receipts, not Otherwise Classified, Army	297	298	298
057–304157 Recoveries under the Foreign Military Sales Program, Air Force	19	41	41
057–321057 General Fund Proprietary Receipts, not Otherwise Classified, Air Force	35	35	36
097–184000 Rent of Equipment and Other Personal Property	....	1	1
097–223600 Sale of Certain Materials in National Defense Stockpile	....	12	12
097–246200 Deposits for Survivor Annuity Benefits	17	21	21
097–265197 Sale of Scrap and Salvage Materials	....	1	1
097–276130 Family Housing Improvement Fund, Downward Reestimates of Subsidies	19	31	....
097–304197 Recoveries under the Foreign Military Sales Program, Defense Agencies	3	5	5
097–321097 General Fund Proprietary Receipts, not Otherwise Classified, Defense Agencies	161	161	162
General Fund Offsetting receipts from the public	744	809	780

Intragovernmental payments:

	2021 actual	2022 est.	2023 est.
017–388517 Undistributed Intragovernmental Payments and Receivables from Cancelled Accounts, Navy	28	45	45
021–388521 Undistributed Intragovernmental Payments and Receivables from Cancelled Accounts, Army	4	45	45
057–388557 Undistributed Intragovernmental Payments and Receivables from Cancelled Accounts, Air Force	56	57	58
097–388597 Undistributed Intragovernmental Payments and Receivables from Cancelled Accounts, Defense Agencies	5	5	5
General Fund Intragovernmental payments	93	152	153

ADMINISTRATIVE PROVISIONS

SEC. 101. *None of the funds made available in this title shall be expended for payments under a cost-plus-a-fixed-fee contract for construction, where cost estimates exceed $25,000, to be performed within the United States, except Alaska, without the specific approval in writing of the Secretary of Defense setting forth the reasons therefor.*

SEC. 102. *Funds made available in this title for construction shall be available for hire of passenger motor vehicles.*

SEC. 103. *Funds made available in this title for construction may be used for advances to the Federal Highway Administration, Department of Transportation, for the construction of access roads as authorized by section 210 of title 23, United States Code, when projects authorized therein are certified as important to the national defense by the Secretary of Defense.*

SEC. 104. *None of the funds made available in this title may be used to begin construction of new bases in the United States for which specific appropriations have not been made.*

SEC. 105. *None of the funds made available in this title shall be used for purchase of land or land easements in excess of 100 percent of the value as determined by the Army Corps of Engineers or the Naval Facilities Engineering Command, except: (1) where there is a determination of value by a Federal court; (2) purchases negotiated by the Attorney General or the designee of the Attorney General; (3) where the estimated value is less than $25,000; or (4) as otherwise determined by the Secretary of Defense to be in the public interest.*

SEC. 106. *None of the funds made available in this title shall be used to: (1) acquire land; (2) provide for site preparation; or (3) install utilities for any family housing, except housing for which funds have been made available in annual Acts making appropriations for military construction.*

SEC. 107. *None of the funds made available in this title for minor construction may be used to transfer or relocate any activity from one base or installation to another, without prior notification to the Committees on Appropriations of both Houses of Congress.*

SEC. 108. *None of the funds made available in this title may be used for the procurement of steel for any construction project or activity for which American steel producers, fabricators, and manufacturers have been denied the opportunity to compete for such steel procurement.*

SEC. 109. *None of the funds available to the Department of Defense for military construction or family housing during the current fiscal year may be used to pay real property taxes in any foreign nation.*

SEC. 110. *None of the funds made available in this title may be used to initiate a new installation overseas without prior notification to the Committees on Appropriations of both Houses of Congress.*

SEC. 111. *None of the funds made available in this title for military construction in the United States territories and possessions in the Pacific and on Kwajalein Atoll, or in countries bordering the Arabian Gulf, may be used to award any contract estimated by the Government to exceed $1,000,000 to a foreign contractor: Provided, That this section shall not be applicable to contract awards for which the lowest responsive and responsible bid of a United States contractor exceeds the lowest responsive and responsible bid of a foreign contractor by greater than 20 percent: Provided further, That this section shall not apply to contract awards for military construction on Kwajalein Atoll for which the lowest responsive and responsible bid is submitted by a Marshallese contractor.*

SEC. 112. *Funds appropriated to the Department of Defense for construction in prior years shall be available for construction authorized for each such military department by the authorizations enacted into law during the current session of Congress.*

SEC. 113. *For military construction or family housing projects that are being completed with funds otherwise expired or lapsed for obligation, expired or lapsed funds may be used to pay the cost of associated supervision, inspection, overhead, engineering and design on those projects and on subsequent claims, if any.*

SEC. 114. Notwithstanding any other provision of law, any funds made available to a military department or defense agency for the construction of military projects may be obligated for a military construction project or contract, or for any portion of such a project or contract, at any time before the end of the fourth fiscal year after the fiscal year for which funds for such project were made available, if the funds obligated for such project: (1) are obligated from funds available for military construction projects; and (2) do not exceed the amount appropriated for such project, plus any amount by which the cost of such project is increased pursuant to law: Provided, That funds may be obligated under this section at any time before the end of fiscal year 2024 for fiscal year 2017 and 2018 military construction projects for which project authorization has not lapsed or for which authorization is extended for fiscal year 2023 by a National Defense Authorization Act.

(INCLUDING TRANSFER OF FUNDS)

SEC. 115. Subject to 30 days prior notification, or 14 days for a notification provided in an electronic medium pursuant to sections 480 and 2883 of title 10, United States Code, to the Committees on Appropriations of both Houses of Congress, such additional amounts as may be determined by the Secretary of Defense may be transferred to: (1) the Department of Defense Family Housing Improvement Fund from amounts appropriated for construction in "Family Housing" accounts, to be merged with and to be available for the same purposes and for the same period of time as amounts appropriated directly to the Fund; or (2) the Department of Defense Military Unaccompanied Housing Improvement Fund from amounts appropriated for construction of military unaccompanied housing in "Military Construction" accounts, to be merged with and to be available for the same purposes and for the same period of time as amounts appropriated directly to the Fund: Provided, That appropriations made available to the Funds shall be available to cover the costs, as defined in section 502(5) of the Congressional Budget Act of 1974, of direct loans or loan guarantees issued by the Department of Defense pursuant to the provisions of subchapter IV of chapter 169 of title 10, United States Code, pertaining to alternative means of acquiring and improving military family housing, military unaccompanied housing, and supporting facilities.

(INCLUDING TRANSFER OF FUNDS)

SEC. 116. In addition to any other transfer authority available to the Department of Defense, amounts may be transferred from the Department of Defense Base Closure Account to the fund established by section 1013(d) of the Demonstration Cities and Metropolitan Development Act of 1966 (42 U.S.C. 3374) to pay for expenses associated with the Homeowners Assistance Program incurred under 42 U.S.C. 3374(a)(1)(A). Any amounts transferred shall be merged with and be available for the same purposes and for the same time period as the fund to which transferred.

SEC. 117. Notwithstanding any other provision of law, funds made available in this title for operation and maintenance of family housing shall be the exclusive source of funds for repair and maintenance of all family housing units, including general or flag officer quarters: Provided, That not more than $35,000 per unit may be spent annually for the maintenance and repair of any general or flag officer quarters without 30 days prior notification, or 14 days for a notification provided in an electronic medium pursuant to sections 480 and 2883 of title 10, United States Code, to the Committees on Appropriations of both Houses of Congress, except that an after-the-fact notification shall be submitted if the limitation is exceeded solely due to costs associated with environmental remediation that could not be reasonably anticipated at the time of the budget submission.

SEC. 118. Amounts contained in the Ford Island Improvement Account established by subsection (h) of section 2814 of title 10, United States Code, are appropriated and shall be available until expended for the purposes specified in subsection (i)(1) of such section or until transferred pursuant to subsection (i)(3) of such section.

(INCLUDING TRANSFER OF FUNDS)

SEC. 119. During the 5-year period after appropriations available in this Act to the Department of Defense for military construction and family housing operation and maintenance and construction have expired for obligation, upon a determination that such appropriations will not be necessary for the liquidation of obligations or for making authorized adjustments to such appropriations for obligations incurred during the period of availability of such appropriations, unobligated balances of such appropriations may be transferred into the appropriation "Foreign Currency Fluctuations, Construction, Defense", to be merged with and to be available for the same time period and for the same purposes as the appropriation to which transferred.

(INCLUDING TRANSFER OF FUNDS)

SEC. 120. For the purposes of this Act, the term "congressional defense committees" means the Committees on Armed Services of the House of Representatives and the Senate, the Subcommittee on Military Construction and Veterans Affairs of the Committee on Appropriations of the Senate, and the Subcommittee on Military Construction and Veterans Affairs of the Committee on Appropriations of the House of Representatives.

SEC. 121. Notwithstanding any other provision of law, the Secretary concerned may waive the percentage or dollar cost limitations applicable to military construction projects or military family housing projects: Provided, That such authority to waive cost limitations may not be used with respect to a military construction project with a total authorized cost greater than $500,000,000 or a military family housing project with a total authorized cost greater than $500,000,000, if that waiver would increase the project cost by more than 50 percent of the total authorized cost of the project: Provided further, That "Secretary concerned" has the meaning provided for in section 101(a) of title 10, United States Code: Provided further, That the authority provided by this section shall remain available until enactment of a National Defense Authorization Act for Fiscal Year 2023.

TITLE VIII—GENERAL PROVISIONS

SEC. 8001. During the current fiscal year, provisions of law prohibiting the payment of compensation to, or employment of, any person not a citizen of the United States shall not apply to personnel of the Department of Defense: Provided, That salary increases granted to direct and indirect hire foreign national employees of the Department of Defense funded by this Act shall not be at a rate in excess of the percentage increase authorized by law for civilian employees of the Department of Defense whose pay is computed under the provisions of section 5332 of title 5, United States Code, or at a rate in excess of the percentage increase provided by the appropriate host nation to its own employees, whichever is higher: Provided further, That this section shall not apply to Department of Defense foreign service national employees serving at United States diplomatic missions whose pay is set by the Department of State under the Foreign Service Act of 1980: Provided further, That the limitations of this provision shall not apply to foreign national employees of the Department of Defense in the Republic of Turkey.

SEC. 8002. No part of any appropriation contained in this Act shall remain available for obligation beyond the current fiscal year, unless expressly so provided herein.

(TRANSFER OF FUNDS)

SEC. 8003. Upon determination by the Secretary of Defense that such action is necessary in the national interest, the Secretary may, with the approval of the Office of Management and Budget, transfer not to exceed $8,000,000,000 of working capital funds of the Department of Defense or funds made available in this Act to the Department of Defense for military functions (except military construction) between such appropriations or funds or any subdivision thereof, to be merged with and to be available for the same purposes, and for the same time period, as the appropriation or fund to which transferred: Provided, That the Secretary of Defense shall notify the Congress promptly of all transfers made pursuant to this authority or any other authority in this Act: Provided further, That transfers among military personnel appropriations shall not be taken into account for purposes of the limitation on the amount of funds that may be transferred under this section.

SEC. 8004. (a) Not later than 60 days after enactment of this Act, the Department of Defense shall submit a report to the congressional defense committees to establish the baseline for application of reprogramming and transfer authorities for fiscal year 2023: Provided, That the report shall include—

(1) a table for each appropriation with a separate column to display the President's budget request, adjustments made by Congress, adjustments due to enacted rescissions, if appropriate, and the fiscal year enacted level;

(2) a delineation in the table for each appropriation both by budget activity and program, project, and activity as detailed in the Budget Appendix; and

(3) an identification of items of special congressional interest.

(b) Notwithstanding section 8003 of this Act, none of the funds provided in this Act shall be available for reprogramming or transfer until the report identified in subsection (a) is submitted to the congressional defense committees, unless the Secretary of Defense certifies in writing to the congressional defense committees that such reprogramming or transfer is necessary as an emergency requirement: Provided, That this subsection shall not apply to transfers from the following appropriations accounts:

(1) "Environmental Restoration, Army";

(2) "Environmental Restoration, Navy";

(3) "Environmental Restoration, Air Force";

(4) "Environmental Restoration, Defense-Wide";

(5) "Environmental Restoration, Formerly Used Defense Sites";

(6) "Drug Interdiction and Counter-drug Activities, Defense"; and

(7) "Shipbuilding and Conversion, Navy: Columbia Class Submarine (AP)" and "Shipbuilding and Conversion, Navy: Columbia Class Submarine" for transfers to the National Sea-Based Deterrence Fund, pursuant to 10 U.S.C. 2218a.

(TRANSFER OF FUNDS)

SEC. 8005. During the current fiscal year, cash balances in working capital funds of the Department of Defense established pursuant to section 2208 of title 10, United States Code, may be maintained in only such amounts as are necessary at any time for cash disbursements to be made from such funds: Provided, That transfers may be made between such funds: Provided further, That transfers may be made between working capital funds and the "Foreign Currency Fluctuations, Defense" appropriation and the "Operation and Maintenance" appropriation accounts in such amounts as may be determined by the Secretary of Defense, with the approval of the Office of Management and Budget, except that such transfers may not be made unless the Secretary of Defense has notified the Congress of the proposed transfer: Provided further, That except in amounts equal to the amounts appropriated to working capital funds in this Act, no obligations may be made against a working capital fund to procure or increase the value of war reserve material inventory, unless the Secretary of Defense has notified the Congress prior to any such obligation.

SEC. 8006. Funds appropriated in title III of this Act may be used for multiyear procurement contracts for the following project: Arleigh Burke Class Guided Missile Destroyer.

SEC. 8007. Within the funds appropriated for the operation and maintenance of the Armed Forces, funds are hereby appropriated pursuant to section 401 of title 10, United States Code, for humanitarian and civic assistance costs under chapter 20 of title 10, United States Code. Such funds may also be obligated for humanitarian and civic assistance costs incidental to authorized operations and pursuant to authority granted in section 401 of title 10, United States Code, and these obligations shall be reported as required by section 401(d) of title 10, United States Code: Provided, That funds available for operation and maintenance shall be available for providing humanitarian and similar assistance by using Civic Action Teams in the Trust Territories of the Pacific Islands and freely associated states of Micronesia, pursuant to the Compact of Free Association as authorized by Public Law 99–239: Provided further, That upon a determination by the Secretary of the Army that such action is beneficial for graduate medical education programs conducted at Army medical facilities located in Hawaii, the Secretary of the Army may authorize the provision of medical services at such facilities and transportation to such facilities, on a nonreimbursable basis, for civilian patients from American Samoa, the Commonwealth of the Northern Mariana Islands, the Marshall Islands, the Federated States of Micronesia, Palau, and Guam.

SEC. 8008. (a) During the current fiscal year, the civilian personnel of the Department of Defense may not be managed solely on the basis of any constraint or limitation in terms of man years, end strength, full-time equivalent positions, or maximum number of employees.

(b) Nothing in this section shall be construed to apply to military (civilian) technicians.

SEC. 8009. None of the funds appropriated by this Act shall be available for the basic pay and allowances of any member of the Army participating as a full-time student and receiving benefits paid by the Secretary of Veterans Affairs from the Department of Defense Education Benefits Fund when time spent as a full-time student is credited toward completion of a service commitment: Provided, That this section shall not apply to those members who have reenlisted with this option prior to October 1, 1987: Provided further, That this section applies only to active components of the Army.

(TRANSFER OF FUNDS)

SEC. 8010. (a) Funds appropriated in title III of this Act for the Department of Defense Pilot Mentor-Protege Program may be transferred to any other appropriation contained in this Act solely for the purpose of implementing a Mentor-Protege Program developmental assistance agreement pursuant to section 831 of the National Defense Authorization Act for Fiscal Year 1991 (Public Law 101–510; 10 U.S.C. 2302 note), as amended, under the authority of this provision or any other transfer authority contained in this Act.

SEC. 8011. None of the funds in this Act may be available for the purchase by the Department of Defense (and its departments and agencies) of welded shipboard anchor and mooring chain 4 inches in diameter and under unless the anchor and mooring chain are manufactured in the United States from components which are substantially manufactured in the United States: Provided, That for the purpose of this section, the term "manufactured" shall include cutting, heat treating, quality control, testing of chain and welding (including the forging and shot blasting process): Provided further, That for the purpose of this section substantially all of the components of anchor and mooring chain shall be considered to be produced or manufactured in the United States if the aggregate cost of the components produced or manufactured in the United States exceeds the aggregate cost of the components produced or manufactured outside the United States: Provided further, That when adequate domestic supplies are not available to meet Department of Defense requirements on a timely basis, the Secretary of the Service responsible for the procurement may waive this restriction on a case-by-case basis by certifying in writing to the Committees on Appropriations of the House of Representatives and the Senate that such an acquisition must be made in order to acquire capability for national security purposes.

SEC. 8012. Funds appropriated by this Act for the Defense Media Activity shall not be used for any national or international political or psychological activities.

SEC. 8013. During the current fiscal year, the Department of Defense is authorized to incur obligations of not to exceed $350,000,000 for purposes specified in section 2350j(c) of title 10, United States Code, in anticipation of receipt of contributions, only from the Government of Kuwait, under that section: Provided, That, upon receipt, such contributions from the Government of Kuwait shall be credited to the appropriations or fund which incurred such obligations.

SEC. 8014. (a) None of the funds appropriated in this Act are available to establish a new Department of Defense (department) federally funded research and development center (FFRDC), either as a new entity, or as a separate entity administrated by an organization managing another FFRDC, or as a nonprofit membership corporation consisting of a consortium of other FFRDCs and other nonprofit entities.

(b) No member of a Board of Directors, Trustees, Overseers, Advisory Group, Special Issues Panel, Visiting Committee, or any similar entity of a defense FFRDC, and no paid consultant to any defense FFRDC, except when acting in a technical advisory capacity, may be compensated for his or her services as a member of such entity, or as a paid consultant by more than one FFRDC in a fiscal year: Provided, That a member of any such entity referred to previously in this subsection shall be allowed travel expenses and per diem as authorized under the Federal Joint Travel Regulations, when engaged in the performance of membership duties.

(c) Notwithstanding any other provision of law, none of the funds available to the department from any source during the current fiscal year may be used by a defense FFRDC, through a fee or other payment mechanism, for construction of new buildings not located on a military installation, for payment of cost sharing for projects funded by Government grants, for absorption of contract overruns, or for certain charitable contributions, not to include employee participation in community service and/or development.

SEC. 8015. None of the funds appropriated or made available in this Act shall be used to procure carbon, alloy, or armor steel plate for use in any Government-owned facility or property under the control of the Department of Defense which were not melted and rolled in the United States or Canada: Provided, That these procurement restrictions shall apply to any and all Federal Supply Class 9515, American Society of Testing and Materials (ASTM) or American Iron and Steel Institute (AISI) specifications of carbon, alloy or armor steel plate: Provided further, That the Secretary of the military department responsible for the procurement may waive this restriction on a case-by-case basis by certifying in writing to the Committees on Appropriations of the House of Representatives and the Senate that adequate domestic supplies are not available to meet Department of Defense requirements on a timely basis and that such an acquisition must be made in order to acquire capability for national security purposes: Provided further, That these restrictions shall not apply to contracts which are in being as of the date of the enactment of this Act.

SEC. 8016. For the purposes of this Act, the term "congressional defense committees" means the Armed Services Committee of the House of Representatives, the Armed Services Committee of the Senate, the Subcommittee on Defense of the Committee on Appropriations of the Senate, and the Subcommittee on Defense of the Committee on Appropriations of the House of Representatives.

SEC. 8017. During the current fiscal year, the Department of Defense may acquire the modification, depot maintenance and repair of aircraft, vehicles and vessels as well as the production of components and other Defense-related articles, through competition between Department of Defense depot maintenance activities and private firms: Provided, That the Senior Acquisition Executive of the military department or Defense Agency concerned, with power of delegation, shall certify that successful bids include comparable estimates of all direct and indirect costs for both public and private bids.

SEC. 8018. (a)

(1) If the Secretary of Defense, after consultation with the United States Trade Representative, determines that a foreign country which is party to an agreement described in paragraph (2) has violated the terms of the agreement by discriminating against certain types of products produced in the United States that are covered by the agreement, the Secretary of Defense shall rescind the Secretary's blanket waiver of the Buy American Act with respect to such types of products produced in that foreign country.

(2) An agreement referred to in paragraph (1) is any reciprocal defense procurement memorandum of understanding, between the United States and a foreign country pursuant to which the Secretary of Defense has prospectively waived the Buy American Act for certain products in that country.

(b) For purposes of this section, the term "Buy American Act" means chapter 83 of title 41, United States Code.

SEC. 8019. During the current fiscal year, amounts contained in the Department of Defense Overseas Military Facility Investment Recovery Account shall be available until expended for the payments specified by section 2687a(b)(2) of title 10, United States Code.

SEC. 8020. (a) Notwithstanding any other provision of law, the Secretary of the Air Force may convey at no cost to the Air Force, without consideration, to Indian tribes located in the States of Nevada, Idaho, North Dakota, South Dakota, Montana, Oregon, Minnesota, and Washington relocatable military housing units located at Grand Forks Air Force Base, Malmstrom Air Force Base, Mountain Home Air Force Base, Ellsworth Air Force Base, and Minot Air Force Base that are excess to the needs of the Air Force.

(b) The Secretary of the Air Force shall convey, at no cost to the Air Force, military housing units under subsection (a) in accordance with the request for such units that are submitted to the Secretary by the Operation Walking Shield Program on behalf of Indian tribes located in the States of Nevada, Idaho, North Dakota, South Dakota, Montana, Oregon, Minnesota, and Washington. Any such conveyance shall be subject to the condition that the housing units shall be removed within a reasonable period of time, as determined by the Secretary.

(c) The Operation Walking Shield Program shall resolve any conflicts among requests of Indian tribes for housing units under subsection (a) before submitting requests to the Secretary of the Air Force under subsection (b).

(d) In this section, the term "Indian tribe" means any recognized Indian tribe included on the current list published by the Secretary of the Interior under section 104 of the Federally Recognized Indian Tribe Act of 1994 (Public Law 103–454; 108 Stat. 4792; 25 U.S.C. 5131).

SEC. 8021. During the current fiscal year, appropriations which are available to the Department of Defense for operation and maintenance may be used to purchase items having an investment item unit cost of not more than $350,000: Provided, That, upon determination by the Secretary of Defense that such action is necessary to meet the operational requirements of a Commander of a Combatant Command engaged in contingency operations overseas, such funds may be used to purchase items having an investment item unit cost of not more than $500,000.

SEC. 8022. None of the funds appropriated by this Act for programs of the Central Intelligence Agency shall remain available for obligation beyond the current fiscal year, except for funds appropriated for the Reserve for Contingencies, which shall remain available until September 30, 2024: Provided, That funds appropriated, transferred, or otherwise credited to the Central Intelligence Agency Central Services Working Capital Fund during this or any prior or subsequent fiscal year shall remain available until expended: Provided further, That any funds appropriated or transferred to the Central Intelligence Agency for advanced research and development acquisition, for agent operations, and for covert action programs authorized by the President under section 503 of the National Security Act of 1947 (50 U.S.C. 3093) shall remain available until September 30, 2024: Provided further, That any funds appropriated or transferred to the Central Intelligence Agency for the construction, improvement, or alteration of facilities, including leased facilities, to be used primarily by personnel of the intelligence community shall remain available until September 30, 2025.

SEC. 8023. (a) None of the funds appropriated in this Act may be expended by an entity of the Department of Defense unless the entity, in expending the funds, complies with the Buy American Act. For purposes of this subsection, the term "Buy American Act" means chapter 83 of title 41, United States Code.

(b) If the Secretary of Defense determines that a person has been convicted of intentionally affixing a label bearing a "Made in America" inscription to any product sold in or shipped to the United States that is not made in America, the Secretary shall determine, in accordance with section 2410f of title 10, United States Code, whether the person should be debarred from contracting with the Department of Defense.

(c) In the case of any equipment or products purchased with appropriations provided under this Act, it is the sense of the Congress that any entity of the Department of Defense, in expending the appropriation, purchase only American-made equipment and products, provided that American-made equipment and products are cost-competitive, quality competitive, and available in a timely fashion.

SEC. 8024. None of the funds appropriated or otherwise made available in this Act may be obligated or expended for assistance to the Democratic People's Republic of Korea unless specifically appropriated for that purpose: Provided, That this restriction shall not apply to any activities incidental to the Defense POW/MIA Accounting Agency mission to recover and identify the remains of United States Armed Forces personnel from the Democratic People's Republic of Korea.

SEC. 8025. Funds appropriated in this Act for operation and maintenance of the Military Departments, Combatant Commands and Defense Agencies shall be available for reimbursement of pay, allowances and other expenses which would otherwise be incurred against appropriations for the National Guard and Reserve when members of the National Guard and Reserve provide intelligence or counter-intelligence support to Combatant Commands, Defense Agencies and Joint Intelligence Activities, including the activities and programs included within the National Intelligence Program and the Military Intelligence Program: Provided, That nothing in this section authorizes deviation from established Reserve and National Guard personnel and training procedures.

SEC. 8026. (a) None of the funds available to the Department of Defense for any fiscal year for drug interdiction or counter-drug activities may be transferred to any other department or agency of the United States except as specifically provided in an appropriations law.

(b) None of the funds available to the Central Intelligence Agency for any fiscal year for drug interdiction or counter-drug activities may be transferred to any other department or agency of the United States except as specifically provided in an appropriations law.

SEC. 8027. None of the funds appropriated by this Act may be used for the procurement of ball and roller bearings other than those produced by a domestic source and of domestic origin: Provided, That the Secretary of the military department responsible for such procurement may waive this restriction on a case-by-case basis by certifying in writing to the Committees on Appropriations of the House of Representatives and the Senate, that adequate domestic supplies are not available to meet Department of Defense requirements on a timely basis and that such an acquisition must be made in order to acquire capability for national security purposes: Provided further, That this restriction shall not apply to the purchase of "commercial items", as defined by section 103 of title 41, United States Code, except that the restriction shall apply to ball or roller bearings purchased as end items.

SEC. 8028. None of the funds in this Act may be used to purchase any supercomputer which is not manufactured in the United States, unless the Secretary of Defense certifies to the congressional defense committees that such an acquisition must be made in order to acquire capability for national security purposes that is not available from United States manufacturers.

SEC. 8029. Notwithstanding any other provision in this Act, the Small Business Innovation Research program and the Small Business Technology Transfer program set-asides shall be taken proportionally from all programs, projects, or activities to the extent they contribute to the extramural budget. The Secretary of each military department, the Director of each Defense Agency, and the head of each other relevant component of the Department of Defense shall submit to the congressional defense committees, concurrent with submission of the budget justification documents to Congress pursuant to section 1105 of title 31, United States Code, a report with a detailed accounting of the Small Business Innovation Research program and the Small Business Technology Transfer program set-asides taken from programs, projects, or activities within such department, agency, or component during the most recently completed fiscal year.

SEC. 8030. None of the funds available to the Department of Defense under this Act shall be obligated or expended to pay a contractor under a contract with the Department of Defense for costs of any amount paid by the contractor to an employee when—

(1) such costs are for a bonus or otherwise in excess of the normal salary paid by the contractor to the employee; and

(2) such bonus is part of restructuring costs associated with a business combination.

(INCLUDING TRANSFER OF FUNDS)

SEC. 8031. During the current fiscal year, no more than $30,000,000 of appropriations made in this Act under the heading "Operation and Maintenance, Defense-Wide" may be transferred to appropriations available for the pay of military personnel, to be merged with, and to be available for the same time period as the appropriations to which transferred, to be used in support of such personnel in connection with support and services for eligible organizations and activities outside the Department of Defense pursuant to section 2012 of title 10, United States Code.

SEC. 8032. During the current fiscal year, in the case of an appropriation account of the Department of Defense for which the period of availability for obligation has expired or which has closed under the provisions of section 1552 of title 31, United States Code, and which has a negative unliquidated or unexpended balance, an obligation or an adjustment of an obligation may be charged to any current appropriation account for the same purpose as the expired or closed account if—

(1) the obligation would have been properly chargeable (except as to amount) to the expired or closed account before the end of the period of availability or closing of that account;

(2) the obligation is not otherwise properly chargeable to any current appropriation account of the Department of Defense; and

(3) in the case of an expired account, the obligation is not chargeable to a current appropriation of the Department of Defense under the provisions of section 1405(b)(8) of the National Defense Authorization Act for Fiscal Year 1991, Public Law 101–510, as amended (31 U.S.C. 1551 note): *Provided*, That in the case of an expired account, if subsequent review or investigation discloses that there was not in fact a negative unliquidated or unexpended balance in the account, any charge to a current account under the authority of this section shall be reversed and recorded against the expired account: *Provided further*, That the total amount charged to a current appropriation under this section may not exceed an amount equal to 1 percent of the total appropriation for that account.

SEC. 8033. (a) Notwithstanding any other provision of law, the Chief of the National Guard Bureau may permit the use of equipment of the National Guard Distance Learning Project by any person or entity on a space-available, reimbursable basis. The Chief of the National Guard Bureau shall establish the amount of reimbursement for such use on a case-by-case basis.

(b) Amounts collected under subsection (a) shall be credited to funds available for the National Guard Distance Learning Project and be available to defray the costs associated with the use of equipment of the project under that subsection. Such funds shall be available for such purposes without fiscal year limitation.

SEC. 8034. None of the funds appropriated in title IV of this Act may be used to procure end-items for delivery to military forces for operational training, operational use or inventory requirements: *Provided*, That this restriction does not apply to end-items used in development, prototyping, and test activities preceding and leading to acceptance for operational use: *Provided further*, That this restriction does not apply to programs funded within the National Intelligence Program: *Provided further*, That the Secretary of Defense may waive this restriction on a case-by-case basis by certifying in writing to the Committees on Appropriations of the House of Representatives and the Senate that it is in the national security interest to do so.

SEC. 8035. (a) The Secretary of Defense may, on a case-by-case basis, waive with respect to a foreign country each limitation on the procurement of defense items from foreign sources provided in law if the Secretary determines that the application of the limitation with respect to that country would invalidate cooperative programs entered into between the Department of Defense and the foreign country, or would invalidate reciprocal trade agreements for the procurement of defense items entered into under section 2531 of title 10, United States Code, and the country does not discriminate against the same or similar defense items produced in the United States for that country.

(b) Subsection (a) applies with respect to—

(1) contracts and subcontracts entered into on or after the date of the enactment of this Act; and

(2) options for the procurement of items that are exercised after such date under contracts that are entered into before such date if the option prices are adjusted for any reason other than the application of a waiver granted under subsection (a).

(c) Subsection (a) does not apply to a limitation regarding construction of public vessels, ball and roller bearings, food, and clothing or textile materials as defined by section XI (chapters 50–65) of the Harmonized Tariff Schedule of the United States and products classified under headings 4010, 4202, 4203, 6401 through 6406, 6505, 7019, 7218 through 7229, 7304.41 through 7304.49, 7306.40, 7502 through 7508, 8105, 8108, 8109, 8211, 8215, and 9404.

SEC. 8036. Notwithstanding any other provision of law, funds appropriated in this Act under the heading "Research, Development, Test and Evaluation, Defense-Wide" for any new start advanced concept technology demonstration project or joint capability demonstration project may only be obligated 45 days after a report, including a description of the project, the planned acquisition and transition strategy and its estimated annual and total cost, has been provided in writing to the congressional defense committees: *Provided*, That the Secretary of Defense may waive this restriction on a case-by-case basis by certifying to the congressional defense committees that it is in the national interest to do so.

SEC. 8037. Notwithstanding section 12310(b) of title 10, United States Code, a service member who is a member of the National Guard serving on full-time National Guard duty under section 502(f) of title 32, United States Code, may perform duties in support of the ground-based elements of the National Ballistic Missile Defense System.

SEC. 8038. None of the funds provided in this Act may be used to transfer to any nongovernmental entity ammunition held by the Department of Defense that has a center-fire cartridge and a United States military nomenclature designation of "armor penetrator", "armor piercing (AP)", "armor piercing incendiary (API)", or "armor-piercing incendiary tracer (API-T)", except to an entity performing demilitarization services for the Department of Defense under a contract that requires the entity to demonstrate to the satisfaction of the Department of Defense that armor piercing projectiles are either: (1) rendered incapable of reuse by the demilitarization process; or (2) used to manufacture ammunition pursuant to a contract with the Department of Defense or the manufacture of ammunition for export pursuant to a License for Permanent Export of Unclassified Military Articles issued by the Department of State.

SEC. 8039. Notwithstanding any other provision of law, the Chief of the National Guard Bureau, or his designee, may waive payment of all or part of the consideration that otherwise would be required under section 2667 of title 10, United States Code, in the case of a lease of personal property for a period not in excess of 1 year to any organization specified in section 508(d) of title 32, United States Code, or any other youth, social, or fraternal nonprofit organization as may be approved by the Chief of the National Guard Bureau, or his designee, on a case-by-case basis.

(INCLUDING TRANSFER OF FUNDS)

SEC. 8040. Of the amounts appropriated in this Act under the heading "Operation and Maintenance, Army", $158,967,374 shall remain available until expended: *Provided*, That, notwithstanding any other provision of law, the Secretary of Defense is authorized to transfer such funds to other activities of the Federal Government: *Provided further*, That the Secretary of Defense is authorized to enter into and carry out contracts for the acquisition of real property, construction, personal services, and operations related to projects carrying out the purposes of this section: *Provided further*, That contracts entered into under the authority of this section may provide for such indemnification as the Secretary determines to be necessary: *Provided further*, That projects authorized by this section shall comply with applicable Federal, State, and local law to the maximum extent consistent with the national security, as determined by the Secretary of Defense.

(INCLUDING TRANSFER OF FUNDS)

SEC. 8041. Of the amounts appropriated in this Act under the headings "Procurement, Defense-Wide" and "Research, Development, Test and Evaluation, Defense-Wide", $500,000,000 shall be for the Israeli Cooperative Programs: *Provided*, That of this amount, $80,000,000 shall be for the Secretary of Defense to provide to the Government of Israel for the procurement of the Iron Dome defense system to counter short-range rocket threats, subject to the U.S.-Israel Iron Dome Procurement Agreement, as amended; $127,000,000 shall be for the Short Range Ballistic Missile Defense (SRBMD) program, including cruise missile defense research and development under the SRBMD program, of which $40,000,000 shall be for co-production activities of SRBMD systems in the United States and in Israel to meet Israel's defense requirements consistent with each nation's laws, regulations, and procedures, subject to the U.S.-Israeli co-production agreement for SRBMD, as amended; $80,000,000 shall be for an upper-tier component to the Israeli Missile Defense Architecture, all of which shall be for co-production activities of Arrow 3 Upper Tier systems in the United States and in Israel to meet Israel's defense requirements consistent with each nation's laws, regulations, and procedures, subject to the U.S.-Israeli co-production agreement for Arrow 3 Upper Tier, as amended; and $173,000,000 shall be for the Arrow System Improvement Program including development of a long range, ground and airborne, detection suite: *Provided further*, That the transfer authority provided under this provision is in addition to any other transfer authority contained in this Act.

SEC. 8042. Of the amounts appropriated in this Act under the heading "Shipbuilding and Conversion, Navy", $1,328,146,000 shall be available until September 30, 2023, to fund prior year shipbuilding program cost increases for the following programs:

(1) FY 2013 Carrier Replacement Program: $461,700,000;
(2) FY 2015 Virginia Class Submarine Program: $46,060,000;
(3) FY 2015 DDG-51 Program: $30,231,000;
(4) FY 2015 Littoral Combat Ship Program: $4,250,000;
(5) FY 2016 DDG-51 Program: $24,238,000;
(6) FY 2016 Virginia Class Submarine Program: $58,642,000;
(7) FY 2016 T-AO Fleet Oiler Program: $9,200,000;
(8) FY 2016 Littoral Combat Ship Program: $18,000,000;
(9) FY 2016 CVN Refueling Overhauls Program: $62,000,000;
(10) FY 2016 Towing, Salvage, and Rescue Ship Program: $11,250,000;
(11) FY 2017 DDG 51 Program: $168,178,000;
(12) FY 2017 LPD-17 Amphibious Transport Dock Program: $17,739,000;
(13) FY 2017 LHA Replacement Program: $19,300,000;
(14) FY 2017 Littoral Combat Ship Program: $29,030,000;
(15) FY 2018 DDG 51 Program: $5,930,000;
(16) FY 2018 Littoral Combat Ship Program: $9,538,000;
(17) FY 2018 T-AO Fleet Oiler Program: $12,500,000;
(18) FY 2018 Towing, Salvage, and Rescue Ship Program: $6,750,000;
(19) FY 2019 Littoral Combat Ship Program: $6,983,000;
(20) FY 2019 T-AO Fleet Oiler Program: $106,400,000;

(21) FY 2019 Towing, Salvage, and Rescue Ship Program: $4,500,000;
(22) FY 2021 Virginia Class Submarine Program: $200,000,000; and
(23) FY 2021 Towing, Salvage, and Rescue Ship Program: $15,727,000.

SEC. 8043. Funds appropriated by this Act, or made available by the transfer of funds in this Act, for intelligence activities are deemed to be specifically authorized by the Congress for purposes of section 504 of the National Security Act of 1947 (50 U.S.C. 3094) during fiscal year 2023 until the enactment of the Intelligence Authorization Act for Fiscal Year 2023.

SEC. 8044. The Secretary of Defense may use up to $650,000,000 of the amounts appropriated or otherwise made available in this Act to the Department of Defense for the rapid acquisition and deployment of supplies and associated support services pursuant to section 806 of the Bob Stump National Defense Authorization Act for Fiscal Year 2003 (Public Law 107–314; 10 U.S.C. 2302 note), but only for the purposes specified in clauses (i), (ii), (iii), and (iv) of subsection (c)(3)(B) of such section and subject to the applicable limits specified in clauses (i), (ii), and (iii) of such subsection and, in the case of clause (iv) of such subsection, subject to a limit of $50,000,000: *Provided*, That the Secretary of Defense shall notify the congressional defense committees promptly of all uses of this authority.

SEC. 8045. None of the funds provided in this Act shall be available for integration of foreign intelligence information unless the information has been lawfully collected and processed during the conduct of authorized foreign intelligence activities: *Provided*, That information pertaining to United States persons shall only be handled in accordance with protections provided in the Fourth Amendment of the United States Constitution as implemented through Executive Order No. 12333.

SEC. 8046. None of the funds appropriated by this Act for programs of the Office of the Director of National Intelligence shall remain available for obligation beyond the current fiscal year, except for funds appropriated for research and technology, which shall remain available until September 30, 2024.

SEC. 8047. For purposes of section 1553(b) of title 31, United States Code, any subdivision of appropriations made in this Act under the heading "Shipbuilding and Conversion, Navy" shall be considered to be for the same purpose as any subdivision under the heading "Shipbuilding and Conversion, Navy" appropriations in any prior fiscal year, and the 1 percent limitation shall apply to the total amount of the appropriation.

SEC. 8048. None of the funds made available by this Act for excess defense articles, assistance under section 333 of title 10, United States Code, or peacekeeping operations for the countries designated annually to be in violation of the standards of the Child Soldiers Prevention Act of 2008 (Public Law 110–457; 22 U.S.C. 2370c–1) may be used to support any military training or operation that includes child soldiers, as defined by the Child Soldiers Prevention Act of 2008, unless such assistance is otherwise permitted under section 404 of the Child Soldiers Prevention Act of 2008.

(INCLUDING TRANSFER OF FUNDS)

SEC. 8049. During the current fiscal year, not to exceed $11,000,000 from each of the appropriations made in title II of this Act for "Operation and Maintenance, Army", "Operation and Maintenance, Navy", and "Operation and Maintenance, Air Force" may be transferred by the military department concerned to its central fund established for Fisher Houses and Suites pursuant to section 2493(d) of title 10, United States Code.

SEC. 8050. (a) None of the funds appropriated or otherwise made available by this Act may be expended for any Federal contract for an amount in excess of $1,000,000, unless the contractor agrees not to—

(1) enter into any agreement with any of its employees or independent contractors that requires, as a condition of employment, that the employee or independent contractor agree to resolve through arbitration any claim under title VII of the Civil Rights Act of 1964 or any tort related to or arising out of sexual assault or harassment, including assault and battery, intentional infliction of emotional distress, false imprisonment, or negligent hiring, supervision, or retention; or

(2) take any action to enforce any provision of an existing agreement with an employee or independent contractor that mandates that the employee or independent contractor resolve through arbitration any claim under title VII of the Civil Rights Act of 1964 or any tort related to or arising out of sexual assault or harassment, including assault and battery, intentional infliction of emotional distress, false imprisonment, or negligent hiring, supervision, or retention.

(b) None of the funds appropriated or otherwise made available by this Act may be expended for any Federal contract unless the contractor certifies that it requires each covered subcontractor to agree not to enter into, and not to take any action to enforce any provision of, any agreement as described in paragraphs (1) and (2) of subsection (a), with respect to any employee or independent contractor performing work related to such subcontract. For purposes of this subsection, a "covered subcontractor" is an entity that has a subcontract in excess of $1,000,000 on a contract subject to subsection (a).

(c) The prohibitions in this section do not apply with respect to a contractor's or subcontractor's agreements with employees or independent contractors that may not be enforced in a court of the United States.

(d) The Secretary of Defense may waive the application of subsection (a) or (b) to a particular contractor or subcontractor for the purposes of a particular contract or subcontract if the Secretary or the Deputy Secretary personally determines that the waiver is necessary to avoid harm to national security interests of the United States, and that the term of the contract or subcontract is not longer than necessary to avoid such harm. The determination shall set forth with specificity the grounds for the waiver and for the contract or subcontract term selected, and shall state any alternatives considered in lieu of a waiver and the reasons each such alternative would not avoid harm to national security interests of the United States. The Secretary of Defense shall transmit to Congress, and simultaneously make public, any determination under this subsection not less than 15 business days before the contract or subcontract addressed in the determination may be awarded.

(INCLUDING TRANSFER OF FUNDS)

SEC. 8051. From within the funds appropriated for operation and maintenance for the Defense Health Program in this Act, up to $168,000,000, shall be available for transfer to the Joint Department of Defense-Department of Veterans Affairs Medical Facility Demonstration Fund in accordance with the provisions of section 1704 of the National Defense Authorization Act for Fiscal Year 2010, Public Law 111–84: *Provided*, That for purposes of section 1704(b), the facility operations funded are operations of the integrated Captain James A. Lovell Federal Health Care Center, consisting of the North Chicago Veterans Affairs Medical Center, the Navy Ambulatory Care Center, and supporting facilities designated as a combined Federal medical facility as described by section 706 of Public Law 110–417: *Provided further*, That additional funds may be transferred from funds appropriated for operation and maintenance for the Defense Health Program to the Joint Department of Defense-Department of Veterans Affairs Medical Facility Demonstration Fund upon written notification by the Secretary of Defense to the Committees on Appropriations of the House of Representatives and the Senate.

SEC. 8052. Appropriations available to the Department of Defense may be used for the purchase of heavy and light armored vehicles for the physical security of personnel or for force protection purposes up to a limit of $450,000 per vehicle, notwithstanding price or other limitations applicable to the purchase of passenger carrying vehicles.

(INCLUDING TRANSFER OF FUNDS)

SEC. 8053. Upon a determination by the Director of National Intelligence that such action is necessary and in the national interest, the Director may, with the approval of the Office of Management and Budget, transfer not to exceed $1,500,000,000 of the funds made available in this Act for the National Intelligence Program.

SEC. 8054. None of the funds made available in this Act may be used for the purchase or manufacture of a flag of the United States unless such flags are treated as covered items under section 2533a(b) of title 10, United States Code.

SEC. 8055. Of the amounts appropriated in this Act for "Shipbuilding and Conversion, Navy", $138,000,000, to remain available for obligation until September 30, 2027, may be used for the purchase of two used sealift vessels for the National Defense Reserve Fleet, established under section 11 of the Merchant Ship Sales Act of 1946 (46 U.S.C. 57100): *Provided*, That such amounts are available for reimbursements to the Ready Reserve Force, Maritime Administration account of the United States Department of Transportation for programs, projects, activities, and expenses related to the National Defense Reserve Fleet: *Provided further*, That notwithstanding 10 U.S.C. 2218 (National Defense Sealift Fund), none of these funds shall be transferred to the National Defense Sealift Fund for execution.

SEC. 8056. None of the funds made available by this Act may be used by the National Security Agency to—

(1) conduct an acquisition pursuant to section 702 of the Foreign Intelligence Surveillance Act of 1978 for the purpose of targeting a United States person; or

(2) acquire, monitor, or store the contents (as such term is defined in section 2510(8) of title 18, United States Code) of any electronic communication of a United States person from a provider of electronic communication services to the public pursuant to section 501 of the Foreign Intelligence Surveillance Act of 1978.

SEC. 8057. Of the amounts appropriated in this Act for "Operation and Maintenance, Navy", $589,325,000, to remain available until expended, may be used for any purposes related to the National Defense Reserve Fleet established under section 11 of the Merchant Ship Sales Act of 1946 (46 U.S.C. 57100): *Provided*, That such amounts are available for reimbursements to the Ready Reserve Force, Maritime Administration account of the United States Department of Transportation for programs, projects, activities, and expenses related to the National Defense Reserve Fleet.

SEC. 8058. (a) None of the funds provided in this Act for the TAO Fleet Oiler program shall be used to award a new contract that provides for the acquisition of the following components unless those components are manufactured in the United States: Auxiliary equipment (including pumps) for shipboard services; propulsion equipment (including engines, reduction gears, and propellers); shipboard cranes; and spreaders for shipboard cranes.

(b) None of the funds provided in this Act for the FFG(X) Frigate program shall be used to award a new contract that provides for the acquisition of the following components unless those components are manufactured in the United States: Air circuit breakers; gyrocompasses; electronic navigation chart systems; steering controls; pumps; propulsion and machinery control systems; totally enclosed lifeboats; auxiliary equipment pumps; shipboard cranes; auxiliary chill water systems; and propulsion propellers: Provided, That the Secretary of the Navy shall incorporate United States manufactured propulsion engines and propulsion reduction gears into the FFG(X) Frigate program beginning not later than with the eleventh ship of the program.

SEC. 8059. None of the funds provided for, or otherwise made available, in this or any other Act, may be obligated or expended by the Secretary of Defense to provide motorized vehicles, aviation platforms, munitions other than small arms and munitions appropriate for customary ceremonial honors, operational military units, or operational military platforms if the Secretary determines that providing such units, platforms, or equipment would undermine the readiness of such units, platforms, or equipment.

SEC. 8060. During fiscal year 2023, the monetary limitation imposed by section 2208(l)(3) of title 10, United States Code may be exceeded by up to $1,000,000,000.

SEC. 8061. (a) Amounts appropriated under title IV of this Act, as detailed in budget activity eight of the tables in the explanatory statement regarding this Act, may be used for expenses for the agile research, development, test and evaluation, procurement, production, modification, and operation and maintenance of digital Software and Digital Technology Pilot programs designated by the Secretary of Defense or in the explanatory statement accompanying this Act.

(b) Software and Digital Technology Pilot Program requirements eligible for funding under this provision include software, electronic tools, systems, applications, resources, acquisition of services, business process re-engineering activities, functional requirements development, technical evaluations, and other activities in direct support of acquiring, developing, deploying, sustaining, enhancing, and modernizing Software and Digital Technology Pilot Programs.

(c) Additional Software and Digital Technology Pilot Programs may be initiated with prior notification to the congressional defense committees.

(d) Removal from Pilot Programs. A system project participating in a Software and Digital Technology Pilot Program may be removed from such Program if the Project has not been successful in meeting criteria established for such Pilot Program by the Secretary of Defense.

SEC. 8062. Supervision and administration costs and costs for design during construction associated with a construction project funded with appropriations available for operation and maintenance, or the "Counter-ISIS Train and Equip Fund" provided in this Act and executed in direct support of military and stability operations to counter the Islamic State of Iraq and Syria, may be obligated at the time a construction contract is awarded: Provided, That, for the purpose of this section, supervision and administration costs and costs for design during construction include all in-house Government costs.

SEC. 8063. From funds made available in title II of this Act, the Secretary of Defense may purchase for use by military and civilian employees of the Department of Defense in the United States Central Command area of responsibility: (1) passenger motor vehicles up to a limit of $75,000 per vehicle; and (2) heavy and light armored vehicles for the physical security of personnel or for force protection purposes up to a limit of $450,000 per vehicle, notwithstanding price or other limitations applicable to the purchase of passenger carrying vehicles.

SEC. 8064. Funds available to the Department of Defense for operation and maintenance may be used, notwithstanding any other provision of law, to provide supplies, services, transportation, including airlift and sealift, and other logistical support to coalition forces supporting military and stability operations to counter the Islamic State of Iraq and Syria: Provided, That the Secretary of Defense shall provide quarterly reports to the congressional defense committees regarding support provided under this section.

SEC. 8065. Of the amounts appropriated in this Act under the heading "Operation and Maintenance, Defense-Wide", for the Defense Security Cooperation Agency, $300,000,000, to remain available until September 30, 2024, shall be for the Ukraine Security Assistance Initiative: Provided, That such funds shall be available to the Secretary of Defense, with the concurrence of the Secretary of State, to provide assistance, including training; equipment; lethal assistance; logistics support, supplies and services; salaries and stipends; sustainment; and intelligence support to the military and national security forces of Ukraine, and to other forces or groups recognized by and under the authority of the Government of Ukraine, including governmental entities within Ukraine, engaged in resisting Russian aggression against Ukraine, for replacement of any weapons or articles provided to the Government of Ukraine from the inventory of the United States, and to recover or dispose of equipment procured using funds made available in this section in this or prior Acts: Provided further, That such funds may be obligated and expended notwithstanding section 1250 of the National Defense Authorization Act for Fiscal Year 2016 (Public Law 114—92): Provided further, That the Secretary of Defense shall, not less than 15 days prior to obligating funds made available in this section (or if the Secretary of Defense determines, on a case-by-case basis, that extraordinary circumstances exist that impact the national security of the United States, as far in advance as is practicable) notify the congressional defense committees in writing of the details of any such obligation: Provided further, That the Secretary of Defense shall, not more than 60 days after such notification is made, inform such committees if such funds have not been obligated and the reasons therefor: Provided further, That the Secretary of Defense shall consult with such committees in advance of the provision of support provided to other forces or groups recognized by and under the authority of the Government of Ukraine: Provided further, That the United States may accept equipment procured using funds made available in this section in this or prior Acts transferred to the security forces of Ukraine and returned by such forces to the United States: Provided further, That equipment procured using funds made available in this section in this or prior Acts, and not yet transferred to the military or national security forces of Ukraine or to other assisted entities, or returned by such forces or other assisted entities to the United States, may be treated as stocks of the Department of Defense upon written notification to the congressional defense committees: Provided further, That the Secretary of Defense shall provide quarterly reports to the congressional defense committees on the use and status of funds made available in this section.

SEC. 8066. Of the amounts appropriated under the heading "Operation and Maintenance, Defense-Wide", for the Defense Security Cooperation Agency, $1,392,920,000, to remain available until September 30, 2024, shall be available for International Security Cooperation Programs and other programs to provide support and assistance to foreign security forces or other groups or individuals to conduct, support or facilitate counterterrorism, crisis response, or building partner capacity programs: Provided, That the Secretary of Defense shall, not less than 15 days prior to obligating funds made available in this section, notify the congressional defense committees in writing of the details of any planned obligation: Provided further, That the Secretary of Defense shall provide quarterly reports to the Committees on Appropriations of the House of Representatives and the Senate on the use and status of funds made available in this section.

SEC. 8067. Of the amounts appropriated under the heading "Operation and Maintenance, Defense-Wide", for the Defense Security Cooperation Agency, $30,000,000, to remain available until September 30, 2024, shall be for payments to reimburse key cooperating nations for logistical, military, and other support, including access, provided to United States military and stability operations to counter the Islamic State of Iraq and Syria: Provided, That such reimbursement payments may be made in such amounts as the Secretary of Defense, with the concurrence of the Secretary of State, and in consultation with the Director of the Office of Management and Budget, may determine, based on documentation determined by the Secretary of Defense to adequately account for the support provided, and such determination is final and conclusive upon the accounting officers of the United States, and 15 days following written notification to the appropriate congressional committees: Provided further, That these funds may be used for the purpose of providing specialized training and procuring supplies and specialized equipment and providing such supplies and loaning such equipment on a non-reimbursable basis to coalition forces supporting United States military and stability operations to counter the Islamic State of Iraq and Syria, and 15 days following written notification to the appropriate congressional committees: Provided further, That the Secretary of Defense shall provide quarterly reports to the Committees on Appropriations of the House of Representatives and the Senate on the use and status of funds made available in this section.

SEC. 8068. Of the amounts appropriated under the heading "Operation and Maintenance, Defense-Wide", for the Defense Security Cooperation Agency, $520,000,000, to remain available until September 30, 2024, shall be available to reimburse Jordan, Lebanon, Egypt, Tunisia, and Oman under section 1226 of the National Defense Authorization Act for Fiscal Year 2016 (22 U.S.C. 2151 note), for enhanced border security: Provided, That the Secretary of Defense shall, not less than 15 days prior to obligating funds made available in this section, notify the congressional defense committees in writing of the details of any planned obligation and the nature of the expenses incurred: *Provided further*, That the Secretary of Defense shall provide quarterly reports to the Committees on Appropriations of the House of Representatives and the Senate on the use and status of funds made available in this section.

SEC. 8069. Equipment procured using funds provided in prior Acts under the heading "Counterterrorism Partnerships Fund" for the program authorized by section 1209 of the Carl Levin and Howard P. "Buck" McKeon National Defense Authorization Act for Fiscal Year 2015 (Public Law 113–291), or under the heading "Iraq Train and Equip Fund" for the program authorized by section 1236 of such Act, and not yet transferred to authorized recipients may be transferred to foreign security forces, irregular forces, groups, or individuals, authorized to receive assistance using amounts provided under the heading "Counter-ISIS Train and Equip Fund" in this Act: *Provided*, That such equipment may be transferred 15 days following written notification to the congressional defense committees.

SEC. 8070. Upon determination by the Secretary of Defense that such action is necessary to address an emergent need related to, or to improve the effectiveness or efficiency of, matters over which the commander of the cyber command has responsibilities under section 167b(d) of title 10, United States Code, the Secretary may, with the approval of the Office of Management and Budget, transfer amounts made available for cyber activities in appropriations in this Act for Operation and Maintenance, Procurement, and Research, Development, Test and Evaluation: *Provided*, That transfers pursuant to this section shall be made in accordance with section 8003 of this Act, as applicable, except that transfers among appropriations pursuant to this section shall not be taken into account for purposes of the limitation on the amount of funds that may be transferred under section 8003.

SEC. 8071. Notwithstanding any provision of this or any prior Act, amounts appropriated for the Space Force in this Act and any prior Acts shall be available for the establishment of field operating agencies for the Space Force.

(INCLUDING TRANSFER OF FUNDS)

SEC. 8072. The Secretary of Defense may transfer funds from any available Department of the Navy appropriation to any available Department of the Navy ship construction appropriation for the purpose of liquidating necessary changes resulting from inflation, market fluctuations, or rate adjustments for any ship construction program appropriated in law: *Provided*, That the Secretary may transfer not to exceed $100,000,000 under the authority provided by this section: *Provided further*, That the Secretary may not transfer any funds until 30 days after the proposed transfer has been reported to the Committees on Appropriations of the House of Representatives and the Senate, unless a response from the Committees is received sooner: *Provided further*, That any funds transferred pursuant to this section shall retain the same period of availability as when originally appropriated: *Provided further*, That the transfer authority provided by this section is in addition to any other transfer authority contained elsewhere in this Act.

SEC. 8073. During the current fiscal year, the Secretary of Defense and Secretaries of the military departments may expend amounts made available for operation and maintenance for any purpose the Secretary concerned determines to be proper with regard to the response to the disruption of the water supply near the Red Hill Bulk Fuel Storage Facility, on Oahu, Hawaii. Such a determination is final and conclusive upon the accounting officers of the United States.

SEC. 8074. Subject to the availability of appropriations and notwithstanding section 2306b of title 10, United States Code, the Secretary of the Navy may enter into a contract or contracts for up to 25 Ship to Shore Connector class crafts and associated material for the Ship to Shore Connector program.

GENERAL PROVISION—THIS TITLE

[SEC. 1301. Notwithstanding any other provision of law, funds provided by this title shall only be for the purposes specified, and shall not be subject to any transfer authority provided by law.] *(Disaster Relief Supplemental Appropriations Act, 2022.)*

[SEC. 2201. Not later than 30 days after the date of enactment of this Act, and every 30 days thereafter through fiscal year 2022, the Secretary of Defense shall provide a written report to the congressional defense committees describing the execution of funds provided in this title, including the amounts obligated and expended, in total and since the previous report; the nature of the costs incurred or services provided by such funds; and any reimbursements or funds transferred by another Federal agency to the Department of Defense which relates to the purpose of the funds provided by this title.]

[SEC. 2202. Notwithstanding any other provision of law, funds provided by this title shall only be for the purposes specified, and shall not be subject to any transfer authority provided by law.]

[SEC. 2203. The Inspector General of the Department of Defense shall carry out reviews of the activities of the Department of Defense to transport and care for Afghans, including but not limited to, the humane treatment and living conditions of Afghans at any Department of Defense facility; the use of funds by the Department of Defense to support such persons, including the monitoring of potential waste, fraud, or abuse of such funds; and any related issues that the Inspector General may direct: *Provided*, That the Inspector General shall provide to the congressional defense committees periodic updates on such oversight efforts and a written report to such committees not later than 60 days after the date of enactment of this Act.]

[SEC. 2204. Title IX of division C of Public Law 116–260 is amended under the heading "Afghanistan Security Forces Fund" by inserting the following before the penultimate proviso: "*Provided further*, That the Secretary of Defense may obligate and expend funds made available under this heading for costs associated with the termination of contracts previously funded with amounts provided under this heading in prior Acts, and to pay valid invoices in satisfaction of liabilities under such contracts for which the applicable prior appropriation cannot be identified:".]

[SEC. 2205. Not later than 90 days after the date of enactment of this Act, the Secretary of Defense, in consultation with the Service Secretaries and the Commander of United States Central Command, shall submit to the congressional defense committees a report regarding the disposition of United States property, equipment, and supplies, including property, equipment, and supplies provided to the Afghanistan National Security Forces, which were destroyed, taken out of Afghanistan, or remain in Afghanistan in connection with the United States military withdrawal: *Provided*, That such report shall include information on the future plans of the Department of Defense regarding any such items.] *(Afghanistan Supplemental Appropriations Act, 2022.)*

[SEC. 1101. Not later than 30 days after the date of enactment of this Act, and every 30 days thereafter through fiscal year 2022, the Secretary of Defense shall provide a written report to the congressional defense committees describing the execution of funds provided in this title, including the amounts obligated and expended, in total and since the previous report; the nature of the costs incurred or services provided by such funds; and any reimbursements or funds transferred by another Federal agency to the Department of Defense which relates to the purpose of the funds provided by this title.]

[SEC. 1102. Notwithstanding any other provision of law, funds provided by this title shall only be for the purposes specified, and shall not be subject to any transfer authority provided by law.] *(Additional Afghanistan Supplemental Appropriations Act, 2022.)*

[SEC. 1501. Each amount appropriated or made available by this Act is in addition to amounts otherwise appropriated for the fiscal year involved.]

[SEC. 1502. No part of any appropriation contained in this Act shall remain available for obligation beyond the current fiscal year unless expressly so provided herein.]

[SEC. 1503. Unless otherwise provided for by this Act, the additional amounts appropriated by this Act to appropriations accounts shall be available under the authorities and conditions applicable to such appropriations accounts for fiscal year 2022.]

[SEC. 1504. Each amount provided by this division is designated by the Congress as being for an emergency requirement pursuant to section 4001(a)(1) and section 4001(b) of S. Con. Res. 14 (117th Congress), the concurrent resolution on the budget for fiscal year 2022.]

[SEC. 1505. Not later than January 15, 2022, the Director of the Office of Management and Budget shall provide to the Committees on Appropriations of the House of Representatives and the Senate a written report on Operation Allies Welcome: *Provided*, That such report shall describe the strategy and transition plan leading to the conclusion of Operation Allies Welcome; a plan, including timeline, for relocating all Afghans currently residing at Department of Defense facilities to longer-term housing; the activities and responsibilities assigned to each Federal agency involved in such strategy and transition plan; and an estimate of the costs from each such agency for carrying out such strategy and transition plan.] *(Additional Afghanistan Supplemental Appropriations Act, 2022.)*

DEPARTMENT OF EDUCATION

OFFICE OF ELEMENTARY AND SECONDARY EDUCATION

Federal Funds

EDUCATION STABILIZATION FUND

Program and Financing (in millions of dollars)

Identification code 091–0251–0–1–501	2021 actual	2022 est.	2023 est.
Obligations by program activity:			
0001 Education Stabilization Fund	229,886	17,805	
0900 Total new obligations, unexpired accounts (object class 41.0)	229,886	17,805	
Budgetary resources:			
Unobligated balance:			
1000 Unobligated balance brought forward, Oct 1	508	18,158	
1011 Unobligated balance transfer from other acct [091–0203]	100		
1021 Recoveries of prior year unpaid obligations	26		
1070 Unobligated balance (total)	634	18,158	
Budget authority:			
Appropriations, discretionary:			
1100 Appropriation	81,880		
1120 Appropriations transferred to other acct [014–2106]	–409		
1131 Unobligated balance of appropriations, permanently reduced		–353	
1160 Appropriation, discretionary (total)	81,471	–353	
Appropriations, mandatory:			
1200 Appropriation	165,959		
1900 Budget authority (total)	247,430	–353	
1930 Total budgetary resources available	248,064	17,805	
Memorandum (non-add) entries:			
1940 Unobligated balance expiring	–20		
1941 Unexpired unobligated balance, end of year	18,158		
Change in obligated balance:			
Unpaid obligations:			
3000 Unpaid obligations, brought forward, Oct 1	18,928	200,174	119,909
3010 New obligations, unexpired accounts	229,886	17,805	
3020 Outlays (gross)	–48,614	–98,070	–86,754
3040 Recoveries of prior year unpaid obligations, unexpired	–26		
3050 Unpaid obligations, end of year	200,174	119,909	33,155
Memorandum (non-add) entries:			
3100 Obligated balance, start of year	18,928	200,174	119,909
3200 Obligated balance, end of year	200,174	119,909	33,155
Budget authority and outlays, net:			
Discretionary:			
4000 Budget authority, gross	81,471	–353	
Outlays, gross:			
4010 Outlays from new discretionary authority	24,951		
4011 Outlays from discretionary balances	14,318	34,229	10,875
4020 Outlays, gross (total)	39,269	34,229	10,875
Mandatory:			
4090 Budget authority, gross	165,959		
Outlays, gross:			
4100 Outlays from new mandatory authority	9,345		
4101 Outlays from mandatory balances		63,841	75,879
4110 Outlays, gross (total)	9,345	63,841	75,879
4180 Budget authority, net (total)	247,430	–353	
4190 Outlays, net (total)	48,614	98,070	86,754

Funds support the following programs authorized and funded in response to the novel coronavirus of 2019 (COVID-19) under the Coronavirus Aid, Relief, and Economic Security Act (the CARES Act); the Coronavirus Response and Relief Supplemental Appropriations Act, 2021; and the American Rescue Plan Act of 2021: the Elementary and Secondary School Emergency Relief Fund, Governors Emergency Education Relief Fund, Discretionary Grants, Emergency Assistance to Nonpublic Schools, Assistance for Homeless Children and Youth; Assistance for the Outlying Areas; and the Higher Education Emergency Relief Fund. Amounts in this schedule reflect balances that are spending out from prior year appropriations.

EDUCATION FOR THE DISADVANTAGED

For carrying out title I and subpart 2 of part B of title II of the Elementary and Secondary Education Act of 1965 (referred to in this Act as "ESEA") and section 418A of the Higher Education Act of 1965 (referred to in this Act as "HEA"), $21,280,551,000, of which $10,340,251,000 shall become available on July 1, 2023, and shall remain available through September 30, 2024, and of which $10,841,177,000 shall become available on October 1, 2023, and shall remain available through September 30, 2024, for academic year 2023–2024: Provided, That $6,459,401,000 shall be for basic grants under section 1124 of the ESEA: Provided further, That up to $5,000,000 of these funds shall be available to the Secretary of Education (referred to in this title as "Secretary") on October 1, 2022, to obtain annually updated local educational agency-level census poverty data from the Bureau of the Census: Provided further, That $1,362,301,000 shall be for concentration grants under section 1124A of the ESEA: Provided further, That $6,357,550,000 shall be for targeted grants under section 1125 of the ESEA: Provided further, That $6,357,550,000 shall be for education finance incentive grants under section 1125A of the ESEA: Provided further, That of the amounts available under the preceding two provisos the Secretary may reserve up to $100,000,000 to pay the costs of voluntary State school funding equity commissions and the costs of voluntary local education agency equity reviews: Provided further, That $30,000,000 shall be for competitive grants to support strong partnerships, which may include those among State educational agencies, local educational agencies and child welfare agencies, to create and implement innovative strategies for improving the education of foster children and youth under part D of title I of the ESEA: Provided further, That the Secretary may reserve up to 10 percent of the amount referred to in the previous proviso to provide technical assistance in the implementation of these grants: Provided further, That $220,000,000 shall be for carrying out subpart 2 of part B of title II: Provided further, That $66,123,000 shall be for carrying out section 418A of the HEA: Provided further, That notwithstanding section 418A(g)(2)(A) of the HEA, the Secretary may reduce the percentage of funds available for a program if the Secretary determines that there are not a sufficient number of high-quality applications for that program.

Note.—A full-year 2022 appropriation for this account was not enacted at the time the Budget was prepared; therefore, the Budget assumes this account is operating under the Continuing Appropriations Act, 2022 (Division A of Public Law 117–43, as amended). The amounts included for 2022 reflect the annualized level provided by the continuing resolution.

Program and Financing (in millions of dollars)

Identification code 091–0900–0–1–501	2021 actual	2022 est.	2023 est.
Obligations by program activity:			
0001 Grants to local educational agencies	16,536	16,536	20,537
0002 State agency programs: Migrants	376	376	376
0003 State agency programs: Neglected, delinquent, and at risk children and youth	48	48	82
0004 Special programs for migrant students	46	46	66
0006 Comprehensive literacy development grants	193	193	192
0007 Innovative approaches to literacy	28	28	28
0900 Total new obligations, unexpired accounts	17,227	17,227	21,281
Budgetary resources:			
Unobligated balance:			
1000 Unobligated balance brought forward, Oct 1	200	202	202
1021 Recoveries of prior year unpaid obligations	2		
1070 Unobligated balance (total)	202	202	202
Budget authority:			
Appropriations, discretionary:			
1100 Appropriation	6,386	6,386	10,439
Advance appropriations, discretionary:			
1170 Advance appropriation	10,841	10,841	10,841
1900 Budget authority (total)	17,227	17,227	21,280
1930 Total budgetary resources available	17,429	17,429	21,482
Memorandum (non-add) entries:			
1941 Unexpired unobligated balance, end of year	202	202	201
Change in obligated balance:			
Unpaid obligations:			
3000 Unpaid obligations, brought forward, Oct 1	12,531	13,584	11,128

327

EDUCATION FOR THE DISADVANTAGED—Continued
Program and Financing—Continued

Identification code 091–0900–0–1–501		2021 actual	2022 est.	2023 est.
3010	New obligations, unexpired accounts	17,227	17,227	21,281
3020	Outlays (gross)	–16,137	–19,683	–17,299
3040	Recoveries of prior year unpaid obligations, unexpired	–2	....	....
3041	Recoveries of prior year unpaid obligations, expired	–35	....	....
3050	Unpaid obligations, end of year	13,584	11,128	15,110
	Memorandum (non-add) entries:			
3100	Obligated balance, start of year	12,531	13,584	11,128
3200	Obligated balance, end of year	13,584	11,128	15,110
	Budget authority and outlays, net:			
	Discretionary:			
4000	Budget authority, gross	17,227	17,227	21,280
	Outlays, gross:			
4010	Outlays from new discretionary authority	5,408	7,843	8,005
4011	Outlays from discretionary balances	10,729	11,840	9,294
4020	Outlays, gross (total)	16,137	19,683	17,299
4180	Budget authority, net (total)	17,227	17,227	21,280
4190	Outlays, net (total)	16,137	19,683	17,299

Summary of Budget Authority and Outlays (in millions of dollars)

	2021 actual	2022 est.	2023 est.
Enacted/requested:			
Budget Authority	17,227	17,227	21,280
Outlays	16,137	19,683	17,299
Legislative proposal, subject to PAYGO:			
Budget Authority	....	....	16,000
Outlays	....	....	640
Total:			
Budget Authority	17,227	17,227	37,280
Outlays	16,137	19,683	17,939

SUMMARY OF PROGRAM LEVEL
(in millions of dollars)

	2021–2022 Academic Year	2022–2023 Academic Year	2023–2024 Academic Year
New Budget Authority	$6,385	$6,385	$26,440
Advance appropriation	10,841	10,841	10,841
Total program level	17,226	17,226	37,281
Change in advance appropriation from the previous year	0	0	0

Grants to local educational agencies.—Funds are allocated via formula for programs that provide academic support to help students in high-poverty schools meet challenging State standards. States assess annually all students in certain grades in at least English language arts, mathematics, and science; develop systems to differentiate among schools on the basis of performance on those assessments and other indicators; provide parents with information on the performance of their child's school; and ensure the development and implementation of support and improvement plans for the lowest-performing schools. The 2023 request would support activities to help school systems address inequities in school funding, including voluntary State school funding equity commissions and voluntary local educational agency equity reviews.

State agency migrant program.—Funds support formula grants to States for educational services to children of migratory farmworkers and fishers, with resources and services for children who have moved within the past 36 months.

State agency neglected, delinquent and at-risk children and youth education program.—Funds support formula grants to States for educational services to neglected or delinquent children and youth in State-run institutions, attending community day programs, and in correctional facilities. The 2023 request would support competitive grants to create and implement innovative strategies for improving the education of foster children and youth.

Special programs for migrant students.—Funds support grants to institutions of higher education and nonprofit organizations that assist migrant students in earning a high school equivalency certificate or in completing their first year of college.

Comprehensive literacy development grants.—Funds support continuation grants to States to provide targeted, evidence-based literacy interventions in high-need schools. States must award subgrants to local educational agencies (LEAs) to support literacy interventions for children from birth through kindergarten entry and for students from kindergarten through grade 12.

Innovative approaches to literacy.—Funds support competitive grants to LEAs, consortia of LEAs, the Bureau of Indian Education, or national nonprofit organizations, to promote literacy programs that support the development of literacy skills in low-income communities. Grantees would develop and implement school library programs and provide high-quality, developmentally appropriate, and up-to-date reading material to children and adolescents in low-income communities.

Object Classification (in millions of dollars)

Identification code 091–0900–0–1–501		2021 actual	2022 est.	2023 est.
	Direct obligations:			
25.1	Advisory and assistance services	5	5	8
25.2	Other services from non-Federal sources	10	10	10
25.3	Other goods and services from Federal sources	....	....	5
25.5	Research and development contracts	2	2	2
25.7	Operation and maintenance of equipment	6	6	2
41.0	Grants, subsidies, and contributions	17,204	17,204	21,254
99.9	Total new obligations, unexpired accounts	17,227	17,227	21,281

EDUCATION FOR THE DISADVANTAGED
(Legislative proposal, subject to PAYGO)

Program and Financing (in millions of dollars)

Identification code 091–0900–4–1–501		2021 actual	2022 est.	2023 est.
	Obligations by program activity:			
0001	Grants to local educational agencies	....	....	16,000
0900	Total new obligations, unexpired accounts (object class 41.0)	....	....	16,000
	Budgetary resources:			
	Budget authority:			
	Appropriations, mandatory:			
1200	Appropriation	....	....	16,000
1930	Total budgetary resources available	....	....	16,000
	Change in obligated balance:			
	Unpaid obligations:			
3010	New obligations, unexpired accounts	....	....	16,000
3020	Outlays (gross)	....	....	–640
3050	Unpaid obligations, end of year	....	....	15,360
	Memorandum (non-add) entries:			
3200	Obligated balance, end of year	....	....	15,360
	Budget authority and outlays, net:			
	Mandatory:			
4090	Budget authority, gross	....	....	16,000
	Outlays, gross:			
4100	Outlays from new mandatory authority	....	....	640
4180	Budget authority, net (total)	....	....	16,000
4190	Outlays, net (total)	....	....	640

Grants to local educational agencies.— The 2023 request includes $16 billion in mandatory funding that, when combined with $20.5 billion in discretionary funding, provides $36.5 billion for the program.

IMPACT AID

For carrying out programs of financial assistance to federally affected schools authorized by title VII of the ESEA, $1,541,112,000, of which $1,394,242,000 shall be for basic support payments under section 7003(b), $48,316,000 shall be for payments for children with disabilities under section 7003(d), $17,406,000, to remain available through September 30, 2024, shall be for construction under section

7007(b), $76,313,000 shall be for Federal property payments under section 7002, and $4,835,000, to remain available until expended, shall be for facilities maintenance under section 7008: Provided, That for purposes of computing the amount of a payment for an eligible local educational agency under section 7003(a) for school year 2022–2023, children enrolled in a school of such agency that would otherwise be eligible for payment under section 7003(a)(1)(B) of such Act, but due to the deployment of both parents or legal guardians, or a parent or legal guardian having sole custody of such children, or due to the death of a military parent or legal guardian while on active duty (so long as such children reside on Federal property as described in section 7003(a)(1)(B)), are no longer eligible under such section, shall be considered as eligible students under such section, provided such students remain in average daily attendance at a school in the same local educational agency they attended prior to their change in eligibility status.

Note.—A full-year 2022 appropriation for this account was not enacted at the time the Budget was prepared; therefore, the Budget assumes this account is operating under the Continuing Appropriations Act, 2022 (Division A of Public Law 117–43, as amended). The amounts included for 2022 reflect the annualized level provided by the continuing resolution.

Program and Financing (in millions of dollars)

Identification code 091–0102–0–1–501		2021 actual	2022 est.	2023 est.
	Obligations by program activity:			
0001	Basic support payments	1,354	1,354	1,394
0002	Payments for children with disabilities	49	49	48
0091	Direct program activities, subtotal	1,403	1,403	1,442
0101	Facilities maintenance	....	7	5
0201	Construction	....	34	18
0301	Payments for Federal property	76	76	76
0900	Total new obligations, unexpired accounts (object class 41.0)	1,479	1,520	1,541
	Budgetary resources:			
	Unobligated balance:			
1000	Unobligated balance brought forward, Oct 1	2	24	5
	Budget authority:			
	Appropriations, discretionary:			
1100	Appropriation	1,501	1,501	1,541
1930	Total budgetary resources available	1,503	1,525	1,546
	Memorandum (non-add) entries:			
1941	Unexpired unobligated balance, end of year	24	5	5
	Change in obligated balance:			
	Unpaid obligations:			
3000	Unpaid obligations, brought forward, Oct 1	246	235	222
3010	New obligations, unexpired accounts	1,479	1,520	1,541
3011	Obligations ("upward adjustments"), expired accounts	210	....	....
3020	Outlays (gross)	–1,490	–1,533	–1,434
3041	Recoveries of prior year unpaid obligations, expired	–210	....	....
3050	Unpaid obligations, end of year	235	222	329
	Memorandum (non-add) entries:			
3100	Obligated balance, start of year	246	235	222
3200	Obligated balance, end of year	235	222	329
	Budget authority and outlays, net:			
	Discretionary:			
4000	Budget authority, gross	1,501	1,501	1,541
	Outlays, gross:			
4010	Outlays from new discretionary authority	1,271	1,333	1,369
4011	Outlays from discretionary balances	219	200	65
4020	Outlays, gross (total)	1,490	1,533	1,434
4180	Budget authority, net (total)	1,501	1,501	1,541
4190	Outlays, net (total)	1,490	1,533	1,434

Impact Aid helps to replace the lost local revenue that would otherwise be available to educate federally connected children. The presence of certain students living on Federal property, such as students who are military dependents or who reside on Indian lands, can place a financial burden on local educational agencies (LEAs) that educate them. The property on which the children live and their parents work is exempt from local property taxes, limiting LEAs' access to a central source of revenue used by most communities to finance education.

Basic support payments.—Payments will be made on behalf of approximately 780,000 federally connected students enrolled in over 1,000 LEAs to assist them in meeting their operation and maintenance costs. Average per-student payments will be approximately $1,720.

Payments for children with disabilities.—Payments in addition to those provided under the Individuals with Disabilities Education Act (IDEA) will be provided on behalf of approximately 52,000 federally connected students with disabilities in approximately 800 LEAs. Average per-student payments will be approximately $930.

Facilities maintenance.—Funds will be used to provide emergency repairs for school facilities that serve military dependents and are owned by the Department of Education. Funds will also be used to transfer the facilities to LEAs.

Construction.—Approximately 7 to 8 construction grants will be awarded competitively to the highest-need Impact Aid LEAs for emergency repairs and modernization of school facilities.

Payments for Federal property.—Payments will be made to approximately 200 local educational agencies in which real property owned by the Federal Government represents 10 percent or more of the assessed value of real property in the local educational agency.

SCHOOL IMPROVEMENT PROGRAMS

For carrying out school improvement activities authorized by part B of title I, part A of title II, subpart 1 of part A of title IV, part B of title IV, part B of title V, and parts B and C of title VI of the ESEA; the McKinney-Vento Homeless Assistance Act; section 203 of the Educational Technical Assistance Act of 2002; the Compact of Free Association Amendments Act of 2003; and the Civil Rights Act of 1964, $5,525,982,000, of which $3,844,541,000 shall become available on July 1, 2023, and remain available through September 30, 2024, and of which $1,681,441,000 shall become available on October 1, 2023, and shall remain available through September 30, 2024, for academic year 2023–2024: Provided, That $378,000,000 shall be for part B of title I: Provided further, That $1,309,673,000 shall be for part B of title IV: Provided further, That $37,397,000 shall be for part B of title VI, which may be used for construction, renovation, and modernization of any public elementary school, secondary school, or structure related to a public elementary school or secondary school that serves a predominantly Native Hawaiian student body, and that the 5 percent limitation in section 6205(b) of the ESEA on the use of funds for administrative purposes shall apply only to direct administrative costs: Provided further, That $36,453,000 shall be for part C of title VI, which shall be awarded on a competitive basis, and may be used for construction, and that the 5 percent limitation in section 6305 of the ESEA on the use of funds for administrative purposes shall apply only to direct administrative costs: Provided further, That $52,000,000 shall be available to carry out section 203 of the Educational Technical Assistance Act of 2002 and the Secretary shall make such arrangements as determined to be necessary to ensure that the Bureau of Indian Education has access to services provided under this section: Provided further, That $24,463,218 shall be available to carry out the Supplemental Education Grants program for the Federated States of Micronesia and the Republic of the Marshall Islands: Provided further, That the Secretary may reserve up to 5 percent of the amount referred to in the previous proviso to provide technical assistance in the implementation of these grants: Provided further, That $202,840,000 shall be for part B of title V: Provided further, That $1,220,000,000 shall be available for grants under subpart 1 of part A of title IV.

Note.—A full-year 2022 appropriation for this account was not enacted at the time the Budget was prepared; therefore, the Budget assumes this account is operating under the Continuing Appropriations Act, 2022 (Division A of Public Law 117–43, as amended). The amounts included for 2022 reflect the annualized level provided by the continuing resolution.

Program and Financing (in millions of dollars)

Identification code 091–1000–0–1–501		2021 actual	2022 est.	2023 est.
	Obligations by program activity:			
0001	Supporting effective instruction State grants	2,137	2,137	2,148
0002	21st century community learning centers	1,259	1,259	1,310
0003	State assessments	369	369	378
0004	Education for homeless children and youths	106	106	110
0005	Native Hawaiians education	66	66	37
0006	Alaska Native education	121	36	36
0007	Training and advisory services	7	7	7
0008	Rural education	188	188	203
0009	Supplemental education grants	16	16	25
0010	Comprehensive centers	52	52	52
0011	Pooled evaluation	12	12	6
0012	Student support and academic enrichment	1,213	1,213	1,220

Office of Elementary and Secondary Education—Continued
Federal Funds—Continued

SCHOOL IMPROVEMENT PROGRAMS—Continued
Program and Financing—Continued

Identification code 091–1000–0–1–501	2021 actual	2022 est.	2023 est.
0900 Total new obligations, unexpired accounts	5,546	5,461	5,532
Budgetary resources:			
Unobligated balance:			
1000 Unobligated balance brought forward, Oct 1	48	116	99
1001 Discretionary unobligated balance brought fwd, Oct 1	48		
Budget authority:			
Appropriations, discretionary:			
1100 Appropriation	3,763	3,763	3,845
Advance appropriations, discretionary:			
1170 Advance appropriation	1,681	1,681	1,681
Appropriations, mandatory:			
1200 Appropriation	170		
1900 Budget authority (total)	5,614	5,444	5,526
1930 Total budgetary resources available	5,662	5,560	5,625
Memorandum (non-add) entries:			
1941 Unexpired unobligated balance, end of year	116	99	93
Change in obligated balance:			
Unpaid obligations:			
3000 Unpaid obligations, brought forward, Oct 1	6,870	7,641	6,129
3010 New obligations, unexpired accounts	5,546	5,461	5,532
3020 Outlays (gross)	–4,763	–6,973	–5,233
3041 Recoveries of prior year unpaid obligations, expired	–12		
3050 Unpaid obligations, end of year	7,641	6,129	6,428
Memorandum (non-add) entries:			
3100 Obligated balance, start of year	6,870	7,641	6,129
3200 Obligated balance, end of year	7,641	6,129	6,428
Budget authority and outlays, net:			
Discretionary:			
4000 Budget authority, gross	5,444	5,444	5,526
Outlays, gross:			
4010 Outlays from new discretionary authority	694	1,084	1,086
4011 Outlays from discretionary balances	4,069	5,788	4,095
4020 Outlays, gross (total)	4,763	6,872	5,181
Mandatory:			
4090 Budget authority, gross	170		
Outlays, gross:			
4101 Outlays from mandatory balances		101	52
4180 Budget authority, net (total)	5,614	5,444	5,526
4190 Outlays, net (total)	4,763	6,973	5,233

Summary of Budget Authority and Outlays (in millions of dollars)

	2021 actual	2022 est.	2023 est.
Enacted/requested:			
Budget Authority	5,614	5,444	5,526
Outlays	4,763	6,973	5,233
Legislative proposal, not subject to PAYGO:			
Budget Authority			1,000
Outlays			20
Total:			
Budget Authority	5,614	5,444	6,526
Outlays	4,763	6,973	5,253

SUMMARY OF PROGRAM LEVEL
(in millions of dollars)

	2021–2022 Academic Year	2022–2023 Academic Year	2023–2024 Academic Year
New Budget Authority	$3,763	$3,763	$3,845
Advance Appropriation	1,681	1,681	1,681
Total program level	5,444	5,444	5,526
Change in advance appropriation over previous year	0	0	0

Supporting effective instruction State grants.—Funds support formula grants to States and local educational agencies (LEAs) to improve teacher and principal effectiveness and ensure the equitable distribution of effective and highly effective teachers and principals.

21st century community learning centers.—Funds support formula grants to States for projects that provide the additional time, support, and enrichment activities needed to improve student achievement.

State assessments.—Funds support formula grants to States to develop and implement assessments that are aligned with college- and career-ready academic standards. Funds could also support audits of State and local assessment systems. A portion of the funds support competitive grants for activities to improve State assessment systems.

Education for homeless children and youths.—Funds support formula grants to States to provide educational and support services that enable homeless children and youth to attend and achieve success in school.

Native Hawaiians education.—Funds support competitive grants to public and private entities to develop or operate innovative projects that enhance the educational services provided to Native Hawaiian children and adults.

Alaska Native education.—Funds support competitive grants to Alaska Native organizations and other public and private organizations to develop or operate innovative projects that enhance the educational services provided to Alaska Native children and adults.

Training and advisory services.—Funds support grants to regional equity assistance centers that provide technical assistance upon request to local educational agencies (LEAs) in addressing educational equity related to issues of race, gender, and national origin.

Rural education.—Funds support formula grants under two programs: the Small, Rural School Achievement program and the Rural and Low-Income School program. The Small, Rural School Achievement program provides rural LEAs with small enrollments with additional formula funds. Funds under the Rural and Low-Income School program, which targets rural LEAs that serve concentrations of poor students, are allocated by formula to States, which in turn allocate funds to eligible LEAs.

Supplemental education grants.—Funds support grants to the Federated States of Micronesia and to the Republic of the Marshall Islands in place of grant programs in which those Freely Associated States no longer participate pursuant to the Compact of Free Association Amendments Act of 2003.

Comprehensive centers.—Funds support 22 comprehensive centers that focus on building State capacity to help school districts and schools meet the requirements of the ESEA.

Student support and academic enrichment grants.—Funds support formula grants to improve academic achievement by increasing the capacity of States and LEAs to provide all students with access to a well-rounded education, to improve school conditions for student learning, and to improve the use of technology.

Object Classification (in millions of dollars)

Identification code 091–1000–0–1–501	2021 actual	2022 est.	2023 est.
Direct obligations:			
25.1 Advisory and assistance services	7	7	7
25.2 Other services from non-Federal sources	24	24	24
25.5 Research and development contracts	1	1	1
25.7 Operation and maintenance of equipment	3	3	3
41.0 Grants, subsidies, and contributions	5,512	5,427	5,497
99.0 Direct obligations	5,547	5,462	5,532
99.5 Adjustment for rounding	–1	–1	
99.9 Total new obligations, unexpired accounts	5,546	5,461	5,532

SCHOOL IMPROVEMENT PROGRAMS
(Legislative proposal, not subject to PAYGO)

Program and Financing (in millions of dollars)

Identification code 091–1000–2–1–501	2021 actual	2022 est.	2023 est.
Obligations by program activity:			
0001 School-based health professionals			1,000
0900 Total new obligations, unexpired accounts (object class 41.0)			1,000
Budgetary resources:			
Budget authority:			
Appropriations, discretionary:			
1100 Appropriation			1,000
1900 Budget authority (total)			1,000

DEPARTMENT OF EDUCATION

		2021 actual	2022 est.	2023 est.
1930	Total budgetary resources available			1,000
	Change in obligated balance:			
	Unpaid obligations:			
3010	New obligations, unexpired accounts			1,000
3020	Outlays (gross)			−20
3050	Unpaid obligations, end of year			980
	Memorandum (non-add) entries:			
3200	Obligated balance, end of year			980
	Budget authority and outlays, net:			
	Discretionary:			
4000	Budget authority, gross			1,000
	Outlays, gross:			
4010	Outlays from new discretionary authority			20
4180	Budget authority, net (total)			1,000
4190	Outlays, net (total)			20

School-based health professionals.—Funds would provide formula grants to State educational agencies, which would then make competitive grants to high-need local educational agencies to support the goal of doubling the number of health professionals, including school counselors, nurses, school psychologists, and social workers, in our Nation's schools.

SAFE SCHOOLS AND CITIZENSHIP EDUCATION

For carrying out activities authorized by subparts 2 and 3 of part F of title IV of the ESEA, $693,000,000: Provided, That $129,000,000 shall be available for section 4631, of which up to $5,000,000, to remain available until expended, shall be for the Project School Emergency Response to Violence (Project SERV) program: Provided further, That $468,000,000 shall be available for section 4625, and up to $10,000,000 of such funds may be used for planning grants: Provided further, That the Secretary may use up to $25,000,000 of the funds in the preceding proviso for grants to local educational agencies to provide integrated student supports designed to improve student social, emotional, physical, and mental health and academic outcomes: Provided further, That the Secretary may reserve up to 2 percent of the funds provided in the second preceding proviso for technical assistance under section 4625 and to grantees funded under the preceding proviso: Provided further, That $96,000,000 shall be available through December 31, 2023, for section 4624.

Note.—A full-year 2022 appropriation for this account was not enacted at the time the Budget was prepared; therefore, the Budget assumes this account is operating under the Continuing Appropriations Act, 2022 (Division A of Public Law 117–43, as amended). The amounts included for 2022 reflect the annualized level provided by the continuing resolution.

Program and Financing (in millions of dollars)

Identification code 091–0203–0–1–501	2021 actual	2022 est.	2023 est.
Obligations by program activity:			
0001 School safety national activities	104	104	129
0002 Full-service community schools	30	30	468
0003 Promise neighborhoods	119	119	96
0500 Direct program activities, subtotal	253	253	693
0900 Total new obligations, unexpired accounts	253	253	693
Budgetary resources:			
Unobligated balance:			
1000 Unobligated balance brought forward, Oct 1	191	55	19
1010 Unobligated balance transfer to other accts [091–0251]	−100		
1070 Unobligated balance (total)	91	55	19
Budget authority:			
Appropriations, discretionary:			
1100 Appropriation	217	217	693
1930 Total budgetary resources available	308	272	712
Memorandum (non-add) entries:			
1941 Unexpired unobligated balance, end of year	55	19	19
Change in obligated balance:			
Unpaid obligations:			
3000 Unpaid obligations, brought forward, Oct 1	309	378	403
3010 New obligations, unexpired accounts	253	253	693
3020 Outlays (gross)	−179	−228	−261
3041 Recoveries of prior year unpaid obligations, expired	−5		
3050 Unpaid obligations, end of year	378	403	835
Memorandum (non-add) entries:			
3100 Obligated balance, start of year	309	378	403
3200 Obligated balance, end of year	378	403	835
Budget authority and outlays, net:			
Discretionary:			
4000 Budget authority, gross	217	217	693
Outlays, gross:			
4010 Outlays from new discretionary authority	1	4	14
4011 Outlays from discretionary balances	178	224	247
4020 Outlays, gross (total)	179	228	261
4180 Budget authority, net (total)	217	217	693
4190 Outlays, net (total)	179	228	261

School safety national activities.—Funds support competitive grants and other discretionary activities to foster safe, secure, and supportive school and community environments conducive to teaching and learning; facilitate emergency management and preparedness as well as recovery from traumatic events; increase the availability of school-based mental health service providers for students; prevent drug use and violence by students; and otherwise improve student well-being. These activities include Project Prevent, a program of grants to local educational agencies to help break the cycle of violence in communities with pervasive violence.

Full-service community schools.—Funds support grants to local educational agencies or the Bureau of Indian Education, in partnership with community-based organizations, nonprofit organizations, or other public or private entities, to provide comprehensive and coordinated academic, social, and health services for students, students' family members, and community members that will result in improved educational outcomes for children in neighborhoods with high rates of poverty, childhood obesity, academic failure, and involvement of community members in the justice system.

Promise neighborhoods.—Funds support competitive grants and other activities for projects designed to improve significantly the educational and developmental outcomes of children within the Nation's most distressed communities, by providing children in the community with access to a cradle-through-college-to-career continuum of academic programs and community supports, including effective schools and services. The 2023 request would continue to support the Administration's Community Violence Intervention initiative by giving priority to applicants for Project Prevent, Full Service Community Schools, and Promise Neighborhoods grantees who propose to incorporate strategies into their projects for reducing gun violence through tools other than incarceration.

Object Classification (in millions of dollars)

Identification code 091–0203–0–1–501	2021 actual	2022 est.	2023 est.
Direct obligations:			
25.1 Advisory and assistance services			10
25.2 Other services from non-Federal sources	3	3	4
25.7 Operation and maintenance of equipment	4	4	4
41.0 Grants, subsidies, and contributions	245	245	675
99.0 Direct obligations	252	252	693
99.5 Adjustment for rounding	1	1	
99.9 Total new obligations, unexpired accounts	253	253	693

INDIAN EDUCATION

For expenses necessary to carry out, to the extent not otherwise provided, title VI, part A of the ESEA, $186,239,000, of which $67,993,000 shall be for subpart 2 of part A of title VI and $7,865,000 shall be for subpart 3 of part A of title VI: Provided, That the 5 percent limitation in sections 6115(d), 6121(e), and 6133(g) of the ESEA on the use of funds for administrative purposes shall apply only to direct administrative costs: Provided further, That the Secretary may make awards under subpart 3 of Part A of title VI without regard to the funding limitation in section 6133(b)(1) of the ESEA: Provided further, That notwithstanding sections 6132(c)(2) and 6133(d)(1) of such Act, the Secretary may make such awards for a period of up to five years.

Note.—A full-year 2022 appropriation for this account was not enacted at the time the Budget was prepared; therefore, the Budget assumes this account is operating under the Continuing

INDIAN EDUCATION—Continued

Appropriations Act, 2022 (Division A of Public Law 117–43, as amended). The amounts included for 2022 reflect the annualized level provided by the continuing resolution.

Program and Financing (in millions of dollars)

Identification code 091–0101–0–1–501	2021 actual	2022 est.	2023 est.
Obligations by program activity:			
0001 Grants to local educational agencies	105	105	105
0002 Special programs for Indian children	68	68	68
0003 National activities	8	8	8
0004 Tribal Education Agencies	....	6	6
0900 Total new obligations, unexpired accounts	181	187	187
Budgetary resources:			
Unobligated balance:			
1000 Unobligated balance brought forward, Oct 1	....	20	14
Budget authority:			
Appropriations, discretionary:			
1100 Appropriation	181	181	186
Appropriations, mandatory:			
1200 Appropriation	20	....	....
1900 Budget authority (total)	201	181	186
1930 Total budgetary resources available	201	201	200
Memorandum (non-add) entries:			
1941 Unexpired unobligated balance, end of year	20	14	13
Change in obligated balance:			
Unpaid obligations:			
3000 Unpaid obligations, brought forward, Oct 1	232	244	202
3010 New obligations, unexpired accounts	181	187	187
3020 Outlays (gross)	–164	–229	–188
3041 Recoveries of prior year unpaid obligations, expired	–5	....	....
3050 Unpaid obligations, end of year	244	202	201
Memorandum (non-add) entries:			
3100 Obligated balance, start of year	232	244	202
3200 Obligated balance, end of year	244	202	201
Budget authority and outlays, net:			
Discretionary:			
4000 Budget authority, gross	181	181	186
Outlays, gross:			
4010 Outlays from new discretionary authority	3	9	9
4011 Outlays from discretionary balances	161	207	172
4020 Outlays, gross (total)	164	216	181
Mandatory:			
4090 Budget authority, gross	20	....	....
Outlays, gross:			
4101 Outlays from mandatory balances	....	13	7
4180 Budget authority, net (total)	201	181	186
4190 Outlays, net (total)	164	229	188

The Indian Education programs support the efforts of local educational agencies (LEAs), Tribes, and Indian organizations to improve teaching and learning for the Nation's American Indian and Alaska Native children.

Grants to local educational agencies.—Formula grants support LEAs in their efforts to enhance and supplement elementary and secondary school programs that serve Indian students, with the goal of ensuring that such programs assist participating students in meeting the same academic standards as all other students.

Special programs for Indian children.—Funds support awards under the Demonstration Grants authority including for Native Youth Community Projects and projects expanding educational opportunity, as well as professional development grants for training Native American teachers and administrators for employment in school districts that serve a high proportion of Indian students.

National activities.—Funds support research, evaluation, data collection, and related activities, grants for Native language immersion schools and programs, and grants to Tribes to create Tribal educational agencies and to expand the capacity of existing Tribal educational agencies through education administrative planning, development, and coordination.

Tribal education agencies.—Funds support awards to Tribal education agencies to improve educational opportunities and achievement of Indian children and youth.

Object Classification (in millions of dollars)

Identification code 091–0101–0–1–501	2021 actual	2022 est.	2023 est.
Direct obligations:			
25.2 Other services from non-Federal sources	3	3	3
25.7 Operation and maintenance of equipment	1	1	1
41.0 Grants, subsidies, and contributions	177	183	183
99.9 Total new obligations, unexpired accounts	181	187	187

OFFICE OF INNOVATION AND IMPROVEMENT

Federal Funds

INNOVATION AND IMPROVEMENT

For carrying out activities authorized by subparts 1, 3 and 4 of part B of title II, and parts C, D, and E and subparts 1 and 4 of part F of title IV of the ESEA, $1,472,000,000: Provided, That $280,500,000 shall be for subparts 1, 3 and 4 of part B of title II and shall be made available without regard to sections 2201, 2231(b) and 2241: Provided further, That $677,500,000 shall be for parts C, D, and E and subpart 4 of part F of title IV, and shall be made available without regard to sections 4311, 4409(a), and 4601 of the ESEA: Provided further, That section 4303(d)(3)(A)(i) shall not apply to the funds available for part C of title IV: Provided further, That of the funds available for part C of title IV, the Secretary shall use not less than $330,000,000 to carry out sections 4303, 4305(a)(2), and 4305(b): Provided further, That the funds for section 4305(b) shall remain available through March 31, 2024: Provided further, That none of the funds available for part C of title IV may be used by the Secretary to make new awards that support any charter school, whether as a grantee or subgrantee or otherwise as a recipient of financing or other financial assistance, that is operated or managed by a for-profit education management organization or other similar for-profit entity, including through a contract with such an organization or entity, except that this proviso does not limit the ability of a charter school to contract with a for-profit entity for discrete purposes other than managing or operating the charter school, such as providing food services or payroll services: Provided further, That notwithstanding section 4601(b), $514,000,000 shall be available through December 31, 2023 for subpart 1 of part F of title IV.

Note.—A full-year 2022 appropriation for this account was not enacted at the time the Budget was prepared; therefore, the Budget assumes this account is operating under the Continuing Appropriations Act, 2022 (Division A of Public Law 117–43, as amended). The amounts included for 2022 reflect the annualized level provided by the continuing resolution.

Program and Financing (in millions of dollars)

Identification code 091–0204–0–1–501	2021 actual	2022 est.	2023 est.
Obligations by program activity:			
0001 Education, innovation and research	192	194	514
0002 Teacher and school leader incentive fund	200	200	150
0003 American history and civics	5	5	11
0004 Supporting effective educator development (SEED)	80	80	80
0005 Charter schools	408	439	440
0006 Magnet schools	109	109	149
0007 Ready to learn programming	30	30	30
0008 Arts in education	31	31	31
0009 Javits gifted and talented education	13	13	13
0010 Statewide family engagement centers	12	12	15
0011 School leader recruitment and support	....	....	40
0799 Total direct obligations	1,080	1,113	1,473
0801 DC schools/SOAR Act	52	53	53
0900 Total new obligations, unexpired accounts	1,132	1,166	1,526
Budgetary resources:			
Unobligated balance:			
1000 Unobligated balance brought forward, Oct 1	296	331	332
Budget authority:			
Appropriations, discretionary:			
1100 Appropriation	1,114	1,114	1,472
Spending authority from offsetting collections, discretionary:			
1700 Collected	53	53	53
1900 Budget authority (total)	1,167	1,167	1,525
1930 Total budgetary resources available	1,463	1,498	1,857
Memorandum (non-add) entries:			
1941 Unexpired unobligated balance, end of year	331	332	331
Change in obligated balance:			
Unpaid obligations:			
3000 Unpaid obligations, brought forward, Oct 1	2,430	2,564	2,301

DEPARTMENT OF EDUCATION

Office of Innovation and Improvement—Continued
Federal Funds—Continued

333

		2021 actual	2022 est.	2023 est.
3010	New obligations, unexpired accounts	1,132	1,166	1,526
3011	Obligations ("upward adjustments"), expired accounts	4		
3020	Outlays (gross)	−946	−1,429	−1,307
3041	Recoveries of prior year unpaid obligations, expired	−56		
3050	Unpaid obligations, end of year	2,564	2,301	2,520
	Memorandum (non-add) entries:			
3100	Obligated balance, start of year	2,430	2,564	2,301
3200	Obligated balance, end of year	2,564	2,301	2,520
	Budget authority and outlays, net:			
	Discretionary:			
4000	Budget authority, gross	1,167	1,167	1,525
	Outlays, gross:			
4010	Outlays from new discretionary authority	19	75	82
4011	Outlays from discretionary balances	927	1,354	1,225
4020	Outlays, gross (total)	946	1,429	1,307
	Offsets against gross budget authority and outlays:			
	Offsetting collections (collected) from:			
4033	Non-Federal sources	−53	−53	−53
4180	Budget authority, net (total)	1,114	1,114	1,472
4190	Outlays, net (total)	893	1,376	1,254

Summary of Budget Authority and Outlays (in millions of dollars)

	2021 actual	2022 est.	2023 est.
Enacted/requested:			
Budget Authority	1,114	1,114	1,472
Outlays	893	1,376	1,254
Legislative proposal, not subject to PAYGO:			
Budget Authority			100
Outlays			2
Total:			
Budget Authority	1,114	1,114	1,572
Outlays	893	1,376	1,256

Education innovation and research.—Funds would support competitive grants for the creation, development, implementation, replication, and scaling up of evidence-based, field-initiated innovations designed to improve student achievement and attainment for high-need students.

Teacher and school leader incentive fund.—Funds would support competitive grants to help eligible entities develop, implement, improve, or expand human capital management systems or performance-based compensation systems in schools served by those entities.

American history and civics.—Funds would support competitive grants to institutions of higher education and other entities with demonstrated expertise to improve the quality of teaching and learning in American history, civics, and government.

Supporting effective educator development (SEED).—Funds would support competitive grants to institutions of higher education, national nonprofit entities, and the BIE to provide educators with evidence-based professional development and to support pathways that allow educators with nontraditional preparation and certification to obtain employment in traditionally underserved local educational agencies.

Charter schools.—Funds would support competitive grants for the opening of new charter schools and the replication and expansion of high-quality charter schools. Funds would also support information dissemination activities and competitive grants to improve charter schools' access to facilities.

Magnet schools.—Funds would support competitive grants to local educational agencies to establish and operate magnet school programs that are part of an approved desegregation plan.

Ready to learn programming.—Funds would support competitive grants to public telecommunications entities to develop and distribute educational video programming and digital content, such as applications and online educational games, for preschool and elementary school children and their parents, caregivers, and teachers to facilitate student academic achievement.

Arts in education.—Funds would support projects and programs to promote arts education for students, including disadvantaged students, through competitive grants to support development and dissemination of instructional materials, programming, and professional development for arts educators.

Javits gifted and talented education.—Funds would support a coordinated program of research, demonstration projects, innovative strategies, and other activities to build and enhance the capacity of elementary and secondary schools to identify gifted and talented students and meet their special educational needs.

Statewide family engagement centers.—Funds would support competitive grants to statewide organizations to carry out parent education and family engagement programs and provide comprehensive technical assistance to State and local educational agencies and organizations that support family-school partnerships.

School leader recruitment and support.—Funds would support grants to improve the recruitment, preparation, placement, support, and retention of effective principals and other school leaders in high-need schools.

Object Classification (in millions of dollars)

Identification code 091–0204–0–1–501	2021 actual	2022 est.	2023 est.
Direct obligations:			
25.2 Other services from non-Federal sources	21	21	22
25.3 Other goods and services from Federal sources	1	1	1
25.5 Research and development contracts	1	1	1
25.7 Operation and maintenance of equipment	1	1	1
41.0 Grants, subsidies, and contributions	1,056	1,089	1,448
99.0 Direct obligations	1,080	1,113	1,473
99.0 Reimbursable obligations	52	53	53
99.9 Total new obligations, unexpired accounts	1,132	1,166	1,526

INNOVATION AND IMPROVEMENT

(Legislative proposal, not subject to PAYGO)

Program and Financing (in millions of dollars)

Identification code 091–0204–2–1–501	2021 actual	2022 est.	2023 est.
Obligations by program activity:			
0001 Fostering diverse schools			100
Budgetary resources:			
Budget authority:			
Appropriations, discretionary:			
1100 Appropriation			100
1930 Total budgetary resources available			100
Change in obligated balance:			
Unpaid obligations:			
3010 New obligations, unexpired accounts			100
3020 Outlays (gross)			−2
3050 Unpaid obligations, end of year			98
Memorandum (non-add) entries:			
3200 Obligated balance, end of year			98
Budget authority and outlays, net:			
Discretionary:			
4000 Budget authority, gross			100
Outlays, gross:			
4010 Outlays from new discretionary authority			2
4180 Budget authority, net (total)			100
4190 Outlays, net (total)			2

Fostering diverse schools.—Funds would support competitive grants to local educational agencies and partner entities for activities to improve racial and socioeconomic diversity in pre-kindergarten through grade twelve.

Object Classification (in millions of dollars)

Identification code 091–0204–2–1–501	2021 actual	2022 est.	2023 est.
Direct obligations:			
25.2 Other services from non-Federal sources			10
41.0 Grants, subsidies, and contributions			90
99.9 Total new obligations, unexpired accounts			100

OFFICE OF ENGLISH LANGUAGE ACQUISITION

Federal Funds

ENGLISH LANGUAGE ACQUISITION

For carrying out part A of title III of the ESEA, $1,075,000,000, which shall become available on July 1, 2023, and shall remain available through September 30, 2024, except that 6.5 percent of such amount shall be available on October 1, 2022, and shall remain available through September 30, 2024, to carry out activities under section 3111(c)(1)(C): Provided, That the Secretary may reserve up to 2 percent of such amount for technical assistance and capacity building: Provided further, That $50,000,000 of the funds made available under this heading shall become available on October 1, 2022, and shall remain available through September 30, 2024 for supplemental awards to State educational agencies in States with local educational agencies that have enrolled at least 100 immigrant children and youth since January 1, 2021, and in States with at least one county where 50 or more unaccompanied children have been released to sponsors since January 1, 2021, from the Department of Health and Human Services, Office of Refugee Resettlement: Provided further, That the Secretary may establish requirements for determining the allocation of such funds.

Note.—A full-year 2022 appropriation for this account was not enacted at the time the Budget was prepared; therefore, the Budget assumes this account is operating under the Continuing Appropriations Act, 2022 (Division A of Public Law 117–43, as amended). The amounts included for 2022 reflect the annualized level provided by the continuing resolution.

Program and Financing (in millions of dollars)

Identification code 091–1300–0–1–501	2021 actual	2022 est.	2023 est.
Obligations by program activity:			
0001 English language acquisition grants	795	797	1,075
Budgetary resources:			
Unobligated balance:			
1000 Unobligated balance brought forward, Oct 1	10	12	12
Budget authority:			
Appropriations, discretionary:			
1100 Appropriation	797	797	1,075
1930 Total budgetary resources available	807	809	1,087
Memorandum (non-add) entries:			
1941 Unexpired unobligated balance, end of year	12	12	12
Change in obligated balance:			
Unpaid obligations:			
3000 Unpaid obligations, brought forward, Oct 1	1,189	1,311	1,222
3010 New obligations, unexpired accounts	795	797	1,075
3020 Outlays (gross)	–672	–886	–804
3041 Recoveries of prior year unpaid obligations, expired	–1		
3050 Unpaid obligations, end of year	1,311	1,222	1,493
Memorandum (non-add) entries:			
3100 Obligated balance, start of year	1,189	1,311	1,222
3200 Obligated balance, end of year	1,311	1,222	1,493
Budget authority and outlays, net:			
Discretionary:			
4000 Budget authority, gross	797	797	1,075
Outlays, gross:			
4010 Outlays from new discretionary authority	3	8	11
4011 Outlays from discretionary balances	669	878	793
4020 Outlays, gross (total)	672	886	804
4180 Budget authority, net (total)	797	797	1,075
4190 Outlays, net (total)	672	886	804

English language acquisition grants.—This program supports formula grants to States to improve services for English Learners. States are accountable for demonstrating that English Learners are making progress toward proficiency in English and meeting the same high State academic standards as all other students. Funds also support national activities, including professional development to increase the supply of high-quality teachers of English Learners and a national information clearinghouse on English language acquisition.

Object Classification (in millions of dollars)

Identification code 091–1300–0–1–501	2021 actual	2022 est.	2023 est.
Direct obligations:			
25.2 Other services from non-Federal sources	2	2	2
25.5 Research and development contracts	3	3	3
25.7 Operation and maintenance of equipment	1	1	1
41.0 Grants, subsidies, and contributions	789	791	1,069
99.0 Direct obligations	795	797	1,075
99.9 Total new obligations, unexpired accounts	795	797	1,075

OFFICE OF SPECIAL EDUCATION AND REHABILITATIVE SERVICES

Federal Funds

SPECIAL EDUCATION

For carrying out the Individuals with Disabilities Education Act (IDEA) and the Special Olympics Sport and Empowerment Act of 2004, $18,130,170,000, of which $8,410,430,000 shall become available on July 1, 2023, and shall remain available through September 30, 2024, and of which $9,283,383,000 shall become available on October 1, 2023, and shall remain available through September 30, 2024, for academic year 2023–2024: Provided, That the amount for section 611(b)(2) of the IDEA shall be equal to the lesser of the amount available for that activity during fiscal year 2022, increased by the amount of inflation as specified in section 619(d)(2)(B) of the IDEA, or the percent change in the funds appropriated under section 611(i) of the IDEA, but not less than the amount for that activity during fiscal year 2022: Provided further, That the Secretary shall, without regard to section 611(d) of the IDEA, distribute to all other States (as that term is defined in section 611(g)(2)), subject to the third proviso, any amount by which a State's allocation under section 611, from funds appropriated under this heading, is reduced under section 612(a)(18)(B), according to the following: 85 percent on the basis of the States' relative populations of children aged 3 through 21 who are of the same age as children with disabilities for whom the State ensures the availability of a free appropriate public education under this part, and 15 percent to States on the basis of the States' relative populations of those children who are living in poverty: Provided further, That the Secretary may not distribute any funds under the previous proviso to any State whose reduction in allocation from funds appropriated under this heading made funds available for such a distribution: Provided further, That the States shall allocate such funds distributed under the second proviso to local educational agencies in accordance with section 611(f): Provided further, That the amount by which a State's allocation under section 611(d) of the IDEA is reduced under section 612(a)(18)(B) and the amounts distributed to States under the previous provisos in fiscal year 2012 or any subsequent year shall not be considered in calculating the awards under section 611(d) for fiscal year 2013 or for any subsequent fiscal years: Provided further, That, notwithstanding the provision in section 612(a)(18)(B) regarding the fiscal year in which a State's allocation under section 611(d) is reduced for failure to comply with the requirement of section 612(a)(18)(A), the Secretary may apply the reduction specified in section 612(a)(18)(B) over a period of consecutive fiscal years, not to exceed 5, until the entire reduction is applied: Provided further, That the Secretary may, in any fiscal year in which a State's allocation under section 611 is reduced in accordance with section 612(a)(18)(B), reduce the amount a State may reserve under section 611(e)(1) by an amount that bears the same relation to the maximum amount described in that paragraph as the reduction under section 612(a)(18)(B) bears to the total allocation the State would have received in that fiscal year under section 611(d) in the absence of the reduction: Provided further, That the Secretary shall either reduce the allocation of funds under section 611 for any fiscal year following the fiscal year for which the State fails to comply with the requirement of section 612(a)(18)(A) as authorized by section 612(a)(18)(B), or seek to recover funds under section 452 of the General Education Provisions Act (20 U.S.C. 1234a): Provided further, That the funds reserved under 611(c) of the IDEA may be used to provide technical assistance to States to improve the capacity of the States to meet the data collection requirements of sections 616 and 618 and to administer and carry out other services and activities to improve data collection, coordination, quality, and use under parts B and C of the IDEA: Provided further, That the Secretary may use funds made available for the State Personnel Development Grants program under part D, subpart 1 of IDEA to evaluate program performance under such subpart: Provided further, That States may use funds reserved for other State-level activities under sections 611(e)(2) and 619(f) of the IDEA to make subgrants to local educational agencies, institutions of higher education, other public agencies, and private non-profit organizations to carry out activities authorized by those sections: Provided further, That, notwithstanding section 643(e)(1) of the IDEA, the Secretary may reserve up to $200,000,000 of the funds appropriated under Part C of the IDEA to provide grants to States that are either carrying out the policy described in sections 632(5)(B)(ii) and 635(c) or are serving at-risk infants and toddlers as defined in section 632(1) and 632(5)(B)(i) in order to facilitate the implementation of such policy: *Provided further,* That, notwithstanding section 643(e)(2)(A) of the IDEA, if 5 or fewer States apply for grants pursuant to section 643(e) of such Act, the Secretary shall provide a grant to each State in an amount equal to the maximum amount described in section 643(e)(2)(B) of such Act: *Provided further,* That if more than 5 States apply for grants pursuant to section 643(e) of the IDEA, the Secretary shall award funds to those States on the basis of the States' relative populations of infants and toddlers except that no such State shall receive a grant in excess of the amount described in section 643(e)(2)(B) of such Act: *Provided further,* That States may use funds allotted under section 643(c) of the IDEA to make subgrants to early intervention service providers to carry out activities authorized by section 638 of IDEA: *Provided further,* That, notwithstanding section 638 of the IDEA, any State receiving a grant under section 633 of the IDEA must reserve not less than ten percent of its award for use in a manner described in a State plan, approved by the Secretary, to ensure equitable access to and participation in Part C services in the State, particularly for populations that have been traditionally underrepresented in the program: *Provided further,* That, notwithstanding section 632(4)(B) of the IDEA, a State receiving a grant under section 633 of the IDEA may establish a system of payments but may not include in that system family fees or out-of-pocket costs to families for early intervention services: *Provided further,* That any State seeking to amend its eligibility criteria under section 635(a)(1) of the IDEA in such a way that would have the effect of reducing the number of infants and families who are eligible under Part C must conduct public participation under section 637(a)(8) of the IDEA at least 24 months prior to implementing such a change: *Provided further,* That, notwithstanding section 638 of the IDEA, a State may use funds it receives under section 633 of the IDEA to offer continued early intervention services to a child who previously received services under Part C of the IDEA from age three until the beginning of the school year following the child's third birthday without regard to the procedures described in section 635(c) of the IDEA: *Provided further,* That, notwithstanding section 643(c) of the IDEA, the Secretary shall allot, from the funds remaining for each fiscal year after the reservation and payments under subsections (a), (b), and (e) of section 643, to each State (as that term is defined in section 643(c)(4)(B)) according to the following: 85 percent on the basis of the State's relative population of infants and toddlers and 15 percent on the basis of the State's relative population of such children who are living in poverty, except that no State shall receive less than 90 percent of the amount it received in the preceding fiscal year: *Provided further,* That, notwithstanding section 638 of the IDEA, a State may use funds appropriated under Part C of the IDEA to conduct child find, public awareness and referral activities for an individual who is expected to become a parent of an infant with a disability (as that term is defined in section 632(5)), as established by medical or other records: *Provided further,* That any State electing to use funds under the preceding proviso shall ensure, that as soon as possible but not later than 45 days after the child's birth, it completes the referral and eligibility process under this part for that child: *Provided further,* That, notwithstanding section 611 of the IDEA, the Secretary may reserve up to $5,000,000 to study issues related to the creation and implementation of a comprehensive system of services and supports for children with disabilities from birth through age five.

Note.—A full-year 2022 appropriation for this account was not enacted at the time the Budget was prepared; therefore, the Budget assumes this account is operating under the Continuing Appropriations Act, 2022 (Division A of Public Law 117–43, as amended). The amounts included for 2022 reflect the annualized level provided by the continuing resolution.

Program and Financing (in millions of dollars)

Identification code 091–0300–0–1–501	2021 actual	2022 est.	2023 est.
Obligations by program activity:			
0001 Grants to States	15,514	12,904	16,259
0002 Preschool grants	598	398	503
0003 Grants for infants and families	703	512	932
0091 Subtotal, State grants	16,815	13,814	17,694
0101 State personnel development	39	39	39
0102 Technical assistance and dissemination	44	54	49
0103 Personnel preparation	90	90	250
0104 Parent information centers	27	27	45
0105 Educational technology, media, and materials	29	29	29
0191 Subtotal, National activities	229	239	412
0201 Special Olympics education program	24	24	24
0900 Total new obligations, unexpired accounts	17,068	14,077	18,130

Budgetary resources:				
	Unobligated balance:			
1000	Unobligated balance brought forward, Oct 1	8	40	33
1001	Discretionary unobligated balance brought fwd, Oct 1	8		
	Budget authority:			
	Appropriations, discretionary:			
1100	Appropriation	4,787	4,787	8,847
	Advance appropriations, discretionary:			
1170	Advance appropriation	9,283	9,283	9,283
	Appropriations, mandatory:			
1200	Appropriation	3,030		
1900	Budget authority (total)	17,100	14,070	18,130
1930	Total budgetary resources available	17,108	14,110	18,163
	Memorandum (non-add) entries:			
1941	Unexpired unobligated balance, end of year	40	33	33
Change in obligated balance:				
	Unpaid obligations:			
3000	Unpaid obligations, brought forward, Oct 1	9,156	13,460	8,959
3010	New obligations, unexpired accounts	17,068	14,077	18,130
3020	Outlays (gross)	–12,757	–18,578	–14,554
3041	Recoveries of prior year unpaid obligations, expired	–7		
3050	Unpaid obligations, end of year	13,460	8,959	12,535
	Memorandum (non-add) entries:			
3100	Obligated balance, start of year	9,156	13,460	8,959
3200	Obligated balance, end of year	13,460	8,959	12,535
Budget authority and outlays, net:				
	Discretionary:			
4000	Budget authority, gross	14,070	14,070	18,130
	Outlays, gross:			
4010	Outlays from new discretionary authority	4,974	6,357	6,552
4011	Outlays from discretionary balances	7,782	9,511	7,747
4020	Outlays, gross (total)	12,756	15,868	14,299
	Mandatory:			
4090	Budget authority, gross	3,030		
	Outlays, gross:			
4100	Outlays from new mandatory authority	1		
4101	Outlays from mandatory balances		2,710	255
4110	Outlays, gross (total)	1	2,710	255
4180	Budget authority, net (total)	17,100	14,070	18,130
4190	Outlays, net (total)	12,757	18,578	14,554

SUMMARY OF IDEA FORMULA GRANTS PROGRAM LEVELS

(in millions of dollars)

	2021–2022 Academic Year	2022–2023 Academic Year	2023–2024 Academic Year
Current Budget Authority	$4,534	$4,534	$8,411
Advance appropriation	9,283	9,283	9,283
Total program level	13,817	13,817	17,694
Change in advance appropriation from the previous year	0	0	0

Grants to States.—Formula grants are provided to States to assist them in providing special education and related services to children with disabilities ages 3 through 21.

Preschool grants.—Formula grants provide additional funds to States to further assist them in providing special education and related services to children with disabilities ages 3 through 5 served under the Grants to States program.

The goal of both the Grants to States and the Preschool grants programs is to improve results for children with disabilities by assisting State and local educational agencies (LEAs) to provide children with disabilities with access to high quality education that will help them meet challenging standards and prepare them for employment and independent living. LEAs may reserve up to 15 percent of the funds they receive under Part B of the Individuals with Disabilities Education Act to provide comprehensive coordinated early intervening services to children age 3 through grade 12.

Grants for infants and families.—Formula grants are provided to assist States to implement statewide systems of coordinated, comprehensive, multi-disciplinary interagency programs to provide early intervention services to children with disabilities, birth through age two, and their families. The goal of this program is to help States provide a comprehensive system of early intervention services that will enhance child and family outcomes.

National activities.—Funds are provided for personnel preparation and development, technical assistance, and other activities to support State ef-

Office of Special Education and Rehabilitative Services—Continued
Federal Funds—Continued

SPECIAL EDUCATION—Continued

forts to improve results for children with disabilities under the State Grants programs. The goal of National Activities is to link States, school systems, and families to best practices to improve results for infants, toddlers, and children with disabilities.

Special Olympics education programs.—Funds are provided to promote the expansion of the Special Olympics and the design and implementation of Special Olympics education programs.

Object Classification (in millions of dollars)

Identification code 091–0300–0–1–501		2021 actual	2022 est.	2023 est.
	Direct obligations:			
25.2	Other services from non-Federal sources	1	1	1
41.0	Grants, subsidies, and contributions	17,067	14,076	18,129
99.0	Direct obligations	17,068	14,077	18,130
99.9	Total new obligations, unexpired accounts	17,068	14,077	18,130

REHABILITATION SERVICES

For carrying out, to the extent not otherwise provided, the Rehabilitation Act of 1973, the Helen Keller National Center Act, and the Randolph-Sheppard Act, $4,125,906,000, of which $3,949,707,000 shall be for grants for vocational rehabilitation services under title I of the Rehabilitation Act: Provided, That the Secretary may use amounts provided in this Act that remain available subsequent to the reallotment of funds to States pursuant to section 110(b) of the Rehabilitation Act for innovative activities aimed at increasing competitive integrated employment as defined in section 7 of such Act for youth and other individuals with disabilities: Provided further, That up to 15 percent of the amounts made available by this or prior Acts for innovative activities as described in the preceding proviso may be used for evaluation and technical assistance related to such activities: Provided further, That States may award subgrants for a portion of the funds to other public and private, nonprofit entities: Provided further, That any funds made available subsequent to reallotment for innovative activities aimed at improving the outcomes of individuals with disabilities shall remain available until September 30, 2024: Provided further, That, notwithstanding the provision in section 111(a)(2)(B) of the Rehabilitation Act regarding a fiscal year in which a States' allotment under section 110(a) is reduced for failure to comply with the requirement of section 111(a)(2)(B), the Secretary may apply the reduction specified in section 111(a)(2)(B) over a period of consecutive fiscal years, not to exceed 5, until the entire reduction is applied: Provided further, That, from amounts provided under this heading, the Secretary shall use $500,000 for a grant to provide training and technical assistance to support implementation of the Randolph-Sheppard Act.

Note.—A full-year 2022 appropriation for this account was not enacted at the time the Budget was prepared; therefore, the Budget assumes this account is operating under the Continuing Appropriations Act, 2022 (Division A of Public Law 117–43, as amended). The amounts included for 2022 reflect the annualized level provided by the continuing resolution.

Program and Financing (in millions of dollars)

Identification code 091–0301–0–1–506		2021 actual	2022 est.	2023 est.
	Obligations by program activity:			
0001	Vocational rehabilitation State grants	3,416	3,684	3,725
0002	Client assistance State grants	13	13	13
0003	Supported employment State grants	23	23	23
0004	Training	29	29	29
0005	Demonstration and Training Programs	6	6	41
0006	Independent living services for older blind individuals	33	33	33
0007	Protection and advocacy of individual rights	18	18	18
0008	Helen Keller National Center	17	17	18
0009	Randolph-Sheppard Vending Facility Program			1
0100	Total direct program	3,555	3,823	3,901
0900	Total new obligations, unexpired accounts	3,555	3,823	3,901
	Budgetary resources:			
	Unobligated balance:			
1012	Unobligated balance transfers between expired and unexpired accounts	130	177	
	Budget authority:			
	Appropriations, discretionary:			
1100	Appropriation	139	139	176
	Appropriations, mandatory:			
1200	Appropriation	3,675	3,719	3,950
1230	Appropriations and/or unobligated balance of appropriations permanently reduced	–209	–212	–225
1260	Appropriations, mandatory (total)	3,466	3,507	3,725
1900	Budget authority (total)	3,605	3,646	3,901
1930	Total budgetary resources available	3,735	3,823	3,901
	Memorandum (non-add) entries:			
1940	Unobligated balance expiring	–180		
	Change in obligated balance:			
	Unpaid obligations:			
3000	Unpaid obligations, brought forward, Oct 1	2,486	3,046	2,103
3010	New obligations, unexpired accounts	3,555	3,823	3,901
3011	Obligations ("upward adjustments"), expired accounts	1		
3020	Outlays (gross)	–2,908	–4,766	–3,819
3041	Recoveries of prior year unpaid obligations, expired	–88		
3050	Unpaid obligations, end of year	3,046	2,103	2,185
	Memorandum (non-add) entries:			
3100	Obligated balance, start of year	2,486	3,046	2,103
3200	Obligated balance, end of year	3,046	2,103	2,185
	Budget authority and outlays, net:			
	Discretionary:			
4000	Budget authority, gross	139	139	176
	Outlays, gross:			
4010	Outlays from new discretionary authority	59	70	88
4011	Outlays from discretionary balances	101	166	71
4020	Outlays, gross (total)	160	236	159
	Mandatory:			
4090	Budget authority, gross	3,466	3,507	3,725
	Outlays, gross:			
4100	Outlays from new mandatory authority	1,093	1,754	1,862
4101	Outlays from mandatory balances	1,655	2,776	1,798
4110	Outlays, gross (total)	2,748	4,530	3,660
4180	Budget authority, net (total)	3,605	3,646	3,901
4190	Outlays, net (total)	2,908	4,766	3,819

Vocational rehabilitation State grants.—The basic State grants program provides Federal matching funds to State vocational rehabilitation (VR) agencies to assist individuals with disabilities to become gainfully employed. Services are tailored to the specific needs of the individual. Priority is given to serving those with the most significant disabilities. In 2021, State VR agencies assisted an estimated 112,445 individuals with disabilities to obtain an employment outcome, about 92 percent of whom were individuals with significant disabilities. VR State Grants is a core program of the workforce development system under the Workforce Innovation and Opportunity Act (WIOA) and a required partner in the one-stop service delivery system for accessing employment and training services. Amendments made by WIOA require State VR agencies to reserve and use at least 15 percent of their Federal grant allotment to support pre-employment transition services for students with disabilities provided in accordance with section 113 of the Rehabilitation Act. Between 1.0 percent and 1.5 percent of the funds appropriated for the VR State grants program must be set aside for the American Indian Vocational Rehabilitation Services Program. The request for the VR State Grants program includes the CPIU adjustment specified in the authorizing statute.

Client assistance State grants.—Formula grants are made to States to provide assistance in informing and advising clients and applicants about benefits available under the Rehabilitation Act and, if requested, to pursue legal or administrative remedies to ensure the protection of the rights of individuals with disabilities.

Supported employment State grants.—Formula grants are made to State VR agencies to provide supported employment services for individuals with the most significant disabilities.

Training.—Grants are made to States and public or nonprofit agencies and organizations, including institutions of higher education, to increase the number of skilled personnel available for employment in the field of rehabilitation and to upgrade the skills of those already employed.

Demonstration and training programs.—Competitive grants and contracts are awarded to expand and improve the provision and effectiveness of programs and services authorized under the Rehabilitation Act or further

DEPARTMENT OF EDUCATION

the purposes of the Act in promoting the employment and independence of individuals with disabilities in the community. Funds are used to support model demonstrations, technical assistance, and projects designed to improve program performance and the delivery of vocational rehabilitation and independent living services.

Independent living services for older individuals who are blind.—Grants are awarded to States to assist individuals over the age of 55 with severe visual disabilities to adjust to their disability and increase their ability to care for their own needs.

Protection and advocacy of individual rights.—Formula grants are made to State protection and advocacy systems to protect the legal and human rights of individuals with disabilities.

Helen Keller National Center for Deaf-Blind Youths and Adults.—The Center provides services to deaf-blind youths and adults and provides training and technical assistance to professional and allied personnel at its national headquarters center and through its regional representatives and affiliate agencies.

Randolph-Sheppard Vending Facility Program.—The Vending Facility program authorized by the Randolph-Sheppard Act provides persons who are blind with remunerative employment and self-support through the operation of vending facilities on federal and other property. This award would support a technical assistance center to provide training and technical assistance to State licensing agencies and blind vendors.

Object Classification (in millions of dollars)

Identification code 091–0301–0–1–506		2021 actual	2022 est.	2023 est.
	Direct obligations:			
25.1	Advisory and assistance services	1	1	1
41.0	Grants, subsidies, and contributions	3,554	3,822	3,900
99.9	Total new obligations, unexpired accounts	3,555	3,823	3,901

AMERICAN PRINTING HOUSE FOR THE BLIND

For carrying out the Act to Promote the Education of the Blind of March 3, 1879, $37,431,000.

Note.—A full-year 2022 appropriation for this account was not enacted at the time the Budget was prepared; therefore, the Budget assumes this account is operating under the Continuing Appropriations Act, 2022 (Division A of Public Law 117–43, as amended). The amounts included for 2022 reflect the annualized level provided by the continuing resolution.

Program and Financing (in millions of dollars)

Identification code 091–0600–0–1–501		2021 actual	2022 est.	2023 est.
	Obligations by program activity:			
0001	American printing house for the blind	34	34	37
0900	Total new obligations, unexpired accounts (object class 41.0)	34	34	37
	Budgetary resources:			
	Budget authority:			
	Appropriations, discretionary:			
1100	Appropriation	34	34	37
1930	Total budgetary resources available	34	34	37
	Change in obligated balance:			
	Unpaid obligations:			
3000	Unpaid obligations, brought forward, Oct 1	11	13	9
3010	New obligations, unexpired accounts	34	34	37
3020	Outlays (gross)	–32	–38	–36
3050	Unpaid obligations, end of year	13	9	10
	Memorandum (non-add) entries:			
3100	Obligated balance, start of year	11	13	9
3200	Obligated balance, end of year	13	9	10
	Budget authority and outlays, net:			
	Discretionary:			
4000	Budget authority, gross	34	34	37
	Outlays, gross:			
4010	Outlays from new discretionary authority	22	26	28
4011	Outlays from discretionary balances	10	12	8

4020	Outlays, gross (total)	32	38	36
4180	Budget authority, net (total)	34	34	37
4190	Outlays, net (total)	32	38	36

The 2023 request supports: the production and distribution of free educational materials for students below the college level who are blind; research related to developing and improving products; and advisory services to consumer organizations on the availability and use of materials. In 2021, the portion of the Federal appropriation allocated to educational materials represented approximately 64 percent of the Printing House's total sales. The full 2021 appropriation represented approximately 69 percent of the Printing House's total actual revenue. The 2023 request is expected to be allocated in a similar manner.

NATIONAL TECHNICAL INSTITUTE FOR THE DEAF

For the National Technical Institute for the Deaf under titles I and II of the Education of the Deaf Act of 1986, $84,500,000: Provided, That from the total amount available, the Institute may at its discretion use funds for the endowment program as authorized under section 207 of such Act.

Note.—A full-year 2022 appropriation for this account was not enacted at the time the Budget was prepared; therefore, the Budget assumes this account is operating under the Continuing Appropriations Act, 2022 (Division A of Public Law 117–43, as amended). The amounts included for 2022 reflect the annualized level provided by the continuing resolution.

Program and Financing (in millions of dollars)

Identification code 091–0601–0–1–502		2021 actual	2022 est.	2023 est.
	Obligations by program activity:			
0001	Operations	112	82	85
0900	Total new obligations, unexpired accounts (object class 41.0)	112	82	85
	Budgetary resources:			
	Budget authority:			
	Appropriations, discretionary:			
1100	Appropriation	93	82	85
	Appropriations, mandatory:			
1200	Appropriation	19		
1900	Budget authority (total)	112	82	85
1930	Total budgetary resources available	112	82	85
	Change in obligated balance:			
	Unpaid obligations:			
3000	Unpaid obligations, brought forward, Oct 1	9	35	10
3010	New obligations, unexpired accounts	112	82	85
3020	Outlays (gross)	–86	–107	–92
3050	Unpaid obligations, end of year	35	10	3
	Memorandum (non-add) entries:			
3100	Obligated balance, start of year	9	35	10
3200	Obligated balance, end of year	35	10	3
	Budget authority and outlays, net:			
	Discretionary:			
4000	Budget authority, gross	93	82	85
	Outlays, gross:			
4010	Outlays from new discretionary authority	81	81	84
4011	Outlays from discretionary balances	5	14	1
4020	Outlays, gross (total)	86	95	85
	Mandatory:			
4090	Budget authority, gross	19		
	Outlays, gross:			
4101	Outlays from mandatory balances		12	7
4180	Budget authority, net (total)	112	82	85
4190	Outlays, net (total)	86	107	92

This program provides postsecondary technical and professional education for individuals who are deaf or hard of hearing, provides training, and conducts applied research into employment-related aspects of deafness. In 2021, the Federal appropriation represented approximately 84 percent of the Institute's operating budget. The 2023 request includes funds that may be used for the Endowment Grant program.

GALLAUDET UNIVERSITY

For the Kendall Demonstration Elementary School, the Model Secondary School for the Deaf, and the partial support of Gallaudet University under titles I and II of the Education of the Deaf Act of 1986, $143,361,000: Provided, That from the total amount available, the University may at its discretion use funds for the endowment program as authorized under section 207 of such Act.

Note.—A full-year 2022 appropriation for this account was not enacted at the time the Budget was prepared; therefore, the Budget assumes this account is operating under the Continuing Appropriations Act, 2022 (Division A of Public Law 117–43, as amended). The amounts included for 2022 reflect the annualized level provided by the continuing resolution.

Program and Financing (in millions of dollars)

Identification code 091–0602–0–1–502	2021 actual	2022 est.	2023 est.
Obligations by program activity:			
0001 Operations	170	140	143
0900 Total new obligations, unexpired accounts (object class 41.0)	170	140	143
Budgetary resources:			
Budget authority:			
Appropriations, discretionary:			
1100 Appropriation	151	140	143
Appropriations, mandatory:			
1200 Appropriation	19		
1900 Budget authority (total)	170	140	143
1930 Total budgetary resources available	170	140	143
Change in obligated balance:			
Unpaid obligations:			
3000 Unpaid obligations, brought forward, Oct 1	23	36	3
3010 New obligations, unexpired accounts	170	140	143
3020 Outlays (gross)	–157	–173	–143
3050 Unpaid obligations, end of year	36	3	3
Memorandum (non-add) entries:			
3100 Obligated balance, start of year	23	36	3
3200 Obligated balance, end of year	36	3	3
Budget authority and outlays, net:			
Discretionary:			
4000 Budget authority, gross	151	140	143
Outlays, gross:			
4010 Outlays from new discretionary authority	136	139	142
4011 Outlays from discretionary balances	21	34	1
4020 Outlays, gross (total)	157	173	143
Mandatory:			
4090 Budget authority, gross	19		
4180 Budget authority, net (total)	170	140	143
4190 Outlays, net (total)	157	173	143

This institution provides undergraduate, continuing education, and graduate programs for students who are deaf, hard of hearing, and hearing. The University also conducts basic and applied research and provides public service programs for persons with hearing loss and persons who work with them.

The University operates the Laurent Clerc National Deaf Education Center, which includes elementary and secondary education programs on the main campus of the University serving students who are deaf or hard of hearing. The Kendall Demonstration Elementary School serves students from birth through grade 8, and the Model Secondary School for the Deaf serves high school students in grades 9 through 12. The Clerc Center also develops and disseminates information on effective educational techniques and strategies for teachers and professionals working with students who are deaf or hard of hearing.

In 2021, the appropriation for Gallaudet represented approximately 72 percent of total revenue for the University. Approximately 24 percent of the Federal appropriation was used to support activities at the Clerc Center, which received nearly 100 percent of its revenue through the appropriation. In addition, the University receives other Federal funds such as student financial aid, vocational rehabilitation, Endowment Grant program income, and competitive grants and contracts. The 2023 request includes funds that may be used for the Endowment Grant program.

OFFICE OF CAREER, TECHNICAL, AND ADULT EDUCATION

Federal Funds

CAREER, TECHNICAL, AND ADULT EDUCATION

For carrying out, to the extent not otherwise provided, the Carl D. Perkins Career and Technical Education Act of 2006 ("Perkins Act") and the Adult Education and Family Literacy Act ("AEFLA"), $2,308,981,000, of which $1,517,981,000 shall become available on July 1, 2023, and shall remain available through September 30, 2024, and of which $791,000,000 shall become available on October 1, 2023, and shall remain available through September 30, 2024: Provided, That $200,000,000 shall be for competitive grants to consortia of local educational agencies, institutions of higher education, and employers to pilot evidence-based strategies to increase the integration and alignment of the last two years of high school and the first two years of postsecondary education to improve postsecondary and career outcomes for all students: Provided further, That of the amounts made available for AEFLA, $38,712,000 shall be for national leadership activities under section 242.

Note.—A full-year 2022 appropriation for this account was not enacted at the time the Budget was prepared; therefore, the Budget assumes this account is operating under the Continuing Appropriations Act, 2022 (Division A of Public Law 117–43, as amended). The amounts included for 2022 reflect the annualized level provided by the continuing resolution.

Program and Financing (in millions of dollars)

Identification code 091–0400–0–1–501	2021 actual	2022 est.	2023 est.
Obligations by program activity:			
0001 Career and Technical Education State Grants	1,334	1,334	1,355
0002 Career and Technical Education National Activities	8	8	215
0091 Subtotal, Career and Technical	1,342	1,342	1,570
0101 Adult Basic and Literacy Education State Grants	675	675	700
0102 Adult Education National Leadership Activities	14	14	39
0191 Subtotal, Adult Education	689	689	739
0900 Total new obligations, unexpired accounts	2,031	2,031	2,309
Budgetary resources:			
Unobligated balance:			
1000 Unobligated balance brought forward, Oct 1	21	20	20
Budget authority:			
Appropriations, discretionary:			
1100 Appropriation	1,240	1,240	1,518
Advance appropriations, discretionary:			
1170 Advance appropriation	790	791	791
1900 Budget authority (total)	2,030	2,031	2,309
1930 Total budgetary resources available	2,051	2,051	2,329
Memorandum (non-add) entries:			
1941 Unexpired unobligated balance, end of year	20	20	20
Change in obligated balance:			
Unpaid obligations:			
3000 Unpaid obligations, brought forward, Oct 1	1,974	2,173	1,861
3010 New obligations, unexpired accounts	2,031	2,031	2,309
3020 Outlays (gross)	–1,827	–2,343	–2,036
3041 Recoveries of prior year unpaid obligations, expired	–5		
3050 Unpaid obligations, end of year	2,173	1,861	2,134
Memorandum (non-add) entries:			
3100 Obligated balance, start of year	1,974	2,173	1,861
3200 Obligated balance, end of year	2,173	1,861	2,134
Budget authority and outlays, net:			
Discretionary:			
4000 Budget authority, gross	2,030	2,031	2,309
Outlays, gross:			
4010 Outlays from new discretionary authority	345	616	630
4011 Outlays from discretionary balances	1,482	1,727	1,406
4020 Outlays, gross (total)	1,827	2,343	2,036
4180 Budget authority, net (total)	2,030	2,031	2,309
4190 Outlays, net (total)	1,827	2,343	2,036

DEPARTMENT OF EDUCATION

SUMMARY OF PROGRAM LEVEL
(in millions of dollars)

	2021–2022 Academic Year	2022–2023 Academic Year	2023–2024 Academic Year
New Budget Authority	$1,240	$1,240	$1,518
Advance Appropriation	791	791	791
Total program level	2,031	2,031	2,309
Change in advance appropriation over previous year	0	0	0

Career and Technical Education:

Career and technical education State grants.—Funds support formula grants to States to expand and improve career and technical education (CTE) in high schools, technical schools, and community colleges under the Carl D. Perkins Career and Technical Education Act of 2006, as amended.

Career and technical education national activities.—Funds support research, development, dissemination, evaluation, assessment, capacity building, and technical assistance activities aimed at improving the quality and effectiveness of CTE programs under the Carl D. Perkins Career and Technical Education Act of 2006, as amended. A new career-connected high schools initiative would support competitive grants to consortia of local educational agencies, institutions of higher education, and employers to increase the integration and alignment of the last two years of high school and the first two years of postsecondary education to improve postsecondary and career outcomes for all students, including students of color and students from low-income backgrounds. Key activities would include dual enrollment in postsecondary-level core content and career-connected coursework; work-based learning opportunities connected to programs of study; attainment of in-demand, career-related credentials; high-quality counseling and career-navigation supports; and educator professional development to support effective integration of academic and career-connected instruction across grades 11–14.

Adult Education:

Adult basic and literacy education State grants.—Funds support formula grants to States to help eliminate functional illiteracy among the Nation's adults, to assist adults in obtaining a high school diploma or its equivalent, and to promote family literacy. A portion of the funds is reserved for formula grants to States to provide English literacy and civics education for immigrants and other limited English proficient adults.

Adult education national leadership activities.—Funds support discretionary activities to evaluate the effectiveness of Federal, State, and local adult education programs, to test and demonstrate methods of improving program quality, and to provide technical assistance to States. The 2023 request would support college bridge programs for adults without a high school diploma or its equivalent and activities to reduce equity gaps for disconnected youth without a high school diploma to help them attain a high school diploma or its equivalent.

Object Classification (in millions of dollars)

Identification code 091–0400–0–1–501	2021 actual	2022 est.	2023 est.
Direct obligations:			
25.1 Advisory and assistance services	15	15	25
25.2 Other services from non-Federal sources	3	3	3
25.3 Other goods and services from Federal sources	1	1	1
41.0 Grants, subsidies, and contributions	2,011	2,011	2,279
99.0 Direct obligations	2,030	2,030	2,308
99.5 Adjustment for rounding	1	1	1
99.9 Total new obligations, unexpired accounts	2,031	2,031	2,309

OFFICE OF POSTSECONDARY EDUCATION

Federal Funds

HIGHER EDUCATION

For carrying out, to the extent not otherwise provided, titles II, III, IV, V, VI, VII, and VIII of the HEA, the Mutual Educational and Cultural Exchange Act of 1961, and section 117 of the Perkins Act, $3,792,802,000: Provided, That notwithstanding any other provision of law, funds made available in this Act to carry out title VI of the HEA and section 102(b)(6) of the Mutual Educational and Cultural Exchange Act of 1961 may be used to support visits and study in foreign countries by individuals who are participating in advanced foreign language training and international studies in areas that are vital to United States national security and who plan to apply their language skills and knowledge of these countries in the fields of government, the professions, or international development: Provided further, That of the funds referred to in the preceding proviso up to 1 percent may be used for program evaluation, national outreach, and information dissemination activities: Provided further, That up to 1.5 percent of the funds made available under chapter 2 of subpart 2 of part A of title IV of the HEA may be used for evaluation: Provided further, That section 313(d) of the HEA shall not apply to an institution of higher education that is eligible to receive funding under section 318 of the HEA: Provided further, That under the Fund for the Improvement of Postsecondary Education, $450,000,000 shall be used to support 4-year institutions that are eligible to receive assistance under sections 316 through 320 of part A of title III, part B of title III, or title V of the HEA to build and expand institutional research and development infrastructure, and $110,000,000 shall be used for grants to eligible States and Tribal Colleges and Universities to implement institutional-level retention and completion reforms that improve student outcomes, including retention, transfer, and completion rates and labor market outcomes: Provided further, That amounts made available for carrying out section 419N of the HEA may be awarded notwithstanding the limitations in section 419N(b)(2) of the HEA.

Note.—A full-year 2022 appropriation for this account was not enacted at the time the Budget was prepared; therefore, the Budget assumes this account is operating under the Continuing Appropriations Act, 2022 (Division A of Public Law 117–43, as amended). The amounts included for 2022 reflect the annualized level provided by the continuing resolution.

Program and Financing (in millions of dollars)

Identification code 091–0201–0–1–502	2021 actual	2022 est.	2023 est.
Obligations by program activity:			
0001 Strengthening institutions	109	109	209
0002 Strengthening tribally controlled colleges and universities	64	66	53
0003 Strengthening Alaska Native and Native Hawaiian-serving institutions	31	33	25
0004 Strengthening historically Black colleges and universities (HBCUs)	416	418	403
0005 Strengthening historically Black graduate institutions	86	87	102
0007 Strengthening predominantly Black institutions	13	28	23
0008 Strengthening Asian American and Native American Pacific Islander-serving institutions	9	10	20
0009 Strengthening Native American-serving nontribal institutions	9	10	12
0010 Minority science and engineering improvement	12	11	18
0011 Strengthening historically Black masters programs	10	13	21
0091 Subtotal, aid for institutional development	759	785	886
0101 Developing Hispanic-serving institutions	147	243	237
0102 Developing Hispanic-serving institution STEM and articulation programs	93		
0103 Promoting baccalaureate opportunities for Hispanic Americans	13	14	29
0104 International education and foreign language studies	76	78	78
0105 Model transition programs for students with intellectual disabilities	13	14	15
0106 Tribally controlled postsecondary career and technical institutions	10	11	11
0191 Subtotal, other aid for institutions	352	360	370
0201 Federal TRIO programs	1,096	1,097	1,298
0202 Gaining early awareness and readiness for undergraduate programs (GEAR UP)	366	368	408
0203 Graduate assistance in areas of national need	22	24	24
0204 Child care access means parents in school	55	55	95
0291 Subtotal, assistance for students	1,539	1,544	1,825
0301 Fund for the improvement of postsecondary education (FIPSE)	40	55	560
0302 Teacher quality partnerships	51	38	132
0303 Hawkins Centers of Excellence			20
0391 Assistance for students, subtotal	91	93	712

Office of Postsecondary Education
Federal Funds   339

HIGHER EDUCATION—Continued
Program and Financing—Continued

Identification code 091–0201–0–1–502	2021 actual	2022 est.	2023 est.
0900 Total new obligations, unexpired accounts	2,741	2,782	3,793
Budgetary resources:			
Unobligated balance:			
1000 Unobligated balance brought forward, Oct 1	25	61	193
1012 Unobligated balance transfers between expired and unexpired accounts	132	132	132
1070 Unobligated balance (total)	157	193	325
Budget authority:			
Appropriations, discretionary:			
1100 Appropriation	2,542	2,542	3,793
Appropriations, mandatory:			
1200 Appropriation	255	255	255
1230 Appropriations and/or unobligated balance of appropriations permanently reduced	–15	–15	–15
1260 Appropriations, mandatory (total)	240	240	240
1900 Budget authority (total)	2,782	2,782	4,033
1930 Total budgetary resources available	2,939	2,975	4,358
Memorandum (non-add) entries:			
1940 Unobligated balance expiring	–137		
1941 Unexpired unobligated balance, end of year	61	193	565
Change in obligated balance:			
Unpaid obligations:			
3000 Unpaid obligations, brought forward, Oct 1	3,867	4,173	4,107
3010 New obligations, unexpired accounts	2,741	2,782	3,793
3020 Outlays (gross)	–2,409	–2,848	–2,985
3041 Recoveries of prior year unpaid obligations, expired	–26		
3050 Unpaid obligations, end of year	4,173	4,107	4,915
Memorandum (non-add) entries:			
3100 Obligated balance, start of year	3,867	4,173	4,107
3200 Obligated balance, end of year	4,173	4,107	4,915
Budget authority and outlays, net:			
Discretionary:			
4000 Budget authority, gross	2,542	2,542	3,793
Outlays, gross:			
4010 Outlays from new discretionary authority	16	76	114
4011 Outlays from discretionary balances	2,169	2,435	2,471
4020 Outlays, gross (total)	2,185	2,511	2,585
Mandatory:			
4090 Budget authority, gross	240	240	240
Outlays, gross:			
4100 Outlays from new mandatory authority		8	8
4101 Outlays from mandatory balances	224	329	392
4110 Outlays, gross (total)	224	337	400
4180 Budget authority, net (total)	2,782	2,782	4,033
4190 Outlays, net (total)	2,409	2,848	2,985

Aid for Institutional Development:

Strengthening institutions.—Funds support planning and development grants for improving academic programs and financial management at schools that enroll high proportions of disadvantaged students and have low per-student expenditures.

Strengthening tribally controlled colleges and universities.—Discretionary and mandatory funds support grants to American Indian tribally controlled colleges and universities with scarce resources to enable them to improve and expand their capacity to serve students and to strengthen management and fiscal operations.

Strengthening Alaska Native and Native Hawaiian-serving institutions.—Discretionary and mandatory funds support Alaska Native and Native Hawaiian-serving institutions to enable them to improve and expand their capacity to serve students and to strengthen management and fiscal operations.

Strengthening historically Black colleges and universities.—Discretionary and mandatory funds support grants to help historically Black undergraduate institutions to improve and expand their capacity to serve students and to strengthen management and fiscal operations.

Strengthening historically Black graduate institutions.—Funds support grants to historically Black graduate institutions to improve and expand their capacity to serve students and to strengthen management and fiscal operations.

Strengthening predominantly Black institutions.—Discretionary and mandatory funds support grants to predominantly Black institutions to improve and expand their capacity to serve students.

Strengthening Asian American- and Native American Pacific Islander-serving institutions.—Discretionary and mandatory funds support grants to help Asian American and Native American Pacific Islander-serving institutions improve and expand their capacity to serve students and to strengthen management and fiscal operations.

Strengthening Native American-serving nontribal institutions.—Discretionary and mandatory funds support grants to help Native American-serving nontribal institutions improve and expand their capacity to serve students and to strengthen management and fiscal operations.

Minority science and engineering improvement.—Funds support grants to predominantly minority institutions to help them make long-range improvements in science and engineering education and to increase the participation of minorities in scientific and technological careers.

Strengthening HBCU Masters program.—Funds support grants to historically Black institutions to improve graduate education opportunities at the Masters level in scientific disciplines in which African Americans are underrepresented.

Aid for Hispanic-serving Institutions:

Developing Hispanic-serving institutions.—Funds support Hispanic-serving institutions to help them improve and expand their capacity to serve students.

Developing Hispanic-serving institutions STEM and articulation programs.—Mandatory funds support Hispanic-serving institutions to help them improve and expand their capacity to serve students with priority given to applications that propose to increase the number of Hispanics and other low-income students attaining degrees in the fields of science, technology, engineering, or mathematics; and to develop model transfer and articulation agreements between 2-year Hispanic-serving institutions and 4-year institutions in such fields.

Promoting postbaccalaureate opportunities for Hispanic Americans.—Discretionary funds support Hispanic-serving institutions to help them expand and improve postbaccalaureate educational opportunities.

Other Aid for Institutions:

International education and foreign language studies programs.—Funds promote the development and improvement of domestic and overseas international and foreign language programs by providing institutional and fellowship grant funding to strengthen the capability and performance of American education in foreign languages and in area and international studies.

Model transition programs for students with intellectual disabilities into higher education.—Funds support grants to institutions of higher education or consortia of such institutions to create or expand high quality, inclusive model comprehensive transition and postsecondary programs for students with intellectual disabilities.

Tribally controlled postsecondary career and technical institutions.—Funds support the operation and improvement of eligible tribally controlled postsecondary career institutions to ensure continued and expanded educational opportunities for Indian students.

Assistance for Students:

Federal TRIO programs.—Funds support postsecondary education outreach and student support services to help individuals from disadvantaged backgrounds prepare for, enter, and complete college and graduate studies.

Gaining early awareness and readiness for undergraduate programs.—Funds support early college preparation and awareness activities at the State and local levels to ensure that low-income elementary and secondary school students are prepared for and pursue postsecondary education.

Graduate assistance in areas of national need.—Funds support fellowships to graduate students of superior ability who have financial need for study in areas of national need.

Child care access means parents in school.—Funds support a program designed to bolster the participation of low-income parents in postsecondary education through the provision of campus-based child care services.

Fund for the improvement of postsecondary education.—Funds support the development of innovative strategies designed to improve college completion, particularly for high-need students.

Teacher quality partnership.—Funds support grants to partnerships including institutions of higher education and local education agencies, among others, to reform pre-baccalaureate teacher preparation programs or create teacher residency programs in high-need local education agencies.

Hawkins centers of excellence.—Funds support a program designed to increase the talent pool of effective minority educators by expanding and reforming teacher education programs at minority-serving institutions.

Pooled evaluation.—Requested authority would enable the Department to reserve up to 0.5 percent of funding annually appropriated for certain Higher Education Act (HEA) programs for rigorous program evaluation, data collection, and analysis of outcome data.

Object Classification (in millions of dollars)

Identification code 091–0201–0–1–502	2021 actual	2022 est.	2023 est.
Direct obligations:			
25.2 Other services from non-Federal sources	6	3	6
25.3 Other goods and services from Federal sources	1	1	1
25.5 Research and development contracts	1	1	....
25.7 Operation and maintenance of equipment	2	2	3
41.0 Grants, subsidies, and contributions	2,731	2,775	3,783
99.9 Total new obligations, unexpired accounts	2,741	2,782	3,793

HOWARD UNIVERSITY

For partial support of Howard University, $311,018,000, of which not less than $3,405,000 shall be for a matching endowment grant pursuant to the Howard University Endowment Act and shall remain available until expended.

Note.—A full-year 2022 appropriation for this account was not enacted at the time the Budget was prepared; therefore, the Budget assumes this account is operating under the Continuing Appropriations Act, 2022 (Division A of Public Law 117–43, as amended). The amounts included for 2022 reflect the annualized level provided by the continuing resolution.

Program and Financing (in millions of dollars)

Identification code 091–0603–0–1–502	2021 actual	2022 est.	2023 est.
Obligations by program activity:			
0001 General support	306	217	227
0002 Howard University Hospital	....	34	84
0900 Total new obligations, unexpired accounts (object class 41.0)	306	251	311
Budgetary resources:			
Budget authority:			
Appropriations, discretionary:			
1100 Appropriation	271	251	311
Appropriations, mandatory:			
1200 Appropriation	35	....	....
1900 Budget authority (total)	306	251	311
1930 Total budgetary resources available	306	251	311
Change in obligated balance:			
Unpaid obligations:			
3000 Unpaid obligations, brought forward, Oct 1	3	11	3
3010 New obligations, unexpired accounts	306	251	311
3020 Outlays (gross)	–298	–259	–311
3050 Unpaid obligations, end of year	11	3	3
Memorandum (non-add) entries:			
3100 Obligated balance, start of year	3	11	3
3200 Obligated balance, end of year	11	3	3
Budget authority and outlays, net:			
Discretionary:			
4000 Budget authority, gross	271	251	311
Outlays, gross:			
4010 Outlays from new discretionary authority	271	248	308
4011 Outlays from discretionary balances	3	11	3
4020 Outlays, gross (total)	274	259	311
Mandatory:			
4090 Budget authority, gross	35	....	....
Outlays, gross:			
4100 Outlays from new mandatory authority	24	....	....
4180 Budget authority, net (total)	306	251	311
4190 Outlays, net (total)	298	259	311

Howard University is a private, nonprofit institution of higher education consisting of 13 schools and colleges. Federal funds are used to provide partial support for University programs as well as for the Howard University Hospital, a teaching facility. In 2022, the Federal appropriation represented approximately 23 percent of the University's revenue and 10 percent of the Hospital's revenue. The 2023 request is expected to be allocated in a similar manner.

The 2023 request would lift the restrictions that prevent Howard University from accessing the HBCU Capital Financing Program.

COLLEGE HOUSING AND ACADEMIC FACILITIES LOANS PROGRAM

For Federal administrative expenses to carry out activities related to existing facility loans pursuant to section 121 of the HEA, $298,000.

HISTORICALLY BLACK COLLEGE AND UNIVERSITY CAPITAL FINANCING PROGRAM ACCOUNT

For the cost of guaranteed loans, $20,150,000, as authorized pursuant to part D of title III of the HEA, which shall remain available through September 30, 2024: Provided, That such costs, including the cost of modifying such loans, shall be as defined in section 502 of the Congressional Budget Act of 1974: Provided further, That these funds are available to subsidize total loan principal, any part of which is to be guaranteed, not to exceed $752,065,725: Provided further, That these funds may be used to support loans to public and private Historically Black Colleges and Universities without regard to the limitations within section 344(a) of the HEA.

In addition, for administrative expenses to carry out the Historically Black College and University Capital Financing Program entered into pursuant to part D of title III of the HEA, $528,000.

Note.—A full-year 2022 appropriation for this account was not enacted at the time the Budget was prepared; therefore, the Budget assumes this account is operating under the Continuing Appropriations Act, 2022 (Division A of Public Law 117–43, as amended). The amounts included for 2022 reflect the annualized level provided by the continuing resolution.

Program and Financing (in millions of dollars)

Identification code 091–0241–0–1–502	2021 actual	2022 est.	2023 est.
Obligations by program activity:			
0001 Forgiveness Modification expenses	136	....	....
Credit program obligations:			
0701 Direct loan subsidy	23	18	8
0703 Subsidy for modifications of direct loans	1,564	....	....
0705 Reestimates of direct loan subsidy	18	242	....
0706 Interest on reestimates of direct loan subsidy	1	42	....
0709 Administrative expenses	....	1	1
0791 Direct program activities, subtotal	1,606	303	9
0900 Total new obligations, unexpired accounts (object class 41.0)	1,742	303	9
Budgetary resources:			
Unobligated balance:			
1000 Unobligated balance brought forward, Oct 1	14	33	63
Budget authority:			
Appropriations, discretionary:			
1100 Appropriation	49	49	21
Appropriations, mandatory:			
1200 Appropriation	2,051	284	....
1900 Budget authority (total)	2,100	333	21
1930 Total budgetary resources available	2,114	366	84
Memorandum (non-add) entries:			
1940 Unobligated balance expiring	–339	....	....
1941 Unexpired unobligated balance, end of year	33	63	75

Office of Postsecondary Education—Continued
Federal Funds—Continued

COLLEGE HOUSING AND ACADEMIC FACILITIES LOANS PROGRAM ACCOUNT—Continued

Program and Financing—Continued

Identification code 091–0241–0–1–502	2021 actual	2022 est.	2023 est.
Change in obligated balance:			
Unpaid obligations:			
3000 Unpaid obligations, brought forward, Oct 1	33	34	42
3010 New obligations, unexpired accounts	1,742	303	9
3020 Outlays (gross)	–1,736	–295	–12
3041 Recoveries of prior year unpaid obligations, expired	–5		
3050 Unpaid obligations, end of year	34	42	39
Memorandum (non-add) entries:			
3100 Obligated balance, start of year	33	34	42
3200 Obligated balance, end of year	34	42	39
Budget authority and outlays, net:			
Discretionary:			
4000 Budget authority, gross	49	49	21
Outlays, gross:			
4010 Outlays from new discretionary authority	6	5	5
4011 Outlays from discretionary balances	17	6	7
4020 Outlays, gross (total)	23	11	12
Mandatory:			
4090 Budget authority, gross	2,051	284	
Outlays, gross:			
4100 Outlays from new mandatory authority	1,713	284	
4180 Budget authority, net (total)	2,100	333	21
4190 Outlays, net (total)	1,736	295	12

Summary of Loan Levels, Subsidy Budget Authority and Outlays by Program (in millions of dollars)

Identification code 091–0241–0–1–502	2021 actual	2022 est.	2023 est.
Direct loan levels supportable by subsidy budget authority:			
115002 Historically Black Colleges and Universities	300	241	270
115999 Total direct loan levels	300	241	270
Direct loan subsidy (in percent):			
132002 Historically Black Colleges and Universities	7.67	7.35	2.68
132999 Weighted average subsidy rate	7.67	7.35	2.68
Direct loan subsidy budget authority:			
133002 Historically Black Colleges and Universities	23	18	8
133999 Total subsidy budget authority	23	18	8
Direct loan subsidy outlays:			
134002 Historically Black Colleges and Universities	1,581	10	11
134999 Total subsidy outlays	1,581	10	11
Direct loan reestimates:			
135001 College housing and academic facilities loans		–2	
135002 Historically Black Colleges and Universities	–189	–6	
135999 Total direct loan reestimates	–189	–8	
Administrative expense data:			
3510 Budget authority	1	1	1
3590 Outlays from new authority	1	1	1

As required by the Federal Credit Reform Act of 1990, this account records the subsidy costs associated with the direct loans obligated and loan guarantees committed in 1992 and beyond, as well as any administrative expenses for the College Housing and Academic Facilities Loans (CHAFL) Program and the Historically Black College and University (HBCU) Capital Financing Program. The subsidy amounts are estimated on a present value basis; the administrative expenses are on a cash basis. These programs are administered separately but consolidated in the Budget for presentation purposes.

College housing and academic facilities loans program.—Funds for this activity pay the Federal costs of administering CHAFL, College Housing Loans (CHL), and Higher Education Facilities Loans (HEFL) programs. Prior to 1994, these programs provided financing for the construction, reconstruction, and renovation of housing, academic, and other educational facilities. Although no new loans have been awarded since 1993, the Department of Education will incur costs for administering the outstanding loans through 2030.

Historically Black college and university (HBCU) capital financing program.—The HBCU Capital Financing Program provides HBCUs with access to capital financing for the repair, renovation, and construction of classrooms, libraries, laboratories, dormitories, instructional equipment, and research instrumentation. The authorizing statute gives the Department authority to enter into insurance agreements with a private for-profit Designated Bonding Authority. The bonding authority issues the loans and maintains an escrow account in which five percent of each institution's principal is deposited. The FAFSA Simplification Act, which was included in the Consolidated Appropriations Act, 2021, signed into law in December 2020, provided authority and funding to discharge debts under the HBCU Capital Financing Program. The Department of Education discharged approximately $1.6 billion of debt provided to HBCUs.

The 2023 request would lift the restrictions that prevent Howard University from accessing the HBCU Capital Financing Program.

Employment Summary

Identification code 091–0241–0–1–502	2021 actual	2022 est.	2023 est.
1001 Direct civilian full-time equivalent employment	3	3	3

COLLEGE HOUSING AND ACADEMIC FACILITIES LOANS FINANCING ACCOUNT

Program and Financing (in millions of dollars)

Identification code 091–4252–0–3–502	2021 actual	2022 est.	2023 est.
Obligations by program activity:			
Credit program obligations:			
0713 Payment of interest to Treasury		1	1
0743 Interest on downward reestimates		2	
0900 Total new obligations, unexpired accounts		3	1
Budgetary resources:			
Unobligated balance:			
1000 Unobligated balance brought forward, Oct 1		–2	
1020 Adjustment of unobligated bal brought forward, Oct 1		2	
Financing authority:			
Spending authority from offsetting collections, mandatory:			
1800 Collected	1	1	1
1825 Spending authority from offsetting collections applied to repay debt	–3		
1850 Spending auth from offsetting collections, mand (total)	–2	1	1
1900 Budget authority (total)	–2	1	1
1930 Total budgetary resources available	–2	1	1
Memorandum (non-add) entries:			
1941 Unexpired unobligated balance, end of year	–2		
Change in obligated balance:			
Unpaid obligations:			
3000 Unpaid obligations, brought forward, Oct 1			2
3010 New obligations, unexpired accounts		3	1
3020 Outlays (gross)		–1	–1
3050 Unpaid obligations, end of year		2	2
Memorandum (non-add) entries:			
3100 Obligated balance, start of year			2
3200 Obligated balance, end of year		2	2
Financing authority and disbursements, net:			
Mandatory:			
4090 Budget authority, gross	–2	1	1
Financing disbursements:			
4110 Outlays, gross (total)		1	1
Offsets against gross financing authority and disbursements:			
Offsetting collections (collected) from:			
4123 Interest repayments	–1	–1	–1
4180 Budget authority, net (total)	–3		
4190 Outlays, net (total)	–1		

DEPARTMENT OF EDUCATION

Status of Direct Loans (in millions of dollars)

Identification code 091–4252–0–3–502		2021 actual	2022 est.	2023 est.
	Cumulative balance of direct loans outstanding:			
1210	Outstanding, start of year	3	3	3
1290	Outstanding, end of year	3	3	3

As required by the Federal Credit Reform Act of 1990, this nonbudgetary account records all cash flows to and from the Government resulting from the College Housing and Academic Facilities loan program. Amounts in this account are a means of financing and are not included in the budget totals.

Balance Sheet (in millions of dollars)

Identification code 091–4252–0–3–502		2020 actual	2021 actual
	ASSETS:		
	Net value of assets related to post-1991 direct loans receivable:		
1401	Direct loans receivable, gross	3	3
1405	Allowance for subsidy cost (-)		
1499	Net present value of assets related to direct loans	3	3
1999	Total assets	3	3
	LIABILITIES:		
2103	Federal liabilities: Debt	3	3
4999	Total liabilities and net position	3	3

COLLEGE HOUSING AND ACADEMIC FACILITIES LOANS LIQUIDATING ACCOUNT

Program and Financing (in millions of dollars)

Identification code 091–0242–0–1–502		2021 actual	2022 est.	2023 est.
	Obligations by program activity:			
	Credit program obligations:			
0713	Payment of interest to Treasury	2	2	2
0900	Total new obligations, unexpired accounts (object class 43.0)	2	2	2
	Budgetary resources:			
	Unobligated balance:			
1000	Unobligated balance brought forward, Oct 1	3	2	
1022	Capital transfer of unobligated balances to general fund	–3	–2	
	Budget authority:			
	Appropriations, mandatory:			
1200	Appropriation	1	9	1
1236	Appropriations applied to repay debt		–8	
1260	Appropriations, mandatory (total)	1	1	1
	Spending authority from offsetting collections, mandatory:			
1800	Collected	5	8	8
1820	Capital transfer of spending authority from offsetting collections to general fund			–5
1825	Spending authority from offsetting collections applied to repay debt	–2	–7	–2
1850	Spending auth from offsetting collections, mand (total)	3	1	1
1900	Budget authority (total)	4	2	2
1930	Total budgetary resources available	4	2	2
	Memorandum (non-add) entries:			
1941	Unexpired unobligated balance, end of year	2		
	Change in obligated balance:			
	Unpaid obligations:			
3000	Unpaid obligations, brought forward, Oct 1	1	1	
3010	New obligations, unexpired accounts	2	2	2
3020	Outlays (gross)	–2	–3	–2
3050	Unpaid obligations, end of year	1		
	Memorandum (non-add) entries:			
3100	Obligated balance, start of year	1	1	
3200	Obligated balance, end of year	1		
	Budget authority and outlays, net:			
	Mandatory:			
4090	Budget authority, gross	4	2	2
	Outlays, gross:			
4100	Outlays from new mandatory authority	2	2	2

Office of Postsecondary Education—Continued
Federal Funds—Continued

343

4101	Outlays from mandatory balances		1	
4110	Outlays, gross (total)	2	3	2
	Offsets against gross budget authority and outlays:			
	Offsetting collections (collected) from:			
4123	Non-Federal sources	–5	–8	–8
4180	Budget authority, net (total)	–1	–6	–6
4190	Outlays, net (total)	–3	–5	–6

Status of Direct Loans (in millions of dollars)

Identification code 091–0242–0–1–502		2021 actual	2022 est.	2023 est.
	Cumulative balance of direct loans outstanding:			
1210	Outstanding, start of year	22	17	9
1251	Repayments: Repayments and prepayments	–2	–8	–2
1264	Other adjustments, net (+ or -)	–3		
1290	Outstanding, end of year	17	9	7

As required by the Federal Credit Reform Act of 1990, the College Housing and Academic Facilities Loans Liquidating Account records all cash flows to and from the Government resulting from direct loans obligated prior to 1992. This account includes loans made under the College Housing and Academic Facilities Loans, College Housing Loans, and Higher Education Facilities Loans programs, which continue to be administered separately.

Balance Sheet (in millions of dollars)

Identification code 091–0242–0–1–502		2020 actual	2021 actual
	ASSETS:		
1101	Federal assets: Fund balances with Treasury	4	3
1601	Direct loans, gross	22	17
1602	Interest receivable	4	4
1603	Allowance for estimated uncollectible loans and interest (-)	–8	–7
1699	Value of assets related to direct loans	18	14
1999	Total assets	22	17
	LIABILITIES:		
	Federal liabilities:		
2103	Debt	10	9
2104	Resources payable to Treasury	16	15
2999	Total liabilities	26	24
	NET POSITION:		
3100	Unexpended appropriations	3	3
3300	Cumulative results of operations	–7	–10
3999	Total net position	–4	–7
4999	Total liabilities and net position	22	17

HISTORICALLY BLACK COLLEGE AND UNIVERSITY CAPITAL FINANCING DIRECT LOAN FINANCING ACCOUNT

Program and Financing (in millions of dollars)

Identification code 091–4255–0–3–502		2021 actual	2022 est.	2023 est.
	Obligations by program activity:			
0004	Interest paid to Treasury (FFB)	21	2	2
0006	Deferment Mod expenses	5		
0007	Public Deferment Payments	2		
0008	CARES Deferment Payments	18		
0009	Forgiveness Mod Expenses	13		
0091	Direct program activities, subtotal	59	2	2
	Credit program obligations:			
0710	Direct loan obligations	300	241	270
0713	Payment of interest to Treasury	9	1	3
0742	Downward reestimates paid to receipt accounts	118	203	
0743	Interest on downward reestimates	89	85	
0791	Direct program activities, subtotal	516	530	273
0900	Total new obligations, unexpired accounts	575	532	275
	Budgetary resources:			
	Unobligated balance:			
1000	Unobligated balance brought forward, Oct 1	177	445	367

HISTORICALLY BLACK COLLEGE AND UNIVERSITY CAPITAL FINANCING DIRECT LOAN FINANCING ACCOUNT—Continued

Program and Financing—Continued

Identification code 091–4255–0–3–502		2021 actual	2022 est.	2023 est.
	Financing authority:			
	Borrowing authority, mandatory:			
1400	Borrowing authority	668	367	752
	Spending authority from offsetting collections, mandatory:			
1800	Collected	1,726	296	17
1825	Spending authority from offsetting collections applied to repay debt	−1,551	−209	−3
1850	Spending auth from offsetting collections, mand (total)	175	87	14
1900	Budget authority (total)	843	454	766
1930	Total budgetary resources available	1,020	899	1,133
	Memorandum (non-add) entries:			
1941	Unexpired unobligated balance, end of year	445	367	858
	Change in obligated balance:			
	Unpaid obligations:			
3000	Unpaid obligations, brought forward, Oct 1	499	548	501
3010	New obligations, unexpired accounts	575	532	275
3020	Outlays (gross)	−526	−579	−221
3050	Unpaid obligations, end of year	548	501	555
	Memorandum (non-add) entries:			
3100	Obligated balance, start of year	499	548	501
3200	Obligated balance, end of year	548	501	555
	Financing authority and disbursements, net:			
	Mandatory:			
4090	Budget authority, gross	843	454	766
	Financing disbursements:			
4110	Outlays, gross (total)	526	579	221
	Offsets against gross financing authority and disbursements:			
	Offsetting collections (collected) from:			
4120	Federal sources (subsidy)	−1,599	−293	−11
4120	Federal sources (FFB)	−48		
4122	Interest on uninvested funds	−12		
4123	Interest repayments	−25	−1	−3
4123	Principal repayments	−42	−2	−3
4130	Offsets against gross budget authority and outlays (total)	−1,726	−296	−17
4160	Budget authority, net (mandatory)	−883	158	749
4170	Outlays, net (mandatory)	−1,200	283	204
4180	Budget authority, net (total)	−883	158	749
4190	Outlays, net (total)	−1,200	283	204

Status of Direct Loans (in millions of dollars)

Identification code 091–4255–0–3–502		2021 actual	2022 est.	2023 est.
	Position with respect to appropriations act limitation on obligations:			
1111	Direct loan obligations from current-year authority	300	241	270
1150	Total direct loan obligations	300	241	270
	Cumulative balance of direct loans outstanding:			
1210	Outstanding, start of year	1,564	160	343
1231	Disbursements: Direct loan disbursements	209	185	221
1251	Repayments: Repayments and prepayments	−67	−2	−3
1264	Other adjustments, net (+ or −)	−1,546		
1290	Outstanding, end of year	160	343	561

As required by the Federal Credit Reform Act of 1990, this non-budgetary account records all cash flows to and from the Federal Government resulting from direct loans obligated in 1996 and beyond. The Federal Financing Bank (FFB) purchases bonds issued by the Historically Black College and University (HBCU) Designated Bonding Authority. Under the policies governing Federal credit programs, bonds purchased by the FFB and supported by the Department of Education with a letter of credit create the equivalent of a Federal direct loan. HBCU bonds are also available for purchase by the private sector, and these will be treated as loan guarantees. However, the Department anticipates that all HBCU loans will be financed by the FFB. The amounts in this account are a means of financing and are not included in the budget totals.

Balance Sheet (in millions of dollars)

Identification code 091–4255–0–3–502		2020 actual	2021 actual
	ASSETS:		
1101	Federal assets: Fund balances with Treasury	215	281
	Net value of assets related to post-1991 direct loans receivable:		
1401	Direct loans receivable, gross	1,564	160
1402	Interest receivable	54	1
1405	Allowance for subsidy cost (−)	−222	−25
1499	Net present value of assets related to direct loans	1,396	136
1901	Other Federal assets: Other assets		
1999	Total assets	1,611	417
	LIABILITIES:		
	Federal liabilities:		
2101	Accounts payable	45	
2102	Interest payable	13	
2103	Debt	1,553	417
2999	Total liabilities	1,611	417
	NET POSITION:		
3300	Cumulative results of operations		
4999	Total liabilities and net position	1,611	417

OFFICE OF FEDERAL STUDENT AID

Federal Funds

STUDENT FINANCIAL ASSISTANCE

For carrying out subparts 1, 3, and 10 of part A, and part C of title IV of the HEA, $26,345,352,000 which shall remain available through September 30, 2024.

The maximum Pell Grant for which a student shall be eligible during award year 2023–2024 shall be $6,335.

Note.—A full-year 2022 appropriation for this account was not enacted at the time the Budget was prepared; therefore, the Budget assumes this account is operating under the Continuing Appropriations Act, 2022 (Division A of Public Law 117–43, as amended). The amounts included for 2022 reflect the annualized level provided by the continuing resolution.

Program and Financing (in millions of dollars)

Identification code 091–0200–0–1–502		2021 actual	2022 est.	2023 est.
	Obligations by program activity:			
0101	Federal Pell grants	27,393	26,726	32,173
0201	Federal supplemental educational opportunity grants (SEOG)	878	884	880
0202	Federal work-study	1,196	1,200	1,190
0291	Campus-based activities - Subtotal	2,074	2,084	2,070
0900	Total new obligations, unexpired accounts (object class 41.0)	29,467	28,810	34,243
	Budgetary resources:			
	Unobligated balance:			
1000	Unobligated balance brought forward, Oct 1	13,129	14,227	15,810
1021	Recoveries of prior year unpaid obligations	33	109	
1070	Unobligated balance (total)	13,162	14,336	15,810
	Budget authority:			
	Appropriations, discretionary:			
1100	Appropriation	24,545	24,545	26,345
1100	Appropriation - Disc Award Inc CHIMP			141
1130	Appropriations permanently reduced		−28	−141
1131	Unobligated balance of appropriations permanently reduced	−500	−500	
1160	Appropriation, discretionary (total)	24,045	24,017	26,345
	Appropriations, mandatory:			
1200	Appropriation	6,555	6,267	6,415
1230	Appropriations and/or unobligated balance of appropriations permanently reduced	−28		
1260	Appropriations, mandatory (total)	6,527	6,267	6,415
1900	Budget authority (total)	30,572	30,284	32,760
1930	Total budgetary resources available	43,734	44,620	48,570
	Memorandum (non-add) entries:			
1940	Unobligated balance expiring	−40		
1941	Unexpired unobligated balance, end of year	14,227	15,810	14,327
	Change in obligated balance:			
	Unpaid obligations:			
3000	Unpaid obligations, brought forward, Oct 1	19,213	19,946	19,728

Code	Description	2021 actual	2022 est.	2023 est.
3010	New obligations, unexpired accounts	29,467	28,810	34,243
3011	Obligations ("upward adjustments"), expired accounts	184		
3020	Outlays (gross)	−28,653	−28,919	−30,601
3040	Recoveries of prior year unpaid obligations, unexpired	−33	−109	
3041	Recoveries of prior year unpaid obligations, expired	−232		
3050	Unpaid obligations, end of year	19,946	19,728	23,370
	Memorandum (non-add) entries:			
3100	Obligated balance, start of year	19,213	19,946	19,728
3200	Obligated balance, end of year	19,946	19,728	23,370
	Budget authority and outlays, net:			
	Discretionary:			
4000	Budget authority, gross	24,045	24,017	26,345
	Outlays, gross:			
4010	Outlays from new discretionary authority	6,719	2,438	3,534
4011	Outlays from discretionary balances	15,312	20,062	17,490
4020	Outlays, gross (total)	22,031	22,500	21,024
	Offsets against gross budget authority and outlays:			
	Offsetting collections (collected) from:			
4033	Non-Federal sources	−3		
	Additional offsets against gross budget authority only:			
4052	Offsetting collections credited to expired accounts	3		
4070	Budget authority, net (discretionary)	24,045	24,017	26,345
4080	Outlays, net (discretionary)	22,028	22,500	21,024
	Mandatory:			
4090	Budget authority, gross	6,527	6,267	6,415
	Outlays, gross:			
4100	Outlays from new mandatory authority	2,121	2,207	2,271
4101	Outlays from mandatory balances	4,501	4,212	7,306
4110	Outlays, gross (total)	6,622	6,419	9,577
	Offsets against gross budget authority and outlays:			
	Offsetting collections (collected) from:			
4123	Non-Federal sources	−17		
	Additional offsets against gross budget authority only:			
4142	Offsetting collections credited to expired accounts	17		
4160	Budget authority, net (mandatory)	6,527	6,267	6,415
4170	Outlays, net (mandatory)	6,605	6,419	9,577
4180	Budget authority, net (total)	30,572	30,284	32,760
4190	Outlays, net (total)	28,633	28,919	30,601

Summary of Budget Authority and Outlays (in millions of dollars)

	2021 actual	2022 est.	2023 est.
Enacted/requested:			
Budget Authority	30,572	30,284	32,760
Outlays	28,633	28,919	30,601
Legislative proposal, subject to PAYGO:			
Budget Authority			6,575
Outlays			2,847
Total:			
Budget Authority	30,572	30,284	39,335
Outlays	28,633	28,919	33,448

Status of Direct Loans (in millions of dollars)

Identification code 091–0200–0–1–502	2021 actual	2022 est.	2023 est.
Cumulative balance of direct loans outstanding:			
1210 Outstanding, start of year	615	664	729
1251 Repayments: Repayments and prepayments	−15	−60	−101
1264 Other adjustments, net (+ or −)	64	125	120
1290 Outstanding, end of year	664	729	748

Notes.—Figures include, in all years, institutional matching share of defaulted notes assigned from institutions to the Education Department.

Funding from the Student Financial Assistance account and related matching funds would provide 8.9 million awards totaling more than $41.2 billion in available aid in award year 2023–2024.

Federal Pell grants.—Pell Grants are the single largest source of grant aid for postsecondary education. Funding for this program is provided from two sources: discretionary and mandatory budget authority provided by the College Cost Reduction and Access Act, as amended, and changes to the Higher Education Act of 1965 made in the Department of Education Appropriations Act of 2021.

In 2023, nearly 6.7 million undergraduates will receive up to $6,335 from the discretionary award and an additional $2,335 from the mandatory add-on to help pay for postsecondary education. Undergraduate students establish eligibility for these grants under award and need determination rules set out in the authorizing statute and annual appropriations act.

The 2023 Budget request includes $24.3 billion in discretionary funding for Pell Grants in 2023, which, when combined with mandatory funding, will support a projected maximum award of $8,670.

Federal supplemental educational opportunity grants (SEOG).—Federal funds are awarded by formula to qualifying institutions, which use these funds to award grants to undergraduate students. While institutions have discretion in awarding these funds, they are required to give priority to Pell Grant recipients and other students with exceptional need. The Federal share of these grants cannot exceed 75 percent of the total grant. The 2023 Budget includes $880 million for SEOG, which would generate $1.25 billion in aid to nearly 1.7 million students.

Federal work-study.—Federal funds are awarded by formula to qualifying institutions, which provide part-time jobs to eligible undergraduate and graduate students. Hourly earnings under this program must be at least the Federal minimum wage. Federal funding, in most cases, pays 75 percent of a student's hourly wages, with the remaining 25 percent paid by the employer. The Federal Work-Study program also requires participating institutions to use at least seven percent of their total funds for students employed in community service jobs.

The 2023 Budget includes $1.19 billion for Work-Study, which would generate $1.21 billion in aid to 620,597 students.

Iraq and Afghanistan service grants.—This program provides non-need-based grants to students whose parent or guardian was a member of the Armed Forces and died in Iraq or Afghanistan as a result of performing military service after September 11, 2001.

Pooled evaluation.—Requested authority in the General Provisions would enable the Department to reserve up to 0.5 percent of funding annually appropriated for certain Higher Education Act (HEA) programs for rigorous program evaluation, data collection, and analysis of outcome data. The authority would not allow the Department to reserve funds appropriated for Pell Grants, but would allow for evaluation of the program with the reserved funds.

Funding tables.—The following tables display student aid funds available, the number of aid awards, average awards, and the unduplicated count of recipients from each Federal student aid program. Loan amounts reflect the amount actually loaned to borrowers, not the Federal cost of these loans. The data in these tables include matching funds wherever appropriate. The 2023 data in these tables reflect the Administration's Budget proposals.

Aid Funds Available for Postsecondary Education and Training

(in thousands of dollars)

	2021	2022	2023
Pell grants	$26,400,480	$26,695,335	$38,714,715
Student loans:			
Subsidized Stafford loans	16,244,711	16,025,387	15,867,580
Unsubsidized Stafford loans (Undergraduates)	18,476,479	18,502,154	18,482,220
Unsubsidized Stafford loans (Graduate students)	27,366,595	27,843,927	27,742,246
Unsubsidized Stafford loans (total)	45,843,074	46,346,081	46,224,466
Parent PLUS loans	10,297,227	10,340,369	10,610,704
Grad PLUS loans	12,071,518	12,317,093	12,480,005
PLUS loans (total)	22,368,745	22,657,462	23,090,709
Consolidation	19,964,715	26,217,008	27,239,740
Student loans, subtotal	104,421,245	111,245,938	112,422,496
Work-study	1,207,681	1,207,681	1,207,681
Supplemental educational opportunity grants	1,251,693	1,251,693	1,251,693
Iraq and Afghanistan service grants	692	692	924
TEACH grants	74,962	75,862	81,148
Total aid available	132,106,312	139,226,759	152,428,215

Number of Aid Awards

(in thousands)

	2021	2022	2023
Pell grants	6,104	6,133	6,657
Subsidized Stafford loans	4,628	4,562	4,515
Unsubsidized Stafford loans (Undergraduates)	4,856	4,816	4,775
Unsubsidized Stafford loans (Graduate students)	1,790	1,800	1,776
Parent PLUS loans	658	650	653
Grad PLUS loans	595	595	593
Consolidation loans	324	380	401

Office of Federal Student Aid—Continued
Federal Funds—Continued

STUDENT FINANCIAL ASSISTANCE—Continued

Number of Aid Awards—Continued

	2021	2022	2023
Work-study	621	621	621
Supplemental educational opportunity grants	1,662	1,662	1,662
Iraq and Afghanistan service grants[1]	0	0	0
TEACH grants	34	34	35
Total awards	21,273	21,254	21,688

[1] Number of recipients is fewer than 1,000.
Note: Numbers may not add due to rounding.

Average Aid Awards
(in whole dollars)

	2021	2022	2023
Pell grants	$4,325	$4,353	$5,816
Subsidized Stafford loans	3,510	3,513	3,514
Unsubsidized Stafford loans (Undergraduates)	3,805	3,842	3,870
Unsubsidized Stafford loans (Graduate students)	15,289	15,472	15,618
Parent PLUS loans	15,640	15,911	16,257
Grad PLUS loans	20,282	20,692	21,028
Consolidation loans	61,616	68,939	67,991
Work-study	1,946	1,946	1,946
Supplemental educational opportunity grants	753	753	753
Iraq and Afghanistan service grants	5,672	5,672	7,574
TEACH grants	2,204	2,204	2,329

Number of Students Aided
(in thousands)

	2021	2022	2023
Unduplicated student count	8,754	8,718	8,910

Administrative Payments to Institutions
(in thousands of dollars)

	2021	2022	2023
Pell grants	$30,520	$30,665	$33,285
Work-study	60,146	60,146	60,146
Supplemental educational opportunity grants	18,891	18,891	18,891

STUDENT FINANCIAL ASSISTANCE
(Legislative proposal, subject to PAYGO)

Program and Financing (in millions of dollars)

Identification code 091–0200–4–1–502	2021 actual	2022 est.	2023 est.
Obligations by program activity:			
0101 Federal Pell grants			6,575
0900 Total new obligations, unexpired accounts (object class 41.0)			6,575
Budgetary resources:			
Budget authority:			
Appropriations, mandatory:			
1200 Appropriation			6,575
1930 Total budgetary resources available			6,575
Change in obligated balance:			
Unpaid obligations:			
3010 New obligations, unexpired accounts			6,575
3020 Outlays (gross)			−2,847
3050 Unpaid obligations, end of year			3,728
Memorandum (non-add) entries:			
3200 Obligated balance, end of year			3,728
Budget authority and outlays, net:			
Mandatory:			
4090 Budget authority, gross			6,575
Outlays, gross:			
4100 Outlays from new mandatory authority			2,847
4180 Budget authority, net (total)			6,575
4190 Outlays, net (total)			2,847

Federal Pell Grants.—The 2023 Budget proposes to increase the mandatory add-on to the maximum Pell Grant from $1,060 to $2,335. With the $900 increase to the discretionary maximum award, the total increase will be $2,175 and the total maximum Pell Grant will be $8,670.

STUDENT AID ADMINISTRATION

For Federal administrative expenses to carry out part D of title I, and subparts 1, 3, 9, and 10 of part A, and parts B, C, D, and E of title IV of the HEA, and subpart 1 of part A of title VII of the Public Health Service Act, $2,654,034,000, to remain available through September 30, 2024.

Note.—A full-year 2022 appropriation for this account was not enacted at the time the Budget was prepared; therefore, the Budget assumes this account is operating under the Continuing Appropriations Act, 2022 (Division A of Public Law 117–43, as amended). The amounts included for 2022 reflect the annualized level provided by the continuing resolution.

Program and Financing (in millions of dollars)

Identification code 091–0202–0–1–502	2021 actual	2022 est.	2023 est.
Obligations by program activity:			
0001 Student aid administration	1,056	1,034	1,188
0002 Servicing activities	906	873	1,466
0900 Total new obligations, unexpired accounts	1,962	1,907	2,654
Budgetary resources:			
Unobligated balance:			
1000 Unobligated balance brought forward, Oct 1	28	64	10
1001 Discretionary unobligated balance brought fwd, Oct 1	28		
1021 Recoveries of prior year unpaid obligations	22		
1070 Unobligated balance (total)	50	64	10
Budget authority:			
Appropriations, discretionary:			
1100 Appropriation	1,884	1,853	2,654
Appropriations, mandatory:			
1200 Appropriation	91		
Spending authority from offsetting collections, discretionary:			
1701 Change in uncollected payments, Federal sources	1		
1900 Budget authority (total)	1,976	1,853	2,654
1930 Total budgetary resources available	2,026	1,917	2,664
Memorandum (non-add) entries:			
1941 Unexpired unobligated balance, end of year	64	10	10
Change in obligated balance:			
Unpaid obligations:			
3000 Unpaid obligations, brought forward, Oct 1	766	888	1,210
3010 New obligations, unexpired accounts	1,962	1,907	2,654
3011 Obligations ("upward adjustments"), expired accounts	3		
3020 Outlays (gross)	−1,804	−1,585	−2,198
3040 Recoveries of prior year unpaid obligations, unexpired	−22		
3041 Recoveries of prior year unpaid obligations, expired	−17		
3050 Unpaid obligations, end of year	888	1,210	1,666
Uncollected payments:			
3060 Uncollected pymts, Fed sources, brought forward, Oct 1		−1	−1
3070 Change in uncollected pymts, Fed sources, unexpired	−1		
3090 Uncollected pymts, Fed sources, end of year	−1	−1	−1
Memorandum (non-add) entries:			
3100 Obligated balance, start of year	766	887	1,209
3200 Obligated balance, end of year	887	1,209	1,665
Budget authority and outlays, net:			
Discretionary:			
4000 Budget authority, gross	1,885	1,853	2,654
Outlays, gross:			
4010 Outlays from new discretionary authority	1,147	1,019	1,421
4011 Outlays from discretionary balances	657	541	747
4020 Outlays, gross (total)	1,804	1,560	2,168
Offsets against gross budget authority and outlays:			
Offsetting collections (collected) from:			
4030 Federal sources		−1	
4033 Non-Federal sources	−1		
4040 Offsets against gross budget authority and outlays (total)	−1	−1	
Additional offsets against gross budget authority only:			
4050 Change in uncollected pymts, Fed sources, unexpired	−1		
4052 Offsetting collections credited to expired accounts	1	1	
4060 Additional offsets against budget authority only (total)		1	
4070 Budget authority, net (discretionary)	1,884	1,853	2,654
4080 Outlays, net (discretionary)	1,803	1,559	2,168
Mandatory:			
4090 Budget authority, gross	91		
Outlays, gross:			
4101 Outlays from mandatory balances		25	30
4180 Budget authority, net (total)	1,975	1,853	2,654
4190 Outlays, net (total)	1,803	1,584	2,198

DEPARTMENT OF EDUCATION

The Department of Education manages Federal student aid programs that will provide $126 billion in new Federal student aid grants and loans (excluding Direct Consolidation Loans) to nearly 9 million students and parents in 2023. The Offices of Postsecondary Education, the Under Secretary, and Federal Student Aid (FSA) are primarily responsible for administering the Federal student financial assistance programs. FSA was created by the Congress in 1998 as a partially independent Performance Based Organization (PBO) with a mandate to improve service to students and other student aid program participants, reduce student aid administration costs, and improve accountability and program integrity.

Object Classification (in millions of dollars)

Identification code 091–0202–0–1–502	2021 actual	2022 est.	2023 est.
Direct obligations:			
Personnel compensation:			
11.1 Full-time permanent	192	204	218
11.3 Other than full-time permanent	8		
11.5 Other personnel compensation	4	4	5
11.9 Total personnel compensation	204	208	223
12.1 Civilian personnel benefits	69	72	82
21.0 Travel and transportation of persons		2	3
23.1 Rental payments to GSA	19	19	18
25.1 Advisory and assistance services	2	1	1
25.2 Other services from non-Federal sources	1,065	955	1,568
25.3 Other goods and services from Federal sources	49	50	52
25.7 Operation and maintenance of equipment	553	600	706
99.0 Direct obligations	1,961	1,907	2,653
99.0 Reimbursable obligations	1		
99.5 Adjustment for rounding			1
99.9 Total new obligations, unexpired accounts	1,962	1,907	2,654

Employment Summary

Identification code 091–0202–0–1–502	2021 actual	2022 est.	2023 est.
1001 Direct civilian full-time equivalent employment	1,551	1,565	1,597

TEACH GRANT PROGRAM ACCOUNT

Program and Financing (in millions of dollars)

Identification code 091–0206–0–1–502	2021 actual	2022 est.	2023 est.
Obligations by program activity:			
Credit program obligations:			
0701 Direct loan subsidy	27	35	39
0703 Subsidy for modifications of direct loans	47	4	
0705 Reestimates of direct loan subsidy	62	53	
0706 Interest on reestimates of direct loan subsidy	16	17	
0900 Total new obligations, unexpired accounts (object class 41.0)	152	109	39
Budgetary resources:			
Budget authority:			
Appropriations, mandatory:			
1200 Appropriation (indefinite) - Loan subsidy	29	37	41
1200 Appropriation (indefinite) - Upward reestimate	78	70	
1200 Appropriation (indefinite) Upward Modification	47	4	
1230 Appropriations and/or unobligated balance of appropriations permanently reduced	–2	–2	–2
1260 Appropriations, mandatory (total)	152	109	39
1930 Total budgetary resources available	152	109	39
Change in obligated balance:			
Unpaid obligations:			
3000 Unpaid obligations, brought forward, Oct 1	9	6	9
3010 New obligations, unexpired accounts	152	109	39
3020 Outlays (gross)	–153	–104	–36
3041 Recoveries of prior year unpaid obligations, expired	–2	–2	–2
3050 Unpaid obligations, end of year	6	9	10
Memorandum (non-add) entries:			
3100 Obligated balance, start of year	9	6	9
3200 Obligated balance, end of year	6	9	10

Office of Federal Student Aid—Continued
Federal Funds—Continued

		2021 actual	2022 est.	2023 est.
	Budget authority and outlays, net:			
	Mandatory:			
4090	Budget authority, gross	152	109	39
	Outlays, gross:			
4100	Outlays from new mandatory authority	146	100	30
4101	Outlays from mandatory balances	7	4	6
4110	Outlays, gross (total)	153	104	36
4180	Budget authority, net (total)	152	109	39
4190	Outlays, net (total)	153	104	36

Summary of Loan Levels, Subsidy Budget Authority and Outlays by Program (in millions of dollars)

Identification code 091–0206–0–1–502	2021 actual	2022 est.	2023 est.
Direct loan levels supportable by subsidy budget authority:			
115001 TEACH Grants	86	82	88
Direct loan subsidy (in percent):			
132001 TEACH Grants	31.72	42.57	44.50
132999 Weighted average subsidy rate	31.72	42.57	44.50
Direct loan subsidy budget authority:			
133001 TEACH Grants	27	35	39
Direct loan subsidy outlays:			
134001 TEACH Grants	75	33	36
Direct loan reestimates:			
135001 TEACH Grants	75	65	

The TEACH Grant program, authorized by the College Cost Reduction and Access Act of 2007, awards annual grants of up to $4,000 to full- or part-time undergraduate and graduate students who agree to teach mathematics, science, foreign languages, bilingual education, special education, or reading at a high-poverty school for not less than four years within eight years of graduation. The program began awarding grants in the 2008–2009 award year. Students must have a grade point average of 3.25 or higher to be eligible to receive a grant. Students who fail to fulfill the service requirements must repay the grants, including interest accrued from the time of award.

Because TEACH Grants turn into loans in cases where the service requirements are not fulfilled, for budget and accounting purposes the program is operated consistent with the requirements of the Federal Credit Reform Act of 1990. This program account records subsidy costs reflecting the net present value of the estimated lifetime Federal program costs for grants awarded in a given fiscal year. Under this approach the subsidy cost reflects the cost of grant awards net of expected future repayments for grants that are converted to loans.

TEACH GRANT FINANCING ACCOUNT

Program and Financing (in millions of dollars)

Identification code 091–4290–0–3–502	2021 actual	2022 est.	2023 est.
Obligations by program activity:			
Credit program obligations:			
0710 Direct loan obligations	86	82	88
0713 Payment of interest to Treasury	20	16	27
0741 Modification savings		2	
0742 Downward reestimates paid to receipt accounts	3	3	
0791 Direct program activities, subtotal	109	103	115
0900 Total new obligations, unexpired accounts	109	103	115
Budgetary resources:			
Unobligated balance:			
1000 Unobligated balance brought forward, Oct 1	1	1	
1021 Recoveries of prior year unpaid obligations	25	7	7
1023 Unobligated balances applied to repay debt	–18	–1	
1024 Unobligated balance of borrowing authority withdrawn	–8	–7	–7
Financing authority:			
Borrowing authority, mandatory:			
1400 Borrowing authority	69	55	52
Spending authority from offsetting collections, mandatory:			
1800 Collected	172	164	112
1801 Change in uncollected payments, Federal sources	–3	1	
1820 Capital transfer of spending authority from offsetting collections for Negative MAT	–2		

TEACH GRANT FINANCING ACCOUNT—Continued
Program and Financing—Continued

Identification code 091–4290–0–3–502	2021 actual	2022 est.	2023 est.
1825 Spending authority from offsetting collections applied to repay debt	–126	–117	–49
1850 Spending auth from offsetting collections, mand (total)	41	48	63
1900 Budget authority (total)	110	103	115
1930 Total budgetary resources available	110	103	115
Memorandum (non-add) entries:			
1941 Unexpired unobligated balance, end of year	1		
Change in obligated balance:			
Unpaid obligations:			
3000 Unpaid obligations, brought forward, Oct 1	89	75	74
3010 New obligations, unexpired accounts	109	103	115
3020 Outlays (gross)	–98	–97	–108
3040 Recoveries of prior year unpaid obligations, unexpired	–25	–7	–7
3050 Unpaid obligations, end of year	75	74	74
Uncollected payments:			
3060 Uncollected pymts, Fed sources, brought forward, Oct 1	–7	–4	–5
3070 Change in uncollected pymts, Fed sources, unexpired	3	–1	
3090 Uncollected pymts, Fed sources, end of year	–4	–5	–5
Memorandum (non-add) entries:			
3100 Obligated balance, start of year	82	71	69
3200 Obligated balance, end of year	71	69	69
Financing authority and disbursements, net:			
Discretionary:			
Additional offsets against gross financing authority only:			
4050 Change in uncollected pymts, Fed sources, unexpired		1	
Mandatory:			
4090 Budget authority, gross	110	103	115
Financing disbursements:			
4110 Outlays, gross (total)	98	97	108
Offsets against gross financing authority and disbursements:			
Offsetting collections (collected) from:			
4120 Upward Reestimate	–78	–69	
4120 Subsidy from Program Account	–28	–31	–36
4120 Upward Modification	–47	–4	
4122 Interest on uninvested funds	–3		
4123 Payment of Principal	–14	–54	–60
4123 Interest Received	–2	–6	–16
4130 Offsets against gross budget authority and outlays (total)	–172	–164	–112
Additional offsets against financing authority only (total):			
4140 Change in uncollected pymts, Fed sources, unexpired	3	–1	
4160 Budget authority, net (mandatory)	–59	–62	3
4170 Outlays, net (mandatory)	–74	–67	–4
4180 Budget authority, net (total)	–59	–61	3
4190 Outlays, net (total)	–74	–67	–4

Status of Direct Loans (in millions of dollars)

Identification code 091–4290–0–3–502	2021 actual	2022 est.	2023 est.
Position with respect to appropriations act limitation on obligations:			
1111 Direct loan obligations from current-year authority	86	82	88
1150 Total direct loan obligations	86	82	88
Cumulative balance of direct loans outstanding:			
1210 Outstanding, start of year	764	783	805
1231 Disbursements: Direct loan disbursements	75	76	81
1251 Repayments: Repayments and prepayments	–15	–54	–61
1264 Other adjustments, net (+ or -)	–41		
1290 Outstanding, end of year	783	805	825

As required by the Federal Credit Reform Act of 1990, this nonbudgetary account records all cash flows to and from the Government resulting from the TEACH Grant program. Amounts in this account are a means of financing and are not included in the budget totals.

Balance Sheet (in millions of dollars)

Identification code 091–4290–0–3–502	2020 actual	2021 actual
ASSETS:		
1101 Federal assets: Fund balances with Treasury	41	40
Net value of assets related to post-1991 direct loans receivable:		
1401 Direct loans receivable, gross	764	783
1402 Interest receivable	88	70
1405 Allowance for subsidy cost (-)	–182	–256
1499 Net present value of assets related to direct loans	670	597
1999 Total assets	711	637
LIABILITIES:		
Federal liabilities:		
2101 Accounts payable		
2103 Debt	711	637
2999 Total liabilities	711	637
NET POSITION:		
3300 Cumulative results of operations		
4999 Total liabilities and net position	711	637

STUDENT FINANCIAL ASSISTANCE DEBT COLLECTION
Special and Trust Fund Receipts (in millions of dollars)

Identification code 091–5557–0–2–502	2021 actual	2022 est.	2023 est.
0100 Balance, start of year			1
Receipts:			
Current law:			
1130 Student Financial Assistance Debt Collection	4	12	16
2000 Total: Balances and receipts	4	12	17
Appropriations:			
Current law:			
2101 Student Financial Assistance Debt Collection	–4	–11	–11
2103 Student Financial Assistance Debt Collection		–1	–1
2132 Student Financial Assistance Debt Collection		1	1
2199 Total current law appropriations	–4	–11	–11
2999 Total appropriations	–4	–11	–11
5099 Balance, end of year		1	6

Program and Financing (in millions of dollars)

Identification code 091–5557–0–2–502	2021 actual	2022 est.	2023 est.
Obligations by program activity:			
0001 Student Financial Assistance Debt Collection	1	3	3
0900 Total new obligations, unexpired accounts (object class 25.2)	1	3	3
Budgetary resources:			
Unobligated balance:			
1000 Unobligated balance brought forward, Oct 1	9	8	12
1022 Capital transfer of unobligated balances to general fund	–4	–3	–3
1070 Unobligated balance (total)	5	5	9
Budget authority:			
Appropriations, mandatory:			
1201 Appropriation (special or trust fund)	4	11	11
1203 Appropriation (previously unavailable)(special or trust)		1	1
1232 Appropriations and/or unobligated balance of appropriations temporarily reduced		–1	–1
1240 Capital transfer of appropriations to general fund		–1	–1
1260 Appropriations, mandatory (total)	4	10	10
1930 Total budgetary resources available	9	15	19
Memorandum (non-add) entries:			
1941 Unexpired unobligated balance, end of year	8	12	16
Change in obligated balance:			
Unpaid obligations:			
3010 New obligations, unexpired accounts	1	3	3
3020 Outlays (gross)	–1	–3	–3
Budget authority and outlays, net:			
Mandatory:			
4090 Budget authority, gross	4	10	10
Outlays, gross:			
4101 Outlays from mandatory balances	1	3	3
4180 Budget authority, net (total)	4	10	10

DEPARTMENT OF EDUCATION

		2021 actual	2022 est.	2023 est.
4190	Outlays, net (total)	1	3	3

FEDERAL STUDENT LOAN RESERVE FUND

Program and Financing (in millions of dollars)

Identification code 091–4257–0–3–502		2021 actual	2022 est.	2023 est.
	Obligations by program activity:			
0102	Obligations, non-Federal	3,916	3,839	1,464
0900	Total new obligations, unexpired accounts (object class 42.0)	3,916	3,839	1,464
	Budgetary resources:			
	Unobligated balance:			
1000	Unobligated balance brought forward, Oct 1	1,943	1,913	971
	Budget authority:			
	Spending authority from offsetting collections, mandatory:			
1800	Collected	3,899	2,897	1,424
1820	Capital transfer of spending authority from offsetting collections to general fund	–13		
1850	Spending auth from offsetting collections, mand (total)	3,886	2,897	1,424
1930	Total budgetary resources available	5,829	4,810	2,395
	Memorandum (non-add) entries:			
1941	Unexpired unobligated balance, end of year	1,913	971	931
	Change in obligated balance:			
	Unpaid obligations:			
3010	New obligations, unexpired accounts	3,916	3,839	1,464
3020	Outlays (gross)	–3,916	–3,839	–1,464
	Budget authority and outlays, net:			
	Mandatory:			
4090	Budget authority, gross	3,886	2,897	1,424
	Outlays, gross:			
4100	Outlays from new mandatory authority	3,837	2,798	1,359
4101	Outlays from mandatory balances	79	1,041	105
4110	Outlays, gross (total)	3,916	3,839	1,464
	Offsets against gross budget authority and outlays:			
	Offsetting collections (collected) from:			
4120	Federal sources	–3,837	–2,897	–1,424
4123	Non-Federal sources	–62		
4130	Offsets against gross budget authority and outlays (total)	–3,899	–2,897	–1,424
4160	Budget authority, net (mandatory)	–13		
4170	Outlays, net (mandatory)	17	942	40
4180	Budget authority, net (total)	–13		
4190	Outlays, net (total)	17	942	40

The Higher Education Amendments of 1998 clarified that reserve funds held by public and non-profit guaranty agencies participating in the Federal Family Education Loan (FFEL) program are Federal property. These reserves are used to pay default claims from FFEL lenders and fees to support agency efforts to avert defaults. The Federal Government reimburses these reserves for default claim payments. The Consolidated Appropriations Act, 2016, increased guaranty agency reinsurance payments from 95 percent of the face value of loans to 100 percent. The following schedule reflects the balances in these guaranty agency funds.

Balance Sheet (in millions of dollars)

Identification code 091–4257–0–3–502		2020 actual	2021 actual
	ASSETS:		
1101	Federal assets: Fund balances with Treasury	1,943	1,943
1999	Total assets	1,943	1,943
	LIABILITIES:		
2104	Federal liabilities: Resources payable to Treasury		
	NET POSITION:		
3300	Cumulative results of operations	1,943	1,943
4999	Total liabilities and net position	1,943	1,943

Office of Federal Student Aid—Continued
Federal Funds—Continued

FEDERAL DIRECT STUDENT LOAN PROGRAM ACCOUNT

Program and Financing (in millions of dollars)

Identification code 091–0243–0–1–502		2021 actual	2022 est.	2023 est.
	Obligations by program activity:			
	Credit program obligations:			
0701	Direct loan subsidy	5,197	9,415	15,314
0703	Subsidy for modifications of direct loans	70,861	12,369	
0705	Reestimates of direct loan subsidy	47,241	22,331	
0706	Interest on reestimates of direct loan subsidy	6,434	4,376	
0900	Total new obligations, unexpired accounts (object class 41.0)	129,733	48,491	15,314
	Budgetary resources:			
	Budget authority:			
	Appropriations, discretionary:			
1100	Appropriation		50	
	Appropriations, mandatory:			
1200	Appropriation (indefinite)	129,733	48,441	15,314
1900	Budget authority (total)	129,733	48,491	15,314
1930	Total budgetary resources available	129,733	48,491	15,314
	Change in obligated balance:			
	Unpaid obligations:			
3000	Unpaid obligations, brought forward, Oct 1	2,046	1,304	1,975
3010	New obligations, unexpired accounts	129,733	48,491	15,314
3020	Outlays (gross)	–130,044	–47,820	–13,811
3041	Recoveries of prior year unpaid obligations, expired	–431		
3050	Unpaid obligations, end of year	1,304	1,975	3,478
	Memorandum (non-add) entries:			
3100	Obligated balance, start of year	2,046	1,304	1,975
3200	Obligated balance, end of year	1,304	1,975	3,478
	Budget authority and outlays, net:			
	Discretionary:			
4000	Budget authority, gross		50	
	Mandatory:			
4090	Budget authority, gross	129,733	48,441	15,314
	Outlays, gross:			
4100	Outlays from new mandatory authority	129,110	47,428	13,135
4101	Outlays from mandatory balances	934	392	676
4110	Outlays, gross (total)	130,044	47,820	13,811
4180	Budget authority, net (total)	129,733	48,491	15,314
4190	Outlays, net (total)	130,044	47,820	13,811

Summary of Loan Levels, Subsidy Budget Authority and Outlays by Program (in millions of dollars)

Identification code 091–0243–0–1–502		2021 actual	2022 est.	2023 est.
	Direct loan levels supportable by subsidy budget authority:			
115001	Stafford	20,070	18,278	18,096
115002	Unsubsidized Stafford	55,953	53,281	53,134
115003	PLUS	23,582	23,830	24,277
115004	Consolidation	22,480	27,548	29,578
115999	Total direct loan levels	122,085	122,937	125,085
	Direct loan subsidy (in percent):			
132001	Stafford	7.40	7.98	12.18
132002	Unsubsidized Stafford	–1.83	2.25	6.57
132003	PLUS	–15.94	–14.15	–10.63
132004	Consolidation	16.51	24.53	32.52
132999	Weighted average subsidy rate	0.34	4.92	10.18
	Direct loan subsidy budget authority:			
133001	Stafford	1,485	1,459	2,204
133002	Unsubsidized Stafford	–1,024	1,199	3,491
133003	PLUS	–3,759	–3,372	–2,581
133004	Consolidation	3,711	6,758	9,619
133999	Total subsidy budget authority	413	6,044	12,733
	Direct loan subsidy outlays:			
134001	Stafford	1,689	1,292	1,746
134002	Unsubsidized Stafford	–466	467	2,453
134003	PLUS	–3,352	–3,374	–2,699
134004	Consolidation	3,717	6,764	9,612
134005	Federal Direct Student Loans	70,811	2,221	
134999	Total subsidy outlays	72,399	7,370	11,112
	Direct loan reestimates:			
135005	Federal Direct Student Loans	52,836	13,005	
135999	Total direct loan reestimates	52,836	13,005	

FEDERAL DIRECT STUDENT LOAN PROGRAM ACCOUNT—Continued

The Federal Government manages two major student loan programs: the Federal Family Education Loan (FFEL) program and the William D. Ford Federal Direct Loan (Direct Loan) program. The Student Aid and Fiscal Responsibility Act eliminated the authorization to originate new FFEL loans; as of July 1, 2010, the Direct Loan program originates all new loans. This narrative outlines the structure of these two programs and provides text tables displaying program cost data; loan volume, subsidy, default, and interest rates; and other descriptive information.

From its inception in 1965 through the end of June 2010, the FFEL program guaranteed almost $899 billion in loans made to postsecondary students and their parents. Although no new FFEL loans have been originated since July 1, 2010, nearly $150 billion of outstanding FFEL loans continue to be serviced by lenders, the Department of Education, and guaranty agencies.

Under the Direct Loan program, the Federal Government provides loan capital through the Treasury while the Department of Education loan origination and servicing is handled by private and not-for-profit loan servicers under performance-based contracts with the Department. The Direct Loan program began operation in award year 1994–1995, originating 7 percent of overall loan volume. In 2023, excluding Consolidation Loans, the Direct Loan program will make $85.01 billion in new loans.

The Direct Loan program currently offers four types of loans: Subsidized Stafford; Unsubsidized Stafford; PLUS; and Consolidation. Loans can be used for qualified educational expenses. Undergraduates with financial need may receive a Subsidized Stafford loan (graduate and professional students are not eligible). The other three loan programs are available to borrowers at all income levels. Interest rates are set annually for loans originated in the upcoming award year based on the 10-year Treasury note; those rates will remain fixed for the life of the loan. For Subsidized Stafford loans available to undergraduates, the interest rate will be equal to the 10-year Treasury note plus 2.05 percent and capped at 8.25 percent. Loans originated in award year 2021–2022 have an interest rate of 3.73 percent. Interest payments for these loans are fully subsidized by the Federal Government while a student is in school and during grace and deferment periods. The interest rate on new Unsubsidized Stafford loans for undergraduate borrowers is the same as that on Subsidized Stafford loans for undergraduates. The Unsubsidized Stafford loan interest rate for graduate and professional students is equal to the 10-year Treasury note plus 3.6 percent and capped at 9.5 percent. Loans originated in award year 2021–2022 have an interest rate of 5.28 percent. The borrower interest rate on PLUS loans to graduate and professional students and parents of undergraduate borrowers is equal to the 10-year Treasury note plus 4.6 percent and capped at 10.5 percent. PLUS loans originated in award year 2021–2022 have an interest rate of 6.28 percent.

Consolidation loans allow borrowers to combine FFEL, Direct Loans, and Perkins Loans, as well as some loans made under the Public Health Service Act. The interest rate for new Consolidation loans equals the weighted average of the interest rate on the loans consolidated, rounded up to the nearest one-eighth of a percent. For most types of Direct Loans, the origination fee is a base rate of 1 percent, but an additional surcharge for sequestration was added in years 2013 to 2021. The base origination fee for PLUS loans is 4 percent, but has included an additional surcharge in years 2013 to 2021. Borrowers may choose from four basic types of repayment plans: standard; graduated; extended (available for qualified borrowers who have outstanding loans of more than $30,000); and income-driven. FFEL borrowers may change repayment plans annually. Direct Loan borrowers may switch between repayment plans at any time. The maximum repayment period is 10 years for standard and graduated plans, as well as the income-sensitive repayment plan that is available only for FFEL loans. Under the current income-driven administrative Pay As You Earn (PAYE) and statutory Income-Based-Repayment (IBR) plans, for new borrowers after 2014, the repayment period is 20 years. Under the current income-driven administrative REPAYE plan, the repayment period is 20 or 25 years depending on whether the borrower has any graduate school loans. And, under the extended, former IBR (for borrowers prior to 2014), and income-contingent repayment plans, the maximum time is 25 years. PAYE and IBR require partial financial hardship in order to qualify for reduced payments and borrowers in those plans have their monthly payments capped at the monthly payment of the 10-year Standard plan. At the end of the repayment term, the borrower's remaining balance is forgiven.

Federal student loans have other benefits. For example, Federal student loans can be discharged when borrowers die, become totally and permanently disabled, or, under some circumstances, declare bankruptcy. In addition, there are several loan forgiveness programs. For example, new borrowers after October 1, 1998, who are employed as teachers in schools serving low-income populations for 5 consecutive, complete school years, qualify for up to $5,000 in loan forgiveness; this benefit is increased to $17,500 for mathematics, science, and special education teachers considered highly qualified under criteria established in the Elementary and Secondary Education Act. In addition, under the Public Service Loan Forgiveness Program, qualifying borrowers who have worked for 10 years full-time for an eligible public service employer, and made 120 qualifying monthly payments after October 1, 2007 in the standard or income-driven plans can have any remaining loan balance forgiven. This benefit is only available in the Direct Loan program, though FFEL borrowers may receive the benefit by taking out a Direct Consolidation Loan. Forgiveness is available for all Direct Loan borrowers, regardless of when they took out their loans.

On Oct. 6, 2021, the Department of Education announced a pandemic-related waiver to the Public Service Loan Forgiveness program statute. The limited waiver impacted student loan borrowers with Direct Loans, those who have already consolidated into the Direct Loan Program, and those who consolidate into the Direct Loan Program by Oct. 31, 2022. Under the new temporary rules, any prior period of repayment will count as a qualifying payment, regardless of loan program, repayment plan, or whether the payment was made in full or on time.

The following tables display performance indicators and program data, including projected overall Direct Loan and FFEL costs.

Federal Budget Authority and Outlays

(in thousands of dollars)

	2021 actual	2022 est.	2023 est.
PROGRAM COST:			
FFEL:			
Liquidating[1]	$0	($142,991)	($212,722)
Program:			
Net Reestimate of Prior Year Costs	3,192,111	9,797,237	0
Net Modification[2]	6,112,293	2,157,407	0
Subtotal, Program	9,304,404	11,954,645	0
Total, FFEL	9,304,404	11,811,654	(212,722)
Direct Loans:			
Program:			
New Net Loan Subsidies	413,686	6,042,991	12,733,042
Net Reestimate of Prior Year Costs	52,835,898	13,004,854	0
Net Modification[3]	70,861,525	2,221,570	0
Total, Direct Loans	124,111,109	21,269,415	12,733,042
Total, FFEL and Direct Loans	133,415,513	33,081,069	12,520,320
PROGRAM COST OUTLAYS:			
FFEL:			
Liquidating[1]	(73,374)	(142,991)	(212,722)
Program:			
Net Reestimate of Prior Year Costs	3,192,111	9,797,237	0
Net Modification[2]	6,112,293	2,157,407	0
Subtotal, Program	9,304,404	11,954,645	0
Total, FFEL	9,231,030	11,811,654	(212,722)
Direct Loans:			
Program:			
Regular	1,587,764	5,146,489	11,111,824
Net Reestimate of Prior Year Costs	52,835,898	13,004,854	0
Net Modification[3]	70,861,525	2,221,570	0
Total, Direct Loans	125,285,187	20,372,914	11,111,824

DEPARTMENT OF EDUCATION

Total, FFEL and Direct Loans	134,516,217	32,184,567	10,899,102

[1] Liquidating account reflects loans made prior to 1992.

[2] FY 2021 reflects costs related to COVID Payment Pause extension and the Total Permanent Disability regulation modification. FY 2022 reflects costs related to the COVID payment pause extension, the shift to Business Process Operations modification, and support for the Federal Student Loan Reserve Fund modification.

[3] FY 2021 reflects costs for COVID Payment Pause, the Total Permanent Disability regulation modification, and the final faith based regulation modification. FY 2022 reflects costs of related to the COVID payment pause extension, and the shift to Business Process Operations modification.

Summary of Default Rates[1]

(expressed as percentages)

	2021 actual	2022 est.	2023 est.
Direct Loans:			
Stafford	25.34	26.23	27.32
Unsubsidized Stafford			
Undergraduate	29.90	31.46	32.23
Graduate/Professional	12.89	14.03	13.62
PLUS			
Parent PLUS	12.80	15.07	15.23
Grad PLUS	10.13	10.27	10.32
Consolidation	16.92	16.47	17.03
Weighted Average, Direct Loans	18.26	18.91	19.18

[1] Default rates displayed in this table, which reflect projected defaults over the life of a loan cohort, are used in developing program cost estimates. The Department uses other rates based on defaults occurring in the first two years of repayment to determine institutional eligibility to participate in Federal loan programs. (The Higher Education Opportunity Act of 2008 changed this requirement to a three-year rate.) These two- and three-year rates tend to be lower than those included in this table.

Selected Program Costs and Offsets

(in thousands of dollars)

	2021 actual	2022 est.	2023 est.
FFEL:			
Payments to lenders:			
Interest benefits	$614,646	$18,476	$5,689
Special allowance payments[1]	(2,405,579)	(401,288)	(174,628)
Default claims	2,783,884	883,238	413,944
Loan discharges	945,929	1,049,017	897,744
Teacher loan forgiveness	40,362	27,375	21,350
Administrative payments to guaranty agencies	81,393	1,015,498	60,680
Fees paid to the Department of Education:			
Loan holder fees	(929,485)	(109,170)	(56,332)
Other Major Transactions:			
Net default collections	(3,026,580)	(3,050,428)	(3,565,594)
Contract collection costs	6,657	8,461	18,409
Federal administrative costs	34,880	34,880	58,552
Net Cash Flow, FFEL	(1,853,893)	(523,941)	(2,320,185)
Ensuring Continued Access to Student Loans (ECASLA):			
Inflows	(6,350,064)	(5,850,929)	(5,482,747)
Outflows	6,483,317	6,412,471	(5,482,747)
Federal administrative costs	104,639	104,639	175,657
Net Cash Flow, ECASLA	237,892	666,180	175,657
Direct Loans:			
Loan disbursements to borrowers	104,802,726	112,471,192	114,619,451
Borrower interest payments	(2,060,947)	(7,749,132)	(27,071,236)
Borrower principal payments	(32,095,343)	(51,324,766)	(76,931,973)
Borrower origination fees	(1,561,562)	(1,613,832)	(1,625,360)
Net default collections	(1,505,442)	(9,769,494)	(10,535,543)
Contract collection costs	456,090	449,828	528,059
Federal administrative costs	750,285	756,724	1,253,853
Net operating cash flows	68,785,806	43,220,520	237,251
Loan capital borrowings from Treasury	(104,802,726)	(112,471,192)	(114,619,451)
Net interest payments to Treasury	28,726,990	29,433,763	29,186,478
Principal payments to Treasury	132,870,843	80,860,862	86,425,417
Subtotal, Treasury activity	56,795,108	(2,176,567)	992,443
Net Cash Flow, Direct Loans	125,580,914	41,043,953	1,229,695

[1] Includes Negative Special Allowance Payments.

Student Loan Program Costs: Analysis of Direct Loans Including Program and Administrative Expenses

(expressed as percentages)

	2021 actual[1]	2022 est.	2023 est.
Direct Loans:			
New Loans:			
Stafford	13.05	7.98	12.18
Unsubsidized Stafford			
Undergraduate	9.37	0.77	4.17
Graduate/Professional	12.01	2.88	8.18
PLUS			
Parent PLUS	−25.34	−36.83	−35.84
Grad PLUS	13.50	4.98	10.77
Subtotal, new loan subsidy	7.65	−0.75	3.37
Federal administrative costs	1.70	1.70	1.70
Subtotal, new loans	9.35	0.95	5.07
Consolidation Loans			
Loan subsidy	22.61	24.53	32.52
Federal administrative costs	0.38	0.38	0.38
Subtotal, consolidation loans	22.99	24.91	32.90
New and Consolidation Loans			
Loan subsidy	10.43	4.91	10.27
Federal administrative costs	1.45	1.45	1.45
Total, Direct Loans	11.88	6.36	11.72

[1] For 2021, the rates are current; these include actual executed rates for 2021 and the effects of re-estimates on those rates.

The table above describes Direct Loan costs on a subsidy rate basis: program costs calculated under the Federal Credit Reform Act of 1990 and comparably projected estimates of Federal administrative costs. As with any long-term projection, the comparison is based on assumed future interest rates, borrower characteristics, administrative costs, and other factors over the life of the loan cohort. To the degree actual conditions differ from projections, estimated subsidy rates will change.

The Federal Credit Reform Act of 1990 requires the cost of existing loan cohorts to be reestimated to reflect changes in actual and assumed borrower behavior, interest rates, and other factors. The following table shows the impact of these reestimates in FFEL and Direct Loans.

Loan Disbursement and Subsidy Costs

(in billions of dollars)

	FFEL	Direct Loans
Original Subsidy Costs	+$77.1	−$113.0
Cumulative Reestimates	−45.9	+164.3
Net Subsidy Costs	+31.1	+51.3
Total Disbursements	+898.7	+1,849.1

For Direct Loans, the net upward reestimate reflects several assumption updates, including changes to the income-driven repayment plan model. Model assumptions affecting the 2021 cohort were also updated. The Direct Loan upward net reestimate for 2022 is primarily due to updated IDR assumptions and discount rates.

Direct Loan Repayment Options

(expressed as percentages)

Subsidies by Repayment Option	2021 actual[1]	2022 est.	2023 est.
Stafford:			
Standard	5.35	−1.80	3.21
Extended	−0.59	−8.02	−4.22
Graduated	2.72	−4.91	−0.33
IDR[2]	31.53	29.13	33.92
Unsubsidized Stafford:			
Standard	−5.66	−17.41	−15.09
Extended	−15.30	−28.23	−27.87
Graduated	−10.91	−23.92	−22.42
IDR	32.02	27.62	34.09
PLUS:			
Standard	−21.77	−33.08	−32.46
Extended	−35.00	−47.74	−48.53
Graduated	−38.90	−51.68	−51.42
IDR	33.41	27.53	34.92
Consolidated:			
Standard	−11.12	−11.12	−7.39
Extended	−40.55	−38.36	−25.10
Graduated	−46.89	−44.15	−30.94
IDR	39.04	38.51	44.85

Direct Loan Repayment Options

(gross volumes in millions of dollars)

Volumes by Repayment Option	2021 actual[1]	2022 est.	2023 est.
Stafford:			
Standard	$9,930	$9,590	$9,683
Extended	416	439	408
Graduated	2,409	2,310	2,352
IDR[2]	5,785	5,940	5,652
Unsubsidized Stafford:			
Standard	20,707	21,403	20,799
Extended	1,789	1,865	1,810
Graduated	5,818	5,795	5,856

Office of Federal Student Aid—Continued
Federal Funds—Continued

FEDERAL DIRECT STUDENT LOAN PROGRAM ACCOUNT—Continued

Direct Loan Repayment Options—Continued

Volumes by Repayment Option	2021 actual[1]	2022 est.	2023 est.
IDR	24,428	24,218	24,669
PLUS:			
Standard	11,719	11,504	12,008
Extended	963	1,039	981
Graduated	2,306	2,597	2,350
IDR	8,537	8,690	8,939
Consolidated:			
Standard	30	21	33
Extended	3,147	3,855	3,682
Graduated	1,210	1,352	1,391
IDR	17,276	22,320	24,472

[1] 2021 rates are current; these include actual executed rates for 2021 and the effects of re-estimates on those rates.
[2] All income-driven plans are included in the IDR category.

FEDERAL DIRECT STUDENT LOAN PROGRAM FINANCING ACCOUNT

Program and Financing (in millions of dollars)

Identification code 091–4253–0–3–502		2021 actual	2022 est.	2023 est.
	Obligations by program activity:			
0301	Consolidation loans-Payment of Orig. Services	13	24	24
0401	Payment of contract collection costs	456	450	528
	Credit program obligations:			
0710	Direct loan obligations	122,086	122,938	125,085
0713	Payment of interest to Treasury	32,957	29,434	29,186
0740	Negative subsidy obligations	4,783	3,372	2,581
0741	Modification savings	....	10,098	....
0742	Downward reestimates paid to receipt accounts	431	13,104	....
0743	Interest on downward reestimates	408	598	....
0791	Direct program activities, subtotal	160,665	179,544	156,852
0900	Total new obligations, unexpired accounts	161,134	180,018	157,404
	Budgetary resources:			
	Unobligated balance:			
1000	Unobligated balance brought forward, Oct 1	3,379	2,080	681
1021	Recoveries of prior year unpaid obligations	15,811	16,048	16,289
1023	Unobligated balances applied to repay debt	–4,984	–2,080	....
1024	Unobligated balance of borrowing authority withdrawn	–13,558	–16,048	–16,289
1033	Recoveries of prior year paid obligations	22	....	....
1070	Unobligated balance (total)	670	....	681
	Financing authority:			
	Appropriations, mandatory:			
1200	Appropriation	182	1,286	....
	Borrowing authority, mandatory:			
1400	Borrowing authority	127,015	141,309	113,079
	Spending authority from offsetting collections, mandatory:			
1800	Collected	171,477	118,276	129,975
1801	Change in uncollected payments, Federal sources	–543	828	760
1820	Capital transfer of spending authority from offsetting collections to general fund	–2,716	–139	....
1825	Spending authority from offsetting collections applied to repay debt	–132,871	–80,861	–86,425
1850	Spending auth from offsetting collections, mand (total)	35,347	38,104	44,310
1900	Budget authority (total)	162,544	180,699	157,389
1930	Total budgetary resources available	163,214	180,699	158,070
	Memorandum (non-add) entries:			
1941	Unexpired unobligated balance, end of year	2,080	681	666
	Change in obligated balance:			
	Unpaid obligations:			
3000	Unpaid obligations, brought forward, Oct 1	58,766	60,334	58,122
3010	New obligations, unexpired accounts	161,134	180,018	157,404
3020	Outlays (gross)	–143,755	–166,182	–144,361
3040	Recoveries of prior year unpaid obligations, unexpired	–15,811	–16,048	–16,289
3050	Unpaid obligations, end of year	60,334	58,122	54,876
	Uncollected payments:			
3060	Uncollected pymts, Fed sources, brought forward, Oct 1	–934	–391	–1,219
3070	Change in uncollected pymts, Fed sources, unexpired	543	–828	–760
3090	Uncollected pymts, Fed sources, end of year	–391	–1,219	–1,979
	Memorandum (non-add) entries:			
3100	Obligated balance, start of year	57,832	59,943	56,903
3200	Obligated balance, end of year	59,943	56,903	52,897

	Financing authority and disbursements, net:			
	Mandatory:			
4090	Budget authority, gross	162,544	180,699	157,389
	Financing disbursements:			
4110	Outlays, gross (total)	143,755	166,182	144,361
	Offsets against gross financing authority and disbursements:			
	Offsetting collections (collected) from:			
4120	Upward reestimate	–47,241	–22,331	....
4120	Upward reestimate, interest	–6,434	–4,376	....
4120	Upward TPD Mod	–18,690	....	....
4120	Upward FY22 Mods	....	–12,319	....
4120	Upward COVID Executive Authority Mod	–51,999	....	....
4120	Upward Faith-Based Mod	–122	....	....
4120	Program Subsidy	–5,558	–8,793	–13,811
4122	Interest on uninvested funds	–4,230	....	....
4123	Repayment of principal, Stafford	–6,084	–12,123	–17,582
4123	Interest received on loans, Stafford	–172	–1,072	–3,587
4123	Origination Fees, Stafford	–166	–170	–168
4123	Other fees, Stafford	–15	....	....
4123	Repayment of principal, Unsubsidized Stafford	–14,875	–27,163	–37,503
4123	Interest received on loans, Unsubsidized Stafford	–938	–2,428	–8,777
4123	Origination Fees, Unsubsidized Stafford	–474	–489	–489
4123	Other fees, Unsubsidized Stafford	–18	....	....
4123	Repayment of principal, PLUS	–7,049	–11,256	–20,400
4123	Interest received on loans, PLUS	–719	–973	–4,792
4123	Origination Fees, PLUS	–922	–955	–968
4123	Other fees, PLUS	–5	....	....
4123	Payment of principal, Consolidation	–5,323	–10,553	–11,983
4123	Interest received on loans, Consolidation	–448	–3,275	–9,915
4123	Other fees, Consolidation	–17	....	....
4130	Offsets against gross budget authority and outlays (total)	–171,499	–118,276	–129,975
	Additional offsets against financing authority only (total):			
4140	Change in uncollected pymts, Fed sources, unexpired	543	–828	–760
4143	Recoveries of prior year paid obligations, unexpired accounts	22	....	....
4150	Additional offsets against budget authority only (total)	565	–828	–760
4160	Budget authority, net (mandatory)	–8,390	61,595	26,654
4170	Outlays, net (mandatory)	–27,744	47,906	14,386
4180	Budget authority, net (total)	–8,390	61,595	26,654
4190	Outlays, net (total)	–27,744	47,906	14,386

Status of Direct Loans (in millions of dollars)

Identification code 091–4253–0–3–502		2021 actual	2022 est.	2023 est.
	STAFFORD			
	Position with respect to appropriations act limitation on obligations:			
1111	Direct loan obligations from current-year authority	20,070	18,279	18,096
1150	Total direct loan obligations	20,070	18,279	18,096
	Cumulative balance of direct loans outstanding:			
1210	Outstanding, start of year	242,061	251,477	254,402
1231	Disbursements: Direct loan disbursements	16,068	16,085	15,890
1251	Repayments: Repayments and prepayments	–6,084	–12,123	–17,582
1261	Adjustments: Capitalized interest	653	36	43
1264	Other adjustments, net (+ or -)	–1,221	–1,073	–873
1290	Outstanding, end of year	251,477	254,402	251,880
	UNSUBSIDIZED STAFFORD			
	Position with respect to appropriations act limitation on obligations:			
1111	Direct loan obligations from current-year authority	55,953	53,281	53,134
1150	Total direct loan obligations	55,953	53,281	53,134
	Cumulative balance of direct loans outstanding:			
1210	Outstanding, start of year	420,709	450,191	468,575
1231	Disbursements: Direct loan disbursements	45,409	46,265	46,255
1251	Repayments: Repayments and prepayments	–14,875	–27,163	–37,503
1261	Adjustments: Capitalized interest	1,135	1,772	3,006
1264	Other adjustments, net (+ or -)	–2,187	–2,490	–2,306
1290	Outstanding, end of year	450,191	468,575	478,027
	PLUS			
	Position with respect to appropriations act limitation on obligations:			
1111	Direct loan obligations from current-year authority	23,582	23,830	24,277
1150	Total direct loan obligations	23,582	23,830	24,277
	Cumulative balance of direct loans outstanding:			
1210	Outstanding, start of year	152,877	167,247	177,825
1231	Disbursements: Direct loan disbursements	21,818	22,583	22,907
1251	Repayments: Repayments and prepayments	–7,049	–11,256	–20,399
1261	Adjustments: Capitalized interest	412	450	916

		2020 actual	2021 actual	2022 est.
1264	Other adjustments, net (+ or -)	–811	–1,199	–1,232
1290	Outstanding, end of year	167,247	177,825	180,017
	CONSOLIDATION			
	Position with respect to appropriations act limitation on obligations:			
1111	Direct loan obligations from current-year authority	22,481	27,548	29,578
1150	Total direct loan obligations	22,481	27,548	29,578
	Cumulative balance of direct loans outstanding:			
1210	Outstanding, start of year	409,169	423,299	437,569
1231	Disbursements: Direct loan disbursements	21,508	27,539	29,568
1251	Repayments: Repayments and prepayments	–5,322	–10,553	–11,982
1264	Other adjustments, net (+ or -)	–2,056	–2,716	–2,585
1290	Outstanding, end of year	423,299	437,569	452,570

As required by the Federal Credit Reform Act of 1990, this nonbudgetary account records all cash flows to and from the Government resulting from Federal Direct Student Loans. Amounts in this account are a means of financing and are not included in the budget totals.

Balance Sheet (in millions of dollars)

Identification code 091–4253–0–3–502	2020 actual	2021 actual
ASSETS:		
Federal assets:		
1101 Fund balances with Treasury	13,483	20,788
Investments in U.S. securities:		
1106 Receivables, net	50,856	20,575
1206 Non-Federal assets: Receivables, net	174	217
Net value of assets related to post-1991 direct loans receivable:		
1401 Direct loans receivable, gross	1,224,816	1,292,214
1402 Interest receivable	92,133	86,486
1405 Allowance for subsidy cost (-)	–216,406	–273,866
1499 Net present value of assets related to direct loans	1,100,543	1,104,834
1901 Other Federal assets: Other assets		
1999 Total assets	1,165,056	1,146,414
LIABILITIES:		
Federal liabilities:		
2101 Accounts payable		
2103 Debt	1,160,099	1,142,195
2105 Other	1,773	303
2201 Non-Federal liabilities: Accounts payable	3,184	3,916
2999 Total liabilities	1,165,056	1,146,414
NET POSITION:		
3300 Cumulative results of operations		
4999 Total liabilities and net position	1,165,056	1,146,414

FEDERAL FAMILY EDUCATION LOAN PROGRAM ACCOUNT

Program and Financing (in millions of dollars)

Identification code 091–0231–0–1–502	2021 actual	2022 est.	2023 est.
Obligations by program activity:			
Credit program obligations:			
0703 Subsidy for modifications of direct loans	2,948	661	
0704 Subsidy for modifications of loan guarantees	3,164	2,044	
0705 Reestimates of direct loan subsidy	940	897	
0706 Interest on reestimates of direct loan subsidy	402	428	
0707 Reestimates of loan guarantee subsidy	1,194	3,866	
0708 Interest on reestimates of loan guarantee subsidy	1,245	4,606	
0900 Total new obligations, unexpired accounts (object class 41.0)	9,893	12,502	
Budgetary resources:			
Budget authority:			
Appropriations, mandatory:			
1200 Appropriation	9,893	12,502	
1930 Total budgetary resources available	9,893	12,502	
Change in obligated balance:			
Unpaid obligations:			
3010 New obligations, unexpired accounts	9,893	12,502	
3020 Outlays (gross)	–9,893	–12,502	

		2021 actual	2022 est.	2023 est.
	Budget authority and outlays, net:			
	Mandatory:			
4090	Budget authority, gross	9,893	12,502	
	Outlays, gross:			
4100	Outlays from new mandatory authority	9,893	12,502	
4180	Budget authority, net (total)	9,893	12,502	
4190	Outlays, net (total)	9,893	12,502	

Summary of Loan Levels, Subsidy Budget Authority and Outlays by Program (in millions of dollars)

Identification code 091–0231–0–1–502	2021 actual	2022 est.	2023 est.
Direct loan subsidy outlays:			
134010 Direct Participation Agreement Reestimates	1,879	131	
134012 Direct Standard Put Reestimates	1,069	76	
134999 Total subsidy outlays	2,948	207	
Direct loan reestimates:			
135010 Direct Participation Agreement Reestimates	838	859	
135012 Direct Standard Put Reestimates	505	467	
135999 Total direct loan reestimates	1,343	1,326	
Guaranteed loan subsidy outlays:			
234006 FFEL Guarantees	3,164	1,950	
234999 Total subsidy outlays	3,164	1,950	
Guaranteed loan reestimates:			
235006 FFEL Guarantees	1,849	8,472	
235999 Total guaranteed loan reestimates	1,849	8,472	

As required by the Federal Credit Reform Act of 1990, this program account records the subsidy costs associated with Federal Family Education Loans (FFEL), formerly guaranteed student loans, committed in 1992 and beyond. Beginning with the 1993 cohort of loans, mandatory administrative costs, specifically contract collection costs, are included in the FFEL subsidy estimates of each year's cohort. Subsidy amounts are estimated on a net present value basis.

A description of the FFEL program and accompanying tables are included under the Federal Direct Student Loan program account.

FEDERAL FAMILY EDUCATION LOAN PROGRAM FINANCING ACCOUNT

Program and Financing (in millions of dollars)

Identification code 091–4251–0–3–502	2021 actual	2022 est.	2023 est.
Obligations by program activity:			
0101 Default claims	516	252	167
0103 Interest benefits	280	15	6
0104 Death, disability, and bankruptcy claims	97	82	44
0105 Teacher loan forgiveness, other write-offs	12		
0107 Contract collection costs	3	3	5
0109 Rehab purchase fee		4	5
0110 Guaranty Agency account maintenance fees	11	17	
0191 Subtotal, Stafford loans	919	373	227
0202 Default claims	614	326	220
0203 Special allowance		1	1
0204 Death, disability, and bankruptcy claims	135	93	66
0205 Teacher loan forgiveness, other write-offs	7		
0207 Contract collection costs	3	3	5
0209 Rehab purchase fee		3	4
0210 Guaranty Agency account maintenance fees	11	13	
0291 Subtotal, Unsubsidized Stafford loans	770	439	296
0301 Default claims	101	43	19
0304 Death, disability, and bankruptcy claims	54	19	15
0307 Contract Collection Costs		1	1
0309 Rehab purchase fee		1	1
0310 Guaranty Agency account maintenance fees	3	1	
0391 Subtotal, PLUS loans	158	65	36
0405 Death, disability, and bankruptcy claims		4	3
0491 Subtotal, SLS loans		4	3
0501 Default claims	1,541	250	8
0502 Special allowance		4	5
0503 Interest benefits	148	1	
0504 Death, disability, and bankruptcy claims	648	840	771
0505 Teacher loan forgiveness, other write-offs	22		
0507 Contract collection costs	4	6	8
0509 Rehab purchase fee		5	5
0510 Guaranty Agency account maintenance fees	54	37	

Office of Federal Student Aid—Continued
Federal Funds—Continued

FEDERAL FAMILY EDUCATION LOAN PROGRAM FINANCING ACCOUNT—Continued
Program and Financing—Continued

Identification code 091–4251–0–3–502	2021 actual	2022 est.	2023 est.
0511 Guaranty Agency Covid Reimbursement	....	949	....
0591 Subtotal, Consolidations loans	2,417	2,092	797
Credit program obligations:			
0713 Payment of interest to Treasury	2,099	1,274	396
0741 Modification savings	....	93	....
0742 Downward reestimates paid to receipt accounts	267	....	....
0743 Interest on downward reestimates	322	....	....
0791 Direct program activities, subtotal	2,688	1,367	396
0900 Total new obligations, unexpired accounts	6,952	4,340	1,755
Budgetary resources:			
Unobligated balance:			
1000 Unobligated balance brought forward, Oct 1	18,734	19,594	29,208
1021 Recoveries of prior year unpaid obligations	826	....	....
1033 Recoveries of prior year paid obligations	236	....	....
1070 Unobligated balance (total)	19,796	19,594	29,208
Financing authority:			
Appropriations, mandatory:			
1200 Appropriation	....	14	....
Borrowing authority, mandatory:			
1400 Borrowing authority	1,430	93	....
Spending authority from offsetting collections, mandatory:			
1800 Collected	12,592	13,892	3,801
1820 Capital transfer of spending authority from offsetting collections to general fund	–359	–45	....
1825 Spending authority from offsetting collections applied to repay debt	–6,913	....	....
1850 Spending auth from offsetting collections, mand (total)	5,320	13,847	3,801
1900 Budget authority (total)	6,750	13,954	3,801
1930 Total budgetary resources available	26,546	33,548	33,009
Memorandum (non-add) entries:			
1941 Unexpired unobligated balance, end of year	19,594	29,208	31,254
Change in obligated balance:			
Unpaid obligations:			
3000 Unpaid obligations, brought forward, Oct 1	1,068	379	382
3010 New obligations, unexpired accounts	6,952	4,340	1,755
3020 Outlays (gross)	–6,815	–4,337	–1,934
3040 Recoveries of prior year unpaid obligations, unexpired	–826	....	....
3050 Unpaid obligations, end of year	379	382	203
Memorandum (non-add) entries:			
3100 Obligated balance, start of year	1,068	379	382
3200 Obligated balance, end of year	379	382	203
Financing authority and disbursements, net:			
Mandatory:			
4090 Budget authority, gross	6,750	13,954	3,801
Financing disbursements:			
4110 Outlays, gross (total)	6,815	4,337	1,934
Offsets against gross financing authority and disbursements:			
Offsetting collections (collected) from:			
4120 Upward reestimate	–1,194	–3,866	....
4120 Interest on upward reestimate	–1,245	–4,606	....
4120 Upward TPD Mod	–2,163	....	....
4120 Upward COVID Executive Authority Mod	–1,001	....	....
4120 Upward CY Mods	....	–2,043	....
4122 Interest on uninvested funds	–1,236	....	....
4123 Stafford recoveries on defaults	–718	–565	–793
4123 Stafford other fees	–22	....	....
4123 Stafford special allowance rebate	–498	–46	–14
4123 Unsubsidized Stafford recoveries on default	–743	–624	–873
4123 Unsubsidized Stafford other fees	–23	....	....
4123 Unsubsidized Stafford special allowance rebate	–696	–120	–45
4123 PLUS recoveries on defaults	–93	–84	–118
4123 PLUS other fees	–3	....	....
4123 PLUS special allowance rebate	–226	–10	–4
4123 SLS recoveries on defaults	–5	–1	–1
4123 Consolidation recoveries on defaults	–1,196	–1,589	–1,781
4123 Consolidation loan holders fee	–930	–109	–56
4123 Consolidation other fees	–37	....	....
4123 Consolidation special allowance rebate	–799	–229	–116
4130 Offsets against gross budget authority and outlays (total)	–12,828	–13,892	–3,801
Additional offsets against financing authority only (total):			
4143 Recoveries of prior year paid obligations, unexpired accounts	236	....	....
4160 Budget authority, net (mandatory)	–5,842	62	....
4170 Outlays, net (mandatory)	–6,013	–9,555	–1,867
4180 Budget authority, net (total)	–5,842	62	....
4190 Outlays, net (total)	–6,013	–9,555	–1,867

Status of Guaranteed Loans (in millions of dollars)

Identification code 091–4251–0–3–502	2021 actual	2022 est.	2023 est.
STAFFORD			
Cumulative balance of guaranteed loans outstanding:			
2210 Outstanding, start of year	15,475	14,605	13,487
2251 Repayments and prepayments	–902	–784	–724
Adjustments:			
2261 Terminations for default that result in loans receivable	–516	–252	–167
2263 Terminations for default that result in claim payments	–97	–82	–44
2264 Other adjustments, net	645	....	....
2290 Outstanding, end of year	14,605	13,487	12,552
Memorandum:			
2299 Guaranteed amount of guaranteed loans outstanding, end of year	14,605	13,487	12,552
Addendum:			
Cumulative balance of defaulted guaranteed loans that result in loans receivable:			
2310 Outstanding, start of year	3,452	3,199	2,726
2331 Disbursements for guaranteed loan claims	516	252	167
2351 Repayments of loans receivable	–718	–565	–793
2361 Write-offs of loans receivable	–97	–260	–189
2364 Other adjustments, net	46	100	100
2390 Outstanding, end of year	3,199	2,726	2,011
UNSUBSIDIZED STAFFORD			
Cumulative balance of guaranteed loans outstanding:			
2210 Outstanding, start of year	19,366	18,301	16,899
2251 Repayments and prepayments	–1,129	–983	–907
Adjustments:			
2261 Terminations for default that result in loans receivable	–614	–326	–220
2263 Terminations for default that result in claim payments	–135	–93	–66
2264 Other adjustments, net	813	....	....
2290 Outstanding, end of year	18,301	16,899	15,706
Memorandum:			
2299 Guaranteed amount of guaranteed loans outstanding, end of year	18,301	16,899	15,706
Addendum:			
Cumulative balance of defaulted guaranteed loans that result in loans receivable:			
2310 Outstanding, start of year	9,385	9,254	8,825
2331 Disbursements for guaranteed loan claims	614	326	220
2351 Repayments of loans receivable	–743	–624	–873
2361 Write-offs of loans receivable	–135	–131	–119
2364 Other adjustments, net	133	....	....
2390 Outstanding, end of year	9,254	8,825	8,053
PLUS			
Cumulative balance of guaranteed loans outstanding:			
2210 Outstanding, start of year	3,000	2,686	2,410
2251 Repayments and prepayments	–175	–144	–129
Adjustments:			
2261 Terminations for default that result in loans receivable	–101	–113	–83
2263 Terminations for default that result in claim payments	–54	–19	–15
2264 Other adjustments, net	16	....	....
2290 Outstanding, end of year	2,686	2,410	2,183
Memorandum:			
2299 Guaranteed amount of guaranteed loans outstanding, end of year	2,686	2,410	2,183
Addendum:			
Cumulative balance of defaulted guaranteed loans that result in loans receivable:			
2310 Outstanding, start of year	37	15	94
2331 Disbursements for guaranteed loan claims	101	113	83
2351 Repayments of loans receivable	–93	–84	–118
2361 Write-offs of loans receivable	–54	–10	–10
2364 Other adjustments, net	24	60	60
2390 Outstanding, end of year	15	94	109
SLS			
Cumulative balance of guaranteed loans outstanding:			
2210 Outstanding, start of year	40	59	52

DEPARTMENT OF EDUCATION

		2020 actual	2021 actual	2022 est.
2251	Repayments and prepayments	–2	–3	–3
	Adjustments:			
2261	Terminations for default that result in loans receivable			
2263	Terminations for default that result in claim payments		–4	–3
2264	Other adjustments, net	21		
2290	Outstanding, end of year	59	52	46
	Memorandum:			
2299	Guaranteed amount of guaranteed loans outstanding, end of year	59	52	46
	Addendum:			
	Cumulative balance of defaulted guaranteed loans that result in loans receivable:			
2310	Outstanding, start of year	281	280	275
2331	Disbursements for guaranteed loan claims			
2351	Repayments of loans receivable	–5	–1	
2361	Write-offs of loans receivable		–4	–3
2364	Other adjustments, net	4		
2390	Outstanding, end of year	280	275	272
	CONSOLIDATION			
	Cumulative balance of guaranteed loans outstanding:			
2210	Outstanding, start of year	89,800	81,610	76,138
2251	Repayments and prepayments	–5,235	–4,382	–4,089
	Adjustments:			
2261	Terminations for default that result in loans receivable	–1,541	–250	–8
2263	Terminations for default that result in claim payments	–648	–840	–771
2264	Other adjustments, net	–766		
2290	Outstanding, end of year	81,610	76,138	71,270
	Memorandum:			
2299	Guaranteed amount of guaranteed loans outstanding, end of year	81,610	76,138	71,270
	Addendum:			
	Cumulative balance of defaulted guaranteed loans that result in loans receivable:			
2310	Outstanding, start of year	19,902	19,865	17,987
2331	Disbursements for guaranteed loan claims	1,541	250	8
2351	Repayments of loans receivable	–1,196	–1,588	–1,781
2361	Write-offs of loans receivable	–648	–840	–770
2364	Other adjustments, net	266	300	250
2390	Outstanding, end of year	19,865	17,987	15,694

As required by the Federal Credit Reform Act of 1990, this nonbudgetary account records all cash flows to and from the Government resulting from Federal Family Education Loans, formerly guaranteed student loans, committed in 1992 and beyond. The amounts in this account are a means of financing and are not included in the budget totals.

Balance Sheet (in millions of dollars)

Identification code 091–4251–0–3–502	2020 actual	2021 actual
ASSETS:		
Federal assets:		
1101 Fund balances with Treasury	19,802	19,972
Investments in U.S. securities:		
1106 Receivables, net	1,522	6,842
1206 Non-Federal assets: Receivables, net	14	5
Net value of assets related to post-1991 acquired defaulted guaranteed loans receivable:		
1501 Defaulted guaranteed loans receivable, gross	33,057	32,613
1502 Interest receivable	9,117	9,298
1505 Allowance for subsidy cost (-)	–22,286	–26,735
1599 Net present value of assets related to defaulted guaranteed loans	19,888	15,176
1901 Other Federal assets: Other assets	2	
1999 Total assets	41,228	41,995
LIABILITIES:		
Federal liabilities:		
2101 Accounts payable	74	
2103 Debt	40,190	34,707
2105 Other		1
Non-Federal liabilities:		
2201 Accounts payable	83	35
2204 Liabilities for loan guarantees	881	7,252
2999 Total liabilities	41,228	41,995
NET POSITION:		
3300 Cumulative results of operations		
4999 Total liabilities and net position	41,228	41,995

TEMPORARY STUDENT LOAN PURCHASE AUTHORITY FINANCING ACCOUNT

Program and Financing (in millions of dollars)

Identification code 091–4453–0–3–502	2021 actual	2022 est.	2023 est.
Obligations by program activity:			
0006 Contract collection costs	20	32	28
Credit program obligations:			
0713 Payment of interest to Treasury	950	963	815
0741 Modification savings		290	
0791 Direct program activities, subtotal	950	1,253	815
0900 Total new obligations, unexpired accounts	970	1,285	843
Budgetary resources:			
Unobligated balance:			
1000 Unobligated balance brought forward, Oct 1	306	67	421
1021 Recoveries of prior year unpaid obligations	2		
1023 Unobligated balances applied to repay debt	–308	–67	
1070 Unobligated balance (total)			421
Financing authority:			
Appropriations, mandatory:			
1200 Appropriation	37	60	
Borrowing authority, mandatory:			
1400 Borrowing authority	31	290	
Spending authority from offsetting collections, mandatory:			
1800 Collected	4,004	3,844	3,490
1825 Spending authority from offsetting collections applied to repay debt	–3,035	–2,488	–2,647
1850 Spending auth from offsetting collections, mand (total)	969	1,356	843
1900 Budget authority (total)	1,037	1,706	843
1930 Total budgetary resources available	1,037	1,706	1,264
Memorandum (non-add) entries:			
1941 Unexpired unobligated balance, end of year	67	421	421
Change in obligated balance:			
Unpaid obligations:			
3000 Unpaid obligations, brought forward, Oct 1	10	5	5
3010 New obligations, unexpired accounts	970	1,285	843
3020 Outlays (gross)	–973	–1,285	–843
3040 Recoveries of prior year unpaid obligations, unexpired	–2		
3050 Unpaid obligations, end of year	5	5	5
Memorandum (non-add) entries:			
3100 Obligated balance, start of year	10	5	5
3200 Obligated balance, end of year	5	5	5
Financing authority and disbursements, net:			
Mandatory:			
4090 Budget authority, gross	1,037	1,706	843
Financing disbursements:			
4110 Outlays, gross (total)	973	1,285	843
Offsets against gross financing authority and disbursements:			
Offsetting collections (collected) from:			
4120 Upward reestimate	–586	–579	
4120 Upward reestimate interest	–252	–280	
4120 FY22 Mods		–421	
4120 Upward COVID Executive Action Mod	–1,879		
4122 Interest on uninvested funds	–57		
4123 Principal repayments	–1,063	–2,303	–2,793
4123 Interest repayments	–165	–261	–697
4123 Fees and other refunds	–2		
4130 Offsets against gross budget authority and outlays (total)	–4,004	–3,844	–3,490
4160 Budget authority, net (mandatory)	–2,967	–2,138	–2,647
4170 Outlays, net (mandatory)	–3,031	–2,559	–2,647
4180 Budget authority, net (total)	–2,967	–2,138	–2,647
4190 Outlays, net (total)	–3,031	–2,559	–2,647

Status of Direct Loans (in millions of dollars)

Identification code 091–4453–0–3–502	2021 actual	2022 est.	2023 est.
Cumulative balance of direct loans outstanding:			
1210 Outstanding, start of year	30,683	29,178	26,759
1251 Repayments: Repayments and prepayments	–1,063	–2,303	–2,793
1264 Other adjustments, net (+ or -)	–442	–116	–107

Office of Federal Student Aid—Continued
Federal Funds—Continued

TEMPORARY STUDENT LOAN PURCHASE AUTHORITY FINANCING ACCOUNT—Continued
Status of Direct Loans—Continued

Identification code 091–4453–0–3–502	2021 actual	2022 est.	2023 est.
1290 Outstanding, end of year	29,178	26,759	23,859

As required by the Federal Credit Reform Act of 1990, this nonbudgetary account records all cash flows to and from the Government resulting from the participation interest program authorized under the Ensuring Continued Access to Student Loans Act of 2008. Amounts in this account are a means of financing and are not included in the budget totals.

Balance Sheet (in millions of dollars)

Identification code 091–4453–0–3–502	2020 actual	2021 actual
ASSETS:		
Federal assets:		
1101 Fund balances with Treasury	316	71
Investments in U.S. securities:		
1106 Receivables, net	1,300	860
Net value of assets related to post-1991 direct loans receivable:		
1401 Direct loans receivable, gross	30,683	29,178
1402 Interest receivable	6,003	5,774
1405 Allowance for subsidy cost (-)	–6,422	–7,315
1499 Net present value of assets related to direct loans	30,264	27,637
1901 Other Federal assets: Other assets	1	1
1999 Total assets	31,881	28,569
LIABILITIES:		
Federal liabilities:		
2101 Accounts payable		
2103 Debt	31,881	28,569
2105 Other		
2201 Non-Federal liabilities: Accounts payable		
2999 Total liabilities	31,881	28,569
NET POSITION:		
3300 Cumulative results of operations		
4999 Total liabilities and net position	31,881	28,569

STUDENT LOAN ACQUISITION ACCOUNT

Program and Financing (in millions of dollars)

Identification code 091–4449–0–3–502	2021 actual	2022 est.	2023 est.
Obligations by program activity:			
0005 Contract collection costs	11	18	16
Credit program obligations:			
0713 Payment of interest to Treasury	447	695	469
0741 Modification savings		164	
0791 Direct program activities, subtotal	447	859	469
0900 Total new obligations, unexpired accounts	458	877	485
Budgetary resources:			
Unobligated balance:			
1000 Unobligated balance brought forward, Oct 1	89	51	241
1021 Recoveries of prior year unpaid obligations	2		
1023 Unobligated balances applied to repay debt	–91	–51	
1070 Unobligated balance (total)			241
Financing authority:			
Appropriations, mandatory:			
1200 Appropriation	20	34	
Borrowing authority, mandatory:			
1400 Borrowing authority	159	164	
Spending authority from offsetting collections, mandatory:			
1800 Collected	2,308	1,980	1,946
1825 Spending authority from offsetting collections applied to repay debt	–1,978	–1,060	–1,460
1850 Spending auth from offsetting collections, mand (total)	330	920	486
1900 Budget authority (total)	509	1,118	486
1930 Total budgetary resources available	509	1,118	727
Memorandum (non-add) entries:			
1941 Unexpired unobligated balance, end of year	51	241	242

	2021 actual	2022 est.	2023 est.
Change in obligated balance:			
Unpaid obligations:			
3000 Unpaid obligations, brought forward, Oct 1	9	5	5
3010 New obligations, unexpired accounts	458	877	485
3020 Outlays (gross)	–460	–877	–485
3040 Recoveries of prior year unpaid obligations, unexpired	–2		
3050 Unpaid obligations, end of year	5	5	5
Memorandum (non-add) entries:			
3100 Obligated balance, start of year	9	5	5
3200 Obligated balance, end of year	5	5	5
Financing authority and disbursements, net:			
Mandatory:			
4090 Budget authority, gross	509	1,118	486
Financing disbursements:			
4110 Outlays, gross (total)	460	877	485
Offsets against gross financing authority and disbursements:			
Offsetting collections (collected) from:			
4120 Upward reestimate	–355	–319	
4120 Upward reestimate interest	–150	–148	
4120 Upward CARES Mod	–1,069		
4120 Upward FY22 Mods		–240	
4122 Interest on uninvested funds	–31		
4123 Principal repayments	–703	–1,131	–1,596
4123 Borrower interest repayments		–142	–350
4130 Offsets against gross budget authority and outlays (total)	–2,308	–1,980	–1,946
4160 Budget authority, net (mandatory)	–1,799	–862	–1,460
4170 Outlays, net (mandatory)	–1,848	–1,103	–1,461
4180 Budget authority, net (total)	–1,799	–862	–1,460
4190 Outlays, net (total)	–1,848	–1,103	–1,461

Status of Direct Loans (in millions of dollars)

Identification code 091–4449–0–3–502	2021 actual	2022 est.	2023 est.
Cumulative balance of direct loans outstanding:			
1210 Outstanding, start of year	16,009	15,238	14,036
1251 Repayments: Repayments and prepayments	–621	–1,131	–1,596
1264 Other adjustments, net (+ or -)	–150	–71	–68
1290 Outstanding, end of year	15,238	14,036	12,372

As required by the Federal Credit Reform Act of 1990, this nonbudgetary account records all cash flows to and from the Government resulting from the standard and short-term Put programs authorized under the Ensuring Continued Access to Student Loans Act of 2008. Amounts in this account are a means of financing and are not included in the budget totals.

Balance Sheet (in millions of dollars)

Identification code 091–4449–0–3–502	2020 actual	2021 actual
ASSETS:		
Federal assets:		
1101 Fund balances with Treasury	98	57
Investments in U.S. securities:		
1106 Receivables, net	740	443
Net value of assets related to post-1991 direct loans receivable:		
1401 Direct loans receivable, gross	16,009	15,238
1402 Interest receivable	2,796	2,715
1405 Allowance for subsidy cost (-)	–4,102	–4,821
1499 Net present value of assets related to direct loans	14,703	13,132
1901 Other Federal assets: Other assets	2	1
1999 Total assets	15,543	13,633
LIABILITIES:		
Federal liabilities:		
2101 Accounts payable		
2103 Debt	15,543	13,633
2105 Other		
2201 Non-Federal liabilities: Accounts payable		
2999 Total liabilities	15,543	13,633
NET POSITION:		
3300 Cumulative results of operations		
4999 Total liabilities and net position	15,543	13,633

DEPARTMENT OF EDUCATION

TEMPORARY STUDENT LOAN PURCHASE AUTHORITY CONDUIT FINANCING ACCOUNT

Program and Financing (in millions of dollars)

Identification code 091–4459–0–3–502	2021 actual	2022 est.	2023 est.
Obligations by program activity:			
0003 Contract collection costs	1	3	3
Credit program obligations:			
0713 Payment of interest to Treasury	42	40	40
0900 Total new obligations, unexpired accounts	43	43	43
Budgetary resources:			
Unobligated balance:			
1000 Unobligated balance brought forward, Oct 1	26	6	
1021 Recoveries of prior year unpaid obligations	10		
1023 Unobligated balances applied to repay debt	–36	–6	
Financing authority:			
Borrowing authority, mandatory:			
1400 Borrowing authority	11	15	
Spending authority from offsetting collections, mandatory:			
1800 Collected	38	28	47
1825 Spending authority from offsetting collections applied to repay debt			–4
1850 Spending auth from offsetting collections, mand (total)	38	28	43
1900 Budget authority (total)	49	43	43
1930 Total budgetary resources available	49	43	43
Memorandum (non-add) entries:			
1941 Unexpired unobligated balance, end of year	6		
Change in obligated balance:			
Unpaid obligations:			
3000 Unpaid obligations, brought forward, Oct 1	11	1	1
3010 New obligations, unexpired accounts	43	43	43
3020 Outlays (gross)	–43	–43	–43
3040 Recoveries of prior year unpaid obligations, unexpired	–10		
3050 Unpaid obligations, end of year	1	1	1
Memorandum (non-add) entries:			
3100 Obligated balance, start of year	11	1	1
3200 Obligated balance, end of year	1	1	1
Financing authority and disbursements, net:			
Mandatory:			
4090 Budget authority, gross	49	43	43
Financing disbursements:			
4110 Outlays, gross (total)	43	43	43
Offsets against gross financing authority and disbursements:			
Offsetting collections (collected) from:			
4122 Interest on uninvested funds	–1		
4123 Principal repayments	–31	–19	–30
4123 Interest repayments	–6	–9	–17
4130 Offsets against gross budget authority and outlays (total)	–38	–28	–47
4160 Budget authority, net (mandatory)	11	15	–4
4170 Outlays, net (mandatory)	5	15	–4
4180 Budget authority, net (total)	11	15	–4
4190 Outlays, net (total)	5	15	–4

Status of Direct Loans (in millions of dollars)

Identification code 091–4459–0–3–502	2021 actual	2022 est.	2023 est.
Cumulative balance of direct loans outstanding:			
1210 Outstanding, start of year	1,389	1,343	1,324
1251 Repayments: Repayments and prepayments	–31	–19	–30
1264 Other adjustments, net (+ or -)	–15		
1290 Outstanding, end of year	1,343	1,324	1,294

As required by the Federal Credit Reform Act of 1990, this nonbudgetary account records all cash flows to and from the Government resulting from the asset-backed commercial paper conduit authorized under the Ensuring Continued Access to Student Loans Act of 2008. Amounts in this account are a means of financing and are not included in the budget totals.

Balance Sheet (in millions of dollars)

Identification code 091–4459–0–3–502	2020 actual	2021 actual
ASSETS:		
1101 Federal assets: Fund balances with Treasury	37	7
Net value of assets related to post-1991 direct loans receivable:		
1401 Direct loans receivable, gross	1,389	1,343
1402 Interest receivable	379	371
1405 Allowance for subsidy cost (-)	–435	–375
1499 Net present value of assets related to direct loans	1,333	1,339
1901 Other Federal assets: Other assets	2	
1999 Total assets	1,372	1,346
LIABILITIES:		
2103 Federal liabilities: Debt	1,372	1,346
2201 Non-Federal liabilities: Accounts payable		
2999 Total liabilities	1,372	1,346
NET POSITION:		
3300 Cumulative results of operations		
4999 Total liabilities and net position	1,372	1,346

FEDERAL FAMILY EDUCATION LOAN LIQUIDATING ACCOUNT

Program and Financing (in millions of dollars)

Identification code 091–0230–0–1–502	2021 actual	2022 est.	2023 est.
Obligations by program activity:			
0101 Interest benefits, net of origination fees	1	3	3
0103 Default claims	9	12	18
0104 Death, disability, and bankruptcy claims	7	8	8
0105 Contract collection costs	1	1	3
0191 Subtotal, Stafford loans	18	24	32
0201 Default claims	1	3	4
0202 Death, disability, and bankruptcy claims	1	1	2
0205 Contract collection costs	1		
0291 Subtotal, PLUS/SLS loans	3	4	6
0900 Total new obligations, unexpired accounts	21	28	38
Budgetary resources:			
Unobligated balance:			
1000 Unobligated balance brought forward, Oct 1	85	74	
1021 Recoveries of prior year unpaid obligations	3	4	
1022 Capital transfer of unobligated balances to general fund	–85	–78	
1033 Recoveries of prior year paid obligations	2		
1070 Unobligated balance (total)	5		
Budget authority:			
Spending authority from offsetting collections, mandatory:			
1800 Collected	90	171	251
1820 Capital transfer of spending authority from offsetting collections to general fund		–143	–213
1850 Spending auth from offsetting collections, mand (total)	90	28	38
1930 Total budgetary resources available	95	28	38
Memorandum (non-add) entries:			
1941 Unexpired unobligated balance, end of year	74		
Change in obligated balance:			
Unpaid obligations:			
3000 Unpaid obligations, brought forward, Oct 1	5	4	
3010 New obligations, unexpired accounts	21	28	38
3020 Outlays (gross)	–19	–28	–38
3040 Recoveries of prior year unpaid obligations, unexpired	–3	–4	
3050 Unpaid obligations, end of year	4		
Memorandum (non-add) entries:			
3100 Obligated balance, start of year	5	4	
3200 Obligated balance, end of year	4		
Budget authority and outlays, net:			
Mandatory:			
4090 Budget authority, gross	90	28	38
Outlays, gross:			
4100 Outlays from new mandatory authority		28	38
4101 Outlays from mandatory balances	19		
4110 Outlays, gross (total)	19	28	38
Offsets against gross budget authority and outlays:			
Offsetting collections (collected) from:			
4123 Fed collections on defaulted loans, Stafford	–78	–154	–226
4123 Other collections, Stafford	–3		
4123 Federal collections on defaulted loans, PLUS/SLS	–11	–17	–25
4130 Offsets against gross budget authority and outlays (total)	–92	–171	–251

Office of Federal Student Aid—Continued
Federal Funds—Continued

FEDERAL FAMILY EDUCATION LOAN LIQUIDATING ACCOUNT—Continued

Program and Financing—Continued

Identification code 091–0230–0–1–502	2021 actual	2022 est.	2023 est.
	Additional offsets against gross budget authority only:			
4143	Recoveries of prior year paid obligations, unexpired accounts	2	....	....
4160	Budget authority, net (mandatory)	....	–143	–213
4170	Outlays, net (mandatory)	–73	–143	–213
4180	Budget authority, net (total)	....	–143	–213
4190	Outlays, net (total)	–73	–143	–213

Status of Guaranteed Loans (in millions of dollars)

Identification code 091–0230–0–1–502	2021 actual	2022 est.	2023 est.
	STAFFORD LOANS			
	Cumulative balance of guaranteed loans outstanding:			
2210	Outstanding, start of year	356	568	534
2251	Repayments and prepayments	–13	–13	–13
	Adjustments:			
2261	Terminations for default that result in loans receivable	–9	–13	–20
2263	Terminations for default that result in claim payments	–7	–8	–9
2264	Other adjustments, net	241	....	....
2290	Outstanding, end of year	568	534	492
	Memorandum:			
2299	Guaranteed amount of guaranteed loans outstanding, end of year	568	534	492
	Addendum:			
	Cumulative balance of defaulted guaranteed loans that result in loans receivable:			
2310	Outstanding, start of year	3,128	3,138	3,049
2331	Disbursements for guaranteed loan claims	9	13	20
2351	Repayments of loans receivable	–65	–94	–71
2361	Write-offs of loans receivable	–7	–8	–9
2364	Other adjustments, net	73	....	....
2390	Outstanding, end of year	3,138	3,049	2,989
	PLUS/SLS LOANS			
	Cumulative balance of guaranteed loans outstanding:			
2210	Outstanding, start of year	38	79	75
2251	Repayments and prepayments	–2	–2	–2
	Adjustments:			
2261	Terminations for default that result in loans receivable	–1	–1	–2
2263	Terminations for default that result in claim payments	–1	–1	–1
2264	Other adjustments, net	45	....	....
2290	Outstanding, end of year	79	75	70
	Memorandum:			
2299	Guaranteed amount of guaranteed loans outstanding, end of year	79	75	70
	Addendum:			
	Cumulative balance of defaulted guaranteed loans that result in loans receivable:			
2310	Outstanding, start of year	498	502	491
2331	Disbursements for guaranteed loan claims	1	1	2
2351	Repayments of loans receivable	–9	–11	–8
2361	Write-offs of loans receivable	–1	–1	–1
2364	Other adjustments, net	13	....	....
2390	Outstanding, end of year	502	491	484

As required by the Federal Credit Reform Act of 1990, this liquidating account records, for this program, all cash flows to and from the Government resulting from guaranteed student loans committed prior to 1992. This account is shown on a cash basis. All new loan activity in this program for 1992 and beyond is recorded in corresponding program and financing accounts.

Balance Sheet (in millions of dollars)

Identification code 091–0230–0–1–502	2020 actual	2021 actual
	ASSETS:		
1101	Federal assets: Fund balances with Treasury	90	78
1701	Defaulted guaranteed loans, gross	3,626	3,640
1702	Interest receivable	5,809	5,738
1703	Allowance for estimated uncollectible loans and interest (-)	–8,249	–8,418
1799	Value of assets related to loan guarantees	1,186	960
1999	Total assets	1,276	1,038
	LIABILITIES:		
2104	Federal liabilities: Resources payable to Treasury	1,275	1,038
	Non-Federal liabilities:		
2201	Accounts payable	....	....
2204	Liabilities for loan guarantees	1	....
2999	Total liabilities	1,276	1,038
	NET POSITION:		
3300	Cumulative results of operations	....	....
4999	Total liabilities and net position	1,276	1,038

Object Classification (in millions of dollars)

Identification code 091–0230–0–1–502	2021 actual	2022 est.	2023 est.
	Direct obligations:			
33.0	Investments and loans	10	15	22
41.0	Grants, subsidies, and contributions	3	4	6
42.0	Insurance claims and indemnities	8	9	10
99.0	Direct obligations	21	28	38
99.9	Total new obligations, unexpired accounts	21	28	38

HEALTH EDUCATION ASSISTANCE LOANS PROGRAM ACCOUNT

Program and Financing (in millions of dollars)

Identification code 091–0247–0–1–502	2021 actual	2022 est.	2023 est.
	Obligations by program activity:			
	Credit program obligations:			
0704	Subsidy for modifications of loan guarantees	1	1	....
0707	Reestimates of loan guarantee subsidy	....	3	....
0708	Interest on reestimates of loan guarantee subsidy	....	11	....
0900	Total new obligations, unexpired accounts (object class 41.0)	1	15	....
	Budgetary resources:			
	Budget authority:			
	Appropriations, mandatory:			
1200	Appropriation	1	15	....
1930	Total budgetary resources available	1	15	....
	Change in obligated balance:			
	Unpaid obligations:			
3010	New obligations, unexpired accounts	1	15	....
3020	Outlays (gross)	–1	–15	....
	Budget authority and outlays, net:			
	Mandatory:			
4090	Budget authority, gross	1	15	....
	Outlays, gross:			
4100	Outlays from new mandatory authority	1	15	....
4180	Budget authority, net (total)	1	15	....
4190	Outlays, net (total)	1	15	....

Summary of Loan Levels, Subsidy Budget Authority and Outlays by Program (in millions of dollars)

Identification code 091–0247–0–1–502	2021 actual	2022 est.	2023 est.
	Guaranteed loan subsidy outlays:			
234001	HEAL Loan Guarantee	1	1	....
	Guaranteed loan reestimates:			
235001	HEAL Loan Guarantee	–25	14	....

Consistent with the Consolidated Appropriations Act, 2014 (P.L. 113–76), the Health Education Assistance Loans (HEAL) program was transferred to the Department of Education from the Department of Health and Human Services in 2014. The Department of Education assumed responsibility for the program and the authority to administer, service, collect, and enforce the program.

The HEAL program guarantees loans from private lenders to health professions students to pay for the costs of their training. As required by the Federal Credit Reform Act of 1990, this account records the subsidy costs

DEPARTMENT OF EDUCATION

associated with HEAL loan guarantees committed in 1992 and beyond (including modifications of HEAL loan guarantees that resulted from obligations or commitments in any year), as well as administrative expenses of the program.

HEALTH EDUCATION ASSISTANCE LOANS FINANCING ACCOUNT

Program and Financing (in millions of dollars)

Identification code 091–4300–0–3–502	2021 actual	2022 est.	2023 est.
Obligations by program activity:			
Credit program obligations:			
0711 Default claim payments on principal		4	4
0713 Payment of interest to Treasury	2	2	2
0715 Default Collection Costs		1	1
0742 Downward reestimates paid to receipt accounts	7		
0743 Interest on downward reestimates	19		
0900 Total new obligations, unexpired accounts	28	7	7
Budgetary resources:			
Unobligated balance:			
1000 Unobligated balance brought forward, Oct 1	13	9	22
1023 Unobligated balances applied to repay debt	–6		
1070 Unobligated balance (total)	7	9	22
Financing authority:			
Borrowing authority, mandatory:			
1400 Borrowing authority	25		
Spending authority from offsetting collections, mandatory:			
1800 Collected	5	20	5
1900 Budget authority (total)	30	20	5
1930 Total budgetary resources available	37	29	27
Memorandum (non-add) entries:			
1941 Unexpired unobligated balance, end of year	9	22	20
Change in obligated balance:			
Unpaid obligations:			
3010 New obligations, unexpired accounts	28	7	7
3020 Outlays (gross)	–28	–7	–6
3050 Unpaid obligations, end of year			1
Memorandum (non-add) entries:			
3200 Obligated balance, end of year			1
Financing authority and disbursements, net:			
Mandatory:			
4090 Budget authority, gross	30	20	5
Financing disbursements:			
4110 Outlays, gross (total)	28	7	6
Offsets against gross financing authority and disbursements:			
Offsetting collections (collected) from:			
4120 Federal sources	–1	–15	
4122 Interest on uninvested funds	–1	–2	–2
4123 Non-Federal sources	–3	–3	–3
4130 Offsets against gross budget authority and outlays (total)	–5	–20	–5
4160 Budget authority, net (mandatory)	25		
4170 Outlays, net (mandatory)	23	–13	1
4180 Budget authority, net (total)	25		
4190 Outlays, net (total)	23	–13	1

Status of Guaranteed Loans (in millions of dollars)

Identification code 091–4300–0–3–502	2021 actual	2022 est.	2023 est.
Position with respect to appropriations act limitation on commitments:			
2143 Uncommitted limitation carried forward			
2150 Total guaranteed loan commitments			
Cumulative balance of guaranteed loans outstanding:			
2210 Outstanding, start of year	60	58	51
2251 Repayments and prepayments	–2	–3	–6
Adjustments:			
2261 Terminations for default that result in loans receivable		–3	–3
2263 Terminations for default that result in claim payments		–1	–1
2264 Other adjustments, net			
2290 Outstanding, end of year	58	51	41

	2021 actual	2022 est.	2023 est.
Memorandum:			
2299 Guaranteed amount of guaranteed loans outstanding, end of year	58	51	41
Addendum:			
Cumulative balance of defaulted guaranteed loans that result in loans receivable:			
2310 Outstanding, start of year	140	136	135
2331 Disbursements for guaranteed loan claims		3	3
2351 Repayments and prepayments	–2	–3	–3
2361 Write-offs of loans receivable		–1	–1
2364 Other adjustments, net	–2		
2390 Outstanding, end of year	136	135	134

As required by the Federal Credit Reform Act of 1990, this nonbudgetary account records all cash flows to and from the Government resulting from the Health Education Assistance Loan program. Amounts in this account are a means of financing and are not included in the budget totals.

Balance Sheet (in millions of dollars)

Identification code 091–4300–0–3–502	2020 actual	2021 actual
ASSETS:		
1101 Federal assets: Fund balances with Treasury	13	8
Net value of assets related to post-1991 acquired defaulted guaranteed loans receivable:		
1501 Defaulted guaranteed loans receivable, gross	140	136
1502 Interest receivable	20	19
1505 Allowance for subsidy cost (-)		74
1599 Net present value of assets related to defaulted guaranteed loans	160	229
1901 Other Federal assets: Other assets	42	
1999 Total assets	215	237
LIABILITIES:		
2103 Federal liabilities: Debt	11	30
Non-Federal liabilities:		
2203 Debt		
2204 Liabilities for loan guarantees	203	206
2999 Total liabilities	214	236
NET POSITION:		
3300 Cumulative results of operations	1	1
4999 Total liabilities and net position	215	237

HEALTH EDUCATION ASSISTANCE LOANS LIQUIDATING ACCOUNT

Program and Financing (in millions of dollars)

Identification code 091–4299–0–3–502	2021 actual	2022 est.	2023 est.
Obligations by program activity:			
Credit program obligations:			
0715 Default Collections Costs		1	1
0900 Total new obligations, unexpired accounts (object class 33.0)		1	1
Budgetary resources:			
Unobligated balance:			
1000 Unobligated balance brought forward, Oct 1	4	2	
1022 Capital transfer of unobligated balances to general fund	–4	–2	
Budget authority:			
Spending authority from offsetting collections, mandatory:			
1800 Collected	2	3	3
1820 Capital transfer of spending authority from offsetting collections to general fund		–2	–2
1850 Spending auth from offsetting collections, mand (total)	2	1	1
1900 Budget authority (total)	2	1	1
1930 Total budgetary resources available	2	1	1
Memorandum (non-add) entries:			
1941 Unexpired unobligated balance, end of year	2		
Change in obligated balance:			
Unpaid obligations:			
3010 New obligations, unexpired accounts		1	1
3020 Outlays (gross)		–1	–1

HEALTH EDUCATION ASSISTANCE LOANS LIQUIDATING ACCOUNT—Continued

Program and Financing—Continued

Identification code 091–4299–0–3–502	2021 actual	2022 est.	2023 est.
Budget authority and outlays, net:			
Mandatory:			
4090 Budget authority, gross	2	1	1
Outlays, gross:			
4100 Outlays from new mandatory authority		1	1
Offsets against gross budget authority and outlays:			
Offsetting collections (collected) from:			
4123 Non-Federal sources	–2	–3	–3
4180 Budget authority, net (total)		–2	–2
4190 Outlays, net (total)	–2	–2	–2

Status of Guaranteed Loans (in millions of dollars)

Identification code 091–4299–0–3–502	2021 actual	2022 est.	2023 est.
Cumulative balance of guaranteed loans outstanding:			
2210 Outstanding, start of year	6	4	3
2251 Repayments and prepayments	–2	–1	–1
Adjustments:			
2261 Terminations for default that result in loans receivable			
2264 Other adjustments, net			
2290 Outstanding, end of year	4	3	2
Memorandum:			
2299 Guaranteed amount of guaranteed loans outstanding, end of year	4	2	2
Addendum:			
Cumulative balance of defaulted guaranteed loans that result in loans receivable:			
2310 Outstanding, start of year	256	252	249
2331 Disbursements for guaranteed loan claims			
2351 Repayments of loans receivable	–2	–3	–3
2361 Write-offs of loans receivable			
2364 Other adjustments, net	–2		
2390 Outstanding, end of year	252	249	246

As required by the Federal Credit Reform Act of 1990, this liquidating account records, for this program, all cash flows to and from the Government resulting from guaranteed Health Education Assistance Loans loans committed prior to 1992. This account is shown on a cash basis. All loan activity in this program for 1992 and beyond is recorded in corresponding program and financing accounts.

Balance Sheet (in millions of dollars)

Identification code 091–4299–0–3–502	2020 actual	2021 actual
ASSETS:		
1101 Federal assets: Fund balances with Treasury	4	2
1701 Defaulted guaranteed loans, gross	256	252
1702 Interest receivable	9	8
1703 Allowance for estimated uncollectible loans and interest (-)	–80	–76
1799 Value of assets related to loan guarantees	185	184
1901 Other Federal assets: Other assets	8	
1999 Total assets	197	186
LIABILITIES:		
2104 Federal liabilities: Resources payable to Treasury	162	158
Non-Federal liabilities:		
2204 Liabilities for loan guarantees	35	36
2207 Other		
2999 Total liabilities	197	194
NET POSITION:		
3300 Cumulative results of operations		–8
4999 Total liabilities and net position	197	186

INSTITUTE OF EDUCATION SCIENCES

Federal Funds

INSTITUTE OF EDUCATION SCIENCES

For carrying out activities authorized by the Education Sciences Reform Act of 2002, the National Assessment of Educational Progress Authorization Act, section 208 of the Educational Technical Assistance Act of 2002, and section 664 of the Individuals with Disabilities Education Act, $662,516,000, which shall remain available through September 30, 2024: *Provided,* That funds available to carry out section 208 of the Educational Technical Assistance Act may be used to link Statewide elementary and secondary data systems with early childhood, postsecondary, and workforce data systems, or to further develop such systems: *Provided further,* That up to $6,000,000 of the funds available to carry out section 208 of the Educational Technical Assistance Act may be used for awards to public or private organizations or agencies to support activities to improve data coordination, quality, and use at the local, State, and national levels.

Note.—A full-year 2022 appropriation for this account was not enacted at the time the Budget was prepared; therefore, the Budget assumes this account is operating under the Continuing Appropriations Act, 2022 (Division A of Public Law 117–43, as amended). The amounts included for 2022 reflect the annualized level provided by the continuing resolution.

Program and Financing (in millions of dollars)

Identification code 091–1100–0–1–503	2021 actual	2022 est.	2023 est.
Obligations by program activity:			
0001 Research, development, and dissemination	187	233	224
0002 Statistics	117	108	105
0003 Regional educational laboratories	56	56	56
0004 National Assessment	146	154	146
0005 National Assessment Governing Board	7	7	7
0006 Research in special education	59	59	61
0007 Statewide longitudinal data systems	35	35	35
0008 Special education studies and evaluations	10	10	10
0100 Total direct program	617	662	644
0799 Total direct obligations	617	662	644
0900 Total new obligations, unexpired accounts	617	662	644
Budgetary resources:			
Unobligated balance:			
1000 Unobligated balance brought forward, Oct 1	108	265	245
1001 Discretionary unobligated balance brought fwd, Oct 1	108	165	
1021 Recoveries of prior year unpaid obligations	4		
1070 Unobligated balance (total)	112	265	245
Budget authority:			
Appropriations, discretionary:			
1100 Appropriation	670	642	663
Appropriations, mandatory:			
1200 Appropriation	100		
1900 Budget authority (total)	770	642	663
1930 Total budgetary resources available	882	907	908
Memorandum (non-add) entries:			
1941 Unexpired unobligated balance, end of year	265	245	264
Change in obligated balance:			
Unpaid obligations:			
3000 Unpaid obligations, brought forward, Oct 1	588	644	691
3010 New obligations, unexpired accounts	617	662	644
3020 Outlays (gross)	–555	–615	–542
3040 Recoveries of prior year unpaid obligations, unexpired	–4		
3041 Recoveries of prior year unpaid obligations, expired	–2		
3050 Unpaid obligations, end of year	644	691	793
Uncollected payments:			
3060 Uncollected pymts, Fed sources, brought forward, Oct 1	–2	–2	–2
3090 Uncollected pymts, Fed sources, end of year	–2	–2	–2
Memorandum (non-add) entries:			
3100 Obligated balance, start of year	586	642	689
3200 Obligated balance, end of year	642	689	791
Budget authority and outlays, net:			
Discretionary:			
4000 Budget authority, gross	670	642	663
Outlays, gross:			
4010 Outlays from new discretionary authority	161	105	108
4011 Outlays from discretionary balances	384	506	415
4020 Outlays, gross (total)	545	611	523

	Mandatory:			
4090	Budget authority, gross	100		
	Outlays, gross:			
4100	Outlays from new mandatory authority	10		
4101	Outlays from mandatory balances		4	19
4110	Outlays, gross (total)	10	4	19
4180	Budget authority, net (total)	770	642	663
4190	Outlays, net (total)	555	615	542

Research, Statistics, and Assessment:

Research, development, and dissemination.—Funds support a diverse portfolio of research, development, and dissemination activities that provide parents, teachers, and schools with evidence-based information on effective educational practices.

Statistics.—Funds support the Department's statistical data collection activities, which are conducted by the National Center for Education Statistics (NCES). NCES collects, analyzes, and disseminates education statistics at all levels, from preschool through postsecondary and adult education, including statistics on international education activities.

Regional educational laboratories.—Funds support a network of 10 regional laboratories that provide expert advice, including training and technical assistance, to help States and school districts apply proven research findings in their school improvement efforts.

Assessment.—Funds support the ongoing National Assessment of Educational Progress (NAEP) and the National Assessment Governing Board (NAGB). NAEP administers assessments to samples of students in order to gather reliable information about educational attainment in important academic areas. NAGB is responsible for formulating NAEP policy; developing student achievement levels; and selecting, consistent with the requirements of the statute, the subjects to be assessed.

Research in special education.—Funds support research to build the evidence base on improving special education and early intervention services and outcomes for infants, toddlers, and children with disabilities.

Statewide longitudinal data systems.—Funds support competitive grant awards to States to foster the design, development, implementation, and use of longitudinal data systems. In addition, funds would support awards to public and private agencies to improve data coordination, quality, and use at the local, State, and national levels.

Special education studies and evaluations.—Funds support studies, evaluations, and assessments related to the implementation of the Individuals with Disabilities Education Act in order to improve special education and early intervention services and outcomes for infants, toddlers, and children with disabilities.

Object Classification (in millions of dollars)

Identification code 091–1100–0–1–503		2021 actual	2022 est.	2023 est.
	Direct obligations:			
	Personnel compensation:			
11.1	Full-time permanent	1	1	1
11.3	Other than full-time permanent	1	1	1
11.9	Total personnel compensation	2	2	2
12.1	Civilian personnel benefits	1	1	1
25.1	Advisory and assistance services	38	44	24
25.2	Other services from non-Federal sources	269	269	279
25.3	Other goods and services from Federal sources	2	2	12
25.5	Research and development contracts	72	72	72
41.0	Grants, subsidies, and contributions	233	272	254
99.9	Total new obligations, unexpired accounts	617	662	644

Employment Summary

Identification code 091–1100–0–1–503	2021 actual	2022 est.	2023 est.
1001 Direct civilian full-time equivalent employment	13	13	13

DEPARTMENTAL MANAGEMENT

Federal Funds

PROGRAM ADMINISTRATION

For carrying out, to the extent not otherwise provided, the Department of Education Organization Act, including rental of conference rooms in the District of Columbia and hire of three passenger motor vehicles, $548,000,000, of which up to $17,500,000, to remain available until expended, shall be available for relocation expenses, and for the renovation and repair of leased buildings: *Provided*, That, from the amount in the preceding proviso, the Secretary may use up to $5,000,000 to support a commission on the future of the teaching profession that addresses the pressing needs of the field, including making the compensation of educators competitive with similarly educated professionals, together with providing for the collection and analysis of labor market data at the State and regional levels on gaps in educators salaries and overall compensation relative to professionals with similar qualifications, including education, skills, and experience: *Provided further*, That, notwithstanding any other provision of law, none of the funds provided by this Act or provided by previous Appropriations Acts to the Department of Education available for obligation or expenditure in the current fiscal year may be used for any activity relating to implementing a reorganization that decentralizes, reduces the staffing level, or alters the responsibilities, structure, authority, or functionality of the Budget Service of the Department of Education, relative to the organization and operation of the Budget Service as in effect on January 1, 2018.

Note.—A full-year 2022 appropriation for this account was not enacted at the time the Budget was prepared; therefore, the Budget assumes this account is operating under the Continuing Appropriations Act, 2022 (Division A of Public Law 117–43, as amended). The amounts included for 2022 reflect the annualized level provided by the continuing resolution.

Special and Trust Fund Receipts (in millions of dollars)

Identification code 091–0800–0–1–503		2021 actual	2022 est.	2023 est.
0100	Balance, start of year		1	2
	Receipts:			
	Current law:			
1130	Contributions	1	1	1
2000	Total: Balances and receipts	1	2	3
5099	Balance, end of year	1	2	3

Program and Financing (in millions of dollars)

Identification code 091–0800–0–1–503		2021 actual	2022 est.	2023 est.
	Obligations by program activity:			
0001	Program administration	448	430	548
	Budgetary resources:			
	Unobligated balance:			
1000	Unobligated balance brought forward, Oct 1	7	23	23
1001	Discretionary unobligated balance brought fwd, Oct 1	7		
	Budget authority:			
	Appropriations, discretionary:			
1100	Appropriation	445	430	548
	Appropriations, mandatory:			
1200	Appropriation	15		
	Spending authority from offsetting collections, discretionary:			
1700	Collected	3		
1701	Change in uncollected payments, Federal sources	1		
1750	Spending auth from offsetting collections, disc (total)	4		
1900	Budget authority (total)	464	430	548
1930	Total budgetary resources available	471	453	571
	Memorandum (non-add) entries:			
1941	Unexpired unobligated balance, end of year	23	23	23
	Change in obligated balance:			
	Unpaid obligations:			
3000	Unpaid obligations, brought forward, Oct 1	176	178	139
3010	New obligations, unexpired accounts	448	430	548
3011	Obligations ("upward adjustments"), expired accounts	1		
3020	Outlays (gross)	–439	–469	–535
3041	Recoveries of prior year unpaid obligations, expired	–8		
3050	Unpaid obligations, end of year	178	139	152
	Uncollected payments:			
3060	Uncollected pymts, Fed sources, brought forward, Oct 1	–2	–2	–2
3070	Change in uncollected pymts, Fed sources, unexpired	–1		
3071	Change in uncollected pymts, Fed sources, expired	1		
3090	Uncollected pymts, Fed sources, end of year	–2	–2	–2

PROGRAM ADMINISTRATION—Continued
Program and Financing—Continued

Identification code 091–0800–0–1–503		2021 actual	2022 est.	2023 est.
	Memorandum (non-add) entries:			
3100	Obligated balance, start of year	174	176	137
3200	Obligated balance, end of year	176	137	150
	Budget authority and outlays, net:			
	Discretionary:			
4000	Budget authority, gross	449	430	548
	Outlays, gross:			
4010	Outlays from new discretionary authority	330	338	439
4011	Outlays from discretionary balances	108	118	96
4020	Outlays, gross (total)	438	456	535
	Offsets against gross budget authority and outlays:			
	Offsetting collections (collected) from:			
4030	Federal sources	–3	–1	....
4040	Offsets against gross budget authority and outlays (total)	–3	–1	....
	Additional offsets against gross budget authority only:			
4050	Change in uncollected pymts, Fed sources, unexpired	–1	....	....
4052	Offsetting collections credited to expired accounts	....	1	....
4060	Additional offsets against budget authority only (total)	–1	1	....
4070	Budget authority, net (discretionary)	445	430	548
4080	Outlays, net (discretionary)	435	455	535
	Mandatory:			
4090	Budget authority, gross	15	....	....
	Outlays, gross:			
4100	Outlays from new mandatory authority	1	....	....
4101	Outlays from mandatory balances	....	13	....
4110	Outlays, gross (total)	1	13	....
4180	Budget authority, net (total)	460	430	548
4190	Outlays, net (total)	436	468	535

The Program Administration account includes the direct Federal costs of providing grants and administering early, elementary, and secondary education; Indian education; English language acquisition; higher education; career, technical, and adult education; special education programs; and programs for persons with disabilities. It also supports assessment, statistics, and research activities.

In addition, this account includes the cost of providing centralized support and administrative services, overall policy development, and strategic planning for the Department. Included in the centralized activities are rent and mail services; telecommunications; contractual services; financial management and accounting, including payments to schools, education agencies and other grant recipients, and preparation of auditable financial statements; information technology services and security; personnel management; personnel security; budget formulation and execution; legal services; congressional and public relations; and intergovernmental affairs. Included in this account is the Department of Education's cost to relocate staff and renovate buildings occupied by Department staff.

Also included in this account are contributions from the public. Contributions not designated for a specific purpose are in the account's Gifts and Bequests Miscellaneous Fund.

Reimbursable program.—Reimbursements to this account are for providing administrative services to other agencies.

Object Classification (in millions of dollars)

Identification code 091–0800–0–1–503		2021 actual	2022 est.	2023 est.
	Direct obligations:			
	Personnel compensation:			
11.1	Full-time permanent	187	200	239
11.3	Other than full-time permanent	19	5	5
11.5	Other personnel compensation	5	5	5
11.9	Total personnel compensation	211	210	249
12.1	Civilian personnel benefits	72	76	90
21.0	Travel and transportation of persons	1	1	3
23.1	Rental payments to GSA	23	28	28
23.3	Communications, utilities, and miscellaneous charges	1	1	1
24.0	Printing and reproduction	....	1	1
25.1	Advisory and assistance services	1	3	4
25.2	Other services from non-Federal sources	29	17	31
25.3	Other goods and services from Federal sources	19	16	16
25.7	Operation and maintenance of equipment	75	72	105
26.0	Supplies and materials	1	2	1
31.0	Equipment	2	2	9
32.0	Land and structures	8	1	10
99.0	Direct obligations	444	430	548
99.5	Adjustment for rounding	4	....	....
99.9	Total new obligations, unexpired accounts	448	430	548

Employment Summary

Identification code 091–0800–0–1–503	2021 actual	2022 est.	2023 est.
1001 Direct civilian full-time equivalent employment	1,624	1,556	1,762

OFFICE FOR CIVIL RIGHTS

For expenses necessary for the Office for Civil Rights, as authorized by section 203 of the Department of Education Organization Act, $161,300,000.

Note.—A full-year 2022 appropriation for this account was not enacted at the time the Budget was prepared; therefore, the Budget assumes this account is operating under the Continuing Appropriations Act, 2022 (Division A of Public Law 117–43, as amended). The amounts included for 2022 reflect the annualized level provided by the continuing resolution.

Program and Financing (in millions of dollars)

Identification code 091–0700–0–1–751		2021 actual	2022 est.	2023 est.
	Obligations by program activity:			
0001	Civil rights	132	131	161
	Budgetary resources:			
	Budget authority:			
	Appropriations, discretionary:			
1100	Appropriation	131	131	161
	Spending authority from offsetting collections, discretionary:			
1701	Change in uncollected payments, Federal sources	1	....	....
1900	Budget authority (total)	132	131	161
1930	Total budgetary resources available	132	131	161
	Change in obligated balance:			
	Unpaid obligations:			
3000	Unpaid obligations, brought forward, Oct 1	37	31	29
3010	New obligations, unexpired accounts	132	131	161
3020	Outlays (gross)	–137	–133	–155
3041	Recoveries of prior year unpaid obligations, expired	–1	....	....
3050	Unpaid obligations, end of year	31	29	35
	Uncollected payments:			
3060	Uncollected pymts, Fed sources, brought forward, Oct 1	....	–1	–1
3070	Change in uncollected pymts, Fed sources, unexpired	–1	....	....
3090	Uncollected pymts, Fed sources, end of year	–1	–1	–1
	Memorandum (non-add) entries:			
3100	Obligated balance, start of year	37	30	28
3200	Obligated balance, end of year	30	28	34
	Budget authority and outlays, net:			
	Discretionary:			
4000	Budget authority, gross	132	131	161
	Outlays, gross:			
4010	Outlays from new discretionary authority	110	110	136
4011	Outlays from discretionary balances	27	23	19
4020	Outlays, gross (total)	137	133	155
	Offsets against gross budget authority and outlays:			
	Offsetting collections (collected) from:			
4030	Federal sources	....	–1	....
	Additional offsets against gross budget authority only:			
4050	Change in uncollected pymts, Fed sources, unexpired	–1	....	....
4052	Offsetting collections credited to expired accounts	....	1	....
4060	Additional offsets against budget authority only (total)	–1	1	....
4070	Budget authority, net (discretionary)	131	131	161
4080	Outlays, net (discretionary)	137	132	155
4180	Budget authority, net (total)	131	131	161
4190	Outlays, net (total)	137	132	155

The Office for Civil Rights is responsible for ensuring that no person is unlawfully discriminated against on the basis of race, color, national origin, sex, disability, or age in the delivery of services or the provision of benefits in programs or activities of schools and institutions receiving financial assistance from the Department of Education. The authorities under which the Office for Civil Rights operates are Title VI of the Civil Rights Act of 1964 (race, color, or national origin discrimination), Title IX of the Education Amendments of 1972 (sex discrimination), Section 504 of the Rehabilitation Act of 1973 (disability discrimination), the Age Discrimination Act of 1975, Title II of the Americans with Disabilities Act of 1990 (whether or not the public entity receives Federal Financial Assistance), and the Boy Scouts of America Equal Access Act of 2002.

Object Classification (in millions of dollars)

Identification code 091–0700–0–1–751		2021 actual	2022 est.	2023 est.
	Direct obligations:			
	Personnel compensation:			
11.1	Full-time permanent	69	70	87
11.3	Other than full-time permanent	2	1	1
11.5	Other personnel compensation	1	1	....
11.9	Total personnel compensation	72	72	88
12.1	Civilian personnel benefits	26	27	34
21.0	Travel and transportation of persons	....	1	1
23.1	Rental payments to GSA	10	10	11
25.2	Other services from non-Federal sources	3	1	1
25.3	Other goods and services from Federal sources	2	3	3
25.7	Operation and maintenance of equipment	18	17	23
99.0	Direct obligations	131	131	161
99.5	Adjustment for rounding	1	....	....
99.9	Total new obligations, unexpired accounts	132	131	161

Employment Summary

Identification code 091–0700–0–1–751	2021 actual	2022 est.	2023 est.
1001 Direct civilian full-time equivalent employment	584	575	676

OFFICE OF INSPECTOR GENERAL

For expenses necessary for the Office of Inspector General, as authorized by section 212 of the Department of Education Organization Act, $76,452,000, of which $2,000,000 shall remain available until expended.

Note.—A full-year 2022 appropriation for this account was not enacted at the time the Budget was prepared; therefore, the Budget assumes this account is operating under the Continuing Appropriations Act, 2022 (Division A of Public Law 117–43, as amended). The amounts included for 2022 reflect the annualized level provided by the continuing resolution.

Program and Financing (in millions of dollars)

Identification code 091–1400–0–1–751		2021 actual	2022 est.	2023 est.
	Obligations by program activity:			
0001	Inspector General	64	72	76
	Budgetary resources:			
	Unobligated balance:			
1000	Unobligated balance brought forward, Oct 1	10	18	9
	Budget authority:			
	Appropriations, discretionary:			
1100	Appropriation	68	63	76
	Appropriations, mandatory:			
1200	Appropriation	5	....	....
1900	Budget authority (total)	73	63	76
1930	Total budgetary resources available	83	81	85
	Memorandum (non-add) entries:			
1940	Unobligated balance expiring	–1	....	....
1941	Unexpired unobligated balance, end of year	18	9	9
	Change in obligated balance:			
	Unpaid obligations:			
3000	Unpaid obligations, brought forward, Oct 1	18	19	19
3010	New obligations, unexpired accounts	64	72	76
3020	Outlays (gross)	–62	–72	–76
3041	Recoveries of prior year unpaid obligations, expired	–1	....	....
3050	Unpaid obligations, end of year	19	19	19
	Memorandum (non-add) entries:			
3100	Obligated balance, start of year	18	19	19
3200	Obligated balance, end of year	19	19	19
	Budget authority and outlays, net:			
	Discretionary:			
4000	Budget authority, gross	68	63	76
	Outlays, gross:			
4010	Outlays from new discretionary authority	49	52	62
4011	Outlays from discretionary balances	13	15	14
4020	Outlays, gross (total)	62	67	76
	Mandatory:			
4090	Budget authority, gross	5	....	....
	Outlays, gross:			
4101	Outlays from mandatory balances	....	5	....
4180	Budget authority, net (total)	73	63	76
4190	Outlays, net (total)	62	72	76

The Office of Inspector General (OIG) is an independent entity within the Department of Education responsible for identifying fraud, waste, abuse, and criminal activity involving the Department's funds, programs, and operations. The OIG conducts independent audits and other reviews to ensure the effectiveness and efficiency of the Department's programs and operations, recommends actions to address systemic weaknesses and improve the Department's programs and operations, and recommends changes needed in Federal laws and regulations.

Object Classification (in millions of dollars)

Identification code 091–1400–0–1–751		2021 actual	2022 est.	2023 est.
	Direct obligations:			
	Personnel compensation:			
11.1	Full-time permanent	27	37	36
11.5	Other personnel compensation	2	1	1
11.9	Total personnel compensation	29	38	37
12.1	Civilian personnel benefits	13	16	16
21.0	Travel and transportation of persons	....	....	2
23.1	Rental payments to GSA	6	6	5
25.1	Advisory and assistance services	1	....	....
25.2	Other services from non-Federal sources	3	3	5
25.3	Other goods and services from Federal sources	3	1	2
25.7	Operation and maintenance of equipment	6	7	8
31.0	Equipment	3	1	1
99.9	Total new obligations, unexpired accounts	64	72	76

Employment Summary

Identification code 091–1400–0–1–751	2021 actual	2022 est.	2023 est.
1001 Direct civilian full-time equivalent employment	228	271	253

DISASTER EDUCATION RECOVERY

Federal Funds

DISASTER EDUCATION RECOVERY

Program and Financing (in millions of dollars)

Identification code 091–0013–0–1–500		2021 actual	2022 est.	2023 est.
	Obligations by program activity:			
0001	Hurricane Education Recovery	13	1,292	67
0900	Total new obligations, unexpired accounts (object class 41.0)	13	1,292	67
	Budgetary resources:			
	Unobligated balance:			
1000	Unobligated balance brought forward, Oct 1	1,293	1,359	67
1021	Recoveries of prior year unpaid obligations	79	....	....
1070	Unobligated balance (total)	1,372	1,359	67
1930	Total budgetary resources available	1,372	1,359	67

DISASTER EDUCATION RECOVERY—Continued
Program and Financing—Continued

Identification code 091–0013–0–1–500	2021 actual	2022 est.	2023 est.
Memorandum (non-add) entries:			
1941 Unexpired unobligated balance, end of year	1,359	67	
Change in obligated balance:			
Unpaid obligations:			
3000 Unpaid obligations, brought forward, Oct 1	680	319	1,061
3010 New obligations, unexpired accounts	13	1,292	67
3020 Outlays (gross)	–295	–550	–493
3040 Recoveries of prior year unpaid obligations, unexpired	–79		
3050 Unpaid obligations, end of year	319	1,061	635
Memorandum (non-add) entries:			
3100 Obligated balance, start of year	680	319	1,061
3200 Obligated balance, end of year	319	1,061	635
Budget authority and outlays, net:			
Discretionary:			
Outlays, gross:			
4011 Outlays from discretionary balances	295	550	493
4180 Budget authority, net (total)			
4190 Outlays, net (total)	295	550	493

Funds support the following six programs authorized under Public Law 115–123: Awards to Eligible Entities for Immediate Aid to Restart School Operations; Temporary Emergency Impact Aid for Displaced Students; Assistance to Local Educational Agencies Serving Homeless Children and Youth enrolled as a result of displacement by a covered disaster or emergency; Project School Emergency Response to Violence activities authorized under section 4631(b) of the Elementary and Secondary Education Act, as amended; Emergency Assistance to Institutions of Higher Education (IHEs) and Students Attending IHEs from an area directly affected by a covered disaster or emergency; and payments to IHEs to help defray the unexpected expenses associated with enrolling students from IHEs at which operations have been disrupted by a covered disaster or emergency. Amounts in this schedule reflect balances that are spending out from prior-year appropriations.

GENERAL FUND RECEIPT ACCOUNTS

(in millions of dollars)

	2021 actual	2022 est.	2023 est.
Offsetting receipts from the public:			
091–143500 General Fund Proprietary Interest Receipts, not Otherwise Classified	4	2	2
091–271810 Federal Family Education Loan Program, Negative Subsidies		547	
091–271830 Federal Family Education Loan Program, Downward Reestimates of Subsidies	589		
091–274130 College Housing and Academic Facilities Loan, Downward Reestimates of Subsidies	207	291	
091–278110 Federal Direct Student Loan Program, Negative Subsidies	3,970	13,744	2,699
091–278130 Federal Direct Student Loan Program, Downward Reestimates of Subsidies	839	13,702	
091–279410 TEACH Grant Program, Negative Subsidies		2	
091–279430 TEACH Grant Program, Downward Reestimates of Subsidies	3	4	
091–279830 Health Education Assistance Loans, Downward Reestimates of Subsidies	25		
091–291500 Repayment of Loans, Capital Contributions, Higher Education Activities	866	771	638
091–322000 All Other General Fund Proprietary Receipts Including Budget Clearing Accounts	130	8	8
General Fund Offsetting receipts from the public	6,633	29,071	3,347
Intragovernmental payments:			
091–388500 Undistributed Intragovernmental Payments and Receivables from Cancelled Accounts	–13		
General Fund Intragovernmental payments	–13		

GENERAL PROVISIONS

SEC. 301. No funds appropriated in this Act may be used to prevent the implementation of programs of voluntary prayer and meditation in the public schools.

(TRANSFER OF FUNDS)

SEC. 302. Not to exceed 1 percent of any discretionary funds (pursuant to the Balanced Budget and Emergency Deficit Control Act of 1985) which are appropriated for the Department of Education in this Act may be transferred between appropriations, but no such appropriation shall be increased by more than 3 percent by any such transfer: Provided, That the transfer authority granted by this section shall not be used to create any new program or to fund any project or activity for which no funds are provided in this Act: Provided further, That the Committees on Appropriations of the House of Representatives and the Senate are notified at least 15 days in advance of any transfer.

SEC. 303. Funds appropriated in this Act and consolidated for evaluation purposes under section 8601(c) of the ESEA shall be available from July 1, 2023, through September 30, 2024.

SEC. 304. (a) An institution of higher education that maintains an endowment fund supported with funds appropriated for title III or V of the HEA for fiscal year 2023 may use the income from that fund to award scholarships to students, subject to the limitation in section 331(c)(3)(B)(i) of the HEA. The use of such income for such purposes, prior to the enactment of this Act, shall be considered to have been an allowable use of that income, subject to that limitation.

(b) Subsection (a) shall be in effect until titles III and V of the HEA are reauthorized.

SEC. 305. Section 114(f) of the HEA (20 U.S.C. 1011c(f)) is amended by striking "2022" and inserting "2023".

SEC. 306. Section 458(a) of the HEA (20 U.S.C. 1087h(a)) is amended in paragraph (4) by striking "2022" and inserting "2023".

(CANCELLATION)

SEC. 307. Of the amounts appropriated under Section 401(b)(7)(A)(iv)(XI) of the Higher Education Act of 1965 (20 U.S.C. 1070a(b)(7)(A)(iv)(XI)) for fiscal year 2023, $141,000,000 are hereby cancelled.

SEC. 308. Of the amounts made available under this title under the heading "Student Aid Administration", $2,300,000 may be used by the Secretary of Education to conduct outreach to borrowers of loans made under part D of title IV of the Higher Education Act of 1965 who may intend to qualify for loan cancellation under section 455(m) of such Act (20 U.S.C. 1087e(m)), to ensure that borrowers are meeting the terms and conditions of such loan cancellation: Provided, That the Secretary shall specifically conduct outreach to assist borrowers who would qualify for loan cancellation under section 455(m) of such Act except that the borrower has made some, or all, of the 120 required payments under a repayment plan that is not described under section 455(m)(A) of such Act, to encourage borrowers to enroll in a qualifying repayment plan: Provided further, That the Secretary shall also communicate to all Direct Loan borrowers the full requirements of section 455(m) of such Act and improve the filing of employment certification by providing improved outreach and information such as outbound calls, electronic communications, ensuring prominent access to program requirements and benefits on each servicer's website, and creating an option for all borrowers to complete the entire payment certification process electronically and on a centralized website.

SEC. 309. None of the funds made available by this Act may be used in contravention of section 203 of the Department of Education Organization Act (20 U.S.C. 3413).

(INCLUDING TRANSFER OF FUNDS)

SEC. 310. Notwithstanding any other provision of law, the Secretary may reserve not more than 0.5 percent from any amount made available in this Act for an HEA program, except for any amounts made available for subpart 1 of part A of title IV of the HEA, to carry out rigorous and independent evaluations and to collect and analyze outcome data for any program authorized by the HEA: Provided, That no funds made available in this Act for the "Student Aid Administration" account shall be subject to the reservation under this section: Provided further, That any funds reserved under this section shall be available through September 30, 2023: Provided further, That if, under any other provision of law, funds are authorized to be reserved or used for evaluation activities with respect to a program or project, the Secretary may also reserve funds for such program or project for the purposes described in this section so long as the total reservation of funds for such program or project does not exceed any statutory limits on such reservations: Provided further, That not later than 10 days prior to the initial obligation of funds reserved under this *section, the Secretary shall submit to the Committees on Appropriations of the Senate and the House of Representatives, the Committee on Health, Education, Labor and Pensions of the Senate, and the Committee on Education and Labor of the House of Representatives a plan that identifies the source and amount of funds reserved under this section, the impact on program grantees if funds are withheld for the purposes of this section, and the activities to be carried out with such funds.*

DEPARTMENT OF ENERGY

NATIONAL NUCLEAR SECURITY ADMINISTRATION
Federal Funds

FEDERAL SALARIES AND EXPENSES

For expenses necessary for Federal Salaries and Expenses in the National Nuclear Security Administration, $496,400,000, to remain available until September 30, 2024, including official reception and representation expenses not to exceed $17,000.

Note.—A full-year 2022 appropriation for this account was not enacted at the time the Budget was prepared; therefore, the Budget assumes this account is operating under the Continuing Appropriations Act, 2022 (Division A of Public Law 117–43, as amended). The amounts included for 2022 reflect the annualized level provided by the continuing resolution.

Program and Financing (in millions of dollars)

Identification code 089–0313–0–1–053		2021 actual	2022 est.	2023 est.
	Obligations by program activity:			
0010	Federal Salaries and Expenses	443	443	496
	Budgetary resources:			
	Unobligated balance:			
1000	Unobligated balance brought forward, Oct 1	27	28	28
1021	Recoveries of prior year unpaid obligations	1		
1070	Unobligated balance (total)	28	28	28
	Budget authority:			
	Appropriations, discretionary:			
1100	Appropriation	443	443	496
1900	Budget authority (total)	443	443	496
1930	Total budgetary resources available	471	471	524
	Memorandum (non-add) entries:			
1941	Unexpired unobligated balance, end of year	28	28	28
	Change in obligated balance:			
	Unpaid obligations:			
3000	Unpaid obligations, brought forward, Oct 1	68	75	65
3010	New obligations, unexpired accounts	443	443	496
3020	Outlays (gross)	–433	–453	–508
3040	Recoveries of prior year unpaid obligations, unexpired	–1		
3041	Recoveries of prior year unpaid obligations, expired	–2		
3050	Unpaid obligations, end of year	75	65	53
	Memorandum (non-add) entries:			
3100	Obligated balance, start of year	68	75	65
3200	Obligated balance, end of year	75	65	53
	Budget authority and outlays, net:			
	Discretionary:			
4000	Budget authority, gross	443	443	496
	Outlays, gross:			
4010	Outlays from new discretionary authority	352	370	415
4011	Outlays from discretionary balances	81	83	93
4020	Outlays, gross (total)	433	453	508
4180	Budget authority, net (total)	443	443	496
4190	Outlays, net (total)	433	453	508

Federal Salaries and Expenses.—This account provides the Federal salaries and other expenses of the National Nuclear Security Administration (NNSA) mission and mission support staff. The Federal Salaries and Expenses appropriation allows for the creation of a well-managed, inclusive, responsive, and accountable organization through the strategic management of human capital and greater integration of budget and performance data. Program direction for Naval Reactors is within that program's account, and program direction for Secure Transportation Asset is within the Weapons Activities account.

Object Classification (in millions of dollars)

Identification code 089–0313–0–1–053		2021 actual	2022 est.	2023 est.
	Direct obligations:			
	Personnel compensation:			
11.1	Full-time permanent	245	245	251
11.3	Other than full-time permanent	2	2	3
11.5	Other personnel compensation	10	10	12
11.9	Total personnel compensation	257	257	266
12.1	Civilian personnel benefits	86	86	95
21.0	Travel and transportation of persons	2	2	2
23.1	Rental payments to GSA	1	1	1
23.3	Communications, utilities, and miscellaneous charges	1	1	2
25.1	Advisory and assistance services	33	33	41
25.2	Other services from non-Federal sources	6	6	9
25.3	Other goods and services from Federal sources	37	37	52
25.4	Operation and maintenance of facilities	18	18	24
26.0	Supplies and materials	1	1	2
32.0	Land and structures	1	1	2
99.9	Total new obligations, unexpired accounts	443	443	496

Employment Summary

Identification code 089–0313–0–1–053		2021 actual	2022 est.	2023 est.
1001	Direct civilian full-time equivalent employment	1,742	1,808	1,934
2001	Reimbursable civilian full-time equivalent employment	2	2	2

NAVAL REACTORS

For Department of Energy expenses necessary for naval reactors activities to carry out the Department of Energy Organization Act (42 U.S.C. 7101 et seq.), including the acquisition (by purchase, condemnation, construction, or otherwise) of real property, plant, and capital equipment, facilities, and facility expansion, $2,081,445,000, to remain available until expended: *Provided*, That of such amount, $58,525,000 shall be available until September 30, 2024, for program direction.

Note.—A full-year 2022 appropriation for this account was not enacted at the time the Budget was prepared; therefore, the Budget assumes this account is operating under the Continuing Appropriations Act, 2022 (Division A of Public Law 117–43, as amended). The amounts included for 2022 reflect the annualized level provided by the continuing resolution.

Program and Financing (in millions of dollars)

Identification code 089–0314–0–1–053		2021 actual	2022 est.	2023 est.
	Obligations by program activity:			
0001	Naval Reactors (Direct)	1,583	1,600	2,091
	Budgetary resources:			
	Unobligated balance:			
1000	Unobligated balance brought forward, Oct 1	15	30	23
1021	Recoveries of prior year unpaid obligations	5		
1070	Unobligated balance (total)	20	30	23
	Budget authority:			
	Appropriations, discretionary:			
1100	Appropriation	1,684	1,684	2,081
1120	Appropriations transferred to other acct [089–0319]	–91	–91	
1160	Appropriation, discretionary (total)	1,593	1,593	2,081
1930	Total budgetary resources available	1,613	1,623	2,104
	Memorandum (non-add) entries:			
1941	Unexpired unobligated balance, end of year	30	23	13
	Change in obligated balance:			
	Unpaid obligations:			
3000	Unpaid obligations, brought forward, Oct 1	1,077	1,186	1,202
3010	New obligations, unexpired accounts	1,583	1,600	2,091
3020	Outlays (gross)	–1,469	–1,584	–1,821
3040	Recoveries of prior year unpaid obligations, unexpired	–5		
3050	Unpaid obligations, end of year	1,186	1,202	1,472
	Memorandum (non-add) entries:			
3100	Obligated balance, start of year	1,077	1,186	1,202
3200	Obligated balance, end of year	1,186	1,202	1,472
	Budget authority and outlays, net:			
	Discretionary:			
4000	Budget authority, gross	1,593	1,593	2,081
	Outlays, gross:			
4010	Outlays from new discretionary authority	666	796	1,040
4011	Outlays from discretionary balances	803	788	781
4020	Outlays, gross (total)	1,469	1,584	1,821
4180	Budget authority, net (total)	1,593	1,593	2,081
4190	Outlays, net (total)	1,469	1,584	1,821

NAVAL REACTORS—Continued

Naval Reactors.—This account funds all naval nuclear propulsion work, beginning with reactor technology development and design, continuing through reactor operation and maintenance, and ending with final disposition of naval spent nuclear fuel. These efforts ensure the safe and reliable operation of reactor plants in nuclear-powered submarines and aircraft carriers, enable continued technology development for future generations of nuclear-powered warships, and supports recapitalization of laboratory facilities and environmental remediation of legacy responsibilities. Due to the crucial nature of nuclear reactor work, Naval Reactors is a centrally managed organization. Federal employees oversee and set policies/procedures for developing new reactor plants and operating existing nuclear plants and the facilities that support these plants.

Object Classification (in millions of dollars)

Identification code 089–0314–0–1–053		2021 actual	2022 est.	2023 est.
	Direct obligations:			
	Personnel compensation:			
11.1	Full-time permanent	34	34	37
11.3	Other than full-time permanent	1	1	2
11.5	Other personnel compensation	1	1	1
11.9	Total personnel compensation	36	36	40
12.1	Civilian personnel benefits	12	12	13
23.3	Communications, utilities, and miscellaneous charges	3	4	6
25.1	Advisory and assistance services	4	5	6
25.2	Other services from non-Federal sources	7	7	8
25.3	Other goods and services from Federal sources	4	4	5
25.4	Operation and maintenance of facilities	1,171	1,179	1,660
31.0	Equipment	10	10	....
32.0	Land and structures	335	342	352
41.0	Grants, subsidies, and contributions	1	1	1
99.9	Total new obligations, unexpired accounts	1,583	1,600	2,091

Employment Summary

Identification code 089–0314–0–1–053	2021 actual	2022 est.	2023 est.
1001 Direct civilian full-time equivalent employment	222	240	246

WEAPONS ACTIVITIES

For Department of Energy expenses, including the purchase, construction, and acquisition of plant and capital equipment and other incidental expenses necessary for atomic energy defense weapons activities in carrying out the purposes of the Department of Energy Organization Act (42 U.S.C. 7101 et seq.), including the acquisition or condemnation of any real property or any facility or for plant or facility acquisition, construction, or expansion, and the purchase of not to exceed one ambulance, for replacement only, $16,486,298,000, to remain available until expended: Provided, That of such amount, $130,070,000 shall be available until September 30, 2024, for program direction.

Note.—A full-year 2022 appropriation for this account was not enacted at the time the Budget was prepared; therefore, the Budget assumes this account is operating under the Continuing Appropriations Act, 2022 (Division A of Public Law 117–43, as amended). The amounts included for 2022 reflect the annualized level provided by the continuing resolution.

Program and Financing (in millions of dollars)

Identification code 089–0240–0–1–053		2021 actual	2022 est.	2023 est.
	Obligations by program activity:			
0001	Weapons Activities (Direct)	14,643	16,117	16,586
0300	Subtotal, Weapons Activities	14,643	16,117	16,586
0799	Total direct obligations	14,643	16,117	16,586
0810	Weapons Activities (Reimbursable)	2,249	2,055	2,122
0900	Total new obligations, unexpired accounts	16,892	18,172	18,708
	Budgetary resources:			
	Unobligated balance:			
1000	Unobligated balance brought forward, Oct 1	136	894	122
1021	Recoveries of prior year unpaid obligations	243	....	....
1033	Recoveries of prior year paid obligations	18	....	....
1070	Unobligated balance (total)	397	894	122
	Budget authority:			
	Appropriations, discretionary:			
1100	Appropriation	15,345	15,345	16,486
	Spending authority from offsetting collections, discretionary:			
1700	Collected	2,036	2,055	2,100
1701	Change in uncollected payments, Federal sources	8	....	....
1750	Spending auth from offsetting collections, disc (total)	2,044	2,055	2,100
1900	Budget authority (total)	17,389	17,400	18,586
1930	Total budgetary resources available	17,786	18,294	18,708
	Memorandum (non-add) entries:			
1941	Unexpired unobligated balance, end of year	894	122	....
	Change in obligated balance:			
	Unpaid obligations:			
3000	Unpaid obligations, brought forward, Oct 1	10,891	12,812	14,949
3010	New obligations, unexpired accounts	16,892	18,172	18,708
3020	Outlays (gross)	–14,728	–16,035	–16,877
3040	Recoveries of prior year unpaid obligations, unexpired	–243	....	....
3050	Unpaid obligations, end of year	12,812	14,949	16,780
	Uncollected payments:			
3060	Uncollected pymts, Fed sources, brought forward, Oct 1	–2,733	–2,741	–2,741
3070	Change in uncollected pymts, Fed sources, unexpired	–8	....	....
3090	Uncollected pymts, Fed sources, end of year	–2,741	–2,741	–2,741
	Memorandum (non-add) entries:			
3100	Obligated balance, start of year	8,158	10,071	12,208
3200	Obligated balance, end of year	10,071	12,208	14,039
	Budget authority and outlays, net:			
	Discretionary:			
4000	Budget authority, gross	17,389	17,400	18,586
	Outlays, gross:			
4010	Outlays from new discretionary authority	6,293	6,816	7,287
4011	Outlays from discretionary balances	8,435	9,219	9,590
4020	Outlays, gross (total)	14,728	16,035	16,877
	Offsets against gross budget authority and outlays:			
	Offsetting collections (collected) from:			
4030	Federal sources	–1,962	–1,951	–1,994
4033	Non-Federal sources	–92	–104	–106
4040	Offsets against gross budget authority and outlays (total)	–2,054	–2,055	–2,100
	Additional offsets against gross budget authority only:			
4050	Change in uncollected pymts, Fed sources, unexpired	–8	....	....
4053	Recoveries of prior year paid obligations, unexpired accounts	18	....	....
4060	Additional offsets against budget authority only (total)	10	....	....
4070	Budget authority, net (discretionary)	15,345	15,345	16,486
4080	Outlays, net (discretionary)	12,674	13,980	14,777
4180	Budget authority, net (total)	15,345	15,345	16,486
4190	Outlays, net (total)	12,674	13,980	14,777

Programs funded within the Weapons Activities appropriation support the Nation's current and future defense posture and its attendant nationwide infrastructure of science, technology, and engineering capabilities. Weapons Activities provides for the maintenance and refurbishment of nuclear weapons to continue sustained confidence in their safety, reliability, and performance; continued investment in scientific, engineering, and manufacturing capabilities to enable certification of the enduring nuclear weapons stockpile; and manufacture of nuclear weapon components. Weapons Activities also provides for continued maintenance and investment in the NNSA nuclear complex to be more responsive and cost effective. The major elements of the program include the following:

Stockpile Management.—Maintains a safe, secure, and effective nuclear weapons stockpile. Activities include extending the expected life of weapons; maintenance, surveillance, assessment, development, and program planning; providing safe and secure dismantlement of nuclear weapons and components; and providing sustainment of needed manufacturing capabilities and capacities, including process improvements and investments focused on increased efficiency of production operations. The FY 2023 Request also includes a new Nuclear Enterprise Assurance (NEA) subprogram, to prevent, detect, and mitigate adversarial subversion risks to the nuclear weapons stockpile and associated design, production, and testing capabilities.

DEPARTMENT OF ENERGY

Production Modernization.—Focuses on the production capabilities of nuclear weapons, including primaries, secondaries, and radiation cases, which are critical to weapon performance.

Stockpile Research, Technology, and Engineering.—Provides the foundation for science-based stockpile decisions, tools, and components; focuses on the most pressing investments the nuclear security enterprise requires to meet Department of Defense warhead needs and schedules; and enables assessment and certification capabilities used throughout the enterprise. Provides the knowledge and expertise needed to maintain confidence in the nuclear weapons stockpile without additional explosive nuclear testing.

Infrastructure and Operations.—Provides the funding required to operate and maintain NNSA facilities and support underlying infrastructure and capabilities at the level necessary to deliver mission results in a safe and secure manner. Modernizes NNSA infrastructure through recapitalization and line-item construction projects.

Defense Nuclear Security.—Provides protection for NNSA personnel, facilities, nuclear weapons, and materials from a full spectrum of threats, ranging from minor security incidents to acts of terrorism. Provides funding for key security program areas at all NNSA facilities.

Secure Transportation Asset.—Provides for the safe, secure transport of nuclear weapons, weapon components, and special nuclear materials to meet mission requirements. The Program Direction subprogram provides for the secure transportation workforce, including the Federal agents.

Information Technology and Cybersecurity.—Provides information technology (IT) and cybersecurity services and solutions for the Nuclear Security Enterprise to accomplish its mission goals and objectives. These services and solutions include commodity IT, unified communications, collaboration tools, mission applications, and cybersecurity oversight and tools.

Object Classification (in millions of dollars)

Identification code 089–0240–0–1–053		2021 actual	2022 est.	2023 est.
	Direct obligations:			
	Personnel compensation:			
11.1	Full-time permanent	49	51	54
11.5	Other personnel compensation	10	12	15
11.9	Total personnel compensation	59	63	69
12.1	Civilian personnel benefits	30	31	34
21.0	Travel and transportation of persons	6	6	8
23.1	Rental payments to GSA	52	53	56
23.3	Communications, utilities, and miscellaneous charges	22	22	24
25.1	Advisory and assistance services	316	376	389
25.2	Other services from non-Federal sources	574	622	680
25.3	Other goods and services from Federal sources	34	35	36
25.4	Operation and maintenance of facilities	10,486	11,731	11,384
25.5	Research and development contracts	127	144	154
25.6	Medical care	5	5	6
25.7	Operation and maintenance of equipment	4	4	6
26.0	Supplies and materials	13	13	15
31.0	Equipment	729	745	924
32.0	Land and structures	2,099	2,176	2,682
41.0	Grants, subsidies, and contributions	87	91	119
99.0	Direct obligations	14,643	16,117	16,586
99.0	Reimbursable obligations	2,249	2,055	2,122
99.9	Total new obligations, unexpired accounts	16,892	18,172	18,708

Employment Summary

Identification code 089–0240–0–1–053	2021 actual	2022 est.	2023 est.
1001 Direct civilian full-time equivalent employment	513	574	572

DEFENSE NUCLEAR NONPROLIFERATION

For Department of Energy expenses, including the purchase, construction, and acquisition of plant and capital equipment and other incidental expenses necessary for defense nuclear nonproliferation activities, in carrying out the purposes of the Department of Energy Organization Act (42 U.S.C. 7101 et seq.), including the ac-quisition or condemnation of any real property or any facility or for plant or facility acquisition, construction, or expansion, $2,346,257,000, to remain available until expended.

Note.—A full-year 2022 appropriation for this account was not enacted at the time the Budget was prepared; therefore, the Budget assumes this account is operating under the Continuing Appropriations Act, 2022 (Division A of Public Law 117–43, as amended). The amounts included for 2022 reflect the annualized level provided by the continuing resolution.

Program and Financing (in millions of dollars)

Identification code 089–0309–0–1–053		2021 actual	2022 est.	2023 est.
	Obligations by program activity:			
0001	Defense Nuclear Nonproliferation (Direct)	2,255	2,360	2,383
0100	Subtotal, obligations by program activity	2,255	2,360	2,383
0799	Total direct obligations	2,255	2,360	2,383
0801	Global material security	6		
0899	Total reimbursable obligations	6		
0900	Total new obligations, unexpired accounts	2,261	2,360	2,383
	Budgetary resources:			
	Unobligated balance:			
1000	Unobligated balance brought forward, Oct 1	451	467	367
1021	Recoveries of prior year unpaid obligations	19		
1033	Recoveries of prior year paid obligations	5		
1070	Unobligated balance (total)	475	467	367
	Budget authority:			
	Appropriations, discretionary:			
1100	Appropriation	2,260	2,260	2,346
1120	Appropriations transferred to other accts [089–0222]	–13		
1160	Appropriation, discretionary (total)	2,247	2,260	2,346
	Spending authority from offsetting collections, discretionary:			
1700	Collected	6		
1900	Budget authority (total)	2,253	2,260	2,346
1930	Total budgetary resources available	2,728	2,727	2,713
	Memorandum (non-add) entries:			
1941	Unexpired unobligated balance, end of year	467	367	330
	Change in obligated balance:			
	Unpaid obligations:			
3000	Unpaid obligations, brought forward, Oct 1	1,463	1,725	1,800
3010	New obligations, unexpired accounts	2,261	2,360	2,383
3020	Outlays (gross)	–1,980	–2,285	–2,254
3040	Recoveries of prior year unpaid obligations, unexpired	–19		
3050	Unpaid obligations, end of year	1,725	1,800	1,929
	Memorandum (non-add) entries:			
3100	Obligated balance, start of year	1,463	1,725	1,800
3200	Obligated balance, end of year	1,725	1,800	1,929
	Budget authority and outlays, net:			
	Discretionary:			
4000	Budget authority, gross	2,253	2,260	2,346
	Outlays, gross:			
4010	Outlays from new discretionary authority	933	1,085	1,126
4011	Outlays from discretionary balances	1,047	1,200	1,128
4020	Outlays, gross (total)	1,980	2,285	2,254
	Offsets against gross budget authority and outlays:			
	Offsetting collections (collected) from:			
4033	Non-Federal sources	–5		
4034	Offsetting governmental collections	–6		
4040	Offsets against gross budget authority and outlays (total)	–11		
	Additional offsets against gross budget authority only:			
4053	Recoveries of prior year paid obligations, unexpired accounts	5		
4070	Budget authority, net (discretionary)	2,247	2,260	2,346
4080	Outlays, net (discretionary)	1,969	2,285	2,254
4180	Budget authority, net (total)	2,247	2,260	2,346
4190	Outlays, net (total)	1,969	2,285	2,254

The Defense Nuclear Nonproliferation (DNN) and the Nuclear Counterterrorism and Incident Response (NCTIR) programs are central to the U.S. strategy to reduce global nuclear security risks. These two programs provide policy and technical leadership to prevent or limit the spread of materials, technology, and expertise related to weapons of mass destruction (WMD); develop technologies that detect the proliferation of WMD worldwide; secure or eliminate inventories of nuclear weapons-related materials and

DEFENSE NUCLEAR NONPROLIFERATION—Continued

infrastructure; and ensure rapid, effective responses to nuclear or radiological incidents and accidents domestically and overseas.

The major elements of the appropriation account include the following:

Material Management and Minimization (M^3).—M^3 programs reduce and, when possible, eliminate weapons-usable nuclear material around the world to achieve permanent threat reduction. This includes minimizing the civilian use of highly enriched uranium (HEU); removing or eliminating nuclear material internationally; and disposing of excess nuclear material in the United States.

Global Material Security (GMS).—GMS programs prevent terrorists and other actors from obtaining nuclear and radioactive materials to use in an improvised nuclear device or a radiological dispersal device by working domestically and with partner countries to improve the security of vulnerable materials and facilities and to build sustainable capacity to deter, detect, and investigate illicit trafficking of these materials. GMS works with countries in bilateral partnerships, and with and through multilateral partners such as the International Atomic Energy Agency (IAEA) and International Criminal Police Organization (Interpol).

Nonproliferation and Arms Control (NPAC).—NPAC programs strengthen nonproliferation and arms control regimes through technology and tool development combined with policy innovation and implementation to prevent proliferation, support peaceful nuclear uses, and enable detection, monitoring and verification missions. NPAC builds the capacity of the IAEA and partner countries to implement international safeguards obligations; leads domestic and international programs implementing U.S. export control obligations; supports the negotiation and implementation of agreements and associated monitoring regimes; and develops approaches and strategies to address emerging nonproliferation and arms control challenges and opportunities.

Defense Nuclear Nonproliferation Research and Development (DNN R&D).—DNN R&D drives the innovation of national and multi-lateral technical capabilities to detect nuclear detonations; foreign nuclear weapons activities; and the presence, movement, or diversion of special nuclear materials. The program also sustains and develops foundational nonproliferation technical competencies that ensure the technical agility needed to support a broad spectrum of U.S. nonproliferation missions and to anticipate threats and build the human capacity to support these missions into the future. DNN R&D leverages the unique facilities and scientific skills of the Department of Energy, academia, and industry to perform research, conduct technology demonstrations, develop prototypes, and produce and deliver sensors for integration into operational systems.

NNSA Bioassurance Program.—The NNSA Bioassurance Program establishes a national security R&D program to anticipate and detect global biological threats and broaden DOE's role in national biodefense. The NNSA contribution complements DOE's support of other departments and U.S. biodefense strategies and plans. The NNSA Bioassurance program will work in close coordination with the Office of Science (DOE/SC) by integrating NNSA's high-security work with DOE/SC's supported "open" science model. The Program will provide the full spectrum of bioassurance capabilities, informed by national security expertise that is drawn from parallel and analogue work on nuclear threats, risks, export controls and licensing, nonproliferation, detection, and verification.

Nonproliferation Construction.—The Nonproliferation Construction Program supports the construction of projects for the dilute and dispose strategy to fulfill the United States' commitment to dispose of 34 metric tons of surplus U.S. weapon-grade plutonium and remove plutonium from the state of South Carolina. The request will complete the final design review and continue the activities required to achieve CD-2/3, *Approval of Performance Baseline and Start of Construction*, to initiate construction on the Surplus Plutonium Disposition (SPD) project. Using available prior year balances, physical termination activities for the Mixed Oxide Fuel Fabrication project were completed in FY 2021 and closeout activities will be completed in FY 2022.

Nuclear Counterterrorism and Incident Response (NCTIR).—The NCTIR Program applies the unique technical expertise of NNSA's nuclear security enterprise to prepare for, prevent, respond to, mitigate, and recover from nuclear or radiological incidents and accidents worldwide. To that end, NCTIR provides scientific understanding of nuclear threat devices, including potential terrorist and proliferant state nuclear capabilities; informs U.S. and international threat reduction policies and regulations; sustains Nuclear Emergency Support Team (NEST) readiness to respond to nuclear and radiological incidents and accidents at home and overseas; provides targeted training to domestic and international partners on nuclear and radiological emergency preparedness and response; and delivers expert analysis and technical capabilities to support national counterproliferation efforts. NCTIR also provides both the structure and processes to ensure a comprehensive and integrated approach to emergency management and continuity of operations, thereby safeguarding the health and safety of workers and the public, protecting the environment, and enhancing the resilience of the Department and the Nation.

Object Classification (in millions of dollars)

Identification code 089–0309–0–1–053		2021 actual	2022 est.	2023 est.
	Direct obligations:			
25.1	Advisory and assistance services	161	161	161
25.2	Other services from non-Federal sources	112	112	112
25.3	Other goods and services from Federal sources	7	7	7
25.4	Operation and maintenance of facilities	1,724	1,825	1,848
25.5	Research and development contracts	1	1	1
25.7	Operation and maintenance of equipment	1	1	1
31.0	Equipment	91	91	91
32.0	Land and structures	139	139	139
41.0	Grants, subsidies, and contributions	19	19	19
99.0	Direct obligations	2,255	2,356	2,379
99.0	Reimbursable obligations	6	4	4
99.9	Total new obligations, unexpired accounts	2,261	2,360	2,383

ENVIRONMENTAL AND OTHER DEFENSE ACTIVITIES

Federal Funds

DEFENSE ENVIRONMENTAL CLEANUP

(INCLUDING TRANSFER OF FUNDS)

For Department of Energy expenses, including the purchase, construction, and acquisition of plant and capital equipment and other expenses necessary for atomic energy defense environmental cleanup activities in carrying out the purposes of the Department of Energy Organization Act (42 U.S.C. 7101 et seq.), including the acquisition or condemnation of any real property or any facility or for plant or facility acquisition, construction, or expansion, $6,914,532,000, to remain available until expended, of which $417,000,000 shall be transferred to the "Uranium Enrichment Decontamination and Decommissioning Fund": Provided, That of such amount, $317,002,000 shall be available until September 30, 2024, for program direction.

Note.—A full-year 2022 appropriation for this account was not enacted at the time the Budget was prepared; therefore, the Budget assumes this account is operating under the Continuing Appropriations Act, 2022 (Division A of Public Law 117–43, as amended). The amounts included for 2022 reflect the annualized level provided by the continuing resolution.

Program and Financing (in millions of dollars)

Identification code 089–0251–0–1–053		2021 actual	2022 est.	2023 est.
	Obligations by program activity:			
0001	Closure Sites	4	5	4
0002	Hanford Site	954	926	818
0003	River Protection - Tank Farm	788	784	806
0004	River Protection - Waste Treatment Plant	906	861	799
0006	Idaho	402	434	379
0007	NNSA Sites	303	328	407
0008	Oak Ridge	442	475	487
0009	Savannah River	1,503	1,532	1,572
0010	Waste Isolation Pilot Plant	406	413	456
0011	Program Support	37	13	103
0012	Safeguards & Security	321	321	310
0013	Technology Development & Demonstration	32	30	25
0014	Program Direction	300	289	317

0015	UED&D Fund Contribution			417
0020	SPRU		15	15
0900	Total new obligations, unexpired accounts	6,398	6,426	6,915
	Budgetary resources:			
	Unobligated balance:			
1000	Unobligated balance brought forward, Oct 1	451	548	560
1021	Recoveries of prior year unpaid obligations	38	12	12
1033	Recoveries of prior year paid obligations	32		
1070	Unobligated balance (total)	521	560	572
	Budget authority:			
	Appropriations, discretionary:			
1100	Appropriation	6,426	6,426	6,915
1120	Appropriations transferred to other accts [089–0222]	–1		
1160	Appropriation, discretionary (total)	6,425	6,426	6,915
1930	Total budgetary resources available	6,946	6,986	7,487
	Memorandum (non-add) entries:			
1941	Unexpired unobligated balance, end of year	548	560	572
	Change in obligated balance:			
	Unpaid obligations:			
3000	Unpaid obligations, brought forward, Oct 1	3,031	3,278	2,516
3010	New obligations, unexpired accounts	6,398	6,426	6,915
3020	Outlays (gross)	–6,111	–7,176	–7,529
3040	Recoveries of prior year unpaid obligations, unexpired	–38	–12	–12
3041	Recoveries of prior year unpaid obligations, expired	–2		
3050	Unpaid obligations, end of year	3,278	2,516	1,890
	Memorandum (non-add) entries:			
3100	Obligated balance, start of year	3,031	3,278	2,516
3200	Obligated balance, end of year	3,278	2,516	1,890
	Budget authority and outlays, net:			
	Discretionary:			
4000	Budget authority, gross	6,425	6,426	6,915
	Outlays, gross:			
4010	Outlays from new discretionary authority	3,493	4,498	4,966
4011	Outlays from discretionary balances	2,618	2,678	2,563
4020	Outlays, gross (total)	6,111	7,176	7,529
	Offsets against gross budget authority and outlays:			
	Offsetting collections (collected) from:			
4033	Non-Federal sources	–32		
4040	Offsets against gross budget authority and outlays (total)	–32		
	Additional offsets against gross budget authority only:			
4053	Recoveries of prior year paid obligations, unexpired accounts	32		
4060	Additional offsets against budget authority only (total)	32		
4070	Budget authority, net (discretionary)	6,425	6,426	6,915
4080	Outlays, net (discretionary)	6,079	7,176	7,529
4180	Budget authority, net (total)	6,425	6,426	6,915
4190	Outlays, net (total)	6,079	7,176	7,529

The Defense Environmental Cleanup program is responsible for protecting human health and the environment by identifying and reducing risks, as well as managing waste and facilities, at sites where the Department carried out defense-related nuclear research and production activities. Those activities resulted in radioactive, hazardous, and mixed-waste contamination requiring remediation, stabilization, decontamination and decommissioning, or some other type of cleanup action. The Budget displays the cleanup program by site and activity.

Closure Sites.—Funds post-closure administration costs after the physical completion of cleanup, including costs for contract closeout and litigation support.

Hanford Site.—Funds cleanup and environmental restoration to protect the Columbia River and surrounding communities. The Hanford site cleanup is managed by two Environmental Management (EM) site offices: the Richland Operations Office and the Office of River Protection.

The Richland Office is responsible for cleanup activities on most of the geographic area making up the Hanford site. The primary cleanup focus is decontamination and decommissioning legacy facilities and characterizing and treating contaminated groundwater.

The Office of River Protection is responsible for the safe storage, retrieval, treatment, immobilization, and disposal of approximately 56 million gallons of radioactive waste stored in 177 underground tanks. It is also responsible for related operation, maintenance, engineering, and construction activities, including those connected to the Waste Treatment and Immobilization Plant being built to solidify the liquid tank waste in a glass form that can be safely stored.

Idaho.—Funds retrieval, treatment, and disposition of nuclear and hazardous wastes and spent nuclear fuel, and legacy site cleanup activities.

NNSA Sites.—Funds the safe and efficient cleanup of the environmental legacy of past operations at National Nuclear Security Administration (NNSA) sites including Nevada National Security Site, Sandia National Laboratories, Lawrence Livermore National Laboratory, Los Alamos National Laboratory and the Separations Process Research Unit. The cleanup strategy follows a risk-informed approach that focuses first on those soil and groundwater contaminant plumes and sources that are the greatest contributors to risk. The overall goal is first to ensure that risks to the public and workers are controlled, then to clean up soil and groundwater using a risk-informed methodology. NNSA is responsible for long-term stewardship of its sites after physical cleanup is completed. Los Alamos legacy cleanup is managed by the EM Los Alamos field office. Funding is included to support the deactivation and decommissioning (D&D) of specific high-risk excess facilities by the Environmental Management program for Lawrence Livermore and Los Alamos National Laboratories.

Oak Ridge.—Funds defense-related cleanup of the three facilities that make up the Oak Ridge site: the East Tennessee Technology Park, the Oak Ridge National Laboratory, and the Y-12 Plant. The overall cleanup strategy is based on surface water considerations, encompassing five distinct watersheds that feed the adjacent Clinch River.

Savannah River Site.—Funds the safe stabilization, treatment, and disposition of legacy nuclear materials, spent nuclear fuel, and waste at the Savannah River site. Key activities include operating the Defense Waste Processing Facility, which is solidifying the high activity liquid waste contained in underground storage tanks, and operation of the Salt Waste Processing Facility, which separates various tank waste components and treats and disposes the low activity liquid waste stream.

Waste Isolation Pilot Plant.—Funds the world's first permitted deep geologic repository for the permanent disposal of radioactive waste, and the Nation's only disposal site for defense-generated transuranic waste. The Waste Isolation Pilot Plant, managed by the Carlsbad Field Office, is an operating facility, supporting the disposal of transuranic waste from waste generator and storage sites across the DOE complex. The Waste Isolation Pilot Plant is crucial to the Department of Energy (DOE) completing its cleanup and closure mission.

Program Direction.—Funds the Federal workforce responsible for the overall direction and administrative support of the EM program, including both Headquarters and field personnel.

Program Support.—Funds management and direction for various cross-cutting EM and DOE initiatives such as science, technology, engineering, and mathematics activities at Minority Serving Institutions and investments in historically underserved communities to support program needs, intergovernmental activities, and analyses and integration activities across DOE in a consistent, responsible, and efficient manner.

Safeguards and Security.—Funds activities to protect against unauthorized access, theft, diversion, loss of custody or destruction of DOE assets, and hostile acts that could cause adverse impacts to fundamental national security or the health and safety of DOE and contractor employees, the public or the environment.

Technology Development and Deployment.—Funds projects managed through Headquarters to address the immediate, near- and long-term technology needs identified by the EM sites, enabling them to accelerate their cleanup schedules, treat orphaned wastes, improve worker safety, and provide technical foundations for the sites' cleanup decisions. These projects focus on maturing and deploying the technologies necessary to accelerate tank waste processing, treatment, and waste loading.

DEFENSE ENVIRONMENTAL CLEANUP—Continued

Object Classification (in millions of dollars)

Identification code 089–0251–0–1–053	2021 actual	2022 est.	2023 est.
Direct obligations:			
Personnel compensation:			
11.1 Full-time permanent	158	159	171
11.3 Other than full-time permanent	2	2	2
11.5 Other personnel compensation	5	5	5
11.9 Total personnel compensation	165	166	178
12.1 Civilian personnel benefits	59	59	64
21.0 Travel and transportation of persons	1	1	1
23.1 Rental payments to GSA	10	10	11
23.2 Rental payments to others	1	1	1
23.3 Communications, utilities, and miscellaneous charges	14	14	15
25.1 Advisory and assistance services	825	829	892
25.2 Other services from non-Federal sources	439	441	475
25.3 Other goods and services from Federal sources	47	47	51
25.4 Operation and maintenance of facilities	3,593	3,609	3,884
25.5 Research and development contracts	4	4	4
25.6 Medical care	16	16	17
25.7 Operation and maintenance of equipment	2	2	2
26.0 Supplies and materials	1	1	1
31.0 Equipment	99	99	107
32.0 Land and structures	1,067	1,072	1,153
41.0 Grants, subsidies, and contributions	55	55	59
99.9 Total new obligations, unexpired accounts	6,398	6,426	6,915

Employment Summary

Identification code 089–0251–0–1–053	2021 actual	2022 est.	2023 est.
1001 Direct civilian full-time equivalent employment	1,213	1,275	1,375

OTHER DEFENSE ACTIVITIES

For Department of Energy expenses, including the purchase, construction, and acquisition of plant and capital equipment and other expenses, necessary for atomic energy defense, other defense activities, and classified activities, in carrying out the purposes of the Department of Energy Organization Act (42 U.S.C. 7101 et seq.), including the acquisition or condemnation of any real property or any facility or for plant or facility acquisition, construction, or expansion, $978,351,000, to remain available until expended: Provided, That of such amount, $331,781,000 shall be available until September 30, 2024, for program direction.

Note.—A full-year 2022 appropriation for this account was not enacted at the time the Budget was prepared; therefore, the Budget assumes this account is operating under the Continuing Appropriations Act, 2022 (Division A of Public Law 117–43, as amended). The amounts included for 2022 reflect the annualized level provided by the continuing resolution.

Program and Financing (in millions of dollars)

Identification code 089–0243–0–1–999	2021 actual	2022 est.	2023 est.
Obligations by program activity:			
0001 Other Defense Activities (Direct)	954	920	988
0100 Subtotal, Direct program activities	954	920	988
0799 Total direct obligations	954	920	988
0810 Other Defense Activities (Reimbursable)	2,008	2,008	2,011
0819 Reimbursable program activities, subtotal	2,008	2,008	2,011
0900 Total new obligations, unexpired accounts	2,962	2,928	2,999
Budgetary resources:			
Unobligated balance:			
1000 Unobligated balance brought forward, Oct 1	56	61	20
1010 Unobligated balance transfer to other accts [047–0616]	....	–1	....
1021 Recoveries of prior year unpaid obligations	105	....	....
1033 Recoveries of prior year paid obligations	1	....	....
1070 Unobligated balance (total)	162	60	20
Budget authority:			
Appropriations, discretionary:			
1100 Appropriation	920	920	978
Spending authority from offsetting collections, discretionary:			
1700 Collected	1,818	1,968	2,011
1701 Change in uncollected payments, Federal sources	123	....	....
1750 Spending auth from offsetting collections, disc (total)	1,941	1,968	2,011
1900 Budget authority (total)	2,861	2,888	2,989
1930 Total budgetary resources available	3,023	2,948	3,009
Memorandum (non-add) entries:			
1941 Unexpired unobligated balance, end of year	61	20	10
Change in obligated balance:			
Unpaid obligations:			
3000 Unpaid obligations, brought forward, Oct 1	2,052	2,124	2,166
3010 New obligations, unexpired accounts	2,962	2,928	2,999
3020 Outlays (gross)	–2,779	–2,886	–3,521
3040 Recoveries of prior year unpaid obligations, unexpired	–105	....	....
3041 Recoveries of prior year unpaid obligations, expired	–6	....	....
3050 Unpaid obligations, end of year	2,124	2,166	1,644
Uncollected payments:			
3060 Uncollected pymts, Fed sources, brought forward, Oct 1	–1,563	–1,603	–1,603
3070 Change in uncollected pymts, Fed sources, unexpired	–123	....	....
3071 Change in uncollected pymts, Fed sources, expired	83	....	....
3090 Uncollected pymts, Fed sources, end of year	–1,603	–1,603	–1,603
Memorandum (non-add) entries:			
3100 Obligated balance, start of year	489	521	563
3200 Obligated balance, end of year	521	563	41
Budget authority and outlays, net:			
Discretionary:			
4000 Budget authority, gross	2,861	2,888	2,989
Outlays, gross:			
4010 Outlays from new discretionary authority	1,207	1,517	1,579
4011 Outlays from discretionary balances	1,572	1,369	1,942
4020 Outlays, gross (total)	2,779	2,886	3,521
Offsets against gross budget authority and outlays:			
Offsetting collections (collected) from:			
4030 Federal sources	–1,793	–1,887	–1,928
4033 Non-Federal sources	–104	–81	–83
4040 Offsets against gross budget authority and outlays (total)	–1,897	–1,968	–2,011
Additional offsets against gross budget authority only:			
4050 Change in uncollected pymts, Fed sources, unexpired	–123	....	....
4052 Offsetting collections credited to expired accounts	78	....	....
4053 Recoveries of prior year paid obligations, unexpired accounts	1	....	....
4060 Additional offsets against budget authority only (total)	–44	....	....
4070 Budget authority, net (discretionary)	920	920	978
4080 Outlays, net (discretionary)	882	918	1,510
4180 Budget authority, net (total)	920	920	978
4190 Outlays, net (total)	882	918	1,510

Environment, Health, Safety and Security Mission Support.—The program supports the Department's health, safety, environment, and security programs to enhance productivity while maintaining the highest standards of safe operation, protection of national assets, and environmental sustainability. The program functions include: policy and guidance development and technical assistance; analysis of health, safety, environment, and security performance; nuclear safety; domestic and international health studies; medical screening programs for former workers; Energy Employee Occupational Illness Compensation Program Act support; quality assurance programs; interface with the Defense Nuclear Facilities Safety Board; national security information programs; and security for the Department's facilities and personnel in the National Capital Area.

Enterprise Assessments.—The program supports the Department's independent assessments of security, cybersecurity, emergency management, and environment, safety and health performance; enforcement of worker safety and health, nuclear safety; and classified information security regulations; and implementation of security and safety professional development and training programs.

Specialized Security Activities.—The program supports national security related analyses requiring highly specialized skills and capabilities.

Legacy Management—The program supports long-term stewardship activities (e.g., groundwater monitoring, disposal cell maintenance, records management, asset management, community outreach and management of natural resources) at sites where active remediation has been completed. In FY 2023, the program will also support strengthening Environmental Justice activities. Lastly, Legacy Management supports post-retirement benefits for former contractor employees.

DEPARTMENT OF ENERGY

Hearings and Appeals.—The Office of Hearings and Appeals adjudicates personnel security cases, as well as whistleblower reprisal complaints filed by DOE contractor employees. The office is the appeal authority in various other areas, including Freedom of Information Act and Privacy Act appeals. In addition, the office decides requests for exception from DOE orders, rules, regulations, and is responsible for the DOE's alternative dispute resolution function.

Defense-Related Administrative Support.—Obligations are included for defense-related administrative support that serves to offset costs attributable to the defense-related programs within the Department of Energy that utilize the department-wide services funded by the Departmental Administration account. These include accounting and information technology department-wide services.

Object Classification (in millions of dollars)

Identification code 089–0243–0–1–999		2021 actual	2022 est.	2023 est.
	Direct obligations:			
	Personnel compensation:			
11.1	Full-time permanent	122	125	125
11.3	Other than full-time permanent	2	2	2
11.5	Other personnel compensation	5	5	5
11.9	Total personnel compensation	129	132	132
12.1	Civilian personnel benefits	45	46	46
21.0	Travel and transportation of persons	1	1	1
23.1	Rental payments to GSA	1	1	1
23.2	Rental payments to others	2	2	2
23.3	Communications, utilities, and miscellaneous charges	7	7	7
25.1	Advisory and assistance services	348	310	360
25.2	Other services from non-Federal sources	56	56	56
25.3	Other goods and services from Federal sources	44	44	44
25.4	Operation and maintenance of facilities	276	276	294
25.7	Operation and maintenance of equipment	4	4	4
26.0	Supplies and materials	1	1	1
31.0	Equipment	10	10	10
32.0	Land and structures	3	3	3
41.0	Grants, subsidies, and contributions	27	27	27
99.0	Direct obligations	954	920	988
99.0	Reimbursable obligations	2,008	2,008	2,011
99.9	Total new obligations, unexpired accounts	2,962	2,928	2,999

Employment Summary

Identification code 089–0243–0–1–999	2021 actual	2022 est.	2023 est.
1001 Direct civilian full-time equivalent employment	871	871	871

DEFENSE NUCLEAR WASTE DISPOSAL

Program and Financing (in millions of dollars)

Identification code 089–0244–0–1–053		2021 actual	2022 est.	2023 est.
	Obligations by program activity:			
0001	Defense Nuclear Waste Disposal (Direct)	1	1	
	Budgetary resources:			
	Unobligated balance:			
1000	Unobligated balance brought forward, Oct 1	2	1	
1930	Total budgetary resources available	2	1	
	Memorandum (non-add) entries:			
1941	Unexpired unobligated balance, end of year	1		
	Change in obligated balance:			
	Unpaid obligations:			
3000	Unpaid obligations, brought forward, Oct 1	3	3	3
3010	New obligations, unexpired accounts	1	1	
3020	Outlays (gross)	–1	–1	–1
3050	Unpaid obligations, end of year	3	3	2
	Memorandum (non-add) entries:			
3100	Obligated balance, start of year	3	3	3
3200	Obligated balance, end of year	3	3	2
	Budget authority and outlays, net:			
	Discretionary:			
	Outlays, gross:			
4011	Outlays from discretionary balances	1	1	1
4180	Budget authority, net (total)			
4190	Outlays, net (total)	1	1	1

The Defense Nuclear Waste Disposal appropriation was established by the Congress as part of the 1993 Energy and Water Development Appropriation (P.L. 102–377), in lieu of payment from the Department of Energy (DOE) into the Nuclear Waste Fund for activities related to the disposal of defense high-level waste from DOE's atomic energy defense activities.

Object Classification (in millions of dollars)

Identification code 089–0244–0–1–053		2021 actual	2022 est.	2023 est.
	Direct obligations:			
25.1	Advisory and assistance services		1	
25.2	Other services from non-Federal sources	1		
99.9	Total new obligations, unexpired accounts	1	1	

ENERGY PROGRAMS

Federal Funds

SCIENCE

For Department of Energy expenses including the purchase, construction, and acquisition of plant and capital equipment, and other expenses necessary for science activities in carrying out the purposes of the Department of Energy Organization Act (42 U.S.C. 7101 et seq.), including the acquisition or condemnation of any real property or any facility or for plant or facility acquisition, construction, or expansion, and purchase of not more than 35 passenger motor vehicles, including one ambulance, for replacement only, $7,799,211,000, to remain available until expended: Provided, That of such amount, $211,211,000 shall be available until September 30, 2024, for program direction.

Note.—A full-year 2022 appropriation for this account was not enacted at the time the Budget was prepared; therefore, the Budget assumes this account is operating under the Continuing Appropriations Act, 2022 (Division A of Public Law 117–43, as amended). The amounts included for 2022 reflect the annualized level provided by the continuing resolution.

Program and Financing (in millions of dollars)

Identification code 089–0222–0–1–251		2021 actual	2022 est.	2023 est.
	Obligations by program activity:			
0001	Basic Energy Sciences	2,221	2,245	2,420
0002	Advanced Scientific Computing Research	985	1,015	1,069
0003	Biological and Environmental Research	728	753	904
0004	High Energy Physics	1,028	1,029	1,122
0005	Nuclear Physics	681	635	739
0006	Fusion Energy Sciences	649	672	723
0007	Science Laboratories Infrastructure	263	240	255
0008	Science Program Direction	193	192	211
0009	Workforce Development for Teachers and Scientists	29	29	41
0010	Safeguards and Security	121	121	190
0011	Small Business Innovation Research	284		
0012	Small Business Technology Transfer	38		
0013	Isotope R&D and Production		78	98
0014	Accelerator R&D and Production		17	27
0799	Total direct obligations	7,220	7,026	7,799
0801	Science (Reimbursable)	622	624	624
0900	Total new obligations, unexpired accounts	7,842	7,650	8,423
	Budgetary resources:			
	Unobligated balance:			
1000	Unobligated balance brought forward, Oct 1	66	59	49
1021	Recoveries of prior year unpaid obligations	93		
1070	Unobligated balance (total)	159	59	49
	Budget authority:			
	Appropriations, discretionary:			
1100	Appropriation	7,026	7,026	7,799
1121	Appropriations transferred from other acct [089–0319]	19		
1121	Appropriations transferred from other acct [089–0309]	13		
1121	Appropriations transferred from other acct [089–0213]	18		
1121	Appropriations transferred from other acct [089–0251]	1		
1121	Appropriations transferred from other acct [089–2250]	1		

SCIENCE—Continued
Program and Financing—Continued

Identification code 089–0222–0–1–251		2021 actual	2022 est.	2023 est.
1121	Appropriations transferred from other acct [089–0321]	80		
1121	Appropriations transferred from other acct [089–0318]	5		
1160	Appropriation, discretionary (total)	7,163	7,026	7,799
	Spending authority from offsetting collections, discretionary:			
1700	Collected	452	614	628
1701	Change in uncollected payments, Federal sources	127		
1750	Spending auth from offsetting collections, disc (total)	579	614	628
1900	Budget authority (total)	7,742	7,640	8,427
1930	Total budgetary resources available	7,901	7,699	8,476
	Memorandum (non-add) entries:			
1941	Unexpired unobligated balance, end of year	59	49	53
	Change in obligated balance:			
	Unpaid obligations:			
3000	Unpaid obligations, brought forward, Oct 1	8,327	8,810	7,877
3010	New obligations, unexpired accounts	7,842	7,650	8,423
3020	Outlays (gross)	−7,265	−8,583	−8,762
3040	Recoveries of prior year unpaid obligations, unexpired	−93		
3041	Recoveries of prior year unpaid obligations, expired	−1		
3050	Unpaid obligations, end of year	8,810	7,877	7,538
	Uncollected payments:			
3060	Uncollected pymts, Fed sources, brought forward, Oct 1	−519	−562	−562
3070	Change in uncollected pymts, Fed sources, unexpired	−127		
3071	Change in uncollected pymts, Fed sources, expired	84		
3090	Uncollected pymts, Fed sources, end of year	−562	−562	−562
	Memorandum (non-add) entries:			
3100	Obligated balance, start of year	7,808	8,248	7,315
3200	Obligated balance, end of year	8,248	7,315	6,976
	Budget authority and outlays, net:			
	Discretionary:			
4000	Budget authority, gross	7,742	7,640	8,427
	Outlays, gross:			
4010	Outlays from new discretionary authority	2,257	2,691	2,967
4011	Outlays from discretionary balances	5,008	5,892	5,795
4020	Outlays, gross (total)	7,265	8,583	8,762
	Offsets against gross budget authority and outlays:			
	Offsetting collections (collected) from:			
4030	Federal sources	−362	−377	−388
4033	Non-Federal sources	−174	−237	−240
4040	Offsets against gross budget authority and outlays (total)	−536	−614	−628
	Additional offsets against gross budget authority only:			
4050	Change in uncollected pymts, Fed sources, unexpired	−127		
4052	Offsetting collections credited to expired accounts	84		
4060	Additional offsets against budget authority only (total)	−43		
4070	Budget authority, net (discretionary)	7,163	7,026	7,799
4080	Outlays, net (discretionary)	6,729	7,969	8,134
4180	Budget authority, net (total)	7,163	7,026	7,799
4190	Outlays, net (total)	6,729	7,969	8,134

The Office of Science (SC) is the nation's largest Federal supporter of basic research in the physical sciences. The SC portfolio has two principal thrusts: direct support of scientific research and direct support of the design, development, construction, and operation of unique, open-access scientific user facilities. SC initiates three new research initiatives to include Energy Earthshots; Funding for Accelerated, Inclusive Research (FAIR); and Accelerate Innovations in Emerging Technologies (Accelerate). The Energy Earthshots initiative will support both small group awards and larger center awards through the Energy Earthshot Research Centers. These centers will bring together multi-investigator, multi-disciplinary teams to address key research challenges at the interface between basic research and applied research and development activities. The FAIR initiative, will target efforts to increase participation and retention of individuals from underrepresented groups in SC research activities. The Accelerate initiative will support scientific research to accelerate the transition of science advances to energy technologies. The request also supports ongoing investments in priority areas including clean energy, microelectronics, critical materials, quantum information science (QIS), artificial intelligence (AI) and machine learning (ML), and exascale computing.

Advanced Scientific Computing Research.—The Advanced Scientific Computing Research (ASCR) program supports research in applied mathematics and computer science; delivers the most advanced computational scientific applications in partnership with disciplinary science; advances computing and networking capabilities; and develops future generations of computing hardware and tools for science, in partnership with the research community and U.S. industry. The strategy to accomplish this has three thrusts: 1) developing, deploying, and maintaining world-class computing and network facilities for science; 2) advancing research in applied mathematics, computer science and advanced networking; and 3) partnering with other DOE and SC programs to advance the use of its high performance computers to drive scientific advances for the Nation in areas such as clean energy and earth systems modeling. The program supports the development, maintenance, and operation of large high-performance computing and network facilities, including the Leadership Computing Facilities at Oak Ridge and Argonne National Laboratories, the National Energy Research Scientific Computing Facility at Lawrence Berkeley National Laboratory, and the Energy Sciences Network.

SC and the National Nuclear Security Administration (NNSA) continue to partner on the Department's Exascale Computing Initiative (ECI) to overcome key exascale challenges in parallelism, energy efficiency, and reliability, with deployment of the Nation's first exascale system in calendar year 2021 and additional exascale systems in calendar years 2022 and 2023. The ECI focuses on delivering advanced simulation through an exascale-capable computing program, emphasizing sustained performance in science and national security mission applications and increased convergence between exascale, AI, and large-data analytic computing.

Basic Energy Sciences.—The Basic Energy Sciences (BES) program supports fundamental research to understand, predict, and ultimately control matter and energy at the electronic, atomic, and molecular levels to provide the foundations for new energy technologies and to support the Department of Energy (DOE) missions in energy, environment, and national security. The research disciplines that BES supports—condensed matter and materials physics, chemistry, geosciences, and aspects of biosciences are those that discover new materials and design new chemical processes that touch virtually every important aspect of energy resources, production, conversion, transmission, storage, efficiency, and waste mitigation.

BES also manages a research portfolio in accelerator physics, x-ray and neutron detectors, and x-ray-optics to explore technology options for developing the next generations of x-ray and neutron sources. On behalf of DOE, BES manages the DOE Established Program to Stimulate Competitive Research (EPSCoR), which supports early-stage energy research in U.S. states and territories that are historically under-represented in federally-supported research.

BES supports twelve scientific user facilities consisting of a complementary set of intense x-ray sources, neutron sources, and research centers for nanoscale science. BES facilities probe materials and chemical systems with ultrahigh spatial, temporal, and energy resolutions to investigate the critical functions of matter and tackle some of the most challenging science questions and urgent national priorities such as the fight against COVID-19. These facilities undergo continual development and upgrade of capabilities, including fabricating new X-ray and neutron experimental stations, improving core facilities, and providing new stand-alone instruments and capabilities. BES also manages construction projects to build new or upgrade existing facilities to provide world-leading tools and instruments to the scientific community and maintain U.S. leadership in the physical sciences.

Biological and Environmental Research.—The Biological and Environmental Research (BER) program supports fundamental research to understand complex biological, biogeochemical, and physical principles of natural systems at scales extending from the genome of microbes and plants to the environmental and ecological processes at the scale of the planet

Earth. BER's support of basic research will contribute to a future of stable, reliable, and resilient energy sources and infrastructures, that will lead to climate solutions, strengthen economic prosperity and assure environmental justice. BER research in biological systems science uses approaches such as genome sequencing, secure biodesign, proteomics, metabolomics, structural biology, and high-resolution imaging and characterization. Integration of this experimental biological information into computational models for iterative testing and validation advances a predictive understanding of biological systems for use in secure, clean, affordable, and reliable energy for adaptation to industry. New efforts in clean energy bio-based materials and foundational bioenergy research underpin new biotechnology and the bioeconomy.

BER research in Earth and environmental systems science is focused on scientific analysis and modeling of the sensitivity and uncertainty of Earth system predictions to atmospheric, cryospheric, oceanic, and biogeochemical processes, with continued support of the Energy Exascale Earth System Model. New Urban Integrated Field Laboratories combine modeling and observations of emerging energy technologies in urban regions, enabling the evaluation of the societal and environmental impacts of current and future energy policies. Augmented planning and implementation continues for a Climate Resilience Center effort, facilitating translations of BER investments in foundational climate research into actionable solutions for impacted communities and addressing the Administration priorities involving climate solutions and environmental justice. Operations and equipment refresh continue at the three BER scientific user facilities: the Joint Genome Institute, the Atmospheric Radiation Measurement Research Facility, and the Environmental Molecular Sciences Laboratory.

Fusion Energy Sciences.—The Fusion Energy Sciences (FES) program mission is to expand the fundamental understanding of matter at very high temperatures and densities and to build the scientific foundation needed to develop a fusion energy source. This is accomplished through the study of plasma, the fourth state of matter, and how it interacts with its surroundings. High-temperature fusion plasmas at hundreds of millions of degrees are being exploited in the laboratory to become the basis for a future clean energy source. Once developed, fusion energy will provide a clean energy source that is well-suited for on- demand, dispatchable electricity production, supplementing intermittent renewables and fission.

The FES program has four elements: 1) Burning Plasma Science: Foundations—The behavior of magnetically confined fusion plasmas is experimentally explored on the DIII-D National Fusion Facility and the National Spherical Torus Experiment-Upgrade (currently under repair), which are national scientific user facilities. Fusion theory and simulation activities predict and interpret the complex behavior of magnetically-confined plasmas. This element also supports partnerships with the private sector through the Innovation Network for Fusion Energy (INFUSE) program and a new milestone-based cost-share fusion enterprise program. In addition, FES will initiate an inertial fusion energy science and technology program; 2) Burning Plasma Science: Long Pulse—U.S. scientists take advantage of international partnerships to conduct research on overseas tokamaks and stellarators with unique capabilities. The element also supports research to develop the nuclear science and novel materials that can harness the power from a burning plasma and withstand the extreme fusion environment; 3) Burning Plasma Science: High Power—This element supports the U.S. Contributions to the International Thermonuclear Experimental Reactor (ITER) Project, the world's first burning plasma experiment, and the initiation of an ITER Research program; and 4) Discovery Plasma Science—This element supports research in Plasma Science & Technology, including plasma astrophysics, high-energy-density laboratory plasmas (HEDLP), and low-temperature plasmas. Besides ITER, FES also manages construction projects to build new or upgrade existing facilities to provide world-leading tools and instruments to the scientific community and maintain U.S. leadership in several areas. These include the Materials Plasma Exposure eXperiment (MPEX) for fusion materials science and the Matter in Extreme Conditions (MEC) Petawatt Upgrade at SLAC National Accelerator Laboratory for HEDLP science.

High Energy Physics.—The High Energy Physics (HEP) program supports fundamental research to understand how the universe works by discovering the elementary constituents of matter and energy, probing the interactions among them, and exploring the basic nature of space and time. A worldwide program of particle physics research is underway to discover what lies beyond the Standard Model of particle physics. Five intertwined science drivers of particle physics provide compelling lines of inquiry that show great promise for discovery: 1) use the Higgs boson as a new tool for discovery; 2) pursue the physics associated with neutrino mass; 3) identify the new physics of dark matter; 4) understand cosmic acceleration, dark energy, and inflation; and 5) explore new particles, interactions and physical principles. The program enables scientific discovery through a strategy organized along three frontiers: 1) The Energy Frontier, where researchers accelerate particles to the highest energies and collide them to produce and study the fundamental constituents of matter; 2) The Intensity Frontier, where researchers use a combination of intense particle beams and highly sensitive detectors to make extremely precise measurements of particle properties, to study some of the rarest particle interactions predicted by the Standard Model, and to search for new physics; and 3) The Cosmic Frontier, where researchers seek to reveal the nature of dark matter and dark energy by using naturally occurring particles to explore new phenomena. The highest-energy particles ever observed have come from cosmic sources, and the ancient light from distant galaxies allows scientists to map the distribution of dark matter and perhaps unravel the nature of dark energy. Investments in Theoretical, Computational, and Interdisciplinary Physics provide the framework to explain experimental observations. Advanced Technology Research and Development (R&D) fosters fundamental and innovative research into particle acceleration and detection techniques and instrumentation, supporting the frontiers and enabling future discovery experiments. HEP supports two particle accelerator scientific user facilities. HEP also manages construction projects to build new or upgrade existing facilities, providing world-leading tools and instruments to the particle physics scientific community.

Nuclear Physics.—The mission of the Nuclear Physics (NP) program is to solve an enduring mystery of the universe-what are the basic constituents of matter and how do they interact to form the elements and the properties we observe? To solve this mystery, NP supports research to discover, explore, and understand all forms of nuclear matter ,including exotic forms that existed in the first moments after the Big Bang. The goal is new knowledge that can benefit commerce, medicine, and national security. Achieving the goal requires support for advanced tools and the scientists and engineers who use them. NP provides ~95% of the support for basic nuclear physics research in the United States. Experimental approaches use large accelerators at national scientific user facilities to collide particles at nearly the speed of light, producing short-lived forms of nuclear matter for investigation. NP currently operates three national user facilities: the Relativistic Heavy Ion Collider, the Continuous Electron Beam Accelerator Facility, and the Argonne Tandem Linac Accelerator Facility. Also three powerful "microscopes" with complementary "resolving powers", which also produce advanced accelerator technology. Other research attempts to understand the theory of the strong nuclear force via Quantum Chromodynamics (QCD). An exciting vision to which NP researchers are making seminal contributions is quantum computing — future computers capable of solving QCD problems intractable with today's capabilities. To maintain U.S. leadership, the Facility for Rare Isotope Beams (FRIB) will begin operations in FY 2022 and will uniquely afford access to 80% of all isotopes predicted to possibly exist in nature, including over 1,000 never produced on earth. The Electron-Ion Collider (EIC) project is under development; when the EIC is completed in the next decade, it will provide unprecedented capability to discover how the mass of everyday objects is dynamically generated by the interaction of quarks and gluons. A targeted program of fundamental symmetries experiments is ongoing, including transformative

SCIENCE—Continued

research to determine whether the elusive neutrino particle is its own antiparticle. The National Nuclear Data Center is supported to collect, evaluate, curate, and disseminate nuclear physics data for basic nuclear physics research and applied nuclear technologies.

Isotope R&D and Production.—The DOE Isotope Program (DOE IP) produces critical radioactive and stable isotopes in short supply for the Nation that no domestic entity has the infrastructure or core competency to produce. Isotopes are high-priority commodities of strategic importance for the Nation and are essential in medical diagnosis and treatment, discovery science, national security and preparedness, industrial processes and manufacturing, space exploration and communications, biology, archeology, quantum science, clean energy, environmental science, and other fields. The DOE IP supports high-priority research on innovative and transformative approaches to isotopes production and processing, such as advanced manufacturing, artificial intelligence and machine learning, and robotics. The DOE IP promotes the development of robust, domestic supply chains of strategic isotopes and ensures national preparedness of critical infrastructure to mitigate risks in supply. The program provides mission readiness for the production and processing of radioactive and stable isotopes that are vital to the missions of many Federal agencies including the National Institutes of Health, National Institute of Standards and Technology, Department of Agriculture, Department of Defense, Department of Homeland Security, NNSA, and DOE SC programs. DOE IP continues to work in close collaboration with all federal organizations to develop strategic plans for isotope production and to establish effective communication to better forecast isotope needs and leverage resources. Construction continues for the Stable Isotope Production and Research Center to expand the stable isotope production capability to meet the demands of the Nation and mitigate dependency on stable isotope supply chains from foreign countries. Investments in QIS and Climate/Clean Energy support technology development for isotopes of interest. The DOE Isotope Traineeship advances workforce development in the field of isotope production and processing, promoting a safe, diverse, equitable and inclusive environment.

Accelerator R&D and Production.—Accelerator R&D and Production (ARDAP) supports cross-cutting basic R&D in accelerator science and technology, access to unique SC accelerator R&D infrastructure, workforce development, and public-private partnerships to advance new technologies for use in SC's scientific facilities and in commercial products. ARDAP supports fundamental research, user facility operations, and production of accelerator technologies in industry, with the aim of ensuring SC and broader U.S. Government have the best scientific instruments available. Reducing supply chain risks by re-shoring critical accelerator technologies is a key part of ARDAP's mission. ARDAP supports early-stage translational research to move advanced accelerator technology out of scientific laboratories and into broader applications in industry, environmental cleanup, medicine, and national security.

Workforce Development for Teachers and Scientists.—The Workforce Development for Teachers and Scientists (WDTS) program mission is to help ensure that DOE has a sustained pipeline of science, technology, engineering, and mathematics workers. This is accomplished through support of undergraduate internships, and graduate thesis research and collaborative faculty research opportunities at the DOE laboratories; and annual, nationwide, middle and high-school science competitions culminating in the National Science Bowl in Washington, D.C. These investments help develop the next generation of scientists and engineers.

Science Laboratories Infrastructure.—The Science Laboratories Infrastructure (SLI) program supports scientific and technological innovation at the SC laboratories by funding and sustaining mission-ready infrastructure and fostering safe and environmentally responsible operations. The program provides state-of-the-art facilities and infrastructure that are flexible, reliable, and sustainable in support of scientific discovery. The SLI program also funds Payments in Lieu of Taxes to local communities around the Argonne, Brookhaven, and Oak Ridge National Laboratories. The SLI program continues to focus on improving infrastructure across the SC national laboratory complex. The FY 2023 request includes funding for eleven on-going SLI construction projects: 1) Princeton Plasma Innovation Center at PPPL; 2) Critical Infrastructure Recovery & Renewal at PPPL; 3) Critical Utilities Rehabilitation Project at BNL; 4) Seismic and Safety Modernization at LBNL; 5) CEBAF Renovation and Expansion at TJNAF; 6) Large Scale Collaboration Center at SLAC; 7) Argonne Utilities Upgrade at ANL; 8) Linear Assets Modernization Project at LBNL; 9) Critical Utilities Infrastructure Revitalization at SLAC; 10) Utilities Infrastructure Project at FNAL; and 11) Biological and Environmental Program Integration Center at LBNL.

Safeguards and Security.—The Safeguards and Security (S&S) program is designed to ensure appropriate security measures are in place to support the SC mission requirement of open scientific research and to protect critical assets within SC laboratories. This is accomplished by providing physical controls that will mitigate possible risks to the laboratories' employees, nuclear and special materials, classified and sensitive information, and facilities. The S&S program also provides funding for cyber security for the laboratories' information technology systems to protect electronic data while enabling the SC mission.

Program Direction.—Science Program Direction supports a highly skilled Federal workforce to develop and oversee SC investments in research and scientific user facilities. SC provides public access to DOE scientific findings to further leverage the Federal science investment and advance the scientific enterprise. SC requires highly skilled scientific and technical program and project managers, as well as experts in areas such as acquisition, finance, legal, construction, and infrastructure management, human resources, and environmental, safety, and health oversight. Oversight of DOE's basic research portfolio, which includes extramural grants and contracts supporting nearly 29,000 researchers located at over 300 institutions and the 17 DOE national laboratories, spanning all fifty states and the District of Columbia and 28 scientific user facilities serving nearly 34,000 users per year, as well as supervision of major construction projects, is a Federal responsibility.

Object Classification (in millions of dollars)

Identification code 089–0222–0–1–251		2021 actual	2022 est.	2023 est.
	Direct obligations:			
	Personnel compensation:			
11.1	Full-time permanent	102	100	111
11.3	Other than full-time permanent	2		
11.5	Other personnel compensation	3		
11.8	Special personal services payments	1		
11.9	Total personnel compensation	108	100	111
12.1	Civilian personnel benefits	37	42	45
23.1	Rental payments to GSA			1
23.2	Rental payments to others			2
23.3	Communications, utilities, and miscellaneous charges	4	4	4
25.1	Advisory and assistance services	29	29	29
25.2	Other services from non-Federal sources	30	30	100
25.3	Other goods and services from Federal sources	12	12	8
25.4	Operation and maintenance of facilities	4,001	3,930	3,694
25.5	Research and development contracts	11	11	11
25.7	Operation and maintenance of equipment	2	2	2
26.0	Supplies and materials	2	2	2
31.0	Equipment	268	249	249
32.0	Land and structures	1,361	1,260	1,234
41.0	Grants, subsidies, and contributions	1,355	1,355	2,307
99.0	Direct obligations	7,220	7,026	7,799
99.0	Reimbursable obligations	622	624	624
99.9	Total new obligations, unexpired accounts	7,842	7,650	8,423

Employment Summary

Identification code 089–0222–0–1–251	2021 actual	2022 est.	2023 est.
1001 Direct civilian full-time equivalent employment	766	766	820

DEPARTMENT OF ENERGY

ADVANCED RESEARCH PROJECTS AGENCY—ENERGY

For Department of Energy expenses necessary in carrying out the activities authorized by section 5012 of the America COMPETES Act (Public Law 110–69), $700,150,000, to remain available until expended: Provided, That of such amount, $57,150,000 shall be available until September 30, 2024, for program direction.

Note.—A full-year 2022 appropriation for this account was not enacted at the time the Budget was prepared; therefore, the Budget assumes this account is operating under the Continuing Appropriations Act, 2022 (Division A of Public Law 117–43, as amended). The amounts included for 2022 reflect the annualized level provided by the continuing resolution.

Program and Financing (in millions of dollars)

Identification code 089–0337–0–1–270	2021 actual	2022 est.	2023 est.
Obligations by program activity:			
0001 ARPA-E Projects	289	392	523
0002 Program Direction	35	35	55
0799 Total direct obligations	324	427	578
0900 Total new obligations, unexpired accounts	324	427	578
Budgetary resources:			
Unobligated balance:			
1000 Unobligated balance brought forward, Oct 1	397	509	510
1021 Recoveries of prior year unpaid obligations	9		
1070 Unobligated balance (total)	406	509	510
Budget authority:			
Appropriations, discretionary:			
1100 Appropriation	427	427	700
Spending authority from offsetting collections, discretionary:			
1701 Change in uncollected payments, Federal sources		1	1
1900 Budget authority (total)	427	428	701
1930 Total budgetary resources available	833	937	1,211
Memorandum (non-add) entries:			
1941 Unexpired unobligated balance, end of year	509	510	633
Change in obligated balance:			
Unpaid obligations:			
3000 Unpaid obligations, brought forward, Oct 1	736	743	803
3010 New obligations, unexpired accounts	324	427	578
3020 Outlays (gross)	–308	–367	–568
3040 Recoveries of prior year unpaid obligations, unexpired	–9		
3050 Unpaid obligations, end of year	743	803	813
Uncollected payments:			
3060 Uncollected pymts, Fed sources, brought forward, Oct 1			–1
3070 Change in uncollected pymts, Fed sources, unexpired		–1	–1
3090 Uncollected pymts, Fed sources, end of year		–1	–2
Memorandum (non-add) entries:			
3100 Obligated balance, start of year	736	743	802
3200 Obligated balance, end of year	743	802	811
Budget authority and outlays, net:			
Discretionary:			
4000 Budget authority, gross	427	428	701
Outlays, gross:			
4010 Outlays from new discretionary authority	23	44	71
4011 Outlays from discretionary balances	285	323	497
4020 Outlays, gross (total)	308	367	568
Offsets against gross budget authority and outlays:			
Offsetting collections (collected) from:			
4030 Federal sources		–1	–1
Additional offsets against gross budget authority only:			
4050 Change in uncollected pymts, Fed sources, unexpired		–1	–1
4052 Offsetting collections credited to expired accounts		1	1
4070 Budget authority, net (discretionary)	427	427	700
4080 Outlays, net (discretionary)	308	366	567
4180 Budget authority, net (total)	427	427	700
4190 Outlays, net (total)	308	366	567

The U.S. Department of Energy's Advanced Research Projects Agency-Energy (ARPA-E) was established by the America COMPETES Act of 2007 (Public Law 110–69), as amended. The mission of ARPA-E is to enhance the economic, climate, and energy security of the United States through the development of advanced technologies that reduce imports of energy from foreign sources; reduce energy-related emissions, including greenhouse gases; improve the energy efficiency of all economic sectors; provide transformative solutions to improve the management, clean-up, and disposal of radioactive waste and spent nuclear fuel; improve the resilience, reliability, and security of infrastructure to produce, deliver, and store energy; mitigate the causes of, reverse the impact of, adapt to, or increase resilience against climate change; and monitor, analyze, and utilize climate emissions data. ARPA-E is expanding its scope to invest in climate-related innovations necessary to achieve net zero climate-inducing emissions by 2050 and address adaptation and resilience due to a changing climate. ARPA-E will ensure that the United States maintains a technological lead in developing and deploying advanced energy technologies. ARPA-E will identify and promote revolutionary advances in energy and climate-related applied sciences, translating scientific discoveries and cutting-edge inventions into technological innovations. It will also accelerate transformational technological advances in areas where industry by itself is not likely to invest due to technical and financial uncertainty. The role of ARPA-E is not to duplicate DOE's basic research and applied programs but to focus on novel early-stage energy research and development with technology applications that can be meaningfully advanced with a small investment over a defined period of time.

Object Classification (in millions of dollars)

Identification code 089–0337–0–1–270	2021 actual	2022 est.	2023 est.
Direct obligations:			
Personnel compensation:			
11.1 Full-time permanent	2	2	3
11.3 Other than full-time permanent	6	8	13
11.9 Total personnel compensation	8	10	16
12.1 Civilian personnel benefits	3	2	3
21.0 Travel and transportation of persons		1	2
25.1 Advisory and assistance services	16	16	26
25.2 Other services from non-Federal sources	19	15	19
25.3 Other goods and services from Federal sources	4	4	8
25.4 Operation and maintenance of facilities	34	56	76
25.5 Research and development contracts	239	323	428
26.0 Supplies and materials	1		
99.0 Direct obligations	324	427	578
99.9 Total new obligations, unexpired accounts	324	427	578

Employment Summary

Identification code 089–0337–0–1–270	2021 actual	2022 est.	2023 est.
1001 Direct civilian full-time equivalent employment	52	64	101

ENERGY SUPPLY AND CONSERVATION

Program and Financing (in millions of dollars)

Identification code 089–0224–0–1–999	2021 actual	2022 est.	2023 est.
Budgetary resources:			
Unobligated balance:			
1000 Unobligated balance brought forward, Oct 1	6	6	6
1930 Total budgetary resources available	6	6	6
Memorandum (non-add) entries:			
1941 Unexpired unobligated balance, end of year	6	6	6
4180 Budget authority, net (total)			
4190 Outlays, net (total)			

NUCLEAR ENERGY

For Department of Energy expenses including the purchase, construction, and acquisition of plant and capital equipment, and other expenses necessary for nuclear energy activities in carrying out the purposes of the Department of Energy Organization Act (42 U.S.C. 7101 et seq.), including the acquisition or condemnation of any real property or any facility or for plant or facility acquisition, construction, or expansion, $1,675,060,000, to remain available until expended: Provided, That of such amount, $85,457,000 shall be available until September 30, 2024, for program direction.

NUCLEAR ENERGY—Continued

Note.—A full-year 2022 appropriation for this account was not enacted at the time the Budget was prepared; therefore, the Budget assumes this account is operating under the Continuing Appropriations Act, 2022 (Division A of Public Law 117–43, as amended). The amounts included for 2022 reflect the annualized level provided by the continuing resolution.

NUCLEAR ENERGY

〔For an additional amount for "Nuclear Energy", $6,000,000,000, to remain available until expended, to carry out activities under the Civil Nuclear Credit Program, as authorized in section 40323 of division D of this Act: *Provided*, That $1,200,000,000, to remain available until expended, shall be made available for fiscal year 2022, $1,200,000,000, to remain available until expended, shall be made available for fiscal year 2023, $1,200,000,000, to remain available until expended, shall be made available for fiscal year 2024, $1,200,000,000, to remain available until expended, shall be made available for fiscal year 2025, and $1,200,000,000, to remain available until expended, shall be made available for fiscal year 2026: *Provided further*, That not later than 90 days after the date of enactment of this Act, the Secretary of Energy shall submit to the House and Senate Committees on Appropriations a detailed spend plan for fiscal year 2022: *Provided further*, That for each fiscal year through 2026, as part of the annual budget submission of the President under section 1105(a) of title 31, United States Code, the Secretary of Energy shall submit a detailed spend plan for that fiscal year: *Provided further*, That up to $36,000,000 of the amount provided under this heading in this Act shall be made available in each of fiscal years 2022 through 2026 for program direction: *Provided further*, That such amount is designated by the Congress as being for an emergency requirement pursuant to section 4112(a) of H. Con. Res. 71 (115th Congress), the concurrent resolution on the budget for fiscal year 2018, and to section 251(b) of the Balanced Budget and Emergency Deficit Control Act of 1985.〕 *(Infrastructure Investments and Jobs Appropriations Act.)*

Program and Financing (in millions of dollars)

Identification code 089–0319–0–1–999	2021 actual	2022 est.	2023 est.
Obligations by program activity:			
0010 Naval Reactors Development	91	91	....
0032 Reactor Concepts RD&D	201	200	135
0034 Advanced Reactors Demonstration Program	374	200	230
0041 Fuel Cycle R&D	279	300	422
0042 University Nuclear Leadership Program	5	5	7
0043 Nuclear Energy Enabling Technologies R&D	115	123	103
0044 Directed R&D & University Programs	....	....	137
0091 Research and Development programs, subtotal	1,065	919	1,034
0301 ORNL Infrastructure Facilities O&M	32	20	....
0350 University Fuel Services	....	12	18
0391 Direct program activities, subtotal	32	32	18
0401 Idaho Facilities Management	280	280	300
0402 Versatile Test Reactor Project	45	45	45
0403 Sample Preparation Laboratory Project	26	26	7
0450 Idaho National Laboratory safeguards and security	151	150	157
0451 International Nuclear Safety	6	5	5
0491 Infrastructure programs, subtotal	508	506	514
0502 Supercritical Transformational Electric Power Generation	4	5	....
0551 Program Direction	69	75	85
0552 International Nuclear Energy Cooperation	1	....	3
0591 Other direct program activities, subtotal	74	80	88
Credit program obligations:			
0739 Civil Nuclear Credit Program	....	1,199	1,199
0791 Direct program activities, subtotal	....	1,199	1,199
0799 Total direct obligations	1,679	2,736	2,853
0801 Nuclear Energy (Reimbursable)	232	240	250
0900 Total new obligations, unexpired accounts	1,911	2,976	3,103
Budgetary resources:			
Unobligated balance:			
1000 Unobligated balance brought forward, Oct 1	309	222	324
1011 Unobligated balance transfer from other acct [072–0306]	6	....	....
1021 Recoveries of prior year unpaid obligations	28	....	....
1070 Unobligated balance (total)	343	222	324
Budget authority:			
Appropriations, discretionary:			
1100 Appropriation	1,508	2,707	1,675
1120 Appropriations transferred to other accts [089–0222]	–19	....	....
1121 Appropriations transferred from other acct [089–0314]	91	91	....
1160 Appropriation, discretionary (total)	1,580	2,798	1,675
Advance appropriations, discretionary:			
1170 Advance appropriation	....	....	1,199
Spending authority from offsetting collections, discretionary:			
1700 Collected	165	280	281
1701 Change in uncollected payments, Federal sources	47	....	....
1750 Spending auth from offsetting collections, disc (total)	212	280	281
1900 Budget authority (total)	1,792	3,078	3,155
1930 Total budgetary resources available	2,135	3,300	3,479
Memorandum (non-add) entries:			
1940 Unobligated balance expiring	–2	....	....
1941 Unexpired unobligated balance, end of year	222	324	376
Change in obligated balance:			
Unpaid obligations:			
3000 Unpaid obligations, brought forward, Oct 1	1,192	1,539	3,013
3010 New obligations, unexpired accounts	1,911	2,976	3,103
3020 Outlays (gross)	–1,535	–1,502	–2,735
3040 Recoveries of prior year unpaid obligations, unexpired	–28	....	....
3041 Recoveries of prior year unpaid obligations, expired	–1	....	....
3050 Unpaid obligations, end of year	1,539	3,013	3,381
Uncollected payments:			
3060 Uncollected pymts, Fed sources, brought forward, Oct 1	–127	–174	–174
3070 Change in uncollected pymts, Fed sources, unexpired	–47	....	....
3090 Uncollected pymts, Fed sources, end of year	–174	–174	–174
Memorandum (non-add) entries:			
3100 Obligated balance, start of year	1,065	1,365	2,839
3200 Obligated balance, end of year	1,365	2,839	3,207
Budget authority and outlays, net:			
Discretionary:			
4000 Budget authority, gross	1,792	3,078	3,155
Outlays, gross:			
4010 Outlays from new discretionary authority	614	1,450	1,031
4011 Outlays from discretionary balances	921	52	1,704
4020 Outlays, gross (total)	1,535	1,502	2,735
Offsets against gross budget authority and outlays:			
Offsetting collections (collected) from:			
4030 Federal sources	–153	–280	–281
4033 Non-Federal sources	–12	....	....
4040 Offsets against gross budget authority and outlays (total)	–165	–280	–281
Additional offsets against gross budget authority only:			
4050 Change in uncollected pymts, Fed sources, unexpired	–47	....	....
4070 Budget authority, net (discretionary)	1,580	2,798	2,874
4080 Outlays, net (discretionary)	1,370	1,222	2,454
4180 Budget authority, net (total)	1,580	2,798	2,874
4190 Outlays, net (total)	1,370	1,222	2,454

The Office of Nuclear Energy (NE) funds a broad range of research and development (R&D) activities and supports Federal nuclear energy R&D infrastructure. The FY 2023 Budget continues programmatic support for advanced reactor R&D activities; fuel cycle R&D; and the safe, environmentally compliant, and cost-effective operation of the Department's facilities vital to nuclear energy R&D activities.

Directed R&D and University Programs.—This program focuses nuclear energy related research and development activities conducted by small businesses and supports university level engineering and science through competitively awarded university led research and development and infrastructure, universities research reactor fuel services, and scholarships and fellowships.

Reactor Concepts Research, Development and Demonstration.—This program conducts R&D on advanced reactor designs and advanced technologies for light water reactors (LWR).

Fuel Cycle Research and Development.—This program conducts R&D on advanced fuel cycle technologies that have the potential to improve resource utilization and energy generation, reduce waste generation, enhance safety, and mitigate risk of proliferation.

Nuclear Energy Enabling Technologies.—This program conducts R&D and strategic infrastructure investments to develop innovative and crosscutting nuclear energy technologies, including investments in modeling and simulation tools and providing access to unique nuclear energy research capabilities through the Nuclear Science User Facilities (NSUF).

Advanced Reactors Demonstration Program.—This program focuses Departmental and non-Federal resources on the development of commercial reactor technologies that may be ready for demonstration and deployment in the mid-term.

Versatile Test Reactor Project.—This program will provide the United States with a fast neutron testing capability to support the development of advanced nuclear reactor technologies. The Versatile Test Reactor (VTR) project will provide a leading edge capability for accelerated testing of advanced nuclear fuels, materials, instrumentation, and sensors.

Infrastructure.—This program manages Department of Energy mission critical facilities at the Idaho National Laboratory (INL), creating a safe and compliant status to support the Department's nuclear energy research and development activities, and testing of naval reactor fuels and reactor core components.

Idaho Sitewide Safeguards and Security.—This program supports the INL complex nuclear facility infrastructure and enables R&D in support of multiple program missions.

International Nuclear Energy Cooperation.—This program leads the Department's international engagement for civil nuclear energy, including analysis, development, and coordination activities.

Program Direction.—This program provides the Federal staffing resources and associated costs required to support the overall direction and execution of NE programs.

In FY 2023, NE will continue to support the Civil Nuclear Credit Program, a $6 billion strategic investment ($1.2 billion for each of five years) through the Bipartisan Infrastructure Law (BIL), to help preserve the existing U.S. reactor fleet and save thousands of high-paying jobs across the country. Under the new program, owners or operators of commercial U.S. reactors can apply for certification to bid on credits to support their continued operations. An application must demonstrate the reactor is projected to close for economic reasons and that closure will lead to a rise in air pollutants and carbon emissions. The program is available for plants that are certified as safe to continue operations and prioritizes plants that use domestically produced fuel.

Object Classification (in millions of dollars)

Identification code 089–0319–0–1–999		2021 actual	2022 est.	2023 est.
	Direct obligations:			
	Personnel compensation:			
11.1	Full-time permanent	33	33	43
11.3	Other than full-time permanent	1	1	1
11.5	Other personnel compensation	1	1	1
11.9	Total personnel compensation	35	35	45
12.1	Civilian personnel benefits	12	12	15
23.3	Communications, utilities, and miscellaneous charges	1	1	1
25.1	Other Contractual Services	10	10	23
25.2	Other services from non-Federal sources	553	590	719
25.3	Other goods and services from Federal sources	12	10	15
25.4	Operation and maintenance of facilities	935	724	766
25.7	Operation and maintenance of equipment	1	1	1
31.0	Equipment	14	15	20
32.0	Land and structures	48	75	85
41.0	Grants, subsidies, and contributions	58	1,263	1,163
99.0	Direct obligations	1,679	2,736	2,853
99.0	Reimbursable obligations	232	240	250
99.9	Total new obligations, unexpired accounts	1,911	2,976	3,103

Employment Summary

Identification code 089–0319–0–1–999	2021 actual	2022 est.	2023 est.
1001 Direct civilian full-time equivalent employment	270	290	394

ELECTRICITY

For Department of Energy expenses including the purchase, construction, and acquisition of plant and capital equipment, and other expenses necessary for electricity activities in carrying out the purposes of the Department of Energy Organization Act (42 U.S.C. 7101 et seq.), including the acquisition or condemnation of any real property or any facility or for plant or facility acquisition, construction, or expansion, $297,386,000, to remain available until expended: Provided, That of such amount, $17,586,000 shall be available until September 30, 2024, for program direction.

Note.—A full-year 2022 appropriation for this account was not enacted at the time the Budget was prepared; therefore, the Budget assumes this account is operating under the Continuing Appropriations Act, 2022 (Division A of Public Law 117–43, as amended). The amounts included for 2022 reflect the annualized level provided by the continuing resolution.

ELECTRICITY

【For an additional amount for "Electricity", $8,100,000,000, to remain available until expended: *Provided*, That of the amount provided under this heading in this Act, $5,000,000,000 shall be for grants under section 40101 of division D of this Act: *Provided further*, That of the funds in the preceding proviso, $1,000,000,000, to remain available until expended, shall be made available for fiscal year 2022, $1,000,000,000, to remain available until expended, shall be made available for fiscal year 2023, $1,000,000,000, to remain available until expended, shall be made available for fiscal year 2024, $1,000,000,000, to remain available until expended, shall be made available for fiscal year 2025, and $1,000,000,000, to remain available until expended, shall be made available for fiscal year 2026: *Provided further*, That of the amount provided under this heading in this Act, $50,000,000 shall be to carry out the Transmission Facilitation Program, including for any administrative expenses of carrying out the program, as authorized in section 40106(d)(3) of division D of this Act: *Provided further*, That of the funds in the preceding proviso, $10,000,000, to remain available until expended, shall be made available for fiscal year 2022, $10,000,000, to remain available until expended, shall be made available for fiscal year 2023, $10,000,000, to remain available until expended, shall be made available for fiscal year 2024, $10,000,000, to remain available until expended, shall be made available for fiscal year 2025, and $10,000,000, to remain available until expended, shall be made available for fiscal year 2026: *Provided further*, That of the amount provided under this heading in this Act and in addition to amounts otherwise made available for this purpose, $3,000,000,000, to remain available until expended, shall be to carry out activities under the Smart Grid Investment Matching Grant Program, as authorized in section 1306 of the Energy Independence and Security Act of 2007 (42 U.S.C. 17386), as amended by section 40107 of division D of this Act: *Provided further*, That of the funds in the preceding proviso, $600,000,000, to remain available until expended, shall be made available for fiscal year 2022, $600,000,000, to remain available until expended, shall be made available for fiscal year 2023, $600,000,000, to remain available until expended, shall be made available for fiscal year 2024, $600,000,000, to remain available until expended, shall be made available for fiscal year 2025, and $600,000,000, to remain available until expended, shall be made available for fiscal year 2026: *Provided further*, That of the amount provided under this heading in this Act, $50,000,000 shall be to carry out an advanced energy security program to secure energy networks, as authorized under section 40125(d) of division D of this Act: *Provided further*, That not later than 90 days after the date of enactment of this Act, the Secretary of Energy shall submit to the House and Senate Committees on Appropriations and the Senate Committee on Energy and Natural Resources and the House Committee on Energy and Commerce a detailed spend plan for fiscal year 2022: *Provided further*, That for each fiscal year through 2026, as part of the annual budget submission of the President under section 1105(a) of title 31, United States Code, the Secretary of Energy shall submit a detailed spend plan for that fiscal year: *Provided further*, That up to three percent of the amounts made available under this heading in each of fiscal years 2022 through 2026 shall be for program direction: *Provided further*, That such amount is designated by the Congress as being for an emergency requirement pursuant to section 4112(a) of H. Con. Res. 71 (115th Congress), the concurrent resolution on the budget for fiscal year 2018, and to section 251(b) of the Balanced Budget and Emergency Deficit Control Act of 1985.】 *(Infrastructure Investments and Jobs Appropriations Act.)*

Program and Financing (in millions of dollars)

Identification code 089–0318–0–1–271		2021 actual	2022 est.	2023 est.
	Obligations by program activity:			
0011	Transmission reliability and resiliency	47	47	37
0012	Resilient distribution systems	47	47	50
0014	Energy Storage	80	80	81
0015	Transformer Resilience and Advanced Components	7	7	23
0017	Cyber Resilient & Security Utility Communication Network			20
0018	Energy Delivery Grid Operations Technology			39
0019	Applied Grid Transformation Solutions			30
0030	Transmission permitting and technical assistance	8	8	
0040	Program Direction	18	18	17
0041	Electricity, Infrastructure Investment and Jobs Act		751	1,608
0799	Total direct obligations	207	958	1,905

Energy Programs—Continued
Federal Funds—Continued

ELECTRICITY—Continued
Program and Financing—Continued

Identification code 089–0318–0–1–271	2021 actual	2022 est.	2023 est.
0900 Total new obligations, unexpired accounts	207	958	1,905
Budgetary resources:			
Unobligated balance:			
1000 Unobligated balance brought forward, Oct 1	12	14	926
1021 Recoveries of prior year unpaid obligations	2		
1070 Unobligated balance (total)	14	14	926
Budget authority:			
Appropriations, discretionary:			
1100 Appropriation	212	212	297
1100 Appropriation		1,658	
1120 Appropriations transferred to other accts [089–0222]	–5		
1160 Appropriation, discretionary (total)	207	1,870	297
Advance appropriations, discretionary:			
1170 Advance appropriation			1,608
Spending authority from offsetting collections, discretionary:			
1700 Collected	1		
1701 Change in uncollected payments, Federal sources	–1		
1900 Budget authority (total)	207	1,870	1,905
1930 Total budgetary resources available	221	1,884	2,831
Memorandum (non-add) entries:			
1941 Unexpired unobligated balance, end of year	14	926	926
Change in obligated balance:			
Unpaid obligations:			
3000 Unpaid obligations, brought forward, Oct 1	286	292	814
3010 New obligations, unexpired accounts	207	958	1,905
3020 Outlays (gross)	–199	–436	–2,072
3040 Recoveries of prior year unpaid obligations, unexpired	–2		
3050 Unpaid obligations, end of year	292	814	647
Uncollected payments:			
3060 Uncollected pymts, Fed sources, brought forward, Oct 1	–2	–1	–1
3070 Change in uncollected pymts, Fed sources, unexpired	1		
3090 Uncollected pymts, Fed sources, end of year	–1	–1	–1
Memorandum (non-add) entries:			
3100 Obligated balance, start of year	284	291	813
3200 Obligated balance, end of year	291	813	646
Budget authority and outlays, net:			
Discretionary:			
4000 Budget authority, gross	207	1,870	1,905
Outlays, gross:			
4010 Outlays from new discretionary authority	20	266	923
4011 Outlays from discretionary balances	179	170	1,149
4020 Outlays, gross (total)	199	436	2,072
Offsets against gross budget authority and outlays:			
Offsetting collections (collected) from:			
4030 Federal sources	–1		
4040 Offsets against gross budget authority and outlays (total)	–1		
Additional offsets against gross budget authority only:			
4050 Change in uncollected pymts, Fed sources, unexpired	1		
4070 Budget authority, net (discretionary)	207	1,870	1,905
4080 Outlays, net (discretionary)	198	436	2,072
4180 Budget authority, net (total)	207	1,870	1,905
4190 Outlays, net (total)	198	436	2,072

The mission of the Office of Electricity (OE) is to drive electric grid modernization and resilience in energy infrastructure. OE leads the Department of Energy's efforts to strengthen, transform, and improve electricity delivery infrastructure so that consumers have access to resilient, secure, and clean sources of energy. OE programs include:

Transmission Reliability and Resilience (TRR).—The TRR program is focused on ensuring the reliability and resilience of the U.S. electric grid through R&D measurement and control of the electricity system, assessing evolving systems needs, identifying pathways to achieve an equitable transition to decarbonization and electrification, and risk assessment to address challenges across integrated energy systems.

Energy Delivery Grid Operations Technology (EDGOT).—EDGOT supports a public private partnership to develop national-scale energy planning and real-time situation awareness capabilities by focusing on developing large, networked communication and data infrastructure across multiple utility boundaries. EDGOT's North America Energy Resilience Model (NAERM) will help transition the current reactive state-of-practice to a new energy planning, investment, and operation paradigm in which we proactively develop infrastructure investment strategies.

Resilient Distribution Systems (RDS).—The RDS program develops transformative technologies, tools, and techniques to modernize the distribution portion of the electric delivery system. RDS activities will help harness emerging sources of energy for balance, reliability, and control: EVs, connected homes and buildings, increasing distributed solar, and energy storage.

Cyber Resilient and Secure Utility Communications Networks (SecureNet).—SecureNet, called Cyber R&D in the FY 2022 request to Congress, addresses energy sector cybersecurity associated with electricity delivery systems. SecureNet will focus on data and physics to redesign grid architecture that exposes the electricity system to cyber threats and will pursue coordinated engagement with DOE's other cyber-related activities.

Energy Storage.—The Energy Storage program, which is included in the Department's Grand Challenge, helps ensure the stability, reliability, and resilience of electricity infrastructure. The request supports emerging technology efforts focused on ultra-low-cost chemistries; a new GSL fellowship program; and continued development of the Rapid Operational Validation Initiative.

Transformer Resilience and Advanced Components (TRAC).—The TRAC program develops innovations for grid hardware that carries, controls, and converts electricity, helping to achieve decarbonization goals, ensure reliability and resilience of electric infrastructure, adapt the electricity delivery system to the evolution of the electric power grid, and provide the foundation to invigorate domestic transformer manufacturing. The request supports field validation of innovative, flexible, and adaptable prototypes for large power transformers (LPTs), which will promote greater standardization to increase grid resilience. TRAC will also address critical research needs for solid-state power substations (SSPS) with an emphasis on advanced materials, embedded intelligence for equipment monitoring, and validation of prototype converter building blocks.

Advanced Grid Transformation Solutions (AGTS).—AGTS is a new program in FY 2023 to address the pressing need for rapidly validating and deploying new systems by integrating technology suites in pilot environments to drive new technology adoption. AGTS will support integrated pilots to show how new technologies can help achieve stakeholder objectives. For each applied demonstration area, AGTS will consult stakeholders ensure that the project scope and outputs will be immediately useful to targeted decisionmakers.

Defense Critical Energy Infrastructure (DCEI) Energy Mission Assurance.—The DCEI Energy Mission Assurance program was funded in FY 2021 to identify, evaluate, prioritize, and assist in developing executable strategies to ensure that critical national defense and security missions have reliable access to power. In FY 2022, DOE proposed to integrate the functions of the DCEI Energy Mission Assurance program into the Office of Cybersecurity, Energy Security, and Emergency Response's suite of activities.

Transmission Permitting & Technical Assistance (TPTA).—The TPTA program worked with electricity system partners and stakeholders to modernize the grid and ensure adequate transmission capacity across the United States. TPTA activities are transferred to the Grid Deployment Office in FY 2023.

Program Direction.—Program Direction provides for the costs associated with the Federal workforce and contractor services that support OE's mission. These costs include salaries, benefits, travel, training, building occupancy, IT systems, and other related expenses.

The Bipartisan Infrastructure Law (BIL) (Infrastructure Investment and Jobs Act, P.L. 117–58) provides additional resources for OE to advance work in: 1) electric grid resilience, 2) technology deployment for enhancing grid flexibility, and 3) modeling energy infrastructure risk. Budgetary projections, including program direction and FTE counts, in the OE account reflect execution of BIL programs appropriated to OE but will be executed through OE, the Office of Cybersecurity, Energy Security, and Emergency Response, and the newly established Grid Deployment Office.

Object Classification (in millions of dollars)

Identification code 089–0318–0–1–271		2021 actual	2022 est.	2023 est.
	Direct obligations:			
	Personnel compensation:			
11.1	Full-time permanent	6	12	18
11.3	Other than full-time permanent	1	2	2
11.9	Total personnel compensation	7	14	20
12.1	Civilian personnel benefits	3	10	8
25.1	Advisory and assistance services	9	69	81
25.2	Other services from non-Federal sources	1	1	9
25.3	Other goods and services from Federal sources	3	6	27
25.4	Operation and maintenance of facilities		48	
25.5	Research and development contracts	161	161	170
32.0	Land and structures	23	23	208
41.0	Grants, subsidies, and contributions		626	1,382
99.0	Direct obligations	207	958	1,905
99.9	Total new obligations, unexpired accounts	207	958	1,905

Employment Summary

Identification code 089–0318–0–1–271		2021 actual	2022 est.	2023 est.
1001	Direct civilian full-time equivalent employment	58	83	124
2001	Reimbursable civilian full-time equivalent employment	4	4	4

GRID DEPLOYMENT OFFICE

For Department of Energy expenses including the purchase, construction, and acquisition of plant and capital equipment, and other expenses necessary for grid deployment in carrying out the purposes of the Department of Energy Organization Act (42 U.S.C. 7101 et seq.), including the acquisition or condemnation of any real property or any facility or for plant or facility acquisition, construction, or expansion, $90,221,000, to remain available until expended: Provided, That of such amount, $5,521,000 shall be available until September 30, 2024, for program direction.

Program and Financing (in millions of dollars)

Identification code 089–2301–0–1–271		2021 actual	2022 est.	2023 est.
	Obligations by program activity:			
0001	Interregional & Offshore Transmission Planning			20
0002	Grid Planning and Development			16
0003	Grid Technical Assistance			30
0004	Wholesale Electricity Marketing TA & Grants			19
0050	Program Direction			5
0900	Total new obligations, unexpired accounts			90
	Budgetary resources:			
	Budget authority:			
	Appropriations, discretionary:			
1100	Appropriation			90
1930	Total budgetary resources available			90
	Change in obligated balance:			
	Unpaid obligations:			
3010	New obligations, unexpired accounts			90
3020	Outlays (gross)			–14
3050	Unpaid obligations, end of year			76
	Memorandum (non-add) entries:			
3200	Obligated balance, end of year			76
	Budget authority and outlays, net:			
	Discretionary:			
4000	Budget authority, gross			90
	Outlays, gross:			
4010	Outlays from new discretionary authority			14
4180	Budget authority, net (total)			90
4190	Outlays, net (total)			14

The newly created Grid Deployment Office (GDO) within the Office of the Under Secretary for Infrastructure serves as the catalyst for the development of new and upgraded high-capacity electric transmission lines nationwide. GDO works with electricity system partners and stakeholders by providing tools, conducting analyses, and improving decision-making processes to modernize and ensure a clean, reliable, resilient, and equitable grid that achieves 100% carbon-free electricity by 2035. Prior to FY 2023, these activities were funded within Electricity. New activities in FY 2023 include Wholesale Electricity Market Technical Assistance and Grants and Interregional and Offshore Transmission Planning.

Additional funding and FTEs for GDO programs provided in the Bipartisan Infrastructure Law are captured in the budgetary projections in, and will be executed through, the Department's Electricity account.

Object Classification (in millions of dollars)

Identification code 089–2301–0–1–271		2021 actual	2022 est.	2023 est.
11.1	Direct obligations: Personnel compensation: Full-time permanent			2
11.9	Total personnel compensation			2
12.1	Civilian personnel benefits			1
23.3	Communications, utilities, and miscellaneous charges			17
24.0	Printing and reproduction			2
25.1	Advisory and assistance services			5
25.2	Other services from non-Federal sources			53
25.3	Other goods and services from Federal sources			5
25.4	Operation and maintenance of facilities			2
25.7	Operation and maintenance of equipment			3
99.9	Total new obligations, unexpired accounts			90

Employment Summary

Identification code 089–2301–0–1–271		2021 actual	2022 est.	2023 est.
1001	Direct civilian full-time equivalent employment			17

TRANSMISSION FACILITATION FUND

Program and Financing (in millions of dollars)

Identification code 089–4380–0–3–271		2021 actual	2022 est.	2023 est.
	Obligations by program activity:			
0010	Loans			200
0020	Capacity contracts			200
0030	Public private partnerships			100
0900	Total new obligations, unexpired accounts			500
	Budgetary resources:			
	Unobligated balance:			
1000	Unobligated balance brought forward, Oct 1			2,500
	Budget authority:			
	Borrowing authority, mandatory:			
1400	Borrowing authority		2,500	
1900	Budget authority (total)		2,500	
1930	Total budgetary resources available		2,500	2,500
	Memorandum (non-add) entries:			
1941	Unexpired unobligated balance, end of year		2,500	2,000
	Change in obligated balance:			
	Unpaid obligations:			
3010	New obligations, unexpired accounts			500
3020	Outlays (gross)			–500
	Budget authority and outlays, net:			
	Mandatory:			
4090	Budget authority, gross		2,500	
	Outlays, gross:			
4101	Outlays from mandatory balances			500
4180	Budget authority, net (total)		2,500	
4190	Outlays, net (total)			500

The Transmission Facilitation Fund was created in section 40106 of the Infrastructure Investment and Jobs Act of 2021 to facilitate the construction

TRANSMISSION FACILITATION FUND—Continued

of electric power transmission lines and related facilities to eligible projects. A borrowing authority of $2.5 billion has been established for the fund to carry out the program.

Object Classification (in millions of dollars)

Identification code 089–4380–0–3–271	2021 actual	2022 est.	2023 est.
Direct obligations:			
33.0 Investments and loans			400
41.0 Grants, subsidies, and contributions			100
99.9 Total new obligations, unexpired accounts			500

CYBERSECURITY, ENERGY SECURITY, AND EMERGENCY RESPONSE

For Department of Energy expenses including the purchase, construction, and acquisition of plant and capital equipment, and other expenses necessary for energy sector cybersecurity, energy security, and emergency response activities in carrying out the purposes of the Department of Energy Organization Act (42 U.S.C. 7101 et seq.), including the acquisition or condemnation of any real property or any facility or for plant or facility acquisition, construction, or expansion, $202,143,000, to remain available until expended: Provided, That of such amount, $25,123,000 shall be available until September 30, 2024, for program direction.

Note.—A full-year 2022 appropriation for this account was not enacted at the time the Budget was prepared; therefore, the Budget assumes this account is operating under the Continuing Appropriations Act, 2022 (Division A of Public Law 117–43, as amended). The amounts included for 2022 reflect the annualized level provided by the continuing resolution.

CYBERSECURITY, ENERGY SECURITY, AND EMERGENCY RESPONSE

[For an additional amount for "Cybersecurity, Energy Security, and Emergency Response", $550,000,000, to remain available until expended: *Provided*, That of the amount provided under this heading in this Act, $250,000,000 shall be to carry out activities under the Cybersecurity for the Energy Sector Research, Development, and Demonstration Program, as authorized in section 40125(b) of division D of this Act: *Provided further*, That of the funds in the preceding proviso, $50,000,000, to remain available until expended, shall be made available for fiscal year 2022, $50,000,000, to remain available until expended, shall be made available for fiscal year 2023, $50,000,000, to remain available until expended, shall be made available for fiscal year 2024, $50,000,000, to remain available until expended, shall be made available for fiscal year 2025, and $50,000,000, to remain available until expended, shall be made available for fiscal year 2026: *Provided further*, That of the amount provided under this heading in this Act, $50,000,000 shall be to carry out activities under the Energy Sector Operational Support for Cyberresilience Program, as authorized in section 40125(c) of division D of this Act: *Provided further*, That of the amount provided under this heading in this Act, $250,000,000, to carry out activities under the Rural and Municipal Utility Advanced Cybersecurity Grant and Technical Assistance Program, as authorized in section 40124 of division D of this Act: *Provided further*, That $50,000,000, to remain available until expended, shall be made available for fiscal year 2022, $50,000,000, to remain available until expended, shall be made available for fiscal year 2023, $50,000,000, to remain available until expended, shall be made available for fiscal year 2024, $50,000,000, to remain available until expended, shall be made available for fiscal year 2025, and $50,000,000, to remain available until expended, shall be made available for fiscal year 2026: *Provided further*, That not later than 90 days after the date of enactment of this Act, the Secretary of Energy shall submit to the House and Senate Committees on Appropriations and the Senate Committee on Energy and Natural Resources and the House Committee on Energy and Commerce a detailed spend plan for fiscal year 2022: *Provided further*, That for each fiscal year through 2026, as part of the annual budget submission of the President under section 1105(a) of title 31, United States Code, the Secretary of Energy shall submit a detailed spend plan for that fiscal year: *Provided further*, That up to three percent of the amounts made available under this heading in this Act in each of fiscal years 2022 through 2026 shall be for program direction: *Provided further*, That such amount is designated by the Congress as being for an emergency requirement pursuant to section 4112(a) of H. Con. Res. 71 (115th Congress), the concurrent resolution on the budget for fiscal year 2018, and to section 251(b) of the Balanced Budget and Emergency Deficit Control Act of 1985.] *(Infrastructure Investments and Jobs Appropriations Act.)*

Program and Financing (in millions of dollars)

Identification code 089–2250–0–1–271	2021 actual	2022 est.	2023 est.
Obligations by program activity:			
0008 Cybersecurity for Energy Delivery Systems	54	54	
0010 Risk Management Technology and Tools (CEDS)			125
0020 Infrastructure security and energy restoration	54	54	
0021 Response and Restoration			24
0022 Information Sharing, Partnerships and Exercises			28
0030 Program direction	13	12	25
0035 CESER, Infrastructure Investment and Jobs Act		68	100
0799 Total direct obligations	121	188	302
0801 Reimbursable work	3	3	3
0900 Total new obligations, unexpired accounts	124	191	305
Budgetary resources:			
Unobligated balance:			
1000 Unobligated balance brought forward, Oct 1	22	64	182
1021 Recoveries of prior year unpaid obligations	8		
1070 Unobligated balance (total)	30	64	182
Budget authority:			
Appropriations, discretionary:			
1100 Appropriation	156	306	202
1120 Appropriations transferred to other acct [089–0222]	–1		
1160 Appropriation, discretionary (total)	155	306	202
Advance appropriations, discretionary:			
1170 Advance appropriation			100
Spending authority from offsetting collections, discretionary:			
1700 Collected	2	3	3
1701 Change in uncollected payments, Federal sources	1		
1750 Spending auth from offsetting collections, disc (total)	3	3	3
1900 Budget authority (total)	158	309	305
1930 Total budgetary resources available	188	373	487
Memorandum (non-add) entries:			
1941 Unexpired unobligated balance, end of year	64	182	182
Change in obligated balance:			
Unpaid obligations:			
3000 Unpaid obligations, brought forward, Oct 1	181	186	194
3010 New obligations, unexpired accounts	124	191	305
3020 Outlays (gross)	–111	–183	–340
3040 Recoveries of prior year unpaid obligations, unexpired	–8		
3050 Unpaid obligations, end of year	186	194	159
Uncollected payments:			
3060 Uncollected pymts, Fed sources, brought forward, Oct 1	–2	–3	–3
3070 Change in uncollected pymts, Fed sources, unexpired	–1		
3090 Uncollected pymts, Fed sources, end of year	–3	–3	–3
Memorandum (non-add) entries:			
3100 Obligated balance, start of year	179	183	191
3200 Obligated balance, end of year	183	191	156
Budget authority and outlays, net:			
Discretionary:			
4000 Budget authority, gross	158	309	305
Outlays, gross:			
4010 Outlays from new discretionary authority	17	81	134
4011 Outlays from discretionary balances	94	102	206
4020 Outlays, gross (total)	111	183	340
Offsets against gross budget authority and outlays:			
Offsetting collections (collected) from:			
4030 Federal sources	–2	–3	–3
4040 Offsets against gross budget authority and outlays (total)	–2	–3	–3
Additional offsets against gross budget authority only:			
4050 Change in uncollected pymts, Fed sources, unexpired	–1		
4070 Budget authority, net (discretionary)	155	306	302
4080 Outlays, net (discretionary)	109	180	337
4180 Budget authority, net (total)	155	306	302
4190 Outlays, net (total)	109	180	337

The Office of Cybersecurity, Energy Security, and Emergency Response (CESER) leads the Department's efforts to secure U.S. energy infrastructure against all hazards, reduce the risks of and impacts from cyber events and other disruptive events, and assists with restoration activities. Programs include:

DEPARTMENT OF ENERGY

Risk Management Tools (RMT).—The RMT program seeks to enhance the reliability and resilience of the Nation's energy infrastructure through near- and long-term activities to strengthen energy sector cybersecurity across the Nation. Working closely with the energy sector and our government partners, RMT focuses on enhancing the speed and effectiveness of threat and vulnerability sharing and accelerating technology and tools to mitigate cyber incidents in today's systems and to develop next-generation resilient energy delivery systems while developing analyses to quantify the resulting relative risk reduction.

Response and Restoration (R&R).—The R&R program coordinates a national effort to secure the U.S. energy infrastructure against all hazards, reduce impacts from disruptive events, and assist industry with restoration activities. R&R delivers a range of capabilities including energy sector emergency response and recovery (including emergency response of a cyber nature); near-real-time situational awareness and information sharing about the status of the energy systems to improve risk management; analysis of evolving threats and hazards to energy infrastructure.

Information Sharing, Partnerships and Exercises (ISPE).—The ISPE program supports energy sector security and resilience in coordination with government and industry partners. By seeding public-private partnerships this program will advance the Department's efforts to support State, Local, Tribal, territory and industry in preparing for, mitigating, and recovering from all threats and hazards facing the U.S. energy sector through information sharing, risk assessments, capacity building in planning and resilience, and targeted training and exercises.

Program Direction.—Program Direction provides for the costs associated with the Federal workforce and contractor services that support CESER's mission. These costs include salaries, benefits, travel, training, building occupancy, IT systems, and other related expenses.

The Bipartisan Infrastructure Law (BIL) (Infrastructure Investment and Jobs Act, P.L. 117–58) provides additional resources for CESER to advance work in: 1) a rural and municipal utility advanced cybersecurity grant and technical assistance program, and 2) enhancing grid security.

Object Classification (in millions of dollars)

Identification code 089–2250–0–1–271		2021 actual	2022 est.	2023 est.
11.1	Direct obligations: Personnel compensation: Full-time permanent	4	7	17
11.9	Total personnel compensation	4	7	17
12.1	Civilian personnel benefits	2	2	4
21.0	Travel and transportation of persons			1
25.1	Advisory and assistance services	13	15	23
25.2	Other services from non-Federal sources	2	3	4
25.3	Other goods and services from Federal sources	1	1	2
25.5	Research and development contracts	99	104	167
41.0	Grants, subsidies, and contributions		56	84
99.0	Direct obligations	121	188	302
99.0	Reimbursable obligations	3	3	3
99.9	Total new obligations, unexpired accounts	124	191	305

Employment Summary

Identification code 089–2250–0–1–271	2021 actual	2022 est.	2023 est.
1001 Direct civilian full-time equivalent employment	21	44	100

ENERGY EFFICIENCY AND RENEWABLE ENERGY

For Department of Energy expenses including the purchase, construction, and acquisition of plant and capital equipment, and other expenses necessary for energy efficiency and renewable energy activities in carrying out the purposes of the Department of Energy Organization Act (42 U.S.C. 7101 et seq.), including the acquisition or condemnation of any real property or any facility or for plant or facility acquisition, construction, or expansion, $4,018,885,000, to remain available until expended: Provided, That of such amount, $224,474,000 shall be available until September 30, 2024, for program direction.

Note.—A full-year 2022 appropriation for this account was not enacted at the time the Budget was prepared; therefore, the Budget assumes this account is operating under the Continuing Appropriations Act, 2022 (Division A of Public Law 117–43, as amended). The amounts included for 2022 reflect the annualized level provided by the continuing resolution.

ENERGY EFFICIENCY AND RENEWABLE ENERGY

[For an additional amount for "Energy Efficiency and Renewable Energy", $16,264,000,000 to remain available until expended: *Provided*, That of the amount provided under this heading in this Act, $250,000,000 shall be for activities for the Energy Efficiency Revolving Loan Fund Capitalization Grant Program, as authorized under section 40502 of division D of this Act: *Provided further*, That of the amount provided under this heading in this Act, $40,000,000 shall be for grants for the Energy Auditor Training Grant Program, as authorized under section 40503 of division D of this Act: *Provided further*, That of the amount provided under the heading in this Act, $225,000,000 shall be for grants for implementing of updated building energy codes, as authorized under section 309 of the Energy Conservation and Production Act (42 U.S.C. 6831 et seq.), as amended by section 40511(a) of division D of this Act: *Provided further*, That of the funds in the preceding proviso, $45,000,000, to remain available until expended, shall be made available for fiscal year 2022, $45,000,000, to remain available until expended, shall be made available for fiscal year 2023, $45,000,000, to remain available until expended, shall be made available for fiscal year 2024, $45,000,000, to remain available until expended, shall be made available for fiscal year 2025, and $45,000,000, to remain available until expended, shall be made available for fiscal year 2026: *Provided further*, That of the amount provided under this heading in this Act, $10,000,000 shall be for Building, Training, and Assessment Centers, as authorized under section 40512 of division D of this Act: *Provided further*, That of the amount provided under this heading in this Act, $10,000,000 shall be for grants for Career Skills Training, as authorized under section 40513 of division D of this Act: *Provided further*, That of the amount provided under this heading in this Act, $150,000,000 shall be for activities for Industrial Research and Assessment Centers, as authorized under subsections (a) through (h) of section 457 of the Energy Independence and Security Act of 2007 (42 U.S.C. 17111 et seq.), as amended by section 40521(b) of division D of this Act: *Provided further*, That of the funds in the preceding proviso, $30,000,000, to remain available until expended, shall be made available for fiscal year 2022, $30,000,000, to remain available until expended, shall be made available for fiscal year 2023, $30,000,000, to remain available until expended, shall be made available for fiscal year 2024, $30,000,000, to remain available until expended, shall be made available for fiscal year 2025, and $30,000,000, to remain available until expended, shall be made available for fiscal year 2026: *Provided further*, That of the amount provided under this heading in this Act, $400,000,000 shall be for activities for Implementation Grants for Industrial Research and Assessment Centers, as authorized under section 457(i) of the Energy Independence and Security Act of 2007 (42 U.S.C. 17111 et seq.), as amended by section 40521(b) of division D of this Act: *Provided further*, That of the funds in the preceding two provisos, $80,000,000, to remain available until expended, shall be made available for fiscal year 2022, $80,000,000, to remain available until expended, shall be made available for fiscal year 2023, $80,000,000, to remain available until expended, shall be made available for fiscal year 2024, $80,000,000, to remain available until expended, shall be made available for fiscal year 2025, and $80,000,000, to remain available until expended, shall be made available for fiscal year 2026: *Provided further*, That of the amount provided under this heading in this Act, $50,000,000 shall be for carrying out activities for Manufacturing Leadership, as authorized under section 40534 of division D of this Act: *Provided further*, That of the amount provided under this heading in this Act, $500,000,000 shall be for grants for Energy Efficiency Improvements and Renewable Energy Improvements at Public School Facilities, as authorized under section 40541 of division D of this Act: *Provided further*, That of the funds in the preceding proviso, $100,000,000, to remain available until expended, shall be made available for fiscal year 2022, $100,000,000, to remain available until expended, shall be made available for fiscal year 2023, $100,000,000, to remain available until expended, shall be made available for fiscal year 2024, $100,000,000, to remain available until expended, shall be made available for fiscal year 2025, and $100,000,000, to remain available until expended, shall be made available for fiscal year 2026: *Provided further*, That of the amount provided under this heading in this Act, $50,000,000 shall be for grants for the Energy Efficiency Materials Pilot Program, as authorized under section 40542 of division D of this Act: *Provided further*, That of the amount provided under this heading in this Act and in addition to amounts otherwise made available for this purpose, $3,500,000,000 shall be for carrying out activities for the Weatherization Assistance Program, as authorized under part A of title IV of the Energy Conservation and Production Act (42 U.S.C. 6861 et seq.): *Provided further*, That of the amount provided under this heading in this Act and in addition to amounts otherwise made available for this purpose, $550,000,000 shall be for carrying out activities for the Energy Efficiency and Conservation Block Grant Program, as authorized under

ENERGY EFFICIENCY AND RENEWABLE ENERGY—Continued

section 542(a) of the Energy Independence and Security Act of 2007 (42 U.S.C. 17152(a)): *Provided further*, That of the amount provided under this heading in this Act, $250,000,000 shall be for grants for the Assisting Federal Facilities with Energy Conservation Technologies Grant Program, as authorized under section 546(b) of the National Energy Conservation Policy Act (42 U.S.C. 8256(b)): *Provided further*, That of the amount provided under this heading in this Act, $10,000,000 shall be for extended product system rebates, as authorized under section 1005 of the Energy Act of 2020 (42 U.S.C. 6311 note; Public Law 116–260): *Provided further*, That of the amount provided under this heading in this Act, $10,000,000 shall be for energy efficient transformer rebates, as authorized under section 1006 of the Energy Act of 2020 (42 U.S.C. 6317 note; Public Law 116–260): *Provided further*, That of the amount provided under this heading in this Act, $3,000,000,000, to remain available until expended, shall be for Battery Material Processing Grants, as authorized under section 40207(b) of division D of this Act: *Provided further*, That of the funds in the preceding proviso, $600,000,000, to remain available until expended, shall be made available for fiscal year 2022, $600,000,000, to remain available until expended, shall be made available for fiscal year 2023, $600,000,000, to remain available until expended, shall be made available for fiscal year 2024, $600,000,000, to remain available until expended, shall be made available for fiscal year 2025, and $600,000,000, to remain available until expended, shall be made available for fiscal year 2026: *Provided further*, That of the amount provided under this heading in this Act, $3,000,000,000 shall be for Battery Manufacturing and Recycling Grants, as authorized under section 40207(c) of division D of this Act: *Provided further*, That of the funds in the preceding proviso, $600,000,000, to remain available until expended, shall be made available for fiscal year 2022, $600,000,000, to remain available until expended, shall be made available for fiscal year 2023, $600,000,000, to remain available until expended, shall be made available for fiscal year 2024, $600,000,000, to remain available until expended, shall be made available for fiscal year 2025, and $600,000,000, to remain available until expended, shall be made available for fiscal year 2026: *Provided further*, That of the amount provided under this heading in this Act, $125,000,000 shall be to carry out activities, as authorized under section 40207(f) of division D of this Act: *Provided further*, That of the amount provided under this heading in this Act, $10,000,000 shall be for a Lithium-Ion Battery Recycling Prize Competition, as authorized under section 40207(e) of division D of this Act: *Provided further*, That of the amount provided under this heading in this Act, $200,000,000 shall be for grants for the Electric Drive Vehicle Battery Recycling and Second-Life Applications Program, as authorized under subsection (k) of section 641 of the Energy Independence and Security Act of 2007 (42 U.S.C. 17231), as amended by section 40208(1) of division D of this Act: *Provided further*, That of the funds in the preceding proviso, $40,000,000, to remain available until expended, shall be made available for fiscal year 2022, $40,000,000, to remain available until expended, shall be made available for fiscal year 2023, $40,000,000, to remain available until expended, shall be made available for fiscal year 2024, $40,000,000, to remain available until expended, shall be made available for fiscal year 2025, and $40,000,000, to remain available until expended, shall be made available for fiscal year 2026: *Provided further*, That of the amount provided under this heading in this Act, $750,000,000 shall be for grants for the Advanced Energy Manufacturing and Recycling Grant Program, as authorized under section 40209 of division D of this Act: *Provided further*, That of the funds in the preceding proviso, $150,000,000, to remain available until expended, shall be made available for fiscal year 2022, $150,000,000, to remain available until expended, shall be made available for fiscal year 2023, $150,000,000, to remain available until expended, shall be made available for fiscal year 2024, $150,000,000, to remain available until expended, shall be made available for fiscal year 2025, and $150,000,000, to remain available until expended, shall be made available for fiscal year 2026: *Provided further*, That of the amount provided under this heading in this Act, $500,000,000 shall be for activities for the Clean Hydrogen Manufacturing Recycling Research, Development, and Demonstration Program, as authorized under section 815 of the Energy Policy Act of 2005 (42 U.S.C. 16151 et seq.), as amended by section 40314 of division D of this Act: *Provided further*, That of the funds in the preceding proviso, $100,000,000, to remain available until expended, shall be made available for fiscal year 2022, $100,000,000, to remain available until expended, shall be made available for fiscal year 2023, $100,000,000, to remain available until expended, shall be made available for fiscal year 2024, $100,000,000, to remain available until expended, shall be made available for fiscal year 2025, and $100,000,000, to remain available until expended, shall be made available for fiscal year 2026: *Provided further*, That of the amount provided under the heading in this Act, $1,000,000,000 shall be for activities for the Clean Hydrogen Electrolysis Program, as authorized under section 816 of the Energy Policy Act of 2005 (42 U.S.C. 16151 et seq.), as amended by section 40314 of division D of this Act: *Provided further*, That of the funds in the preceding proviso, $200,000,000, to remain available until expended, shall be made available for fiscal year 2022, $200,000,000, to remain available until expended, shall be made available for fiscal year 2023, $200,000,000, to remain available until expended, shall be made available for fiscal year 2024, $200,000,000, to remain available until expended, shall be made available for fiscal year 2025, and $200,000,000, to remain available until expended, shall be made available for fiscal year 2026: *Provided further*, That of the amount provided under this heading in this Act, $500,000,000 shall be for carrying out activities for the State Energy Program, as authorized under part D of title III of the Energy Policy and Conservation Act (42 U.S.C. 6321 et seq.), as amended by section 40109 of division D of this Act: *Provided further*, That of the amount provided under this heading in this Act, $125,000,000 shall be for carrying out activities under section 242 of the Energy Policy Act of 2005 (42 U.S.C. 15881), as amended by section 40331 of division D of this Act: *Provided further*, That of the amount provided under this heading in this Act, $75,000,000 shall be for carrying out activities under section 243 of the Energy Policy Act of 2005 (42 U.S.C. 15882), as amended by section 40332 of division D of this Act: *Provided further*, That of the amount provided under this heading in this Act, $553,600,000 shall be for activities for Hydroelectric Incentives, as authorized under section 247 of the Energy Policy Act of 2005 (Public Law 109–58; 119 Stat. 674), as amended by section 40333(a) of division D of this Act: *Provided further*, That of the funds in the preceding proviso, $276,800,000, to remain available until expended, shall be made available for fiscal year 2022, $276,800,000, to remain available until expended, shall be made available for fiscal year 2023: *Provided further*, That of the amount provided under the heading in this Act, $10,000,000 shall be for activities for the Pumped Storage Hydropower Wind and Solar Integration and System Reliability Initiative, as authorized under section 3201 of the Energy Policy Act of 2020 (42 U.S.C. 17232), as amended by section 40334 of division D of this Act: *Provided further*, That of the amount provided under this heading in this Act, $36,000,000 shall be for carrying out activities, as authorized under section 634 of the Energy Independence and Security Act of 2007 (42 U.S.C. 17213): *Provided further*, That of the amount provided under this heading in this Act, $70,400,000 shall be for carrying out activities, as authorized under section 635 of the Energy Independence and Security Act of 2007 (42 U.S.C.17214): *Provided further*, That of the amount provided under this heading in this Act, $40,000,000 shall be for carrying out activities for the National Marine Energy Centers, as authorized under section 636 of the Energy Independence and Security Act of 2007 (42 U.S.C. 17215): *Provided further*, That of the amount provided under this heading in this Act, $84,000,000 shall be for carrying out activities under section 615(d) of the Energy Independence and Security Act of 2007 (42 U.S.C. 17194(d)): *Provided further*, That of the amount provided under this heading in this Act, $60,000,000 shall be for carrying out activities for the Wind Energy Technology Program, as authorized under section 3003(b)(2) of the Energy Act of 2020 (42 U.S.C. 16237(b)(2)): *Provided further*, That of the amount provided under this heading in this Act, $40,000,000 shall be for carrying out activities for the Wind Energy Technology Recycling Research, Development, and Demonstration Program, as authorized under section 3003(b)(4) of the Energy Act of 2020 (42 U.S.C. 16237(b)(4)): *Provided further*, That of the amount provided under this heading in this Act, $40,000,000 shall be for carrying out activities under section 3004(b)(2) of the Energy Act of 2020 (42 U.S.C. 16238(b)(2)): *Provided further*, That of the amount provided under this heading in this Act, $20,000,000 shall be for carrying out activities under section 3004(b)(3) of the Energy Act of 2020 (42 U.S.C. 16238(b)(3)): *Provided further*, That of the amount provided under this heading in this Act, $20,000,000 shall be for carrying out activities under section 3004(b)(4) of the Energy Act of 2020 (42 U.S.C. 16238(b)(4)): *Provided further*, That not later than 90 days after the date of enactment of this Act, the Secretary of Energy shall submit to the House and Senate Committees on Appropriations and the Senate Committee on Energy and Natural Resources and the House Committee on Energy and Commerce a detailed spend plan for fiscal year 2022: *Provided further*, That for each fiscal year through 2026, as part of the annual budget submission of the President under section 1105(a) of title 31, United States Code, the Secretary of Energy shall submit a detailed spend plan for that fiscal year: *Provided further*, That up to three percent of the amounts made available under this heading in this Act in each of fiscal years 2022 through 2026 shall be for program direction: *Provided further*, That such amount is designated by the Congress as being for an emergency requirement pursuant to section 4112(a) of H. Con. Res. 71 (115th Congress), the concurrent resolution on the budget for fiscal year 2018, and to section 251(b) of the Balanced Budget and Emergency Deficit Control Act of 1985.] *(Infrastructure Investments and Jobs Appropriations Act.)*

DEPARTMENT OF ENERGY

Program and Financing (in millions of dollars)

Identification code 089–0321–0–1–270	2021 actual	2022 est.	2023 est.
Obligations by program activity:			
0001 Vehicle Technologies	313	313	477
0002 Bioenergy Technologies	254	254	339
0003 Hydrogen & Fuel Cell Technologies	110	110	136
0091 Sustainable Transportation, subtotal	677	677	952
0101 Solar Energy	338	338	645
0102 Wind Energy	116	116	365
0103 Water Power	137	137	172
0104 Geothermal Technologies	65	65	124
0105 Renewable Energy Integration			14
0191 Renewable Electricity, subtotal	656	656	1,320
0201 Advanced Manufacturing	413	413	608
0202 Building Technologies	303	303	410
0203 Weatherization & Intergovernmental Activities	353	353	
0204 Federal Energy Management Program	26	26	
0291 Energy Efficiency, subtotal	1,095	1,095	1,018
0301 Program Direction & Support	157	157	197
0302 Strategic Programs	16	16	66
0303 Facilities & Infrastructure	130	130	302
0391 EERE Corporate Support, subtotal	303	303	565
0401 Infrastructure Investment and Jobs Act		1,033	2,000
0799 Total direct obligations	2,731	3,764	5,855
0810 Energy Efficiency and Renewable Energy (Reimbursable)	171	168	168
0900 Total new obligations, unexpired accounts	2,902	3,932	6,023
Budgetary resources:			
Unobligated balance:			
1000 Unobligated balance brought forward, Oct 1	720	809	8,209
1021 Recoveries of prior year unpaid obligations	40	90	90
1033 Recoveries of prior year paid obligations	1		
1070 Unobligated balance (total)	761	899	8,299
Budget authority:			
Appropriations, discretionary:			
1100 Appropriation	2,864	2,864	4,019
1100 Appropriation [Infrastructure Investment and Jobs Act of 2021]		8,199	
1120 Appropriations transferred to other accts [089–0222]	–80		
1131 Unobligated balance of appropriations permanently reduced	–2	–2	
1160 Appropriation, discretionary (total)	2,782	11,061	4,019
Advance appropriations, discretionary:			
1170 Advance appropriation [Infrastructure Investment and Jobs Act]			2,220
Spending authority from offsetting collections, discretionary:			
1700 Collected	158	181	181
1701 Change in uncollected payments, Federal sources	10		
1750 Spending auth from offsetting collections, disc (total)	168	181	181
1900 Budget authority (total)	2,950	11,242	6,420
1930 Total budgetary resources available	3,711	12,141	14,719
Memorandum (non-add) entries:			
1941 Unexpired unobligated balance, end of year	809	8,209	8,696
Change in obligated balance:			
Unpaid obligations:			
3000 Unpaid obligations, brought forward, Oct 1	4,131	4,636	5,584
3010 New obligations, unexpired accounts	2,902	3,932	6,023
3020 Outlays (gross)	–2,357	–2,894	–8,138
3040 Recoveries of prior year unpaid obligations, unexpired	–40	–90	–90
3050 Unpaid obligations, end of year	4,636	5,584	3,379
Uncollected payments:			
3060 Uncollected pymts, Fed sources, brought forward, Oct 1	–77	–87	–87
3070 Change in uncollected pymts, Fed sources, unexpired	–10		
3090 Uncollected pymts, Fed sources, end of year	–87	–87	–87
Memorandum (non-add) entries:			
3100 Obligated balance, start of year	4,054	4,549	5,497
3200 Obligated balance, end of year	4,549	5,497	3,292
Budget authority and outlays, net:			
Discretionary:			
4000 Budget authority, gross	2,950	11,242	6,420
Outlays, gross:			
4010 Outlays from new discretionary authority	304	1,405	1,012
4011 Outlays from discretionary balances	2,053	1,489	7,126
4020 Outlays, gross (total)	2,357	2,894	8,138
Offsets against gross budget authority and outlays:			
Offsetting collections (collected) from:			
4030 Federal sources	–72	–81	–81
4033 Non-Federal sources	–87	–100	–100
4040 Offsets against gross budget authority and outlays (total)	–159	–181	–181
Additional offsets against gross budget authority only:			
4050 Change in uncollected pymts, Fed sources, unexpired	–10		
4053 Recoveries of prior year paid obligations, unexpired accounts	1		
4060 Additional offsets against budget authority only (total)	–9		
4070 Budget authority, net (discretionary)	2,782	11,061	6,239
4080 Outlays, net (discretionary)	2,198	2,713	7,957
4180 Budget authority, net (total)	2,782	11,061	6,239
4190 Outlays, net (total)	2,198	2,713	7,957

The Office of Energy Efficiency and Renewable Energy (EERE) accelerates the research, development, demonstration, and deployment (RDD&D) of technologies and solutions to equitably transition America to net-zero greenhouse gas (GHG) emissions economy-wide no later than 2050, creating good paying jobs, and ensuring the clean energy economy benefits all Americans.

To achieve this mission, EERE invests in clean energy technologies that are ready to be demonstrated and deployed, as well as research and development (R&D) activities that advance early stage technologies with a clear path to deployment. EERE's investments focus on five strategic priority areas: decarbonizing the electricity sector, decarbonizing transportation across all modes, decarbonizing energy-intensive industries, reducing the carbon footprint of buildings, and enabling net-zero agricultural production of biofuels.

EERE works in a unified and coordinated way with its state and local partners to accelerate a just, equitable transition to a clean energy economy and ensure that the office's investments benefit everyone, especially those in underserved or pollution over-burdened communities and workers and communities impacted by the energy transition. The office is organized into four pillars, with three technical pillars designed to advance cross-technology solutions, and a Corporate Program pillar that serves as the central organization for all EERE products, services, processes, and systems.

Sustainable Transportation Pillar.—Supports RDD&D efforts to decarbonize transportation across all modes to enable the following: vehicle electrification; commercially viable hydrogen fuel cell trucks; sustainable aviation fuel from biomass; and waste carbon resources and low-GHG options for off-road vehicles, rail, and maritime transport. Many newly-proposed investments in this pillar are directly focused on deployment or demonstration of technology to show viable commercial paths, including a number of programmatic performance milestones by 2030 related to decarbonizing transportation across all modes. The Budget also supports hydrogen use for industrial decarbonization and energy storage, including sustainable biomass to achieve reduced GHG from the agricultural sector.

Renewable Power Pillar.—Supports RDD&D efforts to reduce the costs and accelerate the integration and utilization of renewable energy technologies as part of a reliable, secure, resilient, and fully decarbonized electric system by 2035 and a net zero economy by 2050. This request drives critical cost reductions and technical improvements in wind, solar, geothermal, and water power technologies to increase the penetration of cost-competitive, non-emitting energy generation resources across the country. Renewable Power also provides new research and technologies to facilitate the siting and integration of the high levels of renewable power generation needed to fully decarbonize the power system, and supports the development of diversified, resilient supply chains for all renewable energy technologies to help ensure the long-lasting security of the U.S. energy supply, which will alson provide thousands of good-paying jobs for American workers. The Budget also includes funding for a new Solar Manufacturing Accelerator, an initiative that partners the Advanced Manufacturing Office in the Energy Efficiency pillar with the Solar Energy Technology Office intended to diversify and strengthen the supply chain for solar energy technologies, as well as enhance the domestic capability to produce technologically ad-

ENERGY EFFICIENCY AND RENEWABLE ENERGY—Continued

vanced solar energy components that avoid supply chains that may be reliant in part on unethically sourced materials or vulnerable foreign supply chains.

Energy Efficiency Pillar.— Supports RDD&D to decarbonize America's homes, buildings, and industrial facilities while also strengthening U.S. manufacturing competitiveness and producing thousands of good-paying jobs. The request includes increased support for demonstration and deployment, as well as high impact R&D of technologies to increase energy efficiency, improve demand flexibility, and reduce on-site emissions from our nation's 125 million homes and commercial buildings to reduce total emissions by 50 percent by 2030 and net-zero by 2050. It also increases investment in RDD&D across the multiple decarbonization technologies and approaches necessary to achieve net-zero emissions by 2050, including industry-specific decarbonization investments focused on the chemicals, iron and steel, cement, and food products industries. In addition, the request includes significant funding increases for public investment in federal, state, and community programs to accelerate investments in decarbonizing all sectors of the U.S. economy, and initiates funding for the Solar Manufacturing Accelerator initiative in partnership with the Solar Energy Technologies Office in the Renewable Power pillar.

Corporate Programs Pillar.—Supports activities to make EERE more efficient and effective. This pillar identifies ways to strengthen EERE's overall performance, organization, budget, laboratory management, operations, human capital, and project management while achieving significant cost savings. This includes support for program direction (e.g., salaries and benefits, support services, working capital fund, etc.) and facilities and infrastructure as part of EERE's stewardship of the National Renewable Energy Laboratory (e.g., general plant projects, general purpose equipment, safeguards and security, and capacity building for Administration priorities).

Budgetary projections, including program direction and FTE counts, in the EERE account reflect execution of Bipartisan Infrastructure Legislation (BIL) programs appropriated to EERE and executed through EERE and three newly established programs: State and Community Energy Programs; Manufacturing and Energy Supply Chains; and Federal Energy Management Program.

In FY 2023, through the EERE appropriation, $2.2 Billion of BIL funding is provided to support the following activities: Electric Drive Vehicle Battery Recycling and Second-Life Applications Program; Clean Hydrogen Electrolysis Program; Clean Hydrogen Manufacturing Recycling Research, Development, and Demonstration Program; Maintaining and Enhancing Hydroelectricity Incentives - Section 247 of the Energy Policy Act of 2005; Implementation Grants for Industrial Research and Assessment Centers; Industrial Research and Assessment Centers; Grants for Energy Efficiency Improvement and Renewable Energy Improvements at Public School Facilities; Grants for Updating Building Energy Codes; Advanced Energy Manufacturing and Recycling GrantProgram; Battery Manufacturing and Recycling Grants; and Battery Material Processing Grants.

Object Classification (in millions of dollars)

Identification code 089–0321–0–1–270		2021 actual	2022 est.	2023 est.
	Direct obligations:			
	Personnel compensation:			
11.1	Full-time permanent	77	87	110
11.3	Other than full-time permanent	2	2	2
11.5	Other personnel compensation	2	2	2
11.9	Total personnel compensation	81	91	114
12.1	Civilian personnel benefits	28	33	41
23.3	Communications, utilities, and miscellaneous charges	2	2	4
25.1	Advisory and assistance services	115	115	200
25.2	Other services from non-Federal sources	12	12	12
25.3	Other goods and services from Federal sources	28	28	30
25.4	Operation and maintenance of facilities	1,404	2,339	3,950
25.5	Research and development contracts	122	122	200
25.7	Operation and maintenance of equipment	1	1	2
26.0	Supplies and materials	1	1	2
31.0	Equipment	20	20	40
41.0	Grants, subsidies, and contributions	917	1,000	1,260
99.0	Direct obligations	2,731	3,764	5,855
99.0	Reimbursable obligations	171	168	168
99.9	Total new obligations, unexpired accounts	2,902	3,932	6,023

Employment Summary

Identification code 089–0321–0–1–270	2021 actual	2022 est.	2023 est.
1001 Direct civilian full-time equivalent employment	594	651	828
2001 Reimbursable civilian full-time equivalent employment	1		

OFFICE OF MANUFACTURING AND ENERGY SUPPLY CHAINS

For Department of Energy expenses including the purchase, construction, and acquisition of plant and capital equipment, and other expenses necessary for manufacturing and energy supply chain activities in carrying out the purposes of the Department of Energy Organization Act (42 U.S.C. 7101 et seq.), including the acquisition or condemnation of any real property or any facility or for plant or facility acquisition, construction, or expansion, $27,424,000, to remain available until expended: Provided, That of such amount, $6,424,000 shall be available until September 30, 2024, for program direction.

Program and Financing (in millions of dollars)

Identification code 089–2291–0–1–270		2021 actual	2022 est.	2023 est.
	Obligations by program activity:			
0001	Facility and Workforce Assistance			18
0002	Energy Sector Industrial Base Technical Assistance			3
0010	Program Direction			6
0900	Total new obligations, unexpired accounts			27
	Budgetary resources:			
	Budget authority:			
	Appropriations, discretionary:			
1100	Appropriation			27
1930	Total budgetary resources available			27
	Change in obligated balance:			
	Unpaid obligations:			
3010	New obligations, unexpired accounts			27
3020	Outlays (gross)			–14
3050	Unpaid obligations, end of year			13
	Memorandum (non-add) entries:			
3200	Obligated balance, end of year			13
	Budget authority and outlays, net:			
	Discretionary:			
4000	Budget authority, gross			27
	Outlays, gross:			
4010	Outlays from new discretionary authority			14
4180	Budget authority, net (total)			27
4190	Outlays, net (total)			14

The newly created Office of Manufacturing and Energy Supply Chains (MESC), within the Office of the Under Secretary for Infrastructure, will train the next generation of energy engineers and conduct energy assessments to identify opportunities to improve productivity and competitiveness, reduce waste, and save energy for small- and medium-sized manufacturers. DOEs Industrial Assessment Centers provide a no-cost assessment, including in-depth evaluations of a facility conducted by engineering faculty with upper class and graduate students from a participating university. This detailed process analysis will generate specific recommendations with estimates of costs, performance, and payback schedules.

These activities were previously funded within Energy Efficiency and Renewable Energy. Additional Bipartisan Infrastructure Law funding and full-time equivalents (FTEs) for the MESC program are captured in the budgetary projections in, and will be executed through, the Department's EERE account.

Object Classification (in millions of dollars)

Identification code 089–2291–0–1–270		2021 actual	2022 est.	2023 est.
11.1	Direct obligations: Personnel compensation: Full-time permanent			1
11.9	Total personnel compensation			1
25.1	Advisory and assistance services			4
25.2	Other services from non-Federal sources			1
25.4	Operation and maintenance of facilities			18
94.0	Financial transfers			3
99.9	Total new obligations, unexpired accounts			27

Employment Summary

Identification code 089–2291–0–1–270		2021 actual	2022 est.	2023 est.
1001	Direct civilian full-time equivalent employment			3

OFFICE OF STATE AND COMMUNITY ENERGY PROGRAMS

For Department of Energy expenses including the purchase, construction, and acquisition of plant and capital equipment, and other expenses necessary for state and community energy activities in carrying out the purposes of the Department of Energy Organization Act (42 U.S.C. 7101 et seq.), including the acquisition or condemnation of any real property or any facility or for plant or facility acquisition, construction, or expansion, $726,897,000, to remain available until expended: Provided, That of such amount, $24,727,000 shall be available until September 30, 2024, for program direction.

Program and Financing (in millions of dollars)

Identification code 089–2292–0–1–270		2021 actual	2022 est.	2023 est.
	Obligations by program activity:			
0002	Weatherization Assistance Program			502
0003	Community Programs			25
0004	State Energy Programs			70
0005	Build Back Better Challenge Grants			105
0010	Program Direction			25
0900	Total new obligations, unexpired accounts			727
	Budgetary resources:			
	Budget authority:			
	Appropriations, discretionary:			
1100	Appropriation			727
1930	Total budgetary resources available			727
	Change in obligated balance:			
	Unpaid obligations:			
3010	New obligations, unexpired accounts			727
3020	Outlays (gross)			–239
3050	Unpaid obligations, end of year			488
	Memorandum (non-add) entries:			
3200	Obligated balance, end of year			488
	Budget authority and outlays, net:			
	Discretionary:			
4000	Budget authority, gross			727
	Outlays, gross:			
4010	Outlays from new discretionary authority			239
4180	Budget authority, net (total)			727
4190	Outlays, net (total)			239

The newly created Office of State and Community Energy Programs (SCEP), within the Office of the Under Secretary for Infrastructure, supports the transition to an equitable clean energy economy by working with community-level implementation partners and State Energy Offices. SCEP manages the Weatherization Assistance Program (WAP), State Energy Program, Local Government Program, and Build Back Better Challenge Grants. SECP was previously funded within the Office of Energy Efficiency and Renewable Energy (EERE). In FY 2023, WAP will launch a Low-Income Home Energy Assistance Program Advantage (LIHEAP Advantage) pilot to retrofit and decarbonize LIHEAP beneficiary homes with efficient electric appliances and systems.

These activities were previously funded within EERE. Additional Bipartisan Infrastructure Law funding and FTEs for SCEP are captured in the budgetary projections in, and will be executed through, the Department's EERE account.

Object Classification (in millions of dollars)

Identification code 089–2292–0–1–270		2021 actual	2022 est.	2023 est.
	Direct obligations:			
	Personnel compensation:			
11.1	Full-time permanent			9
11.3	Other than full-time permanent			1
11.5	Other personnel compensation			1
11.9	Total personnel compensation			11
12.1	Civilian personnel benefits			3
21.0	Travel and transportation of persons			2
23.1	Rental payments to GSA			1
23.3	Communications, utilities, and miscellaneous charges			1
25.1	Advisory and assistance services			44
25.2	Other services from non-Federal sources			2
25.3	Other goods and services from Federal sources			1
41.0	Grants, subsidies, and contributions			662
99.9	Total new obligations, unexpired accounts			727

Employment Summary

Identification code 089–2292–0–1–270		2021 actual	2022 est.	2023 est.
1001	Direct civilian full-time equivalent employment			75

FEDERAL ENERGY MANAGEMENT PROGRAM

For Department of Energy expenses including the purchase, construction, and acquisition of plant and capital equipment, and other expenses necessary for federal energy management activities in carrying out the purposes of the Department of Energy Organization Act (42 U.S.C. 7101 et seq.), including the acquisition or condemnation of any real property or any facility or for plant or facility acquisition, construction, or expansion, $169,661,000, to remain available until expended: Provided, That of such amount, $14,511,000 shall be available until September 30, 2024, for program direction.

Program and Financing (in millions of dollars)

Identification code 089–2293–0–1–270		2021 actual	2022 est.	2023 est.
	Obligations by program activity:			
0001	Federal Energy Management			38
0002	Federal Energy Efficiency Fund			60
0003	Net Zero Laboratory Initiative			57
0010	Program Direction			15
0900	Total new obligations, unexpired accounts			170
	Budgetary resources:			
	Budget authority:			
	Appropriations, discretionary:			
1100	Appropriation			170
1930	Total budgetary resources available			170
	Change in obligated balance:			
	Unpaid obligations:			
3010	New obligations, unexpired accounts			170
3020	Outlays (gross)			–68
3050	Unpaid obligations, end of year			102
	Memorandum (non-add) entries:			
3200	Obligated balance, end of year			102
	Budget authority and outlays, net:			
	Discretionary:			
4000	Budget authority, gross			170
	Outlays, gross:			
4010	Outlays from new discretionary authority			68
4180	Budget authority, net (total)			170
4190	Outlays, net (total)			68

FEDERAL ENERGY MANAGEMENT PROGRAM—Continued

The newly created Office of Federal Energy Management Program (FEMP), within the Office of the Under Secretary for Infrastructure, helps Federal agencies meet sustainability goals by providing technical assistance, financial assistance, training, and other resources. FEMP works with stakeholders to enable Federal agencies to identify affordable solutions, facilitate public-private partnerships, and provide energy leadership to the country through government best practices. FEMP was previously funded within the Office of Energy Efficiency and Renewable Energy (EERE). In FY 2023, the program will launch the Net-Zero Labs Initiative to competitively select clean energy deployment and decarbonization projects across the National Laboratories. These investments will create good paying jobs while driving progress toward the Administrations climate goals, including the Presidents goal of 80 percent carbon pollution-free electricity by 2030.

Additional Bipartisan Infrastructure Law funding and FTEs for FEMP are captured in the budgetary projections in, and will be executed through the Department's EERE account.

Object Classification (in millions of dollars)

Identification code 089–2293–0–1–270		2021 actual	2022 est.	2023 est.
	Direct obligations:			
	Personnel compensation:			
11.1	Full-time permanent			3
11.3	Other than full-time permanent			1
11.5	Other personnel compensation			1
11.9	Total personnel compensation			5
12.1	Civilian personnel benefits			1
21.0	Travel and transportation of persons			1
23.1	Rental payments to GSA			1
23.3	Communications, utilities, and miscellaneous charges			1
25.1	Advisory and assistance services			5
25.4	Operation and maintenance of facilities			96
41.0	Grants, subsidies, and contributions			60
99.9	Total new obligations, unexpired accounts			170

Employment Summary

Identification code 089–2293–0–1–270	2021 actual	2022 est.	2023 est.
1001 Direct civilian full-time equivalent employment			47

GLOBAL CLEAN ENERGY MANUFACTURING

(Legislative proposal, subject to PAYGO)

Program and Financing (in millions of dollars)

Identification code 089–2302–4–1–270	2021 actual	2022 est.	2023 est.
Obligations by program activity:			
0010 Clean Energy Manufacturing Programs			196
0020 Program Direction			4
0900 Total new obligations, unexpired accounts			200
Budgetary resources:			
Budget authority:			
Appropriations, mandatory:			
1200 Appropriation			200
1930 Total budgetary resources available			200
Change in obligated balance:			
Unpaid obligations:			
3010 New obligations, unexpired accounts			200
3020 Outlays (gross)			–40
3050 Unpaid obligations, end of year			160
Memorandum (non-add) entries:			
3200 Obligated balance, end of year			160
Budget authority and outlays, net:			
Mandatory:			
4090 Budget authority, gross			200
Outlays, gross:			
4100 Outlays from new mandatory authority			40
4180 Budget authority, net (total)			200
4190 Outlays, net (total)			40

The Budget proposes a $1 billion mandatory investment to launch a Global Clean Energy Manufacturing effort that would build resilient supply chains for climate and clean energy equipment through engagement with allies, enabling an effective global response to the climate crisis while creating economic opportunities for the U.S. to increase its share of the global clean technology market.

Object Classification (in millions of dollars)

Identification code 089–2302–4–1–270	2021 actual	2022 est.	2023 est.
Direct obligations:			
11.1 Personnel compensation: Full-time permanent			1
25.1 Advisory and assistance services			3
25.4 Operation and maintenance of facilities			80
25.5 Research and development contracts			56
41.0 Grants, subsidies, and contributions			60
99.9 Total new obligations, unexpired accounts			200

Employment Summary

Identification code 089–2302–4–1–270	2021 actual	2022 est.	2023 est.
1001 Direct civilian full-time equivalent employment			8

OFFICE OF TECHNOLOGY TRANSITIONS

For Department of Energy expenses in carrying out the activities of the Office of Technology Transitions, $21,558,000, to remain available until September 30, 2028: Provided, That of such amount, $13,183,000 shall be available until September 30, 2024, for program direction.

Note.—A full-year 2022 appropriation for this account was not enacted at the time the Budget was prepared; therefore, the Budget assumes this account is operating under the Continuing Appropriations Act, 2022 (Division A of Public Law 117–43, as amended). The amounts included for 2022 reflect the annualized level provided by the continuing resolution.

Program and Financing (in millions of dollars)

Identification code 089–0346–0–1–276	2021 actual	2022 est.	2023 est.
Obligations by program activity:			
0010 Technology transition activities			9
0040 Program direction			13
0900 Total new obligations, unexpired accounts			22
Budgetary resources:			
Budget authority:			
Appropriations, discretionary:			
1100 Appropriation			22
1930 Total budgetary resources available			22
Change in obligated balance:			
Unpaid obligations:			
3010 New obligations, unexpired accounts			22
3020 Outlays (gross)			–11
3050 Unpaid obligations, end of year			11
Memorandum (non-add) entries:			
3200 Obligated balance, end of year			11
Budget authority and outlays, net:			
Discretionary:			
4000 Budget authority, gross			22
Outlays, gross:			
4010 Outlays from new discretionary authority			11
4180 Budget authority, net (total)			22
4190 Outlays, net (total)			11

The mission of the Office of Technology Transitions (OTT) is to expand the commercial and public impact of the Department of Energy's investments. OTT serves a multi-disciplinary role across the Research, Development, Demonstration, and Deployment (RDD&D) continuum to support

DEPARTMENT OF ENERGY

the transition of our technologies to the market. OTT does so by providing public-private partnering support, market-informed analytics, and commercial adoption risk assessments. OTT manages DOE's ongoing lab-to-market and other technology commercialization activities, including the statutory Technology Commercialization Fund, the Energy I-Corps, the Energy Program for Innovation Clusters (EPIC), and the Lab Partnering Service. OTT stewards DOE technology transition activities, including policy reform, data collection and analyses, industry stakeholder convenings, and amplification of DOE technology transfer success stories across the DOE—including programs, field offices, and the National Laboratories and Production Facilities—as well as engaging with other Federal agencies to improve awareness of the benefits of engaging the DOE research enterprise.

Object Classification (in millions of dollars)

Identification code 089–0346–0–1–276	2021 actual	2022 est.	2023 est.
11.1 Direct obligations: Personnel compensation: Full-time permanent			4
11.9 Total personnel compensation			4
12.1 Civilian personnel benefits			1
25.1 Advisory and assistance services			4
25.2 Other services from non-Federal sources			6
25.3 Other goods and services from Federal sources			3
25.4 Operation and maintenance of facilities			4
99.9 Total new obligations, unexpired accounts			22

Employment Summary

Identification code 089–0346–0–1–276	2021 actual	2022 est.	2023 est.
1001 Direct civilian full-time equivalent employment			39

OFFICE OF CLEAN ENERGY DEMONSTRATIONS

For Department of Energy expenses, including the purchase, construction, and acquisition of plant and capital equipment and other expenses necessary for clean energy demonstrations in carrying out the purposes of the Department of Energy Organization Act (42 U.S.C. 7101 et seq.), including the acquisition or condemnation of any real property or any facility or for plant or facility acquisition, construction, or expansion, $214,052,000, to remain available until expended: *Provided*, That of such amount, $25,000,000 shall be available until September 30, 2024, for program direction.

Note.—A full-year 2022 appropriation for this account was not enacted at the time the Budget was prepared; therefore, the Budget assumes this account is operating under the Continuing Appropriations Act, 2022 (Division A of Public Law 117–43, as amended). The amounts included for 2022 reflect the annualized level provided by the continuing resolution.

OFFICE OF CLEAN ENERGY DEMONSTRATIONS

⟦For an additional amount for "Office of Clean Energy Demonstrations", $21,456,000,000, to remain available until expended: *Provided*, That the Office of Clean Energy Demonstrations, as authorized by section 41201 of division D of this Act, shall conduct administrative and project management responsibilities for the demonstration projects provided for under this heading in this Act: *Provided further*, That the Office of Clean Energy Demonstrations shall consult and coordinate with technology-specific program offices to ensure alignment of technology goals and avoid unnecessary duplication: *Provided further*, That of the amount provided under this heading in this Act and in addition to amounts otherwise made available for this purpose, $355,000,000 shall be to carry out the Energy Storage Demonstration Pilot Grant Program, as authorized under section 3201(c) of the Energy Act of 2020 (42 U.S.C. 17232(c)): *Provided further*, That of the funds in the preceding proviso, $88,750,000, to remain available until expended, shall be made available for fiscal year 2022, $88,750,000, to remain available until expended, shall be made available for fiscal year 2023, $88,750,000, to remain available until expended, shall be made available for fiscal year 2024, $88,750,000, to remain available until expended, shall be made available for fiscal year 2025: *Provided further*, That of the amount provided under this heading in this Act and in addition to amounts otherwise made available for this purpose, $150,000,000 to carry out the Long-duration Demonstration Initiative and Joint Program, as authorized under section 3201(d) of the Energy Act of 2020 (42 U.S.C. 17232(d)): *Provided further*, That of the funds in the preceding proviso, $37,500,000, to remain available until expended, shall be made available for fiscal year 2022, $37,500,000, to remain available until expended, shall be made available for fiscal year 2023, $37,500,000, to remain available until expended, shall be made available for fiscal year 2024, $37,500,000, to remain available until expended, shall be made available for fiscal year 2025: *Provided further*, That of the amount provided under this heading in this Act and in addition to amounts otherwise made available for this purpose, $2,477,000,000 shall be to carry out the Advanced Reactor Demonstration Program, as authorized under section 959A of the Energy Policy Act of 2005 (42 U.S.C. 16279a): *Provided further*, That of the funds in the preceding proviso, $677,000,000, to remain available until expended, shall be made available for fiscal year 2022, $600,000,000, to remain available until expended, shall be made available for fiscal year 2023, $600,000,000, to remain available until expended, shall be made available for fiscal year 2024, $600,000,000, to remain available until expended, shall be made available for fiscal year 2025: *Provided further*, That funds in the preceding proviso shall be for projects selected prior to the date of enactment of this Act: *Provided further*, That of the amount provided under this heading in this Act and in addition to amounts otherwise made available for this purpose, $937,000,000 shall be to carry out the Carbon Capture Large-scale Pilot Projects, as authorized under section 962(b)(2)(B) of the Energy Policy Act of 2005 (42 U.S.C. 16292(b)(2)(B)): *Provided further*, That of the funds in the preceding proviso, $387,000,000, to remain available until expended, shall be made available for fiscal year 2022, $200,000,000, to remain available until expended, shall be made available for fiscal year 2023, $200,000,000, to remain available until expended, shall be made available for fiscal year 2024, $150,000,000, to remain available until expended, shall be made available for fiscal year 2025: *Provided further*, That of the amount provided under this heading in this Act and in addition to amounts otherwise made available for this purpose, $2,537,000,000 shall be for the Carbon Capture Demonstration Projects Program, as authorized under section 962(b)(2)(C) of the Energy Policy Act of 2005 (42 U.S.C. 16292(b)(2)(C)): *Provided further*, That of the funds in the preceding proviso, $937,000,000, to remain available until expended, shall be made available for fiscal year 2022, $500,000,000, to remain available until expended, shall be made available for fiscal year 2023, $500,000,000, to remain available until expended, shall be made available for fiscal year 2024, $600,000,000, to remain available until expended, shall be made available for fiscal year 2025: *Provided further*, That of the amount provided under this heading in this Act and in addition to amounts otherwise made available for this purpose, $500,000,000 shall be to carry out Industrial Emission Demonstration Projects, as authorized under section 454(d)(3) of the Energy Independence and Security Act of 2007 (42 U.S.C. 17113(d)(3)): *Provided further*, That of the funds in the preceding proviso, $100,000,000, to remain available until expended, shall be made available for fiscal year 2022, $100,000,000, to remain available until expended, shall be made available for fiscal year 2023, $150,000,000, to remain available until expended, shall be made available for fiscal year 2024, $150,000,000, to remain available until expended, shall be made available for fiscal year 2025: *Provided further*, That of the amount provided under this heading in this Act and in addition to amounts otherwise made available for this purpose, $500,000,000 shall be to carry out the Clean Energy Demonstration Program on Current and Former Mine Land, as authorized under section 40342 of division D of this Act: *Provided further*, That of the funds in the preceding proviso, $100,000,000, to remain available until expended, shall be made available for fiscal year 2022, $100,000,000, to remain available until expended, shall be made available for fiscal year 2023, $100,000,000, to remain available until expended, shall be made available for fiscal year 2024, $100,000,000, to remain available until expended, shall be made available for fiscal year 2025, and $100,000,000, to remain available until expended, shall be made available for fiscal year 2026: *Provided further*, That of the amount provided under this heading in this Act, $8,000,000,000 shall be made for Regional Clean Hydrogen Hubs, as authorized under section 813 of the Energy Policy Act of 2005 (42 U.S.C. 16151 et seq.), as amended by section 40314 of division D of this Act: *Provided further*, That of the funds in the preceding proviso, $1,600,000,000, to remain available until expended, shall be made available for fiscal year 2022, $1,600,000,000, to remain available until expended, shall be made available for fiscal year 2023, $1,600,000,000, to remain available until expended, shall be made available for fiscal year 2024, $1,600,000,000, to remain available until expended, shall be made available for fiscal year 2025, and $1,600,000,000, to remain available until expended, shall be made available for fiscal year 2026: *Provided further*, That of the amount provided under this heading in this Act, $5,000,000,000 shall be for grants for the Program Upgrading Our Electric Grid and Ensuring Reliability and Resiliency, as authorized under section 40103(b) of division D of this Act: *Provided further*, That of the funds in the preceding proviso, $1,000,000,000, to remain available until expended, shall be made available for fiscal year 2022, $1,000,000,000, to remain available until expended, shall be made available for fiscal year 2023, $1,000,000,000, to remain available until expended, shall be made available for fiscal year 2024, $1,000,000,000, to remain available until expended, shall be made available for

OFFICE OF CLEAN ENERGY DEMONSTRATIONS—Continued

fiscal year 2025, and $1,000,000,000, to remain available until expended, shall be made available for fiscal year 2026: *Provided further*, That of the amount provided under this heading in this Act, $1,000,000,000 shall be to carry out activities for energy improvement in rural and remote areas, as authorized under section 40103(c) of division D of this Act: *Provided further*, That of the funds in the preceding proviso, $200,000,000, to remain available until expended, shall be made available for fiscal year 2022, $200,000,000, to remain available until expended, shall be made available for fiscal year 2023, $200,000,000, to remain available until expended, shall be made available for fiscal year 2024, $200,000,000, to remain available until expended, shall be made available for fiscal year 2025, and $200,000,000, to remain available until expended, shall be made available for fiscal year 2026: *Provided further*, That not later than 90 days after the date of enactment of this Act, the Secretary of Energy shall submit to the House and Senate Committees on Appropriations a detailed spend plan for fiscal year 2022: *Provided further*, That for each fiscal year through 2026, as part of the annual budget submission of the President under section 1105(a) of title 31, United States Code, the Secretary of Energy shall submit a detailed spend plan for that fiscal year: *Provided further*, That up to three percent of the amounts made available under this heading in this Act in each of fiscal years 2022 through 2026 shall be for program direction: *Provided further*, That such amount is designated by the Congress as being for an emergency requirement pursuant to section 4112(a) of H. Con. Res. 71 (115th Congress), the concurrent resolution on the budget for fiscal year 2018, and to section 251(b) of the Balanced Budget and Emergency Deficit Control Act of 1985.] *(Infrastructure Investments and Jobs Appropriations Act.)*

Program and Financing (in millions of dollars)

Identification code 089–2297–0–1–270	2021 actual	2022 est.	2023 est.
Obligations by program activity:			
0010 Clean Energy Demonstrations			112
0011 Program Direction			20
0013 Energy Improvement in Rural and Remote Areas		55	99
0015 Regional Clean Hydrogen Hubs		19	114
0017 Clean Energy Demonstration Program on Current and Former Mine Land		4	57
0019 Energy Storage Demonstration Pilot Grant Program		3	21
0021 Long-duration Demonstration Initiative and Joint Program		35	30
0023 Advanced Reactor Demonstration Program		303	456
0025 Carbon Capture Demonstration Projects Program		10	272
0027 Carbon Capture Large-scale Pilot Projects		24	277
0029 Industrial Emission Demonstration Projects		3	76
0031 Upgrading Our Electric Grid and Ensuring Reliability and Resiliency		154	713
0033 Program Direction - IIJA		62	100
0900 Total new obligations, unexpired accounts		672	2,347
Budgetary resources:			
Unobligated balance:			
1000 Unobligated balance brought forward, Oct 1			4,451
Budget authority:			
Appropriations, discretionary:			
1100 Appropriation		5,123	214
Advance appropriations, discretionary:			
1170 Advance appropriation			4,423
1900 Budget authority (total)		5,123	4,637
1930 Total budgetary resources available		5,123	9,088
Memorandum (non-add) entries:			
1941 Unexpired unobligated balance, end of year		4,451	6,741
Change in obligated balance:			
Unpaid obligations:			
3000 Unpaid obligations, brought forward, Oct 1			268
3010 New obligations, unexpired accounts		672	2,347
3020 Outlays (gross)		–404	–1,104
3050 Unpaid obligations, end of year		268	1,511
Memorandum (non-add) entries:			
3100 Obligated balance, start of year			268
3200 Obligated balance, end of year		268	1,511
Budget authority and outlays, net:			
Discretionary:			
4000 Budget authority, gross		5,123	4,637
Outlays, gross:			
4010 Outlays from new discretionary authority		404	386
4011 Outlays from discretionary balances			718
4020 Outlays, gross (total)		404	1,104
4180 Budget authority, net (total)		5,123	4,637
4190 Outlays, net (total)		404	1,104

The FY 2023 request includes funding for the Office of Clean Energy Demonstrations (OCED), which was authorized and established through the Bipartisan Infrastructure Law (BIL). OCED's mission is to deliver clean energy technology demonstration projects at scale in partnership with the private sector to accelerate deployment, market adoption, and the equitable transition to a decarbonized energy system by 2035.

OCED is a technology-neutral office with expertise in large-scale energy project management and finance that leverages the existing technical expertise throughout the Department of Energy (DOE). OCED investments are part of a clear progression and transition between the research, development, and demonstration projects within the DOE technology offices and initial deployments supported by the private sector or DOE Loan Programs Offices, ensuring continuity of DOE support for clean energy technologies and systems. Funding decisions are made to support scalable outcomes leading to commercialization and deployment for greenhouse gas reductions, job creation, and achieving environmental justice and Justice40 Initiative priorities.

In FY 2023, OCED will support new demonstrations related to the integration of renewable and distributed energy systems. The goal of this new investment area is to support demonstration programs to address integration issues of renewable energy onto the transmission and distribution grids. Additionally, OCED will provide additional support for the Advanced Reactor Demonstration Program, as part of DOE's consolidation of support for these demonstration projects into OCED from the Office of Nuclear Energy (NE). This investment will complement the $2.48 billion provided in BIL to continue these important projects.

In addition to the activities supported through OCED's annual appropriations, the organization will continue to support clean energy demonstrations through its execution of funding provided to OCED in BIL.

Object Classification (in millions of dollars)

Identification code 089–2297–0–1–270	2021 actual	2022 est.	2023 est.
Direct obligations:			
Personnel compensation:			
11.1 Full-time permanent		15	28
11.3 Other than full-time permanent		1	1
11.5 Other personnel compensation		1	1
11.9 Total personnel compensation		17	30
12.1 Civilian personnel benefits		5	8
21.0 Travel and transportation of persons		2	3
23.3 Communications, utilities, and miscellaneous charges		2	4
25.1 Advisory and assistance services		100	200
25.2 Other services from non-Federal sources		10	20
25.3 Other goods and services from Federal sources		5	10
25.4 Operation and maintenance of facilities		195	600
25.5 Research and development contracts		65	100
26.0 Supplies and materials		1	2
41.0 Grants, subsidies, and contributions		270	1,370
99.9 Total new obligations, unexpired accounts		672	2,347

Employment Summary

Identification code 089–2297–0–1–270	2021 actual	2022 est.	2023 est.
1001 Direct civilian full-time equivalent employment		121	224

OFFICE OF INDIAN ENERGY POLICY AND PROGRAMS

For necessary expenses for Indian Energy activities in carrying out the purposes of the Department of Energy Organization Act (42 U.S.C. 7101 et seq.), $150,039,000 to remain available until expended: Provided, That, of the amount appropriated under this heading, $20,303,000 shall be available until September 30, 2024, for program direction.

Note.—A full-year 2022 appropriation for this account was not enacted at the time the Budget was prepared; therefore, the Budget assumes this account is operating under the Continuing Appropriations Act, 2022 (Division A of Public Law 117–43, as amended). The amounts included for 2022 reflect the annualized level provided by the continuing resolution.

DEPARTMENT OF ENERGY

Program and Financing (in millions of dollars)

Identification code 089–0342–0–1–271	2021 actual	2022 est.	2023 est.
Obligations by program activity:			
0010 Direct program activity	33	32	122
Budgetary resources:			
Unobligated balance:			
1000 Unobligated balance brought forward, Oct 1	21	10	
Budget authority:			
Appropriations, discretionary:			
1100 Appropriation	22	22	150
1930 Total budgetary resources available	43	32	150
Memorandum (non-add) entries:			
1941 Unexpired unobligated balance, end of year	10		28
Change in obligated balance:			
Unpaid obligations:			
3000 Unpaid obligations, brought forward, Oct 1	11	33	46
3010 New obligations, unexpired accounts	33	32	122
3020 Outlays (gross)	–11	–19	–110
3050 Unpaid obligations, end of year	33	46	58
Memorandum (non-add) entries:			
3100 Obligated balance, start of year	11	33	46
3200 Obligated balance, end of year	33	46	58
Budget authority and outlays, net:			
Discretionary:			
4000 Budget authority, gross	22	22	150
Outlays, gross:			
4010 Outlays from new discretionary authority	1	1	90
4011 Outlays from discretionary balances	10	18	20
4020 Outlays, gross (total)	11	19	110
4180 Budget authority, net (total)	22	22	150
4190 Outlays, net (total)	11	19	110

Office of Indian Energy Policy and Programs (IE).—Directs, fosters, coordinates, and implements energy planning, education, management, and financial assistance programs that assist Tribes with clean energy development and infrastructure, capacity building, energy costs, and electrification of Indian lands and homes. IE coordinates programmatic activity across the Department related to development of clean energy resources on Indian lands, and works with other Federal government agencies, Indian Tribes, and Tribal organizations to promote Indian energy policies and initiatives. Through financial and technical assistance IE will empower American Indian and Alaskan Native nations to lead the transition to 100% clean energy, seven generation planning, and addressing energy access and energy poverty in Indian Country. A key focus will be on assisting Tribal Colleges and Universities to power their instituitons with clean energy.

Object Classification (in millions of dollars)

Identification code 089–0342–0–1–271	2021 actual	2022 est.	2023 est.
11.1 Direct obligations: Personnel compensation: Full-time permanent	1	1	4
11.9 Total personnel compensation	1	1	4
12.1 Civilian personnel benefits	1	1	1
25.1 Advisory and assistance services	3	2	4
25.2 Other services from non-Federal sources	1	1	1
25.4 Operation and maintenance of facilities	1	1	1
41.0 Grants, subsidies, and contributions	26	26	111
99.9 Total new obligations, unexpired accounts	33	32	122

Employment Summary

Identification code 089–0342–0–1–271	2021 actual	2022 est.	2023 est.
1001 Direct civilian full-time equivalent employment	10	10	29

NON-DEFENSE ENVIRONMENTAL CLEANUP

For Department of Energy expenses, including the purchase, construction, and acquisition of plant and capital equipment and other expenses necessary for non-defense environmental cleanup activities in carrying out the purposes of the Department of Energy Organization Act (42 U.S.C. 7101 et seq.), including the acquisition or condemnation of any real property or any facility or for plant or facility acquisition, construction, or expansion, and the purchase of one zero emission passenger motor vehicle, $323,249,000, to remain available until expended: Provided, That, in addition, fees collected pursuant to subsection (b)(1) of section 6939f of title 42, United States Code, and deposited under this heading in fiscal year 2023 pursuant to section 309 of title III of division C of Public Law 116–94 are appropriated, to remain available until expended, for mercury storage costs: Provided further, That of the amount appropriated under this heading, $123,438,000 shall be derived from the United States Enrichment Corporation Fund, to remain available until expended.

Note.—A full-year 2022 appropriation for this account was not enacted at the time the Budget was prepared; therefore, the Budget assumes this account is operating under the Continuing Appropriations Act, 2022 (Division A of Public Law 117–43, as amended). The amounts included for 2022 reflect the annualized level provided by the continuing resolution.

Program and Financing (in millions of dollars)

Identification code 089–0315–0–1–271	2021 actual	2022 est.	2023 est.
Obligations by program activity:			
0002 Fast Flux Test Facility	3	3	3
0003 Gaseous Diffusion Plants	117	115	123
0004 Small Sites	118	111	105
0005 West Valley Demonstration Project	88	88	90
0006 Management and Storage of Elemental Mercury	1	2	2
0799 Total direct obligations	327	319	323
0801 Non-defense Environmental Cleanup (Reimbursable)	41	35	35
0900 Total new obligations, unexpired accounts	368	354	358
Budgetary resources:			
Unobligated balance:			
1000 Unobligated balance brought forward, Oct 1	8	4	4
1021 Recoveries of prior year unpaid obligations	4		
1070 Unobligated balance (total)	12	4	4
Budget authority:			
Appropriations, discretionary:			
1100 Appropriation	319	319	200
Spending authority from offsetting collections, discretionary:			
1700 Collected	41	35	35
1711 Spending authority from offsetting collections transferred from other accounts [486–4054]			123
1750 Spending auth from offsetting collections, disc (total)	41	35	158
1900 Budget authority (total)	360	354	358
1930 Total budgetary resources available	372	358	362
Memorandum (non-add) entries:			
1941 Unexpired unobligated balance, end of year	4	4	4
Change in obligated balance:			
Unpaid obligations:			
3000 Unpaid obligations, brought forward, Oct 1	269	284	144
3010 New obligations, unexpired accounts	368	354	358
3020 Outlays (gross)	–349	–494	–430
3040 Recoveries of prior year unpaid obligations, unexpired	–4		
3050 Unpaid obligations, end of year	284	144	72
Memorandum (non-add) entries:			
3100 Obligated balance, start of year	269	284	144
3200 Obligated balance, end of year	284	144	72
Budget authority and outlays, net:			
Discretionary:			
4000 Budget authority, gross	360	354	358
Outlays, gross:			
4010 Outlays from new discretionary authority	193	258	298
4011 Outlays from discretionary balances	156	236	132
4020 Outlays, gross (total)	349	494	430
Offsets against gross budget authority and outlays:			
Offsetting collections (collected) from:			
4030 Federal sources	–1		
4033 Non-Federal sources	–40	–35	–35
4040 Offsets against gross budget authority and outlays (total)	–41	–35	–35
4070 Budget authority, net (discretionary)	319	319	323
4080 Outlays, net (discretionary)	308	459	395
4180 Budget authority, net (total)	319	319	323
4190 Outlays, net (total)	308	459	395

NON-DEFENSE ENVIRONMENTAL CLEANUP—Continued

The Non-Defense Environmental Cleanup program includes funds to manage and clean up sites used for civilian energy research and non-defense-related activities. These activities resulted in radioactive, hazardous, and mixed waste contamination that requires remediation, stabilization, or some other type of corrective action, as well as the decontamination and decommissioning of former research and production buildings and supporting infrastructure. The budget displays the cleanup program by site and activity.

West Valley Demonstration Project.—Funds waste disposition, building decontamination, and removal of non-essential facilities in the near-term.

Gaseous Diffusion Plants.—Funds surveillance and maintenance of the former Uranium Program facilities and manages legacy polychlorinated biphenyl contamination. The program also includes the operation of two depleted uranium hexafluoride conversion facilities at Paducah, Kentucky, and Portsmouth, Ohio, which are converting the depleted uranium hexafluoride into a more stable form for reuse or disposition.

Fast Flux Test Facility.—Funds the long-term surveillance and maintenance and eventual decontamination and decommissioning of the Fast Flux Test Facility, constructed and operated from the 1960s through 1980s.

Small Sites.—Funds cleanup, closure, and post-closure environmental activities at a number of geographic sites across the nation, including the Energy Technology Engineering Center and Moab, as well as non-defense activities at Idaho. Some sites are associated with other Department of Energy programs, particularly the Office of Science, and will have continuing missions after EM completes the cleanup. Others will transition to the Office of Legacy Management or private-sector entities for post-closure activities.

Object Classification (in millions of dollars)

Identification code 089–0315–0–1–271		2021 actual	2022 est.	2023 est.
	Direct obligations:			
25.1	Advisory and assistance services	4	4	4
25.2	Other services from non-Federal sources	17	16	17
25.3	Other goods and services from Federal sources	1	1	1
25.4	Operation and maintenance of facilities	300	293	296
32.0	Land and structures	4	4	4
41.0	Grants, subsidies, and contributions	1	1	1
99.0	Direct obligations	327	319	323
99.0	Reimbursable obligations	41	35	35
99.9	Total new obligations, unexpired accounts	368	354	358

FOSSIL ENERGY AND CARBON MANAGEMENT

For Department of Energy expenses necessary in carrying out fossil energy and carbon management research and development activities, under the authority of the Department of Energy Organization Act (42 U.S.C. 7101 et seq.), including the acquisition of interest, including defeasible and equitable interests in any real property or any facility or for plant or facility acquisition or expansion, and for conducting inquiries, technological investigations and research concerning the extraction, processing, use, and disposal of mineral substances without objectionable social and environmental costs (30 U.S.C. 3, 1602, and 1603), $893,160,000, to remain available until expended: Provided, That such amount $70,291,000 shall be available until September 30, 2024, for program direction.

Note.—A full-year 2022 appropriation for this account was not enacted at the time the Budget was prepared; therefore, the Budget assumes this account is operating under the Continuing Appropriations Act, 2022 (Division A of Public Law 117–43, as amended). The amounts included for 2022 reflect the annualized level provided by the continuing resolution.

FOSSIL ENERGY AND CARBON MANAGEMENT

[For an additional amount for "Fossil Energy and Carbon Management", $7,497,140,781, to remain available until expended: *Provided*, That the amount provided under this heading in this Act, $310,140,781 shall be to carry out activities under the Carbon Utilization Program, as authorized in section 969A of the Energy Policy Act of 2005 (42 U.S.C. 16298a), as amended by section 40302 of division D of this Act: *Provided further*, That of the funds in the preceding proviso, $41,000,000, to remain available until expended, shall be made available for fiscal year 2022, $65,250,000, to remain available until expended, shall be made available for fiscal year 2023, $66,562,500, to remain available until expended, shall be made available for fiscal year 2024, $67,940,625, to remain available until expended, shall be made available for fiscal year 2025, and $69,387,656, to remain available until expended, shall be made available for fiscal year 2026: *Provided further*, That of the amount provided under this heading in this Act, $100,000,000 shall be used to carry out the front-end engineering and design program out activities under the Carbon Capture Technology Program, as authorized in section 962 of the Energy Policy Act of 2005 (42 U.S.C. 16292), as amended by section 40303 of division D of this Act: *Provided further*, That of the funds in the preceding proviso, $20,000,000, to remain available until expended, shall be made available for fiscal year 2022, $20,000,000, to remain available until expended, shall be made available for fiscal year 2023, $20,000,000, to remain available until expended, shall be made available for fiscal year 2024, $20,000,000, to remain available until expended, shall be made available for fiscal year 2025, and $20,000,000, to remain available until expended, shall be made available for fiscal year 2026: *Provided further*, That of the amount provided under this heading in this Act, $2,500,000,000 shall be to carry out activities for the Carbon Storage Validation and Testing, as authorized section 963 of the Energy Policy Act of 2005 (42 U.S.C. 16293), as amended by section 40305 of division D of this Act: *Provided further*, That of the funds in the preceding proviso, $500,000,000, to remain available until expended, shall be made available for fiscal year 2022, $500,000,000, to remain available until expended, shall be made available for fiscal year 2023, $500,000,000, to remain available until expended, shall be made available for fiscal year 2024, $500,000,000, to remain available until expended, shall be made available for fiscal year 2025, and $500,000,000, to remain available until expended, shall be made available for fiscal year 2026: *Provided further*, That of the amount provided under this heading in this Act, $3,500,000,000 shall be to carry out a program to develop four regional clean direct air capture hubs, as authorized under section 969D of the Energy Policy Act of 2005 (42 U.S.C. 16298d), as amended by section 40308 of division D of this Act: *Provided further*, That of the funds in the preceding proviso, $700,000,000, to remain available until expended, shall be made available for fiscal year 2022, $700,000,000, to remain available until expended, shall be made available for fiscal year 2023, $700,000,000, to remain available until expended, shall be made available for fiscal year 2024, $700,000,000, to remain available until expended, shall be made available for fiscal year 2025, and $700,000,000, to remain available until expended, shall be made available for fiscal year 2026: *Provided further*, That of the amount provided under this heading in this Act and in addition to amounts otherwise made available for this purpose, $15,000,000 shall be for precommercial direct air capture technology prize competitions, as authorized under section 969D(e)(2)(A) of the Energy Policy Act of 2005 (42 U.S.C. 16298d(e)(2)(A)): *Provided further*, That of the amount provided under this heading in this Act and in addition to amounts otherwise made available for this purpose, $100,000,000 shall be for commercial direct air capture technology prize competitions, as authorized under section 969D(e)(2)(B) of the Energy Policy Act of 2005 (42 U.S.C. 16298d(e)(2)(B)): *Provided further*, That for amounts identified in the preceding proviso, the Secretary shall enter pre-construction commitments with selected projects for future awards for qualified carbon dioxide capture: *Provided further*, That of the amount provided under this heading in this Act, $140,000,000 shall be for a Rare Earth Elements Demonstration Facility, as authorized under section 7001 of the Energy Act of 2020 (42 U.S.C. 13344), as amended by section 40205 of division D of this Act: *Provided further*, That the amount provided under this heading in this Act and in addition to amounts otherwise made available for this purpose, $127,000,000 shall be to carry out rare earth mineral security activities, as authorized under section 7001(a) of the Energy Act of 2020 (42 U.S.C. 13344(a)): *Provided further*, That of the funds in the preceding proviso, $23,000,000, to remain available until expended, shall be made available for fiscal year 2022, $24,200,000, to remain available until expended, shall be made available for fiscal year 2023, $25,400,000, to remain available until expended, shall be made available for fiscal year 2024, $26,600,000, to remain available until expended, shall be made available for fiscal year 2025, and $27,800,000, to remain available until expended, shall be made available for fiscal year 2026: *Provided further*, That of the amount provided under this heading in this Act and in addition to amounts otherwise made available for this purpose, $600,000,000 shall be to carry out critical material innovation, efficiency, and alternatives activities under section 7002(g) of the Energy Act of 2020 (30 U.S.C. 1606(g)): *Provided further*, That of the funds in the preceding proviso, $230,000,000, to remain available until expended, shall be made available for fiscal year 2022, $100,000,000, to remain available until expended, shall be made available for fiscal year 2023, $135,000,000, to remain available until expended, shall be made available for fiscal year 2024, $135,000,000, to remain available until expended, shall be made available for fiscal year 2025: *Provided further*, That of the amount provided under this heading in this Act and in addition to amounts otherwise made available for this purpose, $75,000,000 shall be for the

DEPARTMENT OF ENERGY

Critical Material Supply Chain Research Facility, as authorized under section 7002(h) of the Energy Act of 2020 (30 U.S.C. 1606(h)): *Provided further*, That of the funds in the preceding proviso, $40,000,000, to remain available until expended, shall be made available for fiscal year 2022, and $35,000,000, to remain available until expended, shall be made available for fiscal year 2023: *Provided further*, That of the amount provided under this heading in this Act, $30,000,000 shall be to carry out activities authorized in section 349(b)(2) of the Energy Policy Act of 2005 (42 U.S.C.15907(b)(2)), as amended by section 40601 of division D of this Act: *Provided further*, That not later than 90 days after the date of enactment of this Act, the Secretary of Energy shall submit to the House and Senate Committees on Appropriations a detailed spend plan for fiscal year 2022: *Provided further*, That for each fiscal year through 2026, as part of the annual budget submission of the President under section 1105(a) of title 31, United States Code, the Secretary of Energy shall submit a detailed spend plan for that fiscal year: *Provided further*, That up to three percent of the amounts made available under this heading in this Act in each of fiscal years 2022 through 2026 shall be for program direction: *Provided further*, That such amount is designated by the Congress as being for an emergency requirement pursuant to section 4112(a) of H. Con. Res. 71 (115th Congress), the concurrent resolution on the budget for fiscal year 2018, and to section 251(b) of the Balanced Budget and Emergency Deficit Control Act of 1985.] *(Infrastructure Investments and Jobs Appropriations Act.)*

Program and Financing (in millions of dollars)

Identification code 089–0213–0–1–271		2021 actual	2022 est.	2023 est.
	Obligations by program activity:			
0002	Carbon Capture	80	126	163
0003	Carbon Storage	74	79	122
0004	Advanced Energy Systems	248	122	67
0005	Cross-Cutting Research	68	72	31
0006	Carbon Utilization		23	50
0007	Carbon Dioxide Removal			65
0008	Carbon Capture, Utilization and Storage	15		
0009	Critical Minerals			40
0010	Carbon Ore Processing			4
0012	Program Direction - Management	66	62	70
0013	Program Direction - NETL R&D	177		
0017	Special Recruitment Program	1	1	1
0018	Emissions Mitigation			54
0019	Emissions Quantification			46
0020	Natural gas technologies	71	57	
0021	Unconventional FE Technologies	44	46	
0022	STEP (Supercritical CO2)	29	14	
0024	NETL Research and Operations		83	83
0025	NETL Infrastructure		55	55
0026	NETL IWG Coal and Power Communities and Economic Revitalization			3
0030	Transformational Coal Pilots		10	
0031	Environmentally Prudent Development			13
0032	Natural Gas Hydrogen Research			26
0799	Total direct obligations	873	750	893
0801	Unavailable	2		
0900	Total new obligations, unexpired accounts	875	750	893
	Budgetary resources:			
	Unobligated balance:			
1000	Unobligated balance brought forward, Oct 1	353	226	2,063
1021	Recoveries of prior year unpaid obligations	13		
1070	Unobligated balance (total)	366	226	2,063
	Budget authority:			
	Appropriations, discretionary:			
1100	Appropriation	750	750	893
1100	Appropriation [IIJA]		1,837	
1120	Appropriations transferred to other accts [089–0222]	–18		
1160	Appropriation, discretionary (total)	732	2,587	893
	Advance appropriations, discretionary:			
1170	Advance appropriation			1,442
	Spending authority from offsetting collections, discretionary:			
1700	Collected	3		
1900	Budget authority (total)	735	2,587	2,335
1930	Total budgetary resources available	1,101	2,813	4,398
	Memorandum (non-add) entries:			
1941	Unexpired unobligated balance, end of year	226	2,063	3,505
	Change in obligated balance:			
	Unpaid obligations:			
3000	Unpaid obligations, brought forward, Oct 1	958	1,121	266
3010	New obligations, unexpired accounts	875	750	893
3020	Outlays (gross)	–699	–1,605	–1,067
3040	Recoveries of prior year unpaid obligations, unexpired	–13		
3050	Unpaid obligations, end of year	1,121	266	92
	Memorandum (non-add) entries:			
3100	Obligated balance, start of year	958	1,121	266
3200	Obligated balance, end of year	1,121	266	92
	Budget authority and outlays, net:			
	Discretionary:			
4000	Budget authority, gross	735	2,587	2,335
	Outlays, gross:			
4010	Outlays from new discretionary authority	143	484	400
4011	Outlays from discretionary balances	556	1,121	667
4020	Outlays, gross (total)	699	1,605	1,067
	Offsets against gross budget authority and outlays:			
	Offsetting collections (collected) from:			
4033	Non-Federal sources	–3	–2	–2
4040	Offsets against gross budget authority and outlays (total)	–3	–2	–2
	Additional offsets against gross budget authority only:			
4052	Offsetting collections credited to expired accounts		2	2
4060	Additional offsets against budget authority only (total)		2	2
4070	Budget authority, net (discretionary)	732	2,587	2,335
4080	Outlays, net (discretionary)	696	1,603	1,065
4180	Budget authority, net (total)	732	2,587	2,335
4190	Outlays, net (total)	696	1,603	1,065

The Fossil Energy and Carbon Management (FECM) office conducts research, development, demonstration and deployment (RDD&D) that focuses on technologies to reduce carbon emissions and other environmental impacts of fossil fuel production and use, particularly the hardest-to-decarbonize applications in the electricity and industrial sectors. Additionally, the program advances technologies on carbon dioxide (CO_2) removal (CDR) to reduce atmospheric and legacy emissions of CO_2, and technologies that convert and durably store CO_2 into value-added products. FECM recognizes that decarbonization is essential to meeting climate goals—100% carbon pollution free electricity by 2035 and net-zero greenhouse gas emissions economy-wide by 2050. FECM is also committed to improving the conditions of communities impacted by the legacy of fossil fuel use and to supporting a healthy economic transition that accelerates the growth of good-paying jobs.

Program activities funded through this account focus on: 1) demonstrating and deploying point source carbon capture; 2) Reducing methane emissions; 3) advancing carbon dioxide removal, conversion, transport, and storage; 4) advancing critical minerals, rare earth elements, and mine remediation; 5) supporting low-carbon industrial supply chains; 6) increasing efficient use of big data and artificial intelligence; 7) accelerating carbon-neutral hydrogen; 8) addressing the Energy Water Nexus; 9) investing in thoughtful transition strategies. Many of these activities are pursued in partnership with the National Energy Technology Laboratory (NETL), which also receives funding from this account.

Object Classification (in millions of dollars)

Identification code 089–0213–0–1–271		2021 actual	2022 est.	2023 est.
	Direct obligations:			
	Personnel compensation:			
11.1	Full-time permanent	66	62	70
11.3	Other than full-time permanent	1		1
11.5	Other personnel compensation	2		2
11.9	Total personnel compensation	69	62	73
12.1	Civilian personnel benefits	25		29
21.0	Other Costs for Transportation of Persons	1		1
23.3	Communications, utilities, and miscellaneous charges	10		10
25.1	Advisory and assistance services	142		153
25.3	Purchase of Goods and Services from Government Accounts	7		10
25.3	Other Contractual Services	2		3
25.4	Operation and maintenance of facilities	74	29	75
25.5	Research and Development	494	630	522
25.7	Operation and maintenance of equipment	5		6
26.0	Supplies and materials	1		2
26.0	Pamphlets, Documents, Subscriptions and Publications	2		3
31.0	Equipment	5	29	6
31.0	Non-Capitalized Personal Property	4		
32.0	Land and structures	30		
41.0	Grants, Subsidies, and Contributions	1		

FOSSIL ENERGY AND CARBON MANAGEMENT—Continued
Object Classification—Continued

Identification code 089–0213–0–1–271		2021 actual	2022 est.	2023 est.
41.0	Other Grants Not Otherwise Classified	1		
99.0	Direct obligations	873	750	893
99.0	Reimbursable obligations	2		
99.9	Total new obligations, unexpired accounts	875	750	893

Employment Summary

Identification code 089–0213–0–1–271		2021 actual	2022 est.	2023 est.
1001	Direct civilian full-time equivalent employment	518	528	565

NATIONAL ENERGY TECHNOLOGY LABORATORY RESEARCH AND DEVELOPMENT

Program and Financing (in millions of dollars)

Identification code 089–2298–0–1–271		2021 actual	2022 est.	2023 est.
	Budgetary resources:			
	Unobligated balance:			
1000	Unobligated balance brought forward, Oct 1		3	3
	Budget authority:			
	Spending authority from offsetting collections, mandatory:			
1800	Collected	3		
1930	Total budgetary resources available	3	3	3
	Memorandum (non-add) entries:			
1941	Unexpired unobligated balance, end of year	3	3	3
	Budget authority and outlays, net:			
	Mandatory:			
4090	Budget authority, gross	3		
	Offsets against gross budget authority and outlays:			
	Offsetting collections (collected) from:			
4120	Federal sources	–3		
4180	Budget authority, net (total)			
4190	Outlays, net (total)	–3		

NAVAL PETROLEUM AND OIL SHALE RESERVES

For Department of Energy expenses necessary to carry out naval petroleum and oil shale reserve activities, $13,004,000, to remain available until expended: Provided, That notwithstanding any other provision of law, unobligated funds remaining from prior years shall be available for all naval petroleum and oil shale reserve activities.

Note.—A full-year 2022 appropriation for this account was not enacted at the time the Budget was prepared; therefore, the Budget assumes this account is operating under the Continuing Appropriations Act, 2022 (Division A of Public Law 117–43, as amended). The amounts included for 2022 reflect the annualized level provided by the continuing resolution.

Program and Financing (in millions of dollars)

Identification code 089–0219–0–1–271		2021 actual	2022 est.	2023 est.
	Obligations by program activity:			
0001	Production and Operations	13	14	13
0799	Total direct obligations	13	14	13
0900	Total new obligations, unexpired accounts (object class 25.4)	13	14	13
	Budgetary resources:			
	Unobligated balance:			
1000	Unobligated balance brought forward, Oct 1	4	4	4
	Budget authority:			
	Appropriations, discretionary:			
1100	Appropriation	13	14	13
1900	Budget authority (total)	13	14	13
1930	Total budgetary resources available	17	18	17
	Memorandum (non-add) entries:			
1941	Unexpired unobligated balance, end of year	4	4	4
	Change in obligated balance:			
	Unpaid obligations:			
3000	Unpaid obligations, brought forward, Oct 1	13	10	5
3010	New obligations, unexpired accounts	13	14	13
3020	Outlays (gross)	–16	–19	–15
3050	Unpaid obligations, end of year	10	5	3
	Memorandum (non-add) entries:			
3100	Obligated balance, start of year	13	10	5
3200	Obligated balance, end of year	10	5	3
	Budget authority and outlays, net:			
	Discretionary:			
4000	Budget authority, gross	13	14	13
	Outlays, gross:			
4010	Outlays from new discretionary authority	2	9	8
4011	Outlays from discretionary balances	14	10	7
4020	Outlays, gross (total)	16	19	15
4180	Budget authority, net (total)	13	14	13
4190	Outlays, net (total)	16	19	15

This account funds environmental activities at Naval Petroleum Reserve 1 (NPR-1) in California (Elk Hills) and Naval Petroleum Reserve 3 (NPR-3) in Wyoming (Teapot Dome). Following the sale of the Government's interests in NPR-1 in California (Elk Hills), post-sale environmental assessment/remediation activities continue to be required by the legally binding agreements under the Corrective Action Consent Agreement with the State of California Department of Toxic Substances Control (DTSC). Program activities encompass execution of a technical baseline, interim measures, environmental sampling and analysis, corrective measures, waste removal and disposal, and confirmatory sampling. In FY 2023, funding will continue ongoing activities to attain release from the remaining environmental findings related to the sale of NPR-1. On January 30, 2015, the Department finalized the sale of the Teapot Dome Oilfield. The Department continues to oversee post-sale remediation activities and ground water sampling for the closure of the landfill in compliance with National Environmental Policy Act and Wyoming Department of Environmental Quality requirements.

Employment Summary

Identification code 089–0219–0–1–271		2021 actual	2022 est.	2023 est.
1001	Direct civilian full-time equivalent employment	2	2	2

STRATEGIC PETROLEUM RESERVE

For Department of Energy expenses necessary for Strategic Petroleum Reserve facility development and operations and program management activities pursuant to the Energy Policy and Conservation Act (42 U.S.C. 6201 et seq.), $214,175,000, to remain available until expended.

Note.—A full-year 2022 appropriation for this account was not enacted at the time the Budget was prepared; therefore, the Budget assumes this account is operating under the Continuing Appropriations Act, 2022 (Division A of Public Law 117–43, as amended). The amounts included for 2022 reflect the annualized level provided by the continuing resolution.

STRATEGIC PETROLEUM RESERVE

[For an additional amount for "Strategic Petroleum Reserve", $43,300,000, to remain available until expended, for necessary expenses related to damages caused by natural disasters.] (Disaster Relief Supplemental Appropriations Act, 2022.)

Program and Financing (in millions of dollars)

Identification code 089–0218–0–1–274		2021 actual	2022 est.	2023 est.
	Obligations by program activity:			
0001	SPR Management	22	20	28
0002	SPR Storage Facilities Development	182	168	164
0003	Emergency Appropriation		43	
0004	Northeast Gasoline Supply Reserve			22
0900	Total new obligations, unexpired accounts	204	231	214

DEPARTMENT OF ENERGY

Energy Programs—Continued
Federal Funds—Continued

	Budgetary resources:	2021 actual	2022 est.	2023 est.
	Unobligated balance:			
1000	Unobligated balance brought forward, Oct 1	34	19	19
1021	Recoveries of prior year unpaid obligations	1		
1070	Unobligated balance (total)	35	19	19
	Budget authority:			
	Appropriations, discretionary:			
1100	Appropriation	188	188	214
1100	Appropriation [Emergency]		43	
1160	Appropriation, discretionary (total)	188	231	214
1930	Total budgetary resources available	223	250	233
	Memorandum (non-add) entries:			
1941	Unexpired unobligated balance, end of year	19	19	19
	Change in obligated balance:			
	Unpaid obligations:			
3000	Unpaid obligations, brought forward, Oct 1	172	152	118
3010	New obligations, unexpired accounts	204	231	214
3020	Outlays (gross)	−223	−265	−236
3040	Recoveries of prior year unpaid obligations, unexpired	−1		
3050	Unpaid obligations, end of year	152	118	96
	Memorandum (non-add) entries:			
3100	Obligated balance, start of year	172	152	118
3200	Obligated balance, end of year	152	118	96
	Budget authority and outlays, net:			
	Discretionary:			
4000	Budget authority, gross	188	231	214
	Outlays, gross:			
4010	Outlays from new discretionary authority	65	125	118
4011	Outlays from discretionary balances	158	140	118
4020	Outlays, gross (total)	223	265	236
4180	Budget authority, net (total)	188	231	214
4190	Outlays, net (total)	223	265	236

The Strategic Petroleum Reserve (SPR) provides strategic and economic security against foreign and domestic disruptions in oil supplies via an emergency stockpile of crude oil. The program fulfills United States obligations under the International Energy Program, which commits the United States to support the International Energy Agency through its coordinated energy emergency response plans and provides a deterrent against energy supply disruptions. The FY 2023 Budget will support the SPR's operational readiness and drawdown capabilities of 4.4 MB/d. The program will perform cavern wellbore testing and maintenance activities to ensure the availability of the SPR's crude oil inventory. The FY 2023 Budget will continue to fund the Northeast Gasoline Supply Reserve which currently holds one million barrels of refined product in reserve.

Object Classification (in millions of dollars)

Identification code 089–0218–0–1–274		2021 actual	2022 est.	2023 est.
	Direct obligations:			
11.1	Personnel compensation: Full-time permanent	12	12	12
12.1	Civilian personnel benefits	4	4	4
23.1	Rental payments to GSA	1	1	1
23.3	Communications, utilities, and miscellaneous charges	3	3	1
25.1	Advisory and assistance services	1	1	1
25.2	Other services from non-Federal sources	33	33	33
25.4	Operation and maintenance of facilities	150	134	162
32.0	Land and structures		43	
99.0	Direct obligations	204	231	214
99.9	Total new obligations, unexpired accounts	204	231	214

Employment Summary

Identification code 089–0218–0–1–274	2021 actual	2022 est.	2023 est.
1001 Direct civilian full-time equivalent employment	110	110	110
2001 Reimbursable civilian full-time equivalent employment	18	18	18

SPR PETROLEUM ACCOUNT

For the acquisition, transportation, and injection of petroleum products, and for other necessary expenses pursuant to the Energy Policy and Conservation Act of 1975, as amended (42 U.S.C. 6201 et seq.), sections 403 and 404 of the Bipartisan Budget Act of 2015 (42 U.S.C. 6241, 6239 note), section 32204 of the Fixing America's Surface Transportation Act (42 U.S.C. 6241 note), and section 30204 of the Bipartisan Budget Act of 2018 (42 U.S.C. 6241 note), $8,000,000, to remain available until expended.

Note.—A full-year 2022 appropriation for this account was not enacted at the time the Budget was prepared; therefore, the Budget assumes this account is operating under the Continuing Appropriations Act, 2022 (Division A of Public Law 117–43, as amended). The amounts included for 2022 reflect the annualized level provided by the continuing resolution.

Program and Financing (in millions of dollars)

Identification code 089–0233–0–1–274		2021 actual	2022 est.	2023 est.
	Obligations by program activity:			
0001	SPR Petroleum Account	3	6	8
	Budgetary resources:			
	Unobligated balance:			
1000	Unobligated balance brought forward, Oct 1	9	9	4
1001	Discretionary unobligated balance brought fwd, Oct 1	4	6	
	Budget authority:			
	Appropriations, discretionary:			
1100	Appropriation	1	1	8
	Spending authority from offsetting collections, discretionary:			
1700	Collected	2		
1900	Budget authority (total)	3	1	8
1930	Total budgetary resources available	12	10	12
	Memorandum (non-add) entries:			
1941	Unexpired unobligated balance, end of year	9	4	4
	Change in obligated balance:			
	Unpaid obligations:			
3000	Unpaid obligations, brought forward, Oct 1	25	22	7
3010	New obligations, unexpired accounts	3	6	8
3020	Outlays (gross)	−6	−21	−5
3050	Unpaid obligations, end of year	22	7	10
	Memorandum (non-add) entries:			
3100	Obligated balance, start of year	25	22	7
3200	Obligated balance, end of year	22	7	10
	Budget authority and outlays, net:			
	Discretionary:			
4000	Budget authority, gross	3	1	8
	Outlays, gross:			
4010	Outlays from new discretionary authority			5
4011	Outlays from discretionary balances	6	21	
4020	Outlays, gross (total)	6	21	5
	Offsets against gross budget authority and outlays:			
	Offsetting collections (collected) from:			
4033	Non-Federal sources	−2		
4040	Offsets against gross budget authority and outlays (total)	−2		
4180	Budget authority, net (total)	1	1	8
4190	Outlays, net (total)	4	21	5

The SPR Petroleum Account funds activities related to the acquisition, transportation, and injection of petroleum products into the Strategic Petroleum Reserve (SPR), as well as costs related to the drawdown, sale, and delivery of petroleum products from the Reserve.

Object Classification (in millions of dollars)

Identification code 089–0233–0–1–274		2021 actual	2022 est.	2023 est.
	Direct obligations:			
23.3	Communications, utilities, and miscellaneous charges	1		1
25.2	Other services from non-Federal sources	2	6	7
99.9	Total new obligations, unexpired accounts	3	6	8

ENERGY SECURITY AND INFRASTRUCTURE MODERNIZATION FUND

Special and Trust Fund Receipts (in millions of dollars)

Identification code 089–5615–0–2–274	2021 actual	2022 est.	2023 est.
0100 Balance, start of year	567		
0198 Reconciliation adjustment	–567		
0199 Balance, start of year			
Receipts:			
Current law:			
1130 Proceeds from Sale of Oil, Energy Security and Infrastructure Modernization Fund	450		
2000 Total: Balances and receipts	450		
Appropriations:			
Current law:			
2101 Energy Security and Infrastructure Modernization Fund	–450		
5099 Balance, end of year			

Program and Financing (in millions of dollars)

Identification code 089–5615–0–2–274	2021 actual	2022 est.	2023 est.
Obligations by program activity:			
0010 Energy security and infrastructure modernization	354	109	
0900 Total new obligations, unexpired accounts (object class 25.4)	354	109	
Budgetary resources:			
Unobligated balance:			
1000 Unobligated balance brought forward, Oct 1	13	109	
Budget authority:			
Appropriations, discretionary:			
1101 Appropriation (special or trust)	450		
1900 Budget authority (total)	450		
1930 Total budgetary resources available	463	109	
Memorandum (non-add) entries:			
1941 Unexpired unobligated balance, end of year	109		
Change in obligated balance:			
Unpaid obligations:			
3000 Unpaid obligations, brought forward, Oct 1	731	975	666
3010 New obligations, unexpired accounts	354	109	
3020 Outlays (gross)	–110	–418	–400
3050 Unpaid obligations, end of year	975	666	266
Memorandum (non-add) entries:			
3100 Obligated balance, start of year	731	975	666
3200 Obligated balance, end of year	975	666	266
Budget authority and outlays, net:			
Discretionary:			
4000 Budget authority, gross	450		
Outlays, gross:			
4011 Outlays from discretionary balances	110	418	400
4180 Budget authority, net (total)	450		
4190 Outlays, net (total)	110	418	400

The Energy Security and Infrastructure Modernization Fund was established in Section 404 of the Bipartisan Budget Act of 2015 to finance modernization of the Strategic Petroleum Reserve (SPR). Revenue raised through sales of SPR crude oil will support Life Extension Phase 2 project investments needed to ensure the SPR can maintain its operational readiness capability, meet its mission requirements, and operate in an environmentally responsible manner. The CARES Act extended the Department's authority to sell oil in support of modernization from FY 2020 to FY 2022, and DOE conducted its final sale in FY 2021, thus no further appropriations are requested in FY 2023. Funds in the ESIM account will be used for the Life Extension Phase II (LE2) SPR infrastructure modernization project.

ENERGY INFORMATION ADMINISTRATION

For Department of Energy expenses necessary in carrying out the activities of the Energy Information Administration, $144,480,000, to remain available until expended.

Note.—A full-year 2022 appropriation for this account was not enacted at the time the Budget was prepared; therefore, the Budget assumes this account is operating under the Continuing Appropriations Act, 2022 (Division A of Public Law 117–43, as amended). The amounts included for 2022 reflect the annualized level provided by the continuing resolution.

Program and Financing (in millions of dollars)

Identification code 089–0216–0–1–276	2021 actual	2022 est.	2023 est.
Obligations by program activity:			
0001 Obligations by Program Activity	127	127	144
Budgetary resources:			
Unobligated balance:			
1000 Unobligated balance brought forward, Oct 1	3	3	3
Budget authority:			
Appropriations, discretionary:			
1100 Appropriation	127	127	144
1930 Total budgetary resources available	130	130	147
Memorandum (non-add) entries:			
1941 Unexpired unobligated balance, end of year	3	3	3
Change in obligated balance:			
Unpaid obligations:			
3000 Unpaid obligations, brought forward, Oct 1	42	44	48
3010 New obligations, unexpired accounts	127	127	144
3020 Outlays (gross)	–125	–123	–139
3050 Unpaid obligations, end of year	44	48	53
Memorandum (non-add) entries:			
3100 Obligated balance, start of year	42	44	48
3200 Obligated balance, end of year	44	48	53
Budget authority and outlays, net:			
Discretionary:			
4000 Budget authority, gross	127	127	144
Outlays, gross:			
4010 Outlays from new discretionary authority	87	89	101
4011 Outlays from discretionary balances	38	34	38
4020 Outlays, gross (total)	125	123	139
4180 Budget authority, net (total)	127	127	144
4190 Outlays, net (total)	125	123	139

The U.S. Energy Information Administration (EIA) is the statistical and analytical agency within the U.S. Department of Energy. EIA collects, analyzes, and disseminates independent and impartial energy information to promote sound policymaking, efficient markets, and public understanding of energy and its interaction with the economy and the environment. As the nation's premier source of energy information, EIA conducts a data collection program covering the full spectrum of energy sources, end uses, and energy flows; generates short- and long-term domestic and international energy forecasts and projections; and performs timely, informative energy analyses. The FY 2023 request enables EIA to continue statistical and analysis activities that produce reports critical to the nation, address emerging information needs such as those identified in the Bipartisan Infrastructure Law (Infrastructure Investment and Jobs Act, P.L. 117–58), and expand EIA's energy consumption survey program to collect new data for the populated U.S. territories.

Object Classification (in millions of dollars)

Identification code 089–0216–0–1–276	2021 actual	2022 est.	2023 est.
Direct obligations:			
Personnel compensation:			
11.1 Full-time permanent	42	42	43
11.3 Other than full-time permanent	1	1	1
11.5 Other personnel compensation	1	1	1
11.9 Total personnel compensation	44	44	45
12.1 Civilian personnel benefits	15	15	16
23.3 Communications, utilities, and miscellaneous charges	3	3	4
25.1 Advisory and assistance services	50	50	59
25.3 Purchase of goods and services from Government Accounts	8	8	9
25.3 Other Contractual Services	1	1	2
26.0 Pamphlets, Documents, Subscriptions and Publications	3	3	4
31.0 Equipment	2	2	3
41.0 Grants, subsidies, and contributions	1	1	2
99.9 Total new obligations, unexpired accounts	127	127	144

Employment Summary

Identification code 089–0216–0–1–276	2021 actual	2022 est.	2023 est.
1001 Direct civilian full-time equivalent employment	316	366	366

FEDERAL ENERGY REGULATORY COMMISSION

SALARIES AND EXPENSES

For expenses necessary for the Federal Energy Regulatory Commission to carry out the provisions of the Department of Energy Organization Act (42 U.S.C. 7101 et seq.), including services as authorized by 5 U.S.C. 3109, official reception and representation expenses not to exceed $3,000, and the hire of passenger motor vehicles, $508,400,000, to remain available until expended: Provided, That notwithstanding any other provision of law, not to exceed $508,400,000 of revenues from fees and annual charges, and other services and collections in fiscal year 2023 shall be retained and used for expenses necessary in this account, and shall remain available until expended: Provided further, That the sum herein appropriated from the general fund shall be reduced as revenues are received during fiscal year 2023 so as to result in a final fiscal year 2023 appropriation from the general fund estimated at not more than $0.

Note.—A full-year 2022 appropriation for this account was not enacted at the time the Budget was prepared; therefore, the Budget assumes this account is operating under the Continuing Appropriations Act, 2022 (Division A of Public Law 117–43, as amended). The amounts included for 2022 reflect the annualized level provided by the continuing resolution.

Program and Financing (in millions of dollars)

Identification code 089–0212–0–1–276	2021 actual	2022 est.	2023 est.
Obligations by program activity:			
0801 Ensure Just and Reasonable Rates, Terms & Conditions	200	195	227
0802 Promote Safe, Reliable, Secure & Efficient Infrastructure	149	144	173
0803 Mission Support through Organizational Excellence	90	88	108
0900 Total new obligations, unexpired accounts	439	427	508
Budgetary resources:			
Unobligated balance:			
1000 Unobligated balance brought forward, Oct 1	52	23	
1021 Recoveries of prior year unpaid obligations	6		
1070 Unobligated balance (total)	58	23	
Budget authority:			
Spending authority from offsetting collections, discretionary:			
1700 Collected	404	404	508
1930 Total budgetary resources available	462	427	508
Memorandum (non-add) entries:			
1941 Unexpired unobligated balance, end of year	23		
Change in obligated balance:			
Unpaid obligations:			
3000 Unpaid obligations, brought forward, Oct 1	91	115	93
3010 New obligations, unexpired accounts	439	427	508
3020 Outlays (gross)	–409	–449	–527
3040 Recoveries of prior year unpaid obligations, unexpired	–6		
3050 Unpaid obligations, end of year	115	93	74
Memorandum (non-add) entries:			
3100 Obligated balance, start of year	91	115	93
3200 Obligated balance, end of year	115	93	74
Budget authority and outlays, net:			
Discretionary:			
4000 Budget authority, gross	404	404	508
Outlays, gross:			
4010 Outlays from new discretionary authority	294	364	457
4011 Outlays from discretionary balances	115	85	70
4020 Outlays, gross (total)	409	449	527
Offsets against gross budget authority and outlays:			
Offsetting collections (collected) from:			
4034 Offsetting governmental collections	–404	–404	–508
4180 Budget authority, net (total)			
4190 Outlays, net (total)	5	45	19
Memorandum (non-add) entries:			
5090 Unexpired unavailable balance, SOY: Offsetting collections	15	15	15
5092 Unexpired unavailable balance, EOY: Offsetting collections	15	15	15

The Federal Energy Regulatory Commission (FERC or the Commission) is an independent agency that regulates the transmission and wholesale sale of electricity and natural gas in interstate commerce, as well as the transportation of oil by pipelines in interstate commerce. FERC also reviews proposals to build interstate natural gas pipelines, natural gas storage projects, and liquefied natural gas (LNG) terminals, and FERC licenses non-federal hydropower projects. The Commission assists consumers in obtaining reliable, safe, secure, and economically efficient energy services at a reasonable cost through appropriate regulatory and market means, and collaborative efforts. Regulated entities pay fees and charges sufficient to recover the Commission's full cost of operations.

Ensure Just and Reasonable Rates, Terms, and Conditions.— In carrying out its regulatory role, FERC uses a range of ratemaking activities, leveraging both regulatory and market means. FERC establishes and applies rules and policies that will result in just, reasonable, and not unduly discriminatory or preferential rates, terms, and conditions of jurisdictional service. The Commission fulfills this responsibility by determining whether FERC rules and policies need to be added or changed, and by analyzing and acting on filings in a fair, clear, and timely manner.

Oversight, surveillance and enforcement are essential complements to the Commission's approach to ensure that rates, terms and conditions of service are just and reasonable and not unduly discriminatory or preferential. The Federal Power Act and the Natural Gas Act, along with other statutory authorities, gives FERC oversight and enforcement responsibilities that focus on promoting compliance of regulated entities and detecting and deterring market manipulation and other market violations. The Commission assesses compliance and financial filings of regulated entities and monitors market activity and explores potential violations.

Ensure Safe, Reliable, and Secure Infrastructure Consistent with the Public Interest.—The Commission plays an important role to promote infrastructure that is safe and reliable, both physically and cyber-secure, and consistent with the public interest. Infrastructure for which FERC approval is required includes interstate natural gas pipelines and storage projects, LNG facilities, and non-federal hydropower. In addition, the Commission has authority to site electric transmission facilities in certain circumstances. The Commission reviews natural gas and hydropower infrastructure proposals to facilitate benefits to the nation. FERC conducts thorough and timely technical review of applications to construct, operate, or modify natural gas and hydropower infrastructure. The Commission also assesses compliance with environmental mitigation conditions in FERC orders during construction and operation of natural gas and hydropower infrastructure.

The Commission also has an important role in minimizing risks to the public associated with FERC-jurisdictional energy infrastructure. FERC conducts comprehensive and timely inspections of hydropower and LNG facilities to ensure compliance. The Commission protects and improves the reliable and secure operation of the Bulk-Power System through mandatory and enforceable reliability standards. The Commission also protects FERC-jurisdictional energy infrastructure through collaboration and sharing of best practices.

Provide Mission Support through Organizational Excellence.—The public interest is best served when the Commission operates in an efficient, responsive and transparent manner. FERC pursues this by maintaining processes and providing services that enable FERC offices to manage resources effectively and efficiently. The Commission also provides tools and services that equip employees to drive success and accomplish the agency's mission. FERC will continue to make investments in its people, information technology (IT) resources, and facilities.

The Commission promotes transparency and equity, open communication, and a high standard of ethics to facilitate trust and understanding of FERC's activities. FERC supports this by maintaining legal and other processes in accordance with the principles of due process, fairness, and integrity. FERC considers matters involving environmental justice and equity consistent with its statutory authority. In particular, the Commission has a strong

FEDERAL ENERGY REGULATORY COMMISSION—Continued

commitment to working with affected communities, including environmental justice communities and landowners who may be directly impacted by Commission decisions on jurisdictional infrastructure proposals. The Commission also promotes understanding, participation, and engagement with the public, stakeholders, Tribes, and jurisdictional entities. The Commission will increase its engagement with the public through its newly established Office of Public Participation.

Object Classification (in millions of dollars)

Identification code 089–0212–0–1–276		2021 actual	2022 est.	2023 est.
	Reimbursable obligations:			
	Personnel compensation:			
11.1	Full-time permanent	194	201	218
11.3	Other than full-time permanent	4	4	4
11.5	Other personnel compensation	6	6	6
11.9	Total personnel compensation	204	211	228
12.1	Civilian personnel benefits	71	76	82
21.0	Travel and transportation of persons	1	2	4
23.1	Rental payments to GSA	32	34	33
23.2	Rental payments to others	1	1	1
23.3	Communications, utilities, and miscellaneous charges	2	3	5
24.0	Printing and reproduction	1	1	2
25.1	Advisory and assistance services	15	17	25
25.2	Other services from non-Federal sources	15	17	19
25.3	Other goods and services from Federal sources	2	2	2
25.4	Operation and maintenance of facilities	2	2	2
25.7	Operation and maintenance of equipment	51	50	58
26.0	Supplies and materials	5	5	5
31.0	Equipment	10	5	34
32.0	Land and structures	27		7
99.0	Reimbursable obligations	439	426	507
99.5	Adjustment for rounding		1	1
99.9	Total new obligations, unexpired accounts	439	427	508

Employment Summary

Identification code 089–0212–0–1–276	2021 actual	2022 est.	2023 est.
2001 Reimbursable civilian full-time equivalent employment	1,455	1,465	1,508

CLEAN COAL TECHNOLOGY

Program and Financing (in millions of dollars)

Identification code 089–0235–0–1–271		2021 actual	2022 est.	2023 est.
	Budgetary resources:			
	Unobligated balance:			
1000	Unobligated balance brought forward, Oct 1	2	2	2
1930	Total budgetary resources available	2	2	2
	Memorandum (non-add) entries:			
1941	Unexpired unobligated balance, end of year	2	2	2
4180	Budget authority, net (total)			
4190	Outlays, net (total)			

The Clean Coal Technology Program was established in the 1980s to perform commercial-scale demonstrations of advanced coal-based technologies. All projects have concluded and only closeout activities remain.

ULTRA-DEEPWATER AND UNCONVENTIONAL NATURAL GAS AND OTHER PETROLEUM RESEARCH FUND

Program and Financing (in millions of dollars)

Identification code 089–5523–0–2–271		2021 actual	2022 est.	2023 est.
	Budgetary resources:			
	Unobligated balance:			
1000	Unobligated balance brought forward, Oct 1	7	7	7
1930	Total budgetary resources available	7	7	7
	Memorandum (non-add) entries:			
1941	Unexpired unobligated balance, end of year	7	7	7
4180	Budget authority, net (total)			
4190	Outlays, net (total)			

The Energy Policy Act of 2005 (Public Law 109–58) created a mandatory Ultra-Deepwater and Unconventional Natural Gas and Other Petroleum Research program beginning in 2007. Subtitle J of Title IX of the Energy Policy Act of 2005 (42 U.S.C. 16371 et seq.) was repealed and all unobligated balances in this account were rescinded by the Bipartisan Budget Control Act of FY 2013.

PAYMENTS TO STATES UNDER FEDERAL POWER ACT

Special and Trust Fund Receipts (in millions of dollars)

Identification code 089–5105–0–2–806		2021 actual	2022 est.	2023 est.
0100	Balance, start of year			
	Receipts:			
	Current law:			
1110	Licenses under Federal Power Act from Public Lands and National Forests, Payment to States (37 1/2%)	6	5	6
2000	Total: Balances and receipts	6	5	6
	Appropriations:			
	Current law:			
2101	Payments to States under Federal Power Act	–6	–5	–6
5099	Balance, end of year			

Program and Financing (in millions of dollars)

Identification code 089–5105–0–2–806		2021 actual	2022 est.	2023 est.
	Obligations by program activity:			
0001	Payments to States under Federal Power Act (Direct)	6	5	6
0900	Total new obligations, unexpired accounts (object class 41.0)	6	5	6
	Budgetary resources:			
	Budget authority:			
	Appropriations, mandatory:			
1201	Appropriation (special or trust fund)	6	5	6
1930	Total budgetary resources available	6	5	6
	Change in obligated balance:			
	Unpaid obligations:			
3000	Unpaid obligations, brought forward, Oct 1	3		
3010	New obligations, unexpired accounts	6	5	6
3020	Outlays (gross)	–9	–5	–6
	Memorandum (non-add) entries:			
3100	Obligated balance, start of year	3		
	Budget authority and outlays, net:			
	Mandatory:			
4090	Budget authority, gross	6	5	6
	Outlays, gross:			
4100	Outlays from new mandatory authority	6	5	6
4101	Outlays from mandatory balances	3		
4110	Outlays, gross (total)	9	5	6
4180	Budget authority, net (total)	6	5	6
4190	Outlays, net (total)	9	5	6

The States are paid 37.5 percent of the receipts from licenses for occupancy and use of national forests and public lands within their boundaries issued by the Federal Energy Regulatory Commission (16 U.S.C. 810).

NORTHEAST HOME HEATING OIL RESERVE

For Department of Energy expenses necessary for Northeast Home Heating Oil Reserve storage, operation, and management activities pursuant to the Energy Policy and Conservation Act (42 U.S.C. 6201 et seq.), $7,000,000, to remain available until expended.

Note.—A full-year 2022 appropriation for this account was not enacted at the time the Budget was prepared; therefore, the Budget assumes this account is operating under the Continuing Appropriations Act, 2022 (Division A of Public Law 117–43, as amended). The amounts included for 2022 reflect the annualized level provided by the continuing resolution.

DEPARTMENT OF ENERGY

Special and Trust Fund Receipts (in millions of dollars)

Identification code 089–5369–0–2–274	2021 actual	2022 est.	2023 est.
0100 Balance, start of year	1	1	1
2000 Total: Balances and receipts	1	1	1
5099 Balance, end of year	1	1	1

Program and Financing (in millions of dollars)

Identification code 089–5369–0–2–274	2021 actual	2022 est.	2023 est.
Obligations by program activity:			
0001 NEHHOR	6	7	7
0900 Total new obligations, unexpired accounts (object class 25.2)	6	7	7
Budgetary resources:			
Unobligated balance:			
1000 Unobligated balance brought forward, Oct 1	5	6	6
Budget authority:			
Appropriations, discretionary:			
1100 Appropriation	7	7	7
1930 Total budgetary resources available	12	13	13
Memorandum (non-add) entries:			
1941 Unexpired unobligated balance, end of year	6	6	6
Change in obligated balance:			
Unpaid obligations:			
3000 Unpaid obligations, brought forward, Oct 1	4	3	1
3010 New obligations, unexpired accounts	6	7	7
3020 Outlays (gross)	–7	–9	–7
3050 Unpaid obligations, end of year	3	1	1
Memorandum (non-add) entries:			
3100 Obligated balance, start of year	4	3	1
3200 Obligated balance, end of year	3	1	1
Budget authority and outlays, net:			
Discretionary:			
4000 Budget authority, gross	7	7	7
Outlays, gross:			
4010 Outlays from new discretionary authority	1	6	6
4011 Outlays from discretionary balances	6	3	1
4020 Outlays, gross (total)	7	9	7
4180 Budget authority, net (total)	7	7	7
4190 Outlays, net (total)	7	9	7

The Northeast Home Heating Oil Reserve (NEHHOR) was established to provide an emergency supply of home heating oil for the Northeast States during times of inventory shortages and significant threats to immediate supply. NEHHOR currently holds one million barrels of ultra-low sulfur diesel oil in reserve.

NUCLEAR WASTE DISPOSAL

For Department of Energy expenses necessary for activities to carry out the purposes of the Nuclear Waste Policy Act of 1982, Public Law 97–425, as amended, $10,205,000, to remain available until expended, to be derived from the Nuclear Waste Fund.

Note.—A full-year 2022 appropriation for this account was not enacted at the time the Budget was prepared; therefore, the Budget assumes this account is operating under the Continuing Appropriations Act, 2022 (Division A of Public Law 117–43, as amended). The amounts included for 2022 reflect the annualized level provided by the continuing resolution.

Special and Trust Fund Receipts (in millions of dollars)

Identification code 089–5227–0–2–271	2021 actual	2022 est.	2023 est.
0100 Balance, start of year	42,172	43,847	45,901
Receipts:			
Current law:			
1130 Nuclear Waste Disposal Fund		371	371
1140 Earnings on Investments, Nuclear Waste Disposal Fund	1,687	1,695	1,773
1199 Total current law receipts	1,687	2,066	2,144
1999 Total receipts	1,687	2,066	2,144
2000 Total: Balances and receipts	43,859	45,913	48,045
Appropriations:			
Current law:			
2101 Nuclear Waste Disposal	–8	–8	–10
2101 Salaries and Expenses	–4	–4	–4
2199 Total current law appropriations	–12	–12	–14
2999 Total appropriations	–12	–12	–14
5099 Balance, end of year	43,847	45,901	48,031

Program and Financing (in millions of dollars)

Identification code 089–5227–0–2–271	2021 actual	2022 est.	2023 est.
Obligations by program activity:			
0001 Interim Storage and Nuclear Waste Fund Oversight	21	28	10
Budgetary resources:			
Unobligated balance:			
1000 Unobligated balance brought forward, Oct 1	3	10	10
Budget authority:			
Appropriations, discretionary:			
1100 Appropriation	20	20	
1101 Appropriation (special or trust)	8	8	10
1160 Appropriation, discretionary (total)	28	28	10
1930 Total budgetary resources available	31	38	20
Memorandum (non-add) entries:			
1941 Unexpired unobligated balance, end of year	10	10	10
Change in obligated balance:			
Unpaid obligations:			
3000 Unpaid obligations, brought forward, Oct 1	4	16	20
3010 New obligations, unexpired accounts	21	28	10
3020 Outlays (gross)	–9	–24	–17
3050 Unpaid obligations, end of year	16	20	13
Memorandum (non-add) entries:			
3100 Obligated balance, start of year	4	16	20
3200 Obligated balance, end of year	16	20	13
Budget authority and outlays, net:			
Discretionary:			
4000 Budget authority, gross	28	28	10
Outlays, gross:			
4010 Outlays from new discretionary authority	8	11	4
4011 Outlays from discretionary balances	1	13	13
4020 Outlays, gross (total)	9	24	17
4180 Budget authority, net (total)	28	28	10
4190 Outlays, net (total)	9	24	17
Memorandum (non-add) entries:			
5000 Total investments, SOY: Federal securities: Par value	54,666	55,319	57,357
5001 Total investments, EOY: Federal securities: Par value	55,319	57,357	59,480

The mission of the Nuclear Waste Fund Oversight program is to ensure the continued safety of the Yucca Mountain site through activities such as security, maintenance, and environmental requirements, and continued oversight for the Nuclear Waste Fund including the fiduciary responsibility under the Nuclear Waste Policy Act of 1982.

Object Classification (in millions of dollars)

Identification code 089–5227–0–2–271	2021 actual	2022 est.	2023 est.
11.1 Direct obligations: Personnel compensation: Full-time permanent		3	4
11.9 Total personnel compensation		3	4
12.1 Civilian personnel benefits		2	2
25.1 Advisory and assistance services	21	23	4
99.9 Total new obligations, unexpired accounts	21	28	10

Employment Summary

Identification code 089–5227–0–2–271	2021 actual	2022 est.	2023 est.
1001 Direct civilian full-time equivalent employment		24	27

URANIUM ENRICHMENT DECONTAMINATION AND DECOMMISSIONING FUND

For Department of Energy expenses necessary in carrying out uranium enrichment facility decontamination and decommissioning, remedial actions, and other activities of title II of the Atomic Energy Act of 1954, and title X, subtitle A, of the Energy Policy Act of 1992, $822,421,000, to be derived from the Uranium Enrichment Decontamination and Decommissioning Fund, to remain available until expended, of which $24,400,000 shall be available in accordance with title X, subtitle A, of the Energy Policy Act of 1992.

Note.—A full-year 2022 appropriation for this account was not enacted at the time the Budget was prepared; therefore, the Budget assumes this account is operating under the Continuing Appropriations Act, 2022 (Division A of Public Law 117–43, as amended). The amounts included for 2022 reflect the annualized level provided by the continuing resolution.

Special and Trust Fund Receipts (in millions of dollars)

Identification code 089–5231–0–2–271	2021 actual	2022 est.	2023 est.
0100 Balance, start of year	565	29	31
Receipts:			
Current law:			
1140 Earnings on Investments, Decontamination and Decommissioning Fund	14	2	2
1140 General Fund Payment - Defense, Decontamination and Decommissioning Fund	....	....	417
1199 Total current law receipts	14	2	419
1999 Total receipts	14	2	419
2000 Total: Balances and receipts	579	31	450
Appropriations:			
Current law:			
2101 Uranium Enrichment Decontamination and Decommissioning Fund	–550	....	–417
5099 Balance, end of year	29	31	33

Program and Financing (in millions of dollars)

Identification code 089–5231–0–2–271	2021 actual	2022 est.	2023 est.
Obligations by program activity:			
0001 Oak Ridge	135	135	93
0002 Paducah	257	240	199
0003 Portsmouth	415	430	480
0004 Pension and Community and Regulatory Support	31	31	25
0005 Title X Uranium/Thorium Reimbursement Program	5	5	25
0900 Total new obligations, unexpired accounts	843	841	822
Budgetary resources:			
Unobligated balance:			
1000 Unobligated balance brought forward, Oct 1	10	10	10
1021 Recoveries of prior year unpaid obligations	1	....	....
1033 Recoveries of prior year paid obligations	1	....	....
1070 Unobligated balance (total)	12	10	10
Budget authority:			
Appropriations, discretionary:			
1101 Appropriation (special or trust)	550	....	417
Spending authority from offsetting collections, discretionary:			
1711 Spending authority from offsetting collections transferred from other accounts [486–4054]	291	841	405
1900 Budget authority (total)	841	841	822
1930 Total budgetary resources available	853	851	832
Memorandum (non-add) entries:			
1941 Unexpired unobligated balance, end of year	10	10	10
Change in obligated balance:			
Unpaid obligations:			
3000 Unpaid obligations, brought forward, Oct 1	306	335	242
3010 New obligations, unexpired accounts	843	841	822
3020 Outlays (gross)	–813	–934	–828
3040 Recoveries of prior year unpaid obligations, unexpired	–1	....	....
3050 Unpaid obligations, end of year	335	242	236
Memorandum (non-add) entries:			
3100 Obligated balance, start of year	306	335	242
3200 Obligated balance, end of year	335	242	236
Budget authority and outlays, net:			
Discretionary:			
4000 Budget authority, gross	841	841	822
Outlays, gross:			
4010 Outlays from new discretionary authority	560	589	576
4011 Outlays from discretionary balances	253	345	252
4020 Outlays, gross (total)	813	934	828
Offsets against gross budget authority and outlays:			
Offsetting collections (collected) from:			
4033 Non-Federal sources	–1	....	....
Additional offsets against gross budget authority only:			
4053 Recoveries of prior year paid obligations, unexpired accounts	1	....	....
4070 Budget authority, net (discretionary)	841	841	822
4080 Outlays, net (discretionary)	812	934	828
4180 Budget authority, net (total)	841	841	822
4190 Outlays, net (total)	812	934	828
Memorandum (non-add) entries:			
5000 Total investments, SOY: Federal securities: Par value	851	344	356
5001 Total investments, EOY: Federal securities: Par value	344	356	356

Decontamination and Decommissioning Activities.—Funds: 1) projects to decontaminate, decommission, and remediate the sites and facilities of the gaseous diffusion plants at Portsmouth, Ohio; Paducah, Kentucky; and East Tennessee Technology Park, Oak Ridge, Tennessee and; 2) pensions and post-retirement medical benefits for active and inactive gaseous diffusion plant workers.

Uranium and Thorium Reimbursement Program.—Provides reimbursement to uranium and thorium licensees for the Government's share of cleanup costs pursuant to Title X of the Energy Policy Act of 1992.

Object Classification (in millions of dollars)

Identification code 089–5231–0–2–271	2021 actual	2022 est.	2023 est.
Direct obligations:			
25.1 Advisory and assistance services	1	1	1
25.2 Other services from non-Federal sources	11	11	11
25.4 Operation and maintenance of facilities	765	763	746
32.0 Land and structures	63	63	61
41.0 Grants, subsidies, and contributions	3	3	3
99.9 Total new obligations, unexpired accounts	843	841	822

ISOTOPE PRODUCTION AND DISTRIBUTION PROGRAM FUND

Program and Financing (in millions of dollars)

Identification code 089–4180–0–3–271	2021 actual	2022 est.	2023 est.
Obligations by program activity:			
0801 Isotope Production and Distribution Reimbursable program	133	126	126
Budgetary resources:			
Unobligated balance:			
1000 Unobligated balance brought forward, Oct 1	21	5	5
Budget authority:			
Spending authority from offsetting collections, discretionary:			
1700 Collected	117	126	126
1930 Total budgetary resources available	138	131	131
Memorandum (non-add) entries:			
1941 Unexpired unobligated balance, end of year	5	5	5
Change in obligated balance:			
Unpaid obligations:			
3000 Unpaid obligations, brought forward, Oct 1	112	132	136
3010 New obligations, unexpired accounts	133	126	126
3020 Outlays (gross)	–113	–122	–144
3050 Unpaid obligations, end of year	132	136	118
Memorandum (non-add) entries:			
3100 Obligated balance, start of year	112	132	136
3200 Obligated balance, end of year	132	136	118
Budget authority and outlays, net:			
Discretionary:			
4000 Budget authority, gross	117	126	126
Outlays, gross:			
4010 Outlays from new discretionary authority	33	38	38
4011 Outlays from discretionary balances	80	84	106
4020 Outlays, gross (total)	113	122	144

DEPARTMENT OF ENERGY

Offsets against gross budget authority and outlays:
Offsetting collections (collected) from:

		2021 actual	2022 est.	2023 est.
4030	Federal sources	–78	–56	–56
4033	Non-Federal sources	–39	–70	–70
4040	Offsets against gross budget authority and outlays (total)	–117	–126	–126
4080	Outlays, net (discretionary)	–4	–4	18
4180	Budget authority, net (total)			
4190	Outlays, net (total)	–4	–4	18

Object Classification (in millions of dollars)

Identification code 089–4180–0–3–271		2021 actual	2022 est.	2023 est.
	Reimbursable obligations:			
25.4	Operation and maintenance of facilities	117	110	110
31.0	Equipment	7	7	7
41.0	Grants, subsidies, and contributions	9	9	9
99.0	Reimbursable obligations	133	126	126
99.9	Total new obligations, unexpired accounts	133	126	126

ADVANCED TECHNOLOGY VEHICLES MANUFACTURING LOAN PROGRAM

For Department of Energy administrative expenses necessary in carrying out the Advanced Technology Vehicles Manufacturing Loan Program, $9,800,000, to remain available until September 30, 2024.

Note.—A full-year 2022 appropriation for this account was not enacted at the time the Budget was prepared; therefore, the Budget assumes this account is operating under the Continuing Appropriations Act, 2022 (Division A of Public Law 117–43, as amended). The amounts included for 2022 reflect the annualized level provided by the continuing resolution.

Program and Financing (in millions of dollars)

Identification code 089–0322–0–1–272		2021 actual	2022 est.	2023 est.
	Obligations by program activity:			
	Credit program obligations:			
0701	Direct loan subsidy		236	1,951
0705	Reestimates of direct loan subsidy	9		
0706	Interest on reestimates of direct loan subsidy	6		
0709	Administrative expenses	5	10	10
0900	Total new obligations, unexpired accounts	20	246	1,961
	Budgetary resources:			
	Unobligated balance:			
1000	Unobligated balance brought forward, Oct 1	4,338	2,429	2,188
	Budget authority:			
	Appropriations, discretionary:			
1100	Appropriation	5	5	10
1131	Unobligated balance of appropriations permanently reduced	–1,908		
1160	Appropriation, discretionary (total)	–1,903	5	10
	Appropriations, mandatory:			
1200	Appropriation	14		
1900	Budget authority (total)	–1,889	5	10
1930	Total budgetary resources available	2,449	2,434	2,198
	Memorandum (non-add) entries:			
1941	Unexpired unobligated balance, end of year	2,429	2,188	237
	Change in obligated balance:			
	Unpaid obligations:			
3000	Unpaid obligations, brought forward, Oct 1	4	3	197
3010	New obligations, unexpired accounts	20	246	1,961
3020	Outlays (gross)	–19	–52	–211
3041	Recoveries of prior year unpaid obligations, expired	–2		
3050	Unpaid obligations, end of year	3	197	1,947
	Memorandum (non-add) entries:			
3100	Obligated balance, start of year	4	3	197
3200	Obligated balance, end of year	3	197	1,947
	Budget authority and outlays, net:			
	Discretionary:			
4000	Budget authority, gross	–1,903	5	10
	Outlays, gross:			
4011	Outlays from discretionary balances	5	52	211
	Mandatory:			
4090	Budget authority, gross	14		
	Outlays, gross:			
4100	Outlays from new mandatory authority	14		
4180	Budget authority, net (total)	–1,889	5	10
4190	Outlays, net (total)	19	52	211

Summary of Loan Levels, Subsidy Budget Authority and Outlays by Program (in millions of dollars)

Identification code 089–0322–0–1–272		2021 actual	2022 est.	2023 est.
	Direct loan levels supportable by subsidy budget authority:			
115001	Advanced Vehicle Manufacturing Loans		4,890	12,829
	Direct loan subsidy (in percent):			
132001	Advanced Vehicle Manufacturing Loans		4.83	15.21
132999	Weighted average subsidy rate	0.00	4.83	15.21
	Direct loan subsidy budget authority:			
133001	Advanced Vehicle Manufacturing Loans		236	1,951
	Direct loan subsidy outlays:			
134001	Advanced Vehicle Manufacturing Loans		47	204
	Direct loan reestimates:			
135001	Advanced Vehicle Manufacturing Loans	14	–11	
	Administrative expense data:			
3580	Outlays from balances	1	5	7

Section 136 of the Energy Independence and Security Act of 2007 (EISA) established a direct loan program to support the development of advanced technology vehicles and associated components in the United States, known as the Advanced Technology Vehicles Manufacturing (ATVM) Loan Program. The ATVM Loan Program provides loans to advanced technology vehicle and part manufacturers for the cost of reequipping, expanding, or establishing manufacturing facilities in the United States to produce advanced technology vehicles or qualified components and for associated engineering integration costs.

The Consolidated Security, Disaster, Assistance, and Continuing Appropriation Act of 2009 appropriated $7.5 billion for credit subsidy costs to support a maximum of $25 billion in loans under the ATVM Loan Program. Per EISA subsection (d)(1), the full credit subsidy cost must be paid using appropriated funds. Currently, the program has $17.7 billion in uncommitted loan authority and $2.4 billion in unobligated credit subsidy available to support new projects.

The Bipartisan Infrastructure Law authorized an expanded scope of advanced technology vehicle modes eligible for ATVM loans, including advanced medium- and heavy-duty vehicles, locomotives, maritime vessels, aircraft, and hyperloop technology. The FY 2023 Budget proposes to enable the use of existing appropriated authority to support projects eligible under the expanded scope.

In FY 2023, LPO requests $9.8 million to originate ATVM direct loans and monitor the program's growing portfolio. While the FY 2023 Budget Request does not request new loan authority, LPO anticipates utilizing all remaining ATVM loan authority by the end of FY 2023—closing approximately $5 billion in loans in FY 2022 and $13 billion in FY 2023.

Object Classification (in millions of dollars)

Identification code 089–0322–0–1–272		2021 actual	2022 est.	2023 est.
	Direct obligations:			
11.1	Personnel compensation: Full-time permanent	2	3	4
12.1	Below threshold		1	2
25.1	Advisory and assistance services	3	3	3
25.3	Other goods and services from Federal sources	1	3	1
41.0	Grants, subsidies, and contributions	14	236	1,951
99.0	Direct obligations	20	246	1,961
99.9	Total new obligations, unexpired accounts	20	246	1,961

Employment Summary

Identification code 089–0322–0–1–272		2021 actual	2022 est.	2023 est.
1001	Direct civilian full-time equivalent employment	13	20	28

ADVANCED TECHNOLOGY VEHICLES MANUFACTURING DIRECT LOAN FINANCING ACCOUNT

Program and Financing (in millions of dollars)

Identification code 089–4579–0–3–272		2021 actual	2022 est.	2023 est.
	Obligations by program activity:			
	Credit program obligations:			
0710	Direct loan obligations		4,890	12,829
0713	Payment of interest to Treasury	14	17	27
0715	Interest paid to FFB	18	13	11
0742	Downward reestimates paid to receipt accounts		8	
0743	Interest on downward reestimates		3	
0900	Total new obligations, unexpired accounts	32	4,931	12,867
	Budgetary resources:			
	Unobligated balance:			
1000	Unobligated balance brought forward, Oct 1	20		194
1023	Unobligated balances applied to repay debt	–20		
1070	Unobligated balance (total)			194
	Financing authority:			
	Borrowing authority, mandatory:			
1400	Borrowing authority	436	4,945	13,009
1422	Borrowing authority applied to repay debt	–429		
1440	Borrowing authority, mandatory (total)	7	4,945	13,009
	Spending authority from offsetting collections, mandatory:			
1800	Collected	201	1,025	264
1801	Change in uncollected payments, Federal sources		189	432
1825	Spending authority from offsetting collections applied to repay debt	–176	–1,034	
1850	Spending auth from offsetting collections, mand (total)	25	180	696
1900	Budget authority (total)	32	5,125	13,705
1930	Total budgetary resources available	32	5,125	13,899
	Memorandum (non-add) entries:			
1941	Unexpired unobligated balance, end of year		194	1,032
	Change in obligated balance:			
	Unpaid obligations:			
3000	Unpaid obligations, brought forward, Oct 1			3,896
3010	New obligations, unexpired accounts	32	4,931	12,867
3020	Outlays (gross)	–32	–1,035	–4,230
3050	Unpaid obligations, end of year		3,896	12,533
	Uncollected payments:			
3060	Uncollected pymts, Fed sources, brought forward, Oct 1			–189
3070	Change in uncollected pymts, Fed sources, unexpired		–189	–432
3090	Uncollected pymts, Fed sources, end of year		–189	–621
	Memorandum (non-add) entries:			
3100	Obligated balance, start of year			3,707
3200	Obligated balance, end of year		3,707	11,912
	Financing authority and disbursements, net:			
	Mandatory:			
4090	Budget authority, gross	32	5,125	13,705
	Financing disbursements:			
4110	Outlays, gross (total)	32	1,035	4,230
	Offsets against gross financing authority and disbursements:			
	Offsetting collections (collected) from:			
4120	Payment from program account	–14	–47	–204
4122	Interest on uninvested funds	–7		–13
4123	Non-Federal sources (interest)	–180	–26	–18
4123	Non-Federal sources (principal)		–947	–3
4123	Other Income - Fees		–5	–26
4130	Offsets against gross budget authority and outlays (total)	–201	–1,025	–264
	Additional offsets against financing authority only (total):			
4140	Change in uncollected pymts, Fed sources, unexpired		–189	–432
4160	Budget authority, net (mandatory)	–169	3,911	13,009
4170	Outlays, net (mandatory)	–169	10	3,966
4180	Budget authority, net (total)	–169	3,911	13,009
4190	Outlays, net (total)	–169	10	3,966

Status of Direct Loans (in millions of dollars)

Identification code 089–4579–0–3–272		2021 actual	2022 est.	2023 est.
	Position with respect to appropriations act limitation on obligations:			
1121	Limitation available from carry-forward	17,719	17,719	12,829
1143	Unobligated limitation carried forward (P.L. 110–329) (–)	–17,719	–12,829	
1150	Total direct loan obligations		4,890	12,829
	Cumulative balance of direct loans outstanding:			
1210	Outstanding, start of year	1,249	1,101	1,149
1231	Disbursements: Direct loan disbursements		995	4,192
1251	Repayments: Repayments and prepayments	–148	–947	–3
1290	Outstanding, end of year	1,101	1,149	5,338

Balance Sheet (in millions of dollars)

Identification code 089–4579–0–3–272		2020 actual	2021 actual
	ASSETS:		
	Federal assets:		
1101	Fund balances with Treasury	20	
	Investments in U.S. securities:		
1106	Receivables, net	34	
	Net value of assets related to post-1991 direct loans receivable:		
1401	Direct loans receivable, gross	1,249	1,101
1402	Interest receivable	1	2
1405	Allowance for subsidy cost (–)	–76	–74
1499	Net present value of assets related to direct loans	1,174	1,029
1999	Total assets	1,228	1,029
	LIABILITIES:		
	Federal liabilities:		
2101	Accounts payable		
2103	Debt	1,208	1,018
2105	Other	20	11
2999	Total liabilities	1,228	1,029
	NET POSITION:		
3300	Cumulative results of operations		
4999	Total upward reestimate subsidy BA [89–0322]	1,228	1,029

TITLE 17 INNOVATIVE TECHNOLOGY LOAN GUARANTEE PROGRAM

For the cost of guaranteed loans, $150,000,000, to remain available until expended, for innovative technology projects as authorized under Title XVII of the Energy Policy Act of 2005: Provided, That such costs, including the cost of modifying such loans, shall be as defined in section 502 of the Congressional Budget Act of 1974: Provided further, That these funds are available in addition to the authority provided in any other Act for the costs to guarantee loans under the heading "Department of Energy—Energy Programs—Title 17 Innovative Technology Loan Guarantee Program": Provided further, That these funds are available to subsidize total loan principal, any part of which is to be guaranteed, not to exceed $5,000,000,000: Provided further, That such sums as are derived from amounts received from borrowers pursuant to section 1702(b) of the Energy Policy Act of 2005 under this heading in prior Acts, shall be collected in accordance with section 502(7) of the Congressional Budget Act of 1974: Provided further, That for necessary administrative expenses of the Title 17 Innovative Technology Loan Guarantee Program, as authorized, $66,206,000 is appropriated, to remain available until September 30, 2024: Provided further, That up to $66,206,000 of fees collected in fiscal year 2023 pursuant to section 1702(h) of the Energy Policy Act of 2005 shall be credited as offsetting collections under this heading and used for necessary administrative expenses in this appropriation and shall remain available until September 30, 2024: Provided further, That to the extent that fees collected in fiscal year 2023 exceed $66,206,000, those excess amounts shall be credited as offsetting collections under this heading and available in future fiscal years only to the extent provided in advance in appropriations Acts: Provided further, That the sum herein appropriated from the general fund shall be reduced (1) as such fees are received during fiscal year 2023 (estimated at $48,000,000) and (2) to the extent that any remaining general fund appropriations can be derived from fees collected in previous fiscal years that are not otherwise appropriated, so as to result in a final fiscal year 2023 appropriation from the general fund estimated at $0: Provided further, That the Department of Energy shall not subordinate any loan obligation to other financing in violation of section 1702 of the Energy Policy Act of 2005 or subordinate any Guaranteed Obligation to any loan or other debt obligations in violation of section 609.10 of title 10, Code of Federal Regulations.

Note.—A full-year 2022 appropriation for this account was not enacted at the time the Budget was prepared; therefore, the Budget assumes this account is operating under the Continuing Appropriations Act, 2022 (Division A of Public Law 117–43, as amended). The amounts included for 2022 reflect the annualized level provided by the continuing resolution.

Program and Financing (in millions of dollars)

Identification code 089–0208–0–1–271	2021 actual	2022 est.	2023 est.
Obligations by program activity:			
Credit program obligations:			
0701 Direct loan subsidy		161	30
0705 Reestimates of direct loan subsidy	262		
0706 Interest on reestimates of direct loan subsidy	34	22	
0709 Administrative expenses	37	59	66
0900 Total new obligations, unexpired accounts	333	242	96
Budgetary resources:			
Unobligated balance:			
1000 Unobligated balance brought forward, Oct 1	682	285	97
Budget authority:			
Appropriations, discretionary:			
1100 Appropriation	29		150
1131 Unobligated balance of appropriations permanently reduced	–392		
1160 Appropriation, discretionary (total)	–363		150
Appropriations, mandatory:			
1200 Appropriation	296	22	
Spending authority from offsetting collections, discretionary:			
1700 Collected	3	53	48
1702 Offsetting collections (previously unavailable)			21
1724 Spending authority from offsetting collections precluded from obligation (limitation on obligations)		–21	–3
1750 Spending auth from offsetting collections, disc (total)	3	32	66
1900 Budget authority (total)	–64	54	216
1930 Total budgetary resources available	618	339	313
Memorandum (non-add) entries:			
1941 Unexpired unobligated balance, end of year	285	97	217
Change in obligated balance:			
Unpaid obligations:			
3000 Unpaid obligations, brought forward, Oct 1	21	25	168
3010 New obligations, unexpired accounts	333	242	96
3020 Outlays (gross)	–328	–99	–239
3041 Recoveries of prior year unpaid obligations, expired	–1		
3050 Unpaid obligations, end of year	25	168	25
Memorandum (non-add) entries:			
3100 Obligated balance, start of year	21	25	168
3200 Obligated balance, end of year	25	168	25
Budget authority and outlays, net:			
Discretionary:			
4000 Budget authority, gross	–360	32	216
Outlays, gross:			
4010 Outlays from new discretionary authority		32	96
4011 Outlays from discretionary balances	32	45	143
4020 Outlays, gross (total)	32	77	239
Offsets against gross budget authority and outlays:			
Offsetting collections (collected) from:			
4033 Non-Federal sources	–3	–53	–48
4040 Offsets against gross budget authority and outlays (total)	–3	–53	–48
Mandatory:			
4090 Budget authority, gross	296	22	
Outlays, gross:			
4100 Outlays from new mandatory authority	296	22	
4180 Budget authority, net (total)	–67	1	168
4190 Outlays, net (total)	325	46	191
Memorandum (non-add) entries:			
5090 Unexpired unavailable balance, SOY: Offsetting collections			21
5092 Unexpired unavailable balance, EOY: Offsetting collections		21	3

Summary of Loan Levels, Subsidy Budget Authority and Outlays by Program (in millions of dollars)

Identification code 089–0208–0–1–271	2021 actual	2022 est.	2023 est.
Direct loan levels supportable by subsidy budget authority:			
115001 Section 1703 FFB Loans		6,025	4,510
115999 Total direct loan levels		6,025	4,510
Direct loan subsidy (in percent):			
132001 Section 1703 FFB Loans		2.67	0.66
132999 Weighted average subsidy rate		2.67	0.66
Direct loan subsidy budget authority:			
133001 Section 1703 FFB Loans		161	30
133999 Total subsidy budget authority		161	30
Direct loan subsidy outlays:			
134001 Section 1703 FFB Loans	–45	15	134
134999 Total subsidy outlays	–45	15	134
Direct loan reestimates:			
135001 Section 1703 FFB Loans	190	–146	
135002 Section 1705 FFB Loans	14	–182	
135999 Total direct loan reestimates	204	–328	
Guaranteed loan reestimates:			
235002 Section 1705 Loan Guarantees	–68	–23	
235999 Total guaranteed loan reestimates	–68	–23	

The Title 17 Innovative Technology Loan Guarantee Program (Title 17), authorized by the Energy Policy Act of 2005 (EPAct of 2005), as amended, allows the Department of Energy (DOE) to provide loan guarantees for innovative energy projects that avoid, reduce, or sequester air pollutants or anthropogenic emissions of greenhouse gases. Eligible technologies include energy efficient and renewable energy systems; advanced fossil and carbon capture, sequestration, utilization and storage systems; energy storage; virtual power plants; and various other clean energy projects.

Through the Title 17 loan guarantee program, the Loan Programs Office (LPO) provides access to debt capital for high-impact, large-scale infrastructure projects and initial commercializations in the United States. Eligible projects must meet air pollutant or greenhouse gases emissions requirements; employ new or significantly improved technologies compared to commercial technologies in service in the United States at the time the guarantee is issued; and offer a reasonable prospect of repayment of the principal and interest on the guaranteed obligation.

As of January 2022, $22.4 billion in loan guarantee authority is available to support projects eligible under Section 1703. In addition, $161 million in appropriated credit subsidy is remaining (from the FY 2011 full-year continuing resolution) that can be used for renewable energy and efficient end-use technology projects.

The Bipartisan Infrastructure Law authorized an expanded scope of projects eligible under Title 17, including domestic critical minerals supply chain and State energy financing institution-backed projects. The FY 2023 Budget proposes to enable the use of existing appropriated authority to support projects eligible under this new authority.

The FY 2023 Budget requests $150,000,000 for credit subsidy and $5 billion in loan guarantee authority to support the full range of projects eligible under Title 17. Available loan authority will increase by $5 billion from $22.4 billion to $27.4 billion. The Department expects to obligate approximately $6 billion of loan authority in FY 2022 and $4.5 billion of loan authority in FY 2023.

The Budget requests $66,206,000 for administrative expenses to operate the Title 17 program. The Department estimates that $48,000,000 will be received from fees pursuant to Section 1702(h) of the Energy Policy Act of 2005 and credited as offsetting collection.

Object Classification (in millions of dollars)

Identification code 089–0208–0–1–271	2021 actual	2022 est.	2023 est.
11.1 Direct obligations: Personnel compensation: Full-time permanent	12	13	15
11.9 Total personnel compensation	12	13	15
12.1 Civilian personnel benefits	4	5	5
21.0 Travel and transportation of persons			2
23.3 Communications, utilities, and miscellaneous charges			1
25.1 Advisory and assistance services	17	34	36
25.2 Other services from non-Federal sources	1	3	2
25.3 Other goods and services from Federal sources	2	3	4
26.0 Supplies and materials	1	1	1
41.0 Grants, subsidies, and contributions	296	183	30
99.0 Direct obligations	333	242	96
99.9 Total new obligations, unexpired accounts	333	242	96

TITLE 17 INNOVATIVE TECHNOLOGY LOAN GUARANTEE PROGRAM—Continued

Employment Summary

Identification code 089–0208–0–1–271	2021 actual	2022 est.	2023 est.
1001 Direct civilian full-time equivalent employment	75	93	97

TITLE 17 INNOVATIVE TECHNOLOGY DIRECT LOAN FINANCING ACCOUNT

Program and Financing (in millions of dollars)

Identification code 089–4455–0–3–271	2021 actual	2022 est.	2023 est.
Obligations by program activity:			
Credit program obligations:			
0710 Direct loan obligations	....	6,025	4,510
0713 Payment of interest to Treasury	25	18	13
0715 Interest paid to FFB	428	223	229
0742 Downward reestimates paid to receipt accounts	92	294	....
0743 Interest on downward reestimates	....	55	....
0900 Total new obligations, unexpired accounts	545	6,615	4,752
Budgetary resources:			
Unobligated balance:			
1000 Unobligated balance brought forward, Oct 1	860	846	916
1023 Unobligated balances applied to repay debt	–384	–140	....
1070 Unobligated balance (total)	476	706	916
Financing authority:			
Borrowing authority, mandatory:			
1400 Borrowing authority	268	6,025	4,638
1422 Borrowing authority applied to repay debt	–162	....	....
1440 Borrowing authority, mandatory (total)	106	6,025	4,638
Spending authority from offsetting collections, mandatory:			
1800 Collected	1,415	852	963
1801 Change in uncollected payments, Federal sources	....	136	–111
1825 Spending authority from offsetting collections applied to repay debt	–606	–188	–16
1850 Spending auth from offsetting collections, mand (total)	809	800	836
1900 Budget authority (total)	915	6,825	5,474
1930 Total budgetary resources available	1,391	7,531	6,390
Memorandum (non-add) entries:			
1941 Unexpired unobligated balance, end of year	846	916	1,638
Change in obligated balance:			
Unpaid obligations:			
3000 Unpaid obligations, brought forward, Oct 1	2,430	838	5,465
3010 New obligations, unexpired accounts	545	6,615	4,752
3020 Outlays (gross)	–2,137	–1,988	–5,289
3050 Unpaid obligations, end of year	838	5,465	4,928
Uncollected payments:			
3060 Uncollected pymts, Fed sources, brought forward, Oct 1	....	....	–136
3070 Change in uncollected pymts, Fed sources, unexpired	....	–136	111
3090 Uncollected pymts, Fed sources, end of year	....	–136	–25
Memorandum (non-add) entries:			
3100 Obligated balance, start of year	2,430	838	5,329
3200 Obligated balance, end of year	838	5,329	4,903
Financing authority and disbursements, net:			
Mandatory:			
4090 Budget authority, gross	915	6,825	5,474
Financing disbursements:			
4110 Outlays, gross (total)	2,137	1,988	5,289
Offsets against gross financing authority and disbursements:			
Offsetting collections (collected) from:			
4120 Payment from program account	–296	–25	–141
4120 Interest on reestimate	....	–22	....
4122 Interest on uninvested funds	–56	–23	–6
4123 Interest payments	–1,063	–328	–362
4123 Principal payments	....	–454	–454
4130 Offsets against gross budget authority and outlays (total)	–1,415	–852	–963
Additional offsets against financing authority only (total):			
4140 Change in uncollected pymts, Fed sources, unexpired	....	–136	111
4160 Budget authority, net (mandatory)	–500	5,837	4,622
4170 Outlays, net (mandatory)	722	1,136	4,326
4180 Budget authority, net (total)	–500	5,837	4,622
4190 Outlays, net (total)	722	1,136	4,326

Status of Direct Loans (in millions of dollars)

Identification code 089–4455–0–3–271	2021 actual	2022 est.	2023 est.
Position with respect to appropriations act limitation on obligations:			
1121 Limitation available from carry-forward	22,422	22,422	21,397
1143 Unobligated limitation carried forward (P.L. xx) (–)	–22,422	–16,397	–16,887
1150 Total direct loan obligations	....	6,025	4,510
Cumulative balance of direct loans outstanding:			
1210 Outstanding, start of year	14,782	15,699	16,716
1231 Disbursements: Direct loan disbursements	1,553	1,389	4,799
1251 Repayments: Repayments and prepayments	–569	–328	–362
1261 Adjustments: Capitalized interest	....	....	17
1264 Other adjustments, net (+ or –) [Payment of capitalized interest]	–67	–44	....
1290 Outstanding, end of year	15,699	16,716	21,170

Balance Sheet (in millions of dollars)

Identification code 089–4455–0–3–271	2020 actual	2021 actual
ASSETS:		
Federal assets:		
1101 Fund balances with Treasury	860	847
Investments in U.S. securities:		
1106 Receivables, net	510	142
1206 Non-Federal assets: Receivables, net	12	12
Net value of assets related to post-1991 direct loans receivable:		
1401 Direct loans receivable, gross	14,782	15,699
1402 Interest receivable	78	72
1405 Allowance for subsidy cost (–)	–872	–462
1499 Net present value of assets related to direct loans	13,988	15,309
1999 Total assets	15,370	16,310
LIABILITIES:		
Federal liabilities:		
2103 Debt	15,148	15,856
2105 Other	222	454
2999 Total liabilities	15,370	16,310
NET POSITION:		
3300 Cumulative results of operations	....	....
4999 Total liabilities and net position	15,370	16,310

CARBON DIOXIDE TRANSPORTATION INFRASTRUCTURE FINANCE AND INNOVATION PROGRAM ACCOUNT

[For an additional amount for "Carbon Dioxide Transportation Infrastructure Finance and Innovation Program Account", $2,100,000,000, to remain available until expended, to carry out activities for the Carbon Dioxide Transportation Infrastructure Finance and Innovation Program, as authorized by subtitle J of title IX of the Energy Policy Act of 2005 (42 U.S.C. 16181 et seq.), as amended by section 40304(a) of division D of this Act: *Provided*, That such costs, including the cost of modifying such loans, shall be as defined in section 502 of the Congressional Budget Act of 1974: *Provided further*, That $3,000,000, to remain available until expended, shall be made available for fiscal year 2022 and $2,097,000,000, to remain available until expended, shall be made available for fiscal year 2023: *Provided further*, That the amount made available under this heading in this Act for fiscal year 2022 shall be for administrative expenses to carry out the loan program: *Provided further*, That the Office of Fossil Energy and Carbon Management shall oversee the Carbon Dioxide Transportation Infrastructure Finance and Innovation program, in consultation and coordination with the Department of Energy's Loan Program Office: *Provided further*, That not later than 270 days after the date of enactment of this Act, the Secretary of Energy shall submit to the House and Senate Committees on Appropriations an analysis of how subsidy rates will be determined for loans financed by appropriations provided under this heading in this Act and an analysis of the process for developing draft regulations for the program, including a crosswalk from the statutory requirements for such program, and a timetable for publishing such regulations: *Provided further*, That for each fiscal year through 2027, the annual budget submission of the President under section 1105(a) of title 31, United States Code, shall include a detailed request for the amount recommended for allocation for the Carbon Dioxide Transportation Finance and Innovation program from amounts provided under this heading in this Act and such detailed request shall include any information required pursuant to the Federal Credit Reform Act of 1990, such as credit subsidy rates, a loan limitation, and necessary administrative expenses to carry

DEPARTMENT OF ENERGY

Energy Programs—Continued
Federal Funds—Continued

405

out the loan program: *Provided further*, That such amount is designated by the Congress as being for an emergency requirement pursuant to section 4112(a) of H. Con. Res. 71 (115th Congress), the concurrent resolution on the budget for fiscal year 2018, and to section 251(b) of the Balanced Budget and Emergency Deficit Control Act of 1985.] *(Infrastructure Investments and Jobs Appropriations Act.)*

Program and Financing (in millions of dollars)

Identification code 089–2300–0–1–271		2021 actual	2022 est.	2023 est.
	Obligations by program activity:			
	Credit program obligations:			
0709	Administrative expenses		2	10
	Budgetary resources:			
	Unobligated balance:			
1000	Unobligated balance brought forward, Oct 1			1
	Budget authority:			
	Appropriations, discretionary:			
1100	Appropriation		3	
	Advance appropriations, discretionary:			
1170	Advance appropriation			2,095
1900	Budget authority (total)		3	2,095
1930	Total budgetary resources available		3	2,096
	Memorandum (non-add) entries:			
1941	Unexpired unobligated balance, end of year		1	2,086
	Change in obligated balance:			
	Unpaid obligations:			
3010	New obligations, unexpired accounts		2	10
3020	Outlays (gross)		–2	–10
	Budget authority and outlays, net:			
	Discretionary:			
4000	Budget authority, gross		3	2,095
	Outlays, gross:			
4010	Outlays from new discretionary authority		2	9
4011	Outlays from discretionary balances			1
4020	Outlays, gross (total)		2	10
4180	Budget authority, net (total)		3	2,095
4190	Outlays, net (total)		2	10

Summary of Loan Levels, Subsidy Budget Authority and Outlays by Program (in millions of dollars)

Identification code 089–2300–0–1–271		2021 actual	2022 est.	2023 est.
	Administrative expense data:			
3510	Budget authority		1	1
3580	Outlays from balances			1
3590	Outlays from new authority		1	

The Carbon Dioxide Transportation Infrastructure Finance and Innovation (CIFIA) Program, established in the Bipartisan Infrastructure Law (Infrastructure Investment and Jobs Act, P.L. 117–58), is authorized to provide loans, loan guarantees, and grants for carbon dioxide transport infrastructure projects. CIFIA supports the manufacturing and expansion of common carrier carbon dioxide transportation infrastructure and associated components, including pipeline, shipping, rail, and other transportation infrastructure. The Office of Fossil Energy and Carbon Management oversees the CIFIA program, in consultation and coordination with DOE's Loan Programs Office.

Object Classification (in millions of dollars)

Identification code 089–2300–0–1–271		2021 actual	2022 est.	2023 est.
11.1	Direct obligations: Personnel compensation: Full-time permanent		1	2
11.9	Total personnel compensation		1	2
25.1	Advisory and assistance services		1	8
99.9	Total new obligations, unexpired accounts		2	10

Employment Summary

Identification code 089–2300–0–1–271	2021 actual	2022 est.	2023 est.
1001 Direct civilian full-time equivalent employment		5	10

TRIBAL ENERGY LOAN GUARANTEE PROGRAM

For Department of Energy administrative expenses necessary in carrying out the Tribal Energy Loan Guarantee Program, $1,860,000, to remain available until September 30, 2024.

Note.—A full-year 2022 appropriation for this account was not enacted at the time the Budget was prepared; therefore, the Budget assumes this account is operating under the Continuing Appropriations Act, 2022 (Division A of Public Law 117–43, as amended). The amounts included for 2022 reflect the annualized level provided by the continuing resolution.

Program and Financing (in millions of dollars)

Identification code 089–0350–0–1–271		2021 actual	2022 est.	2023 est.
	Obligations by program activity:			
	Credit program obligations:			
0702	Loan guarantee subsidy		4	1
0709	Administrative expenses	2	2	2
0900	Total new obligations, unexpired accounts	2	6	3
	Budgetary resources:			
	Unobligated balance:			
1000	Unobligated balance brought forward, Oct 1	11	11	7
	Budget authority:			
	Appropriations, discretionary:			
1100	Appropriation	2	2	2
1930	Total budgetary resources available	13	13	9
	Memorandum (non-add) entries:			
1941	Unexpired unobligated balance, end of year	11	7	6
	Change in obligated balance:			
	Unpaid obligations:			
3000	Unpaid obligations, brought forward, Oct 1	1	2	5
3010	New obligations, unexpired accounts	2	6	3
3020	Outlays (gross)	–1	–3	–5
3050	Unpaid obligations, end of year	2	5	3
	Memorandum (non-add) entries:			
3100	Obligated balance, start of year	1	2	5
3200	Obligated balance, end of year	2	5	3
	Budget authority and outlays, net:			
	Discretionary:			
4000	Budget authority, gross	2	2	2
	Outlays, gross:			
4010	Outlays from new discretionary authority		2	2
4011	Outlays from discretionary balances	1	1	3
4020	Outlays, gross (total)	1	3	5
4180	Budget authority, net (total)	2	2	2
4190	Outlays, net (total)	1	3	5

Summary of Loan Levels, Subsidy Budget Authority and Outlays by Program (in millions of dollars)

Identification code 089–0350–0–1–271		2021 actual	2022 est.	2023 est.
	Guaranteed loan levels supportable by subsidy budget authority:			
215001	Tribal Energy Loan Guarantees		735	465
	Guaranteed loan subsidy (in percent):			
232001	Tribal Energy Loan Guarantees		0.56	0.31
232999	Weighted average subsidy rate	0.00	0.56	0.31
	Guaranteed loan subsidy budget authority:			
233001	Tribal Energy Loan Guarantees		4	1
	Guaranteed loan subsidy outlays:			
234001	Tribal Energy Loan Guarantees		1	2

The Tribal Energy Loan Guarantee Program (TELGP) provides access to debt capital for tribal ownership of energy projects and activities that support economic development and tribal sovereignty. TELGP is authorized pursuant to section 2602 of the Energy Policy Act of 1992, as amended by the Energy Policy Act of 2005, to make available up to $2 billion in partial loan guarantees. The Consolidated Appropriations Act, 2017, (H.R. 244,

TRIBAL ENERGY LOAN GUARANTEE PROGRAM—Continued

Public Law 115–31) appropriated $8.5 million to cover the credit subsidy costs associated with the $2 billion in available loan authority.

The FY 2023 Budget proposes $1,860,000 in Administrative Expenses to continue outreach and originating activities and to monitor the expected portfolio of TELGP projects. This funding level allows the Loan Programs Office to help achieve the Administration's objectives of a carbon-pollution free electric sector by 2035 and net-zero emissions, economy-wide, by 2050, supporting placed-based initiatives including energy community and Justice40 investments.

Object Classification (in millions of dollars)

Identification code 089–0350–0–1–271		2021 actual	2022 est.	2023 est.
	Direct obligations:			
25.1	Advisory and assistance services	2	1	1
41.0	Grants, subsidies, and contributions		4	1
99.0	Direct obligations	2	5	2
99.5	Adjustment for rounding		1	1
99.9	Total new obligations, unexpired accounts	2	6	3

Employment Summary

Identification code 089–0350–0–1–271		2021 actual	2022 est.	2023 est.
1001	Direct civilian full-time equivalent employment		5	5

TRIBAL INDIAN ENERGY RESOURCE DEVELOPMENT LOAN GUARANTEE FINANCING ACCOUNT

Program and Financing (in millions of dollars)

Identification code 089–4370–0–3–271		2021 actual	2022 est.	2023 est.
	Obligations by program activity:			
	Credit program obligations:			
0711	Default claim payments on principal		1	4
0900	Total new obligations, unexpired accounts		1	4
	Budgetary resources:			
	Unobligated balance:			
1000	Unobligated balance brought forward, Oct 1			3
	Financing authority:			
	Spending authority from offsetting collections, mandatory:			
1800	Collected		1	2
1801	Change in uncollected payments, Federal sources		3	1
1850	Spending auth from offsetting collections, mand (total)		4	3
1930	Total budgetary resources available		4	6
	Memorandum (non-add) entries:			
1941	Unexpired unobligated balance, end of year		3	2
	Change in obligated balance:			
	Unpaid obligations:			
3010	New obligations, unexpired accounts		1	4
3020	Outlays (gross)		–1	–4
	Uncollected payments:			
3060	Uncollected pymts, Fed sources, brought forward, Oct 1			–3
3070	Change in uncollected pymts, Fed sources, unexpired		–3	–1
3090	Uncollected pymts, Fed sources, end of year		–3	–4
	Memorandum (non-add) entries:			
3100	Obligated balance, start of year			–3
3200	Obligated balance, end of year		–3	–4
	Financing authority and disbursements, net:			
	Mandatory:			
4090	Budget authority, gross		4	3
	Financing disbursements:			
4110	Outlays, gross (total)		1	4
	Offsets against gross financing authority and disbursements:			
	Offsetting collections (collected) from:			
4120	Program Fund Collections		–1	–2
	Additional offsets against financing authority only (total):			
4140	Change in uncollected pymts, Fed sources, unexpired		–3	–1
4170	Outlays, net (mandatory)			2
4180	Budget authority, net (total)			
4190	Outlays, net (total)			2

Status of Guaranteed Loans (in millions of dollars)

Identification code 089–4370–0–3–271		2021 actual	2022 est.	2023 est.
	Position with respect to appropriations act limitation on commitments:			
2121	Limitation available from carry-forward	2,000	2,000	1,265
2142	Uncommitted loan guarantee limitation			
2143	Uncommitted limitation carried forward	–2,000	–1,265	–800
2150	Total guaranteed loan commitments		735	465
2199	Guaranteed amount of guaranteed loan commitments		662	419
	Cumulative balance of guaranteed loans outstanding:			
2210	Outstanding, start of year			112
2231	Disbursements of new guaranteed loans		113	369
2251	Repayments and prepayments			
	Adjustments:			
2261	Terminations for default that result in loans receivable			
2263	Terminations for default that result in claim payments		–1	
2290	Outstanding, end of year		112	481
	Memorandum:			
2299	Guaranteed amount of guaranteed loans outstanding, end of year		102	434
	Addendum:			
	Cumulative balance of defaulted guaranteed loans that result in loans receivable:			
2310	Outstanding, start of year			1
2331	Disbursements for guaranteed loan claims		1	4
2351	Repayments of loans receivable			–1
2390	Outstanding, end of year		1	4

TITLE 17 INNOVATIVE TECHNOLOGY GUARANTEED LOAN FINANCING ACCOUNT

Program and Financing (in millions of dollars)

Identification code 089–4577–0–3–271		2021 actual	2022 est.	2023 est.
	Obligations by program activity:			
	Credit program obligations:			
0711	Default claim payments on principal		24	4
0712	Default claim payments on interest		5	5
0742	Downward reestimates paid to receipt accounts	49	16	
0743	Interest on downward reestimates	19	6	
0900	Total new obligations, unexpired accounts	68	51	9
	Budgetary resources:			
	Unobligated balance:			
1000	Unobligated balance brought forward, Oct 1	193	129	81
	Financing authority:			
	Spending authority from offsetting collections, mandatory:			
1800	Collected	4	3	18
1900	Budget authority (total)	4	3	18
1930	Total budgetary resources available	197	132	99
	Memorandum (non-add) entries:			
1941	Unexpired unobligated balance, end of year	129	81	90
	Change in obligated balance:			
	Unpaid obligations:			
3000	Unpaid obligations, brought forward, Oct 1		1	1
3010	New obligations, unexpired accounts	68	51	9
3020	Outlays (gross)	–67	–51	–9
3050	Unpaid obligations, end of year	1	1	1
	Uncollected payments:			
3060	Uncollected pymts, Fed sources, brought forward, Oct 1	–9	–9	–9
3090	Uncollected pymts, Fed sources, end of year	–9	–9	–9
	Memorandum (non-add) entries:			
3100	Obligated balance, start of year	–9	–8	–8
3200	Obligated balance, end of year	–8	–8	–8
	Financing authority and disbursements, net:			
	Mandatory:			
4090	Budget authority, gross	4	3	18
	Financing disbursements:			
4110	Outlays, gross (total)	67	51	9

	Offsets against gross financing authority and disbursements:			
	Offsetting collections (collected) from:			
4122	Interest on uninvested funds	–4	–3	–3
4123	Principal payments			–12
4123	Interest Payments			–3
4130	Offsets against gross budget authority and outlays (total)	–4	–3	–18
4170	Outlays, net (mandatory)	63	48	–9
4180	Budget authority, net (total)			
4190	Outlays, net (total)	63	48	–9

Status of Guaranteed Loans (in millions of dollars)

Identification code 089–4577–0–3–271		2021 actual	2022 est.	2023 est.
	Position with respect to appropriations act limitation on commitments:			
2121	Limitation available from carry-forward			
2143	Uncommitted limitation carried forward			
2150	Total guaranteed loan commitments			
	Cumulative balance of guaranteed loans outstanding:			
2210	Outstanding, start of year	2,000	1,888	1,782
2231	Disbursements of new guaranteed loans			
2251	Repayments and prepayments	–112	–82	–103
2261	Adjustments: Terminations for default that result in loans receivable		–24	–4
2290	Outstanding, end of year	1,888	1,782	1,675
	Memorandum:			
2299	Guaranteed amount of guaranteed loans outstanding, end of year	1,522	1,438	1,352
	Addendum:			
	Cumulative balance of defaulted guaranteed loans that result in loans receivable:			
2310	Outstanding, start of year			29
2331	Disbursements for guaranteed loan claims		24	4
2351	Repayments of loans receivable			–14
2364	Other adjustments, net		5	5
2390	Outstanding, end of year		29	24

Balance Sheet (in millions of dollars)

Identification code 089–4577–0–3–271		2020 actual	2021 actual
	ASSETS:		
	Federal assets:		
1101	Fund balances with Treasury	184	121
	Investments in U.S. securities:		
1106	Receivables, net		
1501	Net value of assets related to post-1991 acquired defaulted guaranteed loans receivable: Defaulted guaranteed loans receivable, gross		
1999	Total assets	184	121
	LIABILITIES:		
	Federal liabilities:		
2101	Accounts payable		
2105	Other	67	23
2204	Non-Federal liabilities: Liabilities for loan guarantees	117	98
2999	Total liabilities	184	121
	NET POSITION:		
3300	Cumulative results of operations		
4999	Total liabilities and net position	184	121

POWER MARKETING ADMINISTRATION

Federal Funds

Operation and Maintenance, Southeastern Power Administration

For expenses necessary for operation and maintenance of power transmission facilities and for marketing electric power and energy, including transmission wheeling and ancillary services, pursuant to section 5 of the Flood Control Act of 1944 (16 U.S.C. 825s), as applied to the southeastern power area, $8,173,000, including official reception and representation expenses in an amount not to exceed $1,500, to remain available until expended: Provided, That notwithstanding 31 U.S.C. 3302 and section 5 of the Flood Control Act of 1944, up to $8,173,000 collected by the Southeastern Power Administration from the sale of power and related services shall be credited to this account as discretionary offsetting collections, to remain available until expended for the sole purpose of funding the annual expenses of the Southeastern Power Administration: Provided further, That the sum herein appropriated for annual expenses shall be reduced as collections are received during the fiscal year so as to result in a final fiscal year 2023 appropriation estimated at not more than $0: Provided further, That notwithstanding 31 U.S.C. 3302, up to $78,696,000 collected by the Southeastern Power Administration pursuant to the Flood Control Act of 1944 to recover purchase power and wheeling expenses shall be credited to this account as offsetting collections, to remain available until expended for the sole purpose of making purchase power and wheeling expenditures: Provided further, That for purposes of this appropriation, annual expenses means expenditures that are generally recovered in the same year that they are incurred (excluding purchase power and wheeling expenses).

Note.—A full-year 2022 appropriation for this account was not enacted at the time the Budget was prepared; therefore, the Budget assumes this account is operating under the Continuing Appropriations Act, 2022 (Division A of Public Law 117–43, as amended). The amounts included for 2022 reflect the annualized level provided by the continuing resolution.

Program and Financing (in millions of dollars)

Identification code 089–0302–0–1–271		2021 actual	2022 est.	2023 est.
	Obligations by program activity:			
0001	Purchase Power and Wheeling	43	53	79
0002	Annual Expenses	8	7	7
0799	Total direct obligations	51	60	86
0900	Total new obligations, unexpired accounts	51	60	86
	Budgetary resources:			
	Unobligated balance:			
1000	Unobligated balance brought forward, Oct 1	19	30	30
	Budget authority:			
	Spending authority from offsetting collections, discretionary:			
1700	Collected	62	60	84
1900	Budget authority (total)	62	60	84
1930	Total budgetary resources available	81	90	114
	Memorandum (non-add) entries:			
1941	Unexpired unobligated balance, end of year	30	30	28
	Change in obligated balance:			
	Unpaid obligations:			
3000	Unpaid obligations, brought forward, Oct 1	4	5	5
3010	New obligations, unexpired accounts	51	60	86
3020	Outlays (gross)	–50	–60	–86
3050	Unpaid obligations, end of year	5	5	5
	Memorandum (non-add) entries:			
3100	Obligated balance, start of year	4	5	5
3200	Obligated balance, end of year	5	5	5
	Budget authority and outlays, net:			
	Discretionary:			
4000	Budget authority, gross	62	60	84
	Outlays, gross:			
4010	Outlays from new discretionary authority	26	58	81
4011	Outlays from discretionary balances	24	2	5
4020	Outlays, gross (total)	50	60	86
	Offsets against gross budget authority and outlays:			
	Offsetting collections (collected) from:			
4033	Non-Federal sources	–62	–60	–84
4040	Offsets against gross budget authority and outlays (total)	–62	–60	–84
4180	Budget authority, net (total)			
4190	Outlays, net (total)	–12		2

The Southeastern Power Administration (Southeastern) markets power generated at 22 U.S. Army Corps of Engineers' hydroelectric generating plants in an eleven State area of the Southeast. Power deliveries are made by means of contracting for use of transmission facilities owned by others.

Southeastern sells wholesale power primarily to publicly and cooperatively owned electric distribution utilities. Southeastern does not own or operate any transmission facilities. Its long-term contracts provide for periodic electric rate adjustments to ensure that the Federal Government recovers the costs of operations and the capital invested in power facilities, with interest, in keeping with statutory requirements. As in past years, the budget continues to provide funding for annual expenses and purchase

Power Marketing Administration—Continued
Federal Funds—Continued

OPERATION AND MAINTENANCE, SOUTHEASTERN POWER ADMINISTRATION—Continued

power and wheeling expenses through discretionary offsetting collections derived from power receipts collected to recover those expenses.

Program Direction.—Provision is made for negotiation and administration of transmission and power contracts, collection of revenues, accounting and budget activities, development of wholesale power rates, amortization of the Federal power investment, energy efficiency and competitiveness program, investigation and planning of proposed water resources projects, scheduling and dispatch of power generation, scheduling storage and release of water, administration of contractual operation requirements, and determination of methods of operating generating plants individually and in coordination with others to obtain maximum utilization of resources.

Purchase Power and Wheeling.—Provision is made for the payment of wheeling fees and for the purchase of electricity in connection with the disposal of power under contracts with utility companies. Customers are encouraged to use alternative funding mechanisms, including customer advances and net billing to finance these activities. Offsetting collections to fund these ongoing operating services are also available up to 53 million in 2022. As of the end of FY 2021, Southeastern's PPW reserve balance was $27 million.

DISCRETIONARY PURCHASE POWER AND WHEELING, SOUTHEASTERN POWER ADMINISTRATION

(in millions of dollars)

	2019 Actual	2020 Actual	2021 Actual	2022 Estimate	2023 Estimate
Limitation to collect, ('up to' ceiling in appropriations language)	55	56	52	53	79
Actual collections	42	46	52	53	79
PPW Unobligated balance brought forward, Oct 1	12	14	18	27	27
Spending authority from offsetting collections	42	46	52	53	79
Obligations incurred	–40	–42	–43	–53	–79
PPW Unobligated balance, end of year	14	18	27	27	27

Reimbursable Program.—The Consolidated Appropriations Act, 2008 (P.L. 110–161) provided Southeastern with authority to accept advance payment from customers for reimbursable work associated with operations and maintenance activities, consistent with those authorized in section 5 of the Flood Control Act of 1944. Funds received from any State, municipality, corporation, association, firm, district, or individual as an advance payment for reimbursable work will be credited to Southeastern's account and remain available until expended.

Object Classification (in millions of dollars)

Identification code 089–0302–0–1–271	2021 actual	2022 est.	2023 est.
Direct obligations:			
11.1 Personnel compensation: Full-time permanent	4	4	4
12.1 Civilian personnel benefits	2	2	2
25.2 Purchase Power and Wheeling	43	53	79
25.2 Other services from non-Federal sources	2	1	1
99.0 Direct obligations	51	60	86
99.9 Total new obligations, unexpired accounts	51	60	86

Employment Summary

Identification code 089–0302–0–1–271	2021 actual	2022 est.	2023 est.
1001 Direct civilian full-time equivalent employment	39	44	44

CONTINUING FUND, SOUTHEASTERN POWER ADMINISTRATION

A continuing fund maintained from receipts from the sale and transmission of electric power in the Southeastern service area is available to defray emergency expenses necessary to ensure continuity of service (16 U.S.C. 825s–2). The fund was last activated in 2018 to finance power purchases associated with heightened demand and cost spikes due to severe cold weather. Consistent with sound business practices, the Southeastern Power Administration has implemented a policy to recover all emergency costs associated with purchased power and wheeling within one year from the time funds are expended.

OPERATION AND MAINTENANCE, SOUTHWESTERN POWER ADMINISTRATION

For expenses necessary for operation and maintenance of power transmission facilities and for marketing electric power and energy, for construction and acquisition of transmission lines, substations and appurtenant facilities, and for administrative expenses, including official reception and representation expenses in an amount not to exceed $1,500 in carrying out section 5 of the Flood Control Act of 1944 (16 U.S.C. 825s), as applied to the Southwestern Power Administration, $53,488,000, to remain available until expended: Provided, That notwithstanding 31 U.S.C. 3302 and section 5 of the Flood Control Act of 1944 (16 U.S.C. 825s), up to $42,880,000 collected by the Southwestern Power Administration from the sale of power and related services shall be credited to this account as discretionary offsetting collections, to remain available until expended, for the sole purpose of funding the annual expenses of the Southwestern Power Administration: Provided further, That the sum herein appropriated for annual expenses shall be reduced as collections are received during the fiscal year so as to result in a final fiscal year 2023 appropriation estimated at not more than $10,608,000: Provided further, That notwithstanding 31 U.S.C. 3302, up to $70,000,000 collected by the Southwestern Power Administration pursuant to the Flood Control Act of 1944 to recover purchase power and wheeling expenses shall be credited to this account as offsetting collections, to remain available until expended for the sole purpose of making purchase power and wheeling expenditures: Provided further, That for purposes of this appropriation, annual expenses means expenditures that are generally recovered in the same year that they are incurred (excluding purchase power and wheeling expenses).

Note.—A full-year 2022 appropriation for this account was not enacted at the time the Budget was prepared; therefore, the Budget assumes this account is operating under the Continuing Appropriations Act, 2022 (Division A of Public Law 117–43, as amended). The amounts included for 2022 reflect the annualized level provided by the continuing resolution.

Program and Financing (in millions of dollars)

Identification code 089–0303–0–1–271	2021 actual	2022 est.	2023 est.
Obligations by program activity:			
0001 Systems operation and maintenance	1	3	2
0003 Construction		10	5
0004 Program direction	3	4	4
0005 Spectrum Relocation		6	
0010 Annual Expenses	34	38	43
0020 Purchase Power and Wheeling	35	52	70
0200 Direct program subtotal	73	113	124
0799 Total direct obligations	73	113	124
0810 Other reimbursable activities		52	52
0899 Total reimbursable obligations		52	52
0900 Total new obligations, unexpired accounts	73	165	176
Budgetary resources:			
Unobligated balance:			
1000 Unobligated balance brought forward, Oct 1	109	128	132
Budget authority:			
Appropriations, discretionary:			
1100 Appropriation	10	10	11
Spending authority from offsetting collections, discretionary:			
1700 Collected	82	159	165
1900 Budget authority (total)	92	169	176
1930 Total budgetary resources available	201	297	308
Memorandum (non-add) entries:			
1941 Unexpired unobligated balance, end of year	128	132	132
Change in obligated balance:			
Unpaid obligations:			
3000 Unpaid obligations, brought forward, Oct 1	151	150	152
3010 New obligations, unexpired accounts	73	165	176
3020 Outlays (gross)	–74	–163	–223
3050 Unpaid obligations, end of year	150	152	105
Memorandum (non-add) entries:			
3100 Obligated balance, start of year	151	150	152
3200 Obligated balance, end of year	150	152	105

Budget authority and outlays, net:			
Discretionary:			
4000 Budget authority, gross	92	169	176
Outlays, gross:			
4010 Outlays from new discretionary authority	25	28	29
4011 Outlays from discretionary balances	49	135	194
4020 Outlays, gross (total)	74	163	223
Offsets against gross budget authority and outlays:			
Offsetting collections (collected) from:			
4030 Federal sources		–6	–6
4033 Non-Federal sources	–82	–153	–159
4040 Offsets against gross budget authority and outlays (total)	–82	–159	–165
4070 Budget authority, net (discretionary)	10	10	11
4080 Outlays, net (discretionary)	–8	4	58
4180 Budget authority, net (total)	10	10	11
4190 Outlays, net (total)	–8	4	58

Southwestern Power Administration (Southwestern) operates in a six-state area marketing and delivering renewable hydroelectric power produced at the U.S. Army Corps of Engineers' dams. Southwestern operates and maintains 1,381 miles of high voltage transmission lines, 26 substations/switching stations, associated power system controls, and communication sites. Southwestern also makes modifications and constructs additions to existing facilities.

Southwestern markets and delivers its power at wholesale rates to 78 municipal utilities, 21 rural electric cooperatives, and 3 military installations. In compliance with statutory requirements, Southwestern's power sales contracts provide for periodic rate adjustments to ensure that the Federal Government recovers all costs of operations, other costs allocated to power, and the capital investments in power facilities, with interest. Southwestern is also responsible for scheduling and dispatching power and negotiating power sales contracts to meet changing customer load requirements. As in past years, the budget continues to provide funding for annual expenses and purchase power and wheeling expenses through discretionary offsetting collections derived from power receipts collected to recover those expenses.

Program Direction.—Provides compensation and all related expenses for personnel who market, deliver, operate, and maintain Southwestern's high-voltage interconnected power system and associated facilities, those that perform cyber and physical security roles, and those that administratively support these functions.

Operations and Maintenance.—Provides essential electrical and communications equipment replacements and upgrades, capitalized moveable equipment, technical services, and supplies and materials necessary for the safe, reliable, and cost effective operation and maintenance of the power system.

Purchase Power and Wheeling.—Provides for the purchase and delivery of energy to meet limited peaking power contractual obligations. Federal power receipts and alternative financing methods, including net billing, and customer advances are used to fund system-purchased power support and other contractual services. Southwestern has implemented a Purchase Power and Wheeling (PPW) risk mitigation strategy to ensure continuous operations during periods of significant drought. The strategy was developed consistent with existing authorities, and with the participation and support of Southwestern's power customers. Under this approach, Southwestern retains receipts from the recovery of purchase power and wheeling expenses within the 'up to' amount specified by Congress. The receipts retained are available until expended and are available only for PPW expenses. As of the end of FY 2021, Southwestern's PPW reserve balance was $86 million. Customers will provide other power resources and/or purchases for the remainder of their firm loads.

DISCRETIONARY PURCHASE POWER AND WHEELING, SOUTHWESTERN POWER ADMINISTRATION

(in millions of dollars)

	2019 Actual	2020 Actual	2021 Actual	2022 Estimate[1]	2023 Estimate[1]
Limitation to collect, ('up to' ceiling in appropriations language)	50	43	34	70	70
Actual collections	36	26	34	70	70
PPW Unobligated balance brought forward, Oct 1	69	86	88	86	104
Spending authority from offsetting collections	36	26	34	70	70
Obligations incurred	–19	–24	–36	–52	–70
PPW Unobligated balance, end of year	86	88	86	104	104

[1] The FY 2022 and FY 2023 Estimates assume spending authority from offsetting collections equals the 'up to' ceiling and that obligations incurred are the same amount as the spending authority for FY 2023. Actual spending authority from offsetting collections and actual obligations will be dependent upon variability in market prices for PPW and hydrological conditions in Southwestern's region, which vary significantly, are largely unpredictable, and can change quickly.

Construction.—Provides for replacement, addition or upgrade of existing infrastructure to sustain reliable delivery of power to its customers, contain annual maintenance costs, and improve overall efficiency.

Reimbursable Program.—This activity involves services provided by Southwestern to others under various types of reimbursable arrangements.

Object Classification (in millions of dollars)

Identification code 089–0303–0–1–271	2021 actual	2022 est.	2023 est.
Direct obligations:			
Personnel compensation:			
11.1 Full-time permanent	18	18	19
11.5 Other personnel compensation	1		
11.9 Total personnel compensation	19	18	19
12.1 Civilian personnel benefits	6	6	6
21.0 Travel and transportation of persons	1	2	2
23.1 Rental payments to GSA		1	1
23.3 Communications, utilities, and miscellaneous charges	1	1	1
25.1 Advisory and assistance services	3		
25.2 Other services from non-Federal sources	3	69	79
25.3 Other goods and services from Federal sources	2	1	1
25.4 Operation and maintenance of facilities	35	4	4
26.0 Supplies and materials	1	2	2
31.0 Equipment	2	9	9
99.0 Direct obligations	73	113	124
99.0 Reimbursable obligations		52	52
99.9 Total new obligations, unexpired accounts	73	165	176

Employment Summary

Identification code 089–0303–0–1–271	2021 actual	2022 est.	2023 est.
1001 Direct civilian full-time equivalent employment	11	11	11
2001 Reimbursable civilian full-time equivalent employment	155	183	183

CONTINUING FUND, SOUTHWESTERN POWER ADMINISTRATION

Program and Financing (in millions of dollars)

Identification code 089–5649–0–2–271	2021 actual	2022 est.	2023 est.
4180 Budget authority, net (total)			
4190 Outlays, net (total)			
Memorandum (non-add) entries:			
5080 Outstanding debt, SOY	–68	–68	–68
5081 Outstanding debt, EOY	–68	–68	–68

A continuing fund, maintained from receipts from the sale and transmission of electric power in the Southwestern Power Administration service area, is available permanently for emergency expenses necessary to ensure continuity of electric service and continuous operation of the facilities. The fund is also available on an ongoing basis to pay for purchase power and wheeling expenses when the Administrator determines that such expenses are necessary to meet contractual obligations for the sale and delivery of power during periods of below-average generation (16 U.S.C. 825s–1 as amended further by Public Law 101–101). The fund was last activated in

Power Marketing Administration—Continued
Federal Funds—Continued

CONTINUING FUND, SOUTHWESTERN POWER ADMINISTRATION—Continued

FY 2009 to repair and replace damaged transmission lines due to an ice storm.

CONSTRUCTION, REHABILITATION, OPERATION AND MAINTENANCE, WESTERN AREA POWER ADMINISTRATION

For carrying out the functions authorized by title III, section 302(a)(1)(E) of the Act of August 4, 1977 (42 U.S.C. 7152), and other related activities including conservation and renewable resources programs as authorized, $299,573,000, including official reception and representation expenses in an amount not to exceed $1,500, to remain available until expended, of which $299,573,000 shall be derived from the Department of the Interior Reclamation Fund: Provided, That notwithstanding 31 U.S.C. 3302, section 5 of the Flood Control Act of 1944 (16 U.S.C. 825s), and section 1 of the Interior Department Appropriation Act, 1939 (43 U.S.C. 392a), up to $200,841,000 collected by the Western Area Power Administration from the sale of power and related services shall be credited to this account as discretionary offsetting collections, to remain available until expended, for the sole purpose of funding the annual expenses of the Western Area Power Administration: Provided further, That the sum herein appropriated for annual expenses shall be reduced as collections are received during the fiscal year so as to result in a final fiscal year 2023 appropriation estimated at not more than $98,732,000, of which $98,732,000 is derived from the Reclamation Fund: Provided further, That notwithstanding 31 U.S.C. 3302, up to $350,083,000 collected by the Western Area Power Administration pursuant to the Flood Control Act of 1944 and the Reclamation Project Act of 1939 to recover purchase power and wheeling expenses shall be credited to this account as offsetting collections, to remain available until expended for the sole purpose of making purchase power and wheeling expenditures: Provided further, That for purposes of this appropriation, annual expenses means expenditures that are generally recovered in the same year that they are incurred (excluding purchase power and wheeling expenses).

Note.—A full-year 2022 appropriation for this account was not enacted at the time the Budget was prepared; therefore, the Budget assumes this account is operating under the Continuing Appropriations Act, 2022 (Division A of Public Law 117–43, as amended). The amounts included for 2022 reflect the annualized level provided by the continuing resolution.

CONSTRUCTION, REHABILITATION, OPERATION AND MAINTENANCE, WESTERN AREA POWER ADMINISTRATION

(INCLUDING TRANSFER OF FUNDS)

[*For an additional amount for "Construction, Rehabilitation, Operation and Maintenance, Western Area Power Administration", $500,000,000, to remain available until expended, for the purchase of power and transmission services: Provided, That the amount made available under this heading in this Act shall be derived from the general fund of the Treasury and shall be reimbursable from amounts collected by the Western Area Power Administration pursuant to the Flood Control Act of 1944 and the Reclamation Project Act of 1939 to recover purchase power and wheeling expenses: Provided further, That such amounts as the Administrator, Western Area Power Administration, deems necessary for the same purposes as outlined above may be transferred to Western Area Power Administration's Colorado River Basins Power Marketing Fund account: Provided further, That such amount is designated by the Congress as being for an emergency requirement pursuant to section 4112(a) of H. Con. Res. 71 (115th Congress), the concurrent resolution on the budget for fiscal year 2018, and to section 251(b) of the Balanced Budget and Emergency Deficit Control Act of 1985.*] *(Infrastructure Investments and Jobs Appropriations Act.)*

Program and Financing (in millions of dollars)

Identification code 089–5068–0–2–271		2021 actual	2022 est.	2023 est.
Obligations by program activity:				
0001	Systems operation and maintenance	46	45	47
0004	Program direction	40	41	43
0010	Annual Expenses	191	194	201
0011	Purchase Power and Wheeling	361	339	350
0091	Direct Program by Activities - Subtotal (1 level)	638	619	641
0100	Total operating expenses	638	619	641
0101	Capital investment	7	3	9
0799	Total direct obligations	645	622	650
0804	Other Reimbursable	356	655	406
0809	Reimbursable program activities, subtotal	356	655	406
0899	Total reimbursable obligations	356	655	406
0900	Total new obligations, unexpired accounts	1,001	1,277	1,056
Budgetary resources:				
	Unobligated balance:			
1000	Unobligated balance brought forward, Oct 1	704	564	892
1021	Recoveries of prior year unpaid obligations	4		
1070	Unobligated balance (total)	708	564	892
	Budget authority:			
	Appropriations, discretionary:			
1100	Appropriation		499	
1101	Appropriation (special or trust)	89	89	99
1160	Appropriation, discretionary (total)	89	588	99
	Spending authority from offsetting collections, discretionary:			
1700	Collected	756	1,017	957
1701	Change in uncollected payments, Federal sources	12		
1750	Spending auth from offsetting collections, disc (total)	768	1,017	957
1900	Budget authority (total)	857	1,605	1,056
1930	Total budgetary resources available	1,565	2,169	1,948
	Memorandum (non-add) entries:			
1941	Unexpired unobligated balance, end of year	564	892	892
Change in obligated balance:				
	Unpaid obligations:			
3000	Unpaid obligations, brought forward, Oct 1	273	301	489
3010	New obligations, unexpired accounts	1,001	1,277	1,056
3020	Outlays (gross)	–969	–1,089	–918
3040	Recoveries of prior year unpaid obligations, unexpired	–4		
3050	Unpaid obligations, end of year	301	489	627
	Uncollected payments:			
3060	Uncollected pymts, Fed sources, brought forward, Oct 1	–42	–54	–54
3070	Change in uncollected pymts, Fed sources, unexpired	–12		
3090	Uncollected pymts, Fed sources, end of year	–54	–54	–54
	Memorandum (non-add) entries:			
3100	Obligated balance, start of year	231	247	435
3200	Obligated balance, end of year	247	435	573
Budget authority and outlays, net:				
	Discretionary:			
4000	Budget authority, gross	857	1,605	1,056
	Outlays, gross:			
4010	Outlays from new discretionary authority	269	595	332
4011	Outlays from discretionary balances	700	494	586
4020	Outlays, gross (total)	969	1,089	918
	Offsets against gross budget authority and outlays:			
	Offsetting collections (collected) from:			
4030	Federal sources	–179	–218	–115
4033	Non-Federal sources	–577	–799	–842
4040	Offsets against gross budget authority and outlays (total)	–756	–1,017	–957
	Additional offsets against gross budget authority only:			
4050	Change in uncollected pymts, Fed sources, unexpired	–12		
4070	Budget authority, net (discretionary)	89	588	99
4080	Outlays, net (discretionary)	213	72	–39
4180	Budget authority, net (total)	89	588	99
4190	Outlays, net (total)	213	72	–39
Memorandum (non-add) entries:				
5080	Outstanding appropriated debt, SOY	–11,645	–11,807	–12,396
5081	Outstanding appropriated debt, EOY	–11,807	–12,396	–12,495

The Western Area Power Administration (WAPA) markets electric power in 15 central and western states from federally owned power plants operated primarily by the Bureau of Reclamation, the Army Corps of Engineers, and the International Boundary and Water Commission. WAPA operates and maintains about 17,000 circuit-miles of high-voltage transmission lines, more than 300 substations/switchyards and associated power system controls, and communication and electrical facilities for 15 separate power projects. WAPA also constructs additions and modifications to existing facilities.

In keeping with statutory requirements, WAPA's long-term power contracts allow for periodic rate adjustments to ensure that the Federal Government recovers costs of operations, other costs allocated to power, and the capital investment in power facilities, with interest.

Power is sold to nearly 700 wholesale customers, including DOE's National Labs, more than two dozen U.S. Department of Defense installations, municipalities, cooperatives, irrigation districts, public utility districts, other State and Federal Government agencies, and private utilities. Receipts are deposited in the Reclamation Fund, the Falcon and Amistad Operating and Maintenance Fund, the General Fund, the Colorado River Dam Fund, and the Colorado River Basins Power Marketing Fund.

As in past years, the budget continues to provide funding for annual expenses and purchase power and wheeling expenses through discretionary offsetting collections derived from power receipts collected to recover those expenses.

Systems Operation and Maintenance.—Provides essential electrical and communication equipment replacements and upgrades, capitalized moveable equipment, technical services, and supplies and materials necessary for safe reliable operation and cost-effective maintenance of the power systems.

Purchase Power and Wheeling.—Provision is made for the payment of wheeling fees and for the purchase of electricity in connection with the distribution of power under contracts with utility companies. Customers are encouraged to contract for power and wheeling on their own, or use alternative funding mechanisms, including customer advances, net billing, and bill crediting to finance these activities. Ongoing operating services are also available on a reimbursable basis.

WAPA has implemented a Purchase Power and Wheeling (PPW) risk mitigation strategy to ensure continuous operations during periods of significant drought. The strategy was developed consistent with existing authorities, and with the participation and support of WAPA power customers. Under this approach, WAPA retains receipts from the recovery of purchase power and wheeling expenses within the 'up to' amount specified by Congress. The receipts retained are available until expended, and are available only for purchase power and wheeling expenses. As of the end of FY 2021, WAPA's PPW reserve balance was $217 million.

DISCRETIONARY PURCHASE POWER AND WHEELING, WESTERN AREA POWER ADMINISTRATION[1]

(in millions of dollars)

	2019 Actual	2020 Actual	2021 Actual	2022 Estimate	2023 Estimate
Limitation to collect, ('up to' ceiling in appropriations language)	225	227	192	192	350
Actual collections	225	171	192	192	350
PPW Unobligated balance brought forward, Oct 1	282	362	386	217	70
Spending authority from offsetting collections	225	171	192	192	350
Obligations incurred	–145	–147	–361	–339	–350
PPW Unobligated balance, end of year (excluding BIL)	362	386	217	70	70
Cumulative application of BIL funding				250	415
PPW Unobligated balance, end of year				320	485

[1] Excludes alternative financing for PPW.

System Construction.—WAPA's construction and rehabilitation activity emphasizes replacement and upgrades of existing infrastructure to sustain reliable power delivery to its customers, to contain annual maintenance costs, and to improve overall operational efficiency. WAPA will continue to participate in joint construction projects with customers to encourage more widespread transmission access.

Program Direction.—Provides compensation and all related expenses for the workforce that operates and maintains WAPA's high-voltage interconnected transmission system (systems operation and maintenance program), and those that plan, design, and supervise the construction of replacements, upgrades, and additions (system construction program) to the transmission facilities.

Reimbursable Program.—This program involves services provided by WAPA to others under various types of reimbursable arrangements. WAPA's reimbursable authority and partnerships also support responses to natural disasters - to restore the energy infrastructure and access to power.

WAPA will continue to spend out of the Colorado River Dam Fund for operations and maintenance activities associated with the Boulder Canyon Project via a reimbursable arrangement with the Interior Department's Bureau of Reclamation. The Colorado River Dam Fund is a revolving fund operated by the Bureau of Reclamation. Authority for WAPA to obligate directly from the Colorado River Dam Fund comes from section 104(a) of the Hoover Power Plant Act of 1984.

The Bipartisan Infrastructure Law (BIL) (Infrastructure Investment and Jobs Act, P.L. 117–58) provided WAPA with additional resources for purchase power and wheeling.

Object Classification (in millions of dollars)

Identification code 089–5068–0–2–271	2021 actual	2022 est.	2023 est.
Direct obligations:			
Personnel compensation:			
11.1 Full-time permanent	81	101	106
11.3 Other than full-time permanent	12	....	....
11.5 Other personnel compensation	11	7	7
11.9 Total personnel compensation	104	108	113
12.1 Civilian personnel benefits	36	35	37
21.0 Travel and transportation of persons	2	8	7
22.0 Transportation of things	2	....	....
23.1 Rental payments to GSA	1	2	1
23.2 Rental payments to others	1	....	....
23.3 Communications, utilities, and miscellaneous charges	4	6	7
25.1 Advisory and assistance services	30	29	29
25.2 Other services from non-Federal sources	396	365	376
25.3 Other goods and services from Federal sources	....	3	3
25.7 Operation and maintenance of equipment	10	9	9
26.0 Supplies and materials	8	10	14
31.0 Equipment	26	25	27
32.0 Land and structures	25	22	27
99.0 Direct obligations	645	622	650
99.0 Reimbursable obligations	356	655	406
99.9 Total new obligations, unexpired accounts	1,001	1,277	1,056

Employment Summary

Identification code 089–5068–0–2–271	2021 actual	2022 est.	2023 est.
1001 Direct civilian full-time equivalent employment	829	852	857
2001 Reimbursable civilian full-time equivalent employment	353	350	344

WESTERN AREA POWER ADMINISTRATION, BORROWING AUTHORITY, RECOVERY ACT

Program and Financing (in millions of dollars)

Identification code 089–4404–0–3–271	2021 actual	2022 est.	2023 est.
Obligations by program activity:			
0102 Transmission Infrastructure Program Projects	....	400	200
0811 Western Area Power Administration, Borrowing Authority, Recovery (Reimbursable)	7	17	19
0900 Total new obligations, unexpired accounts	7	417	219
Budgetary resources:			
Unobligated balance:			
1000 Unobligated balance brought forward, Oct 1	14	13	13
1001 Discretionary unobligated balance brought fwd, Oct 1	5	4	....
Budget authority:			
Borrowing authority, mandatory:			
1400 Borrowing authority	....	424	212
1421 Borrowing authority temporarily reduced	....	–24	–12
1440 Borrowing authority, mandatory (total)	....	400	200
Spending authority from offsetting collections, discretionary:			
1700 Collected	3	12	13
Spending authority from offsetting collections, mandatory:			
1800 Collected	3	5	6
1900 Budget authority (total)	6	417	219
1930 Total budgetary resources available	20	430	232
Memorandum (non-add) entries:			
1941 Unexpired unobligated balance, end of year	13	13	13

WESTERN AREA POWER ADMINISTRATION, BORROWING AUTHORITY, RECOVERY ACT—Continued

Program and Financing—Continued

Identification code 089–4404–0–3–271	2021 actual	2022 est.	2023 est.
Change in obligated balance:			
Unpaid obligations:			
3000 Unpaid obligations, brought forward, Oct 1	20	20	103
3010 New obligations, unexpired accounts	7	417	219
3020 Outlays (gross)	–7	–334	–259
3050 Unpaid obligations, end of year	20	103	63
Memorandum (non-add) entries:			
3100 Obligated balance, start of year	20	20	103
3200 Obligated balance, end of year	20	103	63
Budget authority and outlays, net:			
Discretionary:			
4000 Budget authority, gross	3	12	13
Outlays, gross:			
4010 Outlays from new discretionary authority		12	13
4011 Outlays from discretionary balances	3	5	
4020 Outlays, gross (total)	3	17	13
Offsets against gross budget authority and outlays:			
Offsetting collections (collected) from:			
4030 Federal sources	–2	–2	–2
4033 Non-Federal sources	–1	–10	–11
4040 Offsets against gross budget authority and outlays (total)	–3	–12	–13
4080 Outlays, net (discretionary)		5	
Mandatory:			
4090 Budget authority, gross	3	405	206
Outlays, gross:			
4100 Outlays from new mandatory authority		301	154
4101 Outlays from mandatory balances	4	16	92
4110 Outlays, gross (total)	4	317	246
Offsets against gross budget authority and outlays:			
Offsetting collections (collected) from:			
4123 Non-Federal sources	–3	–5	–6
4180 Budget authority, net (total)		400	200
4190 Outlays, net (total)	1	317	240

The American Recovery and Reinvestment Act of 2009 (the Act) provided Western Area Power Administration (WAPA) borrowing authority for the purpose of constructing, financing, facilitating, planning, operating, maintaining, or studying construction of new or upgraded electric power transmission lines and related facilities with at least one terminus within the area served by WAPA, and for delivering or facilitating the delivery of power generated by renewable energy resources. This authority to borrow from the United States Treasury is available to WAPA on a permanent, indefinite basis, with the amount of borrowing outstanding not to exceed $3.25 billion at any one time. WAPA established the Transmission Infrastructure Program (TIP) to manage and administer this borrowing authority and its related program requirements.

Object Classification (in millions of dollars)

Identification code 089–4404–0–3–271	2021 actual	2022 est.	2023 est.
25.2 Direct obligations: Other services from non-Federal sources		400	200
99.0 Direct obligations		400	200
Reimbursable obligations:			
11.1 Personnel compensation: Full-time permanent	1	2	2
25.2 Other services from non-Federal sources	4	12	10
43.0 Interest and dividends	2	3	7
99.0 Reimbursable obligations	7	17	19
99.9 Total new obligations, unexpired accounts	7	417	219

Employment Summary

Identification code 089–4404–0–3–271	2021 actual	2022 est.	2023 est.
2001 Reimbursable civilian full-time equivalent employment	5	11	12

EMERGENCY FUND, WESTERN AREA POWER ADMINISTRATION

Program and Financing (in millions of dollars)

Identification code 089–5069–0–2–271	2021 actual	2022 est.	2023 est.
Budgetary resources:			
Unobligated balance:			
1000 Unobligated balance brought forward, Oct 1	1	1	1
1930 Total budgetary resources available	1	1	1
Memorandum (non-add) entries:			
1941 Unexpired unobligated balance, end of year	1	1	1
4180 Budget authority, net (total)			
4190 Outlays, net (total)			
Memorandum (non-add) entries:			
5080 Outstanding debt, SOY	–55	–55	–55
5081 Outstanding debt, EOY	–55	–55	–55

An emergency fund maintained from receipts from the sale and transmission of electric power is available to defray expenses necessary to ensure continuity of service. The fund was last activated in fiscal year 2010 to repair and replace damaged transmission lines due to severe winter storm conditions.

FALCON AND AMISTAD OPERATING AND MAINTENANCE FUND

For operation, maintenance, and emergency costs for the hydroelectric facilities at the Falcon and Amistad Dams, $6,330,000, to remain available until expended, and to be derived from the Falcon and Amistad Operating and Maintenance Fund of the Western Area Power Administration, as provided in section 2 of the Act of June 18, 1954 (68 Stat. 255): Provided, That notwithstanding the provisions of that Act and of 31 U.S.C. 3302, up to $6,102,000 collected by the Western Area Power Administration from the sale of power and related services from the Falcon and Amistad Dams shall be credited to this account as discretionary offsetting collections, to remain available until expended for the sole purpose of funding the annual expenses of the hydroelectric facilities of these Dams and associated Western Area Power Administration activities: Provided further, That the sum herein appropriated for annual expenses shall be reduced as collections are received during the fiscal year so as to result in a final fiscal year 2023 appropriation estimated at not more than $228,000: Provided further, That for purposes of this appropriation, annual expenses means expenditures that are generally recovered in the same year that they are incurred: Provided further, That for fiscal year 2023, the Administrator of the Western Area Power Administration may accept up to $1,598,000 in funds contributed by United States power customers of the Falcon and Amistad Dams for deposit into the Falcon and Amistad Operating and Maintenance Fund, and such funds shall be available for the purpose for which contributed in like manner as if said sums had been specifically appropriated for such purpose: Provided further, That any such funds shall be available without further appropriation and without fiscal year limitation for use by the Commissioner of the United States Section of the International Boundary and Water Commission for the sole purpose of operating, maintaining, repairing, rehabilitating, replacing, or upgrading the hydroelectric facilities at these Dams in accordance with agreements reached between the Administrator, Commissioner, and the power customers.

Note.—A full-year 2022 appropriation for this account was not enacted at the time the Budget was prepared; therefore, the Budget assumes this account is operating under the Continuing Appropriations Act, 2022 (Division A of Public Law 117–43, as amended). The amounts included for 2022 reflect the annualized level provided by the continuing resolution.

Special and Trust Fund Receipts (in millions of dollars)

Identification code 089–5178–0–2–271	2021 actual	2022 est.	2023 est.
0100 Balance, start of year	11	11	11
2000 Total: Balances and receipts	11	11	11
5099 Balance, end of year	11	11	11

Program and Financing (in millions of dollars)

Identification code 089–5178–0–2–271	2021 actual	2022 est.	2023 est.
Obligations by program activity:			
0001 Annual Expenses	5	6	6
0100 Direct program activities, subtotal	5	6	6

		2021 actual	2022 est.	2023 est.
0802	Reimbursable program activity - Alternative Financing	1	2	2
0899	Total reimbursable obligations	1	2	2
0900	Total new obligations, unexpired accounts	6	8	8
	Budgetary resources:			
	Unobligated balance:			
1000	Unobligated balance brought forward, Oct 1	2	3	3
	Budget authority:			
	Spending authority from offsetting collections, discretionary:			
1700	Offsetting collections	7	8	8
1930	Total budgetary resources available	9	11	11
	Memorandum (non-add) entries:			
1941	Unexpired unobligated balance, end of year	3	3	3
	Change in obligated balance:			
	Unpaid obligations:			
3000	Unpaid obligations, brought forward, Oct 1	5	5	3
3010	New obligations, unexpired accounts	6	8	8
3020	Outlays (gross)	−6	−10	−8
3050	Unpaid obligations, end of year	5	3	3
	Memorandum (non-add) entries:			
3100	Obligated balance, start of year	5	5	3
3200	Obligated balance, end of year	5	3	3
	Budget authority and outlays, net:			
	Discretionary:			
4000	Budget authority, gross	7	8	8
	Outlays, gross:			
4010	Outlays from new discretionary authority	1	5	5
4011	Outlays from discretionary balances	5	5	3
4020	Outlays, gross (total)	6	10	8
	Offsets against gross budget authority and outlays:			
	Offsetting collections (collected) from:			
4033	Non-Federal sources	−7	−8	−8
4180	Budget authority, net (total)			
4190	Outlays, net (total)	−1	2	

Pursuant to section 2 of the Act of June 18, 1954, as amended, Western Area Power Administration is requesting funding for the Falcon and Amistad Operating and Maintenance Fund to defray operations, maintenance, and emergency (OM&E) expenses for the hydroelectric facilities at Falcon and Amistad Dams on the Rio Grande River. Most of these funds will be made available to the United States Section of the International Boundary and Water Commission through a reimbursable agreement. Within the fund, $200,000 is for an emergency reserve that will remain unobligated unless unanticipated expenses arise. The budget provides funding for annual expenses through discretionary offsetting collections derived from power receipts collected to recover those expenses. The budget also provides authority to use customer advances. The contributed customer funds will finance the capital replacement requirements of the projects.

Object Classification (in millions of dollars)

Identification code 089–5178–0–2–271		2021 actual	2022 est.	2023 est.
25.3	Direct obligations: Other goods and services from Federal sources	5	6	6
99.0	Reimbursable obligations	1	2	2
99.9	Total new obligations, unexpired accounts	6	8	8

COLORADO RIVER BASINS POWER MARKETING FUND, WESTERN AREA POWER ADMINISTRATION

Program and Financing (in millions of dollars)

Identification code 089–4452–0–3–271		2021 actual	2022 est.	2023 est.
	Obligations by program activity:			
0801	Program direction	73	74	79
0802	Equipment, Contracts and Related Expenses	193	163	179
0900	Total new obligations, unexpired accounts	266	237	258
	Budgetary resources:			
	Unobligated balance:			
1000	Unobligated balance brought forward, Oct 1	142	91	91
	Budget authority:			
	Spending authority from offsetting collections, discretionary:			
1700	Collected	236	258	267
1710	Spending authority from offsetting collections transferred to other accounts [014–4081]	−21	−21	
1720	Capital transfer of spending authority from offsetting collections to general fund			−9
1750	Spending auth from offsetting collections, disc (total)	215	237	258
1930	Total budgetary resources available	357	328	349
	Memorandum (non-add) entries:			
1941	Unexpired unobligated balance, end of year	91	91	91
	Change in obligated balance:			
	Unpaid obligations:			
3000	Unpaid obligations, brought forward, Oct 1	53	68	113
3010	New obligations, unexpired accounts	266	237	258
3020	Outlays (gross)	−251	−192	−243
3050	Unpaid obligations, end of year	68	113	128
	Uncollected payments:			
3060	Uncollected pymts, Fed sources, brought forward, Oct 1	−1	−1	−1
3090	Uncollected pymts, Fed sources, end of year	−1	−1	−1
	Memorandum (non-add) entries:			
3100	Obligated balance, start of year	52	67	112
3200	Obligated balance, end of year	67	112	127
	Budget authority and outlays, net:			
	Discretionary:			
4000	Budget authority, gross	215	237	258
	Outlays, gross:			
4010	Outlays from new discretionary authority	67	53	58
4011	Outlays from discretionary balances	184	139	185
4020	Outlays, gross (total)	251	192	243
	Offsets against gross budget authority and outlays:			
	Offsetting collections (collected) from:			
4030	Federal sources	−5	−5	−5
4033	Non-Federal sources	−231	−253	−262
4040	Offsets against gross budget authority and outlays (total)	−236	−258	−267
4070	Budget authority, net (discretionary)	−21	−21	−9
4080	Outlays, net (discretionary)	15	−66	−24
4180	Budget authority, net (total)	−21	−21	−9
4190	Outlays, net (total)	15	−66	−24

Western Area Power Administration's (WAPA) operation and maintenance (O&M) and power marketing expenses for the Colorado River Storage Project, the Seedskadee Project, the Dolores Project, the Olmsted Replacement Project, and the Fort Peck Project are financed from power revenues.

Colorado River Storage Project.—WAPA markets power and operates and maintains the power transmission facilities of the Colorado River Storage Project consisting of four major storage units: Glen Canyon on the Colorado River in Arizona, Flaming Gorge on the Green River in Utah, Navajo on the San Juan River in New Mexico, and the Wayne N. Aspinall unit on the Gunnison River in Colorado.

Seedskadee Project.—This project includes WAPA's expenses for O&M, power marketing, and transmission of hydroelectric power from the Fontenelle Dam power plant in southwestern Wyoming.

Dolores Project.—This project includes WAPA's expenses for O&M, power marketing, and transmission of hydroelectric power from power plants at McPhee Dam and Towaoc Canal in southwestern Colorado.

Fort Peck Project.—Revenues collected by WAPA are used to defray operation and maintenance and power marketing expenses associated with the power generation and transmission facilities of the Fort Peck Project, and WAPA operates and maintains the transmission system and performs power marketing functions.

Olmsted Replacement Project.—This project includes WAPA's expenses for power marketing of hydroelectric power from the Olmsted Power Plant in Northern Utah.

Equipment, Contracts and Related Expenses.—WAPA operates and maintains approximately 4,000 miles of transmission lines, substations, switchyards, communications, and control equipment associated with this

COLORADO RIVER BASINS POWER MARKETING FUND, WESTERN AREA POWER ADMINISTRATION—Continued

fund. Wholesale power is provided to utilities over interconnected high-voltage transmission systems. In keeping with statutory requirements, long-term power contracts provide for periodic rate adjustments to ensure that the Federal Government recovers all costs of O&M, and all capital invested in power, with interest. This activity provides for the supplies, materials, services, capital equipment replacements, and additions, including communications and control equipment, purchase power, transmission and wheeling services, and interest payments to the U.S. Treasury.

Program Direction.—The personnel compensation and related expenses for all these activities are quantified under Program Direction.

Object Classification (in millions of dollars)

Identification code 089–4452–0–3–271		2021 actual	2022 est.	2023 est.
	Reimbursable obligations:			
	Personnel compensation:			
11.1	Full-time permanent	33	34	39
11.5	Other personnel compensation	5	5	3
11.9	Total personnel compensation	38	39	42
12.1	Civilian personnel benefits	13	13	13
21.0	Travel and transportation of persons	1	2	2
22.0	Transportation of things	1	1	2
23.1	Rental payments to GSA		1	1
23.3	Communications, utilities, and miscellaneous charges	2	2	2
25.1	Advisory and assistance services	8	7	9
25.2	Other services from non-Federal sources	143	115	131
25.3	Other goods and services from Federal sources	22	29	29
25.7	Operation and maintenance of equipment	16	5	3
26.0	Supplies and materials	2	4	3
31.0	Equipment	5	5	9
32.0	Land and structures	15	12	9
43.0	Interest and dividends		2	3
99.9	Total new obligations, unexpired accounts	266	237	258

Employment Summary

Identification code 089–4452–0–3–271	2021 actual	2022 est.	2023 est.
2001 Reimbursable civilian full-time equivalent employment	294	308	308

BONNEVILLE POWER ADMINISTRATION FUND

Expenditures from the Bonneville Power Administration Fund, established pursuant to Public Law 93–454, are approved for the Colville Tribes Residents Fish Hatchery Expansion, Chief Joseph Hatchery Water Quality Project, and Umatilla Hatchery Facility Project, and, in addition, for official reception and representation expenses in an amount not to exceed $5,000: Provided, That during fiscal year 2023, no new direct loan obligations may be made.

Note.—A full-year 2022 appropriation for this account was not enacted at the time the Budget was prepared; therefore, the Budget assumes this account is operating under the Continuing Appropriations Act, 2022 (Division A of Public Law 117–43, as amended). The amounts included for 2022 reflect the annualized level provided by the continuing resolution.

Program and Financing (in millions of dollars)

Identification code 089–4045–0–3–271		2021 actual	2022 est.	2023 est.
	Obligations by program activity:			
0801	Power business line	1,089	889	912
0802	Residential exchange	250	259	259
0803	Bureau of Reclamation	150	152	153
0804	Corp of Engineers	236	253	253
0805	Colville settlement / Spokane settlement	25	28	27
0806	U.S. Fish & Wildlife	31	33	29
0807	Planning council	11	12	12
0808	Fish and Wildlife	241	247	247
0809	Reimbursable program activities, subtotal	2,033	1,873	1,892
0811	Transmission business line	494	508	515
0812	Conservation and energy efficiency	145	156	151
0813	Interest	187	162	165
0814	Pension and health benefits	33	31	32
0819	Reimbursable program activities, subtotal	859	857	863
0821	Power business line	202	264	281
0822	Transmission services	348	476	497
0824	Fish and Wildlife	42	43	43
0825	Capital Equipment	26	22	21
0826	Projects funded in advance	63	56	61
0829	Reimbursable program activities, subtotal	681	861	903
0900	Total new obligations, unexpired accounts	3,573	3,591	3,658
	Budgetary resources:			
	Unobligated balance:			
1000	Unobligated balance brought forward, Oct 1	11	9	522
1023	Unobligated balances applied to repay debt		–1	–514
1070	Unobligated balance (total)	11	8	8
	Budget authority:			
	Borrowing authority, mandatory:			
1400	Borrowing authority	737	805	842
	Contract authority, mandatory:			
1600	Contract authority	2,379		
	Spending authority from offsetting collections, mandatory:			
1800	Collected	3,763	3,999	3,969
1801	Change in uncollected payments, Federal sources	–33		
1802	Offsetting collections (previously unavailable)	8	7	7
1823	New and/or unobligated balance of spending authority from offsetting collections temporarily reduced	–7	–7	–7
1825	Spending authority from offsetting collections applied to repay debt	–757	–699	–734
1826	Spending authority from offsetting collections applied to liquidate contract authority	–2,519		
1850	Spending auth from offsetting collections, mand (total)	455	3,300	3,235
1900	Budget authority (total)	3,571	4,105	4,077
1930	Total budgetary resources available	3,582	4,113	4,085
	Memorandum (non-add) entries:			
1941	Unexpired unobligated balance, end of year	9	522	427
	Change in obligated balance:			
	Unpaid obligations:			
3000	Unpaid obligations, brought forward, Oct 1	3,380	3,444	3,444
3010	New obligations, unexpired accounts	3,573	3,591	3,658
3020	Outlays (gross)	–3,509	–3,591	–3,660
3050	Unpaid obligations, end of year	3,444	3,444	3,442
	Uncollected payments:			
3060	Uncollected pymts, Fed sources, brought forward, Oct 1	–349	–316	–316
3070	Change in uncollected pymts, Fed sources, unexpired	33		
3090	Uncollected pymts, Fed sources, end of year	–316	–316	–316
	Memorandum (non-add) entries:			
3100	Obligated balance, start of year	3,031	3,128	3,128
3200	Obligated balance, end of year	3,128	3,128	3,126
	Budget authority and outlays, net:			
	Mandatory:			
4090	Budget authority, gross	3,571	4,105	4,077
	Outlays, gross:			
4100	Outlays from new mandatory authority	3,341	3,391	3,460
4101	Outlays from mandatory balances	168	200	200
4110	Outlays, gross (total)	3,509	3,591	3,660
	Offsets against gross budget authority and outlays:			
	Offsetting collections (collected) from:			
4120	Federal sources	–51	–90	–90
4123	Non-Federal sources	–3,712	–3,909	–3,879
4130	Offsets against gross budget authority and outlays (total)	–3,763	–3,999	–3,969
	Additional offsets against gross budget authority only:			
4140	Change in uncollected pymts, Fed sources, unexpired	33		
4160	Budget authority, net (mandatory)	–159	106	108
4170	Outlays, net (mandatory)	–254	–408	–309
4180	Budget authority, net (total)	–159	106	108
4190	Outlays, net (total)	–254	–408	–309
	Memorandum (non-add) entries:			
5000	Total investments, SOY: Federal securities: Par value	491		
5052	Obligated balance, SOY: Contract authority	2,519	2,379	2,379
5053	Obligated balance, EOY: Contract authority	2,379	2,379	2,379
5090	Unexpired unavailable balance, SOY: Offsetting collections	8	7	7
5092	Unexpired unavailable balance, EOY: Offsetting collections	7	7	7

Status of Direct Loans (in millions of dollars)

Identification code 089–4045–0–3–271	2021 actual	2022 est.	2023 est.
Cumulative balance of direct loans outstanding:			
1210 Outstanding, start of year	2	2	2

1290 Outstanding, end of year 2 2 2

Bonneville Power Administration (BPA) is a Federal electric power marketing agency in the Pacific Northwest. BPA markets hydroelectric power from 21 multipurpose water resource projects of the U.S. Army Corps of Engineers and 10 projects of the U.S. Bureau of Reclamation, plus some energy from non-Federal generating projects in the region. These generating resources and BPA's transmission system are operated as an integrated power system with operating and financial results combined and reported as the Federal Columbia River Power System (FCRPS). BPA provides about 50 percent of the region's electric energy supply and about three-fourths of the region's high-voltage electric power transmission capacity.

BPA is responsible for meeting the net firm power requirements of its requesting customers through a variety of means, including energy conservation programs, acquisition of renewable and other resources, and power exchanges with utilities both in and outside the region.

BPA finances its operations with a business-type budget under the Government Corporation Control Act, 31 U.S.C. 9101–10, on the basis of the self-financing authority provided by the Federal Columbia River Transmission System Act of 1974 (Transmission Act) (Public Law 93–454) and the U.S. Treasury borrowing authority provided by the Transmission Act, the Pacific Northwest Electric Power Planning and Conservation Act (Pacific Northwest Power Act) (Public Law 96–501) for energy conservation, renewable energy resources, capital fish facilities, and other purposes, the American Recovery and Reinvestment Act of 2009 (Public Law 111–5), Infrastructure Investment and Jobs Act of 2021 (section 40110) (Public Law 117–58), and other legislation. Authority to borrow from the U.S. Treasury is available to the BPA on a permanent, indefinite basis. The amount of U.S. Treasury borrowing outstanding at any time cannot exceed $17.70 billion. BPA finances its approximate $4.4 billion annual cost of operations and investments primarily using power and transmission revenues and loans from the U.S. Treasury.

Operating Expenses—Transmission Services.—Provides for operating over 15,100 circuit miles of high-voltage transmissions lines and 262 substations, and for maintaining the facilities and equipment of the Bonneville transmission system in 2023.

Power Services.—Provides for the planning, contractual acquisition and oversight of reliable, cost effective resources. These resources are needed to serve BPA's portion of the region's forecasted net electric load requirements. This activity also includes protection, mitigation and enhancement of fish and wildlife affected by hydroelectric facilities on the Columbia River and its tributaries in accordance with the Pacific Northwest Power Act. This activity provides for payment of the operation and maintenance (O&M) costs allocated to power the 31 U.S. Army Corps of Engineers and U.S. Bureau of Reclamation hydro projects, amortization on the capital investment in power generating facilities, and irrigation assistance at U.S. Bureau of Reclamation facilities. This activity also provides for the planning, contractual acquisition and oversight of reliable, cost effective conservation. It also provides for extending the benefits of low-cost Federal power to the residential and small farm customers of investor-owned and publicly owned utilities, in accordance with the Pacific Northwest Power Act and for activities of the Pacific Northwest Electric Power and Conservation Planning Council required by the Pacific Northwest Power Act.

Interest.—Provides for payments to the U.S. Treasury for interest on U.S. Treasury borrowings to finance BPA's capital investments under $17.70 billion of U.S. Treasury borrowing authority provided by the Transmission Act; the Pacific Northwest Power Act for energy conservation, renewable energy resources, capital fish facilities, and other purposes; the American Recovery and Reinvestment Act of 2009; Infrastructure Investment and Jobs Act of 2021, and other legislation. This interest category also includes interest on U.S. Army Corps of Engineers, BPA and U.S. Bureau of Reclamation appropriated debt.

Capital Investments—Transmission Services.—Provides for the planning, design and construction of transmission lines, substation and control system additions, replacements, and enhancements to the FCRPS transmission system for a reliable, efficient and cost-effective regional transmission system. Provides for planning, design, and construction work to repair or replace existing transmission lines, substations, control systems, and general facilities of the FCRPS transmission system.

Power Services.—Provides for direct funding of additions, improvements, and replacements at existing Federal hydroelectric projects in the Northwest. It also provides for capital investments to implement environmental activities, and protect, mitigate, and enhance fish and wildlife affected by hydroelectric facilities on the Columbia River and its tributaries, in accordance with the Pacific Northwest Power Act. This activity provides for the planning, contractual acquisition and oversight of reliable, cost effective conservation.

Capital Equipment/Capitalized Bond Premium.—Provides for capital information technologies, office furniture and equipment, and software capital development in support of all BPA programs. It also provides for bond premiums incurred for refinancing of bonds.

Total Capital Obligations.—The 2023 capital obligations are estimated to be $842.5 million.

Contingencies.—Although contingencies are not specifically funded, the need may arise to provide for purchase of power in low-water years; for repair and/or replacement of facilities affected by natural and man-made emergencies, including the resulting additional costs for contracting, construction, and operation and maintenance work; for unavoidable increased costs for the planned program due to necessary but unforeseen adjustments, including engineering and design changes, contractor and other claims and relocations; or for payment of a retrospective premium adjustment in excess nuclear property insurance.

Financing.—The Transmission Act provides for the use by BPA of all receipts, collections, and recoveries in cash from all sources, including the sale of bonds, to finance the annual budget programs of BPA. These receipts result primarily from the sale of power and transmission services. The Transmission Act also provides for authority to borrow from the U.S. Treasury at rates comparable to borrowings at open market rates for similar issues. BPA has $17.70 billion of U.S. Treasury borrowing authority provided by the Transmission Act; the Pacific Northwest Power Act for energy conservation, renewable energy resources, capital fish facilities, and other purposes; the American Recovery and Reinvestment Act of 2009; Infrastructure Investment and Jobs Act of 2021, and other legislation. At the end of 2021, BPA had outstanding bonds with the U.S. Treasury of $5,629 million. At the end of 2021, BPA also had $7,191.1 million of non-Federal debt outstanding, including Energy Northwest bonds. BPA will rely primarily on its U.S. Treasury borrowing authority to finance capital projects, but may also elect to use cash reserves generated by revenues from customers or seek third party financing sources when feasible to finance some of these investments.

In 2021, BPA made payments to the Treasury of $1,049 million and also expects to make payments of $935 million in 2022 and $971 million in 2023. The 2023 payment is expected to be distributed as follows: interest on bonds and appropriations ($192 million), amortization ($734 million), and other ($45 million). BPA also received credits totaling approximately $111 million applied against its Treasury payments in 2021 of which $90.6 million reflected amounts diverted to fish mitigation efforts, but not allocable to power, in the Columbia and Snake River systems.

BPA, with input from its stakeholders, considers other strategies to sustain funding for its infrastructure investment requirements as well. BPA's Financial Plan defines strategies and policies for guiding how BPA will manage risk and variability of electricity markets and water years. It also describes how BPA will continue to manage to ensure it meets its Treasury repayment responsibilities.

Direct Loans.—During 2023, no new direct loan obligations may be made.

Operating Results.—Total revenues are forecast at approximately $3.9 billion in 2023.

BONNEVILLE POWER ADMINISTRATION FUND—Continued

It should be noted that BPA's revenue forecasts are based on several critical assumptions about both the supply of and demand for Federal energy. During the operating year, deviation from the conditions assumed in a rate case may result in a variation in actual revenues of several hundred million dollars from the forecast.

Consistent with Administration policy, BPA will continue to fully recover, from the sale of electric power and transmission, funds sufficient to cover the full cost of Civil Service Retirement System and Post-Retirement Health Benefits for its employees. The entire cost of BPA and the power share of FCRPS U.S. Army Corps of Engineers and U.S. Bureau of Reclamation employees working under the Federal Employees Retirement System is fully recovered in wholesale electric power and transmission rates.

Balance Sheet (in millions of dollars)

Identification code 089–4045–0–3–271		2020 actual	2021 actual
	ASSETS:		
	Federal assets:		
1101	Fund balances with Treasury	55	780
	Investments in U.S. securities:		
1106	Receivables, net	493	
1206	Non-Federal assets: Receivables, net	348	336
1601	Direct loans, gross		
1605	Accounts receivable from foreclosed property		
1699	Value of assets related to direct loans		
	Other Federal assets:		
1801	Cash and other monetary assets		20
1802	Inventories and related properties	108	110
1803	Property, plant and equipment, net	7,581	7,739
1901	Other assets	13,457	13,125
1999	Total assets	22,042	22,110
	LIABILITIES:		
	Federal liabilities:		
2102	Interest payable	84	62
2103	Debt	7,888	5,700
	Non-Federal liabilities:		
2201	Accounts payable	390	524
2203	Debt	5,023	5,043
2207	Other	8,657	10,781
2999	Total liabilities	22,042	22,110
	NET POSITION:		
3300	Cumulative results of operations		
4999	Total liabilities and net position	22,042	22,110

Object Classification (in millions of dollars)

Identification code 089–4045–0–3–271		2021 actual	2022 est.	2023 est.
	Reimbursable obligations:			
11.1	Personnel compensation: Full-time permanent	344	346	352
12.1	Civilian personnel benefits	164	165	168
21.0	Travel and transportation of persons	1	1	1
22.0	Transportation of things	1	1	1
23.2	Rental payments to others	34	34	34
23.3	Communications, utilities, and miscellaneous charges	10	10	10
25.1	Advisory and assistance services	131	132	134
25.2	Other services from non-Federal sources	2,415	2,426	2,471
25.5	Research and development contracts	2	4	4
26.0	Supplies and materials	24	24	25
31.0	Equipment	85	85	87
32.0	Land and structures	79	79	81
41.0	Grants, subsidies, and contributions	47	47	48
43.0	Interest and dividends	236	237	242
99.9	Total new obligations, unexpired accounts	3,573	3,591	3,658

Employment Summary

Identification code 089–4045–0–3–271		2021 actual	2022 est.	2023 est.
1001	Direct civilian full-time equivalent employment	2,825	3,000	3,000

DEPARTMENTAL ADMINISTRATION

Federal Funds

DEPARTMENTAL ADMINISTRATION

For salaries and expenses of the Department of Energy necessary for departmental administration in carrying out the purposes of the Department of Energy Organization Act (42 U.S.C. 7101 et seq.), $497,781,000, to remain available until September 30, 2024, including the hire of zero emission passenger motor vehicles and supporting charging or fueling infrastructure, and official reception and representation expenses not to exceed $30,000, plus such additional amounts as necessary to cover increases in the estimated amount of cost of work for others notwithstanding the provisions of the Anti-Deficiency Act (31 U.S.C. 1511 et seq.): Provided, That such increases in cost of work are offset by revenue increases of the same or greater amount: Provided further, That moneys received by the Department for miscellaneous revenues estimated to total $100,578,000 in fiscal year 2023 may be retained and used for operating expenses within this account, as authorized by section 201 of Public Law 95–238, notwithstanding the provisions of 31 U.S.C. 3302: Provided further, That the sum herein appropriated shall be reduced as collections are received during the fiscal year so as to result in a final fiscal year 2023 appropriation from the general fund estimated at not more than $397,203,000.

Note.—A full-year 2022 appropriation for this account was not enacted at the time the Budget was prepared; therefore, the Budget assumes this account is operating under the Continuing Appropriations Act, 2022 (Division A of Public Law 117–43, as amended). The amounts included for 2022 reflect the annualized level provided by the continuing resolution.

Program and Financing (in millions of dollars)

Identification code 089–0228–0–1–276		2021 actual	2022 est.	2023 est.
	Obligations by program activity:			
0003	Office of the Secretary	5	5	7
0004	Office of Congressional and Intergovernmental Affairs	5	6	7
0005	Office of Public Affairs	5	5	6
0006	General Counsel	35	38	44
0008	Economic Impact and Diversity	11	11	34
0009	Chief Financial Officer	8	10	62
0010	Chief Information Officer			63
0011	Human Capital Management	24	24	34
0012	Indian Energy Policy	1		
0013	Office of Policy	10	10	31
0014	International Affairs	27	27	62
0015	Office of Small and Disadvantaged Business Utilization	4	4	4
0018	Management	56	58	86
0020	Project Management Oversight and Assessment	12	13	14
0025	Office of Technology Transitions	19	13	
0030	Artificial Intelligence Technology Office	2	2	3
0045	Strategic partnership projects	9	16	16
0050	CARES Act IT Supplemental	9		
0799	Total direct obligations	242	242	473
0801	Departmental Administration (Reimbursable)	6	6	6
0900	Total new obligations, unexpired accounts	248	248	479
	Budgetary resources:			
	Unobligated balance:			
1000	Unobligated balance brought forward, Oct 1	84	85	91
1001	Discretionary unobligated balance brought fwd, Oct 1	83		
1020	Adjustment of unobligated bal brought forward, Oct 1	1		
1021	Recoveries of prior year unpaid obligations	4		
1070	Unobligated balance (total)	89	85	91
	Budget authority:			
	Appropriations, discretionary:			
1100	Appropriation	190	159	397
	Spending authority from offsetting collections, discretionary:			
1700	Collected	72	95	101
1701	Change in uncollected payments, Federal sources	8		
1750	Spending auth from offsetting collections, disc (total)	80	95	101
1900	Budget authority (total)	270	254	498
1930	Total budgetary resources available	359	339	589
	Memorandum (non-add) entries:			
1940	Unobligated balance expiring	–26		
1941	Unexpired unobligated balance, end of year	85	91	110
	Change in obligated balance:			
	Unpaid obligations:			
3000	Unpaid obligations, brought forward, Oct 1	118	100	116
3010	New obligations, unexpired accounts	248	248	479
3020	Outlays (gross)	–257	–232	–395
3040	Recoveries of prior year unpaid obligations, unexpired	–4		

3041	Recoveries of prior year unpaid obligations, expired	–5		
3050	Unpaid obligations, end of year	100	116	200
	Uncollected payments:			
3060	Uncollected pymts, Fed sources, brought forward, Oct 1	–3	–12	–12
3061	Adjustments to uncollected pymts, Fed sources, brought forward, Oct 1	–1		
3070	Change in uncollected pymts, Fed sources, unexpired	–8		
3090	Uncollected pymts, Fed sources, end of year	–12	–12	–12
	Memorandum (non-add) entries:			
3100	Obligated balance, start of year	114	88	104
3200	Obligated balance, end of year	88	104	188
	Budget authority and outlays, net:			
	Discretionary:			
4000	Budget authority, gross	270	254	498
	Outlays, gross:			
4010	Outlays from new discretionary authority	160	133	313
4011	Outlays from discretionary balances	97	99	82
4020	Outlays, gross (total)	257	232	395
	Offsets against gross budget authority and outlays:			
	Offsetting collections (collected) from:			
4030	Federal sources	–32	–40	–41
4033	Non-Federal sources	–40	–55	–60
4040	Offsets against gross budget authority and outlays (total)	–72	–95	–101
	Additional offsets against gross budget authority only:			
4050	Change in uncollected pymts, Fed sources, unexpired	–8		
4060	Additional offsets against budget authority only (total)	–8		
4070	Budget authority, net (discretionary)	190	159	397
4080	Outlays, net (discretionary)	185	137	294
4180	Budget authority, net (total)	190	159	397
4190	Outlays, net (total)	185	137	294

Office of the Secretary (OSE).—Directs and leads the management of the Department and provides policy guidance to line and staff organizations in the accomplishment of DOE's mission. In FY 2023, OSE will stand up a Central Climate Change Coordination team responsible to coordinate activities across DOE and other National Climate Task Force agencies.

Congressional and Intergovernmental Affairs (CI).—Responsible for DOE's liaison, communication, coordinating, directing, and promoting the Department's policies and legislative initiatives with Congress, State, territorial, Tribal and local government officials, and other Federal agencies.

Public Affairs (PA).—Responsible for directing and managing the Department's policies and initiatives with the public, news media, and other stakeholders. PA serves as the Department's chief spokesperson with the news media, shapes initiatives aimed at educating the press and public about DOE issues, builds and maintains the Energy.gov platform.

General Counsel (GC).—Responsible for providing legal services to all Department offices, and for determining the Department's authoritative position on any question of law with respect to all Department offices and programs, except for those belonging exclusively to the Federal Energy Regulatory Commission. GC is responsible for the coordination and clearance of proposed legislation affecting energy policy and Department activities. GC administers and monitors standards of conduct requirements, conducts patent program and intellectual property activities, and coordinates rulemaking actions of the Department with other Federal agencies.

Economic Impact and Diversity (ED).—Develops and executes DOE policies to implement applicable statutes and Executive Orders that impact diversity goals affecting equal employment opportunities, minority businesses, minority educational institutions, and historically underrepresented communities. ED identifies ways of ensuring that underrepresented populations are afforded an opportunity to participate fully in DOE programs. ED serves as central coordinator and departmental subject matter expert on equity and justice across the DOE complex and labs. Additionally, ED's Office of Civil Rights and Diversity will directly oversees Equal Employment Opportunity (EEO) complaint processing for the entire enterprise (except for NNSA), as well as directly overseeing the affirmative employment and diversity and inclusion functions for the entire complex (except for NNSA and the PMAs).

Chief Financial Officer (CFO).—Assures the effective management and financial integrity of DOE programs, activities, and resources by developing, implementing, and monitoring DOE-wide policies and systems in the areas of budget administration, finance and accounting, internal controls and financial policy, corporate financial systems, and strategic planning.

Chief Information Officer (CIO).—Provides advice and assistance to the Secretary and other senior managers to ensure that information technology is acquired and information resources are managed in a manner that complies with Administration policies and procedures and statutory requirements. In FY 2023 significant investments will continue to address Cyber vulnerabilities identified as a result of SolarWinds incident of December 2020, implementation of Executive Order 14028 focusing on zero trust architecture, enhanced logging, security licensing, universal encryption, and multifactor authentication.

Chief Human Capital Officer (HC).—Provides DOE leadership on the impact and use of policies, proposals, programs, partnership agreements and relationships related to all aspects of human capital management. HC seeks solutions that address workforce issues in the areas of recruiting, hiring, motivating, succession planning, competency development, training and learning, retention, and diversity.

Office of Policy (OP).—Serves as the principal policy office advising the Secretary of Energy and performing priority policy analyses across the Department's activities, focused on technology; infrastructure; state, local, and tribal activities; and energy jobs, and Arctic Energy coordination.

International Affairs (IA).—Advises Departmental leadership on strategic implementation of U.S. international energy policy and supports DOE's mission to ensure America's security and prosperity by addressing its energy, environmental, and climate challenges through innovative science and technology solutions. IA develops and leads the Department's bilateral and multilateral R&D cooperation, connecting DOE's program offices to advantageous international relationships. IA is the Department lead on fulfilling the Agency's requirements on the Committee of Foreign Investment in the U.S., including the expanded responsibilities derived from the Foreign Investment Risk Review Modernization Act of 2018. In FY 2023, IA will invest in the Net Zero World Initiative, DOE's signature contribution to the Presidents Build Back Better World Initiative, providing comprehensive technology and investment roadmaps to help key large emitters across the globe achieve net zero emissions by 2050.

Office of Small and Disadvantaged Business Utilization (OSDBU).—Responsible for maximizing contracting and subcontracting opportunities for small businesses interested in doing business with the Department. A primary responsibility of OSDBU is to work in partnership with Departmental program elements to achieve prime and subcontracting small business goals set forth by statute and the U.S. Small Business Administration.

Office of Management (MA).—Provides DOE with centralized direction and oversight for the full range of management, procurement and administrative services. MA is responsible for contract management policy development and oversight, acquisition and contract administration, and delivery of procurement services to DOE headquarters organizations. MA activities include the management of headquarters facilities, Department-wide implementation of Federal sustainability goals, purchase or lease of Zero Emission Vehicles (ZEVs) within agency-owned vehicle fleets or as part of a transition from GSA-leased gas-powered vehicles to GSA-leased ZEVs, and related charging infrastructure and program costs.

Project Management Oversight and Assessment (PM).—Provides DOE corporate oversight, managerial leadership and assistance in developing and implementing DOE-wide policies, procedures, programs, and management systems pertaining to project management, and manages the project management career development program for DOE's Federal Project Directors. PM also provides independent oversight of Environmental Management's portfolio of capital asset projects that are $100 million or greater, including all activities involved with on-site cost, schedule, technical and management status reviews, as well as analyzing and reporting performance

DEPARTMENTAL ADMINISTRATION—Continued

progress of the projects. PM will also provide cost estimating and program evaluation.

Strategic Partnership Programs (SPP).—Covers the cost of work performed under orders placed with the Department by non-DOE entities that are precluded by law from making advance payments and certain revenue programs. Reimbursement of these costs is made through deposits of offsetting collections to this account.

Office of Technology Transitions (OTT).—Facilitates accessibility of DOE's capabilities and technologies for private sector commercialization. OTT serves a multi-disciplinary role, providing management of DOE's ongoing tech-to-market activities, including the statutory Technology Commercialization Fund. OTT coordinates DOE technology transition activities, including policy reform, data collection and analyses, industry stakeholder convenings, and amplification of DOE technology transfer success stories across the DOE—including programs, field offices, and the National Labs and Production Facilities—as well as engaging with other Federal agencies to improve awareness of the benefits of engaging the DOE research enterprise. In FY 2023, OTT is requested as a separate appropriation.

Artificial Intelligence Technology Office (AITO).— Coordinates Artificial Intelligence capabilities utilization and research throughout the Department.

Object Classification (in millions of dollars)

Identification code 089–0228–0–1–276		2021 actual	2022 est.	2023 est.
	Direct obligations:			
	Personnel compensation:			
11.1	Full-time permanent	83	83	96
11.3	Other than full-time permanent	9	9	11
11.5	Other personnel compensation	2	2	3
11.9	Total personnel compensation	94	94	110
12.1	Civilian personnel benefits	30	30	34
21.0	Travel and transportation of persons	1	1	5
23.3	Communications, utilities, and miscellaneous charges	11	11	11
25.1	Advisory and assistance services	24	24	60
25.2	Other services from non-Federal sources	15	15	51
25.3	Other goods and services from Federal sources	34	34	107
25.4	Operation and maintenance of facilities	18	18	69
25.7	Other Contractual Services	1	1	1
31.0	Equipment	5	5	5
41.0	Grants, subsidies, and contributions	9	9	20
99.0	Direct obligations	242	242	473
99.0	Reimbursable obligations	6	6	6
99.9	Total new obligations, unexpired accounts	248	248	479

Employment Summary

Identification code 089–0228–0–1–276	2021 actual	2022 est.	2023 est.
1001 Direct civilian full-time equivalent employment	623	623	733
2001 Reimbursable civilian full-time equivalent employment	7	7	7

OFFICE OF THE INSPECTOR GENERAL

For expenses necessary for the Office of the Inspector General in carrying out the provisions of the Inspector General Act of 1978, $106,808,000, to remain available until September 30, 2024.

Note.—A full-year 2022 appropriation for this account was not enacted at the time the Budget was prepared; therefore, the Budget assumes this account is operating under the Continuing Appropriations Act, 2022 (Division A of Public Law 117–43, as amended). The amounts included for 2022 reflect the annualized level provided by the continuing resolution.

Program and Financing (in millions of dollars)

Identification code 089–0236–0–1–276		2021 actual	2022 est.	2023 est.
	Obligations by program activity:			
0001	Office of the Inspector General	60	60	107
0002	Inspector General, Infrastructure Investment and Jobs Act		19	
0799	Total direct obligations	60	79	107
0801	Reimbursable program activity	2		
0900	Total new obligations, unexpired accounts	62	79	107
	Budgetary resources:			
	Unobligated balance:			
1000	Unobligated balance brought forward, Oct 1	6	4	2
	Budget authority:			
	Appropriations, discretionary:			
1100	Appropriation	58	58	107
1100	Appropriation, Infrastructure Investment and Jobs Act		19	
1160	Appropriation, discretionary (total)	58	77	107
	Advance appropriations, discretionary:			
1170	Advance appropriation			12
	Spending authority from offsetting collections, discretionary:			
1700	Collected			2
1701	Change in uncollected payments, Federal sources	2		
1750	Spending auth from offsetting collections, disc (total)	2		2
1900	Budget authority (total)	60	77	121
1930	Total budgetary resources available	66	81	123
	Memorandum (non-add) entries:			
1941	Unexpired unobligated balance, end of year	4	2	16
	Change in obligated balance:			
	Unpaid obligations:			
3000	Unpaid obligations, brought forward, Oct 1	5	8	13
3010	New obligations, unexpired accounts	62	79	107
3020	Outlays (gross)	–59	–74	–114
3050	Unpaid obligations, end of year	8	13	6
	Uncollected payments:			
3060	Uncollected pymts, Fed sources, brought forward, Oct 1		–2	–2
3070	Change in uncollected pymts, Fed sources, unexpired	–2		
3090	Uncollected pymts, Fed sources, end of year	–2	–2	–2
	Memorandum (non-add) entries:			
3100	Obligated balance, start of year	5	6	11
3200	Obligated balance, end of year	6	11	4
	Budget authority and outlays, net:			
	Discretionary:			
4000	Budget authority, gross	60	77	121
	Outlays, gross:			
4010	Outlays from new discretionary authority	49	65	102
4011	Outlays from discretionary balances	10	9	12
4020	Outlays, gross (total)	59	74	114
	Offsets against gross budget authority and outlays:			
	Offsetting collections (collected) from:			
4030	Federal sources			–2
	Additional offsets against gross budget authority only:			
4050	Change in uncollected pymts, Fed sources, unexpired	–2		
4070	Budget authority, net (discretionary)	58	77	119
4080	Outlays, net (discretionary)	59	74	112
4180	Budget authority, net (total)	58	77	119
4190	Outlays, net (total)	59	74	112

The Office of Inspector General (OIG) provides Department-wide (including the National Nuclear Security Administration and the Federal Energy Regulatory Commission) audit, inspection, and investigative functions to identify and recommend corrections for management and administrative deficiencies, which create conditions for existing or potential instances of fraud, waste, abuse or violations of law. The audit function provides financial and performance audits of programs and operations. The inspection function provides independent inspection and analysis of the performance of programs and operations. The investigative function provides for the detection and investigation of improper and illegal activities involving programs, personnel, and operations. Through these efforts, the OIG identifies opportunities for cost savings and operational efficiency; identifies programs that are not meeting performance expectations; recovers monies to the Department and the Treasury as a result of civil and criminal prosecutions; and identifies ways to make Departmental programs safer and more secure.

DEPARTMENT OF ENERGY

Object Classification (in millions of dollars)

Identification code 089–0236–0–1–276		2021 actual	2022 est.	2023 est.
	Direct obligations:			
	Personnel compensation:			
11.1	Full-time permanent	33	33	33
11.3	Other than full-time permanent	1	1	1
11.5	Other personnel compensation	2	2	2
11.9	Total personnel compensation	36	36	36
12.1	Civilian personnel benefits	15	15	15
25.1	Advisory and assistance services	2	2	2
25.2	Other services from non-Federal sources	2	21	49
25.3	Other goods and services from Federal sources	4	4	4
31.0	Equipment	1	1	1
99.0	Direct obligations	60	79	107
99.0	Reimbursable obligations	2		
99.9	Total new obligations, unexpired accounts	62	79	107

Employment Summary

Identification code 089–0236–0–1–276	2021 actual	2022 est.	2023 est.
1001 Direct civilian full-time equivalent employment	287	287	287
2001 Reimbursable civilian full-time equivalent employment	1		

WORKING CAPITAL FUND

Program and Financing (in millions of dollars)

Identification code 089–4563–0–4–276		2021 actual	2022 est.	2023 est.
	Obligations by program activity:			
0802	Project management and career development program	2	2	2
0810	Supplies	1	1	2
0812	Copying Services	3	3	4
0813	Printing and graphics	4	4	5
0814	Building Occupancy (Rent, Operations & Maintenance)	140	140	117
0815	Corporate Business Systems	38	38	49
0816	Mail and Transportation Services	4	4	4
0817	Financial Statement Audits	9	9	12
0818	Procurement Management	9	9	16
0820	Telecommunication	30	30	38
0821	Overseas Presence	13	13	16
0822	Interagency Transfers	8	8	9
0823	Health Services	1	1	2
0825	Corporate Training Services	3	3	3
0826	A-123 / Internal Controls	1	1	2
0827	Pension Studies	1	1	1
0900	Total new obligations, unexpired accounts	267	267	282
	Budgetary resources:			
	Unobligated balance:			
1000	Unobligated balance brought forward, Oct 1	68	49	58
1021	Recoveries of prior year unpaid obligations	2		
1033	Recoveries of prior year paid obligations	1		
1070	Unobligated balance (total)	71	49	58
	Budget authority:			
	Spending authority from offsetting collections, discretionary:			
1700	Collected	245	276	276
1930	Total budgetary resources available	316	325	334
	Memorandum (non-add) entries:			
1941	Unexpired unobligated balance, end of year	49	58	52
	Change in obligated balance:			
	Unpaid obligations:			
3000	Unpaid obligations, brought forward, Oct 1	139	138	2
3010	New obligations, unexpired accounts	267	267	282
3020	Outlays (gross)	–266	–403	–276
3040	Recoveries of prior year unpaid obligations, unexpired	–2		
3050	Unpaid obligations, end of year	138	2	8
	Memorandum (non-add) entries:			
3100	Obligated balance, start of year	139	138	2
3200	Obligated balance, end of year	138	2	8
	Budget authority and outlays, net:			
	Discretionary:			
4000	Budget authority, gross	245	276	276
	Outlays, gross:			
4010	Outlays from new discretionary authority	106	265	265
4011	Outlays from discretionary balances	160	138	11
4020	Outlays, gross (total)	266	403	276
	Offsets against gross budget authority and outlays:			
	Offsetting collections (collected) from:			
4030	Federal sources	–246	–276	–276
	Additional offsets against gross budget authority only:			
4053	Recoveries of prior year paid obligations, unexpired accounts	1		
4080	Outlays, net (discretionary)	20	127	
4180	Budget authority, net (total)			
4190	Outlays, net (total)	20	127	

The Department's Working Capital Fund (WCF) provides the following shared services: rent and building operations, telecommunications, cybersecurity, automated office systems including the Standard Accounting and Reporting System, Strategic Integrated Procurement Enterprise System, payment processing, payroll and personnel processing, administrative services, training and health services, overseas representation, interagency transfers, procurement management, audits, and controls for financial reporting. The WCF assists the Department in improving operational efficiency.

Object Classification (in millions of dollars)

Identification code 089–4563–0–4–276		2021 actual	2022 est.	2023 est.
	Reimbursable obligations:			
	Personnel compensation:			
11.1	Full-time permanent	11	11	12
11.3	Other than full-time permanent	1	1	1
11.5	Other personnel compensation	1	1	1
11.8	Special personal services payments	2	2	2
11.9	Total personnel compensation	15	15	16
12.1	Civilian personnel benefits	5	5	5
21.0	Travel and transportation of persons	1	1	1
22.0	Transportation of things	1	1	1
23.1	Rental payments to GSA	69	69	73
23.3	Communications, utilities, and miscellaneous charges	21	21	23
24.0	Printing and reproduction	3	3	3
25.1	Advisory and assistance services	39	39	41
25.2	Other services from non-Federal sources	14	14	15
25.3	Other goods and services from Federal sources	51	51	54
25.4	Operation and maintenance of facilities	39	39	41
25.7	Operation and maintenance of equipment	1	1	1
26.0	Supplies and materials	1	1	1
31.0	Equipment	1	1	1
32.0	Land and structures	6	6	6
99.0	Reimbursable obligations	267	267	282
99.9	Total new obligations, unexpired accounts	267	267	282

Employment Summary

Identification code 089–4563–0–4–276	2021 actual	2022 est.	2023 est.
2001 Reimbursable civilian full-time equivalent employment	99	99	107

GENERAL FUND RECEIPT ACCOUNTS

(in millions of dollars)

		2021 actual	2022 est.	2023 est.
Offsetting receipts from the public:				
089–089400	Fees and Recoveries, Federal Energy Regulatory Commission	31	9	9
089–143500	General Fund Proprietary Interest Receipts, not Otherwise Classified	4	4	4
089–223400	Sale of Strategic Petroleum Reserve Oil	644	2,930	2,049
089–224500	Sale and Transmission of Electric Energy, Falcon Dam	1	1	1
089–224700	Sale and Transmission of Electric Energy, Southwestern Power Administration	85	7	6
089–224800	Sale and Transmission of Electric Energy, Southeastern Power Administration	151	177	176
089–224900	Sale of Power and Other Utilities, not Otherwise Classified		10	10

General Fund Receipt Accounts—Continued

		2021 actual	2022 est.	2023 est.
089–267910	Title 17 Innovative Technology Loan Guarantees, Negative Subsidies	45	10	7
089–279530	DOE ATVM Direct Loans Downward Reestimate Account		11	
089–279730	DOE Loan Guarantees Downward Reestimate Account	160	372	
089–288900	Repayments on Miscellaneous Recoverable Costs, not Otherwise Classified	33	31	32
089–322000	All Other General Fund Proprietary Receipts Including Budget Clearing Accounts	35	18	14
General Fund Offsetting receipts from the public		1,189	3,580	2,308
Intragovernmental payments:				
089–388500	Undistributed Intragovernmental Payments and Receivables from Cancelled Accounts	–3		
General Fund Intragovernmental payments		–3		

GENERAL PROVISIONS—DEPARTMENT OF ENERGY

SEC. 301. (a) No appropriation, funds, or authority made available by this title for the Department of Energy shall be used to initiate or resume any program, project, or activity or to prepare or initiate Requests For Proposals or similar arrangements (including Requests for Quotations, Requests for Information, and Funding Opportunity Announcements) for a program, project, or activity if the program, project, or activity has not been funded by Congress.

(b)

(1) Unless the Secretary of Energy notifies the Committees on Appropriations of both Houses of Congress at least 3 full business days in advance, none of the funds made available in this title may be used to—

(A) make a grant allocation or discretionary grant award totaling $1,000,000 or more;

(B) make a discretionary contract award or Other Transaction Agreement totaling $1,000,000 or more, including a contract covered by the Federal Acquisition Regulation;

(C) issue a letter of intent to make an allocation, award, or Agreement in excess of the limits in subparagraph (A) or (B); or

(D) announce publicly the intention to make an allocation, award, or Agreement in excess of the limits in subparagraph (A) or (B).

(2) The Secretary of Energy shall submit to the Committees on Appropriations of both Houses of Congress within 15 days of the conclusion of each quarter a report detailing each grant allocation or discretionary grant award totaling less than $1,000,000 provided during the previous quarter.

(3) The notification required by paragraph (1) and the report required by paragraph (2) shall include the recipient of the award, the amount of the award, the fiscal year for which the funds for the award were appropriated, the account and program, project, or activity from which the funds are being drawn, the title of the award, and a brief description of the activity for which the award is made.

(c) The Department of Energy may not, with respect to any program, project, or activity that uses budget authority made available in this title under the heading "Department of Energy—Energy Programs", enter into a multiyear contract, award a multiyear grant, or enter into a multiyear cooperative agreement unless—

(1) the contract, grant, or cooperative agreement is funded for the full period of performance as anticipated at the time of award; or

(2) the contract, grant, or cooperative agreement includes a clause conditioning the Federal Government's obligation on the availability of future year budget authority and the Secretary notifies the Committees on Appropriations of both Houses of Congress at least 3 days in advance.

(d) The amounts made available by this title may be reprogrammed for any program, project, or activity, and the Department shall notify the Committees on Appropriations of both Houses of Congress at least 30 days prior to the use of any proposed reprogramming that would cause any program, project, or activity funding level to increase or decrease by more than $5,000,000 or 10 percent, whichever is less, during the time period covered by this Act.

(e) None of the funds provided in this title shall be available for obligation or expenditure through a reprogramming of funds that—

(1) creates, initiates, or eliminates a program, project, or activity;

(2) increases funds or personnel for any program, project, or activity for which funds are denied or restricted by this Act; or

(3) reduces funds that are directed to be used for a specific program, project, or activity by this Act.

(f)

(1) The Secretary of Energy may waive any requirement or restriction in this section that applies to the use of funds made available for the Department of Energy if compliance with such requirement or restriction would pose a substantial risk to human health, the environment, welfare, or national security.

(2) The Secretary of Energy shall notify the Committees on Appropriations of both Houses of Congress of any waiver under paragraph (1) as soon as practicable, but not later than 3 days after the date of the activity to which a requirement or restriction would otherwise have applied. Such notice shall include an explanation of the substantial risk under paragraph (1) that permitted such waiver.

(g) The unexpended balances of prior appropriations provided for activities in this Act may be available to the same appropriation accounts for such activities established pursuant to this title. Available balances may be merged with funds in the applicable established accounts and thereafter may be accounted for as one fund for the same time period as originally enacted.

SEC. 302. Funds appropriated by this or any other Act, or made available by the transfer of funds in this Act, for intelligence activities are deemed to be specifically authorized by the Congress for purposes of section 504 of the National Security Act of 1947 (50 U.S.C. 3094) during fiscal year 2023 until the enactment of the Intelligence Authorization Act for fiscal year 2023.

SEC. 303. None of the funds made available in this title shall be used for the construction of facilities classified as high-hazard nuclear facilities under 10 CFR Part 830 unless independent oversight is conducted by the Office of Enterprise Assessments to ensure the project is in compliance with nuclear safety requirements.

SEC. 304. None of the funds made available in this title may be used to approve critical decision–2 or critical decision–3 under Department of Energy Order 413.3B, or any successive departmental guidance, for construction projects where the total project cost exceeds $100,000,000, until a separate independent cost estimate has been developed for the project for that critical decision.

SEC. 305. Notwithstanding section 161 of the Energy Policy and Conservation Act (42 U.S.C. 6241), upon a determination by the President in this fiscal year that a regional supply shortage of refined petroleum product of significant scope and duration exists, that a severe increase in the price of refined petroleum product will likely result from such shortage, and that a draw down and sale of refined petroleum product would assist directly and significantly in reducing the adverse impact of such shortage, the Secretary of Energy may draw down and sell refined petroleum product from the Strategic Petroleum Reserve. Proceeds from a sale under this section shall be deposited into the SPR Petroleum Account established in section 167 of the Energy Policy and Conservation Act (42 U.S.C. 6247), and such amounts shall be available for obligation, without fiscal year limitation, consistent with that section.

SEC. 306. Subparagraphs (B) and (C) of section 40401(a)(2) of Public Law 117–58, paragraph (3) of section 16512(r) of title 42, United States Code, and section (l) of section 17013 of title 42, United States Code, shall not apply for fiscal year 2023.

TITLE V—GENERAL PROVISIONS

(INCLUDING TRANSFER OF FUNDS)

SEC. 501. None of the funds appropriated by this Act may be used in any way, directly or indirectly, to influence congressional action on any legislation or appropriation matters pending before Congress, other than to communicate to Members of Congress as described in 18 U.S.C. 1913.

SEC. 502. None of the funds made available by this Act may be used in contravention of Executive Order No. 12898 of February 11, 1994 (Federal Actions to Address Environmental Justice in Minority Populations and Low-Income Populations).

SEC. 503. (a) None of the funds made available in this Act may be used to maintain or establish a computer network unless such network blocks the viewing, downloading, and exchanging of pornography.

(b) Nothing in subsection (a) shall limit the use of funds necessary for any Federal, State, Tribal, or local law enforcement agency or any other entity carrying out criminal investigations, prosecution, or adjudication activities.

SEC. 504. Of the unavailable collections currently in the United States Enrichment Corporation Fund, $405,421,000 shall be transferred to and merged with the Uranium Enrichment Decontamination and Decommissioning Fund and shall be available only to the extent provided in advance in appropriations Acts.

GENERAL PROVISIONS—DEPARTMENT OF ENERGY

[(INCLUDING TRANSFER OF FUNDS)]

[SEC. 301. Notwithstanding section 3304 of title 5, United States Code, and without regard to the provisions of sections 3309 through 3318 of such title 5, the Secretary of Energy, upon a determination that there is a severe shortage of candidates or a critical hiring need for particular positions to carry out the Department of Energy activities funded under this title, may, from within the funds provided to the Department of Energy under this title, recruit and directly appoint highly qualified individuals into the competitive service: *Provided*, That such authority shall not apply to positions in the Excepted Service or the Senior Executive Service: *Provided further*, That any action authorized herein shall be consistent with the merit principles of section 2301 of such title 5, and the Department shall comply with the public notice requirements of section 3327 of such title 5: *Provided further*, That the authority under this section shall terminate on September 30, 2027: *Provided further*, That 180 days after the date of enactment of this Act, the Secretary of Energy shall submit to the House and Senate Committees on Appropriations an estimate of the number of highly qualified individuals it expects to hire under the authority provided in this section.]

[SEC. 302. Up to one-tenth of one percent of each amount appropriated to the Department of Energy in this title may be transferred to "Departmental Administration" to be used for additional management and mission support for funds made available to the Department of Energy in this title in this Act.]

[SEC. 303. One-tenth of one percent of the amounts made available to the Department of Energy under each heading in this title in this Act in each of fiscal years 2022 through 2026 shall be transferred to the Office of the Inspector General of the Department of Energy to oversee the funds made available to the Department of Energy in this title in this Act.] *(Infrastructure Investments and Jobs Appropriations Act.)*

DEPARTMENT OF HEALTH AND HUMAN SERVICES

FOOD AND DRUG ADMINISTRATION
Federal Funds
SALARIES AND EXPENSES
(INCLUDING TRANSFERS OF FUNDS)

For necessary expenses of the Food and Drug Administration, including hire and purchase of passenger motor vehicles; for payment of space rental and related costs pursuant to Public Law 92–313 for programs and activities of the Food and Drug Administration which are included in this Act; for rental of special purpose space in the District of Columbia or elsewhere; in addition to amounts appropriated to the FDA Innovation Account, for carrying out the activities described in section 1002(b)(4) of the 21st Century Cures Act (Public Law 114–255); for miscellaneous and emergency expenses of enforcement activities, authorized and approved by the Secretary and to be accounted for solely on the Secretary's certificate, not to exceed $25,000; and notwithstanding section 521 of Public Law 107–188; $4,416,025,000: Provided, That of the amount provided under this heading, $32,238,000 shall be derived from animal drug user fees authorized by 21 U.S.C. 379j–12, and shall be credited to this account and remain available until expended; $29,459,000 shall be derived from generic new animal drug user fees authorized by 21 U.S.C. 379j–21, and shall be credited to this account and remain available until expended; $712,000,000 shall be derived from tobacco product user fees authorized by 21 U.S.C. 387s, and shall be credited to this account and remain available until expended: Provided further, That in addition to and notwithstanding any other provision under this heading, amounts collected for animal drug user fees and generic new animal drug user fees that exceed the respective fiscal year 2023 limitations are appropriated and shall be credited to this account and remain available until expended: Provided further, That fees derived from animal drug and generic new animal drug assessments for fiscal year 2023, including any such fees collected prior to fiscal year 2023 but credited for fiscal year 2023, shall be subject to the fiscal year 2023 limitations: Provided further, That the Secretary may accept payment during fiscal year 2023 of user fees specified under this heading and authorized for fiscal year 2024, prior to the due date for such fees, and that amounts of such fees assessed for fiscal year 2024 for which the Secretary accepts payment in fiscal year 2023 shall not be included in amounts under this heading: Provided further, That none of these funds shall be used to develop, establish, or operate any program of user fees authorized by 31 U.S.C. 9701: Provided further, That of the total amount appropriated under this heading, $20,000,000 shall be available until September 30, 2025, for the Oncology Center of Excellence to develop and review research, advance regulatory policy, support clinical review of submissions to the Food and Drug Administration related to medical products intended to diagnose or treat cancer, and conduct education and outreach partnerships, in addition to any other amounts available for such purposes: Provided further, That not to exceed $25,000 of this amount shall be for official reception and representation expenses, not otherwise provided for, as determined by the Commissioner: Provided further, That any transfer of funds pursuant to section 770(n) of the Federal Food, Drug, and Cosmetic Act (21 U.S.C. 379dd(n)) shall only be from amounts made available under this heading for other activities: Provided further, That of the amounts that are made available under this heading for "other activities", and that are not derived from user fees, $1,500,000 shall be transferred to and merged with the appropriation for "Department of Health and Human Services—Office of Inspector General" for oversight of the programs and operations of the Food and Drug Administration and shall be in addition to funds otherwise made available for oversight of the Food and Drug Administration: Provided further, That funds may be transferred from one specified activity to another with the prior notification to the Committees on Appropriations of both Houses of Congress.

In addition, mammography user fees authorized by 42 U.S.C. 263b, export certification user fees authorized by 21 U.S.C. 381, priority review user fees authorized by 21 U.S.C. 360n and 360ff, food and feed recall fees, food reinspection fees, and voluntary qualified importer program fees authorized by 21 U.S.C. 379j–31, outsourcing facility fees authorized by 21 U.S.C. 379j–62, prescription drug wholesale distributor licensing and inspection fees authorized by 21 U.S.C. 353(e)(3), third-party logistics provider licensing and inspection fees authorized by 21 U.S.C. 360eee–3(c)(1), third-party auditor fees authorized by 21 U.S.C. 384d(c)(8), medical countermeasure priority review voucher user fees authorized by 21 U.S.C. 360bbb–4a, and fees relating to over-the-counter monograph drugs authorized by 21 U.S.C. 379j–72 shall be credited to this account, to remain available until expended.

BUILDINGS AND FACILITIES

For plans, construction, repair, improvement, extension, alteration, demolition, and purchase of fixed equipment or facilities of or used by the Food and Drug Administration, where not otherwise provided, $30,788,000, to remain available until expended.

Note.—A full-year 2022 appropriation for this account was not enacted at the time the Budget was prepared; therefore, the Budget assumes this account is operating under the Continuing Appropriations Act, 2022 (Division A of Public Law 117–43, as amended). The amounts included for 2022 reflect the annualized level provided by the continuing resolution.

Special and Trust Fund Receipts (in millions of dollars)

Identification code 075–9911–0–1–554		2021 actual	2022 est.	2023 est.
0100	Balance, start of year			1
	Receipts:			
	Current law:			
1130	Cooperative Research and Development Agreements, FDA	2	3	3
2000	Total: Balances and receipts	2	3	4
	Appropriations:			
	Current law:			
2101	Salaries and Expenses	–2	–2	–2
5099	Balance, end of year		1	2

Program and Financing (in millions of dollars)

Identification code 075–9911–0–1–554		2021 actual	2022 est.	2023 est.
	Obligations by program activity:			
0001	Foods	1,099	1,099	1,220
0002	Human Drugs	689	689	790
0003	Devices and Radiological Health	408	408	466
0004	National Center for Toxicological Research	67	67	79
0005	FDA Other Activities (FDA Headquarters)	193	194	228
0006	FDA Other Rent and Rent Related Activities (Including White Oak Consolidation)	144	130	156
0007	FDA GSA Rental Payments	153	168	166
0008	FDA Buildings and Facilities	11	13	31
0009	Cooperative Research and Development (CRADA)	2	2	2
0010	Animal Drugs and Food	192	192	242
0011	Biologics	254	254	275
0012	Food and Drug Safety (no-year)	1		
0015	CURES Activities		50	50
0017	Opioids - IMF	2		
0018	FDA HCFAC Wedge Fund	6		
0019	Coronavirus Emergency Funding Supplemental	209		
0020	FDA User Fees (Non Federal Fund)	2,847	2,870	864
0022	Seafood Safety Studies-GP Sec. 765	1		
0023	Cancer Moonshot			20
0799	Total direct obligations	6,278	6,136	4,589
0802	FDA Reimbursable program (Federal sources)	32	32	35
0899	Total reimbursable obligations	32	32	35
0900	Total new obligations, unexpired accounts	6,310	6,168	4,624
	Budgetary resources:			
	Unobligated balance:			
1000	Unobligated balance brought forward, Oct 1	1,131	1,486	1,453
1001	Discretionary unobligated balance brought fwd, Oct 1	1,122		
1021	Recoveries of prior year unpaid obligations	111		
1033	Recoveries of prior year paid obligations	1		
1070	Unobligated balance (total)	1,243	1,486	1,453
	Budget authority:			
	Appropriations, discretionary:			
1100	Appropriation	3,271	3,215	3,673
1120	Appropriations transferred to other accts [075–0128]	–2	–2	–2
1121	Appropriations transferred from other acct [075–5629]		50	50
1160	Appropriation, discretionary (total)	3,269	3,263	3,721
	Appropriations, mandatory:			
1200	Appropriation	500		
1201	Appropriation (special or trust fund)	2	2	2
1260	Appropriations, mandatory (total)	502	2	2
	Spending authority from offsetting collections, discretionary:			
1700	Collected	2,917	2,870	864
1700	Collected		5	
1701	Change in uncollected payments, Federal sources	5	–5	
1702	Offsetting collections (previously unavailable)	903		

SALARIES AND EXPENSES—Continued

Program and Financing—Continued

Identification code 075–9911–0–1–554		2021 actual	2022 est.	2023 est.
1724	Spending authority from offsetting collections precluded from obligation (limitation on obligations)	–1,049		
1750	Spending auth from offsetting collections, disc (total)	2,776	2,870	864
	Spending authority from offsetting collections, mandatory:			
1800	Collected	10		
1801	Change in uncollected payments, Federal sources	–3		
1850	Spending auth from offsetting collections, mand (total)	7		
1900	Budget authority (total)	6,554	6,135	4,587
1930	Total budgetary resources available	7,797	7,621	6,040
	Memorandum (non-add) entries:			
1940	Unobligated balance expiring	–1		
1941	Unexpired unobligated balance, end of year	1,486	1,453	1,416
	Change in obligated balance:			
	Unpaid obligations:			
3000	Unpaid obligations, brought forward, Oct 1	3,042	3,099	2,011
3010	New obligations, unexpired accounts	6,310	6,168	4,624
3011	Obligations ("upward adjustments"), expired accounts	182		
3020	Outlays (gross)	–6,125	–7,256	–4,493
3040	Recoveries of prior year unpaid obligations, unexpired	–111		
3041	Recoveries of prior year unpaid obligations, expired	–199		
3050	Unpaid obligations, end of year	3,099	2,011	2,142
	Uncollected payments:			
3060	Uncollected pymts, Fed sources, brought forward, Oct 1	–62	–55	–50
3070	Change in uncollected pymts, Fed sources, unexpired	–2	5	
3071	Change in uncollected pymts, Fed sources, expired	9		
3090	Uncollected pymts, Fed sources, end of year	–55	–50	–50
	Memorandum (non-add) entries:			
3100	Obligated balance, start of year	2,980	3,044	1,961
3200	Obligated balance, end of year	3,044	1,961	2,092
	Budget authority and outlays, net:			
	Discretionary:			
4000	Budget authority, gross	6,045	6,133	4,585
	Outlays, gross:			
4010	Outlays from new discretionary authority	3,707	4,934	3,213
4011	Outlays from discretionary balances	2,391	1,404	1,236
4020	Outlays, gross (total)	6,098	6,338	4,449
	Offsets against gross budget authority and outlays:			
	Offsetting collections (collected) from:			
4030	Federal sources:	–35	–5	
4033	Non-Federal sources:	–2,918	–2,870	–864
4040	Offsets against gross budget authority and outlays (total)	–2,953	–2,875	–864
	Additional offsets against gross budget authority only:			
4050	Change in uncollected pymts, Fed sources, unexpired	–5	5	
4052	Offsetting collections credited to expired accounts	35		
4053	Recoveries of prior year paid obligations, unexpired accounts	1		
4060	Additional offsets against budget authority only (total)	31	5	
4070	Budget authority, net (discretionary)	3,123	3,263	3,721
4080	Outlays, net (discretionary)	3,145	3,463	3,585
	Mandatory:			
4090	Budget authority, gross	509	2	2
	Outlays, gross:			
4100	Outlays from new mandatory authority	25	2	2
4101	Outlays from mandatory balances	2	916	42
4110	Outlays, gross (total)	27	918	44
	Offsets against gross budget authority and outlays:			
	Offsetting collections (collected) from:			
4120	Federal sources:	–9		
4123	Non-Federal sources:	–1		
4130	Offsets against gross budget authority and outlays (total)	–10		
	Additional offsets against gross budget authority only:			
4140	Change in uncollected pymts, Fed sources, unexpired	3		
4160	Budget authority, net (mandatory)	502	2	2
4170	Outlays, net (mandatory)	17	918	44
4180	Budget authority, net (total)	3,625	3,265	3,723
4190	Outlays, net (total)	3,162	4,381	3,629
	Memorandum (non-add) entries:			
5090	Unexpired unavailable balance, SOY: Offsetting collections	946	1,092	1,092
5092	Unexpired unavailable balance, EOY: Offsetting collections	1,092	1,092	1,092

Summary of Budget Authority and Outlays (in millions of dollars)

	2021 actual	2022 est.	2023 est.
Enacted/requested:			
Budget Authority	3,625	3,265	3,723
Outlays	3,162	4,381	3,629
Legislative proposal, subject to PAYGO:			
Budget Authority			1,630
Outlays			424
Total:			
Budget Authority	3,625	3,265	5,353
Outlays	3,162	4,381	4,053

The Food and Drug Administration (FDA) promotes and protects public health by overseeing the safety, efficacy, quality, and security of human and veterinary drugs, biological products, medical devices, foods, cosmetics, and products that emit radiation. FDA also has responsibility for regulating the manufacturing, marketing, and distribution of tobacco products to protect public health and to reduce tobacco use by minors. FDA advances public health by helping to advance innovations that make medicines more effective, safe, and affordable and by helping the public get the accurate, science-based information they need to use medicines and foods to maintain and improve their health. FDA supports the Nation's counterterrorism capability by ensuring the security of the food supply and by fostering the development of medical products and countermeasures to respond to deliberate and naturally emerging public health threats. The FY 2023 Budget includes $6.8 billion in total resources for FDA. The Budget invests in priority activities including inspections modernization, critical food safety efforts, medical device cybersecurity, public health employee pay costs, alternative methods to animal testing, and Cancer Moonshot.

Object Classification (in millions of dollars)

Identification code 075–9911–0–1–554		2021 actual	2022 est.	2023 est.
	Direct obligations:			
	Personnel compensation:			
11.1	Full-time permanent	1,815	1,849	1,958
11.3	Other than full-time permanent	176	179	188
11.5	Other personnel compensation	134	136	144
11.7	Military personnel	165	168	173
11.8	Special personal services payments	2	2	2
11.9	Total personnel compensation	2,292	2,334	2,465
12.1	Civilian personnel benefits	763	768	812
12.2	Military personnel benefits	20	21	21
21.0	Travel and transportation of persons	45	44	18
22.0	Transportation of things	4	4	5
23.1	Rental payments to GSA	216	237	88
23.3	Communications, utilities, and miscellaneous charges	22	20	24
24.0	Printing and reproduction	2	2	2
25.1	Advisory and assistance services	93	93	40
25.2	Other services from non-Federal sources	964	893	377
25.3	Other goods and services from Federal sources	933	922	391
25.4	Operation and maintenance of facilities	97	94	42
25.5	Research and development contracts	169	116	49
25.7	Operation and maintenance of equipment	77	99	42
26.0	Supplies and materials	74	68	29
31.0	Equipment	26	36	16
32.0	Land and structures	128	70	30
41.0	Grants, subsidies, and contributions	320	314	137
42.0	Insurance claims and indemnities	1	1	1
44.0	Refunds	32		
99.0	Direct obligations	6,278	6,136	4,589
99.0	Reimbursable obligations	32	32	35
99.9	Total new obligations, unexpired accounts	6,310	6,168	4,624

Employment Summary

Identification code 075–9911–0–1–554		2021 actual	2022 est.	2023 est.
1001	Direct civilian full-time equivalent employment	16,075	15,692	16,221
1101	Direct military average strength employment	1,097	1,097	1,099
2001	Reimbursable civilian full-time equivalent employment	41	41	41
2101	Reimbursable military average strength employment	3	3	3
3001	Allocation account civilian full-time equivalent employment	34	34	34
3101	Allocation account military average strength employment	2	2	2

DEPARTMENT OF HEALTH AND HUMAN SERVICES

SALARIES AND EXPENSES
(Legislative proposal, not subject to PAYGO)

Contingent upon the enactment of authorizing legislation establishing fees under 21 U.S.C. 387s with respect to products deemed under 21 U.S.C. 387a(b) but not specified in 21 U.S.C. 387s(b)(2)(B), the Secretary shall assess and collect such fees, which shall be credited to this account and remain available until expended, in addition to amounts otherwise derived from fees authorized under 21 U.S.C. 387s.

In addition, contingent upon the enactment of authorizing legislation, the Secretary shall charge a fee for prescription drug review activities, medical device review activities, biosimilar biological products review activities, and human generic drugs review activities: Provided, That fees of $1,224,132,000 for prescription drug reviews shall be credited to this account and remain available until expended; fees of $248,342,000 for medical device reviews shall be credited to this account and remain available until expended; fees of $550,449,000 for human generic drug reviews shall be credited to this account and remain available until expended; and fees of $40,841,000 for biosimilar biological product reviews shall be credited to this account and remain available until expended: Provided further, That, in addition to and notwithstanding any other provision under this heading, amounts collected for prescription drug user fees, medical device user fees, biosimilar biological product user fees, and human generic drug user fees that exceed the respective fiscal year 2023 limitations are appropriated and shall be credited to this account and remain available until expended: Provided further, That fees derived from prescription drug reviews, medical device reviews, biosimilar biological products reviews, and human generic drugs reviews for fiscal year 2023 received during fiscal year 2023, including any such fees assessed prior to fiscal year 2023 but credited for fiscal year 2023, shall be subject to the fiscal year 2023 limitations: Provided further, That the Secretary may accept payment during fiscal year 2023 of user fees specified in this paragraph and authorized for fiscal year 2024, prior to the due date for such fees, and that amounts of such fees assessed for fiscal year 2024 for which the Secretary accepts payment in fiscal year 2023 shall not be included in amounts in this paragraph.

Program and Financing (in millions of dollars)

Identification code 075–9911–2–1–554	2021 actual	2022 est.	2023 est.
Obligations by program activity:			
0801 FDA Reimbursable program (User fees)			2,163
0899 Total reimbursable obligations			2,163
Budgetary resources:			
Budget authority:			
Spending authority from offsetting collections, discretionary:			
1700 Collected			2,163
1900 Budget authority (total)			2,163
1930 Total budgetary resources available			2,163
Change in obligated balance:			
Unpaid obligations:			
3010 New obligations, unexpired accounts			2,163
3020 Outlays (gross)			–2,163
Budget authority and outlays, net:			
Discretionary:			
4000 Budget authority, gross			2,163
Outlays, gross:			
4010 Outlays from new discretionary authority			2,163
Offsets against gross budget authority and outlays:			
Offsetting collections (collected) from:			
4033 Non-Federal sources			–2,163
4040 Offsets against gross budget authority and outlays (total)			–2,163
4180 Budget authority, net (total)			
4190 Outlays, net (total)			

The FY 2023 Budget proposes additional resources including an estimated $550 million for the human generic drug program, $41 million for biosimilars, $1.2 billion in prescription drug user fees, and $248 million in medical device user fees. In FY 2022, Congress will consider proposed legislation to reauthorize PDUFA, MDUFA, GDUFA, and BsUFA. The Budget proposes legislation that authorizes the collection and spending of these fees subject to appropriations. The Budget also includes a legislative proposal to increase the user fee collected in support of the tobacco program by $100 million and adds electronic nicotine delivery system manufacturers and importers as entities subject to the user fees.

Object Classification (in millions of dollars)

Identification code 075–9911–2–1–554	2021 actual	2022 est.	2023 est.
Reimbursable obligations:			
21.0 Travel and transportation of persons			32
23.1 Rental payments to GSA			151
25.1 Advisory and assistance services			69
25.2 Other services from non-Federal sources			648
25.3 Other goods and services from Federal sources			673
25.4 Operation and maintenance of facilities			71
25.5 Research and development contracts			84
25.7 Operation and maintenance of equipment			72
26.0 Supplies and materials			51
31.0 Equipment			27
32.0 Land and structures			52
41.0 Grants, subsidies, and contributions			233
99.0 Reimbursable obligations			2,163
99.9 Total new obligations, unexpired accounts			2,163

SALARIES AND EXPENSES
(Legislative proposal, subject to PAYGO)

Program and Financing (in millions of dollars)

Identification code 075–9911–4–1–554	2021 actual	2022 est.	2023 est.
Obligations by program activity:			
0023 Pandemic Preparedness			1,630
0799 Total direct obligations			1,630
Budgetary resources:			
Budget authority:			
Appropriations, mandatory:			
1200 Appropriation			1,630
1900 Budget authority (total)			1,630
1930 Total budgetary resources available			1,630
Change in obligated balance:			
Unpaid obligations:			
3010 New obligations, unexpired accounts			1,630
3020 Outlays (gross)			–424
3050 Unpaid obligations, end of year			1,206
Memorandum (non-add) entries:			
3200 Obligated balance, end of year			1,206
Budget authority and outlays, net:			
Mandatory:			
4090 Budget authority, gross			1,630
Outlays, gross:			
4100 Outlays from new mandatory authority			424
4180 Budget authority, net (total)			1,630
4190 Outlays, net (total)			424

The FY 2023 Budget includes FDAs contributions to the HHS Pandemic Preparedness Plan, and reflects the activities and corresponding spending amounts needed for FDA to achieve the Departments preparedness vision. The FY 2023 Budget will expand and modernize FDAs regulatory capacity, IT, laboratory infrastructure, including strengthening the personal protective equipment supply chain by building analytics and creating predictive modeling capabilities. FDA will also focus on clinical evaluation of vaccines and therapeutics that target high-profile viral families and speed development of diagnostics, including expansion of test validation capacity and development of common performance standards. The Budget will also support FDAs work with its international partners to strengthen foreign inspections, harmonize premarket review of vaccines, therapeutics, diagnostics and reducing zoonotic pathogen spillover.

Object Classification (in millions of dollars)

Identification code 075–9911–4–1–554	2021 actual	2022 est.	2023 est.
Direct obligations:			
21.0 Travel and transportation of persons			24

Food and Drug Administration—Continued
Federal Funds—Continued

SALARIES AND EXPENSES—Continued
Object Classification—Continued

Identification code 075–9911–4–1–554		2021 actual	2022 est.	2023 est.
23.1	Rental payments to GSA			114
25.1	Advisory and assistance services			52
25.2	Other services from non-Federal sources			488
25.3	Other goods and services from Federal sources			508
25.4	Operation and maintenance of facilities			54
25.5	Research and development contracts			63
25.7	Operation and maintenance of equipment			54
26.0	Supplies and materials			38
31.0	Equipment			20
32.0	Land and structures			39
41.0	Grants, subsidies, and contributions			176
99.0	Direct obligations			1,630
99.9	Total new obligations, unexpired accounts			1,630

FDA WORKING CAPITAL FUND

Program and Financing (in millions of dollars)

Identification code 075–4613–0–4–554		2021 actual	2022 est.	2023 est.
	Obligations by program activity:			
0001	Direct program activity		324	324
0801	Reimbursable program activity	654	295	295
0900	Total new obligations, unexpired accounts	654	619	619
	Budgetary resources:			
	Unobligated balance:			
1000	Unobligated balance brought forward, Oct 1	32	22	22
1021	Recoveries of prior year unpaid obligations	8		
1070	Unobligated balance (total)	40	22	22
	Budget authority:			
	Spending authority from offsetting collections, discretionary:			
1700	Collected	634	619	619
1701	Change in uncollected payments, Federal sources	2		
1750	Spending auth from offsetting collections, disc (total)	636	619	619
1900	Budget authority (total)	636	619	619
1930	Total budgetary resources available	676	641	641
	Memorandum (non-add) entries:			
1941	Unexpired unobligated balance, end of year	22	22	22
	Change in obligated balance:			
	Unpaid obligations:			
3000	Unpaid obligations, brought forward, Oct 1	237	243	
3010	New obligations, unexpired accounts	654	619	619
3020	Outlays (gross)	–640	–862	–619
3040	Recoveries of prior year unpaid obligations, unexpired	–8		
3050	Unpaid obligations, end of year	243		
	Uncollected payments:			
3060	Uncollected pymts, Fed sources, brought forward, Oct 1		–2	–2
3070	Change in uncollected pymts, Fed sources, unexpired	–2		
3090	Uncollected pymts, Fed sources, end of year	–2	–2	–2
	Memorandum (non-add) entries:			
3100	Obligated balance, start of year	237	241	–2
3200	Obligated balance, end of year	241	–2	–2
	Budget authority and outlays, net:			
	Discretionary:			
4000	Budget authority, gross	636	619	619
	Outlays, gross:			
4010	Outlays from new discretionary authority	426	619	619
4011	Outlays from discretionary balances	214	243	
4020	Outlays, gross (total)	640	862	619
	Offsets against gross budget authority and outlays:			
	Offsetting collections (collected) from:			
4030	Federal sources	–634	–619	–619
	Additional offsets against gross budget authority only:			
4050	Change in uncollected pymts, Fed sources, unexpired	–2		
4080	Outlays, net (discretionary)	6	243	
4180	Budget authority, net (total)			
4190	Outlays, net (total)	6	243	

Object Classification (in millions of dollars)

Identification code 075–4613–0–4–554		2021 actual	2022 est.	2023 est.
	Direct obligations:			
	Personnel compensation:			
11.1	Full-time permanent		74	74
11.3	Other than full-time permanent		1	1
11.5	Other personnel compensation		2	2
11.7	Military personnel		1	1
11.9	Total personnel compensation		78	78
12.1	Civilian personnel benefits		26	26
12.2	Military personnel benefits		1	1
21.0	Travel and transportation of persons		1	1
23.3	Communications, utilities, and miscellaneous charges		6	6
24.0	Printing and reproduction		1	1
25.1	Advisory and assistance services		15	15
25.2	Other services from non-Federal sources		77	77
25.3	Other goods and services from Federal sources		54	54
25.4	Operation and maintenance of facilities		3	3
25.7	Operation and maintenance of equipment		56	56
26.0	Supplies and materials		4	4
31.0	Equipment		1	1
42.0	Insurance claims and indemnities		1	1
99.0	Direct obligations		324	324
	Reimbursable obligations:			
	Personnel compensation:			
11.1	Full-time permanent	149	58	58
11.3	Other than full-time permanent	3	1	1
11.5	Other personnel compensation	5	1	1
11.7	Military personnel	2	1	1
11.9	Total personnel compensation	159	61	61
12.1	Civilian personnel benefits	58	20	20
21.0	Travel and transportation of persons	3	1	1
23.3	Communications, utilities, and miscellaneous charges	11	5	5
24.0	Printing and reproduction	2	1	1
25.1	Advisory and assistance services	32	12	12
25.2	Other services from non-Federal sources	126	63	63
25.3	Other goods and services from Federal sources	110	81	81
25.4	Operation and maintenance of facilities	1	2	2
25.7	Operation and maintenance of equipment	128	44	44
26.0	Supplies and materials	6	3	3
31.0	Equipment	9		
32.0	Land and structures	9		
41.0	Grants, subsidies, and contributions		1	1
43.0	Interest and dividends		1	1
99.0	Reimbursable obligations	654	295	295
99.9	Total new obligations, unexpired accounts	654	619	619

Employment Summary

Identification code 075–4613–0–4–554		2021 actual	2022 est.	2023 est.
1001	Direct civilian full-time equivalent employment	1,224	1,224	1,224
1101	Direct military average strength employment	13	13	13

PAYMENT TO THE FDA INNOVATION ACCOUNT, CURES ACT

Program and Financing (in millions of dollars)

Identification code 075–0148–0–1–554		2021 actual	2022 est.	2023 est.
	Obligations by program activity:			
0001	Direct program activity	70	50	50
0900	Total new obligations, unexpired accounts (object class 94.0)	70	50	50
	Budgetary resources:			
	Budget authority:			
	Appropriations, mandatory:			
1200	Appropriation	70	50	50
1930	Total budgetary resources available	70	50	50
	Change in obligated balance:			
	Unpaid obligations:			
3010	New obligations, unexpired accounts	70	50	50
3020	Outlays (gross)	–70	–50	–50

DEPARTMENT OF HEALTH AND HUMAN SERVICES

Food and Drug Administration—Continued
Federal Funds—Continued

427

	Budget authority and outlays, net: Mandatory:	2021 actual	2022 est.	2023 est.
4090	Budget authority, gross	70	50	50
	Outlays, gross:			
4100	Outlays from new mandatory authority	70	50	50
4180	Budget authority, net (total)	70	50	50
4190	Outlays, net (total)	70	50	50

This account, and a related special receipt account, were established to support the execution structure necessary to implement the 21st Century Cures Act.

FDA INNOVATION ACCOUNT, CURES ACT

(INCLUDING TRANSFER OF FUNDS)

For necessary expenses to carry out the purposes described under section 1002(b)(4) of the 21st Century Cures Act, in addition to amounts available for such purposes under the heading "Salaries and Expenses", $50,000,000, to remain available until expended: Provided, That amounts appropriated in this paragraph are appropriated pursuant to section 1002(b)(3) of the 21st Century Cures Act, are to be derived from amounts transferred under section 1002(b)(2)(A) of such Act, and may be transferred by the Commissioner of Food and Drugs to the appropriation for "Department of Health and Human Services Food and Drug Administration Salaries and Expenses" solely for the purposes provided in such Act: Provided further, That upon a determination by the Commissioner that funds transferred pursuant to the previous proviso are not necessary for the purposes provided, such amounts may be transferred back to the account: Provided further, That such transfer authority is in addition to any other transfer authority provided by law.

Note.—A full-year 2022 appropriation for this account was not enacted at the time the Budget was prepared; therefore, the Budget assumes this account is operating under the Continuing Appropriations Act, 2022 (Division A of Public Law 117–43, as amended). The amounts included for 2022 reflect the annualized level provided by the continuing resolution.

Special and Trust Fund Receipts (in millions of dollars)

Identification code 075–5629–0–2–554	2021 actual	2022 est.	2023 est.
0100 Balance, start of year			
Receipts:			
Current law:			
1140 General Fund Payment, FDA Innovation, CURES Act	70	50	50
2000 Total: Balances and receipts	70	50	50
Appropriations:			
Current law:			
2101 FDA Innovation, Cures Act	–70	–50	–50
5099 Balance, end of year			

Program and Financing (in millions of dollars)

Identification code 075–5629–0–2–554	2021 actual	2022 est.	2023 est.
Obligations by program activity:			
0001 New Obligations for CURES Activities	69		
Budgetary resources:			
Unobligated balance:			
1000 Unobligated balance brought forward, Oct 1	48	49	49
Budget authority:			
Appropriations, discretionary:			
1101 Appropriation (special or trust)	70	50	50
1120 Appropriations transferred to other acct [075–9911]		–50	–50
1160 Appropriation, discretionary (total)	70		
1930 Total budgetary resources available	118	49	49
Memorandum (non-add) entries:			
1941 Unexpired unobligated balance, end of year	49	49	49
Change in obligated balance:			
Unpaid obligations:			
3000 Unpaid obligations, brought forward, Oct 1	49	54	3
3010 New obligations, unexpired accounts	69		
3020 Outlays (gross)	–64	–51	
3050 Unpaid obligations, end of year	54	3	3
Memorandum (non-add) entries:			
3100 Obligated balance, start of year	49	54	3
3200 Obligated balance, end of year	54	3	3

	Budget authority and outlays, net: Discretionary:	2021 actual	2022 est.	2023 est.
4000	Budget authority, gross	70		
	Outlays, gross:			
4010	Outlays from new discretionary authority	25		
4011	Outlays from discretionary balances	39	51	
4020	Outlays, gross (total)	64	51	
4180	Budget authority, net (total)	70		
4190	Outlays, net (total)	64	51	

The 21st Century Cures Act was enacted into law on December 13, 2016. The Act includes authorities FDA can use to help modernize drug, biological product, and device product development and review and to create greater efficiencies and predictability in product development and review.

Object Classification (in millions of dollars)

Identification code 075–5629–0–2–554	2021 actual	2022 est.	2023 est.
Direct obligations:			
Personnel compensation:			
11.1 Full-time permanent	14		
11.3 Other than full-time permanent	2		
11.5 Other personnel compensation	1		
11.7 Military personnel	1		
11.9 Total personnel compensation	18		
12.1 Civilian personnel benefits	6		
25.1 Advisory and assistance services	5		
25.2 Other services from non-Federal sources	16		
25.3 Other goods and services from Federal sources	5		
25.5 Research and development contracts	4		
25.7 Operation and maintenance of equipment	1		
26.0 Supplies and materials	1		
41.0 Grants, subsidies, and contributions	13		
99.9 Total new obligations, unexpired accounts	69		

Employment Summary

Identification code 075–5629–0–2–554	2021 actual	2022 est.	2023 est.
1001 Direct civilian full-time equivalent employment	120		
1101 Direct military average strength employment	7		

REVOLVING FUND FOR CERTIFICATION AND OTHER SERVICES

Program and Financing (in millions of dollars)

Identification code 075–4309–0–3–554	2021 actual	2022 est.	2023 est.
Obligations by program activity:			
0801 Revolving Fund for Certification and Other Services (Reimbursable)	9	11	11
Budgetary resources:			
Unobligated balance:			
1000 Unobligated balance brought forward, Oct 1	2	1	1
Budget authority:			
Spending authority from offsetting collections, mandatory:			
1800 Collected	8	11	11
1802 Offsetting collections (previously unavailable)	1	1	1
1823 New and/or unobligated balance of spending authority from offsetting collections temporarily reduced	–1	–1	–1
1850 Spending auth from offsetting collections, mand (total)	8	11	11
1900 Budget authority (total)	8	11	11
1930 Total budgetary resources available	10	12	12
Memorandum (non-add) entries:			
1941 Unexpired unobligated balance, end of year	1	1	1
Change in obligated balance:			
Unpaid obligations:			
3000 Unpaid obligations, brought forward, Oct 1	5	5	1
3010 New obligations, unexpired accounts	9	11	11
3020 Outlays (gross)	–9	–15	–10
3050 Unpaid obligations, end of year	5	1	2
Memorandum (non-add) entries:			
3100 Obligated balance, start of year	5	5	1
3200 Obligated balance, end of year	5	1	2

Revolving Fund for Certification and Other Services—Continued
Program and Financing—Continued

Identification code 075–4309–0–3–554	2021 actual	2022 est.	2023 est.
Budget authority and outlays, net:			
Mandatory:			
4090 Budget authority, gross	8	11	11
Outlays, gross:			
4100 Outlays from new mandatory authority	6	10	10
4101 Outlays from mandatory balances	3	5	
4110 Outlays, gross (total)	9	15	10
Offsets against gross budget authority and outlays:			
Offsetting collections (collected) from:			
4123 Non-Federal sources	–8	–11	–11
4180 Budget authority, net (total)			
4190 Outlays, net (total)	1	4	–1
Memorandum (non-add) entries:			
5090 Unexpired unavailable balance, SOY: Offsetting collections	1	1	1
5092 Unexpired unavailable balance, EOY: Offsetting collections	1	1	1

FDA certifies color additives for use in foods, drugs, and cosmetics. It also lists color additives for use in foods, drugs, medical devices, and cosmetics. These services are financed wholly by fees paid by the industries affected.

Object Classification (in millions of dollars)

Identification code 075–4309–0–3–554	2021 actual	2022 est.	2023 est.
Reimbursable obligations:			
11.1 Personnel compensation: Full-time permanent	4	6	6
12.1 Civilian personnel benefits	1	1	1
23.1 Rental payments to GSA	1	1	1
25.7 Operation and maintenance of equipment	1	1	1
32.0 Land and structures	2	2	2
99.9 Total new obligations, unexpired accounts	9	11	11

Employment Summary

Identification code 075–4309–0–3–554	2021 actual	2022 est.	2023 est.
2001 Reimbursable civilian full-time equivalent employment	41	37	37

HEALTH RESOURCES AND SERVICES ADMINISTRATION
Federal Funds

Primary Health Care

For carrying out titles II and III of the Public Health Service Act (referred to in this Act as the "PHS Act") with respect to primary health care and the Native Hawaiian Health Care Act of 1988, $1,839,022,000: *Provided*, That no more than $1,000,000 shall be available until expended for carrying out the provisions of section 224(o) of the PHS Act: *Provided further*, That no more than $120,000,000 shall be available until expended for carrying out subsections (g) through (n) and (q) of section 224 of the PHS Act, and for expenses incurred by the Department of Health and Human Services (referred to in this Act as "HHS") pertaining to administrative claims made under such law.

Health Workforce

For carrying out titles III, VII, and VIII of the PHS Act with respect to the health workforce, sections 1128E and 1921 of the Social Security Act, and the Health Care Quality Improvement Act of 1986, $1,619,884,000: *Provided*, That section 751(j)(2) and 762(k) of the PHS Act and the proportional funding amounts in paragraphs (1) through (4) of section 756(f) of the PHS Act shall not apply to funds made available under this heading: *Provided further*, That for any program operating under section 751 of the PHS Act on or before January 1, 2009, the Secretary of Health and Human Services (referred to in this title as the "Secretary") may hereafter waive any of the requirements contained in sections 751(d)(2)(A) and 751(d)(2)(B) of such Act for the full project period of a grant under such section: *Provided further*, That fees collected for the disclosure of information under section 427(b) of the Health Care Quality Improvement Act of 1986 and sections 1128E(d)(2) and 1921 of the Social Security Act shall be sufficient to recover the full costs of operating the programs authorized by such sections and shall remain available until expended for the National Practitioner Data Bank: *Provided further*, That funds transferred to this account to carry out section 846 and subpart 3 of part D of title III of the PHS Act may be used to make prior year adjustments to awards made under such section and subpart: *Provided further*, That section 756(c) of the PHS Act shall apply to paragraphs (1) through (4) of section 756(a) of the PHS Act: *Provided further*, That $210,000,000 shall remain available until expended for the purposes of providing primary health services, assigning National Health Service Corps ("NHSC") participants to expand the delivery of substance use disorder treatment services, notwithstanding the assignment priorities and limitations under sections 333(a)(1)(D), 333(b), and 333A(a)(1)(B)(ii) of the PHS Act, and making payments under the NHSC Loan Repayment Program under section 338B of such Act: *Provided further*, That within the amount made available in the previous proviso, $15,000,000 shall remain available until expended for the purposes of making payments under the NHSC Loan Repayment Program under section 338B of the PHS Act to individuals participating in such program who provide primary health services in Indian Health Service facilities, Tribally-Operated 638 Health Programs, and Urban Indian Health Programs (as those terms are defined by the Secretary), notwithstanding the assignment priorities and limitations under section 333(b) of such Act: *Provided further*, That within the amount made available in the proviso preceding the previous proviso, $25,000,000 shall remain available until expended for the purposes of making loan repayment awards to mental and behavioral health providers, including peer support specialists, in accordance with section 338B of the PHS Act, notwithstanding the assignment priorities and limitations under sections 333(a)(1)(D), 333(b), 333A(a)(1)(B)(ii), and 334 of the PHS Act: *Provided further*, That for purposes of the previous three provisos, section 331(a)(3)(D) of the PHS Act shall be applied as if the term "primary health services" includes clinical substance use disorder treatment services, including those provided by masters level, licensed substance use disorder treatment counselors , and services provided by certified peer support specialists: *Provided further*, That funds made available under this heading may be used to make grants to establish or expand optional community-based nurse practitioner fellowship programs that are accredited or in the accreditation process, with a preference for those in Federally Qualified Health Centers, for practicing postgraduate nurse practitioners in primary care or behavioral health.

Maternal and Child Health

For carrying out titles III, XI, XII, and XIX of the PHS Act with respect to maternal and child health and title V of the Social Security Act, $1,272,930,000: *Provided*, That notwithstanding sections 502(a)(1) and 502(b)(1) of the Social Security Act, not more than $351,116,000 shall be available for carrying out special projects of regional and national significance pursuant to section 501(a)(2) of such Act and $10,276,000 shall be available for projects described in subparagraphs (A) through (F) of section 501(a)(3) of such Act.

Ryan White HIV/AIDS Program

For carrying out title XXVI of the PHS Act with respect to the Ryan White HIV/AIDS program, $2,654,781,000, of which $2,010,881,000 shall remain available to the Secretary through September 30, 2025, for parts A and B of title XXVI of the PHS Act, and of which not less than $900,313,000 shall be for State AIDS Drug Assistance Programs under the authority of section 2616 or 311(c) of such Act; and of which $290,000,000, to remain available until expended, shall be available to the Secretary for carrying out a program of grants and contracts under title XXVI or section 311(c) of such Act focused on ending the nationwide HIV/AIDS epidemic, with any grants issued under such section 311(c) administered in conjunction with title XXVI of the PHS Act, including the limitation on administrative expenses.

Health Systems

For carrying out titles III and XII of the PHS Act with respect to health care systems, and the Stem Cell Therapeutic and Research Act of 2005, $94,009,000, of which $122,000 shall be available until expended for facilities renovations and other facilities-related expenses of the National Hansen's Disease Program.

Rural Health

For carrying out titles III and IV of the PHS Act with respect to rural health, section 427(a) of the Federal Coal Mine Health and Safety Act of 1969, and sections 711 and 1820 of the Social Security Act, $373,709,000, of which $57,509,000 from general revenues, notwithstanding section 1820(j) of the Social Security Act, shall be available for carrying out the Medicare rural hospital flexibility grants program: *Provided*, That of the funds made available under this heading for Medicare rural hospital flexibility grants, up to $20,942,000 shall be available for the Small Rural Hospital Improvement Grant Program for quality improvement and adoption of health information technology and up to $1,000,000 shall be to carry out section 1820(g)(6) of the Social Security Act, with funds provided for grants under section

DEPARTMENT OF HEALTH AND HUMAN SERVICES

1820(g)(6) available for the purchase and implementation of telehealth services and other efforts to improve health care coordination for rural veterans between rural providers and the Department of Veterans Affairs electronic health record system: Provided further, That notwithstanding section 338J(k) of the PHS Act, $12,500,000 shall be available for State Offices of Rural Health: Provided further, That $12,700,000 shall remain available through September 30, 2025, to support the Rural Residency Development Program.

FAMILY PLANNING

For carrying out the program under title X of the PHS Act to provide for voluntary family planning projects, $400,000,000: Provided, That amounts provided to said projects under such title shall not be expended for abortions, that all pregnancy counseling shall be nondirective, and that such amounts shall not be expended for any activity (including the publication or distribution of literature) that in any way tends to promote public support or opposition to any legislative proposal or candidate for public office.

HRSA-WIDE ACTIVITIES AND PROGRAM SUPPORT

For carrying out title III of the Public Health Service Act and for cross-cutting activities and program support for activities funded in other appropriations included in this Act for the Health Resources and Services Administration, $230,709,000, of which $44,500,000 shall be for expenses necessary for the Office for the Advancement of Telehealth, including grants, contracts, and cooperative agreements for the advancement of telehealth activities: Provided, That funds made available under this heading may be used to supplement program support funding provided under the headings "Primary Health Care", "Health Workforce", "Maternal and Child Health", "Ryan White HIV/AIDS Program", "Health Systems", and "Rural Health".

Note.—A full-year 2022 appropriation for this account was not enacted at the time the Budget was prepared; therefore, the Budget assumes this account is operating under the Continuing Appropriations Act, 2022 (Division A of Public Law 117–43, as amended). The amounts included for 2022 reflect the annualized level provided by the continuing resolution.

Program and Financing (in millions of dollars)

Identification code 075–0350–0–1–550		2021 actual	2022 est.	2023 est.
	Obligations by program activity:			
0005	Primary Health Care (Health Centers, Free Clinics)	1,640	1,684	1,839
0010	Primary Health Care (Mandatory)	11,395	4,013	3,905
0015	Health Workforce	1,317	1,240	1,620
0020	Health Workforce (Mandatory)	920	1,129	412
0025	Maternal and Child Health	972	1,000	1,273
0030	Maternal and Child Health (Mandatory)	21	22	6
0035	Ryan White HIV/AIDS	2,441	2,428	2,655
0040	Health Systems	127	94	94
0045	Rural Health	339	326	374
0050	Family Planning	286	286	400
0051	Family Planning (Mandatory)	2	48	
0055	HRSA Program Management	155	155	169
0056	FQHCs/Rural Health Clinics (Support Act)	6	2	
0057	340B Drug Pricing Program/Office of Pharmacy Affairs		10	17
0058	Telehealth		34	44
0091	Direct program activities, subtotal	19,621	12,471	12,808
0300	Total direct programs	19,621	12,471	12,808
	Credit program obligations:			
0702	Loan guarantee subsidy	1	2	2
0799	Total direct obligations	19,622	12,473	12,810
0801	Health Resources and Services (Reimbursable)	108	101	101
0899	Total reimbursable obligations	108	101	101
0900	Total new obligations, unexpired accounts	19,730	12,574	12,911
	Budgetary resources:			
	Unobligated balance:			
1000	Unobligated balance brought forward, Oct 1	443	1,746	766
1001	Discretionary unobligated balance brought fwd, Oct 1	256	215	
1010	Unobligated balance transfer to other accts [015–5606]	–5	–5	–5
1021	Recoveries of prior year unpaid obligations	59		
1070	Unobligated balance (total)	497	1,741	761
	Budget authority:			
	Appropriations, discretionary:			
1100	Appropriation	7,207	7,207	8,485
1120	Appropriations transferred to other acct [075–1503]	–22		
1160	Appropriation, discretionary (total)	7,185	7,207	8,485
	Appropriations, mandatory:			
1200	Appropriation	4,451	4,443	4,443
1200	Appropriation [American Rescue Plan]	9,280		

		2021 actual	2022 est.	2023 est.
1230	Appropriations and/or unobligated balance of appropriations permanently reduced		–120	–120
1260	Appropriations, mandatory (total)	13,731	4,323	4,323
	Spending authority from offsetting collections, discretionary:			
1700	Collected	22	39	39
1701	Change in uncollected payments, Federal sources	10		
1750	Spending auth from offsetting collections, disc (total)	32	39	39
	Spending authority from offsetting collections, mandatory:			
1800	Offsetting collections (cash)(HPSL&NSL)	32	30	30
1802	Offsetting collections (previously unavailable)	5	2	2
1823	New and/or unobligated balance of spending authority from offsetting collections temporarily reduced	–2	–2	–2
1850	Spending auth from offsetting collections, mand (total)	35	30	30
1900	Budget authority (total)	20,983	11,599	12,877
1930	Total budgetary resources available	21,480	13,340	13,638
	Memorandum (non-add) entries:			
1940	Unobligated balance expiring	–4		
1941	Unexpired unobligated balance, end of year	1,746	766	727
	Change in obligated balance:			
	Unpaid obligations:			
3000	Unpaid obligations, brought forward, Oct 1	10,501	16,456	11,590
3010	New obligations, unexpired accounts	19,730	12,574	12,911
3011	Obligations ("upward adjustments"), expired accounts	24		
3020	Outlays (gross)	–13,665	–17,440	–15,110
3040	Recoveries of prior year unpaid obligations, unexpired	–59		
3041	Recoveries of prior year unpaid obligations, expired	–75		
3050	Unpaid obligations, end of year	16,456	11,590	9,391
	Uncollected payments:			
3060	Uncollected pymts, Fed sources, brought forward, Oct 1	–17	–18	–18
3070	Change in uncollected pymts, Fed sources, unexpired	–10		
3071	Change in uncollected pymts, Fed sources, expired	9		
3090	Uncollected pymts, Fed sources, end of year	–18	–18	–18
	Memorandum (non-add) entries:			
3100	Obligated balance, start of year	10,484	16,438	11,572
3200	Obligated balance, end of year	16,438	11,572	9,373
	Budget authority and outlays, net:			
	Discretionary:			
4000	Budget authority, gross	7,217	7,246	8,524
	Outlays, gross:			
4010	Outlays from new discretionary authority	2,173	2,368	2,772
4011	Outlays from discretionary balances	5,342	5,509	5,567
4020	Outlays, gross (total)	7,515	7,877	8,339
	Offsets against gross budget authority and outlays:			
	Offsetting collections (collected) from:			
4030	Federal sources	–11	–10	–10
4033	Non-Federal sources	–36	–29	–29
4040	Offsets against gross budget authority and outlays (total)	–47	–39	–39
	Additional offsets against gross budget authority only:			
4050	Change in uncollected pymts, Fed sources, unexpired	–10		
4052	Offsetting collections credited to expired accounts	25		
4060	Additional offsets against budget authority only (total)	15		
4070	Budget authority, net (discretionary)	7,185	7,207	8,485
4080	Outlays, net (discretionary)	7,468	7,838	8,300
	Mandatory:			
4090	Budget authority, gross	13,766	4,353	4,353
	Outlays, gross:			
4100	Outlays from new mandatory authority	2,546	1,856	1,856
4101	Outlays from mandatory balances	3,604	7,707	4,915
4110	Outlays, gross (total)	6,150	9,563	6,771
	Offsets against gross budget authority and outlays:			
	Offsetting collections (collected) from:			
4123	Non-Federal sources	–32	–30	–30
4180	Budget authority, net (total)	20,919	11,530	12,808
4190	Outlays, net (total)	13,586	17,371	15,041
	Memorandum (non-add) entries:			
5090	Unexpired unavailable balance, SOY: Offsetting collections	5	2	2
5092	Unexpired unavailable balance, EOY: Offsetting collections	2	2	2
5103	Unexpired unavailable balance, SOY: Fulfilled purpose	1	1	
5104	Unexpired unavailable balance, EOY: Fulfilled purpose	1		

Summary of Loan Levels, Subsidy Budget Authority and Outlays by Program (in millions of dollars)

Identification code 075–0350–0–1–550	2021 actual	2022 est.	2023 est.
Guaranteed loan levels supportable by subsidy budget authority:			
215001 Health centers: Facilities renovation loan guarantee levels	27	72	72

HEALTH RESOURCES AND SERVICES—Continued
Summary of Loan Levels, Subsidy Budget Authority and Outlays by Program—Continued

Identification code 075–0350–0–1–550		2021 actual	2022 est.	2023 est.
215999	Total loan guarantee levels	27	72	72
	Guaranteed loan subsidy (in percent):			
232001	Health centers: Facilities renovation loan guarantee levels	2.78	2.93	2.89
232999	Weighted average subsidy rate	2.78	2.93	2.89
	Guaranteed loan subsidy budget authority:			
233001	Health centers: Facilities renovation loan guarantee levels	1	2	2
233999	Total subsidy budget authority	1	2	2

Resources displayed here support grants and contracts managed by Health Resources and Services Administration (HRSA). These activities include support for Health Centers, treatment and care for those living with HIV/AIDS, health workforce training, maternal and child health care services, promotion of organ and bone marrow donation, rural health activities, and the medical malpractice claims funds, which pay malpractice claims filed against employees of federally-supported health centers and free clinics. HRSA is also responsible for oversight of the 340B Drug Discount Program.

HRSA administers the following revolving loan programs: Health Professions Student Loans (HPSL), Nursing Student Loans (NSL), Primary Care Loans (PCL) and Loans for Disadvantaged Students (LDS). These programs are financed through revolving accounts (Federal Capital Contribution) and do not receive annual appropriations. Through these revolving fund accounts, funds are awarded to institutions that in turn provide loans to individual students. As borrowers pay back loans, the program's revolving account gets replenished, and the collected funds are then used to give out new loans in the following academic years. If the program's revolving account has excess funds that will not be used to provide new loans, these excess funds are returned to HRSA. Funds returned to HRSA are then awarded to programs that are in need of additional funds. The information below reflects Academic Year 2020–2021 data reported in the FY 2021 Annual Operating Report.

Health Professions Revolving Loan Programs

Program	Federal Capital Contribution Account Balance
HPSL	437,467,092
NSL	193,842,531
PCL	155,862,233
LDS	215,701,393
Total	1,002,873,249

Object Classification (in millions of dollars)

Identification code 075–0350–0–1–550		2021 actual	2022 est.	2023 est.
	Direct obligations:			
	Personnel compensation:			
11.1	Full-time permanent	234	240	293
11.3	Other than full-time permanent	6	6	6
11.5	Other personnel compensation	7	8	8
11.7	Military personnel	27	27	28
11.9	Total personnel compensation	274	281	335
12.1	Civilian personnel benefits	85	88	105
12.2	Military personnel benefits	3	3	3
13.0	Benefits for former personnel	2	2	2
23.1	Rental payments to GSA	25	25	25
23.3	Communications, utilities, and miscellaneous charges	6	4	4
25.1	Advisory and assistance services	27	27	31
25.2	Other services from non-Federal sources	337	306	302
25.3	Other goods and services from Federal sources	536	328	308
25.4	Operation and maintenance of facilities	1	1	1
25.6	Medical care	3	3	2
25.7	Operation and maintenance of equipment	4	4	4
26.0	Supplies and materials	1	1	1
31.0	Equipment	13	13	13
41.0	Grants, subsidies, and contributions	18,232	11,279	11,565
42.0	Insurance claims and indemnities	73	108	108
99.0	Direct obligations	19,622	12,473	12,809
99.0	Reimbursable obligations	108	101	102
99.9	Total new obligations, unexpired accounts	19,730	12,574	12,911

Employment Summary

Identification code 075–0350–0–1–550		2021 actual	2022 est.	2023 est.
1001	Direct civilian full-time equivalent employment	2,022	2,022	2,561
1101	Direct military average strength employment	170	170	171
2001	Reimbursable civilian full-time equivalent employment	56	56	56
2101	Reimbursable military average strength employment	3	3	3

VACCINE INJURY COMPENSATION

Program and Financing (in millions of dollars)

Identification code 075–0320–0–1–551		2021 actual	2022 est.	2023 est.
	Budgetary resources:			
	Unobligated balance:			
1000	Unobligated balance brought forward, Oct 1	35	36	36
1033	Recoveries of prior year paid obligations	1		
1070	Unobligated balance (total)	36	36	36
1930	Total budgetary resources available	36	36	36
	Memorandum (non-add) entries:			
1941	Unexpired unobligated balance, end of year	36	36	36
	Budget authority and outlays, net:			
	Mandatory:			
	Offsets against gross budget authority and outlays:			
	Offsetting collections (collected) from:			
4123	Non-Federal sources	–1		
	Additional offsets against gross budget authority only:			
4143	Recoveries of prior year paid obligations, unexpired accounts	1		
4170	Outlays, net (mandatory)	–1		
4180	Budget authority, net (total)			
4190	Outlays, net (total)	–1		

The Vaccine Injury Compensation Program was established pursuant to Public Law 99–660 and Public Law 100–203 and serves as a source of funds to pay claims for compensation for vaccine related injury or death. Payment of claims associated with vaccine related injury or death occurring before October 1, 1988, are financed from the General Fund and are reflected in this account. Given sufficient carry-over funds from prior years' appropriations to pay for the balance of the pre–1988 claims yet to be adjudicated, no appropriation is requested to cover payment of pre–1988 claims. By statute, no new claims are accepted for this account. Payment of claims associated with vaccine related injury or death occurring after October 1, 1988, are reflected in the Vaccine Injury Compensation Program trust fund account.

COVERED COUNTERMEASURE PROCESS FUND

For carrying out section 319F–4 of the PHS Act, $15,000,000, to remain available until expended.

Note.—A full-year 2022 appropriation for this account was not enacted at the time the Budget was prepared; therefore, the Budget assumes this account is operating under the Continuing Appropriations Act, 2022 (Division A of Public Law 117–43, as amended). The amounts included for 2022 reflect the annualized level provided by the continuing resolution.

Program and Financing (in millions of dollars)

Identification code 075–0343–0–1–551		2021 actual	2022 est.	2023 est.
	Obligations by program activity:			
0001	Claims		5	6
0103	Admin Expense	3	4	9
0900	Total new obligations, unexpired accounts	3	9	15

DEPARTMENT OF HEALTH AND HUMAN SERVICES

Budgetary resources:
Unobligated balance:

		2021 actual	2022 est.	2023 est.
1000	Unobligated balance brought forward, Oct 1	1	2	
1011	Unobligated balance transfer from other acct [075–0140]	4	7	
1070	Unobligated balance (total)	5	9	

Budget authority:
Appropriations, discretionary:

1100	Appropriation			15
1930	Total budgetary resources available	5	9	15

Memorandum (non-add) entries:

1941	Unexpired unobligated balance, end of year	2		

Change in obligated balance:
Unpaid obligations:

3000	Unpaid obligations, brought forward, Oct 1	1	2	9
3010	New obligations, unexpired accounts	3	9	15
3020	Outlays (gross)	–2	–2	–11
3050	Unpaid obligations, end of year	2	9	13

Memorandum (non-add) entries:

3100	Obligated balance, start of year	1	2	9
3200	Obligated balance, end of year	2	9	13

Budget authority and outlays, net:
Discretionary:

4000	Budget authority, gross			15

Outlays, gross:

4010	Outlays from new discretionary authority			11
4011	Outlays from discretionary balances	2	2	
4020	Outlays, gross (total)	2	2	11
4180	Budget authority, net (total)			15
4190	Outlays, net (total)	2	2	11

The Covered Countermeasure Process Fund is established pursuant to the Public Health Service (PHS) Act, as amended by Division C of Public Law 109–148, to serve as a source of funds to pay for compensation for injuries, illnesses or death, or losses resulting from the administration to or use by an individual of a covered countermeasure for which a Secretarial Declaration has been issued, pursuant to section 319F-3(b) of the PHS Act. Additionally, authority is provided to address any unexpected claims that may arise under the Smallpox Emergency Personnel Protection Act of 2003 (P.L. 108–20).

Object Classification (in millions of dollars)

Identification code 075–0343–0–1–551		2021 actual	2022 est.	2023 est.
	Direct obligations:			
11.1	Personnel compensation: Full-time permanent			4
25.2	Other services from non-Federal sources	2	2	
42.0	Insurance claims and indemnities		6	11
99.0	Direct obligations	2	8	15
99.5	Adjustment for rounding	1	1	
99.9	Total new obligations, unexpired accounts	3	9	15

Employment Summary

Identification code 075–0343–0–1–551		2021 actual	2022 est.	2023 est.
1001	Direct civilian full-time equivalent employment	2	2	36
1101	Direct military average strength employment	2	2	6

MATERNAL, INFANT, AND EARLY CHILDHOOD HOME VISITING PROGRAMS

Program and Financing (in millions of dollars)

Identification code 075–0321–0–1–551		2021 actual	2022 est.	2023 est.
	Obligations by program activity:			
0010	Maternal, Infant, and Early Childhood Home Visiting Programs	441	504	
	Budgetary resources:			
	Unobligated balance:			
1000	Unobligated balance brought forward, Oct 1	24	127	
1021	Recoveries of prior year unpaid obligations	17		

Health Resources and Services Administration—Continued
Federal Funds—Continued

431

		2021 actual	2022 est.	2023 est.
1070	Unobligated balance (total)	41	127	

Budget authority:
Appropriations, mandatory:

1200	Appropriation	400	400	
1200	Appropriation [American Rescue Plan]	150		
1230	Appropriations and/or unobligated balance of appropriations permanently reduced	–23	–23	
1260	Appropriations, mandatory (total)	527	377	
1930	Total budgetary resources available	568	504	

Memorandum (non-add) entries:

1941	Unexpired unobligated balance, end of year	127		

Change in obligated balance:
Unpaid obligations:

3000	Unpaid obligations, brought forward, Oct 1	747	801	859
3010	New obligations, unexpired accounts	441	504	
3020	Outlays (gross)	–370	–446	–450
3040	Recoveries of prior year unpaid obligations, unexpired	–17		
3050	Unpaid obligations, end of year	801	859	409

Memorandum (non-add) entries:

3100	Obligated balance, start of year	747	801	859
3200	Obligated balance, end of year	801	859	409

Budget authority and outlays, net:
Mandatory:

4090	Budget authority, gross	527	377	

Outlays, gross:

4100	Outlays from new mandatory authority	11	9	
4101	Outlays from mandatory balances	359	437	450
4110	Outlays, gross (total)	370	446	450
4180	Budget authority, net (total)	527	377	
4190	Outlays, net (total)	370	446	450

Summary of Budget Authority and Outlays (in millions of dollars)

	2021 actual	2022 est.	2023 est.
Enacted/requested:			
Budget Authority	527	377	
Outlays	370	446	450
Legislative proposal, subject to PAYGO:			
Budget Authority			467
Outlays			19
Total:			
Budget Authority	527	377	467
Outlays	370	446	469

The Maternal, Infant and Early Childhood Home Visiting Program provides comprehensive services for at risk communities. These activities are administered by HRSA.

Object Classification (in millions of dollars)

Identification code 075–0321–0–1–551		2021 actual	2022 est.	2023 est.
11.1	Direct obligations: Personnel compensation: Full-time permanent	5	5	
11.9	Total personnel compensation	5	5	
12.1	Civilian personnel benefits	2	2	
25.1	Advisory and assistance services	30	30	
41.0	Grants, subsidies, and contributions	404	467	
99.9	Total new obligations, unexpired accounts	441	504	

Employment Summary

Identification code 075–0321–0–1–551		2021 actual	2022 est.	2023 est.
1001	Direct civilian full-time equivalent employment	38	38	
1101	Direct military average strength employment	3	3	

MATERNAL, INFANT, AND EARLY CHILDHOOD HOME VISITING PROGRAMS—Continued
MATERNAL, INFANT, AND EARLY CHILDHOOD HOME VISITING PROGRAMS
(Legislative proposal, subject to PAYGO)

Program and Financing (in millions of dollars)

Identification code 075–0321–4–1–551	2021 actual	2022 est.	2023 est.
Obligations by program activity:			
0010 Maternal, Infant, and Early Childhood Home Visiting Programs			467
Budgetary resources:			
Budget authority:			
Appropriations, mandatory:			
1200 Appropriation			467
1930 Total budgetary resources available			467
Change in obligated balance:			
Unpaid obligations:			
3010 New obligations, unexpired accounts			467
3020 Outlays (gross)			–19
3050 Unpaid obligations, end of year			448
Memorandum (non-add) entries:			
3200 Obligated balance, end of year			448
Budget authority and outlays, net:			
Mandatory:			
4090 Budget authority, gross			467
Outlays, gross:			
4100 Outlays from new mandatory authority			19
4180 Budget authority, net (total)			467
4190 Outlays, net (total)			19

The Budget extends for five years and increases funding for the Maternal, Infant, and Early Childhood Home Visiting (MIECHV) Program.

Object Classification (in millions of dollars)

Identification code 075–0321–4–1–551	2021 actual	2022 est.	2023 est.
11.1 Direct obligations: Personnel compensation: Full-time permanent			5
11.9 Total personnel compensation			5
12.1 Civilian personnel benefits			2
25.1 Advisory and assistance services			30
41.0 Grants, subsidies, and contributions			430
99.9 Total new obligations, unexpired accounts			467

Employment Summary

Identification code 075–0321–4–1–551	2021 actual	2022 est.	2023 est.
1001 Direct civilian full-time equivalent employment			52
1101 Direct military average strength employment			3

HEALTH CENTER GUARANTEED LOAN FINANCING ACCOUNT

Program and Financing (in millions of dollars)

Identification code 075–4442–0–3–551	2021 actual	2022 est.	2023 est.
Budgetary resources:			
Unobligated balance:			
1000 Unobligated balance brought forward, Oct 1	1	2	2
Financing authority:			
Spending authority from offsetting collections, mandatory:			
1800 Collected	1		
1930 Total budgetary resources available	2	2	2
Memorandum (non-add) entries:			
1941 Unexpired unobligated balance, end of year	2	2	2
Financing authority and disbursements, net:			
Mandatory:			
4090 Budget authority, gross	1		
Offsets against gross financing authority and disbursements:			
Offsetting collections (collected) from:			
4122 Interest on uninvested funds	–1		
4180 Budget authority, net (total)			
4190 Outlays, net (total)	–1		

Status of Guaranteed Loans (in millions of dollars)

Identification code 075–4442–0–3–551	2021 actual	2022 est.	2023 est.
Position with respect to appropriations act limitation on commitments:			
2111 Guaranteed loan commitments from current-year authority			
2121 Limitation available from carry-forward	886	859	787
2143 Uncommitted limitation carried forward	–859	–787	–715
2150 Total guaranteed loan commitments	27	72	72
2199 Guaranteed amount of guaranteed loan commitments	21	58	58
Cumulative balance of guaranteed loans outstanding:			
2210 Outstanding, start of year	27	51	112
2231 Disbursements of new guaranteed loans	27	72	72
2251 Repayments and prepayments	–3	–10	–10
Adjustments:			
2263 Terminations for default that result in claim payments		–1	
2264 Other adjustments, net			
2290 Outstanding, end of year	51	112	174
Memorandum:			
2299 Guaranteed amount of guaranteed loans outstanding, end of year	39	87	137

Public Law 104–299, Public Law 104–208, and Public Law 115–141 authorize Health Resources and Services Administration (HRSA) to guarantee up to $1 billion in private loans to health centers for the costs of developing and operating managed care networks or plans and for the construction, renovation, and modernization of medical facilities. The program account for this activity is displayed in the Health Resources and Services account (75–0350) as a line in the program and financing schedule.

Balance Sheet (in millions of dollars)

Identification code 075–4442–0–3–551	2020 actual	2021 actual
ASSETS:		
1101 Federal assets: Fund balances with Treasury	1	1
1999 Total assets	1	1
LIABILITIES:		
2204 Non-Federal liabilities: Liabilities for loan guarantees	1	1
NET POSITION:		
3300 Cumulative results of operations		
4999 Total liabilities and net position	1	1

MEDICAL FACILITIES GUARANTEE AND LOAN FUND

Status of Direct Loans (in millions of dollars)

Identification code 075–9931–0–3–551	2021 actual	2022 est.	2023 est.
Cumulative balance of direct loans outstanding:			
1210 Outstanding, start of year	5	5	5
1290 Outstanding, end of year	5	5	5

Titles VI and XVI of the PHS Act established a loan and loan guarantee fund for medical facilities with a maximum amount allowable for the Government's liability. Direct loans were made available for public facilities and guaranteed loans for private, nonprofit facilities. Funds under this authority were established in the amount of $50 million for use in fulfilling guarantees in the event of default, $30 million as a revolving fund for direct loans, and an amount for interest subsidy payments on guaranteed loans.

Balance Sheet (in millions of dollars)

Identification code 075–9931–0–3–551	2020 actual	2021 actual
ASSETS:		
1601 Direct loans, gross	5	5
1999 Total assets	5	5

DEPARTMENT OF HEALTH AND HUMAN SERVICES

LIABILITIES:

2201	Non-Federal liabilities: Accounts payable		5	5
	NET POSITION:			
3100	Unexpended appropriations			
3300	Cumulative results of operations			
3999	Total net position			
4999	Total liabilities and net position		5	5

Trust Funds

VACCINE INJURY COMPENSATION PROGRAM TRUST FUND

For payments from the Vaccine Injury Compensation Program Trust Fund (the "Trust Fund"), such sums as may be necessary for claims associated with vaccine-related injury or death with respect to vaccines administered after September 30, 1988, pursuant to subtitle 2 of title XXI of the PHS Act, to remain available until expended: Provided, That for necessary administrative expenses, not to exceed $26,200,000 shall be available from the Trust Fund to the Secretary.

Note.—A full-year 2022 appropriation for this account was not enacted at the time the Budget was prepared; therefore, the Budget assumes this account is operating under the Continuing Appropriations Act, 2022 (Division A of Public Law 117–43, as amended). The amounts included for 2022 reflect the annualized level provided by the continuing resolution.

Special and Trust Fund Receipts (in millions of dollars)

Identification code 075–8175–0–7–551		2021 actual	2022 est.	2023 est.
0100	Balance, start of year	3,965	4,060	4,202
	Receipts:			
	Current law:			
1110	Deposits, Vaccine Injury Compensation Trust Fund	313	329	326
1140	Interest and Profits on Investments, Vaccine Injury Compensation Trust Fund	59	102	117
1199	Total current law receipts	372	431	443
1999	Total receipts	372	431	443
2000	Total: Balances and receipts	4,337	4,491	4,645
	Appropriations:			
	Current law:			
2101	Vaccine Injury Compensation Program Trust Fund	–38	–38	–68
2101	Vaccine Injury Compensation Program Trust Fund	–334	–251	–256
2135	Vaccine Injury Compensation Program Trust Fund	85		
2199	Total current law appropriations	–287	–289	–324
2999	Total appropriations	–287	–289	–324
4030	Vaccine Injury Compensation Program Trust Fund	10		
5099	Balance, end of year	4,060	4,202	4,321

Program and Financing (in millions of dollars)

Identification code 075–8175–0–7–551		2021 actual	2022 est.	2023 est.
	Obligations by program activity:			
0001	Compensation: Claims for post - FY 1989 injuries	249	251	256
0103	Claims processing (Claims Court)	10	10	10
0104	Claims processing (HRSA)	11	11	26
0105	Claims processing (Dept. of Justice)	17	17	32
0191	Direct program activities, subtotal	38	38	68
0900	Total new obligations, unexpired accounts	287	289	324
	Budgetary resources:			
	Unobligated balance:			
1021	Recoveries of prior year unpaid obligations	2		
1033	Recoveries of prior year paid obligations	8		
1035	Unobligated balance of appropriations withdrawn	–10		
	Budget authority:			
	Appropriations, discretionary:			
1101	Appropriation (special or trust)	38	38	68
	Appropriations, mandatory:			
1201	Appropriation (special or trust fund)	334	251	256
1235	Appropriations precluded from obligation (special or trust)	–85		
1260	Appropriations, mandatory (total)	249	251	256
1900	Budget authority (total)	287	289	324
1930	Total budgetary resources available	287	289	324

Identification code 075–8175–0–7–551		2021 actual	2022 est.	2023 est.
	Change in obligated balance:			
	Unpaid obligations:			
3000	Unpaid obligations, brought forward, Oct 1	18	20	1
3010	New obligations, unexpired accounts	287	289	324
3020	Outlays (gross)	–283	–308	–324
3040	Recoveries of prior year unpaid obligations, unexpired	–2		
3050	Unpaid obligations, end of year	20	1	1
	Memorandum (non-add) entries:			
3100	Obligated balance, start of year	18	20	1
3200	Obligated balance, end of year	20	1	1
	Budget authority and outlays, net:			
	Discretionary:			
4000	Budget authority, gross	38	38	68
	Outlays, gross:			
4010	Outlays from new discretionary authority	28	38	68
4011	Outlays from discretionary balances	9	9	
4020	Outlays, gross (total)	37	47	68
	Mandatory:			
4090	Budget authority, gross	249	251	256
	Outlays, gross:			
4100	Outlays from new mandatory authority	246	251	256
4101	Outlays from mandatory balances		10	
4110	Outlays, gross (total)	246	261	256
	Offsets against gross budget authority and outlays:			
	Offsetting collections (collected) from:			
4123	Non-Federal sources	–8		
	Additional offsets against gross budget authority only:			
4143	Recoveries of prior year paid obligations, unexpired accounts	8		
4160	Budget authority, net (mandatory)	249	251	256
4170	Outlays, net (mandatory)	238	261	256
4180	Budget authority, net (total)	287	289	324
4190	Outlays, net (total)	275	308	324
	Memorandum (non-add) entries:			
5000	Total investments, SOY: Federal securities: Par value	3,967	4,054	4,234
5001	Total investments, EOY: Federal securities: Par value	4,054	4,234	4,421

The Vaccine Injury Compensation Program was established pursuant to Public Law 99–660 and Public Law 100–203 and serves as a source of funds to pay claims for compensation for vaccine-related injury or death. This account reflects payments for claims for vaccine-related injury or death occurring after October 1, 1988.

Object Classification (in millions of dollars)

Identification code 075–8175–0–7–551		2021 actual	2022 est.	2023 est.
	Direct obligations:			
11.1	Personnel compensation: Full-time permanent	2	2	4
12.1	Civilian personnel benefits	1	1	1
25.3	Other goods and services from Federal sources	7	7	7
42.0	Insurance claims and indemnities	277	279	312
99.9	Total new obligations, unexpired accounts	287	289	324

Employment Summary

Identification code 075–8175–0–7–551		2021 actual	2022 est.	2023 est.
1001	Direct civilian full-time equivalent employment	14	14	26
1101	Direct military average strength employment	5	5	6

INDIAN HEALTH SERVICE

Federal Funds

INDIAN HEALTH SERVICES

Note.—A full-year 2022 appropriation for this account was not enacted at the time the Budget was prepared; therefore, the Budget assumes this account is operating under the Continuing Appropriations Act, 2022 (Division A of Public Law 117–43, as amended). The amounts included for 2022 reflect the annualized level provided by the continuing resolution.

Indian Health Services—Continued

Program and Financing (in millions of dollars)

Identification code 075–0390–0–1–551	2021 actual	2022 est.	2023 est.
Obligations by program activity:			
0001 Clinical services	7,826	6,225	6,225
0002 Preventive health	326	235	235
0003 Urban health	57	76	76
0004 Indian health professions	60	80	80
0005 Tribal management	1	1	1
0006 Direct operations	153	54	54
0007 Self-governance	6	6	6
0009 Diabetes funds	137	150	150
0799 Total direct obligations	8,566	6,827	6,827
0801 Indian Health Services (Reimbursable)	1,893	1,860	1,860
0900 Total new obligations, unexpired accounts	10,459	8,687	8,687
Budgetary resources:			
Unobligated balance:			
1000 Unobligated balance brought forward, Oct 1	2,109	4,753	2,126
1001 Discretionary unobligated balance brought fwd, Oct 1	2,064		
1021 Recoveries of prior year unpaid obligations	285		
1070 Unobligated balance (total)	2,394	4,753	2,126
Budget authority:			
Appropriations, discretionary:			
1100 Appropriation	4,301	4,346	6,262
1121 Appropriations transferred from other acct [075–0943]	210		
1121 Appropriations transferred from other acct [075–0140]	790		
1160 Appropriation, discretionary (total)	5,301	4,346	6,262
Appropriations, mandatory:			
1200 Appropriation (Diabetes)	150	150	150
1200 Appropriation (American Rescue Plan)	5,494		
1230 Appropriations and/or unobligated balance of appropriations permanently reduced		−3	−3
1260 Appropriations, mandatory (total)	5,644	147	147
Spending authority from offsetting collections, discretionary:			
1700 Collected	1,884	1,567	1,868
1701 Change in uncollected payments, Federal sources	7		
1750 Spending auth from offsetting collections, disc (total)	1,891	1,567	1,868
1900 Budget authority (total)	12,836	6,060	8,277
1930 Total budgetary resources available	15,230	10,813	10,403
Memorandum (non-add) entries:			
1940 Unobligated balance expiring	−18		
1941 Unexpired unobligated balance, end of year	4,753	2,126	1,716
Change in obligated balance:			
Unpaid obligations:			
3000 Unpaid obligations, brought forward, Oct 1	1,384	1,758	1,299
3010 New obligations, unexpired accounts	10,459	8,687	8,687
3011 Obligations ("upward adjustments"), expired accounts	21		
3020 Outlays (gross)	−9,812	−9,146	−8,179
3040 Recoveries of prior year unpaid obligations, unexpired	−285		
3041 Recoveries of prior year unpaid obligations, expired	−9		
3050 Unpaid obligations, end of year	1,758	1,299	1,807
Uncollected payments:			
3060 Uncollected pymts, Fed sources, brought forward, Oct 1	−106	−113	−113
3070 Change in uncollected pymts, Fed sources, unexpired	−7		
3090 Uncollected pymts, Fed sources, end of year	−113	−113	−113
Memorandum (non-add) entries:			
3100 Obligated balance, start of year	1,278	1,645	1,186
3200 Obligated balance, end of year	1,645	1,186	1,694
Budget authority and outlays, net:			
Discretionary:			
4000 Budget authority, gross	7,192	5,913	8,130
Outlays, gross:			
4010 Outlays from new discretionary authority	5,086	5,478	7,504
4011 Outlays from discretionary balances	1,521	774	522
4020 Outlays, gross (total)	6,607	6,252	8,026
Offsets against gross budget authority and outlays:			
Offsetting collections (collected) from:			
4030 Federal sources	−259	−299	−436
4033 Non-Federal sources	−1,627	−1,268	−1,432
4040 Offsets against gross budget authority and outlays (total)	−1,886	−1,567	−1,868
Additional offsets against gross budget authority only:			
4050 Change in uncollected pymts, Fed sources, unexpired	−7		
4052 Offsetting collections credited to expired accounts	2		
4060 Additional offsets against budget authority only (total)	−5		
4070 Budget authority, net (discretionary)	5,301	4,346	6,262
4080 Outlays, net (discretionary)	4,721	4,685	6,158
Mandatory:			
4090 Budget authority, gross	5,644	147	147
Outlays, gross:			
4100 Outlays from new mandatory authority	3,103	141	141
4101 Outlays from mandatory balances	102	2,753	12
4110 Outlays, gross (total)	3,205	2,894	153
4180 Budget authority, net (total)	10,945	4,493	6,409
4190 Outlays, net (total)	7,926	7,579	6,311

The Indian Health Services account provides medical care, public health services, and health professions training opportunities to American Indians and Alaska Natives. The Budget proposes to shift the four IHS accounts from discretionary to mandatory.

Object Classification (in millions of dollars)

Identification code 075–0390–0–1–551	2021 actual	2022 est.	2023 est.
Direct obligations:			
Personnel compensation:			
11.1 Full-time permanent	422	336	336
11.3 Other than full-time permanent	18	14	14
11.5 Other personnel compensation	97	77	77
11.7 Military personnel	63	50	50
11.9 Total personnel compensation	600	477	477
12.1 Civilian personnel benefits	181	144	144
12.2 Military personnel benefits	13	10	10
13.0 Benefits for former personnel	13	10	10
21.0 Travel and transportation of persons	5	4	4
21.0 Patient travel	59	47	47
22.0 Transportation of things	11	9	9
23.1 Rental payments to GSA	29	23	23
23.2 Rental payments to others	16	13	13
23.3 Communications, utilities, and miscellaneous charges	31	25	25
25.1 Advisory and assistance services	9	7	7
25.2 Other services from non-Federal sources	311	248	248
25.3 Other goods and services from Federal sources	194	155	155
25.4 Operation and maintenance of facilities	4	3	3
25.6 Medical care	790	634	634
25.8 Subsistence and support of persons	115	92	92
26.0 Supplies and materials	180	143	143
31.0 Equipment	44	35	35
32.0 Land and structures	24	19	19
41.0 Grants, subsidies, and contributions	5,936	4,728	4,728
42.0 Insurance claims and indemnities	1	1	1
99.0 Direct obligations	8,566	6,827	6,827
99.0 Reimbursable obligations	1,893	1,860	1,860
99.9 Total new obligations, unexpired accounts	10,459	8,687	8,687

Employment Summary

Identification code 075–0390–0–1–551	2021 actual	2022 est.	2023 est.
1001 Direct civilian full-time equivalent employment	6,797	6,761	6,900
1101 Direct military average strength employment	732	721	736
2001 Reimbursable civilian full-time equivalent employment	6,146	6,114	6,239
2101 Reimbursable military average strength employment	661	651	665

INDIAN HEALTH SERVICES

(Legislative proposal, not subject to PAYGO)

Program and Financing (in millions of dollars)

Identification code 075–0390–2–1–551	2021 actual	2022 est.	2023 est.
Budgetary resources:			
Budget authority:			
Appropriations, discretionary:			
1100 Appropriation			−6,262
Appropriations, mandatory:			
1200 Appropriation			6,262
Budget authority and outlays, net:			
Discretionary:			
4000 Budget authority, gross			−6,262
Outlays, gross:			
4010 Outlays from new discretionary authority			−5,636

/ DEPARTMENT OF HEALTH AND HUMAN SERVICES

		2021 actual	2022 est.	2023 est.
	Mandatory:			
4090	Budget authority, gross			6,262
	Outlays, gross:			
4100	Outlays from new mandatory authority			5,636
4180	Budget authority, net (total)			
4190	Outlays, net (total)			

CONTRACT SUPPORT COSTS

Note.—A full-year 2022 appropriation for this account was not enacted at the time the Budget was prepared; therefore, the Budget assumes this account is operating under the Continuing Appropriations Act, 2022 (Division A of Public Law 117–43, as amended). The amounts included for 2022 reflect the annualized level provided by the continuing resolution.

Program and Financing (in millions of dollars)

Identification code 075–0344–0–1–551	2021 actual	2022 est.	2023 est.
Obligations by program activity:			
0001 Contract Support Costs	1,182	1,142	1,142
Budgetary resources:			
Budget authority:			
Appropriations, discretionary:			
1100 Appropriation	1,182	1,142	1,142
1900 Budget authority (total)	1,182	1,142	1,142
1930 Total budgetary resources available	1,182	1,142	1,142
Change in obligated balance:			
Unpaid obligations:			
3000 Unpaid obligations, brought forward, Oct 1	130	321	
3010 New obligations, unexpired accounts	1,182	1,142	1,142
3011 Obligations ("upward adjustments"), expired accounts	79		
3020 Outlays (gross)	–1,033	–1,463	–1,142
3041 Recoveries of prior year unpaid obligations, expired	–37		
3050 Unpaid obligations, end of year	321		
Memorandum (non-add) entries:			
3100 Obligated balance, start of year	130	321	
3200 Obligated balance, end of year	321		
Budget authority and outlays, net:			
Discretionary:			
4000 Budget authority, gross	1,182	1,142	1,142
Outlays, gross:			
4010 Outlays from new discretionary authority	956	1,142	1,142
4011 Outlays from discretionary balances	77	321	
4020 Outlays, gross (total)	1,033	1,463	1,142
4180 Budget authority, net (total)	1,182	1,142	1,142
4190 Outlays, net (total)	1,033	1,463	1,142

The Contract Support Costs account provides for the reasonable and allowable costs for direct program expenses for the operation of, and any additional administrative or other expense related to, the overhead incurred by tribes and tribal organizations who operate health programs through self-determination contracts and compacts. The Budget proposes to shift the four IHS accounts from discretionary to mandatory.

Object Classification (in millions of dollars)

Identification code 075–0344–0–1–551	2021 actual	2022 est.	2023 est.
Direct obligations:			
25.3 Other goods and services from Federal sources	266	251	257
41.0 Grants, subsidies, and contributions	916	891	885
99.9 Total new obligations, unexpired accounts	1,182	1,142	1,142

CONTRACT SUPPORT COSTS

(Legislative proposal, not subject to PAYGO)

Program and Financing (in millions of dollars)

Identification code 075–0344–2–1–551	2021 actual	2022 est.	2023 est.
Budgetary resources:			
Budget authority:			
Appropriations, discretionary:			
1100 Appropriation			–1,142
Appropriations, mandatory:			
1200 Appropriation			1,142
Budget authority and outlays, net:			
Discretionary:			
4000 Budget authority, gross			–1,142
Outlays, gross:			
4010 Outlays from new discretionary authority			–1,142
Mandatory:			
4090 Budget authority, gross			1,142
Outlays, gross:			
4100 Outlays from new mandatory authority			1,142
4180 Budget authority, net (total)			
4190 Outlays, net (total)			

PAYMENTS FOR TRIBAL LEASES

Note.—A full-year 2022 appropriation for this account was not enacted at the time the Budget was prepared; therefore, the Budget assumes this account is operating under the Continuing Appropriations Act, 2022 (Division A of Public Law 117–43, as amended). The amounts included for 2022 reflect the annualized level provided by the continuing resolution.

Program and Financing (in millions of dollars)

Identification code 075–0200–0–1–551	2021 actual	2022 est.	2023 est.
Obligations by program activity:			
0001 Payments for Tribal Leases	123	150	150
0900 Total new obligations, unexpired accounts (object class 41.0)	123	150	150
Budgetary resources:			
Unobligated balance:			
1000 Unobligated balance brought forward, Oct 1		16	16
Budget authority:			
Appropriations, discretionary:			
1100 Appropriation	139	150	150
1930 Total budgetary resources available	139	166	166
Memorandum (non-add) entries:			
1941 Unexpired unobligated balance, end of year	16	16	16
Change in obligated balance:			
Unpaid obligations:			
3000 Unpaid obligations, brought forward, Oct 1		13	
3010 New obligations, unexpired accounts	123	150	150
3020 Outlays (gross)	–110	–163	–150
3050 Unpaid obligations, end of year	13		
Memorandum (non-add) entries:			
3100 Obligated balance, start of year		13	
3200 Obligated balance, end of year	13		
Budget authority and outlays, net:			
Discretionary:			
4000 Budget authority, gross	139	150	150
Outlays, gross:			
4010 Outlays from new discretionary authority	110	150	150
4011 Outlays from discretionary balances		13	
4020 Outlays, gross (total)	110	163	150
4180 Budget authority, net (total)	139	150	150
4190 Outlays, net (total)	110	163	150

The Payments for Tribal Leases account provides for the reasonable and allowable costs for leases with a Tribe or tribal organization for a building owned or leased by the tribe or tribal organization that is used for administration or delivery of services under the Indian Self-Determination and Education Assistance Act. The Budget proposes to shift the four IHS accounts from discretionary to mandatory.

PAYMENTS FOR TRIBAL LEASES—Continued

PAYMENTS FOR TRIBAL LEASES

(Legislative proposal, not subject to PAYGO)

Program and Financing (in millions of dollars)

Identification code 075–0200–2–1–551	2021 actual	2022 est.	2023 est.
Budgetary resources:			
Budget authority:			
Appropriations, discretionary:			
1100 .... Appropriation			–150
Appropriations, mandatory:			
1200 .... Appropriation			150
Budget authority and outlays, net:			
Discretionary:			
4000 .... Budget authority, gross			–150
Outlays, gross:			
4010 .... Outlays from new discretionary authority			–150
Mandatory:			
4090 .... Budget authority, gross			150
Outlays, gross:			
4100 .... Outlays from new mandatory authority			150
4180 .... Budget authority, net (total)			
4190 .... Outlays, net (total)			

INDIAN HEALTH FACILITIES

Note.—A full-year 2022 appropriation for this account was not enacted at the time the Budget was prepared; therefore, the Budget assumes this account is operating under the Continuing Appropriations Act, 2022 (Division A of Public Law 117–43, as amended). The amounts included for 2022 reflect the annualized level provided by the continuing resolution.

INDIAN HEALTH FACILITIES

(INCLUDING TRANSFERS OF FUNDS)

[For an additional amount for "Indian Health Facilities", $3,500,000,000, to remain available until expended, for the provision of domestic and community sanitation facilities for Indians, as authorized by section 7 of the Act of August 5, 1954 (68 Stat. 674): *Provided*, That $700,000,000, to remain available until expended, shall be made available for fiscal year 2022, $700,000,000, to remain available until expended, shall be made available for fiscal year 2023, $700,000,000, to remain available until expended, shall be made available for fiscal year 2024, $700,000,000, to remain available until expended, shall be made available for fiscal year 2025, and $700,000,000, to remain available until expended, shall be made available for fiscal year 2026: *Provided further*, That of the amounts made available under this heading, up to $2,200,000,000 shall be for projects that exceed the economical unit cost and shall be available until expended: *Provided further*, That up to three percent of the amounts made available in each fiscal year shall be for salaries, expenses, and administration: *Provided further*, That one-half of one percent of the amounts made available under this heading in this Act in each fiscal years 2022 through 2026 shall be transferred to the Office of Inspector General of the Department of Health and Human Services for oversight of funding provided to the Department of Health and Human Services in this title in this Act: *Provided further*, That no funds available to the Indian Health Service for salaries, expenses, administration, and oversight shall be available for contracts, grants, compacts, or cooperative agreements under the provisions of the Indian Self-Determination and Education Assistance Act as amended: *Provided further*, That funds under this heading made available to Tribes and Tribal organizations under the Indian Self-Determination and Education Assistance Act (25 U.S.C. 5301 et seq.) shall be available on a one-time basis, are nonrecurring, and shall not be part of the amount required by section 106 of the Indian Self-Determination and Education Assistance Act (25 U.S.C. 5325), and shall only be used for the purposes identified in this heading: *Provided further*, That not later than 90 days after the date of enactment of this Act, the Secretary of Health and Human Services shall submit to the House and Senate Committees on Appropriations a detailed spend plan for fiscal year 2022: *Provided further*, That for each fiscal year through 2026, as part of the annual budget submission of the President under section 1105(a) of title 31, United States Code, the Secretary of Health and Human Services shall submit a detailed spend plan for that fiscal year: *Provided further*, That such amount is designated by the Congress as being for an emergency requirement pursuant to section 4112(a) of H. Con. Res. 71 (115th Congress), the concurrent resolution on the budget for fiscal year 2018, and to section 251(b) of the Balanced Budget and Emergency Deficit Control Act of 1985.] *(Infrastructure Investments and Jobs Appropriations Act.)*

Special and Trust Fund Receipts (in millions of dollars)

Identification code 075–0391–0–1–551	2021 actual	2022 est.	2023 est.
0100 Balance, start of year			
Receipts:			
Current law:			
1130 .... Rent and Charges for Quarters, Indian Health Service	10	9	9
2000 Total: Balances and receipts	10	9	9
Appropriations:			
Current law:			
2101 .... Indian Health Facilities	–10	–9	–9
5099 Balance, end of year			

Program and Financing (in millions of dollars)

Identification code 075–0391–0–1–551	2021 actual	2022 est.	2023 est.
Obligations by program activity:			
0001 Maintenance	190	168	168
0002 Sanitation Facilities Construction	219	193	193
0003 Facilities and environmental health	293	259	259
0004 Equipment	27	24	24
0005 Health Care Facilities Construction	142	125	125
0100 Total direct program	871	769	769
0799 Total direct obligations	871	769	769
0801 Indian Health Facilities (Reimbursable)	105	57	57
0900 Total new obligations, unexpired accounts	976	826	826
Budgetary resources:			
Unobligated balance:			
1000 Unobligated balance brought forward, Oct 1	944	1,620	2,481
1001 Discretionary unobligated balance brought fwd, Oct 1	931		
1021 Recoveries of prior year unpaid obligations	32		
1070 Unobligated balance (total)	976	1,620	2,481
Budget authority:			
Appropriations, discretionary:			
1100 .... Appropriation	918	1,619	1,567
Advance appropriations, discretionary:			
1170 .... Advance appropriation			696
Appropriations, mandatory:			
1200 .... Appropriation (American Rescue Plan)	600		
1201 .... Appropriation (special or trust fund)	10	9	9
1260 Appropriations, mandatory (total)	610	9	9
Spending authority from offsetting collections, discretionary:			
1700 .... Collected	92	59	59
1900 Budget authority (total)	1,620	1,687	2,331
1930 Total budgetary resources available	2,596	3,307	4,812
Memorandum (non-add) entries:			
1941 Unexpired unobligated balance, end of year	1,620	2,481	3,986
Change in obligated balance:			
Unpaid obligations:			
3000 Unpaid obligations, brought forward, Oct 1	892	947	908
3010 New obligations, unexpired accounts	976	826	826
3020 Outlays (gross)	–889	–865	–1,705
3040 Recoveries of prior year unpaid obligations, unexpired	–32		
3050 Unpaid obligations, end of year	947	908	29
Uncollected payments:			
3060 Uncollected pymts, Fed sources, brought forward, Oct 1	–18	–18	–18
3090 Uncollected pymts, Fed sources, end of year	–18	–18	–18
Memorandum (non-add) entries:			
3100 Obligated balance, start of year	874	929	890
3200 Obligated balance, end of year	929	890	11
Budget authority and outlays, net:			
Discretionary:			
4000 Budget authority, gross	1,010	1,678	2,322
Outlays, gross:			
4010 Outlays from new discretionary authority	349	684	807
4011 Outlays from discretionary balances	352	88	805
4020 Outlays, gross (total)	701	772	1,612
Offsets against gross budget authority and outlays:			
Offsetting collections (collected) from:			
4030 Federal sources	–92	–59	–59
4040 Offsets against gross budget authority and outlays (total)	–92	–59	–59
Mandatory:			
4090 Budget authority, gross	610	9	9

DEPARTMENT OF HEALTH AND HUMAN SERVICES

		2021 actual	2022 est.	2023 est.
	Outlays, gross:			
4100	Outlays from new mandatory authority	183	9	9
4101	Outlays from mandatory balances	5	84	84
4110	Outlays, gross (total)	188	93	93
4180	Budget authority, net (total)	1,528	1,628	2,272
4190	Outlays, net (total)	797	806	1,646

The Indian Health Facilities account supports construction, repair and improvement, equipment, and environmental health and facilities support for the Indian Health Service. The Budget proposes to shift the four IHS accounts from discretionary to mandatory.

Object Classification (in millions of dollars)

Identification code 075–0391–0–1–551	2021 actual	2022 est.	2023 est.
Direct obligations:			
Personnel compensation:			
11.1 Full-time permanent	56	49	49
11.3 Other than full-time permanent	3	3	3
11.5 Other personnel compensation	4	4	4
11.7 Military personnel	28	25	25
11.9 Total personnel compensation	91	81	81
12.1 Civilian personnel benefits	22	19	19
12.2 Military personnel benefits	2	2	2
21.0 Travel and transportation of persons	2	2	2
22.0 Transportation of things	4	4	4
23.1 Rental payments to GSA	4	4	4
23.3 Communications, utilities, and miscellaneous charges	13	11	11
25.1 Advisory and assistance services	3	3	3
25.2 Other services from non-Federal sources	178	157	157
25.3 Other goods and services from Federal sources	2	2	2
25.4 Operation and maintenance of facilities	144	127	127
25.7 Operation and maintenance of equipment	89	78	78
25.8 Subsistence and support of persons	2	2	2
26.0 Supplies and materials	7	6	6
31.0 Equipment	64	57	57
32.0 Land and structures	29	25	25
41.0 Grants, subsidies, and contributions	215	189	189
99.0 Direct obligations	871	769	769
99.0 Reimbursable obligations	105	57	57
99.9 Total new obligations, unexpired accounts	976	826	826

Employment Summary

Identification code 075–0391–0–1–551	2021 actual	2022 est.	2023 est.
1001 Direct civilian full-time equivalent employment	960	955	975
1101 Direct military average strength employment	203	200	204
2001 Reimbursable civilian full-time equivalent employment	46	46	47

INDIAN HEALTH FACILITIES

(Legislative proposal, not subject to PAYGO)

Program and Financing (in millions of dollars)

Identification code 075–0391–2–1–551	2021 actual	2022 est.	2023 est.
Budgetary resources:			
Budget authority:			
Appropriations, discretionary:			
1100 Appropriation			–1,567
Appropriations, mandatory:			
1200 Appropriation			1,567
Budget authority and outlays, net:			
Discretionary:			
4000 Budget authority, gross			–1,567
Outlays, gross:			
4010 Outlays from new discretionary authority			–470
Mandatory:			
4090 Budget authority, gross			1,567
Outlays, gross:			
4100 Outlays from new mandatory authority			470
4180 Budget authority, net (total)			
4190 Outlays, net (total)			

FUNDING FOR INDIAN HEALTH SERVICES

(Legislative proposal, subject to PAYGO)

The Budget proposes to shift the four IHS accounts from discretionary to mandatory. After FY 2023, IHS funding would grow to keep pace with healthcare costs and population growth and gradually close longstanding service and facility shortfalls. The net score forgoes discretionary funding for mandatory to provide IHS stable and predictable funding.

CENTERS FOR DISEASE CONTROL AND PREVENTION
Federal Funds

CDC-WIDE ACTIVITIES AND PROGRAM SUPPORT

(INCLUDING TRANSFER OF FUNDS)

To carry out titles II, III, IV, VII, XI, XV, XVII, XIX, XXI, XXIII, XXVI, and XXVIII of the Public Health Service Act (PHS Act), sections 101, 102, 103, 201, 202, 203, 301, and 501 of the Federal Mine Safety and Health Act, section 13 of the Mine Improvement and New Emergency Response Act, sections 20, 21, and 22 of the Occupational Safety and Health Act, titles II and IV of the Immigration and Nationality Act, section 501 of the Refugee Education Assistance Act, and for expenses necessary to support activities related to countering potential biological, nuclear, radiological, and chemical threats to civilian populations, $9,620,961,000; of which $128,421,000 shall remain available through September 30, 2024 for international HIV/AIDS; $353,200,000 shall remain available through September 30, 2025 for global public health protection; $600,000,000 shall remain available through September 30, 2024 for public health infrastructure and capacity; and $50,000,000 shall remain available through September 30, 2024 for forecasting epidemics and outbreak analytics: Provided, That funds may be used for purchase and insurance of official motor vehicles in foreign countries: Provided further, That of the amounts made available under this heading, up to $1,000,000 shall remain available until expended to pay for the transportation, medical care, treatment, and other related costs of persons quarantined or isolated under Federal or State quarantine law: Provided further, That funds made available under this heading may be available for making grants under section 1509 of the PHS Act for not less than 21 States, tribes, or tribal organizations: Provided further, That of the funds made available under this heading, $15,000,000 shall be available to continue and expand community specific extension and outreach programs to combat obesity in counties with the highest levels of obesity: Provided further, That the proportional funding requirements under section 1503(a) of the PHS Act shall not apply to funds made available under this heading: Provided further, That of the amounts appropriated under this heading up to $3,000,000 may remain available until expended for carrying out the Vessel Sanitation Program, to the extent that user fee collections are insufficient: Provided further, That of the amounts appropriated under this heading, $55,000,000 shall remain available until September 30, 2027, for costs related to the acquisition of real property, equipment, construction, installation, demolition, and renovation of facilities: Provided further, That funds made available in this or any prior Act that for the acquisition of real property or for construction or improvement of facilities shall be available to make improvements on non-federally owned property, provided that any improvements that are not adjacent to federally owned property do not exceed $2,500,000, and that the primary benefit of such improvements accrues to CDC: Provided further, That funds previously set-aside by CDC for repair and upgrade of the Lake Lynn Experimental Mine and Laboratory shall be used to acquire a replacement mine safety research facility: Provided further, That in addition, the prior year unobligated balance of any amounts assigned to former employees in accounts of CDC made available for Individual Learning Accounts shall be credited to and merged with the amounts made available for buildings and facilities to support the replacement of the mine safety research facility: Provided further, That paragraphs (1) through (3) of subsection (b) of section 2821 of the PHS Act shall not apply to funds appropriated under this heading: Provided further, That of the amounts made available under this heading, $35,000,000, to remain available until expended, shall be available to the Director of the CDC for deposit in the Infectious Diseases Rapid Response Reserve Fund established by section 231 of division B of Public Law 115–245: Provided further, That funds appropriated under this heading may be used to support a contract for the operation and maintenance of an aircraft in direct support of activities throughout CDC to ensure the agency is prepared to address public health preparedness emergencies: Provided further, That any amounts made available by this Act to the Centers for Disease Control and Prevention may be used to support the salaries and expenses of any CDC employee or fellow responding to an emergency or other urgent public health crisis: Provided further, That employees of CDC or the Public Health Service, both civilian and commissioned

Centers for Disease Control and Prevention—Continued
Federal Funds—Continued

CDC-WIDE ACTIVITIES AND PROGRAM SUPPORT—Continued

officers, detailed to States, municipalities, or other organizations under authority of section 214 of the PHS Act, or in overseas assignments, shall be treated as non-Federal employees for reporting purposes only and shall not be included within any personnel ceiling applicable to the Agency, Service, or HHS during the period of detail or assignment: *Provided further*, That CDC may use up to $10,000 from amounts appropriated to CDC in this Act for official reception and representation expenses when specifically approved by the Director of CDC: *Provided further*, That in addition, such sums as may be derived from authorized user fees, which shall be credited to the appropriation charged with the cost thereof: *Provided further*, That with respect to the previous proviso, authorized user fees from the Vessel Sanitation Program and the Respirator Certification Program shall be available through September 30, 2024: *Provided further*, That in addition to amounts provided herein, $7,000,000 for lead poisoning prevention and $143,540,000 for health statistics shall be made available from amounts available under section 241 of the PHS Act.

ENERGY EMPLOYEES OCCUPATIONAL ILLNESS COMPENSATION PROGRAM

For necessary expenses to administer the Energy Employees Occupational Illness Compensation Program Act, $55,358,000, to remain available until expended: *Provided*, That this amount shall be available consistent with the provision regarding administrative expenses in section 151(b) of division B, title I of Public Law 106–554.

Note.—A full-year 2022 appropriation for this account was not enacted at the time the Budget was prepared; therefore, the Budget assumes this account is operating under the Continuing Appropriations Act, 2022 (Division A of Public Law 117–43, as amended). The amounts included for 2022 reflect the annualized level provided by the continuing resolution.

【CDC-WIDE ACTIVITIES AND PROGRAM SUPPORT】

【For an additional amount for "CDC-Wide Activities and Program Support", $21,500,000, for support of Operation Allies Welcome, to remain available until September 30, 2022, for medical support, screening, and other related public health activities related to Afghan arrivals and refugees.】 *(Afghanistan Supplemental Appropriations Act, 2022.)*

【CDC-WIDE ACTIVITIES AND PROGRAM SUPPORT】

【For an additional amount for "CDC-Wide Activities and Program Support", $8,000,000, to remain available until September 30, 2022, for support of Operation Allies Welcome for medical support, screening, and other related public health activities related to Afghan arrivals and refugees.】 *(Additional Afghanistan Supplemental Appropriations Act, 2022.)*

Special and Trust Fund Receipts (in millions of dollars)

Identification code 075–0943–0–1–999		2021 actual	2022 est.	2023 est.
0100	Balance, start of year			1
	Receipts:			
	Current law:			
1130	Cooperative Research and Development Agreements, Centers for Disease Control	2	2	2
2000	Total: Balances and receipts	2	2	3
	Appropriations:			
	Current law:			
2101	CDC-wide Activities and Program Support	–2	–1	–1
5099	Balance, end of year		1	2

Program and Financing (in millions of dollars)

Identification code 075–0943–0–1–999		2021 actual	2022 est.	2023 est.
	Obligations by program activity:			
0001	Birth Defects, Developmental Disabilities, Disability and Health (0958)	167	168	
0002	CDC-Wide Activities and Program Support (0943)	15,286	274	9,621
0004	Chronic Disease Prevention and Health Promotion (0948)	1,296	1,277	
0005	Emerging and Zoonotic Infectious Diseases (0949)	644	648	
0006	Energy Employee Illness Occupational Compensation Program Act (EEOICPA) (0954)	53	50	
0007	Environmental Health (0947)	222	223	
0008	Global Health (0955)	604	592	
0012	HIV/AIDS, Viral Hepatitis, STD and TB Prevention (0950)	1,309	1,314	
0013	Immunization and Respiratory Diseases (0951)	815	821	
0015	Injury Prevention and Control (0952)	680	683	
0016	Occupational Safety and Health (0953)	344	345	
0019	Public Health Preparedness and Response (0956)	840	842	
0020	Public Health Scientific Services (0959)	590	592	
0021	Cooperative Research and Development Agreements (CRADA) (5146)	1		
0022	Ebola (Emergency pursuant to 2011 BCA)	1		
0024	CDC-Wide Activities and Program Support (User and Other Similar Fees)	127		
0799	Total direct obligations	22,979	7,829	9,621
0802	CDC-Wide Activities and Program Support (Reimbursable)	252	653	668
0809	Reimbursable program activities, subtotal	252	653	668
0900	Total new obligations, unexpired accounts	23,231	8,482	10,289
	Budgetary resources:			
	Unobligated balance:			
1000	Unobligated balance brought forward, Oct 1	3,158	7,711	7,274
1001	Discretionary unobligated balance brought fwd, Oct 1	3,066		
1010	Unobligated balance transfer to other accts [075–0140]	–544		
1021	Recoveries of prior year unpaid obligations	77		
1070	Unobligated balance (total)	2,691	7,711	7,274
	Budget authority:			
	Appropriations, discretionary:			
1100	Appropriation	15,683	6,965	9,621
1120	Appropriations transferred to other acct [075–0390]	–210		
1120	Appropriations transferred to other acct [075–1503]	–21		
1120	Appropriations transferred to other acct [075–0945]	–10	–10	–35
1121	Appropriations transferred from other acct [075–0116]		856	
1160	Appropriation, discretionary (total)	15,442	7,811	9,586
	Appropriations, mandatory:			
1200	Appropriation (075–0954 - EEOICPA)	55	55	55
1200	Appropriation (075–0943 American Rescue Plan)	11,520		
1201	Appropriation (075–5146 CRADA)	2	1	1
1221	Appropriations transferred from other acct PPHF [075–0116]	856		903
1230	Appropriations and/or unobligated balance of appropriations permanently reduced	–5	–5	–4
1260	Appropriations, mandatory (total)	12,428	51	955
	Spending authority from offsetting collections, discretionary:			
1700	Collected	291	181	185
1701	Change in uncollected payments, Federal sources	92		
1750	Spending auth from offsetting collections, disc (total)	383	181	185
	Spending authority from offsetting collections, mandatory:			
1800	Collected	4	2	2
1900	Budget authority (total)	28,257	8,045	10,728
1930	Total budgetary resources available	30,948	15,756	18,002
	Memorandum (non-add) entries:			
1940	Unobligated balance expiring	–6		
1941	Unexpired unobligated balance, end of year	7,711	7,274	7,713
	Change in obligated balance:			
	Unpaid obligations:			
3000	Unpaid obligations, brought forward, Oct 1	10,155	21,997	15,164
3010	New obligations, unexpired accounts	23,231	8,482	10,289
3011	Obligations ("upward adjustments"), expired accounts	35		
3020	Outlays (gross)	–11,153	–15,315	–12,298
3040	Recoveries of prior year unpaid obligations, unexpired	–77		
3041	Recoveries of prior year unpaid obligations, expired	–194		
3050	Unpaid obligations, end of year	21,997	15,164	13,155
	Uncollected payments:			
3060	Uncollected pymts, Fed sources, brought forward, Oct 1	–130	–144	–144
3070	Change in uncollected pymts, Fed sources, unexpired	–92		
3071	Change in uncollected pymts, Fed sources, expired	78		
3090	Uncollected pymts, Fed sources, end of year	–144	–144	–144
	Memorandum (non-add) entries:			
3100	Obligated balance, start of year	10,025	21,853	15,020
3200	Obligated balance, end of year	21,853	15,020	13,011
	Budget authority and outlays, net:			
	Discretionary:			
4000	Budget authority, gross	15,825	7,992	9,771
	Outlays, gross:			
4010	Outlays from new discretionary authority	3,630	2,135	2,600
4011	Outlays from discretionary balances	6,157	7,581	7,430
4020	Outlays, gross (total)	9,787	9,716	10,030
	Offsets against gross budget authority and outlays:			
	Offsetting collections (collected) from:			
4030	Federal sources	–359	–181	–185
4033	Non-Federal sources	–12		
4040	Offsets against gross budget authority and outlays (total)	–371	–181	–185
	Additional offsets against gross budget authority only:			
4050	Change in uncollected pymts, Fed sources, unexpired	–92		
4052	Offsetting collections credited to expired accounts	80		
4060	Additional offsets against budget authority only (total)	–12		
4070	Budget authority, net (discretionary)	15,442	7,811	9,586

DEPARTMENT OF HEALTH AND HUMAN SERVICES

Centers for Disease Control and Prevention—Continued
Federal Funds—Continued

		2021 actual	2022 est.	2023 est.
4080	Outlays, net (discretionary)	9,416	9,535	9,845
	Mandatory:			
4090	Budget authority, gross	12,432	53	957
	Outlays, gross:			
4100	Outlays from new mandatory authority	617	41	223
4101	Outlays from mandatory balances	749	5,558	2,045
4110	Outlays, gross (total)	1,366	5,599	2,268
	Offsets against gross budget authority and outlays:			
	Offsetting collections (collected) from:			
4123	Non-Federal sources	–4	–2	–2
4180	Budget authority, net (total)	27,870	7,862	10,541
4190	Outlays, net (total)	10,778	15,132	12,111

Summary of Budget Authority and Outlays (in millions of dollars)

	2021 actual	2022 est.	2023 est.
Enacted/requested:			
Budget Authority	27,870	7,862	10,541
Outlays	10,778	15,132	12,111
Legislative proposal, subject to PAYGO:			
Budget Authority			30,088
Outlays			8,432
Total:			
Budget Authority	27,870	7,862	40,629
Outlays	10,778	15,132	20,543

The Centers for Disease Control and Prevention (CDC) works to protect the health and safety of all Americans. The agency has played a key role in protecting Americans from recent health emergencies including COVID-19, opioid overdose, Zika, and H1N1. Key programs of the CDC include immunization and respiratory diseases; HIV/AIDS, viral hepatitis, STD, and tuberculosis prevention; emerging and zoonotic infectious diseases; chronic disease prevention and health promotion; public health and scientific services; injury prevention and control; environmental health; global health; programs that reduce the occurrence of birth defects and developmental disabilities; public health preparedness and emergency response; and cross-cutting CDC-wide activities and program support, including public health infrastructure. The FY 2023 Budget continues to increase foundational investments in core public health capacities that are essential prepare for and response to public health emergencies and to the effective and efficient functioning of public health system. These include a request for $600 million for dedicated funding to invest in public health infrastructure and capacity, and $50 million to support the Center for Forecasting and Outbreak Analytics, which will sustain efforts begun in FY 2021 with COVID-19 emergency supplemental appropriations. The FY 2023 Budget also provides $310 million for CDC to undertake the fourth year of the Ending the HIV Epidemic in the U.S. initiative, and $200 million to continue CDC's Public Health Data Modernization efforts. The FY 2023 Budget provides $353 million for global public health protection activities to protect Americans through partnerships and other activities that support public health capacity improvements in countries at risk for uncontrolled outbreaks of infectious diseases. In addition, the FY 2023 Budget includes several policy proposals to allow CDC to more efficiently respond to public health emergencies, including a proposal to modernize CDC's budget structure by consolidating the existing 13 Treasury accounts, including "Buildings and Facilities", into a single "CDC-Wide Activities and Program Support" account. Nearly all existing budget lines are maintained within the proposed single account structure.

Object Classification (in millions of dollars)

Identification code 075–0943–0–1–999		2021 actual	2022 est.	2023 est.
	Direct obligations:			
	Personnel compensation:			
11.1	Full-time permanent	851	887	1,110
11.3	Other than full-time permanent	138	103	135
11.5	Other personnel compensation	70	47	64
11.6	Military personnel - basic allowance for housing	1	1	1
11.7	Military personnel	93	89	118
11.8	Special personal services payments	4	3	4
11.9	Total personnel compensation	1,157	1,130	1,432
12.1	Civilian personnel benefits	371	347	469
12.2	Military personnel benefits	29	30	38
21.0	Travel and transportation of persons	20	11	14
22.0	Transportation of things	9	7	11
23.1	Rental payments to GSA	4	6	6
23.3	Communications, utilities, and miscellaneous charges	4	5	5
24.0	Printing and reproduction	2	3	3
25.1	Advisory and assistance services	2,517	755	1,090
25.2	Other services from non-Federal sources	79	83	90
25.3	Other goods and services from Federal sources	5,374	1,062	1,117
25.4	Operation and maintenance of facilities	16	17	31
25.5	Research and development contracts	30	32	34
25.6	Medical care	5	5	6
25.7	Operation and maintenance of equipment	54	30	46
26.0	Supplies and materials	128	37	74
31.0	Equipment	82	59	76
32.0	Land and structures	1	2	26
41.0	Grants, subsidies, and contributions	13,097	4,208	5,053
99.0	Direct obligations	22,979	7,829	9,621
99.0	Reimbursable obligations	252	653	668
99.9	Total new obligations, unexpired accounts	23,231	8,482	10,289

Employment Summary

Identification code 075–0943–0–1–999		2021 actual	2022 est.	2023 est.
1001	Direct civilian full-time equivalent employment	9,241	10,953	10,412
1101	Direct military average strength employment	743	774	741
2001	Reimbursable civilian full-time equivalent employment	286	251	252
2101	Reimbursable military average strength employment	27	27	26

CDC-WIDE ACTIVITIES AND PROGRAM SUPPORT

(Legislative proposal, subject to PAYGO)

Program and Financing (in millions of dollars)

Identification code 075–0943–4–1–999		2021 actual	2022 est.	2023 est.
	Obligations by program activity:			
0001	CDC-Wide Activities and Program Support (0943)			30,088
	Budgetary resources:			
	Budget authority:			
	Appropriations, mandatory:			
1200	Appropriation			30,088
1900	Budget authority (total)			30,088
1930	Total budgetary resources available			30,088
	Change in obligated balance:			
	Unpaid obligations:			
3010	New obligations, unexpired accounts			30,088
3020	Outlays (gross)			–8,432
3050	Unpaid obligations, end of year			21,656
	Memorandum (non-add) entries:			
3200	Obligated balance, end of year			21,656
	Budget authority and outlays, net:			
	Mandatory:			
4090	Budget authority, gross			30,088
	Outlays, gross:			
4100	Outlays from new mandatory authority			8,432
4180	Budget authority, net (total)			30,088
4190	Outlays, net (total)			8,432

The FY 2023 Budget for CDC establishes a new Vaccines for Adults (VFA) program, which will provide uninsured adults with access to all vaccines recommended by the Advisory Committee on Immunization Practices (ACIP) at no cost. As a complement to the successful Vaccines for Children (VFC) program, the VFA program will reduce disparities in vaccine coverage and promote infrastructure for broad access to routine and outbreak vaccines. The FY 2023 Budget also includes mandatory funding for significant investments in pandemic preparedness and biodefense across HHS, including CDC. These investments will allow CDC to transform medical defenses, ensure situational awareness, strengthen public health systems and build core capabilities.

CDC-WIDE ACTIVITIES AND PROGRAM SUPPORT—Continued

Object Classification (in millions of dollars)

Identification code 075–0943–4–1–999		2021 actual	2022 est.	2023 est.
	Direct obligations:			
21.0	Travel and transportation of persons			32
22.0	Transportation of things			1
23.3	Communications, utilities, and miscellaneous charges			1
25.1	Advisory and assistance services			5,443
25.2	Other services from non-Federal sources			40
25.3	Other goods and services from Federal sources			745
25.4	Operation and maintenance of facilities			9
25.5	Research and development contracts			15
25.6	Medical care			2
25.7	Operation and maintenance of equipment			66
26.0	Supplies and materials			2,023
31.0	Equipment			82
41.0	Grants, subsidies, and contributions			21,629
99.9	Total new obligations, unexpired accounts			30,088

BUILDINGS AND FACILITIES

Note.—A full-year 2022 appropriation for this account was not enacted at the time the Budget was prepared; therefore, the Budget assumes this account is operating under the Continuing Appropriations Act, 2022 (Division A of Public Law 117–43, as amended). The amounts included for 2022 reflect the annualized level provided by the continuing resolution.

Program and Financing (in millions of dollars)

Identification code 075–0960–0–1–551		2021 actual	2022 est.	2023 est.
	Obligations by program activity:			
0001	CDC Buildings and Facilities (0960)		30	30
	Budgetary resources:			
	Unobligated balance:			
1000	Unobligated balance brought forward, Oct 1	376	377	377
1021	Recoveries of prior year unpaid obligations	1		
1070	Unobligated balance (total)	377	377	377
	Budget authority:			
	Appropriations, discretionary:			
1100	Appropriation		30	30
1930	Total budgetary resources available	407	407	377
	Memorandum (non-add) entries:			
1941	Unexpired unobligated balance, end of year	377	377	377
	Change in obligated balance:			
	Unpaid obligations:			
3000	Unpaid obligations, brought forward, Oct 1	59	33	33
3010	New obligations, unexpired accounts	30	30	
3020	Outlays (gross)	–55	–30	–29
3040	Recoveries of prior year unpaid obligations, unexpired	–1		
3050	Unpaid obligations, end of year	33	33	4
	Memorandum (non-add) entries:			
3100	Obligated balance, start of year	59	33	33
3200	Obligated balance, end of year	33	33	4
	Budget authority and outlays, net:			
	Discretionary:			
4000	Budget authority, gross		30	30
	Outlays, gross:			
4010	Outlays from new discretionary authority	1	12	
4011	Outlays from discretionary balances	54	18	29
4020	Outlays, gross (total)	55	30	29
4180	Budget authority, net (total)		30	30
4190	Outlays, net (total)	55	30	29

Buildings and Facilities funds support renovations to existing buildings, as well as repair and improvements (e.g., laboratory ventilation upgrades, structural repairs, roof replacements, and electrical and mechanical repairs) necessary to restore, maintain, and improve CDC's assets. The FY 2023 Budget includes several policy proposals to allow CDC to more efficiently respond to public health emergencies, including a proposal to modernize CDC's budget structure by consolidating the existing 13 Treasury accounts, including "Buildings and Facilities", into a single "CDC-Wide Activities and Program Support" account.

Object Classification (in millions of dollars)

Identification code 075–0960–0–1–551		2021 actual	2022 est.	2023 est.
	Direct obligations:			
25.1	Advisory and assistance services	1	2	
25.4	Operation and maintenance of facilities	6	10	
31.0	Equipment	1		
32.0	Land and structures	22	18	
99.9	Total new obligations, unexpired accounts	30	30	

CDC WORKING CAPITAL FUND

Program and Financing (in millions of dollars)

Identification code 075–4553–0–4–551		2021 actual	2022 est.	2023 est.
	Obligations by program activity:			
0801	CDC Working Capital Fund (Reimbursable)	735	671	671
	Budgetary resources:			
	Unobligated balance:			
1000	Unobligated balance brought forward, Oct 1	125	232	232
1021	Recoveries of prior year unpaid obligations	19		
1070	Unobligated balance (total)	144	232	232
	Budget authority:			
	Spending authority from offsetting collections, discretionary:			
1700	Collected	823	671	671
1900	Budget authority (total)	823	671	671
1930	Total budgetary resources available	967	903	903
	Memorandum (non-add) entries:			
1941	Unexpired unobligated balance, end of year	232	232	232
	Change in obligated balance:			
	Unpaid obligations:			
3000	Unpaid obligations, brought forward, Oct 1	239	292	217
3010	New obligations, unexpired accounts	735	671	671
3020	Outlays (gross)	–663	–746	–671
3040	Recoveries of prior year unpaid obligations, unexpired	–19		
3050	Unpaid obligations, end of year	292	217	217
	Uncollected payments:			
3060	Uncollected pymts, Fed sources, brought forward, Oct 1	–2	–2	–2
3090	Uncollected pymts, Fed sources, end of year	–2	–2	–2
	Memorandum (non-add) entries:			
3100	Obligated balance, start of year	237	290	215
3200	Obligated balance, end of year	290	215	215
	Budget authority and outlays, net:			
	Discretionary:			
4000	Budget authority, gross	823	671	671
	Outlays, gross:			
4010	Outlays from new discretionary authority	464	443	443
4011	Outlays from discretionary balances	199	303	228
4020	Outlays, gross (total)	663	746	671
	Offsets against gross budget authority and outlays:			
	Offsetting collections (collected) from:			
4030	Federal sources	–823	–671	–671
4180	Budget authority, net (total)			
4190	Outlays, net (total)	–160	75	

Implemented in fiscal year 2014, CDC's Working Capital Fund has extended availability and serves as the funding mechanism to finance centralized business services support across CDC. Services rendered under the fund are performed at pre-established rates that are used to cover the full cost of operations and future investments. Contributions are collected for services, thereby creating market-like incentives to maximize efficiency and quality.

DEPARTMENT OF HEALTH AND HUMAN SERVICES

Object Classification (in millions of dollars)

Identification code 075–4553–0–4–551		2021 actual	2022 est.	2023 est.
	Reimbursable obligations:			
	Personnel compensation:			
11.1	Full-time permanent	163	149	150
11.3	Other than full-time permanent	6	5	5
11.5	Other personnel compensation	6	5	5
11.7	Military personnel	4	4	3
11.9	Total personnel compensation	179	163	163
12.1	Civilian personnel benefits	64	58	59
12.2	Military personnel benefits	1	1	1
22.0	Transportation of things	1	1	1
23.1	Rental payments to GSA	34	31	31
23.3	Communications, utilities, and miscellaneous charges	23	21	21
25.1	Advisory and assistance services	114	104	106
25.2	Other services from non-Federal sources	49	45	44
25.3	Other goods and services from Federal sources	119	109	109
25.4	Operation and maintenance of facilities	79	72	73
25.7	Operation and maintenance of equipment	57	52	50
31.0	Equipment	12	11	10
32.0	Land and structures	3	3	3
99.9	Total new obligations, unexpired accounts	735	671	671

Employment Summary

Identification code 075–4553–0–4–551	2021 actual	2022 est.	2023 est.
2001 Reimbursable civilian full-time equivalent employment	1,604	1,620	1,635
2101 Reimbursable military average strength employment	25	27	27

INFECTIOUS DISEASES RAPID RESPONSE RESERVE FUND

Program and Financing (in millions of dollars)

Identification code 075–0945–0–1–551		2021 actual	2022 est.	2023 est.
	Obligations by program activity:			
0001	Direct program activity	18	10	35
	Budgetary resources:			
	Unobligated balance:			
1000	Unobligated balance brought forward, Oct 1	601	594	594
1021	Recoveries of prior year unpaid obligations	1		
1070	Unobligated balance (total)	602	594	594
	Budget authority:			
	Appropriations, discretionary:			
1121	Appropriations transferred from other acct [075–0943]	10	10	35
1930	Total budgetary resources available	612	604	629
	Memorandum (non-add) entries:			
1941	Unexpired unobligated balance, end of year	594	594	594
	Change in obligated balance:			
	Unpaid obligations:			
3000	Unpaid obligations, brought forward, Oct 1	37	26	5
3010	New obligations, unexpired accounts	18	10	35
3020	Outlays (gross)	–28	–31	–26
3040	Recoveries of prior year unpaid obligations, unexpired	–1		
3050	Unpaid obligations, end of year	26	5	14
	Memorandum (non-add) entries:			
3100	Obligated balance, start of year	37	26	5
3200	Obligated balance, end of year	26	5	14
	Budget authority and outlays, net:			
	Discretionary:			
4000	Budget authority, gross	10	10	35
	Outlays, gross:			
4010	Outlays from new discretionary authority		6	22
4011	Outlays from discretionary balances	28	25	4
4020	Outlays, gross (total)	28	31	26
4180	Budget authority, net (total)	10	10	35
4190	Outlays, net (total)	28	31	26

The FY 2023 Budget provides $35 million for the Infectious Diseases Rapid Response Reserve Fund within the Centers for Disease Control and Prevention. This Fund will provide the ability to respond efficiently and rapidly to emerging infectious disease threats or outbreaks.

Object Classification (in millions of dollars)

Identification code 075–0945–0–1–551		2021 actual	2022 est.	2023 est.
	Direct obligations:			
21.0	Travel and transportation of persons	1	2	2
25.1	Advisory and assistance services	3		19
25.3	Other goods and services from Federal sources	2	5	11
26.0	Supplies and materials	1	1	1
31.0	Equipment	1	2	2
41.0	Grants, subsidies, and contributions	10		
99.9	Total new obligations, unexpired accounts	18	10	35

TOXIC SUBSTANCES AND ENVIRONMENTAL PUBLIC HEALTH

For necessary expenses for the Agency for Toxic Substances and Disease Registry (ATSDR) in carrying out activities set forth in sections 104(i) and 111(c)(4) of the Comprehensive Environmental Response, Compensation, and Liability Act of 1980 (CERCLA) and section 3019 of the Solid Waste Disposal Act, $85,020,000: Provided, That notwithstanding any other provision of law, in lieu of performing a health assessment under section 104(i)(6) of CERCLA, the Administrator of ATSDR may conduct other appropriate health studies, evaluations, or activities, including, without limitation, biomedical testing, clinical evaluations, medical monitoring, and referral to accredited healthcare providers: Provided further, That in performing any such health assessment or health study, evaluation, or activity, the Administrator of ATSDR shall not be bound by the deadlines in section 104(i)(6)(A) of CERCLA: Provided further, That none of the funds appropriated under this heading shall be available for ATSDR to issue in excess of 40 toxicological profiles pursuant to section 104(i) of CERCLA during fiscal year 2023, and existing profiles may be updated as necessary.

Note.—A full-year 2022 appropriation for this account was not enacted at the time the Budget was prepared; therefore, the Budget assumes this account is operating under the Continuing Appropriations Act, 2022 (Division A of Public Law 117–43, as amended). The amounts included for 2022 reflect the annualized level provided by the continuing resolution.

Program and Financing (in millions of dollars)

Identification code 075–0944–0–1–551		2021 actual	2022 est.	2023 est.
	Obligations by program activity:			
0001	Agency for Toxic Substances and Disease Registry, Toxic Substance (Direct)	96	78	85
0801	Agency for Toxic Substances and Disease Registry, Toxic Substance (Reimbursable)	7	14	14
0900	Total new obligations, unexpired accounts	103	92	99
	Budgetary resources:			
	Unobligated balance:			
1000	Unobligated balance brought forward, Oct 1	33	29	18
	Budget authority:			
	Appropriations, discretionary:			
1100	Appropriation	78	78	85
1121	Appropriations transferred from other acct [097–0100]	15		
1160	Appropriation, discretionary (total)	93	78	85
	Spending authority from offsetting collections, discretionary:			
1700	Collected	5	3	
1701	Change in uncollected payments, Federal sources	2		
1750	Spending auth from offsetting collections, disc (total)	7	3	
1900	Budget authority (total)	100	81	85
1930	Total budgetary resources available	133	110	103
	Memorandum (non-add) entries:			
1940	Unobligated balance expiring	–1		
1941	Unexpired unobligated balance, end of year	29	18	4
	Change in obligated balance:			
	Unpaid obligations:			
3000	Unpaid obligations, brought forward, Oct 1	78	81	53
3010	New obligations, unexpired accounts	103	92	99
3011	Obligations ("upward adjustments"), expired accounts	2		
3020	Outlays (gross)	–97	–120	–79
3041	Recoveries of prior year unpaid obligations, expired	–5		
3050	Unpaid obligations, end of year	81	53	73
	Uncollected payments:			
3060	Uncollected pymts, Fed sources, brought forward, Oct 1	–7	–6	–6
3070	Change in uncollected pymts, Fed sources, unexpired	–2		
3071	Change in uncollected pymts, Fed sources, expired	3		

Centers for Disease Control and Prevention—Continued
Federal Funds—Continued

TOXIC SUBSTANCES AND ENVIRONMENTAL PUBLIC HEALTH—Continued

Program and Financing—Continued

Identification code 075–0944–0–1–551	2021 actual	2022 est.	2023 est.
3090 Uncollected pymts, Fed sources, end of year	–6	–6	–6
Memorandum (non-add) entries:			
3100 Obligated balance, start of year	71	75	47
3200 Obligated balance, end of year	75	47	67
Budget authority and outlays, net:			
Discretionary:			
4000 Budget authority, gross	100	81	85
Outlays, gross:			
4010 Outlays from new discretionary authority	51	53	55
4011 Outlays from discretionary balances	43	67	24
4020 Outlays, gross (total)	94	120	79
Offsets against gross budget authority and outlays:			
Offsetting collections (collected) from:			
4030 Federal sources	–8	–3	
4040 Offsets against gross budget authority and outlays (total)	–8	–3	
Additional offsets against gross budget authority only:			
4050 Change in uncollected pymts, Fed sources, unexpired	–2		
4052 Offsetting collections credited to expired accounts	3		
4060 Additional offsets against budget authority only (total)	1		
4070 Budget authority, net (discretionary)	93	78	85
4080 Outlays, net (discretionary)	86	117	79
Mandatory:			
Outlays, gross:			
4101 Outlays from mandatory balances	3		
4180 Budget authority, net (total)	93	78	85
4190 Outlays, net (total)	89	117	79

Object Classification (in millions of dollars)

Identification code 075–0944–0–1–551	2021 actual	2022 est.	2023 est.
Direct obligations:			
Personnel compensation:			
11.1 Full-time permanent	23	22	21
11.3 Other than full-time permanent	1	1	1
11.5 Other personnel compensation	1	1	1
11.7 Military personnel	4	4	4
11.9 Total personnel compensation	29	28	27
12.1 Civilian personnel benefits	9	7	8
25.1 Advisory and assistance services	12	3	11
25.2 Other services from non-Federal sources	3	1	2
25.3 Other goods and services from Federal sources	13	12	12
25.7 Operation and maintenance of equipment	1		
31.0 Equipment	3	2	2
41.0 Grants, subsidies, and contributions	26	25	23
99.0 Direct obligations	96	78	85
99.0 Reimbursable obligations	7	14	14
99.9 Total new obligations, unexpired accounts	103	92	99

Employment Summary

Identification code 075–0944–0–1–551	2021 actual	2022 est.	2023 est.
1001 Direct civilian full-time equivalent employment	198	194	194
1101 Direct military average strength employment	30	30	30
2001 Reimbursable civilian full-time equivalent employment	1	2	2
2101 Reimbursable military average strength employment	1	1	1

WORLD TRADE CENTER HEALTH PROGRAM FUND

Program and Financing (in millions of dollars)

Identification code 075–0946–0–1–551	2021 actual	2022 est.	2023 est.
Obligations by program activity:			
0001 World Trade Center Health Program—Federal Share (CDC/NIOSH)	506	577	710
0002 World Trade Center Health Program—NYC	56	64	79
0900 Total new obligations, unexpired accounts	562	641	789
Budgetary resources:			
Unobligated balance:			
1000 Unobligated balance brought forward, Oct 1	928	973	908
1021 Recoveries of prior year unpaid obligations	5		
1033 Recoveries of prior year paid obligations	45		
1070 Unobligated balance (total)	978	973	908
Budget authority:			
Appropriations, mandatory:			
1200 Appropriation (WTC (CDC Direct))	457	518	535
1200 Appropriation (WTC—NYC DHSS—CDC)	51	58	59
1260 Appropriations, mandatory (total)	508	576	594
Spending authority from offsetting collections, mandatory:			
1800 Collected	49		
1900 Budget authority (total)	557	576	594
1930 Total budgetary resources available	1,535	1,549	1,502
Memorandum (non-add) entries:			
1941 Unexpired unobligated balance, end of year	973	908	713
Change in obligated balance:			
Unpaid obligations:			
3000 Unpaid obligations, brought forward, Oct 1	255	239	439
3010 New obligations, unexpired accounts	562	641	789
3020 Outlays (gross)	–573	–441	–520
3040 Recoveries of prior year unpaid obligations, unexpired	–5		
3050 Unpaid obligations, end of year	239	439	708
Memorandum (non-add) entries:			
3100 Obligated balance, start of year	255	239	439
3200 Obligated balance, end of year	239	439	708
Budget authority and outlays, net:			
Mandatory:			
4090 Budget authority, gross	557	576	594
Outlays, gross:			
4100 Outlays from new mandatory authority		265	273
4101 Outlays from mandatory balances	573	176	247
4110 Outlays, gross (total)	573	441	520
Offsets against gross budget authority and outlays:			
Offsetting collections (collected) from:			
4123 Non-Federal sources	–94		
Additional offsets against gross budget authority only:			
4143 Recoveries of prior year paid obligations, unexpired accounts	45		
4160 Budget authority, net (mandatory)	508	576	594
4170 Outlays, net (mandatory)	479	441	520
4180 Budget authority, net (total)	508	576	594
4190 Outlays, net (total)	479	441	520

HHS, along with CDC, began implementing provisions of the James Zadroga 9/11 Health and Compensation Act of 2010 (P.L. 111–347) on July 1, 2011, to provide monitoring and treatment benefits to eligible responders and survivors. CDC serves as the Program Administrator for the World Trade Center (WTC) Health Program. The WTC Health Program provides quality care for WTC-related health conditions, conducts WTC research, and maintains a health registry to collect data on victims of the September 11, 2001, terrorist attacks. The WTC Health Program has been extended through FY 2090 under the James Zadroga 9/11 Health and Compensation Reauthorization Act of 2015 (P.L. 114–113, Division O, Title III). The amounts included for 2022 and 2023 in the Budget reflect estimated Federal obligations for the WTC Health Program.

Object Classification (in millions of dollars)

Identification code 075–0946–0–1–551	2021 actual	2022 est.	2023 est.
Direct obligations:			
Personnel compensation:			
11.1 Full-time permanent	5	5	8
11.3 Other than full-time permanent	1	1	1
11.7 Military personnel	1	1	1
11.9 Total personnel compensation	7	7	10
12.1 Civilian personnel benefits	2	2	3
25.1 Advisory and assistance services	25	50	39
25.3 Other goods and services from Federal sources	14	17	21
25.4 Operation and maintenance of facilities		1	
25.6 Medical care	114	137	170
31.0 Equipment	2	2	2
41.0 Grants, subsidies, and contributions	16	30	24
42.0 Insurance claims and indemnities	382	395	520

		2021 actual	2022 est.	2023 est.
99.9	Total new obligations, unexpired accounts	562	641	789

Employment Summary

Identification code 075–0946–0–1–551	2021 actual	2022 est.	2023 est.
1001 Direct civilian full-time equivalent employment	52	52	62
1101 Direct military average strength employment	7	7	7

NATIONAL INSTITUTES OF HEALTH
Federal Funds

NATIONAL CANCER INSTITUTE

For carrying out section 301 and title IV of the PHS Act with respect to cancer, $6,497,851,000, of which up to $30,000,000 may be used for facilities repairs and improvements at the National Cancer Institute—Frederick Federally Funded Research and Development Center in Frederick, Maryland.

NATIONAL HEART, LUNG, AND BLOOD INSTITUTE

For carrying out section 301 and title IV of the PHS Act with respect to cardiovascular, lung, and blood diseases, and blood and blood products, $3,822,961,000.

NATIONAL INSTITUTE OF DENTAL AND CRANIOFACIAL RESEARCH

For carrying out section 301 and title IV of the PHS Act with respect to dental and craniofacial diseases, $513,191,000.

NATIONAL INSTITUTE OF DIABETES AND DIGESTIVE AND KIDNEY DISEASES

For carrying out section 301 and title IV of the PHS Act with respect to diabetes and digestive and kidney disease, $2,206,080,000.

NATIONAL INSTITUTE OF NEUROLOGICAL DISORDERS AND STROKE

For carrying out section 301 and title IV of the PHS Act with respect to neurological disorders and stroke, $2,543,043,000.

NATIONAL INSTITUTE OF ALLERGY AND INFECTIOUS DISEASES

For carrying out section 301 and title IV of the PHS Act with respect to allergy and infectious diseases, $6,268,313,000.

NATIONAL INSTITUTE OF GENERAL MEDICAL SCIENCES

For carrying out section 301 and title IV of the PHS Act with respect to general medical sciences, $3,097,557,000, of which $1,271,505,000 shall be from funds available under section 241 of the PHS Act: Provided, That not less than $410,644,000 is provided for the Institutional Development Awards program.

EUNICE KENNEDY SHRIVER NATIONAL INSTITUTE OF CHILD HEALTH AND HUMAN DEVELOPMENT

For carrying out section 301 and title IV of the PHS Act with respect to child health and human development, $1,674,941,000.

NATIONAL EYE INSTITUTE

For carrying out section 301 and title IV of the PHS Act with respect to eye diseases and visual disorders, $853,355,000.

NATIONAL INSTITUTE OF ENVIRONMENTAL HEALTH SCIENCES

For carrying out section 301 and title IV of the PHS Act with respect to environmental health sciences, $932,056,000.

NATIONAL INSTITUTE OF ENVIRONMENTAL HEALTH SCIENCES

For necessary expenses for the National Institute of Environmental Health Sciences in carrying out activities set forth in section 311(a) of the Comprehensive Environmental Response, Compensation, and Liability Act of 1980 (42 U.S.C. 9660(a)) and section 126(g) of the Superfund Amendments and Reauthorization Act of 1986, $83,035,000.

NATIONAL INSTITUTE ON AGING

For carrying out section 301 and title IV of the PHS Act with respect to aging, $4,011,413,000.

NATIONAL INSTITUTE OF ARTHRITIS AND MUSCULOSKELETAL AND SKIN DISEASES

For carrying out section 301 and title IV of the PHS Act with respect to arthritis and musculoskeletal and skin diseases, $676,254,000.

NATIONAL INSTITUTE ON DEAFNESS AND OTHER COMMUNICATION DISORDERS

For carrying out section 301 and title IV of the PHS Act with respect to deafness and other communication disorders, $508,704,000.

NATIONAL INSTITUTE OF NURSING RESEARCH

For carrying out section 301 and title IV of the PHS Act with respect to nursing research, $198,670,000.

NATIONAL INSTITUTE ON ALCOHOL
EFFECTS AND ALCOHOL-ASSOCIATED DISORDERS

For carrying out section 301 and title IV of the PHS Act with respect to alcohol misuse, alcohol use disorder, and other alcohol-associated disorders, $566,725,000.

NATIONAL INSTITUTE ON DRUGS AND ADDICTION

For carrying out section 301 and title IV of the PHS Act with respect to drugs and addiction, $1,843,326,000.

NATIONAL INSTITUTE OF MENTAL HEALTH

For carrying out section 301 and title IV of the PHS Act with respect to mental health, $1,985,828,000.

NATIONAL HUMAN GENOME RESEARCH INSTITUTE

For carrying out section 301 and title IV of the PHS Act with respect to human genome research, $629,154,000.

NATIONAL INSTITUTE OF BIOMEDICAL IMAGING AND BIOENGINEERING

For carrying out section 301 and title IV of the PHS Act with respect to biomedical imaging and bioengineering research, $419,493,000.

NATIONAL CENTER FOR COMPLEMENTARY AND INTEGRATIVE HEALTH

For carrying out section 301 and title IV of the PHS Act with respect to complementary and integrative health, $183,368,000.

NATIONAL INSTITUTE ON MINORITY HEALTH AND HEALTH DISPARITIES

For carrying out section 301 and title IV of the PHS Act with respect to minority health and health disparities research, $659,817,000.

JOHN E. FOGARTY INTERNATIONAL CENTER

For carrying out the activities of the John E. Fogarty International Center (described in subpart 2 of part E of title IV of the PHS Act), $95,801,000.

NATIONAL LIBRARY OF MEDICINE

For carrying out section 301 and title IV of the PHS Act with respect to health information communications, $471,998,000: Provided, That of the amounts available for improvement of information systems, $4,000,000 shall be available until September 30, 2024: Provided further, That in fiscal year 2023, the National Library of Medicine may enter into personal services contracts for the provision of services in facilities owned, operated, or constructed under the jurisdiction of the National Institutes of Health (referred to in this title as "NIH").

NATIONAL CENTER FOR ADVANCING TRANSLATIONAL SCIENCES

For carrying out section 301 and title IV of the PHS Act with respect to translational sciences, $873,654,000: Provided, That up to $90,000,000 shall be available to implement section 480 of the PHS Act, relating to the Cures Acceleration Network: Provided further, That at least $599,349,000 is provided to the Clinical and Translational Sciences Awards program.

OFFICE OF THE DIRECTOR
(INCLUDING TRANSFER OF FUNDS)

For carrying out the responsibilities of the Office of the Director, NIH, $2,302,065,000: Provided, That funding shall be available for the purchase of not to exceed 29 passenger motor vehicles for replacement only: Provided further, That all funds credited to the NIH Management Fund shall remain available for one fiscal year after the fiscal year in which they are deposited: Provided further, That $645,939,000 shall be available for the Common Fund established under section 402A(c)(1) of the PHS Act: Provided further, That of the funds provided, $10,000 shall be for official reception and representation expenses when specifically approved by the Director of the NIH: Provided further, That the Office of AIDS Research within the Office of the Director of the NIH may spend up to $8,000,000 to make grants for construction or renovation of facilities as provided for in section 2354(a)(5)(B) of the PHS Act: Provided further, That up to $30,000,000 shall be used to carry out section 404I of the PHS Act (42 U.S.C. 283k) with respect to the National Primate Research Centers and Caribbean Primate Research Center: Provided further, That $5,000,000 shall be transferred to and merged with the ap-

NATIONAL INSTITUTES OF HEALTH—Continued

propriation for the "Office of Inspector General" for oversight of grant programs and operations of the NIH, including agency efforts to ensure the integrity of its grant application evaluation and selection processes, and shall be in addition to funds otherwise made available for oversight of the NIH: Provided further, That the funds provided in the previous proviso may be transferred from one specified activity to another with 15 days prior notification to the Committees on Appropriations of the House of Representatives and the Senate: Provided further, That the Inspector General shall consult with the Committees on Appropriations of the House of Representatives and the Senate before submitting to the Committees an audit plan for fiscal years 2023 and 2024 no later than 30 days after the date of enactment of this Act: Provided further, That amounts available under this heading are also available to establish, operate, and support the Research Policy Board authorized by section 2034(f) of the 21st Century Cures Act.

In addition to other funds appropriated for the Common Fund established under section 402A(c) of the PHS Act, $12,600,000 is appropriated to the Common Fund from the 10-year Pediatric Research Initiative Fund described in section 9008 of title 26, United States Code, for the purpose of carrying out section 402(b)(7)(B)(ii) of the PHS Act (relating to pediatric research), as authorized in the Gabriella Miller Kids First Research Act.

BUILDINGS AND FACILITIES

For the study of, construction of, demolition of, renovation of, and acquisition of equipment for, facilities of or used by NIH, including the acquisition of real property, $300,000,000, to remain available through September 30, 2027.

ADVANCED RESEARCH PROJECTS AGENCY FOR HEALTH

For carrying out section 301 and title IV of the PHS Act with respect to advanced research projects for health, $5,000,000,000, to remain available through September 30, 2025.

Note.—A full-year 2022 appropriation for this account was not enacted at the time the Budget was prepared; therefore, the Budget assumes this account is operating under the Continuing Appropriations Act, 2022 (Division A of Public Law 117–43, as amended). The amounts included for 2022 reflect the annualized level provided by the continuing resolution.

Special and Trust Fund Receipts (in millions of dollars)

Identification code 075–9915–0–1–552		2021 actual	2022 est.	2023 est.
0100	Balance, start of year	....	....	....
	Receipts:			
	Current law:			
1130	Cooperative Research and Development Agreements, NIH	54	82	82
2000	Total: Balances and receipts	54	82	82
	Appropriations:			
	Current law:			
2101	National Institutes of Health	−54	−82	−82
5099	Balance, end of year	....	....	....

Program and Financing (in millions of dollars)

Identification code 075–9915–0–1–552		2021 actual	2022 est.	2023 est.
	Obligations by program activity:			
0001	National Cancer Institute (0849)	6,670	6,748	6,714
0002	National Heart, Lung, and Blood Institute (0872)	3,673	3,696	3,823
0003	National Institute of Dental and Craniofacial Research (0873)	483	485	513
0004	National Institute of Diabetes and Digestive and Kidney Disease (0884)	2,125	2,132	2,206
0005	National Institute of Neurological Disorders and Stroke (0886)	2,491	2,534	2,768
0006	National Institute of Allergy and Infectious Diseases (0885)	6,421	6,599	6,268
0007	National Institute of General Medical Sciences (0851)	1,715	1,720	1,826
0008	National Institute of Child Health and Human Development (0844)	1,588	1,590	1,675
0009	National Eye Institute (0887)	833	836	853
0010	National Institute of Environmental Health Sciences (0862)	896	898	1,015
0011	National Institute on Aging (0843)	3,888	3,899	4,012
0012	National Institute of Arthritis and Musculoskeletal and Skin Disease (0888)	632	634	676
0013	National Institute on Deafness and Other Communication Disorder (0890)	497	498	509
0014	National Institute of Mental Health (0892)	2,100	2,106	2,211
0015	National Institute on Drug Abuse (0893)	1,476	1,480	1,843
0016	National Institute on Alcohol Abuse and Alcoholism (0894)	553	555	567
0017	National Institute of Nursing Research (0889)	174	175	199
0018	National Human Genome Research Institute (0891)	614	616	629
0019	National Institute of Biomedical Imaging and Bioengineering (0898)	523	429	419
0021	National Center for Complementary and Integrative Health (0896)	154	154	183
0022	National Institute on Minority Health and Health Disparities (0897)	389	391	660
0023	John E. Fogarty International Center (0819)	84	84	96
0024	National Library of Medicine (0807)	463	465	472
0025	NIH Office of the Director (0846)	2,695	2,479	2,310
0026	NIH Buildings and facilities (0838)	180	200	300
0027	NIH Cooperative Research and Development Agreements	47	82	82
0028	National Center for Advancing Translational Sciences (0875)	866	858	874
0029	Advanced Research Projects Agency for Health	....	....	5,000
0031	Type 1 Diabetes	104	433	141
0799	Total direct obligations	42,334	42,776	48,844
0801	NIH Reimbursable - Other	5,229	5,400	5,555
0802	NIH Royalties	100	96	96
0809	Reimbursable program activities, subtotal	5,329	5,496	5,651
0899	Total reimbursable obligations	5,329	5,496	5,651
0900	Total new obligations, unexpired accounts	47,663	48,272	54,495
	Budgetary resources:			
	Unobligated balance:			
1000	Unobligated balance brought forward, Oct 1	3,304	2,131	975
1001	Discretionary unobligated balance brought fwd, Oct 1	2,948	....	....
1010	Unobligated balance transfer to other accts [075–0140]	−773	....	....
1021	Recoveries of prior year unpaid obligations	193	....	....
1033	Recoveries of prior year paid obligations	4	....	....
1070	Unobligated balance (total)	2,728	2,131	975
	Budget authority:			
	Appropriations, discretionary:			
1100	Appropriation	42,352	41,103	47,947
1120	Appropriations transferred to other acct [075–1503]	−1,186	....	....
1120	Appropriations transferred to other acct [075–0128]	−5	−5	−5
1121	Appropriations transferred from other acct [075–5628]	295	295	666
1121	Appropriations transferred from other acct [075–5736]	13	4	13
1160	Appropriation, discretionary (total)	41,469	41,397	48,621
	Appropriations, mandatory:			
1200	Appropriation	150	150	150
1201	Appropriation (special or trust fund)	54	82	82
1230	Appropriations and/or unobligated balance of appropriations permanently reduced	....	−9	−9
1260	Appropriations, mandatory (total)	204	223	223
	Spending authority from offsetting collections, discretionary:			
1700	Collected	4,996	5,496	5,651
1701	Change in uncollected payments, Federal sources	401	....	....
1750	Spending auth from offsetting collections, disc (total)	5,397	5,496	5,651
	Spending authority from offsetting collections, mandatory:			
1800	Collected	2	....	....
1900	Budget authority (total)	47,072	47,116	54,495
1930	Total budgetary resources available	49,800	49,247	55,470
	Memorandum (non-add) entries:			
1940	Unobligated balance expiring	−6	....	....
1941	Unexpired unobligated balance, end of year	2,131	975	975
	Change in obligated balance:			
	Unpaid obligations:			
3000	Unpaid obligations, brought forward, Oct 1	46,468	49,673	51,475
3010	New obligations, unexpired accounts	47,663	48,272	54,495
3011	Obligations ("upward adjustments"), expired accounts	478	....	....
3020	Outlays (gross)	−43,880	−46,470	−47,826
3040	Recoveries of prior year unpaid obligations, unexpired	−193	....	....
3041	Recoveries of prior year unpaid obligations, expired	−863	....	....
3050	Unpaid obligations, end of year	49,673	51,475	58,144
	Uncollected payments:			
3060	Uncollected pymts, Fed sources, brought forward, Oct 1	−969	−796	−796
3070	Change in uncollected pymts, Fed sources, unexpired	−401	....	....
3071	Change in uncollected pymts, Fed sources, expired	574	....	....
3090	Uncollected pymts, Fed sources, end of year	−796	−796	−796
	Memorandum (non-add) entries:			
3100	Obligated balance, start of year	45,499	48,877	50,679
3200	Obligated balance, end of year	48,877	50,679	57,348
	Budget authority and outlays, net:			
	Discretionary:			
4000	Budget authority, gross	46,866	46,893	54,272
	Outlays, gross:			
4010	Outlays from new discretionary authority	13,060	11,919	12,801
4011	Outlays from discretionary balances	30,664	34,373	34,795
4020	Outlays, gross (total)	43,724	46,292	47,596

DEPARTMENT OF HEALTH AND HUMAN SERVICES

National Institutes of Health—Continued
Federal Funds—Continued

445

		2021 actual	2022 est.	2023 est.
	Offsets against gross budget authority and outlays:			
	Offsetting collections (collected) from:			
4030	Federal sources	−5,359	−5,496	−5,651
4033	Non-Federal sources	−223		
4040	Offsets against gross budget authority and outlays (total)	−5,582	−5,496	−5,651
	Additional offsets against gross budget authority only:			
4050	Change in uncollected pymts, Fed sources, unexpired	−401		
4052	Offsetting collections credited to expired accounts	582		
4053	Recoveries of prior year paid obligations, unexpired accounts	4		
4060	Additional offsets against budget authority only (total)	185		
4070	Budget authority, net (discretionary)	41,469	41,397	48,621
4080	Outlays, net (discretionary)	38,142	40,796	41,945
	Mandatory:			
4090	Budget authority, gross	206	223	223
	Outlays, gross:			
4100	Outlays from new mandatory authority	13	25	25
4101	Outlays from mandatory balances	143	153	205
4110	Outlays, gross (total)	156	178	230
	Offsets against gross budget authority and outlays:			
	Offsetting collections (collected) from:			
4123	Non-Federal sources	−2		
4180	Budget authority, net (total)	41,673	41,620	48,844
4190	Outlays, net (total)	38,296	40,974	42,175

Summary of Budget Authority and Outlays (in millions of dollars)

	2021 actual	2022 est.	2023 est.
Enacted/requested:			
Budget Authority	41,673	41,620	48,844
Outlays	38,296	40,974	42,175
Legislative proposal, subject to PAYGO:			
Budget Authority			12,050
Outlays			362
Total:			
Budget Authority	41,673	41,620	60,894
Outlays	38,296	40,974	42,537

This program funds biomedical research and research training. These accounts will continue to be appropriated separately and are displayed in a consolidated format to improve the readability of the presentation. The FY 2023 Budget continues to fund a new Advanced Research Projects Agency for Health within the National Institutes of Health, as first proposed in the FY 2022 Budget. With an initial focus on cancer and other diseases such as diabetes and Alzheimer's, ARPA-H would drive transformational innovation in health research and speed application and implementation of health breakthroughs.

Object Classification (in millions of dollars)

Identification code 075–9915–0–1–552		2021 actual	2022 est.	2023 est.
	Direct obligations:			
	Personnel compensation:			
11.1	Full-time permanent	1,144	1,222	1,313
11.3	Other than full-time permanent	587	616	651
11.5	Other personnel compensation	71	75	78
11.7	Military personnel	13	14	15
11.8	Special personal services payments	221	229	239
11.9	Total personnel compensation	2,036	2,156	2,296
12.1	Civilian personnel benefits	656	726	772
12.2	Military personnel benefits	11	12	13
21.0	Travel and transportation of persons	8	10	11
22.0	Transportation of things	8	9	8
23.1	Rental payments to GSA	31	32	30
23.3	Communications, utilities, and miscellaneous charges	12	12	12
25.1	Advisory and assistance services	1,425	1,407	1,445
25.2	Other services from non-Federal sources	1,880	1,560	1,586
25.3	Other goods and services from Federal sources	3,024	3,082	3,140
25.4	Operation and maintenance of facilities	49	235	46
25.5	Research and development contracts	1,695	1,659	1,652
25.6	Medical care	43	45	44
25.7	Operation and maintenance of equipment	176	176	181
26.0	Supplies and materials	273	295	267
31.0	Equipment	176	239	235
32.0	Land and structures	160	149	218
41.0	Grants, subsidies, and contributions	30,671	30,972	36,888
99.0	Direct obligations	42,334	42,776	48,844
99.0	Reimbursable obligations	5,329	5,496	5,651
99.9	Total new obligations, unexpired accounts	47,663	48,272	54,495

Employment Summary

Identification code 075–9915–0–1–552	2021 actual	2022 est.	2023 est.
1001 Direct civilian full-time equivalent employment	13,617	14,669	15,181
1101 Direct military average strength employment	132	134	136
2001 Reimbursable civilian full-time equivalent employment	4,574	4,782	4,895
2101 Reimbursable military average strength employment	85	90	90

NATIONAL INSTITUTES OF HEALTH

(Legislative proposal, subject to PAYGO)

Program and Financing (in millions of dollars)

Identification code 075–9915–4–1–552		2021 actual	2022 est.	2023 est.
	Obligations by program activity:			
0001	Prepare for pandemic and biological threats			12,050
0900	Total new obligations, unexpired accounts (object class 25.5)			12,050
	Budgetary resources:			
	Budget authority:			
	Appropriations, mandatory:			
1200	Appropriation			12,050
1930	Total budgetary resources available			12,050
	Change in obligated balance:			
	Unpaid obligations:			
3010	New obligations, unexpired accounts			12,050
3020	Outlays (gross)			−362
3050	Unpaid obligations, end of year			11,688
	Memorandum (non-add) entries:			
3200	Obligated balance, end of year			11,688
	Budget authority and outlays, net:			
	Mandatory:			
4090	Budget authority, gross			12,050
	Outlays, gross:			
4100	Outlays from new mandatory authority			362
4180	Budget authority, net (total)			12,050
4190	Outlays, net (total)			362

The 2023 Budget includes mandatory funding to support research and development of vaccines, diagnostics, and therapeutics against high priority viral families, biosafety and biosecurity, and expanded laboratory capacity and clinical trial infrastructure as part of investments across HHS to ensure national readiness for potential future pandemic threats.

PAYMENT TO THE NIH INNOVATION ACCOUNT, CURES ACT

Program and Financing (in millions of dollars)

Identification code 075–0147–0–1–552		2021 actual	2022 est.	2023 est.
	Obligations by program activity:			
0001	Payment to NIH Innovation (object class 94.0)	404	496	1,085
0900	Total new obligations, unexpired accounts (object class 94.0)	404	496	1,085
	Budgetary resources:			
	Budget authority:			
	Appropriations, mandatory:			
1200	Appropriation	404	496	1,085
1930	Total budgetary resources available	404	496	1,085
	Change in obligated balance:			
	Unpaid obligations:			
3010	New obligations, unexpired accounts	404	496	1,085
3020	Outlays (gross)	−404	−496	−1,085
	Budget authority and outlays, net:			
	Mandatory:			
4090	Budget authority, gross	404	496	1,085

PAYMENT TO THE NIH INNOVATION ACCOUNT, CURES ACT—Continued

Program and Financing—Continued

Identification code 075–0147–0–1–552	2021 actual	2022 est. *	2023 est.
Outlays, gross:			
4100 Outlays from new mandatory authority	404	496	1,085
4180 Budget authority, net (total)	404	496	1,085
4190 Outlays, net (total)	404	496	1,085

This account, and a related special fund receipt account, were established to support the execution structure necessary to implement the 21st Century Cures Act.

NIH INNOVATION ACCOUNT, CURES ACT

(INCLUDING TRANSFER OF FUNDS)

For necessary expenses to carry out the purposes described in section 1001(b)(4) of the 21st Century Cures Act, in addition to amounts available for such purposes in the appropriations provided to the NIH in this Act, $1,085,000,000, to remain available until expended: Provided, That such amounts are appropriated pursuant to section 1001(b)(3) of such Act, are to be derived from amounts transferred under section 1001(b)(2)(A) of such Act, and may be transferred by the Director of the National Institutes of Health to other accounts of the National Institutes of Health solely for the purposes provided in such Act: Provided further, That upon a determination by the Director that funds transferred pursuant to the previous proviso are not necessary for the purposes provided, such amounts may be transferred back to the Account: Provided further, That the transfer authority provided under this heading is in addition to any other transfer authority provided by law.

Note.—A full-year 2022 appropriation for this account was not enacted at the time the Budget was prepared; therefore, the Budget assumes this account is operating under the Continuing Appropriations Act, 2022 (Division A of Public Law 117–43, as amended). The amounts included for 2022 reflect the annualized level provided by the continuing resolution.

Special and Trust Fund Receipts (in millions of dollars)

Identification code 075–5628–0–2–552	2021 actual	2022 est.	2023 est.
0100 Balance, start of year			92
Receipts:			
Current law:			
1140 General Fund Payment, NIH Innovation, CURES Act	404	496	1,085
2000 Total: Balances and receipts	404	496	1,177
Appropriations:			
Current law:			
2101 NIH Innovation, Cures Act	–404	–404	–1,085
5099 Balance, end of year		92	92

Program and Financing (in millions of dollars)

Identification code 075–5628–0–2–552	2021 actual	2022 est.	2023 est.
Obligations by program activity:			
0001 CURES obligations	96	185	419
Budgetary resources:			
Unobligated balance:			
1000 Unobligated balance brought forward, Oct 1	63	76	
Budget authority:			
Appropriations, discretionary:			
1101 Appropriation (special or trust)	404	404	1,085
1120 Appropriations transferred to other acct [075–9915]	–295	–295	–666
1160 Appropriation, discretionary (total)	109	109	419
1930 Total budgetary resources available	172	185	419
Memorandum (non-add) entries:			
1941 Unexpired unobligated balance, end of year	76		
Change in obligated balance:			
Unpaid obligations:			
3000 Unpaid obligations, brought forward, Oct 1	246	174	219
3010 New obligations, unexpired accounts	96	185	419
3020 Outlays (gross)	–168	–140	–203
3050 Unpaid obligations, end of year	174	219	435
Memorandum (non-add) entries:			
3100 Obligated balance, start of year	246	174	219
3200 Obligated balance, end of year	174	219	435
Budget authority and outlays, net:			
Discretionary:			
4000 Budget authority, gross	109	109	419
Outlays, gross:			
4010 Outlays from new discretionary authority		19	76
4011 Outlays from discretionary balances	168	121	127
4020 Outlays, gross (total)	168	140	203
4180 Budget authority, net (total)	109	109	419
4190 Outlays, net (total)	168	140	203

The 21st Century Cures Act was enacted into law on December 13, 2016. The 21st Century Cures Act authorizes $4.8 billion over 10 years for four NIH Innovation Projects and includes amendments to the Public Health Service Act to advance Precision Medicine and other high-priority NIH activities. Amounts appropriated into the NIH Innovation Account are either transferred to the individual institutes and centers or obligated directly in the NIH Innovation Account.

Object Classification (in millions of dollars)

Identification code 075–5628–0–2–552	2021 actual	2022 est.	2023 est.
Direct obligations:			
25.1 Advisory and assistance services	2	2	
25.3 Other goods and services from Federal sources	6	4	7
25.5 Research and development contracts			15
41.0 Grants, subsidies, and contributions	88	179	397
99.9 Total new obligations, unexpired accounts	96	185	419

10-YEAR PEDIATRIC RESEARCH INITIATIVE FUND

Special and Trust Fund Receipts (in millions of dollars)

Identification code 075–5736–0–2–552	2021 actual	2022 est.	2023 est.
0100 Balance, start of year	17	4	
Receipts:			
Current law:			
1140 Transfers from Presidential Election Campaign Fund			21
2000 Total: Balances and receipts	17	4	21
Appropriations:			
Current law:			
2101 10-Year Pediatric Research Initiative Fund	–13	–4	–13
5099 Balance, end of year	4		8

Program and Financing (in millions of dollars)

Identification code 075–5736–0–2–552	2021 actual	2022 est.	2023 est.
Budgetary resources:			
Budget authority:			
Appropriations, discretionary:			
1101 Appropriation (special or trust)	13	4	13
1120 Appropriations transferred to other accts [075–9915]	–13	–4	–13
4180 Budget authority, net (total)			
4190 Outlays, net (total)			

This special fund was created by the Gabriella Miller Kids First Research Act, enacted on April 3, 2014. This fund receives transfers from the Presidential Election Campaign Fund, which are then appropriated to the NIH Common Fund to support pediatric research.

SUBSTANCE USE AND MENTAL HEALTH SERVICES ADMINISTRATION

Federal Funds

MENTAL HEALTH

For carrying out titles III, V, and XIX of the PHS Act with respect to mental health, and the Protection and Advocacy for Individuals with Mental Illness Act, $4,182,687,000: Provided further, That notwithstanding section 520A(f)(2) of the

DEPARTMENT OF HEALTH AND HUMAN SERVICES

Substance Use And Mental Health Services Administration—Continued
Federal Funds—Continued

447

PHS Act, no funds appropriated for carrying out section 520A shall be available for carrying out section 1971 of the PHS Act: *Provided further,* That in addition to amounts provided herein, $21,039,000 shall be available under section 241 of the PHS Act to supplement funds otherwise available for mental health activities and to carry out subpart I of part B of title XIX of the PHS Act to fund section 1920(b) technical assistance, national data, data collection and evaluation activities, and further that the total available under this Act for section 1920(b) activities shall not exceed 5 percent of the amounts appropriated for subpart I of part B of title XIX: *Provided further,* That of the funds made available under this heading for subpart I of part B of title XIX of the PHS Act, not less than 10 percent shall be used to support evidence-based crisis systems: *Provided further,* That up to 10 percent of the amounts made available to carry out the Children's Mental Health Services program may be used to carry out demonstration grants or contracts for early interventions with persons not more than 25 years of age at clinical high risk of developing a first episode of psychosis: *Provided further,* That section 520E(b)(2) of the PHS Act shall not apply to funds appropriated in this Act for fiscal year 2023: *Provided further,* That $552,500,000 shall be available until September 30, 2024 for grants to communities and community organizations who meet criteria for Certified Community Behavioral Health Clinics pursuant to section 223(a) of Public Law 113–93: *Provided further,* That none of the funds provided for section 1911 of the PHS Act shall be subject to section 241 of such Act: *Provided further,* That of the funds made available under this heading, $21,420,000 shall be to carry out section 224 of the Protecting Access to Medicare Act of 2014 (Public Law 113–93; 42 U.S.C. 290aa 22 note). *Provided further,* That notwithstanding sections 1911(b) and 1912 of the PHS Act, amounts made available under this heading for subpart I of part B of title XIX of such Act shall also be available to support evidence-based programs that address early intervention and prevention of mental disorders among at-risk children and adults: *Provided further,* That States shall expend at least 10 percent of the amount each receives for carrying out section 1911 of the PHS Act to support evidence-based programs that address early intervention and prevention of mental disorders for at-risk youth and adults: *Provided further,* That notwithstanding section 1912 of the PHS Act, the plan described in such section and section 1911(b) of the PHS Act shall also include the evidence-based programs described in the previous proviso pursuant to plan criteria established by the Secretary.

SUBSTANCE USE SERVICES

For carrying out titles III and V of the PHS Act with respect to substance use treatment and title XIX of such Act with respect to substance use treatment and prevention, and the SUPPORT for Patients and Communities Act, $5,493,243,000: *Provided,* That $2,000,000,000 shall be for State Opioid Response Grants for carrying out activities pertaining to opioids and stimulants undertaken by the State agency responsible for administering the substance use prevention and treatment block grant under subpart II of part B of title XIX of the PHS Act (42 U.S.C. 300x–21 et seq.): *Provided further,* That of such amount $75,000,000 shall be made available to Indian Tribes or tribal organizations: *Provided further,* That 15 percent of the remaining amount shall be for the States with the highest mortality rate related to opioid use disorders: *Provided further,* That of the amounts provided for State Opioid Response Grants not more than 2 percent shall be available for Federal administrative expenses, training, technical assistance, and evaluation: *Provided further,* That of the amount not reserved by the previous three provisos, the Secretary shall make allocations to States, territories, and the District of Columbia according to a formula using national survey results that the Secretary determines are the most objective and reliable measure of drug use and drug-related deaths: *Provided further,* That prevention and treatment activities funded through such grants may include education, treatment (including the provision of medication), behavioral health services for individuals in treatment programs, referral to treatment services, recovery support, and medical screening associated with such treatment: *Provided further,* That each State, as well as the District of Columbia, shall receive not less than $4,000,000: *Provided further,* That in addition to amounts provided herein, the following amounts shall be available under section 241 of the PHS Act: (1) $79,200,000 to supplement funds otherwise available for substance use treatment activities to carry out subpart II of part B of title XIX of the PHS Act to fund section 1935(b) technical assistance, national data, data collection and evaluation activities, and further that the total available under this Act for section 1935(b) activities shall not exceed 5 percent of the amounts appropriated for subpart II of part B of title XIX; and (2) $2,000,000 to evaluate substance use treatment programs: *Provided further,* That for purposes of calculating the HIV set-aside under subpart II of part B of title XIX, the rate of cases of HIV shall be used instead of the rate of cases of AIDS: *Provided further,* That each State that receives funds appropriated under this heading in this Act for carrying out subpart II of part B of title XIX of the PHS Act shall expend not less than 10 percent of such funds for recovery support services: *Provided further,* That none of the funds provided for section 1921 of the PHS Act or State Opioid Response Grants shall be subject to section 241 of such Act.

SUBSTANCE USE PREVENTION SERVICES

For carrying out titles III and V of the PHS Act with respect to substance use prevention, $311,912,000.

HEALTH SURVEILLANCE AND PROGRAM SUPPORT

For program support and cross-cutting activities that supplement activities funded under the headings "Mental Health", "Substance Use Services", and "Substance Use Prevention Services" in carrying out titles III, V, and XIX of the PHS Act and the Protection and Advocacy for Individuals with Mental Illness Act in the Substance Use and Mental Health Services Administration, $149,645,000: *Provided,* That in addition to amounts provided herein, $31,428,000 shall be available under section 241 of the PHS Act to supplement funds available to carry out national surveys on drug use and mental health, to collect and analyze program data, and to conduct public awareness and technical assistance activities: *Provided further,* That, in addition, fees may be collected for the costs of publications, data, data tabulations, and data analysis completed under title V of the PHS Act and provided to a public or private entity upon request, which shall be credited to this appropriation and shall remain available until expended for such purposes: *Provided further,* That amounts made available in this Act for carrying out section 501(o) of the PHS Act shall remain available through September 30, 2023: *Provided further,* That funds made available under this heading may be used to supplement program support funding provided under the headings "Mental Health", "Substance Use Services", and "Substance Use Prevention Services".

Note.—A full-year 2022 appropriation for this account was not enacted at the time the Budget was prepared; therefore, the Budget assumes this account is operating under the Continuing Appropriations Act, 2022 (Division A of Public Law 117–43, as amended). The amounts included for 2022 reflect the annualized level provided by the continuing resolution.

Program and Financing (in millions of dollars)

Identification code 075–1362–0–1–551		2021 actual	2022 est.	2023 est.
	Obligations by program activity:			
0006	Mental Health	3,274	1,870	4,183
0007	Substance Use Services	5,190	3,774	5,493
0008	Substance Use Prevention	208	208	312
0009	Health Surveillance and Program Support	4,384	129	150
0011	SAMHSA Prevention Fund	12	12	12
0100	Total, direct program	13,068	5,993	10,150
0799	Total direct obligations	13,068	5,993	10,150
0802	SAMHSA Reimbursables	189	269	269
0810	SAMHSA Reimbursable: PHS Evaluation	129	134	134
0899	Total reimbursable obligations	318	403	403
0900	Total new obligations, unexpired accounts	13,386	6,396	10,553
	Budgetary resources:			
	Unobligated balance:			
1000	Unobligated balance brought forward, Oct 1	6	655	630
1021	Recoveries of prior year unpaid obligations	59		
1070	Unobligated balance (total)	65	655	630
	Budget authority:			
	Appropriations, discretionary:			
1100	Appropriation	10,120	5,948	10,137
1120	Appropriations transferred to other acct [075–1503]	–18		
1121	Appropriations transferred from other acct [075–0116]		12	
1160	Appropriation, discretionary (total)	10,102	5,960	10,137
	Appropriations, mandatory:			
1200	Appropriation [COVID]	3,560		
1221	Appropriations transferred from the Prevention and Public Health Fund [075–0116]	12		12
1260	Appropriations, mandatory (total)	3,572		12
	Spending authority from offsetting collections, discretionary:			
1700	Collected	36	411	177
1701	Change in uncollected payments, Federal sources	283		
1750	Spending auth from offsetting collections, disc (total)	319	411	177
1900	Budget authority (total)	13,993	6,371	10,326
1930	Total budgetary resources available	14,058	7,026	10,956
	Memorandum (non-add) entries:			
1940	Unobligated balance expiring	–17		
1941	Unexpired unobligated balance, end of year	655	630	403
	Change in obligated balance:			
	Unpaid obligations:			
3000	Unpaid obligations, brought forward, Oct 1	8,568	15,527	13,262
3010	New obligations, unexpired accounts	13,386	6,396	10,553

SUBSTANCE USE AND MENTAL HEALTH SERVICES ADMINISTRATION—Continued

Program and Financing—Continued

Identification code 075–1362–0–1–551		2021 actual	2022 est.	2023 est.
3011	Obligations ("upward adjustments"), expired accounts	29		
3020	Outlays (gross)	−6,087	−8,661	−10,509
3040	Recoveries of prior year unpaid obligations, unexpired	−59		
3041	Recoveries of prior year unpaid obligations, expired	−310		
3050	Unpaid obligations, end of year	15,527	13,262	13,306
	Uncollected payments:			
3060	Uncollected pymts, Fed sources, brought forward, Oct 1	−449	−556	−556
3070	Change in uncollected pymts, Fed sources, unexpired	−283		
3071	Change in uncollected pymts, Fed sources, expired	176		
3090	Uncollected pymts, Fed sources, end of year	−556	−556	−556
	Memorandum (non-add) entries:			
3100	Obligated balance, start of year	8,119	14,971	12,706
3200	Obligated balance, end of year	14,971	12,706	12,750
	Budget authority and outlays, net:			
	Discretionary:			
4000	Budget authority, gross	10,421	6,371	10,314
	Outlays, gross:			
4010	Outlays from new discretionary authority	1,165	1,956	3,186
4011	Outlays from discretionary balances	4,906	5,979	6,606
4020	Outlays, gross (total)	6,071	7,935	9,792
	Offsets against gross budget authority and outlays:			
	Offsetting collections (collected) from:			
4030	Federal sources	−169	−409	−175
4033	Non-Federal sources	−8	−2	−2
4040	Offsets against gross budget authority and outlays (total)	−177	−411	−177
	Additional offsets against gross budget authority only:			
4050	Change in uncollected pymts, Fed sources, unexpired	−283		
4052	Offsetting collections credited to expired accounts	141		
4060	Additional offsets against budget authority only (total)	−142		
4070	Budget authority, net (discretionary)	10,102	5,960	10,137
4080	Outlays, net (discretionary)	5,894	7,524	9,615
	Mandatory:			
4090	Budget authority, gross	3,572		12
	Outlays, gross:			
4100	Outlays from new mandatory authority	4		4
4101	Outlays from mandatory balances	12	726	713
4110	Outlays, gross (total)	16	726	717
4180	Budget authority, net (total)	13,674	5,960	10,149
4190	Outlays, net (total)	5,910	8,250	10,332

Summary of Budget Authority and Outlays (in millions of dollars)

	2021 actual	2022 est.	2023 est.
Enacted/requested:			
Budget Authority	13,674	5,960	10,149
Outlays	5,910	8,250	10,332
Legislative proposal, subject to PAYGO:			
Budget Authority			413
Outlays			124
Total:			
Budget Authority	13,674	5,960	10,562
Outlays	5,910	8,250	10,456

This program provides Federal support to strengthen the capacity of the Nation's health care delivery system to provide effective substance misuse prevention, addiction treatment, and mental health services for people at risk for or experiencing substance use disorders or mental illness. SAMHSA builds partnerships with States, communities, tribal organizations, and private not-for-profit organizations to enhance health and reduce the adverse impact of substance *misuse* and mental illness on America's communities.

Object Classification (in millions of dollars)

Identification code 075–1362–0–1–551		2021 actual	2022 est.	2023 est.
	Direct obligations:			
	Personnel compensation:			
11.1	Full-time permanent	48	48	50
11.3	Other than full-time permanent	2	2	2
11.5	Other personnel compensation	1	1	1
11.7	Military personnel	3	4	4
11.9	Total personnel compensation	54	55	57
12.1	Civilian personnel benefits	15	16	17
12.2	Military personnel benefits	2	2	2
21.0	Travel and transportation of persons	1	1	1
23.1	Rental payments to GSA	5	5	7
23.3	Communications, utilities, and miscellaneous charges	1	1	1
24.0	Printing and reproduction	1	1	1
25.1	Advisory and assistance services	36	37	38
25.2	Other services from non-Federal sources	84	94	193
25.3	Other goods and services from Federal sources	24	25	33
25.4	Operation and maintenance of facilities	1	1	1
26.0	Supplies and materials	1	1	1
41.0	Grants, subsidies, and contributions	12,843	5,754	9,798
99.0	Direct obligations	13,068	5,993	10,150
99.0	Reimbursable obligations	318	403	403
99.9	Total new obligations, unexpired accounts	13,386	6,396	10,553

Employment Summary

Identification code 075–1362–0–1–551		2021 actual	2022 est.	2023 est.
1001	Direct civilian full-time equivalent employment	400	462	568
1101	Direct military average strength employment	29	30	31
2001	Reimbursable civilian full-time equivalent employment	40	148	117
2101	Reimbursable military average strength employment	3	10	9

SUBSTANCE USE AND MENTAL HEALTH SERVICES ADMINISTRATION

(Legislative proposal, subject to PAYGO)

Program and Financing (in millions of dollars)

Identification code 075–1362–4–1–551		2021 actual	2022 est.	2023 est.
	Obligations by program activity:			
0006	Mental Health			413
0100	Total, direct program			413
0900	Total new obligations, unexpired accounts (object class 41.0)			413
	Budgetary resources:			
	Budget authority:			
	Appropriations, mandatory:			
1200	Appropriation [CHMC]			413
1930	Total budgetary resources available			413
	Change in obligated balance:			
	Unpaid obligations:			
3010	New obligations, unexpired accounts			413
3020	Outlays (gross)			−124
3050	Unpaid obligations, end of year			289
	Memorandum (non-add) entries:			
3200	Obligated balance, end of year			289
	Budget authority and outlays, net:			
	Mandatory:			
4090	Budget authority, gross			413
	Outlays, gross:			
4100	Outlays from new mandatory authority			124
4180	Budget authority, net (total)			413
4190	Outlays, net (total)			124

The Community Mental Health Centers will expand access and improve the quality of services available to people with serious mental illness (SMI) and serious emotional disorders (SED).

AGENCY FOR HEALTHCARE RESEARCH AND QUALITY

Federal Funds

HEALTHCARE RESEARCH AND QUALITY

For carrying out titles III and IX of the PHS Act, part A of title XI of the Social Security Act, and section 1013 of the Medicare Prescription Drug, Improvement, and Modernization Act of 2003, $376,091,000: Provided, That section 947(c) of the PHS Act shall not apply in fiscal year 2023: Provided further, That, in addition to amounts provided herein, $39,800,000 shall be available to this appropriation, for the purposes under this heading, from amounts provided pursuant to section 241 of the PHS Act: Provided further, That in addition, amounts received from Freedom

DEPARTMENT OF HEALTH AND HUMAN SERVICES

Centers for Medicare and Medicaid Services
Federal Funds

449

of Information Act fees, reimbursable and interagency agreements, and the sale of data shall be credited to this appropriation and shall remain available until September 30, 2024.

Note.—A full-year 2022 appropriation for this account was not enacted at the time the Budget was prepared; therefore, the Budget assumes this account is operating under the Continuing Appropriations Act, 2022 (Division A of Public Law 117–43, as amended). The amounts included for 2022 reflect the annualized level provided by the continuing resolution.

Program and Financing (in millions of dollars)

Identification code 075–1700–0–1–552		2021 actual	2022 est.	2023 est.
	Obligations by program activity:			
0001	Research on Health Costs, Quality and Outcomes	193	195	229
0002	Medical Expenditure Panel Survey	72	72	72
0003	AHRQ Program Support	71	71	75
0799	Total direct obligations	336	338	376
0803	Research on Health Costs, Quality and Outcomes (Reimbursable)	21	31	60
0805	AHRQ Program Support (Reimbursable)		2	1
0899	Total reimbursable obligations	21	33	61
0900	Total new obligations, unexpired accounts	357	371	437
	Budgetary resources:			
	Unobligated balance:			
1000	Unobligated balance brought forward, Oct 1	15	17	2
1001	Discretionary unobligated balance brought fwd, Oct 1	6		
	Budget authority:			
	Appropriations, discretionary:			
1100	Appropriation	338	338	376
1120	Appropriations transferred to other acct [075–1503]	–1		
1160	Appropriation, discretionary (total)	337	338	376
	Spending authority from offsetting collections, discretionary:			
1700	Collected	1	1	1
1701	Change in uncollected payments, Federal sources	13	17	60
1750	Spending auth from offsetting collections, disc (total)	14	18	61
	Spending authority from offsetting collections, mandatory:			
1800	Collected	8		
1900	Budget authority (total)	359	356	437
1930	Total budgetary resources available	374	373	439
	Memorandum (non-add) entries:			
1941	Unexpired unobligated balance, end of year	17	2	2
	Change in obligated balance:			
	Unpaid obligations:			
3000	Unpaid obligations, brought forward, Oct 1	339	335	353
3010	New obligations, unexpired accounts	357	371	437
3020	Outlays (gross)	–355	–353	–419
3041	Recoveries of prior year unpaid obligations, expired	–6		
3050	Unpaid obligations, end of year	335	353	371
	Uncollected payments:			
3060	Uncollected pymts, Fed sources, brought forward, Oct 1	–28	–24	–25
3070	Change in uncollected pymts, Fed sources, unexpired	–13	–17	–60
3071	Change in uncollected pymts, Fed sources, expired	17	16	16
3090	Uncollected pymts, Fed sources, end of year	–24	–25	–69
	Memorandum (non-add) entries:			
3100	Obligated balance, start of year	311	311	328
3200	Obligated balance, end of year	311	328	302
	Budget authority and outlays, net:			
	Discretionary:			
4000	Budget authority, gross	351	356	437
	Outlays, gross:			
4010	Outlays from new discretionary authority	136	136	193
4011	Outlays from discretionary balances	213	217	226
4020	Outlays, gross (total)	349	353	419
	Offsets against gross budget authority and outlays:			
	Offsetting collections (collected) from:			
4030	Federal sources	–18	–17	–60
4030	Federal sources		–1	–1
4040	Offsets against gross budget authority and outlays (total)	–18	–18	–61
	Additional offsets against gross budget authority only:			
4050	Change in uncollected pymts, Fed sources, unexpired	–13	–17	–60
4052	Offsetting collections credited to expired accounts	17	17	60
4060	Additional offsets against budget authority only (total)	4		
4070	Budget authority, net (discretionary)	337	338	376
4080	Outlays, net (discretionary)	331	335	358
	Mandatory:			
4090	Budget authority, gross	8		
	Outlays, gross:			
4101	Outlays from mandatory balances	6		
	Offsets against gross budget authority and outlays:			
	Offsetting collections (collected) from:			
4123	Non-Federal sources	–8		
4180	Budget authority, net (total)	337	338	376
4190	Outlays, net (total)	329	335	358

AHRQ's mission is to produce evidence to make health care safer, higher quality, more accessible, equitable, and affordable, and to work within the U.S. Department of Health and Human Services and with other partners to make sure that the evidence is understood and used.

Object Classification (in millions of dollars)

Identification code 075–1700–0–1–552		2021 actual	2022 est.	2023 est.
	Direct obligations:			
	Personnel compensation:			
11.1	Full-time permanent	33	34	36
11.3	Other than full-time permanent	4	4	4
11.5	Other personnel compensation	1	1	2
11.7	Military personnel	1	1	1
11.9	Total personnel compensation	39	40	43
12.1	Civilian personnel benefits	13	13	14
23.1	Rental payments to GSA	3	3	3
25.2	Other services from non-Federal sources	9	9	9
25.3	Other goods and services from Federal sources	23	23	18
25.5	Research and development contracts	132	132	124
41.0	Grants, subsidies, and contributions	117	118	165
99.0	Direct obligations	336	338	376
99.0	Reimbursable obligations	21	33	61
99.9	Total new obligations, unexpired accounts	357	371	437

Employment Summary

Identification code 075–1700–0–1–552		2021 actual	2022 est.	2023 est.
1001	Direct civilian full-time equivalent employment	257	257	264
1101	Direct military average strength employment	5	5	5
2001	Reimbursable civilian full-time equivalent employment	2	2	2
3001	Allocation account civilian full-time equivalent employment	6	6	24

CENTERS FOR MEDICARE AND MEDICAID SERVICES
Federal Funds

GRANTS TO STATES FOR MEDICAID

For carrying out, except as otherwise provided, titles XI and XIX of the Social Security Act, $367,357,090,000, to remain available until expended.

In addition, for carrying out such titles after May 31, 2023, for the last quarter of fiscal year 2023 for unanticipated costs incurred for the current fiscal year, such sums as may be necessary, to remain available until expended.

In addition, for carrying out such titles for the first quarter of fiscal year 2024, $197,580,474,000, to remain available until expended.

Payment under such title XIX may be made for any quarter with respect to a State plan or plan amendment in effect during such quarter, if submitted in or prior to such quarter and approved in that or any subsequent quarter.

Note.—A full-year 2022 appropriation for this account was not enacted at the time the Budget was prepared; therefore, the Budget assumes this account is operating under the Continuing Appropriations Act, 2022 (Division A of Public Law 117–43, as amended). The amounts included for 2022 reflect the annualized level provided by the continuing resolution.

Program and Financing (in millions of dollars)

Identification code 075–0512–0–1–551		2021 actual	2022 est.	2023 est.
	Obligations by program activity:			
0001	Medicaid Vendor Payments	531,284	584,922	555,251
0002	State and local administration	24,509	22,954	23,649
0003	Vaccines for Children	3,806	5,555	5,609
0799	Total direct obligations	559,599	613,431	584,509
0900	Total new obligations, unexpired accounts (object class 41.0)	559,599	613,431	584,509

Centers for Medicare and Medicaid Services—Continued
Federal Funds—Continued

GRANTS TO STATES FOR MEDICAID—Continued

Program and Financing—Continued

Identification code 075–0512–0–1–551	2021 actual	2022 est.	2023 est.
Budgetary resources:			
Unobligated balance:			
1000 Unobligated balance brought forward, Oct 1	311	418	
1021 Recoveries of prior year unpaid obligations	27,081	52,757	49,991
1033 Recoveries of prior year paid obligations	11,781		
1070 Unobligated balance (total)	39,173	53,175	49,991
Budget authority:			
Appropriations, mandatory:			
1200 Appropriation	379,581	409,923	367,357
Advance appropriations, mandatory:			
1270 Advance appropriation	139,903	148,732	165,722
Spending authority from offsetting collections, mandatory:			
1800 Collected	1,126	1,601	1,439
1801 Change in uncollected payments, Federal sources	234		
1850 Spending auth from offsetting collections, mand (total)	1,360	1,601	1,439
1900 Budget authority (total)	520,844	560,256	534,518
1930 Total budgetary resources available	560,017	613,431	584,509
Memorandum (non-add) entries:			
1941 Unexpired unobligated balance, end of year	418		
Change in obligated balance:			
Unpaid obligations:			
3000 Unpaid obligations, brought forward, Oct 1	72,293	71,316	68,551
3010 New obligations, unexpired accounts	559,599	613,431	584,509
3020 Outlays (gross)	–533,495	–563,439	–537,216
3040 Recoveries of prior year unpaid obligations, unexpired	–27,081	–52,757	–49,991
3050 Unpaid obligations, end of year	71,316	68,551	65,853
Uncollected payments:			
3060 Uncollected pymts, Fed sources, brought forward, Oct 1	–1,084	–1,318	–1,318
3070 Change in uncollected pymts, Fed sources, unexpired	–234		
3090 Uncollected pymts, Fed sources, end of year	–1,318	–1,318	–1,318
Memorandum (non-add) entries:			
3100 Obligated balance, start of year	71,209	69,998	67,233
3200 Obligated balance, end of year	69,998	67,233	64,535
Budget authority and outlays, net:			
Mandatory:			
4090 Budget authority, gross	520,844	560,256	534,518
Outlays, gross:			
4100 Outlays from new mandatory authority	504,507	545,879	534,518
4101 Outlays from mandatory balances	28,988	17,560	2,698
4110 Outlays, gross (total)	533,495	563,439	537,216
Offsets against gross budget authority and outlays:			
Offsetting collections (collected) from:			
4120 Federal sources	–1,126	–1,601	–1,439
4123 Non-Federal sources	–11,781		
4130 Offsets against gross budget authority and outlays (total)	–12,907	–1,601	–1,439
Additional offsets against gross budget authority only:			
4140 Change in uncollected pymts, Fed sources, unexpired	–234		
4143 Recoveries of prior year paid obligations, unexpired accounts	11,781		
4150 Additional offsets against budget authority only (total)	11,547		
4160 Budget authority, net (mandatory)	519,484	558,655	533,079
4170 Outlays, net (mandatory)	520,588	561,838	535,777
4180 Budget authority, net (total)	519,484	558,655	533,079
4190 Outlays, net (total)	520,588	561,838	535,777

Summary of Budget Authority and Outlays (in millions of dollars)

	2021 actual	2022 est.	2023 est.
Enacted/requested:			
Budget Authority	519,484	558,655	533,079
Outlays	520,588	561,838	535,777
Legislative proposal, not subject to PAYGO:			
Budget Authority			–18
Outlays			–18
Legislative proposal, subject to PAYGO:			
Budget Authority			134
Outlays			134
Total:			
Budget Authority	519,484	558,655	533,195
Outlays	520,588	561,838	535,893

Medicaid assists States in providing medical care to their low-income populations by granting Federal matching payments under title XIX of the Social Security Act to States with approved plans.

Medicaid estimates assume budget authority for expenses that are incurred but not reported (IBNR).

Authorized as part of title XIX, Vaccines for Children (VFC) finances the purchase of vaccines for low-income, eligible children. VFC is administered by the Centers for Disease Control and Prevention and is funded entirely by the Federal Government.

Vaccines for Children

(in millions of dollars)

Obligations	2021	2022	2023
Vaccine Purchase	3,570	5,292	5,267
Vaccine Stockpile	10	11	99
Ordering, Distribution, and Operations	226	252	242
Total Obligations	3,806	5,555	5,608

GRANTS TO STATES FOR MEDICAID

(Legislative proposal, not subject to PAYGO)

Program and Financing (in millions of dollars)

Identification code 075–0512–2–1–551	2021 actual	2022 est.	2023 est.
Obligations by program activity:			
0001 Medicaid Vendor Payments			–18
0799 Total direct obligations			–18
0900 Total new obligations, unexpired accounts (object class 41.0)			–18
Budgetary resources:			
Budget authority:			
Appropriations, mandatory:			
1200 Appropriation			–18
1900 Budget authority (total)			–18
1930 Total budgetary resources available			–18
Change in obligated balance:			
Unpaid obligations:			
3010 New obligations, unexpired accounts			–18
3020 Outlays (gross)			18
Budget authority and outlays, net:			
Mandatory:			
4090 Budget authority, gross			–18
Outlays, gross:			
4100 Outlays from new mandatory authority			–18
4180 Budget authority, net (total)			–18
4190 Outlays, net (total)			–18

This schedule reflects the non-PAYGO impacts on Medicaid resulting from the proposed allocation adjustment for the Social Security Administration. Please refer to the narrative in the Limitation on Administrative Expenses (Social Security Administration) account for more information.

GRANTS TO STATES FOR MEDICAID

(Legislative proposal, subject to PAYGO)

Program and Financing (in millions of dollars)

Identification code 075–0512–4–1–551	2021 actual	2022 est.	2023 est.
Obligations by program activity:			
0001 Medicaid Vendor Payments			134
0799 Total direct obligations			134
0900 Total new obligations, unexpired accounts (object class 41.0)			134
Budgetary resources:			
Budget authority:			
Appropriations, mandatory:			
1200 Appropriation			134
1900 Budget authority (total)			134
1930 Total budgetary resources available			134

DEPARTMENT OF HEALTH AND HUMAN SERVICES

Change in obligated balance:
Unpaid obligations:

3010	New obligations, unexpired accounts			134
3020	Outlays (gross)			−134

Budget authority and outlays, net:
Mandatory:

4090	Budget authority, gross			134
	Outlays, gross:			
4100	Outlays from new mandatory authority			134
4180	Budget authority, net (total)			134
4190	Outlays, net (total)			134

This schedule reflects the Administration's Medicaid proposals.

STATE GRANTS AND DEMONSTRATIONS

Program and Financing (in millions of dollars)

Identification code 075–0516–0–1–551	2021 actual	2022 est.	2023 est.
Obligations by program activity:			
0012 Medicaid integrity program	76	107	115
0018 Money follows the person (MFP) demonstration	414	765	819
0019 MFP evaluations and technical support	2	2	2
0023 Grants to improve outreach and enrollment	20	52	9
0028 Demo to increase substance use provider under the Medicaid Program	1	1	
0029 Community-based mobile crisis intervention services	15		
0799 Total direct obligations	528	927	945
0900 Total new obligations, unexpired accounts	528	927	945
Budgetary resources:			
Unobligated balance:			
1000 Unobligated balance brought forward, Oct 1	798	788	665
1012 Unobligated balance transfers between expired and unexpired accounts	268	292	
1021 Recoveries of prior year unpaid obligations	16		
1070 Unobligated balance (total)	1,082	1,080	665
Budget authority:			
Appropriations, mandatory:			
1200 Appropriation	531	543	547
1230 Appropriations and/or unobligated balance of appropriations permanently reduced	−5	−31	−32
1260 Appropriations, mandatory (total)	526	512	515
1900 Budget authority (total)	526	512	515
1930 Total budgetary resources available	1,608	1,592	1,180
Memorandum (non-add) entries:			
1940 Unobligated balance expiring	−292		
1941 Unexpired unobligated balance, end of year	788	665	235
Change in obligated balance:			
Unpaid obligations:			
3000 Unpaid obligations, brought forward, Oct 1	418	531	1,094
3010 New obligations, unexpired accounts	528	927	945
3020 Outlays (gross)	−359	−364	−531
3040 Recoveries of prior year unpaid obligations, unexpired	−16		
3041 Recoveries of prior year unpaid obligations, expired	−40		
3050 Unpaid obligations, end of year	531	1,094	1,508
Memorandum (non-add) entries:			
3100 Obligated balance, start of year	418	531	1,094
3200 Obligated balance, end of year	531	1,094	1,508
Budget authority and outlays, net:			
Mandatory:			
4090 Budget authority, gross	526	512	515
Outlays, gross:			
4100 Outlays from new mandatory authority	32	42	51
4101 Outlays from mandatory balances	327	322	480
4110 Outlays, gross (total)	359	364	531
4180 Budget authority, net (total)	526	512	515
4190 Outlays, net (total)	359	364	531

Summary of Budget Authority and Outlays (in millions of dollars)

	2021 actual	2022 est.	2023 est.
Enacted/requested:			
Budget Authority	526	512	515
Outlays	359	364	531
Legislative proposal, subject to PAYGO:			
Budget Authority			545
Outlays			545
Total:			
Budget Authority	526	512	1,060
Outlays	359	364	1,076

State Grants and Demonstrations includes funding for grant programs enacted in several legislative authorities, including the Ticket to Work and Work Incentives Improvement Act of 1999 (P.L. 106–170), the Medicare Prescription Drug, Improvement, and Modernization Act of 2003 (P.L. 108–173), the Deficit Reduction Act of 2005 (P.L. 109–171), the Children's Health Insurance Program Reauthorization Act of 2009 (P.L. 111–3), the Patient Protection and Affordable Care Act (P.L. 111–148), the Health Care and Education Reconciliation Act of 2010 (P.L. 111–152), the Protecting Access to Medicare Act of 2014 (P.L. 113–93), and the Medicare Access and CHIP Reauthorization Act of 2015 (P.L. 114–10). The account also includes funding for grant programs enacted in the HEALTHY KIDS Act (P.L. 115–120), the Advancing Chronic Care, Extenders, and Social Services Act (P.L. 115–123), the Substance Use-Disorder Prevention that Promotes Opioid Recovery and Treatment for Patients and Communities Act (P.L. 115–271), the Medicaid Extenders Act of 2019 (P.L. 116–3), the Medicaid Services Investment and Accountability Act of 2019 (P.L. 116–16), the Sustaining Excellence in Medicaid Act of 2019 (P.L. 116–39), the Continuing Appropriations Act, 2020, the Health Extenders Act of 2019 (P.L. 116–59), the Further Consolidated Appropriation Act, 2020 (P.L. 116–94), the Consolidated Appropriations Act, 2021 (P.L. 116–260), and the American Rescue Plan Act of 2021 (P.L. 117–2).

Object Classification (in millions of dollars)

Identification code 075–0516–0–1–551	2021 actual	2022 est.	2023 est.
11.1 Direct obligations: Personnel compensation: Full-time permanent - Medicaid Integrity Program	35	39	39
11.9 Total personnel compensation	35	39	39
12.1 Civilian personnel benefits - Medicaid Integrity Program	9	9	9
41.0 Grants, subsidies, and contributions - Medicaid Integrity Program	32	59	67
41.0 Grants, subsidies, and contributions - Money follows the person (MFP) demonstrations	414	765	819
41.0 Grants, subsidies, and contributions - MFP evaluations and technical support	2	2	2
41.0 Grants, subsidies, and contributions - Grants to improve outreach and enrollment	20	52	9
41.0 Grants, subsidies, and contributions - Demo to increase substance use provider capacity under Medicaid	1	1	
41.0 Grants, subsidies, and contributions - Community-based mobile crisis intervention services	15		
99.0 Direct obligations	528	927	945
99.9 Total new obligations, unexpired accounts	528	927	945

Employment Summary

Identification code 075–0516–0–1–551	2021 actual	2022 est.	2023 est.
1001 Direct civilian full-time equivalent employment	218	240	240
1101 Direct military average strength employment	6	6	6

STATE GRANTS AND DEMONSTRATIONS

(Legislative proposal, subject to PAYGO)

Program and Financing (in millions of dollars)

Identification code 075–0516–4–1–551	2021 actual	2022 est.	2023 est.
Obligations by program activity:			
0027 Demonstration Programs to Improve Mental Health Services			45
0030 Establish performance bonus fund to improve behavioral health in Medicaid			500
0799 Total direct obligations			545
0900 Total new obligations, unexpired accounts			545

Centers for Medicare and Medicaid Services—Continued
Federal Funds—Continued

STATE GRANTS AND DEMONSTRATIONS—Continued

Program and Financing—Continued

Identification code 075–0516–4–1–551		2021 actual	2022 est.	2023 est.
	Budgetary resources:			
	Budget authority:			
	Appropriations, mandatory:			
1200	Appropriation			545
1900	Budget authority (total)			545
1930	Total budgetary resources available			545
	Change in obligated balance:			
	Unpaid obligations:			
3010	New obligations, unexpired accounts			545
3020	Outlays (gross)			–545
	Budget authority and outlays, net:			
	Mandatory:			
4090	Budget authority, gross			545
	Outlays, gross:			
4100	Outlays from new mandatory authority			545
4180	Budget authority, net (total)			545
4190	Outlays, net (total)			545

This schedule reflects the Administration's State Grants and Demonstrations proposals.

Object Classification (in millions of dollars)

Identification code 075–0516–4–1–551		2021 actual	2022 est.	2023 est.
	Direct obligations:			
41.0	Grants, subsidies, and contributions - Demos to Improve Mental Health			45
41.0	Grants, subsidies, and contributions - Establish performance bonus fund to improve behavioral health in Medicaid			500
99.0	Direct obligations			545
99.9	Total new obligations, unexpired accounts			545

PAYMENTS TO THE HEALTH CARE TRUST FUNDS

For payment to the Federal Hospital Insurance Trust Fund and the Federal Supplementary Medical Insurance Trust Fund, as provided under sections 217(g), 1844, and 1860D-16 of the Social Security Act, sections 103(c) and 111(d) of the Social Security Amendments of 1965, section 278(d)(3) of Public Law 97–248, and for administrative expenses incurred pursuant to section 201(g) of the Social Security Act, $548,130,000,000.

In addition, for making matching payments under section 1844 and benefit payments under section 1860D-16 of the Social Security Act that were not anticipated in budget estimates, such sums as may be necessary.

Note.—A full-year 2022 appropriation for this account was not enacted at the time the Budget was prepared; therefore, the Budget assumes this account is operating under the Continuing Appropriations Act, 2022 (Division A of Public Law 117–43, as amended). The amounts included for 2022 reflect the annualized level provided by the continuing resolution.

Program and Financing (in millions of dollars)

Identification code 075–0580–0–1–571		2021 actual	2022 est.	2023 est.
	Obligations by program activity:			
0001	Federal contribution to match premiums (SMI)	335,479	384,646	434,348
0002	Part D benefits (Rx Drug)	96,290	100,969	111,800
0003	Part D Federal administration (Rx Drug)	882	882	600
0004	General Fund Transfers to HI	1,327	1,360	1,376
0006	Federal Bureau of Investigation (HCFAC)	148	153	157
0007	Federal payments from taxation of OASDI benefits (HI)	24,975	32,439	35,072
0008	Criminal fines (HCFAC)	68	34	21
0009	Civil penalties and damages (HCFAC—DOJ and CMS administration)	15	53	54
0010	Asset Forfeiture	135	33	34
0011	State Low Income Determinations	5	5	5
0900	Total new obligations, unexpired accounts	459,324	520,574	583,467
	Budgetary resources:			
	Budget authority:			
	Appropriations, mandatory:			
1200	Appropriation (definite, annual)	439,514	487,862	548,129
1200	Appropriation (indefinite, annual)	13,514		
1200	Appropriation (permanent, Taxation of OASDI)	24,975	32,439	35,072
1200	Appropriation (permanent, annual, HCFAC - FBI)	148	153	157
1200	Appropriation (permanent, HCFAC)	218	120	109
1200	Appropriation (definite, annual, CAA Section 101)	3,000		
1260	Appropriations, mandatory (total)	481,369	520,574	583,467
1930	Total budgetary resources available	481,369	520,574	583,467
	Memorandum (non-add) entries:			
1940	Unobligated balance expiring	–22,045		
	Change in obligated balance:			
	Unpaid obligations:			
3000	Unpaid obligations, brought forward, Oct 1	16,873	16,385	72,968
3010	New obligations, unexpired accounts	459,324	520,574	583,467
3020	Outlays (gross)	–444,202	–463,991	–506,496
3041	Recoveries of prior year unpaid obligations, expired	–15,610		
3050	Unpaid obligations, end of year	16,385	72,968	149,939
	Memorandum (non-add) entries:			
3100	Obligated balance, start of year	16,873	16,385	72,968
3200	Obligated balance, end of year	16,385	72,968	149,939
	Budget authority and outlays, net:			
	Mandatory:			
4090	Budget authority, gross	481,369	520,574	583,467
	Outlays, gross:			
4100	Outlays from new mandatory authority	443,922	447,606	478,338
4101	Outlays from mandatory balances	280	16,385	28,158
4110	Outlays, gross (total)	444,202	463,991	506,496
	Offsets against gross budget authority and outlays:			
	Offsetting collections (collected) from:			
4120	Federal sources	–22		
4123	Non-Federal sources	–4,507		
4130	Offsets against gross budget authority and outlays (total)	–4,529		
	Additional offsets against gross budget authority only:			
4142	Offsetting collections credited to expired accounts	4,529		
4160	Budget authority, net (mandatory)	481,369	520,574	583,467
4170	Outlays, net (mandatory)	439,673	463,991	506,496
4180	Budget authority, net (total)	481,369	520,574	583,467
4190	Outlays, net (total)	439,673	463,991	506,496

Payments are made to the Federal Hospital Insurance and Federal Supplementary Medical Insurance trust funds from the general fund of the Treasury to finance Medicare's medical and drug benefits for beneficiaries and administrative expenses that are properly chargeable to the general fund.

Object Classification (in millions of dollars)

Identification code 075–0580–0–1–571		2021 actual	2022 est.	2023 est.
	Direct obligations:			
41.0	Grants, subsidies, and contributions	361,506	519,214	582,091
42.0	Insurance claims and indemnities (HI Uninsured Federal)	95	82	52
94.0	Financial transfers (Federal admin)	97,723	1,278	1,324
99.9	Total new obligations, unexpired accounts	459,324	520,574	583,467

QUALITY IMPROVEMENT ORGANIZATIONS

Program and Financing (in millions of dollars)

Identification code 075–0519–0–1–571		2021 actual	2022 est.	2023 est.
	Obligations by program activity:			
0001	QIO Clinical Quality Improvement		144	90
0003	QIO Support Contracts	422	453	475
0004	QIO Administration	69	75	76
0005	American Rescue Plan Act - SNF Infection Control Support		200	
0900	Total new obligations, unexpired accounts	491	872	641
	Budgetary resources:			
	Unobligated balance:			
1000	Unobligated balance brought forward, Oct 1		200	

DEPARTMENT OF HEALTH AND HUMAN SERVICES

Centers for Medicare and Medicaid Services—Continued
Federal Funds—Continued

453

		2021 actual	2022 est.	2023 est.
	Budget authority:			
	Appropriations, mandatory:			
1200	Appropriation	200	....	....
	Spending authority from offsetting collections, mandatory:			
1800	Collected	172	311	174
1801	Change in uncollected payments, Federal sources	469	361	467
1850	Spending auth from offsetting collections, mand (total)	641	672	641
1900	Budget authority (total)	841	672	641
1930	Total budgetary resources available	841	872	641
	Memorandum (non-add) entries:			
1940	Unobligated balance expiring	–150		
1941	Unexpired unobligated balance, end of year	200		
	Change in obligated balance:			
	Unpaid obligations:			
3000	Unpaid obligations, brought forward, Oct 1	1,105	928	928
3010	New obligations, unexpired accounts	491	872	641
3011	Obligations ("upward adjustments"), expired accounts	69		
3020	Outlays (gross)	–645	–872	–641
3041	Recoveries of prior year unpaid obligations, expired	–92		
3050	Unpaid obligations, end of year	928	928	928
	Uncollected payments:			
3060	Uncollected pymts, Fed sources, brought forward, Oct 1	–2,005	–1,887	–2,248
3070	Change in uncollected pymts, Fed sources, unexpired	–469	–361	–467
3071	Change in uncollected pymts, Fed sources, expired	587		
3090	Uncollected pymts, Fed sources, end of year	–1,887	–2,248	–2,715
	Memorandum (non-add) entries:			
3100	Obligated balance, start of year	–900	–959	–1,320
3200	Obligated balance, end of year	–959	–1,320	–1,787
	Budget authority and outlays, net:			
	Mandatory:			
4090	Budget authority, gross	841	672	641
	Outlays, gross:			
4100	Outlays from new mandatory authority	176	203	247
4101	Outlays from mandatory balances	469	669	394
4110	Outlays, gross (total)	645	872	641
	Offsets against gross budget authority and outlays:			
	Offsetting collections (collected) from:			
4120	Federal sources	–642	–672	–641
	Additional offsets against gross budget authority only:			
4140	Change in uncollected pymts, Fed sources, unexpired	–469	–361	–467
4142	Offsetting collections credited to expired accounts	470	361	467
4150	Additional offsets against budget authority only (total)	1		
4160	Budget authority, net (mandatory)	200		
4170	Outlays, net (mandatory)	3	200	
4180	Budget authority, net (total)	200		
4190	Outlays, net (total)	3	200	

Part B of title XI of the Social Security Act, as amended by the Peer Review Improvement Act of 1982 (P.L. 97–248), provides the statutory authority for the Medicare Quality Improvement Organization (QIO) Program. The mission of the program is to promote the effectiveness, efficiency, economy, and quality of services delivered to Medicare beneficiaries and to ensure that those services are reasonable and necessary. The program is funded through transfers from the Medicare Hospital Insurance Trust Fund and the Medicare Supplementary Medical Insurance Trust Fund. In FY 2012, a Treasury account specific to the QIO Program was established to improve budgetary operations.

Object Classification (in millions of dollars)

Identification code 075–0519–0–1–571		2021 actual	2022 est.	2023 est.
	Direct obligations:			
	Personnel compensation:			
11.1	Full-time permanent	33	39	39
11.5	Other personnel compensation	1	1	1
11.7	Military personnel	1	1	1
11.9	Total personnel compensation	35	41	41
12.1	Civilian personnel benefits	12	12	12
23.1	Rental payments to GSA	4	4	4
25.2	Other services from non-Federal sources	418	762	562
25.3	Other goods and services from Federal sources	13	33	13
25.4	Operation and maintenance of facilities	9	20	9
99.9	Total new obligations, unexpired accounts	491	872	641

Employment Summary

Identification code 075–0519–0–1–571		2021 actual	2022 est.	2023 est.
1001	Direct civilian full-time equivalent employment	264	253	262
1101	Direct military average strength employment	6	6	8

PROGRAM MANAGEMENT

For carrying out, except as otherwise provided, titles XI, XVIII, XIX, and XXI of the Social Security Act, titles XIII and XXVII of the PHS Act, the Clinical Laboratory Improvement Amendments of 1988, and other responsibilities of the Centers for Medicare & Medicaid Services, not to exceed $4,346,985,000, to be transferred from the Federal Hospital Insurance Trust Fund and the Federal Supplementary Medical Insurance Trust Fund, as authorized by section 201(g) of the Social Security Act; together with all funds collected in accordance with section 353 of the PHS Act and section 1857(e)(2) of the Social Security Act, funds retained by the Secretary pursuant to section 1893(h) of the Social Security Act, and such sums as may be collected from authorized user fees and the sale of data, which shall be credited to this account and remain available until expended: Provided, That all funds derived in accordance with 31 U.S.C. 9701 from organizations established under title XIII of the PHS Act shall be credited to and available for carrying out the purposes of this appropriation: Provided further, That the Secretary is directed to collect fees in fiscal year 2023 from Medicare Advantage organizations pursuant to section 1857(e)(2) of the Social Security Act and from eligible organizations with risk-sharing contracts under section 1876 of that Act pursuant to section 1876(k)(4)(D) of that Act: Provided further, That of the amount made available under this heading, $494,261,000 shall remain available until September 30, 2024, and shall be available for the Survey and Certification Program.

Note.—A full-year 2022 appropriation for this account was not enacted at the time the Budget was prepared; therefore, the Budget assumes this account is operating under the Continuing Appropriations Act, 2022 (Division A of Public Law 117–43, as amended). The amounts included for 2022 reflect the annualized level provided by the continuing resolution.

Program and Financing (in millions of dollars)

Identification code 075–0511–0–1–550		2021 actual	2022 est.	2023 est.
	Obligations by program activity:			
0001	Program operations	2,772	2,785	2,957
0002	Federal administration	769	773	896
0003	State survey and certification	426	397	494
0004	Research, demonstrations, and evaluation projects	20	20	
0007	ARRA Medicare/Medicaid HIT	19	22	19
0009	Other Mandatory Program Activity	106	101	88
0100	Total direct program	4,112	4,098	4,454
0799	Total direct obligations	4,112	4,098	4,454
0801	Clinical laboratory improvement amendments	72	78	78
0802	Sale of data	27	20	20
0803	Coordination of benefits	43	38	40
0804	Medicare advantage/Prescription drug plan	96	96	109
0805	Provider enrollment	27	73	74
0806	Recovery audit contractors	133	204	204
0808	Marketplace User Fees	1,729	1,879	1,723
0810	Risk Adjustment Administrative Expenses	47	53	51
0813	Other reimbursable program activity	37	56	59
0899	Total reimbursable obligations	2,211	2,497	2,358
0900	Total new obligations, unexpired accounts	6,323	6,595	6,812
	Budgetary resources:			
	Unobligated balance:			
1000	Unobligated balance brought forward, Oct 1	3,214	4,639	4,690
1001	Discretionary unobligated balance brought fwd, Oct 1	182		
1020	Adjustment of unobligated bal brought forward, Oct 1	651		
1021	Recoveries of prior year unpaid obligations	67		
1070	Unobligated balance (total)	3,932	4,639	4,690
	Budget authority:			
	Appropriations, mandatory:			
1200	Appropriation (General Fund Total)	503	3	3
	Spending authority from offsetting collections, discretionary:			
1700	Collected	1,768	4,055	4,428
1701	Change in uncollected payments, Federal sources	2,279		
1710	Spending authority from offsetting collections transferred to other accounts [075–1503]	–12		
1750	Spending auth from offsetting collections, disc (total)	4,035	4,055	4,428

Centers for Medicare and Medicaid Services—Continued
Federal Funds—Continued

PROGRAM MANAGEMENT—Continued

Program and Financing—Continued

Identification code 075–0511–0–1–550		2021 actual	2022 est.	2023 est.
	Spending authority from offsetting collections, mandatory:			
1800	Collected	2,584	2,620	2,465
1801	Change in uncollected payments, Federal sources	–45	....	....
1802	Offsetting collections (previously unavailable)	95	96	99
1823	New and/or unobligated balance of spending authority from offsetting collections temporarily reduced	–97	–128	–146
1850	Spending auth from offsetting collections, mand (total)	2,537	2,588	2,418
1900	Budget authority (total)	7,075	6,646	6,849
1930	Total budgetary resources available	11,007	11,285	11,539
	Memorandum (non-add) entries:			
1940	Unobligated balance expiring	–45	....	....
1941	Unexpired unobligated balance, end of year	4,639	4,690	4,727
	Change in obligated balance:			
	Unpaid obligations:			
3000	Unpaid obligations, brought forward, Oct 1	4,717	4,893	4,408
3010	New obligations, unexpired accounts	6,323	6,595	6,812
3011	Obligations ("upward adjustments"), expired accounts ...	31	....	....
3020	Outlays (gross)	–5,927	–7,080	–6,820
3040	Recoveries of prior year unpaid obligations, unexpired	–67	....	....
3041	Recoveries of prior year unpaid obligations, expired	–184	....	....
3050	Unpaid obligations, end of year	4,893	4,408	4,400
	Uncollected payments:			
3060	Uncollected pymts, Fed sources, brought forward, Oct 1 ...	–4,810	–5,465	–5,465
3061	Adjustments to uncollected pymts, Fed sources, brought forward, Oct 1	–651	....	....
3070	Change in uncollected pymts, Fed sources, unexpired	–2,234	....	....
3071	Change in uncollected pymts, Fed sources, expired	2,230	....	....
3090	Uncollected pymts, Fed sources, end of year	–5,465	–5,465	–5,465
	Memorandum (non-add) entries:			
3100	Obligated balance, start of year	–744	–572	–1,057
3200	Obligated balance, end of year	–572	–1,057	–1,065
	Budget authority and outlays, net:			
	Discretionary:			
4000	Budget authority, gross	4,035	4,055	4,428
	Outlays, gross:			
4010	Outlays from new discretionary authority	1,663	2,068	2,255
4011	Outlays from discretionary balances	2,186	2,198	2,065
4020	Outlays, gross (total)	3,849	4,266	4,320
	Offsets against gross budget authority and outlays:			
	Offsetting collections (collected) from:			
4030	Federal sources	–3,738	–3,975	–4,346
4033	Non-Federal sources	–38	–80	–82
4040	Offsets against gross budget authority and outlays (total)	–3,776	–4,055	–4,428
	Additional offsets against gross budget authority only:			
4050	Change in uncollected pymts, Fed sources, unexpired	–2,279	....	....
4052	Offsetting collections credited to expired accounts	2,008	....	....
4060	Additional offsets against budget authority only (total)	–271	....	....
4070	Budget authority, net (discretionary)	–12	....	....
4080	Outlays, net (discretionary)	73	211	–108
	Mandatory:			
4090	Budget authority, gross	3,040	2,591	2,421
	Outlays, gross:			
4100	Outlays from new mandatory authority	24	1,270	1,174
4101	Outlays from mandatory balances	2,054	1,544	1,326
4110	Outlays, gross (total)	2,078	2,814	2,500
	Offsets against gross budget authority and outlays:			
	Offsetting collections (collected) from:			
4120	Federal sources	–738	–63	–68
4123	Non-Federal sources	–1,850	–2,557	–2,397
4130	Offsets against gross budget authority and outlays (total)	–2,588	–2,620	–2,465
	Additional offsets against gross budget authority only:			
4140	Change in uncollected pymts, Fed sources, unexpired	45	....	....
4142	Offsetting collections credited to expired accounts	4	....	....
4150	Additional offsets against budget authority only (total)	49	....	....
4160	Budget authority, net (mandatory)	501	–29	–44
4170	Outlays, net (mandatory)	–510	194	35
4180	Budget authority, net (total)	489	–29	–44
4190	Outlays, net (total)	–437	405	–73
	Memorandum (non-add) entries:			
5090	Unexpired unavailable balance, SOY: Offsetting collections	224	219	251
5091	Expiring unavailable balance: Offsetting collections	–7	....	....
5092	Unexpired unavailable balance, EOY: Offsetting collections	219	251	298
5093	Expired unavailable balance, SOY: Offsetting collections	115	122	122
5095	Expired unavailable balance, EOY: Offsetting collections	115	122	122

Summary of Budget Authority and Outlays (in millions of dollars)

	2021 actual	2022 est.	2023 est.
Enacted/requested:			
Budget Authority	489	–29	–44
Outlays	–437	405	–73
Legislative proposal, subject to PAYGO:			
Budget Authority			300
Outlays			50
Total:			
Budget Authority	489	–29	256
Outlays	–437	405	–23

Program management activities include funding for program operations, survey and certification, the Clinical Laboratory Improvement Amendments (CLIA), Medicare Advantage, Medicare Part D coordination of benefits, recovery audit contracts, and other administrative costs.

Object Classification (in millions of dollars)

Identification code 075–0511–0–1–550		2021 actual	2022 est.	2023 est.
	Direct obligations:			
	Personnel compensation:			
11.1	Full-time permanent	409	408	443
11.3	Other than full-time permanent	11	11	12
11.5	Other personnel compensation	9	9	10
11.7	Military personnel	14	14	15
11.9	Total personnel compensation	443	442	480
12.1	Civilian personnel benefits	186	185	202
12.2	Military personnel benefits	8	8	9
21.0	Travel and transportation of persons	1	1	1
23.1	Rental payments to GSA	4	4	4
23.3	Communications, utilities, and miscellaneous charges	8	8	9
24.0	Printing and reproduction	56	56	61
25.2	Other services from non-Federal sources	2,831	2,820	3,065
25.3	Other goods and services from Federal sources	145	145	157
25.6	Medical care	393	392	426
25.7	Operation and maintenance of equipment	21	21	23
41.0	Grants, subsidies, and contributions	16	16	17
99.0	Direct obligations	4,112	4,098	4,454
99.0	Reimbursable obligations	2,211	2,497	2,358
99.9	Total new obligations, unexpired accounts	6,323	6,595	6,812

Employment Summary

Identification code 075–0511–0–1–550		2021 actual	2022 est.	2023 est.
1001	Direct civilian full-time equivalent employment	4,075	4,106	4,394
1001	Direct civilian full-time equivalent employment	56	35	26
1101	Direct military average strength employment	130	130	125
2001	Reimbursable civilian full-time equivalent employment	460	555	576
2101	Reimbursable military average strength employment	21	21	21

PROGRAM MANAGEMENT

(Legislative proposal, subject to PAYGO)

Program and Financing (in millions of dollars)

Identification code 075–0511–4–1–550		2021 actual	2022 est.	2023 est.
	Obligations by program activity:			
0001	Program operations			300
0100	Total direct program			300
0799	Total direct obligations			300
0900	Total new obligations, unexpired accounts (object class 25.2)			300
	Budgetary resources:			
	Budget authority:			
	Appropriations, mandatory:			
1200	Appropriation (General Fund Total)			300
1900	Budget authority (total)			300

DEPARTMENT OF HEALTH AND HUMAN SERVICES

1930	Total budgetary resources available				300
	Change in obligated balance:				
	Unpaid obligations:				
3010	New obligations, unexpired accounts				300
3020	Outlays (gross)				−50
3050	Unpaid obligations, end of year				250
	Memorandum (non-add) entries:				
3200	Obligated balance, end of year				250
	Budget authority and outlays, net:				
	Mandatory:				
4090	Budget authority, gross				300
	Outlays, gross:				
4100	Outlays from new mandatory authority				50
4180	Budget authority, net (total)				300
4190	Outlays, net (total)				50

This display includes resources to implement HHS's legislative proposals in the FY 2023 Budget.

———

CHILDREN'S HEALTH INSURANCE FUND

Program and Financing (in millions of dollars)

Identification code 075–0515–0–1–551	2021 actual	2022 est.	2023 est.
Obligations by program activity:			
0001 Grants to states and US territories	18,144	19,218	18,686
0002 CHIP Redistribution Funds	1		
0003 Child health quality	7	12	16
0900 Total new obligations, unexpired accounts (object class 41.0)	18,152	19,230	18,702
Budgetary resources:			
Unobligated balance:			
1000 Unobligated balance brought forward, Oct 1	12,251	10,328	10,998
1011 Unobligated balance transfer from other acct [075–5551]	1		
1033 Recoveries of prior year paid obligations	84		
1070 Unobligated balance (total)	12,336	10,328	10,998
Budget authority:			
Appropriations, discretionary:			
1131 Unobligated balance of appropriations permanently reduced		−2,000	
1134 Appropriations precluded from obligation		−4,000	−12,315
1160 Appropriation, discretionary (total)		−6,000	−12,315
Appropriations, mandatory:			
1200 Appropriation	24,800	25,900	25,900
1202 Appropriation (previously unavailable)			4,000
1230 75-X-0515 - Appropriations and/or unobligated balance of appropriations permanently reduced	−2,000		
1230 75-21-0515 - Appropriations and/or unobligated balance of appropriations permanently reduced	−1,000		
1260 Appropriations, mandatory (total)	21,800	25,900	29,900
1900 Budget authority (total)	21,800	19,900	17,585
1930 Total budgetary resources available	34,136	30,228	28,583
Memorandum (non-add) entries:			
1940 Unobligated balance expiring	−5,656		
1941 Unexpired unobligated balance, end of year	10,328	10,998	9,881
Change in obligated balance:			
Unpaid obligations:			
3000 Unpaid obligations, brought forward, Oct 1	6,809	8,729	11,346
3010 New obligations, unexpired accounts	18,152	19,230	18,702
3020 Outlays (gross)	−16,177	−16,613	−16,168
3041 Recoveries of prior year unpaid obligations, expired	−55		
3050 Unpaid obligations, end of year	8,729	11,346	13,880
Memorandum (non-add) entries:			
3100 Obligated balance, start of year	6,809	8,729	11,346
3200 Obligated balance, end of year	8,729	11,346	13,880
Budget authority and outlays, net:			
Discretionary:			
4000 Budget authority, gross		−6,000	−12,315
Mandatory:			
4090 Budget authority, gross	21,800	25,900	29,900
Outlays, gross:			
4100 Outlays from new mandatory authority	9,671	7,892	4,417
4101 Outlays from mandatory balances	6,506	8,721	11,751

Centers for Medicare and Medicaid Services—Continued
Federal Funds—Continued

4110	Outlays, gross (total)	16,177	16,613	16,168
	Offsets against gross budget authority and outlays:			
	Offsetting collections (collected) from:			
4123	Non-Federal sources:	−84		
	Additional offsets against gross budget authority only:			
4143	Recoveries of prior year paid obligations, unexpired accounts	84		
4160	Budget authority, net (mandatory)	21,800	25,900	29,900
4170	Outlays, net (mandatory)	16,093	16,613	16,168
4180	Budget authority, net (total)	21,800	19,900	17,585
4190	Outlays, net (total)	16,093	16,613	16,168

Summary of Budget Authority and Outlays (in millions of dollars)

	2021 actual	2022 est.	2023 est.
Enacted/requested:			
Budget Authority	21,800	19,900	17,585
Outlays	16,093	16,613	16,168
Legislative proposal, subject to PAYGO:			
Outlays			−230
Total:			
Budget Authority	21,800	19,900	17,585
Outlays	16,093	16,613	15,938

The Balanced Budget Act of 1997 (P.L. 105–33) established the Children's Health Insurance Program (CHIP) under title XXI of the Social Security Act. Title XXI provides Federal matching funds to States to enable them to extend coverage to uninsured children from low-income families. States are able to use title XXI funds for obtaining health benefit coverage for uninsured children through a separate CHIP program, a CHIP Medicaid expansion program, or a combination of both. The Children's Health Insurance Program Reauthorization Act of 2009 (P.L. 111–3, CHIPRA) reauthorized the CHIP program and appropriated funding for CHIP through fiscal year 2013. CHIPRA made some modifications to the program, including increased funding for States and territories, and support for child health quality and outreach activities. CHIPRA also created a contingency fund in a separate account to assist States who project spending above their available allocated CHIP funds. The Patient Protection and Affordable Care Act of 2010 (P.L. 111–148) and the Medicare Access and CHIP Reauthorization Act of 2015 (P.L. 114–10) extended CHIP funding through fiscal year 2015 and 2017, respectively. The HEALTHY KIDS Act (P.L. 115–120) and the Advancing Chronic Care, Extenders, and Social Services Act (P.L. 115–123) extended CHIP funding through fiscal year 2023 and 2027, respectively.

CHILDREN'S HEALTH INSURANCE FUND

(Legislative proposal, subject to PAYGO)

Program and Financing (in millions of dollars)

Identification code 075–0515–4–1–551	2021 actual	2022 est.	2023 est.
Change in obligated balance:			
Unpaid obligations:			
3020 Outlays (gross)			230
3050 Unpaid obligations, end of year			230
Memorandum (non-add) entries:			
3200 Obligated balance, end of year			230
Budget authority and outlays, net:			
Mandatory:			
Outlays, gross:			
4101 Outlays from mandatory balances			−230
4180 Budget authority, net (total)			
4190 Outlays, net (total)			−230

CENTER FOR MEDICARE AND MEDICAID INNOVATION

Program and Financing (in millions of dollars)

Identification code 075–0522–0–1–551		2021 actual	2022 est.	2023 est.
	Obligations by program activity:			
0001	Administration	330	390	379
0002	Innovation Activities	370	376	377
0900	Total new obligations, unexpired accounts	700	766	756
	Budgetary resources:			
	Unobligated balance:			
1000	Unobligated balance brought forward, Oct 1	10,460	9,835	9,069
1021	Recoveries of prior year unpaid obligations	75		
1070	Unobligated balance (total)	10,535	9,835	9,069
1930	Total budgetary resources available	10,535	9,835	9,069
	Memorandum (non-add) entries:			
1941	Unexpired unobligated balance, end of year	9,835	9,069	8,313
	Change in obligated balance:			
	Unpaid obligations:			
3000	Unpaid obligations, brought forward, Oct 1	1,028	925	743
3010	New obligations, unexpired accounts	700	766	756
3020	Outlays (gross)	–728	–948	–737
3040	Recoveries of prior year unpaid obligations, unexpired	–75		
3050	Unpaid obligations, end of year	925	743	762
	Memorandum (non-add) entries:			
3100	Obligated balance, start of year	1,028	925	743
3200	Obligated balance, end of year	925	743	762
	Budget authority and outlays, net:			
	Mandatory:			
	Outlays, gross:			
4101	Outlays from mandatory balances	728	948	737
4180	Budget authority, net (total)			
4190	Outlays, net (total)	728	948	737

The Center for Medicare and Medicaid Innovation ("Innovation Center") was established by section 1115A of the Social Security Act (as added by section 3021 of the Patient Protection and Affordable Care Act). The Innovation Center is tasked with testing innovative payment and service delivery models to reduce program expenditures while preserving or enhancing the quality of care provided to individuals under Medicare, Medicaid, or the Children's Health Insurance Program (CHIP). The statute provides $10 billion in mandatory funding for these purposes for fiscal years 2011 through 2019 and each subsequent 10-year fiscal period (beginning with the 10-year fiscal period beginning with fiscal year 2020).

Object Classification (in millions of dollars)

Identification code 075–0522–0–1–551		2021 actual	2022 est.	2023 est.
	Direct obligations:			
	Personnel compensation:			
11.1	Full-time permanent	83	101	103
11.3	Other than full-time permanent	2	3	3
11.5	Other personnel compensation	1	1	2
11.7	Military personnel	2	2	2
11.9	Total personnel compensation	88	107	110
12.1	Civilian personnel benefits	22	26	27
12.2	Military personnel benefits	1	1	1
23.1	Rental payments to GSA	2	3	3
25.2	Other services from non-Federal sources	510	538	522
25.3	Other goods and services from Federal sources	6	7	7
25.4	Operation and maintenance of facilities	2	3	3
41.0	Grants, subsidies, and contributions	69	80	82
99.0	Direct obligations	700	765	755
99.5	Adjustment for rounding		1	1
99.9	Total new obligations, unexpired accounts	700	766	756

Employment Summary

Identification code 075–0522–0–1–551		2021 actual	2022 est.	2023 est.
1001	Direct civilian full-time equivalent employment	507	497	497
1101	Direct military average strength employment	16	16	16

CHILD ENROLLMENT CONTINGENCY FUND

Special and Trust Fund Receipts (in millions of dollars)

Identification code 075–5551–0–2–551		2021 actual	2022 est.	2023 est.
0100	Balance, start of year	6,093	13,999	14,000
	Receipts:			
	Current law:			
1140	Interest, Child Enrollment Contingency Fund	14	21	29
2000	Total: Balances and receipts	6,107	14,020	14,029
	Appropriations:			
	Current law:			
2101	Child Enrollment Contingency Fund	–14	–20	–29
2103	Child Enrollment Contingency Fund	–6,093	–14,000	–14,000
2135	Child Enrollment Contingency Fund		14,000	19,860
2135	Child Enrollment Contingency Fund	9,087		
2199	Total current law appropriations	2,980	–20	5,831
2999	Total appropriations	2,980	–20	5,831
4030	Child Enrollment Contingency Fund	4,912		
5099	Balance, end of year	13,999	14,000	19,860

Program and Financing (in millions of dollars)

Identification code 075–5551–0–2–551		2021 actual	2022 est.	2023 est.
	Budgetary resources:			
	Unobligated balance:			
1000	Unobligated balance brought forward, Oct 1	4,913	1,980	7,180
1010	Unobligated balance transfer to other accts [075–0515]	–1		
1035	Unobligated balance precluded from obligation (limitation on obligations)(special and trust)	–4,912		
1070	Unobligated balance (total)		1,980	7,180
	Budget authority:			
	Appropriations, discretionary:			
1135	Appropriations precluded from obligation (special or trust)		–14,000	–19,860
	Appropriations, mandatory:			
1200	Appropriation	4,960	5,180	1,980
1201	Appropriation (special or trust fund)	14	20	29
1203	Appropriation (previously unavailable)(special or trust)	6,093	14,000	14,000
1235	Appropriations precluded from obligation (special or trust)	–9,087		
1260	Appropriations, mandatory (total)	1,980	19,200	16,009
1900	Budget authority (total)	1,980	5,200	–3,851
1930	Total budgetary resources available	1,980	7,180	3,329
	Memorandum (non-add) entries:			
1941	Unexpired unobligated balance, end of year	1,980	7,180	3,329
	Change in obligated balance:			
	Unpaid obligations:			
3000	Unpaid obligations, brought forward, Oct 1	309	309	309
3050	Unpaid obligations, end of year	309	309	309
	Memorandum (non-add) entries:			
3100	Obligated balance, start of year	309	309	309
3200	Obligated balance, end of year	309	309	309
	Budget authority and outlays, net:			
	Discretionary:			
4000	Budget authority, gross		–14,000	–19,860
	Mandatory:			
4090	Budget authority, gross	1,980	19,200	16,009
4180	Budget authority, net (total)	1,980	5,200	–3,851
4190	Outlays, net (total)			

The Children's Health Insurance Program Reauthorization Act of 2009 (P.L. 111–3) established the Child Enrollment Contingency Fund under title XXI of the Social Security Act. Beginning in 2009, a State may qualify for a Contingency Fund payment if it projects a funding shortfall for the fiscal year and if its average monthly child enrollment exceeds its target average number of enrollees for the fiscal year. The Patient Protection and Affordable Care Act of 2010 (P.L. 111–148) and the Medicare Access and CHIP Reauthorization Act of 2015 (P.L. 114–10) extended the Contingency

DEPARTMENT OF HEALTH AND HUMAN SERVICES

Fund through fiscal years 2015 and 2017, respectively. The HEALTHY KIDS Act (P.L. 115–120) and the Advancing Chronic Care, Extenders, and Social Services Act (P.L. 115–123) extended the Contingency Fund through FY 2023 and FY 2027, respectively.

The Fund receives an appropriation equal to 20 percent of the CHIP national allotment appropriation under section 2104(a) of the Social Security Act. The Contingency Fund is invested in interest bearing securities of the United States, and the income derived from these investments constitutes a part of the fund.

MEDICARE HEALTH INFORMATION TECHNOLOGY INCENTIVE PAYMENTS, RECOVERY ACT

Program and Financing (in millions of dollars)

Identification code 075–0508–0–1–551		2021 actual	2022 est.	2023 est.
	Obligations by program activity:			
0801	Incentive payments to hospitals	53	56	5
0900	Total new obligations, unexpired accounts (object class 42.0)	53	56	5
	Budgetary resources:			
	Unobligated balance:			
1000	Unobligated balance brought forward, Oct 1	59	1	1
1020	Adjustment of unobligated bal brought forward, Oct 1	–59		
1021	Recoveries of prior year unpaid obligations	2		
1070	Unobligated balance (total)	2	1	1
	Budget authority:			
	Spending authority from offsetting collections, mandatory:			
1800	Collected from the HI Trust Fund	49	56	5
1801	Change in uncollected payments, Federal sources	3		
1850	Spending auth from offsetting collections, mand (total)	52	56	5
1930	Total budgetary resources available	54	57	6
	Memorandum (non-add) entries:			
1941	Unexpired unobligated balance, end of year	1	1	1
	Change in obligated balance:			
	Unpaid obligations:			
3000	Unpaid obligations, brought forward, Oct 1	14	19	19
3010	New obligations, unexpired accounts	53	56	5
3020	Outlays (gross)	–46	–56	–24
3040	Recoveries of prior year unpaid obligations, unexpired	–2		
3050	Unpaid obligations, end of year	19	19	
	Uncollected payments:			
3060	Uncollected pymts, Fed sources, brought forward, Oct 1	–59	–3	–3
3061	Adjustments to uncollected pymts, Fed sources, brought forward, Oct 1	59		
3070	Change in uncollected pymts, Fed sources, unexpired	–3		
3090	Uncollected pymts, Fed sources, end of year	–3	–3	–3
	Memorandum (non-add) entries:			
3100	Obligated balance, start of year	14	16	16
3200	Obligated balance, end of year	16	16	–3
	Budget authority and outlays, net:			
	Mandatory:			
4090	Budget authority, gross	52	56	5
	Outlays, gross:			
4100	Outlays from new mandatory authority	36	37	5
4101	Outlays from mandatory balances	10	19	19
4110	Outlays, gross (total)	46	56	24
	Offsets against gross budget authority and outlays:			
	Offsetting collections (collected) from:			
4120	Federal sources	–49	–56	–5
	Additional offsets against gross budget authority only:			
4140	Change in uncollected pymts, Fed sources, unexpired	–3		
4170	Outlays, net (mandatory)	–3		19
4180	Budget authority, net (total)			
4190	Outlays, net (total)	–3		19

RATE REVIEW GRANTS

Program and Financing (in millions of dollars)

Identification code 075–0112–0–1–551		2021 actual	2022 est.	2023 est.
	Obligations by program activity:			
0001	Premium rate review grants	20		11
0900	Total new obligations, unexpired accounts (object class 41.0)	20		11
	Budgetary resources:			
	Unobligated balance:			
1000	Unobligated balance brought forward, Oct 1	8	10	11
1020	Adjustment of unobligated bal brought forward, Oct 1	17	1	
1021	Recoveries of prior year unpaid obligations	5	1	
1070	Unobligated balance (total)	30	11	11
1930	Total budgetary resources available	30	11	11
	Memorandum (non-add) entries:			
1941	Unexpired unobligated balance, end of year	10	11	
	Change in obligated balance:			
	Unpaid obligations:			
3000	Unpaid obligations, brought forward, Oct 1	9	21	14
3010	New obligations, unexpired accounts	20		11
3020	Outlays (gross)	–3	–6	–5
3040	Recoveries of prior year unpaid obligations, unexpired	–5	–1	
3050	Unpaid obligations, end of year	21	14	20
	Memorandum (non-add) entries:			
3100	Obligated balance, start of year	9	21	14
3200	Obligated balance, end of year	21	14	20
	Budget authority and outlays, net:			
	Mandatory:			
	Outlays, gross:			
4101	Outlays from mandatory balances	3	6	5
4180	Budget authority, net (total)			
4190	Outlays, net (total)	3	6	5

The Patient Protection and Affordable Care Act (P.L. 111–148) added section 2794 to the Public Health Service Act and provided that the Secretary carry out a program to award grants to States for a five-year period beginning in fiscal year 2010. The program provided $250 million in grants to help States develop or enhance their current rate review activities from 2010 through 2014, with remaining unobligated balances subsequently available for state implementation of consumer protections and other insurance reform activities consistent with section 2794(c)(2)(B).

PRE-EXISTING CONDITION INSURANCE PLAN PROGRAM

Program and Financing (in millions of dollars)

Identification code 075–0113–0–1–551		2021 actual	2022 est.	2023 est.
	Obligations by program activity:			
0001	Pre-Existing Condition Insurance Plan Program (Direct)	60		
0002	Administration		68	14
0799	Total direct obligations	60	68	14
0900	Total new obligations, unexpired accounts (object class 25.2)	60	68	14
	Budgetary resources:			
	Unobligated balance:			
1000	Unobligated balance brought forward, Oct 1	141	83	15
1021	Recoveries of prior year unpaid obligations	2		
1070	Unobligated balance (total)	143	83	15
1930	Total budgetary resources available	143	83	15
	Memorandum (non-add) entries:			
1941	Unexpired unobligated balance, end of year	83	15	1
	Change in obligated balance:			
	Unpaid obligations:			
3000	Unpaid obligations, brought forward, Oct 1	71	75	93
3010	New obligations, unexpired accounts	60	68	14
3020	Outlays (gross)	–54	–50	–48
3040	Recoveries of prior year unpaid obligations, unexpired	–2		
3050	Unpaid obligations, end of year	75	93	59

Centers for Medicare and Medicaid Services—Continued
Federal Funds—Continued

PRE-EXISTING CONDITION INSURANCE PLAN PROGRAM—Continued

Program and Financing—Continued

Identification code 075–0113–0–1–551		2021 actual	2022 est.	2023 est.
	Memorandum (non-add) entries:			
3100	Obligated balance, start of year	71	75	93
3200	Obligated balance, end of year	75	93	59
	Budget authority and outlays, net:			
	Mandatory:			
	Outlays, gross:			
4101	Outlays from mandatory balances	54	50	48
4180	Budget authority, net (total)			
4190	Outlays, net (total)	54	50	48

This account funded the Pre-Existing Condition Insurance Plan program (PCIP), which made health insurance available to people who had been unable to purchase insurance due to a pre-existing condition. Enrollees paid monthly premiums similar to those charged in the commercial individual market, and the Federal government paid for remaining costs that exceeded enrollee contributions. The funding for this program, including operating costs, was provided in the Patient Protection and Affordable Care Act (P.L. 111–148). The PCIP program ended in fiscal year 2014, and outlays in subsequent fiscal years reflect program close out and claims run out costs, as well as allowable administrative costs in the current year.

EARLY RETIREE REINSURANCE PROGRAM

Program and Financing (in millions of dollars)

Identification code 075–0114–0–1–551		2021 actual	2022 est.	2023 est.
	Budgetary resources:			
	Unobligated balance:			
1000	Unobligated balance brought forward, Oct 1	32	32	36
1021	Recoveries of prior year unpaid obligations		4	
1070	Unobligated balance (total)	32	36	36
1930	Total budgetary resources available	32	36	36
	Memorandum (non-add) entries:			
1941	Unexpired unobligated balance, end of year	32	36	36
	Change in obligated balance:			
	Unpaid obligations:			
3000	Unpaid obligations, brought forward, Oct 1	4	4	
3040	Recoveries of prior year unpaid obligations, unexpired		–4	
3050	Unpaid obligations, end of year	4		
	Memorandum (non-add) entries:			
3100	Obligated balance, start of year	4	4	
3200	Obligated balance, end of year	4		
4180	Budget authority, net (total)			
4190	Outlays, net (total)			

The Patient Protection and Affordable Care Act (P.L. 111–148) authorized and appropriated $5 billion for the Early Retiree Reinsurance Program (ERRP). By statute, ERRP sunset on January 1, 2014, and is no longer providing reimbursements to plan sponsors.

AFFORDABLE INSURANCE EXCHANGE GRANTS

Program and Financing (in millions of dollars)

Identification code 075–0115–0–1–551		2021 actual	2022 est.	2023 est.
	Obligations by program activity:			
0002	Administration		20	
0900	Total new obligations, unexpired accounts (object class 41.0)		20	
	Budgetary resources:			
	Budget authority:			
	Appropriations, mandatory:			
1200	Appropriation		20	
1930	Total budgetary resources available		20	

		2021 actual	2022 est.	2023 est.
	Change in obligated balance:			
	Unpaid obligations:			
3000	Unpaid obligations, brought forward, Oct 1		20	10
3010	New obligations, unexpired accounts	20		
3020	Outlays (gross)		–10	–10
3050	Unpaid obligations, end of year	20	10	
	Memorandum (non-add) entries:			
3100	Obligated balance, start of year		20	10
3200	Obligated balance, end of year	20	10	
	Budget authority and outlays, net:			
	Mandatory:			
4090	Budget authority, gross	20		
	Outlays, gross:			
4101	Outlays from mandatory balances		10	10
4180	Budget authority, net (total)	20		
4190	Outlays, net (total)		10	10

Section 1311 of the Patient Protection and Affordable Care Act (P.L. 111–148) provided amounts necessary to enable the Secretary to award grants to States to implement Health Insurance Exchanges beginning no later than March 23, 2011, and allowed for renewal of grants through January 1, 2015. The final round of grants was awarded to States in December 2014. The American Rescue Plan Act of 2021 (P.L. 117–2) created a grant program for state-based Marketplaces established under section 1311(b) of the Patient Protection and Affordable Care Act. $20 million has been appropriated and is available until September 30, 2022 to enable state-based Marketplaces to modernize or update any system, program, or technology required to be compliant with applicable federal requirements.

COST-SHARING REDUCTIONS

Program and Financing (in millions of dollars)

Identification code 075–0126–0–1–551		2021 actual	2022 est.	2023 est.
	Obligations by program activity:			
0001	Cost Sharing Reductions		7,877	5,733
0002	Basic Health Program		1,886	1,669
0900	Total new obligations, unexpired accounts (object class 41.0)		9,763	7,402
	Budgetary resources:			
	Budget authority:			
	Appropriations, mandatory:			
1200	Appropriation		10,353	7,849
1230	Appropriations and/or unobligated balance of appropriations permanently reduced		–590	–447
1260	Appropriations, mandatory (total)		9,763	7,402
1900	Budget authority (total)		9,763	7,402
1930	Total budgetary resources available		9,763	7,402
	Change in obligated balance:			
	Unpaid obligations:			
3010	New obligations, unexpired accounts		9,763	7,402
3020	Outlays (gross)		–9,763	–7,402
	Budget authority and outlays, net:			
	Mandatory:			
4090	Budget authority, gross		9,763	7,402
	Outlays, gross:			
4100	Outlays from new mandatory authority		9,763	7,402
4180	Budget authority, net (total)		9,763	7,402
4190	Outlays, net (total)		9,763	7,402

Summary of Budget Authority and Outlays (in millions of dollars)

	2021 actual	2022 est.	2023 est.
Enacted/requested:			
Budget Authority		9,763	7,402
Outlays		9,763	7,402
Legislative proposal, subject to PAYGO:			
Budget Authority			9
Outlays			9
Total:			
Budget Authority		9,763	7,411

DEPARTMENT OF HEALTH AND HUMAN SERVICES

Centers for Medicare and Medicaid Services—Continued
Federal Funds—Continued

		2021 actual	2022 est.	2023 est.
	Outlays		9,763	7,411

Under current law, insurers are required to offer reduced cost-sharing to eligible, low-income consumers. The classification of CSRs as an entitlement pursuant to BBEDCA does not determine legal entitlement to a payment or benefit or availability of funding.

COST-SHARING REDUCTIONS

(Legislative proposal, subject to PAYGO)

Program and Financing (in millions of dollars)

Identification code 075–0126–4–1–551		2021 actual	2022 est.	2023 est.
	Obligations by program activity:			
0001	Cost Sharing Reductions			9
0900	Total new obligations, unexpired accounts (object class 41.0)			9
	Budgetary resources:			
	Budget authority:			
	Appropriations, mandatory:			
1200	Appropriation			10
1230	Appropriations and/or unobligated balance of appropriations permanently reduced			–1
1260	Appropriations, mandatory (total)			9
1930	Total budgetary resources available			9
	Change in obligated balance:			
	Unpaid obligations:			
3010	New obligations, unexpired accounts			9
3020	Outlays (gross)			–9
	Budget authority and outlays, net:			
	Mandatory:			
4090	Budget authority, gross			9
	Outlays, gross:			
4100	Outlays from new mandatory authority			9
4180	Budget authority, net (total)			9
4190	Outlays, net (total)			9

The proposals build on existing consumer protections and improve access to behavioral health services by doing the following: requiring coverage of three behavioral health visits and three primary care visits without cost-sharing; limiting utilization management controls for behavioral health; amending MHPAEA to authorize the Secretaries to regulate behavioral health network adequacy for all plans and issuers; and creating a new standard for parity in behavioral health based on comparative analysis of reimbursement rates.

RISK ADJUSTMENT PROGRAM PAYMENTS

Special and Trust Fund Receipts (in millions of dollars)

Identification code 075–5733–0–2–551		2021 actual	2022 est.	2023 est.
0100	Balance, start of year	348	393	360
	Receipts:			
	Current law:			
1110	Receipts, Risk Adjustment Program	6,887	6,311	6,318
2000	Total: Balances and receipts	7,235	6,704	6,678
	Appropriations:			
	Current law:			
2101	Risk Adjustment Program Payments	–6,887	–6,311	–6,318
2103	Risk Adjustment Program Payments	–348	–393	–360
2132	Risk Adjustment Program Payments	393	360	360
2199	Total current law appropriations	–6,842	–6,344	–6,318
2999	Total appropriations	–6,842	–6,344	–6,318
5099	Balance, end of year	393	360	360

Program and Financing (in millions of dollars)

Identification code 075–5733–0–2–551		2021 actual	2022 est.	2023 est.
	Obligations by program activity:			
0001	Risk Adjustment Program Payments (Direct)	6,341	6,344	6,318
0900	Total new obligations, unexpired accounts (object class 41.0)	6,341	6,344	6,318
	Budgetary resources:			
	Unobligated balance:			
1000	Unobligated balance brought forward, Oct 1	410	911	911
	Budget authority:			
	Appropriations, mandatory:			
1201	Appropriation (special or trust fund)	6,887	6,311	6,318
1203	Appropriation (previously unavailable)(special or trust)	348	393	360
1232	Appropriations and/or unobligated balance of appropriations temporarily reduced	–393	–360	–360
1260	Appropriations, mandatory (total)	6,842	6,344	6,318
1930	Total budgetary resources available	7,252	7,255	7,229
	Memorandum (non-add) entries:			
1941	Unexpired unobligated balance, end of year	911	911	911
	Change in obligated balance:			
	Unpaid obligations:			
3000	Unpaid obligations, brought forward, Oct 1	3,054	2,420	
3010	New obligations, unexpired accounts	6,341	6,344	6,318
3020	Outlays (gross)	–6,975	–8,764	–6,318
3050	Unpaid obligations, end of year	2,420		
	Memorandum (non-add) entries:			
3100	Obligated balance, start of year	3,054	2,420	
3200	Obligated balance, end of year	2,420		
	Budget authority and outlays, net:			
	Mandatory:			
4090	Budget authority, gross	6,842	6,344	6,318
	Outlays, gross:			
4100	Outlays from new mandatory authority	3,511	6,344	6,318
4101	Outlays from mandatory balances	3,464	2,420	
4110	Outlays, gross (total)	6,975	8,764	6,318
4180	Budget authority, net (total)	6,842	6,344	6,318
4190	Outlays, net (total)	6,975	8,764	6,318

Section 1343 of the Patient Protection and Affordable Care Act (P.L. 111–148) established a permanent risk adjustment program for non-grandfathered plans in the individual and small group markets. Risk adjustment is budget neutral within each state and market, such that charges collected from plans with lower than average actuarial risk are used to make payments to plans with higher than average actuarial risk. Risk adjustment may be operated by a State, or by the Federal government in the event a State chooses not to operate risk adjustment. Payments and charges are made in the year following the plan year for which they are calculated.

TRANSITIONAL REINSURANCE PROGRAM

Special and Trust Fund Receipts (in millions of dollars)

Identification code 075–5735–0–2–551		2021 actual	2022 est.	2023 est.
0100	Balance, start of year			
	Receipts:			
	Current law:			
1110	Contributions, Transitional Reinsurance Program	1		
2000	Total: Balances and receipts	1		
	Appropriations:			
	Current law:			
2101	Transitional Reinsurance Program	–1		
5099	Balance, end of year			

Program and Financing (in millions of dollars)

Identification code 075–5735–0–2–551		2021 actual	2022 est.	2023 est.
	Obligations by program activity:			
0001	Transitional reinsurance payments		14	

TRANSITIONAL REINSURANCE PROGRAM—Continued

Program and Financing—Continued

Identification code 075–5735–0–2–551	2021 actual	2022 est.	2023 est.
0900 Total new obligations, unexpired accounts (object class 41.0)		14	
Budgetary resources:			
Unobligated balance:			
1000 Unobligated balance brought forward, Oct 1	7	14	
1033 Recoveries of prior year paid obligations	6		
1070 Unobligated balance (total)	13	14	
Budget authority:			
Appropriations, mandatory:			
1201 Appropriation (special or trust fund)	1		
1930 Total budgetary resources available	14	14	
Memorandum (non-add) entries:			
1941 Unexpired unobligated balance, end of year	14		
Change in obligated balance:			
Unpaid obligations:			
3000 Unpaid obligations, brought forward, Oct 1	212	212	
3010 New obligations, unexpired accounts		14	
3020 Outlays (gross)		–226	
3050 Unpaid obligations, end of year	212		
Memorandum (non-add) entries:			
3100 Obligated balance, start of year	212	212	
3200 Obligated balance, end of year	212		
Budget authority and outlays, net:			
Mandatory:			
4090 Budget authority, gross	1		
Outlays, gross:			
4101 Outlays from mandatory balances		226	
Offsets against gross budget authority and outlays:			
Offsetting collections (collected) from:			
4123 Non-Federal sources	–6		
Additional offsets against gross budget authority only:			
4143 Recoveries of prior year paid obligations, unexpired accounts	6		
4160 Budget authority, net (mandatory)	1		
4170 Outlays, net (mandatory)	–6	226	
4180 Budget authority, net (total)	1		
4190 Outlays, net (total)	–6	226	

Section 1341 of the Patient Protection and Affordable Care Act (P.L. 111–148) established a transitional three-year reinsurance program to minimize the impact of high-cost enrollees in plans in the individual market for plan years 2014, 2015, and 2016. The Centers for Medicare & Medicaid Services assessed contributing entities a per enrollee fee to fund the reinsurance program and made payments to issuers in the individual market for enrollees whose medical costs exceed a certain threshold, up to a reinsurance cap. Reinsurance collections and payments were made in the year following the plan year for which they were applicable. Reinsurance collections ended in FY 2019 and outlays in subsequent fiscal years reflect remaining payments, refunds, and allowable administrative activities.

CONSUMER OPERATED AND ORIENTED PLAN PROGRAM CONTINGENCY FUND

Program and Financing (in millions of dollars)

Identification code 075–0524–0–1–551	2021 actual	2022 est.	2023 est.
Obligations by program activity:			
Credit program obligations:			
0705 Reestimates of direct loan subsidy		1	
0900 Total new obligations, unexpired accounts (object class 25.2)		1	
Budgetary resources:			
Budget authority:			
Appropriations, mandatory:			
1200 Appropriation		1	
1930 Total budgetary resources available		1	
Change in obligated balance:			
Unpaid obligations:			
3000 Unpaid obligations, brought forward, Oct 1	2	1	
3010 New obligations, unexpired accounts		1	
3020 Outlays (gross)	–1	–2	
3050 Unpaid obligations, end of year	1		
Memorandum (non-add) entries:			
3100 Obligated balance, start of year	2	1	
3200 Obligated balance, end of year	1		
Budget authority and outlays, net:			
Mandatory:			
4090 Budget authority, gross		1	
Outlays, gross:			
4100 Outlays from new mandatory authority		1	
4101 Outlays from mandatory balances	1	1	
4110 Outlays, gross (total)	1	2	
4180 Budget authority, net (total)		1	
4190 Outlays, net (total)	1	2	

Summary of Loan Levels, Subsidy Budget Authority and Outlays by Program (in millions of dollars)

Identification code 075–0524–0–1–551	2021 actual	2022 est.	2023 est.
Direct loan reestimates:			
135001 Startup Loans	–10	–6	
135002 Solvency Loans	–36	2	
135999 Total direct loan reestimates	–46	–4	

The Consumer Operated and Oriented Plan Contingency Fund was established by the American Taxpayer Relief Act of 2012 (P.L. 112–240). This fund provides assistance and oversight to qualified nonprofit health insurance issuers that have been awarded loans or grants under section 1322 of the Patient Protection and Affordable Care Act (P.L. 111–148).

CONSUMER OPERATED AND ORIENTED PLAN PROGRAM ACCOUNT

Program and Financing (in millions of dollars)

Identification code 075–0118–0–1–551	2021 actual	2022 est.	2023 est.
Obligations by program activity:			
Credit program obligations:			
0705 Reestimates of direct loan subsidy		6	
0706 Interest on reestimates of direct loan subsidy		2	
0709 Administrative expenses	1		
0900 Total new obligations, unexpired accounts (object class 25.2)	1	8	
Budgetary resources:			
Unobligated balance:			
1000 Unobligated balance brought forward, Oct 1	1		
Budget authority:			
Appropriations, mandatory:			
1200 Appropriation		8	
1900 Budget authority (total)		8	
1930 Total budgetary resources available	1	8	
Change in obligated balance:			
Unpaid obligations:			
3000 Unpaid obligations, brought forward, Oct 1	1	1	
3010 New obligations, unexpired accounts	1	8	
3020 Outlays (gross)	–1	–9	
3050 Unpaid obligations, end of year	1		
Memorandum (non-add) entries:			
3100 Obligated balance, start of year	1	1	
3200 Obligated balance, end of year	1		
Budget authority and outlays, net:			
Mandatory:			
4090 Budget authority, gross		8	
Outlays, gross:			
4100 Outlays from new mandatory authority		8	
4101 Outlays from mandatory balances	1	1	
4110 Outlays, gross (total)	1	9	
4180 Budget authority, net (total)		8	
4190 Outlays, net (total)	1	9	

DEPARTMENT OF HEALTH AND HUMAN SERVICES

Summary of Loan Levels, Subsidy Budget Authority and Outlays by Program (in millions of dollars)

Identification code 075–0118–0–1–551		2021 actual	2022 est.	2023 est.
	Direct loan reestimates:			
135002	Startup Loans	–77	–30	
135003	Solvency Loans	–219	7	
135999	Total direct loan reestimates	–296	–23	

Section 1322 of the Patient Protection and Affordable Care Act (P.L. 111–148) authorized and appropriated funding for the Consumer Operated and Oriented Plan (CO-OP) Program. The CO-OP Program fosters the creation of qualified nonprofit health insurance issuers that operate with a strong consumer focus to offer qualified health plans in the individual and small group markets in the States. The Secretary awarded loans to qualified nonprofit issuers to fund start-up costs and reserves, which enabled qualified issuers to meet state solvency requirements. The Secretary issued the final round of loans in December 2014.

CONSUMER OPERATED AND ORIENTED PLAN FINANCING ACCOUNT

Program and Financing (in millions of dollars)

Identification code 075–4418–0–3–551		2021 actual	2022 est.	2023 est.
	Obligations by program activity:			
	Credit program obligations:			
0713	Payment of interest to Treasury	8	8	8
0742	Downward reestimates paid to receipt accounts	249	27	
0743	Interest on downward reestimates	47	3	
0900	Total new obligations, unexpired accounts	304	38	8
	Budgetary resources:			
	Unobligated balance:			
1000	Unobligated balance brought forward, Oct 1	24	7	4
	Financing authority:			
	Borrowing authority, mandatory:			
1400	Borrowing authority	284	27	3
	Spending authority from offsetting collections, mandatory:			
1800	Collected	66	51	6
1825	Spending authority from offsetting collections applied to repay debt	–63	–43	
1850	Spending auth from offsetting collections, mand (total)	3	8	6
1900	Budget authority (total)	287	35	9
1930	Total budgetary resources available	311	42	13
	Memorandum (non-add) entries:			
1941	Unexpired unobligated balance, end of year	7	4	5
	Change in obligated balance:			
	Unpaid obligations:			
3000	Unpaid obligations, brought forward, Oct 1			38
3010	New obligations, unexpired accounts	304	38	8
3020	Outlays (gross)	–304		
3050	Unpaid obligations, end of year		38	46
	Memorandum (non-add) entries:			
3100	Obligated balance, start of year			38
3200	Obligated balance, end of year		38	46
	Financing authority and disbursements, net:			
	Mandatory:			
4090	Budget authority, gross	287	35	9
	Financing disbursements:			
4110	Outlays, gross (total)	304		
	Offsets against gross financing authority and disbursements:			
	Offsetting collections (collected) from:			
4120	Federal sources		–7	
4122	Interest on uninvested funds		–3	–6
4123	Non-Federal sources	–66	–41	
4130	Offsets against gross budget authority and outlays (total)	–66	–51	–6
4160	Budget authority, net (mandatory)	221	–16	3
4170	Outlays, net (mandatory)	238	–51	–6
4180	Budget authority, net (total)	221	–16	3
4190	Outlays, net (total)	238	–51	–6

Centers for Medicare and Medicaid Services—Continued
Federal Funds—Continued 461

Status of Direct Loans (in millions of dollars)

Identification code 075–4418–0–3–551		2021 actual	2022 est.	2023 est.
	Cumulative balance of direct loans outstanding:			
1210	Outstanding, start of year	1,893	1,812	1,771
1251	Repayments: Repayments and prepayments		–41	
1263	Write-offs for default: Direct loans	–81		–94
1290	Outstanding, end of year	1,812	1,771	1,677

Balance Sheet (in millions of dollars)

Identification code 075–4418–0–3–551		2020 actual	2021 actual
	ASSETS:		
	Federal assets:		
1101	Fund balances with Treasury	9	6
	Investments in U.S. securities:		
1106	Receivables, net	259	7
	Net value of assets related to post-1991 direct loans receivable:		
1401	Direct loans receivable, gross	1,893	1,812
1402	Interest receivable	25	41
1405	Allowance for subsidy cost (-)	–1,778	–1,467
1499	Net present value of assets related to direct loans	140	386
1999	Total assets	408	399
	LIABILITIES:		
2103	Federal liabilities: Debt	408	399
	NET POSITION:		
3300	Cumulative results of operations		
4999	Total liabilities and net position	408	399

CONSUMER OPERATED AND ORIENTED PLAN PROGRAM CONTINGENCY FUND FINANCING ACCOUNT

Program and Financing (in millions of dollars)

Identification code 075–4482–0–3–551		2021 actual	2022 est.	2023 est.
	Obligations by program activity:			
	Credit program obligations:			
0713	Payment of interest to Treasury	2	2	2
0742	Downward reestimates paid to receipt accounts	40	5	
0743	Interest on downward reestimates	6	1	
0900	Total new obligations, unexpired accounts	48	8	2
	Budgetary resources:			
	Unobligated balance:			
1000	Unobligated balance brought forward, Oct 1	1	4	11
	Financing authority:			
	Borrowing authority, mandatory:			
1400	Borrowing authority	47	6	2
	Spending authority from offsetting collections, mandatory:			
1800	Collected	9	11	112
1825	Spending authority from offsetting collections applied to repay debt	–5	–2	–112
1850	Spending auth from offsetting collections, mand (total)	4	9	
1900	Budget authority (total)	51	15	2
1930	Total budgetary resources available	52	19	13
	Memorandum (non-add) entries:			
1941	Unexpired unobligated balance, end of year	4	11	11
	Change in obligated balance:			
	Unpaid obligations:			
3000	Unpaid obligations, brought forward, Oct 1			8
3010	New obligations, unexpired accounts	48	8	2
3020	Outlays (gross)	–48		
3050	Unpaid obligations, end of year		8	10
	Memorandum (non-add) entries:			
3100	Obligated balance, start of year			8
3200	Obligated balance, end of year		8	10
	Financing authority and disbursements, net:			
	Mandatory:			
4090	Budget authority, gross	51	15	2
	Financing disbursements:			
4110	Outlays, gross (total)	48		

Centers for Medicare and Medicaid Services—Continued
Federal Funds—Continued

CONSUMER OPERATED AND ORIENTED PLAN PROGRAM CONTINGENCY FUND FINANCING ACCOUNT—Continued

Program and Financing—Continued

Identification code 075–4482–0–3–551	2021 actual	2022 est.	2023 est.
Offsets against gross financing authority and disbursements:			
Offsetting collections (collected) from:			
4120 Federal sources		–2	
4123 Non-Federal sources	–9	–9	–112
4130 Offsets against gross budget authority and outlays (total)	–9	–11	–112
4160 Budget authority, net (mandatory)	42	4	–110
4170 Outlays, net (mandatory)	39	–11	–112
4180 Budget authority, net (total)	42	4	–110
4190 Outlays, net (total)	39	–11	–112

Status of Direct Loans (in millions of dollars)

Identification code 075–4482–0–3–551	2021 actual	2022 est.	2023 est.
Cumulative balance of direct loans outstanding:			
1210 Outstanding, start of year	480	471	347
1251 Repayments: Repayments and prepayments		–6	–12
1263 Write-offs for default: Direct loans	–9	–118	–118
1290 Outstanding, end of year	471	347	217

Balance Sheet (in millions of dollars)

Identification code 075–4482–0–3–551	2020 actual	2021 actual
ASSETS:		
Federal assets:		
1101 Fund balances with Treasury	5	5
Investments in U.S. securities:		
1106 Receivables, net	5	2
1206 Non-Federal assets: Receivables, net		
Net value of assets related to post-1991 direct loans receivable:		
1401 Direct loans receivable, gross	480	471
1402 Interest receivable	5	9
1405 Allowance for subsidy cost (-)	–429	–378
1499 Net present value of assets related to direct loans	56	102
1999 Total assets	66	109
LIABILITIES:		
Federal liabilities:		
2103 Debt	65	108
2104 Resources payable to Treasury		
2207 Non-Federal liabilities: Other		
2999 Total liabilities	65	108
NET POSITION:		
3300 Cumulative results of operations	1	1
4999 Total liabilities and net position	66	109

MENTAL HEALTH PARITY ENFORCEMENT GRANTS

(Legislative proposal, subject to PAYGO)

Program and Financing (in millions of dollars)

Identification code 075–0521–4–1–551	2021 actual	2022 est.	2023 est.
Obligations by program activity:			
0001 Mental Health Parity Enforcement Grants			125
0900 Total new obligations, unexpired accounts (object class 41.0)			125
Budgetary resources:			
Budget authority:			
Appropriations, mandatory:			
1200 Appropriation			125
1930 Total budgetary resources available			125
Change in obligated balance:			
Unpaid obligations:			
3010 New obligations, unexpired accounts			125
3020 Outlays (gross)			–10
3050 Unpaid obligations, end of year			115

Memorandum (non-add) entries:			
3200 Obligated balance, end of year			115
Budget authority and outlays, net:			
Mandatory:			
4090 Budget authority, gross			125
Outlays, gross:			
4100 Outlays from new mandatory authority			10
4180 Budget authority, net (total)			125
4190 Outlays, net (total)			10

This proposal provides $125 million in mandatory funding in FY 2023, available for a period of five fiscal years, for grants to states to enforce mental health parity requirements. This proposal would allow any funds from grants that are not expended by the states at the end of the five fiscal years to remain available to the HHS Secretary to make additional mental health parity grants.

MEDICARE INVESTMENTS

(Legislative proposal, subject to PAYGO)

Program and Financing (in millions of dollars)

Identification code 999–9068–4–1–571	2021 actual	2022 est.	2023 est.
Obligations by program activity:			
0001 Direct program activity			70
0900 Total new obligations, unexpired accounts (object class 92.0)			70
Budgetary resources:			
Budget authority:			
Appropriations, mandatory:			
1200 Appropriation			70
1930 Total budgetary resources available			70
Change in obligated balance:			
Unpaid obligations:			
3010 New obligations, unexpired accounts			70
3020 Outlays (gross)			–70
Budget authority and outlays, net:			
Mandatory:			
4090 Budget authority, gross			70
Outlays, gross:			
4100 Outlays from new mandatory authority			70
4180 Budget authority, net (total)			70
4190 Outlays, net (total)			70

The Budget proposes investments in Medicare that strengthen mental health services, enhance Medicare beneficiary access to vaccines, and address gaps in physician incentive payments. This reflects the combined policy impacts of these investments and is net of premiums and other offsetting collections.

Trust Funds

FEDERAL HOSPITAL INSURANCE TRUST FUND

Special and Trust Fund Receipts (in millions of dollars)

Identification code 075–8005–0–7–571	2021 actual	2022 est.	2023 est.
0100 Balance, start of year	95,439	92,022	118,682
0198 Reconciliation adjustment	–44		
0199 Balance, start of year	95,395	92,022	118,682
Receipts:			
Current law:			
1110 FHI Trust Fund, Transfers from General Fund (FICA Taxes)	273,479	305,903	320,963
1110 FHI Trust Fund, Receipts from Railroad Retirement Board	552	527	536
1110 FHI Trust Fund, Transfers from General Fund (SECA Taxes)	20,787	22,205	21,840
1110 FHI Trust Fund, Civil Penalties and Damages	385	598	629
1130 FHI Trust Fund, Other Proprietary Interest from the Public	1	2	2
1130 FHI Trust Fund, Basic Premium, Medicare Advantage	293	419	461
1130 FHI Trust Fund, Medicare Refunds	27,966	28,016	7,394
1130 Affordable Care Act Medicare Shared Savings Models (HI)	79	48	48

DEPARTMENT OF HEALTH AND HUMAN SERVICES

Centers for Medicare and Medicaid Services—Continued
Trust Funds—Continued

463

		2021 actual	2022 est.	2023 est.
1130	FHI Trust Fund, Premiums Collected for Uninsured Individuals not Otherwise Eligible	4,141	4,742	4,911
1140	FHI Trust Fund, Federal Employer Contributions (FICA)	4,283	4,442	4,603
1140	FHI Trust Fund, Postal Service Employer Contributions (FICA)	597	620	660
1140	FHI Trust Fund, Interest Received by Trust Funds	2,438	2,911	3,313
1140	FHI Trust Fund, Taxation on OASDI Benefits	24,975	32,439	35,072
1140	FHI Trust Fund, Payment from the General Fund for Health Care Fraud and Abuse Control Account	148	153	157
1140	FHI Trust Fund, Transfers from General Fund (criminal Fines)	67	19	21
1140	FHI Trust Fund, Transfers from General Fund (civil Monetary Penalties)	69	53	54
1140	FHI Trust Fund, Transfers from General Fund (asset Forfeitures)	135	33	34
1140	FHI Trust Fund, Interest Payments by Railroad Retirement Board	16	10	14
1140	FHI Trust Fund, Payments from the General Fund (uninsured and Program Management)	1,298	929	993
1199	Total current law receipts	361,709	404,069	401,705
	Proposed:			
1210	FHI Trust Fund, Transfers from General Fund (FICA Taxes)			–4
1210	FHI Trust Fund, Transfers from General Fund (FICA Taxes)			–938
1299	Total proposed receipts			–942
1999	Total receipts	361,709	404,069	400,763
2000	Total: Balances and receipts	457,104	496,091	519,445
	Appropriations:			
	Current law:			
2101	Federal Hospital Insurance Trust Fund	–2,802	–2,802	–3,056
2101	Federal Hospital Insurance Trust Fund	–356,721	–399,022	–397,259
2101	Health Care Fraud and Abuse Control Account	–807	–807	–899
2101	Health Care Fraud and Abuse Control Account	–1,415	–1,364	–2,322
2103	Federal Hospital Insurance Trust Fund	–4,006	–2,917	–19,045
2103	Health Care Fraud and Abuse Control Account		–51	–54
2132	Federal Hospital Insurance Trust Fund	31	2,917	8,146
2132	Health Care Fraud and Abuse Control Account		23	54
2135	Federal Hospital Insurance Trust Fund	786	26,614	
2199	Total current law appropriations	–364,934	–377,409	–414,435
	Proposed:			
2201	Health Care Fraud and Abuse Control Account			1,141
2999	Total appropriations	–364,934	–377,409	–413,294
3098	Federal Hospital Insurance Trust Fund	–81		
5098	Reconciliation adjustment	–67		
5099	Balance, end of year	92,022	118,682	106,151

Program and Financing (in millions of dollars)

Identification code 075–8005–0–7–571		2021 actual	2022 est.	2023 est.
	Obligations by program activity:			
0001	Benefit payments, HI	382,161	371,741	407,507
0002	HIT Incentive Payments	6	5	
0003	Administration, HI	2,924	2,950	3,218
0004	Quality improvement organizations, HI	385	513	489
0799	Total direct obligations	385,476	375,209	411,214
0900	Total new obligations, unexpired accounts	385,476	375,209	411,214
	Budgetary resources:			
	Unobligated balance:			
1000	Unobligated balance brought forward, Oct 1			1
1021	Recoveries of prior year unpaid obligations	17		
1026	Adjustment for change in allocation of trust fund limitation or foreign exchange valuation	81		
1033	Recoveries of prior year paid obligations	22,666		
1070	Unobligated balance (total)	22,764		1
	Budget authority:			
	Appropriations, discretionary:			
1101	Appropriation (special or trust)	2,802	2,802	3,056
	Appropriations, mandatory:			
1201	Appropriation (special or trust fund)	356,721	399,022	397,259
1203	Appropriation (previously unavailable)(special or trust)	4,006	2,917	19,045
1232	Appropriations and/or unobligated balance of appropriations temporarily reduced (Sequester)	–31	–2,917	–8,146
1235	Appropriations precluded from obligation (special or trust)	–786	–26,614	
1260	Appropriations, mandatory (total)	359,910	372,408	408,158
1900	Budget authority (total)	362,712	375,210	411,214
1930	Total budgetary resources available	385,476	375,210	411,215

		2021 actual	2022 est.	2023 est.
	Memorandum (non-add) entries:			
1941	Unexpired unobligated balance, end of year		1	1
	Change in obligated balance:			
	Unpaid obligations:			
3000	Unpaid obligations, brought forward, Oct 1	36,279	41,570	41,429
3001	Adjustments to unpaid obligations, brought forward, Oct 1	183		
3010	New obligations, unexpired accounts	385,476	375,209	411,214
3020	Outlays (gross)	–380,351	–375,350	–411,075
3040	Recoveries of prior year unpaid obligations, unexpired	–17		
3050	Unpaid obligations, end of year	41,570	41,429	41,568
	Memorandum (non-add) entries:			
3100	Obligated balance, start of year	36,462	41,570	41,429
3200	Obligated balance, end of year	41,570	41,429	41,568
	Budget authority and outlays, net:			
	Discretionary:			
4000	Budget authority, gross	2,802	2,802	3,056
	Outlays, gross:			
4010	Outlays from new discretionary authority	1,927	1,781	1,877
4011	Outlays from discretionary balances	842	1,142	1,040
4020	Outlays, gross (total)	2,769	2,923	2,917
	Mandatory:			
4090	Budget authority, gross	359,910	372,408	408,158
	Outlays, gross:			
4100	Outlays from new mandatory authority	323,782	332,730	362,511
4101	Outlays from mandatory balances	53,800	39,697	45,647
4110	Outlays, gross (total)	377,582	372,427	408,158
	Offsets against gross budget authority and outlays:			
	Offsetting collections (collected) from:			
4123	Non-Federal sources	–22,666		
	Additional offsets against gross budget authority only:			
4143	Recoveries of prior year paid obligations, unexpired accounts	22,666		
4160	Budget authority, net (mandatory)	359,910	372,408	408,158
4170	Outlays, net (mandatory)	354,916	372,427	408,158
4180	Budget authority, net (total)	362,712	375,210	411,214
4190	Outlays, net (total)	357,685	375,350	411,075
	Memorandum (non-add) entries:			
5000	Total investments, SOY: Federal securities: Par value	133,735	136,168	161,934
5001	Total investments, EOY: Federal securities: Par value	136,168	161,934	150,548

The Hospital Insurance (HI) program funds the costs of hospital and related care for individuals age 65 or older and for eligible disabled persons.

Status of Funds (in millions of dollars)

Identification code 075–8005–0–7–571		2021 actual	2022 est.	2023 est.
	Unexpended balance, start of year:			
0100	Balance, start of year	134,361	136,267	162,551
0999	Total balance, start of year	134,361	136,267	162,551
	Cash income during the year:			
	Current law:			
	Receipts:			
1110	FHI Trust Fund, Transfers from General Fund (FICA Taxes)	273,479	305,903	320,963
1110	FHI Trust Fund, Receipts from Railroad Retirement Board	552	527	536
1110	FHI Trust Fund, Transfers from General Fund (SECA Taxes)	20,787	22,205	21,840
1110	FHI Trust Fund, Civil Penalties and Damages	385	598	629
1130	FHI Trust Fund, Basic Premium, Medicare Advantage	293	419	461
1130	FHI Trust Fund, Medicare Refunds	27,966	28,016	7,394
1130	Affordable Care Act Medicare Shared Savings Models (HI)	79	48	48
1130	FHI Trust Fund, Premiums Collected for Uninsured Individuals not Otherwise Eligible	4,141	4,742	4,911
1130	Federal Hospital Insurance Trust Fund	22,666		
1150	FHI Trust Fund, Interest Received by Trust Funds	2,438	2,911	3,313
1150	FHI Trust Fund, Other Proprietary Interest from the Public	1	2	2
1150	FHI Trust Fund, Interest Payments by Railroad Retirement Board	16	10	14
1160	FHI Trust Fund, Federal Employer Contributions (FICA)	4,283	4,442	4,603
1160	FHI Trust Fund, Postal Service Employer Contributions (FICA)	597	620	660
1160	FHI Trust Fund, Taxation on OASDI Benefits	24,975	32,439	35,072
1160	FHI Trust Fund, Payment from the General Fund for Health Care Fraud and Abuse Control Account	148	153	157

Centers for Medicare and Medicaid Services—Continued
Trust Funds—Continued

FEDERAL HOSPITAL INSURANCE TRUST FUND—Continued
Status of Funds—Continued

Identification code 075–8005–0–7–571		2021 actual	2022 est.	2023 est.
1160	FHI Trust Fund, Transfers from General Fund (criminal Fines)	67	19	21
1160	FHI Trust Fund, Transfers from General Fund (civil Monetary Penalties)	69	53	54
1160	FHI Trust Fund, Transfers from General Fund (asset Forfeitures)	135	33	34
1160	FHI Trust Fund, Payments from the General Fund (uninsured and Program Management)	1,298	929	993
1199	Income under present law	384,375	404,069	401,705
	Proposed:			
1210	FHI Trust Fund, Transfers from General Fund (FICA Taxes)			–938
1210	FHI Trust Fund, Transfers from General Fund (FICA Taxes)			–4
1299	Income proposed			–942
1999	Total cash income	384,375	404,069	400,763
	Cash outgo during year:			
	Current law:			
2100	Federal Hospital Insurance Trust Fund [Budget Acct]	–380,351	–375,350	–411,075
2100	Health Care Fraud and Abuse Control Account [Budget Acct]	–2,119	–2,435	–3,261
2199	Outgo under current law	–382,470	–377,785	–414,336
	Proposed:			
2200	Health Care Fraud and Abuse Control Account			1,141
2299	Outgo under proposed legislation			1,141
2999	Total cash outgo (-)	–382,470	–377,785	–413,195
	Surplus or deficit:			
3110	Excluding interest	–550	23,361	–15,761
3120	Interest	2,455	2,923	3,329
3199	Subtotal, surplus or deficit	1,905	26,284	–12,432
3298	Reconciliation adjustment	1		
3299	Total adjustments	1		
3999	Total change in fund balance	1,906	26,284	–12,432
	Unexpended balance, end of year:			
4100	Uninvested balance (net), end of year	99	617	–429
4200	Federal Hospital Insurance Trust Fund	136,168	161,934	150,548
4999	Total balance, end of year	136,267	162,551	150,119

Object Classification (in millions of dollars)

Identification code 075–8005–0–7–571		2021 actual	2022 est.	2023 est.
	Direct obligations:			
25.3	Other goods and services from Federal sources	2		
41.0	Payment for Quality Improvement Organization (QIO) activities	385	513	489
42.0	Insurance claims and indemnities (benefits)	377,232	371,746	407,507
94.0	Financial transfers	7,857	2,950	3,218
99.9	Total new obligations, unexpired accounts	385,476	375,209	411,214

Employment Summary

Identification code 075–8005–0–7–571		2021 actual	2022 est.	2023 est.
1001	Direct civilian full-time equivalent employment	1	1	1

HEALTH CARE FRAUD AND ABUSE CONTROL ACCOUNT

In addition to amounts otherwise available for program integrity and program management, $899,000,000, to remain available through September 30, 2024, to be transferred from the Federal Hospital Insurance Trust Fund and the Federal Supplementary Medical Insurance Trust Fund, as authorized by section 201(g) of the Social Security Act, of which $692,174,000 shall be for the Centers for Medicare & Medicaid Services program integrity activities, of which $109,612,000 shall be for the Department of Health and Human Services Office of Inspector General to carry out fraud and abuse activities authorized by section 1817(k)(3) of such Act, and of which $97,214,000 shall be for the Department of Justice to carry out fraud and abuse activities authorized by section 1817(k)(3) of such Act: Provided, That the report required by section 1817(k)(5) of the Social Security Act for fiscal year 2023 shall include measures of the operational efficiency and impact on fraud, waste, and abuse in the Medicare, Medicaid, and CHIP programs for the funds provided by this appropriation: Provided further, That of the amount provided under this heading, $323,000,000 is provided to meet the terms of a concurrent resolution on the budget for health care fraud and abuse control activities, and $576,000,000 is additional new budget authority specified for purposes of a concurrent resolution on the budget for additional health care fraud and abuse control activities: Provided further, That the Secretary shall provide not less than $20,000,000 from amounts made available under this heading and amounts made available for fiscal year 2023 under section 1817(k)(3)(A) of the Social Security Act for the Senior Medicare Patrol program to combat health care fraud and abuse.

Note.—A full-year 2022 appropriation for this account was not enacted at the time the Budget was prepared; therefore, the Budget assumes this account is operating under the Continuing Appropriations Act, 2022 (Division A of Public Law 117–43, as amended). The amounts included for 2022 reflect the annualized level provided by the continuing resolution.

Program and Financing (in millions of dollars)

Identification code 075–8393–0–7–571		2021 actual	2022 est.	2023 est.
	Obligations by program activity:			
0001	Medicare integrity program	1,036	963	1,002
0002	FBI fraud and abuse control	156	153	157
0003	Other fraud and abuse control	325	323	331
0005	Undistributed Savings, Medicare SSA CDRs		–47	–287
0006	Undistributed Medicare and Medicaid baseline impact attributable to HCFAC Cap/Allocation Adjustment			1,119
0091	Total Mandatory	1,517	1,392	2,322
0101	CMS discretionary	682	616	692
0102	Other discretionary	191	191	207
0191	Total Discretionary	873	807	899
0900	Total new obligations, unexpired accounts	2,390	2,199	3,221
	Budgetary resources:			
	Unobligated balance:			
1000	Unobligated balance brought forward, Oct 1	557	417	417
1001	Discretionary unobligated balance brought fwd, Oct 1	218		
1021	Recoveries of prior year unpaid obligations	36		
1070	Unobligated balance (total)	593	417	417
	Budget authority:			
	Appropriations, discretionary:			
1101	Appropriation (special or trust)	807	807	899
	Appropriations, mandatory:			
1201	Appropriation (special or trust fund)	1,415	1,364	2,322
1203	Appropriation (previously unavailable)(special or trust)		51	54
1232	Appropriations and/or unobligated balance of appropriations temporarily reduced		–23	–54
1260	Appropriations, mandatory (total)	1,415	1,392	2,322
1900	Budget authority (total)	2,222	2,199	3,221
1930	Total budgetary resources available	2,815	2,616	3,638
	Memorandum (non-add) entries:			
1940	Unobligated balance expiring	–8		
1941	Unexpired unobligated balance, end of year	417	417	417
	Special and non-revolving trust funds:			
1951	Unobligated balance expiring	8		
1952	Expired unobligated balance, start of year	69	71	71
1953	Expired unobligated balance, end of year	63	71	71
	Change in obligated balance:			
	Unpaid obligations:			
3000	Unpaid obligations, brought forward, Oct 1	2,062	2,267	2,031
3010	New obligations, unexpired accounts	2,390	2,199	3,221
3020	Outlays (gross)	–2,119	–2,435	–3,261
3040	Recoveries of prior year unpaid obligations, unexpired	–36		
3041	Recoveries of prior year unpaid obligations, expired	–30		
3050	Unpaid obligations, end of year	2,267	2,031	1,991
	Memorandum (non-add) entries:			
3100	Obligated balance, start of year	2,062	2,267	2,031
3200	Obligated balance, end of year	2,267	2,031	1,991
	Budget authority and outlays, net:			
	Discretionary:			
4000	Budget authority, gross	807	807	899
	Outlays, gross:			
4010	Outlays from new discretionary authority	176	322	359
4011	Outlays from discretionary balances	602	530	540
4020	Outlays, gross (total)	778	852	899
	Mandatory:			
4090	Budget authority, gross	1,415	1,392	2,322

DEPARTMENT OF HEALTH AND HUMAN SERVICES

Centers for Medicare and Medicaid Services—Continued
Trust Funds—Continued

		2021 actual	2022 est.	2023 est.
	Outlays, gross:			
4100	Outlays from new mandatory authority	513	661	1,550
4101	Outlays from mandatory balances	828	922	812
4110	Outlays, gross (total)	1,341	1,583	2,362
4180	Budget authority, net (total)	2,222	2,199	3,221
4190	Outlays, net (total)	2,119	2,435	3,261

Summary of Budget Authority and Outlays (in millions of dollars)

	2021 actual	2022 est.	2023 est.
Enacted/requested:			
Budget Authority	2,222	2,199	3,221
Outlays	2,119	2,435	3,261
Legislative proposal, not subject to PAYGO:			
Budget Authority			–1,141
Outlays			–1,141
Total:			
Budget Authority	2,222	2,199	2,080
Outlays	2,119	2,435	2,120

The Health Insurance Portability and Accountability Act of 1996 (P.L. 104–191) established the Health Care Fraud and Abuse Control (HCFAC) account within the Federal Hospital Insurance Trust Fund and appropriated funds from the Trust Fund to the HCFAC account for specified health care fraud and abuse control activities of the Department of Health and Human Services (HHS), the Department of Justice, and other agencies.

The Budget includes a discretionary request for efforts to safeguard Centers for Medicare and Medicaid Services (CMS) program integrity that will supplement other CMS program integrity funds. See additional discussion in the Budget Process chapter in the *Analytical Perspectives* volume.

Object Classification (in millions of dollars)

Identification code 075–8393–0–7–571		2021 actual	2022 est.	2023 est.
	Direct obligations:			
	Personnel compensation:			
11.1	Full-time permanent (CMS)	64	65	65
11.3	Other Than Full-Time Permanent	1	1	1
11.5	Other Personnel Compensation	1	1	1
11.7	Military Personnel	1	1	1
11.9	Total personnel compensation	67	68	68
12.1	Civilian Personnel Benefits (CMS)	19	19	19
12.2	Military Personnel Benefits	1	1	1
23.1	Rental Payments to GSA	14	14	14
23.3	Communications, Utilities, and Miscellaneous Charges	5	5	5
25.2	Other Services from Non-Federal Sources	1,238	1,157	1,236
25.3	Other Goods and Services from Federal Sources	38	36	38
25.4	Operation and Maintenance of Facilities	5	5	5
25.6	Medical Care (CMS)	309	290	309
92.0	Undistributed (SSA CDR Medicare baseline Savings)		–47	–287
92.0	Undistributed (Medicare baseline impact attributable to HCFAC Cap/Allocation Adjustment)			1,119
94.0	Financial Transfers	694	651	694
99.9	Total new obligations, unexpired accounts	2,390	2,199	3,221

Employment Summary

Identification code 075–8393–0–7–571	2021 actual	2022 est.	2023 est.
1001 Direct civilian full-time equivalent employment	472	522	522
1101 Direct military average strength employment	13	13	13

HEALTH CARE FRAUD AND ABUSE CONTROL ACCOUNT

(Legislative proposal, not subject to PAYGO)

Program and Financing (in millions of dollars)

Identification code 075–8393–2–7–571		2021 actual	2022 est.	2023 est.
	Obligations by program activity:			
0005	Undistributed Savings, Medicare SSA CDRs			–22
0006	Undistributed Medicare and Medicaid baseline impact attributable to HCFAC Cap/Allocation Adjustment			–1,119
0091	Total Mandatory			–1,141
0900	Total new obligations, unexpired accounts			–1,141

		2021 actual	2022 est.	2023 est.
	Budgetary resources:			
	Budget authority:			
	Appropriations, mandatory:			
1201	Appropriation (special or trust fund)			–1,141
1900	Budget authority (total)			–1,141
1930	Total budgetary resources available			–1,141
	Change in obligated balance:			
	Unpaid obligations:			
3010	New obligations, unexpired accounts			–1,141
3020	Outlays (gross)			1,141
	Budget authority and outlays, net:			
	Mandatory:			
4090	Budget authority, gross			–1,141
	Outlays, gross:			
4100	Outlays from new mandatory authority			–1,141
4180	Budget authority, net (total)			–1,141
4190	Outlays, net (total)			–1,141

This schedule reflects the non-PAYGO impacts on Medicare and Medicaid spending resulting from the proposed allocation adjustment to further support the Centers for Medicare and Medicaid Services (CMS) program integrity work. This additional investment results in savings to the Medicare and Medicaid programs. This schedule also reflects the non-PAYGO impacts on Medicare resulting from the proposed allocation adjustment for the Social Security Administration. Please refer to the narrative in the Limitation on Administrative Expenses (Social Security Administration) account for more information.

Object Classification (in millions of dollars)

Identification code 075–8393–2–7–571		2021 actual	2022 est.	2023 est.
	Direct obligations:			
92.0	Undistributed (SSA CDR Medicare baseline Savings)			–22
92.0	Undistributed (Medicare baseline impact attributable to HCFAC Cap/Allocation Adjustment)			–1,119
99.9	Total new obligations, unexpired accounts			–1,141

FEDERAL SUPPLEMENTARY MEDICAL INSURANCE TRUST FUND

Special and Trust Fund Receipts (in millions of dollars)

Identification code 075–8004–0–7–571		2021 actual	2022 est.	2023 est.
0100	Balance, start of year	52,946	132,486	150,908
0198	Rounding adjustment	1		
0199	Balance, start of year	52,947	132,486	150,908
	Receipts:			
	Current law:			
1110	Fee on Branded Prescription Pharmaceutical Manufacturers and Importers, SMI	2,790	2,660	1,581
1130	Other Proprietary Interest from the Public, FSMI Fund	1	3	3
1130	Gifts, Medicare Prescription Drug Accounts, FSMI		413	567
1130	Premiums Collected for Medicare Prescription Drug Account, FSMI	5,604	5,745	5,906
1130	Payments from States, Medicare Prescription Drug Account, FSMI	11,859	12,708	13,975
1130	Basic Premium, Medicare Advantage, FSMI Trust Fund	399	556	611
1130	Gifts, FSMI Fund		1	1
1130	Medicare Refunds, SMI	16,026	16,076	5,419
1130	Affordable Care Act Medicare Shared Savings Models, SMI	112	45	45
1130	Premiums Collected for the Aged, FSMI Fund	98,508	115,794	130,466
1130	Premiums Collected for the Disabled, FSMI Fund	13,862	14,626	15,544
1140	Federal Contributions, FSMI Fund	330,973	339,627	375,698
1140	Interest Received by Trust Fund, FSMI Fund	2,053	3,138	3,740
1140	Federal Contribution, State Low-income Determinations, Prescription Drug Account, FSMI		5	5
1140	Interest, Medicare Prescription Drug Account, FSMI	46	50	65
1140	Federal Contribution for Admin. Contribution for Admin. Costs, Prescription Drug Account, FSMI	882	882	500
1140	Federal Contributions for Benefits, Prescription Drug Account, SMI	81,181	89,850	93,961
1140	Miscellaneous Federal Payments, Federal Supplementary Medical Insurance Trust Fund	1	1	1
1199	Total current law receipts	564,297	602,180	648,088

Centers for Medicare and Medicaid Services—Continued
Trust Funds—Continued

FEDERAL SUPPLEMENTARY MEDICAL INSURANCE TRUST FUND—Continued

Special and Trust Fund Receipts—Continued

Identification code 075–8004–0–7–571		2021 actual	2022 est.	2023 est.
1999	Total receipts	564,297	602,180	648,088
2000	Total: Balances and receipts	617,244	734,666	798,996
	Appropriations:			
	Current law:			
2101	Federal Supplementary Medical Insurance Trust Fund	–3,265	–3,301	–4,173
2101	Federal Supplementary Medical Insurance Trust Fund	–461,390	–491,549	–529,785
2101	Medicare Prescription Drug Account, Federal Supplementary Insurance Trust Fund	–881	–878	–596
2101	Medicare Prescription Drug Account, Federal Supplementary Insurance Trust Fund	–98,759	–108,362	–113,916
2103	Federal Supplementary Medical Insurance Trust Fund	–4,305	–3,588	–10,187
2132	Federal Supplementary Medical Insurance Trust Fund	11	3,588	10,187
2132	Medicare Prescription Drug Account, Federal Supplementary Insurance Trust Fund		103	382
2135	Federal Supplementary Medical Insurance Trust Fund	85,895	20,229	21,324
2199	Total current law appropriations	–482,694	–583,758	–626,764
2999	Total appropriations	–482,694	–583,758	–626,764
3098	Federal Supplementary Medical Insurance Trust Fund	–145		
5098	Reconciliation adjustment	–1,919		
5099	Balance, end of year	132,486	150,908	172,232

Program and Financing (in millions of dollars)

Identification code 075–8004–0–7–571		2021 actual	2022 est.	2023 est.
	Obligations by program activity:			
0001	Benefit payments, SMI	428,627	469,848	506,799
0002	Transfer to Medicaid for payment of SMI premiums	1,360	1,314	1,434
0004	Administration, SMI	3,058	3,301	4,249
0005	Quality Improvement Organizations, SMI	126	159	152
0799	Total direct obligations	433,171	474,622	512,634
0900	Total new obligations, unexpired accounts	433,171	474,622	512,634
	Budgetary resources:			
	Unobligated balance:			
1000	Unobligated balance brought forward, Oct 1		1	
1021	Recoveries of prior year unpaid obligations	5		
1026	Adjustment for change in allocation of trust fund limitation or foreign exchange valuation	145		
1033	Recoveries of prior year paid obligations	14,810		
1070	Unobligated balance (total)	14,960	1	
	Budget authority:			
	Appropriations, discretionary:			
1101	Appropriation (special or trust)	3,265	3,301	4,173
	Appropriations, mandatory:			
1201	Appropriation (special or trust fund)	461,390	491,549	529,785
1203	Appropriation (previously unavailable)(special or trust)	4,305	3,588	10,187
1232	Appropriations and/or unobligated balance of appropriations temporarily reduced	–11	–3,588	–10,187
1235	Appropriations precluded from obligation (special or trust)	–85,895	–20,229	–21,324
1236	Appropriations applied to repay debt	–10,539		
1260	Appropriations, mandatory (total)	369,250	471,320	508,461
	Borrowing authority, mandatory:			
1400	Borrowing authority	45,697		
1900	Budget authority (total)	418,212	474,621	512,634
1930	Total budgetary resources available	433,172	474,622	512,634
	Memorandum (non-add) entries:			
1941	Unexpired unobligated balance, end of year	1		
	Change in obligated balance:			
	Unpaid obligations:			
3000	Unpaid obligations, brought forward, Oct 1	29,334	32,812	32,622
3001	Adjustments to unpaid obligations, brought forward, Oct 1	2,060		
3010	New obligations, unexpired accounts	433,171	474,622	512,634
3020	Outlays (gross)	–431,748	–474,812	–512,446
3040	Recoveries of prior year unpaid obligations, unexpired	–5		
3050	Unpaid obligations, end of year	32,812	32,622	32,810
	Memorandum (non-add) entries:			
3100	Obligated balance, start of year	31,394	32,812	32,622
3200	Obligated balance, end of year	32,812	32,622	32,810

	Budget authority and outlays, net:			
	Discretionary:			
4000	Budget authority, gross	3,265	3,301	4,173
	Outlays, gross:			
4010	Outlays from new discretionary authority	1,902	2,160	2,566
4011	Outlays from discretionary balances	1,661	1,291	1,419
4020	Outlays, gross (total)	3,563	3,451	3,985
	Mandatory:			
4090	Budget authority, gross	414,947	471,320	508,461
	Outlays, gross:			
4100	Outlays from new mandatory authority	386,045	440,774	475,337
4101	Outlays from mandatory balances	42,140	30,587	33,124
4110	Outlays, gross (total)	428,185	471,361	508,461
	Offsets against gross budget authority and outlays:			
	Offsetting collections (collected) from:			
4123	Non-Federal sources	–14,810		
	Additional offsets against gross budget authority only:			
4143	Recoveries of prior year paid obligations, unexpired accounts	14,810		
4160	Budget authority, net (mandatory)	414,947	471,320	508,461
4170	Outlays, net (mandatory)	413,375	471,361	508,461
4180	Budget authority, net (total)	418,212	474,621	512,634
4190	Outlays, net (total)	416,938	474,812	512,446
	Memorandum (non-add) entries:			
5000	Total investments, SOY: Federal securities: Par value	87,477	170,677	156,727
5001	Total investments, EOY: Federal securities: Par value	170,677	156,727	179,051
5080	Outstanding debt, SOY	–1,154	–36,312	–36,312
5081	Outstanding debt, EOY	–36,312	–36,312	–36,312
5082	Borrowing	–45,697		

The Supplementary Medical Insurance (SMI) program is a voluntary program that affords protection against the costs of physician care and certain other medical services. The program also covers treatment of end-stage renal disease for eligible enrollees. SMI costs are generally financed by premium payments from enrollees and contributions from the general revenues.

Status of Funds (in millions of dollars)

Identification code 075–8004–0–7–571		2021 actual	2022 est.	2023 est.
	Unexpended balance, start of year:			
0100	Balance, start of year	88,909	137,647	157,689
0999	Total balance, start of year	88,909	137,647	157,689
	Cash income during the year:			
	Current law:			
	Receipts:			
1110	Fee on Branded Prescription Pharmaceutical Manufacturers and Importers, SMI	2,790	2,660	1,581
1130	Gifts, Medicare Prescription Drug Accounts, FSMI		413	567
1130	Premiums Collected for Medicare Prescription Drug Account, FSMI	5,604	5,745	5,906
1130	Payments from States, Medicare Prescription Drug Account, FSMI	11,859	12,708	13,975
1130	Basic Premium, Medicare Advantage, FSMI Trust Fund	399	556	611
1130	Gifts, FSMI Fund		1	1
1130	Medicare Refunds, SMI	16,026	16,076	5,419
1130	Affordable Care Act Medicare Shared Savings Models, SMI	112	45	45
1130	Premiums Collected for the Aged, FSMI Fund	98,508	115,794	130,466
1130	Premiums Collected for the Disabled, FSMI Fund	13,862	14,626	15,544
1130	Federal Supplementary Medical Insurance Trust Fund	14,810		
1130	Medicare Prescription Drug Account, Federal Supplementary Insurance Trust Fund	2		
1150	Interest Received by Trust Fund, FSMI Fund	2,053	3,138	3,740
1150	Other Proprietary Interest from the Public, FSMI Fund	1	3	3
1150	Interest, Medicare Prescription Drug Account, FSMI	46	50	65
1160	Federal Contributions, FSMI Fund	330,973	339,627	375,698
1160	Federal Contribution, State Low-income Determinations, Prescription Drug Account, FSMI		5	5
1160	Federal Contribution for Admin. Contribution for Admin. Costs, Prescription Drug Account, FSMI	882	882	500
1160	Federal Contributions for Benefits, Prescription Drug Account, SMI	81,181	89,850	93,961
1160	Miscellaneous Federal Payments, Federal Supplementary Medical Insurance Trust Fund	1	1	1
1160	Medicare Prescription Drug Account, Federal Supplementary Insurance Trust Fund		1,807	
1199	Income under present law	579,109	603,987	648,088
1999	Total cash income	579,109	603,987	648,088

DEPARTMENT OF HEALTH AND HUMAN SERVICES

Centers for Medicare and Medicaid Services—Continued
Trust Funds—Continued
467

		2021 actual	2022 est.	2023 est.
	Cash outgo during year: Current law:			
2100	Federal Supplementary Medical Insurance Trust Fund [Budget Acct]	−431,748	−474,812	−512,446
2100	Medicare Prescription Drug Account, Federal Supplementary Insurance Trust Fund [Budget Acct]	−98,621	−109,133	−114,107
2199	Outgo under current law	−530,369	−583,945	−626,553
2999	Total cash outgo (−)	−530,369	−583,945	−626,553
	Surplus or deficit:			
3110	Excluding interest	46,640	16,851	17,727
3120	Interest	2,100	3,191	3,808
3199	Subtotal, surplus or deficit	48,740	20,042	21,535
3298	Reconciliation adjustment	−2	....	....
3299	Total adjustments	−2	....	....
3999	Total change in fund balance	48,738	20,042	21,535
	Unexpended balance, end of year:			
4100	Uninvested balance (net), end of year	−33,030	962	173
4200	Federal Supplementary Medical Insurance Trust Fund	170,677	156,727	179,051
4999	Total balance, end of year	137,647	157,689	179,224

Object Classification (in millions of dollars)

Identification code 075–8004–0–7–571		2021 actual	2022 est.	2023 est.
	Direct obligations:			
11.1	Personnel compensation: Full-time permanent	1	1	1
41.0	Payment for Quality Improvement Organization (QIO) activity	126	159	152
42.0	Insurance claims and indemnities	426,494	471,161	508,233
94.0	Financial transfers	6,550	3,301	4,248
99.0	Direct obligations	433,171	474,622	512,634
99.9	Total new obligations, unexpired accounts	433,171	474,622	512,634

Employment Summary

Identification code 075–8004–0–7–571	2021 actual	2022 est.	2023 est.
1001 Direct civilian full-time equivalent employment	5	1	1

MEDICARE PRESCRIPTION DRUG ACCOUNT, FEDERAL SUPPLEMENTARY INSURANCE TRUST FUND

Program and Financing (in millions of dollars)

Identification code 075–8308–0–7–571		2021 actual	2022 est.	2023 est.
	Obligations by program activity:			
0001	Prescription Drug Benefits	98,760	108,228	112,793
0002	Administrative Costs	882	882	600
0799	Total direct obligations	99,642	109,110	113,393
0801	Reimbursable program activity	1,807	....	....
0900	Total new obligations, unexpired accounts	101,449	109,110	113,393
	Budgetary resources:			
	Unobligated balance:			
1000	Unobligated balance brought forward, Oct 1	....	....	27
1033	Recoveries of prior year paid obligations	2	....	....
1070	Unobligated balance (total)	2	....	27
	Budget authority:			
	Appropriations, discretionary:			
1101	Appropriation (special or trust)	881	878	596
	Appropriations, mandatory:			
1201	Appropriation (special or trust fund)	98,759	108,362	113,916
1232	Appropriations and/or unobligated balance of appropriations temporarily reduced	....	−103	−382
1260	Appropriations, mandatory (total)	98,759	108,259	113,534
	Spending authority from offsetting collections, mandatory:			
1800	Collected	....	1,807	....
1801	Change in uncollected payments, Federal sources	1,807	−1,807	....
1850	Spending auth from offsetting collections, mand (total)	1,807	....	....
1900	Budget authority (total)	101,447	109,137	114,130
1930	Total budgetary resources available	101,449	109,137	114,157
	Memorandum (non-add) entries:			
1941	Unexpired unobligated balance, end of year	....	27	764
	Change in obligated balance:			
	Unpaid obligations:			
3000	Unpaid obligations, brought forward, Oct 1	14,230	17,061	17,038
3001	Adjustments to unpaid obligations, brought forward, Oct 1	3	....	....
3010	New obligations, unexpired accounts	101,449	109,110	113,393
3020	Outlays (gross)	−98,621	−109,133	−114,107
3050	Unpaid obligations, end of year	17,061	17,038	16,324
	Uncollected payments:			
3060	Uncollected pymts, Fed sources, brought forward, Oct 1	−6,448	−8,255	−6,448
3070	Change in uncollected pymts, Fed sources, unexpired	−1,807	1,807	....
3090	Uncollected pymts, Fed sources, end of year	−8,255	−6,448	−6,448
	Memorandum (non-add) entries:			
3100	Obligated balance, start of year	7,785	8,806	10,590
3200	Obligated balance, end of year	8,806	10,590	9,876
	Budget authority and outlays, net:			
	Discretionary:			
4000	Budget authority, gross	881	878	596
	Outlays, gross:			
4010	Outlays from new discretionary authority	364	520	390
4011	Outlays from discretionary balances	159	351	183
4020	Outlays, gross (total)	523	871	573
	Mandatory:			
4090	Budget authority, gross	100,566	108,259	113,534
	Outlays, gross:			
4100	Outlays from new mandatory authority	85,220	91,592	100,532
4101	Outlays from mandatory balances	12,878	16,670	13,002
4110	Outlays, gross (total)	98,098	108,262	113,534
	Offsets against gross budget authority and outlays:			
	Offsetting collections (collected) from:			
4120	Federal sources:	....	−1,807	....
4123	Non-Federal sources	−2	....	....
4130	Offsets against gross budget authority and outlays (total)	−2	−1,807	....
	Additional offsets against gross budget authority only:			
4140	Change in uncollected pymts, Fed sources, unexpired	−1,807	1,807	....
4143	Recoveries of prior year paid obligations, unexpired accounts	2	....	....
4150	Additional offsets against budget authority only (total)	−1,805	1,807	....
4160	Budget authority, net (mandatory)	98,759	108,259	113,534
4170	Outlays, net (mandatory)	98,096	106,455	113,534
4180	Budget authority, net (total)	99,640	109,137	114,130
4190	Outlays, net (total)	98,619	107,326	114,107

Since January 2006, Medicare beneficiaries have had the opportunity to enroll in a comprehensive voluntary prescription drug benefit.

Object Classification (in millions of dollars)

Identification code 075–8308–0–7–571		2021 actual	2022 est.	2023 est.
	Direct obligations:			
25.2	Other services from non-Federal sources	882	882	600
42.0	Insurance claims and indemnities	98,760	108,228	112,793
99.0	Direct obligations	99,642	109,110	113,393
99.0	Reimbursable obligations	1,807	....	....
99.9	Total new obligations, unexpired accounts	101,449	109,110	113,393

Employment Summary

Identification code 075–8308–0–7–571	2021 actual	2022 est.	2023 est.
1001 Direct civilian full-time equivalent employment	4	4	4

ADMINISTRATION FOR CHILDREN AND FAMILIES
Federal Funds
TEMPORARY ASSISTANCE FOR NEEDY FAMILIES

Program and Financing (in millions of dollars)

Identification code 075–1552–0–1–609		2021 actual	2022 est.	2023 est.
	Obligations by program activity:			
0001	State family assistance grant	16,437	16,343	16,343
0002	Territories - family assistance grants	78	78	78
0006	Tribal work programs	4	8	8
0009	Healthy marriage and responsible fatherhood grants	147	149	149
0010	Evaluation Funding and What Works Clearinghouse	43	45	45
0011	Census Bureau Research	10	10	10
0012	Pandemic Emergency Assistance	995	1	1
0900	Total new obligations, unexpired accounts	17,714	16,634	16,634
	Budgetary resources:			
	Unobligated balance:			
1000	Unobligated balance brought forward, Oct 1		5	94
	Budget authority:			
	Appropriations, mandatory:			
1200	Appropriation	17,739	16,739	16,739
1230	Appropriations and/or unobligated balance of appropriations permanently reduced	–1	–1	–1
1260	Appropriations, mandatory (total)	17,738	16,738	16,738
1900	Budget authority (total)	17,738	16,738	16,738
1930	Total budgetary resources available	17,738	16,743	16,832
	Memorandum (non-add) entries:			
1940	Unobligated balance expiring	–19	–15	–15
1941	Unexpired unobligated balance, end of year	5	94	183
	Change in obligated balance:			
	Unpaid obligations:			
3000	Unpaid obligations, brought forward, Oct 1	9,449	11,776	11,373
3010	New obligations, unexpired accounts	17,714	16,634	16,634
3011	Obligations ("upward adjustments"), expired accounts	2		
3020	Outlays (gross)	–15,383	–17,037	–16,517
3041	Recoveries of prior year unpaid obligations, expired	–6		
3050	Unpaid obligations, end of year	11,776	11,373	11,490
	Memorandum (non-add) entries:			
3100	Obligated balance, start of year	9,449	11,776	11,373
3200	Obligated balance, end of year	11,776	11,373	11,490
	Budget authority and outlays, net:			
	Mandatory:			
4090	Budget authority, gross	17,738	16,738	16,738
	Outlays, gross:			
4100	Outlays from new mandatory authority	10,032	9,813	9,813
4101	Outlays from mandatory balances	5,351	7,224	6,704
4110	Outlays, gross (total)	15,383	17,037	16,517
4180	Budget authority, net (total)	17,738	16,738	16,738
4190	Outlays, net (total)	15,383	17,037	16,517

This account provides funding for the Temporary Assistance for Needy Families (TANF) block grant and related activities authorized by the Personal Responsibility and Work Opportunity Reconciliation Act of 1996 (P.L. 104–193), as amended by the Deficit Reduction Act of 2005 (P.L. 109–171). TANF's authorization was most recently extended in the Continuing Appropriations Act of 2022 (P. L. 117–70).

Object Classification (in millions of dollars)

Identification code 075–1552–0–1–609		2021 actual	2022 est.	2023 est.
11.1	Direct obligations: Personnel compensation: Full-time permanent	14	9	9
11.9	Total personnel compensation	14	9	9
12.1	Civilian personnel benefits	1	1	1
23.1	Rental payments to GSA	1	1	1
25.1	Advisory and assistance services	49	48	48
25.2	Other services from non-Federal sources	24	23	23
25.3	Other goods and services from Federal sources	7	6	6
25.4	Operation and maintenance of facilities	1	1	1
41.0	Grants, subsidies, and contributions	17,617	16,545	16,545
99.9	Total new obligations, unexpired accounts	17,714	16,634	16,634

Employment Summary

Identification code 075–1552–0–1–609		2021 actual	2022 est.	2023 est.
1001	Direct civilian full-time equivalent employment	98	102	102

CONTINGENCY FUND

Program and Financing (in millions of dollars)

Identification code 075–1522–0–1–609		2021 actual	2022 est.	2023 est.
	Obligations by program activity:			
0001	Contingency Fund for State Welfare Programs	608	608	608
0900	Total new obligations, unexpired accounts (object class 41.0)	608	608	608
	Budgetary resources:			
	Budget authority:			
	Appropriations, mandatory:			
1200	Appropriation	608	608	608
1930	Total budgetary resources available	608	608	608
	Change in obligated balance:			
	Unpaid obligations:			
3000	Unpaid obligations, brought forward, Oct 1	8	23	25
3010	New obligations, unexpired accounts	608	608	608
3011	Obligations ("upward adjustments"), expired accounts	14		
3020	Outlays (gross)	–604	–606	–604
3041	Recoveries of prior year unpaid obligations, expired	–3		
3050	Unpaid obligations, end of year	23	25	29
	Memorandum (non-add) entries:			
3100	Obligated balance, start of year	8	23	25
3200	Obligated balance, end of year	23	25	29
	Budget authority and outlays, net:			
	Mandatory:			
4090	Budget authority, gross	608	608	608
	Outlays, gross:			
4100	Outlays from new mandatory authority	596	598	596
4101	Outlays from mandatory balances	8	8	8
4110	Outlays, gross (total)	604	606	604
	Offsets against gross budget authority and outlays:			
	Offsetting collections (collected) from:			
4123	Non-Federal sources	–14		
	Additional offsets against gross budget authority only:			
4142	Offsetting collections credited to expired accounts	14		
4160	Budget authority, net (mandatory)	608	608	608
4170	Outlays, net (mandatory)	590	606	604
4180	Budget authority, net (total)	608	608	608
4190	Outlays, net (total)	590	606	604

The TANF Contingency Fund provides a funding reserve of $608 million to assist states that meet certain criteria related to the state's unemployment rate and Supplemental Nutrition Assistance Program (SNAP) caseload. In order to qualify for contingency funds, States must also meet a higher maintenance-of-effort requirement of 100 percent of historical expenditures. The authorization for the Contingency Fund was most recently extended in the Contining Appropriations Act of 2022 (P.L. 117–70).

PAYMENTS TO STATES FOR CHILD SUPPORT ENFORCEMENT AND FAMILY SUPPORT PROGRAMS

For carrying out, except as otherwise provided, titles I, IV-D, X, XI, XIV, and XVI of the Social Security Act and the Act of July 5, 1960, $2,883,000,000, to remain available until expended; and for such purposes for the first quarter of fiscal year 2024, $1,300,000,000, to remain available until expended.

For carrying out, after May 31 of the current fiscal year, except as otherwise provided, titles I, IV-D, X, XI, XIV, and XVI of the Social Security Act and the Act of July 5, 1960, for the last 3 months of the current fiscal year for unanticipated costs, incurred for the current fiscal year, such sums as may be necessary.

Note.—A full-year 2022 appropriation for this account was not enacted at the time the Budget was prepared; therefore, the Budget assumes this account is operating under the Continuing Appropriations Act, 2022 (Division A of Public Law 117–43, as amended). The amounts included for 2022 reflect the annualized level provided by the continuing resolution.

DEPARTMENT OF HEALTH AND HUMAN SERVICES

Administration for Children and Families—Continued
Federal Funds—Continued

Program and Financing (in millions of dollars)

Identification code 075–1501–0–1–609	2021 actual	2022 est.	2023 est.
Obligations by program activity:			
0001 State child support administrative costs	3,940	3,691	3,675
0002 Child support incentive payments	600	600	655
0003 Access and visitation grants	10	10	10
0091 Subtotal, child support enforcement	4,550	4,301	4,340
0102 Payments to territories	66	53	33
0103 Repatriation	9	11	10
0191 Subtotal, other payments	75	64	43
0799 Total direct obligations	4,625	4,365	4,383
0801 Offset obligations (CSE grants to States)		2	
0900 Total new obligations, unexpired accounts	4,625	4,367	4,383
Budgetary resources:			
Unobligated balance:			
1000 Unobligated balance brought forward, Oct 1	1	111	138
1021 Recoveries of prior year unpaid obligations	809	200	200
1033 Recoveries of prior year paid obligations	25		
1037 Unobligated balance of appropriations withdrawn	–540		
1070 Unobligated balance (total)	295	311	338
Budget authority:			
Appropriations, mandatory:			
1200 Appropriation	3,039	2,795	2,883
1230 Appropriations and/or unobligated balance of appropriations permanently reduced		–1	–1
1260 Appropriations, mandatory (total)	3,039	2,794	2,882
Advance appropriations, mandatory:			
1270 Advance appropriation	1,400	1,400	1,300
Spending authority from offsetting collections, mandatory:			
1800 Collected	2		
1900 Budget authority (total)	4,441	4,194	4,182
1930 Total budgetary resources available	4,736	4,505	4,520
Memorandum (non-add) entries:			
1941 Unexpired unobligated balance, end of year	111	138	137
Change in obligated balance:			
Unpaid obligations:			
3000 Unpaid obligations, brought forward, Oct 1	1,804	1,435	1,486
3010 New obligations, unexpired accounts	4,625	4,367	4,383
3020 Outlays (gross)	–4,185	–4,116	–4,122
3040 Recoveries of prior year unpaid obligations, unexpired	–809	–200	–200
3050 Unpaid obligations, end of year	1,435	1,486	1,547
Memorandum (non-add) entries:			
3100 Obligated balance, start of year	1,804	1,435	1,486
3200 Obligated balance, end of year	1,435	1,486	1,547
Budget authority and outlays, net:			
Mandatory:			
4090 Budget authority, gross	4,441	4,194	4,182
Outlays, gross:			
4100 Outlays from new mandatory authority	3,761	3,543	3,523
4101 Outlays from mandatory balances	424	573	599
4110 Outlays, gross (total)	4,185	4,116	4,122
Offsets against gross budget authority and outlays:			
Offsetting collections (collected) from:			
4123 Non-Federal sources	–27		
Additional offsets against gross budget authority only:			
4143 Recoveries of prior year paid obligations, unexpired accounts	25		
4160 Budget authority, net (mandatory)	4,439	4,194	4,182
4170 Outlays, net (mandatory)	4,158	4,116	4,122
4180 Budget authority, net (total)	4,439	4,194	4,182
4190 Outlays, net (total)	4,158	4,116	4,122

This account provides for payments to States for child support enforcement and other family support programs, including access and visitation programs for families. The Federal share of child support collections is returned to the Treasury in a receipt account.

Object Classification (in millions of dollars)

Identification code 075–1501–0–1–609	2021 actual	2022 est.	2023 est.
Direct obligations:			
25.1 Advisory and assistance services		1	1
25.2 Other services from non-Federal sources	6	7	7
41.0 Grants, subsidies, and contributions	4,619	4,359	4,375
99.0 Direct obligations	4,625	4,367	4,383
99.9 Total new obligations, unexpired accounts	4,625	4,367	4,383

LOW INCOME HOME ENERGY ASSISTANCE

For carrying out subsections (b) and (d) of section 2602 of the Low-Income Home Energy Assistance Act of 1981 (42 U.S.C. 8621 et seq.), $3,975,304,000: Provided, That notwithstanding section 2609A(a) of such Act, not more than $20,500,000 may be reserved by the Secretary of Health and Human Services for technical assistance, training, and monitoring of program activities for compliance with internal controls, policies and procedures and the Secretary may, in addition to the authorities provided in section 2609A(a)(1), use such funds through contracts with private entities that do not qualify as nonprofit organizations: Provided further, That all but $760,000,000 of the amount appropriated under this heading shall be allocated as though the total appropriation for such payments for fiscal year 2023 was less than $1,975,000,000: Provided further, That, after applying all applicable provisions of section 2604 of such Act and the previous proviso, each State or territory that would otherwise receive an allocation that is less than 97 percent of the amount that it received under this heading for fiscal year 2022 from amounts appropriated in the Department of Health and Human Services Appropriations Act for such fiscal year shall have its allocation increased to that 97 percent level, with the portions of other States' and territories' allocations that would exceed 100 percent of the amounts they respectively received in such fashion for fiscal year 2022 being ratably reduced: Provided further, That notwithstanding any provision of the Low-Income Home Energy Assistance Act of 1981 (42 U.S.C. 8621 et seq.), of the amounts received by a State, territory, or Tribe under this heading for fiscal year 2023, not more than 2.7% of such amounts may be used for the activities described in section 2912 of the American Rescue Plan Act of 2021 (Public Law 117–2): Provided further, That of the total amount of funds available to a State, territory, or Tribe for the activities described in section 2912 of the American Rescue Plan Act, not more than 15% of such amounts shall be available for administrative expenses.

Note.—A full-year 2022 appropriation for this account was not enacted at the time the Budget was prepared; therefore, the Budget assumes this account is operating under the Continuing Appropriations Act, 2022 (Division A of Public Law 117–43, as amended). The amounts included for 2022 reflect the annualized level provided by the continuing resolution.

LOW INCOME HOME ENERGY ASSISTANCE

[For an additional amount for "Low Income Home Energy Assistance", $500,000,000, to remain available through September 30, 2026, for making payments under subsection (b) of section 2602 of the Low-Income Home Energy Assistance Act of 1981 (42 U.S.C. 8621 et seq.): *Provided*, That $100,000,000, to remain available until September 30, 2026, shall be made available in fiscal year 2022, $100,000,000, to remain available until September 30, 2026, shall be made available in fiscal year 2023, $100,000,000, to remain available until September 30, 2026, shall be made available in fiscal year 2024, $100,000,000, to remain available until September 30, 2026, shall be made available in fiscal year 2025, and $100,000,000, to remain available until September 30, 2026, shall be made available in fiscal year 2026: *Provided further*, That, of the amount available for obligation in a fiscal year under this heading in this Act, $50,000,000 shall be allocated as though the total appropriation for such payments for such fiscal year was less than $1,975,000,000: *Provided further*, That such amount is designated by the Congress as being for an emergency requirement pursuant to section 4112(a) of H. Con. Res. 71 (115th Congress), the concurrent resolution on the budget for fiscal year 2018, and to section 251(b) of the Balanced Budget and Emergency Deficit Control Act of 1985.] *(Infrastructure Investments and Jobs Appropriations Act.)*

Program and Financing (in millions of dollars)

Identification code 075–1502–0–1–609	2021 actual	2022 est.	2023 est.
Obligations by program activity:			
0001 LIHEAP Block Grant	8,214	3,850	4,075
Budgetary resources:			
Unobligated balance:			
1000 Unobligated balance brought forward, Oct 1	1		
1012 Unobligated balance transfers between expired and unexpired accounts	1		
1070 Unobligated balance (total)	2		

469

Administration for Children and Families—Continued
Federal Funds—Continued

LOW INCOME HOME ENERGY ASSISTANCE—Continued

Program and Financing—Continued

Identification code 075–1502–0–1–609	2021 actual	2022 est.	2023 est.
Budget authority:			
Appropriations, discretionary:			
1100 Appropriation	3,750	3,850	3,975
1120 Appropriations transferred to other acct [075–1503]	–38		
1160 Appropriation, discretionary (total)	3,712	3,850	3,975
Advance appropriations, discretionary:			
1170 Advance appropriation			100
Appropriations, mandatory:			
1200 Appropriation	4,500		
1900 Budget authority (total)	8,212	3,850	4,075
1930 Total budgetary resources available	8,214	3,850	4,075
Change in obligated balance:			
Unpaid obligations:			
3000 Unpaid obligations, brought forward, Oct 1	2,383	6,145	4,335
3010 New obligations, unexpired accounts	8,214	3,850	4,075
3011 Obligations ("upward adjustments"), expired accounts	1		
3020 Outlays (gross)	–4,417	–5,660	–6,317
3041 Recoveries of prior year unpaid obligations, expired	–36		
3050 Unpaid obligations, end of year	6,145	4,335	2,093
Memorandum (non-add) entries:			
3100 Obligated balance, start of year	2,383	6,145	4,335
3200 Obligated balance, end of year	6,145	4,335	2,093
Budget authority and outlays, net:			
Discretionary:			
4000 Budget authority, gross	3,712	3,850	4,075
Outlays, gross:			
4010 Outlays from new discretionary authority	2,243	2,462	2,567
4011 Outlays from discretionary balances	1,915	1,626	1,388
4020 Outlays, gross (total)	4,158	4,088	3,955
Mandatory:			
4090 Budget authority, gross	4,500		
Outlays, gross:			
4100 Outlays from new mandatory authority	259		
4101 Outlays from mandatory balances		1,572	2,362
4110 Outlays, gross (total)	259	1,572	2,362
4180 Budget authority, net (total)	8,212	3,850	4,075
4190 Outlays, net (total)	4,417	5,660	6,317

LIHEAP provides federally funded assistance to low-income households via State, territory, and tribal governments for the purpose of managing costs associated with home energy bills and energy crises, as well as weatherization and minor energy-related home repairs.

Object Classification (in millions of dollars)

Identification code 075–1502–0–1–609	2021 actual	2022 est.	2023 est.
Direct obligations:			
11.1 Personnel compensation: Full-time permanent			2
25.1 Advisory and assistance services		2	7
25.2 Other services from non-Federal sources			3
25.3 Other goods and services from Federal sources	1	1	9
41.0 Grants, subsidies, and contributions	8,211	3,847	4,054
99.9 Total new obligations, unexpired accounts	8,214	3,850	4,075

Employment Summary

Identification code 075–1502–0–1–609	2021 actual	2022 est.	2023 est.
1001 Direct civilian full-time equivalent employment			11

REFUGEE AND ENTRANT ASSISTANCE

(INCLUDING TRANSFER OF FUNDS)

For necessary expenses for refugee and entrant assistance activities authorized by section 414 of the Immigration and Nationality Act and section 501 of the Refugee Education Assistance Act of 1980, and for carrying out section 462 of the Homeland Security Act of 2002, section 235 of the William Wilberforce Trafficking Victims Protection Reauthorization Act of 2008, the Trafficking Victims Protection Act of 2000 ("TVPA"), and the Torture Victims Relief Act of 1998, $6,327,843,000, of which $6,261,346,000 shall remain available through September 30, 2025 for carrying out such sections 414, 501, 462, and 235: Provided, That amounts available under this heading to carry out the TVPA shall also be available for research and evaluation with respect to activities under such Act: Provided further, That the limitation in section 204 of this Act regarding transfers increasing any appropriation shall apply to transfers to appropriations under this heading by substituting "15 percent" for "3 percent": Provided further, That the contribution of funds requirement under section 235(c)(6)(C)(iii) of the William Wilberforce Trafficking Victims Protection Reauthorization Act of 2008 shall not apply to funds made available under this heading.

Note.—A full-year 2022 appropriation for this account was not enacted at the time the Budget was prepared; therefore, the Budget assumes this account is operating under the Continuing Appropriations Act, 2022 (Division A of Public Law 117–43, as amended). The amounts included for 2022 reflect the annualized level provided by the continuing resolution.

REFUGEE AND ENTRANT ASSISTANCE

【*For an additional amount for "Refugee and Entrant Assistance", $1,680,000,000, to remain available until September 30, 2023, for support of Operation Allies Welcome for carrying out refugee and entrant assistance activities in support of citizens or nationals of Afghanistan paroled into the United States under section 212(d)(5) of the Immigration and Nationality Act and citizens or nationals of Afghanistan for whom such refugee and entrant assistance activities are authorized: Provided, That amounts made available under this heading in this Act may be used for grants or contracts with qualified nonprofit organizations to provide culturally and linguistically appropriate services, including wrap-around services during temporary housing and after resettlement, housing assistance, medical assistance, legal assistance, and case management assistance: Provided further, That the Director of the Office of Refugee Resettlement, in carrying out section 412(c)(1)(A) of the Immigration and Nationality Act with amounts made available under this heading in this Act, may allocate such amounts among the States in a manner that accounts for the most current data available.*】 *(Afghanistan Supplemental Appropriations Act, 2022.)*

REFUGEE AND ENTRANT ASSISTANCE

【*For an additional amount for "Refugee and Entrant Assistance", $1,263,728,000, to remain available until September 30, 2023, for support of Operation Allies Welcome for carrying out refugee and entrant assistance activities in support of citizens or nationals of Afghanistan paroled into the United States under section 212(d)(5) of the Immigration and Nationality Act and citizens or nationals of Afghanistan for whom such refugee and entrant assistance activities are authorized: Provided, That amounts made available under this heading in this Act may be used for grants or contracts with qualified nonprofit organizations to provide culturally and linguistically appropriate services, including wrap-around services during temporary housing and after resettlement, housing assistance, medical assistance, legal assistance, education services, and case management assistance: Provided further, That the Director of the Office of Refugee Resettlement, in carrying out section 412(c)(1)(A) of the Immigration and Nationality Act with amounts made available under this heading in this Act, may allocate such amounts among the States in a manner that accounts for the most current data available.*】 *(Additional Afghanistan Supplemental Appropriations Act, 2022.)*

Program and Financing (in millions of dollars)

Identification code 075–1503–0–1–609	2021 actual	2022 est.	2023 est.
Obligations by program activity:			
0001 Refugee Support Services (RSS) and Transitional & Medical Services (TAMS)	561	561	1,360
0002 Assistance for treatment of torture victims	27	17	27
0003 Unaccompanied Children	6,866	6,361	4,901
0005 Trafficking Victims program	40	29	39
0799 Total direct obligations	7,494	6,968	6,327
0801 Reimbursable program activity	56	56	56
0900 Total new obligations, unexpired accounts	7,550	7,024	6,383
Budgetary resources:			
Unobligated balance:			
1000 Unobligated balance brought forward, Oct 1	1,418	543	3,456
1021 Recoveries of prior year unpaid obligations	445		
1033 Recoveries of prior year paid obligations	1		
1070 Unobligated balance (total)	1,864	543	3,456
Budget authority:			
Appropriations, discretionary:			
1100 Base Appropriation	1,935	8,954	6,328
1121 Appropriations transferred from other acct [075–1502]	38		
1121 Appropriations transferred from other acct [075–9912]	2		

DEPARTMENT OF HEALTH AND HUMAN SERVICES

Administration for Children and Families—Continued
Federal Funds—Continued

		2021 actual	2022 est.	2023 est.
1121	Appropriations transferred from other acct [075–1515]	33		
1121	Appropriations transferred from other acct [075–0140]	858		
1121	Appropriations transferred from other acct [075–1700]	1		
1121	Appropriations transferred from other acct [075–0943]	21		
1121	Appropriations transferred from other acct [075–0350]	22		
1121	Appropriations transferred from other acct [075–1362]	18		
1121	Appropriations transferred from other acct [075–9915]	1,186		
1121	Appropriations transferred from other acct [075–0142]	7		
1160	Appropriation, discretionary (total)	4,121	8,954	6,328
	Spending authority from offsetting collections, discretionary:			
1700	Collected	44		
1711	Spending authority from offsetting collections transferred from other accounts [075–0511]	12		
1750	Spending auth from offsetting collections, disc (total)	56		
	Spending authority from offsetting collections, mandatory:			
1800	Collected	1,077	983	
1801	Change in uncollected payments, Federal sources	983		
1850	Spending auth from offsetting collections, mand (total)	2,060	983	
1900	Budget authority (total)	6,237	9,937	6,328
1930	Total budgetary resources available	8,101	10,480	9,784
	Memorandum (non-add) entries:			
1940	Unobligated balance expiring	–8		
1941	Unexpired unobligated balance, end of year	543	3,456	3,401
	Change in obligated balance:			
	Unpaid obligations:			
3000	Unpaid obligations, brought forward, Oct 1	2,603	3,374	2,135
3010	New obligations, unexpired accounts	7,550	7,024	6,383
3011	Obligations ("upward adjustments"), expired accounts	2	151	
3020	Outlays (gross)	–6,231	–8,414	–5,545
3040	Recoveries of prior year unpaid obligations, unexpired	–445		
3041	Recoveries of prior year unpaid obligations, expired	–105		
3050	Unpaid obligations, end of year	3,374	2,135	2,973
	Uncollected payments:			
3060	Uncollected pymts, Fed sources, brought forward, Oct 1	–7	–990	–990
3070	Change in uncollected pymts, Fed sources, unexpired	–983		
3090	Uncollected pymts, Fed sources, end of year	–990	–990	–990
	Memorandum (non-add) entries:			
3100	Obligated balance, start of year	2,596	2,384	1,145
3200	Obligated balance, end of year	2,384	1,145	1,983
	Budget authority and outlays, net:			
	Discretionary:			
4000	Budget authority, gross	4,177	8,954	6,328
	Outlays, gross:			
4010	Outlays from new discretionary authority	2,590	5,405	2,848
4011	Outlays from discretionary balances	2,383	1,062	2,422
4020	Outlays, gross (total)	4,973	6,467	5,270
	Offsets against gross budget authority and outlays:			
	Offsetting collections (collected) from:			
4030	Federal sources	–44		
4033	Non-Federal sources	–2		
4040	Offsets against gross budget authority and outlays (total)	–46		
	Additional offsets against gross budget authority only:			
4052	Offsetting collections credited to expired accounts	1		
4053	Recoveries of prior year paid obligations, unexpired accounts	1		
4060	Additional offsets against budget authority only (total)	2		
4070	Budget authority, net (discretionary)	4,133	8,954	6,328
4080	Outlays, net (discretionary)	4,927	6,467	5,270
	Mandatory:			
4090	Budget authority, gross	2,060	983	
	Outlays, gross:			
4100	Outlays from new mandatory authority	1,258	442	
4101	Outlays from mandatory balances		1,505	275
4110	Outlays, gross (total)	1,258	1,947	275
	Offsets against gross budget authority and outlays:			
	Offsetting collections (collected) from:			
4120	Federal sources	–1,077	–983	
	Additional offsets against gross budget authority only:			
4140	Change in uncollected pymts, Fed sources, unexpired	–983		
4170	Outlays, net (mandatory)	181	964	275
4180	Budget authority, net (total)	4,133	8,954	6,328
4190	Outlays, net (total)	5,108	7,431	5,545

Summary of Budget Authority and Outlays (in millions of dollars)

	2021 actual	2022 est.	2023 est.
Enacted/requested:			
Budget Authority	4,133	8,954	6,328
Outlays	5,108	7,431	5,545
Legislative proposal, subject to PAYGO:			
Budget Authority			1,813
Outlays			816
Total:			
Budget Authority	4,133	8,954	8,141
Outlays	5,108	7,431	6,361

This account provides funds to States and non-governmental organizations to administer the refugee and entrant assistance programs. Funds support cash and medical assistance and social services for refugees, asylees, and other arrivals eligible for refugee benefits. The account also includes funding for the care and placement of unaccompanied children, and for the rehabilitation of victims of torture and human trafficking. The appropriations request should be $6,327,843,000.

Object Classification (in millions of dollars)

Identification code 075–1503–0–1–609

		2021 actual	2022 est.	2023 est.
	Direct obligations:			
	Personnel compensation:			
11.1	Full-time permanent	20	23	31
11.7	Military personnel	2	2	3
11.9	Total personnel compensation	22	25	34
12.1	Civilian personnel benefits	5	8	11
12.2	Military personnel benefits	1	1	2
23.1	Rental payments to GSA	7	7	7
25.1	Advisory and assistance services	16	16	16
25.2	Other services from non-Federal sources	3,564	3,032	2,378
25.3	Other goods and services from Federal sources	2,533	2,533	2,533
25.4	Operation and maintenance of facilities	1	1	1
41.0	Grants, subsidies, and contributions	1,345	1,345	1,345
99.0	Direct obligations	7,494	6,968	6,327
99.0	Reimbursable obligations	56	56	56
99.9	Total new obligations, unexpired accounts	7,550	7,024	6,383

Employment Summary

Identification code 075–1503–0–1–609

		2021 actual	2022 est.	2023 est.
1001	Direct civilian full-time equivalent employment	193	193	259
1101	Direct military average strength employment	21	21	21

REFUGEE AND ENTRANT ASSISTANCE

(Legislative proposal, subject to PAYGO)

Program and Financing (in millions of dollars)

Identification code 075–1503–4–1–609

		2021 actual	2022 est.	2023 est.
	Obligations by program activity:			
0003	Unaccompanied Children - Contingency Fund			1,547
0004	Unaccompanied Children - Legal Services			266
0900	Total new obligations, unexpired accounts (object class 41.0)			1,813
	Budgetary resources:			
	Budget authority:			
	Appropriations, mandatory:			
1200	Appropriation			1,813
1900	Budget authority (total)			1,813
1930	Total budgetary resources available			1,813
	Change in obligated balance:			
	Unpaid obligations:			
3010	New obligations, unexpired accounts			1,813
3020	Outlays (gross)			–816
3050	Unpaid obligations, end of year			997
	Memorandum (non-add) entries:			
3200	Obligated balance, end of year			997

REFUGEE AND ENTRANT ASSISTANCE—Continued
Program and Financing—Continued

Identification code 075–1503–4–1–609	2021 actual	2022 est.	2023 est.
Budget authority and outlays, net:			
Mandatory:			
4090 Budget authority, gross			1,813
Outlays, gross:			
4100 Outlays from new mandatory authority			816
4180 Budget authority, net (total)			1,813
4190 Outlays, net (total)			816

The Budget proposes a mandatory contingency fund authorized in fiscal years 2023 through 2025 that provides additional funding during months of high referrals of unaccompanied children (UC), as well as mandatory funding for scaling-up UC legal representation towards a goal of achieving universal representation.

PROMOTING SAFE AND STABLE FAMILIES

For carrying out, except as otherwise provided, section 436 of the Social Security Act, $345,000,000 and, for carrying out, except as otherwise provided, section 437 of such Act, $106,000,000: Provided, That of the funds available to carry out section 437, $60,000,000 shall be allocated consistent with subsections (b) through (d) of such section: Provided further, That of the funds available to carry out section 437, to assist in meeting the requirements described in section 471(e)(4)(C), $30,000,000 shall be for grants to each State, territory, and Indian tribe operating title IV-E plans for developing, enhancing, or evaluating kinship navigator programs, as described in section 427(a)(1) of such Act and $9,000,000, in addition to funds otherwise appropriated in section 476 for such purposes, shall be for the Family First Clearinghouse and to support evaluation and technical assistance relating to the evaluation of child and family services: Provided further, That, of the funds available to carry out section 437, $7,000,000 shall be for competitive grants to regional partnerships as described in section 437(f), and shall be in addition to any other funds appropriated for such purposes: Provided further, That section 437(b)(1) shall be applied to amounts in the previous proviso by substituting "5 percent" for "3.3 percent", and notwithstanding section 436(b)(1), such reserved amounts may be used for identifying, establishing, and disseminating practices to meet the criteria specified in section 471(e)(4)(C): Provided further, That the reservation in section 437(b)(2) and the limitations in section 437(d) shall not apply to funds specified in the second proviso: Provided further, That the minimum grant award for kinship navigator programs in the case of States and territories shall be $200,000, and, in the case of tribes, shall be $25,000.

Note.—A full-year 2022 appropriation for this account was not enacted at the time the Budget was prepared; therefore, the Budget assumes this account is operating under the Continuing Appropriations Act, 2022 (Division A of Public Law 117–43, as amended). The amounts included for 2022 reflect the annualized level provided by the continuing resolution.

Program and Financing (in millions of dollars)

Identification code 075–1512–0–1–506	2021 actual	2022 est.	2023 est.
Obligations by program activity:			
0001 Grants to States and Tribes	455	376	376
0002 Research, training and technical assistance	6	10	10
0003 State court improvement activities	30	31	31
0004 Family Connection Grants	1	2	2
0005 Personal Responsibility Education (PREP)	82	73	73
0006 Sexual Risk Abstinence Education (SRAE)	72	70	70
0007 Family Rec. & Reunification	1	3	3
0008 Foster Family Home 1822	2		
0009 Family First Transition Act 2021	3		
0900 Total new obligations, unexpired accounts	652	565	565
Budgetary resources:			
Unobligated balance:			
1000 Unobligated balance brought forward, Oct 1	56	49	34
1021 Recoveries of prior year unpaid obligations	2		
1033 Recoveries of prior year paid obligations	3		
1070 Unobligated balance (total)	61	49	34
Budget authority:			
Appropriations, discretionary:			
1100 Appropriation	83	83	106
Appropriations, mandatory:			
1200 Appropriation	580	495	495
1230 Appropriations and/or unobligated balance of appropriations permanently reduced	–20	–28	–28
1260 Appropriations, mandatory (total)	560	467	467
1900 Budget authority (total)	643	550	573
1930 Total budgetary resources available	704	599	607
Memorandum (non-add) entries:			
1940 Unobligated balance expiring	–3		
1941 Unexpired unobligated balance, end of year	49	34	42
Change in obligated balance:			
Unpaid obligations:			
3000 Unpaid obligations, brought forward, Oct 1	1,235	1,318	1,111
3010 New obligations, unexpired accounts	652	565	565
3011 Obligations ("upward adjustments"), expired accounts	1		
3020 Outlays (gross)	–536	–772	–802
3040 Recoveries of prior year unpaid obligations, unexpired	–2		
3041 Recoveries of prior year unpaid obligations, expired	–32		
3050 Unpaid obligations, end of year	1,318	1,111	874
Memorandum (non-add) entries:			
3100 Obligated balance, start of year	1,235	1,318	1,111
3200 Obligated balance, end of year	1,318	1,111	874
Budget authority and outlays, net:			
Discretionary:			
4000 Budget authority, gross	83	83	106
Outlays, gross:			
4010 Outlays from new discretionary authority	22	20	25
4011 Outlays from discretionary balances	65	63	73
4020 Outlays, gross (total)	87	83	98
Mandatory:			
4090 Budget authority, gross	560	467	467
Outlays, gross:			
4100 Outlays from new mandatory authority	104	73	65
4101 Outlays from mandatory balances	345	616	639
4110 Outlays, gross (total)	449	689	704
Offsets against gross budget authority and outlays:			
Offsetting collections (collected) from:			
4123 Non-Federal sources	–3		
Additional offsets against gross budget authority only:			
4143 Recoveries of prior year paid obligations, unexpired accounts	3		
4160 Budget authority, net (mandatory)	560	467	467
4170 Outlays, net (mandatory)	446	689	704
4180 Budget authority, net (total)	643	550	573
4190 Outlays, net (total)	533	772	802

Summary of Budget Authority and Outlays (in millions of dollars)

	2021 actual	2022 est.	2023 est.
Enacted/requested:			
Budget Authority	643	550	573
Outlays	533	772	802
Legislative proposal, subject to PAYGO:			
Budget Authority			300
Outlays			78
Total:			
Budget Authority	643	550	873
Outlays	533	772	880

This account provides funds for a broad range of child welfare services, including family preservation and support services and grants to increase the well-being of and improve the permanency outcomes for children affected by substance abuse, through Promoting Safe and Stable Families. It also includes the Sexual Risk Avoidance Education program and the Personal Responsibility Education Program (PREP).

Object Classification (in millions of dollars)

Identification code 075–1512–0–1–506	2021 actual	2022 est.	2023 est.
Direct obligations:			
11.1 Personnel compensation: Full-time permanent	2	2	2
25.1 Advisory and assistance services	15	14	14
25.3 Other goods and services from Federal sources	13	15	15
41.0 Grants, subsidies, and contributions	622	534	534
99.9 Total new obligations, unexpired accounts	652	565	565

DEPARTMENT OF HEALTH AND HUMAN SERVICES

Employment Summary

Identification code 075–1512–0–1–506	2021 actual	2022 est.	2023 est.
1001 Direct civilian full-time equivalent employment	24	19	20

PROMOTING SAFE AND STABLE FAMILIES
(Legislative proposal, subject to PAYGO)

Program and Financing (in millions of dollars)

Identification code 075–1512–4–1–506	2021 actual	2022 est.	2023 est.
Obligations by program activity:			
0001 Grants to States and Tribes			220
0003 State court improvement activities			30
0010 Legal Services			50
0900 Total new obligations, unexpired accounts			300
Budgetary resources:			
Budget authority:			
Appropriations, mandatory:			
1200 Appropriation			300
1930 Total budgetary resources available			300
Change in obligated balance:			
Unpaid obligations:			
3010 New obligations, unexpired accounts			300
3020 Outlays (gross)			–78
3050 Unpaid obligations, end of year			222
Memorandum (non-add) entries:			
3200 Obligated balance, end of year			222
Budget authority and outlays, net:			
Mandatory:			
4090 Budget authority, gross			300
Outlays, gross:			
4100 Outlays from new mandatory authority			78
4180 Budget authority, net (total)			300
4190 Outlays, net (total)			78

The Budget proposes to increase funding for Promoting Safe and Stable Families by $300 million per year and to create a new set-aside to increase access to legal services for children and families involved in the child welfare system.

Object Classification (in millions of dollars)

Identification code 075–1512–4–1–506	2021 actual	2022 est.	2023 est.
Direct obligations:			
11.1 Personnel compensation: Full-time permanent			2
25.1 Advisory and assistance services			10
25.3 Other goods and services from Federal sources			12
41.0 Grants, subsidies, and contributions			276
99.9 Total new obligations, unexpired accounts			300

Employment Summary

Identification code 075–1512–4–1–506	2021 actual	2022 est.	2023 est.
1001 Direct civilian full-time equivalent employment			14

CHILD CARE ENTITLEMENT TO STATES

Program and Financing (in millions of dollars)

Identification code 075–1550–0–1–609	2021 actual	2022 est.	2023 est.
Obligations by program activity:			
0001 Mandatory child care	1,177	1,177	1,177
0002 Matching child care	2,164	2,164	2,164
0003 Child Care Training and technical assistance	17	17	17
0004 Child care tribal grants	100	100	100
0005 Child Care Research	17	17	17
0006 Child Care Territory Grants	75	75	75
0900 Total new obligations, unexpired accounts	3,550	3,550	3,550
Budgetary resources:			
Budget authority:			
Appropriations, mandatory:			
1200 Appropriation	3,550	3,550	3,550
1930 Total budgetary resources available	3,550	3,550	3,550
Change in obligated balance:			
Unpaid obligations:			
3000 Unpaid obligations, brought forward, Oct 1	1,170	1,517	1,829
3010 New obligations, unexpired accounts	3,550	3,550	3,550
3011 Obligations ("upward adjustments"), expired accounts	3		
3020 Outlays (gross)	–3,154	–3,238	–3,415
3041 Recoveries of prior year unpaid obligations, expired	–52		
3050 Unpaid obligations, end of year	1,517	1,829	1,964
Memorandum (non-add) entries:			
3100 Obligated balance, start of year	1,170	1,517	1,829
3200 Obligated balance, end of year	1,517	1,829	1,964
Budget authority and outlays, net:			
Mandatory:			
4090 Budget authority, gross	3,550	3,550	3,550
Outlays, gross:			
4100 Outlays from new mandatory authority	2,230	2,229	2,229
4101 Outlays from mandatory balances	924	1,009	1,186
4110 Outlays, gross (total)	3,154	3,238	3,415
Offsets against gross budget authority and outlays:			
Offsetting collections (collected) from:			
4123 Non-Federal sources	–3		
Additional offsets against gross budget authority only:			
4142 Offsetting collections credited to expired accounts	3		
4160 Budget authority, net (mandatory)	3,550	3,550	3,550
4170 Outlays, net (mandatory)	3,151	3,238	3,415
4180 Budget authority, net (total)	3,550	3,550	3,550
4190 Outlays, net (total)	3,151	3,238	3,415

This account provides child care subsidies for low-income working families and was established by the Personal Responsibility and Work Opportunity Reconciliation Act of 1996 (P.L. 104–193), as amended by the American Rescue Plan Act of 2021 (P.L. 117–002).

Object Classification (in millions of dollars)

Identification code 075–1550–0–1–609	2021 actual	2022 est.	2023 est.
Direct obligations:			
25.1 Advisory and assistance services	15	15	15
25.3 Other goods and services from Federal sources	6	6	6
41.0 Grants, subsidies, and contributions	3,529	3,529	3,529
99.9 Total new obligations, unexpired accounts	3,550	3,550	3,550

CHILD CARE ENTITLEMENT TO STATES
(Legislative proposal, subject to PAYGO)

The Child Care Entitlement to States includes a new allocation of up to of one half of one percent of the program funds for resources to effectively administer the Child Care and Development Fund. Funds can be used for Federal administrative expenses to carry out section 418 of the Social Security Act.

PAYMENTS TO STATES FOR THE CHILD CARE AND DEVELOPMENT BLOCK GRANT

For carrying out the Child Care and Development Block Grant Act of 1990 ("CCDBG Act"), $7,562,000,000 shall be used to supplement, not supplant State general revenue funds for child care assistance for low-income families: Provided, That technical assistance under section 658I(a)(3) of such Act may be provided directly, or through the use of contracts, grants, cooperative agreements, or interagency agreements: Provided further, That all funds made available to carry out section 418 of the Social Security Act (42 U.S.C. 618), including funds appropriated for that purpose in such section 418 or any other provision of law, shall be subject to the reservation of funds authority in paragraphs (4) and (5) of section 658O(a) of the CCDBG Act: Provided further, That in addition to the amounts required to be reserved by the Secretary under section 658O(a)(2)(A) of such Act, $177,330,000 shall be for Indian tribes and tribal organizations: Provided further, That of the amounts made available under this heading, the Secretary may reserve up to 0.5

PAYMENTS TO STATES FOR THE CHILD CARE AND DEVELOPMENT BLOCK GRANT—Continued

percent for Federal administrative expenses: *Provided further*, That of the total amount of funds made available to carry out section 418 of the Social Security Act (42 U.S.C. 618), including funds appropriated for that purpose in such section or any other provision of law, the Secretary may reserve up to 0.5 percent of such funds for Federal administrative expenses to carry out such section.

Program and Financing (in millions of dollars)

Identification code 075–1515–0–1–609		2021 actual	2022 est.	2023 est.
	Obligations by program activity:			
0001	Child Care Block Grant Payments to States	5,849	5,881	7,524
0002	Child Care Block Grant Payments to States [Disaster supplemental]	1	....	....
0003	Child Care Block Grant Payments to States [CARES supplemental]	8	....	....
0004	Child Care Research and Evaluation Fund	30	30	38
0005	Child Care Block Grant Payments to States [CRRSA]	9,985	....	....
0006	Child Care Block Grant Payments to States (ARP)	14,990	....	....
0007	Child Care Stabilization Fund [ARP]	23,975	....	....
0900	Total new obligations, unexpired accounts	54,838	5,911	7,562
	Budgetary resources:			
	Unobligated balance:			
1000	Unobligated balance brought forward, Oct 1	10	50	50
1012	Unobligated balance transfers between expired and unexpired accounts	1	....	....
1070	Unobligated balance (total)	11	50	50
	Budget authority:			
	Appropriations, discretionary:			
1100	Appropriation	15,911	5,911	7,562
1120	Appropriations transferred to other acct [075–1503]	–33	....	....
1160	Appropriation, discretionary (total)	15,878	5,911	7,562
	Appropriations, mandatory:			
1200	Appropriation	39,000	....	....
1900	Budget authority (total)	54,878	5,911	7,562
1930	Total budgetary resources available	54,889	5,961	7,612
	Memorandum (non-add) entries:			
1940	Unobligated balance expiring	–1	....	....
1941	Unexpired unobligated balance, end of year	50	50	50
	Change in obligated balance:			
	Unpaid obligations:			
3000	Unpaid obligations, brought forward, Oct 1	6,407	49,106	31,146
3010	New obligations, unexpired accounts	54,838	5,911	7,562
3020	Outlays (gross)	–12,121	–23,871	–24,050
3041	Recoveries of prior year unpaid obligations, expired	–18	....	....
3050	Unpaid obligations, end of year	49,106	31,146	14,658
	Memorandum (non-add) entries:			
3100	Obligated balance, start of year	6,407	49,106	31,146
3200	Obligated balance, end of year	49,106	31,146	14,658
	Budget authority and outlays, net:			
	Discretionary:			
4000	Budget authority, gross	15,878	5,911	7,562
	Outlays, gross:			
4010	Outlays from new discretionary authority	6,169	2,536	3,025
4011	Outlays from discretionary balances	4,451	7,005	6,611
4020	Outlays, gross (total)	10,620	9,541	9,636
	Mandatory:			
4090	Budget authority, gross	39,000	....	....
	Outlays, gross:			
4100	Outlays from new mandatory authority	1,501	....	....
4101	Outlays from mandatory balances	....	14,330	14,414
4110	Outlays, gross (total)	1,501	14,330	14,414
4180	Budget authority, net (total)	54,878	5,911	7,562
4190	Outlays, net (total)	12,121	23,871	24,050

This program provides grants to States for child care subsidies for low-income working families and activities to improve child care quality.

Object Classification (in millions of dollars)

Identification code 075–1515–0–1–609		2021 actual	2022 est.	2023 est.
	Direct obligations:			
11.1	Personnel compensation: Full-time permanent	3	4	11
12.1	Civilian personnel benefits	1	1	4
23.3	Communications, utilities, and miscellaneous charges	1	1	1
25.1	Advisory and assistance services	63	53	60
25.3	Other goods and services from Federal sources	10	10	10
41.0	Grants, subsidies, and contributions	54,760	5,842	7,476
99.9	Total new obligations, unexpired accounts	54,838	5,911	7,562

Employment Summary

Identification code 075–1515–0–1–609		2021 actual	2022 est.	2023 est.
1001	Direct civilian full-time equivalent employment	32	33	92

SOCIAL SERVICES BLOCK GRANT

For making grants to States pursuant to section 2002 of the Social Security Act, $1,700,000,000: *Provided,* That notwithstanding subparagraph (B) of section 404(d)(2) of such Act, the applicable percent specified under such subparagraph for a State to carry out State programs pursuant to title XX-A of such Act shall be 10 percent.

Note.—A full-year 2022 appropriation for this account was not enacted at the time the Budget was prepared; therefore, the Budget assumes this account is operating under the Continuing Appropriations Act, 2022 (Division A of Public Law 117–43, as amended). The amounts included for 2022 reflect the annualized level provided by the continuing resolution.

Program and Financing (in millions of dollars)

Identification code 075–1534–0–1–506		2021 actual	2022 est.	2023 est.
	Obligations by program activity:			
0001	Social Services Block Grant	1,603	1,603	1,603
0002	Health Profession Opportunity Grants	3	2	....
0900	Total new obligations, unexpired accounts	1,606	1,605	1,603
	Budgetary resources:			
	Unobligated balance:			
1000	Unobligated balance brought forward, Oct 1	30	32	30
	Budget authority:			
	Appropriations, mandatory:			
1200	Appropriation	1,718	1,700	1,700
1230	Appropriations and/or unobligated balance of appropriations permanently reduced	–97	–97	–97
1260	Appropriations, mandatory (total)	1,621	1,603	1,603
1930	Total budgetary resources available	1,651	1,635	1,633
	Memorandum (non-add) entries:			
1940	Unobligated balance expiring	–13	....	....
1941	Unexpired unobligated balance, end of year	32	30	30
	Change in obligated balance:			
	Unpaid obligations:			
3000	Unpaid obligations, brought forward, Oct 1	500	435	404
3010	New obligations, unexpired accounts	1,606	1,605	1,603
3020	Outlays (gross)	–1,655	–1,636	–1,627
3041	Recoveries of prior year unpaid obligations, expired	–16	....	....
3050	Unpaid obligations, end of year	435	404	380
	Memorandum (non-add) entries:			
3100	Obligated balance, start of year	500	435	404
3200	Obligated balance, end of year	435	404	380
	Budget authority and outlays, net:			
	Mandatory:			
4090	Budget authority, gross	1,621	1,603	1,603
	Outlays, gross:			
4100	Outlays from new mandatory authority	1,280	1,253	1,253
4101	Outlays from mandatory balances	375	383	374
4110	Outlays, gross (total)	1,655	1,636	1,627
4180	Budget authority, net (total)	1,621	1,603	1,603
4190	Outlays, net (total)	1,655	1,636	1,627

The Social Services Block Grant (SSBG) account includes funding for SSBG (for a broad array of social services for children and adults.

Object Classification (in millions of dollars)

Identification code 075–1534–0–1–506		2021 actual	2022 est.	2023 est.
	Direct obligations:			
11.1	Personnel compensation: Full-time permanent	1	1	....

DEPARTMENT OF HEALTH AND HUMAN SERVICES

Administration for Children and Families—Continued
Federal Funds—Continued

475

		2021 actual	2022 est.	2023 est.
25.1	Advisory and assistance services	2	1	
41.0	Grants, subsidies, and contributions	1,603	1,603	1,603
99.9	Total new obligations, unexpired accounts	1,606	1,605	1,603

Employment Summary

Identification code 075–1534–0–1–506	2021 actual	2022 est.	2023 est.
1001 Direct civilian full-time equivalent employment	7	6	

CHILDREN AND FAMILIES SERVICES PROGRAMS

For carrying out, except as otherwise provided, the Runaway and Homeless Youth Act, the Head Start Act, the Every Student Succeeds Act, the Child Abuse Prevention and Treatment Act, sections 303 and 313 of the Family Violence Prevention and Services Act, the Native American Programs Act of 1974, title II of the Child Abuse Prevention and Treatment and Adoption Reform Act of 1978 (adoption opportunities), part B-1 of title IV and sections 429, 473A, 477(i), 1110, 1114A, and 1115 of the Social Security Act, and the Community Services Block Grant Act ("CSBG Act"); and for necessary administrative expenses to carry out titles I, IV, V, X, XI, XIV, XVI, and XX-A of the Social Security Act, the Act of July 5, 1960, and section 2204 of the American Rescue Plan Act of 2021, $15,311,822,000, of which $75,000,000, to remain available through September 30, 2024, shall be for grants to States for adoption and legal guardianship incentive payments, as defined by section 473A of the Social Security Act and may be made for adoptions and legal guardianships completed before September 30, 2023: Provided, That $12,203,454,000 shall be for making payments under the Head Start Act, including for Early Head Start-Child Care Partnerships, and, of which, notwithstanding section 640 of such Act:

(1) $505,359,000 shall be available for a cost of living adjustment, and with respect to any continuing appropriations act, funding available for a cost of living adjustment shall not be construed as an authority or condition under this Act;

(2) $25,000,000 shall be available for allocation by the Secretary to supplement activities described in paragraphs (7)(B) and (9) of section 641(c) of the Head Start Act under the Designation Renewal System, established under the authority of sections 641(c)(7), 645A(b)(12), and 645A(d) of such Act, and such funds shall not be included in the calculation of "base grant" in subsequent fiscal years, as such term is used in section 640(a)(7)(A) of such Act;

(3) $950,000,000, in addition to funds otherwise available for such purposes under section 640 of the Head Start Act, shall be available through September 30, 2024, for awards to eligible entities for Head Start and Early Head Start programs and to entities defined as eligible under section 645A(d) of such Act for high quality infant and toddler care through Early Head Start - Child Care Partnerships, and for training and technical assistance for such activities: Provided further, That of the funds made available in this subparagraph, up to $21,000,000 shall be available to the Secretary for the administrative costs of carrying out this subparagraph: Provided further, That, of the funds made available in this subparagraph, $650,000,000 shall be prioritized for Early Head Start - Child Care Partnerships and for training and technical assistance for such activities: Provided further, That the Secretary shall ensure that areas of greatest need are prioritized for funding made available in this subparagraph;

(4) $4,000,000 shall be available for the purposes of maintaining the Tribal Colleges and Universities Head Start Partnership Program consistent with section 648(g) of such Act; and

(5) $21,000,000 shall be available to supplement funding otherwise available for research, evaluation, and Federal administrative costs:

Provided further, That the Secretary may reduce the reservation of funds under section 640(a)(2)(C) of such Act in lieu of reducing the reservation of funds under sections 640(a)(2)(B), 640(a)(2)(D), and 640(a)(2)(E) of such Act: Provided further, That $450,000,000 shall be available until December 31, 2023 for carrying out sections 9212 and 9213 of the Every Student Succeeds Act: Provided further, That up to 3 percent of the funds in the preceding proviso shall be available for technical assistance and evaluation related to grants awarded under such section 9212: Provided further, That $789,834,000 shall be for making payments under the CSBG Act: Provided further, That $35,615,000 shall be for section 680 of the CSBG Act, of which not less than $23,615,000 shall be for section 680(a)(2) and not less than $12,000,000 shall be for section 680(a)(3)(B) of such Act: Provided further, That, notwithstanding section 675C(a)(3) of the CSBG Act, to the extent Community Services Block Grant funds are distributed as grant funds by a State to an eligible entity as provided under such Act, and have not been expended by such entity, they shall remain with such entity for carryover into the next fiscal year for expenditure by such entity consistent with program purposes: Provided further, That the Secretary shall establish procedures regarding the disposition of intangible assets and program income that permit such assets acquired with, and program income derived from, grant funds authorized under section 680 of the CSBG Act to become the sole property of such grantees after a period of not more than 12 years after the end of the grant period for any activity consistent with section 680(a)(2)(A) of the CSBG Act: Provided further, That intangible assets in the form of loans, equity investments and other debt instruments, and program income may be used by grantees for any eligible purpose consistent with section 680(a)(2)(A) of the CSBG Act: Provided further, That these procedures shall apply to such grant funds made available after November 29, 1999: Provided further, That funds appropriated for section 680(a)(2) of the CSBG Act shall be available for financing construction and rehabilitation and loans or investments in private business enterprises owned by community development corporations: Provided further, That $491,869,000 shall be for carrying out section 303(a) of the Family Violence Prevention and Services Act, of which $7,000,000 shall be allocated notwithstanding section 303(a)(2) of such Act for carrying out section 309 of such Act, and of which $6,750,000 shall be for necessary administrative expenses to carry out such Act and section 2204 of the American Rescue Plan Act of 2021, in addition to amounts otherwise available for such purposes: Provided further, That the percentages specified in section 112(a)(2) of the Child Abuse Prevention and Treatment Act shall not apply to funds appropriated under this heading: Provided further, That $8,000,000 shall be for a human services case management system for federally declared disasters, to include a comprehensive national case management contract and Federal costs of administering the system: Provided further, That up to $2,000,000 shall be for improving the Public Assistance Reporting Information System, including grants to States to support data collection for a study of the system's effectiveness.

CHILDREN AND FAMILIES SERVICES PROGRAMS

[*For an additional amount for "Children and Families Services Programs", $7,773,000, to remain available until September 30, 2022, for support of Operation Allies Welcome for necessary administrative expenses to carry out refugee and entrant assistance activities in support of citizens or nationals of Afghanistan.*] *(Afghanistan Supplemental Appropriations Act, 2022.)*

Program and Financing (in millions of dollars)

Identification code 075–1536–0–1–506		2021 actual	2022 est.	2023 est.
Obligations by program activity:				
0101	Head Start	12,509	10,748	12,203
0102	Preschool Development Grants	280	517	450
0103	Runaway and homeless youth (basic centers)	60	64	71
0104	Transitional living	57	53	58
0106	Education grants to reduce sexual abuse of runaway youth	20	20	21
0109	Child abuse State grants	190	90	125
0110	Child abuse discretionary activities	35	35	42
0111	Community-based child abuse prevention	309	63	90
0112	Child welfare services	269	269	279
0113	Child welfare training, research, or demonstration projects	19	19	121
0114	Adoption opportunities	44	44	46
0116	Adoption and Legal Guardianship Incentives	52	98	75
0117	Independent living education and training vouchers	48	43	48
0124	Native American programs	76	57	63
0125	Social services and income maintenance research	8	8	69
0128	ACF Federal administration	212	219	234
0131	Disaster human services case management	2	2	8
0191	Direct program activities, subtotal	14,190	12,349	14,003
0301	Community services block grant	832	745	754
0303	Rural community facilities	10	10	12
0304	Community economic development	20	20	24
0305	Low Income Household Drinking Water & Wastewater Emergency Assistance	1,127	10	
0308	Domestic violence hotline	13	13	27
0309	Family violence prevention and services	378	438	492
0391	Direct program activities, subtotal	2,380	1,236	1,309
0400	Total, direct program	16,570	13,585	15,312
0799	Total direct obligations	16,570	13,585	15,312
0801	Children and Families Services Programs (Reimbursable)	15	34	34
0809	Reimbursable program activities, subtotal	15	34	34
0900	Total new obligations, unexpired accounts	16,585	13,619	15,346
Budgetary resources:				
Unobligated balance:				
1000	Unobligated balance brought forward, Oct 1	820	540	5
1012	Unobligated balance transfers between expired and unexpired accounts		4		

CHILDREN AND FAMILIES SERVICES PROGRAMS—Continued

Program and Financing—Continued

Identification code 075–1536–0–1–506	2021 actual	2022 est.	2023 est.
1021 Recoveries of prior year unpaid obligations	65		
1070 Unobligated balance (total)	889	540	5
Budget authority:			
Appropriations, discretionary:			
1100 Appropriation	13,929	13,049	15,312
Appropriations, mandatory:			
1200 Appropriation	2,320		
Spending authority from offsetting collections, discretionary:			
1700 Collected	3	23	23
1701 Change in uncollected payments, Federal sources	1		
1750 Spending auth from offsetting collections, disc (total)	4	23	23
Spending authority from offsetting collections, mandatory:			
1800 Collected	3	11	11
1801 Change in uncollected payments, Federal sources	10	1	1
1850 Spending auth from offsetting collections, mand (total)	13	12	12
1900 Budget authority (total)	16,266	13,084	15,347
1930 Total budgetary resources available	17,155	13,624	15,352
Memorandum (non-add) entries:			
1940 Unobligated balance expiring	−30		
1941 Unexpired unobligated balance, end of year	540	5	6
Change in obligated balance:			
Unpaid obligations:			
3000 Unpaid obligations, brought forward, Oct 1	12,204	15,296	14,091
3010 New obligations, unexpired accounts	16,585	13,619	15,346
3011 Obligations ("upward adjustments"), expired accounts	20		
3020 Outlays (gross)	−13,219	−14,824	−15,300
3040 Recoveries of prior year unpaid obligations, unexpired	−65		
3041 Recoveries of prior year unpaid obligations, expired	−229		
3050 Unpaid obligations, end of year	15,296	14,091	14,137
Uncollected payments:			
3060 Uncollected pymts, Fed sources, brought forward, Oct 1	−23	−26	−27
3070 Change in uncollected pymts, Fed sources, unexpired	−11	−1	−1
3071 Change in uncollected pymts, Fed sources, expired	8		
3090 Uncollected pymts, Fed sources, end of year	−26	−27	−28
Memorandum (non-add) entries:			
3100 Obligated balance, start of year	12,181	15,270	14,064
3200 Obligated balance, end of year	15,270	14,064	14,109
Budget authority and outlays, net:			
Discretionary:			
4000 Budget authority, gross	13,933	13,072	15,335
Outlays, gross:			
4010 Outlays from new discretionary authority	4,532	4,495	5,294
4011 Outlays from discretionary balances	8,622	9,747	9,414
4020 Outlays, gross (total)	13,154	14,242	14,708
Offsets against gross budget authority and outlays:			
Offsetting collections (collected) from:			
4030 Federal sources	−3	−23	−23
4033 Non-Federal sources	−4		
4040 Offsets against gross budget authority and outlays (total)	−7	−23	−23
Additional offsets against gross budget authority only:			
4050 Change in uncollected pymts, Fed sources, unexpired	−1		
4052 Offsetting collections credited to expired accounts	4		
4060 Additional offsets against budget authority only (total)	3		
4070 Budget authority, net (discretionary)	13,929	13,049	15,312
4080 Outlays, net (discretionary)	13,147	14,219	14,685
Mandatory:			
4090 Budget authority, gross	2,333	12	12
Outlays, gross:			
4100 Outlays from new mandatory authority	61	12	12
4101 Outlays from mandatory balances	4	570	580
4110 Outlays, gross (total)	65	582	592
Offsets against gross budget authority and outlays:			
Offsetting collections (collected) from:			
4120 Federal sources	−6	−12	−12
Additional offsets against gross budget authority only:			
4140 Change in uncollected pymts, Fed sources, unexpired	−10	−1	−1
4142 Offsetting collections credited to expired accounts	3	1	1
4150 Additional offsets against budget authority only (total)	−7		
4160 Budget authority, net (mandatory)	2,320		
4170 Outlays, net (mandatory)	59	570	580
4180 Budget authority, net (total)	16,249	13,049	15,312
4190 Outlays, net (total)	13,206	14,789	15,265

The request totals $15.3 billion, including $12.2 billion for Head Start, and provides assistance to children, families, and communities through partnerships with States and local community agencies.

Object Classification (in millions of dollars)

Identification code 075–1536–0–1–506	2021 actual	2022 est.	2023 est.
Direct obligations:			
Personnel compensation:			
11.1 Full-time permanent	120	123	121
11.3 Other than full-time permanent	5	5	4
11.5 Other personnel compensation	2	2	2
11.7 Military personnel	1	1	1
11.9 Total personnel compensation	128	131	128
12.1 Civilian personnel benefits	44	43	45
21.0 Travel and transportation of persons			2
23.1 Rental payments to GSA	5	5	10
23.3 Communications, utilities, and miscellaneous charges	1	1	2
25.1 Advisory and assistance services	144	144	305
25.2 Other services from non-Federal sources	13	13	19
25.3 Other goods and services from Federal sources	209	209	85
25.4 Operation and maintenance of facilities	5	5	5
26.0 Supplies and materials			1
31.0 Equipment	3	3	1
41.0 Grants, subsidies, and contributions	16,018	13,031	14,709
99.0 Direct obligations	16,570	13,585	15,312
99.0 Reimbursable obligations	15	34	34
99.9 Total new obligations, unexpired accounts	16,585	13,619	15,346

Employment Summary

Identification code 075–1536–0–1–506	2021 actual	2022 est.	2023 est.
1001 Direct civilian full-time equivalent employment	1,071	1,049	1,017
1101 Direct military average strength employment	4	4	4
2001 Reimbursable civilian full-time equivalent employment	9	10	10

CHILDREN'S RESEARCH AND TECHNICAL ASSISTANCE

Program and Financing (in millions of dollars)

Identification code 075–1553–0–1–609	2021 actual	2022 est.	2023 est.
Obligations by program activity:			
0001 Training and technical assistance	13	12	12
0002 Federal parent locator service	24	23	23
0799 Total direct obligations	37	35	35
0801 Federal Parent Locator Service reimbursable	28	38	38
0899 Total reimbursable obligations	28	38	38
0900 Total new obligations, unexpired accounts	65	73	73
Budgetary resources:			
Unobligated balance:			
1000 Unobligated balance brought forward, Oct 1	7	8	10
1021 Recoveries of prior year unpaid obligations	4		
1070 Unobligated balance (total)	11	8	10
Budget authority:			
Appropriations, mandatory:			
1200 Appropriation	37	37	37
1230 Appropriations and/or unobligated balance of appropriations permanently reduced	−2	−2	−2
1260 Appropriations, mandatory (total)	35	35	35
Spending authority from offsetting collections, mandatory:			
1800 Collected	27	40	40
1802 Offsetting collections (previously unavailable)	1	1	1
1823 New and/or unobligated balance of spending authority from offsetting collections temporarily reduced	−1	−1	−1
1850 Spending auth from offsetting collections, mand (total)	27	40	40
1900 Budget authority (total)	62	75	75
1930 Total budgetary resources available	73	83	85
Memorandum (non-add) entries:			
1941 Unexpired unobligated balance, end of year	8	10	12

DEPARTMENT OF HEALTH AND HUMAN SERVICES

Administration for Children and Families—Continued
Federal Funds—Continued

477

		2021 actual	2022 est.	2023 est.
	Change in obligated balance:			
	Unpaid obligations:			
3000	Unpaid obligations, brought forward, Oct 1	20	10	9
3010	New obligations, unexpired accounts	65	73	73
3020	Outlays (gross)	−71	−74	−73
3040	Recoveries of prior year unpaid obligations, unexpired	−4		
3050	Unpaid obligations, end of year	10	9	9
	Uncollected payments:			
3060	Uncollected pymts, Fed sources, brought forward, Oct 1	−6	−6	−6
3090	Uncollected pymts, Fed sources, end of year	−6	−6	−6
	Memorandum (non-add) entries:			
3100	Obligated balance, start of year	14	4	3
3200	Obligated balance, end of year	4	3	3
	Budget authority and outlays, net:			
	Mandatory:			
4090	Budget authority, gross	62	75	75
	Outlays, gross:			
4100	Outlays from new mandatory authority	49	59	59
4101	Outlays from mandatory balances	22	15	14
4110	Outlays, gross (total)	71	74	73
	Offsets against gross budget authority and outlays:			
	Offsetting collections (collected) from:			
4120	Federal sources	−9	−12	−12
4123	Non-Federal sources	−18	−28	−28
4130	Offsets against gross budget authority and outlays (total)	−27	−40	−40
4160	Budget authority, net (mandatory)	35	35	35
4170	Outlays, net (mandatory)	44	34	33
4180	Budget authority, net (total)	35	35	35
4190	Outlays, net (total)	44	34	33
	Memorandum (non-add) entries:			
5090	Unexpired unavailable balance, SOY: Offsetting collections	1	1	1
5092	Unexpired unavailable balance, EOY: Offsetting collections	1	1	1

This account provides funding for research and technical assistance activities established by the Personal Responsibility and Work Opportunity Reconciliation Act of 1996 (P.L. 104–193), as amended by the Deficit Reduction Act of 2005 (P.L. 109–171).

Object Classification (in millions of dollars)

Identification code 075–1553–0–1–609		2021 actual	2022 est.	2023 est.
	Direct obligations:			
11.1	Personnel compensation: Full-time permanent	9	10	10
12.1	Civilian personnel benefits	3	3	3
23.1	Rental payments to GSA	4	4	4
25.3	Other goods and services from Federal sources	7	4	4
25.7	Operation and maintenance of equipment	14	14	14
99.0	Direct obligations	37	35	35
99.0	Reimbursable obligations	28	38	38
99.9	Total new obligations, unexpired accounts	65	73	73

Employment Summary

Identification code 075–1553–0–1–609	2021 actual	2022 est.	2023 est.
1001 Direct civilian full-time equivalent employment	66	76	82

PAYMENTS FOR FOSTER CARE AND PERMANENCY

For carrying out, except as otherwise provided, title IV-E of the Social Security Act, $7,606,000,000.

For carrying out, except as otherwise provided, title IV-E of the Social Security Act, for the first quarter of fiscal year 2024, $3,200,000,000.

For carrying out, after May 31 of the current fiscal year, except as otherwise provided, section 474 of title IV-E of the Social Security Act, for the last 3 months of the current fiscal year for unanticipated costs, incurred for the current fiscal year, such sums as may be necessary.

Note.—A full-year 2022 appropriation for this account was not enacted at the time the Budget was prepared; therefore, the Budget assumes this account is operating under the Continuing Appropriations Act, 2022 (Division A of Public Law 117–43, as amended). The amounts included for 2022 reflect the annualized level provided by the continuing resolution.

Program and Financing (in millions of dollars)

Identification code 075–1545–0–1–609		2021 actual	2022 est.	2023 est.
	Obligations by program activity:			
0001	Foster care	5,788	6,032	6,189
0002	Independent living	547	143	143
0004	Adoption assistance	3,641	4,046	4,128
0005	Guardianship	249	317	345
0006	Technical Assistance and Implementation Services for Tribal Programs	3	3	3
0007	Prevention Services Technical Assistance	1	1	1
0900	Total new obligations, unexpired accounts	10,229	10,542	10,809
	Budgetary resources:			
	Unobligated balance:			
1000	Unobligated balance brought forward, Oct 1		99	95
1012	Unobligated balance transfers between expired and unexpired accounts	4		
1020	Adjustment of unobligated bal brought forward, Oct 1	654		
1070	Unobligated balance (total)	658	99	95
	Budget authority:			
	Appropriations, mandatory:			
1200	Appropriation	7,417	7,541	7,611
1230	Appropriations and/or unobligated balance of appropriations permanently reduced	−2	−3	−3
1260	Appropriations, mandatory (total)	7,415	7,538	7,608
	Advance appropriations, mandatory:			
1270	Advance appropriation	3,000	3,000	3,200
1900	Budget authority (total)	10,415	10,538	10,808
1930	Total budgetary resources available	11,073	10,637	10,903
	Memorandum (non-add) entries:			
1940	Unobligated balance expiring	−745		
1941	Unexpired unobligated balance, end of year	99	95	94
	Change in obligated balance:			
	Unpaid obligations:			
3000	Unpaid obligations, brought forward, Oct 1	1,618	1,984	1,836
3010	New obligations, unexpired accounts	10,229	10,542	10,809
3011	Obligations ("upward adjustments"), expired accounts	84		
3020	Outlays (gross)	−9,713	−10,690	−10,206
3041	Recoveries of prior year unpaid obligations, expired	−234		
3050	Unpaid obligations, end of year	1,984	1,836	2,439
	Memorandum (non-add) entries:			
3100	Obligated balance, start of year	1,618	1,984	1,836
3200	Obligated balance, end of year	1,984	1,836	2,439
	Budget authority and outlays, net:			
	Mandatory:			
4090	Budget authority, gross	10,415	10,538	10,808
	Outlays, gross:			
4100	Outlays from new mandatory authority	8,357	8,913	9,140
4101	Outlays from mandatory balances	1,356	1,777	1,066
4110	Outlays, gross (total)	9,713	10,690	10,206
4180	Budget authority, net (total)	10,415	10,538	10,808
4190	Outlays, net (total)	9,713	10,690	10,206

Summary of Budget Authority and Outlays (in millions of dollars)

	2021 actual	2022 est.	2023 est.
Enacted/requested:			
Budget Authority	10,415	10,538	10,808
Outlays	9,713	10,690	10,206
Legislative proposal, subject to PAYGO:			
Budget Authority		161	444
Outlays		161	444
Total:			
Budget Authority	10,415	10,699	11,252
Outlays	9,713	10,851	10,650

This account provides formula grants for Foster Care, Adoption Assistance, Guardianship Assistance Program, Foster Care Prevention Services, and the Chafee Program for Successful Transition to Adulthood, as well as technical assistance and implementation services for tribal programs.

Foster Care—The proposed level will support eligible low-income children who must be placed outside the home. An average of 225,600 children per month are estimated to be served in FY 2023.

PAYMENTS FOR FOSTER CARE AND PERMANENCY—Continued

Adoption Assistance—The proposed funding level will support subsidies for families adopting eligible low-income children with special needs. An average of 523,300 children per month are estimated to be served in FY 2023.

Guardianship Assistance Program—The proposed funding level will provide payments for relatives taking legal guardianship of eligible children who have been in foster care. An average of 67,800 children per month are estimated to be served in FY 2023.

Object Classification (in millions of dollars)

Identification code 075–1545–0–1–609		2021 actual	2022 est.	2023 est.
	Direct obligations:			
21.0	Travel and transportation of persons	1	1	1
23.1	Rental payments to GSA	1	1	1
25.1	Advisory and assistance services	34	42	46
25.2	Other services from non-Federal sources	1	1	1
41.0	Grants, subsidies, and contributions	10,192	10,497	10,760
99.9	Total new obligations, unexpired accounts	10,229	10,542	10,809

Employment Summary

Identification code 075–1545–0–1–609		2021 actual	2022 est.	2023 est.
1001	Direct civilian full-time equivalent employment	3	3	3

PAYMENTS FOR FOSTER CARE AND PERMANENCY

(Legislative proposal, subject to PAYGO)

Program and Financing (in millions of dollars)

Identification code 075–1545–4–1–609		2021 actual	2022 est.	2023 est.
	Obligations by program activity:			
0001	Foster care		161	344
0002	Independent living			100
0900	Total new obligations, unexpired accounts (object class 41.0)		161	444
	Budgetary resources:			
	Budget authority:			
	Appropriations, mandatory:			
1200	Appropriation		161	444
1900	Budget authority (total)		161	444
1930	Total budgetary resources available		161	444
	Change in obligated balance:			
	Unpaid obligations:			
3010	New obligations, unexpired accounts		161	444
3020	Outlays (gross)		–161	–444
	Budget authority and outlays, net:			
	Mandatory:			
4090	Budget authority, gross		161	444
	Outlays, gross:			
4100	Outlays from new mandatory authority		161	444
4180	Budget authority, net (total)		161	444
4190	Outlays, net (total)		161	444

The Budget proposes to increase reimbursement rates for the Prevention Services and Kinship Navigator programs. The Budget also proposes to increase reimbursement rates in the foster care and guardianship assistance programs for children placed with kin and to reduce reimbursement rates for children placed in most congregate care settings. The Budget proposes to increase Chafee funding by $100 million per year and add flexibilities in the program. Finally, the Budget proposes to amend title IV-E to prohibit states and contractors from discriminating against prospective foster or adoptive parents or children in foster care or being considered for adoption on the basis of their religious beliefs, sexual orientation, gender identity, gender expression, or sex.

ADMINISTRATION FOR COMMUNITY LIVING

Federal Funds

AGING AND DISABILITY SERVICES PROGRAMS

(INCLUDING TRANSFER OF FUNDS)

For carrying out, to the extent not otherwise provided, the Older Americans Act of 1965 ("OAA"), the RAISE Family Caregivers Act, the Supporting Grandparents Raising Grandchildren Act, titles III and XXIX of the PHS Act, sections 1252 and 1253 of the PHS Act, section 119 of the Medicare Improvements for Patients and Providers Act of 2008, title XX-B of the Social Security Act, the Developmental Disabilities Assistance and Bill of Rights Act of 2000, parts 2 and 5 of subtitle D of title II of the Help America Vote Act of 2002, the Assistive Technology Act of 1998, titles II and VII (and section 14 with respect to such titles) of the Rehabilitation Act of 1973, and for Department-wide coordination of policy and program activities that assist individuals with disabilities, $2,930,491,000, together with $55,242,000 to be transferred from the Federal Hospital Insurance Trust Fund and the Federal Supplementary Medical Insurance Trust Fund to carry out section 4360 of the Omnibus Budget Reconciliation Act of 1990: Provided, That, in addition to amounts provided herein, $27,503,000 shall be available to this appropriation, for the purposes under this heading, from amounts provided pursuant to section 241 of the PHS Act: Provided further, That of amounts made available under this heading to carry out section 321 of the OAA, up to one percent shall be available for grants to develop and implement evidence-based practices to enhance home and community-based supportive services: Provided further, That of amounts made available under this heading to carry out sections 311, 331, and 336 of the OAA, up to one percent of such amounts shall be available for developing and implementing evidence-based practices for enhancing senior nutrition, including medically-tailored meals: Provided further, That notwithstanding any other provision of this Act, funds made available under this heading to carry out section 311 of the OAA may be transferred to the Secretary of Agriculture in accordance with such section: Provided further, That notwithstanding section 206(h) of the OAA, up to one percent of amounts appropriated to carry out programs authorized under title III of such Act shall be available for conducting evaluations: Provided further, That up to five percent of the funds provided for adult protective services grants under section 2042 of title XX of the Social Security Act may be used to make grants to Tribes and Tribal Organizations: Provided further, That up to $1.5 million of funds made available under this heading for aging network support activities under sections 202, 215, and 411 of the OAA and up to $1.5 million of funds made available under this heading for projects of national significance under subtitle E of title I of the Developmental Disabilities Assistance and Bill of Rights Act of 2000 may be merged and used for demonstration grants that benefit both older individuals and individuals with any type of disability: Provided further, That none of the funds made available under this heading may be used by an eligible system (as defined in section 102 of the Protection and Advocacy for Individuals with Mental Illness Act (42 U.S.C. 10802)) to continue to pursue any legal action in a Federal or State court on behalf of an individual or group of individuals with a developmental disability (as defined in section 102(8)(A) of the Developmental Disabilities and Assistance and Bill of Rights Act of 2000 (20 U.S.C. 15002(8)(A)) that is attributable to a mental impairment (or a combination of mental and physical impairments), that has as the requested remedy the closure of State operated intermediate care facilities for people with intellectual or developmental disabilities, unless reasonable public notice of the action has been provided to such individuals (or, in the case of mental incapacitation, the legal guardians who have been specifically awarded authority by the courts to make healthcare and residential decisions on behalf of such individuals) who are affected by such action, within 90 days of instituting such legal action, which informs such individuals (or such legal guardians) of their legal rights and how to exercise such rights consistent with current Federal Rules of Civil Procedure: Provided further, That the limitations in the immediately preceding proviso shall not apply in the case of an individual who is neither competent to consent nor has a legal guardian, nor shall the proviso apply in the case of individuals who are a ward of the State or subject to public guardianship.

Program and Financing (in millions of dollars)

Identification code 075–0142–0–1–506		2021 actual	2022 est.	2023 est.
	Obligations by program activity:			
0101	Aging Services Programs	3,495	1,872	2,308
0102	ACL Program Administration	41	41	57
0103	Integrated Aging and Disability Services Programs	46	54	68
0104	Disability Services Programs	324	316	380
0105	National Institute on Disability, Independent Living & Rehab Research	113	113	119

DEPARTMENT OF HEALTH AND HUMAN SERVICES

Departmental Management
Federal Funds

0300	Total, direct program	4,019	2,396	2,932
0799	Total direct obligations	4,019	2,396	2,932
0801	ACL Reimbursable Programs	112	109	110
0802	PHS Evaluation: Disability Reimbursable (Collected)	....	....	28
0899	Total reimbursable obligations	112	109	138
0900	Total new obligations, unexpired accounts	4,131	2,505	3,070
	Budgetary resources:			
	Unobligated balance:			
1000	Unobligated balance brought forward, Oct 1	17	220	59
1021	Recoveries of prior year unpaid obligations	1		
1070	Unobligated balance (total)	18	220	59
	Budget authority:			
	Appropriations, discretionary:			
1100	Appropriation	2,481	2,207	2,930
1120	Appropriations transferred to other acct [012–3507]	–1	–1	
1120	Appropriations transferred to other acct [075–1503]	–7		
1121	Appropriations transferred from other acct [075–0116] ...	....	28	
1160	Appropriation, discretionary (total)	2,473	2,234	2,930
	Appropriations, mandatory:			
1200	Appropriation	1,720		
1221	PPHF Appropriations transferred from other accounts [075–0116]	28		28
1260	Appropriations, mandatory (total)	1,748		28
	Spending authority from offsetting collections, discretionary:			
1701	Change in uncollected payments, Federal sources	75	75	77
	Spending authority from offsetting collections, mandatory:			
1800	Collected		35	35
1801	Change in uncollected payments, Federal sources	38		
1850	Spending auth from offsetting collections, mand (total)	38	35	35
1900	Budget authority (total)	4,334	2,344	3,070
1930	Total budgetary resources available	4,352	2,564	3,129
	Memorandum (non-add) entries:			
1940	Unobligated balance expiring	–1		
1941	Unexpired unobligated balance, end of year	220	59	59
	Change in obligated balance:			
	Unpaid obligations:			
3000	Unpaid obligations, brought forward, Oct 1	2,534	3,979	2,605
3010	New obligations, unexpired accounts	4,131	2,505	3,070
3011	Obligations ("upward adjustments"), expired accounts ...	3		
3020	Outlays (gross)	–2,664	–3,879	–3,778
3040	Recoveries of prior year unpaid obligations, unexpired ...	–1		
3041	Recoveries of prior year unpaid obligations, expired	–24		
3050	Unpaid obligations, end of year	3,979	2,605	1,897
	Uncollected payments:			
3060	Uncollected pymts, Fed sources, brought forward, Oct 1 ...	–187	–297	–372
3070	Change in uncollected pymts, Fed sources, unexpired ...	–113	–75	–77
3071	Change in uncollected pymts, Fed sources, expired	3		
3090	Uncollected pymts, Fed sources, end of year	–297	–372	–449
	Memorandum (non-add) entries:			
3100	Obligated balance, start of year	2,347	3,682	2,233
3200	Obligated balance, end of year	3,682	2,233	1,448
	Budget authority and outlays, net:			
	Discretionary:			
4000	Budget authority, gross	2,548	2,309	3,007
	Outlays, gross:			
4010	Outlays from new discretionary authority	878	1,381	1,802
4011	Outlays from discretionary balances	1,729	988	922
4020	Outlays, gross (total)	2,607	2,369	2,724
	Offsets against gross budget authority and outlays:			
	Offsetting collections (collected) from:			
4030	Federal sources	–2	–75	–77
	Additional offsets against gross budget authority only:			
4050	Change in uncollected pymts, Fed sources, unexpired ...	–75	–75	–77
4052	Offsetting collections credited to expired accounts	2	75	77
4060	Additional offsets against budget authority only (total) ...	–73		
4070	Budget authority, net (discretionary)	2,473	2,234	2,930
4080	Outlays, net (discretionary)	2,605	2,294	2,647
	Mandatory:			
4090	Budget authority, gross	1,786	35	63
	Outlays, gross:			
4100	Outlays from new mandatory authority	12	7	7
4101	Outlays from mandatory balances	45	1,503	1,047
4110	Outlays, gross (total)	57	1,510	1,054
	Offsets against gross budget authority and outlays:			
	Offsetting collections (collected) from:			
4120	Federal sources		–35	–35
	Additional offsets against gross budget authority only:			
4140	Change in uncollected pymts, Fed sources, unexpired ...	–38		
4160	Budget authority, net (mandatory)	1,748		28
4170	Outlays, net (mandatory)	57	1,475	1,019
4180	Budget authority, net (total)	4,221	2,234	2,958
4190	Outlays, net (total)	2,662	3,769	3,666

This account funds formula and discretionary grants that provide home and community-based services and supports to assist older adults and people of all ages with disabilities to live independently and to fully participate in their communities. ACL works with states, localities, tribal organizations, nonprofit organizations, businesses and families, and through networks of aging and disability organizations, to provide these services and supports which include nutrition, supportive, caregiver, independent living, and protection and advocacy services.

Object Classification (in millions of dollars)

Identification code 075–0142–0–1–506	2021 actual	2022 est.	2023 est.
Direct obligations:			
11.1 Personnel compensation: Full-time permanent	23	24	31
12.1 Civilian personnel benefits	8	8	10
23.1 Rental payments to GSA	3	3	3
25.1 Advisory and assistance services	50	52	57
41.0 Grants, subsidies, and contributions	3,935	2,309	2,830
99.0 Direct obligations	4,019	2,396	2,931
99.0 Reimbursable obligations	112	109	139
99.9 Total new obligations, unexpired accounts	4,131	2,505	3,070

Employment Summary

Identification code 075–0142–0–1–506	2021 actual	2022 est.	2023 est.
1001 Direct civilian full-time equivalent employment	171	175	219
2001 Reimbursable civilian full-time equivalent employment ...	12	12	12

DEPARTMENTAL MANAGEMENT

Federal Funds

GENERAL DEPARTMENTAL MANAGEMENT

For necessary expenses, not otherwise provided, for general departmental management, including hire of six passenger motor vehicles, and for carrying out titles III, XVII, XXI, and section 229 of the PHS Act, the United States-Mexico Border Health Commission Act, and health or human services research and evaluation activities, including such activities that are similar to activities carried out by other components of the Department, $579,839,000, together with $85,228,000 from the amounts available under section 241 of the PHS Act : Provided, That of this amount, $58,400,000 shall be for minority AIDS prevention and treatment activities: Provided further, That of the funds made available under this heading, $111,000,000 shall be for making competitive contracts and grants to public and private entities to fund medically accurate and age appropriate programs that reduce teen pregnancy and for the Federal costs associated with administering and evaluating such contracts and grants, of which not more than 10 percent of the available funds shall be for training and technical assistance, evaluation, outreach, and additional program support activities, and of the remaining amount 75 percent shall be for replicating programs that have been proven effective through rigorous evaluation to reduce teenage pregnancy, behavioral risk factors underlying teenage pregnancy, or other associated risk factors, and 25 percent shall be available for research and demonstration grants to develop, replicate, refine, and test additional models and innovative strategies for preventing teenage pregnancy: Provided further, That of the amounts provided under this heading from amounts available under section 241 of the PHS Act, $7,700,000 shall be available to carry out evaluations (including longitudinal evaluations) of teenage pregnancy prevention approaches: Provided further, That funds provided in this Act for embryo adoption activities may be used to provide to individuals adopting embryos, through grants and other mechanisms, medical and administrative services deemed necessary for such adoptions: Provided further, That such services shall be provided consistent with 42 CFR 59.5(a)(4): Provided further, That of the funds made available under this heading, $5,000,000 shall be

GENERAL DEPARTMENTAL MANAGEMENT—Continued

for carrying out prize competitions sponsored by the Office of the Secretary to accelerate innovation in the prevention, diagnosis, and treatment of kidney diseases (as authorized by section 24 of the Stevenson-Wydler Technology Innovation Act of 1980 (15 U.S.C. 3719)).

Note.—A full-year 2022 appropriation for this account was not enacted at the time the Budget was prepared; therefore, the Budget assumes this account is operating under the Continuing Appropriations Act, 2022 (Division A of Public Law 117–43, as amended). The amounts included for 2022 reflect the annualized level provided by the continuing resolution.

Program and Financing (in millions of dollars)

Identification code 075–9912–0–1–551		2021 actual	2022 est.	2023 est.
	Obligations by program activity:			
0001	GDM Direct	486	486	580
0100	Direct, subtotal	486	486	580
0802	GDM Reimbursable (collected)	189	189	181
0803	PHS Evaluation Reimbursable (Collected)	65	65	86
0809	Reimbursable program activities, subtotal	254	254	267
0811	OGC HCFAC Mandatory (R)	7	7	10
0812	ASPE PTAC Mandatory (R)	4	4	5
0813	ASPA/CDC/ PSA Mandatory (R)	22	22	
0814	ASPE Equity Mandatory (R)	1	1	
0816	OASH OCCHE Mandatory (R)	1	1	
0819	Reimbursable program activities, subtotal	35	35	15
0899	Total reimbursable obligations	289	289	282
0900	Total new obligations, unexpired accounts	775	775	862
	Budgetary resources:			
	Unobligated balance:			
1000	Unobligated balance brought forward, Oct 1	39	56	55
1001	Discretionary unobligated balance brought fwd, Oct 1	1		
1011	Unobligated balance transfer from other acct [075–0116]	3		
1021	Recoveries of prior year unpaid obligations	13		
1070	Unobligated balance (total)	55	56	55
	Budget authority:			
	Appropriations, discretionary:			
1100	Appropriation [GDM Direct]	486	486	580
1120	Appropriations transferred — other accts [075–1503]	–2		
1160	Appropriation, discretionary (total)	484	486	580
	Spending authority from offsetting collections, discretionary:			
1700	Collected	102	254	267
1701	Change in uncollected payments, Federal sources	156		
1711	Spending authority from offsetting collections transferred from other accounts [075–0139]	1		
1750	Spending auth from offsetting collections, disc (total)	259	254	267
	Spending authority from offsetting collections, mandatory:			
1800	Collected	40	35	15
1801	Change in uncollected payments, Federal sources	–6		
1850	Spending auth from offsetting collections, mand (total)	34	35	15
1900	Budget authority (total)	777	775	862
1930	Total budgetary resources available	832	831	917
	Memorandum (non-add) entries:			
1940	Unobligated balance expiring	–1	–1	
1941	Unexpired unobligated balance, end of year	56	55	55
	Change in obligated balance:			
	Unpaid obligations:			
3000	Unpaid obligations, brought forward, Oct 1	563	562	518
3010	New obligations, unexpired accounts	775	775	862
3011	Obligations ("upward adjustments"), expired accounts	13		
3020	Outlays (gross)	–743	–819	–803
3040	Recoveries of prior year unpaid obligations, unexpired	–13		
3041	Recoveries of prior year unpaid obligations, expired	–33		
3050	Unpaid obligations, end of year	562	518	577
	Uncollected payments:			
3060	Uncollected pymts, Fed sources, brought forward, Oct 1	–280	–301	–301
3070	Change in uncollected pymts, Fed sources, unexpired	–150		
3071	Change in uncollected pymts, Fed sources, expired	129		
3090	Uncollected pymts, Fed sources, end of year	–301	–301	–301
	Memorandum (non-add) entries:			
3100	Obligated balance, start of year	283	261	217
3200	Obligated balance, end of year	261	217	276
	Budget authority and outlays, net:			
	Discretionary:			
4000	Budget authority, gross	743	740	847
	Outlays, gross:			
4010	Outlays from new discretionary authority	369	354	402
4011	Outlays from discretionary balances	338	377	386
4020	Outlays, gross (total)	707	731	788
	Offsets against gross budget authority and outlays:			
	Offsetting collections (collected) from:			
4030	Federal sources:	–227	–254	–267
4033	Non-Federal sources:	–1		
4040	Offsets against gross budget authority and outlays (total)	–228	–254	–267
	Additional offsets against gross budget authority only:			
4050	Change in uncollected pymts, Fed sources, unexpired	–156		
4052	Offsetting collections credited to expired accounts	126		
4060	Additional offsets against budget authority only (total)	–30		
4070	Budget authority, net (discretionary)	485	486	580
4080	Outlays, net (discretionary)	479	477	521
	Mandatory:			
4090	Budget authority, gross	34	35	15
	Outlays, gross:			
4100	Outlays from new mandatory authority	8	35	15
4101	Outlays from mandatory balances	28	53	
4110	Outlays, gross (total)	36	88	15
	Offsets against gross budget authority and outlays:			
	Offsetting collections (collected) from:			
4120	Federal sources:	–40	–35	–15
	Additional offsets against gross budget authority only:			
4140	Change in uncollected pymts, Fed sources, unexpired	6		
4170	Outlays, net (mandatory)	–4	53	
4180	Budget authority, net (total)	485	486	580
4190	Outlays, net (total)	475	530	521

Note.—The reimbursable program (HCFAC) in the General Department Management (GDM) account reflects estimates of the allocation for 2023. The actual allocation is determined annually.

General Departmental Management (GDM) funds activities that provide leadership, policy, legal, and administrative guidance to HHS components and support research to develop policy initiatives and improve existing HHS programs. GDM also funds the activities of the Office of the Assistant Secretary for Health, including adolescent health, disease prevention and health promotion, physical fitness and sports, minority health, research integrity, women's health, and programs funded through the Prevention and Public Health Fund.

Object Classification (in millions of dollars)

Identification code 075–9912–0–1–551		2021 actual	2022 est.	2023 est.
	Direct obligations:			
	Personnel compensation:			
11.1	Full-time permanent	85	85	108
11.3	Other than full-time permanent	4	4	4
11.5	Other personnel compensation	1	1	1
11.7	Military personnel	2	2	4
11.9	Total personnel compensation	92	92	117
12.1	Civilian personnel benefits	33	33	44
12.2	Military personnel benefits	1	1	1
21.0	Travel and transportation of persons	1	1	1
23.1	Rental payments to GSA	21	21	22
23.3	Communications, utilities, and miscellaneous charges	2	2	1
24.0	Printing and reproduction	1	1	1
25.1	Advisory and assistance services	41	41	37
25.2	Other services from non-Federal sources	25	25	35
25.3	Other goods and services from Federal sources	126	126	140
25.4	Operation and maintenance of facilities	2	2	11
25.7	Operation and maintenance of equipment	2	2	3
26.0	Supplies and materials	1	1	1
31.0	Equipment	1	1	2
41.0	Grants, subsidies, and contributions	137	137	164
99.0	Direct obligations	486	486	580
99.0	Reimbursable obligations	289	289	282
99.9	Total new obligations, unexpired accounts	775	775	862

Employment Summary

Identification code 075–9912–0–1–551	2021 actual	2022 est.	2023 est.
1001 Direct civilian full-time equivalent employment	751	799	950

DEPARTMENT OF HEALTH AND HUMAN SERVICES

Departmental Management—Continued
Federal Funds—Continued

481

		2021 actual	2022 est.	2023 est.
1101	Direct military average strength employment	26	38	43
2001	Reimbursable civilian full-time equivalent employment	544	552	591
2101	Reimbursable military average strength employment	6	11	12

OFFICE FOR CIVIL RIGHTS

For expenses necessary for the Office for Civil Rights, $60,250,000.

Note.—A full-year 2022 appropriation for this account was not enacted at the time the Budget was prepared; therefore, the Budget assumes this account is operating under the Continuing Appropriations Act, 2022 (Division A of Public Law 117–43, as amended). The amounts included for 2022 reflect the annualized level provided by the continuing resolution.

Program and Financing (in millions of dollars)

Identification code 075–0135–0–1–751		2021 actual	2022 est.	2023 est.
	Obligations by program activity:			
0001	Office for Civil Rights (Direct)	39	39	60
0801	Office for Civil Rights (Reimbursable)	18	20	21
0900	Total new obligations, unexpired accounts	57	59	81
	Budgetary resources:			
	Unobligated balance:			
1000	Unobligated balance brought forward, Oct 1	62	53	43
1021	Recoveries of prior year unpaid obligations	2		
1070	Unobligated balance (total)	64	53	43
	Budget authority:			
	Appropriations, discretionary:			
1100	Appropriation	39	39	60
	Spending authority from offsetting collections, mandatory:			
1800	Collected	7	10	10
1802	Offsetting collections (previously unavailable)		1	1
1823	New and/or unobligated balance of spending authority from offsetting collections temporarily reduced		−1	−1
1850	Spending auth from offsetting collections, mand (total)	7	10	10
1900	Budget authority (total)	46	49	70
1930	Total budgetary resources available	110	102	113
	Memorandum (non-add) entries:			
1941	Unexpired unobligated balance, end of year	53	43	32
	Change in obligated balance:			
	Unpaid obligations:			
3000	Unpaid obligations, brought forward, Oct 1	18	22	33
3010	New obligations, unexpired accounts	57	59	81
3020	Outlays (gross)	−51	−48	−74
3040	Recoveries of prior year unpaid obligations, unexpired	−2		
3050	Unpaid obligations, end of year	22	33	40
	Memorandum (non-add) entries:			
3100	Obligated balance, start of year	18	22	33
3200	Obligated balance, end of year	22	33	40
	Budget authority and outlays, net:			
	Discretionary:			
4000	Budget authority, gross	39	39	60
	Outlays, gross:			
4010	Outlays from new discretionary authority	29	31	48
4011	Outlays from discretionary balances	6	5	12
4020	Outlays, gross (total)	35	36	60
	Mandatory:			
4090	Budget authority, gross	7	10	10
	Outlays, gross:			
4100	Outlays from new mandatory authority		2	2
4101	Outlays from mandatory balances	16	10	12
4110	Outlays, gross (total)	16	12	14
	Offsets against gross budget authority and outlays:			
	Offsetting collections (collected) from:			
4123	Non-Federal sources	−7	−10	−10
4180	Budget authority, net (total)	39	39	60
4190	Outlays, net (total)	44	38	64
	Memorandum (non-add) entries:			
5090	Unexpired unavailable balance, SOY: Offsetting collections	1	1	1
5092	Unexpired unavailable balance, EOY: Offsetting collections	1	1	1

The Office for Civil Rights funds activities that carry out the Department's civil rights, nondiscrimination, health information privacy, and security compliance programs.

Object Classification (in millions of dollars)

Identification code 075–0135–0–1–751		2021 actual	2022 est.	2023 est.
	Direct obligations:			
	Personnel compensation:			
11.1	Full-time permanent	15	17	29
11.3	Other than full-time permanent			1
11.5	Other personnel compensation	1	1	1
11.9	Total personnel compensation	16	18	31
12.1	Civilian personnel benefits	5	6	10
21.0	Travel and transportation of persons			1
23.1	Rental payments to GSA	4	4	4
25.2	Other services from non-Federal sources	2	3	5
25.3	Other goods and services from Federal sources	11	7	8
25.4	Operation and maintenance of facilities		1	
31.0	Equipment	1		1
99.0	Direct obligations	39	39	60
99.0	Reimbursable obligations	18	20	21
99.9	Total new obligations, unexpired accounts	57	59	81

Employment Summary

Identification code 075–0135–0–1–751		2021 actual	2022 est.	2023 est.
1001	Direct civilian full-time equivalent employment	126	140	231
1101	Direct military average strength employment	1	1	1
2001	Reimbursable civilian full-time equivalent employment	54	49	49

OFFICE OF THE NATIONAL COORDINATOR FOR HEALTH INFORMATION TECHNOLOGY

From amounts made available pursuant to section 241 of the PHS Act, $103,614,000 shall be for expenses necessary for the Office of the National Coordinator for Health Information Technology, including for grants, contracts, and cooperative agreements for the development and advancement of interoperable health information technology.

Note.—A full-year 2022 appropriation for this account was not enacted at the time the Budget was prepared; therefore, the Budget assumes this account is operating under the Continuing Appropriations Act, 2022 (Division A of Public Law 117–43, as amended). The amounts included for 2022 reflect the annualized level provided by the continuing resolution.

Program and Financing (in millions of dollars)

Identification code 075–0130–0–1–551		2021 actual	2022 est.	2023 est.
	Obligations by program activity:			
0001	Health information technology (IT)	62	62	
0799	Total direct obligations	62	62	
0801	Office of the National Coordinator for Health IT (ONC): Reimbursable	4	4	4
0802	ONC Reimbursable program activity: PHS Evaluation			104
0899	Total reimbursable obligations	4	4	108
0900	Total new obligations, unexpired accounts	66	66	108
	Budgetary resources:			
	Unobligated balance:			
1000	Unobligated balance brought forward, Oct 1	11	19	40
1021	Recoveries of prior year unpaid obligations	8		
1070	Unobligated balance (total)	19	19	40
	Budget authority:			
	Appropriations, discretionary:			
1100	Appropriation	62	62	
	Spending authority from offsetting collections, discretionary:			
1700	Collected	1	25	104
1701	Change in uncollected payments, Federal sources	3		
1750	Spending auth from offsetting collections, disc (total)	4	25	104
1900	Budget authority (total)	66	87	104
1930	Total budgetary resources available	85	106	144
	Memorandum (non-add) entries:			
1941	Unexpired unobligated balance, end of year	19	40	36
	Change in obligated balance:			
	Unpaid obligations:			
3000	Unpaid obligations, brought forward, Oct 1	54	42	27
3010	New obligations, unexpired accounts	66	66	108

OFFICE OF THE NATIONAL COORDINATOR FOR HEALTH INFORMATION TECHNOLOGY—Continued

Program and Financing—Continued

Identification code 075–0130–0–1–551	2021 actual	2022 est.	2023 est.
3011 Obligations ("upward adjustments"), expired accounts	1	....	....
3020 Outlays (gross)	−69	−81	−74
3040 Recoveries of prior year unpaid obligations, unexpired	−8	....	....
3041 Recoveries of prior year unpaid obligations, expired	−2	....	....
3050 Unpaid obligations, end of year	42	27	61
Uncollected payments:			
3060 Uncollected pymts, Fed sources, brought forward, Oct 1	−9	−7	−7
3070 Change in uncollected pymts, Fed sources, unexpired	−3	....	....
3071 Change in uncollected pymts, Fed sources, expired	5	....	....
3090 Uncollected pymts, Fed sources, end of year	−7	−7	−7
Memorandum (non-add) entries:			
3100 Obligated balance, start of year	45	35	20
3200 Obligated balance, end of year	35	20	54
Budget authority and outlays, net:			
Discretionary:			
4000 Budget authority, gross	66	87	104
Outlays, gross:			
4010 Outlays from new discretionary authority	43	65	57
4011 Outlays from discretionary balances	26	16	17
4020 Outlays, gross (total)	69	81	74
Offsets against gross budget authority and outlays:			
Offsetting collections (collected) from:			
4030 Federal sources:	−6	−25	−104
4040 Offsets against gross budget authority and outlays (total)	−6	−25	−104
Additional offsets against gross budget authority only:			
4050 Change in uncollected pymts, Fed sources, unexpired	−3	....	....
4052 Offsetting collections credited to expired accounts	5	....	....
4060 Additional offsets against budget authority only (total)	2	....	....
4070 Budget authority, net (discretionary)	62	62	....
4080 Outlays, net (discretionary)	63	56	−30
4180 Budget authority, net (total)	62	62	....
4190 Outlays, net (total)	63	56	−30

This program supports coordination, leadership, and development of Federal health information technology activities and Federal initiatives for the nationwide advancement of private and secure interoperable health information technology, in cooperation with participants in the health sector. The Office of the National Coordinator for Health Information Technology was authorized in title XXX of the PHS Act as added by the Health Information Technology for Economic and Clinical Health (HITECH) Act (P.L. 111–5, Title XIII) and the 21st Century Cures Act (P.L. 114–255), for the purpose of addressing strategic planning, coordination, and the analysis of key technical, economic and other issues related to the public and private adoption of health information technology.

Object Classification (in millions of dollars)

Identification code 075–0130–0–1–551	2021 actual	2022 est.	2023 est.
Direct obligations:			
Personnel compensation:			
11.1 Full-time permanent	22	22	....
11.5 Other personnel compensation	2	2	....
11.9 Total personnel compensation	24	24	....
12.1 Civilian personnel benefits	8	8	....
23.1 Rental payments to GSA	2	2	....
25.2 Other services from non-Federal sources	12	12	....
25.3 Other goods and services from Federal sources	11	11	....
41.0 Grants, subsidies, and contributions	6	6	....
99.0 Direct obligations	63	63	....
99.0 Reimbursable obligations	4	4	108
99.5 Adjustment for rounding	−1	−1	....
99.9 Total new obligations, unexpired accounts	66	66	108

Employment Summary

Identification code 075–0130–0–1–551	2021 actual	2022 est.	2023 est.
1001 Direct civilian full-time equivalent employment	180	180	180

MEDICARE HEARINGS AND APPEALS

For expenses necessary for Medicare hearings and appeals in the Office of the Secretary, $196,000,000 shall remain available until September 30,2024, to be transferred in appropriate part from the Federal Hospital Insurance Trust Fund and the Federal Supplementary Medical Insurance Trust Fund.

Note.—A full-year 2022 appropriation for this account was not enacted at the time the Budget was prepared; therefore, the Budget assumes this account is operating under the Continuing Appropriations Act, 2022 (Division A of Public Law 117–43, as amended). The amounts included for 2022 reflect the annualized level provided by the continuing resolution.

Program and Financing (in millions of dollars)

Identification code 075–0139–0–1–551	2021 actual	2022 est.	2023 est.
Obligations by program activity:			
0001 Medicare Hearings and Appeals (Direct)	208	192	196
0799 Total direct obligations	208	192	196
Budgetary resources:			
Unobligated balance:			
1000 Unobligated balance brought forward, Oct 1	48	40	40
1021 Recoveries of prior year unpaid obligations	5	....	....
1070 Unobligated balance (total)	53	40	40
Budget authority:			
Spending authority from offsetting collections, discretionary:			
1700 Collected	187	192	196
1701 Change in uncollected payments, Federal sources	10	....	....
1710 Spending authority from offsetting collections transferred to other accounts [075–0120]	−1	....	....
1750 Spending auth from offsetting collections, disc (total)	196	192	196
1900 Budget authority (total)	196	192	196
1930 Total budgetary resources available	249	232	236
Memorandum (non-add) entries:			
1940 Unobligated balance expiring	−1	....	....
1941 Unexpired unobligated balance, end of year	40	40	40
Change in obligated balance:			
Unpaid obligations:			
3000 Unpaid obligations, brought forward, Oct 1	45	40	2
3010 New obligations, unexpired accounts	208	192	196
3011 Obligations ("upward adjustments"), expired accounts	1	....	....
3020 Outlays (gross)	−203	−230	−196
3040 Recoveries of prior year unpaid obligations, unexpired	−5	....	....
3041 Recoveries of prior year unpaid obligations, expired	−6	....	....
3050 Unpaid obligations, end of year	40	2	2
Uncollected payments:			
3060 Uncollected pymts, Fed sources, brought forward, Oct 1	−92	−96	−96
3070 Change in uncollected pymts, Fed sources, unexpired	−10	....	....
3071 Change in uncollected pymts, Fed sources, expired	6	....	....
3090 Uncollected pymts, Fed sources, end of year	−96	−96	−96
Memorandum (non-add) entries:			
3100 Obligated balance, start of year	−47	−56	−94
3200 Obligated balance, end of year	−56	−94	−94
Budget authority and outlays, net:			
Discretionary:			
4000 Budget authority, gross	196	192	196
Outlays, gross:			
4010 Outlays from new discretionary authority	131	192	196
4011 Outlays from discretionary balances	72	....	....
4020 Outlays, gross (total)	203	192	196
Offsets against gross budget authority and outlays:			
Offsetting collections (collected) from:			
4030 Federal sources	−187	−192	−196
Additional offsets against gross budget authority only:			
4050 Change in uncollected pymts, Fed sources, unexpired	−10	....	....
4060 Additional offsets against budget authority only (total)	−10	....	....
4070 Budget authority, net (discretionary)	−1	....	....
4080 Outlays, net (discretionary)	16	....	....

DEPARTMENT OF HEALTH AND HUMAN SERVICES

Departmental Management—Continued
Federal Funds—Continued

483

		2021 actual	2022 est.	2023 est.
	Mandatory: Outlays, gross:			
4101	Outlays from mandatory balances		38	
4180	Budget authority, net (total)	−1		
4190	Outlays, net (total)	16	38	

This appropriation funds the operations of the Office of Medicare Hearings and Appeals (OMHA), as authorized by the Medicare Prescription Drug, Improvement, and Modernization Act of 2003, and the Medicare appeals related operations of the Departmental Appeals Board (DAB). OMHA provides an independent and impartial forum for the adjudication of claims brought by or on behalf of Medicare beneficiaries related to their benefits and care. The Departmental Appeals Board for Medicare provides final HHS administrative review of claims for Medicare entitlement, payment, and coverage.

Object Classification (in millions of dollars)

Identification code 075–0139–0–1–551	2021 actual	2022 est.	2023 est.
Direct obligations:			
Personnel compensation:			
11.1 Full-time permanent	117	108	101
11.5 Other personnel compensation		2	2
11.9 Total personnel compensation	117	110	103
12.1 Civilian personnel benefits	41	39	37
23.1 Rental payments to GSA	12	11	10
23.3 Communications, utilities, and miscellaneous charges	8	7	14
24.0 Printing and reproduction	1	1	1
25.1 Advisory and assistance services			2
25.2 Other services from non-Federal sources	17	12	12
25.3 Other goods and services from Federal sources	9	11	15
25.4 Operation and maintenance of facilities	1	1	1
25.7 Operation and maintenance of equipment	2		
26.0 Supplies and materials			1
99.0 Direct obligations	208	192	196
99.9 Total new obligations, unexpired accounts	208	192	196

Employment Summary

Identification code 075–0139–0–1–551	2021 actual	2022 est.	2023 est.
1001 Direct civilian full-time equivalent employment	1,228	1,090	1,025

PUBLIC HEALTH AND SOCIAL SERVICES EMERGENCY FUND

For expenses necessary to support activities related to countering potential biological, nuclear, radiological, chemical, and cybersecurity threats to civilian populations, and for other public health emergencies, $1,687,610,000, of which $828,380,000 shall remain available through September 30, 2024, for expenses necessary to support advanced research and development pursuant to section 319L of the PHS Act and other administrative expenses of the Biomedical Advanced Research and Development Authority: Provided, That funds provided under this heading for the purpose of acquisition of security countermeasures shall be in addition to any other funds available for such purpose: Provided further, That products purchased with funds provided under this heading may, at the discretion of the Secretary, be deposited in the Strategic National Stockpile pursuant to section 319F-2 of the PHS Act: Provided further, That $5,000,000 of the amounts made available to support emergency operations shall remain available through September 30, 2025: Provided further, That $132,801,000 of the amounts made available to support coordination of the development, production, and distribution of vaccines, therapeutics, and other medical countermeasures shall remain available through September 30, 2024.

For expenses necessary for procuring security countermeasures (as defined in section 319F-2(c)(1)(B) of the PHS Act), $770,000,000, to remain available until expended.

For expenses necessary to carry out section 319F-2(a) of the PHS Act, $975,000,000, to remain available until expended.

For an additional amount for expenses necessary to prepare for or respond to an influenza pandemic, $382,000,000; of which $347,000,000 shall be available until expended, for activities including the development and purchase of vaccine, antivirals, necessary medical supplies, diagnostics, and other surveillance tools: Provided, That notwithstanding section 496(b) of the PHS Act, funds may be used for the construction or renovation of privately owned facilities for the production of pandemic influenza vaccines and other biologics, if the Secretary finds such construction or renovation necessary to secure sufficient supplies of such vaccines or biologics.

Program and Financing (in millions of dollars)

Identification code 075–0140–0–1–551	2021 actual	2022 est.	2023 est.
Obligations by program activity:			
0001 Public Health and Social Services Emergency Fund	117,764	97,439	3,815
0100 Direct program activities, subtotal	117,764	97,439	3,815
0801 Reimbursable program (FEMA)	135	135	140
0802 Reimbursable program activity (OPP)	3	3	2
0899 Total reimbursable obligations	138	138	142
0900 Total new obligations, unexpired accounts	117,902	97,577	3,957
Budgetary resources:			
Unobligated balance:			
1000 Unobligated balance brought forward, Oct 1	86,561	95,631	1,056
1001 Discretionary unobligated balance brought fwd, Oct 1	86,548		
1010 Unobligated balance transfer to other accts [075–0343]	−4	−7	
1011 Unobligated balance transfer from other acct [075–0943]	544		
1011 Unobligated balance transfer from other acct [075–0846]	581		
1011 Unobligated balance transfer from other acct [075–0849]	114		
1011 Unobligated balance transfer from other acct [075–0898]	78		
1021 Recoveries of prior year unpaid obligations	4,334		
1033 Recoveries of prior year paid obligations	1,541		
1070 Unobligated balance (total)	93,749	95,624	1,056
Budget authority:			
Appropriations, discretionary:			
1100 Appropriation	51,192	2,847	3,815
1120 Appropriations transferred to other acct [075–1503]	−858		
1120 Appropriations transferred to other acct [075–0390]	−790		
1160 Appropriation, discretionary (total)	49,544	2,847	3,815
Appropriations, mandatory:			
1200 Appropriation	70,110		
Spending authority from offsetting collections, discretionary:			
1700 Collected	2	162	165
1701 Change in uncollected payments, Federal sources	135		
1750 Spending auth from offsetting collections, disc (total)	137	162	165
1900 Budget authority (total)	119,791	3,009	3,980
1930 Total budgetary resources available	213,540	98,633	5,036
Memorandum (non-add) entries:			
1940 Unobligated balance expiring	−7		
1941 Unexpired unobligated balance, end of year	95,631	1,056	1,079
Change in obligated balance:			
Unpaid obligations:			
3000 Unpaid obligations, brought forward, Oct 1	38,868	80,077	109,794
3010 New obligations, unexpired accounts	117,902	97,577	3,957
3011 Obligations ("upward adjustments"), expired accounts	37		
3020 Outlays (gross)	−72,302	−67,860	−21,715
3040 Recoveries of prior year unpaid obligations, unexpired	−4,334		
3041 Recoveries of prior year unpaid obligations, expired	−94		
3050 Unpaid obligations, end of year	80,077	109,794	92,036
Uncollected payments:			
3060 Uncollected pymts, Fed sources, brought forward, Oct 1	−272	−332	−332
3070 Change in uncollected pymts, Fed sources, unexpired	−135		
3071 Change in uncollected pymts, Fed sources, expired	75		
3090 Uncollected pymts, Fed sources, end of year	−332	−332	−332
Memorandum (non-add) entries:			
3100 Obligated balance, start of year	38,596	79,745	109,462
3200 Obligated balance, end of year	79,745	109,462	91,704
Budget authority and outlays, net:			
Discretionary:			
4000 Budget authority, gross	49,681	3,009	3,980
Outlays, gross:			
4010 Outlays from new discretionary authority	7,917	644	1,028
4011 Outlays from discretionary balances	59,361	41,182	6,665
4020 Outlays, gross (total)	67,278	41,826	7,693
Offsets against gross budget authority and outlays:			
Offsetting collections (collected) from:			
4030 Federal sources	−98	−162	−165
4033 Non-Federal sources	−1,551		
4040 Offsets against gross budget authority and outlays (total)	−1,649	−162	−165
Additional offsets against gross budget authority only:			
4050 Change in uncollected pymts, Fed sources, unexpired	−135		
4052 Offsetting collections credited to expired accounts	106		

PUBLIC HEALTH AND SOCIAL SERVICES EMERGENCY FUND—Continued

Program and Financing—Continued

Identification code 075–0140–0–1–551		2021 actual	2022 est.	2023 est.
4053	Recoveries of prior year paid obligations, unexpired accounts	1,541	....	....
4060	Additional offsets against budget authority only (total)	1,512	....	....
4070	Budget authority, net (discretionary)	49,544	2,847	3,815
4080	Outlays, net (discretionary)	65,629	41,664	7,528
	Mandatory:			
4090	Budget authority, gross	70,110	....	....
	Outlays, gross:			
4100	Outlays from new mandatory authority	5,022	....	....
4101	Outlays from mandatory balances	2	26,034	14,022
4110	Outlays, gross (total)	5,024	26,034	14,022
4180	Budget authority, net (total)	119,654	2,847	3,815
4190	Outlays, net (total)	70,653	67,698	21,550

Summary of Budget Authority and Outlays (in millions of dollars)

	2021 actual	2022 est.	2023 est.
Enacted/requested:			
Budget Authority	119,654	2,847	3,815
Outlays	70,653	67,698	21,550
Legislative proposal, subject to PAYGO:			
Budget Authority	....	....	40,019
Outlays	....	....	6,003
Total:			
Budget Authority	119,654	2,847	43,834
Outlays	70,653	67,698	27,553

The Public Health and Social Services Emergency Fund (PHSSEF) provides resources to support a comprehensive program to prepare for the health and medical consequences of bioterrorism or other public health emergencies. This account includes funding for the Office of the Assistant Secretary for Preparedness and Response (ASPR), as authorized by the Pandemic and All-Hazards Preparedness and Advancing Innovation Act of 2019. Funds will be used for hospital preparedness and other emergency preparedness activities including the National Disaster Medical System and National Biodefense Strategy implementation. The PHSSEF continues to support the advanced development, procurement, and stockpiling of biodefense and pandemic influenza countermeasures.

The PHSSEF also supports the HHS Cybersecurity program, National Security and Strategic Information programs, the U.S. Public Health Service Commissioned Corps, and the Medical Reserve Corps.

Object Classification (in millions of dollars)

Identification code 075–0140–0–1–551		2021 actual	2022 est.	2023 est.
	Direct obligations:			
	Personnel compensation:			
11.1	Full-time permanent	149	123	183
11.3	Other than full-time permanent	19	16	14
11.5	Other personnel compensation	11	9	1
11.7	Military personnel	18	15	15
11.8	Special personal services payments	1	1	1
11.9	Total personnel compensation	198	164	214
12.1	Civilian personnel benefits	48	40	55
12.2	Military personnel benefits	6	5	7
21.0	Travel and transportation of persons	9	7	12
22.0	Transportation of things	205	169	7
23.1	Rental payments to GSA	9	7	7
23.2	Rental payments to others	11	9	16
23.3	Communications, utilities, and miscellaneous charges	7	6	4
24.0	Printing and reproduction	1	1	1
25.1	Advisory and assistance services	8,119	6,686	263
25.2	Other services from non-Federal sources	35,561	29,513	1,001
25.3	Other goods and services from Federal sources	34,746	28,730	1,020
25.4	Operation and maintenance of facilities	5	4	6
25.5	Research and development contracts	529	437	17
25.6	Medical care	11	9	1
25.7	Operation and maintenance of equipment	99	82	33
26.0	Supplies and materials	1,321	1,092	43
31.0	Equipment	150	124	5
32.0	Land and structures	9	7	1
41.0	Grants, subsidies, and contributions	36,718	30,345	1,100
42.0	Insurance claims and indemnities	1	1	1
43.0	Interest and dividends	1	1	1
99.0	Direct obligations	117,764	97,439	3,815
99.0	Reimbursable obligations	138	138	142
99.9	Total new obligations, unexpired accounts	117,902	97,577	3,957

Employment Summary

Identification code 075–0140–0–1–551		2021 actual	2022 est.	2023 est.
1001	Direct civilian full-time equivalent employment	1,102	1,214	1,649
1101	Direct military average strength employment	114	94	197

PUBLIC HEALTH AND SOCIAL SERVICES EMERGENCY FUND

(Legislative proposal, subject to PAYGO)

Program and Financing (in millions of dollars)

Identification code 075–0140–4–1–551		2021 actual	2022 est.	2023 est.
	Obligations by program activity:			
0001	Prepare for pandemic and biological threats	....	....	40,019
0100	Direct program activities, subtotal	....	....	40,019
0900	Total new obligations, unexpired accounts (object class 25.5)	....	....	40,019
	Budgetary resources:			
	Budget authority:			
	Appropriations, mandatory:			
1200	Appropriation	....	....	40,019
1930	Total budgetary resources available	....	....	40,019
	Change in obligated balance:			
	Unpaid obligations:			
3010	New obligations, unexpired accounts	....	....	40,019
3020	Outlays (gross)	....	....	–6,003
3050	Unpaid obligations, end of year	....	....	34,016
	Memorandum (non-add) entries:			
3200	Obligated balance, end of year	....	....	34,016
	Budget authority and outlays, net:			
	Mandatory:			
4090	Budget authority, gross	....	....	40,019
	Outlays, gross:			
4100	Outlays from new mandatory authority	....	....	6,003
4180	Budget authority, net (total)	....	....	40,019
4190	Outlays, net (total)	....	....	6,003

The 2023 Budget includes mandatory funding for significant investments in pandemic preparedness across HHS, including the Office of the Assistant Secretary for Preparedness and Response. These investments will support advanced development and manufacturing of vaccines, therapeutics, and diagnostics for high priority viral families and scale up manufacturing capacity for medical countermeasures.

DEFENSE PRODUCTION ACT MEDICAL SUPPLIES ENHANCEMENT

Program and Financing (in millions of dollars)

Identification code 075–0150–0–1–551		2021 actual	2022 est.	2023 est.
	Obligations by program activity:			
0001	Direct program activity	689	5,800	900
	Budgetary resources:			
	Unobligated balance:			
1000	Unobligated balance brought forward, Oct 1	....	9,311	3,511
	Budget authority:			
	Appropriations, mandatory:			
1200	Appropriation	10,000	....	....
1930	Total budgetary resources available	10,000	9,311	3,511
	Memorandum (non-add) entries:			
1941	Unexpired unobligated balance, end of year	9,311	3,511	2,611
	Change in obligated balance:			
	Unpaid obligations:			
3000	Unpaid obligations, brought forward, Oct 1	....	637	637

DEPARTMENT OF HEALTH AND HUMAN SERVICES

Departmental Management—Continued
Federal Funds—Continued

485

		2021 actual	2022 est.	2023 est.
3010	New obligations, unexpired accounts	689	5,800	900
3020	Outlays (gross)	–52	–5,800	–500
3050	Unpaid obligations, end of year	637	637	1,037
	Memorandum (non-add) entries:			
3100	Obligated balance, start of year	....	637	637
3200	Obligated balance, end of year	637	637	1,037
	Budget authority and outlays, net:			
	Mandatory:			
4090	Budget authority, gross	10,000	....	....
	Outlays, gross:			
4100	Outlays from new mandatory authority	52	....	....
4101	Outlays from mandatory balances	....	5,800	500
4110	Outlays, gross (total)	52	5,800	500
4180	Budget authority, net (total)	10,000	....	....
4190	Outlays, net (total)	52	5,800	500

Defense Production Act Medical Supplies Enhancement includes funds appropriated by the American Rescue Plan Act of 2021 to carry out titles I, III, and VII of the Defense Production Act to enhance the emergency medical supply of materials necessary to respond to public health emergencies and disasters. Funds will be used for the purchase, production and distribution of medical supplies, such as testing and personal protective equipment, and equipment, including durable medical equipment, related to combating the COVID-19 pandemic. After September 30, 2022, funds may be used for any other activity necessary to meet critical public health needs of the United States, with respect to any pathogen that the President has determined has the potential for creating a public health emergency.

Object Classification (in millions of dollars)

Identification code 075–0150–0–1–551	2021 actual	2022 est.	2023 est.
Direct obligations:			
25.1 Advisory and assistance services	14	118	18
25.2 Other services from non-Federal sources	9	76	11
25.3 Other goods and services from Federal sources	506	4,259	662
32.0 Land and structures	160	1,347	209
99.9 Total new obligations, unexpired accounts	689	5,800	900

PREP FOR ALL TO END THE HIV EPIDEMIC

(Legislative proposal, subject to PAYGO)

Program and Financing (in millions of dollars)

Identification code 075–0151–4–1–551	2021 actual	2022 est.	2023 est.
Obligations by program activity:			
0001 Direct program activity	....	....	237
0900 Total new obligations, unexpired accounts (object class 25.6)	....	....	237
Budgetary resources:			
Budget authority:			
Appropriations, mandatory:			
1200 Appropriation	....	....	237
1930 Total budgetary resources available	....	....	237
Change in obligated balance:			
Unpaid obligations:			
3010 New obligations, unexpired accounts	....	....	237
3020 Outlays (gross)	....	....	–213
3050 Unpaid obligations, end of year	....	....	24
Memorandum (non-add) entries:			
3200 Obligated balance, end of year	....	....	24
Budget authority and outlays, net:			
Mandatory:			
4090 Budget authority, gross	....	....	237
Outlays, gross:			
4100 Outlays from new mandatory authority	....	....	213
4180 Budget authority, net (total)	....	....	237
4190 Outlays, net (total)	....	....	213

This national program creates a financing delivery system to guarantee PrEP at no cost for all uninsured and underinsured individuals, provide essential wrap-around services through States, IHS and tribal entities, and localities, and establish a network of community providers to reach underserved areas and populations. Together, these investments will help support the National HIV/AIDS Strategy (2022–2025) commitment to a 75 percent reduction in HIV infection by 2025.

MENTAL HEALTH TRANSFORMATION FUND

(Legislative proposal, subject to PAYGO)

Program and Financing (in millions of dollars)

Identification code 075–0136–4–1–551	2021 actual	2022 est.	2023 est.
Obligations by program activity:			
0001 Direct program activity	....	....	750
0900 Total new obligations, unexpired accounts (object class 41.0)	....	....	750
Budgetary resources:			
Budget authority:			
Appropriations, mandatory:			
1200 Appropriation	....	....	7,500
1930 Total budgetary resources available	....	....	7,500
Memorandum (non-add) entries:			
1941 Unexpired unobligated balance, end of year	....	....	6,750
Change in obligated balance:			
Unpaid obligations:			
3010 New obligations, unexpired accounts	....	....	750
3020 Outlays (gross)	....	....	–750
Budget authority and outlays, net:			
Mandatory:			
4090 Budget authority, gross	....	....	7,500
Outlays, gross:			
4100 Outlays from new mandatory authority	....	....	750
4180 Budget authority, net (total)	....	....	7,500
4190 Outlays, net (total)	....	....	750

The fund will support innovative, transformational initiatives to improve system capacity, connect more people to the care they need, and create a continuum of support by promoting wellness and recovery. These programs will prioritize sustainability, integration, leverage existing capacity, and support new models of care, including hub-and-spoke models.

TRANSFERS FROM THE PATIENT-CENTERED OUTCOMES RESEARCH TRUST FUND

Program and Financing (in millions of dollars)

Identification code 075–0145–0–1–552	2021 actual	2022 est.	2023 est.
Obligations by program activity:			
0001 AHRQ	63	105	111
0002 Office of the Secretary	....	26	28
0900 Total new obligations, unexpired accounts	63	131	139
Budgetary resources:			
Unobligated balance:			
1000 Unobligated balance brought forward, Oct 1	261	318	323
1021 Recoveries of prior year unpaid obligations	5	....	....
1070 Unobligated balance (total)	266	318	323
Budget authority:			
Spending authority from offsetting collections, mandatory:			
1800 Collected	115	136	144
1930 Total budgetary resources available	381	454	467
Memorandum (non-add) entries:			
1941 Unexpired unobligated balance, end of year	318	323	328
Change in obligated balance:			
Unpaid obligations:			
3000 Unpaid obligations, brought forward, Oct 1	101	91	74
3010 New obligations, unexpired accounts	63	131	139
3020 Outlays (gross)	–68	–148	–133

Departmental Management—Continued
Federal Funds—Continued

TRANSFERS FROM THE PATIENT-CENTERED OUTCOMES RESEARCH TRUST FUND—Continued

Program and Financing—Continued

Identification code 075–0145–0–1–552		2021 actual	2022 est.	2023 est.
3040	Recoveries of prior year unpaid obligations, unexpired	–5	....	....
3050	Unpaid obligations, end of year	91	74	80
	Memorandum (non-add) entries:			
3100	Obligated balance, start of year	101	91	74
3200	Obligated balance, end of year	91	74	80
	Budget authority and outlays, net:			
	Mandatory:			
4090	Budget authority, gross	115	136	144
	Outlays, gross:			
4100	Outlays from new mandatory authority	....	4	4
4101	Outlays from mandatory balances	68	144	129
4110	Outlays, gross (total)	68	148	133
	Offsets against gross budget authority and outlays:			
	Offsetting collections (collected) from:			
4120	Federal sources	–115	–136	–144
4180	Budget authority, net (total)	....	....	....
4190	Outlays, net (total)	–47	12	–11

Public Law 111–148 established the Patient-Centered Outcomes Research Trust Fund (PCORTF). Beginning in FY 2011, a total of 20 percent of the funds appropriated or credited to the PCORTF was transferred each year to the Department of Health and Human Services (HHS). In FY 2020, PCORTF was extended through FY 2029. As authorized in section 937 of the Public Health Service Act, HHS will disseminate research findings from the Patient-Centered Outcomes Research Institute and other government-funded comparative clinical effectiveness research and coordinate Federal health programs to build research and data capacity for comparative clinical effectiveness research. Transferred funds were distributed to the Secretary of HHS and the Agency for Healthcare Research and Quality to carry out these activities.

Object Classification (in millions of dollars)

Identification code 075–0145–0–1–552		2021 actual	2022 est.	2023 est.
	Direct obligations:			
25.3	Other goods and services from Federal sources	38	105	111
41.0	Grants, subsidies, and contributions	25	26	28
99.9	Total new obligations, unexpired accounts	63	131	139

Employment Summary

Identification code 075–0145–0–1–552		2021 actual	2022 est.	2023 est.
1001	Direct civilian full-time equivalent employment	4	....	....

NONRECURRING EXPENSES FUND

Program and Financing (in millions of dollars)

Identification code 075–0125–0–1–551		2021 actual	2022 est.	2023 est.
	Obligations by program activity:			
0001	Nonrecurring Expenses Fund Projects	372	1,029	509
	Budgetary resources:			
	Unobligated balance:			
1000	Unobligated balance brought forward, Oct 1	1,191	1,458	804
1012	Unobligated balance transfers between expired and unexpired accounts	997	750	750
1021	Recoveries of prior year unpaid obligations	17	....	....
1070	Unobligated balance (total)	2,205	2,208	1,554
	Budget authority:			
	Appropriations, discretionary:			
1131	Unobligated balance of appropriations permanently reduced	–375	–375	–500
1930	Total budgetary resources available	1,830	1,833	1,054
	Memorandum (non-add) entries:			
1941	Unexpired unobligated balance, end of year	1,458	804	545
	Change in obligated balance:			
	Unpaid obligations:			
3000	Unpaid obligations, brought forward, Oct 1	728	785	1,315
3010	New obligations, unexpired accounts	372	1,029	509
3020	Outlays (gross)	–298	–499	–184
3040	Recoveries of prior year unpaid obligations, unexpired	–17	....	....
3050	Unpaid obligations, end of year	785	1,315	1,640
	Memorandum (non-add) entries:			
3100	Obligated balance, start of year	728	785	1,315
3200	Obligated balance, end of year	785	1,315	1,640
	Budget authority and outlays, net:			
	Discretionary:			
4000	Budget authority, gross	–375	–375	–500
	Outlays, gross:			
4010	Outlays from new discretionary authority	....	–101	–135
4011	Outlays from discretionary balances	298	600	319
4020	Outlays, gross (total)	298	499	184
4180	Budget authority, net (total)	–375	–375	–500
4190	Outlays, net (total)	298	499	184

The Nonrecurring Expenses Fund is a no-year account that receives transfers of expired unobligated balances from discretionary accounts prior to cancellation. The Fund is used for capital acquisition, including facilities infrastructure and information technology infrastructure.

Object Classification (in millions of dollars)

Identification code 075–0125–0–1–551		2021 actual	2022 est.	2023 est.
	Direct obligations:			
23.1	Rental payments to GSA	1	3	1
25.1	Advisory and assistance services	7	19	10
25.2	Other services from non-Federal sources	19	53	26
25.4	Operation and maintenance of facilities	6	17	8
25.7	Operation and maintenance of equipment	18	49	25
32.0	Land and structures	321	888	439
99.0	Direct obligations	372	1,029	509
99.9	Total new obligations, unexpired accounts	372	1,029	509

Employment Summary

Identification code 075–0125–0–1–551		2021 actual	2022 est.	2023 est.
1001	Direct civilian full-time equivalent employment	4	4	4

HEALTH INSURANCE REFORM IMPLEMENTATION FUND

Program and Financing (in millions of dollars)

Identification code 075–0119–0–1–551		2021 actual	2022 est.	2023 est.
	Budgetary resources:			
	Unobligated balance:			
1000	Unobligated balance brought forward, Oct 1	4	6	6
1021	Recoveries of prior year unpaid obligations	2	....	....
1070	Unobligated balance (total)	6	6	6
1930	Total budgetary resources available	6	6	6
	Memorandum (non-add) entries:			
1941	Unexpired unobligated balance, end of year	6	6	6
	Change in obligated balance:			
	Unpaid obligations:			
3000	Unpaid obligations, brought forward, Oct 1	14	12	10
3020	Outlays (gross)	....	–2	–2
3040	Recoveries of prior year unpaid obligations, unexpired	–2	....	....
3050	Unpaid obligations, end of year	12	10	8
	Memorandum (non-add) entries:			
3100	Obligated balance, start of year	14	12	10
3200	Obligated balance, end of year	12	10	8

DEPARTMENT OF HEALTH AND HUMAN SERVICES

Departmental Management—Continued
Federal Funds—Continued

487

		2021 actual	2022 est.	2023 est.
	Budget authority and outlays, net:			
	Mandatory:			
	Outlays, gross:			
4101	Outlays from mandatory balances		2	2
4180	Budget authority, net (total)			
4190	Outlays, net (total)		2	2

Section 1005 of the Health Care and Education Reconciliation Act of 2010 (P.L. 111–152) appropriated $1,000,000,000 to the Health Insurance Reform Implementation Fund within the Department of Health and Human Services. The Fund shall be used for Federal administrative expenses necessary to carry out the requirements of the Patient Protection and Affordable Care Act of 2010 (P.L. 111–148) and the Health Care and Education Reconciliation Act of 2010.

NO SURPRISES IMPLEMENTATION FUND

Program and Financing (in millions of dollars)

Identification code 075–0127–0–1–551		2021 actual	2022 est.	2023 est.
	Obligations by program activity:			
0001	Direct program activity	63	144	138
	Budgetary resources:			
	Unobligated balance:			
1000	Unobligated balance brought forward, Oct 1		437	293
	Budget authority:			
	Appropriations, mandatory:			
1200	Appropriation	500		
1930	Total budgetary resources available	500	437	293
	Memorandum (non-add) entries:			
1941	Unexpired unobligated balance, end of year	437	293	155
	Change in obligated balance:			
	Unpaid obligations:			
3000	Unpaid obligations, brought forward, Oct 1		54	54
3010	New obligations, unexpired accounts	63	144	138
3020	Outlays (gross)	–9	–144	–138
3050	Unpaid obligations, end of year	54	54	54
	Memorandum (non-add) entries:			
3100	Obligated balance, start of year		54	54
3200	Obligated balance, end of year	54	54	54
	Budget authority and outlays, net:			
	Mandatory:			
4090	Budget authority, gross	500		
	Outlays, gross:			
4100	Outlays from new mandatory authority	9		
4101	Outlays from mandatory balances		144	138
4110	Outlays, gross (total)	9	144	138
4180	Budget authority, net (total)	500		
4190	Outlays, net (total)	9	144	138

Section 118 of the No Surprises Act (P.L. 116–260) appropriated $500,000,000 to the No Surprises Implementation Fund within the Department of Health and Human Services. The Fund shall be used for implementation expenses necessary to carry out the requirements of the No Surprises Act and Title II Transparency provisions for the Department of Health and Human Services, the Department of Labor, and the Department of the Treasury.

Object Classification (in millions of dollars)

Identification code 075–0127–0–1–551		2021 actual	2022 est.	2023 est.
	Direct obligations:			
11.1	Personnel compensation: Full-time permanent	5	11	11
12.1	Civilian personnel benefits	2	5	5
21.0	Travel and transportation of persons	2	5	4
25.1	Advisory and assistance services	1	2	2
25.2	Other services from non-Federal sources	53	121	116
99.9	Total new obligations, unexpired accounts	63	144	138

Employment Summary

Identification code 075–0127–0–1–551	2021 actual	2022 est.	2023 est.
1001 Direct civilian full-time equivalent employment	64	209	209

PREVENTION AND PUBLIC HEALTH FUND

Program and Financing (in millions of dollars)

Identification code 075–0116–0–1–551		2021 actual	2022 est.	2023 est.
	Budgetary resources:			
	Unobligated balance:			
1000	Unobligated balance brought forward, Oct 1	6	3	50
1010	Unobligated balance transfer to other accts [075–0120]	–3		
1070	Unobligated balance (total)	3	3	50
	Budget authority:			
	Appropriations, discretionary:			
1120	Appropriations transferred to other acct [075–0142]		–28	
1120	Appropriations transferred to other acct [075–0943]		–856	
1120	Appropriations transferred to other acct [075–1362]		–12	
1160	Appropriation, discretionary (total)		–896	
	Appropriations, mandatory:			
1200	Appropriation	950	1,000	1,000
1220	Appropriations transferred to other accts [075–0142]	–28		–28
1220	Appropriations transferred to other accts [075–0943]	–856		–903
1220	Appropriations transferred to other accts [075–1362]	–12		–12
1230	Appropriations and/or unobligated balance of appropriations permanently reduced [SEQ]	–54	–57	–57
1260	Appropriations, mandatory (total)		943	
1900	Budget authority (total)		47	
1930	Total budgetary resources available	3	50	50
	Memorandum (non-add) entries:			
1941	Unexpired unobligated balance, end of year	3	50	50
	Budget authority and outlays, net:			
	Discretionary:			
4000	Budget authority, gross		–896	
	Mandatory:			
4090	Budget authority, gross		943	
4180	Budget authority, net (total)		47	
4190	Outlays, net (total)			

The Prevention and Public Health Fund supports prevention and public health activities. In FY 2023, $943 million is available to support a range of public health efforts intended to prevent disease and reduce health care costs. The Secretary has authority to transfer to accounts within HHS.

PREGNANCY ASSISTANCE FUND

Program and Financing (in millions of dollars)

Identification code 075–0117–0–1–551		2021 actual	2022 est.	2023 est.
	Change in obligated balance:			
	Unpaid obligations:			
3000	Unpaid obligations, brought forward, Oct 1	6	1	
3020	Outlays (gross)	–3	–1	
3041	Recoveries of prior year unpaid obligations, expired	–2		
3050	Unpaid obligations, end of year	1		
	Memorandum (non-add) entries:			
3100	Obligated balance, start of year	6	1	
3200	Obligated balance, end of year	1		
	Budget authority and outlays, net:			
	Mandatory:			
	Outlays, gross:			
4101	Outlays from mandatory balances	3	1	
4180	Budget authority, net (total)			
4190	Outlays, net (total)	3	1	

This appropriation funds competitive grants to States to assist pregnant and parenting teens and women. Annual funding for this program expired

Departmental Management—Continued
Federal Funds—Continued

PREGNANCY ASSISTANCE FUND—Continued

at the end of FY 2019. The Budget does request an extension of this program.

SECTION 241 EVALUATION TRANSACTIONS ACCOUNT

Program and Financing (in millions of dollars)

Identification code 075–3902–0–1–552		2021 actual	2022 est.	2023 est.
	Obligations by program activity:			
0801	Section 241 Evaluation Transactions Account (Reimbursable)	541	555	633
0809	Reimbursable program activities, subtotal	541	555	633
0900	Total new obligations, unexpired accounts (object class 25.3)	541	555	633
	Budgetary resources:			
	Budget authority:			
	Spending authority from offsetting collections, discretionary:			
1700	Collected	27	555	633
1701	Change in uncollected payments, Federal sources	514		
1750	Spending auth from offsetting collections, disc (total)	541	555	633
1930	Total budgetary resources available	541	555	633
	Change in obligated balance:			
	Unpaid obligations:			
3000	Unpaid obligations, brought forward, Oct 1	936	845	793
3010	New obligations, unexpired accounts	541	555	633
3020	Outlays (gross)	–618	–607	–685
3041	Recoveries of prior year unpaid obligations, expired	–14		
3050	Unpaid obligations, end of year	845	793	741
	Uncollected payments:			
3060	Uncollected pymts, Fed sources, brought forward, Oct 1	–936	–844	–844
3070	Change in uncollected pymts, Fed sources, unexpired	–514		
3071	Change in uncollected pymts, Fed sources, expired	606		
3090	Uncollected pymts, Fed sources, end of year	–844	–844	–844
	Memorandum (non-add) entries:			
3100	Obligated balance, start of year		1	–51
3200	Obligated balance, end of year	1	–51	–103
	Budget authority and outlays, net:			
	Discretionary:			
4000	Budget authority, gross	541	555	633
	Outlays, gross:			
4010	Outlays from new discretionary authority	27	555	633
4011	Outlays from discretionary balances	591	52	52
4020	Outlays, gross (total)	618	607	685
	Offsets against gross budget authority and outlays:			
	Offsetting collections (collected) from:			
4030	Federal sources	–618	–555	–633
4040	Offsets against gross budget authority and outlays (total)	–618	–555	–633
	Additional offsets against gross budget authority only:			
4050	Change in uncollected pymts, Fed sources, unexpired	–514		
4052	Offsetting collections credited to expired accounts	591		
4060	Additional offsets against budget authority only (total)	77		
4080	Outlays, net (discretionary)		52	52
4180	Budget authority, net (total)			
4190	Outlays, net (total)		52	52

The Public Health Service (PHS) Act Evaluation Transactions account supports the execution of section 241 of the PHS Act.

PROGRAM SUPPORT CENTER

Federal Funds

RETIREMENT PAY AND MEDICAL BENEFITS FOR COMMISSIONED OFFICERS

For retirement pay and medical benefits of Public Health Service Commissioned Officers as authorized by law, for payments under the Retired Serviceman's Family Protection Plan and Survivor Benefit Plan, and for medical care of dependents and retired personnel under the Dependents' Medical Care Act, such amounts as may be required during the current fiscal year.

Note.—A full-year 2022 appropriation for this account was not enacted at the time the Budget was prepared; therefore, the Budget assumes this account is operating under the Continuing Appropriations Act, 2022 (Division A of Public Law 117–43, as amended). The amounts included for 2022 reflect the annualized level provided by the continuing resolution.

Program and Financing (in millions of dollars)

Identification code 075–0379–0–1–551		2021 actual	2022 est.	2023 est.
	Obligations by program activity:			
0001	Retirement payments	657	550	573
0002	Survivors' benefits		35	36
0003	Medical care		104	101
0900	Total new obligations, unexpired accounts	657	689	710
	Budgetary resources:			
	Budget authority:			
	Appropriations, mandatory:			
1200	Appropriation	657	689	710
1930	Total budgetary resources available	657	689	710
	Change in obligated balance:			
	Unpaid obligations:			
3000	Unpaid obligations, brought forward, Oct 1	91	84	34
3010	New obligations, unexpired accounts	657	689	710
3011	Obligations ("upward adjustments"), expired accounts	12		
3020	Outlays (gross)	–659	–739	–708
3041	Recoveries of prior year unpaid obligations, expired	–17		
3050	Unpaid obligations, end of year	84	34	36
	Memorandum (non-add) entries:			
3100	Obligated balance, start of year	91	84	34
3200	Obligated balance, end of year	84	34	36
	Budget authority and outlays, net:			
	Mandatory:			
4090	Budget authority, gross	657	689	710
	Outlays, gross:			
4100	Outlays from new mandatory authority	596	655	674
4101	Outlays from mandatory balances	63	84	34
4110	Outlays, gross (total)	659	739	708
	Offsets against gross budget authority and outlays:			
	Offsetting collections (collected) from:			
4123	Non-Federal sources	–3		
	Additional offsets against gross budget authority only:			
4142	Offsetting collections credited to expired accounts	3		
4160	Budget authority, net (mandatory)	657	689	710
4170	Outlays, net (mandatory)	656	739	708
4180	Budget authority, net (total)	657	689	710
4190	Outlays, net (total)	656	739	708

The number of beneficiaries using the Commissioned Corps system is estimated as follows:

Retirement Pay, Survivor Benefits, and Medical Benefits

	2021	2022	2023
Active Duty:			
HHS	4,394	4,814	4,845
DOJ, BOP	645	613	610
Homeland Security	548	576	563
EPA	47	47	43
All Other	341	345	331
Total Active Duty*	5975	6,395	6,392
Retirees & Survivors:			
Retirees	6,380	6,500	6,300
Retiree family members and survivors	1,120	1,100	1,100
Total Retirement Pay	7,500	7,600	7,400
Total Beneficiaries (active duty, retirees, survivors)	13,475	13,995	13,697

This activity funds annuities of retired Public Health Service (PHS) commissioned officers and survivors of retirees, and medical benefits for active duty PHS commissioned officers, retirees, and dependents of members and retirees of the PHS Commissioned Corps.

*The total active duty levels reflect base FTEs plus the supplementals.

Object Classification (in millions of dollars)

Identification code 075–0379–0–1–551		2021 actual	2022 est.	2023 est.
	Direct obligations:			
13.0	Benefits for former personnel	561	585	609

DEPARTMENT OF HEALTH AND HUMAN SERVICES

		2021 actual	2022 est.	2023 est.
25.6	Medical care	96	104	101
99.9	Total new obligations, unexpired accounts	657	689	710

HHS ACCRUAL CONTRIBUTION TO THE UNIFORMED SERVICES RETIREE HEALTH CARE FUND

Program and Financing (in millions of dollars)

Identification code 075–0170–0–1–551	2021 actual	2022 est.	2023 est.
Obligations by program activity:			
0001 Medicare eligible accruals	30	36	37
0900 Total new obligations, unexpired accounts (object class 12.2)	30	36	37
Budgetary resources:			
Budget authority:			
Appropriations, discretionary:			
1100 Appropriation	30	36	37
1900 Budget authority (total)	30	36	37
1930 Total budgetary resources available	30	36	37
Change in obligated balance:			
Unpaid obligations:			
3010 New obligations, unexpired accounts	30	36	37
3020 Outlays (gross)	–30	–36	–37
Budget authority and outlays, net:			
Discretionary:			
4000 Budget authority, gross	30	36	37
Outlays, gross:			
4010 Outlays from new discretionary authority	30	36	37
4180 Budget authority, net (total)	30	36	37
4190 Outlays, net (total)	30	36	37

The cost of medical benefits for Medicare-eligible beneficiaries is paid from the Department of Defense Medicare-Eligible Retiree Health Care Fund (10 U.S.C., ch. 56). Beginning in 2006, permanent indefinite authority is provided for a discretionary appropriation of the annual accrual payment into this fund (P.L. No. 108–375, section 725).

DEBT COLLECTION FUND

Program and Financing (in millions of dollars)

Identification code 075–5745–0–2–551	2021 actual	2022 est.	2023 est.
Obligations by program activity:			
0801 Reimbursable program activity	8	15	10
Budgetary resources:			
Unobligated balance:			
1000 Unobligated balance brought forward, Oct 1	4	5	
Budget authority:			
Spending authority from offsetting collections, discretionary:			
1700 Collected	10	10	10
1701 Change in uncollected payments, Federal sources	–1		
1750 Spending auth from offsetting collections, disc (total)	9	10	10
1930 Total budgetary resources available	13	15	10
Memorandum (non-add) entries:			
1941 Unexpired unobligated balance, end of year	5		
Change in obligated balance:			
Unpaid obligations:			
3000 Unpaid obligations, brought forward, Oct 1	5	3	9
3010 New obligations, unexpired accounts	8	15	10
3020 Outlays (gross)	–10	–9	–2
3050 Unpaid obligations, end of year	3	9	17
Uncollected payments:			
3060 Uncollected pymts, Fed sources, brought forward, Oct 1	–1		
3070 Change in uncollected pymts, Fed sources, unexpired	1		
Memorandum (non-add) entries:			
3100 Obligated balance, start of year	4	3	9
3200 Obligated balance, end of year	3	9	17

Program Support Center—Continued
Federal Funds—Continued

		2021 actual	2022 est.	2023 est.
Budget authority and outlays, net:				
Discretionary:				
4000	Budget authority, gross	9	10	10
Outlays, gross:				
4010	Outlays from new discretionary authority	6	1	1
4011	Outlays from discretionary balances	4	8	1
4020	Outlays, gross (total)	10	9	2
Offsets against gross budget authority and outlays:				
Offsetting collections (collected) from:				
4030	Federal sources	–10	–10	–10
Additional offsets against gross budget authority only:				
4050	Change in uncollected pymts, Fed sources, unexpired	1		
4080	Outlays, net (discretionary)		–1	–8
4180	Budget authority, net (total)			
4190	Outlays, net (total)		–1	–8

Object Classification (in millions of dollars)

Identification code 075–5745–0–2–551	2021 actual	2022 est.	2023 est.
11.1 Reimbursable obligations: Personnel compensation: Full-time permanent	2	2	2
11.9 Total personnel compensation	2	2	2
12.1 Civilian personnel benefits	1	1	1
25.1 Advisory and assistance services	5	12	7
99.9 Total new obligations, unexpired accounts	8	15	10

Employment Summary

Identification code 075–5745–0–2–551	2021 actual	2022 est.	2023 est.
2001 Reimbursable civilian full-time equivalent employment	18	25	25

HEALTH ACTIVITIES FUNDS

Program and Financing (in millions of dollars)

Identification code 075–9913–0–1–551	2021 actual	2022 est.	2023 est.
Budgetary resources:			
Unobligated balance:			
1000 Unobligated balance brought forward, Oct 1	1	1	1
1930 Total budgetary resources available	1	1	1
Memorandum (non-add) entries:			
1941 Unexpired unobligated balance, end of year	1	1	1
4180 Budget authority, net (total)			
4190 Outlays, net (total)			

HHS SERVICE AND SUPPLY FUND

Program and Financing (in millions of dollars)

Identification code 075–9941–0–4–551	2021 actual	2022 est.	2023 est.
Obligations by program activity:			
0801 Program Support Center	424	573	506
0802 OS activities	636	728	902
0900 Total new obligations, unexpired accounts	1,060	1,301	1,408
Budgetary resources:			
Unobligated balance:			
1000 Unobligated balance brought forward, Oct 1	198	265	1,162
1021 Recoveries of prior year unpaid obligations	117	250	250
1070 Unobligated balance (total)	315	515	1,412
Budget authority:			
Spending authority from offsetting collections, discretionary:			
1700 Collected	956	1,948	1,948
1701 Change in uncollected payments, Federal sources	54		
1750 Spending auth from offsetting collections, disc (total)	1,010	1,948	1,948
1930 Total budgetary resources available	1,325	2,463	3,360
Memorandum (non-add) entries:			
1941 Unexpired unobligated balance, end of year	265	1,162	1,952

490

Program Support Center—Continued
Federal Funds—Continued

HHS SERVICE AND SUPPLY FUND—Continued

Program and Financing—Continued

Identification code 075–9941–0–4–551	2021 actual	2022 est.	2023 est.
Change in obligated balance:			
Unpaid obligations:			
3000 Unpaid obligations, brought forward, Oct 1	788	792	546
3010 New obligations, unexpired accounts	1,060	1,301	1,408
3020 Outlays (gross)	–939	–1,297	–1,703
3040 Recoveries of prior year unpaid obligations, unexpired	–117	–250	–250
3050 Unpaid obligations, end of year	792	546	1
Uncollected payments:			
3060 Uncollected pymts, Fed sources, brought forward, Oct 1	–406	–460	–460
3070 Change in uncollected pymts, Fed sources, unexpired	–54		
3090 Uncollected pymts, Fed sources, end of year	–460	–460	–460
Memorandum (non-add) entries:			
3100 Obligated balance, start of year	382	332	86
3200 Obligated balance, end of year	332	86	–459
Budget authority and outlays, net:			
Discretionary:			
4000 Budget authority, gross	1,010	1,948	1,948
Outlays, gross:			
4010 Outlays from new discretionary authority	690	981	980
4011 Outlays from discretionary balances	249	316	723
4020 Outlays, gross (total)	939	1,297	1,703
Offsets against gross budget authority and outlays:			
Offsetting collections (collected) from:			
4030 Federal sources	–954	–1,948	–1,948
4033 Non-Federal sources	–2		
4040 Offsets against gross budget authority and outlays (total)	–956	–1,948	–1,948
Additional offsets against gross budget authority only:			
4050 Change in uncollected pymts, Fed sources, unexpired	–54		
4080 Outlays, net (discretionary)	–17	–651	–245
4180 Budget authority, net (total)			
4190 Outlays, net (total)	–17	–651	–245

The HHS Service and Supply Fund (SSF) provides a wide range of logistical and support services to components of the Department and other Federal agencies. The Program Support Center includes activities, such as personnel and payroll support, information technology, financial management operations, and administrative services, including acquisitions management, building and property management, telecommunication services, medical supplies repackaging and distribution services, and the Federal Occupational Health Service. The Office of the Secretary activities include the Service and Supply Fund Manager's Office, departmental contracts, audit resolutions, Commissioned Corps force management, web management, claims, acquisition integration and modernization, acquisition reform, small business consolidation, grants tracking, the physical security component of the Department's implementation of Homeland Security Presidential Directive 12, and commercial services management.

Most Commissioned Corps officers work for agencies in the Department of Health and Human Services and are reflected in the agencies' personnel summaries. However, some officers are assigned to other Federal agencies. The allocation account section in the following personnel summary shows officers assigned to other agencies, which are paid directly by that agency, either through an allocation account or by directly citing that agency's appropriation.

Object Classification (in millions of dollars)

Identification code 075–9941–0–4–551	2021 actual	2022 est.	2023 est.
Reimbursable obligations:			
Personnel compensation:			
11.1 Full-time permanent	118	138	177
11.3 Other than full-time permanent	4	5	6
11.5 Other personnel compensation	4	5	6
11.7 Military personnel	7	9	11
11.8 Special personal services payments	14	15	
11.9 Total personnel compensation	147	172	200
12.1 Civilian personnel benefits	42	49	61
12.2 Military personnel benefits	1	2	2
21.0 Travel and transportation of persons		4	4
22.0 Transportation of things	2	1	6
23.1 Rental payments to GSA	21	14	22
23.3 Communications, utilities, and miscellaneous charges	24	31	34
24.0 Printing and reproduction	1	3	4
25.1 Advisory and assistance services	19	30	36
25.2 Other services from non-Federal sources	339	554	480
25.3 Other goods and services from Federal sources	175	160	207
25.4 Operation and maintenance of facilities	17	7	12
25.6 Medical care	12	11	15
25.7 Operation and maintenance of equipment	194	179	216
26.0 Supplies and materials	23	25	33
31.0 Equipment	43	59	76
99.9 Total new obligations, unexpired accounts	1,060	1,301	1,408

Employment Summary

Identification code 075–9941–0–4–551	2021 actual	2022 est.	2023 est.
2001 Reimbursable civilian full-time equivalent employment	1,020	1,331	1,426
2101 Reimbursable military average strength employment	42	64	64
3101 Allocation account military average strength employment	1,534	1,534	1,504

Trust Funds

MISCELLANEOUS TRUST FUNDS

Special and Trust Fund Receipts (in millions of dollars)

Identification code 075–9971–0–7–551	2021 actual	2022 est.	2023 est.
0100 Balance, start of year		1	3
Receipts:			
Current law:			
1130 Contributions, Indian Health Facilities	3	3	3
1130 Contributions, N.I.H., Unconditional Gift Fund	5	3	3
1130 Centers for Disease Control, Gifts and Donations	21	26	26
1130 Contributions, N.I.H., Conditional Gift Fund	44	40	40
1130 Contributions to the Indian Health Service Gift Fund		1	1
1140 Interest, Miscellaneous Trust Funds	1	1	1
1199 Total current law receipts	74	74	74
1999 Total receipts	74	74	74
2000 Total: Balances and receipts	74	75	77
Appropriations:			
Current law:			
2101 Miscellaneous Trust Funds	–73	–72	–72
5099 Balance, end of year	1	3	5

Program and Financing (in millions of dollars)

Identification code 075–9971–0–7–551	2021 actual	2022 est.	2023 est.
Obligations by program activity:			
0002 Gifts	57	62	62
0003 Contributions, Indian Health Facilities	3	6	6
0900 Total new obligations, unexpired accounts	60	68	68
Budgetary resources:			
Unobligated balance:			
1000 Unobligated balance brought forward, Oct 1	185	204	216
1021 Recoveries of prior year unpaid obligations	3	8	8
1033 Recoveries of prior year paid obligations	3		
1070 Unobligated balance (total)	191	212	224
Budget authority:			
Appropriations, mandatory:			
1201 Appropriation (special or trust fund)	73	72	72
1930 Total budgetary resources available	264	284	296
Memorandum (non-add) entries:			
1941 Unexpired unobligated balance, end of year	204	216	228
Change in obligated balance:			
Unpaid obligations:			
3000 Unpaid obligations, brought forward, Oct 1	97	88	60
3010 New obligations, unexpired accounts	60	68	68
3020 Outlays (gross)	–66	–88	–84
3040 Recoveries of prior year unpaid obligations, unexpired	–3	–8	–8
3050 Unpaid obligations, end of year	88	60	36
Memorandum (non-add) entries:			
3100 Obligated balance, start of year	97	88	60

DEPARTMENT OF HEALTH AND HUMAN SERVICES

Office of the Inspector General
Federal Funds

		2021 actual	2022 est.	2023 est.
3200	Obligated balance, end of year	88	60	36
	Budget authority and outlays, net:			
	Mandatory:			
4090	Budget authority, gross	73	72	72
	Outlays, gross:			
4100	Outlays from new mandatory authority	12	26	26
4101	Outlays from mandatory balances	54	62	58
4110	Outlays, gross (total)	66	88	84
	Offsets against gross budget authority and outlays:			
	Offsetting collections (collected) from:			
4123	Non-Federal sources	−3		
	Additional offsets against gross budget authority only:			
4143	Recoveries of prior year paid obligations, unexpired accounts	3		
4160	Budget authority, net (mandatory)	73	72	72
4170	Outlays, net (mandatory)	63	88	84
4180	Budget authority, net (total)	73	72	72
4190	Outlays, net (total)	63	88	84
	Memorandum (non-add) entries:			
5000	Total investments, SOY: Federal securities: Par value	31	29	29
5001	Total investments, EOY: Federal securities: Par value	29	29	29

Gifts to the Public Health Service are for the benefit of patients and for research. Contributions are made for the construction, improvement, extension, and provision of sanitation facilities.

Object Classification (in millions of dollars)

Identification code 075–9971–0–7–551		2021 actual	2022 est.	2023 est.
	Direct obligations:			
	Personnel compensation:			
11.1	Full-time permanent	3	3	3
11.3	Other than full-time permanent	1	1	1
11.8	Special personal services payments	2	2	2
11.9	Total personnel compensation	6	6	6
12.1	Civilian personnel benefits	1	1	1
25.1	Advisory and assistance services	6	7	7
25.2	Other services from non-Federal sources	11	12	12
25.3	Other goods and services from Federal sources	5	6	6
25.5	Research and development contracts	2	2	2
25.6	Medical care	1	1	1
26.0	Supplies and materials	7	8	8
31.0	Equipment	1	1	1
41.0	Grants, subsidies, and contributions	20	24	24
99.9	Total new obligations, unexpired accounts	60	68	68

Employment Summary

Identification code 075–9971–0–7–551	2021 actual	2022 est.	2023 est.
1001 Direct civilian full-time equivalent employment	43	43	43
1101 Direct military average strength employment	2	2	2

OFFICE OF THE INSPECTOR GENERAL

Federal Funds

OFFICE OF INSPECTOR GENERAL

For expenses necessary for the Office of Inspector General, including the hire of passenger motor vehicles for investigations, in carrying out the provisions of the Inspector General Act of 1978, $106,329,000: Provided, That of such amount, necessary sums shall be available for providing protective services to the Secretary and investigating non-payment of child support cases for which non-payment is a Federal offense under 18 U.S.C. 228: Provided further, That, of the amount appropriated under this heading, $5,300,000 shall be available through September 30, 2024, for activities authorized under section 3022 of the Public Health Service Act (42 U.S.C. 300jj–52) relating to information blocking.

Note.—A full-year 2022 appropriation for this account was not enacted at the time the Budget was prepared; therefore, the Budget assumes this account is operating under the Continuing Appropriations Act, 2022 (Division A of Public Law 117–43, as amended). The amounts included for 2022 reflect the annualized level provided by the continuing resolution.

Program and Financing (in millions of dollars)

Identification code 075–0128–0–1–551		2021 actual	2022 est.	2023 est.
	Obligations by program activity:			
0001	Office of Inspector General (Direct)	90	90	90
0801	Office of Inspector General HCFAC Trust Fund	253	228	228
0802	Office of Inspector General (Direct Reimbursable)	23	21	21
0803	Office of Inspector General HCFAC Discretionary	99	101	99
0899	Total reimbursable obligations	375	350	348
0900	Total new obligations, unexpired accounts	465	440	438
	Budgetary resources:			
	Unobligated balance:			
1000	Unobligated balance brought forward, Oct 1	53	162	146
1001	Discretionary unobligated balance brought fwd, Oct 1	15		
1021	Recoveries of prior year unpaid obligations	6		
1070	Unobligated balance (total)	59	162	146
	Budget authority:			
	Appropriations, discretionary:			
1100	Appropriation	80	84	106
1121	Appropriations transferred from other acct [075–9911]	2	2	2
1121	Appropriations transferred from other acct [075–9915]	5	5	5
1160	Appropriation, discretionary (total)	87	91	113
	Advance appropriations, discretionary:			
1170	Advance appropriation			4
	Appropriations, mandatory:			
1200	Appropriation	10		
	Spending authority from offsetting collections, discretionary:			
1700	Collected	100	111	111
1701	Change in uncollected payments, Federal sources	14		
1750	Spending auth from offsetting collections, disc (total)	114	111	111
	Spending authority from offsetting collections, mandatory:			
1800	Collected	219	222	222
1801	Change in uncollected payments, Federal sources	144		
1802	Offsetting collections (previously unavailable)		1	1
1823	New and/or unobligated balance of spending authority from offsetting collections temporarily reduced		−1	−1
1850	Spending auth from offsetting collections, mand (total)	363	222	222
1900	Budget authority (total)	574	424	450
1930	Total budgetary resources available	633	586	596
	Memorandum (non-add) entries:			
1940	Unobligated balance expiring	−6		
1941	Unexpired unobligated balance, end of year	162	146	158
	Change in obligated balance:			
	Unpaid obligations:			
3000	Unpaid obligations, brought forward, Oct 1	89	105	72
3010	New obligations, unexpired accounts	465	440	438
3011	Obligations ("upward adjustments"), expired accounts	1		
3020	Outlays (gross)	−442	−473	−448
3040	Recoveries of prior year unpaid obligations, unexpired	−6		
3041	Recoveries of prior year unpaid obligations, expired	−2		
3050	Unpaid obligations, end of year	105	72	62
	Uncollected payments:			
3060	Uncollected pymts, Fed sources, brought forward, Oct 1	−93	−243	−243
3070	Change in uncollected pymts, Fed sources, unexpired	−158		
3071	Change in uncollected pymts, Fed sources, expired	8		
3090	Uncollected pymts, Fed sources, end of year	−243	−243	−243
	Memorandum (non-add) entries:			
3100	Obligated balance, start of year	−4	−138	−171
3200	Obligated balance, end of year	−138	−171	−181
	Budget authority and outlays, net:			
	Discretionary:			
4000	Budget authority, gross	201	202	228
	Outlays, gross:			
4010	Outlays from new discretionary authority	170	183	208
4011	Outlays from discretionary balances	33	18	18
4020	Outlays, gross (total)	203	201	226
	Offsets against gross budget authority and outlays:			
	Offsetting collections (collected) from:			
4030	Federal sources	−107	−111	−111
	Additional offsets against gross budget authority only:			
4050	Change in uncollected pymts, Fed sources, unexpired	−14		
4052	Offsetting collections credited to expired accounts	7		
4060	Additional offsets against budget authority only (total)	−7		
4070	Budget authority, net (discretionary)	87	91	117
4080	Outlays, net (discretionary)	96	90	115

OFFICE OF INSPECTOR GENERAL—Continued
Program and Financing—Continued

Identification code 075–0128–0–1–551	2021 actual	2022 est.	2023 est.
Mandatory:			
4090 Budget authority, gross	373	222	222
Outlays, gross:			
4100 Outlays from new mandatory authority	182	202	202
4101 Outlays from mandatory balances	57	70	20
4110 Outlays, gross (total)	239	272	222
Offsets against gross budget authority and outlays:			
Offsetting collections (collected) from:			
4120 Federal sources	–210	–221	–221
4123 Non-Federal sources	–9	–12	–12
4130 Offsets against gross budget authority and outlays (total)	–219	–233	–233
Additional offsets against gross budget authority only:			
4140 Change in uncollected pymts, Fed sources, unexpired	–144		
4142 Offsetting collections credited to expired accounts		11	11
4150 Additional offsets against budget authority only (total)	–144	11	11
4160 Budget authority, net (mandatory)	10		
4170 Outlays, net (mandatory)	20	39	–11
4180 Budget authority, net (total)	97	91	117
4190 Outlays, net (total)	116	129	104

The mission of the Office of Inspector General (OIG) is to protect the integrity of the U.S. Department of Health and Human Services (HHS) programs and the health and welfare of the people they serve. As established by the Inspector General Act of 1978, OIG is an independent and objective organization that fights fraud, waste, and abuse and promotes efficiency, economy, and effectiveness in HHS programs and operations. OIG works to ensure that Federal dollars are used appropriately and that HHS programs well serve the people that use them. OIG fulfills its mission through a broad range of audits, evaluations, investigations, and enforcement and compliance activities. In addition to discretionary appropriations, OIG receives funds through the Health Care Fraud and Abuse Control (HCFAC) account created by the Health Insurance Portability and Accountability Act of 1996.

Object Classification (in millions of dollars)

Identification code 075–0128–0–1–551	2021 actual	2022 est.	2023 est.
Direct obligations:			
Personnel compensation:			
11.1 Full-time permanent	40	40	40
11.3 Other than full-time permanent	1	1	1
11.5 Other personnel compensation	1	1	1
11.9 Total personnel compensation	42	42	42
12.1 Civilian personnel benefits	16	16	15
21.0 Travel and transportation of persons	2	2	2
22.0 Transportation of things	1	1	1
23.1 Rental payments to GSA	6	6	6
23.3 Communications, utilities, and miscellaneous charges	1	1	1
25.2 Other services from non-Federal sources	15	15	15
25.3 Other goods and services from Federal sources	2	2	2
25.4 Operation and maintenance of facilities	1	1	1
31.0 Equipment	4	4	4
99.0 Direct obligations	90	90	89
99.0 Reimbursable obligations	375	350	349
99.9 Total new obligations, unexpired accounts	465	440	438

Employment Summary

Identification code 075–0128–0–1–551	2021 actual	2022 est.	2023 est.
1001 Direct civilian full-time equivalent employment	1,624	1,599	1,638
2001 Reimbursable civilian full-time equivalent employment	10	10	10

GENERAL FUND RECEIPT ACCOUNTS
(in millions of dollars)

	2021 actual	2022 est.	2023 est.
Offsetting receipts from the public:			
075–143500 General Fund Proprietary Interest Receipts, not Otherwise Classified	203	203	203
075–267403 Consumer Operated and Oriented Plan Direct Loan Program, Downward Reestimate of Subsidies	342	36	
075–310700 Federal Share of Child Support Collections	887	699	575
075–322000 All Other General Fund Proprietary Receipts Including Budget Clearing Accounts	1,019	34	34
General Fund Offsetting receipts from the public	2,451	972	812
Intragovernmental payments:			
075–388500 Undistributed Intragovernmental Payments and Receivables from Cancelled Accounts	–10		
General Fund Intragovernmental payments	–10		

GENERAL PROVISIONS

SEC. 201. Funds appropriated in this title shall be available for not to exceed $50,000 for official reception and representation expenses when specifically approved by the Secretary.

SEC. 202. None of the funds appropriated in this title shall be used to pay the salary of an individual, through a grant or other extramural mechanism, at a rate in excess of Executive Level II: Provided, That this section shall not apply to the Head Start program.

SEC. 203. Notwithstanding section 241(a) of the PHS Act, such portion as the Secretary shall determine, but not more than 2.55 percent, of any amounts appropriated for programs authorized under such Act shall be made available for the evaluation (directly, or by grants or contracts) and the implementation and effectiveness of programs funded in this title.

(TRANSFER OF FUNDS)

SEC. 204. Not to exceed 1 percent of any discretionary funds (pursuant to the Balanced Budget and Emergency Deficit Control Act of 1985) which are appropriated for the current fiscal year for HHS in this Act may be transferred between appropriations, but no such appropriation shall be increased by more than 3 percent by any such transfer: Provided, That the transfer authority granted by this section shall not be used to create any new program or to fund any project or activity for which no funds are provided in this Act: Provided further, That the Committees on Appropriations of the House of Representatives and the Senate are notified at least 15 days in advance of any transfer.

SEC. 205. In lieu of the timeframe specified in section 338E(c)(2) of the PHS Act, terminations described in such section may occur up to 60 days after the effective date of a contract awarded in fiscal year 2023 under section 338B of such Act, or at any time if the individual who has been awarded such contract has not received funds due under the contract.

SEC. 206. None of the funds appropriated in this Act may be made available to any entity under title X of the PHS Act unless the applicant for the award certifies to the Secretary that it encourages family participation in the decision of minors to seek family planning services and that it provides counseling to minors on how to resist attempts to coerce minors into engaging in sexual activities.

SEC. 207. Notwithstanding any other provision of law, no provider of services under title X of the PHS Act shall be exempt from any State law requiring notification or the reporting of child abuse, child molestation, sexual abuse, rape, or incest.

SEC. 208. None of the funds appropriated by this Act (including funds appropriated to any trust fund) may be used to carry out the Medicare Advantage program if the Secretary denies participation in such program to an otherwise eligible entity (including a Provider Sponsored Organization) because the entity informs the Secretary that it will not provide, pay for, provide coverage of, or provide referrals for abortions: Provided, That the Secretary shall make appropriate prospective adjustments to the capitation payment to such an entity (based on an actuarially sound estimate of the expected costs of providing the service to such entity's enrollees): Provided further, That nothing in this section shall be construed to change the Medicare program's coverage for such services and a Medicare Advantage organization described in this section shall be responsible for informing enrollees where to obtain information about all Medicare covered services.

SEC. 209. None of the funds made available in this title may be used, in whole or in part, to advocate or promote gun control.

SEC. 210. In order for HHS to carry out international health activities, including HIV/AIDS and other infectious disease, chronic and environmental disease, and other health activities abroad during fiscal year 2023:

(1) The Secretary may exercise authority equivalent to that available to the Secretary of State in section 2(c) of the State Department Basic Authorities Act of 1956. The Secretary shall consult with the Secretary of State and relevant Chief of Mission to ensure that the authority provided in this section is exercised in a manner consistent with section 207 of the Foreign Service Act of 1980 and other applicable statutes administered by the Department of State.

(2) The Secretary is authorized to provide such funds by advance or reimbursement to the Secretary of State as may be necessary to pay the costs of acquisition, lease, alteration, renovation, and management of facilities outside of the United States for the use of HHS. The Department of State shall cooperate fully with the Secretary to ensure that HHS has secure, safe, functional facilities that comply with applicable regulation governing location, setback, and other facilities requirements and serve the purposes established by this Act. The Secretary is authorized, in consultation with the Secretary of State, through grant or cooperative agreement, to make available to public or nonprofit private institutions or agencies in participating foreign countries, funds to acquire, lease, alter, or renovate facilities in those countries as necessary to conduct programs of assistance for international health activities, including activities relating to HIV/AIDS and other infectious diseases, chronic and environmental diseases, and other health activities abroad.

(3) The Secretary is authorized to provide to personnel appointed or assigned by the Secretary to serve abroad, allowances and benefits similar to those provided under chapter 9 of title I of the Foreign Service Act of 1980, and 22 U.S.C. 4081 through 4086 and subject to such regulations prescribed by the Secretary. The Secretary is further authorized to provide locality-based comparability payments (stated as a percentage) up to the amount of the locality-based comparability payment (stated as a percentage) that would be payable to such personnel under section 5304 of title 5, United States Code if such personnel's official duty station were in the District of Columbia. Leaves of absence for personnel under this subsection shall be on the same basis as that provided under subchapter I of chapter 63 of title 5, United States Code, or section 903 of the Foreign Service Act of 1980, to individuals serving in the Foreign Service.

(TRANSFER OF FUNDS)

SEC. 211. The Director of the NIH, jointly with the Director of the Office of AIDS Research, may transfer up to 3 percent among institutes and centers from the total amounts identified by these two Directors as funding for research pertaining to the human immunodeficiency virus: Provided, That the Committees on Appropriations of the House of Representatives and the Senate are notified at least 15 days in advance of any transfer.

(TRANSFER OF FUNDS)

SEC. 212. Of the amounts made available in this Act for NIH, the amount for research related to the human immunodeficiency virus, as jointly determined by the Director of NIH and the Director of the Office of AIDS Research, shall be made available to the "Office of AIDS Research" account. The Director of the Office of AIDS Research shall transfer from such account amounts necessary to carry out section 2353(d)(3) of the PHS Act.

SEC. 213. (a) AUTHORITY.—Notwithstanding any other provision of law, the Director of NIH ("Director") may use funds authorized under section 402(b)(12) of the PHS Act to enter into transactions (other than contracts, cooperative agreements, or grants) to carry out research identified pursuant to or research and activities described in such section 402(b)(12).

(b) PEER REVIEW.—In entering into transactions under subsection (a), the Director may utilize such peer review procedures (including consultation with appropriate scientific experts) as the Director determines to be appropriate to obtain assessments of scientific and technical merit. Such procedures shall apply to such transactions in lieu of the peer review and advisory council review procedures that would otherwise be required under sections 301(a)(3), 405(b)(1)(B), 405(b)(2), 406(a)(3)(A), 492, and 494 of the PHS Act.

(TRANSFER OF FUNDS)

SEC. 214. Not to exceed 1 percent of funds appropriated by this Act to the offices, institutes, and centers of the National Institutes of Health may be transferred to and merged with funds appropriated under the heading "National Institutes of Health-Buildings and Facilities": Provided, That the use of such transferred funds shall be subject to a centralized prioritization and governance process: Provided further, That the Director of the National Institutes of Health shall notify the Committees on Appropriations of the House of Representatives and the Senate at least 15 days in advance of any such transfer: Provided further, That this transfer authority is in addition to any other transfer authority provided by law.

(TRANSFER OF FUNDS)

SEC. 215. Of the amounts made available for NIH, 1 percent of the amount made available for National Research Service Awards ("NRSA") shall be made available to the Administrator of the Health Resources and Services Administration to make NRSA awards for research in primary medical care to individuals affiliated with entities who have received grants or contracts under sections 736, 739, or 747 of the PHS Act, and 1 percent of the amount made available for NRSA shall be made available to the Director of the Agency for Healthcare Research and Quality to make NRSA awards for health service research.

SEC. 216. (a) The Biomedical Advanced Research and Development Authority ("BARDA") may enter into a contract, for more than one but no more than 10 program years, for purchase of research services or of security countermeasures, as that term is defined in section 319F-2(c)(1)(B) of the PHS Act (42 U.S.C. 247d–6b(c)(1)(B)), if—

(1) funds are available and obligated—

(A) for the full period of the contract or for the first fiscal year in which the contract is in effect; and

(B) for the estimated costs associated with a necessary termination of the contract; and

(2) the Secretary determines that a multi-year contract will serve the best interests of the Federal Government by encouraging full and open competition or promoting economy in administration, performance, and operation of BARDA's programs.

(b) A contract entered into under this section—

(1) shall include a termination clause as described by subsection (c) of section 3903 of title 41, United States Code; and

(2) shall be subject to the congressional notice requirement stated in subsection (d) of such section.

SEC. 217. Effective during the period beginning on November 1, 2015 and ending January 1, 2024, any provision of law that refers (including through cross-reference to another provision of law) to the current recommendations of the United States Preventive Services Task Force with respect to breast cancer screening, mammography, and prevention shall be administered by the Secretary involved as if—

(1) such reference to such current recommendations were a reference to the recommendations of such Task Force with respect to breast cancer screening, mammography, and prevention last issued before 2009; and

(2) such recommendations last issued before 2009 applied to any screening mammography modality under section 1861(jj) of the Social Security Act (42 U.S.C. 1395x(jj)).

(TRANSFER OF FUNDS)

SEC. 218. The NIH Director may transfer funds for opioid addiction, opioid alternatives, stimulant misuse and addiction, pain management, and addiction treatment to other Institutes and Centers of the NIH to be used for the same purpose 15 days after notifying the Committees on Appropriations of the House of Representatives and the Senate: Provided, That the transfer authority provided in the previous proviso is in addition to any other transfer authority provided by law.

SEC. 219. Funds appropriated in this Act that are available for salaries and expenses of employees of the Department of Health and Human Services shall also be available to pay travel and related expenses of such an employee or of a member of his or her family, when such employee is assigned to duty, in the United States or in a U.S. territory, during a period and in a location that are the subject of a determination of a public health emergency under section 319 of the Public Health Service Act and such travel is necessary to obtain medical care for an illness, injury, or medical condition that cannot be adequately addressed in that location at that time. For purposes of this section, the term "U.S. territory" means Guam, the Commonwealth of Puerto Rico, the Northern Mariana Islands, the Virgin Islands, American Samoa, or the Trust Territory of the Pacific Islands.

SEC. 220. The Department of Health and Human Services may accept donations from the private sector, nongovernmental organizations, and other groups independent of the Federal Government for the care of unaccompanied alien children (as defined in section 462(g)(2) of the Homeland Security Act of 2002 (6 U.S.C. 279(g)(2))) in the care of the Office of Refugee Resettlement of the Administration for Children and Families, including monetary donations, medical goods, and services, which may include early childhood developmental screenings, school supplies, toys, clothing, and any other items and services intended to promote the wellbeing of such children.

SEC. 221. None of the funds made available in this Act under the heading "Department of Health and Human Services—Administration for Children and Families—Refugee and Entrant Assistance" may be obligated to a grantee or contractor to house unaccompanied alien children (as such term is defined in section 462(g)(2) of the Homeland Security Act of 2002 (6 U.S.C. 279(g)(2))) in any facility that is not State-licensed for the care of unaccompanied alien children, except in the case that the Secretary determines that housing unaccompanied alien children in such a facility is necessary on a temporary basis due to an influx of such children or an emergency, provided that—

(1) the terms of the grant or contract for the operations of any such facility that remains in operation for more than six consecutive months shall require compliance with—

(A) the same requirements as licensed placements, as listed in Exhibit 1 of the Flores Settlement Agreement that the Secretary determines are applicable to non-State licensed facilities; and

(B) staffing ratios of one (1) on-duty Youth Care Worker for every eight (8) children or youth during waking hours, one (1) on-duty Youth Care Worker for every sixteen (16) children or youth during sleeping hours, and clinician ratios to children (including mental health providers) as required in grantee cooperative agreements;

(2) the Secretary may grant a 60-day waiver for a contractor's or grantee's non-compliance with paragraph (1) if the Secretary certifies and provides a report to Congress on the contractor's or grantee's good-faith efforts and progress towards compliance;

(3) not more than four consecutive waivers under paragraph (2) may be granted to a contractor or grantee with respect to a specific facility;

(4) ORR shall ensure full adherence to the monitoring requirements set forth in section 5.5 of its Policies and Procedures Guide as of May 15, 2019;

(5) for any such unlicensed facility in operation for more than three consecutive months, ORR shall conduct a minimum of one comprehensive monitoring visit during the first three months of operation, with quarterly monitoring visits thereafter; and

(6) not later than 60 days after the date of enactment of this Act, ORR shall brief the Committees on Appropriations of the House of Representatives and the Senate outlining the requirements of ORR for influx facilities including any requirement listed in paragraph (1)(A) that the Secretary has determined are not applicable to non-State licensed facilities.

SEC. 222. In addition to the existing Congressional notification for formal site assessments of potential influx facilities, the Secretary shall notify the Committees on Appropriations of the House of Representatives and the Senate at least 15 days before operationalizing an unlicensed facility, and shall (1) specify whether the facility is hard-sided or soft-sided, and (2) provide analysis that indicates that, in the absence of the influx facility, the likely outcome is that unaccompanied alien children will remain in the custody of the Department of Homeland Security for longer than 72 hours or that unaccompanied alien children will be otherwise placed in danger. Within 60 days of bringing such a facility online, and monthly thereafter, the Secretary shall provide to the Committees on Appropriations of the House of Representatives and the Senate a report detailing the total number of children in care at the facility, the average length of stay and average length of care of children at the facility, and, for any child that has been at the facility for more than 60 days, their length of stay and reason for delay in release.

SEC. 223. None of the funds made available in this Act may be used to prevent a United States Senator or Member of the House of Representatives from entering, for the purpose of conducting oversight, any facility in the United States used for the purpose of maintaining custody of, or otherwise housing, unaccompanied alien children (as defined in section 462(g)(2) of the Homeland Security Act of 2002 (6 U.S.C. 279(g)(2))), provided that such Senator or Member has coordinated the oversight visit with the Office of Refugee Resettlement not less than two business days in advance to ensure that such visit would not interfere with the operations (including child welfare and child safety operations) of such facility.

SEC. 224. Funds appropriated in this Act that are available for salaries and expenses of employees of the Centers for Disease Control and Prevention shall also be available for the primary and secondary schooling of eligible dependents of personnel stationed in a U.S. territory as defined in section 219 of this Act at costs not in excess of those paid for or reimbursed by the Department of Defense.

(CANCELLATION)

SEC. 225. Of the unobligated balances in the "Nonrecurring Expenses Fund" established in section 223 of division G of Public Law 110–161, $500,000,000 are hereby permanently cancelled not later than September 30, 2023.

SEC. 226. For purposes of any transfer to appropriations under the heading "Department of Health and Human Services—Office of the Secretary—Public Health and Social Services Emergency Fund", section 204 of this Act shall be applied by substituting "10 percent" for "3 percent".

SEC. 227. For fiscal year 2023, the notification requirements described in sections 1804(a) and 1851(d) of the Social Security Act may be fulfilled by the Secretary in a manner similar to that described in paragraphs (1) and (2) of section 1806(c) of such Act.

SEC. 228.

Section 340B of the Public Health Service Act (42 U.S.C. 256b) is amended
(a) in subsection (a)(5)(C)—

(1) by striking "A covered entity shall permit" and inserting "(i) DUPLICATE DISCOUNTS AND DRUG RESALE. A covered entity shall permit"; and

(2) by inserting at the end the following:

"(ii) USE OF SAVINGS. A covered entity shall permit the Secretary to audit, at the Secretary's expense, the records of the entity to determine how net income from purchases under this section are used by the covered entity."

"(iii) RECORDS RETENTION. Covered entities shall retain such records and provide such records and reports as deemed necessary by the Secretary for carrying out this subparagraph.".

(b) by adding at the end the following new subsection:

"(f) REGULATIONS. The Secretary may promulgate such regulations as the Secretary determines appropriate to carry out the provisions of this section.".

(INCLUDING TRANSFER OF FUNDS)

SEC. 229. (a) The Secretary may reserve not more than 0.25 percent from each appropriation made in this Act to the accounts of the Administration for Children and Families identified in subsection (b) in order to administer and carry out evaluations of any of the programs or activities that are funded under such accounts. Funds reserved under this section may be transferred to the "Children and Families Services Programs" account for use by the Assistant Secretary for the Administration for Children and Families and shall remain available until expended: Provided, That funds reserved under this section shall not be available for obligation unless the Assistant Secretary submits a plan to the Committees on Appropriations of the House of Representatives and the Senate describing the evaluations to be carried out 15 days in advance of any such transfer.

(b) The accounts referred to in subsection (a) are: "Low Income Home Energy Assistance", "Refugee and Entrant Assistance", "Payments to States for the Child Care and Development Block Grant", and "Children and Families Services Programs".

SEC. 230. (a) PREMIUM PAY AUTHORITY. If services performed by a Department of Health and Human Services employee during a public health emergency declared under section 319 of the Public Health Service Act are determined by the Secretary of Health and Human Services to be primarily related to preparation for, prevention of, or response to such public health emergency, any premium pay that is provided for such services shall be exempted from the aggregate of basic pay and premium pay calculated under section 5547(a) of title 5, United States Code, and any other provision of law limiting the aggregate amount of premium pay payable on a biweekly or calendar year basis.

(b) OVERTIME AUTHORITY. Any overtime that is provided for such services described in subsection (a) shall be exempted from any annual limit on the amount of overtime payable in a calendar or fiscal year.

(c) APPLICABILITY OF AGGREGATE LIMITATION ON PAY. In determining, for purposes of section 5307 of title 5, United States Code, whether an employee's total pay exceeds the annual rate payable under such section, the Secretary of Health and Human Services shall not include pay exempted under this section.

(d) LIMITATION OF PAY AUTHORITY. Pay exempted from otherwise applicable limits under subsection (a) shall not cause the aggregate pay earned for the calendar year in which the exempted pay is earned to exceed the rate of basic pay payable for a position at level II of the Executive Schedule under section 5313 of title 5, United States Code.

(e) DANGER PAY FOR SERVICE IN PUBLIC HEALTH EMERGENCIES. The Secretary of Health and Human Services may grant a danger pay allowance under section 5928 of title 5, United States Code, without regard to the conditions of the first sentence of such section, for work that is performed by a Department of Health and Human Services employee during a public health emergency declared under section 319 of the Public Health Service Act that the Secretary determines is primarily related to preparation for, prevention of, or response to such public health emergency and is performed under conditions that threaten physical harm or imminent danger to the health or well-being of the employee.

(f) EFFECTIVE DATE. This section shall take effect as if enacted on September 30, 2021.

SEC. 231. Section 2813 of the Public Health Service Act (42 U.S.C. 300hh–15) is amended—

(1) by redesignating subsection (i) as subsection (j); and

(2) by inserting after subsection (h) the following new subsection:

"(i) TORT CLAIMS AND WORK INJURY COMPENSATION COVERAGE FOR CORPS VOLUNTEERS.—

"(1) IN GENERAL. If under section 223 and regulations pursuant to such section; and through an agreement entered into in accordance with such regulations, the Secretary accepts, from an individual in the Corps, services for a specified period that are volunteer and without compensation other than reasonable reimbursement or allowance for expenses actually incurred, such individual shall, during such period, have the coverages described in paragraphs (2) and (3).

"(2) FEDERAL TORT CLAIMS ACT COVERAGE. Such individual shall, while performing such services during such period—

"(A) be deemed to be an employee of the Department of Health and Human Services, for purposes of claims under sections 1346(b) and 2672 of title 28, United States Code, for money damages for personal injury, including death, resulting from performance of functions under such agreement; and

"(B) be deemed to be an employee of the Public Health Service performing medical, surgical, dental, or related functions, for purposes of having the remedy provided by such sections of title 28 be exclusive of any other civil action or proceeding by reason of the same subject matter against such individual or against the estate of such individual.

"(3) COMPENSATION FOR WORK INJURIES. Such individual shall, while performing such services during such period, be deemed to be an employee of the Department of Health and Human Services, and an injury sustained by such an individual shall be deemed 'in the performance of duty', for purposes of chapter 81 of title 5, United States Code, pertaining to compensation for work injuries.".

SEC. 232. Notwithstanding any other provision of law, the Secretary of Health and Human Services may use $5,000,000 of the amounts appropriated under the heading "Department of Health and Human Services—Office of the Secretary—General Departmental Management" to supplement funds otherwise available to the Secretary for the hire and purchase of zero emission passenger motor vehicles and supporting charging or fueling infrastructure, and to cover other costs related to electrifying the motor vehicle fleet within HHS: Provided, That supporting charging or fueling infrastructure installed in a parking area with such funds shall be deemed personal property under the control and custody of the component of the Department of Health and Human Services managing such parking area.

SEC. 233. Section 402A(d) of the Public Health Service Act (42 U.S.C. 282a(d)) is amended—

(1) in the first sentence by striking "under subsection (a)" and inserting "to carry out this title"; and

(2) in the second sentence by striking "account under subsection (a)(1)".

SEC. 234. The Secretary of Health and Human Services may waive penalties and administrative requirements in title XXVI of the Public Health Service Act for awards under such title from amounts provided under the heading "Department of Health and Human Services—Health Resources and Services Administration" in this or any other appropriations Act for this fiscal year, including amounts made available to such heading by transfer.

SEC. 235. None of the funds made available by this Act from the Federal Hospital Insurance Trust Fund or the Federal Supplemental Medical Insurance Trust Fund, or transferred from other accounts funded by this Act to the "Centers for Medicare and Medicaid Services—Program Management" account, may be used for payments under section 1342(b)(1) of Public Law 111–148 (relating to risk corridors).

SEC. 236. (a) Amounts made available to the Department of Health and Human Services in this or any other Act under the heading "Administration for Children and Families—Refugee and Entrant Assistance" may in this fiscal year and hereafter be used to provide, including through grants, contracts, or cooperative agreements, mental health and other supportive services, including access to legal services, to children, parents, and legal guardians who were separated at the United States-Mexico border between January 20, 2017, and January 20, 2021: Provided, That such services shall also be available to immediate family members of such individuals if such family members are in the United States and in the same household: Provided further, That amounts made available to the Department of Health and Human Services for refugee and entrant assistance activities in any other provision of law may be used to carry out the purposes of this section: Provided further, That the Secretary of Health and Human Services may identify the children, parents, and legal guardians eligible to receive mental health and other supportive services described under this section through reference to the identified members of the classes, and their minor children, in the class-action lawsuits Ms. J.P. v. Barr and Ms. L. v. ICE; Provided further, the Secretary has sole discretion to identify the individuals who will receive services under this section due to their status as immediate family members residing in the same household of class members or class members' minor children, and such identification shall not be subject to judicial review.

(b) Notwithstanding any other provision of law, in this fiscal year and hereafter, individuals identified in subsection (a), including immediate family members of such individuals residing in the same household if such immediate family members are identified by the Secretary in accordance with such subsection, shall be eligible for resettlement assistance, entitlement programs, and other benefits available to refugees admitted under section 207 of the Immigration and Nationality Act (8 U.S.C. 1157) to the same extent, and for the same periods of time, as such refugees.

SEC. 237. During this fiscal year, an Operating or Staff Division in HHS may enter into a reimbursable agreement with another major organizational unit within HHS or of another agency under which the ordering agency or unit delegates to the servicing agency or unit the authority and funding to issue a grant or cooperative agreement on its behalf: Provided, That the head of the ordering agency or unit must certify that amounts are available and that the order is in the best interests of the United States Government: Provided further, That funding may be provided by way of advance or reimbursement, as deemed appropriate by the ordering agency or unit, with proper adjustments of estimated amounts provided in advance to be made based on actual costs: Provided further, That an agreement made under this section obligates an appropriation of the ordering agency or unit, including for costs to administer such grant or cooperative agreement, and such obligation shall be deemed to be an obligation for any purpose of law: Provided further, That an agreement made under this section may be performed for a period that extends beyond the current fiscal year.

SEC. 238. Section 317G of the Public Health Service Act (42 U.S.C. 247b–8) is amended by adding at the end the following: "The Secretary may, no later than 120 days after the end of an individual's participation in such a fellowship or training program, and without regard to any provision in title 5 of the United State Code governing appointments in the competitive service, appoint a participant in such a fellowship or training program to a term or permanent position in the Centers for Disease Control and Prevention.".

SEC. 239. In the event of a public health emergency declared by the Secretary of Health and Human Services under section 319 of the Public Health Service Act, or where the Secretary determines that there is a significant potential for such an emergency to exist that will affect national security or the health and security of United States citizens domestically or internationally, the Director of the Centers for Disease Control and Prevention may enter into transactions other than contracts, grants, and cooperative agreements that are directly related to preparing for or responding to such emergency or potential emergency.

SEC. 240. (a) The Public Health Service Act (42 U.S.C. 201 et seq.), the Controlled Substances Act (21 U.S.C. 801 et seq.), the Comprehensive Smoking Education Act (15 U.S.C. 1331 et seq.), the Comprehensive Addiction and Recovery Act of 2016 (Public Law 114–198), the Drug Abuse Prevention, Treatment, and Rehabilitation Act (21 U.S.C. 1101 et seq.), the Omnibus Crime Control and Safe Streets Act of 1968 (34 U.S.C. 10101 et seq.), and title 5 of the United States Code are each amended—

(1) by striking "National Institute on Drug Abuse" each place it appears and inserting "National Institute on Drugs and Addiction"; and

(2) by striking "National Advisory Council on Drug Abuse" each place it appears and inserting "National Advisory Council on Drugs and Addiction".

(b) Title IV of the Public Health Service Act (42 U.S.C. 281 et seq.) is amended—

(1) in section 464H(b)(5), by striking "National Institute of Drug Abuse" and inserting "National Institute on Drugs and Addiction";

(2) in sections 464L, 464M(a), 464O, and 494A, by striking "drug abuse" each place it appears and inserting "drug use";

(3) in section 464L(a), by striking "treatment of drug abusers" and inserting "treatment of drug addiction";

(4) in section 464M(a), by striking "prevention of such abuse" and inserting "prevention of such use";

(5) in section 464N—

(A) in the section heading, by striking "DRUG ABUSE RESEARCH CENTERS" and inserting "DRUGS AND ADDICTION RESEARCH CENTERS";

(B) in subsection (a)—

(i) in matter preceding paragraph (1), by striking "National Drug Abuse Research Centers" and inserting "National Drugs and Addiction Research Centers"; and

(ii) in paragraph (1)(C), by striking "treatment of drug abuse" and inserting "treatment of drug addiction"; and

(C) in subsection (c)—

(i) by striking "DRUG ABUSE AND ADDICTION RESEARCH" and inserting "DRUGS AND ADDICTION RESEARCH CENTERS";

(ii) in paragraph (1), by striking "National Drug Abuse Treatment Clinical Trials Network" and inserting "National Drug Addiction Treatment Clinical Trials Network"; and

(iii) in paragraph (2)(H), by striking "reasons that individuals abuse drugs, or refrain from abusing drugs" and inserting "reasons that individuals use drugs or refrain from using drugs"; and

(6) in section 464P—

(A) in subsection (a)—

(i) in paragraph (1), by striking "drug abuse treatments" and inserting "drug addiction treatments"; and

(ii) in paragraph (6), by striking "treatment of drug abuse" and inserting "treatment of drug addiction"; and

(B) in subsection (d)—

(i) by striking "disease of drug abuse" and inserting "disease of drug addiction";

(ii) by striking "abused drugs" each place it appears and inserting "addictive drugs"; and

(iii) by striking "drugs of abuse" and inserting "drugs of addiction".

(c) Section 464N of the Public Health Service Act (42 U.S.C. 285o–2), as amended by subsection (b)(5), is further amended by striking "drug abuse" each place it appears and inserting "drug use".

(d) Any reference in any law, regulation, map, document, paper, or other record of the United States to the National Institute on Drug Abuse shall be considered to be a reference to the National Institute on Drugs and Addiction.

SEC. 241. (a) The Public Health Service Act (42 U.S.C. 201 et seq.) and the Comprehensive Alcohol Abuse and Alcoholism Prevention, Treatment, and Rehabilitation Act of 1970 (42 U.S.C. 4541 et seq.) are each amended—

(1) by striking "National Institute on Alcohol Abuse and Alcoholism" each place it appears and inserting "National Institute on Alcohol Effects and Alcohol-Associated Disorders"; and

(2) by striking "National Advisory Council on Alcohol Abuse and Alcoholism" each place it appears and inserting "National Advisory Council on Alcohol Effects and Alcohol-Associated Disorders".

(b) Title IV of the Public Health Service Act (42 U.S.C. 281 et seq.) is amended—

(1) in section 464H—

(A) in subsection (a)—

(i) by striking "prevention of alcohol abuse" and inserting "prevention of alcohol misuse"; and

(ii) by striking "treatment of alcoholism" and inserting "treatment of alcohol-associated disorders"; and

(B) in subsection (b)—

(i) in paragraph (3)—

(I) in subparagraph (A), by striking "alcohol abuse and domestic violence" and inserting "alcohol misuse and domestic violence";

(II) in subparagraph (D), by striking "abuse of alcohol" and inserting "misuse of alcohol";

(III) by striking subparagraph (E) and inserting "(E) the effect of social pressures, legal requirements regarding the use of alcoholic beverages, the cost of such beverages, and the economic status and education of users of such beverages on the incidence of alcohol misuse, alcohol use disorder, and other alcohol-associated disorders,"; and

(ii) in paragraph (5), by striking "impact of alcohol abuse" and inserting "impact of alcohol misuse";

(2) in sections 464H(b), 464I, and 494A, by striking "alcohol abuse and alcoholism" each place it appears and inserting "alcohol misuse, alcohol use disorder, and other alcohol-associated disorders";

(3) in sections 464H(b) and 464J(a), by striking "alcoholism and alcohol abuse" each place it appears and inserting "alcohol misuse, alcohol use disorder, and other alcohol-associated disorders"; and

(4) in section 464J(a)—

(A) by striking "alcoholism and other alcohol problems" each place it appears and inserting "alcohol misuse, alcohol use disorder, and other alcohol-associated disorders";

(B) in the matter preceding paragraph (1), by striking "interdisciplinary research related to alcoholism" and inserting "interdisciplinary research related to alcohol-associated disorders"; and

(C) in paragraph (1)(E), by striking "alcohol problems" each place it appears and inserting "alcohol misuse, alcohol use disorder, and other alcohol-associated disorders".

(c) Any reference in any law, regulation, map, document, paper, or other record of the United States to the National Institute on Alcohol Abuse and Alcoholism shall be considered to be a reference to the National Institute on Alcohol Effects and Alcohol-Associated Disorders.

SEC. 242. (a) The Public Health Service Act (42 U.S.C. 201 et seq.) is amended—

(1) by striking "Substance Abuse and Mental Health Services Administration" each place it appears and inserting "Substance Use And Mental Health Services Administration";

(2) by striking "Center for Substance Abuse Treatment" each place it appears and inserting "Center for Substance Use Services"; and

(3) by striking "Center for Substance Abuse Prevention" each place it appears and inserting "Center for Substance Use Prevention Services".

(b) Title V of the Public Health Service Act (42 U.S.C. 290aa et seq.) is amended—

(1) in the title heading, by striking "SUBSTANCE ABUSE AND MENTAL HEALTH SERVICES ADMINISTRATION" and inserting "SUBSTANCE USE AND MENTAL HEALTH SERVICES ADMINISTRATION";

(2) in section 501—

(A) in the section heading, by striking "SUBSTANCE ABUSE AND MENTAL HEALTH SERVICES ADMINISTRATION" and inserting "SUBSTANCE USE AND MENTAL HEALTH SERVICES ADMINISTRATION"; and

(B) in subsection (a), by striking "(hereafter referred to in this title as the Administration)" and inserting "(hereafter referred to in this title as SAMHSA or the Administration)";

(3) in section 507, in the section heading, by striking "CENTER FOR SUBSTANCE ABUSE TREATMENT" and inserting "CENTER FOR SUBSTANCE USE SERVICES";

(4) in section 513(a), in the subsection heading, by striking "CENTER FOR SUBSTANCE ABUSE TREATMENT" and inserting "CENTER FOR SUBSTANCE USE SERVICES"; and

(5) in section 515, in the section heading, by striking "CENTER FOR SUBSTANCE ABUSE PREVENTION" and inserting "CENTER FOR SUBSTANCE USE PREVENTION SERVICES".

(c) Section 1932(b)(3) of the Public Health Service Act (42 U.S.C. 300x–32(b)(3)) is amended in the paragraph heading by striking "CENTER FOR SUBSTANCE ABUSE PREVENTION" and inserting "CENTER FOR SUBSTANCE USE PREVENTION SERVICES".

(d) Section 1935(b)(2) of the Public Health Service Act (42 U.S.C. 300x–35(b)(2)) is amended in the paragraph heading by striking "CENTER FOR SUBSTANCE ABUSE PREVENTION" and inserting "CENTER FOR SUBSTANCE USE PREVENTION SERVICES".

(e) The Indian Alcohol and Substance Abuse Prevention and Treatment Act of 1986 (25 U.S.C. 2401 et seq.) is amended by striking "Substance Abuse and Mental Health Services Administration" each place it appears and inserting "Substance use And Mental Health Services Administration".

(f) The Social Security Act is amended in sections 1861, 1866F, and 1945 (42 U.S.C. 1395x, 1395cc–6, 1396w–4) by striking "Substance Abuse and Mental Health Services Administration" each place it appears and inserting "Substance use And Mental Health Services Administration".

(g) Section 105(a)(7)(C)(i)(III) of the Child Abuse Prevention and Treatment Act (42 U.S.C. 5106a(7)(C)(i)(III)) is amended by striking "Substance Abuse and Mental Health Services Administration" and inserting "Substance use And Mental Health Services Administration".

(h)

(1) Except as provided in paragraph (2), any reference in any law, regulation, map, document, paper, or other record of the United States to the Substance Abuse and Mental Health Services Administration, the Center for Substance Abuse Treatment of such Administration, or the Center for Substance Abuse Prevention of such Administration shall be considered to be a reference to the Substance use And Mental Health Services Administration, the Center for Substance Use Services of such Administration, or the Center for Substance Use Prevention Services of such Administration, respectively.

(2) Paragraph (1) shall not be construed to alter or affect section 6001(d) of the 21st Century Cures Act (42 U.S.C. 290aa note), providing that a reference to the Administrator of the Substance Abuse and Mental Health Services Administration shall be construed to be a reference to the Assistant Secretary for Mental Health and Substance Use.

GENERAL PROVISION—THIS TITLE

〖SEC. 2301. (a) Not later than 45 days after the date of enactment of this Act, the Secretary of Health and Human Services, the Secretary of State, and the Secretary of Homeland Security shall jointly submit a strategy on Afghan evacuee resettlement to the appropriate congressional committees and leadership describing agency roles and responsibilities, vetting, immigration status of each Afghan, and anticipated costs associated with implementing such strategy.

(b) DEFINITION OF AFGHAN EVACUEE.—In this section, the term "Afghan evacuee" means a person whose evacuation from Afghanistan to the United States, or a location overseas controlled by the United States, was facilitated by the United States as part of Operation Allies Refuge.〗

(Afghanistan Supplemental Appropriations Act, 2022.)

DEPARTMENT OF HOMELAND SECURITY

The Department of Homeland Security's (DHS) mission is to safeguard the American people, our homeland, and our values with honor and integrity. Threats to our safety and security are constantly evolving and require continuous risk assessments and adaptive strategies to effectively address them. The men and women at DHS demonstrate agility and dedication to our mission by protecting our Nation from threats by land, sea, air, and cyber.

As in the 2022 President's Budget, the 2023 President's Budget continues the proposed reorganization of the United States Coast Guard's (USCG) Program, Project, and Activity (PPA) structure. In May 2017, Congress passed the Consolidated Appropriations Act, 2017 reorganizing DHS's appropriations and PPAs into the DHS Common Appropriations Structure (CAS). While USCG adopted the new CAS appropriations, it maintained a Legacy PPA structure. The 2022 President's Budget reorganizes the PPA structure to fully transition USCG to a CAS-aligned PPA structure.

OFFICE OF THE SECRETARY AND EXECUTIVE MANAGEMENT

Federal Funds

OPERATIONS AND SUPPORT

For necessary expenses of the Office of the Secretary and for executive management for operations and support, $291,180,000; of which $3,048,000, to remain available until September 30, 2024, shall be for the Medical Information Exchange: Provided, That not to exceed $30,000 shall be for official reception and representation expenses.

Note.—A full-year 2022 appropriation for this account was not enacted at the time the Budget was prepared; therefore, the Budget assumes this account is operating under the Continuing Appropriations Act, 2022 (Division A of Public Law 117–43, as amended). The amounts included for 2022 reflect the annualized level provided by the continuing resolution.

OPERATIONS AND SUPPORT

[For an additional amount for "Operations and Support", $147,456,000, to remain available until September 30, 2022, for necessary expenses in support of Operation Allies Welcome, including the provision of staffing and support services for Safe Havens: *Provided*, That amounts provided under this heading in this Act may be transferred by the Secretary of Homeland Security to other appropriations in the Department of Homeland Security only for necessary expenses of Operation Allies Welcome and not for any other purpose: *Provided further*, That amounts made available under this heading in this Act shall be available in addition to any other appropriations available for the same purpose, including appropriations available pursuant to the authority of section 506(a)(2) of the Foreign Assistance Act of 1961: *Provided further*, That, beginning not later than January 31, 2022, the Office of the Secretary shall report monthly to the Committees on Appropriations of the Senate and the House of Representatives on the use of transfer authority provided under this heading in this Act.] *(Additional Afghanistan Supplemental Appropriations Act, 2022.)*

Program and Financing (in millions of dollars)

Identification code 070–0100–0–1–751		2021 actual	2022 est.	2023 est.
Obligations by program activity:				
0011	Operations and Engagement	73	75	81
0012	Strategy, Policy, and Plans	51	51	74
0013	Management and Oversight	65	55	136
0014	Afghanistan Supplemental Appropriations Act		147	
0100	Subtotal, Direct Programs	189	328	291
0799	Total direct obligations	189	328	291
0882	CAS - OSEM O&S Reimbursable program activity	15	25	23
0889	Reimbursable program activities, subtotal	15	25	23
0900	Total new obligations, unexpired accounts	204	353	314
Budgetary resources:				
Unobligated balance:				
1000	Unobligated balance brought forward, Oct 1	6	7	7
1012	Unobligated balance transfers between expired and unexpired accounts	1		
1070	Unobligated balance (total)	7	7	7
Budget authority:				
Appropriations, discretionary:				
1100	Appropriation - CAS OSEM	181	181	291
1100	Appropriation - OAW		147	
1121	Appropriations transferred from other acct [070–0550]	8		
1121	Appropriations transferred from other acct [070–0112]	1		
1131	Unobligated balance of appropriations permanently reduced	–1		
1160	Appropriation, discretionary (total)	189	328	291
Spending authority from offsetting collections, discretionary:				
1700	Collected - CAS - OSEM O&S	10	25	21
1701	Change in uncollected payments, Federal sources	5		
1750	Spending auth from offsetting collections, disc (total)	15	25	21
1900	Budget authority (total)	204	353	312
1930	Total budgetary resources available	211	360	319
Memorandum (non-add) entries:				
1941	Unexpired unobligated balance, end of year	7	7	5
Change in obligated balance:				
Unpaid obligations:				
3000	Unpaid obligations, brought forward, Oct 1	78	92	86
3010	New obligations, unexpired accounts	204	353	314
3011	Obligations ("upward adjustments"), expired accounts	2		
3020	Outlays (gross)	–186	–359	–313
3041	Recoveries of prior year unpaid obligations, expired	–6		
3050	Unpaid obligations, end of year	92	86	87
Uncollected payments:				
3060	Uncollected pymts, Fed sources, brought forward, Oct 1	–10	–6	–6
3070	Change in uncollected pymts, Fed sources, unexpired	–5		
3071	Change in uncollected pymts, Fed sources, expired	9		
3090	Uncollected pymts, Fed sources, end of year	–6	–6	–6
Memorandum (non-add) entries:				
3100	Obligated balance, start of year	68	86	80
3200	Obligated balance, end of year	86	80	81
Budget authority and outlays, net:				
Discretionary:				
4000	Budget authority, gross	204	353	312
Outlays, gross:				
4010	Outlays from new discretionary authority	132	289	239
4011	Outlays from discretionary balances	54	70	74
4020	Outlays, gross (total)	186	359	313
Offsets against gross budget authority and outlays:				
Offsetting collections (collected) from:				
4030	Federal sources	–18	–25	–21
4040	Offsets against gross budget authority and outlays (total)	–18	–25	–21
Additional offsets against gross budget authority only:				
4050	Change in uncollected pymts, Fed sources, unexpired	–5		
4052	Offsetting collections credited to expired accounts	8		
4060	Additional offsets against budget authority only (total)	3		
4070	Budget authority, net (discretionary)	189	328	291
4080	Outlays, net (discretionary)	168	334	292
4180	Budget authority, net (total)	189	328	291
4190	Outlays, net (total)	168	334	292

The Office of the Secretary and Executive Management directs and leads management of the Department and provides policy guidance to operating bureaus within the organization; plans and executes departmental strategies to accomplish agency objectives and provides central leadership to the Department. Offices supported by resources from this appropriation include: the Office of the Secretary; the Office of Strategy, Policy, and Plans; the Office of Public Affairs; the Office of Legislative Affairs; the Office of the General Counsel; the Office of Health Security and Resilience; the Office for Civil Rights and Civil Liberties; the Office of the Citizenship and Immigration Services Ombudsman; the Office of the Immigration Detention Ombudsman; the Privacy Office; and the Office of Partnership and Engagement.

The Operations and Support appropriation funds support the costs incurred for the day-to-day operation and maintenance of the organization, including,

498   Office of the Secretary and Executive Management—Continued
Federal Funds—Continued
                                                                         THE BUDGET FOR FISCAL YEAR 2023

OPERATIONS AND SUPPORT—Continued

but not limited to, salaries, services, supplies, utilities, travel, training, and transportation, as well as minor procurement, construction, and improvement projects.

Object Classification (in millions of dollars)

Identification code 070–0100–0–1–751		2021 actual	2022 est.	2023 est.
	Direct obligations:			
	Personnel compensation:			
11.1	Full-time permanent	75	81	133
11.3	Other than full-time permanent	8	5	3
11.5	Other personnel compensation	3	1	....
11.8	Special personal services payments	....	1	3
11.9	Total personnel compensation	86	88	139
12.1	Civilian personnel benefits	28	29	44
21.0	Travel and transportation of persons	3	5	12
23.1	Rental payments to GSA	....	2	1
25.1	Advisory and assistance services	45	28	45
25.2	Other services from non-Federal sources	16	13	15
25.3	Other goods and services from Federal sources	6	161	32
25.4	Operation and maintenance of facilities	3	....	....
25.7	Operation and maintenance of equipment	....	....	1
26.0	Supplies and materials	1	1	1
31.0	Equipment	1	1	1
99.0	Direct obligations	189	328	291
99.0	Reimbursable obligations	15	25	23
99.9	Total new obligations, unexpired accounts	204	353	314

Employment Summary

Identification code 070–0100–0–1–751	2021 actual	2022 est.	2023 est.
1001 Direct civilian full-time equivalent employment	591	763	915
2001 Reimbursable civilian full-time equivalent employment	43	67	67

FEDERAL ASSISTANCE

(INCLUDING TRANSFERS OF FUNDS)

For necessary expenses of the Office of the Secretary and for executive management for Federal assistance through grants, contracts, cooperative agreements, and other activities, $25,000,000, which shall be transferred to the Federal Emergency Management Agency, of which $20,000,000 shall be for targeted violence and terrorism prevention grants and of which $5,000,000 shall be for an Alternatives to Detention Case Management pilot program, to remain available until September 30, 2024: Provided, That the amounts made available for the pilot program shall be awarded to nonprofit organizations and local governments and administered by a National Board, which shall be chaired by the Officer for Civil Rights and Civil Liberties, for the purposes of providing case management services, including but not limited to: mental health services; human and sex trafficking screening; legal orientation programs; cultural orientation programs; connections to social services; and for individuals who will be removed, reintegration services: Provided further, That such services shall be provided to each individual enrolled into the U.S. Immigration and Customs Enforcement Alternatives to Detention program in the geographic areas served by the pilot program: Provided further, That any such individual may opt out of receiving such services after providing written informed consent: Provided further, That not to exceed $350,000 shall be for the administrative costs of the Department of Homeland Security for the pilot program.

Note.—A full-year 2022 appropriation for this account was not enacted at the time the Budget was prepared; therefore, the Budget assumes this account is operating under the Continuing Appropriations Act, 2022 (Division A of Public Law 117–43, as amended). The amounts included for 2022 reflect the annualized level provided by the continuing resolution.

Program and Financing (in millions of dollars)

Identification code 070–0416–0–1–751	2021 actual	2022 est.	2023 est.
Budgetary resources:			
Budget authority:			
Appropriations, discretionary:			
1100 Appropriation	25	25	25
1120 Appropriations transferred to other acct [070–0413]	–25	–25	–25
4180 Budget authority, net (total)	....	....	....
4190 Outlays, net (total)	....	....	....

Trust Funds

GIFTS AND DONATIONS

Program and Financing (in millions of dollars)

Identification code 070–8244–0–7–453	2021 actual	2022 est.	2023 est.
Obligations by program activity:			
0001 Direct program activity	1	....	....
0900 Total new obligations, unexpired accounts (object class 25.3)	1	....	....
Budgetary resources:			
Unobligated balance:			
1000 Unobligated balance brought forward, Oct 1	4	3	3
1930 Total budgetary resources available	4	3	3
Memorandum (non-add) entries:			
1941 Unexpired unobligated balance, end of year	3	3	3
Change in obligated balance:			
Unpaid obligations:			
3000 Unpaid obligations, brought forward, Oct 1	90	42	17
3010 New obligations, unexpired accounts	1	....	....
3020 Outlays (gross)	–49	–25	–5
3050 Unpaid obligations, end of year	42	17	12
Memorandum (non-add) entries:			
3100 Obligated balance, start of year	90	42	17
3200 Obligated balance, end of year	42	17	12
Budget authority and outlays, net:			
Discretionary:			
Outlays, gross:			
4011 Outlays from discretionary balances	49	25	5
4180 Budget authority, net (total)	....	....	....
4190 Outlays, net (total)	49	25	5

The Gifts and Donations account represents contributions to the Department from outside sources to facilitate the work of the Department.

MANAGEMENT DIRECTORATE

Federal Funds

OPERATIONS AND SUPPORT

For necessary expenses of the Management Directorate for operations and support, including for the purchase or lease of zero emission passenger motor vehicles and supporting charging or fueling infrastructure, $1,753,425,000; of which $76,000,000 shall remain available until September 30, 2024: Provided, That not to exceed $2,000 shall be for official reception and representation expenses.

Note.—A full-year 2022 appropriation for this account was not enacted at the time the Budget was prepared; therefore, the Budget assumes this account is operating under the Continuing Appropriations Act, 2022 (Division A of Public Law 117–43, as amended). The amounts included for 2022 reflect the annualized level provided by the continuing resolution.

Program and Financing (in millions of dollars)

Identification code 070–0112–0–1–999	2021 actual	2022 est.	2023 est.
Obligations by program activity:			
0001 Under Secretary for Management	14	....	....
0012 CAS - Immediate Office of the Under Secretary of Management	4	5	6
0013 CAS - Office of the Chief Readiness Support Officer	187	179	320
0014 CAS - Office of the Chief Human Capital Officer	134	129	152
0015 CAS - Office of the Chief Security Officer	134	135	189
0016 CAS - Chief Procurement Officer	107	106	93
0017 CAS - Office of the Chief Financial Officer	90	89	112
0018 CAS - Office of the Chief Information Officer	499	501	631
0019 CAS - Office of Biometric Identity Management	252	254	229
0020 CAS - Office of Program Accountability and Risk Management	....	....	21
0021 COVID Supplemental	120	....	....
0799 Total direct obligations	1,541	1,398	1,753
0801 USM/CFO Reimbursable program activity	106	154	154

DEPARTMENT OF HOMELAND SECURITY

Management Directorate—Continued
Federal Funds—Continued

		2021 actual	2022 est.	2023 est.
0802	CIO Reimbursable program activity	100	119	119
0899	Total reimbursable obligations	206	273	273
0900	Total new obligations, unexpired accounts	1,747	1,671	2,026
	Budgetary resources:			
	Unobligated balance:			
1000	Unobligated balance brought forward, Oct 1	364	261	266
1001	Discretionary unobligated balance brought fwd, Oct 1	139		
1011	Unobligated balance transfer from other acct [070–0566]	1		
1011	Unobligated balance transfer from other acct [070–0521]	1		
1012	Unobligated balance transfers between expired and unexpired accounts	2		
1021	Recoveries of prior year unpaid obligations	25	5	5
1033	Recoveries of prior year paid obligations	3		
1070	Unobligated balance (total)	396	266	271
	Budget authority:			
	Appropriations, discretionary:			
1100	Appropriation	1,398	1,398	1,753
1120	Appropriations transferred to other acct [070–0100]	–1		
1121	Appropriations transferred from other acct [070–0406]	10		
1131	Unobligated balance of appropriations permanently reduced	–1		
1160	Appropriation, discretionary (total)	1,406	1,398	1,753
	Spending authority from offsetting collections, discretionary:			
1700	Collected	63	94	94
1701	Change in uncollected payments, Federal sources	144	179	179
1750	Spending auth from offsetting collections, disc (total)	207	273	273
1900	Budget authority (total)	1,613	1,671	2,026
1930	Total budgetary resources available	2,009	1,937	2,297
	Memorandum (non-add) entries:			
1940	Unobligated balance expiring	–1		
1941	Unexpired unobligated balance, end of year	261	266	271
	Change in obligated balance:			
	Unpaid obligations:			
3000	Unpaid obligations, brought forward, Oct 1	954	1,008	824
3010	New obligations, unexpired accounts	1,747	1,671	2,026
3011	Obligations ("upward adjustments"), expired accounts	33		
3020	Outlays (gross)	–1,626	–1,830	–2,059
3040	Recoveries of prior year unpaid obligations, unexpired	–25	–5	–5
3041	Recoveries of prior year unpaid obligations, expired	–75	–20	–20
3050	Unpaid obligations, end of year	1,008	824	766
	Uncollected payments:			
3060	Uncollected pymts, Fed sources, brought forward, Oct 1	–154	–206	–405
3070	Change in uncollected pymts, Fed sources, unexpired	–144	–179	–179
3071	Change in uncollected pymts, Fed sources, expired	92	–20	–20
3090	Uncollected pymts, Fed sources, end of year	–206	–405	–604
	Memorandum (non-add) entries:			
3100	Obligated balance, start of year	800	802	419
3200	Obligated balance, end of year	802	419	162
	Budget authority and outlays, net:			
	Discretionary:			
4000	Budget authority, gross	1,613	1,671	2,026
	Outlays, gross:			
4010	Outlays from new discretionary authority	997	1,081	1,354
4011	Outlays from discretionary balances	622	749	705
4020	Outlays, gross (total)	1,619	1,830	2,059
	Offsets against gross budget authority and outlays:			
	Offsetting collections (collected) from:			
4030	Federal sources	–145	–94	–94
4033	Non-Federal sources	–2		
4040	Offsets against gross budget authority and outlays (total)	–147	–94	–94
	Additional offsets against gross budget authority only:			
4050	Change in uncollected pymts, Fed sources, unexpired	–144	–179	–179
4052	Offsetting collections credited to expired accounts	81		
4053	Recoveries of prior year paid obligations, unexpired accounts	3		
4060	Additional offsets against budget authority only (total)	–60	–179	–179
4070	Budget authority, net (discretionary)	1,406	1,398	1,753
4080	Outlays, net (discretionary)	1,472	1,736	1,965
	Mandatory:			
	Outlays, gross:			
4101	Outlays from mandatory balances	7		
4180	Budget authority, net (total)	1,406	1,398	1,753
4190	Outlays, net (total)	1,479	1,736	1,965

The Management Directorate provides enterprise leadership and management and business administration services, as well as biometric and identity management services. These can include financial management, acquisition oversight, workforce management, physical and personnel security requirements, administrative supplies and services, non-programmatic information technology, day-to-day management of headquarters-related property and assets, daily communication costs, and other general day-to-day management and administration. The Management Directorate includes the following offices: Immediate Office of the Under Secretary for Management; Office of the Chief Readiness Support Officer; Office of the Chief Human Capital Officer; Office of the Chief Procurement Officer; Office of the Chief Financial Officer; Office of the Chief Information Officer; Office of the Chief Security Officer; Office of Biometric Identity Management, and the Office of Program Accountability and Risk Management. The Office of the Chief Information Officer includes $9 million for the Homeland Security Infrastructure Program; this program is functionally classified as 051 (Department of Defense-military).

Object Classification (in millions of dollars)

Identification code 070–0112–0–1–999		2021 actual	2022 est.	2023 est.
	Direct obligations:			
	Personnel compensation:			
11.1	Full-time permanent	254	254	308
11.3	Other than full-time permanent	7	7	2
11.5	Other personnel compensation	7	7	5
11.9	Total personnel compensation	268	268	315
12.1	Civilian personnel benefits	91	91	106
21.0	Travel and transportation of persons	1	1	3
23.1	Rental payments to GSA	123	123	135
23.3	Communications, utilities, and miscellaneous charges	2	2	8
25.1	Advisory and assistance services	373	346	338
25.2	Other services from non-Federal sources	70	70	211
25.3	Other goods and services from Federal sources	158	158	383
25.4	Operation and maintenance of facilities	4	4	12
25.5	Research and development contracts			31
25.7	Operation and maintenance of equipment	298	195	196
26.0	Supplies and materials	126	113	2
31.0	Equipment	27	27	13
99.0	Direct obligations	1,541	1,398	1,753
99.0	Reimbursable obligations	206	273	273
99.9	Total new obligations, unexpired accounts	1,747	1,671	2,026

Employment Summary

Identification code 070–0112–0–1–999	2021 actual	2022 est.	2023 est.
1001 Direct civilian full-time equivalent employment	1,958	2,281	2,350
2001 Reimbursable civilian full-time equivalent employment	15	5	5

PROCUREMENT, CONSTRUCTION, AND IMPROVEMENTS

For necessary expenses of the Management Directorate for procurement, construction, and improvements, $572,378,000, of which $182,378,000 shall remain available until September 30, 2025; and of which $390,000,000 shall remain available until September 30, 2027.

Note.—A full-year 2022 appropriation for this account was not enacted at the time the Budget was prepared; therefore, the Budget assumes this account is operating under the Continuing Appropriations Act, 2022 (Division A of Public Law 117–43, as amended). The amounts included for 2022 reflect the annualized level provided by the continuing resolution.

Program and Financing (in millions of dollars)

Identification code 070–0406–0–1–751		2021 actual	2022 est.	2023 est.
	Obligations by program activity:			
0001	CAS - Construction and Facility Improvements	6	55	390
0002	CAS - Mission Support Assets and Infrastructure	23	20	15
0004	CAS - Mission Support Assets and Infrastructure - FSM	70	100	114
0005	CAS - Mission Support Assets and Infrastructure - HRIT	14	10	15
0008	OBIM - HART	46	30	38
0799	Total direct obligations	159	215	572

PROCUREMENT, CONSTRUCTION, AND IMPROVEMENTS—Continued

Program and Financing—Continued

Identification code 070–0406–0–1–751	2021 actual	2022 est.	2023 est.
0900 Total new obligations, unexpired accounts	159	215	572
Budgetary resources:			
Unobligated balance:			
1000 Unobligated balance brought forward, Oct 1	182	234	269
1011 Unobligated balance transfer from other acct [047–0616]	....	35	16
1021 Recoveries of prior year unpaid obligations	5	....	....
1033 Recoveries of prior year paid obligations	1	....	....
1070 Unobligated balance (total)	188	269	285
Budget authority:			
Appropriations, discretionary:			
1100 Appropriation	215	215	572
1120 Appropriations transferred to other acct [070–0112]	–8	....	....
1120 Appropriations transferred to other acct [070–0112]	–2	....	....
1160 Appropriation, discretionary (total)	205	215	572
1900 Budget authority (total)	205	215	572
1930 Total budgetary resources available	393	484	857
Memorandum (non-add) entries:			
1941 Unexpired unobligated balance, end of year	234	269	285
Change in obligated balance:			
Unpaid obligations:			
3000 Unpaid obligations, brought forward, Oct 1	189	214	282
3010 New obligations, unexpired accounts	159	215	572
3020 Outlays (gross)	–128	–147	–256
3040 Recoveries of prior year unpaid obligations, unexpired	–5	....	....
3041 Recoveries of prior year unpaid obligations, expired	–1	....	....
3050 Unpaid obligations, end of year	214	282	598
Memorandum (non-add) entries:			
3100 Obligated balance, start of year	189	214	282
3200 Obligated balance, end of year	214	282	598
Budget authority and outlays, net:			
Discretionary:			
4000 Budget authority, gross	205	215	572
Outlays, gross:			
4010 Outlays from new discretionary authority	22	39	117
4011 Outlays from discretionary balances	106	108	139
4020 Outlays, gross (total)	128	147	256
Offsets against gross budget authority and outlays:			
Offsetting collections (collected) from:			
4030 Federal sources	–1	....	....
4040 Offsets against gross budget authority and outlays (total)	–1	....	....
Additional offsets against gross budget authority only:			
4053 Recoveries of prior year paid obligations, unexpired accounts	1	....	....
4060 Additional offsets against budget authority only (total)	1	....	....
4070 Budget authority, net (discretionary)	205	215	572
4080 Outlays, net (discretionary)	127	147	256
4180 Budget authority, net (total)	205	215	572
4190 Outlays, net (total)	127	147	256

The Management Directorate's Procurement, Construction, and Improvements (PC&I) appropriation provides the support necessary for the planning, operational development, engineering, and purchase of one or more assets prior to sustainment. Information technology included in the PC&I account provides useful software and hardware in an operational environment, including non-tangible assets. The PC&I budget also includes funding for construction and facilities improvements, including the National Capital Region Consolidation project, necessary for the planning, operational development, and engineering prior to sustainment.

Object Classification (in millions of dollars)

Identification code 070–0406–0–1–751	2021 actual	2022 est.	2023 est.
Direct obligations:			
25.1 Advisory and assistance services	87	18	21
25.2 Other services from non-Federal sources	15	....	102
25.3 Other goods and services from Federal sources	5	193	273
25.4 Operation and maintenance of facilities	2	....	2
25.7 Operation and maintenance of equipment	3	....	15
26.0 Supplies and materials	....	3	3
31.0 Equipment	47	1	16
32.0 Land and structures	....	....	140
99.9 Total new obligations, unexpired accounts	159	215	572

FEDERAL PROTECTIVE SERVICE

The revenues and collections of security fees credited to this account shall be available until expended for necessary expenses related to the protection of federally owned and leased buildings and for the operations of the Federal Protective Service.

Note.—A full-year 2022 appropriation for this account was not enacted at the time the Budget was prepared; therefore, the Budget assumes this account is operating under the Continuing Appropriations Act, 2022 (Division A of Public Law 117–43, as amended). The amounts included for 2022 reflect the annualized level provided by the continuing resolution.

Program and Financing (in millions of dollars)

Identification code 070–0542–0–1–804	2021 actual	2022 est.	2023 est.
Obligations by program activity:			
0801 Federal Protective Service (Reimbursable)	35	....	....
0802 CAS - FPS Operations	404	393	457
0803 CAS - Countermeasures	1,234	1,260	1,656
0900 Total new obligations, unexpired accounts	1,673	1,653	2,113
Budgetary resources:			
Unobligated balance:			
1000 Unobligated balance brought forward, Oct 1	429	565	634
1021 Recoveries of prior year unpaid obligations	47	32	32
1033 Recoveries of prior year paid obligations	8	2	2
1070 Unobligated balance (total)	484	599	668
Budget authority:			
Spending authority from offsetting collections, discretionary:			
1700 Collected	1,727	1,653	2,078
1701 Change in uncollected payments, Federal sources	27	35	35
1750 Spending auth from offsetting collections, disc (total)	1,754	1,688	2,113
1930 Total budgetary resources available	2,238	2,287	2,781
Memorandum (non-add) entries:			
1941 Unexpired unobligated balance, end of year	565	634	668
Change in obligated balance:			
Unpaid obligations:			
3000 Unpaid obligations, brought forward, Oct 1	604	728	336
3010 New obligations, unexpired accounts	1,673	1,653	2,113
3020 Outlays (gross)	–1,502	–2,013	–2,028
3040 Recoveries of prior year unpaid obligations, unexpired	–47	–32	–32
3050 Unpaid obligations, end of year	728	336	389
Uncollected payments:			
3060 Uncollected pymts, Fed sources, brought forward, Oct 1	–550	–577	–612
3070 Change in uncollected pymts, Fed sources, unexpired	–27	–35	–35
3090 Uncollected pymts, Fed sources, end of year	–577	–612	–647
Memorandum (non-add) entries:			
3100 Obligated balance, start of year	54	151	–276
3200 Obligated balance, end of year	151	–276	–258
Budget authority and outlays, net:			
Discretionary:			
4000 Budget authority, gross	1,754	1,688	2,113
Outlays, gross:			
4010 Outlays from new discretionary authority	1,183	1,350	1,690
4011 Outlays from discretionary balances	319	663	338
4020 Outlays, gross (total)	1,502	2,013	2,028
Offsets against gross budget authority and outlays:			
Offsetting collections (collected) from:			
4030 Federal sources	–1,729	–1,653	–2,078
4033 Non-Federal sources	–6	–2	–2
4040 Offsets against gross budget authority and outlays (total)	–1,735	–1,655	–2,080
Additional offsets against gross budget authority only:			
4050 Change in uncollected pymts, Fed sources, unexpired	–27	–35	–35
4053 Recoveries of prior year paid obligations, unexpired accounts	8	2	2
4060 Additional offsets against budget authority only (total)	–19	–33	–33
4080 Outlays, net (discretionary)	–233	358	–52
4180 Budget authority, net (total)	....	....	....
4190 Outlays, net (total)	–233	358	–52

DEPARTMENT OF HOMELAND SECURITY

The Federal Protective Service (FPS) protects Federal facilities and those who occupy them by conducting law enforcement and protective security services, and leveraging access to the intelligence and information resources of Federal, State, local, tribal, territorial, and private sector partners. FPS conducts Facility Security Assessments and recommends appropriate countermeasures, ensures stakeholder threat awareness training, and oversees a large contract for a Protective Security Officer workforce. These services provide a comprehensive risk-based approach to facility protection that allows FPS to prioritize its operations to prevent, detect, assess, respond to, and disrupt criminal and other incidents that endanger the Federal community.

Object Classification (in millions of dollars)

Identification code 070–0542–0–1–804	2021 actual	2022 est.	2023 est.
Reimbursable obligations:			
Personnel compensation:			
11.1 Full-time permanent	137	147	148
11.3 Other than full-time permanent	3		
11.5 Other personnel compensation	17	26	26
11.9 Total personnel compensation	157	173	174
12.1 Civilian personnel benefits	57	54	54
21.0 Travel and transportation of persons	7	13	18
22.0 Transportation of things	14	3	4
23.1 Rental payments to GSA	35	26	35
23.3 Communications, utilities, and miscellaneous charges	18	8	13
25.1 Advisory and assistance services	28	46	63
25.2 Other services from non-Federal sources	1,309	1,216	1,613
25.3 Other goods and services from Federal sources	3	62	65
25.4 Operation and maintenance of facilities		1	1
25.7 Operation and maintenance of equipment	32	31	46
25.8 Subsistence and support of persons	1	1	1
26.0 Supplies and materials	6	3	4
31.0 Equipment	6	13	18
32.0 Land and structures		3	4
99.9 Total new obligations, unexpired accounts	1,673	1,653	2,113

Employment Summary

Identification code 070–0542–0–1–804	2021 actual	2022 est.	2023 est.
2001 Reimbursable civilian full-time equivalent employment	1,673	1,506	1,529

OFFICE OF BIOMETRIC IDENTITY MANAGEMENT

Program and Financing (in millions of dollars)

Identification code 070–0521–0–1–751	2021 actual	2022 est.	2023 est.
Obligations by program activity:			
0001 System development and deployment	16	19	
0900 Total new obligations, unexpired accounts (object class 31.0)	16	19	
Budgetary resources:			
Unobligated balance:			
1000 Unobligated balance brought forward, Oct 1	17		
1010 Unobligated balance transfer to other accts [070–0530]	–2		
1010 Unobligated balance transfer to other accts [070–0112]	–1		
1021 Recoveries of prior year unpaid obligations	2	19	
1070 Unobligated balance (total)	16	19	
1930 Total budgetary resources available	16	19	
Change in obligated balance:			
Unpaid obligations:			
3000 Unpaid obligations, brought forward, Oct 1	37	36	5
3010 New obligations, unexpired accounts	16	19	
3020 Outlays (gross)	–14	–31	
3040 Recoveries of prior year unpaid obligations, unexpired	–2	–19	
3041 Recoveries of prior year unpaid obligations, expired	–1		
3050 Unpaid obligations, end of year	36	5	5
Memorandum (non-add) entries:			
3100 Obligated balance, start of year	37	36	5
3200 Obligated balance, end of year	36	5	5

Management Directorate—Continued
Federal Funds—Continued 501

	2021 actual	2022 est.	2023 est.
Budget authority and outlays, net:			
Discretionary:			
Outlays, gross:			
4011 Outlays from discretionary balances	14	31	
4180 Budget authority, net (total)			
4190 Outlays, net (total)	14	31	

The Office of Biometric Identity Management (OBIM) provides biometric identification services to help Federal, State, and local government partners identify people accurately to determine if they pose a risk to the United States. This program supplies the technology for collecting and storing biometric data. The program shares information, provides analysis, updates biometric and terrorist watch lists, and ensures the integrity of the data. OBIM is the lead DHS identity management service provider and works to ensure that the Homeland is safe, secure, and resilient. OBIM serves as a single authoritative biometric service provider, with cross-cutting responsibilities to serve DHS Components and other mission partners, such as the Department of Justice, the Department of State, and the Department of Defense; State, local, and tribal law enforcement; the Intelligence Community; and foreign government partners.

WORKING CAPITAL FUND

Program and Financing (in millions of dollars)

Identification code 070–4640–0–4–751	2021 actual	2022 est.	2023 est.
Budgetary resources:			
Unobligated balance:			
1000 Unobligated balance brought forward, Oct 1	71	83	111
1021 Recoveries of prior year unpaid obligations	20	28	28
1070 Unobligated balance (total)	91	111	139
Budget authority:			
Spending authority from offsetting collections, discretionary:			
1700 Collected	138		
1701 Change in uncollected payments, Federal sources	–146		
1750 Spending auth from offsetting collections, disc (total)	–8		
1930 Total budgetary resources available	83	111	139
Memorandum (non-add) entries:			
1941 Unexpired unobligated balance, end of year	83	111	139
Change in obligated balance:			
Unpaid obligations:			
3000 Unpaid obligations, brought forward, Oct 1	219	73	29
3020 Outlays (gross)	–126	–16	
3040 Recoveries of prior year unpaid obligations, unexpired	–20	–28	–28
3050 Unpaid obligations, end of year	73	29	1
Uncollected payments:			
3060 Uncollected pymts, Fed sources, brought forward, Oct 1	–323	–177	–177
3070 Change in uncollected pymts, Fed sources, unexpired	146		
3090 Uncollected pymts, Fed sources, end of year	–177	–177	–177
Memorandum (non-add) entries:			
3100 Obligated balance, start of year	–104	–104	–148
3200 Obligated balance, end of year	–104	–148	–176
Budget authority and outlays, net:			
Discretionary:			
4000 Budget authority, gross	–8		
Outlays, gross:			
4011 Outlays from discretionary balances	126	16	
Offsets against gross budget authority and outlays:			
Offsetting collections (collected) from:			
4030 Federal sources	–138		
4040 Offsets against gross budget authority and outlays (total)	–138		
Additional offsets against gross budget authority only:			
4050 Change in uncollected pymts, Fed sources, unexpired	146		
4060 Additional offsets against budget authority only (total)	146		
4080 Outlays, net (discretionary)	–12	16	
4180 Budget authority, net (total)			
4190 Outlays, net (total)	–12	16	

The Department of Homeland Security (DHS) and the Working Capital Fund (WCF) Governance Board decided to dissolve the WCF in 2021. This decision was reached after conducting strategic reviews of the WCF

WORKING CAPITAL FUND—Continued

Governance criteria and discussions within the Management Directorate on their business strategy for providing services to their customer base. As a result, no funds are included in the 2023 Budget. All activities were removed from the WCF with base transfers in 2021. DHS Components will transfer funds to the servicing Management lines of business for Fee-for-Service and Government-Wide Mandated Services. The WCF remains in existence to liquidate pre-existing obligations that occurred against the fund and wind down activities.

ANALYSIS AND OPERATIONS
Federal Funds

OPERATIONS AND SUPPORT

For necessary expenses of the Office of Intelligence and Analysis and the Office of Homeland Security Situational Awareness for operations and support, $341,159,000, of which $119,792,000 shall remain available until September 30, 2024: Provided, That not to exceed $3,825 shall be for official reception and representation expenses and not to exceed $2,000,000 is available for facility needs associated with secure space at fusion centers, including improvements to buildings.

Note.—A full-year 2022 appropriation for this account was not enacted at the time the Budget was prepared; therefore, the Budget assumes this account is operating under the Continuing Appropriations Act, 2022 (Division A of Public Law 117–43, as amended). The amounts included for 2022 reflect the annualized level provided by the continuing resolution.

Program and Financing (in millions of dollars)

Identification code 070–0115–0–1–751	2021 actual	2022 est.	2023 est.
Obligations by program activity:			
0001 Analysis and Operations	291	298	341
0801 Analysis and Operations (Reimbursable)	23	31	41
0900 Total new obligations, unexpired accounts	314	329	382
Budgetary resources:			
Unobligated balance:			
1000 Unobligated balance brought forward, Oct 1	4	21	7
1021 Recoveries of prior year unpaid obligations	5		
1070 Unobligated balance (total)	9	21	7
Budget authority:			
Appropriations, discretionary:			
1100 Appropriation	299	298	341
1121 Appropriations transferred from other acct [070–0550]	6		
1160 Appropriation, discretionary (total)	305	298	341
Spending authority from offsetting collections, discretionary:			
1700 Collected	32	31	41
1701 Change in uncollected payments, Federal sources	–9	–14	
1750 Spending auth from offsetting collections, disc (total)	23	17	41
1900 Budget authority (total)	328	315	382
1930 Total budgetary resources available	337	336	389
Memorandum (non-add) entries:			
1940 Unobligated balance expiring	–2		
1941 Unexpired unobligated balance, end of year	21	7	7
Change in obligated balance:			
Unpaid obligations:			
3000 Unpaid obligations, brought forward, Oct 1	178	158	184
3010 New obligations, unexpired accounts	314	329	382
3011 Obligations ("upward adjustments"), expired accounts	3		
3020 Outlays (gross)	–324	–303	–317
3040 Recoveries of prior year unpaid obligations, unexpired	–5		
3041 Recoveries of prior year unpaid obligations, expired	–8		
3050 Unpaid obligations, end of year	158	184	249
Uncollected payments:			
3060 Uncollected pymts, Fed sources, brought forward, Oct 1	–53	–38	–24
3070 Change in uncollected pymts, Fed sources, unexpired	9	14	
3071 Change in uncollected pymts, Fed sources, expired	6		
3090 Uncollected pymts, Fed sources, end of year	–38	–24	–24
Memorandum (non-add) entries:			
3100 Obligated balance, start of year	125	120	160
3200 Obligated balance, end of year	120	160	225
Budget authority and outlays, net:			
Discretionary:			
4000 Budget authority, gross	328	315	382
Outlays, gross:			
4010 Outlays from new discretionary authority	202	157	190
4011 Outlays from discretionary balances	122	146	127
4020 Outlays, gross (total)	324	303	317
Offsets against gross budget authority and outlays:			
Offsetting collections (collected) from:			
4030 Federal sources	–39	–45	–41
4033 Non-Federal sources	–1		
4040 Offsets against gross budget authority and outlays (total)	–40	–45	–41
Additional offsets against gross budget authority only:			
4050 Change in uncollected pymts, Fed sources, unexpired	9	14	
4052 Offsetting collections credited to expired accounts	8	14	
4060 Additional offsets against budget authority only (total)	17	28	
4070 Budget authority, net (discretionary)	305	298	341
4080 Outlays, net (discretionary)	284	258	276
4180 Budget authority, net (total)	305	298	341
4190 Outlays, net (total)	284	258	276

Analysis and Operations (A&O) provides resources supporting the Office of Intelligence and Analysis (I&A) and the Office of Homeland Security Situational Awareness (OSA), formerly known as the Office of Operations Coordination (OPS). This funding includes both National Intelligence Program (NIP) and non-NIP resources. Even though these two offices are different and distinct in their missions, they work closely together and collaborate with other departmental component agencies and related Federal agencies, as well as State, local, tribal, foreign, and private-sector partners, to improve intelligence analysis, information sharing, incident management support, and situational awareness. I&A's mission is to equip the Homeland Security Enterprise with the timely intelligence and information it needs to keep the homeland safe, secure, and resilient. I&A is the interface between the Intelligence Community (IC) and Federal, State, local, and private sector homeland security partners, providing strategic analyses, warning, and actionable intelligence, ensuring departmental leadership, components, law enforcement, and IC partners have the tools they need to confront and disrupt terrorist threats. I&A's unique mission within the IC blends national intelligence with Department of Homeland Security (DHS) component and other stakeholder source data, providing homeland security-centric analysis. The Under Secretary for Intelligence and Analysis leads (I&A) is the Department's Chief Intelligence Officer responsible for overseeing the DHS Intelligence Enterprise. The Under Secretary is also responsible for implementing the National Strategy on Information Sharing across the Department. The mission of OSA is to provide information sharing, situational awareness, and a common operating picture, enabling execution of the Secretary's responsibilities across the Homeland Security Enterprise. OSA plays a pivotal role in the DHS mission to lead the unified national effort to secure America by facilitating the Secretary's responsibilities across the full spectrum of incident management efforts (i.e., prevention, protection, response and recovery). OSA provides situational awareness, assessments, and facilitates operational information sharing with all DHS components, as well as for Federal, State, local, tribal, private sector, and international partners. OSA supports the DHS mission by partnering with other Homeland Security Enterprise partners and by maintaining 24/7 operation of the National Operations Center (NOC), enabling multi-agency fusion of law enforcement, national intelligence, emergency response, and private sector reporting.

Object Classification (in millions of dollars)

Identification code 070–0115–0–1–751	2021 actual	2022 est.	2023 est.
Direct obligations:			
Personnel compensation:			
11.1 Full-time permanent	106	105	126
11.5 Other personnel compensation	7	2	2
11.8 Special personal services payments	3	3	3
11.9 Total personnel compensation	116	110	131
12.1 Civilian personnel benefits	39	33	41

DEPARTMENT OF HOMELAND SECURITY

ADMINISTRATIVE PROVISIONS

		2021 actual	2022 est.	2023 est.
21.0	Travel and transportation of persons	2	4	4
23.1	Rental payments to GSA	1	1	1
25.1	Advisory and assistance services	72	101	124
25.3	Other goods and services from Federal sources	12	16	11
25.7	Operation and maintenance of equipment	48	23	22
26.0	Supplies and materials	1	1	1
31.0	Equipment	....	9	6
99.0	Direct obligations	291	298	341
99.0	Reimbursable obligations	23	31	41
99.9	Total new obligations, unexpired accounts	314	329	382

Employment Summary

Identification code 070–0115–0–1–751	2021 actual	2022 est.	2023 est.
1001 Direct civilian full-time equivalent employment	910	853	949
2001 Reimbursable civilian full-time equivalent employment	7	9	9

OFFICE OF THE INSPECTOR GENERAL

Federal Funds

OPERATIONS AND SUPPORT

For necessary expenses of the Office of the Inspector General for operations and support, $214,879,000: Provided, That not to exceed $300,000 may be used for certain confidential operational expenses, including the payment of informants, to be expended at the direction of the Inspector General.

Note.—A full-year 2022 appropriation for this account was not enacted at the time the Budget was prepared; therefore, the Budget assumes this account is operating under the Continuing Appropriations Act, 2022 (Division A of Public Law 117–43, as amended). The amounts included for 2022 reflect the annualized level provided by the continuing resolution.

Program and Financing (in millions of dollars)

Identification code 070–0200–0–1–751		2021 actual	2022 est.	2023 est.
	Obligations by program activity:			
0002	CAS - Mission Support	196	202	215
0799	Total direct obligations	196	202	215
0801	Operating Expenses (Reimbursable)	13	18	18
0900	Total new obligations, unexpired accounts	209	220	233
	Budgetary resources:			
	Unobligated balance:			
1000	Unobligated balance brought forward, Oct 1	11	7	3
1001	Discretionary unobligated balance brought fwd, Oct 1	9	4	....
1021	Recoveries of prior year unpaid obligations	2	....	....
1070	Unobligated balance (total)	13	7	3
	Budget authority:			
	Appropriations, discretionary:			
1100	Appropriation	190	190	215
1121	Appropriations transferred from other acct [070–0530]	....	1	....
1121	Appropriations transferred from other acct [070–0613]	....	1	....
1121	Appropriations transferred from other acct [070–4236]	....	2	....
1121	Appropriations transferred from other acct [070–0702]	....	1	....
1121	Appropriations transferred from other acct [070–0413]	....	3	....
1160	Appropriation, discretionary (total)	190	198	215
	Advance appropriations, discretionary:			
1173	Advance appropriations transferred from other accounts [070–0413]	....	....	1
1173	Advance appropriations transferred from other accounts [070–4236]	....	....	2
1173	Advance appropriations transferred from other accounts [070–0702]	....	....	1
1180	Advanced appropriation, discretionary (total)	....	....	4
	Spending authority from offsetting collections, discretionary:			
1700	Collected	13	18	18
1900	Budget authority (total)	203	216	237
1930	Total budgetary resources available	216	223	240
	Memorandum (non-add) entries:			
1941	Unexpired unobligated balance, end of year	7	3	7
	Change in obligated balance:			
	Unpaid obligations:			
3000	Unpaid obligations, brought forward, Oct 1	70	64	50
3010	New obligations, unexpired accounts	209	220	233
3020	Outlays (gross)	–209	–234	–232
3040	Recoveries of prior year unpaid obligations, unexpired	–2	....	....
3041	Recoveries of prior year unpaid obligations, expired	–4	....	....
3050	Unpaid obligations, end of year	64	50	51
	Uncollected payments:			
3060	Uncollected pymts, Fed sources, brought forward, Oct 1	–10	–10	–10
3090	Uncollected pymts, Fed sources, end of year	–10	–10	–10
	Memorandum (non-add) entries:			
3100	Obligated balance, start of year	60	54	40
3200	Obligated balance, end of year	54	40	41
	Budget authority and outlays, net:			
	Discretionary:			
4000	Budget authority, gross	203	216	237
	Outlays, gross:			
4010	Outlays from new discretionary authority	166	173	193
4011	Outlays from discretionary balances	43	61	39
4020	Outlays, gross (total)	209	234	232
	Offsets against gross budget authority and outlays:			
	Offsetting collections (collected) from:			
4030	Federal sources	–12	–18	–18
4033	Non-Federal sources	–1	....	....
4040	Offsets against gross budget authority and outlays (total)	–13	–18	–18
4070	Budget authority, net (discretionary)	190	198	219
4080	Outlays, net (discretionary)	196	216	214
4180	Budget authority, net (total)	190	198	219
4190	Outlays, net (total)	196	216	214

The Operations and Support appropriation provides the funds necessary for the operations, mission support, and associated management and administration costs for the Office of Inspector General (OIG). The OIG conducts and supervises audits, inspections, and investigations relating to the programs and operations of the Department; promotes economy, efficiency, and effectiveness; and prevents and detects fraud, waste, and abuse in the Department's programs and operations.

Object Classification (in millions of dollars)

Identification code 070–0200–0–1–751		2021 actual	2022 est.	2023 est.
	Direct obligations:			
	Personnel compensation:			
11.1	Full-time permanent	90	96	99
11.3	Other than full-time permanent	1	3	3
11.5	Other personnel compensation	6	6	9
11.9	Total personnel compensation	97	105	111
12.1	Civilian personnel benefits	40	42	45
21.0	Travel and transportation of persons	1	1	1
23.1	Rental payments to GSA	11	11	11
23.3	Communications, utilities, and miscellaneous charges	4	4	4
25.1	Advisory and assistance services	25	25	22
25.2	Other services from non-Federal sources	1	1	1
25.3	Other goods and services from Federal sources	5	4	7
25.7	Operation and maintenance of equipment	6	4	5
26.0	Supplies and materials	1	1	1
31.0	Equipment	5	4	7
99.0	Direct obligations	196	202	215
99.0	Reimbursable obligations	13	18	18
99.9	Total new obligations, unexpired accounts	209	220	233

Employment Summary

Identification code 070–0200–0–1–751	2021 actual	2022 est.	2023 est.
1001 Direct civilian full-time equivalent employment	723	769	778

ADMINISTRATIVE PROVISIONS

SEC. 101. (a) The Secretary of Homeland Security shall submit a report not later than October 15, 2023, to the Inspector General of the Department of Homeland Security listing all grants and contracts awarded by any means other than full and open competition during fiscal years 2022 or 2023.

(b) The Inspector General shall review the report required by subsection (a) to assess departmental compliance with applicable laws and regulations and report

the results of that review to the Committees on Appropriations of the Senate and the House of Representatives not later than February 15, 2024.

SEC. 102. Not later than 30 days after the last day of each month, the Chief Financial Officer of the Department of Homeland Security shall submit to the Committees on Appropriations of the Senate and the House of Representatives a monthly budget and staffing report that includes total obligations of the Department for that month and for the fiscal year at the appropriation and program, project, and activity levels, by the source year of the appropriation.

SEC. 103. The Secretary of Homeland Security shall require that all contracts of the Department of Homeland Security that provide award fees link such fees to successful acquisition outcomes, which shall be specified in terms of cost, schedule, and performance.

SEC. 104. (a) The Secretary of Homeland Security, in consultation with the Secretary of the Treasury, shall notify the Committees on Appropriations of the Senate and the House of Representatives of any proposed transfers of funds available under section 9705(g)(4)(B) of title 31, United States Code, from the Department of the Treasury Forfeiture Fund to any agency within the Department of Homeland Security.

(b) None of the funds identified for such a transfer may be obligated until the Committees on Appropriations of the Senate and the House of Representatives are notified of the proposed transfer.

SEC. 105. All official costs associated with the use of Government aircraft by Department of Homeland Security personnel to support official travel of the Secretary and the Deputy Secretary shall be paid from amounts made available for the Office of the Secretary.

SEC. 106. Section 107 of the Department of Homeland Security Appropriations Act, 2018 (division F of Public Law 115–141), related to visa overstay data and border security metrics, shall apply in fiscal year 2023, except that the reference to "this Act" shall be treated as referring to this Act, and the reference to "2017" shall be treated as referring to "2022".

U.S. CUSTOMS AND BORDER PROTECTION

Federal Funds

OPERATIONS AND SUPPORT

For necessary expenses of U.S. Customs and Border Protection for operations and support, including the transportation of unaccompanied minor aliens; the provision of air and marine support to Federal, State, local, and international agencies in the enforcement or administration of laws enforced by the Department of Homeland Security; at the discretion of the Secretary of Homeland Security, the provision of such support to Federal, State, and local agencies in other law enforcement and emergency humanitarian efforts; the purchase and lease of up to 7,500 (6,500 for replacement only) police-type vehicles; the purchase, maintenance, or operation of marine vessels, aircraft, and unmanned aerial systems; and contracting with individuals for personal services abroad; $14,459,625,000; of which $3,274,000 shall be derived from the Harbor Maintenance Trust Fund for administrative expenses related to the collection of the Harbor Maintenance Fee pursuant to section 9505(c)(3) of the Internal Revenue Code of 1986 (26 U.S.C. 9505(c)(3)) and notwithstanding section 1511(e)(1) of the Homeland Security Act of 2002 (6 U.S.C. 551(e)(1)); of which $500,000,000 shall be available until September 30, 2024; and of which such sums as become available in the Customs User Fee Account, except sums subject to section 13031(f)(3) of the Consolidated Omnibus Budget Reconciliation Act of 1985 (19 U.S.C. 58c(f)(3)), shall be derived from that account: Provided, That not to exceed $34,425 shall be for official reception and representation expenses: Provided further, That not to exceed $150,000 shall be available for payment for rental space in connection with preclearance operations: Provided further, That not to exceed $2,000,000 shall be for awards of compensation to informants, to be accounted for solely under the certificate of the Secretary of Homeland Security.

Note.—A full-year 2022 appropriation for this account was not enacted at the time the Budget was prepared; therefore, the Budget assumes this account is operating under the Continuing Appropriations Act, 2022 (Division A of Public Law 117–43, as amended). The amounts included for 2022 reflect the annualized level provided by the continuing resolution.

OPERATIONS AND SUPPORT

[For an additional amount for "Operations and Support", $330,000,000, to remain available until September 30, 2026, for furniture, fixtures, and equipment for the land ports of entry modernized with funding provided to the General Services Administration in this Act: Provided, That such amount is designated by the Congress as being for an emergency requirement pursuant to section 4112(a) of H. Con. Res. 71 (115th Congress), the concurrent resolution on the budget for fiscal year 2018, and to section 251(b) of the Balanced Budget and Emergency Deficit Control Act of 1985.] (Infrastructure Investments and Jobs Appropriations Act.)

Special and Trust Fund Receipts (in millions of dollars)

Identification code 070–0530–0–1–751		2021 actual	2022 est.	2023 est.
0100	Balance, start of year	1,021	991	1,147
0198	Rounding adjustment	–1		
0199	Balance, start of year	1,020	991	1,147
	Receipts:			
	Current law:			
1120	Immigration User Fee	264	530	778
1120	Land Border Inspection Fee	28	36	63
1120	Fines and Penalties, Immigration Enforcement Account		1	1
1120	Customs Conveyance, Passenger, and Other Fees	57	209	336
1120	Customs Conveyance, Passenger, and Other Fees	70	65	69
1120	Customs Conveyance, Passenger, and Other Fees	156	297	463
1120	US Customs User Fees Account, Merchandise Processing	90	92	67
1120	US Customs User Fees Account, Merchandise Processing	2,885	2,947	3,375
1120	Customs Fees, Inflation Adjustment	15	23	142
1120	Customs Fees, Inflation Adjustment	13	20	23
1130	Fees, Customs and Border Protection Services at User Fee Facilities	18	10	21
1199	Total current law receipts	3,596	4,230	5,338
1999	Total receipts	3,596	4,230	5,338
2000	Total: Balances and receipts	4,616	5,221	6,485
	Appropriations:			
	Current law:			
2101	Operations and Support	–46	–135	–135
2101	Operations and Support	–16	–10	–21
2101	Operations and Support	–2,975	–2,947	–3,375
2101	Operations and Support	–96	–209	–336
2101	Operations and Support	–28	–36	–63
2101	Operations and Support	–218	–395	–643
2101	Operations and Support	–117	–265	–413
2101	Operations and Support	–70	–58	–62
2101	Operations and Support	–28	–40	–58
2101	Operations and Support		–1	–1
2103	Operations and Support	–6	–3	–3
2103	Operations and Support	–56	–28	–45
2132	Operations and Support	3	8	8
2132	Operations and Support	28	45	70
2199	Total current law appropriations	–3,625	–4,074	–5,077
2999	Total appropriations	–3,625	–4,074	–5,077
5099	Balance, end of year	991	1,147	1,408

Program and Financing (in millions of dollars)

Identification code 070–0530–0–1–751		2021 actual	2022 est.	2023 est.
	Obligations by program activity:			
0004	CAS - Mission Support	2,157	1,860	2,089
0005	CAS - Border Security Operations	5,528	4,854	5,490
0006	CAS - Trade and Travel Operations	7,090	8,124	7,599
0007	CAS - Integrated Operations	1,250	1,161	1,538
0799	Total direct obligations	16,025	15,999	16,716
0801	Reimbursable activity	1,011	1,306	1,991
0900	Total new obligations, unexpired accounts	17,036	17,305	18,707
	Budgetary resources:			
	Unobligated balance:			
1000	Unobligated balance brought forward, Oct 1	846	404	246
1001	Discretionary unobligated balance brought fwd, Oct 1	358	231	
1010	Unobligated balance transfer to other accts [011–5512]	–12		
1011	Unobligated balance transfer from other acct [070–0400]	3		
1011	Unobligated balance transfer from other acct [070–0410]	4		
1011	Unobligated balance transfer from other acct [070–0413]	17		
1011	Unobligated balance transfer from other acct [070–0521]	2		
1011	Unobligated balance transfer from other acct [070–0532]	207		
1011	Unobligated balance transfer from other acct [070–0544]	2		
1011	Unobligated balance transfer from other acct [070–0550]	4		
1011	Unobligated balance transfer from other acct [070–0610]	21		
1011	Unobligated balance transfer from other acct [070–0613]	60		
1011	Unobligated balance transfer from other acct [070–0716]	2		
1012	Unobligated balance transfers between expired and unexpired accounts	13		
1021	Recoveries of prior year unpaid obligations	53	104	82
1033	Recoveries of prior year paid obligations	1	7	4
1070	Unobligated balance (total)	1,223	515	332
	Budget authority:			
	Appropriations, discretionary:			
1100	Appropriation	9,931	9,958	11,082

DEPARTMENT OF HOMELAND SECURITY

U.S. Customs and Border Protection—Continued
Federal Funds—Continued

505

1100	Appropriation IIJA	....	330	....
1100	Appropriation Section 541	....	840	....
1101	Appropriation (Small Airports)	16	10	21
1101	Appropriation (COBRA - MPF)	2,975	2,947	3,375
1101	Appropriation (COBRA - FTA)	96	209	336
1101	Appropriation (Harbor Maintenance Fee)	3	3	3
1120	Appropriations transferred to other acct [070–0200] ...	....	–1	....
1121	Appropriations transferred from other acct [070–0300]	1	....	....
1121	Appropriations transferred from other acct [070–0410]	3	....	....
1121	Appropriations transferred from other acct [070–0550]	25	....	....
1121	Appropriations transferred from other acct [070–0532]	69	....	....
1121	Appropriations transferred from other acct [070–0610]	8	....	....
1160	Appropriation, discretionary (total)	13,127	14,296	14,817
	Appropriations, mandatory:			
1200	Appropriation-FY 2021 Enacted 541 CHIMP	840	....	....
1201	Appropriation (Land Border)	28	36	63
1201	Appropriation (IUF)	218	395	643
1201	Appropriation (COBRA)	117	265	413
1201	Appropriation (COBRA - ECCF)	70	58	62
1201	Appropriation (COBRA - FAST Act)	28	40	58
1201	Appropriation (Immigration Enforcement Fines)	....	1	1
1203	Appropriation (previously unavailable)(special or trust) ...	56	28	45
1221	Appropriations transferred from other acct [012–1600]	533	189	417
1232	Appropriations and/or unobligated balance of appropriations temporarily reduced	–28	–45	–70
1235	Appropriations precluded from obligation (special or trust)	–137	–137	–137
1260	Appropriations, mandatory (total)	1,725	830	1,495
	Spending authority from offsetting collections, discretionary:			
1700	Collected	933	1,496	1,792
1701	Change in uncollected payments, Federal sources	431	411	437
1750	Spending auth from offsetting collections, disc (total)	1,364	1,907	2,229
	Spending authority from offsetting collections, mandatory:			
1811	Spending authority from offsetting collections transferred from other accounts [018–4020]	3	3	5
1900	Budget authority (total)	16,219	17,036	18,546
1930	Total budgetary resources available	17,442	17,551	18,878
	Memorandum (non-add) entries:			
1940	Unobligated balance expiring	–2	....	....
1941	Unexpired unobligated balance, end of year	404	246	171
	Change in obligated balance:			
	Unpaid obligations:			
3000	Unpaid obligations, brought forward, Oct 1	3,761	3,930	4,004
3010	New obligations, unexpired accounts	17,036	17,305	18,707
3011	Obligations ("upward adjustments"), expired accounts ...	55	50	50
3020	Outlays (gross)	–16,604	–17,107	–18,447
3040	Recoveries of prior year unpaid obligations, unexpired	–53	–104	–82
3041	Recoveries of prior year unpaid obligations, expired ...	–265	–70	–70
3050	Unpaid obligations, end of year	3,930	4,004	4,162
	Uncollected payments:			
3060	Uncollected pymts, Fed sources, brought forward, Oct 1	–283	–564	–905
3070	Change in uncollected pymts, Fed sources, unexpired	–431	–411	–437
3071	Change in uncollected pymts, Fed sources, expired ...	150	70	70
3090	Uncollected pymts, Fed sources, end of year	–564	–905	–1,272
	Memorandum (non-add) entries:			
3100	Obligated balance, start of year	3,478	3,366	3,099
3200	Obligated balance, end of year	3,366	3,099	2,890
	Budget authority and outlays, net:			
	Discretionary:			
4000	Budget authority, gross	14,491	16,203	17,046
	Outlays, gross:			
4010	Outlays from new discretionary authority	11,616	12,831	13,597
4011	Outlays from discretionary balances	2,975	3,393	3,439
4020	Outlays, gross (total)	14,591	16,224	17,036
	Offsets against gross budget authority and outlays:			
	Offsetting collections (collected) from:			
4030	Federal sources	–925	–1,519	–1,845
4033	Non-Federal sources	–120	–132	–100
4040	Offsets against gross budget authority and outlays (total)	–1,045	–1,651	–1,945
	Additional offsets against gross budget authority only:			
4050	Change in uncollected pymts, Fed sources, unexpired	–431	–411	–437
4052	Offsetting collections credited to expired accounts	111	148	149
4053	Recoveries of prior year paid obligations, unexpired accounts	1	7	4
4060	Additional offsets against budget authority only (total)	–319	–256	–284
4070	Budget authority, net (discretionary)	13,127	14,296	14,817
4080	Outlays, net (discretionary)	13,546	14,573	15,091
	Mandatory:			
4090	Budget authority, gross	1,728	833	1,500
	Outlays, gross:			
4100	Outlays from new mandatory authority	1,656	673	1,154
4101	Outlays from mandatory balances	357	210	257
4110	Outlays, gross (total)	2,013	883	1,411
4180	Budget authority, net (total)	14,855	15,129	16,317
4190	Outlays, net (total)	15,559	15,456	16,502

U.S. Customs and Border Protection (CBP) works to secure America's borders, while facilitating legitimate trade and travel. CBP is responsible for inspecting travelers at the land, sea, and air ports-of-entry (POEs) for immigration, customs, and agriculture compliance, as well as interdicting illegal entrants between the POEs. CBP enforces the laws regarding admission of foreign-born persons into the United States; identifies and apprehends aliens; and ensures that all goods and persons entering and exiting the United States do so legally. CBP's over 60,000 highly trained employees ensure that the agency performs its mission with vigilance, integrity, and professionalism.

The Operations and Support appropriation funds necessary operations, mission support, and associated management and administrative costs. Major programs include:

Border Security Operations.—This program funds activities designed to protect the Nation through the coordinated use of Border Patrol Agents, technology, and air and marine forces to detect, interdict, and prevent acts of terrorism and the unlawful movement of people, illegal drugs, and other contraband toward or across the borders of the United States. These activities contribute to securing America's Southwest, Northern, and Coastal borders. Through the coordinated use of operational capabilities and assets of the U.S. Border Patrol and Air and Marine Operations, CBP prevents terrorism and terrorist weapons, illegal aliens, smugglers, narcotics, and other contraband from moving across the borders of the United States.

Trade and Travel Operations.—This program funds the mitigation of terrorist threats and the prevention of contraband from entering the U.S. while facilitating the legal flow of people and trade. CBP achieves this mission by deploying CBP officers to the POEs and by using a combination of technology, intelligence, risk information, targeting, and international cooperation to screen inbound international cargo and travelers and, in targeted border areas, to screen departing export cargo. Additional attention to outbound travel along areas of the Southwest border helps prevent the exit of money and weapons for illegal purposes. CBP has extended a zone of security beyond the United States' physical borders through bilateral cooperation with other nations, private-sector partnerships, expanded targeting, and advance scrutiny of information on people and products coming into the U.S.

Integrated Operations.—This program captures the activities to establish the foundation for an integrated, all-hazards planning framework helping to mitigate routine emergencies, catastrophic events and interruptions of border security operations both at and between the ports of entry. Activities funded in the program operate at the national level and are not limited to a specific geographical area. Integrated Operations include funding for command and control, coordination, occupational health and safety, and information and situational awareness for multiple CBP mission programs.

Mission Support.—This program captures activities that are standardized across the Department of Homeland Security that provide enterprise leadership, management, and/or business administration services and describes the capabilities and activities that support the day-to-day management and back office functions enabling both CBP and the Department to operate efficiently and effectively. Key capabilities include conducting agency planning and performance management; managing finances; managing the agency workforce to include recruiting, hiring, screening, equipping, and training new employees; providing physical and personnel security; acquiring goods and services; managing information technology; managing agency property and assets; managing agency communications; managing legal affairs; and providing general management and administration.

U.S. Customs and Border Protection—Continued
Federal Funds—Continued

OPERATIONS AND SUPPORT—Continued

Object Classification (in millions of dollars)

Identification code 070–0530–0–1–751		2021 actual	2022 est.	2023 est.
	Direct obligations:			
	Personnel compensation:			
11.1	Full-time permanent	5,953	5,942	6,232
11.3	Other than full-time permanent	8	8	7
11.5	Other personnel compensation	1,280	1,280	1,336
11.8	Special personal services payments	21	20	20
11.9	Total personnel compensation	7,262	7,250	7,595
12.1	Civilian personnel benefits	3,782	3,779	3,947
13.0	Benefits for former personnel	1	1	1
21.0	Travel and transportation of persons	143	143	147
22.0	Transportation of things	16	16	16
23.1	Rental payments to GSA	616	616	643
23.2	Rental payments to others	41	41	42
23.3	Communications, utilities, and miscellaneous charges	142	142	147
24.0	Printing and reproduction	6	6	5
25.1	Advisory and assistance services	73	73	75
25.2	Other services from non-Federal sources	1,693	1,692	1,767
25.3	Other goods and services from Federal sources	240	240	250
25.4	Operation and maintenance of facilities	307	307	320
25.6	Medical care	160	160	166
25.7	Operation and maintenance of equipment	308	307	320
25.8	Subsistence and support of persons	334	332	346
26.0	Supplies and materials	367	365	380
31.0	Equipment	488	486	507
32.0	Land and structures	30	29	29
42.0	Insurance claims and indemnities	5	4	4
44.0	Refunds	10	9	8
91.0	Unvouchered	1	1	1
99.0	Direct obligations	16,025	15,999	16,716
99.0	Reimbursable obligations	1,011	1,306	1,991
99.9	Total new obligations, unexpired accounts	17,036	17,305	18,707

Employment Summary

Identification code 070–0530–0–1–751		2021 actual	2022 est.	2023 est.
1001	Direct civilian full-time equivalent employment	52,075	49,549	50,912
2001	Reimbursable civilian full-time equivalent employment	10,655	9,403	9,794

OPERATIONS AND SUPPORT

(Legislative proposal, subject to PAYGO)

The Budget proposes to extend the collection of customs fees established by the Consolidated Omnibus Budget Reconciliation Act of 1985 (COBRA, P.L. 99272), the Merchandise Processing Fee (MPF) established by the Omnibus Reconciliation Act of 1986 (P.L. 99509), and the Express Consignment Courier Facilities (ECCF) fee created under the Trade Act of 2002 (P.L. 107210) beyond their current expiration date of September 30, 2031 to September 30, 2032. The Budget also proposes to make permanent the MPF rate increase (from 0.21 percent ad valorem to 0.3464 percent ad valorem) enacted in Section 503 of the U.S.-Korea Free Trade Agreement Implementation Act (P.L. 11241).

BORDER SECURITY FENCING, INFRASTRUCTURE, AND TECHNOLOGY

Program and Financing (in millions of dollars)

Identification code 070–0533–0–1–751		2021 actual	2022 est.	2023 est.
	Obligations by program activity:			
0002	Development and Deployment	1		19
	Budgetary resources:			
	Unobligated balance:			
1000	Unobligated balance brought forward, Oct 1	28	27	18
1021	Recoveries of prior year unpaid obligations	15	6	1
1070	Unobligated balance (total)	43	33	19
	Budget authority:			
	Appropriations, discretionary:			
1131	Unobligated balance of appropriations permanently reduced	–15	–15	
1930	Total budgetary resources available	28	18	19

	Memorandum (non-add) entries:			
1941	Unexpired unobligated balance, end of year	27	18	

	Change in obligated balance:			
	Unpaid obligations:			
3000	Unpaid obligations, brought forward, Oct 1	93	57	21
3010	New obligations, unexpired accounts	1		19
3011	Obligations ("upward adjustments"), expired accounts	5		
3020	Outlays (gross)	–24	–30	–30
3040	Recoveries of prior year unpaid obligations, unexpired	–15	–6	–1
3041	Recoveries of prior year unpaid obligations, expired	–3		
3050	Unpaid obligations, end of year	57	21	9
	Memorandum (non-add) entries:			
3100	Obligated balance, start of year	93	57	21
3200	Obligated balance, end of year	57	21	9

	Budget authority and outlays, net:			
	Discretionary:			
4000	Budget authority, gross	–15	–15	
	Outlays, gross:			
4011	Outlays from discretionary balances	24	30	30
	Offsets against gross budget authority and outlays:			
	Offsetting collections (collected) from:			
4030	Federal sources	–4		
4040	Offsets against gross budget authority and outlays (total)	–4		
	Additional offsets against gross budget authority only:			
4052	Offsetting collections credited to expired accounts	4		
4060	Additional offsets against budget authority only (total)	4		
4070	Budget authority, net (discretionary)	–15	–15	
4080	Outlays, net (discretionary)	20	30	30
4180	Budget authority, net (total)	–15	–15	
4190	Outlays, net (total)	20	30	30

Object Classification (in millions of dollars)

Identification code 070–0533–0–1–751		2021 actual	2022 est.	2023 est.
	Direct obligations:			
25.2	Other services from non-Federal sources			14
25.3	Other goods and services from Federal sources			3
31.0	Equipment	1		2
99.9	Total new obligations, unexpired accounts	1		19

AUTOMATION MODERNIZATION, CUSTOMS AND BORDER PROTECTION

Program and Financing (in millions of dollars)

Identification code 070–0531–0–1–751		2021 actual	2022 est.	2023 est.
	Obligations by program activity:			
0001	No Year Carryover	4	3	
0799	Total direct obligations	4	3	
	Budgetary resources:			
	Unobligated balance:			
1000	Unobligated balance brought forward, Oct 1	1		
1021	Recoveries of prior year unpaid obligations	3	3	
1070	Unobligated balance (total)	4	3	
1930	Total budgetary resources available	4	3	
	Change in obligated balance:			
	Unpaid obligations:			
3000	Unpaid obligations, brought forward, Oct 1	6	4	2
3010	New obligations, unexpired accounts	4	3	
3011	Obligations ("upward adjustments"), expired accounts	1		
3020	Outlays (gross)	–2	–2	–1
3040	Recoveries of prior year unpaid obligations, unexpired	–3	–3	
3041	Recoveries of prior year unpaid obligations, expired	–2		
3050	Unpaid obligations, end of year	4	2	1
	Memorandum (non-add) entries:			
3100	Obligated balance, start of year	6	4	2
3200	Obligated balance, end of year	4	2	1

DEPARTMENT OF HOMELAND SECURITY

U.S. Customs and Border Protection—Continued
Federal Funds—Continued

Budget authority and outlays, net:
Discretionary:
Outlays, gross:

		2021 actual	2022 est.	2023 est.
4011	Outlays from discretionary balances		2	2	1
4180	Budget authority, net (total)				
4190	Outlays, net (total)		2	2	1

Object Classification (in millions of dollars)

Identification code 070–0531–0–1–751	2021 actual	2022 est.	2023 est.
Direct obligations:			
25.3 Other goods and services from Federal sources		3	2	
31.0 Equipment		1	1	
99.0 Direct obligations		4	3	
99.9 Total new obligations, unexpired accounts		4	3	

PROCUREMENT, CONSTRUCTION, AND IMPROVEMENTS

For necessary expenses of U.S. Customs and Border Protection for procurement, construction, and improvements, including procurement of marine vessels, aircraft, and unmanned aerial systems, $440,280,000; of which $294,921,000 shall remain available until September 30, 2025; and of which $145,359,000 shall remain available until September 30, 2027.

Note.—A full-year 2022 appropriation for this account was not enacted at the time the Budget was prepared; therefore, the Budget assumes this account is operating under the Continuing Appropriations Act, 2022 (Division A of Public Law 117–43, as amended). The amounts included for 2022 reflect the annualized level provided by the continuing resolution.

PROCUREMENT, CONSTRUCTION, AND IMPROVEMENTS

⟦For an additional amount for "Procurement, Construction, and Improvements", $100,000,000, to remain available until September 30, 2026, for land port of entry construction, modernization, and sustainment: *Provided*, That not later than 90 days after the date of enactment of this Act, the Department shall submit to the House and Senate Committees on Appropriations a detailed spend plan for the amount made available under this heading in this Act: *Provided further*, That such amount is designated by the Congress as being for an emergency requirement pursuant to section 4112(a) of H. Con. Res. 71 (115th Congress), the concurrent resolution on the budget for fiscal year 2018, and to section 251(b) of the Balanced Budget and Emergency Deficit Control Act of 1985.⟧ *(Infrastructure Investments and Jobs Appropriations Act.)*

Program and Financing (in millions of dollars)

Identification code 070–0532–0–1–751	2021 actual	2022 est.	2023 est.
Obligations by program activity:			
0002 Program Oversight	2		
0003 Facilities Construction and Sustainment	8		
0007 CAS - Mission Support Assets and Infrastructure	506	40	62
0008 CAS - Border Security Assets and Infrastructure	226	796	905
0009 CAS - Trade and Travel Assets and Infrastructure	527	76	119
0010 CAS - Integrated Operations Assets and Infrastructure	131	158	266
0012 CAS - Construction and Facility Improvements	73	261	335
0799 Total direct obligations	1,473	1,331	1,687
0801 Reimbursable program activity	3	3	5
0900 Total new obligations, unexpired accounts	1,476	1,334	1,692
Budgetary resources:			
Unobligated balance:			
1000 Unobligated balance brought forward, Oct 1	1,099	2,485	3,529
1010 Unobligated balance transfer to other accts [070–0530]	–207		
1010 Unobligated balance transfer to other accts [070–0862]	–20		
1011 Unobligated balance transfer from other acct [047–0616]	6		
1021 Recoveries of prior year unpaid obligations	1,337	465	475
1070 Unobligated balance (total)	2,215	2,950	4,004
Budget authority:			
Appropriations, discretionary:			
1100 Appropriation	1,840	1,940	440
1120 Appropriations transferred to other acct [070–0530]	–69		
1131 Unobligated balance of appropriations permanently reduced	–33	–33	
1160 Appropriation, discretionary (total)	1,738	1,907	440
Spending authority from offsetting collections, discretionary:			
1700 Collected	2	5	5
1701 Change in uncollected payments, Federal sources	6	1	1
1750 Spending auth from offsetting collections, disc (total)	8	6	6
1900 Budget authority (total)	1,746	1,913	446
1930 Total budgetary resources available	3,961	4,863	4,450
Memorandum (non-add) entries:			
1941 Unexpired unobligated balance, end of year	2,485	3,529	2,758
Change in obligated balance:			
Unpaid obligations:			
3000 Unpaid obligations, brought forward, Oct 1	4,682	3,007	1,553
3010 New obligations, unexpired accounts	1,476	1,334	1,692
3011 Obligations ("upward adjustments"), expired accounts	1		
3020 Outlays (gross)	–1,811	–2,323	–1,916
3040 Recoveries of prior year unpaid obligations, unexpired	–1,337	–465	–475
3041 Recoveries of prior year unpaid obligations, expired	–4		
3050 Unpaid obligations, end of year	3,007	1,553	854
Uncollected payments:			
3060 Uncollected pymts, Fed sources, brought forward, Oct 1	–3	–9	–10
3070 Change in uncollected pymts, Fed sources, unexpired	–6	–1	–1
3090 Uncollected pymts, Fed sources, end of year	–9	–10	–11
Memorandum (non-add) entries:			
3100 Obligated balance, start of year	4,679	2,998	1,543
3200 Obligated balance, end of year	2,998	1,543	843
Budget authority and outlays, net:			
Discretionary:			
4000 Budget authority, gross	1,746	1,913	446
Outlays, gross:			
4010 Outlays from new discretionary authority	90	621	134
4011 Outlays from discretionary balances	1,721	1,702	1,782
4020 Outlays, gross (total)	1,811	2,323	1,916
Offsets against gross budget authority and outlays:			
Offsetting collections (collected) from:			
4030 Federal sources	–2	–5	–5
4040 Offsets against gross budget authority and outlays (total)	–2	–5	–5
Additional offsets against gross budget authority only:			
4050 Change in uncollected pymts, Fed sources, unexpired	–6	–1	–1
4060 Additional offsets against budget authority only (total)	–6	–1	–1
4070 Budget authority, net (discretionary)	1,738	1,907	440
4080 Outlays, net (discretionary)	1,809	2,318	1,911
4180 Budget authority, net (total)	1,738	1,907	440
4190 Outlays, net (total)	1,809	2,318	1,911

The U.S. Customs and Border Protection (CBP) Procurement, Construction, and Improvements (PC&I) appropriation provides the funds necessary for the planning, operational development, engineering, and purchase of one or more assets prior to sustainment. The funding within this account enables investments in border security technology, aircraft, marine vessels, tactical infrastructure, information technology systems, and other acquisitions. PC&I funding also supports the construction and modernization of critical facilities and associated infrastructure. These investments enable CBP to accomplish its complex mission of protecting the border while facilitating lawful trade, travel, and immigration.

Object Classification (in millions of dollars)

Identification code 070–0532–0–1–751	2021 actual	2022 est.	2023 est.
Direct obligations:			
21.0 Travel and transportation of persons	1	1	1
22.0 Transportation of things	2	1	1
23.1 Rental payments to GSA	1	1	1
23.3 Communications, utilities, and miscellaneous charges	2	1	1
25.1 Advisory and assistance services	2	2	2
25.2 Other services from non-Federal sources	780	708	896
25.3 Other goods and services from Federal sources	68	60	77
25.4 Operation and maintenance of facilities	4	3	3
25.7 Operation and maintenance of equipment	5	4	4
26.0 Supplies and materials	22	19	24
31.0 Equipment	431	392	501
32.0 Land and structures	155	139	176
99.0 Direct obligations	1,473	1,331	1,687
99.0 Reimbursable obligations	3	3	5

U.S. Customs and Border Protection—Continued
Federal Funds—Continued

PROCUREMENT, CONSTRUCTION, AND IMPROVEMENTS—Continued

Object Classification—Continued

Identification code 070–0532–0–1–751	2021 actual	2022 est.	2023 est.
99.9 Total new obligations, unexpired accounts	1,476	1,334	1,692

AIR AND MARINE INTERDICTION, OPERATIONS, MAINTENANCE, AND PROCUREMENT

Program and Financing (in millions of dollars)

Identification code 070–0544–0–1–751	2021 actual	2022 est.	2023 est.
Obligations by program activity:			
0001 Operations and Maintenance	9	2	
0002 Procurement		4	
0799 Total direct obligations	9	6	
0900 Total new obligations, unexpired accounts (object class 25.2)	9	6	
Budgetary resources:			
Unobligated balance:			
1000 Unobligated balance brought forward, Oct 1	7	1	
1010 Unobligated balance transfer to other accts [070–0530]	–2		
1021 Recoveries of prior year unpaid obligations	5	5	
1070 Unobligated balance (total)	10	6	
1930 Total budgetary resources available	10	6	
Memorandum (non-add) entries:			
1941 Unexpired unobligated balance, end of year	1		
Change in obligated balance:			
Unpaid obligations:			
3000 Unpaid obligations, brought forward, Oct 1	36	26	16
3010 New obligations, unexpired accounts	9	6	
3011 Obligations ("upward adjustments"), expired accounts	1		
3020 Outlays (gross)	–10	–11	–15
3040 Recoveries of prior year unpaid obligations, unexpired	–5	–5	
3041 Recoveries of prior year unpaid obligations, expired	–5		
3050 Unpaid obligations, end of year	26	16	1
Uncollected payments:			
3060 Uncollected pymts, Fed sources, brought forward, Oct 1	–1	–1	–1
3090 Uncollected pymts, Fed sources, end of year	–1	–1	–1
Memorandum (non-add) entries:			
3100 Obligated balance, start of year	35	25	15
3200 Obligated balance, end of year	25	15	
Budget authority and outlays, net:			
Discretionary:			
Outlays, gross:			
4011 Outlays from discretionary balances	10	11	15
4180 Budget authority, net (total)			
4190 Outlays, net (total)	10	11	15

ENHANCED INSPECTIONAL SERVICES

Program and Financing (in millions of dollars)

Identification code 070–4363–0–3–751	2021 actual	2022 est.	2023 est.
Obligations by program activity:			
0801 Enhanced Inspectional Services (Reimbursable)	16	31	32
Budgetary resources:			
Unobligated balance:			
1000 Unobligated balance brought forward, Oct 1	5	4	4
Budget authority:			
Spending authority from offsetting collections, discretionary:			
1700 Collected	15	31	32
1930 Total budgetary resources available	20	35	36
Memorandum (non-add) entries:			
1941 Unexpired unobligated balance, end of year	4	4	4
Change in obligated balance:			
Unpaid obligations:			
3000 Unpaid obligations, brought forward, Oct 1	3	3	
3010 New obligations, unexpired accounts	16	31	32
3020 Outlays (gross)	–16	–34	–32
3050 Unpaid obligations, end of year	3		
Memorandum (non-add) entries:			
3100 Obligated balance, start of year	3	3	
3200 Obligated balance, end of year	3		
Budget authority and outlays, net:			
Discretionary:			
4000 Budget authority, gross	15	31	32
Outlays, gross:			
4010 Outlays from new discretionary authority	11	31	32
4011 Outlays from discretionary balances	5	3	
4020 Outlays, gross (total)	16	34	32
Offsets against gross budget authority and outlays:			
Offsetting collections (collected) from:			
4033 Non-Federal sources	–15	–31	–32
4180 Budget authority, net (total)			
4190 Outlays, net (total)	1	3	

Under Section 481 of the Cross-Border Trade Enhancement Act of 2016 (P.L. 114–279), the Commissioner of Customs and Border Protection (CBP) may approve requests from interested parties to reimburse CBP for enhanced inspectional services. Subjected to limitations, CBP is authorized to receive reimbursement from corporations, Government agencies, and other interested parties for certain inspection services in the air, land, and sea environments at domestic locations. This allows CBP to provide services to requesting parties that it could not provide in the absence of reimbursement. The Enhanced Inspectional Services account is used to manage funds associated with reimbursable agreements with external parties.

Object Classification (in millions of dollars)

Identification code 070–4363–0–3–751	2021 actual	2022 est.	2023 est.
Reimbursable obligations:			
Personnel compensation:			
11.1 Full-time permanent	1	2	3
11.5 Other personnel compensation	7	17	17
11.9 Total personnel compensation	8	19	20
12.1 Civilian personnel benefits	4	8	8
25.2 Other services from non-Federal sources	4	4	4
99.9 Total new obligations, unexpired accounts	16	31	32

Employment Summary

Identification code 070–4363–0–3–751	2021 actual	2022 est.	2023 est.
2001 Reimbursable civilian full-time equivalent employment	59		

REFUNDS, TRANSFERS, AND EXPENSES OF OPERATION, PUERTO RICO

Special and Trust Fund Receipts (in millions of dollars)

Identification code 070–5687–0–2–806	2021 actual	2022 est.	2023 est.
0100 Balance, start of year	13	17	13
Receipts:			
Current law:			
1110 Deposits, Duties, and Taxes, Puerto Rico	301	225	225
2000 Total: Balances and receipts	314	242	238
Appropriations:			
Current law:			
2101 Refunds, Transfers, and Expenses of Operation, Puerto Rico	–301	–225	–225
2103 Refunds, Transfers, and Expenses of Operation, Puerto Rico	–13	–17	–13
2132 Refunds, Transfers, and Expenses of Operation, Puerto Rico	17	13	13
2199 Total current law appropriations	–297	–229	–225
2999 Total appropriations	–297	–229	–225
5099 Balance, end of year	17	13	13

DEPARTMENT OF HOMELAND SECURITY

Program and Financing (in millions of dollars)

Identification code 070–5687–0–2–806	2021 actual	2022 est.	2023 est.
Obligations by program activity:			
0001 Refunds, Transfers, and Expenses of Operation, Puerto Rico (Direct)	300	225	225
0100 Direct program activities, subtotal	300	225	225
Budgetary resources:			
Unobligated balance:			
1000 Unobligated balance brought forward, Oct 1	73	79	83
1021 Recoveries of prior year unpaid obligations	9		
1070 Unobligated balance (total)	82	79	83
Budget authority:			
Appropriations, mandatory:			
1201 Appropriation (special or trust fund)	301	225	225
1203 Appropriation (previously unavailable)(special or trust)	13	17	13
1232 Appropriations and/or unobligated balance of appropriations temporarily reduced	–17	–13	–13
1260 Appropriations, mandatory (total)	297	229	225
1930 Total budgetary resources available	379	308	308
Memorandum (non-add) entries:			
1941 Unexpired unobligated balance, end of year	79	83	83
Change in obligated balance:			
Unpaid obligations:			
3000 Unpaid obligations, brought forward, Oct 1	273	438	343
3010 New obligations, unexpired accounts	300	225	225
3020 Outlays (gross)	–126	–320	–219
3040 Recoveries of prior year unpaid obligations, unexpired	–9		
3050 Unpaid obligations, end of year	438	343	349
Memorandum (non-add) entries:			
3100 Obligated balance, start of year	273	438	343
3200 Obligated balance, end of year	438	343	349
Budget authority and outlays, net:			
Mandatory:			
4090 Budget authority, gross	297	229	225
Outlays, gross:			
4100 Outlays from new mandatory authority	100	116	112
4101 Outlays from mandatory balances	26	204	107
4110 Outlays, gross (total)	126	320	219
4180 Budget authority, net (total)	297	229	225
4190 Outlays, net (total)	126	320	219

Per 48 U.S.C. 740, duties and taxes collected by U.S. Customs and Border Protection (CBP) in the Commonwealth of Puerto Rico are deposited in a mandatory trust called the Puerto Rico Trust Fund (PRTF). CBP is authorized to reimburse costs incurred in performing commercial operations related to duty and tax collections in the Commonwealth with revenues available in PRTF. After recovering the costs of those activities, accounting for any outstanding liabilities (i.e., custodial liabilities, refunds, and drawback activity), and executing another use of available revenue agreed upon between the Commonwealth and U.S. Immigration and Customs Enforcement, available collections are transferred to Puerto Rico's Treasury (Hacienda) to be expended by the Government of Puerto Rico, as established by law.

Object Classification (in millions of dollars)

Identification code 070–5687–0–2–806	2021 actual	2022 est.	2023 est.
Direct obligations:			
Personnel compensation:			
11.1 Full-time permanent	28	24	30
11.5 Other personnel compensation	1	1	2
11.9 Total personnel compensation	29	25	32
12.1 Civilian personnel benefits	17	13	19
21.0 Travel and transportation of persons			1
22.0 Transportation of things	1		3
23.1 Rental payments to GSA	2	2	2
23.2 Rental payments to others		1	
23.3 Communications, utilities, and miscellaneous charges	1	1	1
25.2 Other services from non-Federal sources	6	6	7
25.3 Other goods and services from Federal sources	39	39	41
25.4 Operation and maintenance of facilities	4	3	5
25.7 Operation and maintenance of equipment	3	3	7
26.0 Supplies and materials	6	2	15
31.0 Equipment	3	2	4
32.0 Land and structures	27	4	
44.0 Refunds	162	124	88
99.9 Total new obligations, unexpired accounts	300	225	225

Employment Summary

Identification code 070–5687–0–2–806	2021 actual	2022 est.	2023 est.
1001 Direct civilian full-time equivalent employment	325	263	263

PAYMENTS TO WOOL MANUFACTURERS

Special and Trust Fund Receipts (in millions of dollars)

Identification code 070–5533–0–2–376	2021 actual	2022 est.	2023 est.
0100 Balance, start of year	1	1	1
2000 Total: Balances and receipts	1	1	1
5099 Balance, end of year	1	1	1

INTERNATIONAL REGISTERED TRAVELER

Special and Trust Fund Receipts (in millions of dollars)

Identification code 070–5543–0–2–751	2021 actual	2022 est.	2023 est.
0100 Balance, start of year			
Receipts:			
Current law:			
1120 International Registered Traveler Program Fund	144	117	204
2000 Total: Balances and receipts	144	117	204
Appropriations:			
Current law:			
2101 International Registered Traveler	–144	–117	–204
5099 Balance, end of year			

Program and Financing (in millions of dollars)

Identification code 070–5543–0–2–751	2021 actual	2022 est.	2023 est.
Obligations by program activity:			
0001 International Registered Traveler (Direct)	194	117	204
Budgetary resources:			
Unobligated balance:			
1000 Unobligated balance brought forward, Oct 1	217	170	170
1021 Recoveries of prior year unpaid obligations	3		
1070 Unobligated balance (total)	220	170	170
Budget authority:			
Appropriations, discretionary:			
1101 Appropriation (special or trust)	144	117	204
1930 Total budgetary resources available	364	287	374
Memorandum (non-add) entries:			
1941 Unexpired unobligated balance, end of year	170	170	170
Change in obligated balance:			
Unpaid obligations:			
3000 Unpaid obligations, brought forward, Oct 1	116	145	44
3010 New obligations, unexpired accounts	194	117	204
3020 Outlays (gross)	–162	–218	–115
3040 Recoveries of prior year unpaid obligations, unexpired	–3		
3050 Unpaid obligations, end of year	145	44	133
Memorandum (non-add) entries:			
3100 Obligated balance, start of year	116	145	44
3200 Obligated balance, end of year	145	44	133
Budget authority and outlays, net:			
Discretionary:			
4000 Budget authority, gross	144	117	204
Outlays, gross:			
4010 Outlays from new discretionary authority	10	49	86

510   U.S. Customs and Border Protection—Continued
       Federal Funds—Continued

INTERNATIONAL REGISTERED TRAVELER—Continued

Program and Financing—Continued

Identification code 070–5543–0–2–751	2021 actual	2022 est.	2023 est.
4011 Outlays from discretionary balances	152	169	29
4020 Outlays, gross (total)	162	218	115
4180 Budget authority, net (total)	144	117	204
4190 Outlays, net (total)	162	218	115

The International Registered Traveler Program is authorized under section 565(3)(A) of the Consolidated Appropriations Act of 2008 (P.L. 110–161). U.S. Customs and Border Protection established Global Entry as an international registered traveler program that incorporates technologies, such as biometrics and e-passports, and security threat assessments to expedite screening and processing of international passengers. Global Entry allows expedited clearance for pre-approved and low-risk travelers upon arrival in the United States. The International Registered Traveler account is used to fund Global Entry program activities.

Object Classification (in millions of dollars)

Identification code 070–5543–0–2–751	2021 actual	2022 est.	2023 est.
Direct obligations:			
Personnel compensation:			
11.1 Full-time permanent	18	14	25
11.5 Other personnel compensation	21	13	22
11.9 Total personnel compensation	39	27	47
12.1 Civilian personnel benefits	10	8	14
21.0 Travel and transportation of persons	1		
23.3 Communications, utilities, and miscellaneous charges	5	3	5
24.0 Printing and reproduction	25	10	18
25.2 Other services from non-Federal sources	79	45	78
25.3 Other goods and services from Federal sources	28	19	33
31.0 Equipment	7	5	9
99.9 Total new obligations, unexpired accounts	194	117	204

Employment Summary

Identification code 070–5543–0–2–751	2021 actual	2022 est.	2023 est.
1001 Direct civilian full-time equivalent employment	204	237	274

ELECTRONIC SYSTEM FOR TRAVEL AUTHORIZATION

Special and Trust Fund Receipts (in millions of dollars)

Identification code 070–5595–0–2–751	2021 actual	2022 est.	2023 est.
0100 Balance, start of year	2		
Receipts:			
Current law:			
1110 Electronic System for Travel Authorization (ESTA) Fees	5	11	51
2000 Total: Balances and receipts	7	11	51
Appropriations:			
Current law:			
2101 Electronic System for Travel Authorization	–5	–11	–51
2103 Electronic System for Travel Authorization	–2	–1	–1
2132 Electronic System for Travel Authorization		1	3
2199 Total current law appropriations	–7	–11	–49
2999 Total appropriations	–7	–11	–49
5099 Balance, end of year			2

Program and Financing (in millions of dollars)

Identification code 070–5595–0–2–751	2021 actual	2022 est.	2023 est.
Obligations by program activity:			
0001 Electronic System for Travel Authorization (ESTA) (Direct)	20	11	51
Budgetary resources:			
Unobligated balance:			
1000 Unobligated balance brought forward, Oct 1	12	2	2
1021 Recoveries of prior year unpaid obligations	3		
1070 Unobligated balance (total)	15	2	2
Budget authority:			
Appropriations, mandatory:			
1201 Appropriation (special or trust fund)	5	11	51
1203 Appropriation (previously unavailable)(special or trust)	2	1	1
1232 Appropriations and/or unobligated balance of appropriations temporarily reduced		–1	–3
1260 Appropriations, mandatory (total)	7	11	49
1930 Total budgetary resources available	22	13	51
Memorandum (non-add) entries:			
1941 Unexpired unobligated balance, end of year	2	2	
Change in obligated balance:			
Unpaid obligations:			
3000 Unpaid obligations, brought forward, Oct 1	34	16	7
3010 New obligations, unexpired accounts	20	11	51
3020 Outlays (gross)	–35	–20	–31
3040 Recoveries of prior year unpaid obligations, unexpired	–3		
3050 Unpaid obligations, end of year	16	7	27
Memorandum (non-add) entries:			
3100 Obligated balance, start of year	34	16	7
3200 Obligated balance, end of year	16	7	27
Budget authority and outlays, net:			
Mandatory:			
4090 Budget authority, gross	7	11	49
Outlays, gross:			
4100 Outlays from new mandatory authority		6	26
4101 Outlays from mandatory balances	35	14	5
4110 Outlays, gross (total)	35	20	31
4180 Budget authority, net (total)	7	11	49
4190 Outlays, net (total)	35	20	31

The Implementing Recommendations of the 9/11 Commission Act of 2007 (P.L. 110–53) required the establishment of an electronic authorization system to pre-screen noncitizens prior to arrival in the United States. This mandate was made operational by the creation of the Electronic System for Travel Authorization (ESTA). ESTA operates under informed compliance, requiring all Visa Waiver Program travelers to obtain authorization prior to travel. The Visa Waiver Program allows visitors to travel to the United States for business or pleasure for 90 days or less without obtaining a visa. This account funds the provision and administration of the ESTA system.

Object Classification (in millions of dollars)

Identification code 070–5595–0–2–751	2021 actual	2022 est.	2023 est.
11.1 Direct obligations: Personnel compensation: Full-time permanent	3	3	12
11.9 Total personnel compensation	3	3	12
12.1 Civilian personnel benefits	1	1	5
23.3 Communications, utilities, and miscellaneous charges	1		1
25.2 Other services from non-Federal sources	12	4	27
25.7 Operation and maintenance of equipment	2	1	5
31.0 Equipment	1	2	1
99.9 Total new obligations, unexpired accounts	20	11	51

Employment Summary

Identification code 070–5595–0–2–751	2021 actual	2022 est.	2023 est.
1001 Direct civilian full-time equivalent employment	33	27	91

ELECTRONIC VISA UPDATE SYSTEM

Special and Trust Fund Receipts (in millions of dollars)

Identification code 070–5703–0–2–751	2021 actual	2022 est.	2023 est.
0100 Balance, start of year			
Receipts:			
Proposed:			
1210 Electronic Visa Update System Fees			47

DEPARTMENT OF HOMELAND SECURITY

		2021 actual	2022 est.	2023 est.
2000	Total: Balances and receipts			47
	Appropriations:			
	Proposed:			
2201	Electronic Visa Update System			−47
5099	Balance, end of year			

ELECTRONIC VISA UPDATE SYSTEM

(Legislative proposal, subject to PAYGO)

Program and Financing (in millions of dollars)

Identification code 070–5703–4–2–751	2021 actual	2022 est.	2023 est.
Obligations by program activity:			
0001 Electronic Visa Update System (direct)			47
0900 Total new obligations, unexpired accounts (object class 25.2)			47
Budgetary resources:			
Budget authority:			
Appropriations, mandatory:			
1201 Appropriation (special or trust fund)			47
1930 Total budgetary resources available			47
Change in obligated balance:			
Unpaid obligations:			
3010 New obligations, unexpired accounts			47
3020 Outlays (gross)			−47
Budget authority and outlays, net:			
Mandatory:			
4090 Budget authority, gross			47
Outlays, gross:			
4100 Outlays from new mandatory authority			47
4180 Budget authority, net (total)			47
4190 Outlays, net (total)			47

The Budget proposes establishing a user fee to cover costs that U.S. Customs and Border Protection incurs to administer the Electronic Visa Update System (EVUS) program. EVUS is an automated system used to determine eligibility to travel to the United States for temporary business or pleasure on a 10-year U.S. visitor visa. EVUS complements the existing visa application process and enhances CBP's ability to make pre-travel admissibility and risk determinations. This account will fund the costs of providing and administering the system.

APEC BUSINESS TRAVEL CARD

Special and Trust Fund Receipts (in millions of dollars)

Identification code 070–5569–0–2–751	2021 actual	2022 est.	2023 est.
0100 Balance, start of year			
Receipts:			
Current law:			
1130 Fees, APEC Business Travel Card	1	1	2
2000 Total: Balances and receipts	1	1	2
Appropriations:			
Current law:			
2101 APEC Business Travel Card	−1	−1	−2
5099 Balance, end of year			

Program and Financing (in millions of dollars)

Identification code 070–5569–0–2–751	2021 actual	2022 est.	2023 est.
Obligations by program activity:			
0801 APEC Business Travel Card	1	1	2
0900 Total new obligations, unexpired accounts (object class 25.2)	1	1	2
Budgetary resources:			
Unobligated balance:			
1000 Unobligated balance brought forward, Oct 1	1	1	1
Budget authority:			
Appropriations, mandatory:			
1201 Appropriation (special or trust fund)	1	1	2

U.S. Customs and Border Protection—Continued
Federal Funds—Continued

511

		2021 actual	2022 est.	2023 est.
1900	Budget authority (total)	1	1	2
1930	Total budgetary resources available	2	2	3
	Memorandum (non-add) entries:			
1941	Unexpired unobligated balance, end of year	1	1	1
	Change in obligated balance:			
	Unpaid obligations:			
3000	Unpaid obligations, brought forward, Oct 1		1	
3010	New obligations, unexpired accounts	1	1	2
3020	Outlays (gross)		−2	−2
3050	Unpaid obligations, end of year	1		
	Memorandum (non-add) entries:			
3100	Obligated balance, start of year		1	
3200	Obligated balance, end of year	1		
	Budget authority and outlays, net:			
	Mandatory:			
4090	Budget authority, gross	1	1	2
	Outlays, gross:			
4100	Outlays from new mandatory authority		1	2
4101	Outlays from mandatory balances		1	
4110	Outlays, gross (total)		2	2
4180	Budget authority, net (total)	1	1	2
4190	Outlays, net (total)		2	2

9–11 RESPONSE AND BIOMETRIC EXIT ACCOUNT

Special and Trust Fund Receipts (in millions of dollars)

Identification code 070–5702–0–2–751	2021 actual	2022 est.	2023 est.
0100 Balance, start of year	2	2	2
Receipts:			
Current law:			
1120 Temporary L-1 Visa Fees, 9–11 Response and Biometric Exit Account	2	7	11
1120 Temporary H-1B Visa Fees, 9–11 Response and Biometric Exit Account	26	23	36
1199 Total current law receipts	28	30	47
1999 Total receipts	28	30	47
2000 Total: Balances and receipts	30	32	49
Appropriations:			
Current law:			
2101 9–11 Response and Biometric Exit Account	−28	−30	−47
2103 9–11 Response and Biometric Exit Account	−2	−2	−2
2132 9–11 Response and Biometric Exit Account	2	2	3
2199 Total current law appropriations	−28	−30	−46
2999 Total appropriations	−28	−30	−46
5099 Balance, end of year	2	2	3

Program and Financing (in millions of dollars)

Identification code 070–5702–0–2–751	2021 actual	2022 est.	2023 est.
Obligations by program activity:			
0001 Direct program activity	39	30	47
Budgetary resources:			
Unobligated balance:			
1000 Unobligated balance brought forward, Oct 1	50	41	41
1021 Recoveries of prior year unpaid obligations	2		
1070 Unobligated balance (total)	52	41	41
Budget authority:			
Appropriations, mandatory:			
1201 Appropriation (special or trust fund)	28	30	47
1203 Appropriation (previously unavailable)(special or trust)	2	2	2
1232 Appropriations and/or unobligated balance of appropriations temporarily reduced	−2	−2	−3
1260 Appropriations, mandatory (total)	28	30	46
1930 Total budgetary resources available	80	71	87
Memorandum (non-add) entries:			
1941 Unexpired unobligated balance, end of year	41	41	40

512   U.S. Customs and Border Protection—Continued
       Federal Funds—Continued   THE BUDGET FOR FISCAL YEAR 2023

9–11 RESPONSE AND BIOMETRIC EXIT ACCOUNT—Continued

Program and Financing—Continued

Identification code 070–5702–0–2–751	2021 actual	2022 est.	2023 est.
Change in obligated balance:			
Unpaid obligations:			
3000 Unpaid obligations, brought forward, Oct 1	35	28	1
3010 New obligations, unexpired accounts	39	30	47
3020 Outlays (gross)	–44	–57	–32
3040 Recoveries of prior year unpaid obligations, unexpired	–2		
3050 Unpaid obligations, end of year	28	1	16
Memorandum (non-add) entries:			
3100 Obligated balance, start of year	35	28	1
3200 Obligated balance, end of year	28	1	16
Budget authority and outlays, net:			
Mandatory:			
4090 Budget authority, gross	28	30	46
Outlays, gross:			
4100 Outlays from new mandatory authority		15	23
4101 Outlays from mandatory balances	44	42	9
4110 Outlays, gross (total)	44	57	32
4180 Budget authority, net (total)	28	30	46
4190 Outlays, net (total)	44	57	32

Division O of the Consolidated Appropriations Act of 2016 (P.L. 114–113) established the 9–11 Response and Biometric Exit Account. Pursuant to the law, amounts in this account shall be available to the Secretary of Homeland Security without further appropriation for implementing the biometric entry and exit system described in section 7208 of the Intelligence Reform and Terrorism Prevention Act of 2004 (8 U.S.C. 1365b).

Object Classification (in millions of dollars)

Identification code 070–5702–0–2–751	2021 actual	2022 est.	2023 est.
Direct obligations:			
23.3 Communications, utilities, and miscellaneous charges	1	1	2
25.2 Other services from non-Federal sources	37	29	45
31.0 Equipment	1		
99.9 Total new obligations, unexpired accounts	39	30	47

Trust Funds

U.S. CUSTOMS REFUNDS, TRANSFERS AND EXPENSES, UNCLAIMED AND ABANDONED GOODS

Special and Trust Fund Receipts (in millions of dollars)

Identification code 070–8789–0–7–751	2021 actual	2022 est.	2023 est.
0100 Balance, start of year			
Receipts:			
Current law:			
1110 Proceeds of the Sales of Unclaimed Abandoned, Seized Goods	1	2	3
2000 Total: Balances and receipts	1	2	3
Appropriations:			
Current law:			
2101 U.S. Customs Refunds, Transfers and Expenses, Unclaimed and Abandoned Goods	–1	–2	–3
5099 Balance, end of year			

Program and Financing (in millions of dollars)

Identification code 070–8789–0–7–751	2021 actual	2022 est.	2023 est.
Obligations by program activity:			
0001 U.S. Customs Refunds, Transfers and Expenses, Unclaimed and Aban (Direct)	2	2	3
Budgetary resources:			
Unobligated balance:			
1000 Unobligated balance brought forward, Oct 1	1	1	1
1021 Recoveries of prior year unpaid obligations	1		
1070 Unobligated balance (total)	2	1	1
Budget authority:			
Appropriations, mandatory:			
1201 Appropriation (special or trust fund)	1	2	3
1930 Total budgetary resources available	3	3	4
Memorandum (non-add) entries:			
1941 Unexpired unobligated balance, end of year	1	1	1
Change in obligated balance:			
Unpaid obligations:			
3000 Unpaid obligations, brought forward, Oct 1	1		
3010 New obligations, unexpired accounts	2	2	3
3020 Outlays (gross)	–2	–2	–3
3040 Recoveries of prior year unpaid obligations, unexpired	–1		
Memorandum (non-add) entries:			
3100 Obligated balance, start of year	1		
Budget authority and outlays, net:			
Mandatory:			
4090 Budget authority, gross	1	2	3
Outlays, gross:			
4100 Outlays from new mandatory authority	1	2	3
4101 Outlays from mandatory balances	1		
4110 Outlays, gross (total)	2	2	3
4180 Budget authority, net (total)	1	2	3
4190 Outlays, net (total)	2	2	3

This account expends proceeds from the auction of unclaimed and abandoned goods, authorized by 19 CFR 127.41.

Object Classification (in millions of dollars)

Identification code 070–8789–0–7–751	2021 actual	2022 est.	2023 est.
Direct obligations:			
25.2 Other services from non-Federal sources	2	1	2
44.0 Refunds		1	1
99.9 Total new obligations, unexpired accounts	2	2	3

U.S. IMMIGRATION AND CUSTOMS ENFORCEMENT

Federal Funds

OPERATIONS AND SUPPORT

For necessary expenses of U.S. Immigration and Customs Enforcement for operations and support, including the purchase and lease of up to 3,790 (2,350 for replacement only) police-type vehicles; overseas vetted units; and maintenance, minor construction, and minor leasehold improvements at owned and leased facilities; $8,002,128,000; of which not less than $6,000,000 shall remain available until expended for efforts to enforce laws against forced child labor; of which $46,696,000 shall remain available until September 30, 2024; of which not less than $1,500,000 is for paid apprenticeships for participants in the Human Exploitation Rescue Operative Child-Rescue Corps; of which not less than $15,000,000 shall be available for investigation of intellectual property rights violations, including operation of the National Intellectual Property Rights Coordination Center; and of which not less than $3,802,229,000 shall be for enforcement, detention, and removal operations, including support for joint processing centers and transportation of unaccompanied minor aliens: Provided, That not to exceed $11,475 shall be for official reception and representation expenses: Provided further, That not to exceed $10,000,000 shall be available until expended for conducting special operations under section 3131 of the Customs Enforcement Act of 1986 (19 U.S.C. 2081): Provided further, That not to exceed $2,000,000 shall be for awards of compensation to informants, to be accounted for solely under the certificate of the Secretary of Homeland Security: Provided further, That not to exceed $11,216,000 shall be available to fund or reimburse other Federal agencies for the costs associated with the care, maintenance, and repatriation of smuggled aliens unlawfully present in the United States.

Note.—A full-year 2022 appropriation for this account was not enacted at the time the Budget was prepared; therefore, the Budget assumes this account is operating under the Continuing Appropriations Act, 2022 (Division A of Public Law 117–43, as amended). The amounts included for 2022 reflect the annualized level provided by the continuing resolution.

Special and Trust Fund Receipts (in millions of dollars)

Identification code 070–0540–0–1–751	2021 actual	2022 est.	2023 est.
0100 Balance, start of year	21	24	26

DEPARTMENT OF HOMELAND SECURITY

U.S. Immigration and Customs Enforcement—Continued
Federal Funds—Continued

513

		2021 actual	2022 est.	2023 est.
0198	Rounding adjustment	−1		
0199	Balance, start of year	20	24	26
	Receipts:			
	Current law:			
1120	Breached Bond Penalties Greater Than $8M, Breached Bond Detention Fund	27	55	55
1120	Student and Exchange Visitor Fee	171	187	187
1120	Detention and Removal Operations Fees			3
1199	Total current law receipts	198	242	245
1999	Total receipts	198	242	245
2000	Total: Balances and receipts	218	266	271
	Appropriations:			
	Current law:			
2101	Operations and Support	−171	−187	−187
2101	Operations and Support	−26	−55	−55
2101	Operations and Support			−3
2103	Operations and Support	−5	−10	−10
2103	Operations and Support	−3	−1	−3
2132	Operations and Support	10	10	11
2132	Operations and Support	1	3	3
2199	Total current law appropriations	−194	−240	−244
2999	Total appropriations	−194	−240	−244
5099	Balance, end of year	24	26	27

Program and Financing (in millions of dollars)

Identification code 070–0540–0–1–751		2021 actual	2022 est.	2023 est.
	Obligations by program activity:			
0001	Immigration and Customs Enforcement (Direct)	373	278	
0002	CAS - Mission Support	1,300	1,304	1,468
0003	CAS - Office of the Principal Legal Advisor	311	314	402
0004	CAS - Homeland Security Investigations	2,136	2,139	2,330
0005	CAS - Enforcement and Removal Operations	4,161	4,119	3,802
0799	Total direct obligations	8,281	8,154	8,002
0801	Immigration and Customs Enforcement (Reimbursable)	218	218	218
0900	Total new obligations, unexpired accounts	8,499	8,372	8,220
	Budgetary resources:			
	Unobligated balance:			
1000	Unobligated balance brought forward, Oct 1	474	371	400
1001	Discretionary unobligated balance brought fwd, Oct 1	131		
1010	Unobligated balance transfer to other accts [070–0545]	−3		
1012	Unobligated balance transfers between expired and unexpired accounts	19		
1021	Recoveries of prior year unpaid obligations	55		
1070	Unobligated balance (total)	545	371	400
	Budget authority:			
	Appropriations, discretionary:			
1100	Base Appropriation	7,876	7,876	8,002
1121	Appropriations transferred from other acct [070–0550]	5		
1121	Appropriations transferred from other acct [011–1070]	2		
1160	Appropriation, discretionary (total)	7,883	7,876	8,002
	Appropriations, mandatory:			
1201	Student and Exchange Visitor Program	171	187	187
1201	Breached Bond Detention Fund	26	55	55
1201	Immigration User Fee	46	135	135
1201	Detention and Removal Operations Fees			3
1203	Student and Exchange Visitor Program (previously unavailable)	5	10	10
1203	Breached Bond Detention Fund (previously unavailable)	3	1	3
1203	Immigration User Fee (previously unavailable)	6	3	3
1232	Appropriations temporarily reduced (Student and Exchange Visitor Program)	−10	−10	−11
1232	Appropriations temporarily reduced (Breached Bond Fund)	−1	−3	−3
1232	Appropriations temporarily reduced (Immigration User Fee)	−3	−8	−8
1260	Appropriations, mandatory (total)	243	370	374
	Spending authority from offsetting collections, discretionary:			
1700	Collected	110	155	155
1701	Change in uncollected payments, Federal sources	117		
1750	Spending auth from offsetting collections, disc (total)	227	155	155
1900	Budget authority (total)	8,353	8,401	8,531
1930	Total budgetary resources available	8,898	8,772	8,931
	Memorandum (non-add) entries:			
1940	Unobligated balance expiring	−28		
1941	Unexpired unobligated balance, end of year	371	400	711
	Change in obligated balance:			
	Unpaid obligations:			
3000	Unpaid obligations, brought forward, Oct 1	2,446	2,426	3,310
3010	New obligations, unexpired accounts	8,499	8,372	8,220
3011	Obligations ("upward adjustments"), expired accounts	68		
3020	Outlays (gross)	−8,346	−7,488	−6,793
3040	Recoveries of prior year unpaid obligations, unexpired	−55		
3041	Recoveries of prior year unpaid obligations, expired	−186		
3050	Unpaid obligations, end of year	2,426	3,310	4,737
	Uncollected payments:			
3060	Uncollected pymts, Fed sources, brought forward, Oct 1	−110	−162	−162
3070	Change in uncollected pymts, Fed sources, unexpired	−117		
3071	Change in uncollected pymts, Fed sources, expired	65		
3090	Uncollected pymts, Fed sources, end of year	−162	−162	−162
	Memorandum (non-add) entries:			
3100	Obligated balance, start of year	2,336	2,264	3,148
3200	Obligated balance, end of year	2,264	3,148	4,575
	Budget authority and outlays, net:			
	Discretionary:			
4000	Budget authority, gross	8,110	8,031	8,157
	Outlays, gross:			
4010	Outlays from new discretionary authority	6,315	4,879	4,956
4011	Outlays from discretionary balances	1,778	2,136	1,576
4020	Outlays, gross (total)	8,093	7,015	6,532
	Offsets against gross budget authority and outlays:			
	Offsetting collections (collected) from:			
4030	Federal sources	−172	−155	−155
4033	Non-Federal sources	−20		
4040	Offsets against gross budget authority and outlays (total)	−192	−155	−155
	Additional offsets against gross budget authority only:			
4050	Change in uncollected pymts, Fed sources, unexpired	−117		
4052	Offsetting collections credited to expired accounts	82		
4060	Additional offsets against budget authority only (total)	−35		
4070	Budget authority, net (discretionary)	7,883	7,876	8,002
4080	Outlays, net (discretionary)	7,901	6,860	6,377
	Mandatory:			
4090	Budget authority, gross	243	370	374
	Outlays, gross:			
4100	Outlays from new mandatory authority	132	183	186
4101	Outlays from mandatory balances	121	290	75
4110	Outlays, gross (total)	253	473	261
4180	Budget authority, net (total)	8,126	8,246	8,376
4190	Outlays, net (total)	8,154	7,333	6,638
	Memorandum (non-add) entries:			
5096	Unexpired unavailable balance, SOY: Appropriations		14	14
5098	Unexpired unavailable balance, EOY: Appropriations		14	14

As the largest investigative arm of the Department of Homeland Security (DHS), U.S. Immigration and Customs Enforcement (ICE) brings a unified and coordinated focus to the enforcement of Federal immigration and customs laws. The President's Budget supports ICE's mission to enforce immigration and customs laws. ICE works to protect the United States and its people by deterring, interdicting, and investigating threats arising from the movement of people and goods into and out of the United States.

The Operations and Support appropriation funds necessary operations, mission support, and associated management and administrative costs. Major programs include:

Homeland Security Investigations (HSI).—Investigates a broad range of domestic and international immigration and customs violations such as human smuggling and trafficking; the smuggling of weapons and other types of contraband including opioids; export enforcement, such as investigating illegal arms exports and exports of dual-use equipment that may threaten national security; financial crimes, such as money laundering, bulk cash smuggling, and other financial crimes; commercial fraud, including intellectual property violations; cybercrimes; child exploitation; identity and immigration benefit fraud; and human rights violations. HSI is also responsible for the collection, analysis, and dissemination of strategic, operational, and tactical intelligence for use by the operational elements of ICE and DHS.

U.S. Immigration and Customs Enforcement—Continued
Federal Funds—Continued

OPERATIONS AND SUPPORT—Continued

Enforcement and Removal Operations (ERO).—Responsible for promoting public safety and national security by identifying, apprehending, and detaining removable noncitizens prior to ensuring their departure from the United States through the fair enforcement of the Nation's immigration laws.

Office of the Principal Legal Advisor.—Serves as the exclusive legal representative for the U.S. Government at immigration court hearings, and provides expert legal counsel to ICE on customs, immigration, labor, and administrative law.

Mission Support.—Manages ICE's financial and human resources, information technology, training for employees and special agents, sensitive property, facilities, and other assets.

Object Classification (in millions of dollars)

Identification code 070–0540–0–1–751		2021 actual	2022 est.	2023 est.
	Direct obligations:			
	Personnel compensation:			
11.1	Full-time permanent	2,161	2,147	2,419
11.3	Other than full-time permanent	17	20	26
11.5	Other personnel compensation	400	400	539
11.8	Special personal services payments	....	....	3
11.9	Total personnel compensation	2,578	2,567	2,987
12.1	Civilian personnel benefits	1,257	1,260	1,292
21.0	Travel and transportation of persons	440	400	447
22.0	Transportation of things	15	15	11
23.1	Rental payments to GSA	336	330	400
23.2	Rental payments to others	13	14	27
23.3	Communications, utilities, and miscellaneous charges	92	92	89
25.1	Advisory and assistance services	590	575	667
25.2	Other services from non-Federal sources	297	280	34
25.3	Other goods and services from Federal sources	113	113	130
25.4	Operation and maintenance of facilities	1,705	1,680	112
25.6	Medical care	255	260	7
25.7	Operation and maintenance of equipment	217	220	163
25.8	Subsistence and support of persons	11	11	1,389
26.0	Supplies and materials	52	52	52
31.0	Equipment	239	218	125
32.0	Land and structures	40	36	41
42.0	Insurance claims and indemnities	29	29	26
91.0	Unvouchered	2	2	3
99.0	Direct obligations	8,281	8,154	8,002
99.0	Reimbursable obligations	218	218	218
99.9	Total new obligations, unexpired accounts	8,499	8,372	8,220

Employment Summary

Identification code 070–0540–0–1–751	2021 actual	2022 est.	2023 est.
1001 Direct civilian full-time equivalent employment	20,282	21,257	21,319
2001 Reimbursable civilian full-time equivalent employment	544	544	544

AUTOMATION MODERNIZATION, IMMIGRATION AND CUSTOMS ENFORCEMENT

Program and Financing (in millions of dollars)

Identification code 070–0543–0–1–751		2021 actual	2022 est.	2023 est.
	Budgetary resources:			
	Unobligated balance:			
1000	Unobligated balance brought forward, Oct 1	1	....	....
	Budget authority:			
	Appropriations, discretionary:			
1131	Unobligated balance of appropriations permanently reduced	–1	....	....
	Change in obligated balance:			
	Unpaid obligations:			
3000	Unpaid obligations, brought forward, Oct 1	2	1	....
3020	Outlays (gross)	–1	–1	....
3050	Unpaid obligations, end of year	1	....	....
	Memorandum (non-add) entries:			
3100	Obligated balance, start of year	2	1	....
3200	Obligated balance, end of year	1	....	....
	Budget authority and outlays, net:			
	Discretionary:			
4000	Budget authority, gross	–1	....	....
	Outlays, gross:			
4011	Outlays from discretionary balances	1	1	....
4180	Budget authority, net (total)	–1	....	....
4190	Outlays, net (total)	1	1	....

PROCUREMENT, CONSTRUCTION, AND IMPROVEMENTS

For necessary expenses of U.S. Immigration and Customs Enforcement for procurement, construction, and improvements, $97,762,000, of which $22,997,000 shall remain available until September 30, 2025, and of which $74,765,000 shall remain available until September 30, 2027.

Note.—A full-year 2022 appropriation for this account was not enacted at the time the Budget was prepared; therefore, the Budget assumes this account is operating under the Continuing Appropriations Act, 2022 (Division A of Public Law 117–43, as amended). The amounts included for 2022 reflect the annualized level provided by the continuing resolution.

Program and Financing (in millions of dollars)

Identification code 070–0545–0–1–751		2021 actual	2022 est.	2023 est.
	Obligations by program activity:			
0002	CAS - Mission Support Assets and Infrastructure	30	30	11
0003	CAS - Operational Communications/Information Technology	17	17	12
0004	CAS - Construction and Facility Improvements	31	31	75
0900	Total new obligations, unexpired accounts	78	78	98
	Budgetary resources:			
	Unobligated balance:			
1000	Unobligated balance brought forward, Oct 1	69	88	107
1011	Unobligated balance transfer from other acct [070–0540]	3	....	....
1070	Unobligated balance (total)	72	88	107
	Budget authority:			
	Appropriations, discretionary:			
1100	Appropriation	97	97	98
1131	Unobligated balance of appropriations permanently reduced	–3	....	....
1160	Appropriation, discretionary (total)	94	97	98
1930	Total budgetary resources available	166	185	205
	Memorandum (non-add) entries:			
1941	Unexpired unobligated balance, end of year	88	107	107
	Change in obligated balance:			
	Unpaid obligations:			
3000	Unpaid obligations, brought forward, Oct 1	94	109	130
3010	New obligations, unexpired accounts	78	78	98
3020	Outlays (gross)	–63	–57	–201
3050	Unpaid obligations, end of year	109	130	27
	Memorandum (non-add) entries:			
3100	Obligated balance, start of year	94	109	130
3200	Obligated balance, end of year	109	130	27
	Budget authority and outlays, net:			
	Discretionary:			
4000	Budget authority, gross	94	97	98
	Outlays, gross:			
4010	Outlays from new discretionary authority	1	....	79
4011	Outlays from discretionary balances	62	57	122
4020	Outlays, gross (total)	63	57	201
4180	Budget authority, net (total)	94	97	98
4190	Outlays, net (total)	63	57	201

Procurement, Construction, and Improvements (PC&I) provides the funds necessary for the planning, operational development, engineering, and purchase of headquarters and field operational and IT assets prior to the sustainment phase. Funding within this account is used for the acquisition and construction of U.S. Immigration and Customs Enforcement (ICE) facilities, as well as for automation modernization activities that strengthen information availability while improving information sharing across the Department of Homeland Security, ICE, and other partner organizations in a fully secure information technology environment.

DEPARTMENT OF HOMELAND SECURITY

Transportation Security Administration — Federal Funds

Object Classification (in millions of dollars)

Identification code 070–0545–0–1–751		2021 actual	2022 est.	2023 est.
	Direct obligations:			
23.2	Rental payments to others	1	1	....
25.1	Advisory and assistance services	14	14	....
25.2	Other services from non-Federal sources	....	....	4
25.7	Operation and maintenance of equipment	1	2	....
31.0	Equipment	32	31	19
32.0	Land and structures	31	30	75
99.0	Direct obligations	79	78	98
99.5	Adjustment for rounding	−1	....	....
99.9	Total new obligations, unexpired accounts	78	78	98

TRANSPORTATION SECURITY ADMINISTRATION

Federal Funds

OPERATIONS AND SUPPORT

For necessary expenses of the Transportation Security Administration for operations and support, $9,542,725,000, to remain available until September 30, 2024: Provided, That not to exceed $7,650 shall be for official reception and representation expenses: Provided further, That security service fees authorized under section 44940 of title 49, United States Code, shall be credited to this appropriation as offsetting collections and shall be available only for aviation security: Provided further, That the sum appropriated under this heading from the general fund shall be reduced on a dollar-for-dollar basis as such offsetting collections are received during fiscal year 2023 so as to result in a final fiscal year appropriation from the general fund estimated at not more than $5,530,282,000.

Note.—A full-year 2022 appropriation for this account was not enacted at the time the Budget was prepared; therefore, the Budget assumes this account is operating under the Continuing Appropriations Act, 2022 (Division A of Public Law 117–43, as amended). The amounts included for 2022 reflect the annualized level provided by the continuing resolution.

Special and Trust Fund Receipts (in millions of dollars)

Identification code 070–0550–0–1–400		2021 actual	2022 est.	2023 est.
0100	Balance, start of year	....	....	....
	Receipts:			
	Current law:			
1130	Unclaimed Checkpoint Money	1	1	1
2000	Total: Balances and receipts	1	1	1
	Appropriations:			
	Current law:			
2101	Operations and Support	−1	−1	−1
5099	Balance, end of year	....	....	....

Program and Financing (in millions of dollars)

Identification code 070–0550–0–1–400		2021 actual	2022 est.	2023 est.
	Obligations by program activity:			
0002	CAS - Mission Support	955	902	1,043
0003	CAS - Aviation Screening Operations	5,415	5,498	6,949
0004	CAS - Other Operations and Enforcement	1,618	1,394	1,550
0799	Total direct obligations	7,988	7,794	9,542
0801	Aviation Security (Reimbursable)	7	7	7
0900	Total new obligations, unexpired accounts	7,995	7,801	9,549
	Budgetary resources:			
	Unobligated balance:			
1000	Unobligated balance brought forward, Oct 1	372	519	1,099
1001	Discretionary unobligated balance brought fwd, Oct 1	363	....	....
1010	Unobligated balance transfer to other accts [070–0530]	−4	....	....
1021	Recoveries of prior year unpaid obligations	31	211	37
1033	Recoveries of prior year paid obligations	36	6	9
1070	Unobligated balance (total)	435	736	1,145
	Budget authority:			
	Appropriations, discretionary:			
1100	Appropriation	6,973	5,425	7,050
1101	Appropriation (special or trust)	1	1	1
1120	Appropriations transferred to other acct [070–0530]	−25	....	....
1120	Appropriations transferred to other acct [070–0400]	−10	....	....
1120	Appropriations transferred to other acct [070–0540]	−5	....	....
1120	Appropriations transferred to other acct [070–0115]	−6	....	....
1120	Appropriations transferred to other acct [070–0100]	−8	....	....
1160	Appropriation, discretionary (total)	6,920	5,426	7,051
	Appropriations, mandatory:			
1200	Appropriation	13	....	....
	Spending authority from offsetting collections, discretionary:			
1700	Offsetting Collections - Passenger Security Fee	846	2,369	2,493
1700	Offsetting Collections - TWIC	65	66	63
1700	Offsetting Collections - HAZMAT CDL	18	19	19
1700	Offsetting Collections - Commercial Aviation and Airport	6	10	10
1700	Offsetting Collections - Air Cargo	5	5	5
1700	Offsetting Collections - Pre-Check	245	250	250
1700	Reimbursables	7	7	7
1701	Change in uncollected payments, Federal sources	8	6	9
1750	Spending auth from offsetting collections, disc (total)	1,200	2,732	2,856
	Spending authority from offsetting collections, mandatory:			
1800	Alien Flight School	4	6	6
1900	Budget authority (total)	8,137	8,164	9,913
1930	Total budgetary resources available	8,572	8,900	11,058
	Memorandum (non-add) entries:			
1940	Unobligated balance expiring	−58	....	....
1941	Unexpired unobligated balance, end of year	519	1,099	1,509
	Change in obligated balance:			
	Unpaid obligations:			
3000	Unpaid obligations, brought forward, Oct 1	1,886	2,041	2,164
3010	New obligations, unexpired accounts	7,995	7,801	9,549
3011	Obligations ("upward adjustments"), expired accounts	4	....	....
3020	Outlays (gross)	−7,776	−7,467	−10,145
3040	Recoveries of prior year unpaid obligations, unexpired	−31	−211	−37
3041	Recoveries of prior year unpaid obligations, expired	−37	....	....
3050	Unpaid obligations, end of year	2,041	2,164	1,531
	Uncollected payments:			
3060	Uncollected pymts, Fed sources, brought forward, Oct 1	−19	−24	−30
3070	Change in uncollected pymts, Fed sources, unexpired	−8	−6	−9
3071	Change in uncollected pymts, Fed sources, expired	3	....	....
3090	Uncollected pymts, Fed sources, end of year	−24	−30	−39
	Memorandum (non-add) entries:			
3100	Obligated balance, start of year	1,867	2,017	2,134
3200	Obligated balance, end of year	2,017	2,134	1,492
	Budget authority and outlays, net:			
	Discretionary:			
4000	Budget authority, gross	8,120	8,158	9,907
	Outlays, gross:			
4010	Outlays from new discretionary authority	6,198	6,687	8,231
4011	Outlays from discretionary balances	1,567	774	1,908
4020	Outlays, gross (total)	7,765	7,461	10,139
	Offsets against gross budget authority and outlays:			
	Offsetting collections (collected) from:			
4030	Federal sources	−17	−6	−9
4033	Non-Federal sources	−83	−7	−7
4034	Offsetting governmental collections	−1,130	−2,719	−2,840
4040	Offsets against gross budget authority and outlays (total)	−1,230	−2,732	−2,856
	Additional offsets against gross budget authority only:			
4050	Change in uncollected pymts, Fed sources, unexpired	−8	−6	−9
4052	Offsetting collections credited to expired accounts	2	....	....
4053	Recoveries of prior year paid obligations, unexpired accounts	36	6	9
4060	Additional offsets against budget authority only (total)	30	....	....
4070	Budget authority, net (discretionary)	6,920	5,426	7,051
4080	Outlays, net (discretionary)	6,535	4,729	7,283
	Mandatory:			
4090	Budget authority, gross	17	6	6
	Outlays, gross:			
4100	Outlays from new mandatory authority	11	2	2
4101	Outlays from mandatory balances	....	4	4
4110	Outlays, gross (total)	11	6	6
	Offsets against gross budget authority and outlays:			
	Offsetting collections (collected) from:			
4124	Offsetting governmental collections	−4	−6	−6
4180	Budget authority, net (total)	6,933	5,426	7,051
4190	Outlays, net (total)	6,542	4,729	7,283

Summary of Budget Authority and Outlays (in millions of dollars)

	2021 actual	2022 est.	2023 est.
Enacted/requested:			
Budget Authority	6,933	5,426	7,051

OPERATIONS AND SUPPORT—Continued
Summary of Budget Authority and Outlays—Continued

	2021 actual	2022 est.	2023 est.
Outlays	6,542	4,729	7,283
Legislative proposal, not subject to PAYGO:			
Budget Authority			–1,520
Outlays			–1,520
Total:			
Budget Authority	6,933	5,426	5,531
Outlays	6,542	4,729	5,763

The Transportation Security Administration (TSA) protects the Nation's transportation systems to ensure freedom of movement for people and commerce. The Operations and Support appropriation funds necessary operation, mission support, and associated management and administrative costs. Major programs include:

Mission Support.—This program supports headquarters offices, human resources, information technology, and major acquisitions to support those efforts.

Aviation Screening Operations.—This program supports the majority of TSA's frontline operations, and includes funding for the Screening Workforce, the National Explosives Detection Canine Team program, Secure Flight, and programs that support screening capabilities, as well as field support for these efforts. Since 2011, TSA has been performing this function through the use of an intelligence-driven risk-based security approach. Risk-based security increases the overall security effectiveness by focusing security resources on higher-risk and unknown travelers, while expanding the process for low risk and known/trusted travelers.

Other Operations and Enforcement.—This program supports: the Inflight Security program, which includes funding for the Federal Air Marshals Service and Federal Flight Deck Officer and Crew Training; Aviation Regulation, which provides law enforcement and regulatory presence at airports to ensure compliance with required security measures and response to security incidents; Air Cargo, which implements statutory requirement for ensuring the security of transportation systems and passengers when cargo is transported by air; Intelligence and the TSA Operations Center, which provides for the review, synthesis, and analysis of transportation specific intelligence; Surface Programs, which protect the surface transportation system (mass transit, freight rail, pipeline, and maritime modes); and vetting programs, which vet various populations requiring access to the transportation network.

Appropriations in this account are partially offset by revenue from related fees.

Object Classification (in millions of dollars)

Identification code 070–0550–0–1–400	2021 actual	2022 est.	2023 est.
Direct obligations:			
Personnel compensation:			
11.1 Full-time permanent	3,222	2,984	4,075
11.3 Other than full-time permanent	339	385	450
11.5 Other personnel compensation	317	350	400
11.8 Special personal services payments	103	103	103
11.9 Total personnel compensation	3,981	3,822	5,028
12.1 Civilian personnel benefits	1,747	1,605	1,947
13.0 Benefits for former personnel	9	9	9
21.0 Travel and transportation of persons	160	267	267
22.0 Transportation of things	1	1	1
23.1 Rental payments to GSA	129	129	129
23.2 Rental payments to others	83	83	83
23.3 Communications, utilities, and miscellaneous charges	67	67	67
24.0 Printing and reproduction	1	1	1
25.1 Advisory and assistance services	500	500	500
25.2 Other services from non-Federal sources	252	252	252
25.3 Other goods and services from Federal sources	366	366	366
25.4 Operation and maintenance of facilities	23	23	23
25.7 Operation and maintenance of equipment	398	398	598
25.8 Subsistence and support of persons	3	3	3
26.0 Supplies and materials	76	76	76
31.0 Equipment	83	83	83
32.0 Land and structures	9	9	9
41.0 Grants, subsidies, and contributions	99	99	99
42.0 Insurance claims and indemnities	1	1	1
99.0 Direct obligations	7,988	7,794	9,542
99.0 Reimbursable obligations	7	7	7
99.9 Total new obligations, unexpired accounts	7,995	7,801	9,549

Employment Summary

Identification code 070–0550–0–1–400	2021 actual	2022 est.	2023 est.
1001 Direct civilian full-time equivalent employment	56,210	55,166	57,435
2001 Reimbursable civilian full-time equivalent employment		3	3

OPERATIONS AND SUPPORT
(Legislative proposal, not subject to PAYGO)

Program and Financing (in millions of dollars)

Identification code 070–0550–2–1–400	2021 actual	2022 est.	2023 est.
Budgetary resources:			
Budget authority:			
Appropriations, discretionary:			
1100 Appropriation			–1,520
Spending authority from offsetting collections, discretionary:			
1700 Offsetting Collections - Passenger Security Fee			1,520
Budget authority and outlays, net:			
Discretionary:			
Offsets against gross budget authority and outlays:			
Offsetting collections (collected) from:			
4034 Offsetting governmental collections:			–1,520
4040 Offsets against gross budget authority and outlays (total)			–1,520
4180 Budget authority, net (total)			–1,520
4190 Outlays, net (total)			–1,520

The purpose of this Budget proposal is to eliminate the annual mandatory deficit reduction deposit at Treasury from the Passenger Security Fee beginning in fiscal year 2023. The amounts would be added to the fee revenue that is treated as offsetting collections against the TSA annual appropriations that fund the security services for which the fee is collected.

SURFACE TRANSPORTATION SECURITY

The Surface Transportation Security account is a legacy appropriation that supports personnel and resources dedicated to evaluating the risk of terrorist attack on surface transportation modes, assessing the standards and procedures to address those risks, and ensuring compliance with regulations and policies.

INTELLIGENCE AND VETTING

Program and Financing (in millions of dollars)

Identification code 070–0557–0–1–400	2021 actual	2022 est.	2023 est.
Budgetary resources:			
Unobligated balance:			
1000 Unobligated balance brought forward, Oct 1	7	7	7
1001 Discretionary unobligated balance brought fwd, Oct 1	5		
1930 Total budgetary resources available	7	7	7
Memorandum (non-add) entries:			
1941 Unexpired unobligated balance, end of year	7	7	7
Change in obligated balance:			
Unpaid obligations:			
3000 Unpaid obligations, brought forward, Oct 1	27	6	
3020 Outlays (gross)	–20	–6	
3041 Recoveries of prior year unpaid obligations, expired	–1		
3050 Unpaid obligations, end of year	6		
Memorandum (non-add) entries:			
3100 Obligated balance, start of year	27	6	
3200 Obligated balance, end of year	6		

DEPARTMENT OF HOMELAND SECURITY

Budget authority and outlays, net:
Discretionary:
Outlays, gross:

		2021 actual	2022 est.	2023 est.
4011	Outlays from discretionary balances	20	6	
4180	Budget authority, net (total)			
4190	Outlays, net (total)	20	6	

The Intelligence and Vetting account is a legacy appropriation that funds TSA's vetting programs, which enhance the interdiction of terrorists and their methods of terrorism by streamlining terrorist-related threat assessments.

TRANSPORTATION SECURITY SUPPORT

Program and Financing (in millions of dollars)

Identification code 070–0554–0–1–400	2021 actual	2022 est.	2023 est.
Change in obligated balance:			
Unpaid obligations:			
3000 Unpaid obligations, brought forward, Oct 1	30	12	
3020 Outlays (gross)	–3	–12	
3041 Recoveries of prior year unpaid obligations, expired	–15		
3050 Unpaid obligations, end of year	12		
Memorandum (non-add) entries:			
3100 Obligated balance, start of year	30	12	
3200 Obligated balance, end of year	12		
Budget authority and outlays, net:			
Discretionary:			
Outlays, gross:			
4011 Outlays from discretionary balances		3	12
4180 Budget authority, net (total)			
4190 Outlays, net (total)		3	12

The Transportation Security Support account is a legacy appropriation that funds TSA mission support functions, such as information technology, human capital services, and headquarters' administration functions.

PROCUREMENT, CONSTRUCTION, AND IMPROVEMENTS

For necessary expenses of the Transportation Security Administration for procurement, construction, and improvements, $119,345,000, to remain available until September 30, 2025.

Note.—A full-year 2022 appropriation for this account was not enacted at the time the Budget was prepared; therefore, the Budget assumes this account is operating under the Continuing Appropriations Act, 2022 (Division A of Public Law 117–43, as amended). The amounts included for 2022 reflect the annualized level provided by the continuing resolution.

Special and Trust Fund Receipts (in millions of dollars)

Identification code 070–0410–0–1–400	2021 actual	2022 est.	2023 est.
0100 Balance, start of year	15	14	14
Receipts:			
Current law:			
1120 Fees, Aviation Security Capital Fund	250	250	250
2000 Total: Balances and receipts	265	264	264
Appropriations:			
Current law:			
2101 Procurement, Construction, and Improvements	–250	–250	–250
2103 Procurement, Construction, and Improvements	–15	–14	–14
2132 Procurement, Construction, and Improvements	14	14	14
2199 Total current law appropriations	–251	–250	–250
2999 Total appropriations	–251	–250	–250
5099 Balance, end of year	14	14	14

Program and Financing (in millions of dollars)

Identification code 070–0410–0–1–400	2021 actual	2022 est.	2023 est.
Obligations by program activity:			
0001 CAS - Aviation Screening Infrastructure	163	134	119
0004 CAS - Aviation Security Capital Fund (mandatory)	489	250	250
0900 Total new obligations, unexpired accounts	652	384	369
Budgetary resources:			
Unobligated balance:			
1000 Unobligated balance brought forward, Oct 1	284	15	15
1001 Discretionary unobligated balance brought fwd, Oct 1	35		
1010 Unobligated balance transfer to other accts [070–0530]	–4		
1021 Recoveries of prior year unpaid obligations	5		
1070 Unobligated balance (total)	285	15	15
Budget authority:			
Appropriations, discretionary:			
1100 Appropriation	134	134	119
1120 Appropriations transferred to other acct [070–0530]	–3		
1160 Appropriation, discretionary (total)	131	134	119
Appropriations, mandatory:			
1201 Appropriation (special or trust fund)	250	250	250
1203 Appropriation (previously unavailable)(special or trust)	15	14	14
1232 Appropriations and/or unobligated balance of appropriations temporarily reduced	–14	–14	–14
1260 Appropriations, mandatory (total)	251	250	250
1900 Budget authority (total)	382	384	369
1930 Total budgetary resources available	667	399	384
Memorandum (non-add) entries:			
1941 Unexpired unobligated balance, end of year	15	15	15
Change in obligated balance:			
Unpaid obligations:			
3000 Unpaid obligations, brought forward, Oct 1	971	1,275	1,098
3010 New obligations, unexpired accounts	652	384	369
3020 Outlays (gross)	–343	–561	–487
3040 Recoveries of prior year unpaid obligations, unexpired	–5		
3050 Unpaid obligations, end of year	1,275	1,098	980
Memorandum (non-add) entries:			
3100 Obligated balance, start of year	971	1,275	1,098
3200 Obligated balance, end of year	1,275	1,098	980
Budget authority and outlays, net:			
Discretionary:			
4000 Budget authority, gross	131	134	119
Outlays, gross:			
4010 Outlays from new discretionary authority	33	47	42
4011 Outlays from discretionary balances	75	249	201
4020 Outlays, gross (total)	108	296	243
Mandatory:			
4090 Budget authority, gross	251	250	250
Outlays, gross:			
4100 Outlays from new mandatory authority	8	3	3
4101 Outlays from mandatory balances	227	262	241
4110 Outlays, gross (total)	235	265	244
4180 Budget authority, net (total)	382	384	369
4190 Outlays, net (total)	343	561	487

The Procurement, Construction, and Improvements (PC&I) Appropriation provides the funds, above certain threshold amounts, necessary for the manufacture, purchase, or enhancement of assets. The funding provides resources to procure and improve equipment and systems that support aviation screening operations, other transportation screening and vetting operations, and other mission support functions. This account includes funding from the Aviation Security Capital Fund (ASCF), which is used for acquisition and installation of checked baggage screening equipment and explosives detection systems, as well as for airport infrastructure modifications.

Object Classification (in millions of dollars)

Identification code 070–0410–0–1–400	2021 actual	2022 est.	2023 est.
Direct obligations:			
25.1 Advisory and assistance services	180	200	200
25.2 Other services from non-Federal sources		1	1
26.0 Supplies and materials		1	1
31.0 Equipment	472	182	167
99.9 Total new obligations, unexpired accounts	652	384	369

RESEARCH AND DEVELOPMENT

For necessary expenses of the Transportation Security Administration for research and development, $33,532,000, to remain available until September 30, 2024.

Note.—A full-year 2022 appropriation for this account was not enacted at the time the Budget was prepared; therefore, the Budget assumes this account is operating under the Continuing Appropriations Act, 2022 (Division A of Public Law 117–43, as amended). The amounts included for 2022 reflect the annualized level provided by the continuing resolution.

Program and Financing (in millions of dollars)

Identification code 070–0802–0–1–400		2021 actual	2022 est.	2023 est.
	Obligations by program activity:			
0001	Research and Development	29	30	33
0900	Total new obligations, unexpired accounts (object class 25.5)	29	30	33
	Budgetary resources:			
	Unobligated balance:			
1000	Unobligated balance brought forward, Oct 1	1	2	2
	Budget authority:			
	Appropriations, discretionary:			
1100	Appropriation	30	30	34
1930	Total budgetary resources available	31	32	36
	Memorandum (non-add) entries:			
1941	Unexpired unobligated balance, end of year	2	2	3
	Change in obligated balance:			
	Unpaid obligations:			
3000	Unpaid obligations, brought forward, Oct 1	28	37	31
3010	New obligations, unexpired accounts	29	30	33
3020	Outlays (gross)	–20	–36	–31
3050	Unpaid obligations, end of year	37	31	33
	Memorandum (non-add) entries:			
3100	Obligated balance, start of year	28	37	31
3200	Obligated balance, end of year	37	31	33
	Budget authority and outlays, net:			
	Discretionary:			
4000	Budget authority, gross	30	30	34
	Outlays, gross:			
4010	Outlays from new discretionary authority	3	10	12
4011	Outlays from discretionary balances	17	26	19
4020	Outlays, gross (total)	20	36	31
4180	Budget authority, net (total)	30	30	34
4190	Outlays, net (total)	20	36	31

The Research and Development appropriation funds necessary technology demonstrations and system development in support of TSA's passenger, baggage, and intermodal screening functions. TSA's research and development activities usually involve inter-agency agreements with established research organizations, such as the Department of Homeland Security Science and Technology Directorate, the Department of Energy, the Naval Sea Systems Command, and other federally funded research and development centers. TSA works directly with industry to test and demonstrate the newest security technologies for transportation infrastructure.

UNITED STATES COAST GUARD

Federal Funds

OPERATIONS AND SUPPORT

For necessary expenses of the Coast Guard for operations and support including the Coast Guard Reserve; purchase or lease of not to exceed 25 passenger motor vehicles, which shall be for replacement only; purchase or lease of small boats for contingent and emergent requirements (at a unit cost of not more than $700,000) and repairs and service-life replacements, not to exceed a total of $31,000,000; purchase, lease, or improvements of boats necessary for overseas deployments and activities; payments pursuant to section 156 of Public Law 97–377 (42 U.S.C. 402 note; 96 Stat. 1920); and recreation and welfare; $9,620,029,000, of which $530,000,000 shall be for defense-related activities; of which $24,500,000 shall be derived from the Oil Spill Liability Trust Fund to carry out the purposes of section 1012(a)(5) of the Oil Pollution Act of 1990 (33 U.S.C. 2712(a)(5)); of which $24,386,000 shall remain available until September 30, 2027, for environmental compliance and restoration; and of which $100,000,000 shall remain available until September 30, 2024: Provided, That not to exceed $23,000 shall be for official reception and representation expenses.

Note.—A full-year 2022 appropriation for this account was not enacted at the time the Budget was prepared; therefore, the Budget assumes this account is operating under the Continuing Appropriations Act, 2022 (Division A of Public Law 117–43, as amended). The amounts included for 2022 reflect the annualized level provided by the continuing resolution.

OPERATIONS AND SUPPORT

⟦*For an additional amount for "Operations and Support", $5,000,000, to remain available until September 30, 2026, for personnel and administrative expenses: Provided, That such amount is designated by the Congress as being for an emergency requirement pursuant to section 4112(a) of H. Con. Res. 71 (115th Congress), the concurrent resolution on the budget for fiscal year 2018, and to section 251(b) of the Balanced Budget and Emergency Deficit Control Act of 1985.*⟧ *(Infrastructure Investments and Jobs Appropriations Act.)*

Program and Financing (in millions of dollars)

Identification code 070–0610–0–1–999		2021 actual	2022 est.	2023 est.
	Obligations by program activity:			
0001	Military Pay and Allowances	4,139		
0002	Civilian Pay and Benefits	1,076		
0003	Training and Recruiting	226		
0004	Operating Funds and Unit Level Maintenance	993		
0005	Centrally Managed Accounts	83		
0006	Intermediate and Depot Level Maintenance	1,842		
0007	Reserve Training	127		
0008	Environmental Compliance and Restoration	17		
0009	Military Personnel		4,760	5,071
0010	Mission Support		406	430
0011	Field Operations		3,373	4,119
0600	Total direct program	8,503	8,539	9,620
0799	Total direct obligations	8,503	8,539	9,620
0801	Operating Expenses (Reimbursable)	204	392	328
0900	Total new obligations, unexpired accounts	8,707	8,931	9,948
	Budgetary resources:			
	Unobligated balance:			
1000	Unobligated balance brought forward, Oct 1	143	73	24
1010	Unobligated balance transfer to other accts [070–0530]	–21		
1012	Unobligated balance transfers between expired and unexpired accounts	21		
1021	Recoveries of prior year unpaid obligations	3		
1070	Unobligated balance (total)	146	73	24
	Budget authority:			
	Appropriations, discretionary:			
1100	Appropriation	8,461	8,466	9,596
1120	Appropriations transferred to other acct [070–0530]	–8		
1160	Appropriation, discretionary (total)	8,453	8,466	9,596
	Spending authority from offsetting collections, discretionary:			
1700	Collected	143	416	352
1701	Change in uncollected payments, Federal sources	97		
1750	Spending auth from offsetting collections, disc (total)	240	416	352
1900	Budget authority (total)	8,693	8,882	9,948
1930	Total budgetary resources available	8,839	8,955	9,972
	Memorandum (non-add) entries:			
1940	Unobligated balance expiring	–59		
1941	Unexpired unobligated balance, end of year	73	24	24
	Change in obligated balance:			
	Unpaid obligations:			
3000	Unpaid obligations, brought forward, Oct 1	2,392	2,437	2,255
3010	New obligations, unexpired accounts	8,707	8,931	9,948
3011	Obligations ("upward adjustments"), expired accounts	89		
3020	Outlays (gross)	–8,570	–9,113	–9,409
3040	Recoveries of prior year unpaid obligations, unexpired	–3		
3041	Recoveries of prior year unpaid obligations, expired	–178		
3050	Unpaid obligations, end of year	2,437	2,255	2,794
	Uncollected payments:			
3060	Uncollected pymts, Fed sources, brought forward, Oct 1	–109	–137	–137
3070	Change in uncollected pymts, Fed sources, unexpired	–97		
3071	Change in uncollected pymts, Fed sources, expired	69		
3090	Uncollected pymts, Fed sources, end of year	–137	–137	–137
	Memorandum (non-add) entries:			
3100	Obligated balance, start of year	2,283	2,300	2,118
3200	Obligated balance, end of year	2,300	2,118	2,657

DEPARTMENT OF HOMELAND SECURITY

United States Coast Guard—Continued
Federal Funds—Continued
519

		2021 actual	2022 est.	2023 est.
	Budget authority and outlays, net:			
	Discretionary:			
4000	Budget authority, gross	8,693	8,882	9,948
	Outlays, gross:			
4010	Outlays from new discretionary authority	6,656	6,836	7,451
4011	Outlays from discretionary balances	1,914	2,277	1,958
4020	Outlays, gross (total)	8,570	9,113	9,409
	Offsets against gross budget authority and outlays:			
	Offsetting collections (collected) from:			
4030	Federal sources	–198	–416	–352
4033	Non-Federal sources	–12		
4040	Offsets against gross budget authority and outlays (total)	–210	–416	–352
	Additional offsets against gross budget authority only:			
4050	Change in uncollected pymts, Fed sources, unexpired	–97		
4052	Offsetting collections credited to expired accounts	67		
4060	Additional offsets against budget authority only (total)	–30		
4070	Budget authority, net (discretionary)	8,453	8,466	9,596
4080	Outlays, net (discretionary)	8,360	8,697	9,057
4180	Budget authority, net (total)	8,453	8,466	9,596
4190	Outlays, net (total)	8,360	8,697	9,057

The Operations and Support account funds the operations of the Coast Guard as it carries out its duties as a maritime, military, multi-mission operating agency and one of the six Armed Forces. To fulfill its mission, the Coast Guard employs multipurpose vessels, aircraft, and shore units, strategically located along the coasts and inland waterways of the United States. This account funds operations and maintenance of these assets, and sustainment of new and existing Coast Guard programs, projects, activities, and personnel. This account also provides funds for Reserve Training and Environmental Compliance and Restoration.

Object Classification (in millions of dollars)

Identification code 070–0610–0–1–999		2021 actual	2022 est.	2023 est.
	Direct obligations:			
	Personnel compensation:			
11.1	Full-time permanent	759	775	884
11.3	Other than full-time permanent	5	5	5
11.5	Other personnel compensation	34	26	30
11.6	Military personnel - basic allowance for housing	895	940	1,000
11.7	Military personnel	2,285	2,372	2,638
11.8	Special personal services payments	8	9	10
11.9	Total personnel compensation	3,986	4,127	4,567
12.1	Civilian personnel benefits	295	291	338
12.2	Military personnel benefits	290	308	347
13.0	Benefits for former personnel	4	4	4
21.0	Travel and transportation of persons	207	261	271
22.0	Transportation of things	116	118	123
23.1	Rental payments to GSA	59	7	57
23.2	Rental payments to others	39	33	37
23.3	Communications, utilities, and miscellaneous charges	192	207	259
24.0	Printing and reproduction	3	3	4
25.1	Advisory and assistance services	167	146	161
25.2	Other services from non-Federal sources	335	416	483
25.3	Other goods and services from Federal sources	147	194	182
25.4	Operation and maintenance of facilities	273	248	290
25.6	Medical care	352	354	397
25.7	Operation and maintenance of equipment	910	768	880
25.8	Subsistence and support of persons	6	4	4
26.0	Supplies and materials	915	675	706
31.0	Equipment	196	324	473
32.0	Land and structures	9	42	34
41.0	Grants, subsidies, and contributions		6	
42.0	Insurance claims and indemnities	2	3	3
99.0	Direct obligations	8,503	8,539	9,620
99.0	Reimbursable obligations	204	392	328
99.9	Total new obligations, unexpired accounts	8,707	8,931	9,948

Employment Summary

Identification code 070–0610–0–1–999		2021 actual	2022 est.	2023 est.
1001	Direct civilian full-time equivalent employment	7,955	8,342	8,677
1101	Direct military average strength employment	40,856	42,016	42,476
2001	Reimbursable civilian full-time equivalent employment	221	160	202
2101	Reimbursable military average strength employment	625	480	477

ENVIRONMENTAL COMPLIANCE AND RESTORATION

Program and Financing (in millions of dollars)

Identification code 070–0611–0–1–304		2021 actual	2022 est.	2023 est.
	Obligations by program activity:			
0001	Environmental Compliance	3		
0900	Total new obligations, unexpired accounts (object class 25.2)	3		
	Budgetary resources:			
	Unobligated balance:			
1000	Unobligated balance brought forward, Oct 1	6	3	3
1930	Total budgetary resources available	6	3	3
	Memorandum (non-add) entries:			
1941	Unexpired unobligated balance, end of year	3	3	3
	Change in obligated balance:			
	Unpaid obligations:			
3000	Unpaid obligations, brought forward, Oct 1	7	6	
3010	New obligations, unexpired accounts	3		
3020	Outlays (gross)	–4	–6	
3050	Unpaid obligations, end of year	6		
	Memorandum (non-add) entries:			
3100	Obligated balance, start of year	7	6	
3200	Obligated balance, end of year	6		
	Budget authority and outlays, net:			
	Discretionary:			
	Outlays, gross:			
4011	Outlays from discretionary balances	4	6	
4180	Budget authority, net (total)			
4190	Outlays, net (total)	4	6	

The Environmental Compliance and Restoration account supports activities to comply with obligations in section 318, chapter 3 of title 14 of the United States Code related to Environmental Compliance and Restoration. This includes environmental cleanup, sustainment, and restoration of current and former contaminated Coast Guard facilities, and engineering remedies for Coast Guard assets, to comply with environmental laws and prevent contamination and environmental damage.

RESERVE TRAINING

The Reserve Training account supports the training of Coast Guard Reserve Forces so they are prepared to provide qualified personnel to augment active duty forces in the event of conflict, national emergency, or natural and manmade disasters. Reservists maintain their readiness through formal training, mobilization exercises, and duty alongside regular Coast Guard members during routine and emergency operations. Reservists will continue to serve as a cost-effective surge force for response to man-made and natural disasters.

PROCUREMENT, CONSTRUCTION, AND IMPROVEMENTS

For necessary expenses of the Coast Guard for procurement, construction, and improvements, including aids to navigation, shore facilities (including facilities at Department of Defense installations used by the Coast Guard), and vessels and aircraft, including equipment related thereto, $1,654,850,000, to remain available until September 30, 2027; of which $20,000,000 shall be derived from the Oil Spill Liability Trust Fund to carry out the purposes of section 1012(a)(5) of the Oil Pollution Act of 1990 (33 U.S.C. 2712(a)(5)).

Note.—A full-year 2022 appropriation for this account was not enacted at the time the Budget was prepared; therefore, the Budget assumes this account is operating under the Continuing Appropriations Act, 2022 (Division A of Public Law 117–43, as amended). The amounts included for 2022 reflect the annualized level provided by the continuing resolution.

PROCUREMENT, CONSTRUCTION, AND IMPROVEMENTS—Continued

PROCUREMENT, CONSTRUCTION, AND IMPROVEMENTS

〔For an additional amount for "Procurement, Construction, and Improvements", $429,000,000, to remain available until September 30, 2026: *Provided*, That of the funds made available under this heading in this Act—〕

〔(1) $131,500,000 shall be for housing, family support, safety, and training facilities, as described in the Coast Guard Fiscal Year 2022 Unfunded Priorities List submitted to Congress on June 29, 2021;〕

〔(2) $158,000,000 shall be for shore construction addressing facility deficiencies, as described in the Coast Guard Fiscal Year 2022 Unfunded Priorities List submitted to Congress on June 29, 2021;〕

〔(3) $19,500,000 shall be for shore construction supporting operational assets and maritime commerce, as described in the Coast Guard Fiscal Year 2022 Unfunded Priorities List submitted to Congress on June 29, 2021; and〕

〔(4) $120,000,000 shall be for construction and improvement of childcare development centers:〕

〔*Provided further*, That not later than 90 days after the date of enactment of this Act, the Department shall submit to the Committees on Appropriations and Commerce, Science, and Transportation of the Senate and the Committees on Appropriations and Transportation and Infrastructure in the House of Representatives a detailed expenditure plan, including a list of project locations under each paragraph in the preceding proviso: *Provided further*, That such amount is designated by the Congress as being for an emergency requirement pursuant to section 4112(a) of H. Con. Res. 71 (115th Congress), the concurrent resolution on the budget for fiscal year 2018, and to section 251(b) of the Balanced Budget and Emergency Deficit Control Act of 1985.〕 *(Infrastructure Investments and Jobs Appropriations Act.)*

Program and Financing (in millions of dollars)

Identification code 070–0613–0–1–403	2021 actual	2022 est.	2023 est.
Obligations by program activity:			
0001 Vessels	984	1,426	1,446
0002 Aircraft	628	236	163
0003 Other Acquisition Programs	80	79	85
0004 Shore Facilities and Aids to Navigation	410	277	386
0600 Total Direct Program	2,102	2,018	2,080
0799 Total direct obligations	2,102	2,018	2,080
0801 Acquisition, Construction, and Improvements (Reimbursable)	50	108	33
0900 Total new obligations, unexpired accounts	2,152	2,126	2,113
Budgetary resources:			
Unobligated balance:			
1000 Unobligated balance brought forward, Oct 1	3,143	3,284	3,958
1010 Unobligated balance transfer to other accts [070–0530]	–60		
1021 Recoveries of prior year unpaid obligations	22		
1033 Recoveries of prior year paid obligations	20		
1070 Unobligated balance (total)	3,125	3,284	3,958
Budget authority:			
Appropriations, discretionary:			
1100 Appropriation	2,244	2,673	1,635
1120 Appropriations transferred to other acct [070–0200]		–1	
1160 Appropriation, discretionary (total)	2,244	2,672	1,635
Spending authority from offsetting collections, discretionary:			
1700 Collected	23	128	53
1701 Change in uncollected payments, Federal sources	53		
1750 Spending auth from offsetting collections, disc (total)	76	128	53
1900 Budget authority (total)	2,320	2,800	1,688
1930 Total budgetary resources available	5,445	6,084	5,646
Memorandum (non-add) entries:			
1940 Unobligated balance expiring	–9		
1941 Unexpired unobligated balance, end of year	3,284	3,958	3,533
Change in obligated balance:			
Unpaid obligations:			
3000 Unpaid obligations, brought forward, Oct 1	4,010	4,441	4,093
3010 New obligations, unexpired accounts	2,152	2,126	2,113
3011 Obligations ("upward adjustments"), expired accounts	14		
3020 Outlays (gross)	–1,693	–2,474	–2,305
3040 Recoveries of prior year unpaid obligations, unexpired	–22		
3041 Recoveries of prior year unpaid obligations, expired	–20		
3050 Unpaid obligations, end of year	4,441	4,093	3,901
Uncollected payments:			
3060 Uncollected pymts, Fed sources, brought forward, Oct 1	–28	–81	–81
3070 Change in uncollected pymts, Fed sources, unexpired	–53		
3090 Uncollected pymts, Fed sources, end of year	–81	–81	–81
Memorandum (non-add) entries:			
3100 Obligated balance, start of year	3,982	4,360	4,012
3200 Obligated balance, end of year	4,360	4,012	3,820
Budget authority and outlays, net:			
Discretionary:			
4000 Budget authority, gross	2,320	2,800	1,688
Outlays, gross:			
4010 Outlays from new discretionary authority	124	395	217
4011 Outlays from discretionary balances	1,569	2,079	2,088
4020 Outlays, gross (total)	1,693	2,474	2,305
Offsets against gross budget authority and outlays:			
Offsetting collections (collected) from:			
4030 Federal sources	–23	–20	–20
4033 Non-Federal sources	–21	–108	–33
4040 Offsets against gross budget authority and outlays (total)	–44	–128	–53
Additional offsets against gross budget authority only:			
4050 Change in uncollected pymts, Fed sources, unexpired	–53		
4052 Offsetting collections credited to expired accounts	1		
4053 Recoveries of prior year paid obligations, unexpired accounts	20		
4060 Additional offsets against budget authority only (total)	–32		
4070 Budget authority, net (discretionary)	2,244	2,672	1,635
4080 Outlays, net (discretionary)	1,649	2,346	2,252
4180 Budget authority, net (total)	2,244	2,672	1,635
4190 Outlays, net (total)	1,649	2,346	2,252

The Procurement, Construction, and Improvements account provides for the acquisition, procurement, construction, rebuilding, and improvement of vessels, aircraft, information management resources, other equipment, shore facilities, and aids to navigation required to execute the Coast Guard's missions and achieve its performance goals. The Coast Guard will continue the recapitalization of boats, major cutters and patrol boats, aircraft, and command, control, communications, computers, intelligence, surveillance and reconnaissance systems. Furthermore, the Coast Guard will continue fleet sustainment projects to enhance and extend the service life of selected existing aircraft and cutters. The Coast Guard will also invest in shore infrastructure as well as repair aging buildings, and other facilities. These vital recapitalization projects will provide the Coast Guard with capabilities necessary to perform its missions.

Object Classification (in millions of dollars)

Identification code 070–0613–0–1–403	2021 actual	2022 est.	2023 est.
Direct obligations:			
21.0 Travel and transportation of persons	5	16	9
23.2 Rental payments to others	2		
23.3 Communications, utilities, and miscellaneous charges	37	1	
25.1 Advisory and assistance services	201	591	319
25.2 Other services from non-Federal sources	114	41	51
25.3 Other goods and services from Federal sources	412	149	235
25.4 Operation and maintenance of facilities	44	80	52
25.7 Operation and maintenance of equipment	37	11	45
25.8 Subsistence and support of persons	1		
26.0 Supplies and materials	127	84	21
31.0 Equipment	883	905	1,312
32.0 Land and structures	239	140	36
99.0 Direct obligations	2,102	2,018	2,080
99.0 Reimbursable obligations	50	108	33
99.9 Total new obligations, unexpired accounts	2,152	2,126	2,113

ALTERATION OF BRIDGES

Program and Financing (in millions of dollars)

Identification code 070–0614–0–1–403	2021 actual	2022 est.	2023 est.
Budgetary resources:			
Unobligated balance:			
1000 Unobligated balance brought forward, Oct 1	2		

DEPARTMENT OF HOMELAND SECURITY

		2021 actual	2022 est.	2023 est.
	Budget authority:			
	Appropriations, discretionary:			
1131	Unobligated balance of appropriations permanently reduced	–2		
	Budget authority and outlays, net:			
	Discretionary:			
4000	Budget authority, gross	–2		
4180	Budget authority, net (total)	–2		
4190	Outlays, net (total)			

The Alteration of Bridges account funds the Federal Government's share of costs for altering or removing bridges determined to be unreasonable obstructions to navigation. Under the Truman-Hobbs Act of 1940 (33 U.S.C. 511–523), the Federal Government shares, with the bridge owner, the cost of altering railroad and publicly-owned highway bridges declared by the Coast Guard to be unreasonable obstructions to navigation.

RESEARCH AND DEVELOPMENT

For necessary expenses of the Coast Guard for research and development; and for maintenance, rehabilitation, lease, and operation of facilities and equipment; $7,476,000, to remain available until September 30, 2025, of which $500,000 shall be derived from the Oil Spill Liability Trust Fund to carry out the purposes of section 1012(a)(5) of the Oil Pollution Act of 1990 (33 U.S.C. 2712(a)(5)): Provided, That there may be credited to and used for the purposes of this appropriation funds received from State and local governments, other public authorities, private sources, and foreign countries for expenses incurred for research, development, testing, and evaluation.

Note.—A full-year 2022 appropriation for this account was not enacted at the time the Budget was prepared; therefore, the Budget assumes this account is operating under the Continuing Appropriations Act, 2022 (Division A of Public Law 117–43, as amended). The amounts included for 2022 reflect the annualized level provided by the continuing resolution.

Program and Financing (in millions of dollars)

Identification code 070–0615–0–1–403		2021 actual	2022 est.	2023 est.
	Obligations by program activity:			
0001	Applied R&D	8	7	7
0801	Research, Development, Test, and Evaluation (Reimbursable)	3	5	5
0900	Total new obligations, unexpired accounts	11	12	12
	Budgetary resources:			
	Unobligated balance:			
1000	Unobligated balance brought forward, Oct 1	6	7	11
	Budget authority:			
	Appropriations, discretionary:			
1100	Appropriation	10	10	7
	Spending authority from offsetting collections, discretionary:			
1700	Collected	2	6	6
1701	Change in uncollected payments, Federal sources	1		
1750	Spending auth from offsetting collections, disc (total)	3	6	6
1900	Budget authority (total)	13	16	13
1930	Total budgetary resources available	19	23	24
	Memorandum (non-add) entries:			
1940	Unobligated balance expiring	–1		
1941	Unexpired unobligated balance, end of year	7	11	12
	Change in obligated balance:			
	Unpaid obligations:			
3000	Unpaid obligations, brought forward, Oct 1	8	7	6
3010	New obligations, unexpired accounts	11	12	12
3020	Outlays (gross)	–11	–13	–14
3041	Recoveries of prior year unpaid obligations, expired	–1		
3050	Unpaid obligations, end of year	7	6	4
	Uncollected payments:			
3060	Uncollected pymts, Fed sources, brought forward, Oct 1	–4	–5	–5
3070	Change in uncollected pymts, Fed sources, unexpired	–1		
3090	Uncollected pymts, Fed sources, end of year	–5	–5	–5
	Memorandum (non-add) entries:			
3100	Obligated balance, start of year	4	2	1
3200	Obligated balance, end of year	2	1	–1

		2021 actual	2022 est.	2023 est.
	Budget authority and outlays, net:			
	Discretionary:			
4000	Budget authority, gross	13	16	13
	Outlays, gross:			
4010	Outlays from new discretionary authority	2	8	7
4011	Outlays from discretionary balances	9	5	7
4020	Outlays, gross (total)	11	13	14
	Offsets against gross budget authority and outlays:			
	Offsetting collections (collected) from:			
4030	Federal sources	–2	–6	–6
	Additional offsets against gross budget authority only:			
4050	Change in uncollected pymts, Fed sources, unexpired	–1		
4070	Budget authority, net (discretionary)	10	10	7
4080	Outlays, net (discretionary)	9	7	8
4180	Budget authority, net (total)	10	10	7
4190	Outlays, net (total)	9	7	8

The Research and Development account provides the funds to develop techniques, methods, hardware, and systems that directly contribute to increasing the productivity and effectiveness of the Coast Guard's missions, as well as expertise and services that enhance pre-acquisition planning and analysis to reduce cost, schedule, and performance risks across multiple acquisition projects.

Object Classification (in millions of dollars)

Identification code 070–0615–0–1–403		2021 actual	2022 est.	2023 est.
	Direct obligations:			
21.0	Travel and transportation of persons		1	1
23.3	Communications, utilities, and miscellaneous charges	1		
25.1	Advisory and assistance services	1	1	1
25.2	Other services from non-Federal sources	1		
25.5	Research and development contracts		3	3
25.7	Operation and maintenance of equipment		1	1
26.0	Supplies and materials	5	1	1
99.0	Direct obligations	8	7	7
99.0	Reimbursable obligations	3	5	5
99.9	Total new obligations, unexpired accounts	11	12	12

MEDICARE-ELIGIBLE RETIREE HEALTH FUND CONTRIBUTION, HOMELAND SECURITY

Program and Financing (in millions of dollars)

Identification code 070–0616–0–1–403		2021 actual	2022 est.	2023 est.
	Obligations by program activity:			
0001	MERHCF	215	241	253
0900	Total new obligations, unexpired accounts (object class 12.2)	215	241	253
	Budgetary resources:			
	Budget authority:			
	Appropriations, discretionary:			
1100	Appropriation	215	241	253
1930	Total budgetary resources available	215	241	253
	Change in obligated balance:			
	Unpaid obligations:			
3010	New obligations, unexpired accounts	215	241	253
3020	Outlays (gross)	–215	–241	–253
	Budget authority and outlays, net:			
	Discretionary:			
4000	Budget authority, gross	215	241	253
	Outlays, gross:			
4010	Outlays from new discretionary authority	215	241	253
4180	Budget authority, net (total)	215	241	253
4190	Outlays, net (total)	215	241	253

The Medicare-Eligible Retiree Health Care Fund Contribution account provides for the cost of medical benefits for Medicare-eligible beneficiaries paid from the Department of Defense Medicare-Eligible Retiree Health Care Fund (10 U.S.C. ch. 56). Permanent indefinite authority is provided

MEDICARE-ELIGIBLE RETIREE HEALTH FUND CONTRIBUTION, HOMELAND SECURITY—Continued

for a discretionary appropriation of the annual accrual payment into this fund (P.L. 108–375).

RETIRED PAY

For retired pay, including the payment of obligations otherwise chargeable to lapsed appropriations for this purpose, payments under the Retired Serviceman's Family Protection and Survivor Benefits Plans, payment for career status bonuses, payment of continuation pay under section 356 of title 37, United States Code, concurrent receipts, combat-related special compensation, and payments for medical care of retired personnel and their dependents under chapter 55 of title 10, United States Code, $2,044,414,000, to remain available until expended.

Note.—A full-year 2022 appropriation for this account was not enacted at the time the Budget was prepared; therefore, the Budget assumes this account is operating under the Continuing Appropriations Act, 2022 (Division A of Public Law 117–43, as amended). The amounts included for 2022 reflect the annualized level provided by the continuing resolution.

Program and Financing (in millions of dollars)

Identification code 070–0602–0–1–403		2021 actual	2022 est.	2023 est.
	Obligations by program activity:			
0001	Retired Pay	1,861	2,009	2,044
	Budgetary resources:			
	Unobligated balance:			
1000	Unobligated balance brought forward, Oct 1	130	139	....
	Budget authority:			
	Appropriations, mandatory:			
1200	Appropriation	1,870	1,870	2,044
1930	Total budgetary resources available	2,000	2,009	2,044
	Memorandum (non-add) entries:			
1941	Unexpired unobligated balance, end of year	139		
	Change in obligated balance:			
	Unpaid obligations:			
3000	Unpaid obligations, brought forward, Oct 1	152	158	296
3010	New obligations, unexpired accounts	1,861	2,009	2,044
3020	Outlays (gross)	−1,855	−1,871	−2,027
3050	Unpaid obligations, end of year	158	296	313
	Memorandum (non-add) entries:			
3100	Obligated balance, start of year	152	158	296
3200	Obligated balance, end of year	158	296	313
	Budget authority and outlays, net:			
	Mandatory:			
4090	Budget authority, gross	1,870	1,870	2,044
	Outlays, gross:			
4100	Outlays from new mandatory authority	1,612	1,684	1,839
4101	Outlays from mandatory balances	243	187	188
4110	Outlays, gross (total)	1,855	1,871	2,027
4180	Budget authority, net (total)	1,870	1,870	2,044
4190	Outlays, net (total)	1,855	1,871	2,027

The Retired Pay account funds the retired pay of military personnel of the Coast Guard and Coast Guard Reserve, members of the former Lighthouse Service, and annuities payable to beneficiaries of retired military personnel under the Retired Serviceman's Family Protection Plan (10 U.S.C. 1431–46) and Survivor Benefits Plans (10 U.S.C. 1447–55); payments for career status bonuses; payment of continuation pay (37 U.S.C. 356); concurrent receipts, and combat-related special compensation under the National Defense Authorization Act, as authorized by law; and payments for medical care of retired personnel and their dependents under the Dependents Medical Care Act (10 U.S.C., ch. 55).

Object Classification (in millions of dollars)

Identification code 070–0602–0–1–403		2021 actual	2022 est.	2023 est.
	Direct obligations:			
12.2	Military personnel benefits	16	20	36
13.0	Benefits for former personnel	1,460	1,586	1,711
23.2	Rental payments to others	....	20	14
25.6	Medical care	347	348	257
26.0	Supplies and materials	38	35	26
99.9	Total new obligations, unexpired accounts	1,861	2,009	2,044

COAST GUARD HOUSING FUND

Special and Trust Fund Receipts (in millions of dollars)

Identification code 070–5710–0–2–403		2021 actual	2022 est.	2023 est.
0100	Balance, start of year	7	8	8
	Receipts:			
	Current law:			
1130	Sale of Real Property, Coast Guard Housing Fund	63	4	4
2000	Total: Balances and receipts	70	12	12
	Appropriations:			
	Current law:			
2101	Coast Guard Housing Fund	−62	−4	−4
5099	Balance, end of year	8	8	8

Program and Financing (in millions of dollars)

Identification code 070–5710–0–2–403		2021 actual	2022 est.	2023 est.
	Obligations by program activity:			
0001	Coast Guard Housing Fund	....	66	4
0900	Total new obligations, unexpired accounts (object class 25.4)	....	66	4
	Budgetary resources:			
	Unobligated balance:			
1000	Unobligated balance brought forward, Oct 1	....	62	....
	Budget authority:			
	Appropriations, discretionary:			
1101	Appropriation (special or trust)	62	4	4
1900	Budget authority (total)	62	4	4
1930	Total budgetary resources available	62	66	4
	Memorandum (non-add) entries:			
1941	Unexpired unobligated balance, end of year	62		
	Change in obligated balance:			
	Unpaid obligations:			
3000	Unpaid obligations, brought forward, Oct 1	....	....	33
3010	New obligations, unexpired accounts	....	66	4
3020	Outlays (gross)	....	−33	−18
3050	Unpaid obligations, end of year	....	33	19
	Memorandum (non-add) entries:			
3100	Obligated balance, start of year	....	....	33
3200	Obligated balance, end of year	....	33	19
	Budget authority and outlays, net:			
	Discretionary:			
4000	Budget authority, gross	62	4	4
	Outlays, gross:			
4010	Outlays from new discretionary authority	....	1	1
4011	Outlays from discretionary balances	....	32	17
4020	Outlays, gross (total)	....	33	18
4180	Budget authority, net (total)	62	4	4
4190	Outlays, net (total)	....	33	18

The Housing Fund, established in 2011, receives deposits of proceeds from the conveyance of property under the administrative control of the Coast Guard. In accordance with 14 U.S.C. 2946, amounts in the fund may be appropriated for certain activities associated with military family housing and military unaccompanied housing.

ABANDONED SEAFARERS FUND

Special and Trust Fund Receipts (in millions of dollars)

Identification code 070–5677–0–2–403		2021 actual	2022 est.	2023 est.
0100	Balance, start of year	5	5	10
	Receipts:			
	Current law:			
1110	Penalties, Abandoned Seafarers Fund	....	5	5

DEPARTMENT OF HOMELAND SECURITY

		2021 actual	2022 est.	2023 est.
2000	Total: Balances and receipts	5	10	15
5099	Balance, end of year	5	10	15

SUPPLY FUND

Program and Financing (in millions of dollars)

Identification code 070–4535–0–4–403		2021 actual	2022 est.	2023 est.
	Obligations by program activity:			
0801	Supply Fund (Reimbursable)	61	114	75
0900	Total new obligations, unexpired accounts (object class 26.0)	61	114	75
	Budgetary resources:			
	Unobligated balance:			
1000	Unobligated balance brought forward, Oct 1	38	39	
1021	Recoveries of prior year unpaid obligations	4		
1070	Unobligated balance (total)	42	39	
	Budget authority:			
	Spending authority from offsetting collections, discretionary:			
1700	Collected	58	75	75
1930	Total budgetary resources available	100	114	75
	Memorandum (non-add) entries:			
1941	Unexpired unobligated balance, end of year	39		
	Change in obligated balance:			
	Unpaid obligations:			
3000	Unpaid obligations, brought forward, Oct 1	10	8	39
3010	New obligations, unexpired accounts	61	114	75
3020	Outlays (gross)	–59	–83	–75
3040	Recoveries of prior year unpaid obligations, unexpired	–4		
3050	Unpaid obligations, end of year	8	39	39
	Memorandum (non-add) entries:			
3100	Obligated balance, start of year	10	8	39
3200	Obligated balance, end of year	8	39	39
	Budget authority and outlays, net:			
	Discretionary:			
4000	Budget authority, gross	58	75	75
	Outlays, gross:			
4010	Outlays from new discretionary authority	52	75	75
4011	Outlays from discretionary balances	7	8	
4020	Outlays, gross (total)	59	83	75
	Offsets against gross budget authority and outlays:			
	Offsetting collections (collected) from:			
4030	Federal sources	–58	–75	–75
4180	Budget authority, net (total)			
4190	Outlays, net (total)	1	8	

The Supply Fund, in accordance with 14 U.S.C. 941, finances the procurement of uniform clothing, commissary provisions, general stores, technical material, and fuel for vessels over 180 feet in length. The fund is normally financed by reimbursements from the sale of goods.

YARD FUND

Program and Financing (in millions of dollars)

Identification code 070–4743–0–4–403		2021 actual	2022 est.	2023 est.
	Obligations by program activity:			
0801	Shipyard activities	133	212	140
	Budgetary resources:			
	Unobligated balance:			
1000	Unobligated balance brought forward, Oct 1	74	72	
1021	Recoveries of prior year unpaid obligations	1		
1070	Unobligated balance (total)	75	72	
	Budget authority:			
	Spending authority from offsetting collections, discretionary:			
1700	Collected	131	140	140
1701	Change in uncollected payments, Federal sources	–1		
1750	Spending auth from offsetting collections, disc (total)	130	140	140
1930	Total budgetary resources available	205	212	140

United States Coast Guard—Continued
Trust Funds

		2021 actual	2022 est.	2023 est.
	Memorandum (non-add) entries:			
1941	Unexpired unobligated balance, end of year	72		
	Change in obligated balance:			
	Unpaid obligations:			
3000	Unpaid obligations, brought forward, Oct 1	33	40	74
3010	New obligations, unexpired accounts	133	212	140
3020	Outlays (gross)	–125	–178	–140
3040	Recoveries of prior year unpaid obligations, unexpired	–1		
3050	Unpaid obligations, end of year	40	74	74
	Uncollected payments:			
3060	Uncollected pymts, Fed sources, brought forward, Oct 1	–7	–6	–6
3070	Change in uncollected pymts, Fed sources, unexpired	1		
3090	Uncollected pymts, Fed sources, end of year	–6	–6	–6
	Memorandum (non-add) entries:			
3100	Obligated balance, start of year	26	34	68
3200	Obligated balance, end of year	34	68	68
	Budget authority and outlays, net:			
	Discretionary:			
4000	Budget authority, gross	130	140	140
	Outlays, gross:			
4010	Outlays from new discretionary authority	69	140	140
4011	Outlays from discretionary balances	56	38	
4020	Outlays, gross (total)	125	178	140
	Offsets against gross budget authority and outlays:			
	Offsetting collections (collected) from:			
4030	Federal sources	–131	–140	–140
	Additional offsets against gross budget authority only:			
4050	Change in uncollected pymts, Fed sources, unexpired	1		
4080	Outlays, net (discretionary)	–6	38	
4180	Budget authority, net (total)			
4190	Outlays, net (total)	–6	38	

The Yard Fund finances the industrial operation of the Coast Guard Yard, Curtis Bay, MD (14 U.S.C. 939). The Yard Fund finances all direct and indirect costs for its operations out of payments from Coast Guard and other agency appropriations that are placed in the fund.

Object Classification (in millions of dollars)

Identification code 070–4743–0–4–403		2021 actual	2022 est.	2023 est.
	Reimbursable obligations:			
	Personnel compensation:			
11.1	Full-time permanent	38	38	38
11.5	Other personnel compensation	10	10	10
11.7	Military personnel	1	1	1
11.9	Total personnel compensation	49	49	49
12.1	Civilian personnel benefits	16	16	16
21.0	Travel and transportation of persons	1	1	1
23.3	Communications, utilities, and miscellaneous charges	1	2	1
25.2	Other services from non-Federal sources		1	
25.4	Operation and maintenance of facilities	4	9	4
26.0	Supplies and materials	54	119	61
31.0	Equipment	8	15	8
99.9	Total new obligations, unexpired accounts	133	212	140

Employment Summary

Identification code 070–4743–0–4–403		2021 actual	2022 est.	2023 est.
2001	Reimbursable civilian full-time equivalent employment	554	630	630
2101	Reimbursable military average strength employment	12	14	14

Trust Funds

AQUATIC RESOURCES TRUST FUND

Special and Trust Fund Receipts (in millions of dollars)

Identification code 070–8147–0–7–403		2021 actual	2022 est.	2023 est.
0100	Balance, start of year	782	758	757
	Receipts:			
	Current law:			
1110	Excise Taxes, Sport Fish Restoration, Aquatic Resources Trust Fund	599	592	599
1110	Customs Duties, Aquatic Resources Trust Fund	86	97	99

524　United States Coast Guard—Continued
Trust Funds—Continued

THE BUDGET FOR FISCAL YEAR 2023

AQUATIC RESOURCES TRUST FUND—Continued

Special and Trust Fund Receipts—Continued

Identification code 070–8147–0–7–403		2021 actual	2022 est.	2023 est.
1140	Earnings on Investments, Aquatic Resources Trust Fund	30	26	28
1199	Total current law receipts	715	715	726
1999	Total receipts	715	715	726
2000	Total: Balances and receipts	1,497	1,473	1,483
	Appropriations:			
	Current law:			
2101	Sport Fish Restoration	–742	–715	–715
2103	Sport Fish Restoration	–27	–29	–28
2103	Boat Safety	–7	–7	–7
2103	Coastal Wetlands Restoration Trust Fund	–5	–5	–5
2132	Sport Fish Restoration	29	28	28
2132	Boat Safety	8	7	7
2132	Coastal Wetlands Restoration Trust Fund	5	5	5
2199	Total current law appropriations	–739	–716	–715
2999	Total appropriations	–739	–716	–715
5099	Balance, end of year	758	757	768

Program and Financing (in millions of dollars)

Identification code 070–8147–0–7–403		2021 actual	2022 est.	2023 est.
4180	Budget authority, net (total)			
4190	Outlays, net (total)			
	Memorandum (non-add) entries:			
5000	Total investments, SOY: Federal securities: Par value	2,083	2,224	2,188
5001	Total investments, EOY: Federal securities: Par value	2,224	2,188	2,340

   The Internal Revenue Code of 1986, as amended by the Transportation Equity Act for the 21st Century and the Safe, Accountable, Flexible, Efficient Transportation Equity Act—A Legacy for Users, provides for the transfer of Highway Trust Fund revenue derived from the motor boat fuel tax and certain other taxes to the Aquatic Resources Trust Fund. In 2005, Title X of P.L. 109–59 changed the name of the Aquatic Resources Trust Fund to the Sport Fish Restoration and Boating Trust Fund. Appropriations are authorized from this fund to meet expenditures for programs specified by law, including sport fish restoration and boating safety activities. Excise tax receipts for the trust fund include motorboat fuel tax receipts, plus receipts from excise taxes on sport fishing equipment, sonar and fish finders, small engine fuels, and import duties on fishing equipment and recreational vessels.

BOAT SAFETY

Program and Financing (in millions of dollars)

Identification code 070–8149–0–7–403		2021 actual	2022 est.	2023 est.
	Obligations by program activity:			
0001	State recreational boating safety programs	125	141	132
0002	Compliance and boating programs	8		
0900	Total new obligations, unexpired accounts	133	141	132
	Budgetary resources:			
	Unobligated balance:			
1000	Unobligated balance brought forward, Oct 1	8	9	
1021	Recoveries of prior year unpaid obligations	2		
1070	Unobligated balance (total)	10	9	
	Budget authority:			
	Appropriations, mandatory:			
1203	Appropriation (previously unavailable)(special or trust)	7	7	7
1221	Appropriations transferred from other acct [014–8151]	133	132	132
1232	Appropriations and/or unobligated balance of appropriations temporarily reduced	–8	–7	–7
1260	Appropriations, mandatory (total)	132	132	132
1930	Total budgetary resources available	142	141	132
	Memorandum (non-add) entries:			
1941	Unexpired unobligated balance, end of year	9		
	Change in obligated balance:			
	Unpaid obligations:			
3000	Unpaid obligations, brought forward, Oct 1	103	133	127
3010	New obligations, unexpired accounts	133	141	132
3020	Outlays (gross)	–101	–147	–132
3040	Recoveries of prior year unpaid obligations, unexpired	–2		
3050	Unpaid obligations, end of year	133	127	127
	Memorandum (non-add) entries:			
3100	Obligated balance, start of year	103	133	127
3200	Obligated balance, end of year	133	127	127
	Budget authority and outlays, net:			
	Mandatory:			
4090	Budget authority, gross	132	132	132
	Outlays, gross:			
4100	Outlays from new mandatory authority	44	54	54
4101	Outlays from mandatory balances	57	93	78
4110	Outlays, gross (total)	101	147	132
4180	Budget authority, net (total)	132	132	132
4190	Outlays, net (total)	101	147	132

   The Boat Safety account provides grants for the development and implementation of a coordinated national recreational boating safety program. Boating safety statistics reflect the success in meeting the program's objectives. Pursuant to 16 U.S.C. 777c, as amended by the Safe, Accountable, Flexible, Efficient Transportation Equity Act—A Legacy for Users (P.L. 109–59), the Boat Safety program receives 18.5 percent of the funds collected in the Sport Fish Restoration and Boating Safety Trust Fund.

Object Classification (in millions of dollars)

Identification code 070–8149–0–7–403		2021 actual	2022 est.	2023 est.
	Direct obligations:			
11.1	Personnel compensation: Full-time permanent	2	2	2
12.1	Civilian personnel benefits	1	1	1
25.2	Other services from non-Federal sources	4	4	3
41.0	Grants, subsidies, and contributions	126	134	126
99.9	Total new obligations, unexpired accounts	133	141	132

Employment Summary

Identification code 070–8149–0–7–403		2021 actual	2022 est.	2023 est.
1001	Direct civilian full-time equivalent employment	18	19	19

TRUST FUND SHARE OF EXPENSES

Program and Financing (in millions of dollars)

Identification code 070–8314–0–7–304		2021 actual	2022 est.	2023 est.
	Obligations by program activity:			
0001	Trust Fund Share of Expenses	24	45	45
0002	Procurement, Construction, and Improvements	20		
0003	Research and Development	1		
0900	Total new obligations, unexpired accounts (object class 94.0)	45	45	45
	Budgetary resources:			
	Budget authority:			
	Appropriations, discretionary:			
1101	Appropriation (special or trust)	45	45	45
1930	Total budgetary resources available	45	45	45
	Change in obligated balance:			
	Unpaid obligations:			
3010	New obligations, unexpired accounts	45	45	45
3020	Outlays (gross)	–45	–45	–45
	Budget authority and outlays, net:			
	Discretionary:			
4000	Budget authority, gross	45	45	45

		2021 actual	2022 est.	2023 est.
	Outlays, gross:			
4010	Outlays from new discretionary authority	45	45	45
4180	Budget authority, net (total)	45	45	45
4190	Outlays, net (total)	45	45	45

The Trust Fund Share of Expenses account provides resources from the Oil Spill Liability Trust Fund for activities authorized in other accounts including: Operations and Support; Procurement, Construction, and Improvements; and Research and Development.

GENERAL GIFT FUND

Special and Trust Fund Receipts (in millions of dollars)

Identification code 070–8533–0–7–403	2021 actual	2022 est.	2023 est.
0100 Balance, start of year			
Receipts:			
Current law:			
1130 General Gift Fund	3	3	3
2000 Total: Balances and receipts	3	3	3
Appropriations:			
Current law:			
2101 General Gift Fund	–3	–3	–3
5099 Balance, end of year			

Program and Financing (in millions of dollars)

Identification code 070–8533–0–7–403	2021 actual	2022 est.	2023 est.
Obligations by program activity:			
0001 Obligations by program activity	3	6	3
0900 Total new obligations, unexpired accounts (object class 26.0)	3	6	3
Budgetary resources:			
Unobligated balance:			
1000 Unobligated balance brought forward, Oct 1	3	3	
Budget authority:			
Appropriations, mandatory:			
1201 Appropriation (special or trust fund)	3	3	3
1930 Total budgetary resources available	6	6	3
Memorandum (non-add) entries:			
1941 Unexpired unobligated balance, end of year	3		
Change in obligated balance:			
Unpaid obligations:			
3000 Unpaid obligations, brought forward, Oct 1		1	3
3010 New obligations, unexpired accounts	3	6	3
3020 Outlays (gross)	–2	–4	–3
3050 Unpaid obligations, end of year	1	3	3
Memorandum (non-add) entries:			
3100 Obligated balance, start of year		1	3
3200 Obligated balance, end of year	1	3	3
Budget authority and outlays, net:			
Mandatory:			
4090 Budget authority, gross	3	3	3
Outlays, gross:			
4100 Outlays from new mandatory authority	2	3	3
4101 Outlays from mandatory balances		1	
4110 Outlays, gross (total)	2	4	3
4180 Budget authority, net (total)	3	3	3
4190 Outlays, net (total)	2	4	3
Memorandum (non-add) entries:			
5000 Total investments, SOY: Federal securities: Par value	2	2	3
5001 Total investments, EOY: Federal securities: Par value	2	3	3

The General Gift Fund, maintained from gifts, devises, or bequests, is used for purposes as specified by the donor in connection with or benefit to the Coast Guard training program, as well as all other programs and activities permitted by law (10 U.S.C. 2601).

OIL SPILL LIABILITY TRUST FUND

Special and Trust Fund Receipts (in millions of dollars)

Identification code 070–8185–0–7–304	2021 actual	2022 est.	2023 est.
0100 Balance, start of year	7,108	7,716	8,397
0198 Rounding adjustment	1		
0199 Balance, start of year	7,109	7,716	8,397
Receipts:			
Current law:			
1110 Excise Taxes, Oil Spill Liability Trust Fund	552	650	670
1110 Fines and Penalties, OSLTF	74	89	88
1130 Recoveries, Oil Spill Liability Trust Fund	66	75	69
1140 Earnings on Investments	70	75	85
1199 Total current law receipts	762	889	912
Proposed:			
1210 Excise Taxes, Oil Spill Liability Trust Fund			108
1999 Total receipts	762	889	1,020
2000 Total: Balances and receipts	7,871	8,605	9,417
Appropriations:			
Current law:			
2101 Oil Spill Research	–15	–15	–15
2101 Inland Oil Spill Programs	–20	–20	–27
2101 Trust Fund Share of Pipeline Safety	–23	–23	–29
2101 Trust Fund Share of Expenses	–45	–45	–45
2101 Maritime Oil Spill Programs	–60	–101	–101
2101 Denali Commission Trust Fund	–3	–4	–4
2103 Maritime Oil Spill Programs	–6	–6	–6
2132 Maritime Oil Spill Programs	6	6	6
2199 Total current law appropriations	–166	–208	–221
2999 Total appropriations	–166	–208	–221
Special and trust fund receipts returned:			
3010 Maritime Oil Spill Programs	6		
5098 Reconciliation adjustment	5		
5099 Balance, end of year	7,716	8,397	9,196

Program and Financing (in millions of dollars)

Identification code 070–8185–0–7–304	2021 actual	2022 est.	2023 est.
4180 Budget authority, net (total)			
4190 Outlays, net (total)			
Memorandum (non-add) entries:			
5000 Total investments, SOY: Federal securities: Par value	7,315	7,833	8,664
5001 Total investments, EOY: Federal securities: Par value	7,833	8,664	9,394

The Oil Spill Liability Trust Fund (OSLTF) is used to finance oil pollution prevention and cleanup activities by various Federal agencies. In accordance with the provisions of the Oil Pollution Act of 1990, the Fund may finance annually up to $50 million of emergency resources and all valid claims from injured parties resulting from oil spills. For Coast Guard, this funds the Trust Fund Share of Expenses and Maritime Oil Spill Programs accounts. The OSLTF is funded by an excise tax on each barrel of oil produced domestically or imported.

Status of Funds (in millions of dollars)

Identification code 070–8185–0–7–304	2021 actual	2022 est.	2023 est.
Unexpended balance, start of year:			
0100 Balance, start of year	7,356	7,963	8,618
0999 Total balance, start of year	7,356	7,963	8,618
Cash income during the year:			
Current law:			
Receipts:			
1110 Excise Taxes, Oil Spill Liability Trust Fund	552	650	670
1110 Fines and Penalties, OSLTF	74	89	88
1130 Recoveries, Oil Spill Liability Trust Fund	66	75	69
1130 Maritime Oil Spill Programs	6		
1150 Earnings on Investments	70	75	85
1160 Inland Oil Spill Programs	23	12	12
1199 Income under present law	791	901	924
Proposed:			
1210 Excise Taxes, Oil Spill Liability Trust Fund			108

OIL SPILL LIABILITY TRUST FUND—Continued
Status of Funds—Continued

Identification code 070–8185–0–7–304	2021 actual	2022 est.	2023 est.
1299 Income proposed	....	....	108
1999 Total cash income	791	901	1,032
Cash outgo during year:			
Current law:			
2100 Oil Spill Research [Budget Acct]	−13	−22	−19
2100 Inland Oil Spill Programs [Budget Acct]	−29	−29	−38
2100 Trust Fund Share of Pipeline Safety [Budget Acct]	−26	−19	−32
2100 Trust Fund Share of Expenses [Budget Acct]	−45	−45	−45
2100 Maritime Oil Spill Programs [Budget Acct]	−67	−125	−101
2100 Denali Commission Trust Fund [Budget Acct]	−4	−6	−8
2199 Outgo under current law	−184	−246	−243
2999 Total cash outgo (−)	−184	−246	−243
Surplus or deficit:			
3110 Excluding interest	537	580	704
3120 Interest	70	75	85
3199 Subtotal, surplus or deficit	607	655	789
3999 Total change in fund balance	607	655	789
Unexpended balance, end of year:			
4100 Uninvested balance (net), end of year	130	−46	13
4200 Oil Spill Liability Trust Fund	7,833	8,664	9,394
4999 Total balance, end of year	7,963	8,618	9,407

MARITIME OIL SPILL PROGRAMS

Program and Financing (in millions of dollars)

Identification code 070–8349–0–7–304	2021 actual	2022 est.	2023 est.
Obligations by program activity:			
0001 Maritime Oil Spill Programs	94	206	101
0002 Payment of claims	8	....	....
0003 Prince William Sound Oil Spill Recovery Institute	1	....	....
0900 Total new obligations, unexpired accounts (object class 25.2)	103	206	101
Budgetary resources:			
Unobligated balance:			
1000 Unobligated balance brought forward, Oct 1	143	105	....
1021 Recoveries of prior year unpaid obligations	5	....	....
1030 Other balances withdrawn to special or trust funds	−6	....	....
1033 Recoveries of prior year paid obligations	6	....	....
1070 Unobligated balance (total)	148	105	....
Budget authority:			
Appropriations, mandatory:			
1201 Appropriation (special or trust fund)	60	101	101
1203 Appropriation (previously unavailable)(special or trust)	6	6	6
1232 Appropriations and/or unobligated balance of appropriations temporarily reduced	−6	−6	−6
1260 Appropriations, mandatory (total)	60	101	101
1900 Budget authority (total)	60	101	101
1930 Total budgetary resources available	208	206	101
Memorandum (non-add) entries:			
1941 Unexpired unobligated balance, end of year	105	....	....
Special and non-revolving trust funds:			
1950 Other balances withdrawn and returned to unappropriated receipts	6	....	....
Change in obligated balance:			
Unpaid obligations:			
3000 Unpaid obligations, brought forward, Oct 1	39	70	151
3010 New obligations, unexpired accounts	103	206	101
3020 Outlays (gross)	−67	−125	−101
3040 Recoveries of prior year unpaid obligations, unexpired	−5	....	....
3050 Unpaid obligations, end of year	70	151	151
Memorandum (non-add) entries:			
3100 Obligated balance, start of year	39	70	151
3200 Obligated balance, end of year	70	151	151
Budget authority and outlays, net:			
Mandatory:			
4090 Budget authority, gross	60	101	101
Outlays, gross:			
4100 Outlays from new mandatory authority	56	63	63
4101 Outlays from mandatory balances	11	62	38
4110 Outlays, gross (total)	67	125	101
Offsets against gross budget authority and outlays:			
Offsetting collections (collected) from:			
4123 Non-Federal sources	−6	....	....
Additional offsets against gross budget authority only:			
4143 Recoveries of prior year paid obligations, unexpired accounts	6	....	....
4160 Budget authority, net (mandatory)	60	101	101
4170 Outlays, net (mandatory)	61	125	101
4180 Budget authority, net (total)	60	101	101
4190 Outlays, net (total)	61	125	101

The Maritime Oil Spill Programs account provides resources from the Oil Spill Liability Trust Fund for costs associated with the cleanup of oil spills. These include emergency costs associated with oil spill cleanup, funding provided to the Prince William Sound Oil Spill Recovery Institute, and the payment of claims to those who suffer harm from oil spills where the responsible party is not identifiable or is without resources. The claims activity in this account will continue to be funded under separate permanent appropriations and are being displayed in a consolidated format to enhance presentation.

UNITED STATES SECRET SERVICE
Federal Funds
OPERATIONS AND SUPPORT

For necessary expenses of the United States Secret Service for operations and support, including purchase of not to exceed 652 vehicles for police-type use; hire of passenger motor vehicles; purchase of motorcycles made in the United States; hire of aircraft; rental of buildings in the District of Columbia; fencing, lighting, guard booths, and other facilities on private or other property not in Government ownership or control, as may be necessary to perform protective functions; conduct of and participation in firearms matches; presentation of awards; conduct of behavioral research in support of protective intelligence and operations; payment in advance for commercial accommodations as may be necessary to perform protective functions; and payment, without regard to section 5702 of title 5, United States Code, of subsistence expenses of employees who are on protective missions, whether at or away from their duty stations; $2,633,596,000; of which $52,296,000 shall remain available until September 30, 2024, and of which $6,000,000 shall be for a grant for activities related to investigations of missing and exploited children; and of which up to $17,000,000 may be for calendar year 2022 premium pay in excess of the annual equivalent of the limitation on the rate of pay contained in section 5547(a) of title 5, United States Code, pursuant to section 2 of the Overtime Pay for Protective Services Act of 2016 (5 U.S.C. 5547 note), as amended by Public Law 116–269: Provided, That not to exceed $19,125 shall be for official reception and representation expenses: Provided further, That not to exceed $100,000 shall be to provide technical assistance and equipment to foreign law enforcement organizations in criminal investigations within the jurisdiction of the United States Secret Service.

Note.—A full-year 2022 appropriation for this account was not enacted at the time the Budget was prepared; therefore, the Budget assumes this account is operating under the Continuing Appropriations Act, 2022 (Division A of Public Law 117–43, as amended). The amounts included for 2022 reflect the annualized level provided by the continuing resolution.

Program and Financing (in millions of dollars)

Identification code 070–0400–0–1–751	2021 actual	2022 est.	2023 est.
Obligations by program activity:			
0001 Mission Support	496	509	623
0002 Protective Operations	1,059	1,022	1,085
0003 Field Operations	727	727	781
0004 Basic and In-Service Training and Professional Development	118	115	145
0799 Total direct obligations	2,400	2,373	2,634
0801 Operating Expenses (Reimbursable)	19	27	27
0900 Total new obligations, unexpired accounts	2,419	2,400	2,661
Budgetary resources:			
Unobligated balance:			
1000 Unobligated balance brought forward, Oct 1	42	35	35
1001 Discretionary unobligated balance brought fwd, Oct 1	21	....	....

		2021 actual	2022 est.	2023 est.
1010	Unobligated balance transfer to other accts [070–0530]	−3		
1011	Unobligated balance transfer from other acct [070–0407]	1		
1012	Unobligated balance transfers between expired and unexpired accounts	5		
1021	Recoveries of prior year unpaid obligations	1		
1033	Recoveries of prior year paid obligations	2		
1070	Unobligated balance (total)	48	35	35
	Budget authority:			
	Appropriations, discretionary:			
1100	Appropriation	2,373	2,373	2,634
1121	Appropriations transferred from other acct [070–0300]	2		
1121	Appropriations transferred from other acct [070–0550]	10		
1131	Unobligated balance of appropriations permanently reduced	−2		
1160	Appropriation, discretionary (total)	2,383	2,373	2,634
	Spending authority from offsetting collections, discretionary:			
1700	Collected	12	27	27
1701	Change in uncollected payments, Federal sources	19		
1750	Spending auth from offsetting collections, disc (total)	31	27	27
1900	Budget authority (total)	2,414	2,400	2,661
1930	Total budgetary resources available	2,462	2,435	2,696
	Memorandum (non-add) entries:			
1940	Unobligated balance expiring	−8		
1941	Unexpired unobligated balance, end of year	35	35	35
	Change in obligated balance:			
	Unpaid obligations:			
3000	Unpaid obligations, brought forward, Oct 1	727	760	207
3010	New obligations, unexpired accounts	2,419	2,400	2,661
3011	Obligations ("upward adjustments"), expired accounts	62		
3020	Outlays (gross)	−2,372	−2,953	−2,635
3040	Recoveries of prior year unpaid obligations, unexpired	−1		
3041	Recoveries of prior year unpaid obligations, expired	−75		
3050	Unpaid obligations, end of year	760	207	233
	Uncollected payments:			
3060	Uncollected pymts, Fed sources, brought forward, Oct 1	−43	−56	−56
3070	Change in uncollected pymts, Fed sources, unexpired	−19		
3071	Change in uncollected pymts, Fed sources, expired	6		
3090	Uncollected pymts, Fed sources, end of year	−56	−56	−56
	Memorandum (non-add) entries:			
3100	Obligated balance, start of year	684	704	151
3200	Obligated balance, end of year	704	151	177
	Budget authority and outlays, net:			
	Discretionary:			
4000	Budget authority, gross	2,414	2,400	2,661
	Outlays, gross:			
4010	Outlays from new discretionary authority	1,883	2,158	2,393
4011	Outlays from discretionary balances	480	795	242
4020	Outlays, gross (total)	2,363	2,953	2,635
	Offsets against gross budget authority and outlays:			
	Offsetting collections (collected) from:			
4030	Federal sources	−27	−27	−27
4033	Non-Federal sources	−24		
4040	Offsets against gross budget authority and outlays (total)	−51	−27	−27
	Additional offsets against gross budget authority only:			
4050	Change in uncollected pymts, Fed sources, unexpired	−19		
4052	Offsetting collections credited to expired accounts	37		
4053	Recoveries of prior year paid obligations, unexpired accounts	2		
4060	Additional offsets against budget authority only (total)	20		
4070	Budget authority, net (discretionary)	2,383	2,373	2,634
4080	Outlays, net (discretionary)	2,312	2,926	2,608
	Mandatory:			
	Outlays, gross:			
4101	Outlays from mandatory balances	9		
4180	Budget authority, net (total)	2,383	2,373	2,634
4190	Outlays, net (total)	2,321	2,926	2,608

The United States Secret Service has statutory authority to carry out two primary missions: protection of the Nation's leaders and investigation of financial and electronic crimes. The Secret Service protects and investigates threats against the President and Vice President, their families, visiting heads of state and government, and other individuals as directed by the President; protects the White House Complex, Vice President's Residence, foreign missions, and other buildings within Washington, D.C.; and manages the security at designated National Special Security Events. The Secret Service also investigates violations of laws relating to counterfeiting of obligations and securities of the United States; financial crimes that include, but are not limited to, access device fraud, financial institution fraud, identity theft, and computer fraud; and computer-based attacks on financial, banking, telecommunications, and other critical infrastructure. Within Secret Service, the Operations and Support appropriation funds necessary operations, mission support, and associated management and administration costs.

Object Classification (in millions of dollars)

Identification code 070–0400–0–1–751	2021 actual	2022 est.	2023 est.
Direct obligations:			
Personnel compensation:			
11.1 Full-time permanent	799	776	1,105
11.3 Other than full-time permanent	23	22	15
11.5 Other personnel compensation	299	290	122
11.9 Total personnel compensation	1,121	1,088	1,242
12.1 Civilian personnel benefits	487	473	550
21.0 Travel and transportation of persons	142	146	146
22.0 Transportation of things	8	8	3
23.1 Rental payments to GSA	121	124	120
23.2 Rental payments to others	4	4	9
23.3 Communications, utilities, and miscellaneous charges	34	35	19
25.1 Advisory and assistance services	91	94	5
25.2 Other services from non-Federal sources	111	114	101
25.3 Other goods and services from Federal sources	61	63	8
25.4 Operation and maintenance of facilities	6	6	3
25.6 Medical care	4	4	
25.7 Operation and maintenance of equipment	45	46	17
26.0 Supplies and materials	39	40	157
31.0 Equipment	85	88	245
32.0 Land and structures	33	34	4
41.0 Grants, subsidies, and contributions	6	6	6
99.0 Direct obligations	2,398	2,373	2,635
99.0 Reimbursable obligations	17	27	27
99.5 Adjustment for rounding	4		−1
99.9 Total new obligations, unexpired accounts	2,419	2,400	2,661

Employment Summary

Identification code 070–0400–0–1–751	2021 actual	2022 est.	2023 est.
1001 Direct civilian full-time equivalent employment	7,443	7,443	8,163
2001 Reimbursable civilian full-time equivalent employment	11	11	11

CONTRIBUTION FOR ANNUITY BENEFITS, UNITED STATES SECRET SERVICE

Program and Financing (in millions of dollars)

Identification code 070–0405–0–1–751	2021 actual	2022 est.	2023 est.
Obligations by program activity:			
0304 Mandatory-DC Annuity	268	268	268
Budgetary resources:			
Unobligated balance:			
1000 Unobligated balance brought forward, Oct 1		3	3
Budget authority:			
Appropriations, mandatory:			
1200 Appropriation	271	268	268
1930 Total budgetary resources available	271	271	271
Memorandum (non-add) entries:			
1941 Unexpired unobligated balance, end of year	3	3	3
Change in obligated balance:			
Unpaid obligations:			
3000 Unpaid obligations, brought forward, Oct 1	21	22	22
3010 New obligations, unexpired accounts	268	268	268
3020 Outlays (gross)	−267	−268	−268
3050 Unpaid obligations, end of year	22	22	22
Memorandum (non-add) entries:			
3100 Obligated balance, start of year	21	22	22
3200 Obligated balance, end of year	22	22	22

528   United States Secret Service—Continued
Federal Funds—Continued
                                                                                     THE BUDGET FOR FISCAL YEAR 2023

CONTRIBUTION FOR ANNUITY BENEFITS, UNITED STATES SECRET SERVICE—Continued

Program and Financing—Continued

Identification code 070–0405–0–1–751	2021 actual	2022 est.	2023 est.
Budget authority and outlays, net:			
Mandatory:			
4090 Budget authority, gross	271	268	268
Outlays, gross:			
4100 Outlays from new mandatory authority	246	247	247
4101 Outlays from mandatory balances	21	21	21
4110 Outlays, gross (total)	267	268	268
4180 Budget authority, net (total)	271	268	268
4190 Outlays, net (total)	267	268	268

This account provides the Secret Service funding for contributions to the District of Columbia's Police and Firefighters Retirement Plan (DC Annuity).

Object Classification (in millions of dollars)

Identification code 070–0405–0–1–751	2021 actual	2022 est.	2023 est.
Direct obligations:			
11.8 Personnel compensation: Special personal services payments	266	266	266
12.1 Civilian personnel benefits	2	2	2
99.9 Total new obligations, unexpired accounts	268	268	268

PROCUREMENT, CONSTRUCTION, AND IMPROVEMENTS

For necessary expenses of the United States Secret Service for procurement, construction, and improvements, $65,888,000, to remain available until September 30, 2025.

Note.—A full-year 2022 appropriation for this account was not enacted at the time the Budget was prepared; therefore, the Budget assumes this account is operating under the Continuing Appropriations Act, 2022 (Division A of Public Law 117–43, as amended). The amounts included for 2022 reflect the annualized level provided by the continuing resolution.

Program and Financing (in millions of dollars)

Identification code 070–0401–0–1–751	2021 actual	2022 est.	2023 est.
Obligations by program activity:			
0006 Protection Assets and Infrastructure	54	52	53
0007 Operational Communications/Information Technology	....	....	3
0008 Construction and Facility Improvements	2	1	10
0900 Total new obligations, unexpired accounts	56	53	66
Budgetary resources:			
Unobligated balance:			
1000 Unobligated balance brought forward, Oct 1	44	41	41
Budget authority:			
Appropriations, discretionary:			
1100 Appropriation	53	53	66
1930 Total budgetary resources available	97	94	107
Memorandum (non-add) entries:			
1941 Unexpired unobligated balance, end of year	41	41	41
Change in obligated balance:			
Unpaid obligations:			
3000 Unpaid obligations, brought forward, Oct 1	131	105	8
3010 New obligations, unexpired accounts	56	53	66
3011 Obligations ("upward adjustments"), expired accounts	1	....	....
3020 Outlays (gross)	–82	–150	–64
3041 Recoveries of prior year unpaid obligations, expired	–1	....	....
3050 Unpaid obligations, end of year	105	8	10
Memorandum (non-add) entries:			
3100 Obligated balance, start of year	131	105	8
3200 Obligated balance, end of year	105	8	10
Budget authority and outlays, net:			
Discretionary:			
4000 Budget authority, gross	53	53	66
Outlays, gross:			
4010 Outlays from new discretionary authority	5	45	56
4011 Outlays from discretionary balances	77	105	8
4020 Outlays, gross (total)	82	150	64
Offsets against gross budget authority and outlays:			
Offsetting collections (collected) from:			
4030 Federal sources	–1	....	....
Additional offsets against gross budget authority only:			
4052 Offsetting collections credited to expired accounts	1	....	....
4070 Budget authority, net (discretionary)	53	53	66
4080 Outlays, net (discretionary)	81	150	64
4180 Budget authority, net (total)	53	53	66
4190 Outlays, net (total)	81	150	64

Procurement, Construction, and Improvements provides funds necessary for the planning, operational development, engineering and purchase of one or more assets prior to sustainment. This account provides necessary funding and investments needed to support the Secret Service's protective and investigation missions.

Object Classification (in millions of dollars)

Identification code 070–0401–0–1–751	2021 actual	2022 est.	2023 est.
Direct obligations:			
25.1 Advisory and assistance services	7	....	....
25.2 Other services from non-Federal sources	6	40	55
25.3 Other goods and services from Federal sources	5	....	....
25.5 Research and development contracts	1	....	....
31.0 Equipment	37	13	1
32.0 Land and structures	....	....	10
99.9 Total new obligations, unexpired accounts	56	53	66

RESEARCH AND DEVELOPMENT

For necessary expenses of the United States Secret Service for research and development, $4,025,000, to remain available until September 30, 2024.

Note.—A full-year 2022 appropriation for this account was not enacted at the time the Budget was prepared; therefore, the Budget assumes this account is operating under the Continuing Appropriations Act, 2022 (Division A of Public Law 117–43, as amended). The amounts included for 2022 reflect the annualized level provided by the continuing resolution.

Program and Financing (in millions of dollars)

Identification code 070–0804–0–1–751	2021 actual	2022 est.	2023 est.
Obligations by program activity:			
0001 Protection	4	12	4
0900 Total new obligations, unexpired accounts (object class 25.2)	4	12	4
Budgetary resources:			
Unobligated balance:			
1000 Unobligated balance brought forward, Oct 1	....	8	8
Budget authority:			
Appropriations, discretionary:			
1100 Appropriation	12	12	4
1930 Total budgetary resources available	12	20	12
Memorandum (non-add) entries:			
1941 Unexpired unobligated balance, end of year	8	8	8
Change in obligated balance:			
Unpaid obligations:			
3000 Unpaid obligations, brought forward, Oct 1	5	4	2
3010 New obligations, unexpired accounts	4	12	4
3020 Outlays (gross)	–5	–14	–5
3050 Unpaid obligations, end of year	4	2	1
Memorandum (non-add) entries:			
3100 Obligated balance, start of year	5	4	2
3200 Obligated balance, end of year	4	2	1
Budget authority and outlays, net:			
Discretionary:			
4000 Budget authority, gross	12	12	4
Outlays, gross:			
4010 Outlays from new discretionary authority	3	10	3
4011 Outlays from discretionary balances	2	4	2
4020 Outlays, gross (total)	5	14	5
4180 Budget authority, net (total)	12	12	4
4190 Outlays, net (total)	5	14	5

Research and Development includes funds necessary for supporting the search for new or refined knowledge and ideas and for the application or use of such knowledge and ideas for the development of new or improved products, processes, or capabilities. This account provides support to the Secret Service's protective and investigative missions.

ADMINISTRATIVE PROVISIONS

SEC. 201. Section 201 of the Department of Homeland Security Appropriations Act, 2018 (division F of Public Law 115–141), related to overtime compensation limitations, shall apply with respect to funds made available in this Act in the same manner as such section applied to funds made available in that Act, except that "fiscal year 2023" shall be substituted for "fiscal year 2018".

SEC. 202. Funding made available under the headings "U.S. Customs and Border Protection—Operations and Support" and "U.S. Customs and Border Protection—Procurement, Construction, and Improvements" shall be available for customs expenses when necessary to maintain operations and prevent adverse personnel actions in Puerto Rico and the U.S. Virgin Islands, in addition to funding provided by sections 740 and 1406i of title 48, United States Code.

SEC. 203. As authorized by section 601(b) of the United States-Colombia Trade Promotion Agreement Implementation Act (Public Law 112–42), fees collected from passengers arriving from Canada, Mexico, or an adjacent island pursuant to section 13031(a)(5) of the Consolidated Omnibus Budget Reconciliation Act of 1985 (19 U.S.C. 58c(a)(5)) shall be available until expended.

SEC. 204. For an additional amount for "U.S. Customs and Border Protection—Operations and Support", $31,000,000, to remain available until expended, to be reduced by amounts collected and credited to this appropriation in fiscal year 2023 from amounts authorized to be collected by section 286(i) of the Immigration and Nationality Act (8 U.S.C. 1356(i)), section 10412 of the Farm Security and Rural Investment Act of 2002 (7 U.S.C. 8311), and section 817 of the Trade Facilitation and Trade Enforcement Act of 2015 (Public Law 114–125), or other such authorizing language: Provided, That to the extent that amounts realized from such collections exceed $31,000,000, those amounts in excess of $31,000,000 shall be credited to this appropriation, to remain available until expended.

SEC. 205. None of the funds made available in this Act for U.S. Customs and Border Protection may be used to prevent an individual not in the business of importing a prescription drug (within the meaning of section 801(g) of the Federal Food, Drug, and Cosmetic Act) from importing a prescription drug from Canada that complies with the Federal Food, Drug, and Cosmetic Act: Provided, That this section shall apply only to individuals transporting on their person a personal-use quantity of the prescription drug, not to exceed a 90-day supply: Provided further, That the prescription drug may not be—

(1) a controlled substance, as defined in section 102 of the Controlled Substances Act (21 U.S.C. 802); or

(2) a biological product, as defined in section 351 of the Public Health Service Act (42 U.S.C. 262).

SEC. 206. Notwithstanding any other provision of law, none of the funds provided in this or any other Act shall be used to approve a waiver of the navigation and vessel-inspection laws pursuant to section 501(b) of title 46, United States Code, for the transportation of crude oil distributed from and to the Strategic Petroleum Reserve until the Secretary of Homeland Security, after consultation with the Secretaries of the Departments of Energy and Transportation and representatives from the United States flag maritime industry, takes adequate measures to ensure the use of United States flag vessels: Provided, That the Secretary shall notify the Committees on Appropriations of the Senate and the House of Representatives, the Committee on Commerce, Science, and Transportation of the Senate, and the Committee on Transportation and Infrastructure of the House of Representatives within 2 business days of any request for waivers of navigation and vessel-inspection laws pursuant to section 501(b) of title 46, United States Code, with respect to such transportation, and the disposition of such requests.

SEC. 207. (a) Beginning on the date of enactment of this Act, the Secretary of Homeland Security shall not—

(1) establish, collect, or otherwise impose any new border crossing fee on individuals crossing the Southern border or the Northern border at a land port of entry; or

(2) conduct any study relating to the imposition of a border crossing fee.

(b) In this section, the term "border crossing fee" means a fee that every pedestrian, cyclist, and driver and passenger of a private motor vehicle is required to pay for the privilege of crossing the Southern border or the Northern border at a land port of entry.

SEC. 208. Not later than 90 days after the date of enactment of this Act, the Secretary of Homeland Security shall submit an expenditure plan for any amounts made available for "U.S. Customs and Border Protection—Procurement, Construction, and Improvements" in this Act and prior Acts to the Committees on Appropriations of the Senate and the House of Representatives: Provided, That no such amounts provided in this Act may be obligated prior to the submission of such plan.

SEC. 209. Federal funds may not be made available for the construction of fencing—

(1) within the Santa Ana Wildlife Refuge;

(2) within the Bentsen-Rio Grande Valley State Park;

(3) within La Lomita Historical park;

(4) within the National Butterfly Center;

(5) within or east of the Vista del Mar Ranch tract of the Lower Rio Grande Valley National Wildlife Refuge; or

(6) within historic cemeteries.

SEC. 210. Funds made available in this Act may be used to alter operations within the National Targeting Center of U.S. Customs and Border Protection: Provided, That none of the funds provided by this Act, provided by previous appropriations Acts that remain available for obligation or expenditure in fiscal year 2023, or provided from any accounts in the Treasury of the United States derived by the collection of fees available to the components funded by this Act, may be used to reduce planned vetting operations at existing locations unless specifically authorized by a statute enacted after the date of enactment of this Act.

SEC. 211. Without regard to the limitation as to time and condition of section 503(d) of this Act, the Secretary may reprogram within and transfer funds to "U.S. Immigration and Customs Enforcement—Operations and Support" as necessary to ensure the detention of aliens prioritized for removal.

SEC. 212. None of the funds provided under the heading "U.S. Immigration and Customs Enforcement—Operations and Support" may be used to continue a delegation of law enforcement authority authorized under section 287(g) of the Immigration and Nationality Act (8 U.S.C. 1357(g)) if the Department of Homeland Security Inspector General determines that the terms of the agreement governing the delegation of authority have been materially violated.

SEC. 213. (a) None of the funds provided under the heading "U.S. Immigration and Customs Enforcement—Operations and Support" may be used to continue any contract for the provision of detention services if the two most recent overall performance evaluations received by the contracted facility are less than "adequate" or the equivalent median score in any subsequent performance evaluation system.

(b) The performance evaluations referenced in subsection (a) shall be conducted by the U.S. Immigration and Customs Enforcement Office of Professional Responsibility.

SEC. 214. The reports required to be submitted under section 218 of the Department of Homeland Security Appropriations Act, 2020 (division D of Public Law 116–93) shall continue to be submitted with respect to the period beginning 15 days after the date of the enactment of this Act and semimonthly thereafter, and each matter required to be included in such report by such section 218 shall apply in the same manner and to the same extent during the period described in this section, except that for purposes of reports submitted with respect to such period described, the following additional requirements shall be treated as being included as subparagraphs (H) through (J) of paragraph (1) of such section 218—

(1) the average lengths of stay, including average post-determination length of stay in the case of detainees described in subparagraph (F), for individuals who remain in detention as of the last date of each such reporting period;

(2) the number who have been in detention, disaggregated by the number of detainees described in subparagraph (F), for each of the following—

(A) over 2 years;

(B) from over 1 year to 2 years;

(C) from over 6 months to 1 year; and

(D) for less than 6 months; and

(3) the number of individuals described in section 115.5 of title 28, Code of Federal Regulations, including the use and duration of solitary confinement for such person.

SEC. 215. The terms and conditions of sections 216 and 217 of the Department of Homeland Security Appropriations Act, 2020 (division D of Public Law 116–93) shall apply to this Act.

SEC. 216. Members of the United States House of Representatives and the United States Senate, including the leadership; the heads of Federal agencies and commissions, including the Secretary, Deputy Secretary, Under Secretaries, and Assistant Secretaries of the Department of Homeland Security; the United States Attorney General, Deputy Attorney General, Assistant Attorneys General, and the United States Attorneys; and senior members of the Executive Office of the President, including the Director of the Office of Management and Budget, shall not be exempt from Federal passenger and baggage screening.

SEC. 217. Any award by the Transportation Security Administration to deploy explosives detection systems shall be based on risk, the airport's current reliance on other screening solutions, lobby congestion resulting in increased security concerns, high injury rates, airport readiness, and increased cost effectiveness.

SEC. 218. Notwithstanding section 44923 of title 49, United States Code, for fiscal year 2023, any funds in the Aviation Security Capital Fund established by section 44923(h) of title 49, United States Code, may be used for the procurement and installation of explosives detection systems or for the issuance of other transaction agreements for the purpose of funding projects described in section 44923(a) of such title.

SEC. 219. Not later than 30 days after the submission of the President's budget proposal, the Administrator of the Transportation Security Administration shall submit to the Committees on Appropriations and Commerce, Science, and Transportation of the Senate and the Committees on Appropriations and Homeland Security in the House of Representatives a single report that fulfills the following requirements:

(1) a Capital Investment Plan that includes a plan for continuous and sustained capital investment in new, and the replacement of aged, transportation security equipment;

(2) the 5-year technology investment plan as required by section 1611 of title XVI of the Homeland Security Act of 2002, as amended by section 3 of the Transportation Security Acquisition Reform Act (Public Law 113–245); and

(3) the Advanced Integrated Passenger Screening Technologies report as required by the Senate Report accompanying the Department of Homeland Security Appropriations Act, 2019 (Senate Report 115–283).

SEC. 220. None of the funds made available by this Act under the heading "Coast Guard—Operations and Support" shall be for expenses incurred for recreational vessels under section 12114 of title 46, United States Code, except to the extent fees are collected from owners of yachts and credited to the appropriation made available by this Act under the heading "Coast Guard—Operations and Support": Provided, That to the extent such fees are insufficient to pay expenses of recreational vessel documentation under such section 12114, and there is a backlog of recreational vessel applications, personnel performing non-recreational vessel documentation functions under subchapter II of chapter 121 of title 46, United States Code, may perform documentation under section 12114.

SEC. 221. Without regard to the limitation as to time and condition of section 503(d) of this Act, after June 30, up to $10,000,000 may be reprogrammed to or from the Military Pay funding category within "Coast Guard—Operations and Support" in accordance with subsection (a) of section 503 of this Act.

SEC. 222. Notwithstanding any other provision of law, the Commandant of the Coast Guard shall submit to the Committees on Appropriations of the Senate and the House of Representatives a future-years capital investment plan as described in the second proviso under the heading "Coast Guard—Acquisition, Construction, and Improvements" in the Department of Homeland Security Appropriations Act, 2015 (Public Law 114–4), which shall be subject to the requirements in the third and fourth provisos under such heading.

SEC. 223. Of the funds made available for defense-related activities under the heading "Coast Guard—Operations and Support", up to $190,000,000 that are used for enduring overseas missions in support of the global fight against terror may be reallocated by program, project, and activity, notwithstanding section 503 of this Act.

SEC. 224. None of the funds in this Act shall be used to reduce the Coast Guard's Operations Systems Center mission or its government-employed or contract staff levels.

SEC. 225. None of the funds appropriated by this Act may be used to conduct, or to implement the results of, a competition under Office of Management and Budget Circular A-76 for activities performed with respect to the Coast Guard National Vessel Documentation Center.

SEC. 226. Funds made available in this Act may be used to alter operations within the Civil Engineering Program of the Coast Guard nationwide, including civil engineering units, facilities design and construction centers, maintenance and logistics commands, and the Coast Guard Academy, except that none of the funds provided in this Act may be used to reduce operations within any civil engineering unit unless specifically authorized by a statute enacted after the date of enactment of this Act.

SEC. 227. Amounts deposited into the Coast Guard Housing Fund in fiscal year 2023 shall be available until expended to carry out the purposes of section 2946 of title 14, United States Code, and shall be in addition to funds otherwise available for such purposes.

SEC. 228. The United States Secret Service is authorized to obligate funds in anticipation of reimbursements from executive agencies, as defined in section 105 of title 5, United States Code, for personnel receiving training sponsored by the James J. Rowley Training Center, except that total obligations at the end of the fiscal year shall not exceed total budgetary resources available under the heading "United States Secret Service—Operations and Support" at the end of the fiscal year.

SEC. 229. None of the funds made available to the United States Secret Service by this Act or by previous appropriations Acts may be made available for the protection of the head of a Federal agency other than the Secretary of Homeland Security: Provided, That the Director of the United States Secret Service may enter into agreements to provide such protection on a fully reimbursable basis.

SEC. 230. For purposes of section 503(a)(3) of this Act, up to $15,000,000 may be reprogrammed within "United States Secret Service—Operations and Support".

SEC. 231. Funding made available in this Act for "United States Secret Service—Operations and Support" is available for travel of United States Secret Service employees on protective missions without regard to the limitations on such expenditures in this or any other Act if the Director of the United States Secret Service or a designee notifies the Committees on Appropriations of the Senate and the House of Representatives 10 or more days in advance, or as early as practicable, prior to such expenditures.

SEC. 232. Funding made available under the headings "U.S. Customs and Border Protection—Operations and Support" and "U.S. Immigration and Customs Enforcement—Operations and Support" may be used to provide or reimburse third-parties for the provision of COVID-19 testing and shelter for the purpose of voluntary isolation of persons encountered by U.S. Customs and Border Protection after entering the United States along the southwest border and deemed inadmissible under section 212(a) of the Immigration and Nationality Act (8 U.S.C. 1182(a)): Provided, That such testing and shelter shall be provided immediately after such persons leave Department of Homeland Security custody: Provided further, That for purposes of this section, funds may only be used in States or jurisdictions that do not have an agreement with the Federal government for the provision or reimbursement of such services.

SEC. 233. The unobligated balances of amounts specified in subsections (a)(1) through (a)(5) of section 230 of division F of the Consolidated Appropriations Act, 2018 (Public Law 115–141), section 230(a)(1) of division A of the Consolidated Appropriations Act, 2019 (Public Law 116–6), section 209(a)(1) of division D of the Consolidated Appropriations Act, 2020 (Public Law 116–93), and section 210 of division F of the Consolidated Appropriations Act, 2021 (Public Law 116–260) shall, in addition to the purposes for which they were originally appropriated, be available for the construction and improvement of roads along the southwest border, the removal and eradication of vegetation along the southwest border that creates obstacles to the detection of illegal entry, remediation and environmental mitigation, including scientific studies, related to border barrier construction, including barrier construction undertaken by the Department of Defense, and the acquisition and deployment of border security technology at and between ports of entry along the southwest border: Provided, That amounts repurposed by this section shall be in addition to any other amounts made available for such purposes.

SEC. 234. Section 230(b) of division F of the Consolidated Appropriations Act, 2018 (Public Law 115–141), section 230(b) of division A of the Consolidated Appropriations Act, 2019 (Public Law 116–6), and section 209(b) of division D of the Consolidated Appropriations Act, 2020 (Public Law 116–93) shall no longer apply.

SEC. 235. The Secretary of Homeland Security may transfer up to $225,000,000 in unobligated balances available from prior appropriations Acts under the heading "U.S. Customs and Border Protection—Procurement, Construction, and Improvements" to the Department of the Interior (including any agency or bureau within the Department of the Interior) or the Forest Service within the Department of Agriculture for the execution of environmental and other mitigation projects or activities, including the acquisition of land and scientific studies, related to the construction of border barriers on the southwest border between fiscal year 2017 and fiscal year 2021 by U.S. Customs and Border Protection and the Department of Defense.

CYBERSECURITY AND INFRASTRUCTURE SECURITY AGENCY

Federal Funds

OPERATIONS AND SUPPORT

For necessary expenses of the Cybersecurity and Infrastructure Security Agency for operations and support, $1,961,613,000, of which $21,424,000 shall remain available until September 30, 2024: Provided, That not to exceed $5,500 shall be for official reception and representation expenses.

Note.—A full-year 2022 appropriation for this account was not enacted at the time the Budget was prepared; therefore, the Budget assumes this account is operating under the Continuing Appropriations Act, 2022 (Division A of Public Law 117-43, as amended). The amounts included for 2022 reflect the annualized level provided by the continuing resolution.

DEPARTMENT OF HOMELAND SECURITY

OPERATIONS AND SUPPORT

[For an additional amount for "Operations and Support", $35,000,000, to remain available until September 30, 2026, for risk management operations and stakeholder engagement and requirements: *Provided*, That such amount is designated by the Congress as being for an emergency requirement pursuant to section 4112(a) of H. Con. Res. 71 (115th Congress), the concurrent resolution on the budget for fiscal year 2018, and to section 251(b) of the Balanced Budget and Emergency Deficit Control Act of 1985.] *(Infrastructure Investments and Jobs Appropriations Act.)*

Program and Financing (in millions of dollars)

Identification code 070–0566–0–1–999		2021 actual	2022 est.	2023 est.
	Obligations by program activity:			
0002	CAS - Mission Support	136	141	223
0003	CAS - Cybersecurity	1,008	919	1,093
0005	CAS - Emergency Communications	116	116	108
0006	CAS - Integrated Operations	177	176	187
0007	CAS - Infrastructure Security	160	163	167
0008	CAS - Risk Management Operations	104	127	112
0009	CAS - Stakeholder Engagement and Requirements	53	55	72
0799	Total direct obligations	1,754	1,697	1,962
0801	Reimbursable program activity	10		
0900	Total new obligations, unexpired accounts	1,764	1,697	1,962
	Budgetary resources:			
	Unobligated balance:			
1000	Unobligated balance brought forward, Oct 1	6	278	284
1010	Unobligated balance transfer to other accts [070–0112]	–1		
1012	Unobligated balance transfers between expired and unexpired accounts	3	2	2
1021	Recoveries of prior year unpaid obligations	1		
1070	Unobligated balance (total)	9	280	286
	Budget authority:			
	Appropriations, discretionary:			
1100	Appropriation	1,662	1,697	1,962
1131	Unobligated balance of appropriations permanently reduced	–2		
1160	Appropriation, discretionary (total)	1,660	1,697	1,962
	Appropriations, mandatory:			
1200	Appropriation	364		
	Spending authority from offsetting collections, discretionary:			
1700	Collected	1	4	
1701	Change in uncollected payments, Federal sources	13		
1750	Spending auth from offsetting collections, disc (total)	14	4	
1900	Budget authority (total)	2,038	1,701	1,962
1930	Total budgetary resources available	2,047	1,981	2,248
	Memorandum (non-add) entries:			
1940	Unobligated balance expiring	–5		
1941	Unexpired unobligated balance, end of year	278	284	286
	Change in obligated balance:			
	Unpaid obligations:			
3000	Unpaid obligations, brought forward, Oct 1	1,053	1,193	1,474
3010	New obligations, unexpired accounts	1,764	1,697	1,962
3011	Obligations ("upward adjustments"), expired accounts	12		
3020	Outlays (gross)	–1,608	–1,416	–1,007
3040	Recoveries of prior year unpaid obligations, unexpired	–1		
3041	Recoveries of prior year unpaid obligations, expired	–27		
3050	Unpaid obligations, end of year	1,193	1,474	2,429
	Uncollected payments:			
3060	Uncollected pymts, Fed sources, brought forward, Oct 1	–26	–24	–24
3070	Change in uncollected pymts, Fed sources, unexpired	–13		
3071	Change in uncollected pymts, Fed sources, expired	15		
3090	Uncollected pymts, Fed sources, end of year	–24	–24	–24
	Memorandum (non-add) entries:			
3100	Obligated balance, start of year	1,027	1,169	1,450
3200	Obligated balance, end of year	1,169	1,450	2,405
	Budget authority and outlays, net:			
	Discretionary:			
4000	Budget authority, gross	1,674	1,701	1,962
	Outlays, gross:			
4010	Outlays from new discretionary authority	819	341	392
4011	Outlays from discretionary balances	781	794	615
4020	Outlays, gross (total)	1,600	1,135	1,007
	Offsets against gross budget authority and outlays:			
	Offsetting collections (collected) from:			
4030	Federal sources	–16	–4	
4033	Non-Federal sources	–2		
4040	Offsets against gross budget authority and outlays (total)	–18	–4	
	Additional offsets against gross budget authority only:			
4050	Change in uncollected pymts, Fed sources, unexpired	–13		
4052	Offsetting collections credited to expired accounts	17		
4060	Additional offsets against budget authority only (total)	4		
4070	Budget authority, net (discretionary)	1,660	1,697	1,962
4080	Outlays, net (discretionary)	1,582	1,131	1,007
	Mandatory:			
4090	Budget authority, gross	364		
	Outlays, gross:			
4100	Outlays from new mandatory authority	8		
4101	Outlays from mandatory balances		281	
4110	Outlays, gross (total)	8	281	
4180	Budget authority, net (total)	2,024	1,697	1,962
4190	Outlays, net (total)	1,590	1,412	1,007

The Cybersecurity and Infrastructure Security Agency (CISA) leads efforts to protect the Nation's critical infrastructure against cyber and physical threats, including terrorist attacks, cyber incidents, natural disasters, and other catastrophic incidents. The Operations and Support Account funds the necessary operations, mission support, and associated management and administration costs for the Agency.

Object Classification (in millions of dollars)

Identification code 070–0566–0–1–999		2021 actual	2022 est.	2023 est.
11.1	Direct obligations: Personnel compensation: Full-time permanent	390	384	400
11.9	Total personnel compensation	390	384	400
12.1	Civilian personnel benefits	129	130	171
23.1	Rental payments to GSA	30	30	30
25.1	Advisory and assistance services	1,170	1,118	1,326
25.3	Other goods and services from Federal sources	35	35	35
99.0	Direct obligations	1,754	1,697	1,962
99.0	Reimbursable obligations	10		
99.9	Total new obligations, unexpired accounts	1,764	1,697	1,962

Employment Summary

Identification code 070–0566–0–1–999	2021 actual	2022 est.	2023 est.
1001 Direct civilian full-time equivalent employment	2,400	2,464	2,740

INFRASTRUCTURE PROTECTION AND INFORMATION SECURITY

Program and Financing (in millions of dollars)

Identification code 070–0565–0–1–054		2021 actual	2022 est.	2023 est.
	Change in obligated balance:			
	Unpaid obligations:			
3000	Unpaid obligations, brought forward, Oct 1	46	6	
3020	Outlays (gross)	–6	–6	
3041	Recoveries of prior year unpaid obligations, expired	–34		
3050	Unpaid obligations, end of year	6		
	Memorandum (non-add) entries:			
3100	Obligated balance, start of year	46	6	
3200	Obligated balance, end of year	6		
	Budget authority and outlays, net:			
	Discretionary:			
	Outlays, gross:			
4011	Outlays from discretionary balances	6	6	
4180	Budget authority, net (total)			
4190	Outlays, net (total)	6	6	

PROCUREMENT, CONSTRUCTION, AND IMPROVEMENTS

For necessary expenses of the Cybersecurity and Infrastructure Security Agency for procurement, construction, and improvements, $545,148,000, to remain available until September 30, 2025.

Note.—A full-year 2022 appropriation for this account was not enacted at the time the Budget was prepared; therefore, the Budget assumes this account is operating under the Continuing Appropriations Act, 2022 (Division A of Public Law 117–43, as amended). The amounts included for 2022 reflect the annualized level provided by the continuing resolution.

Program and Financing (in millions of dollars)

Identification code 070–0412–0–1–999	2021 actual	2022 est.	2023 est.
Obligations by program activity:			
0001 CAS - Cybersecurity	426	350	450
0002 CAS - Emergency Communications	46	61	61
0005 CAS - Infrastructure Protection	6	7	7
0006 CAS - Construction Facilities and Improvements			27
0900 Total new obligations, unexpired accounts	478	418	545
Budgetary resources:			
Unobligated balance:			
1000 Unobligated balance brought forward, Oct 1	21	195	130
1001 Discretionary unobligated balance brought fwd, Oct 1	21		
1021 Recoveries of prior year unpaid obligations	13		
1070 Unobligated balance (total)	34	195	130
Budget authority:			
Appropriations, discretionary:			
1100 Appropriation	353	353	545
Appropriations, mandatory:			
1200 Appropriation	286		
1900 Budget authority (total)	639	353	545
1930 Total budgetary resources available	673	548	675
Memorandum (non-add) entries:			
1941 Unexpired unobligated balance, end of year	195	130	130
Change in obligated balance:			
Unpaid obligations:			
3000 Unpaid obligations, brought forward, Oct 1	423	441	714
3010 New obligations, unexpired accounts	478	418	545
3020 Outlays (gross)	–446	–145	–375
3040 Recoveries of prior year unpaid obligations, unexpired	–13		
3041 Recoveries of prior year unpaid obligations, expired	–1		
3050 Unpaid obligations, end of year	441	714	884
Memorandum (non-add) entries:			
3100 Obligated balance, start of year	423	441	714
3200 Obligated balance, end of year	441	714	884
Budget authority and outlays, net:			
Discretionary:			
4000 Budget authority, gross	353	353	545
Outlays, gross:			
4010 Outlays from new discretionary authority	162	71	108
4011 Outlays from discretionary balances	284	74	212
4020 Outlays, gross (total)	446	145	320
Mandatory:			
4090 Budget authority, gross	286		
Outlays, gross:			
4101 Outlays from mandatory balances			55
4180 Budget authority, net (total)	639	353	545
4190 Outlays, net (total)	446	145	375

Procurement, Construction, and Improvements (PC&I) provides the funds necessary for the manufacture, purchase, or enhancement of one or more assets prior to sustainment. This funding supports the investments needed to enhance the security and resilience of infrastructure against terrorist attacks, cyber events, and natural disasters. Secure and resilient infrastructure is essential for national security, economic vitality, and public health and safety. This includes activities to understand and manage risk from natural disaster.

Object Classification (in millions of dollars)

Identification code 070–0412–0–1–999	2021 actual	2022 est.	2023 est.
Direct obligations:			
25.1 Advisory and assistance services	231	240	367
25.3 Other goods and services from Federal sources	247	178	178
99.9 Total new obligations, unexpired accounts	478	418	545

RESEARCH AND DEVELOPMENT

For necessary expenses of the Cybersecurity and Infrastructure Security Agency for research and development, $3,931,000, to remain available until September 30, 2024.

Note.—A full-year 2022 appropriation for this account was not enacted at the time the Budget was prepared; therefore, the Budget assumes this account is operating under the Continuing Appropriations Act, 2022 (Division A of Public Law 117–43, as amended). The amounts included for 2022 reflect the annualized level provided by the continuing resolution.

Program and Financing (in millions of dollars)

Identification code 070–0805–0–1–054	2021 actual	2022 est.	2023 est.
Obligations by program activity:			
0004 CAS - Risk Management R&D	12	4	3
0005 CAS - Infrastructure Security R&D	1	1	1
0900 Total new obligations, unexpired accounts (object class 25.5)	13	5	4
Budgetary resources:			
Unobligated balance:			
1000 Unobligated balance brought forward, Oct 1	8	3	7
Budget authority:			
Appropriations, discretionary:			
1100 Appropriation	9	9	4
1930 Total budgetary resources available	17	12	11
Memorandum (non-add) entries:			
1940 Unobligated balance expiring	–1		
1941 Unexpired unobligated balance, end of year	3	7	7
Change in obligated balance:			
Unpaid obligations:			
3000 Unpaid obligations, brought forward, Oct 1	15	17	11
3010 New obligations, unexpired accounts	13	5	4
3020 Outlays (gross)	–10	–11	–12
3041 Recoveries of prior year unpaid obligations, expired	–1		
3050 Unpaid obligations, end of year	17	11	3
Memorandum (non-add) entries:			
3100 Obligated balance, start of year	15	17	11
3200 Obligated balance, end of year	17	11	3
Budget authority and outlays, net:			
Discretionary:			
4000 Budget authority, gross	9	9	4
Outlays, gross:			
4010 Outlays from new discretionary authority		5	2
4011 Outlays from discretionary balances	10	6	10
4020 Outlays, gross (total)	10	11	12
4180 Budget authority, net (total)	9	9	4
4190 Outlays, net (total)	10	11	12

Research and Development includes the funds necessary for supporting the search for new or refined knowledge and ideas, and for the application or use of such knowledge and ideas for the development of new or improved products, processes, or capabilities. These resources fund capability development in support of the Cybersecurity and Infrastructure Security Agency's (CISA) infrastructure security and analytics initiatives.

CYBERSECURITY RESPONSE AND RECOVERY FUND

Note.—A full-year 2022 appropriation for this account was not enacted at the time the Budget was prepared; therefore, the Budget assumes this account is operating under the Continuing Appropriations Act, 2022 (Division A of Public Law 117–43, as amended). The amounts included for 2022 reflect the annualized level provided by the continuing resolution.

CYBERSECURITY RESPONSE AND RECOVERY FUND

[For an additional amount for "Cybersecurity Response and Recovery Fund", $100,000,000, to remain available until September 30, 2028, for cyber response and recovery, as authorized by subtitle C of the Homeland Security Act of 2002, as amended by this Act: *Provided*, That $20,000,000, to remain available until September 30, 2028, shall be made available for fiscal year 2022, $20,000,000, to remain available until September 30, 2028, shall be made available for fiscal year 2023, $20,000,000, to remain available until September 30, 2028, shall be made available for fiscal year 2024, $20,000,000, to remain available until September 30, 2028, shall be made available for fiscal year 2025, and $20,000,000, to remain available until September 30, 2028, shall be made available for fiscal year 2026: *Provided further,* That amounts provided under this heading in this Act shall be available only upon a declaration of a significant incident by the Secretary of Homeland Security pursuant to section 2233 of the Homeland Security Act of 2002, as amended by this Act: *Provided further,* That the Cybersecurity and Infrastructure Security Agency shall provide to the Committees on Appropriations and Homeland Security and Governmental Affairs of the Senate and the Committees on Appropriations and Oversight and Reform of the House of Representatives monthly reports, to be submitted not later than the tenth business day following the end of each month, on the status of funds made available under this heading in this Act, including an accounting of the most recent funding allocation estimates, obligations, expenditures, and unobligated funds, delineated by significant incident, as defined in section 2232 of the Homeland Security Act of 2002, as amended by this Act: *Provided further,* That such amount is designated by the Congress as being for an emergency requirement pursuant to section 4112(a) of H. Con. Res. 71 (115th Congress), the concurrent resolution on the budget for fiscal year 2018, and to section 251(b) of the Balanced Budget and Emergency Deficit Control Act of 1985.] *(Infrastructure Investments and Jobs Appropriations Act.)*

Program and Financing (in millions of dollars)

Identification code 070–1911–0–1–054	2021 actual	2022 est.	2023 est.
Obligations by program activity:			
0001 Direct program activity		20	20
0900 Total new obligations, unexpired accounts (object class 25.1)		20	20
Budgetary resources:			
Budget authority:			
Appropriations, discretionary:			
1100 Appropriation		20	
Advance appropriations, discretionary:			
1170 Advance appropriation			20
1900 Budget authority (total)		20	20
1930 Total budgetary resources available		20	20
Change in obligated balance:			
Unpaid obligations:			
3000 Unpaid obligations, brought forward, Oct 1			16
3010 New obligations, unexpired accounts		20	20
3020 Outlays (gross)		–4	–14
3050 Unpaid obligations, end of year		16	22
Memorandum (non-add) entries:			
3100 Obligated balance, start of year			16
3200 Obligated balance, end of year		16	22
Budget authority and outlays, net:			
Discretionary:			
4000 Budget authority, gross		20	20
Outlays, gross:			
4010 Outlays from new discretionary authority		4	10
4011 Outlays from discretionary balances			4
4020 Outlays, gross (total)		4	14
4180 Budget authority, net (total)		20	20
4190 Outlays, net (total)		4	14

The Cybersecurity and Infrastructure Security Agency's (CISA) Cyber Response and Recovery Fund (CRRF) appropriation ensures that funding is available to CISA to respond to a catastrophic cyber event. This account was authorized and appropriated in the Infrastructure Improvements and Jobs Act.

OFFICE OF HEALTH AFFAIRS

Federal Funds

OPERATIONS AND SUPPORT

Program and Financing (in millions of dollars)

Identification code 070–0117–0–1–453	2021 actual	2022 est.	2023 est.
Change in obligated balance:			
Unpaid obligations:			
3000 Unpaid obligations, brought forward, Oct 1	27	10	1
3011 Obligations ("upward adjustments"), expired accounts	1		
3020 Outlays (gross)	–5	–9	
3041 Recoveries of prior year unpaid obligations, expired	–13		
3050 Unpaid obligations, end of year	10	1	1
Uncollected payments:			
3060 Uncollected pymts, Fed sources, brought forward, Oct 1	–3	–3	–3
3090 Uncollected pymts, Fed sources, end of year	–3	–3	–3
Memorandum (non-add) entries:			
3100 Obligated balance, start of year	24	7	–2
3200 Obligated balance, end of year	7	–2	–2
Budget authority and outlays, net:			
Discretionary:			
Outlays, gross:			
4011 Outlays from discretionary balances	5	9	
4180 Budget authority, net (total)			
4190 Outlays, net (total)	5	9	

FEDERAL EMERGENCY MANAGEMENT AGENCY

Federal Funds

FEDERAL ASSISTANCE

For activities of the Federal Emergency Management Agency for Federal assistance through grants, contracts, cooperative agreements, and other activities, $3,530,489,000, which shall be allocated as follows:

(1) $616,186,000 for the State Homeland Security Grant Program under section 2004 of the Homeland Security Act of 2002 (6 U.S.C. 605), of which $90,000,000 shall be for Operation Stonegarden, $15,000,000 shall be for Tribal Homeland Security Grants under section 2005 of the Homeland Security Act of 2002 (6 U.S.C. 606), and $180,000,000 shall be for organizations (as described under section 501(c)(3) of the Internal Revenue Code of 1986 and exempt from tax under section 501(a) of such code) determined by the Secretary of Homeland Security to be at high risk of a terrorist attack: Provided, That notwithstanding subsection (c)(4) of such section 2004, for fiscal year 2022, the Commonwealth of Puerto Rico shall make available to local and tribal governments amounts provided to the Commonwealth of Puerto Rico under this paragraph in accordance with subsection (c)(1) of such section 2004: Provided further, That up to 1 percent of the total amount of funding made available under this paragraph may be made available to other offices within the Federal Emergency Management Agency to carry out evaluations of programs and activities receiving funds under this paragraph.

(2) $711,184,000 for the Urban Area Security Initiative under section 2003 of the Homeland Security Act of 2002 (6 U.S.C. 604), of which $180,000,000 shall be for organizations (as described under section 501(c)(3) of the Internal Revenue Code of 1986 and exempt from tax under section 501(a) of such code) determined by the Secretary of Homeland Security to be at high risk of a terrorist attack: Provided, That up to 1 percent of the total amount of funding made available under this paragraph may be made available to other offices within the Federal Emergency Management Agency to carry out evaluations of programs and activities receiving funds under this paragraph.

(3) $100,000,000 for Public Transportation Security Assistance, Railroad Security Assistance, and Over-the-Road Bus Security Assistance under sections 1406, 1513, and 1532 of the Implementing Recommendations of the 9/11 Commission Act of 2007 (6 U.S.C. 1135, 1163, and 1182), of which $10,000,000 shall be for Amtrak security and $2,000,000 shall be for Over-the-Road Bus Security: Provided, That such public transportation security assistance shall be provided directly to public transportation agencies.

(4) $100,000,000 for Port Security Grants in accordance with section 70107 of title 46, United States Code.

(5) $740,000,000, to remain available until September 30, 2024, of which $370,000,000 shall be for Assistance to Firefighter Grants and $370,000,000 shall be for Staffing for Adequate Fire and Emergency Response Grants under sections 33 and 34 respectively of the Federal Fire Prevention and Control Act of 1974 (15 U.S.C. 2229 and 2229a).

(6) $355,000,000 for emergency management performance grants under the National Flood Insurance Act of 1968 (42 U.S.C. 4001 et seq.), the Robert T. Stafford Disaster Relief and Emergency Assistance Act (42 U.S.C. 5121), the Earthquake Hazards Reduction Act of 1977 (42 U.S.C. 7701), section 762 of title 6, United States Code, and Reorganization Plan No. 3 of 1978 (5 U.S.C. App.).

(7) $350,000,000 for necessary expenses for Flood Hazard Mapping and Risk Analysis, in addition to and to supplement any other sums appropriated under the National Flood Insurance Fund, and such additional sums as may be provided by

FEDERAL ASSISTANCE—Continued

States or other political subdivisions for cost-shared mapping activities under section 1360(f)(2) of the National Flood Insurance Act of 1968 (42 U.S.C. 4101(f)(2)), to remain available until expended.

(8) $12,000,000 for Regional Catastrophic Preparedness Grants.

(9) $154,000,000 for the emergency food and shelter program under title III of the McKinney-Vento Homeless Assistance Act (42 U.S.C. 11331), to remain available until expended, of which $24,000,000 shall be for the purposes of providing humanitarian relief to families and individuals encountered by the Department of Homeland Security: Provided, That not to exceed 3.5 percent shall be for total administrative costs.

(10) $80,000,000, to remain available until September 30, 2024, for a critical infrastructure cyber grant program to provide financial assistance to public and private entities to implement risk reduction strategies and capabilities to protect critical infrastructure from cyberattacks.

(11) $312,119,000 to sustain current operations for training, exercises, technical assistance, and other programs.

Note.—A full-year 2022 appropriation for this account was not enacted at the time the Budget was prepared; therefore, the Budget assumes this account is operating under the Continuing Appropriations Act, 2022 (Division A of Public Law 117–43, as amended). The amounts included for 2022 reflect the annualized level provided by the continuing resolution.

FEDERAL ASSISTANCE

[For an additional amount for "Federal Assistance", $50,000,000, to remain available until September 30, 2022, for emergency management performance grants under the National Flood Insurance Act of 1968 (42 U.S.C. 4001 et seq.), the Robert T. Stafford Disaster Relief and Emergency Assistance Act (42 U.S.C. 5121), the Earthquake Hazards Reduction Act of 1977 (42 U.S.C. 7701), section 762 of title 6, United States Code, and Reorganization Plan No. 3 of 1978 (5 U.S.C. App.).] *(Disaster Relief Supplemental Appropriations Act, 2022.)*

FEDERAL ASSISTANCE

[(INCLUDING TRANSFER OF FUNDS)]

[For an additional amount for "Federal Assistance", $2,233,000,000, which shall be allocated as follows:]

[(1) $500,000],[000, to remain available until expended, for grants pursuant to section 205 of the Robert T. Stafford Disaster Relief and Emergency Assistance Act (42 U.S.C. 5135): *Provided*, That $100,000,000, to remain available until expended, shall be made available for fiscal year 2022, $100,000,000, to remain available until expended, shall be made available for fiscal year 2023, $100,000,000, to remain available until expended, shall be made available for fiscal year 2024, $100,000,000, to remain available until expended, shall be made available for fiscal year 2025, and $100,000,000, to remain available until expended, shall be made available for fiscal year 2026: *Provided further*, That in addition to amounts made available for administrative expenses under section 205(d)(2) of the Robert T. Stafford Disaster Relief and Emergency Assistance Act (42 U.S.C. 5135(d)(2)), no more than 3 percent of the amounts made available in fiscal year 2022, 3 percent of the amounts made available in fiscal year 2023, and 3 percent of the amounts made available in each of fiscal years 2024 through 2026 under this paragraph in this Act may be transferred to "Federal Emergency Management Agency—Operations and Support" for salaries and expenses.]

[(2) $733,000,000, to remain available until expended: *Provided*, That $148,000,000 of the amounts made available under this paragraph in this Act shall be for grants to States pursuant to section 8(e) of the National Dam Safety Program Act (33 U.S.C. 467f(e)): *Provided further*, That $585,000,000 of the amounts made available under this paragraph in this Act shall be for grants to States pursuant to section 8A of the National Dam Safety Program Act (33 U.S.C. 467f-2), of which no less than $75,000,000 shall be for the removal of dams: *Provided further*, That dam removal projects shall include written consent of the dam owner, if ownership is established: *Provided further*, That in addition to amounts made available for administrative expenses, no more than 3 percent of the amounts made available under this paragraph in this Act may be transferred to "Federal Emergency Management Agency—Operations and Support" for salaries and expenses.]

[(3) $1,000,000,000 to remain available until expended, for grants to states, local, tribal, and territorial governments for improvement to cybersecurity and critical infrastructure, as authorized by section 2218 of the Homeland Security Act of 2002, as amended by this Act: *Provided*, That $200,000,000, to remain available until expended, shall be made available for fiscal year 2022, $400,000,000, to remain available until expended, shall be made available for fiscal year 2023, $300,000,000, to remain available until expended, shall be made available for fiscal year 2024, and $100,000,000, to remain available until expended, shall be made available for fiscal year 2025: *Provided further*, That no more than 3 percent of the amounts made available in each of fiscal years 2022 through 2025 under this paragraph in this Act may be transferred to "Federal Emergency Management Agency—Operations and Support" for salaries and expenses: *Provided*, That such amount is designated by the Congress as being for an emergency requirement pursuant to section 4112(a) of H. Con. Res. 71 (115th Congress), the concurrent resolution on the budget for fiscal year 2018, and to section 251(b) of the Balanced Budget and Emergency Deficit Control Act of 1985.] *(Infrastructure Investments and Jobs Appropriations Act.)*

Program and Financing (in millions of dollars)

Identification code 070–0413–0–1–999	2021 actual	2022 est.	2023 est.
Obligations by program activity:			
0001 CAS - Grants	3,713	3,587	4,116
0002 CAS - Education, Training, and Exercises (incl USFA)	287	288	312
0799 Total direct obligations	4,000	3,875	4,428
0900 Total new obligations, unexpired accounts	4,000	3,875	4,428
Budgetary resources:			
Unobligated balance:			
1000 Unobligated balance brought forward, Oct 1	1,021	1,222	1,760
1010 Unobligated balance transfer to other accts [070–0530]	–17		
1021 Recoveries of prior year unpaid obligations	4		
1070 Unobligated balance (total)	1,008	1,222	1,760
Budget authority:			
Appropriations, discretionary:			
1100 CAS - Grants	3,020	3,020	3,218
1100 CAS - Education, Training, and Exercises	288	288	312
1100 Supp Approp for IIJA—Cybersecurity Grant Program (PL 117–58)		200	
1100 Supp Approp for IIJA—STORM Act (PL 117–58)		100	
1100 Supp Approp for IIJA—Dam Safety & Removal Program (PL 117–58)		733	
1100 Emergency Approp for EMPG (PL 117–43)		50	
1120 Appropriations transferred to other acct [070–0200]		–3	
1121 Appropriations transferred from other acct [070–0416]	25	25	25
1160 Appropriation, discretionary (total)	3,333	4,413	3,555
Advance appropriations, discretionary:			
1170 Advance appropriation - STORM Act			100
1170 Advance appropriation - Cybersecurity Grant Program			400
1172 Advance appropriations transferred to other accounts [070–0200]			–1
1180 Advanced appropriation, discretionary (total)			499
Appropriations, mandatory:			
1200 Supp Approp for American Rescue Plan Act of 2021—EFS	510		
1200 Supp Approp for American Rescue Plan Act of 2021—AFG	100		
1200 Supp Approp for American Rescue Plan Act of 2021—SAFER	200		
1200 Supp Approp for American Rescue Plan Act of 2021—EMPG	100		
1260 Appropriations, mandatory (total)	910		
1900 Budget authority (total)	4,243	4,413	4,054
1930 Total budgetary resources available	5,251	5,635	5,814
Memorandum (non-add) entries:			
1940 Unobligated balance expiring	–29		
1941 Unexpired unobligated balance, end of year	1,222	1,760	1,386
Change in obligated balance:			
Unpaid obligations:			
3000 Unpaid obligations, brought forward, Oct 1	6,939	8,097	8,214
3010 New obligations, unexpired accounts	4,000	3,875	4,428
3011 Obligations ("upward adjustments"), expired accounts	7		
3020 Outlays (gross)	–2,797	–3,758	–3,752
3030 Unpaid obligations transferred to other accts [069–0700]	–10		
3040 Recoveries of prior year unpaid obligations, unexpired	–4		
3041 Recoveries of prior year unpaid obligations, expired	–38		
3050 Unpaid obligations, end of year	8,097	8,214	8,890
Uncollected payments:			
3060 Uncollected pymts, Fed sources, brought forward, Oct 1	–1	–1	–1
3090 Uncollected pymts, Fed sources, end of year	–1	–1	–1
Memorandum (non-add) entries:			
3100 Obligated balance, start of year	6,938	8,096	8,213
3200 Obligated balance, end of year	8,096	8,213	8,889
Budget authority and outlays, net:			
Discretionary:			
4000 Budget authority, gross	3,333	4,413	4,054

DEPARTMENT OF HOMELAND SECURITY

Federal Emergency Management Agency—Continued
Federal Funds—Continued

535

	Outlays, gross:			
4010	Outlays from new discretionary authority	100	171	206
4011	Outlays from discretionary balances	2,616	3,195	3,252
4020	Outlays, gross (total)	2,716	3,366	3,458
	Offsets against gross budget authority and outlays:			
	Offsetting collections (collected) from:			
4030	Federal sources	–1		
4040	Offsets against gross budget authority and outlays (total)	–1		
	Additional offsets against gross budget authority only:			
4052	Offsetting collections credited to expired accounts	1		
4060	Additional offsets against budget authority only (total)	1		
4070	Budget authority, net (discretionary)	3,333	4,413	4,054
4080	Outlays, net (discretionary)	2,715	3,366	3,458
	Mandatory:			
4090	Budget authority, gross	910		
	Outlays, gross:			
4100	Outlays from new mandatory authority	81		
4101	Outlays from mandatory balances		392	294
4110	Outlays, gross (total)	81	392	294
4180	Budget authority, net (total)	4,243	4,413	4,054
4190	Outlays, net (total)	2,796	3,758	3,752

Federal Assistance provides monetary and non-monetary support to non-Federal Emergency Management Agency (FEMA) entities. Support may be provided in the form of grants or grant agreements, cooperative agreements, non-cash contributions, and other Federal support, but does not include amounts received as reimbursement for services rendered to individuals. Through a variety of programs, FEMA provides for grants, training, exercises, and other support to assist Federal agencies, States, territories, and tribal and local jurisdictions to prevent, protect against, mitigate, respond to, and recover from terrorism and natural disasters.

Grants: FEMA provides State and local preparedness grants that focus on building and sustaining the 32 core capabilities associated with the five mission areas described in the National Preparedness Goal. These grants include: 1) the State Homeland Security Grant Program, including Operation Stonegarden, Tribal Homeland Security Grants, and the Nonprofit Security Grant Program, which supports the implementation of State homeland security strategies to address identified planning, organization, equipment, training, and exercise needs to prevent, protect against, mitigate, respond to, and recover from acts of terrorism and other catastrophic events; 2) the Urban Area Security Initiative, including the Nonprofit Security Grant Program, which addresses the unique risk-driven and capabilities-based planning, organization, equipment, training, and exercise needs of high-threat, high-density urban areas based on capability targets identified during the Threat Hazard Identification and Risk Assessment process; 3) the Transit Security Grant Program for public transportation security assistance and railroad security assistance, which supports owners and operators of transit systems, including intra-city bus, commuter bus, ferries, and all forms of passenger rail, to protect critical surface transportation infrastructure and the traveling public from acts of terrorism and to increase the resilience of transit infrastructure; 4) the Port Security Grant Program, which improves port-wide maritime security risk management, enhances maritime domain awareness, supports maritime security training and exercises, and maintains and/or reestablishes maritime security mitigation protocols that support port recovery and resiliency capabilities; 5) Firefighter Assistance Grants, including the Assistance to Firefighter Grant and the Staffing for Adequate Fire and Emergency Response grants, which provide direct assistance to local fire departments for investments to improve their ability to safeguard the lives of firefighting personnel and members of the public in the event of a terrorist attack or other major incident; 6) Emergency Management Performance Grants, which provides funding on a formula basis to all 56 States and Territories to achieve target levels of capability in catastrophic planning and emergency management; 7) the Flood Hazard Mapping and Risk Analysis program, which drives national actions to reduce flood risk by addressing flood hazard data update needs, supporting local government hazard mitigation planning, and providing the flood risk data needed to manage the NFIP's financial exposure; 8) the Regional Catastrophic Preparedness Grant program which builds regional capacity to manage catastrophic incidents by improving and expanding collaboration for catastrophic incident preparedness; 9) the High Risk Damn Safety program which provides technical, planning, design, and construction assistance in the form of grants for rehabilitation of eligible high hazard potential damns; 10) the Emergency Food and Shelter grant program which provides funds to nonprofit and governmental organizations at the local level to supplement their programs for emergency food and shelter; and 11) a critical infrastructure cyber grant program to provide financial assistance to public and private entities to implement risk reduction strategies and capabilities to protect critical infrastructure from cyber-attacks.

Education, Training, and Exercises Programs: FEMA provides specialized training to emergency responders and supports development, execution, and evaluation of exercises to test the Nation's preparedness for all hazards. These programs include: 1) the National Exercise Program, which designs, coordinates, conducts, and evaluates exercises that rigorously test the Nation's ability to perform missions and functions that prevent, protect against, respond to, recover from, and mitigate all hazards; 2) the Center for Domestic Preparedness, which provides specialized all-hazards preparedness training to State, local, and tribal emergency responders on skills tied to national priorities, in particular those related to Weapons of Mass Destruction; 3) the Emergency Management Institute, which provides training to Federal, State, local, tribal, volunteer, public, and private sector officials to strengthen emergency management core competencies, knowledge, and skills, thus improving the Nation's capability to prepare for, protect against, respond to, recover from, and mitigate all hazards; 4) the National Domestic Preparedness Consortium, which provides first responders with a comprehensive, all-hazards training program that includes a focus on weapons of mass destruction, Chemical, Biological, Radiological, Nuclear, and Explosive (CBRNE) agents, natural hazards, and natural disasters aimed to improve their capacity to prevent, protect against, respond to, and recover from all hazards events including acts of terrorism; 5) the Continuing Training Grants, which provides funding via cooperative agreements to partners to develop and deliver training to prepare communities to prevent, protect against, mitigate, respond to, and recover from acts to terrorism and natural, man-made, and technological hazards; 6) the Center for Homeland Defense and Security, which develops and offers educational resources to the entire homeland security enterprise; and 7) the U.S. Fire Administration, which promotes fire awareness, safety, and risk reduction across communities and prepares the Nation's first responders through ongoing training in evaluating and minimizing community risk, improving protection of critical infrastructure, and preparing to respond to all-hazard emergencies.

Object Classification (in millions of dollars)

Identification code 070–0413–0–1–999	2021 actual	2022 est.	2023 est.
Direct obligations:			
Personnel compensation:			
11.1 Full-time permanent	33	34	50
11.5 Other personnel compensation	1	2	4
11.9 Total personnel compensation	34	36	54
12.1 Civilian personnel benefits	12	12	14
21.0 Travel and transportation of persons	2	7	7
23.3 Communications, utilities, and miscellaneous charges	4	4	4
25.1 Advisory and assistance services	119	25	25
25.2 Other services from non-Federal sources	172	316	323
25.3 Other goods and services from Federal sources	2	2	2
25.4 Operation and maintenance of facilities	11	11	11
25.7 Operation and maintenance of equipment	4	4	4
26.0 Supplies and materials	1	1	1
31.0 Equipment	5	5	5
32.0 Land and structures	4	4	4
41.0 Grants, subsidies, and contributions	3,630	3,448	3,974
99.0 Direct obligations	4,000	3,875	4,428
99.9 Total new obligations, unexpired accounts	4,000	3,875	4,428

Federal Emergency Management Agency—Continued
Federal Funds—Continued

FEDERAL ASSISTANCE—Continued

Employment Summary

Identification code 070–0413–0–1–999	2021 actual	2022 est.	2023 est.
1001 Direct civilian full-time equivalent employment	332	370	383

OPERATIONS AND SUPPORT

For necessary expenses of the Federal Emergency Management Agency for operations and support, $1,378,232,000: *Provided*, That not to exceed $2,250 shall be for official reception and representation expenses.

Note.—A full-year 2022 appropriation for this account was not enacted at the time the Budget was prepared; therefore, the Budget assumes this account is operating under the Continuing Appropriations Act, 2022 (Division A of Public Law 117–43, as amended). The amounts included for 2022 reflect the annualized level provided by the continuing resolution.

OPERATIONS AND SUPPORT

[For an additional amount for "Operations and Support", $67,000,000, to remain available until September 30, 2026, for Federal agency dam safety activities and assistance to States under sections 7 through 12 of the National Dam Safety Program Act (33 U.S.C. 467e through 467h): *Provided*, That such amount is designated by the Congress as being for an emergency requirement pursuant to section 4112(a) of H. Con. Res. 71 (115th Congress), the concurrent resolution on the budget for fiscal year 2018, and to section 251(b) of the Balanced Budget and Emergency Deficit Control Act of 1985.] *(Infrastructure Investments and Jobs Appropriations Act.)*

Program and Financing (in millions of dollars)

Identification code 070–0700–0–1–999	2021 actual	2022 est.	2023 est.
Obligations by program activity:			
0001 CAS - Mission Support	529	508	591
0002 CAS - Regional Operations	175	175	202
0003 CAS - Mitigation	44	48	84
0004 CAS - Preparedness and Protection	160	155	233
0005 CAS - Response and Recovery	248	248	276
0799 Total direct obligations	1,156	1,134	1,386
0801 Salaries and Expenses (Reimbursable)	36	36	36
0900 Total new obligations, unexpired accounts	1,192	1,170	1,422
Budgetary resources:			
Unobligated balance:			
1000 Unobligated balance brought forward, Oct 1	15	....	62
1011 Unobligated balance transfer from other acct [070–0702]	9	....	....
1012 Unobligated balance transfers between expired and unexpired accounts	1	....	....
1021 Recoveries of prior year unpaid obligations	5	....	....
1070 Unobligated balance (total)	30	....	62
Budget authority:			
Appropriations, discretionary:			
1100 Appropriation	1,129	1,129	1,378
1100 Supp Approp for IIJA - Dam Safety and Removal Program (PL 117–58)	....	67	....
1120 Appropriations transferred to other acct [070–0414]	–1	....	....
1131 Unobligated balance of appropriations permanently reduced	–1	....	....
1160 Appropriation, discretionary (total)	1,127	1,196	1,378
Spending authority from offsetting collections, discretionary:			
1700 Collected	26	36	36
1701 Change in uncollected payments, Federal sources	10	....	....
1750 Spending auth from offsetting collections, disc (total)	36	36	36
1900 Budget authority (total)	1,163	1,232	1,414
1930 Total budgetary resources available	1,193	1,232	1,476
Memorandum (non-add) entries:			
1940 Unobligated balance expiring	–1	....	....
1941 Unexpired unobligated balance, end of year	....	62	54
Change in obligated balance:			
Unpaid obligations:			
3000 Unpaid obligations, brought forward, Oct 1	568	563	459
3010 New obligations, unexpired accounts	1,192	1,170	1,422
3011 Obligations ("upward adjustments"), expired accounts	27	....	....
3020 Outlays (gross)	–1,178	–1,274	–1,329
3040 Recoveries of prior year unpaid obligations, unexpired	–5	....	....
3041 Recoveries of prior year unpaid obligations, expired	–41	....	....
3050 Unpaid obligations, end of year	563	459	552
Uncollected payments:			
3060 Uncollected pymts, Fed sources, brought forward, Oct 1	–29	–11	–11
3070 Change in uncollected pymts, Fed sources, unexpired	–10	....	....
3071 Change in uncollected pymts, Fed sources, expired	28	....	....
3090 Uncollected pymts, Fed sources, end of year	–11	–11	–11
Memorandum (non-add) entries:			
3100 Obligated balance, start of year	539	552	448
3200 Obligated balance, end of year	552	448	541
Budget authority and outlays, net:			
Discretionary:			
4000 Budget authority, gross	1,163	1,232	1,414
Outlays, gross:			
4010 Outlays from new discretionary authority	795	767	928
4011 Outlays from discretionary balances	383	507	401
4020 Outlays, gross (total)	1,178	1,274	1,329
Offsets against gross budget authority and outlays:			
Offsetting collections (collected) from:			
4030 Federal sources	–52	–36	–36
4040 Offsets against gross budget authority and outlays (total)	–52	–36	–36
Additional offsets against gross budget authority only:			
4050 Change in uncollected pymts, Fed sources, unexpired	–10	....	....
4052 Offsetting collections credited to expired accounts	26	....	....
4060 Additional offsets against budget authority only (total)	16	....	....
4070 Budget authority, net (discretionary)	1,127	1,196	1,378
4080 Outlays, net (discretionary)	1,126	1,238	1,293
4180 Budget authority, net (total)	1,127	1,196	1,378
4190 Outlays, net (total)	1,126	1,238	1,293

Operations and Support funds the Federal Emergency Management Agency's core mission: development and maintenance of an integrated, nationwide capability to prepare for, mitigate, respond to, and recover from the consequences of terrorist attacks and other major disasters and emergencies, in partnership with other Federal agencies, State, local, tribal, and territorial (SLTT) governments, volunteer organizations, and the private sector. Activities supported by this account incorporate the essential command and control functions, mitigate long-term risks, ensure the continuity and restoration of essential services and functions, and provide leadership to build, sustain, and improve the coordination and delivery of support to citizens and State, local, tribal, and territorial governments.

Object Classification (in millions of dollars)

Identification code 070–0700–0–1–999	2021 actual	2022 est.	2023 est.
Direct obligations:			
Personnel compensation:			
11.1 Full-time permanent	428	440	528
11.5 Other personnel compensation	13	13	16
11.9 Total personnel compensation	441	453	544
12.1 Civilian personnel benefits	152	156	187
21.0 Travel and transportation of persons	2	1	2
23.1 Rental payments to GSA	46	47	69
23.3 Communications, utilities, and miscellaneous charges	32	23	27
24.0 Printing and reproduction	1	1	1
25.1 Advisory and assistance services	132	133	177
25.2 Other services from non-Federal sources	169	178	223
25.3 Other goods and services from Federal sources	8	7	7
25.4 Operation and maintenance of facilities	38	29	32
25.7 Operation and maintenance of equipment	46	33	39
26.0 Supplies and materials	10	7	8
31.0 Equipment	28	20	24
32.0 Land and structures	1	1	1
41.0 Grants, subsidies, and contributions	50	45	45
99.0 Direct obligations	1,156	1,134	1,386
99.0 Reimbursable obligations	36	36	36
99.9 Total new obligations, unexpired accounts	1,192	1,170	1,422

Employment Summary

Identification code 070–0700–0–1–999	2021 actual	2022 est.	2023 est.
1001 Direct civilian full-time equivalent employment	3,603	3,799	4,201

DEPARTMENT OF HOMELAND SECURITY

Federal Emergency Management Agency—Continued
Federal Funds—Continued

537

		2021 actual	2022 est.	2023 est.
2001	Reimbursable civilian full-time equivalent employment	30	30	30

STATE AND LOCAL PROGRAMS

Program and Financing (in millions of dollars)

Identification code 070–0560–0–1–453		2021 actual	2022 est.	2023 est.
	Change in obligated balance:			
	Unpaid obligations:			
3000	Unpaid obligations, brought forward, Oct 1	132	53	3
3011	Obligations ("upward adjustments"), expired accounts	2		
3020	Outlays (gross)	–62	–50	
3041	Recoveries of prior year unpaid obligations, expired	–19		
3050	Unpaid obligations, end of year	53	3	3
	Memorandum (non-add) entries:			
3100	Obligated balance, start of year	132	53	3
3200	Obligated balance, end of year	53	3	3
	Budget authority and outlays, net:			
	Discretionary:			
	Outlays, gross:			
4011	Outlays from discretionary balances	62	50	
4180	Budget authority, net (total)			
4190	Outlays, net (total)	62	50	

RADIOLOGICAL EMERGENCY PREPAREDNESS PROGRAM

Program and Financing (in millions of dollars)

Identification code 070–0715–0–1–453		2021 actual	2022 est.	2023 est.
	Obligations by program activity:			
0801	Radiological Emergency Preparedness	37	36	36
	Budgetary resources:			
	Unobligated balance:			
1000	Unobligated balance brought forward, Oct 1	8	10	10
1021	Recoveries of prior year unpaid obligations	5	3	1
1070	Unobligated balance (total)	13	13	11
	Budget authority:			
	Spending authority from offsetting collections, discretionary:			
1700	Collected	33	33	33
1702	Offsetting collections (previously unavailable)	34	33	33
1724	Spending authority from offsetting collections precluded from obligation (limitation on obligations)	–33	–33	–33
1750	Spending auth from offsetting collections, disc (total)	34	33	33
1930	Total budgetary resources available	47	46	44
	Memorandum (non-add) entries:			
1941	Unexpired unobligated balance, end of year	10	10	8
	Change in obligated balance:			
	Unpaid obligations:			
3000	Unpaid obligations, brought forward, Oct 1	16	14	15
3010	New obligations, unexpired accounts	37	36	36
3020	Outlays (gross)	–33	–32	–32
3040	Recoveries of prior year unpaid obligations, unexpired	–5	–3	–1
3041	Recoveries of prior year unpaid obligations, expired	–1		
3050	Unpaid obligations, end of year	14	15	18
	Memorandum (non-add) entries:			
3100	Obligated balance, start of year	16	14	15
3200	Obligated balance, end of year	14	15	18
	Budget authority and outlays, net:			
	Discretionary:			
4000	Budget authority, gross	34	33	33
	Outlays, gross:			
4010	Outlays from new discretionary authority		19	19
4011	Outlays from discretionary balances	33	13	13
4020	Outlays, gross (total)	33	32	32
	Offsets against gross budget authority and outlays:			
	Offsetting collections (collected) from:			
4030	Federal sources	–2	–2	–2
4033	Non-Federal sources	–31	–31	–31
4040	Offsets against gross budget authority and outlays (total)	–33	–33	–33
4070	Budget authority, net (discretionary)	1		
4080	Outlays, net (discretionary)		–1	–1
4180	Budget authority, net (total)	1		
4190	Outlays, net (total)		–1	–1
	Memorandum (non-add) entries:			
5090	Unexpired unavailable balance, SOY: Offsetting collections	34	33	33
5092	Unexpired unavailable balance, EOY: Offsetting collections	33	33	33

The Radiological Emergency Preparedness Program assists State, local, and tribal governments in the development of off-site radiological emergency preparedness plans within the emergency planning zones of Nuclear Regulatory Commission (NRC) licensed commercial nuclear power facilities. The fund is financed from fees assessed and collected from the NRC licensees to cover the costs for radiological emergency planning, preparedness, and response activities in the following year, as authorized in the Administrative Provisions, Sec. 308.

Object Classification (in millions of dollars)

Identification code 070–0715–0–1–453		2021 actual	2022 est.	2023 est.
	Reimbursable obligations:			
11.1	Personnel compensation: Full-time permanent	14	14	14
12.1	Civilian personnel benefits	7	7	7
21.0	Travel and transportation of persons	2	2	2
23.1	Rental payments to GSA	1	1	1
23.3	Communications, utilities, and miscellaneous charges	1	1	1
25.2	Other services from non-Federal sources	11	10	10
25.4	Operation and maintenance of facilities	1	1	1
99.9	Total new obligations, unexpired accounts	37	36	36

Employment Summary

Identification code 070–0715–0–1–453		2021 actual	2022 est.	2023 est.
2001	Reimbursable civilian full-time equivalent employment	126	138	137

DISASTER RELIEF FUND

For necessary expenses in carrying out the Robert T. Stafford Disaster Relief and Emergency Assistance Act (42 U.S.C. 5121 et seq.), $19,740,000,000, to remain available until expended, which shall be for major disasters declared pursuant to the Robert T. Stafford Disaster Relief and Emergency Assistance Act (42 U.S.C. 5121 et seq.).

DISASTER RELIEF FUND

[(INCLUDING TRANSFER OF FUNDS)]

[For an additional amount for "Disaster Relief Fund", $1,000,000,000, to remain available until expended, in addition to any amounts set aside pursuant to section 203(i) of the Robert T. Stafford Disaster Relief and Emergency Assistance Act (42 U.S.C. 5133), for grants pursuant to such section: *Provided*, That $200,000,000, to remain available until expended, shall be made available for fiscal year 2022, $200,000,000, to remain available until expended, shall be made available for fiscal year 2023, $200,000,000, to remain available until expended, shall be made available for fiscal year 2024, $200,000,000, to remain available until expended, shall be made available for fiscal year 2025, and $200,000,000, to remain available until expended, shall be made available for fiscal year 2026: *Provided further*, That no more than $16,500,000 of the amounts made available in each of fiscal years 2022 through 2026 under this heading in this Act may be transferred to "Federal Emergency Management Agency—Operations and Support" for salaries and expenses: *Provided further*, That such amount is designated by the Congress as being for an emergency requirement pursuant to section 4112(a) of H. Con. Res. 71 (115th Congress), the concurrent resolution on the budget for fiscal year 2018, and to section 251(b) of the Balanced Budget and Emergency Deficit Control Act of 1985.] *(Infrastructure Investments and Jobs Appropriations Act.)*

Program and Financing (in millions of dollars)

Identification code 070–0702–0–1–453		2021 actual	2022 est.	2023 est.
	Obligations by program activity:			
0003	Base/Non Major Disasters	891	886	720
0004	Disaster Relief	32,553	21,762	25,298

Disaster Relief Fund—Continued

Program and Financing—Continued

Identification code 070–0702–0–1–453	2021 actual	2022 est.	2023 est.
0005 PDM/BRIC	157	388	545
0007 ARPA	25,336	21,274	3,390
0799 Total direct obligations	58,937	44,310	29,953
0801 Reimbursable program activity	199		
0900 Total new obligations, unexpired accounts	59,136	44,310	29,953
Budgetary resources:			
Unobligated balance:			
1000 Unobligated balance brought forward, Oct 1	15,823	33,998	10,014
1001 Discretionary unobligated balance brought fwd, Oct 1	15,823		
1010 Unobligated balance transfer to other accts [070–0703]	–4	–257	
1010 Unobligated balance transfer to other accts [070–0700]	–9		
1010 Unobligated balance transfer to other accts [070–0414]	–7		
1011 Unobligated balance transfer from other acct [072–1035]	8		
1011 Unobligated balance transfer from other acct [016–0179]	1	6	
1021 Recoveries of prior year unpaid obligations	7,687	3,300	
1033 Recoveries of prior year paid obligations	345	1	
1070 Unobligated balance (total)	23,844	37,048	10,014
Budget authority:			
Appropriations, discretionary:			
1100 Appropriation	19,142	17,342	19,740
1120 Appropriations transferred to other acct [070–0703]	–33	–66	
1120 Appropriations transferred to other acct [070–0200]		–1	
1160 Appropriation, discretionary (total)	19,109	17,275	19,740
Advance appropriations, discretionary:			
1170 Advance appropriation			200
1172 Advance appropriations transferred to other accounts [070–0200]			–1
1180 Advanced appropriation, discretionary (total)			199
Appropriations, mandatory:			
1200 Appropriation	50,000		
Spending authority from offsetting collections, discretionary:			
1700 Collected	180	1	
1701 Change in uncollected payments, Federal sources	1		
1750 Spending auth from offsetting collections, disc (total)	181	1	
1900 Budget authority (total)	69,290	17,276	19,939
1930 Total budgetary resources available	93,134	54,324	29,953
Memorandum (non-add) entries:			
1941 Unexpired unobligated balance, end of year	33,998	10,014	
Change in obligated balance:			
Unpaid obligations:			
3000 Unpaid obligations, brought forward, Oct 1	57,670	66,137	70,932
3010 New obligations, unexpired accounts	59,136	44,310	29,953
3020 Outlays (gross)	–42,952	–36,215	–29,073
3040 Recoveries of prior year unpaid obligations, unexpired	–7,687	–3,300	
3041 Recoveries of prior year unpaid obligations, expired	–30		
3050 Unpaid obligations, end of year	66,137	70,932	71,812
Uncollected payments:			
3060 Uncollected pymts, Fed sources, brought forward, Oct 1	–1,126	–2	–2
3070 Change in uncollected pymts, Fed sources, unexpired	–1		
3071 Change in uncollected pymts, Fed sources, expired	1,125		
3090 Uncollected pymts, Fed sources, end of year	–2	–2	–2
Memorandum (non-add) entries:			
3100 Obligated balance, start of year	56,544	66,135	70,930
3200 Obligated balance, end of year	66,135	70,930	71,810
Budget authority and outlays, net:			
Discretionary:			
4000 Budget authority, gross	19,290	17,276	19,939
Outlays, gross:			
4010 Outlays from new discretionary authority	1,247	3,415	3,948
4011 Outlays from discretionary balances	33,055	17,290	13,916
4020 Outlays, gross (total)	34,302	20,705	17,864
Offsets against gross budget authority and outlays:			
Offsetting collections (collected) from:			
4030 Federal sources	–1,402	–1	
4033 Non-Federal sources	–217	–1	
4040 Offsets against gross budget authority and outlays (total)	–1,619	–2	
Additional offsets against gross budget authority only:			
4050 Change in uncollected pymts, Fed sources, unexpired	–1		
4052 Offsetting collections credited to expired accounts	1,094		
4053 Recoveries of prior year paid obligations, unexpired accounts	345	1	
4060 Additional offsets against budget authority only (total)	1,438	1	
4070 Budget authority, net (discretionary)	19,109	17,275	19,939
4080 Outlays, net (discretionary)	32,683	20,703	17,864
Mandatory:			
4090 Budget authority, gross	50,000		
Outlays, gross:			
4100 Outlays from new mandatory authority	8,650		
4101 Outlays from mandatory balances		15,510	11,209
4110 Outlays, gross (total)	8,650	15,510	11,209
4180 Budget authority, net (total)	69,109	17,275	19,939
4190 Outlays, net (total)	41,333	36,213	29,073

Through the Disaster Relief Fund (DRF), the Federal Emergency Management Agency (FEMA) provides a significant portion of the total Federal response to Presidentially-declared major disasters and emergencies that overwhelm State and tribal resources, pursuant to the Robert T. Stafford Disaster Relief and Emergency Act, P.L. 93–288 (as amended), 42 U.S. Code sections 5121–5207. Primary assistance programs include Federal disaster support to individuals and households, public assistance, and hazard mitigation assistance which includes such activities as the repair and restoration of State, local, tribal, territorial, and nonprofit disaster damaged infrastructure, financial assistance to eligible disaster survivors, and funding to rebuild in a way that reduces or mitigates future disaster losses in communities.

The 2023 DRF funds requested under the disaster relief Major Disaster Allocation consist of five principal components: (1) catastrophic obligations; (2) non-catastrophic obligations; (3) recoveries; (4) the set-aside for the Building Resilient Infrastructure in Communities (BRIC) grant program; and (5) a reserve. Funds required for the catastrophic category, defined as events greater than $500 million, are based on FEMA spend plans for all past declared catastrophic events and do not include funds for new catastrophic events that may occur in 2023. It is assumed that any new catastrophic event in 2023 will be funded through a future supplemental funding request. The non-catastrophic amount is based on an approach that uses the 10-year average for non-catastrophic events to provide a more realistic projection of non-catastrophic needs in 2023.

The DRF base request supports the 10-year average for the costs associated with emergency declarations, pre-disaster surge activities, and fire management assistance grants. The base also includes funds for projected yearly disaster readiness and support activities. The 2023 DRF base requirements will be funded through available carryover balances from 2022.

Object Classification (in millions of dollars)

Identification code 070–0702–0–1–453	2021 actual	2022 est.	2023 est.
Direct obligations:			
Personnel compensation:			
11.1 Full-time permanent	716	900	875
11.3 Other than full-time permanent	243	275	200
11.5 Other personnel compensation	140	180	90
11.9 Total personnel compensation	1,099	1,355	1,165
12.1 Civilian personnel benefits	320	232	166
13.0 Benefits for former personnel	13	9	6
21.0 Travel and transportation of persons	181	131	94
22.0 Transportation of things	99	87	62
23.1 Rental payments to GSA	24	19	19
23.2 Rental payments to others	63	45	45
23.3 Communications, utilities, and miscellaneous charges	40	29	21
24.0 Printing and reproduction	1	1	1
25.1 Advisory and assistance services	122	88	63
25.2 Other services from non-Federal sources	2,128	1,544	1,104
25.3 Other goods and services from Federal sources	5,256	3,812	2,726
25.4 Operation and maintenance of facilities	89	65	46
25.6 Medical care	56	40	29
25.7 Operation and maintenance of equipment	30	22	16
25.8 Subsistence and support of persons	4	3	2
26.0 Supplies and materials	168	227	162
31.0 Equipment	70	74	53
41.0 Grants, subsidies, and contributions	49,173	36,527	24,173
99.0 Direct obligations	58,936	44,310	29,953
99.0 Reimbursable obligations	199		

DEPARTMENT OF HOMELAND SECURITY

Federal Emergency Management Agency—Continued
Federal Funds—Continued

539

		2021 actual	2022 est.	2023 est.
99.5	Adjustment for rounding	1		
99.9	Total new obligations, unexpired accounts	59,136	44,310	29,953

Employment Summary

Identification code 070–0702–0–1–453	2021 actual	2022 est.	2023 est.
1001 Direct civilian full-time equivalent employment	11,624	8,428	9,501

FLOOD HAZARD MAPPING AND RISK ANALYSIS PROGRAM

Program and Financing (in millions of dollars)

Identification code 070–0500–0–1–453		2021 actual	2022 est.	2023 est.
	Budgetary resources:			
	Unobligated balance:			
1000	Unobligated balance brought forward, Oct 1	4	7	7
1021	Recoveries of prior year unpaid obligations	3		
1070	Unobligated balance (total)	7	7	7
1930	Total budgetary resources available	7	7	7
	Memorandum (non-add) entries:			
1941	Unexpired unobligated balance, end of year	7	7	7
	Change in obligated balance:			
	Unpaid obligations:			
3000	Unpaid obligations, brought forward, Oct 1	29	12	
3020	Outlays (gross)	–14	–12	
3040	Recoveries of prior year unpaid obligations, unexpired	–3		
3050	Unpaid obligations, end of year	12		
	Memorandum (non-add) entries:			
3100	Obligated balance, start of year	29	12	
3200	Obligated balance, end of year	12		
	Budget authority and outlays, net:			
	Discretionary:			
	Outlays, gross:			
4011	Outlays from discretionary balances	14	12	
4180	Budget authority, net (total)			
4190	Outlays, net (total)	14	12	

NATIONAL FLOOD INSURANCE FUND

For activities under the National Flood Insurance Act of 1968 (42 U.S.C. 4001 et seq.), the Flood Disaster Protection Act of 1973 (42 U.S.C. 4001 et seq.), the Biggert-Waters Flood Insurance Reform Act of 2012 (Public Law 112–141, 126 Stat. 916), and the Homeowner Flood Insurance Affordability Act of 2014 (Public Law 113–89; 128 Stat. 1020), $225,000,000, to remain available until September 30, 2024, which shall be derived from offsetting amounts collected under section 1308(d) of the National Flood Insurance Act of 1968 (42 U.S.C. 4015(d)); of which $18,500,000 shall be available for mission support associated with flood management; and of which $206,500,000 shall be available for flood plain management and flood mapping: Provided, That any additional fees collected pursuant to section 1308(d) of the National Flood Insurance Act of 1968 (42 U.S.C. 4015(d)) shall be credited as offsetting collections to this account, to be available for flood plain management and flood mapping: Provided further, That in fiscal year 2023, no funds shall be available from the National Flood Insurance Fund under section 1310 of the National Flood Insurance Act of 1968 (42 U.S.C. 4017) in excess of—

(1) $223,770,000 for operating expenses and salaries and expenses associated with flood insurance operations;

(2) $960,647,000 for commissions and taxes of agents;

(3) such sums as are necessary for interest on Treasury borrowings; and

(4) $175,000,000, which shall remain available until expended, for flood mitigation actions and for flood mitigation assistance under section 1366 of the National Flood Insurance Act of 1968 (42 U.S.C. 4104c), notwithstanding sections 1366(e) and 1310(a)(7) of such Act (42 U.S.C. 4104c(e), 4017):

Provided further, That the amounts collected under section 102 of the Flood Disaster Protection Act of 1973 (42 U.S.C. 4012a) and section 1366(e) of the National Flood Insurance Act of 1968 (42 U.S.C. 4104c(e)), shall be deposited in the National Flood Insurance Fund to supplement other amounts specified as available for section 1366 of the National Flood Insurance Act of 1968, notwithstanding section 102(f)(8), section 1366(e) of the National Flood Insurance Act of 1968, and paragraphs (1) through (3) of section 1367(b) of such Act (42 U.S.C. 4012a(f)(8), 4104c(e), 4104d(b)(1)–(3)): Provided further, That total administrative costs shall not exceed 4 percent of the total appropriation: Provided further, That up to $5,000,000 is available to carry out section 24 of the Homeowner Flood Insurance Affordability Act of 2014 (42 U.S.C. 4033).

Note.—A full-year 2022 appropriation for this account was not enacted at the time the Budget was prepared; therefore, the Budget assumes this account is operating under the Continuing Appropriations Act, 2022 (Division A of Public Law 117–43, as amended). The amounts included for 2022 reflect the annualized level provided by the continuing resolution.

NATIONAL FLOOD INSURANCE FUND

[For an additional amount for "National Flood Insurance Fund", $3,500,000,000, to be derived from the General Fund of the Treasury, to remain available until expended, for flood mitigation actions and for flood mitigation assistance under section 1366 of the National Flood Insurance Act of 1968 (42 U.S.C. 4104c), notwithstanding sections 1366(e), 1310(a)(7), and 1367 of such Act (42 U.S.C.4104c(e), 4017(a)(7), 4104d), in addition to any other funds available for this purpose: Provided, That $700,000,000, to remain available until expended, shall be made available for fiscal year 2022, $700,000,000, to remain available until expended, shall be made available for fiscal year 2023, $700,000,000, to remain available until expended, shall be made available for fiscal year 2024, $700,000,000, to remain available until expended, shall be made available for fiscal year 2025, and $700,000,000, to remain available until expended, shall be made available for fiscal year 2026: Provided further, That notwithstanding section 1366(d) of the National Flood Insurance Act of 1968 (42 U.S.C. 4104c(d)), the Administrator of the Federal Emergency Management Agency may also use amounts made available under subsection (a) to provide flood mitigation assistance under section 1366 of that Act (42 U.S.C. 4104c) for mitigation activities in an amount up to 90 percent of all eligible costs for a property—]

[(1) located within a census tract with a Centers for Disease Control and Prevention Social Vulnerability Index score of not less than 0.5001; or]

[(2) that serves as a primary residence for individuals with a household income of not more than 100 percent of the applicable area median income:]

[Provided further, That such amount is designated by the Congress as being for an emergency requirement pursuant to section 4112(a) of H. Con. Res. 71 (115th Congress), the concurrent resolution on the budget for fiscal year 2018, and to section 251(b) of the Balanced Budget and Emergency Deficit Control Act of 1985.] (Infrastructure Investments and Jobs Appropriations Act.)

Program and Financing (in millions of dollars)

Identification code 070–4236–0–3–453		2021 actual	2022 est.	2023 est.
	Obligations by program activity:			
0001	Flood Mitigation Assistance Grant		9	88
0801	NFIP Mandatory	3,717	3,778	5,800
0802	Mission Support (Discretionary)	18	16	19
0803	Floodplain Management and Flood Mapping (Discretionary)	224	214	222
0899	Total reimbursable obligations	3,959	4,008	6,041
0900	Total new obligations, unexpired accounts	3,959	4,017	6,129
	Budgetary resources:			
	Unobligated balance:			
1000	Unobligated balance brought forward, Oct 1	4,375	4,228	4,702
1001	Discretionary unobligated balance brought fwd, Oct 1	139		
1021	Recoveries of prior year unpaid obligations	89		
1070	Unobligated balance (total)	4,464	4,228	4,702
	Budget authority:			
	Appropriations, discretionary:			
1100	Appropriation		700	
1120	Appropriations transferred to other acct [070–0200]		–2	
1160	Appropriation, discretionary (total)		698	
	Advance appropriations, discretionary:			
1170	Advance appropriation			700
1172	Advance appropriations transferred to other accounts [070–0200]			–2
1180	Advanced appropriation, discretionary (total)			698
	Spending authority from offsetting collections, discretionary:			
1700	Collected	201	215	225
	Spending authority from offsetting collections, mandatory:			
1800	Offsetting collections	3,521	3,563	3,420
1802	Offsetting collections (previously unavailable)	90	89	74
1823	New and/or unobligated balance of spending authority from offsetting collections temporarily reduced	–89	–74	–74
1850	Spending auth from offsetting collections, mand (total)	3,522	3,578	3,420
1900	Budget authority (total)	3,723	4,491	4,343

540   Federal Emergency Management Agency—Continued
Federal Funds—Continued

NATIONAL FLOOD INSURANCE FUND—Continued

Program and Financing—Continued

Identification code 070–4236–0–3–453		2021 actual	2022 est.	2023 est.
1930	Total budgetary resources available	8,187	8,719	9,045
	Memorandum (non-add) entries:			
1941	Unexpired unobligated balance, end of year	4,228	4,702	2,916
	Change in obligated balance:			
	Unpaid obligations:			
3000	Unpaid obligations, brought forward, Oct 1	1,406	2,089	1,732
3010	New obligations, unexpired accounts	3,959	4,017	6,129
3020	Outlays (gross)	–3,187	–4,374	–4,213
3040	Recoveries of prior year unpaid obligations, unexpired	–89		
3050	Unpaid obligations, end of year	2,089	1,732	3,648
	Memorandum (non-add) entries:			
3100	Obligated balance, start of year	1,406	2,089	1,732
3200	Obligated balance, end of year	2,089	1,732	3,648
	Budget authority and outlays, net:			
	Discretionary:			
4000	Budget authority, gross	201	913	923
	Outlays, gross:			
4010	Outlays from new discretionary authority	115	136	142
4011	Outlays from discretionary balances	74	82	156
4020	Outlays, gross (total)	189	218	298
	Offsets against gross budget authority and outlays:			
	Offsetting collections (collected) from:			
4033	Non-Federal sources	–201	–215	–225
	Mandatory:			
4090	Budget authority, gross	3,522	3,578	3,420
	Outlays, gross:			
4100	Outlays from new mandatory authority	2,355	2,865	2,736
4101	Outlays from mandatory balances	643	1,291	1,179
4110	Outlays, gross (total)	2,998	4,156	3,915
	Offsets against gross budget authority and outlays:			
	Offsetting collections (collected) from:			
4123	Non-Federal sources	–3,521	–3,563	–3,420
4180	Budget authority, net (total)	1	713	698
4190	Outlays, net (total)	–535	596	568
	Memorandum (non-add) entries:			
5090	Unexpired unavailable balance, SOY: Offsetting collections	90	89	74
5092	Unexpired unavailable balance, EOY: Offsetting collections	89	74	74

Summary of Budget Authority and Outlays (in millions of dollars)

	2021 actual	2022 est.	2023 est.
Enacted/requested:			
Budget Authority	1	713	698
Outlays	–535	596	568
Legislative proposal, subject to PAYGO:			
Budget Authority			45
Outlays			45
Total:			
Budget Authority	1	713	743
Outlays	–535	596	613

The Federal Government provides flood insurance through the National Flood Insurance Program (NFIP), which is administered by the Federal Emergency Management Agency (FEMA). Flood insurance is available to homeowners and businesses in communities that have adopted and enforce appropriate floodplain management measures. Coverage is limited to buildings and their contents. At the end of 2021, the program had approximately 4.9 million policies in nearly 22,400 communities with approximately $1.3 trillion of insurance in force.

The program uses a multi-pronged strategy for reducing future flood damage. The NFIP offers flood mitigation assistance grants for projects that reduce or eliminate the risk of flood damages to buildings insured by the NFIP. In addition, flood mitigation assistance grants targeted toward repetitive and severe repetitive loss properties not only help owners of high-risk property, but through acquisition, relocation, or elevation also reduce the disproportionate drain on the National Flood Insurance Fund these properties cause. FEMA works to ensure that the flood mitigation grant program is closely integrated with other FEMA mitigation grant programs, resulting in better coordination and communication with State and local governments. Further, through the Community Rating System, FEMA adjusts premium rates to encourage community and State mitigation activities beyond those required by the NFIP. A study conducted in 2014 shows these efforts, in addition to the minimum NFIP requirements for floodplain management, can yield over $1.9 billion annually in avoided flood claims.

In 2023, FEMA continues to put the NFIP on a more sustainable financial footing by signaling the true cost associated with living in a floodplain, through premium increases for policies which are priced at less than full risk.

Object Classification (in millions of dollars)

Identification code 070–4236–0–3–453		2021 actual	2022 est.	2023 est.
	Direct obligations:			
11.3	Personnel compensation: Other than full-time permanent		1	3
25.2	Other services from non-Federal sources		8	8
41.0	Grants, subsidies, and contributions			77
99.0	Direct obligations		9	88
	Reimbursable obligations:			
	Personnel compensation:			
11.1	Full-time permanent	59	59	60
11.5	Other personnel compensation	1	1	1
11.9	Total personnel compensation	60	60	61
12.1	Civilian personnel benefits	14	14	14
23.1	Rental payments to GSA	8	8	8
23.3	Communications, utilities, and miscellaneous charges	3	3	3
24.0	Printing and reproduction	2	2	2
25.1	Advisory and assistance services	181	181	181
25.2	Other services from non-Federal sources	1,167	1,137	1,144
25.4	Operation and maintenance of facilities	1	1	1
25.7	Operation and maintenance of equipment	1	1	1
31.0	Equipment	1	1	1
41.0	Grants, subsidies, and contributions	253	253	253
42.0	Insurance claims and indemnities	1,911	2,058	4,050
43.0	Interest and dividends	357	289	322
99.0	Reimbursable obligations	3,959	4,008	6,041
99.9	Total new obligations, unexpired accounts	3,959	4,017	6,129

Employment Summary

Identification code 070–4236–0–3–453	2021 actual	2022 est.	2023 est.
2001 Reimbursable civilian full-time equivalent employment	440	517	567

NATIONAL FLOOD INSURANCE FUND

(Legislative proposal, not subject to PAYGO)

The purpose of this 2023 Budget proposal is to remedy the recognized need to provide affordable assistance to certain households, which otherwise might not participate at all, as FEMA puts the National Flood Insurance Program (NFIP) on a more sustainable financial footing. The Budget proposal moves this forward by indicating to households the true cost of living in a floodplain. With this information, FEMA will still undertake a targeted means-tested assistance program, which is to offer premium assistance based on income or ability to pay, rather than just location or date of construction. Overall, this proposal is expected to increase the number of policy holders and covered properties, and so help make obtaining and maintaining flood insurance more affordable.

NATIONAL FLOOD INSURANCE FUND

(Legislative proposal, subject to PAYGO)

Program and Financing (in millions of dollars)

Identification code 070–4236–4–3–453		2021 actual	2022 est.	2023 est.
	Obligations by program activity:			
0801	NFIP Mandatory			45
0899	Total reimbursable obligations			45
0900	Total new obligations, unexpired accounts (object class 42.0)			45

DEPARTMENT OF HOMELAND SECURITY

Federal Emergency Management Agency—Continued
Federal Funds—Continued

541

	Budgetary resources:			
	Budget authority:			
	Appropriations, mandatory:			
1200	Appropriation	....	....	45
	Spending authority from offsetting collections, mandatory:			
1800	Offsetting collections	....	....	–37
1802	Offsetting collections (previously unavailable)	....	....	37
1823	New and/or unobligated balance of spending authority from offsetting collections temporarily reduced	....	....	–37
1850	Spending auth from offsetting collections, mand (total)	....	....	–37
1900	Budget authority (total)	....	....	8
1930	Total budgetary resources available	....	....	8
	Memorandum (non-add) entries:			
1941	Unexpired unobligated balance, end of year	....	....	–37
	Change in obligated balance:			
	Unpaid obligations:			
3010	New obligations, unexpired accounts	....	....	45
3020	Outlays (gross)	....	....	–8
3050	Unpaid obligations, end of year	....	....	37
	Memorandum (non-add) entries:			
3200	Obligated balance, end of year	....	....	37
	Budget authority and outlays, net:			
	Mandatory:			
4090	Budget authority, gross	....	....	8
	Outlays, gross:			
4100	Outlays from new mandatory authority	....	....	8
	Offsets against gross budget authority and outlays:			
	Offsetting collections (collected) from:			
4123	Non-Federal sources	....	....	37
4180	Budget authority, net (total)	....	....	45
4190	Outlays, net (total)	....	....	45

The purpose of this 2023 Budget proposal is to remedy the recognized need to provide affordable assistance to certain households, which otherwise might not participate at all, as FEMA puts the National Flood Insurance Program (NFIP) on a more sustainable financial footing. The Budget proposal moves this forward by indicating to households the true cost of living in a floodplain. With this information, FEMA will still undertake a targeted means-tested assistance program, which is to offer premium assistance based on income or ability to pay, rather than just location or date of construction. Overall, this proposal is expected to increase the number of policy holders and covered properties, and so help make obtaining and maintaining flood insurance more affordable.

NATIONAL FLOOD INSURANCE RESERVE FUND

Special and Trust Fund Receipts (in millions of dollars)

Identification code 070–5701–0–2–453	2021 actual	2022 est.	2023 est.
0100 Balance, start of year	....	....	....
Receipts:			
Current law:			
1130 Fees, National Flood Insurance Reserve Fund	961	969	941
1140 Earnings on Investments, National Flood Insurance Reserve Fund	38	26	54
1199 Total current law receipts	999	995	995
Proposed:			
1230 Fees, National Flood Insurance Reserve Fund	....	....	2
1999 Total receipts	999	995	997
2000 Total: Balances and receipts	999	995	997
Appropriations:			
Current law:			
2101 National Flood Insurance Reserve Fund	–999	–995	–995
Proposed:			
2201 National Flood Insurance Reserve Fund	....	....	–2
2999 Total appropriations	–999	–995	–997
5099 Balance, end of year	....	....	....

Program and Financing (in millions of dollars)

Identification code 070–5701–0–2–453	2021 actual	2022 est.	2023 est.
Obligations by program activity:			
0001 NFIP Obligations from Reserve Fund	444	371	371
0900 Total new obligations, unexpired accounts (object class 42.0)	444	371	371
Budgetary resources:			
Unobligated balance:			
1000 Unobligated balance brought forward, Oct 1	1,875	2,430	3,054
Budget authority:			
Appropriations, mandatory:			
1201 Appropriation (special or trust fund)	999	995	995
1930 Total budgetary resources available	2,874	3,425	4,049
Memorandum (non-add) entries:			
1941 Unexpired unobligated balance, end of year	2,430	3,054	3,678
Change in obligated balance:			
Unpaid obligations:			
3000 Unpaid obligations, brought forward, Oct 1	276	328	511
3010 New obligations, unexpired accounts	444	371	371
3020 Outlays (gross)	–392	–188	–591
3050 Unpaid obligations, end of year	328	511	291
Memorandum (non-add) entries:			
3100 Obligated balance, start of year	276	328	511
3200 Obligated balance, end of year	328	511	291
Budget authority and outlays, net:			
Mandatory:			
4090 Budget authority, gross	999	995	995
Outlays, gross:			
4100 Outlays from new mandatory authority	199	26	54
4101 Outlays from mandatory balances	193	162	537
4110 Outlays, gross (total)	392	188	591
4180 Budget authority, net (total)	999	995	995
4190 Outlays, net (total)	392	188	591
Memorandum (non-add) entries:			
5000 Total investments, SOY: Federal securities: Par value	1,645	1,342	3,055
5001 Total investments, EOY: Federal securities: Par value	1,342	3,055	3,679

Summary of Budget Authority and Outlays (in millions of dollars)

	2021 actual	2022 est.	2023 est.
Enacted/requested:			
Budget Authority	999	995	995
Outlays	392	188	591
Legislative proposal, subject to PAYGO:			
Budget Authority	....	....	2
Total:			
Budget Authority	999	995	997
Outlays	392	188	591

As directed by the Biggert-Waters Flood Insurance Reform Act of 2012, FEMA has established the National Flood Insurance Reserve Fund for the National Flood Insurance Program to meet expected future obligations of the program, to include payment of claims, claims adjustment expenses, the purchase of reinsurance, and the repayment of outstanding debt owed to the U.S. Treasury, including interest.

NATIONAL FLOOD INSURANCE RESERVE FUND

(Legislative proposal, subject to PAYGO)

Program and Financing (in millions of dollars)

Identification code 070–5701–4–2–453	2021 actual	2022 est.	2023 est.
Budgetary resources:			
Budget authority:			
Appropriations, mandatory:			
1201 Appropriation (special or trust fund)	....	....	2
1930 Total budgetary resources available	....	....	2
Memorandum (non-add) entries:			
1941 Unexpired unobligated balance, end of year	....	....	2
Budget authority and outlays, net:			
Mandatory:			
4090 Budget authority, gross	....	....	2

Federal Emergency Management Agency—Continued
Federal Funds—Continued

NATIONAL FLOOD INSURANCE RESERVE FUND—Continued
Program and Financing—Continued

Identification code 070–5701–4–2–453	2021 actual	2022 est.	2023 est.
4180 Budget authority, net (total)			2
4190 Outlays, net (total)			
Memorandum (non-add) entries:			
5001 Total investments, EOY: Federal securities: Par value			2

The purpose of this 2023 Budget proposal is to remedy the recognized need to provide affordable assistance to certain households, which otherwise might not participate at all, as FEMA puts the National Flood Insurance Program (NFIP) on a more sustainable financial footing. The Budget proposal moves this forward by indicating to households the true cost of living in a floodplain. With this information, FEMA will still undertake a targeted means-tested assistance program, which is to offer premium assistance based on income or ability to pay, rather than just location or date of construction. Overall, this proposal is expected to increase the number of policy holders and covered properties, and so help make obtaining and maintaining flood insurance more affordable. This proposal will increase collections into the Reserve Fund.

NATIONAL PRE-DISASTER MITIGATION FUND
Program and Financing (in millions of dollars)

Identification code 070–0716–0–1–453	2021 actual	2022 est.	2023 est.
Obligations by program activity:			
0001 Pre-disaster mitigation	6	11	
0900 Total new obligations, unexpired accounts (object class 41.0)	6	11	
Budgetary resources:			
Unobligated balance:			
1000 Unobligated balance brought forward, Oct 1	9	18	7
1010 Unobligated balance transfer to other accts [070–0530]	–2		
1021 Recoveries of prior year unpaid obligations	17		
1070 Unobligated balance (total)	24	18	7
1930 Total budgetary resources available	24	18	7
Memorandum (non-add) entries:			
1941 Unexpired unobligated balance, end of year	18	7	7
Change in obligated balance:			
Unpaid obligations:			
3000 Unpaid obligations, brought forward, Oct 1	141	99	60
3010 New obligations, unexpired accounts	6	11	
3020 Outlays (gross)	–31	–50	–49
3040 Recoveries of prior year unpaid obligations, unexpired	–17		
3050 Unpaid obligations, end of year	99	60	11
Memorandum (non-add) entries:			
3100 Obligated balance, start of year	141	99	60
3200 Obligated balance, end of year	99	60	11
Budget authority and outlays, net:			
Discretionary:			
Outlays, gross:			
4011 Outlays from discretionary balances	31	50	49
4180 Budget authority, net (total)			
4190 Outlays, net (total)	31	50	49

EMERGENCY FOOD AND SHELTER
Program and Financing (in millions of dollars)

Identification code 070–0707–0–1–605	2021 actual	2022 est.	2023 est.
Change in obligated balance:			
Unpaid obligations:			
3000 Unpaid obligations, brought forward, Oct 1	2		
3020 Outlays (gross)	–2		

Memorandum (non-add) entries:			
3100 Obligated balance, start of year	2		
Budget authority and outlays, net:			
Discretionary:			
Outlays, gross:			
4011 Outlays from discretionary balances	2		
4180 Budget authority, net (total)			
4190 Outlays, net (total)	2		

DISASTER ASSISTANCE DIRECT LOAN PROGRAM ACCOUNT
Program and Financing (in millions of dollars)

Identification code 070–0703–0–1–453	2021 actual	2022 est.	2023 est.
Obligations by program activity:			
Credit program obligations:			
0701 Direct loan subsidy	122	30	42
0703 Subsidy for modifications of direct loans		85	
0705 Reestimates of direct loan subsidy	5	15	
0706 Interest on reestimates of direct loan subsidy	1	2	
0709 Administrative expenses	5	5	
0900 Total new obligations, unexpired accounts	133	137	42
Budgetary resources:			
Unobligated balance:			
1000 Unobligated balance brought forward, Oct 1	272	192	395
1011 Unobligated balance transfer from other acct [070–0702]	4	257	
1021 Recoveries of prior year unpaid obligations	10		
1070 Unobligated balance (total)	286	449	395
Budget authority:			
Appropriations, discretionary:			
1121 Appropriations transferred from other acct [070–0702]	33	66	
Appropriations, mandatory:			
1200 Appropriation	6	17	
1900 Budget authority (total)	39	83	
1930 Total budgetary resources available	325	532	395
Memorandum (non-add) entries:			
1941 Unexpired unobligated balance, end of year	192	395	353
Change in obligated balance:			
Unpaid obligations:			
3000 Unpaid obligations, brought forward, Oct 1	126	87	43
3010 New obligations, unexpired accounts	133	137	42
3020 Outlays (gross)	–162	–181	–49
3040 Recoveries of prior year unpaid obligations, unexpired	–10		
3050 Unpaid obligations, end of year	87	43	36
Memorandum (non-add) entries:			
3100 Obligated balance, start of year	126	87	43
3200 Obligated balance, end of year	87	43	36
Budget authority and outlays, net:			
Discretionary:			
4000 Budget authority, gross	33	66	
Outlays, gross:			
4010 Outlays from new discretionary authority		66	
4011 Outlays from discretionary balances	156	98	49
4020 Outlays, gross (total)	156	164	49
Mandatory:			
4090 Budget authority, gross	6	17	
Outlays, gross:			
4100 Outlays from new mandatory authority	6	17	
4180 Budget authority, net (total)	39	83	
4190 Outlays, net (total)	162	181	49

Summary of Loan Levels, Subsidy Budget Authority and Outlays by Program (in millions of dollars)

Identification code 070–0703–0–1–453	2021 actual	2022 est.	2023 est.
Direct loan levels supportable by subsidy budget authority:			
115002 Community Disaster Loan Program	151	38	54
115999 Total direct loan levels	151	38	54
Direct loan subsidy (in percent):			
132002 Community Disaster Loan Program	80.39	77.74	78.94
132999 Weighted average subsidy rate	80.39	77.74	78.94
Direct loan subsidy budget authority:			
133002 Community Disaster Loan Program	122	30	42

DEPARTMENT OF HOMELAND SECURITY

		2021 actual	2022 est.	2023 est.
133999	Total subsidy budget authority	122	30	42
	Direct loan subsidy outlays:			
134002	Community Disaster Loan Program	134	134	38
134003	Special Community Disaster Loans	20	27	11
134999	Total subsidy outlays	154	161	49
	Direct loan reestimates:			
135002	Community Disaster Loan Program	3	8	
135003	Special Community Disaster Loans	2	8	
135999	Total direct loan reestimates	5	16	
	Administrative expense data:			
3510	Budget authority	5		
3580	Outlays from balances	2	3	

Disaster assistance loans authorized by the Robert T. Stafford Disaster Relief and Emergency Assistance Act (42 U.S.C. 5121 et seq.) includes two programs: 1) section 319 authorizes for direct loans to States for the non-Federal portion of cost-shared Stafford Act programs; and 2) section 417 authorizes direct community disaster loans to local governments that incurred substantial loss of tax and other revenues as a result of a major disaster and require financial assistance in order to perform governmental functions.

Object Classification (in millions of dollars)

Identification code 070–0703–0–1–453		2021 actual	2022 est.	2023 est.
	Direct obligations:			
25.2	Other services from non-Federal sources	5	5	
33.0	Investments and loans	128	132	42
99.0	Direct obligations	133	137	42
99.9	Total new obligations, unexpired accounts	133	137	42

DISASTER ASSISTANCE DIRECT LOAN FINANCING ACCOUNT

Program and Financing (in millions of dollars)

Identification code 070–4234–0–3–453		2021 actual	2022 est.	2023 est.
	Obligations by program activity:			
	Credit program obligations:			
0710	Direct loan obligations	151	38	54
0713	Payment of interest to Treasury	3		
0742	Downward reestimates paid to receipt accounts	1	1	
0791	Direct program activities, subtotal	155	39	54
0900	Total new obligations, unexpired accounts	155	39	54
	Budgetary resources:			
	Financing authority:			
	Borrowing authority, mandatory:			
1400	Borrowing authority	32	10	12
	Spending authority from offsetting collections, mandatory:			
1800	Collected	169	178	49
1801	Change in uncollected payments, Federal sources	–32	–47	–7
1825	Spending authority from offsetting collections applied to repay debt	–14	–102	
1850	Spending auth from offsetting collections, mand (total)	123	29	42
1900	Budget authority (total)	155	39	54
1930	Total budgetary resources available	155	39	54
	Change in obligated balance:			
	Unpaid obligations:			
3000	Unpaid obligations, brought forward, Oct 1	135	99	45
3010	New obligations, unexpired accounts	155	39	54
3020	Outlays (gross)	–191	–93	–60
3050	Unpaid obligations, end of year	99	45	39
	Uncollected payments:			
3060	Uncollected pymts, Fed sources, brought forward, Oct 1	–115	–83	–36
3070	Change in uncollected pymts, Fed sources, unexpired	32	47	7
3090	Uncollected pymts, Fed sources, end of year	–83	–36	–29
	Memorandum (non-add) entries:			
3100	Obligated balance, start of year	20	16	9
3200	Obligated balance, end of year	16	9	10

Federal Emergency Management Agency—Continued
Federal Funds—Continued

		2021 actual	2022 est.	2023 est.
	Financing authority and disbursements, net:			
	Mandatory:			
4090	Budget authority, gross	155	39	54
	Financing disbursements:			
4110	Outlays, gross (total)	191	93	60
	Offsets against gross financing authority and disbursements:			
	Offsetting collections (collected) from:			
4120	Federal sources	–160	–178	–49
4122	Interest on uninvested funds	–1		
4123	Non-Federal sources- Principal	–8		
4130	Offsets against gross budget authority and outlays (total)	–169	–178	–49
	Additional offsets against financing authority only (total):			
4140	Change in uncollected pymts, Fed sources, unexpired	32	47	7
4160	Budget authority, net (mandatory)	18	–92	12
4170	Outlays, net (mandatory)	22	–85	11
4180	Budget authority, net (total)	18	–92	12
4190	Outlays, net (total)	22	–85	11

Status of Direct Loans (in millions of dollars)

Identification code 070–4234–0–3–453		2021 actual	2022 est.	2023 est.
	Position with respect to appropriations act limitation on obligations:			
1121	Limitation available from carry-forward	168	55	71
1143	Unobligated limitation carried forward (P.L. xx) (-)	–17	–17	–17
1150	Total direct loan obligations	151	38	54
	Cumulative balance of direct loans outstanding:			
1210	Outstanding, start of year	655	833	83
1231	Disbursements: Direct loan disbursements	187	92	60
1251	Repayments: Repayments and prepayments	–8		
1264	Other adjustments, net (+ or -)	–1	–842	–23
1290	Outstanding, end of year	833	83	120

Balance Sheet (in millions of dollars)

Identification code 070–4234–0–3–453		2020 actual	2021 actual
	ASSETS:		
	Federal assets:		
1101	Fund balances with Treasury		
	Investments in U.S. securities:		
1106	Receivables, net	6	85
	Net value of assets related to post-1991 direct loans receivable:		
1401	Direct loans receivable, gross	655	833
1402	Interest receivable	20	38
1405	Allowance for subsidy cost (-)	–609	–863
1499	Net present value of assets related to direct loans	66	8
1999	Total assets	72	93
	LIABILITIES:		
	Federal liabilities:		
2103	Debt	71	93
2105	Other	1	
2207	Non-Federal liabilities: Other		
2999	Total liabilities	72	93
	NET POSITION:		
3300	Cumulative results of operations		
4999	Total liabilities and net position	72	93

PROCUREMENT, CONSTRUCTION, AND IMPROVEMENTS

For necessary expenses of the Federal Emergency Management Agency for procurement, construction, and improvements, $190,319,000, of which $123,425,000 shall remain available until September 30, 2025, and of which $66,894,000 shall remain available until September 30, 2027.

Note.—A full-year 2022 appropriation for this account was not enacted at the time the Budget was prepared; therefore, the Budget assumes this account is operating under the Continuing Appropriations Act, 2022 (Division A of Public Law 117–43, as amended). The amounts included for 2022 reflect the annualized level provided by the continuing resolution.

Program and Financing (in millions of dollars)

Identification code 070–0414–0–1–999		2021 actual	2022 est.	2023 est.
	Obligations by program activity:			
0001	CAS - Operational Communications/Information Technology	12	10	9

Federal Emergency Management Agency—Continued
Federal Funds—Continued

PROCUREMENT, CONSTRUCTION, AND IMPROVEMENTS—Continued

Program and Financing—Continued

Identification code 070–0414–0–1–999	2021 actual	2022 est.	2023 est.
0002 CAS - Construction and Facility Improvements	50	31	66
0003 CAS - Mission Support Assets and Infrastructure	49	41	115
0900 Total new obligations, unexpired accounts	111	82	190
Budgetary resources:			
Unobligated balance:			
1000 Unobligated balance brought forward, Oct 1	35	37	61
1011 Unobligated balance transfer from other acct [070–0702]	7		
1070 Unobligated balance (total)	42	37	61
Budget authority:			
Appropriations, discretionary:			
1100 CAS - Operational Communications/Information Technology	12	12	9
1100 CAS - Construction and Facility Improvements	47	47	66
1100 CAS - Mission Support Assets and Infrastructure	47	47	115
1121 Appropriations transferred from other acct [070–0700]	1		
1160 Appropriation, discretionary (total)	107	106	190
1930 Total budgetary resources available	149	143	251
Memorandum (non-add) entries:			
1940 Unobligated balance expiring	–1		
1941 Unexpired unobligated balance, end of year	37	61	61
Change in obligated balance:			
Unpaid obligations:			
3000 Unpaid obligations, brought forward, Oct 1	152	141	96
3010 New obligations, unexpired accounts	111	82	190
3020 Outlays (gross)	–121	–127	–128
3041 Recoveries of prior year unpaid obligations, expired	–1		
3050 Unpaid obligations, end of year	141	96	158
Memorandum (non-add) entries:			
3100 Obligated balance, start of year	152	141	96
3200 Obligated balance, end of year	141	96	158
Budget authority and outlays, net:			
Discretionary:			
4000 Budget authority, gross	107	106	190
Outlays, gross:			
4010 Outlays from new discretionary authority	21	14	36
4011 Outlays from discretionary balances	100	113	92
4020 Outlays, gross (total)	121	127	128
4180 Budget authority, net (total)	107	106	190
4190 Outlays, net (total)	121	127	128

Procurement, Construction, and Improvements (PC&I) provides funds necessary for the Federal Emergency Management Agency's (FEMA) major investments in information technology, communication, facilities, and infrastructure that support operations essential to FEMA's mission. The PC&I appropriation consists of three programs, projects, and activities:

Operational Communications/Information Technology.—The 2023 request includes funding for FEMA's investments in communications infrastructure, IT systems, and equipment that are directly used by field offices and personnel and have multi-mission frontline applications.

Construction and Facility Improvements.—The 2023 request includes funding for major construction and improvements for FEMA's land and facility investments above the real property threshold set for minor construction in Operations and Support and Federal Assistance appropriations.

Mission Support Assets and Infrastructure.—The 2023 request includes funding for the design, implementation, and integration of new solutions for major FEMA systems and data management that support the Agency's mission.

Object Classification (in millions of dollars)

Identification code 070–0414–0–1–999	2021 actual	2022 est.	2023 est.
Direct obligations:			
25.1 Advisory and assistance services	18	10	12
25.2 Other services from non-Federal sources	41	30	102
25.4 Operation and maintenance of facilities	2	2	
25.7 Operation and maintenance of equipment	2	2	
31.0 Equipment	3	3	9
32.0 Land and structures	45	35	67
99.0 Direct obligations	111	82	190
99.9 Total new obligations, unexpired accounts	111	82	190

ADMINISTRATIVE PROVISIONS

SEC. 301. Funds made available under the heading "Cybersecurity and Infrastructure Security Agency—Operations and Support" may be made available for the necessary expenses of carrying out the competition specified in section 2(e) of Executive Order No. 13870 (May 2, 2019), including the provision of monetary and non-monetary awards for Federal civilian employees and members of the uniformed services, the necessary expenses for the honorary recognition of any award recipients, and activities to encourage participation in the competition, including promotional items: Provided, That any awards made pursuant to this section shall be of the same type and amount as those authorized under sections 4501 through 4505 of title 5, United States Code.

SEC. 302. Notwithstanding section 2008(a)(12) of the Homeland Security Act of 2002 (6 U.S.C. 609(a)(12)) or any other provision of law, not more than 5 percent of the amount of a grant made available in paragraphs (1) through (4) under "Federal Emergency Management Agency—Federal Assistance", may be used by the grantee for expenses directly related to administration of the grant.

SEC. 303. Except for grants under the Nonprofit Security Grant Program, applications for grants under the heading "Federal Emergency Management Agency—Federal Assistance", for paragraphs (1) through (4), shall be made available to eligible applicants not later than 60 days after the date of enactment of this Act, eligible applicants shall submit applications not later than 80 days after the grant announcement, and the Administrator of the Federal Emergency Management Agency shall act within 65 days after the receipt of an application.

SEC. 304. Under the heading "Federal Emergency Management Agency—Federal Assistance", for grants under paragraphs (1) through (4), (8), and (9), the Administrator of the Federal Emergency Management Agency shall brief the Committees on Appropriations of the Senate and the House of Representatives 5 full business days in advance of announcing publicly the intention of making an award.

SEC. 305. Under the heading "Federal Emergency Management Agency—Federal Assistance", for grants under paragraphs (1) and (2), the installation of communications towers is not considered construction of a building or other physical facility.

SEC. 306. The reporting requirements in paragraphs (1) and (2) under the heading "Federal Emergency Management Agency—Disaster Relief Fund" in the Department of Homeland Security Appropriations Act, 2015 (Public Law 114–4) shall be applied in fiscal year 2023 with respect to budget year 2024 and current fiscal year 2023, respectively—

(1) in paragraph (1) by substituting "fiscal year 2024" for "fiscal year 2016"; and

(2) in paragraph (2) by inserting "business" after "fifth".

SEC. 307. In making grants under the heading "Federal Emergency Management Agency—Federal Assistance", for Staffing for Adequate Fire and Emergency Response grants, the Administrator of the Federal Emergency Management Agency may grant waivers from the requirements in subsections (a)(1)(A), (a)(1)(B), (a)(1)(E), (c)(1), (c)(2), and (c)(4) of section 34 of the Federal Fire Prevention and Control Act of 1974 (15 U.S.C. 2229a).

SEC. 308. The aggregate charges assessed during fiscal year 2023, as authorized in title III of the Departments of Veterans Affairs and Housing and Urban Development, and Independent Agencies Appropriations Act, 1999 (42 U.S.C. 5196e), shall not be less than 100 percent of the amounts anticipated by the Department of Homeland Security to be necessary for its Radiological Emergency Preparedness Program for the next fiscal year: Provided, That the methodology for assessment and collection of fees shall be fair and equitable and shall reflect costs of providing such services, including administrative costs of collecting such fees: Provided further, That such fees shall be deposited in a Radiological Emergency Preparedness Program account as offsetting collections and will become available for authorized purposes on October 1, 2023, and remain available until expended.

SEC. 309. Any balances of funds appropriated in any prior Act for activities funded by National Predisaster Mitigation Fund under section 203 of the Robert T. Stafford Disaster Relief and Emergency Assistance Act (42 U.S.C. 5133) (as in effect on the day before the date of enactment of section 1234 of division D of Public Law 115–254) may be transferred to and merged for all purposes with the funds set aside pursuant to subsection (i)(1) of section 203 of the Robert T. Stafford Disaster Relief and Emergency Assistance Act (42 U.S.C. 5133), as in effect on the date of the enactment of this section.

DEPARTMENT OF HOMELAND SECURITY

Citizenship and Immigration Services
Federal Funds
545

SEC. 310. In making grants under the heading "Federal Emergency Management Agency—Federal Assistance", for Assistance to Firefighter Grants, the Administrator of the Federal Emergency Management Agency may waive subsection (k) of section 33 of the Federal Fire Prevention and Control Act of 1974 (15 U.S.C. 2229).

SEC. 311. Amounts made available in paragraphs (1) and (2) under the heading "Federal Emergency Management Agency—Federal Assistance" in this title specifically for organizations as described under section 501(c)(3) of the Internal Revenue Code of 1986 and exempt from tax under section 501(a) of such code may be used to award grants to entities otherwise eligible to receive grants under those paragraphs should insufficient qualified applications be received or approved by August 30, 2023: Provided, That no grants may be awarded under this section unless the Committees on Appropriations of the Senate and the House of Representatives are notified at least 5 days in advance of such awards.

CITIZENSHIP AND IMMIGRATION SERVICES

Federal Funds

OPERATIONS AND SUPPORT

For necessary expenses of U.S. Citizenship and Immigration Services for operations and support, including for the E-Verify Program, information technology and cybersecurity, application processing, the reduction of backlogs within USCIS asylum, field, and service center offices, additional support for asylum adjudication workloads, and support of the refugee program, $903,622,000: Provided, That such amounts shall be in addition to any other amounts made available for such purposes, and shall not be construed to require any reduction of any fee described in section 286(m) of the Immigration and Nationality Act (8 U.S.C. 1356(m)).

Note.—A full-year 2022 appropriation for this account was not enacted at the time the Budget was prepared; therefore, the Budget assumes this account is operating under the Continuing Appropriations Act, 2022 (Division A of Public Law 117–43, as amended). The amounts included for 2022 reflect the annualized level provided by the continuing resolution.

Program and Financing (in millions of dollars)

Identification code 070–0300–0–1–751		2021 actual	2022 est.	2023 est.
	Obligations by program activity:			
0001	Citizenship and Immigration Services (Direct)	112	....	....
0002	CAS - Employment Status Verification	....	117	110
0003	Application Processing	....	250	765
0004	Information Technology and Cybersecurity	....	....	29
0799	Total direct obligations	112	367	904
0900	Total new obligations, unexpired accounts	112	367	904
	Budgetary resources:			
	Unobligated balance:			
1000	Unobligated balance brought forward, Oct 1	2	4	4
1012	Unobligated balance transfers between expired and unexpired accounts	9		
1021	Recoveries of prior year unpaid obligations	2		
1070	Unobligated balance (total)	13	4	4
	Budget authority:			
	Appropriations, discretionary:			
1100	Appropriation	118	367	904
1120	Appropriations transferred to other accts [070–0530]	–1		
1120	Appropriations transferred to other acct [070–0400]	–2		
1131	Unobligated balance of appropriations permanently reduced	–9		
1160	Appropriation, discretionary (total)	106	367	904
1930	Total budgetary resources available	119	371	908
	Memorandum (non-add) entries:			
1940	Unobligated balance expiring	–3		
1941	Unexpired unobligated balance, end of year	4	4	4
	Change in obligated balance:			
	Unpaid obligations:			
3000	Unpaid obligations, brought forward, Oct 1	48	48	187
3010	New obligations, unexpired accounts	112	367	904
3020	Outlays (gross)	–98	–228	–622
3040	Recoveries of prior year unpaid obligations, unexpired	–2		
3041	Recoveries of prior year unpaid obligations, expired	–12		
3050	Unpaid obligations, end of year	48	187	469
	Memorandum (non-add) entries:			
3100	Obligated balance, start of year	48	48	187
3200	Obligated balance, end of year	48	187	469

	Budget authority and outlays, net:			
	Discretionary:			
4000	Budget authority, gross	106	367	904
	Outlays, gross:			
4010	Outlays from new discretionary authority	67	175	430
4011	Outlays from discretionary balances	31	53	192
4020	Outlays, gross (total)	98	228	622
4180	Budget authority, net (total)	106	367	904
4190	Outlays, net (total)	98	228	622

The mission of U.S. Citizenship and Immigration Services (USCIS) is to adjudicate and grant immigration and citizenship benefits, provide accurate and useful information to applicants and petitioners, and promote an awareness and understanding of citizenship in support of immigrant integration, while also protecting the integrity of our Nation's immigration system. USCIS approves millions of immigration benefit applications each year, ranging from work authorization and lawful permanent residency to asylum and refugee status. The Budget continues to invest in technology to improve and automate business operations, eliminate paper-based processing, improve information sharing, and enhance USCIS' ability to identify and prevent immigration benefit fraud.

The Budget assumes that USCIS will continue to be funded primarily through fees on the applications and petitions it adjudicates.

Within USCIS' appropriated funding, Operations and Support funds necessary operations, mission support, and associated management and administration costs, including for the E-Verify program, asylum adjudications, support for the refugee program, information technology and cybersecurity, application processing, and backlog reduction efforts.

Object Classification (in millions of dollars)

Identification code 070–0300–0–1–751		2021 actual	2022 est.	2023 est.
	Direct obligations:			
	Personnel compensation:			
11.1	Full-time permanent	27	143	347
11.3	Other than full-time permanent			3
11.5	Other personnel compensation	1	1	71
11.9	Total personnel compensation	28	144	421
12.1	Civilian personnel benefits	10	26	107
21.0	Travel and transportation of persons			58
22.0	Transportation of things			1
23.1	Rental payments to GSA	7	8	6
23.2	Rental payments to others			9
23.3	Communications, utilities, and miscellaneous charges	1	1	1
24.0	Printing and reproduction			1
25.1	Advisory and assistance services	11	56	107
25.2	Other services from non-Federal sources		30	87
25.3	Other goods and services from Federal sources	4	4	14
25.4	Operation and maintenance of facilities			1
25.7	Operation and maintenance of equipment	5	5	51
26.0	Supplies and materials		18	3
31.0	Equipment	44	74	37
99.0	Direct obligations	110	366	904
99.5	Adjustment for rounding	2	1	
99.9	Total new obligations, unexpired accounts	112	367	904

Employment Summary

Identification code 070–0300–0–1–751	2021 actual	2022 est.	2023 est.
1001 Direct civilian full-time equivalent employment	270	1,351	3,014

PROCUREMENT, CONSTRUCTION, AND IMPROVEMENTS

Program and Financing (in millions of dollars)

Identification code 070–0407–0–1–751		2021 actual	2022 est.	2023 est.
	Obligations by program activity:			
0001	Citizenship and Immigration Services (Direct)	1		
0900	Total new obligations, unexpired accounts (object class 31.0)	1		

Citizenship and Immigration Services—Continued
Federal Funds—Continued

PROCUREMENT, CONSTRUCTION, AND IMPROVEMENTS—Continued

Program and Financing—Continued

Identification code 070–0407–0–1–751	2021 actual	2022 est.	2023 est.
Budgetary resources:			
Unobligated balance:			
1000 Unobligated balance brought forward, Oct 1	10	1	1
1010 Unobligated balance transfer to other accts [070–0400]	–1		
1021 Recoveries of prior year unpaid obligations	2		
1070 Unobligated balance (total)	11	1	1
Budget authority:			
Appropriations, discretionary:			
1131 Unobligated balance of appropriations permanently reduced	–8		
1930 Total budgetary resources available	3	1	1
Memorandum (non-add) entries:			
1940 Unobligated balance expiring	–1		
1941 Unexpired unobligated balance, end of year	1	1	1
Change in obligated balance:			
Unpaid obligations:			
3000 Unpaid obligations, brought forward, Oct 1	5	1	1
3010 New obligations, unexpired accounts	1		
3020 Outlays (gross)	–3		
3040 Recoveries of prior year unpaid obligations, unexpired	–2		
3050 Unpaid obligations, end of year	1	1	1
Memorandum (non-add) entries:			
3100 Obligated balance, start of year	5	1	1
3200 Obligated balance, end of year	1	1	1
Budget authority and outlays, net:			
Discretionary:			
4000 Budget authority, gross	–8		
Outlays, gross:			
4011 Outlays from discretionary balances	3		
4180 Budget authority, net (total)	–8		
4190 Outlays, net (total)	3		

The Procurement, Construction, and Improvements appropriation provides the funds necessary for the planning, operational development, engineering, and purchases associated with the U.S. Citizenship and Immigration Service's employment eligibility verification program. U.S. Citizenship and Immigration Services does not request funds for Procurement, Construction, and Improvements in 2023 due to the program having achieved Full Operational Capability.

FEDERAL ASSISTANCE

For necessary expenses of U.S. Citizenship and Immigration Services for Federal assistance for the Citizenship and Integration Grant Program, $10,000,000.

Note.—A full-year 2022 appropriation for this account was not enacted at the time the Budget was prepared; therefore, the Budget assumes this account is operating under the Continuing Appropriations Act, 2022 (Division A of Public Law 117–43, as amended). The amounts included for 2022 reflect the annualized level provided by the continuing resolution.

Program and Financing (in millions of dollars)

Identification code 070–0408–0–1–751	2021 actual	2022 est.	2023 est.
Obligations by program activity:			
0001 Citizenship and Integration Grant Program	10	10	10
0900 Total new obligations, unexpired accounts (object class 41.0)	10	10	10
Budgetary resources:			
Budget authority:			
Appropriations, discretionary:			
1100 Appropriation	10	10	10
1930 Total budgetary resources available	10	10	10
Change in obligated balance:			
Unpaid obligations:			
3000 Unpaid obligations, brought forward, Oct 1	16	18	18
3010 New obligations, unexpired accounts	10	10	10
3020 Outlays (gross)	–8	–10	–10
3050 Unpaid obligations, end of year	18	18	18
Memorandum (non-add) entries:			
3100 Obligated balance, start of year	16	18	18
3200 Obligated balance, end of year	18	18	18
Budget authority and outlays, net:			
Discretionary:			
4000 Budget authority, gross	10	10	10
Outlays, gross:			
4011 Outlays from discretionary balances	8	10	10
4180 Budget authority, net (total)	10	10	10
4190 Outlays, net (total)	8	10	10

The U.S. Citizenship and Immigration Services (USCIS) Federal Assistance appropriations provides funding for the Citizenship and Integration Grant Program. The goal of the program is to expand the availability of high-quality citizenship preparation services for lawful permanent residents across the nation and to provide opportunities for lawful permanent residents to gain the knowledge and skills necessary to integrate into the fabric of American society. USCIS awards grant funding on a competitive basis to organizations that provide citizenship preparation and naturalization application services to lawful permanent residents, including former refugees and asylees.

IMMIGRATION EXAMINATIONS FEE

Special and Trust Fund Receipts (in millions of dollars)

Identification code 070–5088–0–2–751	2021 actual	2022 est.	2023 est.
0100 Balance, start of year	226	269	245
Receipts:			
Current law:			
1120 Immigration Examination Fee	4,713	4,291	4,293
2000 Total: Balances and receipts	4,939	4,560	4,538
Appropriations:			
Current law:			
2101 Immigration Examinations Fee	–4,713	–4,291	–4,293
2103 Immigration Examinations Fee	–226	–269	–245
2132 Immigration Examinations Fee	269	245	245
2199 Total current law appropriations	–4,670	–4,315	–4,293
2999 Total appropriations	–4,670	–4,315	–4,293
5099 Balance, end of year	269	245	245

Program and Financing (in millions of dollars)

Identification code 070–5088–0–2–751	2021 actual	2022 est.	2023 est.
Obligations by program activity:			
0001 Citizenship and Immigration Services	4,302	4,751	5,004
0002 Operation Allies Welcome		193	
0799 Total direct obligations	4,302	4,944	5,004
0801 Reimbursable program activity	58	75	75
0900 Total new obligations, unexpired accounts	4,360	5,019	5,079
Budgetary resources:			
Unobligated balance:			
1000 Unobligated balance brought forward, Oct 1	1,033	1,533	1,172
1021 Recoveries of prior year unpaid obligations	114	76	76
1033 Recoveries of prior year paid obligations	9		
1070 Unobligated balance (total)	1,156	1,609	1,248
Budget authority:			
Appropriations, discretionary:			
1120 Appropriations transferred to other acct [015–0339]		–4	–4
Appropriations, mandatory:			
1200 Appropriation [Operations Allies Welcome]		193	
1201 Immigration Examinations Fee Account	4,713	4,291	4,293
1203 Appropriation (previously unavailable)(special or trust)	226	269	245
1220 Appropriations transferred to other acct [015–0339]	–4		
1232 Appropriations and/or unobligated balance of appropriations temporarily reduced	–269	–245	–245
1260 Appropriations, mandatory (total)	4,666	4,508	4,293
Spending authority from offsetting collections, mandatory:			
1800 Collected	62	75	75
1801 Change in uncollected payments, Federal sources	10		
1802 Offsetting collections (previously unavailable)	3	4	1

DEPARTMENT OF HOMELAND SECURITY

Citizenship and Immigration Services—Continued
Federal Funds—Continued

547

		2021 actual	2022 est.	2023 est.
1823	New and/or unobligated balance of spending authority from offsetting collections temporarily reduced	−4	−1	−1
1850	Spending auth from offsetting collections, mand (total)	71	78	75
1900	Budget authority (total)	4,737	4,582	4,364
1930	Total budgetary resources available	5,893	6,191	5,612
	Memorandum (non-add) entries:			
1941	Unexpired unobligated balance, end of year	1,533	1,172	533
	Change in obligated balance:			
	Unpaid obligations:			
3000	Unpaid obligations, brought forward, Oct 1	961	1,070	1,574
3010	New obligations, unexpired accounts	4,360	5,019	5,079
3020	Outlays (gross)	−4,137	−4,439	−4,436
3040	Recoveries of prior year unpaid obligations, unexpired	−114	−76	−76
3050	Unpaid obligations, end of year	1,070	1,574	2,141
	Uncollected payments:			
3060	Uncollected pymts, Fed sources, brought forward, Oct 1	−19	−29	−29
3070	Change in uncollected pymts, Fed sources, unexpired	−10		
3090	Uncollected pymts, Fed sources, end of year	−29	−29	−29
	Memorandum (non-add) entries:			
3100	Obligated balance, start of year	942	1,041	1,545
3200	Obligated balance, end of year	1,041	1,545	2,112
	Budget authority and outlays, net:			
	Discretionary:			
4000	Budget authority, gross		−4	−4
	Outlays, gross:			
4010	Outlays from new discretionary authority		−4	−4
	Mandatory:			
4090	Budget authority, gross	4,737	4,586	4,368
	Outlays, gross:			
4100	Outlays from new mandatory authority	3,549	3,226	3,080
4101	Outlays from mandatory balances	588	1,217	1,360
4110	Outlays, gross (total)	4,137	4,443	4,440
	Offsets against gross budget authority and outlays:			
	Offsetting collections (collected) from:			
4120	Federal sources	−59	−63	−63
4123	Non-Federal sources	−12	−12	−12
4130	Offsets against gross budget authority and outlays (total)	−71	−75	−75
	Additional offsets against gross budget authority only:			
4140	Change in uncollected pymts, Fed sources, unexpired	−10		
4143	Recoveries of prior year paid obligations, unexpired accounts	9		
4150	Additional offsets against budget authority only (total)	−1		
4160	Budget authority, net (mandatory)	4,665	4,511	4,293
4170	Outlays, net (mandatory)	4,066	4,368	4,365
4180	Budget authority, net (total)	4,665	4,507	4,289
4190	Outlays, net (total)	4,066	4,364	4,361
	Memorandum (non-add) entries:			
5090	Unexpired unavailable balance, SOY: Offsetting collections	3		
5092	Unexpired unavailable balance, EOY: Offsetting collections	4		

The Immigration Examinations Fee Account (IEFA) is authorized via Section 286(m) of the Immigration and Nationality Act (8 U.S.C. 1356(m)) and is the primary funding source for USCIS. IEFA provides the resources to: strengthen and effectively administer the immigration system; strengthen national security safeguards and combat fraud; and reinforce quality and consistency in administering immigration benefits.

Object Classification (in millions of dollars)

Identification code 070–5088–0–2–751	2021 actual	2022 est.	2023 est.
Direct obligations:			
Personnel compensation:			
11.1 Full-time permanent	1,704	1,953	1,977
11.3 Other than full-time permanent	9	14	15
11.5 Other personnel compensation	58	83	89
11.9 Total personnel compensation	1,771	2,050	2,081
12.1 Civilian personnel benefits	643	737	746
13.0 Benefits for former personnel	1		
21.0 Travel and transportation of persons	4	38	21
22.0 Transportation of things	10	12	11
23.1 Rental payments to GSA	274	308	286
23.2 Rental payments to others	1	1	1
23.3 Communications, utilities, and miscellaneous charges	66	53	53
24.0 Printing and reproduction	8	8	8
25.1 Advisory and assistance services	673	664	701
25.2 Other services from non-Federal sources	32	66	54
25.3 Other goods and services from Federal sources	297	424	456
25.4 Operation and maintenance of facilities	2	3	3
25.7 Operation and maintenance of equipment	109	101	108
26.0 Supplies and materials	14	18	15
31.0 Equipment	361	408	406
32.0 Land and structures	31	49	49
42.0 Insurance claims and indemnities	3	4	4
99.0 Direct obligations	4,300	4,944	5,003
99.0 Reimbursable obligations	60	75	75
99.5 Adjustment for rounding			1
99.9 Total new obligations, unexpired accounts	4,360	5,019	5,079

Employment Summary

Identification code 070–5088–0–2–751	2021 actual	2022 est.	2023 est.
1001 Direct civilian full-time equivalent employment	18,107	18,649	18,713

H-1B Nonimmigrant Petitioner Account

Special and Trust Fund Receipts (in millions of dollars)

Identification code 070–5106–0–2–751	2021 actual	2022 est.	2023 est.
0100 Balance, start of year	174	27	14
0198 Rounding adjustment	−1		
0199 Balance, start of year	173	27	14
Receipts:			
Current law:			
1120 H-1B Nonimmigrant Petitioner Account	384	388	397
2000 Total: Balances and receipts	557	415	411
Appropriations:			
Current law:			
2101 Training and Employment Services	−267	−194	−199
2101 State Unemployment Insurance and Employment Service Operations	−27	−19	−20
2101 H-1B Nonimmigrant Petitioner Account	−27	−20	−20
2101 STEM Education	−213	−162	−159
2103 Training and Employment Services	−11	−15	−11
2103 State Unemployment Insurance and Employment Service Operations	−1	−2	−1
2103 H-1B Nonimmigrant Petitioner Account	−1	−2	−1
2103 STEM Education	−9	−9	−9
2132 Training and Employment Services	15	11	11
2132 State Unemployment Insurance and Employment Service Operations	2	1	1
2132 H-1B Nonimmigrant Petitioner Account	1	1	1
2132 STEM Education	9	9	9
2199 Total current law appropriations	−529	−401	−398
2999 Total appropriations	−529	−401	−398
5098 Reconciliation adjustment	−1		
5099 Balance, end of year	27	14	13

Program and Financing (in millions of dollars)

Identification code 070–5106–0–2–751	2021 actual	2022 est.	2023 est.
Obligations by program activity:			
0001 Citizenship and Immigration Services	14	15	20
Budgetary resources:			
Unobligated balance:			
1000 Unobligated balance brought forward, Oct 1	13	18	16
Budget authority:			
Appropriations, discretionary:			
1131 Unobligated balance of appropriations permanently reduced		−8	
Appropriations, mandatory:			
1201 Appropriation (special or trust fund)	27	20	20
1203 Appropriation (previously unavailable)(special or trust)	1	2	1
1230 Appropriations and/or unobligated balance of appropriations permanently reduced	−8		
1232 Appropriations and/or unobligated balance of appropriations temporarily reduced	−1	−1	−1
1260 Appropriations, mandatory (total)	19	21	20
1900 Budget authority (total)	19	13	20
1930 Total budgetary resources available	32	31	36

Citizenship and Immigration Services—Continued
Federal Funds—Continued

H-1B NONIMMIGRANT PETITIONER ACCOUNT—Continued
Program and Financing—Continued

Identification code 070–5106–0–2–751	2021 actual	2022 est.	2023 est.
Memorandum (non-add) entries:			
1941 Unexpired unobligated balance, end of year	18	16	16
Change in obligated balance:			
Unpaid obligations:			
3000 Unpaid obligations, brought forward, Oct 1	2	6	....
3010 New obligations, unexpired accounts	14	15	20
3020 Outlays (gross)	–10	–21	–20
3050 Unpaid obligations, end of year	6	....	....
Memorandum (non-add) entries:			
3100 Obligated balance, start of year	2	6	....
3200 Obligated balance, end of year	6	....	....
Budget authority and outlays, net:			
Discretionary:			
4000 Budget authority, gross	....	–8	....
Mandatory:			
4090 Budget authority, gross	19	21	20
Outlays, gross:			
4100 Outlays from new mandatory authority	8	15	14
4101 Outlays from mandatory balances	2	6	6
4110 Outlays, gross (total)	10	21	20
4180 Budget authority, net (total)	19	13	20
4190 Outlays, net (total)	10	21	20

The H-1B Nonimmigrant Petitioner Fee Account was established by Section 286(s) of the Immigration and Nationality Act (8 U.S.C. 1356(s)), and amended by the American Competitiveness and Workforce Improvement Act of 1998 (ACWIA), Public Law 105–277, Division C, Title IV, 112 Stat. 2681. The ACWIA fee was reauthorized and made permanent by the L-1 Visa and H-1B Visa Reform Act of 2004 (part of the Consolidated Appropriations Act, 2005, Public Law 108–447, 118 Stat. 2809, 3351–61 (2004)). The account supports activities related to the processing of petitions for nonimmigrant workers in the H-1B visa classification.

Object Classification (in millions of dollars)

Identification code 070–5106–0–2–751	2021 actual	2022 est.	2023 est.
Direct obligations:			
23.3 Communications, utilities, and miscellaneous charges	1	2	2
25.1 Advisory and assistance services	13	13	18
99.0 Direct obligations	14	15	20
99.9 Total new obligations, unexpired accounts	14	15	20

H-1B AND L FRAUD PREVENTION AND DETECTION ACCOUNT

Special and Trust Fund Receipts (in millions of dollars)

Identification code 070–5389–0–2–751	2021 actual	2022 est.	2023 est.
0100 Balance, start of year	8	8	12
Receipts:			
Current law:			
1120 H-1B and L Fraud Prevention and Detection Account	121	146	150
2000 Total: Balances and receipts	129	154	162
Appropriations:			
Current law:			
2101 H-1 B and L Fraud Prevention and Detection	–40	–49	–50
2101 H&L Fraud Prevention and Detection Fee	–40	–45	–45
2101 H-1B and L Fraud Prevention and Detection Account	–40	–49	–50
2103 H-1 B and L Fraud Prevention and Detection	–2	–2	–3
2103 H&L Fraud Prevention and Detection Fee	–3	–3	–3
2103 H-1B and L Fraud Prevention and Detection Account	–2	–3	–3
2132 H-1 B and L Fraud Prevention and Detection	2	3	3
2132 H&L Fraud Prevention and Detection Fee	3	3	3
2132 H-1B and L Fraud Prevention and Detection Account	2	3	3
2199 Total current law appropriations	–120	–142	–145
2999 Total appropriations	–120	–142	–145
5098 Reconciliation adjustment	–1	....	....
5099 Balance, end of year	8	12	17

Program and Financing (in millions of dollars)

Identification code 070–5389–0–2–751	2021 actual	2022 est.	2023 est.
Obligations by program activity:			
0001 Citizenship and Immigration Services	37	53	54
Budgetary resources:			
Unobligated balance:			
1000 Unobligated balance brought forward, Oct 1	14	19	15
1021 Recoveries of prior year unpaid obligations	2	....	....
1070 Unobligated balance (total)	16	19	15
Budget authority:			
Appropriations, mandatory:			
1201 Appropriation (special or trust fund)	40	49	50
1203 Appropriation (previously unavailable)(special or trust)	2	3	3
1232 Appropriations and/or unobligated balance of appropriations temporarily reduced	–2	–3	–3
1260 Appropriations, mandatory (total)	40	49	50
1900 Budget authority (total)	40	49	50
1930 Total budgetary resources available	56	68	65
Memorandum (non-add) entries:			
1941 Unexpired unobligated balance, end of year	19	15	11
Change in obligated balance:			
Unpaid obligations:			
3000 Unpaid obligations, brought forward, Oct 1	18	19	23
3010 New obligations, unexpired accounts	37	53	54
3020 Outlays (gross)	–34	–49	–50
3040 Recoveries of prior year unpaid obligations, unexpired	–2	....	....
3050 Unpaid obligations, end of year	19	23	27
Memorandum (non-add) entries:			
3100 Obligated balance, start of year	18	19	23
3200 Obligated balance, end of year	19	23	27
Budget authority and outlays, net:			
Mandatory:			
4090 Budget authority, gross	40	49	50
Outlays, gross:			
4100 Outlays from new mandatory authority	21	31	35
4101 Outlays from mandatory balances	13	18	15
4110 Outlays, gross (total)	34	49	50
4180 Budget authority, net (total)	40	49	50
4190 Outlays, net (total)	34	49	50

The Fraud Prevention and Detection Account (FPDA) is authorized via Section 286(v) of the Immigration and Nationality Act (8 U.S.C. 1356(v)) and the L-1 Visa and H-1B Visa Reform Act of 2004 (part of P.L. 108–447). FPDA supports the operations, mission support, and associated management and administration (M&A) costs related to preventing and detecting fraud in the adjudication of all immigration benefit types.

Object Classification (in millions of dollars)

Identification code 070–5389–0–2–751	2021 actual	2022 est.	2023 est.
Direct obligations:			
Personnel compensation:			
11.1 Full-time permanent	12	19	19
11.5 Other personnel compensation	....	....	1
11.9 Total personnel compensation	12	19	20
12.1 Civilian personnel benefits	5	7	7
21.0 Travel and transportation of persons	....	1	1
22.0 Transportation of things	....	1	1
23.3 Communications, utilities, and miscellaneous charges	2	2	2
25.1 Advisory and assistance services	....	4	4
25.7 Operation and maintenance of equipment	....	1	1
31.0 Equipment	17	18	17
99.0 Direct obligations	36	53	53
99.5 Adjustment for rounding	1	....	1
99.9 Total new obligations, unexpired accounts	37	53	54

DEPARTMENT OF HOMELAND SECURITY

Federal Law Enforcement Training Center
Federal Funds

549

Employment Summary

Identification code 070–5389–0–2–751	2021 actual	2022 est.	2023 est.
1001 Direct civilian full-time equivalent employment	171	176	176

FEDERAL LAW ENFORCEMENT TRAINING CENTER

Federal Funds

OPERATIONS AND SUPPORT

For necessary expenses of the Federal Law Enforcement Training Centers for operations and support, including the purchase of not to exceed 117 vehicles for police-type use and hire of passenger motor vehicles, and services as authorized by section 3109 of title 5, United States Code, $355,247,000, of which $66,665,000 shall remain available until September 30, 2024: Provided, That not to exceed $7,180 shall be for official reception and representation expenses.

Note.—A full-year 2022 appropriation for this account was not enacted at the time the Budget was prepared; therefore, the Budget assumes this account is operating under the Continuing Appropriations Act, 2022 (Division A of Public Law 117–43, as amended). The amounts included for 2022 reflect the annualized level provided by the continuing resolution.

Program and Financing (in millions of dollars)

Identification code 070–0509–0–1–751	2021 actual	2022 est.	2023 est.
Obligations by program activity:			
0001 CAS - Mission Support	30	30	32
0002 CAS - Law Enforcement Training	241	256	290
0003 CAS - Minor Construction and Maintenance	34	28	33
0799 Total direct obligations	305	314	355
0801 Operations and Support (Reimbursable)	115	200	203
0900 Total new obligations, unexpired accounts	420	514	558
Budgetary resources:			
Unobligated balance:			
1000 Unobligated balance brought forward, Oct 1	8	17	18
1012 Unobligated balance transfers between expired and unexpired accounts	1		
1021 Recoveries of prior year unpaid obligations	1	1	1
1070 Unobligated balance (total)	10	18	19
Budget authority:			
Appropriations, discretionary:			
1100 Appropriation	314	314	355
1120 Appropriations transferred to other acct [070–0510]	–1		
1160 Appropriation, discretionary (total)	313	314	355
Spending authority from offsetting collections, discretionary:			
1700 Collected	82	162	164
1701 Change in uncollected payments, Federal sources	33	38	39
1750 Spending auth from offsetting collections, disc (total)	115	200	203
1900 Budget authority (total)	428	514	558
1930 Total budgetary resources available	438	532	577
Memorandum (non-add) entries:			
1940 Unobligated balance expiring	–1		
1941 Unexpired unobligated balance, end of year	17	18	19
Change in obligated balance:			
Unpaid obligations:			
3000 Unpaid obligations, brought forward, Oct 1	83	106	83
3010 New obligations, unexpired accounts	420	514	558
3011 Obligations ("upward adjustments"), expired accounts	1		
3020 Outlays (gross)	–390	–531	–552
3040 Recoveries of prior year unpaid obligations, unexpired	–1	–1	–1
3041 Recoveries of prior year unpaid obligations, expired	–7	–5	–5
3050 Unpaid obligations, end of year	106	83	83
Uncollected payments:			
3060 Uncollected pymts, Fed sources, brought forward, Oct 1	–22	–36	–69
3070 Change in uncollected pymts, Fed sources, unexpired	–33	–38	–39
3071 Change in uncollected pymts, Fed sources, expired	19	5	5
3090 Uncollected pymts, Fed sources, end of year	–36	–69	–103
Memorandum (non-add) entries:			
3100 Obligated balance, start of year	61	70	14
3200 Obligated balance, end of year	70	14	–20
Budget authority and outlays, net:			
Discretionary:			
4000 Budget authority, gross	428	514	558
Outlays, gross:			
4010 Outlays from new discretionary authority	247	442	480
4011 Outlays from discretionary balances	143	89	72
4020 Outlays, gross (total)	390	531	552
Offsets against gross budget authority and outlays:			
Offsetting collections (collected) from:			
4030 Federal sources	–96	–198	–201
4033 Non-Federal sources	–2	–2	–2
4040 Offsets against gross budget authority and outlays (total)	–98	–200	–203
Additional offsets against gross budget authority only:			
4050 Change in uncollected pymts, Fed sources, unexpired	–33	–38	–39
4052 Offsetting collections credited to expired accounts	16	38	39
4060 Additional offsets against budget authority only (total)	–17		
4070 Budget authority, net (discretionary)	313	314	355
4080 Outlays, net (discretionary)	292	331	349
4180 Budget authority, net (total)	313	314	355
4190 Outlays, net (total)	292	331	349

The Federal Law Enforcement Training Centers (FLETC) serves as an interagency law enforcement training organization for over 100 participating organizations, providing the necessary facilities, equipment, and support services to conduct basic, advanced, specialized, and refresher training for Federal law enforcement personnel. FLETC personnel conduct the instructional programs for basic law enforcement recruits and some advanced training based on agency requests. Additionally, FLETC provides advanced training tuition-free, or at a reduced cost, to State, local, rural, tribal, and territorial law enforcement officers at all four of its campuses, through export training deliveries, and through distance learning on a space-available basis. In cooperation with the Department of State, FLETC delivers training at International Law Enforcement Academies (ILEA) in Gaborone, Botswana; Bangkok, Thailand; Budapest, Hungary; Roswell, New Mexico; San Salvador, El Salvador; and the Regional Training Center in Accra, Ghana. Additionally, FLETC holds the Director position managing the ILEAs in Gaborone, Botswana and Budapest, Hungary. FLETC provides other training and assistance internationally in collaboration with and in support of U.S. embassies. FLETC also hosts authorized and vetted international students for training programs at FLETC facilities in the United States on a space-available and fully reimbursable basis.

FLETC's Operations and Support account funds necessary operations, mission support, and associated management and administrative costs. In addition, this account includes the funding and activities that are associated with minor construction, maintenance, and improvement projects.

Object Classification (in millions of dollars)

Identification code 070–0509–0–1–751	2021 actual	2022 est.	2023 est.
Direct obligations:			
Personnel compensation:			
11.1 Full-time permanent	99	101	103
11.3 Other than full-time permanent	2	2	3
11.5 Other personnel compensation	7	7	9
11.9 Total personnel compensation	108	110	115
12.1 Civilian personnel benefits	45	46	49
21.0 Travel and transportation of persons	5	5	7
23.3 Communications, utilities, and miscellaneous charges	10	11	13
24.0 Printing and reproduction	1	1	2
25.1 Advisory and assistance services	6	6	8
25.2 Other services from non-Federal sources	13	13	17
25.3 Other goods and services from Federal sources	1	1	2
25.4 Operation and maintenance of facilities	32	33	36
25.6 Medical care	5	5	7
25.7 Operation and maintenance of equipment	25	25	27
25.8 Subsistence and support of persons	1	1	2
26.0 Supplies and materials	17	19	24
31.0 Equipment	19	19	23
32.0 Land and structures	18	19	23
99.0 Direct obligations	306	314	355
99.0 Reimbursable obligations	114	200	203
99.9 Total new obligations, unexpired accounts	420	514	558

Federal Law Enforcement Training Center—Continued
Federal Funds—Continued

Operations and Support—Continued
Employment Summary

Identification code 070–0509–0–1–751	2021 actual	2022 est.	2023 est.
1001 Direct civilian full-time equivalent employment	1,021	1,021	1,085
2001 Reimbursable civilian full-time equivalent employment	204	204	207

PROCUREMENT, CONSTRUCTION, AND IMPROVEMENTS

For necessary expenses of the Federal Law Enforcement Training Centers for procurement, construction, and improvements, $41,300,000, to remain available until September 30, 2027, for acquisition of necessary additional real property and facilities, construction and ongoing maintenance, facility improvements and related expenses of the Federal Law Enforcement Training Centers.

Note.—A full-year 2022 appropriation for this account was not enacted at the time the Budget was prepared; therefore, the Budget assumes this account is operating under the Continuing Appropriations Act, 2022 (Division A of Public Law 117–43, as amended). The amounts included for 2022 reflect the annualized level provided by the continuing resolution.

Program and Financing (in millions of dollars)

Identification code 070–0510–0–1–751	2021 actual	2022 est.	2023 est.
Obligations by program activity:			
0001 CAS – Procurement, Construction, and Improvements (Direct)	71	26	41
0799 Total direct obligations	71	26	41
0801 Procurement, Construction, and Improvements (Reimbursable)	79	39	10
0900 Total new obligations, unexpired accounts	150	65	51
Budgetary resources:			
Unobligated balance:			
1000 Unobligated balance brought forward, Oct 1	167	65	65
1021 Recoveries of prior year unpaid obligations	1	1	1
1070 Unobligated balance (total)	168	66	66
Budget authority:			
Appropriations, discretionary:			
1100 Appropriation	26	26	41
1121 Appropriations transferred from other acct [070–0509]	1		
1160 Appropriation, discretionary (total)	27	26	41
Spending authority from offsetting collections, discretionary:			
1700 Collected	39	45	20
1701 Change in uncollected payments, Federal sources	–19	–6	–10
1750 Spending auth from offsetting collections, disc (total)	20	39	10
1900 Budget authority (total)	47	65	51
1930 Total budgetary resources available	215	131	117
Memorandum (non-add) entries:			
1940 Unobligated balance expiring		–1	–1
1941 Unexpired unobligated balance, end of year	65	65	65
Change in obligated balance:			
Unpaid obligations:			
3000 Unpaid obligations, brought forward, Oct 1	87	126	98
3010 New obligations, unexpired accounts	150	65	51
3011 Obligations ("upward adjustments"), expired accounts		1	1
3020 Outlays (gross)	–110	–93	–64
3040 Recoveries of prior year unpaid obligations, unexpired	–1	–1	–1
3050 Unpaid obligations, end of year	126	98	85
Uncollected payments:			
3060 Uncollected pymts, Fed sources, brought forward, Oct 1	–149	–103	–94
3070 Change in uncollected pymts, Fed sources, unexpired	19	6	10
3071 Change in uncollected pymts, Fed sources, expired	27	3	3
3090 Uncollected pymts, Fed sources, end of year	–103	–94	–81
Memorandum (non-add) entries:			
3100 Obligated balance, start of year	–62	23	4
3200 Obligated balance, end of year	23	4	4
Budget authority and outlays, net:			
Discretionary:			
4000 Budget authority, gross	47	65	51
Outlays, gross:			
4010 Outlays from new discretionary authority	12	8	6
4011 Outlays from discretionary balances	98	85	58
4020 Outlays, gross (total)	110	93	64
Offsets against gross budget authority and outlays:			
Offsetting collections (collected) from:			
4030 Federal sources	–66	–47	–32
Additional offsets against gross budget authority only:			
4050 Change in uncollected pymts, Fed sources, unexpired	19	6	10
4052 Offsetting collections credited to expired accounts	27	2	12
4060 Additional offsets against budget authority only (total)	46	8	22
4070 Budget authority, net (discretionary)	27	26	41
4080 Outlays, net (discretionary)	44	46	32
4180 Budget authority, net (total)	27	26	41
4190 Outlays, net (total)	44	46	32

The Federal Law Enforcement Training Centers' (FLETC) Procurement, Construction, and Improvement (PC&I) account funds the purchase, building, manufacturing, or assemblage of one or more end items that create, extend or enhance FLETC's existing capabilities. Funds provided through this account support the procurement, construction, and/or improvements of personal property end items with an individual cost of $250,000 or more, and real property end items with an individual cost of $2 million or more. Language in the President's Budget authorizes FLETC to receive reimbursements in the PC&I account, and also authorizes reimbursements to FLETC from U.S. Government agencies for the construction of special use facilities. The language also authorizes the acquisition of necessary additional real property and facilities, construction and ongoing maintenance, facility improvements and related expenses of the Federal Law Enforcement Training Centers.

Object Classification (in millions of dollars)

Identification code 070–0510–0–1–751	2021 actual	2022 est.	2023 est.
32.0 Direct obligations: Land and structures	71	26	41
99.0 Direct obligations	71	26	41
99.0 Reimbursable obligations	79	39	10
99.9 Total new obligations, unexpired accounts	150	65	51

SCIENCE AND TECHNOLOGY
Federal Funds

OPERATIONS AND SUPPORT

For necessary expenses of the Science and Technology Directorate for operations and support, including the purchase or lease of not to exceed 5 vehicles, $353,107,000, of which $201,397,000 shall remain available until September 30, 2024: Provided, That not to exceed $10,000 shall be for official reception and representation expenses.

Note.—A full-year 2022 appropriation for this account was not enacted at the time the Budget was prepared; therefore, the Budget assumes this account is operating under the Continuing Appropriations Act, 2022 (Division A of Public Law 117–43, as amended). The amounts included for 2022 reflect the annualized level provided by the continuing resolution.

Program and Financing (in millions of dollars)

Identification code 070–0800–0–1–751	2021 actual	2022 est.	2023 est.
Obligations by program activity:			
0002 Research, Development, Acquisition, and Operations	2		
0003 CAS – Mission Support	122	123	152
0004 CAS – Laboratory Facilities	118	123	127
0005 CAS – Acquistion and Operations Analysis	55	57	74
0799 Total direct obligations	297	303	353
0801 Research, Development, Acquisitions and Operations (Reimbursable)	50	34	34
0900 Total new obligations, unexpired accounts	347	337	387
Budgetary resources:			
Unobligated balance:			
1000 Unobligated balance brought forward, Oct 1	54	58	55
1021 Recoveries of prior year unpaid obligations	7		
1070 Unobligated balance (total)	61	58	55

DEPARTMENT OF HOMELAND SECURITY

Science and Technology—Continued
Federal Funds—Continued
551

		2021 actual	2022 est.	2023 est.
	Budget authority:			
	Appropriations, discretionary:			
1100	Appropriation	303	303	353
	Spending authority from offsetting collections, discretionary:			
1700	Collected	19	31	31
1701	Change in uncollected payments, Federal sources	23		
1750	Spending auth from offsetting collections, disc (total)	42	31	31
1900	Budget authority (total)	345	334	384
1930	Total budgetary resources available	406	392	439
	Memorandum (non-add) entries:			
1940	Unobligated balance expiring	–1		
1941	Unexpired unobligated balance, end of year	58	55	52
	Change in obligated balance:			
	Unpaid obligations:			
3000	Unpaid obligations, brought forward, Oct 1	355	318	256
3010	New obligations, unexpired accounts	347	337	387
3011	Obligations ("upward adjustments"), expired accounts	6		
3020	Outlays (gross)	–359	–399	–410
3040	Recoveries of prior year unpaid obligations, unexpired	–7		
3041	Recoveries of prior year unpaid obligations, expired	–24		
3050	Unpaid obligations, end of year	318	256	233
	Uncollected payments:			
3060	Uncollected pymts, Fed sources, brought forward, Oct 1	–90	–112	–112
3070	Change in uncollected pymts, Fed sources, unexpired	–23		
3071	Change in uncollected pymts, Fed sources, expired	1		
3090	Uncollected pymts, Fed sources, end of year	–112	–112	–112
	Memorandum (non-add) entries:			
3100	Obligated balance, start of year	265	206	144
3200	Obligated balance, end of year	206	144	121
	Budget authority and outlays, net:			
	Discretionary:			
4000	Budget authority, gross	345	334	384
	Outlays, gross:			
4010	Outlays from new discretionary authority	137	161	190
4011	Outlays from discretionary balances	222	238	220
4020	Outlays, gross (total)	359	399	410
	Offsets against gross budget authority and outlays:			
	Offsetting collections (collected) from:			
4030	Federal sources	–20	–29	–29
4033	Non-Federal sources	–1	–2	–2
4040	Offsets against gross budget authority and outlays (total)	–21	–31	–31
	Additional offsets against gross budget authority only:			
4050	Change in uncollected pymts, Fed sources, unexpired	–23		
4052	Offsetting collections credited to expired accounts	2		
4060	Additional offsets against budget authority only (total)	–21		
4070	Budget authority, net (discretionary)	303	303	353
4080	Outlays, net (discretionary)	338	368	379
4180	Budget authority, net (total)	303	303	353
4190	Outlays, net (total)	338	368	379

The Operations and Support (O&S) appropriation for the Science and Technology Directorate (S&T) provides funding to ensure delivery of advanced technology solutions to Department of Homeland Security (DHS) Components and first responders. This appropriation also supports Systems Engineering, Standards, and Test and Evaluation (T&E) to ensure that S&T and DHS Components develop effective technologies that work in the operational environment. This includes costs necessary for operations and support activities to advance S&T's mission, as well as salaries and benefits, and operating costs for five laboratory facilities.

Object Classification (in millions of dollars)

Identification code 070–0800–0–1–751		2021 actual	2022 est.	2023 est.
	Direct obligations:			
	Personnel compensation:			
11.1	Full-time permanent	64	61	74
11.3	Other than full-time permanent	2	6	7
11.5	Other personnel compensation	3	2	2
11.8	Special personal services payments	3	3	4
11.9	Total personnel compensation	72	72	87
12.1	Civilian personnel benefits	23	23	30
21.0	Travel and transportation of persons		1	1
23.1	Rental payments to GSA	2	1	1
23.2	Rental payments to others			2
23.3	Communications, utilities, and miscellaneous charges	1		1
25.1	Advisory and assistance services	104	154	168
25.2	Other services from non-Federal sources	2	3	5
25.3	Other goods and services from Federal sources	25	29	33
25.4	Operation and maintenance of facilities	47	3	3
25.5	Research and development contracts	5		
25.7	Operation and maintenance of equipment	6	8	9
26.0	Supplies and materials	2	1	2
31.0	Equipment	5	8	10
32.0	Land and structures	3		
41.0	Grants, subsidies, and contributions			1
99.0	Direct obligations	297	303	353
99.0	Reimbursable obligations	50	34	34
99.9	Total new obligations, unexpired accounts	347	337	387

Employment Summary

Identification code 070–0800–0–1–751	2021 actual	2022 est.	2023 est.
1001 Direct civilian full-time equivalent employment	433	499	540

PROCUREMENT, CONSTRUCTION, AND IMPROVEMENTS

For necessary expenses of the Science and Technology Directorate for procurement, construction, and improvements, $89,466,000, to remain available until September 30, 2027.

Note.—A full-year 2022 appropriation for this account was not enacted at the time the Budget was prepared; therefore, the Budget assumes this account is operating under the Continuing Appropriations Act, 2022 (Division A of Public Law 117–43, as amended). The amounts included for 2022 reflect the annualized level provided by the continuing resolution.

Program and Financing (in millions of dollars)

Identification code 070–0415–0–1–751		2021 actual	2022 est.	2023 est.
	Obligations by program activity:			
0001	Laboratory Facilities	11	19	89
	Budgetary resources:			
	Unobligated balance:			
1000	Unobligated balance brought forward, Oct 1		8	8
	Budget authority:			
	Appropriations, discretionary:			
1100	Appropriation	19	19	89
1930	Total budgetary resources available	19	27	97
	Memorandum (non-add) entries:			
1941	Unexpired unobligated balance, end of year	8	8	8
	Change in obligated balance:			
	Unpaid obligations:			
3000	Unpaid obligations, brought forward, Oct 1		11	11
3010	New obligations, unexpired accounts	11	19	89
3020	Outlays (gross)		–19	–38
3050	Unpaid obligations, end of year	11	11	62
	Memorandum (non-add) entries:			
3100	Obligated balance, start of year		11	11
3200	Obligated balance, end of year	11	11	62
	Budget authority and outlays, net:			
	Discretionary:			
4000	Budget authority, gross	19	19	89
	Outlays, gross:			
4010	Outlays from new discretionary authority		6	27
4011	Outlays from discretionary balances		13	11
4020	Outlays, gross (total)		19	38
4180	Budget authority, net (total)	19	19	89
4190	Outlays, net (total)		19	38

S&T's Procurement, Construction, & Improvements (PC&I) appropriation supports requirements to ensure laboratory infrastructure remains aligned to S&T mission requirements. PC&I funding allows S&T to make essential investments in construction, expansion, maintenance, modernization, or removal as necessary to support requirements generated by DHS Components. In addition, PC&I funding allows S&T the ability to invest in equipment and information technology to ensure that S&T laboratories maintain accreditation.

Science and Technology—Continued
Federal Funds—Continued

PROCUREMENT, CONSTRUCTION, AND IMPROVEMENTS—Continued

Object Classification (in millions of dollars)

Identification code 070–0415–0–1–751		2021 actual	2022 est.	2023 est.
	Direct obligations:			
25.1	Advisory and assistance services	3	6	2
25.3	Other goods and services from Federal sources	3	3	....
25.5	Research and development contracts	....	1	1
26.0	Supplies and materials	....	1	1
31.0	Equipment	....	3	36
32.0	Land and structures	5	5	49
99.9	Total new obligations, unexpired accounts	11	19	89

RESEARCH AND DEVELOPMENT

For necessary expenses of the Science and Technology Directorate for research and development, $458,718,000, to remain available until September 30, 2025.

Note.—A full-year 2022 appropriation for this account was not enacted at the time the Budget was prepared; therefore, the Budget assumes this account is operating under the Continuing Appropriations Act, 2022 (Division A of Public Law 117–43, as amended). The amounts included for 2022 reflect the annualized level provided by the continuing resolution.

RESEARCH AND DEVELOPMENT

[For an additional amount for "Research and Development", $157,500,000, to remain available until September 30, 2026, for critical infrastructure security and resilience research, development, test, and evaluation: *Provided*, That the funds made available under this heading in this Act may be used for—]

[(1) special event risk assessments rating planning tools;]

[(2) electromagnetic pulse and geo-magnetic disturbance resilience capabilities;]

[(3) positioning, navigation, and timing capabilities;]

[(4) public safety and violence prevention to evaluate soft target security, including countering improvised explosive device events and protection of U.S. critical infrastructure; and]

[(5) research supporting security testing capabilities relating to telecommunications equipment, industrial control systems, and open source software:]

[*Provided further*, That not later than 90 days after the date of enactment of this Act, the Department shall submit to the House and Senate Committees on Appropriations a detailed spend plan for the amount made available under this heading in this Act: *Provided further*, That such amount is designated by the Congress as being for an emergency requirement pursuant to section 4112(a) of H. Con. Res. 71 (115th Congress), the concurrent resolution on the budget for fiscal year 2018, and to section 251(b) of the Balanced Budget and Emergency Deficit Control Act of 1985.] *(Infrastructure Investments and Jobs Appropriations Act.)*

Program and Financing (in millions of dollars)

Identification code 070–0803–0–1–751		2021 actual	2022 est.	2023 est.
	Obligations by program activity:			
0001	CAS - Research, Development and Innovation	395	399	408
0002	CAS - University Programs	38	45	51
0799	Total direct obligations	433	444	459
0801	Research and Development (Reimbursable)	45	45	45
0900	Total new obligations, unexpired accounts	478	489	504
	Budgetary resources:			
	Unobligated balance:			
1000	Unobligated balance brought forward, Oct 1	169	186	319
1021	Recoveries of prior year unpaid obligations	30	....	....
1070	Unobligated balance (total)	199	186	319
	Budget authority:			
	Appropriations, discretionary:			
1100	Appropriation	444	602	459
	Spending authority from offsetting collections, discretionary:			
1700	Collected	35	20	20
1701	Change in uncollected payments, Federal sources	–13	....	....
1750	Spending auth from offsetting collections, disc (total)	22	20	20
1900	Budget authority (total)	466	622	479
1930	Total budgetary resources available	665	808	798
	Memorandum (non-add) entries:			
1940	Unobligated balance expiring	–1	....	....
1941	Unexpired unobligated balance, end of year	186	319	294

	Change in obligated balance:	2021 actual	2022 est.	2023 est.
	Unpaid obligations:			
3000	Unpaid obligations, brought forward, Oct 1	696	669	630
3010	New obligations, unexpired accounts	478	489	504
3020	Outlays (gross)	–469	–528	–221
3040	Recoveries of prior year unpaid obligations, unexpired	–30	....	....
3041	Recoveries of prior year unpaid obligations, expired	–6	....	....
3050	Unpaid obligations, end of year	669	630	913
	Uncollected payments:			
3060	Uncollected pymts, Fed sources, brought forward, Oct 1	–113	–76	–76
3070	Change in uncollected pymts, Fed sources, unexpired	13	....	....
3071	Change in uncollected pymts, Fed sources, expired	24	....	....
3090	Uncollected pymts, Fed sources, end of year	–76	–76	–76
	Memorandum (non-add) entries:			
3100	Obligated balance, start of year	583	593	554
3200	Obligated balance, end of year	593	554	837
	Budget authority and outlays, net:			
	Discretionary:			
4000	Budget authority, gross	466	622	479
	Outlays, gross:			
4010	Outlays from new discretionary authority	38	95	50
4011	Outlays from discretionary balances	431	433	171
4020	Outlays, gross (total)	469	528	221
	Offsets against gross budget authority and outlays:			
	Offsetting collections (collected) from:			
4030	Federal sources	–59	–20	–20
	Additional offsets against gross budget authority only:			
4050	Change in uncollected pymts, Fed sources, unexpired	13	....	....
4052	Offsetting collections credited to expired accounts	24	....	....
4060	Additional offsets against budget authority only (total)	37	....	....
4070	Budget authority, net (discretionary)	444	602	459
4080	Outlays, net (discretionary)	410	508	201
4180	Budget authority, net (total)	444	602	459
4190	Outlays, net (total)	410	508	201

S&T's Research and Development (R&D) appropriation provides funds for basic, applied, and developmental research supporting state-of-the-art technology and solutions to meet the needs of DHS Components and the first responder community. R&D activities also include technology demonstrations, university and industry partnerships, and technology transfer and commercialization. Funds also support critical homeland security-related research and education at U.S. colleges and universities to address high-priority, DHS-related issues and to enhance long term homeland security capabilities.

Object Classification (in millions of dollars)

Identification code 070–0803–0–1–751		2021 actual	2022 est.	2023 est.
	Direct obligations:			
21.0	Travel and transportation of persons	....	1	1
25.1	Advisory and assistance services	51	51	66
25.2	Other services from non-Federal sources	....	2	2
25.3	Other goods and services from Federal sources	7	4	6
25.5	Research and development contracts	339	348	337
25.7	Operation and maintenance of equipment	1	1	1
31.0	Equipment	1	....	....
41.0	Grants, subsidies, and contributions	34	37	46
99.0	Direct obligations	433	444	459
99.0	Reimbursable obligations	45	45	45
99.9	Total new obligations, unexpired accounts	478	489	504

COUNTERING WEAPONS OF MASS DESTRUCTION OFFICE

Federal Funds

OPERATIONS AND SUPPORT

For necessary expenses of the Countering Weapons of Mass Destruction Office for operations and support, $151,970,000, of which $50,446,000 shall remain available until September 30, 2024: Provided, That not to exceed $2,250 shall be for official reception and representation expenses.

DEPARTMENT OF HOMELAND SECURITY

Note.—A full-year 2022 appropriation for this account was not enacted at the time the Budget was prepared; therefore, the Budget assumes this account is operating under the Continuing Appropriations Act, 2022 (Division A of Public Law 117–43, as amended). The amounts included for 2022 reflect the annualized level provided by the continuing resolution.

Program and Financing (in millions of dollars)

Identification code 070–0861–0–1–751		2021 actual	2022 est.	2023 est.
	Obligations by program activity:			
0003	Capability and Operational Support	95	101	66
0004	Mission Support	80	83	86
0799	Total direct obligations	175	184	152
0801	Reimbursable program activity	10		
0900	Total new obligations, unexpired accounts	185	184	152
	Budgetary resources:			
	Unobligated balance:			
1000	Unobligated balance brought forward, Oct 1		4	1
1012	Unobligated balance transfers between expired and unexpired accounts	1		
1070	Unobligated balance (total)	1	4	1
	Budget authority:			
	Appropriations, discretionary:			
1100	Appropriation	180	180	152
1131	Unobligated balance of appropriations permanently reduced	–1		
1160	Appropriation, discretionary (total)	179	180	152
	Spending authority from offsetting collections, discretionary:			
1700	Collected	9	1	
1701	Change in uncollected payments, Federal sources	1		
1750	Spending auth from offsetting collections, disc (total)	10	1	
1900	Budget authority (total)	189	181	152
1930	Total budgetary resources available	190	185	153
	Memorandum (non-add) entries:			
1940	Unobligated balance expiring	–1		
1941	Unexpired unobligated balance, end of year	4	1	1
	Change in obligated balance:			
	Unpaid obligations:			
3000	Unpaid obligations, brought forward, Oct 1	144	148	117
3010	New obligations, unexpired accounts	185	184	152
3011	Obligations ("upward adjustments"), expired accounts	1		
3020	Outlays (gross)	–178	–215	–160
3041	Recoveries of prior year unpaid obligations, expired	–4		
3050	Unpaid obligations, end of year	148	117	109
	Uncollected payments:			
3060	Uncollected pymts, Fed sources, brought forward, Oct 1		–1	
3070	Change in uncollected pymts, Fed sources, unexpired	–1		
3071	Change in uncollected pymts, Fed sources, expired		1	
3090	Uncollected pymts, Fed sources, end of year	–1		
	Memorandum (non-add) entries:			
3100	Obligated balance, start of year	144	147	117
3200	Obligated balance, end of year	147	117	109
	Budget authority and outlays, net:			
	Discretionary:			
4000	Budget authority, gross	189	181	152
	Outlays, gross:			
4010	Outlays from new discretionary authority	89	85	71
4011	Outlays from discretionary balances	89	130	89
4020	Outlays, gross (total)	178	215	160
	Offsets against gross budget authority and outlays:			
	Offsetting collections (collected) from:			
4030	Federal sources	–10	–1	
4033	Non-Federal sources	–1		
4040	Offsets against gross budget authority and outlays (total)	–11	–1	
	Additional offsets against gross budget authority only:			
4050	Change in uncollected pymts, Fed sources, unexpired	–1		
4052	Offsetting collections credited to expired accounts	2		
4060	Additional offsets against budget authority only (total)	1		
4070	Budget authority, net (discretionary)	179	180	152
4080	Outlays, net (discretionary)	167	214	160
4180	Budget authority, net (total)	179	180	152
4190	Outlays, net (total)	167	214	160

The Countering Weapons of Mass Destruction Office's (CWMD) Operations and Support account provides funds to support the development of counter WMD capabilities through strategic planning and analysis; test and evaluation of chemical, biological, and radiological/nuclear detection technologies; and assisting DHS operational components and other agencies in defining requirements necessary to achieve their mission. Additionally, O&S funding provides for the day-to-day operation of the CWMD Office.

Object Classification (in millions of dollars)

Identification code 070–0861–0–1–751		2021 actual	2022 est.	2023 est.
	Direct obligations:			
	Personnel compensation:			
11.1	Full-time permanent	34	35	36
11.3	Other than full-time permanent	1	1	1
11.5	Other personnel compensation	1	1	1
11.8	Special personal services payments		4	4
11.9	Total personnel compensation	36	41	42
12.1	Civilian personnel benefits	11	12	13
21.0	Travel and transportation of persons		1	1
25.1	Advisory and assistance services	31	43	41
25.2	Other services from non-Federal sources	2	7	11
25.3	Other goods and services from Federal sources	56	27	23
25.4	Operation and maintenance of facilities	33	33	
25.5	Research and development contracts	3	1	1
25.7	Operation and maintenance of equipment	2	7	7
26.0	Supplies and materials	1	9	9
31.0	Equipment		3	4
99.0	Direct obligations	175	184	152
99.0	Reimbursable obligations	10		
99.9	Total new obligations, unexpired accounts	185	184	152

Employment Summary

Identification code 070–0861–0–1–751		2021 actual	2022 est.	2023 est.
1001	Direct civilian full-time equivalent employment	287	279	252
2001	Reimbursable civilian full-time equivalent employment		25	23

RESEARCH AND DEVELOPMENT

For necessary expenses of the Countering Weapons of Mass Destruction Office for research and development, $82,515,000, to remain available until September 30, 2025.

Note.—A full-year 2022 appropriation for this account was not enacted at the time the Budget was prepared; therefore, the Budget assumes this account is operating under the Continuing Appropriations Act, 2022 (Division A of Public Law 117–43, as amended). The amounts included for 2022 reflect the annualized level provided by the continuing resolution.

Program and Financing (in millions of dollars)

Identification code 070–0860–0–1–751		2021 actual	2022 est.	2023 est.
	Obligations by program activity:			
0009	Transformational Research and Development	21	24	37
0010	Technical Forensics	8	7	
0012	Detection Capability Development	22	24	46
0013	Rapid Capabilities	6	10	
0900	Total new obligations, unexpired accounts	57	65	83
	Budgetary resources:			
	Unobligated balance:			
1000	Unobligated balance brought forward, Oct 1	32	44	44
1021	Recoveries of prior year unpaid obligations	4		
1070	Unobligated balance (total)	36	44	44
	Budget authority:			
	Appropriations, discretionary:			
1100	Appropriation	65	65	83
1900	Budget authority (total)	65	65	83
1930	Total budgetary resources available	101	109	127
	Memorandum (non-add) entries:			
1941	Unexpired unobligated balance, end of year	44	44	44
	Change in obligated balance:			
	Unpaid obligations:			
3000	Unpaid obligations, brought forward, Oct 1	131	92	91

RESEARCH AND DEVELOPMENT—Continued

Program and Financing—Continued

Identification code 070–0860–0–1–751	2021 actual	2022 est.	2023 est.
3010 New obligations, unexpired accounts	57	65	83
3011 Obligations ("upward adjustments"), expired accounts	1		
3020 Outlays (gross)	–87	–66	–83
3040 Recoveries of prior year unpaid obligations, unexpired	–4		
3041 Recoveries of prior year unpaid obligations, expired	–6		
3050 Unpaid obligations, end of year	92	91	91
Memorandum (non-add) entries:			
3100 Obligated balance, start of year	131	92	91
3200 Obligated balance, end of year	92	91	91
Budget authority and outlays, net:			
Discretionary:			
4000 Budget authority, gross	65	65	83
Outlays, gross:			
4010 Outlays from new discretionary authority	4	13	17
4011 Outlays from discretionary balances	83	53	66
4020 Outlays, gross (total)	87	66	83
4180 Budget authority, net (total)	65	65	83
4190 Outlays, net (total)	87	66	83

The Countering Weapons of Mass Destruction Office's (CWMD) Research and Development account provides funds to identify, explore, and demonstrate new technologies and capabilities that will help enable the Department of Homeland Security and its partners to prevent, protect against, respond to, and mitigate chemical, biological, radiological and nuclear threats and incidents. CWMD works closely with operational customers to ensure the effective transition of new technologies to the field. Funding in this account supports basic, applied, and developmental projects that prioritize the delivery of capability into the hands of the operator.

Object Classification (in millions of dollars)

Identification code 070–0860–0–1–751	2021 actual	2022 est.	2023 est.
Direct obligations:			
25.1 Advisory and assistance services	6	8	10
25.3 Other goods and services from Federal sources	38	40	45
25.5 Research and development contracts	1	3	6
31.0 Equipment	5	6	9
41.0 Grants, subsidies, and contributions	7	8	13
99.0 Direct obligations	57	65	83
99.9 Total new obligations, unexpired accounts	57	65	83

PROCUREMENT, CONSTRUCTION, AND IMPROVEMENTS

For necessary expenses of the Countering Weapons of Mass Destruction Office for procurement, construction, and improvements, $55,304,000, to remain available until September 30, 2025.

Note.—A full-year 2022 appropriation for this account was not enacted at the time the Budget was prepared; therefore, the Budget assumes this account is operating under the Continuing Appropriations Act, 2022 (Division A of Public Law 117–43, as amended). The amounts included for 2022 reflect the annualized level provided by the continuing resolution.

Program and Financing (in millions of dollars)

Identification code 070–0862–0–1–751	2021 actual	2022 est.	2023 est.
Obligations by program activity:			
0006 Large Scale Detection Systems	106	85	46
0007 Portable Detection Systems	40	26	9
0008 Integrated Operations Assets and Infrastructure	13		
0799 Total direct obligations	159	111	55
0900 Total new obligations, unexpired accounts	159	111	55
Budgetary resources:			
Unobligated balance:			
1000 Unobligated balance brought forward, Oct 1	125	74	50
1011 Unobligated balance transfer from other acct [070–0532]	20		
1021 Recoveries of prior year unpaid obligations	3		
1070 Unobligated balance (total)	148	74	50
Budget authority:			
Appropriations, discretionary:			
1100 Appropriation	87	87	55
1900 Budget authority (total)	87	87	55
1930 Total budgetary resources available	235	161	105
Memorandum (non-add) entries:			
1940 Unobligated balance expiring	–2		
1941 Unexpired unobligated balance, end of year	74	50	50
Change in obligated balance:			
Unpaid obligations:			
3000 Unpaid obligations, brought forward, Oct 1	98	168	84
3010 New obligations, unexpired accounts	159	111	55
3011 Obligations ("upward adjustments"), expired accounts	1		
3020 Outlays (gross)	–83	–195	–74
3040 Recoveries of prior year unpaid obligations, unexpired	–3		
3041 Recoveries of prior year unpaid obligations, expired	–4		
3050 Unpaid obligations, end of year	168	84	65
Memorandum (non-add) entries:			
3100 Obligated balance, start of year	98	168	84
3200 Obligated balance, end of year	168	84	65
Budget authority and outlays, net:			
Discretionary:			
4000 Budget authority, gross	87	87	55
Outlays, gross:			
4010 Outlays from new discretionary authority	1	35	22
4011 Outlays from discretionary balances	82	160	52
4020 Outlays, gross (total)	83	195	74
Offsets against gross budget authority and outlays:			
Offsetting collections (collected) from:			
4033 Non-Federal sources	–1		
4040 Offsets against gross budget authority and outlays (total)	–1		
Additional offsets against gross budget authority only:			
4052 Offsetting collections credited to expired accounts	1		
4060 Additional offsets against budget authority only (total)	1		
4070 Budget authority, net (discretionary)	87	87	55
4080 Outlays, net (discretionary)	82	195	74
4180 Budget authority, net (total)	87	87	55
4190 Outlays, net (total)	82	195	74

The Countering Weapons of Mass Destruction Office's (CWMD) Procurement, Construction, and Improvements account provides funds for the acquisition and deployment of nuclear, radiological, chemical, and biological systems to support Department of Homeland Security operational components such as U.S. Customs and Border Protection. CWMD utilizes an integrated lifecycle approach in the management of these systems, and achieves efficiencies through a centralized acquisition process. Funding in this account supports the acquisition and deployment of enhanced Radiation Portal Monitors to begin recapitalization of the fleet; other programs to support scanning of cargo entering the Nation; and procurement of chemical, biological, and radiological equipment that can be carried, worn, or easily moved to support operational end-users.

Object Classification (in millions of dollars)

Identification code 070–0862–0–1–751	2021 actual	2022 est.	2023 est.
Direct obligations:			
25.1 Advisory and assistance services	75	6	5
25.2 Other services from non-Federal sources		5	
25.3 Other goods and services from Federal sources	46	26	14
31.0 Equipment	38	74	36
99.9 Total new obligations, unexpired accounts	159	111	55

FEDERAL ASSISTANCE

For necessary expenses of the Countering Weapons of Mass Destruction Office for Federal assistance through grants, contracts, cooperative agreements, and other activities, $139,183,000, to remain available until September 30, 2025.

Note.—A full-year 2022 appropriation for this account was not enacted at the time the Budget was prepared; therefore, the Budget assumes this account is operating under the Continuing Appropriations Act, 2022 (Division A of Public Law 117–43, as amended). The amounts included for 2022 reflect the annualized level provided by the continuing resolution.

DEPARTMENT OF HOMELAND SECURITY

Program and Financing (in millions of dollars)

Identification code 070–0411–0–1–999	2021 actual	2022 est.	2023 est.
Obligations by program activity:			
0004 Training, Exercises, and Readiness	18	23	20
0005 Securing the Cities	42	29	35
0006 Biological Support	35	33	85
0799 Total direct obligations	95	85	140
0900 Total new obligations, unexpired accounts	95	85	140
Budgetary resources:			
Unobligated balance:			
1000 Unobligated balance brought forward, Oct 1	34	16	1
1021 Recoveries of prior year unpaid obligations	6		
1033 Recoveries of prior year paid obligations	2		
1070 Unobligated balance (total)	42	16	1
Budget authority:			
Appropriations, discretionary:			
1100 Appropriation	70	70	139
1900 Budget authority (total)	70	70	139
1930 Total budgetary resources available	112	86	140
Memorandum (non-add) entries:			
1940 Unobligated balance expiring	–1		
1941 Unexpired unobligated balance, end of year	16	1	
Change in obligated balance:			
Unpaid obligations:			
3000 Unpaid obligations, brought forward, Oct 1	125	162	68
3010 New obligations, unexpired accounts	95	85	140
3011 Obligations ("upward adjustments"), expired accounts	2		
3020 Outlays (gross)	–52	–179	–101
3040 Recoveries of prior year unpaid obligations, unexpired	–6		
3041 Recoveries of prior year unpaid obligations, expired	–2		
3050 Unpaid obligations, end of year	162	68	107
Memorandum (non-add) entries:			
3100 Obligated balance, start of year	125	162	68
3200 Obligated balance, end of year	162	68	107
Budget authority and outlays, net:			
Discretionary:			
4000 Budget authority, gross	70	70	139
Outlays, gross:			
4010 Outlays from new discretionary authority	10	33	64
4011 Outlays from discretionary balances	42	146	37
4020 Outlays, gross (total)	52	179	101
Offsets against gross budget authority and outlays:			
Offsetting collections (collected) from:			
4033 Non-Federal sources	–2		
4040 Offsets against gross budget authority and outlays (total)	–2		
Additional offsets against gross budget authority only:			
4053 Recoveries of prior year paid obligations, unexpired accounts	2		
4070 Budget authority, net (discretionary)	70	70	139
4080 Outlays, net (discretionary)	50	179	101
4180 Budget authority, net (total)	70	70	139
4190 Outlays, net (total)	50	179	101

The Countering Weapons of Mass Destruction Office (CWMD) Federal Assistance account provides the funds for outreach efforts necessary to ensure Federal, State, local, territorial, and tribal (FSLTT) and international partners have the access and resources to support the threat detection mission. FSLTT support is focused on detecting devices or materials prior to their entry into the United States and maximizing the probability of an encounter prior to WMD materials reaching potential targets. The Federal Assistance account provides resources for the Nation's biodetection system. The funds support early warning and preparedness for biological and chemical events.

Object Classification (in millions of dollars)

Identification code 070–0411–0–1–999	2021 actual	2022 est.	2023 est.
Direct obligations:			
25.1 Advisory and assistance services	2	21	45
25.2 Other services from non-Federal sources		3	3
25.3 Other goods and services from Federal sources	9	9	3
25.4 Operation and maintenance of facilities	15		
25.7 Operation and maintenance of equipment			4
26.0 Supplies and materials			22
31.0 Equipment	8	8	18
41.0 Grants, subsidies, and contributions	61	44	45
99.0 Direct obligations	95	85	140
99.9 Total new obligations, unexpired accounts	95	85	140

ADMINISTRATIVE PROVISIONS

SEC. 401. Notwithstanding any other provision of law, funds otherwise made available to U.S. Citizenship and Immigration Services may be used to acquire, operate, equip, and dispose of up to 5 vehicles, for replacement only, for areas where the Administrator of General Services does not provide vehicles for lease: Provided, That the Director of U.S. Citizenship and Immigration Services may authorize employees who are assigned to those areas to use such vehicles to travel between the employees' residences and places of employment.

SEC. 402. None of the funds appropriated by this Act may be used to process or approve a competition under Office of Management and Budget Circular A–76 for services provided by employees (including employees serving on a temporary or term basis) of U.S. Citizenship and Immigration Services of the Department of Homeland Security who are known as Immigration Information Officers, Immigration Service Analysts, Contact Representatives, Investigative Assistants, or Immigration Services Officers.

SEC. 403. The terms and conditions of section 403 of the Department of Homeland Security Appropriations Act, 2020 (division D of Public Law 116–93) shall apply to this Act.

SEC. 404. The Director of the Federal Law Enforcement Training Centers is authorized to distribute funds to Federal law enforcement agencies for expenses incurred participating in training accreditation.

SEC. 405. The Federal Law Enforcement Training Accreditation Board, including representatives from the Federal law enforcement community and non-Federal accreditation experts involved in law enforcement training, shall lead the Federal law enforcement training accreditation process to continue the implementation of measuring and assessing the quality and effectiveness of Federal law enforcement training programs, facilities, and instructors.

SEC. 406. The Director of the Federal Law Enforcement Training Centers may accept transfers to its "Procurement, Construction, and Improvements" account from Government agencies requesting the construction of special use facilities, as authorized by the Economy Act (31 U.S.C. 1535(b)): Provided, That such transfers may include transfers of funds from the Immigration Examinations Fee Account described in section 286(m) of the Immigration and Nationality Act (8 U.S.C. 1356(m)) that the Director of U.S. Citizenship and Immigration Services determines necessary to support U.S. Citizenship and Immigration Services training programs: Provided further, That the Federal Law Enforcement Training Centers maintain administrative control and ownership upon completion of such facilities.

SEC. 407. The functions of the Federal Law Enforcement Training Centers instructor staff shall be classified as inherently governmental for purposes of the Federal Activities Inventory Reform Act of 1998 (31 U.S.C. 501 note).

SEC. 408. Notwithstanding the seventh proviso under the heading "Immigration and Naturalization Service—Salaries and Expenses" in Public Law 105–119 (relating to FD-258 fingerprint cards), or any other provision of law, funds made available to U.S. Citizenship and Immigration Services by this or any other Act may be used for the collection and use of biometrics taken at a U.S. Citizenship and Immigration Services Application Support Center that is overseen virtually by U.S. Citizenship and Immigration Services personnel using appropriate technology.

SEC. 409. Notwithstanding section 286(n) of the Immigration and Nationality Act (8 U.S.C. 1356(n)), the Director of U.S. Citizenship and Immigration Services may use not more than $2,500 of amounts deposited in the Immigration Examinations Fee Account for official reception and representation expenses in fiscal year 2023.

GENERAL FUND RECEIPT ACCOUNTS

(in millions of dollars)

	2021 actual	2022 est.	2023 est.
Governmental receipts:			
070–083400 Breached Bond Penalties	8	8	8
070–242600 Temporary L-1 Visa Fee Increase	2	16	11
070–242700 Temporary H-1B Visa Fee Increase	26	49	48

General Fund Receipt Accounts—Continued

		2021 actual	2022 est.	2023 est.
General Fund Governmental receipts		36	73	67
Offsetting receipts from the public:				
070–031100	Tonnage Duty Increases	30	27	29
070–090000	Passenger Security Fees Returned to the General Fund	1,440	1,480	1,520
070–090000	Passenger Security Fees Returned to the General Fund: Legislative proposal, subject to PAYGO	....	....	–1,520
070–143500	General Fund Proprietary Interest Receipts, not Otherwise Classified	54	22	22
070–242100	Marine Safety Fees	17	17	18
070–274030	Disaster Assistance, Downward Reestimates	1	1	....
070–322000	All Other General Fund Proprietary Receipts Including Budget Clearing Accounts	13	....	....
General Fund Offsetting receipts from the public		1,555	1,547	69
Intragovernmental payments:				
070–388500	Undistributed Intragovernmental Payments and Receivables from Cancelled Accounts	17	....	....
General Fund Intragovernmental payments		17	....	....

GENERAL PROVISIONS
(INCLUDING TRANSFERS OF FUNDS)

SEC. 501. No part of any appropriation contained in this Act shall remain available for obligation beyond the current fiscal year unless expressly so provided herein.

SEC. 502. Subject to the requirements of section 503 of this Act, the unexpended balances of prior appropriations provided for activities in this Act may be transferred to appropriation accounts for such activities established pursuant to this Act, may be merged with funds in the applicable established accounts, and thereafter may be accounted for as one fund for the same time period as originally enacted.

SEC. 503. (a) None of the funds provided by this Act, provided by previous appropriations Acts to the components in or transferred to the Department of Homeland Security that remain available for obligation or expenditure in fiscal year 2023, or provided from any accounts in the Treasury of the United States derived by the collection of fees available to the components funded by this Act, shall be available for obligation or expenditure through a reprogramming of funds that—

(1) creates or eliminates a program, project, or activity, or increases funds for any program, project, or activity for which funds have been denied or restricted by the Congress;

(2) contracts out any function or activity presently performed by Federal employees or any new function or activity proposed to be performed by Federal employees in the President's budget proposal for fiscal year 2023 for the Department of Homeland Security;

(3) augments funding for existing programs, projects, or activities in excess of $5,000,000 or 10 percent, whichever is less;

(4) reduces funding for any program, project, or activity, or numbers of personnel, by 10 percent or more; or

(5) results from any general savings from a reduction in personnel that would result in a change in funding levels for programs, projects, or activities as approved by the Congress.

(b) Subsection (a) shall not apply if the Committees on Appropriations of the Senate and the House of Representatives are notified at least 15 days in advance of such reprogramming.

(c) Up to 5 percent of any appropriation made available for the current fiscal year for the Department of Homeland Security by this Act or provided by previous appropriations Acts may be transferred between such appropriations if the Committees on Appropriations of the Senate and the House of Representatives are notified at least 30 days in advance of such transfer, but no such appropriation, except as otherwise specifically provided, shall be increased by more than 10 percent by such transfer.

(d) Notwithstanding subsections (a), (b), and (c), no funds shall be reprogrammed within or transferred between appropriations based upon an initial notification provided after June 30, except in extraordinary circumstances that imminently threaten the safety of human life or the protection of property.

(e) The notification thresholds and procedures set forth in subsections (a), (b), (c), and (d) shall apply to any use of deobligated balances of funds provided in previous Department of Homeland Security Appropriations Acts that remain available for obligation in the current year.

(f) Notwithstanding subsection (c), the Secretary of Homeland Security may transfer to the fund established by 8 U.S.C. 1101 note, up to $20,000,000 from appropriations available to the Department of Homeland Security: Provided, That the Secretary shall notify the Committees on Appropriations of the Senate and the House of Representatives at least 5 days in advance of such transfer.

SEC. 504. Section 504 of the Department of Homeland Security Appropriations Act, 2017 (division F of Public Law 115–31), related to the operations of a working capital fund, shall apply with respect to funds made available in this Act in the same manner as such section applied to funds made available in that Act: Provided, That funds from such working capital fund may be obligated and expended in anticipation of reimbursements from components of the Department of Homeland Security.

SEC. 505. Except as otherwise specifically provided by law, not to exceed 50 percent of unobligated balances remaining available at the end of fiscal year 2023, as recorded in the financial records at the time of a reprogramming notification, but not later than June 30, 2024, from appropriations for "Operations and Support" for fiscal year 2023 in this Act shall remain available through September 30, 2024, in the account and for the purposes for which the appropriations were provided: Provided, That prior to the obligation of such funds, a notification shall be submitted to the Committees on Appropriations of the Senate and the House of Representatives in accordance with section 503 of this Act.

SEC. 506. Funds made available by this Act for intelligence activities are deemed to be specifically authorized by the Congress for purposes of section 504 of the National Security Act of 1947 (50 U.S.C. 414) during fiscal year 2023 until the enactment of an Act authorizing intelligence activities for fiscal year 2023.

SEC. 507. (a) The Secretary of Homeland Security, or the designee of the Secretary, shall notify the Committees on Appropriations of the Senate and the House of Representatives at least 3 full business days in advance of—

(1) making or awarding a grant allocation or grant in excess of $1,000,000;

(2) making or awarding a contract, other transaction agreement, or task or delivery order on a Department of Homeland Security multiple award contract, or to issue a letter of intent totaling in excess of $4,000,000;

(3) awarding a task or delivery order requiring an obligation of funds in an amount greater than $10,000,000 from multi-year Department of Homeland Security funds;

(4) making a sole-source grant award; or

(5) announcing publicly the intention to make or award items under paragraph (1), (2), (3), or (4), including a contract covered by the Federal Acquisition Regulation.

(b) If the Secretary of Homeland Security determines that compliance with this section would pose a substantial risk to human life, health, or safety, an award may be made without notification, and the Secretary shall notify the Committees on Appropriations of the Senate and the House of Representatives not later than 5 full business days after such an award is made or letter issued.

(c) A notification under this section—

(1) may not involve funds that are not available for obligation; and

(2) shall include the amount of the award; the fiscal year for which the funds for the award were appropriated; the type of contract; and the account from which the funds are being drawn.

SEC. 508. Notwithstanding any other provision of law, no agency shall purchase, construct, or lease any additional facilities, except within or contiguous to existing locations, to be used for the purpose of conducting Federal law enforcement training without advance notification to the Committees on Appropriations of the Senate and the House of Representatives, except that the Federal Law Enforcement Training Centers is authorized to obtain the temporary use of additional facilities by lease, contract, or other agreement for training that cannot be accommodated in existing Centers' facilities.

SEC. 509. None of the funds appropriated or otherwise made available by this Act may be used for expenses for any construction, repair, alteration, or acquisition project for which a prospectus otherwise required under chapter 33 of title 40, United States Code, has not been approved, except that necessary funds may be expended for each project for required expenses for the development of a proposed prospectus.

SEC. 510. Sections 520, 522, and 530 of the Department of Homeland Security Appropriations Act, 2008 (division E of Public Law 110–161; 121 Stat. 2073 and 2074) shall apply with respect to funds made available in this Act in the same manner as such sections applied to funds made available in that Act.

SEC. 511. None of the funds made available in this Act may be used in contravention of the applicable provisions of the Buy American Act: Provided, That for purposes of the preceding sentence, the term "Buy American Act" means chapter 83 of title 41, United States Code.

SEC. 512. None of the funds made available in this Act may be used to amend the oath of allegiance required by section 337 of the Immigration and Nationality Act (8 U.S.C. 1448).

SEC. 513.

(a) None of the funds provided or otherwise made available in this Act shall be available to carry out section 872 of the Homeland Security Act of 2002 (6 U.S.C. 452) unless explicitly authorized by the Congress.

(b) Subsection (a) shall not apply to—

(1) the use of such section 872 to establish an office within the Office of the Secretary that shall, for departmental workforce health and safety, medical, and public health functions and activities—

(A) develop departmental policies;

(B) establish standards;

(C) provide technical assistance and operational support;

(D) conduct oversight; and

(E) serve as the primary liaison and coordinator; and

(2) the reallocation to an office established under paragraph (1) of

(A) the position and responsibilities of the Chief Medical Officer and related personnel from the Countering Weapons of Mass Destruction Office;

(B) the personnel, functions, and responsibilities related to departmental workforce health and medical activities from the Under Secretary for Management as authorized in section 710 of the Homeland Security Act, and related safety activities; and

(C) the responsibility of carrying out the program authorized by section 528 of the Homeland Security Act and related personnel.

(c) The Secretary of Homeland Security may transfer funds made available in this Act under the headings "Management Directorate" and "Countering Weapons of Mass Destruction Office" consistent with the establishment of the office and the reallocations of functions, positions, and responsibilities described in subsection (b).

(d) The Secretary shall submit a notification to the Committees on Appropriations of the Senate and the House of Representatives, the Committee on Homeland Security of the House of Representatives, and the Homeland Security and Governmental Affairs Committee of the Senate at least 15 days prior to the establishment of the office described in subsection (b).

(e) The functions of the office described in subsection (b) shall not include chemical, biological, radiological, and nuclear programs of the Countering Weapons of Mass Destruction Office and the transfer of funds described in subsection (c) shall not include funding appropriated for such programs.

SEC. 514. None of the funds made available in this Act may be used for planning, testing, piloting, or developing a national identification card.

SEC. 515. None of the funds made available in this Act may be used for first-class travel by the employees of agencies funded by this Act in contravention of sections 301–10.122 through 301–10.124 of title 41, Code of Federal Regulations.

SEC. 516. None of the funds made available in this Act may be used to employ workers described in section 274A(h)(3) of the Immigration and Nationality Act (8 U.S.C. 1324a(h)(3)).

SEC. 517. Notwithstanding any other provision of this Act, none of the funds appropriated or otherwise made available by this Act may be used to pay award or incentive fees for contractor performance that has been judged to be below satisfactory performance or performance that does not meet the basic requirements of a contract.

SEC. 518. None of the funds appropriated or otherwise made available by this Act may be used by the Department of Homeland Security to enter into any Federal contract unless such contract is entered into in accordance with the requirements of subtitle I of title 41, United States Code, or chapter 137 of title 10, United States Code, and the Federal Acquisition Regulation, unless such contract is otherwise authorized by statute to be entered into without regard to the above referenced statutes.

SEC. 519. (a) None of the funds made available in this Act may be used to maintain or establish a computer network unless such network blocks the viewing, downloading, and exchanging of pornography.

(b) Nothing in subsection (a) shall limit the use of funds necessary for any Federal, State, tribal, or local law enforcement agency or any other entity carrying out criminal investigations, prosecution, or adjudication activities.

SEC. 520. None of the funds made available in this Act may be used by a Federal law enforcement officer to facilitate the transfer of an operable firearm to an individual if the Federal law enforcement officer knows or suspects that the individual is an agent of a drug cartel unless law enforcement personnel of the United States continuously monitor or control the firearm at all times.

SEC. 521. None of the funds made available in this Act may be used to pay for the travel to or attendance of more than 50 employees of a single component of the Department of Homeland Security, who are stationed in the United States, at a single international conference unless the Secretary of Homeland Security, or a designee, determines that such attendance is in the national interest and notifies the Committees on Appropriations of the Senate and the House of Representatives within at least 10 days of that determination and the basis for that determination: Provided, That for purposes of this section the term "international conference" shall mean a conference occurring outside of the United States attended by representatives of the United States Government and of foreign governments, international organizations, or nongovernmental organizations: Provided further, That the total cost to the Department of Homeland Security of any such conference shall not exceed $500,000: Provided further, That employees who attend a conference virtually without travel away from their permanent duty station within the United States shall not be counted for purposes of this section, and the prohibition contained in this section shall not apply to payments for the costs of attendance for such employees.

SEC. 522. None of the funds made available in this Act may be used to reimburse any Federal department or agency for its participation in a National Special Security Event.

SEC. 523. None of the funds made available to the Department of Homeland Security by this or any other Act may be obligated for any structural pay reform that affects more than 100 full-time positions or costs more than $5,000,000 in a single year unless it has been explicitly justified to the Congress in budget justification materials and subsequently enacted by Congress, or if not so justified and enacted, before the end of the 30-day period beginning on the date on which the Secretary of Homeland Security submits to Congress a notification that includes—

(1) the number of full-time positions affected by such change;

(2) funding required for such change for the current year and through the Future Years Homeland Security Program;

(3) justification for such change; and

(4) an analysis of compensation alternatives to such change that were considered by the Department.

SEC. 524. (a) Any agency receiving funds made available in this Act shall, subject to subsections (b) and (c), post on the public website of that agency any report required to be submitted by the Committees on Appropriations of the Senate and the House of Representatives in this Act, upon the determination by the head of the agency that it shall serve the national interest.

(b) Subsection (a) shall not apply to a report if—

(1) the public posting of the report compromises homeland or national security; or

(2) the report contains proprietary information.

(c) The head of the agency posting such report shall do so only after such report has been made available to the Committees on Appropriations of the Senate and the House of Representatives for not less than 45 days except as otherwise specified in law.

SEC. 525. (a) Funding provided in this Act for "Operations and Support" may be used for minor procurement, construction, and improvements.

(b) For purposes of subsection (a), "minor" refers to end items with a unit cost of $250,000 or less for personal property, and $2,000,000 or less for real property.

SEC. 526. None of the funds made available by this Act may be obligated or expended to implement the Arms Trade Treaty until the Senate approves a resolution of ratification for the Treaty.

SEC. 527. The authority provided by section 532 of the Department of Homeland Security Appropriations Act, 2018 (Public Law 115–141) regarding primary and secondary schooling of dependents shall continue in effect during fiscal year 2023.

SEC. 528. (a) Section 831 of the Homeland Security Act of 2002 (6 U.S.C. 391) shall be applied—

(1) In subsection (a), by substituting "September 30, 2023," for "September 30, 2017,"; and

(2) In subsection (c)(1), by substituting "September 30, 2023," for "September 30, 2017".

(b) The Secretary of Homeland Security, under the authority of section 831 of the Homeland Security Act of 2002 (6 U.S.C. 391(a)), may carry out prototype projects under sections 4002 and 4003 of title 10, United States Code, and the Secretary shall perform the functions of the Secretary of Defense as prescribed.

(c) The Secretary of Homeland Security under section 831 of the Homeland Security Act of 2002 (6 U.S.C. 391(d)) may use the definition of nontraditional government contractor as defined in section 4003(e) of title 10, United States Code.

SEC. 529. (a) None of the funds appropriated or otherwise made available to the Department of Homeland Security by this Act may be used to prevent any of the following persons from entering, for the purpose of conducting oversight, any facility operated by or for the Department of Homeland Security used to detain or otherwise house aliens, or to make any temporary modification at any such facility that in any way alters what is observed by a visiting member of Congress or such designated employee, compared to what would be observed in the absence of such modification:

(1) A Member of Congress.

(2) An employee of the United States House of Representatives or the United States Senate designated by such a Member for the purposes of this section.

(b) Nothing in this section may be construed to require a Member of Congress to provide prior notice of the intent to enter a facility described in subsection (a) for the purpose of conducting oversight.

(c) With respect to individuals described in subsection (a)(2), the Department of Homeland Security may require that a request be made at least 24 hours in advance of an intent to enter a facility described in subsection (a).

SEC. 530. *(a) Except as provided in subsection (b), none of the funds made available in this Act may be used to place restraints on a woman in the custody of the Department of Homeland Security (including during transport, in a detention facility, or at an outside medical facility) who is pregnant or in post-delivery recuperation.*

(b) Subsection (a) shall not apply with respect to a pregnant woman if—

(1) an appropriate official of the Department of Homeland Security makes an individualized determination that the woman—

(A) is a serious flight risk, and such risk cannot be prevented by other means; or

(B) poses an immediate and serious threat to harm herself or others that cannot be prevented by other means; or

(2) a medical professional responsible for the care of the pregnant woman determines that the use of therapeutic restraints is appropriate for the medical safety of the woman.

(c) If a pregnant woman is restrained pursuant to subsection (b), only the safest and least restrictive restraints, as determined by the appropriate medical professional treating the woman, may be used. In no case may restraints be used on a woman who is in active labor or delivery, and in no case may a pregnant woman be restrained in a face-down position with four-point restraints, on her back, or in a restraint belt that constricts the area of the pregnancy. A pregnant woman who is immobilized by restraints shall be positioned, to the maximum extent feasible, on her left side.

SEC. 531. *(a) None of the funds made available by this Act may be used to destroy any document, recording, or other record pertaining to any—*

(1) death of,

(2) potential sexual assault or abuse perpetrated against, or

(3) allegation of abuse, criminal activity, or disruption committed by

an individual held in the custody of the Department of Homeland Security.

(b) The records referred to in subsection (a) shall be made available, in accordance with applicable laws and regulations, and Federal rules governing disclosure in litigation, to an individual who has been charged with a crime, been placed into segregation, or otherwise punished as a result of an allegation described in paragraph (3), upon the request of such individual.

SEC. 532. *Section 519 of division F of Public Law 114–113, regarding a prohibition on funding for any position designated as a Principal Federal Official, shall apply with respect to any Federal funds in the same manner as such section applied to funds made available in that Act.*

SEC. 533. *The personnel, supplies, or equipment of any component of the Department of Homeland Security may be deployed to support activities of the Department of Homeland Security related to a significant rise in undocumented migrants at the southwest border and related activities, and for the enforcement of immigration and customs laws, detention and removals of undocumented migrants crossing the border unlawfully, and investigations without reimbursement as jointly agreed by the detailing components.*

SEC. 534. *Notwithstanding section 503 of this Act, up to 5 percent of any appropriation made available for the current fiscal year for the Department of Homeland Security by this Act may be transferred to the Department's "Information Technology Modernization Fund", as authorized by section 1077(b)(1) of title X of division A of the National Defense Authorization Act for Fiscal Year 2018 (Public Law 115–91): Provided, That amounts transferred pursuant to this section shall remain available through the end of the third fiscal year after the fiscal year in which the transfer is made: Provided further, That the Committees on Appropriations of the Senate and the House of Representatives shall be notified at least three days in advance of any transfer made pursuant to this section.*

SEC. 535. *Section 1901(e) of the Homeland Security Act of 2002 (6 U.S.C. 591(e)) is repealed.*

GENERAL PROVISION—THIS TITLE

[SEC. 1601. (a) Repayments of the remaining balances of all loans, as of September 30, 2021, by the Federal Emergency Management Agency under section 417 of the Robert T. Stafford Disaster Relief and Emergency Assistance Act (42 U.S.C. 5184) are hereby cancelled.

(b) Of the unobligated balances available to the Department of Homeland Security for "Federal Emergency Management Agency—Disaster Relief Fund", such sums as are necessary may be transferred to the Disaster Assistance Direct Loan Program Account for carrying out subsection (a).

(c) Each amount repurposed or transferred by this section that was previously designated by the Congress as an emergency requirement or as being for disaster relief pursuant to the Balanced Budget and Emergency Deficit Control Act of 1985 or a concurrent resolution on the budget is designated by the Congress as an emergency requirement pursuant to section 4001(a)(1) and section 4001(b), or as being for disaster relief pursuant to section 4004(b)(6) and section 4005(f), respectively, of S. Con. Res. 14 (117th Congress), the concurrent resolution on the budget for fiscal year 2022.]

(Disaster Relief Supplemental Appropriations Act, 2022.)

GENERAL PROVISION—THIS TITLE

[SEC. 501. One-quarter of one percent of the amounts made available under each heading in this title in this Act in each of fiscal years 2022 through 2026 shall be transferred to the Office of the Inspector General of the Department of the Homeland Security for oversight of funding provided to the Department of Homeland Security in this title in this Act.] *(Infrastructure Investments and Jobs Appropriations Act.)*

DEPARTMENT OF HOUSING AND URBAN DEVELOPMENT

PUBLIC AND INDIAN HOUSING PROGRAMS
Federal Funds
TENANT-BASED RENTAL ASSISTANCE

For activities and assistance for the provision of tenant-based rental assistance authorized under the United States Housing Act of 1937, as amended (42 U.S.C. 1437 et seq.) (in this title "the Act"), not otherwise provided for, $28,130,000,000, to remain available until expended, which shall be available on October 1, 2022 (in addition to the $4,000,000,000 previously appropriated under this heading that shall be available on October 1, 2022), and $4,000,000,000, to remain available until expended, which shall be available on October 1, 2023: Provided, That the amounts made available under this heading are provided as follows:

(1) $26,234,000,000 shall be available for renewals of expiring section 8 tenant-based annual contributions contracts (including renewals of enhanced vouchers under any provision of law authorizing such assistance under section 8(t) of the Act) and including renewal of other special purpose incremental vouchers: Provided, That notwithstanding any other provision of law, from amounts provided under this paragraph and any carryover, the Secretary for the calendar year 2023 funding cycle shall provide renewal funding for each public housing agency based on validated voucher management system (VMS) leasing and cost data for the prior calendar year and by applying an inflation factor as established by the Secretary, by notice published in the Federal Register, and by making any necessary adjustments for the costs associated with the first-time renewal of vouchers under this paragraph including tenant protection and Choice Neighborhoods vouchers: Provided further, That costs associated with any forgone increases in tenant rent payments due to the implementation of rent incentives as authorized pursuant to waivers or alternative requirements of the Jobs-Plus initiative as described under the heading "Self-Sufficiency Programs" shall be renewed: Provided further, That the Secretary shall, to the extent necessary to stay within the amount specified under this paragraph (except as otherwise modified under this paragraph), prorate each public housing agency's allocation otherwise established pursuant to this paragraph: Provided further, That except as provided in the following provisos, the entire amount specified under this paragraph (except as otherwise modified under this paragraph) shall be obligated to the public housing agencies based on the allocation and pro rata method described above: Provided further, That the Secretary may extend the notification period with the prior written notification to the House and Senate Committees on Appropriations: Provided further, That public housing agencies participating in the MTW demonstration shall be funded in accordance with the requirements of the MTW demonstration program or their MTW agreements, if any, and shall be subject to the same pro rata adjustments under the previous provisos: Provided further, That the Secretary may offset public housing agencies' calendar year 2023 allocations based on the excess amounts of public housing agencies' net restricted assets accounts, including HUD-held programmatic reserves (in accordance with VMS data in calendar year 2022 that is verifiable and complete), as determined by the Secretary: Provided further, That public housing agencies participating in the MTW demonstration shall also be subject to the offset, as determined by the Secretary, from the agencies' calendar year 2023 MTW funding allocation: Provided further, That the Secretary shall use any offset referred to in the previous two provisos throughout the calendar year to prevent the termination of rental assistance for families as the result of insufficient funding, as determined by the Secretary, to avoid or reduce the proration of renewal funding allocations, and to enable public housing agencies operating their existing housing choice voucher programs with high utilization rates and a demonstrated capacity to serve additional families, as determined by the Secretary, to assist more families: Provided further, That the Secretary may also reallocate authorized units from public housing agencies with a history of significant under-leasing and utilization to public housing agencies that meet the requirements of the previous proviso to receive funds to assist more families and that have under lease all, or nearly all, of their authorized units: Provided further, That such reallocations shall be made in accordance with terms and conditions established by the Secretary by notice: Provided further, That the Secretary may utilize unobligated balances, including recaptures and carryover, remaining from prior year appropriations (excluding special purpose vouchers), notwithstanding the purposes for which such amounts were appropriated, to avoid or reduce the proration of renewal funding allocations: Provided further, That up to $100,000,000 shall be available only: (1) for adjustments in the allocations for public housing agencies, after application for an adjustment by a public housing agency that experienced a significant increase, as determined by the Secretary, in renewal costs of vouchers resulting from unforeseen circumstances or from portability under section 8(r) of the Act; (2) for vouchers that were not in use during the previous 12-month period in order to be available to meet a commitment pursuant to section 8(o)(13) of the Act, or an adjustment for a funding obligation not yet expended in the previous calendar year for a MTW-eligible activity to develop affordable housing for an agency added to the MTW demonstration under the expansion authority provided in section 239 of the Transportation, Housing and Urban Development, and Related Agencies Appropriations Act, 2016 (division L of Public Law 114–113); (3) for adjustments for costs associated with HUD-Veterans Affairs Supportive Housing (HUD-VASH) vouchers; (4) for public housing agencies that despite taking reasonable cost savings measures, as determined by the Secretary, would otherwise be required to terminate rental assistance for families as a result of insufficient funding; (5) for adjustments for withheld payments for months in the previous calendar year that were subsequently paid by the public housing agency after the agency's actual costs were validated; and (6) for public housing agencies that have experienced increased costs or loss of units in an area for which the President declared a disaster under title IV of the Robert T. Stafford Disaster Relief and Emergency Assistance Act (42 U.S.C. 5170 et seq.): Provided further, That the Secretary shall allocate amounts under the previous proviso based on need, as determined by the Secretary: Provided further, That of the total amount provided under this paragraph, up to $50,000,000 shall be available to supplement funds transferred from the heading "Public Housing Fund" to fund contracts for properties converting from assistance under Section 9 of the United States Housing Act of 1937 (42 U.S.C. 1437g) under the heading "Rental Assistance Demonstration" in title II of the Transportation, Housing and Urban Development, and Related Agencies Appropriations Act, 2012 (division C of Public Law 112–55) to further long-term financial stability and promote the energy or water efficiency, climate resilience, or preservation of such properties; Provided further, That the amounts under the previous proviso may also be available, without additional competition, for cooperative agreements with Participating Administrative Entities that have been previously or newly selected under section 513(b) of the Multifamily Assisted Housing Reform and Affordability Act of 1997 (42 U.S.C. 1437f note) to provide direct support, including carrying out due diligence and underwriting functions for owners and for technical assistance activities, on conditions established by the Secretary for small properties and owners entering into any conversion contract under the First Component;

(2) $220,000,000 shall be for section 8 rental assistance for relocation and replacement of housing units that are demolished or disposed of pursuant to section 18 of the Act, conversion of section 23 projects to assistance under section 8, the family unification program under section 8(x) of the Act, relocation of witnesses (including victims of violent crimes) in connection with efforts to combat crime in public and assisted housing pursuant to a request from a law enforcement or prosecution agency, enhanced vouchers under any provision of law authorizing such assistance under section 8(t) of the Act, Choice Neighborhood vouchers, mandatory and voluntary conversions, and tenant protection assistance including replacement and relocation assistance or for project-based assistance to prevent the displacement of unassisted elderly tenants currently residing in section 202 properties financed between 1959 and 1974 that are refinanced pursuant to Public Law 106–569, as amended, or under the authority as provided under this Act: Provided, That up to $20,000,000 of the amounts made available under this paragraph may be to provide replacement tenant protection assistance to low-income tenants assisted under section 521 of title V of the Housing Act of 1949 (42 U.S.C. 1471 et seq.), upon the determination and referral by the Secretary of the Department of Agriculture that section 521 assistance is no longer available to protect such tenants due to maturity, prepayment, or foreclosure of loans under section 514 or section 515 of such Act (42 U.S.C. 1484 and 1485): Provided further, That when a public housing development is submitted for demolition or disposition under section 18 of the Act, the Secretary may provide section 8 rental assistance when the units pose an imminent health and safety risk to residents: Provided further, That the Secretary may provide section 8 rental assistance from amounts made available under this paragraph for units assisted under a project-based subsidy contract funded under the "Project-Based Rental Assistance" heading under this title where the owner has received a Notice of Default and the units pose an imminent health and safety risk to residents: Provided further, That to the extent that the Secretary determines that such units are not feasible for continued rental assistance payments or transfer of the subsidy contract associated with such units to another project or projects and owner or owners, any remaining amounts associated with such units under such contract shall be recaptured and such recaptured amounts, in an amount equal to the cost of rental assistance provided pursuant to the previous proviso, up to the total amounts recaptured, shall be transferred to and merged with amounts under this paragraph: Provided further, That of the amounts made available under this paragraph, no less than

Tenant-Based Rental Assistance—Continued

$5,000,000 may be available to provide tenant protection assistance, not otherwise provided under this paragraph, to residents residing in low vacancy areas and who may have to pay rents greater than 30 percent of household income, as the result of: (A) the maturity of a HUD-insured, HUD-held or section 202 loan that requires the permission of the Secretary prior to loan prepayment; (B) the expiration of a rental assistance contract for which the tenants are not eligible for enhanced voucher or tenant protection assistance under existing law; or (C) the expiration of affordability restrictions accompanying a mortgage or preservation program administered by the Secretary: Provided further, That such tenant protection assistance made available under the previous proviso may be provided under the authority of section 8(t) or section 8(o)(13) of the Act: Provided further, That any tenant protection voucher made available from amounts under this paragraph shall not be reissued by any public housing agency, except the replacement vouchers as defined by the Secretary by notice, when the initial family that received any such voucher no longer receives such voucher, and the authority for any public housing agency to issue any such voucher shall cease to exist: Provided further, That the Secretary may only provide replacement vouchers for units that were occupied within the previous 24 months that cease to be available as assisted housing, subject only to the availability of funds;

(3) $3,014,000,000 shall be for administrative and other expenses of public housing agencies in administering the section 8 tenant-based rental assistance program, of which up to $10,000,000 shall be available to the Secretary to allocate to public housing agencies that need additional funds to administer their section 8 programs, including fees associated with section 8 tenant protection rental assistance, the administration of disaster related vouchers, HUD-VASH vouchers, and other special purpose incremental vouchers: Provided, That no less than $3,004,000,000 of the amount provided in this paragraph shall be allocated to public housing agencies for the calendar year 2023 funding cycle based on section 8(q) of the Act (and related Appropriation Act provisions) as in effect immediately before the enactment of the Quality Housing and Work Responsibility Act of 1998 (Public Law 105–276): Provided further, That if the amounts made available under this paragraph are insufficient to pay the amounts determined under the previous proviso, the Secretary may decrease the amounts allocated to agencies by a uniform percentage applicable to all agencies receiving funding under this paragraph or may, to the extent necessary to provide full payment of amounts determined under the previous proviso, utilize unobligated balances, including recaptures and carryover, remaining from funds appropriated to the Department of Housing and Urban Development under this heading from prior fiscal years, excluding special purpose vouchers, notwithstanding the purposes for which such amounts were appropriated: Provided further, That all public housing agencies participating in the MTW demonstration shall be funded in accordance with the requirements of the MTW demonstration program or their MTW agreements, if any, and shall be subject to the same uniform percentage decrease as under the previous proviso: Provided further, That amounts provided under this paragraph shall be only for activities related to the provision of tenant-based rental assistance authorized under section 8, including related development activities;

(4) $667,000,000 for the renewal of tenant-based assistance contracts under section 811 of the Cranston-Gonzalez National Affordable Housing Act (42 U.S.C. 8013), including necessary administrative expenses: Provided, That up to $10,000,000 shall be available only (1) for adjustments in the allocation for public housing agencies, after applications for an adjustment by a public housing agency that experienced a significant increase, as determined by the Secretary, in Mainstream renewal costs resulting from unforeseen circumstances, and (2) for public housing agencies that despite taking reasonable cost saving measures, as determined by the Secretary, would otherwise be required to terminate the rental assistance for Mainstream families as a result of insufficient funding: Provided further, That the Secretary shall allocate amounts under the previous proviso based on need, as determined by the Secretary: Provided further, That upon turnover, section 811 special purpose vouchers funded under this heading in this or prior Acts, or under any other heading in prior Acts, shall be provided to non-elderly persons with disabilities;

(5) Of the amounts provided under paragraph (1) up to $5,000,000 shall be for rental assistance and associated administrative fees for Tribal HUD-VASH to serve Native American veterans that are homeless or at-risk of homelessness living on or near a reservation or other Indian areas: Provided, That such amount shall be made available for renewal grants to recipients that received assistance under prior Acts under the Tribal HUD-VASH program: Provided further, That the Secretary shall be authorized to specify criteria for renewal grants, including data on the utilization of assistance reported by grant recipients: Provided further, That such assistance shall be administered in accordance with program requirements under the Native American Housing Assistance and Self-Determination Act of 1996 and modeled after the HUD-VASH program: Provided further, That the Secretary shall be authorized to waive, or specify alternative requirements for any provision of any statute or regulation that the Secretary administers in connection with the use of funds made available under this paragraph (except for requirements related to fair housing, nondiscrimination, labor standards, and the environment), upon a finding by the Secretary that any such waivers or alternative requirements are necessary for the effective delivery and administration of such assistance: Provided further, That grant recipients shall report to the Secretary on utilization of such rental assistance and other program data, as prescribed by the Secretary: Provided further, That the Secretary may reallocate, as determined by the Secretary, amounts returned or recaptured from awards under the Tribal HUD-VASH program under prior Acts to existing recipients under the Tribal HUD-VASH program;

(6) $1,550,000,000 shall be made available for new incremental voucher assistance under section 8(o) of the Act, to be allocated pursuant to a method, as determined by the Secretary, which may include a formula that may include such factors as severe cost burden, overcrowding, substandard housing for very low-income renters, homelessness, and administrative capacity, where such allocation method shall include both rural and urban areas: Provided, That the Secretary may specify additional terms and conditions to ensure that public housing agencies provide vouchers for use by survivors of domestic violence, dating violence, sexual assault, stalking, or human trafficking, or individuals and families who are homeless, as defined in section 103(a) of the McKinney-Vento Homeless Assistance Act (42 U.S.C. 11302(a)), or at risk of homelessness, as defined in section 401(1) of such Act (42 U.S.C. 11360(1));

(7) $445,000,000 shall be for mobility-related services, as defined by the Secretary, for voucher families with children modeled after services provided in connection with the mobility demonstration authorized under section 235 of division G of the Consolidated Appropriations Act, 2019 (42 U.S.C. 1437f note; Public Law 116–6): Provided, That the Secretary shall make funding available to public housing agencies on a competitive basis and shall give preference to public housing agencies with higher concentrations of voucher families with children residing in high-poverty neighborhoods: Provided further, That the Secretary may recapture from the public housing agencies unused balances based on utilization of such awards and reallocate such amounts to any other public housing agency or agencies based on need for such mobility-related services as identified under such competition; and

(8) the Secretary shall separately track all special purpose vouchers funded under this heading: Provided, That the Secretary may waive, or specify alternative requirements for, any provision of any statute or regulation that the Secretary administers in connection with the use of funds made available for new incremental voucher assistance or renewals for the Mainstream program, the HUD-VASH program (in consultation with the Secretary of the Department of Veterans Affairs), and the family unification program (including the Foster Youth to Independence program) in this and prior Acts (except for requirements related to fair housing, nondiscrimination, labor standards, and the environment), upon a finding by the Secretary that any such waivers or alternative requirements are necessary for the effective delivery and administration of voucher assistance in such respective programs.

Note.—A full-year 2022 appropriation for this account was not enacted at the time the Budget was prepared; therefore, the Budget assumes this account is operating under the Continuing Appropriations Act, 2022 (Division A of Public Law 117–43, as amended). The amounts included for 2022 reflect the annualized level provided by the continuing resolution.

Program and Financing (in millions of dollars)

Identification code 086–0302–0–1–604		2021 actual	2022 est.	2023 est.
	Obligations by program activity:			
0001	Tenant Protection	143	157	220
0002	Administrative Fees	2,103	2,356	3,014
0006	Contract Renewals	22,935	23,338	26,234
0007	Rental Assistance Demonstration	61	66	46
0008	Veterans Affairs Supportive Housing Vouchers	47	88	
0013	Section 811 Mainstream Vouchers	428	447	667
0014	Family Unification Program	18	53	
0015	Tribal HUD VASH	4	13	
0016	Family Mobility Demonstration	46	4	
0017	Contract Renewals (CARES Act)	157		
0019	Homeless Vouchers - Domestic Violence		86	
0020	Contract Renewals - (ARP Act)	786	215	671
0021	Administrative Fees - (ARP Act)	357	35	50
0022	Allocation Adjustments for CY 2021 - (ARP Act)	16	17	
0023	Mobility Related Services			445
0024	Incremental Vouchers			1,550
0029	Rental Assistance Demonstration for Section 202		4	2

DEPARTMENT OF HOUSING AND URBAN DEVELOPMENT

Public and Indian Housing Programs—Continued
Federal Funds—Continued

561

		2021 actual	2022 est.	2023 est.
0900	Total new obligations, unexpired accounts (object class 41.0)	27,101	26,879	32,899
	Budgetary resources:			
	Unobligated balance:			
1000	Unobligated balance brought forward, Oct 1	872	4,598	3,552
1001	Discretionary unobligated balance brought fwd, Oct 1	872		
1011	Unobligated balance transfer from other acct [086–0320]		1	
1020	Adjustment of unobligated bal brought forward, Oct 1	–29		
1021	Recoveries of prior year unpaid obligations	7		
1033	Recoveries of prior year paid obligations	29		
1070	Unobligated balance (total)	879	4,599	3,552
	Budget authority:			
	Appropriations, discretionary:			
1100	Appropriation	21,777	21,777	28,130
1121	Appropriations transferred from other acct [086–0320]		3	2
1121	Appropriations transferred from other acct [086–0481]	63	52	46
1160	Appropriation, discretionary (total)	21,840	21,832	28,178
	Advance appropriations, discretionary:			
1170	Advance appropriation	4,000	4,000	4,000
	Appropriations, mandatory:			
1200	Appropriation	4,980		
1900	Budget authority (total)	30,820	25,832	32,178
1930	Total budgetary resources available	31,699	30,431	35,730
	Memorandum (non-add) entries:			
1941	Unexpired unobligated balance, end of year	4,598	3,552	2,831
	Change in obligated balance:			
	Unpaid obligations:			
3000	Unpaid obligations, brought forward, Oct 1	4,826	6,530	6,766
3001	Adjustments to unpaid obligations, brought forward, Oct 1	29		
3010	New obligations, unexpired accounts	27,101	26,879	32,899
3020	Outlays (gross)	–25,419	–26,643	–31,619
3040	Recoveries of prior year unpaid obligations, unexpired	–7		
3050	Unpaid obligations, end of year	6,530	6,766	8,046
	Memorandum (non-add) entries:			
3100	Obligated balance, start of year	4,855	6,530	6,766
3200	Obligated balance, end of year	6,530	6,766	8,046
	Budget authority and outlays, net:			
	Discretionary:			
4000	Budget authority, gross	25,840	25,832	32,178
	Outlays, gross:			
4010	Outlays from new discretionary authority	21,723	21,926	27,137
4011	Outlays from discretionary balances	3,328	4,025	3,905
4020	Outlays, gross (total)	25,051	25,951	31,042
	Offsets against gross budget authority and outlays:			
	Offsetting collections (collected) from:			
4033	Non-Federal sources	–29		
	Additional offsets against gross budget authority only:			
4053	Recoveries of prior year paid obligations, unexpired accounts	29		
4070	Budget authority, net (discretionary)	25,840	25,832	32,178
4080	Outlays, net (discretionary)	25,022	25,951	31,042
	Mandatory:			
4090	Budget authority, gross	4,980		
	Outlays, gross:			
4100	Outlays from new mandatory authority	368		
4101	Outlays from mandatory balances		692	577
4110	Outlays, gross (total)	368	692	577
4180	Budget authority, net (total)	30,820	25,832	32,178
4190	Outlays, net (total)	25,390	26,643	31,619

The Budget provides $32.1 billion for the Tenant-Based Rental Assistance (TBRA) program (also known as the Housing Choice Voucher program), which is the Federal Government's largest income-targeted rental assistance program. The program currently provides housing assistance to around 2.3 million extremely low- to very low-income families to rent decent, safe, and sanitary housing in the private market. About 2,100 state and local Public Housing Authorities (PHAs) administer the Housing Choice Voucher program.

The Budget provides $26.2 billion in contract renewals to continue to assist families in calendar year 2023. This includes $50 million for the Rental Assistance Demonstration to further long-term financial stability and promote the energy or water efficiency, climate resilience, or preservation of properties that convert to Project-Based Vouchers.

The Budget includes $667 million for the renewal of Section 811 mainstream housing vouchers for persons with disabilities, including the first-time renewal of new mainstream vouchers allocated in 2022, and associated administrative fees, as well as a new set-aside to provide adjustments to PHAs as a result of significant increases in mainstream renewal costs resulting from unforeseen circumstances and to prevent the termination of assistance for mainstream families should there be insufficient funding.

The Budget also requests the following: $3.0 billion in PHA administrative fees to support core functions such as admitting households, conducting housing quality inspections, and completing tenant income certifications; $220 million for tenant protection vouchers, which are provided to families who may have to relocate due to actions beyond their control, such as a public housing demolition or redevelopment, and when private owners of multi-family developments choose to leave the project-based program or convert to long-term Section 8 contracts, including up to $20 million that may be used to assist low-income tenants referred by the Secretary of the Department of Argriculture (USDA) when section 521 assistance is no longer available to protect tenants due to the maturity, prepayment, or foreclosure of a section 514 or 515 loan, as part of the Budget's proposal to decouple USDA section 521 rental assistance from section 514 or 515 mortgage loans; and up to $5 million for the renewal of vouchers by Tribes under the Tribal Housing and Department of Housing and Urban Development and Department of Veterans Affairs Supportive Housing program, to serve Native American veterans who are homeless or at risk of homelessness and living in and around designated tribal areas.

In addition, the Budget includes $1.6 billion for new incremental vouchers for 200,000 additional households, including those who are experiencing or at risk of homelessness or fleeing or attempting to flee domestic violence, dating violence, sexual assault, stalking, or human trafficking. The Budget also includes $445 million for Mobility Services, which will provide funding for services to better enable families with children to move to areas of higher opportunity.

HOUSING CERTIFICATE FUND

(INCLUDING CANCELLATIONS)

Unobligated balances, including recaptures and carryover, remaining from funds appropriated to the Department of Housing and Urban Development under this heading, the heading "Annual Contributions for Assisted Housing" and the heading "Project-Based Rental Assistance", for fiscal year 2023 and prior years may be used for renewal of or amendments to section 8 project-based contracts and for performance-based contract administrators, notwithstanding the purposes for which such funds were appropriated: Provided, That any obligated balances of contract authority from fiscal year 1974 and prior fiscal years that have been terminated are hereby permanently cancelled: Provided further, That amounts heretofore recaptured, or recaptured during the current fiscal year, from section 8 project-based contracts from source years fiscal year 1975 through fiscal year 1987 are hereby permanently cancelled, and an amount of additional new budget authority, equivalent to the amount permanently cancelled is hereby appropriated, to remain available until expended, for the purposes set forth under this heading, in addition to amounts otherwise available.

Note.—A full-year 2022 appropriation for this account was not enacted at the time the Budget was prepared; therefore, the Budget assumes this account is operating under the Continuing Appropriations Act, 2022 (Division A of Public Law 117–43, as amended). The amounts included for 2022 reflect the annualized level provided by the continuing resolution.

Program and Financing (in millions of dollars)

Identification code 086–0319–0–1–604	2021 actual	2022 est.	2023 est.
Obligations by program activity:			
0002 Contract Administrators	6	25	20
0900 Total new obligations, unexpired accounts (object class 41.0)	6	25	20
Budgetary resources:			
Unobligated balance:			
1000 Unobligated balance brought forward, Oct 1	72	75	52
1020 Adjustment of unobligated bal brought forward, Oct 1	–1		
1021 Recoveries of prior year unpaid obligations	12	10	10

HOUSING CERTIFICATE FUND—Continued

Program and Financing—Continued

Identification code 086–0319–0–1–604		2021 actual	2022 est.	2023 est.
1029	Other balances withdrawn to Treasury	–3	–8	–8
1033	Recoveries of prior year paid obligations	1		
1070	Unobligated balance (total)	81	77	54
	Budget authority:			
	Appropriations, discretionary:			
1100	Appropriation	13	15	15
1131	Unobligated balance of appropriations permanently reduced (HCF funds)	–13	–15	–15
1930	Total budgetary resources available	81	77	54
	Memorandum (non-add) entries:			
1941	Unexpired unobligated balance, end of year	75	52	34
	Change in obligated balance:			
	Unpaid obligations:			
3000	Unpaid obligations, brought forward, Oct 1	55	28	18
3001	Adjustments to unpaid obligations, brought forward, Oct 1	1		
3010	New obligations, unexpired accounts	6	25	20
3020	Outlays (gross)	–22	–25	–20
3040	Recoveries of prior year unpaid obligations, unexpired	–12	–10	–10
3050	Unpaid obligations, end of year	28	18	8
	Memorandum (non-add) entries:			
3100	Obligated balance, start of year	56	28	18
3200	Obligated balance, end of year	28	18	8
	Budget authority and outlays, net:			
	Discretionary:			
	Outlays, gross:			
4011	Outlays from discretionary balances	22	25	20
	Offsets against gross budget authority and outlays:			
	Offsetting collections (collected) from:			
4033	Non-Federal sources	–1		
	Additional offsets against gross budget authority only:			
4053	Recoveries of prior year paid obligations, unexpired accounts	1		
4080	Outlays, net (discretionary)	21	25	20
4180	Budget authority, net (total)			
4190	Outlays, net (total)	21	25	20

Until 2005, the Housing Certificate Fund provided funding to both the project-based and tenant-based components of the Section 8 program. Project-Based Rental Assistance (PBRA) and Tenant-Based Rental Assistance are now funded in separate accounts. The Housing Certificate Fund retains and recovers balances from the previous years' appropriations and uses those balances to support PBRA contract renewals, amendments, and administration.

PUBLIC HOUSING CAPITAL FUND

Program and Financing (in millions of dollars)

Identification code 086–0304–0–1–604		2021 actual	2022 est.	2023 est.
	Obligations by program activity:			
0001	Capital Grants (Modernization)	2	10	
0003	Emergency/Disaster Reserve	11		
0004	Emergency/Disaster Reserve (Receivership PHAs)	35		
0006	Resident Opportunities and Supportive Services	3		
0007	Administrative Receivership	1	1	
0008	Financial and Physical Assessment Support	6	4	
0011	Safety and Security	18		
0012	Lead-Based Paint Hazards	32		
0013	Other Health Hazards	20		
0900	Total new obligations, unexpired accounts (object class 41.0)	128	15	
	Budgetary resources:			
	Unobligated balance:			
1000	Unobligated balance brought forward, Oct 1	140	15	
1001	Discretionary unobligated balance brought fwd, Oct 1	138		
1020	Adjustment of unobligated bal brought forward, Oct 1	–1		
1021	Recoveries of prior year unpaid obligations	2		
1033	Recoveries of prior year paid obligations	2		
1070	Unobligated balance (total)	143	15	
1930	Total budgetary resources available	143	15	
	Memorandum (non-add) entries:			
1941	Unexpired unobligated balance, end of year	15		
	Change in obligated balance:			
	Unpaid obligations:			
3000	Unpaid obligations, brought forward, Oct 1	5,745	3,779	1,972
3001	Adjustments to unpaid obligations, brought forward, Oct 1	1		
3010	New obligations, unexpired accounts	128	15	
3020	Outlays (gross)	–2,087	–1,822	–942
3040	Recoveries of prior year unpaid obligations, unexpired	–2		
3041	Recoveries of prior year unpaid obligations, expired	–6		
3050	Unpaid obligations, end of year	3,779	1,972	1,030
	Memorandum (non-add) entries:			
3100	Obligated balance, start of year	5,746	3,779	1,972
3200	Obligated balance, end of year	3,779	1,972	1,030
	Budget authority and outlays, net:			
	Discretionary:			
	Outlays, gross:			
4011	Outlays from discretionary balances	2,087	1,822	942
	Offsets against gross budget authority and outlays:			
	Offsetting collections (collected) from:			
4033	Non-Federal sources	–2		
	Additional offsets against gross budget authority only:			
4053	Recoveries of prior year paid obligations, unexpired accounts	2		
4060	Additional offsets against budget authority only (total)	2		
4080	Outlays, net (discretionary)	2,085	1,822	942
4180	Budget authority, net (total)			
4190	Outlays, net (total)	2,085	1,822	942

The Consolidated Appropriations Act, 2021 (P.L. 116–260) combined the Public Housing Capital Fund and the Public Housing Operating Fund into the new Public Housing Fund. The Public Housing Capital Fund continues to make obligations and outlays from funds appropriated in 2020 and earlier.

PUBLIC HOUSING OPERATING FUND

Program and Financing (in millions of dollars)

Identification code 086–0163–0–1–604		2021 actual	2022 est.	2023 est.
	Obligations by program activity:			
0001	PH Formula Grants	469	3	
0003	Shortfall Prevention	25		
0900	Total new obligations, unexpired accounts (object class 41.0)	494	3	
	Budgetary resources:			
	Unobligated balance:			
1000	Unobligated balance brought forward, Oct 1	497	3	
1020	Adjustment of unobligated bal brought forward, Oct 1	–2		
1021	Recoveries of prior year unpaid obligations	1		
1033	Recoveries of prior year paid obligations	2		
1070	Unobligated balance (total)	498	3	
1930	Total budgetary resources available	498	3	
	Memorandum (non-add) entries:			
1940	Unobligated balance expiring	–1		
1941	Unexpired unobligated balance, end of year	3		
	Change in obligated balance:			
	Unpaid obligations:			
3000	Unpaid obligations, brought forward, Oct 1	1,337	207	3
3001	Adjustments to unpaid obligations, brought forward, Oct 1	4		
3010	New obligations, unexpired accounts	494	3	
3020	Outlays (gross)	–1,624	–207	–3
3040	Recoveries of prior year unpaid obligations, unexpired	–1		
3041	Recoveries of prior year unpaid obligations, expired	–3		
3050	Unpaid obligations, end of year	207	3	
	Memorandum (non-add) entries:			
3100	Obligated balance, start of year	1,341	207	3
3200	Obligated balance, end of year	207	3	

DEPARTMENT OF HOUSING AND URBAN DEVELOPMENT

Public and Indian Housing Programs—Continued
Federal Funds—Continued

	Budget authority and outlays, net:			
	Discretionary:			
	Outlays, gross:			
4011	Outlays from discretionary balances	1,624	207	3
	Offsets against gross budget authority and outlays:			
	Offsetting collections (collected) from:			
4033	Non-Federal sources	–4		
	Additional offsets against gross budget authority only:			
4052	Offsetting collections credited to expired accounts	2		
4053	Recoveries of prior year paid obligations, unexpired accounts	2		
4060	Additional offsets against budget authority only (total)	4		
4080	Outlays, net (discretionary)	1,620	207	3
4180	Budget authority, net (total)			
4190	Outlays, net (total)	1,620	207	3

The Consolidated Appropriations Act, 2021 (P.L. 116–260) combined the Public Housing Capital Fund and the Public Housing Operating Fund into the new Public Housing Fund. The Public Housing Operating Fund continues to make obligations and outlays from funds appropriated in 2020 and earlier.

PUBLIC HOUSING FUND

For 2023 payments to public housing agencies for the operation and management of public housing, as authorized by section 9(e) of the United States Housing Act of 1937 (42 U.S.C. 1437g(e)) (the "Act"), and to carry out capital and management activities for public housing agencies, as authorized under section 9(d) of the Act (42 U.S.C. 1437g(d)), $8,780,000,000, to remain available until September 30, 2026: Provided, That the amounts made available under this heading are provided as follows:

(1) $5,035,000,000 shall be available to the Secretary to allocate pursuant to the Operating Fund formula at part 990 of title 24, Code of Federal Regulations, for 2023 payments: Provided, That the amount of any forgone increases in tenant rent payments due to the implementation of rent incentives as authorized pursuant to waivers or alternative requirements of the Jobs-Plus initiative as described under the heading "Self-Sufficiency Programs" shall be factored into the PHA's general operating fund eligibility pursuant to such formula;

(2) $25,000,000 shall be available to the Secretary to allocate pursuant to a need-based application process notwithstanding section 203 of this title and not subject to such Operating Fund formula to public housing agencies that experience, or are at risk of, financial shortfalls, as determined by the Secretary: Provided, That after all such shortfall needs are met, the Secretary may distribute any remaining funds to all public housing agencies on a pro-rata basis pursuant to such Operating Fund formula;

(3) $3,200,000,000 shall be available to the Secretary to allocate pursuant to the Capital Fund formula at section 905.400 of title 24, Code of Federal Regulations: Provided, That from the funds made available under this paragraph, the Secretary shall provide bonus awards in fiscal year 2023 to public housing agencies that are designated high performers;

(4) $40,000,000 shall be available for the Secretary to make grants, notwithstanding section 203 of this title, to public housing agencies for emergency capital needs, including safety and security measures necessary to address crime and drug-related activity, as well as needs resulting from unforeseen or unpreventable emergencies and natural disasters excluding Presidentially declared emergencies and natural disasters under the Robert T. Stafford Disaster Relief and Emergency Act (42 U.S.C. 5121 et seq.) occurring in fiscal year 2023: Provided, That of the amount made available under this paragraph, not less than $20,000,000 shall be for safety and security measures: Provided further, That in addition to the amount in the previous proviso for such safety and security measures, any amounts that remain available, after all applications received on or before September 30, 2024, for emergency capital needs have been processed, shall be allocated to public housing agencies for such safety and security measures;

(5) $25,000,000 shall be for competitive grants to public housing agencies to evaluate and reduce lead-based paint hazards in public housing by carrying out the activities of risk assessments, abatement, and interim controls (as those terms are defined in section 1004 of the Residential Lead-Based Paint Hazard Reduction Act of 1992 (42 U.S.C. 4851b)): Provided, That for purposes of environmental review, a grant under this paragraph shall be considered funds for projects or activities under title I of the United States Housing Act of 1937 (42 U.S.C. 1437 et seq.) for purposes of section 26 of such Act (42 U.S.C. 1437x) and shall be subject to the regulations implementing such section;

(6) $60,000,000 shall be available for competitive grants to public housing agencies to evaluate and reduce housing-related hazards including carbon monoxide, radon and mold in public housing: Provided, That for purposes of environmental review, grants under this paragraph shall be considered funds for projects or activities under title I of the United States Housing Act of 1937 (42 U.S.C. 1437 et seq.) for purposes of section 26 of such Act (42 U.S.C. 1437x) and shall be subject to the regulations implementing such section: Provided further, That amounts made available under this paragraph shall be combined with any amounts remaining from amounts made available under this paragraph for Healthy Homes Initiative grants in prior Acts and shall be used in accordance with the purposes and requirements under this paragraph;

(7) $45,000,000 shall be to support the costs of administrative and judicial receiverships and for competitive grants to PHAs in receivership, designated troubled or substandard, or otherwise at risk, as determined by the Secretary, for costs associated with public housing asset improvement, in addition to other amounts for that purpose provided under any heading under this title;

(8) $50,000,000 shall be to support ongoing public housing financial and physical assessment activities; and

(9) $300,000,000 shall be available to improve the energy or water efficiency or climate resilience of public housing, including for competitive grants to public housing agencies for capital improvements to achieve such purposes: Provided, That for purposes of environmental review, grants under this paragraph shall be considered funds for projects or activities under title I of the United States Housing Act of 1937 (42 U.S.C. 1437 et seq.) for purposes of section 26 of such Act (42 U.S.C. 1437x) and shall be subject to the regulations implementing such section: Provided further, That of the amounts made available under this paragraph, up to $24,000,000 shall be available for utility benchmarking, including research and evaluations, technical assistance, and contracts, of which up to $9,000,000 may be transferred to and merged with amounts made available under the heading "Information Technology Fund" to develop systems and tools necessary to collect and analyze PHA utility benchmarking data;

Provided further, That notwithstanding any other provision of law or regulation, during fiscal year 2023, the Secretary of Housing and Urban Development may not delegate to any Department official other than the Deputy Secretary and the Assistant Secretary for Public and Indian Housing any authority under paragraph (2) of section 9(j) of the Act regarding the extension of the time periods under such section: Provided further, That for purposes of such section 9(j), the term "obligate" means, with respect to amounts, that the amounts are subject to a binding agreement that will result in outlays, immediately or in the future: Provided further, That a public housing agency may use operating reserve funds or any amounts allocated to such agency pursuant to the Operating or Capital Fund formulas from amounts made available in this and prior Acts for any eligible activities under sections 9(d)(1) and 9(e)(1) of the United States Housing Act of 1937 (42 U.S.C. 1437g(d)(1) and (e)(1)).

Note.—A full-year 2022 appropriation for this account was not enacted at the time the Budget was prepared; therefore, the Budget assumes this account is operating under the Continuing Appropriations Act, 2022 (Division A of Public Law 117–43, as amended). The amounts included for 2022 reflect the annualized level provided by the continuing resolution.

Program and Financing (in millions of dollars)

Identification code 086–0481–0–1–604		2021 actual	2022 est.	2023 est.
	Obligations by program activity:			
0001	Operating Formula Grants	4,321	4,781	5,007
0002	Shortfall Prevention	25	25	25
0003	Capital Formula Grants	2,710	2,738	3,142
0004	Emergency and Disaster Grants	19	20	20
0005	Emergency and Disaster Grants (Receivership and Monitor)	45	45	
0006	Safety and Security Grants	10	10	20
0007	Lead-Based Paint Hazards Grants	20	25	25
0008	Healthy Homes Grants		35	60
0009	Financial and Physical Assessment	1	23	50
0010	Administrative & Judicial Receivership, Grants to Troubled PHAs		15	45
0011	Radon Testing and Mitigation Demonstration		4	
0012	Utilities Benchmarking			24
0013	Energy Efficiency and Climate Resilience Grants			276
0900	Total new obligations, unexpired accounts (object class 41.0)	7,151	7,721	8,694
	Budgetary resources:			
	Unobligated balance:			
1000	Unobligated balance brought forward, Oct 1		536	536
	Budget authority:			
	Appropriations, discretionary:			
1100	Appropriation	7,806	7,806	8,780
1120	Appropriations transferred to other acct [086–0302]	–63	–52	–46

PUBLIC HOUSING FUND—Continued

Program and Financing—Continued

Identification code 086–0481–0–1–604		2021 actual	2022 est.	2023 est.
1120	Appropriations transferred to other acct [086–0303]	–56	–33	–40
1120	Appropriations transferred to other acct [086–4586]			–9
1160	Appropriation, discretionary (total)	7,687	7,721	8,685
1930	Total budgetary resources available	7,687	8,257	9,221
	Memorandum (non-add) entries:			
1941	Unexpired unobligated balance, end of year	536	536	527
	Change in obligated balance:			
	Unpaid obligations:			
3000	Unpaid obligations, brought forward, Oct 1		3,578	5,556
3010	New obligations, unexpired accounts	7,151	7,721	8,694
3020	Outlays (gross)	–3,573	–5,743	–6,902
3050	Unpaid obligations, end of year	3,578	5,556	7,348
	Memorandum (non-add) entries:			
3100	Obligated balance, start of year		3,578	5,556
3200	Obligated balance, end of year	3,578	5,556	7,348
	Budget authority and outlays, net:			
	Discretionary:			
4000	Budget authority, gross	7,687	7,721	8,685
	Outlays, gross:			
4010	Outlays from new discretionary authority	3,573	3,586	3,762
4011	Outlays from discretionary balances		2,157	3,140
4020	Outlays, gross (total)	3,573	5,743	6,902
4180	Budget authority, net (total)	7,687	7,721	8,685
4190	Outlays, net (total)	3,573	5,743	6,902

The Budget provides $8.78 billion for the Public Housing Fund to carry out capital and management activities in the Public Housing program. The budget allocates $5 billion to Public Housing Agencies (PHAs) for the costs of operating public housing. The Budget includes $25 million for need-based assistance to PHAs that are at risk of financial shortfalls. The Budget also allocates $3.2 billion to PHAs for capital needs and modernization. The Budget includes $40 million available to PHAs for emergency capital needs resulting from emergencies and natural disasters, which includes $20 million for safety and security measures necessary to address crime and drug-related activity. The Budget includes $25 million for competitive grants to PHAs to evaluate and reduce lead-based paint hazards in public housing. The Budget also includes $60 million for competitive grants to public housing agencies to evaluate and reduce housing-based hazards including fire safety, carbon monoxide, radon, and mold. The Budget includes $45 million to support the costs of administrative and judicial receiverships and for competitive grants to PHAs in receivership, designated troubled or substandard, or otherwise at risk, for costs associated with public housing asset improvement. The Budget also includes $50 million for ongoing financial and physical assessment activities.

The Budget includes $276 million for competitive grants for capital improvements to improve energy or water efficiency or climate resilience of public housing. The Budget also includes $24 million for utility benchmarking, including contract support and technical assistance.

CHOICE NEIGHBORHOODS INITIATIVE

For competitive grants under the Choice Neighborhoods Initiative (subject to section 24 of the United States Housing Act of 1937 (42 U.S.C. 1437v) unless otherwise specified under this heading), for transformation, rehabilitation, and replacement housing needs of both public and HUD-assisted housing and to transform neighborhoods of poverty into functioning, sustainable mixed income neighborhoods with appropriate services, schools, public assets, transportation and access to jobs, $250,000,000, to remain available until September 30, 2026: Provided, That grant funds may be used for resident and community services, community development, and affordable housing needs in the community, and for conversion of vacant or foreclosed properties to affordable housing: Provided further, That the use of funds made available under this heading shall not be deemed to be for public housing notwithstanding section 3(b)(1) of such Act: Provided further, That grantees shall commit to an additional period of affordability determined by the Secretary of not fewer than 20 years: Provided further, That the Secretary may specify a period of affordability that is less than 20 years with respect to homeownership units developed with grants from amounts made available under this heading: Provided further, That grantees shall provide a match in State, local, other Federal or private funds: Provided further, That grantees may include local governments, Tribal entities, public housing agencies, and nonprofit organizations: Provided further, That for-profit developers may apply jointly with a public entity: Provided further, That for purposes of environmental review, a grantee shall be treated as a public housing agency under section 26 of the United States Housing Act of 1937 (42 U.S.C. 1437x), and grants made with amounts available under this heading shall be subject to the regulations issued by the Secretary to implement such section: Provided further, That of the amount provided under this heading, not less than $100,000,000 shall be awarded to public housing agencies: Provided further, That such grantees shall create partnerships with other local organizations, including assisted housing owners, service agencies, and resident organizations: Provided further, That the Secretary shall consult with the Secretaries of Education, Labor, Transportation, Health and Human Services, Agriculture, and Commerce, the Attorney General, and the Administrator of the Environmental Protection Agency to coordinate and leverage other appropriate Federal resources: Provided further, That not more than $5,000,000 of funds made available under this heading may be provided as grants to undertake comprehensive local planning with input from residents and the community: Provided further, That not more than $10,000,000 of the funds made available under this heading shall be available, in addition to amounts otherwise available for such purposes, for planning and implementation grants, notwithstanding section 203 of this title, to support the revitalization of communities with public or HUD-assisted housing in close proximity to Superfund sites, notwithstanding the limitation on planning under the previous proviso: Provided further, That communities selected under this program shall not be ineligible for participation in the Choice Neighborhoods Initiative due to their selection under this program: Provided further, That the Secretary shall define eligible activities for such grant assistance, which may include permitting grantees to provide assistance to businesses and nonprofit organizations to carry out economic development and job creation or job retention activities: Provided further, That the Secretary shall be authorized to waive, or specify alternative requirements for any provision of such section 24 that the Secretary administers in connection with the use of funds for this program (except for requirements related to fair housing, nondiscrimination, labor standards, and the environment), upon a finding by the Secretary that any such waivers or alternative requirements are necessary for the effective delivery and administration of such assistance: Provided further, That unobligated balances, including recaptures, remaining from funds appropriated under the heading "Revitalization of Severely Distressed Public Housing (HOPE VI)" in fiscal year 2011 and prior fiscal years may be used for purposes under this heading, notwithstanding the purposes for which such amounts were appropriated: Provided further, That notwithstanding section 24(o) of the United States Housing Act of 1937 (42 U.S.C. 1437v(o)), the Secretary may, until September 30, 2023, obligate any available unobligated balances made available under this heading in this or any prior Act.

Note.—A full-year 2022 appropriation for this account was not enacted at the time the Budget was prepared; therefore, the Budget assumes this account is operating under the Continuing Appropriations Act, 2022 (Division A of Public Law 117–43, as amended). The amounts included for 2022 reflect the annualized level provided by the continuing resolution.

Program and Financing (in millions of dollars)

Identification code 086–0349–0–1–604		2021 actual	2022 est.	2023 est.
	Obligations by program activity:			
0001	Choice Neighborhoods Grants	165	200	240
0002	Remediation and Revitalization of Contaminated Lands Fund (RECLAIM)			10
0900	Total new obligations, unexpired accounts (object class 41.0)	165	200	250
	Budgetary resources:			
	Unobligated balance:			
1000	Unobligated balance brought forward, Oct 1	189	224	224
	Budget authority:			
	Appropriations, discretionary:			
1100	Appropriation	200	200	250
1930	Total budgetary resources available	389	424	474
	Memorandum (non-add) entries:			
1941	Unexpired unobligated balance, end of year	224	224	224
	Change in obligated balance:			
	Unpaid obligations:			
3000	Unpaid obligations, brought forward, Oct 1	545	638	694
3010	New obligations, unexpired accounts	165	200	250

DEPARTMENT OF HOUSING AND URBAN DEVELOPMENT

Public and Indian Housing Programs—Continued
Federal Funds—Continued

565

		2021 actual	2022 est.	2023 est.
3020	Outlays (gross)	–72	–144	–155
3050	Unpaid obligations, end of year	638	694	789
	Memorandum (non-add) entries:			
3100	Obligated balance, start of year	545	638	694
3200	Obligated balance, end of year	638	694	789
	Budget authority and outlays, net:			
	Discretionary:			
4000	Budget authority, gross	200	200	250
	Outlays, gross:			
4011	Outlays from discretionary balances	72	144	155
4180	Budget authority, net (total)	200	200	250
4190	Outlays, net (total)	72	144	155

The Budget requests $250 million for Choice Neighborhoods to continue the transformation of neighborhoods of concentrated poverty into sustainable, mixed-income neighborhoods with well-functioning services, schools, public assets, transportation, and access to jobs. The goal of the program is to transform distressed neighborhoods and improve the quality of life of current and future residents by coordinating and concentrating neighborhood investments from multiple sources. HUD will allocate up to $5 million for 10 to 12 Planning Grants and the remaining $235 million will fund four to six Implementation Grants.

In addition, the Budget includes $10 million under Choice Neighborhoods to fund the pilot Revitalization and Empowerment of Communities near Contaminated Lands through Assistance, Investment, and Mitigation (RECLAIM) program. The program will support community-driven efforts to revitalize distressed neighborhoods that contain public and/or HUD-assisted housing and are located on or near Superfund sites. RECLAIM leverages a coordinated interagency effort to identify, cleanup, and improve these sites by concentrating Federal resources. HUD will provide planning and implementation grants for pilot communities to improve health and safety, generate economic opportunities, and preserve or create affordable housing.

REVITALIZATION OF SEVERELY DISTRESSED PUBLIC HOUSING (HOPE VI)

Program and Financing (in millions of dollars)

Identification code 086–0218–0–1–604	2021 actual	2022 est.	2023 est.
Obligations by program activity:			
0001 HOPE VI/Choice Neighborhoods Grants	1		
0900 Total new obligations, unexpired accounts (object class 41.0)	1		
Budgetary resources:			
Unobligated balance:			
1000 Unobligated balance brought forward, Oct 1	1		
1020 Adjustment of unobligated bal brought forward, Oct 1	–1		
1033 Recoveries of prior year paid obligations	1		
1070 Unobligated balance (total)	1		
1930 Total budgetary resources available	1		
Change in obligated balance:			
Unpaid obligations:			
3000 Unpaid obligations, brought forward, Oct 1	15	15	10
3001 Adjustments to unpaid obligations, brought forward, Oct 1	1		
3010 New obligations, unexpired accounts	1		
3020 Outlays (gross)	–2	–5	–5
3050 Unpaid obligations, end of year	15	10	5
Memorandum (non-add) entries:			
3100 Obligated balance, start of year	16	15	10
3200 Obligated balance, end of year	15	10	5
Budget authority and outlays, net:			
Discretionary:			
Outlays, gross:			
4011 Outlays from discretionary balances	2	5	5
Offsets against gross budget authority and outlays:			
Offsetting collections (collected) from:			
4033 Non-Federal sources	–1		
Additional offsets against gross budget authority only:			
4053 Recoveries of prior year paid obligations, unexpired accounts	1		
4080 Outlays, net (discretionary)	1	5	5
4180 Budget authority, net (total)			
4190 Outlays, net (total)	1	5	5

The HOPE VI program has accomplished its goal of contributing to the demolition of approximately 100,000 severely distressed Public Housing units. The Budget proposes no additional funds for this program. Instead, the Budget builds on the success of HOPE VI with the Choice Neighborhoods program, which makes a broad range of transformative investments in high-poverty neighborhoods where Public Housing and other HUD-assisted housing is located.

SELF-SUFFICIENCY PROGRAMS

For activities and assistance related to Self-Sufficiency Programs, to remain available until September 30, 2026, $175,000,000: Provided, That the amounts made available under this heading are provided as follows:

(1) $120,000,000 shall be for the Family Self-Sufficiency program to support family self-sufficiency coordinators under section 23 of the United States Housing Act of 1937 (42 U.S.C. 1437u), to promote the development of local strategies to coordinate the use of assistance under sections 8 and 9 of such Act with public and private resources, and enable eligible families to achieve economic independence and self-sufficiency: Provided, That the Secretary may, by Federal Register notice, waive or specify alternative requirements under subsections (b)(3), (b)(4), (b)(5), or (c)(1) of section 23 of such Act in order to facilitate the operation of a unified self-sufficiency program for individuals receiving assistance under different provisions of such Act, as determined by the Secretary: Provided further, That owners or sponsors of a multifamily property receiving project-based rental assistance under section 8 of such Act may voluntarily make a Family Self-Sufficiency program available to the assisted tenants of such property in accordance with procedures established by the Secretary: Provided further, That such procedures established pursuant to the previous proviso shall permit participating tenants to accrue escrow funds in accordance with section 23(d)(2) of such Act and shall allow owners to use funding from residual receipt accounts to hire coordinators for their own Family Self-Sufficiency program;

(2) $35,000,000 shall be for the Resident Opportunity and Self-Sufficiency program to provide for supportive services, service coordinators, and congregate services as authorized by section 34 of the United States Housing Act of 1937 (42 U.S.C. 1437z–6) and the Native American Housing Assistance and Self-Determination Act of 1996 (25 U.S.C. 4101 et seq.); and

(3) $20,000,000 shall be for a Jobs-Plus initiative, modeled after the Jobs-Plus demonstration: Provided, That funding provided under this paragraph shall be available for competitive grants to public housing authorities or owners or sponsors of multifamily properties receiving project-based rental assistance under section 8, that, in partnership with local workforce investment boards established under section 107 of the Workforce Innovation and Opportunity Act of 2014 (29 U.S.C. 3122), and other agencies and organizations provide support to help public housing residents, or tenants residing in units assisted under a project-based section 8 contract (including section 8(o)(13) of the United States Housing Act of 1937), obtain employment or increase earnings, or both: Provided further, That applicants must demonstrate the ability to provide services to such residents or tenants, partner with workforce investment boards, and leverage service dollars: Provided further, That the Secretary may allow public housing agencies to request exemptions from rent and income limitation requirements under sections 3 and 6 of the United States Housing Act of 1937 (42 U.S.C. 1437a, 1437d), as necessary to implement the Jobs-Plus program, on such terms and conditions as the Secretary may approve upon a finding by the Secretary that any such waivers or alternative requirements are necessary for the effective implementation of the Jobs-Plus initiative as a voluntary program for residents: Provided further, That the Secretary shall publish by notice in the Federal Register any waivers or alternative requirements pursuant to the preceding proviso no later than 10 days before the effective date of such notice: Provided further, That the costs of any rent incentives as authorized pursuant to such waivers or alternative requirements shall not be charged against the competitive grant amounts made available under this paragraph.

Note.—A full-year 2022 appropriation for this account was not enacted at the time the Budget was prepared; therefore, the Budget assumes this account is operating under the Continuing Appropriations Act, 2022 (Division A of Public Law 117–43, as amended). The amounts included for 2022 reflect the annualized level provided by the continuing resolution.

SELF-SUFFICIENCY PROGRAMS—Continued

Program and Financing (in millions of dollars)

Identification code 086–0350–0–1–604	2021 actual	2022 est.	2023 est.
Obligations by program activity:			
0001 Family Self-Sufficiency	80	105	120
0002 Jobs-Plus Initiative	28	15	20
0003 Resident Opportunity and Self-Sufficiency	34	35	35
0900 Total new obligations, unexpired accounts (object class 41.0)	142	155	175
Budgetary resources:			
Unobligated balance:			
1000 Unobligated balance brought forward, Oct 1	130	143	143
Budget authority:			
Appropriations, discretionary:			
1100 Appropriation	155	155	175
1930 Total budgetary resources available	285	298	318
Memorandum (non-add) entries:			
1941 Unexpired unobligated balance, end of year	143	143	143
Change in obligated balance:			
Unpaid obligations:			
3000 Unpaid obligations, brought forward, Oct 1	35	96	107
3010 New obligations, unexpired accounts	142	155	175
3020 Outlays (gross)	–81	–144	–160
3050 Unpaid obligations, end of year	96	107	122
Memorandum (non-add) entries:			
3100 Obligated balance, start of year	35	96	107
3200 Obligated balance, end of year	96	107	122
Budget authority and outlays, net:			
Discretionary:			
4000 Budget authority, gross	155	155	175
Outlays, gross:			
4011 Outlays from discretionary balances	81	144	160
4180 Budget authority, net (total)	155	155	175
4190 Outlays, net (total)	81	144	160

The Budget requests $175 million for the Self-Sufficiency Programs account, which includes $120 million for the Family Self-Sufficiency (FSS) program, $35 million for Resident Opportunity and Self-Sufficiency (ROSS) and $20 million for the Jobs Plus Initiative.

NATIVE AMERICAN PROGRAMS
(INCLUDING CANCELLATIONS)

For activities and assistance authorized under title I of the Native American Housing Assistance and Self-Determination Act of 1996 (NAHASDA) (25 U.S.C. 4111 et seq.), title I of the Housing and Community Development Act of 1974 with respect to Indian tribes (42 U.S.C. 5306(a)(1)), and related training and technical assistance, $1,000,000,000, to remain available until September 30, 2027: Provided, That the amounts made available under this heading are provided as follows:

(1) $772,000,000 shall be available for the Native American Housing Block Grants program, as authorized under title I of NAHASDA: Provided, That, notwithstanding NAHASDA, to determine the amount of the allocation under title I of such Act for each Indian tribe, the Secretary shall apply the formula under section 302 of NAHASDA with the need component based on single-race census data and with the need component based on multi-race census data, and the amount of the allocation for each Indian tribe shall be the greater of the two resulting allocation amounts;

(2) $150,000,000 shall be available for competitive grants under the Native American Housing Block Grants program, as authorized under title I of NAHASDA: Provided, That the Secretary shall obligate such amount for competitive grants to eligible recipients authorized under NAHASDA that apply for funds: Provided further, That in awarding such amount, the Secretary shall consider need and administrative capacity, shall give priority to projects that will spur construction and rehabilitation of housing, and may give priority to projects that improve water or energy efficiency or increase climate or disaster resilience for housing units owned, operated, or assisted by eligible recipients authorized under NAHASDA: Provided further, That any funds transferred for the necessary costs of administering and overseeing the obligation and expenditure of such amounts in prior Acts may also be used for the necessary costs of administering and overseeing such amounts;

(3) $1,000,000 shall be for the cost of guaranteed notes and other obligations, as authorized by title VI of NAHASDA: Provided, That such costs, including the cost of modifying such notes and other obligations, shall be as defined in section 502 of the Congressional Budget Act of 1974, as amended: Provided further, That funds made available in this and prior Acts for the cost of such guaranteed notes and other obligations, that are unobligated, including recaptures and carryover, are available to subsidize the total principal amount of any notes and other obligations, any part of which is to be guaranteed, not to exceed $50,000,000, to remain available until September 30, 2024: Provided further, That any remaining loan guarantee limitation authorized for this program in fiscal year 2020 or prior fiscal years is hereby permanently cancelled;

(4) $70,000,000 shall be available for grants to Indian tribes for carrying out the Indian Community Development Block Grant program under title I of the Housing and Community Development Act of 1974, notwithstanding section 106(a)(1) of such Act, of which, notwithstanding any other provision of law (including section 203 of this Act), up to $4,000,000 may be used for emergencies that constitute imminent threats to health and safety: Provided, That not to exceed 20 percent of any grant made with funds appropriated under this paragraph shall be expended for planning and management development and administration; and

(5) $7,000,000, in addition to amounts otherwise available for such purpose, shall be available for providing training and technical assistance to Indian tribes, Indian housing authorities, and tribally designated housing entities, to support the inspection of Indian housing units, contract expertise, and for training and technical assistance related to funding provided under this heading and other headings under this Act for the needs of Native American families and Indian country: Provided, That of the funds made available under this paragraph, not less than $2,000,000 shall be available for a national organization as authorized under section 703 of NAHASDA (25 U.S.C. 4212): Provided further, That amounts made available under this paragraph may be used, contracted, or competed as determined by the Secretary: Provided further, That notwithstanding the provisions of the Federal Grant and Cooperative Agreements Act of 1977 (31 U.S.C. 6301–6308), the amounts made available under this paragraph may be used by the Secretary to enter into cooperative agreements with public and private organizations, agencies, institutions, and other technical assistance providers to support the administration of negotiated rulemaking under section 106 of NAHASDA (25 U.S.C. 4116), the administration of the allocation formula under section 302 of NAHASDA (25 U.S.C. 4152), and the administration of performance tracking and reporting under section 407 of NAHASDA (25 U.S.C. 4167).

Note.—A full-year 2022 appropriation for this account was not enacted at the time the Budget was prepared; therefore, the Budget assumes this account is operating under the Continuing Appropriations Act, 2022 (Division A of Public Law 117–43, as amended). The amounts included for 2022 reflect the annualized level provided by the continuing resolution.

Program and Financing (in millions of dollars)

Identification code 086–0313–0–1–604	2021 actual	2022 est.	2023 est.
Obligations by program activity:			
0010 Indian Housing Block Grants	648	651	772
0011 Technical Assistance	5	5	7
0015 National and Regional Organizations	2	4	2
0016 Indian Community Development Block Grant	4	145	72
0018 Indian Housing Block Grant (CARES Act)	1		
0019 Indian Community Development Block Grant (CARES Act)	3		2
0020 Indian Housing Competitive Grants	96	195	150
0021 Indian Housing Block Grant (ARP Act)	219	231	
0022 Indian Community Development Block Grant (ARP Act)		280	
0023 Technical Assistance (ARP Act)	10		
0091 Direct program activities, subtotal	988	1,511	1,005
Credit program obligations:			
0702 Loan guarantee subsidy	1	1	1
0791 Direct program activities, subtotal	1	1	1
0900 Total new obligations, unexpired accounts (object class 41.0)	989	1,512	1,006
Budgetary resources:			
Unobligated balance:			
1000 Unobligated balance brought forward, Oct 1	127	703	16
1001 Discretionary unobligated balance brought fwd, Oct 1	127		
1020 Adjustment of unobligated bal brought forward, Oct 1	–3		
1033 Recoveries of prior year paid obligations	3		
1070 Unobligated balance (total)	127	703	16
Budget authority:			
Appropriations, discretionary:			
1100 Appropriation	825	825	1,000
Appropriations, mandatory:			
1200 Appropriation [ARP Act]	740		

DEPARTMENT OF HOUSING AND URBAN DEVELOPMENT

Public and Indian Housing Programs—Continued
Federal Funds—Continued

		2021 actual	2022 est.	2023 est.
1900	Budget authority (total)	1,565	825	1,000
1930	Total budgetary resources available	1,692	1,528	1,016
	Memorandum (non-add) entries:			
1941	Unexpired unobligated balance, end of year	703	16	10
	Change in obligated balance:			
	Unpaid obligations:			
3000	Unpaid obligations, brought forward, Oct 1	1,379	1,538	1,692
3001	Adjustments to unpaid obligations, brought forward, Oct 1	3	....	....
3010	New obligations, unexpired accounts	989	1,512	1,006
3020	Outlays (gross)	–833	–1,358	–1,119
3050	Unpaid obligations, end of year	1,538	1,692	1,579
	Memorandum (non-add) entries:			
3100	Obligated balance, start of year	1,382	1,538	1,692
3200	Obligated balance, end of year	1,538	1,692	1,579
	Budget authority and outlays, net:			
	Discretionary:			
4000	Budget authority, gross	825	825	1,000
	Outlays, gross:			
4010	Outlays from new discretionary authority	239	289	350
4011	Outlays from discretionary balances	586	588	621
4020	Outlays, gross (total)	825	877	971
	Offsets against gross budget authority and outlays:			
	Offsetting collections (collected) from:			
4033	Non-Federal sources	–3	....	....
	Additional offsets against gross budget authority only:			
4053	Recoveries of prior year paid obligations, unexpired accounts	3	....	....
4070	Budget authority, net (discretionary)	825	825	1,000
4080	Outlays, net (discretionary)	822	877	971
	Mandatory:			
4090	Budget authority, gross	740	....	....
	Outlays, gross:			
4100	Outlays from new mandatory authority	8	....	....
4101	Outlays from mandatory balances	....	481	148
4110	Outlays, gross (total)	8	481	148
4180	Budget authority, net (total)	1,565	825	1,000
4190	Outlays, net (total)	830	1,358	1,119

Summary of Loan Levels, Subsidy Budget Authority and Outlays by Program (in millions of dollars)

Identification code 086–0313–0–1–604	2021 actual	2022 est.	2023 est.
Guaranteed loan levels supportable by subsidy budget authority:			
215001 Title VI Indian Federal Guarantees Program	19	12	12
Guaranteed loan subsidy (in percent):			
232001 Title VI Indian Federal Guarantees Program	6.39	5.55	5.63
232999 Weighted average subsidy rate	6.39	5.55	5.63
Guaranteed loan subsidy budget authority:			
233001 Title VI Indian Federal Guarantees Program	1	1	1
Guaranteed loan subsidy outlays:			
234001 Title VI Indian Federal Guarantees Program	1	1	1
Guaranteed loan reestimates:			
235001 Title VI Indian Federal Guarantees Program	–1	....	....

The Budget requests $1 billion for the Native American Programs account, which supports a wide range of affordable housing activities in Indian Country through grants and loan guarantees to recipients representing almost 600 Indian Tribes. The Budget requests $922 million for the Indian Housing Block Grant program ($772 million for formula grants and $150 million for competitive grants that may be used to make homes in Indian Country more energy efficient and further climate resilience); $70 million for the Indian Community Development Block Grant program; and $7 million for training and technical assistance. The Budget also requests $1 million in program funds to support up to $50 million in new loan guarantees for affordable housing construction and related community development projects through the Title VI program.

TITLE VI INDIAN FEDERAL GUARANTEES FINANCING ACCOUNT

Program and Financing (in millions of dollars)

Identification code 086–4244–0–3–604	2021 actual	2022 est.	2023 est.
Obligations by program activity:			
Credit program obligations:			
0742 Downward reestimates paid to receipt accounts	1	....	....
0900 Total new obligations, unexpired accounts	1	....	....
Budgetary resources:			
Unobligated balance:			
1000 Unobligated balance brought forward, Oct 1	3	3	4
Financing authority:			
Spending authority from offsetting collections, mandatory:			
1800 Collected	....	1	1
1801 Change in uncollected payments, Federal sources	1	....	....
1850 Spending auth from offsetting collections, mand (total)	1	1	1
1930 Total budgetary resources available	4	4	5
Memorandum (non-add) entries:			
1941 Unexpired unobligated balance, end of year	3	4	5
Change in obligated balance:			
Unpaid obligations:			
3010 New obligations, unexpired accounts	1	....	....
3020 Outlays (gross)	–1	....	....
Uncollected payments:			
3060 Uncollected pymts, Fed sources, brought forward, Oct 1	–2	–3	–3
3070 Change in uncollected pymts, Fed sources, unexpired	–1	....	....
3090 Uncollected pymts, Fed sources, end of year	–3	–3	–3
Memorandum (non-add) entries:			
3100 Obligated balance, start of year	–2	–3	–3
3200 Obligated balance, end of year	–3	–3	–3
Financing authority and disbursements, net:			
Mandatory:			
4090 Budget authority, gross	1	1	1
Financing disbursements:			
4110 Outlays, gross (total)	1	....	....
Offsets against gross financing authority and disbursements:			
Offsetting collections (collected) from:			
4120 Federal sources	....	–1	–1
Additional offsets against financing authority only (total):			
4140 Change in uncollected pymts, Fed sources, unexpired	–1	....	....
4170 Outlays, net (mandatory)	1	....	–1
4180 Budget authority, net (total)	....	....	....
4190 Outlays, net (total)	1	–1	–1

Status of Guaranteed Loans (in millions of dollars)

Identification code 086–4244–0–3–604	2021 actual	2022 est.	2023 est.
Position with respect to appropriations act limitation on commitments:			
2111 Guaranteed loan commitments from current-year authority	19	12	12
2121 Limitation available from carry-forward	....	....	....
2142 Uncommitted loan guarantee limitation	....	....	....
2143 Uncommitted limitation carried forward	....	....	....
2150 Total guaranteed loan commitments	19	12	12
2199 Guaranteed amount of guaranteed loan commitments	19	12	12
Cumulative balance of guaranteed loans outstanding:			
2210 Outstanding, start of year	67	67	70
2231 Disbursements of new guaranteed loans	....	12	12
2251 Repayments and prepayments	....	–9	–11
2263 Adjustments: Terminations for default that result in claim payments	....	....	....
2290 Outstanding, end of year	67	70	71
Memorandum:			
2299 Guaranteed amount of guaranteed loans outstanding, end of year	67	70	71

Balance Sheet (in millions of dollars)

Identification code 086–4244–0–3–604	2020 actual	2021 actual
ASSETS:		
1101 Federal assets: Fund balances with Treasury	1	1
1999 Total assets	1	1

Public and Indian Housing Programs—Continued
Federal Funds—Continued

TITLE VI INDIAN FEDERAL GUARANTEES FINANCING ACCOUNT—Continued
Balance Sheet—Continued

Identification code 086–4244–0–3–604	2020 actual	2021 actual
LIABILITIES:		
2204 Non-Federal liabilities: Liabilities for loan guarantees	1	1
NET POSITION:		
3300 Cumulative results of operations		
4999 Total liabilities and net position	1	1

NATIVE HAWAIIAN HOUSING BLOCK GRANT

For the Native Hawaiian Housing Block Grant program, as authorized under title VIII of the Native American Housing Assistance and Self-Determination Act of 1996 (25 U.S.C. 4221 et seq.), $10,000,000, to remain available until September 30, 2027: Provided, That notwithstanding section 812(b) of such Act, the Department of Hawaiian Home Lands may not invest grant amounts made available under this heading in investment securities and other obligations: Provided further, That amounts made available under this heading in this and prior fiscal years may be used to provide rental assistance to eligible Native Hawaiian families both on and off the Hawaiian Home Lands, notwithstanding any other provision of law.

Note.—A full-year 2022 appropriation for this account was not enacted at the time the Budget was prepared; therefore, the Budget assumes this account is operating under the Continuing Appropriations Act, 2022 (Division A of Public Law 117–43, as amended). The amounts included for 2022 reflect the annualized level provided by the continuing resolution.

Program and Financing (in millions of dollars)

Identification code 086–0235–0–1–604		2021 actual	2022 est.	2023 est.
	Obligations by program activity:			
0001	Native Hawaiian Housing Block Grant	2	2	10
0013	Native Hawaiian Housing Block Grant (ARP Act)	5		
0900	Total new obligations, unexpired accounts (object class 41.0)	7	2	10
	Budgetary resources:			
	Budget authority:			
	Appropriations, discretionary:			
1100	Appropriation	2	2	10
	Appropriations, mandatory:			
1200	Appropriation (ARP Act)	5		
1900	Budget authority (total)	7	2	10
1930	Total budgetary resources available	7	2	10
	Change in obligated balance:			
	Unpaid obligations:			
3000	Unpaid obligations, brought forward, Oct 1	18	17	13
3010	New obligations, unexpired accounts	7	2	10
3020	Outlays (gross)	–8	–6	–5
3050	Unpaid obligations, end of year	17	13	18
	Memorandum (non-add) entries:			
3100	Obligated balance, start of year	18	17	13
3200	Obligated balance, end of year	17	13	18
	Budget authority and outlays, net:			
	Discretionary:			
4000	Budget authority, gross	2	2	10
	Outlays, gross:			
4011	Outlays from discretionary balances	4	5	5
	Mandatory:			
4090	Budget authority, gross	5		
	Outlays, gross:			
4100	Outlays from new mandatory authority	4		
4101	Outlays from mandatory balances		1	
4110	Outlays, gross (total)	4	1	
4180	Budget authority, net (total)	7	2	10
4190	Outlays, net (total)	8	6	5

The Native Hawaiian Housing Block Grant (NHHBG) program provides funds to carry out affordable housing activities, including rental assistance both on and off the Hawaiian home lands, for eligible low-income Native Hawaiian families. The Hawaiian Department of Hawaiian Home Lands is the sole recipient of NHHBG funds. The Budget requests $10 million for this program.

INDIAN HOUSING LOAN GUARANTEE FUND PROGRAM ACCOUNT
(INCLUDING CANCELLATIONS)

For the cost of guaranteed loans, as authorized by section 184 of the Housing and Community Development Act of 1992 (12 U.S.C. 1715z–13a), $5,521,000, to remain available until expended: Provided, That such costs, including the costs of modifying such loans, shall be as defined in section 502 of the Congressional Budget Act of 1974: Provided further, That funds made available in this and prior Acts for the cost of guaranteed loans, as authorized by section 184 of the Housing and Community Development Act of 1992 (12 U.S.C. 1715z–13a), that are unobligated, including recaptures and carryover, are available to subsidize total loan principal, any part of which is to be guaranteed, up to $1,400,000,000, to remain available until September 30, 2024: Provided further, That any remaining loan guarantee limitation authorized under this heading in fiscal year 2020 or prior fiscal years is hereby permanently cancelled: Provided further, That any amounts determined by the Secretary to be unavailable are hereby returned to the General Fund of the Treasury of the United States.

Note.—A full-year 2022 appropriation for this account was not enacted at the time the Budget was prepared; therefore, the Budget assumes this account is operating under the Continuing Appropriations Act, 2022 (Division A of Public Law 117–43, as amended). The amounts included for 2022 reflect the annualized level provided by the continuing resolution.

Program and Financing (in millions of dollars)

Identification code 086–0223–0–1–371		2021 actual	2022 est.	2023 est.
	Obligations by program activity:			
	Credit program obligations:			
0702	Loan guarantee subsidy	3	3	4
0707	Reestimates of loan guarantee subsidy	17		
0708	Interest on reestimates of loan guarantee subsidy	3		
0709	Administrative expenses		1	1
0900	Total new obligations, unexpired accounts (object class 41.0)	23	4	5
	Budgetary resources:			
	Unobligated balance:			
1000	Unobligated balance brought forward, Oct 1	9	8	6
1029	Other balances withdrawn to Treasury			–2
1070	Unobligated balance (total)	9	8	4
	Budget authority:			
	Appropriations, discretionary:			
1100	Appropriation	2	2	6
	Appropriations, mandatory:			
1200	Appropriation	20		
1900	Budget authority (total)	22	2	6
1930	Total budgetary resources available	31	10	10
	Memorandum (non-add) entries:			
1941	Unexpired unobligated balance, end of year	8	6	5
	Change in obligated balance:			
	Unpaid obligations:			
3000	Unpaid obligations, brought forward, Oct 1		1	1
3010	New obligations, unexpired accounts	23	4	5
3020	Outlays (gross)	–22	–4	–4
3050	Unpaid obligations, end of year	1	1	2
	Memorandum (non-add) entries:			
3100	Obligated balance, start of year		1	1
3200	Obligated balance, end of year	1	1	2
	Budget authority and outlays, net:			
	Discretionary:			
4000	Budget authority, gross	2	2	6
	Outlays, gross:			
4010	Outlays from new discretionary authority			1
4011	Outlays from discretionary balances	2	4	3
4020	Outlays, gross (total)	2	4	4
	Mandatory:			
4090	Budget authority, gross	20		
	Outlays, gross:			
4100	Outlays from new mandatory authority	20		
4180	Budget authority, net (total)	22	2	6
4190	Outlays, net (total)	22	4	4

DEPARTMENT OF HOUSING AND URBAN DEVELOPMENT

Public and Indian Housing Programs—Continued
Federal Funds—Continued

569

Summary of Budget Authority and Outlays (in millions of dollars)

	2021 actual	2022 est.	2023 est.
Enacted/requested:			
Budget Authority	22	2	6
Outlays	22	4	4
Legislative proposal, not subject to PAYGO:			
Outlays			1
Total:			
Budget Authority	22	2	6
Outlays	22	4	5

Summary of Loan Levels, Subsidy Budget Authority and Outlays by Program (in millions of dollars)

Identification code 086–0223–0–1–371		2021 actual	2022 est.	2023 est.
	Guaranteed loan levels supportable by subsidy budget authority:			
215001	Indian Housing Loan Guarantee	863	823	840
	Guaranteed loan subsidy (in percent):			
232001	Indian Housing Loan Guarantee	0.30	0.33	0.50
232999	Weighted average subsidy rate	0.30	0.33	0.50
	Guaranteed loan subsidy budget authority:			
233001	Indian Housing Loan Guarantee	3	3	4
	Guaranteed loan subsidy outlays:			
234001	Indian Housing Loan Guarantee	2	3	3
	Guaranteed loan reestimates:			
235001	Indian Housing Loan Guarantee	3	–65	
	Administrative expense data:			
3510	Budget authority	1	1	1

The Indian Housing Loan Guarantee program (also known as the Section 184 program) provides access to private mortgage financing for Native Americans, Indian Tribes and their tribally-designated housing entities that could otherwise face barriers due to the unique legal status of Indian trust land. The Budget requests $5.5 million in program funds to support up to $1.4 billion in new loan guarantees for this program.

INDIAN HOUSING LOAN GUARANTEE FUND PROGRAM ACCOUNT

(Legislative proposal, not subject to PAYGO)

Program and Financing (in millions of dollars)

Identification code 086–0223–2–1–371		2021 actual	2022 est.	2023 est.
	Obligations by program activity:			
	Credit program obligations:			
0702	Loan guarantee subsidy			2
0900	Total new obligations, unexpired accounts (object class 41.0)			2
	Memorandum (non-add) entries:			
1941	Unexpired unobligated balance, end of year			–2
	Change in obligated balance:			
	Unpaid obligations:			
3010	New obligations, unexpired accounts			2
3020	Outlays (gross)			–1
3050	Unpaid obligations, end of year			1
	Memorandum (non-add) entries:			
3200	Obligated balance, end of year			1
	Budget authority and outlays, net:			
	Discretionary:			
	Outlays, gross:			
4011	Outlays from discretionary balances			1
4180	Budget authority, net (total)			
4190	Outlays, net (total)			1

Summary of Loan Levels, Subsidy Budget Authority and Outlays by Program (in millions of dollars)

Identification code 086–0223–2–1–371		2021 actual	2022 est.	2023 est.
	Guaranteed loan levels supportable by subsidy budget authority:			
215001	Indian Housing Loan Guarantee			264
	Guaranteed loan subsidy (in percent):			
232001	Indian Housing Loan Guarantee			0.50
	Guaranteed loan subsidy budget authority:			
233001	Indian Housing Loan Guarantee			2
	Guaranteed loan subsidy outlays:			
234001	Indian Housing Loan Guarantee			1

The Budget reflects additional obligations and outlays associated with a legislative proposal to amend the Section 184 authorizing statute to permit HUD to expand the program service area to all Tribal members regardless of where they purchase a home.

INDIAN HOUSING LOAN GUARANTEE FUND FINANCING ACCOUNT

Program and Financing (in millions of dollars)

Identification code 086–4104–0–3–604		2021 actual	2022 est.	2023 est.
	Obligations by program activity:			
	Credit program obligations:			
0711	Default claim payments on principal	9	20	30
0715	Property preservation costs		1	1
0742	Downward reestimates paid to receipt accounts	13	58	
0743	Interest on downward reestimates	4	7	
0900	Total new obligations, unexpired accounts	26	86	31
	Budgetary resources:			
	Unobligated balance:			
1000	Unobligated balance brought forward, Oct 1	153	144	93
1020	Adjustment of unobligated bal brought forward, Oct 1	–12		
1023	Unobligated balances applied to repay debt	–18		
1070	Unobligated balance (total)	123	144	93
	Financing authority:			
	Spending authority from offsetting collections, mandatory:			
1800	Collected	46	35	35
1801	Change in uncollected payments, Federal sources	1		
1850	Spending auth from offsetting collections, mand (total)	47	35	35
1900	Budget authority (total)	47	35	35
1930	Total budgetary resources available	170	179	128
	Memorandum (non-add) entries:			
1941	Unexpired unobligated balance, end of year	144	93	97
	Change in obligated balance:			
	Unpaid obligations:			
3000	Unpaid obligations, brought forward, Oct 1	1		
3010	New obligations, unexpired accounts	26	86	31
3020	Outlays (gross)	–27	–86	–31
	Uncollected payments:			
3060	Uncollected pymts, Fed sources, brought forward, Oct 1	–1	–2	–2
3070	Change in uncollected pymts, Fed sources, unexpired	–1		
3090	Uncollected pymts, Fed sources, end of year	–2	–2	–2
	Memorandum (non-add) entries:			
3100	Obligated balance, start of year		–2	–2
3200	Obligated balance, end of year	–2	–2	–2
	Financing authority and disbursements, net:			
	Mandatory:			
4090	Budget authority, gross	47	35	35
	Financing disbursements:			
4110	Outlays, gross (total)	27	86	31
	Offsets against gross financing authority and disbursements:			
	Offsetting collections (collected) from:			
4120	Federal sources: Payments from program account	–21	–4	–4
4122	Interest on uninvested funds	–4		
4123	Non-Federal sources	–21	–31	–31
4130	Offsets against gross budget authority and outlays (total)	–46	–35	–35
	Additional offsets against financing authority only (total):			
4140	Change in uncollected pymts, Fed sources, unexpired	–1		
4170	Outlays, net (mandatory)	–19	51	–4
4180	Budget authority, net (total)			
4190	Outlays, net (total)	–19	51	–4

Status of Guaranteed Loans (in millions of dollars)

Identification code 086–4104–0–3–604		2021 actual	2022 est.	2023 est.
	Position with respect to appropriations act limitation on commitments:			
2111	Guaranteed loan commitments from current-year authority	863	823	840
2121	Limitation available from carry-forward			
2143	Uncommitted limitation carried forward			
2150	Total guaranteed loan commitments	863	823	840
2199	Guaranteed amount of guaranteed loan commitments	863	823	840
	Cumulative balance of guaranteed loans outstanding:			
2210	Outstanding, start of year	4,702	4,362	4,938

Public and Indian Housing Programs—Continued
Federal Funds—Continued

INDIAN HOUSING LOAN GUARANTEE FUND FINANCING ACCOUNT—Continued

Status of Guaranteed Loans—Continued

Identification code 086–4104–0–3–604	2021 actual	2022 est.	2023 est.
2231 Disbursements of new guaranteed loans	692	800	800
2251 Repayments and prepayments	–1,023	–204	–220
Adjustments:			
2263 Terminations for default that result in claim payments	–9	–20	–27
2264 Other adjustments, net			
2290 Outstanding, end of year	4,362	4,938	5,491
Memorandum:			
2299 Guaranteed amount of guaranteed loans outstanding, end of year	4,362	4,838	5,291

Balance Sheet (in millions of dollars)

Identification code 086–4104–0–3–604	2020 actual	2021 actual
ASSETS:		
Federal assets:		
1101 Fund balances with Treasury	141	141
Investments in U.S. securities:		
1106 Receivables, net	1	1
1504 Net value of assets related to post-1991 acquired defaulted guaranteed loans receivable: Foreclosed property	7	9
1999 Total assets	149	151
LIABILITIES:		
2103 Federal liabilities: Debt Payable to Treasury	19	
Non-Federal liabilities:		
2201 Accounts payable		
2204 Liabilities for loan guarantees	122	141
2207 Unearned revenues and advances	7	9
2999 Total liabilities	148	150
NET POSITION:		
3300 Cumulative results of operations	1	1
4999 Total liabilities and net position	149	151

INDIAN HOUSING LOAN GUARANTEE FUND FINANCING ACCOUNT

(Legislative proposal, not subject to PAYGO)

Program and Financing (in millions of dollars)

Identification code 086–4104–2–3–604	2021 actual	2022 est.	2023 est.
Budgetary resources:			
Financing authority:			
Spending authority from offsetting collections, mandatory:			
1800 Collected			1
1900 Budget authority (total)			1
1930 Total budgetary resources available			1
Memorandum (non-add) entries:			
1941 Unexpired unobligated balance, end of year			1
Financing authority and disbursements, net:			
Mandatory:			
4090 Budget authority, gross			1
Offsets against gross financing authority and disbursements:			
Offsetting collections (collected) from:			
4120 Federal sources: Payments from program account			–1
4180 Budget authority, net (total)			
4190 Outlays, net (total)			–1

Status of Guaranteed Loans (in millions of dollars)

Identification code 086–4104–2–3–604	2021 actual	2022 est.	2023 est.
Position with respect to appropriations act limitation on commitments:			
2111 Guaranteed loan commitments from current-year authority			264
2121 Limitation available from carry-forward			
2143 Uncommitted limitation carried forward			
2150 Total guaranteed loan commitments			264
2199 Guaranteed amount of guaranteed loan commitments			264
Cumulative balance of guaranteed loans outstanding:			
2210 Outstanding, start of year			
2231 Disbursements of new guaranteed loans			164
2251 Repayments and prepayments			

Adjustments:			
2263 Terminations for default that result in claim payments			
2264 Other adjustments, net			
2290 Outstanding, end of year			164
Memorandum:			
2299 Guaranteed amount of guaranteed loans outstanding, end of year			

NATIVE HAWAIIAN HOUSING LOAN GUARANTEE FUND PROGRAM ACCOUNT

(INCLUDING CANCELLATIONS)

New commitments to guarantee loans, as authorized by section 184A of the Housing and Community Development Act of 1992 (12 U.S.C. 1715z–13b), any part of which is to be guaranteed, shall not exceed $28,000,000 in total loan principal, to remain available until September 30, 2024: Provided, That the Secretary may enter into commitments to guarantee loans used for refinancing: Provided further, That any unobligated balances, including recaptures and carryover, remaining from amounts made available under this heading in prior Acts and any remaining loan guarantee limitation associated with such amounts in such prior Acts are hereby permanently cancelled.

Note.—A full-year 2022 appropriation for this account was not enacted at the time the Budget was prepared; therefore, the Budget assumes this account is operating under the Continuing Appropriations Act, 2022 (Division A of Public Law 117–43, as amended). The amounts included for 2022 reflect the annualized level provided by the continuing resolution.

Program and Financing (in millions of dollars)

Identification code 086–0233–0–1–371	2021 actual	2022 est.	2023 est.
Obligations by program activity:			
Credit program obligations:			
0708 Interest on reestimates of loan guarantee subsidy	1		
0900 Total new obligations, unexpired accounts (object class 41.0)	1		
Budgetary resources:			
Unobligated balance:			
1000 Unobligated balance brought forward, Oct 1	6	6	6
Budget authority:			
Appropriations, discretionary:			
1131 Unobligated balance of appropriations permanently reduced			–6
Appropriations, mandatory:			
1200 Appropriation	1		
1900 Budget authority (total)	1		–6
1930 Total budgetary resources available	7	6	
Memorandum (non-add) entries:			
1941 Unexpired unobligated balance, end of year	6	6	
Change in obligated balance:			
Unpaid obligations:			
3010 New obligations, unexpired accounts	1		
3020 Outlays (gross)	–1		
Budget authority and outlays, net:			
Discretionary:			
4000 Budget authority, gross			–6
Mandatory:			
4090 Budget authority, gross	1		
Outlays, gross:			
4100 Outlays from new mandatory authority	1		
4180 Budget authority, net (total)	1		–6
4190 Outlays, net (total)	1		

Summary of Loan Levels, Subsidy Budget Authority and Outlays by Program (in millions of dollars)

Identification code 086–0233–0–1–371	2021 actual	2022 est.	2023 est.
Guaranteed loan levels supportable by subsidy budget authority:			
215001 Native Hawaiian Housing Loan Guarantees	19	19	20
Guaranteed loan subsidy (in percent):			
232001 Native Hawaiian Housing Loan Guarantees	–.15	–.19	–.35
232999 Weighted average subsidy rate	–.15	–.19	–.35
Guaranteed loan reestimates:			
235001 Native Hawaiian Housing Loan Guarantees	–2	–2	

DEPARTMENT OF HOUSING AND URBAN DEVELOPMENT

The Native Hawaiian Housing Loan Guarantee program (also known as the Section 184A program) provides access to private mortgage financing to Native Hawaiian families who are eligible to reside on Hawaiian home lands and would otherwise face barriers to acquiring such financing because of the unique legal status of the Hawaiian home lands. Since 2017, this program has operated on a negative subsidy basis, but the Budget requests $28 million in loan guarantee commitment authority to continue supporting these loans.

NATIVE HAWAIIAN HOUSING LOAN GUARANTEE FUND FINANCING ACCOUNT

Program and Financing (in millions of dollars)

Identification code 086–4351–0–3–371	2021 actual	2022 est.	2023 est.
Obligations by program activity:			
Credit program obligations:			
0711 Default claim payments on principal		2	2
0742 Downward reestimates paid to receipt accounts	3	2	
0743 Interest on downward reestimates		1	
0900 Total new obligations, unexpired accounts	3	5	2
Budgetary resources:			
Unobligated balance:			
1000 Unobligated balance brought forward, Oct 1	4	2	
1023 Unobligated balances applied to repay debt	–1		
1070 Unobligated balance (total)	3	2	
Financing authority:			
Borrowing authority, mandatory:			
1400 Borrowing authority			3
Spending authority from offsetting collections, mandatory:			
1800 Collected	2		2
1900 Budget authority (total)	2	3	2
1930 Total budgetary resources available	5	5	2
Memorandum (non-add) entries:			
1941 Unexpired unobligated balance, end of year	2		
Change in obligated balance:			
Unpaid obligations:			
3010 New obligations, unexpired accounts	3	5	2
3020 Outlays (gross)	–3	–5	–2
Financing authority and disbursements, net:			
Mandatory:			
4090 Budget authority, gross	2	3	2
Financing disbursements:			
4110 Outlays, gross (total)	3	5	2
Offsets against gross financing authority and disbursements:			
Offsetting collections (collected) from:			
4120 Federal sources	–2		
4123 Non-Federal sources			–2
4130 Offsets against gross budget authority and outlays (total)	–2		–2
4160 Budget authority, net (mandatory)			3
4170 Outlays, net (mandatory)	1	5	
4180 Budget authority, net (total)			3
4190 Outlays, net (total)	1	5	

Status of Guaranteed Loans (in millions of dollars)

Identification code 086–4351–0–3–371	2021 actual	2022 est.	2023 est.
Position with respect to appropriations act limitation on commitments:			
2111 Guaranteed loan commitments from current-year authority			20
2121 Limitation available from carry-forward	200	181	
2143 Uncommitted limitation carried forward	–181	–162	
2150 Total guaranteed loan commitments	19	19	20
2199 Guaranteed amount of guaranteed loan commitments	19	19	20
Cumulative balance of guaranteed loans outstanding:			
2210 Outstanding, start of year	115	112	120
2231 Disbursements of new guaranteed loans	16	17	17
2251 Repayments and prepayments	–19	–6	–7
Adjustments:			
2263 Terminations for default that result in claim payments		–3	–2
2264 Other adjustments, net			
2290 Outstanding, end of year	112	120	128
Memorandum:			
2299 Guaranteed amount of guaranteed loans outstanding, end of year	112	120	128

Balance Sheet (in millions of dollars)

Identification code 086–4351–0–3–371	2020 actual	2021 actual
ASSETS:		
1101 Federal assets: Fund balances with Treasury	4	1
1504 Net value of assets related to post-1991 acquired defaulted guaranteed loans receivable: Foreclosed property	2	3
1999 Total assets	6	4
LIABILITIES:		
2103 Federal liabilities: Debt payable to Treasury	1	
2204 Non-Federal liabilities: Liabilities for loan guarantees	5	4
2999 Total liabilities	6	4
NET POSITION:		
3300 Cumulative results of operations		
4999 Total liabilities and net position	6	4

COMMUNITY PLANNING AND DEVELOPMENT

Federal Funds

COMMUNITY DEVELOPMENT FUND

For carrying out the community development block grant program under title I of the Housing and Community Development Act of 1974, as amended (42 U.S.C. 5301 et seq.) (in this heading "the Act"), $3,770,000,000, to remain available until September 30, 2025, unless otherwise specified: Provided, That unless explicitly provided for under this heading, not to exceed 20 percent of any grant made with funds made available under this heading shall be expended for planning and management development and administration: Provided further, That a metropolitan city, urban county, unit of general local government, or insular area that directly or indirectly receives funds under this heading may not sell, trade, or otherwise transfer all or any portion of such funds to another such entity in exchange for any other funds, credits, or non-Federal considerations, but shall use such funds for activities eligible under title I of the Act: Provided further, That notwithstanding section 105(e)(1) of the Act, no funds made available under this heading may be provided to a for-profit entity for an economic development project under section 105(a)(17) unless such project has been evaluated and selected in accordance with guidelines required under subsection (e)(2) of section 105: Provided further, That of the amount provided under this heading, $195,000,000 shall be for up to 100 grants to state and local governments for additional activities under such title I for the identification and removal of barriers to revitalization faced by underserved communities in deteriorating or deteriorated neighborhoods with the greatest need, as determined by the Secretary: Provided further, That the Secretary shall establish by notice a formula identifying the neighborhoods eligible for such additional assistance, based on factors that may include the number or relative share of persons in poverty, the number or relative share of persons in poverty in areas with concentrated poverty or concentrated vacancy, and other factors: Provided further, That a state or local government responsible for carrying out title I activities within the eligible neighborhood shall be given the opportunity to apply for such assistance: Provided further, That such amounts shall not be subject to the limitation in the first proviso: Provided further, That in administering such amounts the Secretary may waive or specify alternative requirements to sections 105 and 106 of the Act (42 U.S.C. 5305 and 5306) except for requirements related to fair housing, nondiscrimination, labor standards, the environment, and requirements that activities benefit persons of low- and moderate-income, upon a finding that such a waiver is necessary to expedite or facilitate the use of such amount: Provided further, That of the amount provided under this heading, $25,000,000 shall be for activities authorized under section 8071 of the SUPPORT for Patients and Communities Act (Public Law 115–271): Provided further, That the funds allocated pursuant to the preceding proviso shall not adversely affect the amount of any formula assistance received by a State under this heading: Provided further, That the Secretary shall allocate the funds for such activities based on the notice establishing the funding formula published in 84 FR 16027 (April 17, 2019).

Note.—A full-year 2022 appropriation for this account was not enacted at the time the Budget was prepared; therefore, the Budget assumes this account is operating under the Continuing Appropriations Act, 2022 (Division A of Public Law 117–43, as amended). The amounts included for 2022 reflect the annualized level provided by the continuing resolution.

COMMUNITY DEVELOPMENT FUND—Continued

COMMUNITY DEVELOPMENT FUND

[(INCLUDING TRANSFERS OF FUNDS)]

[For an additional amount for "Community Development Fund", $5,000,000,000, to remain available until expended, for necessary expenses for activities authorized under title I of the Housing and Community Development Act of 1974 (42 U.S.C. 5301 et seq.) related to disaster relief, long-term recovery, restoration of infrastructure and housing, economic revitalization, and mitigation, in the most impacted and distressed areas resulting from a major disaster that occurred in 2020 or 2021 pursuant to the Robert T. Stafford Disaster Relief and Emergency Assistance Act (42 U.S.C. 5121 et seq.): *Provided*, That amounts made available under this heading in this Act shall be awarded directly to the State, unit of general local government, or Indian tribe (as such term is defined in section 102 of the Housing and Community Development Act of 1974 (42 U.S.C. 5302)) at the discretion of the Secretary: *Provided further*, That the Secretary shall allocate, using the best available data, an amount equal to the total estimate for unmet needs for qualifying disasters under this heading in this Act: *Provided further*, That any final allocation for the total estimate for unmet need made available under the preceding proviso shall include an additional amount of 15 percent of such estimate for additional mitigation: *Provided further*, That of the amounts made available under this heading in this Act, no less than $1,610,000,000 shall be allocated for major declared disasters that occurred in 2020 within 30 days of the date of enactment of this Act: *Provided further*, That the Secretary shall not prohibit the use of amounts made available under this heading in this Act for non-Federal share as authorized by section 105(a)(9) of the Housing and Community Development Act of 1974 (42 U.S.C. 5305(a)(9)): *Provided further*, That of the amounts made available under this heading in this Act, grantees may establish grant programs to assist small businesses for working capital purposes to aid in recovery: *Provided further*, That as a condition of drawing funds for any activity other than general administration, the Secretary shall certify in advance that such grantee has in place proficient financial controls and procurement processes and has established adequate procedures to prevent any duplication of benefits as defined by section 312 of the Robert T. Stafford Disaster Relief and Emergency Assistance Act (42 U.S.C. 5155), to ensure timely expenditure of funds, to maintain comprehensive websites regarding all disaster recovery activities assisted with amounts made available under this heading in this Act, and to detect and prevent waste, fraud, and abuse of funds: *Provided further*, That with respect to any such duplication of benefits, the Secretary shall act in accordance with section 1210 of Public Law 115–254 (132 Stat. 3442) and section 312 of the Robert T. Stafford Disaster Relief and Emergency Assistance Act (42 U.S.C. 5155): *Provided further*, That the Secretary shall require grantees to maintain on a public website information containing common reporting criteria established by the Department that permits individuals and entities awaiting assistance and the general public to see how all grant funds are used, including copies of all relevant procurement documents, including grantee administrative contracts and details of ongoing procurement processes, as determined by the Secretary: *Provided further*, That prior to the obligation of funds a grantee shall submit a plan to the Secretary for approval detailing the proposed use of all funds, including criteria for eligibility and how the use of these funds will address long-term recovery and restoration of infrastructure and housing, economic revitalization, and mitigation in the most impacted and distressed areas: *Provided further*, That such funds may not be used for activities reimbursable by, or for which funds are made available by, the Federal Emergency Management Agency or the Army Corps of Engineers: *Provided further*, That funds allocated under this heading in this Act shall not be considered relevant to the non-disaster formula allocations made pursuant to section 106 of the Housing and Community Development Act of 1974 (42 U.S.C. 5306): *Provided further*, That a State, unit of general local government, or Indian tribe may use up to 5 percent of its allocation for administrative costs related to a major disaster under this heading in this Act and for the same purposes in prior and future Acts and such amounts shall be available for any eligible administrative costs without regard to a particular disaster: *Provided further*, That in administering the amounts made available under this heading in this Act, the Secretary of Housing and Urban Development may waive, or specify alternative requirements for, any provision of any statute or regulation that the Secretary administers in connection with the obligation by the Secretary or the use by the recipient of these funds (except for requirements related to fair housing, nondiscrimination, labor standards, and the environment), if the Secretary finds that good cause exists for the waiver or alternative requirement and such waiver or alternative requirement would not be inconsistent with the overall purpose of title I of the Housing and Community Development Act of 1974: *Provided further*, That, notwithstanding the preceding proviso, recipients of funds provided under this heading in this Act that use such funds to supplement Federal assistance provided under section 402, 403, 404, 406, 407, 408(c)(4), or 502 of the Robert T. Stafford Disaster Relief and Emergency Assistance Act (42 U.S.C. 5121 et seq.) may adopt, without review or public comment, any environmental review, approval, or permit performed by a Federal agency, and such adoption shall satisfy the responsibilities of the recipient with respect to such environmental review, approval or permit: *Provided further*, That, notwithstanding section 104(g)(2) of the Housing and Community Development Act of 1974 (42 U.S.C. 5304(g)(2)), the Secretary or a State may, upon receipt of a request for release of funds and certification, immediately approve the release of funds for an activity or project assisted under this heading in this Act if the recipient has adopted an environmental review, approval or permit under the preceding proviso or the activity or project is categorically excluded from review under the National Environmental Policy Act of 1969 (42 U.S.C. 4321 et seq.): *Provided further*, That the Secretary shall publish via notice in the Federal Register or on the website of the Department any waiver, or alternative requirement, to any statute or regulation that the Secretary administers pursuant to title I of the Housing and Community Development Act of 1974 no later than 5 days before the effective date of such waiver or alternative requirement: *Provided further*, That the Secretary is authorized to approve the use of amounts made available under this heading in this Act or a prior or future Act for activities authorized under title I of the Housing and Community Development Act of 1974 (42 U.S.C. 5301 et seq.) related to unmet recovery needs in the most impacted and distressed areas resulting from a major disaster in this Act or in a prior or future Act to be used interchangeably and without limitation for the same activities in the most impacted and distressed areas resulting from other major disasters assisted under this Act or a prior or future Act when such areas overlap and when the use of the funds will address unmet recovery needs of both disasters: *Provided further*, That, until the Secretary publishes a Federal Register Notice establishing the requirements for the previous proviso, grantees that received grants under the same heading for 2017, 2018 or 2019 disasters may submit for approval revised plans for the use of funds related to those major disasters to expand the eligible beneficiaries of existing programs contained in such previously approved plans to include those impacted by disasters in 2020 or 2021: *Provided further*, That of the amounts made available under this heading in this Act, up to $7,000,000 shall be made available for capacity building and technical assistance, including assistance on contracting and procurement, to support States, units of general local government, or Indian tribes, and subrecipients that receive allocations for disaster recovery pursuant to the authority under this heading in this Act and allocations for disaster recovery in any prior or future Acts: *Provided further*, That of the amounts made available under this heading in this Act, up to $5,500,000 shall be transferred to "Department of Housing and Urban Development—Program Office Salaries and Expenses—Community Planning and Development" for necessary costs, including information technology costs, of administering and overseeing the obligation and expenditure of amounts made available under the heading "Community Development Fund" in this Act or any prior or future Act that makes amounts available for purposes related to major disasters under such heading.] *(Disaster Relief Supplemental Appropriations Act, 2022.)*

Program and Financing (in millions of dollars)

Identification code 086–0162–0–1–451		2021 actual	2022 est.	2023 est.
	Obligations by program activity:			
0001	Community Development Formula Grants	4,175	3,461	4,194
0011	Disaster Assistance	23,284	5,072	2,943
0015	Recovery Housing (SUPPORT)	8	45	25
0016	Community Development Formula Grants (CARES Act)	3,187	45	....
0017	Community Development Grants Technical Assistance (CARES Act)	5	....	....
0018	Historically Underserved Communities	....	....	138
0900	Total new obligations, unexpired accounts (object class 41.0)	30,659	8,623	7,300
	Budgetary resources:			
	Unobligated balance:			
1000	Unobligated balance brought forward, Oct 1	30,935	3,751	3,597
1020	Adjustment of unobligated bal brought forward, Oct 1	–57	....	....
1021	Recoveries of prior year unpaid obligations	1	....	....
1033	Recoveries of prior year paid obligations	57	....	....
1070	Unobligated balance (total)	30,936	3,751	3,597
	Budget authority:			
	Appropriations, discretionary:			
1100	Appropriation	3,475	3,475	3,770
1100	Appropriation	....	5,000	....
1120	Appropriations transferred to other acct [086–0338]	....	–6	....
1160	Appropriation, discretionary (total)	3,475	8,469	3,770
1930	Total budgetary resources available	34,411	12,220	7,367
	Memorandum (non-add) entries:			
1940	Unobligated balance expiring	–1	....	....

DEPARTMENT OF HOUSING AND URBAN DEVELOPMENT

Community Planning and Development—Continued
Federal Funds—Continued

573

1941	Unexpired unobligated balance, end of year	3,751	3,597	67
	Change in obligated balance:			
	Unpaid obligations:			
3000	Unpaid obligations, brought forward, Oct 1	26,381	50,259	48,114
3001	Adjustments to unpaid obligations, brought forward, Oct 1	67		
3010	New obligations, unexpired accounts	30,659	8,623	7,300
3020	Outlays (gross)	−6,826	−10,768	−10,942
3040	Recoveries of prior year unpaid obligations, unexpired	−1		
3041	Recoveries of prior year unpaid obligations, expired	−21		
3050	Unpaid obligations, end of year	50,259	48,114	44,472
	Memorandum (non-add) entries:			
3100	Obligated balance, start of year	26,448	50,259	48,114
3200	Obligated balance, end of year	50,259	48,114	44,472
	Budget authority and outlays, net:			
	Discretionary:			
4000	Budget authority, gross	3,475	8,469	3,770
	Outlays, gross:			
4010	Outlays from new discretionary authority	36	35	38
4011	Outlays from discretionary balances	6,790	10,733	10,904
4020	Outlays, gross (total)	6,826	10,768	10,942
	Offsets against gross budget authority and outlays:			
	Offsetting collections (collected) from:			
4033	Non-Federal sources	−67		
	Additional offsets against gross budget authority only:			
4052	Offsetting collections credited to expired accounts	10		
4053	Recoveries of prior year paid obligations, unexpired accounts	57		
4060	Additional offsets against budget authority only (total)	67		
4070	Budget authority, net (discretionary)	3,475	8,469	3,770
4080	Outlays, net (discretionary)	6,759	10,768	10,942
4180	Budget authority, net (total)	3,475	8,469	3,770
4190	Outlays, net (total)	6,759	10,768	10,942

The Community Development Fund account contains the following programs:

Community Development Block Grant (CDBG).—The CDBG program provides formula grants to States, local governments, and Insular Areas to benefit mainly low- to moderate-income persons, and support a wide range of community and economic development activities, such as public infrastructure improvements (which account for approximately 36 percent of all CDBG funds), housing rehabilitation and construction (approximately 24 percent of funds), job creation and retention, and public services. After $7 million is allocated to Insular Areas, seventy percent of CDBG formula grants are distributed to mainly urban areas (entitlement communities), and 30 percent are distributed to States (non-entitlement communities). The Budget requests a total of $3.77 billion, of which $3.55 billion is funding for the CDBG program, and $195 million is for targeted CDBG activities aimed at removing barriers to revitalization in approximately 100 of the most underserved neighborhoods in the United States.

Indian Community Development Block Grant (ICDBG).—The Budget requests ICDBG in the Native American Programs account.

CDBG Disaster Recovery (CDBG-DR).—This account also contains a substantial amount of appropriated CDBG-DR funding provided to communities impacted by major disasters.

Recovery Housing (SUPPORT).—The Budget requests $25 million for activities authorized under the SUPPORT for Patients and Communities Act. This formula program is allocated to states and the District of Columbia to provide temporary housing for individuals recovering from substance use disorders, including opioids.

COMMUNITY DEVELOPMENT LOAN GUARANTEES PROGRAM ACCOUNT

Subject to section 502 of the Congressional Budget Act of 1974 (2 U.S.C. 661a), during fiscal year 2023, commitments to guarantee loans under section 108 of the Housing and Community Development Act of 1974 (42 U.S.C. 5308), any part of which is guaranteed, shall not exceed a total principal amount of $300,000,000, notwithstanding any aggregate limitation on outstanding obligations guaranteed in subsection (k) of such section 108: Provided, That the Secretary shall collect fees from borrowers, notwithstanding subsection (m) of such section 108, to result in a credit subsidy cost of zero for guaranteeing such loans, and any such fees shall be collected in accordance with section 502(7) of the Congressional Budget Act of 1974: Provided further, That such commitment authority funded by fees may be used to guarantee, or make commitments to guarantee, notes or other obligations issued by any State on behalf of non-entitlement communities in the State in accordance with the requirements of such section 108: Provided further, That any State receiving such a guarantee or commitment under the preceding proviso shall distribute all funds subject to such guarantee to the units of general local government in nonentitlement areas that received the commitment.

Note.—A full-year 2022 appropriation for this account was not enacted at the time the Budget was prepared; therefore, the Budget assumes this account is operating under the Continuing Appropriations Act, 2022 (Division A of Public Law 117–43, as amended). The amounts included for 2022 reflect the annualized level provided by the continuing resolution.

Program and Financing (in millions of dollars)

Identification code 086–0198–0–1–451		2021 actual	2022 est.	2023 est.
	Obligations by program activity:			
	Credit program obligations:			
0707	Reestimates of loan guarantee subsidy		2	
0900	Total new obligations, unexpired accounts (object class 41.0)		2	
	Budgetary resources:			
	Budget authority:			
	Appropriations, mandatory:			
1200	Appropriation		2	
1900	Budget authority (total)		2	
1930	Total budgetary resources available		2	
	Change in obligated balance:			
	Unpaid obligations:			
3010	New obligations, unexpired accounts		2	
3020	Outlays (gross)		−2	
	Budget authority and outlays, net:			
	Mandatory:			
4090	Budget authority, gross		2	
	Outlays, gross:			
4100	Outlays from new mandatory authority		2	
4180	Budget authority, net (total)		2	
4190	Outlays, net (total)		2	

Summary of Loan Levels, Subsidy Budget Authority and Outlays by Program (in millions of dollars)

Identification code 086–0198–0–1–451		2021 actual	2022 est.	2023 est.
	Guaranteed loan levels supportable by subsidy budget authority:			
215003	Section 108 Community Development Loan Guarantee (Fee)	81	200	300
215999	Total loan guarantee levels	81	200	300
	Guaranteed loan subsidy (in percent):			
232003	Section 108 Community Development Loan Guarantee (Fee)	0.00	0.00	0.00
232999	Weighted average subsidy rate	0.00	0.00	0.00
	Guaranteed loan reestimates:			
235001	Section 108 Community Development Loan Guarantee	1	−3	
235003	Section 108 Community Development Loan Guarantee (Fee)	−1	−1	
235999	Total guaranteed loan reestimates		−4	

The Community Development Loan Guarantee Program (Section 108) supports economic development projects, housing rehabilitation, and the rehabilitation, construction, or installation of public facilities for the benefit of low and moderate-income persons or to aid in the prevention or elimination of slums and blight. The Budget requests $300 million in new loan guarantee authority for Section 108 for 2023.

COMMUNITY DEVELOPMENT LOAN GUARANTEES FINANCING ACCOUNT

Program and Financing (in millions of dollars)

Identification code 086–4096–0–3–451		2021 actual	2022 est.	2023 est.
	Obligations by program activity:			
	Credit program obligations:			
0742	Downward reestimates paid to receipt accounts		1	3
0743	Interest on downward reestimates		1	1

COMMUNITY DEVELOPMENT LOAN GUARANTEES FINANCING ACCOUNT—Continued

Program and Financing—Continued

Identification code 086–4096–0–3–451	2021 actual	2022 est.	2023 est.
0900 Total new obligations, unexpired accounts	2	4	....
Budgetary resources:			
Unobligated balance:			
1000 Unobligated balance brought forward, Oct 1	6	7	8
Financing authority:			
Spending authority from offsetting collections, mandatory:			
1800 Collected	3	5	5
1930 Total budgetary resources available	9	12	13
Memorandum (non-add) entries:			
1941 Unexpired unobligated balance, end of year	7	8	13
Change in obligated balance:			
Unpaid obligations:			
3010 New obligations, unexpired accounts	2	4	....
3020 Outlays (gross)	–2	–4	....
Financing authority and disbursements, net:			
Mandatory:			
4090 Budget authority, gross	3	5	5
Financing disbursements:			
4110 Outlays, gross (total)	2	4	....
Offsets against gross financing authority and disbursements:			
Offsetting collections (collected) from:			
4120 Federal Sources: Payments from Program Account	–2	....	....
4123 Non-Federal sources	–1	–5	–5
4130 Offsets against gross budget authority and outlays (total)	–3	–5	–5
4170 Outlays, net (mandatory)	–1	–1	–5
4180 Budget authority, net (total)	....	....	....
4190 Outlays, net (total)	–1	–1	–5

Status of Guaranteed Loans (in millions of dollars)

Identification code 086–4096–0–3–451	2021 actual	2022 est.	2023 est.
Position with respect to appropriations act limitation on commitments:			
2111 Guaranteed loan commitments from current-year authority	81	200	300
2121 Limitation available from carry-forward	....	....	....
2142 Uncommitted loan guarantee limitation	....	....	....
2143 Uncommitted limitation carried forward	....	....	....
2150 Total guaranteed loan commitments	81	200	300
2199 Guaranteed amount of guaranteed loan commitments	81	200	300
Cumulative balance of guaranteed loans outstanding:			
2210 Outstanding, start of year	987	843	769
2231 Disbursements of new guaranteed loans	41	95	145
2251 Repayments and prepayments	–185	–169	–165
2290 Outstanding, end of year	843	769	749
Memorandum:			
2299 Guaranteed amount of guaranteed loans outstanding, end of year	843	769	749

Balance Sheet (in millions of dollars)

Identification code 086–4096–0–3–451	2020 actual	2021 actual
ASSETS:		
1101 Federal assets: Fund balances with Treasury	6	7
1999 Total assets	6	7
LIABILITIES:		
Non-Federal liabilities:		
2204 Liabilities for loan guarantees	3	4
2207 Other	....	....
2999 Total liabilities	3	4
NET POSITION:		
3300 Cumulative results of operations	3	3
4999 Total liabilities and net position	6	7

COMMUNITY DEVELOPMENT LOAN GUARANTEES LIQUIDATING ACCOUNT

Program and Financing (in millions of dollars)

Identification code 086–4097–0–3–451	2021 actual	2022 est.	2023 est.
Change in obligated balance:			
Uncollected payments:			
3060 Uncollected pymts, Fed sources, brought forward, Oct 1	–3	....	....
3061 Adjustments to uncollected pymts, Fed sources, brought forward, Oct 1	3	....	....
4180 Budget authority, net (total)	....	....	....
4190 Outlays, net (total)	....	....	....

Status of Guaranteed Loans (in millions of dollars)

Identification code 086–4097–0–3–451	2021 actual	2022 est.	2023 est.
Cumulative balance of guaranteed loans outstanding:			
2210 Outstanding, start of year	1	....	....
2251 Repayments and prepayments	....	....	....
2264 Adjustments: Other adjustments, net	–1	....	....
2290 Outstanding, end of year	....	....	....
Memorandum:			
2299 Guaranteed amount of guaranteed loans outstanding, end of year	....	....	....

Balance Sheet (in millions of dollars)

Identification code 086–4097–0–3–451	2020 actual	2021 actual
ASSETS:		
Federal assets:		
1101 Fund balances with Treasury	–3	....
Investments in U.S. securities:		
1106 Receivables, net	....	....
1206 Non-Federal assets: Receivables, net	3	....
1605 Accounts receivable from foreclosed property	3	....
1606 Foreclosed property	....	....
1699 Value of assets related to direct loans	3	....
1999 Total assets	3	....

HOME INVESTMENT PARTNERSHIPS PROGRAM

For the HOME Investment Partnerships program, as authorized under title II of the Cranston-Gonzalez National Affordable Housing Act, as amended (42 U.S.C. 12721 et seq.), $1,950,000,000, to remain available until September 30, 2026: Provided, That of the amount made available under this heading, up to $100,000,000 shall be for awards to States and insular areas for assistance to homebuyers as authorized under section 212(a)(1) of such Act (42 U.S.C. 12742(a)(1)), in addition to amounts otherwise available for such purpose: Provided further, That amounts made available under the preceding proviso shall be allocated in the same manner as amounts under this heading, except that amounts that would have been reserved and allocated to units of general local government within the State pursuant to section 217 of such Act (42 U.S.C. 12747) shall be provided to the State: Provided further, That the Secretary may waive or specify alternative requirements for any provision of such Act in connection with the use of amounts made available under the previous two provisos (except for requirements related to fair housing, nondiscrimination, labor standards, and the environment) upon a finding that any such waivers or alternative requirements are necessary to expedite or facilitate the use of amounts awarded pursuant to the preceding provisos: Provided further, That notwithstanding section 231(b) of such Act (42 U.S.C. 12771(b)), all unobligated balances remaining from amounts recaptured pursuant to such section that remain available until expended shall be combined with amounts made available under this heading and allocated in accordance with the formula under section 217(b)(1)(A) of such Act (42 U.S.C. 12747(b)(1)(A)): Provided further, That section 218(g) of such Act (42 U.S.C. 12748(g)) shall not apply with respect to the right of a jurisdiction to draw funds from its HOME Investment Trust Fund that otherwise expired or would expire in 2016, 2017, 2018, 2019, 2020, 2021, 2022, 2023, 2024, or 2025 under that section: Provided further, That section 231(b) of such Act (42 U.S.C. 12771(b)) shall not apply to any uninvested funds that otherwise were deducted or would be deducted from the line of credit in the participating jurisdiction's HOME Investment Trust Fund in 2018, 2019, 2020, 2021, 2022, 2023, 2024, or 2025 under that section.

DEPARTMENT OF HOUSING AND URBAN DEVELOPMENT

Community Planning and Development—Continued
Federal Funds—Continued

Note.—A full-year 2022 appropriation for this account was not enacted at the time the Budget was prepared; therefore, the Budget assumes this account is operating under the Continuing Appropriations Act, 2022 (Division A of Public Law 117–43, as amended). The amounts included for 2022 reflect the annualized level provided by the continuing resolution.

Program and Financing (in millions of dollars)

Identification code 086–0205–0–1–604	2021 actual	2022 est.	2023 est.
Obligations by program activity:			
0001 HOME Investment Partnership Program	1,573	1,247	1,800
0015 Homeless Assistance and Supportive Services Program (ARP)	4,925		
0016 Technical Assistance (ARP)	10	15	
0900 Total new obligations, unexpired accounts (object class 41.0)	6,508	1,262	1,800
Budgetary resources:			
Unobligated balance:			
1000 Unobligated balance brought forward, Oct 1	458	249	337
1020 Adjustment of unobligated bal brought forward, Oct 1	–1		
1021 Recoveries of prior year unpaid obligations	2		
1033 Recoveries of prior year paid obligations	1		
1070 Unobligated balance (total)	460	249	337
Budget authority:			
Appropriations, discretionary:			
1100 Appropriation	1,350	1,350	1,950
Appropriations, mandatory:			
1200 Appropriation	4,950		
1900 Budget authority (total)	6,300	1,350	1,950
1930 Total budgetary resources available	6,760	1,599	2,287
Memorandum (non-add) entries:			
1940 Unobligated balance expiring	–3		
1941 Unexpired unobligated balance, end of year	249	337	487
Change in obligated balance:			
Unpaid obligations:			
3000 Unpaid obligations, brought forward, Oct 1	3,782	9,416	8,711
3001 Adjustments to unpaid obligations, brought forward, Oct	1		
3010 New obligations, unexpired accounts	6,508	1,262	1,800
3020 Outlays (gross)	–864	–1,967	–2,775
3040 Recoveries of prior year unpaid obligations, unexpired	–2		
3041 Recoveries of prior year unpaid obligations, expired	–9		
3050 Unpaid obligations, end of year	9,416	8,711	7,736
Memorandum (non-add) entries:			
3100 Obligated balance, start of year	3,783	9,416	8,711
3200 Obligated balance, end of year	9,416	8,711	7,736
Budget authority and outlays, net:			
Discretionary:			
4000 Budget authority, gross	1,350	1,350	1,950
Outlays, gross:			
4010 Outlays from new discretionary authority	1	7	10
4011 Outlays from discretionary balances	863	1,316	1,428
4020 Outlays, gross (total)	864	1,323	1,438
Offsets against gross budget authority and outlays:			
Offsetting collections (collected) from:			
4033 Non-Federal sources	–1		
Additional offsets against gross budget authority only:			
4053 Recoveries of prior year paid obligations, unexpired accounts	1		
4060 Additional offsets against budget authority only (total)	1		
4070 Budget authority, net (discretionary)	1,350	1,350	1,950
4080 Outlays, net (discretionary)	863	1,323	1,438
Mandatory:			
4090 Budget authority, gross	4,950		
Outlays, gross:			
4101 Outlays from mandatory balances		644	1,337
4180 Budget authority, net (total)	6,300	1,350	1,950
4190 Outlays, net (total)	863	1,967	2,775

The Budget requests $1.95 billion for the HOME Investment Partnerships program (HOME). The HOME program provides annual formula grant assistance to States and units of local government to increase the supply of affordable housing and expand homeownership for low-income persons through the acquisition, new construction, and rehabilitation of affordable renter- and owner-occupied housing, as well as the provision of tenant-based rental assistance. Over time, the requested HOME funding is estimated to result in the production of approximately 41,000 units of affordable housing and support over 15,000 low-income households with tenant-based rental assistance. In addition, the request includes a $100 million set-aside for a FirstHOME Downpayment initiative to States and insular areas to better ensure sustainable homeownership.

HOMELESS ASSISTANCE GRANTS

For assistance under title IV of the McKinney-Vento Homeless Assistance Act (42 U.S.C. 11360 et seq.), $3,576,000,000, to remain available until September 30, 2025: Provided, That of the amounts made available under this heading—

(1) not less than $290,000,000 shall be for the Emergency Solutions Grants program authorized under subtitle B of such title IV (42 U.S.C. 11371 et seq.) ;

(2) up to $3,197,000,000 shall be for the Continuum of Care program authorized under subtitle C of such title IV (42 U.S.C. 11381 et seq.) and the Rural Housing Stability Assistance programs authorized under subtitle D of such title IV (42 U.S.C. 11408): Provided, That the Secretary shall prioritize funding under the Continuum of Care program to continuums of care that have demonstrated a capacity to reallocate funding from lower performing projects to higher performing projects: Provided further, That the Secretary shall provide incentives to create projects that coordinate with housing providers and healthcare organizations to provide permanent supportive housing and rapid re-housing services: Provided further, That the Secretary may establish by notice an alternative maximum amount for administrative costs related to the requirements described in sections 402(f)(1) and 402(f)(2) of subtitle A of such title IV of no more than 5 percent or $50,000, whichever is greater, notwithstanding the 3 percent limitation in section 423(a)(10) of such subtitle C: Provided further, That of the amounts made available for the Continuum of Care program under this paragraph, not less than $52,000,000 shall be for grants for new rapid re-housing projects and supportive service projects providing coordinated entry, and for eligible activities that the Secretary determines to be critical in order to assist survivors of domestic violence, dating violence, sexual assault, stalking, or human trafficking: Provided further, That amounts made available for the Continuum of Care program under this heading in this Act and any remaining unobligated balances from prior Acts may be used to competitively or non-competitively renew or replace grants for youth homeless demonstration projects under the Continuum of Care program, notwithstanding any conflict with the requirements of the Continuum of Care program;

(3) up to $7,000,000 shall be for the national homeless data analysis project: Provided, That notwithstanding the provisions of the Federal Grant and Cooperative Agreements Act of 1977 (31 U.S.C. 6301–6308), the amounts made available under this paragraph and any remaining unobligated balances under this heading for such purposes in prior Acts may be used by the Secretary to enter into cooperative agreements with such entities as may be determined by the Secretary, including public and private organizations, agencies, and institutions; and

(4) not less than $82,000,000 shall be to implement projects to demonstrate how a comprehensive approach to serving homeless youth, age 24 and under, in up to 25 communities with a priority for communities with substantial rural populations in up to eight locations, can dramatically reduce youth homelessness: Provided, That of the amount made available under this paragraph, up to $10,000,000 shall be to provide technical assistance on improving system responses to youth homelessness, and collection, analysis, use, and reporting of data and performance measures under the comprehensive approaches to serve homeless youth, in addition to and in coordination with other technical assistance funds provided under this title: Provided further, That the Secretary may use up to 10 percent of the amount made available under the previous proviso to build the capacity of current technical assistance providers or to train new technical assistance providers with verifiable prior experience with systems and programs for youth experiencing homelessness: Provided further, That youth aged 24 and under seeking assistance under this heading shall not be required to provide third party documentation to establish their eligibility under subsection (a) or (b) of section 103 of the McKinney-Vento Homeless Assistance Act (42 U.S.C. 11302) to receive services: Provided further, That unaccompanied youth aged 24 and under or families headed by youth aged 24 and under who are living in unsafe situations may be served by youth-serving providers funded under this heading: Provided further, That persons eligible under section 103(a)(5) of the McKinney-Vento Homeless Assistance Act may be served by any project funded under this heading to provide both transitional housing and rapid re-housing:

Provided, That for all matching funds requirements applicable to funds made available under this heading for this fiscal year and prior fiscal years, a grantee may use (or could have used) as a source of match funds other funds administered by the Secretary and other Federal agencies unless there is (or was) a specific statutory prohibition on any such use of any such funds: Provided further, That

HOMELESS ASSISTANCE GRANTS—Continued

none of the funds made available under this heading shall be available to provide funding for new projects, except for projects created through reallocation, unless the Secretary determines that the continuum of care has demonstrated that projects are evaluated and ranked based on the degree to which they improve the continuum of care's system performance: *Provided further,* That any unobligated amounts remaining from funds made available under this heading in fiscal year 2012 and prior years for project-based rental assistance for rehabilitation projects with 10-year grant terms may be used for purposes under this heading, notwithstanding the purposes for which such funds were appropriated: *Provided further,* That unobligated balances, including recaptures and carryover, remaining from funds transferred to or appropriated under this heading in fiscal year 2019 or prior years, except for rental assistance amounts that were recaptured and made available until expended, shall be available for the current purposes authorized under this heading in addition to the purposes for which such funds originally were appropriated.

Note.—A full-year 2022 appropriation for this account was not enacted at the time the Budget was prepared; therefore, the Budget assumes this account is operating under the Continuing Appropriations Act, 2022 (Division A of Public Law 117–43, as amended). The amounts included for 2022 reflect the annualized level provided by the continuing resolution.

Program and Financing (in millions of dollars)

Identification code 086–0192–0–1–604	2021 actual	2022 est.	2023 est.
Obligations by program activity:			
0001 Continuum of Care	2,531	2,519	2,818
0002 Emergency Solutions Grants—Formula	355	260	290
0003 National Homeless Data Analysis Project	1	13	7
0005 Youth Demonstration	79	155	82
0007 Victims of Domestic Violence	24	50	50
0008 Emergency Solutions Grants (CARES Act)	2,271		
0009 Emergency Solutions Grants Technical Assistance (CARES Act)	18		
0799 Total direct obligations	5,279	2,997	3,247
0900 Total new obligations, unexpired accounts (object class 41.0)	5,279	2,997	3,247
Budgetary resources:			
Unobligated balance:			
1000 Unobligated balance brought forward, Oct 1	5,217	3,395	3,549
1012 Unobligated balance transfers between expired and unexpired accounts	398	151	150
1020 Adjustment of unobligated bal brought forward, Oct 1	–2		
1021 Recoveries of prior year unpaid obligations	65		
1033 Recoveries of prior year paid obligations	2		
1070 Unobligated balance (total)	5,680	3,546	3,699
Budget authority:			
Appropriations, discretionary:			
1100 Appropriation	3,072	3,000	3,576
1131 Unobligated balance of appropriations permanently reduced	–72		
1160 Appropriation, discretionary (total)	3,000	3,000	3,576
1900 Budget authority (total)	3,000	3,000	3,576
1930 Total budgetary resources available	8,680	6,546	7,275
Memorandum (non-add) entries:			
1940 Unobligated balance expiring	–6		
1941 Unexpired unobligated balance, end of year	3,395	3,549	4,028
Change in obligated balance:			
Unpaid obligations:			
3000 Unpaid obligations, brought forward, Oct 1	4,791	6,745	4,282
3001 Adjustments to unpaid obligations, brought forward, Oct 1	4		
3010 New obligations, unexpired accounts	5,279	2,997	3,247
3020 Outlays (gross)	–3,219	–5,460	–3,319
3040 Recoveries of prior year unpaid obligations, unexpired	–65		
3041 Recoveries of prior year unpaid obligations, expired	–45		
3050 Unpaid obligations, end of year	6,745	4,282	4,210
Memorandum (non-add) entries:			
3100 Obligated balance, start of year	4,795	6,745	4,282
3200 Obligated balance, end of year	6,745	4,282	4,210
Budget authority and outlays, net:			
Discretionary:			
4000 Budget authority, gross	3,000	3,000	3,576
Outlays, gross:			
4010 Outlays from new discretionary authority		3	4
4011 Outlays from discretionary balances	3,219	5,457	3,315
4020 Outlays, gross (total)	3,219	5,460	3,319
Offsets against gross budget authority and outlays:			
Offsetting collections (collected) from:			
4033 Non-Federal sources	–4		
4040 Offsets against gross budget authority and outlays (total)	–4		
Additional offsets against gross budget authority only:			
4052 Offsetting collections credited to expired accounts	2		
4053 Recoveries of prior year paid obligations, unexpired accounts	2		
4060 Additional offsets against budget authority only (total)	4		
4070 Budget authority, net (discretionary)	3,000	3,000	3,576
4080 Outlays, net (discretionary)	3,215	5,460	3,319
4180 Budget authority, net (total)	3,000	3,000	3,576
4190 Outlays, net (total)	3,215	5,460	3,319

The Homeless Assistance Grants account provides funds for the Emergency Solutions Grant (ESG) and Continuum of Care (CoC) programs. These programs, which award funds through formula and competitive processes, enable localities to shape and implement comprehensive, flexible, coordinated approaches to address the multiple issues of homelessness, including chronic homelessness, veteran homelessness, and homelessness among families and youth.

The Budget provides a total of $3.576 billion for a wide range of activities to assist homeless persons and prevent future occurrences of homelessness. The Budget supports $3.197 billion for the CoC program to fund competitive renewals and new projects for target populations, including not less than $52 million for rapid re-housing projects and other assistance to serve people fleeing domestic violence, dating violence, sexual assault, stalking, or human trafficking. The Budget also provides $290 million for ESG formula funding for communities to address emergency needs such as emergency shelter, street outreach, essential services, homelessness prevention, and rapid rehousing; not less than $82 million to implement projects serving homeless youth; and $7 million for the National Homeless Data Analysis Project.

HOUSING OPPORTUNITIES FOR PERSONS WITH AIDS

For carrying out the Housing Opportunities for Persons with AIDS program, as authorized by the AIDS Housing Opportunity Act (42 U.S.C. 12901 et seq.), $455,000,000, to remain available until September 30, 2024, except that amounts allocated pursuant to section 854(c)(5) of such Act shall remain available until September 30, 2025.

Note.—A full-year 2022 appropriation for this account was not enacted at the time the Budget was prepared; therefore, the Budget assumes this account is operating under the Continuing Appropriations Act, 2022 (Division A of Public Law 117–43, as amended). The amounts included for 2022 reflect the annualized level provided by the continuing resolution.

Program and Financing (in millions of dollars)

Identification code 086–0308–0–1–604	2021 actual	2022 est.	2023 est.
Obligations by program activity:			
0001 HOPWA Formula Grants	478	337	454
0002 HOPWA Competitive Grants	27	66	79
0004 HOPWA Formula Grants (Cares Act)	16		
0900 Total new obligations, unexpired accounts (object class 41.0)	521	403	533
Budgetary resources:			
Unobligated balance:			
1000 Unobligated balance brought forward, Oct 1	240	149	176
Budget authority:			
Appropriations, discretionary:			
1100 Appropriation	430	430	455
1900 Budget authority (total)	430	430	455
1930 Total budgetary resources available	670	579	631
Memorandum (non-add) entries:			
1941 Unexpired unobligated balance, end of year	149	176	98
Change in obligated balance:			
Unpaid obligations:			
3000 Unpaid obligations, brought forward, Oct 1	626	771	717
3001 Adjustments to unpaid obligations, brought forward, Oct 1	1		
3010 New obligations, unexpired accounts	521	403	533

DEPARTMENT OF HOUSING AND URBAN DEVELOPMENT

		2021	2022	2023
3020	Outlays (gross)	−376	−457	−427
3041	Recoveries of prior year unpaid obligations, expired	−1		
3050	Unpaid obligations, end of year	771	717	823
	Memorandum (non-add) entries:			
3100	Obligated balance, start of year	627	771	717
3200	Obligated balance, end of year	771	717	823
	Budget authority and outlays, net:			
	Discretionary:			
4000	Budget authority, gross	430	430	455
	Outlays, gross:			
4010	Outlays from new discretionary authority		4	5
4011	Outlays from discretionary balances	376	453	422
4020	Outlays, gross (total)	376	457	427
	Offsets against gross budget authority and outlays:			
	Offsetting collections (collected) from:			
4033	Non-Federal sources	−1		
	Additional offsets against gross budget authority only:			
4052	Offsetting collections credited to expired accounts	1		
4070	Budget authority, net (discretionary)	430	430	455
4080	Outlays, net (discretionary)	375	457	427
4180	Budget authority, net (total)	430	430	455
4190	Outlays, net (total)	375	457	427

The Budget provides $455 million for the Housing Opportunities for Persons With AIDS (HOPWA) program. HOPWA funding provides States and localities with resources to devise long-term comprehensive strategies for providing housing and supportive services to meet the housing needs of persons living with HIV/AIDS and their families.

Ninety percent of HOPWA funds is distributed to States and eligible metropolitan areas according to a formula, and the remaining ten percent is awarded competitively to States, local governments, and private nonprofit entities. The HOPWA formula, which was updated in 2016, allocates funds based on cases of persons living with HIV/AIDS and is adjusted for an area's fair market rent and poverty rates to further ensure HOPWA funds are focused on areas that have the most need. The updated formula became effective in 2017 with a five-year stop-loss/stop-gain period and is fully implemented as of fiscal year 2022. HUD continues to work closely with formula grantees through a comprehensive technical assistance initiative to support communities in implementing the local strategies developed during that five-year phase-in period to manage HOPWA formula changes. The Budget also proposes to not prioritize renewals in its competition so that funds are able to better support more evidence-based service delivery models, address current community needs, and fund innovative projects that support the administration's goals of ending the HIV epidemic by 2030.

SELF-HELP AND ASSISTED HOMEOWNERSHIP OPPORTUNITY PROGRAM

For the Self-Help and Assisted Homeownership Opportunity Program, as authorized under section 11 of the Housing Opportunity Program Extension Act of 1996 (42 U.S.C. 12805 note), and for related activities and assistance, $60,000,000, to remain available until September 30, 2025: Provided, That of the total amount made available under this heading, $10,000,000 shall be for the Self-Help Homeownership Opportunity Program as authorized under such section 11: Provided further, That of the total amount made available under this heading, $41,000,000 shall be for the second, third, and fourth capacity building entities specified in section 4(a) of the HUD Demonstration Act of 1993 (42 U.S.C. 9816 note), of which not less than $5,000,000 shall be for rural capacity building activities: Provided further, That for purposes of awarding grants from amounts provided in the previous proviso, the Secretary may enter into multiyear agreements, as appropriate, subject to the availability of annual appropriations: Provided further, That of the total amount made available under this heading, $5,000,000 shall be for capacity building by national rural housing organizations having experience assessing national rural conditions and providing financing, training, technical assistance, information, and research to local nonprofit organizations, local governments, and Indian Tribes serving high need rural communities: Provided further, That of the total amount provided under this heading, $4,000,000, shall be made available for a program to rehabilitate and modify the homes of disabled or low-income veterans, as authorized under section 1079 of Public Law 113–291.

Note.—A full-year 2022 appropriation for this account was not enacted at the time the Budget was prepared; therefore, the Budget assumes this account is operating under the Continuing Appropriations Act, 2022 (Division A of Public Law 117–43, as amended). The amounts included for 2022 reflect the annualized level provided by the continuing resolution.

Program and Financing (in millions of dollars)

Identification code 086–0176–0–1–604	2021 actual	2022 est.	2023 est.
Obligations by program activity:			
0001 Self Help Housing Opportunity Program	10	10	10
0002 Capacity Building	36	41	41
0003 Rural Capacity Building	10	5	5
0007 Veteran Home Rehab and Mod Pilot	4	5	4
0900 Total new obligations, unexpired accounts (object class 41.0)	60	61	60
Budgetary resources:			
Unobligated balance:			
1000 Unobligated balance brought forward, Oct 1	65	65	64
Budget authority:			
Appropriations, discretionary:			
1100 Appropriation	60	60	60
1930 Total budgetary resources available	125	125	124
Memorandum (non-add) entries:			
1941 Unexpired unobligated balance, end of year	65	64	64
Change in obligated balance:			
Unpaid obligations:			
3000 Unpaid obligations, brought forward, Oct 1	118	132	134
3010 New obligations, unexpired accounts	60	61	60
3020 Outlays (gross)	−46	−59	−50
3050 Unpaid obligations, end of year	132	134	144
Memorandum (non-add) entries:			
3100 Obligated balance, start of year	118	132	134
3200 Obligated balance, end of year	132	134	144
Budget authority and outlays, net:			
Discretionary:			
4000 Budget authority, gross	60	60	60
Outlays, gross:			
4011 Outlays from discretionary balances	46	59	50
4180 Budget authority, net (total)	60	60	60
4190 Outlays, net (total)	46	59	50

The Budget requests $60 million for the Self-Help and Assisted Homeownership Opportunity Program (SHOP) account. The Budget includes $10 million for SHOP, as authorized by Section 11 of the Housing Opportunity Program Extension Act of 1996, to award grants to eligible non-profit organizations to assist low-income homebuyers willing to contribute "sweat equity" toward the construction of their houses.

The Budget provides $41 million for Capacity Building for Community Development and Affordable Housing Program. The program is authorized by Section 4 of the HUD Demonstration Act of 1993 to develop the capacity and ability of community development corporations (CDCs) and community housing organizations (CHDOs) to undertake community development and affordable housing projects and programs.

The Budget provides $5 million for the Rural Capacity Building Program which awards funds to national organizations to enhance the capacity and ability of local governments, Indian Tribes, housing development organizations, rural CDCs, and rural CHDOs, to carry out community development and affordable housing activities that benefit low- and moderate-income families and persons in rural areas.

Conducted in partnership with the U.S. Department of Veterans Affairs, the Budget includes $4 million for the Veterans Housing Rehabilitation and Modification Pilot Program to rehabilitate and modify the homes of disabled and low-income veterans.

NEIGHBORHOOD STABILIZATION PROGRAM

Program and Financing (in millions of dollars)

Identification code 086–0344–0–1–451	2021 actual	2022 est.	2023 est.
Obligations by program activity:			
0003 Disaster Assistance		1	

Community Planning and Development—Continued
Federal Funds—Continued

NEIGHBORHOOD STABILIZATION PROGRAM—Continued
Program and Financing—Continued

Identification code 086–0344–0–1–451	2021 actual	2022 est.	2023 est.
0900 Total new obligations, unexpired accounts (object class 41.0)	....	1	....
Budgetary resources:			
Unobligated balance:			
1000 Unobligated balance brought forward, Oct 1	1	1	....
1930 Total budgetary resources available	1	1	....
Memorandum (non-add) entries:			
1941 Unexpired unobligated balance, end of year	1	....	....
Change in obligated balance:			
Unpaid obligations:			
3000 Unpaid obligations, brought forward, Oct 1	148	133	117
3010 New obligations, unexpired accounts	....	1	....
3020 Outlays (gross)	–15	–17	–16
3050 Unpaid obligations, end of year	133	117	101
Memorandum (non-add) entries:			
3100 Obligated balance, start of year	148	133	117
3200 Obligated balance, end of year	133	117	101
Budget authority and outlays, net:			
Mandatory:			
Outlays, gross:			
4101 Outlays from mandatory balances	15	17	16
4180 Budget authority, net (total)	....	....	....
4190 Outlays, net (total)	15	17	16

This account reports the remaining balances and outlays related to $3.92 billion in Neighborhood Stabilization Program (NSP) funds authorized by the Housing and Economic Recovery Act of 2008, and $1 billion in NSP funds authorized by the Dodd-Frank Financial Reform and Consumer Protection Act of 2010.

PERMANENT SUPPORTIVE HOUSING
Program and Financing (in millions of dollars)

Identification code 086–0342–0–1–604	2021 actual	2022 est.	2023 est.
Change in obligated balance:			
Unpaid obligations:			
3000 Unpaid obligations, brought forward, Oct 1	5	5	....
3020 Outlays (gross)	....	–5	....
3050 Unpaid obligations, end of year	5	....	....
Memorandum (non-add) entries:			
3100 Obligated balance, start of year	5	5	....
3200 Obligated balance, end of year	5	....	....
Budget authority and outlays, net:			
Discretionary:			
Outlays, gross:			
4011 Outlays from discretionary balances	....	5	....
4180 Budget authority, net (total)	....	....	....
4190 Outlays, net (total)	....	5	....

This account reports the remaining outlays from the Supplemental Appropriations Act, 2008 (Public Law 110–252), which provided permanent supportive housing assistance and project-based vouchers to the Louisiana Recovery Authority. These previously funded projects and vouchers are eligible for renewal under the Homeless Assistance Grants and Tenant-Based Rental Assistance accounts.

BROWNFIELDS REDEVELOPMENT
Program and Financing (in millions of dollars)

Identification code 086–0314–0–1–451	2021 actual	2022 est.	2023 est.
Change in obligated balance:			
Unpaid obligations:			
3000 Unpaid obligations, brought forward, Oct 1	5	5	4
3020 Outlays (gross)	....	–1	–1
3050 Unpaid obligations, end of year	5	4	3
Memorandum (non-add) entries:			
3100 Obligated balance, start of year	5	5	4
3200 Obligated balance, end of year	5	4	3
Budget authority and outlays, net:			
Discretionary:			
Outlays, gross:			
4011 Outlays from discretionary balances	....	1	1
4180 Budget authority, net (total)	....	....	....
4190 Outlays, net (total)	....	1	1

The Budget requests no funding for the Brownfields Economic Development Initiative (BEDI), which was a competitive grant program designed to assist cities with the redevelopment of brownfield sites for the purposes of economic development and job creation. The Consolidated and Further Continuing Appropriations Act, 2015 (Public Law 113–235) rescinded all unobligated balances of BEDI as of the end of fiscal year 2016.

RURAL HOUSING AND ECONOMIC DEVELOPMENT
Program and Financing (in millions of dollars)

Identification code 086–0324–0–1–604	2021 actual	2022 est.	2023 est.
Budgetary resources:			
Unobligated balance:			
1000 Unobligated balance brought forward, Oct 1	1	1	1
1930 Total budgetary resources available	1	1	1
Memorandum (non-add) entries:			
1941 Unexpired unobligated balance, end of year	1	1	1
4180 Budget authority, net (total)	....	....	....
4190 Outlays, net (total)	....	....	....

The Budget does not provide funding for the Rural Housing and Economic Development (RHED) program. RHED was created to support housing and economic development activities in rural communities. The Consolidated Appropriations Act, 2016 (Public Law 114–113) rescinded all unobligated balances of RHED funds remaining in the account as of the end of 2016.

REVOLVING FUND (LIQUIDATING PROGRAMS)

The Revolving Fund (liquidating programs) was established by the Independent Offices Appropriations Act of 1955 for the efficient liquidation of assets acquired under a number of housing and urban development programs, all of which are no longer active. For example, the Section 312 loan program portfolio, which provided first and junior lien financing at below market interest rates for the rehabilitation of homes in low-income neighborhoods, constituted a large portion of the account activities but has not originated new loans for over 20 years. The operational expenses are financed from a permanent, indefinite appropriation to administer the remaining repayments of loans, recaptures, and lien releases in the portfolio. Any remaining unobligated balances in the account are returned to the Treasury annually.

Balance Sheet (in millions of dollars)

Identification code 086–4015–0–3–451	2020 actual	2021 actual
ASSETS:		
1101 Federal assets: Fund balances with Treasury	....	....
1601 Direct loans, gross	....	....
1603 Allowance for estimated uncollectible loans and interest (-)	....	....
1604 Direct loans and interest receivable, net	....	....
1606 Foreclosed property	....	....
1699 Value of assets related to direct loans	....	....
1999 Total assets	....	....
LIABILITIES:		
2207 Non-Federal liabilities: Other	....	....

Trust Funds

HOUSING TRUST FUND

Special and Trust Fund Receipts (in millions of dollars)

Identification code 086–8560–0–7–604	2021 actual	2022 est.	2023 est.
0100 Balance, start of year	19	41	42
Receipts:			
Current law:			
1130 Affordable Housing Allocation, Housing Trust Fund	711	740	393
2000 Total: Balances and receipts	730	781	435
Appropriations:			
Current law:			
2101 Housing Trust Fund	–711	–740	–393
2103 Housing Trust Fund	–19	–41	–42
2132 Housing Trust Fund	41	42	22
2199 Total current law appropriations	–689	–739	–413
2999 Total appropriations	–689	–739	–413
5099 Balance, end of year	41	42	22

Program and Financing (in millions of dollars)

Identification code 086–8560–0–7–604	2021 actual	2022 est.	2023 est.
Obligations by program activity:			
0001 Housing Trust Fund Grants	698	635	511
0900 Total new obligations, unexpired accounts (object class 41.0)	698	635	511
Budgetary resources:			
Unobligated balance:			
1000 Unobligated balance brought forward, Oct 1	108	105	209
1020 Adjustment of unobligated bal brought forward, Oct 1	–4		
1021 Recoveries of prior year unpaid obligations	6		
1033 Recoveries of prior year paid obligations	4		
1070 Unobligated balance (total)	114	105	209
Budget authority:			
Appropriations, mandatory:			
1201 Appropriation (special or trust fund)	711	740	393
1203 Appropriation (previously unavailable)(special or trust)	19	41	42
1232 Appropriations and/or unobligated balance of appropriations temporarily reduced	–41	–42	–22
1260 Appropriations, mandatory (total)	689	739	413
1930 Total budgetary resources available	803	844	622
Memorandum (non-add) entries:			
1941 Unexpired unobligated balance, end of year	105	209	111
Change in obligated balance:			
Unpaid obligations:			
3000 Unpaid obligations, brought forward, Oct 1	837	1,316	1,707
3001 Adjustments to unpaid obligations, brought forward, Oct 1	4		
3010 New obligations, unexpired accounts	698	635	511
3020 Outlays (gross)	–217	–244	–361
3040 Recoveries of prior year unpaid obligations, unexpired	–6		
3050 Unpaid obligations, end of year	1,316	1,707	1,857
Memorandum (non-add) entries:			
3100 Obligated balance, start of year	841	1,316	1,707
3200 Obligated balance, end of year	1,316	1,707	1,857
Budget authority and outlays, net:			
Mandatory:			
4090 Budget authority, gross	689	739	413
Outlays, gross:			
4101 Outlays from mandatory balances	217	244	361
Offsets against gross budget authority and outlays:			
Offsetting collections (collected) from:			
4123 Non-Federal sources	–4		

NET POSITION:

3100 Unexpended appropriations		14	14
3300 Cumulative results of operations		–14	–14
3999 Total net position			
4999 Total liabilities and net position			

Additional offsets against gross budget authority only:			
4143 Recoveries of prior year paid obligations, unexpired accounts	4		
4160 Budget authority, net (mandatory)	689	739	413
4170 Outlays, net (mandatory)	213	244	361
4180 Budget authority, net (total)	689	739	413
4190 Outlays, net (total)	213	244	361

The Housing Trust Fund was authorized by section 1131 of the Housing and Economic Recovery Act of 2008 (Public Law 110–289), which directed the account to be funded from assessments on Fannie Mae and Freddie Mac. The Budget estimates that $393 million will be allocated in 2023 to the Housing Trust Fund to provide grants to States to increase and preserve the supply of affordable rental housing and homeownership opportunities for extremely low-income families. Funds will be distributed by formula to States to be used primarily for the construction, preservation, and rehabilitation of affordable rental housing for extremely low-income families, with up to ten percent of the funding available for similar eligible activities that support homeownership, and up to ten percent available for grantee administrative costs.

HOUSING PROGRAMS

Federal Funds

PROJECT-BASED RENTAL ASSISTANCE

For activities and assistance for the provision of project-based subsidy contracts under the United States Housing Act of 1937 (42 U.S.C. 1437 et seq.) ("the Act"), not otherwise provided for, $14,600,000,000, to remain available until expended, shall be available on October 1, 2022 (in addition to the $400,000,000 previously appropriated under this heading that became available October 1, 2022), and $400,000,000, to remain available until expended, shall be available on October 1, 2023: Provided, That the amounts made available under this heading shall be available for expiring or terminating section 8 project-based subsidy contracts (including section 8 moderate rehabilitation contracts), for amendments to section 8 project-based subsidy contracts (including section 8 moderate rehabilitation contracts), for contracts entered into pursuant to section 441 of the McKinney-Vento Homeless Assistance Act (42 U.S.C. 11401), for renewal of section 8 contracts for units in projects that are subject to approved plans of action under the Emergency Low Income Housing Preservation Act of 1987 or the Low-Income Housing Preservation and Resident Homeownership Act of 1990, and for administrative and other expenses associated with project-based activities and assistance funded under this heading: Provided further, That the amount of any forgone increases in tenant rent payments due to the implementation of rent incentives as authorized pursuant to waivers or alternative requirements of the Jobs-Plus initiative as described under the heading "Self-Sufficiency Programs" shall be factored into housing assistance payments under project-based subsidy contracts: Provided further, That of the total amounts provided under this heading, not to exceed $375,000,000 shall be available for performance-based contract administrators or contractors for section 8 project-based assistance, for carrying out 42 U.S.C. 1437(f): Provided further, That the Secretary may also use such amounts in the previous proviso for performance-based contract administrators or contractors for the administration of: interest reduction payments pursuant to section 236(a) of the National Housing Act (12 U.S.C. 1715z–1(a)); rent supplement payments pursuant to section 101 of the Housing and Urban Development Act of 1965 (12 U.S.C. 1701s); section 236(f)(2) rental assistance payments (12 U.S.C. 1715z–1(f)(2)); project rental assistance contracts for the elderly under section 202(c)(2) of the Housing Act of 1959 (12 U.S.C. 1701q); project rental assistance contracts for supportive housing for persons with disabilities under section 811(d)(2) of the Cranston-Gonzalez National Affordable Housing Act (42 U.S.C. 8013(d)(2)); project assistance contracts pursuant to section 202(h) of the Housing Act of 1959 (Public Law 86–372; 73 Stat. 667); and loans under section 202 of the Housing Act of 1959 (Public Law 86–372; 73 Stat. 667): Provided further, That amounts recaptured under this heading, the heading "Annual Contributions for Assisted Housing", or the heading "Housing Certificate Fund", may be used for renewals of or amendments to section 8 project-based contracts or for performance-based contract administrators or contractors, notwithstanding the purposes for which such amounts were appropriated: Provided further, That, notwithstanding any other provision of law, upon the request of the Secretary, project funds that are held in residual receipts accounts for any project subject to a section 8 project-based Housing Assistance Payments contract that authorizes the Department or a housing finance agency to require that surplus project funds be deposited

PROJECT-BASED RENTAL ASSISTANCE—Continued

in an interest-bearing residual receipts account and that are in excess of an amount to be determined by the Secretary, shall be remitted to the Department and deposited in this account, to be available until expended: Provided further, That amounts deposited pursuant to the previous proviso shall be available in addition to the amount otherwise provided by this heading for uses authorized under this heading: Provided further, That of the total amount provided under this heading, up to $50,000,000 shall be available to supplement funds transferred from the heading "Public Housing Fund" to fund contracts for properties converting from assistance under section 9 of the United States Housing Act of 1937 (42 U.S.C. 1437g) under the heading "Rental Assistance Demonstration" in the Department of Housing and Urban Development Appropriations Act, 2012 (title II of division C of Public Law 112–55) to further long-term financial stability and promote the energy or water efficiency, climate resilience, or preservation of such properties: Provided further, That the amounts under the previous proviso may also be available, without additional competition, for cooperative agreements with Participating Administrative Entities that have been previously or newly selected under section 513(b) of the Multifamily Assisted Housing Reform and Affordability Act of 1997 (42 U.S.C. 1437f note) (MAHRAA) to provide direct support, including carrying out due diligence and underwriting functions for owners and for technical assistance activities, on conditions established by the Secretary for small properties and owners entering into any conversion contract under the First Component: Provided further, That of the total amount provided under this heading, up to $10,000,000 shall be available to supplement funds transferred from the heading "Housing for the Elderly" to fund contracts for properties converting from assistance under section 202(c)(2) of the Housing Act of 1959 (12 U.S.C. 1701q(c)(2)) under the heading "Rental Assistance Demonstration" in the Department of Housing and Urban Development Appropriations Act, 2012 (title II of division C of Public Law 112–55) to further long-term financial stability and promote the energy or water efficiency, climate resilience, or preservation of such properties: Provided further, That the amounts under the previous proviso may also be available, without additional competition, for cooperative agreements with Participating Administrative Entities that have been previously or newly selected under section 513(b) of MAHRAA to provide direct support, including carrying out due diligence and underwriting functions for owners and for technical assistance activities, on conditions established by the Secretary for small properties and owners entering into any conversion contract under the Second Component: Provided further, That of the total amounts provided under this heading, not to exceed $275,000,000 shall be available for rent adjustments as added by section 234 of this Act, of which no less than $25,000,000 of such amounts shall be available for adjustments added by section 234(b) necessary to address health and safety deficiencies: Provided further, That up to 2 percent of the total amount made available in the previous proviso shall be for administrative contract costs, including for carrying out due diligence and underwriting functions for evaluating owners' requests and for technical assistance activities: Provided further, That of the total amounts provided under this heading, not to exceed $31,000,000 shall be available for budget-based adjustments for service coordinators for the elderly: Provided further, That any additional amounts for rent adjustments or supplemental contract funding authorized under the seven previous provisos shall be combined with other amounts obligated to such contracts and the combined total amount shall be available for all purposes under such contracts.

Note.—A full-year 2022 appropriation for this account was not enacted at the time the Budget was prepared; therefore, the Budget assumes this account is operating under the Continuing Appropriations Act, 2022 (Division A of Public Law 117–43, as amended). The amounts included for 2022 reflect the annualized level provided by the continuing resolution.

Program and Financing (in millions of dollars)

Identification code 086–0303–0–1–604	2021 actual	2022 est.	2023 est.
Obligations by program activity:			
0001 Contract Renewals	12,886	13,082	14,325
0002 RAD Contract Renewals	56	81	80
0003 Section 8 Amendments	40	55	20
0004 Contract Administrators	350	350	375
0006 Tenant Education and Outreach		10	
0007 Contract Renewals (CARES Act)	19		
0008 Mod Rehab and SRO Renewals	223	160	204
0009 Post-M2M Rent Adjustments			40
0010 Health and Safety Rent Adjustments			10
0900 Total new obligations, unexpired accounts (object class 41.0)	13,574	13,738	15,054
Budgetary resources:			
Unobligated balance:			
1000 Unobligated balance brought forward, Oct 1	369	371	204
1011 Unobligated balance transfer from other acct [086–0320]		2	
1020 Adjustment of unobligated bal brought forward, Oct 1	–3		
1021 Recoveries of prior year unpaid obligations	55	56	56
1033 Recoveries of prior year paid obligations	3		
1070 Unobligated balance (total)	424	429	260
Budget authority:			
Appropriations, discretionary:			
1100 Appropriation	13,065	13,065	14,600
1121 Appropriations transferred from other acct [086–0320]		15	17
1121 Appropriations transferred from other acct [086–0481]	56	33	40
1160 Appropriation, discretionary (total)	13,121	13,113	14,657
Advance appropriations, discretionary:			
1170 Advance appropriation	400	400	400
1900 Budget authority (total)	13,521	13,513	15,057
1930 Total budgetary resources available	13,945	13,942	15,317
Memorandum (non-add) entries:			
1941 Unexpired unobligated balance, end of year	371	204	263
Change in obligated balance:			
Unpaid obligations:			
3000 Unpaid obligations, brought forward, Oct 1	4,318	4,295	4,388
3001 Adjustments to unpaid obligations, brought forward, Oct 1	3		
3010 New obligations, unexpired accounts	13,574	13,738	15,054
3020 Outlays (gross)	–13,545	–13,589	–14,517
3040 Recoveries of prior year unpaid obligations, unexpired	–55	–56	–56
3050 Unpaid obligations, end of year	4,295	4,388	4,869
Memorandum (non-add) entries:			
3100 Obligated balance, start of year	4,321	4,295	4,388
3200 Obligated balance, end of year	4,295	4,388	4,869
Budget authority and outlays, net:			
Discretionary:			
4000 Budget authority, gross	13,521	13,513	15,057
Outlays, gross:			
4010 Outlays from new discretionary authority	9,305	8,923	9,927
4011 Outlays from discretionary balances	4,240	4,666	4,590
4020 Outlays, gross (total)	13,545	13,589	14,517
Offsets against gross budget authority and outlays:			
Offsetting collections (collected) from:			
4033 Non-Federal sources	–3		
Additional offsets against gross budget authority only:			
4053 Recoveries of prior year paid obligations, unexpired accounts	3		
4070 Budget authority, net (discretionary)	13,521	13,513	15,057
4080 Outlays, net (discretionary)	13,542	13,589	14,517
4180 Budget authority, net (total)	13,521	13,513	15,057
4190 Outlays, net (total)	13,542	13,589	14,517

The Budget requests $15 billion for Project-Based Rental Assistance (PBRA), of which $400 million is requested as an advance appropriation to become available in 2024. The PBRA program assists approximately 1.2 million extremely low- to low-income households in obtaining decent, safe, and sanitary housing in private accommodations. PBRA serves families, elderly, and disabled households and provides transitional housing for the homeless through the McKinney-Vento SRO program. Through this funding, the Department of Housing and Urban Development (HUD) supports approximately 17,200 contracts with private owners of multifamily housing by paying the difference between a portion of a household's income and the approved market-based rent for a housing unit. The Budget continues to support the program's calendar year funding cycle and provides 12 months of funding for all contracts.

Program activities include the following:

Contract Renewals and Amendments.—These activities provide funding for HUD to renew expiring contracts and amend contracts that have not expired but require additional funding for HUD to meet remaining payment obligations. Appropriations for these activities are supplemented with recoveries of excess balances remaining on expired contracts that utilized less resources than anticipated during their initial terms. This appropriation includes $60 million for the Rental Assistance Demonstration to further long-term financial stability and promote the energy or water efficiency or climate resilience of properties converting to project-based assistance.

Contract Administrators.—The Budget requests $375 million for contract administration. This activity funds the local level administration of the program through HUD agreements with performance-based contract administrators or other supportive services contractors.

Rent Adjustments for Select Properties.—For at-risk post-Mark to Market Section 8 properties and other PBRA properties with health and safety deficiencies, the budget includes $275 million to allow budget-based rent adjustments to facilitate rehabilitation and sustainable operation of the properties, consistent with program requirements that the property rents remain at or below comparable market rents.

Service Coordinators.—This budget includes $31 million to support budget based rent increases to cover the costs of service coordinators to help elderly residents stay healthy and age in place.

HOUSING FOR THE ELDERLY

(INCLUDING TRANSFER OF FUNDS)

For capital advances, including amendments to capital advance contracts, for housing for the elderly, as authorized by section 202 of the Housing Act of 1959 (12 U.S.C. 1701q), for project rental assistance for the elderly under section 202(c)(2) of such Act, including amendments to contracts for such assistance and renewal of expiring contracts for such assistance for up to a 5-year term, for senior preservation rental assistance contracts, including renewals, as authorized by section 811(e) of the American Homeownership and Economic Opportunity Act of 2000 (12 U.S.C. 1701q note), and for supportive services associated with the housing, $966,000,000, to remain available until September 30, 2026: Provided, That of the amount made available under this heading, up to $120,000,000 shall be for service coordinators and the continuation of existing congregate service grants for residents of assisted housing projects: Provided further, That the Secretary may enter into new project-based subsidy contracts, which shall be renewable under section 524 of the Multi-family Assisted Housing Reform and Affordability Act of 1997, using the resources made available under the heading "Project-Based Rental Assistance" to support projects awarded new capital advance awards: Provided further, That, from amounts made available under this heading for project rental assistance contracts, the Secretary shall transfer to and merge with amounts available under the heading "Project-Based Rental Assistance" an amount equal to the total cost of the new incremental project-based subsidy contracts executed under the authority of the previous proviso: Provided further, That amounts made available under this heading shall be available for Real Estate Assessment Center inspections and inspection-related activities associated with section 202 projects: Provided further, That the Secretary may waive the provisions of section 202 governing the terms and conditions of project rental assistance, except that the initial contract term for such assistance shall not exceed 5 years in duration: Provided further, That upon request of the Secretary, project funds that are held in residual receipts accounts for any project subject to a section 202 project rental assistance contract, and that upon termination of such contract are in excess of an amount to be determined by the Secretary, shall be remitted to the Department and deposited in this account, to remain available until September 30, 2026: Provided further, That amounts deposited in this account pursuant to the previous proviso shall be available, in addition to the amounts otherwise provided by this heading, for the purposes authorized under this heading: Provided further, That unobligated balances, including recaptures and carryover, remaining from funds transferred to or appropriated under this heading shall be available for the current purposes authorized under this heading in addition to the purposes for which such funds originally were appropriated.

Note.—A full-year 2022 appropriation for this account was not enacted at the time the Budget was prepared; therefore, the Budget assumes this account is operating under the Continuing Appropriations Act, 2022 (Division A of Public Law 117–43, as amended). The amounts included for 2022 reflect the annualized level provided by the continuing resolution.

Program and Financing (in millions of dollars)

Identification code 086–0320–0–1–604	2021 actual	2022 est.	2023 est.
Obligations by program activity:			
0001 Capital Advance and Expenses	146	153	161
0002 PRAC Renewal/Amendment	674	678	692
0003 Service Coordinators/Congregate Services	98	105	112
0005 Senior Preservation Rental Assistance Contracts (SPRAC) Amendments	19	23	26
0007 Supportive Services/IWISH Demonstration		14	
0008 Aging in Place Home Modifications and Repairs	20		
0044 PRAC Renewal/Amendment (CARES Act)	5	15	
0045 Service Coordinators/Congregate Services (CARES Act)	4	6	
0900 Total new obligations, unexpired accounts (object class 41.0)	966	994	991
Budgetary resources:			
Unobligated balance:			
1000 Unobligated balance brought forward, Oct 1	330	227	68
1010 Unobligated balance transfer to other accts [086–0302]		–1	
1010 Unobligated balance transfer to other accts [086–0303]		–2	
1021 Recoveries of prior year unpaid obligations	6	1	1
1070 Unobligated balance (total)	336	225	69
Budget authority:			
Appropriations, discretionary:			
1100 Appropriation	855	855	966
1120 Appropriations transferred to other acct [086–0302]		–3	–2
1120 Appropriations transferred to other acct [086–0303]		–15	–17
1160 Appropriation, discretionary (total)	855	837	947
Spending authority from offsetting collections, discretionary:			
1700 Collected	3		
1900 Budget authority (total)	858	837	947
1930 Total budgetary resources available	1,194	1,062	1,016
Memorandum (non-add) entries:			
1940 Unobligated balance expiring	–1		
1941 Unexpired unobligated balance, end of year	227	68	25
Change in obligated balance:			
Unpaid obligations:			
3000 Unpaid obligations, brought forward, Oct 1	691	863	998
3010 New obligations, unexpired accounts	966	994	991
3020 Outlays (gross)	–786	–858	–1,048
3040 Recoveries of prior year unpaid obligations, unexpired	–6	–1	–1
3041 Recoveries of prior year unpaid obligations, expired	–2		
3050 Unpaid obligations, end of year	863	998	940
Memorandum (non-add) entries:			
3100 Obligated balance, start of year	691	863	998
3200 Obligated balance, end of year	863	998	940
Budget authority and outlays, net:			
Discretionary:			
4000 Budget authority, gross	858	837	947
Outlays, gross:			
4010 Outlays from new discretionary authority	323	268	379
4011 Outlays from discretionary balances	463	590	669
4020 Outlays, gross (total)	786	858	1,048
Offsets against gross budget authority and outlays:			
Offsetting collections (collected) from:			
4033 Non-Federal sources	–3		
4040 Offsets against gross budget authority and outlays (total)	–3		
4180 Budget authority, net (total)	855	837	947
4190 Outlays, net (total)	783	858	1,048

The Housing for the Elderly Program (Section 202) supports the construction and operation of supportive housing for very low-income elderly households, including the frail elderly. The Budget provides $966 million for this program, including $742 million to renew and amend operating subsidy contracts for existing Section 202 housing including Senior Preservation Rental Assistance Contracts, $100 million for Capital Advances and new operating subsidy to increase the supply of affordable housing for seniors, $120 million to support service coordinators who work on-site to help residents obtain critical services, and $4 million for property inspections and other related expenses.

HOUSING FOR PERSONS WITH DISABILITIES

For capital advances, including amendments to capital advance contracts, for supportive housing for persons with disabilities, as authorized by section 811 of the Cranston-Gonzalez National Affordable Housing Act (42 U.S.C. 8013), for project rental assistance for supportive housing for persons with disabilities under section 811(d)(2) of such Act, for project assistance contracts pursuant to subsection (h) of section 202 of the Housing Act of 1959, as added by section 205(a) of the Housing and Community Development Amendments of 1978 (Public Law 95–557: 92 Stat. 2090), including amendments to contracts for such assistance and renewal of expiring contracts for such assistance for up to a 5-year term, for project rental assistance to State housing finance agencies and other appropriate entities as authorized under section 811(b)(3) of the Cranston-Gonzalez National Affordable Housing Act, and for supportive services associated with the housing for persons with disabilities as authorized by section 811(b)(1) of such Act, $287,700,000, to remain available until

Housing Programs—Continued
Federal Funds—Continued

HOUSING FOR PERSONS WITH DISABILITIES—Continued

September 30, 2026: Provided, That amounts made available under this heading shall be available for Real Estate Assessment Center inspections and inspection-related activities associated with section 811 projects: Provided further, That, upon the request of the Secretary, project funds that are held in residual receipts accounts for any project subject to a section 811 project rental assistance contract, and that upon termination of such contract are in excess of an amount to be determined by the Secretary, shall be remitted to the Department and deposited in this account, to remain available until September 30, 2026: Provided further, That amounts deposited in this account pursuant to the previous proviso shall be available in addition to the amounts otherwise provided by this heading for the purposes authorized under this heading: Provided further, That unobligated balances, including recaptures and carryover, remaining from funds transferred to or appropriated under this heading shall be used for the current purposes authorized under this heading in addition to the purposes for which such funds originally were appropriated.

Note.—A full-year 2022 appropriation for this account was not enacted at the time the Budget was prepared; therefore, the Budget assumes this account is operating under the Continuing Appropriations Act, 2022 (Division A of Public Law 117–43, as amended). The amounts included for 2022 reflect the annualized level provided by the continuing resolution.

Program and Financing (in millions of dollars)

Identification code 086–0237–0–1–604	2021 actual	2022 est.	2023 est.
Obligations by program activity:			
0001 Capital Advance and Expenses	131	142	82
0002 PRAC/PAC Renewals and Amendments	184	190	205
0004 State Housing Project Rental Assistance	....	....	23
0044 PRAC/PAC Renewals and Amendments (CARES Act)	1	9	....
0900 Total new obligations, unexpired accounts (object class 41.0)	316	341	310
Budgetary resources:			
Unobligated balance:			
1000 Unobligated balance brought forward, Oct 1	232	148	38
1021 Recoveries of prior year unpaid obligations	2	1	1
1070 Unobligated balance (total)	234	149	39
Budget authority:			
Appropriations, discretionary:			
1100 Appropriation	227	227	288
Spending authority from offsetting collections, discretionary:			
1700 Collected	3	3	....
1900 Budget authority (total)	230	230	288
1930 Total budgetary resources available	464	379	327
Memorandum (non-add) entries:			
1941 Unexpired unobligated balance, end of year	148	38	17
Change in obligated balance:			
Unpaid obligations:			
3000 Unpaid obligations, brought forward, Oct 1	396	496	538
3010 New obligations, unexpired accounts	316	341	310
3020 Outlays (gross)	–214	–298	–372
3040 Recoveries of prior year unpaid obligations, unexpired	–2	–1	–1
3050 Unpaid obligations, end of year	496	538	475
Memorandum (non-add) entries:			
3100 Obligated balance, start of year	396	496	538
3200 Obligated balance, end of year	496	538	475
Budget authority and outlays, net:			
Discretionary:			
4000 Budget authority, gross	230	230	288
Outlays, gross:			
4010 Outlays from new discretionary authority	39	43	49
4011 Outlays from discretionary balances	175	255	323
4020 Outlays, gross (total)	214	298	372
Offsets against gross budget authority and outlays:			
Offsetting collections (collected) from:			
4033 Non-Federal sources	–3	–3	....
4180 Budget authority, net (total)	227	227	288
4190 Outlays, net (total)	211	295	372

The Housing for Persons With Disabilities Program (Section 811) supports the development and operation of supportive housing for very low-income people with disabilities. The Budget provides $287.7 million for this program, including $205 million to renew and amend operating subsidy contracts for existing Section 811 housing, $80 million for Capital Advances and new operating subsidy and State Project Rental Assistance to expand the supply of affordable housing for low-income persons with disabilities, and up to $2.7 million for property inspections and other related expenses.

OTHER ASSISTED HOUSING PROGRAMS

Program and Financing (in millions of dollars)

Identification code 086–0206–0–1–999	2021 actual	2022 est.	2023 est.
Budgetary resources:			
Unobligated balance:			
1000 Unobligated balance brought forward, Oct 1	97	84	84
1033 Recoveries of prior year paid obligations	1	....	....
1070 Unobligated balance (total)	98	84	84
Budget authority:			
Appropriations, discretionary:			
1131 Unobligated balance of appropriations permanently reduced	–14	....	....
1900 Budget authority (total)	–14	....	....
1930 Total budgetary resources available	84	84	84
Memorandum (non-add) entries:			
1941 Unexpired unobligated balance, end of year	84	84	84
Change in obligated balance:			
Unpaid obligations:			
3000 Unpaid obligations, brought forward, Oct 1	274	209	149
3020 Outlays (gross)	–65	–60	–55
3050 Unpaid obligations, end of year	209	149	94
Memorandum (non-add) entries:			
3100 Obligated balance, start of year	274	209	149
3200 Obligated balance, end of year	209	149	94
Budget authority and outlays, net:			
Discretionary:			
4000 Budget authority, gross	–14	....	....
Outlays, gross:			
4011 Outlays from discretionary balances	65	60	55
Offsets against gross budget authority and outlays:			
Offsetting collections (collected) from:			
4033 Non-Federal sources, 01	–1	....	....
4040 Offsets against gross budget authority and outlays (total)	–1	....	....
Additional offsets against gross budget authority only:			
4053 Recoveries of prior year paid obligations, unexpired accounts	1	....	....
4070 Budget authority, net (discretionary)	–14	....	....
4080 Outlays, net (discretionary)	64	60	55
4180 Budget authority, net (total)	–14	....	....
4190 Outlays, net (total)	64	60	55

The Other Assisted Housing Programs account contains the programs listed below:

Rent Supplement.—Rent Supplement assistance payments support assisted units for qualified low-income tenants.

Section 235.—The Housing and Urban-Rural Recovery Act of 1983 (Public Law 98–181) authorized a restructured Section 235 (Homeownership Assistance) program that provided homeowners a ten-year interest reduction subsidy on their mortgages.

Section 236.—The Housing and Urban Development Act of 1968, as amended, authorized the Section 236 Rental Housing Assistance Program, which subsidizes the monthly mortgage payment that an owner of a rental or cooperative project is required to make. This interest subsidy reduces rents for lower income tenants. Some Section 236 properties also have rental assistance contracts with the Department of Housing and Urban Development (HUD) through the Rental Assistance Payment (RAP) program.

In 2019, HUD converted the last remaining Rent Supplement and RAP properties to long-term, project-based Section 8 contracts, using the Rental Assistance Demonstration program.

RENTAL HOUSING ASSISTANCE FUND

Program and Financing (in millions of dollars)

Identification code 086–4041–0–3–604	2021 actual	2022 est.	2023 est.
Budgetary resources:			
Unobligated balance:			
1000 Unobligated balance brought forward, Oct 1	15	16	17
Budget authority:			
Spending authority from offsetting collections, mandatory:			
1800 Collected	1	1	1
1930 Total budgetary resources available	16	17	18
Memorandum (non-add) entries:			
1941 Unexpired unobligated balance, end of year	16	17	18
Budget authority and outlays, net:			
Mandatory:			
4090 Budget authority, gross	1	1	1
Offsets against gross budget authority and outlays:			
Offsetting collections (collected) from:			
4123 Non-Federal sources	–1	–1	–1
4180 Budget authority, net (total)			
4190 Outlays, net (total)	–1	–1	–1
Memorandum (non-add) entries:			
5090 Unexpired unavailable balance, SOY: Offsetting collections	1	1	1
5092 Unexpired unavailable balance, EOY: Offsetting collections	1	1	1

As authorized by the Housing and Urban Development Act of 1968, the Rental Housing Assistance Fund collects funds which are in excess of the established basic rents for units in Section 236 subsidized projects. Funds in this account remain available to pay refunds of excess rental charges.

FLEXIBLE SUBSIDY FUND

Program and Financing (in millions of dollars)

Identification code 086–4044–0–3–604	2021 actual	2022 est.	2023 est.
Budgetary resources:			
Unobligated balance:			
1000 Unobligated balance brought forward, Oct 1	590	614	645
Budget authority:			
Spending authority from offsetting collections, discretionary:			
1700 Collected	24	31	37
1930 Total budgetary resources available	614	645	682
Memorandum (non-add) entries:			
1941 Unexpired unobligated balance, end of year	614	645	682
Budget authority and outlays, net:			
Discretionary:			
4000 Budget authority, gross	24	31	37
Offsets against gross budget authority and outlays:			
Offsetting collections (collected) from:			
4033 Non-Federal sources	–24	–31	–37
4040 Offsets against gross budget authority and outlays (total)	–24	–31	–37
4180 Budget authority, net (total)			
4190 Outlays, net (total)	–24	–31	–37
Memorandum (non-add) entries:			
5090 Unexpired unavailable balance, SOY: Offsetting collections	2	2	2
5092 Unexpired unavailable balance, EOY: Offsetting collections	2	2	2

Status of Direct Loans (in millions of dollars)

Identification code 086–4044–0–3–604	2021 actual	2022 est.	2023 est.
Cumulative balance of direct loans outstanding:			
1210 Outstanding, start of year	290	268	244
1251 Repayments: Repayments and prepayments	–18	–24	–22
1264 Other adjustments: net (+ or -)	–4		
1290 Outstanding, end of year	268	244	222

The Flexible Subsidy Fund assisted financially troubled subsidized projects under certain Federal Housing Administration (FHA) authorities. The subsidies were intended to prevent potential losses to the FHA fund resulting from project insolvency and to preserve these projects as a viable source of housing for low- and moderate-income tenants. Priority was given to projects with Federal insurance-in-force and then to those with mortgages that had been assigned to the Department.

Balance Sheet (in millions of dollars)

Identification code 086–4044–0–3–604	2020 actual	2021 actual
ASSETS:		
1101 Federal assets: Fund balances with Treasury	592	615
1601 Direct loans, gross	290	267
1602 Interest receivable	47	44
1603 Allowance for estimated uncollectible loans and interest (-)	–50	–58
1699 Value of assets related to direct loans	287	253
1999 Total assets	879	868
NET POSITION:		
3100 Unexpended appropriations		
3300 Cumulative results of operations	879	868
3999 Total net position	879	868
4999 Total liabilities and net position	879	868

GREEN RETROFIT PROGRAM FOR MULTIFAMILY HOUSING, RECOVERY ACT

Summary of Loan Levels, Subsidy Budget Authority and Outlays by Program (in millions of dollars)

Identification code 086–0306–0–1–604	2021 actual	2022 est.	2023 est.
Direct loan reestimates:			
135001 Energy Retrofit Loans	–6	–5	

The Green Retrofit Program offered grants and loans to owners of eligible Department of Housing and Urban Development (HUD) assisted multifamily housing properties to fund green retrofits, which are intended to reduce ongoing utility consumption, benefit resident health, and benefit the environment. This program was funded under Title XII of the American Recovery and Reinvestment Act of 2009 (Public Law 111–5), and the authority to make new awards has expired. All loan cash flows are recorded in the corresponding financing account (86–4589).

GREEN RETROFIT PROGRAM FOR MULTIFAMILY HOUSING FINANCING ACCOUNT

Program and Financing (in millions of dollars)

Identification code 086–4589–0–3–604	2021 actual	2022 est.	2023 est.
Obligations by program activity:			
Credit program obligations:			
0742 Downward reestimates paid to receipt accounts	4	3	
0743 Interest on downward reestimates	2	2	
0900 Total new obligations, unexpired accounts	6	5	
Budgetary resources:			
Unobligated balance:			
1000 Unobligated balance brought forward, Oct 1	3		
Financing authority:			
Spending authority from offsetting collections, mandatory:			
1800 Collected	3	5	5
1900 Budget authority (total)	3	5	5
1930 Total budgetary resources available	6	5	5
Memorandum (non-add) entries:			
1941 Unexpired unobligated balance, end of year			5
Change in obligated balance:			
Unpaid obligations:			
3010 New obligations, unexpired accounts	6	5	
3020 Outlays (gross)	–6	–5	
Financing authority and disbursements, net:			
Mandatory:			
4090 Budget authority, gross	3	5	5
Financing disbursements:			
4110 Outlays, gross (total)	6	5	

584   Housing Programs—Continued
       Federal Funds—Continued   THE BUDGET FOR FISCAL YEAR 2023

GREEN RETROFIT PROGRAM FOR MULTIFAMILY HOUSING FINANCING ACCOUNT—Continued

Program and Financing—Continued

Identification code 086–4589–0–3–604	2021 actual	2022 est.	2023 est.
Offsets against gross financing authority and disbursements:			
Offsetting collections (collected) from:			
4123 Non-Federal sources	–3	–5	–5
4180 Budget authority, net (total)	....	....	....
4190 Outlays, net (total)	3	....	–5

Status of Direct Loans (in millions of dollars)

Identification code 086–4589–0–3–604	2021 actual	2022 est.	2023 est.
Cumulative balance of direct loans outstanding:			
1210 Outstanding, start of year	41	36	31
1251 Repayments: Repayments and prepayments	–5	–5	–5
1290 Outstanding, end of year	36	31	26

Balance Sheet (in millions of dollars)

Identification code 086–4589–0–3–604	2020 actual	2021 actual
ASSETS:		
1101 Federal assets: Fund balances with Treasury	3	....
Net value of assets related to post-1991 direct loans receivable:		
1401 Direct loans receivable, gross	41	36
1402 Interest receivable	1	1
1405 Allowance for subsidy cost (–)	–33	–27
1499 Net present value of assets related to direct loans	9	10
1999 Total assets	12	10
LIABILITIES:		
Federal liabilities:		
2103 Debt	10	10
2105 Other	2	....
2999 Total liabilities	12	10
NET POSITION:		
3300 Cumulative results of operations	....	....
4999 Total liabilities and net position	12	10

GREEN AND RESILIENT RETROFIT PROGRAM FOR MULTIFAMILY HOUSING

For a demonstration program to improve the energy or water efficiency or climate resilience of multifamily properties modeled after the Green Retrofit Program for Multifamily Housing, $250,000,000, to remain available until September 30, 2026: Provided, That such demonstration program amounts shall be for grants or for the cost of direct loans to properties receiving project-based assistance pursuant to section 202 of the Housing Act of 1959 (12 U.S.C. 1701q), section 811 of the Cranston-Gonzalez National Affordable Housing Act (42 U.S.C. 8013), section 811 of the American Homeownership and Economic Opportunity Act of 2000 (12 U.S.C. 1701q note), section 8 of the United States Housing Act of 1937 (42 U.S.C. 1437 et seq.) (excluding section 8(o)(13) of such Act), or properties converting to a project-based subsidy contract under section 8 of the United States Housing Act of 1937 (excluding section 8(o)(13) of such Act) through the Rental Assistance Demonstration: Provided further, That the costs of such loans, including the cost of modifying such loans, shall be as defined in section 502 of the Congressional Budget Act of 1974: Provided further, That the Secretary may subsidize gross obligations for the principal amount of direct loans not to exceed $400,000,000, to remain available until September 30, 2026: Provided further, That up to $31,500,000 of the amount made available under this heading shall be for data collection and utility consumption benchmarking of properties eligible for grants or direct loans under this demonstration program, of which $5,000,000 may be transferred to and merged with amounts made available under the heading "Information Technology Fund" for information technology systems and tools necessary for the collection and analysis of such utility benchmarking data: Provided further, That up to $11,000,000 of the amount made available under this heading shall be for administrative contract costs for the demonstration program and benchmarking, including for carrying out property and energy or water assessment, due diligence, and underwriting functions for such demonstration program: Provided further, That such amounts may also be available, without additional competition, for cooperative agreements with Participating Administrative Entities that have been previously or newly selected under section 513(b) of the Multifamily Assisted Housing Reform and Affordability Act of 1997 (42 U.S.C. 1437f note) ("MAHRAA") to provide direct support and technical assistance for owners on conditions established by the Secretary for any grant or loan authorized under this heading: Provided further, That grants or loans authorized under this heading may be provided through the policies, procedures, contracts, and transactional infrastructure of the authorized programs administered by the Office of Multifamily Housing Programs, Office of Housing, of the Department of Housing and Urban Development: Provided further, That the Secretary may waive or specify alternative requirements for any provision of any statute or regulation that the Secretary administers in connection with the use of the amounts made available under this heading for the demonstration (except for requirements related to fair housing, nondiscrimination, labor standards, and the environment), upon a finding by the Secretary that such waivers or alternative requirements are necessary to expedite or facilitate the use of such amounts.

Note.—A full-year 2022 appropriation for this account was not enacted at the time the Budget was prepared; therefore, the Budget assumes this account is operating under the Continuing Appropriations Act, 2022 (Division A of Public Law 117–43, as amended). The amounts included for 2022 reflect the annualized level provided by the continuing resolution.

Program and Financing (in millions of dollars)

Identification code 086–0482–0–1–604	2021 actual	2022 est.	2023 est.
Obligations by program activity:			
0001 Green and Resilient Grants	....	....	140
0002 Green and Resilient Program Benchmarking	....	....	26
0003 Administrative Contracts	....	....	11
0091 Direct program activities, subtotal	....	....	177
Credit program obligations:			
0701 Direct loan subsidy	....	....	68
0900 Total new obligations, unexpired accounts (object class 41.0)	....	....	245
Budgetary resources:			
Budget authority:			
Appropriations, discretionary:			
1100 Appropriation	....	....	250
1120 Appropriations transferred to other acct [086–4586]	....	....	–5
1160 Appropriation, discretionary (total)	....	....	245
1930 Total budgetary resources available	....	....	245
Change in obligated balance:			
Unpaid obligations:			
3010 New obligations, unexpired accounts	....	....	245
3020 Outlays (gross)	....	....	–112
3050 Unpaid obligations, end of year	....	....	133
Memorandum (non-add) entries:			
3200 Obligated balance, end of year	....	....	133
Budget authority and outlays, net:			
Discretionary:			
4000 Budget authority, gross	....	....	245
Outlays, gross:			
4010 Outlays from new discretionary authority	....	....	112
4180 Budget authority, net (total)	....	....	245
4190 Outlays, net (total)	....	....	112

Summary of Loan Levels, Subsidy Budget Authority and Outlays by Program (in millions of dollars)

Identification code 086–0482–0–1–604	2021 actual	2022 est.	2023 est.
Direct loan levels supportable by subsidy budget authority:			
115001 Baseline and Standard Enhancements	....	....	38
115003 High Impact Green Housing	....	....	150
115999 Total direct loan levels	....	....	188
Direct loan subsidy (in percent):			
132001 Baseline and Standard Enhancements	....	....	20.00
132003 High Impact Green Housing	....	....	40.00
132999 Weighted average subsidy rate	....	....	35.96
Direct loan subsidy budget authority:			
133001 Baseline and Standard Enhancements	....	....	8
133003 High Impact Green Housing	....	....	60
133999 Total subsidy budget authority	....	....	68
Direct loan subsidy outlays:			
134001 Baseline and Standard Enhancements	....	....	8
134003 High Impact Green Housing	....	....	60
134999 Total subsidy outlays	....	....	68

DEPARTMENT OF HOUSING AND URBAN DEVELOPMENT

The Green and Resilient Retrofit Program would provide funding to owners of Multifamily-assisted properties to rehabilitate these properties to be more energy and water efficient, healthier, and more resilient to extreme weather events. This increased investment will improve the stock of affordable housing available to many low- and extremely low-income families, often from marginalized communities. This program would support climate resilience, reduce the likelihood of catastrophic damage from future disasters, reduce energy and water consumption, and improve indoor air quality. The Budget requests $250 million for grants and loans for properties currently assisted under Project-Based Rental Assistance, Housing for the Elderly, and Housing for Persons with Disabilities, including $31.5 million for data collection and utility consumption benchmarking of properties across multifamily housing.

GREEN AND RESILIENT RETROFIT PROGRAM FOR MULTIFAMILY HOUSING, FINANCING ACCOUNT

Program and Financing (in millions of dollars)

Identification code 086–4616–0–3–604	2021 actual	2022 est.	2023 est.
Obligations by program activity:			
Credit program obligations:			
0710 Direct loan obligations			188
0713 Payment of interest to Treasury			3
0900 Total new obligations, unexpired accounts			191
Budgetary resources:			
Financing authority:			
Borrowing authority, mandatory:			
1400 Borrowing authority			119
Spending authority from offsetting collections, mandatory:			
1800 Collected			72
1900 Budget authority (total)			191
1930 Total budgetary resources available			191
Change in obligated balance:			
Unpaid obligations:			
3010 New obligations, unexpired accounts			191
3020 Outlays (gross)			–191
Financing authority and disbursements, net:			
Mandatory:			
4090 Budget authority, gross			191
Financing disbursements:			
4110 Outlays, gross (total)			191
Offsets against gross financing authority and disbursements:			
Offsetting collections (collected) from:			
4120 Federal sources - payment from program account			–68
4123 Repayment of principal			–3
4123 Interest payments			–1
4130 Offsets against gross budget authority and outlays (total)			–72
4160 Budget authority, net (mandatory)			119
4170 Outlays, net (mandatory)			119
4180 Budget authority, net (total)			119
4190 Outlays, net (total)			119

Status of Direct Loans (in millions of dollars)

Identification code 086–4616–0–3–604	2021 actual	2022 est.	2023 est.
Position with respect to appropriations act limitation on obligations:			
1111 Direct loan obligations from current-year authority			188
1150 Total direct loan obligations			188

HOUSING COUNSELING ASSISTANCE

For contracts, grants, and other assistance excluding loans, as authorized under section 106 of the Housing and Urban Development Act of 1968, as amended, $65,900,000, to remain available until September 30, 2024, including up to $4,900,000 for administrative contract services: Provided, That funds shall be used for providing counseling and advice to tenants and homeowners, both current and prospective, with respect to property maintenance, financial management or literacy, and such other matters as may be appropriate to assist them in improving their housing conditions, meeting their financial needs, and fulfilling the responsibilities of tenancy or homeownership; for program administration; and for housing counselor training: Provided further, That for purposes of awarding grants from amounts provided under this heading, the Secretary may enter into multiyear agreements, as appropriate, subject to the availability of annual appropriations.

Note.—A full-year 2022 appropriation for this account was not enacted at the time the Budget was prepared; therefore, the Budget assumes this account is operating under the Continuing Appropriations Act, 2022 (Division A of Public Law 117–43, as amended). The amounts included for 2022 reflect the annualized level provided by the continuing resolution.

Program and Financing (in millions of dollars)

Identification code 086–0156–0–1–604	2021 actual	2022 est.	2023 est.
Obligations by program activity:			
0001 Housing Counseling Assistance	2	110	61
0002 Administrative Contract Services	2	3	5
0004 Housing Counseling Eviction Prevention Grants		20	
0900 Total new obligations, unexpired accounts	4	133	66
Budgetary resources:			
Unobligated balance:			
1000 Unobligated balance brought forward, Oct 1	3	77	22
Budget authority:			
Appropriations, discretionary:			
1100 Appropriation	78	78	66
1930 Total budgetary resources available	81	155	88
Memorandum (non-add) entries:			
1941 Unexpired unobligated balance, end of year	77	22	22
Change in obligated balance:			
Unpaid obligations:			
3000 Unpaid obligations, brought forward, Oct 1	65	23	103
3010 New obligations, unexpired accounts	4	133	66
3020 Outlays (gross)	–45	–53	–101
3041 Recoveries of prior year unpaid obligations, expired	–1		
3050 Unpaid obligations, end of year	23	103	68
Memorandum (non-add) entries:			
3100 Obligated balance, start of year	65	23	103
3200 Obligated balance, end of year	23	103	68
Budget authority and outlays, net:			
Discretionary:			
4000 Budget authority, gross	78	78	66
Outlays, gross:			
4010 Outlays from new discretionary authority		4	3
4011 Outlays from discretionary balances	45	49	98
4020 Outlays, gross (total)	45	53	101
4180 Budget authority, net (total)	78	78	66
4190 Outlays, net (total)	45	53	101

The Housing Counseling Assistance Program provides: 1) comprehensive housing counseling services to eligible homeowners and tenants through grants, oversight, and technical assistance; and 2) training to housing counselors and staff of government or non-profit entities that participate in HUD's Housing Counseling program. Eligible Housing Counseling program services include group education and individualized housing counseling on pre- and post-purchase homeownership budgeting and financial management, reverse mortgage counseling, homelessness prevention, rental counseling, and avoiding discrimination, foreclosure, and eviction. The objectives of the Housing Counseling program include overcoming barriers to stable and affordable housing; expanding sustainable homeownership and rental opportunities; preventing foreclosure and eviction; and deterring discrimination, scams, and fraud.

The Budget includes $65.9 million for this program, of which $61 million is intended to fund grants to HUD-approved Housing Counseling agencies for direct services and to develop training for HUD-approved housing counselors.

HOUSING COUNSELING ASSISTANCE—Continued

Object Classification (in millions of dollars)

Identification code 086–0156–0–1–604		2021 actual	2022 est.	2023 est.
	Direct obligations:			
25.2	Other services from non-Federal sources	2	3	5
41.0	Grants, subsidies, and contributions	2	130	61
99.9	Total new obligations, unexpired accounts	4	133	66

MUTUAL MORTGAGE INSURANCE PROGRAM ACCOUNT

New commitments to guarantee single family loans insured under the Mutual Mortgage Insurance Fund shall not exceed $400,000,000,000, to remain available until September 30, 2024: Provided, That during fiscal year 2023, obligations to make direct loans to carry out the purposes of section 204(g) of the National Housing Act, as amended, shall not exceed $1,000,000: Provided further, That the foregoing amount in the previous proviso shall be for loans to nonprofit and governmental entities in connection with sales of single family real properties owned by the Secretary and formerly insured under the Mutual Mortgage Insurance Fund: Provided further, That for administrative contract expenses of the Federal Housing Administration, $165,000,000, to remain available until September 30, 2024: Provided further, That of the amount in the previous proviso, up to $15,000,000, to remain available until September 30, 2025, shall be for the cost of guaranteed loans to support a pilot of new loan products, which may include mortgagee and borrower incentives designed to lower barriers to homeownership, notwithstanding the limitations on eligibility in section 203(b) of the National Housing Act: Provided further, That such costs in the previous proviso, including the costs of modifying such loans, shall be as defined in section 502 of the Congressional Budget Act of 1974: Provided further, That notwithstanding the limitation in the first sentence of section 255(g) of the National Housing Act (12 U.S.C. 1715z–20(g)), during fiscal year 2023 the Secretary may insure and enter into new commitments to insure mortgages under section 255 of the National Housing Act.

Note.—A full-year 2022 appropriation for this account was not enacted at the time the Budget was prepared; therefore, the Budget assumes this account is operating under the Continuing Appropriations Act, 2022 (Division A of Public Law 117–43, as amended). The amounts included for 2022 reflect the annualized level provided by the continuing resolution.

Program and Financing (in millions of dollars)

Identification code 086–0183–0–1–371		2021 actual	2022 est.	2023 est.
	Obligations by program activity:			
	Credit program obligations:			
0702	Loan guarantee subsidy			15
0707	Reestimates of loan guarantee subsidy	2,754	662	
0708	Interest on reestimates of loan guarantee subsidy	215	468	
0709	Administrative expenses	151	130	159
0900	Total new obligations, unexpired accounts	3,120	1,260	174
	Budgetary resources:			
	Unobligated balance:			
1000	Unobligated balance brought forward, Oct 1	40	21	23
1011	Unobligated balance transfer from other acct [086–0236]	2,969	1,130	
1021	Recoveries of prior year unpaid obligations	4	2	2
1070	Unobligated balance (total)	3,013	1,153	25
	Budget authority:			
	Appropriations, discretionary:			
1100	Appropriation - Administrative Expenses	130	130	150
1100	Appropriation - Credit Subsidy			15
1160	Appropriation, discretionary (total)	130	130	165
1900	Budget authority (total)	130	130	165
1930	Total budgetary resources available	3,143	1,283	190
	Memorandum (non-add) entries:			
1940	Unobligated balance expiring	–2		
1941	Unexpired unobligated balance, end of year	21	23	16
	Change in obligated balance:			
	Unpaid obligations:			
3000	Unpaid obligations, brought forward, Oct 1	131	144	155
3010	New obligations, unexpired accounts	3,120	1,260	174
3011	Obligations ("upward adjustments"), expired accounts	2		
3020	Outlays (gross)	–3,095	–1,246	–130
3040	Recoveries of prior year unpaid obligations, unexpired	–4	–2	–2
3041	Recoveries of prior year unpaid obligations, expired	–10	–1	–2
3050	Unpaid obligations, end of year	144	155	195
	Memorandum (non-add) entries:			
3100	Obligated balance, start of year	131	144	155
3200	Obligated balance, end of year	144	155	195
	Budget authority and outlays, net:			
	Discretionary:			
4000	Budget authority, gross	130	130	165
	Outlays, gross:			
4010	Outlays from new discretionary authority	34	29	42
4011	Outlays from discretionary balances	92	87	88
4020	Outlays, gross (total)	126	116	130
	Mandatory:			
	Outlays, gross:			
4101	Outlays from mandatory balances	2,969	1,130	
4180	Budget authority, net (total)	130	130	165
4190	Outlays, net (total)	3,095	1,246	130

Summary of Loan Levels, Subsidy Budget Authority and Outlays by Program (in millions of dollars)

Identification code 086–0183–0–1–371		2021 actual	2022 est.	2023 est.
	Guaranteed loan levels supportable by subsidy budget authority:			
215002	MMI Fund	344,464	326,000	225,000
215004	MMI HECM	21,330	23,900	26,430
215008	Home Equity Accelerator Loan			3,409
215999	Total loan guarantee levels	365,794	349,900	254,839
	Guaranteed loan subsidy (in percent):			
232002	MMI Fund	–3.36	–2.69	–3.05
232004	MMI HECM	–2.39	–2.54	–4.19
232008	Home Equity Accelerator Loan			0.44
232999	Weighted average subsidy rate	–3.30	–2.68	–3.12
	Guaranteed loan subsidy budget authority:			
233002	MMI Fund	–11,574	–8,769	–6,863
233004	MMI HECM	–510	–607	–1,107
233008	Home Equity Accelerator Loan			15
233999	Total subsidy budget authority	–12,084	–9,376	–7,955
	Guaranteed loan subsidy outlays:			
234002	MMI Fund	–11,481	–8,769	–6,863
234004	MMI HECM	–510	–607	–1,107
234008	Home Equity Accelerator Loan			8
234999	Total subsidy outlays	–11,991	–9,376	–7,962
	Guaranteed loan reestimates:			
235002	MMI Fund	–3,434	–13,323	
235004	MMI HECM	–9,344	–5,393	
235999	Total guaranteed loan reestimates	–12,778	–18,716	
	Administrative expense data:			
3510	Budget authority	130	130	130
3580	Outlays from balances	92	87	86
3590	Outlays from new authority	34	29	30

The Federal Housing Administration (FHA) provides mortgage insurance for the purchase, refinance and rehabilitation of single-family homes. FHA mortgage insurance is designed to encourage lenders to make credit available to borrowers whom the conventional market does not adequately serve, including first-time homebuyers, minorities, lower-income families and residents of underserved areas (central cities and rural areas). Historically, FHA has also provided countercyclical support in times of economic crisis. For budgetary purposes, the Mutual Mortgage Insurance (MMI) Fund is separated into three risk categories: forward loans, Home Equity Conversion Mortgages (HECMs), and a proposed Home Equity Accelerator Loan (HEAL) pilot. Forward programs guarantee loans for standard single-family purchases and refinances (Section 203(b) program), home improvements (Section 203(k) program) and condominiums. HECMs, also known as reverse mortgages, enable elderly homeowners to borrow against the equity in their homes without having to make repayments during their lifetime. HEAL, a new positive subsidy pilot, would offer loan products designed to lower barriers to homeownership for first-generation and/or low-wealth first-time homebuyers.

The Budget requests $165 million for the MMI Program account. This includes $150 million in administrative expenses to support a range of FHA functions, such as loan underwriting, claims processing and risk

DEPARTMENT OF HOUSING AND URBAN DEVELOPMENT

Housing Programs—Continued
Federal Funds—Continued

587

monitoring. Additionally, the Budget provides $15 million in credit subsidy for the new HEAL pilot.

The Budget also requests a limitation of $400 billion on loan guarantees for the MMI Fund. The Budget projects insurance of $225 billion in forward mortgages, $26.4 billion in HECMs, and $3.4 billion in HEAL pilot loans, with additional commitment authority available in case these amounts are exceeded during execution.

Object Classification (in millions of dollars)

Identification code 086–0183–0–1–371		2021 actual	2022 est.	2023 est.
	Direct obligations:			
25.2	Other services from non-Federal sources	151	130	159
41.0	Grants, subsidies, and contributions	2,754	662	15
43.0	Interest and dividends	215	468	....
99.9	Total new obligations, unexpired accounts	3,120	1,260	174

FHA-MUTUAL MORTGAGE INSURANCE GUARANTEED LOAN FINANCING ACCOUNT

Program and Financing (in millions of dollars)

Identification code 086–4587–0–3–371		2021 actual	2022 est.	2023 est.
	Obligations by program activity:			
0003	Other capital investment & operating expenses	4,923	7,625	3,408
	Credit program obligations:			
0711	Default claim payments on principal	4,883	7,563	3,381
0712	Default claim payments on interest	84	130	158
0713	Payment of interest to Treasury	2,088	1,848	1,968
0740	Negative subsidy obligations	12,084	9,376	7,970
0742	Downward reestimates paid to receipt accounts	12,985	17,529	....
0743	Interest on downward reestimates	2,762	2,317	....
0791	Direct program activities, subtotal	34,886	38,763	13,477
0900	Total new obligations, unexpired accounts	39,809	46,388	16,885
	Budgetary resources:			
	Unobligated balance:			
1000	Unobligated balance brought forward, Oct 1	8,537	6,394	261
1021	Recoveries of prior year unpaid obligations	488	419	487
1033	Recoveries of prior year paid obligations	52	....	....
1070	Unobligated balance (total)	9,077	6,813	748
	Financing authority:			
	Borrowing authority, mandatory:			
1400	Borrowing authority	19,647	25,000	8,600
	Spending authority from offsetting collections, mandatory:			
1800	Offsetting collections	22,604	16,936	16,640
1825	Spending authority from offsetting collections applied to repay debt	–5,125	–2,100	–2,100
1850	Spending auth from offsetting collections, mand (total)	17,479	14,836	14,540
1900	Budget authority (total)	37,126	39,836	23,140
1930	Total budgetary resources available	46,203	46,649	23,888
	Memorandum (non-add) entries:			
1941	Unexpired unobligated balance, end of year	6,394	261	7,003
	Change in obligated balance:			
	Unpaid obligations:			
3000	Unpaid obligations, brought forward, Oct 1	1,746	1,467	25,853
3010	New obligations, unexpired accounts	39,809	46,388	16,885
3020	Outlays (gross)	–39,600	–21,583	–19,376
3040	Recoveries of prior year unpaid obligations, unexpired	–488	–419	–487
3050	Unpaid obligations, end of year	1,467	25,853	22,875
	Memorandum (non-add) entries:			
3100	Obligated balance, start of year	1,746	1,467	25,853
3200	Obligated balance, end of year	1,467	25,853	22,875
	Financing authority and disbursements, net:			
	Mandatory:			
4090	Budget authority, gross	37,126	39,836	23,140
	Financing disbursements:			
4110	Outlays, gross (total)	39,600	21,583	19,376
	Offsets against gross financing authority and disbursements:			
	Offsetting collections (collected) from:			
4120	Upward Reestimate from Program Account	–2,969	–1,130	....
4120	Credit Subsidy	....	....	–8
4122	Interest on uninvested funds	–402	–401	–435
4123	Fees and premiums	–14,626	–14,324	–14,318
4123	Recoveries on defaults	–4,607	–1,081	–1,879
4123	Repayment of Excess Claims	–52	....	....
4130	Offsets against gross budget authority and outlays (total)	–22,656	–16,936	–16,640
	Additional offsets against financing authority only (total):			
4143	Recoveries of prior year paid obligations, unexpired accounts	52	....	....
4160	Budget authority, net (mandatory)	14,522	22,900	6,500
4170	Outlays, net (mandatory)	16,944	4,647	2,736
4180	Budget authority, net (total)	14,522	22,900	6,500
4190	Outlays, net (total)	16,944	4,647	2,736

Status of Guaranteed Loans (in millions of dollars)

Identification code 086–4587–0–3–371		2021 actual	2022 est.	2023 est.
	Position with respect to appropriations act limitation on commitments:			
2111	Guaranteed loan commitments from current-year authority	400,000	400,000	400,000
2121	Limitation available from carry-forward	400,000	400,000	400,000
2142	Uncommitted loan guarantee limitation	–34,206	–50,100	–145,161
2143	Uncommitted limitation carried forward	–400,000	–400,000	–400,000
2150	Total guaranteed loan commitments	365,794	349,900	254,839
2199	Guaranteed amount of guaranteed loan commitments	365,794	349,900	254,839
	Cumulative balance of guaranteed loans outstanding:			
2210	Outstanding, start of year	1,311,279	1,252,407	1,388,729
2231	Disbursements of new guaranteed loans	365,794	349,900	253,134
2251	Repayments and prepayments	–419,783	–197,935	–183,768
	Adjustments:			
2261	Terminations for default that result in loans receivable	–4,078	–8,654	–7,185
2262	Terminations for default that result in acquisition of property	–590	–1,286	–1,190
2263	Terminations for default that result in claim payments	–215	–5,703	–6,624
2264	Other adjustments, net	....	....	....
2290	Outstanding, end of year	1,252,407	1,388,729	1,443,096
	Memorandum:			
2299	Guaranteed amount of guaranteed loans outstanding, end of year	1,252,407	1,388,729	1,443,096
	Addendum:			
	Cumulative balance of defaulted guaranteed loans that result in loans receivable:			
2310	Outstanding, start of year	31,608	35,130	39,536
2331	Disbursements for guaranteed loan claims	4,078	8,654	7,185
2351	Repayments of loans receivable	–556	–1,032	–1,103
2361	Write-offs of loans receivable	....	–3,216	–2,141
2364	Other adjustments, net	....	....	....
2390	Outstanding, end of year	35,130	39,536	43,477

Balance Sheet (in millions of dollars)

Identification code 086–4587–0–3–371		2020 actual	2021 actual
	ASSETS:		
	Federal assets:		
1101	Fund balances with Treasury	10,283	7,861
	Investments in U.S. securities:		
1106	Receivables, net	3,356	1,993
1206	Non-Federal assets: Receivables, net	848	1,272
	Net value of assets related to post-1991 acquired defaulted guaranteed loans receivable:		
1501	Defaulted guaranteed loans receivable, gross	31,608	35,130
1502	Interest receivable	13,943	15,653
1504	Foreclosed property	696	449
1505	Allowance for subsidy cost (-)	–13,095	–13,788
1599	Net value of assets related to defaulted guaranteed loan	33,152	37,444
	Other Federal assets:		
1801	Cash and other monetary assets	6	60
1901	Other assets	....	....
1999	Total assets	47,645	48,630
	LIABILITIES:		
	Federal liabilities:		
2101	Accounts payable	1	....
2103	Federal liabilities, Debt	42,686	57,208
2105	Other	13,596	8,884
	Non-Federal liabilities:		
2201	Accounts payable	444	433
2204	Liabilities for loan guarantees	–9,479	–18,258
2207	Other	397	363
2999	Total liabilities	47,645	48,630

FHA-MUTUAL MORTGAGE INSURANCE GUARANTEED LOAN FINANCING ACCOUNT—Continued

Balance Sheet—Continued

Identification code 086–4587–0–3–371	2020 actual	2021 actual
NET POSITION:		
3300 Cumulative results of operations	....	....
3300 Total other	....	....
3999 Total net position	....	....
4999 Total liabilities and net position	47,645	48,630

FHA-MUTUAL MORTGAGE INSURANCE CAPITAL RESERVE ACCOUNT

Program and Financing (in millions of dollars)

Identification code 086–0236–0–1–371	2021 actual	2022 est.	2023 est.
Budgetary resources:			
Unobligated balance:			
1000 Unobligated balance brought forward, Oct 1	68,903	92,309	123,024
1010 Unobligated balance transfer to other accts [086–0183]	–2,969	–1,130	....
1011 Unobligated balance transfer from other acct [086–4070]	....	23	....
1070 Unobligated balance (total)	65,934	91,202	123,024
Budget authority:			
Spending authority from offsetting collections, mandatory:			
1800 Offsetting collections (negative subsidy)	11,991	9,376	7,970
1800 Offsetting collections (interest on investments)	–1,587	2,600	1,043
1800 Offsetting collections (downward reestimate)	15,747	19,846	....
1801 Change in uncollected payments, Federal sources	224	....	....
1850 Spending auth from offsetting collections, mand (total)	26,375	31,822	9,013
1930 Total budgetary resources available	92,309	123,024	132,037
Memorandum (non-add) entries:			
1941 Unexpired unobligated balance, end of year	92,309	123,024	132,037
Change in obligated balance:			
Uncollected payments:			
3060 Uncollected pymts, Fed sources, brought forward, Oct 1	–324	–548	–548
3070 Change in uncollected pymts, Fed sources, unexpired	–224	....	....
3090 Uncollected pymts, Fed sources, end of year	–548	–548	–548
Memorandum (non-add) entries:			
3100 Obligated balance, start of year	–324	–548	–548
3200 Obligated balance, end of year	–548	–548	–548
Budget authority and outlays, net:			
Discretionary:			
Offsets against gross budget authority and outlays:			
Offsetting collections (collected) from:			
4030 Federal sources	–11,991	–9,376	–7,970
Mandatory:			
4090 Budget authority, gross	26,375	31,822	9,013
Offsets against gross budget authority and outlays:			
Offsetting collections (collected) from:			
4120 Federal Sources: Downward Reestimate	–15,747	–19,846	....
4121 Interest on Federal securities	1,587	–2,600	–1,043
4130 Offsets against gross budget authority and outlays (total)	–14,160	–22,446	–1,043
Additional offsets against gross budget authority only:			
4140 Change in uncollected pymts, Fed sources, unexpired	–224	....	....
4160 Budget authority, net (mandatory)	11,991	9,376	7,970
4170 Outlays, net (mandatory)	–14,160	–22,446	–1,043
4180 Budget authority, net (total)	....	....	....
4190 Outlays, net (total)	–26,151	–31,822	–9,013
Memorandum (non-add) entries:			
5000 Total investments, SOY: Federal securities: Par value	67,937	94,132	122,494
5001 Total investments, EOY: Federal securities: Par value	94,132	122,494	131,354

The Capital Reserve account is the ultimate depository for all net budgetary resources collected by MMI Fund programs. Negative credit subsidy receipts from new loan guarantees and downward reestimates, as well as interest earnings on Treasury investments, are recorded in this account. This account has no authority to obligate funds, but transfers balances of budget authority as necessary to the MMI Program account for the cost of upward credit subsidy reestimates and the MMI Liquidating account for obligations of that account.

Balance Sheet (in millions of dollars)

Identification code 086–0236–0–1–371	2020 actual	2021 actual
ASSETS:		
Federal assets:		
1101 Fund balances with Treasury	650	944
Investments in U.S. securities:		
1102 Treasury securities, net	69,246	97,342
1106 Receivables, net	13,596	8,884
1999 Total assets	83,492	107,170
LIABILITIES:		
Federal liabilities:		
2101 Accounts payable	....	....
2105 Other	3,356	5,297
2999 Total liabilities	3,356	5,297
NET POSITION:		
3300 Cumulative results of operations	80,136	101,873
4999 Total liabilities and net position	83,492	107,170

FHA-MUTUAL MORTGAGE AND COOPERATIVE HOUSING INSURANCE FUNDS LIQUIDATING ACCOUNT

Program and Financing (in millions of dollars)

Identification code 086–4070–0–3–371	2021 actual	2022 est.	2023 est.
Obligations by program activity:			
0103 Acquisition of real properties	....	14	....
0107 Capitalized Expenses	4	3	5
0108 Loss mitigation activities	....	2	....
0191 Total capital investment	4	19	5
0202 Other Operation expenses	2	3	3
0900 Total new obligations, unexpired accounts	6	22	8
Budgetary resources:			
Unobligated balance:			
1000 Unobligated balance brought forward, Oct 1	30	34	....
1010 Unobligated balance transfer to other accts [086–0236]	....	–23	....
1021 Recoveries of prior year unpaid obligations	5	5	5
1070 Unobligated balance (total)	35	16	5
Budget authority:			
Spending authority from offsetting collections, mandatory:			
1800 Collected	5	6	6
1930 Total budgetary resources available	40	22	11
Memorandum (non-add) entries:			
1941 Unexpired unobligated balance, end of year	34	....	3
Change in obligated balance:			
Unpaid obligations:			
3000 Unpaid obligations, brought forward, Oct 1	150	146	145
3010 New obligations, unexpired accounts	6	22	8
3020 Outlays (gross)	–5	–18	–17
3040 Recoveries of prior year unpaid obligations, unexpired	–5	–5	–5
3050 Unpaid obligations, end of year	146	145	131
Memorandum (non-add) entries:			
3100 Obligated balance, start of year	150	146	145
3200 Obligated balance, end of year	146	145	131
Budget authority and outlays, net:			
Mandatory:			
4090 Budget authority, gross	5	6	6
Outlays, gross:			
4100 Outlays from new mandatory authority	2	3	2
4101 Outlays from mandatory balances	3	15	15
4110 Outlays, gross (total)	5	18	17
Offsets against gross budget authority and outlays:			
Offsetting collections (collected) from:			
4123 Non-Federal sources - Fees & Premiums	–4	–3	–3
4123 Non-Federal sources - Recoveries on Defaults	–1	–3	–3
4130 Offsets against gross budget authority and outlays (total)	–5	–6	–6
4170 Outlays, net (mandatory)	....	12	11
4180 Budget authority, net (total)	....	....	....

DEPARTMENT OF HOUSING AND URBAN DEVELOPMENT

Housing Programs—Continued
Federal Funds—Continued

589

Identification code 086–4070–0–3–371		2021 actual	2022 est.	2023 est.
4190	Outlays, net (total)	....	12	11

Status of Guaranteed Loans (in millions of dollars)

Identification code 086–4070–0–3–371		2021 actual	2022 est.	2023 est.
	Cumulative balance of guaranteed loans outstanding:			
2210	Outstanding, start of year	17	....	....
2251	Repayments and prepayments	–17	....	....
2262	Adjustments: Terminations for default that result in acquisition of property	....	....	....
2290	Outstanding, end of year	....	....	....
	Memorandum:			
2299	Guaranteed amount of guaranteed loans outstanding, end of year	....	....	....
	Addendum:			
	Cumulative balance of defaulted guaranteed loans that result in loans receivable:			
2310	Outstanding, start of year	15	15	14
2331	Disbursements for guaranteed loan claims	....	....	....
2351	Repayments of loans receivable	....	....	....
2361	Write-offs of loans receivable	....	–1	–1
2390	Outstanding, end of year	15	14	13

Balance Sheet (in millions of dollars)

Identification code 086–4070–0–3–371		2020 actual	2021 actual
	ASSETS:		
1101	Federal assets: Fund balances with Treasury	180	178
1206	Non-Federal assets: Receivables, net	1	....
1701	Defaulted guaranteed loans, gross	15	15
1703	Allowance for estimated uncollectible loans and interest (-)	–1	–1
1704	Defaulted guaranteed loans and interest receivable, net	14	14
1705	Accounts receivable from foreclosed property	....	....
1706	Foreclosed property	1	....
1799	Value of assets related to loan guarantees	15	14
	Other Federal assets:		
1801	Cash and other monetary assets	....	....
1901	Other assets	....	....
1999	Total assets	196	192
	LIABILITIES:		
	Non-Federal liabilities:		
2201	Accounts payable	144	144
2204	Liabilities for loan guarantees	....	....
2207	Unearned revenue and advances, and other	22	21
2999	Total liabilities	166	165
	NET POSITION:		
3300	Cumulative results of operations	30	27
4999	Total liabilities and net position	196	192

Object Classification (in millions of dollars)

Identification code 086–4070–0–3–371		2021 actual	2022 est.	2023 est.
	Direct obligations:			
25.2	Other services from non-Federal sources	2	3	3
32.0	Land and structures	4	3	5
42.0	Insurance claims and indemnities	....	16	....
99.9	Total new obligations, unexpired accounts	6	22	8

HOME OWNERSHIP PRESERVATION EQUITY FUND PROGRAM ACCOUNT

Program and Financing (in millions of dollars)

Identification code 086–0343–0–1–371		2021 actual	2022 est.	2023 est.
	Budgetary resources:			
	Unobligated balance:			
1000	Unobligated balance brought forward, Oct 1	7	7	7
1930	Total budgetary resources available	7	7	7
	Memorandum (non-add) entries:			
1941	Unexpired unobligated balance, end of year	7	7	7
4180	Budget authority, net (total)	....	....	....
4190	Outlays, net (total)	....	....	....

Summary of Loan Levels, Subsidy Budget Authority and Outlays by Program (in millions of dollars)

Identification code 086–0343–0–1–371		2021 actual	2022 est.	2023 est.
	Guaranteed loan reestimates:			
235001	HOPE for Homeowners Loan Guarantees	–1	–1	....

The HOPE for Homeowners program was created by the Housing and Economic Recovery Act of 2008 to help homeowners at risk of default and foreclosure refinance into affordable, sustainable loans. Under the program, eligible homeowners refinanced their current mortgage loans into a new mortgage insured by FHA. The program ended on September 30, 2011. In 2016, excess HOPE Bond proceeds in the amount of $455 million were transferred to the HOPE Reserve Fund, and used to retire the HOPE Bonds. Remaining HOPE Bond activity is shown in the HOPE Reserve Fund.

HOME OWNERSHIP PRESERVATION EQUITY FUND FINANCING ACCOUNT

Program and Financing (in millions of dollars)

Identification code 086–4353–0–3–371		2021 actual	2022 est.	2023 est.
	Obligations by program activity:			
0003	Other Investment & Operating Expenses	1	1	1
	Credit program obligations:			
0711	Default claim payments on principal	1	1	1
0742	Downward reestimates paid to receipt accounts	1	1	....
0791	Direct program activities, subtotal	2	2	1
0900	Total new obligations, unexpired accounts	3	3	2
	Budgetary resources:			
	Unobligated balance:			
1000	Unobligated balance brought forward, Oct 1	3	2	1
1021	Recoveries of prior year unpaid obligations	1	....	....
1070	Unobligated balance (total)	4	2	1
	Financing authority:			
	Spending authority from offsetting collections, mandatory:			
1800	Collected	1	2	2
1900	Budget authority (total)	1	2	2
1930	Total budgetary resources available	5	4	3
	Memorandum (non-add) entries:			
1941	Unexpired unobligated balance, end of year	2	1	1
	Change in obligated balance:			
	Unpaid obligations:			
3000	Unpaid obligations, brought forward, Oct 1	2	2	4
3010	New obligations, unexpired accounts	3	3	2
3020	Outlays (gross)	–2	–1	–1
3040	Recoveries of prior year unpaid obligations, unexpired	–1	....	....
3050	Unpaid obligations, end of year	2	4	5
	Memorandum (non-add) entries:			
3100	Obligated balance, start of year	2	2	4
3200	Obligated balance, end of year	2	4	5
	Financing authority and disbursements, net:			
	Mandatory:			
4090	Budget authority, gross	1	2	2
	Financing disbursements:			
4110	Outlays, gross (total)	2	1	1
	Offsets against gross financing authority and disbursements:			
	Offsetting collections (collected) from:			
4122	Interest on uninvested funds	....	–1	–1
4123	Premiums	–1	–1	–1
4130	Offsets against gross budget authority and outlays (total)	–1	–2	–2
4170	Outlays, net (mandatory)	1	–1	–1
4180	Budget authority, net (total)	....	....	....
4190	Outlays, net (total)	1	–1	–1

HOME OWNERSHIP PRESERVATION EQUITY FUND FINANCING ACCOUNT—Continued

Status of Guaranteed Loans (in millions of dollars)

Identification code 086–4353–0–3–371		2021 actual	2022 est.	2023 est.
	Position with respect to appropriations act limitation on commitments:			
2143	Uncommitted limitation carried forward	....	....	....
2150	Total guaranteed loan commitments	....	....	....
	Cumulative balance of guaranteed loans outstanding:			
2210	Outstanding, start of year	48	46	44
2251	Repayments and prepayments	–1	–1	–1
	Adjustments:			
2261	Terminations for default that result in loans receivable	....	....	....
2262	Terminations for default that result in acquisition of property	....	....	....
2263	Terminations for default that result in claim payments	–1	–1	–1
2290	Outstanding, end of year	46	44	42
	Memorandum:			
2299	Guaranteed amount of guaranteed loans outstanding, end of year	46	44	42
	Addendum:			
	Cumulative balance of defaulted guaranteed loans that result in loans receivable:			
2310	Outstanding, start of year	6	6	6
2331	Disbursements for guaranteed loan claims	....	....	....
2390	Outstanding, end of year	6	6	6

Balance Sheet (in millions of dollars)

Identification code 086–4353–0–3–371		2020 actual	2021 actual
	ASSETS:		
1101	Federal assets: Fund balances with Treasury	5	5
	Net value of assets related to post-1991 acquired defaulted guaranteed loans receivable:		
1501	Defaulted guaranteed loans receivable, gross	6	6
1504	Foreclosed property	....	....
1505	Allowance for subsidy cost (–)	–3	–3
1599	Net present value of assets related to defaulted guaranteed loans	3	3
1999	Total assets	8	8
	LIABILITIES:		
2204	Non-Federal liabilities: Liabilities for loan guarantees	8	8
	NET POSITION:		
3300	Cumulative results of operations	....	....
4999	Total liabilities and net position	8	8

EMERGENCY HOMEOWNERS' RELIEF FUND

Summary of Loan Levels, Subsidy Budget Authority and Outlays by Program (in millions of dollars)

Identification code 086–0407–0–1–371		2021 actual	2022 est.	2023 est.
	Direct loan reestimates:			
135001	Emergency Homeowners' Relief	–4	–1	....

The Emergency Homeowners Loan Program (EHLP), which expired in 2011, provided emergency mortgage assistance to homeowners who were unemployed or underemployed due to economic or medical conditions. This account reflects no new obligations but displays the liquidation of prior year obligations.

EMERGENCY HOMEOWNERS' RELIEF FINANCING ACCOUNT

Program and Financing (in millions of dollars)

Identification code 086–4357–0–3–371		2021 actual	2022 est.	2023 est.
	Obligations by program activity:			
	Credit program obligations:			
0742	Downward reestimates paid to receipt accounts	3	1	....
0743	Interest on downward reestimates	1	....	....
0900	Total new obligations, unexpired accounts	4	1	....
	Budgetary resources:			
	Unobligated balance:			
1000	Unobligated balance brought forward, Oct 1	1	....	....
	Financing authority:			
	Borrowing authority, mandatory:			
1400	Borrowing authority	2	....	....
	Spending authority from offsetting collections, mandatory:			
1800	Collected	1	1	1
1900	Budget authority (total)	3	1	1
1930	Total budgetary resources available	4	1	1
	Memorandum (non-add) entries:			
1941	Unexpired unobligated balance, end of year	....	....	1
	Change in obligated balance:			
	Unpaid obligations:			
3010	New obligations, unexpired accounts	4	1	....
3020	Outlays (gross)	–4	–1	....
	Financing authority and disbursements, net:			
	Mandatory:			
4090	Budget authority, gross	3	1	1
	Financing disbursements:			
4110	Outlays, gross (total)	4	1	....
	Offsets against gross financing authority and disbursements:			
	Offsetting collections (collected) from:			
4123	Repayments of principal, net	–1	–1	–1
4180	Budget authority, net (total)	2	....	....
4190	Outlays, net (total)	3	....	–1

Status of Direct Loans (in millions of dollars)

Identification code 086–4357–0–3–371		2021 actual	2022 est.	2023 est.
	Cumulative balance of direct loans outstanding:			
1210	Outstanding, start of year	56	54	53
1251	Repayments: Repayments and prepayments	–1	–1	–1
1264	Other adjustments, net (+ or –)	–1	....	....
1290	Outstanding, end of year	54	53	52

Balance Sheet (in millions of dollars)

Identification code 086–4357–0–3–371		2020 actual	2021 actual
	ASSETS:		
1101	Federal assets: Fund balances with Treasury	....	....
	Net value of assets related to post-1991 direct loans receivable:		
1401	Direct loans receivable, gross	56	54
1405	Allowance for subsidy cost (–)	–56	–53
1499	Net present value of assets related to direct loans	....	1
1999	Total assets	....	1
	LIABILITIES:		
2103	Federal liabilities: Debt payable to Treasury	....	1
4999	Total Liabilities and Net Position	....	1

GENERAL AND SPECIAL RISK PROGRAM ACCOUNT

New commitments to guarantee loans insured under the General and Special Risk Insurance Funds, as authorized by sections 238 and 519 of the National Housing Act (12 U.S.C. 1715z–3 and 1735c), shall not exceed $35,000,000,000 in total loan principal, any part of which is to be guaranteed, to remain available until September 30, 2024: Provided, That during fiscal year 2023, gross obligations for the principal amount of direct loans, as authorized by sections 204(g), 207(l), 238, and 519(a) of the National Housing Act, shall not exceed $1,000,000, which shall be for loans to nonprofit and governmental entities in connection with the sale of single family real properties owned by the Secretary and formerly insured under such Act.

Note.—A full-year 2022 appropriation for this account was not enacted at the time the Budget was prepared; therefore, the Budget assumes this account is operating under the Continuing Appropriations Act, 2022 (Division A of Public Law 117–43, as amended). The amounts included for 2022 reflect the annualized level provided by the continuing resolution.

Program and Financing (in millions of dollars)

Identification code 086–0200–0–1–371	2021 actual	2022 est.	2023 est.
Obligations by program activity:			
Credit program obligations:			
0705 Reestimates of direct loan subsidy	277		
0706 Interest on reestimates of direct loan subsidy		62	
0707 Reestimates of loan guarantee subsidy	1,508	459	
0708 Interest on reestimates of loan guarantee subsidy	212	118	
0900 Total new obligations, unexpired accounts	1,997	639	
Budgetary resources:			
Unobligated balance:			
1000 Unobligated balance brought forward, Oct 1	2	2	2
Budget authority:			
Appropriations, mandatory:			
1200 Appropriation	1,997	639	
1900 Budget authority (total)	1,997	639	
1930 Total budgetary resources available	1,999	641	2
Memorandum (non-add) entries:			
1941 Unexpired unobligated balance, end of year	2	2	2
Change in obligated balance:			
Unpaid obligations:			
3010 New obligations, unexpired accounts	1,997	639	
3020 Outlays (gross)	–1,997	–639	
Budget authority and outlays, net:			
Mandatory:			
4090 Budget authority, gross	1,997	639	
Outlays, gross:			
4100 Outlays from new mandatory authority	1,997	639	
4180 Budget authority, net (total)	1,997	639	
4190 Outlays, net (total)	1,997	639	

Summary of Loan Levels, Subsidy Budget Authority and Outlays by Program (in millions of dollars)

Identification code 086–0200–0–1–371	2021 actual	2022 est.	2023 est.
Direct loan levels supportable by subsidy budget authority:			
115002 FFB Risk Sharing		2,000	1,496
115999 Total direct loan levels		2,000	1,496
Direct loan subsidy (in percent):			
132002 FFB Risk Sharing		–9.23	–8.13
132999 Weighted average subsidy rate		–9.23	–8.13
Direct loan subsidy budget authority:			
133002 FFB Risk Sharing		–185	–122
133999 Total subsidy budget authority		–185	–122
Direct loan subsidy outlays:			
134002 FFB Risk Sharing	–41	–48	–161
134999 Total subsidy outlays	–41	–48	–161
Direct loan reestimates:			
135002 FFB Risk Sharing	185	–164	
135999 Total direct loan reestimates	185	–164	
Guaranteed loan levels supportable by subsidy budget authority:			
215001 Apartment New Construction / Substantial Rehab	3,805	3,928	3,143
215003 Tax Credits	5,478	5,522	5,522
215005 Apartment Refinances	20,944	16,772	11,956
215008 Housing Finance Agency Risk Sharing	631	337	303
215010 Residential Care Facilities	116	123	125
215011 Residential Care Facility Refinances	4,549	4,814	4,812
215012 Hospitals	1,447	642	642
215013 Other Rental	421	260	195
215017 Title 1 Property Improvement	26	30	50
215018 Title 1 Manufactured Housing	1	1	1
215999 Total loan guarantee levels	37,418	32,429	26,749
Guaranteed loan subsidy (in percent):			
232001 Apartment New Construction / Substantial Rehab	–1.19	–1.32	–.90
232003 Tax Credits	–2.27	–2.52	–2.17
232005 Apartment Refinances	–2.37	–2.88	–2.25
232008 Housing Finance Agency Risk Sharing	–1.32	–2.27	–1.56
232010 Residential Care Facilities	–6.32	–6.51	–5.80
232011 Residential Care Facility Refinances	–2.70	–3.50	–2.27
232012 Hospitals	–5.81	–5.37	–5.73
232013 Other Rental	–2.27	–3.34	–2.64
232017 Title 1 Property Improvement	–2.45	–1.69	–1.60
232018 Title 1 Manufactured Housing	–6.20	–6.21	–6.15
232999 Weighted average subsidy rate	–2.40	–2.78	–2.17
Guaranteed loan subsidy budget authority:			
233001 Apartment New Construction / Substantial Rehab	–45	–52	–28
233003 Tax Credits	–124	–139	–120
233005 Apartment Refinances	–497	–483	–269
233008 Housing Finance Agency Risk Sharing	–8	–8	–5
233010 Residential Care Facilities	–7	–8	–7
233011 Residential Care Facility Refinances	–123	–168	–109
233012 Hospitals	–84	–34	–37
233013 Other Rental	–9	–9	–5
233017 Title 1 Property Improvement	–1	–1	–1
233018 Title 1 Manufactured Housing	–1		
233999 Total subsidy budget authority	–899	–902	–581
Guaranteed loan subsidy outlays:			
234001 Apartment New Construction / Substantial Rehab	–43	–46	–32
234003 Tax Credits	–99	–134	–121
234005 Apartment Refinances	–526	–391	–297
234008 Housing Finance Agency Risk Sharing	–6	–5	–6
234010 Residential Care Facilities	–2	–12	–7
234011 Residential Care Facility Refinances	–130	–129	–121
234012 Hospitals	–98	–10	–36
234013 Other Rental	–6	–8	–7
234017 Title 1 Property Improvement	–1	–1	–1
234999 Total subsidy outlays	–911	–736	–628
Guaranteed loan reestimates:			
235001 Apartment New Construction / Substantial Rehab	211	–124	
235003 Tax Credits	233	–17	
235005 Apartment Refinances	126	35	
235008 Housing Finance Agency Risk Sharing	–1		
235010 Residential Care Facilities	8	–4	
235011 Residential Care Facility Refinances	216	16	
235012 Hospitals	–2	–92	
235013 Other Rental	5	7	
235017 Title 1 Property Improvement	1	1	
235018 Title 1 Manufactured Housing	2		
235023 GI/SRI Reestimates	–1,465	–2,676	
235999 Total guaranteed loan reestimates	–666	–2,854	

The Federal Housing Administration's General Insurance and Special Risk Insurance (GI/SRI) programs provide mortgage insurance for a variety of purposes, including financing for the development and rehabilitation of multifamily housing, residential care facilities, and hospitals. The Budget requests a limitation of $35 billion on loan guarantees for the GI/SRI Fund. GI/SRI's mortgage insurance programs are designed to operate without the need for subsidy appropriations, with fees set higher than anticipated losses. Therefore, the Budget does not request an appropriation of new credit subsidy funds.

GI/SRI programs guarantee loans at 100 percent, with three exceptions where other parties guarantee a portion of the loan: Housing Finance Agency Risk Sharing, Qualified Participating Entity Risk Sharing, and Federal Financing Bank Risk Sharing.

Object Classification (in millions of dollars)

Identification code 086–0200–0–1–371	2021 actual	2022 est.	2023 est.
Direct obligations:			
41.0 Grants, subsidies, and contributions	1,785	459	
41.0 Interest	212	180	
99.9 Total new obligations, unexpired accounts	1,997	639	

FHA–GENERAL AND SPECIAL RISK GUARANTEED LOAN FINANCING ACCOUNT

Program and Financing (in millions of dollars)

Identification code 086–4077–0–3–371	2021 actual	2022 est.	2023 est.
Obligations by program activity:			
0003 Other capital investments and operating expenses	3	107	107
0014 Contract Costs		30	30
0091 Direct program activities, subtotal	3	137	137
Credit program obligations:			
0711 Default claim payments on principal	1,627	1,256	1,375
0712 Default claim payments on interest	574	471	841
0713 Payment of interest to Treasury	398	596	596
0740 Negative subsidy obligations	899	902	581
0742 Downward reestimates paid to receipt accounts	1,224	1,872	

Housing Programs—Continued
Federal Funds—Continued

FHA-GENERAL AND SPECIAL RISK GUARANTEED LOAN FINANCING ACCOUNT—Continued

Program and Financing—Continued

Identification code 086–4077–0–3–371	2021 actual	2022 est.	2023 est.
0743 Interest on downward reestimates	1,161	1,560	....
0791 Direct program activities, subtotal	5,883	6,657	3,393
0900 Total new obligations, unexpired accounts	5,886	6,794	3,530
Budgetary resources:			
Unobligated balance:			
1000 Unobligated balance brought forward, Oct 1	5,952	3,938	1,116
1021 Recoveries of prior year unpaid obligations	55	50	50
1033 Recoveries of prior year paid obligations	6	7	7
1070 Unobligated balance (total)	6,013	3,995	1,173
Financing authority:			
Borrowing authority, mandatory:			
1400 Borrowing authority	1,688	2,639	2,639
1400 Borrowing authority	29	15	15
1440 Borrowing authority, mandatory (total)	1,717	2,654	2,654
Spending authority from offsetting collections, mandatory:			
1800 Collected	3,844	2,117	1,551
1825 Spending authority from offsetting collections applied to repay debt	–1,750	–856	–856
1850 Spending auth from offsetting collections, mand (total)	2,094	1,261	695
1900 Budget authority (total)	3,811	3,915	3,349
1930 Total budgetary resources available	9,824	7,910	4,522
Memorandum (non-add) entries:			
1941 Unexpired unobligated balance, end of year	3,938	1,116	992
Change in obligated balance:			
Unpaid obligations:			
3000 Unpaid obligations, brought forward, Oct 1	603	557	3,708
3010 New obligations, unexpired accounts	5,886	6,794	3,530
3020 Outlays (gross)	–5,877	–3,593	–3,593
3040 Recoveries of prior year unpaid obligations, unexpired	–55	–50	–50
3050 Unpaid obligations, end of year	557	3,708	3,595
Memorandum (non-add) entries:			
3100 Obligated balance, start of year	603	557	3,708
3200 Obligated balance, end of year	557	3,708	3,595
Financing authority and disbursements, net:			
Mandatory:			
4090 Budget authority, gross	3,811	3,915	3,349
Financing disbursements:			
4110 Outlays, gross (total)	5,877	3,593	3,593
Offsets against gross financing authority and disbursements:			
Offsetting collections (collected) from:			
4120 Upward reestimate from program account	–1,720	–577	....
4122 Interest on uninvested funds	–241	–287	–287
4123 Fees and premiums	–859	–963	–859
4123 Recoveries on HUD-Held Notes	–866	–278	–11
4123 Title I recoveries	–7	–1	....
4123 Single family property recoveries	–152	–5	–8
4123 Gross Proceeds from Mortgage Note Sales	–2	–3	–383
4123 Non-Federal Resources-other	–3	–10	–10
4130 Offsets against gross budget authority and outlays (total)	–3,850	–2,124	–1,558
Additional offsets against financing authority only (total):			
4143 Recoveries of prior year paid obligations, unexpired accounts	6	7	7
4160 Budget authority, net (mandatory)	–33	1,798	1,798
4170 Outlays, net (mandatory)	2,027	1,469	2,035
4180 Budget authority, net (total)	–33	1,798	1,798
4190 Outlays, net (total)	2,027	1,469	2,035

Status of Guaranteed Loans (in millions of dollars)

Identification code 086–4077–0–3–371	2021 actual	2022 est.	2023 est.
Position with respect to appropriations act limitation on commitments:			
2111 Guaranteed loan commitments from current-year authority	30,000	30,000	35,000
2121 Limitation available from carry-forward	30,000	22,582	20,153
2142 Uncommitted loan guarantee limitation	....	....	....
2143 Uncommitted limitation carried forward	–22,582	–20,153	–28,404
2150 Total guaranteed loan commitments	37,418	32,429	26,749
2199 Guaranteed amount of guaranteed loan commitments	37,090	32,409	26,500
Cumulative balance of guaranteed loans outstanding:			
2210 Outstanding, start of year	168,249	173,383	186,528
2231 Disbursements of new guaranteed loans	36,259	32,429	28,404
2251 Repayments and prepayments	–28,975	–16,957	–16,165
Adjustments:			
2261 Terminations for default that result in loans receivable	–1,186	–1,789	–1,649
2262 Terminations for default that result in acquisition of property	–41	–3	–2
2263 Terminations for default that result in claim payments	–923	–535	–273
2290 Outstanding, end of year	173,383	186,528	196,843
Memorandum:			
2299 Guaranteed amount of guaranteed loans outstanding, end of year	168,999	180,000	190,000
Addendum:			
Cumulative balance of defaulted guaranteed loans that result in loans receivable:			
2310 Outstanding, start of year	6,489	7,150	7,230
2331 Disbursements for guaranteed loan claims	1,186	1,789	1,649
2351 Repayments of loans receivable	–524	–1,708	–1,873
2361 Write-offs of loans receivable	–1	–1	–1
2390 Outstanding, end of year	7,150	7,230	7,005

Balance Sheet (in millions of dollars)

Identification code 086–4077–0–3–371	2020 actual	2021 actual
ASSETS:		
Federal assets:		
1101 Fund balances with Treasury	6,554	4,494
Investments in U.S. securities:		
1106 Receivables, net	676	463
Non-Federal assets:		
1201 Investments in non-Federal securities, net	....	....
1206 Receivables, net	41	41
Net value of assets related to post-1991 acquired defaulted guaranteed loans receivable:		
1501 Defaulted guaranteed loans receivable, gross	6,489	7,150
1502 Interest receivable	3,564	3,972
1504 Foreclosed property	118	176
1505 Allowance for subsidy cost (-)	–3,651	–3,493
1599 Net value of assets related to defaulted guaranteed loan	6,520	7,805
Other Federal assets:		
1801 Cash and other monetary assets	6	–1
1901 Other assets	....	....
1999 Total assets	13,797	12,802
LIABILITIES:		
Federal liabilities:		
2103 Debt	8,980	8,946
2105 Other	1,267	3,239
Non-Federal liabilities:		
2201 Accounts payable	170	157
2204 Liabilities for loan guarantees	3,287	349
2207 Other	93	111
2999 Total liabilities	13,797	12,802
NET POSITION:		
3300 Cumulative results of operations	....	....
4999 Total liabilities and net position	13,797	12,802

FHA-GENERAL AND SPECIAL RISK DIRECT LOAN FINANCING ACCOUNT

Program and Financing (in millions of dollars)

Identification code 086–4105–0–3–371	2021 actual	2022 est.	2023 est.
Obligations by program activity:			
0003 Other capital investments and operating expenses	....	1	1
Credit program obligations:			
0710 Direct loan obligations	....	2,000	1,496
0713 Payment of interest to Treasury	5	6	6
0715 Payment of Interest to FFB	80	57	57
0716 Payment of interest differential	....	1	1
0717 Direct Loans - SF Property Disposition	....	1	1
0740 Negative subsidy obligations	....	185	122
0742 Downward reestimates paid to receipt accounts	226	....	....
0743 Interest on downward reestimates	92	....	....
0791 Direct program activities, subtotal	177	2,476	1,683

DEPARTMENT OF HOUSING AND URBAN DEVELOPMENT

Housing Programs—Continued
Federal Funds—Continued   **593**

0900	Total new obligations, unexpired accounts	177	2,477	1,684
	Budgetary resources:			
	Unobligated balance:			
1000	Unobligated balance brought forward, Oct 1	169	376	354
1020	Adjustment of unobligated bal brought forward, Oct 1	–1		
1021	Recoveries of prior year unpaid obligations	59	40	49
1070	Unobligated balance (total)	227	416	403
	Financing authority:			
	Borrowing authority, mandatory:			
1400	Borrowing authority - Treasury	29	300	300
1400	Borrowing authority - FFB		2,000	1,496
1440	Borrowing authority, mandatory (total)	29	2,300	1,796
	Spending authority from offsetting collections, mandatory:			
1800	Collected	390	210	152
1825	Spending authority from offsetting collections applied to repay debt	–93	–95	–102
1850	Spending auth from offsetting collections, mand (total)	297	115	50
1900	Budget authority (total)	326	2,415	1,846
1930	Total budgetary resources available	553	2,831	2,249
	Memorandum (non-add) entries:			
1941	Unexpired unobligated balance, end of year	376	354	565
	Change in obligated balance:			
	Unpaid obligations:			
3000	Unpaid obligations, brought forward, Oct 1	511	116	1,990
3001	Adjustments to unpaid obligations, brought forward, Oct 1	1		
3010	New obligations, unexpired accounts	177	2,477	1,684
3020	Outlays (gross)	–514	–563	–563
3040	Recoveries of prior year unpaid obligations, unexpired	–59	–40	–49
3050	Unpaid obligations, end of year	116	1,990	3,062
	Memorandum (non-add) entries:			
3100	Obligated balance, start of year	512	116	1,990
3200	Obligated balance, end of year	116	1,990	3,062
	Financing authority and disbursements, net:			
	Mandatory:			
4090	Budget authority, gross	326	2,415	1,846
	Financing disbursements:			
4110	Outlays, gross (total)	514	563	563
	Offsets against gross financing authority and disbursements:			
	Offsetting collections (collected) from:			
4120	Upward reestimate from program account	–277	–62	
4122	Interest on uninvested funds	–9	–1	–1
4123	Repayment of Principal	–104	–97	–104
4123	DL Interest Payments		–48	–45
4123	Loan Guarantee Fees		–2	–2
4130	Offsets against gross budget authority and outlays (total)	–390	–210	–152
4160	Budget authority, net (mandatory)	–64	2,205	1,694
4170	Outlays, net (mandatory)	124	353	411
4180	Budget authority, net (total)	–64	2,205	1,694
4190	Outlays, net (total)	124	353	411

Status of Direct Loans (in millions of dollars)

Identification code 086–4105–0–3–371	2021 actual	2022 est.	2023 est.
Position with respect to appropriations act limitation on obligations:			
1111 Direct loan obligations from current-year authority		2,000	1,496
1150 Total direct loan obligations		2,000	1,496
Cumulative balance of direct loans outstanding:			
1210 Outstanding, start of year	2,364	2,630	2,533
1231 Disbursements: Direct loan disbursements	296		
1251 Repayments: Repayments and prepayments	–30	–97	–104
1290 Outstanding, end of year	2,630	2,533	2,429

Balance Sheet (in millions of dollars)

Identification code 086–4105–0–3–371	2020 actual	2021 actual
ASSETS:		
Federal assets:		
1101 Fund balances with Treasury	113	222
Investments in U.S. securities:		
1106 Receivables, net	3	
Net value of assets related to post-1991 direct loans receivable:		
1401 Direct loans receivable, gross	2,364	2,630
1402 Interest receivable	6	6
1405 Allowance for subsidy cost (–)	317	284
1499 Net present value of assets related to direct loans	2,687	2,920
1999 Total assets	2,803	3,142
LIABILITIES:		
Federal liabilities:		
2102 Interest payable		6
2103 Debt	2,520	2,747
2105 Other	276	388
Non-Federal liabilities:		
2204 Liabilities for loan guarantees	7	
2207 Other		1
2999 Total liabilities	2,803	3,142
NET POSITION:		
3300 Cumulative results of operations		
4999 Total liabilities and net position	2,803	3,142

FHA–GENERAL AND SPECIAL RISK INSURANCE FUNDS LIQUIDATING ACCOUNT

Program and Financing (in millions of dollars)

Identification code 086–4072–0–3–371	2021 actual	2022 est.	2023 est.
Obligations by program activity:			
0110 Capitalized Expenses	1	3	3
0111 HUD Held Notes Escrow Activity	12	15	15
0113 Other	3	4	4
0900 Total new obligations, unexpired accounts	16	22	22
Budgetary resources:			
Unobligated balance:			
1000 Unobligated balance brought forward, Oct 1	125	170	60
1021 Recoveries of prior year unpaid obligations	8	10	10
1022 Capital transfer of unobligated balances to general fund	–125	–170	–60
1070 Unobligated balance (total)	8	10	10
Budget authority:			
Appropriations, mandatory:			
1200 Appropriation	25	25	25
Spending authority from offsetting collections, mandatory:			
1800 Collected	153	47	25
1900 Budget authority (total)	178	72	50
1930 Total budgetary resources available	186	82	60
Memorandum (non-add) entries:			
1941 Unexpired unobligated balance, end of year	170	60	38
Change in obligated balance:			
Unpaid obligations:			
3000 Unpaid obligations, brought forward, Oct 1	68	62	57
3010 New obligations, unexpired accounts	16	22	22
3020 Outlays (gross)	–14	–17	–17
3040 Recoveries of prior year unpaid obligations, unexpired	–8	–10	–10
3050 Unpaid obligations, end of year	62	57	52
Uncollected payments:			
3060 Uncollected pymts, Fed sources, brought forward, Oct 1	–1	–1	–1
3090 Uncollected pymts, Fed sources, end of year	–1	–1	–1
Memorandum (non-add) entries:			
3100 Obligated balance, start of year	67	61	56
3200 Obligated balance, end of year	61	56	51
Budget authority and outlays, net:			
Mandatory:			
4090 Budget authority, gross	178	72	50
Outlays, gross:			
4100 Outlays from new mandatory authority	10	7	7
4101 Outlays from mandatory balances	4	10	10
4110 Outlays, gross (total)	14	17	17
Offsets against gross budget authority and outlays:			
Offsetting collections (collected) from:			
4123 Non-Federal sources - Other	–153	–47	–25
4180 Budget authority, net (total)	25	25	25
4190 Outlays, net (total)	–139	–30	–8

Status of Guaranteed Loans (in millions of dollars)

Identification code 086–4072–0–3–371	2021 actual	2022 est.	2023 est.
Cumulative balance of guaranteed loans outstanding:			
2210 Outstanding, start of year	162	162	119

Housing Programs—Continued
Federal Funds—Continued

FHA-General and Special Risk Insurance Funds Liquidating Account—Continued

Status of Guaranteed Loans—Continued

Identification code 086–4072–0–3–371		2021 actual	2022 est.	2023 est.
2251	Repayments and prepayments	....	–43	–17
	Adjustments:			
2261	Terminations for default that result in loans receivable	....	....	....
2262	Terminations for default that result in acquisition of property	....	....	....
2290	Outstanding, end of year	162	119	102
	Memorandum:			
2299	Guaranteed amount of guaranteed loans outstanding, end of year	....	....	....
	Addendum:			
	Cumulative balance of defaulted guaranteed loans that result in loans receivable:			
2310	Outstanding, start of year	1,370	1,258	1,254
2331	Disbursements for guaranteed loan claims	....	....	....
2351	Repayments of loans receivable	–112	–4	–4
2390	Outstanding, end of year	1,258	1,254	1,250

Balance Sheet (in millions of dollars)

Identification code 086–4072–0–3–371		2020 actual	2021 actual
	ASSETS:		
	Federal assets:		
1101	Fund balances with Treasury	192	231
	Investments in U.S. securities:		
1102	Treasury securities, par	....	....
1206	Non-Federal assets: Receivables, net	1	2
1701	Defaulted guaranteed loans, gross	1,370	1,258
1702	Interest receivable	264	264
1703	Allowance for estimated uncollectible loans and interest (–)	–683	–637
1704	Defaulted guaranteed loans and interest receivable, net	951	885
1705	Accounts receivable from foreclosed property	....	....
1706	Foreclosed property	....	....
1799	Value of assets related to loan guarantees	951	885
1901	Other Federal assets: Other assets	....	....
1999	Total assets	1,144	1,118
	LIABILITIES:		
	Non-Federal liabilities:		
2201	Accounts payable	10	10
2204	Liabilities for loan guarantees	....	....
2207	Other	–67	–67
2999	Total liabilities	–57	–57
	NET POSITION:		
3100	Unexpended appropriations	278	303
3300	Cumulative results of operations	923	871
3999	Total net position	1,201	1,174
4999	Total liabilities and net position	1,144	1,117

Object Classification (in millions of dollars)

Identification code 086–4072–0–3–371		2021 actual	2022 est.	2023 est.
	Direct obligations:			
32.0	Land and structures	1	3	3
33.0	Investments and loans	15	19	19
99.9	Total new obligations, unexpired accounts	16	22	22

FHA-Loan Guarantee Recovery Fund Financing Account

Program and Financing (in millions of dollars)

Identification code 086–4106–0–3–371		2021 actual	2022 est.	2023 est.
	Budgetary resources:			
	Unobligated balance:			
1000	Unobligated balance brought forward, Oct 1	7	8	8
	Financing authority:			
	Spending authority from offsetting collections, mandatory:			
1800	Collected	1	....	....
1930	Total budgetary resources available	8	8	8
	Memorandum (non-add) entries:			
1941	Unexpired unobligated balance, end of year	8	8	8
	Financing authority and disbursements, net:			
	Mandatory:			
4090	Budget authority, gross	1	....	....
	Offsets against gross financing authority and disbursements:			
	Offsetting collections (collected) from:			
4122	Interest on uninvested funds	–1	....	....
4180	Budget authority, net (total)	....	....	....
4190	Outlays, net (total)	–1	....	....

Status of Guaranteed Loans (in millions of dollars)

Identification code 086–4106–0–3–371		2021 actual	2022 est.	2023 est.
	Position with respect to appropriations act limitation on commitments:			
2111	Guaranteed loan commitments from current-year authority	....	....	....
2150	Total guaranteed loan commitments	....	....	....
	Cumulative balance of guaranteed loans outstanding:			
2210	Outstanding, start of year	3	....	....
2251	Repayments and prepayments	–3	....	....
2290	Outstanding, end of year	....	....	....
	Memorandum:			
2299	Guaranteed amount of guaranteed loans outstanding, end of year	....	....	....

Section 4 of the Church Arson Prevention Act of 1996 (Public Law 104–155), entitled "Loan Guarantee Recovery Fund," authorizes the Secretary of Housing and Urban Development to guarantee loans made by financial institutions to assist certain non-profit organizations that were damaged as a result of acts of arson or terrorism.

Balance Sheet (in millions of dollars)

Identification code 086–4106–0–3–371		2020 actual	2021 actual
	ASSETS:		
1101	Federal assets: Fund balances with Treasury	7	7
1999	Total assets	7	7
	LIABILITIES:		
	Non-Federal liabilities:		
2204	Liabilities for loan guarantees	7	7
2207	Other	....	....
2999	Total liabilities	7	7
4999	Total liabilities and net position	7	7

Housing for the Elderly or Handicapped Fund Liquidating Account

Program and Financing (in millions of dollars)

Identification code 086–4115–0–3–371		2021 actual	2022 est.	2023 est.
	Obligations by program activity:			
0102	Loan Management, Liquidations and Property Dispositions	2	3	3
0900	Total new obligations, unexpired accounts (object class 32.0)	2	3	3
	Budgetary resources:			
	Unobligated balance:			
1000	Unobligated balance brought forward, Oct 1	177	136	....
1021	Recoveries of prior year unpaid obligations	1	....	....
1022	Capital transfer of unobligated balances to general fund	–177	–136	....
1070	Unobligated balance (total)	1	....	....
	Budget authority:			
	Spending authority from offsetting collections, mandatory:			
1800	Collected	137	115	96
1820	Capital transfer of spending authority from offsetting collections to general fund	....	–112	–93

DEPARTMENT OF HOUSING AND URBAN DEVELOPMENT

Housing Programs—Continued
Trust Funds 595

		2021 actual	2022 est.	2023 est.
1850	Spending auth from offsetting collections, mand (total)	137	3	3
1930	Total budgetary resources available	138	3	3
	Memorandum (non-add) entries:			
1941	Unexpired unobligated balance, end of year	136		
	Change in obligated balance:			
	Unpaid obligations:			
3000	Unpaid obligations, brought forward, Oct 1	4	3	2
3010	New obligations, unexpired accounts	2	3	3
3020	Outlays (gross)	−2	−4	−4
3040	Recoveries of prior year unpaid obligations, unexpired	−1		
3050	Unpaid obligations, end of year	3	2	1
	Memorandum (non-add) entries:			
3100	Obligated balance, start of year	4	3	2
3200	Obligated balance, end of year	3	2	1
	Budget authority and outlays, net:			
	Mandatory:			
4090	Budget authority, gross	137	3	3
	Outlays, gross:			
4100	Outlays from new mandatory authority		3	3
4101	Outlays from mandatory balances	2	1	1
4110	Outlays, gross (total)	2	4	4
	Offsets against gross budget authority and outlays:			
	Offsetting collections (collected) from:			
4123	Non-Federal sources	−137	−115	−96
4180	Budget authority, net (total)		−112	−93
4190	Outlays, net (total)	−135	−111	−92

Status of Direct Loans (in millions of dollars)

Identification code 086–4115–0–3–371	2021 actual	2022 est.	2023 est.
Cumulative balance of direct loans outstanding:			
1210 Outstanding, start of year	545	449	369
1251 Repayments: Repayments and prepayments	−96	−80	−67
1290 Outstanding, end of year	449	369	302

Balance Sheet (in millions of dollars)

Identification code 086–4115–0–3–371	2020 actual	2021 actual
ASSETS:		
1101 Federal assets: Fund balances with Treasury	180	139
1206 Non-Federal assets: Interest Receivable: Public		
1601 Direct loans, gross	545	449
1602 Interest receivable	10	10
1603 Allowance for estimated uncollectible loans and interest (−)	−11	−8
1699 Value of assets related to direct loans	544	451
1999 Total assets	724	590
LIABILITIES:		
Non-Federal liabilities:		
2201 Accounts payable	2	3
2207 Other		
2999 Total liabilities	2	3
NET POSITION:		
3100 Unexpended Appropriations	3	3
3300 Revolving Fund: Cumulative results of operations	719	584
3999 Total net position	722	587
4999 Total liabilities and net position	724	590

PAYMENT TO MANUFACTURED HOUSING FEES TRUST FUND

For necessary expenses as authorized by the National Manufactured Housing Construction and Safety Standards Act of 1974 (42 U.S.C. 5401 et seq.), up to $14,000,000, to remain available until expended, of which $14,000,000 shall be derived from the Manufactured Housing Fees Trust Fund (established under section 620(e) of such Act (42 U.S.C. 5419(e)): Provided, That not to exceed the total amount appropriated under this heading shall be available from the general fund of the Treasury to the extent necessary to incur obligations and make expenditures pending the receipt of collections to the Fund pursuant to section 620 of such Act: Provided further, That the amount made available under this heading from the general fund shall be reduced as such collections are received during fiscal year 2023 so as to result in a final fiscal year 2023 appropriation from the general fund estimated at zero, and fees pursuant to such section 620 shall be modified as necessary to ensure such a final fiscal year 2023 appropriation: Provided further, That for the dispute resolution and installation programs, the Secretary may assess and collect fees from any program participant: Provided further, That such collections shall be deposited into the Trust Fund, and the Secretary, as provided herein, may use such collections, as well as fees collected under section 620 of such Act, for necessary expenses of such Act: Provided further, That, notwithstanding the requirements of section 620 of such Act, the Secretary may carry out responsibilities of the Secretary under such Act through the use of approved service providers that are paid directly by the recipients of their services.

Note.—A full-year 2022 appropriation for this account was not enacted at the time the Budget was prepared; therefore, the Budget assumes this account is operating under the Continuing Appropriations Act, 2022 (Division A of Public Law 117–43, as amended). The amounts included for 2022 reflect the annualized level provided by the continuing resolution.

Trust Funds

MANUFACTURED HOUSING FEES TRUST FUND

Special and Trust Fund Receipts (in millions of dollars)

Identification code 086–8119–0–7–376	2021 actual	2022 est.	2023 est.
0100 Balance, start of year	14	18	21
Receipts:			
Current law:			
1120 Mobile Home Inspection and Monitoring Fees, Manufactured Housing Fee Trust Fund	17	16	16
2000 Total: Balances and receipts	31	34	37
Appropriations:			
Current law:			
2101 Manufactured Housing Fees Trust Fund	−13	−13	−14
5099 Balance, end of year	18	21	23

Program and Financing (in millions of dollars)

Identification code 086–8119–0–7–376	2021 actual	2022 est.	2023 est.
Obligations by program activity:			
0002 Manufactured Housing Program Costs	11	13	14
Budgetary resources:			
Unobligated balance:			
1000 Unobligated balance brought forward, Oct 1	7	9	9
Budget authority:			
Appropriations, discretionary:			
1101 Appropriation (special or trust)	13	13	14
1930 Total budgetary resources available	20	22	23
Memorandum (non-add) entries:			
1941 Unexpired unobligated balance, end of year	9	9	9
Change in obligated balance:			
Unpaid obligations:			
3000 Unpaid obligations, brought forward, Oct 1	11	12	13
3010 New obligations, unexpired accounts	11	13	14
3020 Outlays (gross)	−10	−12	−14
3050 Unpaid obligations, end of year	12	13	13
Memorandum (non-add) entries:			
3100 Obligated balance, start of year	11	12	13
3200 Obligated balance, end of year	12	13	13
Budget authority and outlays, net:			
Discretionary:			
4000 Budget authority, gross	13	13	14
Outlays, gross:			
4010 Outlays from new discretionary authority	1	2	2
4011 Outlays from discretionary balances	9	10	12
4020 Outlays, gross (total)	10	12	14
4180 Budget authority, net (total)	13	13	14
4190 Outlays, net (total)	10	12	14

The National Manufactured Housing Construction and Safety Standards Act of 1974, as amended, authorizes the development and enforcement of appropriate standards for the construction, design, installation, and performance of manufactured homes to assure their quality, durability, affordability, and safety. All manufactured homes produced since the standards took effect in 1976 must comply with Federal construction and safety standards. Fees are charged to the manufacturers for each transportable section produced

Housing Programs—Continued
Trust Funds—Continued

MANUFACTURED HOUSING FEES TRUST FUND—Continued

to offset the expenses incurred by the Department in carrying out the responsibilities under the authorizing legislation. The Budget proposes to fully fund the $14 million cost of authorized activities with these fees.

Thirty-three States participate in the program under Department of Housing and Urban Development (HUD) approved State compliance plans and are partially reimbursed by HUD for their activities. HUD administers a compliance program for the remaining 17 States. HUD coordinates the Manufactured Housing Consensus Committee to recommend revisions to and interpretations of the manufactured housing standards and regulations. HUD also develops and implements model standards for installation of manufactured housing, as well as an installation enforcement program. HUD administers installation enforcement programs in 14 States and oversees HUD-approved programs in 36 States. Finally, HUD administers a dispute resolution program for manufactured housing homeowners, retailers, installers, and manufacturers in 24 States and oversees HUD-approved dispute resolution programs in 26 States.

Object Classification (in millions of dollars)

Identification code 086–8119–0–7–376		2021 actual	2022 est.	2023 est.
	Direct obligations:			
25.1	Advisory and assistance services	8	8	9
41.0	Grants, subsidies, and contributions	3	5	5
99.9	Total new obligations, unexpired accounts	11	13	14

HOUSING SUPPLY

Federal Funds

HOUSING SUPPLY FUND

(Legislative proposal, subject to PAYGO)

Program and Financing (in millions of dollars)

Identification code 086–0500–4–1–604		2021 actual	2022 est.	2023 est.
	Obligations by program activity:			
0001	Affordable Housing Production Grants			5,000
0002	Grants to Reduce Affordable Housing Barriers			1,000
0900	Total new obligations, unexpired accounts (object class 41.0)			6,000
	Budgetary resources:			
	Budget authority:			
	Appropriations, mandatory:			
1200	Appropriation (Affordable Housing Production Grants)			5,000
1200	Appropriation (Grants to Reduce Affordable Housing Barriers)			2,000
1260	Appropriations, mandatory (total)			7,000
1930	Total budgetary resources available			7,000
	Memorandum (non-add) entries:			
1941	Unexpired unobligated balance, end of year			1,000
	Change in obligated balance:			
	Unpaid obligations:			
3010	New obligations, unexpired accounts			6,000
3020	Outlays (gross)			–700
3050	Unpaid obligations, end of year			5,300
	Memorandum (non-add) entries:			
3200	Obligated balance, end of year			5,300
	Budget authority and outlays, net:			
	Mandatory:			
4090	Budget authority, gross			7,000
	Outlays, gross:			
4100	Outlays from new mandatory authority			700
4180	Budget authority, net (total)			7,000
4190	Outlays, net (total)			700

To address the critical shortage of affordable housing in communities throughout the Nation, the Budget proposes $50 billion in mandatory funding and additional Low-Income Housing Tax Credits to address market gaps, increase housing supply, and help to stabilize housing prices over the long-term. In HUD specifically, the proposal includes a new $35 billion Housing Supply Fund. The Fund will contain $25 billion for affordable housing production grants to state and local housing finance agencies and their partners to provide grants, revolving loan funds, and other streamlined financing tools. The Fund will also provide $10 billion in grants to advance state and local jurisdictions' efforts to remove barriers to affordable housing development, including funding for housing-related infrastructure.

GOVERNMENT NATIONAL MORTGAGE ASSOCIATION

The Government National Mortgage Association (GNMA) was established by Federal charter in 1968. It is a wholly-owned Government corporation within HUD. It was established to support Federal housing initiatives by providing liquidity to the secondary mortgage market and to attract capital from the global capital markets for the Nation's mortgage markets. Its primary function is to guarantee the timely payment of principal and interest on mortgage-backed securities (MBS) that are backed by loans insured or guaranteed by FHA, the Department of Veterans Affairs, Rural Development in the Department of Agriculture, and HUD's Office of Public and Indian Housing.

Federal Funds

GUARANTEES OF MORTGAGE-BACKED SECURITIES PASS-THROUGH ASSISTANCE

Program and Financing (in millions of dollars)

Identification code 086–0480–0–1–371		2021 actual	2022 est.	2023 est.
	Obligations by program activity:			
0801	Pass-Through Assistance	2		
0900	Total new obligations, unexpired accounts (object class 33.0)	2		
	Budgetary resources:			
	Unobligated balance:			
1000	Unobligated balance brought forward, Oct 1	11,697	3,000	
1010	Unobligated balance transfer to other accts [086–0238]		–3,000	
1020	Adjustment of unobligated bal brought forward, Oct 1	–8,700		
1070	Unobligated balance (total)	2,997		
	Budget authority:			
	Spending authority from offsetting collections, mandatory:			
1800	Collected	5		
1900	Budget authority (total)	5		
1930	Total budgetary resources available	3,002		
	Memorandum (non-add) entries:			
1941	Unexpired unobligated balance, end of year	3,000		
	Change in obligated balance:			
	Unpaid obligations:			
3010	New obligations, unexpired accounts	2		
3020	Outlays (gross)	–2		
	Budget authority and outlays, net:			
	Mandatory:			
4090	Budget authority, gross	5		
	Outlays, gross:			
4101	Outlays from mandatory balances	2		
	Offsets against gross budget authority and outlays:			
	Offsetting collections (collected) from:			
4123	Non-Federal sources	–5		
4180	Budget authority, net (total)			
4190	Outlays, net (total)	–3		

DEPARTMENT OF HOUSING AND URBAN DEVELOPMENT

GUARANTEES OF MORTGAGE-BACKED SECURITIES CAPITAL RESERVE ACCOUNT

Program and Financing (in millions of dollars)

Identification code 086–0238–0–1–371		2021 actual	2022 est.	2023 est.
	Budgetary resources:			
	Unobligated balance:			
1000	Unobligated balance brought forward, Oct 1	10,721	14,170	21,114
1010	Unobligated balance transfer to other accts [086–0186]	–1,600	–500	–500
1011	Unobligated balance transfer from other acct [086–4240]	2,000	500	500
1011	Unobligated balance transfer from other acct [086–4238]	1	....	....
1011	Unobligated balance transfer from other acct [086–0480]	....	3,000	....
1070	Unobligated balance (total)	11,122	17,170	21,114
	Budget authority:			
	Spending authority from offsetting collections, mandatory:			
1800	Offsetting collections (negative subsidy)	2,893	2,699	2,090
1800	Offsetting collections (interest on investments)	5	26	72
1800	Offsetting collections (interest on loans)	150	150	150
1800	Offsetting collections (downward reestimate)	....	1,069	....
1850	Spending auth from offsetting collections, mand (total)	3,048	3,944	2,312
1930	Total budgetary resources available	14,170	21,114	23,426
	Memorandum (non-add) entries:			
1941	Unexpired unobligated balance, end of year	14,170	21,114	23,426
	Budget authority and outlays, net:			
	Discretionary:			
	Offsets against gross budget authority and outlays:			
	Offsetting collections (collected) from:			
4030	Federal sources	–2,893	–2,699	–2,090
4040	Offsets against gross budget authority and outlays (total)	–2,893	–2,699	–2,090
	Mandatory:			
4090	Budget authority, gross	3,048	3,944	2,312
	Offsets against gross budget authority and outlays:			
	Offsetting collections (collected) from:			
4120	Federal sources	–150	–1,219	–150
4121	Interest on Federal securities	–5	–26	–72
4130	Offsets against gross budget authority and outlays (total)	–155	–1,245	–222
4160	Budget authority, net (mandatory)	2,893	2,699	2,090
4170	Outlays, net (mandatory)	–155	–1,245	–222
4180	Budget authority, net (total)	....	....	....
4190	Outlays, net (total)	–3,048	–3,944	–2,312
	Memorandum (non-add) entries:			
5000	Total investments, SOY: Federal securities: Par value	8,400	14,171	21,114
5001	Total investments, EOY: Federal securities: Par value	14,171	21,114	23,426

This mandatory account earns interest on Treasury investments and is the eventual depository for all budgetary resources collected by the Government National Mortgage Association (GNMA), including negative subsidy receipts from new security guarantees, downward reestimates and loan repayments from the Financing account. This account has no authority to obligate funds but transfers resources to the GNMA Program account as necessary for mandatory spending authorized in that account.

GUARANTEES OF MORTGAGE-BACKED SECURITIES LOAN GUARANTEE PROGRAM ACCOUNT

New commitments to issue guarantees to carry out the purposes of section 306 of the National Housing Act, as amended (12 U.S.C. 1721(g)), shall not exceed $900,000,000,000, to remain available until September 30, 2024: Provided, That $42,400,000, to remain available until September 30, 2024, to be derived from fees credited as offsetting collections to this account, including balances of fees collected and credited in prior fiscal years, shall be available for necessary salaries and expenses of the Office of Government National Mortgage Association: Provided further, That receipts from Commitment and Multiclass fees collected pursuant to title III of the National Housing Act (12 U.S.C. 1716 et seq.) shall be credited as offsetting collections to this account.

Note.—A full-year 2022 appropriation for this account was not enacted at the time the Budget was prepared; therefore, the Budget assumes this account is operating under the Continuing Appropriations Act, 2022 (Division A of Public Law 117–43, as amended). The amounts included for 2022 reflect the annualized level provided by the continuing resolution.

Program and Financing (in millions of dollars)

Identification code 086–0186–0–1–371		2021 actual	2022 est.	2023 est.
	Obligations by program activity:			
	Credit program obligations:			
0707	Reestimates of loan guarantee subsidy	1,608	....	....
0708	Interest on reestimates of loan guarantee subsidy	41	....	....
0709	Administrative expenses	295	555	549
0799	Total direct obligations	1,944	555	549
0801	Servicing Expenses	95	100	100
0900	Total new obligations, unexpired accounts	2,039	655	649
	Budgetary resources:			
	Unobligated balance:			
1000	Unobligated balance brought forward, Oct 1	639	266	174
1001	Discretionary unobligated balance brought fwd, Oct 1	12	10	....
1011	Unobligated balance transfer from other acct [086–0238]	1,600	500	500
1020	Adjustment of unobligated bal brought forward, Oct 1	–2	....	....
1021	Recoveries of prior year unpaid obligations	31	25	....
1070	Unobligated balance (total)	2,268	791	674
	Budget authority:			
	Spending authority from offsetting collections, discretionary:			
1700	Collected	272	222	241
1724	Spending authority from offsetting collections precluded from obligation (limitation on obligations)	–235	–185	–199
1750	Spending auth from offsetting collections, disc (total)	37	37	42
	Spending authority from offsetting collections, mandatory:			
1800	Collected	....	1	1
1900	Budget authority (total)	37	38	43
1930	Total budgetary resources available	2,305	829	717
	Memorandum (non-add) entries:			
1941	Unexpired unobligated balance, end of year	266	174	68
	Change in obligated balance:			
	Unpaid obligations:			
3000	Unpaid obligations, brought forward, Oct 1	669	744	929
3001	Adjustments to unpaid obligations, brought forward, Oct 1	2	....	....
3010	New obligations, unexpired accounts	2,039	655	649
3020	Outlays (gross)	–1,935	–445	–496
3040	Recoveries of prior year unpaid obligations, unexpired	–31	–25	....
3050	Unpaid obligations, end of year	744	929	1,082
	Memorandum (non-add) entries:			
3100	Obligated balance, start of year	671	744	929
3200	Obligated balance, end of year	744	929	1,082
	Budget authority and outlays, net:			
	Discretionary:			
4000	Budget authority, gross	37	37	42
	Outlays, gross:			
4010	Outlays from new discretionary authority	27	37	42
4011	Outlays from discretionary balances	6	7	3
4020	Outlays, gross (total)	33	44	45
	Offsets against gross budget authority and outlays:			
	Offsetting collections (collected) from:			
4033	Non-Federal sources	–272	–222	–241
	Mandatory:			
4090	Budget authority, gross	....	1	1
	Outlays, gross:			
4100	Outlays from new mandatory authority	....	1	1
4101	Outlays from mandatory balances	1,902	400	450
4110	Outlays, gross (total)	1,902	401	451
	Offsets against gross budget authority and outlays:			
	Offsetting collections (collected) from:			
4123	Non-Federal sources	....	–1	–1
4180	Budget authority, net (total)	–235	–185	–199
4190	Outlays, net (total)	1,663	222	254
	Memorandum (non-add) entries:			
5090	Unexpired unavailable balance, SOY: Offsetting collections	1,035	1,270	1,455
5092	Unexpired unavailable balance, EOY: Offsetting collections	1,270	1,455	1,654

Summary of Loan Levels, Subsidy Budget Authority and Outlays by Program (in millions of dollars)

Identification code 086–0186–0–1–371	2021 actual	2022 est.	2023 est.
Guaranteed loan levels supportable by subsidy budget authority:			
215001 Guarantees of Mortgage-Backed Securities	933,213	710,206	614,659
215999 Total loan guarantee levels	933,213	710,206	614,659

Government National Mortgage Association—Continued
Federal Funds—Continued

GUARANTEES OF MORTGAGE-BACKED SECURITIES LOAN GUARANTEE PROGRAM ACCOUNT—Continued

Summary of Loan Levels, Subsidy Budget Authority and Outlays by Program—Continued

Identification code 086–0186–0–1–371	2021 actual	2022 est.	2023 est.
Guaranteed loan subsidy (in percent):			
232001 Guarantees of Mortgage-Backed Securities	–.31	–.38	–.34
232999 Weighted average subsidy rate	–.31	–.38	–.34
Guaranteed loan subsidy budget authority:			
233001 Guarantees of Mortgage-Backed Securities	–2,893	–2,699	–2,090
233999 Total subsidy budget authority	–2,893	–2,699	–2,090
Guaranteed loan subsidy outlays:			
234001 Guarantees of Mortgage-Backed Securities	–2,893	–2,699	–2,090
234999 Total subsidy outlays	–2,893	–2,699	–2,090
Guaranteed loan reestimates:			
235001 Guarantees of Mortgage-Backed Securities	1,649	–1,069	
235999 Total guaranteed loan reestimates	1,649	–1,069	
Administrative expense data:			
3510 Budget authority	37	37	42
3590 Outlays from new authority	27	37	42

The Budget requests commitment authority for GNMA to guarantee $900 billion in new MBS and provides $42.4 million in spending authority from offsetting collections (Commitment and Multiclass Fees) for the salaries and expenses of GNMA.

Object Classification (in millions of dollars)

Identification code 086–0186–0–1–371	2021 actual	2022 est.	2023 est.
Direct obligations:			
Personnel compensation:			
11.1 Full-time permanent	23	28	30
11.3 Other than full-time permanent	2	2	2
11.9 Total personnel compensation	25	30	32
12.1 Civilian personnel benefits	8	13	14
25.2 Other services from non-Federal sources	260	511	500
25.3 Other goods and services from Federal sources	2	1	3
41.0 Grants, subsidies, and contributions	1,608		
43.0 Interest and dividends	41		
99.0 Direct obligations	1,944	555	549
99.0 Reimbursable obligations	95	100	100
99.9 Total new obligations, unexpired accounts	2,039	655	649

Employment Summary

Identification code 086–0186–0–1–371	2021 actual	2022 est.	2023 est.
1001 Direct civilian full-time equivalent employment	154	191	198

GUARANTEES OF MORTGAGE-BACKED SECURITIES FINANCING ACCOUNT

Program and Financing (in millions of dollars)

Identification code 086–4240–0–3–371	2021 actual	2022 est.	2023 est.
Obligations by program activity:			
0003 Advances and other	65	1,654	172
0004 Preservation of collateral	508	605	515
0005 Payment of Interest on Borrowings	150	150	150
0091 Subtotal—Advances and Operating Expenses	723	2,409	837
Credit program obligations:			
0740 Negative subsidy obligations	2,893	2,699	2,090
0742 Downward reestimates paid to receipt accounts		1,045	
0743 Interest on downward reestimates		24	
0791 Direct program activities, subtotal	2,893	3,768	2,090
0900 Total new obligations, unexpired accounts	3,616	6,177	2,927
Budgetary resources:			
Unobligated balance:			
1000 Unobligated balance brought forward, Oct 1	7,858	5,778	2,288
1010 Unobligated balance transfer to other accts [086–0238]	–2,000	–500	–500
1020 Adjustment of unobligated bal brought forward, Oct 1	–1		
1070 Unobligated balance (total)	5,857	5,278	1,788
Financing authority:			
Spending authority from offsetting collections, mandatory:			
1800 Collected	3,537	3,187	1,422
1930 Total budgetary resources available	9,394	8,465	3,210
Memorandum (non-add) entries:			
1941 Unexpired unobligated balance, end of year	5,778	2,288	283
Change in obligated balance:			
Unpaid obligations:			
3000 Unpaid obligations, brought forward, Oct 1	1,493	1,967	3,714
3010 New obligations, unexpired accounts	3,616	6,177	2,927
3020 Outlays (gross)	–3,142	–4,430	–3,612
3050 Unpaid obligations, end of year	1,967	3,714	3,029
Uncollected payments:			
3060 Uncollected pymts, Fed sources, brought forward, Oct 1	–1		
3061 Adjustments to uncollected pymts, Fed sources, brought forward, Oct 1	1		
Memorandum (non-add) entries:			
3100 Obligated balance, start of year	1,493	1,967	3,714
3200 Obligated balance, end of year	1,967	3,714	3,029
Financing authority and disbursements, net:			
Mandatory:			
4090 Budget authority, gross	3,537	3,187	1,422
Financing disbursements:			
4110 Outlays, gross (total)	3,142	4,430	3,612
Offsets against gross financing authority and disbursements:			
Offsetting collections (collected) from:			
4120 Federal sources	–1,649		
4123 Guarantee Fees	–1,395	–1,133	–901
4123 Repayment of advances	–48	–200	–51
4123 Non-Federal sources	–445	–1,854	–470
4130 Offsets against gross budget authority and outlays (total)	–3,537	–3,187	–1,422
4170 Outlays, net (mandatory)	–395	1,243	2,190
4180 Budget authority, net (total)			
4190 Outlays, net (total)	–395	1,243	2,190

Status of Guaranteed Loans (in millions of dollars)

Identification code 086–4240–0–3–371	2021 actual	2022 est.	2023 est.
Position with respect to appropriations act limitation on commitments:			
2111 Guaranteed loan commitments from current-year authority	1,300,000	1,300,000	900,000
2121 Limitation available from carry-forward	222,641	523,545	945,814
2142 Uncommitted loan guarantee limitation	–65,883	–167,525	–270,915
2143 Uncommitted limitation carried forward	–523,545	–945,814	–960,240
2150 Total guaranteed loan commitments	933,213	710,206	614,659
2199 Guaranteed amount of guaranteed loan commitments	933,213	710,206	614,659
Cumulative balance of guaranteed loans outstanding:			
2210 Outstanding, start of year	2,117,699	2,125,591	2,151,490
2231 Disbursements of new guaranteed loans	934,009	710,206	614,659
2251 Repayments and prepayments	–926,117	–684,307	–692,645
2290 Outstanding, end of year	2,125,591	2,151,490	2,073,504
Memorandum:			
2299 Guaranteed amount of guaranteed loans outstanding, end of year	2,125,591	2,151,490	2,073,504
Addendum:			
Cumulative balance of defaulted guaranteed loans that result in loans receivable:			
2310 Outstanding, start of year	2,178	1,902	1,502
2331 Disbursements for guaranteed loan claims	35	1,661	210
2351 Repayments of loans receivable	–371	–2,054	–521
2361 Write-offs of loans receivable	–1		
2364 Other adjustments, net	61	–7	–38
2390 Outstanding, end of year	1,902	1,502	1,153

Balance Sheet (in millions of dollars)

Identification code 086–4240–0–3–371	2020 actual	2021 actual
ASSETS:		
Federal assets:		
1101 Fund balances with Treasury	9,351	7,746
Investments in U.S. securities:		
1106 Receivables, net	1	
1206 Non-Federal assets: Receivables, net	169	159

DEPARTMENT OF HOUSING AND URBAN DEVELOPMENT

Policy Development and Research
Federal Funds — 599

1401	Net value of assets related to post-1991 direct loans receivable: Direct loans receivable, gross		
	Net value of assets related to post-1991 acquired defaulted guaranteed loans receivable:		
1501	Defaulted guaranteed loans receivable, gross	2,103	1,855
1504	Foreclosed property	75	47
1505	Allowance for subsidy cost (-)		
1599	Net present value of assets related to defaulted guaranteed loans	2,178	1,902
1801	Other Federal assets: Cash and other monetary assets	30	36
1999	Total assets	11,729	9,843
	LIABILITIES: Non-Federal liabilities:		
2201	Accounts payable	1	5
2207	Other	1,525	205
2999	Total liabilities	1,526	210
	NET POSITION:		
3100	Unexpended appropriations		
3300	Cumulative results of operations	10,203	9,633
3999	Total net position	10,203	9,633
4999	Total liabilities and net position	11,729	9,843

GUARANTEES OF MORTGAGE-BACKED SECURITIES LIQUIDATING ACCOUNT

Program and Financing (in millions of dollars)

Identification code 086–4238–0–3–371	2021 actual	2022 est.	2023 est.
Obligations by program activity:			
0002 Operating expenses			
0002 Operating expenses		1	1
0900 Total new obligations, unexpired accounts (object class 25.2)		1	1
Budgetary resources:			
Unobligated balance:			
1000 Unobligated balance brought forward, Oct 1	101	100	100
1010 Unobligated balance transfer to other accts [086–0238]	–1		
1070 Unobligated balance (total)	100	100	100
Budget authority:			
Spending authority from offsetting collections, mandatory:			
1800 Collected		1	1
1930 Total budgetary resources available	100	101	101
Memorandum (non-add) entries:			
1941 Unexpired unobligated balance, end of year	100	100	100
Change in obligated balance:			
Unpaid obligations:			
3000 Unpaid obligations, brought forward, Oct 1	23	23	22
3010 New obligations, unexpired accounts		1	1
3020 Outlays (gross)		–2	–2
3050 Unpaid obligations, end of year	23	22	21
Memorandum (non-add) entries:			
3100 Obligated balance, start of year	23	23	22
3200 Obligated balance, end of year	23	22	21
Budget authority and outlays, net:			
Mandatory:			
4090 Budget authority, gross		1	1
Outlays, gross:			
4101 Outlays from mandatory balances		2	2
Offsets against gross budget authority and outlays:			
Offsetting collections (collected) from:			
4121 Interest on Federal securities		–1	–1
4180 Budget authority, net (total)			
4190 Outlays, net (total)		1	1
Memorandum (non-add) entries:			
5000 Total investments, SOY: Federal securities: Par value	124	123	122
5001 Total investments, EOY: Federal securities: Par value	123	122	121

Balance Sheet (in millions of dollars)

Identification code 086–4238–0–3–371	2020 actual	2021 actual
ASSETS:		
Federal assets:		
Investments in U.S. securities:		
1102 Treasury securities, par	124	123
1106 Receivables, net		
1601 Direct loans, gross		
1603 Allowance for estimated uncollectible loans and interest (-)		
1699 Value of assets related to direct loans		
1901 Other Federal assets: Other assets		
1999 Total assets	124	123
LIABILITIES:		
Non-Federal liabilities:		
2201 Accounts payable	23	23
2207 Other		
2999 Total liabilities	23	23
NET POSITION:		
3100 Unexpended appropriations		
3300 Cumulative results of operations	101	100
3999 Total net position	101	100
4999 Total liabilities and net position	124	123

POLICY DEVELOPMENT AND RESEARCH

Federal Funds

RESEARCH AND TECHNOLOGY

For contracts, grants, and necessary expenses of programs of research and studies relating to housing and urban problems, not otherwise provided for, as authorized by title V of the Housing and Urban Development Act of 1970 (12 U.S.C. 1701z–1 et seq.), including carrying out the functions of the Secretary of Housing and Urban Development under section 1(a)(1)(i) of Reorganization Plan No. 2 of 1968, and for technical assistance, $145,000,000, to remain available until September 30, 2024: *Provided*, That with respect to amounts made available under this heading, notwithstanding section 203 of this title, the Secretary may enter into cooperative agreements with philanthropic entities, other Federal agencies, State or local governments and their agencies, Indian Tribes, tribally designated housing entities, or colleges or universities for research projects: *Provided further*, That with respect to the preceding proviso, such partners to the cooperative agreements shall contribute at least a 50 percent match toward the cost of the project: *Provided further*, That for non-competitive agreements entered into in accordance with the preceding two provisos, the Secretary shall comply with section 2(b) of the Federal Funding Accountability and Transparency Act of 2006 (Public Law 109–282, 31 U.S.C. note) in lieu of compliance with section 102(a)(4)(C) of the Department of Housing and Urban Development Reform Act of 1989 (42 U.S.C. 3545(a)(4)(C)) with respect to documentation of award decisions.

Note.—A full-year 2022 appropriation for this account was not enacted at the time the Budget was prepared; therefore, the Budget assumes this account is operating under the Continuing Appropriations Act, 2022 (Division A of Public Law 117–43, as amended). The amounts included for 2022 reflect the annualized level provided by the continuing resolution.

Program and Financing (in millions of dollars)

Identification code 086–0108–0–1–451	2021 actual	2022 est.	2023 est.
Obligations by program activity:			
0001 Contracts, Grants and Cooperative Agreements	61	62	61
0002 Research and Demonstrations	18	17	14
0003 Technical Assistance	36	33	33
0799 Total direct obligations	115	112	108
0801 BJA Pay for Success Evaluation	1		
0802 Technical Assistance for ERA	3		
0899 Total reimbursable obligations	4		
0900 Total new obligations, unexpired accounts	119	112	108
Budgetary resources:			
Unobligated balance:			
1000 Unobligated balance brought forward, Oct 1	52	47	42
1012 Unobligated balance transfers between expired and unexpired accounts	7		

RESEARCH AND TECHNOLOGY—Continued
Program and Financing—Continued

Identification code 086–0108–0–1–451		2021 actual	2022 est.	2023 est.
1021	Recoveries of prior year unpaid obligations	....	2	2
1070	Unobligated balance (total)	59	49	44
	Budget authority:			
	Appropriations, discretionary:			
1100	Appropriation	105	105	145
	Spending authority from offsetting collections, discretionary:			
1700	Collected	3	....	....
1900	Budget authority (total)	108	105	145
1930	Total budgetary resources available	167	154	189
	Memorandum (non-add) entries:			
1940	Unobligated balance expiring	−1	....	....
1941	Unexpired unobligated balance, end of year	47	42	81
	Change in obligated balance:			
	Unpaid obligations:			
3000	Unpaid obligations, brought forward, Oct 1	107	142	154
3001	Adjustments to unpaid obligations, brought forward, Oct 1	7	....	....
3010	New obligations, unexpired accounts	119	112	108
3011	Obligations ("upward adjustments"), expired accounts	2	....	....
3020	Outlays (gross)	−84	−98	−127
3040	Recoveries of prior year unpaid obligations, unexpired	....	−2	−2
3041	Recoveries of prior year unpaid obligations, expired	−9	....	....
3050	Unpaid obligations, end of year	142	154	133
	Memorandum (non-add) entries:			
3100	Obligated balance, start of year	114	142	154
3200	Obligated balance, end of year	142	154	133
	Budget authority and outlays, net:			
	Discretionary:			
4000	Budget authority, gross	108	105	145
	Outlays, gross:			
4010	Outlays from new discretionary authority	39	42	58
4011	Outlays from discretionary balances	45	56	69
4020	Outlays, gross (total)	84	98	127
	Offsets against gross budget authority and outlays:			
	Offsetting collections (collected) from:			
4030	Federal sources	−11	....	....
	Additional offsets against gross budget authority only:			
4052	Offsetting collections credited to expired accounts	8	....	....
4060	Additional offsets against budget authority only (total)	8	....	....
4070	Budget authority, net (discretionary)	105	105	145
4080	Outlays, net (discretionary)	73	98	127
4180	Budget authority, net (total)	105	105	145
4190	Outlays, net (total)	73	98	127

The Housing and Urban Development Act of 1970 directs the Secretary to undertake programs of research, studies, testing, and demonstrations related to the Department of Housing and Urban Development's (HUD) mission. These functions are carried out by HUD's Office of Policy Development and Research (PD&R) through in-house analysis by staff; contracts with industry, nonprofit research organizations, and educational institutions; and cooperative agreements with educational, governmental, and philanthropic entities. In addition, centralized technical assistance for the Department is supported through this account; these funds enable HUD to support its partners with better coordinated, cross-program technical assistance rather than conventional, program-specific assistance.

The Budget requests $145 million for HUD's Research and Technology (R&T) program. R&T investments support HUD's enterprise-wide commitment to integrate evidence and cross-disciplinary intelligence throughout program policy, management, and operations. The request consists of $70 million for core research support, surveys, data infrastructure, and knowledge management (i.e., research dissemination); $25 million for research, evaluations, and demonstrations; and $50 million for technical assistance.

Object Classification (in millions of dollars)

Identification code 086–0108–0–1–451		2021 actual	2022 est.	2023 est.
	Direct obligations:			
25.1	Advisory and assistance services	61	62	61
41.0	Grants, subsidies, and contributions	54	50	47
99.0	Direct obligations	115	112	108
99.0	Reimbursable obligations	4	....	....
99.9	Total new obligations, unexpired accounts	119	112	108

FAIR HOUSING AND EQUAL OPPORTUNITY
Federal Funds
FAIR HOUSING ACTIVITIES

For contracts, grants, and other assistance, not otherwise provided for, as authorized by title VIII of the Civil Rights Act of 1968 (42 U.S.C. 3601 et seq.), and section 561 of the Housing and Community Development Act of 1987 (42 U.S.C. 3616a), $86,000,000, to remain available until September 30, 2024: Provided, That notwithstanding section 3302 of title 31, United States Code, the Secretary may assess and collect fees to cover the costs of the Fair Housing Training Academy, and may use such funds to develop on-line courses and provide such training: Provided further, That none of the funds made available under this heading may be used to lobby the executive or legislative branches of the Federal Government in connection with a specific contract, grant, or loan: Provided further, That of the funds made available under this heading, $1,000,000 shall be available to the Secretary for the creation and promotion of translated materials and other programs that support the assistance of persons with limited English proficiency in utilizing the services provided by the Department of Housing and Urban Development.

Note.—A full-year 2022 appropriation for this account was not enacted at the time the Budget was prepared; therefore, the Budget assumes this account is operating under the Continuing Appropriations Act, 2022 (Division A of Public Law 117–43, as amended). The amounts included for 2022 reflect the annualized level provided by the continuing resolution.

Program and Financing (in millions of dollars)

Identification code 086–0144–0–1–751		2021 actual	2022 est.	2023 est.
	Obligations by program activity:			
0001	Fair Housing Assistance	23	24	31
0002	Fair Housing Initiatives	10	92	56
0003	Limited English Proficiency	....	1	1
0005	National Fair Housing Training Academy	2	2	2
0006	Fair Housing Initiatives (CARES Act)	1	....	....
0008	Fair Housing Initiatives (ARP Act)	....	19	....
0900	Total new obligations, unexpired accounts	36	138	90
	Budgetary resources:			
	Unobligated balance:			
1000	Unobligated balance brought forward, Oct 1	17	73	9
1001	Discretionary unobligated balance brought fwd, Oct 1	17	....	....
	Budget authority:			
	Appropriations, discretionary:			
1100	Appropriation	73	73	86
	Appropriations, mandatory:			
1200	Appropriation (ARP)	19	....	....
	Spending authority from offsetting collections, discretionary:			
1700	Collected	....	1	1
1900	Budget authority (total)	92	74	87
1930	Total budgetary resources available	109	147	96
	Memorandum (non-add) entries:			
1941	Unexpired unobligated balance, end of year	73	9	6
	Change in obligated balance:			
	Unpaid obligations:			
3000	Unpaid obligations, brought forward, Oct 1	102	71	123
3010	New obligations, unexpired accounts	36	138	90
3020	Outlays (gross)	−66	−86	−86
3041	Recoveries of prior year unpaid obligations, expired	−1	....	....
3050	Unpaid obligations, end of year	71	123	127
	Memorandum (non-add) entries:			
3100	Obligated balance, start of year	102	71	123
3200	Obligated balance, end of year	71	123	127
	Budget authority and outlays, net:			
	Discretionary:			
4000	Budget authority, gross	73	74	87
	Outlays, gross:			
4010	Outlays from new discretionary authority	4	5	5
4011	Outlays from discretionary balances	62	81	73
4020	Outlays, gross (total)	66	86	78

DEPARTMENT OF HOUSING AND URBAN DEVELOPMENT

Office of Lead Hazard Control and Healthy Homes
Federal Funds

601

		2021 actual	2022 est.	2023 est.
	Offsets against gross budget authority and outlays:			
	Offsetting collections (collected) from:			
4033	Non-Federal sources		−1	−1
	Mandatory:			
4090	Budget authority, gross	19		
	Outlays, gross:			
4101	Outlays from mandatory balances			8
4180	Budget authority, net (total)	92	73	86
4190	Outlays, net (total)	66	85	85

The Budget requests $86 million for fair housing activities to support efforts to end housing discrimination. Of the amount requested, $26 million is for the Fair Housing Assistance Program (FHAP); $56 million is for the Fair Housing Initiatives Program (FHIP); $3 million is for the National Fair Housing Training Academy (NFHTA); and $1 million is for the Limited English Proficiency Initiative (LEPI).

FHAP provides funding to State and local agencies to assure prompt and effective processing of complaints under substantially equivalent State and local fair housing laws. To be eligible for assistance through FHAP, an agency must administer a fair housing law that HUD has certified as substantially equivalent to the Federal Fair Housing Act.

FHIP provides funding to States and local governments, and to public and private non-profit organizations, that administer programs to prevent or eliminate discriminatory housing practices through enforcement, education, and outreach. These grants allow the organizations to provide fair housing enforcement through testing in the rental and sales markets, to file fair housing complaints to HUD, and to conduct investigations. Further, the education and outreach activities these organizations conduct also help to educate the public, housing providers, and local governments about their rights and responsibilities under the Fair Housing Act.

The NFHTA provides comprehensive fair housing and civil rights training for investigators, local agencies, educators, attorneys, industry representatives, and other housing industry professionals.

LEPI provides funds for oral interpretation and written translation services, which help make HUD programs and activities accessible to people who are not proficient in English.

Object Classification (in millions of dollars)

Identification code 086–0144–0–1–751		2021 actual	2022 est.	2023 est.
	Direct obligations:			
25.1	Advisory and assistance services	2	2	2
41.0	Grants, subsidies, and contributions	34	136	88
99.9	Total new obligations, unexpired accounts	36	138	90

OFFICE OF LEAD HAZARD CONTROL AND HEALTHY HOMES

Federal Funds

LEAD HAZARD REDUCTION

(INCLUDING TRANSFER OF FUNDS)

For the Lead Hazard Reduction Program, as authorized by section 1011 of the Residential Lead-Based Paint Hazard Reduction Act of 1992, and for related activities and assistance, $400,000,000, to remain available until September 30, 2025, of which $85,000,000 shall be for the Healthy Homes Initiative, pursuant to sections 501 and 502 of the Housing and Urban Development Act of 1970, which shall include research, studies, testing, and demonstration efforts, including education and outreach concerning lead-based paint poisoning and other housing-related diseases and hazards, and mitigating housing-related health and safety hazards in housing of low-income families: Provided, That for purposes of environmental review, pursuant to the National Environmental Policy Act of 1969 (42 U.S.C. 4321 et seq.) and other provisions of law that further the purposes of such Act, a grant under the Healthy Homes Initiative, or the Lead Technical Studies program, or other demonstrations or programs under this heading or under prior appropriations Acts for such purposes under this heading, shall be considered to be funds for a special project for purposes of section 305(c) of the Multifamily Housing Property Disposition Reform Act of 1994: Provided further, That not less than $105,000,000 of the amounts made available under this heading for the award of grants pursuant to section 1011 of the Residential Lead-Based Paint Hazard Reduction Act of 1992 shall be provided to areas with the highest lead-based paint abatement needs: Provided further, That of the amount made available for the Healthy Homes Initiative, $5,000,000 shall be for the implementation of projects in up to five communities that are served by both the Healthy Homes Initiative and the Department of Energy weatherization programs to demonstrate whether the coordination of Healthy Homes remediation activities with weatherization activities achieves cost savings and better outcomes in improving the safety and quality of homes: Provided further, That each applicant for a grant or cooperative agreement under this heading shall certify adequate capacity that is acceptable to the Secretary to carry out the proposed use of funds pursuant to a notice of funding availability: Provided further, That of the amounts made available for the Healthy Homes Initiative, $10,000,000 shall be for a program established by the Secretary to make grants to experienced non-profit organizations, States, local governments, or public housing agencies for safety and functional home modification repairs and renovations to meet the needs of low-income elderly homeowners to enable them to remain in their primary residence: Provided further, That of the total amount made available under the previous proviso, no less than $5,000,000 shall be available to meet such needs in communities with substantial rural populations: Provided further, That amounts made available under this heading, except for amounts in the previous two provisos, in this or prior appropriations Acts, still remaining available, may be used for any purpose under this heading notwithstanding the purpose for which such amounts were appropriated if a program competition is undersubscribed and there are other program competitions under this heading that are oversubscribed: Provided further, That $5,000,000 of the amounts made available under this heading shall be for a radon testing and mitigation resident safety demonstration program (the radon demonstration) in public housing: Provided further, That the testing method, mitigation method, or action level used under the radon demonstration shall be as specified by applicable state or local law, if such a law is more protective of human health of the environment than the method or level specified by the Secretary: Provided further, That the Secretary shall conduct a demonstration to harmonize income eligibility criteria for grants under this heading in this and prior Acts with the income eligibility criteria of certain other Federal programs: Provided further, That, for purposes of such demonstration, the Secretary may establish income eligibility criteria for such grants using income eligibility criteria of any program administered by the Secretary, the Department of Energy weatherization assistance program (42 U.S.C. 6851 et seq.), the Department of Health and Human Services low income home energy assistance program (42 U.S.C. 8621 et seq.), and the Department of Veterans Affairs supportive services for veteran families program (38 U.S.C. 2044): Provided further, That up to $2,000,000 of the amounts made available under this heading may be transferred to the heading "Research and Technology" for the purposes of conducting research and studies and for use in accordance with the provisos under that heading for non-competitive agreements.

Note.—A full-year 2022 appropriation for this account was not enacted at the time the Budget was prepared; therefore, the Budget assumes this account is operating under the Continuing Appropriations Act, 2022 (Division A of Public Law 117–43, as amended). The amounts included for 2022 reflect the annualized level provided by the continuing resolution.

Program and Financing (in millions of dollars)

Identification code 086–0174–0–1–451		2021 actual	2022 est.	2023 est.
	Obligations by program activity:			
0001	Lead-Based Paint Hazard Reduction Grants and Demo	78	513	305
0003	Healthy Homes Grants and Support	30	162	75
0004	Lead Technical Studies and Support	4	5	5
0005	Lead-Based Paint Hazard Reduction Neighborhood Grants		23	
0007	Radon Testing And Remediation			5
0009	Aging in Place Home Modification Grants	10	10	10
0900	Total new obligations, unexpired accounts (object class 41.0)	122	713	400
	Budgetary resources:			
	Unobligated balance:			
1000	Unobligated balance brought forward, Oct 1	133	371	18
	Budget authority:			
	Appropriations, discretionary:			
1100	Appropriation	360	360	400
1930	Total budgetary resources available	493	731	418
	Memorandum (non-add) entries:			
1941	Unexpired unobligated balance, end of year	371	18	18
	Change in obligated balance:			
	Unpaid obligations:			
3000	Unpaid obligations, brought forward, Oct 1	712	732	1,166
3010	New obligations, unexpired accounts	122	713	400

Office of Lead Hazard Control and Healthy Homes—Continued
Federal Funds—Continued

LEAD HAZARD REDUCTION—Continued

Program and Financing—Continued

Identification code 086–0174–0–1–451		2021 actual	2022 est.	2023 est.
3020	Outlays (gross)	–90	–279	–347
3041	Recoveries of prior year unpaid obligations, expired	–12	....	....
3050	Unpaid obligations, end of year	732	1,166	1,219
	Memorandum (non-add) entries:			
3100	Obligated balance, start of year	712	732	1,166
3200	Obligated balance, end of year	732	1,166	1,219
	Budget authority and outlays, net:			
	Discretionary:			
4000	Budget authority, gross	360	360	400
	Outlays, gross:			
4010	Outlays from new discretionary authority	....	7	8
4011	Outlays from discretionary balances	90	272	339
4020	Outlays, gross (total)	90	279	347
4180	Budget authority, net (total)	360	360	400
4190	Outlays, net (total)	90	279	347

The primary purpose of the Lead-Based Paint Hazard Control Grant program is to reduce the exposure of young children to lead-based paint and other environmental hazards in their homes, including protecting them from permanent developmental problems and asthma, and exposure to pesticides and carbon monoxide.

The program plays a critical role in addressing the number one environmental disease impacting children: lead poisoning. The Budget requests $400 million, including $305 million for the Department of Housing and Urban Development's (HUD) Lead Hazard Control Grants and Lead Hazard Reduction Demonstration Program; $85 million for the Healthy Homes Program, of which $10 million will be for safety and functional home modification repairs and renovations for low-income elderly homeowners; $5 million for a radon testing and mitigation demonstration program; and $5 million for lead-based paint technical studies and support. The Budget includes an appropriations provision that would allow the transfer of unobligated balances and recaptured funds from undersubscribed competitive programs to other competitive programs experiencing oversubscription.

The Lead Hazard Control Grant Program provides grants of $1 million to $5 million to State and local governments and Indian Tribes for control of lead-based paint hazards in pre-1978 private unassisted rental and owner-occupied housing of low-income families. The grants are also designed to facilitate the development of a housing maintenance and rehabilitation workforce trained in lead-safe work practices and a certified hazard evaluation and control industry. In awarding grants HUD promotes the use of new low-cost approaches to hazard control that can be replicated across the nation.

The Healthy Homes program enables HUD to assess and control housing-related hazards that contribute to diseases and injuries of children and other vulnerable populations. With funding from this program, grantees implement and evaluate methods for controlling two or more housing-related diseases through a single intervention. Healthy Homes funding is also used to provide technical support and training and assist in the completion of national surveys and other studies. In addition, the program conducts education and outreach to help State, local and non-governmental agencies, housing industry stakeholders, and the public understand the health and housing relationship and identify and address housing-related health and safety hazards.

The Office of Lead Hazard Control and Healthy Homes will continue its lead-based paint technical studies and support activities, which include public education; support for State and local agencies, private property owners, HUD programs and field offices, and professional organizations; technical studies to improve program policy and implementation; quality control to ensure that the evaluation and control of lead-based paint hazards is done properly in HUD-assisted housing; and development of standards, technical guidance, regulations, and improved testing and hazard control methods.

MANAGEMENT AND ADMINISTRATION
Federal Funds

EXECUTIVE OFFICES

For necessary salaries and expenses for Executive Offices, which shall be comprised of the offices of the Secretary, Deputy Secretary, Adjudicatory Services, Congressional and Intergovernmental Relations, Public Affairs, Small and Disadvantaged Business Utilization, and the Center for Faith-Based and Neighborhood Partnerships, $18,000,000, to remain available until September 30, 2024: Provided, That not to exceed $25,000 of the amount made available under this heading shall be available to the Secretary of Housing and Urban Development (referred to in this title as "the Secretary") for official reception and representation expenses as the Secretary may determine.

Note.—A full-year 2022 appropriation for this account was not enacted at the time the Budget was prepared; therefore, the Budget assumes this account is operating under the Continuing Appropriations Act, 2022 (Division A of Public Law 117–43, as amended). The amounts included for 2022 reflect the annualized level provided by the continuing resolution.

Program and Financing (in millions of dollars)

Identification code 086–0332–0–1–604		2021 actual	2022 est.	2023 est.
	Obligations by program activity:			
0001	Personnel Compensation	8	13	15
0002	Benefits	3	3	5
0003	Non-Personnel Costs	2	3	3
0900	Total new obligations, unexpired accounts	13	19	23
	Budgetary resources:			
	Unobligated balance:			
1000	Unobligated balance brought forward, Oct 1	4	8	6
	Budget authority:			
	Appropriations, discretionary:			
1100	Appropriation	17	17	18
1930	Total budgetary resources available	21	25	24
	Memorandum (non-add) entries:			
1941	Unexpired unobligated balance, end of year	8	6	1
	Change in obligated balance:			
	Unpaid obligations:			
3000	Unpaid obligations, brought forward, Oct 1	1	1	....
3010	New obligations, unexpired accounts	13	19	23
3020	Outlays (gross)	–13	–20	–20
3050	Unpaid obligations, end of year	1	....	3
	Memorandum (non-add) entries:			
3100	Obligated balance, start of year	1	1	....
3200	Obligated balance, end of year	1	....	3
	Budget authority and outlays, net:			
	Discretionary:			
4000	Budget authority, gross	17	17	18
	Outlays, gross:			
4010	Outlays from new discretionary authority	9	14	14
4011	Outlays from discretionary balances	4	6	6
4020	Outlays, gross (total)	13	20	20
4180	Budget authority, net (total)	17	17	18
4190	Outlays, net (total)	13	20	20

The Executive Offices account funds salaries and expenses (S&E) for executive management offices, including the Offices of the Secretary; Deputy Secretary; Congressional and Intergovernmental Relations; Public Affairs; Adjudicatory Services; Center for Faith-Based and Neighborhood Partnerships; and Small and Disadvantaged Business Utilization. The Budget requests $18 million for this account.

Object Classification (in millions of dollars)

Identification code 086–0332–0–1–604		2021 actual	2022 est.	2023 est.
	Direct obligations:			
11.1	Personnel compensation: Full-time permanent	8	13	15
12.1	Civilian personnel benefits	3	3	5
25.2	Other services from non-Federal sources	1	1	1

DEPARTMENT OF HOUSING AND URBAN DEVELOPMENT

Management and Administration—Continued
Federal Funds—Continued   603

		2021 actual	2022 est.	2023 est.
25.3	Other goods and services from Federal sources	1	2	2
99.9	Total new obligations, unexpired accounts	13	19	23

Employment Summary

Identification code 086–0332–0–1–604	2021 actual	2022 est.	2023 est.
1001 Direct civilian full-time equivalent employment	60	97	111

ADMINISTRATIVE SUPPORT OFFICES

For necessary salaries and expenses for Administrative Support Offices, $690,900,000, to remain available until September 30, 2024: Provided, That of the sums appropriated under this heading—

(1) $97,000,000 shall be available for the Office of the Chief Financial Officer;

(2) $126,100,000 shall be available for the Office of the General Counsel;

(3) $326,400,000 shall be available for the Office of Administration (which includes the Office of the Chief Administrative Officer, the Office of the Chief Human Capital Officer, and the Office of the Chief Procurement Officer);

(4) $66,200,000 shall be available for the Office of Field Policy and Management;

(5) $5,000,000 shall be available for the Office of Equal Employment and Equity Advancement; and

(6) $70,200,000 shall be available for the Office of the Chief Information Officer: Provided further, That funds made available under this heading may be used for necessary administrative and non-administrative expenses of the Department, not otherwise provided for, including purchase of uniforms, or allowances therefor, as authorized by sections 5901 and 5902 of title 5, United States Code; hire of passenger motor vehicles; and services as authorized by section 3109 of title 5, United States Code: Provided further, That funds made available under this heading and the heading "Program Offices" may be available for office and conference room modifications and other costs to support workplace and workforce needs of the Department, including information technology needs, in addition to amounts otherwise available for such purposes: Provided further, That notwithstanding any other provision of law, funds appropriated under this heading may be used for advertising and promotional activities that directly support program activities funded in this title.

Note.—A full-year 2022 appropriation for this account was not enacted at the time the Budget was prepared; therefore, the Budget assumes this account is operating under the Continuing Appropriations Act, 2022 (Division A of Public Law 117–43, as amended). The amounts included for 2022 reflect the annualized level provided by the continuing resolution.

Program and Financing (in millions of dollars)

Identification code 086–0335–0–1–999	2021 actual	2022 est.	2023 est.
Obligations by program activity:			
0001 Personnel Compensation	239	270	314
0002 Benefits	89	96	109
0003 Non-Personnel Costs	249	265	285
0004 CARES Act	24		
0799 Total direct obligations	601	631	708
0801 Reimbursable program activity	4	4	4
0900 Total new obligations, unexpired accounts	605	635	712
Budgetary resources:			
Unobligated balance:			
1000 Unobligated balance brought forward, Oct 1	74	64	26
1021 Recoveries of prior year unpaid obligations	3		
1033 Recoveries of prior year paid obligations	1	10	
1070 Unobligated balance (total)	78	74	26
Budget authority:			
Appropriations, discretionary:			
1100 Appropriation	577	577	691
1121 Appropriations transferred from other acct [086–0479]	3		
1160 Appropriation, discretionary (total)	580	577	691
Spending authority from offsetting collections, discretionary:			
1700 Collected	4		
1701 Change in uncollected payments, Federal sources	10	10	
1750 Spending auth from offsetting collections, disc (total)	14	10	
1900 Budget authority (total)	594	587	691
1930 Total budgetary resources available	672	661	717
Memorandum (non-add) entries:			
1940 Unobligated balance expiring	–3		
1941 Unexpired unobligated balance, end of year	64	26	5
Change in obligated balance:			
Unpaid obligations:			
3000 Unpaid obligations, brought forward, Oct 1	170	190	193
3010 New obligations, unexpired accounts	605	635	712
3011 Obligations ("upward adjustments"), expired accounts	2		
3020 Outlays (gross)	–574	–632	–774
3040 Recoveries of prior year unpaid obligations, unexpired	–3		
3041 Recoveries of prior year unpaid obligations, expired	–10		
3050 Unpaid obligations, end of year	190	193	131
Uncollected payments:			
3060 Uncollected pymts, Fed sources, brought forward, Oct 1		–10	–20
3070 Change in uncollected pymts, Fed sources, unexpired	–10	–10	
3090 Uncollected pymts, Fed sources, end of year	–10	–20	–20
Memorandum (non-add) entries:			
3100 Obligated balance, start of year	170	180	173
3200 Obligated balance, end of year	180	173	111
Budget authority and outlays, net:			
Discretionary:			
4000 Budget authority, gross	594	587	691
Outlays, gross:			
4010 Outlays from new discretionary authority	442	500	587
4011 Outlays from discretionary balances	132	132	187
4020 Outlays, gross (total)	574	632	774
Offsets against gross budget authority and outlays:			
Offsetting collections (collected) from:			
4030 Federal sources	–4	–10	
4033 Non-Federal sources	–1		
4040 Offsets against gross budget authority and outlays (total)	–5	–10	
Additional offsets against gross budget authority only:			
4050 Change in uncollected pymts, Fed sources, unexpired	–10	–10	
4053 Recoveries of prior year paid obligations, unexpired accounts	1	10	
4060 Additional offsets against budget authority only (total)	–9		
4070 Budget authority, net (discretionary)	580	577	691
4080 Outlays, net (discretionary)	569	622	774
4180 Budget authority, net (total)	580	577	691
4190 Outlays, net (total)	569	622	774

The Administrative Support Offices account funds S&E for offices that perform central Departmental functions, including the Offices of the Chief Financial Officer; Administration (including the Office of the Chief Administrative Officer, the Office of the Chief Human Capital Officer, and the Office of the Chief Procurement Officer); General Counsel; Field Policy and Management; Equal Employment and Equity Advancement; and Chief Information Officer. The Budget requests $690.9 million for this account.

Object Classification (in millions of dollars)

Identification code 086–0335–0–1–999	2021 actual	2022 est.	2023 est.
Direct obligations:			
Personnel compensation:			
11.1 Full-time permanent	236	263	306
11.3 Other than full-time permanent	1	1	1
11.5 Other personnel compensation	5	6	7
11.9 Total personnel compensation	242	270	314
12.1 Civilian personnel benefits	89	96	108
13.0 Benefits for former personnel	1	1	1
21.0 Travel and transportation of persons	1	1	5
23.1 Rental payments to GSA	112	108	111
23.3 Communications, utilities, and miscellaneous charges	13	15	17
24.0 Printing and reproduction	1	1	1
25.1 Advisory and assistance services	70	71	76
25.2 Other services from non-Federal sources	20	21	23
25.3 Other goods and services from Federal sources	37	38	41
25.4 Operation and maintenance of facilities	1	1	1
25.7 Operation and maintenance of equipment	2		
26.0 Supplies and materials	1	1	2
31.0 Equipment	8	6	7
32.0 Land and structures	2		
42.0 Insurance claims and indemnities	1	1	1
99.0 Direct obligations	601	631	708
99.0 Reimbursable obligations	4	4	4
99.9 Total new obligations, unexpired accounts	605	635	712

604　Management and Administration—Continued
　　　Federal Funds—Continued

THE BUDGET FOR FISCAL YEAR 2023

ADMINISTRATIVE SUPPORT OFFICES—Continued

Employment Summary

Identification code 086–0335–0–1–999	2021 actual	2022 est.	2023 est.
1001 Direct civilian full-time equivalent employment	1,880	1,886	2,163

PROGRAM OFFICES

For necessary salaries and expenses for Program Offices, $1,087,200,000, to remain available until September 30, 2024: Provided, That of the sums appropriated under this heading—

(1) $285,900,000 shall be available for the Office of Public and Indian Housing;

(2) $154,100,000 shall be available for the Office of Community Planning and Development;

(3) $488,500,000 shall be available for the Office of Housing;

(4) $41,600,000 shall be available for the Office of Policy Development and Research;

(5) $105,800,000 shall be available for the Office of Fair Housing and Equal Opportunity; and

(6) $11,300,000 shall be available for the Office of Lead Hazard Control and Healthy Homes.

Note.—A full-year 2022 appropriation for this account was not enacted at the time the Budget was prepared; therefore, the Budget assumes this account is operating under the Continuing Appropriations Act, 2022 (Division A of Public Law 117–43, as amended). The amounts included for 2022 reflect the annualized level provided by the continuing resolution.

Program and Financing (in millions of dollars)

Identification code 086–0479–0–1–999	2021 actual	2022 est.	2023 est.
Obligations by program activity:			
0001　Personnel Compensation	614	663	748
0002　Benefits	214	230	259
0003　Non-Personnel Costs	69	54	85
0004　PIH CARES Act	5		
0005　CPD CARES Act	3		
0006　CPD HOME American Rescue Plan		13	1
0007　FHEO American Rescue Plan	1		
0008　PIH ONAP American Rescue Plan		5	
0009　PIH TBRA American Rescue Plan	12	7	1
0900　Total new obligations, unexpired accounts	918	972	1,094
Budgetary resources:			
Unobligated balance:			
1000　Unobligated balance brought forward, Oct 1	62	114	48
1001　Discretionary unobligated balance brought fwd, Oct 1	62	51	
Budget authority:			
Appropriations, discretionary:			
1100　Appropriation	905	905	1,087
1120　Appropriations transferred to other acct [086–0335]	–3		
1160　Appropriation, discretionary (total)	902	905	1,087
Appropriations, mandatory:			
1200　Appropriation [CPD HOME American Rescue Plan]	50		
1200　Appropriation [FHEO American Rescue Plan]	1		
1200　Appropriation [PIH ONAP American Rescue Plan]	5		
1200　Appropriation [PIH TBRA American Rescue Plan]	20		
1260　Appropriations, mandatory (total)	76		
Spending authority from offsetting collections, discretionary:			
1700　Collected	1	1	
1900　Budget authority (total)	979	906	1,087
1930　Total budgetary resources available	1,041	1,020	1,135
Memorandum (non-add) entries:			
1940　Unobligated balance expiring	–9		
1941　Unexpired unobligated balance, end of year	114	48	41
Change in obligated balance:			
Unpaid obligations:			
3000　Unpaid obligations, brought forward, Oct 1	51	96	62
3010　New obligations, unexpired accounts	918	972	1,094
3020　Outlays (gross)	–873	–1,006	–1,116
3050　Unpaid obligations, end of year	96	62	40
Uncollected payments:			
3060　Uncollected pymts, Fed sources, brought forward, Oct 1	–1	–1	–1
3090　Uncollected pymts, Fed sources, end of year	–1	–1	–1
Memorandum (non-add) entries:			
3100　Obligated balance, start of year	50	95	61
3200　Obligated balance, end of year	95	61	39
Budget authority and outlays, net:			
Discretionary:			
4000　Budget authority, gross	903	906	1,087
Outlays, gross:			
4010　Outlays from new discretionary authority	779	869	1,044
4011　Outlays from discretionary balances	94	113	57
4020　Outlays, gross (total)	873	982	1,101
Offsets against gross budget authority and outlays:			
Offsetting collections (collected) from:			
4030　Federal sources	–1	–1	
Mandatory:			
4090　Budget authority, gross	76		
Outlays, gross:			
4101　Outlays from mandatory balances		24	15
4180　Budget authority, net (total)	978	905	1,087
4190　Outlays, net (total)	872	1,005	1,116

The Program Offices account funds S&E for six program offices, including the Offices of Housing; Public and Indian Housing; Community Planning and Development; Policy Development and Research; Fair Housing and Equal Opportunity; and Lead Hazard Control and Healthy Homes. The Budget requests $1.1 billion for this account.

Object Classification (in millions of dollars)

Identification code 086–0479–0–1–999	2021 actual	2022 est.	2023 est.
Direct obligations:			
Personnel compensation:			
11.1　Full-time permanent	597	651	726
11.3　Other than full-time permanent	4	4	5
11.5　Other personnel compensation	15	16	18
11.9　Total personnel compensation	616	671	749
12.1　Civilian personnel benefits	214	230	259
21.0　Travel and transportation of persons		3	5
25.1　Advisory and assistance services	2	2	2
25.2　Other services from non-Federal sources	23	19	23
25.3　Other goods and services from Federal sources	56	47	56
41.0　Grants, subsidies, and contributions	7		
99.9　Total new obligations, unexpired accounts	918	972	1,094

Employment Summary

Identification code 086–0479–0–1–999	2021 actual	2022 est.	2023 est.
1001 Direct civilian full-time equivalent employment	5,223	5,389	5,854

PUBLIC AND INDIAN HOUSING

Program and Financing (in millions of dollars)

Identification code 086–0337–0–1–604	2021 actual	2022 est.	2023 est.
Obligations by program activity:			
0004　Non-Personnel Expenses	1		
0900　Total new obligations, unexpired accounts (object class 25.3)	1		
Budgetary resources:			
Unobligated balance:			
1000　Unobligated balance brought forward, Oct 1	1		
1930　Total budgetary resources available	1		
Change in obligated balance:			
Unpaid obligations:			
3000　Unpaid obligations, brought forward, Oct 1	4	3	
3010　New obligations, unexpired accounts	1		
3011　Obligations ("upward adjustments"), expired accounts	2		
3020　Outlays (gross)	–2	–3	
3041　Recoveries of prior year unpaid obligations, expired	–2		
3050　Unpaid obligations, end of year	3		
Memorandum (non-add) entries:			
3100　Obligated balance, start of year	4	3	
3200　Obligated balance, end of year	3		

DEPARTMENT OF HOUSING AND URBAN DEVELOPMENT

Management and Administration—Continued
Federal Funds—Continued

	Budget authority and outlays, net: Discretionary: Outlays, gross:			
4011	Outlays from discretionary balances		2	3
4180	Budget authority, net (total)			
4190	Outlays, net (total)		2	3

The Budget requests S&E funding for six program offices, including the Office of Public and Indian Housing (PIH), in a consolidated Program Offices account (086–0479). This account reflects pre–2020 S&E funding for PIH.

COMMUNITY PLANNING AND DEVELOPMENT

Program and Financing (in millions of dollars)

Identification code 086–0338–0–1–451	2021 actual	2022 est.	2023 est.
Obligations by program activity:			
0001 Personnel Compensation	2		
0002 Benefits	1		
0007 Disaster Relief Admin		2	5
0900 Total new obligations, unexpired accounts	3	2	5
Budgetary resources:			
Unobligated balance:			
1000 Unobligated balance brought forward, Oct 1	26	23	27
Budget authority:			
Appropriations, discretionary:			
1121 Appropriations transferred from other acct [086–0162]		6	
1930 Total budgetary resources available	26	29	27
Memorandum (non-add) entries:			
1941 Unexpired unobligated balance, end of year	23	27	22
Change in obligated balance:			
Unpaid obligations:			
3000 Unpaid obligations, brought forward, Oct 1	2	2	2
3010 New obligations, unexpired accounts	3	2	5
3020 Outlays (gross)	–3	–2	–6
3050 Unpaid obligations, end of year	2	2	1
Memorandum (non-add) entries:			
3100 Obligated balance, start of year	2	2	2
3200 Obligated balance, end of year	2	2	1
Budget authority and outlays, net:			
Discretionary:			
4000 Budget authority, gross		6	
Outlays, gross:			
4011 Outlays from discretionary balances	3	2	6
4180 Budget authority, net (total)		6	
4190 Outlays, net (total)	3	2	6

The Budget requests S&E funding for six program offices, including the Office of Community Planning and Development, in a consolidated Program Offices account (086–0479). This account primarily reflects budgetary resources available for administration of CDBG-DR grants.

Object Classification (in millions of dollars)

Identification code 086–0338–0–1–451	2021 actual	2022 est.	2023 est.
Direct obligations:			
Personnel compensation:			
11.1 Full-time permanent	2	2	2
11.5 Other personnel compensation	1		1
11.9 Total personnel compensation	3	2	3
12.1 Civilian personnel benefits			1
21.0 Travel and transportation of persons			1
99.9 Total new obligations, unexpired accounts	3	2	5

Employment Summary

Identification code 086–0338–0–1–451	2021 actual	2022 est.	2023 est.
1001 Direct civilian full-time equivalent employment	20	17	25

HOUSING

Program and Financing (in millions of dollars)

Identification code 086–0334–0–1–604	2021 actual	2022 est.	2023 est.
Change in obligated balance:			
Unpaid obligations:			
3000 Unpaid obligations, brought forward, Oct 1	2	2	
3011 Obligations ("upward adjustments"), expired accounts	2		
3020 Outlays (gross)	–1	–2	
3041 Recoveries of prior year unpaid obligations, expired	–1		
3050 Unpaid obligations, end of year	2		
Memorandum (non-add) entries:			
3100 Obligated balance, start of year	2	2	
3200 Obligated balance, end of year	2		
Budget authority and outlays, net:			
Discretionary:			
Outlays, gross:			
4011 Outlays from discretionary balances	1	2	
Offsets against gross budget authority and outlays:			
Offsetting collections (collected) from:			
4033 Non-Federal sources	–2		
4040 Offsets against gross budget authority and outlays (total)	–2		
Additional offsets against gross budget authority only:			
4052 Offsetting collections credited to expired accounts	2		
4060 Additional offsets against budget authority only (total)	2		
4080 Outlays, net (discretionary)	–1	2	
4180 Budget authority, net (total)			
4190 Outlays, net (total)	–1	2	

The Budget requests S&E funding for six program offices, including the Office of Housing, in a consolidated Program Offices account (086–0479). This account reflects pre–2020 S&E funding for the Office of Housing.

FAIR HOUSING AND EQUAL OPPORTUNITY

Program and Financing (in millions of dollars)

Identification code 086–0340–0–1–751	2021 actual	2022 est.	2023 est.
Change in obligated balance:			
Unpaid obligations:			
3000 Unpaid obligations, brought forward, Oct 1	2		
3011 Obligations ("upward adjustments"), expired accounts	1		
3020 Outlays (gross)	–1		
3041 Recoveries of prior year unpaid obligations, expired	–2		
Memorandum (non-add) entries:			
3100 Obligated balance, start of year	2		
Budget authority and outlays, net:			
Discretionary:			
Outlays, gross:			
4011 Outlays from discretionary balances	1		
4180 Budget authority, net (total)			
4190 Outlays, net (total)	1		

The Budget requests S&E funding for six program offices, including the Office of Fair Housing and Equal Opportunity (FHEO), in a consolidated Program Offices account (086–0479). This account reflects pre–2020 S&E funding for FHEO.

Management and Administration—Continued
Federal Funds—Continued

SALARIES AND EXPENSES

Program and Financing (in millions of dollars)

Identification code 086–0143–0–1–999		2021 actual	2022 est.	2023 est.
	Obligations by program activity:			
0803	FEMA Mission Assignments	1	....	....
0900	Total new obligations, unexpired accounts (object class 25.2)	1	....	....
	Budgetary resources:			
	Unobligated balance:			
1000	Unobligated balance brought forward, Oct 1	5	5	5
	Budget authority:			
	Spending authority from offsetting collections, discretionary:			
1700	Collected	1	....	....
1900	Budget authority (total)	1	....	....
1930	Total budgetary resources available	6	5	5
	Memorandum (non-add) entries:			
1941	Unexpired unobligated balance, end of year	5	5	5
	Change in obligated balance:			
	Unpaid obligations:			
3000	Unpaid obligations, brought forward, Oct 1	....	....	1
3010	New obligations, unexpired accounts	1	....	....
3020	Outlays (gross)	....	–1	....
3050	Unpaid obligations, end of year	1	....	....
	Uncollected payments:			
3060	Uncollected pymts, Fed sources, brought forward, Oct 1	–3	–3	–3
3090	Uncollected pymts, Fed sources, end of year	–3	–3	–3
	Memorandum (non-add) entries:			
3100	Obligated balance, start of year	–3	–2	–3
3200	Obligated balance, end of year	–2	–3	–3
	Budget authority and outlays, net:			
	Discretionary:			
4000	Budget authority, gross	1	....	....
	Outlays, gross:			
4011	Outlays from discretionary balances	....	1	....
	Offsets against gross budget authority and outlays:			
	Offsetting collections (collected) from:			
4030	Federal sources	–1	....	....
4180	Budget authority, net (total)	....	....	....
4190	Outlays, net (total)	–1	1	....

This account primarily supports S&E for Departmental personnel responding to disasters. Resources are derived from reimbursable agreements such as FEMA Mission Assignments.

OFFICE OF INSPECTOR GENERAL

For necessary salaries and expenses of the Office of Inspector General in carrying out the Inspector General Act of 1978, as amended, $149,000,000: Provided, That the Inspector General shall have independent authority over all personnel and acquisition issues within this office.

Note.—A full-year 2022 appropriation for this account was not enacted at the time the Budget was prepared; therefore, the Budget assumes this account is operating under the Continuing Appropriations Act, 2022 (Division A of Public Law 117–43, as amended). The amounts included for 2022 reflect the annualized level provided by the continuing resolution.

Program and Financing (in millions of dollars)

Identification code 086–0189–0–1–451		2021 actual	2022 est.	2023 est.
	Obligations by program activity:			
0001	OIG Salaries and Benefits	103	105	113
0002	OIG Non-Personnel Costs	39	32	36
0004	Hurricane Sandy and Other Disaster related activities	1	1	2
0005	CARES Act	1	2	2
0900	Total new obligations, unexpired accounts	144	140	153
	Budgetary resources:			
	Unobligated balance:			
1000	Unobligated balance brought forward, Oct 1	20	9	6
	Budget authority:			
	Appropriations, discretionary:			
1100	Appropriation	137	137	149
1930	Total budgetary resources available	157	146	155
	Memorandum (non-add) entries:			
1940	Unobligated balance expiring	–4	....	....
1941	Unexpired unobligated balance, end of year	9	6	2
	Change in obligated balance:			
	Unpaid obligations:			
3000	Unpaid obligations, brought forward, Oct 1	26	30	26
3010	New obligations, unexpired accounts	144	140	153
3011	Obligations ("upward adjustments"), expired accounts	5	....	....
3020	Outlays (gross)	–140	–142	–147
3041	Recoveries of prior year unpaid obligations, expired	–5	–2	–2
3050	Unpaid obligations, end of year	30	26	30
	Memorandum (non-add) entries:			
3100	Obligated balance, start of year	26	30	26
3200	Obligated balance, end of year	30	26	30
	Budget authority and outlays, net:			
	Discretionary:			
4000	Budget authority, gross	137	137	149
	Outlays, gross:			
4010	Outlays from new discretionary authority	113	114	124
4011	Outlays from discretionary balances	27	28	23
4020	Outlays, gross (total)	140	142	147
4180	Budget authority, net (total)	137	137	149
4190	Outlays, net (total)	140	142	147

The Office of the Inspector General (OIG) provides independent and objective reviews of the integrity, efficiency and effectiveness of HUD programs and operations. Through various activities, the OIG seeks to promote efficiency and effectiveness, detect and deter fraud and abuse, investigate allegations of misconduct by HUD employees and review and make recommendations regarding existing and proposed legislation and regulations affecting HUD. The Budget includes $149 million for the OIG's agency-wide audit and investigative functions.

Object Classification (in millions of dollars)

Identification code 086–0189–0–1–451		2021 actual	2022 est.	2023 est.
	Direct obligations:			
	Personnel compensation:			
11.1	Full-time permanent	73	77	83
11.5	Other personnel compensation	2	1	1
11.9	Total personnel compensation	75	78	84
12.1	Civilian personnel benefits	30	30	33
21.0	Travel and transportation of persons	....	....	2
23.1	Rental payments to GSA	7	7	7
25.1	Advisory and assistance services	25	20	22
31.0	Equipment	7	5	5
99.9	Total new obligations, unexpired accounts	144	140	153

Employment Summary

Identification code 086–0189–0–1–451		2021 actual	2022 est.	2023 est.
1001	Direct civilian full-time equivalent employment	518	520	535

INFORMATION TECHNOLOGY FUND

For the development, modernization, and enhancement of, modifications to, and infrastructure for Department-wide and program-specific information technology systems, for the continuing operation and maintenance of both Department-wide and program-specific information systems, and for program-related maintenance activities, $382,000,000, of which $339,000,000 shall remain available until September 30, 2024, and of which $43,000,000 shall remain available until September 30, 2026: Provided, That any amounts transferred to this Fund under this Act shall remain available until September 30, 2026: Provided further, That any amounts transferred to this Fund from amounts appropriated by previously enacted appropriations Acts may be used for the purposes specified under this Fund, in addition to any other information technology purposes for which such amounts were appropriated.

Note.—A full-year 2022 appropriation for this account was not enacted at the time the Budget was prepared; therefore, the Budget assumes this account is operating under the Continuing Appropriations Act, 2022 (Division A of Public Law 117–43, as amended). The amounts included for 2022 reflect the annualized level provided by the continuing resolution.

DEPARTMENT OF HOUSING AND URBAN DEVELOPMENT

Management and Administration—Continued
Federal Funds—Continued

Program and Financing (in millions of dollars)

Identification code 086–4586–0–4–451		2021 actual	2022 est.	2023 est.
	Obligations by program activity:			
0001	Information Technology Expenses	319	336	409
	Budgetary resources:			
	Unobligated balance:			
1000	Unobligated balance brought forward, Oct 1	44	53	27
1021	Recoveries of prior year unpaid obligations	28	10	10
1070	Unobligated balance (total)	72	63	37
	Budget authority:			
	Appropriations, discretionary:			
1100	Appropriation	300	300	382
1121	Appropriations transferred from other acct [086–0481]	....	....	9
1121	Appropriations transferred from other acct [086–0482]	....	....	5
1160	Appropriation, discretionary (total)	300	300	396
1900	Budget authority (total)	300	300	396
1930	Total budgetary resources available	372	363	433
	Memorandum (non-add) entries:			
1941	Unexpired unobligated balance, end of year	53	27	24
	Change in obligated balance:			
	Unpaid obligations:			
3000	Unpaid obligations, brought forward, Oct 1	324	260	251
3010	New obligations, unexpired accounts	319	336	409
3020	Outlays (gross)	–344	–335	–377
3040	Recoveries of prior year unpaid obligations, unexpired	–28	–10	–10
3041	Recoveries of prior year unpaid obligations, expired	–11	....	....
3050	Unpaid obligations, end of year	260	251	273
	Memorandum (non-add) entries:			
3100	Obligated balance, start of year	324	260	251
3200	Obligated balance, end of year	260	251	273
	Budget authority and outlays, net:			
	Discretionary:			
4000	Budget authority, gross	300	300	396
	Outlays, gross:			
4010	Outlays from new discretionary authority	113	168	222
4011	Outlays from discretionary balances	231	167	155
4020	Outlays, gross (total)	344	335	377
4180	Budget authority, net (total)	300	300	396
4190	Outlays, net (total)	344	335	377

The Information Technology (IT) Fund provides for the infrastructure, systems, and services that support Department of Housing and Urban Development (HUD) programs, which include all of HUD's mortgage insurance liabilities, rental subsidies, formula grants, and competitive grants. The Budget provides $382 million for the development, modernization, enhancement, operation, and maintenance of HUD's IT infrastructure and systems. It excludes end-user IT devices and wireless support, which are requested within HUD's Working Capital Fund account.

Object Classification (in millions of dollars)

Identification code 086–4586–0–4–451		2021 actual	2022 est.	2023 est.
	Direct obligations:			
25.7	Operation and maintenance of equipment	286	290	353
31.0	Equipment	33	46	56
99.9	Total new obligations, unexpired accounts	319	336	409

WORKING CAPITAL FUND

(INCLUDING TRANSFER OF FUNDS)

For the working capital fund (referred to in this paragraph as the "Fund"), established pursuant to section 7(f) of the Department of Housing and Urban Development Act (42 U.S.C. 3535(f)), amounts transferred, including reimbursements, to the Fund under this heading shall be available, without fiscal year limitation, for any expenses necessary for the maintenance and operation of the Department that the Secretary finds to be desirable in the interest of economy and efficiency: Provided, That expenses of operation under such section 7(f) shall include operational reserves.

Note.—A full-year 2022 appropriation for this account was not enacted at the time the Budget was prepared; therefore, the Budget assumes this account is operating under the Continuing Appropriations Act, 2022 (Division A of Public Law 117–43, as amended). The amounts included for 2022 reflect the annualized level provided by the continuing resolution.

Program and Financing (in millions of dollars)

Identification code 086–4598–0–4–604		2021 actual	2022 est.	2023 est.
	Obligations by program activity:			
0805	WCF Program - Reimb	61	63	78
	Budgetary resources:			
	Unobligated balance:			
1000	Unobligated balance brought forward, Oct 1	8	17	17
1021	Recoveries of prior year unpaid obligations	1	....	....
1070	Unobligated balance (total)	9	17	17
	Budget authority:			
	Spending authority from offsetting collections, discretionary:			
1700	Collected	47	63	78
1701	Change in uncollected payments, Federal sources	22	....	....
1750	Spending auth from offsetting collections, disc (total)	69	63	78
1900	Budget authority (total)	69	63	78
1930	Total budgetary resources available	78	80	95
	Memorandum (non-add) entries:			
1941	Unexpired unobligated balance, end of year	17	17	17
	Change in obligated balance:			
	Unpaid obligations:			
3000	Unpaid obligations, brought forward, Oct 1	14	22	21
3010	New obligations, unexpired accounts	61	63	78
3020	Outlays (gross)	–52	–64	–73
3040	Recoveries of prior year unpaid obligations, unexpired	–1	....	....
3050	Unpaid obligations, end of year	22	21	26
	Uncollected payments:			
3060	Uncollected pymts, Fed sources, brought forward, Oct 1	–5	–27	–27
3070	Change in uncollected pymts, Fed sources, unexpired	–22	....	....
3090	Uncollected pymts, Fed sources, end of year	–27	–27	–27
	Memorandum (non-add) entries:			
3100	Obligated balance, start of year	9	–5	–6
3200	Obligated balance, end of year	–5	–6	–1
	Budget authority and outlays, net:			
	Discretionary:			
4000	Budget authority, gross	69	63	78
	Outlays, gross:			
4010	Outlays from new discretionary authority	32	43	53
4011	Outlays from discretionary balances	20	21	20
4020	Outlays, gross (total)	52	64	73
	Offsets against gross budget authority and outlays:			
	Offsetting collections (collected) from:			
4030	Federal sources	–47	–63	–78
	Additional offsets against gross budget authority only:			
4050	Change in uncollected pymts, Fed sources, unexpired	–22	....	....
4080	Outlays, net (discretionary)	5	1	–5
4180	Budget authority, net (total)	....	....	....
4190	Outlays, net (total)	5	1	–5

The Working Capital Fund (WCF) is used to fund agency-wide goods and services that enhance the efficiency and economy of the Department's operations. The WCF is revolving in nature and fully recovers its operational costs. Amounts transferred/reimbursed to the Fund are derived from S&E accounts.

Object Classification (in millions of dollars)

Identification code 086–4598–0–4–604		2021 actual	2022 est.	2023 est.
	Reimbursable obligations:			
11.1	Personnel compensation: Full-time permanent	1	2	3
12.1	Civilian personnel benefits	1	1	2
25.2	Other services from non-Federal sources	1	1	1
25.3	Other goods and services from Federal sources	58	59	72
99.0	Reimbursable obligations	61	63	78
99.9	Total new obligations, unexpired accounts	61	63	78

WORKING CAPITAL FUND—Continued

Employment Summary

Identification code 086–4598–0–4–604	2021 actual	2022 est.	2023 est.
2001 Reimbursable civilian full-time equivalent employment	11	13	21

TRANSFORMATION INITIATIVE

Program and Financing (in millions of dollars)

Identification code 086–0402–0–1–451	2021 actual	2022 est.	2023 est.
Change in obligated balance:			
Unpaid obligations:			
3000 Unpaid obligations, brought forward, Oct 1	3		
3020 Outlays (gross)	–1		
3041 Recoveries of prior year unpaid obligations, expired	–2		
Memorandum (non-add) entries:			
3100 Obligated balance, start of year	3		
Budget authority and outlays, net:			
Discretionary:			
Outlays, gross:			
4011 Outlays from discretionary balances	1		
4180 Budget authority, net (total)			
4190 Outlays, net (total)	1		

This account reports the remaining balances and outlays for the Transformation Initiative, which received funding from 2010 to 2014 to increase investments in research and evaluation, program demonstrations, technical assistance, and information technology.

GENERAL FUND RECEIPT ACCOUNTS
(in millions of dollars)

	2021 actual	2022 est.	2023 est.
Offsetting receipts from the public:			
086–267810 Green Retrofit Program for Multifamily Housing, Downward Reestimates of Subsidies	6	5	
086–269430 Emergency Homeowners' Relief Fund, Downward Reestimates	4	1	
086–269530 Home Ownership Preservation Equity Fund, Downward Reestimates of Subsidies	1	1	
086–271910 FHA-General and Special Risk, Negative Subsidies	951	784	789
086–271930 FHA-General and Special Risk, Downward Reestimates of Subsidies	2,477	3,658	
086–274330 Indian Housing Loan Guarantees, Downward Reestimates of Subsidies	17	65	
086–276230 Title VI Indian Loan Guarantee Downward Reestimate	1		
086–277330 Community Development Loan Guarantees, Downward Reestimates	2	4	
086–279930 Native Hawaiian Housing Loan Guarantees, Downward Reestimates of Subsidies	3	2	
086–322000 All Other General Fund Proprietary Receipts Including Budget Clearing Accounts	5	12	12
General Fund Offsetting receipts from the public	3,467	4,533	801
Intragovernmental payments:			
086–388510 Undistributed Intragovernmental Payments	2	5	5
General Fund Intragovernmental payments	2	5	5

GENERAL PROVISIONS—DEPARTMENT OF HOUSING AND URBAN DEVELOPMENT

(INCLUDING TRANSFERS OF FUNDS)
(INCLUDING CANCELLATIONS)

SEC. 201. Fifty percent of the amounts of budget authority, or in lieu thereof 50 percent of the cash amounts associated with such budget authority, that are recaptured from projects described in section 1012(a) of the Stewart B. McKinney Homeless Assistance Amendments Act of 1988 (42 U.S.C. 1437f note) shall be cancelled or in the case of cash, shall be remitted to the Treasury, and such amounts of budget authority or cash recaptured and not cancelled or remitted to the Treasury shall be used by State housing finance agencies or local governments or local housing agencies with projects approved by the Secretary of Housing and Urban Development for which settlement occurred after January 1, 1992, in accordance with such section. Notwithstanding the previous sentence, the Secretary may award up to 15 percent of the budget authority or cash recaptured and not cancelled or remitted to the Treasury to provide project owners with incentives to refinance their project at a lower interest rate.

SEC. 202. None of the funds made available by this Act may be used to investigate or prosecute under the Fair Housing Act any otherwise lawful activity engaged in by one or more persons, including the filing or maintaining of a nonfrivolous legal action, that is engaged in solely for the purpose of achieving or preventing action by a Government official or entity, or a court of competent jurisdiction.

SEC. 203. Except as explicitly provided in law, any grant, cooperative agreement or other assistance made pursuant to title II of this Act shall be made on a competitive basis and in accordance with section 102 of the Department of Housing and Urban Development Reform Act of 1989 (42 U.S.C. 3545).

SEC. 204. Funds of the Department of Housing and Urban Development subject to the Government Corporation Control Act or section 402 of the Housing Act of 1950 shall be available, without regard to the limitations on administrative expenses, for legal services on a contract or fee basis, and for utilizing and making payment for services and facilities of the Federal National Mortgage Association, Government National Mortgage Association, Federal Home Loan Mortgage Corporation, Federal Financing Bank, Federal Reserve banks or any member thereof, Federal Home Loan banks, and any insured bank within the meaning of the Federal Deposit Insurance Corporation Act, as amended (12 U.S.C. 1811–1).

SEC. 205. Corporations and agencies of the Department of Housing and Urban Development which are subject to the Government Corporation Control Act are hereby authorized to make such expenditures, within the limits of funds and borrowing authority available to each such corporation or agency and in accordance with law, and to make such contracts and commitments without regard to fiscal year limitations as provided by section 104 of such Act as may be necessary in carrying out the programs set forth in the budget for 2023 for such corporation or agency except as hereinafter provided: Provided, That collections of these corporations and agencies may be used for new loan or mortgage purchase commitments only to the extent expressly provided for in this Act (unless such loans are in support of other forms of assistance provided for in this or prior appropriations Acts), except that this proviso shall not apply to the mortgage insurance or guaranty operations of these corporations, or where loans or mortgage purchases are necessary to protect the financial interest of the United States Government.

SEC. 206. (a) Notwithstanding any other provision of law, subject to the conditions listed under this section, for fiscal years 2023 and 2024, the Secretary of Housing and Urban Development may authorize the transfer of some or all project-based assistance, debt held or insured by the Secretary and statutorily required low-income and very low-income use restrictions if any, associated with one or more multifamily housing project or projects to another multifamily housing project or projects.

(b) PHASED TRANSFERS.—Transfers of project-based assistance under this section may be done in phases to accommodate the financing and other requirements related to rehabilitating or constructing the project or projects to which the assistance is transferred, to ensure that such project or projects meet the standards under subsection (c).

(c) The transfer authorized in subsection (a) is subject to the following conditions:
(1) NUMBER AND BEDROOM SIZE OF UNITS.—
(A) For occupied units in the transferring project: The number of low-income and very low-income units and the configuration (i.e., bedroom size) provided by the transferring project shall be no less than when transferred to the receiving project or projects and the net dollar amount of Federal assistance provided to the transferring project shall remain the same in the receiving project or projects.
(B) For unoccupied units in the transferring project: The Secretary may authorize a reduction in the number of dwelling units in the receiving project or projects to allow for a reconfiguration of bedroom sizes to meet current market demands, as determined by the Secretary and provided there is no increase in the project-based assistance budget authority.
(2) The transferring project shall, as determined by the Secretary, be either physically obsolete or economically nonviable, or be reasonably expected to become economically nonviable when complying with state or Federal requirements for community integration and reduced concentration of individuals with disabilities.
(3) The receiving project or projects shall meet or exceed applicable physical standards established by the Secretary.

(4) The owner or mortgagor of the transferring project shall notify and consult with the tenants residing in the transferring project and provide a certification of approval by all appropriate local governmental officials.

(5) The tenants of the transferring project who remain eligible for assistance to be provided by the receiving project or projects shall not be required to vacate their units in the transferring project or projects until new units in the receiving project are available for occupancy.

(6) The Secretary determines that this transfer is in the best interest of the tenants.

(7) If either the transferring project or the receiving project or projects meets the condition specified in subsection (d)(2)(A), any lien on the receiving project resulting from additional financing obtained by the owner shall be subordinate to any FHA-insured mortgage lien transferred to, or placed on, such project by the Secretary, except that the Secretary may waive this requirement upon determination that such a waiver is necessary to facilitate the financing of acquisition, construction, and/or rehabilitation of the receiving project or projects.

(8) If the transferring project meets the requirements of subsection (d)(2), the owner or mortgagor of the receiving project or projects shall execute and record either a continuation of the existing use agreement or a new use agreement for the project where, in either case, any use restrictions in such agreement are of no lesser duration than the existing use restrictions.

(9) The transfer does not increase the cost (as defined in section 502 of the Congressional Budget Act of 1974(2 U.S.C. 661a)) of any FHA-insured mortgage, except to the extent that appropriations are provided in advance for the amount of any such increased cost.

(d) For purposes of this section—

(1) the terms "low-income" and "very low-income" shall have the meanings provided by the statute and/or regulations governing the program under which the project is insured or assisted;

(2) the term "multifamily housing project" means housing that meets one of the following conditions—

(A) housing that is subject to a mortgage insured under the National Housing Act;

(B) housing that has project-based assistance attached to the structure including projects undergoing mark to market debt restructuring under the Multifamily Assisted Housing Reform and Affordability Housing Act;

(C) housing that is assisted under section 202 of the Housing Act of 1959 (12 U.S.C. 1701q);

(D) housing that is assisted under section 202 of the Housing Act of 1959 (12 U.S.C. 1701q), as such section existed before the enactment of the Cranston-Gonzales National Affordable Housing Act;

(E) housing that is assisted under section 811 of the Cranston-Gonzales National Affordable Housing Act (42 U.S.C. 8013); or

(F) housing or vacant land that is subject to a use agreement;

(3) the term "project-based assistance" means—

(A) assistance provided under section 8(b) of the United States Housing Act of 1937 (42 U.S.C. 1437f(b));

(B) assistance for housing constructed or substantially rehabilitated pursuant to assistance provided under section 8(b)(2) of such Act (as such section existed immediately before October 1, 1983);

(C) rent supplement payments under section 101 of the Housing and Urban Development Act of 1965 (12 U.S.C. 1701s);

(D) interest reduction payments under section 236 and/or additional assistance payments under section 236(f)(2) of the National Housing Act (12 U.S.C. 1715z–1);

(E) assistance payments made under section 202(c)(2) of the Housing Act of 1959 (12 U.S.C. 1701q(c)(2)); and

(F) assistance payments made under section 811(d)(2) of the Cranston-Gonzalez National Affordable Housing Act (42 U.S.C. 8013(d)(2));

(4) the term "receiving project or projects" means the multifamily housing project or projects to which some or all of the project-based assistance, debt, and statutorily required low-income and very low-income use restrictions are to be transferred;

(5) the term "transferring project" means the multifamily housing project which is transferring some or all of the project-based assistance, debt, and the statutorily required low-income and very low-income use restrictions to the receiving project or projects; and

(6) the term "Secretary" means the Secretary of Housing and Urban Development.

(e) RESEARCH REPORT.—*The Secretary shall conduct an evaluation of the transfer authority under this section, including the effect of such transfers on the operational efficiency, contract rents, physical and financial conditions, and long-term preservation of the affected properties.*

SEC. 207. *(a) No assistance shall be provided under section 8 of the United States Housing Act of 1937 (42 U.S.C. 1437f) to any individual who—*

(1) is enrolled as a student at an institution of higher education (as defined under section 102 of the Higher Education Act of 1965 (20 U.S.C. 1002));

(2) is under 24 years of age;

(3) is not a veteran;

(4) is unmarried;

(5) does not have a dependent child;

(6) is not a person with disabilities, as such term is defined in section 3(b)(3)(E) of the United States Housing Act of 1937 (42 U.S.C. 1437a(b)(3)(E)) and was not receiving assistance under such section 8 as of November 30, 2005;

(7) is not a youth who left foster care at age 14 or older and is at risk of becoming homeless; and

(8) is not otherwise individually eligible, or has parents who, individually or jointly, are not eligible, to receive assistance under section 8 of the United States Housing Act of 1937 (42 U.S.C. 1437f).

(b) For purposes of determining the eligibility of a person to receive assistance under section 8 of the United States Housing Act of 1937 (42 U.S.C. 1437f), any financial assistance (in excess of amounts received for tuition and any other required fees and charges) that an individual receives under the Higher Education Act of 1965 (20 U.S.C. 1001 et seq.), from private sources, or from an institution of higher education (as defined under section 102 of the Higher Education Act of 1965 (20 U.S.C. 1002)), shall be considered income to that individual, except for a person over the age of 23 with dependent children.

SEC. 208. *The funds made available for Native Alaskans under paragraph (1) under the heading "Native American Programs" in title II of this Act shall be allocated to the same Native Alaskan housing block grant recipients that received funds in fiscal year 2005, and only such recipients shall be eligible to apply for funds made available under paragraph (2) of such heading.*

SEC. 209. *Notwithstanding any other provision of law, in fiscal year 2023, in managing and disposing of any multifamily property that is owned or has a mortgage held by the Secretary of Housing and Urban Development, and during the process of foreclosure on any property with a contract for rental assistance payments under section 8 of the United States Housing Act of 1937 (42 U.S.C. 1437f) or any other Federal programs, the Secretary shall maintain any rental assistance payments under section 8 of the United States Housing Act of 1937 and other programs that are attached to any dwelling units in the property. To the extent the Secretary determines, in consultation with the tenants and the local government that such a multifamily property owned or having a mortgage held by the Secretary is not feasible for continued rental assistance payments under such section 8 or other programs, based on consideration of (1) the costs of rehabilitating and operating the property and all available Federal, State, and local resources, including rent adjustments under section 524 of the Multifamily Assisted Housing Reform and Affordability Act of 1997 ("MAHRAA") (42 U.S.C. 1437f note), and (2) environmental conditions that cannot be remedied in a cost-effective fashion, the Secretary may, in consultation with the tenants of that property, contract for project-based rental assistance payments with an owner or owners of other existing housing properties, or provide other rental assistance. The Secretary shall also take appropriate steps to ensure that project-based contracts remain in effect prior to foreclosure, subject to the exercise of contractual abatement remedies to assist relocation of tenants for imminent major threats to health and safety after written notice to and informed consent of the affected tenants and use of other available remedies, such as partial abatements or receivership. After disposition of any multifamily property described in this section, the contract and allowable rent levels on such properties shall be subject to the requirements under section 524 of MAHRAA.*

SEC. 210. *Public housing agencies that own and operate 400 or fewer public housing units may elect to be exempt from any asset management requirement imposed by the Secretary in connection with the operating fund rule: Provided, That an agency seeking a discontinuance of a reduction of subsidy under the operating fund formula shall not be exempt from asset management requirements.*

SEC. 211. *With respect to the use of amounts provided in this Act and in future Acts for the operation, capital improvement, and management of public housing as authorized by sections 9(d) and 9(e) of the United States Housing Act of 1937 (42 U.S.C. 1437g(d),(e)), the Secretary shall not impose any requirement or guideline relating to asset management that restricts or limits in any way the use of capital funds for central office costs pursuant to paragraph (1) or (2) of section 9(g) of the United States Housing Act of 1937 (42 U.S.C. 1437g(g)(1), (2)): Provided, That a public housing agency may not use capital funds authorized under section 9(d) for activities that are eligible under section 9(e) for assistance with amounts from the* operating fund in excess of the amounts permitted under paragraph (1) or (2) of section 9(g).

SEC. 212. No official or employee of the Department of Housing and Urban Development shall be designated as an allotment holder unless the Office of the Chief Financial Officer has determined that such allotment holder has implemented an adequate system of funds control and has received training in funds control procedures and directives. The Chief Financial Officer shall ensure that there is a trained allotment holder for each HUD appropriation under the accounts "Executive Offices", "Administrative Support Offices", "Program Offices", "Government National Mortgage Association—Guarantees of Mortgage-Backed Securities Loan Guarantee Program Account", and "Office of Inspector General" within the Department of Housing and Urban Development.

SEC. 213. The Secretary shall, for fiscal year 2023, notify the public through the Federal Register and other means, as determined appropriate, of the issuance of a notice of the availability of assistance or notice of funding opportunity (NOFO) for any program or discretionary fund administered by the Secretary that is to be competitively awarded. Notwithstanding any other provision of law, for fiscal year 2023, the Secretary may make the NOFO available only on the Internet at the appropriate Government website or through other electronic media, as determined by the Secretary.

SEC. 214. The Secretary is authorized to transfer up to 10 percent or $5,000,000, whichever is less, of funds appropriated for any office under the headings "Administrative Support Offices" or "Program Offices" to any other such office : Provided, That the Secretary shall provide notification to the House and Senate Committees on Appropriations three business days in advance of any such transfers: Provided further, That no appropriation for any such office shall be increased or decreased by more than 10 percent or $5,000,000, whichever is less, unless such Committees are notified in writing ten business days in advance of any such transfers.

SEC. 215. (a) Any entity receiving housing assistance payments shall maintain decent, safe, and sanitary conditions, as determined by the Secretary, and comply with any standards under applicable State or local laws, rules, ordinances, or regulations relating to the physical condition of any property covered under a housing assistance payment contract.

(b) The Secretary shall take action under subsection (c) when a multifamily housing project with a contract under section 8 of the United States Housing Act of 1937 (42 U.S.C. 1437f) or a contract for similar project-based assistance—

(1) receives a Uniform Physical Condition Standards (UPCS) score of 59 or less; or

(2) fails to certify in writing to the Secretary within 3 days that all Exigent Health and Safety deficiencies identified by the inspector at the project have been corrected.

(3) Such requirements shall apply to insured and noninsured projects with assistance attached to the units under section 8 of the United States Housing Act of 1937 (42 U.S.C. 1437f), but shall not apply to such units assisted under section 8(o)(13) of such Act (42 U.S.C. 1437f(o)(13)) or to public housing units assisted with capital or operating funds under section 9 of the United States Housing Act of 1937 (42 U.S.C. 1437g).

(c)

(1) Within 15 days of the issuance of the Real Estate Assessment Center ("REAC") inspection, the Secretary shall provide the owner with a Notice of Default with a specified timetable, determined by the Secretary, for correcting all deficiencies. The Secretary shall provide a copy of the Notice of Default to the tenants, the local government, any mortgagees, and any contract administrator. If the owner's appeal results in a UPCS score of 60 or above, the Secretary may withdraw the Notice of Default.

(2) At the end of the time period for correcting all deficiencies specified in the Notice of Default, if the owner fails to fully correct such deficiencies, the Secretary may—

(A) require immediate replacement of project management with a management agent approved by the Secretary;

(B) impose civil money penalties, which shall be used solely for the purpose of supporting safe and sanitary conditions at applicable properties, as designated by the Secretary, with priority given to the tenants of the property affected by the penalty;

(C) abate the section 8 contract, including partial abatement, as determined by the Secretary, until all deficiencies have been corrected;

(D) pursue transfer of the project to an owner, approved by the Secretary under established procedures, who will be obligated to promptly make all required repairs and to accept renewal of the assistance contract if such renewal is offered;

(E) transfer the existing section 8 contract to another project or projects and owner or owners;

(F) pursue exclusionary sanctions, including suspensions or debarments from Federal programs;

(G) seek judicial appointment of a receiver to manage the property and cure all project deficiencies or seek a judicial order of specific performance requiring the owner to cure all project deficiencies;

(H) work with the owner, lender, or other related party to stabilize the property in an attempt to preserve the property through compliance, transfer of ownership, or an infusion of capital provided by a third-party that requires time to effectuate; or

(I) take any other regulatory or contractual remedies available as deemed necessary and appropriate by the Secretary.

(d) The Secretary shall take appropriate steps to ensure that project-based contracts remain in effect, subject to the exercise of contractual abatement remedies to assist relocation of tenants for major threats to health and safety after written notice to the affected tenants. To the extent the Secretary determines, in consultation with the tenants and the local government, that the property is not feasible for continued rental assistance payments under such section 8 or other programs, based on consideration of—

(1) the costs of rehabilitating and operating the property and all available Federal, State, and local resources, including rent adjustments under section 524 of the Multifamily Assisted Housing Reform and Affordability Act of 1997 ("MAHRAA"); and

(2) environmental conditions that cannot be remedied in a cost-effective fashion, the Secretary may contract for project-based rental assistance payments with an owner or owners of other existing housing properties, or provide other rental assistance.

(e) The Secretary shall report quarterly on all properties covered by this section that are assessed through the Real Estate Assessment Center and have UPCS physical inspection scores of less than 60 or have received an unsatisfactory management and occupancy review within the past 36 months. The report shall include—

(1) identification of the enforcement actions being taken to address such conditions, including imposition of civil money penalties and termination of subsidies, and identification of properties that have such conditions multiple times;

(2) identification of actions that the Department of Housing and Urban Development is taking to protect tenants of such identified properties; and

(3) any administrative or legislative recommendations to further improve the living conditions at properties covered under a housing assistance payment contract.

This report shall be submitted to the Senate and House Committees on Appropriations not later than 30 days after the enactment of this Act, and on the first business day of each Federal fiscal year quarter thereafter while this section remains in effect.

SEC. 216. None of the funds made available by this Act, or any other Act, for purposes authorized under section 8 (only with respect to the tenant-based rental assistance program) and section 9 of the United States Housing Act of 1937 (42 U.S.C. 1437 et seq.), may be used by any public housing agency for any amount of salary, including bonuses, for the chief executive officer of which, or any other official or employee of which, that exceeds the annual rate of basic pay payable for a position at level IV of the Executive Schedule at any time during any public housing agency fiscal year 2023.

SEC. 217. None of the funds made available in this Act shall be used by the Federal Housing Administration, the Government National Mortgage Association, or the Department of Housing and Urban Development to insure, securitize, or establish a Federal guarantee of any mortgage or mortgage backed security that refinances or otherwise replaces a mortgage that has been subject to eminent domain condemnation or seizure, by a State, municipality, or any other political subdivision of a State.

SEC. 218. None of the funds made available by this Act may be used to terminate the status of a unit of general local government as a metropolitan city (as defined in section 102 of the Housing and Community Development Act of 1974 (42 U.S.C. 5302)) with respect to grants under section 106 of such Act (42 U.S.C. 5306).

SEC. 219. Amounts made available by this Act that are appropriated, allocated, advanced on a reimbursable basis, or transferred to the Office of Policy Development and Research of the Department of Housing and Urban Development and functions thereof, for research, evaluation, or statistical purposes, and that are unexpended at the time of completion of a contract, grant, or cooperative agreement, may be deobligated and shall immediately become available and may be reobligated in that fiscal year or the subsequent fiscal year for the research, evaluation, or statistical purposes for which the amounts are made available to that Office subject to reprogramming requirements in section 226 of this Act.

SEC. 220. None of the funds provided in this Act or any other Act may be used for awards, including performance, special act, or spot, for any employee of the Department of Housing and Urban Development subject to administrative discipline (including suspension from work), in this fiscal year, but this prohibition shall not be effective prior to the effective date of any such administrative discipline or after any final decision over-turning such discipline.

SEC. 221. With respect to grant amounts awarded under the heading "Homeless Assistance Grants" for fiscal years 2015 through 2023 for the Continuum of Care (CoC) program as authorized under subtitle C of title IV of the McKinney-Vento Homeless Assistance Act, costs paid by program income of grant recipients may count toward meeting the recipient's matching requirements, provided the costs are eligible CoC costs that supplement the recipient's CoC program.

SEC. 222. (a) From amounts made available under this title under the heading "Homeless Assistance Grants", the Secretary may award 1-year transition grants to recipients of funds for activities under subtitle C of the McKinney-Vento Homeless Assistance Act (42 U.S.C. 11381 et seq.) to transition from one Continuum of Care program component to another.

(b) In order to be eligible to receive a transition grant, the funding recipient must have the consent of the continuum of care and meet standards determined by the Secretary.

SEC. 223. The Promise Zone designations and Promise Zone Designation Agreements entered into pursuant to such designations, made by the Secretary in prior fiscal years, shall remain in effect in accordance with the terms and conditions of such agreements.

SEC. 224. Any public housing agency designated as a Moving to Work agency pursuant to section 239 of division L of Public Law 114–113 (42 U.S.C. 1437f note; 129 Stat. 2897) may, upon such designation, use funds (except for special purpose funding, including special purpose vouchers) previously allocated to any such public housing agency under section 8 or 9 of the United States Housing Act of 1937, including any reserve funds held by the public housing agency or funds held by the Department of Housing and Urban Development, pursuant to the authority for use of section 8 or 9 funding provided under such section and section 204 of title II of the Departments of Veterans Affairs and Housing and Urban Development and Independent Agencies Appropriations Act, 1996 (Public Law 104–134; 110 Stat. 1321–28), notwithstanding the purposes for which such funds were appropriated.

SEC. 225. None of the amounts made available by this Act may be used to prohibit any public housing agency under receivership or the direction of a Federal monitor from applying for, receiving, or using funds made available under the heading "Public Housing Fund" for competitive grants to evaluate and reduce lead-based paint hazards in this Act or that remain available and not awarded from prior Acts, or be used to prohibit a public housing agency from using such funds to carry out any required work pursuant to a settlement agreement, consent decree, voluntary agreement, or similar document for a violation of the Lead Safe Housing or Lead Disclosure Rules.

SEC. 226. Except as otherwise provided in this Act, and unless the House and Senate Committees on Appropriations are consulted 15 days in advance of any reprogramming and are notified in writing 10 days in advance of such reprogramming, none of the funds provided in this title, provided by previous appropriations Acts to the Department of Housing and Urban Development that remain available for obligation or expenditure in fiscal year 2023, or provided from any accounts in the Treasury derived by the collection of fees and available to the Department of Housing and Urban Development, shall be available for obligation or expenditure through a reprogramming of funds that—

(a) for Program and Information Technology funds—

(1) initiates or creates a new program, project, or activity;

(2) eliminates a program, project, or activity;

(3) increases funds for any program, project, or activity for which funds have been denied or restricted by the Congress;

(4) proposes to use funds directed for a specific activity by either the House or Senate Committees on Appropriations for a different purpose;

(5) augments existing programs, projects, or activities in excess of $5,000,000 or 10 percent, whichever is less; or

(6) reduces existing programs, projects, or activities by $5,000,000 or 10 percent, whichever is less;

(b) for Salaries and Expenses funds—

(1) assigns personnel or hires to support the creation of a new program, project, or activity not previously included in the President's budget;

(2) increases the personnel or other resources for any program, project, or activity for which funds have been denied or restricted by the Congress;

(3) relocates or closes an office;

(4) reorganizes an office, which shall include the transfer of any function from one office to another office.

SEC. 227. Not later than 60 days after the date of enactment of this Act, the Department of Housing and Urban Development shall submit a report to the Committees on Appropriations of the Senate and of the House of Representatives to establish the baseline for application of reprogramming and transfer authorities for the current fiscal year: Provided, That such report shall include—

(a) a table for each appropriation with a separate column to display the prior year enacted level, the President's budget request, adjustments made by Congress, adjustments due to enacted rescissions, if appropriate, and the fiscal year enacted level;

(b) for program funds, a delineation in the table for each appropriation and its respective prior year enacted level by program, project, and activity as detailed in the budget appendix for the respective appropriation; and

(c) for salaries and expenses, an organizational chart for each office that includes detail to the branch level, and clearly identifies those "offices" to which section 226(b) shall be applied.

SEC. 228. (a) Funds previously made available in the Consolidated and Further Continuing Appropriations Act, 2015 (Public Law 113–235) for the "Choice Neighborhoods Initiative" that were available for obligation through fiscal year 2017 are to remain available through fiscal year 2023 for the liquidation of valid obligations incurred in fiscal years 2015 through 2017.

(b) Funds previously made available in the Consolidated Appropriations Act, 2016 (Public Law 114–113) for the "Choice Neighborhoods Initiative" that were available for obligation through fiscal year 2018 are to remain available through fiscal year 2024 for the liquidation of valid obligations incurred in fiscal years 2016 through 2018.

(c) Funds previously made available in the Consolidated Appropriations Act, 2017 (Public Law 115–31) for the "Choice Neighborhoods Initiative" that were available for obligation through fiscal year 2019 are to remain available through fiscal year 2025 for the liquidation of valid obligations incurred in fiscal years 2017 through 2019.

(d) Funds previously made available in the Consolidated Appropriations Act, 2018 (Public Law 115–141) for the "Choice Neighborhoods Initiative" that were available for obligation through fiscal year 2020 are to remain available through fiscal year 2026 for the liquidation of valid obligations incurred in fiscal years 2018 through 2020.

(e) Funds previously made available in the Consolidated Appropriations Act, 2019 (Public Law 116–6) for the "Choice Neighborhoods Initiative" that were available for obligation through fiscal year 2021 are to remain available through fiscal year 2027 for the liquidation of valid obligations incurred in fiscal years 2019 through 2021.

(f) Funds previously made available in the Further Consolidated Appropriations Act, 2020 (Public Law 116–94) for the "Choice Neighborhoods Initiative" that were available for obligation through fiscal year 2022 are to remain available through fiscal year 2028 for the liquidation of valid obligations incurred in fiscal years 2020 through 2022.

(g) Funds previously made available in the Consolidated Appropriations Act, 2021 (Public Law 116–260) for the "Choice Neighborhoods Initiative" that were available for obligation through fiscal year 2023 are to remain available through fiscal year 2029 for the liquidation of valid obligations incurred in fiscal years 2021 through 2023.

(h)

(1) This section shall become effective immediately upon enactment of this Act.

(2) If this Act is enacted after September 30, 2022, subsection (a) shall be applied as if it were in effect on September 30, 2022.

SEC. 229. Section 239 of the Department of Housing and Urban Development Appropriations Act, 2016 (Public Law 114–113; 129 Stat. 2897) is amended by striking "7-year period" and inserting "10-year period" in the fifth sentence.

SEC. 230. Paragraph (6) of section 542(c) of the Housing and Community Development Act of 1992 (12 U.S.C. 1715z–22(c)) is amended in its title by deleting "Prohibition on" and by revising the text of paragraph (6) to read as follows: "The Government National Mortgage Association may, at the discretion of the Secretary, securitize any multifamily loan insured under this subsection, provided that, notwithstanding any other provision, any successors and assigns of the risk share partner (including the holders of credit instruments issued under a trust mortgage or deed of trust pursuant to which such holders act by and through a trustee therein named) shall not assume any obligation under the risk-sharing agreement and may assign any defaulted loan to the Federal Housing Administration in exchange for payment of the full mortgage insurance claim. The risk-sharing agreement must provide for reimbursement to the Secretary by the risk share partner(s) for either all or a portion of the losses incurred on the loans insured. The originating Housing Finance Agency cannot assign or otherwise be relieved of its risk share obligations under the risk-sharing agreement.".

SEC. 231. Of the amounts made available for salaries and expenses under all accounts under this title (except for the Office of Inspector General account), a total of up to $10,000,000 may be transferred to and merged with amounts made available in the "Information Technology Fund" account under this title.

SEC. 232. The language under the heading "Rental Assistance Demonstration" in the Department of Housing and Urban Development Appropriations Act, 2012 (Public Law 112–55), as most recently amended by Public Law 115–141, is further amended—

(a) in the initial undesignated matter, by striking "and 'Public Housing Operating Fund'" and inserting ", 'Public Housing Operating Fund', and 'Public Housing Fund'";

(b) in the second proviso, by striking "until September 30, 2024" and inserting "for fiscal year 2012 and thereafter";

(c) by striking the fourth proviso and inserting the following new provisos: "Provided further, That at properties with assistance under section 9 of the Act requesting to partially convert such assistance, and where an event under section 18 of the Act occurs that results in the eligibility for tenant protection vouchers under section 8(o) of the Act, the Secretary may convert the tenant protection voucher assistance to assistance under a project-based subsidy contract under section 8 of the Act, which shall be eligible for renewal under section 524 of the Multifamily Assisted Housing Reform and Affordability Act of 1997, or assistance under section 8(o)(13) of the Act, so long as the property meets any additional requirements established by the Secretary to facilitate conversion: Provided further, That to facilitate the conversion of assistance under the previous proviso, the Secretary may transfer an amount equal to the total amount that would have been allocated for tenant protection voucher assistance for properties that have requested such conversions from amounts made available for tenant protection voucher assistance under the heading 'Tenant-Based Rental Assistance' to the heading 'Project-Based Rental Assistance': Provided further, That at properties with assistance previously converted hereunder to assistance under the heading "Project-Based Rental Assistance," which are also separately assisted under section 8(o)(13) of the Act, the Secretary may, with the consent of the public housing agency and owner, terminate such project-based subsidy contracts and immediately enter into one new project-based subsidy contract under section 8 of the Act, which shall be eligible for renewal under section 524 of the Multifamily Assisted Housing Reform and Affordability Act of 1997, subject to the requirement that any residents assisted under section 8(o)(13) of the Act at the time of such termination of such project-based subsidy contract shall retain all rights accrued under section 8(o)(13)(E) of the Act under the new project-based subsidy contract and section 8(o)(13)(F)(iv) of the Act shall not apply: Provided further, That to carry out the previous proviso, the Secretary may transfer from the heading "Tenant-Based Rental Assistance" to the heading "Project-Based Rental Assistance" an amount equal to the amounts associated with such terminating contract under section 8(o)(13) of the Act:";

(d) in the thirteenth proviso, as reordered above, by—

(1) inserting "'Public Housing Fund', 'Self-Sufficiency Programs', 'Family Self-Sufficiency'" following "'Public Housing Operating Fund',"; and

(2) inserting "or the ongoing availability of services for residents" after "effective conversion of assistance under the demonstration";

(e) by striking the twenty-first proviso, as reordered above, and inserting the following new provisos: "Provided further, That conversions of assistance under the following provisos herein shall be considered as the 'Second Component' and shall be authorized for fiscal year 2012 and thereafter: Provided further, That owners of properties assisted under section 101 of the Housing and Urban Development Act of 1965, section 236(f)(2) of the National Housing Act, or section 8(e)(2) of the United States Housing Act of 1937, for which an event after October 1, 2006 has caused or results in the termination of rental assistance or affordability restrictions and the issuance of tenant protection vouchers under section 8(o) of the Act shall be eligible, subject to requirements established by the Secretary, for conversion of assistance available for such vouchers or assistance contracts to assistance under a long term project-based subsidy contract under section 8 of the Act: Provided further, That owners of properties with a project rental assistance contract under section 202(c)(2) of the Housing Act of 1959 shall be eligible, subject to requirements established by the Secretary, including but not limited to the subordination, restructuring, or both, of any capital advance documentation, including any note, mortgage, use agreement or other agreements, evidencing or securing a capital advance previously provided by the Secretary under section 202(c)(1) of the Housing Act of 1959 as necessary to facilitate the conversion of assistance while maintaining the affordability period and the designation of the property as serving elderly persons, and tenant consultation procedures, for conversion of assistance available for such assistance contracts to assistance under a long term project-based subsidy contract under section 8 of the Act: Provided further, That owners of properties with a senior preservation rental assistance contract under section 811 of the American Homeownership and Economic Opportunity Act of 2000 (12 U.S.C. 1701q note), shall be eligible, subject to requirements established by the Secretary as necessary to facilitate the conversion of assistance while maintaining the affordability period and the designation of the property as serving elderly families, and tenant consultation procedures, for conversion of assistance available for such assistance contracts to assistance under a long term project-based subsidy contract under section 8 of the Act: Provided further, That owners of properties with a project rental assistance contract under section 811(d)(2) of the Cranston-Gonzalez National Affordable Housing Act, shall be eligible, subject to requirements established by the Secretary, including but not limited to the subordination, restructuring, or both, of any capital advance documentation, including any note, mortgage, use agreement or other agreements, evidencing or securing a capital advance previously provided by the Secretary under section 811(d)(2) of the Cranston-Gonzalez National Affordable Housing Act as necessary to facilitate the conversion of assistance while maintaining the affordability period and the designation of the property as serving persons with disabilities, and tenant consultation procedures, for conversion of assistance contracts to assistance under a long term project-based subsidy contract under section 8 of the Act: Provided further, That long term project-based subsidy contracts under section 8 of the Act which are established under this Second Component shall have a term of no less than 20 years, with rent adjustments only by an operating cost factor established by the Secretary, which shall be eligible for renewal under section 524 of the Multifamily Assisted Housing Reform and Affordability Act of 1997 (42 U.S.C. 1437f note), or, subject to agreement of the administering public housing agency, to assistance under section 8(o)(13) of the Act, to which the limitation under subparagraph (B) of section 8(o)(13) of the Act shall not apply and for which the Secretary may waive or alter the provisions of subparagraphs (C) and (D) of section 8(o)(13) of the Act:";

(f) after the twenty-seventh proviso, as reordered above, by inserting the following new proviso: "Provided further, That the Secretary may waive or alter the requirements of section 8(c)(1)(A) of the Act for contracts provided to properties converting assistance from section 202(c)(2) of the Housing Act of 1959 as necessary to ensure the ongoing provision and coordination of services or to avoid a reduction in project subsidy:"; and

(g) in the thirty-third proviso, as reordered above, by—

(1) striking "heading 'Housing for the Elderly'" and inserting "headings 'Housing for the Elderly' and 'Housing for Persons with Disabilities'"; and

(2) striking "any section 202 project rental assistance contract conversions" and inserting "the conversion of assistance from section 202(c)(2) of the Housing Act of 1959, section 811 of the American Homeownership and Economic Opportunity Act of 2000, or section 811(d)(2) of the Cranston-Gonzalez National Affordable Housing Act".

SEC. 233. Funds previously made available in the Consolidated Appropriations Act, 2019 (Public Law 116–6) for "Lead Hazard Reduction" that were available for obligation through fiscal year 2020 are to remain available through fiscal year 2027 for the liquidation of valid obligations incurred in fiscal years 2019 through 2020.

SEC. 234. MARK-TO-MARKET AMENDMENTS. The Multifamily Assisted Housing Reform and Affordability Act of 1997 (42 U.S.C. 1437f note) is amended—

(a) in section 515, by adding at the end the following new subsection:

"(d) RENT ADJUSTMENTS AND SUBSEQUENT RENEWALS. After the initial renewal of a section 8 contract pursuant to this section and notwithstanding any other provision of law or contract regarding the adjustment of rents or subsequent renewal of such contract for a project, including such a provision in section 514 or this section, in the case of a project subject to any restrictions imposed pursuant to sections 514 or this section, the Secretary may, not more often than once every 10 years, adjust such rents or renew such contracts at rent levels that are equal to the lesser of budget-based rents or comparable market rents for the market area upon the request of an owner or purchaser who—

"(1) demonstrates that—

"(A) project income is insufficient to operate and maintain the project, as determined by the Secretary; or

"(B) the rent adjustment or renewal contract is necessary to support commercially reasonable financing (including any required debt service coverage and replacement reserve) for rehabilitation necessary to ensure the long-term sustainability of the project, as determined by the Secretary; and

"(2) agrees to—

"(A) extend the affordability and use restrictions required under 514(e)(6) for an additional twenty years; and

"(B) enter into a binding commitment to continue to renew such contract for and during such extended term, provided that after the affordability and use restrictions required under 514(e)(6) have been maintained for a term of 30 years:

"(i) an owner with a contract for which rent levels were set at the time of its initial renewal under section 514(g)(2) shall request that the Secretary renew such contract under section 524 for and during such extended term; and

"(ii) an owner with a contract for which rent levels were set at the time of its initial renewal under section 514(g)(1) may request that the Secretary renew such contract under section 524.";

(b) in section 524, by adding at the end the following new subsection:

"(h) RENT ADJUSTMENTS TO ADDRESS DISTRESS. In the case of a section 8 contract that will be eligible for renewal under this section when it expires or terminates, notwithstanding any provision of contract or law regarding the adjustment of rents, including such a provision in this section, the Secretary may adjust such rents, subject to the availability of funds for such rent adjustments, to rent levels that are equal to the lesser of budget-based rents or comparable market rents for the market area at the request of an owner or purchaser who demonstrates that such rent adjustment is needed to address project health and safety deficiencies and that—

"(1) project income is insufficient to operate and maintain the project, as determined by the Secretary; or

"(2) the rent adjustment is necessary to support commercially reasonable financing (including any required debt service coverage and replacement reserve) for rehabilitation necessary to ensure the long-term sustainability of the project, as determined by the Secretary."; and

(c) in section 579, by striking "October 1, 2022" each place it appears and inserting in lieu thereof "October 1, 2027".

SEC. 235. Notwithstanding any other provision of law, if the Secretary determines, for any prior formula grant allocation administered by the Secretary under a program under the headings "Public and Indian Housing", "Community Planning and Development", or "Housing Programs" in this title, that a recipient received an allocation greater than the amount such recipient should have received for a formula allocation cycle pursuant to applicable statutes and regulations, the Secretary may adjust for any such funding error in the next applicable formula allocation cycle by—

(a) offsetting each such recipient's formula allocation (if eligible for a formula allocation in the next applicable formula allocation cycle) by the amount of any such funding error; and

(b) reallocating any available balances that are attributable to the offset to the recipient or recipients that would have been allocated additional funds in the formula allocation cycle in which any such error occurred (if such recipient or recipients are eligible for a formula allocation in the next applicable formula allocation cycle) in an amount proportionate to such recipient's eligibility under the next applicable formula allocation cycle formula:

Provided, That all offsets and reallocations from such available balances shall be recorded against funds available for the next applicable formula allocation cycle: Provided further, That the term "next applicable formula allocation cycle" means the first formula allocation cycle for a program that is reasonably available for correction following such a Secretarial determination: Provided further, That if, upon request by a recipient and giving consideration to all Federal resources available to the recipient for the same grant purposes, the Secretary determines that the offset in a next applicable formula allocation cycle would critically impair the recipient's ability to accomplish the purpose of the formula grant, the Secretary may adjust for the funding error across two or more formula allocation cycles.

SEC. 236. Public housing agencies may not renew rental assistance contracts under the moderate rehabilitation program under section 8(e)(2) of the United States Housing Act of 1937 (42 U.S.C. 1437f(e)(2)) or the moderate rehabilitation single room occupancy program under section 441 of the McKinney-Vento Homeless Assistance Act (42 U.S.C. 11401) after September 30, 2027.

SEC. 237. (a) With respect to the funds made available for the Continuum of Care program authorized under subtitle C of title IV of the McKinney-Vento Homeless Assistance Act (42 U.S.C. 11381 et seq.) under the heading "Homeless Assistance Grants" in the Department of Housing and Urban Development Appropriations Act, 2021 (Public Law 116–260), under section 231 of the Department of Housing and Urban Development Appropriations Act, 2020 (42 U.S.C. 11364a), or in this title, Title VI of the Civil Rights Act of 1964 (42 U.S.C. 2000d et seq.) and Title VIII of the Civil Rights Act of 1968 (42 U.S.C. 3601 et seq.) shall not apply to applications by or awards for projects to be carried out—

(1) on or off reservation or trust lands for awards made to Indian tribes or tribally designated housing entities; or

(2) on reservation or trust lands for awards made to eligible entities as defined in section 401 of the McKinney-Vento Homeless-Assistance Act (42 U.S.C. 11360).

(b) With respect to funds made available for the Continuum of Care program authorized under subtitle C of title IV of the McKinney-Vento Homeless Assistance Act (42 U.S.C. 11381 et seq.) under the heading "Homeless Assistance Grants" in this title or under section 231 of the Department of Housing and Urban Development Appropriations Act, 2020 (42 U.S.C. 11364a)—

(1) applications for projects to be carried out on reservations or trust land shall contain a certification of consistency with an approved Indian housing plan developed under section 102 of the Native American Housing Assistance and Self-Determination Act (NAHASDA) (25 U.S.C. 4112), notwithstanding section 106 of the Cranston-Gonzalez National Affordable Housing Act (42 U.S.C. 12706) and section 403 of the McKinney-Vento Homeless Assistance Act (42 U.S.C. 11361);

(2) Indian tribes and tribally designated housing entities that are recipients of awards for projects on reservations or trust land shall certify that they are following an approved housing plan developed under section 102 of NAHASDA (25 U.S.C. 4112); and

(3) a collaborative applicant for a Continuum of Care whose geographic area includes only reservation and trust land is not required to meet the requirement in section 402(f)(2) of the McKinney-Vento Homeless Assistance Act (42 U.S.C. 11360a(f)(2)).

SEC. 238. Of the amounts made available under the heading "Project-Based Rental Assistance" in prior Acts, up to $1,300,000 may be transferred to Treasury Account 86-X-0148 for the liquidation of obligations incurred in fiscal year 2018 in connection with the continued provision of interest reduction payments authorized under section 236 of the National Housing Act (12 U.S.C. 1715z–1).

DEPARTMENT OF THE INTERIOR

LAND AND MINERALS MANAGEMENT

Bureau of Land Management

The Bureau of Land Management (BLM) is charged with the multiple use management of natural resources on approximately 245 million acres of surface estate of public land, about one-eighth of the land in the United States. The BLM also administers approximately 700 million acres of onshore Federal mineral estate underlying the BLM and other surface ownerships. In addition, the BLM has trust responsibilities on 56 million acres of Indian trust lands for mineral operations and cadastral (land) surveys. The lands managed by the BLM provide important natural resources, recreational and scenic values to the American people, as well as resource commodities and revenue to the Federal Government, States, and counties. It is the mission of the BLM to sustain the health, diversity, and productivity of the public lands for the use and enjoyment of present and future generations.

Federal Funds

Management of Lands and Resources

For necessary expenses for protection, use, improvement, development, disposal, cadastral surveying, classification, acquisition of easements and other interests in lands, and performance of other functions, including maintenance of facilities, as authorized by law, in the management of lands and their resources under the jurisdiction of the Bureau of Land Management, including the general administration of the Bureau, and assessment of mineral potential of public lands pursuant to section 1010(a) of Public Law 96–487 (16 U.S.C. 3150(a)), $1,427,939,000, to remain available until September 30, 2024; of which $76,355,000 for annual maintenance and deferred maintenance programs and $153,100,000 for the wild horse and burro program, as authorized by Public Law 92–195 (16 U.S.C. 1331 et seq.), shall remain available until expended: Provided, That amounts in the fee account of the BLM Permit Processing Improvement Fund may be used for any bureau-related expenses associated with the processing of oil and gas applications for permits to drill and related use of authorizations: Provided further, That of the amounts made available under this heading, up to $1,000,000 shall be made available for the purposes described in section 122(e)(1)(A) of division G of Public Law 115–31 (43 U.S.C. 1748c(e)(1)(A)).

In addition, $51,020,000, to remain available until expended, is for conducting oil and gas inspection activities, to be reduced by amounts collected by the Bureau and credited to this appropriation derived from onshore oil and gas inspection fees that the Bureau shall collect, as provided for in this Act; and $39,696,000 is for Mining Law Administration program operations, including the cost of administering the mining claim fee program, to remain available until expended, to be reduced by amounts collected by the Bureau and credited to this appropriation from mining claim maintenance fees and location fees that are hereby authorized for fiscal year 2023, so as to result in a final appropriation estimated at not more than $1,427,939,000, and $2,000,000, to remain available until expended, from communication site rental fees established by the Bureau for the cost of administering communication site activities.

Note.—A full-year 2022 appropriation for this account was not enacted at the time the Budget was prepared; therefore, the Budget assumes this account is operating under the Continuing Appropriations Act, 2022 (Division A of Public Law 117–43, as amended). The amounts included for 2022 reflect the annualized level provided by the continuing resolution.

Management of Lands and Resources

⟦*For an additional amount for "Management of Lands and Resources", $1,192,000, to remain available until expended, for necessary expenses related to the consequences of calendar year 2019, 2020, and 2021 wildfires, hurricanes and other natural disasters.*⟧ *(Disaster Relief Supplemental Appropriations Act, 2022.)*

Program and Financing (in millions of dollars)

Identification code 014–1109–0–1–302		2021 actual	2022 est.	2023 est.
	Obligations by program activity:			
0011	Land resources	263	231	231
0012	Wildlife and fisheries	7	8	8
0013	Threatened and endangered species	1	1	1
0014	Recreation management	79	76	76
0015	Energy and minerals	207	204	204
0016	Realty and ownership management	83	79	79
0017	Resource protection	139	132	132
0018	Transportation and facilities maintenance	126	174	174
0020	Workforce and organizational support	178	166	166
0021	Aquatic resources management	57	54	54
0022	Wildlife habitat management	133	124	124
0030	National Monuments & NCA	46	41	41
0799	Total direct obligations	1,319	1,290	1,290
0801	Management of Lands and Resources (Reimbursable)	18	18	18
0802	Communication site rental fees (R)	3	2	2
0803	Mining law administration (R)	43	41	41
0805	Cadastral reimbursable program	8	7	7
0899	Total reimbursable obligations	72	68	68
0900	Total new obligations, unexpired accounts	1,391	1,358	1,358
	Budgetary resources:			
	Unobligated balance:			
1000	Unobligated balance brought forward, Oct 1	228	177	157
1021	Recoveries of prior year unpaid obligations	64	45	45
1070	Unobligated balance (total)	292	222	202
	Budget authority:			
	Appropriations, discretionary:			
1100	Appropriation	1,221	1,221	1,428
1100	Appropriation - Disaster Relief Supplemental [P.L. 117–43]		1	
1131	Unobligated balance of appropriations permanently reduced	–13	–1	
1160	Appropriation, discretionary (total)	1,208	1,221	1,428
	Spending authority from offsetting collections, discretionary:			
1700	Offsetting collections (Mining law and Comm Sites)	44	40	40
1700	Offsetting collections (Economy Act)	28	32	32
1700	Offsetting Collections (O&G Inspection Fees)			51
1701	Change in uncollected payments, Federal sources	–4		
1750	Spending auth from offsetting collections, disc (total)	68	72	123
1900	Budget authority (total)	1,276	1,293	1,551
1930	Total budgetary resources available	1,568	1,515	1,753
	Memorandum (non-add) entries:			
1941	Unexpired unobligated balance, end of year	177	157	395
	Change in obligated balance:			
	Unpaid obligations:			
3000	Unpaid obligations, brought forward, Oct 1	692	757	544
3010	New obligations, unexpired accounts	1,391	1,358	1,358
3020	Outlays (gross)	–1,261	–1,526	–1,530
3040	Recoveries of prior year unpaid obligations, unexpired	–64	–45	–45
3041	Recoveries of prior year unpaid obligations, expired	–1		
3050	Unpaid obligations, end of year	757	544	327
	Uncollected payments:			
3060	Uncollected pymts, Fed sources, brought forward, Oct 1	–37	–33	–33
3070	Change in uncollected pymts, Fed sources, unexpired	4		
3090	Uncollected pymts, Fed sources, end of year	–33	–33	–33
	Memorandum (non-add) entries:			
3100	Obligated balance, start of year	655	724	511
3200	Obligated balance, end of year	724	511	294
	Budget authority and outlays, net:			
	Discretionary:			
4000	Budget authority, gross	1,276	1,293	1,551
	Outlays, gross:			
4010	Outlays from new discretionary authority	755	974	1,181
4011	Outlays from discretionary balances	506	552	349
4020	Outlays, gross (total)	1,261	1,526	1,530
	Offsets against gross budget authority and outlays:			
	Offsetting collections (collected) from:			
4030	Federal sources	–28	–32	–32
4033	Non-Federal sources	–44	–40	–40
4033	Non-Federal sources			–51
4040	Offsets against gross budget authority and outlays (total)	–72	–72	–123
	Additional offsets against gross budget authority only:			
4050	Change in uncollected pymts, Fed sources, unexpired	4		
4070	Budget authority, net (discretionary)	1,208	1,221	1,428
4080	Outlays, net (discretionary)	1,189	1,454	1,407
4180	Budget authority, net (total)	1,208	1,221	1,428
4190	Outlays, net (total)	1,189	1,454	1,407

MANAGEMENT OF LANDS AND RESOURCES—Continued
Program and Financing—Continued

Identification code 014–1109–0–1–302	2021 actual	2022 est.	2023 est.
Memorandum (non-add) entries:			
5090 Unexpired unavailable balance, SOY: Offsetting collections	4	4	4
5092 Unexpired unavailable balance, EOY: Offsetting collections	4	4	4

Land resources.—Provides for the integrated management of public land resources, including forestry, rangeland, and cultural resources, as well as wild horses and burros.

Wildlife and aquatic habitat management.—This activity encompasses programs that provide for the maintenance, improvement, or enhancement of wildlife habitats; the protection, conservation, consultation, recovery, and evaluation of populations and habitats of threatened, endangered and special status animal and plant species; as well as the management of water resources and riparian and wetlands areas, as part of the management of public lands and ecosystems.

Recreation management.—Provides for management and protection of recreational resource values, designated and potential wilderness areas, visitor services, and collection and expenditure of recreation user fees.

Energy and minerals management.—Provides for the management of: onshore oil, gas, and coal in line with the requirements of Executive Orders 13990 and 14008; renewable energy resources such as wind, solar, and geothermal energy; other leasable minerals and mineral materials activities; and the administration of encumbrances on the mineral estate on Federal and Indian lands. These programs also address needed remediation and reclamation of abandoned or orphaned oil and gas wells on BLM lands. The 2023 Budget continues to fund oil and gas management activities through a combination of direct appropriations and permanent appropriations authorized by the National Defense Authorization Act of 2015. The 2023 Budget proposes to offset the costs of oil and gas inspection activities through revenue from new inspection fees similar to those already in place for offshore operations.

Realty and ownership management.—Provides for management and non-reimbursable processing of authorizations and compliance for realty actions and rights-of-way (including Alaska), administration of land title records and completion of cadastral surveys on public lands.

Communication site management.—This program grants and administers authorizations for communications sites; develops site management plans to guide users and analyze the impacts of communication structures on the sites and the surrounding lands; and conducts facility compliance inspections. Program costs are expected to be fully offset by site rental fees in 2023.

Resource protection.—Provides for management of the land use planning and National Environmental Policy Act processes, including assessment and monitoring activities. Also ensures the health and safety of users of the public lands through remediation of abandoned mine lands and protection from criminal and other unlawful activities; mitigation of the effects of hazardous material and/or waste and physical safety hazards.

Transportation and facilities management.—Provides for construction and maintenance of administrative and recreation sites, roads, trails, bridges and dams, including compliance with building codes and standards and environmental protection requirements. These funds allow for the systematic management of facilities with critical health and safety concerns, and ensure the protection of natural and cultural resources and the environment. The Bureau of Land Management funds all construction and deferred maintenance projects from this activity, including those on the Oregon and California grant lands.

National Conservation Lands.—Provides for the management of National Monuments, National Conservation Areas, and other Congressional conservation designations in the National Conservation Lands. The program provides for the recurring operational (base) budgets of these units.

Workforce and organizational support.—Provides for the management of bureau business practices, such as human resources, Equal Employment Opportunity, financial resources, procurement, property, information technology, and fixed costs.

Mining law administration.—Provides for exploration and development of minerals on public lands pursuant to the General Mining Law of 1872, including validity examinations, patent application reviews, enforcement of environmental and bonding requirements, and recordation of mining claims. Program costs are expected to be fully offset by claim maintenance and other fees in 2023.

Funding requested in this account will complement the Civilian Climate Corps and will develop the next generation of conservation workers and create a new pathway to good-paying jobs.

Object Classification (in millions of dollars)

Identification code 014–1109–0–1–302	2021 actual	2022 est.	2023 est.
Direct obligations:			
Personnel compensation:			
11.1 Full-time permanent	436	436	436
11.3 Other than full-time permanent	13	13	13
11.5 Other personnel compensation	23	23	23
11.9 Total personnel compensation	472	472	472
12.1 Civilian personnel benefits	151	151	151
21.0 Travel and transportation of persons	6	6	6
22.0 Transportation of things	5	5	5
23.1 Rental payments to GSA	31	31	31
23.2 Rental payments to others	31	31	31
23.3 Communications, utilities, and miscellaneous charges	27	25	25
24.0 Printing and reproduction	1	1	1
25.1 Advisory and assistance services	45	40	40
25.2 Other services from non-Federal sources	226	226	226
25.3 Other goods and services from Federal sources	126	106	106
25.4 Operation and maintenance of facilities	24	24	24
25.5 Research and development contracts	3	3	3
25.7 Operation and maintenance of equipment	17	17	17
26.0 Supplies and materials	30	30	30
31.0 Equipment	19	17	17
32.0 Land and structures	33	33	33
41.0 Grants, subsidies, and contributions	69	69	69
42.0 Insurance claims and indemnities	3	3	3
99.0 Direct obligations	1,319	1,290	1,290
99.0 Reimbursable obligations	72	68	68
99.9 Total new obligations, unexpired accounts	1,391	1,358	1,358

Employment Summary

Identification code 014–1109–0–1–302	2021 actual	2022 est.	2023 est.
1001 Direct civilian full-time equivalent employment	5,371	5,433	5,651
2001 Reimbursable civilian full-time equivalent employment	362	362	368
3001 Allocation account civilian full-time equivalent employment	2,318	2,624	2,986

OREGON AND CALIFORNIA GRANT LANDS

For expenses necessary for management, protection, and development of resources and for construction, operation, and maintenance of access roads, reforestation, and other improvements on the revested Oregon and California Railroad grant lands, on other Federal lands in the Oregon and California land-grant counties of Oregon, and on adjacent rights-of-way; and acquisition of lands or interests therein, including existing connecting roads on or adjacent to such grant lands; $128,696,000, to remain available until expended: Provided, That 25 percent of the aggregate of all receipts during the current fiscal year from the revested Oregon and California Railroad grant lands is hereby made a charge against the Oregon and California land-grant fund and shall be transferred to the General Fund in the Treasury in accordance with the second paragraph of subsection (b) of title II of the Act of August 28, 1937 (43 U.S.C. 2605).

Note.—A full-year 2022 appropriation for this account was not enacted at the time the Budget was prepared; therefore, the Budget assumes this account is operating under the Continuing Appropriations Act, 2022 (Division A of Public Law 117–43, as amended). The amounts included for 2022 reflect the annualized level provided by the continuing resolution.

Program and Financing (in millions of dollars)

Identification code 014–1116–0–1–302		2021 actual	2022 est.	2023 est.
	Obligations by program activity:			
0004	Western Oregon Resource Management	105	105	105
0005	Western Oregon Data Systems Operation & Management	2	2	2
0006	Western Oregon National Monuments & NCA	1	1	1
0007	Western Oregon Transportation and Facilities Maintenance	11	10	10
0900	Total new obligations, unexpired accounts	119	118	118
	Budgetary resources:			
	Unobligated balance:			
1000	Unobligated balance brought forward, Oct 1	3	4	6
1021	Recoveries of prior year unpaid obligations	5	5	5
1070	Unobligated balance (total)	8	9	11
	Budget authority:			
	Appropriations, discretionary:			
1100	Appropriation	115	115	129
1930	Total budgetary resources available	123	124	140
	Memorandum (non-add) entries:			
1941	Unexpired unobligated balance, end of year	4	6	22
	Change in obligated balance:			
	Unpaid obligations:			
3000	Unpaid obligations, brought forward, Oct 1	43	48	40
3010	New obligations, unexpired accounts	119	118	118
3020	Outlays (gross)	–109	–121	–128
3040	Recoveries of prior year unpaid obligations, unexpired	–5	–5	–5
3050	Unpaid obligations, end of year	48	40	25
	Memorandum (non-add) entries:			
3100	Obligated balance, start of year	43	48	40
3200	Obligated balance, end of year	48	40	25
	Budget authority and outlays, net:			
	Discretionary:			
4000	Budget authority, gross	115	115	129
	Outlays, gross:			
4010	Outlays from new discretionary authority	83	92	103
4011	Outlays from discretionary balances	26	29	25
4020	Outlays, gross (total)	109	121	128
4180	Budget authority, net (total)	115	115	129
4190	Outlays, net (total)	109	121	128

Western Oregon resources management.—Provides for the management of approximately 2.4 million acres of lands that are primarily forested ecosystems in western Oregon. These lands support a number of resource activities including timber management, grazing management, and recreation management. In support of these activities, the Bureau of Land Management (BLM) is involved in improving critical watersheds, restoring wildlife and fish habitat, providing recreation opportunities, and preserving cultural resources.

Western Oregon information and resource data systems.—Provides for the acquisition, operation, and maintenance of the automated data support systems and spatial data systems required for management of the Oregon and California programs.

Western Oregon transportation and facilities maintenance.—Provides for annual maintenance activities of the transportation system, office buildings, warehouse and storage structures, shops, greenhouses, and recreation sites necessary to assure public safety and effective management of the lands in western Oregon. The BLM funds deferred maintenance projects on Oregon and California Grant Lands from the Management of Lands and Resources appropriation.

Western Oregon acquisition.—Provides for the necessary acquisition of easements and road-use agreements to facilitate timber sale and administrative site access for general resource management purposes and for monitoring and fee collection of timber hauling on government controlled roads. This activity also provides for transportation planning, survey, and design of access and other resource management roads.

Western Oregon National Conservation Lands.—Provides for the management of National Monuments, National Conservation Areas, and other Congressional conservation designations on the National Conservation Lands. The program provides for the recurring operational (base) budgets of these National Conservation Lands units.

Object Classification (in millions of dollars)

Identification code 014–1116–0–1–302		2021 actual	2022 est.	2023 est.
	Direct obligations:			
	Personnel compensation:			
11.1	Full-time permanent	51	51	51
11.3	Other than full-time permanent	4	4	4
11.5	Other personnel compensation	2	2	2
11.9	Total personnel compensation	57	57	57
12.1	Civilian personnel benefits	18	18	18
23.3	Communications, utilities, and miscellaneous charges	4	4	4
25.1	Advisory and assistance services	2	2	2
25.2	Other services from non-Federal sources	20	20	20
25.3	Other goods and services from Federal sources	8	7	7
25.4	Operation and maintenance of facilities	1	1	1
25.7	Operation and maintenance of equipment	2	2	2
26.0	Supplies and materials	2	2	2
31.0	Equipment	2	2	2
41.0	Grants, subsidies, and contributions	3	3	3
99.9	Total new obligations, unexpired accounts	119	118	118

Employment Summary

Identification code 014–1116–0–1–302		2021 actual	2022 est.	2023 est.
1001	Direct civilian full-time equivalent employment	590	617	658

ABANDONED WELL REMEDIATION FUND

Program and Financing (in millions of dollars)

Identification code 014–2640–0–1–302		2021 actual	2022 est.	2023 est.
	Obligations by program activity:			
0001	Abandoned Well Remediation Fund (Direct)	1		
0900	Total new obligations, unexpired accounts (object class 25.2)	1		
	Budgetary resources:			
	Unobligated balance:			
1000	Unobligated balance brought forward, Oct 1		2	2
1021	Recoveries of prior year unpaid obligations	3		
1070	Unobligated balance (total)	3	2	2
1930	Total budgetary resources available	3	2	2
	Memorandum (non-add) entries:			
1941	Unexpired unobligated balance, end of year	2	2	2
	Change in obligated balance:			
	Unpaid obligations:			
3000	Unpaid obligations, brought forward, Oct 1	3	1	
3010	New obligations, unexpired accounts	1		
3020	Outlays (gross)		–1	
3040	Recoveries of prior year unpaid obligations, unexpired	–3		
3050	Unpaid obligations, end of year	1		
	Memorandum (non-add) entries:			
3100	Obligated balance, start of year	3	1	
3200	Obligated balance, end of year	1		
	Budget authority and outlays, net:			
	Mandatory:			
	Outlays, gross:			
4101	Outlays from mandatory balances		1	
4180	Budget authority, net (total)			
4190	Outlays, net (total)		1	

Abandoned Well Remediation Fund.—Section 10, paragraph (b) of Public Law 113–40, 127 Stat. 545, provided mandatory appropriated funds to remediate, reclaim, and close abandoned oil and gas wells on current or former National Petroleum Reserve land in 2014, 2015, and 2019. The account remains open as BLM continues to complete work and execute funds.

LAND ACQUISITION

Note.—A full-year 2022 appropriation for this account was not enacted at the time the Budget was prepared; therefore, the Budget assumes this account is operating under the Continuing Appropriations Act, 2022 (Division A of Public Law 117–43, as amended). The amounts included for 2022 reflect the annualized level provided by the continuing resolution.

Program and Financing (in millions of dollars)

Identification code 014–5033–0–2–302		2021 actual	2022 est.	2023 est.
	Obligations by program activity:			
0001	Land acquisition	7	22	22
0002	Acquisition management	2		
0900	Total new obligations, unexpired accounts	9	22	22
	Budgetary resources:			
	Unobligated balance:			
1000	Unobligated balance brought forward, Oct 1	94	141	176
1001	Discretionary unobligated balance brought fwd, Oct 1	94		
1010	Unobligated balance transfer to other accts [014–9925]	–5		
1070	Unobligated balance (total)	89	141	176
	Budget authority:			
	Appropriations, discretionary:			
1131	Unobligated balance of appropriations permanently reduced	–5	–5	
	Appropriations, mandatory:			
1201	Appropriation (special or trust fund)	66	66	71
1203	Appropriation (previously unavailable)(special or trust)			4
1232	Appropriations and/or unobligated balance of appropriations temporarily reduced		–4	–4
1260	Appropriations, mandatory (total)	66	62	71
1900	Budget authority (total)	61	57	71
1930	Total budgetary resources available	150	198	247
	Memorandum (non-add) entries:			
1941	Unexpired unobligated balance, end of year	141	176	225
	Change in obligated balance:			
	Unpaid obligations:			
3000	Unpaid obligations, brought forward, Oct 1	3	3	10
3010	New obligations, unexpired accounts	9	22	22
3020	Outlays (gross)	–9	–15	–31
3050	Unpaid obligations, end of year	3	10	1
	Memorandum (non-add) entries:			
3100	Obligated balance, start of year	3	3	10
3200	Obligated balance, end of year	3	10	1
	Budget authority and outlays, net:			
	Discretionary:			
4000	Budget authority, gross	–5	–5	
	Outlays, gross:			
4011	Outlays from discretionary balances	9	6	11
	Mandatory:			
4090	Budget authority, gross	66	62	71
	Outlays, gross:			
4100	Outlays from new mandatory authority		9	13
4101	Outlays from mandatory balances			7
4110	Outlays, gross (total)		9	20
4180	Budget authority, net (total)	61	57	71
4190	Outlays, net (total)	9	15	31

This appropriation provides for the acquisition of lands or interests in lands, by purchase, easement or exchange, when necessary for public access and recreation use, preservation of open space, resource protection, and/or other purposes related to the management of public lands. Beginning in 2021, BLM land acquisition is funded with permanent appropriations through the Land and Water Conservation Fund. The 2023 budget invests funding in projects that substantially conserve or protect against threats to resources, improve public access to outdoor recreation opportunities, and have strong local partner engagement and support.

Object Classification (in millions of dollars)

Identification code 014–5033–0–2–302		2021 actual	2022 est.	2023 est.
	Direct obligations:			
11.1	Personnel compensation: Full-time permanent	1	1	1
25.2	Other services from non-Federal sources	1	1	1
32.0	Land and structures	7	20	20
99.9	Total new obligations, unexpired accounts	9	22	22

Employment Summary

Identification code 014–5033–0–2–302	2021 actual	2022 est.	2023 est.
1001 Direct civilian full-time equivalent employment	13	14	14

RANGE IMPROVEMENTS

For rehabilitation, protection, and acquisition of lands and interests therein, and improvement of Federal rangelands pursuant to section 401 of the Federal Land Policy and Management Act of 1976 (43 U.S.C. 1751), notwithstanding any other Act, sums equal to 50 percent of all moneys received during the prior fiscal year under sections 3 and 15 of the Taylor Grazing Act (43 U.S.C. 315b, 315m) and the amount designated for range improvements from grazing fees and mineral leasing receipts from Bankhead-Jones lands transferred to the Department of the Interior pursuant to law, but not less than $10,000,000, to remain available until expended: Provided, That not to exceed $600,000 shall be available for administrative expenses.

Note.—A full-year 2022 appropriation for this account was not enacted at the time the Budget was prepared; therefore, the Budget assumes this account is operating under the Continuing Appropriations Act, 2022 (Division A of Public Law 117–43, as amended). The amounts included for 2022 reflect the annualized level provided by the continuing resolution.

Special and Trust Fund Receipts (in millions of dollars)

Identification code 014–5132–0–2–302		2021 actual	2022 est.	2023 est.
0100	Balance, start of year	6	6	7
0198	Rounding adjustment	–1		
0199	Balance, start of year	5	6	7
	Receipts:			
	Current law:			
1130	Grazing Fees for Range Improvements, Taylor Grazing Act, As Amended	7	8	8
2000	Total: Balances and receipts	12	14	15
	Appropriations:			
	Current law:			
2101	Range Improvements	–7	–8	–8
2132	Range Improvements	1	1	1
2199	Total current law appropriations	–6	–7	–7
2999	Total appropriations	–6	–7	–7
5099	Balance, end of year	6	7	8

Program and Financing (in millions of dollars)

Identification code 014–5132–0–2–302		2021 actual	2022 est.	2023 est.
	Obligations by program activity:			
0001	Public Lands Improvements	7	8	8
0002	Farm Tenant Act Lands Improvements	1	1	1
0900	Total new obligations, unexpired accounts	8	9	9
	Budgetary resources:			
	Unobligated balance:			
1000	Unobligated balance brought forward, Oct 1	10	11	11
	Budget authority:			
	Appropriations, mandatory:			
1200	Appropriation (General Fund)	3	2	2
1201	Appropriation (special or trust fund)	7	8	8
1232	Appropriations and/or unobligated balance of appropriations temporarily reduced	–1	–1	–1
1260	Appropriations, mandatory (total)	9	9	9
1930	Total budgetary resources available	19	20	20
	Memorandum (non-add) entries:			
1941	Unexpired unobligated balance, end of year	11	11	11
	Change in obligated balance:			
	Unpaid obligations:			
3000	Unpaid obligations, brought forward, Oct 1	5	5	4
3010	New obligations, unexpired accounts	8	9	9
3020	Outlays (gross)	–8	–10	–10
3050	Unpaid obligations, end of year	5	4	3
	Memorandum (non-add) entries:			
3100	Obligated balance, start of year	5	5	4

DEPARTMENT OF THE INTERIOR

Land and Minerals Management—Continued
Bureau of Land Management—Continued
619

		2021 actual	2022 est.	2023 est.
3200	Obligated balance, end of year	5	4	3
	Budget authority and outlays, net:			
	Mandatory:			
4090	Budget authority, gross	9	9	9
	Outlays, gross:			
4100	Outlays from new mandatory authority	2	4	4
4101	Outlays from mandatory balances	6	6	6
4110	Outlays, gross (total)	8	10	10
4180	Budget authority, net (total)	9	9	9
4190	Outlays, net (total)	8	10	10

This appropriation is derived from a percentage of receipts from grazing of livestock on the public lands and from grazing and mineral leasing receipts on Bankhead-Jones Farm Tenant Act lands transferred from the Department of Agriculture by various Executive Orders. These funds are used for the planning, construction, development, and monitoring of range improvements.

Object Classification (in millions of dollars)

Identification code 014–5132–0–2–302	2021 actual	2022 est.	2023 est.
Direct obligations:			
11.1 Personnel compensation: Full-time permanent	2	3	3
12.1 Civilian personnel benefits	1	1	1
25.2 Other services from non-Federal sources	2	2	2
26.0 Supplies and materials	1	1	1
32.0 Land and structures	1	1	1
41.0 Grants, subsidies, and contributions	1	1	1
99.9 Total new obligations, unexpired accounts	8	9	9

Employment Summary

Identification code 014–5132–0–2–302	2021 actual	2022 est.	2023 est.
1001 Direct civilian full-time equivalent employment	21	23	25

SERVICE CHARGES, DEPOSITS, AND FORFEITURES

For administrative expenses and other costs related to processing application documents and other authorizations for use and disposal of public lands and resources, for costs of providing copies of official public land documents, for monitoring construction, operation, and termination of facilities in conjunction with use authorizations, and for rehabilitation of damaged property, such amounts as may be collected under Public Law 94–579 (43 U.S.C. 1701 et seq.), and under section 28 of the Mineral Leasing Act (30 U.S.C. 185), to remain available until expended: Provided, That notwithstanding any provision to the contrary of section 305(a) of Public Law 94–579 (43 U.S.C. 1735(a)), any moneys that have been or will be received pursuant to that section, whether as a result of forfeiture, compromise, or settlement, if not appropriate for refund pursuant to section 305(c) of that Act (43 U.S.C. 1735(c)), shall be available and may be expended under the authority of this Act by the Secretary of the Interior to improve, protect, or rehabilitate any public lands administered through the Bureau of Land Management which have been damaged by the action of a resource developer, purchaser, permittee, or any unauthorized person, without regard to whether all moneys collected from each such action are used on the exact lands damaged which led to the action: Provided further, That any such moneys that are in excess of amounts needed to repair damage to the exact land for which funds were collected may be used to repair other damaged public lands.

Note.—A full-year 2022 appropriation for this account was not enacted at the time the Budget was prepared; therefore, the Budget assumes this account is operating under the Continuing Appropriations Act, 2022 (Division A of Public Law 117–43, as amended). The amounts included for 2022 reflect the annualized level provided by the continuing resolution.

Special and Trust Fund Receipts (in millions of dollars)

Identification code 014–5017–0–2–302	2021 actual	2022 est.	2023 est.
0100 Balance, start of year			
Receipts:			
Current law:			
1130 Service Charges, Deposits, and Forfeitures, BLM	32	28	34
2000 Total: Balances and receipts	32	28	34
Appropriations:			
Current law:			
2101 Service Charges, Deposits, and Forfeitures	–32	–28	–34
5099 Balance, end of year			

Program and Financing (in millions of dollars)

Identification code 014–5017–0–2–302	2021 actual	2022 est.	2023 est.
Obligations by program activity:			
0001 Right-of-way processing	10	10	11
0004 Energy and minerals cost recovery	2	3	3
0005 Wild horse and burro cost recover	2	1	1
0006 Repair of damaged lands	5	5	6
0007 Cost recoverable realty		1	1
0008 Recreation cost recovery	1	3	3
0009 Copy fees	1	1	1
0011 Trans Alaska Pipeline Authority	2	2	2
0900 Total new obligations, unexpired accounts	23	26	28
Budgetary resources:			
Unobligated balance:			
1000 Unobligated balance brought forward, Oct 1	73	63	64
1021 Recoveries of prior year unpaid obligations	1		
1070 Unobligated balance (total)	74	63	64
Budget authority:			
Appropriations, discretionary:			
1101 Appropriation (special or trust)	32	28	34
1131 Unobligated balance of appropriations permanently reduced	–20	–1	
1160 Appropriation, discretionary (total)	12	27	34
1930 Total budgetary resources available	86	90	98
Memorandum (non-add) entries:			
1941 Unexpired unobligated balance, end of year	63	64	70
Change in obligated balance:			
Unpaid obligations:			
3000 Unpaid obligations, brought forward, Oct 1	9	9	20
3010 New obligations, unexpired accounts	23	26	28
3020 Outlays (gross)	–22	–15	–20
3040 Recoveries of prior year unpaid obligations, unexpired	–1		
3050 Unpaid obligations, end of year	9	20	28
Memorandum (non-add) entries:			
3100 Obligated balance, start of year	9	9	20
3200 Obligated balance, end of year	9	20	28
Budget authority and outlays, net:			
Discretionary:			
4000 Budget authority, gross	12	27	34
Outlays, gross:			
4010 Outlays from new discretionary authority	6	8	10
4011 Outlays from discretionary balances	16	7	10
4020 Outlays, gross (total)	22	15	20
4180 Budget authority, net (total)	12	27	34
4190 Outlays, net (total)	22	15	20

This appropriation is derived from: 1) revenues received to offset administrative and other costs incurred to process applications for rights-of-way, and the monitoring of construction, operation, and termination of rights-of-ways; 2) recovery of costs associated with the adopt-a-horse program; 3) revenues received for rehabilitation of damages to lands, resources, and facilities; 4) fees for processing specified categories of realty actions under the Federal Land Policy and Management Act of 1976; 5) deposits received from contractors in lieu of completing contract requirements such as slash burning and timber extension expenses; 6) fees for costs of reproduction and administrative services involved in providing requested copies of materials; 7) fixed fees for energy and minerals lease applications, assignments, and transfers; 8) costs of processing applications and administering permits, including environmental analysis and monitoring of special recreation permits; and, 9) rents received for permits to conduct filming and photography on public lands that rise above casual use. The Bureau of Land Management will continue to seek new opportunities to recover costs of services provided to benefiting public land users to reduce the need for direct appropriations from the Treasury.

Land and Minerals Management—Continued
Bureau of Land Management—Continued

SERVICE CHARGES, DEPOSITS, AND FORFEITURES—Continued

Object Classification (in millions of dollars)

Identification code 014–5017–0–2–302	2021 actual	2022 est.	2023 est.
Direct obligations:			
Personnel compensation:			
11.1 Full-time permanent	10	11	12
11.5 Other personnel compensation	1	1	1
11.9 Total personnel compensation	11	12	13
12.1 Civilian personnel benefits	3	3	3
25.1 Advisory and assistance services	1	1	1
25.2 Other services from non-Federal sources	2	3	4
25.3 Other goods and services from Federal sources	2	3	3
26.0 Supplies and materials	1	1	1
41.0 Grants, subsidies, and contributions	3	3	3
99.9 Total new obligations, unexpired accounts	23	26	28

Employment Summary

Identification code 014–5017–0–2–302	2021 actual	2022 est.	2023 est.
1001 Direct civilian full-time equivalent employment	125	131	140

PERMANENT OPERATING FUNDS

Special and Trust Fund Receipts (in millions of dollars)

Identification code 014–9926–0–2–302	2021 actual	2022 est.	2023 est.
0100 Balance, start of year	76	71	91
Receipts:			
Current law:			
1130 Deposits for Road Maintenance and Reconstruction	4	4	4
1130 Rents and Charges for Quarters, Bureau of Land Management, Interior	1	1	1
1130 Forest Ecosystem Health and Recovery, Disposal of Salvage Timber	9	12	12
1130 Land Sales, Southern Nevada Public Land Management	93	349	384
1130 Timber Sale Pipeline Restoration Fund	2	5	5
1130 Recreation Enhancement Fee, BLM	27	28	28
1130 Rent from Mineral Leases, Permit Processing Improvement Fund	5	5	5
1130 Oil and Gas Permit Processing Fee - 85%	56	56	56
1140 Earnings on Investments, Southern Nevada Public Land Management	3	1	6
1199 Total current law receipts	200	461	501
1999 Total receipts	200	461	501
2000 Total: Balances and receipts	276	532	592
Appropriations:			
Current law:			
2101 Permanent Operating Funds	–27	–27	–28
2101 Permanent Operating Funds	–9	–12	–12
2101 Permanent Operating Funds	–2	–5	–5
2101 Permanent Operating Funds	–4	–4	–4
2101 Permanent Operating Funds	–96	–349	–384
2101 Permanent Operating Funds		–1	–6
2101 Permanent Operating Funds	–61	–56	–55
2101 Permanent Operating Funds	–1	–1	–1
2101 Permanent Operating Funds	–1		
2103 Permanent Operating Funds	–14	–10	–24
2132 Permanent Operating Funds	10	24	26
2199 Total current law appropriations	–205	–441	–493
2999 Total appropriations	–205	–441	–493
5099 Balance, end of year	71	91	99

Program and Financing (in millions of dollars)

Identification code 014–9926–0–2–302	2021 actual	2022 est.	2023 est.
Obligations by program activity:			
0001 Forest ecosystem health and recovery fund	7	8	8
0002 Recreation fee demonstration	27	26	26
0003 Expenses, road maintenance deposits	4	7	7
0004 Timber sale pipeline restoration fund	3	3	3
0005 Southern Nevada public land sales (85)	27	83	83
0008 Lincoln County Lands Act	1	2	2
0013 Operation and maintenance of quarters	1	1	1
0014 Permit Processing Improvement Fund	35	47	47
0019 Washington County, Utah Land Acquisition Account		1	1
0900 Total new obligations, unexpired accounts	105	178	178
Budgetary resources:			
Unobligated balance:			
1000 Unobligated balance brought forward, Oct 1	1,139	1,240	1,503
1021 Recoveries of prior year unpaid obligations	1		
1070 Unobligated balance (total)	1,140	1,240	1,503
Budget authority:			
Appropriations, mandatory:			
1201 Recreation fee demonstration program	27	27	28
1201 Forest ecosystem health and recovery fund	9	12	12
1201 Timber sales pipeline restoration fund	2	5	5
1201 Expenses, road maintenance deposits	4	4	4
1201 S. Nevada public land management	96	349	384
1201 S. Nevada public land management-interest earned		1	6
1201 Permit processing improvement fund	61	56	55
1201 Operation and maintenance of quarters	1	1	1
1201 Federal Lands Disposal Account	1		
1203 Appropriation (previously unavailable)(special or trust)	14	10	24
1232 Appropriations and/or unobligated balance of appropriations temporarily reduced	–10	–24	–26
1260 Appropriations, mandatory (total)	205	441	493
1900 Budget authority (total)	205	441	493
1930 Total budgetary resources available	1,345	1,681	1,996
Memorandum (non-add) entries:			
1941 Unexpired unobligated balance, end of year	1,240	1,503	1,818
Change in obligated balance:			
Unpaid obligations:			
3000 Unpaid obligations, brought forward, Oct 1	132	101	126
3010 New obligations, unexpired accounts	105	178	178
3020 Outlays (gross)	–135	–153	–224
3040 Recoveries of prior year unpaid obligations, unexpired	–1		
3050 Unpaid obligations, end of year	101	126	80
Memorandum (non-add) entries:			
3100 Obligated balance, start of year	132	101	126
3200 Obligated balance, end of year	101	126	80
Budget authority and outlays, net:			
Mandatory:			
4090 Budget authority, gross	205	441	493
Outlays, gross:			
4100 Outlays from new mandatory authority	11	58	74
4101 Outlays from mandatory balances	124	95	150
4110 Outlays, gross (total)	135	153	224
4180 Budget authority, net (total)	205	441	493
4190 Outlays, net (total)	135	153	224
Memorandum (non-add) entries:			
5000 Total investments, SOY: Federal securities: Par value	1,043	1,089	1,240
5001 Total investments, EOY: Federal securities: Par value	1,089	1,240	6,020

Permanent operating funds accounts include:

Operations and maintenance of quarters.—Funds in this account are used to maintain and repair the Bureau of Land Management (BLM) employee-occupied quarters from which rental charges are collected. Agencies are required to collect rental charges from employees who occupy Government-owned housing and quarters. This housing is provided only in isolated areas or where an employee is required to live on-site at a Federally owned facility or reservation.

Forest ecosystems health and recovery.—The Forest Ecosystems Health and Recovery Fund was established as a permanent appropriation in the FY 1993 Interior Appropriations Act (Public Law 102–381). This authority was subsequently amended to temporarily expand the use of the Fund to cover additional forest health and recovery activities. A five-year reauthorization of the FEHRF was included in the FY 2015 Consolidated and Further Continuing Appropriations Act (Public Law 113–235) and expired at the end of FY 2020. The Consolidated Appropriations Act, 2021 (Public Law 116–260) included a one-year extension of the authority for the FEHRF to continue to be used for the broader forest health and recovery activities. The FY 2023 President's budget proposes a one-year extension of this authority (through September 30, 2023). Without this reauthorization, funds in the FEHRF could only be used for the limited purposes provided for in the original FEHRF authorization. Funds in this account are derived from revenue generated from the Federal share of receipts from the sale of salvage timber from the Oregon and California grant lands, public domain lands, and Coos Bay Wagon Road lands. Pursuant to Public Law 102–381, as amended, this account was established to allow the BLM to more efficiently and effectively address forest health issues. Funds can be used for other forest health purposes, including vegetation and density control treatments.

Timber sale pipeline restoration fund.—This Fund provides for the deposit and use of fees collected by the BLM for sales of timber authorized by section 2001(k) of Public Law 104–19. Of the total deposited into this account, 75 percent is to be used for the preparation of timber sales to fill the timber pipeline on lands administered by the BLM, and 25 percent is to be used to address recreation projects on the BLM lands.

Stewardship contract product sales.—Stewardship contracting improves, maintains, or restores forest and rangeland health; restores or maintains water quality; improves fish and wildlife habitat; reestablishes native plant species and increases their resilience to insects and disease; and reduces hazardous fuels that pose risks to communities and ecosystem values. With stewardship contracting, the BLM may apply the value of timber or other forest products removed as an offset against the cost of services received, and monies from a contract may be retained by the BLM. These monies are available for expenditure without further appropriation at project sites.

Expenses, road maintenance deposits.—Users of certain roads under the BLM's jurisdiction make deposits for maintenance purposes. Moneys collected are appropriated for necessary road maintenance. Moneys collected on Oregon and California grant lands are available only for those lands (43 U.S.C. 1762(c), 43 U.S.C. 1735(b)).

Federal Lands Recreation Enhancement Act, BLM.—The Federal Lands Recreation Enhancement Act (FLREA) was enacted on December 8, 2004, as part of the Consolidated Appropriations Act for 2005. All recreation fee receipts collected under this authority at BLM sites are deposited in the Recreation Fee account. The BLM returns 100 percent of these receipts back to the site where the fees were generated. The budget proposes appropriations language to extend the program through October 1, 2024.

Operations and acquisitions in Nevada from land sale receipts.—Pursuant to the Southern Nevada Public Land Management Act (SNPLMA) (Public Law 105–263), 85 percent of receipts from sales of public domain lands in southern Nevada are used to acquire environmentally sensitive lands in Nevada; make capital improvements to areas administered by the National Park Service, the U.S. Fish and Wildlife Service and BLM in Clark County, Nevada; develop a multi-species habitat plan in Clark County, Nevada; develop parks, trails and natural areas and implement other conservation initiatives in Clark County, Nevada; and reimburse the BLM for costs incurred arranging sales and exchanges under the Act.

Lincoln County Land Sales Act.—Public Law 106–298 authorizes the Secretary to dispose of certain lands in Lincoln County, Nevada, and distribute the proceeds as follows: five percent to the State of Nevada; 10 percent to the county; and 85 percent to an interest bearing account available for expenditure without further appropriation to be used by the Secretary of the Interior to acquire environmentally sensitive lands in the State of Nevada, for identification and management of unique archaeological resources, for development of a multi-species habitat conservation plan in the county, and for other specified administrative purposes.

White Pine County Land Sales Act.—Public Law 109–432 authorizes the Secretary to dispose of certain lands in White Pine County, Nevada, and to distribute the proceeds as follows: five percent to the State of Nevada; 10 percent to the county; and 85 percent to an account available for expenditure without further appropriation for the management of archaeological resources, wilderness protection, recreation activities, preparation of a management plan, reimbursement for sale costs, and other purposes.

Leases from Naval Petroleum Reserve No 2.—The 2005 Energy Policy Act established this Fund for environmental investigation and restoration on that site located in Kern County, California. A portion of revenue from new leases on the site is authorized to be deposited to this account. In 2008, it was certified that sufficient funds had been collected to cover the cost of the cleanup and other expenses and no more deposits were to be made to the Fund. New revenue from site operations is distributed under the Mineral Leasing Act.

BLM Permit Processing Improvement Fund.—The 2005 Energy Policy Act, as amended by the National Defense Authorization Act for Fiscal Year 2015, established pilot offices to improve interagency coordination in processing onshore Federal oil and gas permits. Fifty-percent of the rents from non-geothermal onshore mineral leases are authorized to be deposited in this Fund and used to facilitate the BLM oil and gas permit processing in these pilot offices. In addition, in 2016 through 2026, fees collected for processing applications for permits to drill will be deposited to this Fund and available for Federal oil and gas permitting activities.

Federal land disposal.—The Federal Land Transaction Facilitation Act, Public Law 106–248 (114 Stat. 613), provided authority for the BLM to sell public lands classified as suitable for disposal under resource management plans in effect at the time of enactment. This law provided that receipts from such sales could be used to acquire non-Federal lands with significant resource values that fall within the boundaries of areas now managed by the Department of the Interior and the U.S. Forest Service. The Federal Land Transaction Facilitation Act was permanently reauthorized by Public Law 115–141, the 2018 Consolidated Appropriations Act.

Owyhee Land Acquisition Account.—The 2009 Omnibus Public Land Management Act, Public Law 111–11 (123 Stat. 1039), provides that the Secretary may sell public land located within the Boise District of the BLM that, as of July 25, 2000, was identified for disposal in appropriate resource management plans. Amounts in the account shall be available to the Secretary, without further appropriation, to purchase land or interests in land in, or adjacent to certain wilderness areas.

Washington County, Utah Land Acquisition Account.—The 2009 Omnibus Public Land Management Act, Public Law 111–11 (123 Stat. 1091), authorizes the sale of public land located within Washington County, Utah, that, as of July 25, 2000, was identified for disposal in appropriate resource management plans. Amounts in the account shall be available to the Secretary, without further appropriation, to purchase land or interests in land, in or adjacent to certain wilderness areas.

Silver Saddle Endowment Account.—The 2009 Omnibus Public Land Management Act, Public Law 111–11 (123 Stat. 1114), requires Carson City, Nevada to deposit twenty-five percent of the difference between what the Secretary of the Interior and the City paid for the 62-acre Bernhard parcel before the Secretary conveys the land to the City. Amounts deposited in the account shall be available to the Secretary, without further appropriation, for the oversight and enforcement of a certain conservation easement.

Carson City Special Account.—The 2009 Omnibus Public Land Management Act, Public Law 111–11 (123 Stat. 1113), authorizes the sale of 158 acres of public land described in the statute. Five percent of the proceeds are paid to the State of Nevada for use for public education. The remainder is deposited to this account and used to acquire environmentally sensitive land or an interest in environmentally sensitive land in Carson City; to cover the cost of surveys and appraisals; and to reimburse the BLM for administrative expenses.

Ojito Land Acquisition.—The Ojito Wilderness Act authorized the sale of land to the Pueblo Indian Tribe and the purchase of land from willing sellers within the State of New Mexico.

Land and Minerals Management—Continued
Bureau of Land Management—Continued

PERMANENT OPERATING FUNDS—Continued
Object Classification (in millions of dollars)

Identification code 014–9926–0–2–302	2021 actual	2022 est.	2023 est.
Direct obligations:			
Personnel compensation:			
11.1 Full-time permanent	42	65	65
11.3 Other than full-time permanent	2	2	2
11.5 Other personnel compensation	3	3	3
11.9 Total personnel compensation	47	70	70
12.1 Civilian personnel benefits	14	14	14
21.0 Travel and transportation of persons	1	1	1
23.3 Communications, utilities, and miscellaneous charges	1	1	1
25.2 Other services from non-Federal sources	9	11	11
25.3 Other goods and services from Federal sources	5	7	7
25.4 Operation and maintenance of facilities	2	3	3
25.7 Operation and maintenance of equipment	1	1	1
26.0 Supplies and materials	3	5	5
31.0 Equipment	1	1	1
32.0 Land and structures	1	1	1
41.0 Grants, subsidies, and contributions	20	63	63
99.9 Total new obligations, unexpired accounts	105	178	178

Employment Summary

Identification code 014–9926–0–2–302	2021 actual	2022 est.	2023 est.
1001 Direct civilian full-time equivalent employment	577	603	613

MISCELLANEOUS PERMANENT PAYMENT ACCOUNTS
Special and Trust Fund Receipts (in millions of dollars)

Identification code 014–9921–0–2–999	2021 actual	2022 est.	2023 est.
0100 Balance, start of year	104	129	126
Receipts:			
Current law:			
1130 Receipts from Grazing, Etc., Public Lands outside Grazing Districts	2	1	1
1130 Receipts from Grazing, Etc., Public Lands within Grazing Districts	1	2	2
1130 Payments to States and Counties from Land Sales	2	....	....
1130 Funds Reserved, Title II Projects on Federal Lands	2	1	1
1130 Sale of Public Lands and Materials	20	....	....
1130 Oregon and California Land-grant Fund	5	....	....
1130 Deposits, Oregon and California Grant Lands	24	31	31
1199 Total current law receipts	56	35	35
1999 Total receipts	56	35	35
2000 Total: Balances and receipts	160	164	161
Appropriations:			
Current law:			
2101 Miscellaneous Permanent Payment Accounts	–2	–1	–1
2101 Miscellaneous Permanent Payment Accounts	–1	–1	–1
2101 Miscellaneous Permanent Payment Accounts	–1	–2	–2
2101 Miscellaneous Permanent Payment Accounts	–24	–31	–31
2101 Miscellaneous Permanent Payment Accounts	–2	–1	–1
2103 Miscellaneous Permanent Payment Accounts	....	–2	....
2132 Miscellaneous Permanent Payment Accounts	2	....	2
2199 Total current law appropriations	–28	–38	–34
2999 Total appropriations	–28	–38	–34
5098 Reconciliation adjustment	–3	....	....
5099 Balance, end of year	129	126	127

Program and Financing (in millions of dollars)

Identification code 014–9921–0–2–999	2021 actual	2022 est.	2023 est.
Obligations by program activity:			
0001 Payments to O&C Counties, Title I/III 5884	23	17	17
0003 Payment to O&C and CBWR Counties, Title II 5485	5	....	....
0004 From grazing fees, etc., public lands outside grazing districts 5016	1	1	1
0005 From grazing fees, etc., public lands within grazing districts 5032	1	2	2
0009 Proceeds from sales 5133	2	1	1
0013 Payments to State and Counties from Nevada Land Sales	....	14	14
0015 Payments to CBWR counties under 1939 statute	....	2	2
0900 Total new obligations, unexpired accounts (object class 41.0)	32	37	37
Budgetary resources:			
Unobligated balance:			
1000 Unobligated balance brought forward, Oct 1	15	11	12
Budget authority:			
Appropriations, mandatory:			
1201 Proceeds of sales-payments to states	2	1	1
1201 Payments from grazing fees outside grazing districts	1	1	1
1201 Payments from grazing fees within grazing districts	1	2	2
1201 Payments to O&C Counties, Title I/III 5884	24	31	31
1201 Payment to O&C and CBWR Counties, Title II 5485	2	1	1
1203 Appropriation (previously unavailable)(special or trust)	....	2	....
1232 Appropriations and/or unobligated balance of appropriations temporarily reduced	–2	....	–2
1260 Appropriations, mandatory (total)	28	38	34
1930 Total budgetary resources available	43	49	46
Memorandum (non-add) entries:			
1941 Unexpired unobligated balance, end of year	11	12	9
Change in obligated balance:			
Unpaid obligations:			
3000 Unpaid obligations, brought forward, Oct 1	1	5	10
3010 New obligations, unexpired accounts	32	37	37
3020 Outlays (gross)	–28	–32	–27
3050 Unpaid obligations, end of year	5	10	20
Memorandum (non-add) entries:			
3100 Obligated balance, start of year	1	5	10
3200 Obligated balance, end of year	5	10	20
Budget authority and outlays, net:			
Mandatory:			
4090 Budget authority, gross	28	38	34
Outlays, gross:			
4100 Outlays from new mandatory authority	....	24	20
4101 Outlays from mandatory balances	28	8	7
4110 Outlays, gross (total)	28	32	27
4180 Budget authority, net (total)	28	38	34
4190 Outlays, net (total)	28	32	27

Miscellaneous permanent payments include:

Payments for Oregon and California and Coos Bay Wagon Road grant lands, receipts.—The Secure Rural Schools and Community Self-Determination Act of 2000 (as amended by P.L. 116–93, the Further Consolidated Appropriations Act, 2020), provides annual revenue sharing payments to the 18 O&C counties. These payments are derived from revenues from Federal activities on O&C lands in the previous fiscal year that were not deposited to permanent operating funds, supplemented by amounts from the General Fund when necessary. The Infrastructure Investment and Jobs Act, P.L. 117–58, amended the Secure Rural Schools and Community Self-Determination Act to extend SRS payments through 2023, with the final payment in 2024. In the absence of this authority, eligible counties would receive funds authorized under the 1937 and 1939 statutes. Payments to the Oregon counties under the 1937 statute would be 50 percent of revenues from O&C grant lands. Payments under the 1939 statute are for lost tax revenue in two Oregon counties and would be roughly 75 percent of all revenues from Coos Bay Wagon Road grant lands.

Payments to States (proceeds of sales).—States are paid five percent of the net proceeds from the sale of public land and public land products (31 U.S.C. 1305).

Payments to States from grazing receipts, etc, public lands outside grazing districts.—States are paid 50 percent of the grazing receipts from public lands outside of grazing districts (43 U.S.C. 315i, 315m).

Payments to States from grazing receipts, etc, public lands within districts.—States are paid 12.5 percent of grazing receipts from public lands inside grazing districts (43 U.S.C. 315b, 315i).

Payments to States from grazing receipts, etc, public lands within grazing districts, miscellaneous.—States are paid specifically determined amounts from grazing receipts derived from miscellaneous lands within grazing districts when payment is not feasible on a percentage basis (43 U.S.C. 315).

Payments to counties, National Grasslands.—Of the revenues received from the use of Bankhead-Jones Act lands administered by the Bureau of Land Management (BLM), 25 percent is paid to the counties in which such lands are situated, for school and road purposes (7 U.S.C. 1012).

Payments to Nevada from receipts on land sales.—Public Law 96–586 authorizes and directs the Secretary to sell not more than 700 acres of public lands per calendar year in and around Las Vegas, Nevada, the proceeds of which are to be used to acquire environmentally sensitive lands in the Lake Tahoe Basin of California and Nevada. Annual revenues are distributed to the State of Nevada (five percent) and the county in which the land is located (10 percent).

Public Law 105–263, as amended by Public Law 107–282, authorizes the disposal through sale of approximately 49,000 acres in Clark County Nevada, the proceeds of which are to be distributed as follows: a) five percent for use in the general education program of the State of Nevada; b) 10 percent for use by the Southern Nevada Water Authority for water treatment and transmission facility infrastructure in Clark County, Nevada; and c) the remaining 85 percent to a special fund administered by the Secretary of the Interior to be used to acquire environmentally sensitive lands in Nevada; make capital improvements to areas administered by the National Park Service, Fish and Wildlife Service, and the BLM in Clark County, Nevada; develop a multi-species habitat plan in Clark County, Nevada; develop parks, trails, and natural areas and implement other conservation initiatives in Clark County, Nevada; and reimburse the BLM for costs incurred arranging sales and exchanges under the Act.

Public Law 106–298 authorizes the sale of certain lands in Lincoln County, Nevada. The proceeds of these sales are to be distributed as follows: a) five percent to the State of Nevada for general education purposes; b) 10 percent to Lincoln County for general purposes with emphasis on supporting schools; and c) the remaining 85 percent to a special fund administered by the Secretary of the Interior to acquire environmentally sensitive lands in the State of Nevada, for identification and management of unique archaeological resources, for development of a multi-species habitat conservation plan in the county, and for other specified administrative purposes.

Cook Inlet Region, Incorporated Account.—This account received funding appropriated by section 9102 of the 1990 Department of Defense Appropriations Act for the acquisition of Federal real properties, improvements on such lands or rights to their use or exploitation, and any personal property related to the land purchased by the Cook Inlet Region, Incorporated as authorized by the provisions of section 12(b) of Public Law 94–204 (43 U.S.C. 1611). The BLM maintains an accounting of the funds used by the Cook Inlet Region, Incorporated to purchase properties.

State 5 Percent Share, Carson City Land Sales.—The 2009 Omnibus Public Land Management Act, Public Law 111–11 (123 Stat. 1113), requires that five percent of proceeds from the sale of 158 acres described in the statute shall be paid to the State of Nevada for general public education purposes.

Helium Fund

Program and Financing (in millions of dollars)

Identification code 014–4053–0–3–306		2021 actual	2022 est.	2023 est.
	Obligations by program activity:			
0801	Production and sales	13	13	13
0802	Transmission and storage	4	4	4
0803	Administration and other expenses	3	3	3
0900	Total new obligations, unexpired accounts	20	20	20
	Budgetary resources:			
	Unobligated balance:			
1000	Unobligated balance brought forward, Oct 1	155	140	116
1021	Recoveries of prior year unpaid obligations	1		
1022	Capital transfer of unobligated balances to general fund	–60	–56	–56
1070	Unobligated balance (total)	96	84	60
	Budget authority:			
	Spending authority from offsetting collections, mandatory:			
1800	Collected	64	52	52
1930	Total budgetary resources available	160	136	112
	Memorandum (non-add) entries:			
1941	Unexpired unobligated balance, end of year	140	116	92
	Change in obligated balance:			
	Unpaid obligations:			
3000	Unpaid obligations, brought forward, Oct 1	16	21	31
3010	New obligations, unexpired accounts	20	20	20
3020	Outlays (gross)	–14	–10	–40
3040	Recoveries of prior year unpaid obligations, unexpired	–1		
3050	Unpaid obligations, end of year	21	31	11
	Memorandum (non-add) entries:			
3100	Obligated balance, start of year	16	21	31
3200	Obligated balance, end of year	21	31	11
	Budget authority and outlays, net:			
	Mandatory:			
4090	Budget authority, gross	64	52	52
	Outlays, gross:			
4100	Outlays from new mandatory authority		10	10
4101	Outlays from mandatory balances	14		30
4110	Outlays, gross (total)	14	10	40
	Offsets against gross budget authority and outlays:			
	Offsetting collections (collected) from:			
4123	Non-Federal sources	–64	–52	–52
4180	Budget authority, net (total)			
4190	Outlays, net (total)	–50	–42	–12

The Helium Act Amendments of 1960, Public Law 86–777 (50 U.S.C. 167), authorized activities necessary to provide sufficient helium to meet the current and foreseeable future needs of essential government activities. The Helium Privatization Act of 1996 (HPA), Public Law 104–273, provided for the eventual privatization of the program and its functions, specifying that once the helium debt is retired, the Helium Production Fund would be dissolved. The debt was repaid at the beginning of 2014. The Helium Stewardship Act of 2013 (HSA), Public Law 113–40, provided for continued operation of the Helium program while facilitating a gradual exit from the helium market. The Helium program consists of: (a) continued storage and transmission of crude helium; (b) oversight of the production of helium on Federal lands; and (c) administration of in-kind and open market crude helium gas sale programs. To minimize impacts to the helium market, the HSA provides a "glide path" from the sales mandated under HPA, increasing the sales price of helium through an auction mechanism and reducing the total volume of helium sold each year until the amount in storage reaches 3.0 billion cubic feet. At that point, the remaining helium will be reserved for Federal users. Additionally, pursuant to HSA BLM transferred all assets for disposal to the General Services Administration (GSA) at the end of FY 2021. The GSA, following its disposal process, will complete marketing, asset valuation, and dispose of all assets on or before September 30, 2023.

Balance Sheet (in millions of dollars)

Identification code 014–4053–0–3–306		2020 actual	2021 actual
	ASSETS:		
1101	Federal assets: Fund balances with Treasury	171	171
1206	Non-Federal assets: Receivables, net	6	6
1605	Accounts receivable from foreclosed property	6	6
	Other Federal assets:		
1802	Inventories and related properties		
1803	Property, plant and equipment, net		
1901	Other assets		
1999	Total assets	183	183
	LIABILITIES:		
	Federal liabilities:		
2103	Debt	21	21
2105	Other		
2201	Non-Federal liabilities: Accounts payable		
2999	Total liabilities	21	21

HELIUM FUND—Continued

Balance Sheet—Continued

Identification code 014–4053–0–3–306	2020 actual	2021 actual
NET POSITION:		
3300 Cumulative results of operations	162	162
4999 Total liabilities and net position	183	183

Object Classification (in millions of dollars)

Identification code 014–4053–0–3–306	2021 actual	2022 est.	2023 est.
Reimbursable obligations:			
Personnel compensation:			
11.1 Full-time permanent	4	4	4
11.3 Other than full-time permanent	1	1	1
11.9 Total personnel compensation	5	5	5
12.1 Civilian personnel benefits	2	2	2
23.2 Rental payments to others	6	6	6
23.3 Communications, utilities, and miscellaneous charges	5	5	5
25.2 Other services from non-Federal sources	1	1	1
25.7 Operation and maintenance of equipment	1	1	1
99.9 Total new obligations, unexpired accounts	20	20	20

Employment Summary

Identification code 014–4053–0–3–306	2021 actual	2022 est.	2023 est.
2001 Reimbursable civilian full-time equivalent employment	44	45	46

WORKING CAPITAL FUND

Program and Financing (in millions of dollars)

Identification code 014–4525–0–4–302	2021 actual	2022 est.	2023 est.
Obligations by program activity:			
0801 Operating expenses	76	216	220
0802 Capital investment	176	51	52
0900 Total new obligations, unexpired accounts	252	267	272
Budgetary resources:			
Unobligated balance:			
1000 Unobligated balance brought forward, Oct 1	188	194	190
Budget authority:			
Spending authority from offsetting collections, discretionary:			
1700 Collected	251	263	269
1701 Change in uncollected payments, Federal sources	7		
1750 Spending auth from offsetting collections, disc (total)	258	263	269
1930 Total budgetary resources available	446	457	459
Memorandum (non-add) entries:			
1941 Unexpired unobligated balance, end of year	194	190	187
Change in obligated balance:			
Unpaid obligations:			
3000 Unpaid obligations, brought forward, Oct 1	50	67	281
3010 New obligations, unexpired accounts	252	267	272
3020 Outlays (gross)	–235	–53	–62
3050 Unpaid obligations, end of year	67	281	491
Uncollected payments:			
3060 Uncollected pymts, Fed sources, brought forward, Oct 1	–6	–13	–13
3070 Change in uncollected pymts, Fed sources, unexpired	–7		
3090 Uncollected pymts, Fed sources, end of year	–13	–13	–13
Memorandum (non-add) entries:			
3100 Obligated balance, start of year	44	54	268
3200 Obligated balance, end of year	54	268	478
Budget authority and outlays, net:			
Discretionary:			
4000 Budget authority, gross	258	263	269
Outlays, gross:			
4010 Outlays from new discretionary authority	37	26	27
4011 Outlays from discretionary balances	198	27	35
4020 Outlays, gross (total)	235	53	62
Offsets against gross budget authority and outlays:			
Offsetting collections (collected) from:			
4030 Federal sources	–250	–263	–269
4033 Non-Federal sources	–1		
4040 Offsets against gross budget authority and outlays (total)	–251	–263	–269
Additional offsets against gross budget authority only:			
4050 Change in uncollected pymts, Fed sources, unexpired	–7		
4080 Outlays, net (discretionary)	–16	–210	–207
4180 Budget authority, net (total)			
4190 Outlays, net (total)	–16	–210	–207

Section 306 of the Federal Land Policy and Management Act of 1976 authorizes a Bureau of Land Management working capital fund. The fund is managed as a self-sustaining revolving fund for purchase and maintenance of vehicles and equipment, purchase of materials for resource conservation projects, purchase of uniforms, and other business-type functions.

Balance Sheet (in millions of dollars)

Identification code 014–4525–0–4–302	2020 actual	2021 actual
ASSETS:		
Federal assets:		
1101 Fund balances with Treasury	233	233
Investments in U.S. securities:		
1106 Receivables, net	7	7
Other Federal assets:		
1801 Cash and other monetary assets		
1802 Inventories and related properties		
1803 Property, plant and equipment, net		
1999 Total assets	240	240
LIABILITIES:		
2105 Federal liabilities: Other		
NET POSITION:		
3300 Cumulative results of operations	240	240
4999 Total liabilities and net position	240	240

Object Classification (in millions of dollars)

Identification code 014–4525–0–4–302	2021 actual	2022 est.	2023 est.
Reimbursable obligations:			
Personnel compensation:			
11.1 Full-time permanent	119	121	124
11.3 Other than full-time permanent	5	6	6
11.5 Other personnel compensation	1	2	2
11.9 Total personnel compensation	125	129	132
12.1 Civilian personnel benefits	53	54	55
25.2 Other services from non-Federal sources	3		
25.7 Operation and maintenance of equipment	5	6	6
26.0 Supplies and materials	26	27	27
31.0 Equipment	40	51	52
99.9 Total new obligations, unexpired accounts	252	267	272

Employment Summary

Identification code 014–4525–0–4–302	2021 actual	2022 est.	2023 est.
2001 Reimbursable civilian full-time equivalent employment	32	33	34

Trust Funds

MISCELLANEOUS TRUST FUNDS

In addition to amounts authorized to be expended under existing laws, there is hereby appropriated such amounts as may be contributed under section 307 of Public Law 94–579 (43 U.S.C. 1737), and such amounts as may be advanced for administrative costs, surveys, appraisals, and costs of making conveyances of omitted lands under section 211(b) of that Act (43 U.S.C. 1721(b)), to remain available until expended.

Note.—A full-year 2022 appropriation for this account was not enacted at the time the Budget was prepared; therefore, the Budget assumes this account is operating under the Continuing Appropriations Act, 2022 (Division A of Public Law 117–43, as amended). The amounts included for 2022 reflect the annualized level provided by the continuing resolution.

DEPARTMENT OF THE INTERIOR

Land and Minerals Management—Continued
Bureau of Ocean Energy Management

625

Special and Trust Fund Receipts (in millions of dollars)

Identification code 014–9971–0–7–302		2021 actual	2022 est.	2023 est.
0100	Balance, start of year			
	Receipts:			
	Current law:			
1130	Contributions and Deposits, BLM	31	22	32
2000	Total: Balances and receipts	31	22	32
	Appropriations:			
	Current law:			
2101	Miscellaneous Trust Funds	–31	–22	–32
5099	Balance, end of year			

Program and Financing (in millions of dollars)

Identification code 014–9971–0–7–302		2021 actual	2022 est.	2023 est.
	Obligations by program activity:			
0001	Resource development FLPMA	14	14	14
0002	Resource development CA OHV	6	6	6
0003	Resource development Taylor Grazing	1	1	1
0004	Public Survey	1	1	1
0005	Sikes Act		1	1
0900	Total new obligations, unexpired accounts	22	23	23
	Budgetary resources:			
	Unobligated balance:			
1000	Unobligated balance brought forward, Oct 1	65	75	74
1021	Recoveries of prior year unpaid obligations	1		
1070	Unobligated balance (total)	66	75	74
	Budget authority:			
	Appropriations, mandatory:			
1201	Appropriation (special or trust fund)	31	22	32
1930	Total budgetary resources available	97	97	106
	Memorandum (non-add) entries:			
1941	Unexpired unobligated balance, end of year	75	74	83
	Change in obligated balance:			
	Unpaid obligations:			
3000	Unpaid obligations, brought forward, Oct 1	15	16	17
3010	New obligations, unexpired accounts	22	23	23
3020	Outlays (gross)	–20	–22	–26
3040	Recoveries of prior year unpaid obligations, unexpired	–1		
3050	Unpaid obligations, end of year	16	17	14
	Memorandum (non-add) entries:			
3100	Obligated balance, start of year	15	16	17
3200	Obligated balance, end of year	16	17	14
	Budget authority and outlays, net:			
	Mandatory:			
4090	Budget authority, gross	31	22	32
	Outlays, gross:			
4100	Outlays from new mandatory authority	6	10	14
4101	Outlays from mandatory balances	14	12	12
4110	Outlays, gross (total)	20	22	26
4180	Budget authority, net (total)	31	22	32
4190	Outlays, net (total)	20	22	26

Current Trust Funds include:

Land and Resource Management Trust Fund.—Provides for the acceptance of contributed money or services for: 1) resource development, protection, and management; 2) conveyance or acquisition of public lands (including omitted lands or islands) to States, their political subdivisions, or individuals; and 3) conducting cadastral surveys, provided that estimated costs are paid prior to project initiation. (The Federal Land Policy and Management Act of 1976 (43 U.S.C. 1721, 1737).) The Sikes Act of 1974, as amended, provides for acceptance of contributions for conservation, restoration, and management of species and their habitats in cooperation with State wildlife agencies (16 U.S.C. 670 et seq.).

Permanent Trust Funds include:

Range improvements.—Acceptance of contributions for rangeland improvements is authorized by the Taylor Grazing Act (43 U.S.C. 315h and 315i). These funds are permanently appropriated as trust funds to the Secretary for uses specified by those Acts.

Public surveys.—Acceptance of contributions for public surveys is authorized by 43 U.S.C. 759, 761, and 31 U.S.C. 1321(a). These contributions are permanently appropriated as trust funds to the Secretary for uses specified by those Acts.

Trustee funds, Alaska townsites.—Amounts received from the sale of Alaska town lots are available for expenses incident to the maintenance and sale of townsites (31 U.S.C. 1321; Comp. Gen. Dec. of Nov. 18, 1935).

Object Classification (in millions of dollars)

Identification code 014–9971–0–7–302		2021 actual	2022 est.	2023 est.
	Direct obligations:			
	Personnel compensation:			
11.1	Full-time permanent	4	4	4
11.3	Other than full-time permanent	1	1	1
11.5	Other personnel compensation	1	1	1
11.9	Total personnel compensation	6	6	6
12.1	Civilian personnel benefits	2	2	2
25.2	Other services from non-Federal sources	4	5	5
25.3	Other goods and services from Federal sources	5	5	5
25.4	Operation and maintenance of facilities	1	1	1
26.0	Supplies and materials	2	2	2
41.0	Grants, subsidies, and contributions	2	2	2
99.9	Total new obligations, unexpired accounts	22	23	23

Employment Summary

Identification code 014–9971–0–7–302		2021 actual	2022 est.	2023 est.
1001	Direct civilian full-time equivalent employment	74	77	82

ADMINISTRATIVE PROVISIONS

The Bureau of Land Management may carry out the operations funded under this Act by direct expenditure, contracts, grants, cooperative agreements, and reimbursable agreements with public and private entities, including with States. Appropriations for the Bureau shall be available for purchase, erection, and dismantlement of temporary structures, and alteration and maintenance of necessary buildings and appurtenant facilities to which the United States has title; up to $100,000 for payments, at the discretion of the Secretary, for information or evidence concerning violations of laws administered by the Bureau; miscellaneous and emergency expenses of enforcement activities authorized or approved by the Secretary and to be accounted for solely on the Secretary's certificate, not to exceed $10,000: Provided, That notwithstanding Public Law 90–620 (44 U.S.C. 501), the Bureau may, under cooperative cost-sharing and partnership arrangements authorized by law, procure printing services from cooperators in connection with jointly produced publications for which the cooperators share the cost of printing either in cash or in services, and the Bureau determines the cooperator is capable of meeting accepted quality standards: Provided further, That projects to be funded pursuant to a written commitment by a State government to provide an identified amount of money in support of the project may be carried out by the Bureau on a reimbursable basis.

BUREAU OF OCEAN ENERGY MANAGEMENT

Federal Funds

OCEAN ENERGY MANAGEMENT

For expenses necessary for granting and administering leases, easements, rights-of-way, and agreements for use for oil and gas, other minerals, energy, and marine-related purposes on the Outer Continental Shelf and approving operations related thereto, as authorized by law; for environmental studies, as authorized by law; for implementing other laws and to the extent provided by Presidential or Secretarial delegation; and for matching grants or cooperative agreements, $237,407,000, of which $192,765,000 is to remain available until September 30, 2024, and of which $44,642,000 is to remain available until expended: Provided, That this total appropriation shall be reduced by amounts collected by the Secretary of the Interior and credited to this appropriation from additions to receipts resulting from increases to lease rental rates in effect on August 5, 1993, and from cost recovery fees from activities conducted by the Bureau of Ocean Energy Management pursuant to the Outer Continental Shelf Lands Act, including studies, assessments, analysis, and

Land and Minerals Management—Continued
Bureau of Ocean Energy Management—Continued

OCEAN ENERGY MANAGEMENT—Continued

miscellaneous administrative activities: Provided further, That the sum herein appropriated shall be reduced as such collections are received during the fiscal year, so as to result in a final fiscal year 2023 appropriation estimated at not more than $192,765,000: Provided further, That not to exceed $3,000 shall be available for reasonable expenses related to promoting volunteer beach and marine cleanup activities.

Note.—A full-year 2022 appropriation for this account was not enacted at the time the Budget was prepared; therefore, the Budget assumes this account is operating under the Continuing Appropriations Act, 2022 (Division A of Public Law 117–43, as amended). The amounts included for 2022 reflect the annualized level provided by the continuing resolution.

Program and Financing (in millions of dollars)

Identification code 014–1917–0–1–302	2021 actual	2022 est.	2023 est.
Obligations by program activity:			
0001 Renewable Energy	26	23	43
0002 Conventional Energy	61	55	60
0003 Environmental Programs	81	67	78
0004 Executive Direction	18	16	19
0006 Marine Minerals	11	9	13
0192 Total direct program	197	170	213
0799 Total direct obligations	197	170	213
0802 RSAs	1	2	2
0900 Total new obligations, unexpired accounts	198	172	215
Budgetary resources:			
Unobligated balance:			
1000 Unobligated balance brought forward, Oct 1	41	37	64
1021 Recoveries of prior year unpaid obligations	3	5	5
1070 Unobligated balance (total)	44	42	69
Budget authority:			
Appropriations, discretionary:			
1100 Appropriation	147	135	193
1131 Unobligated balance of appropriations permanently reduced	–2	–2	....
1160 Appropriation, discretionary (total)	145	133	193
Spending authority from offsetting collections, discretionary:			
1700 Collected - Offsetting Collections (Rents & Cost Recoveries)	46	58	45
1700 Collected - RSAs	1	2	2
1701 Change in uncollected payments, Federal sources	1	1	1
1750 Spending auth from offsetting collections, disc (total)	48	61	48
1900 Budget authority (total)	193	194	241
1930 Total budgetary resources available	237	236	310
Memorandum (non-add) entries:			
1940 Unobligated balance expiring	–2	....	....
1941 Unexpired unobligated balance, end of year	37	64	95
Change in obligated balance:			
Unpaid obligations:			
3000 Unpaid obligations, brought forward, Oct 1	114	128	155
3010 New obligations, unexpired accounts	198	172	215
3020 Outlays (gross)	–181	–140	–230
3040 Recoveries of prior year unpaid obligations, unexpired	–3	–5	–5
3050 Unpaid obligations, end of year	128	155	135
Uncollected payments:			
3060 Uncollected pymts, Fed sources, brought forward, Oct 1	–1	–2	–3
3070 Change in uncollected pymts, Fed sources, unexpired	–1	–1	–1
3090 Uncollected pymts, Fed sources, end of year	–2	–3	–4
Memorandum (non-add) entries:			
3100 Obligated balance, start of year	113	126	152
3200 Obligated balance, end of year	126	152	131
Budget authority and outlays, net:			
Discretionary:			
4000 Budget authority, gross	193	194	241
Outlays, gross:			
4010 Outlays from new discretionary authority	106	110	149
4011 Outlays from discretionary balances	75	30	81
4020 Outlays, gross (total)	181	140	230
Offsets against gross budget authority and outlays:			
Offsetting collections (collected) from:			
4030 Federal sources: RSAs	–1	–2	–2
4033 Non-Federal sources - OCS offsetting collections-rents & cost rec fees; contributions; Bond Forfeitures	–46	–58	–45
4040 Offsets against gross budget authority and outlays (total)	–47	–60	–47
Additional offsets against gross budget authority only:			
4050 Change in uncollected pymts, Fed sources, unexpired	–1	–1	–1
4070 Budget authority, net (discretionary)	145	133	193
4080 Outlays, net (discretionary)	134	80	183
4180 Budget authority, net (total)	145	133	193
4190 Outlays, net (total)	134	80	183
Memorandum (non-add) entries:			
5090 Unexpired unavailable balance, SOY: Offsetting collections	5	5	5
5092 Unexpired unavailable balance, EOY: Offsetting collections	5	5	5

The Bureau of Ocean Energy Management (BOEM) manages the exploration and development of the nation's offshore energy and marine mineral resources on the U.S. Outer Continental Shelf (OCS). BOEM's work supports Administration efforts, including creating good paying jobs as the Nation transitions to a clean energy future, advancing energy security, and supporting economic prosperity and the reliability and affordability of domestic clean energy. BOEM oversees development of renewable energy resources such as offshore wind, wave and ocean currents; vast deposits of oil and natural gas; and non-energy minerals. BOEM's goal is to balance economic development, energy security, and environmental protection through responsible and transparent management of offshore resources based on the best available science. To carry out this mission, BOEM: supports renewable energy leasing and development; provides OCS oil and gas planning, leasing and oversight, including inventories of oil and gas reserves, resource and economic evaluation, review and administration of oil and gas exploration and development plans, geological and geophysical (G&G) permitting, and financial assurance and risk management; conveys sand and gravel resources; and conducts National Environmental Policy Act (NEPA) analysis and environmental studies.

The Ocean Energy Management account includes the following budget activities: Renewable Energy, Conventional Energy, Marine Minerals, Environmental Programs, and Executive Direction.

Renewable Energy.—Supports the Administration's commitment to deepen and diversify the Nation's energy portfolio by accelerating offshore renewable energy production in response to EO 14008. Oversees renewable energy program development and implementation, including: identification of wind energy areas; environmental and compliance work; competitive and noncompetitive leasing actions; review of site assessment plans, and construction and operations plans; and consultation with Tribal Nations, State and local governments, Federal agencies, and other stakeholders.

Conventional Energy.—Manages OCS oil and gas development in line with the requirements of Executive Orders 13990 and 14008. BOEM activities include: developing the National OCS Oil and Gas Leasing Program; implementing the lease sale process; administering leases; protecting the Federal Government from financial risks related to natural resource development; reviewing exploration and development plans and geological and geophysical permit applications; developing and maintaining the OCS cadastre; and conducting technical and economic resource evaluation and fair market value determination. In conducting these activities, BOEM fosters environmental justice; actively involves Tribal Nations, the public and stakeholders; and addresses the challenges posed by climate change.

Marine Minerals.—Manages non-energy minerals on the OCS and conveys, on a noncompetitive basis, the rights to those resources to Federal, State, and local government agencies for shore protection, beach and wetlands restoration projects, or for use in construction projects funded or authorized by the Federal Government. Facilitates access to and manages these crucial OCS resources to support resilient coasts, natural disaster preparedness, and protection of shoreline infrastructure vital to the Nation's security, economy, and ecosystems. Funding supports mineral resource exploration and leasing activities, coordination with governmental partners, engagement of stakeholders, and scientific research to improve decision-making and risk management.

Environmental Programs.—Advances Administration priorities by ensuring that science and environmental protection are foremost considerations

DEPARTMENT OF THE INTERIOR

Land and Minerals Management—Continued
Bureau of Safety and Environmental Enforcement   627

in BOEM decision-making, fostering conservation of natural and cultural resources, combating climate change, and advancing environmental justice. Informs decision-makers and the public about the potential impacts of OCS energy and mineral activities on the marine, coastal, and human environment. Develops the environmental impact statements and environmental assessments needed to consider the potential environmental impacts of proposed actions in accordance with the National Environmental Protection Act, the OCS Lands Act, and numerous other environmental statutes, regulations, and executive orders. Funding supports scientific research needed to inform policy decisions regarding energy and mineral development on the OCS.

Executive Direction.—Funds bureau-wide leadership, direction, management, coordination, communication strategies, outreach, and regulatory development. This includes budget management, administrative services management, bureau-wide information technology management and governance, congressional and public affairs, policy analysis, regulations, overseeing official documents, international affairs, and Freedom of Information Act activities.

Object Classification (in millions of dollars)

Identification code 014–1917–0–1–302		2021 actual	2022 est.	2023 est.
	Direct obligations:			
11.1	Personnel compensation: Full-time permanent	71	61	77
12.1	Civilian personnel benefits	26	23	28
21.0	Travel and transportation of persons			1
24.0	Printing and reproduction	1	1	1
25.2	Other services from non-Federal sources	27	23	29
25.3	Other goods and services from Federal sources	58	50	62
31.0	Equipment	2	2	2
41.0	Grants, subsidies, and contributions	12	10	13
99.0	Direct obligations	197	170	213
99.0	Reimbursable obligations	1	2	2
99.9	Total new obligations, unexpired accounts	198	172	215

Employment Summary

Identification code 014–1917–0–1–302		2021 actual	2022 est.	2023 est.
1001	Direct civilian full-time equivalent employment	575	610	677

BUREAU OF SAFETY AND ENVIRONMENTAL ENFORCEMENT

Federal Funds

OFFSHORE SAFETY AND ENVIRONMENTAL ENFORCEMENT

For expenses necessary for the regulation of operations related to leases, easements, rights-of-way, and agreements for use for oil and gas, other minerals, energy, and marine-related purposes on the Outer Continental Shelf, as authorized by law; for enforcing and implementing laws and regulations as authorized by law and to the extent provided by Presidential or Secretarial delegation; and for matching grants or cooperative agreements, $195,350,000, of which $142,378,000 is to remain available until September 30, 2024, and of which $52,972,000 is to remain available until expended, including $30,000,000 for offshore decommissioning activities: Provided, That this total appropriation shall be reduced by amounts collected by the Secretary of the Interior and credited to this appropriation from additions to receipts resulting from increases to lease rental rates in effect on August 5, 1993, and from cost recovery fees from activities conducted by the Bureau of Safety and Environmental Enforcement pursuant to the Outer Continental Shelf Lands Act, including studies, assessments, analysis, and miscellaneous administrative activities: Provided further, That the sum herein appropriated shall be reduced as such collections are received during the fiscal year, so as to result in a final fiscal year 2023 appropriation estimated at not more than $172,378,000.

For an additional amount, $50,736,000, to remain available until expended, to be reduced by amounts collected by the Secretary and credited to this appropriation, which shall be derived from non-refundable inspection fees collected in fiscal year 2023, as provided in this Act: Provided, That to the extent that amounts realized from such inspection fees exceed $50,736,000, the amounts realized in excess of $50,736,000 shall be credited to this appropriation and remain available until expended: Provided further, That for fiscal year 2023, not less than 50 percent of the inspection fees expended by the Bureau of Safety and Environmental Enforcement will be used to fund personnel and mission-related costs to expand capacity and expedite the orderly development, subject to environmental safeguards, of the Outer Continental Shelf pursuant to the Outer Continental Shelf Lands Act (43 U.S.C. 1331 et seq.), including the review of applications for permits to drill.

Note.—A full-year 2022 appropriation for this account was not enacted at the time the Budget was prepared; therefore, the Budget assumes this account is operating under the Continuing Appropriations Act, 2022 (Division A of Public Law 117–43, as amended). The amounts included for 2022 reflect the annualized level provided by the continuing resolution.

OFFSHORE SAFETY AND ENVIRONMENTAL ENFORCEMENT

〚*For an additional amount for "Offshore Safety and Environmental Enforcement", $223,000, to remain available until expended, for necessary expenses related to the consequences of calendar year 2019, 2020 and 2021 wildfires, hurricanes and natural disasters.*〛 *(Disaster Relief Supplemental Appropriations Act, 2022.)*

Program and Financing (in millions of dollars)

Identification code 014–1700–0–1–302		2021 actual	2022 est.	2023 est.
	Obligations by program activity:			
0001	Environmental Enforcement	5	5	5
0002	Operations, Safety and Regulation	161	177	171
0003	Administrative Operations	19	20	19
0004	Executive Direction	16	16	18
0006	Offshore Decommissioning			30
0192	Total direct program	201	218	243
0799	Total direct obligations	201	218	243
0802	Reimbursable Service Agreements	51	76	44
0900	Total new obligations, unexpired accounts	252	294	287
	Budgetary resources:			
	Unobligated balance:			
1000	Unobligated balance brought forward, Oct 1	89	91	24
1021	Recoveries of prior year unpaid obligations	9		
1070	Unobligated balance (total)	98	91	24
	Budget authority:			
	Appropriations, discretionary:			
1100	Appropriation	137	122	172
1131	Unobligated balance of appropriations permanently reduced	–10	–10	
1160	Appropriation, discretionary (total)	127	112	172
	Spending authority from offsetting collections, discretionary:			
1700	Offsetting Collections (Cost Recovery)	4	5	5
1700	Offsetting Collections (Rental Receipts)	19	24	18
1700	Collected (Inspection Fee)	34	43	51
1700	Reimbursable Service Agreements	44	43	37
1701	Change in uncollected payments, Federal sources	17		
1750	Spending auth from offsetting collections, disc (total)	118	115	111
1900	Budget authority (total)	245	227	283
1930	Total budgetary resources available	343	318	307
	Memorandum (non-add) entries:			
1941	Unexpired unobligated balance, end of year	91	24	20
	Change in obligated balance:			
	Unpaid obligations:			
3000	Unpaid obligations, brought forward, Oct 1	100	111	150
3010	New obligations, unexpired accounts	252	294	287
3020	Outlays (gross)	–231	–255	–285
3040	Recoveries of prior year unpaid obligations, unexpired	–9		
3041	Recoveries of prior year unpaid obligations, expired	–1		
3050	Unpaid obligations, end of year	111	150	152
	Uncollected payments:			
3060	Uncollected pymts, Fed sources, brought forward, Oct 1	–27	–44	–44
3070	Change in uncollected pymts, Fed sources, unexpired	–17		
3090	Uncollected pymts, Fed sources, end of year	–44	–44	–44
	Memorandum (non-add) entries:			
3100	Obligated balance, start of year	73	67	106
3200	Obligated balance, end of year	67	106	108
	Budget authority and outlays, net:			
	Discretionary:			
4000	Budget authority, gross	245	227	283
	Outlays, gross:			
4010	Outlays from new discretionary authority	139	155	198
4011	Outlays from discretionary balances	92	100	87
4020	Outlays, gross (total)	231	255	285

OFFSHORE SAFETY AND ENVIRONMENTAL ENFORCEMENT—Continued

Program and Financing—Continued

Identification code 014–1700–0–1–302	2021 actual	2022 est.	2023 est.
Offsets against gross budget authority and outlays:			
Offsetting collections (collected) from:			
4030 Federal sources	–44	–43	–37
4033 Non-Federal sources	–57	–72	–74
4040 Offsets against gross budget authority and outlays (total)	–101	–115	–111
Additional offsets against gross budget authority only:			
4050 Change in uncollected pymts, Fed sources, unexpired	–17		
4060 Additional offsets against budget authority only (total)	–17		
4070 Budget authority, net (discretionary)	127	112	172
4080 Outlays, net (discretionary)	130	140	174
4180 Budget authority, net (total)	127	112	172
4190 Outlays, net (total)	130	140	174
Memorandum (non-add) entries:			
5090 Unexpired unavailable balance, SOY: Offsetting collections	6	6	6
5092 Unexpired unavailable balance, EOY: Offsetting collections	6	6	6

The Bureau of Safety and Environmental Enforcement (BSEE) was established on October 1, 2011, to ensure the safe and environmentally responsible exploration, development, production, and conservation of the Nation's offshore energy resources. BSEE uses its full range of authorities, policies, and tools to ensure safety, oil spill preparedness, environmental stewardship, and appropriate development of offshore oil, natural gas, and renewable energy resources. The Bureau continues to improve its mission processes and staff capabilities to keep pace with the continued innovation in Outer Continental Shelf (OCS) exploration and production. To fulfill its mission, BSEE must adapt and respond to changes in both the renewable energy and oil and gas sectors throughout the lifecycle of offshore energy development. BSEE is committed to continually improving the effectiveness of its safety management systems program and compliance assurance functions such as the inspection program, enhancing its permitting processes around greater quality assurance and consistency, ensuring high levels of preparedness in the event of oil spills, and addressing requirements for an expanded OCS renewable energy program. BSEE's work supports Administration efforts to create good paying jobs as the Nation transitions to a clean energy future. The Offshore Safety and Environmental Enforcement (OSEE) account is BSEE's primary operating account and funds the following activities: Operations, Safety, and Regulation; Environmental Enforcement; Administrative Operations; Executive Direction; and Offshore Decommissioning.

Operations, Safety, and Regulation.—Funds reviews of OCS oil and gas permit applications and offshore wind industry submittals; inspections of OCS facilities, including critical high-risk activities; offshore operator oil spill planning and preparedness compliance; investigations; enforcement; audit programs; annual operator performance reviews; verification of oil and gas production levels to help ensure the public receives a fair return; research supporting the analysis of emerging technologies, standards and regulatory review and development activities; and technical training.

Environmental Enforcement.—Funds environmental compliance staff and operational support required to: manage compliance verification and enforcement of environmental standards placed on OCS operations; ensure BSEE's compliance with NEPA, the Endangered Species Act (ESA), and the National Historic Preservation Act (NHPA) for Bureau permitting; conduct specialized inspections of air and water quality requirements, and other environmental mitigation measures; and oversee coordination and engagement for Tribal consultation requirements, and other environmental Acts, regulations, and policies.

Administrative Operations.—Funds general administration programs, equal employment opportunity services, emergency management, finance, human resources, procurement, and information management. BSEE also provides administrative services, such as human resources, procurement, and finance, to the Bureau of Ocean Energy Management (BOEM) and other entities within the Department on a reimbursable basis.

Executive Direction.—Funds bureau-wide leadership, direction, management, coordination, communications strategies, and outreach. This includes functions such as budget, congressional and public affairs, and policy and analysis.

Offshore Decommissioning.—Funds according to regulatory standards, the proper maintenance, monitoring, and decommissioning of orphaned wells, pipelines, and structures left on the OCS for which there is no remaining liable party.

Object Classification (in millions of dollars)

Identification code 014–1700–0–1–302	2021 actual	2022 est.	2023 est.
Direct obligations:			
11.1 Personnel compensation: Full-time permanent	77	82	82
12.1 Civilian personnel benefits	27	28	28
23.1 Rental payments to GSA	10	10	10
25.1 Advisory and assistance services	10	10	10
25.2 Other services from non-Federal sources	40	50	75
25.3 Other goods and services from Federal sources	11	12	12
25.5 Research and development contracts	12	10	10
25.7 Operation and maintenance of equipment	8	9	9
31.0 Equipment	2	3	3
41.0 Grants, subsidies, and contributions	4	4	4
99.0 Direct obligations	201	218	243
99.0 Reimbursable obligations	50	76	44
99.5 Adjustment for rounding	1		
99.9 Total new obligations, unexpired accounts	252	294	287

Employment Summary

Identification code 014–1700–0–1–302	2021 actual	2022 est.	2023 est.
1001 Direct civilian full-time equivalent employment	656	734	778
2001 Reimbursable civilian full-time equivalent employment	102	125	125

Trust Funds

OIL SPILL RESEARCH

For necessary expenses to carry out title I, section 1016; title IV, sections 4202 and 4303; title VII; and title VIII, section 8201 of the Oil Pollution Act of 1990, $15,099,000, which shall be derived from the Oil Spill Liability Trust Fund, to remain available until expended.

Note.—A full-year 2022 appropriation for this account was not enacted at the time the Budget was prepared; therefore, the Budget assumes this account is operating under the Continuing Appropriations Act, 2022 (Division A of Public Law 117–43, as amended). The amounts included for 2022 reflect the annualized level provided by the continuing resolution.

Program and Financing (in millions of dollars)

Identification code 014–8370–0–7–302	2021 actual	2022 est.	2023 est.
Obligations by program activity:			
0001 Oil Spill Research (Direct)	19	21	17
Budgetary resources:			
Unobligated balance:			
1000 Unobligated balance brought forward, Oct 1	17	13	7
Budget authority:			
Appropriations, discretionary:			
1101 Appropriation (special or trust)	15	15	15
1930 Total budgetary resources available	32	28	22
Memorandum (non-add) entries:			
1941 Unexpired unobligated balance, end of year	13	7	5
Change in obligated balance:			
Unpaid obligations:			
3000 Unpaid obligations, brought forward, Oct 1	17	23	22
3010 New obligations, unexpired accounts	19	21	17
3020 Outlays (gross)	–13	–22	–19
3050 Unpaid obligations, end of year	23	22	20
Memorandum (non-add) entries:			
3100 Obligated balance, start of year	17	23	22

DEPARTMENT OF THE INTERIOR

Land and Minerals Management—Continued
Office of Surface Mining Reclamation and Enforcement — 629

		2021 actual	2022 est.	2023 est.
3200	Obligated balance, end of year	23	22	20
	Budget authority and outlays, net:			
	Discretionary:			
4000	Budget authority, gross	15	15	15
	Outlays, gross:			
4010	Outlays from new discretionary authority	3	8	8
4011	Outlays from discretionary balances	10	14	11
4020	Outlays, gross (total)	13	22	19
4180	Budget authority, net (total)	15	15	15
4190	Outlays, net (total)	13	22	19

The Oil Pollution Act of 1990 authorizes use of the Oil Spill Liability Trust Fund, established by section 9509 of the Internal Revenue Code of 1986. The Oil Spill Research appropriation is drawn from the Oil Spill Liability Trust Fund and funds: 1) oil spill prevention, abatement, planning, preparedness, and response functions for all facilities seaward of the coastline of the United States that handle, store, or transport oil; 2) oil spill research; and 3) Ohmsett—the National Oil Spill Response Research and Renewable Energy Test Facility.

Object Classification (in millions of dollars)

Identification code 014–8370–0–7–302		2021 actual	2022 est.	2023 est.
	Direct obligations:			
11.1	Personnel compensation: Full-time permanent	2	3	3
12.1	Civilian personnel benefits	1	1	1
25.2	Other services from non-Federal sources	12	13	9
25.5	Research and development contracts	4	4	4
99.9	Total new obligations, unexpired accounts	19	21	17

Employment Summary

Identification code 014–8370–0–7–302	2021 actual	2022 est.	2023 est.
1001 Direct civilian full-time equivalent employment	18	22	23

OFFICE OF SURFACE MINING RECLAMATION AND ENFORCEMENT

Federal Funds

REGULATION AND TECHNOLOGY

For necessary expenses to carry out the provisions of the Surface Mining Control and Reclamation Act of 1977, Public Law 95–87, $122,076,000, to remain available until September 30, 2024, of which $65,000,000 shall be available for state and tribal regulatory grants: Provided, That appropriations for the Office of Surface Mining Reclamation and Enforcement may provide for the travel and per diem expenses of State and tribal personnel attending Office of Surface Mining Reclamation and Enforcement sponsored training.

In addition, for costs to review, administer, and enforce permits issued by the Office pursuant to section 507 of Public Law 95–87 (30 U.S.C. 1257), $40,000, to remain available until expended: Provided, That fees assessed and collected by the Office pursuant to such section 507 shall be credited to this account as discretionary offsetting collections, to remain available until expended: Provided further, That the sum herein appropriated from the general fund shall be reduced as collections are received during the fiscal year, so as to result in a fiscal year 2023 appropriation estimated at not more than $122,076,000.

Note.—A full-year 2022 appropriation for this account was not enacted at the time the Budget was prepared; therefore, the Budget assumes this account is operating under the Continuing Appropriations Act, 2022 (Division A of Public Law 117–43, as amended). The amounts included for 2022 reflect the annualized level provided by the continuing resolution.

Program and Financing (in millions of dollars)

Identification code 014–1801–0–1–302		2021 actual	2022 est.	2023 est.
	Obligations by program activity:			
0002	Environmental protection	85	85	88
0003	Technology development and transfer	14	14	15
0004	Financial management	1	1	1
0005	Executive direction and administration	13	13	15
0900	Total new obligations, unexpired accounts	113	113	119

	Budgetary resources:			
	Unobligated balance:			
1000	Unobligated balance brought forward, Oct 1	39	22	5
1021	Recoveries of prior year unpaid obligations	2	3	3
1070	Unobligated balance (total)	41	25	8
	Budget authority:			
	Appropriations, discretionary:			
1100	Appropriation	118	118	122
1131	Unobligated balance of appropriations permanently reduced	–25	–25	
1160	Appropriation, discretionary (total)	93	93	122
	Spending authority from offsetting collections, discretionary:			
1700	Collected	1		
1900	Budget authority (total)	94	93	122
1930	Total budgetary resources available	135	118	130
	Memorandum (non-add) entries:			
1941	Unexpired unobligated balance, end of year	22	5	11
	Change in obligated balance:			
	Unpaid obligations:			
3000	Unpaid obligations, brought forward, Oct 1	56	57	62
3010	New obligations, unexpired accounts	113	113	119
3020	Outlays (gross)	–105	–105	–108
3040	Recoveries of prior year unpaid obligations, unexpired	–2	–3	–3
3041	Recoveries of prior year unpaid obligations, expired	–5		
3050	Unpaid obligations, end of year	57	62	70
	Memorandum (non-add) entries:			
3100	Obligated balance, start of year	56	57	62
3200	Obligated balance, end of year	57	62	70
	Budget authority and outlays, net:			
	Discretionary:			
4000	Budget authority, gross	94	93	122
	Outlays, gross:			
4010	Outlays from new discretionary authority	49	40	52
4011	Outlays from discretionary balances	56	65	56
4020	Outlays, gross (total)	105	105	108
	Offsets against gross budget authority and outlays:			
	Offsetting collections (collected) from:			
4033	Non-Federal sources	–1		
4040	Offsets against gross budget authority and outlays (total)	–1		
4180	Budget authority, net (total)	93	93	122
4190	Outlays, net (total)	104	105	108

Environmental protection.—This activity funds functions that directly contribute to ensuring the environment is protected during surface coal mining operations. It also addresses activities to ensure coal operators adequately reclaim the land after mining is completed.

Under this activity, the Office of Surface Mining Reclamation and Enforcement provides grants and support to States to operate enforcement programs on State and private lands under the terms of the Surface Mining Control and Reclamation Act of 1977. This activity also provides for the operation of enforcement programs in States without their own regulatory program and on Federal and Indian lands, as well as Federal oversight of the State regulatory programs.

Technology development and transfer.—This activity provides funding to enhance the technical skills that States and Indian Tribes need to operate their regulatory programs. It provides training and technical tools, such as the Coal Information Management System, to States and Indian Tribes to solve problems related to the environmental effects of coal mining and technical assistance to address specific coal mining issues.

Financial management.—This activity provides resources for managing, accounting, processing collections, and pursuing delinquent civil penalties. This includes developing and maintaining information management systems that support these functions and enhance the agency's ability to deny new mining permits to applicants with unabated State or Federal violations. This activity also includes accounting for and reporting on grants awarded to States and Tribes for regulatory purposes.

Executive direction and administration.—This activity provides funding for executive direction, general administrative support, and the acquisition of certain agency-wide common services, such as rent, telephones, and postage.

630 **Land and Minerals Management**—Continued
  Office of Surface Mining Reclamation and Enforcement—Continued   THE BUDGET FOR FISCAL YEAR 2023

REGULATION AND TECHNOLOGY—Continued

Object Classification (in millions of dollars)

Identification code 014–1801–0–1–302		2021 actual	2022 est.	2023 est.
	Direct obligations:			
11.1	Personnel compensation: Full-time permanent	26	29	30
12.1	Civilian personnel benefits	9	9	9
21.0	Travel and transportation of persons	....	2	2
23.1	Rental payments to GSA	2	2	2
23.2	Rental payments to others	....	4	4
25.2	Other services from non-Federal sources	8	6	6
26.0	Supplies and materials	....	1	1
31.0	Equipment	1	1	1
41.0	Grants, subsidies, and contributions	67	59	64
99.9	Total new obligations, unexpired accounts	113	113	119

Employment Summary

Identification code 014–1801–0–1–302	2021 actual	2022 est.	2023 est.
1001 Direct civilian full-time equivalent employment	237	298	312

ABANDONED MINE RECLAMATION FUND

For necessary expenses to carry out title IV of the Surface Mining Control and Reclamation Act of 1977, Public Law 95–87, $34,142,000, to be derived from receipts of the Abandoned Mine Reclamation Fund and to remain available until expended: Provided, That pursuant to Public Law 97–365, the Department of the Interior is authorized to use up to 20 percent from the recovery of the delinquent debt owed to the United States Government to pay for contracts to collect these debts: Provided further, That funds made available under title IV of Public Law 95–87 may be used for any required non-Federal share of the cost of projects funded by the Federal Government for the purpose of environmental restoration related to treatment or abatement of acid mine drainage from abandoned mines: Provided further, That such projects must be consistent with the purposes and priorities of the Surface Mining Control and Reclamation Act: Provided further, That amounts provided under this heading may be used for the travel and per diem expenses of State and tribal personnel attending Office of Surface Mining Reclamation and Enforcement sponsored training.

In addition, $115,000,000, to remain available until expended, for grants to States and federally recognized Indian Tribes for reclamation of abandoned mine lands and other related activities : Provided, That such additional amount shall be used for economic and community development in conjunction with the priorities in section 403(a) of the Surface Mining Control and Reclamation Act of 1977 (30 U.S.C. 1233(a)): Provided further, That of such additional amount, $75,000,000 shall be distributed in equal amounts to the three Appalachian States with the greatest amount of unfunded needs to meet the priorities described in paragraphs (1) and (2) of such section, $30,000,000 shall be distributed in equal amounts to the three Appalachian States with the subsequent greatest amount of unfunded needs to meet such priorities, and $10,000,000 shall be for grants to federally recognized Indian Tribes without regard to their status as certified or uncertified under the Surface Mining Control and Reclamation Act of 1977 (30 U.S.C. 1233(a)), for reclamation of abandoned mine lands and other related activities and shall be used for economic and community development in conjunction with the priorities in section 403(a) of the Surface Mining Control and Reclamation Act of 1977: Provided further, That such additional amount shall be allocated to States and Indian Tribes within 60 days after the date of enactment of this Act.

Note.—A full-year 2022 appropriation for this account was not enacted at the time the Budget was prepared; therefore, the Budget assumes this account is operating under the Continuing Appropriations Act, 2022 (Division A of Public Law 117–43, as amended). The amounts included for 2022 reflect the annualized level provided by the continuing resolution.

ABANDONED MINE RECLAMATION FUND

〔(INCLUDING TRANSFERS OF FUNDS)〕

〔*For an additional amount to be deposited in the "Abandoned Mine Reclamation Fund", $11,293,000,000, to remain available until expended, to carry out section 40701 of division D of this Act: Provided, That of the amount provided under this heading in this Act, $25,000,000, to remain available until expended, shall be to carry out activities as authorized in section 40701(g) of division D of this Act: Provided further, That up to 3 percent of the amounts made available under this heading in this Act shall be for salaries, expenses, and administration: Provided further, That one-half of one percent of the amounts made available under this* heading in this Act shall be transferred to the Office of Inspector General of the Department of the Interior for oversight of funding provided to the Department of the Interior in this title in this Act: *Provided further,* That such amount is designated by the Congress as being for an emergency requirement pursuant to section 4112(a) of H. Con. Res. 71 (115th Congress), the concurrent resolution on the budget for fiscal year 2018, and to section 251(b) of the Balanced Budget and Emergency Deficit Control Act of 1985.〕 *(Infrastructure Investments and Jobs Appropriations Act.)*

Special and Trust Fund Receipts (in millions of dollars)

Identification code 014–5015–0–2–999		2021 actual	2022 est.	2023 est.
0100	Balance, start of year	2,308	2,276	2,220
	Receipts:			
	Current law:			
1110	Abandoned Mine Reclamation Fund, Reclamation Fees	112	92	84
1140	Earnings on Investments, Abandoned Mine Reclamation Fund	24	5	82
1199	Total current law receipts	136	97	166
1999	Total receipts	136	97	166
2000	Total: Balances and receipts	2,444	2,373	2,386
	Appropriations:			
	Current law:			
2101	Abandoned Mine Reclamation Fund	–25	–25	–34
2101	Abandoned Mine Reclamation Fund	–29	–19	–82
2101	Abandoned Mine Reclamation Fund	–122	–116	–101
2132	Abandoned Mine Reclamation Fund	7	7	6
2199	Total current law appropriations	–169	–153	–211
2999	Total appropriations	–169	–153	–211
5098	Rounding adjustment	1	....	....
5099	Balance, end of year	2,276	2,220	2,175

Program and Financing (in millions of dollars)

Identification code 014–5015–0–2–999		2021 actual	2022 est.	2023 est.
	Obligations by program activity:			
0001	Environmental Restoration	68	127	177
0002	Technology development and transfer	4	4	4
0003	Financial management	6	6	6
0004	Executive direction and administration	7	7	7
0005	AML funded Grants to States	132	127	127
0006	UMWA and other benefits	29	19	82
0007	2022 Bipartisan Infrastructure Law (P.L. 117–58)	....	727	743
0900	Total new obligations, unexpired accounts	246	1,017	1,146
	Budgetary resources:			
	Unobligated balance:			
1000	Unobligated balance brought forward, Oct 1	150	201	10,709
1001	Discretionary unobligated balance brought fwd, Oct 1	126	....	....
1021	Recoveries of prior year unpaid obligations	23	25	25
1070	Unobligated balance (total)	173	226	10,734
	Budget authority:			
	Appropriations, discretionary:			
1100	Appropriation (Economic Development)	115	115	115
1100	Appropriation (Bipartisan Infrastructure Law)	....	11,293	....
1101	Appropriation (special or trust)	25	25	34
1120	Appropriations transferred to other acct [014–0104]	....	–56	....
1131	Unobligated balance of appropriations permanently reduced	–10	–5	....
1160	Appropriation, discretionary (total)	130	11,372	149
	Appropriations, mandatory:			
1201	Appropriation (AML & RAMP transfers to UMWA)	29	19	82
1201	Appropriation (AML grants to states)	122	116	101
1232	Appropriations and/or unobligated balance of appropriations temporarily reduced	–7	–7	–6
1260	Appropriations, mandatory (total)	144	128	177
1900	Budget authority (total)	274	11,500	326
1930	Total budgetary resources available	447	11,726	11,060
	Memorandum (non-add) entries:			
1941	Unexpired unobligated balance, end of year	201	10,709	9,914
	Change in obligated balance:			
	Unpaid obligations:			
3000	Unpaid obligations, brought forward, Oct 1	596	580	1,292
3010	New obligations, unexpired accounts	246	1,017	1,146
3020	Outlays (gross)	–239	–280	–463

DEPARTMENT OF THE INTERIOR

Land and Minerals Management—Continued
Office of Surface Mining Reclamation and Enforcement—Continued

631

		2021 actual	2022 est.	2023 est.
3040	Recoveries of prior year unpaid obligations, unexpired	–23	–25	–25
3050	Unpaid obligations, end of year	580	1,292	1,950
	Memorandum (non-add) entries:			
3100	Obligated balance, start of year	596	580	1,292
3200	Obligated balance, end of year	580	1,292	1,950
	Budget authority and outlays, net:			
	Discretionary:			
4000	Budget authority, gross	130	11,372	149
	Outlays, gross:			
4010	Outlays from new discretionary authority	15	16	22
4011	Outlays from discretionary balances	64	117	244
4020	Outlays, gross (total)	79	133	266
	Mandatory:			
4090	Budget authority, gross	144	128	177
	Outlays, gross:			
4100	Outlays from new mandatory authority	11	38	98
4101	Outlays from mandatory balances	149	109	99
4110	Outlays, gross (total)	160	147	197
4180	Budget authority, net (total)	274	11,500	326
4190	Outlays, net (total)	239	280	463
	Memorandum (non-add) entries:			
5000	Total investments, SOY: Federal securities: Par value	2,633	2,572	12,966
5001	Total investments, EOY: Federal securities: Par value	2,572	12,966	12,141

Environmental restoration.—This activity funds those functions that contribute to reclaiming lands affected by past coal mining practices. This activity provides discretionary funding for the Federal reclamation program for watershed restoration projects and for the evaluation of State and tribal reclamation programs that now receive mandatory funding for reclamation activities. This activity also provides for the operation of Federal reclamation programs for activities in those States without their own reclamation programs.

Technology development and transfer.—This activity provides funding to enhance the technical skills States and Indian Tribes need to operate their reclamation programs. The Office of Surface Mining Reclamation and Enforcement (OSMRE) provides training and technical assistance on mining and reclamation-related problems.

Financial management.—This activity provides funds to identify, notify, collect, and audit fees from coal operators for the Abandoned Mine Reclamation Fund. The OSMRE seeks to maximize voluntary compliance with the Surface Mining Control and Reclamation Act's reclamation fee provisions. This activity also includes accounting for and reporting on grants awarded to States and Tribes for reclamation activities.

Executive direction and administration.—This activity provides funding for executive direction, general administrative support, and the acquisition of certain agency-wide common services such as rent, telephones, and postage.

Funds in this account support the Administration's efforts to address the needs of coal communities by reclaiming formerly mined lands so that they can be repurposed for beneficial economic uses, providing local, good-paying union jobs for skilled technicians and operators in some of the hardest hit communities in the Nation. The Budget provides $115 million for the AML Economic Revitalization grant program to support Appalachian States and qualified Tribes with AML reclamation in conjunction with economic and community development activities.

Status of Funds (in millions of dollars)

Identification code 014–5015–0–2–999		2021 actual	2022 est.	2023 est.
	Unexpended balance, start of year:			
0100	Balance, start of year	2,600	2,941	2,697
0298	Reconciliation adjustment	454		
0999	Total balance, start of year	3,054	2,941	2,697
	Cash income during the year:			
	Current law:			
	Receipts:			
1110	Abandoned Mine Reclamation Fund, Reclamation Fees	112	92	84
1150	Earnings on Investments, Abandoned Mine Reclamation Fund	24	5	82
1199	Income under present law	136	97	166
1999	Total cash income	136	97	166
	Cash outgo during year:			
	Current law:			
2100	Abandoned Mine Reclamation Fund [Budget Acct]	–239	–280	–463
2199	Outgo under current law	–239	–280	–463
2999	Total cash outgo (-)	–239	–280	–463
	Surplus or deficit:			
3110	Excluding interest	–127	–188	–379
3120	Interest	24	5	82
3199	Subtotal, surplus or deficit	–103	–183	–297
3220	Abandoned Mine Reclamation Fund	–10	–5	
3230	Abandoned Mine Reclamation Fund		–56	
3299	Total adjustments	–10	–61	
3999	Total change in fund balance	–113	–244	–297
	Unexpended balance, end of year:			
4100	Uninvested balance (net), end of year	369	–10,269	–9,741
4200	Abandoned Mine Reclamation Fund	2,572	12,966	12,141
4999	Total balance, end of year	2,941	2,697	2,400

Object Classification (in millions of dollars)

Identification code 014–5015–0–2–999	2021 actual	2022 est.	2023 est.
Direct obligations:			
11.1 Personnel compensation: Full-time permanent	12	15	17
12.1 Civilian personnel benefits	5	6	9
23.1 Rental payments to GSA	1	1	1
25.2 Other services from non-Federal sources	4	16	19
31.0 Equipment	1	2	4
41.0 Grants, subsidies, and contributions	223	977	1,096
99.9 Total new obligations, unexpired accounts	246	1,017	1,146

Employment Summary

Identification code 014–5015–0–2–999	2021 actual	2022 est.	2023 est.
1001 Direct civilian full-time equivalent employment	113	100	115

PAYMENTS TO STATES IN LIEU OF COAL FEE RECEIPTS

Program and Financing (in millions of dollars)

Identification code 014–1803–0–1–999	2021 actual	2022 est.	2023 est.
Obligations by program activity:			
0003 In Lieu Payments to Certified States and Tribes	39	36	27
0900 Total new obligations, unexpired accounts (object class 41.0)	39	36	27
Budgetary resources:			
Unobligated balance:			
1000 Unobligated balance brought forward, Oct 1	2	4	12
1021 Recoveries of prior year unpaid obligations	3	8	8
1070 Unobligated balance (total)	5	12	20
Budget authority:			
Appropriations, mandatory:			
1200 Appropriation	40	38	29
1230 Appropriations and/or unobligated balance of appropriations permanently reduced	–2	–2	–2
1260 Appropriations, mandatory (total)	38	36	27
1930 Total budgetary resources available	43	48	47
Memorandum (non-add) entries:			
1941 Unexpired unobligated balance, end of year	4	12	20
Change in obligated balance:			
Unpaid obligations:			
3000 Unpaid obligations, brought forward, Oct 1	403	354	271
3010 New obligations, unexpired accounts	39	36	27
3020 Outlays (gross)	–85	–111	–84
3040 Recoveries of prior year unpaid obligations, unexpired	–3	–8	–8
3050 Unpaid obligations, end of year	354	271	206
Memorandum (non-add) entries:			
3100 Obligated balance, start of year	403	354	271

Land and Minerals Management—Continued
Federal Funds—Continued

PAYMENTS TO STATES IN LIEU OF COAL FEE RECEIPTS—Continued

Program and Financing—Continued

Identification code 014–1803–0–1–999		2021 actual	2022 est.	2023 est.
3200	Obligated balance, end of year	354	271	206
	Budget authority and outlays, net:			
	Mandatory:			
4090	Budget authority, gross	38	36	27
	Outlays, gross:			
4101	Outlays from mandatory balances	85	111	84
4180	Budget authority, net (total)	38	36	27
4190	Outlays, net (total)	85	111	84

The Surface Mining Reclamation and Enforcement Act of 1977 (30 U.S.C. 1243), as amended, authorizes mandatory Treasury payments to all States and Tribes equivalent to their share of the accumulated balance of the Abandoned Mine Reclamation Fund. The payments also return half of annual coal fee collections to States and Tribes that have certified completion of their abandoned coal mine reclamation programs.

SUPPLEMENTAL PAYMENTS TO UMWA PLANS

Program and Financing (in millions of dollars)

Identification code 014–1804–0–1–999		2021 actual	2022 est.	2023 est.
	Obligations by program activity:			
0001	Supplemental Payments to UMWA Benefit Plans	388	331	340
0002	Payments to the 1974 UMWA Pension Plan	322	381	381
0900	Total new obligations, unexpired accounts (object class 25.2)	710	712	721
	Budgetary resources:			
	Budget authority:			
	Appropriations, mandatory:			
1200	Appropriation	710	712	721
1930	Total budgetary resources available	710	712	721
	Change in obligated balance:			
	Unpaid obligations:			
3010	New obligations, unexpired accounts	710	712	721
3020	Outlays (gross)	–710	–712	–721
	Budget authority and outlays, net:			
	Mandatory:			
4090	Budget authority, gross	710	712	721
	Outlays, gross:			
4100	Outlays from new mandatory authority	710	712	721
4180	Budget authority, net (total)	710	712	721
4190	Outlays, net (total)	710	712	721

The Surface Mining Reclamation and Enforcement Act of 1977 (30 U.S.C. 1243), as amended by the Tax Relief and Health Care Act of 2006 (Public Law 109–432), the Bipartisan Miners Act of 2019 (Division M of Public Law 116–94), and the American Miner Benefits Improvement Act of 2020 (Division Y of Public Law 116–260), authorizes mandatory Treasury payments to three United Mine Workers of America (UMWA) retiree health benefit plans (the Combined Benefit Fund, the 1992 Plan, and the 1993 Plan), to the extent that other Federal funding sources do not meet the plans' expenditure needs, and to the 1974 UMWA Pension Plan, subject to certain limitations. Interest earned on Abandoned Mine Land trust fund balances is available for transfer to cover funding shortfalls in the health benefit plans; unobligated balances in the Fund are used to generate interest for this purpose.

WATER AND SCIENCE

BUREAU OF RECLAMATION

Appropriations to the Bureau of Reclamation are made from the General Fund and from certain special funds in the Treasury. Projects funded from the General Fund include the Colorado River Basin Project and the Colorado River Storage Project, among others. Special funds include the Reclamation Fund, the Central Valley Project Restoration Fund, the Colorado River Dam Fund, and the Recreation, Entrance, and User Fee account. Non-Federal entities also advance funds for operation and maintenance and provide funds under the Contributed Funds Act.

Of the Bureau's special funds, the Reclamation Fund consists of repayments and other revenues from water and power users; receipts from the sale, lease, and rental of Federal lands; and certain oil and mineral revenues. It can finance program activities authorized under "Reclamation Law" that directly benefit the 17 Western States. The Central Valley Project Restoration Fund consists of revenues from project beneficiaries. The Colorado River Dam Fund generates revenue from the sale of Boulder Canyon Project power.

The 2023 estimates are summarized by source as follows (in millions of dollars):

	Total Appropriations	General Fund	Reclamation Fund	CVP Restoration Fund	Other
Appropriated Funds:					
Water and Related Resources (net)	1239	98	1141		
Transferred from Water and Related Resources to Lower and Upper Colorado Basin Funds and Aging Infrastructure	31	31			
California Bay-Delta Restoration	33	33			
Policy and Administration	65		65		
Working Capital Fund	0				
Loan Program	0	0			
Central Valley Project Restoration Fund	46			46	
Gross Current Authority	1414	162	1206	46	0
Central Valley Project Restoration Fund, current offset	–46			–46	
Net Current Authority	1368	162	1206	0	0
Loan Liquidating Account	–1				–1
Colorado River Dam Fund	106				106
Reclamation Trust Fund	1				1
San Joaquin Restoration Fund	14				14
Reclamation Water Settlements Fund	124				124
Federal Lands Recreation Enhancement Act	2				2
Aging Infrastruction Account	2				2
Total Permanent Appropriations	248	0	0	0	248
Grand Total	1616	162	1206	0	248

Federal Funds

BUREAU OF RECLAMATION

The following appropriations shall be expended to execute authorized functions of the Bureau of Reclamation:

WATER AND RELATED RESOURCES

(INCLUDING TRANSFERS OF FUNDS)

For management, development, and restoration of water and related natural resources and for related activities, including the operation, maintenance, and rehabilitation of reclamation and other facilities, participation in fulfilling related Federal responsibilities to Native Americans, and related grants to, and cooperative and other agreements with, State and local governments, federally recognized Indian Tribes, and others, $1,270,376,000, to remain available until expended, of which $22,165,000 shall be available for transfer to the Upper Colorado River Basin Fund and $7,584,000 shall be available for transfer to the Lower Colorado River Basin Development Fund; of which such amounts as may be necessary may be advanced to the Colorado River Dam Fund: Provided, That $500,000 shall be available for transfer into the Aging Infrastructure Account established by section 9603(d)(1) of the Omnibus Public Land Management Act of 2009, as amended (43 U.S.C. 510b(d)(1)): Provided further, That such transfers may be increased or decreased within the overall appropriation under this heading: Provided further, That of the total appropriated, the amount for program activities that can be financed by the Reclamation Fund, the Water Storage Enhancement Receipts account established by section 4011(e) of Public Law 114–322, or the Bureau of Reclamation special fee account established by 16 U.S.C. 6806 shall be derived from that Fund or ac-

WATER AND RELATED RESOURCES

〖For an additional amount for "Water and Related Resources", $210,000,000, to remain available until expended: *Provided*, That of such amount, $200,000,000 shall be available for activities to address drought, as determined by the Secretary of the Interior: *Provided further*, That of the amount made available under this heading in this Act, $10,000,000 shall be for fire remediation and suppression emergency assistance related to wildfires: *Provided further*, That the Commissioner shall provide a monthly report directly to the Committees on Appropriations of the House of Representatives and the Senate detailing the allocation and obligation of these funds, beginning not later than 60 days after the date of enactment of this Act.〗 *(Disaster Relief Supplemental Appropriations Act, 2022.)*

WATER AND RELATED RESOURCES

〖(INCLUDING TRANSFER OF FUNDS)〗

〖For an additional amount for "Water and Related Resources", $8,300,000,000, to remain available until expended: *Provided*, That $1,660,000,000, to remain available until expended, shall be made available for fiscal year 2022, $1,660,000,000, to remain available until expended, shall be made available for fiscal year 2023, $1,660,000,000, to remain available until expended, shall be made available for fiscal year 2024, $1,660,000,000, to remain available until expended, shall be made available for fiscal year 2025, $1,660,000,000, to remain available until expended, shall be made available for fiscal year 2026: *Provided further*, That of the amount provided under this heading in this Act for fiscal years 2022 through 2026, $1,150,000,000 shall be for water storage, groundwater storage, and conveyance projects in accordance with section 40902 of division D of this Act: *Provided further*, That of the funds identified in the preceding proviso, $100,000,000 shall be available for small surface water and ground water storage projects authorized in section 40903 of division D of this Act: *Provided further*, That of the amount provided under this heading in this Act, $3,200,000,000 shall be available for transfer into the Aging Infrastructure Account established by section 9603(d)(1) of the Omnibus Public Land Management Act of 2009, as amended (43 U.S.C. 510b(d)(1)): *Provided further*, That of the funds identified in the preceding proviso, $100,000,000 shall be made available for reserved or transferred works that have suffered a critical failure, in accordance with section 40904(a) of division D of this Act, and $100,000,000 shall be made available for dam rehabilitation, reconstruction, or replacement in accordance with section 40904(b) of division D of this Act: *Provided further*, That of the amount provided under this heading in this Act for fiscal years 2022 through 2026, $1,000,000,000 shall be for rural water projects that have been authorized by an Act of Congress before July 1, 2021, in accordance with the Reclamation Rural Water Supply Act of 2006 (43 U.S.C. 2401 et seq.): *Provided further*, That of the amount provided under this heading in this Act for fiscal years 2022 through 2026, $1,000,000,000 shall be for water recycling and reuse projects: *Provided further*, That of the funds identified in the preceding proviso, $550,000,000 shall be for water recycling and reuse projects authorized in accordance with the Reclamation Wastewater and Groundwater Study and Facilities Act (42 U.S.C. 390h et seq.), as described in section 40901(4)(A) of division D of this Act, and $450,000,000 shall be for large-scale water recycling and reuse projects in accordance with section 40905 of division D of this Act: *Provided further*, That of the amount provided under this heading in this Act for fiscal years 2022 through 2026, $250,000,000 shall be for water desalination projects in accordance with the Water Desalinization Act of 1996 (42 U.S.C. 10301 note; Public Law 104–298), as described in section 40901(5) of division D of this Act: *Provided further*, That of the amount provided under this heading in this Act for fiscal years 2022 through 2026, $500,000,000 shall be for the safety of dams program, in accordance with the Reclamation Safety of Dams Act of 1978 (43 U.S.C. 506 et seq.): *Provided further*, That of the amount provided under this heading in this Act for fiscal years 2022 through 2026, $400,000,000 shall be for WaterSMART Grants in accordance with section 9504 of the Omnibus Public Land Management Act of 2009 (42 U.S.C. 10364): *Provided further*, That of the funds identified in the preceding proviso, $100,000,000 shall be for projects that would improve the condition of a natural feature or nature-based feature, as described in section 40901(7) of division D of this Act: *Provided further*, That of the amount provided under this heading in this Act for fiscal years 2022 through 2026, $300,000,000 shall be for implementing the drought contingency plan consistent with the obligations of the Secretary under the Colorado River Drought Contingency Plan Authorization Act (Public Law 116–14; 133 Stat. 850), as described in section 40901(8) of division D of this Act: *Provided further*, That of the funds identified in the preceding proviso, $50,000,000 shall be for use in accordance with the Drought Contingency Plan for the Upper Colorado River Basin: *Provided further*, That of the amount provided under this heading in this Act for fiscal years 2022 through 2026, $100,000,000 shall be to provide financial assistance for watershed management projects in accordance with subtitle A of title VI of the Omnibus Public Land Management Act of 2009 (16 U.S.C. 1015 et seq.): *Provided further*, That of the amount provided under this heading in this Act for fiscal years 2022 through 2026, $250,000,000 shall be for design, study and construction of aquatic ecosystem restoration and protection projects in accordance with section 1109 of the Consolidated Appropriations Act, 2021: *Provided further*, That of the amount provided under this heading in this Act for fiscal years 2022 through 2026, $100,000,000 shall be for multi-benefit projects to improve watershed health in accordance with section 40907 of division D of this Act: *Provided further*, That of the amounts provided under this heading in this Act for fiscal years 2022 through 2026, $50,000,000 shall be for endangered species recovery and conservation programs in the Colorado River Basin in accordance with Public Law 106–392, title XVIII of Public Law 102–575, and subtitle E of title IX of Public Law 111–11: *Provided further*, That up to three percent of the amounts made available under this heading in this Act in each of fiscal years 2022 through 2026 shall be for program administration and policy expenses: *Provided further*, That not later than 60 days after the date of enactment of this Act, the Secretary of the Interior shall submit to the House and Senate Committees on Appropriations a detailed spend plan, including a list of project locations of the preceding proviso, to be funded for fiscal year 2022: *Provided further*, That beginning not later than 120 days after the enactment of this Act, the Secretary of the Interior shall provide a monthly report to the Committees on Appropriations of the House of Representatives and the Senate detailing the allocation and obligation of the funds provided under this heading in this Act: *Provided further*, That for fiscal years 2023 through 2026, as part of the annual budget submission of the President under section 1105(a) of title 31, United States Code, the Secretary of the Interior shall submit a detailed spend plan for those fiscal years, including a list of project locations: *Provided further*, That such amount is designated by the Congress as being for an emergency requirement pursuant to section 4112(a) of H. Con. Res. 71 (115th Congress), the concurrent resolution on the budget for fiscal year 2018, and to section 251(b) of the Balanced Budget and Emergency Deficit Control Act of 1985.〗 *(Infrastructure Investments and Jobs Appropriations Act.)*

Special and Trust Fund Receipts (in millions of dollars)

Identification code 014–0680–0–1–301		2021 actual	2022 est.	2023 est.
0100	Balance, start of year	158	233	311
	Receipts:			
	Current law:			
1130	Recreation Enhancement Fee Program	1	2	2
1130	Water Storage Enhancement Receipts	75	78	
1199	Total current law receipts	76	80	2
1999	Total receipts	76	80	2
2000	Total: Balances and receipts	234	313	313
	Appropriations:			
	Current law:			
2101	Water and Related Resources	–1	–2	–2
5099	Balance, end of year	233	311	311

Program and Financing (in millions of dollars)

Identification code 014–0680–0–1–301		2021 actual	2022 est.	2023 est.
	Obligations by program activity:			
0001	Facility operations	310	503	339
0002	Facility maintenance and rehabilitation	275	406	333
0003	Water and energy management and development	570	949	334
0004	Fish and wildlife management and development	195	258	188
0005	Land management and development	44	67	47
0006	Restoration of Federal Assets (Disaster Supplemental P.L. 116–20)		3	
0007	CARES Act Supplemental (P.L. 116–20)	7		
0008	2022 Disaster Supplemental (P.L. 117–43)		210	

Water and Science—Continued
Bureau of Reclamation—Continued

WATER AND RELATED RESOURCES—Continued
Program and Financing—Continued

Identification code 014–0680–0–1–301	2021 actual	2022 est.	2023 est.
0009 2022 Bipartisan Infrastructure Law (P.L. 117–58)	....	1,560	1,020
0100 Total direct program	1,401	3,956	2,261
0799 Total direct obligations	1,401	3,956	2,261
0801 Water and Related Resources (Reimbursable)	361	745	353
0900 Total new obligations, unexpired accounts	1,762	4,701	2,614
Budgetary resources:			
Unobligated balance:			
1000 Unobligated balance brought forward, Oct 1	1,453	1,634	575
1001 Discretionary unobligated balance brought fwd, Oct 1	1,385	1,009	....
1021 Recoveries of prior year unpaid obligations	61	....	....
1070 Unobligated balance (total)	1,514	1,634	575
Budget authority:			
Appropriations, discretionary:			
1100 Appropriation	242	235	129
1100 Appropriation - Disaster Relief Supplemental (P.L. 117–43)	....	210	....
1100 Appropriation - Bipartisan Infrastructure Law (P.L. 117–58)	....	1,660	....
1101 Appropriation (special or trust)	1,279	1,286	1,141
1120 Appropriations transferred to other accts [014–4081]	–39	....	–22
1120 Appropriations transferred to other accts [014–4079]	–6	....	–8
1120 Appropriations transferred to other acct [014–5668]	–26	....	....
1120 Appropriations transferred to other acct [014–5624]	....	–100	–1
1160 Appropriation, discretionary (total)	1,450	3,291	1,239
Advance appropriations, discretionary:			
1170 Advance appropriation - Bipartisan Infrastructure Law (P.L. 117–58)	....	....	1,660
1172 Advance appropriations transferred to other accounts [014–5624]	....	....	–640
1180 Advanced appropriation, discretionary (total)	....	....	1,020
Appropriations, mandatory:			
1201 Appropriation (special or trust fund)	1	2	2
Spending authority from offsetting collections, discretionary:			
1700 Collected	400	349	353
1701 Change in uncollected payments, Federal sources	32	....	....
1750 Spending auth from offsetting collections, disc (total)	432	349	353
1900 Budget authority (total)	1,883	3,642	2,614
1930 Total budgetary resources available	3,397	5,276	3,189
Memorandum (non-add) entries:			
1940 Unobligated balance expiring	–1	....	....
1941 Unexpired unobligated balance, end of year	1,634	575	575
Change in obligated balance:			
Unpaid obligations:			
3000 Unpaid obligations, brought forward, Oct 1	1,456	1,723	2,809
3010 New obligations, unexpired accounts	1,762	4,701	2,614
3020 Outlays (gross)	–1,434	–3,615	–3,025
3040 Recoveries of prior year unpaid obligations, unexpired	–61	....	....
3050 Unpaid obligations, end of year	1,723	2,809	2,398
Uncollected payments:			
3060 Uncollected pymts, Fed sources, brought forward, Oct 1	–329	–361	–361
3070 Change in uncollected pymts, Fed sources, unexpired	–32	....	....
3090 Uncollected pymts, Fed sources, end of year	–361	–361	–361
Memorandum (non-add) entries:			
3100 Obligated balance, start of year	1,127	1,362	2,448
3200 Obligated balance, end of year	1,362	2,448	2,037
Budget authority and outlays, net:			
Discretionary:			
4000 Budget authority, gross	1,882	3,640	2,612
Outlays, gross:			
4010 Outlays from new discretionary authority	504	2,184	1,567
4011 Outlays from discretionary balances	929	1,360	1,456
4020 Outlays, gross (total)	1,433	3,544	3,023
Offsets against gross budget authority and outlays:			
Offsetting collections (collected) from:			
4030 Federal sources	–203	–217	–216
4033 Non-Federal sources	–197	–132	–137
4040 Offsets against gross budget authority and outlays (total)	–400	–349	–353
Additional offsets against gross budget authority only:			
4050 Change in uncollected pymts, Fed sources, unexpired	–32	....	....
4070 Budget authority, net (discretionary)	1,450	3,291	2,259
4080 Outlays, net (discretionary)	1,033	3,195	2,670
Mandatory:			
4090 Budget authority, gross	1	2	2
Outlays, gross:			
4100 Outlays from new mandatory authority	....	2	....
4101 Outlays from mandatory balances	1	69	....
4110 Outlays, gross (total)	1	71	2
4180 Budget authority, net (total)	1,451	3,293	2,261
4190 Outlays, net (total)	1,034	3,266	2,672

Summary of Budget Authority and Outlays (in millions of dollars)

	2021 actual	2022 est.	2023 est.
Enacted/requested:			
Budget Authority	1,451	3,293	2,261
Outlays	1,034	3,266	2,672
Legislative proposal, subject to PAYGO:			
Budget Authority	....	....	34
Outlays	....	....	20
Total:			
Budget Authority	1,451	3,293	2,295
Outlays	1,034	3,266	2,692

The Water and Related Resources account supports the development, management, and restoration of water and related resources in the 17 Western States. The account includes funds to operate, maintain, and rehabilitate existing water and power facilities; protect public safety; conduct studies and perform work to improve the reliability of water and related resources; and provide financial assistance for various projects, water conservation, and fish and wildlife activities. Work funded through the account will support environmental justice for communities that have been left behind.

Work is done in partnership and cooperation with non-Federal entities and other Federal agencies to reduce conflict, facilitate solutions to complex water issues, and stretch limited water supplies.

Object Classification (in millions of dollars)

Identification code 014–0680–0–1–301	2021 actual	2022 est.	2023 est.
Direct obligations:			
Personnel compensation:			
11.1 Full-time permanent	174	228	234
11.3 Other than full-time permanent	3	3	3
11.5 Other personnel compensation	12	16	16
11.9 Total personnel compensation	189	247	253
12.1 Civilian personnel benefits	54	73	74
21.0 Travel and transportation of persons	3	3	3
23.1 Rental payments to GSA	1	1	1
23.2 Rental payments to others	1	1	1
23.3 Communications, utilities, and miscellaneous charges	15	15	16
25.2 Other services from non-Federal sources	758	3,226	1,517
26.0 Supplies and materials	9	9	9
31.0 Equipment	10	10	10
32.0 Land and structures	65	67	68
41.0 Grants, subsidies, and contributions	294	302	307
99.0 Direct obligations	1,399	3,954	2,259
99.0 Reimbursable obligations	361	745	353
99.5 Adjustment for rounding	2	2	2
99.9 Total new obligations, unexpired accounts	1,762	4,701	2,614

Employment Summary

Identification code 014–0680–0–1–301	2021 actual	2022 est.	2023 est.
1001 Direct civilian full-time equivalent employment	1,586	2,057	2,057
2001 Reimbursable civilian full-time equivalent employment	676	683	683
3001 Allocation account civilian full-time equivalent employment	2	5	5
3001 Allocation account civilian full-time equivalent employment	....	2	2
3001 Allocation account civilian full-time equivalent employment	8	....	....
3001 Allocation account civilian full-time equivalent employment	1	....	....
3001 Allocation account civilian full-time equivalent employment	1	....	....

WATER AND RELATED RESOURCES

(Legislative proposal, subject to PAYGO)

Program and Financing (in millions of dollars)

Identification code 014–0680–4–1–301	2021 actual	2022 est.	2023 est.
Obligations by program activity:			
0010 IWRSC O&MR			34
0100 Total direct program			34
0799 Total direct obligations			34
0900 Total new obligations, unexpired accounts (object class 25.2)			34
Budgetary resources:			
Budget authority:			
Appropriations, mandatory:			
1221 Appropriations transferred from other acct [014–2699]			34
1930 Total budgetary resources available			34
Change in obligated balance:			
Unpaid obligations:			
3010 New obligations, unexpired accounts			34
3020 Outlays (gross)			–20
3050 Unpaid obligations, end of year			14
Memorandum (non-add) entries:			
3200 Obligated balance, end of year			14
Budget authority and outlays, net:			
Mandatory:			
4090 Budget authority, gross			34
Outlays, gross:			
4100 Outlays from new mandatory authority			20
4180 Budget authority, net (total)			34
4190 Outlays, net (total)			20

The 2023 President's Budget Request proposes legislation to address the ongoing Operation, Maintenance, and Repair requirements associated with four enacted Indian Water Rights Settlements managed by the Bureau of Reclamation. These annual requirements are associated with the Ak Chin Indian Water Rights Settlement Project, the Animas-La Plata Project (Colorado Ute Settlement), the Columbia and Snake River Salmon Recovery Project (Nez Perce Settlement), and the Navajo-Gallup Water Supply Project.

The proposal provides $34.0 million annually over ten years to cover these requirements. Funds would be deposited into the Indian Water Rights Settlement Completion Fund and shall transfer to the Bureau of Reclamation for implementation.

CALIFORNIA BAY-DELTA RESTORATION

(INCLUDING TRANSFERS OF FUNDS)

For carrying out activities authorized by the Water Supply, Reliability, and Environmental Improvement Act, consistent with plans to be approved by the Secretary of the Interior, $33,000,000, to remain available until expended, of which such amounts as may be necessary to carry out such activities may be transferred to appropriate accounts of other participating Federal agencies to carry out authorized purposes: Provided, That funds appropriated herein may be used for the Federal share of the costs of CALFED Program management: Provided further, That CALFED implementation shall be carried out in a balanced manner with clear performance measures demonstrating concurrent progress in achieving the goals and objectives of the Program.

Note.—A full-year 2022 appropriation for this account was not enacted at the time the Budget was prepared; therefore, the Budget assumes this account is operating under the Continuing Appropriations Act, 2022 (Division A of Public Law 117–43, as amended). The amounts included for 2022 reflect the annualized level provided by the continuing resolution.

Program and Financing (in millions of dollars)

Identification code 014–0687–0–1–301	2021 actual	2022 est.	2023 est.
Obligations by program activity:			
0001 California Bay-Delta Restoration (Direct)	32	35	33
Budgetary resources:			
Unobligated balance:			
1000 Unobligated balance brought forward, Oct 1	1	2	
Budget authority:			
Appropriations, discretionary:			
1100 Appropriation	33	33	33
1930 Total budgetary resources available	34	35	33
Memorandum (non-add) entries:			
1941 Unexpired unobligated balance, end of year	2		
Change in obligated balance:			
Unpaid obligations:			
3000 Unpaid obligations, brought forward, Oct 1	70	71	76
3010 New obligations, unexpired accounts	32	35	33
3020 Outlays (gross)	–31	–30	–33
3050 Unpaid obligations, end of year	71	76	76
Memorandum (non-add) entries:			
3100 Obligated balance, start of year	70	71	76
3200 Obligated balance, end of year	71	76	76
Budget authority and outlays, net:			
Discretionary:			
4000 Budget authority, gross	33	33	33
Outlays, gross:			
4010 Outlays from new discretionary authority	10	12	12
4011 Outlays from discretionary balances	21	18	21
4020 Outlays, gross (total)	31	30	33
4180 Budget authority, net (total)	33	33	33
4190 Outlays, net (total)	31	30	33

This account funds activities that are consistent with the CALFED Bay-Delta Program, a collaborative effort involving State and Federal agencies and representatives of California's urban, agricultural, and environmental communities. The goals of the program are to improve fish and wildlife habitat, water supply reliability, water quality, and levee integrity in the San Francisco Bay-San Joaquin River Delta, the principal hub of California's water distribution system.

Object Classification (in millions of dollars)

Identification code 014–0687–0–1–301	2021 actual	2022 est.	2023 est.
Direct obligations:			
11.1 Personnel compensation: Full-time permanent	3	4	4
12.1 Civilian personnel benefits	1	1	1
25.2 Other services from non-Federal sources	8	9	7
41.0 Grants, subsidies, and contributions	19	20	20
99.0 Direct obligations	31	34	32
99.5 Adjustment for rounding	1	1	1
99.9 Total new obligations, unexpired accounts	32	35	33

Employment Summary

Identification code 014–0687–0–1–301	2021 actual	2022 est.	2023 est.
1001 Direct civilian full-time equivalent employment	25	31	31

TAOS SETTLEMENT FUND

Program and Financing (in millions of dollars)

Identification code 014–2638–0–1–301	2021 actual	2022 est.	2023 est.
Obligations by program activity:			
0001 Taos Settlement Fund (Direct)		1	
0900 Total new obligations, unexpired accounts (object class 25.2)		1	
Budgetary resources:			
Unobligated balance:			
1000 Unobligated balance brought forward, Oct 1	1	1	
1930 Total budgetary resources available	1	1	
Memorandum (non-add) entries:			
1941 Unexpired unobligated balance, end of year	1		

TAOS SETTLEMENT FUND—Continued
Program and Financing—Continued

Identification code 014–2638–0–1–301		2021 actual	2022 est.	2023 est.
	Change in obligated balance:			
	Unpaid obligations:			
3000	Unpaid obligations, brought forward, Oct 1	15	15	
3010	New obligations, unexpired accounts		1	
3020	Outlays (gross)		–16	
3050	Unpaid obligations, end of year	15		
	Memorandum (non-add) entries:			
3100	Obligated balance, start of year	15	15	
3200	Obligated balance, end of year	15		
	Budget authority and outlays, net:			
	Mandatory:			
	Outlays, gross:			
4101	Outlays from mandatory balances			16
4180	Budget authority, net (total)			
4190	Outlays, net (total)			16

This account covers certain expenses associated with Mutual-Benefit Projects funding authorized by the Taos Pueblo Indian Water Rights Settlement Act contained in Title V of the Claims Resolution Act of 2010 (Public Law 111–291).

AGING INFRASTRUCTURE ACCOUNT

Special and Trust Fund Receipts (in millions of dollars)

Identification code 014–5624–0–2–301		2021 actual	2022 est.	2023 est.
0100	Balance, start of year			
	Receipts:			
	Current law:			
1130	Repayment of Reimbursement Costs, Aging Infrastructure Account			2
2000	Total: Balances and receipts			2
	Appropriations:			
	Current law:			
2101	Aging Infrastructure Account			–2
5099	Balance, end of year			

Program and Financing (in millions of dollars)

Identification code 014–5624–0–2–301		2021 actual	2022 est.	2023 est.
	Obligations by program activity:			
0001	Aging Infrastructure Account (Direct)			3
0002	2022 Bipartisan Infrastructure Law (P.L. 117–58)		100	640
0900	Total new obligations, unexpired accounts (object class 25.2)		100	643
	Budgetary resources:			
	Budget authority:			
	Appropriations, discretionary:			
1121	Appropriations transferred from other acct [014–0680]		100	1
	Advance appropriations, discretionary:			
1173	Advance appropriations transferred from other accounts [014–0680]			640
	Appropriations, mandatory:			
1201	Appropriation (special or trust fund)			2
1900	Budget authority (total)		100	643
1930	Total budgetary resources available		100	643
	Change in obligated balance:			
	Unpaid obligations:			
3000	Unpaid obligations, brought forward, Oct 1			40
3010	New obligations, unexpired accounts		100	643
3020	Outlays (gross)		–60	–426
3050	Unpaid obligations, end of year		40	257
	Memorandum (non-add) entries:			
3100	Obligated balance, start of year			40
3200	Obligated balance, end of year		40	257

	Budget authority and outlays, net:			
	Discretionary:			
4000	Budget authority, gross		100	641
	Outlays, gross:			
4010	Outlays from new discretionary authority		60	385
4011	Outlays from discretionary balances			40
4020	Outlays, gross (total)		60	425
	Mandatory:			
4090	Budget authority, gross			2
	Outlays, gross:			
4100	Outlays from new mandatory authority			1
4180	Budget authority, net (total)		100	643
4190	Outlays, net (total)		60	426

This account provides funds to, and provides for the extended repayment of the funds by, a transferred works operating entity or project beneficiary responsible for repayment of reimbursable costs for the conduct of extraordinary operation and maintenance work at a project facility as authorized by Title XI of the Consolidated Appropriations Act, 2021 (Public Law 116–260) and Title IX of the Infrastructure Investment and Jobs Act, 2021 (Public Law 117–58).

RECLAMATION WATER SETTLEMENTS FUND

Special and Trust Fund Receipts (in millions of dollars)

Identification code 014–5593–0–2–301		2021 actual	2022 est.	2023 est.
0100	Balance, start of year			
	Receipts:			
	Current law:			
1130	Reclamation Water Settlements Fund	120	120	120
1140	Earnings on Investments, Reclamation Water Settlement Fund	1	4	4
1199	Total current law receipts	121	124	124
1999	Total receipts	121	124	124
2000	Total: Balances and receipts	121	124	124
	Appropriations:			
	Current law:			
2101	Reclamation Water Settlements Fund	–121	–124	–124
5099	Balance, end of year			

Program and Financing (in millions of dollars)

Identification code 014–5593–0–2–301		2021 actual	2022 est.	2023 est.
	Obligations by program activity:			
0001	Reclamation Water Settlements Fund (Direct)	19	178	190
	Budgetary resources:			
	Unobligated balance:			
1000	Unobligated balance brought forward, Oct 1	265	367	313
	Budget authority:			
	Appropriations, mandatory:			
1201	Appropriation (special or trust fund)	121	124	124
1930	Total budgetary resources available	386	491	437
	Memorandum (non-add) entries:			
1941	Unexpired unobligated balance, end of year	367	313	247
	Change in obligated balance:			
	Unpaid obligations:			
3000	Unpaid obligations, brought forward, Oct 1	16	18	71
3010	New obligations, unexpired accounts	19	178	190
3020	Outlays (gross)	–17	–125	–185
3050	Unpaid obligations, end of year	18	71	76
	Memorandum (non-add) entries:			
3100	Obligated balance, start of year	16	18	71
3200	Obligated balance, end of year	18	71	76
	Budget authority and outlays, net:			
	Mandatory:			
4090	Budget authority, gross	121	124	124
	Outlays, gross:			
4100	Outlays from new mandatory authority		53	48
4101	Outlays from mandatory balances	17	72	137
4110	Outlays, gross (total)	17	125	185

DEPARTMENT OF THE INTERIOR

Water and Science—Continued
Bureau of Reclamation—Continued   637

		2021 actual	2022 est.	2023 est.
4180	Budget authority, net (total)	121	124	124
4190	Outlays, net (total)	17	125	185
	Memorandum (non-add) entries:			
5000	Total investments, SOY: Federal securities: Par value	243	364	323
5001	Total investments, EOY: Federal securities: Par value	364	323	249

This account funds expenses associated with Indian water rights settlements under the Navajo-Gallup Water Supply Project, other projects as authorized by the Omnibus Public Land Management Act of 2009 (P.L. 111–11), the Claims Resolution Act of 2010 (P.L. 111–291), and the Water Infrastructure Improvements for the Nation Act of 2016 (P.L. 114–322). The Secretary may expend money from the Fund to implement a settlement agreement approved by the Congress that resolves, in whole or in part, litigation involving the United States, if the settlement agreement or implementing legislation requires the Bureau of Reclamation to provide financial assistance for, or plan, design, and construct: A) water supply infrastructure; or B) a project: (i) to rehabilitate a water delivery system to conserve water; or (ii) to restore fish and wildlife habitat or otherwise improve environmental conditions associated with or affected by, or located within the same river basin as a Federal reclamation project that is in existence on the date of enactment of this Act.

Object Classification (in millions of dollars)

Identification code 014–5593–0–2–301	2021 actual	2022 est.	2023 est.
Direct obligations:			
25.2 Other services from non-Federal sources	....	5	5
32.0 Land and structures	19	19	19
41.0 Grants, subsidies, and contributions	....	154	166
99.9 Total new obligations, unexpired accounts	19	178	190

BLACKFEET WATER SETTLEMENT IMPLEMENTATION FUND

Program and Financing (in millions of dollars)

Identification code 014–5668–0–2–301	2021 actual	2022 est.	2023 est.
Budgetary resources:			
Unobligated balance:			
1000 Unobligated balance brought forward, Oct 1	44	70	70
Budget authority:			
Appropriations, discretionary:			
1121 Appropriations transferred from other acct [014–0680]	26	....	....
1930 Total budgetary resources available	70	70	70
Memorandum (non-add) entries:			
1941 Unexpired unobligated balance, end of year	70	70	70
Budget authority and outlays, net:			
Discretionary:			
4000 Budget authority, gross	26	....	....
4180 Budget authority, net (total)	26	....	....
4190 Outlays, net (total)	....	....	....
Memorandum (non-add) entries:			
5000 Total investments, SOY: Federal securities: Par value	44	70	70
5001 Total investments, EOY: Federal securities: Par value	70	70	70

This account covers multiple construction components associated with the Blackfeet Water Rights Settlement Act contained in Title III, Subtitle G of the Water Infrastructure Improvements for the Nation Act of 2016 (Public Law 114–322).

RECLAMATION FUND

Special and Trust Fund Receipts (in millions of dollars)

Identification code 014–5000–0–2–301	2021 actual	2022 est.	2023 est.
0100 Balance, start of year	17,689	18,114	18,982
Receipts:			
Current law:			
1130 Reclamation Fund, Miscellaneous Interest	17	12	12
1130 Reclamation Fund, Royalties on Natural Resources	1,369	2,135	1,974
1130 Reclamation Fund, Sale of Timber and Other Products	1	1	1
1130 Reclamation Fund, Other Proprietary Receipts from the Public	179	71	71
1130 Reclamation Fund, Sale of Public Domain	17	14	14
1130 Reclamation Fund, All Other, Sale of Electric Energy, Bonneville Power Administration	1	5	2
1130 Reclamation Fund, All Other, Sale of Power and Other Utilities (WAPA)	270	65	81
1199 Total current law receipts	1,854	2,303	2,155
1999 Total receipts	1,854	2,303	2,155
2000 Total: Balances and receipts	19,543	20,417	21,137
Appropriations:			
Current law:			
2101 Water and Related Resources	–1,279	–1,286	–1,141
2101 Policy and Administration	–60	–60	–65
2101 Construction, Rehabilitation, Operation and Maintenance, Western Area Power Administration	–89	–89	–99
2199 Total current law appropriations	–1,428	–1,435	–1,305
2999 Total appropriations	–1,428	–1,435	–1,305
Special and trust fund receipts returned:			
3010 Policy and Administration	1	....	....
3010 Policy and Administration	1	....	....
5098 Reconciliation adjustment	–3	....	....
5099 Balance, end of year	18,114	18,982	19,832

This fund is derived from repayments and other revenues from water and power users, together with certain receipts from the sale, lease, and rental of Federal lands in the 17 Western States and certain oil and mineral revenues. Receipts deposited are made available by the Congress through annual appropriations acts.

POLICY AND ADMINISTRATION

For expenses necessary for policy, administration, and related functions in the Office of the Commissioner, the Denver office, and offices in the six regions of the Bureau of Reclamation, to remain available until September 30, 2024, $65,079,000, to be derived from the Reclamation Fund and be nonreimbursable as provided in 43 U.S.C. 377: Provided, That no part of any other appropriation in this Act shall be available for activities or functions budgeted as policy and administration expenses.

Note.—A full-year 2022 appropriation for this account was not enacted at the time the Budget was prepared; therefore, the Budget assumes this account is operating under the Continuing Appropriations Act, 2022 (Division A of Public Law 117–43, as amended). The amounts included for 2022 reflect the annualized level provided by the continuing resolution.

Program and Financing (in millions of dollars)

Identification code 014–5065–0–2–301	2021 actual	2022 est.	2023 est.
Obligations by program activity:			
0001 Policy and Administration (Direct)	55	76	65
0002 CARES Act Supplemental (P.L. 1116–138)	6	....	....
0900 Total new obligations, unexpired accounts	61	76	65
Budgetary resources:			
Unobligated balance:			
1000 Unobligated balance brought forward, Oct 1	16	16	....
1021 Recoveries of prior year unpaid obligations	1	....	....
1070 Unobligated balance (total)	17	16	....
Budget authority:			
Appropriations, discretionary:			
1101 Appropriation (special or trust)	60	60	65
1930 Total budgetary resources available	77	76	65
Memorandum (non-add) entries:			
1941 Unexpired unobligated balance, end of year	16	....	....
Special and non-revolving trust funds:			
1950 Other balances withdrawn and returned to unappropriated receipts	1	....	....
1952 Expired unobligated balance, start of year	2	1	1
1953 Expired unobligated balance, end of year	1	1	1
1954 Unobligated balance canceling	1	....	....
Change in obligated balance:			
Unpaid obligations:			
3000 Unpaid obligations, brought forward, Oct 1	8	10	8

638 Water and Science—Continued
Bureau of Reclamation—Continued

THE BUDGET FOR FISCAL YEAR 2023

POLICY AND ADMINISTRATION—Continued

Program and Financing—Continued

Identification code 014–5065–0–2–301	2021 actual	2022 est.	2023 est.
3010 New obligations, unexpired accounts	61	76	65
3020 Outlays (gross)	–58	–78	–64
3040 Recoveries of prior year unpaid obligations, unexpired	–1		
3050 Unpaid obligations, end of year	10	8	9
Memorandum (non-add) entries:			
3100 Obligated balance, start of year	8	10	8
3200 Obligated balance, end of year	10	8	9
Budget authority and outlays, net:			
Discretionary:			
4000 Budget authority, gross	60	60	65
Outlays, gross:			
4010 Outlays from new discretionary authority	45	51	55
4011 Outlays from discretionary balances	13	27	9
4020 Outlays, gross (total)	58	78	64
4180 Budget authority, net (total)	60	60	65
4190 Outlays, net (total)	58	78	64

This account supports the direction and management of all Reclamation activities as performed by the Commissioner's office and the six regional offices. Charges attributable to individual projects or specific beneficiaries, including the costs of related administrative and technical services, are covered under other Bureau of Reclamation accounts.

Object Classification (in millions of dollars)

Identification code 014–5065–0–2–301	2021 actual	2022 est.	2023 est.
Direct obligations:			
Personnel compensation:			
11.1 Full-time permanent	26	41	42
11.3 Other than full-time permanent	1	1	1
11.5 Other personnel compensation	1	1	1
11.9 Total personnel compensation	28	43	44
12.1 Civilian personnel benefits	8	12	12
23.1 Rental payments to GSA	1	1	1
25.2 Other services from non-Federal sources	23	19	7
99.0 Direct obligations	60	75	64
99.5 Adjustment for rounding	1	1	1
99.9 Total new obligations, unexpired accounts	61	76	65

Employment Summary

Identification code 014–5065–0–2–301	2021 actual	2022 est.	2023 est.
1001 Direct civilian full-time equivalent employment	175	276	276

CENTRAL VALLEY PROJECT RESTORATION FUND

For carrying out the programs, projects, plans, habitat restoration, improvement, and acquisition provisions of the Central Valley Project Improvement Act, such sums as may be collected in fiscal year 2023 in the Central Valley Project Restoration Fund pursuant to sections 3407(d), 3404(c)(3), and 3405(f) of Public Law 102–575, to remain available until expended: Provided, That the Bureau of Reclamation is directed to assess and collect the full amount of the additional mitigation and restoration payments authorized by section 3407(d) of Public Law 102–575: Provided further, That none of the funds made available under this heading may be used for the acquisition or leasing of water for in-stream purposes if the water is already committed to in-stream purposes by a court adopted decree or order.

Note.—A full-year 2022 appropriation for this account was not enacted at the time the Budget was prepared; therefore, the Budget assumes this account is operating under the Continuing Appropriations Act, 2022 (Division A of Public Law 117–43, as amended). The amounts included for 2022 reflect the annualized level provided by the continuing resolution.

Special and Trust Fund Receipts (in millions of dollars)

Identification code 014–5173–0–2–301	2021 actual	2022 est.	2023 est.
0100 Balance, start of year	6		
Receipts:			
Current law:			
1130 Central Valley Project Restoration Fund, Revenue	39	56	46
2000 Total: Balances and receipts	45	56	46
Appropriations:			
Current law:			
2101 Central Valley Project Restoration Fund	–45	–56	–46
5099 Balance, end of year			

Program and Financing (in millions of dollars)

Identification code 014–5173–0–2–301	2021 actual	2022 est.	2023 est.
Obligations by program activity:			
0001 Central Valley Project Restoration Fund (Direct)	43	60	46
Budgetary resources:			
Unobligated balance:			
1000 Unobligated balance brought forward, Oct 1		4	
1021 Recoveries of prior year unpaid obligations	2		
1070 Unobligated balance (total)	2	4	
Budget authority:			
Appropriations, discretionary:			
1101 Appropriation (special fund, restoration fund, 3407(d))	45	56	46
1930 Total budgetary resources available	47	60	46
Memorandum (non-add) entries:			
1941 Unexpired unobligated balance, end of year	4		
Change in obligated balance:			
Unpaid obligations:			
3000 Unpaid obligations, brought forward, Oct 1	113	113	81
3010 New obligations, unexpired accounts	43	60	46
3020 Outlays (gross)	–41	–92	–52
3040 Recoveries of prior year unpaid obligations, unexpired	–2		
3050 Unpaid obligations, end of year	113	81	75
Memorandum (non-add) entries:			
3100 Obligated balance, start of year	113	113	81
3200 Obligated balance, end of year	113	81	75
Budget authority and outlays, net:			
Discretionary:			
4000 Budget authority, gross	45	56	46
Outlays, gross:			
4010 Outlays from new discretionary authority	9	20	16
4011 Outlays from discretionary balances	32	72	36
4020 Outlays, gross (total)	41	92	52
4180 Budget authority, net (total)	45	56	46
4190 Outlays, net (total)	41	92	52

This fund was established to carry out the provisions of the Central Valley Project Improvement Act—to provide funding from project beneficiaries for habitat restoration, improvement and acquisition, and other fish and wildlife restoration activities in the Central Valley Project area of California. Resources are derived from donations, revenues from voluntary water transfers, and tiered water pricing. The account is also financed through additional mitigation and restoration payments collected on an annual basis from project beneficiaries.

Object Classification (in millions of dollars)

Identification code 014–5173–0–2–301	2021 actual	2022 est.	2023 est.
Direct obligations:			
11.1 Personnel compensation: Full-time permanent	2	2	2
12.1 Civilian personnel benefits	1	1	1
23.3 Communications, utilities, and miscellaneous charges	6	6	6
25.2 Other services from non-Federal sources	13	29	15
32.0 Land and structures	4	4	4
41.0 Grants, subsidies, and contributions	16	17	17
99.0 Direct obligations	42	59	45
99.5 Adjustment for rounding	1	1	1
99.9 Total new obligations, unexpired accounts	43	60	46

DEPARTMENT OF THE INTERIOR

Water and Science—Continued
Bureau of Reclamation—Continued

Employment Summary

Identification code 014–5173–0–2–301	2021 actual	2022 est.	2023 est.
1001 Direct civilian full-time equivalent employment	16	18	18

COLORADO RIVER DAM FUND, BOULDER CANYON PROJECT

Special and Trust Fund Receipts (in millions of dollars)

Identification code 014–5656–0–2–301	2021 actual	2022 est.	2023 est.
0100 Balance, start of year			
Receipts:			
Current law:			
1130 Revenues, Colorado River Dam Fund, Boulder Canyon Project	83	104	106
2000 Total: Balances and receipts	83	104	106
Appropriations:			
Current law:			
2101 Colorado River Dam Fund, Boulder Canyon Project	–83	–104	–106
5099 Balance, end of year			

Program and Financing (in millions of dollars)

Identification code 014–5656–0–2–301	2021 actual	2022 est.	2023 est.
Obligations by program activity:			
0001 Facility operations	57	77	71
0002 Facility maintenance and rehabilitation	18	20	19
0003 Water and Energy Management and Development	11	13	13
0900 Total new obligations, unexpired accounts	86	110	103
Budgetary resources:			
Unobligated balance:			
1000 Unobligated balance brought forward, Oct 1	65	64	57
1021 Recoveries of prior year unpaid obligations	3		
1022 Capital transfer of unobligated balances to general fund		–1	–1
1070 Unobligated balance (total)	68	63	56
Budget authority:			
Appropriations, mandatory:			
1201 Appropriation (special or trust fund)	83	104	106
1240 Capital transfer of appropriations to general fund	–1		
1260 Appropriations, mandatory (total)	82	104	106
1930 Total budgetary resources available	150	167	162
Memorandum (non-add) entries:			
1941 Unexpired unobligated balance, end of year	64	57	59
Change in obligated balance:			
Unpaid obligations:			
3000 Unpaid obligations, brought forward, Oct 1	16	26	44
3010 New obligations, unexpired accounts	86	110	103
3020 Outlays (gross)	–73	–92	–102
3040 Recoveries of prior year unpaid obligations, unexpired	–3		
3050 Unpaid obligations, end of year	26	44	45
Memorandum (non-add) entries:			
3100 Obligated balance, start of year	16	26	44
3200 Obligated balance, end of year	26	44	45
Budget authority and outlays, net:			
Mandatory:			
4090 Budget authority, gross	82	104	106
Outlays, gross:			
4100 Outlays from new mandatory authority		59	60
4101 Outlays from mandatory balances	73	33	42
4110 Outlays, gross (total)	73	92	102
4180 Budget authority, net (total)	82	104	106
4190 Outlays, net (total)	73	92	102

Revenues from the sale of Boulder Canyon Project power are placed in this Fund and are available without further appropriation to pay the operation and maintenance costs of the project including those of the Western Area Power Administration for power marketing, transmission, operation, maintenance, and rehabilitation; to pay interest on amounts advanced from the Treasury; to pay annually not more than $300,000 each to Arizona and Nevada; and to repay advances from the Treasury for construction and other purposes. The rates charged for Boulder Canyon power also include certain amounts for transfer to the Lower Colorado River Basin Development Fund.

Object Classification (in millions of dollars)

Identification code 014–5656–0–2–301	2021 actual	2022 est.	2023 est.
Direct obligations:			
Personnel compensation:			
11.1 Full-time permanent	20	25	26
11.5 Other personnel compensation	2	3	3
11.9 Total personnel compensation	22	28	29
12.1 Civilian personnel benefits	6	8	8
25.2 Other services from non-Federal sources	54	70	62
26.0 Supplies and materials	1	1	1
41.0 Grants, subsidies, and contributions	1	1	1
99.0 Direct obligations	84	108	101
99.5 Adjustment for rounding	2	2	2
99.9 Total new obligations, unexpired accounts	86	110	103

Employment Summary

Identification code 014–5656–0–2–301	2021 actual	2022 est.	2023 est.
1001 Direct civilian full-time equivalent employment	180	218	218

SAN JOAQUIN RESTORATION FUND

Special and Trust Fund Receipts (in millions of dollars)

Identification code 014–5537–0–2–301	2021 actual	2022 est.	2023 est.
0100 Balance, start of year			
Receipts:			
Current law:			
1130 San Joaquin River Restoration Fund Receipts	3	13	14
2000 Total: Balances and receipts	3	13	14
Appropriations:			
Current law:			
2101 San Joaquin Restoration Fund	–3	–13	–14
5099 Balance, end of year			

Program and Financing (in millions of dollars)

Identification code 014–5537–0–2–301	2021 actual	2022 est.	2023 est.
Obligations by program activity:			
0001 San Joaquin Restoration Fund (Direct)	3	253	14
Budgetary resources:			
Unobligated balance:			
1000 Unobligated balance brought forward, Oct 1	240	240	
Budget authority:			
Appropriations, mandatory:			
1201 Appropriation (special or trust fund)	3	13	14
1900 Budget authority (total)	3	13	14
1930 Total budgetary resources available	243	253	14
Memorandum (non-add) entries:			
1941 Unexpired unobligated balance, end of year	240		
Change in obligated balance:			
Unpaid obligations:			
3000 Unpaid obligations, brought forward, Oct 1	3	3	8
3010 New obligations, unexpired accounts	3	253	14
3020 Outlays (gross)	–3	–248	–13
3050 Unpaid obligations, end of year	3	8	9
Memorandum (non-add) entries:			
3100 Obligated balance, start of year	3	3	8
3200 Obligated balance, end of year	3	8	9
Budget authority and outlays, net:			
Mandatory:			
4090 Budget authority, gross	3	13	14
Outlays, gross:			
4100 Outlays from new mandatory authority		4	5

Water and Science—Continued
Bureau of Reclamation—Continued

SAN JOAQUIN RESTORATION FUND—Continued

Program and Financing—Continued

Identification code 014–5537–0–2–301		2021 actual	2022 est.	2023 est.
4101	Outlays from mandatory balances	3	244	8
4110	Outlays, gross (total)	3	248	13
4180	Budget authority, net (total)	3	13	14
4190	Outlays, net (total)	3	248	13

This account receives funding (user fees and repayment receipts) from the Friant Division long-term water contractors and other Federal and non-Federal sources to implement the provisions described in the settlement for the National Resources Defense Council et al. v. Rodgers lawsuit. The settlement's two primary goals are: 1) to restore and maintain fish populations in "good condition" in the main stem of the San Joaquin River below Friant Dam to the confluence of the Merced River, including naturally reproducing and self-sustaining populations of salmon and other fish; and 2) to reduce or avoid adverse water supply impacts to all of the Friant Division long-term contractors that may result from the Interim Flows and Restoration Flows provided for in the Settlement.

Object Classification (in millions of dollars)

Identification code 014–5537–0–2–301		2021 actual	2022 est.	2023 est.
	Direct obligations:			
11.1	Personnel compensation: Full-time permanent		3	3
12.1	Civilian personnel benefits		1	1
25.2	Other services from non-Federal sources	2	218	7
41.0	Grants, subsidies, and contributions		30	2
99.0	Direct obligations	2	252	13
99.5	Adjustment for rounding	1	1	1
99.9	Total new obligations, unexpired accounts	3	253	14

Employment Summary

Identification code 014–5537–0–2–301		2021 actual	2022 est.	2023 est.
1001	Direct civilian full-time equivalent employment	2	22	22

LOWER COLORADO RIVER BASIN DEVELOPMENT FUND

Program and Financing (in millions of dollars)

Identification code 014–4079–0–3–301		2021 actual	2022 est.	2023 est.
	Obligations by program activity:			
0801	Facility operation	62	60	62
0802	Water & energy management & development	40	75	48
0900	Total new obligations, unexpired accounts	102	135	110
	Budgetary resources:			
	Unobligated balance:			
1000	Unobligated balance brought forward, Oct 1	289	302	284
1001	Discretionary unobligated balance brought fwd, Oct 1	1	1	
1021	Recoveries of prior year unpaid obligations	26		
1022	Capital transfer of unobligated balances to general fund		–1	–1
1070	Unobligated balance (total)	315	301	283
	Budget authority:			
	Appropriations, discretionary:			
1121	Appropriations transferred from other acct [014–0680]	6		8
	Spending authority from offsetting collections, mandatory:			
1800	Collected	91	118	89
1801	Change in uncollected payments, Federal sources	–7		
1802	Offsetting collections (previously unavailable)		1	1
1823	New and/or unobligated balance of spending authority from offsetting collections temporarily reduced	–1	–1	
1850	Spending auth from offsetting collections, mand (total)	83	118	90
1900	Budget authority (total)	89	118	98
1930	Total budgetary resources available	404	419	381
	Memorandum (non-add) entries:			
1941	Unexpired unobligated balance, end of year	302	284	271
	Change in obligated balance:			
	Unpaid obligations:			
3000	Unpaid obligations, brought forward, Oct 1	42	26	75
3010	New obligations, unexpired accounts	102	135	110
3020	Outlays (gross)	–92	–86	–124
3040	Recoveries of prior year unpaid obligations, unexpired	–26		
3050	Unpaid obligations, end of year	26	75	61
	Uncollected payments:			
3060	Uncollected pymts, Fed sources, brought forward, Oct 1	–7		
3070	Change in uncollected pymts, Fed sources, unexpired	7		
	Memorandum (non-add) entries:			
3100	Obligated balance, start of year	35	26	75
3200	Obligated balance, end of year	26	75	61
	Budget authority and outlays, net:			
	Discretionary:			
4000	Budget authority, gross	6		8
	Outlays, gross:			
4010	Outlays from new discretionary authority			5
4011	Outlays from discretionary balances	8		
4020	Outlays, gross (total)	8		5
	Mandatory:			
4090	Budget authority, gross	83	118	90
	Outlays, gross:			
4100	Outlays from new mandatory authority		41	31
4101	Outlays from mandatory balances	84	45	88
4110	Outlays, gross (total)	84	86	119
	Offsets against gross budget authority and outlays:			
	Offsetting collections (collected) from:			
4120	Federal sources	–15		
4121	Interest on Federal securities		–1	–1
4123	Non-Federal sources	–76	–117	–88
4130	Offsets against gross budget authority and outlays (total)	–91	–118	–89
	Additional offsets against gross budget authority only:			
4140	Change in uncollected pymts, Fed sources, unexpired	7		
4160	Budget authority, net (mandatory)	–1		1
4170	Outlays, net (mandatory)	–7	–32	30
4180	Budget authority, net (total)	5		9
4190	Outlays, net (total)	1	–32	35
	Memorandum (non-add) entries:			
5000	Total investments, SOY: Federal securities: Par value	323	326	386
5001	Total investments, EOY: Federal securities: Par value	326	386	446
5090	Unexpired unavailable balance, SOY: Offsetting collections		1	1
5092	Unexpired unavailable balance, EOY: Offsetting collections	1	1	

Ongoing construction costs of the Central Arizona project are financed through appropriations transferred to this Fund. Revenues from the operation and repayment, including interest, of project facilities are available without further appropriation. A portion of the revenues from the Boulder Canyon power and Parker-Davis projects are also transferred to this Fund. Use of the revenues are authorized for operation and maintenance expenses, for a share of Colorado River salinity control projects, and for other purposes defined in the Colorado River Basin Project Act as amended by the Arizona Water Settlements Act, Public Law 108–451.

Object Classification (in millions of dollars)

Identification code 014–4079–0–3–301		2021 actual	2022 est.	2023 est.
	Reimbursable obligations:			
11.1	Personnel compensation: Full-time permanent	3	3	3
12.1	Civilian personnel benefits	1	1	1
32.0	Land and structures	23	31	25
41.0	Grants, subsidies, and contributions	74	99	80
99.0	Reimbursable obligations	101	134	109
99.5	Adjustment for rounding	1	1	1
99.9	Total new obligations, unexpired accounts	102	135	110

Employment Summary

Identification code 014–4079–0–3–301		2021 actual	2022 est.	2023 est.
2001	Reimbursable civilian full-time equivalent employment	23	22	22

DEPARTMENT OF THE INTERIOR

UPPER COLORADO RIVER BASIN FUND

Program and Financing (in millions of dollars)

Identification code 014–4081–0–3–301		2021 actual	2022 est.	2023 est.
	Obligations by program activity:			
0801	Facility operation	76	75	63
0802	Facility maintenance & rehabilitation	39	30	33
0803	Water & energy management & development	62	68	6
0804	Fish & wildlife management & development	28	43	36
0805	Land management & development	5	5	1
0900	Total new obligations, unexpired accounts	210	221	139
	Budgetary resources:			
	Unobligated balance:			
1000	Unobligated balance brought forward, Oct 1	158	201	106
1001	Discretionary unobligated balance brought fwd, Oct 1	2	2	
1021	Recoveries of prior year unpaid obligations	2		
1022	Capital transfer of unobligated balances to general fund		–4	–4
1070	Unobligated balance (total)	160	197	102
	Budget authority:			
	Appropriations, discretionary:			
1121	Appropriations transferred from other acct [014–0680]	39		22
	Spending authority from offsetting collections, discretionary:			
1711	Spending authority from offsetting collections transferred from other accounts [089–4452]		21	
	Spending authority from offsetting collections, mandatory:			
1800	Collected	210	109	117
1811	Spending authority from offsetting collections transferred from other accounts [089–4452]	21		
1820	Capital transfer of spending authority from offsetting collections to general fund	–19		
1850	Spending auth from offsetting collections, mand (total)	212	109	117
1900	Budget authority (total)	251	130	139
1930	Total budgetary resources available	411	327	241
	Memorandum (non-add) entries:			
1941	Unexpired unobligated balance, end of year	201	106	102
	Change in obligated balance:			
	Unpaid obligations:			
3000	Unpaid obligations, brought forward, Oct 1	278	248	188
3010	New obligations, unexpired accounts	210	221	139
3020	Outlays (gross)	–238	–281	–131
3040	Recoveries of prior year unpaid obligations, unexpired	–2		
3050	Unpaid obligations, end of year	248	188	196
	Memorandum (non-add) entries:			
3100	Obligated balance, start of year	278	248	188
3200	Obligated balance, end of year	248	188	196
	Budget authority and outlays, net:			
	Discretionary:			
4000	Budget authority, gross	39	21	22
	Outlays, gross:			
4010	Outlays from new discretionary authority		13	13
4011	Outlays from discretionary balances	81	69	8
4020	Outlays, gross (total)	81	82	21
	Mandatory:			
4090	Budget authority, gross	212	109	117
	Outlays, gross:			
4100	Outlays from new mandatory authority		33	35
4101	Outlays from mandatory balances	157	166	75
4110	Outlays, gross (total)	157	199	110
	Offsets against gross budget authority and outlays:			
	Offsetting collections (collected) from:			
4120	Federal sources	–85	–1	–1
4123	Non-Federal sources	–125	–108	–116
4130	Offsets against gross budget authority and outlays (total)	–210	–109	–117
4160	Budget authority, net (mandatory)	2		
4170	Outlays, net (mandatory)	–53	90	–7
4180	Budget authority, net (total)	41	21	22
4190	Outlays, net (total)	28	172	14

Ongoing construction costs of the Colorado River Storage project are financed through appropriations transferred to this account. Revenues from the operation of project facilities are available without further appropriation for operation and maintenance expenses and for capital repayment to the General Fund.

Water and Science—Continued
Bureau of Reclamation—Continued

Object Classification (in millions of dollars)

Identification code 014–4081–0–3–301		2021 actual	2022 est.	2023 est.
	Reimbursable obligations:			
	Personnel compensation:			
11.1	Full-time permanent	24	11	11
11.5	Other personnel compensation	2	1	1
11.9	Total personnel compensation	26	12	12
12.1	Civilian personnel benefits	7	3	3
32.0	Land and structures	64	74	44
41.0	Grants, subsidies, and contributions	112	131	79
99.0	Reimbursable obligations	209	220	138
99.5	Adjustment for rounding	1	1	1
99.9	Total new obligations, unexpired accounts	210	221	139

Employment Summary

Identification code 014–4081–0–3–301	2021 actual	2022 est.	2023 est.
2001 Reimbursable civilian full-time equivalent employment	214	97	97

WORKING CAPITAL FUND

Program and Financing (in millions of dollars)

Identification code 014–4524–0–4–301		2021 actual	2022 est.	2023 est.
	Obligations by program activity:			
0801	Information resources management	41	50	45
0803	Administrative expenses	317	369	346
0804	Technical expenses	172	199	185
0900	Total new obligations, unexpired accounts	530	618	576
	Budgetary resources:			
	Unobligated balance:			
1000	Unobligated balance brought forward, Oct 1	144	149	94
1021	Recoveries of prior year unpaid obligations	3		
1070	Unobligated balance (total)	147	149	94
	Budget authority:			
	Spending authority from offsetting collections, discretionary:			
1700	Collected	536	563	576
1701	Change in uncollected payments, Federal sources	–4		
1750	Spending auth from offsetting collections, disc (total)	532	563	576
1930	Total budgetary resources available	679	712	670
	Memorandum (non-add) entries:			
1941	Unexpired unobligated balance, end of year	149	94	94
	Change in obligated balance:			
	Unpaid obligations:			
3000	Unpaid obligations, brought forward, Oct 1	59	66	135
3010	New obligations, unexpired accounts	530	618	576
3020	Outlays (gross)	–520	–549	–574
3040	Recoveries of prior year unpaid obligations, unexpired	–3		
3050	Unpaid obligations, end of year	66	135	137
	Uncollected payments:			
3060	Uncollected pymts, Fed sources, brought forward, Oct 1	–83	–79	–79
3070	Change in uncollected pymts, Fed sources, unexpired	4		
3090	Uncollected pymts, Fed sources, end of year	–79	–79	–79
	Memorandum (non-add) entries:			
3100	Obligated balance, start of year	–24	–13	56
3200	Obligated balance, end of year	–13	56	58
	Budget authority and outlays, net:			
	Discretionary:			
4000	Budget authority, gross	532	563	576
	Outlays, gross:			
4010	Outlays from new discretionary authority		507	518
4011	Outlays from discretionary balances	520	42	56
4020	Outlays, gross (total)	520	549	574
	Offsets against gross budget authority and outlays:			
	Offsetting collections (collected) from:			
4030	Federal sources	–534	–561	–574
4033	Non-Federal sources	–2	–2	–2
4040	Offsets against gross budget authority and outlays (total)	–536	–563	–576

WORKING CAPITAL FUND—Continued
Program and Financing—Continued

Identification code 014–4524–0–4–301	2021 actual	2022 est.	2023 est.
Additional offsets against gross budget authority only:			
4050 Change in uncollected pymts, Fed sources, unexpired	4	....	....
4080 Outlays, net (discretionary)	–16	–14	–2
4180 Budget authority, net (total)	....	....	....
4190 Outlays, net (total)	–16	–14	–2

This revolving fund enables Reclamation to recover the costs of administrative and technical services and of facilities used by its programs and by others and accumulate funds to finance capital equipment purchases.

Object Classification (in millions of dollars)

Identification code 014–4524–0–4–301	2021 actual	2022 est.	2023 est.
Reimbursable obligations:			
Personnel compensation:			
11.1 Full-time permanent	236	191	195
11.3 Other than full-time permanent	6	6	6
11.5 Other personnel compensation	7	5	5
11.9 Total personnel compensation	249	202	206
12.1 Civilian personnel benefits	79	66	67
21.0 Travel and transportation of persons	1	1	1
23.1 Rental payments to GSA	16	17	17
23.2 Rental payments to others	2	2	2
23.3 Communications, utilities, and miscellaneous charges	6	6	6
25.2 Other services from non-Federal sources	152	298	251
26.0 Supplies and materials	5	5	5
31.0 Equipment	18	19	19
41.0 Grants, subsidies, and contributions	1	1	1
99.0 Reimbursable obligations	529	617	575
99.5 Adjustment for rounding	1	1	1
99.9 Total new obligations, unexpired accounts	530	618	576

Employment Summary

Identification code 014–4524–0–4–301	2021 actual	2022 est.	2023 est.
2001 Reimbursable civilian full-time equivalent employment	2,294	1,848	1,848

BUREAU OF RECLAMATION LOAN PROGRAM ACCOUNT

Under the Small Reclamation Projects Act, loans and grants can be made to non-Federal organizations for construction of small water resource projects.

As required by the Federal Credit Reform Act of 1990, the Reclamation loan program account records the subsidy costs associated with the direct loans obligated in 1992 and beyond, as well as administrative expenses of this program. The subsidy amounts are estimated on a present value basis and the administrative expenses are estimated on a cash basis.

No funds are requested for the Reclamation loan program for direct loans or for loan program administration for 2023.

BUREAU OF RECLAMATION DIRECT LOAN FINANCING ACCOUNT

Program and Financing (in millions of dollars)

Identification code 014–4547–0–3–301	2021 actual	2022 est.	2023 est.
Obligations by program activity:			
Credit program obligations:			
0713 Payment of interest to Treasury	2	....	....
0900 Total new obligations, unexpired accounts	2	....	....
Budgetary resources:			
Financing authority:			
Spending authority from offsetting collections, mandatory:			
1800 Collected	3	3	3
1825 Spending authority from offsetting collections applied to repay debt	–1	–3	–3
1850 Spending auth from offsetting collections, mand (total)	2	....	....
1900 Budget authority (total)	2	....	....
1930 Total budgetary resources available	2	....	....
Change in obligated balance:			
Unpaid obligations:			
3010 New obligations, unexpired accounts	2	....	....
3020 Outlays (gross)	–2	....	....
Financing authority and disbursements, net:			
Mandatory:			
4090 Budget authority, gross	2	....	....
Financing disbursements:			
4110 Outlays, gross (total)	2	....	....
Offsets against gross financing authority and disbursements:			
Offsetting collections (collected) from:			
4123 Repayments of principal	–3	–2	–2
4123 Interest received on loans	....	–1	–1
4130 Offsets against gross budget authority and outlays (total)	–3	–3	–3
4160 Budget authority, net (mandatory)	–1	–3	–3
4170 Outlays, net (mandatory)	–1	–3	–3
4180 Budget authority, net (total)	–1	–3	–3
4190 Outlays, net (total)	–1	–3	–3

Status of Direct Loans (in millions of dollars)

Identification code 014–4547–0–3–301	2021 actual	2022 est.	2023 est.
Cumulative balance of direct loans outstanding:			
1210 Outstanding, start of year	29	27	25
1251 Repayments: Repayments and prepayments	–2	–2	–2
1290 Outstanding, end of year	27	25	23

As required by the Federal Credit Reform Act of 1990, the Reclamation direct loan financing account is a non-budgetary account for recording all cash flows to and from the Government resulting from direct loans obligated in 1992 and beyond. The amounts in this account are a means of financing and are not included in budget totals.

Balance Sheet (in millions of dollars)

Identification code 014–4547–0–3–301	2020 actual	2021 actual
ASSETS:		
Net value of assets related to post-1991 direct loans receivable:		
1401 Direct loans receivable, gross	29	27
1405 Allowance for subsidy cost (-)	–1	–1
1499 Net present value of assets related to direct loans	28	26
1999 Total assets	28	26
LIABILITIES:		
2103 Federal liabilities: Debt	28	26
NET POSITION:		
3300 Cumulative results of operations	....	....
4999 Total liabilities and net position	28	26

BUREAU OF RECLAMATION LOAN LIQUIDATING ACCOUNT

Program and Financing (in millions of dollars)

Identification code 014–0667–0–1–301	2021 actual	2022 est.	2023 est.
Budgetary resources:			
Budget authority:			
Spending authority from offsetting collections, mandatory:			
1800 Collected	1	1	1
1820 Capital transfer of spending authority from offsetting collections to general fund	–1	–1	–1
Budget authority and outlays, net:			
Mandatory:			
Offsets against gross budget authority and outlays:			
Offsetting collections (collected) from:			
4123 Non-Federal sources	–1	–1	–1
4180 Budget authority, net (total)	–1	–1	–1

Identification code 014–0667–0–1–301		2021 actual	2022 est.	2023 est.
4190	Outlays, net (total)	–1	–1	–1

Status of Direct Loans (in millions of dollars)

Identification code 014–0667–0–1–301		2021 actual	2022 est.	2023 est.
	Cumulative balance of direct loans outstanding:			
1210	Outstanding, start of year	13	12	11
1251	Repayments: Repayments and prepayments	–1	–1	–1
1290	Outstanding, end of year	12	11	10

As required by the Federal Credit Reform Act of 1990, the Reclamation loan liquidating account records all cash flows to and from the Government resulting from direct loans obligated prior to 1992. All loans obligated in 1992, or thereafter, are recorded in loan program account No. 14–0685–0–1–301 and loan program financing account No. 14–4547–0–3–301.

Balance Sheet (in millions of dollars)

Identification code 014–0667–0–1–301		2020 actual	2021 actual
	ASSETS:		
1601	Direct loans, gross	13	12
1603	Allowance for estimated uncollectible loans and interest (-)	–7	–7
1699	Value of assets related to direct loans	6	5
1999	Total assets	6	5
	LIABILITIES:		
2104	Federal liabilities: Resources payable to Treasury	6	5
	NET POSITION:		
3300	Cumulative results of operations		
4999	Total liabilities and net position	6	5

Trust Funds
RECLAMATION TRUST FUNDS

Special and Trust Fund Receipts (in millions of dollars)

Identification code 014–8070–0–7–301		2021 actual	2022 est.	2023 est.
0100	Balance, start of year			
	Receipts:			
	Current law:			
1130	Deposits, Reclamation Trust Funds		1	1
2000	Total: Balances and receipts		1	1
	Appropriations:			
	Current law:			
2101	Reclamation Trust Funds		–1	–1
5099	Balance, end of year			

Program and Financing (in millions of dollars)

Identification code 014–8070–0–7–301		2021 actual	2022 est.	2023 est.
	Obligations by program activity:			
0001	Reclamation Trust Funds (Direct)	27	1	1
0900	Total new obligations, unexpired accounts (object class 25.2)	27	1	1
	Budgetary resources:			
	Unobligated balance:			
1000	Unobligated balance brought forward, Oct 1	28	1	1
	Budget authority:			
	Appropriations, mandatory:			
1201	Appropriation (special or trust fund)		1	1
1930	Total budgetary resources available	28	2	2
	Memorandum (non-add) entries:			
1941	Unexpired unobligated balance, end of year	1	1	1
	Change in obligated balance:			
	Unpaid obligations:			
3010	New obligations, unexpired accounts	27	1	1
3020	Outlays (gross)	–27	–1	–1

		2021 actual	2022 est.	2023 est.
	Budget authority and outlays, net:			
	Mandatory:			
4090	Budget authority, gross		1	1
	Outlays, gross:			
4101	Outlays from mandatory balances	27	1	1
4180	Budget authority, net (total)		1	1
4190	Outlays, net (total)	27	1	1

The Bureau of Reclamation performs work on various projects and activities with funding provided by non-Federal entities under 43 U.S.C. 395 and 396.

Employment Summary

Identification code 014–8070–0–7–301		2021 actual	2022 est.	2023 est.
1001	Direct civilian full-time equivalent employment		1	1

ADMINISTRATIVE PROVISION

Appropriations for the Bureau of Reclamation shall be available for purchase and replacement of motor vehicles and to provide supporting charging or fueling infrastructure.

CENTRAL UTAH PROJECT
Federal Funds

CENTRAL UTAH PROJECT COMPLETION ACCOUNT

For carrying out activities authorized by the Central Utah Project Completion Act, $20,000,000, to remain available until expended, of which $5,000,000 shall be deposited into the Utah Reclamation Mitigation and Conservation Account for use by the Utah Reclamation Mitigation and Conservation Commission: Provided, That of the amount provided under this heading, $1,600,000 shall be available until September 30, 2024, for expenses necessary in carrying out related responsibilities of the Secretary of the Interior: Provided further, That for fiscal year 2023, of the amount made available to the Commission under this Act or any other Act, the Commission may use an amount not to exceed $1,880,000 for administrative expenses.

Note.—A full-year 2022 appropriation for this account was not enacted at the time the Budget was prepared; therefore, the Budget assumes this account is operating under the Continuing Appropriations Act, 2022 (Division A of Public Law 117–43, as amended). The amounts included for 2022 reflect the annualized level provided by the continuing resolution.

CENTRAL UTAH PROJECT COMPLETION ACCOUNT

[For an additional amount for "Central Utah Project Completion Account", $10,000,000 to be deposited into the Utah Reclamation Mitigation and Conservation Account for use by the Utah Reclamation Mitigation and Conservation Commission, to remain available until expended, for expenses necessary in carrying out fire remediation activities for wildfires.] *(Disaster Relief Supplemental Appropriations Act, 2022.)*

CENTRAL UTAH PROJECT COMPLETION ACCOUNT

[For an additional amount for "Central Utah Project Completion Account", $50,000,000, to remain available until expended, of which $10,000,000 shall be deposited into the Utah Reclamation Mitigation and Conservation Account for use by the Utah Reclamation Mitigation and Conservation Commission: *Provided*, That such amount is designated by the Congress as being for an emergency requirement pursuant to section 4112(a) of H. Con. Res. 71 (115th Congress), the concurrent resolution on the budget for fiscal year 2018, and to section 251(b) of the Balanced Budget and Emergency Deficit Control Act of 1985.] *(Infrastructure Investments and Jobs Appropriations Act.)*

Program and Financing (in millions of dollars)

Identification code 014–0787–0–1–301		2021 actual	2022 est.	2023 est.
	Obligations by program activity:			
0001	Central Utah project construction	14	54	10
0003	Fish and Wildlife	3	3	4
0004	Program administration	2	2	1
0900	Total new obligations, unexpired accounts	19	59	15

CENTRAL UTAH PROJECT COMPLETION ACCOUNT—Continued
Program and Financing—Continued

Identification code 014–0787–0–1–301	2021 actual	2022 est.	2023 est.
Budgetary resources:			
Unobligated balance:			
1000 Unobligated balance brought forward, Oct 1	1	1	1
Budget authority:			
Appropriations, discretionary:			
1100 Appropriation	21	21	20
1100 Appropriation - Disaster Relief Supplemental [P.L. 117–43]		10	
1100 Appropriation - Bipartisan Infrastructure Law [P.L. 117–58]		50	
1120 Appropriations transferred to other accts [014–5174]	–2	–22	–5
1160 Appropriation, discretionary (total)	19	59	15
1930 Total budgetary resources available	20	60	16
Memorandum (non-add) entries:			
1941 Unexpired unobligated balance, end of year	1	1	1
Change in obligated balance:			
Unpaid obligations:			
3000 Unpaid obligations, brought forward, Oct 1	1	2	3
3010 New obligations, unexpired accounts	19	59	15
3020 Outlays (gross)	–18	–58	–15
3050 Unpaid obligations, end of year	2	3	3
Memorandum (non-add) entries:			
3100 Obligated balance, start of year	1	2	3
3200 Obligated balance, end of year	2	3	3
Budget authority and outlays, net:			
Discretionary:			
4000 Budget authority, gross	19	59	15
Outlays, gross:			
4010 Outlays from new discretionary authority	17	56	13
4011 Outlays from discretionary balances	1	2	2
4020 Outlays, gross (total)	18	58	15
4180 Budget authority, net (total)	19	59	15
4190 Outlays, net (total)	18	58	15

Titles II through VI of Public Law 102–575 authorize the completion of the Central Utah Project through construction and related activities, including the mitigation, conservation, and enhancement of fish and wildlife and recreational resources. Funds are requested in this account for: the Central Utah Water Conservancy District; transfer to the Utah Reclamation Mitigation and Conservation Commission; and to carry out related responsibilities of the Secretary.

Object Classification (in millions of dollars)

Identification code 014–0787–0–1–301	2021 actual	2022 est.	2023 est.
Direct obligations:			
25.2 Other services from non-Federal sources	14	54	10
25.3 Other goods and services from Federal sources	2	2	2
41.0 Grants, subsidies, and contributions	3	3	3
99.9 Total new obligations, unexpired accounts	19	59	15

UTAH RECLAMATION MITIGATION AND CONSERVATION ACCOUNT
Special and Trust Fund Receipts (in millions of dollars)

Identification code 014–5174–0–2–301	2021 actual	2022 est.	2023 est.
0100 Balance, start of year	139	120	120
Receipts:			
Current law:			
1140 Interest on Principal, Utah Mitigation and Conservation Fund	–9	7	7
2000 Total: Balances and receipts	130	127	127
Appropriations:			
Current law:			
2101 Utah Reclamation Mitigation and Conservation Account	–10	–7	–7
2103 Utah Reclamation Mitigation and Conservation Account	–1	–1	–1
2132 Utah Reclamation Mitigation and Conservation Account	1	1	1
2199 Total current law appropriations	–10	–7	–7
2999 Total appropriations	–10	–7	–7
5099 Balance, end of year	120	120	120

Program and Financing (in millions of dollars)

Identification code 014–5174–0–2–301	2021 actual	2022 est.	2023 est.
Obligations by program activity:			
0001 Utah Reclamation Mitigation and Conservation	3	7	1
0002 Title IV Interest on Investment	10	7	7
0900 Total new obligations, unexpired accounts	13	14	8
Budgetary resources:			
Unobligated balance:			
1000 Unobligated balance brought forward, Oct 1	4	3	18
1001 Discretionary unobligated balance brought fwd, Oct 1	1		
Budget authority:			
Appropriations, discretionary:			
1121 Appropriations transferred from other acct [014–0787]	2	22	5
Appropriations, mandatory:			
1201 Appropriation (special or trust fund)	10	7	7
1203 Appropriation (previously unavailable)(special or trust)	1	1	1
1232 Appropriations and/or unobligated balance of appropriations temporarily reduced	–1	–1	–1
1260 Appropriations, mandatory (total)	10	7	7
1900 Budget authority (total)	12	29	12
1930 Total budgetary resources available	16	32	30
Memorandum (non-add) entries:			
1941 Unexpired unobligated balance, end of year	3	18	22
Change in obligated balance:			
Unpaid obligations:			
3000 Unpaid obligations, brought forward, Oct 1	8	10	7
3010 New obligations, unexpired accounts	13	14	8
3020 Outlays (gross)	–11	–17	–15
3050 Unpaid obligations, end of year	10	7	
Memorandum (non-add) entries:			
3100 Obligated balance, start of year	8	10	7
3200 Obligated balance, end of year	10	7	
Budget authority and outlays, net:			
Discretionary:			
4000 Budget authority, gross	2	22	5
Outlays, gross:			
4010 Outlays from new discretionary authority	1	7	2
4011 Outlays from discretionary balances		1	5
4020 Outlays, gross (total)	1	8	7
Mandatory:			
4090 Budget authority, gross	10	7	7
Outlays, gross:			
4100 Outlays from new mandatory authority	2	7	6
4101 Outlays from mandatory balances	8	2	2
4110 Outlays, gross (total)	10	9	8
4180 Budget authority, net (total)	12	29	12
4190 Outlays, net (total)	11	17	15
Memorandum (non-add) entries:			
5000 Total investments, SOY: Federal securities: Par value	138	120	120
5001 Total investments, EOY: Federal securities: Par value	120	120	120

The Utah Reclamation Mitigation and Conservation account was established under Title IV of Public Law 102–575 for contributions from the State of Utah, the Federal Government (through the Secretary of the Interior and the Western Area Power Administration), and project beneficiaries (the Conservancy District). The requirement for contributions from the State, the Secretary, and the Conservancy District ended in 2001. The requirement for contributions from the Western Area Power Administration ended in 2013. Funds are deposited into the account as principal and may not be expended for any purpose. Interest earned annually on the account is available for expenditure, without further appropriations, by the Utah Reclamation Mitigation and Conservation Commission, which has the option to use the funds for the mitigation, conservation, and enhancement of fish and wildlife and recreational resources, or to reinvest the funds into the account as principal.

DEPARTMENT OF THE INTERIOR

Object Classification (in millions of dollars)

Identification code 014–5174–0–2–301	2021 actual	2022 est.	2023 est.
Direct obligations:			
11.1 Personnel compensation: Full-time permanent	1	1	1
25.2 Other services from non-Federal sources	11	11	6
25.3 Other goods and services from Federal sources	1	2	1
99.9 Total new obligations, unexpired accounts	13	14	8

Employment Summary

Identification code 014–5174–0–2–301	2021 actual	2022 est.	2023 est.
1001 Direct civilian full-time equivalent employment	10	10	10

UNITED STATES GEOLOGICAL SURVEY

Federal Funds

SURVEYS, INVESTIGATIONS, AND RESEARCH

For expenses necessary for the United States Geological Survey to perform surveys, investigations, and research covering topography, geology, hydrology, biology, and the mineral and water resources of the United States, its territories and possessions, and other areas as authorized by 43 U.S.C. 31, 1332, and 1340; classify lands as to their mineral and water resources; give engineering supervision to power permittees and Federal Energy Regulatory Commission licensees; administer the minerals exploration program (30 U.S.C. 641); conduct inquiries into the economic conditions affecting mining and materials processing industries (30 U.S.C. 3, 21a, and 1603; 50 U.S.C. 98g(a)(1)) and related purposes as authorized by law; and to publish and disseminate data relative to the foregoing activities; $1,711,344,000, to remain available until September 30, 2024; of which $92,274,000 shall remain available until expended for satellite operations; and of which $74,840,000 shall be available until expended for deferred maintenance and capital improvement projects that exceed $100,000 in cost: Provided, That none of the funds provided for the ecosystem research activity shall be used to conduct new surveys on private property, unless specifically authorized in writing by the property owner: Provided further, That no part of this appropriation shall be used to pay more than one-half the cost of topographic mapping or water resources data collection and investigations carried on in cooperation with States and municipalities.

Note.—A full-year 2022 appropriation for this account was not enacted at the time the Budget was prepared; therefore, the Budget assumes this account is operating under the Continuing Appropriations Act, 2022 (Division A of Public Law 117–43, as amended). The amounts included for 2022 reflect the annualized level provided by the continuing resolution.

SURVEYS, INVESTIGATIONS, AND RESEARCH

[For an additional amount for "Surveys, Investigations, and Research", $26,284,000, to remain available until expended, for necessary expenses related to the consequences of calendar year 2019, 2020, and 2021 wildfires, hurricanes and other natural disasters.] *(Disaster Relief Supplemental Appropriations Act, 2022.)*

SURVEYS, INVESTIGATIONS, AND RESEARCH

(INCLUDING TRANSFERS OF FUNDS)

[For an additional amount for "Surveys, Investigations, and Research", $510,668,000, to remain available until expended, for the Secretary of the Interior to carry out activities authorized in sections 40201, 40204, and 41003(a) of division D of this Act: *Provided*, That amounts made available under this heading in this Act shall be allocated as follows:]

[(1) $320,000,000 to carry out section 40201 of division D of this Act: *Provided*, That $64,000,000, to remain available until September 30, 2024, shall be made available for fiscal year 2022, $64,000,000, to remain available until September 30, 2025, shall be made available for fiscal year 2023, $64,000,000, to remain available until September 30, 2026, shall be made available for fiscal year 2024, $64,000,000, to remain available until September 30, 2027, shall be made available for fiscal year 2025, and $64,000,000, to remain available until September 30, 2028, shall be made available for fiscal year 2026;]

[(2) $167,000,000, to remain available until expended, for fiscal year 2022 to carry out section 40204 of division D of this Act;]

[(3) $23,668,000 to carry out section 41003(a) of division D of this Act: *Provided*, That $8,668,000, to remain available until September 30, 2024, shall be made available for fiscal year 2022, $5,000,000, to remain available until September 30, 2025, shall be made available for fiscal year 2023, $5,000,000, to remain available until September 30, 2026, shall be made available for fiscal year 2024, and $5,000,000, to remain available until September 30, 2027, shall be made available for fiscal year 2025:]

[*Provided further*, That amounts provided under this heading in this Act shall be in addition to amounts otherwise available for such purposes: *Provided further*, That one-half of one percent of the amounts made available under this heading in this Act in each of fiscal years 2022 through 2026 shall be transferred to the Office of Inspector General of the Department of the Interior for oversight of funding provided to the Department of the Interior in this title in this Act: *Provided further*, That such amount is designated by the Congress as being for an emergency requirement pursuant to section 4112(a) of H. Con. Res. 71 (115th Congress), the concurrent resolution on the budget for fiscal year 2018, and to section 251(b) of the Balanced Budget and Emergency Deficit Control Act of 1985.] *(Infrastructure Investments and Jobs Appropriations Act.)*

Program and Financing (in millions of dollars)

Identification code 014–0804–0–1–306	2021 actual	2022 est.	2023 est.
Obligations by program activity:			
0001 Ecosystems	264	260	366
0004 Natural Hazards	175	178	217
0005 Water Resources	255	265	300
0006 Core Science Systems	255	253	341
0007 Science Support	95	98	124
0008 Facilities	118	261	160
0009 Energy and Mineral Resources	90	89	143
0091 Direct program activities, subtotal	1,252	1,404	1,651
0101 Restoration of Federal Assets (Hurricane Supplemental P.L. 115–123)	3	2	
0102 Restoration of Federal Assets (Disaster Supplemental P.L. 116–20)	15	9	55
0103 2022 Disaster Supplemental (P.L. 117–43)		11	10
0104 2022 Bipartisan Infrastructure Law (P.L. 117–58)		60	228
0191 Direct program activities, subtotal	18	82	293
0799 Total direct obligations	1,270	1,486	1,944
0801 Surveys, Investigations, and Research (Reimbursable)	571	571	571
0900 Total new obligations, unexpired accounts	1,841	2,057	2,515
Budgetary resources:			
Unobligated balance:			
1000 Unobligated balance brought forward, Oct 1	814	901	996
1001 Discretionary unobligated balance brought fwd, Oct 1	789	878	
1021 Recoveries of prior year unpaid obligations	10		
1070 Unobligated balance (total)	824	901	996
Budget authority:			
Appropriations, discretionary:			
1100 Appropriation	1,316	1,316	1,711
1100 Appropriation - 2022 Disaster Supplemental [P.L. 117–43]		26	
1100 Appropriation - 2022 Bipartisan Infrastructure Law [P.L. 117–58]		240	
1120 Appropriations transferred to other acct [014–0104]		–1	
1160 Appropriation, discretionary (total)	1,316	1,581	1,711
Advance appropriations, discretionary:			
1170 Advance appropriation			69
Spending authority from offsetting collections, discretionary:			
1700 Collected	532	571	571
1701 Change in uncollected payments, Federal sources	71		
1750 Spending auth from offsetting collections, disc (total)	603	571	571
1900 Budget authority (total)	1,919	2,152	2,351
1930 Total budgetary resources available	2,743	3,053	3,347
Memorandum (non-add) entries:			
1940 Unobligated balance expiring	–1		
1941 Unexpired unobligated balance, end of year	901	996	832
Change in obligated balance:			
Unpaid obligations:			
3000 Unpaid obligations, brought forward, Oct 1	564	606	931
3010 New obligations, unexpired accounts	1,841	2,057	2,515
3011 Obligations ("upward adjustments"), expired accounts	1		
3020 Outlays (gross)	–1,785	–1,732	–2,304
3040 Recoveries of prior year unpaid obligations, unexpired	–10		
3041 Recoveries of prior year unpaid obligations, expired	–5		
3050 Unpaid obligations, end of year	606	931	1,142
Uncollected payments:			
3060 Uncollected pymts, Fed sources, brought forward, Oct 1	–728	–774	–774
3070 Change in uncollected pymts, Fed sources, unexpired	–71		
3071 Change in uncollected pymts, Fed sources, expired	25		

SURVEYS, INVESTIGATIONS, AND RESEARCH—Continued
Program and Financing—Continued

Identification code 014–0804–0–1–306		2021 actual	2022 est.	2023 est.
3090	Uncollected pymts, Fed sources, end of year	–774	–774	–774
	Memorandum (non-add) entries:			
3100	Obligated balance, start of year	–164	–168	157
3200	Obligated balance, end of year	–168	157	368
	Budget authority and outlays, net:			
	Discretionary:			
4000	Budget authority, gross	1,919	2,152	2,351
	Outlays, gross:			
4010	Outlays from new discretionary authority	1,161	1,579	1,897
4011	Outlays from discretionary balances	622	151	405
4020	Outlays, gross (total)	1,783	1,730	2,302
	Offsets against gross budget authority and outlays:			
	Offsetting collections (collected) from:			
4030	Federal sources	–319	–325	–325
4033	Non-Federal sources	–238	–246	–246
4040	Offsets against gross budget authority and outlays (total)	–557	–571	–571
	Additional offsets against gross budget authority only:			
4050	Change in uncollected pymts, Fed sources, unexpired	–71		
4052	Offsetting collections credited to expired accounts	25		
4060	Additional offsets against budget authority only (total)	–46		
4070	Budget authority, net (discretionary)	1,316	1,581	1,780
4080	Outlays, net (discretionary)	1,226	1,159	1,731
	Mandatory:			
	Outlays, gross:			
4101	Outlays from mandatory balances	2	2	2
4180	Budget authority, net (total)	1,316	1,581	1,780
4190	Outlays, net (total)	1,228	1,161	1,733

The U.S. Geological Survey (USGS) monitors, analyzes, and predicts current and evolving Earth-system interactions and delivers actionable information at scales and timeframes relevant to decision makers. USGS provides science about natural hazards, natural resources, ecosystems and environmental health, and the effects of climate and land-use change.

Ecosystems.—The USGS Ecosystems Mission Area is the biological research arm of Interior and provides science to ensure America's ecosystems are managed sustainably and biological resources in wild and urban spaces are conserved now and into the future. Scientists examine the consequences of climate and environmental change, effects of management actions on communities, lands and species, and risks of and solutions to harmful invasive species, wildlife diseases, and contaminants in the environment.

Energy and Mineral Resources.—The USGS Energy and Mineral Resources Mission Area is the Nation's primary source of impartial scientific information on domestic and global geologic resources and their supply chains. The Nation relies on a variety of energy and mineral resources to power homes and businesses and to manufacture products and technologies from phones to vehicles. The mission area conducts research on the full life cycle of these resources, including the Nation's domestic resources and global trade relationships; carbon storage potential and critical mineral supply chains essential to sustainable energy transitions; environmental and socioeconomic effects of geologic resource occurrence, extraction, use, wastes, and demands on water supplies; and supply, demand, and trade of mineral commodities. The mission area provides science to inform economic, technological, national security, and geopolitical strategies and decisions, as well as sustainable natural resource management and the development of infrastructure and new technologies.

Natural Hazards.—The USGS Natural Hazards Mission Area plays a critical role in providing policymakers and the public with a clear understanding of potential threats from natural hazards, societal vulnerability to these threats, and strategies for improving resilience to earthquakes, volcanic eruptions, landslides, floods, hurricanes, geomagnetic storms, tsunamis, and wildfires. This mission area also includes USGS activities that characterize and assess coastal and marine hazards, processes, conditions, change, and vulnerability. The USGS Natural Hazards mission area works with partners and stakeholders to define and mitigate hazards risks, build an understanding of natural hazard processes, and characterize potential impacts on human activity and health, the economy, and the changing environment.

Water Resources.—The USGS Water Resources Mission Area is the Nation's primary Federal source of information about water resources. To fulfill this responsibility, the USGS Water Resources mission area monitors and assesses the amount and characteristics of the Nation's water resources, assesses sources and behavior of contaminants in the water environment, and develops tools to improve management and understanding of water resources. This work supports Federal, State, tribal, and municipal government decisions in managing water resources for domestic, agricultural, commercial, industrial, recreational, and ecological uses; protects and enhances water resources for human health, aquatic health, and environmental quality; minimizes loss of life and property as a result of water-related natural hazards, such as floods, droughts, and land movement; and contributes to sustainable stewardship and development of the Nation's resources for the benefit of present and future generations.

Core Science Systems.—The USGS Core Science Systems Mission Area fulfills the USGS' role as the National civilian mapping agency —a 143 year legacy since its establishment in 1879. The USGS conducts detailed surveys and distributes high-quality and highly accurate topographic, geologic, hydrographic, and biogeographic maps and remotely sensed data and analyses to the public. Mapping accuracy enabled by cutting-edge technologies allows precise planning for: recreational use on public lands; collaborative conservation with Department of the Interior partners; critical mineral resource assessments; renewable energy development; transportation and pipeline infrastructure projects; urban planning and development; land change and flood prediction at regional, local, and neighborhood scales; emergency response; and hazards mitigation. The USGS Core Science Systems Mission Area is the Federal steward of this high-quality geospatial and remote sensing data, and provides access to the public through The National Map, the Federal GeoPlatform, the National Land Cover Database, the National Geologic Map Database, the USGS Earth Explorer, and the National Biogeographic Map, and the Protected Areas Database of the United States. The USGS also operates Landsat satellites and data systems necessary to understand, monitor, and detect changes that affect the Nation's natural and agricultural resources, economy, public safety and national security, and historical heritage.

Science Support.—The USGS Science Support Mission Area provides functions essential to support the USGS mission such as: scientific integrity processes; sharing and communicating science findings; purchasing science equipment and field supplies; executing science agreements with partners; contracting for support scientists and researchers; budget formulation; human resources; safety training; hazardous waste management; and information technology, which supports the scientific process and information management of scientific data. Science Support also provides bureau-wide executive direction and coordination, communication, business administration, and financial management.

Facilities.—The USGS Facilities Mission Area provides safe, functional workspace, laboratories, and facilities for the USGS to accomplish its scientific mission. The mission area provides rental payments and operation and maintenance for properties and deferred maintenance and capital improvement for owned assets.

Reimbursable Program.—This program includes reimbursements from non-Federal sources (States, Tribes, and municipalities) for cooperative efforts; proceeds from the sale of copies of photographs and records and the sale of personal property; reimbursements from permittees and licensees of the Federal Energy Regulatory Commission; and reimbursements from foreign countries and international organizations for technical assistance. The USGS also receives reimbursements from other Federal agencies for mission-related work performed at the request of the financing agency.

Object Classification (in millions of dollars)

Identification code 014–0804–0–1–306		2021 actual	2022 est.	2023 est.
	Direct obligations:			
	Personnel compensation:			
11.1	Full-time permanent	400	413	481
11.3	Other than full-time permanent	46	48	56
11.5	Other personnel compensation	20	21	24
11.9	Total personnel compensation	466	482	561
12.1	Civilian personnel benefits	175	185	210
21.0	Travel and transportation of persons	6	6	7
22.0	Transportation of things	2	2	2
23.1	Rental payments to GSA	55	60	68
23.2	Rental payments to others	3	3	3
23.3	Communications, utilities, and miscellaneous charges	21	21	21
24.0	Printing and reproduction	1	1	1
25.1	Advisory and assistance services	60	78	60
25.2	Other services from non-Federal sources	142	146	380
25.3	Other goods and services from Federal sources	95	96	96
25.4	Operation and maintenance of facilities	17	12	12
25.5	Research and development contracts	3	31	40
25.7	Operation and maintenance of equipment	20	20	41
26.0	Supplies and materials	21	22	23
31.0	Equipment	56	58	63
32.0	Land and structures	5	130	202
41.0	Grants, subsidies, and contributions	122	133	154
99.0	Direct obligations	1,270	1,486	1,944
99.0	Reimbursable obligations	571	571	571
99.9	Total new obligations, unexpired accounts	1,841	2,057	2,515

Employment Summary

Identification code 014–0804–0–1–306		2021 actual	2022 est.	2023 est.
1001	Direct civilian full-time equivalent employment	4,571	4,619	5,203
2001	Reimbursable civilian full-time equivalent employment	3,008	3,008	3,008
3001	Allocation account civilian full-time equivalent employment	47	24	24

WORKING CAPITAL FUND

Program and Financing (in millions of dollars)

Identification code 014–4556–0–4–306		2021 actual	2022 est.	2023 est.
	Obligations by program activity:			
0801	Working capital fund	109	114	101
	Budgetary resources:			
	Unobligated balance:			
1000	Unobligated balance brought forward, Oct 1	164	172	156
1021	Recoveries of prior year unpaid obligations	2		
1070	Unobligated balance (total)	166	172	156
	Budget authority:			
	Spending authority from offsetting collections, discretionary:			
1700	Collected	115	98	90
1930	Total budgetary resources available	281	270	246
	Memorandum (non-add) entries:			
1941	Unexpired unobligated balance, end of year	172	156	145
	Change in obligated balance:			
	Unpaid obligations:			
3000	Unpaid obligations, brought forward, Oct 1	35	61	87
3010	New obligations, unexpired accounts	109	114	101
3020	Outlays (gross)	–81	–88	–88
3040	Recoveries of prior year unpaid obligations, unexpired	–2		
3050	Unpaid obligations, end of year	61	87	100
	Memorandum (non-add) entries:			
3100	Obligated balance, start of year	35	61	87
3200	Obligated balance, end of year	61	87	100
	Budget authority and outlays, net:			
	Discretionary:			
4000	Budget authority, gross	115	98	90
	Outlays, gross:			
4010	Outlays from new discretionary authority	42	44	40
4011	Outlays from discretionary balances	39	44	48
4020	Outlays, gross (total)	81	88	88
	Offsets against gross budget authority and outlays:			
	Offsetting collections (collected) from:			
4030	Federal sources	–114	–98	–90
4033	Non-Federal sources	–1		
4040	Offsets against gross budget authority and outlays (total)	–115	–98	–90
4080	Outlays, net (discretionary)	–34	–10	–2
4180	Budget authority, net (total)			
4190	Outlays, net (total)	–34	–10	–2

The Working Capital Fund allows for efficient financial management of U.S. Geological Survey activities including telecommunications investments; acquisition, replacement, and enhancement of scientific equipment; facilities, publications, General Service Administration Buildings delegation operations and laboratory operations; modernization and equipment replacement; and drilling and training services.

Balance Sheet (in millions of dollars)

Identification code 014–4556–0–4–306		2020 actual	2021 actual
	ASSETS:		
1101	Federal assets: Fund balances with Treasury	140	140
1803	Other Federal assets: Property, plant and equipment, net	37	37
1999	Total assets	177	177
	LIABILITIES:		
2201	Non-Federal liabilities: Accounts payable	3	3
	NET POSITION:		
3300	Cumulative results of operations	174	174
4999	Total liabilities and net position	177	177

Object Classification (in millions of dollars)

Identification code 014–4556–0–4–306		2021 actual	2022 est.	2023 est.
	Reimbursable obligations:			
	Personnel compensation:			
11.1	Full-time permanent	8	9	8
11.5	Other personnel compensation	1	1	1
11.9	Total personnel compensation	9	10	9
12.1	Civilian personnel benefits	4	4	3
23.1	Rental payments to GSA	1	1	1
23.3	Communications, utilities, and miscellaneous charges	1	1	1
25.2	Other services from non-Federal sources	11	8	7
25.3	Other goods and services from Federal sources	10	13	12
25.4	Operation and maintenance of facilities	10	13	10
25.7	Operation and maintenance of equipment	6	5	5
26.0	Supplies and materials	6	6	5
31.0	Equipment	32	33	30
32.0	Land and structures	19	20	18
99.9	Total new obligations, unexpired accounts	109	114	101

Employment Summary

Identification code 014–4556–0–4–306		2021 actual	2022 est.	2023 est.
2001	Reimbursable civilian full-time equivalent employment	105	105	105

Trust Funds

CONTRIBUTED FUNDS

Special and Trust Fund Receipts (in millions of dollars)

Identification code 014–8562–0–7–306		2021 actual	2022 est.	2023 est.
0100	Balance, start of year			
	Receipts:			
	Current law:			
1130	Contributed Funds, Geological Survey	1	2	1
2000	Total: Balances and receipts	1	2	1
	Appropriations:			
	Current law:			
2101	Contributed Funds	–1	–2	–1
5099	Balance, end of year			

CONTRIBUTED FUNDS—Continued

Program and Financing (in millions of dollars)

Identification code 014–8562–0–7–306	2021 actual	2022 est.	2023 est.
Obligations by program activity:			
0801 Donations and contributed funds	1	2	1
0900 Total new obligations, unexpired accounts (object class 99.5)	1	2	1
Budgetary resources:			
Unobligated balance:			
1000 Unobligated balance brought forward, Oct 1	3	3	3
Budget authority:			
Appropriations, mandatory:			
1201 Appropriation (special or trust fund)	1	2	1
1930 Total budgetary resources available	4	5	4
Memorandum (non-add) entries:			
1941 Unexpired unobligated balance, end of year	3	3	3
Change in obligated balance:			
Unpaid obligations:			
3010 New obligations, unexpired accounts	1	2	1
3020 Outlays (gross)	–1	–2	–1
Budget authority and outlays, net:			
Mandatory:			
4090 Budget authority, gross	1	2	1
Outlays, gross:			
4100 Outlays from new mandatory authority		1	
4101 Outlays from mandatory balances	1	1	1
4110 Outlays, gross (total)	1	2	1
4180 Budget authority, net (total)	1	2	1
4190 Outlays, net (total)	1	2	1

Funds in this account are provided by States, local governments, and private organizations (pursuant to 43 U.S.C. 36c). This appropriation (a permanent, indefinite, special fund) makes these funds available to the U.S. Geological Survey (USGS) to perform the work desired by the contributor and the USGS. Research and development, data collection and analysis, and services are undertaken when such activities are of mutual interest and benefit and assist USGS in accomplishing its mandated purposes.

Employment Summary

Identification code 014–8562–0–7–306	2021 actual	2022 est.	2023 est.
1001 Direct civilian full-time equivalent employment	4	4	4

ADMINISTRATIVE PROVISIONS

From within the amount appropriated for activities of the United States Geological Survey such sums as are necessary shall be available for contracting for the furnishing of topographic maps and for the making of geophysical or other specialized surveys when it is administratively determined that such procedures are in the public interest; construction and maintenance of necessary buildings and appurtenant facilities; acquisition of lands for gauging stations, observation wells, and seismic equipment; expenses of the United States National Committee for Geological Sciences; and payment of compensation and expenses of persons employed by the Survey duly appointed to represent the United States in the negotiation and administration of interstate compacts: Provided, That activities funded by appropriations herein made may be accomplished through the use of contracts, grants, or cooperative agreements as defined in section 6302 of title 31, United States Code: Provided further, That the United States Geological Survey may enter into contracts or cooperative agreements directly with individuals or indirectly with institutions or nonprofit organizations, without regard to 41 U.S.C. 6101, for the temporary or intermittent services of students or recent graduates, who shall be considered employees for the purpose of chapters 57 and 81 of title 5, United States Code, relating to compensation for travel and work injuries, and chapter 171 of title 28, United States Code, relating to tort claims, but shall not be considered to be Federal employees for any other purposes: Provided further, That the United States Geological Survey is authorized to enter into a direct lease agreement for space as part of a Cooperative Science Agreement and may record obligations under such lease agreement on a year-by-year basis.

FISH AND WILDLIFE AND PARKS

UNITED STATES FISH AND WILDLIFE SERVICE

Federal Funds

RESOURCE MANAGEMENT

For necessary expenses of the United States Fish and Wildlife Service, as authorized by law, and for scientific and economic studies, general administration, and for the performance of other authorized functions related to such resources, $1,745,122,000, to remain available until September 30, 2024: Provided, That not to exceed $23,946,000 shall be used for implementing subsections (a), (b), (c), and (e) of section 4 of the Endangered Species Act of 1973 (16 U.S.C. 1533) (except for processing petitions, developing and issuing proposed and final regulations, and taking any other steps to implement actions described in subsection (c)(2)(A), (c)(2)(B)(i), or (c)(2)(B)(ii)).

Note.—A full-year 2022 appropriation for this account was not enacted at the time the Budget was prepared; therefore, the Budget assumes this account is operating under the Continuing Appropriations Act, 2022 (Division A of Public Law 117–43, as amended). The amounts included for 2022 reflect the annualized level provided by the continuing resolution.

RESOURCE MANAGEMENT

[(INCLUDING TRANSFERS OF FUNDS)]

[*For an additional amount for "Resource Management", $455,000,000, to remain available until expended: Provided, That $91,000,000, to remain available until expended, shall be made available for fiscal year 2022, $91,000,000, to remain available until expended, shall be made available for fiscal year 2023, $91,000,000, to remain available until expended, shall be made available for fiscal year 2024, $91,000,000, to remain available until expended, shall be made available for fiscal year 2025, and $91,000,000, to remain available until expended, shall be made available for fiscal year 2026: Provided further, That of the funds made available under this heading in this Act, the following amounts shall be for the following purposes in equal amounts for each of fiscal years 2022 through 2026, and shall be in addition to amounts otherwise made available for such purpose—*]

[(1) $255,000,000 shall be for the following regional ecosystem restoration purposes—]

[(A) $26,000,000 shall be for Delaware River Basin Conservation Act;]

[(B) $162,000,000 shall be for Klamath Basin restoration activities, including habitat restoration, planning, design, engineering, environmental compliance, fee acquisition, infrastructure development, construction, operations and maintenance, improvements, and expansion, as necessary, on lands currently leased by the U.S. Fish and Wildlife Service for conservation and recovery of endangered species;]

[(C) $17,000,000 shall be for implementing section 5(d)(2) of the Lake Tahoe Restoration Act; and]

[(D) $50,000,000 shall be for sagebrush steppe ecosystem;]

[(2) $200,000,000 shall be for restoring fish and wildlife passage by removing in-stream barriers and providing technical assistance under the National Fish Passage Program:]

[*Provided further, That one-half of one percent of the amounts made available under this heading in this Act in each of fiscal years 2022 through 2026 shall be transferred to the Office of Inspector General of the Department of the Interior for oversight of funding provided to the Department of the Interior in this title in this Act: Provided further, That nothing under this heading in this Act shall be construed as providing any new authority to remove, breach, or otherwise alter the operations of a Federal hydropower dam and dam removal projects shall include written consent of the dam owner, if ownership is established: Provided further, That such amount is designated by the Congress as being for an emergency requirement pursuant to section 4112(a) of H. Con. Res. 71 (115th Congress), the concurrent resolution on the budget for fiscal year 2018, and to section 251(b) of the Balanced Budget and Emergency Deficit Control Act of 1985.*] *(Infrastructure Investments and Jobs Appropriations Act.)*

Program and Financing (in millions of dollars)

Identification code 014–1611–0–1–302	2021 actual	2022 est.	2023 est.
Obligations by program activity:			
0001 Ecological Services	273	307	309
0002 National Wildlife Refuge System	503	578	581
0004 Conservation and Enforcement	177	192	193

DEPARTMENT OF THE INTERIOR

Fish and Wildlife and Parks—Continued
United States Fish and Wildlife Service—Continued

649

0005	Fisheries and Aquatic Resource Conservation	204	237	238
0006	Habitat Conservation	70	80	80
0007	Cooperative Landscape Conservation	12	17	17
0008	General Operations	135	172	173
0009	Science Support	15	29	29
0010	USMCA Supplemental (P.L. 116–113)	1	2	2
0011	American Rescue Plan (P.L. 117–2)	37	37	37
0012	2022 Bipartisan Infrastructure Law (P.L. 117–58)		10	73
0100	Subtotal, direct program	1,427	1,661	1,732
0799	Total direct obligations	1,427	1,661	1,732
0801	Great Lakes Restoration Initiative	50	54	54
0802	Reimbursable program activity all other	203	220	220
0899	Total reimbursable obligations	253	274	274
0900	Total new obligations, unexpired accounts	1,680	1,935	2,006
	Budgetary resources:			
	Unobligated balance:			
1000	Unobligated balance brought forward, Oct 1	386	551	375
1001	Discretionary unobligated balance brought fwd, Oct 1	386	483	
1021	Recoveries of prior year unpaid obligations	18	19	18
1070	Unobligated balance (total)	404	570	393
	Budget authority:			
	Appropriations, discretionary:			
1100	Appropriation	1,380	1,380	1,745
1100	Appropriation - Bipartisan Infrastructure Law [P.L. 117–58]		91	
1160	Appropriation, discretionary (total)	1,380	1,471	1,745
	Advance appropriations, discretionary:			
1170	Advance appropriation			91
	Appropriations, mandatory:			
1200	Appropriation [American Rescue Plan]	105		
	Spending authority from offsetting collections, discretionary:			
1700	Collected	270	269	269
1700	Collected - NWRS Cost Recovery [CHIMP]			1
1701	Change in uncollected payments, Federal sources	72		
1750	Spending auth from offsetting collections, disc (total)	342	269	270
1900	Budget authority (total)	1,827	1,740	2,106
1930	Total budgetary resources available	2,231	2,310	2,499
	Memorandum (non-add) entries:			
1941	Unexpired unobligated balance, end of year	551	375	493
	Change in obligated balance:			
	Unpaid obligations:			
3000	Unpaid obligations, brought forward, Oct 1	745	839	894
3010	New obligations, unexpired accounts	1,680	1,935	2,006
3011	Obligations ("upward adjustments"), expired accounts	2		
3020	Outlays (gross)	–1,562	–1,861	–2,041
3040	Recoveries of prior year unpaid obligations, unexpired	–18	–19	–18
3041	Recoveries of prior year unpaid obligations, expired	–8		
3050	Unpaid obligations, end of year	839	894	841
	Uncollected payments:			
3060	Uncollected pymts, Fed sources, brought forward, Oct 1	–360	–432	–432
3070	Change in uncollected pymts, Fed sources, unexpired	–72		
3090	Uncollected pymts, Fed sources, end of year	–432	–432	–432
	Memorandum (non-add) entries:			
3100	Obligated balance, start of year	385	407	462
3200	Obligated balance, end of year	407	462	409
	Budget authority and outlays, net:			
	Discretionary:			
4000	Budget authority, gross	1,722	1,740	2,106
	Outlays, gross:			
4010	Outlays from new discretionary authority	873	1,079	1,367
4011	Outlays from discretionary balances	689	767	644
4020	Outlays, gross (total)	1,562	1,846	2,011
	Offsets against gross budget authority and outlays:			
	Offsetting collections (collected) from:			
4030	Federal sources	–214	–200	–200
4033	Non-Federal sources	–56	–69	–70
4040	Offsets against gross budget authority and outlays (total)	–270	–269	–270
	Additional offsets against gross budget authority only:			
4050	Change in uncollected pymts, Fed sources, unexpired	–72		
4060	Additional offsets against budget authority only (total)	–72		
4070	Budget authority, net (discretionary)	1,380	1,471	1,836
4080	Outlays, net (discretionary)	1,292	1,577	1,741
	Mandatory:			
4090	Budget authority, gross	105		
	Outlays, gross:			
4101	Outlays from mandatory balances		15	30
4180	Budget authority, net (total)	1,485	1,471	1,836
4190	Outlays, net (total)	1,292	1,592	1,771

Ecological Services.—The Service conserves, protects, and enhances fish, wildlife, plants, and their habitat by working with private landowners, States, Tribes, non-governmental organizations, and other Federal agencies. These partnership activities help protect and recover species listed under the Endangered Species Act and work to make the listing of additional species unnecessary. Financial assistance is provided to private landowners to restore or improve habitat for endangered species and other at-risk species. Technical assistance helps prevent or minimize potential conflicts between development projects and imperiled species.

Habitat Conservation.—Through technical and financial assistance, the Service promotes the protection, conservation, and restoration of the Nation's fish and wildlife resources. These conservation activities are accomplished through a voluntary citizen and community based stewardship program with partners on private lands. Conserving the Nation's coastal trust resources is accomplished through collaboration with others on public and private lands.

National Wildlife Refuge System.—The Service maintains the National Wildlife Refuge System consisting of 567 refuges, waterfowl production areas in 212 counties managed by 38 wetland management districts, 49 wildlife coordination areas, and seven national monuments. The National Wildlife Refuge System administers this network of lands and waters to conserve and restore fish, wildlife, plants, and their habitats, for the benefit of present and future generations of Americans.

Conservation and Enforcement.—The Service directs and coordinates national migratory bird programs to protect and enhance populations and habitat of more than 1,000 species of birds. Grants and partnerships are key to these programs, such as Joint Ventures that implement the North American Waterfowl Management Plan. The Service Law Enforcement program investigates wildlife crimes, regulates wildlife trade, helps Americans understand and obey wildlife protection laws, and works in partnership with international, State, and Tribal counterparts to conserve wildlife resources. The Service, through the International Affairs Program, works with domestic and international partners to promote a coordinated strategy to protect, restore, and enhance the world's diverse wildlife and their habitats, with a focus on species of international concern.

Fish and Aquatic Conservation.—The Fish and Aquatic Conservation Program consists of a network of 71 National Fish Hatcheries, one historic National Fish Hatchery, six Fish Health Centers, seven Fish Technology Centers, 51 Fish and Wildlife Conservation Offices, and the Aquatic Animal Drug Approval Partnership Program. Working with partners, the program recovers, restores and maintains fish and other aquatic resources at self-sustaining levels; provides technical assistance to States, Tribes and others; and supports Federal mitigation programs for the benefit of the American public.

Cooperative Landscape Conservation.—The Cooperative Landscape Program works with States to deliver conservation on a landscape scale and build collaborative approaches to conservation through coalitions with States and other partners.

Science Support.—Science Support provides funding for applied science directed at high impact questions of concern to management of fish and wildlife resources. This science provides information to inform resource management decisions to best manage species at healthy and sustainable levels.

General Operations.—Funding for the Service's general operations provides policy guidance, program coordination, and administrative services to all of the Fish and Wildlife Service's programs. The funds also support the National Conservation Training Center and projects through the National Fish and Wildlife Foundation to restore and enhance fish and wildlife populations.

Fish and Wildlife and Parks—Continued
United States Fish and Wildlife Service—Continued

RESOURCE MANAGEMENT—Continued

Funding requested in this account will complement the Civilian Climate Corps and will develop the next generation of conservation workers and create a new pathway to good-paying jobs.

Object Classification (in millions of dollars)

Identification code 014–1611–0–1–302		2021 actual	2022 est.	2023 est.
	Direct obligations:			
	Personnel compensation:			
11.1	Full-time permanent	546	628	655
11.3	Other than full-time permanent	20	23	24
11.5	Other personnel compensation	28	30	32
11.9	Total personnel compensation	594	681	711
12.1	Civilian personnel benefits	248	280	293
21.0	Travel and transportation of persons	5	12	12
22.0	Transportation of things	4	5	5
23.1	Rental payments to GSA	39	55	57
23.2	Rental payments to others	1	3	3
23.3	Communications, utilities, and miscellaneous charges	25	29	30
24.0	Printing and reproduction	3	3	4
25.1	Advisory and assistance services	14	19	20
25.2	Other services from non-Federal sources	66	80	83
25.3	Other goods and services from Federal sources	57	71	74
25.4	Operation and maintenance of facilities	27	31	32
25.6	Medical care		1	1
25.7	Operation and maintenance of equipment	15	19	19
26.0	Supplies and materials	44	52	54
31.0	Equipment	42	57	59
32.0	Land and structures	35	38	40
41.0	Grants, subsidies, and contributions	206	225	234
42.0	Insurance claims and indemnities	1	1	1
99.0	Direct obligations	1,426	1,662	1,732
99.0	Reimbursable obligations	254	273	274
99.9	Total new obligations, unexpired accounts	1,680	1,935	2,006

Employment Summary

Identification code 014–1611–0–1–302		2021 actual	2022 est.	2023 est.
1001	Direct civilian full-time equivalent employment	6,396	6,516	7,454
2001	Reimbursable civilian full-time equivalent employment	848	848	848
3001	Allocation account civilian full-time equivalent employment	593	631	709

◆

CONSTRUCTION

For construction, improvement, acquisition, or removal of buildings and other facilities required in the conservation, management, investigation, protection, and utilization of fish and wildlife resources, and the acquisition of lands and interests therein; $46,418,000, to remain available until expended: Provided, That such amounts are available for the modernization of field communication capabilities, in addition to amounts otherwise made available for such purpose.

Note.—A full-year 2022 appropriation for this account was not enacted at the time the Budget was prepared; therefore, the Budget assumes this account is operating under the Continuing Appropriations Act, 2022 (Division A of Public Law 117–43, as amended). The amounts included for 2022 reflect the annualized level provided by the continuing resolution.

CONSTRUCTION

[For an additional amount for "Construction", $58,227,000, to remain available until expended, for necessary expenses related to the consequences of calendar year 2019, 2020, and 2021 wildfires, hurricanes and other natural disasters.] *(Disaster Relief Supplemental Appropriations Act, 2022.)*

Program and Financing (in millions of dollars)

Identification code 014–1612–0–1–302		2021 actual	2022 est.	2023 est.
	Obligations by program activity:			
0001	Line item construction projects	8	10	13
0002	Nationwide engineering service	5	6	6
0003	Bridge, dam and seismic safety	7	3	3
0007	Restoration of Federal Assets (Hurricane Supplemental P.L. 115–123)	12	10	3
0008	Construction Deferred Maintenance	28	5	12
0009	Restoration of Federal Assets (Disaster Supplemental P.L. 116–20)	16	5	5
0010	2022 Disaster Supplemental (P.L. 117–43)		15	15
0100	Total, Direct program	76	54	57
0799	Total direct obligations	76	54	57
0801	Construction (Reimbursable)		1	1
0900	Total new obligations, unexpired accounts	76	55	58
	Budgetary resources:			
	Unobligated balance:			
1000	Unobligated balance brought forward, Oct 1	122	74	97
1010	Unobligated balance transfer to other accts [014–5648]	–1		
1021	Recoveries of prior year unpaid obligations	11	1	1
1070	Unobligated balance (total)	132	75	98
	Budget authority:			
	Appropriations, discretionary:			
1100	Appropriation	18	18	46
1100	Appropriation - Disaster Relief Supplemental [P.L. 117–43]		58	
1160	Appropriation, discretionary (total)	18	76	46
	Spending authority from offsetting collections, discretionary:			
1700	Collected	1	1	1
1701	Change in uncollected payments, Federal sources	–1		
1750	Spending auth from offsetting collections, disc (total)		1	1
1900	Budget authority (total)	18	77	47
1930	Total budgetary resources available	150	152	145
	Memorandum (non-add) entries:			
1941	Unexpired unobligated balance, end of year	74	97	87
	Change in obligated balance:			
	Unpaid obligations:			
3000	Unpaid obligations, brought forward, Oct 1	233	210	172
3010	New obligations, unexpired accounts	76	55	58
3020	Outlays (gross)	–88	–92	–101
3040	Recoveries of prior year unpaid obligations, unexpired	–11	–1	–1
3050	Unpaid obligations, end of year	210	172	128
	Uncollected payments:			
3060	Uncollected pymts, Fed sources, brought forward, Oct 1	–1		
3070	Change in uncollected pymts, Fed sources, unexpired	1		
	Memorandum (non-add) entries:			
3100	Obligated balance, start of year	232	210	172
3200	Obligated balance, end of year	210	172	128
	Budget authority and outlays, net:			
	Discretionary:			
4000	Budget authority, gross	18	77	47
	Outlays, gross:			
4010	Outlays from new discretionary authority	5	5	10
4011	Outlays from discretionary balances	83	87	91
4020	Outlays, gross (total)	88	92	101
	Offsets against gross budget authority and outlays:			
	Offsetting collections (collected) from:			
4030	Federal sources	–1	–1	–1
4040	Offsets against gross budget authority and outlays (total)	–1	–1	–1
	Additional offsets against gross budget authority only:			
4050	Change in uncollected pymts, Fed sources, unexpired	1		
4070	Budget authority, net (discretionary)	18	76	46
4080	Outlays, net (discretionary)	87	91	100
4180	Budget authority, net (total)	18	76	46
4190	Outlays, net (total)	87	91	100

The Construction activity provides funding for projects that focus on construction and rehabilitation, environmental compliance, pollution abatement, hazardous materials cleanup, and seismic safety for facilities on Fish and Wildlife Service lands. This also includes repair and inspection of the Service's dams and bridges. This activity also provides funding for modernization of field communications capability. These projects are needed to accomplish the management objectives and purposes of these structures, protect and enhance natural resources, and fulfill the Service's mission.

Object Classification (in millions of dollars)

Identification code 014–1612–0–1–302		2021 actual	2022 est.	2023 est.
	Direct obligations:			
11.1	Personnel compensation: Full-time permanent	5	5	4
12.1	Civilian personnel benefits	2	2	2
23.1	Rental payments to GSA		1	
25.2	Other services from non-Federal sources		1	

DEPARTMENT OF THE INTERIOR

Fish and Wildlife and Parks—Continued
United States Fish and Wildlife Service—Continued

651

		2021 actual	2022 est.	2023 est.
25.3	Other goods and services from Federal sources	12	....	9
25.4	Operation and maintenance of facilities	23	22	17
25.7	Operation and maintenance of equipment	1	....	1
26.0	Supplies and materials	....	1	....
31.0	Equipment	....	1	....
32.0	Land and structures	19	15	15
41.0	Grants, subsidies, and contributions	14	7	10
99.0	Direct obligations	76	55	58
99.9	Total new obligations, unexpired accounts	76	55	58

Employment Summary

Identification code 014–1612–0–1–302	2021 actual	2022 est.	2023 est.
1001 Direct civilian full-time equivalent employment	46	48	51

STATE AND TRIBAL WILDLIFE GRANTS

For wildlife conservation grants to States and to the District of Columbia, Puerto Rico, Guam, the United States Virgin Islands, the Northern Mariana Islands, American Samoa, and Indian tribes under the provisions of the Fish and Wildlife Act of 1956 and the Fish and Wildlife Coordination Act, for the development and implementation of programs for the benefit of wildlife and their habitat, including species that are not hunted or fished, $82,362,000, to remain available until expended: Provided, That of the amount provided herein, $8,000,000 is for a competitive grant program for Indian tribes not subject to the remaining provisions of this appropriation: Provided further, That $10,362,000 is for a competitive grant program to implement approved plans for States, territories, and other jurisdictions and at the discretion of affected States, the regional Associations of fish and wildlife agencies, not subject to the remaining provisions of this appropriation: Provided further, That the Secretary shall, after deducting $18,362,000 and administrative expenses, apportion the amount provided herein in the following manner: (1) to the District of Columbia and to the Commonwealth of Puerto Rico, each a sum equal to not more than one-half of 1 percent thereof; and (2) to Guam, American Samoa, the United States Virgin Islands, and the Commonwealth of the Northern Mariana Islands, each a sum equal to not more than one-fourth of 1 percent thereof: Provided further, That the Secretary of the Interior shall apportion the remaining amount in the following manner: (1) one-third of which is based on the ratio to which the land area of such State bears to the total land area of all such States; and (2) two-thirds of which is based on the ratio to which the population of such State bears to the total population of all such States: Provided further, That the amounts apportioned under this paragraph shall be adjusted equitably so that no State shall be apportioned a sum which is less than 1 percent of the amount available for apportionment under this paragraph for any fiscal year or more than 5 percent of such amount: Provided further, That the Federal share of planning grants shall not exceed 75 percent of the total costs of such projects and the Federal share of implementation grants shall not exceed 65 percent of the total costs of such projects: Provided further, That the non-Federal share of such projects may not be derived from Federal grant programs: Provided further, That any amount apportioned in 2023 to any State, territory, or other jurisdiction that remains unobligated as of September 30, 2024, shall be reapportioned, together with funds appropriated in 2025, in the manner provided herein.

Note.—A full-year 2022 appropriation for this account was not enacted at the time the Budget was prepared; therefore, the Budget assumes this account is operating under the Continuing Appropriations Act, 2022 (Division A of Public Law 117–43, as amended). The amounts included for 2022 reflect the annualized level provided by the continuing resolution.

Program and Financing (in millions of dollars)

Identification code 014–5474–0–2–302	2021 actual	2022 est.	2023 est.
Obligations by program activity:			
0001 State wildlife grants	55	60	65
0002 State competitive grants	7	8	8
0003 Tribal Wildlife Grants	6	4	4
0004 Administration	4	4	4
0900 Total new obligations, unexpired accounts	72	76	81
Budgetary resources:			
Unobligated balance:			
1000 Unobligated balance brought forward, Oct 1	50	51	51
1010 Unobligated balance transfer to other accts [014–5648]	–2	....	....
1021 Recoveries of prior year unpaid obligations	3	4	4
1070 Unobligated balance (total)	51	55	55
Budget authority:			
Appropriations, discretionary:			
1100 Appropriation	72	72	82
1930 Total budgetary resources available	123	127	137
Memorandum (non-add) entries:			
1941 Unexpired unobligated balance, end of year	51	51	56
Change in obligated balance:			
Unpaid obligations:			
3000 Unpaid obligations, brought forward, Oct 1	122	130	132
3010 New obligations, unexpired accounts	72	76	81
3020 Outlays (gross)	–61	–70	–76
3040 Recoveries of prior year unpaid obligations, unexpired	–3	–4	–4
3050 Unpaid obligations, end of year	130	132	133
Memorandum (non-add) entries:			
3100 Obligated balance, start of year	122	130	132
3200 Obligated balance, end of year	130	132	133
Budget authority and outlays, net:			
Discretionary:			
4000 Budget authority, gross	72	72	82
Outlays, gross:			
4010 Outlays from new discretionary authority	16	16	18
4011 Outlays from discretionary balances	45	54	58
4020 Outlays, gross (total)	61	70	76
4180 Budget authority, net (total)	72	72	82
4190 Outlays, net (total)	61	70	76

The State and Tribal Wildlife Grants program provides funds to States, Commonwealths, the District of Columbia, and Territories, and to federally-recognized Tribes to stabilize, restore, enhance, and protect species and their habitats that are of conservation concern. For States, this is primarily through a formula-based apportionment. Additionally, a competitive program for States uses a merit-based process to fund outcome-oriented, results-based projects. At the discretion of affected States, the competitive program may be used by regional associations of State fish and wildlife agencies. The Tribal Wildlife Grant program supports federally-recognized Tribes in the development and implementation of conservation programs for the benefit of wildlife and their habitats, including species of Tribal cultural or traditional importance.

Object Classification (in millions of dollars)

Identification code 014–5474–0–2–302	2021 actual	2022 est.	2023 est.
Direct obligations:			
11.1 Personnel compensation: Full-time permanent	2	2	2
12.1 Civilian personnel benefits	1	1	1
25.1 Advisory and assistance services	....	1	1
25.3 Other goods and services from Federal sources	1	1	1
41.0 Grants, subsidies, and contributions	68	71	76
99.9 Total new obligations, unexpired accounts	72	76	81

Employment Summary

Identification code 014–5474–0–2–302	2021 actual	2022 est.	2023 est.
1001 Direct civilian full-time equivalent employment	15	18	18

MULTINATIONAL SPECIES CONSERVATION FUND

For expenses necessary to carry out the African Elephant Conservation Act (16 U.S.C. 4201 et seq.), the Asian Elephant Conservation Act of 1997 (16 U.S.C. 4261 et seq.), the Rhinoceros and Tiger Conservation Act of 1994 (16 U.S.C. 5301 et seq.), the Great Ape Conservation Act of 2000 (16 U.S.C. 6301 et seq.), and the Marine Turtle Conservation Act of 2004 (16 U.S.C. 6601 et seq.), $19,000,000, to remain available until expended.

Note.—A full-year 2022 appropriation for this account was not enacted at the time the Budget was prepared; therefore, the Budget assumes this account is operating under the Continuing Appropriations Act, 2022 (Division A of Public Law 117–43, as amended). The amounts included for 2022 reflect the annualized level provided by the continuing resolution.

MULTINATIONAL SPECIES CONSERVATION FUND—Continued

Program and Financing (in millions of dollars)

Identification code 014–1652–0–1–302	2021 actual	2022 est.	2023 est.
Obligations by program activity:			
0001 African elephant	2	4	4
0002 Asian elephant	1	5	4
0003 Rhinoceros and tiger	1	7	7
0004 Great ape conservation	1	3	3
0005 Marine turtle	1	3	3
0006 Multinational Species Semi Postal Stamp Act (Direct)	....	1	1
0900 Total new obligations, unexpired accounts (object class 41.0)	6	23	22
Budgetary resources:			
Unobligated balance:			
1000 Unobligated balance brought forward, Oct 1	18	31	27
1001 Discretionary unobligated balance brought fwd, Oct 1	18	30	....
Budget authority:			
Appropriations, discretionary:			
1100 Appropriation	18	18	19
Spending authority from offsetting collections, mandatory:			
1800 Collected	1	1	1
1900 Budget authority (total)	19	19	20
1930 Total budgetary resources available	37	50	47
Memorandum (non-add) entries:			
1941 Unexpired unobligated balance, end of year	31	27	25
Change in obligated balance:			
Unpaid obligations:			
3000 Unpaid obligations, brought forward, Oct 1	2	5	13
3010 New obligations, unexpired accounts	6	23	22
3020 Outlays (gross)	–3	–15	–21
3050 Unpaid obligations, end of year	5	13	14
Memorandum (non-add) entries:			
3100 Obligated balance, start of year	2	5	13
3200 Obligated balance, end of year	5	13	14
Budget authority and outlays, net:			
Discretionary:			
4000 Budget authority, gross	18	18	19
Outlays, gross:			
4010 Outlays from new discretionary authority	....	5	6
4011 Outlays from discretionary balances	3	9	14
4020 Outlays, gross (total)	3	14	20
Mandatory:			
4090 Budget authority, gross	1	1	1
Outlays, gross:			
4101 Outlays from mandatory balances	....	1	1
Offsets against gross budget authority and outlays:			
Offsetting collections (collected) from:			
4120 Federal sources	....	–1	–1
4123 Non-Federal sources	–1	....	....
4130 Offsets against gross budget authority and outlays (total)	–1	–1	–1
4170 Outlays, net (mandatory)	–1	....	....
4180 Budget authority, net (total)	18	18	19
4190 Outlays, net (total)	2	14	20

African Elephant Conservation Program.—Provides technical and financial assistance to protect African elephants and their habitats, including elephant population management, public education, and anti-poaching activities.

Rhinoceros and Tiger Conservation Program.—Provides conservation grants to protect rhinoceros and tiger populations and their habitats within African and Asian countries.

Asian Elephant Conservation Program.—Provides financial assistance for Asian elephant conservation projects to protect elephant populations and their habitats within 13 range countries.

Great Ape Conservation Program.—Provides assistance for conservation and protection of chimpanzee, gorilla, orangutan, bonobo, and gibbon populations.

Marine Turtle Conservation Program.—Provides financial assistance for projects, public education, and the conservation of marine turtles and their nesting habitats.

Vanishing Species Semipostal Stamp.—The Multinational Species Conservation Fund Semipostal Stamp Act of 2010, as amended, requires the United States Postal Service to issue and sell, at a premium, a Multinational Species Conservation Funds Semipostal stamp. The proceeds of this stamp are transferred to the Service to help operations supported by the Multinational Species Conservation Funds.

Employment Summary

Identification code 014–1652–0–1–302	2021 actual	2022 est.	2023 est.
1001 Direct civilian full-time equivalent employment	2	4	5

NEOTROPICAL MIGRATORY BIRD CONSERVATION

For expenses necessary to carry out the Neotropical Migratory Bird Conservation Act (16 U.S.C. 6101 et seq.), $7,910,000, to remain available until expended.

Note.—A full-year 2022 appropriation for this account was not enacted at the time the Budget was prepared; therefore, the Budget assumes this account is operating under the Continuing Appropriations Act, 2022 (Division A of Public Law 117–43, as amended). The amounts included for 2022 reflect the annualized level provided by the continuing resolution.

Program and Financing (in millions of dollars)

Identification code 014–1696–0–1–302	2021 actual	2022 est.	2023 est.
Obligations by program activity:			
0001 Neotropical Migratory Bird	5	5	8
0900 Total new obligations, unexpired accounts (object class 41.0)	5	5	8
Budgetary resources:			
Budget authority:			
Appropriations, discretionary:			
1100 Appropriation	5	5	8
1930 Total budgetary resources available	5	5	8
Change in obligated balance:			
Unpaid obligations:			
3000 Unpaid obligations, brought forward, Oct 1	9	10	9
3010 New obligations, unexpired accounts	5	5	8
3020 Outlays (gross)	–4	–6	–6
3050 Unpaid obligations, end of year	10	9	11
Memorandum (non-add) entries:			
3100 Obligated balance, start of year	9	10	9
3200 Obligated balance, end of year	10	9	11
Budget authority and outlays, net:			
Discretionary:			
4000 Budget authority, gross	5	5	8
Outlays, gross:			
4010 Outlays from new discretionary authority	1	2	2
4011 Outlays from discretionary balances	3	4	4
4020 Outlays, gross (total)	4	6	6
4180 Budget authority, net (total)	5	5	8
4190 Outlays, net (total)	4	6	6

Funds in this account provide grants to conserve migratory bird populations in the United States, Canada, Latin America, and the Caribbean pursuant to the Neotropical Migratory Bird Conservation Act (16 U.S.C. 6101 et seq.).

Employment Summary

Identification code 014–1696–0–1–302	2021 actual	2022 est.	2023 est.
1001 Direct civilian full-time equivalent employment	1	1	1

LAND ACQUISITION

Program and Financing (in millions of dollars)

Identification code 014–5020–0–2–302	2021 actual	2022 est.	2023 est.
Obligations by program activity:			
0001 Land Acquisition Management	13	14	14
0002 Exchanges	1	2	2

DEPARTMENT OF THE INTERIOR

Fish and Wildlife and Parks—Continued
United States Fish and Wildlife Service—Continued

653

		2021 actual	2022 est.	2023 est.
0003	Emergencies, Hardships, and Inholdings	7	6	6
0004	Highlands Conservation Act	8	15	15
0005	Land Acquisitions	28	30	35
0006	Sportsmen and Recreational Access	6	4	4
0100	Total, direct program	63	71	76
0799	Total direct obligations	63	71	76
0900	Total new obligations, unexpired accounts	63	71	76
	Budgetary resources:			
	Unobligated balance:			
1000	Unobligated balance brought forward, Oct 1	69	120	159
1001	Discretionary unobligated balance brought fwd, Oct 1	69	36	
1010	Unobligated balance transfer to other accts [014–5648]	–1		
1021	Recoveries of prior year unpaid obligations	3	3	3
1070	Unobligated balance (total)	71	123	162
	Budget authority:			
	Appropriations, mandatory:			
1201	Appropriation (special or trust fund)	112	112	115
1203	Appropriation (previously unavailable)(special or trust)			6
1232	Appropriations and/or unobligated balance of appropriations temporarily reduced		–6	–7
1260	Appropriations, mandatory (total)	112	106	114
	Spending authority from offsetting collections, discretionary:			
1700	Collected		1	1
1900	Budget authority (total)	112	107	115
1930	Total budgetary resources available	183	230	277
	Memorandum (non-add) entries:			
1941	Unexpired unobligated balance, end of year	120	159	201
	Change in obligated balance:			
	Unpaid obligations:			
3000	Unpaid obligations, brought forward, Oct 1	52	61	58
3010	New obligations, unexpired accounts	63	71	76
3020	Outlays (gross)	–51	–71	–112
3040	Recoveries of prior year unpaid obligations, unexpired	–3	–3	–3
3050	Unpaid obligations, end of year	61	58	19
	Uncollected payments:			
3060	Uncollected pymts, Fed sources, brought forward, Oct 1	–1	–1	–1
3090	Uncollected pymts, Fed sources, end of year	–1	–1	–1
	Memorandum (non-add) entries:			
3100	Obligated balance, start of year	51	60	57
3200	Obligated balance, end of year	60	57	18
	Budget authority and outlays, net:			
	Discretionary:			
4000	Budget authority, gross		1	1
	Outlays, gross:			
4010	Outlays from new discretionary authority		1	1
4011	Outlays from discretionary balances	35	25	20
4020	Outlays, gross (total)	35	26	21
	Offsets against gross budget authority and outlays:			
	Offsetting collections (collected) from:			
4030	Federal sources		–1	–1
	Mandatory:			
4090	Budget authority, gross	112	106	114
	Outlays, gross:			
4100	Outlays from new mandatory authority	16	33	35
4101	Outlays from mandatory balances		12	56
4110	Outlays, gross (total)	16	45	91
4180	Budget authority, net (total)	112	106	114
4190	Outlays, net (total)	51	70	111

Federal Land Acquisition funds are used to protect areas that have native fish or wildlife values and provide natural resource benefits over a broad geographical area. Funds in this account also cover acquisition management activities, such as title fees and land surveys. The U.S. Fish and Wildlife Service places emphasis on acquiring important fish, wildlife, and plant habitat for the conservation of listed endangered and threatened species, implementing the North American Waterfowl Management Plan, and conserving migratory birds of conservation concern. The Federal Land Acquisition program uses alternative and innovative conservation tools, including conservation easements, and implements projects that have the input and participation of the affected local communities and stakeholders. The U.S. Fish and Wildlife Service is not requesting discretionary funding for this account.

The Great American Outdoors Act (P.L. 116–152) makes funds deposited into the Land and Water Conservation Fund available for expenditure without further appropriation or fiscal year limitation while providing that the U.S. Fish and Wildlife Service shall submit to Congress detailed account, program, and project allocations made available under the statute.

Object Classification (in millions of dollars)

Identification code 014–5020–0–2–302	2021 actual	2022 est.	2023 est.
Direct obligations:			
11.1 Personnel compensation: Full-time permanent	6	6	6
12.1 Civilian personnel benefits	2	2	2
23.1 Rental payments to GSA	1	1	1
25.1 Advisory and assistance services	1	1	1
25.2 Other services from non-Federal sources	2	2	2
25.3 Other goods and services from Federal sources	3	3	3
32.0 Land and structures	41	46	51
41.0 Grants, subsidies, and contributions	8	10	10
99.0 Direct obligations	64	71	76
99.5 Adjustment for rounding	–1		
99.9 Total new obligations, unexpired accounts	63	71	76

Employment Summary

Identification code 014–5020–0–2–302	2021 actual	2022 est.	2023 est.
1001 Direct civilian full-time equivalent employment	62	70	70

LANDOWNER INCENTIVE PROGRAM

The Landowner Incentive Program provided cost-shared, competitive grants to States, Commonwealths, the District of Columbia, Territories, and Tribes to create, supplement or expand upon new or ongoing landowner incentive programs. These programs provided technical and financial assistance to private landowners to help them protect and manage imperiled species and their habitat, while continuing to engage in traditional land use or working conservation practices. The program was phased out in 2008 and minimal balances remain in this account.

MIGRATORY BIRD CONSERVATION ACCOUNT

Special and Trust Fund Receipts (in millions of dollars)

Identification code 014–5137–0–2–303	2021 actual	2022 est.	2023 est.
0100 Balance, start of year	5	7	5
Receipts:			
Current law:			
1110 Migratory Bird Hunting Stamps	22	22	22
1110 Custom Duties on Arms and Ammunition	82	50	50
1110 Migratory Birds Hunting Stamps (Conservation Easements)	15	15	15
1199 Total current law receipts	119	87	87
1999 Total receipts	119	87	87
2000 Total: Balances and receipts	124	94	92
Appropriations:			
Current law:			
2101 Migratory Bird Conservation Account	–119	–87	–87
2103 Migratory Bird Conservation Account	–5	–7	–5
2132 Migratory Bird Conservation Account	7	5	5
2199 Total current law appropriations	–117	–89	–87
2999 Total appropriations	–117	–89	–87
5099 Balance, end of year	7	5	5

Program and Financing (in millions of dollars)

Identification code 014–5137–0–2–303	2021 actual	2022 est.	2023 est.
Obligations by program activity:			
0001 Printing and Sale of Duck Stamps		1	1

MIGRATORY BIRD CONSERVATION ACCOUNT—Continued
Program and Financing—Continued

Identification code 014–5137–0–2–303	2021 actual	2022 est.	2023 est.
0002 Acquisition of Land and Easements	115	93	87
0900 Total new obligations, unexpired accounts	115	94	88
Budgetary resources:			
Unobligated balance:			
1000 Unobligated balance brought forward, Oct 1	15	18	14
1021 Recoveries of prior year unpaid obligations	1	1	1
1070 Unobligated balance (total)	16	19	15
Budget authority:			
Appropriations, mandatory:			
1201 Appropriation (special or trust fund)	119	87	87
1203 Appropriation (previously unavailable)(special or trust)	5	7	5
1232 Appropriations and/or unobligated balance of appropriations temporarily reduced	–7	–5	–5
1260 Appropriations, mandatory (total)	117	89	87
1930 Total budgetary resources available	133	108	102
Memorandum (non-add) entries:			
1941 Unexpired unobligated balance, end of year	18	14	14
Change in obligated balance:			
Unpaid obligations:			
3000 Unpaid obligations, brought forward, Oct 1	43	48	54
3010 New obligations, unexpired accounts	115	94	88
3020 Outlays (gross)	–109	–87	–90
3040 Recoveries of prior year unpaid obligations, unexpired	–1	–1	–1
3050 Unpaid obligations, end of year	48	54	51
Memorandum (non-add) entries:			
3100 Obligated balance, start of year	43	48	54
3200 Obligated balance, end of year	48	54	51
Budget authority and outlays, net:			
Mandatory:			
4090 Budget authority, gross	117	89	87
Outlays, gross:			
4100 Outlays from new mandatory authority	71	54	52
4101 Outlays from mandatory balances	38	33	38
4110 Outlays, gross (total)	109	87	90
4180 Budget authority, net (total)	117	89	87
4190 Outlays, net (total)	109	87	90

Funds deposited into this account include import duties on arms and ammunition and receipts in excess of U.S. Postal Service expenses from the sale of Migratory Bird Hunting and Conservation Stamps, also known as Duck Stamps. These funds are used to acquire land and water for migratory bird refuges and waterfowl production areas. In addition, any funds reverted from the States within the Federal Aid in Wildlife Restoration Fund are available for this purpose. The Federal Duck Stamp Act (P.L. 113–264) increased the price of Duck Stamps from $15 to $25, with the $10 increase to be dedicated to the acquisition of conservation easements for conservation of migratory birds.

Object Classification (in millions of dollars)

Identification code 014–5137–0–2–303	2021 actual	2022 est.	2023 est.
Direct obligations:			
11.1 Personnel compensation: Full-time permanent	7	6	6
12.1 Civilian personnel benefits	3	2	2
25.2 Other services from non-Federal sources	1	1	1
25.3 Other goods and services from Federal sources	3	3	3
32.0 Land and structures	101	82	76
99.9 Total new obligations, unexpired accounts	115	94	88

Employment Summary

Identification code 014–5137–0–2–303	2021 actual	2022 est.	2023 est.
1001 Direct civilian full-time equivalent employment	79	79	79

NORTH AMERICAN WETLANDS CONSERVATION FUND

For expenses necessary to carry out the provisions of the North American Wetlands Conservation Act (16 U.S.C. 4401 et seq.), $46,500,000, to remain available until expended.

Note.—A full-year 2022 appropriation for this account was not enacted at the time the Budget was prepared; therefore, the Budget assumes this account is operating under the Continuing Appropriations Act, 2022 (Division A of Public Law 117–43, as amended). The amounts included for 2022 reflect the annualized level provided by the continuing resolution.

Special and Trust Fund Receipts (in millions of dollars)

Identification code 014–5241–0–2–302	2021 actual	2022 est.	2023 est.
0100 Balance, start of year	7	7	7
2000 Total: Balances and receipts	7	7	7
5099 Balance, end of year	7	7	7

Program and Financing (in millions of dollars)

Identification code 014–5241–0–2–302	2021 actual	2022 est.	2023 est.
Obligations by program activity:			
0003 Wetlands conservation projects	52	49	49
Budgetary resources:			
Unobligated balance:			
1000 Unobligated balance brought forward, Oct 1	15	10	10
1001 Discretionary unobligated balance brought fwd, Oct 1	10	6	
1021 Recoveries of prior year unpaid obligations		2	2
1070 Unobligated balance (total)	15	12	12
Budget authority:			
Appropriations, discretionary:			
1100 Appropriation	47	47	47
1900 Budget authority (total)	47	47	47
1930 Total budgetary resources available	62	59	59
Memorandum (non-add) entries:			
1941 Unexpired unobligated balance, end of year	10	10	10
Change in obligated balance:			
Unpaid obligations:			
3000 Unpaid obligations, brought forward, Oct 1	84	96	95
3010 New obligations, unexpired accounts	52	49	49
3020 Outlays (gross)	–40	–48	–49
3040 Recoveries of prior year unpaid obligations, unexpired		–2	–2
3050 Unpaid obligations, end of year	96	95	93
Memorandum (non-add) entries:			
3100 Obligated balance, start of year	84	96	95
3200 Obligated balance, end of year	96	95	93
Budget authority and outlays, net:			
Discretionary:			
4000 Budget authority, gross	47	47	47
Outlays, gross:			
4010 Outlays from new discretionary authority	3	7	7
4011 Outlays from discretionary balances	29	38	40
4020 Outlays, gross (total)	32	45	47
Mandatory:			
Outlays, gross:			
4101 Outlays from mandatory balances	8	3	2
4180 Budget authority, net (total)	47	47	47
4190 Outlays, net (total)	40	48	49

Funds deposited into this account include direct appropriations and fines, penalties, and forfeitures collected under the authority of the Migratory Bird Treaty Act (16 U.S.C. 707). The North American Wetlands Conservation Fund supports wetlands conservation projects approved by the Migratory Bird Conservation Commission. Interest on obligations held in the Federal Aid in Wildlife Restoration Fund is also available for this purpose. In addition, a portion of receipts to the Sport Fish Restoration Account is also available for coastal wetlands conservation projects.

These projects help fulfill the habitat protection, restoration, and enhancement goals of the North American Waterfowl Management Plan and the Tripartite Agreement among Mexico, Canada, and the United States. These projects may involve partnerships with public agencies and private entities, with non-Federal matching contributions, for the long-term conservation

DEPARTMENT OF THE INTERIOR

of habitat for migratory birds and other fish and wildlife, including species that are listed, or are candidates to be listed, under the Endangered Species Act (16 U.S.C. 1531).

Wetlands conservation projects include obtaining a real property interest in lands or waters, including water rights; the restoration, management or enhancement of habitat; and training and development for conservation management in Mexico. Funding may be provided for assistance for wetlands conservation projects in Canada or Mexico.

Object Classification (in millions of dollars)

Identification code 014–5241–0–2–302	2021 actual	2022 est.	2023 est.
Direct obligations:			
11.1 Personnel compensation: Full-time permanent	1	1	1
32.0 Land and structures	1	1	1
41.0 Grants, subsidies, and contributions	50	47	47
99.9 Total new obligations, unexpired accounts	52	49	49

Employment Summary

Identification code 014–5241–0–2–302	2021 actual	2022 est.	2023 est.
1001 Direct civilian full-time equivalent employment	7	7	7

COOPERATIVE ENDANGERED SPECIES CONSERVATION FUND

For expenses necessary to carry out section 6 of the Endangered Species Act of 1973 (16 U.S.C. 1535), $23,702,000, to remain available until expended, which shall be derived from the Cooperative Endangered Species Conservation Fund.

Note.—A full-year 2022 appropriation for this account was not enacted at the time the Budget was prepared; therefore, the Budget assumes this account is operating under the Continuing Appropriations Act, 2022 (Division A of Public Law 117–43, as amended). The amounts included for 2022 reflect the annualized level provided by the continuing resolution.

Special and Trust Fund Receipts (in millions of dollars)

Identification code 014–5143–0–2–302	2021 actual	2022 est.	2023 est.
0100 Balance, start of year	692	743	815
Receipts:			
Current law:			
1140 Payment from the General Fund, Cooperative Endangered Species Conservation Fund	75	96	83
2000 Total: Balances and receipts	767	839	898
Appropriations:			
Current law:			
2101 Cooperative Endangered Species Conservation Fund	–24	–24	–24
5099 Balance, end of year	743	815	874

Program and Financing (in millions of dollars)

Identification code 014–5143–0–2–302	2021 actual	2022 est.	2023 est.
Obligations by program activity:			
0001 Conservation Grants to States	21	15	13
0002 HCP Planning Assistance Grants	7	4	8
0004 Administration	4	4	4
0005 HCP Land Acquisition Grants to States	1	20	5
0006 Species Recovery Land Acquisition	2	12	3
0007 Payment to special fund unavailable receipt account	75	96	83
0900 Total new obligations, unexpired accounts	110	151	116
Budgetary resources:			
Unobligated balance:			
1000 Unobligated balance brought forward, Oct 1	76	93	93
1001 Discretionary unobligated balance brought fwd, Oct 1	76	82	
1021 Recoveries of prior year unpaid obligations	10	14	14
1070 Unobligated balance (total)	86	107	107
Budget authority:			
Appropriations, discretionary:			
1101 Appropriation LWCF special fund [145005]	20	20	
1101 Appropriation CESCF special fund [145143]	24	24	24
1131 Unobligated balance of appropriations permanently reduced	–13	–13	
1160 Appropriation, discretionary (total)	31	31	24
Appropriations, mandatory:			
1200 Appropriation	75	96	83
1201 Appropriation (special or trust fund)	11	11	30
1203 Appropriation (previously unavailable)(special or trust)			1
1232 Appropriations and/or unobligated balance of appropriations temporarily reduced		–1	–2
1260 Appropriations, mandatory (total)	86	106	112
1900 Budget authority (total)	117	137	136
1930 Total budgetary resources available	203	244	243
Memorandum (non-add) entries:			
1941 Unexpired unobligated balance, end of year	93	93	127
Change in obligated balance:			
Unpaid obligations:			
3000 Unpaid obligations, brought forward, Oct 1	132	110	98
3010 New obligations, unexpired accounts	110	151	116
3020 Outlays (gross)	–122	–149	–149
3040 Recoveries of prior year unpaid obligations, unexpired	–10	–14	–14
3050 Unpaid obligations, end of year	110	98	51
Memorandum (non-add) entries:			
3100 Obligated balance, start of year	132	110	98
3200 Obligated balance, end of year	110	98	51
Budget authority and outlays, net:			
Discretionary:			
4000 Budget authority, gross	31	31	24
Outlays, gross:			
4010 Outlays from new discretionary authority	1		2
4011 Outlays from discretionary balances	46	49	51
4020 Outlays, gross (total)	47	49	53
Mandatory:			
4090 Budget authority, gross	86	106	112
Outlays, gross:			
4100 Outlays from new mandatory authority	75	98	90
4101 Outlays from mandatory balances		2	6
4110 Outlays, gross (total)	75	100	96
4180 Budget authority, net (total)	117	137	136
4190 Outlays, net (total)	122	149	149

The Cooperative Endangered Species Conservation Fund provides grants to States and U.S. Territories for species and habitat conservation actions on non-Federal lands, including habitat acquisition, conservation planning, habitat restoration, status surveys, captive propagation and reintroduction, research, and education for species that are listed or are candidates for listing, as threatened or endangered. These activities support recovery efforts and Habitat Conservation Plans in partnership with local governments and other interested parties to protect species. Appropriations to this account have been financed by both the Land and Water Conservation Fund and the Cooperative Endangered Species Conservation Fund. The latter is an unavailable receipt account that receives a transfer from the General Fund of the U.S. Treasury equal to five percent of receipts deposited to the Federal Aid in Wildlife and Sport Fish Restoration accounts plus Lacey Act receipts over $500,000. Funds made available for grants from the Cooperative Endangered Species Conservation Fund are subject to annual appropriations from Congress. The Great American Outdoors Act, enacted in 2020, provides mandatory funding for the Land and Water Conservation Fund (LWCF). The 2023 President's Budget proposes to allocate mandatory LWCF to support land acquisition activities associated with this program.

Object Classification (in millions of dollars)

Identification code 014–5143–0–2–302	2021 actual	2022 est.	2023 est.
Direct obligations:			
11.1 Personnel compensation: Full-time permanent	1	1	1
25.3 Other goods and services from Federal sources	2	2	2
25.7 Operation and maintenance of equipment	1	1	1
41.0 Grants, subsidies, and contributions	31	51	29
94.0 Financial transfers	75	96	83
99.0 Direct obligations	110	151	116
99.9 Total new obligations, unexpired accounts	110	151	116

Fish and Wildlife and Parks—Continued
United States Fish and Wildlife Service—Continued

COOPERATIVE ENDANGERED SPECIES CONSERVATION FUND—Continued

Employment Summary

Identification code 014–5143–0–2–302	2021 actual	2022 est.	2023 est.
1001 Direct civilian full-time equivalent employment	9	9	9

NATIONAL WILDLIFE REFUGE FUND

Note.—A full-year 2022 appropriation for this account was not enacted at the time the Budget was prepared; therefore, the Budget assumes this account is operating under the Continuing Appropriations Act, 2022 (Division A of Public Law 117–43, as amended). The amounts included for 2022 reflect the annualized level provided by the continuing resolution.

Special and Trust Fund Receipts (in millions of dollars)

Identification code 014–5091–0–2–806	2021 actual	2022 est.	2023 est.
0100 Balance, start of year			
Receipts:			
Current law:			
1130 National Wildlife Refuge Fund	7	8	8
2000 Total: Balances and receipts	7	8	8
Appropriations:			
Current law:			
2101 National Wildlife Refuge Fund	–7	–8	–8
5099 Balance, end of year			

Program and Financing (in millions of dollars)

Identification code 014–5091–0–2–806	2021 actual	2022 est.	2023 est.
Obligations by program activity:			
0001 Expenses for sales	3	3	2
0003 Payments to counties	17	17	5
0900 Total new obligations, unexpired accounts	20	20	7
Budgetary resources:			
Unobligated balance:			
1000 Unobligated balance brought forward, Oct 1	4	4	5
Budget authority:			
Appropriations, discretionary:			
1100 Appropriation	13	13	
Appropriations, mandatory:			
1201 Appropriation (special or trust fund)	7	8	8
1900 Budget authority (total)	20	21	8
1930 Total budgetary resources available	24	25	13
Memorandum (non-add) entries:			
1941 Unexpired unobligated balance, end of year	4	5	6
Change in obligated balance:			
Unpaid obligations:			
3000 Unpaid obligations, brought forward, Oct 1	1	1	1
3010 New obligations, unexpired accounts	20	20	7
3020 Outlays (gross)	–20	–20	–8
3050 Unpaid obligations, end of year	1	1	
Memorandum (non-add) entries:			
3100 Obligated balance, start of year	1	1	1
3200 Obligated balance, end of year	1	1	
Budget authority and outlays, net:			
Discretionary:			
4000 Budget authority, gross	13	13	
Outlays, gross:			
4010 Outlays from new discretionary authority	13	13	
Mandatory:			
4090 Budget authority, gross	7	8	8
Outlays, gross:			
4100 Outlays from new mandatory authority	5	6	6
4101 Outlays from mandatory balances	2	1	2
4110 Outlays, gross (total)	7	7	8
4180 Budget authority, net (total)	20	21	8
4190 Outlays, net (total)	20	20	8

The Refuge Revenue Sharing Act (16 U.S.C. 715s) authorizes the Service to make payments to counties in which Fish and Wildlife Service fee lands are located, from the revenues resulting from the sale of products from Service lands, less expenses for producing the revenue and activities related to revenue sharing. The 2023 Budget does not propose to supplement revenues with discretionary funding.

Object Classification (in millions of dollars)

Identification code 014–5091–0–2–806	2021 actual	2022 est.	2023 est.
Direct obligations:			
26.0 Supplies and materials	1	1	1
41.0 Grants, subsidies, and contributions	18	19	6
99.0 Direct obligations	19	20	7
99.5 Adjustment for rounding	1		
99.9 Total new obligations, unexpired accounts	20	20	7

Employment Summary

Identification code 014–5091–0–2–806	2021 actual	2022 est.	2023 est.
1001 Direct civilian full-time equivalent employment	4	4	4

RECREATION ENHANCEMENT FEE PROGRAM, FWS

Special and Trust Fund Receipts (in millions of dollars)

Identification code 014–5252–0–2–303	2021 actual	2022 est.	2023 est.
0100 Balance, start of year			
Receipts:			
Current law:			
1130 Recreation Enhancement Fee, Fish and Wildlife Service	7	7	7
2000 Total: Balances and receipts	7	7	7
Appropriations:			
Current law:			
2101 Recreation Enhancement Fee Program, FWS	–7	–7	–7
5099 Balance, end of year			

Program and Financing (in millions of dollars)

Identification code 014–5252–0–2–303	2021 actual	2022 est.	2023 est.
Obligations by program activity:			
0001 Recreation Enhancement Fee Program	5	6	6
Budgetary resources:			
Unobligated balance:			
1000 Unobligated balance brought forward, Oct 1	15	17	18
Budget authority:			
Appropriations, mandatory:			
1201 Appropriation (special or trust fund)	7	7	7
1930 Total budgetary resources available	22	24	25
Memorandum (non-add) entries:			
1941 Unexpired unobligated balance, end of year	17	18	19
Change in obligated balance:			
Unpaid obligations:			
3000 Unpaid obligations, brought forward, Oct 1	2	2	2
3010 New obligations, unexpired accounts	5	6	6
3020 Outlays (gross)	–5	–6	–7
3050 Unpaid obligations, end of year	2	2	1
Memorandum (non-add) entries:			
3100 Obligated balance, start of year	2	2	2
3200 Obligated balance, end of year	2	2	1
Budget authority and outlays, net:			
Mandatory:			
4090 Budget authority, gross	7	7	7
Outlays, gross:			
4100 Outlays from new mandatory authority	5	4	4
4101 Outlays from mandatory balances		2	3
4110 Outlays, gross (total)	5	6	7
4180 Budget authority, net (total)	7	7	7
4190 Outlays, net (total)	5	6	7

The Federal Lands Recreation Enhancement Act (FLREA) was passed on December 8, 2004, as part of the Omnibus Appropriations bill for 2005.

Approximately 164 Fish and Wildlife Service sites collect entrance fees and other receipts. All receipts are deposited into a recreation fee account of which at least 80 percent is returned to the collecting site.

The recreation fee program supports user generated cost recovery for the operation and maintenance of recreation areas, visitor services improvements, and habitat enhancement projects on Federal lands. Fees are used primarily at the site to improve visitor access, enhance public safety and security, address maintenance needs, enhance resource protection, and cover the costs of collection. Recreation fees are often used at Service sites to fund student intern and various youth programs focusing on hunting, fishing, wildlife observation, wildlife photography, environmental education, and environmental interpretation. Section 423 of Division G of the Consolidated Appropriations Act, 2021 (P.L. 116–260) extended FLREA through 2022. The 2023 budget includes appropriations language to extend FLREA through October 1, 2024.

Object Classification (in millions of dollars)

Identification code 014–5252–0–2–303		2021 actual	2022 est.	2023 est.
	Direct obligations:			
	Personnel compensation:			
11.1	Full-time permanent	1	1	1
11.3	Other than full-time permanent		1	1
11.9	Total personnel compensation	1	2	2
25.3	Other goods and services from Federal sources	1	1	1
26.0	Supplies and materials	1	1	1
32.0	Land and structures	1	1	1
41.0	Grants, subsidies, and contributions	1	1	1
99.9	Total new obligations, unexpired accounts	5	6	6

Employment Summary

Identification code 014–5252–0–2–303		2021 actual	2022 est.	2023 est.
1001	Direct civilian full-time equivalent employment	23	30	30

FEDERAL AID IN WILDLIFE RESTORATION

Special and Trust Fund Receipts (in millions of dollars)

Identification code 014–5029–0–2–303		2021 actual	2022 est.	2023 est.
0100	Balance, start of year	741	1,204	963
	Receipts:			
	Current law:			
1110	Excise Taxes, Federal Aid to Wildlife Restoration Fund	1,162	895	902
1140	Earnings on Investments, Federal Aid to Wildlife Restoration Fund	27	25	28
1199	Total current law receipts	1,189	920	930
1999	Total receipts	1,189	920	930
2000	Total: Balances and receipts	1,930	2,124	1,893
	Appropriations:			
	Current law:			
2101	Federal Aid in Wildlife Restoration	–729	–1,187	–923
2103	Federal Aid in Wildlife Restoration	–39	–42	–68
2132	Federal Aid in Wildlife Restoration	42	68	53
2199	Total current law appropriations	–726	–1,161	–938
2999	Total appropriations	–726	–1,161	–938
5099	Balance, end of year	1,204	963	955

Program and Financing (in millions of dollars)

Identification code 014–5029–0–2–303		2021 actual	2022 est.	2023 est.
	Obligations by program activity:			
0003	Multi-state conservation grant program	8	6	6
0004	Administration	12	13	13
0005	Wildlife restoration grants	722	1,025	953
0006	NAWCF (interest used for grants)	50	38	35
0007	Section 10 hunter education	8	8	8
0900	Total new obligations, unexpired accounts	800	1,090	1,015
	Budgetary resources:			
	Unobligated balance:			
1000	Unobligated balance brought forward, Oct 1	356	344	473
1021	Recoveries of prior year unpaid obligations	62	58	58
1070	Unobligated balance (total)	418	402	531
	Budget authority:			
	Appropriations, mandatory:			
1201	Appropriation (special or trust fund)	729	1,187	923
1203	Appropriation (previously unavailable)(special or trust)	39	42	68
1232	Appropriations and/or unobligated balance of appropriations temporarily reduced	–42	–68	–53
1260	Appropriations, mandatory (total)	726	1,161	938
1930	Total budgetary resources available	1,144	1,563	1,469
	Memorandum (non-add) entries:			
1941	Unexpired unobligated balance, end of year	344	473	454
	Change in obligated balance:			
	Unpaid obligations:			
3000	Unpaid obligations, brought forward, Oct 1	1,000	1,025	1,225
3010	New obligations, unexpired accounts	800	1,090	1,015
3020	Outlays (gross)	–713	–832	–959
3040	Recoveries of prior year unpaid obligations, unexpired	–62	–58	–58
3050	Unpaid obligations, end of year	1,025	1,225	1,223
	Memorandum (non-add) entries:			
3100	Obligated balance, start of year	1,000	1,025	1,225
3200	Obligated balance, end of year	1,025	1,225	1,223
	Budget authority and outlays, net:			
	Mandatory:			
4090	Budget authority, gross	726	1,161	938
	Outlays, gross:			
4100	Outlays from new mandatory authority	182	239	195
4101	Outlays from mandatory balances	531	593	764
4110	Outlays, gross (total)	713	832	959
4180	Budget authority, net (total)	726	1,161	938
4190	Outlays, net (total)	713	832	959
	Memorandum (non-add) entries:			
5000	Total investments, SOY: Federal securities: Par value	2,060	2,540	2,602
5001	Total investments, EOY: Federal securities: Par value	2,540	2,602	2,588

The Federal Aid in Wildlife Restoration Act (16 U.S.C. 669 et seq.), also known as the Pittman-Robertson Wildlife Restoration Act, created a program to fund the selection, restoration, rehabilitation and improvement of wildlife habitat, hunter education and safety, and wildlife management research. Under the program, States, Puerto Rico, Guam, the Virgin Islands, American Samoa, and the Northern Mariana Islands are allocated funds from an excise tax on sporting arms and ammunition, handguns, and a tax on certain archery equipment. States are reimbursed up to 75 percent of the cost of approved wildlife and hunter education projects.

The Wildlife and Sport Fish Restoration Programs Improvement Act (P.L. 106–408) amends the Pittman-Robertson Wildlife Restoration Act and authorizes a Multistate Conservation Grant Program, as well as the Firearm and Bow Hunter Education and Safety Program that provides grants to the States.

The Target Practice and Marksmanship Training Support Act (P.L. 116–17) amends the Pittman-Robertson Wildlife Restoration Act to define a public target range and offers States alternatives for funding specific activities related to public target ranges.

Object Classification (in millions of dollars)

Identification code 014–5029–0–2–303		2021 actual	2022 est.	2023 est.
	Direct obligations:			
11.1	Personnel compensation: Full-time permanent	6	6	6
12.1	Civilian personnel benefits	2	2	2
25.1	Advisory and assistance services		1	1
25.3	Other goods and services from Federal sources	3	3	3
25.7	Operation and maintenance of equipment	1		
32.0	Land and structures	4	6	6
41.0	Grants, subsidies, and contributions	784	1,072	997
99.9	Total new obligations, unexpired accounts	800	1,090	1,015

658

Fish and Wildlife and Parks—Continued
United States Fish and Wildlife Service—Continued

FEDERAL AID IN WILDLIFE RESTORATION—Continued

Employment Summary

Identification code 014–5029–0–2–303	2021 actual	2022 est.	2023 est.
1001 Direct civilian full-time equivalent employment	54	53	60

COASTAL IMPACT ASSISTANCE

Program and Financing (in millions of dollars)

Identification code 014–5579–0–2–306	2021 actual	2022 est.	2023 est.
Obligations by program activity:			
0001 Administration	....	1	1
0900 Total new obligations, unexpired accounts (object class 25.1)	....	1	1
Budgetary resources:			
Unobligated balance:			
1000 Unobligated balance brought forward, Oct 1	5	5	4
1930 Total budgetary resources available	5	5	4
Memorandum (non-add) entries:			
1941 Unexpired unobligated balance, end of year	5	4	3
Change in obligated balance:			
Unpaid obligations:			
3010 New obligations, unexpired accounts	....	1	1
3020 Outlays (gross)	....	–1	–1
Budget authority and outlays, net:			
Mandatory:			
Outlays, gross:			
4101 Outlays from mandatory balances	....	1	1
4180 Budget authority, net (total)	....	....	....
4190 Outlays, net (total)	....	1	1

The Energy Policy Act (P.L. 109–58) amends section 31 of the Outer Continental Shelf (OCS) Lands Act (43 U.S.C. 1356 et seq.) to require that for each of the fiscal years 2007 through 2010, $250,000,000 in OCS revenues be distributed each year to coastal States that have submitted approved coastal impact assistance plans. The formula for distribution is based on the amount of qualified OCS revenues generated off the coastline of each producing State. In addition, 35 percent of each State's allocable share is to be distributed to coastal political subdivisions based on population, coastline, and distance to applicable OCS leases. In 2011, administration of this program was transferred from the Bureau of Ocean Energy Management, Regulation, and Enforcement to the Fish and Wildlife Service.

Employment Summary

Identification code 014–5579–0–2–306	2021 actual	2022 est.	2023 est.
1001 Direct civilian full-time equivalent employment	....	1	1

MISCELLANEOUS PERMANENT APPROPRIATIONS

Special and Trust Fund Receipts (in millions of dollars)

Identification code 014–9927–0–2–302	2021 actual	2022 est.	2023 est.
0100 Balance, start of year	....	....	....
Receipts:			
Current law:			
1130 Rents and Charges for Quarters, Fish and Wildlife Service	4	5	4
1198 Rounding adjustment	1	....	....
1199 Total current law receipts	5	5	4
1999 Total receipts	5	5	4
2000 Total: Balances and receipts	5	5	4
Appropriations:			
Current law:			
2101 Miscellaneous Permanent Appropriations	–5	–5	–4

THE BUDGET FOR FISCAL YEAR 2023

5099 Balance, end of year	....	....	....

Program and Financing (in millions of dollars)

Identification code 014–9927–0–2–302	2021 actual	2022 est.	2023 est.
Obligations by program activity:			
0001 Miscellaneous Permanents	5	4	4
Budgetary resources:			
Unobligated balance:			
1000 Unobligated balance brought forward, Oct 1	9	9	10
Budget authority:			
Appropriations, mandatory:			
1201 Appropriation (special or trust fund)	5	5	4
1930 Total budgetary resources available	14	14	14
Memorandum (non-add) entries:			
1941 Unexpired unobligated balance, end of year	9	10	10
Change in obligated balance:			
Unpaid obligations:			
3000 Unpaid obligations, brought forward, Oct 1	1	2	2
3010 New obligations, unexpired accounts	5	4	4
3020 Outlays (gross)	–4	–4	–5
3050 Unpaid obligations, end of year	2	2	1
Memorandum (non-add) entries:			
3100 Obligated balance, start of year	1	2	2
3200 Obligated balance, end of year	2	2	1
Budget authority and outlays, net:			
Mandatory:			
4090 Budget authority, gross	5	5	4
Outlays, gross:			
4100 Outlays from new mandatory authority	2	2	2
4101 Outlays from mandatory balances	2	2	3
4110 Outlays, gross (total)	4	4	5
4180 Budget authority, net (total)	5	5	4
4190 Outlays, net (total)	4	4	5

Operation and maintenance of quarters.—Revenue from the rental of Government quarters is deposited in this account for use in the operation and maintenance of such quarters for the Fish and Wildlife Service, pursuant to Public Law 98–473, Section 320; 98 Stat. 1874, as amended.

Proceeds from sales, water resources development projects.—Receipts collected from the sale of timber and crops from National Wildlife Refuge System lands leased or licensed from the Department of the Army may be used to pay the costs of production of the timber and crops and for managing wildlife habitat, 16 U.S.C. 460(d).

Lahontan Valley and Pyramid Lake Fish and Wildlife Fund.—Under the Truckee-Carson Pyramid Lake Water Rights Settlement Act, the Lahontan Valley and Pyramid Lake Fish and Wildlife Fund receives revenues and donations from non-Federal parties to support the restoration and enhancement of wetlands in the Lahontan Valley and to restore and protect the Pyramid Lake fishery. Revenues received from the Bureau of Reclamation's Washoe Project in excess of operation and maintenance costs for the Stampede Reservoir are available without further appropriation. Donations made for express purposes and State cost-sharing funds are available without further appropriation. The Secretary of the Interior is also authorized to deposit proceeds from the sale of certain lands and interests in lands into the Pyramid Lake Fish and Wildlife Fund.

Community Partnership Enhancement.—Under the National Wildlife Refuge System Volunteer and Community Partnership Enhancement Act (P.L. 105–242, dated October 5, 1998), the Service is authorized to enter into cooperative agreements with nonprofit organizations, academic institutions, or State and local governments to construct, operate, maintain, or improve refuge facilities and services, and to promote volunteer outreach and education programs.

Object Classification (in millions of dollars)

Identification code 014–9927–0–2–302	2021 actual	2022 est.	2023 est.
Direct obligations:			
23.3 Communications, utilities, and miscellaneous charges	1	1	1

		2021 actual	2022 est.	2023 est.
25.2	Other services from non-Federal sources	1	1	1
25.4	Operation and maintenance of facilities	1	1	1
26.0	Supplies and materials	1	1	1
32.0	Land and structures	1		
99.9	Total new obligations, unexpired accounts	5	4	4

Employment Summary

Identification code 014–9927–0–2–302	2021 actual	2022 est.	2023 est.
1001 Direct civilian full-time equivalent employment	2	4	4

Trust Funds

SPORT FISH RESTORATION

Program and Financing (in millions of dollars)

Identification code 014–8151–0–7–303	2021 actual	2022 est.	2023 est.
Obligations by program activity:			
0001 Payments to States for sport fish restoration	419	430	440
0003 North American wetlands conservation grants	19	18	17
0004 Coastal wetlands conservation grants	27	22	20
0006 Administration	12	13	12
0007 National communication & outreach	14	14	12
0009 Multi-State conservation activities	3	4	3
0010 Marine Fisheries Commissions & Boating Council	1	1	1
0011 Boating Infrastructure Improvement	37	33	30
0900 Total new obligations, unexpired accounts	532	535	535
Budgetary resources:			
Unobligated balance:			
1000 Unobligated balance brought forward, Oct 1	214	238	233
1021 Recoveries of prior year unpaid obligations	43	36	36
1070 Unobligated balance (total)	257	274	269
Budget authority:			
Appropriations, mandatory:			
1201 Appropriation (special or trust fund)	742	715	715
1203 Appropriation (previously unavailable)(special or trust)	27	29	28
1220 Appropriations transferred to other accts [096–8333]	–94	–90	–90
1220 Appropriations transferred to other accts [070–8149]	–133	–132	–132
1232 Appropriations and/or unobligated balance of appropriations temporarily reduced	–29	–28	–28
1260 Appropriations, mandatory (total)	513	494	493
1930 Total budgetary resources available	770	768	762
Memorandum (non-add) entries:			
1941 Unexpired unobligated balance, end of year	238	233	227
Change in obligated balance:			
Unpaid obligations:			
3000 Unpaid obligations, brought forward, Oct 1	549	622	668
3010 New obligations, unexpired accounts	532	535	535
3020 Outlays (gross)	–416	–453	–481
3040 Recoveries of prior year unpaid obligations, unexpired	–43	–36	–36
3050 Unpaid obligations, end of year	622	668	686
Memorandum (non-add) entries:			
3100 Obligated balance, start of year	549	622	668
3200 Obligated balance, end of year	622	668	686
Budget authority and outlays, net:			
Mandatory:			
4090 Budget authority, gross	513	494	493
Outlays, gross:			
4100 Outlays from new mandatory authority	154	129	128
4101 Outlays from mandatory balances	262	324	353
4110 Outlays, gross (total)	416	453	481
4180 Budget authority, net (total)	513	494	493
4190 Outlays, net (total)	416	453	481

The Federal Aid in Sport Fish Restoration Act, also known as the Dingell-Johnson Sport Fish Restoration Act (16 U.S.C. 777 et seq.), created a fishery resources, conservation, and restoration program funded by excise taxes on fishing equipment and certain other sport fish related products and fuel.

The Wildlife and Sport Fish Restoration Programs Improvement Act (P.L. 106–408) amends the Dingell-Johnson Sport Fish Restoration Act and authorizes a Multistate Conservation Grant Program. It also provides funding for several fisheries commissions and the Sport Fishing and Boating Partnership Council.

The Sport Fish Restoration Act specifies that the net deposits made into the Sport Fish Restoration and Boating Safety Trust Fund, minus the distributions for administrative expenses for the Fish and Wildlife Service and the United States Coast Guard, special commissions, and the Boating Council, be distributed to support the following:

The Coastal Wetlands Planning, Protection, and Restoration Act (16 U.S.C. 3951 et seq.).—18.673 percent of net deposits, or amounts collected in small engine fuels excise taxes as provided by 26 U.S.C. 9504(b), whichever is greater, are to be made available and distributed as follows: 70 percent to the U.S. Army Corps of Engineers for priority project and conservation planning activities in Louisiana; 15 percent to the Fish and Wildlife Service for coastal wetlands conservation grants; and 15 percent to the Fish and Wildlife Service for wetlands conservation projects per the North American Wetlands Conservation Act (16 U.S.C. 4407).

Boating Safety Programs.—17.315 percent of net deposits are to be made available to the United States Coast Guard for State recreational boating safety programs.

Boating Infrastructure Improvement.—Four percent of net deposits are to be made available to the Secretary of the Interior to make grants to 1) States, as determined through a competitive award process, for the development and maintenance of facilities for transient non-trailerable recreational vessels 26 feet or longer, or 2) States, Commonwealths, the District of Columbia and Territories, as determined through a competitive award process, to carry out projects for the construction, renovation, operation, and maintenance of pumpout stations and waste reception facilities, as well as for educational programs on proper disposal of sewage. Not more than 75 percent of the four percent shall be available for grants under either of the award processes referenced in this paragraph.

National Outreach and Communications Programs.—Two percent of net deposits are to be made available to the Secretary of the Interior to develop national and State outreach plans to promote safe fishing and boating opportunities and the conservation of aquatic resources.

Grants to States.—58.012 percent of net deposits are provided to the States, Puerto Rico, Guam, the Virgin Islands, American Samoa, the Northern Mariana Islands, and the District of Columbia for up to 75 percent of the cost of approved projects including: research into fisheries problems, surveys and inventories of fish populations, acquisition and improvement of fish habitat, and provision of access for public use and $3 million is reserved for Multistate Conservation Activities.

The Infrastructure Investment and Jobs Act (P.L. 117–58) amends Section 3 and 4 of the Federal Aid in Sport Fish Restoration Act, changing the amounts available for administration and extending the funding authorization for Coastal Wetlands Planning, Protection, and Restoration Act, Boating Infrastructure Improvement, and the National Outreach and Communications program through FY 2026.

Object Classification (in millions of dollars)

Identification code 014–8151–0–7–303	2021 actual	2022 est.	2023 est.
Direct obligations:			
11.1 Personnel compensation: Full-time permanent	6	6	6
12.1 Civilian personnel benefits	2	2	2
23.1 Rental payments to GSA	1	1	1
25.3 Other goods and services from Federal sources	3	3	3
25.7 Operation and maintenance of equipment	1	1	1
32.0 Land and structures	1		
41.0 Grants, subsidies, and contributions	518	522	522
99.9 Total new obligations, unexpired accounts	532	535	535

SPORT FISH RESTORATION—Continued

Employment Summary

Identification code 014–8151–0–7–303	2021 actual	2022 est.	2023 est.
1001 Direct civilian full-time equivalent employment	51	50	55

CONTRIBUTED FUNDS

Special and Trust Fund Receipts (in millions of dollars)

Identification code 014–8216–0–7–302	2021 actual	2022 est.	2023 est.
0100 Balance, start of year			
Receipts:			
Current law:			
1130 Deposits, Contributed Funds, Fish and Wildlife Service	3	5	5
2000 Total: Balances and receipts	3	5	5
Appropriations:			
Current law:			
2101 Contributed Funds	–3	–5	–5
5099 Balance, end of year			

Program and Financing (in millions of dollars)

Identification code 014–8216–0–7–302	2021 actual	2022 est.	2023 est.
Obligations by program activity:			
0001 Contributed Funds	4	4	4
Budgetary resources:			
Unobligated balance:			
1000 Unobligated balance brought forward, Oct 1	17	16	17
Budget authority:			
Appropriations, mandatory:			
1201 Appropriation (special or trust fund)	3	5	5
1930 Total budgetary resources available	20	21	22
Memorandum (non-add) entries:			
1941 Unexpired unobligated balance, end of year	16	17	18
Change in obligated balance:			
Unpaid obligations:			
3000 Unpaid obligations, brought forward, Oct 1	3	2	1
3010 New obligations, unexpired accounts	4	4	4
3020 Outlays (gross)	–5	–5	–5
3050 Unpaid obligations, end of year	2	1	
Memorandum (non-add) entries:			
3100 Obligated balance, start of year	3	2	1
3200 Obligated balance, end of year	2	1	
Budget authority and outlays, net:			
Mandatory:			
4090 Budget authority, gross	3	5	5
Outlays, gross:			
4100 Outlays from new mandatory authority	1	1	1
4101 Outlays from mandatory balances	4	4	4
4110 Outlays, gross (total)	5	5	5
4180 Budget authority, net (total)	3	5	5
4190 Outlays, net (total)	5	5	5

Donated funds support activities such as endangered species projects, refuge and fish hatchery operations and maintenance, and migratory bird conservation and invasive species mitigation projects.

Object Classification (in millions of dollars)

Identification code 014–8216–0–7–302	2021 actual	2022 est.	2023 est.
11.1 Direct obligations: Personnel compensation: Full-time permanent	1	1	1
11.9 Total personnel compensation	1	1	1
26.0 Supplies and materials	1	1	1
41.0 Grants, subsidies, and contributions	1	1	1
99.0 Direct obligations	3	3	3
99.5 Adjustment for rounding	1	1	1
99.9 Total new obligations, unexpired accounts	4	4	4

Employment Summary

Identification code 014–8216–0–7–302	2021 actual	2022 est.	2023 est.
1001 Direct civilian full-time equivalent employment	18	18	18

ADMINISTRATIVE PROVISIONS

The United States Fish and Wildlife Service may carry out the operations of Service programs by direct expenditure, contracts, grants, cooperative agreements and reimbursable agreements with public and private entities. Appropriations and funds available to the United States Fish and Wildlife Service shall be available for repair of damage to public roads within and adjacent to reservation areas caused by operations of the Service; options for the purchase of land at not to exceed one dollar for each option; facilities incident to such public recreational uses on conservation areas as are consistent with their primary purpose; and the maintenance and improvement of aquaria, buildings, and other facilities under the jurisdiction of the Service and to which the United States has title, and which are used pursuant to law in connection with management, and investigation of fish and wildlife resources: Provided, That notwithstanding 44 U.S.C. 501, the Service may, under cooperative cost sharing and partnership arrangements authorized by law, procure printing services from cooperators in connection with jointly produced publications for which the cooperators share at least one-half the cost of printing either in cash or services and the Service determines the cooperator is capable of meeting accepted quality standards: Provided further, That the Service may accept donated aircraft as replacements for existing aircraft: Provided further, That notwithstanding 31 U.S.C. 3302, all fees collected for non-toxic shot review and approval shall be deposited under the heading "United States Fish and Wildlife Service—Resource Management" and shall be available to the Secretary, without further appropriation, to be used for expenses of processing of such non-toxic shot type or coating applications and revising regulations as necessary, and shall remain available until expended: Provided further, That the second proviso under the heading "United States Fish and Wildlife Service—Resource Management" in title I of division E of Public Law 112–74 (16 U.S.C. 742l–1) is amended by striking "2012" and inserting "2023" and striking "$400,000" and inserting "$750,000".

The Secretary may recover costs for response, assessment, and damages to Service resources from the unauthorized actions of private parties, including non-compliance with Service-issued permits, or for costs as otherwise provided by Federal, State, or local law, regulation, or court order as a result of the destruction, loss of, or injury to any living or non-living Service resource: Provided, That such damages may include compensation for the cost of replacing, restoring, or acquiring the equivalent of the damaged Service resource; the value of any significant loss of use of a Service resource pending its restoration, replacement, or the acquisition of an equivalent resource; or the value of the Service resource in the event the resource cannot be restored, replaced or re-acquired: Provided further, That response costs as described herein may include the following actions: preventing, minimizing, or abating destruction or loss of, or injury to, a Service resource; abating or minimizing the imminent risk of such destruction, loss, or injury; or monitoring the ongoing effects of any incident causing such destruction, loss, or injury: Provided further, That any instrumentality, including but not limited to a vessel, vehicle, aircraft, or other equipment or mechanism that destroys, causes the loss of, or injures any living or non-living Service resource or which causes the Secretary to undertake actions to prevent, minimize, or abate destruction, loss of, injury, or risk to such resource shall be liable in rem to the United States for response costs and damages resulting from such destruction, loss, injury, or risk to the same extent as a person would be liable under the same or similar circumstances: Provided further, That in addition to any other authority to accept donations, the Secretary may accept donations of money or services to meet expected, immediate, or ongoing response costs and damages: Provided further, That amounts and damages recovered by the Secretary for response and assessment costs, and donations collected pursuant to this provision, shall be credited to the "United States Fish and Wildlife Service—Resource Management" account, and shall remain available until expended for response costs and damage assessments conducted; restoration, replacement, or acquisition of Service resources; and monitoring and studying Service resources.

NATIONAL PARK SERVICE

Federal Funds

OPERATION OF THE NATIONAL PARK SYSTEM

For expenses necessary for the management, operation, and maintenance of areas and facilities administered by the National Park Service and for the general administration of the National Park Service, $3,089,856,000, to remain available until September 30, 2024, of which $11,661,000 shall be for planning and interagency coordination in support of Everglades restoration and $135,980,000 shall be for maintenance, repair, or rehabilitation projects for constructed assets and $188,184,000 shall be for cyclic maintenance projects for constructed assets and cultural resources and $5,000,000 shall be for uses authorized by section 101122 of title 54, United States Code: Provided, That funds appropriated under this heading in this Act are available for the purposes of section 5 of Public Law 95–348: Provided further, That notwithstanding section 9 of the 400 Years of African-American History Commission Act (36 U.S.C. note prec. 101; Public Law 115–102), as amended, $3,300,000 of the funds provided under this heading shall be made available for the purposes specified by that Act: Provided further, That sections (7)(b) and (8) of that Act shall be amended by striking "July 1, 2022" and inserting "July 1, 2024".

In addition, for purposes described in section 2404 of Public Law 116–9, an amount equal to the amount deposited in this fiscal year into the National Park Medical Services Fund established pursuant to such section of such Act, to remain available until expended, shall be derived from such Fund.

Note.—A full-year 2022 appropriation for this account was not enacted at the time the Budget was prepared; therefore, the Budget assumes this account is operating under the Continuing Appropriations Act, 2022 (Division A of Public Law 117–43, as amended). The amounts included for 2022 reflect the annualized level provided by the continuing resolution.

Special and Trust Fund Receipts (in millions of dollars)

Identification code 014–1036–0–1–303	2021 actual	2022 est.	2023 est.
0100 Balance, start of year	1	1	1
2000 Total: Balances and receipts	1	1	1
5099 Balance, end of year	1	1	1

Program and Financing (in millions of dollars)

Identification code 014–1036–0–1–303	2021 actual	2022 est.	2023 est.
Obligations by program activity:			
0001 Park management	2,520	2,520	2,872
0002 External administrative costs	196	196	218
0799 Total direct obligations	2,716	2,716	3,090
0801 Operation of the National Park System (Reimbursable)	31	34	34
0900 Total new obligations, unexpired accounts	2,747	2,750	3,124
Budgetary resources:			
Unobligated balance:			
1000 Unobligated balance brought forward, Oct 1	151	114	77
1021 Recoveries of prior year unpaid obligations	4		
1070 Unobligated balance (total)	155	114	77
Budget authority:			
Appropriations, discretionary:			
1100 Appropriation	2,688	2,688	3,090
1120 Appropriations transferred to other acct [239–2780]	–8	–8	
1120 Appropriations transferred to other acct [247–5721]	–3	–3	–3
1121 Appropriations transferred from other acct [014–5762]	1	2	2
1160 Appropriation, discretionary (total)	2,678	2,679	3,089
Spending authority from offsetting collections, discretionary:			
1700 Collected	34	34	34
1900 Budget authority (total)	2,712	2,713	3,123
1930 Total budgetary resources available	2,867	2,827	3,200
Memorandum (non-add) entries:			
1940 Unobligated balance expiring	–6		
1941 Unexpired unobligated balance, end of year	114	77	76
Change in obligated balance:			
Unpaid obligations:			
3000 Unpaid obligations, brought forward, Oct 1	757	878	865
3010 New obligations, unexpired accounts	2,747	2,750	3,124
3011 Obligations ("upward adjustments"), expired accounts	2		
3020 Outlays (gross)	–2,595	–2,763	–3,048
3040 Recoveries of prior year unpaid obligations, unexpired	–4		
3041 Recoveries of prior year unpaid obligations, expired	–29		
3050 Unpaid obligations, end of year	878	865	941
Memorandum (non-add) entries:			
3100 Obligated balance, start of year	757	878	865
3200 Obligated balance, end of year	878	865	941
Budget authority and outlays, net:			
Discretionary:			
4000 Budget authority, gross	2,712	2,713	3,123
Outlays, gross:			
4010 Outlays from new discretionary authority	2,012	2,043	2,351
4011 Outlays from discretionary balances	583	720	697
4020 Outlays, gross (total)	2,595	2,763	3,048
Offsets against gross budget authority and outlays:			
Offsetting collections (collected) from:			
4033 Non-Federal sources	–34	–34	–34
4180 Budget authority, net (total)	2,678	2,679	3,089
4190 Outlays, net (total)	2,561	2,729	3,014

The National Park Service administers 423 units and over 85 million acres of land in 50 States, the District of Columbia, Puerto Rico, the U.S. Virgin Islands, Guam, Samoa, and the Northern Marianas. This annual appropriation funds the operation of areas and facilities administered under the National Park System through two budget activities. Funds within this appropriation are available for one year, with the exception of funds for repair and rehabilitation, cyclic maintenance, cooperative restoration of the Everglades, and uses authorized by section 101122 of title 54, United States Code, which are available for two years. The FY 2023 Budget proposes all appropriations in this account be made available for two years. This account contains reimbursable activity such as recovery of costs associated with special use permits.

The first activity, Park Management, covers the management and operation of park areas, and is divided into five subactivities that represent functional areas:

Resource stewardship.—Encompasses resource management operations that provide for the protection and preservation of unique natural, cultural, and historical features of units of the National Park System.

Visitor services.—Includes operations that provide orientation, educational, and interpretive programs to enhance the visitor's park experience. It also provides for the efficient management of commercial services for the benefit of visitors and the protection of resources.

Park protection.—Provides for the protection of park resources, visitors, and staff. Funding supports law enforcement operations, including the United States Park Police, that reduce vandalism and other destruction of park resources, safety, and public health operations.

Facility operations and maintenance.—Encompasses the maintenance and protection of buildings, other facilities, lands, and other government investments.

Park support.—Covers the management, supervision, and administrative operations for park areas and partnerships.

The second activity, External Administrative Costs, funds costs which are largely determined by organizations outside the National Park Service and for which funding requirements are less flexible. The requirements for these costs are mandated in accordance with applicable laws. To promote the efficient performance of the National Park Service, these costs are most effectively managed on a centralized basis.

Object Classification (in millions of dollars)

Identification code 014–1036–0–1–303	2021 actual	2022 est.	2023 est.
Direct obligations:			
Personnel compensation:			
11.1 Full-time permanent	931	949	1,078
11.3 Other than full-time permanent	92	93	111
11.5 Other personnel compensation	68	69	71
11.9 Total personnel compensation	1,091	1,111	1,260
12.1 Civilian personnel benefits	477	484	545
21.0 Travel and transportation of persons	14	30	30
22.0 Transportation of things	9	10	10
23.1 Rental payments to GSA	46	60	60
23.2 Rental payments to others	13	12	14
23.3 Communications, utilities, and miscellaneous charges	93	88	102
24.0 Printing and reproduction	4	4	5

OPERATION OF THE NATIONAL PARK SYSTEM—Continued

Object Classification—Continued

Identification code 014–1036–0–1–303		2021 actual	2022 est.	2023 est.
25.1	Advisory and assistance services	17	16	19
25.2	Other services from non-Federal sources	181	171	199
25.3	Other goods and services from Federal sources	198	186	216
25.4	Operation and maintenance of facilities	189	179	208
25.5	Research and development contracts	2	2	2
25.6	Medical care	1	1	1
25.7	Operation and maintenance of equipment	47	45	52
26.0	Supplies and materials	113	107	124
31.0	Equipment	60	57	66
32.0	Land and structures	62	59	68
41.0	Grants, subsidies, and contributions	98	93	108
42.0	Insurance claims and indemnities	1	1	1
99.0	Direct obligations	2,716	2,716	3,090
99.0	Reimbursable obligations	31	34	34
99.9	Total new obligations, unexpired accounts	2,747	2,750	3,124

Employment Summary

Identification code 014–1036–0–1–303		2021 actual	2022 est.	2023 est.
1001	Direct civilian full-time equivalent employment	14,370	14,490	15,860
2001	Reimbursable civilian full-time equivalent employment	277	277	277
3001	Allocation account civilian full-time equivalent employment	761	773	860
3001	Allocation account civilian full-time equivalent employment	6	6	6

CENTENNIAL CHALLENGE

For expenses necessary to carry out the provisions of section 101701 of title 54, United States Code, relating to challenge cost share agreements, $15,000,000, to remain available until expended, for Centennial Challenge projects and programs: Provided, That not less than 50 percent of the total cost of each project or program shall be derived from non-Federal sources in the form of donated cash, assets, or a pledge of donation guaranteed by an irrevocable letter of credit.

Note.—A full-year 2022 appropriation for this account was not enacted at the time the Budget was prepared; therefore, the Budget assumes this account is operating under the Continuing Appropriations Act, 2022 (Division A of Public Law 117–43, as amended). The amounts included for 2022 reflect the annualized level provided by the continuing resolution.

Program and Financing (in millions of dollars)

Identification code 014–2645–0–1–303		2021 actual	2022 est.	2023 est.
	Obligations by program activity:			
0001	Centennial Challenge	13	13	18
0801	Centennial Challenge (Reimbursable)		1	5
0900	Total new obligations, unexpired accounts	13	14	23
	Budgetary resources:			
	Unobligated balance:			
1000	Unobligated balance brought forward, Oct 1	60	67	72
1001	Discretionary unobligated balance brought fwd, Oct 1	52		
	Budget authority:			
	Appropriations, discretionary:			
1100	Appropriation	15	15	15
	Spending authority from offsetting collections, mandatory:			
1800	Collected	5	4	4
1900	Budget authority (total)	20	19	19
1930	Total budgetary resources available	80	86	91
	Memorandum (non-add) entries:			
1941	Unexpired unobligated balance, end of year	67	72	68
	Change in obligated balance:			
	Unpaid obligations:			
3000	Unpaid obligations, brought forward, Oct 1	8	8	3
3010	New obligations, unexpired accounts	13	14	23
3020	Outlays (gross)	–13	–19	–19
3050	Unpaid obligations, end of year	8	3	7
	Memorandum (non-add) entries:			
3100	Obligated balance, start of year	8	8	3
3200	Obligated balance, end of year	8	3	7
	Budget authority and outlays, net:			
	Discretionary:			
4000	Budget authority, gross	15	15	15
	Outlays, gross:			
4010	Outlays from new discretionary authority		11	11
4011	Outlays from discretionary balances	13	4	4
4020	Outlays, gross (total)	13	15	15
	Mandatory:			
4090	Budget authority, gross	5	4	4
	Outlays, gross:			
4101	Outlays from mandatory balances		4	4
	Offsets against gross budget authority and outlays:			
	Offsetting collections (collected) from:			
4123	Non-Federal sources	–5	–4	–4
4180	Budget authority, net (total)	15	15	15
4190	Outlays, net (total)	8	15	15

Centennial Challenge funds are used to complete projects with partner donations. All Federal funds must be matched on a 50/50 basis, derived from non-Federal sources in the form of cash, assets, or a pledge of donation guaranteed by an irrevocable letter of credit. Projects are administered under existing National Park Service partnership authorities.

Object Classification (in millions of dollars)

Identification code 014–2645–0–1–303		2021 actual	2022 est.	2023 est.
	Direct obligations:			
11.3	Personnel compensation: Other than full-time permanent	1	1	1
25.2	Other services from non-Federal sources	2	2	2
25.4	Operation and maintenance of facilities	5	5	9
32.0	Land and structures	1	1	5
41.0	Grants, subsidies, and contributions	4	4	5
99.0	Direct obligations	13	13	22
99.0	Reimbursable obligations		1	1
99.9	Total new obligations, unexpired accounts	13	14	23

Employment Summary

Identification code 014–2645–0–1–303		2021 actual	2022 est.	2023 est.
1001	Direct civilian full-time equivalent employment	17	17	17

VISITOR EXPERIENCE IMPROVEMENTS FUND

Program and Financing (in millions of dollars)

Identification code 014–4488–0–3–303		2021 actual	2022 est.	2023 est.
	Obligations by program activity:			
0801	Visitor Experience Improvements Fund		6	5
0900	Total new obligations, unexpired accounts (object class 25.2)		6	5
	Budgetary resources:			
	Unobligated balance:			
1000	Unobligated balance brought forward, Oct 1			5
	Budget authority:			
	Appropriations, mandatory:			
1221	Appropriations transferred from other acct [014–9924]		10	
	Spending authority from offsetting collections, mandatory:			
1800	Collected		1	3
1900	Budget authority (total)		11	3
1930	Total budgetary resources available		11	8
	Memorandum (non-add) entries:			
1941	Unexpired unobligated balance, end of year		5	3
	Change in obligated balance:			
	Unpaid obligations:			
3000	Unpaid obligations, brought forward, Oct 1			1
3010	New obligations, unexpired accounts		6	5
3020	Outlays (gross)		–5	–6
3050	Unpaid obligations, end of year		1	
	Memorandum (non-add) entries:			
3100	Obligated balance, start of year			1
3200	Obligated balance, end of year		1	

Budget authority and outlays, net:

		2021 actual	2022 est.	2023 est.
	Mandatory:			
4090	Budget authority, gross	....	11	3
	Outlays, gross:			
4100	Outlays from new mandatory authority	....	5	2
4101	Outlays from mandatory balances	....	....	4
4110	Outlays, gross (total)	....	5	6
	Offsets against gross budget authority and outlays:			
	Offsetting collections (collected) from:			
4123	Non-Federal sources	....	–1	–3
4180	Budget authority, net (total)	....	10	....
4190	Outlays, net (total)	....	4	3

The Visitor Experience Improvements Authority (VEIA) Revolving Fund provides for the administration of commercial services contracts, and related professional services contracts, for the operation and expansion of commercial visitor facilities and visitor services programs. This includes expenses necessary for the management, improvement, enhancement, operation, construction, and maintenance of commercial visitor services facilities. Funds will also be used to make payments for possessory interest and leasehold surrender interest in existing commercial services contracts awarded under separate authorities. VEIA is designated as a revolving fund pursuant to Title VII of the National Park Service Centennial Act of 2016 (P.L. 114–289). The authority provides the National Park Service with the tools to improve commercial visitor facilities and services. The Visitor Experience Improvement Authority expires on December 16, 2023. In order to continue executing the program, which was paused due to the impacts of the COVID-19 pandemic on the hospitality industry, the FY 2023 Budget proposes to extend the authority by two years to implement new regulations being promulgated by the NPS and to enter into and execute contracts.

NATIONAL RECREATION AND PRESERVATION

For expenses necessary to carry out recreation programs, natural programs, cultural programs, heritage partnership programs, environmental compliance and review, international park affairs, and grant administration, not otherwise provided for, $74,581,000, to remain available until September 30, 2024.

Note.—A full-year 2022 appropriation for this account was not enacted at the time the Budget was prepared; therefore, the Budget assumes this account is operating under the Continuing Appropriations Act, 2022 (Division A of Public Law 117–43, as amended). The amounts included for 2022 reflect the annualized level provided by the continuing resolution.

Program and Financing (in millions of dollars)

Identification code 014–1042–0–1–303	2021 actual	2022 est.	2023 est.
Obligations by program activity:			
0002 Natural programs	16	17	16
0003 Cultural programs	31	34	32
0006 International park affairs	2	2	2
0008 Heritage partnership programs	24	22	23
0799 Total direct obligations	73	75	73
0801 National Recreation and Preservation (Reimbursable)	4	4	4
0900 Total new obligations, unexpired accounts	77	79	77
Budgetary resources:			
Unobligated balance:			
1000 Unobligated balance brought forward, Oct 1	8	9	8
Budget authority:			
Appropriations, discretionary:			
1100 Appropriation	74	74	75
Spending authority from offsetting collections, discretionary:			
1700 Collected	4	4	4
1900 Budget authority (total)	78	78	79
1930 Total budgetary resources available	86	87	87
Memorandum (non-add) entries:			
1941 Unexpired unobligated balance, end of year	9	8	10
Change in obligated balance:			
Unpaid obligations:			
3000 Unpaid obligations, brought forward, Oct 1	58	64	59
3010 New obligations, unexpired accounts	77	79	77
3020 Outlays (gross)	–70	–84	–81
3041 Recoveries of prior year unpaid obligations, expired	–1	....	....
3050 Unpaid obligations, end of year	64	59	55
Memorandum (non-add) entries:			
3100 Obligated balance, start of year	58	64	59
3200 Obligated balance, end of year	64	59	55
Budget authority and outlays, net:			
Discretionary:			
4000 Budget authority, gross	78	78	79
Outlays, gross:			
4010 Outlays from new discretionary authority	36	52	53
4011 Outlays from discretionary balances	34	32	28
4020 Outlays, gross (total)	70	84	81
Offsets against gross budget authority and outlays:			
Offsetting collections (collected) from:			
4033 Non-Federal sources	–4	–4	–4
4040 Offsets against gross budget authority and outlays (total)	–4	–4	–4
4180 Budget authority, net (total)	74	74	75
4190 Outlays, net (total)	66	80	77

The National Recreation and Preservation appropriation covers a broad range of activities relating to preservation of natural, cultural and historic resources, and environmental compliance. These programs provide a central point at the Federal level for recreation and preservation planning; the coordination of Federal and State policies, procedures and guidelines; and the administration of technical and financial assistance to international, Federal, State, and local governments and private organizations. This appropriation is comprised of the following five budget activities:

Natural Programs.—Increases river and trail opportunities through Rivers, Trails, and Conservation Assistance, State and local technical assistance and Chesapeake Bay Gateways and Water Trails grants; creates river conservation and recreational opportunities that are compatible with continuing and future operations of hydropower facilities, fulfills National Park Service responsibilities under the Federal Power Act, and protects park resources through the Hydropower Recreation Assistance Program; manages the National Natural Landmark program; and provides technical assistance to State and local governments and transfers surplus real property to local governments for recreation uses.

Cultural Programs.—Manages the National Register of Historic Places; reviews and certifies applications for Federal Tax Credits for Historic Preservation as a reimbursable activity; conducts cultural resources management planning through the National Historic Landmarks program, the Historic American Buildings Survey, the Historic American Engineering Record and the Historic American Landscapes Survey programs; and advances the application of science and technology in historic preservation and provides information distribution and skills training in the preservation and conservation of the Nation's significant historic and cultural resources through the National Center for Preservation Technology and Training. This program activity also supports the American Battlefield Protection Program Assistance Grants program, the Japanese American Confinement Site Grants program, the Native American Graves Protection and Repatriation Grants program, the 9/11 Memorial Act Grants program, and the American Indian and Native Hawaiian Art & Culture Grants. This activity also includes relevant grant administration funding. .

Environmental Compliance and Review.—Provides review and commentary on environmental impact statements, Federal licensing, permit applications, and other actions that may impact areas of National Park Service jurisdiction.

International Park Affairs.—Coordinates international assistance programs and the exchange and support functions that complement the Service's domestic role.

Heritage Partnership Programs.—Provides financial and technical assistance to Congressionally designated national heritage areas, managed by private or State organizations to promote the conservation of natural, historic, scenic, and cultural resources.

NATIONAL RECREATION AND PRESERVATION—Continued

Object Classification (in millions of dollars)

Identification code 014–1042–0–1–303		2021 actual	2022 est.	2023 est.
	Direct obligations:			
	Personnel compensation:			
11.1	Full-time permanent	19	20	21
11.3	Other than full-time permanent	1	1	1
11.5	Other personnel compensation	2	2	2
11.9	Total personnel compensation	22	23	24
12.1	Civilian personnel benefits	8	8	8
25.2	Other services from non-Federal sources	3	3	3
25.3	Other goods and services from Federal sources	1	1	1
26.0	Supplies and materials		1	1
41.0	Grants, subsidies, and contributions	39	39	36
99.0	Direct obligations	73	75	73
99.0	Reimbursable obligations	4	4	4
99.9	Total new obligations, unexpired accounts	77	79	77

Employment Summary

Identification code 014–1042–0–1–303	2021 actual	2022 est.	2023 est.
1001 Direct civilian full-time equivalent employment	200	200	201
2001 Reimbursable civilian full-time equivalent employment	21	21	21

URBAN PARK AND RECREATION FUND

The Urban Park Recreation Recovery Act of 1978 authorizes matching grants and technical assistance to eligible economically distressed urban communities to revitalize and improve recreation opportunities. The program provides direct Federal grants to local governments to rehabilitate existing indoor and outdoor recreation facilities; to demonstrate innovative ways to enhance park and recreation opportunities; and to develop local Recovery Action Plans to identify needs, priorities and strategies for revitalization of the total recreation system. No funds are requested for this program in FY 2023.

CONSTRUCTION

For construction, improvements, repair, or replacement of physical facilities, and compliance and planning for programs and areas administered by the National Park Service, $279,340,000, to remain available until expended: Provided, That notwithstanding any other provision of law, for any project initially funded in fiscal year 2023 with a future phase indicated in the National Park Service 5-Year Line Item Construction Plan, a single procurement may be issued which includes the full scope of the project: Provided further, That the solicitation and contract shall contain the clause availability of funds found at 48 CFR 52.232–18: Provided further, That National Park Service Donations, Park Concessions Franchise Fees, and Recreation Fees may be made available for the cost of adjustments and changes within the original scope of effort for projects funded by the National Park Service Construction appropriation: Provided further, That the Secretary of the Interior shall notify the Committees on Appropriations, in accordance with current reprogramming thresholds, prior to making any charges authorized under this heading: Provided further, That amounts provided under this heading are available for the modernization of field communication capabilities, in addition to amounts otherwise made available for such purpose.

Note.—A full-year 2022 appropriation for this account was not enacted at the time the Budget was prepared; therefore, the Budget assumes this account is operating under the Continuing Appropriations Act, 2022 (Division A of Public Law 117–43, as amended). The amounts included for 2022 reflect the annualized level provided by the continuing resolution.

CONSTRUCTION

⟦*For an additional amount for "Construction", $229,472,000, to remain available until expended, for necessary expenses related to the consequences of calendar year 2019, 2020, and 2021 wildfires, hurricanes and other natural disasters.*⟧ *(Disaster Relief Supplemental Appropriations Act, 2022.)*

Program and Financing (in millions of dollars)

Identification code 014–1039–0–1–303		2021 actual	2022 est.	2023 est.
	Obligations by program activity:			
0001	Line item construction and maintenance	192	235	254
0002	Special programs	22	28	28
0003	Construction planning	18	25	25
0005	Construction program management and operations	44	42	42
0006	Management planning	12	12	12
0007	Restoration of Federal Assets (Hurricane Supplemental P.L. 115–123)	50	40	10
0008	Restoration of Federal Assets (Disaster Supplemental P.L. 116–20)	7	20	20
0009	Disaster Relief Supplemental [P.L. 117–43]		60	80
0799	Total direct obligations	345	462	471
0801	Construction (and Major Maintenance) (Reimbursable)	109	139	139
0900	Total new obligations, unexpired accounts	454	601	610
	Budgetary resources:			
	Unobligated balance:			
1000	Unobligated balance brought forward, Oct 1	843	706	642
1001	Discretionary unobligated balance brought fwd, Oct 1	823	598	
1021	Recoveries of prior year unpaid obligations	9		
1070	Unobligated balance (total)	852	706	642
	Budget authority:			
	Appropriations, discretionary:			
1100	Appropriation	224	453	279
	Spending authority from offsetting collections, discretionary:			
1700	Collected	125	125	125
1701	Change in uncollected payments, Federal sources	–41	–41	–41
1750	Spending auth from offsetting collections, disc (total)	84	84	84
1900	Budget authority (total)	308	537	363
1930	Total budgetary resources available	1,160	1,243	1,005
	Memorandum (non-add) entries:			
1941	Unexpired unobligated balance, end of year	706	642	395
	Change in obligated balance:			
	Unpaid obligations:			
3000	Unpaid obligations, brought forward, Oct 1	480	521	481
3010	New obligations, unexpired accounts	454	601	610
3020	Outlays (gross)	–404	–641	–646
3040	Recoveries of prior year unpaid obligations, unexpired	–9		
3050	Unpaid obligations, end of year	521	481	445
	Uncollected payments:			
3060	Uncollected pymts, Fed sources, brought forward, Oct 1	–192	–151	–110
3070	Change in uncollected pymts, Fed sources, unexpired	41	41	41
3090	Uncollected pymts, Fed sources, end of year	–151	–110	–69
	Memorandum (non-add) entries:			
3100	Obligated balance, start of year	288	370	371
3200	Obligated balance, end of year	370	371	376
	Budget authority and outlays, net:			
	Discretionary:			
4000	Budget authority, gross	308	537	363
	Outlays, gross:			
4010	Outlays from new discretionary authority	38	135	109
4011	Outlays from discretionary balances	356	491	527
4020	Outlays, gross (total)	394	626	636
	Offsets against gross budget authority and outlays:			
	Offsetting collections (collected) from:			
4030	Federal sources	–89	–89	–89
4033	Non-Federal sources	–36	–36	–36
4040	Offsets against gross budget authority and outlays (total)	–125	–125	–125
	Additional offsets against gross budget authority only:			
4050	Change in uncollected pymts, Fed sources, unexpired	41	41	41
4070	Budget authority, net (discretionary)	224	453	279
4080	Outlays, net (discretionary)	269	501	511
	Mandatory:			
	Outlays, gross:			
4101	Outlays from mandatory balances	10	15	10
4180	Budget authority, net (total)	224	453	279
4190	Outlays, net (total)	279	516	521

The Construction appropriation provides support to several National Park Service mission goals, including preserving park resources, providing for visitor enjoyment, and improving organizational effectiveness. In addition, this account contains activity related to reimbursable agreements.

The Construction appropriation is composed of five budget activities:

Line item construction.—This activity provides for the construction, rehabilitation, and replacement of facilities needed to accomplish the management objectives approved for each park.

Special programs.—This activity includes Emergency and Unscheduled Projects, Employee Housing, Dam Safety, and Equipment Replacement.

Construction planning.—This activity includes the project planning function to prepare working drawings, specification documents, and contracts needed to construct or rehabilitate National Park Service facilities.

Construction program management and operations.—This activity provides centralized design and engineering management services, as well as contracting services for park construction projects.

Management planning.—Under this activity, funding is used to prepare and update Unit Management Plans. The plans guide National Park Service actions for the protection, use, development, and management of each park unit. Funding also is used to conduct studies of alternatives for the protection of areas that may have potential for addition to the National Park System and for environmental impact planning and compliance.

Object Classification (in millions of dollars)

Identification code 014–1039–0–1–303	2021 actual	2022 est.	2023 est.
Direct obligations:			
Personnel compensation:			
11.1 Full-time permanent	32	32	34
11.3 Other than full-time permanent	2	2	2
11.5 Other personnel compensation	2	2	2
11.9 Total personnel compensation	36	36	38
12.1 Civilian personnel benefits	13	13	13
21.0 Travel and transportation of persons	1	4	4
23.3 Communications, utilities, and miscellaneous charges	1	2	2
25.1 Advisory and assistance services	1	1	1
25.2 Other services from non-Federal sources	53	80	82
25.3 Other goods and services from Federal sources	14	20	21
25.4 Operation and maintenance of facilities	83	139	141
25.7 Operation and maintenance of equipment	3	8	8
26.0 Supplies and materials	1	5	4
31.0 Equipment	15	21	22
32.0 Land and structures	115	115	117
41.0 Grants, subsidies, and contributions	9	13	13
42.0 Insurance claims and indemnities	....	5	5
99.0 Direct obligations	345	462	471
99.0 Reimbursable obligations	109	139	139
99.9 Total new obligations, unexpired accounts	454	601	610

Employment Summary

Identification code 014–1039–0–1–303	2021 actual	2022 est.	2023 est.
1001 Direct civilian full-time equivalent employment	330	328	330
2001 Reimbursable civilian full-time equivalent employment	423	423	423
3001 Allocation account civilian full-time equivalent employment	118	146	146

LAND ACQUISITION AND STATE ASSISTANCE

Note.—A full-year 2022 appropriation for this account was not enacted at the time the Budget was prepared; therefore, the Budget assumes this account is operating under the Continuing Appropriations Act, 2022 (Division A of Public Law 117–43, as amended). The amounts included for 2022 reflect the annualized level provided by the continuing resolution.

Program and Financing (in millions of dollars)

Identification code 014–5035–0–2–303	2021 actual	2022 est.	2023 est.
Obligations by program activity:			
0001 Land acquisition	18	50	50
0002 Land acquisition administration	5	....	....
0005 Grants to States	174	125	76
0006 GAOA - Federal Land Acquisition	7	44	44
0007 GAOA - State Assistance	9	475	475
0008 GAOA - American Battlefield Protection Program	....	10	20
0900 Total new obligations, unexpired accounts	213	704	665

Budgetary resources:				
Unobligated balance:				
1000	Unobligated balance brought forward, Oct 1	724	1,040	846
1001	Discretionary unobligated balance brought fwd, Oct 1	498	353	....
1010	Unobligated balance transfer to other accts [014–5648]	–11	....	....
1021	Recoveries of prior year unpaid obligations	6	....	....
1070	Unobligated balance (total)	719	1,040	846
Budget authority:				
Appropriations, discretionary:				
1131	Unobligated balance of appropriations permanently reduced	–23	–21	....
Appropriations, mandatory:				
1201	Appropriation (special or trust fund) GOMESA	88	89	125
1201	Appropriation (special or trust fund) GAOA LWCF	474	474	447
1203	Appropriation (previously unavailable)(special or trust)	....	....	27
1232	Appropriations and/or unobligated balance of appropriations temporarily reduced	–5	–5	–7
1232	Appropriations and/or unobligated balance of appropriations temporarily reduced	....	–27	–25
1260	Appropriations, mandatory (total)	557	531	567
1900	Budget authority (total)	534	510	567
1930	Total budgetary resources available	1,253	1,550	1,413
Memorandum (non-add) entries:				
1941	Unexpired unobligated balance, end of year	1,040	846	748
Change in obligated balance:				
Unpaid obligations:				
3000	Unpaid obligations, brought forward, Oct 1	319	419	760
3010	New obligations, unexpired accounts	213	704	665
3020	Outlays (gross)	–107	–363	–383
3040	Recoveries of prior year unpaid obligations, unexpired	–6	....	....
3050	Unpaid obligations, end of year	419	760	1,042
Memorandum (non-add) entries:				
3100	Obligated balance, start of year	319	419	760
3200	Obligated balance, end of year	419	760	1,042
Budget authority and outlays, net:				
Discretionary:				
4000	Budget authority, gross	–23	–21	....
Outlays, gross:				
4011	Outlays from discretionary balances	77	177	161
Mandatory:				
4090	Budget authority, gross	557	531	567
Outlays, gross:				
4100	Outlays from new mandatory authority	....	65	64
4101	Outlays from mandatory balances	30	121	158
4110	Outlays, gross (total)	30	186	222
4180	Budget authority, net (total)	534	510	567
4190	Outlays, net (total)	107	363	383
Memorandum (non-add) entries:				
5052	Obligated balance, SOY: Contract authority	70	70	70
5053	Obligated balance, EOY: Contract authority	70	70	70
5099	Unexpired unavailable balance, SOY: Contract authority	14	14	14
5100	Unexpired unavailable balance, EOY: Contract authority	14	14	14

The Land Acquisition and State Assistance appropriation uses permanent funding derived from the Land and Water Conservation Fund to support National Park Service land acquisition activities and provide grants to States for the purchase and development of land for outdoor recreation activities. The Great American Outdoors Act (P.L. 116–152) makes funds deposited into the Land and Water Conservation Fund available for expenditure without further appropriation or fiscal year limitation while providing that the National Park Service shall submit to Congress detailed account, program and project allocations made available under the statute.

In addition, the Gulf of Mexico Energy Security Act of 2006 (P.L. 109–432) allows a portion of the revenue collected from certain oil and gas leases in the Gulf of Mexico Outer Continental Shelf (OCS) to be deposited to the Land and Water Conservation Fund and distributed to States in accordance with the Land and Water Conservation Act of 1965. The National Park Service portion of the revenue is 12.5 percent of total qualified OCS revenues. These OCS receipts became available for expenditure as mandatory funding beginning in 2009. The Consolidated Appropriations Act, 2021 (P.L. 116–260) permits the use of up to three percent of the amounts authorized to be disbursed for costs of administration per the statute.

LAND ACQUISITION AND STATE ASSISTANCE—Continued

The Land Acquisition and State Assistance program is composed of the following budget activities:

Federal land acquisition.—Provides for the acquisition of land and interests in land to preserve and protect, for public use and enjoyment, the historic, scenic, natural, and recreational values of congressionally authorized areas within the National Park System.

State conservation grants.—Provides matching grants to States and local units of government for the acquisition and development of land and facilities that provide the public access to new opportunities to engage in outdoor recreation. The program includes both traditional formula and competitive grant programs for States.

American Battlefield Protection Program.—The American Battlefield Protection Program awards grants for the acquisition, modernization and restoration of American battlefields. The program supports the protection of battlefield lands associated with the Revolutionary War, the Civil War, and the War of 1812 and it aids State and local governments and non-profit organizations acquire or otherwise preserve these important cultural resources for recreational access and education.

Object Classification (in millions of dollars)

Identification code 014–5035–0–2–303		2021 actual	2022 est.	2023 est.
	Direct obligations:			
	Personnel compensation:			
11.1	Full-time permanent	11	4	7
11.3	Other than full-time permanent	1		
11.9	Total personnel compensation	12	4	7
12.1	Civilian personnel benefits	4	2	3
25.1	Advisory and assistance services		1	1
25.2	Other services from non-Federal sources		3	3
25.3	Other goods and services from Federal sources	2		
32.0	Land and structures	6		
32.0	Land and structures	5	40	39
41.0	Grants, subsidies, and contributions	184	654	612
99.9	Total new obligations, unexpired accounts	213	704	665

Employment Summary

Identification code 014–5035–0–2–303	2021 actual	2022 est.	2023 est.
1001 Direct civilian full-time equivalent employment	108	142	183

NATIONAL PARK MEDICAL SERVICES FUND

Special and Trust Fund Receipts (in millions of dollars)

Identification code 014–5762–0–2–303		2021 actual	2022 est.	2023 est.
0100	Balance, start of year			
	Receipts:			
	Current law:			
1130	Fees, National Park Medical Services Fund	1	2	2
2000	Total: Balances and receipts	1	2	2
	Appropriations:			
	Current law:			
2101	National Park Medical Services Fund	–1	–2	–2
5099	Balance, end of year			

Program and Financing (in millions of dollars)

Identification code 014–5762–0–2–303		2021 actual	2022 est.	2023 est.
	Budgetary resources:			
	Budget authority:			
	Appropriations, discretionary:			
1101	Appropriation (special or trust)	1	2	2
1120	Appropriations transferred to other acct [014–1036]	–1	–2	–2
4180	Budget authority, net (total)			
4190	Outlays, net (total)			

The National Park Medical Services Fund was established in the John D. Dingell, Jr. Conservation, Management, And Recreation Act (Public Law 116–9). The Fund consists of fees collected for medical services provided to persons in units of the National Park System or for medical services provided by National Park Service personnel outside units of the National Park System and donations to the Fund. Amounts deposited into the Fund are available, to the extent provided in advance by Acts of appropriation, for units of the National Park System to provide medical services. Funds may also be used to obtain and improve medical facilities, equipment, vehicles, and other needs as well as prepare needs assessments or other programmatic analyses and management plans for medical services programs.

RECREATION FEE PERMANENT APPROPRIATIONS

Special and Trust Fund Receipts (in millions of dollars)

Identification code 014–9928–0–2–303		2021 actual	2022 est.	2023 est.
0100	Balance, start of year	2	2	2
	Receipts:			
	Current law:			
1130	Recreation Enhancement Fee, National Park System	313	321	329
2000	Total: Balances and receipts	315	323	331
	Appropriations:			
	Current law:			
2101	Recreation Fee Permanent Appropriations	–313	–321	–329
2103	Recreation Fee Permanent Appropriations	–2	–2	–2
2132	Recreation Fee Permanent Appropriations	2	2	2
2199	Total current law appropriations	–313	–321	–329
2999	Total appropriations	–313	–321	–329
5099	Balance, end of year	2	2	2

Program and Financing (in millions of dollars)

Identification code 014–9928–0–2–303		2021 actual	2022 est.	2023 est.
	Obligations by program activity:			
0001	Recreational Fee Program	272	384	409
0002	Transportation systems fund	15	15	
0799	Total direct obligations	287	399	409
0801	Reimbursable program activity	10	10	10
0900	Total new obligations, unexpired accounts	297	409	419
	Budgetary resources:			
	Unobligated balance:			
1000	Unobligated balance brought forward, Oct 1	381	415	342
1021	Recoveries of prior year unpaid obligations	8	5	5
1070	Unobligated balance (total)	389	420	347
	Budget authority:			
	Appropriations, mandatory:			
1201	Appropriation (special or trust fund)	313	321	329
1203	Appropriation (previously unavailable)(special or trust)	2	2	2
1232	Appropriations and/or unobligated balance of appropriations temporarily reduced	–2	–2	–2
1260	Appropriations, mandatory (total)	313	321	329
	Spending authority from offsetting collections, mandatory:			
1800	Collected	10	10	10
1900	Budget authority (total)	323	331	339
1930	Total budgetary resources available	712	751	686
	Memorandum (non-add) entries:			
1941	Unexpired unobligated balance, end of year	415	342	267
	Change in obligated balance:			
	Unpaid obligations:			
3000	Unpaid obligations, brought forward, Oct 1	170	183	295
3010	New obligations, unexpired accounts	297	409	419
3020	Outlays (gross)	–276	–292	–308
3040	Recoveries of prior year unpaid obligations, unexpired	–8	–5	–5
3050	Unpaid obligations, end of year	183	295	401
	Memorandum (non-add) entries:			
3100	Obligated balance, start of year	170	183	295
3200	Obligated balance, end of year	183	295	401

DEPARTMENT OF THE INTERIOR

Fish and Wildlife and Parks—Continued
National Park Service—Continued

667

		2021 actual	2022 est.	2023 est.
	Budget authority and outlays, net:			
	Mandatory:			
4090	Budget authority, gross	323	331	339
	Outlays, gross:			
4100	Outlays from new mandatory authority		74	76
4101	Outlays from mandatory balances	276	218	232
4110	Outlays, gross (total)	276	292	308
	Offsets against gross budget authority and outlays:			
	Offsetting collections (collected) from:			
4123	Non-Federal sources	−10	−10	−10
4180	Budget authority, net (total)	313	321	329
4190	Outlays, net (total)	266	282	298

Recreation fee program.—The National Park Service (NPS) and other land management agencies operate a fee program that allows parks and other units to collect admission and user fees in accordance with the Federal Lands Recreation Enhancement Act (FLREA). Section 423 of Division G of the Consolidated Appropriations Act, 2021 (P.L. 116–260) extended FLREA through 2022. The FY 2023 Budget includes appropriations language to extend authority for FLREA through October 1, 2024.

Net proceeds are used to provide benefits and services to the visitor throughout the National Park System. Up to 80 percent may be retained for use by the collecting park and the remainder retained for discretionary, Service-wide use by the National Park Service Director. Proceeds from the sale of the America the Beautiful passes, which allow access to all public lands that charge fees for a year, are distributed among the Federal land management agencies which offer them for sale, including the National Park Service, the Bureau of Land Management, the U.S. Fish and Wildlife Service, the Bureau of Reclamation, and the U.S. Forest Service, as determined by the Secretaries of the Department of the Interior and the Department of Agriculture in accordance with Public Law 108–447. The National Park Service Centennial Act (P.L. 114–289) established in the National Park Foundation, a Second Century Endowment for NPS projects and activities, funded through offsetting collections from the first $10 million collected in each fiscal year, generated from the America the Beautiful Senior Pass.

Deed-restricted parks fee program.—Park units where admission fees may not be collected by reason of deed restrictions retain any other recreation fees collected and use them for certain park operation purposes in accordance with Public Law 105–327. This law applies to Great Smoky Mountains National Park, Lincoln Home National Historic Site, and Abraham Lincoln Birthplace National Historic Site.

Transportation systems fund.—Fees charged for public use of transportation services at parks are retained and used by each collecting park for costs associated with the transportation systems in accordance with section 501 of Public Law 105–391.

Payment for tax losses on land acquired for Grand Teton National Park.—Revenues received from fees collected from visitors are used to compensate the State of Wyoming for tax losses on Grand Teton National Park lands (16 U.S.C. 406d–3).

Object Classification (in millions of dollars)

Identification code 014–9928–0–2–303		2021 actual	2022 est.	2023 est.
	Direct obligations:			
	Personnel compensation:			
11.1	Full-time permanent	42	43	44
11.3	Other than full-time permanent	34	35	36
11.5	Other personnel compensation	5	5	5
11.9	Total personnel compensation	81	83	85
12.1	Civilian personnel benefits	23	24	24
21.0	Travel and transportation of persons	1	1	1
22.0	Transportation of things	1	2	2
23.3	Communications, utilities, and miscellaneous charges	5	8	8
24.0	Printing and reproduction	2	4	4
25.1	Advisory and assistance services	3	6	6
25.2	Other services from non-Federal sources	42	66	68
25.3	Other goods and services from Federal sources	10	17	18
25.4	Operation and maintenance of facilities	52	82	83
25.7	Operation and maintenance of equipment	15	23	24
26.0	Supplies and materials	11	19	20
31.0	Equipment	6	9	9
32.0	Land and structures	22	35	36
41.0	Grants, subsidies, and contributions	13	20	21
99.0	Direct obligations	287	399	409
99.0	Reimbursable obligations	10	10	10
99.9	Total new obligations, unexpired accounts	297	409	419

Employment Summary

Identification code 014–9928–0–2–303	2021 actual	2022 est.	2023 est.
1001 Direct civilian full-time equivalent employment	1,618	1,618	1,618

HISTORIC PRESERVATION FUND

For expenses necessary in carrying out the National Historic Preservation Act (division A of subtitle III of title 54, United States Code), $151,800,000, to be derived from the Historic Preservation Fund and to remain available until September 30, 2024, of which $25,000,000 shall be for Save America's Treasures grants for preservation of nationally significant sites, structures and artifacts as authorized by section 7303 of the Omnibus Public Land Management Act of 2009 (54 U.S.C. 3089): Provided, That an individual Save America's Treasures grant shall be matched by non-Federal funds: Provided further, That individual projects shall only be eligible for one grant: Provided further, That all projects to be funded shall be approved by the Secretary of the Interior, who shall provide notification to the House and Senate Committees on Appropriations: Provided further, That of the funds provided for the Historic Preservation Fund, $1,000,000 is for competitive grants for the survey and nomination of properties to the National Register of Historic Places and as National Historic Landmarks associated with communities currently under-represented, as determined by the Secretary, $26,125,000 is for competitive grants to preserve the sites and stories of the Civil Rights movement; $10,000,000 is for grants to Historically Black Colleges and Universities; $10,000,000 is for competitive grants for the restoration of historic properties of national, State, and local significance listed on or eligible for inclusion on the National Register of Historic Places, to be made without imposing the usage or direct grant restrictions of section 101(e)(3) (54 U.S.C. 302904) of the National Historical Preservation Act: Provided further, That such competitive grants shall be made without imposing the matching requirements in section 302902(b)(3) of title 54, United States Code to States and Indian tribes as defined in chapter 3003 of such title, Native Hawaiian organizations, local governments, including Certified Local Governments, and non-profit organizations.

Note.—A full-year 2022 appropriation for this account was not enacted at the time the Budget was prepared; therefore, the Budget assumes this account is operating under the Continuing Appropriations Act, 2022 (Division A of Public Law 117–43, as amended). The amounts included for 2022 reflect the annualized level provided by the continuing resolution.

Special and Trust Fund Receipts (in millions of dollars)

Identification code 014–5140–0–2–303		2021 actual	2022 est.	2023 est.
0100	Balance, start of year	3,424	3,430	3,436
	Receipts:			
	Current law:			
1130	Historic Preservation Fund, Rent Receipts, Outer Continental Shelf Lands	150	150	150
2000	Total: Balances and receipts	3,574	3,580	3,586
	Appropriations:			
	Current law:			
2101	Historic Preservation Fund	−144	−144	−152
5099	Balance, end of year	3,430	3,436	3,434

Program and Financing (in millions of dollars)

Identification code 014–5140–0–2–303		2021 actual	2022 est.	2023 est.
	Obligations by program activity:			
0001	Grants-in-aid	103	130	139
0002	Save America's Treasures grants	16	25	50
0004	Grants to States and Territories (Hurricane Supplemental P.L. 116–20)		1	
0900	Total new obligations, unexpired accounts	119	156	189
	Budgetary resources:			
	Unobligated balance:			
1000	Unobligated balance brought forward, Oct 1	54	79	67

HISTORIC PRESERVATION FUND—Continued
Program and Financing—Continued

Identification code 014–5140–0–2–303		2021 actual	2022 est.	2023 est.
	Budget authority:			
	Appropriations, discretionary:			
1101	Appropriation (special fund, definite) HPF	144	144	152
1930	Total budgetary resources available	198	223	219
	Memorandum (non-add) entries:			
1941	Unexpired unobligated balance, end of year	79	67	30
	Special and non-revolving trust funds:			
1952	Expired unobligated balance, start of year	3	3	3
1953	Expired unobligated balance, end of year	3	3	3
	Change in obligated balance:			
	Unpaid obligations:			
3000	Unpaid obligations, brought forward, Oct 1	257	290	261
3010	New obligations, unexpired accounts	119	156	189
3020	Outlays (gross)	–85	–185	–185
3041	Recoveries of prior year unpaid obligations, expired	–1		
3050	Unpaid obligations, end of year	290	261	265
	Memorandum (non-add) entries:			
3100	Obligated balance, start of year	257	290	261
3200	Obligated balance, end of year	290	261	265
	Budget authority and outlays, net:			
	Discretionary:			
4000	Budget authority, gross	144	144	152
	Outlays, gross:			
4010	Outlays from new discretionary authority	13	69	73
4011	Outlays from discretionary balances	72	116	112
4020	Outlays, gross (total)	85	185	185
4180	Budget authority, net (total)	144	144	152
4190	Outlays, net (total)	85	185	185

The Historic Preservation Fund appropriation includes grant programs to facilitate the preservation of the Nation's historic and cultural resources. This appropriation provides grants-in-aid to States, Territories, Indian Tribes, and Historically Black Colleges and Universities. Grants-in-aid to States and local governments require a 40 percent funding match; grants to Tribes do not require matching funds. In addition to the traditional grants-in-aid described above, the account includes competitive grant programs. This includes grants for the survey and nomination of properties associated with communities currently underrepresented in the National Register and as National Historic Landmarks, and grants to preserve the sites and stories of the Civil Rights Movement.

Object Classification (in millions of dollars)

Identification code 014–5140–0–2–303		2021 actual	2022 est.	2023 est.
	Direct obligations:			
25.3	Other goods and services from Federal sources	6	6	15
41.0	Grants, subsidies, and contributions	113	150	174
99.9	Total new obligations, unexpired accounts	119	156	189

Employment Summary

Identification code 014–5140–0–2–303		2021 actual	2022 est.	2023 est.
1001	Direct civilian full-time equivalent employment	4	4	4

OTHER PERMANENT APPROPRIATIONS

Special and Trust Fund Receipts (in millions of dollars)

Identification code 014–9924–0–2–303		2021 actual	2022 est.	2023 est.
0100	Balance, start of year	2	2	2
	Receipts:			
	Current law:			
1130	Rents and Charges for Quarters, National Park Service	23	23	24
1130	Rental Payments, Park Buildings Lease and Maintenance Fund	10	10	11
1130	Concession Improvement Accounts Deposit	12	12	12
1130	User Fees for Filming and Photography on Public Lands		1	1
1130	Park Concessions Franchise Fees	82	101	107
1199	Total current law receipts	127	147	155
1999	Total receipts	127	147	155
2000	Total: Balances and receipts	129	149	157
	Appropriations:			
	Current law:			
2101	Other Permanent Appropriations	–127	–147	–155
5099	Balance, end of year	2	2	2

Program and Financing (in millions of dollars)

Identification code 014–9924–0–2–303		2021 actual	2022 est.	2023 est.
	Obligations by program activity:			
0001	Operation and maintenance of quarters	24	29	25
0003	Park concessions franchise fees	54	106	119
0005	Rental Payments, Park Buildings Lease and Maintenance Fund	5	20	16
0006	Concessions improvements accounts	11	12	12
0007	Contribution for annuity benefits for USPP	36	42	40
0008	Filming and Photography Special Use Fee Program		2	2
0900	Total new obligations, unexpired accounts	130	211	214
	Budgetary resources:			
	Unobligated balance:			
1000	Unobligated balance brought forward, Oct 1	263	299	267
1021	Recoveries of prior year unpaid obligations	2		
1070	Unobligated balance (total)	265	299	267
	Budget authority:			
	Appropriations, mandatory:			
1200	Appropriation	41	42	40
1201	Appropriation (special or trust fund)	127	147	155
1220	Appropriations transferred to other acct [014–4488]		–10	
1260	Appropriations, mandatory (total)	168	179	195
1900	Budget authority (total)	168	179	195
1930	Total budgetary resources available	433	478	462
	Memorandum (non-add) entries:			
1940	Unobligated balance expiring	–4		
1941	Unexpired unobligated balance, end of year	299	267	248
	Change in obligated balance:			
	Unpaid obligations:			
3000	Unpaid obligations, brought forward, Oct 1	54	42	72
3010	New obligations, unexpired accounts	130	211	214
3020	Outlays (gross)	–140	–181	–194
3040	Recoveries of prior year unpaid obligations, unexpired	–2		
3050	Unpaid obligations, end of year	42	72	92
	Memorandum (non-add) entries:			
3100	Obligated balance, start of year	54	42	72
3200	Obligated balance, end of year	42	72	92
	Budget authority and outlays, net:			
	Mandatory:			
4090	Budget authority, gross	168	179	195
	Outlays, gross:			
4100	Outlays from new mandatory authority	36	161	176
4101	Outlays from mandatory balances	104	20	18
4110	Outlays, gross (total)	140	181	194
4180	Budget authority, net (total)	168	179	195
4190	Outlays, net (total)	140	181	194

Park concessions franchise fees.—Franchise fees for concessioner activities in the National Park System (NPS) are deposited in this account and used for certain park operations activities in accordance with section 407 of Public Law 105–391. By law, 20 percent of franchise fees collected are used to support activities throughout the National Park System and 80 percent are retained and used by each collecting park unit for visitor services and for purposes of funding high-priority and urgently necessary resource management programs and operations. The National Park Service Centennial Act (P.L. 114–289), establishes a new concessions contracting authority within NPS, which is described under the Visitor Experience Improvements Fund account.

Concessions improvement accounts.—National Park Service agreements with private concessioners providing visitor services within national parks can require concessioners to deposit a portion of gross receipts or a fixed sum of money in a separate bank account. A concessioner may expend funds from such an account with the approval of the park superintendent for improvements to facilities that directly support concession visitor services but would not otherwise be funded through the appropriations process. Concessioners do not accrue possessory interests from improvements funded through these accounts.

Park buildings lease and maintenance fund.—Rental payments for leases to use buildings and associated property in the National Park System are deposited in this account and used for infrastructure needs at park units in accordance with section 802 of Public Law 105–391.

Operation and maintenance of quarters.—Revenues from the rental of Government-owned quarters to park employees are deposited in this account and used to operate and maintain the quarters.

Filming and photography special use fees.—In limited circumstances, the National Park Service may issue permits and retain associated fees to use park lands and facilities for commercial filming, still photography, and similar activities.

Contributions to U.S. Park Police annuity benefits.—Necessary costs of benefit payments to annuitants under the pension program for United States Park Police officers hired prior to January 1, 1984, established under Public Law 85–157, are paid from the General Fund of the Treasury to the extent the payments exceed deductions from salaries of active duty employees in the program. Permanent funding for such payments was provided in the Department of the Interior and Related Agencies Appropriations Act, 2002. Before 2002, such payments were funded from appropriations made annually to the National Park Service.

Delaware Water Gap, Route 209 Operations.—The Delaware Water Gap National Recreation Area Improvement Act, section 4(b) of Public Law 109–156, as amended by Public Law 115–101, directs the Department of the Interior to establish a fee and permit program for the use of Highway 209 by commercial vehicles. All fees received are set aside in a special account and made available for the administration and enforcement of the program, including registering vehicles, issuing permits and vehicle identification stickers, and personnel costs. The FY 2023 Budget proposes to further amend section 4(b) of Public Law 109–156 by extending statutory authority through FY 2023.

Object Classification (in millions of dollars)

Identification code 014–9924–0–2–303		2021 actual	2022 est.	2023 est.
	Direct obligations:			
	Personnel compensation:			
11.1	Full-time permanent	13	13	14
11.3	Other than full-time permanent	7	8	8
11.5	Other personnel compensation	1	1	1
11.9	Total personnel compensation	21	22	23
12.1	Civilian personnel benefits	6	7	7
21.0	Travel and transportation of persons		1	1
23.3	Communications, utilities, and miscellaneous charges	5	6	6
25.1	Advisory and assistance services	11	16	15
25.2	Other services from non-Federal sources	56	89	91
25.3	Other goods and services from Federal sources	1	4	4
25.4	Operation and maintenance of facilities	5	30	31
25.6	Medical care		6	6
25.7	Operation and maintenance of equipment	2	3	3
26.0	Supplies and materials	10	12	12
31.0	Equipment	4	5	5
32.0	Land and structures	6	6	6
41.0	Grants, subsidies, and contributions	3	4	4
99.9	Total new obligations, unexpired accounts	130	211	214

Employment Summary

Identification code 014–9924–0–2–303	2021 actual	2022 est.	2023 est.
1001 Direct civilian full-time equivalent employment	353	353	353

Trust Funds

Construction (Trust Fund)

Parkway construction project funds have been derived from the Highway Trust Fund through appropriations to liquidate contract authority, which has been provided under section 104(a)(8) of the Federal Aid Highway Act of 1978, title I of Public Law 95–599, as amended, and appropriations language, which has made the contract authority and the appropriations available until expended.

Miscellaneous Trust Funds

Special and Trust Fund Receipts (in millions of dollars)

Identification code 014–9972–0–7–303		2021 actual	2022 est.	2023 est.
0100	Balance, start of year			
	Receipts:			
	Current law:			
1130	Donations to National Park Service	61	51	51
1140	Earnings on Investments, Donations to National Park Service		1	1
1199	Total current law receipts	61	52	52
1999	Total receipts	61	52	52
2000	Total: Balances and receipts	61	52	52
	Appropriations:			
	Current law:			
2101	Miscellaneous Trust Funds	–61	–52	–52
5099	Balance, end of year			

Program and Financing (in millions of dollars)

Identification code 014–9972–0–7–303		2021 actual	2022 est.	2023 est.
	Obligations by program activity:			
0001	Donations to National Park Service	57	71	62
	Budgetary resources:			
	Unobligated balance:			
1000	Unobligated balance brought forward, Oct 1	86	91	72
1021	Recoveries of prior year unpaid obligations	1		
1070	Unobligated balance (total)	87	91	72
	Budget authority:			
	Appropriations, mandatory:			
1201	Appropriation (special or trust fund)	61	52	52
1930	Total budgetary resources available	148	143	124
	Memorandum (non-add) entries:			
1941	Unexpired unobligated balance, end of year	91	72	62
	Change in obligated balance:			
	Unpaid obligations:			
3000	Unpaid obligations, brought forward, Oct 1	32	40	55
3010	New obligations, unexpired accounts	57	71	62
3020	Outlays (gross)	–48	–56	–56
3040	Recoveries of prior year unpaid obligations, unexpired	–1		
3050	Unpaid obligations, end of year	40	55	61
	Memorandum (non-add) entries:			
3100	Obligated balance, start of year	32	40	55
3200	Obligated balance, end of year	40	55	61
	Budget authority and outlays, net:			
	Mandatory:			
4090	Budget authority, gross	61	52	52
	Outlays, gross:			
4100	Outlays from new mandatory authority		26	26
4101	Outlays from mandatory balances	48	30	30
4110	Outlays, gross (total)	48	56	56
4180	Budget authority, net (total)	61	52	52

Fish and Wildlife and Parks—Continued
Trust Funds—Continued

MISCELLANEOUS TRUST FUNDS—Continued

Program and Financing—Continued

Identification code 014–9972–0–7–303	2021 actual	2022 est.	2023 est.
4190 Outlays, net (total)	48	56	56

National Park Service, donations.—The Secretary of the Interior accepts and uses donated moneys for the purposes of the National Park System (54 U.S.C. 101101), as designated by the donor when stated.

Preservation, Birthplace of Abraham Lincoln, National Park Service.—This Fund consists of an endowment established by the Lincoln Farm Association. The interest therefrom is available for preservation of the Abraham Lincoln Birthplace National Historic Site, Kentucky (16 U.S.C. 211, 212).

Object Classification (in millions of dollars)

Identification code 014–9972–0–7–303		2021 actual	2022 est.	2023 est.
	Direct obligations:			
	Personnel compensation:			
11.1	Full-time permanent	5	5	5
11.3	Other than full-time permanent	5	6	6
11.5	Other personnel compensation	1	1	1
11.9	Total personnel compensation	11	12	12
12.1	Civilian personnel benefits	3	3	3
23.3	Communications, utilities, and miscellaneous charges	1	1	1
25.2	Other services from non-Federal sources	10	10	10
25.3	Other goods and services from Federal sources		2	2
25.4	Operation and maintenance of facilities	15	20	15
25.7	Operation and maintenance of equipment		1	1
26.0	Supplies and materials	2	4	4
31.0	Equipment	1	3	1
32.0	Land and structures	8	8	7
41.0	Grants, subsidies, and contributions	6	7	6
99.9	Total new obligations, unexpired accounts	57	71	62

Employment Summary

Identification code 014–9972–0–7–303	2021 actual	2022 est.	2023 est.
1001 Direct civilian full-time equivalent employment	208	208	208

ADMINISTRATIVE PROVISIONS

(INCLUDING TRANSFER OF FUNDS)

In addition to other uses set forth in section 101917(c)(2) of title 54, United States Code, franchise fees credited to a sub-account shall be available for expenditure by the Secretary, without further appropriation, for use at any unit within the National Park System to extinguish or reduce liability for Possessory Interest or leasehold surrender interest. Such funds may only be used for this purpose to the extent that the benefitting unit anticipated franchise fee receipts over the term of the contract at that unit exceed the amount of funds used to extinguish or reduce liability. Franchise fees at the benefitting unit shall be credited to the sub-account of the originating unit over a period not to exceed the term of a single contract at the benefitting unit, in the amount of funds so expended to extinguish or reduce liability.

For the costs of administration of the Land and Water Conservation Fund grants authorized by section 105(a)(2)(B) of the Gulf of Mexico Energy Security Act of 2006 (Public Law 109–432), the National Park Service may retain up to 3 percent of the amounts which are authorized to be disbursed under such section, such retained amounts to remain available until expended.

National Park Service funds may be transferred to the Federal Highway Administration (FHWA), Department of Transportation, for purposes authorized under 23 U.S.C. 203. Transfers may include a reasonable amount for FHWA administrative support costs.

INDIAN AFFAIRS

BUREAU OF INDIAN AFFAIRS

Federal Funds

OPERATION OF INDIAN PROGRAMS

(INCLUDING TRANSFERS OF FUNDS)

For expenses necessary for the operation of Indian programs, as authorized by law, including the Snyder Act of November 2, 1921 (25 U.S.C. 13) and the Indian Self-Determination and Education Assistance Act of 1975 (25 U.S.C. 5301 et seq.), $2,082,036,000, to remain available until September 30, 2024, except as otherwise provided herein; of which not to exceed $8,500 may be for official reception and representation expenses; of which not to exceed $77,994,000 shall be for welfare assistance payments: Provided, That in cases of designated Federal disasters, the Secretary of the Interior may exceed such cap for welfare payments from the amounts provided herein, to provide for disaster relief to Indian communities affected by the disaster: Provided further, That federally recognized Indian tribes and tribal organizations of federally recognized Indian tribes may use their tribal priority allocations for unmet welfare assistance costs: Provided further, That not to exceed $87,386,000 shall remain available until expended for housing improvement, road maintenance, attorney fees, litigation support, land records improvement, land acquisition, and the Navajo-Hopi Settlement Program: Provided further, That any forestry funds allocated to a federally recognized tribe which remain unobligated as of September 30, 2024, may be transferred during fiscal year 2025 to an Indian forest land assistance account established for the benefit of the holder of the funds within the holder's trust fund account: Provided further, That any such unobligated balances not so transferred shall expire on September 30, 2025: Provided further, That in order to enhance the safety of Bureau field employees, the Bureau may use funds to purchase uniforms or other identifying articles of clothing for personnel: Provided further, That the Bureau of Indian Affairs may accept transfers of funds from United States Customs and Border Protection to supplement any other funding available for reconstruction or repair of roads owned by the Bureau of Indian Affairs as identified on the National Tribal Transportation Facility Inventory, 23 U.S.C. 202(b)(1): Provided further, That section 5 of the Indian Reorganization Act of June 18, 1934 (25 U.S.C. 5108) shall be applied by substituting "$10,000,000" for "$2,000,000".

Note.—A full-year 2022 appropriation for this account was not enacted at the time the Budget was prepared; therefore, the Budget assumes this account is operating under the Continuing Appropriations Act, 2022 (Division A of Public Law 117–43, as amended). The amounts included for 2022 reflect the annualized level provided by the continuing resolution.

OPERATION OF INDIAN PROGRAMS

(INCLUDING TRANSFERS OF FUNDS)

[For an additional amount for "Operation of Indian Programs", $216,000,000, to remain available until expended for tribal climate resilience, adaptation, and community relocation planning, design, and implementation of projects which address the varying climate challenges facing tribal communities across the country: *Provided*, That of the funds in the preceding proviso, $43,200,000, to remain available until expended, shall be made available for fiscal year 2022, $43,200,000, to remain available until expended, shall be made available for fiscal year 2023, $43,200,000, to remain available until expended shall be made available for fiscal year 2024, $43,200,000, to remain available until expended, shall be made available for fiscal year 2025, and $43,200,000, to remain available until expended, shall be made available for fiscal year 2026: *Provided further*, That of the funds made available under the preceding proviso for fiscal years 2022 through 2026, $130,000,000 shall be for community relocation, and $86,000,000 shall be for tribal climate resilience and adaptation projects: *Provided further*, That up to 3 percent of the amounts made available under this heading in this Act in each of fiscal years 2022 through 2026 shall be for salaries, expenses, and administration: *Provided further*, That one-half of one percent of the amounts made available under this heading in this Act in each of fiscal years 2022 through 2026 shall be transferred to the Office of Inspector General of the Department of the Interior for oversight of funding provided to the Department of the Interior in this title in this Act: *Provided further*, That awards made under subsection (d) to Tribes and Tribal organizations under the Indian Self-Determination and Education Assistance Act (25 U.S.C. 5301 et seq.) shall be considered non-recurring and shall not be part of the amount required by section 106 of the Indian Self-Determination and Education Assistance Act (25 U.S.C. 5325), and such funds shall only be used for the purposes identified in this section: *Provided further*, That such amount is designated by the Congress as being for an emergency requirement pursuant to section 4112(a) of H. Con. Res. 71 (115th Congress), the concurrent resolution on the budget for fiscal year 2018, and to section 251(b) of the Balanced Budget and Emergency Deficit Control Act of 1985.] *(Infrastructure Investments and Jobs Appropriations Act.)*

DEPARTMENT OF THE INTERIOR

Program and Financing (in millions of dollars)

Identification code 014–2100–0–1–999	2021 actual	2022 est.	2023 est.
Obligations by program activity:			
0007 Tribal Government	318	304	304
0008 Human services	171	136	136
0009 Trust - Natural resources management	246	275	275
0010 Trust - Real estate services	129	124	124
0011 Education	46		
0012 Public safety and justice	423	490	490
0013 Community and economic development	37	37	37
0014 Executive direction and administrative services	248	235	235
0015 CARES ACT SUPPLEMENTAL (P.L. 116–136)	33		
0016 American Rescue Plan (P.L. 117–2)	708	500	500
0799 Total direct obligations	2,359	2,101	2,101
0807 Operation of Indian Programs (Reimbursable)	114	211	211
0899 Total reimbursable obligations	114	211	211
0900 Total new obligations, unexpired accounts	2,473	2,312	2,312
Budgetary resources:			
Unobligated balance:			
1000 Unobligated balance brought forward, Oct 1	373	558	202
1011 Unobligated balance transfer from other acct [014–2106]	3		
1012 Unobligated balance transfers between expired and unexpired accounts	10	14	14
1021 Recoveries of prior year unpaid obligations	10	2	2
1070 Unobligated balance (total)	396	574	218
Budget authority:			
Appropriations, discretionary:			
1100 Appropriation	1,617	1,660	2,082
1121 Appropriations transferred from other acct [014–2106]	50		
1121 Appropriations transferred from other acct [014–0102]	2		
1160 Appropriation, discretionary (total)	1,669	1,660	2,082
Advance appropriations, discretionary:			
1170 Advance appropriation			43
Appropriations, mandatory:			
1200 Appropriation American Rescue Plan (P.L. 117–2)	900		
Spending authority from offsetting collections, discretionary:			
1700 Collected	61	280	280
1701 Change in uncollected payments, Federal sources	6		
1750 Spending auth from offsetting collections, disc (total)	67	280	280
1900 Budget authority (total)	2,636	1,940	2,405
1930 Total budgetary resources available	3,032	2,514	2,623
Memorandum (non-add) entries:			
1940 Unobligated balance expiring	–1		
1941 Unexpired unobligated balance, end of year	558	202	311
Change in obligated balance:			
Unpaid obligations:			
3000 Unpaid obligations, brought forward, Oct 1	419	699	841
3010 New obligations, unexpired accounts	2,473	2,312	2,312
3011 Obligations ("upward adjustments"), expired accounts	3		
3020 Outlays (gross)	–2,174	–2,168	–2,319
3040 Recoveries of prior year unpaid obligations, unexpired	–10	–2	–2
3041 Recoveries of prior year unpaid obligations, expired	–12		
3050 Unpaid obligations, end of year	699	841	832
Uncollected payments:			
3060 Uncollected pymts, Fed sources, brought forward, Oct 1	–40	–43	–43
3070 Change in uncollected pymts, Fed sources, unexpired	–6		
3071 Change in uncollected pymts, Fed sources, expired	3		
3090 Uncollected pymts, Fed sources, end of year	–43	–43	–43
Memorandum (non-add) entries:			
3100 Obligated balance, start of year	379	656	798
3200 Obligated balance, end of year	656	798	789
Budget authority and outlays, net:			
Discretionary:			
4000 Budget authority, gross	1,736	1,940	2,405
Outlays, gross:			
4010 Outlays from new discretionary authority	1,200	1,319	1,624
4011 Outlays from discretionary balances	499	579	585
4020 Outlays, gross (total)	1,699	1,898	2,209
Offsets against gross budget authority and outlays:			
Offsetting collections (collected) from:			
4030 Federal sources	–61	–280	–280
4033 Non-Federal sources	–8		
4040 Offsets against gross budget authority and outlays (total)	–69	–280	–280
Additional offsets against gross budget authority only:			
4050 Change in uncollected pymts, Fed sources, unexpired	–6		
4052 Offsetting collections credited to expired accounts	8		
4060 Additional offsets against budget authority only (total)	2		
4070 Budget authority, net (discretionary)	1,669	1,660	2,125
4080 Outlays, net (discretionary)	1,630	1,618	1,929
Mandatory:			
4090 Budget authority, gross	900		
Outlays, gross:			
4100 Outlays from new mandatory authority	475		
4101 Outlays from mandatory balances		270	110
4110 Outlays, gross (total)	475	270	110
4180 Budget authority, net (total)	2,569	1,660	2,125
4190 Outlays, net (total)	2,105	1,888	2,039

The Operation of Indian Programs appropriation consists of a wide range of services and benefits provided to federally recognized Indian Tribes, Alaska Native groups, and individual American Indians and Alaska Natives, to fulfill Federal trust and treaty responsibilities and support tribal self-determination. The Budget reflects broad increases within this account, including to empower tribal communities, address the impacts of climate change, create economic opportunities, enhance public safety, and advance environmental justice for tribal communities that have been left behind.

This account covers expenses associated with the following activities:

Tribal Government.—This activity promotes the sovereignty of federally recognized Indian Tribes by supporting and assisting them in the development and maintenance of strong and stable governments capable of administering quality programs and developing economies. This activity also provides for the maintenance of Bureau of Indian Affairs (BIA) roads and bridges.

Human Services.—This activity provides funding for social services, welfare assistance, and Indian Child Welfare Act programs. The objective of this activity is to improve the quality of life for individual Indians who live on or near Indian reservations and to help protect children, the elderly, and disabled from abuse and neglect.

Trust: Natural Resources Management.—This activity provides for the management, development, and protection of Indian trust land and natural resource assets and related treaty rights. This activity also provides funding to address the impacts of climate change. Natural resource programs in Indian Country include agriculture, forestry, water, fish, wildlife, and parks, and energy and minerals.

Trust: Real Estate.—This activity promotes cooperative efforts with landowners for the optimal utilization, development, and enhancement of trust and restricted Federal Indian-owned lands. The activity includes general real estate services, probate, land title and records, environmental compliance, and other trust services and rights protection.

Public Safety and Justice.—This activity funds law enforcement activities in Indian Country in over 25 States. Programs under this activity include investigative, police, and detention services; tribal courts; fire protection; implementation of the Violence Against Women Act; and facilities maintenance.

Community and Economic Development.—This activity promotes the economic vitality of American Indians and Alaska Natives through job placement and training, economic development, and community development programs.

Executive Direction and Administrative Services.—This activity supports the management of finance, budget, acquisition, and property functions, as well as information technology resources, personnel services, facilities management, payment of General Services Administration rentals and direct rentals, and intra-governmental payments. Significant portions of Indian Affairs activities are executed under contracts or compacts with federally recognized Indian Tribes to run tribal and Federal programs. Funding also supports BIA or Bureau of Indian Education oversight and technical assistance for these activities in the central and regional offices.

OPERATION OF INDIAN PROGRAMS—Continued

Object Classification (in millions of dollars)

Identification code 014–2100–0–1–999	2021 actual	2022 est.	2023 est.
Direct obligations:			
Personnel compensation:			
11.1 Full-time permanent	208	150	150
11.3 Other than full-time permanent	2	99	99
11.5 Other personnel compensation	25	20	20
11.9 Total personnel compensation	235	269	269
12.1 Civilian personnel benefits	91	100	100
13.0 Benefits for former personnel	1	1	1
21.0 Travel and transportation of persons	5	15	15
22.0 Transportation of things	1	2	2
23.1 Rental payments to GSA	20	21	21
23.2 Rental payments to others	18	16	16
23.3 Communications, utilities, and miscellaneous charges	14	35	35
24.0 Printing and reproduction	....	1	1
25.1 Advisory and assistance services	16	3	3
25.2 Other services from non-Federal sources	1,709	1,033	1,033
25.3 Other goods and services from Federal sources	116	90	90
25.4 Operation and maintenance of facilities	5	12	12
25.5 ADP Contracts	....	2	2
25.6 Medical care	....	1	1
25.7 Operation and maintenance of equipment	9	15	15
26.0 Supplies and materials	13	34	34
31.0 Equipment	23	33	33
32.0 Land and structures	6	1	1
41.0 Grants, subsidies, and contributions	77	417	417
99.0 Direct obligations	2,359	2,101	2,101
99.0 Reimbursable obligations	114	211	211
99.9 Total new obligations, unexpired accounts	2,473	2,312	2,312

Employment Summary

Identification code 014–2100–0–1–999	2021 actual	2022 est.	2023 est.
1001 Direct civilian full-time equivalent employment	2,843	2,843	3,005
2001 Reimbursable civilian full-time equivalent employment	184	36	37
3001 Allocation account civilian full-time equivalent employment	429	490	576

CONTRACT SUPPORT COSTS

For payments to tribes and tribal organizations for contract support costs associated with Indian Self-Determination and Education Assistance Act agreements with the Bureau of Indian Affairs and the Bureau of Indian Education for fiscal year 2023, such sums as may be necessary, which shall be available for obligation through September 30, 2024: Provided, That notwithstanding any other provision of law, no amounts made available under this heading shall be available for transfer to another budget account.

Note.—A full-year 2022 appropriation for this account was not enacted at the time the Budget was prepared; therefore, the Budget assumes this account is operating under the Continuing Appropriations Act, 2022 (Division A of Public Law 117–43, as amended). The amounts included for 2022 reflect the annualized level provided by the continuing resolution.

Program and Financing (in millions of dollars)

Identification code 014–2240–0–1–999	2021 actual	2022 est.	2023 est.
Obligations by program activity:			
0007 Tribal Government	315	253	310
0100 Direct program activities, subtotal	315	253	310
Budgetary resources:			
Unobligated balance:			
1000 Unobligated balance brought forward, Oct 1	....	1	95
1040 Adjustment to prior year indefinite appropriation in subsequent fiscal year	83	....	....
1070 Unobligated balance (total)	83	1	95
Budget authority:			
Appropriations, discretionary:			
1100 Appropriation	233	347	409
1930 Total budgetary resources available	316	348	504
Memorandum (non-add) entries:			
1941 Unexpired unobligated balance, end of year	1	95	194

	2021 actual	2022 est.	2023 est.
Change in obligated balance:			
Unpaid obligations:			
3000 Unpaid obligations, brought forward, Oct 1	49	147	79
3010 New obligations, unexpired accounts	315	253	310
3020 Outlays (gross)	–217	–321	–380
3050 Unpaid obligations, end of year	147	79	9
Memorandum (non-add) entries:			
3100 Obligated balance, start of year	49	147	79
3200 Obligated balance, end of year	147	79	9
Budget authority and outlays, net:			
Discretionary:			
4000 Budget authority, gross	233	347	409
Outlays, gross:			
4010 Outlays from new discretionary authority	129	201	237
4011 Outlays from discretionary balances	88	120	143
4020 Outlays, gross (total)	217	321	380
4180 Budget authority, net (total)	233	347	409
4190 Outlays, net (total)	217	321	380

The Contract Support Costs account provides payments to Tribes for the administrative costs associated with executing tribal self-determination contracts and self-governance compacts under the Indian Self-Determination and Education Assistance Act. Payments are available for direct and indirect contract support costs. Indirect contract support costs are those incurred for a Tribe's or tribal organization's common services, including, but not limited to, insurance and audits. Direct contract support costs include program-specific costs such as unemployment taxes and workers compensation insurance. The account also supports costs associated with executing or administering new and/or expanded self-determination contracts. The 2023 Budget proposes to continue to manage this account as an indefinite appropriation to ensure the availability of full funding to meet contract support costs requirements for the fiscal year.

Object Classification (in millions of dollars)

Identification code 014–2240–0–1–999	2021 actual	2022 est.	2023 est.
Direct obligations:			
25.2 Other services from non-Federal sources	310	240	297
41.0 Grants, subsidies, and contributions	5	13	13
99.9 Total new obligations, unexpired accounts	315	253	310

CONTRACT SUPPORT COSTS

(Legislative proposal, not subject to PAYGO)

Program and Financing (in millions of dollars)

Identification code 014–2240–2–1–999	2021 actual	2022 est.	2023 est.
Budgetary resources:			
Budget authority:			
Appropriations, discretionary:			
1100 Appropriation	....	....	–409
Appropriations, mandatory:			
1200 Appropriation	....	....	409
Budget authority and outlays, net:			
Discretionary:			
4000 Budget authority, gross	....	....	–409
Outlays, gross:			
4010 Outlays from new discretionary authority	....	....	–237
Mandatory:			
4090 Budget authority, gross	....	....	409
Outlays, gross:			
4100 Outlays from new mandatory authority	....	....	237
4180 Budget authority, net (total)			
4190 Outlays, net (total)			

The 2023 Budget proposes to reclassify Contract Support Costs funding from discretionary to mandatory beginning in 2023. Specifically, the Budget proposes that beginning in 2023, the Indian Affairs Contract Support Costs account will continue to be funded through the Appropriations process but will be reclassified as mandatory funding for the purposes of scoring. This account will continue as an indefinite appropriation to ensure the availability of full funding to meet Contract Support Costs requirements for the fiscal year.

PAYMENTS FOR TRIBAL LEASES

For payments to tribes and tribal organizations for leases pursuant to section 105(l) of the Indian Self-Determination and Education Assistance Act (25 U.S.C. 5324(l)) for fiscal year 2023, such sums as may be necessary, which shall be available for obligation through September 30, 2024: Provided, That notwithstanding any other provision of law, no amounts made available under this heading shall be available for transfer to another budget account.

Note.—A full-year 2022 appropriation for this account was not enacted at the time the Budget was prepared; therefore, the Budget assumes this account is operating under the Continuing Appropriations Act, 2022 (Division A of Public Law 117–43, as amended). The amounts included for 2022 reflect the annualized level provided by the continuing resolution.

Program and Financing (in millions of dollars)

Identification code 014–0200–0–1–999		2021 actual	2022 est.	2023 est.
	Obligations by program activity:			
0001	Lease Payments	10	37	55
0900	Total new obligations, unexpired accounts (object class 25.2)	10	37	55
	Budgetary resources:			
	Budget authority:			
	Appropriations, discretionary:			
1100	Appropriation	10	37	55
1930	Total budgetary resources available	10	37	55
	Change in obligated balance:			
	Unpaid obligations:			
3000	Unpaid obligations, brought forward, Oct 1			4
3010	New obligations, unexpired accounts	10	37	55
3020	Outlays (gross)	–6	–41	–55
3050	Unpaid obligations, end of year		4	
	Memorandum (non-add) entries:			
3100	Obligated balance, start of year			4
3200	Obligated balance, end of year		4	
	Budget authority and outlays, net:			
	Discretionary:			
4000	Budget authority, gross	10	37	55
	Outlays, gross:			
4010	Outlays from new discretionary authority	6	37	55
4011	Outlays from discretionary balances		4	
4020	Outlays, gross (total)	6	41	55
4180	Budget authority, net (total)	10	37	55
4190	Outlays, net (total)	6	41	55

The Payments for Tribal Leases account provides for the reasonable and allowable costs for leases with a Tribe or tribal organization for a building owned or leased by the Tribe or tribal organization used for administration or to deliver services under Section 105(l) of the Indian Self-Determination and Education Assistance Act. The 2023 Budget proposes to continue to manage this account as an indefinite appropriation to ensure the full availability of budget authority needed for such lease agreements. Funding from the account would be used for either Bureau of Indian Affairs or Bureau of Indian Education Section 105(l) lease costs.

PAYMENTS FOR TRIBAL LEASES

(Legislative proposal, not subject to PAYGO)

Program and Financing (in millions of dollars)

Identification code 014–0200–2–1–999		2021 actual	2022 est.	2023 est.
	Budgetary resources:			
	Budget authority:			
	Appropriations, discretionary:			
1100	Appropriation			–55
	Appropriations, mandatory:			
1200	Appropriation			55
	Budget authority and outlays, net:			
	Discretionary:			
4000	Budget authority, gross			–55
	Outlays, gross:			
4010	Outlays from new discretionary authority			–55
	Mandatory:			
4090	Budget authority, gross			55
	Outlays, gross:			
4100	Outlays from new mandatory authority			55
4180	Budget authority, net (total)			
4190	Outlays, net (total)			

The 2023 Budget proposes to reclassify Payments for Tribal Leases funding from discretionary to mandatory beginning in 2023. Specifically, the Budget proposes that beginning in 2023, the Indian Affairs Payments for Tribal Leases account will continue to be funded through the Appropriations process but will be reclassified as mandatory funding for the purposes of scoring. This account will continue as an indefinite appropriation to ensure the availability of full funding to meet Indian Self-Determination and Education Assistance Act Section 105(l) lease requirements for the fiscal year.

CONSTRUCTION

(INCLUDING TRANSFER OF FUNDS)

For construction, repair, improvement, and maintenance of irrigation and power systems, buildings, utilities, and other facilities, including architectural and engineering services by contract; acquisition of lands, and interests in lands; and preparation of lands for farming, and for construction of the Navajo Indian Irrigation Project pursuant to Public Law 87–483; $205,732,000, to remain available until expended: Provided, That such amounts as may be available for the construction of the Navajo Indian Irrigation Project may be transferred to the Bureau of Reclamation: Provided further, That any funds provided for the Safety of Dams program pursuant to the Act of November 2, 1921 (25 U.S.C. 13), shall be made available on a nonreimbursable basis: Provided further, That this appropriation may be reimbursed from the Bureau of Trust Funds Administration appropriation for the appropriate share of construction costs for space expansion needed in agency offices to meet trust reform implementation: Provided further, That of the funds made available under this heading, $10,000,000 shall be derived from the Indian Irrigation Fund established by section 3211 of the WIIN Act (Public Law 114–322; 130 Stat. 1749): Provided further, That amounts provided under this heading are available for the modernization of Federal field communication capabilities, in addition to amounts otherwise made available for such purpose.

Note.—A full-year 2022 appropriation for this account was not enacted at the time the Budget was prepared; therefore, the Budget assumes this account is operating under the Continuing Appropriations Act, 2022 (Division A of Public Law 117–43, as amended). The amounts included for 2022 reflect the annualized level provided by the continuing resolution.

CONSTRUCTION

[*For an additional amount for "Construction", $452,000, to remain available until expended, for necessary expenses related to the consequences of calendar year 2019, 2020, and 2021 wildfires, hurricanes and other natural disasters.*] *(Disaster Relief Supplemental Appropriations Act, 2022.)*

CONSTRUCTION

(INCLUDING TRANSFERS OF FUNDS)

[*For an additional amount for "Construction", $250,000,000, to remain available until expended, for construction, repair, improvement, and maintenance of irrigation and power systems, safety of dams, water sanitation, and other facilities: Provided, That any funds provided for the Safety of Dams program pursuant to the Act of November 2, 1921 (25 U.S.C. 13), shall be made available on a nonreimbursable basis: Provided further, That $50,000,000, to remain available until expended, shall be made available for fiscal year 2022, $50,000,000, to remain available until expended, shall be made available for fiscal year 2023, $50,000,000, to remain available until expended, shall be made available for fiscal year 2024, $50,000,000, to remain available until expended, shall be made available for fiscal year 2025, and $50,000,000, to remain available until expended, shall be made available for fiscal year 2026: Provided further, That of the funds made available under this heading in this Act for fiscal years 2022 through 2026—*]

[(1) *Not less than $50,000,000 shall be for addressing irrigation and power systems; and*]

Indian Affairs—Continued
Bureau of Indian Affairs—Continued

CONSTRUCTION—Continued

[(2) $200,000,000 shall be for safety of dams, water sanitation, and other facilities:]

[*Provided further*, That up to 3 percent of the amounts made available under this heading in this Act in each of fiscal years 2022 through 2026 shall be for salaries, expenses, and administration: *Provided further*, That one-half of one percent of the amounts made available under this heading in this Act in each of fiscal years 2022 through 2026 shall be transferred to the Office of Inspector General of the Department of the Interior for oversight of funding provided to the Department of the Interior in this title in this Act: *Provided further*, That such amount is designated by the Congress as being for an emergency requirement pursuant to section 4112(a) of H. Con. Res. 71 (115th Congress), the concurrent resolution on the budget for fiscal year 2018, and to section 251(b) of the Balanced Budget and Emergency Deficit Control Act of 1985.] *(Infrastructure Investments and Jobs Appropriations Act.)*

Program and Financing (in millions of dollars)

Identification code 014–2301–0–1–452		2021 actual	2022 est.	2023 est.
	Obligations by program activity:			
0001	Education construction	30		
0002	Public safety and justice construction	71	8	8
0003	Resource management construction	50	79	79
0004	Other Program Construction	17	8	8
0005	BOR Allocation Account	3	2	2
0799	Total direct obligations	171	97	97
0807	Construction (Reimbursable)	1	2	2
0900	Total new obligations, unexpired accounts	172	99	99
	Budgetary resources:			
	Unobligated balance:			
1000	Unobligated balance brought forward, Oct 1	435	394	506
1021	Recoveries of prior year unpaid obligations	2	24	24
1070	Unobligated balance (total)	437	418	530
	Budget authority:			
	Appropriations, discretionary:			
1100	Appropriation	119	169	196
1121	Appropriations transferred from other acct [014–5639]	10	10	10
1160	Appropriation, discretionary (total)	129	179	206
	Advance appropriations, discretionary:			
1170	Advance appropriation			50
	Spending authority from offsetting collections, discretionary:			
1700	Collected		8	8
1900	Budget authority (total)	129	187	264
1930	Total budgetary resources available	566	605	794
	Memorandum (non-add) entries:			
1941	Unexpired unobligated balance, end of year	394	506	695
	Change in obligated balance:			
	Unpaid obligations:			
3000	Unpaid obligations, brought forward, Oct 1	142	194	107
3010	New obligations, unexpired accounts	172	99	99
3020	Outlays (gross)	–118	–162	–169
3040	Recoveries of prior year unpaid obligations, unexpired	–2	–24	–24
3050	Unpaid obligations, end of year	194	107	13
	Memorandum (non-add) entries:			
3100	Obligated balance, start of year	142	194	107
3200	Obligated balance, end of year	194	107	13
	Budget authority and outlays, net:			
	Discretionary:			
4000	Budget authority, gross	129	187	264
	Outlays, gross:			
4010	Outlays from new discretionary authority	20	45	63
4011	Outlays from discretionary balances	98	117	106
4020	Outlays, gross (total)	118	162	169
	Offsets against gross budget authority and outlays:			
	Offsetting collections (collected) from:			
4030	Federal sources		–8	–8
4040	Offsets against gross budget authority and outlays (total)		–8	–8
4180	Budget authority, net (total)	129	179	256
4190	Outlays, net (total)	118	154	161

Public safety and justice construction.—This activity provides for the planning, design, improvement, repair, replacement, and construction of law enforcement and detention center facilities on Indian lands.

Resources management construction.—This activity provides for the construction, extension, and rehabilitation of irrigation projects, dams, and related power systems on Indian reservations.

Other program construction.—This activity provides for the improvement and repair of Indian Affairs' regional and agency facilities, the telecommunications system, field communications, drinking and wastewater infrastructure, the facilities management system, and construction program management.

Object Classification (in millions of dollars)

Identification code 014–2301–0–1–452		2021 actual	2022 est.	2023 est.
11.1	Direct obligations: Personnel compensation: Full-time permanent	4	4	4
11.9	Total personnel compensation	4	4	4
12.1	Civilian personnel benefits	2	2	2
23.3	Communications, utilities, and miscellaneous charges	1	1	1
25.1	Advisory and assistance services	9	9	9
25.2	Other services from non-Federal sources	118	44	44
25.3	Other goods and services from Federal sources	9	9	9
25.4	Operation and maintenance of facilities	9	9	9
25.7	Operation and maintenance of equipment	3	3	3
31.0	Equipment	1	1	1
32.0	Land and structures	9	9	9
41.0	Grants, subsidies, and contributions	6	6	6
99.0	Direct obligations	171	97	97
99.0	Reimbursable obligations	1	2	2
99.9	Total new obligations, unexpired accounts	172	99	99

Employment Summary

Identification code 014–2301–0–1–452	2021 actual	2022 est.	2023 est.
1001 Direct civilian full-time equivalent employment	41	41	41
2001 Reimbursable civilian full-time equivalent employment	2	2	2
3001 Allocation account civilian full-time equivalent employment	128	128	128

HIGH-HAZARD INDIAN DAM SAFETY DEFERRED MAINTENANCE FUND

Special and Trust Fund Receipts (in millions of dollars)

Identification code 014–5637–0–2–452	2021 actual	2022 est.	2023 est.
0100 Balance, start of year	2	2	2
2000 Total: Balances and receipts	2	2	2
5099 Balance, end of year	2	2	2

Program and Financing (in millions of dollars)

Identification code 014–5637–0–2–452		2021 actual	2022 est.	2023 est.
	Budgetary resources:			
	Budget authority:			
	Appropriations, discretionary:			
1100	Appropriation	23	23	23
1134	Appropriations precluded from obligation	–23	–23	–23
4180	Budget authority, net (total)			
4190	Outlays, net (total)			
	Memorandum (non-add) entries:			
5000	Total investments, SOY: Federal securities: Par value	93	116	120
5001	Total investments, EOY: Federal securities: Par value	116	120	124
5096	Unexpired unavailable balance, SOY: Appropriations	91	114	114
5098	Unexpired unavailable balance, EOY: Appropriations	114	137	137

LOW-HAZARD INDIAN DAM SAFETY DEFERRED MAINTENANCE FUND

Special and Trust Fund Receipts (in millions of dollars)

Identification code 014–5638–0–2–452	2021 actual	2022 est.	2023 est.
0100 Balance, start of year	1	1	1

DEPARTMENT OF THE INTERIOR

Indian Affairs—Continued
Bureau of Indian Affairs—Continued

675

Identification code 014–5638–0–2–452		2021 actual	2022 est.	2023 est.
2000	Total: Balances and receipts	1	1	1
5099	Balance, end of year	1	1	1

Program and Financing (in millions of dollars)

Identification code 014–5638–0–2–452		2021 actual	2022 est.	2023 est.
	Budgetary resources:			
	Budget authority:			
	Appropriations, discretionary:			
1100	Appropriation	10	10	10
1134	Appropriations precluded from obligation	–10	–10	–10
4180	Budget authority, net (total)			
4190	Outlays, net (total)			
	Memorandum (non-add) entries:			
5000	Total investments, SOY: Federal securities: Par value	41	51	53
5001	Total investments, EOY: Federal securities: Par value	51	53	55
5096	Unexpired unavailable balance, SOY: Appropriations	40	50	50
5098	Unexpired unavailable balance, EOY: Appropriations	50	60	60

INDIAN IRRIGATION FUND

Special and Trust Fund Receipts (in millions of dollars)

Identification code 014–5639–0–2–452		2021 actual	2022 est.	2023 est.
0100	Balance, start of year	1	....	1
	Receipts:			
	Current law:			
1140	Earnings on Investments, Indian Irrigation Fund	....	2	2
2000	Total: Balances and receipts	1	2	3
	Appropriations:			
	Current law:			
2101	Indian Irrigation Fund	–1	–1	–1
5099	Balance, end of year	....	1	2

Program and Financing (in millions of dollars)

Identification code 014–5639–0–2–452		2021 actual	2022 est.	2023 est.
	Budgetary resources:			
	Budget authority:			
	Appropriations, discretionary:			
1100	Appropriation	35	35	35
1101	Appropriation (special or trust)	1	1	1
1102	Appropriation (previously unavailable)	9	9	9
1120	Appropriations transferred to other acct [014–2301]	–10	–10	–10
1134	Appropriations precluded from obligation	–35	–35	–35
4180	Budget authority, net (total)			
4190	Outlays, net (total)			
	Memorandum (non-add) entries:			
5000	Total investments, SOY: Federal securities: Par value	123	149	155
5001	Total investments, EOY: Federal securities: Par value	149	155	161
5096	Unexpired unavailable balance, SOY: Appropriations	123	187	187
5098	Unexpired unavailable balance, EOY: Appropriations	158	222	222

WHITE EARTH SETTLEMENT FUND

Program and Financing (in millions of dollars)

Identification code 014–2204–0–1–452		2021 actual	2022 est.	2023 est.
	Obligations by program activity:			
0001	Payments for White Earth Settlement	....	2	2
0900	Total new obligations, unexpired accounts (object class 41.0)	....	2	2
	Budgetary resources:			
	Unobligated balance:			
1000	Unobligated balance brought forward, Oct 1	1	1	1
	Budget authority:			
	Appropriations, mandatory:			
1200	Appropriation	....	2	2
1930	Total budgetary resources available	1	3	3

		2021 actual	2022 est.	2023 est.
	Memorandum (non-add) entries:			
1941	Unexpired unobligated balance, end of year	1	1	1
	Change in obligated balance:			
	Unpaid obligations:			
3010	New obligations, unexpired accounts	....	2	2
3020	Outlays (gross)	....	–2	–2
	Budget authority and outlays, net:			
	Mandatory:			
4090	Budget authority, gross	....	2	2
	Outlays, gross:			
4100	Outlays from new mandatory authority	....	2	2
4180	Budget authority, net (total)	....	2	2
4190	Outlays, net (total)	....	2	2

The White Earth Reservation Land Settlement Act of 1985 (P.L. 99–264) authorizes the payment of funds to eligible allottees or heirs of the White Earth Reservation in Minnesota, as determined by the Secretary of the Interior. The payment of funds shall be treated as the final judgment, award, or compromise settlement under the provisions of Title 31, United States Code, section 1304.

INDIAN LAND AND WATER CLAIM SETTLEMENTS AND MISCELLANEOUS PAYMENTS TO INDIANS

For payments and necessary administrative expenses for implementation of Indian land and water claim settlements pursuant to Public Laws 99–264, 114–322, and 116–260 and for implementation of other land and water rights settlements, $825,000, to remain available until expended.

Note.—A full-year 2022 appropriation for this account was not enacted at the time the Budget was prepared; therefore, the Budget assumes this account is operating under the Continuing Appropriations Act, 2022 (Division A of Public Law 117–43, as amended). The amounts included for 2022 reflect the annualized level provided by the continuing resolution.

Program and Financing (in millions of dollars)

Identification code 014–2303–0–1–452		2021 actual	2022 est.	2023 est.
	Obligations by program activity:			
0001	White Earth	....	1	1
0025	Navajo Nation Water Resources Development Trust Fund	....	4	4
0027	Navajo Water Settlement	9	29	15
0028	Under the reporting threshold	....	1	1
0034	Aamodt	....	15	....
0035	Yurok Land Settlement	....	8	....
0036	Aamodt Litigation Settlement - Mandatory	....	3	....
0037	Blackfeet Water Settlement	45	....	....
0900	Total new obligations, unexpired accounts	54	61	21
	Budgetary resources:			
	Unobligated balance:			
1000	Unobligated balance brought forward, Oct 1	56	48	33
	Budget authority:			
	Appropriations, discretionary:			
1100	Appropriation	46	46	1
1900	Budget authority (total)	46	46	1
1930	Total budgetary resources available	102	94	34
	Memorandum (non-add) entries:			
1941	Unexpired unobligated balance, end of year	48	33	13
	Change in obligated balance:			
	Unpaid obligations:			
3000	Unpaid obligations, brought forward, Oct 1	10	10	27
3010	New obligations, unexpired accounts	54	61	21
3020	Outlays (gross)	–54	–44	–24
3050	Unpaid obligations, end of year	10	27	24
	Memorandum (non-add) entries:			
3100	Obligated balance, start of year	10	10	27
3200	Obligated balance, end of year	10	27	24
	Budget authority and outlays, net:			
	Discretionary:			
4000	Budget authority, gross	46	46	1
	Outlays, gross:			
4010	Outlays from new discretionary authority	45	23	....
4011	Outlays from discretionary balances	9	21	24
4020	Outlays, gross (total)	54	44	24

Indian Affairs—Continued
Bureau of Indian Affairs—Continued

INDIAN LAND AND WATER CLAIM SETTLEMENTS AND MISCELLANEOUS PAYMENTS TO INDIANS—Continued

Program and Financing—Continued

Identification code 014–2303–0–1–452	2021 actual	2022 est.	2023 est.
4180 Budget authority, net (total)	46	46	1
4190 Outlays, net (total)	54	44	24

This account covers expenses associated with the following authorized activities.

Land settlements:

White Earth Reservation Land Settlement Act (P.L. 99–264).—Funds are used to investigate and verify questionable transfers of land by which individual Indian allottees, or their heirs, were divested of ownership and to achieve the payment of compensation to said allottees or heirs in accordance with the Act. A major portion of work is contracted under Public Law 93–638, as amended, to the White Earth Reservation Business Committee.

Water settlements:

In FY 2023, the following enacted Indian Water Rights settlements are eligible for mandatory funding authorized in the Infrastructure Investment and Jobs Act, P.L. 117–58 (30 U.S.C. 1245) through the Indian Water Settlements Completion Fund.

Montana Water Rights Protection Act. (P.L. 116–260).—Funds are used for payments to the Selis Qlispe Ksanka Trust Fund authorized by the settlement Act to implement the water rights compact among the Confederated Salish and Kootenai Tribes of the Flathead Indian Reservation, United States, and State of Montana. The Compact includes rehabilitation and modernization of the Flathead Indian Irrigation Project and associated mitigation, reclamation, and restoration activities, among other things. Consistent with P.L. 116–260, appropriated funds will be transferred to the Selis Qlipse Ksanka Trust Fund.

Navajo-Utah Water Right Settlement (P.L. 116–260).—Funds are used for payments to the Navajo-Utah Settlement Trust Fund as authorized by the settlement Act to implement the Navajo Utah Water Rights Settlement Agreement entered into among the Navajo Nation, United States, and State of Utah. Amounts from the Trust Fund will be used by the Nation for planning, design, construction, operations, and maintenance of Navajo water development projects for domestic municipal water supply, including distribution infrastructure, and agricultural water conservation.

Blackfeet Water Rights Settlement (P.L. 114–322).—Funds are used for payments to the Blackfeet Settlement Trust Fund for use by the Tribe for administration of Tribal water rights and energy development projects; water, storage, and development projects; to assist the Tribe in paying operations, maintenance, and replacement costs for infrastructure projects funded by the settlement compact, and for other purposes the Act authorizes for the Trust Fund.

White Mountain Apache Tribe Water Rights Quantification Act of 2010 (P.L. 111–291).—Funds are used for payments to the WMAT Settlement Fund established in the Act for use by the Tribe for fish production, including hatcheries; rehabilitation of recreational lakes and existing irrigation systems; water-related economic development projects; and protection, restoration, and economic development of forest and watershed health.

Miscellaneous Payments to Indians:

Truckee River Operating Agreement (P.L. 101–618).—Funds are used to pay the BIA share of ongoing payments for the Truckee River Operating Agreement authorized in Section 205 of the Truckee-Carson-Pyramid Lake Water Settlement Act for services provided to implement the settlement.

Object Classification (in millions of dollars)

Identification code 014–2303–0–1–452	2021 actual	2022 est.	2023 est.
Direct obligations:			
25.2 Other services from non-Federal sources	9	10	1
41.0 Grants, subsidies, and contributions	45	51	20
99.9 Total new obligations, unexpired accounts	54	61	21

INDIAN WATER RIGHTS SETTLEMENT COMPLETION FUND

Program and Financing (in millions of dollars)

Identification code 014–2699–0–1–452	2021 actual	2022 est.	2023 est.
Obligations by program activity:			
0001 Indian Water Rights Completion Fund		250	250
0900 Total new obligations, unexpired accounts (object class 41.0)		250	250
Budgetary resources:			
Unobligated balance:			
1000 Unobligated balance brought forward, Oct 1			2,250
Budget authority:			
Appropriations, mandatory:			
1200 Appropriation		2,500	
1900 Budget authority (total)		2,500	
1930 Total budgetary resources available		2,500	2,250
Memorandum (non-add) entries:			
1941 Unexpired unobligated balance, end of year		2,250	2,000
Change in obligated balance:			
Unpaid obligations:			
3010 New obligations, unexpired accounts		250	250
3020 Outlays (gross)		–250	–250
Budget authority and outlays, net:			
Mandatory:			
4090 Budget authority, gross		2,500	
Outlays, gross:			
4100 Outlays from new mandatory authority		250	
4101 Outlays from mandatory balances			250
4110 Outlays, gross (total)		250	250
4180 Budget authority, net (total)		2,500	
4190 Outlays, net (total)		250	250

The Infrastructure Investment and Jobs Act, Public Law 117–58, established the Indian Water Rights Settlement Completion Fund for transfer to funds or accounts authorized to receive discretionary appropriations, or to satisfy other obligations identified by the Secretary of the Interior, under an Indian water settlement approved and authorized by an Act of Congress before the date of enactment of the Act, November 15, 2021. The Act provides $2.5 billion in mandatory funding to be deposited in the Fund to remain available until expended.

INDIAN WATER RIGHTS SETTLEMENT COMPLETION FUND

(Legislative proposal, subject to PAYGO)

Program and Financing (in millions of dollars)

Identification code 014–2699–4–1–452	2021 actual	2022 est.	2023 est.
Budgetary resources:			
Budget authority:			
Appropriations, mandatory:			
1200 Appropriation			34
1220 Appropriations transferred to other acct [014–0680]			–34
4180 Budget authority, net (total)			
4190 Outlays, net (total)			

The 2023 Budget proposes legislation to address the ongoing Operation, Maintenance, and Repair requirements associated with four enacted Indian Water Rights Settlements managed by the Bureau of Reclamation. These annual requirements are associated with the Ak Chin Indian Water Rights Settlement Project, the Animas-La Plata Project (Colorado Ute Settlement), the Columbia and Snake River Salmon Recovery Project (Nez Perce Settlement), and the Navajo-Gallup Water Supply Project.

The proposal provides $34.0 million annually over ten years to cover these requirements. Funds would be deposited into the Indian Water Rights

Settlement Completion Fund and shall transfer to the Bureau of Reclamation for implementation.

INDIAN LAND CONSOLIDATION

For the acquisition of fractional interests to further land consolidation as authorized under the Indian Land Consolidation Act Amendments of 2000 (Public Law 106–462), and the American Indian Probate Reform Act of 2004 (Public Law 108–374), $80,000,000, to remain available until expended: Provided, That any provision of the Indian Land Consolidation Act Amendments of 2000 (Public Law 106–462) that requires or otherwise relates to application of a lien shall not apply to the acquisitions funded herein.

Note.—A full-year 2022 appropriation for this account was not enacted at the time the Budget was prepared; therefore, the Budget assumes this account is operating under the Continuing Appropriations Act, 2022 (Division A of Public Law 117–43, as amended). The amounts included for 2022 reflect the annualized level provided by the continuing resolution.

Program and Financing (in millions of dollars)

Identification code 014–2103–0–1–452	2021 actual	2022 est.	2023 est.
Obligations by program activity:			
0001 Indian Land Consolidation		4	40
0801 Indian Land Consolidation (Reimbursable)			4
0900 Total new obligations, unexpired accounts		4	44
Budgetary resources:			
Budget authority:			
Appropriations, discretionary:			
1100 Appropriation			80
Spending authority from offsetting collections, discretionary:			
1700 Collected		4	4
1900 Budget authority (total)		4	84
1930 Total budgetary resources available		4	84
Memorandum (non-add) entries:			
1941 Unexpired unobligated balance, end of year			40
Change in obligated balance:			
Unpaid obligations:			
3010 New obligations, unexpired accounts		4	44
3020 Outlays (gross)		–4	–44
Budget authority and outlays, net:			
Discretionary:			
4000 Budget authority, gross		4	84
Outlays, gross:			
4010 Outlays from new discretionary authority		4	44
Offsets against gross budget authority and outlays:			
Offsetting collections (collected) from:			
4030 Federal sources		–4	–4
4040 Offsets against gross budget authority and outlays (total)		–4	–4
4180 Budget authority, net (total)			80
4190 Outlays, net (total)			40

This appropriation was established in 1999 and received appropriations between 1999–2010 to fund a program to consolidate fractional interests in Indian lands. Funds were used to purchase small interests in parcels of land from willing individual Indian landowners and convey those interests to the Tribe on whose reservation the land is located. Current funding activity in this account reflects ongoing legacy activities funded through reimbursable work. This program is authorized under the Indian Land Consolidation Act Amendments of 2000 (P.L. 106–462), the American Indian Probate Reform Act of 2004 (P.L. 108–374) and other authorities.

Indian Land Consolidation.—The 2022 Budget proposed to reestablish the Indian Land Consolidation Program with modifications. The reestablished program will consolidate fractional interests in Indian lands. Funds will be used to purchase small interests in parcels of land from willing individual Indian landowners and convey those interests to the Tribe on whose reservation the land is located. Consolidation of these interests is expected to reduce the Government's cost for managing Indian lands and promote conservation on these lands. This program is authorized under the Indian Land Consolidation Act Amendments of 2000 (P.L. 106–462), the American Indian Probate Reform Act of 2004 (P.L. 108–374), and other authorities. This program is independent of the Land Buy Back Program for Tribal Nations, and any provision of the Indian Land Consolidation Act Amendments of 2000 (P.L. 106–462) that requires or otherwise relates to application of a lien shall not apply to the acquisitions funded by this account.

Object Classification (in millions of dollars)

Identification code 014–2103–0–1–452	2021 actual	2022 est.	2023 est.
Direct obligations:			
11.1 Personnel compensation: Full-time permanent			1
32.0 Land and structures		4	39
99.0 Direct obligations		4	40
99.0 Reimbursable obligations			4
99.9 Total new obligations, unexpired accounts		4	44

Employment Summary

Identification code 014–2103–0–1–452	2021 actual	2022 est.	2023 est.
1001 Direct civilian full-time equivalent employment			21

INDIAN WATER RIGHTS AND HABITAT ACQUISITION PROGRAM

Program and Financing (in millions of dollars)

Identification code 014–5505–0–2–303	2021 actual	2022 est.	2023 est.
Budgetary resources:			
Unobligated balance:			
1000 Unobligated balance brought forward, Oct 1	3	3	3
1930 Total budgetary resources available	3	3	3
Memorandum (non-add) entries:			
1941 Unexpired unobligated balance, end of year	3	3	3
4180 Budget authority, net (total)			
4190 Outlays, net (total)			

Funds were requested in 2003 for the settlement of the water claims of the Shivwits Band of the Paiute Indian Tribe of Utah. Public Law 106–263 specifies the use of the Land and Water Conservation Fund for the implementation of the water rights and habitat acquisition program.

OPERATION AND MAINTENANCE OF QUARTERS

Special and Trust Fund Receipts (in millions of dollars)

Identification code 014–5051–0–2–452	2021 actual	2022 est.	2023 est.
0100 Balance, start of year			
Receipts:			
Current law:			
1130 Rents and Charges for Quarters, Bureau of Indian Affairs	6	6	6
2000 Total: Balances and receipts	6	6	6
Appropriations:			
Current law:			
2101 Operation and Maintenance of Quarters	–6	–6	–6
5099 Balance, end of year			

Program and Financing (in millions of dollars)

Identification code 014–5051–0–2–452	2021 actual	2022 est.	2023 est.
Obligations by program activity:			
0001 Operations and maintenance	6	6	6
Budgetary resources:			
Unobligated balance:			
1000 Unobligated balance brought forward, Oct 1	7	7	7
Budget authority:			
Appropriations, mandatory:			
1201 Appropriation (special or trust fund)	6	6	6
1930 Total budgetary resources available	13	13	13

678   Indian Affairs—Continued
       Bureau of Indian Affairs—Continued

OPERATION AND MAINTENANCE OF QUARTERS—Continued

Program and Financing—Continued

Identification code 014–5051–0–2–452	2021 actual	2022 est.	2023 est.
Memorandum (non-add) entries:			
1941 Unexpired unobligated balance, end of year	7	7	7
Change in obligated balance:			
Unpaid obligations:			
3000 Unpaid obligations, brought forward, Oct 1	1	1	
3010 New obligations, unexpired accounts	6	6	6
3020 Outlays (gross)	–6	–7	–6
3050 Unpaid obligations, end of year	1		
Memorandum (non-add) entries:			
3100 Obligated balance, start of year	1	1	
3200 Obligated balance, end of year	1		
Budget authority and outlays, net:			
Mandatory:			
4090 Budget authority, gross	6	6	6
Outlays, gross:			
4100 Outlays from new mandatory authority	3	6	6
4101 Outlays from mandatory balances	3	1	
4110 Outlays, gross (total)	6	7	6
4180 Budget authority, net (total)	6	6	6
4190 Outlays, net (total)	6	7	6

Public Law 88–459 (Federal Employees Quarters and Facilities Act of 1964) is the basic authority under which the Secretary utilizes funds from the rental of quarters to defray the costs of operation and maintenance incidental to the employee quarters program. Public Law 98–473 established a special fund, to remain available until expended, for the operation and maintenance of quarters.

Object Classification (in millions of dollars)

Identification code 014–5051–0–2–452	2021 actual	2022 est.	2023 est.
Direct obligations:			
Personnel compensation:			
11.1 Full-time permanent	1	1	1
11.3 Other than full-time permanent	1	1	1
11.9 Total personnel compensation	2	2	2
12.1 Civilian personnel benefits	1	1	1
23.3 Communications, utilities, and miscellaneous charges	1	1	1
25.4 Operation and maintenance of facilities	1	1	1
26.0 Supplies and materials	1	1	1
99.0 Direct obligations	6	6	6
99.9 Total new obligations, unexpired accounts	6	6	6

Employment Summary

Identification code 014–5051–0–2–452	2021 actual	2022 est.	2023 est.
1001 Direct civilian full-time equivalent employment	40	40	40

MISCELLANEOUS PERMANENT APPROPRIATIONS

Special and Trust Fund Receipts (in millions of dollars)

Identification code 014–9925–0–2–452	2021 actual	2022 est.	2023 est.
0100 Balance, start of year	5	5	7
Receipts:			
Current law:			
1130 Deposits, Operation and Maintenance, Indian Irrigation Systems	39	39	39
1130 Alaska Resupply Program		1	1
1130 Power Revenues, Indian Irrigation Projects	74	74	76
1140 Earnings on Investments, Operation and Maintenance, Indian Irrigation Systems		1	1
1140 Earnings on Investments, Indian Irrigation Projects		1	1
1199 Total current law receipts	113	116	118
1999 Total receipts	113	116	118
2000 Total: Balances and receipts	118	121	125
Appropriations:			
Current law:			
2101 Miscellaneous Permanent Appropriations	–114	–115	–115
2103 Miscellaneous Permanent Appropriations	–1	–1	–1
2132 Miscellaneous Permanent Appropriations	2	2	2
2199 Total current law appropriations	–113	–114	–114
2999 Total appropriations	–113	–114	–114
5099 Balance, end of year	5	7	11

Program and Financing (in millions of dollars)

Identification code 014–9925–0–2–452	2021 actual	2022 est.	2023 est.
Obligations by program activity:			
0002 Operation and maintenance, Indian irrigation systems	37	36	36
0003 Power systems, Indian irrigation projects	88	73	73
0004 Alaska resupply program	2	2	2
0900 Total new obligations, unexpired accounts	127	111	111
Budgetary resources:			
Unobligated balance:			
1000 Unobligated balance brought forward, Oct 1	76	84	89
1011 Unobligated balance transfer from other acct [014–5035]	11		
1011 Unobligated balance transfer from other acct [014–5020]	1		
1011 Unobligated balance transfer from other acct [014–5474]	2		
1011 Unobligated balance transfer from other acct [014–5033]	5		
1011 Unobligated balance transfer from other acct [014–1612]	1		
1021 Recoveries of prior year unpaid obligations	2	2	2
1070 Unobligated balance (total)	98	86	91
Budget authority:			
Appropriations, mandatory:			
1201 Appropriation (special or trust fund)	114	115	115
1203 Appropriation (previously unavailable)(special or trust)	1	1	1
1232 Appropriations and/or unobligated balance of appropriations temporarily reduced	–2	–2	–2
1260 Appropriations, mandatory (total)	113	114	114
1900 Budget authority (total)	113	114	114
1930 Total budgetary resources available	211	200	205
Memorandum (non-add) entries:			
1941 Unexpired unobligated balance, end of year	84	89	94
Change in obligated balance:			
Unpaid obligations:			
3000 Unpaid obligations, brought forward, Oct 1	26	34	30
3010 New obligations, unexpired accounts	127	111	111
3020 Outlays (gross)	–117	–113	–114
3040 Recoveries of prior year unpaid obligations, unexpired	–2	–2	–2
3050 Unpaid obligations, end of year	34	30	25
Memorandum (non-add) entries:			
3100 Obligated balance, start of year	26	34	30
3200 Obligated balance, end of year	34	30	25
Budget authority and outlays, net:			
Discretionary:			
Outlays, gross:			
4011 Outlays from discretionary balances	4		
Mandatory:			
4090 Budget authority, gross	113	114	114
Outlays, gross:			
4100 Outlays from new mandatory authority	60	58	58
4101 Outlays from mandatory balances	53	55	56
4110 Outlays, gross (total)	113	113	114
4180 Budget authority, net (total)	113	114	114
4190 Outlays, net (total)	117	113	114
Memorandum (non-add) entries:			
5000 Total investments, SOY: Federal securities: Par value	75	83	91
5001 Total investments, EOY: Federal securities: Par value	83	91	99

Claims and treaty obligations.—Payments are made to fulfill treaty obligations with the Senecas of New York (Act of February 19, 1831), the Six Nations of New York (Act of November 11, 1794), and the Pawnees of Oklahoma (the treaty of September 24, 1857).

Operation and maintenance, Indian irrigation systems.—Revenues derived from charges for operation and maintenance of Indian irrigation projects are used to defray in part the cost of operating and maintaining

DEPARTMENT OF THE INTERIOR

these projects (25 U.S.C. 162a (The Act of November 4, 1983), 60 Stat. 895, P.L. 98–146).

Power systems, Indian irrigation projects.—Revenues collected from the sale of electric power by the Colorado River and Flathead power systems are used to operate and maintain those systems (25 U.S.C. 162a (The Act of November 4, 1983), 60 Stat. 895; 65 Stat. 254, P.L. 98–146). This activity also includes Cochiti Wet Field Solution funds that were transferred from the Corps of Engineers to pay for operation and maintenance, repair, and replacement of the on-going drainage system (P.L. 102–358).

Alaska resupply program.—Revenues collected from operation of the Alaska Resupply Program are used to operate and maintain this program (P.L. 77–457, 56 Stat. 95).

Object Classification (in millions of dollars)

Identification code 014–9925–0–2–452		2021 actual	2022 est.	2023 est.
	Direct obligations:			
	Personnel compensation:			
11.1	Full-time permanent	17	17	17
11.5	Other personnel compensation	3	3	3
11.9	Total personnel compensation	20	20	20
12.1	Civilian personnel benefits	7	7	7
23.3	Communications, utilities, and miscellaneous charges	5	5	5
25.1	Advisory and assistance services	23	23	23
25.2	Other services from non-Federal sources	53	40	40
25.3	Other goods and services from Federal sources	3	3	3
25.4	Operation and maintenance of facilities	2	2	2
25.7	Operation and maintenance of equipment	2	2	2
26.0	Supplies and materials	5	5	5
32.0	Land and structures	3	3	3
41.0	Grants, subsidies, and contributions	4	1	1
99.9	Total new obligations, unexpired accounts	127	111	111

Employment Summary

Identification code 014–9925–0–2–452	2021 actual	2022 est.	2023 est.
1001 Direct civilian full-time equivalent employment	268	268	267

Indian Direct Loan Financing Account

Program and Financing (in millions of dollars)

Identification code 014–4416–0–3–452		2021 actual	2022 est.	2023 est.
	Obligations by program activity:			
	Credit program obligations:			
0715	Other (Rounding)		1	1
0900	Total new obligations, unexpired accounts		1	1
	Budgetary resources:			
	Financing authority:			
	Spending authority from offsetting collections, mandatory:			
1800	Collected	1	1	1
1825	Spending authority from offsetting collections applied to repay debt	–1		
1850	Spending auth from offsetting collections, mand (total)		1	1
1900	Budget authority (total)		1	1
1930	Total budgetary resources available		1	1
	Change in obligated balance:			
	Unpaid obligations:			
3000	Unpaid obligations, brought forward, Oct 1	1		
3010	New obligations, unexpired accounts		1	1
3020	Outlays (gross)	–1	–1	–1
	Memorandum (non-add) entries:			
3100	Obligated balance, start of year	1		
	Financing authority and disbursements, net:			
	Mandatory:			
4090	Budget authority, gross		1	1
	Financing disbursements:			
4110	Outlays, gross (total)	1	1	1

Indian Affairs—Continued
Bureau of Indian Affairs—Continued   679

	Offsets against gross financing authority and disbursements:			
	Offsetting collections (collected) from:			
4120	Federal sources	–1		
4123	Collections of loans		–1	–1
4130	Offsets against gross budget authority and outlays (total)	–1	–1	–1
4160	Budget authority, net (mandatory)	–1		
4180	Budget authority, net (total)	–1		
4190	Outlays, net (total)			

Status of Direct Loans (in millions of dollars)

Identification code 014–4416–0–3–452	2021 actual	2022 est.	2023 est.
Cumulative balance of direct loans outstanding:			
1210 Outstanding, start of year	2	2	2
1290 Outstanding, end of year	2	2	2

Balance Sheet (in millions of dollars)

Identification code 014–4416–0–3–452		2020 actual	2021 actual
	ASSETS:		
	Federal assets:		
	Investments in U.S. securities:		
1106	Receivables, net	1	1
	Net value of assets related to post-1991 direct loans receivable:		
1401	Direct loans receivable, gross	2	2
1405	Allowance for subsidy cost (-)	2	2
1499	Net present value of assets related to direct loans	4	4
1999	Total assets	5	5
	LIABILITIES:		
	Federal liabilities:		
2103	Debt	5	5
2104	Resources payable to Treasury		
2999	Total liabilities	5	5
	NET POSITION:		
3300	Cumulative results of operations		
4999	Total liabilities and net position	5	5

Revolving Fund for Loans Liquidating Account

Status of Direct Loans (in millions of dollars)

Identification code 014–4409–0–3–452	2021 actual	2022 est.	2023 est.
Cumulative balance of direct loans outstanding:			
1210 Outstanding, start of year	1	1	1
1290 Outstanding, end of year	1	1	1

Balance Sheet (in millions of dollars)

Identification code 014–4409–0–3–452		2020 actual	2021 actual
	ASSETS:		
1601	Direct loans, gross	1	1
1602	Interest receivable		
1603	Allowance for estimated uncollectible loans and interest (-)		
1699	Value of assets related to direct loans	1	1
1999	Total assets	1	1
	LIABILITIES:		
2104	Federal liabilities: Resources payable to Treasury	1	1
	NET POSITION:		
3300	Cumulative results of operations		
4999	Total liabilities and net position	1	1

Indian Guaranteed Loan Program Account

For the cost of guaranteed loans and insured loans, $13,884,000, to remain available until September 30, 2024, of which $2,680,000 is for administrative expenses, as authorized by the Indian Financing Act of 1974: Provided, That such costs, including the cost of modifying such loans, shall be as defined in section 502

INDIAN GUARANTEED LOAN PROGRAM ACCOUNT—Continued

of the Congressional Budget Act of 1974: Provided further, That these funds are available to subsidize total loan principal, any part of which is to be guaranteed or insured, not to exceed $103,456,940.

Note.—A full-year 2022 appropriation for this account was not enacted at the time the Budget was prepared; therefore, the Budget assumes this account is operating under the Continuing Appropriations Act, 2022 (Division A of Public Law 117–43, as amended). The amounts included for 2022 reflect the annualized level provided by the continuing resolution.

Program and Financing (in millions of dollars)

Identification code 014–2628–0–1–452		2021 actual	2022 est.	2023 est.
	Obligations by program activity:			
	Credit program obligations:			
0702	Loan guarantee subsidy	10	10	10
0705	Reestimates of direct loan subsidy	1	1	
0707	Reestimates of loan guarantee subsidy	3	2	
0709	Administrative expenses	2	3	2
0900	Total new obligations, unexpired accounts	16	16	12
	Budgetary resources:			
	Budget authority:			
	Appropriations, discretionary:			
1100	Appropriation	12	12	14
	Appropriations, mandatory:			
1200	Appropriation	4	4	
1900	Budget authority (total)	16	16	14
1930	Total budgetary resources available	16	16	14
	Memorandum (non-add) entries:			
1941	Unexpired unobligated balance, end of year			2
	Change in obligated balance:			
	Unpaid obligations:			
3000	Unpaid obligations, brought forward, Oct 1	11	10	16
3010	New obligations, unexpired accounts	16	16	12
3020	Outlays (gross)	–15	–10	–5
3041	Recoveries of prior year unpaid obligations, expired	–2		
3050	Unpaid obligations, end of year	10	16	23
	Memorandum (non-add) entries:			
3100	Obligated balance, start of year	11	10	16
3200	Obligated balance, end of year	10	16	23
	Budget authority and outlays, net:			
	Discretionary:			
4000	Budget authority, gross	12	12	14
	Outlays, gross:			
4010	Outlays from new discretionary authority	6	2	3
4011	Outlays from discretionary balances	5	4	2
4020	Outlays, gross (total)	11	6	5
	Mandatory:			
4090	Budget authority, gross	4	4	
	Outlays, gross:			
4100	Outlays from new mandatory authority	4	4	
4180	Budget authority, net (total)	16	16	14
4190	Outlays, net (total)	15	10	5

Summary of Loan Levels, Subsidy Budget Authority and Outlays by Program (in millions of dollars)

Identification code 014–2628–0–1–452		2021 actual	2022 est.	2023 est.
	Direct loan reestimates:			
135001	Indian Direct Loans	1	1	
	Guaranteed loan levels supportable by subsidy budget authority:			
215001	Indian Guaranteed Loans	78	101	101
215002	Indian Insured Loans	5	2	2
215999	Total loan guarantee levels	83	103	103
	Guaranteed loan subsidy (in percent):			
232001	Indian Guaranteed Loans	12.30	9.87	7.48
232002	Indian Insured Loans	12.75	9.51	6.27
232999	Weighted average subsidy rate	12.33	9.86	7.46
	Guaranteed loan subsidy budget authority:			
233001	Indian Guaranteed Loans	10	10	9
233002	Indian Insured Loans	1		1
233999	Total subsidy budget authority	11	10	10
	Guaranteed loan subsidy outlays:			
234001	Indian Guaranteed Loans	9	1	3
234999	Total subsidy outlays	9	1	3
	Guaranteed loan reestimates:			
235001	Indian Guaranteed Loans	–22	–23	
235999	Total guaranteed loan reestimates	–22	–23	
	Administrative expense data:			
3510	Budget authority	1	1	1
3590	Outlays from new authority		1	1

As required by the Federal Credit Reform Act of 1990, this account supports the subsidy costs associated with guaranteed and insured loans committed in 1992 and beyond (including modifications of loan guarantees that resulted from obligations or commitments in any year), as well as administrative expenses of this program including improvements to information technology systems.

Object Classification (in millions of dollars)

Identification code 014–2628–0–1–452		2021 actual	2022 est.	2023 est.
	Direct obligations:			
25.3	Other goods and services from Federal sources	2	3	2
41.0	Grants, subsidies, and contributions	14	13	10
99.9	Total new obligations, unexpired accounts	16	16	12

INDIAN GUARANTEED LOAN FINANCING ACCOUNT

Program and Financing (in millions of dollars)

Identification code 014–4415–0–3–452		2021 actual	2022 est.	2023 est.
	Obligations by program activity:			
0003	Interest supplement payments		2	2
	Credit program obligations:			
0711	Default claim payments on principal		2	2
0712	Default claim payments on interest		1	1
0742	Downward reestimates paid to receipt accounts	18	21	
0743	Interest on downward reestimates	7	4	
0791	Direct program activities, subtotal	25	28	3
0900	Total new obligations, unexpired accounts	25	30	5
	Budgetary resources:			
	Unobligated balance:			
1000	Unobligated balance brought forward, Oct 1	96	88	58
	Financing authority:			
	Spending authority from offsetting collections, mandatory:			
1800	Collected	18	3	3
1801	Change in uncollected payments, Federal sources	–1		
1825	Spending authority from offsetting collections applied to repay debt		–3	–3
1850	Spending auth from offsetting collections, mand (total)	17		
1900	Budget authority (total)	17		
1930	Total budgetary resources available	113	88	58
	Memorandum (non-add) entries:			
1941	Unexpired unobligated balance, end of year	88	58	53
	Change in obligated balance:			
	Unpaid obligations:			
3000	Unpaid obligations, brought forward, Oct 1			25
3010	New obligations, unexpired accounts	25	30	5
3020	Outlays (gross)	–25	–5	–5
3050	Unpaid obligations, end of year		25	25
	Uncollected payments:			
3060	Uncollected pymts, Fed sources, brought forward, Oct 1	–11	–10	–10
3070	Change in uncollected pymts, Fed sources, unexpired	1		
3090	Uncollected pymts, Fed sources, end of year	–10	–10	–10
	Memorandum (non-add) entries:			
3100	Obligated balance, start of year	–11	–10	15
3200	Obligated balance, end of year	–10	15	15
	Financing authority and disbursements, net:			
	Mandatory:			
4090	Budget authority, gross	17		
	Financing disbursements:			
4110	Outlays, gross (total)	25	5	5

DEPARTMENT OF THE INTERIOR

Indian Affairs—Continued
Bureau of Indian Affairs—Continued

		2021 actual	2022 est.	2023 est.
	Offsets against gross financing authority and disbursements:			
	Offsetting collections (collected) from:			
4120	Payments from program account	–12	–3	–3
4122	Interest on uninvested funds	–2		
4123	Non-Federal sources	–4		
4130	Offsets against gross budget authority and outlays (total)	–18	–3	–3
	Additional offsets against financing authority only (total):			
4140	Change in uncollected pymts, Fed sources, unexpired	1		
4160	Budget authority, net (mandatory)		–3	–3
4170	Outlays, net (mandatory)	7	2	2
4180	Budget authority, net (total)		–3	–3
4190	Outlays, net (total)	7	2	2

Status of Guaranteed Loans (in millions of dollars)

Identification code 014–4415–0–3–452		2021 actual	2022 est.	2023 est.
	Position with respect to appropriations act limitation on commitments:			
2111	Guaranteed loan commitments from current-year authority	83	103	103
2150	Total guaranteed loan commitments	83	103	103
2199	Guaranteed amount of guaranteed loan commitments	75		
	Cumulative balance of guaranteed loans outstanding:			
2210	Outstanding, start of year	478	515	524
2231	Disbursements of new guaranteed loans	37	93	93
2251	Repayments and prepayments		–82	–82
2261	Adjustments: Terminations for default that result in loans receivable		–2	–2
2290	Outstanding, end of year	515	524	533
	Memorandum:			
2299	Guaranteed amount of guaranteed loans outstanding, end of year	515	478	478
	Addendum:			
	Cumulative balance of defaulted guaranteed loans that result in loans receivable:			
2310	Outstanding, start of year	37	37	38
2331	Disbursements for guaranteed loan claims		2	2
2351	Repayments of loans receivable		–1	–1
2361	Write-offs of loans receivable			
2390	Outstanding, end of year	37	38	39

Balance Sheet (in millions of dollars)

Identification code 014–4415–0–3–452		2020 actual	2021 actual
	ASSETS:		
	Federal assets:		
1101	Fund balances with Treasury	78	78
	Investments in U.S. securities:		
1106	Receivables, net	2	2
	Net value of assets related to post-1991 acquired defaulted guaranteed loans receivable:		
1501	Defaulted guaranteed loans receivable, gross	1	37
1502	Interest receivable		
1505	Allowance for subsidy cost (-)	–1	–37
1599	Net present value of assets related to defaulted guaranteed loans		
1901	Other Federal assets: Upward Subsidy Reestimate Receivable		
1999	Total assets	80	80
	LIABILITIES:		
	Federal liabilities:		
2103	Debt		
2105	Other-Downward Reestimate	25	25
2204	Non-Federal liabilities: Liabilities for loan guarantees	55	55
2999	Total liabilities	80	80
	NET POSITION:		
3300	Cumulative results of operations		
4999	Total liabilities and net position	80	80

INDIAN LOAN GUARANTY AND INSURANCE FUND LIQUIDATING ACCOUNT

Status of Guaranteed Loans (in millions of dollars)

Identification code 014–4410–0–3–452		2021 actual	2022 est.	2023 est.
	Addendum:			
	Cumulative balance of defaulted guaranteed loans that result in loans receivable:			
2310	Outstanding, start of year	1	1	1
2351	Repayments of loans receivable			
2390	Outstanding, end of year	1	1	1

Balance Sheet (in millions of dollars)

Identification code 014–4410–0–3–452		2020 actual	2021 actual
	ASSETS:		
1701	Defaulted guaranteed loans, gross	1	1
1702	Interest receivable		
1703	Allowance for estimated uncollectible loans and interest (-)		
1799	Value of assets related to loan guarantees	1	1
1999	Total assets	1	1

SELIS-QLISPE KSANKA SETTLEMENT TRUST FUND

Program and Financing (in millions of dollars)

Identification code 014–5740–0–2–452		2021 actual	2022 est.	2023 est.
	Obligations by program activity:			
0001	CSKT Water Settlement	90	90	90
0900	Total new obligations, unexpired accounts (object class 94.0)	90	90	90
	Budgetary resources:			
	Budget authority:			
	Appropriations, mandatory:			
1200	Appropriation	90	90	90
1930	Total budgetary resources available	90	90	90
	Change in obligated balance:			
	Unpaid obligations:			
3010	New obligations, unexpired accounts	90	90	90
3020	Outlays (gross)	–90	–90	–90
	Budget authority and outlays, net:			
	Mandatory:			
4090	Budget authority, gross	90	90	90
	Outlays, gross:			
4100	Outlays from new mandatory authority	90	90	90
4180	Budget authority, net (total)	90	90	90
4190	Outlays, net (total)	90	90	90

The Selis-Qlispe Ksanka Settlement Trust Fund was established in the Montana Water Rights Protection Act (P.L. 116–260). The Act settles claims to water rights in Montana for the Confederated Salish and Kootenai Tribes of the Flathead Indian Reservation. The Act authorizes annual payments of $90,000,000 to the Trust Fund out of any Funds in the Treasury not otherwise appropriated starting in fiscal year 2021 through fiscal year 2030 for a total of $900,000,000. The Act also authorizes discretionary appropriations of $1,000,000,000 for deposit in the Trust Fund. The Trust Fund includes two accounts: the Salish and Kootenai Compact Account and the Salish and Kootenai Settlement implementation Account. Funds deposited into the account are adjusted to reflect fluctuations in costs occurring after the date of enactment of the act up to the day of deposit to the Fund. The Trust Fund is interest bearing.

Indian Affairs—Continued
Bureau of Indian Education

Trust Funds

GIFTS AND DONATIONS, BUREAU OF INDIAN AFFAIRS

Special and Trust Fund Receipts (in millions of dollars)

Identification code 014–8361–0–7–501	2021 actual	2022 est.	2023 est.
0100 Balance, start of year			
Receipts:			
Current law:			
1130 Gifts and Donations, Bureau of Indian Affairs	1	1	1
2000 Total: Balances and receipts	1	1	1
Appropriations:			
Current law:			
2101 Gifts and Donations, Bureau of Indian Affairs	–1	–1	–1
5099 Balance, end of year			

Program and Financing (in millions of dollars)

Identification code 014–8361–0–7–501	2021 actual	2022 est.	2023 est.
Obligations by program activity:			
0001 Gifts and Donations, Bureau of Indian Affairs (Direct)	1	1	1
0900 Total new obligations, unexpired accounts (object class 11.3)	1	1	1
Budgetary resources:			
Unobligated balance:			
1000 Unobligated balance brought forward, Oct 1	3	3	3
Budget authority:			
Appropriations, mandatory:			
1201 Appropriation (special or trust fund)	1	1	1
1930 Total budgetary resources available	4	4	4
Memorandum (non-add) entries:			
1941 Unexpired unobligated balance, end of year	3	3	3
Change in obligated balance:			
Unpaid obligations:			
3000 Unpaid obligations, brought forward, Oct 1		1	
3010 New obligations, unexpired accounts	1	1	1
3020 Outlays (gross)		–2	–1
3050 Unpaid obligations, end of year	1		
Memorandum (non-add) entries:			
3100 Obligated balance, start of year		1	
3200 Obligated balance, end of year	1		
Budget authority and outlays, net:			
Mandatory:			
4090 Budget authority, gross	1	1	1
Outlays, gross:			
4100 Outlays from new mandatory authority		1	1
4101 Outlays from mandatory balances		1	
4110 Outlays, gross (total)		2	1
4180 Budget authority, net (total)	1	1	1
4190 Outlays, net (total)		2	1

Donations and contributed funds.—The Secretary of the Interior may accept donations of funds or other property, and may use the donated property in accordance with the terms of the donation in furtherance of any program authorized by other provision of law for the benefit of Indians (25 U.S.C. 5341).

Employment Summary

Identification code 014–8361–0–7–501	2021 actual	2022 est.	2023 est.
1001 Direct civilian full-time equivalent employment	7	7	7

BUREAU OF INDIAN EDUCATION
Federal Funds

OPERATION OF INDIAN EDUCATION PROGRAMS

For expenses necessary for the operation of Indian education programs, as authorized by law, including the Snyder Act of November 2, 1921 (25 U.S.C. 13), the Indian Self-Determination and Education Assistance Act of 1975 (25 U.S.C. 5301 et seq.), the Education Amendments of 1978 (25 U.S.C. 2001–2019), and the Tribally Controlled Schools Act of 1988 (25 U.S.C. 2501 et seq.), $1,155,634,000, to remain available until September 30, 2024, except as otherwise provided herein: *Provided*, That federally recognized Indian tribes and tribal organizations of federally recognized Indian tribes may use their tribal priority allocations for unmet welfare assistance costs: *Provided further*, That not to exceed $848,425,000 for school operations costs of Bureau-funded schools and other education programs shall become available on July 1, 2023, and shall remain available until September 30, 2024: *Provided further*, That notwithstanding any other provision of law, including but not limited to the Indian Self-Determination Act of 1975 (25 U.S.C. 5301 et seq.) and section 1128 of the Education Amendments of 1978 (25 U.S.C. 2008), not to exceed $97,453,000 within and only from such amounts made available for school operations shall be available for administrative cost grants associated with grants approved prior to July 1, 2023: *Provided further*, That in order to enhance the safety of Bureau field employees, the Bureau may use funds to purchase uniforms or other identifying articles of clothing for personnel.

Note.—A full-year 2022 appropriation for this account was not enacted at the time the Budget was prepared; therefore, the Budget assumes this account is operating under the Continuing Appropriations Act, 2022 (Division A of Public Law 117–43, as amended). The amounts included for 2022 reflect the annualized level provided by the continuing resolution.

Program and Financing (in millions of dollars)

Identification code 014–2106–0–1–501	2021 actual	2022 est.	2023 est.
Obligations by program activity:			
0001 Education	923	800	800
0002 CARES ACT SUPPLEMENTAL (P.L. 116–136)	358		
0003 American Rescue Plan (P.L. 117–2)	564	450	450
0100 Direct program activities, subtotal	1,845	1,250	1,250
0799 Total direct obligations	1,845	1,250	1,250
0807 OIEP Reimbursable	190	12	12
0808 CARES ACT SUPPLEMENTAL (P.L. 116–136)	6		
0809 Reimbursable program activities, subtotal	196	12	12
0899 Total reimbursable obligations	196	12	12
0900 Total new obligations, unexpired accounts	2,041	1,262	1,262
Budgetary resources:			
Unobligated balance:			
1000 Unobligated balance brought forward, Oct 1	491	951	869
1001 Discretionary unobligated balance brought fwd, Oct 1	491		
1010 Unobligated balance transfer to other accts [014–2100]	–3		
1021 Recoveries of prior year unpaid obligations	6		
1070 Unobligated balance (total)	494	951	869
Budget authority:			
Appropriations, discretionary:			
1100 Appropriation	973	973	1,156
1120 Appropriations transferred to other acct [014–2100]	–50		
1121 Appropriations transferred from other acct [091–0251]	409		
1160 Appropriation, discretionary (total)	1,332	973	1,156
Appropriations, mandatory:			
1200 Appropriation American Rescue Plan (P.L. 117–2)	850		
Spending authority from offsetting collections, discretionary:			
1700 Collected	196	108	108
1701 Change in uncollected payments, Federal sources	120	99	99
1750 Spending auth from offsetting collections, disc (total)	316	207	207
1900 Budget authority (total)	2,498	1,180	1,363
1930 Total budgetary resources available	2,992	2,131	2,232
Memorandum (non-add) entries:			
1941 Unexpired unobligated balance, end of year	951	869	970
Change in obligated balance:			
Unpaid obligations:			
3000 Unpaid obligations, brought forward, Oct 1	143	238	344
3010 New obligations, unexpired accounts	2,041	1,262	1,262
3020 Outlays (gross)	–1,940	–1,156	–1,442
3040 Recoveries of prior year unpaid obligations, unexpired	–6		
3050 Unpaid obligations, end of year	238	344	164
Uncollected payments:			
3060 Uncollected pymts, Fed sources, brought forward, Oct 1	–99	–219	–318
3070 Change in uncollected pymts, Fed sources, unexpired	–120	–99	–99
3090 Uncollected pymts, Fed sources, end of year	–219	–318	–417
Memorandum (non-add) entries:			
3100 Obligated balance, start of year	44	19	26
3200 Obligated balance, end of year	19	26	–253

DEPARTMENT OF THE INTERIOR

Indian Affairs—Continued
Bureau of Indian Education—Continued

683

		2021 actual	2022 est.	2023 est.
	Budget authority and outlays, net:			
	Discretionary:			
4000	Budget authority, gross	1,648	1,180	1,363
	Outlays, gross:			
4010	Outlays from new discretionary authority	808	596	669
4011	Outlays from discretionary balances	597	394	645
4020	Outlays, gross (total)	1,405	990	1,314
	Offsets against gross budget authority and outlays:			
	Offsetting collections (collected) from:			
4030	Federal sources	–182	–104	–104
4033	Non-Federal sources	–14	–4	–4
4040	Offsets against gross budget authority and outlays (total)	–196	–108	–108
	Additional offsets against gross budget authority only:			
4050	Change in uncollected pymts, Fed sources, unexpired	–120	–99	–99
4070	Budget authority, net (discretionary)	1,332	973	1,156
4080	Outlays, net (discretionary)	1,209	882	1,206
	Mandatory:			
4090	Budget authority, gross	850		
	Outlays, gross:			
4100	Outlays from new mandatory authority	535		
4101	Outlays from mandatory balances		166	128
4110	Outlays, gross (total)	535	166	128
4180	Budget authority, net (total)	2,182	973	1,156
4190	Outlays, net (total)	1,744	1,048	1,334

The Operation of Indian Education Programs appropriation consists of a wide range of education-related services and benefits provided to federally recognized Indian Tribes, individual American Indians and Alaska Natives, and Bureau of Indian Education-funded schools. This includes 169 elementary and secondary schools either operated by the Bureau of Indian Education or Tribes, 14 dormitories, two post-secondary schools, and eligible tribal colleges and universities.

This account covers expenses associated with the following activities: elementary, secondary, and post-secondary school operations; other education programs for Native children; scholarships; adult education programs; education program management; and facilities operation and maintenance.

Object Classification (in millions of dollars)

Identification code 014–2106–0–1–501		2021 actual	2022 est.	2023 est.
	Direct obligations:			
	Personnel compensation:			
11.1	Full-time permanent	37	37	37
11.3	Other than full-time permanent	124	124	124
11.5	Other personnel compensation	7	7	7
11.9	Total personnel compensation	168	168	168
12.1	Civilian personnel benefits	57	57	57
21.0	Travel and transportation of persons	1	1	1
23.3	Communications, utilities, and miscellaneous charges	27	27	27
25.1	Advisory and assistance services	8	8	8
25.2	Other services from non-Federal sources	123	123	123
25.3	Other goods and services from Federal sources	7	7	7
25.4	Operation and maintenance of facilities	7	7	7
25.7	Operation and maintenance of equipment	6	6	6
26.0	Supplies and materials	24	24	24
31.0	Equipment	29	29	29
32.0	Land and structures	2	2	2
41.0	Grants, subsidies, and contributions	1,386	791	791
99.0	Direct obligations	1,845	1,250	1,250
99.0	Reimbursable obligations	196	12	12
99.9	Total new obligations, unexpired accounts	2,041	1,262	1,262

Employment Summary

Identification code 014–2106–0–1–501	2021 actual	2022 est.	2023 est.
1001 Direct civilian full-time equivalent employment	2,346	2,346	2,682
2001 Reimbursable civilian full-time equivalent employment	378	526	531

EDUCATION CONSTRUCTION

For construction, repair, improvement, and maintenance of buildings, utilities, and other facilities necessary for the operation of Indian education programs, including architectural and engineering services by contract; acquisition of lands, and interests in lands; $420,102,000 to remain available until expended: Provided, That in order to ensure timely completion of construction projects, the Secretary of the Interior may assume control of a project and all funds related to the project, if, not later than 18 months after the date of the enactment of this Act, any Public Law 100–297 (25 U.S.C. 2501, et seq.) grantee receiving funds appropriated in this Act or in any prior Act, has not completed the planning and design phase of the project and commenced construction.

Note.—A full-year 2022 appropriation for this account was not enacted at the time the Budget was prepared; therefore, the Budget assumes this account is operating under the Continuing Appropriations Act, 2022 (Division A of Public Law 117–43, as amended). The amounts included for 2022 reflect the annualized level provided by the continuing resolution.

Program and Financing (in millions of dollars)

Identification code 014–2105–0–1–452		2021 actual	2022 est.	2023 est.
	Obligations by program activity:			
0001	Education Obligations	60	190	290
	Budgetary resources:			
	Unobligated balance:			
1000	Unobligated balance brought forward, Oct 1	223	427	501
	Budget authority:			
	Appropriations, discretionary:			
1100	Appropriation	264	264	420
1930	Total budgetary resources available	487	691	921
	Memorandum (non-add) entries:			
1941	Unexpired unobligated balance, end of year	427	501	631
	Change in obligated balance:			
	Unpaid obligations:			
3000	Unpaid obligations, brought forward, Oct 1	24	51	31
3010	New obligations, unexpired accounts	60	190	290
3020	Outlays (gross)	–33	–210	–314
3050	Unpaid obligations, end of year	51	31	7
	Memorandum (non-add) entries:			
3100	Obligated balance, start of year	24	51	31
3200	Obligated balance, end of year	51	31	7
	Budget authority and outlays, net:			
	Discretionary:			
4000	Budget authority, gross	264	264	420
	Outlays, gross:			
4010	Outlays from new discretionary authority	13	132	210
4011	Outlays from discretionary balances	20	78	104
4020	Outlays, gross (total)	33	210	314
4180	Budget authority, net (total)	264	264	420
4190	Outlays, net (total)	33	210	314

The Education Construction program supports the Bureau of Indian Education (BIE) by renovating or replacing schools and dormitories to provide an environment conducive to quality educational achievement and improved opportunities for Indian students. The program provides safe, functional, energy-efficient, and accessible facilities to students attending BIE-funded schools and dormitories.

Object Classification (in millions of dollars)

Identification code 014–2105–0–1–452		2021 actual	2022 est.	2023 est.
11.1	Direct obligations: Personnel compensation: Full-time permanent	1	1	1
11.9	Total personnel compensation	1	1	1
12.1	Civilian personnel benefits	1	1	1
25.1	Advisory and assistance services	1	1	1
25.2	Other services from non-Federal sources	30	100	175
25.4	Operation and maintenance of facilities	1	1	1
25.7	Operation and maintenance of equipment	1	1	1
32.0	Land and structures	1	1	1
41.0	Grants, subsidies, and contributions	24	84	109
99.9	Total new obligations, unexpired accounts	60	190	290

EDUCATION CONSTRUCTION—Continued

Employment Summary

Identification code 014–2105–0–1–452	2021 actual	2022 est.	2023 est.
1001 Direct civilian full-time equivalent employment	11	11	14

ADMINISTRATIVE PROVISIONS

The Bureau of Indian Affairs and the Bureau of Indian Education may carry out the operation of Indian programs by direct expenditure, contracts, cooperative agreements, compacts, and grants, either directly or in cooperation with States and other organizations.

Notwithstanding Public Law 87–279 (25 U.S.C. 15), the Bureau of Indian Affairs may contract for services in support of the management, operation, and maintenance of the Power Division of the San Carlos Irrigation Project.

Notwithstanding any other provision of law, no funds available to the Bureau of Indian Affairs or the Bureau of Indian Education for central office oversight and Executive Direction and Administrative Services (except Executive Direction and Administrative Services funding for Tribal Priority Allocations, regional offices, and facilities operations and maintenance) shall be available for contracts, grants, compacts, or cooperative agreements with the Bureau of Indian Affairs or the Bureau of Indian Education under the provisions of the Indian Self-Determination Act or the Tribal Self-Governance Act of 1994 (Public Law 103–413).

In the event any tribe returns appropriations made available by this Act to the Bureau of Indian Affairs or the Bureau of Indian Education, this action shall not diminish the Federal Government's trust responsibility to that tribe, or the government-to-government relationship between the United States and that tribe, or that tribe's ability to access future appropriations.

Notwithstanding any other provision of law, no funds available to the Bureau of Indian Education, other than the amounts provided herein for assistance to public schools under 25 U.S.C. 452 et seq., shall be available to support the operation of any elementary or secondary school in the State of Alaska.

No funds available to the Bureau of Indian Education shall be used to support expanded grades for any school or dormitory beyond the grade structure in place or approved by the Secretary of the Interior at each school in the Bureau of Indian Education school system as of October 1, 1995, except that the Secretary of the Interior may waive this prohibition to support expansion of up to one additional grade when the Secretary determines such waiver is needed to support accomplishment of the mission of the Bureau of Indian Education, or more than one grade to expand the elementary grade structure for Bureau-funded schools with a K-2 grade structure on October 1, 1996. Appropriations made available in this or any prior Act for schools funded by the Bureau shall be available, in accordance with the Bureau's funding formula, only to the schools in the Bureau school system as of September 1, 1996, and to any school or school program that was reinstated in fiscal year 2012. Funds made available under this Act may not be used to establish a charter school at a Bureau-funded school (as that term is defined in section 1141 of the Education Amendments of 1978 (25 U.S.C. 2021)), except that a charter school that is in existence on the date of the enactment of this Act and that has operated at a Bureau-funded school before September 1, 1999, may continue to operate during that period, but only if the charter school pays to the Bureau a pro rata share of funds to reimburse the Bureau for the use of the real and personal property (including buses and vans), the funds of the charter school are kept separate and apart from Bureau funds, and the Bureau does not assume any obligation for charter school programs of the State in which the school is located if the charter school loses such funding. Employees of Bureau-funded schools sharing a campus with a charter school and performing functions related to the charter school's operation and employees of a charter school shall not be treated as Federal employees for purposes of chapter 171 of title 28, United States Code.

Notwithstanding any other provision of law, including section 113 of title I of appendix C of Public Law 106–113, if in fiscal year 2003 or 2004 a grantee received indirect and administrative costs pursuant to a distribution formula based on section 5(f) of Public Law 101–301, the Secretary shall continue to distribute indirect and administrative cost funds to such grantee using the section 5(f) distribution formula.

Funds available under this Act may not be used to establish satellite locations of schools in the Bureau school system as of September 1, 1996, except that the Secretary may waive this prohibition in order for an Indian tribe to provide language and cultural immersion educational programs for non-public schools located within the jurisdictional area of the tribal government which exclusively serve tribal members, do not include grades beyond those currently served at the existing Bureau-funded school, provide an educational environment with educator presence and academic facilities comparable to the Bureau-funded school, comply with all applicable Tribal, Federal, or State health and safety standards, and the Americans with Disabilities Act, and demonstrate the benefits of establishing operations at a satellite location in lieu of incurring extraordinary costs, such as for transportation or other impacts to students such as those caused by busing students extended distances: Provided, That no funds available under this Act may be used to fund operations, maintenance, rehabilitation, construction, or other facilities-related costs for such assets that are not owned by the Bureau: Provided further, That the term "satellite school" means a school location physically separated from the existing Bureau school by more than 50 miles but that forms part of the existing school in all other respects.

Funds made available for Tribal Priority Allocations within Operation of Indian Programs and Operation of Indian Education Programs may be used to execute requested adjustments in tribal priority allocations initiated by an Indian Tribe.

BUREAU OF TRUST FUNDS ADMINISTRATION

Federal Funds

FEDERAL TRUST PROGRAMS

(INCLUDING TRANSFER OF FUNDS)

For the operation of trust programs for Indians by direct expenditure, contracts, cooperative agreements, compacts, and grants, $112,675,000, to remain available until expended, of which not to exceed $17,867,000 from this or any other Act, may be available for settlement support: Provided, That funds for trust management improvements and litigation support may, as needed, be transferred to or merged with the Bureau of Indian Affairs, "Operation of Indian Programs" and Bureau of Indian Education, "Operation of Indian Education Programs" accounts; the Office of the Solicitor, "Salaries and Expenses" account; and the Office of the Secretary, "Departmental Operations" account: Provided further, That funds made available through contracts or grants obligated during fiscal year 2023, as authorized by the Indian Self-Determination Act of 1975 (25 U.S.C. 5301 et seq.), shall remain available until expended by the contractor or grantee: Provided further, That notwithstanding any other provision of law, the Secretary shall not be required to provide a quarterly statement of performance for any Indian trust account that has not had activity for at least 15 months and has a balance of $15 or less: Provided further, That the Secretary shall issue an annual account statement and maintain a record of any such accounts and shall permit the balance in each such account to be withdrawn upon the express written request of the account holder: Provided further, That not to exceed $100,000 is available for the Secretary to make payments to correct administrative errors of either disbursements from or deposits to Individual Indian Money or Tribal accounts after September 30, 2002: Provided further, That erroneous payments that are recovered shall be credited to and remain available in this account for this purpose: Provided further, That the Secretary shall not be required to reconcile Special Deposit Accounts with a balance of less than $500 unless the Bureau of Trust Funds Administration receives proof of ownership from a Special Deposit Accounts claimant: Provided further, That notwithstanding section 102 of the American Indian Trust Fund Management Reform Act of 1994 (Public Law 103–412) or any other provision of law, the Secretary may aggregate the trust accounts of individuals whose whereabouts are unknown for a continuous period of at least 5 years and shall not be required to generate periodic statements of performance for the individual accounts: Provided further, That with respect to the eighth proviso, the Secretary shall continue to maintain sufficient records to determine the balance of the individual accounts, including any accrued interest and income, and such funds shall remain available to the individual account holders.

Note.—A full-year 2022 appropriation for this account was not enacted at the time the Budget was prepared; therefore, the Budget assumes this account is operating under the Continuing Appropriations Act, 2022 (Division A of Public Law 117–43, as amended). The amounts included for 2022 reflect the annualized level provided by the continuing resolution.

Program and Financing (in millions of dollars)

Identification code 014–0120–0–1–808	2021 actual	2022 est.	2023 est.
Obligations by program activity:			
0001 Program operations, support, and improvements	113	106	111
0002 Executive direction	2	2	2
0799 Total direct obligations	115	108	113
0900 Total new obligations, unexpired accounts	115	108	113
Budgetary resources:			
Unobligated balance:			
1000 Unobligated balance brought forward, Oct 1	23	27	27

DEPARTMENT OF THE INTERIOR

Indian Affairs—Continued
Bureau of Trust Funds Administration—Continued 685

		2021 actual	2022 est.	2023 est.
1021	Recoveries of prior year unpaid obligations	9		
1070	Unobligated balance (total)	32	27	27
	Budget authority:			
	Appropriations, discretionary:			
1100	Appropriation	108	108	113
	Spending authority from offsetting collections, discretionary:			
1700	Collected	2		
1900	Budget authority (total)	110	108	113
1930	Total budgetary resources available	142	135	140
	Memorandum (non-add) entries:			
1941	Unexpired unobligated balance, end of year	27	27	27
	Change in obligated balance:			
	Unpaid obligations:			
3000	Unpaid obligations, brought forward, Oct 1	38	41	20
3010	New obligations, unexpired accounts	115	108	113
3020	Outlays (gross)	–103	–129	–111
3040	Recoveries of prior year unpaid obligations, unexpired	–9		
3050	Unpaid obligations, end of year	41	20	22
	Memorandum (non-add) entries:			
3100	Obligated balance, start of year	38	41	20
3200	Obligated balance, end of year	41	20	22
	Budget authority and outlays, net:			
	Discretionary:			
4000	Budget authority, gross	110	108	113
	Outlays, gross:			
4010	Outlays from new discretionary authority	72	97	102
4011	Outlays from discretionary balances	31	32	9
4020	Outlays, gross (total)	103	129	111
	Offsets against gross budget authority and outlays:			
	Offsetting collections (collected) from:			
4030	Federal sources	–2		
4180	Budget authority, net (total)	108	108	113
4190	Outlays, net (total)	101	129	111

To provide financial Trust services to Indian Tribes, individual American Indians, and Alaska Natives, the 2023 Budget requests funds for the Bureau of Trust Funds Administration (BTFA) within the Office of the Assistant Secretary—Indian Affairs.

Executive Direction.—This activity supports BTFA staff and the Bureau's responsibilities and authorities for Indian trust fund management.

Trust Operations and Program Operations.—This activity supports the management and investment of approximately $6.2 billion held in trust for Indian Tribes and individual Indians. Responsibilities include accurate and timely posting of collections, investment and disbursement of funds, and providing timely financial information to Indian Tribes and individual Indian money account holders.

Object Classification (in millions of dollars)

Identification code 014–0120–0–1–808	2021 actual	2022 est.	2023 est.
Direct obligations:			
Personnel compensation:			
11.1 Full-time permanent	39	39	39
11.3 Other than full-time permanent	1	1	2
11.5 Other personnel compensation	2	1	2
11.9 Total personnel compensation	42	41	43
12.1 Civilian personnel benefits	15	14	15
23.1 Rental payments to GSA	3	3	3
23.3 Communications, utilities, and miscellaneous charges	2	1	1
25.1 Advisory and assistance services	5	5	5
25.2 Other services from non-Federal sources	27	27	28
25.3 Other goods and services from Federal sources	16	15	16
25.7 Operation and maintenance of equipment	1	1	1
99.0 Direct obligations	111	107	112
99.0 Reimbursable obligations	1	1	1
99.5 Adjustment for rounding	3		
99.9 Total new obligations, unexpired accounts	115	108	113

Employment Summary

Identification code 014–0120–0–1–808	2021 actual	2022 est.	2023 est.
1001 Direct civilian full-time equivalent employment	391	417	422
2001 Reimbursable civilian full-time equivalent employment	3	3	3

TRIBAL SPECIAL FUND

Special and Trust Fund Receipts (in millions of dollars)

Identification code 014–5265–0–2–452	2021 actual	2022 est.	2023 est.
0100	Balance, start of year			
	Receipts:			
	Current law:			
1130	Interest on Investments in GSEs, Tribal Special Fund	10	10	11
1130	Return of Principal from Private Sector Investments, Tribal Special Fund	77	79	80
1199	Total current law receipts	87	89	91
1999	Total receipts	87	89	91
2000	Total: Balances and receipts	87	89	91
	Appropriations:			
	Current law:			
2101	Tribal Special Fund	–87	–89	–91
5099	Balance, end of year			

Program and Financing (in millions of dollars)

Identification code 014–5265–0–2–452	2021 actual	2022 est.	2023 est.
Obligations by program activity:			
0001 Tribal Special Fund (Direct)	102	89	91
0900 Total new obligations, unexpired accounts (object class 41.0)	102	89	91
Budgetary resources:			
Unobligated balance:			
1000 Unobligated balance brought forward, Oct 1	94	79	79
Budget authority:			
Appropriations, mandatory:			
1201 Appropriation (special or trust fund)	87	89	91
1930 Total budgetary resources available	181	168	170
Memorandum (non-add) entries:			
1941 Unexpired unobligated balance, end of year	79	79	79
Change in obligated balance:			
Unpaid obligations:			
3010 New obligations, unexpired accounts	102	89	91
3020 Outlays (gross)	–102	–89	–91
Budget authority and outlays, net:			
Mandatory:			
4090 Budget authority, gross	87	89	91
Outlays, gross:			
4100 Outlays from new mandatory authority		89	91
4101 Outlays from mandatory balances	102		
4110 Outlays, gross (total)	102	89	91
4180 Budget authority, net (total)	87	89	91
4190 Outlays, net (total)	102	89	91
Memorandum (non-add) entries:			
5000 Total investments, SOY: Federal securities: Par value	94	79	74
5001 Total investments, EOY: Federal securities: Par value	79	74	76
5010 Total investments, SOY: non-Fed securities: Market value	429	437	444
5011 Total investments, EOY: non-Fed securities: Market value	437	444	446

The Tribal Special Fund includes the following accounts: Tribal Economic Recovery Fund which consists of the Three Affiliated Fort Berthold Trust Fund and the Standing Rock Trust Fund, Papago Cooperative Fund, Ute Tribe Trust Fund, Pyramid Lake Indian Reservation Trust Fund, San Luis Rey Water Authority Trust Fund, and Cochiti Wetfields. More detailed information on specific accounts is provided in the budget justification for the Bureau of Trust Funds Administration.

Tribal trust funds are deposited into a consolidated account in the U.S. Department of the Treasury pursuant to: 1) general or specific acts of the Congress and 2) Federal management of tribal real properties, the titles to which are held in trust for the Tribes by the United States. These funds are available to respective tribal groups for various purposes, under various

Indian Affairs—Continued
Federal Funds—Continued

TRIBAL SPECIAL FUND—Continued

acts of the Congress, and may be subject to the provisions of tribal constitutions, bylaws, charters, and resolutions of the various Tribes, bands, or groups.

TRUST LAND CONSOLIDATION FUND

Program and Financing (in millions of dollars)

Identification code 014–5670–0–2–452		2021 actual	2022 est.	2023 est.
	Obligations by program activity:			
0001	Land Purchases	66	48	....
0003	Administration	....	11	2
0900	Total new obligations, unexpired accounts	66	59	2
	Budgetary resources:			
	Unobligated balance:			
1000	Unobligated balance brought forward, Oct 1	57	61	67
1021	Recoveries of prior year unpaid obligations	70	65	....
1070	Unobligated balance (total)	127	126	67
1930	Total budgetary resources available	127	126	67
	Memorandum (non-add) entries:			
1941	Unexpired unobligated balance, end of year	61	67	65
	Change in obligated balance:			
	Unpaid obligations:			
3000	Unpaid obligations, brought forward, Oct 1	109	30	24
3010	New obligations, unexpired accounts	66	59	2
3020	Outlays (gross)	–75	....	–1
3040	Recoveries of prior year unpaid obligations, unexpired	–70	–65	....
3050	Unpaid obligations, end of year	30	24	25
	Memorandum (non-add) entries:			
3100	Obligated balance, start of year	109	30	24
3200	Obligated balance, end of year	30	24	25
	Budget authority and outlays, net:			
	Mandatory:			
	Outlays, gross:			
4101	Outlays from mandatory balances	75	....	1
4180	Budget authority, net (total)	....	....	....
4190	Outlays, net (total)	75	....	1

The Individual Indian Money Account Litigation Settlement (P.L. 111–291) established a trust land consolidation Fund for the buy-back and consolidation of fractionated interests in parcels of land from individual Indian landowners. The Fund also covers administrative costs to undertake the process of acquiring fractionated interests and associated trust reform activities not to exceed 15 percent of the Fund. The acquisition of fractionated interests is authorized under the Indian Land Consolidation Act Amendments of 2000 (P.L. 106–462), and the American Indian Probate Reform Act of 2004 (P.L. 108–374). The Settlement provides additional authority for the acquisition of interests held by persons who cannot be located after engaging in extensive efforts to notify them and locate them for a five-year period. The Settlement was finalized on November 24, 2012 and in accordance with the terms of the legislation, these funds remain available for ten years from the date of the Settlement. The funds are scheduled to expire in November, 2022. In FY 2022 and in early FY 2023, the program will commence an orderly shutdown of the program to fulfill the requirements of the Settlement. This account is managed by the Bureau of Trust Funds Administration.

Object Classification (in millions of dollars)

Identification code 014–5670–0–2–452		2021 actual	2022 est.	2023 est.
	Direct obligations:			
11.1	Personnel compensation: Full-time permanent	1	1	....
12.1	Civilian personnel benefits	1	1	....
25.2	Other services from non-Federal sources	4	4	....
25.3	Other goods and services from Federal sources	60	53	2
99.9	Total new obligations, unexpired accounts	66	59	2

Employment Summary

Identification code 014–5670–0–2–452		2021 actual	2022 est.	2023 est.
1001	Direct civilian full-time equivalent employment	12	10	....

INDIAN EDUCATION SCHOLARSHIP HOLDING FUND

The Individual Indian Money Account Litigation Settlement (P.L. 111–291) established this Fund to provide Indian land owners with an additional incentive to sell their fractionated interests, given that the market value associated with highly fractionated interests would be quite low in many cases. Program contributions reached the maximum of $60 million in 2017 and were transferred from the Trust Land Consolidation Fund to this Fund for higher education scholarships for American Indians and Alaska Natives to be administered as described in the Settlement agreement. This account is managed by the Bureau of Trust Funds Administration.

Trust Funds

TRIBAL TRUST FUND

Special and Trust Fund Receipts (in millions of dollars)

Identification code 014–8030–0–7–452		2021 actual	2022 est.	2023 est.
0100	Balance, start of year	....	....	....
	Receipts:			
	Current law:			
1130	Interest on Investments in GSEs, Tribal Trust Fund	3	3	3
1130	Return of Principal from Private Sector Investments, Tribal Trust Fund	13	13	14
1130	Miscellaneous Sales of Assets, Tribal Trust Fund	135	138	142
1199	Total current law receipts	151	154	159
1999	Total receipts	151	154	159
2000	Total: Balances and receipts	151	154	159
	Appropriations:			
	Current law:			
2101	Tribal Trust Fund	–151	–154	–159
5099	Balance, end of year	....	....	....

Program and Financing (in millions of dollars)

Identification code 014–8030–0–7–452		2021 actual	2022 est.	2023 est.
	Obligations by program activity:			
0001	Tribal Trust Fund (Direct)	160	154	159
0900	Total new obligations, unexpired accounts (object class 41.0)	160	154	159
	Budgetary resources:			
	Unobligated balance:			
1000	Unobligated balance brought forward, Oct 1	104	95	95
	Budget authority:			
	Appropriations, mandatory:			
1201	Appropriation (special or trust fund)	151	154	159
1930	Total budgetary resources available	255	249	254
	Memorandum (non-add) entries:			
1941	Unexpired unobligated balance, end of year	95	95	95
	Change in obligated balance:			
	Unpaid obligations:			
3010	New obligations, unexpired accounts	160	154	159
3020	Outlays (gross)	–160	–154	–159
	Budget authority and outlays, net:			
	Mandatory:			
4090	Budget authority, gross	151	154	159
	Outlays, gross:			
4100	Outlays from new mandatory authority	....	143	148
4101	Outlays from mandatory balances	160	11	11
4110	Outlays, gross (total)	160	154	159
4180	Budget authority, net (total)	151	154	159
4190	Outlays, net (total)	160	154	159

DEPARTMENT OF THE INTERIOR

Departmental Offices

	Memorandum (non-add) entries:			
5000	Total investments, SOY: Federal securities: Par value	104	96	74
5001	Total investments, EOY: Federal securities: Par value	96	74	76
5010	Total investments, SOY: non-Fed securities: Market value	129	229	228
5011	Total investments, EOY: non-Fed securities: Market value	229	228	230

The Tribal Trust Fund includes the following accounts: Funds Contributed for Advancement of the Indian Race, Bequest of George C. Edgeter Fund, Ella M. Franklin Fund, Josephine Lambert Fund, Orrie Shaw Fund, Welmas Endowment Fund, Arizona Intertribal Trust Fund, Navajo Trust Fund, Chippewa Cree Tribal Trust Fund, Shivwits Band of Paiute Indians Trust Fund, Northern Cheyenne Trust Fund, Crow Creek Sioux Tribe Infrastructure Development Trust Fund, and Lower Brule Infrastructure Fund. More detailed information on specific accounts is provided in the budget justification for the Bureau of Trust Funds Administration.

Tribal trust funds are deposited into a consolidated account in the U.S. Department of the Treasury pursuant to: 1) general or specific Acts of the Congress and 2) Federal management of tribal real properties, the titles to which are held in trust for the Tribes by the United States. These funds are available to respective tribal groups for various purposes, under various acts of the Congress, and may be subject to the provisions of tribal constitutions, bylaws, charters, and resolutions of the various Tribes, bands, or groups.

DEPARTMENTAL OFFICES

Federal Funds

DEPARTMENTAL OPERATIONS

(INCLUDING TRANSFER OF FUNDS)

For necessary expenses for management of the Department of the Interior and for grants and cooperative agreements, as authorized by law, $146,530,000, to remain available until September 30, 2024; of which not to exceed $15,000 may be for official reception and representation expenses; of which up to $1,000,000 shall be available for workers compensation payments and unemployment compensation payments associated with the orderly closure of the United States Bureau of Mines; and of which $14,295,000 for Indian land, mineral, and resource valuation activities shall remain available until expended: Provided, That funds for Indian land, mineral, and resource valuation activities may, as needed, be transferred to and merged with the Bureau of Indian Affairs "Operation of Indian Programs" and Bureau of Indian Education "Operation of Indian Education Programs" accounts and the Bureau of Trust Funds Administration "Federal Trust Programs" account: Provided further, That funds made available through contracts or grants obligated during fiscal year 2023, as authorized by the Indian Self-Determination Act of 1975 (25 U.S.C. 5301 et seq.), shall remain available until expended by the contractor or grantee.

Note.—A full-year 2022 appropriation for this account was not enacted at the time the Budget was prepared; therefore, the Budget assumes this account is operating under the Continuing Appropriations Act, 2022 (Division A of Public Law 117–43, as amended). The amounts included for 2022 reflect the annualized level provided by the continuing resolution.

DEPARTMENTAL OPERATIONS

[(INCLUDING TRANSFERS OF FUNDS)]

[For an additional amount for "Departmental Operations", $905,000,000, to remain available until expended, for the Secretary of the Interior to carry out activities, as authorized in section 40804 of division D of this Act: *Provided*, That $337,000,000, to remain available until expended, shall be made available for fiscal year 2022, $142,000,000, to remain available until expended, shall be made available for fiscal year 2023, $142,000,000, to remain available until expended, shall be made available for fiscal year 2024, $142,000,000, to remain available until expended, shall be made available for fiscal year 2025, and $142,000,000, to remain available until expended, shall be made available for fiscal year 2026: *Provided further*, That the Secretary may transfer the funds provided under this heading in this Act to any other account in the Department of the Interior to carry out such purposes: *Provided further*, That the Secretary of the Interior and the Secretary of Agriculture, acting through the Chief of the Forest Service, may authorize the transfer of funds provided under this heading in this Act between the Departments for the purpose of carrying out activities as authorized in section 40804(b)(1) of division D of this Act: *Provided further*, That up to 3 percent of the amounts made available under this heading in this Act in each of fiscal years 2022 through 2026 shall be for salaries, expenses, and administration: *Provided further*, That one-half of one percent of the amounts made available under this heading in this Act in each of fiscal years 2022 through 2026 shall be transferred to the Office of Inspector General of the Department of the Interior for oversight of funding provided to the Department of the Interior in this title in this Act: *Provided further*, That such amount is designated by the Congress as being for an emergency requirement pursuant to section 4112(a) of H. Con. Res. 71 (115th Congress), the concurrent resolution on the budget for fiscal year 2018, and to section 251(b) of the Balanced Budget and Emergency Deficit Control Act of 1985.] *(Infrastructure Investments and Jobs Appropriations Act.)*

Program and Financing (in millions of dollars)

Identification code 014–0102–0–1–306		2021 actual	2022 est.	2023 est.
	Obligations by program activity:			
0012	Leadership and Administration	102	110	122
0013	Management Services	17	34	40
0015	Disaster Relief Appropriations Act, 2013	1	1	1
0018	CARES Act Supplemental P.L. 116–136	151		
0019	2022 Bipartisan Infrastructure Law (P.L. 117–58)		138	241
0100	Direct program subtotal	271	283	404
0799	Total direct obligations	271	283	404
0804	Leadership and Administration	88	73	73
0805	Management Services	5	8	8
0899	Total reimbursable obligations	93	81	81
0900	Total new obligations, unexpired accounts	364	364	485
	Budgetary resources:			
	Unobligated balance:			
1000	Unobligated balance brought forward, Oct 1	199	45	226
1021	Recoveries of prior year unpaid obligations	4	2	2
1070	Unobligated balance (total)	203	47	228
	Budget authority:			
	Appropriations, discretionary:			
1100	Appropriation	121	121	147
1100	Appropriation - Bipartisan Infrastructure Law (P.L. 117–58)		337	
1120	Appropriations transferred to other acct - BIA [014–2100]	–2		
1120	Appropriations transferred to other acct - OIG [014–0104]		–2	
1160	Appropriation, discretionary (total)	119	456	147
	Advance appropriations, discretionary:			
1170	Advance appropriation			142
1172	Advance appropriations transferred to other accounts - OIG [014–0104]			–1
1180	Advanced appropriation, discretionary (total)			141
	Appropriations, mandatory:			
1201	Appropriation (GAOA P.L. 116–152)	19	19	19
1202	Appropriation (previously unavailable)			1
1232	Appropriations and/or unobligated balance of appropriations temporarily reduced		–1	–1
1260	Appropriations, mandatory (total)	19	18	19
	Spending authority from offsetting collections, discretionary:			
1700	Collected	69	53	53
1701	Change in uncollected payments, Federal sources	17	16	16
1722	Unobligated balance of spending authority from offsetting collections permanently reduced	–17		
1750	Spending auth from offsetting collections, disc (total)	69	69	69
1900	Budget authority (total)	207	543	376
1930	Total budgetary resources available	410	590	604
	Memorandum (non-add) entries:			
1940	Unobligated balance expiring	–1		
1941	Unexpired unobligated balance, end of year	45	226	119
	Change in obligated balance:			
	Unpaid obligations:			
3000	Unpaid obligations, brought forward, Oct 1	67	143	233
3010	New obligations, unexpired accounts	364	364	485
3011	Obligations ("upward adjustments"), expired accounts	15		
3020	Outlays (gross)	–295	–271	–321
3040	Recoveries of prior year unpaid obligations, unexpired	–4	–2	–2
3041	Recoveries of prior year unpaid obligations, expired	–4	–1	–1
3050	Unpaid obligations, end of year	143	233	394
	Uncollected payments:			
3060	Uncollected pymts, Fed sources, brought forward, Oct 1	–25	–44	–60
3070	Change in uncollected pymts, Fed sources, unexpired	–17	–16	–16
3071	Change in uncollected pymts, Fed sources, expired	–2		
3090	Uncollected pymts, Fed sources, end of year	–44	–60	–76

Departmental Offices—Continued

SALARIES AND EXPENSES—Continued
Program and Financing—Continued

Identification code 014–0102–0–1–306	2021 actual	2022 est.	2023 est.
Memorandum (non-add) entries:			
3100 Obligated balance, start of year	42	99	173
3200 Obligated balance, end of year	99	173	318
Budget authority and outlays, net:			
Discretionary:			
4000 Budget authority, gross	188	525	357
Outlays, gross:			
4010 Outlays from new discretionary authority	149	138	143
4011 Outlays from discretionary balances	134	112	159
4020 Outlays, gross (total)	283	250	302
Offsets against gross budget authority and outlays:			
Offsetting collections (collected) from:			
4030 Federal sources	–81	–62	–62
Additional offsets against gross budget authority only:			
4050 Change in uncollected pymts, Fed sources, unexpired	–17	–16	–16
4052 Offsetting collections credited to expired accounts	12	9	9
4060 Additional offsets against budget authority only (total)	–5	–7	–7
4070 Budget authority, net (discretionary)	102	456	288
4080 Outlays, net (discretionary)	202	188	240
Mandatory:			
4090 Budget authority, gross	19	18	19
Outlays, gross:			
4100 Outlays from new mandatory authority	12	16	17
4101 Outlays from mandatory balances		5	2
4110 Outlays, gross (total)	12	21	19
4180 Budget authority, net (total)	121	474	307
4190 Outlays, net (total)	214	209	259

This appropriation supports the functions of the Office of the Secretary of the Interior, including executive-level leadership, policy, guidance, and coordination of the responsibilities carried out by its bureaus and offices. In addition, the appropriation supports programmatic functions carried out by the Office of the Secretary including mineral revenue modeling, the Take Pride in America program, the Department's quasi-judicial and appellate responsibilities, and the Appraisal and Valuation Services Office. The appropriation also provides for workers' and unemployment compensation payments for former Bureau of Mines employees.

Object Classification (in millions of dollars)

Identification code 014–0102–0–1–306	2021 actual	2022 est.	2023 est.
Direct obligations:			
Personnel compensation:			
11.1 Full-time permanent - Direct	67	63	76
11.1 Full-time permanent - Allocation		2	5
11.3 Other than full-time permanent	7	5	5
11.5 Other personnel compensation	5	3	3
11.9 Total personnel compensation	79	73	89
12.1 Civilian personnel benefits	26	23	27
21.0 Travel and transportation of persons	1	1	1
22.0 Transportation of things	1	1	1
23.1 Rental payments to GSA	2	2	3
23.2 Rental payments to others	2	1	1
23.3 Communications, utilities, and miscellaneous charges	6	1	1
25.1 Advisory and assistance services	5	2	2
25.2 Other services from non-Federal sources	18	25	83
25.3 Other goods and services from Federal sources	55	76	92
25.4 Operation and maintenance of facilities	21		
25.7 Operation and maintenance of equipment	6	1	1
26.0 Supplies and materials	8	1	1
31.0 Equipment	19	1	1
32.0 Land and structures	7	1	1
41.0 Grants, subsidies, and contributions	14	74	100
99.0 Direct obligations	270	283	404
99.0 Reimbursable obligations	94	81	81
99.9 Total new obligations, unexpired accounts	364	364	485

Employment Summary

Identification code 014–0102–0–1–306	2021 actual	2022 est.	2023 est.
1001 Direct civilian full-time equivalent employment	471	497	545
2001 Reimbursable civilian full-time equivalent employment	252	283	288
3001 Allocation account civilian full-time equivalent employment	44	50	50

MINERAL LEASING AND ASSOCIATED PAYMENTS

Special and Trust Fund Receipts (in millions of dollars)

Identification code 014–5003–0–2–999	2021 actual	2022 est.	2023 est.
0100 Balance, start of year	80	108	151
Receipts:			
Current law:			
1130 Receipts from Mineral Leasing, Public Lands	1,886	2,625	2,427
2000 Total: Balances and receipts	1,966	2,733	2,578
Appropriations:			
Current law:			
2101 Mineral Leasing and Associated Payments	–1,886	–2,625	–2,427
2103 Mineral Leasing and Associated Payments	–79	–107	–150
2132 Mineral Leasing and Associated Payments	107	150	138
2199 Total current law appropriations	–1,858	–2,582	–2,439
2999 Total appropriations	–1,858	–2,582	–2,439
5099 Balance, end of year	108	151	139

Program and Financing (in millions of dollars)

Identification code 014–5003–0–2–999	2021 actual	2022 est.	2023 est.
Obligations by program activity:			
0001 Mineral Leasing and Associated Payments (Direct)	1,858	2,582	2,439
0900 Total new obligations, unexpired accounts (object class 41.0)	1,858	2,582	2,439
Budgetary resources:			
Unobligated balance:			
1000 Unobligated balance brought forward, Oct 1	2	2	2
Budget authority:			
Appropriations, mandatory:			
1201 Appropriation (special or trust fund)	1,886	2,625	2,427
1203 Appropriation (previously unavailable)(special or trust)	79	107	150
1232 Appropriations and/or unobligated balance of appropriations temporarily reduced	–107	–150	–138
1260 Appropriations, mandatory (total)	1,858	2,582	2,439
1900 Budget authority (total)	1,858	2,582	2,439
1930 Total budgetary resources available	1,860	2,584	2,441
Memorandum (non-add) entries:			
1941 Unexpired unobligated balance, end of year	2	2	2
Change in obligated balance:			
Unpaid obligations:			
3010 New obligations, unexpired accounts	1,858	2,582	2,439
3020 Outlays (gross)	–1,858	–2,582	–2,439
Budget authority and outlays, net:			
Mandatory:			
4090 Budget authority, gross	1,858	2,582	2,439
Outlays, gross:			
4100 Outlays from new mandatory authority	1,858	2,582	2,439
4180 Budget authority, net (total)	1,858	2,582	2,439
4190 Outlays, net (total)	1,858	2,582	2,439

Under the Mineral Leasing Act (MLA), States receive fifty percent of Federal revenues generated from mineral production occurring on Federal lands within that State's boundaries. Alaska is the exception, receiving a 90 percent share of receipts from Federal mineral leasing in that State. Separate statutes cover revenue sharing payments from the National Petroleum Reserve-Alaska and the 1002 Area of the Arctic National Wildlife Refuge, where the traditional MLA fifty-percent state share applies. To partially cover the costs of administering the Federal mineral leasing program, the Bipartisan Budget Act of 2013 permanently amended the MLA to deduct two percent from the required payments to States under the Act.

DEPARTMENT OF THE INTERIOR

These payments are administered by Interior's Office of Natural Resources Revenue.

NATIONAL PETROLEUM RESERVE, ALASKA

Special and Trust Fund Receipts (in millions of dollars)

Identification code 014–5045–0–2–806	2021 actual	2022 est.	2023 est.
0100 Balance, start of year	12	6	7
Receipts:			
Current law:			
1130 Receipts from Oil and Gas Leases, National Petroleum Reserve in Alaska, MMS	8	22	26
2000 Total: Balances and receipts	20	28	33
Appropriations:			
Current law:			
2101 National Petroleum Reserve, Alaska	–15	–22	–26
2132 National Petroleum Reserve, Alaska	1	1	1
2199 Total current law appropriations	–14	–21	–25
2999 Total appropriations	–14	–21	–25
5099 Balance, end of year	6	7	8

Program and Financing (in millions of dollars)

Identification code 014–5045–0–2–806	2021 actual	2022 est.	2023 est.
Obligations by program activity:			
0001 National Petroleum Reserve, Alaska (Direct)	14	21	25
0900 Total new obligations, unexpired accounts (object class 41.0)	14	21	25
Budgetary resources:			
Budget authority:			
Appropriations, mandatory:			
1201 Appropriation (special or trust fund)	15	22	26
1232 Appropriations and/or unobligated balance of appropriations temporarily reduced	–1	–1	–1
1260 Appropriations, mandatory (total)	14	21	25
1930 Total budgetary resources available	14	21	25
Change in obligated balance:			
Unpaid obligations:			
3010 New obligations, unexpired accounts	14	21	25
3020 Outlays (gross)	–14	–21	–25
Budget authority and outlays, net:			
Mandatory:			
4090 Budget authority, gross	14	21	25
Outlays, gross:			
4100 Outlays from new mandatory authority	14	21	25
4180 Budget authority, net (total)	14	21	25
4190 Outlays, net (total)	14	21	25

Payments to Alaska from oil and gas leasing in the National Petroleum Reserve-Alaska (NPR-A).—Public Law 96–514 requires that 50 percent of all Federal revenues received from oil and gas leasing in the NPR-A be paid to the State of Alaska. These payments are administered by Interior's Office of Natural Resources Revenue.

PAYMENT TO ALASKA, ARCTIC NATIONAL WILDLIFE REFUGE

Special and Trust Fund Receipts (in millions of dollars)

Identification code 014–5488–0–2–806	2021 actual	2022 est.	2023 est.
0100 Balance, start of year			
Receipts:			
Current law:			
1130 Arctic National Wildlife Refuge, Rent, Royalties and Bonuses, (Alaska Share)	8	2	11
2000 Total: Balances and receipts	8	2	11
Appropriations:			
Current law:			
2101 Payment to Alaska, Arctic National Wildlife Refuge	–8	–2	–11
2132 Payment to Alaska, Arctic National Wildlife Refuge			1
2199 Total current law appropriations	–8	–2	–10
2999 Total appropriations	–8	–2	–10
5099 Balance, end of year			1

Program and Financing (in millions of dollars)

Identification code 014–5488–0–2–806	2021 actual	2022 est.	2023 est.
Obligations by program activity:			
0001 Payment to Alaska, Arctic National Wildlife Refuge	8	2	10
0900 Total new obligations, unexpired accounts (object class 41.0)	8	2	10
Budgetary resources:			
Budget authority:			
Appropriations, mandatory:			
1201 Appropriation (special or trust fund)	8	2	11
1232 Appropriations and/or unobligated balance of appropriations temporarily reduced			–1
1260 Appropriations, mandatory (total)	8	2	10
1930 Total budgetary resources available	8	2	10
Change in obligated balance:			
Unpaid obligations:			
3010 New obligations, unexpired accounts	8	2	10
3020 Outlays (gross)	–8	–2	–10
Budget authority and outlays, net:			
Mandatory:			
4090 Budget authority, gross	8	2	10
Outlays, gross:			
4100 Outlays from new mandatory authority	8	2	10
4180 Budget authority, net (total)	8	2	10
4190 Outlays, net (total)	8	2	10

In accordance with Section 20001 of the 2017 Tax Cuts and Jobs Act (P.L. 115–97), the State of Alaska will receive 50 percent of Federal revenues generated from mineral production occurring in the 1002 Area of the Coastal Plain of the Arctic National Wildlife Refuge (ANWR). These payments will be administered by the Office of Natural Resources Revenue.

LEASES OF LANDS ACQUIRED FOR FLOOD CONTROL, NAVIGATION, AND ALLIED PURPOSES

Special and Trust Fund Receipts (in millions of dollars)

Identification code 014–5248–0–2–302	2021 actual	2022 est.	2023 est.
0100 Balance, start of year	15	17	20
Receipts:			
Current law:			
1130 Leases of Lands Acquired for Flood Control, Navigation, and Allied Purposes	43	46	42
2000 Total: Balances and receipts	58	63	62
Appropriations:			
Current law:			
2101 Leases of Lands Acquired for Flood Control, Navigation, and Allied Purposes	–43	–46	–42
2132 Leases of Lands Acquired for Flood Control, Navigation, and Allied Purposes	2	3	2
2199 Total current law appropriations	–41	–43	–40
2999 Total appropriations	–41	–43	–40
5099 Balance, end of year	17	20	22

Program and Financing (in millions of dollars)

Identification code 014–5248–0–2–302	2021 actual	2022 est.	2023 est.
Obligations by program activity:			
0001 Leases of Lands Acquired for Flood Control, Navigation, and Alli (Direct)	41	43	40
0900 Total new obligations, unexpired accounts (object class 41.0)	41	43	40

LEASES OF LANDS ACQUIRED FOR FLOOD CONTROL, NAVIGATION, AND ALLIED PURPOSES—Continued

Program and Financing—Continued

Identification code 014–5248–0–2–302	2021 actual	2022 est.	2023 est.
Budgetary resources:			
Budget authority:			
Appropriations, mandatory:			
1201 Appropriation (special or trust fund)	43	46	42
1232 Appropriations and/or unobligated balance of appropriations temporarily reduced	–2	–3	–2
1260 Appropriations, mandatory (total)	41	43	40
1930 Total budgetary resources available	41	43	40
Change in obligated balance:			
Unpaid obligations:			
3010 New obligations, unexpired accounts	41	43	40
3020 Outlays (gross)	–41	–43	–40
Budget authority and outlays, net:			
Mandatory:			
4090 Budget authority, gross	41	43	40
Outlays, gross:			
4100 Outlays from new mandatory authority	41	43	40
4180 Budget authority, net (total)	41	43	40
4190 Outlays, net (total)	41	43	40

According to the Flood Control Act of 1936 (33 U.S.C. 701 et seq.), 75 percent of revenue collected in the Treasury from the leasing of lands acquired by the United States for flood control, navigation, and allied purposes, is to be shared with the State in which it was collected. These funds are to be expended as the State legislature may prescribe for the benefit of the public schools and roads in the county from which the revenue was collected, or for defraying other expenses of county government. These expenses include public obligations of levee and drainage districts for flood control and drainage improvements. Payments are administered by Interior's Office of Natural Resources Revenue.

NATIONAL FORESTS FUND, PAYMENT TO STATES

Special and Trust Fund Receipts (in millions of dollars)

Identification code 014–5243–0–2–302	2021 actual	2022 est.	2023 est.
0100 Balance, start of year	3	3	4
Receipts:			
Current law:			
1130 National Forests Fund, Payments to States	5	9	9
2000 Total: Balances and receipts	8	12	13
Appropriations:			
Current law:			
2101 National Forests Fund, Payment to States	–5	–9	–9
2132 National Forests Fund, Payment to States		1	1
2199 Total current law appropriations	–5	–8	–8
2999 Total appropriations	–5	–8	–8
5099 Balance, end of year	3	4	5

Program and Financing (in millions of dollars)

Identification code 014–5243–0–2–302	2021 actual	2022 est.	2023 est.
Obligations by program activity:			
0001 National Forests Fund, Payment to States (Direct)	5	8	8
0900 Total new obligations, unexpired accounts (object class 41.0)	5	8	8
Budgetary resources:			
Budget authority:			
Appropriations, mandatory:			
1201 Appropriation (special or trust fund)	5	9	9
1232 Appropriations and/or unobligated balance of appropriations temporarily reduced		–1	–1
1260 Appropriations, mandatory (total)	5	8	8
1930 Total budgetary resources available	5	8	8
Change in obligated balance:			
Unpaid obligations:			
3010 New obligations, unexpired accounts	5	8	8
3020 Outlays (gross)	–5	–8	–8
Budget authority and outlays, net:			
Mandatory:			
4090 Budget authority, gross	5	8	8
Outlays, gross:			
4100 Outlays from new mandatory authority	5	8	8
4180 Budget authority, net (total)	5	8	8
4190 Outlays, net (total)	5	8	8

Since May 23, 1908 (16 U.S.C. 499), 25 percent of the revenues collected from onshore mineral leasing and production on national forest lands have been paid to the State in which the national forest resides. A State's payment is based on national forest acreage. Where a national forest is situated in several States, an individual State payment is proportionate to its area within that particular national forest. These payments are administered by Interior's Office of Natural Resources Revenue.

GEOTHERMAL LEASE REVENUES, PAYMENT TO COUNTIES

Special and Trust Fund Receipts (in millions of dollars)

Identification code 014–5574–0–2–806	2021 actual	2022 est.	2023 est.
0100 Balance, start of year			
Receipts:			
Current law:			
1130 Geothermal Lease Revenues, County Share	5	5	5
2000 Total: Balances and receipts	5	5	5
Appropriations:			
Current law:			
2101 Geothermal Lease Revenues, Payment to Counties	–5	–5	–5
5099 Balance, end of year			

Program and Financing (in millions of dollars)

Identification code 014–5574–0–2–806	2021 actual	2022 est.	2023 est.
Obligations by program activity:			
0001 Geothermal Lease Revenues, Payment to Counties (Direct)	5	5	5
0900 Total new obligations, unexpired accounts (object class 41.0)	5	5	5
Budgetary resources:			
Budget authority:			
Appropriations, mandatory:			
1201 Appropriation (special or trust fund)	5	5	5
1930 Total budgetary resources available	5	5	5
Change in obligated balance:			
Unpaid obligations:			
3010 New obligations, unexpired accounts	5	5	5
3020 Outlays (gross)	–5	–5	–5
Budget authority and outlays, net:			
Mandatory:			
4090 Budget authority, gross	5	5	5
Outlays, gross:			
4100 Outlays from new mandatory authority	5	5	5
4180 Budget authority, net (total)	5	5	5
4190 Outlays, net (total)	5	5	5

The Energy Policy Act of 2005 (P.L. 109–58) amended section 20 of the Geothermal Steam Act of 1970 (30 U.S.C. 1019 et seq.) to provide that for the revenues collected from geothermal leasing, 50 percent of the revenues are to be paid to the State and 25 percent are to be paid to the county in which the leased lands or geothermal resources are located. Payments are administered by Interior's Office of Natural Resources Revenue.

DEPARTMENT OF THE INTERIOR

STATES SHARE FROM CERTAIN GULF OF MEXICO LEASES

Special and Trust Fund Receipts (in millions of dollars)

Identification code 014–5535–0–2–302	2021 actual	2022 est.	2023 est.
0100 Balance, start of year	314	333	456
Receipts:			
Current law:			
1130 Outer Continental Shelf Rentals and Bonuses, State Share from Certain Gulf of Mexico Leases	54	146	9
1130 Outer Continental Shelf Royalties	214	230	366
1199 Total current law receipts	268	376	375
1999 Total receipts	268	376	375
2000 Total: Balances and receipts	582	709	831
Appropriations:			
Current law:			
2101 States Share from Certain Gulf of Mexico Leases	–264	–268	–376
2132 States Share from Certain Gulf of Mexico Leases	15	15	21
2199 Total current law appropriations	–249	–253	–355
2999 Total appropriations	–249	–253	–355
5099 Balance, end of year	333	456	476

Program and Financing (in millions of dollars)

Identification code 014–5535–0–2–302	2021 actual	2022 est.	2023 est.
Obligations by program activity:			
0001 States Share from Certain Gulf of Mexico Leases (Direct)	249	253	355
0900 Total new obligations, unexpired accounts (object class 41.0)	249	253	355
Budgetary resources:			
Budget authority:			
Appropriations, mandatory:			
1201 Appropriation (special or trust fund)	264	268	376
1232 Appropriations and/or unobligated balance of appropriations temporarily reduced	–15	–15	–21
1260 Appropriations, mandatory (total)	249	253	355
1930 Total budgetary resources available	249	253	355
Change in obligated balance:			
Unpaid obligations:			
3010 New obligations, unexpired accounts	249	253	355
3020 Outlays (gross)	–249	–253	–355
Budget authority and outlays, net:			
Mandatory:			
4090 Budget authority, gross	249	253	355
Outlays, gross:			
4100 Outlays from new mandatory authority	249	253	355
4180 Budget authority, net (total)	249	253	355
4190 Outlays, net (total)	249	253	355

The Gulf of Mexico Energy Security Act of 2006 (GOMESA, P.L. 109–432) provides that 37.5 percent of Outer Continental Shelf revenues from certain leases, in most cases subject to an annual payment cap, be distributed to four coastal States (Alabama, Louisiana, Mississippi, and Texas) and their local governments based on a complex allocation formula. These payments are administered by Interior's Office of Natural Resources Revenue.

ENVIRONMENTAL IMPROVEMENT AND RESTORATION FUND

Special and Trust Fund Receipts (in millions of dollars)

Identification code 014–5425–0–2–302	2021 actual	2022 est.	2023 est.
0100 Balance, start of year	1,523	1,541	1,554
Receipts:			
Current law:			
1140 Interest Earned, Environmental Improvement and Restoration Fund	25	9	11
1140 Interest Earned, Environmental Improvement and Restoration Fund		9	11
1199 Total current law receipts	25	18	22
1999 Total receipts	25	18	22
2000 Total: Balances and receipts	1,548	1,559	1,576
Appropriations:			
Current law:			
2101 Environmental Improvement and Restoration Fund	–7	–5	–2
5099 Balance, end of year	1,541	1,554	1,574

Program and Financing (in millions of dollars)

Identification code 014–5425–0–2–302	2021 actual	2022 est.	2023 est.
4180 Budget authority, net (total)			
4190 Outlays, net (total)			
Memorandum (non-add) entries:			
5000 Total investments, SOY: Federal securities: Par value	1,542	1,560	1,569
5001 Total investments, EOY: Federal securities: Par value	1,560	1,569	1,581

Title IV of the Department of the Interior and Related Agencies Appropriation Act, 1998 (P.L. 105–83) established the Environmental Improvement and Restoration Fund account. As required by law, 50 percent of the principal and 50 percent of the interest from the Alaska Escrow account are deposited into the Environmental Improvement and Restoration Fund. The law requires that the corpus of the Fund be invested. Twenty percent of the interest earned by the Fund is permanently appropriated to the Department of Commerce, and the unappropriated balance of interest remains in the Fund, subject to appropriation. At this time, no budget authority is requested.

LAND AND WATER CONSERVATION FUND

Special and Trust Fund Receipts (in millions of dollars)

Identification code 014–5005–0–2–303	2021 actual	2022 est.	2023 est.
0100 Balance, start of year	22,484	22,472	22,544
0198 Rounding adjustment	1		
0199 Balance, start of year	22,485	22,472	22,544
Receipts:			
Current law:			
1110 Land and Water Conservation Fund, Motorboat Fuels Tax	1	1	1
1130 Outer Continental Shelf Royalties, LWCF Share from Certain Gulf of Mexico Leases		77	94
1130 Land and Water Conservation Fund, Rent Receipts, Outer Continental Shelf Lands	1	900	382
1130 Land and Water Conservation Fund, Royalty Receipts, Outer Continental Shelf	887		518
1130 Outer Continental Shelf Rents and Bonuses, LWCF Share from Certain Gulf of Mexico Leases	89	49	3
1130 Land and Water Conservation Fund, Surplus Property Sales	12	6	6
1199 Total current law receipts	990	1,033	1,004
1999 Total receipts	990	1,033	1,004
2000 Total: Balances and receipts	23,475	23,505	23,548
Appropriations:			
Current law:			
2101 State and Private Forestry	–94	–94	–94
2101 Land Acquisition	–1	–1	–1
2101 Land Acquisition	–124	–124	–124
2101 Land Acquisition	–66	–66	–71
2101 Land Acquisition	–112	–112	–115
2101 Cooperative Endangered Species Conservation Fund	–20	–20	
2101 Cooperative Endangered Species Conservation Fund	–11	–11	–30
2101 Land Acquisition and State Assistance	–88	–89	–125
2101 Land Acquisition and State Assistance	–474	–474	–447
2101 Salaries and Expenses	–19	–19	–19
2102 Salaries and Expenses			–1
2103 State and Private Forestry			–5
2103 Land Acquisition			–4
2103 Land Acquisition			–6
2103 Land Acquisition and State Assistance			–27
2132 State and Private Forestry		5	5
2132 Land Acquisition		4	4
2132 Land Acquisition		6	7
2132 Cooperative Endangered Species Conservation Fund		1	2
2132 Land Acquisition and State Assistance	5	5	7

Departmental Offices—Continued
Federal Funds—Continued

LAND AND WATER CONSERVATION FUND—Continued

Special and Trust Fund Receipts—Continued

Identification code 014–5005–0–2–303	2021 actual	2022 est.	2023 est.
2132 Land Acquisition and State Assistance	....	27	25
2132 Salaries and Expenses	....	1	1
2199 Total current law appropriations	–1,004	–961	–1,018
2999 Total appropriations	–1,004	–961	–1,018
5098 Rounding adjustment	1	....	....
5099 Balance, end of year	22,472	22,544	22,530

ADMINISTRATIVE PROVISIONS

For fiscal year 2023, up to $400,000 of the payments authorized by chapter 69 of title 31, United States Code, may be retained for administrative expenses of the Payments in Lieu of Taxes Program: Provided, That the amounts provided under this Act specifically for the Payments in Lieu of Taxes program are the only amounts available for payments authorized under chapter 69 of title 31, United States Code: Provided further, That in the event the sums appropriated for any fiscal year for payments pursuant to this chapter are insufficient to make the full payments authorized by that chapter to all units of local government, then the payment to each local government shall be made proportionally: Provided further, That the Secretary may make adjustments to payment to individual units of local government to correct for prior overpayments or underpayments: Provided further, That no payment shall be made pursuant to that chapter to otherwise eligible units of local government if the computed amount of the payment is less than $100.

The Office of the Secretary provides for the administration of the Payments in Lieu of Taxes program, which makes payments to counties and other units of local government for lands within their boundaries administered by the Bureau of Land Management, U.S. Forest Service, the National Park Service, the Fish and Wildlife Service, and certain other agencies. Funding for the program is in a separate account within Department-Wide programs.

INSULAR AFFAIRS

The Secretary of the Interior is charged with the responsibility of promoting the economic and political development of those insular areas which are under U.S. jurisdiction and within the responsibility of the Department of the Interior. The Secretary originates and implements Federal policy for the U.S. territories; guides and coordinates certain operating programs and construction projects; provides information services and technical assistance; coordinates certain Federal programs and services provided to the freely associated states, and participates in foreign policy and defense matters concerning the U.S. territories and the freely associated states.

Federal Funds

TRUST TERRITORY OF THE PACIFIC ISLANDS

Until October 1, 1994, the United States exercised jurisdiction over the Trust Territory of the Pacific Islands according to the terms of the 1947 Trusteeship Agreement between the United States and the Security Council of the United Nations. These responsibilities were carried out by the Department of the Interior.

The Department of the Interior is seeking no additional appropriations for the Trust Territory of the Pacific Islands. Compacts of Free Association have been implemented with the Federated States of Micronesia, the Republic of the Marshall Islands, and the Republic of Palau.

Remaining funds in the Trust Territory of the Pacific Islands account are being used to improve basic economic information and financial management capabilities in the insular areas; address compact impact related issues; and also for brown tree snake control.

COMPACT OF FREE ASSOCIATION

For grants and necessary expenses, $8,463,000, to remain available until expended, as provided for in sections 221(a)(2) and 233 of the Compact of Free Association for the Republic of Palau; and section 221(a)(2) of the Compacts of Free Association for the Government of the Republic of the Marshall Islands and the Federated States of Micronesia, as authorized by Public Law 99–658 and Public Law 108–188: Provided, That of the funds appropriated under this heading, $5,000,000 is for deposit into the Compact Trust Fund of the Republic of the Marshall Islands as compensation authorized by Public Law 108–188 for adverse financial and economic impacts.

Note.—A full-year 2022 appropriation for this account was not enacted at the time the Budget was prepared; therefore, the Budget assumes this account is operating under the Continuing Appropriations Act, 2022 (Division A of Public Law 117–43, as amended). The amounts included for 2022 reflect the annualized level provided by the continuing resolution.

Program and Financing (in millions of dollars)

Identification code 014–0415–0–1–808	2021 actual	2022 est.	2023 est.
Obligations by program activity:			
0001 Federal services assistance	9	8	8
0002 Enewetak	1	1	1
0091 Direct program activities, subtotal	10	9	9
0101 Palau Compact Extension, mandatory	2	....	....
0192 Subtotal	12	9	9
0201 Assistance to the Marshall Islands	74	80	81
0202 Assistance to the Federated States of Micronesia	110	116	118
0204 Compact Impact	30	30	30
0205 Judical Training/FEMA	1	1	1
0291 Subtotal, permanent indefinite	215	227	230
0799 Total direct obligations	227	236	239
0801 Compact of Free Association (Reimbursable)	17	17	17
0900 Total new obligations, unexpired accounts	244	253	256
Budgetary resources:			
Unobligated balance:			
1000 Unobligated balance brought forward, Oct 1	305	320	328
1001 Discretionary unobligated balance brought fwd, Oct 1	1	....	....
1021 Recoveries of prior year unpaid obligations	6	9	9
1070 Unobligated balance (total)	311	329	337
Budget authority:			
Appropriations, discretionary:			
1100 Appropriation	8	8	8
Appropriations, mandatory:			
1200 Appropriation	227	226	229
Spending authority from offsetting collections, discretionary:			
1700 Collected	18	18	24
1900 Budget authority (total)	253	252	261
1930 Total budgetary resources available	564	581	598
Memorandum (non-add) entries:			
1941 Unexpired unobligated balance, end of year	320	328	342
Change in obligated balance:			
Unpaid obligations:			
3000 Unpaid obligations, brought forward, Oct 1	72	89	85
3010 New obligations, unexpired accounts	244	253	256
3011 Obligations ("upward adjustments"), expired accounts	4	....	....
3020 Outlays (gross)	–222	–248	–257
3040 Recoveries of prior year unpaid obligations, unexpired	–6	–9	–9
3041 Recoveries of prior year unpaid obligations, expired	–3	....	....
3050 Unpaid obligations, end of year	89	85	75
Memorandum (non-add) entries:			
3100 Obligated balance, start of year	72	89	85
3200 Obligated balance, end of year	89	85	75
Budget authority and outlays, net:			
Discretionary:			
4000 Budget authority, gross	26	26	32
Outlays, gross:			
4010 Outlays from new discretionary authority	7	9	9
4011 Outlays from discretionary balances	20	16	17
4020 Outlays, gross (total)	27	25	26

		2021 actual	2022 est.	2023 est.
	Offsets against gross budget authority and outlays:			
	Offsetting collections (collected) from:			
4030	Federal sources	−18	−18	−24
4040	Offsets against gross budget authority and outlays (total)	−18	−18	−24
	Mandatory:			
4090	Budget authority, gross	227	226	229
	Outlays, gross:			
4100	Outlays from new mandatory authority	173	189	191
4101	Outlays from mandatory balances	22	34	40
4110	Outlays, gross (total)	195	223	231
4180	Budget authority, net (total)	235	234	237
4190	Outlays, net (total)	204	230	233

The peoples of the Republic of the Marshall Islands, the Federated States of Micronesia and the Republic of Palau approved Compacts of Free Association negotiated by the United States and their governments. The Compact of Free Association Act of 1985 (P.L. 99–239) constituted the necessary authorizing legislation to make annual payments to the Republic of the Marshall Islands and the Federated States of Micronesia. Payments began in 1987 and continued through 2003 when the original economic assistance package expired. The Compact of Free Association Amendments Act of 2003 (P.L. 108–188), continues financial assistance to the Federated States of Micronesia and the Republic of the Marshall Islands through 2023. The Compact of Free Association for the Republic of Palau was enacted on November 14, 1986 as Public Law 99–658, and was implemented on October 1, 1994. Financial assistance provisions under the Compact of Free Association with the Republic of Palau were set to expire on September 30, 2009, however, under the 2010 Compact Review Agreement (CRA) the United States agreed to provide continued economic assistance to the Government of Palau through 2024.

Object Classification (in millions of dollars)

Identification code 014–0415–0–1–808		2021 actual	2022 est.	2023 est.
	Direct obligations:			
25.3	Other goods and services from Federal sources	3	3	3
41.0	Grants, subsidies, and contributions	224	233	236
99.0	Direct obligations	227	236	239
99.0	Reimbursable obligations	17	17	17
99.9	Total new obligations, unexpired accounts	244	253	256

PAYMENTS TO THE UNITED STATES TERRITORIES, FISCAL ASSISTANCE

Program and Financing (in millions of dollars)

Identification code 014–0418–0–1–806		2021 actual	2022 est.	2023 est.
	Obligations by program activity:			
0001	Advance payments to Guam of estimated U.S. income tax collections	76	80	80
0002	Advance payments to the Virgin Islands of estimated U.S. excise tax collections	294	300	300
0900	Total new obligations, unexpired accounts (object class 41.0)	370	380	380
	Budgetary resources:			
	Budget authority:			
	Appropriations, mandatory:			
1200	Appropriation	370	380	380
1930	Total budgetary resources available	370	380	380
	Change in obligated balance:			
	Unpaid obligations:			
3010	New obligations, unexpired accounts	370	380	380
3020	Outlays (gross)	−370	−380	−380
	Budget authority and outlays, net:			
	Mandatory:			
4090	Budget authority, gross	370	380	380
	Outlays, gross:			
4100	Outlays from new mandatory authority	370	380	380
4180	Budget authority, net (total)	370	380	380
4190	Outlays, net (total)	370	380	380

Public Law 95–348 requires that certain revenues collected by the U.S. Treasury involving Guam and the Virgin Islands (income taxes withheld and excise taxes) be paid prior to the start of the fiscal year of collection. The 2023 Budget includes funds for these advance payments.

ASSISTANCE TO TERRITORIES

For expenses necessary for assistance to territories under the jurisdiction of the Department of the Interior and other jurisdictions identified in section 104(e) of Public Law 108–188, $117,257,000, of which: (1) $107,040,000 shall remain available until expended for territorial assistance, including general technical assistance, maintenance assistance, disaster assistance, coral reef initiative and natural resources activities, and brown tree snake control and research; grants to the judiciary in American Samoa for compensation and expenses, as authorized by law (48 U.S.C. 1661(c)); grants to the Government of American Samoa, in addition to current local revenues, for construction and support of governmental functions; grants to the Government of the Virgin Islands, as authorized by law; grants to the Government of Guam, as authorized by law; and grants to the Government of the Northern Mariana Islands, as authorized by law (Public Law 94–241; 90 Stat. 272); and (2) $10,217,000 shall be available until September 30, 2024, for salaries and expenses of the Office of Insular Affairs: Provided, That all financial transactions of the territorial and local governments herein provided for, including such transactions of all agencies or instrumentalities established or used by such governments, may be audited by the Government Accountability Office, at its discretion, in accordance with chapter 35 of title 31, United States Code: Provided further, That Northern Mariana Islands Covenant grant funding shall be provided according to those terms of the Agreement of the Special Representatives on Future United States Financial Assistance for the Northern Mariana Islands approved by Public Law 104–134: Provided further, That the funds for the program of operations and maintenance improvement are appropriated to institutionalize routine operations and maintenance improvement of capital infrastructure with territorial participation and cost sharing to be determined by the Secretary based on the grantee's commitment to timely maintenance of its capital assets: Provided further, That any appropriation for disaster assistance under this heading in this Act or previous appropriations Acts may be used as non-Federal matching funds for the purpose of hazard mitigation grants provided pursuant to section 404 of the Robert T. Stafford Disaster Relief and Emergency Assistance Act (42 U.S.C. 5170c).

Note.—A full-year 2022 appropriation for this account was not enacted at the time the Budget was prepared; therefore, the Budget assumes this account is operating under the Continuing Appropriations Act, 2022 (Division A of Public Law 117–43, as amended). The amounts included for 2022 reflect the annualized level provided by the continuing resolution.

Program and Financing (in millions of dollars)

Identification code 014–0412–0–1–808		2021 actual	2022 est.	2023 est.
	Obligations by program activity:			
0009	Office of Insular Affairs	8	9	10
0010	Technical assistance	24	22	22
0015	Coral Reef Initiative & Natural Resources	3	3	4
0017	Maintenance assistance fund	5	4	4
0018	American Samoa operations grants	25	24	24
0019	Brown Treesnake	4	4	4
0021	Energizing Insular Communities	9	9	15
0031	Compact Impact Discretionary	4	4	6
0035	CARES Act Supplemental (P.L. 116–136)	12		
0091	Direct subtotal, discretionary	94	79	89
0101	Capital Improvement Program, Mandatory	29	28	28
0900	Total new obligations, unexpired accounts	123	107	117
	Budgetary resources:			
	Unobligated balance:			
1000	Unobligated balance brought forward, Oct 1	18	6	10
1001	Discretionary unobligated balance brought fwd, Oct 1	16	3	
1021	Recoveries of prior year unpaid obligations	4	4	9
1070	Unobligated balance (total)	22	10	19
	Budget authority:			
	Appropriations, discretionary:			
1100	Appropriation	79	79	89
	Appropriations, mandatory:			
1200	Appropriation	28	28	28
1900	Budget authority (total)	107	107	117
1930	Total budgetary resources available	129	117	136

ASSISTANCE TO TERRITORIES—Continued

Program and Financing—Continued

Identification code 014–0412–0–1–808		2021 actual	2022 est.	2023 est.
	Memorandum (non-add) entries:			
1941	Unexpired unobligated balance, end of year	6	10	19
	Change in obligated balance:			
	Unpaid obligations:			
3000	Unpaid obligations, brought forward, Oct 1	237	261	213
3010	New obligations, unexpired accounts	123	107	117
3020	Outlays (gross)	–95	–151	–134
3040	Recoveries of prior year unpaid obligations, unexpired	–4	–4	–9
3050	Unpaid obligations, end of year	261	213	187
	Memorandum (non-add) entries:			
3100	Obligated balance, start of year	237	261	213
3200	Obligated balance, end of year	261	213	187
	Budget authority and outlays, net:			
	Discretionary:			
4000	Budget authority, gross	79	79	89
	Outlays, gross:			
4010	Outlays from new discretionary authority	35	40	44
4011	Outlays from discretionary balances	42	85	63
4020	Outlays, gross (total)	77	125	107
	Mandatory:			
4090	Budget authority, gross	28	28	28
	Outlays, gross:			
4100	Outlays from new mandatory authority		1	1
4101	Outlays from mandatory balances	18	25	26
4110	Outlays, gross (total)	18	26	27
4180	Budget authority, net (total)	107	107	117
4190	Outlays, net (total)	95	151	134

This appropriation provides support for basic government operations for those insular areas requiring such support, capital infrastructure improvements, special program and economic development assistance, and technical assistance.

Pursuant to section 118 of Public Law 104–134, $27.7 million in mandatory covenant capital improvement program grant funding may be allocated to high priority needs in the U.S. Territories and freely associated states.

Object Classification (in millions of dollars)

Identification code 014–0412–0–1–808		2021 actual	2022 est.	2023 est.
	Direct obligations:			
11.1	Personnel compensation: Full-time permanent	3	3	3
12.1	Civilian personnel benefits	1	1	1
25.2	Other services from non-Federal sources	3	3	3
25.3	Other goods and services from Federal sources	9	9	12
41.0	Grants, subsidies, and contributions	106	91	98
99.0	Direct obligations	122	107	117
99.5	Adjustment for rounding	1		
99.9	Total new obligations, unexpired accounts	123	107	117

Employment Summary

Identification code 014–0412–0–1–808	2021 actual	2022 est.	2023 est.
1001 Direct civilian full-time equivalent employment	29	36	36

ASSISTANCE TO AMERICAN SAMOA DIRECT LOAN FINANCING ACCOUNT

Program and Financing (in millions of dollars)

Identification code 014–4163–0–3–806		2021 actual	2022 est.	2023 est.
	Obligations by program activity:			
	Credit program obligations:			
0713	Payment of interest to Treasury	1	1	1
0900	Total new obligations, unexpired accounts	1	1	1

	Budgetary resources:			
	Financing authority:			
	Spending authority from offsetting collections, mandatory:			
1800	Collected	1	1	1
1930	Total budgetary resources available	1	1	1
	Change in obligated balance:			
	Unpaid obligations:			
3010	New obligations, unexpired accounts	1	1	1
3020	Outlays (gross)	–1	–1	–1
	Financing authority and disbursements, net:			
	Mandatory:			
4090	Budget authority, gross	1	1	1
	Financing disbursements:			
4110	Outlays, gross (total)	1	1	1
	Offsets against gross financing authority and disbursements:			
	Offsetting collections (collected) from:			
4123	Non-Federal sources - interest payments fr. Am. Samoa	–1	–1	–1
4180	Budget authority, net (total)			
4190	Outlays, net (total)			

Status of Direct Loans (in millions of dollars)

Identification code 014–4163–0–3–806		2021 actual	2022 est.	2023 est.
	Cumulative balance of direct loans outstanding:			
1210	Outstanding, start of year	14	14	14
1251	Repayments: Repayments	–1	–1	–1
1261	Adjustments: Capitalized interest	1	1	1
1290	Outstanding, end of year	14	14	14

In 2000, the American Samoa Government (ASG) was authorized to borrow $18.6 million from the U.S. Treasury in order to reduce significant past due debts to vendors. Repayment of the loan is secured and accomplished with funds, as they become due and payable to ASG from the Escrow Account established under the terms and conditions of the Tobacco Master Settlement Agreement. The ASG agreed to significant financial reforms as a prerequisite to receiving the loan proceeds.

Balance Sheet (in millions of dollars)

Identification code 014–4163–0–3–806		2020 actual	2021 actual
	ASSETS:		
	Net value of assets related to post-1991 direct loans receivable:		
1401	Direct loans receivable, gross	14	14
1405	Allowance for subsidy cost (-)	–5	–5
1499	Net present value of assets related to direct loans	9	9
1999	Total assets	9	9
	LIABILITIES:		
2103	Federal liabilities: Debt	8	8
	NET POSITION:		
3300	Cumulative results of operations	1	1
4999	Total liabilities and net position	9	9

ADMINISTRATIVE PROVISIONS

(INCLUDING TRANSFER OF FUNDS)

At the request of the Governor of Guam, the Secretary may transfer discretionary funds or mandatory funds provided under section 104(e) of Public Law 108–188 and Public Law 104–134, that are allocated for Guam, to the Secretary of Agriculture for the subsidy cost of direct or guaranteed loans, plus not to exceed three percent of the amount of the subsidy transferred for the cost of loan administration, for the purposes authorized by the Rural Electrification Act of 1936 and section 306(a)(1) of the Consolidated Farm and Rural Development Act for construction and repair projects in Guam, and such funds shall remain available until expended: Provided, That such costs, including the cost of modifying such loans, shall be as defined in section 502 of the Congressional Budget Act of 1974: Provided further, That such loans or loan guarantees may be made without regard to the population of the area, credit elsewhere requirements, and restrictions on the types of eligible entities under the Rural Electrification Act of 1936 and section 306(a)(1) of the Consolidated Farm and Rural Development Act: Provided further, That any funds transferred to the

DEPARTMENT OF THE INTERIOR

OFFICE OF THE SOLICITOR

Federal Funds

SALARIES AND EXPENSES

For necessary expenses of the Office of the Solicitor, $102,050,000, to remain available until September 30, 2024.

Note.—A full-year 2022 appropriation for this account was not enacted at the time the Budget was prepared; therefore, the Budget assumes this account is operating under the Continuing Appropriations Act, 2022 (Division A of Public Law 117–43, as amended). The amounts included for 2022 reflect the annualized level provided by the continuing resolution.

Program and Financing (in millions of dollars)

Identification code 014–0107–0–1–306		2021 actual	2022 est.	2023 est.
	Obligations by program activity:			
0001	Salaries and Expenses (Direct)	87	87	102
0801	Salaries and Expenses (Reimbursable)	21	23	23
0900	Total new obligations, unexpired accounts	108	110	125
	Budgetary resources:			
	Budget authority:			
	Appropriations, discretionary:			
1100	Appropriation	87	87	102
	Spending authority from offsetting collections, discretionary:			
1700	Collected	19	23	23
1701	Change in uncollected payments, Federal sources	2		
1750	Spending auth from offsetting collections, disc (total)	21	23	23
1900	Budget authority (total)	108	110	125
1930	Total budgetary resources available	108	110	125
	Change in obligated balance:			
	Unpaid obligations:			
3000	Unpaid obligations, brought forward, Oct 1	9	10	7
3010	New obligations, unexpired accounts	108	110	125
3011	Obligations ("upward adjustments"), expired accounts	1		
3020	Outlays (gross)	–107	–113	–124
3041	Recoveries of prior year unpaid obligations, expired	–1		
3050	Unpaid obligations, end of year	10	7	8
	Uncollected payments:			
3060	Uncollected pymts, Fed sources, brought forward, Oct 1	–3	–2	–2
3070	Change in uncollected pymts, Fed sources, unexpired	–2		
3071	Change in uncollected pymts, Fed sources, expired	3		
3090	Uncollected pymts, Fed sources, end of year	–2	–2	–2
	Memorandum (non-add) entries:			
3100	Obligated balance, start of year	6	8	5
3200	Obligated balance, end of year	8	5	6
	Budget authority and outlays, net:			
	Discretionary:			
4000	Budget authority, gross	108	110	125
	Outlays, gross:			
4010	Outlays from new discretionary authority	99	104	118
4011	Outlays from discretionary balances	8	9	6
4020	Outlays, gross (total)	107	113	124
	Offsets against gross budget authority and outlays:			
	Offsetting collections (collected) from:			
4030	Federal sources	–23	–23	–23
4040	Offsets against gross budget authority and outlays (total)	–23	–23	–23
	Additional offsets against gross budget authority only:			
4050	Change in uncollected pymts, Fed sources, unexpired	–2		
4052	Offsetting collections credited to expired accounts	4		
4060	Additional offsets against budget authority only (total)	2		
4070	Budget authority, net (discretionary)	87	87	102
4080	Outlays, net (discretionary)	84	90	101
4180	Budget authority, net (total)	87	87	102
4190	Outlays, net (total)	84	90	101

The Office of the Solicitor (Office) provides legal advice and counsel to the Secretary, the Secretariat, and all constituent bureaus and offices of the Department of the Interior. All attorneys employed in the Department for the purposes of providing legal services are under the supervision of the Solicitor, except the Justices of American Samoa and the attorneys in the Office of Congressional and Legislative Affairs, Office of Inspector General, and the Office of Hearings and Appeals. Additionally, the Office administers the Department's ethics program and manages Freedom of Information Act programs. The Office is comprised of headquarters staff, located in Washington, DC and 16 regional and field offices.

Object Classification (in millions of dollars)

Identification code 014–0107–0–1–306		2021 actual	2022 est.	2023 est.
	Direct obligations:			
	Personnel compensation:			
11.1	Full-time permanent	51	51	61
11.3	Other than full-time permanent	1	1	1
11.5	Other personnel compensation	2	2	2
11.9	Total personnel compensation	54	54	64
12.1	Civilian personnel benefits	18	18	22
23.1	Rental payments to GSA	3	4	4
23.3	Communications, utilities, and miscellaneous charges	1	1	1
25.1	Advisory and assistance services	2	2	2
25.2	Other services from non-Federal sources	1	1	1
25.3	Other goods and services from Federal sources	7	7	8
99.0	Direct obligations	86	87	102
99.0	Reimbursable obligations	21	23	23
99.5	Adjustment for rounding	1		
99.9	Total new obligations, unexpired accounts	108	110	125

Employment Summary

Identification code 014–0107–0–1–306		2021 actual	2022 est.	2023 est.
1001	Direct civilian full-time equivalent employment	390	386	416
2001	Reimbursable civilian full-time equivalent employment	94	99	99
3001	Allocation account civilian full-time equivalent employment	42	42	52

OFFICE OF INSPECTOR GENERAL

Federal Funds

SALARIES AND EXPENSES

For necessary expenses of the Office of Inspector General, $76,870,000, to remain available until September 30, 2024.

Note.—A full-year 2022 appropriation for this account was not enacted at the time the Budget was prepared; therefore, the Budget assumes this account is operating under the Continuing Appropriations Act, 2022 (Division A of Public Law 117–43, as amended). The amounts included for 2022 reflect the annualized level provided by the continuing resolution.

Program and Financing (in millions of dollars)

Identification code 014–0104–0–1–306		2021 actual	2022 est.	2023 est.
	Obligations by program activity:			
0001	Salaries and Expenses (Direct)	57	62	77
0005	2022 Bipartisan Infrastructure Law (P.L. 117–58)		1	4
0799	Total direct obligations	57	63	81
0801	Salaries and Expenses (Reimbursable)	3	3	2
0900	Total new obligations, unexpired accounts	60	66	83
	Budgetary resources:			
	Unobligated balance:			
1000	Unobligated balance brought forward, Oct 1	7	8	87
	Budget authority:			
	Appropriations, discretionary:			
1100	Appropriation	59	59	77
1121	Appropriations transferred from Office of the Secretary [014–0102]		2	
1121	Appropriations transferred from U.S. Geological Survey [014–0804]		1	
1121	Appropriations transferred from Energy Community Revitalization Program [014–2641]		23	
1121	Appropriations transferred from Wildland Fire Management [014–1125]		2	
1121	Appropriations transferred from OSMRE [014–5015]		56	
1160	Appropriation, discretionary (total)	59	143	77

Departmental Offices—Continued
Federal Funds—Continued

SALARIES AND EXPENSES—Continued

Program and Financing—Continued

Identification code 014–0104–0–1–306	2021 actual	2022 est.	2023 est.
Advance appropriations, discretionary:			
1173 Advance appropriations transferred from Office of the Secretary [014–0102]			1
1173 Advance appropriations transferred from Wildland Fire Management [014–1125]			1
1180 Advanced appropriation, discretionary (total)			2
Spending authority from offsetting collections, discretionary:			
1700 Collected	2	2	2
1900 Budget authority (total)	61	145	81
1930 Total budgetary resources available	68	153	168
Memorandum (non-add) entries:			
1941 Unexpired unobligated balance, end of year	8	87	85
Change in obligated balance:			
Unpaid obligations:			
3000 Unpaid obligations, brought forward, Oct 1	4	5	4
3010 New obligations, unexpired accounts	60	66	83
3020 Outlays (gross)	–59	–67	–82
3050 Unpaid obligations, end of year	5	4	5
Uncollected payments:			
3060 Uncollected pymts, Fed sources, brought forward, Oct 1	–1	–1	–1
3090 Uncollected pymts, Fed sources, end of year	–1	–1	–1
Memorandum (non-add) entries:			
3100 Obligated balance, start of year	3	4	3
3200 Obligated balance, end of year	4	3	4
Budget authority and outlays, net:			
Discretionary:			
4000 Budget authority, gross	61	145	81
Outlays, gross:			
4010 Outlays from new discretionary authority	51	59	74
4011 Outlays from discretionary balances	8	8	8
4020 Outlays, gross (total)	59	67	82
Offsets against gross budget authority and outlays:			
Offsetting collections (collected) from:			
4030 Federal sources	–2	–2	–2
4180 Budget authority, net (total)	59	143	79
4190 Outlays, net (total)	57	65	80

The mission of the Office of Inspector General is to provide independent oversight to promote accountability, integrity, economy, efficiency, and effectiveness within the U.S. Department of the Interior. This mission is achieved by conducting independent investigations, audits, inspections, and evaluations and by reporting our findings of fraud, waste, abuse, or mismanagement along with recommendations for improvement.

Object Classification (in millions of dollars)

Identification code 014–0104–0–1–306	2021 actual	2022 est.	2023 est.
Direct obligations:			
Personnel compensation:			
11.1 Full-time permanent	32	35	45
11.5 Other personnel compensation	3	3	3
11.9 Total personnel compensation	35	38	48
12.1 Civilian personnel benefits	14	15	18
21.0 Travel and transportation of persons		1	2
23.1 Rental payments to GSA	1	2	2
25.2 Other services from non-Federal sources	1	1	3
25.3 Other goods and services from Federal sources	4	4	6
25.7 Operation and maintenance of equipment	1	1	1
31.0 Equipment	1	1	1
99.0 Direct obligations	57	63	81
99.0 Reimbursable obligations	3	3	2
99.9 Total new obligations, unexpired accounts	60	66	83

Employment Summary

Identification code 014–0104–0–1–306	2021 actual	2022 est.	2023 est.
1001 Direct civilian full-time equivalent employment	247	258	322
2001 Reimbursable civilian full-time equivalent employment	15	15	12

NATIONAL INDIAN GAMING COMMISSION

Federal Funds

SALARIES AND EXPENSES

Program and Financing (in millions of dollars)

Identification code 014–0118–0–1–806	2021 actual	2022 est.	2023 est.
Obligations by program activity:			
0801 Salaries and Expenses (Reimbursable)	2	2	2
0900 Total new obligations, unexpired accounts (object class 25.2)	2	2	2
Budgetary resources:			
Unobligated balance:			
1000 Unobligated balance brought forward, Oct 1	2	2	2
Budget authority:			
Spending authority from offsetting collections, discretionary:			
1700 Collected	2	2	2
1930 Total budgetary resources available	4	4	4
Memorandum (non-add) entries:			
1941 Unexpired unobligated balance, end of year	2	2	2
Change in obligated balance:			
Unpaid obligations:			
3010 New obligations, unexpired accounts	2	2	2
3020 Outlays (gross)	–2	–2	–2
Budget authority and outlays, net:			
Discretionary:			
4000 Budget authority, gross	2	2	2
Outlays, gross:			
4010 Outlays from new discretionary authority	1	2	2
4011 Outlays from discretionary balances	1		
4020 Outlays, gross (total)	2	2	2
Offsets against gross budget authority and outlays:			
Offsetting collections (collected) from:			
4033 Non-Federal sources	–2	–2	–2
4180 Budget authority, net (total)			
4190 Outlays, net (total)			

The National Indian Gaming Commission conducts background investigations of individuals and entities with a financial interest in, or management responsibility for, potential management contracts. Tribes may also submit fingerprint cards to the Commission for processing by the Federal Bureau of Investigation and the Commission may charge a fee to process fingerprint cards on behalf of the Tribes. The Commission is reimbursed from the potential contractors to conduct these background investigations and also for fingerprint processing costs.

NATIONAL INDIAN GAMING COMMISSION, GAMING ACTIVITY FEES

Special and Trust Fund Receipts (in millions of dollars)

Identification code 014–5141–0–2–806	2021 actual	2022 est.	2023 est.
0100 Balance, start of year	1	1	1
Receipts:			
Current law:			
1110 National Indian Gaming Commission, Gaming Activity Fees	20	21	25
2000 Total: Balances and receipts	21	22	26
Appropriations:			
Current law:			
2101 National Indian Gaming Commission, Gaming Activity Fees	–20	–21	–25
2103 National Indian Gaming Commission, Gaming Activity Fees	–1	–1	–1
2132 National Indian Gaming Commission, Gaming Activity Fees	1	1	1
2199 Total current law appropriations	–20	–21	–25
2999 Total appropriations	–20	–21	–25

| 5099 | Balance, end of year | 1 | 1 | 1 |

Program and Financing (in millions of dollars)

Identification code 014–5141–0–2–806	2021 actual	2022 est.	2023 est.
Obligations by program activity:			
0001 National Indian Gaming Commission, Gaming Activity Fees (Direct)	21	24	24
Budgetary resources:			
Unobligated balance:			
1000 Unobligated balance brought forward, Oct 1	9	8	5
Budget authority:			
Appropriations, mandatory:			
1201 Appropriation (special or trust fund)	20	21	25
1203 Appropriation (previously unavailable)(special or trust)	1	1	1
1232 Appropriations and/or unobligated balance of appropriations temporarily reduced	–1	–1	–1
1260 Appropriations, mandatory (total)	20	21	25
1930 Total budgetary resources available	29	29	30
Memorandum (non-add) entries:			
1941 Unexpired unobligated balance, end of year	8	5	6
Change in obligated balance:			
Unpaid obligations:			
3000 Unpaid obligations, brought forward, Oct 1	4	6	8
3010 New obligations, unexpired accounts	21	24	24
3020 Outlays (gross)	–19	–22	–22
3050 Unpaid obligations, end of year	6	8	10
Memorandum (non-add) entries:			
3100 Obligated balance, start of year	4	6	8
3200 Obligated balance, end of year	6	8	10
Budget authority and outlays, net:			
Mandatory:			
4090 Budget authority, gross	20	21	25
Outlays, gross:			
4100 Outlays from new mandatory authority	10	14	17
4101 Outlays from mandatory balances	9	8	5
4110 Outlays, gross (total)	19	22	22
4180 Budget authority, net (total)	20	21	25
4190 Outlays, net (total)	19	22	22

The Indian Gaming Regulatory Act (IGRA) established the National Indian Gaming Commission (NIGC) as an independent Federal regulatory agency within the Department of the Interior. The purpose of the IGRA and the NIGC is to support and promote tribal economic development, self-sufficiency and strong tribal governments through the operation of gaming on Indian lands. The Commission collaborates with Tribes to monitor and regulate gaming activities conducted on Indian Lands to ensure that gaming operations are conducted with integrity and that Tribes are the primary beneficiaries of gaming revenues. IGRA authorizes the Commission to assess and collect fees on tribal gaming revenues to cover agency operating costs.

Object Classification (in millions of dollars)

Identification code 014–5141–0–2–806	2021 actual	2022 est.	2023 est.
Direct obligations:			
11.1 Personnel compensation: Full-time permanent	13	15	15
12.1 Civilian personnel benefits	4	5	5
23.1 Rental payments to GSA	2	2	2
25.3 Other goods and services from Federal sources	2	2	2
99.9 Total new obligations, unexpired accounts	21	24	24

Employment Summary

Identification code 014–5141–0–2–806	2021 actual	2022 est.	2023 est.
1001 Direct civilian full-time equivalent employment	108	129	129

DEPARTMENT-WIDE PROGRAMS

Federal Funds

OFFICE OF NATURAL RESOURCES REVENUE

For necessary expenses for management of the collection and disbursement of royalties, fees, and other mineral revenue proceeds, and for grants and cooperative agreements, as authorized by law, $174,977,000, to remain available until September 30, 2024; of which $69,751,000 shall remain available until expended for the purpose of mineral revenue management activities: Provided, That notwithstanding any other provision of law, $15,000 shall be available for refunds of overpayments in connection with certain Indian leases in which the Secretary of the Interior concurred with the claimed refund due, to pay amounts owed to Indian allottees or tribes, or to correct prior unrecoverable erroneous payments.

Note.—A full-year 2022 appropriation for this account was not enacted at the time the Budget was prepared; therefore, the Budget assumes this account is operating under the Continuing Appropriations Act, 2022 (Division A of Public Law 117–43, as amended). The amounts included for 2022 reflect the annualized level provided by the continuing resolution.

Program and Financing (in millions of dollars)

Identification code 014–1113–0–1–306	2021 actual	2022 est.	2023 est.
Obligations by program activity:			
0001 Office of Natural Resources Revenue	157	147	174
0100 Direct program activities, subtotal	157	147	174
0801 Office of Natural Resources Revenue [Reimbursable]		1	1
0900 Total new obligations, unexpired accounts	157	148	175
Budgetary resources:			
Unobligated balance:			
1000 Unobligated balance brought forward, Oct 1	13	9	11
1021 Recoveries of prior year unpaid obligations	2	1	1
1070 Unobligated balance (total)	15	10	12
Budget authority:			
Appropriations, discretionary:			
1100 Appropriation	148	148	175
Spending authority from offsetting collections, discretionary:			
1700 Collected	2	1	1
1701 Change in uncollected payments, Federal sources	1		
1750 Spending auth from offsetting collections, disc (total)	3	1	1
1900 Budget authority (total)	151	149	176
1930 Total budgetary resources available	166	159	188
Memorandum (non-add) entries:			
1941 Unexpired unobligated balance, end of year	9	11	13
Change in obligated balance:			
Unpaid obligations:			
3000 Unpaid obligations, brought forward, Oct 1	53	65	48
3010 New obligations, unexpired accounts	157	148	175
3020 Outlays (gross)	–143	–164	–173
3040 Recoveries of prior year unpaid obligations, unexpired	–2	–1	–1
3050 Unpaid obligations, end of year	65	48	49
Uncollected payments:			
3060 Uncollected pymts, Fed sources, brought forward, Oct 1		–1	–1
3070 Change in uncollected pymts, Fed sources, unexpired	–1		
3090 Uncollected pymts, Fed sources, end of year	–1	–1	–1
Memorandum (non-add) entries:			
3100 Obligated balance, start of year	53	64	47
3200 Obligated balance, end of year	64	47	48
Budget authority and outlays, net:			
Discretionary:			
4000 Budget authority, gross	151	149	176
Outlays, gross:			
4010 Outlays from new discretionary authority	95	116	137
4011 Outlays from discretionary balances	48	48	36
4020 Outlays, gross (total)	143	164	173
Offsets against gross budget authority and outlays:			
Offsetting collections (collected) from:			
4030 Federal sources	–2	–1	–1
Additional offsets against gross budget authority only:			
4050 Change in uncollected pymts, Fed sources, unexpired	–1		
4070 Budget authority, net (discretionary)	148	148	175
4080 Outlays, net (discretionary)	141	163	172
4180 Budget authority, net (total)	148	148	175
4190 Outlays, net (total)	141	163	172

OFFICE OF NATURAL RESOURCES REVENUE—Continued

The Office of Natural Resources Revenue (ONRR) is responsible for ensuring revenue from Federal and Indian mineral leases is effectively, efficiently, and accurately collected, accounted for, analyzed, audited, and disbursed to recipients in a timely manner. ONRR revenue distributions are made to States, Tribes, individual Indian mineral royalty owners, and U.S. Treasury accounts.

Object Classification (in millions of dollars)

Identification code 014–1113–0–1–306		2021 actual	2022 est.	2023 est.
	Direct obligations:			
	Personnel compensation:			
11.1	Full-time permanent	61	60	60
11.3	Other than full-time permanent	1	1	1
11.5	Other personnel compensation	2	1	2
11.9	Total personnel compensation	64	62	63
12.1	Civilian personnel benefits	23	21	23
23.1	Rental payments to GSA	3	3	3
25.1	Advisory and assistance services	28	18	41
25.2	Other services from non-Federal sources	2	2	2
25.3	Other goods and services from Federal sources	12	14	14
25.4	Operation and maintenance of facilities	1	1	1
25.7	Operation and maintenance of equipment	13	13	15
31.0	Equipment	....	1	....
41.0	Grants, subsidies, and contributions	11	12	12
99.0	Direct obligations	157	147	174
99.0	Reimbursable obligations	....	1	1
99.9	Total new obligations, unexpired accounts	157	148	175

Employment Summary

Identification code 014–1113–0–1–306	2021 actual	2022 est.	2023 est.
1001 Direct civilian full-time equivalent employment	573	600	608
2001 Reimbursable civilian full-time equivalent employment	6	5	5

PAYMENTS IN LIEU OF TAXES

For necessary expenses for payments authorized by Chapter 69 of title 31, United States Code, $535,000,000.

Note.—A full-year 2022 appropriation for this account was not enacted at the time the Budget was prepared; therefore, the Budget assumes this account is operating under the Continuing Appropriations Act, 2022 (Division A of Public Law 117–43, as amended). The amounts included for 2022 reflect the annualized level provided by the continuing resolution.

Program and Financing (in millions of dollars)

Identification code 014–1114–0–1–806		2021 actual	2022 est.	2023 est.
	Obligations by program activity:			
0001	Payments in Lieu of Taxes (Direct)	530	525	535
0900	Total new obligations, unexpired accounts (object class 41.0)	530	525	535
	Budgetary resources:			
	Budget authority:			
	Appropriations, discretionary:			
1100	Appropriations, discretionary	....	525	535
	Appropriations, mandatory:			
1200	Appropriation	530	....	....
1900	Budget authority (total)	530	525	535
1930	Total budgetary resources available	530	525	535
	Change in obligated balance:			
	Unpaid obligations:			
3010	New obligations, unexpired accounts	530	525	535
3020	Outlays (gross)	–530	–525	–535
	Budget authority and outlays, net:			
	Discretionary:			
4000	Budget authority, gross	....	525	535
	Outlays, gross:			
4010	Outlays from new discretionary authority	....	525	535
	Mandatory:			
4090	Budget authority, gross	530	....	....
	Outlays, gross:			
4100	Outlays from new mandatory authority	530	....	....
4180	Budget authority, net (total)	530	525	535
4190	Outlays, net (total)	530	525	535

Public Law 94–565 (31 U.S.C. 6901–07), as amended, authorizes Payments in Lieu of Taxes ("PILT payments") to counties and other units of local government for lands within their boundaries administered by the Bureau of Land Management, the National Park Service, the Fish and Wildlife Service, and the Bureau of Reclamation. Additionally, PILT payments cover Federal lands administered by the U.S. Forest Service, U.S. Army Corps of Engineers, and the Utah Reclamation Mitigation and Conservation Commission. The PILT payment formula is based on a number of factors, including the amount of Federal land within an eligible unit of local government, its population, and certain other Federal payments the local government may receive.

From the inception of the PILT program in 1977 through 2007, PILT funding was subject to annual appropriations. The Emergency Economic Stabilization Act of 2008 provided a five-year (FYs 2008–2012) mandatory funding stream for PILT at the full authorization levels calculated using the existing PILT formula. The Moving Ahead for Progress in the 21st Century Act (P.L. 112–141) extended the mandatory authorization through 2013, and the Agricultural Act of 2014 (P.L. 113–79) extended the mandatory authorization through 2014. The Carl Levin and Howard P. "Buck" McKeon National Defense Authorization Act for Fiscal Year 2015 and the Consolidated and Further Continuing Appropriations Act (P.L. 113–235) extended PILT payment authority through 2015 with a combination of discretionary and mandatory funds. The Consolidated Appropriations Act of 2016 (P.L. 114–113) provided discretionary PILT funding within the Office of the Secretary, Departmental Operations account to extend payment authority through 2016. The Consolidated Appropriations Act, 2017 (P.L. 115–31) provided discretionary PILT funding within Department-wide Programs. Congressional appropriations for 2018 (P.L. 115–141), 2019 (P.L. 116–6), 2020 (P.L. 116–94), and 2021 (P.L. 116–260) each provided PILT funding at the full authorized levels. The Extending Government Funding and Delivering Emergency Assistance Act; Division A, Continuing Appropriations Act of 2022 (P.L. 117–43; as amended by P.L. 117–70 and P.L. 117–86) extended PILT payment authority through March 11, 2022. The 2023 Budget proposes discretionary funding for PILT payments within Department-wide Programs.

Employment Summary

Identification code 014–1114–0–1–806	2021 actual	2022 est.	2023 est.
1001 Direct civilian full-time equivalent employment	1	2	2

CENTRAL HAZARDOUS MATERIALS FUND

For necessary expenses of the Department of the Interior and any of its component offices and bureaus for the response action, including associated activities, performed pursuant to the Comprehensive Environmental Response, Compensation, and Liability Act (42 U.S.C. 9601 et seq.), $10,064,000, to remain available until expended.

Note.—A full-year 2022 appropriation for this account was not enacted at the time the Budget was prepared; therefore, the Budget assumes this account is operating under the Continuing Appropriations Act, 2022 (Division A of Public Law 117–43, as amended). The amounts included for 2022 reflect the annualized level provided by the continuing resolution.

Program and Financing (in millions of dollars)

Identification code 014–1121–0–1–304		2021 actual	2022 est.	2023 est.
	Obligations by program activity:			
0001	Remedial Action	10	10	10
0801	Central Hazardous Materials Fund (Reimbursable)	5	5	5
0900	Total new obligations, unexpired accounts	15	15	15

DEPARTMENT OF THE INTERIOR

		2021 actual	2022 est.	2023 est.
	Budgetary resources:			
	Unobligated balance:			
1000	Unobligated balance brought forward, Oct 1	22	20	21
1021	Recoveries of prior year unpaid obligations	1	1	1
1070	Unobligated balance (total)	23	21	22
	Budget authority:			
	Appropriations, discretionary:			
1100	Appropriation	10	10	10
	Spending authority from offsetting collections, discretionary:			
1700	Collected	2	5	5
1900	Budget authority (total)	12	15	15
1930	Total budgetary resources available	35	36	37
	Memorandum (non-add) entries:			
1941	Unexpired unobligated balance, end of year	20	21	22
	Change in obligated balance:			
	Unpaid obligations:			
3000	Unpaid obligations, brought forward, Oct 1	22	25	14
3010	New obligations, unexpired accounts	15	15	15
3020	Outlays (gross)	−11	−25	−15
3040	Recoveries of prior year unpaid obligations, unexpired	−1	−1	−1
3050	Unpaid obligations, end of year	25	14	13
	Memorandum (non-add) entries:			
3100	Obligated balance, start of year	22	25	14
3200	Obligated balance, end of year	25	14	13
	Budget authority and outlays, net:			
	Discretionary:			
4000	Budget authority, gross	12	15	15
	Outlays, gross:			
4010	Outlays from new discretionary authority	3	6	6
4011	Outlays from discretionary balances	8	19	9
4020	Outlays, gross (total)	11	25	15
	Offsets against gross budget authority and outlays:			
	Offsetting collections (collected) from:			
4033	Non-Federal sources	−2	−5	−5
4180	Budget authority, net (total)	10	10	10
4190	Outlays, net (total)	9	20	10

The Comprehensive Environmental Response, Compensation and Liability Act, as amended (42 U.S.C. 9601 et seq.) authorizes the President to investigate and clean up releases of hazardous substances. Under Executive Order 12580, the Secretary of the Interior is vested with the authority to address releases or threatened releases of hazardous substances on lands under the Department's jurisdiction, custody or control. The Central Hazardous Materials Fund is used to fund remedial investigations and cleanup of hazardous waste sites on such lands and to enable the Department to pursue potentially responsible parties for recovery of costs. The Fund is authorized to collect and retain within this account amounts recovered from responsible parties.

Object Classification (in millions of dollars)

Identification code 014–1121–0–1–304		2021 actual	2022 est.	2023 est.
	Direct obligations:			
	Personnel compensation:			
11.1	Full-time permanent - Direct	1	1	1
11.1	Full-time permanent - Allocation	1	1	1
11.9	Total personnel compensation	2	2	2
12.1	Civilian personnel benefits	1	1	1
25.2	Other services from non-Federal sources	6	6	6
25.3	Other goods and services from Federal sources	1	1	1
99.0	Direct obligations	10	10	10
99.0	Reimbursable obligations	5	5	5
99.9	Total new obligations, unexpired accounts	15	15	15

Employment Summary

Identification code 014–1121–0–1–304	2021 actual	2022 est.	2023 est.
1001 Direct civilian full-time equivalent employment	4	4	4

NATURAL RESOURCE DAMAGE ASSESSMENT AND RESTORATION

NATURAL RESOURCE DAMAGE ASSESSMENT FUND

To conduct natural resource damage assessment, restoration activities, and onshore oil spill preparedness by the Department of the Interior necessary to carry out the provisions of the Comprehensive Environmental Response, Compensation, and Liability Act (42 U.S.C. 9601 et seq.), the Federal Water Pollution Control Act (33 U.S.C. 1251 et seq.), the Oil Pollution Act of 1990 (33 U.S.C. 2701 et seq.), and 54 U.S.C. 100721 et seq., $8,059,000, to remain available until expended.

Note.—A full-year 2022 appropriation for this account was not enacted at the time the Budget was prepared; therefore, the Budget assumes this account is operating under the Continuing Appropriations Act, 2022 (Division A of Public Law 117–43, as amended). The amounts included for 2022 reflect the annualized level provided by the continuing resolution.

Special and Trust Fund Receipts (in millions of dollars)

Identification code 014–1618–0–1–302		2021 actual	2022 est.	2023 est.
0100	Balance, start of year		1	1
	Receipts:			
	Current law:			
1130	Natural Resources Damages from Legal Actions	568	597	597
1140	Natural Resources Damages from Legal Actions, EOI	6	10	12
1199	Total current law receipts	574	607	609
1999	Total receipts	574	607	609
2000	Total: Balances and receipts	574	608	610
	Appropriations:			
	Current law:			
2101	Natural Resource Damage Assessment Fund	−573	−607	−609
5099	Balance, end of year	1	1	1

Program and Financing (in millions of dollars)

Identification code 014–1618–0–1–302		2021 actual	2022 est.	2023 est.
	Obligations by program activity:			
0001	Damage assessments	7	6	6
0002	Prince William Sound restoration	6	3	3
0003	Other restoration	228	300	300
0004	Program management	4	4	4
0005	Onshore oil spill preparedness		1	1
0900	Total new obligations, unexpired accounts	245	314	314
	Budgetary resources:			
	Unobligated balance:			
1000	Unobligated balance brought forward, Oct 1	2,009	2,136	2,376
1001	Discretionary unobligated balance brought fwd, Oct 1	12		
1010	Unobligated balance transfer to other accts [013–4316]	−193	−50	−50
1010	Unobligated balance transfer to other accts [012–4368]	−13	−4	−4
1021	Recoveries of prior year unpaid obligations	2	1	1
1070	Unobligated balance (total)	1,805	2,083	2,323
	Budget authority:			
	Appropriations, discretionary:			
1100	Appropriation	8	8	8
	Appropriations, mandatory:			
1201	Appropriation (special or trust fund)	573	607	609
1220	Appropriations transferred to other acct [013–4316]	−4	−6	−6
1220	Appropriations transferred to other acct [068–4365]	−1	−2	−2
1260	Appropriations, mandatory (total)	568	599	601
1900	Budget authority (total)	576	607	609
1930	Total budgetary resources available	2,381	2,690	2,932
	Memorandum (non-add) entries:			
1941	Unexpired unobligated balance, end of year	2,136	2,376	2,618
	Change in obligated balance:			
	Unpaid obligations:			
3000	Unpaid obligations, brought forward, Oct 1	99	81	146
3010	New obligations, unexpired accounts	245	314	314
3020	Outlays (gross)	−261	−248	−304
3040	Recoveries of prior year unpaid obligations, unexpired	−2	−1	−1
3050	Unpaid obligations, end of year	81	146	155
	Memorandum (non-add) entries:			
3100	Obligated balance, start of year	99	81	146
3200	Obligated balance, end of year	81	146	155
	Budget authority and outlays, net:			
	Discretionary:			
4000	Budget authority, gross	8	8	8

NATURAL RESOURCE DAMAGE ASSESSMENT AND RESTORATION—Continued

Program and Financing—Continued

Identification code 014–1618–0–1–302	2021 actual	2022 est.	2023 est.
	Outlays, gross:			
4010	Outlays from new discretionary authority	6	6	6
4011	Outlays from discretionary balances	2	2	2
4020	Outlays, gross (total)	8	8	8
	Mandatory:			
4090	Budget authority, gross	568	599	601
	Outlays, gross:			
4100	Outlays from new mandatory authority	10	48	48
4101	Outlays from mandatory balances	243	192	248
4110	Outlays, gross (total)	253	240	296
4180	Budget authority, net (total)	576	607	609
4190	Outlays, net (total)	261	248	304
	Memorandum (non-add) entries:			
5000	Total investments, SOY: Federal securities: Par value	1,896	2,025	2,250
5001	Total investments, EOY: Federal securities: Par value	2,025	2,250	2,400

Under the Natural Resource Damage Assessment and Restoration Fund (Restoration Fund), natural resource damage assessments are performed to provide the basis for claims against responsible parties for the restoration of injured natural resources. Funds are appropriated to conduct damage assessments, provide restoration support, prepare for response to potential inland oil spills, and for program management. In addition, funds will be received for the restoration of damaged resources and other activities and for natural resource damage assessments from responsible parties through cooperative assessment agreements, negotiated settlements, or other legal actions by the Department of the Interior. Responsible parties may also provide in-kind services to restore injured natural resources.

Restoration activities include: 1) the replacement and enhancement of affected resources; 2) acquisition of equivalent resources and services; and, 3) long-term environmental monitoring and research programs directed to the prevention, containment, and amelioration of hazardous substances and oil spill sites.

The Restoration Fund operates as a Department-wide program, incorporating the interdisciplinary expertise of its various bureaus and offices. Natural resource damage assessments and the restoration of injured natural resources are authorized by the Comprehensive Environmental Response, Compensation, and Liability Act, as amended (42 U.S.C. 9601 et seq.), Federal Water Pollution Control Act, as amended (33 U.S.C. 1251 et seq.), the Oil Pollution Act of 1990 (33 U.S.C. 2701 et seq.), and the System Unit Resource Protection Act (54 U.S.C. 100721). Since 1992, amounts received by the United States and its State and tribal co-trustee partners from responsible parties for restoration or reimbursement in settlement of natural resource damages may be deposited in the Fund and shall accrue interest.

Object Classification (in millions of dollars)

Identification code 014–1618–0–1–302	2021 actual	2022 est.	2023 est.
	Direct obligations:			
	Personnel compensation:			
11.1	Full-time permanent - Direct	2	2	2
11.1	Full-time permanent - Allocation	7	8	8
11.3	Other than full-time permanent - Allocation	2	...	...
11.9	Total personnel compensation	11	10	10
12.1	Civilian personnel benefits - Allocation	3	3	3
12.1	Civilian personnel benefits - Direct	1	1	1
25.1	Advisory and assistance services - Allocation	1	1	1
25.2	Other services from non-Federal sources - Allocation	7	1	1
25.3	Other goods and services from Federal sources - Direct	1	1	1
25.3	Other goods and services from Federal sources - Allocation	1	2	2
31.0	Equipment - Allocation	1	1	1
32.0	Land and structures - Allocation	2	2	2
41.0	Grants, subsidies, and contributions - Allocation	24	25	25
42.0	Insurance claims and indemnities - Direct	193	267	267
99.0	Direct obligations	245	314	314

99.9	Total new obligations, unexpired accounts	245	314	314

Employment Summary

Identification code 014–1618–0–1–302	2021 actual	2022 est.	2023 est.
1001	Direct civilian full-time equivalent employment	18	18	18

EXXON VALDEZ RESTORATION PROGRAM

The 2023 Budget reflects the receipts, transfers, and mandatory spending by the Department of the Interior associated with the civil and criminal settlements resulting from the 1989 *Exxon Valdez* oil spill in the Prince William Sound and surrounding areas. Funding from the settlements, including interest, is provided to Federal and State of Alaska natural resource trustee agencies to restore the natural resources and services damaged by the spill. The *Exxon Valdez* Oil Spill Trustee Council consists of three State and three Federal trustees who oversee restoration of the injured ecosystem through the use of civil settlement funds. The criminal settlement funds are managed separately by the Federal and Alaska State governments, but are coordinated with the Council.

WILDLAND FIRE MANAGEMENT

(INCLUDING TRANSFERS OF FUNDS)

For necessary expenses for fire preparedness, fire suppression operations, fire science and research, emergency rehabilitation, fuels management activities, and rural fire assistance by the Department of the Interior, $1,199,630,000, to remain available until expended, of which not to exceed $10,000,000 shall be for the renovation or construction of fire facilities: Provided, That such funds are also available for repayment of advances to other appropriation accounts from which funds were previously transferred for such purposes: Provided further, That of the funds provided $304,344,000 is for fuels management activities: Provided further, That of the funds provided $20,470,000 is for burned area rehabilitation: Provided further, That persons hired pursuant to 43 U.S.C. 1469 may be furnished subsistence and lodging without cost from funds available from this appropriation: Provided further, That notwithstanding 42 U.S.C. 1856d, sums received by a bureau or office of the Department of the Interior for fire protection rendered pursuant to 42 U.S.C. 1856 et seq., protection of United States property, may be credited to the appropriation from which funds were expended to provide that protection, and are available without fiscal year limitation: Provided further, That using the amounts designated under this title of this Act, the Secretary of the Interior may enter into procurement contracts, grants, or cooperative agreements, for fuels management activities, and for training and monitoring associated with such fuels management activities on Federal land, or on adjacent non-Federal land for activities that benefit resources on Federal land: Provided further, That the costs of implementing any cooperative agreement between the Federal Government and any non-Federal entity may be shared, as mutually agreed on by the affected parties: Provided further, That notwithstanding requirements of the Competition in Contracting Act, the Secretary, for purposes of fuels management activities, may obtain maximum practicable competition among: (1) local private, nonprofit, or cooperative entities; (2) Youth Conservation Corps crews, Public Lands Corps (Public Law 109–154), or related partnerships with State, local, or nonprofit youth groups; (3) small or micro-businesses; or (4) other entities that will hire or train locally a significant percentage, defined as 50 percent or more, of the project workforce to complete such contracts: Provided further, That in implementing this section, the Secretary shall develop written guidance to field units to ensure accountability and consistent application of the authorities provided herein: Provided further, That funds appropriated under this heading may be used to reimburse the United States Fish and Wildlife Service and the National Marine Fisheries Service for the costs of carrying out their responsibilities under the Endangered Species Act of 1973 (16 U.S.C. 1531 et seq.) to consult and conference, as required by section 7 of such Act, in connection with wildland fire management activities: Provided further, That the Secretary of the Interior may use wildland fire appropriations to enter into leases of real property with local governments, at or below fair market value, to construct capitalized improvements for fire facilities on such leased properties, including but not limited to fire guard stations, retardant stations, and other initial attack and fire support facilities, and to make advance payments for any such lease or for construction activity associated with the lease: Provided further, That the Secretary of the Interior and the Secretary

DEPARTMENT OF THE INTERIOR

of Agriculture may authorize the transfer of funds appropriated for wildland fire management, in an aggregate amount not to exceed $50,000,000, between the Departments when such transfers would facilitate and expedite wildland fire management programs and projects: *Provided further,* That funds provided for wildfire suppression shall be available for support of Federal emergency response actions: *Provided further,* That funds appropriated under this heading shall be available for assistance to or through the Department of State in connection with forest and rangeland research, technical information, and assistance in foreign countries, and, with the concurrence of the Secretary of State, shall be available to support forestry, wildland fire management, and related natural resource activities outside the United States and its territories and possessions, including technical assistance, education and training, and cooperation with United States and international organizations: *Provided further,* That of the funds provided under this heading $383,657,000 is provided as the average costs for wildfire suppression operations to meet the terms of a concurrent resolution on the budget.

Note.—A full-year 2022 appropriation for this account was not enacted at the time the Budget was prepared; therefore, the Budget assumes this account is operating under the Continuing Appropriations Act, 2022 (Division A of Public Law 117–43, as amended). The amounts included for 2022 reflect the annualized level provided by the continuing resolution.

WILDLAND FIRE MANAGEMENT

[(INCLUDING TRANSFER OF FUNDS)]

[For an additional amount for "Wildland Fire Management", $100,000,000, to remain available until expended, for necessary expenses related to wildfires]: *Provided,* That of the amounts provided under this heading in this Act, $55,000,000 shall be for hazardous fuels management activities: *Provided further,* That of the amounts provided under this heading in this Act, $45,000,000, shall be for burned area recovery.] *(Disaster Relief Supplemental Appropriations Act, 2022.)*

WILDLAND FIRE MANAGEMENT

[(INCLUDING TRANSFERS OF FUNDS)]

[For an additional amount for "Wildland Fire Management", $1,458,000,000, to remain available until expended: *Provided,* That $407,600,000, to remain available until expended, shall be made available for fiscal year 2022, $262,600,000, to remain available until expended, shall be made available for fiscal year 2023, $262,600,000, to remain available until expended, shall be made available for fiscal year 2024, $262,600,000, to remain available until expended, shall be made available for fiscal year 2025, and $262,600,000, to remain available until expended, shall be made available for fiscal year 2026: *Provided further,* That of the funds made available under this heading in this Act, the following amounts shall be for the following purposes for the following fiscal years—]

([1])[$1,055,000,000 for the Secretary of the Interior to carry out activities for the Department of the Interior, as authorized in section 40803 of division D of this Act, including fuels management activities, of which $327,000,000, to remain available until expended, shall be made available for fiscal year 2022 and $182,000,000, to remain available until expended, shall be made available for each of fiscal years 2023 through 2026;]

[(2) In addition to amounts made available in paragraph (1) for fuels management activities, $35,600,000 for each of fiscal years 2022 through 2026 for such purpose; and]

[(3) In addition to amounts made available in paragraph (1) for burned area rehabilitation, $45,000,000 for each of fiscal years 2022 through 2026 for such purpose:]

[*Provided further,* That up to $2,000,000 for each of fiscal years 2022 through 2026 from funds made available in paragraphs (2) and (3) of the preceding proviso shall be for implementation of the Tribal Forestry Protection Act, as amended (Public Law 108–278): *Provided further,* That the Secretary may transfer the funds provided under this heading in this Act to any other account in the Department of the Interior to carry out such purposes: *Provided further,* That funds appropriated under this heading in this Act may be transferred to the United States Fish and Wildlife Service and the National Marine Fisheries Service for the costs of carrying out their responsibilities under the Endangered Species Act of 1973 (16 U.S.C. 1531 et seq.) to consult and conference, as required by section 7 of such Act, in connection with wildland fire management activities: *Provided further,* That up to 3 percent of the amounts made available under this heading in this Act in each of fiscal years 2022 through 2026 shall be for salaries, expenses, and administration: *Provided further,* That one-half of one percent of the amounts made available under this heading in this Act in each of fiscal years 2022 through 2026 shall be transferred to the Office of Inspector General of the Department of the Interior for oversight of funding provided to the Department of the Interior in this title in this Act: *Provided further,* That such amount is designated by the Congress as being for an emergency requirement pursuant to section 4112(a) of H. Con. Res. 71 (115th Congress), the concurrent resolution on the budget for fiscal year 2018, and to section 251(b) of the Balanced Budget and Emergency Deficit Control Act of 1985.] *(Infrastructure Investments and Jobs Appropriations Act.)*

Program and Financing (in millions of dollars)

Identification code 014–1125–0–1–302		2021 actual	2022 est.	2023 est.
	Obligations by program activity:			
0002	Preparedness	348	350	450
0004	Fire suppression operations	411	400	384
0006	Fuels Management	228	225	285
0008	Burned area rehabilitation	22	23	25
0009	Facilities Construction and Maintenance	17	20	20
0010	Joint Fire Science	3	3	4
0011	Wildfire Suppression Cap Adjustment	238	252	285
0012	2022 Disaster Supplemental (P.L. 117–43)		40	40
0013	2022 Bipartisan Infrastructure Law (P.L. 117–58)		185	350
0799	Total direct obligations	1,267	1,498	1,843
0801	Fire reimbursable	63	82	82
0900	Total new obligations, unexpired accounts	1,330	1,580	1,925
	Budgetary resources:			
	Unobligated balance:			
1000	Unobligated balance brought forward, Oct 1	122	132	443
1011	Unobligated balance transfer from other acct [014–0130]	232	282	295
1021	Recoveries of prior year unpaid obligations	26	30	30
1070	Unobligated balance (total)	380	444	768
	Budget authority:			
	Appropriations, discretionary:			
1100	Appropriation	609	609	816
1100	Appropriation - Fire Suppression	384	384	384
1100	Appropriation - Disaster Relief Supplemental [P.L. 117–43]		100	
1100	Appropriation - Bipartisan Infrastructure Law [P.L. 117–58]		407	
1120	Appropriations transferred to other acct [014–0104]		–2	
1121	Appropriations transferred from other acct [012–1106]	1		
1121	Appropriations transferred from other acct [012–1115]	2		
1121	Appropriations transferred from other acct [014–0130]	28		
1121	Appropriations transferred from other acct [012–1122]	1		
1160	Appropriation, discretionary (total)	1,025	1,498	1,200
	Advance appropriations, discretionary:			
1170	Advance appropriation			263
1172	Advance appropriations transferred to other accounts [014–0104]			–1
1180	Advanced appropriation, discretionary (total)			262
	Spending authority from offsetting collections, discretionary:			
1700	Collected	58	75	75
1701	Change in uncollected payments, Federal sources	–1	6	3
1750	Spending auth from offsetting collections, disc (total)	57	81	78
1900	Budget authority (total)	1,082	1,579	1,540
1930	Total budgetary resources available	1,462	2,023	2,308
	Memorandum (non-add) entries:			
1941	Unexpired unobligated balance, end of year	132	443	383
	Change in obligated balance:			
	Unpaid obligations:			
3000	Unpaid obligations, brought forward, Oct 1	357	363	491
3010	New obligations, unexpired accounts	1,330	1,580	1,925
3020	Outlays (gross)	–1,298	–1,422	–1,651
3040	Recoveries of prior year unpaid obligations, unexpired	–26	–30	–30
3050	Unpaid obligations, end of year	363	491	735
	Uncollected payments:			
3060	Uncollected pymts, Fed sources, brought forward, Oct 1	–34	–33	–39
3070	Change in uncollected pymts, Fed sources, unexpired	1	–6	–3
3090	Uncollected pymts, Fed sources, end of year	–33	–39	–42
	Memorandum (non-add) entries:			
3100	Obligated balance, start of year	323	330	452
3200	Obligated balance, end of year	330	452	693
	Budget authority and outlays, net:			
	Discretionary:			
4000	Budget authority, gross	1,082	1,579	1,540
	Outlays, gross:			
4010	Outlays from new discretionary authority	793	960	1,185
4011	Outlays from discretionary balances	505	462	466
4020	Outlays, gross (total)	1,298	1,422	1,651
	Offsets against gross budget authority and outlays:			
	Offsetting collections (collected) from:			
4030	Federal sources	–25	–16	–15

WILDLAND FIRE MANAGEMENT—Continued
Program and Financing—Continued

Identification code 014–1125–0–1–302		2021 actual	2022 est.	2023 est.
4033	Non-Federal sources	–33	–59	–60
4040	Offsets against gross budget authority and outlays (total)	–58	–75	–75
	Additional offsets against gross budget authority only:			
4050	Change in uncollected pymts, Fed sources, unexpired	1	–6	–3
4070	Budget authority, net (discretionary)	1,025	1,498	1,462
4080	Outlays, net (discretionary)	1,240	1,347	1,576
4180	Budget authority, net (total)	1,025	1,498	1,462
4190	Outlays, net (total)	1,240	1,347	1,576

Preparedness.—Funds the non-emergency and predictable aspects of the Department of the Interior's (DOI) wildland fire program, including the initial attack suppression action on wildfires. Preparedness includes readiness, operational planning, oversight, procurement, training, supervision, and deployment of wildland fire suppression personnel and equipment prior to wildland fire occurrence, and rural fire readiness, in which assistance is provided to local cooperators to enhance their capacity to protect remote communities and natural resources. It also includes activities related to program monitoring and evaluation, and integration of fire into land-use planning.

Suppression Operations.—Funds the emergency and unpredictable aspects of DOI's wildland fire management program. Suppression operations include the total spectrum of management actions taken on wildland fires in a safe, cost-effective manner, considering public benefits and values to be protected consistent with resource objectives and land management plans. This activity includes emergency actions taken during and immediately following a wildfire to stabilize the soil and structures to prevent erosion, floods, landslides, and further resource damage. Generally, emergency stabilization actions may be performed within one year of containment of a fire; however, exceptions to this time limit are allowed under certain circumstances. In fiscal years 2010 through 2017, funding for the ten-year average of inflation-adjusted suppression obligations was split between the FLAME Wildfire Suppression Reserve Fund and this appropriation. The 2023 Budget request fully funds suppression operations at the ten-year average of obligations as reported in the 2015 President's Budget, in accordance with the Consolidated Appropriations Act, 2018 (P.L. 115–141). This Act also amended the Balanced Budget and Emergency Deficit Control Act to provide additional new budget authority for fiscal years 2020 through 2027. This additional budget authority is provided in the Wildfire Suppression Operations Reserve Fund account and made available subject to the requirements in P.L. 115–141. This additional new budget authority will help ensure that adequate resources are available to the Departments of the Interior and Agriculture to fight wildland fires, protect communities, and safeguard human life during the most severe wildland fire seasons. The DOI and Forest Service wildland fire management programs will continue to strengthen oversight and accountability of suppression spending and use risk management principles to guide decision-making at the strategic, program, and operational levels.

Fuels Management.—Funds the application of fuels treatments aimed at mitigating risk to communities and their values, including areas in the wildland urban interface. This activity may also conduct treatments that improve the integrity and resilience of our forests and rangelands. The Fuels Management activity will contribute to community adaptation to fire and improve the ability to safely and appropriately respond to wildfire. Funding for the Fuels Management activity covers the planning, operational aspects, and monitoring of fuels treatments. The program will utilize such treatment methods as prescribed fire, mechanical, chemical, and biological treatments or a combination of methods.

Other Operations.—Funds all other aspects of the wildland fire management program, which includes Fire Facilities Construction and Maintenance, Burned Area Rehabilitation, and Joint Fire Science. The Fire Facilities Construction and Maintenance program funds construction and maintenance of facilities to house firefighters and equipment used in wildland firefighting and fuels management activities. The Burned Area Rehabilitation program begins the recovery process for lands and resources damaged by wildland fires that would not return to fire adapted conditions without intervention. Soil stabilization and the introduction of native and other desirable plant species are employed for up to three years, or up to five years under certain circumstances, following containment of a fire to return severely-burned areas to appropriate fire regimes and resource conditions. The Joint Fire Science subactivity funds the Department's share of the Joint Fire Science program, an interagency partnership that sponsors and delivers applied research to assist field managers with fuels treatment, post-fire rehabilitation, smoke management and many other related topics.

Object Classification (in millions of dollars)

Identification code 014–1125–0–1–302		2021 actual	2022 est.	2023 est.
	Direct obligations:			
	Personnel compensation:			
11.1	Full-time permanent - direct	4	6	7
11.1	Full-time permanent - allocation	208	255	285
11.3	Other than full-time permanent - allocation	22	26	30
11.5	Other personnel compensation - allocation	157	168	185
11.5	Other personnel compensation - direct	1	1	1
11.8	Special personal services payments - allocation	43	45	47
11.9	Total personnel compensation	435	501	555
12.1	Civilian personnel benefits - direct	2	3	4
12.1	Civilian personnel benefits - allocation	113	130	153
21.0	Travel and transportation of persons - allocation	34	39	45
22.0	Transportation of things - allocation	3	4	5
23.2	Rental payments to others - allocation	8	9	10
23.3	Communications, utilities, and miscellaneous charges - allocation	42	44	50
23.3	Communications, utilities, and miscellaneous charges - direct	2	3	4
25.1	Advisory and assistance services - direct	5	6	7
25.1	Advisory and assistance services - allocation	2	3	4
25.2	Other services from non-Federal sources - allocation	362	430	550
25.3	Other goods and services from Federal sources - direct	9	11	13
25.3	Other goods and services from Federal sources - allocation	93	102	123
25.4	Operation and maintenance of facilities - allocation	4	6	8
25.6	Medical care - allocation	4	6	8
25.7	Operation and maintenance of equipment - allocation	8	9	11
25.8	Subsistence and support of persons - allocation	1	2	3
26.0	Supplies and materials - allocation	56	70	95
31.0	Equipment - allocation	21	25	30
32.0	Land and structures - allocation	9	10	15
41.0	Grants, subsidies, and contributions - allocation	54	85	150
99.0	Direct obligations	1,267	1,498	1,843
99.0	Reimbursable obligations	63	82	82
99.9	Total new obligations, unexpired accounts	1,330	1,580	1,925

Employment Summary

Identification code 014–1125–0–1–302	2021 actual	2022 est.	2023 est.
1001 Direct civilian full-time equivalent employment	30	37	39

FLAME WILDFIRE SUPPRESSION RESERVE FUND

In 2010 through 2017, amounts in the FLAME Fund included the portion of the ten-year average of suppression obligations, adjusted for inflation, intended to support the most severe, complex, and threatening fires. The Secretary is authorized to permit transfers from this account to cover these extreme fire events. The Secretary may also transfer funds in the event DOI has exhausted its suppression resources due to an active fire season. Funds have not been appropriated to the FLAME account since 2017, and remaining FLAME balances were transferred to the Wildland Fire Management account in 2018.

WILDFIRE SUPPRESSION OPERATIONS RESERVE FUND

(INCLUDING TRANSFERS OF FUNDS)

In addition to the amounts provided under the heading "Department of the Interior—Department-Wide Programs—Wildland Fire Management" for wildfire suppression operations, $340,000,000, to remain available until transferred, is additional new budget authority in excess of the average costs for wildfire suppression operations for purposes of a concurrent resolution on the budget: Provided, That such amounts may be transferred to and merged with amounts made available under the headings "Department of Agriculture—Forest Service—Wildland Fire Management" and "Department of the Interior—Department-Wide Programs—Wildland Fire Management" for wildfire suppression operations in the fiscal year in which such amounts are transferred: Provided further, That amounts may be transferred to the "Wildland Fire Management" accounts in the Department of Agriculture or the Department of the Interior only upon the notification of the House and Senate Committees on Appropriations that all wildfire suppression operations funds appropriated under that heading in this and prior appropriations Acts to the agency to which the funds will be transferred will be obligated within 30 days: Provided further, That the transfer authority provided under this heading is in addition to any other transfer authority provided by law.

Note.—A full-year 2022 appropriation for this account was not enacted at the time the Budget was prepared; therefore, the Budget assumes this account is operating under the Continuing Appropriations Act, 2022 (Division A of Public Law 117–43, as amended). The amounts included for 2022 reflect the annualized level provided by the continuing resolution.

Program and Financing (in millions of dollars)

Identification code 014–0130–0–1–302		2021 actual	2022 est.	2023 est.
	Budgetary resources:			
	Unobligated balance:			
1000	Unobligated balance brought forward, Oct 1	232	282	310
1010	Unobligated balance transfer to other accts [014–1125]	–232	–282	–295
1070	Unobligated balance (total)			15
	Budget authority:			
	Appropriations, discretionary:			
1100	Appropriation	310	310	340
1120	Appropriations transferred to other acct [014–1125]	–28		
1160	Appropriation, discretionary (total)	282	310	340
1930	Total budgetary resources available	282	310	355
	Memorandum (non-add) entries:			
1941	Unexpired unobligated balance, end of year	282	310	355
	Budget authority and outlays, net:			
	Discretionary:			
4000	Budget authority, gross	282	310	340
4180	Budget authority, net (total)	282	310	340
4190	Outlays, net (total)			

Suppression Operations.—In addition to the amounts provided under the heading "Department of the Interior-Department-Wide Programs-Wildland Fire Management" for wildfire suppression operations, the Consolidated Appropriations Act, 2018 (P.L. 115–141) amended the Balanced Budget and Emergency Deficit Control Act to provide additional budget authority for fiscal years 2020 through 2027. This budget authority is available for fire suppression requirements in a severe fire season when annual appropriations are close to depletion. The additional budget authority will help ensure adequate resources are available to the Departments of the Interior and Agriculture to fight wildland fires, protect communities, and safeguard human life during the most severe wildland fire seasons.

WORKING CAPITAL FUND

For the operation and maintenance of a departmental financial and business management system, data management and information technology improvements of general benefit to the Department, cybersecurity, and the consolidation of facilities and operations throughout the Department, $118,746,000, to remain available until expended: Provided, That none of the funds appropriated in this Act or any other Act may be used to establish reserves in the Working Capital Fund account other than for accrued annual leave and depreciation of equipment without prior notice to the Committees on Appropriations of the House of Representatives and the Senate: Provided further, That the Secretary of the Interior may assess reasonable charges to State, local, and tribal government employees for training services provided by the National Indian Program Training Center, other than training related to Public Law 93–638: Provided further, That the Secretary may lease or otherwise provide space and related facilities, equipment, or professional services of the National Indian Program Training Center to State, local and tribal government employees or persons or organizations engaged in cultural, educational, or recreational activities (as defined in section 3306(a) of title 40, United States Code) at the prevailing rate for similar space, facilities, equipment, or services in the vicinity of the National Indian Program Training Center: Provided further, That all funds received pursuant to the two preceding provisos shall be credited to this account, shall be available until expended, and shall be used by the Secretary for necessary expenses of the National Indian Program Training Center: Provided further, That the Secretary may enter into grants and cooperative agreements to support the Office of Natural Resource Revenue's collection and disbursement of royalties, fees, and other mineral revenue proceeds, as authorized by law.

Note.—A full-year 2022 appropriation for this account was not enacted at the time the Budget was prepared; therefore, the Budget assumes this account is operating under the Continuing Appropriations Act, 2022 (Division A of Public Law 117–43, as amended). The amounts included for 2022 reflect the annualized level provided by the continuing resolution.

Program and Financing (in millions of dollars)

Identification code 014–4523–0–4–306		2021 actual	2022 est.	2023 est.
	Obligations by program activity:			
0001	Enterprise Initiatives (Discretionary)	64	61	119
0002	Spectrum (Mandatory)	1	1	2
0100	Direct program activities, subtotal	65	62	121
0799	Total direct obligations	65	62	121
0807	WCF Reimbursable Activities	1,035	981	1,035
0809	Reimbursable program activities, subtotal	1,035	981	1,035
0900	Total new obligations, unexpired accounts	1,100	1,043	1,156
	Budgetary resources:			
	Unobligated balance:			
1000	Unobligated balance brought forward, Oct 1	221	265	473
1001	Discretionary unobligated balance brought fwd, Oct 1	217		
1021	Recoveries of prior year unpaid obligations	73	66	66
1070	Unobligated balance (total)	294	331	539
	Budget authority:			
	Appropriations, discretionary:			
1100	Appropriation	61	61	119
	Spending authority from offsetting collections, discretionary:			
1700	Collected	969	1,180	1,180
1701	Change in uncollected payments, Federal sources	41	–56	–56
1750	Spending auth from offsetting collections, disc (total)	1,010	1,124	1,124
1900	Budget authority (total)	1,071	1,185	1,243
1930	Total budgetary resources available	1,365	1,516	1,782
	Memorandum (non-add) entries:			
1941	Unexpired unobligated balance, end of year	265	473	626
	Change in obligated balance:			
	Unpaid obligations:			
3000	Unpaid obligations, brought forward, Oct 1	422	456	217
3010	New obligations, unexpired accounts	1,100	1,043	1,156
3020	Outlays (gross)	–993	–1,216	–1,234
3040	Recoveries of prior year unpaid obligations, unexpired	–73	–66	–66
3050	Unpaid obligations, end of year	456	217	73
	Uncollected payments:			
3060	Uncollected pymts, Fed sources, brought forward, Oct 1	–287	–328	–272
3070	Change in uncollected pymts, Fed sources, unexpired	–41	56	56
3090	Uncollected pymts, Fed sources, end of year	–328	–272	–216
	Memorandum (non-add) entries:			
3100	Obligated balance, start of year	135	128	–55
3200	Obligated balance, end of year	128	–55	–143
	Budget authority and outlays, net:			
	Discretionary:			
4000	Budget authority, gross	1,071	1,185	1,243
	Outlays, gross:			
4010	Outlays from new discretionary authority	597	837	874
4011	Outlays from discretionary balances	383	379	360
4020	Outlays, gross (total)	980	1,216	1,234
	Offsets against gross budget authority and outlays:			
	Offsetting collections (collected) from:			
4030	Federal sources	–950	–1,169	–1,169
4033	Non-Federal sources	–19	–11	–11

Departmental Offices—Continued
Department-Wide Programs—Continued

WORKING CAPITAL FUND—Continued
Program and Financing—Continued

Identification code 014–4523–0–4–306		2021 actual	2022 est.	2023 est.
4040	Offsets against gross budget authority and outlays (total)	–969	–1,180	–1,180
	Additional offsets against gross budget authority only:			
4050	Change in uncollected pymts, Fed sources, unexpired	–41	56	56
4070	Budget authority, net (discretionary)	61	61	119
4080	Outlays, net (discretionary)	11	36	54
	Mandatory:			
	Outlays, gross:			
4101	Outlays from mandatory balances	13		
4180	Budget authority, net (total)	61	61	119
4190	Outlays, net (total)	24	36	54
	Memorandum (non-add) entries:			
5096	Unexpired unavailable balance, SOY: Appropriations	3	3	3
5098	Unexpired unavailable balance, EOY: Appropriations	3	3	3

The Working Capital Fund finances services and activities that can be performed more effectively and efficiently in a centralized manner, including business services provided by the Interior Business Center (IBC). Activities financed through the Fund include information technology and security, systems hosting and help desk services, Departmental news and information, aircraft services, central reproduction, supplies and health services, and safety and health initiatives. Departmental administrative systems hosted through the Fund include the Federal Personnel and Payroll System and the Financial and Business Management System (FBMS). The IBC provides financial management, acquisition, and human resources services as well as payroll services to other agencies as one of the Government-wide shared service providers selected by the Office of Personnel Management. Through the National Indian Program Training Center, a component of Department of the Interior (DOI) University, the Working Capital Fund provides training courses and other services related to Indian culture, law and programs to Federal Government employees. The appropriated portion of the Working Capital Fund includes funding for FBMS operations and maintenance, and enhancements; strengthening cybersecurity and the IT supply chain, improving data management; evaluating program effectiveness; and modernizing Interior's law enforcement records management system and field communications infrastructure.

Object Classification (in millions of dollars)

Identification code 014–4523–0–4–306		2021 actual	2022 est.	2023 est.
	Direct obligations:			
11.1	Personnel compensation: Full-time permanent	11	11	14
12.1	Civilian personnel benefits	4	3	4
23.3	Communications, utilities, and miscellaneous charges	7	3	8
25.1	Advisory and assistance services	3	2	4
25.2	Other services from non-Federal sources	24	22	63
25.3	Other goods and services from Federal sources	4	12	18
25.7	Operation and maintenance of equipment	11	9	10
99.0	Direct obligations	64	62	121
	Reimbursable obligations:			
	Personnel compensation:			
11.1	Full-time permanent	132	129	129
11.3	Other than full-time permanent	3	2	2
11.5	Other personnel compensation	4	3	3
11.9	Total personnel compensation	139	134	134
12.1	Civilian personnel benefits	118	123	123
21.0	Travel and transportation of persons	1	3	3
23.1	Rental payments to GSA	29	30	30
23.2	Rental payments to others	3	3	3
23.3	Communications, utilities, and miscellaneous charges	142	105	123
24.0	Printing and reproduction	1		
25.1	Advisory and assistance services	117	90	112
25.2	Other services from non-Federal sources	275	261	274
25.3	Other goods and services from Federal sources	137	153	154
25.4	Operation and maintenance of facilities	11	11	11
25.6	Medical care	1	1	1
25.7	Operation and maintenance of equipment	51	54	54
26.0	Supplies and materials	4	6	6
31.0	Equipment	6	7	7
99.0	Reimbursable obligations	1,035	981	1,035

| 99.5 | Adjustment for rounding | 1 | | |
| 99.9 | Total new obligations, unexpired accounts | 1,100 | 1,043 | 1,156 |

Employment Summary

Identification code 014–4523–0–4–306		2021 actual	2022 est.	2023 est.
1001	Direct civilian full-time equivalent employment	84	91	101
2001	Reimbursable civilian full-time equivalent employment	1,223	1,283	1,297

INTERIOR FRANCHISE FUND

Program and Financing (in millions of dollars)

Identification code 014–4529–0–4–306		2021 actual	2022 est.	2023 est.
	Obligations by program activity:			
0801	Reimbursable Activity	1,223	1,134	1,085
	Budgetary resources:			
	Unobligated balance:			
1000	Unobligated balance brought forward, Oct 1	111	57	4
1021	Recoveries of prior year unpaid obligations	73	101	101
1070	Unobligated balance (total)	184	158	105
	Budget authority:			
	Spending authority from offsetting collections, discretionary:			
1700	Collected	1,311	1,114	1,114
1701	Change in uncollected payments, Federal sources	–215	–134	–134
1750	Spending auth from offsetting collections, disc (total)	1,096	980	980
1900	Budget authority (total)	1,096	980	980
1930	Total budgetary resources available	1,280	1,138	1,085
	Memorandum (non-add) entries:			
1941	Unexpired unobligated balance, end of year	57	4	
	Change in obligated balance:			
	Unpaid obligations:			
3000	Unpaid obligations, brought forward, Oct 1	1,014	958	1,011
3010	New obligations, unexpired accounts	1,223	1,134	1,085
3020	Outlays (gross)	–1,206	–980	–1,039
3040	Recoveries of prior year unpaid obligations, unexpired	–73	–101	–101
3050	Unpaid obligations, end of year	958	1,011	956
	Uncollected payments:			
3060	Uncollected pymts, Fed sources, brought forward, Oct 1	–637	–422	–288
3070	Change in uncollected pymts, Fed sources, unexpired	215	134	134
3090	Uncollected pymts, Fed sources, end of year	–422	–288	–154
	Memorandum (non-add) entries:			
3100	Obligated balance, start of year	377	536	723
3200	Obligated balance, end of year	536	723	802
	Budget authority and outlays, net:			
	Discretionary:			
4000	Budget authority, gross	1,096	980	980
	Outlays, gross:			
4010	Outlays from new discretionary authority	238	323	323
4011	Outlays from discretionary balances	968	657	716
4020	Outlays, gross (total)	1,206	980	1,039
	Offsets against gross budget authority and outlays:			
	Offsetting collections (collected) from:			
4030	Federal sources	–1,311	–1,114	–1,114
4040	Offsets against gross budget authority and outlays (total)	–1,311	–1,114	–1,114
	Additional offsets against gross budget authority only:			
4050	Change in uncollected pymts, Fed sources, unexpired	215	134	134
4080	Outlays, net (discretionary)	–105	–134	–75
4180	Budget authority, net (total)			
4190	Outlays, net (total)	–105	–134	–75

The Interior Franchise Fund (IFF) was established by the Government Management Reform Act (P.L. 103–356) as amended, and provides acquisition management and administrative services to the Department of the Interior and other Federal agencies on a competitive, fee basis. Operating costs for the IFF are funded fully by the fees collected in exchange for the services provided.

Object Classification (in millions of dollars)

Identification code 014–4529–0–4–306		2021 actual	2022 est.	2023 est.
	Reimbursable obligations:			
	Personnel compensation:			
11.1	Full-time permanent	14	14	16
11.5	Other personnel compensation	1	....	....
11.9	Total personnel compensation	15	14	16
12.1	Civilian personnel benefits	5	6	6
21.0	Travel and transportation of persons	2	2	2
23.1	Rental payments to GSA	1	2	2
23.3	Communications, utilities, and miscellaneous charges	1	1	2
25.1	Advisory and assistance services	364	335	359
25.2	Other services from non-Federal sources	645	567	443
25.3	Other goods and services from Federal sources	15	24	23
25.4	Operation and maintenance of facilities	6	4	6
25.5	Research and development contracts	103	105	146
25.7	Operation and maintenance of equipment	11	6	11
31.0	Equipment	18	11	11
41.0	Grants, subsidies, and contributions	37	57	58
99.0	Reimbursable obligations	1,223	1,134	1,085
99.9	Total new obligations, unexpired accounts	1,223	1,134	1,085

Employment Summary

Identification code 014–4529–0–4–306	2021 actual	2022 est.	2023 est.
2001 Reimbursable civilian full-time equivalent employment	113	109	109

NATIONAL PARKS AND PUBLIC LAND LEGACY RESTORATION FUND

Special and Trust Fund Receipts (in millions of dollars)

Identification code 014–5715–0–2–302		2021 actual	2022 est.	2023 est.
0100	Balance, start of year	....	....	94
	Receipts:			
	Current law:			
1140	Earnings on Investments, National Parks and Public Land Legacy Restoration Fund	....	4	5
2000	Total: Balances and receipts	....	4	99
	Appropriations:			
	Current law:			
2101	National Parks and Public Land Legacy Restoration Fund	....	–2	–5
2102	National Parks and Public Land Legacy Restoration Fund	....	....	–92
2132	National Parks and Public Land Legacy Restoration Fund	....	92	92
2199	Total current law appropriations	....	90	–5
2999	Total appropriations	....	90	–5
5099	Balance, end of year	....	94	94

Program and Financing (in millions of dollars)

Identification code 014–5715–0–2–302		2021 actual	2022 est.	2023 est.
	Obligations by program activity:			
0001	Great American Outdoors Act (P.L. 116–152)	751	1,438	1,874
	Budgetary resources:			
	Unobligated balance:			
1000	Unobligated balance brought forward, Oct 1	....	864	951
	Budget authority:			
	Appropriations, mandatory:			
1200	Appropriation	1,900	1,900	1,900
1201	Appropriation (special or trust fund)	....	2	5
1202	Appropriation (previously unavailable)	....	....	92
1220	Appropriations transferred to other acct [012–5716]	–285	–285	–285
1232	Appropriations and/or unobligated balance of appropriations temporarily reduced	....	–92	–92
1260	Appropriations, mandatory (total)	1,615	1,525	1,620
1930	Total budgetary resources available	1,615	2,389	2,571
	Memorandum (non-add) entries:			
1941	Unexpired unobligated balance, end of year	864	951	697
	Change in obligated balance:			
	Unpaid obligations:			
3000	Unpaid obligations, brought forward, Oct 1	....	652	885
3010	New obligations, unexpired accounts	751	1,438	1,874
3020	Outlays (gross)	–99	–1,205	–1,223
3050	Unpaid obligations, end of year	652	885	1,536
	Memorandum (non-add) entries:			
3100	Obligated balance, start of year	....	652	885
3200	Obligated balance, end of year	652	885	1,536
	Budget authority and outlays, net:			
	Mandatory:			
4090	Budget authority, gross	1,615	1,525	1,620
	Outlays, gross:			
4100	Outlays from new mandatory authority	99	150	201
4101	Outlays from mandatory balances	....	1,055	1,022
4110	Outlays, gross (total)	99	1,205	1,223
4180	Budget authority, net (total)	1,615	1,525	1,620
4190	Outlays, net (total)	99	1,205	1,223
	Memorandum (non-add) entries:			
5000	Total investments, SOY: Federal securities: Par value	....	1,660	1,901
5001	Total investments, EOY: Federal securities: Par value	1,660	1,901	2,291

The Great American Outdoors Act (P.L. 116–152) established the National Parks and Public Land Legacy Restoration Fund to reduce deferred maintenance at the Department of the Interior and the U.S. Forest Service. The Fund supports restoration of deteriorating assets through an allocation of 70 percent to the National Park Service, 5 percent to the U.S. Fish and Wildlife Service, 5 percent to the Bureau of Land Management, 5 percent to the Bureau of Indian Education, and 15 percent to the U.S. Forest Service. The Fund is supported by the deposit of 50 percent of all Federal energy development revenue from the prior year that would otherwise be credited or deposited as miscellaneous receipts to the Treasury, subject to an annual limit of $1.9 billion for five years (2021–2025). The Departments of the Interior and Agriculture annually submit projects to Congress, execute projects, and monitor results/program performance. This Fund makes a significant investment in the facilities which support the important missions of the Department of the Interior and the U.S. Forest Service and help maintain America's national treasures for future generations.

Object Classification (in millions of dollars)

Identification code 014–5715–0–2–302		2021 actual	2022 est.	2023 est.
	Direct obligations:			
	Personnel compensation:			
11.1	Full-time permanent (allocation)	5	13	14
11.3	Other than full-time permanent	....	7	15
11.9	Total personnel compensation	5	20	29
12.1	Civilian personnel benefits (allocation)	2	8	11
21.0	Travel and transportation of persons	....	2	2
22.0	Transportation of things	....	1	1
25.1	Advisory and assistance services	....	7	7
25.2	Other services from non-Federal sources	61	66	81
25.3	Other goods and services from Federal sources	34	58	70
25.4	Operation and maintenance of facilities	73	138	171
26.0	Supplies and materials	1	4	4
31.0	Equipment	....	1	1
32.0	Land and structures	573	1,133	1,497
99.0	Direct obligations	749	1,438	1,874
99.5	Adjustment for rounding	2	....	....
99.9	Total new obligations, unexpired accounts	751	1,438	1,874

ENERGY COMMUNITY REVITALIZATION PROGRAM

(INCLUDING TRANSFERS OF FUNDS)

For necessary expenses of the Department of the Interior to inventory, assess, decommission, reclaim, respond to hazardous substance releases, remediate lands pursuant to section 40704 of Public Law 117–58 (30 U.S.C. 1245), and carry out the purposes of section 349 of the Energy Policy Act of 2005 (42 U.S.C. 15907), as amended, $65,000,000, to remain available until expended: Provided, That such amount shall be in addition to amounts otherwise available for such purposes: Provided further, That amounts appropriated under this heading are available for program management and oversight of these activities: Provided further, That the

Energy Community Revitalization Program—Continued

Secretary may transfer the funds provided under this heading in this Act to any other account in the Department to carry out such purposes, and may expend such funds directly, or through grants: Provided further, That these amounts are not available to fulfill Comprehensive Environmental Response, Compensation, and Liability Act (CERCLA) obligations agreed to in settlement or imposed by a court, whether for payment of funds or for work to be performed.

Note.—A full-year 2022 appropriation for this account was not enacted at the time the Budget was prepared; therefore, the Budget assumes this account is operating under the Continuing Appropriations Act, 2022 (Division A of Public Law 117–43, as amended). The amounts included for 2022 reflect the annualized level provided by the continuing resolution.

Energy Community Revitalization Program

[(INCLUDING TRANSFERS OF FUNDS)]

[For an additional amount for Department-Wide Programs, $4,677,000,000, to remain available until expended, for an Energy Community Revitalization program to carry out orphaned well site plugging, remediation, and restoration activities authorized in section 349 of the Energy Policy Act of 2005 (42 U.S.C. 15907), as amended by section 40601 of division D of this Act: *Provided*, That of the funds made available under this heading in this Act, the following amounts shall be for the following purposes—]

[(1) $250,000,000, to remain available until September 30, 2030, shall be to carry out activities authorized in section 349(b) of the Energy Policy Act of 2005 (42 U.S.C. 15907(b)), as amended by section 40601 of division D of this Act;]

[(2) $775,000,000, to remain available until September 30, 2030, shall be to carry out activities authorized in section 349(c)(3) of the Energy Policy Act of 2005 (42 U.S.C. 15907(c)(3)), as amended by section 40601 of division D of this Act;]

[(3) $2,000,000,000, to remain available until September 30, 2030, shall be to carry out activities authorized in section 349(c)(4) of the Energy Policy Act of 2005 (42 U.S.C. 15907(c)(4)), as amended by section 40601 of division D of this Act;]

[(4) $1,500,000,000, to remain available until September 30, 2030, shall be to carry out activities authorized in section 349(c)(5) of the Energy Policy Act of 2005 (42 U.S.C. 15907(c)(5)), as amended by section 40601 of division D of this Act;]

[(5) $150,000,000, to remain available until September 30, 2030, shall be to carry out activities authorized in section 349(d) of the Energy Policy Act of 2005 (42 U.S.C.15907(d)), as amended by section 40601 of division D of this Act;]

[*Provided further*, That of the amount provided under this heading in this Act, $2,000,000 shall be provided by the Secretary through a cooperative agreement with the Interstate Oil and Gas Compact Commission to carry out the consultations authorized in section 349 of the Energy Policy Act of 2005 (42 U.S.C. 15907), as amended by section 40601 of division D of this Act: *Provided further*, That amounts provided under this heading in this Act shall be in addition to amounts otherwise available for such purposes: *Provided further*, That amounts provided under this heading in this Act are not available to fulfill Comprehensive Environmental Response, Compensation, and Liability Act (CERCLA) obligations agreed to in settlement or imposed by a court, whether for payment of funds or for work to be performed: *Provided further*, That the Secretary may transfer the funds provided under this heading in this Act to any other account in the Department of the Interior to carry out such purposes: *Provided further*, That the Secretary may transfer funds made available in paragraph (1) of the first proviso under this heading to the Secretary of Agriculture, acting through the Chief of the Forest Service, to carry out such purposes: *Provided further*, That up to 3 percent of the amounts made available under this heading in this Act shall be for salaries, expenses, and administration: *Provided further*, That one-half of one percent of the amounts made available under this heading in this Act shall be transferred to the Office of Inspector General of the Department of the Interior for oversight of funding provided to the Department of the Interior in this title in this Act: *Provided further*, That such amount is designated by the Congress as being for an emergency requirement pursuant to section 4112(a) of H. Con. Res. 71 (115th Congress), the concurrent resolution on the budget for fiscal year 2018, and to section 251(b) of the Balanced Budget and Emergency Deficit Control Act of 1985.] *(Infrastructure Investments and Jobs Appropriations Act.)*

Program and Financing (in millions of dollars)

Identification code 014–2641–0–1–302	2021 actual	2022 est.	2023 est.
Obligations by program activity:			
0001 State Grants			35
0002 Tribal Grants			10
0003 Federal Program			18
0004 Program Management			2
0011 2022 Bipartisan Infrastructure Law (P.L. 117–58)		823	1,043
0900 Total new obligations, unexpired accounts		823	1,108
Budgetary resources:			
Unobligated balance:			
1000 Unobligated balance brought forward, Oct 1			3,831
Budget authority:			
Appropriations, discretionary:			
1100 Appropriation		4,677	65
1120 Appropriations transferred to other acct - OIG [014–0104]		–23	
1160 Appropriation, discretionary (total)		4,654	65
1930 Total budgetary resources available		4,654	3,896
Memorandum (non-add) entries:			
1941 Unexpired unobligated balance, end of year		3,831	2,788
Change in obligated balance:			
Unpaid obligations:			
3000 Unpaid obligations, brought forward, Oct 1			776
3010 New obligations, unexpired accounts		823	1,108
3020 Outlays (gross)		–47	–491
3050 Unpaid obligations, end of year		776	1,393
Memorandum (non-add) entries:			
3100 Obligated balance, start of year			776
3200 Obligated balance, end of year		776	1,393
Budget authority and outlays, net:			
Discretionary:			
4000 Budget authority, gross		4,654	65
Outlays, gross:			
4010 Outlays from new discretionary authority		47	26
4011 Outlays from discretionary balances			465
4020 Outlays, gross (total)		47	491
4180 Budget authority, net (total)		4,654	65
4190 Outlays, net (total)		47	491

The 2023 budget includes appropriated funds for the Energy Community Revitalization Program (ECRP) for programs and activities authorized by Section 40704 of P.L. 117–58 (30 U.S.C. 1245) and Section 349 of the Energy Policy Act of 2005 (42 U.S.C. 15907), as amended. The ECRP provides grants to States and Tribal communities impacted by abandoned hard rock mining and orphaned oil and gas wells. The program provides resources to States and Tribes to address the sites where the companies that created them have left and are no longer viable to address the needed cleanup and closure. This program will create jobs in these communities to repair the damage from these legacy activities and in doing so, improve the environment, restore water quality, and make the community safer.

In addition, the ECRP provides critical funding to address the hundreds of thousands of abandoned hardrock mines and orphan oil and gas wells scattered across Federal lands. The Federal program assists Interior bureaus to inventory, assess, and prioritize these sites for cleanup. The primary focus of 2023 requested funds will be to remediate abandoned hardrock mines posing the highest risks to the environment and physical safety on Department lands. The ECRP is also responsible for executing funds made available for orphaned oil and gas well activities enacted in the Infrastructure Investment and Jobs Act (P.L. 117–58).

Object Classification (in millions of dollars)

Identification code 014–2641–0–1–302	2021 actual	2022 est.	2023 est.
Direct obligations:			
Personnel compensation:			
11.1 Full-time permanent - Direct		1	2
11.1 Full-time permanent - Allocation			2
11.9 Total personnel compensation		1	4
12.1 Civilian personnel benefits			1
25.1 Advisory and assistance services		2	
25.2 Other services from non-Federal sources		41	125
25.3 Other goods and services from Federal sources		2	8
41.0 Grants, subsidies, and contributions		777	970
99.9 Total new obligations, unexpired accounts		823	1,108

Employment Summary

Identification code 014–2641–0–1–302	2021 actual	2022 est.	2023 est.
1001 Direct civilian full-time equivalent employment		3	14

ADMINISTRATIVE PROVISION

There is hereby authorized for acquisition from available resources within the Working Capital Fund, aircraft which may be obtained by donation, purchase, or through available excess surplus property: *Provided,* That existing aircraft being replaced may be sold, with proceeds derived or trade-in value used to offset the purchase price for the replacement aircraft.

GENERAL FUND RECEIPT ACCOUNTS
(in millions of dollars)

	2021 actual	2022 est.	2023 est.
Offsetting receipts from the public:			
014–143500 General Fund Proprietary Interest Receipts, not Otherwise Classified	25	14	14
014–181100 Rent and Bonuses from Land Leases for Resource Exploration and Extraction	16	23	25
014–182000 Rent and Bonuses on Outer Continental Shelf Lands		3,669	
014–202000 Royalties on Outer Continental Shelf Lands	2,820	5,490	4,835
014–202500 Arctic National Wildlife Refuge (ANWR) Oil and Gas Leasing Revenues, Federal Share	8	2	11
014–203200 Hardrock Mining Holding Fee	59	27	31
014–203900 Royalties on Natural Resources, not Otherwise Classified	456	602	559
014–222900 Sale of Timber, Wildlife and Other Natural Land Products, not Otherwise Classified	20	15	15
014–248400 Receipts from Grazing Fees, Federal Share	4	6	6
014–272930 Indian Loan Guarantee, Downward Reestimates of Subsidies	25	25	
014–322000 All Other General Fund Proprietary Receipts Including Budget Clearing Accounts	107	93	94
General Fund Offsetting receipts from the public	3,540	9,966	5,590
Intragovernmental payments:			
014–388500 Undistributed Intragovernmental Payments and Receivables from Cancelled Accounts	–42	25	25
General Fund Intragovernmental payments	–42	25	25

GENERAL PROVISIONS
(INCLUDING TRANSFERS OF FUNDS)

EMERGENCY TRANSFER AUTHORITY—INTRA-BUREAU

SEC. 101. Appropriations made in this title shall be available for expenditure or transfer (within each bureau or office), with the approval of the Secretary of the Interior, for the emergency reconstruction, replacement, or repair of aircraft, buildings, utilities, or other facilities or equipment damaged or destroyed by fire, flood, storm, or other unavoidable causes: *Provided,* That no funds shall be made available under this authority until funds specifically made available to the Department of the Interior for emergencies shall have been exhausted: *Provided further,* That it is the sense of the Congress that all funds used pursuant to this section should be replenished by a supplemental appropriation, to be requested as promptly as possible.

EMERGENCY TRANSFER AUTHORITY—DEPARTMENT-WIDE

SEC. 102. The Secretary of the Interior may authorize the expenditure or transfer of any no year appropriation in this title, in addition to the amounts included in the budget programs of the several agencies, for the suppression or emergency prevention of wildland fires on or threatening lands under the jurisdiction of the Department of the Interior; for the emergency rehabilitation of burned-over lands under its jurisdiction; for emergency actions related to potential or actual earthquakes, floods, volcanoes, storms, or other unavoidable causes; for contingency planning subsequent to actual oil spills; for response and natural resource damage assessment activities related to actual oil spills or releases of hazardous substances into the environment; for the prevention, suppression, and control of actual or potential grasshopper and Mormon cricket outbreaks on lands under the jurisdiction of the Secretary, pursuant to the authority in section 417(b) of Public Law 106–224 (7 U.S.C. 7717(b)); for emergency reclamation projects under section 410 of Public Law 95–87; and shall transfer, from any no year funds available to the Office of Surface Mining Reclamation and Enforcement, such funds as may be necessary to permit assumption of regulatory authority in the event a primacy State is not carrying out the regulatory provisions of the Surface Mining Act: *Provided,* That appropriations made in this title for wildland fire operations shall be available for the payment of obligations incurred during the preceding fiscal year, and for reimbursement to other Federal agencies for destruction of vehicles, aircraft, or other equipment in connection with their use for wildland fire operations, with such reimbursement to be credited to appropriations currently available at the time of receipt thereof: *Provided further,* That for wildland fire operations, no funds shall be made available under this authority until the Secretary determines that funds appropriated for "wildland fire suppression" shall be exhausted within 30 days: *Provided further,* That it is the sense of the Congress that all funds used pursuant to this section should be replenished by a supplemental appropriation, to be requested as promptly as possible: *Provided further,* That such replenishment funds shall be used to reimburse, on a pro rata basis, accounts from which emergency funds were transferred.

AUTHORIZED USE OF FUNDS

SEC. 103. Appropriations made to the Department of the Interior in this title shall be available for services as authorized by section 3109 of title 5, United States Code, when authorized by the Secretary of the Interior, in total amount not to exceed $500,000; purchase and replacement of motor vehicles, including specially equipped law enforcement vehicles and zero emission passenger motor vehicles and supporting charging or fueling infrastructure; hire, maintenance, and operation of aircraft; hire of passenger motor vehicles, including zero emission passenger motor vehicles and supporting charging or fueling infrastructure; purchase of reprints; payment for telephone service in private residences in the field, when authorized under regulations approved by the Secretary; and the payment of dues, when authorized by the Secretary, for library membership in societies or associations which issue publications to members only or at a price to members lower than to subscribers who are not members.

AUTHORIZED USE OF FUNDS, INDIAN TRUST MANAGEMENT

SEC. 104. Appropriations made in this Act under the headings Bureau of Indian Affairs and Bureau of Indian Education, and Bureau of Trust Funds Administration and any unobligated balances from prior appropriations Acts made under the same headings shall be available for expenditure or transfer for Indian trust management and reform activities. Total funding for settlement support activities shall not exceed amounts specifically designated in this Act for such purpose. The Secretary shall notify the House and Senate Committees on Appropriations within 60 days of the expenditure or transfer of any funds under this section, including the amount expended or transferred and how the funds will be used.

REDISTRIBUTION OF FUNDS, BUREAU OF INDIAN AFFAIRS

SEC. 105. Notwithstanding any other provision of law, the Secretary of the Interior is authorized to redistribute any Tribal Priority Allocation funds, including tribal base funds, to alleviate tribal funding inequities by transferring funds to address identified, unmet needs, dual enrollment, overlapping service areas or inaccurate distribution methodologies. No tribe shall receive a reduction in Tribal Priority Allocation funds of more than 10 percent in fiscal year 2023. Under circumstances of dual enrollment, overlapping service areas or inaccurate distribution methodologies, the 10 percent limitation does not apply.

ELLIS, GOVERNORS, AND LIBERTY ISLANDS

SEC. 106. Notwithstanding any other provision of law, the Secretary of the Interior is authorized to acquire lands, waters, or interests therein, including the use of all or part of any pier, dock, or landing within the State of New York and the State of New Jersey, for the purpose of operating and maintaining facilities in the support of transportation and accommodation of visitors to Ellis, Governors, and Liberty Islands, and of other program and administrative activities, by donation or with appropriated funds, including franchise fees (and other monetary consideration), or by exchange; and the Secretary is authorized to negotiate and enter into leases, subleases, concession contracts, or other agreements for the use of such facilities on such terms and conditions as the Secretary may determine reasonable: *Provided,* That for the purposes of 54 U.S.C. 200306(a), such lands, waters, or interests therein shall be considered to be within the exterior boundary of a System unit authorized or established.

OUTER CONTINENTAL SHELF INSPECTION FEES

SEC. 107. (a) In fiscal year 2023, the Secretary of the Interior shall collect a non-refundable inspection fee, which shall be deposited in the "Offshore Safety and Environmental Enforcement" account, from the designated operator for facilities subject to inspection under 43 U.S.C. 1348(c).

(b) Annual fees shall be collected for facilities that are above the waterline, excluding drilling rigs, and are in place at the start of the fiscal year. Fees for fiscal year 2023 shall be—

(1) $11,725 for facilities with no wells, but with processing equipment or gathering lines;

(2) $18,984 for facilities with 1 to 10 wells, with any combination of active or inactive wells; and

(3) $35,176 for facilities with more than 10 wells, with any combination of active or inactive wells.

(c) Fees shall be assessed for facilities that are above the waterline, excluding drilling rigs, and require follow-up inspections. Fees for fiscal year 2023 shall be—

(1) $5,863 for facilities with no wells, but with processing or gathering lines;

(2) $9,492 for facilities with 1 to 10 wells, with any combination of active or inactive wells; and

(3) $17,588 for facilities with more than 10 wells, with any combination of active or inactive wells.

(d) Fees for drilling rigs shall be assessed for all inspections completed in fiscal year 2023. Fees for fiscal year 2023 shall be—

(1) $34,059 per inspection for rigs operating in water depths of 500 feet or more; and

(2) $18,649 per inspection for rigs operating in water depths of less than 500 feet.

(e) Fees for inspection of well operations conducted via non-rig units as outlined in title 30 CFR 250 subparts D, E, F, and Q shall be assessed for all inspections completed in fiscal year 2023. Fees for fiscal year 2023 shall be—

(1) $13,260 per inspection for non-rig units operating in water depths of 2,500 feet or more;

(2) $11,530 per inspection for non-rig units operating in water depths between 500 and 2,499 feet; and

(3) $4,470 per inspection for non-rig units operating in water depths of less than 500 feet.

(f) The Secretary shall bill designated operators under subsection (b) quarterly, with payment required within 30 days of billing. The Secretary shall bill designated operators under subsections (c) and (d) within 30 days of the end of the month in which the inspection occurred, with payment required within 30 days of billing. The Secretary shall bill designated operators under subsection (e) with payment required by the end of the following quarter.

CONTRACTS AND AGREEMENTS FOR WILD HORSE AND BURRO HOLDING FACILITIES

SEC. 108. *Notwithstanding any other provision of this Act, the Secretary of the Interior may enter into multiyear cooperative agreements with nonprofit organizations and other appropriate entities, and may enter into multiyear contracts in accordance with the provisions of section 3903 of title 41, United States Code (except that the 5-year term restriction in subsection (a) shall not apply), for the long-term care and maintenance of excess wild free roaming horses and burros by such organizations or entities on private land. Such cooperative agreements and contracts may not exceed 10 years, subject to renewal at the discretion of the Secretary.*

MASS MARKING OF SALMONIDS

SEC. 109. *The United States Fish and Wildlife Service shall, in carrying out its responsibilities to protect threatened and endangered species of salmon, implement a system of mass marking of salmonid stocks, intended for harvest, that are released from federally operated or federally financed hatcheries including but not limited to fish releases of coho, chinook, and steelhead species. Marked fish must have a visible mark that can be readily identified by commercial and recreational fishers.*

CONTRACTS AND AGREEMENTS WITH INDIAN AFFAIRS

SEC. 110. *Notwithstanding any other provision of law, during fiscal year 2023, in carrying out work involving cooperation with State, local, and tribal governments or any political subdivision thereof, Indian Affairs may record obligations against accounts receivable from any such entities, except that total obligations at the end of the fiscal year shall not exceed total budgetary resources available at the end of the fiscal year.*

DEPARTMENT OF THE INTERIOR EXPERIENCED SERVICES PROGRAM

SEC. 111. *(a) Notwithstanding any other provision of law relating to Federal grants and cooperative agreements, the Secretary of the Interior is authorized to make grants to, or enter into cooperative agreements with, private nonprofit organizations designated by the Secretary of Labor under title V of the Older Americans Act of 1965 to utilize the talents of older Americans in programs authorized by other provisions of law administered by the Secretary and consistent with such provisions of law.*

(b) Prior to awarding any grant or agreement under subsection (a), the Secretary shall ensure that the agreement would not—

(1) result in the displacement of individuals currently employed by the Department, including partial displacement through reduction of non-overtime hours, wages, or employment benefits;

(2) result in the use of an individual under the Department of the Interior Experienced Services Program for a job or function in a case in which a Federal employee is in a layoff status from the same or substantially equivalent job within the Department; or

(3) affect existing contracts for services.

SEPARATION OF ACCOUNTS

SEC. 112. *The Secretary of the Interior, in order to implement an orderly transition to separate accounts of the Bureau of Indian Affairs and the Bureau of Indian Education, may transfer funds among and between the successor offices and bureaus affected by the reorganization only in conformance with the reprogramming guidelines described in this Act.*

INTERAGENCY MOTOR POOL

SEC. 113. *Notwithstanding any other provision of law or Federal regulation, federally recognized Indian tribes or authorized tribal organizations that receive Tribally-Controlled School Grants pursuant to Public Law 100–297 may obtain interagency motor vehicles and related services for performance of any activities carried out under such grants to the same extent as if they were contracting under the Indian Self-Determination and Education Assistance Act.*

DECOMMISSIONING ACCOUNT

SEC. 114. *The fifth and sixth provisos under the amended heading "Royalty and Offshore Minerals Management" for the Minerals Management Service in Public Law 101–512 (104 Stat. 1926, as amended) (43 U.S.C. 1338a) are further amended by striking and replacing them with— "Provided further, That notwithstanding section 3302 of title 31, any moneys hereafter received as a result of the forfeiture of a bond or other security by an Outer Continental Shelf permittee, lessee, or right-of-way holder that does not fulfill the requirements of its permit, lease, or right-of-way or does not comply with the regulations of the Secretary, or as a bankruptcy distribution or settlement associated with such failure or noncompliance, shall be credited to a separate account established in the Treasury for decommissioning activities and shall be available to the Bureau of Ocean Energy Management without further appropriation or fiscal year limitation to cover the cost to the United States of any improvement, protection, rehabilitation, or decommissioning work rendered necessary by the action or inaction that led to the forfeiture or bankruptcy distribution or settlement, to remain available until expended: Provided further, That amounts deposited into the decommissioning account may be allocated to the Bureau of Safety and Environmental Enforcement for such costs: Provided further, That any moneys received for such costs currently held in the Ocean Energy Management account shall be transferred to the decommissioning account: Provided further, That any portion of the moneys so credited shall be returned to the bankruptcy estate, permittee, lessee, or right-of-way holder to the extent that the money is in excess of the amount expended in performing the work necessitated by the action or inaction which led to their receipt or, if the bond or security was forfeited for failure to pay the civil penalty, in excess of the civil penalty imposed.".*

INDIAN REORGANIZATION ACT

SEC. 115. *(a) MODIFICATION.*

(1) In general. The first sentence of section 19 of the Act of June 18, 1934 (commonly known as the "Indian Reorganization Act") (25 U.S.C. 5129), is amended—

(A) by striking "The term" and inserting "Effective beginning on June 18, 1934, the term"; and

(B) by striking "any recognized Indian tribe now under Federal jurisdiction" and inserting "any federally recognized Indian tribe".

(2) EFFECTIVE DATE. The amendments made by paragraph (1) shall take effect as if included in the Act of June 18, 1934 (commonly known as the "Indian Reorganization Act") (25 U.S.C. 5129), on the date of enactment of that Act.

(b) RATIFICATION AND CONFIRMATION OF ACTIONS. Any action taken by the Secretary of the Interior pursuant to the Act of June 18, 1934 (commonly known as the "Indian Reorganization Act") (25 U.S.C. 5101 et seq.) for any Indian tribe that was federally recognized on the date of the action is ratified and confirmed, to the extent such action is subjected to challenge based on whether the Indian tribe was federally recognized or under Federal jurisdiction on June 18, 1934, as if the action had, by prior act of Congress, been specifically authorized and directed.

(c) EFFECT ON OTHER LAWS.

(1) In general, nothing in this section or the amendments made by this section affects

(A) the application or effect of any Federal law other than the Act of June 18, 1934 (25 U.S.C. 5101 et seq.) (as amended by subsection (a)); or

(B) any limitation on the authority of the Secretary of the Interior under any Federal law or regulation other than the Act of June 18, 1934 (25 U.S.C. 5101 et seq.) (as so amended).

(2) REFERENCES IN OTHER LAWS. An express reference to the Act of June 18, 1934 (25 U.S.C. 5101 et seq.) contained in any other Federal law shall be considered to be a reference to that Act as amended by subsection (a).

EXTENSION OF ALYCE SPOTTED BEAR AND WALTER SOBOLEFF COMMISSION ON NATIVE AMERICAN CHILDREN REPORTING DEADLINE

SEC. 116. Section 3(f) of Public Law 114–244 is amended by striking "3 years" and inserting "5 years".

NATIONAL HERITAGE AREAS AND CORRIDORS

SEC. 117. (a) Section 126 of Public Law 98–398, as amended (98 Stat. 1456; 120 Stat. 1853), is further amended by striking "the date that is 15 years after the date of enactment of this section" and inserting "September 30, 2024".

(b) Section 10 of Public Law 99–647, as amended (100 Stat. 3630; 104 Stat. 1018; 120 Stat. 1858; 128 Stat. 3804), is further amended by striking "2021" and inserting "2024".

(c) Section 12 of Public Law 100–692, as amended (102 Stat. 4558; 112 Stat. 3258; 123 Stat. 1292; 127 Stat. 420; 128 Stat. 314; 128 Stat. 3801), is further amended—

(1) in subsection (c)(1), by striking "2021" and inserting "2024"; and
(2) in subsection (d), by striking "2021" and inserting "2024".

(d) Section 106(b) of Public Law 103–449, as amended (108 Stat. 4755; 113 Stat. 1726; 123 Stat. 1291; 128 Stat. 3802), is further amended by striking "2021" and inserting "2024".

(e) Division II of Public Law 104–333 (54 U.S.C. 320101 note), as amended, is further amended by striking "2021" each place it appears in the following sections and inserting "2024":

(1) in subsection 107 (110 Stat. 4244; 127 Stat. 420; 128 Stat. 314; 128 Stat. 3801);
(2) in subsection 408 (110 Stat. 4256; 127 Stat. 420; 128 Stat. 314; 128 Stat. 3801);
(3) in subsection 507 (110 Stat. 4260; 127 Stat. 420; 128 Stat. 314; 128 Stat. 3801);
(4) in subsection 707 (110 Stat. 4267; 127 Stat. 420; 128 Stat. 314; 128 Stat. 3801);
(5) in subsection 809 (110 Stat. 4275; 122 Stat. 826; 127 Stat. 420; 128 Stat. 314; 128 Stat. 3801);
(6) in subsection 910 (110 Stat. 4281; 127 Stat. 420; 128 Stat. 314; 128 Stat. 3801);
(7) in subsection 310 (110 Stat. 4252; 127 Stat. 420; 128 Stat. 314; 129 Stat. 2551; 132 Stat. 661; 133 Stat. 778);
(8) in subsection 607 (110 Stat. 4264; 127 Stat. 420; 128 Stat. 314; 129 Stat. 2551; 132 Stat. 661; 133 Stat. 778–779); and
(9) in subsection 208 (110 Stat. 4248; 127 Stat. 420; 128 Stat. 314; 129 Stat. 2551; 132 Stat. 661; 133 Stat. 778).

(f) Section 109 of Public Law 105–355, as amended (112 Stat. 3252; 128 Stat. 3802), is further amended by striking "2021" and inserting "2024".

(g) Public Law 106–278 (54 U.S.C. 320101 note), as amended, is further amended:

(1) in section 108 (114 Stat. 818; 127 Stat. 420; 128 Stat. 314; 128 Stat. 3802) by striking "2021" and inserting "2024"; and
(2) in section 209 (114 Stat. 824; 128 Stat. 3802) by striking "2021" and inserting "2024".

(h) Sec. 157(i) of Public Law 106–291, as amended (114 Stat. 967; 128 Stat. 3802), is further amended by striking "2021" and inserting "2024".

(i) Section 7 of Public Law 106–319, as amended (114 Stat. 1284; 128 Stat. 3802), is further amended by striking "2021" and inserting "2024".

(j) Section 811 of Title VIII of Appendix D of Public Law 106–554, as amended (114 Stat. 2763, 2763A-295; 128 Stat. 3802), is further amended by striking "2021" and inserting "2024".

(k) Section 140(j) Public Law 108–108, as amended (117 Stat. 1274; 131 Stat. 461; 132 Stat. 661; 133 Stat. 778), is further amended by striking "2021" and inserting "2024".

(l) Title II of Public Law 109–338 (54 U.S.C. 320101 note; 120 Stat. 1787–1845), as amended, is further amended:

(1) in each of sections 208, 221, 240, 260, 269, 289, 291J, 295L and 297H by striking "the date that is 15 years after the date of enactment of this Act" and inserting "September 30, 2024"; and
(2) in section 280B by striking "the day occurring 15 years after the date of the enactment of this subtitle" and inserting "September 30, 2024".

(m) Section 810(a)(1) of Title VIII of Division B of Appendix D of Public Law 106–554, as amended (114 Stat. 2763; 123 Stat. 1295; 131 Stat. 461; 133 Stat. 2714), is further amended by striking "$14,000,000" and inserting "$16,000,000".

(n) Section 125(a) of Title IV of Public Law 109–338 (120 Stat. 1853) is amended by striking "$10,000,000" and inserting "$12,000,000".

(o) Section 210(a) of Title II of Public Law 106–278 (114 Stat. 824) is amended by striking "$10,000,000" and inserting "$12,000,000".

(p) Section 804(j) of division B of H.R. 5666 (Appendix D) as enacted into law by section 1(a)(4) of Public Law 106–554, as amended (54 U.S.C. 320101 note; 114 Stat. 2763, 2763A-295; 123 Stat. 1294; 128 Stat. 3802; 131 Stat. 461; 131 Stat. 2714), is further amended by striking "September 30, 2021" and inserting "September 30, 2037".

(q) Section 295D(d) of Public Law 109–338, as amended (54 U.S.C. 320101 note; 120 Stat. 1833; 130 Stat. 962), is further amended by striking "15 years after the date of enactment of this Act" and inserting "on September 30, 2037".

(r) Section 109(a) of title I of Public Law 103–449, as amended (108 Stat. 4755; 113 Stat. 1726; 123 Stat. 1291; 128 Stat. 3802, 133 Stat. 2714,), is further amended by striking "17,000,000" and inserting "19,000,000".

(s) Section 409(a) of division II of Public Law 104–333, as amended (54 U.S.C. 320101 note; 110 Stat. 4256; 127 Stat. 420; 128 Stat. 314; 128 Stat. 3801), is further amended by striking "20,000,000" and inserting "22,000,000".

(t) Section 608(a) of division II of Public Law 104–333, as amended (54 U.S.C. 320101 note; 110 Stat. 4264; 127 Stat. 420; 128 Stat. 314; 129 Stat. 2551; 132 Stat. 661; 133 Stat. 2714), is further amended by striking "17,000,000" and inserting "19,000,000".

(u) Section 157(h)(1) of Public Law 106–291, as amended (114 Stat. 967; 128 Stat. 3802), is further amended by striking "15,000,000" and inserting "17,000,000".

(v) Title IV of Public Law 110–229, as amended (54 U.S.C. 320101 note), is further amended in section 411 (122 Stat. 802), section 432 (112 Stat. 809), and section 451 (122 Stat. 818, 133 Stat. 768) by striking "the date that is 15 years after the date of the enactment of this subtitle" each place it appears and by striking "September 30, 2024" each place it appears.

(w) Section 512 of title V of division J of Public Law 108–447, as amended (54 U.S.C. 320101 note; 118 Stat. 3361, 123 Stat. 1204, 133 Stat. 2713), is further amended by striking "2022" and inserting "2024".

(x) Section 608 of title VI of Public Law 108–447, as amended (54 U.S.C. 320101 note; 118 Stat. 3368, 133 Stat. 768, 133 Stat. 2714), is further amended by striking "2022" and inserting "2024".

STUDY FOR SELMA TO MONTGOMERY NATIONAL HISTORIC TRAIL

SEC. 118. (a) STUDY.—The Secretary of the Interior (Secretary) shall conduct a study to evaluate—

(1) resources associated with the 1965 Voting Rights March from Selma to Montgomery not currently part of the Selma to Montgomery National Historic Trail (Trail) (16 U.S.C. 1244(a)(20)) that would be appropriate for addition to the Trail; and
(2) the potential designation of the Trail as a unit of the National Park System instead of, or in addition to, remaining a designated part of the National Trails System.

(b) REPORT.—Not later than one year after the date on which funds are made available for the study, the Secretary shall submit to the Committee on Natural Resources of the House of Representatives and the Committee on Energy and Natural Resources of the Senate a report that describes the results of the study and the conclusions and recommendations of the study.

(c) LAND ACQUISITION.—The Secretary is authorized, subject to the availability of appropriations and at her discretion, to acquire property or interests therein located in the city of Selma, Alabama and generally depicted on the map entitled "Selma to Montgomery NHT Proposed Addition" numbered 628/177376 and dated September 14, 2021, with the consent of the owner, for the benefit of the Selma to Montgomery National Historic Trail and to further the purposes for which the trail has been established.

DELAWARE WATER GAP AUTHORITY

SEC. 119. Section 4(b) of The Delaware Water Gap National Recreation Area Improvement Act, as amended by section 1 of Public Law 115–101, is further amended by striking "2021" and inserting "2023".

VISITOR EXPERIENCE IMPROVEMENT AUTHORITY

SEC. 120. Section 101938 of title 54, United States Code, is amended by striking "7" and inserting "9".

LOWELL NATIONAL HISTORIC PARK

SEC. 121. Section 103(a) of Public Law 95–290 (16 U.S.C. 410cc–13; 92 Stat. 292) is amended by striking subsection (1) and redesignating subsection (2) as subsection (1).

LAND AND WATER CONSERVATION FUND FINANCIAL ASSISTANCE TO STATES

SEC. 122. Notwithstanding any other provision of law, for expenses necessary to directly carry out the Financial Assistance to States provisions of the Land and

Water Conservation Act of 1965, as amended (54 U.S.C. 200305), in lieu of State assistance program indirect costs (as described in 2 C.F.R. 200), the National Park Service may retain up to 7 percent of the State Conservation Grants assistance program to disperse to States, the District of Columbia, and insular areas, as matching grants to support state program administrative costs.

ONSHORE OIL AND GAS INSPECTION FEE

SEC. 123. Onshore Oil and Gas Inspection Fees.—

(a) The designated operator under each oil and gas lease on Federal or Indian lands, or under each unit and communitization agreement that includes one or more such Federal or Indian leases, that is subject to inspection under section 108(b) of the Federal Oil and Gas Royalty Management Act of 1982 (30 U.S.C. 1718(b)) and that is in force at the start of fiscal year 2022 shall pay a nonrefundable annual inspection fee that the Bureau of Land Management (BLM) shall collect and deposit in the Management of Lands and Resources account.

(b) Fees for fiscal year 2023 shall be—

(1) $1,560 for each lease or unit or communitization agreement with 1 to 10 wells, with any combination of active or inactive wells;

(2) $7,000 for each lease or unit or communitization agreement with 11 to 50 wells, with any combination of active or inactive wells; and

(3) $14,000 for each lease or unit or communitization agreement with more than 50 wells, with any combination of active or inactive wells.

(c) BLM shall bill designated operators within 60 days of enactment of this Act, with payment required within 30 days of billing.

(d) Penalty.—If the designated operator fails to pay the full amount of the fee as prescribed in this section, the Secretary may, in addition to utilizing any other applicable enforcement authority, assess civil penalties against the operator in the same manner as if this section were a mineral leasing law as defined in paragraph (8) of section 3 of Public Law 97–451 (30 U.S.C 1702(8)), as amended.

(e) Exemption for tribal operators.—An operator that is a Tribe or is controlled by a Tribe is not subject to subsection (a) with respect to a lease, unit, or communitization agreement that is located entirely on the lands of such Tribe.

GENERAL PROVISIONS—DEPARTMENT OF THE INTERIOR

SEC. 201. (a) None of the funds provided in title II of this Act for Water and Related Resources, or provided by previous or subsequent appropriations Acts to the agencies or entities funded in title II of this Act for Water and Related Resources that remain available for obligation or expenditure in fiscal year 2023, shall be available for obligation or expenditure through a reprogramming of funds that—

(1) initiates or creates a new program, project, or activity;

(2) eliminates a program, project, or activity;

(3) increases funds for any program, project, or activity for which funds have been denied or restricted by this Act, unless notice has been transmitted to the Committees on Appropriations of both Houses of Congress;

(4) restarts or resumes any program, project or activity for which funds are not provided in this Act, unless notice has been transmitted to the Committees on Appropriations of both Houses of Congress;

(5) transfers funds in excess of the following limits, unless notice has been transmitted to the Committees on Appropriations of both Houses of Congress:

(A) 15 percent for any program, project or activity for which $2,000,000 or more is available at the beginning of the fiscal year; or

(B) $400,000 for any program, project or activity for which less than $2,000,000 is available at the beginning of the fiscal year;

(6) transfers more than $500,000 from either the Facilities Operation, Maintenance, and Rehabilitation category or the Resources Management and Development category to any program, project, or activity in the other category, unless notice has been transmitted to the Committees on Appropriations of both Houses of Congress; or

(7) transfers, where necessary to discharge legal obligations of the Bureau of Reclamation, more than $5,000,000 to provide adequate funds for settled contractor claims, increased contractor earnings due to accelerated rates of operations, and real estate deficiency judgments, unless notice has been transmitted to the Committees on Appropriations of both Houses of Congress.

(b) Subsection (a)(5) shall not apply to any transfer of funds within the Facilities Operation, Maintenance, and Rehabilitation category.

(c) For purposes of this section, the term "transfer" means any movement of funds into or out of a program, project, or activity.

(d) The Bureau of Reclamation shall submit reports on a quarterly basis to the Committees on Appropriations of both Houses of Congress detailing all the funds reprogrammed between programs, projects, activities, or categories of funding. The first quarterly report shall be submitted not later than 60 days after the date of enactment of this Act.

SEC. 202. (a) None of the funds appropriated or otherwise made available by this Act may be used to determine the final point of discharge for the interceptor drain for the San Luis Unit until development by the Secretary of the Interior and the State of California of a plan, which shall conform to the water quality standards of the State of California as approved by the Administrator of the Environmental Protection Agency, to minimize any detrimental effect of the San Luis drainage waters.

(b) The costs of the Kesterson Reservoir Cleanup Program and the costs of the San Joaquin Valley Drainage Program shall be classified by the Secretary of the Interior as reimbursable or nonreimbursable and collected until fully repaid pursuant to the "Cleanup Program—Alternative Repayment Plan" and the "SJVDP—Alternative Repayment Plan" described in the report entitled "Repayment Report, Kesterson Reservoir Cleanup Program and San Joaquin Valley Drainage Program, February 1995", prepared by the Department of the Interior, Bureau of Reclamation. Any future obligations of funds by the United States relating to, or providing for, drainage service or drainage studies for the San Luis Unit shall be fully reimbursable by San Luis Unit beneficiaries of such service or studies pursuant to Federal reclamation law.

SEC. 203. Section 9504(e) of the Omnibus Public Land Management Act of 2009 (42 U.S.C. 10364(e)) is amended by striking "$610,000,000" and inserting "$760,000,000".

SEC. 204. Title I of Public Law 108–361 (the CALFED Bay-Delta Authorization Act) (118 Stat. 1681), as amended by section 4007(k) of Public Law 114–322, shall be applied by substituting "2023" for "2021" each place it appears.

SEC. 205. Section 9106(g)(2) of Public Law 111–11 (Omnibus Public Land Management Act of 2009) shall be applied by substituting "2023" for "2021".

SEC. 206. (a) Section 104(c) of the Reclamation States Emergency Drought Relief Act of 1991 (43 U.S.C. 2214(c)) shall be applied by substituting "2023" for "2021".

(b) Section 301 of the Reclamation States Emergency Drought Relief Act of 1991 (43 U.S.C. 2241) shall be applied by substituting "2023" for "2021".

SEC. 207. Section 1101(d) of the Reclamation Projects Authorization and Adjustment Act of 1992 (Public Law 102–575) is amended by striking "$10,000,000" and inserting "$13,000,000".

SEC. 208. Section 103(f)(4)(A) of Public Law 108–361 (the CALFED Bay-Delta Authorization Act) (118 Stat. 1681) is amended by striking "$25,000,000" and inserting "$30,000,000".

TITLE IV—GENERAL PROVISIONS

(INCLUDING TRANSFERS OF FUNDS)

RESTRICTION ON USE OF FUNDS

SEC. 401. No part of any appropriation contained in this Act shall be available for any activity or the publication or distribution of literature that in any way tends to promote public support or opposition to any legislative proposal on which Congressional action is not complete other than to communicate to Members of Congress as described in 18 U.S.C. 1913.

OBLIGATION OF APPROPRIATIONS

SEC. 402. No part of any appropriation contained in this Act shall remain available for obligation beyond the current fiscal year unless expressly so provided herein.

DISCLOSURE OF ADMINISTRATIVE EXPENSES

SEC. 403. The amount and basis of estimated overhead charges, deductions, reserves, or holdbacks, including working capital fund charges, from programs, projects, activities and subactivities to support government-wide, departmental, agency, or bureau administrative functions or headquarters, regional, or central operations shall be presented in annual budget justifications to the Committees on Appropriations of the House of Representatives and the Senate. Changes to such estimates shall be presented to the Committees on Appropriations

MINING APPLICATIONS

SEC. 404. (a) LIMITATION OF FUNDS.—None of the funds appropriated or otherwise made available pursuant to this Act shall be obligated or expended to accept or process applications for a patent for any mining or mill site claim located under the general mining laws.

(b) EXCEPTIONS.—Subsection (a) shall not apply if the Secretary of the Interior determines that, for the claim concerned: (1) a patent application was filed with the Secretary on or before September 30, 1994; and (2) all requirements established under sections 2325 and 2326 of the Revised Statutes (30 U.S.C. 29 and 30) for vein or lode claims, sections 2329, 2330, 2331, and 2333 of the Revised Statutes (30 U.S.C. 35, 36, and 37) for placer claims, and section 2337 of the Revised Statutes (30 U.S.C. 42) for mill site claims, as the case may be, were fully complied with by the applicant by that date.

(c) REPORT.—On September 30, 2024, the Secretary of the Interior shall file with the House and Senate Committees on Appropriations and the Committee on Natural Resources of the House and the Committee on Energy and Natural Resources of the Senate a report on actions taken by the Department under the plan submitted pursuant to section 314(c) of the Department of the Interior and Related Agencies Appropriations Act, 1997 (Public Law 104–208).

(d) MINERAL EXAMINATIONS.—In order to process patent applications in a timely and responsible manner, upon the request of a patent applicant, the Secretary of the Interior shall allow the applicant to fund a qualified third-party contractor to be selected by the Director of the Bureau of Land Management to conduct a mineral examination of the mining claims or mill sites contained in a patent application as set forth in subsection (b). The Bureau of Land Management shall have the sole responsibility to choose and pay the third-party contractor in accordance with the standard procedures employed by the Bureau of Land Management in the retention of third-party contractors.

CONTRACT SUPPORT COSTS, PRIOR YEAR LIMITATION

SEC. 405. Sections 405 and 406 of division F of the Consolidated and Further Continuing Appropriations Act, 2015 (Public Law 113–235) shall continue in effect in fiscal years 2023 and 2024.

CONTRACT SUPPORT COSTS, FISCAL YEAR 2023 AND 2024 LIMITATION

SEC. 406. Amounts provided by this Act for fiscal years 2023 and 2024 under the headings "Contract Support Costs" are the only amounts available for contract support costs arising out of self-determination or self-governance contracts, grants, compacts, or annual funding agreements for each such fiscal year: Provided, That such amounts provided by this Act are not available for payment of claims for contract support costs for prior years, or for repayments of payments for settlements or judgments awarding contract support costs for prior years: Provided further, That notwithstanding any other provision of law, funds appropriated under the headings "Contract Support Costs" in this or prior Acts shall remain available for disbursement until any claims relating to such amounts and submitted under chapter 71 of title 41, United States Code, are resolved.

FOREST MANAGEMENT PLANS

SEC. 407. The Secretary of Agriculture shall not be considered to be in violation of subparagraph 6(f)(5)(A) of the Forest and Rangeland Renewable Resources Planning Act of 1974 (16 U.S.C. 1604(f)(5)(A)) solely because more than 15 years have passed without revision of the plan for a unit of the National Forest System. Nothing in this section exempts the Secretary from any other requirement of the Forest and Rangeland Renewable Resources Planning Act (16 U.S.C. 1600 et seq.) or any other law: Provided, That if the Secretary is not acting expeditiously and in good faith, within the funding available, to revise a plan for a unit of the National Forest System, this section shall be void with respect to such plan and a court of proper jurisdiction may order completion of the plan on an accelerated basis.

PROHIBITION WITHIN NATIONAL MONUMENTS

SEC. 408. No funds provided in this Act may be expended to conduct preleasing, leasing and related activities under either the Mineral Leasing Act (30 U.S.C. 181 et seq.) or the Outer Continental Shelf Lands Act (43 U.S.C. 1331 et seq.) within the boundaries of a National Monument established pursuant to the Act of June 8, 1906 (16 U.S.C. 431 et seq.) as such boundary existed on January 20, 2001, except where such activities are allowed under the Presidential proclamation establishing such monument.

LIMITATION ON TAKINGS

SEC. 409. Unless otherwise provided herein, no funds appropriated in this Act for the acquisition of lands or interests in lands may be expended for the filing of declarations of taking or complaints in condemnation without notice to the House and Senate Committees on Appropriations: Provided, That this provision shall not apply to funds appropriated to implement the Everglades National Park Protection and Expansion Act of 1989, or to funds appropriated for Federal assistance to the State of Florida to acquire lands for Everglades restoration purposes.

PROHIBITION ON NO-BID CONTRACTS

SEC. 410. None of the funds appropriated or otherwise made available by this Act to executive branch agencies may be used to enter into any Federal contract unless such contract is entered into in accordance with the requirements of Chapter 33 of title 41, United States Code, or Chapter 137 of title 10, United States Code, and the Federal Acquisition Regulation, unless—

(1) Federal law specifically authorizes a contract to be entered into without regard for these requirements, including formula grants for States, or federally recognized Indian tribes;

(2) such contract is authorized by the Indian Self-Determination and Education Assistance Act (Public Law 93–638, 25 U.S.C. 450 et seq.) or by any other Federal laws that specifically authorize a contract within an Indian tribe as defined in section 4(e) of that Act (25 U.S.C. 450b(e)); or

(3) such contract was awarded prior to the date of enactment of this Act.

POSTING OF REPORTS

SEC. 411. (a) Any agency receiving funds made available in this Act, shall, subject to subsections (b) and (c), post on the public website of that agency any report required to be submitted by the Congress in this or any other Act, upon the determination by the head of the agency that it shall serve the national interest.

(b) Subsection (a) shall not apply to a report if—

(1) the public posting of the report compromises national security; or

(2) the report contains proprietary information.

(c) The head of the agency posting such report shall do so only after such report has been made available to the requesting Committee or Committees of Congress for no less than 45 days.

NATIONAL ENDOWMENT FOR THE ARTS GRANT GUIDELINES

SEC. 412. Of the funds provided to the National Endowment for the Arts—

(1) The Chairperson shall only award a grant to an individual if such grant is awarded to such individual for a literature fellowship, National Heritage Fellowship, or American Jazz Masters Fellowship.

(2) The Chairperson shall establish procedures to ensure that no funding provided through a grant, except a grant made to a State or local arts agency, or regional group, may be used to make a grant to any other organization or individual to conduct activity independent of the direct grant recipient. Nothing in this subsection shall prohibit payments made in exchange for goods and services.

(3) No grant shall be used for seasonal support to a group, unless the application is specific to the contents of the season, including identified programs or projects.

NATIONAL ENDOWMENT FOR THE ARTS PROGRAM PRIORITIES

SEC. 413. (a) In providing services or awarding financial assistance under the National Foundation on the Arts and the Humanities Act of 1965 from funds appropriated under this Act, the Chairperson of the National Endowment for the Arts shall ensure that priority is given to providing services or awarding financial assistance for projects, productions, workshops, or programs that serve underserved populations.

(b) In this section:

(1) The term "underserved population" means a population of individuals, including urban minorities, who have historically been outside the purview of arts and humanities programs due to factors such as a high incidence of income below the poverty line or to geographic isolation.

(2) The term "poverty line" means the poverty line (as defined by the Office of Management and Budget, and revised annually in accordance with section 673(2) of the Community Services Block Grant Act (42 U.S.C. 9902(2))) applicable to a family of the size involved.

(c) In providing services and awarding financial assistance under the National Foundation on the Arts and Humanities Act of 1965 with funds appropriated by this Act, the Chairperson of the National Endowment for the Arts shall ensure that priority is given to providing services or awarding financial assistance for projects, productions, workshops, or programs that will encourage public knowledge, education, understanding, and appreciation of the arts.

(d) With funds appropriated by this Act to carry out section 5 of the National Foundation on the Arts and Humanities Act of 1965—

(1) the Chairperson shall establish a grant category for projects, productions, workshops, or programs that are of national impact or availability or are able to tour several States;

(2) the Chairperson shall not make grants exceeding 15 percent, in the aggregate, of such funds to any single State, excluding grants made under the authority of paragraph (1);

(3) the Chairperson shall report to the Congress annually and by State, on grants awarded by the Chairperson in each grant category under section 5 of such Act; and

(4) the Chairperson shall encourage the use of grants to improve and support community-based music performance and education.

STATUS OF BALANCES OF APPROPRIATIONS

SEC. 414. The Department of the Interior, the Environmental Protection Agency, the Forest Service, and the Indian Health Service shall provide the Committees on Appropriations of the House of Representatives and Senate quarterly reports on the status of balances of appropriations including all uncommitted, committed, and unobligated funds in each program and activity within 60 days of enactment of this Act.

EXTENSION OF GRAZING PERMITS

SEC. 415. The terms and conditions of section 325 of Public Law 108–108 (117 Stat. 1307), regarding grazing permits issued by the Forest Service on any lands not subject to administration under section 402 of the Federal Lands Policy and Management Act (43 U.S.C. 1752), shall remain in effect for fiscal year 2023.

FUNDING PROHIBITION

SEC. 416. (a) None of the funds made available in this Act may be used to maintain or establish a computer network unless such network is designed to block access to pornography websites.

(b) Nothing in subsection (a) shall limit the use of funds necessary for any Federal, State, tribal, or local law enforcement agency or any other entity carrying out criminal investigations, prosecution, or adjudication activities.

HUMANE TRANSFER AND TREATMENT OF ANIMALS

SEC. 417. (a) Notwithstanding any other provision of law, the Secretary of the Interior, with respect to land administered by the Bureau of Land Management, or the Secretary of Agriculture, with respect to land administered by the Forest Service (referred to in this section as the "Secretary concerned"), may transfer excess wild horses and burros that have been removed from land administered by the Secretary concerned to other Federal, State, and local government agencies for use as work animals.

(b) The Secretary concerned may make a transfer under subsection (a) immediately on the request of a Federal, State, or local government agency.

(c) An excess wild horse or burro transferred under subsection (a) shall lose status as a wild free-roaming horse or burro (as defined in section 2 of Public Law 92–195 (commonly known as the "Wild Free-Roaming Horses and Burros Act") (16 U.S.C. 1332)).

(d) A Federal, State, or local government agency receiving an excess wild horse or burro pursuant to subsection (a) shall not—

(1) destroy the horse or burro in a manner that results in the destruction of the horse or burro into a commercial product;

(2) sell or otherwise transfer the horse or burro in a manner that results in the destruction of the horse or burro for processing into a commercial product; or

(3) euthanize the horse or burro, except on the recommendation of a licensed veterinarian in a case of severe injury, illness, or advanced age.

(e) Amounts appropriated by this Act shall not be available for—

(1) the destruction of any healthy, unadopted, and wild horse or burro under the jurisdiction of the Secretary concerned (including a contractor); or

(2) the sale of a wild horse or burro that results in the destruction of the wild horse or burro for processing into a commercial product.

FOREST SERVICE FACILITY REALIGNMENT AND ENHANCEMENT AUTHORIZATION EXTENSION

SEC. 418. Section 503(f) of Public Law 109–54 (16 U.S.C. 580d note) shall be applied by substituting "September 30, 2023" for "September 30, 2019".

LOCAL COOPERATOR TRAINING AGREEMENTS AND TRANSFERS OF EXCESS EQUIPMENT AND SUPPLIES FOR WILDFIRES

SEC. 419. The Secretary of the Interior is authorized to enter into grants and cooperative agreements with volunteer fire departments, rural fire departments, rangeland fire protection associations, and similar organizations to provide for wildland fire training and equipment, including supplies and communication devices. Notwithstanding section 121(c) of title 40, United States Code, or section 521 of title 40, United States Code, the Secretary is further authorized to transfer title to excess Department of the Interior firefighting equipment no longer needed to carry out the functions of the Department's wildland fire management program to such organizations.

RECREATION FEES

SEC. 420. Section 810 of the Federal Lands Recreation Enhancement Act (16 U.S.C. 6809) shall be applied by substituting "October 1, 2024" for "September 30, 2019".

LOCAL CONTRACTORS

SEC. 421. Section 412 of division E of Public Law 112–74 shall be applied by substituting "fiscal year 2023" for "fiscal year 2019", and by inserting the following proviso before the last proviso: "Provided further, That all laborers and mechanics employed by contractors and subcontractors on projects funded directly by or assisted in whole or in part by and through the Federal Government pursuant to this section shall be paid wages at rates not less than those prevailing on projects of a character similar in the locality as determined by the Secretary of Labor in accordance with subchapter IV of chapter 31 of title 40, United States Code: Provided further, That the materials used by the contractor or subcontractor are substantially manufactured, mined, and produced in the United States in accordance with chapter 83 of title 41, United States Code (commonly known as the Buy American Act): Provided further, That for each skilled craft employed on any applicable construction project under this section, demonstrate an ability to use and commit to use individuals enrolled in a registered apprenticeship program, which such individuals shall, to the greatest extent practicable, constitute not less than 20 percent of the individuals working on such project: Provided further, That all contractors and subcontractors of the eligible entity receiving grant funds shall not require mandatory arbitration for any dispute involving a worker engaged in a service for the contractor or subcontractor under this section: Provided further, That for construction projects where the total cost to the Federal Government is $25,000,000 or more, contractors or subcontractors, to the greatest extent practicable, be a party to a project labor agreement or require contractors and subcontractors to consent to a project labor agreement: Provided further, That any contractor or subcontractor awarded contracts, grants, or cooperative agreements under this section must have an explicit neutrality policy on any issue involving the organization of employees of the contractor or subcontractor, and all contractors and subcontractors, for purposes of collective bargaining:".

SHASTA-TRINITY MARINA FEE AUTHORITY AUTHORIZATION EXTENSION

SEC. 422. Section 422 of division F of Public Law 110–161 (121 Stat 1844), as amended, shall be applied by substituting "fiscal year 2023" for "fiscal year 2019".

INTERPRETIVE ASSOCIATION AUTHORIZATION EXTENSION

SEC. 423. Section 426 of division G of Public Law 113–76 (16 U.S.C. 565a–1 note) shall be applied by substituting "September 30, 2023" for "September 30, 2019".

PUERTO RICO SCHOOLING AUTHORIZATION EXTENSION

SEC. 424. The authority provided by the 19th unnumbered paragraph under heading "Administrative Provisions, Forest Service" in title III of Public Law 109–54, as amended, shall be applied by substituting "fiscal year 2023" for "fiscal year 2019".

FOREST BOTANICAL PRODUCTS FEE COLLECTION AUTHORIZATION EXTENSION

SEC. 425. Section 339 of the Department of the Interior and Related Agencies Appropriations Act, 2000 (as enacted into law by Public Law 106–113; 16 U.S.C. 528 note), as amended by section 335(6) of Public Law 108–108 and section 432 of Public Law 113–76, shall be applied by substituting "fiscal year 2023" for "fiscal year 2019".

CHACO CANYON

SEC. 426. None of the funds made available by this Act may be used to accept a nomination for oil and gas leasing under 43 CFR 3120.3 et seq, or to offer for oil and gas leasing, any Federal lands within the withdrawal area identified on the map of the Chaco Culture National Historical Park prepared by the Bureau of Land Management and dated April 2, 2019.

TRIBAL LEASES

SEC. 427. Notwithstanding any other provision of law, in the case of any lease under section 105(l) of the Indian Self-Determination and Education Assistance Act (25 U.S.C. 5324(l)), the initial lease term shall commence no earlier than the date of receipt of the lease proposal.

FOREST ECOSYSTEM HEALTH AND RECOVERY FUND

SEC. 428. The authority provided under the heading "Forest Ecosystem Health and Recovery Fund" in title I of Public Law 111–88, as amended by section 117 of division F of Public Law 113–235, shall be applied by substituting "fiscal year 2023" for "fiscal year 2020" each place it appears.

TIMBER SALE REQUIREMENTS

SEC. 429. No timber sale in Alaska's Region 10 shall be advertised if the indicated rate is deficit (defined as the value of the timber is not sufficient to cover all logging and stumpage costs and provide a normal profit and risk allowance under the Forest Service's appraisal process) when appraised using a residual value appraisal. The western red cedar timber from those sales which is surplus to the needs of the domestic processors in Alaska, shall be made available to domestic processors in the contiguous 48 United States at prevailing domestic prices. All additional western red cedar volume not sold to Alaska or contiguous 48 United States domestic processors may be exported to foreign markets at the election of the timber sale holder. All Alaska yellow cedar may be sold at prevailing export prices at the election of the timber sale holder.

TRANSFER AUTHORITY TO FEDERAL HIGHWAY ADMINISTRATION FOR THE NATIONAL PARKS AND PUBLIC LAND LEGACY RESTORATION FUND

SEC. 430. Funds provided by this Act or any other Act that are subject to the allocations in 54 U.S.C. 200402(e)(1) may be further allocated or reallocated to the Federal Highway Administration for transportation projects of the covered agencies defined in 54 U.S.C. 200401(2).

WILD AND SCENIC RIVERS COMPREHENSIVE RIVER MANAGEMENT PLANS

SEC. 431. The Secretary of Agriculture shall not be considered to be in violation of section 3(d)(1) of the Wild and Scenic Rivers Act (16 U.S.C. 1274(d)(1)) for not completing a comprehensive river management plan within 3 full fiscal years after the date of designation, except the comprehensive river management plan must be completed or appropriately updated not later than the completion of the next applicable forest plan revision.

FACILITIES RENOVATION FOR URBAN INDIAN ORGANIZATIONS TO THE EXTENT AUTHORIZED FOR OTHER GOVERNMENT CONTRACTORS

SEC. 432. The Secretary of Health and Human Services may authorize an urban Indian organization (as defined in section 4 of the Indian Health Care Improvement Act (25 U.S.C. 1603) that is awarded a grant or contract under title V of that Act

(25 U.S.C. 1651 et seq.) to use funds provided in such grant or contract for minor renovations to facilities or construction or expansion of facilities, including leased facilities, to assist the urban Indian organization in meeting or maintaining standards issued by Federal or State governments or by accreditation organizations.

TIMBER EXPORT

SEC. 433. The Secretary of Agriculture shall not be required to issue regulations under section 495 of the Forest Resources Conservation and Shortage Relief Act of 1997 (16 U.S.C. 620f) for the fiscal year ending on September 30, 2023.

ROAD CONSTRUCTION

SEC. 434. Section 8206(a) of the Agriculture Act of 2014 (16 U.S.C. 2113a(a)(4)(B)(i)) is amended by inserting "or Bureau of Land Management managed" after "National Forest System".

GENERAL PROVISION—THIS TITLE

[SEC. 1701. (a)

(1) If services performed by the designated employees under paragraph (2) of this subsection at the Department of the Interior or the Department of Agriculture during 2021 are determined by the Secretary of the Interior or the Secretary of Agriculture, as applicable, to be primarily related to emergency wildland fire suppression activities, any premium pay for such services shall be disregarded in calculating the aggregate of such employee's basic pay and premium pay for purposes of a limitation under section 5547(a) of title 5, United States Code, or under any other provision of law, whether such employee's pay is paid on a bi-weekly or calendar year basis. Any services during 2021 that generate payments payable in 2022 shall be disregarded in applying this subsection.

(2) The premium pay waiver under paragraph (1) of this subsection shall apply to individuals serving as wildland firefighters and as fire management response officials, including regional fire directors, deputy regional fire directors, agency officials who directly oversee fire operations, and fire management officers, and individuals serving on incident management teams (IMTs), at the National Interagency Fire Center (NIFC), at Geographic Area Coordinating Centers (GACCs), and at Operations centers.

(3) The Departments of the Interior and Agriculture shall provide a report to Congress detailing the number of positions, including by occupation, grade, and the aggregate pay by type of pay for each individual who receives pay authorized under subsection (a)(1).

(b) Any overtime pay for services described in subsection (a) that is payable under an authority outside of title 5, United States Code, shall be disregarded in calculating any annual limit on the amount of overtime pay payable in 2021.

(c) Any pay that is disregarded under either subsection (a) or (b) shall be disregarded in calculating such employee's aggregate pay for purposes of applying the limitation in section 5307 of title 5, United States Code, during 2021.

(d)

(1) Pay that is disregarded under subsection (a) or (b) shall not cause the aggregate of the employee's basic pay and premium pay for the applicable calendar year to exceed the rate of basic pay payable for a position at level II of the Executive Schedule under section 5313 of title 5, United States Code, as in effect at the end of such calendar year.

(2) For purposes of applying this subsection to an employee who would otherwise be subject to the premium pay limits established under section 5547 of title 5, United States Code, "premium pay" means the premium pay paid under the provisions of law cited in section 5547(a).

(3) For purposes of applying this subsection to an employee under a premium pay limit established under an authority other than section 5547 of title 5, United States Code, the agency responsible for administering such limit shall determine what payments are considered premium pay.

(4) For the purpose of applying this subsection, "basic pay" includes any applicable locality-based comparability payment under section 5304 of title 5, United States Code, any applicable special rate supplement under section 5305 of such title, or any equivalent payment under a similar provision of law.

(e) This section shall take effect as if enacted on January 1, 2021.

(f) If application of this section results in the payment of additional premium pay to a covered employee of a type that is normally creditable as basic pay for retirement or any other purpose, that additional pay shall not—

(1) be considered to be basic pay of the covered employee for any purpose; or

(2) be used in computing a lump-sum payment to the covered employee for accumulated and accrued annual leave under section 5551 or section 5552 of title 5, United States Code, or other similar provision of law.

(g) Not later than 45 days after the date of enactment of this Act, the Secretary of the Interior and Secretary of Agriculture shall jointly provide to the Committees on Appropriations of the House of Representatives and the Senate, the Senate Committee on Agriculture Nutrition and Forestry, the House of Representatives Committee on Agriculture, the Senate Committee on Energy and Natural Resources, the House of Representatives Committee on Natural Resources, Senate Committee on Homeland Security and Governmental Affairs, and the House of Representatives Committee on Oversight and Reform, a framework to modernize the wildland firefighting workforce beginning in fiscal year 2022.]

(Disaster Relief Supplemental Appropriations Act, 2022.)

[SEC. 601. Not later than 90 days after the date of enactment of this Act, the Secretary of the Interior shall submit to the House and Senate Committees on Appropriations a detailed spend plan for the funds provided to the Department of the Interior in this title in this Act for fiscal year 2022, and for each fiscal year through 2026, as part of the annual budget submission of the President under section 1105(a) of title 31, United States Code, the Secretary of the Interior shall submit a detailed spend plan for the funds provided to the Department of the Interior in this title in this Act for that fiscal year.] *(Infrastructure Investments and Jobs Appropriations Act.)*

DEPARTMENT OF JUSTICE

GENERAL ADMINISTRATION
Federal Funds

SALARIES AND EXPENSES

For expenses necessary for the administration of the Department of Justice, $196,531,000, of which $6,000,000 shall remain available until September 30, 2024, and of which not to exceed $4,000,000 for security and construction of Department of Justice facilities shall remain available until expended.

Note.—A full-year 2022 appropriation for this account was not enacted at the time the Budget was prepared; therefore, the Budget assumes this account is operating under the Continuing Appropriations Act, 2022 (Division A of Public Law 117–43, as amended). The amounts included for 2022 reflect the annualized level provided by the continuing resolution.

Program and Financing (in millions of dollars)

Identification code 015–0129–0–1–999		2021 actual	2022 est.	2023 est.
	Obligations by program activity:			
0002	Department Leadership	116	18	36
0003	Intergovernmental Relations and External Affairs		11	17
0004	Executive Support and Professional Responsibility		16	19
0005	Justice Management Division		74	122
0799	Total direct obligations	116	119	194
0801	Salaries and Expenses (Reimbursable)	26	26	40
0900	Total new obligations, unexpired accounts	142	145	234
	Budgetary resources:			
	Unobligated balance:			
1000	Unobligated balance brought forward, Oct 1	10	18	37
1012	Unobligated balance transfers between expired and unexpired accounts	3		
1070	Unobligated balance (total)	13	18	37
	Budget authority:			
	Appropriations, discretionary:			
1100	Appropriation	124	124	197
	Spending authority from offsetting collections, discretionary:			
1700	Collected	14	40	40
1701	Change in uncollected payments, Federal sources	14		
1750	Spending auth from offsetting collections, disc (total)	28	40	40
1900	Budget authority (total)	152	164	237
1930	Total budgetary resources available	165	182	274
	Memorandum (non-add) entries:			
1940	Unobligated balance expiring	–5		
1941	Unexpired unobligated balance, end of year	18	37	40
	Change in obligated balance:			
	Unpaid obligations:			
3000	Unpaid obligations, brought forward, Oct 1	22	22	2
3010	New obligations, unexpired accounts	142	145	234
3011	Obligations ("upward adjustments"), expired accounts	2		
3020	Outlays (gross)	–142	–165	–225
3041	Recoveries of prior year unpaid obligations, expired	–2		
3050	Unpaid obligations, end of year	22	2	11
	Uncollected payments:			
3060	Uncollected pymts, Fed sources, brought forward, Oct 1	–17	–21	–21
3070	Change in uncollected pymts, Fed sources, unexpired	–14		
3071	Change in uncollected pymts, Fed sources, expired	10		
3090	Uncollected pymts, Fed sources, end of year	–21	–21	–21
	Memorandum (non-add) entries:			
3100	Obligated balance, start of year	5	1	–19
3200	Obligated balance, end of year	1	–19	–10
	Budget authority and outlays, net:			
	Discretionary:			
4000	Budget authority, gross	152	164	237
	Outlays, gross:			
4010	Outlays from new discretionary authority	124	139	200
4011	Outlays from discretionary balances	18	26	25
4020	Outlays, gross (total)	142	165	225
	Offsets against gross budget authority and outlays:			
	Offsetting collections (collected) from:			
4030	Federal sources	–25	–40	–40
4040	Offsets against gross budget authority and outlays (total)	–25	–40	–40
	Additional offsets against gross budget authority only:			
4050	Change in uncollected pymts, Fed sources, unexpired	–14		
4052	Offsetting collections credited to expired accounts	11		
4060	Additional offsets against budget authority only (total)	–3		
4070	Budget authority, net (discretionary)	124	124	197
4080	Outlays, net (discretionary)	117	125	185
4180	Budget authority, net (total)	124	124	197
4190	Outlays, net (total)	117	125	185

Program Direction and Policy Coordination.—The Attorney General of the United States is responsible for leading the Department of Justice in accomplishing its missions. The Attorney General is assisted by the Deputy Attorney General, the Associate Attorney General, Department policy-level officials, and the Justice Management Division. The General Administration appropriation provides the resources for the programs and operations of the Attorney General, the Deputy Attorney General, the Associate Attorney General and their Offices, several Senior Policy Offices, and the Justice Management Division.

Object Classification (in millions of dollars)

Identification code 015–0129–0–1–999		2021 actual	2022 est.	2023 est.
	Direct obligations:			
	Personnel compensation:			
11.1	Full-time permanent	52	52	75
11.3	Other than full-time permanent	4	4	4
11.5	Other personnel compensation	1	1	2
11.9	Total personnel compensation	57	57	81
12.1	Civilian personnel benefits	19	19	25
21.0	Travel and transportation of persons	1	1	1
23.1	Rental payments to GSA	18	21	27
23.2	Rental payments to others	1	1	1
23.3	Communications, utilities, and miscellaneous charges	2	2	4
25.1	Advisory and assistance services	4	4	
25.2	Other services from non-Federal sources	1	1	17
25.3	Other goods and services from Federal sources	8	8	22
25.4	Operation and maintenance of facilities	1	1	1
25.7	Operation and maintenance of equipment	2	2	2
26.0	Supplies and materials	2	2	2
31.0	Equipment			11
99.0	Direct obligations	116	119	194
99.0	Reimbursable obligations	26	26	40
99.9	Total new obligations, unexpired accounts	142	145	234

Employment Summary

Identification code 015–0129–0–1–999	2021 actual	2022 est.	2023 est.
1001 Direct civilian full-time equivalent employment	394	394	591
2001 Reimbursable civilian full-time equivalent employment	69	64	64

JUSTICE INFORMATION SHARING TECHNOLOGY

(INCLUDING TRANSFER OF FUNDS)

For necessary expenses for information sharing technology, including planning, development, deployment and departmental direction, $153,057,000, to remain available until expended: Provided, That the Attorney General may transfer up to $40,000,000 to this account, from funds available to the Department of Justice for information technology, to remain available until expended, for enterprise-wide information technology initiatives: Provided further, That the transfer authority in the preceding proviso is in addition to any other transfer authority contained in this Act: Provided further, That any transfer pursuant to the first proviso shall be treated as a reprogramming under section 504 of this Act and shall not be available for obligation or expenditure except in compliance with the procedures set forth in that section.

Note.—A full-year 2022 appropriation for this account was not enacted at the time the Budget was prepared; therefore, the Budget assumes this account is operating under the Continuing Appropriations Act, 2022 (Division A of Public Law 117–43, as amended). The amounts included for 2022 reflect the annualized level provided by the continuing resolution.

General Administration—Continued
Federal Funds—Continued

JUSTICE INFORMATION SHARING TECHNOLOGY—Continued

Program and Financing (in millions of dollars)

Identification code 015–0134–0–1–751	2021 actual	2022 est.	2023 est.
Obligations by program activity:			
0001 Justice Information Sharing Technology	38	34	153
0801 Justice Information Sharing Technology (Reimbursable)	19	50	50
0900 Total new obligations, unexpired accounts	57	84	203
Budgetary resources:			
Unobligated balance:			
1000 Unobligated balance brought forward, Oct 1	52	55	55
1001 Discretionary unobligated balance brought fwd, Oct 1	49		
1011 Unobligated balance transfer from other acct [015–0409]	4		
1021 Recoveries of prior year unpaid obligations	8		
1033 Recoveries of prior year paid obligations	2		
1070 Unobligated balance (total)	66	55	55
Budget authority:			
Appropriations, discretionary:			
1100 Appropriation	34	34	153
Spending authority from offsetting collections, discretionary:			
1700 Collected	41	50	50
1701 Change in uncollected payments, Federal sources	–29		
1750 Spending auth from offsetting collections, disc (total)	12	50	50
1900 Budget authority (total)	46	84	203
1930 Total budgetary resources available	112	139	258
Memorandum (non-add) entries:			
1941 Unexpired unobligated balance, end of year	55	55	55
Change in obligated balance:			
Unpaid obligations:			
3000 Unpaid obligations, brought forward, Oct 1	41	32	16
3010 New obligations, unexpired accounts	57	84	203
3020 Outlays (gross)	–58	–100	–206
3040 Recoveries of prior year unpaid obligations, unexpired	–8		
3050 Unpaid obligations, end of year	32	16	13
Uncollected payments:			
3060 Uncollected pymts, Fed sources, brought forward, Oct 1	–77	–48	–48
3070 Change in uncollected pymts, Fed sources, unexpired	29		
3090 Uncollected pymts, Fed sources, end of year	–48	–48	–48
Memorandum (non-add) entries:			
3100 Obligated balance, start of year	–36	–16	–32
3200 Obligated balance, end of year	–16	–32	–35
Budget authority and outlays, net:			
Discretionary:			
4000 Budget authority, gross	46	84	203
Outlays, gross:			
4010 Outlays from new discretionary authority	30	80	186
4011 Outlays from discretionary balances	28	20	20
4020 Outlays, gross (total)	58	100	206
Offsets against gross budget authority and outlays:			
Offsetting collections (collected) from:			
4030 Federal sources	–43	–50	–50
Additional offsets against gross budget authority only:			
4050 Change in uncollected pymts, Fed sources, unexpired	29		
4053 Recoveries of prior year paid obligations, unexpired accounts	2		
4060 Additional offsets against budget authority only (total)	31		
4070 Budget authority, net (discretionary)	34	34	153
4080 Outlays, net (discretionary)	15	50	156
4180 Budget authority, net (total)	34	34	153
4190 Outlays, net (total)	15	50	156

The Justice Information Sharing Technology (JIST) appropriation provides resources to the Department of Justice (DOJ) Chief Information Officer (CIO) to ensure progress towards DOJ's strategic goals in supporting agents, attorneys, analysts, and administrative staffs across the world in support of their missions. The CIO is also responsible for ensuring these and other IT investments align with DOJ's overall IT strategy, as well as its technical reference and enterprise architectures. JIST resources will fund the following programs in FY 2023: cybersecurity, IT transformation, IT architecture and oversight, and innovation engineering.

Cybersecurity.—Enhancing DOJ's cybersecurity posture remains a top priority for the Department and its leadership, as DOJ supports a wide range of missions, including national security, law enforcement investigations, prosecution, and incarceration. The systems supporting these critical missions must secure sensitive information, enable critical mission workflows, and protect the integrity of data and information guiding vital decisions.

IT Transformation.—IT transformation is an ongoing commitment to evolve DOJ's IT environment by driving toward shared commodity infrastructure services and seeking simplified design and implementation of tools to advance the mission. These efforts allow DOJ to shift from custom, government-owned solutions, to advanced industry-leading offerings at competitive pricing. The OCIO recognizes modernization as an ongoing activity, requiring IT strategies to adapt as technology changes.

IT Architecture and Oversight.—OCIO provides guidance on IT objectives and serves as a central aggregation point for reporting on activities from across components to help ensure compliance with enterprise architecture (EA) requirements from OMB and the Government Accountability Office. OCIO provides support to a wide range of IT planning, governance, and oversight processes such as IT investment management and Capital Planning and Investment Control (CPIC), as well as the DOJ Investment Review Council and Investment Review Board, which allow OCIO to ensure alignment of investments across the Department. The EA repository contains information on all departmental system, aligns investments to these systems, and maintains the Department's IT asset inventory in compliance with OMB Circular A-130. Oversight of the DOJ's IT environment by the CIO is vital given the role of technology in supporting DOJ's varied legal, investigative, and administrative missions. JIST resources fund the DOJ-wide IT architecture governance and oversight responsibilities of the OCIO. These efforts support the CIO's responsibilities in complying with FITARA, the Clinger-Cohen Act, and other applicable laws, regulations and Executive Orders covering Federal information technology management.

Innovation Engineering.—OCIO facilitates adoption of new and innovative technologies to support DOJ mission requirements. By creating partnerships with DOJ components, Federal agencies, and industry for the exploration of these new technologies, OCIO is responsible for leading the ideation, design, planning, and execution of enterprise-wide IT innovations to enhance DOJ user experiences, while ensuring alignment with DOJ architectures and strategic priorities.

Object Classification (in millions of dollars)

Identification code 015–0134–0–1–751	2021 actual	2022 est.	2023 est.
Direct obligations:			
11.1 Personnel compensation: Full-time permanent	5	5	7
12.1 Civilian personnel benefits	1	1	2
23.1 Rental payments to GSA	1	1	1
23.3 Communications, utilities, and miscellaneous charges			1
25.1 Advisory and assistance services	11	13	115
25.2 Other services from non-Federal sources	1	1	
25.3 Other goods and services from Federal sources		6	17
25.7 Operation and maintenance of equipment	18		
31.0 Equipment	1	7	10
99.0 Direct obligations	38	34	153
99.0 Reimbursable obligations	19	50	50
99.9 Total new obligations, unexpired accounts	57	84	203

Employment Summary

Identification code 015–0134–0–1–751	2021 actual	2022 est.	2023 est.
1001 Direct civilian full-time equivalent employment	32	32	48

DEPARTMENT OF JUSTICE

TACTICAL LAW ENFORCEMENT WIRELESS COMMUNICATIONS

Program and Financing (in millions of dollars)

Identification code 015–0132–0–1–751	2021 actual	2022 est.	2023 est.
Budgetary resources:			
Unobligated balance:			
1000 Unobligated balance brought forward, Oct 1	1	1	1
1930 Total budgetary resources available	1	1	1
Memorandum (non-add) entries:			
1941 Unexpired unobligated balance, end of year	1	1	1
4180 Budget authority, net (total)			
4190 Outlays, net (total)			

In 2013, operational and maintenance funding for legacy radio networks was transferred back to the participating components. The management of this program shifted to the Federal Bureau of Investigation, including resources for developing new technologies, as well as improving and upgrading radio infrastructure. The transfer of activities is complete.

EXECUTIVE OFFICE FOR IMMIGRATION REVIEW

(INCLUDING TRANSFER OF FUNDS)

For expenses necessary for the administration of immigration-related activities of the Executive Office for Immigration Review, $1,354,889,000, of which $4,000,000 shall be derived by transfer from the Executive Office for Immigration Review fees deposited in the "Immigration Examinations Fee" account: Provided, That of the amounts made available under this heading, $125,000,000 shall remain available until expended, of which $75,000,000 shall be available for necessary build-out and modifications of courtroom space: Provided further, That, of the amounts made available under this heading, not less than $223,371,000 shall be for Legal Access Programs activities, of which $150,000,000 shall remain available until expended to make grants and enter into contracts or cooperative agreements to provide legal representation: Provided further, That not more than 3 percent of the funds made available for legal representation in the previous proviso shall be available for necessary administrative expenses.

Note.—A full-year 2022 appropriation for this account was not enacted at the time the Budget was prepared; therefore, the Budget assumes this account is operating under the Continuing Appropriations Act, 2022 (Division A of Public Law 117–43, as amended). The amounts included for 2022 reflect the annualized level provided by the continuing resolution.

Program and Financing (in millions of dollars)

Identification code 015–0339–0–1–751	2021 actual	2022 est.	2023 est.
Obligations by program activity:			
0001 Executive Office for Immigration Review (EOIR)	763	761	1,230
0799 Total direct obligations	763	765	891
0801 Executive Office for Immigration Review (EOIR) Reimb	5	24	24
0809 Reimbursable program activities, subtotal	5	24	24
0900 Total new obligations, unexpired accounts	768	785	1,254
Budgetary resources:			
Unobligated balance:			
1000 Unobligated balance brought forward, Oct 1	19	7	
1012 Unobligated balance transfers between expired and unexpired accounts	18	20	
1070 Unobligated balance (total)	37	27	
Budget authority:			
Appropriations, discretionary:			
1100 Appropriation	730	730	1,351
1121 Appropriations transferred from other acct [070–5088]	4	4	4
1160 Appropriation, discretionary (total)	734	734	1,355
Spending authority from offsetting collections, discretionary:			
1701 Change in uncollected payments, Federal sources	5	24	24
1900 Budget authority (total)	739	758	1,379
1930 Total budgetary resources available	776	785	1,379
Memorandum (non-add) entries:			
1940 Unobligated balance expiring	–1		
1941 Unexpired unobligated balance, end of year	7		125
Change in obligated balance:			
Unpaid obligations:			
3000 Unpaid obligations, brought forward, Oct 1	226	321	236
3010 New obligations, unexpired accounts	768	785	1,254
3011 Obligations ("upward adjustments"), expired accounts	13		
3020 Outlays (gross)	–660	–870	–1,375
3041 Recoveries of prior year unpaid obligations, expired	–26		
3050 Unpaid obligations, end of year	321	236	115
Uncollected payments:			
3060 Uncollected pymts, Fed sources, brought forward, Oct 1		–5	–29
3070 Change in uncollected pymts, Fed sources, unexpired	–5	–24	–24
3090 Uncollected pymts, Fed sources, end of year	–5	–29	–53
Memorandum (non-add) entries:			
3100 Obligated balance, start of year	226	316	207
3200 Obligated balance, end of year	316	207	62
Budget authority and outlays, net:			
Discretionary:			
4000 Budget authority, gross	739	758	1,379
Outlays, gross:			
4010 Outlays from new discretionary authority	528	677	1,230
4011 Outlays from discretionary balances	132	193	145
4020 Outlays, gross (total)	660	870	1,375
Offsets against gross budget authority and outlays:			
Offsetting collections (collected) from:			
4030 Federal sources	–3	–22	–22
4033 Non-Federal sources	–2	–2	–2
4040 Offsets against gross budget authority and outlays (total)	–5	–24	–24
Additional offsets against gross budget authority only:			
4050 Change in uncollected pymts, Fed sources, unexpired	–5	–24	–24
4052 Offsetting collections credited to expired accounts	5	24	24
4070 Budget authority, net (discretionary)	734	734	1,355
4080 Outlays, net (discretionary)	655	846	1,351
4180 Budget authority, net (total)	734	734	1,355
4190 Outlays, net (total)	655	846	1,351

Summary of Budget Authority and Outlays (in millions of dollars)

	2021 actual	2022 est.	2023 est.
Enacted/requested:			
Budget Authority	734	734	1,355
Outlays	655	846	1,351
Legislative proposal, subject to PAYGO:			
Budget Authority			450
Outlays			68
Total:			
Budget Authority	734	734	1,805
Outlays	655	846	1,419

The Executive Office for Immigration Review (EOIR) was created on January 9, 1983 through an internal Department of Justice (DOJ) reorganization that combined the Board of Immigration Appeals (BIA) with the Immigration Judge function. In addition to establishing EOIR as a separate agency within DOJ, this reorganization made the Immigration Courts independent of the agency charged with enforcement of Federal immigration laws. Under delegated authority from the Attorney General, EOIR conducts immigration court proceedings, appellate reviews, and administrative hearings. The Office of the Chief Administrative Hearing Officer was added in 1987. EOIR is headed by a Director, appointed by the Attorney General, who oversees approximately 70 Immigration Courts nationwide, the BIA, and the headquarters organization located in Falls Church.

Object Classification (in millions of dollars)

Identification code 015–0339–0–1–751	2021 actual	2022 est.	2023 est.
Direct obligations:			
Personnel compensation:			
11.1 Full-time permanent	214	214	336
11.3 Other than full-time permanent	47	47	76
11.5 Other personnel compensation	3	3	8
11.9 Total personnel compensation	264	264	420
12.1 Civilian personnel benefits	93	93	114
21.0 Travel and transportation of persons	1	1	7
22.0 Transportation of things	1	1	1
23.1 Rental payments to GSA	61	75	90
23.2 Rental payments to others	1	1	
23.3 Communications, utilities, and miscellaneous charges	6	6	21
24.0 Printing and reproduction	1	1	2
25.1 Advisory and assistance services	88	90	129

EXECUTIVE OFFICE FOR IMMIGRATION REVIEW—Continued

Object Classification—Continued

Identification code 015–0339–0–1–751		2021 actual	2022 est.	2023 est.
25.2	Other services from non-Federal sources	74	74	115
25.3	Other purchases & Svcs from Gov't accounts	8	8	33
25.4	Operation and maintenance of facilities	25	25	28
25.7	Operation and maintenance of equipment	80	79	73
26.0	Supplies and materials	2	2	8
31.0	Equipment	35	19	70
32.0	Land and structures	23	21	95
41.0	Grants, subsidies, and contributions			23
42.0	Insurance claims and indemnities		1	1
99.0	Direct obligations	763	761	1,230
99.0	Reimbursable obligations	5	24	24
99.9	Total new obligations, unexpired accounts	768	785	1,254

Employment Summary

Identification code 015–0339–0–1–751		2021 actual	2022 est.	2023 est.
1001	Direct civilian full-time equivalent employment	2,277	2,621	3,539

EXECUTIVE OFFICE FOR IMMIGRATION REVIEW

(Legislative proposal, subject to PAYGO)

Program and Financing (in millions of dollars)

Identification code 015–0339–4–1–751		2021 actual	2022 est.	2023 est.
	Obligations by program activity:			
0001	Executive Office for Immigration Review (EOIR)			68
	Budgetary resources:			
	Budget authority:			
	Appropriations, mandatory:			
1200	Appropriation			450
1930	Total budgetary resources available			450
	Memorandum (non-add) entries:			
1941	Unexpired unobligated balance, end of year			382
	Change in obligated balance:			
	Unpaid obligations:			
3010	New obligations, unexpired accounts			68
3020	Outlays (gross)			−68
	Budget authority and outlays, net:			
	Mandatory:			
4090	Budget authority, gross			450
	Outlays, gross:			
4100	Outlays from new mandatory authority			68
4180	Budget authority, net (total)			450
4190	Outlays, net (total)			68

The 2023 Budget proposes a mandatory investment of $4.5 billion in the Executive Office for Immigration Review over a 10-year period to make grants, enter into contracts or cooperative agreements to provide legal representation to individuals and families in the immigration system.

Object Classification (in millions of dollars)

Identification code 015–0339–4–1–751		2021 actual	2022 est.	2023 est.
11.1	Direct obligations: Personnel compensation: Full-time permanent			3
11.9	Total personnel compensation			3
12.1	Civilian personnel benefits			1
23.3	Communications, utilities, and miscellaneous charges			1
25.3	Other purchases & Svcs from Gov't accounts			1
31.0	Equipment			1
41.0	Grants, subsidies, and contributions			61
99.0	Direct obligations			68
99.9	Total new obligations, unexpired accounts			68

Employment Summary

Identification code 015–0339–4–1–751		2021 actual	2022 est.	2023 est.
1001	Direct civilian full-time equivalent employment			26

OFFICE OF INSPECTOR GENERAL

For necessary expenses of the Office of Inspector General, $135,856,000, including not to exceed $10,000 to meet unforeseen emergencies of a confidential character: Provided, That not to exceed $6,000,000 shall remain available until September 30, 2024.

Note.—A full-year 2022 appropriation for this account was not enacted at the time the Budget was prepared; therefore, the Budget assumes this account is operating under the Continuing Appropriations Act, 2022 (Division A of Public Law 117–43, as amended). The amounts included for 2022 reflect the annualized level provided by the continuing resolution.

Program and Financing (in millions of dollars)

Identification code 015–0328–0–1–751		2021 actual	2022 est.	2023 est.
	Obligations by program activity:			
0001	Office of Inspector General (Direct)	107	111	146
0801	Office of Inspector General (Reimbursable)	26	26	16
0900	Total new obligations, unexpired accounts	133	137	162
	Budgetary resources:			
	Unobligated balance:			
1000	Unobligated balance brought forward, Oct 1	24	28	36
	Budget authority:			
	Appropriations, discretionary:			
1100	Appropriation	111	111	136
1121	Appropriations transferred from other acct [015–5041]	10	10	10
1160	Appropriation, discretionary (total)	121	121	146
	Spending authority from offsetting collections, discretionary:			
1700	Collected	12	24	24
1700	Collected			1
1700	Collected			11
1701	Change in uncollected payments, Federal sources	5		
1750	Spending auth from offsetting collections, disc (total)	17	24	36
1900	Budget authority (total)	138	145	182
1930	Total budgetary resources available	162	173	218
	Memorandum (non-add) entries:			
1940	Unobligated balance expiring	−1		
1941	Unexpired unobligated balance, end of year	28	36	56
	Change in obligated balance:			
	Unpaid obligations:			
3000	Unpaid obligations, brought forward, Oct 1	20	26	17
3010	New obligations, unexpired accounts	133	137	162
3011	Obligations ("upward adjustments"), expired accounts	5	5	5
3020	Outlays (gross)	−129	−151	−177
3041	Recoveries of prior year unpaid obligations, expired	−3		
3050	Unpaid obligations, end of year	26	17	7
	Uncollected payments:			
3060	Uncollected pymts, Fed sources, brought forward, Oct 1	−29	−27	−27
3070	Change in uncollected pymts, Fed sources, unexpired	−5		
3071	Change in uncollected pymts, Fed sources, expired	7		
3090	Uncollected pymts, Fed sources, end of year	−27	−27	−27
	Memorandum (non-add) entries:			
3100	Obligated balance, start of year	−9	−1	−10
3200	Obligated balance, end of year	−1	−10	−20
	Budget authority and outlays, net:			
	Discretionary:			
4000	Budget authority, gross	138	145	182
	Outlays, gross:			
4010	Outlays from new discretionary authority	113	126	158
4011	Outlays from discretionary balances	16	25	19
4020	Outlays, gross (total)	129	151	177
	Offsets against gross budget authority and outlays:			
	Offsetting collections (collected) from:			
4030	Federal sources	−22	−24	−36
4040	Offsets against gross budget authority and outlays (total)	−22	−24	−36
	Additional offsets against gross budget authority only:			
4050	Change in uncollected pymts, Fed sources, unexpired	−5		
4052	Offsetting collections credited to expired accounts	10		

DEPARTMENT OF JUSTICE

		2021 actual	2022 est.	2023 est.
4060	Additional offsets against budget authority only (total)	5		
4070	Budget authority, net (discretionary)	121	121	146
4080	Outlays, net (discretionary)	107	127	141
4180	Budget authority, net (total)	121	121	146
4190	Outlays, net (total)	107	127	141

The Office of the Inspector General (OIG) was statutorily established in the Department of Justice on April 14, 1989. The OIG investigates alleged violations of criminal and civil laws, regulations, and ethical standards arising from the conduct of the Department's employees. The OIG provides leadership and assists management in promoting integrity, economy, efficiency, and effectiveness within the Department and in its financial, contractual, and grant relationships with others. By statute, the OIG also reports to the Attorney General, the Congress, and the public on a semiannual basis regarding its significant activities.

The Audit Division is responsible for independent audits and reviews of Department organizations, programs, functions, computer security and information technology systems, and financial statement audits. The Audit Division also conducts or reviews external audits of expenditures made under Department contracts, grants, and other agreements.

The Investigations Division investigates allegations of civil rights violations, bribery, fraud, abuse and violations of other laws, rules, and procedures that govern Department employees, contractors, and grantees. This Division also develops these cases for criminal prosecution, civil action, or administrative action. In some instances, the OIG refers allegations to components within the Department and requests notification of their findings and of any disciplinary action taken.

The Evaluation and Inspections Division conducts program and management reviews that involve on-site inspection, statistical analysis, and other techniques to review Department programs and activities and makes recommendations for improvement.

The Oversight and Review Division investigates allegations of significant interest to the American public and the Congress, and of vital importance to the Department.

The Office of the General Counsel provides legal advice to OIG management and staff. It also drafts memoranda on issues of law; prepares administrative subpoenas; represents the OIG in personnel, contractual, ethical, and legal matters; and responds to Freedom of Information Act requests.

The Management and Planning Division provides advice to OIG senior leadership on administrative and fiscal policy, and assists OIG components in the areas of budget formulation and execution, security, personnel, training, travel, procurement, property management, telecommunications, records management, quality assurance, internal controls, and general support.

The Information Technology Division executes the OIG's IT strategic vision and goals by directing technology and business process integration, network administration, implementation of computer hardware and software, cybersecurity, applications development, programming services, policy formulation, and other mission-support activities.

Object Classification (in millions of dollars)

Identification code 015–0328–0–1–751		2021 actual	2022 est.	2023 est.
	Direct obligations:			
	Personnel compensation:			
11.1	Full-time permanent	54	59	73
11.3	Other than full-time permanent	1	1	3
11.5	Other personnel compensation	5	4	5
11.9	Total personnel compensation	60	64	81
12.1	Civilian personnel benefits	24	25	36
21.0	Travel and transportation of persons	1	1	2
23.1	Rental payments to GSA	9	9	11
23.3	Communications, utilities, and miscellaneous charges	1	1	2
25.1	Advisory and assistance services	2	2	2
25.3	Other goods and services from Federal sources	5	5	4
25.4	Operation and maintenance of facilities	1	1	1
25.7	Operation and maintenance of equipment	1	1	1
26.0	Supplies and materials	1	1	2
31.0	Equipment	2	1	4

General Administration—Continued
Federal Funds—Continued

		2021 actual	2022 est.	2023 est.
99.0	Direct obligations	107	111	146
99.0	Reimbursable obligations	26	26	16
99.9	Total new obligations, unexpired accounts	133	137	162

Employment Summary

Identification code 015–0328–0–1–751	2021 actual	2022 est.	2023 est.
1001 Direct civilian full-time equivalent employment	466	529	550
2001 Reimbursable civilian full-time equivalent employment	68	20	20

WORKING CAPITAL FUND

Program and Financing (in millions of dollars)

Identification code 015–4526–0–4–751		2021 actual	2022 est.	2023 est.
	Obligations by program activity:			
0001	Direct - Debt Collection Management	284	286	286
0002	Direct - Capital Investment and Proceeds	37	43	43
0799	Total direct obligations	321	329	329
0801	Financial and employee data	318	288	288
0802	Data Processing and Telecommunications	604	566	566
0803	Space Management	672	680	680
0805	Human Resources	32	35	35
0806	Debt Collection Management	1		
0807	Mail and Publication Services	74	87	87
0810	Security Services	59	63	63
0899	Total reimbursable obligations	1,760	1,719	1,719
0900	Total new obligations, unexpired accounts	2,081	2,048	2,048
	Budgetary resources:			
	Unobligated balance:			
1000	Unobligated balance brought forward, Oct 1	718	756	568
1012	Unobligated balance transfers between expired and unexpired accounts	119		
1021	Recoveries of prior year unpaid obligations	97		
1033	Recoveries of prior year paid obligations	16		
1070	Unobligated balance (total)	950	756	568
	Budget authority:			
	Spending authority from offsetting collections, discretionary:			
1700	Collected	1,916	2,048	2,048
1701	Change in uncollected payments, Federal sources	52		
1702	Offsetting collections (previously unavailable)	107		
1722	Unobligated balance of spending authority from offsetting collections permanently reduced	–188	–188	–100
1750	Spending auth from offsetting collections, disc (total)	1,887	1,860	1,948
1900	Budget authority (total)	1,887	1,860	1,948
1930	Total budgetary resources available	2,837	2,616	2,516
	Memorandum (non-add) entries:			
1941	Unexpired unobligated balance, end of year	756	568	468
	Change in obligated balance:			
	Unpaid obligations:			
3000	Unpaid obligations, brought forward, Oct 1	561	545	188
3010	New obligations, unexpired accounts	2,081	2,048	2,048
3020	Outlays (gross)	–2,000	–2,405	–1,948
3040	Recoveries of prior year unpaid obligations, unexpired	–97		
3050	Unpaid obligations, end of year	545	188	288
	Uncollected payments:			
3060	Uncollected pymts, Fed sources, brought forward, Oct 1	–537	–589	–589
3070	Change in uncollected pymts, Fed sources, unexpired	–52		
3090	Uncollected pymts, Fed sources, end of year	–589	–589	–589
	Memorandum (non-add) entries:			
3100	Obligated balance, start of year	24	–44	–401
3200	Obligated balance, end of year	–44	–401	–301
	Budget authority and outlays, net:			
	Discretionary:			
4000	Budget authority, gross	1,887	1,860	1,948
	Outlays, gross:			
4010	Outlays from new discretionary authority	1,732	1,860	1,948
4011	Outlays from discretionary balances	268	545	
4020	Outlays, gross (total)	2,000	2,405	1,948
	Offsets against gross budget authority and outlays:			
	Offsetting collections (collected) from:			
4030	Federal sources	–1,712	–2,048	–2,048

General Administration—Continued
Federal Funds—Continued

WORKING CAPITAL FUND—Continued

Program and Financing—Continued

Identification code 015–4526–0–4–751		2021 actual	2022 est.	2023 est.
4033	Non-Federal sources	–220		
4040	Offsets against gross budget authority and outlays (total)	–1,932	–2,048	–2,048
	Additional offsets against gross budget authority only:			
4050	Change in uncollected pymts, Fed sources, unexpired	–52		
4053	Recoveries of prior year paid obligations, unexpired accounts	16		
4060	Additional offsets against budget authority only (total)	–36		
4070	Budget authority, net (discretionary)	–81	–188	–100
4080	Outlays, net (discretionary)	68	357	–100
4180	Budget authority, net (total)	–81	–188	–100
4190	Outlays, net (total)	68	357	–100
	Memorandum (non-add) entries:			
5090	Unexpired unavailable balance, SOY: Offsetting collections	107		

The Working Capital Fund finances, on a reimbursable basis, those administrative services that can be performed more efficiently at the Department level.

Object Classification (in millions of dollars)

Identification code 015–4526–0–4–751		2021 actual	2022 est.	2023 est.
	Direct obligations:			
	Personnel compensation:			
11.1	Full-time permanent	74	91	91
11.3	Other than full-time permanent	16	11	11
11.5	Other personnel compensation	1	1	1
11.9	Total personnel compensation	91	103	103
12.1	Civilian personnel benefits	31	40	40
21.0	Travel and transportation of persons		6	6
23.1	Rental payments to GSA	17	7	7
23.3	Communications, utilities, and miscellaneous charges	1	1	1
25.1	Advisory and assistance services	88	80	80
25.2	Other services from non-Federal sources	42	47	47
25.3	Other goods and services from Federal sources	37	39	39
25.4	Operation and maintenance of facilities	3		
25.7	Operation and maintenance of equipment	5	1	1
26.0	Supplies and materials		1	1
31.0	Equipment	6	4	4
99.0	Direct obligations	321	329	329
	Reimbursable obligations:			
	Personnel compensation:			
11.1	Full-time permanent	68	54	54
11.3	Other than full-time permanent	1	6	6
11.5	Other personnel compensation	2	14	14
11.9	Total personnel compensation	71	74	74
12.1	Civilian personnel benefits	22	23	23
21.0	Travel and transportation of persons	1	2	2
23.1	Rental payments to GSA	587	627	627
23.2	Rental payments to others	2	3	3
23.3	Communications, utilities, and miscellaneous charges	138	14	14
25.1	Advisory and assistance services	169	108	108
25.2	Other services from non-Federal sources	58	62	62
25.3	Other goods and services from Federal sources	244	423	423
25.4	Operation and maintenance of facilities	79	72	72
25.7	Operation and maintenance of equipment	378	307	307
26.0	Supplies and materials	1	1	1
31.0	Equipment	10	3	3
99.0	Reimbursable obligations	1,760	1,719	1,719
99.9	Total new obligations, unexpired accounts	2,081	2,048	2,048

Employment Summary

Identification code 015–4526–0–4–751		2021 actual	2022 est.	2023 est.
1001	Direct civilian full-time equivalent employment	630	709	709
2001	Reimbursable civilian full-time equivalent employment	448	534	534

UNITED STATES PAROLE COMMISSION

Federal Funds

SALARIES AND EXPENSES

For necessary expenses of the United States Parole Commission as authorized, $14,591,000: Provided, That, notwithstanding any other provision of law, upon the expiration of a term of office of a Commissioner, the Commissioner may continue to act until a successor has been appointed.

Note.—A full-year 2022 appropriation for this account was not enacted at the time the Budget was prepared; therefore, the Budget assumes this account is operating under the Continuing Appropriations Act, 2022 (Division A of Public Law 117–43, as amended). The amounts included for 2022 reflect the annualized level provided by the continuing resolution.

Program and Financing (in millions of dollars)

Identification code 015–1061–0–1–751		2021 actual	2022 est.	2023 est.
	Obligations by program activity:			
0001	Determination of parole of prisoners and supervision of parolees	11	14	15
	Budgetary resources:			
	Budget authority:			
	Appropriations, discretionary:			
1100	Appropriation	14	14	15
1930	Total budgetary resources available	14	14	15
	Memorandum (non-add) entries:			
1940	Unobligated balance expiring	–3		
	Change in obligated balance:			
	Unpaid obligations:			
3000	Unpaid obligations, brought forward, Oct 1	3	3	2
3010	New obligations, unexpired accounts	11	14	15
3020	Outlays (gross)	–11	–15	–15
3050	Unpaid obligations, end of year	3	2	2
	Memorandum (non-add) entries:			
3100	Obligated balance, start of year	3	3	2
3200	Obligated balance, end of year	3	2	2
	Budget authority and outlays, net:			
	Discretionary:			
4000	Budget authority, gross	14	14	15
	Outlays, gross:			
4010	Outlays from new discretionary authority	9	12	13
4011	Outlays from discretionary balances	2	3	2
4020	Outlays, gross (total)	11	15	15
4180	Budget authority, net (total)	14	14	15
4190	Outlays, net (total)	11	15	15

The United States Parole Commission is responsible for 1) making parole release and revocation decisions for all parole-eligible Federal and District of Columbia Code offenders; 2) setting and enforcing the conditions of supervised release for District of Columbia Code offenders; 3) making release decisions for United States citizens convicted of a crime in another country who voluntarily return to the United States for service of sentence; 4) performing parole-related functions for certain military and State offenders; and 5) exercising decision-making authority over State offenders who are on the State probation or parole, and are transferred to Federal authorities under the witness security program.

The Parole Commission works to reduce offender recidivism rates by implementing new revocation guidelines and establishing alternatives to incarceration for low-risk, non-violent offenders. In addition, the Commission seeks to improve the rehabilitation process by monitoring an effective offender supervision program through U.S. and District of Columbia probation officers, and through research studies that evaluate the effectiveness of offender supervision programs. The Parole Commission has oversight responsibility for the supervision of District of Columbia parolees and supervised releases under the National Capital Revitalization and Self-Government Improvement Act (P.L. 105–33).

Object Classification (in millions of dollars)

Identification code 015–1061–0–1–751		2021 actual	2022 est.	2023 est.
11.1	Direct obligations: Personnel compensation: Full-time permanent	5	7	7
11.9	Total personnel compensation	5	7	7
12.1	Civilian personnel benefits	2	2	3
23.1	Rental payments to GSA	2	2	2
25.2	Other services from non-Federal sources	1	2	2
25.3	Other goods and services from Federal sources	1	1	1
99.9	Total new obligations, unexpired accounts	11	14	15

Employment Summary

Identification code 015–1061–0–1–751		2021 actual	2022 est.	2023 est.
1001	Direct civilian full-time equivalent employment	41	47	47

LEGAL ACTIVITIES AND U.S. MARSHALS
Federal Funds

SALARIES AND EXPENSES, GENERAL LEGAL ACTIVITIES

(INCLUDING TRANSFER OF FUNDS)

For expenses necessary for the legal activities of the Department of Justice, not otherwise provided for, including not to exceed $20,000 for expenses of collecting evidence, to be expended under the direction of, and to be accounted for solely under the certificate of, the Attorney General; the administration of pardon and clemency petitions; and rent of private or Government-owned space in the District of Columbia, $1,164,266,000, of which not to exceed $50,000,000 for litigation support contracts and information technology projects, including cybersecurity and hardening of critical networks, shall remain available until expended: Provided, That of the amount provided for INTERPOL Washington dues payments, not to exceed $685,000 shall remain available until expended: Provided further, That of the total amount appropriated, not to exceed $9,000 shall be available to INTERPOL Washington for official reception and representation expenses: Provided further, That of the total amount appropriated, not to exceed $9,000 shall be available to the Criminal Division for official reception and representation expenses: Provided further, That notwithstanding section 205 of this Act, upon a determination by the Attorney General that emergent circumstances require additional funding for litigation activities of the Civil Division, the Attorney General may transfer such amounts to "Salaries and Expenses, General Legal Activities" from available appropriations for the current fiscal year for the Department of Justice, as may be necessary to respond to such circumstances: Provided further, That any transfer pursuant to the preceding proviso shall be treated as a reprogramming under section 504 of this Act and shall not be available for obligation or expenditure except in compliance with the procedures set forth in that section: Provided further, That of the amount appropriated, such sums as may be necessary shall be available to the Civil Rights Division for salaries and expenses associated with the election monitoring program under the Voting Rights Act of 1965 (52 U.S.C. 10301 et seq.) and other federal statutes enforced by the Civil Rights Division that protect the right to vote, including the Help America Vote Act of 2002 (Public Law 107–252), National Voter Registration Act of 1993 (Public Law 103–31), Uniformed and Overseas Citizens Absentee Voting Act (Public Law 99–410), Civil Rights Act of 1870 (Act of May 31, 1870, ch. 114), Civil Rights Act of 1957 (Public Law 85–315), Civil Rights Act of 1960 (Public Law 86–449), Civil Rights Act of 1964 (Public Law 88–352), and Americans with Disabilities Act of 1990 (Public Law 101–336), and to reimburse the Office of Personnel Management for such salaries and expenses: Provided further, That any funds provided under this heading in prior year appropriations acts that remain available to the Civil Rights Division for the election monitoring program may be used for the purposes in the preceding proviso: Provided further, That of the amounts provided under this heading for the election monitoring program, $3,390,000 shall remain available until expended.

In addition, for reimbursement of expenses of the Department of Justice associated with processing cases under the National Childhood Vaccine Injury Act of 1986, $31,738,000, to be appropriated from the Vaccine Injury Compensation Trust Fund and to remain available until expended.

Note.—A full-year 2022 appropriation for this account was not enacted at the time the Budget was prepared; therefore, the Budget assumes this account is operating under the Continuing Appropriations Act, 2022 (Division A of Public Law 117–43, as amended). The amounts included for 2022 reflect the annualized level provided by the continuing resolution.

Program and Financing (in millions of dollars)

Identification code 015–0128–0–1–999		2021 actual	2022 est.	2023 est.
Obligations by program activity:				
0001	Conduct of Supreme Court proceedings and review of appellate	14	14	15
0002	General tax matters	110	112	121
0003	Criminal matters	240	241	265
0004	Claims, customs, and general civil matters	380	389	433
0005	Land, natural resources, and Indian matters	118	118	160
0006	Legal opinions	9	9	11
0007	Civil rights matters	164	184	222
0008	INTERPOL Washington	35	36	42
0009	Office of Pardon Attorney	4	5	22
0010	Office for Access to Justice			10
0799	Total direct obligations	1,074	1,108	1,301
0880	Salaries and Expenses, General Legal Activities (Offsetting Collections)	234	742	742
0889	Reimbursable program activities, subtotal	234	742	742
0900	Total new obligations, unexpired accounts	1,308	1,850	2,043
Budgetary resources:				
Unobligated balance:				
1000	Unobligated balance brought forward, Oct 1	46	71	27
1001	Discretionary unobligated balance brought fwd, Oct 1	39		
1012	Unobligated balance transfers between expired and unexpired accounts	13		
1021	Recoveries of prior year unpaid obligations	5		
1070	Unobligated balance (total)	64	71	27
Budget authority:				
Appropriations, discretionary:				
1100	Appropriation	960	960	1,164
Spending authority from offsetting collections, discretionary:				
1700	Collected	184	742	742
1700	Collected		70	84
1700	Collected [Transfer from 068–8145]			18
1701	Change in uncollected payments, Federal sources	145		
1750	Spending auth from offsetting collections, disc (total)	329	812	844
Spending authority from offsetting collections, mandatory:				
1800	Collected	27	34	34
1801	Change in uncollected payments, Federal sources	7		
1850	Spending auth from offsetting collections, mand (total)	34	34	34
1900	Budget authority (total)	1,323	1,806	2,042
1930	Total budgetary resources available	1,387	1,877	2,069
Memorandum (non-add) entries:				
1940	Unobligated balance expiring	–8		
1941	Unexpired unobligated balance, end of year	71	27	26
Change in obligated balance:				
Unpaid obligations:				
3000	Unpaid obligations, brought forward, Oct 1	389	392	313
3010	New obligations, unexpired accounts	1,308	1,850	2,043
3011	Obligations ("upward adjustments"), expired accounts	18		
3020	Outlays (gross)	–1,274	–1,929	–2,010
3040	Recoveries of prior year unpaid obligations, unexpired	–5		
3041	Recoveries of prior year unpaid obligations, expired	–44		
3050	Unpaid obligations, end of year	392	313	346
Uncollected payments:				
3060	Uncollected pymts, Fed sources, brought forward, Oct 1	–355	–308	–308
3070	Change in uncollected pymts, Fed sources, unexpired	–152		
3071	Change in uncollected pymts, Fed sources, expired	199		
3090	Uncollected pymts, Fed sources, end of year	–308	–308	–308
Memorandum (non-add) entries:				
3100	Obligated balance, start of year	34	84	5
3200	Obligated balance, end of year	84	5	38
Budget authority and outlays, net:				
Discretionary:				
4000	Budget authority, gross	1,289	1,772	2,008
Outlays, gross:				
4010	Outlays from new discretionary authority	966	1,541	1,747
4011	Outlays from discretionary balances	280	209	228
4020	Outlays, gross (total)	1,246	1,750	1,975
Offsets against gross budget authority and outlays:				
Offsetting collections (collected) from:				
4030	Federal sources	–360	–812	–826
4030	Federal sources [Transfer from 068–8145]			–18
4033	Non-Federal sources	–5		

SALARIES AND EXPENSES, GENERAL LEGAL ACTIVITIES—Continued

Program and Financing—Continued

Identification code 015–0128–0–1–999		2021 actual	2022 est.	2023 est.
4040	Offsets against gross budget authority and outlays (total)	–365	–812	–844
	Additional offsets against gross budget authority only:			
4050	Change in uncollected pymts, Fed sources, unexpired	–145	....	....
4052	Offsetting collections credited to expired accounts	181	....	....
4060	Additional offsets against budget authority only (total)	36	....	....
4070	Budget authority, net (discretionary)	960	960	1,164
4080	Outlays, net (discretionary)	881	938	1,131
	Mandatory:			
4090	Budget authority, gross	34	34	34
	Outlays, gross:			
4100	Outlays from new mandatory authority	22	30	30
4101	Outlays from mandatory balances	6	149	5
4110	Outlays, gross (total)	28	179	35
	Offsets against gross budget authority and outlays:			
	Offsetting collections (collected) from:			
4120	Federal sources	–27	–34	–34
	Additional offsets against gross budget authority only:			
4140	Change in uncollected pymts, Fed sources, unexpired	–7	....	....
4170	Outlays, net (mandatory)	1	145	1
4180	Budget authority, net (total)	960	960	1,164
4190	Outlays, net (total)	882	1,083	1,132

The following Department legal activities are financed from this appropriation:

Supreme Court Proceedings and Appellate Matters.—The Office of the Solicitor General conducts substantially all litigation on behalf of the United States and its agencies in the Supreme Court of the United States, approves decisions to appeal and seek further review in cases involving the United States in the lower Federal courts, and supervises the handling of litigation in the Federal appellate courts.

General Tax Matters.—The mission of the Tax Division is to enforce the nation's tax laws fully, fairly, and consistently, through both criminal and civil litigation, in order to promote voluntary compliance with the tax laws, maintain public confidence in the integrity of the tax system, and promote the sound development of the law.

Criminal Matters.—The Criminal Division develops, enforces, and supervises the application of all Federal criminal laws, except those specifically assigned to other divisions. The mission of the Criminal Division is to identify and respond to critical and emerging national and international criminal threats, and to lead the enforcement, regulatory, and intelligence communities in a coordinated nationwide response to reduce those threats.

Claims, Customs, and General Civil Matters.—The Civil Division represents the Federal Government in civil litigation to defend Federal statutes, regulations, and policies, and to avoid payment of unjustified monetary claims. It also investigates and pursues perpetrators of financial, economic, health care, and other forms of fraud to recover billions of dollars owed to the Federal Government. Examples of non-monetary litigation include the defense of thousands of challenges to immigration enforcement decisions and to Federal activities involving counterterrorism, as well as enforcement of consumer protection laws.

Environment and Natural Resource Matters.—The Environment and Natural Resources Division enforces the Nation's civil and criminal environmental laws and defends environmental challenges to Government action. Additionally, the Division represents the United States in virtually all matters concerning the use and development of the Nation's natural resources and public lands, wildlife protection, Indian rights and claims, worker safety, animal welfare, and the acquisition of Federal property.

Legal Opinions.—The Office of Legal Counsel provides written opinions and oral advice in response to requests from the Counsel to the President, the various agencies of the executive branch, and offices within the Department, including the offices of the Attorney General and Deputy Attorney General.

Civil Rights Matters.—This program enforces the Nation's Federal civil rights laws. Through the enforcement of a wide range of anti-discrimination laws, the Division gives meaning to our Nation's promise of equal opportunity. The Division works to uphold and defend the civil and constitutional rights of all individuals, particularly some of the most vulnerable members of our society. The Division enforces Federal statutes that prohibit discrimination and provide a remedy for constitutional violations.

INTERPOL Washington.—This program is the United States National Central Bureau and designated representative to INTERPOL on behalf of the Attorney General. Its mission includes, but is not limited to, facilitating international police cooperation; transmitting criminal justice, humanitarian, and other law enforcement related information between U.S. law enforcement authorities and their foreign counterparts; and coordinating and integrating information for investigations of an international nature.

Office of The Pardon Attorney.—The Office of the Pardon Attorney (OPA) receives and evaluates clemency petitions for federal crimes and prepares letters of advice for the President for each application with approval from the Deputy Attorney General. In addition, OPA responds to inquiries concerning executive clemency petitions and the clemency process from applicants, their legal representatives, members of the public, and Members of Congress; prepares all necessary documents to effect the President's decision to grant or deny clemency; and provides advisory services to White House Counsel concerning executive clemency procedures.

Office for Access to Justice.—The Office for Access to Justice helps the justice system efficiently deliver outcomes that are fair and accessible to all, irrespective of wealth and status by working with Federal agencies and state, local, and tribal justice system stakeholders to increase access to legal assistance and to improve the justice delivery systems that serve people who are unable to afford lawyers.

Reimbursable Programs.—This reflects reimbursable funding for the following:

  Civil Division.—For litigating cases under the National Childhood Vaccine Injury Act, and for litigating a number of extraordinarily large cases on behalf of the United States;

  Criminal Division.—For activities related to healthcare fraud and drug prosecutions, international training programs, and asset forfeiture related activities;

  Environment and Natural Resources Division.—From numerous client agencies for personnel, automated litigation support, and litigation consultant services for a variety of environmental, natural resource, land acquisition, and Native American cases, including from the Environmental Protection Agency for Superfund enforcement litigation; and,

  Civil Rights Division.—For activities related to the Division's Complaint Adjudication Office and Health Care Fraud activities.

Object Classification (in millions of dollars)

Identification code 015–0128–0–1–999		2021 actual	2022 est.	2023 est.
	Direct obligations:			
	Personnel compensation:			
11.1	Full-time permanent	450	450	527
11.3	Other than full-time permanent	54	54	54
11.5	Other personnel compensation	12	12	12
11.8	Special personal services payments	3	3	3
11.9	Total personnel compensation	519	519	596
12.1	Civilian personnel benefits	170	170	215
21.0	Travel and transportation of persons	5	5	5
22.0	Transportation of things	1	1	1
23.1	Rental payments to GSA	109	109	120
23.2	Rental payments to others	4	4	4
23.3	Communications, utilities, and miscellaneous charges	13	13	13
24.0	Printing and reproduction	1	1	1
25.1	Advisory and assistance services	120	153	200
25.2	Other services from non-Federal sources	12	12	13
25.3	Other goods and services from Federal sources	41	41	46
25.4	Operation and maintenance of facilities	24	24	26
25.7	Operation and maintenance of equipment	24	24	26
26.0	Supplies and materials	3	3	3
31.0	Equipment	14	14	14
41.0	Grants, subsidies, and contributions	15	15	18
99.0	Direct obligations	1,075	1,108	1,301
99.0	Reimbursable obligations	233	742	742

DEPARTMENT OF JUSTICE

Legal Activities and U.S. Marshals—Continued
Federal Funds—Continued

	2021 actual	2022 est.	2023 est.
99.9 Total new obligations, unexpired accounts	1,308	1,850	2,043

Employment Summary

Identification code 015–0128–0–1–999	2021 actual	2022 est.	2023 est.
1001 Direct civilian full-time equivalent employment	3,334	3,576	3,984
2001 Reimbursable civilian full-time equivalent employment	462	515	600

SALARIES AND EXPENSES, ANTITRUST DIVISION

For expenses necessary for the enforcement of antitrust and kindred laws, $273,006,000, to remain available until expended, of which not to exceed $5,000 shall be available for official reception and representation expenses: Provided, That notwithstanding any other provision of law, fees collected for premerger notification filings under the Hart-Scott-Rodino Antitrust Improvements Act of 1976 (15 U.S.C. 18a), regardless of the year of collection (and estimated to be $274,500,000 in fiscal year 2023), shall be retained and used for necessary expenses in this appropriation, and shall remain available until expended: Provided further, That the sum herein appropriated from the general fund shall be reduced as such offsetting collections are received during fiscal year 2023, so as to result in a final fiscal year 2023 appropriation from the general fund estimated at $0.

Note.—A full-year 2022 appropriation for this account was not enacted at the time the Budget was prepared; therefore, the Budget assumes this account is operating under the Continuing Appropriations Act, 2022 (Division A of Public Law 117–43, as amended). The amounts included for 2022 reflect the annualized level provided by the continuing resolution.

Program and Financing (in millions of dollars)

Identification code 015–0319–0–1–752	2021 actual	2022 est.	2023 est.
Obligations by program activity:			
0001 Antitrust	182	233	287
0801 Salaries and Expenses, Antitrust Division (Reimbursable)	1	1	
0900 Total new obligations, unexpired accounts	183	234	287
Budgetary resources:			
Unobligated balance:			
1000 Unobligated balance brought forward, Oct 1	6	61	64
1021 Recoveries of prior year unpaid obligations	1		
1070 Unobligated balance (total)	7	61	64
Budget authority:			
Spending authority from offsetting collections, discretionary:			
1700 Collected	237	237	237
1900 Budget authority (total)	237	237	237
1930 Total budgetary resources available	244	298	301
Memorandum (non-add) entries:			
1941 Unexpired unobligated balance, end of year	61	64	14
Change in obligated balance:			
Unpaid obligations:			
3000 Unpaid obligations, brought forward, Oct 1	37	53	49
3010 New obligations, unexpired accounts	183	234	287
3020 Outlays (gross)	–166	–238	–213
3040 Recoveries of prior year unpaid obligations, unexpired	–1		
3050 Unpaid obligations, end of year	53	49	123
Uncollected payments:			
3060 Uncollected pymts, Fed sources, brought forward, Oct 1	–2	–2	–2
3090 Uncollected pymts, Fed sources, end of year	–2	–2	–2
Memorandum (non-add) entries:			
3100 Obligated balance, start of year	35	51	47
3200 Obligated balance, end of year	51	47	121
Budget authority and outlays, net:			
Discretionary:			
4000 Budget authority, gross	237	237	237
Outlays, gross:			
4010 Outlays from new discretionary authority	142	185	185
4011 Outlays from discretionary balances	24	53	28
4020 Outlays, gross (total)	166	238	213
Offsets against gross budget authority and outlays:			
Offsetting collections (collected) from:			
4033 Non-Federal sources	–237	–237	–237
4040 Offsets against gross budget authority and outlays (total)	–237	–237	–237
4180 Budget authority, net (total)			
4190 Outlays, net (total)	–71	1	–24

Summary of Budget Authority and Outlays (in millions of dollars)

	2021 actual	2022 est.	2023 est.
Enacted/requested:			
Outlays	–71	1	–24
Legislative proposal, not subject to PAYGO:			
Outlays			–8
Total:			
Outlays	–71	1	–32

The Antitrust Division administers and enforces antitrust and related statutes. This program primarily involves the investigation of suspected violations of the antitrust laws, the conduct of civil and criminal proceedings in the Federal courts, and the maintenance of competitive conditions.

The Department of Justice Antitrust Division and the Federal Trade Commission (FTC) are responsible for reviewing corporate mergers to ensure they do not promote anticompetitive practices. Revenue collected from pre-merger filing fees, known as Hart-Scott-Rodino fees, are collected by the FTC and split evenly between the two agencies. In 2023, the Antitrust Division will continue to collect filing fees for pre-merger notifications and will retain these fees for expenditure in support of its programs.

Object Classification (in millions of dollars)

Identification code 015–0319–0–1–752	2021 actual	2022 est.	2023 est.
Direct obligations:			
Personnel compensation:			
11.1 Full-time permanent	68	94	117
11.3 Other than full-time permanent	12	17	20
11.5 Other personnel compensation	2	2	2
11.8 Special personal services payments	1	1	1
11.9 Total personnel compensation	83	114	140
12.1 Civilian personnel benefits	27	39	48
21.0 Travel and transportation of persons		1	1
23.1 Rental payments to GSA	23	24	29
23.3 Communications, utilities, and miscellaneous charges	1	1	2
25.1 Advisory and assistance services	9	12	17
25.2 Other services from non-Federal sources	6	7	10
25.3 Other goods and services from Federal sources	4	12	16
25.4 Operation and maintenance of facilities	3	4	3
25.7 Operation and maintenance of equipment	12	9	11
26.0 Supplies and materials	2	2	2
31.0 Equipment	1	1	5
32.0 Land and structures	11	7	3
99.0 Direct obligations	182	233	287
99.0 Reimbursable obligations	1	1	
99.9 Total new obligations, unexpired accounts	183	234	287

Employment Summary

Identification code 015–0319–0–1–752	2021 actual	2022 est.	2023 est.
1001 Direct civilian full-time equivalent employment	602	773	1,022

SALARIES AND EXPENSES, ANTITRUST DIVISION

(Legislative proposal, not subject to PAYGO)

Program and Financing (in millions of dollars)

Identification code 015–0319–2–1–752	2021 actual	2022 est.	2023 est.
Obligations by program activity:			
0001 Antitrust			30
Budgetary resources:			
Budget authority:			
Spending authority from offsetting collections, discretionary:			
1700 Collected			38
1900 Budget authority (total)			38
1930 Total budgetary resources available			38
Memorandum (non-add) entries:			
1941 Unexpired unobligated balance, end of year			8

SALARIES AND EXPENSES, ANTITRUST DIVISION—Continued
Program and Financing—Continued

Identification code 015–0319–2–1–752	2021 actual	2022 est.	2023 est.
Change in obligated balance:			
Unpaid obligations:			
3010 New obligations, unexpired accounts			30
3020 Outlays (gross)			–30
Budget authority and outlays, net:			
Discretionary:			
4000 Budget authority, gross			38
Outlays, gross:			
4010 Outlays from new discretionary authority			30
Offsets against gross budget authority and outlays:			
Offsetting collections (collected) from:			
4033 Non-Federal sources			–38
4040 Offsets against gross budget authority and outlays (total)			–38
4180 Budget authority, net (total)			
4190 Outlays, net (total)			–8

Object Classification (in millions of dollars)

Identification code 015–0319–2–1–752	2021 actual	2022 est.	2023 est.
Direct obligations:			
25.3 Other goods and services from Federal sources			17
31.0 Equipment			13
99.0 Direct obligations			30
99.9 Total new obligations, unexpired accounts			30

SALARIES AND EXPENSES, UNITED STATES ATTORNEYS

For necessary expenses of the Offices of the United States Attorneys, including inter-governmental and cooperative agreements, $2,772,350,000: Provided, That of the total amount appropriated, not to exceed $19,600 shall be available for official reception and representation expenses: Provided further, That not to exceed $40,000,000 shall remain available until expended: Provided further, That each United States Attorney shall establish or participate in a task force on human trafficking.

Note.—A full-year 2022 appropriation for this account was not enacted at the time the Budget was prepared; therefore, the Budget assumes this account is operating under the Continuing Appropriations Act, 2022 (Division A of Public Law 117–43, as amended). The amounts included for 2022 reflect the annualized level provided by the continuing resolution.

Program and Financing (in millions of dollars)

Identification code 015–0322–0–1–752	2021 actual	2022 est.	2023 est.
Obligations by program activity:			
0002 Criminal	1,831	1,764	2,100
0003 Civil	580	557	639
0004 Legal Education	21	21	33
0799 Total direct obligations	2,432	2,342	2,772
0801 Salaries and Expenses, United States Attorneys (Reimbursable)	58	64	64
0900 Total new obligations, unexpired accounts	2,490	2,406	2,836
Budgetary resources:			
Unobligated balance:			
1000 Unobligated balance brought forward, Oct 1	88	120	156
1001 Discretionary unobligated balance brought fwd, Oct 1	76		
1012 Unobligated balance transfers between expired and unexpired accounts	55		
1021 Recoveries of prior year unpaid obligations	9		
1033 Recoveries of prior year paid obligations	2		
1070 Unobligated balance (total)	154	120	156
Budget authority:			
Appropriations, discretionary:			
1100 Appropriation	2,342	2,342	2,772
1121 Appropriations transferred from other acct [011–1070]	1		
1160 Appropriation, discretionary (total)	2,343	2,342	2,772
Spending authority from offsetting collections, discretionary:			
1700 Collected	73	71	71
1700 Collected - HCFAC Discretionary		29	29
1701 Change in uncollected payments, Federal sources	14		
1750 Spending auth from offsetting collections, disc (total)	87	100	100
Spending authority from offsetting collections, mandatory:			
1800 Collected	32		
1801 Change in uncollected payments, Federal sources	–3		
1850 Spending auth from offsetting collections, mand (total)	29		
1900 Budget authority (total)	2,459	2,442	2,872
1930 Total budgetary resources available	2,613	2,562	3,028
Memorandum (non-add) entries:			
1940 Unobligated balance expiring	–3		
1941 Unexpired unobligated balance, end of year	120	156	192
Change in obligated balance:			
Unpaid obligations:			
3000 Unpaid obligations, brought forward, Oct 1	502	526	268
3010 New obligations, unexpired accounts	2,490	2,406	2,836
3011 Obligations ("upward adjustments"), expired accounts	14		
3020 Outlays (gross)	–2,421	–2,664	–2,746
3040 Recoveries of prior year unpaid obligations, unexpired	–9		
3041 Recoveries of prior year unpaid obligations, expired	–50		
3050 Unpaid obligations, end of year	526	268	358
Uncollected payments:			
3060 Uncollected pymts, Fed sources, brought forward, Oct 1	–132	–126	–126
3070 Change in uncollected pymts, Fed sources, unexpired	–11		
3071 Change in uncollected pymts, Fed sources, expired	17		
3090 Uncollected pymts, Fed sources, end of year	–126	–126	–126
Memorandum (non-add) entries:			
3100 Obligated balance, start of year	370	400	142
3200 Obligated balance, end of year	400	142	232
Budget authority and outlays, net:			
Discretionary:			
4000 Budget authority, gross	2,430	2,442	2,872
Outlays, gross:			
4010 Outlays from new discretionary authority	2,055	2,138	2,512
4011 Outlays from discretionary balances	332	500	234
4020 Outlays, gross (total)	2,387	2,638	2,746
Offsets against gross budget authority and outlays:			
Offsetting collections (collected) from:			
4030 Federal sources	–89	–100	–100
4033 Non-Federal sources	–1		
4040 Offsets against gross budget authority and outlays (total)	–90	–100	–100
Additional offsets against gross budget authority only:			
4050 Change in uncollected pymts, Fed sources, unexpired	–14		
4052 Offsetting collections credited to expired accounts	17		
4060 Additional offsets against budget authority only (total)	3		
4070 Budget authority, net (discretionary)	2,343	2,342	2,772
4080 Outlays, net (discretionary)	2,297	2,538	2,646
Mandatory:			
4090 Budget authority, gross	29		
Outlays, gross:			
4100 Outlays from new mandatory authority	29		
4101 Outlays from mandatory balances	5	26	
4110 Outlays, gross (total)	34	26	
Offsets against gross budget authority and outlays:			
Offsetting collections (collected) from:			
4120 Federal sources	–32		
4123 Non-Federal sources	–2		
4130 Offsets against gross budget authority and outlays (total)	–34		
Additional offsets against gross budget authority only:			
4140 Change in uncollected pymts, Fed sources, unexpired	3		
4143 Recoveries of prior year paid obligations, unexpired accounts	2		
4150 Additional offsets against budget authority only (total)	5		
4170 Outlays, net (mandatory)		26	
4180 Budget authority, net (total)	2,343	2,342	2,772
4190 Outlays, net (total)	2,297	2,564	2,646

There are 94 United States Attorneys' Offices located throughout the United States, Puerto Rico, the Virgin Islands, Guam, and the Northern Mariana Islands. The 93 U.S. Attorneys (Guam and the Northern Mariana Islands are under the direction of a single U.S. Attorney) prosecute criminal offenses against the United States, represent the Government in civil actions in which the United States is concerned, and initiate proceedings for the collection of fines, penalties, and forfeitures owed to the United States.

DEPARTMENT OF JUSTICE

Object Classification (in millions of dollars)

Identification code 015–0322–0–1–752		2021 actual	2022 est.	2023 est.
	Direct obligations:			
	Personnel compensation:			
11.1	Full-time permanent	1,114	1,175	1,222
11.3	Other than full-time permanent	97	94	151
11.5	Other personnel compensation	30	35	37
11.8	Special personal services payments	2	3	1
11.9	Total personnel compensation	1,243	1,307	1,411
12.1	Civilian personnel benefits	443	442	507
21.0	Travel and transportation of persons	8	9	21
22.0	Transportation of things	....	....	1
23.1	Rental payments to GSA	256	260	265
23.2	Rental payments to others	6	6	6
23.3	Communications, utilities, and miscellaneous charges	29	32	34
24.0	Printing and reproduction	1	1	1
25.1	Advisory and assistance services	115	58	168
25.2	Other services from non-Federal sources	33	35	40
25.3	Purchases from Govt Accts	75	56	92
25.4	Operation and maintenance of facilities	88	24	48
25.7	Operation and maintenance of equipment	68	75	73
26.0	Supplies and materials	10	11	11
31.0	Equipment	53	25	93
32.0	Land and structures	3	....	....
42.0	Insurance claims and indemnities	1	1	1
99.0	Direct obligations	2,432	2,342	2,772
99.0	Reimbursable obligations	58	64	64
99.9	Total new obligations, unexpired accounts	2,490	2,406	2,836

Employment Summary

Identification code 015–0322–0–1–752	2021 actual	2022 est.	2023 est.
1001 Direct civilian full-time equivalent employment	10,347	10,381	11,034
2001 Reimbursable civilian full-time equivalent employment	418	490	490

SALARIES AND EXPENSES, FOREIGN CLAIMS SETTLEMENT COMMISSION

For expenses necessary to carry out the activities of the Foreign Claims Settlement Commission, including services as authorized by section 3109 of title 5, United States Code, $2,504,000.

Note.—A full-year 2022 appropriation for this account was not enacted at the time the Budget was prepared; therefore, the Budget assumes this account is operating under the Continuing Appropriations Act, 2022 (Division A of Public Law 117–43, as amended). The amounts included for 2022 reflect the annualized level provided by the continuing resolution.

Program and Financing (in millions of dollars)

Identification code 015–0100–0–1–153		2021 actual	2022 est.	2023 est.
	Obligations by program activity:			
0001	Foreign Claims	2	2	3
	Budgetary resources:			
	Budget authority:			
	Appropriations, discretionary:			
1100	Appropriation	2	2	3
1930	Total budgetary resources available	2	2	3
	Change in obligated balance:			
	Unpaid obligations:			
3000	Unpaid obligations, brought forward, Oct 1	1	....	....
3010	New obligations, unexpired accounts	2	2	3
3020	Outlays (gross)	–2	–2	–3
3041	Recoveries of prior year unpaid obligations, expired	–1	....	....
	Memorandum (non-add) entries:			
3100	Obligated balance, start of year	1	....	....
	Budget authority and outlays, net:			
	Discretionary:			
4000	Budget authority, gross	2	2	3
	Outlays, gross:			
4010	Outlays from new discretionary authority	2	2	3
4180	Budget authority, net (total)	2	2	3
4190	Outlays, net (total)	2	2	3

The Foreign Claims Settlement Commission adjudicates the claims of United States nationals (individuals and corporations) for losses and injuries caused by foreign governments, pursuant to the International Claims Settlement Act of 1949 and other statutes. In 2023, the Commission will continue to administer the Albania Claims Program in accordance with the 1995 United States-Albanian Claims Settlement Agreement.

Object Classification (in millions of dollars)

Identification code 015–0100–0–1–153		2021 actual	2022 est.	2023 est.
	Direct obligations:			
11.1	Personnel compensation: Full-time permanent	1	1	1
12.1	Civilian personnel benefits	....	....	1
25.3	Other goods and services from Federal sources	1	1	1
99.9	Total new obligations, unexpired accounts	2	2	3

Employment Summary

Identification code 015–0100–0–1–153	2021 actual	2022 est.	2023 est.
1001 Direct civilian full-time equivalent employment	7	9	9

UNITED STATES MARSHALS SERVICE

SALARIES AND EXPENSES

For necessary expenses of the United States Marshals Service, $1,807,138,000, of which not to exceed $20,000 shall be available for official reception and representation expenses, and not to exceed $25,000,000 shall remain available until expended.

Note.—A full-year 2022 appropriation for this account was not enacted at the time the Budget was prepared; therefore, the Budget assumes this account is operating under the Continuing Appropriations Act, 2022 (Division A of Public Law 117–43, as amended). The amounts included for 2022 reflect the annualized level provided by the continuing resolution.

Program and Financing (in millions of dollars)

Identification code 015–0324–0–1–752		2021 actual	2022 est.	2023 est.
	Obligations by program activity:			
0002	Judicial and Courthouse Security	505	514	620
0003	Fugitive Apprehension	601	587	735
0004	Prisoner Security and Transportation	269	264	299
0005	Protection of Witnesses	65	63	71
0006	Tactical Operations	64	68	82
0799	Total direct obligations	1,504	1,496	1,807
0801	Salaries and Expenses, United States Marshals Service (Reimbursable)	37	44	44
0900	Total new obligations, unexpired accounts	1,541	1,540	1,851
	Budgetary resources:			
	Unobligated balance:			
1000	Unobligated balance brought forward, Oct 1	14	16	56
1001	Discretionary unobligated balance brought fwd, Oct 1	7	....	....
1012	Unobligated balance transfers between expired and unexpired accounts	25	25	....
1021	Recoveries of prior year unpaid obligations	3	5	....
1033	Recoveries of prior year paid obligations	5	....	....
1070	Unobligated balance (total)	47	46	56
	Budget authority:			
	Appropriations, discretionary:			
1100	Appropriation	1,496	1,496	1,807
1120	Appropriations transferred to other acct [015–1020]	–12	....	....
1121	Appropriations transferred from other acct [011–1070]	1	....	....
1160	Appropriation, discretionary (total)	1,485	1,496	1,807
	Appropriations, mandatory:			
1221	Appropriations transferred from other acct [011–5512]	....	3	8
	Spending authority from offsetting collections, discretionary:			
1700	Collected	25	44	44
1701	Change in uncollected payments, Federal sources	16	7	7
1750	Spending auth from offsetting collections, disc (total)	41	51	51
1900	Budget authority (total)	1,526	1,550	1,866
1930	Total budgetary resources available	1,573	1,596	1,922
	Memorandum (non-add) entries:			
1940	Unobligated balance expiring	–16	....	....

Legal Activities and U.S. Marshals—Continued
Federal Funds—Continued

UNITED STATES MARSHALS SERVICE—Continued

Program and Financing—Continued

Identification code 015–0324–0–1–752		2021 actual	2022 est.	2023 est.
1941	Unexpired unobligated balance, end of year	16	56	71
	Change in obligated balance:			
	Unpaid obligations:			
3000	Unpaid obligations, brought forward, Oct 1	293	291	144
3010	New obligations, unexpired accounts	1,541	1,540	1,851
3011	Obligations ("upward adjustments"), expired accounts	22		
3020	Outlays (gross)	–1,537	–1,682	–1,838
3040	Recoveries of prior year unpaid obligations, unexpired	–3	–5	
3041	Recoveries of prior year unpaid obligations, expired	–25		
3050	Unpaid obligations, end of year	291	144	157
	Uncollected payments:			
3060	Uncollected pymts, Fed sources, brought forward, Oct 1	–6	–17	–24
3070	Change in uncollected pymts, Fed sources, unexpired	–16	–7	–7
3071	Change in uncollected pymts, Fed sources, expired	5		
3090	Uncollected pymts, Fed sources, end of year	–17	–24	–31
	Memorandum (non-add) entries:			
3100	Obligated balance, start of year	287	274	120
3200	Obligated balance, end of year	274	120	126
	Budget authority and outlays, net:			
	Discretionary:			
4000	Budget authority, gross	1,526	1,547	1,858
	Outlays, gross:			
4010	Outlays from new discretionary authority	1,301	1,392	1,672
4011	Outlays from discretionary balances	233	286	155
4020	Outlays, gross (total)	1,534	1,678	1,827
	Offsets against gross budget authority and outlays:			
	Offsetting collections (collected) from:			
4030	Federal sources	–26	–44	–44
4033	Non-Federal sources	–9	–7	–7
4034	Offsetting governmental collections	–1		
4040	Offsets against gross budget authority and outlays (total)	–36	–51	–51
	Additional offsets against budget authority only:			
4050	Change in uncollected pymts, Fed sources, unexpired	–16	–7	–7
4052	Offsetting collections credited to expired accounts	6	7	7
4053	Recoveries of prior year paid obligations, unexpired accounts	5		
4060	Additional offsets against budget authority only (total)	–5		
4070	Budget authority, net (discretionary)	1,485	1,496	1,807
4080	Outlays, net (discretionary)	1,498	1,627	1,776
	Mandatory:			
4090	Budget authority, gross		3	8
	Outlays, gross:			
4100	Outlays from new mandatory authority			8
4101	Outlays from mandatory balances	3	4	3
4110	Outlays, gross (total)	3	4	11
4180	Budget authority, net (total)	1,485	1,499	1,815
4190	Outlays, net (total)	1,501	1,631	1,787

The Federal Government is represented by a United States Marshal in each of the 94 judicial districts. The primary mission of the United States Marshals Service (USMS) is to protect, defend, and enforce the American justice system by securing Federal court facilities and ensuring the safety of judges and other court personnel; apprehending fugitives and non-compliant sex offenders; exercising custody of Federal prisoners, and providing for their security and transportation from arrest to incarceration; ensuring the safety of protected government witnesses and their families; executing Federal warrants and court orders; managing seized assets acquired through illegal means; and providing custody, management, and disposal of forfeited assets. The USMS is the principal support force in the Federal judicial system and an integral part of the Federal law enforcement community.

Other Federal funds are derived from the Administrative Office of the U.S. Courts for the Judicial Facility Security Program, the Assets Forfeiture Fund for seized assets management and disposal, the Fees and Expenses of Witnesses appropriation for security and relocation of protected witnesses, the Organized Crime Drug Enforcement Task Forces Program for multi-agency drug investigations, and the Department of Health and Human Services for protecting the Strategic National Stockpile. Non-Federal funds are derived from State and local governments for witness protection and the transportation of prisoners pursuant to State writs, as well as fees collected from service of civil process and sales associated with judicial orders.

For 2023, the USMS requests program increases totaling $137.8 million. These program increases support the Administration's goals of keeping our country safe by protecting national security, countering domestic terrorism, combating violent crime, and fighting violent drug trafficking gangs and cartels. To strengthen USMS district offices, respond to increasing workload, and fight violent crime, including fugitive apprehension and enforcement operations, the USMS requests $64.5 million; requested funding will also be used to establish a national recruitment and strategic outreach branch that will facilitate hiring and diversity by attracting the highest caliber applicants. To update USMS information technology infrastructure, the USMS requests $11.7 million to transition on-premise hardware to the cloud and expand the capabilities of the USMS-proprietary SHIELD operational mobile application to incorporate judicial security functionality. To further strengthen judicial security, the USMS requests $5.0 million to update Physical Access Control Systems in Federal courthouses. To support the implementation of the Task Force Officer and Deputy U.S. Marshal body worn camera program, the USMS requests $42.5 million; requested funding will enhance the video management solution and provide necessary personnel for program development, implementation, oversight, management, and external reporting. Finally, the USMS requests $14.1 million to address increased operational requirements related to the transfer of felony cases from Oklahoma state jurisdiction to Federal courts following the U.S. Supreme Court decision in *McGirt v. Oklahoma*.

Object Classification (in millions of dollars)

Identification code 015–0324–0–1–752		2021 actual	2022 est.	2023 est.
	Direct obligations:			
	Personnel compensation:			
11.1	Full-time permanent	497	503	557
11.3	Other than full-time permanent	14	15	15
11.5	Other personnel compensation	98	109	119
11.8	Special personal services payments	7	7	7
11.9	Total personnel compensation	616	634	698
12.1	Civilian personnel benefits	310	320	366
21.0	Travel and transportation of persons	24	24	33
22.0	Transportation of things	1	1	3
23.1	Rental payments to GSA	200	202	210
23.2	Rental payments to others	13	20	20
23.3	Communications, utilities, and miscellaneous charges	24	24	26
24.0	Printing and reproduction			1
25.1	Advisory and assistance services	40	34	47
25.2	Other services from non-Federal sources	25	25	72
25.3	Other goods and services from Federal sources	75	68	82
25.4	Operation and maintenance of facilities	25	25	26
25.7	Operation and maintenance of equipment	58	49	51
25.8	Subsistence and support of persons			1
26.0	Supplies and materials	28	27	34
31.0	Equipment	51	31	125
32.0	Land and structures	13	11	11
42.0	Insurance claims and indemnities	1	1	1
99.0	Direct obligations	1,504	1,496	1,807
99.0	Reimbursable obligations	37	44	44
99.9	Total new obligations, unexpired accounts	1,541	1,540	1,851

Employment Summary

Identification code 015–0324–0–1–752	2021 actual	2022 est.	2023 est.
1001 Direct civilian full-time equivalent employment	4,976	5,039	5,345
2001 Reimbursable civilian full-time equivalent employment	121	150	139

CONSTRUCTION

For construction in space that is controlled, occupied, or utilized by the United States Marshals Service for prisoner holding and related support, $19,260,000, to remain available until expended.

DEPARTMENT OF JUSTICE

Legal Activities and U.S. Marshals—Continued
Federal Funds—Continued 727

Note.—A full-year 2022 appropriation for this account was not enacted at the time the Budget was prepared; therefore, the Budget assumes this account is operating under the Continuing Appropriations Act, 2022 (Division A of Public Law 117–43, as amended). The amounts included for 2022 reflect the annualized level provided by the continuing resolution.

Program and Financing (in millions of dollars)

Identification code 015–0133–0–1–751		2021 actual	2022 est.	2023 est.
	Obligations by program activity:			
0001	Construction	18	15	19
	Budgetary resources:			
	Unobligated balance:			
1000	Unobligated balance brought forward, Oct 1	9	8	11
1021	Recoveries of prior year unpaid obligations	2	3	3
1070	Unobligated balance (total)	11	11	14
	Budget authority:			
	Appropriations, discretionary:			
1100	Appropriation	15	15	19
1930	Total budgetary resources available	26	26	33
	Memorandum (non-add) entries:			
1941	Unexpired unobligated balance, end of year	8	11	14
	Change in obligated balance:			
	Unpaid obligations:			
3000	Unpaid obligations, brought forward, Oct 1	67	59	29
3010	New obligations, unexpired accounts	18	15	19
3020	Outlays (gross)	–24	–42	–18
3040	Recoveries of prior year unpaid obligations, unexpired	–2	–3	–3
3050	Unpaid obligations, end of year	59	29	27
	Memorandum (non-add) entries:			
3100	Obligated balance, start of year	67	59	29
3200	Obligated balance, end of year	59	29	27
	Budget authority and outlays, net:			
	Discretionary:			
4000	Budget authority, gross	15	15	19
	Outlays, gross:			
4010	Outlays from new discretionary authority		1	1
4011	Outlays from discretionary balances	24	41	17
4020	Outlays, gross (total)	24	42	18
4180	Budget authority, net (total)	15	15	19
4190	Outlays, net (total)	24	42	18

The Construction appropriation provides resources to modify spaces controlled, occupied, and/or utilized by the United States Marshals Service for prisoner holding and related support.

For 2023, the USMS requests program increases totaling $4.3 million. To increase base funding for USMS construction projects including congressionally approved new courthouses, critical courthouse renovations, and unscheduled maintenance, the USMS requests $2 million. To establish funding for the Capital Security Program, the USMS requests $2.3 million; requested funding will improve physical security in older courthouses occupied by the Federal judiciary and the USMS by separating circulation areas for the public, judiciary, and detainees.

Object Classification (in millions of dollars)

Identification code 015–0133–0–1–751		2021 actual	2022 est.	2023 est.
	Direct obligations:			
25.4	Operation and maintenance of facilities	1	1	2
31.0	Equipment	1	2	2
32.0	Land and structures	16	12	15
99.9	Total new obligations, unexpired accounts	18	15	19

FEDERAL PRISONER DETENTION

For necessary expenses related to United States prisoners in the custody of the United States Marshals Service as authorized by section 4013 of title 18, United States Code, $2,129,789,000, to remain available until expended: Provided, That not to exceed $20,000,000 shall be considered "funds appropriated for State and local law enforcement assistance" pursuant to section 4013(b) of title 18, United States Code: Provided further, That the United States Marshals Service shall be responsible for managing the Justice Prisoner and Alien Transportation System.

Note.—A full-year 2022 appropriation for this account was not enacted at the time the Budget was prepared; therefore, the Budget assumes this account is operating under the Continuing Appropriations Act, 2022 (Division A of Public Law 117–43, as amended). The amounts included for 2022 reflect the annualized level provided by the continuing resolution.

Program and Financing (in millions of dollars)

Identification code 015–1020–0–1–752		2021 actual	2022 est.	2023 est.
	Obligations by program activity:			
0001	Federal Prisoner Detention	2,196	2,172	2,130
0100	Direct program activities, subtotal	2,196	2,172	2,130
	Budgetary resources:			
	Unobligated balance:			
1000	Unobligated balance brought forward, Oct 1	27	36	70
1021	Recoveries of prior year unpaid obligations	21	34	15
1070	Unobligated balance (total)	48	70	85
	Budget authority:			
	Appropriations, discretionary:			
1100	Appropriation	2,047	2,172	2,130
1100	Appropriation - Emergency pursuant to 2011 Budget Control Act	125		
1121	Appropriations transferred from other acct [015–0324]	12		
1160	Appropriation, discretionary (total)	2,184	2,172	2,130
1900	Budget authority (total)	2,184	2,172	2,130
1930	Total budgetary resources available	2,232	2,242	2,215
	Memorandum (non-add) entries:			
1941	Unexpired unobligated balance, end of year	36	70	85
	Change in obligated balance:			
	Unpaid obligations:			
3000	Unpaid obligations, brought forward, Oct 1	332	327	346
3010	New obligations, unexpired accounts	2,196	2,172	2,130
3020	Outlays (gross)	–2,180	–2,119	–2,226
3040	Recoveries of prior year unpaid obligations, unexpired	–21	–34	–15
3050	Unpaid obligations, end of year	327	346	235
	Memorandum (non-add) entries:			
3100	Obligated balance, start of year	332	327	346
3200	Obligated balance, end of year	327	346	235
	Budget authority and outlays, net:			
	Discretionary:			
4000	Budget authority, gross	2,184	2,172	2,130
	Outlays, gross:			
4010	Outlays from new discretionary authority	1,845	1,846	1,810
4011	Outlays from discretionary balances	335	273	416
4020	Outlays, gross (total)	2,180	2,119	2,226
4180	Budget authority, net (total)	2,184	2,172	2,130
4190	Outlays, net (total)	2,180	2,119	2,226

The Federal Prisoner Detention (FPD) appropriation is responsible for the costs associated with the care of Federal detainees in the custody of the United States Marshals Service (USMS). The USMS must ensure the safe, secure, and humane confinement of persons in its custody while allowing unimpeded prisoner transportation operations. The FPD appropriation provides for housing, subsistence, transportation, medical care, and medical guard service of Federal detainees in State, local, and private facilities.

The Federal Government utilizes various methods to house detainees. The USMS acquires detention bed space for Federal detainees through several means, using the most appropriate method to maximize efficiency and effectiveness for the Government:

    1) Federally-owned and managed detention facilities, where the Government has paid for construction and operation of the facility, funded through the Federal Bureau of Prisons (BOP) appropriation;

    2) Intergovernmental Agreements (IGAs) with State and local jurisdictions, whose excess prison and jail bed capacity is utilized via a negotiated daily rate paid to those jurisdictions; and

    3) Private performance-based contract facilities, where an individual daily rate or contract minimum rate is paid. In response to the President's Executive Order (EO) 14006, "*Reforming Our Incarceration System to*

Legal Activities and U.S. Marshals—Continued
Federal Funds—Continued

FEDERAL PRISONER DETENTION—Continued

Eliminate the Use of Privately Operated Criminal Detention Facilities," the USMS began the process of discontinuing its private detention facility contracts in March 2021.

Over 80 percent of the USMS detainee population placed in government facilities will be housed under IGAs.

For 2023, the USMS requests one program increase of $106.2 million. Due to uncertainties regarding the COVID-19 pandemic and an ongoing backlog of sentenced prisoners awaiting transfer to BOP facilities, the request supplements the USMS projected detention funding requirement to allow for unforeseen upward adjustments to current cost estimates. This request increases the probability the FPD appropriation will have sufficient funding in FY 2023.

Object Classification (in millions of dollars)

Identification code 015–1020–0–1–752		2021 actual	2022 est.	2023 est.
	Direct obligations:			
	Personnel compensation:			
11.1	Full-time permanent	3	3	5
11.5	Other personnel compensation	....	1	....
11.8	Special personal services payments	1	1	1
11.9	Total personnel compensation	4	5	6
12.1	Civilian personnel benefits	1	1	2
21.0	Travel and transportation of persons	1	2	2
23.1	Rental payments to GSA	1	1	1
23.3	Communications, utilities, and miscellaneous charges	1	....	2
25.1	Advisory and assistance services	5	7	7
25.2	Other services from non-Federal sources	....	....	1
25.3	Other goods and services from Federal sources	136	95	95
25.4	Operation and maintenance of facilities	9	10	10
25.6	Medical care	111	108	148
25.7	Operation and maintenance of equipment	2	2	2
25.8	Subsistence and support of persons	1,924	1,934	1,846
26.0	Supplies and materials	1	1	1
31.0	Equipment	....	6	7
99.9	Total new obligations, unexpired accounts	2,196	2,172	2,130

Employment Summary

Identification code 015–1020–0–1–752	2021 actual	2022 est.	2023 est.
1001 Direct civilian full-time equivalent employment	25	30	42

FEES AND EXPENSES OF WITNESSES

For fees and expenses of witnesses, for expenses of contracts for the procurement and supervision of expert witnesses, for private counsel expenses, including advances, and for expenses of foreign counsel, $270,000,000, to remain available until expended, of which not to exceed $16,000,000 is for construction of buildings for protected witness safesites; not to exceed $3,000,000 is for the purchase and maintenance of armored and other vehicles for witness security caravans; and not to exceed $35,000,000 is for the purchase, installation, maintenance, and upgrade of secure telecommunications equipment and a secure automated information network to store and retrieve the identities and locations of protected witnesses: Provided, That amounts made available under this heading may not be transferred pursuant to section 205 of this Act.

Note.—A full-year 2022 appropriation for this account was not enacted at the time the Budget was prepared; therefore, the Budget assumes this account is operating under the Continuing Appropriations Act, 2022 (Division A of Public Law 117–43, as amended). The amounts included for 2022 reflect the annualized level provided by the continuing resolution.

Program and Financing (in millions of dollars)

Identification code 015–0311–0–1–752		2021 actual	2022 est.	2023 est.
	Obligations by program activity:			
0001	Fees and expenses of witnesses	256	256	206
0002	Protection of witnesses	66	66	47
0003	Private counsel	3	3	6
0004	Foreign counsel	16	16	9
0005	Alternative Dispute Resolution	2	2	2
0900	Total new obligations, unexpired accounts	343	343	270

	Budgetary resources:			
	Unobligated balance:			
1000	Unobligated balance brought forward, Oct 1	247	250	162
1021	Recoveries of prior year unpaid obligations	91	....	....
1070	Unobligated balance (total)	338	250	162
	Budget authority:			
	Appropriations, mandatory:			
1200	Appropriation	270	270	270
1230	Appropriations and/or unobligated balance of appropriations permanently reduced	–15	–15	–15
1260	Appropriations, mandatory (total)	255	255	255
1930	Total budgetary resources available	593	505	417
	Memorandum (non-add) entries:			
1941	Unexpired unobligated balance, end of year	250	162	147

	Change in obligated balance:			
	Unpaid obligations:			
3000	Unpaid obligations, brought forward, Oct 1	423	436	477
3010	New obligations, unexpired accounts	343	343	270
3020	Outlays (gross)	–239	–302	–295
3040	Recoveries of prior year unpaid obligations, unexpired	–91	....	....
3050	Unpaid obligations, end of year	436	477	452
	Memorandum (non-add) entries:			
3100	Obligated balance, start of year	423	436	477
3200	Obligated balance, end of year	436	477	452

	Budget authority and outlays, net:			
	Mandatory:			
4090	Budget authority, gross	255	255	255
	Outlays, gross:			
4100	Outlays from new mandatory authority	106	174	174
4101	Outlays from mandatory balances	133	128	121
4110	Outlays, gross (total)	239	302	295
4180	Budget authority, net (total)	255	255	255
4190	Outlays, net (total)	239	302	295

This appropriation is used to pay fees and expenses of witnesses who appear on behalf of the Government in litigation in which the United States is a party. The United States Attorneys, the United States Marshals Service, and the Department's six litigating divisions are served by this appropriation.

Fees and Expenses of Witnesses.—Pays the fees and expenses associated with the presentation of testimony on behalf of the United States for fact witnesses who testify as to events or facts about which they have personal knowledge, and for expert witnesses who provide technical or scientific testimony. This program also pays the fees of physicians and psychiatrists who examine accused persons upon order of the court to determine their mental competency.

Protection of Witnesses.—Pays subsistence and other costs to ensure the safety of Government witnesses whose testimony on behalf of the United States places them or their families in jeopardy.

Victim Compensation Fund.—Pays restitution to any victim of a crime committed by a protected witness who causes or threatens death or serious bodily injury.

Private Counsel.—Pays private counsel retained to represent Government employees who are sued, charged, or subpoenaed for actions taken while performing their official duties (private counsel expenditures may be authorized for congressional testimony as well as for litigation in instances where Government counsel is precluded from representing the employee or private counsel is otherwise appropriate).

Foreign Counsel.—Allows the Civil Division, which is authorized to oversee litigation in foreign courts, to pay legal expenses of foreign counsel, retained and supervised by the Department of Justice, who represent the United States in cases filed in foreign courts.

Alternative Dispute Resolution.—Pays the costs of providing Alternative Dispute Resolution (ADR) services in instances wherein the Department has taken the initiative to use such services and wherein the courts have directed the parties to attempt a settlement using mediation or some other ADR process.

Object Classification (in millions of dollars)

Identification code 015–0311–0–1–752		2021 actual	2022 est.	2023 est.
11.8	Direct obligations: Personnel compensation: Fees and expenses of witnesses	251	251	203
11.9	Total personnel compensation	251	251	203
21.0	Per diem in lieu of subsistence	4	4	9
23.1	Rental payments to GSA	6	6	
25.1	Advisory and assistance services	11	11	8
25.2	Other services from non-Federal sources			2
25.3	Other goods and services from Federal sources	2	2	3
25.4	Operation and maintenance of facilities	1	1	
25.7	Operation and maintenance of equipment	1	1	
25.8	Subsistence and support of persons	66	66	45
31.0	Equipment	1	1	
99.9	Total new obligations, unexpired accounts	343	343	270

SALARIES AND EXPENSES, COMMUNITY RELATIONS SERVICE

(INCLUDING TRANSFER OF FUNDS)

For necessary expenses of the Community Relations Service, $25,024,000: Provided, That notwithstanding section 205 of this Act, upon a determination by the Attorney General that emergent circumstances require additional funding for conflict resolution and violence prevention activities of the Community Relations Service, the Attorney General may transfer such amounts to the Community Relations Service, from available appropriations for the current fiscal year for the Department of Justice, as may be necessary to respond to such circumstances: Provided further, That any transfer pursuant to the preceding proviso shall be treated as a reprogramming under section 504 of this Act and shall not be available for obligation or expenditure except in compliance with the procedures set forth in that section.

Note.—A full-year 2022 appropriation for this account was not enacted at the time the Budget was prepared; therefore, the Budget assumes this account is operating under the Continuing Appropriations Act, 2022 (Division A of Public Law 117–43, as amended). The amounts included for 2022 reflect the annualized level provided by the continuing resolution.

Program and Financing (in millions of dollars)

Identification code 015–0500–0–1–752		2021 actual	2022 est.	2023 est.
	Obligations by program activity:			
0001	Community Relations Service	15	18	25
	Budgetary resources:			
	Unobligated balance:			
1000	Unobligated balance brought forward, Oct 1		1	1
	Budget authority:			
	Appropriations, discretionary:			
1100	Appropriation	18	18	25
1930	Total budgetary resources available	18	19	26
	Memorandum (non-add) entries:			
1940	Unobligated balance expiring	–2		
1941	Unexpired unobligated balance, end of year	1	1	1
	Change in obligated balance:			
	Unpaid obligations:			
3000	Unpaid obligations, brought forward, Oct 1	9	8	3
3010	New obligations, unexpired accounts	15	18	25
3020	Outlays (gross)	–15	–23	–23
3041	Recoveries of prior year unpaid obligations, expired	–1		
3050	Unpaid obligations, end of year	8	3	5
	Memorandum (non-add) entries:			
3100	Obligated balance, start of year	9	8	3
3200	Obligated balance, end of year	8	3	5
	Budget authority and outlays, net:			
	Discretionary:			
4000	Budget authority, gross	18	18	25
	Outlays, gross:			
4010	Outlays from new discretionary authority	9	15	21
4011	Outlays from discretionary balances	6	8	2
4020	Outlays, gross (total)	15	23	23
4180	Budget authority, net (total)	18	18	25
4190	Outlays, net (total)	15	23	23

The Community Relations Service provides assistance to State and local communities in the prevention and resolution of tension, violence, and civil disorders relating to actual or perceived discrimination on the basis of race, color, or national origin. The Service also works with communities to employ strategies to prevent and respond to bias and hate crimes committed on the basis of actual or perceived race, color, national origin, gender, gender identity, sexual orientation, religion, or disability. The 2023 Budget will allow CRS to expand its mediation and conciliation services to communities experiencing conflict.

Object Classification (in millions of dollars)

Identification code 015–0500–0–1–752		2021 actual	2022 est.	2023 est.
	Direct obligations:			
11.1	Personnel compensation: Full-time permanent	4	5	11
12.1	Civilian personnel benefits	1	2	3
23.1	Rental payments to GSA	3	3	3
23.3	Communications, utilities, and miscellaneous charges	1	2	2
25.1	Advisory and assistance services	1	1	1
25.3	Other goods and services from Federal sources	5	5	5
99.9	Total new obligations, unexpired accounts	15	18	25

Employment Summary

Identification code 015–0500–0–1–752		2021 actual	2022 est.	2023 est.
1001	Direct civilian full-time equivalent employment	28	54	118

INDEPENDENT COUNSEL

Program and Financing (in millions of dollars)

Identification code 015–0327–0–1–752		2021 actual	2022 est.	2023 est.
	Obligations by program activity:			
0001	Investigations and prosecutions as authorized by Congress	4	4	4
	Budgetary resources:			
	Budget authority:			
	Appropriations, mandatory:			
1200	Appropriation	4	4	4
1930	Total budgetary resources available	4	4	4
	Change in obligated balance:			
	Unpaid obligations:			
3000	Unpaid obligations, brought forward, Oct 1		3	1
3010	New obligations, unexpired accounts	4	4	4
3020	Outlays (gross)	–1	–6	–4
3050	Unpaid obligations, end of year	3	1	1
	Memorandum (non-add) entries:			
3100	Obligated balance, start of year		3	1
3200	Obligated balance, end of year	3	1	1
	Budget authority and outlays, net:			
	Mandatory:			
4090	Budget authority, gross	4	4	4
	Outlays, gross:			
4100	Outlays from new mandatory authority	1	3	3
4101	Outlays from mandatory balances		3	1
4110	Outlays, gross (total)	1	6	4
4180	Budget authority, net (total)	4	4	4
4190	Outlays, net (total)	1	6	4

A permanent appropriation is available to fund independent and special counsel activities (28 U.S.C. 591 note). In recent years, special counsels have been appointed to investigate allegations that senior Executive Branch officials violated Federal law. This permanent appropriation is used to fund such investigations.

Legal Activities and U.S. Marshals—Continued
Federal Funds—Continued

INDEPENDENT COUNSEL—Continued

Object Classification (in millions of dollars)

Identification code 015–0327–0–1–752	2021 actual	2022 est.	2023 est.
11.1 Direct obligations: Personnel compensation: Full-time permanent	2	2	2
11.9 Total personnel compensation	2	2	2
25.3 Other goods and services from Federal sources	1	1	1
25.7 Operation and maintenance of equipment	1	1	1
99.9 Total new obligations, unexpired accounts	4	4	4

Employment Summary

Identification code 015–0327–0–1–752	2021 actual	2022 est.	2023 est.
1001 Direct civilian full-time equivalent employment	4	4	4

VICTIMS COMPENSATION FUND

Program and Financing (in millions of dollars)

Identification code 015–0139–0–1–754	2021 actual	2022 est.	2023 est.
Obligations by program activity:			
0001 Victims Compensation	1,851	1,993	1,992
0002 Management and Administration	46	63	36
0900 Total new obligations, unexpired accounts	1,897	2,056	2,028
Budgetary resources:			
Unobligated balance:			
1000 Unobligated balance brought forward, Oct 1	333	....	....
Budget authority:			
Appropriations, mandatory:			
1200 Appropriation	1,567	2,060	2,030
1230 Appropriations and/or unobligated balance of appropriations permanently reduced	–3	–4	–2
1260 Appropriations, mandatory (total)	1,564	2,056	2,028
1900 Budget authority (total)	1,564	2,056	2,028
1930 Total budgetary resources available	1,897	2,056	2,028
Change in obligated balance:			
Unpaid obligations:			
3000 Unpaid obligations, brought forward, Oct 1	12	65	88
3010 New obligations, unexpired accounts	1,897	2,056	2,028
3020 Outlays (gross)	–1,844	–2,033	–2,026
3050 Unpaid obligations, end of year	65	88	90
Memorandum (non-add) entries:			
3100 Obligated balance, start of year	12	65	88
3200 Obligated balance, end of year	65	88	90
Budget authority and outlays, net:			
Mandatory:			
4090 Budget authority, gross	1,564	2,056	2,028
Outlays, gross:			
4100 Outlays from new mandatory authority	1,500	1,971	2,026
4101 Outlays from mandatory balances	344	62	....
4110 Outlays, gross (total)	1,844	2,033	2,026
4180 Budget authority, net (total)	1,564	2,056	2,028
4190 Outlays, net (total)	1,844	2,033	2,026

Public Law 114–113 provided $4.6 billion starting in 2017 for the settlement of claims related to the September 11th attacks. Per Section 410, a new Treasury account was established called the "Victims Compensation Fund." This fund is available for the settlement of claim determinations issued after December 17, 2015. After all claims in the September 11th Victim Compensation Fund were resolved, $813 million in remaining funding became available in the new Victims Compensation Fund.

On July 29, 2019, the President signed into law the Never Forget the Heroes: James Zadroga, Ray Pfeifer, and Luis Alvarez Permanent Authorization of the September 11th Victim Compensation Fund, Public Law 116–34. The Act extends the VCF's claim filing deadline to October 1, 2090, and appropriates such funds as may be necessary in each fiscal year through fiscal year 2092 to pay all eligible claims.

Object Classification (in millions of dollars)

Identification code 015–0139–0–1–754	2021 actual	2022 est.	2023 est.
Direct obligations:			
11.1 Personnel compensation: Full-time permanent	4	6	5
12.1 Civilian personnel benefits	2	2	2
23.3 Communications, utilities, and miscellaneous charges	1	1	....
25.1 Advisory and assistance services	37	53	27
25.3 Other goods and services from Federal sources	2	1	2
42.0 Insurance claims and indemnities	1,851	1,993	1,992
99.9 Total new obligations, unexpired accounts	1,897	2,056	2,028

Employment Summary

Identification code 015–0139–0–1–754	2021 actual	2022 est.	2023 est.
1001 Direct civilian full-time equivalent employment	32	37	37

UNITED STATES VICTIMS OF STATE SPONSORED TERRORISM FUND

Special and Trust Fund Receipts (in millions of dollars)

Identification code 015–5608–0–2–754	2021 actual	2022 est.	2023 est.
0100 Balance, start of year	1	1	1
Receipts:			
Current law:			
1110 Fines, Penalties, and Forfeitures, United States Victims of State Sponsored Terrorism Fund	43	171	170
1140 Earnings on Investments, United States Victims of State Sponsored Terrorism Fund	....	1	1
1199 Total current law receipts	43	172	171
1999 Total receipts	43	172	171
2000 Total: Balances and receipts	44	173	172
Appropriations:			
Current law:			
2101 United States Victims of State Sponsored Terrorism Fund	–42	–172	–170
2103 United States Victims of State Sponsored Terrorism Fund	....	–1	–1
2132 United States Victims of State Sponsored Terrorism Fund	....	1	1
2199 Total current law appropriations	–42	–172	–170
2999 Total appropriations	–42	–172	–170
5098 Rounding adjustment	–1	....	....
5099 Balance, end of year	1	1	2

Program and Financing (in millions of dollars)

Identification code 015–5608–0–2–754	2021 actual	2022 est.	2023 est.
Obligations by program activity:			
0001 Victim Compensation	....	3	....
0002 Management and Administration	4	7	7
0900 Total new obligations, unexpired accounts	4	10	7
Budgetary resources:			
Unobligated balance:			
1000 Unobligated balance brought forward, Oct 1	175	213	375
Budget authority:			
Appropriations, mandatory:			
1201 Appropriation (special or trust fund)	42	172	170
1203 Appropriation (previously unavailable)(special or trust)	....	1	1
1232 Appropriations and/or unobligated balance of appropriations temporarily reduced	....	–1	–1
1260 Appropriations, mandatory (total)	42	172	170
1930 Total budgetary resources available	217	385	545
Memorandum (non-add) entries:			
1941 Unexpired unobligated balance, end of year	213	375	538
Change in obligated balance:			
Unpaid obligations:			
3000 Unpaid obligations, brought forward, Oct 1	3	3	3
3010 New obligations, unexpired accounts	4	10	7

DEPARTMENT OF JUSTICE

Legal Activities and U.S. Marshals—Continued
Federal Funds—Continued

731

		2021 actual	2022 est.	2023 est.
3020	Outlays (gross)	−4	−10	−7
3050	Unpaid obligations, end of year	3	3	3
	Memorandum (non-add) entries:			
3100	Obligated balance, start of year	3	3	3
3200	Obligated balance, end of year	3	3	3
	Budget authority and outlays, net:			
	Mandatory:			
4090	Budget authority, gross	42	172	170
	Outlays, gross:			
4100	Outlays from new mandatory authority		7	7
4101	Outlays from mandatory balances	4	3	
4110	Outlays, gross (total)	4	10	7
4180	Budget authority, net (total)	42	172	170
4190	Outlays, net (total)	4	10	7
	Memorandum (non-add) entries:			
5000	Total investments, SOY: Federal securities: Par value	168	168	168
5001	Total investments, EOY: Federal securities: Par value	168	168	61

The Consolidated Appropriations Act, 2016 established the United States Victims of State Sponsored Terrorism Fund (VSSTF) as an effort to improve the availability of compensation for certain U.S. victims of state sponsored terrorism. VSSTF is managed by the Criminal Division's Money Laundering and Asset Recovery Section.

Object Classification (in millions of dollars)

Identification code 015–5608–0–2–754		2021 actual	2022 est.	2023 est.
	Direct obligations:			
11.1	Personnel compensation: Full-time permanent	1	1	1
25.1	Advisory and assistance services	3	6	6
42.0	Insurance claims and indemnities		3	
99.9	Total new obligations, unexpired accounts	4	10	7

Employment Summary

Identification code 015–5608–0–2–754	2021 actual	2022 est.	2023 est.
1001 Direct civilian full-time equivalent employment	6	6	6

UNITED STATES TRUSTEE SYSTEM FUND

For necessary expenses of the United States Trustee Program, as authorized, $260,277,000, to remain available until expended: Provided, That, notwithstanding any other provision of law, deposits to the United States Trustee System Fund and amounts herein appropriated shall be available in such amounts as may be necessary to pay refunds due depositors: Provided further, That, notwithstanding any other provision of law, fees deposited into the Fund pursuant to section 589a of title 28, United States Code (with the exception of those fees to be transferred pursuant to section 589a(f)(1)(B) and (C)), shall be retained and used for necessary expenses in this appropriation and shall remain available until expended: Provided further, That to the extent that fees deposited into the Fund in fiscal year 2023, net of amounts necessary to pay refunds due depositors, exceed $260,277,000, those excess amounts (with the exception of those fees to be transferred pursuant to section 589a(f)(1)(B) and (C)) shall be available in future fiscal years only to the extent provided in advance in appropriations Acts: Provided further, That the sum herein appropriated from the general fund shall be reduced (1) as such fees are received during fiscal year 2023, net of amounts necessary to pay refunds due depositors, and (2) to the extent that any remaining general fund appropriations can be derived from amounts deposited in the Fund in previous fiscal years that are not otherwise appropriated, so as to result in a final fiscal year 2023 appropriation from the general fund estimated at $0.

Note.—A full-year 2022 appropriation for this account was not enacted at the time the Budget was prepared; therefore, the Budget assumes this account is operating under the Continuing Appropriations Act, 2022 (Division A of Public Law 117–43, as amended). The amounts included for 2022 reflect the annualized level provided by the continuing resolution.

Special and Trust Fund Receipts (in millions of dollars)

Identification code 015–5073–0–2–752		2021 actual	2022 est.	2023 est.
0100	Balance, start of year	233	370	370
	Receipts:			
	Current law:			
1120	Fees for Bankruptcy Oversight, U.S. Trustees System	369	232	301
1140	Earnings on Investments, U.S. Trustees System			1
1199	Total current law receipts	369	232	302
1999	Total receipts	369	232	302
2000	Total: Balances and receipts	602	602	672
	Appropriations:			
	Current law:			
2101	United States Trustee System Fund	−369	−232	−260
2135	United States Trustee System Fund	137		
2199	Total current law appropriations	−232	−232	−260
2999	Total appropriations	−232	−232	−260
5099	Balance, end of year	370	370	412

Program and Financing (in millions of dollars)

Identification code 015–5073–0–2–752		2021 actual	2022 est.	2023 est.
	Obligations by program activity:			
0001	United States Trustee System Fund (Direct)	241	246	261
	Budgetary resources:			
	Unobligated balance:			
1000	Unobligated balance brought forward, Oct 1	7	11	
1010	Unobligated balance transfer to other accts [010–5116]		−15	
1021	Recoveries of prior year unpaid obligations	13	4	
1070	Unobligated balance (total)	20		
	Budget authority:			
	Appropriations, discretionary:			
1101	Appropriation (special or trust)	369	232	260
1135	Appropriations precluded from obligation (special or trust)	−137		
1160	Appropriation, discretionary (total)	232	232	260
1900	Budget authority (total)	232	232	260
1930	Total budgetary resources available	252	232	260
	Memorandum (non-add) entries:			
1941	Unexpired unobligated balance, end of year	11		
	Change in obligated balance:			
	Unpaid obligations:			
3000	Unpaid obligations, brought forward, Oct 1	70	52	59
3010	New obligations, unexpired accounts	241	246	261
3020	Outlays (gross)	−246	−235	−265
3040	Recoveries of prior year unpaid obligations, unexpired	−13	−4	
3050	Unpaid obligations, end of year	52	59	55
	Memorandum (non-add) entries:			
3100	Obligated balance, start of year	70	52	59
3200	Obligated balance, end of year	52	59	55
	Budget authority and outlays, net:			
	Discretionary:			
4000	Budget authority, gross	232	232	260
	Outlays, gross:			
4010	Outlays from new discretionary authority	208	204	229
4011	Outlays from discretionary balances	38	31	36
4020	Outlays, gross (total)	246	235	265
4180	Budget authority, net (total)	232	232	260
4190	Outlays, net (total)	246	235	265
	Memorandum (non-add) entries:			
5000	Total investments, SOY: Federal securities: Par value	157	236	215
5001	Total investments, EOY: Federal securities: Par value	236	215	234
	Unfunded deficiencies:			
7000	Unfunded deficiency, start of year			−14
	Change in deficiency during the year:			
7010	New deficiency		−14	−1
7020	Unfunded deficiency, end of year		−14	−15

The United States Trustee Program (USTP or Program) supervises the administration of bankruptcy cases and private trustees in the Federal Bankruptcy Courts and litigates against fraud and abuse in the system by debtors, creditors, attorneys, bankruptcy petition preparers, and others. The Bankruptcy Judges, U.S. Trustees and Family Farmer Bankruptcy Act of

UNITED STATES TRUSTEE SYSTEM FUND—Continued

1986 (P.L. 99–554) expanded the pilot trustee program to a 21 region, nationwide program encompassing 88 judicial districts (bankruptcy cases filed in Alabama and North Carolina are administered by the Administrative Office of the U.S. Courts). The Bankruptcy Abuse Prevention and Consumer Protection Act of 2005, (P.L. 109–8) expanded the Program's responsibilities to include, among other things, means testing, credit counseling/debtor education, and debtor audits. The August 2019 enactment of the Small Business Reorganization Act (P.L. 116–54) gave the Program additional responsibilities regarding small business debtors.

USTP appropriations are offset primarily by revenues deposited into the United States Trustee System Fund from filing fees paid by consumer and business debtors as well as quarterly fees based on disbursements made by most chapter 11 debtors. In October 2017, the Bankruptcy Judgeship Act of 2017 (P.L. 115–72) was enacted, adjusting quarterly fees for the largest chapter 11 debtors beginning January 1, 2018 and through September 30, 2022, depending on the balance of the Fund. Following the enactment of the Bankruptcy Administration Improvement Act (BAIA), (P.L. 116–325) in January 2021, quarterly fees were further amended beginning April 1, 2021 through December 31, 2025. The BAIA reduces quarterly fees paid in almost all chapter 11 cases, does not increase quarterly fees for any case, and simplifies the fee structure. Under the new law, the USTP's FY 2023 appropriation is anticipated to be fully offset by bankruptcy fees collected and on deposit in the United States Trustee System Fund. Further, the law continues funding for bankruptcy judgeships and uses surplus fees for additional private chapter 7 bankruptcy trustee compensation.

Object Classification (in millions of dollars)

Identification code 015–5073–0–2–752		2021 actual	2022 est.	2023 est.
	Direct obligations:			
	Personnel compensation:			
11.1	Full-time permanent	114	116	132
11.3	Other than full-time permanent	8	8	10
11.5	Other personnel compensation	2	2	2
11.9	Total personnel compensation	124	126	144
12.1	Civilian personnel benefits	46	47	54
21.0	Travel and transportation of persons			1
23.1	Rental payments to GSA	24	25	25
23.3	Communications, utilities, and miscellaneous charges	7	6	7
25.1	Advisory and assistance services	7	8	3
25.2	Other services from non-Federal sources	1	1	1
25.3	Other goods and services from Federal sources	16	14	10
25.4	Operation and maintenance of facilities	3	4	4
25.7	Operation and maintenance of equipment	2	5	4
26.0	Supplies and materials	1	1	1
31.0	Equipment	7	8	5
32.0	Land and structures	3	1	2
99.9	Total new obligations, unexpired accounts	241	246	261

Employment Summary

Identification code 015–5073–0–2–752	2021 actual	2022 est.	2023 est.
1001 Direct civilian full-time equivalent employment	991	996	1,092
2001 Reimbursable civilian full-time equivalent employment	1	1	1

ASSETS FORFEITURE FUND

For expenses authorized by subparagraphs (B), (F), and (G) of section 524(c)(1) of title 28, United States Code, $20,514,000, to be derived from the Department of Justice Assets Forfeiture Fund.

Note.—A full-year 2022 appropriation for this account was not enacted at the time the Budget was prepared; therefore, the Budget assumes this account is operating under the Continuing Appropriations Act, 2022 (Division A of Public Law 117–43, as amended). The amounts included for 2022 reflect the annualized level provided by the continuing resolution.

Special and Trust Fund Receipts (in millions of dollars)

Identification code 015–5042–0–2–752		2021 actual	2022 est.	2023 est.
0100	Balance, start of year	101	79	153
	Receipts:			
	Current law:			
1110	Forfeited Cash and Proceeds from the Sale of Forfeited Property, Assets Forfeiture Fund	1,383	1,072	1,055
1140	Interest and Profit on Investment, Department of Justice Assets Forfeiture Fund	40	3	3
1199	Total current law receipts	1,423	1,075	1,058
1999	Total receipts	1,423	1,075	1,058
2000	Total: Balances and receipts	1,524	1,154	1,211
	Appropriations:			
	Current law:			
2101	Assets Forfeiture Fund	–21	–21	–21
2101	Assets Forfeiture Fund	–1,403	–954	–954
2103	Assets Forfeiture Fund	–101	–80	–54
2132	Assets Forfeiture Fund	80		
2132	Assets Forfeiture Fund		54	54
2199	Total current law appropriations	–1,445	–1,001	–975
2999	Total appropriations	–1,445	–1,001	–975
5099	Balance, end of year	79	153	236

Program and Financing (in millions of dollars)

Identification code 015–5042–0–2–752		2021 actual	2022 est.	2023 est.
	Obligations by program activity:			
0001	Assets Forfeiture Fund (Direct)	1,626	1,434	1,420
0801	Assets Forfeiture Fund (Reimbursable)	17	18	20
0900	Total new obligations, unexpired accounts	1,643	1,452	1,440
	Budgetary resources:			
	Unobligated balance:			
1000	Unobligated balance brought forward, Oct 1	1,158	1,084	726
1001	Discretionary unobligated balance brought fwd, Oct 1	2		
1021	Recoveries of prior year unpaid obligations	95	75	75
1033	Recoveries of prior year paid obligations	10		
1070	Unobligated balance (total)	1,263	1,159	801
	Budget authority:			
	Appropriations, discretionary:			
1101	Appropriation (special or trust)	21	21	21
1130	Appropriations permanently reduced			–100
1160	Appropriation, discretionary (total)	21	21	–79
	Appropriations, mandatory:			
1201	Appropriation (special or trust fund)	1,403	954	954
1203	Appropriation (previously unavailable)(special or trust)	101	80	54
1232	Appropriations and/or unobligated balance of appropriations temporarily reduced	–80		
1232	Appropriations and/or unobligated balance of appropriations temporarily reduced (sequester)		–54	–54
1260	Appropriations, mandatory (total)	1,424	980	954
	Spending authority from offsetting collections, mandatory:			
1800	Collected	17	18	20
1801	Change in uncollected payments, Federal sources	2		
1850	Spending auth from offsetting collections, mand (total)	19	18	20
1900	Budget authority (total)	1,464	1,019	895
1930	Total budgetary resources available	2,727	2,178	1,696
	Memorandum (non-add) entries:			
1941	Unexpired unobligated balance, end of year	1,084	726	256
	Change in obligated balance:			
	Unpaid obligations:			
3000	Unpaid obligations, brought forward, Oct 1	2,253	1,129	1,234
3010	New obligations, unexpired accounts	1,643	1,452	1,440
3020	Outlays (gross)	–2,672	–1,272	–1,035
3040	Recoveries of prior year unpaid obligations, unexpired	–95	–75	–75
3050	Unpaid obligations, end of year	1,129	1,234	1,564
	Uncollected payments:			
3060	Uncollected pymts, Fed sources, brought forward, Oct 1	–24	–26	–26
3070	Change in uncollected pymts, Fed sources, unexpired	–2		
3090	Uncollected pymts, Fed sources, end of year	–26	–26	–26
	Memorandum (non-add) entries:			
3100	Obligated balance, start of year	2,229	1,103	1,208

DEPARTMENT OF JUSTICE

Legal Activities and U.S. Marshals—Continued
Federal Funds—Continued

733

		1,103	1,208	1,538
3200	Obligated balance, end of year	1,103	1,208	1,538
	Budget authority and outlays, net:			
	Discretionary:			
4000	Budget authority, gross	21	21	–79
	Outlays, gross:			
4010	Outlays from new discretionary authority	12	8	–52
4011	Outlays from discretionary balances	7	12	12
4020	Outlays, gross (total)	19	20	–40
	Mandatory:			
4090	Budget authority, gross	1,443	998	974
	Outlays, gross:			
4100	Outlays from new mandatory authority	1,333	584	570
4101	Outlays from mandatory balances	1,320	668	505
4110	Outlays, gross (total)	2,653	1,252	1,075
	Offsets against gross budget authority and outlays:			
	Offsetting collections (collected) from:			
4120	Federal sources	–18	–18	–20
4123	Non-Federal sources	–9		
4130	Offsets against gross budget authority and outlays (total)	–27	–18	–20
	Additional offsets against gross budget authority only:			
4140	Change in uncollected pymts, Fed sources, unexpired	–2		
4143	Recoveries of prior year paid obligations, unexpired accounts	10		
4150	Additional offsets against budget authority only (total)	8		
4160	Budget authority, net (mandatory)	1,424	980	954
4170	Outlays, net (mandatory)	2,626	1,234	1,055
4180	Budget authority, net (total)	1,445	1,001	875
4190	Outlays, net (total)	2,645	1,254	1,015
	Memorandum (non-add) entries:			
5000	Total investments, SOY: Federal securities: Par value	3,224	1,339	1,340
5001	Total investments, EOY: Federal securities: Par value	1,339	1,340	1,341

The Comprehensive Crime Control Act of 1984 established the Assets Forfeiture Fund (AFF) as a repository for forfeited cash and the proceeds of sales of forfeited property under any law enforced and administered by the Department of Justice in accordance with 28 U.S.C. 524(c). Authorities of the AFF have been amended by various public laws enacted since 1984. Under current law, authority to use the AFF for certain investigative expenses shall be specified in annual appropriations acts. Expenses necessary to seize, detain, inventory, safeguard, maintain, advertise, or sell property under seizure are funded through a permanent, indefinite appropriation. In addition, beginning in 1993, other general expenses of managing and operating the assets forfeiture program are paid from the permanent, indefinite portion of the AFF. Once all expenses are covered, the balance is maintained to meet ongoing expenses of the program. Excess unobligated balances may also be allocated by the Attorney General in accordance with 28 U.S.C. 524(c)(8)(E). The 2023 Budget proposes a cancellation of unobligated balances of $100 million.

Object Classification (in millions of dollars)

Identification code 015–5042–0–2–752	2021 actual	2022 est.	2023 est.
	Direct obligations:			
11.1	Personnel compensation: Full-time permanent	46	49	52
12.1	Civilian personnel benefits	17	18	19
21.0	Travel and transportation of persons	3	3	3
22.0	Transportation of things	3	3	3
23.1	Rental payments to GSA	18	18	18
23.2	Rental payments to others	1	1	1
23.3	Communications, utilities, and miscellaneous charges	29	30	30
25.1	Advisory and assistance services	148	148	148
25.2	Other services from non-Federal sources	1,254	1,057	1,039
25.3	Other goods and services from Federal sources	59	59	59
25.4	Operation and maintenance of facilities	1	1	1
25.7	Operation and maintenance of equipment	39	39	39
26.0	Supplies and materials	3	3	3
31.0	Equipment	5	5	5
99.0	Direct obligations	1,626	1,434	1,420
99.0	Reimbursable obligations	17	18	20
99.9	Total new obligations, unexpired accounts	1,643	1,452	1,440

Employment Summary

Identification code 015–5042–0–2–752	2021 actual	2022 est.	2023 est.
1001	Direct civilian full-time equivalent employment	95	113	113
1001	Direct civilian full-time equivalent employment	23	34	36
1001	Direct civilian full-time equivalent employment	4	4	4
1001	Direct civilian full-time equivalent employment	47	57	57
1001	Direct civilian full-time equivalent employment	1	4	4
1001	Direct civilian full-time equivalent employment	178	202	202

JUSTICE PRISONER AND ALIEN TRANSPORTATION SYSTEM FUND, U.S. MARSHALS

Program and Financing (in millions of dollars)

Identification code 015–4575–0–4–752	2021 actual	2022 est.	2023 est.
	Obligations by program activity:			
0801	Justice Prisoner and Alien Transportation System Fund, U.S. Marshals (Reimbursable)	74	71	69
	Budgetary resources:			
	Unobligated balance:			
1000	Unobligated balance brought forward, Oct 1	33	30	37
1021	Recoveries of prior year unpaid obligations		2	
1070	Unobligated balance (total)	33	32	37
	Budget authority:			
	Spending authority from offsetting collections, discretionary:			
1700	Collected	71	76	76
1930	Total budgetary resources available	104	108	113
	Memorandum (non-add) entries:			
1941	Unexpired unobligated balance, end of year	30	37	44
	Change in obligated balance:			
	Unpaid obligations:			
3000	Unpaid obligations, brought forward, Oct 1	5	30	23
3010	New obligations, unexpired accounts	74	71	69
3020	Outlays (gross)	–49	–76	–86
3040	Recoveries of prior year unpaid obligations, unexpired		–2	
3050	Unpaid obligations, end of year	30	23	6
	Uncollected payments:			
3060	Uncollected pymts, Fed sources, brought forward, Oct 1	–2	–2	–2
3090	Uncollected pymts, Fed sources, end of year	–2	–2	–2
	Memorandum (non-add) entries:			
3100	Obligated balance, start of year	3	28	21
3200	Obligated balance, end of year	28	21	4
	Budget authority and outlays, net:			
	Discretionary:			
4000	Budget authority, gross	71	76	76
	Outlays, gross:			
4010	Outlays from new discretionary authority	12	68	68
4011	Outlays from discretionary balances	37	8	18
4020	Outlays, gross (total)	49	76	86
	Offsets against gross budget authority and outlays:			
	Offsetting collections (collected) from:			
4030	Federal sources	–71	–76	–76
4040	Offsets against gross budget authority and outlays (total)	–71	–76	–76
4180	Budget authority, net (total)			
4190	Outlays, net (total)	–22		10

The Justice Prisoner and Alien Transportation System (JPATS) is responsible for transporting the majority of Federal detainees and prisoners in the custody of the United States Marshals Service or the Bureau of Prisons. JPATS transports both pretrial detainees and sentenced prisoners via coordinated air and ground systems without sacrificing the safety of the public, Federal employees, or those in custody. JPATS also transports detainees and prisoners on a reimbursable space-available basis for the Department of Defense, other participating Federal departments, and State and local agencies. Customers are billed based on the number of flight hours and the number of seats used to move their detainees/prisoners.

JUSTICE PRISONER AND ALIEN TRANSPORTATION SYSTEM FUND, U.S. MARSHALS—Continued

Object Classification (in millions of dollars)

Identification code 015–4575–0–4–752		2021 actual	2022 est.	2023 est.
	Reimbursable obligations:			
	Personnel compensation:			
11.1	Full-time permanent	10	12	12
11.5	Other personnel compensation	1	1	1
11.8	Special personal services payments	4	....	5
11.9	Total personnel compensation	15	13	18
12.1	Civilian personnel benefits	4	5	5
21.0	Travel and transportation of persons	....	1	1
23.1	Rental payments to GSA	1	1	1
23.3	Communications, utilities, and miscellaneous charges	4	6	6
25.1	Advisory and assistance services	....	1	1
25.2	Other services from non-Federal sources	....	1	....
25.3	Other goods and services from Federal sources	1	1	1
25.4	Operation and maintenance of facilities	....	....	1
25.7	Operation and maintenance of equipment	13	18	19
25.8	Subsistence and support of persons	....	7	....
26.0	Supplies and materials	11	14	15
31.0	Equipment	25	3	1
99.9	Total new obligations, unexpired accounts	74	71	69

Employment Summary

Identification code 015–4575–0–4–752		2021 actual	2022 est.	2023 est.
2001	Reimbursable civilian full-time equivalent employment	96	113	113

NATIONAL SECURITY DIVISION

Federal Funds

SALARIES AND EXPENSES

(INCLUDING TRANSFER OF FUNDS)

For expenses necessary to carry out the activities of the National Security Division, $133,512,000, of which not to exceed $5,000,000 for information technology systems shall remain available until expended: Provided, That notwithstanding section 205 of this Act, upon a determination by the Attorney General that emergent circumstances require additional funding for the activities of the National Security Division, the Attorney General may transfer such amounts to this heading from available appropriations for the current fiscal year for the Department of Justice, as may be necessary to respond to such circumstances: Provided further, That any transfer pursuant to the preceding proviso shall be treated as a reprogramming under section 504 of this Act and shall not be available for obligation or expenditure except in compliance with the procedures set forth in that section.

Note.—A full-year 2022 appropriation for this account was not enacted at the time the Budget was prepared; therefore, the Budget assumes this account is operating under the Continuing Appropriations Act, 2022 (Division A of Public Law 117–43, as amended). The amounts included for 2022 reflect the annualized level provided by the continuing resolution.

Program and Financing (in millions of dollars)

Identification code 015–1300–0–1–751		2021 actual	2022 est.	2023 est.
	Obligations by program activity:			
0001	National Security Division	106	117	134
0801	Salaries and Expenses (Reimbursable)	2	....	....
0900	Total new obligations, unexpired accounts	108	117	134
	Budgetary resources:			
	Unobligated balance:			
1000	Unobligated balance brought forward, Oct 1	6	7	9
1012	Unobligated balance transfers between expired and unexpired accounts	1	....	....
1070	Unobligated balance (total)	7	7	9
	Budget authority:			
	Appropriations, discretionary:			
1100	Appropriation	117	117	134
	Spending authority from offsetting collections, discretionary:			
1700	Collected	1	2	2
1701	Change in uncollected payments, Federal sources	2	....	....
1750	Spending auth from offsetting collections, disc (total)	3	2	2
1900	Budget authority (total)	120	119	136
1930	Total budgetary resources available	127	126	145
	Memorandum (non-add) entries:			
1940	Unobligated balance expiring	–12	....	....
1941	Unexpired unobligated balance, end of year	7	9	11
	Change in obligated balance:			
	Unpaid obligations:			
3000	Unpaid obligations, brought forward, Oct 1	14	21	6
3010	New obligations, unexpired accounts	108	117	134
3020	Outlays (gross)	–99	–132	–134
3041	Recoveries of prior year unpaid obligations, expired	–2	....	....
3050	Unpaid obligations, end of year	21	6	6
	Uncollected payments:			
3060	Uncollected pymts, Fed sources, brought forward, Oct 1	–6	–7	–7
3070	Change in uncollected pymts, Fed sources, unexpired	–2	....	....
3071	Change in uncollected pymts, Fed sources, expired	1	....	....
3090	Uncollected pymts, Fed sources, end of year	–7	–7	–7
	Memorandum (non-add) entries:			
3100	Obligated balance, start of year	8	14	–1
3200	Obligated balance, end of year	14	–1	–1
	Budget authority and outlays, net:			
	Discretionary:			
4000	Budget authority, gross	120	119	136
	Outlays, gross:			
4010	Outlays from new discretionary authority	89	106	121
4011	Outlays from discretionary balances	10	26	13
4020	Outlays, gross (total)	99	132	134
	Offsets against gross budget authority and outlays:			
	Offsetting collections (collected) from:			
4030	Federal sources	–1	–2	–2
4040	Offsets against gross budget authority and outlays (total)	–1	–2	–2
	Additional offsets against gross budget authority only:			
4050	Change in uncollected pymts, Fed sources, unexpired	–2	....	....
4060	Additional offsets against budget authority only (total)	–2	....	....
4070	Budget authority, net (discretionary)	117	117	134
4080	Outlays, net (discretionary)	98	130	132
4180	Budget authority, net (total)	117	117	134
4190	Outlays, net (total)	98	130	132

The Mission of the National Security Division (NSD) is to protect the United States from threats to our national security by pursuing justice through the law. NSD strengthens the Department's core national security functions by providing strategic national security policy coordination and development. NSD combines counterterrorism, counterintelligence, export control, and cyber prosecutors with attorneys who oversee the Department's foreign intelligence/counterintelligence operations, as well as attorneys who provide policy and legal advice on a wide range of national security issues. For 2023, NSD is requesting $134 million to protect and defend the United States against the full range of national security threats, consistent with the rule of law.

Object Classification (in millions of dollars)

Identification code 015–1300–0–1–751		2021 actual	2022 est.	2023 est.
	Direct obligations:			
	Personnel compensation:			
11.1	Full-time permanent	47	55	60
11.3	Other than full-time permanent	1	2	2
11.5	Other personnel compensation	1	2	2
11.8	Special personal services payments	1	1	1
11.9	Total personnel compensation	50	60	64
12.1	Civilian personnel benefits	17	24	22
21.0	Travel and transportation of persons	....	....	1
23.1	Rental payments to GSA	14	14	14
25.1	Advisory and assistance services	3	3	4
25.2	Other services from non-Federal sources	....	....	2
25.3	Other goods and services from Federal sources	16	10	15
25.4	Operation and maintenance of facilities	1	1	....
25.7	Operation and maintenance of equipment	1	1	3
31.0	Equipment	3	3	7
99.0	Direct obligations	105	116	132
99.0	Reimbursable obligations	2	....	....
99.5	Adjustment for rounding	1	1	2

DEPARTMENT OF JUSTICE   Interagency Law Enforcement
                                                                                                                                                              Federal Funds   735

99.9	Total new obligations, unexpired accounts	108	117	134

Employment Summary

Identification code 015–1300–0–1–751	2021 actual	2022 est.	2023 est.
1001 Direct civilian full-time equivalent employment	324	336	364

RADIATION EXPOSURE COMPENSATION

Federal Funds

PAYMENT TO RADIATION EXPOSURE COMPENSATION TRUST FUND

Program and Financing (in millions of dollars)

Identification code 015–0333–0–1–054		2021 actual	2022 est.	2023 est.
	Obligations by program activity:			
0001	Payment to radiation exposure compensation trust fund	70	70	20
0900	Total new obligations, unexpired accounts (object class 25.2)	70	70	20
	Budgetary resources:			
	Budget authority:			
	Appropriations, mandatory:			
1200	Appropriation	70	70	20
1930	Total budgetary resources available	70	70	20
	Change in obligated balance:			
	Unpaid obligations:			
3010	New obligations, unexpired accounts	70	70	20
3020	Outlays (gross)	–70	–70	–20
	Budget authority and outlays, net:			
	Mandatory:			
4090	Budget authority, gross	70	70	20
	Outlays, gross:			
4100	Outlays from new mandatory authority	70	70	20
4180	Budget authority, net (total)	70	70	20
4190	Outlays, net (total)	70	70	20

Trust Funds

RADIATION EXPOSURE COMPENSATION TRUST FUND

Special and Trust Fund Receipts (in millions of dollars)

Identification code 015–8116–0–7–054		2021 actual	2022 est.	2023 est.
0100	Balance, start of year			
	Receipts:			
	Current law:			
1140	Payment from the General Fund, Radiation Exposure Compensation Trust Fund	70	70	20
2000	Total: Balances and receipts	70	70	20
	Appropriations:			
	Current law:			
2101	Radiation Exposure Compensation Trust Fund	–70	–70	–20
5099	Balance, end of year			

Program and Financing (in millions of dollars)

Identification code 015–8116–0–7–054		2021 actual	2022 est.	2023 est.
	Obligations by program activity:			
0001	Payments to RECA claimants	50	100	20
0900	Total new obligations, unexpired accounts (object class 41.0)	50	100	20
	Budgetary resources:			
	Unobligated balance:			
1000	Unobligated balance brought forward, Oct 1	10	30	
	Budget authority:			
	Appropriations, mandatory:			
1201	Appropriation (special or trust fund)	70	70	20
1930	Total budgetary resources available	80	100	20

	Memorandum (non-add) entries:			
1941	Unexpired unobligated balance, end of year		30	
	Change in obligated balance:			
	Unpaid obligations:			
3000	Unpaid obligations, brought forward, Oct 1		2	4
3010	New obligations, unexpired accounts	50	100	20
3020	Outlays (gross)	–48	–98	–20
3050	Unpaid obligations, end of year	2	4	4
	Memorandum (non-add) entries:			
3100	Obligated balance, start of year		2	4
3200	Obligated balance, end of year	2	4	4
	Budget authority and outlays, net:			
	Mandatory:			
4090	Budget authority, gross	70	70	20
	Outlays, gross:			
4100	Outlays from new mandatory authority	48	70	20
4101	Outlays from mandatory balances		28	
4110	Outlays, gross (total)	48	98	20
4180	Budget authority, net (total)	70	70	20
4190	Outlays, net (total)	48	98	20

The Radiation Exposure Compensation Act (RECA), as amended, authorizes payments to individuals exposed to radiation as a result of atmospheric nuclear tests or uranium mining, milling, or transport. RECA workload is included with the workload of the Civil Division.

INTERAGENCY LAW ENFORCEMENT

Federal Funds

INTERAGENCY CRIME AND DRUG ENFORCEMENT

For necessary expenses for the identification, investigation, and prosecution of individuals associated with the most significant drug trafficking organizations, transnational organized crime, and money laundering organizations not otherwise provided for, to include inter-governmental agreements with State and local law enforcement agencies engaged in the investigation and prosecution of individuals involved in transnational organized crime and drug trafficking, $550,458,000, of which $50,000,000 shall remain available until expended: Provided, That any amounts obligated from appropriations under this heading may be used under authorities available to the organizations reimbursed from this appropriation.

Note.—A full-year 2022 appropriation for this account was not enacted at the time the Budget was prepared; therefore, the Budget assumes this account is operating under the Continuing Appropriations Act, 2022 (Division A of Public Law 117–43, as amended). The amounts included for 2022 reflect the annualized level provided by the continuing resolution.

Program and Financing (in millions of dollars)

Identification code 015–0323–0–1–751		2021 actual	2022 est.	2023 est.
	Obligations by program activity:			
0001	Investigations	381	381	381
0003	Prosecution	169	169	169
0799	Total direct obligations	550	550	550
0801	Interagency Crime and Drug Enforcement (Reimbursable)	9		
0900	Total new obligations, unexpired accounts	559	550	550
	Budgetary resources:			
	Unobligated balance:			
1000	Unobligated balance brought forward, Oct 1	29	24	27
1021	Recoveries of prior year unpaid obligations	8	3	3
1033	Recoveries of prior year paid obligations			19
1070	Unobligated balance (total)	37	27	49
	Budget authority:			
	Appropriations, discretionary:			
1100	Appropriation	550	550	550
	Spending authority from offsetting collections, discretionary:			
1700	Collected	1		
1701	Change in uncollected payments, Federal sources	1		3
1750	Spending auth from offsetting collections, disc (total)	2		3
1900	Budget authority (total)	552	550	553
1930	Total budgetary resources available	589	577	602
	Memorandum (non-add) entries:			
1940	Unobligated balance expiring	–6		

INTERAGENCY CRIME AND DRUG ENFORCEMENT—Continued
Program and Financing—Continued

Identification code 015–0323–0–1–751	2021 actual	2022 est.	2023 est.
1941 Unexpired unobligated balance, end of year	24	27	52
Change in obligated balance:			
Unpaid obligations:			
3000 Unpaid obligations, brought forward, Oct 1	124	119	115
3010 New obligations, unexpired accounts	559	550	550
3011 Obligations ("upward adjustments"), expired accounts	2		
3020 Outlays (gross)	–555	–551	–556
3040 Recoveries of prior year unpaid obligations, unexpired	–8	–3	–3
3041 Recoveries of prior year unpaid obligations, expired	–3		
3050 Unpaid obligations, end of year	119	115	106
Uncollected payments:			
3060 Uncollected pymts, Fed sources, brought forward, Oct 1	–6	–6	–12
3070 Change in uncollected pymts, Fed sources, unexpired	–1		–3
3071 Change in uncollected pymts, Fed sources, expired	1	–6	3
3090 Uncollected pymts, Fed sources, end of year	–6	–12	–12
Memorandum (non-add) entries:			
3100 Obligated balance, start of year	118	113	103
3200 Obligated balance, end of year	113	103	94
Budget authority and outlays, net:			
Discretionary:			
4000 Budget authority, gross	552	550	553
Outlays, gross:			
4010 Outlays from new discretionary authority	483	412	414
4011 Outlays from discretionary balances	72	139	142
4020 Outlays, gross (total)	555	551	556
Offsets against gross budget authority and outlays:			
Offsetting collections (collected) from:			
4030 Federal sources	–2		–48
4040 Offsets against gross budget authority and outlays (total)	–2		–48
Additional offsets against gross budget authority only:			
4050 Change in uncollected pymts, Fed sources, unexpired	–1		–3
4052 Offsetting collections credited to expired accounts	1		29
4053 Recoveries of prior year paid obligations, unexpired accounts			19
4060 Additional offsets against budget authority only (total)			45
4070 Budget authority, net (discretionary)	550	550	550
4080 Outlays, net (discretionary)	553	551	508
4180 Budget authority, net (total)	550	550	550
4190 Outlays, net (total)	553	551	508

The Organized Crime Drug Enforcement Task Forces (OCDETF) program identifies, disrupts, and dismantles major domestic and transnational criminal organizations (TCOs) that engage in drug trafficking, violence, and money laundering activities which threaten the public safety and economic and national security of the United States. OCDETF accomplishes this mission by synthesizing the resources and expertise of 11 Federal law enforcement agency members, the Department of Justice's Criminal Division, United States Attorneys' Offices, and State and local law enforcement. The OCDETF task force approach effectively coordinates two primary activities: investigation and prosecution.

Investigation.—This activity includes resources for the direct investigative, intelligence, and support activities of OCDETF's multi-agency task forces, focusing on the disruption and dismantlement of major TCOs. Organizations participating under the Investigations function are the Drug Enforcement Administration, Federal Bureau of Investigation, Internal Revenue Service, Bureau of Alcohol, Tobacco, Firearms and Explosives, U.S. Coast Guard, U.S. Marshals Service, U.S. Secret Service, U.S. Postal Inspection Service, and Homeland Security Investigations. This activity also includes resources for the OCDETF Fusion Center (OFC), a multi-agency intelligence center which analyzes fused law enforcement financial and human intelligence information. The OFC produces actionable intelligence for use by OCDETF member agencies to disrupt and dismantle major criminal organizations and their supporting financial structures. In addition, the OFC creates strategic intelligence products that enhance TCO threat analyses and support national strategic efforts against transnational organ-

ized crime. OCDETF also maintains 19 Co-Located Strike Forces and supports transnational organized crime investigations through its International Organized Crime Intelligence and Operations Center (IOC-2). IOC-2 is a multi-agency intelligence center with a mission to significantly disrupt and dismantle those international criminal organizations posing the greatest threat to the United States. Multiple Federal agencies participate in IOC-2 activities and related investigations.

Prosecution.—This activity includes resources for the prosecution of cases generated through the investigative efforts of task force agents. Litigation efforts are intended to dismantle in their entirety those major transnational criminal organizations engaged in the highest levels of drug trafficking, violence, and money laundering by targeting the leaders of these organizations. This includes activities designed to secure the seizure and forfeiture of the assets of these enterprises. Participating agencies are the U.S. Attorneys and the Department of Justice's Criminal Division.

Object Classification (in millions of dollars)

Identification code 015–0323–0–1–751	2021 actual	2022 est.	2023 est.
Direct obligations:			
Personnel compensation:			
11.1 Full-time permanent	388	364	349
11.3 Other than full-time permanent	8	8	8
11.5 Other personnel compensation	23	23	24
11.9 Total personnel compensation	419	395	381
12.1 Civilian personnel benefits	108	96	92
21.0 Travel and transportation of persons	6	6	6
23.1 Rental payments to GSA	3	3	3
23.2 Rental payments to others	3	3	3
23.3 Communications, utilities, and miscellaneous charges	2	2	2
25.1 Advisory and assistance services		1	1
25.3 Other goods and services from Federal sources	9	36	54
31.0 Equipment		8	8
99.0 Direct obligations	550	550	550
99.0 Reimbursable obligations	9		
99.9 Total new obligations, unexpired accounts	559	550	550

Employment Summary

Identification code 015–0323–0–1–751	2021 actual	2022 est.	2023 est.
1001 Direct civilian full-time equivalent employment	2,702	2,573	2,456

FEDERAL BUREAU OF INVESTIGATION

Federal Funds

SALARIES AND EXPENSES

For necessary expenses of the Federal Bureau of Investigation for detection, investigation, and prosecution of crimes against the United States, $10,741,678,000, of which not to exceed $216,900,000 shall remain available until expended: Provided, That not to exceed $284,000 shall be available for official reception and representation expenses.

Note.—A full-year 2022 appropriation for this account was not enacted at the time the Budget was prepared; therefore, the Budget assumes this account is operating under the Continuing Appropriations Act, 2022 (Division A of Public Law 117–43, as amended). The amounts included for 2022 reflect the annualized level provided by the continuing resolution.

〖SALARIES AND EXPENSES〗

〖For an additional amount for "Salaries and Expenses", $50,000,000, to remain available until September 30, 2022, for investigative activities associated with Afghan resettlement operations〗. *(Afghanistan Supplemental Appropriations Act, 2022.)*

Program and Financing (in millions of dollars)

Identification code 015–0200–0–1–999	2021 actual	2022 est.	2023 est.
Obligations by program activity:			
0001 Intelligence	1,862	1,532	1,813
0002 Counterterrorism/Counterintelligence	4,014	3,460	4,034
0003 Criminal Enterprises and Federal Crimes	3,584	3,073	3,512
0004 Criminal Justice Services	611	242	524
0008 CJIS and COVID-19 Funding	84		

DEPARTMENT OF JUSTICE

Federal Bureau of Investigation—Continued
Federal Funds—Continued

737

0009	Afghanistan Supplemental	....	50	....
0091	Direct program activities, subtotal	10,155	8,357	9,883
0201	Intelligence	....	266	183
0202	Counterterrorism/Counterintelligence	....	423	302
0203	Criminal Enterprises and Federal Crimes	....	317	240
0204	Criminal Justice Services	....	356	134
0291	Direct program activities, subtotal	....	1,362	859
0300	Direct program activities, subtotal	10,155	9,719	10,742
0799	Total direct obligations	10,155	9,719	10,742
0801	Salaries and Expenses (Reimbursable)	923	1,045	1,045
0900	Total new obligations, unexpired accounts	11,078	10,764	11,787
	Budgetary resources:			
	Unobligated balance:			
1000	Unobligated balance brought forward, Oct 1	907	878	1,053
1001	Discretionary unobligated balance brought fwd, Oct 1	657	....	....
1012	Unobligated balance transfers between expired and unexpired accounts	112		
1021	Recoveries of prior year unpaid obligations	39	....	....
1033	Recoveries of prior year paid obligations	1	....	....
1070	Unobligated balance (total)	1,059	878	1,053
	Budget authority:			
	Appropriations, discretionary:			
1100	Appropriation	9,928	9,749	10,742
1100	Appropriation	....	50	....
1121	Appropriations transferred from other acct [011–1070]	2	....	....
1131	Unobligated balance of appropriations permanently reduced	–80	–80	....
1160	Appropriation, discretionary (total)	9,850	9,719	10,742
	Appropriations, mandatory:			
1221	Appropriations transferred from other acct [011–5512]	4	42	52
	Spending authority from offsetting collections, discretionary:			
1700	Collected	763	1,033	1,055
1701	Change in uncollected payments, Federal sources	188	....	....
1750	Spending auth from offsetting collections, disc (total)	951	1,033	1,055
	Spending authority from offsetting collections, mandatory:			
1800	Collected	144	145	145
1801	Change in uncollected payments, Federal sources	3	....	....
1850	Spending auth from offsetting collections, mand (total)	147	145	145
1900	Budget authority (total)	10,952	10,939	11,994
1930	Total budgetary resources available	12,011	11,817	13,047
	Memorandum (non-add) entries:			
1940	Unobligated balance expiring	–55	....	....
1941	Unexpired unobligated balance, end of year	878	1,053	1,260
	Change in obligated balance:			
	Unpaid obligations:			
3000	Unpaid obligations, brought forward, Oct 1	2,974	3,029	2,513
3010	New obligations, unexpired accounts	11,078	10,764	11,787
3011	Obligations ("upward adjustments"), expired accounts	89	....	....
3020	Outlays (gross)	–10,892	–11,280	–11,793
3040	Recoveries of prior year unpaid obligations, unexpired	–39	....	....
3041	Recoveries of prior year unpaid obligations, expired	–181	....	....
3050	Unpaid obligations, end of year	3,029	2,513	2,507
	Uncollected payments:			
3060	Uncollected pymts, Fed sources, brought forward, Oct 1	–570	–570	–570
3070	Change in uncollected pymts, Fed sources, unexpired	–191	....	....
3071	Change in uncollected pymts, Fed sources, expired	191	....	....
3090	Uncollected pymts, Fed sources, end of year	–570	–570	–570
	Memorandum (non-add) entries:			
3100	Obligated balance, start of year	2,404	2,459	1,943
3200	Obligated balance, end of year	2,459	1,943	1,937
	Budget authority and outlays, net:			
	Discretionary:			
4000	Budget authority, gross	10,801	10,752	11,797
	Outlays, gross:			
4010	Outlays from new discretionary authority	8,027	8,618	9,434
4011	Outlays from discretionary balances	2,678	2,481	2,165
4020	Outlays, gross (total)	10,705	11,099	11,599
	Offsets against gross budget authority and outlays:			
	Offsetting collections (collected) from:			
4030	Federal sources	–754	–1,033	–1,055
4033	Non-Federal sources	–208	....	....
4040	Offsets against gross budget authority and outlays (total)	–962	–1,033	–1,055
	Additional offsets against gross budget authority only:			
4050	Change in uncollected pymts, Fed sources, unexpired	–188	....	....
4052	Offsetting collections credited to expired accounts	198	....	....
4053	Recoveries of prior year paid obligations, unexpired accounts	1	....	....
4060	Additional offsets against budget authority only (total)	11	....	....
4070	Budget authority, net (discretionary)	9,850	9,719	10,742
4080	Outlays, net (discretionary)	9,743	10,066	10,544
	Mandatory:			
4090	Budget authority, gross	151	187	197
	Outlays, gross:			
4100	Outlays from new mandatory authority	....	181	189
4101	Outlays from mandatory balances	187	....	5
4110	Outlays, gross (total)	187	181	194
	Offsets against gross budget authority and outlays:			
	Offsetting collections (collected) from:			
4120	Federal sources	–144	–145	–145
	Additional offsets against gross budget authority only:			
4140	Change in uncollected pymts, Fed sources, unexpired	–3	....	....
4160	Budget authority, net (mandatory)	4	42	52
4170	Outlays, net (mandatory)	43	36	49
4180	Budget authority, net (total)	9,854	9,761	10,794
4190	Outlays, net (total)	9,786	10,102	10,593

The mission of the Federal Bureau of Investigation (FBI) is to protect the American people and uphold the Constitution of the United States.

The FBI's enterprise strategy includes several integrated components. The vision outlines the FBI's desired strategic position, which it aims to accomplish by continuously evolving to mitigate existing threats and anticipate future threats. To focus efforts across the enterprise, the FBI developed strategic objectives, operational mission priorities, through its Integrated Program Management process.

The FBI is headed by a Director, who is appointed by the President and confirmed by the Senate. FBI Headquarters, located in Washington, DC, provides centralized operational, policy, and administrative support to FBI investigations. The FBI operates 56 field offices in major U.S. cities and approximately 350 resident agencies (RAs) throughout the country. RAs are satellite offices that allow the FBI to maintain a presence in and serve local communities. The FBI also operates 63 Legal Attache offices and 29 sub-offices in 73 foreign countries around the world. Additionally, there are several specialized facilities and analytical centers within the FBI that are located across the country, such as the Criminal Justice Information Services Division in Clarksburg, WV; the Terrorist Explosive Device Analytical Center and Hazardous Devices School in Huntsville, AL; and the FBI Academy and Laboratory at Quantico, VA.

A number of FBI activities are carried out on reimbursable bases. For example, the FBI is reimbursed for its participation in the Organized Crime Drug Enforcement Task Force program and by other Federal agencies for certain intelligence and investigative services, such as pre-employment background inquiries and fingerprint and name checks. The FBI is also authorized to conduct fingerprint and name checks for certain non-Federal agencies.

For 2023, the FBI is requesting $10.7 billion in Salaries and Expenses funding. Specifically, the FBI requests program increases of $52.0 million to bolster its cyber investigative program, $48.8 million to counter acts of mass violence and threats to public safety, $42.2 million to address core counterintelligence needs and other national security priorities, $20.6 million to combat crime and corruption, $17.8 million to bolster its Civil Rights program, $36.9 million to defend the organization against cybersecurity threats, $16.9 million to bolster the organization's IT networks, $27.4 million to support the implementation of the organization's body-worn camera program for FBI Special Agents, $39.4 million to support the substantial personnel, structural, and security requirements of newly constructed buildings in Huntsville, Alabama, and $22.5 million to address increased responsibilities in Oklahoma stemming from the Supreme Court's *McGirt v. Oklahoma* decision.

SALARIES AND EXPENSES—Continued
Object Classification (in millions of dollars)

Identification code 015–0200–0–1–999		2021 actual	2022 est.	2023 est.
	Direct obligations:			
	Personnel compensation:			
11.1	Full-time permanent	3,557	3,594	3,922
11.3	Other than full-time permanent	43	....	1
11.5	Other personnel compensation	443	456	500
11.8	Special personal services payments	1	....	1
11.9	Total personnel compensation	4,044	4,050	4,424
12.1	Civilian personnel benefits	1,931	1,877	2,182
13.0	Benefits for former personnel	1	....	....
21.0	Travel and transportation of persons	129	153	133
22.0	Transportation of things	11	....	3
23.1	Rental payments to GSA	685	692	713
23.2	Rental payments to others	96	35	31
23.3	Communications, utilities, and miscellaneous charges	174	214	125
24.0	Printing and reproduction	5	1	3
25.1	Advisory and assistance services	1,158	720	939
25.2	Other services from non-Federal sources	529	756	864
25.3	Other goods and services from Federal sources	119	116	113
25.4	Operation and maintenance of facilities	232	214	201
25.5	Research and development contracts	6	18	13
25.6	Medical care	....	....	1
25.7	Operation and maintenance of equipment	299	350	265
25.8	Subsistence and support of persons	1	1	1
26.0	Supplies and materials	188	103	202
31.0	Equipment	469	419	505
32.0	Land and structures	69	....	21
41.0	Grants, subsidies, and contributions	2	....	3
42.0	Insurance claims and indemnities	7	....	....
99.0	Direct obligations	10,155	9,719	10,742
99.0	Reimbursable obligations	923	1,045	1,045
99.9	Total new obligations, unexpired accounts	11,078	10,764	11,787

Employment Summary

Identification code 015–0200–0–1–999		2021 actual	2022 est.	2023 est.
1001	Direct civilian full-time equivalent employment	33,852	33,852	35,264
2001	Reimbursable civilian full-time equivalent employment	1,431	1,431	1,546

CONSTRUCTION

For necessary expenses, to include the cost of equipment, furniture, and information technology requirements, related to construction or acquisition of buildings, facilities, and sites by purchase, or as otherwise authorized by law; conversion, modification, and extension of federally owned buildings; preliminary planning and design of projects; and operation and maintenance of secure work environment facilities and secure networking capabilities, $61,895,000, to remain available until expended.

Note.—A full-year 2022 appropriation for this account was not enacted at the time the Budget was prepared; therefore, the Budget assumes this account is operating under the Continuing Appropriations Act, 2022 (Division A of Public Law 117–43, as amended). The amounts included for 2022 reflect the annualized level provided by the continuing resolution.

Program and Financing (in millions of dollars)

Identification code 015–0203–0–1–751		2021 actual	2022 est.	2023 est.
	Obligations by program activity:			
0006	Secure Work Environment Program	53	50	49
0011	Quantico	1	12	13
0014	Terrorists Explosive Devices Analytical Center	2	....	....
0020	21st Century Facilities	123	....	....
0900	Total new obligations, unexpired accounts	179	62	62
	Budgetary resources:			
	Unobligated balance:			
1000	Unobligated balance brought forward, Oct 1	921	1,314	1,818
1021	Recoveries of prior year unpaid obligations	6	....	....
1070	Unobligated balance (total)	927	1,314	1,818
	Budget authority:			
	Appropriations, discretionary:			
1100	Appropriation	566	566	62
1900	Budget authority (total)	566	566	62
1930	Total budgetary resources available	1,493	1,880	1,880
	Memorandum (non-add) entries:			
1941	Unexpired unobligated balance, end of year	1,314	1,818	1,818
	Change in obligated balance:			
	Unpaid obligations:			
3000	Unpaid obligations, brought forward, Oct 1	560	386	420
3010	New obligations, unexpired accounts	179	62	62
3020	Outlays (gross)	–347	–28	–482
3040	Recoveries of prior year unpaid obligations, unexpired	–6	....	....
3050	Unpaid obligations, end of year	386	420	....
	Memorandum (non-add) entries:			
3100	Obligated balance, start of year	560	386	420
3200	Obligated balance, end of year	386	420	....
	Budget authority and outlays, net:			
	Discretionary:			
4000	Budget authority, gross	566	566	62
	Outlays, gross:			
4010	Outlays from new discretionary authority	....	28	3
4011	Outlays from discretionary balances	347	....	479
4020	Outlays, gross (total)	347	28	482
4180	Budget authority, net (total)	566	566	62
4190	Outlays, net (total)	347	28	482

For 2023, the FBI is requesting a total of $61.9 million in Construction funding for the Secure Work Environment program and for renovations at the FBI Academy in Quantico, Virginia.

The Administration also recognizes the critical need for a new FBI headquarters. The J. Edgar Hoover building can no longer support the long-term mission of the FBI. The Administration has begun a multi-year process of constructing a modern, secure suburban facility from which the FBI can continue its mission to protect the American people. During the next year, FBI and GSA will work to identify a location to construct a Federally-owned, modern and secure facility for at least 7,500 personnel in the suburbs. Over the next year, FBI and GSA will finalize an updated program of requirements for a secure suburban campus, including the final number of personnel, to inform a 2024 Budget request for funding for the new facility. GSA will also begin initial steps to acquire, if necessary, the site for the new suburban location. Additionally, FBI and GSA will work to identify a Federally-owned location in the District of Columbia to support a presence of approximately 750–1,000 FBI personnel that would support day-to-day FBI engagement with DOJ headquarters, the White House, and Congress.

Object Classification (in millions of dollars)

Identification code 015–0203–0–1–751		2021 actual	2022 est.	2023 est.
	Direct obligations:			
23.3	Communications, utilities, and miscellaneous charges	5	....	....
25.1	Advisory and assistance services	41	....	....
25.2	Other services from non-Federal sources	12	....	....
25.4	Operation and maintenance of facilities	27	2	2
25.7	Operation and maintenance of equipment	5	....	....
26.0	Supplies and materials	1	1	1
31.0	Equipment	52	49	49
32.0	Land and structures	36	10	10
99.9	Total new obligations, unexpired accounts	179	62	62

DRUG ENFORCEMENT ADMINISTRATION

Federal Funds

SALARIES AND EXPENSES

For necessary expenses of the Drug Enforcement Administration, including not to exceed $70,000 to meet unforeseen emergencies of a confidential character pursuant to section 530C of title 28, United States Code; and expenses for conducting drug education and training programs, including travel and related expenses for participants in such programs and the distribution of items of token value that promote the goals of such programs, $2,523,116,000, of which not to exceed $75,000,000 shall remain available until expended and not to exceed $90,000 shall be available for official reception and representation expenses: Provided, That, notwithstanding section 3672 of Public Law 106–310, up to $10,000,000 may be used to reimburse

DEPARTMENT OF JUSTICE

Drug Enforcement Administration—Continued
Federal Funds—Continued

States, units of local government, Indian Tribal Governments, other public entities, and multi-jurisdictional or regional consortia thereof for expenses incurred to clean up and safely dispose of substances associated with clandestine methamphetamine laboratories, conversion and extraction operations, tableting operations, or laboratories and processing operations for fentanyl and fentanyl-related substances which may present a danger to public health or the environment: *Provided further*, That of the amounts appropriated under this heading, not to exceed $50,000 shall be available in fiscal year 2023 for expenses associated with the celebration of the 50th anniversary of the Drug Enforcement Administration.

Note.—A full-year 2022 appropriation for this account was not enacted at the time the Budget was prepared; therefore, the Budget assumes this account is operating under the Continuing Appropriations Act, 2022 (Division A of Public Law 117–43, as amended). The amounts included for 2022 reflect the annualized level provided by the continuing resolution.

Program and Financing (in millions of dollars)

Identification code 015–1100–0–1–751		2021 actual	2022 est.	2023 est.
	Obligations by program activity:			
0002	International Enforcement	464	465	476
0003	Domestic Enforcement	2,012	1,978	2,153
0004	State and Local Assistance	13	12	13
0799	Total direct obligations	2,489	2,455	2,642
0801	Reimbursable	21	38	34
0900	Total new obligations, unexpired accounts	2,510	2,493	2,676
	Budgetary resources:			
	Unobligated balance:			
1000	Unobligated balance brought forward, Oct 1	240	167	697
1001	Discretionary unobligated balance brought fwd, Oct 1	85		
1012	Unobligated balance transfers between expired and unexpired accounts	62	75	75
1021	Recoveries of prior year unpaid obligations	4		
1033	Recoveries of prior year paid obligations			72
1070	Unobligated balance (total)	306	242	844
	Budget authority:			
	Appropriations, discretionary:			
1100	Appropriation	2,336	2,336	2,523
1121	Appropriations transferred from other acct [011–1070]	15		
1160	Appropriation, discretionary (total)	2,351	2,336	2,523
	Appropriations, mandatory:			
1221	Appropriations transferred from other acct [011–5512]	11	8	8
	Spending authority from offsetting collections, discretionary:			
1700	Collected	20	480	435
1701	Change in uncollected payments, Federal sources	–4	124	136
1750	Spending auth from offsetting collections, disc (total)	16	604	571
1900	Budget authority (total)	2,378	2,948	3,102
1930	Total budgetary resources available	2,684	3,190	3,946
	Memorandum (non-add) entries:			
1940	Unobligated balance expiring	–7		
1941	Unexpired unobligated balance, end of year	167	697	1,270
	Change in obligated balance:			
	Unpaid obligations:			
3000	Unpaid obligations, brought forward, Oct 1	640	646	627
3010	New obligations, unexpired accounts	2,510	2,493	2,676
3011	Obligations ("upward adjustments"), expired accounts	28	214	2
3020	Outlays (gross)	–2,451	–2,726	–3,080
3040	Recoveries of prior year unpaid obligations, unexpired	–4		
3041	Recoveries of prior year unpaid obligations, expired	–77		
3050	Unpaid obligations, end of year	646	627	225
	Uncollected payments:			
3060	Uncollected pymts, Fed sources, brought forward, Oct 1	–46	–29	–40
3070	Change in uncollected pymts, Fed sources, unexpired	4	–124	–136
3071	Change in uncollected pymts, Fed sources, expired	13	113	129
3090	Uncollected pymts, Fed sources, end of year	–29	–40	–47
	Memorandum (non-add) entries:			
3100	Obligated balance, start of year	594	617	587
3200	Obligated balance, end of year	617	587	178
	Budget authority and outlays, net:			
	Discretionary:			
4000	Budget authority, gross	2,367	2,940	3,094
	Outlays, gross:			
4010	Outlays from new discretionary authority	1,843	2,356	2,463
4011	Outlays from discretionary balances	565	322	584
4020	Outlays, gross (total)	2,408	2,678	3,047
	Offsets against gross budget authority and outlays:			
	Offsetting collections (collected) from:			
4030	Federal sources	–32	–548	–572
4033	Non-Federal sources	–8	–9	–8
4040	Offsets against gross budget authority and outlays (total)	–40	–557	–580
	Additional offsets against gross budget authority only:			
4050	Change in uncollected pymts, Fed sources, unexpired	4	–124	–136
4052	Offsetting collections credited to expired accounts	20	77	73
4053	Recoveries of prior year paid obligations, unexpired accounts			72
4060	Additional offsets against budget authority only (total)	24	–47	9
4070	Budget authority, net (discretionary)	2,351	2,336	2,523
4080	Outlays, net (discretionary)	2,368	2,121	2,467
	Mandatory:			
4090	Budget authority, gross	11	8	8
	Outlays, gross:			
4100	Outlays from new mandatory authority		8	8
4101	Outlays from mandatory balances	43	40	25
4110	Outlays, gross (total)	43	48	33
4180	Budget authority, net (total)	2,362	2,344	2,531
4190	Outlays, net (total)	2,411	2,169	2,500

The Drug Enforcement Administration's (DEA) mission is to enforce the controlled substances laws and regulations of the United States. DEA's major focus is the disruption and dismantlement of Priority Target Organizations (PTOs)—domestic and international drug trafficking and money laundering organizations having a significant impact on drug availability in the United States. The DEA emphasizes PTOs with links to organizations on the Attorney General's Consolidated Priority Organization Target list, which represents the "Most Wanted" drug trafficking and money laundering organizations believed to be primarily responsible for the United States' illicit drug supply, including heroin. The DEA also considers it a high priority to target the financial infrastructure of major drug trafficking organizations, and members of the financial community who facilitate the laundering of their proceeds. In FY 2021, the DEA denied drug traffickers $48.8 billion in revenue through the seizure of both assets and drugs.

The DEA's primary focus has always been and continues to be enforcing the nation's drug laws. However, we recognize that community outreach and support are important not only in preventing drug misuse, but also in developing community connections that assist enforcement efforts. The DEA's community outreach efforts provide websites, publications, exhibits, educational programs, presentations, and collaboration through the domestic field divisions and in partnerships with dozens of Federal, state, and local organizations that have the common cause of preventing substance misuse.

The DEA has 238 domestic offices organized in 23 divisions throughout the United States. Internationally, the DEA has 92 offices in 69 countries and is responsible for coordinating and pursuing U.S. drug investigations abroad. Federal, State, local, and international partnerships continue to play an important role in DEA's enforcement efforts. For nearly 43 years, the DEA has led a task force program that today includes approximately 3,000 task force officers participating in 379 task forces. DEA's Special Operations Division (SOD) and the El Paso Intelligence Center (EPIC) are vital resources for Federal, State, and local law enforcement. Additionally, through the Office of National Security Intelligence (ONSI), the DEA ensures that national security information obtained in the course of conducting its drug law enforcement mission is expeditiously shared with the Intelligence Community.

DEA's activities are divided into three decision units:

Domestic Enforcement.—Through effective enforcement efforts and associated support functions, the DEA disrupts and dismantles the leadership, command, control, and infrastructure of major drug trafficking syndicates, criminal organizations, and violent drug trafficking groups that threaten the United States. This decision unit contains most of DEA's resources, domestic enforcement groups, State and local task forces, other Federal and local task forces, intelligence groups, and all the support functions essential to accomplishing their mission. DEA's objectives for Domestic Enforcement include:

SALARIES AND EXPENSES—Continued

—Identifying and targeting the national/regional organizations most responsible for the domestic distribution and manufacture of illicit drugs;

—Systematically disrupting or dismantling targeted organizations by arresting/convicting their leaders and facilitators, seizing and forfeiting their assets, targeting their money laundering operations, and destroying their command and control networks; and,

—Working with international offices to dismantle domestic organizations directly affiliated with Transnational Criminal Organizations

International Enforcement.—The DEA works with its foreign counterparts to attack the vulnerabilities in the leadership, production, transportation, communications, finance, and distribution sectors of major international drug trafficking organizations. DEA's objectives for International Enforcement include:

—Identifying and targeting the most significant international drug and chemical trafficking organizations;

—Disrupting and dismantling the networks, financial infrastructures, operations, and resource bases of targeted international drug and chemical trafficking organizations; and

—Preventing drug trafficking organizations from funding terrorist organizations and activities.

State and Local Assistance.—The DEA provides clandestine laboratory training and meets the hazardous waste cleanup needs of the U.S. law enforcement community. The DEA supports State and local law enforcement with assistance and training so that State and local agencies can better address the environmental threat of clandestine laboratories in their communities. As a result, DEA's nationwide contracts, container program, and established training programs allow the DEA to provide State and local clandestine lab and hazardous environment cleanup and training assistance in a cost-effective manner.

For 2023, the DEA requests $31.1 million to transform how the DEA exploits, stores, and integrates data to enhance its investigations; $19.8 million to establish an agency-wide Body Worn Camera program; $8.0 million for cyber investigative support; $3.0 million to implement Cybersecurity Maturity Model improvements; and $3.3 million to provide additional staffing support to the DEA's Tulsa, Oklahoma Resident Office in response to Supreme Court's decision in *McGirt v. Oklahoma*.

Object Classification (in millions of dollars)

Identification code 015–1100–0–1–751		2021 actual	2022 est.	2023 est.
	Direct obligations:			
	Personnel compensation:			
11.1	Full-time permanent	643	689	729
11.3	Other than full-time permanent	9	3	7
11.5	Other personnel compensation	145	123	130
11.9	Total personnel compensation	797	815	866
12.1	Civilian personnel benefits	510	459	498
21.0	Travel and transportation of persons	17	38	41
22.0	Transportation of things	11	14	14
23.1	Rental payments to GSA	264	199	213
23.2	Rental payments to others	7	37	34
23.3	Communications, utilities, and miscellaneous charges	61	64	65
24.0	Printing and reproduction	1	1	3
25.1	Advisory and assistance services	235	131	143
25.2	Other services from non-Federal sources	96	240	262
25.3	Other goods and services from Federal sources	95	116	122
25.4	Operation and maintenance of facilities	40	30	30
25.5	Research and development contracts	1	1	1
25.6	Medical care	1	1	1
25.7	Operation and maintenance of equipment	150	95	98
25.8	Subsistence and support of persons	....	18	18
26.0	Supplies and materials	55	53	53
31.0	Equipment	118	95	117
32.0	Land and structures	29	47	62
42.0	Insurance claims and indemnities	1	1	1
99.0	Direct obligations	2,489	2,455	2,642
99.0	Reimbursable obligations	21	38	34
99.9	Total new obligations, unexpired accounts	2,510	2,493	2,676

Employment Summary

Identification code 015–1100–0–1–751		2021 actual	2022 est.	2023 est.
1001	Direct civilian full-time equivalent employment	6,240	6,449	6,547
2001	Reimbursable civilian full-time equivalent employment	971	11	11

CONSTRUCTION

Note.—A full-year 2022 appropriation for this account was not enacted at the time the Budget was prepared; therefore, the Budget assumes this account is operating under the Continuing Appropriations Act, 2022 (Division A of Public Law 117–43, as amended). The amounts included for 2022 reflect the annualized level provided by the continuing resolution.

Program and Financing (in millions of dollars)

Identification code 015–1101–0–1–751		2021 actual	2022 est.	2023 est.
	Obligations by program activity:			
0006	Direct program activity	....	50	50
0900	Total new obligations, unexpired accounts (object class 32.0)	....	50	50
	Budgetary resources:			
	Unobligated balance:			
1000	Unobligated balance brought forward, Oct 1	....	50	50
	Budget authority:			
	Appropriations, discretionary:			
1100	Appropriation	50	50	....
1930	Total budgetary resources available	50	100	50
	Memorandum (non-add) entries:			
1941	Unexpired unobligated balance, end of year	50	50	
	Change in obligated balance:			
	Unpaid obligations:			
3010	New obligations, unexpired accounts	....	50	50
3020	Outlays (gross)	....	–50	–20
3050	Unpaid obligations, end of year	....	....	30
	Memorandum (non-add) entries:			
3200	Obligated balance, end of year	....	....	30
	Budget authority and outlays, net:			
	Discretionary:			
4000	Budget authority, gross	50	50	....
	Outlays, gross:			
4010	Outlays from new discretionary authority	....	30	....
4011	Outlays from discretionary balances	....	20	20
4020	Outlays, gross (total)	....	50	20
4180	Budget authority, net (total)	50	50	....
4190	Outlays, net (total)	....	50	20

DIVERSION CONTROL FEE ACCOUNT

Special and Trust Fund Receipts (in millions of dollars)

Identification code 015–5131–0–2–751		2021 actual	2022 est.	2023 est.
0100	Balance, start of year	25	31	86
	Receipts:			
	Current law:			
1120	Diversion Control Fee Account, DEA	549	566	585
2000	Total: Balances and receipts	574	597	671
	Appropriations:			
	Current law:			
2101	Diversion Control Fee Account	–549	–511	–581
2103	Diversion Control Fee Account	–25	–31	–31
2132	Diversion Control Fee Account	31	31	31
2199	Total current law appropriations	–543	–511	–581
2999	Total appropriations	–543	–511	–581
5099	Balance, end of year	31	86	90

DEPARTMENT OF JUSTICE

Program and Financing (in millions of dollars)

Identification code 015–5131–0–2–751	2021 actual	2022 est.	2023 est.
Obligations by program activity:			
0001 Diversion Control	544	511	581
Budgetary resources:			
Unobligated balance:			
1000 Unobligated balance brought forward, Oct 1	24	39	50
1021 Recoveries of prior year unpaid obligations	15	10	16
1070 Unobligated balance (total)	39	49	66
Budget authority:			
Appropriations, mandatory:			
1201 Appropriation (special or trust fund)	549	511	581
1203 Appropriation (previously unavailable)(special or trust)	25	31	31
1232 Appropriations and/or unobligated balance of appropriations temporarily reduced	–31	–31	–31
1260 Appropriations, mandatory (total)	543	511	581
Spending authority from offsetting collections, mandatory:			
1800 Collected	1	1	1
1900 Budget authority (total)	544	512	582
1930 Total budgetary resources available	583	561	648
Memorandum (non-add) entries:			
1941 Unexpired unobligated balance, end of year	39	50	67
Change in obligated balance:			
Unpaid obligations:			
3000 Unpaid obligations, brought forward, Oct 1	97	98	143
3010 New obligations, unexpired accounts	544	511	581
3020 Outlays (gross)	–528	–456	–526
3040 Recoveries of prior year unpaid obligations, unexpired	–15	–10	–16
3050 Unpaid obligations, end of year	98	143	182
Memorandum (non-add) entries:			
3100 Obligated balance, start of year	97	98	143
3200 Obligated balance, end of year	98	143	182
Budget authority and outlays, net:			
Mandatory:			
4090 Budget authority, gross	544	512	582
Outlays, gross:			
4100 Outlays from new mandatory authority	432	387	382
4101 Outlays from mandatory balances	96	69	144
4110 Outlays, gross (total)	528	456	526
Offsets against gross budget authority and outlays:			
Offsetting collections (collected) from:			
4120 Federal sources	–1	–1	–1
4180 Budget authority, net (total)	543	511	581
4190 Outlays, net (total)	527	455	525

Public Law 102–395 established the Diversion Control Fee Account in 1993. Fees charged by the Drug Enforcement Administration (DEA) under the Diversion Control Program are set at a level that ensures the recovery of the full costs of operating this program. By carrying out the mandates of the Controlled Substances Act (CSA), the DEA ensures that adequate supplies of controlled drugs are available to meet legitimate medical, scientific, industrial, and export needs, while preventing, detecting, and eliminating diversion of these substances to illicit traffic. The CSA requires physicians, pharmacists, and chemical companies to register with the DEA in order to distribute or manufacture controlled substances or listed chemicals. The registrant community, physicians, prescribers, and pharmacists, can be seen as the first line of defense against the opioid epidemic now facing the United States. The engagement and education of these community members can help in reducing the overprescribing of opioids and the prevention of abuse and illicit use. Investigations conducted by the Diversion Control Program fall into two distinct categories: the diversion of legitimately manufactured pharmaceutical controlled substances and the diversion of controlled chemicals (List I and II) used in the illicit manufacture of controlled substances. DEA's objectives for diversion control include:

—Identifying and targeting those responsible for the diversion of pharmaceutical controlled substances through traditional investigation and cybercrime initiatives to systematically disrupt and dismantle those entities involved in diversion schemes;

—Supporting the registrant population with improved technology, including e-commerce and customer support, while maintaining cooperation, support, and assistance from the regulated industry;

—Educating the public on the dangers of prescription drug abuse and proactive enforcement measures to combat emerging drug trends; and,

—Ensuring an adequate and uninterrupted supply of pharmaceutical controlled substances and listed chemicals to meet legitimate medical, commercial, and scientific needs.

Object Classification (in millions of dollars)

Identification code 015–5131–0–2–751	2021 actual	2022 est.	2023 est.
Direct obligations:			
Personnel compensation:			
11.1 Full-time permanent	204	190	216
11.3 Other than full-time permanent	2	2	2
11.5 Other personnel compensation	15	14	16
11.9 Total personnel compensation	221	206	234
12.1 Civilian personnel benefits	85	85	96
21.0 Travel and transportation of persons	3	8	9
22.0 Transportation of things	1	3	3
23.1 Rental payments to GSA	42	35	39
23.2 Rental payments to others	1	1	1
23.3 Communications, utilities, and miscellaneous charges	8	9	11
24.0 Printing and reproduction	5	9	10
25.1 Advisory and assistance services	102	56	68
25.2 Other services from non-Federal sources	17	38	43
25.3 Other goods and services from Federal sources	13	11	13
25.4 Operation and maintenance of facilities	6	5	5
25.7 Operation and maintenance of equipment	20	28	12
26.0 Supplies and materials	5	2	9
31.0 Equipment	11	11	28
32.0 Land and structures	4	4	
99.9 Total new obligations, unexpired accounts	544	511	581

Employment Summary

Identification code 015–5131–0–2–751	2021 actual	2022 est.	2023 est.
1001 Direct civilian full-time equivalent employment	1,811	1,967	2,064

BUREAU OF ALCOHOL, TOBACCO, FIREARMS, AND EXPLOSIVES

Federal Funds

SALARIES AND EXPENSES

For necessary expenses of the Bureau of Alcohol, Tobacco, Firearms and Explosives, for training of State and local law enforcement agencies with or without reimbursement, including training in connection with the training and acquisition of canines for explosives and fire accelerants detection; and for provision of laboratory assistance to State and local law enforcement agencies, with or without reimbursement, $1,732,528,000, of which not to exceed $36,000 shall be for official reception and representation expenses, not to exceed $1,000,000 shall be available for the payment of attorneys' fees as provided by section 924(d)(2) of title 18, United States Code, and not to exceed $25,000,000 shall remain available until expended: Provided, That none of the funds appropriated herein shall be available to investigate or act upon applications for relief from Federal firearms disabilities under section 925(c) of title 18, United States Code: Provided further, That such funds shall be available to investigate and act upon applications filed by corporations for relief from Federal firearms disabilities under section 925(c) of title 18, United States Code: Provided further, That no funds made available by this or any other Act may be used to transfer the functions, missions, or activities of the Bureau of Alcohol, Tobacco, Firearms and Explosives to other agencies or Departments.

Note.—A full-year 2022 appropriation for this account was not enacted at the time the Budget was prepared; therefore, the Budget assumes this account is operating under the Continuing Appropriations Act, 2022 (Division A of Public Law 117–43, as amended). The amounts included for 2022 reflect the annualized level provided by the continuing resolution.

742   Bureau of Alcohol, Tobacco, Firearms, and Explosives—Continued
        Federal Funds—Continued   THE BUDGET FOR FISCAL YEAR 2023

SALARIES AND EXPENSES—Continued

Program and Financing (in millions of dollars)

Identification code 015–0700–0–1–751	2021 actual	2022 est.	2023 est.
Obligations by program activity:			
0006 Law Enforcement Operations	1,137	1,182	1,374
0007 Investigative Support Services	349	353	407
0192 Total Direct Program	1,486	1,535	1,781
0799 Total direct obligations	1,486	1,535	1,781
0801 Salaries and Expenses (Reimbursable)	79	145	145
0900 Total new obligations, unexpired accounts	1,565	1,680	1,926
Budgetary resources:			
Unobligated balance:			
1000 Unobligated balance brought forward, Oct 1	171	154	122
1001 Discretionary unobligated balance brought fwd, Oct 1	25		
1010 Unobligated balance transfer to other accts [011–5512]	–15		
1012 Unobligated balance transfers between expired and unexpired accounts	14	15	15
1021 Recoveries of prior year unpaid obligations	3	4	4
1070 Unobligated balance (total)	173	173	141
Budget authority:			
Appropriations, discretionary:			
1100 Appropriation	1,484	1,484	1,733
Spending authority from offsetting collections, discretionary:			
1700 Collected	59	145	145
1701 Change in uncollected payments, Federal sources	7		
1750 Spending auth from offsetting collections, disc (total)	66	145	145
1900 Budget authority (total)	1,550	1,629	1,878
1930 Total budgetary resources available	1,723	1,802	2,019
Memorandum (non-add) entries:			
1940 Unobligated balance expiring	–4		
1941 Unexpired unobligated balance, end of year	154	122	93
Change in obligated balance:			
Unpaid obligations:			
3000 Unpaid obligations, brought forward, Oct 1	354	383	419
3010 New obligations, unexpired accounts	1,565	1,680	1,926
3011 Obligations ("upward adjustments"), expired accounts	5		
3020 Outlays (gross)	–1,514	–1,640	–1,865
3040 Recoveries of prior year unpaid obligations, unexpired	–3	–4	–4
3041 Recoveries of prior year unpaid obligations, expired	–24		
3050 Unpaid obligations, end of year	383	419	476
Uncollected payments:			
3060 Uncollected pymts, Fed sources, brought forward, Oct 1	–89	–76	–76
3070 Change in uncollected pymts, Fed sources, unexpired	–7		
3071 Change in uncollected pymts, Fed sources, expired	20		
3090 Uncollected pymts, Fed sources, end of year	–76	–76	–76
Memorandum (non-add) entries:			
3100 Obligated balance, start of year	265	307	343
3200 Obligated balance, end of year	307	343	400
Budget authority and outlays, net:			
Discretionary:			
4000 Budget authority, gross	1,550	1,629	1,878
Outlays, gross:			
4010 Outlays from new discretionary authority	1,243	1,436	1,653
4011 Outlays from discretionary balances	269	189	192
4020 Outlays, gross (total)	1,512	1,625	1,845
Offsets against gross budget authority and outlays:			
Offsetting collections (collected) from:			
4030 Federal sources	–78	–145	–145
4033 Non-Federal sources	–2		
4040 Offsets against gross budget authority and outlays (total)	–80	–145	–145
Additional offsets against gross budget authority only:			
4050 Change in uncollected pymts, Fed sources, unexpired	–7		
4052 Offsetting collections credited to expired accounts	21		
4060 Additional offsets against budget authority only (total)	14		
4070 Budget authority, net (discretionary)	1,484	1,484	1,733
4080 Outlays, net (discretionary)	1,432	1,480	1,700
Mandatory:			
Outlays, gross:			
4101 Outlays from mandatory balances	2	15	20
4180 Budget authority, net (total)	1,484	1,484	1,733
4190 Outlays, net (total)	1,434	1,495	1,720

The Bureau of Alcohol, Tobacco, Firearms, and Explosives (ATF) is the U.S. law enforcement agency dedicated to protecting our Nation from the illicit use of firearms and explosives in violent crime and acts of terrorism. The ATF protects our communities from violent criminals and criminal organizations by investigating and preventing the illegal use and trafficking of firearms, the illegal use and improper storage of explosives, acts of arson and bombings, and the illegal diversion of alcohol and tobacco products. The ATF regulates the firearms and explosives industries from manufacture and/or importation through retail sale to ensure that Federal Firearms Licensees and Federal Explosives Licensees and permitees conduct business in compliance with all applicable laws and regulations.

For FY 2023, the ATF requests $123.2 million for targeted efforts to fight violent crime and promote gun safety, which includes $20.1 million for Industry Operations Investigator support for regulatory enforcement and diversion control; $53.7 million for Combating Gun Violence; $21.2 million for the National Integrated Ballistics Information Network and Crime Gun Intelligence; $14.4 million for modernization of the National Tracing Center; and $13.7 million to enhance community policing efforts through the Body Worn Camera Program.

Object Classification (in millions of dollars)

Identification code 015–0700–0–1–751	2021 actual	2022 est.	2023 est.
Direct obligations:			
Personnel compensation:			
11.1 Full-time permanent	554	587	655
11.3 Other than full-time permanent	2	2	5
11.5 Other personnel compensation	76	77	86
11.9 Total personnel compensation	632	666	746
12.1 Civilian personnel benefits	305	313	337
21.0 Travel and transportation of persons	23	23	27
22.0 Transportation of things	2	2	3
23.1 Rental payments to GSA	96	103	104
23.3 Communications, utilities, and miscellaneous charges	29	29	33
24.0 Printing and reproduction	1	1	2
25.2 Other services from non-Federal sources	21	24	31
25.2 Other services from non-Federal sources	178	200	283
25.3 Other goods and services from Federal sources	28	26	32
25.7 Operation and maintenance of equipment	74	72	75
26.0 Supplies and materials	27	25	30
31.0 Equipment	41	35	59
32.0 Land and structures	28	15	18
42.0 Insurance claims and indemnities	1	1	1
99.0 Direct obligations	1,486	1,535	1,781
99.0 Reimbursable obligations	79	145	145
99.9 Total new obligations, unexpired accounts	1,565	1,680	1,926

Employment Summary

Identification code 015–0700–0–1–751	2021 actual	2022 est.	2023 est.
1001 Direct civilian full-time equivalent employment	4,981	5,066	5,316
2001 Reimbursable civilian full-time equivalent employment	3	3	3

FEDERAL PRISON SYSTEM

Federal Funds

SALARIES AND EXPENSES

(INCLUDING TRANSFER OF FUNDS)

For necessary expenses of the Federal Prison System for the administration, operation, and maintenance of Federal penal and correctional institutions, and for the provision of technical assistance and advice on corrections related issues to foreign governments, $8,005,951,000: Provided, That not less than $409,483,000 shall be for the programs and activities authorized by the First Step Act of 2018 (Public Law 115–391): Provided further, That the Director of the Federal Prison System shall transfer not less than 2 percent of the funds in the preceding proviso, to be merged with the appropriation for "Research, Evaluation and Statistics" for the National Institute of Justice to carry out evaluations of programs and activities related to the First Step Act of 2018: Provided further, That the Attorney General may transfer to the Department of Health and Human Services such amounts as

DEPARTMENT OF JUSTICE

Federal Prison System—Continued
Federal Funds—Continued
743

may be necessary for direct expenditures by that Department for medical relief for inmates of Federal penal and correctional institutions: Provided further, That the Director of the Federal Prison System, where necessary, may enter into contracts with a fiscal agent or fiscal intermediary claims processor to determine the amounts payable to persons who, on behalf of the Federal Prison System, furnish health services to individuals committed to the custody of the Federal Prison System: Provided further, That not to exceed $5,400 shall be available for official reception and representation expenses: Provided further, That not to exceed $50,000,000 shall remain available until expended for necessary operations: Provided further, That, of the amounts provided for contract confinement, not to exceed $20,000,000 shall remain available until expended to make payments in advance for grants, contracts and reimbursable agreements, and other expenses: Provided further, That the Director of the Federal Prison System may accept donated property and services relating to the operation of the prison card program from a not-for-profit entity which has operated such program in the past, notwithstanding the fact that such not-for-profit entity furnishes services under contracts to the Federal Prison System relating to the operation of pre-release services, halfway houses, or other custodial facilities.

Note.—A full-year 2022 appropriation for this account was not enacted at the time the Budget was prepared; therefore, the Budget assumes this account is operating under the Continuing Appropriations Act, 2022 (Division A of Public Law 117–43, as amended). The amounts included for 2022 reflect the annualized level provided by the continuing resolution.

Program and Financing (in millions of dollars)

Identification code 015–1060–0–1–753	2021 actual	2022 est.	2023 est.
Obligations by program activity:			
0001 Inmate Care and Programs	2,910	2,925	3,182
0002 Institution Security and Administration	3,408	3,493	3,650
0003 Contract Confinement	843	963	839
0004 Management and Administration	303	327	327
0005 Discretionary, Emergency pursuant to 2011 Budget Control Act	261		
0091 Total operating expenses	7,725	7,708	7,998
0101 Capital investment: Institutional improvements	127		
0192 Total direct program	7,852	7,708	7,998
0799 Total direct obligations	7,852	7,708	7,998
0801 Salaries and Expenses (Reimbursable)	10	15	15
0900 Total new obligations, unexpired accounts	7,862	7,723	8,013
Budgetary resources:			
Unobligated balance:			
1000 Unobligated balance brought forward, Oct 1	2	110	110
1012 Unobligated balance transfers between expired and unexpired accounts	50		
1070 Unobligated balance (total)	52	110	110
Budget authority:			
Appropriations, discretionary:			
1100 Appropriation	7,708	7,708	8,006
1100 Appropriation, Discretionary, Emergency pursuant to 2011 Budget Control Act	300		
1120 Appropriations transferred to other acct [015–1003]	–13		
1120 Appropriations transferred to other acct [015–0401]			–8
1160 Appropriation, discretionary (total)	7,995	7,708	7,998
Spending authority from offsetting collections, discretionary:			
1700 Collected	16	15	15
1701 Change in uncollected payments, Federal sources	2		
1750 Spending auth from offsetting collections, disc (total)	18	15	15
1900 Budget authority (total)	8,013	7,723	8,013
1930 Total budgetary resources available	8,065	7,833	8,123
Memorandum (non-add) entries:			
1940 Unobligated balance expiring	–93		
1941 Unexpired unobligated balance, end of year	110	110	110
Change in obligated balance:			
Unpaid obligations:			
3000 Unpaid obligations, brought forward, Oct 1	960	1,166	1,417
3010 New obligations, unexpired accounts	7,862	7,723	8,013
3011 Obligations ("upward adjustments"), expired accounts	24		
3020 Outlays (gross)	–7,630	–7,472	–7,878
3041 Recoveries of prior year unpaid obligations, expired	–50		
3050 Unpaid obligations, end of year	1,166	1,417	1,552
Uncollected payments:			
3060 Uncollected pymts, Fed sources, brought forward, Oct 1	–3	–4	–4
3070 Change in uncollected pymts, Fed sources, unexpired	–2		
3071 Change in uncollected pymts, Fed sources, expired	1		
3090 Uncollected pymts, Fed sources, end of year	–4	–4	–4
Memorandum (non-add) entries:			
3100 Obligated balance, start of year	957	1,162	1,413
3200 Obligated balance, end of year	1,162	1,413	1,548
Budget authority and outlays, net:			
Discretionary:			
4000 Budget authority, gross	8,013	7,723	8,013
Outlays, gross:			
4010 Outlays from new discretionary authority	6,824	6,460	6,757
4011 Outlays from discretionary balances	806	1,012	1,121
4020 Outlays, gross (total)	7,630	7,472	7,878
Offsets against gross budget authority and outlays:			
Offsetting collections (collected) from:			
4030 Federal sources	–17		
4033 Non-Federal sources	–1	–15	–15
4040 Offsets against gross budget authority and outlays (total)	–18	–15	–15
Additional offsets against gross budget authority only:			
4050 Change in uncollected pymts, Fed sources, unexpired	–2		
4052 Offsetting collections credited to expired accounts	2		
4070 Budget authority, net (discretionary)	7,995	7,708	7,998
4080 Outlays, net (discretionary)	7,612	7,457	7,863
4180 Budget authority, net (total)	7,995	7,708	7,998
4190 Outlays, net (total)	7,612	7,457	7,863

This appropriation will provide for the custody and care of a projected average daily population of over 153,000 offenders, and for the maintenance and operation of 122 penal institutions, regional offices, and a central office located in Washington, D.C. The appropriation also finances the incarceration of sentenced Federal prisoners in State and local jails and other facilities for short periods of time. An average daily population of about 16,000 prisoners will be in contract facilities in 2023. The Federal Prison System (FPS) also receives reimbursements for the daily care and maintenance of State and local offenders, for utilities used by Federal Prison Industries, Inc., for staff housing, and for meals purchased by FPS staff at institutions.

Inmate Care and Programs.—This activity covers the costs of all food, medical supplies, clothing, welfare services, release clothing, transportation, gratuities, staff salaries (including salaries of Health Resources and Services Administration commissioned officers), and operational costs of functions directly related to providing inmate care. This decision unit also finances the costs of GED classes and other educational programs, vocational training, drug treatment, religious programs, psychological services, and other inmate programs such as Life Connections.

Institution Security and Administration.—This activity covers costs associated with the maintenance of facilities and institution security. This activity finances institution maintenance, motor pool operations, powerhouse operations, institution security, and other administrative functions.

Contract Confinement.—This activity provides for the confinement of sentenced Federal offenders in a Government-owned, contractor-operated facility, and State, local, and private contract facilities. It also provides for the care of Federal prisoners in contract community residential centers and covers the costs associated with management and oversight of contract confinement functions.

Management and Administration.—This activity covers all costs associated with general administration and provides funding for the central office, regional offices, and staff training centers. Also included are oversight functions of the executive staff and regional and central office program managers in the areas of: budget development and execution; financial management; procurement and property management; human resource management; inmate systems management; safety; legal counsel; research and evaluation; and systems support.

For 2023, the BOP requests a total of $409 million in base funding to continue robustly implementing the First Step Act. The full and timely implementation of the First Step Act remains a priority for the BOP. Also, this request includes a total of $48.7 million in program increases for: Security Camera Systems Upgrade ($15.6 million), this request will allow the BOP to begin the upgrade of security camera systems throughout BOP institutions, enhance institution safety and security by eliminating blind spots and improving video quality, provide for wide-range area coverage and clear picture image for enhanced internal security, criminal prosecutions

SALARIES AND EXPENSES—Continued

and public safety; and McGirt Resources ($33.1 million), this request will allow the BOP to improve its readiness for potential needs associated with the Supreme Courts recent *McGirt v Oklahoma* decision. In addition, the 2023 Budget supports a transfer of no less than 2 percent from the Federal Bureau of Prisons (BOP) First Step Act funding to support NIJ's research and evaluation of First Step Act related programs and activities.

Object Classification (in millions of dollars)

Identification code 015–1060–0–1–753		2021 actual	2022 est.	2023 est.
	Direct obligations:			
	Personnel compensation:			
11.1	Full-time permanent	2,655	2,785	2,933
11.3	Other than full-time permanent	6	5	5
11.5	Other personnel compensation	376	441	442
11.9	Total personnel compensation	3,037	3,231	3,380
12.1	Civilian personnel benefits	1,728	1,733	1,788
13.0	Benefits for former personnel	2	2	2
21.0	Travel and transportation of persons	21	35	35
22.0	Transportation of things	8	12	12
23.1	Rental payments to GSA	29	29	30
23.2	Rental payments to others	3	3	3
23.3	Communications, utilities, and miscellaneous charges	277	293	298
24.0	Printing and reproduction	1	1	1
25.2	Other services from non-Federal sources	1,841	1,649	1,716
26.0	Supplies and materials	528	667	680
31.0	Equipment	128	44	44
32.0	Land and structures	1	1	1
41.0	Grants, subsidies, and contributions	4	3	3
42.0	Insurance claims and indemnities	4	5	5
43.0	Interest and dividends	240		
99.0	Direct obligations	7,852	7,708	7,998
99.0	Reimbursable obligations	10	15	15
99.9	Total new obligations, unexpired accounts	7,862	7,723	8,013

Employment Summary

Identification code 015–1060–0–1–753	2021 actual	2022 est.	2023 est.
1001 Direct civilian full-time equivalent employment	35,210	35,161	36,566

BUILDINGS AND FACILITIES

For planning, acquisition of sites, and construction of new facilities; purchase and acquisition of facilities and remodeling, and equipping of such facilities for penal and correctional use, including all necessary expenses incident thereto, by contract or force account; and constructing, remodeling, and equipping necessary buildings and facilities at existing penal and correctional institutions, including all necessary expenses incident thereto, by contract or force account, $179,300,000, to remain available until expended: Provided, That labor of United States prisoners may be used for work performed under this appropriation.

(CANCELLATION)

Of the unobligated balances from prior year appropriations available under this heading, $886,456,000 are hereby permanently cancelled: Provided, That no amounts may be cancelled from amounts that were designated by the Congress as an emergency requirement pursuant to a concurrent resolution on the budget or the Balanced Budget and Emergency Deficit Control Act of 1985, as amended.

Note.—A full-year 2022 appropriation for this account was not enacted at the time the Budget was prepared; therefore, the Budget assumes this account is operating under the Continuing Appropriations Act, 2022 (Division A of Public Law 117–43, as amended). The amounts included for 2022 reflect the annualized level provided by the continuing resolution.

Program and Financing (in millions of dollars)

Identification code 015–1003–0–1–753		2021 actual	2022 est.	2023 est.
	Obligations by program activity:			
0001	New construction	2	2	2
0002	Modernization and Repair	144	125	177
0900	Total new obligations, unexpired accounts	146	127	179

		2021 actual	2022 est.	2023 est.
	Budgetary resources:			
	Unobligated balance:			
1000	Unobligated balance brought forward, Oct 1	968	962	962
	Budget authority:			
	Appropriations, discretionary:			
1100	Appropriation	127	127	179
1121	Appropriations transferred from other acct [015–1060]	13		
1131	Unobligated balance of appropriations permanently reduced			–886
1160	Appropriation, discretionary (total)	140	127	–707
1930	Total budgetary resources available	1,108	1,089	255
	Memorandum (non-add) entries:			
1941	Unexpired unobligated balance, end of year	962	962	76
	Change in obligated balance:			
	Unpaid obligations:			
3000	Unpaid obligations, brought forward, Oct 1	83	104	108
3010	New obligations, unexpired accounts	146	127	179
3020	Outlays (gross)	–125	–123	–82
3050	Unpaid obligations, end of year	104	108	205
	Memorandum (non-add) entries:			
3100	Obligated balance, start of year	83	104	108
3200	Obligated balance, end of year	104	108	205
	Budget authority and outlays, net:			
	Discretionary:			
4000	Budget authority, gross	140	127	–707
	Outlays, gross:			
4010	Outlays from new discretionary authority		13	18
4011	Outlays from discretionary balances	125	110	64
4020	Outlays, gross (total)	125	123	82
4180	Budget authority, net (total)	140	127	–707
4190	Outlays, net (total)	125	123	82

New Construction.—This activity includes the costs associated with land and building acquisition, new prison construction, and land payments for the Federal Transfer Center in Oklahoma City, which serves as a Bureau-wide transfer and processing center. For 2023, the Budget requests $2.0 million for new construction base program funding, and proposes a cancellation of $867.5 million in prior years' unobligated new construction balances.

Modernization and Repair of Existing Facilities.—This activity includes costs associated with rehabilitation, modernization, and renovation of Bureau-owned buildings and other structures in order to meet legal requirements and accommodate correctional programs. For 2023, the Budget requests $177.3 million to help address critical major projects and reduce the backlog of unfunded rehabilitation, modernization, and renovation projects. The Budget also includes a proposed cancellation of $19 million in prior year unobligated modernization and repair balances.

Object Classification (in millions of dollars)

Identification code 015–1003–0–1–753		2021 actual	2022 est.	2023 est.
	Direct obligations:			
11.1	Personnel compensation: Full-time permanent	4	4	4
12.1	Civilian personnel benefits	2	2	2
21.0	Travel and transportation of persons	1	1	1
23.3	Communications, utilities, and miscellaneous charges	1	1	1
25.2	Other services from non-Federal sources	99	90	142
26.0	Supplies and materials	18	22	22
31.0	Equipment	11	5	5
32.0	Land and structures	10	2	2
99.9	Total new obligations, unexpired accounts	146	127	179

Employment Summary

Identification code 015–1003–0–1–753	2021 actual	2022 est.	2023 est.
1001 Direct civilian full-time equivalent employment	39	49	59

FEDERAL PRISON INDUSTRIES, INCORPORATED

The Federal Prison Industries, Incorporated, is hereby authorized to make such expenditures within the limits of funds and borrowing authority available, and in

DEPARTMENT OF JUSTICE

accord with the law, and to make such contracts and commitments without regard to fiscal year limitations as provided by section 9104 of title 31, United States Code, as may be necessary in carrying out the program set forth in the budget for the current fiscal year for such corporation.

LIMITATION ON ADMINISTRATIVE EXPENSES, FEDERAL PRISON INDUSTRIES, INCORPORATED

Not to exceed $2,700,000 of the funds of the Federal Prison Industries, Incorporated, shall be available for its administrative expenses, and for services as authorized by section 3109 of title 5, United States Code, to be computed on an accrual basis to be determined in accordance with the corporation's current prescribed accounting system, and such amounts shall be exclusive of depreciation, payment of claims, and expenditures which such accounting system requires to be capitalized or charged to cost of commodities acquired or produced, including selling and shipping expenses, and expenses in connection with acquisition, construction, operation, maintenance, improvement, protection, or disposition of facilities and other property belonging to the corporation or in which it has an interest.

Note.—A full-year 2022 appropriation for this account was not enacted at the time the Budget was prepared; therefore, the Budget assumes this account is operating under the Continuing Appropriations Act, 2022 (Division A of Public Law 117–43, as amended). The amounts included for 2022 reflect the annualized level provided by the continuing resolution.

Program and Financing (in millions of dollars)

Identification code 015–4500–0–4–753	2021 actual	2022 est.	2023 est.
Obligations by program activity:			
0804 Federal Prison Industries	573	750	765
0809 Reimbursable program activities, subtotal	573	750	765
Budgetary resources:			
Unobligated balance:			
1000 Unobligated balance brought forward, Oct 1	91	179	179
Budget authority:			
Spending authority from offsetting collections, discretionary:			
1700 Collected	3	3	3
Spending authority from offsetting collections, mandatory:			
1800 Collected	659	747	747
1801 Change in uncollected payments, Federal sources	–1		
1850 Spending auth from offsetting collections, mand (total)	658	747	747
1900 Budget authority (total)	661	750	750
1930 Total budgetary resources available	752	929	929
Memorandum (non-add) entries:			
1941 Unexpired unobligated balance, end of year	179	179	164
Change in obligated balance:			
Unpaid obligations:			
3000 Unpaid obligations, brought forward, Oct 1	242	161	
3010 New obligations, unexpired accounts	573	750	765
3020 Outlays (gross)	–654	–911	–750
3050 Unpaid obligations, end of year	161		15
Uncollected payments:			
3060 Uncollected pymts, Fed sources, brought forward, Oct 1	–35	–34	–34
3070 Change in uncollected pymts, Fed sources, unexpired	1		
3090 Uncollected pymts, Fed sources, end of year	–34	–34	–34
Memorandum (non-add) entries:			
3100 Obligated balance, start of year	207	127	–34
3200 Obligated balance, end of year	127	–34	–19
Budget authority and outlays, net:			
Discretionary:			
4000 Budget authority, gross	3	3	3
Outlays, gross:			
4010 Outlays from new discretionary authority		3	3
Mandatory:			
4090 Budget authority, gross	658	747	747
Outlays, gross:			
4100 Outlays from new mandatory authority	573	747	747
4101 Outlays from mandatory balances	81	161	
4110 Outlays, gross (total)	654	908	747
Offsets against gross budget authority and outlays:			
Offsetting collections (collected) from:			
4120 Federal sources	–660	–747	–747
4121 Interest on Federal securities	–2	–3	–3
4130 Offsets against gross budget authority and outlays (total)	–662	–750	–750
Additional offsets against gross budget authority only:			
4140 Change in uncollected pymts, Fed sources, unexpired	1		
4160 Budget authority, net (mandatory)	–3	–3	–3
4170 Outlays, net (mandatory)	–8	158	–3
4180 Budget authority, net (total)			
4190 Outlays, net (total)	–8	161	
Memorandum (non-add) entries:			
5000 Total investments, SOY: Federal securities: Par value	287	277	270
5001 Total investments, EOY: Federal securities: Par value	277	270	260

Federal Prison Industries, Inc. (FPI), was created by the Congress in 1934 and is a wholly-owned Government corporation. Its mission is to employ and train Federal inmates through a diversified work program providing products and services to other Federal agencies. These operations are conducted in a self-sustaining manner so as to maximize meaningful inmate employment opportunities and minimize the effects of competition on private industry and labor. Employment provides inmates with work, occupational knowledge and skills, plus money for personal expenses and family assistance.

FPI operates as a revolving fund and does not receive an annual appropriation. The majority of revenues are derived from the sale of products and services to other Federal Departments, agencies, and bureaus. Operating expenses such as the cost of raw materials and supplies, inmate wages, staff salaries, and capital expenditures are applied against these revenues resulting in operating income or loss, which is reapplied toward operating costs for future production. In this regard, FPI makes capital investments in buildings and improvements, machinery, and equipment as necessary in the conduct of its industrial operation.

In order to increase inmate work opportunities, FPI continues to explore opportunities with commercial customers. In the Consolidated and Further Continuing Appropriations Act, 2012 (P.L. 112–55), FPI received two new authorities to increase inmate employment. The first enables FPI to recapture work that would otherwise be performed outside of the United States, also known as repatriation. The second authorized FPI to participate in the Prison Industries Enhancement Certification Program, which allows FPI to partner with commercial businesses under a strict set of conditions to manufacture and sell prison-made goods in interstate commerce.

Object Classification (in millions of dollars)

Identification code 015–4500–0–4–753	2021 actual	2022 est.	2023 est.
Reimbursable obligations:			
Personnel compensation:			
11.1 Full-time permanent	94	75	78
11.5 Other personnel compensation	2	2	2
11.8 Special personal services payments		37	38
11.9 Total personnel compensation	96	114	118
12.1 Civilian personnel benefits	33	39	40
21.0 Travel and transportation of persons	2	3	3
22.0 Transportation of things	1	2	2
23.2 Rental payments to others	1	1	1
23.3 Communications, utilities, and miscellaneous charges	9	12	12
24.0 Printing and reproduction	1	1	1
25.2 Other services from non-Federal sources	12	13	13
26.0 Supplies and materials	402	555	565
31.0 Equipment	16	10	10
99.9 Total new obligations, unexpired accounts	573	750	765

Employment Summary

Identification code 015–4500–0–4–753	2021 actual	2022 est.	2023 est.
2001 Reimbursable civilian full-time equivalent employment	699	753	753

Trust Funds

COMMISSARY FUNDS, FEDERAL PRISONS (TRUST REVOLVING FUND)

Program and Financing (in millions of dollars)

Identification code 015–8408–0–8–753	2021 actual	2022 est.	2023 est.
Obligations by program activity:			
0801 Commissary Funds, Federal Prisons (trust Revolving Fund) (Reimbursable)	336	359	375
Budgetary resources:			
Unobligated balance:			
1000 Unobligated balance brought forward, Oct 1	52	128	128
Budget authority:			
Spending authority from offsetting collections, mandatory:			
1800 Collected	409	359	375
1801 Change in uncollected payments, Federal sources	3		
1802 Offsetting collections (previously unavailable)	4	4	4
1823 New and/or unobligated balance of spending authority from offsetting collections temporarily reduced	–4	–4	–4
1850 Spending auth from offsetting collections, mand (total)	412	359	375
1930 Total budgetary resources available	464	487	503
Memorandum (non-add) entries:			
1941 Unexpired unobligated balance, end of year	128	128	128
Change in obligated balance:			
Unpaid obligations:			
3000 Unpaid obligations, brought forward, Oct 1	30	16	
3010 New obligations, unexpired accounts	336	359	375
3020 Outlays (gross)	–350	–375	–359
3050 Unpaid obligations, end of year	16		16
Uncollected payments:			
3060 Uncollected pymts, Fed sources, brought forward, Oct 1	–8	–11	–11
3070 Change in uncollected pymts, Fed sources, unexpired	–3		
3090 Uncollected pymts, Fed sources, end of year	–11	–11	–11
Memorandum (non-add) entries:			
3100 Obligated balance, start of year	22	5	–11
3200 Obligated balance, end of year	5	–11	5
Budget authority and outlays, net:			
Mandatory:			
4090 Budget authority, gross	412	359	375
Outlays, gross:			
4100 Outlays from new mandatory authority		359	359
4101 Outlays from mandatory balances	350	16	
4110 Outlays, gross (total)	350	375	359
Offsets against gross budget authority and outlays:			
Offsetting collections (collected) from:			
4120 Federal sources	–407		
4123 Non-Federal sources	–2	–359	–375
4130 Offsets against gross budget authority and outlays (total)	–409	–359	–375
Additional offsets against gross budget authority only:			
4140 Change in uncollected pymts, Fed sources, unexpired	–3		
4170 Outlays, net (mandatory)	–59	16	–16
4180 Budget authority, net (total)			
4190 Outlays, net (total)	–59	16	–16
Memorandum (non-add) entries:			
5090 Unexpired unavailable balance, SOY: Offsetting collections	4	4	4
5092 Unexpired unavailable balance, EOY: Offsetting collections	4	4	4

Budget Program.—The Commissary Fund consists of the operation of commissaries for the inmates as an earned privilege.

Financing.—Profits are derived from the sale of goods and services to inmates. Sales for 2023 are estimated at $375 million. Adequate working capital is assured from retained earnings.

Operating Results.—Profits received are used for programs, goods, and services for the benefit of inmates.

Object Classification (in millions of dollars)

Identification code 015–8408–0–8–753	2021 actual	2022 est.	2023 est.
Reimbursable obligations:			
Personnel compensation:			
11.1 Full-time permanent	49	49	49
11.5 Other personnel compensation	1	1	1
11.8 Special personal services payments	20	20	20
11.9 Total personnel compensation	70	70	70
12.1 Civilian personnel benefits	33	33	33
25.2 Other services from non-Federal sources	16	16	16
26.0 Supplies and materials	214	237	253
31.0 Equipment	3	3	3
99.9 Total new obligations, unexpired accounts	336	359	375

Employment Summary

Identification code 015–8408–0–8–753	2021 actual	2022 est.	2023 est.
2001 Reimbursable civilian full-time equivalent employment	665	665	665

OFFICE OF JUSTICE PROGRAMS

Federal Funds

RESEARCH, EVALUATION AND STATISTICS

For grants, contracts, cooperative agreements, and other assistance authorized by title I of the Omnibus Crime Control and Safe Streets Act of 1968 (Public Law 90–351) ("title I of the 1968 Act"); the Violent Crime Control and Law Enforcement Act of 1994 (Public Law 103–322) ("the 1994 Act"); the Juvenile Justice and Delinquency Prevention Act of 1974 (Public Law 93–415) ("the 1974 Act"); the PROTECT Act (Public Law 108–21) ; the Justice for All Act of 2004 (Public Law 108–405); the Violence Against Women and Department of Justice Reauthorization Act of 2005 (Public Law 109–162) ("the 2005 Act"); the Victims of Child Abuse Act of 1990 (title II of Public Law 101–647); the Second Chance Act of 2007 (Public Law 110–199); the Victims of Crime Act of 1984 (chapter XIV of title II of Public Law 98–473); the Adam Walsh Child Protection and Safety Act of 2006 (Public Law 109–248) ("the Adam Walsh Act"); the PROTECT Our Children Act of 2008 (Public Law 110–401); subtitle C of title II of the Homeland Security Act of 2002 (Public Law 107–296) ("the 2002 Act"); the Prison Rape Elimination Act of 2003 (Public Law 108–79) ("PREA"); the NICS Improvement Amendments Act of 2007 (Public Law 110–180); the Violence Against Women Reauthorization Act of 2013 (Public Law 113–4) ("the VAW 2013 Act"); the Comprehensive Addiction and Recovery Act of 2016 (Public Law 114–198); the First Step Act of 2018 (Public Law 115–391); 28 U.S.C. 530C; and other programs, $88,000,000, to remain available until expended, of which—

(1) $45,000,000 is for criminal justice statistics programs, and other activities, as authorized by part C of title I of the 1968 Act, and for civil justice statistics programs; and

(2) $43,000,000 is for research, development, and evaluation programs, and other activities as authorized by part B of title I of the 1968 Act and subtitle C of title II of the 2002 Act, and for activities authorized by or consistent with the First Step Act of 2018, of which $10,000,000 is for research targeted toward developing a better understanding of the domestic radicalization phenomenon, and advancing evidence-based strategies for effective intervention and prevention; $1,000,000 is for research to study the root causes of school violence to include the impact and effectiveness of grants made under the STOP School Violence Act; and $2,000,000 is for research on violence against American Indians/Alaska Natives or otherwise affecting indigenous communities, in connection with extractive industry activities.

Note.—A full-year 2022 appropriation for this account was not enacted at the time the Budget was prepared; therefore, the Budget assumes this account is operating under the Continuing Appropriations Act, 2022 (Division A of Public Law 117–43, as amended). The amounts included for 2022 reflect the annualized level provided by the continuing resolution.

Program and Financing (in millions of dollars)

Identification code 015–0401–0–1–754	2021 actual	2022 est.	2023 est.
Obligations by program activity:			
0001 National Institute of Justice	15	21	29
0002 Bureau of Justice Statistics	29	38	42
0004 Regional Information Sharing System	32		
0011 Management and Administration	13	6	5
0013 Research on Domestic Radicalization		6	9
0014 Research, Evaluation, and Statistics Set-aside	25		80
0019 Research on School Safety		1	1
0024 Research to Reduce Trauma for Child Pornography Victims		1	
0025 National Model for Reducing Incarceration Rates		4	
0026 Research on Counter-Unmanned Aerial Systems (C-UAS)		2	
0027 Data Collection on Police Suicide		3	
0028 Violence Against Natives at Extraction Sites			2

DEPARTMENT OF JUSTICE

Office of Justice Programs—Continued
Federal Funds—Continued

747

0029	FIRST STEP Act Evaluation activities (transfer from BOP)	....	....	8
0799	Total direct obligations	114	82	176
0801	Programmatic Reimbursable	2	....	19
0802	Management & Administration Reimbursable	267	266	273
0899	Total reimbursable obligations	269	266	292
0900	Total new obligations, unexpired accounts	383	348	468
	Budgetary resources:			
	Unobligated balance:			
1000	Unobligated balance brought forward, Oct 1	14	92	79
1021	Recoveries of prior year unpaid obligations	21	....	....
1033	Recoveries of prior year paid obligations	1	....	....
1070	Unobligated balance (total)	36	92	79
	Budget authority:			
	Appropriations, discretionary:			
1100	Appropriation	82	82	88
1121	Appropriations transferred from other acct [015–0404]	38	....	61
1121	Appropriations transferred from other acct [015–0405]	7	....	19
1121	Appropriations transferred from other acct [015–0409]	3	3	4
1121	Appropriations transferred from other acct [015–0406]	40	40	40
1121	Appropriations transferred from other acct [015–1060]	....	....	8
1131	Unobligated balance of appropriations permanently reduced	–5	–5	–2
1160	Appropriation, discretionary (total)	165	120	218
	Spending authority from offsetting collections, discretionary:			
1700	Collected	284	215	250
1701	Change in uncollected payments, Federal sources	–10	....	....
1750	Spending auth from offsetting collections, disc (total)	274	215	250
1900	Budget authority (total)	439	335	468
1930	Total budgetary resources available	475	427	547
	Memorandum (non-add) entries:			
1941	Unexpired unobligated balance, end of year	92	79	79
	Change in obligated balance:			
	Unpaid obligations:			
3000	Unpaid obligations, brought forward, Oct 1	433	333	13
3010	New obligations, unexpired accounts	383	348	468
3020	Outlays (gross)	–462	–668	–468
3040	Recoveries of prior year unpaid obligations, unexpired	–21	....	....
3050	Unpaid obligations, end of year	333	13	13
	Uncollected payments:			
3060	Uncollected pymts, Fed sources, brought forward, Oct 1	–84	–74	–74
3070	Change in uncollected pymts, Fed sources, unexpired	10	....	....
3090	Uncollected pymts, Fed sources, end of year	–74	–74	–74
	Memorandum (non-add) entries:			
3100	Obligated balance, start of year	349	259	–61
3200	Obligated balance, end of year	259	–61	–61
	Budget authority and outlays, net:			
	Discretionary:			
4000	Budget authority, gross	439	335	468
	Outlays, gross:			
4010	Outlays from new discretionary authority	256	335	468
4011	Outlays from discretionary balances	206	333	....
4020	Outlays, gross (total)	462	668	468
	Offsets against gross budget authority and outlays:			
	Offsetting collections (collected) from:			
4030	Federal sources	–284	–215	–250
4033	Non-Federal sources:	–1	....	....
4040	Offsets against gross budget authority and outlays (total)	–285	–215	–250
	Additional offsets against gross budget authority only:			
4050	Change in uncollected pymts, Fed sources, unexpired	10	....	....
4053	Recoveries of prior year paid obligations, unexpired accounts	1	....	....
4060	Additional offsets against budget authority only (total)	11	....	....
4070	Budget authority, net (discretionary)	165	120	218
4080	Outlays, net (discretionary)	177	453	218
4180	Budget authority, net (total)	165	120	218
4190	Outlays, net (total)	177	453	218

The 2023 Budget requests $88 million for the Office of Justice Programs (OJP) Research, Evaluation, and Statistics appropriation. This appropriation provides nationwide support for criminal justice professionals and decision-makers through programs that provide grants, contracts, and cooperative agreements for research, development, and evaluation, and support development and dissemination of quality and relevant statistical and scientific information. The information and technologies developed through OJP's research and statistical programs improve the efficiency and effectiveness of criminal justice programs at all levels of government.

Research, Development, and Evaluation Program. - The 2023 Budget proposes a total of $43 million for the National Institute of Justice (NIJ) to support high-quality research, development, and evaluation in the forensic, social, and physical sciences. Of this funding, at least $1 million will be dedicated to school safety research and $10 million will support research on domestic radicalization, and $2 million will research violence against American Indians and Alaskan Natives at extractive industry sites. In addition, the 2023 Budget supports a transfer of no less than 2 percent from the Federal Bureau of Prisons (BOP) First Step Act funding to support NIJ's research and evaluation of First Step Act related programs and activities.

Criminal Justice Statistics Program. - The 2023 Budget proposes $45 million for the Bureau of Justice Statistics (BJS) to carryout national statistical collections supporting data-driven approaches to reduce and prevent crime and to assist state, local and tribal governments in enhancing their statistical capabilities, including improving criminal history records and information systems. Current programs provide statistics on: victimization, corrections, law enforcement, Federal justice systems, prosecution and adjudication (courts), criminal histories and recidivism, and tribal communities.

2.5% Research, Evaluation and Statistics Set Aside. - The 2023 Budget requests a set-aside of up to 2.5 percent for research, evaluation, and statistics. The set-aside amount from OJP discretionary programs supports the base programs for NIJ and BJS.

Management and Administration. - The 2023 Budget proposes a total Management and Administration funding level of $274.2 million for OJP, supporting 757 total FTE.

Object Classification (in millions of dollars)

Identification code 015–0401–0–1–754	2021 actual	2022 est.	2023 est.
Direct obligations:			
11.1 Personnel compensation: Full-time permanent	8	6	13
25.1 Advisory and assistance services	14	10	21
25.3 Other goods and services from Federal sources	48	34	73
41.0 Grants, subsidies, and contributions	44	32	69
99.0 Direct obligations	114	82	176
99.0 Reimbursable obligations	269	266	292
99.9 Total new obligations, unexpired accounts	383	348	468

Employment Summary

Identification code 015–0401–0–1–754	2021 actual	2022 est.	2023 est.
1001 Direct civilian full-time equivalent employment	619	619	747

STATE AND LOCAL LAW ENFORCEMENT ASSISTANCE

(INCLUDING TRANSFER OF FUNDS)

For grants, contracts, cooperative agreements, and other assistance authorized by the Violent Crime Control and Law Enforcement Act of 1994 (Public Law 103–322) ("the 1994 Act"); title I of the Omnibus Crime Control and Safe Streets Act of 1968 (Public Law 90–351) ("title I of the 1968 Act"); the Justice for All Act of 2004 (Public Law 108–405); the Victims of Child Abuse Act of 1990 (title II of Public Law 101–647) ("the 1990 Act"); the Trafficking Victims Protection Reauthorization Act of 2005 (Public Law 109–164) ("the TVPRA of 2005"); the Violence Against Women and Department of Justice Reauthorization Act of 2005 (Public Law 109–162) ("the 2005 Act"); the Adam Walsh Child Protection and Safety Act of 2006 (Public Law 109–248) ("the Adam Walsh Act"); the Victims of Trafficking and Violence Protection Act of 2000 (Public Law 106–386) ("the Victims of Trafficking Act"); the NICS Improvement Amendments Act of 2007 (Public Law 110–180); subtitle C of title II of the Homeland Security Act of 2002 (Public Law 107–296) ("the 2002 Act"); the Prison Rape Elimination Act of 2003 (Public Law 108–79) ("PREA"); the Public Safety Officer Medal of Valor Act of 2001 (Public Law

STATE AND LOCAL LAW ENFORCEMENT ASSISTANCE—Continued

107–12); the Second Chance Act of 2007 (Public Law 110–199); the Prioritizing Resources and Organization for Intellectual Property Act of 2008 (Public Law 110–403) ("the PRO-IP Act"); the Victims of Crime Act of 1984 (chapter XIV of title II of Public Law 98–473) ("the 1984 Act"); the Violence Against Women Reauthorization Act of 2013 (Public Law 113–4) ("the VAW 2013 Act"); the Comprehensive Addiction and Recovery Act of 2016 (Public Law 114–198) ("CARA"); the Project Safe Neighborhoods Grant Program Authorization Act of 2018 (Public Law 115–185) ("the PSN Grant Act of 2018"); the Matthew Shepard and James Byrd, Jr. Hate Crimes Prevention Act (Public Law 111–84); title II of Kristen's Act (title II of Public Law 106–468, as amended); 28 U.S.C. 530C; and 36 U.S.C. 220531 ("the Keep Young Athletes Safe Act"); and other programs, $2,518,000,000, to remain available until expended as follows—

(1) $533,500,000 for the Edward Byrne Memorial Justice Assistance Grant program as authorized by title I of the 1968 Act, including subpart 1 of part E of such title (except that section 1001(c), and the special rules for Puerto Rico under section 505(g), of such title shall not apply for purposes of this Act), of which, notwithstanding such subpart 1—

(A) $13,000,000 is for an Officer Robert Wilson III memorial initiative on Preventing Violence Against Law Enforcement and Ensuring Officer Resilience and Survivability (VALOR);

(B) $10,000,000 is for an initiative to support evidence-based policing;

(C) $10,000,000 is for an initiative to enhance prosecutorial decision-making;

(D) $5,000,000 is for the operationalization, maintenance, and expansion of the National Missing and Unidentified Persons System;

(E) $10,000,000 is for a grant program for State and local law enforcement to provide officer training on responding to individuals with mental illness or disabilities;

(F) $2,000,000 is for a student loan repayment assistance program pursuant to part JJ of title I of the 1968 Act, as amended;

(G) $15,500,000 is for prison rape prevention and prosecution grants to States and units of local government, and other programs, as authorized by PREA;

(H) $3,000,000 is for the Missing Americans Alert Program (title XXIV of the 1994 Act, as amended by Kevin and Avonte's Law of 2018 (division Q of Public Law 115–141));

(I) $4,000,000 is for the establishment, operation, maintenance, or other support of one or more national centers on forensics ;

(J) $40,000,000 is for the project safe neighborhoods program, including as authorized by the PSN Grant Act of 2018 ;

(K) $12,000,000 is for the Capital Litigation Improvement Grant Program, as authorized by title IV of the Justice for All Act of 2004, and for grants for wrongful conviction review;

(L) $14,000,000 is for community-based violence prevention initiatives;

(M) $3,000,000 is for a national center for restorative justice;

(N) $1,000,000 is for the Ashanti Alert Communications Network as authorized by title II of Kristen's Act, and for related planning, implementation and other support activities;

(O) $3,500,000 is for a grant program to replicate and support family-based alternative sentencing programs;

(P) $1,000,000 is for a grant program to support child advocacy training in post-secondary education;

(Q) $7,000,000 is for a rural violent crime initiative, including assistance for law enforcement;

(R) $2,000,000 is for grants to States and units of local government to deploy managed access systems to combat contraband cell phone use in prison;

(S) $2,000,000 is for grants for development of child-friendly family visitation spaces in correctional facilities; and

(T) $20,000,000 is for a grant program to provide law enforcement officer training on racial profiling, de-escalation, and duty to intervene;

(2) $90,000,000 for victim services programs for victims of trafficking, as authorized by section 107(b)(2) of the Victims of Trafficking Act, by the TVPRA of 2005, or by the VAW 2013 Act, and related activities such as investigations and prosecutions;

(3) $13,000,000 for a grant program to prevent and address economic, high technology, white collar, and Internet crime, including as authorized by section 401 of the PRO-IP Act, of which not more than $2,500,000 is for intellectual property enforcement grants (including as authorized by such section 401), and $2,000,000 is for grants to develop databases on Internet of Things device capabilities and to build and execute training modules for law enforcement;

(4) $20,000,000 for sex offender management assistance, as authorized by the Adam Walsh Act, and related activities;

(5) $30,000,000 for the Patrick Leahy Bulletproof Vest Partnership Grant Program, as authorized by section 2501 of title I of the 1968 Act: Provided, That $1,500,000 is transferred directly to the National Institute of Standards and Technology's Office of Law Enforcement Standards for research, testing, and evaluation programs;

(6) $1,000,000 for the National Sex Offender Public Website;

(7) $89,000,000 for grants to States to upgrade criminal and mental health records for the National Instant Criminal Background Check System: Provided, That, to the extent warranted by meritorious applications, priority shall be given to applications for awards under the authority of the NICS Improvement Amendments Act of 2007 (Public Law 110–180), and no less than $25,000,000 shall be awarded under such authority;

(8) $35,000,000 for Paul Coverdell Forensic Sciences Improvement Grants under part BB of title I of the 1968 Act;

(9) $147,000,000 for DNA-related and forensic programs and activities, of which—

(A) $112,000,000 is for the purposes authorized under section 2 of the DNA Analysis Backlog Elimination Act of 2000 (Public Law 106–546) (the Debbie Smith DNA Backlog Grant Program): Provided, That up to 4 percent of funds made available under this paragraph may be used for the purposes described in the DNA Training and Education for Law Enforcement, Correctional Personnel, and Court Officers program (Public Law 108–405, section 303);

(B) $19,000,000 for other local, State, and Federal forensic activities;

(C) $12,000,000 is for the purposes described in section 412 of the Justice for All Act of 2004 (the Kirk Bloodsworth Post-Conviction DNA Testing Grant Program; and

(D) $4,000,000 is for Sexual Assault Forensic Exam Program grants, including as authorized by section 304 of Public Law 108–405;

(10) $100,000,000 for a community-based program to improve the response to sexual assault, and apply enhanced approaches and techniques to reduce violent crime, including assistance for investigation and prosecution of related cold cases;

(11) $14,000,000 for the court-appointed special advocate program, as authorized by section 217 of the 1990 Act;

(12) $50,000,000 for assistance to Indian tribes;

(13) $125,000,000 for offender reentry programs and research, including as authorized by the Second Chance Act of 2007, of which, notwithstanding such Act, not to exceed—

(A) $8,000,000 is for a program to improve State, local, and Tribal probation or parole supervision efforts and strategies;

(B) $5,000,000 is for children of incarcerated parents demonstration programs to enhance and maintain parental and family relationships for incarcerated parents as a reentry or recidivism reduction strategy; and

(C) $5,000,000 is for additional replication sites that implement programs such as the Project HOPE Opportunity Probation with Enforcement model that employ swift and certain sanctions in probation:

Provided, That up to $7,500,000 of funds made available in this paragraph may be used for performance-based awards for Pay for Success projects, of which up to $5,000,000 shall be for Pay for Success programs implementing the Permanent Supportive Housing Model and reentry housing;

(14) $418,000,000 for comprehensive opioid abuse reduction activities, including as authorized by CARA, and for the following programs, which shall address opioid, stimulant, and substance abuse reduction consistent with underlying program authorities—

(A) $95,000,000 for Drug Courts, as authorized by part EE of title I of the 1968 Act, without regard to section 2952 of such title or the limitation of section 2951(a)(1) thereof relating to violent offenders;

(B) $40,000,000 for mental health courts and adult and juvenile collaboration program grants, as authorized by parts V and HH of title I of the 1968 Act, notwithstanding section 2991(e) of such title;

(C) $35,000,000 for grants for Residential Substance Abuse Treatment for State Prisoners, as authorized by part S of title I of the 1968 Act;

(D) $25,000,000 for a veterans treatment courts program, and for other services for veterans in the criminal justice system;

(E) $33,000,000 for a program to monitor prescription drugs and scheduled listed chemical products; and

(F) $190,000,000 for a comprehensive opioid, stimulant, and substance abuse program;

(15) $2,500,000 for a competitive grant program authorized by the Keep Young Athletes Safe Act (36 U.S.C. 220531);

(16) $82,000,000 for grants to be administered by the Bureau of Justice Assistance for purposes authorized under the STOP School Violence Act;

DEPARTMENT OF JUSTICE

Office of Justice Programs—Continued
Federal Funds—Continued

749

(17) $3,000,000 for grants to State and local law enforcement agencies for the expenses associated with the investigation and prosecution of criminal offenses, involving civil rights, including as authorized by the Emmett Till Unsolved Civil Rights Crimes Reauthorization Act of 2016 (Public Law 114–325);

(18) $10,000,000 for grants to conduct educational outreach and training on hate crimes and to investigate and prosecute hate crimes, including as authorized by section 4704 of the Matthew Shepard and James Byrd, Jr. Hate Crimes Prevention Act (Public Law 111–84);

(19) $95,000,000 for initiatives to improve police-community relations, of which $35,000,000 is for a competitive matching grant program for purchases of body-worn cameras and related expenses for State, local, and Tribal law enforcement; $35,000,000 is for a justice reinvestment initiative, for activities related to criminal justice reform and recidivism reduction; and $25,000,000 is for an Edward Byrne Memorial criminal justice innovation program;

(20) $10,000,000 for emergency law enforcement assistance for events occurring during or after fiscal year 2023, as authorized by section 609M of the Justice Assistance Act of 1984 (34 U.S.C. 50101);

(21) $250,000,000 for a community violence intervention initiative;

(22) $40,000,000 for an incentivization program for red flag and gun licensing laws;

(23) $10,000,000 for a pilot program for gun buyback and relinquishment;

(24) $25,000,000 for a public defender improvement program;

(25) $20,000,000 for regional sexual assault investigative training academies and related activities;

(26) $5,000,000 for grants to combat hate crimes, including as authorized by section 5 of the COVID-19 Hate Crimes Act (Public Law 117–13) (the Jabara-Heyer NO HATE Act); and

(27) $300,000,000 for the Accelerating Justice System Reform (AJSR) initiative: Provided, That, if a unit of local government uses any of the funds made available under this heading to increase the number of law enforcement officers, the unit of local government will achieve a net gain in the number of law enforcement officers who perform non-administrative public sector safety service.

Note.—A full-year 2022 appropriation for this account was not enacted at the time the Budget was prepared; therefore, the Budget assumes this account is operating under the Continuing Appropriations Act, 2022 (Division A of Public Law 117–43, as amended). The amounts included for 2022 reflect the annualized level provided by the continuing resolution.

Program and Financing (in millions of dollars)

Identification code 015–0404–0–1–754		2021 actual	2022 est.	2023 est.
	Obligations by program activity:			
0001	State Criminal Alien Assistance Program	....	478	....
0002	Adam Walsh Act Implementation	2	36	18
0007	Justice Assistance Grants	286	363	326
0009	Residential Substance Abuse Treatment	30	32	29
0010	Drug Court Program	1	158	86
0011	Community Trust Initiative: Justice Reinvestment Initiative	....	64	31
0012	Victims of Trafficking	1	168	86
0013	Prescription Drug Monitoring Program	4	60	28
0014	Prison Rape Prevention and Prosecution Program	3	25	15
0015	Capital Litigation Improvement Grant Program	....	12	11
0016	Justice and Mental Health Collaborations	1	64	35
0017	National Sex Offender Public Website	....	2	1
0018	Project Hope Opportunity Probation with Enforcement (HOPE)	....	7	5
0019	Bulletproof Vest Partnership	26	30	26
0021	Strategies for Policing Innovation (Smart Policing)	....	14	9
0022	National Criminal Records History Improvement Program (NCHIP)	29	79	58
0023	Innovative Prosecution Solutions Initiative (Smart Prosecution)	....	14	9
0029	Court Appointed Special Advocate (CASA)	....	24	12
0031	National Instant Criminal Background Check System (NICS) Act Record Improvement Pgm (NARIP)	12	35	23
0035	Post-conviction DNA Testing grants	....	13	10
0038	Sexual Assault Forensic Exam Program grants	....	8	3
0043	Project Safe Neighborhoods	....	38	38
0044	DNA Initiative - DNA Related and Forensic Programs and Activities	4	210	112
0045	Coverdell Forensic Science Grants	....	62	31
0050	Second Chance Act/Offender Reentry	1	141	104
0053	Missing Alzheimer's Patient Alert Program (Kevin and Avonte's Law)	....	6	3
0056	Economic, High-tech, White Collar, and Internet Crime Prevention	....	14	7
0077	VALOR Initiative	....	22	12
0081	Community Based Crime Reduction Program (Byrne Criminal Justice Innovation)	1	39	22
0082	Tribal Assistance	2	84	46
0084	John R. Justice Student Loan Repayment Program	2	2	2
0088	Intellectual Property Enforcement Program	....	4	2
0089	Management and Administration	133	133	139
0091	Direct program activities, subtotal	538	2,441	1,339
0103	Veterans Treatment Courts	....	45	20
0108	Sexual Assault Kit Initiative (SAKI) (Community Teams to Reduce the SAK Backlog)	1	90	90
0115	Community Trust Initiative: Body-Worn Camera (BWC) Partnership Program	....	62	31
0116	National Missing and Unidentified Persons System	2	2	5
0117	Emergency Federal Law Enforcement Assistance	1	....	9
0122	Natl. Training Center to Improve Police Responses to People with Mental Illness	....	14	9
0132	Comprehensive Opioid Abuse Program (COAP)	8	355	180
0137	Innovations in Supervision (Smart Probation)	....	12	7
0139	Pay for Success	....	14	7
0140	Children of Incarcerated Parents Demo Grants	....	10	5
0141	Keep Young Athletes Safe	2	2	2
0143	STOP School Violence Act	2	154	76
0153	Community-Based Violence Prevention Initiatives	1	26	13
0155	Managed Access Systems (Combatting Contraband Cell Phone Use in Prisons)	....	4	2
0156	Emmett Till Unsolved Civil Rights Crimes Program	....	4	3
0159	State, Local, and Federal Forensic Activities	8	28	16
0160	National Center for Restorative Justice	3	3	3
0162	National Center on Forensics	....	7	4
0163	Ashanti Alert Network	....	2	1
0164	Family Alternative Sentencing Pilot Program	....	5	3
0165	Child Advocacy Training	....	2	1
0166	Rural Violent Crime Initiative	....	13	6
0167	Family Friendly Visitation Spaces in Prisons/Jails	....	4	2
0168	Internet of Things	....	4	2
0169	Matthew Shepard and James Byrd, Jr. Hate Crimes Prevention Grants Program	....	9	9
0170	Training on Racial Profiling and De-escalation	....	....	19
0171	Community Violence Intervention	....	....	231
0172	Gun Buyback and Relinquishment Program	....	....	10
0174	Incentivization Program for Red Flag and Gun Licensing Laws	....	....	37
0175	Public Defender Improvement Program	....	....	22
0176	Regional Sexual Assault Investigative Training Academies	....	....	18
0178	Khalid Jabara and Heather Heyer NO HATE Act Program	....	....	4
0179	Accelerating Justice System Reform	....	....	269
0191	Direct program activities, subtotal	28	871	1,116
0799	Total direct obligations	566	3,312	2,455
0801	State and Local Law Enforcement Assistance (Reimbursable)	4	....	....
0900	Total new obligations, unexpired accounts	570	3,312	2,455
	Budgetary resources:			
	Unobligated balance:			
1000	Unobligated balance brought forward, Oct 1	348	1,573	56
1021	Recoveries of prior year unpaid obligations	34	....	10
1033	Recoveries of prior year paid obligations	1	2	....
1070	Unobligated balance (total)	383	1,575	66
	Budget authority:			
	Appropriations, discretionary:			
1100	Appropriation	1,915	1,914	2,518
1120	Appropriations transferred to NIST [013–0500]	–2	–2	–2
1120	Appropriations transferred to OJP RES 2% Set-Aside [015–0401]	–38	....	–61
1131	Unobligated balance of appropriations permanently reduced	–119	–119	–66
1160	Appropriation, discretionary (total)	1,756	1,793	2,389
	Spending authority from offsetting collections, discretionary:			
1700	Collected	2	....	....
1701	Change in uncollected payments, Federal sources	2	....	....
1750	Spending auth from offsetting collections, disc (total)	4	....	....
1900	Budget authority (total)	1,760	1,793	2,389
1930	Total budgetary resources available	2,143	3,368	2,455
	Memorandum (non-add) entries:			
1941	Unexpired unobligated balance, end of year	1,573	56	....
	Change in obligated balance:			
	Unpaid obligations:			
3000	Unpaid obligations, brought forward, Oct 1	3,983	3,250	4,170
3010	New obligations, unexpired accounts	570	3,312	2,455
3020	Outlays (gross)	–1,269	–2,392	–2,485
3040	Recoveries of prior year unpaid obligations, unexpired	–34	....	–10
3050	Unpaid obligations, end of year	3,250	4,170	4,130
	Uncollected payments:			
3060	Uncollected pymts, Fed sources, brought forward, Oct 1	–2	–4	–4

STATE AND LOCAL LAW ENFORCEMENT ASSISTANCE—Continued

Program and Financing—Continued

Identification code 015–0404–0–1–754	2021 actual	2022 est.	2023 est.
3070 Change in uncollected pymts, Fed sources, unexpired	–2		
3090 Uncollected pymts, Fed sources, end of year	–4	–4	–4
Memorandum (non-add) entries:			
3100 Obligated balance, start of year	3,981	3,246	4,166
3200 Obligated balance, end of year	3,246	4,166	4,126
Budget authority and outlays, net:			
Discretionary:			
4000 Budget authority, gross	1,760	1,793	2,389
Outlays, gross:			
4010 Outlays from new discretionary authority	135	395	525
4011 Outlays from discretionary balances	1,134	1,997	1,960
4020 Outlays, gross (total)	1,269	2,392	2,485
Offsets against gross budget authority and outlays:			
Offsetting collections (collected) from:			
4030 Federal sources	–2	–2	
4033 Non-Federal sources	–1		
4040 Offsets against gross budget authority and outlays (total)	–3	–2	
Additional offsets against gross budget authority only:			
4050 Change in uncollected pymts, Fed sources, unexpired	–2		
4053 Recoveries of prior year paid obligations, unexpired accounts	1	2	
4060 Additional offsets against budget authority only (total)	–1	2	
4070 Budget authority, net (discretionary)	1,756	1,793	2,389
4080 Outlays, net (discretionary)	1,266	2,390	2,485
4180 Budget authority, net (total)	1,756	1,793	2,389
4190 Outlays, net (total)	1,266	2,390	2,485

The 2023 Budget requests $2.518 billion for the Office of Justice Programs' (OJP) State and Local Law Enforcement Assistance appropriation. State, local, and tribal law enforcement and criminal justice professionals are responsible for the majority of the Nation's day-to-day crime prevention and control activities. The programs supported by this account help OJP partners throughout the Nation to advance work that promotes civil rights, increases access to justice, supports crime victims, protects the public from crime and evolving threats, and builds trust between law enforcement and the community. These programs include a combination of formula and discretionary grant programs, coupled with robust training and technical assistance activities designed to address the most pressing crime-related challenges of confronting the criminal justice system. Priority programs in the 2023 Budget will promote criminal and juvenile justice system reform, advance innovation and the use of science, research, and statistics, prevent and reduce violent crime, combat the growing threat of hate crimes, and identify and promote services to victims. They include:

Byrne Justice Assistance Grants (JAG).—The Byrne Justice Assistance Grants program awards grants to state, local, and tribal governments to support a broad range of activities that prevent and control crime, including: law enforcement programs; prosecution and court programs; prevention and education programs; corrections and community corrections programs; drug treatment programs; and planning, evaluation, and technology improvement programs. The 2023 Budget proposes $533.5 million for this program. Included in this amount is $40 million for Project Safe Neighborhoods, which supports expanding the nationwide initiative that identifies the most pressing state and local violent crime problems and develops comprehensive strategies to address and prevent them. In addition, as part of the Byrne JAG program, the 2023 Budget continues to invest in the Community-Based Violence Prevention Initiative ($14 million), the Capital Litigation Improvement Program ($12 million), Training to Improve Racial Profiling, De-escalation, and Duty to Intervene Program ($20 million), the Prison Rape Elimination Act Implementation Program ($15.5 million), Strategies for Policing Innovation ($10 million), and Innovative Prosecution Solutions Initiative ($10 million), and the VALOR Initiative ($13 million).

Promoting Criminal Justice System Reform and Enhancing Civil Rights.—The 2023 Budget directs funding to criminal justice system reform efforts, including efforts to address systemic inequities and build community trust with law enforcement. The 2023 Budget supports a wide range of programs addressing these issues, including $300 million for a new Accelerating Justice System Reform initiative, which provides state, local, and tribal governments with additional resources to invest in addressing the root cause of crime, including gun crime and other violent crime.

Preventing and Reducing Violent Crime through Community Based Programs.—The 2023 Budget proposes to fund programs that help communities find evidence-based approaches to reduce crime and improve public safety, including $250 million for Community Violence Intervention Initiative, which provides communities with funding to plan localized intervention programs to reduce violence and $82 million for the STOP School Violence Act program.

Assisting Communities, Law Enforcement, and Criminal Justice Agencies in Countering the Growing Threat of Hate Crime.—The Budget requests funding for new and existing programs focused on addressing hate-crimes, including $10 million for the Matthew Shepard and James Byrd, Jr. Hate Crimes Prevention Grants Program, $5 million for the new Khalid Jabara and Heather Heyer NO HATE Act Program, and $3 million for the Emmett Till Unsolved Civil Rights Crimes Act Program.

Preventing and Reducing Gun Violence.—The 2023 Budget continues investments in proven strategies that will reduce gun violence while respecting the rights of law-abiding gun owners. The 2023 Budget requests $40 million for the Incentivization Program for Red Flag and Gun Licensing Laws and $10 million for the Gun Buyback and Relinquishment Program.

Comprehensive Addiction Recovery Act (CARA).—The 2023 Budget requests $418 million for continued support for programs authorized by the Comprehensive Addiction Recovery Act, including $190 million for OJP's Comprehensive Opioid and Stimulant and Substance Abuse Program (COSSAP), which aims to reduce substance abuse and the number of overdose fatalities. The 2023 Budget also requests $95 million for the Drug Court Program, which provides an alternative to incarceration to addicted offenders who enter the criminal justice system, addressing their addiction through treatment and recovery support services and subsequently reducing recidivism. Other CARA-authorized programs requested in the budget include: Veterans Treatment Courts ($25 million), Residential Substance Abuse Treatment ($35 million), Justice and Mental Health Collaborations ($40 million), and the Prescription Drug Monitoring Program ($33 million).

Second Chance Act Program.—This program provides grants to establish and expand various adult and juvenile offender reentry programs and funds related research. Successful reintegration will reduce rates of criminal recidivism, thus increasing public safety. The 2023 Budget proposes $125 million for this program. Of this total, $8 million is to help states, localities, and tribes develop comprehensive, innovative probation and parole supervision programs and $5 million is for the Children of Incarcerated Parents Demonstration Grant Program.

Combatting Sexual Assault and Human Trafficking.—The 2023 Budget continues investments in several programs that assist state, local, and tribal governments in improving their response to sexual assault and eliminating forensic evidence analysis backlogs related to these cases. The 2023 Budget requests $100 million for the Sexual Assault Kit Initiative and $20 million for a regional training program to improve investigation of and response to sexual assault. The 2023 Budget also requests $90 million to support human trafficking grant programs, including support for comprehensive and specialized services for human trafficking victims.

Accelerating Justice System Reform.—The Budget will propose to create a new grant program, Accelerating Justice System Reform, which provides state, local, and tribal governments with additional resources for crime prevention. This program will be supported with a total of $15 billion, with $300 million in discretionary resources in 2023, and then $14.7 billion in mandatory resources beginning in 2024.

Object Classification (in millions of dollars)

Identification code 015–0404–0–1–754		2021 actual	2022 est.	2023 est.
	Direct obligations:			
25.1	Advisory and assistance services	29	31	23
25.3	Other goods and services from Federal sources	134	136	101
25.7	Operation and maintenance of equipment	1	2	1
41.0	Grants, subsidies, and contributions	402	3,143	2,330
99.0	Direct obligations	566	3,312	2,455
99.0	Reimbursable obligations	4		
99.9	Total new obligations, unexpired accounts	570	3,312	2,455

COMMUNITY ORIENTED POLICING SERVICES

COMMUNITY ORIENTED POLICING SERVICES PROGRAMS

(INCLUDING TRANSFER OF FUNDS)

For activities authorized by the Violent Crime Control and Law Enforcement Act of 1994 (Public Law 103–322); the Omnibus Crime Control and Safe Streets Act of 1968 ("the 1968 Act"); the Violence Against Women and Department of Justice Reauthorization Act of 2005 (Public Law 109–162) ("the 2005 Act"); the American Law Enforcement Heroes Act of 2017 (Public Law 115–37); the Law Enforcement Mental Health and Wellness Act (Public Law 115–113) ("the LEMHW Act"); the SUPPORT for Patients and Communities Act (Public Law 115–271); and the Supporting and Treating Officers In Crisis Act of 2019 (Public Law 116–32) ("the STOIC Act"), $651,000,000, to remain available until expended: Provided, That any balances made available through prior year deobligations shall only be available in accordance with section 504 of this Act: Provided further, That of the amount provided under this heading—

(1) $537,000,000 is for grants under section 1701 of title I of the 1968 Act (34 U.S.C. 10381) for the hiring and rehiring of additional career law enforcement officers under part Q of such title notwithstanding section 1701(h) (34 U.S.C. 10381(h)), section 1701(i) (34 U.S.C. 10381(i)), and 1704(c) (34 U.S.C. 10384(c)) of such title: Provided, That, notwithstanding section 1704(c) of such title (34 U.S.C. 10384(c)), funding for hiring or rehiring a career law enforcement officer may not exceed $125,000 unless the Director of the Office of Community Oriented Policing Services grants a waiver from this limitation: Provided further, That within the amounts appropriated under this paragraph, $40,000,000 is for improving Tribal law enforcement, including hiring, equipment, training, anti-methamphetamine activities, and anti-opioid activities: Provided further, That of the amounts appropriated under this paragraph, $40,000,000 is for regional information sharing activities, as authorized by part M of title I of the 1968 Act, which shall be transferred to and merged with "Research, Evaluation, and Statistics" for administration by the Office of Justice Programs: Provided further, That within the amounts appropriated under this paragraph, no less than $6,000,000 is to support the Tribal Access Program: Provided further, That within the amounts appropriated under this paragraph, $8,000,000 is for training, peer mentoring, mental health program activities, and other support services as authorized under the LEMHW Act and STOIC Act: Provided further, That within the amounts appropriated under this paragraph, $12,000,000 is for community policing development activities in furtherance of section 1701 of title I of the 1968 Act (34 U.S.C. 10381): Provided further, That within the amounts appropriated under this paragraph, $20,000,000 is for the collaborative reform model of technical assistance in furtherance of section 1701 of title I of the 1968 Act (34 U.S.C. 10381): Provided further, That within the amounts appropriated under this paragraph, $23,000,000 is for furthering evidence- and practice-based programs that promote organizational reform, legitimacy, and justice in policing;

(2) $11,000,000 is for activities authorized by the POLICE Act of 2016 (Public Law 114–199);

(3) $15,000,000 is for competitive grants to State law enforcement agencies in States with high seizures of precursor chemicals, finished methamphetamine, laboratories, and laboratory dump seizures: Provided, That funds appropriated under this paragraph shall be utilized for investigative purposes to locate or investigate illicit activities, including precursor diversion, laboratories, or methamphetamine traffickers;

(4) $35,000,000 is for competitive grants to statewide law enforcement agencies in States with high rates of primary treatment admissions for heroin and other opioids: Provided, That these funds shall be utilized for investigative purposes to locate or investigate illicit activities, including activities related to the distribution of heroin or unlawful distribution of prescription opioids, or unlawful heroin and prescription opioid traffickers through statewide collaboration; and

(5) $53,000,000 is for competitive grants to be administered by the Community Oriented Policing Services Office for purposes authorized under the STOP School Violence Act (title V of division S of Public Law 115–141).

(CANCELLATION)

Of the unobligated balances from prior year appropriations available under this heading, $15,000,000 are hereby permanently cancelled: Provided, That no amounts may be cancelled from amounts that were designated by the Congress as an emergency requirement pursuant to a concurrent resolution on the budget or the Balanced Budget and Emergency Deficit Control Act of 1985, as amended.

Note.—A full-year 2022 appropriation for this account was not enacted at the time the Budget was prepared; therefore, the Budget assumes this account is operating under the Continuing Appropriations Act, 2022 (Division A of Public Law 117–43, as amended). The amounts included for 2022 reflect the annualized level provided by the continuing resolution.

Program and Financing (in millions of dollars)

Identification code 015–0406–0–1–754		2021 actual	2022 est.	2023 est.
	Obligations by program activity:			
0007	Management and administration	32	35	35
0008	Tribal Law Enforcement	26	36	36
0009	COPS Hiring Program	30	403	403
0010	School Safety Program		52	52
0012	COPS Anti-Methamphetamine Program	13	13	13
0013	Anti-Heroin Task Forces	31	31	31
0016	Preparing for Active Shooter Situations	10	11	11
0799	Total direct obligations	142	581	581
0900	Total new obligations, unexpired accounts	142	581	581
	Budgetary resources:			
	Unobligated balance:			
1000	Unobligated balance brought forward, Oct 1	34	250	
1021	Recoveries of prior year unpaid obligations	28		15
1033	Recoveries of prior year paid obligations	7		
1070	Unobligated balance (total)	69	250	15
	Budget authority:			
	Appropriations, discretionary:			
1100	Appropriation	386	386	651
1120	Appropriations transferred to other acct [015–0401]	–40	–40	–40
1131	Unobligated balance of appropriations permanently reduced	–15	–15	–15
1160	Appropriation, discretionary (total)	331	331	596
	Spending authority from offsetting collections, discretionary:			
1701	Change in uncollected payments, Federal sources	–8		
1900	Budget authority (total)	323	331	596
1930	Total budgetary resources available	392	581	611
	Memorandum (non-add) entries:			
1941	Unexpired unobligated balance, end of year	250		30
	Change in obligated balance:			
	Unpaid obligations:			
3000	Unpaid obligations, brought forward, Oct 1	770	699	911
3010	New obligations, unexpired accounts	142	581	581
3020	Outlays (gross)	–185	–369	–537
3040	Recoveries of prior year unpaid obligations, unexpired	–28		–15
3050	Unpaid obligations, end of year	699	911	940
	Uncollected payments:			
3060	Uncollected pymts, Fed sources, brought forward, Oct 1	–8		
3070	Change in uncollected pymts, Fed sources, unexpired	8		
	Memorandum (non-add) entries:			
3100	Obligated balance, start of year	762	699	911
3200	Obligated balance, end of year	699	911	940
	Budget authority and outlays, net:			
	Discretionary:			
4000	Budget authority, gross	323	331	596
	Outlays, gross:			
4010	Outlays from new discretionary authority	20	53	229
4011	Outlays from discretionary balances	165	316	308
4020	Outlays, gross (total)	185	369	537

COMMUNITY ORIENTED POLICING SERVICES—Continued
Program and Financing—Continued

Identification code 015–0406–0–1–754	2021 actual	2022 est.	2023 est.
Offsets against gross budget authority and outlays:			
Offsetting collections (collected) from:			
4030 Federal sources	–6		
4033 Non-Federal sources	–1		
4040 Offsets against gross budget authority and outlays (total)	–7		
Additional offsets against gross budget authority only:			
4050 Change in uncollected pymts, Fed sources, unexpired	8		
4053 Recoveries of prior year paid obligations, unexpired accounts	7		
4060 Additional offsets against budget authority only (total)	15		
4070 Budget authority, net (discretionary)	331	331	596
4080 Outlays, net (discretionary)	178	369	537
4180 Budget authority, net (total)	331	331	596
4190 Outlays, net (total)	178	369	537

Summary of Budget Authority and Outlays (in millions of dollars)

	2021 actual	2022 est.	2023 est.
Enacted/requested:			
Budget Authority	331	331	596
Outlays	178	369	537
Legislative proposal, subject to PAYGO:			
Budget Authority			2,175
Outlays			870
Total:			
Budget Authority	331	331	2,771
Outlays	178	369	1,407

The Community Oriented Policing Services (COPS) Office advances the practice of community policing by the Nation's state and local law enforcement agencies through information sharing and grant resources. COPS develops programs that respond directly to the emerging needs of law enforcement agencies to shift focus from reacting to preventing crime and disorder.

To advance this mission, COPS develops training and technical assistance to enhance law enforcement officers problem-solving and community interaction skills, promotes collaboration between law enforcement and community members to develop innovative initiatives to prevent crime, and provides cost-effective service delivery to grantees to support community policing. COPS awards grants to hire community policing professionals, develop and test innovative policing strategies, and provide training and technical assistance to community members, local government leaders, and all levels of law enforcement. Since 1994, the COPS Office has invested more than $14 billion to help advance community policing, supporting over 13,000 of the Nation's 18,000 law enforcement agencies.

The 2023 Presidents Budget requests $651 million for COPS programs, including $537 million for the COPS Hiring Program. Within this amount, $40 million is for tribal law enforcement; $35 million is for Community Policing Development and the Just Policing Program; $20 million is for collaborative reform; and $6 million is for the Tribal Access Program.

The Budget additionally proposes to implement reforms that seek to more closely align the COPS Hiring program with evidence-based strategies to reduce violent crime in partnership with communities. This includes new priorities for jurisdictions that support Community Violence Intervention (CVI) programs, for jurisdictions that seek to hire officers to engage directly with CVI teams and other community stakeholders to ensure those groups are involved in strategic operations and planning, and for jurisdictions seeking to implement hiring practices to help agencies mirror the racial diversity of the communities that they serve.

Object Classification (in millions of dollars)

Identification code 015–0406–0–1–754	2021 actual	2022 est.	2023 est.
11.1 Direct obligations: Personnel compensation: Full-time permanent	10	10	10
11.9 Total personnel compensation	10	10	10
12.1 Civilian personnel benefits	3	3	3
23.1 Rental payments to GSA	3	3	3
23.3 Communications, utilities, and miscellaneous charges	3	3	3
25.1 Advisory and assistance services	2	2	2
25.2 Other services from non-Federal sources	2	2	2
25.3 Other goods and services from Federal sources	13	15	15
41.0 Grants, subsidies, and contributions	106	543	543
99.0 Direct obligations	142	581	581
99.9 Total new obligations, unexpired accounts	142	581	581

Employment Summary

Identification code 015–0406–0–1–754	2021 actual	2022 est.	2023 est.
1001 Direct civilian full-time equivalent employment	71	72	72

COMMUNITY ORIENTED POLICING SERVICES
(Legislative proposal, subject to PAYGO)

Program and Financing (in millions of dollars)

Identification code 015–0406–4–1–754	2021 actual	2022 est.	2023 est.
Obligations by program activity:			
0007 Management and administration			53
0009 COPS Hiring Program			2,122
0799 Total direct obligations			2,175
0900 Total new obligations, unexpired accounts			2,175
Budgetary resources:			
Budget authority:			
Appropriations, mandatory:			
1200 Appropriation			2,175
1930 Total budgetary resources available			2,175
Change in obligated balance:			
Unpaid obligations:			
3010 New obligations, unexpired accounts			2,175
3020 Outlays (gross)			–870
3050 Unpaid obligations, end of year			1,305
Memorandum (non-add) entries:			
3200 Obligated balance, end of year			1,305
Budget authority and outlays, net:			
Mandatory:			
4090 Budget authority, gross			2,175
Outlays, gross:			
4100 Outlays from new mandatory authority			870
4180 Budget authority, net (total)			2,175
4190 Outlays, net (total)			870

The Budget proposes $12.8 billion over a five-year period for the COPS Hiring Program.

Object Classification (in millions of dollars)

Identification code 015–0406–4–1–754	2021 actual	2022 est.	2023 est.
11.1 Direct obligations: Personnel compensation: Full-time permanent			10
11.9 Total personnel compensation			10
12.1 Civilian personnel benefits			4
21.0 Travel and transportation of persons			4
23.1 Rental payments to GSA			2
23.3 Communications, utilities, and miscellaneous charges			15
25.1 Advisory and assistance services			6
25.2 Other services from non-Federal sources			12
41.0 Grants, subsidies, and contributions			2,122
99.0 Direct obligations			2,175
99.9 Total new obligations, unexpired accounts			2,175

DEPARTMENT OF JUSTICE

Employment Summary

Identification code 015–0406–4–1–754	2021 actual	2022 est.	2023 est.
1001 Direct civilian full-time equivalent employment			53

GUN CRIME PREVENTION STRATEGIC FUND
(Legislative proposal, subject to PAYGO)

Program and Financing (in millions of dollars)

Identification code 015–0424–4–1–754	2021 actual	2022 est.	2023 est.
Obligations by program activity:			
0001 Gun Crime Prevention Strategic Grants			882
0002 Management and Administration			2
0900 Total new obligations, unexpired accounts			884
Budgetary resources:			
Budget authority:			
Appropriations, mandatory:			
1200 Appropriation			884
1930 Total budgetary resources available			884
Change in obligated balance:			
Unpaid obligations:			
3010 New obligations, unexpired accounts			884
3020 Outlays (gross)			–194
3050 Unpaid obligations, end of year			690
Memorandum (non-add) entries:			
3200 Obligated balance, end of year			690
Budget authority and outlays, net:			
Mandatory:			
4090 Budget authority, gross			884
Outlays, gross:			
4100 Outlays from new mandatory authority			194
4180 Budget authority, net (total)			884
4190 Outlays, net (total)			194

The Budget will propose to create a new grant program, the Gun Crime Prevention Strategic Fund, which provides states and localities with comprehensive resources to invest in law enforcement and crime prevention.

Object Classification (in millions of dollars)

Identification code 015–0424–4–1–754	2021 actual	2022 est.	2023 est.
Direct obligations:			
12.1 Civilian personnel benefits			2
25.1 Advisory and assistance services			3
41.0 Grants, subsidies, and contributions			879
99.9 Total new obligations, unexpired accounts			884

Employment Summary

Identification code 015–0424–4–1–754	2021 actual	2022 est.	2023 est.
1001 Direct civilian full-time equivalent employment			10

OFFICE ON VIOLENCE AGAINST WOMEN

VIOLENCE AGAINST WOMEN PREVENTION AND PROSECUTION PROGRAMS
(INCLUDING TRANSFER OF FUNDS)

For grants, contracts, cooperative agreements, and other assistance for the prevention and prosecution of violence against women, as authorized by the Omnibus Crime Control and Safe Streets Act of 1968 (34 U.S.C. 10101 et seq.) ("the 1968 Act"); the Violent Crime Control and Law Enforcement Act of 1994 (Public Law 103–322) ("the 1994 Act"); the Victims of Child Abuse Act of 1990 (Public Law 101–647) ("the 1990 Act"); the Prosecutorial Remedies and Other Tools to end the Exploitation of Children Today Act of 2003 (Public Law 108–21); the Juvenile Justice and Delinquency Prevention Act of 1974 (34 U.S.C. 11101 et seq.) ("the 1974 Act"); the Victims of Trafficking and Violence Protection Act of 2000 (Public Law 106–386) ("the 2000 Act"); the Violence Against Women and Department of Justice Reauthorization Act of 2005 (Public Law 109–162) ("the 2005 Act"); the Violence Against Women Reauthorization Act of 2013 (Public Law 113–4) ("the 2013 Act"); the Rape Survivor Child Custody Act of 2015 (Public Law 114–22) ("the 2015 Act"); and the Abolish Human Trafficking Act (Public Law 115–392); and for related victims services, $1,000,000,000, to remain available until expended: *Provided*, That except as otherwise provided by law, not to exceed 5 percent of funds made available under this heading may be used for expenses related to evaluation, training, and technical assistance: *Provided further*, That of the amount provided—

(1) $326,000,000 is for grants to combat violence against women, as authorized by part T of the 1968 Act;

(2) $100,000,000 is for transitional housing assistance grants for victims of domestic violence, dating violence, stalking, or sexual assault as authorized by section 40299 of the 1994 Act;

(3) $3,500,000 is for the National Institute of Justice and the Bureau of Justice Statistics for research, evaluation, and statistics of violence against women and related issues addressed by grant programs of the Office on Violence Against Women, which shall be transferred to "Research, Evaluation and Statistics" for administration by the Office of Justice Programs;

(4) $18,000,000 is for a grant program to provide services to advocate for and respond to youth victims of domestic violence, dating violence, sexual assault, and stalking; assistance to children and youth exposed to such violence; programs to engage men and youth in preventing such violence; and assistance to middle and high school students through education and other services related to such violence: *Provided*, That unobligated balances available for the programs authorized by sections 41201, 41204, and 41303 of the 1994 Act, prior to its amendment by the 2013 Act, shall be available for this program: *Provided further*, That 10 percent of the total amount available for this grant program shall be available for grants under the program authorized by section 2015 of the 1968 Act: *Provided further*, That the definitions and grant conditions in section 40002 of the 1994 Act shall apply to this program;

(5) $10,000,000 is for a grant program to engage men and youth in preventing domestic violence, dating violence, sexual assault, and stalking: *Provided*, That unobligated balances available for the programs authorized by section 41305 of the 1994 Act, prior to its amendment by the 2013 Act, shall be available for this program: *Provided further*, That 10 percent of the total amount available for this grant program shall be available for grants under the program authorized by section 2015 of the 1968 Act: *Provided further*, That the definitions and grant conditions in section 40002 of the 1994 Act shall apply to this program;

(6) $83,000,000 is for grants to encourage arrest policies as authorized by part U of Title I of the 1968 Act, of which up to $4,000,000 is for a homicide reduction initiative; up to $8,000,000 is for a domestic violence firearms lethality reduction initiative; $25,000,000 is for an initiative to promote effective policing and prosecution responses to domestic violence, dating violence, sexual assault, and stalking, including evaluation of the effectiveness of funded interventions; and $3,000,000 is for an initiative to enhance prosecution and investigation of online abuse and harassment: *Provided*, That subsections 2101(c) and (d) of the 1968 Act shall not apply to these initiatives;

(7) $100,000,000 is for sexual assault victims assistance, as authorized by section 41601 of the 1994 Act;

(8) $47,500,000 is for rural domestic violence and child abuse enforcement assistance grants, as authorized by section 40295 of the 1994 Act;

(9) $40,000,000 is for grants to reduce violent crimes against women on campus, as authorized by section 304 of the 2005 Act but not subject to the restrictions of section 304(a)(2) of such act, of which $20,000,000 is for grants to Historically Black Colleges and Universities, Hispanic-Serving Institutions, and Tribal colleges;

(10) $100,000,000 is for legal assistance for victims, as authorized by section 1201 of the 2000 Act;

(11) $10,000,000 is for enhanced training and services to end violence against and abuse of women in later life, as authorized by section 40801 of the 1994 Act;

(12) $28,000,000 is for grants to support families in the justice system, as authorized by section 1301 of the 2000 Act: *Provided*, That unobligated balances available for the programs authorized by section 1301 of the 2000 Act and section 41002 of the 1994 Act, prior to their amendment by the 2013 Act, shall be available for this program;

(13) $17,500,000 is for education and training to end violence against and abuse of women with disabilities, as authorized by section 1402 of the 2000 Act;

(14) $1,000,000 is for the National Resource Center on Workplace Responses to assist victims of domestic violence, as authorized by section 41501 of the 1994 Act;

Office of Justice Programs—Continued
Federal Funds—Continued

OFFICE ON VIOLENCE AGAINST WOMEN—Continued

(15) $1,000,000 is for analysis and research on violence against Indian women, including as authorized by section 904 of the 2005 Act: Provided, That such funds may be transferred to "Research, Evaluation and Statistics" for administration by the Office of Justice Programs;

(16) $500,000 is for a national clearinghouse that provides training and technical assistance on issues relating to sexual assault of American Indian and Alaska Native women;

(17) $5,500,000 is for grants to assist Tribal Governments in exercising special domestic violence criminal jurisdiction, as authorized by section 904 of the 2013 Act: Provided, That the grant conditions in section 40002(b) of the 1994 Act shall apply to this program;

(18) $25,000,000 is for a grant program to support restorative justice responses to domestic violence, dating violence, sexual assault, and stalking, including evaluations of those responses: Provided, That the definitions and grant conditions in section 40002 of the 1994 Act shall apply to this program;

(19) $7,000,000 is for an initiative to support transgender victims of domestic violence, dating violence, sexual assault, and stalking, including through the provision of technical assistance: Provided, That the definitions and grant conditions in section 40002 of the 1994 Act shall apply to this initiative;

(20) $4,000,000 is for a National Deaf Services Line to provide remote services to Deaf victims of domestic violence, dating violence, sexual assault, and stalking: Provided, That the definitions and grant conditions in section 40002 of the 1994 Act shall apply to this service line;

(21) $10,000,000 is for an initiative to build the capacity of community-based organizations that serve victims of domestic violence, dating violence, sexual assault, and stalking in culturally specific and other underserved communities to apply for and manage federal grant funding: Provided, That the definitions and grant conditions in section 40002 of the 1994 Act shall apply to this initiative;

(22) $35,000,000 is for culturally specific services for victims, as authorized by section 121 of the 2005 Act;

(23) $10,000,000 is for grants for outreach and services to underserved populations, as authorized by section 120 of the 2005 Act;

(24) $5,000,000 is to address emerging issues related to violence against women: Provided, That the grant conditions in section 40002(b) of the 1994 Act shall apply to this initiative;

(25) $3,000,000 is for an initiative to support tribal prosecutors to be cross-designated as Tribal Special Assistant United States Attorneys: Provided, That the definitions and grant conditions in section 40002 of the 1994 Act shall apply to this initiative;

(26) $1,500,000 is for the purposes authorized under the 2015 Act; and

(27) $8,000,000 is for an initiative to provide financial assistance to victims, including evaluation of the effectiveness of funded projects; Provided that the definitions and grant conditions in section 40002 of the 1994 Act shall apply to this initiative.

(CANCELLATION)

Of the unobligated balances from prior year appropriations available under this heading, $15,000,000 are hereby permanently cancelled: Provided, That no amounts may be cancelled from amounts that were designated by the Congress as an emergency requirement pursuant to a concurrent resolution on the budget or the Balanced Budget and Emergency Deficit Control Act of 1985, as amended.

Note.—A full-year 2022 appropriation for this account was not enacted at the time the Budget was prepared; therefore, the Budget assumes this account is operating under the Continuing Appropriations Act, 2022 (Division A of Public Law 117–43, as amended). The amounts included for 2022 reflect the annualized level provided by the continuing resolution.

Program and Financing (in millions of dollars)

Identification code 015–0409–0–1–754		2021 actual	2022 est.	2023 est.
	Obligations by program activity:			
0002	Grants to Combat Violence Against Women (STOP)	206	209	310
0003	Research and Evaluation of Violence Against Women (NIJ)	3	3	4
0004	Management and administration	24	26	35
0005	Transitional Housing	40	40	98
0006	Consolidated Youth Oriented Program	11	11	17
0007	Grants to Encourage Arrest Policies	46	46	82
0008	Rural Domestic Violence and Child Abuse Enforcement Assistance	43	43	45
0009	Legal Assistance Program	44	44	96
0010	Tribal Special Domestic Violence Criminal Jurisdiction	1	1	5
0011	Campus Violence	19	19	39
0012	Disabilities Program	5	5	17
0013	Elder Program	3	3	10
0014	Sexual Assault Services	41	41	98
0016	Indian Country - Sexual Assault Clearinghouse	1	....	....
0017	National Resource Center on Workplace Responses	1	1	1
0018	Research on Violence Against Indian Women	1	1	1
0020	Rape Survivor Child Custody Act Program	1	1	2
0021	Justice for Families	17	17	27
0022	Engaging Men and Youth in Prevention	....	....	9
0023	National Deaf Services	....	....	4
0024	Restorative Justice	....	....	25
0025	Supporting Transgender Victims	....	....	7
0026	Culturally-Specific services	....	....	33
0027	Community-based Organizational Capacity Building program	....	....	10
0028	Underserved Populations Program	....	....	9
0029	Emerging Issues in Violence Against Women	....	....	5
0030	Tribal Special Assistant United States Attorneys	....	....	3
0031	Financial Assistance Program	....	....	8
0799	Total direct obligations	507	511	1,000
0888	Reimbursable program activity	1	....	....
0889	Reimbursable program activities, subtotal	1	....	....
0900	Total new obligations, unexpired accounts	508	511	1,000
	Budgetary resources:			
	Unobligated balance:			
1000	Unobligated balance brought forward, Oct 1	33	36	49
1010	Unobligated balance transfer to other accts [015–0134]	–4	....	....
1021	Recoveries of prior year unpaid obligations	2	11	11
1070	Unobligated balance (total)	31	47	60
	Budget authority:			
	Appropriations, discretionary:			
1100	Appropriation	79	79	1,000
1120	Appropriations transferred to other accts [015–0401]	–3	–3	–4
1121	Appropriations transferred from other acct [015–5041]	435	435	....
1131	Unobligated balance of appropriations permanently reduced	....	....	–15
1160	Appropriation, discretionary (total)	511	511	981
	Spending authority from offsetting collections, discretionary:			
1701	Change in uncollected payments, Federal sources	2	2	2
1900	Budget authority (total)	513	513	983
1930	Total budgetary resources available	544	560	1,043
	Memorandum (non-add) entries:			
1941	Unexpired unobligated balance, end of year	36	49	43
	Change in obligated balance:			
	Unpaid obligations:			
3000	Unpaid obligations, brought forward, Oct 1	1,188	1,285	1,104
3010	New obligations, unexpired accounts	508	511	1,000
3020	Outlays (gross)	–409	–681	–515
3040	Recoveries of prior year unpaid obligations, unexpired	–2	–11	–11
3050	Unpaid obligations, end of year	1,285	1,104	1,578
	Uncollected payments:			
3060	Uncollected pymts, Fed sources, brought forward, Oct 1	–9	–11	–13
3070	Change in uncollected pymts, Fed sources, unexpired	–2	–2	–2
3090	Uncollected pymts, Fed sources, end of year	–11	–13	–15
	Memorandum (non-add) entries:			
3100	Obligated balance, start of year	1,179	1,274	1,091
3200	Obligated balance, end of year	1,274	1,091	1,563
	Budget authority and outlays, net:			
	Discretionary:			
4000	Budget authority, gross	513	513	983
	Outlays, gross:			
4010	Outlays from new discretionary authority	20	22	27
4011	Outlays from discretionary balances	389	659	488
4020	Outlays, gross (total)	409	681	515
	Additional offsets against gross budget authority only:			
4050	Change in uncollected pymts, Fed sources, unexpired	–2	–2	–2
4060	Additional offsets against budget authority only (total)	–2	–2	–2
4180	Budget authority, net (total)	511	511	981
4190	Outlays, net (total)	409	681	515

The mission of the Office on Violence Against Women (OVW) is to provide Federal leadership in developing the Nation's capacity to reduce domestic violence, dating violence, sexual assault, and stalking through the implementation of the Violence Against Women Act (VAWA).

Since its inception in 1995, OVW has awarded over $9.0 billion in grants and cooperative agreements, and has launched a multifaceted approach to implementing VAWA. By forging state, local, and tribal partnerships among police, prosecutors, judges, victim advocates, health care providers, faith leaders, organizations that serve culturally specific and underserved communities and others, OVW grant programs help provide victims with the protection and services they need to pursue safe and healthy lives, while simultaneously enabling communities to hold offenders accountable for their violence.

The 2023 Budget proposes $1 billion for programs administered by OVW to prevent and respond to violence against women, including domestic violence, dating violence, sexual assault, and stalking. The language reflects that this entire amount is requested as directly appropriated funding and eliminates a funding transfer from the Crime Victims Fund.

Object Classification (in millions of dollars)

Identification code 015–0409–0–1–754		2021 actual	2022 est.	2023 est.
	Direct obligations:			
	Personnel compensation:			
11.1	Full-time permanent	7	9	15
11.3	Other than full-time permanent	1	1	1
11.9	Total personnel compensation	8	10	16
12.1	Civilian personnel benefits	3	4	5
23.1	Rental payments to GSA	2	3	2
25.1	Advisory and assistance services	10	10	4
25.2	Other services from non-Federal sources	1	1	1
25.3	Other goods and services from Federal sources	5	5	7
41.0	Grants, subsidies, and contributions	478	478	965
99.0	Direct obligations	507	511	1,000
99.0	Reimbursable obligations	1	....	....
99.9	Total new obligations, unexpired accounts	508	511	1,000

Employment Summary

Identification code 015–0409–0–1–754	2021 actual	2022 est.	2023 est.
1001 Direct civilian full-time equivalent employment	64	75	133

JUVENILE JUSTICE PROGRAMS

For grants, contracts, cooperative agreements, and other assistance authorized by the Juvenile Justice and Delinquency Prevention Act of 1974 (Public Law 93–415) ("the 1974 Act"); title I of the Omnibus Crime Control and Safe Streets Act of 1968 (Public Law 90–351) ("title I of the 1968 Act"); the Violent Crime Control and Law Enforcement Act of 1994 (Public Law 103–322) ("the 1994 Act"); the Violence Against Women and Department of Justice Reauthorization Act of 2005 (Public Law 109–162) ("the 2005 Act"); the PROTECT Act (Public Law 108–21); the Victims of Child Abuse Act of 1990 (title II of Public Law 101–647) ("the 1990 Act"); the Adam Walsh Child Protection and Safety Act of 2006 (Public Law 109–248) ("the Adam Walsh Act"); the PROTECT Our Children Act of 2008 (Public Law 110–401) ("the 2008 Act"); the Violence Against Women Reauthorization Act of 2013 (Public Law 113–4) ("the VAW 2013 Act"); the Justice for All Reauthorization Act of 2016 (Public Law 114–324); the Victims of Crime Act of 1984 (chapter XIV of title II of Public Law 98–473) ("the 1984 Act"); the Comprehensive Addiction and Recovery Act of 2016 (Public Law 114–198); and 28 U.S.C. 530C; and for other juvenile justice programs, $760,000,000, to remain available until expended as follows—

(1) $157,000,000 for programs authorized by section 221 of the 1974 Act: Provided, That of the amounts provided under this paragraph, $500,000 shall be for a competitive demonstration grant program to support emergency planning among State, local, and Tribal juvenile justice residential facilities;

(2) $120,000,000 for youth mentoring programs;

(3) $117,000,000 for delinquency prevention, of which, pursuant to 28 U.S.C. 530C(a)—

(A) $10,000,000 shall be for grants to prevent trafficking of girls;

(B) $30,000,000 shall be for the Tribal Youth Program;

(C) $500,000 shall be for an Internet site providing information and resources on children of incarcerated parents;

(D) $20,000,000 shall be for competitive programs focusing on girls in the juvenile justice system;

(E) $16,000,000 shall be for an initiative relating to youth affected by opioids, stimulants, and other substance abuse; and

(F) $30,000,000 shall be for an initiative relating to children exposed to violence;

(4) $50,000,000 for programs authorized by the 1990 Act;

(5) $120,000,000 for missing and exploited children programs, including as authorized by sections 404(b) and 405(a) of the 1974 Act (except that section 102(b)(4)(B) of the 2008 Act shall not apply for purposes of this Act);

(6) $6,000,000 for child abuse training programs for judicial personnel and practitioners, as authorized by section 222 of the 1990 Act;

(7) $40,000,000 for a program to improve juvenile indigent defense;

(8) $100,000,000 for an initiative relating to alternatives to youth incarceration;

(9) $30,000,000 for an initiative to promote juvenile justice and child welfare collaboration;

(10) $15,000,000 for a program to reduce barriers related to juvenile and criminal records for youth; and

(11) $5,000,000 for a hate crime prevention and intervention initiative for youth: Provided, That not more than 10 percent of each amount may be used for research, evaluation, and statistics activities related to juvenile justice and delinquency prevention: Provided further, That not more than 2 percent of each amount designated, other than as expressly authorized by statute, may be used for training and technical assistance related to juvenile justice and delinquency prevention: Provided further, That funds made available for juvenile justice and delinquency prevention activities pursuant to the two preceding provisos may be used without regard to the authorizations associated with the underlying sources of those funds: Provided further, That the three preceding provisos shall not apply to paragraphs (3), (5), and (7) through (11).

Note.—A full-year 2022 appropriation for this account was not enacted at the time the Budget was prepared; therefore, the Budget assumes this account is operating under the Continuing Appropriations Act, 2022 (Division A of Public Law 117–43, as amended). The amounts included for 2022 reflect the annualized level provided by the continuing resolution.

Program and Financing (in millions of dollars)

Identification code 015–0405–0–1–754		2021 actual	2022 est.	2023 est.
	Obligations by program activity:			
0001	Part B: Formula Grants	5	125	139
0002	Youth Mentoring	1	169	107
0003	Delinquency Prevention Program (Title V - Local Delinq. Prevention Incentive Grants)	1	27	4
0004	Victims of Child Abuse	4	50	45
0009	Tribal Youth Program	1	17	28
0011	Emergency Planning - Juvenile Detention Facilities	....	2	1
0013	Missing and Exploited Children	1	173	107
0014	Child Abuse Training for Judicial Personnel and Practitioners	....	6	6
0015	Management and Administration	27	25	45
0017	Girls in the Juvenile Justice System	....	5	19
0018	Children of Incarcerated Parents Web Portal	1	1	1
0021	Indigent Defense Initiative— Improving Juvenile Indigent Defense Program	....	4	36
0023	Opioid Affected Youth Initiative	....	18	15
0024	Children Exposed to Violence	....	14	28
0025	Prevention of Trafficking of Girls	....	3	9
0026	Alternatives to Youth Incarceration Initiative	....	....	89
0028	Eliminating Records-Related Barriers to Youth Success	....	....	13
0029	Juvenile Justice and Child Welfare Collaboration Initiative	....	....	27
0030	Youth-Focused Hate Crime Prevention and Intervention Initiative	....	....	5
0799	Total direct obligations	41	639	724
0801	Juvenile Justice Programs (Reimbursable)	6	6	....
0900	Total new obligations, unexpired accounts	47	645	724
	Budgetary resources:			
	Unobligated balance:			
1000	Unobligated balance brought forward, Oct 1	15	313	17
1021	Recoveries of prior year unpaid obligations	2	....	....
1033	Recoveries of prior year paid obligations	1	....	....
1070	Unobligated balance (total)	18	313	17
	Budget authority:			
	Appropriations, discretionary:			
1100	Appropriation	346	346	760
1120	Appropriations transferred to OJP RES 2% Set-Aside [015–0401]	–7	....	–19
1131	Unobligated balance of appropriations permanently reduced	–3	–3	–7
1160	Appropriation, discretionary (total)	336	343	734
	Spending authority from offsetting collections, discretionary:			
1700	Collected	7	6	....
1701	Change in uncollected payments, Federal sources	–1	....	....
1750	Spending auth from offsetting collections, disc (total)	6	6	....
1900	Budget authority (total)	342	349	734

Juvenile Justice Programs—Continued
Program and Financing—Continued

Identification code 015–0405–0–1–754		2021 actual	2022 est.	2023 est.
1930	Total budgetary resources available	360	662	751
	Memorandum (non-add) entries:			
1941	Unexpired unobligated balance, end of year	313	17	27
	Change in obligated balance:			
	Unpaid obligations:			
3000	Unpaid obligations, brought forward, Oct 1	598	402	623
3010	New obligations, unexpired accounts	47	645	724
3020	Outlays (gross)	–241	–424	–423
3040	Recoveries of prior year unpaid obligations, unexpired	–2		
3050	Unpaid obligations, end of year	402	623	924
	Uncollected payments:			
3060	Uncollected pymts, Fed sources, brought forward, Oct 1	–2	–1	–1
3070	Change in uncollected pymts, Fed sources, unexpired	1		
3090	Uncollected pymts, Fed sources, end of year	–1	–1	–1
	Memorandum (non-add) entries:			
3100	Obligated balance, start of year	596	401	622
3200	Obligated balance, end of year	401	622	923
	Budget authority and outlays, net:			
	Discretionary:			
4000	Budget authority, gross	342	349	734
	Outlays, gross:			
4010	Outlays from new discretionary authority	28	58	112
4011	Outlays from discretionary balances	213	366	311
4020	Outlays, gross (total)	241	424	423
	Offsets against gross budget authority and outlays:			
	Offsetting collections (collected) from:			
4030	Federal sources	–7	–6	
4033	Non-Federal sources	–1		
4040	Offsets against gross budget authority and outlays (total)	–8	–6	
	Additional offsets against gross budget authority only:			
4050	Change in uncollected pymts, Fed sources, unexpired	1		
4053	Recoveries of prior year paid obligations, unexpired accounts	1		
4060	Additional offsets against budget authority only (total)	2		
4070	Budget authority, net (discretionary)	336	343	734
4080	Outlays, net (discretionary)	233	418	423
4180	Budget authority, net (total)	336	343	734
4190	Outlays, net (total)	233	418	423

The 2023 Budget requests $760 million for the Office of Justice Programs (OJP) Juvenile Justice Programs to support State, local, tribal, and community efforts to develop and implement effective crime and delinquency prevention programs, develop and implement effective and innovative juvenile justice programs, ensure fairness and equitable treatment for all juveniles in contact with the justice system, provide appropriate reentry services for youth returning to their communities after detention in secure correctional facilities, and effectively address crimes against children and young people. The 2023 Budget requests $157 million for the Part B: Formula Grants Program, which is the core program that supports State, local, and tribal efforts to improve the fairness and responsiveness of the juvenile justice system and to ensure appropriate accountability of the juvenile offender. The 2023 Budget requests $117 million for Delinquency Prevention programs, including $30 million for the Children Exposed to Violence Awareness and Intervention Initiative and $20 million for the Girls in the Juvenile Justice System Program. The 2023 Budget also invests in new juvenile justice programs, requesting $15 million for the Eliminating Records-Related Barriers to Youth Success Program to aid justice-system-involved youth in setting aside (i.e. expunging, sealing, or vacating) their records to help bolster reentry success, $30 million for a new Juvenile Justice and Child Welfare Collaboration Initiative that will assist communities in supporting dual status youth who have come into contact with both the juvenile justice system and the child welfare system, and $5 million for a Youth-Focused Hate Crime Prevention and Intervention Initiative to combat hate crimes. The 2023 Budget maintains support for priority programs, including $100 million to support community-based alternatives to youth incarceration, $40 million for the Improving Juvenile Indigent Defense Program, $120 million for the Missing and Exploited Children Program (MECP), $120 million for Youth Mentoring, and $50 million for the Victims of Child Abuse Act program.

Object Classification (in millions of dollars)

Identification code 015–0405–0–1–754		2021 actual	2022 est.	2023 est.
	Direct obligations:			
25.1	Advisory and assistance services	8	8	9
25.3	Other goods and services from Federal sources	27	27	31
41.0	Grants, subsidies, and contributions	6	604	684
99.0	Direct obligations	41	639	724
99.0	Reimbursable obligations	6	6	
99.9	Total new obligations, unexpired accounts	47	645	724

PUBLIC SAFETY OFFICER BENEFITS
(INCLUDING TRANSFER OF FUNDS)

For payments and expenses authorized under section 1001(a)(4) of title I of the Omnibus Crime Control and Safe Streets Act of 1968, such sums as are necessary (including amounts for administrative costs), to remain available until expended; and $34,800,000 for payments authorized by section 1201(b) of such Act and for educational assistance authorized by section 1218 of such Act, to remain available until expended: Provided, That notwithstanding section 205 of this Act, upon a determination by the Attorney General that emergent circumstances require additional funding for such disability and education payments, the Attorney General may transfer such amounts to "Public Safety Officer Benefits" from available appropriations for the Department of Justice as may be necessary to respond to such circumstances: Provided further, That any transfer pursuant to the preceding proviso shall be treated as a reprogramming under section 504 of this Act and shall not be available for obligation or expenditure except in compliance with the procedures set forth in that section.

Note.—A full-year 2022 appropriation for this account was not enacted at the time the Budget was prepared; therefore, the Budget assumes this account is operating under the Continuing Appropriations Act, 2022 (Division A of Public Law 117–43, as amended). The amounts included for 2022 reflect the annualized level provided by the continuing resolution.

Program and Financing (in millions of dollars)

Identification code 015–0403–0–1–754		2021 actual	2022 est.	2023 est.
	Obligations by program activity:			
0001	Public Safety Officers Discretionary Disability and Education Benefit Payments	9	23	33
0002	Public Safety Officers Death Mandatory Payments	113	119	181
0003	Management and Administration (discretionary funding only)		10	13
0900	Total new obligations, unexpired accounts	122	152	227
	Budgetary resources:			
	Unobligated balance:			
1000	Unobligated balance brought forward, Oct 1	13	28	20
	Budget authority:			
	Appropriations, discretionary:			
1100	Appropriation	25	25	35
	Appropriations, mandatory:			
1200	Appropriation	113	119	192
1230	Appropriations and/or unobligated balance of appropriations permanently reduced	–1		
1260	Appropriations, mandatory (total)	112	119	192
1900	Budget authority (total)	137	144	227
1930	Total budgetary resources available	150	172	247
	Memorandum (non-add) entries:			
1941	Unexpired unobligated balance, end of year	28	20	20
	Change in obligated balance:			
	Unpaid obligations:			
3000	Unpaid obligations, brought forward, Oct 1	47	83	12
3010	New obligations, unexpired accounts	122	152	227
3020	Outlays (gross)	–86	–223	–227
3050	Unpaid obligations, end of year	83	12	12
	Memorandum (non-add) entries:			
3100	Obligated balance, start of year	47	83	12

DEPARTMENT OF JUSTICE

Office of Justice Programs—Continued
Federal Funds—Continued

757

		2021 actual	2022 est.	2023 est.
3200	Obligated balance, end of year	83	12	12
	Budget authority and outlays, net:			
	Discretionary:			
4000	Budget authority, gross	25	25	35
	Outlays, gross:			
4010	Outlays from new discretionary authority	7	25	35
4011	Outlays from discretionary balances	1		
4020	Outlays, gross (total)	8	25	35
	Mandatory:			
4090	Budget authority, gross	112	119	192
	Outlays, gross:			
4100	Outlays from new mandatory authority	52	119	192
4101	Outlays from mandatory balances	26	79	
4110	Outlays, gross (total)	78	198	192
4180	Budget authority, net (total)	137	144	227
4190	Outlays, net (total)	86	223	227

The 2023 Budget requests $226.8 million for the Office of Justice Programs' Public Safety Officers' Benefits (PSOB) Program, of which $192 million is a mandatory appropriation for death benefits and $34.8 million is a discretionary appropriation for disability and education benefits. This appropriation supports programs that provide benefits to public safety officers who are severely injured in the line of duty and to the families and survivors of public safety officers killed or mortally injured in the line of duty. These programs represent the continuation of a partnership between the Department of Justice, national public safety organizations, and public safety agencies at the state, local, and tribal levels. The PSOB program oversees three types of benefits:

Death Benefits.—This program provides a one-time financial benefit to survivors of public safety officers whose deaths resulted from injuries sustained in the line of duty.

Disability Benefits.—This program offers a one-time financial benefit to public safety officers permanently disabled by catastrophic injuries sustained in the line of duty.

Education Benefits.—This program provides financial support for higher education expenses to the eligible spouses and children of public safety officers killed or permanently disabled in the line of duty.

Object Classification (in millions of dollars)

Identification code 015–0403–0–1–754		2021 actual	2022 est.	2023 est.
	Direct obligations:			
25.1	Advisory and assistance services	5	6	9
25.3	Other goods and services from Federal sources	11	13	19
42.0	Insurance claims and indemnities	106	133	199
99.9	Total new obligations, unexpired accounts	122	152	227

CRIME VICTIMS FUND

Special and Trust Fund Receipts (in millions of dollars)

Identification code 015–5041–0–2–754		2021 actual	2022 est.	2023 est.
0100	Balance, start of year	4,370	3,134	2,619
	Receipts:			
	Current law:			
1110	Fines, Penalties, and Forfeitures, Crime Victims Fund	774	1,500	1,750
2000	Total: Balances and receipts	5,144	4,634	4,369
	Appropriations:			
	Current law:			
2101	Crime Victims Fund	–774	–1,500	–1,750
2103	Crime Victims Fund	–4,370	–2,778	–2,406
2103	Crime Victims Fund		–356	–213
2132	Crime Victims Fund	356	213	223
2135	Crime Victims Fund		2,406	2,396
2135	Crime Victims Fund	2,778		
2199	Total current law appropriations	–2,010	–2,015	–1,750
2999	Total appropriations	–2,010	–2,015	–1,750
5099	Balance, end of year	3,134	2,619	2,619

Program and Financing (in millions of dollars)

Identification code 015–5041–0–2–754		2021 actual	2022 est.	2023 est.
	Obligations by program activity:			
0001	Crime victims grants and assistance	1,369	1,365	1,485
0002	Management and administration	90	88	88
0003	HHS	17	17	17
0006	Tribal Victims Assistance Grants	101	100	100
0007	Victim Advocate Program			50
0799	Total direct obligations	1,577	1,570	1,740
0801	Crime Victims Fund Reimbursable Program Activity	2	3	
0900	Total new obligations, unexpired accounts	1,579	1,573	1,740
	Budgetary resources:			
	Unobligated balance:			
1000	Unobligated balance brought forward, Oct 1	53	60	60
1021	Recoveries of prior year unpaid obligations	17		
1033	Recoveries of prior year paid obligations	2		
1070	Unobligated balance (total)	72	60	60
	Budget authority:			
	Appropriations, discretionary:			
1120	Appropriations transferred to other acct [015–0409]		–435	
1120	Appropriations transferred to other acct [015–0328]		–10	–10
1135	Appropriations precluded from obligation (special or trust)		–2,406	–2,396
1160	Appropriation, discretionary (total)		–2,851	–2,406
	Appropriations, mandatory:			
1201	Appropriation (special or trust fund)	774	1,500	1,750
1203	Appropriation (unavailable balances)	4,370	2,778	2,406
1203	Appropriation (previously unavailable)(special or trust)		356	213
1220	Appropriations transferred to other acct OVW [015–0409]	–435		
1220	Appropriations transferred to Inspector General [015–0328]	–10		
1232	Appropriations and/or unobligated balance of appropriations temporarily reduced	–356	–213	–223
1235	Appropriations precluded from obligation (special or trust)	–2,778		
1260	Appropriations, mandatory (total)	1,565	4,421	4,146
	Spending authority from offsetting collections, discretionary:			
1700	Collected		7	
1701	Change in uncollected payments, Federal sources	2	–4	
1750	Spending auth from offsetting collections, disc (total)	2	3	
1900	Budget authority (total)	1,567	1,573	1,740
1930	Total budgetary resources available	1,639	1,633	1,800
	Memorandum (non-add) entries:			
1941	Unexpired unobligated balance, end of year	60	60	60
	Change in obligated balance:			
	Unpaid obligations:			
3000	Unpaid obligations, brought forward, Oct 1	7,223	6,196	2,299
3010	New obligations, unexpired accounts	1,579	1,573	1,740
3020	Outlays (gross)	–2,589	–5,470	–1,880
3040	Recoveries of prior year unpaid obligations, unexpired	–17		
3050	Unpaid obligations, end of year	6,196	2,299	2,159
	Uncollected payments:			
3060	Uncollected pymts, Fed sources, brought forward, Oct 1	–2	–4	
3070	Change in uncollected pymts, Fed sources, unexpired	–2	4	
3090	Uncollected pymts, Fed sources, end of year	–4		
	Memorandum (non-add) entries:			
3100	Obligated balance, start of year	7,221	6,192	2,299
3200	Obligated balance, end of year	6,192	2,299	2,159
	Budget authority and outlays, net:			
	Discretionary:			
4000	Budget authority, gross	2	–2,848	–2,406
	Outlays, gross:			
4010	Outlays from new discretionary authority		–1,137	–962
4011	Outlays from discretionary balances			–713
4020	Outlays, gross (total)		–1,137	–1,675
	Offsets against gross budget authority and outlays:			
	Offsetting collections (collected) from:			
4030	Federal sources		–7	
	Additional offsets against gross budget authority only:			
4050	Change in uncollected pymts, Fed sources, unexpired	–2	4	
4070	Budget authority, net (discretionary)		–2,851	–2,406
4080	Outlays, net (discretionary)		–1,144	–1,675

CRIME VICTIMS FUND—Continued
Program and Financing—Continued

Identification code 015–5041–0–2–754	2021 actual	2022 est.	2023 est.
Mandatory:			
4090 Budget authority, gross	1,565	4,421	4,146
Outlays, gross:			
4100 Outlays from new mandatory authority	139	1,640	1,524
4101 Outlays from mandatory balances	2,450	4,967	2,031
4110 Outlays, gross (total)	2,589	6,607	3,555
Offsets against gross budget authority and outlays:			
Offsetting collections (collected) from:			
4123 Non-Federal sources	–2		
Additional offsets against gross budget authority only:			
4143 Recoveries of prior year paid obligations, unexpired accounts	2		
4160 Budget authority, net (mandatory)	1,565	4,421	4,146
4170 Outlays, net (mandatory)	2,587	6,607	3,555
4180 Budget authority, net (total)	1,565	1,570	1,740
4190 Outlays, net (total)	2,587	5,463	1,880

The Crime Victims Fund (CVF) provides formula grants to states and territories to support compensation and services for victims of crime. CVF funding also supports training, technical assistance, and demonstration grants designed to improve the capabilities and capacity of victims services providers throughout the Nation. The Fund is financed by collections of fines, penalty assessments, and bond forfeitures from defendants convicted of Federal crimes. The 2023 Budget proposes to provide $1.75 billion from collections and balances for crime victim compensation, services, and related needs. Of this amount, $50 million is also proposed to support a new victim advocate program and up to $87.5 million for the Office for Victims of Crime for Tribal Victims Assistance Grants.

The proposed obligation cap level will prevent the depletion of the Fund. The 2023 Budget also eliminates the funding transfer to the Office on Violence Against Women (OVW) that has been included as part of the CVF appropriations language in recent years. The elimination of this set aside will provide more victim assistance and compensation dollars to the states, and more support for grant programs to address issues critical to the Administration, such as improving the accessibility of services to victims in underserved communities and expanding hospital-based services to crime victims. Additionally, in 2020, OVC established a 60-month grant period for Tribes funded under the tribal set-aside from the CVF. This longer project period, which effectively allows tribal grantees more time to drawn down and expend grant funds, will continue to provide Tribes some flexibility in using their existing grant funds to mediate the reduction in the Tribal set-aside.

Object Classification (in millions of dollars)

Identification code 015–5041–0–2–754	2021 actual	2022 est.	2023 est.
Direct obligations:			
25.1 Advisory and assistance services	27	35	35
25.3 Other goods and services from Federal sources	170	170	170
25.7 Operation and maintenance of equipment	58	58	58
41.0 Grants, subsidies, and contributions	1,321	1,306	1,476
42.0 Insurance claims and indemnities	1	1	1
99.0 Direct obligations	1,577	1,570	1,740
99.0 Reimbursable obligations	2	3	
99.9 Total new obligations, unexpired accounts	1,579	1,573	1,740

DOMESTIC TRAFFICKING VICTIMS' FUND
Special and Trust Fund Receipts (in millions of dollars)

Identification code 015–5606–0–2–754	2021 actual	2022 est.	2023 est.
0100 Balance, start of year			
Receipts:			
Current law:			
1110 Fines, Penalties, and Forfeitures, Domestic Trafficking Victims' Fund	1	2	2
2000 Total: Balances and receipts	1	2	2
Appropriations:			
Current law:			
2101 Domestic Trafficking Victims' Fund	–1	–2	–2
5099 Balance, end of year			

Program and Financing (in millions of dollars)

Identification code 015–5606–0–2–754	2021 actual	2022 est.	2023 est.
Obligations by program activity:			
0001 Domestic Trafficking Victims		11	7
0100 Direct program activities, subtotal		11	7
0900 Total new obligations, unexpired accounts (object class 41.0)		11	7
Budgetary resources:			
Unobligated balance:			
1000 Unobligated balance brought forward, Oct 1		6	2
1011 Unobligated balance transfer from other acct [075–0360]	5	5	5
1070 Unobligated balance (total)	5	11	7
Budget authority:			
Appropriations, mandatory:			
1201 Appropriation (special or trust fund)	1	2	2
1900 Budget authority (total)	1	2	2
1930 Total budgetary resources available	6	13	9
Memorandum (non-add) entries:			
1941 Unexpired unobligated balance, end of year	6	2	2
Change in obligated balance:			
Unpaid obligations:			
3000 Unpaid obligations, brought forward, Oct 1	15	11	13
3010 New obligations, unexpired accounts		11	7
3020 Outlays (gross)	–4	–9	–2
3050 Unpaid obligations, end of year	11	13	18
Memorandum (non-add) entries:			
3100 Obligated balance, start of year	15	11	13
3200 Obligated balance, end of year	11	13	18
Budget authority and outlays, net:			
Mandatory:			
4090 Budget authority, gross	1	2	2
Outlays, gross:			
4101 Outlays from mandatory balances	4	9	2
4180 Budget authority, net (total)	1	2	2
4190 Outlays, net (total)	4	9	2

The Justice for Victims of Trafficking Act of 2015 (Public Law 11422) created the Domestic Victims of Trafficking Fund (DVTF) and authorizes grants to expand and improve services for victims of trafficking in the U.S. and victims of child pornography as authorized by the Victims of Child Abuse Act of 1990, the Trafficking Victims Protection Act of 2000, and the Trafficking Victims Protection Reauthorization Act of 2005. All programs supported by DVTF are administered by the Office of Justice Programs in consultation with the Department of Health and Human Services. The 2023 Budget proposes a total of $6.5 million (including $5 million in funding transferred from the Department of Health and Human Services and $1.5 million in collections from the Federal court system) to support grants under this program.

GENERAL FUND RECEIPT ACCOUNTS
(in millions of dollars)

	2021 actual	2022 est.	2023 est.
Governmental receipts:			
015–085400 Registration Fees, DEA	15	15	15
015–087000 Chapter Eleven Filing Fees, Bankruptcy, Department of Justice	5	5	5
General Fund Governmental receipts	20	20	20

Offsetting receipts from the public:

015-143500	General Fund Proprietary Interest Receipts, not Otherwise Classified		1	1
015-322000	All Other General Fund Proprietary Receipts Including Budget Clearing Accounts	589	525	525
General Fund Offsetting receipts from the public		589	526	526
Intragovernmental payments:				
015-388500	Undistributed Intragovernmental Payments and Receivables from Cancelled Accounts	−234	104	104
General Fund Intragovernmental payments		−234	104	104

GENERAL PROVISIONS—DEPARTMENT OF JUSTICE

(INCLUDING TRANSFER OF FUNDS)
(INCLUDING CANCELLATION OF FUNDS)

SEC. 201. In addition to amounts otherwise made available in this title for official reception and representation expenses, a total of not to exceed $50,000 from funds appropriated to the Department of Justice in this title shall be available to the Attorney General for official reception and representation expenses.

SEC. 202. None of the funds appropriated by this title shall be available to pay for an abortion, except where the life of the mother would be endangered if the fetus were carried to term, or in the case of rape or incest: Provided, That should this prohibition be declared unconstitutional by a court of competent jurisdiction, this section shall be null and void.

SEC. 203. None of the funds appropriated under this title shall be used to require any person to perform, or facilitate in any way the performance of, any abortion.

SEC. 204. Nothing in the preceding section shall remove the obligation of the Director of the Bureau of Prisons to provide escort services necessary for a female inmate to receive such service outside the Federal facility: Provided, That nothing in this section in any way diminishes the effect of section 203 intended to address the philosophical beliefs of individual employees of the Bureau of Prisons.

SEC. 205. Not to exceed 5 percent of any appropriation made available for the current fiscal year for the Department of Justice in this Act may be transferred between such appropriations, but no such appropriation, except as otherwise specifically provided, shall be increased by more than 10 percent by any such transfers: Provided, That any transfer pursuant to this section shall be treated as a reprogramming of funds under section 504 of this Act and shall not be available for obligation except in compliance with the procedures set forth in that section.

SEC. 206. None of the funds made available under this title may be used by the Federal Bureau of Prisons or the United States Marshals Service for the purpose of transporting an individual who is a prisoner pursuant to conviction for crime under State or Federal law and is classified as a maximum or high security prisoner, other than to a prison or other facility certified by the Federal Bureau of Prisons as appropriately secure for housing such a prisoner.

SEC. 207. (a) None of the funds appropriated by this Act may be used by Federal prisons to purchase cable television services, or to rent or purchase audiovisual or electronic media or equipment used primarily for recreational purposes.

(b) Subsection (a) does not preclude the rental, maintenance, or purchase of audiovisual or electronic media or equipment for inmate training, religious, or educational programs.

SEC. 208. The notification thresholds and procedures set forth in section 504 of this Act shall apply to deviations from the amounts designated for specific activities in this Act and in the explanatory statement that accompanies this Act, and to any use of deobligated balances of funds provided under this title in previous years.

SEC. 209. None of the funds appropriated by this Act may be used to plan for, begin, continue, finish, process, or approve a public-private competition under the Office of Management and Budget Circular A-76 or any successor administrative regulation, directive, or policy for work performed by employees of the Bureau of Prisons or of Federal Prison Industries, Incorporated.

SEC. 210. At the discretion of the Attorney General, and in addition to any amounts that otherwise may be available (or authorized to be made available) by law, with respect to funds appropriated by this title under the headings "Research, Evaluation and Statistics", "State and Local Law Enforcement Assistance", and "Juvenile Justice Programs"—

(1) up to 2 percent of funds made available for grant or reimbursement programs may be used by the Office of Justice Programs to provide training and technical assistance; and

(2) up to 2.5 percent of funds made available for grant or reimbursement programs, except for amounts appropriated specifically for research, evaluation, or statistical programs administered by the National Institute of Justice and the Bureau of Justice Statistics, shall be transferred to and merged with funds provided to the National Institute of Justice and the Bureau of Justice Statistics, to be used by them for research, evaluation, or statistical purposes, without regard to the authorizations for such grant or reimbursement programs.

SEC. 211. Upon request by a grantee for whom the Attorney General has determined there is a fiscal hardship, the Attorney General may, with respect to funds appropriated in this or any other Act making appropriations for fiscal years 2020 through 2023 for the following programs, waive the following requirements:

(1) For the adult and juvenile offender State and local reentry demonstration projects under part FF of title I of the Omnibus Crime Control and Safe Streets Act of 1968, the requirements under section 2976(g)(1) of such part.

(2) For grants to protect inmates and safeguard communities as authorized by section 6 of the Prison Rape Elimination Act of 2003, the requirements of section 6(c)(3) of such Act.

SEC. 212. Notwithstanding any other provision of law, section 20109(a) of subtitle A of title II of the Violent Crime Control and Law Enforcement Act of 1994 (34 U.S.C. 12109(a)) shall not apply to amounts made available by this or any other Act.

SEC. 213. None of the funds made available under this Act, other than for the national instant criminal background check system established under section 103 of the Brady Handgun Violence Prevention Act (34 U.S.C. 40901), may be used by a Federal law enforcement officer to facilitate the transfer of an operable firearm to an individual if the Federal law enforcement officer knows or suspects that the individual is an agent of a drug cartel, unless law enforcement personnel of the United States continuously monitor or control the firearm at all times.

SEC. 214. Discretionary funds that are made available in this Act for the Office of Justice Programs may be used to participate in Performance Partnership Pilots authorized under such authorities as have been enacted for Performance Partnership Pilots in appropriations acts in prior fiscal years and the current fiscal year.

SEC. 215. Notwithstanding any other provision of law, amounts deposited or available in the Fund established by section 1402 of chapter XIV of title II of Public Law 98–473 (34 U.S.C. 20101) in any fiscal year in excess of $1,750,000,000 shall not be available for obligation until the following fiscal year: Provided, That notwithstanding section 1402(d) of such Act, of the amounts available from the Fund for obligation: (1) $10,000,000 shall be transferred to the Department of Justice Office of Inspector General and remain available until expended for oversight and auditing purposes associated with this section; (2) up to 5 percent shall be available to the Office for Victims of Crime for grants, consistent with the requirements of the Victims of Crime Act, to Indian tribes to improve services for victims of crime; and (3) $50,000,000 is for a victim advocate program.

SEC. 216. In this fiscal year, amounts credited to and made available in the Department of Justice Working Capital Fund as an offsetting collection pursuant to section 11013 of Public Law 107–273 shall be so credited and available as provided in that section.

SEC. 217. The following provisos are repealed:

(a) the first and fifth provisos included under the heading "Department of Justice—Bureau of Alcohol, Tobacco, Firearms and Explosives—Salaries and Expenses" in the Department of Justice Appropriations Act, 2013 (Title II, Division B, Public Law 113–6); and

(b) the sixth proviso included under the heading "Department of Justice—Bureau of Alcohol, Tobacco, Firearms and Explosives—Salaries and Expenses" in each of the following Acts: the Department of Justice Appropriations Act, 2012 (Title II, Division B, Public Law 112–55); the Department of Justice Appropriations Act, 2010 (Title II, Division B, Public Law 111–117); the Department of Justice Appropriations Act, 2009 (Title II, Division B, Public Law 111–8); the Department of Justice Appropriations Act, 2008 (Title II, Division B, Public Law 110–161); the Department of Justice Appropriations Act, 2006 (Title I, Public Law 109–108); and the Department of Justice Appropriations Act, 2005 (Title I, Division B, Public Law 108–447).

SEC. 218. Section 3201 of Public Law 101–647, as amended (28 U.S.C. 509 note), is hereby amended:

(1) by striking "or the Immigration and Naturalization Service" and inserting "the Federal Prison System, the Bureau of Alcohol, Tobacco, Firearms and Explosives, or the United States Marshals Service"; and

(2) by striking "$25,000" and inserting "$50,000".

(CANCELLATIONS)

SEC. 219. Of the unobligated balances available from prior year appropriations to the Office of Justice Programs, $75,000,000 are hereby permanently cancelled: Provided, That no amounts may be cancelled from amounts that were designated by the Congress as an emergency requirement pursuant to the Concurrent Resolution on the Budget or the Balanced Budget and Emergency Deficit Control Act of 1985, as amended.

SEC. 220. Of the unobligated balances available in the Working Capital Fund, $100,000,000 are hereby permanently cancelled: Provided, That no amounts may be cancelled from amounts that were designated by the Congress as an emergency requirement pursuant to the Concurrent Resolution on the Budget or the Balanced Budget and Emergency Deficit Control Act of 1985, as amended.

SEC. 221. Of the unobligated balances available in the Department of Justice Assets Forfeiture Fund, established by section 524 of title 28, United States Code, $100,000,000 shall be permanently cancelled not later than September 30, 2023: Provided, That no amounts may be cancelled from amounts that were designated by the Congress as an emergency requirement pursuant to a concurrent resolution on the budget or the Balanced Budget and Emergency Deficit Control Act of 1985, as amended.

DEPARTMENT OF LABOR

EMPLOYMENT AND TRAINING ADMINISTRATION
Federal Funds

TRAINING AND EMPLOYMENT SERVICES

For necessary expenses of the Workforce Innovation and Opportunity Act (referred to in this Act as "WIOA") and the National Apprenticeship Act, $4,410,999,000, plus reimbursements, shall be available. Of the amounts provided:

(1) for grants to States for adult employment and training activities, youth activities, and dislocated worker employment and training activities, $3,019,102,000 as follows:

(A) $899,987,000 for adult employment and training activities, of which $187,987,000 shall be available for the period July 1, 2023 through June 30, 2024, and of which $712,000,000 shall be available for the period October 1, 2023 through June 30, 2024;

(B) $963,837,000 for youth activities, which shall be available for the period April 1, 2023 through June 30, 2024; and

(C) $1,155,278,000 for dislocated worker employment and training activities, of which $295,278,000 shall be available for the period July 1, 2023 through June 30, 2024, and of which $860,000,000 shall be available for the period October 1, 2023 through June 30, 2024:

Provided, That the funds available for allotment to outlying areas to carry out subtitle B of title I of the WIOA shall not be subject to the requirements of section 127(b)(1)(B)(ii) of such Act: Provided further, That notwithstanding the requirements of the WIOA, outlying areas may submit a single application for a consolidated grant that awards funds that would otherwise be available to such areas to carry out the activities described in subtitle B of title I of the WIOA: Provided further, That such application shall be submitted to the Secretary at such time, in such manner, and containing such information as the Secretary may require: Provided futher, That outlying areas awarded a consolidated grant described in the preceding provisos may use the funds for any of the programs and activities authorized under subtitle B of title I of the WIOA, subject to approval of the application and such reporting requirements issued by the Secretary; and

(2) for national programs, $1,391,897,000 as follows:

(A) $527,386,000 for the dislocated workers assistance national reserve, of which $327,386,000 shall be available for the period July 1, 2023 through September 30, 2024, and of which $200,000,000 shall be available for the period October 1, 2023 through September 30, 2024: Provided further, That funds provided to carry out section 132(a)(2)(A) of the WIOA may be used to provide assistance to a State for statewide or local use in order to address cases where there have been worker dislocations across multiple sectors or across multiple local areas and such workers remain dislocated; coordinate the State workforce development plan with emerging economic development needs; and train such eligible dislocated workers: Provided further, That funds provided to carry out sections 168(b) and 169(c) of the WIOA may be used for technical assistance and demonstration projects, respectively, that provide assistance to new entrants in the workforce and incumbent workers: Provided further, That notwithstanding section 168(b) of the WIOA, of the funds provided under this subparagraph, the Secretary of Labor (referred to in this title as "Secretary") may reserve not more than 10 percent of such funds to provide technical assistance and carry out additional activities related to the transition to the WIOA: Provided further, That of the funds provided under this subparagraph, $335,000,000 shall be for training and employment assistance under sections 168(b), 169(c) (notwithstanding the 10 percent limitation in such section) and 170 of the WIOA as follows:

(i) $35,000,000 shall be for workers in the Appalachian region, as defined by 40 U.S.C. 14102(a)(1) and workers in the Lower Mississippi, as defined in section 4(2) of the Delta Development Act (Public Law 100–460, 102 Stat. 2246; 7 U.S.C. 2009aa(2));

(ii) $100,000,000 shall be for the purpose of developing, offering, or improving educational or career training programs at community colleges, defined as public institutions of higher education, as described in section 101(a) of the Higher Education Act of 1965 and at which the associate's degree is primarily the highest degree awarded, with other eligible institutions of higher education, as defined in section 101(a) of the Higher Education Act of 1965, eligible to participate through consortia, with community colleges as the lead grantee: Provided, That the Secretary shall follow the requirements for the program in House Report 116–62 and in the explanatory statement accompanying this Act: Provided further, That any grant funds used for apprenticeships shall be used to support only apprenticeship programs registered under the National Apprenticeship Act and as referred to in section 3(7)(B) of the WIOA;

(iii) $100,000,000 shall be for training and employment assistance for workers in communities that have experienced job losses due to dislocations in industries related to fossil fuel extraction or energy production;

(iv) $100,000,000 shall be for grants, contracts, or cooperative agreements to industry or sector partnerships to expand employment and training activities in high-skill, high-wage, or in-demand sectors and occupations for dislocated workers and other unemployed or underemployed workers, individuals with barriers to employment, new entrants to the workforce, or incumbent workers; and for grants, contracts, or cooperative agreements or other assistance to State boards or local boards to support the creation or expansion of industry or sector partnerships in local areas with high percentages of dislocated workers or individuals with barriers to employment;

(B) $63,800,000 for Native American programs under section 166 of the WIOA, which shall be available for the period July 1, 2023 through June 30, 2024;

(C) $96,711,000 for migrant and seasonal farmworker programs under section 167 of the WIOA, including $89,315,000 for formula grants (of which not less than 70 percent shall be for employment and training services), $6,429,000 for migrant and seasonal housing (of which not less than 70 percent shall be for permanent housing), and $967,000 for other discretionary purposes, which shall be available for the period April 1, 2023 through June 30, 2024: Provided, That notwithstanding any other provision of law or related regulation, the Department of Labor shall take no action limiting the number or proportion of eligible participants receiving related assistance services or discouraging grantees from providing such services: Provided further, That notwithstanding the definition of "eligible seasonal farmworker" in section 167(i)(3)(A) of the WIOA relating to an individual being "low-income", an individual is eligible for migrant and seasonal farmworker programs under section 167 of the WIOA under that definition if, in addition to meeting the requirements of clauses (i) and (ii) of section 167(i)(3)(A), such individual is a member of a family with a total family income equal to or less than 150 percent of the poverty line;

(D) $145,000,000 for YouthBuild activities as described in section 171 of the WIOA, which shall be available for the period April 1, 2023 through June 30, 2024;

(E) $150,000,000 for ex-offender activities, under the authority of section 169 of the WIOA, which shall be available for the period April 1, 2023 through June 30, 2024: Provided, That of this amount, $25,000,000 shall be for competitive grants to national and regional intermediaries for activities that prepare for employment young adults with criminal records, young adults who have been justice system-involved, or young adults who have dropped out of school or other educational programs, with a priority for projects serving high-crime, high-poverty areas;

(F) $6,000,000 for the Workforce Data Quality Initiative, under the authority of section 169 of the WIOA, which shall be available for the period July 1, 2023 through June 30, 2024;

(G) $303,000,000 to expand opportunities through apprenticeships only registered under the National Apprenticeship Act and as referred to in section 3(7)(B) of the WIOA, to be available to the Secretary to carry out activities through grants, cooperative agreements, contracts and other arrangements, with States and other appropriate entities, including equity intermediaries and business and labor industry partner intermediaries, which shall be available for the period July 1, 2023 through June 30, 2024;

(H) $75,000,000 for a National Youth Employment Program, under the authority of section 169 of the WIOA, including the expansion of summer and year-round job opportunities for disadvantaged youth, which shall be available for the period April 1, 2023 through June 30, 2024;

(I) $10,000,000 for a national training program for veterans, members of the armed forces who are separating from active duty, and the spouses of veterans and such members, focused on training related to employment in clean energy sectors and occupations, under the authority of section 169 of the WIOA, which shall be available for the period July 1, 2023 through June 30, 2024; and

(J) $15,000,000 for employment and training activities for youth related to high-quality employment opportunities in industry sectors or occupations related to climate resilience or mitigation, to be provided through grants, contracts, or cooperative agreements to State or local public agencies or private nonprofit entities, and which may include paid work experiences in public agencies (notwithstanding section 194(10) of the WIOA), private nonprofit entities, or pre-apprenticeship and registered apprenticeship programs, and other appropriate activities in coordination with climate resilience or mitigation activities undertaken by other Federal agencies under the authority of section 169 of the WIOA, which shall be available for the period July 1, 2023 through June 30, 2024.

762   Employment and Training Administration—Continued
Federal Funds—Continued

THE BUDGET FOR FISCAL YEAR 2023

TRAINING AND EMPLOYMENT SERVICES—Continued

Note.—A full-year 2022 appropriation for this account was not enacted at the time the Budget was prepared; therefore, the Budget assumes this account is operating under the Continuing Appropriations Act, 2022 (Division A of Public Law 117–43, as amended). The amounts included for 2022 reflect the annualized level provided by the continuing resolution.

Program and Financing (in millions of dollars)

Identification code 016–0174–0–1–504		2021 actual	2022 est.	2023 est.
	Obligations by program activity:			
0001	Adult Employment and Training Activities	864	861	900
0003	Dislocated Worker Employment and Training Activities	1,349	1,412	1,441
0005	Youth Activities	1,013	1,020	1,060
0008	Reintegration of Ex-Offenders	98	100	100
0010	Native Americans	56	55	64
0011	Migrant and Seasonal Farmworkers	97	94	97
0015	H-1B Job Training Grants	191		198
0017	Data Quality Initiative	6	12	
0024	Apprenticeship Grants	176	187	180
0799	Total direct obligations	3,850	3,741	4,040
0900	Total new obligations, unexpired accounts	3,850	3,741	4,040
	Budgetary resources:			
	Unobligated balance:			
1000	Unobligated balance brought forward, Oct 1	811	546	431
1001	Discretionary unobligated balance brought fwd, Oct 1	519	450	
1010	Unobligated balance transfer to other accts [016–0172]	–1		
1010	Unobligated balance transfer to other accts [016–0165]		–2	
1021	Recoveries of prior year unpaid obligations	23		
1070	Unobligated balance (total)	833	544	431
	Budget authority:			
	Appropriations, discretionary:			
1100	Appropriation	1,891	1,891	2,639
1106	Reappropriation			24
1120	Appropriations transferred to other acct [016–4601]			–24
1120	Appropriations transferred to other acct [016–0172]	–1		
1131	Unobligated balance of appropriations permanently reduced		–228	
1160	Appropriation, discretionary (total)	1,890	1,663	2,639
	Advance appropriations, discretionary:			
1170	Advance appropriation	1,772	1,772	1,772
1172	Advance appropriations transferred to DM-CEO [016–0165]	–1	–5	
1172	Advance appropriations transferred to ETA PA [016–0172]	–1		
1180	Advanced appropriation, discretionary (total)	1,770	1,767	1,772
	Appropriations, mandatory:			
1201	Appropriation (H-1B Skills Training)	267	194	199
1203	Appropriation (previously unavailable)(special or trust)	11	15	11
1230	Appropriations and/or unobligated balance of appropriations permanently reduced	–360		
1232	Appropriations and/or unobligated balance of appropriations temporarily reduced	–15	–11	–11
1260	Appropriations, mandatory (total)	–97	198	199
1900	Budget authority (total)	3,563	3,628	4,610
1930	Total budgetary resources available	4,396	4,172	5,041
	Memorandum (non-add) entries:			
1941	Unexpired unobligated balance, end of year	546	431	1,001
	Change in obligated balance:			
	Unpaid obligations:			
3000	Unpaid obligations, brought forward, Oct 1	4,619	5,030	3,891
3010	New obligations, unexpired accounts	3,850	3,741	4,040
3011	Obligations ("upward adjustments"), expired accounts	1		
3020	Outlays (gross)	–3,361	–4,880	–3,893
3040	Recoveries of prior year unpaid obligations, unexpired	–23		
3041	Recoveries of prior year unpaid obligations, expired	–56		
3050	Unpaid obligations, end of year	5,030	3,891	4,038
	Memorandum (non-add) entries:			
3100	Obligated balance, start of year	4,619	5,030	3,891
3200	Obligated balance, end of year	5,030	3,891	4,038
	Budget authority and outlays, net:			
	Discretionary:			
4000	Budget authority, gross	3,660	3,430	4,411
	Outlays, gross:			
4010	Outlays from new discretionary authority	774	1,037	1,090
4011	Outlays from discretionary balances	2,479	3,653	2,562
4020	Outlays, gross (total)	3,253	4,690	3,652
	Mandatory:			
4090	Budget authority, gross	–97	198	199
	Outlays, gross:			
4101	Outlays from mandatory balances	108	190	241
4180	Budget authority, net (total)	3,563	3,628	4,610
4190	Outlays, net (total)	3,361	4,880	3,893

Enacted in 2014, the Workforce Innovation and Opportunity Act (WIOA) is the primary authorization for this appropriation account. The Act is intended to provide job seekers and workers with the labor market information, job search assistance, and training they need to get and keep good jobs, and to provide employers with skilled workers. Funds appropriated for this account generally are available on a July to June program year basis, and include substantial advance appropriation amounts. This account includes:

Adult employment and training activities.—Grants to provide financial assistance to States and territories to design and operate training and employment assistance programs for adults, including low-income individuals and public assistance recipients.

Youth activities.—Grants to support a wide range of activities and services to prepare low-income youth for academic and employment success, including summer and year-round jobs. The program links academic and occupational learning with youth development activities.

Dislocated worker employment and training activities.—Grants to provide reemployment services and retraining assistance to individuals dislocated from their employment. Includes competitive grants for POWER+, which will support community-led workforce transition, layoff aversion, job creation, and other strategic initiatives designed to ensure economic prosperity for workers and job seekers in the coal, oil, and gas industries. Also includes sector-based training grants to provide workers with in-demand training that leads to high-quality jobs. Also includes grants that will strengthen community colleges' capacity to provide effective training programs.

Reentry Employment Opportunities.—Supports activities authorized under section 169 of the WIOA to help individuals exiting incarceration make a successful transition to community life and long-term employment through mentoring, job training, and other services. The Department also provides competitive grants for a range of young adults who have been involved with the criminal justice system or who left high school before graduation, particularly those in high-poverty, high-crime areas, with similar services. The Administration intends to devote funds to test and replicate evidence-based strategies for serving individuals leaving incarceration. The Department of Labor will continue to coordinate closely with the Department of Justice and other relevant Agencies in carrying out this program.

Apprenticeship.—Activities that support and expand Registered Apprenticeship programs at the state and local levels through a range of activities, such as state-specific outreach strategies, partnerships, economic development strategies, and expanded access to apprenticeship opportunities for under-represented populations through pre-apprenticeships and career pathways.

YouthBuild.—Grants to provide academic training and occupational skills training, mentoring, and supportive services to eligible at-risk youth, with a specific focus on attaining construction skills through building or rehabilitating affordable housing for low-income or homeless families in their own neighborhoods.

Indian and Native American Program.—Grants to provide employment, education, intensive training, and supportive services to tribes, tribal consortia, and nonprofit Indian organizations.

Migrant and Seasonal Farmworkers.—Grants to provide employment and training services to migrant and seasonal farmworkers (MSFW) and their dependents. The program provides career, training, housing assistance, youth, and other related assistance services to MSFWs.

National Youth Employment Program.—Competitive grants to operate summer and year-round youth employment programs through partnerships with employers in high demand industries and occupations. In addition to employment, programs will provide supportive services, such as transportation and childcare, necessary for youth participation in summer and year-round employment programs and will connect youth with additional skill-building opportunities that enable them to enter on-ramps to careers.

Veterans' Clean Energy Training.—Competitive grants to prepare eligible veterans, transitioning service members, and spouses of veterans and transitioning service members for careers in clean energy sectors and occupations.

Civilian Climate Corps.—A multi-Departmental initiative to mobilize the next generation of conservation and resilience workers and maximize the creation of accessible training opportunities and good jobs.

Object Classification (in millions of dollars)

Identification code 016–0174–0–1–504		2021 actual	2022 est.	2023 est.
	Direct obligations:			
25.1	Advisory and assistance services	5	56	
25.2	Other services from non-Federal sources	57		36
25.3	Other goods and services from Federal sources	5		
25.7	Operation and maintenance of equipment	20		
31.0	Equipment	1		
41.0	Grants, subsidies, and contributions	3,762	3,685	4,004
99.0	Direct obligations	3,850	3,741	4,040
99.9	Total new obligations, unexpired accounts	3,850	3,741	4,040

JOB CORPS

(INCLUDING TRANSFER OF FUNDS)

To carry out subtitle C of title I of the WIOA, including Federal administrative expenses, the purchase and hire of passenger motor vehicles, the construction, alteration, and repairs of buildings and other facilities, and the purchase of real property for training centers as authorized by the WIOA, $1,778,964,000, plus reimbursements, as follows:

(1) $1,603,011,000 for Job Corps Operations, which shall be available for the period July 1, 2023 through June 30, 2024: Provided, That the Secretary may transfer up to 3 percent of such funds for construction, rehabilitation, and acquisition of Job Corps Centers: Provided further, That any funds transferred pursuant to the preceding provision shall be available for obligation through June 30, 2026: Provided further, That the Committees on Appropriations of the House of Representatives and the Senate shall be notified at least 15 days in advance of any such transfer;

(2) $133,000,000 for construction, rehabilitation and acquisition of Job Corps Centers, which shall be available for the period July 1, 2023 through June 30, 2026, and which may include the acquisition, maintenance, and repair of major items of equipment; and

(3) $42,953,000 for necessary expenses of Job Corps, which shall be available for obligation for the period October 1, 2022 through September 30, 2023:

Provided, That no funds from any other appropriation shall be used to provide meal services at or for Job Corps centers.

Note.—A full-year 2022 appropriation for this account was not enacted at the time the Budget was prepared; therefore, the Budget assumes this account is operating under the Continuing Appropriations Act, 2022 (Division A of Public Law 117–43, as amended). The amounts included for 2022 reflect the annualized level provided by the continuing resolution.

Program and Financing (in millions of dollars)

Identification code 016–0181–0–1–504		2021 actual	2022 est.	2023 est.
	Obligations by program activity:			
0001	Operations	1,630	1,639	1,642
0002	Construction, Rehabilitation, and Acquisition (CRA)	208	78	97
0003	Administration	32	32	43
0900	Total new obligations, unexpired accounts	1,870	1,749	1,782
	Budgetary resources:			
	Unobligated balance:			
1000	Unobligated balance brought forward, Oct 1	1,311	1,220	1,218
1010	Unobligated balance transfer to other accts [016–0165]	–1	–2	
1012	Unobligated balance transfers between expired and unexpired accounts	–1		
1021	Recoveries of prior year unpaid obligations	32		
1070	Unobligated balance (total)	1,341	1,218	1,218
	Budget authority:			
	Appropriations, discretionary:			
1100	Appropriation	1,749	1,749	1,779
1106	Reappropriation			9
1120	Appropriations transferred to other acct [016–4601]			–9
1160	Appropriation, discretionary (total)	1,749	1,749	1,779
	Spending authority from offsetting collections, discretionary:			
1700	Collected	2		
1900	Budget authority (total)	1,751	1,749	1,779
1930	Total budgetary resources available	3,092	2,967	2,997
	Memorandum (non-add) entries:			
1940	Unobligated balance expiring	–2		
1941	Unexpired unobligated balance, end of year	1,220	1,218	1,215
	Change in obligated balance:			
	Unpaid obligations:			
3000	Unpaid obligations, brought forward, Oct 1	1,130	1,333	1,409
3010	New obligations, unexpired accounts	1,870	1,749	1,782
3011	Obligations ("upward adjustments"), expired accounts	20		
3020	Outlays (gross)	–1,595	–1,673	–1,718
3040	Recoveries of prior year unpaid obligations, unexpired	–32		
3041	Recoveries of prior year unpaid obligations, expired	–60		
3050	Unpaid obligations, end of year	1,333	1,409	1,473
	Memorandum (non-add) entries:			
3100	Obligated balance, start of year	1,130	1,333	1,409
3200	Obligated balance, end of year	1,333	1,409	1,473
	Budget authority and outlays, net:			
	Discretionary:			
4000	Budget authority, gross	1,751	1,749	1,779
	Outlays, gross:			
4010	Outlays from new discretionary authority	112	190	199
4011	Outlays from discretionary balances	1,483	1,483	1,519
4020	Outlays, gross (total)	1,595	1,673	1,718
	Offsets against gross budget authority and outlays:			
	Offsetting collections (collected) from:			
4030	Federal sources	–2		
4033	Non-Federal sources	–4		
4040	Offsets against gross budget authority and outlays (total)	–6		
	Additional offsets against gross budget authority only:			
4052	Offsetting collections credited to expired accounts	4		
4070	Budget authority, net (discretionary)	1,749	1,749	1,779
4080	Outlays, net (discretionary)	1,589	1,673	1,718
4180	Budget authority, net (total)	1,749	1,749	1,779
4190	Outlays, net (total)	1,589	1,673	1,718

Established in 1964 as part of the Economic Opportunity Act and authorized by the Workforce Innovation and Opportunity Act of 2014 (P.L. 113–128, Title 1, Subtitle C, section 141), Job Corps is the nation's largest federally-funded, primarily residential, training program for at-risk youth. Job Corps provides economically disadvantaged youth with academic, career technical and marketable skills to enter the workforce, enroll in post-secondary education, or enlist in the military. Job Corps participants must be economically disadvantaged youth, between the ages of 16–24, and meet one or more of the following criteria: basic skills deficient; a school dropout; homeless, a runaway, or a foster child; a parent; or in need of additional education, vocational training, or intensive counseling and related assistance in order to participate successfully in regular schoolwork or to secure and hold employment.

Large and small businesses, nonprofit organizations, Native American organizations and Alaskan Native corporations manage and operate the majority of the Job Corps centers through contractual agreements with the Department of Labor, while the remaining centers are operated through an interagency agreement with the U.S. Department of Agriculture.

Object Classification (in millions of dollars)

Identification code 016–0181–0–1–504		2021 actual	2022 est.	2023 est.
	Direct obligations:			
	Personnel compensation:			
11.1	Full-time permanent	80	79	85
11.3	Other than full-time permanent	1	1	1
11.5	Other personnel compensation		2	1
11.9	Total personnel compensation	81	82	87
12.1	Civilian personnel benefits	36	34	38

JOB CORPS—Continued
Object Classification—Continued

Identification code 016–0181–0–1–504		2021 actual	2022 est.	2023 est.
13.0	Benefits for former personnel	1	....	....
21.0	Travel and transportation of persons	1	1	1
22.0	Transportation of things	1	....	....
23.1	Rental payments to GSA	1	1	1
23.2	Rental payments to others	9	9	9
23.3	Communications, utilities, and miscellaneous charges	8	11	11
25.1	Advisory and assistance services	27	27	27
25.2	Other services from non-Federal sources	1,447	1,452	1,454
25.3	Other goods and services from Federal sources	34	30	33
25.4	Operation and maintenance of facilities	46	40	49
26.0	Supplies and materials	14	11	12
31.0	Equipment	3	1	2
32.0	Land and structures	159	38	48
41.0	Grants, subsidies, and contributions	2	12	10
99.0	Direct obligations	1,870	1,749	1,782
99.9	Total new obligations, unexpired accounts	1,870	1,749	1,782

Employment Summary

Identification code 016–0181–0–1–504		2021 actual	2022 est.	2023 est.
1001	Direct civilian full-time equivalent employment	124	140	170

COMMUNITY SERVICE EMPLOYMENT FOR OLDER AMERICANS

To carry out title V of the Older Americans Act of 1965 (referred to in this Act as "OAA"), $405,000,000, which shall be available for the period April 1, 2023 through June 30, 2024, and may be recaptured and reobligated in accordance with section 517(c) of the OAA.

Note.—A full-year 2022 appropriation for this account was not enacted at the time the Budget was prepared; therefore, the Budget assumes this account is operating under the Continuing Appropriations Act, 2022 (Division A of Public Law 117–43, as amended). The amounts included for 2022 reflect the annualized level provided by the continuing resolution.

Program and Financing (in millions of dollars)

Identification code 016–0175–0–1–504		2021 actual	2022 est.	2023 est.
	Obligations by program activity:			
0001	National programs	464	417	405
	Budgetary resources:			
	Unobligated balance:			
1000	Unobligated balance brought forward, Oct 1	55	2	....
1010	Unobligated balance transfer to other accts [016–0172]	–2	....	....
1012	Unobligated balance transfers between expired and unexpired accounts	9	10	....
1070	Unobligated balance (total)	62	12	....
	Budget authority:			
	Appropriations, discretionary:			
1100	Appropriation	405	405	405
1120	Appropriations transferred to other acct [016–0172]	–1	....	....
1160	Appropriation, discretionary (total)	404	405	405
1930	Total budgetary resources available	466	417	405
	Memorandum (non-add) entries:			
1941	Unexpired unobligated balance, end of year	2	....	....
	Change in obligated balance:			
	Unpaid obligations:			
3000	Unpaid obligations, brought forward, Oct 1	308	370	340
3010	New obligations, unexpired accounts	464	417	405
3020	Outlays (gross)	–391	–447	–405
3041	Recoveries of prior year unpaid obligations, expired	–11	....	....
3050	Unpaid obligations, end of year	370	340	340
	Memorandum (non-add) entries:			
3100	Obligated balance, start of year	308	370	340
3200	Obligated balance, end of year	370	340	340
	Budget authority and outlays, net:			
	Discretionary:			
4000	Budget authority, gross	404	405	405
	Outlays, gross:			
4010	Outlays from new discretionary authority	60	77	77
4011	Outlays from discretionary balances	331	370	328
4020	Outlays, gross (total)	391	447	405
4180	Budget authority, net (total)	404	405	405
4190	Outlays, net (total)	391	447	405

Community Service Employment for Older Americans (CSEOA) is a community service and work-based job training program for older Americans. Authorized by Title IV of the Older Americans Act, as amended, and reauthorized in 2020 (P.L. 116–131), the program provides training for low-income, unemployed seniors ages 55 and older. Participants gain work experience in a variety of community service activities at non-profit and public facilities, including schools, hospitals, day-care centers, and senior centers. The program provides over 40 million community service hours to public and non-profit agencies, allowing them to enhance and provide needed services.

Object Classification (in millions of dollars)

Identification code 016–0175–0–1–504		2021 actual	2022 est.	2023 est.
	Direct obligations:			
25.2	Other services from non-Federal sources	5	10	....
25.7	Operation and maintenance of equipment	4	....	1
41.0	Grants, subsidies, and contributions	455	407	404
99.9	Total new obligations, unexpired accounts	464	417	405

FEDERAL UNEMPLOYMENT BENEFITS AND ALLOWANCES

For payments during fiscal year 2023 of trade adjustment benefit payments and allowances under part I of subchapter B of chapter 2 of title II of the Trade Act of 1974, and section 246 of that Act; and for training, employment and case management services, allowances for job search and relocation, and related State administrative expenses under part II of subchapter B of chapter 2 of title II of the Trade Act of 1974, and including benefit payments, allowances, training, employment and case management services, and related State administration provided pursuant to section 231(a) of the Trade Adjustment Assistance Extension Act of 2011, and sections 405(a) and 406 of the Trade Preferences Extension Act of 2015, $494,400,000 together with such amounts as may be necessary to be charged to the subsequent appropriation for payments for any period subsequent to September 15, 2023: Provided, That notwithstanding section 502 of this Act, any part of the appropriation provided under this heading may remain available for obligation beyond the current fiscal year pursuant to the authorities of section 245(c) of the Trade Act of 1974 (19 U.S.C. 2317(c)): Provided further, That the termination provisions in sections 246(b) and 285(a) of the Trade Act of 1974, as amended, including the application of those provisions described in paragraphs (4) and (7) of section 406(a) of the Trade Preferences Extension Act of 2015, shall not apply.

Note.—A full-year 2022 appropriation for this account was not enacted at the time the Budget was prepared; therefore, the Budget assumes this account is operating under the Continuing Appropriations Act, 2022 (Division A of Public Law 117–43, as amended). The amounts included for 2022 reflect the annualized level provided by the continuing resolution.

Program and Financing (in millions of dollars)

Identification code 016–0326–0–1–999		2021 actual	2022 est.	2023 est.
	Obligations by program activity:			
0001	Trade Adjustment Assistance benefits	58	140	219
0002	Trade Adjustment Assistance training and other activities	370	224	266
0005	Wage Insurance Payments	13	13	9
0900	Total new obligations, unexpired accounts (object class 41.0)	441	377	494
	Budgetary resources:			
	Unobligated balance:			
1000	Unobligated balance brought forward, Oct 1	....	1	133
	Budget authority:			
	Appropriations, mandatory:			
1200	Appropriation	634	540	494
1230	Appropriations and/or unobligated balance of appropriations permanently reduced	–36	–31	–28
1260	Appropriations, mandatory (total)	598	509	466
1900	Budget authority (total)	598	509	466

1930	Total budgetary resources available	598	510	599
	Memorandum (non-add) entries:			
1940	Unobligated balance expiring	−156		
1941	Unexpired unobligated balance, end of year	1	133	105
	Change in obligated balance:			
	Unpaid obligations:			
3000	Unpaid obligations, brought forward, Oct 1	1,071	1,031	532
3010	New obligations, unexpired accounts	441	377	494
3020	Outlays (gross)	−214	−474	−406
3041	Recoveries of prior year unpaid obligations, expired	−267	−402	−402
3050	Unpaid obligations, end of year	1,031	532	218
	Memorandum (non-add) entries:			
3100	Obligated balance, start of year	1,071	1,031	532
3200	Obligated balance, end of year	1,031	532	218
	Budget authority and outlays, net:			
	Mandatory:			
4090	Budget authority, gross	598	509	466
	Outlays, gross:			
4100	Outlays from new mandatory authority	52	281	226
4101	Outlays from mandatory balances	162	193	180
4110	Outlays, gross (total)	214	474	406
4180	Budget authority, net (total)	598	509	466
4190	Outlays, net (total)	214	474	406

The Federal Unemployment Benefits and Allowances (FUBA) account funds the Trade Adjustment Assistance (TAA) for Workers program, which provides income support through Trade Readjustment Allowances (TRA); funding for training, employment and case management services, job search allowances, and relocation allowances through Training and Other Activities; and wage supplements through Alternative/Reemployment Trade Adjustment Assistance (A/RTAA). $494,400,000 will fund these activities of the TAA program in Fiscal Year 2023, assuming a continuation of the reversion program currently in effect.

STATE UNEMPLOYMENT INSURANCE AND EMPLOYMENT SERVICE OPERATIONS

For authorized administrative expenses, $107,066,000, together with not to exceed $4,151,107,000 which may be expended from the Employment Security Administration Account in the Unemployment Trust Fund ("the Trust Fund"), of which—

(1) $3,184,635,000 from the Trust Fund is for grants to States for the administration of State unemployment insurance laws as authorized under title III of the Social Security Act (including not less than $375,000,000 to carry out reemployment services and eligibility assessments under section 306 of such Act, any claimants of regular compensation, as defined in such section, including those who are profiled as most likely to exhaust their benefits, may be eligible for such services and assessments: Provided, That of such amount, $117,000,000 is specified for grants under section 306 of the Social Security Act and $258,000,000 is additional new budget authority specified for purposes of the budgetary adjustments under section 314(g) of the Congressional Budget Act of 1974; and $9,000,000 for continued support of the Unemployment Insurance Integrity Center of Excellence), the administration of unemployment insurance for Federal employees and for ex-service members as authorized under 5 U.S.C. 8501–8523, and the administration of trade readjustment allowances, reemployment trade adjustment assistance, and alternative trade adjustment assistance under the Trade Act of 1974 and under section 231(a) of the Trade Adjustment Assistance Extension Act of 2011, and sections 405(a) and 406 of the Trade Preferences Extension Act of 2015 (except that the termination provisions in sections 246(b) and 285(a) of the Trade Act of 1974, as amended, including the application of those provisions described in paragraphs (4) and (7) of section 406 of the Trade Preferences Extension Act of 2015, shall not apply), and shall be available for obligation by the States through December 31, 2023, except that funds used for automation shall be available for Federal obligation through December 31, 2023, and for State obligation through September 30, 2025, or, if the automation is being carried out through consortia of States, for State obligation through September 30, 2029, and for expenditure through September 30, 2030, and funds for competitive grants awarded to States for improved operations and to conduct in-person reemployment and eligibility assessments and unemployment insurance improper payment reviews and provide reemployment services and referrals to training, as appropriate, shall be available for Federal obligation through December 31, 2023 (except that funds for outcome payments pursuant to section 306(f)(2) of the Social Security Act shall be available for Federal obligation through March 31, 2024), and for obligation by the States through September 30, 2025, and funds for the Unemployment Insurance Integrity Center of Excellence shall be available for obligation by the State through September 30, 2024, and funds used for unemployment insurance workloads experienced through September 30, 2023 shall be available for Federal obligation through December 31, 2023;

(2) $168,174,000 from the Trust Fund is for national activities necessary to support the administration of the Federal-State unemployment insurance system;

(3) $677,449,000 from the Trust Fund, together with $21,413,000 from the General Fund of the Treasury, is for grants to States in accordance with section 6 of the Wagner-Peyser Act, and shall be available for Federal obligation for the period July 1, 2023 through June 30, 2024;

(4) $22,318,000 from the Trust Fund is for national activities of the Employment Service, including administration of the work opportunity tax credit under section 51 of the Internal Revenue Code of 1986 (including assisting States in adopting or modernizing information technology for use in the processing of certification requests), and the provision of technical assistance and staff training under the Wagner-Peyser Act;

(5) $98,531,000 from the Trust Fund is for the administration of foreign labor certifications and related activities under the Immigration and Nationality Act and related laws, of which $70,249,000 shall be available for the Federal administration of such activities, and $28,282,000 shall be available for grants to States for the administration of such activities; and

(6) $85,653,000 from the General Fund is to provide workforce information, national electronic tools, and one-stop system building under the Wagner-Peyser Act and shall be available for Federal obligation for the period July 1, 2023 through June 30, 2024, of which up to $9,800,000 shall be used to carry out research and demonstration projects related to testing effective ways to promote greater labor force participation of people with disabilities: Provided, That the Secretary may transfer amounts made available for research and demonstration projects under this paragraph to the "Office of Disability Employment Policy" account for such purposes:

Provided, That to the extent that the Average Weekly Insured Unemployment ("AWIU") for fiscal year 2023 is projected by the Department of Labor to exceed 1,778,000, an additional $28,600,000 from the Trust Fund shall be available for obligation for every 100,000 increase in the AWIU level (including a pro rata amount for any increment less than 100,000) to carry out title III of the Social Security Act: Provided further, That funds appropriated in this Act that are allotted to a State to carry out activities under title III of the Social Security Act may be used by such State to assist other States in carrying out activities under such title III if the other States include areas that have suffered a major disaster declared by the President under the Robert T. Stafford Disaster Relief and Emergency Assistance Act: Provided further, That the Secretary may use funds appropriated for grants to States under title III of the Social Security Act to make payments on behalf of States for the use of the National Directory of New Hires under section 453(j)(8) of such Act: Provided further, That the Secretary may use funds appropriated for grants to States under title III of the Social Security Act to make payments on behalf of States to the entity operating the State Information Data Exchange System: Provided further, That funds appropriated in this Act which are used to establish a national one-stop career center system, or which are used to support the national activities of the Federal-State unemployment insurance, employment service, or immigration programs, may be obligated in contracts, grants, or agreements with States and non-State entities: Provided further, That States awarded competitive grants for improved operations under title III of the Social Security Act, or awarded grants to support the national activities of the Federal-State unemployment insurance system, may award subgrants to other States and non-State entities under such grants, subject to the conditions applicable to the grants: Provided further, That funds appropriated under this Act for activities authorized under title III of the Social Security Act and the Wagner-Peyser Act may be used by States to fund integrated Unemployment Insurance and Employment Service automation efforts, notwithstanding cost allocation principles prescribed under the final rule entitled "Uniform Administrative Requirements, Cost Principles, and Audit Requirements for Federal Awards" at part 200 of title 2, Code of Federal Regulations: Provided further, That the Secretary, at the request of a State participating in a consortium with other States, may reallot funds allotted to such State under title III of the Social Security Act to other States participating in the consortium or to the entity operating the Unemployment Insurance Information Technology Support Center in order to carry out activities that benefit the administration of the unemployment compensation law of the State making the request: Provided further, That the Secretary may collect fees for the costs associated with additional data collection, analyses, and reporting services relating to the National Agricultural Workers Survey requested by State and local governments, public and private institutions of higher education, and nonprofit organizations and may utilize such sums, in accordance with the provisions of 29 U.S.C. 9a, for the National Ag-

Employment and Training Administration—Continued
Federal Funds—Continued

STATE UNEMPLOYMENT INSURANCE AND EMPLOYMENT SERVICE
OPERATIONS—Continued

ricultural Workers Survey infrastructure, methodology, and data to meet the information collection and reporting needs of such entities, which shall be credited to this appropriation and shall remain available until September 30, 2024, for such purposes.

Note.—A full-year 2022 appropriation for this account was not enacted at the time the Budget was prepared; therefore, the Budget assumes this account is operating under the Continuing Appropriations Act, 2022 (Division A of Public Law 117–43, as amended). The amounts included for 2022 reflect the annualized level provided by the continuing resolution.

Program and Financing (in millions of dollars)

Identification code 016–0179–0–1–999	2021 actual	2022 est.	2023 est.
Obligations by program activity:			
0001 UI State Admin, RESEA, and EUC Admin	4,000	2,721	3,185
0002 UI National Activities	18	18	168
0010 ES Grants to States	668	670	699
0011 ES National Activities	22	22	22
0012 Workforce Information	62	90	86
0014 Foreign Labor Certification	78	78	99
0015 H-1B Fees	17	27	20
0016 CARES Act	3,595	802	....
0017 UI Fraud - ARP	141	773	800
0799 Total direct obligations	8,601	5,201	5,079
0801 Reimbursable program DUA administration	10	51	51
0803 Reimbursable program NAWS surveys	1	2	2
0899 Total reimbursable obligations	11	53	53
0900 Total new obligations, unexpired accounts	8,612	5,254	5,132
Budgetary resources:			
Unobligated balance:			
1000 Unobligated balance brought forward, Oct 1	97	1,990	1,081
1001 Discretionary unobligated balance brought fwd, Oct 1	85	125	
1010 Unobligated balance transfer to ETA PA [016–0172]	–3		
1010 Unobligated balance transfer to Disaster Relief Fund [070–0702]	–1	–6	
1010 Unobligated balance transfer to DOL CEO [016–0165]		–5	
1021 Recoveries of prior year unpaid obligations	1	27	
1070 Unobligated balance (total)	94	2,006	1,081
Budget authority:			
Appropriations, discretionary:			
1100 Appropriation	84	84	107
1130 Appropriations permanently reduced		–8	
1160 Appropriation, discretionary (total)	84	76	107
Appropriations, mandatory:			
1200 Appropriation	1,994		
1201 Appropriation (H-1B Fees)	27	19	20
1203 Appropriation (previously unavailable)(special or trust)	1	2	1
1230 Appropriations and/or unobligated balance of appropriations permanently reduced	–8		
1232 Appropriations and/or unobligated balance of appropriations temporarily reduced	–2	–1	–1
1260 Appropriations, mandatory (total)	2,012	20	20
Spending authority from offsetting collections, discretionary:			
1700 Collected	4,719	3,431	4,203
1701 Change in uncollected payments, Federal sources	98		
1750 Spending auth from offsetting collections, disc (total)	4,817	3,431	4,203
Spending authority from offsetting collections, mandatory:			
1800 Offsetting collections [EUC Admin and CARES]	2,355	802	
1801 Change in uncollected payments, Federal sources	1,240		
1850 Spending auth from offsetting collections, mand (total)	3,595	802	
1900 Budget authority (total)	10,508	4,329	4,330
1930 Total budgetary resources available	10,602	6,335	5,411
Memorandum (non-add) entries:			
1941 Unexpired unobligated balance, end of year	1,990	1,081	279
Change in obligated balance:			
Unpaid obligations:			
3000 Unpaid obligations, brought forward, Oct 1	3,571	5,108	3,853
3010 New obligations, unexpired accounts	8,612	5,254	5,132
3011 Obligations ("upward adjustments"), expired accounts	6		
3020 Outlays (gross)	–7,070	–6,482	–5,244
3040 Recoveries of prior year unpaid obligations, unexpired	–1	–27	
3041 Recoveries of prior year unpaid obligations, expired	–10		
3050 Unpaid obligations, end of year	5,108	3,853	3,741
Uncollected payments:			
3060 Uncollected pymts, Fed sources, brought forward, Oct 1	–2,779	–4,035	–4,035
3070 Change in uncollected pymts, Fed sources, unexpired	–1,338		
3071 Change in uncollected pymts, Fed sources, expired	82		
3090 Uncollected pymts, Fed sources, end of year	–4,035	–4,035	–4,035
Memorandum (non-add) entries:			
3100 Obligated balance, start of year	792	1,073	–182
3200 Obligated balance, end of year	1,073	–182	–294
Budget authority and outlays, net:			
Discretionary:			
4000 Budget authority, gross	4,901	3,507	4,310
Outlays, gross:			
4010 Outlays from new discretionary authority	2,510	2,120	2,689
4011 Outlays from discretionary balances	2,182	2,195	1,437
4020 Outlays, gross (total)	4,692	4,315	4,126
Offsets against gross budget authority and outlays:			
Offsetting collections (collected) from:			
4030 Federal sources [ES Grants to States]	–649	–649	–677
4030 Federal sources [ES Natl Activities]	–22	–22	–22
4030 Federal sources [FLC Fed Admin]	–58	–58	–70
4030 Federal sources [FLC State Grants]	–20	–20	–28
4030 Federal sources [NAWS]	–1	–2	–2
4030 Federal sources [UI Admin/Natl Activities]	–3,831	–2,429	–2,978
4030 Federal sources [RESEA]	–200	–200	–375
4030 Federal sources [DUA]	–10	–51	–51
4040 Offsets against gross budget authority and outlays (total)	–4,791	–3,431	–4,203
Additional offsets against gross budget authority only:			
4050 Change in uncollected pymts, Fed sources, unexpired	–98		
4052 Offsetting collections credited to expired accounts	72		
4060 Additional offsets against budget authority only (total)	–26		
4070 Budget authority, net (discretionary)	84	76	107
4080 Outlays, net (discretionary)	–99	884	–77
Mandatory:			
4090 Budget authority, gross	5,607	822	20
Outlays, gross:			
4100 Outlays from new mandatory authority	6	762	20
4101 Outlays from mandatory balances	2,372	1,405	1,098
4110 Outlays, gross (total)	2,378	2,167	1,118
Offsets against gross budget authority and outlays:			
Offsetting collections (collected) from:			
4120 Federal sources	–2,355	–802	
Additional offsets against gross budget authority only:			
4140 Change in uncollected pymts, Fed sources, unexpired	–1,240		
4160 Budget authority, net (mandatory)	2,012	20	20
4170 Outlays, net (mandatory)	23	1,365	1,118
4180 Budget authority, net (total)	2,096	96	127
4190 Outlays, net (total)	–76	2,249	1,041

Unemployment compensation.—State administration amounts provide administrative grants to State agencies that pay unemployment compensation to eligible workers and collect State unemployment taxes from employers. These agencies also pay unemployment benefits to former Federal personnel and ex-servicemembers as well as trade readjustment allowances to eligible individuals. State administration amounts also provide administrative grants to State agencies to improve the integrity and financial stability of the unemployment compensation program through a comprehensive performance management system, UI Performs. The purpose is to effect continuous improvement in State performance and implement activities designed to reduce errors and prevent fraud, waste, and abuse in the payment of unemployment compensation benefits and the collection of unemployment taxes. National activities relating to the Federal-State unemployment insurance programs are conducted through contracts or agreements with the State agencies or non-State entities. A workload contingency reserve is included in State administration to meet increases in the costs of administering the program resulting from increases in the number of unemployment claims filed and paid. The appropriation automatically provides additional funds whenever unemployment claim workloads increase above levels specified in the appropriations language.

UNEMPLOYMENT COMPENSATION PROGRAM STATISTICS

	2020 actual	2021 actual	2022 est.	2023 est.
Basic workload (in thousands):				
Employer tax accounts	8,691	9,092	9,257	9,250
Employee wage items recorded	697,089	710,207	717,439	735,677
Initial claims taken	65,266	38,959	16,144	13,060
Weeks claimed	473,886	264,487	109,865	91,875

Nonmonetary determinations	8,539	10,268	8,265	7,080
Appeals	1,136	1,504	1,339	1,141
Covered employment	134,758	139,779	144,633	146,830

Employment service.—The public employment service is a nationwide system providing no-fee employment services to job-seekers and employers. State employment service activities are financed by grants provided by formula to States. Funding allotments are provided annually on a Program Year basis beginning July 1 and ending June 30 of the following year.

Employment service activities serving national needs are conducted through specific reimbursable agreements between the States and the Federal Government under the Wagner-Peyser Act, as amended, and other legislation. States also receive funding under this activity for administration of the Work Opportunity Tax Credit, as well as for amortization payments for those States that had independent retirement plans prior to 1980 in their State employment service agencies.

EMPLOYMENT SERVICE PROGRAM STATISTICS

	2020 actual	2021 est.	2022 est.	2023 est.
Number of Participants Served	2,437,906	2,445,445	2,445,445	2,550,591

Foreign Labor Certification.—This activity provides for the administration and operation of the foreign labor certification programs within the Employment and Training Administration. Under these programs, U.S. employers that can demonstrate a shortage of qualified, available U.S. workers and no adverse impact on similarly situated U.S. workers may seek the Secretary of Labor's certification as a first step in the multi-agency process required to hire a foreign worker to fill critical permanent or temporary vacancies. Major programs include the permanent, H-2A temporary agricultural, H-2B temporary non-agricultural, CW-1 temporary, and H-1B temporary highly skilled worker visas. The account is divided into Federal and State activities.

Federal Administration.—Federal Administration provides leadership, policy, budget, program operations including staffing (Federal and contractors), information technology, three national processing center facilities, and operational direction to Federal activities supporting the effective and efficient administration of foreign labor certification programs.

State grants.—State grants provides grants to State workforce agencies in 50 States and 5 U.S. territories funding employment-related activities required for the administration of Federal foreign labor certification programs. Activities include State Workforce Agency posting and circulation of job orders and other assistance to employers in the recruitment of U.S. workers, processing of employer requests for prevailing wage determinations for the permanent and temporary programs, State safety inspection of housing provided by employers to workers, and State development of prevailing wage and prevailing practice surveys used to set wages and standards in a defined geographic area.

Workforce Information, Electronic Tools, and System Building.—These funds are used to support the joint Federal-State efforts to improve the comprehensive American Job Center system authorized under the Workforce Innovation and Opportunity Act. This system provides workers and employers with quick and easy access to a wide array of enhanced career development and labor market information services. A portion of these funds supports a joint initiative between the Employment and Training Administration and the Office of Disability Employment Policy to improve the accessibility and accountability of the public workforce development system for individuals with disabilities.

National Agricultural Workers Survey fee.—The Department of Labor conducts the National Agricultural Workers Survey (NAWS), which collects information annually about the demographic, employment, and health characteristics of the U.S. crop labor force. The information is obtained directly from farm workers through face-to-face interviews.

Object Classification (in millions of dollars)

Identification code 016–0179–0–1–999		2021 actual	2022 est.	2023 est.
	Direct obligations:			
	Personnel compensation:			
11.1	Full-time permanent	22	45	53
11.5	Other personnel compensation	1	1	1
11.9	Total personnel compensation	23	46	54
12.1	Civilian personnel benefits	9	19	22
23.1	Rental payments to GSA	3	3	3
25.1	Advisory and assistance services	19	18	18
25.2	Other services from non-Federal sources	19	57	47
25.3	Other goods and services from Federal sources	30	72	87
25.4	Operation and maintenance of facilities			1
25.7	Operation and maintenance of equipment	9	16	18
41.0	Grants, subsidies, and contributions	7,879	4,970	4,829
42.0	Insurance claims and indemnities	610		
99.0	Direct obligations	8,601	5,201	5,079
99.0	Reimbursable obligations	11	53	53
99.9	Total new obligations, unexpired accounts	8,612	5,254	5,132

Employment Summary

Identification code 016–0179–0–1–999		2021 actual	2022 est.	2023 est.
1001	Direct civilian full-time equivalent employment	159	250	284
1001	Direct civilian full-time equivalent employment	35	44	44

PAYMENTS TO THE UNEMPLOYMENT TRUST FUND

Program and Financing (in millions of dollars)

Identification code 016–0178–0–1–603		2021 actual	2022 est.	2023 est.
	Obligations by program activity:			
0010	Payments to EUCA	169,386		
0012	Payments to ESAA	4,969	850	
0013	Payments to the FUA	6,569		
0900	Total new obligations, unexpired accounts (object class 94.0)	180,924	850	
	Budgetary resources:			
	Budget authority:			
	Appropriations, mandatory:			
1200	Appropriation (indefinite)	180,924	850	
1930	Total budgetary resources available	180,924	850	
	Change in obligated balance:			
	Unpaid obligations:			
3010	New obligations, unexpired accounts	180,924	850	
3020	Outlays (gross)	–180,924	–850	
	Budget authority and outlays, net:			
	Mandatory:			
4090	Budget authority, gross	180,924	850	
	Outlays, gross:			
4100	Outlays from new mandatory authority	180,924	850	
4180	Budget authority, net (total)	180,924	850	
4190	Outlays, net (total)	180,924	850	

This account provides for general fund financing of extended unemployment benefit programs under certain statutes. It is also the mechanism used to make general fund reimbursements for some or all of the benefits and administrative costs incurred for temporary Federal programs. These funds are transferred from the Payments to the Unemployment Trust Fund account to a receipt account in the Unemployment Trust Fund (UTF) so that resources may be transferred to the Employment Security Administration Account in the UTF for administrative costs, or to the Extended Unemployment Compensation Account or the Federal Unemployment Account in the UTF for benefit costs.

SHORT TIME COMPENSATION PROGRAMS

Program and Financing (in millions of dollars)

Identification code 016–0168–0–1–603	2021 actual	2022 est.	2023 est.
Obligations by program activity:			
0001 Grants	....	1	....
0002 Benefits	651	....	....
0900 Total new obligations, unexpired accounts	651	1	....
Budgetary resources:			
Unobligated balance:			
1000 Unobligated balance brought forward, Oct 1	1	1	....
Budget authority:			
Appropriations, mandatory:			
1200 Appropriation	651	....	....
1900 Budget authority (total)	651	....	....
1930 Total budgetary resources available	652	1	....
Memorandum (non-add) entries:			
1941 Unexpired unobligated balance, end of year	1	....	....
Change in obligated balance:			
Unpaid obligations:			
3000 Unpaid obligations, brought forward, Oct 1	419	381	332
3010 New obligations, unexpired accounts	651	1	....
3020 Outlays (gross)	–689	–50	–50
3050 Unpaid obligations, end of year	381	332	282
Memorandum (non-add) entries:			
3100 Obligated balance, start of year	419	381	332
3200 Obligated balance, end of year	381	332	282
Budget authority and outlays, net:			
Mandatory:			
4090 Budget authority, gross	651	....	....
Outlays, gross:			
4101 Outlays from mandatory balances	689	50	50
4180 Budget authority, net (total)	651	....	....
4190 Outlays, net (total)	689	50	50

The Coronavirus Aid, Relief, and Economic Security Act (Public Law 116–136) provided as an incentive for states to enact state Short-Time Compensation (STC) programs and promote the use of STC, 100 percent reimbursement of STC benefit costs paid under state law for weeks ending on or before December 31, 2020. The Continued Assistance for Unemployed Workers Act of 2020 (Public Law 116–260) extended the 100 percent STC reimbursements to include weeks of unemployment ending on or before March 14, 2021, and the American Rescue Plan Act (Public Law 117–2) further extended the 100 percent STC reimbursements to include weeks of unemployment ending on or before September 6, 2021. Grant funding was also available to states whose permanent STC laws meet the Federal definition.

Object Classification (in millions of dollars)

Identification code 016–0168–0–1–603	2021 actual	2022 est.	2023 est.
Direct obligations:			
41.0 Grants, subsidies, and contributions	....	1	....
42.0 Insurance claims and indemnities	651	....	....
99.9 Total new obligations, unexpired accounts	651	1	....

FEDERAL ADDITIONAL UNEMPLOYMENT COMPENSATION PROGRAM, RECOVERY

Program and Financing (in millions of dollars)

Identification code 016–1800–0–1–603	2021 actual	2022 est.	2023 est.
Obligations by program activity:			
0001 Federal Additional Unemployment Compensation Program, Recovery (Direct)	187,295	47	....
0900 Total new obligations, unexpired accounts (object class 42.0)	187,295	47	....
Budgetary resources:			
Unobligated balance:			
1029 Other balances withdrawn to Treasury	–2	....	....
1033 Recoveries of prior year paid obligations	2	....	....
Budget authority:			
Appropriations, mandatory:			
1200 Appropriation	187,295	47	....
1900 Budget authority (total)	187,295	47	....
1930 Total budgetary resources available	187,295	47	....
Change in obligated balance:			
Unpaid obligations:			
3000 Unpaid obligations, brought forward, Oct 1	4,284	28,879	23,036
3010 New obligations, unexpired accounts	187,295	47	....
3020 Outlays (gross)	–162,700	–5,890	–4,630
3050 Unpaid obligations, end of year	28,879	23,036	18,406
Memorandum (non-add) entries:			
3100 Obligated balance, start of year	4,284	28,879	23,036
3200 Obligated balance, end of year	28,879	23,036	18,406
Budget authority and outlays, net:			
Mandatory:			
4090 Budget authority, gross	187,295	47	....
Outlays, gross:			
4100 Outlays from new mandatory authority	162,699	47	....
4101 Outlays from mandatory balances	1	5,843	4,630
4110 Outlays, gross (total)	162,700	5,890	4,630
Offsets against gross budget authority and outlays:			
Offsetting collections (collected) from:			
4123 Non-Federal sources	–2	....	....
Additional offsets against gross budget authority only:			
4143 Recoveries of prior year paid obligations, unexpired accounts	2	....	....
4160 Budget authority, net (mandatory)	187,295	47	....
4170 Outlays, net (mandatory)	162,698	5,890	4,630
4180 Budget authority, net (total)	187,295	47	....
4190 Outlays, net (total)	162,698	5,890	4,630

This account provides mandatory general revenue funding for Federal Pandemic Unemployment Compensation (FPUC), a temporary program established under the Coronavirus Aid, Relief, and Economic Security Act (Public Law 116–136). This program paid a supplement of $600 on every week of unemployment compensation through July 31, 2020. It was then reauthorized by the Continued Assistance for Unemployed Workers Act of 2020 (Public Law 116–260) and modified to provide $300 per week in supplemental benefits for weeks of unemployment beginning after December 26, 2020, and ending on or before March 14, 2021. In addition to reestablishing the FPUC program, the Continued Assistance for Unemployed Workers Act of 2020 established the Mixed Earners Unemployment Compensation (MEUC) program, which paid a $100 supplemental to certain claimants with self-employment income for weeks of unemployment ending on or before March 14, 2021. The FAUC account also provides funding for the MEUC program. The American Rescue Plan Act (Public Law 117–2) extended the FPUC program at $300 per week and the MEUC program at $100 per week for certain claimants for weeks of unemployment ending on or before September 6, 2021.

ADVANCES TO THE UNEMPLOYMENT TRUST FUND AND OTHER FUNDS

For repayable advances to the Unemployment Trust Fund as authorized by sections 905(d) and 1203 of the Social Security Act, and to the Black Lung Disability Trust Fund as authorized by section 9501(c)(1) of the Internal Revenue Code of 1986; and for nonrepayable advances to the revolving fund established by section 901(e) of the Social Security Act, to the Unemployment Trust Fund as authorized by 5 U.S.C. 8509, and to the "Federal Unemployment Benefits and Allowances" account, such sums as may be necessary, which shall be available for obligation through September 30, 2024.

Note.—A full-year 2022 appropriation for this account was not enacted at the time the Budget was prepared; therefore, the Budget assumes this account is operating under the Continuing Appropriations Act, 2022 (Division A of Public Law 117–43, as amended). The amounts included for 2022 reflect the annualized level provided by the continuing resolution.

This appropriation makes available funding for repayable advances (loans) to two accounts in the Unemployment Trust Fund (UTF): the Extended

Unemployment Compensation Account (EUCA) which pays the Federal share of extended unemployment benefits, and the Federal Unemployment Account (FUA) which makes loans to States to fund unemployment benefits. In addition, the account has provided repayable advances to the Black Lung Disability Trust Fund (BLDTF) when its balances proved insufficient to make payments from that account. The BLDTF now has authority to borrow directly from the Treasury under the trust fund debt restructuring provisions of Public Law 110–343. Repayable advances are shown as borrowing authority within the UTF or the BLDTF, and they do not appear as budget authority or outlays in the Advances to the Unemployment Trust Fund and Other Funds account.

This appropriation also makes available funding as needed for nonrepayable advances to the Federal Employees Compensation Account (FECA) to pay the costs of unemployment compensation for former Federal employees and ex-servicemembers, and to the Federal Unemployment Benefits and Allowances (FUBA) account to pay the costs of benefits and services under the Trade Adjustment Assistance (TAA) for Workers program. These advances are shown as budget authority and outlays in the Advances account. The 2014 appropriations language included new authority for nonrepayable advances to the revolving fund for the Employment Security Administration Account (ESAA) in the UTF. In turn, this revolving fund may provide repayable, interest-bearing advances to the ESAA if it runs short of funds, and the borrowing authority will enable the ESAA to cover its obligations despite seasonal variations in the account's receipts.

The Department estimates that $3 billion will be borrowed during Fiscal Year 2022 and an additional $3 billion will be borrowed in Fiscal Year 2023. Detail on the nonrepayable advances is provided above; detail on the repayable advances is shown separately in the UTF or the BLDTF.

To address the potential need for significant and somewhat unpredictable advances to various accounts, the Congress appropriates such sums as necessary for advances to all of the potential recipient accounts. The Fiscal Year 2023 request continues this authority.

PROGRAM ADMINISTRATION

For expenses of administering employment and training programs, $153,793,000, together with not to exceed $68,840,000 which may be expended from the Employment Security Administration Account in the Unemployment Trust Fund.

Note.—A full-year 2022 appropriation for this account was not enacted at the time the Budget was prepared; therefore, the Budget assumes this account is operating under the Continuing Appropriations Act, 2022 (Division A of Public Law 117–43, as amended). The amounts included for 2022 reflect the annualized level provided by the continuing resolution.

Program and Financing (in millions of dollars)

Identification code 016–0172–0–1–504		2021 actual	2022 est.	2023 est.
Obligations by program activity:				
0003	Workforce security	46	43	59
0004	Apprenticeship training, employer and labor services	36	36	49
0005	Executive direction	9	9	11
0006	Training & Employment Services	75	71	104
0007	ARP Act	1	5	2
0008	CARES Act	2	1	
0799	Total direct obligations	169	165	225
0803	Reimbursable programs (DUA/E-grants/VOPAR/VRAP)	5	9	9
0900	Total new obligations, unexpired accounts	174	174	234
Budgetary resources:				
Unobligated balance:				
1000	Unobligated balance brought forward, Oct 1	7	15	9
1001	Discretionary unobligated balance brought fwd, Oct 1	7	15	
1011	Unobligated balance transfer from ETA SUIESO [016–0179]	3		
1011	Unobligated balance transfer from CSEOA [016–0175]	2		
1011	Unobligated balance transfer from TES Multi-Year Acct [016–0174]	1		
1070	Unobligated balance (total)	13	15	9
Budget authority:				
Appropriations, discretionary:				
1100	Appropriation	109	109	154
1121	Appropriations transferred from other acct ETA CSEOA [016–0175]	1		
1121	Appropriations transferred from other acct ETA TES [016–0174]	1		
1160	Appropriation, discretionary (total)	111	109	154
Advance appropriations, discretionary:				
1173	Advance appropriations transferred from TES Advance from FY 2020 [016–0174]	1		
Appropriations, mandatory:				
1200	Appropriation	8		
Spending authority from offsetting collections, discretionary:				
1700	Offsetting collections (UTF)	50	50	69
1700	Collected [DUA/eGrants/Grants Management/TA to PA]	5	9	9
1701	Change in uncollected payments, Federal sources	1		
1750	Spending auth from offsetting collections, disc (total)	56	59	78
1900	Budget authority (total)	176	168	232
1930	Total budgetary resources available	189	183	241
Memorandum (non-add) entries:				
1941	Unexpired unobligated balance, end of year	15	9	7
Change in obligated balance:				
Unpaid obligations:				
3000	Unpaid obligations, brought forward, Oct 1	15	26	17
3010	New obligations, unexpired accounts	174	174	234
3011	Obligations ("upward adjustments"), expired accounts	1		
3020	Outlays (gross)	–163	–183	–228
3041	Recoveries of prior year unpaid obligations, expired	–1		
3050	Unpaid obligations, end of year	26	17	23
Uncollected payments:				
3060	Uncollected pymts, Fed sources, brought forward, Oct 1	–4	–5	–5
3070	Change in uncollected pymts, Fed sources, unexpired	–1		
3090	Uncollected pymts, Fed sources, end of year	–5	–5	–5
Memorandum (non-add) entries:				
3100	Obligated balance, start of year	11	21	12
3200	Obligated balance, end of year	21	12	18
Budget authority and outlays, net:				
Discretionary:				
4000	Budget authority, gross	168	168	232
Outlays, gross:				
4010	Outlays from new discretionary authority	151	158	218
4011	Outlays from discretionary balances	12	23	10
4020	Outlays, gross (total)	163	181	228
Offsets against gross budget authority and outlays:				
Offsetting collections (collected) from:				
4030	Federal sources	–55	–59	–78
4040	Offsets against gross budget authority and outlays (total)	–55	–59	–78
Additional offsets against gross budget authority only:				
4050	Change in uncollected pymts, Fed sources, unexpired	–1		
4060	Additional offsets against budget authority only (total)	–1		
4070	Budget authority, net (discretionary)	112	109	154
4080	Outlays, net (discretionary)	108	122	150
Mandatory:				
4090	Budget authority, gross	8		
Outlays, gross:				
4101	Outlays from mandatory balances		2	
4180	Budget authority, net (total)	120	109	154
4190	Outlays, net (total)	108	124	150

This account provides for the Federal administration of Employment and Training Administration programs.

Training and Employment services.—Training and Employment services provides leadership, policy direction and administration for a decentralized system of grants to State and local governments. The account also provides Federally administered programs for job training and employment assistance for low-income adults, youth, and dislocated workers; training and employment services to special targeted groups; settlement of trade adjustment petitions; and related program operations support activities.

Workforce security.—Provides leadership and policy direction for the administration of the comprehensive nationwide public employment service system; oversees unemployment insurance programs in each State; supports a one-stop career center network, including a comprehensive system of collecting, analyzing and disseminating labor market information; and includes related program operations support activities.

Employment and Training Administration—Continued
Federal Funds—Continued

PROGRAM ADMINISTRATION—Continued

Office of Apprenticeship.—Bolstering Registered Apprenticeship programs across the U.S. and ensuring that historically underrepresented groups have access. Oversees the administration of a Federal-State apprenticeship structure that registers apprenticeship training programs meeting national standards. Provides outreach to employers and labor organizations to promote and develop high-quality apprenticeship programs.

Executive direction.—Provides leadership and policy direction for all training and employment services programs and activities and provides for related program operations support, including research, evaluations, and demonstrations.

Object Classification (in millions of dollars)

Identification code 016–0172–0–1–504		2021 actual	2022 est.	2023 est.
	Direct obligations:			
	Personnel compensation:			
11.1	Full-time permanent	71	75	91
11.3	Other than full-time permanent	2		
11.5	Other personnel compensation	2	2	2
11.9	Total personnel compensation	75	77	93
12.1	Civilian personnel benefits	26	26	33
21.0	Travel and transportation of persons		1	1
23.1	Rental payments to GSA	9	10	10
25.2	Other services from non-Federal sources	4	3	1
25.3	Other goods and services from Federal sources	44	39	78
25.7	Operation and maintenance of equipment	11	9	9
99.0	Direct obligations	169	165	225
99.0	Reimbursable obligations	5	9	9
99.9	Total new obligations, unexpired accounts	174	174	234

Employment Summary

Identification code 016–0172–0–1–504	2021 actual	2022 est.	2023 est.
1001 Direct civilian full-time equivalent employment	611	623	671
2001 Reimbursable civilian full-time equivalent employment	30	36	36

FOREIGN LABOR CERTIFICATION PROCESSING

Special and Trust Fund Receipts (in millions of dollars)

Identification code 016–5507–0–2–505	2021 actual	2022 est.	2023 est.
0100 Balance, start of year			
Receipts:			
Proposed:			
1220 Foreign Labor Certification Processing Fee			4
2000 Total: Balances and receipts			4
Appropriations:			
Proposed:			
2201 Foreign Labor Certification Processing			–4
5099 Balance, end of year			

FOREIGN LABOR CERTIFICATION PROCESSING

(Legislative proposal, subject to PAYGO)

Program and Financing (in millions of dollars)

Identification code 016–5507–4–2–505		2021 actual	2022 est.	2023 est.
	Obligations by program activity:			
0001	Fees for PERM, H-2A, H-2B, PW, CW1			4
	Budgetary resources:			
	Budget authority:			
	Appropriations, mandatory:			
1201	Appropriation (special or trust fund)			4
1900	Budget authority (total)			4
1930	Total budgetary resources available			4

	Change in obligated balance:			
	Unpaid obligations:			
3010	New obligations, unexpired accounts			4
3020	Outlays (gross)			–4
	Budget authority and outlays, net:			
	Mandatory:			
4090	Budget authority, gross			4
	Outlays, gross:			
4100	Outlays from new mandatory authority			4
4180	Budget authority, net (total)			4
4190	Outlays, net (total)			4

The Budget proposes authorizing legislation to establish and retain fees to cover the costs of operating the foreign labor certification programs. For several employment-based visa categories, the foreign labor certification programs help ensure that employers proposing to hire foreign workers have verified that there are an insufficient number of able, willing, and qualified U.S. workers available for the job and that the foreign workers will be appropriately compensated and not disadvantage similarly employed U.S. workers. The ability to charge fees in these programs would give the Department a more reliable, workload-based funding source for this function, similar to the fee-based funding structure in place at the Department of Homeland Security. The proposal would reduce reliance on annual discretionary appropriations and impose the cost of operations on the employers that use and most benefit from the foreign labor certification programs.

The proposal would authorize the Department to charge fees for its prevailing wage determinations, permanent labor certification program, H-2B nonagricultural workers program, and CW-1 Northern Mariana Islands transitional workers program, as well as retain and adjust the fees already collected for H-2A labor certifications, which are currently deposited in the U.S. Treasury's General Fund. The fee levels, including possible expedited processing fees, would be set via regulation to ensure that the amounts are subject to review and reflect the cost to DOL of operating the programs. Given the DOL Office of the Inspector General's (OIG) important role in investigating fraud and abuse, the proposal also includes a mechanism to provide funding for OIG's work in the foreign labor certification programs.

Object Classification (in millions of dollars)

Identification code 016–5507–4–2–505		2021 actual	2022 est.	2023 est.
	Direct obligations:			
11.1	Personnel compensation: Full-time permanent			3
12.1	Civilian personnel benefits			1
99.9	Total new obligations, unexpired accounts			4

Employment Summary

Identification code 016–5507–4–2–505	2021 actual	2022 est.	2023 est.
1001 Direct civilian full-time equivalent employment			19

Trust Funds

UNEMPLOYMENT TRUST FUND

Special and Trust Fund Receipts (in millions of dollars)

Identification code 016–8042–0–7–999	2021 actual	2022 est.	2023 est.
0100 Balance, start of year	34,090	33,830	17,431
Receipts:			
Current law:			
1110 General Taxes, FUTA, Unemployment Trust Fund	6,141	6,563	7,682
1110 Unemployment Trust Fund, State Accounts, Deposits by States	50,350	51,138	46,708
1110 Unemployment Trust Fund, Deposits by Railroad Retirement Board	111	279	318
1130 CMIA Interest, Unemployment Trust Fund	2	2	2
1130 Interest on Unemployment Insurance Loans to States, Federal Unemployment Account, Unemployment Trust Fund	57	623	577
1140 Deposits by Federal Agencies to the Federal Employees Compensation Account, Unemployment Trust Fund	563	549	483

DEPARTMENT OF LABOR

Employment and Training Administration—Continued
Trust Funds—Continued

		2021 actual	2022 est.	2023 est.
1140	Payments from the General Fund for Administrative Cost for Extended Unemployment Benefit, Unemployment Trust Fund	177,203	850	
1140	Unemployment Trust Fund, Interest and Profits on Investments in Public Debt Securities	1,281	1,241	1,026
1199	Total current law receipts	235,708	61,245	56,796
1999	Total receipts	235,708	61,245	56,796
2000	Total: Balances and receipts	269,798	95,075	74,227
	Appropriations:			
	Current law:			
2101	Unemployment Trust Fund	−5,190	−3,761	−4,563
2101	Unemployment Trust Fund	−230,407	−57,913	−33,756
2101	Railroad Unemployment Insurance Trust Fund	−20	−20	−20
2101	Railroad Unemployment Insurance Trust Fund	−100	−255	−294
2103	Unemployment Trust Fund	−2,537	−16,127	−10,242
2103	Railroad Unemployment Insurance Trust Fund	−3		
2103	Railroad Unemployment Insurance Trust Fund	−25	−44	−75
2132	Unemployment Trust Fund	389	115	45
2135	Unemployment Trust Fund	1,860		
2135	Railroad Unemployment Insurance Trust Fund	6		
2135	Railroad Unemployment Insurance Trust Fund	50	71	248
2199	Total current law appropriations	−235,977	−77,934	−48,657
	Proposed:			
2201	Unemployment Trust Fund		290	474
2999	Total appropriations	−235,977	−77,644	−48,183
5098	Adjustment to reconcile to budgetary accounting	9		
5099	Balance, end of year	33,830	17,431	26,044

Program and Financing (in millions of dollars)

Identification code 016–8042–0–7–999	2021 actual	2022 est.	2023 est.
Obligations by program activity:			
0001 Benefit payments by States	211,932	54,954	32,040
0002 Federal employees' unemployment compensation [FECA]	512	691	457
0003 State administrative expenses [ES Grants to States, ES Nat'l Actv, UI, and RESEA]	4,730	3,431	4,053
0010 Direct expenses [PA, FLC, OIG, SOL, and BLS]	202	202	242
0011 Reimbursements to the Department of the Treasury	102	97	105
0020 Veterans employment and training	259	259	268
0021 Interest on FUTA refunds	1,163	1,031	680
0023 EUC, CARES Admin, FFCRA [from PUTF]	2,985	850	
0024 FUA and EUCA advances for Extended Benefits	33,000	3,000	3,000
0900 Total new obligations, unexpired accounts	254,885	64,515	40,845
Budgetary resources:			
Budget authority:			
Appropriations, discretionary:			
1101 Appropriation (special or trust)	5,190	3,761	4,563
Appropriations, mandatory:			
1201 Appropriation (special or trust fund)	230,407	57,913	33,756
1203 Appropriation (previously unavailable)(special or trust)	2,537	16,127	10,242
1232 Appropriations and/or unobligated balance of appropriations temporarily reduced	−389	−115	−45
1235 Appropriations precluded from obligation (special or trust)	−1,860		
1236 Appropriations applied to repay debt	−14,000	−16,000	−10,500
1260 Appropriations, mandatory (total)	216,695	57,925	33,453
Borrowing authority, mandatory:			
1400 Borrowing authority	33,000	3,000	3,000
1421 Borrowing authority temporarily reduced		−171	−171
1440 Borrowing authority, mandatory (total)	33,000	2,829	2,829
1900 Budget authority (total)	254,885	64,515	40,845
1930 Total budgetary resources available	254,885	64,515	40,845
Change in obligated balance:			
Unpaid obligations:			
3000 Unpaid obligations, brought forward, Oct 1	16,127	39,955	29,187
3010 New obligations, unexpired accounts	254,885	64,515	40,845
3020 Outlays (gross)	−231,057	−75,283	−46,869
3050 Unpaid obligations, end of year	39,955	29,187	23,163
Memorandum (non-add) entries:			
3100 Obligated balance, start of year	16,127	39,955	29,187
3200 Obligated balance, end of year	39,955	29,187	23,163
Budget authority and outlays, net:			
Discretionary:			
4000 Budget authority, gross	5,190	3,761	4,563
Outlays, gross:			
4010 Outlays from new discretionary authority	5,190	2,470	3,079
4011 Outlays from discretionary balances	1,840	3,243	1,489
4020 Outlays, gross (total)	7,030	5,713	4,568
Mandatory:			
4090 Budget authority, gross	249,695	60,754	36,282
Outlays, gross:			
4100 Outlays from new mandatory authority	208,977	60,320	36,273
4101 Outlays from mandatory balances	15,050	9,250	6,028
4110 Outlays, gross (total)	224,027	69,570	42,301
4180 Budget authority, net (total)	254,885	64,515	40,845
4190 Outlays, net (total)	231,057	75,283	46,869
Memorandum (non-add) entries:			
5000 Total investments, SOY: Federal securities Federal Accounts: Par value	50,515	53,135	13,649
5000 Total investments, SOY: Federal securities State Accounts: Par value			45,214
5001 Total investments, EOY: Federal securities Federal Accounts: Par value	53,135	13,649	13,164
5001 Total investments, EOY: Federal securities State Accounts: Par value		45,214	55,477
5080 Outstanding debt, SOY	−36,000	−55,000	−42,000
5081 Outstanding debt, EOY	−55,000	−42,000	−34,336
5082 Borrowing	−33,000	−3,000	−2,836

Summary of Budget Authority and Outlays (in millions of dollars)

	2021 actual	2022 est.	2023 est.
Enacted/requested:			
Budget Authority	254,885	64,515	40,845
Outlays	231,057	75,283	46,869
Legislative proposal, not subject to PAYGO:			
Budget Authority		−290	−474
Outlays		−290	−474
Total:			
Budget Authority	254,885	64,225	40,371
Outlays	231,057	74,993	46,395

The financial transactions of the Federal-State and railroad unemployment insurance systems are made through the Unemployment Trust Fund (UTF). The UTF has two accounts for the railroad unemployment insurance system but for the Federal-State unemployment insurance system there are 57 separate accounts: one for each of the 50 states, three jurisdictions (District of Columbia, Puerto Rico, Virgin Islands) and four Federal accounts. The state and jurisdiction accounts receive funds from a state unemployment insurance payroll tax which is used to pay benefits. The Federal Unemployment Tax Act (FUTA) payroll tax provides funds for two of the Federal accounts — the Employment Security Administration Account (ESAA) and the Extended Unemployment Compensation Account (EUCA) — while the remaining two, the Federal Unemployment Account (FUA) and the Federal Employees Compensation Account (FEC Account), are revolving accounts.

Except for FEC Account balances, funds on deposit in the UTF accounts are invested in Government securities until needed for payment of benefits or administrative expenses. The FUTA payroll tax is deposited in the ESAA which retains 80 percent of the deposit and pays the costs of Federal and State administration of the unemployment insurance system, veterans' employment services, surveys of wages and employment, foreign labor certifications and about 97 percent of the costs of the Employment Service. The other 20 percent of FUTA is transferred to the EUCA which pays for certain extended benefit (EB) payments. During periods of high State unemployment, there is a stand-by program of EB, financed one-half by State unemployment taxes and one-half by the FUTA payroll tax.

The UTF also provides repayable advances (loans) from the FUA to States and jurisdictions when the balances in their individual accounts are insufficient to pay benefits. Federal accounts in the UTF may receive repayable and nonrepayable advances from the general fund when they have insufficient balances to make advances to States, pay the Federal share of extended unemployment benefits, or pay for State and Federal administrative costs.

UNEMPLOYMENT TRUST FUND—Continued

The FEC Account in the UTF provides funds to States for unemployment compensation benefits paid to eligible former Federal civilian personnel, Postal Service employees, and ex-servicemembers. In turn, the various Federal agencies reimburse the FEC Account for benefits paid to their former employees. The FEC Account is not funded out of Federal unemployment taxes. Any additional resources necessary to assure that the FEC Account can make the required payments to States are provided from the Advances to the Unemployment Trust Fund and Other Funds appropriation.

Both the benefit payments and administrative expenses of the separate unemployment insurance program for railroad employees are paid from the UTF, and receipts from a tax on railroad payrolls are deposited into the program's accounts in the UTF to meet expenses.

Status of Funds (in millions of dollars)

Identification code 016–8042–0–7–999		2021 actual	2022 est.	2023 est.
	Unexpended balance, start of year:			
0100	Balance, start of year	14,228	18,674	4,621
0298	Adjustment for loan for TAFS 060X8051 from TAFS 060X8011	–22		
0999	Total balance, start of year	14,206	18,674	4,621
	Cash income during the year:			
	Current law:			
	Receipts:			
1110	General Taxes, FUTA, Unemployment Trust Fund	6,141	6,563	7,682
1110	Unemployment Trust Fund, State Accounts, Deposits by States	50,350	51,138	46,708
1110	Unemployment Trust Fund, State Accounts, Deposits by States			
1110	Unemployment Trust Fund, Deposits by Railroad Retirement Board	111	279	318
*1130	Railroad Unemployment Insurance Trust Fund	17	15	15
1150	CMIA Interest, Unemployment Trust Fund	2	2	2
1150	Unemployment Trust Fund, Interest and Profits on Investments in Public Debt Securities	1,281	1,241	1,026
1150	Interest on Unemployment Insurance Loans to States, Federal Unemployment Account, Unemployment Trust Fund	57	623	577
1160	Deposits by Federal Agencies to the Federal Employees Compensation Account, Unemployment Trust Fund	563	549	483
1160	Payments from the General Fund for Administrative Cost for Extended Unemployment Benefit, Unemployment Trust Fund	177,203	850	
1160	Railroad Unemployment Insurance Trust Fund	1		
1199	Income under present law	235,726	61,260	56,811
	Proposed:			
1210	Unemployment Trust Fund, State Accounts, Deposits by States			
1299	Income proposed			
1999	Total cash income	235,726	61,260	56,811
	Cash outgo during year:			
	Current law:			
2100	Unemployment Trust Fund [Budget Acct]	–231,057	–75,283	–46,869
2100	Railroad Unemployment Insurance Trust Fund [Budget Acct]	–197	–161	–149
2199	Outgo under current law	–231,254	–75,444	–47,018
	Proposed:			
2200	Unemployment Trust Fund		290	474
2299	Outgo under proposed legislation		290	474
2999	Total cash outgo (-)	–231,254	–75,154	–46,544
	Surplus or deficit:			
3110	Excluding interest	3,132	–15,760	8,662
3120	Interest	1,340	1,866	1,605
3199	Subtotal, surplus or deficit	4,472	–13,894	10,267
3220	Railroad Unemployment Insurance Trust Fund		–7	
3230	Railroad Unemployment Insurance Trust Fund	81		
3230	Railroad Unemployment Insurance Trust Fund		–107	
3298	Adjustment to reconcile	–85	–45	
3299	Total adjustments	–4	–159	
3999	Total change in fund balance	4,468	–14,053	10,267
	Unexpended balance, end of year:			
4100	Uninvested balance (net), end of year	–34,461	–54,242	–53,753
4200	Unemployment Trust Fund	53,135	58,863	68,641
4999	Total balance, end of year	18,674	4,621	14,888

Object Classification (in millions of dollars)

Identification code 016–8042–0–7–999		2021 actual	2022 est.	2023 est.
	Direct obligations:			
25.3	Reimbursements to Department of the Treasury	102	97	105
42.0	FECA (Federal Employee) Benefits	512	691	457
42.0	State unemployment benefits	198,210	54,954	32,040
43.0	Interest and dividends	885	1,031	680
94.0	ETA-PA, BLS, FLC	196	196	236
94.0	Veterans employment and training	259	259	268
94.0	Payments to States for administrative expenses	4,730	3,431	4,053
94.0	Departmental Management [OIG, SOL]	6	6	6
94.0	FUA and EUCA advances for Extended Benefits	33,000	3,000	3,000
94.0	EUC/CARES Admin PUTF	2,985	850	
94.0	Repayment of debt	14,000		
99.9	Total new obligations, unexpired accounts	254,885	64,515	40,845

UNEMPLOYMENT TRUST FUND

(Legislative proposal, not subject to PAYGO)

Program and Financing (in millions of dollars)

Identification code 016–8042–2–7–999		2021 actual	2022 est.	2023 est.
	Obligations by program activity:			
0001	Benefit payments by States		–290	–474
0900	Total new obligations, unexpired accounts (object class 42.0)		–290	–474
	Budgetary resources:			
	Budget authority:			
	Appropriations, mandatory:			
1201	Appropriation (special or trust fund)		–290	–474
1900	Budget authority (total)		–290	–474
1930	Total budgetary resources available		–290	–474
	Change in obligated balance:			
	Unpaid obligations:			
3010	New obligations, unexpired accounts		–290	–474
3020	Outlays (gross)		290	474
	Budget authority and outlays, net:			
	Mandatory:			
4090	Budget authority, gross		–290	–474
	Outlays, gross:			
4100	Outlays from new mandatory authority		–290	–474
4180	Budget authority, net (total)		–290	–474
4190	Outlays, net (total)		–290	–474

The Bipartisan Budget Act of 2018 (P.L. 115–123) amended the Social Security Act and permanently authorized the Reemployment Services and Eligibility Assessments (RESEA) program, authorizing $117 million in annual base funding, plus an allocation adjustment level, previously referred to as a discretionary cap adjustment. The allocation adjustment level provides for an increasing level of funding up to a specified amount each year. Multiple research studies have found that the RESEA service delivery model leads to reduced unemployment insurance durations, and thereby benefit savings, among other improvements in employment outcomes.

The FY 2023 President's Budget includes projected savings generated by the allocation adjustment funding from the operation of RESEA. These savings are based on the projected reduction in claimant durations due to the RESEA provisions and the associated benefits savings due to fewer weeks paid. The savings also indirectly impact state unemployment tax revenues, as state tax collections are largely determined by benefit outlays and trust fund reserves, and lower benefit outlays translate into slightly lower tax rates and collections over the 10-year projection period.

EMPLOYEE BENEFITS SECURITY ADMINISTRATION

Federal Funds

SALARIES AND EXPENSES

For necessary expenses for the Employee Benefits Security Administration, $233,867,000, of which up to $3,000,000 shall be available until expended for the procurement of expert witnesses for enforcement litigation.

DEPARTMENT OF LABOR

Employee Benefits Security Administration—Continued
Federal Funds—Continued

Note.—A full-year 2022 appropriation for this account was not enacted at the time the Budget was prepared; therefore, the Budget assumes this account is operating under the Continuing Appropriations Act, 2022 (Division A of Public Law 117–43, as amended). The amounts included for 2022 reflect the annualized level provided by the continuing resolution.

Program and Financing (in millions of dollars)

Identification code 016–1700–0–1–601		2021 actual	2022 est.	2023 est.
	Obligations by program activity:			
0001	Enforcement and participant assistance	147	146	192
0002	Policy and compliance assistance	27	27	33
0003	Executive leadership, program oversight and administration	7	7	9
0004	CARES Act	1		
0005	Expert Witness	1	1	
0006	American Rescue Plan Act	9	1	
0799	Total direct obligations	192	182	234
0801	Reimbursable obligations	7	8	8
0900	Total new obligations, unexpired accounts	199	190	242
	Budgetary resources:			
	Unobligated balance:			
1000	Unobligated balance brought forward, Oct 1	2	1	
1001	Discretionary unobligated balance brought fwd, Oct 1	2		
	Budget authority:			
	Appropriations, discretionary:			
1100	Appropriation	181	181	234
	Appropriations, mandatory:			
1200	American Rescue Plan Act	10		
	Spending authority from offsetting collections, discretionary:			
1700	Collected: Federal Sources	5	8	8
1701	Change in uncollected payments, Federal sources	2		
1750	Spending auth from offsetting collections, disc (total)	7	8	8
1900	Budget authority (total)	198	189	242
1930	Total budgetary resources available	200	190	242
	Memorandum (non-add) entries:			
1941	Unexpired unobligated balance, end of year	1		
	Change in obligated balance:			
	Unpaid obligations:			
3000	Unpaid obligations, brought forward, Oct 1	28	29	45
3010	New obligations, unexpired accounts	199	190	242
3011	Obligations ("upward adjustments"), expired accounts	1		
3020	Outlays (gross)	–198	–174	–228
3041	Recoveries of prior year unpaid obligations, expired	–1		
3050	Unpaid obligations, end of year	29	45	59
	Uncollected payments:			
3060	Uncollected pymts, Fed sources, brought forward, Oct 1	–2	–2	–2
3070	Change in uncollected pymts, Fed sources, unexpired	–2		
3071	Change in uncollected pymts, Fed sources, expired	2		
3090	Uncollected pymts, Fed sources, end of year	–2	–2	–2
	Memorandum (non-add) entries:			
3100	Obligated balance, start of year	26	27	43
3200	Obligated balance, end of year	27	43	57
	Budget authority and outlays, net:			
	Discretionary:			
4000	Budget authority, gross	188	189	242
	Outlays, gross:			
4010	Outlays from new discretionary authority	166	142	181
4011	Outlays from discretionary balances	27	27	47
4020	Outlays, gross (total)	193	169	228
	Offsets against gross budget authority and outlays:			
	Offsetting collections (collected) from:			
4030	Federal sources	–7	–8	–8
4040	Offsets against gross budget authority and outlays (total)	–7	–8	–8
	Additional offsets against gross budget authority only:			
4050	Change in uncollected pymts, Fed sources, unexpired	–2		
4052	Offsetting collections credited to expired accounts	2		
4070	Budget authority, net (discretionary)	181	181	234
4080	Outlays, net (discretionary)	186	161	220
	Mandatory:			
4090	Budget authority, gross	10		
	Outlays, gross:			
4100	Outlays from new mandatory authority	5		
4101	Outlays from mandatory balances		5	
4110	Outlays, gross (total)	5	5	
4180	Budget authority, net (total)	191	181	234
4190	Outlays, net (total)	191	166	220

Summary of Budget Authority and Outlays (in millions of dollars)

	2021 actual	2022 est.	2023 est.
Enacted/requested:			
Budget Authority	191	181	234
Outlays	191	166	220
Legislative proposal, subject to PAYGO:			
Budget Authority			2
Outlays			2
Total:			
Budget Authority	191	181	236
Outlays	191	166	222

Employee Benefits Security Programs[2].—Conducts criminal and civil investigations to ensure compliance with the fiduciary provisions of the Employee Retirement Income Security Act (ERISA) and the Federal Employees' Retirement System Act (FERSA). Assures compliance with applicable reporting, disclosure and other requirements of ERISA as well as accounting, auditing, and actuarial standards. Discloses required plan filings to the public. Provides information, technical, and compliance assistance to benefit plan professionals and participants and to the general public. Conducts policy, research, and legislative analysis on pension, health, and other employee benefit issues. Provides compliance assistance to employers and plan officials. Develops regulations and interpretations. Issues individual and class exemptions from regulations. Provides leadership, policy direction, strategic planning, and administrative guidance in the support of the Department's ERISA responsibilities.

EMPLOYEE BENEFITS AND SECURITY PROGRAMS[2]	2021 Actual	2022 est.[1]	2023 est.
Investigations conducted	1,280	N/A	N/A[3]
Participant benefit recoveries and plan assets restored	$2,531,005,000[4]	$1,107,110,000	$1,178,450,000
Major case monetary recoveries per major case staff day	$112,103	$87,394	$67,864
Monetary recoveries on major cases closed per staff day	$100,940	$67,066	$58,864
Other non-major civil cases closed or referred for litigation within 18 months	81.0%	76.0%	76.0%
Inquiries received	175,986	175,000	175,000
Reporting compliance reviews	3,415	3,600	3,750
Exemptions, determinations, interpretations and regulations issued	3,997	4,215	4,432[5]
Average days to process exemption requests	313	350	350

[1] Reflects estimates prior to FY 2022 full year appropriations.

[2] Employee Benefits Security Programs encompass three budget activities to include: (1) Enforcement and Participant Assistance; (2) Policy and Compliance Assistance; and (3) Executive Leadership, Program Oversight and Administration.

[3] The agency continues its efforts to enhance the quality and impact of its investigations and has placed special emphasis on Major Case monetary recoveries, as well as the impact of its investigations (e.g., the amounts recovered for plan participants and beneficiaries). While the agency will continue to report the total number of investigations conducted, it will no longer make projections of the raw number of investigations.

[4] Reflects over $2.17 billion in participant benefit recoveries, $165.8 million in plan assets restored, $108.4 million in participant health plan recoveries, $50.8 million in distributions for abandoned plans, and over $34 million for Voluntary Fiduciary Correction Program recoveries.

[5] Includes Multiple Employer Welfare Arrangement (MEWA) registrations and individual exemptions.

Object Classification (in millions of dollars)

Identification code 016–1700–0–1–601		2021 actual	2022 est.	2023 est.
	Direct obligations:			
	Personnel compensation:			
11.1	Full-time permanent	87	93	111
11.3	Other than full-time permanent	1	1	1
11.5	Other personnel compensation	2	2	2
11.9	Total personnel compensation	90	96	114
12.1	Civilian personnel benefits	32	33	46
21.0	Travel and transportation of persons		1	2
23.1	Rental payments to GSA	11	10	11
23.3	Communications, utilities, and miscellaneous charges			1
24.0	Printing and reproduction		1	1
25.1	Advisory and assistance services	1		2
25.2	Other services from non-Federal sources	11	4	13
25.3	Other goods and services from Federal sources	44	35	30
25.5	Research and development contracts	1	1	1
25.7	Operation and maintenance of equipment			11
26.0	Supplies and materials	1	1	1
31.0	Equipment			1
99.0	Direct obligations	192	182	234
99.0	Reimbursable obligations	7	8	8
99.9	Total new obligations, unexpired accounts	199	190	242

773

Employee Benefits Security Administration—Continued
Federal Funds—Continued

SALARIES AND EXPENSES—Continued

Employment Summary

Identification code 016–1700–0–1–601	2021 actual	2022 est.	2023 est.
1001 Direct civilian full-time equivalent employment	789	777	978

SALARIES AND EXPENSES
(Legislative proposal, subject to PAYGO)

Program and Financing (in millions of dollars)

Identification code 016–1700–4–1–601	2021 actual	2022 est.	2023 est.
Obligations by program activity:			
0009 Mental Health Parity and Addiction Equity Act			2
0799 Total direct obligations			2
Budgetary resources:			
Budget authority:			
Appropriations, mandatory:			
1200 Mental Health Parity and Addiction Equity Act			2
1930 Total budgetary resources available			2
Change in obligated balance:			
Unpaid obligations:			
3010 New obligations, unexpired accounts			2
3020 Outlays (gross)			–2
Budget authority and outlays, net:			
Mandatory:			
4090 Budget authority, gross			2
Outlays, gross:			
4100 Outlays from new mandatory authority			2
4180 Budget authority, net (total)			2
4190 Outlays, net (total)			2

The FY 2023 Budget proposes to provide the Department with $275,000,000 over 10 years, in mandatory funding for EBSA and SOL, to increase capacity for the agency to perform audits related to mental health and substance abuse (including investigating reimbursement rates as Non-Quantitative Treatment Limitations) and take action against non-compliant actors. These enhanced oversight and compliance efforts would increase the number of large group market health plans and issuers that are complying with the mental health parity requirements under the Mental Health Parity and Addiction Equity Act. Additionally, the Budget proposes to authorize EBSA to assess civil monetary penalties for parity violations.

Object Classification (in millions of dollars)

Identification code 016–1700–4–1–601	2021 actual	2022 est.	2023 est.
11.1 Direct obligations: Personnel compensation: Full-time permanent			1
11.9 Total personnel compensation			1
25.7 Operation and maintenance of equipment			1
99.0 Direct obligations			2
99.9 Total new obligations, unexpired accounts			2

Employment Summary

Identification code 016–1700–4–1–601	2021 actual	2022 est.	2023 est.
1001 Direct civilian full-time equivalent employment			7

PENSION BENEFIT GUARANTY CORPORATION

Federal Funds

PENSION BENEFIT GUARANTY CORPORATION FUND

The Pension Benefit Guaranty Corporation ("Corporation") is authorized to make such expenditures, including financial assistance authorized by subtitle E of title IV of the Employee Retirement Income Security Act of 1974, within limits of funds and borrowing authority available to the Corporation, and in accord with law, and to make such contracts and commitments without regard to fiscal year limitations, as provided by 31 U.S.C. 9104, as may be necessary in carrying out the program, including associated administrative expenses, through September 30, 2023, for the Corporation: Provided, That none of the funds available to the Corporation for fiscal year 2023 shall be available for obligations for administrative expenses in excess of $493,314,000: Provided further, That to the extent that the number of new plan participants in plans terminated by the Corporation exceeds 100,000 in fiscal year 2023, an amount not to exceed an additional $9,200,000 shall be available through September 30, 2027, for obligations for administrative expenses for every 20,000 additional terminated participants: Provided further, That obligations in excess of the amounts provided for administrative expenses in this paragraph may be incurred and shall be available through September 30, 2027 for obligation for unforeseen and extraordinary pre-termination or termination expenses or extraordinary multiemployer program related expenses after approval by the Office of Management and Budget and notification of the Committees on Appropriations of the House of Representatives and the Senate: Provided further, That an additional amount shall be available for obligation through September 30, 2027 to the extent the Corporation's expenses exceed $250,000 for the provision of credit or identity monitoring to affected individuals upon suffering a security incident or privacy breach, not to exceed an additional $100 per affected individual.

Note.—A full-year 2022 appropriation for this account was not enacted at the time the Budget was prepared; therefore, the Budget assumes this account is operating under the Continuing Appropriations Act, 2022 (Division A of Public Law 117–43, as amended). The amounts included for 2022 reflect the annualized level provided by the continuing resolution.

Program and Financing (in millions of dollars)

Identification code 016–4204–0–3–601	2021 actual	2022 est.	2023 est.
Obligations by program activity:			
0080 Multiemployer, Administrative Expenses [Special Financial Assistance]		27	16
0081 Multiemployer [Special Financial Assistance]	4	55,000	23,418
0192 Direct program activities, subtotal	4	55,027	23,434
0799 Total direct obligations	4	55,027	23,434
0801 Single-employer benefit payment	6,179	7,140	7,344
0802 Multiemployer financial assistance	230	190	214
0806 Administrative Expenses	459	457	493
0807 Investment Management Fees	119	138	140
0899 Total reimbursable obligations	6,987	7,925	8,191
0900 Total new obligations, unexpired accounts	6,991	62,952	31,625
Budgetary resources:			
Unobligated balance:			
1000 Unobligated balance brought forward, Oct 1	45,205	48,821	53,726
Budget authority:			
Appropriations, mandatory:			
1200 Appropriation [Special Financial Assistance]		55,000	23,418
1200 Appropriation [Special Financial Assistance (Administrative Exp.)]	4	27	16
1202 Appropriation (previously unavailable)			2
1232 Appropriations and/or unobligated balance of appropriations temporarily reduced		–2	–1
1260 Appropriations, mandatory (total)	4	55,025	23,435
Spending authority from offsetting collections, mandatory:			
1800 Collected	10,609	12,832	13,990
1802 Offsetting collections (previously unavailable)	8	8	8
1823 New and/or unobligated balance of spending authority from offsetting collections temporarily reduced	–8	–8	–8
1850 Spending auth from offsetting collections, mand (total)	10,609	12,832	13,990
1900 Budget authority (total)	10,613	67,857	37,425
1930 Total budgetary resources available	55,818	116,678	91,151
Memorandum (non-add) entries:			
1940 Unobligated balance expiring	–6		
1941 Unexpired unobligated balance, end of year	48,821	53,726	59,526
Change in obligated balance:			
Unpaid obligations:			
3000 Unpaid obligations, brought forward, Oct 1	360	387	11
3010 New obligations, unexpired accounts	6,991	62,952	31,625
3020 Outlays (gross)	–6,964	–63,328	–31,625
3050 Unpaid obligations, end of year	387	11	11
Memorandum (non-add) entries:			
3100 Obligated balance, start of year	360	387	11
3200 Obligated balance, end of year	387	11	11

DEPARTMENT OF LABOR

Pension Benefit Guaranty Corporation—Continued
Federal Funds—Continued

	Budget authority and outlays, net:			
	Mandatory:			
4090	Budget authority, gross	10,613	67,857	37,425
	Outlays, gross:			
4100	Outlays from new mandatory authority	6,724	62,941	31,625
4101	Outlays from mandatory balances	240	387	
4110	Outlays, gross (total)	6,964	63,328	31,625
	Offsets against gross budget authority and outlays:			
	Offsetting collections (collected) from:			
4120	Federal sources (Treasury Dept Reimbursable Agreement)	–1		
4121	Cash Investment Receipts	–575	–1,275	–1,404
4123	Non-Federal sources	–10,033	–11,557	–12,584
4123	Non-Federal sources			–2
4130	Offsets against gross budget authority and outlays (total)	–10,609	–12,832	–13,990
4160	Budget authority, net (mandatory)	4	55,025	23,435
4170	Outlays, net (mandatory)	–3,645	50,496	17,635
4180	Budget authority, net (total)	4	55,025	23,435
4190	Outlays, net (total)	–3,645	50,496	17,635
	Memorandum (non-add) entries:			
5000	Total investments, SOY: Federal securities: Par value	45,553	50,323	55,232
5001	Total investments, EOY: Federal securities: Par value	50,323	55,232	61,029
5090	Unexpired unavailable balance, SOY: Offsetting collections	8	8	8
5092	Unexpired unavailable balance, EOY: Offsetting collections	8	8	8
5096	Unexpired unavailable balance, SOY: Appropriations			2
5098	Unexpired unavailable balance, EOY: Appropriations		2	1

The Pension Benefit Guaranty Corporation (PBGC or the Corporation) is a Federal corporation established under the Employee Retirement Income Security Act of 1974, as amended. It guarantees payment of basic pension benefits earned by over 33,000,000 of America's workers and retirees participating in more than 25,000 private-sector defined benefit pension plans. The Single-Employer Program protects about 22,7000,000 workers and retirees in about 23,900 pension plans. The Multiemployer Program protects about 10,900,000 workers and retirees in about 1,360 pension plans. The Corporation's two insurance programs are legally separate and operationally and financially independent.

The Single-Employer Program is financed by insurance premiums, investment income, and recoveries from companies formerly responsible for the plans. Congress sets PBGC premium rates.

The Multiemployer Program is financed by premiums and investment income. The American Rescue Plan (ARP) Act of 2021 - a historic law passed by Congress and signed by President Biden on March 11, 2021 - established the Special Financial Assistance (SFA) Program for certain financially troubled multiemployer plans. The SFA Program is financed by general taxpayer funds provided by the U.S. Treasury.

PBGC is requesting $493,314,000 in spending authority for administrative expenses in 2023. The request includes spending authority of $9,979,000 for Strengthening Cybersecurity and Modernization of Enterprise Systems, $3,973,000 for Implementing Federal Safety and Security Protocols, $11,473,000 for Cost-of-Living Adjustments, $4,600,000 for Modernizing Enterprise Risk Management Capabilities and Strengthening Internal Control, and (-$2,000,000) program decrease for a one-time cost to upgrade Oracles Federal Financial eBusiness Suite applications.

Plan Preservation Efforts.—PBGC works to preserve plans and keep pension promises in the hands of the employers who make them. When companies undertake major transactions that might threaten their ability to pay pensions, PBGC negotiates protections for their pension plans. PBGC encouraged companies, both in bankruptcy and otherwise, to preserve their plans that were at risk. In 2021, PBGC:

—Paid $230,000,000 in financial assistance to 109 insolvent multiemployer plans covering 80,786 participants receiving guaranteed benefits;

—Performed audits of seven multiemployer plans covering nearly 10,000 participants to evaluate the timeliness and accuracy of benefit payments to all participants, compliance with laws and regulations, and the effectiveness and efficiency in management of the remaining assets in terminated and insolvent plans.

Stepping in to Insure Pensions When Plans Fail.—When plans do fail, PBGC steps in to ensure that basic benefits continue to be paid. Over the years, PBGC has become responsible for almost 1,500,000 current and future retirees in trusteed pension plans. In 2021, PBGC:

—Paid $6,400,000,000 in benefits to 970,000 retirees in single-employer plans; and

—Performed standard termination audits of single-employer plans that resulted in additional payments of $2,600,000 to 1,462 people.

Single-employer benefit payments.—Through its Single-Employer Program, PBGC is directly responsible for the benefits of about 1,500,000 current and future retirees in trusteed pension plans. The Single-Employer Program covers defined benefit pension plans that generally are sponsored by a single employer. When an under-funded single-employer plan terminates, PBGC steps in to pay participants' benefits up to legal limits set by law. This typically happens when the employer sponsoring an underfunded plan goes bankrupt, ceases operation, or can no longer afford to keep the plan going. PBGC takes over the plan's assets, administration, and payment of benefits up to the legal limits. In some instances, plans can choose to voluntarily terminate by filing a standard termination if the plan has enough money to pay all benefits owed to participants. In FY 2021, PBGC:

— Took responsibility for 47 single-employer plans that provide the pension benefits to an additional 34,000 workers and retirees;

— Protected 99,345 single-employer plan participants from employers emerging from bankruptcy.

Multiemployer financial assistance.—The Multiemployer Program covers about 10,900,000 participants in about 1,360 insured plans. A multiemployer plan is a pension plan sponsored by two or more unrelated employers under collective bargaining agreements with one or more unions. Multiemployer plans cover most unionized workers in the trucking, retail food, construction, mining, garment, and other industries. If a PBGC-insured multiemployer plan is unable to pay guaranteed benefits when due, PBGC provides insolvent multiemployer plans with financial assistance, in the statutorily required form of loans, sufficient to pay PBGC guaranteed benefits and reasonable administrative expenses.

Under the SFA Program, PBGC expects to provide financial assistance to more than 250 eligible plans covering over 3,000,000 people. PBGC provides one-time payments to eligible plans to enable them to pay benefits at the plan level.

Investment management fees.—PBGC contracts with professional financial services corporations to manage Trust Fund assets in accordance with an investment strategy approved by PBGC's Board of Directors. Investment management fees are driven by the amount of assets under management. They are a direct, programmatic expense required to maintain the Trust Fund which supports single-employer benefit payments.

Consolidated Administrative Budget.—PBGC's administrative budget comprises all expenditures and operations that support:

—Benefit payments to pension plan participants;

—Financial assistance to distressed multiemployer pension plans; and

—Stewardship and accountability.

These operations include premium collections, pre-trusteeship work, efforts to preserve pension plans, recovery of assets from former plan sponsors, and pension insurance program protection activities. This area also covers the expenditures that support activities related to trusteeship; plan asset management (excluding investment management fees) and trust accounting; as well as benefit payments and administration services. Finally, this area includes the administrative functions covering procurement, financial management, human resources, facilities management, communications, legal support, and information technology infrastructure. These funds support the operations of the Participant and Plan Sponsor Advocate. They also support the required functions and efforts of the Office of the Inspector General, including training and participation in Council of the Inspectors General on Integrity and Efficiency (CIGIE) activities.

Pension Benefit Guaranty Corporation—Continued
Federal Funds—Continued

PENSION BENEFIT GUARANTY CORPORATION FUND—Continued

Object Classification (in millions of dollars)

Identification code 016–4204–0–3–601	2021 actual	2022 est.	2023 est.
Direct obligations:			
11.1 Personnel compensation: Full-time permanent		7	7
12.1 Civilian personnel benefits		3	3
25.2 Other services from non-Federal sources		15	6
31.0 Equipment		2	
33.0 Investments and loans		55,000	23,418
99.0 Direct obligations		55,027	23,434
Reimbursable obligations:			
Personnel compensation:			
11.1 Full-time permanent	119	121	128
11.3 Other than full-time permanent	3	3	3
11.5 Other personnel compensation	4	4	4
11.9 Total personnel compensation	126	128	135
12.1 Civilian personnel benefits	43	43	47
21.0 Travel and transportation of persons		1	1
23.2 Rental payments to others	30	24	24
23.3 Communications, utilities, and miscellaneous charges	4	5	5
25.1 Advisory and assistance services	119	138	140
25.2 Other services from non-Federal sources	235	243	264
25.3 Other goods and services from Federal sources	9	10	14
26.0 Supplies and materials	1	1	1
31.0 Equipment	15	2	2
33.0 Investments and loans	230	190	214
42.0 Insurance claims and indemnities	6,179	7,140	7,344
99.0 Reimbursable obligations	6,991	7,925	8,191
99.9 Total new obligations, unexpired accounts	6,991	62,952	31,625

Employment Summary

Identification code 016–4204–0–3–601	2021 actual	2022 est.	2023 est.
1001 Direct civilian full-time equivalent employment		44	44
2001 Reimbursable civilian full-time equivalent employment	938	924	940

PENSION BENEFIT GUARANTY CORPORATION FUND

(Legislative proposal, subject to PAYGO)

The Budget calls for the repeal of the provision accelerating FY 2026 premiums into FY 2025. This provision creates unnecessary confusion and burden on insured plans because they are forced to pay premiums early for just one year. The provision will also create additional accounting and management costs for both the plans and PBGC given the high likelihood of late payments. Repealing this provision will be budget neutral, enhance compliance, and avoid unnecessary administrative costs for pension plans and the PBGC.

OFFICE OF WORKERS' COMPENSATION PROGRAMS

Federal Funds

SALARIES AND EXPENSES

For necessary expenses for the Office of Workers' Compensation Programs, $143,772,000, together with $2,205,000 which may be expended from the Special Fund in accordance with sections 39(c), 44(d), and 44(j) of the Longshore and Harbor Workers' Compensation Act.

Note.—A full-year 2022 appropriation for this account was not enacted at the time the Budget was prepared; therefore, the Budget assumes this account is operating under the Continuing Appropriations Act, 2022 (Division A of Public Law 117–43, as amended). The amounts included for 2022 reflect the annualized level provided by the continuing resolution.

Program and Financing (in millions of dollars)

Identification code 016–0163–0–1–505	2021 actual	2022 est.	2023 est.
Obligations by program activity:			
0003 Federal programs for workers' compensation	115	115	144
0004 American Rescue Plan Act	11	19	
0799 Total direct obligations	126	134	144
0801 Trust Funds, Federal Programs for Workers' Compensation	40	41	44
0900 Total new obligations, unexpired accounts	166	175	188
Budgetary resources:			
Unobligated balance:			
1000 Unobligated balance brought forward, Oct 1		20	1
Budget authority:			
Appropriations, discretionary:			
1100 Appropriation	115	115	144
Appropriations, mandatory:			
1200 American Rescue Plan Act	30		
Spending authority from offsetting collections, discretionary:			
1700 Collected	41	41	44
1900 Budget authority (total)	186	156	188
1930 Total budgetary resources available	186	176	189
Memorandum (non-add) entries:			
1941 Unexpired unobligated balance, end of year	20	1	1
Change in obligated balance:			
Unpaid obligations:			
3000 Unpaid obligations, brought forward, Oct 1	11	16	17
3010 New obligations, unexpired accounts	166	175	188
3011 Obligations ("upward adjustments"), expired accounts	1		
3020 Outlays (gross)	–161	–174	–186
3041 Recoveries of prior year unpaid obligations, expired	–1		
3050 Unpaid obligations, end of year	16	17	19
Memorandum (non-add) entries:			
3100 Obligated balance, start of year	11	16	17
3200 Obligated balance, end of year	16	17	19
Budget authority and outlays, net:			
Discretionary:			
4000 Budget authority, gross	156	156	188
Outlays, gross:			
4010 Outlays from new discretionary authority	144	145	174
4011 Outlays from discretionary balances	9	10	12
4020 Outlays, gross (total)	153	155	186
Offsets against gross budget authority and outlays:			
Offsetting collections (collected) from:			
4030 Federal sources	–39	–41	–44
4034 Offsetting governmental collections	–2		
4040 Offsets against gross budget authority and outlays (total)	–41	–41	–44
4070 Budget authority, net (discretionary)	115	115	144
4080 Outlays, net (discretionary)	112	114	142
Mandatory:			
4090 Budget authority, gross	30		
Outlays, gross:			
4100 Outlays from new mandatory authority	8		
4101 Outlays from mandatory balances		19	
4110 Outlays, gross (total)	8	19	
4180 Budget authority, net (total)	145	115	144
4190 Outlays, net (total)	120	133	142

The Office of Workers' Compensation Programs (OWCP) administers the Federal Employees' Compensation Act (FECA), the Longshore and Harbor Workers' Compensation Act, the Energy Employees Occupational Illness Compensation Program Act (EEOICPA), and the Black Lung Benefits Act (Black Lung). These programs ensure that eligible disabled and injured workers or their survivors receive compensation and medical benefits and a range of services, including vocational rehabilitation, supervision of medical care, and technical and advisory counseling, to which they are entitled.

Object Classification (in millions of dollars)

Identification code 016–0163–0–1–505	2021 actual	2022 est.	2023 est.
Direct obligations:			
Personnel compensation:			
11.1 Full-time permanent	62	79	87
11.3 Other than full-time permanent	1		
11.5 Other personnel compensation	1	1	1
11.9 Total personnel compensation	64	80	88
12.1 Civilian personnel benefits	25	30	33
23.1 Rental payments to GSA	8	6	6
23.3 Communications, utilities, and miscellaneous charges	1	1	1
25.2 Other services from non-Federal sources	1	1	1
25.3 Other goods and services from Federal sources	20	12	13
25.7 Operation and maintenance of equipment	6	3	1
26.0 Supplies and materials	1	1	1
99.0 Direct obligations	126	134	144

DEPARTMENT OF LABOR

Office of Workers' Compensation Programs—Continued
Federal Funds—Continued

777

		2021 actual	2022 est.	2023 est.
99.0	Reimbursable obligations	40	41	44
99.9	Total new obligations, unexpired accounts	166	175	188

Employment Summary

Identification code 016–0163–0–1–505	2021 actual	2022 est.	2023 est.
1001 Direct civilian full-time equivalent employment	770	931	948

SPECIAL BENEFITS

(INCLUDING TRANSFER OF FUNDS)

For the payment of compensation, benefits, and expenses (except administrative expenses not otherwise authorized by law) accruing during the current or any prior fiscal year authorized by 5 U.S.C. 81; continuation of benefits as provided for under the heading "Civilian War Benefits" in the Federal Security Agency Appropriation Act, 1947; the Employees' Compensation Commission Appropriation Act, 1944; section 5(f) of the War Claims Act (50 U.S.C. App. 2012); obligations incurred under the War Hazards Compensation Act (42 U.S.C. 1701 et seq.); and 50 percent of the additional compensation and benefits required by section 10(h) of the Longshore and Harbor Workers' Compensation Act, $250,000,000, together with such amounts as may be necessary to be charged to the subsequent year appropriation for the payment of compensation and other benefits for any period subsequent to August 15 of the current year, for deposit into and to assume the attributes of the Employees' Compensation Fund established under 5 U.S.C. 8147(a): Provided, That amounts appropriated may be used under 5 U.S.C. 8104 by the Secretary to reimburse an employer, who is not the employer at the time of injury, for portions of the salary of a re-employed, disabled beneficiary: Provided further, That balances of reimbursements unobligated on September 30, 2022, shall remain available until expended for the payment of compensation, benefits, and expenses: Provided further, That in addition there shall be transferred to this appropriation from the Postal Service and from any other corporation or instrumentality required under 5 U.S.C. 8147(c) to pay an amount for its fair share of the cost of administration, such sums as the Secretary determines to be the cost of administration for employees of such fair share entities through September 30, 2023: Provided further, That of those funds transferred to this account from the fair share entities to pay the cost of administration of the Federal Employees' Compensation Act, $81,752,000 shall be made available to the Secretary as follows:

(1) For enhancement and maintenance of automated data processing systems operations and telecommunications systems, $27,727,000;

(2) For automated workload processing operations, including document imaging, centralized mail intake, and medical bill processing, $26,125,000;

(3) For periodic roll disability management and medical review, $26,126,000;

(4) For program integrity, $1,774,000; and

(5) The remaining funds shall be paid into the Treasury as miscellaneous receipts: Provided further, That the Secretary may require that any person filing a notice of injury or a claim for benefits under 5 U.S.C. 81, or the Longshore and Harbor Workers' Compensation Act, provide as part of such notice and claim, such identifying information (including Social Security account number) as such regulations may prescribe.

Note.—A full-year 2022 appropriation for this account was not enacted at the time the Budget was prepared; therefore, the Budget assumes this account is operating under the Continuing Appropriations Act, 2022 (Division A of Public Law 117–43, as amended). The amounts included for 2022 reflect the annualized level provided by the continuing resolution.

Program and Financing (in millions of dollars)

Identification code 016–1521–0–1–600	2021 actual	2022 est.	2023 est.
Obligations by program activity:			
0001 Longshore and harbor workers' compensation benefits	2	2	2
0002 Federal Employees' Compensation Act benefits	237	242	248
0799 Total direct obligations	239	244	250
0801 Federal Employees' Compensation Act benefits	2,734	2,488	2,541
0802 FECA Fair Share (administrative expenses)	80	81	82
0899 Total reimbursable obligations	2,814	2,569	2,623
0900 Total new obligations, unexpired accounts	3,053	2,813	2,873
Budgetary resources:			
Unobligated balance:			
1000 Unobligated balance brought forward, Oct 1	1,588	1,539	1,735
Budget authority:			
Appropriations, mandatory:			
1200 Appropriation	239	244	250
Spending authority from offsetting collections, mandatory:			
1800 Collected	2,765	2,765	2,798
1900 Budget authority (total)	3,004	3,009	3,048
1930 Total budgetary resources available	4,592	4,548	4,783
Memorandum (non-add) entries:			
1941 Unexpired unobligated balance, end of year	1,539	1,735	1,910
Change in obligated balance:			
Unpaid obligations:			
3000 Unpaid obligations, brought forward, Oct 1	229	251	138
3010 New obligations, unexpired accounts	3,053	2,813	2,873
3020 Outlays (gross)	–3,031	–2,926	–2,913
3050 Unpaid obligations, end of year	251	138	98
Uncollected payments:			
3060 Uncollected pymts, Fed sources, brought forward, Oct 1	–27	–27	–27
3090 Uncollected pymts, Fed sources, end of year	–27	–27	–27
Memorandum (non-add) entries:			
3100 Obligated balance, start of year	202	224	111
3200 Obligated balance, end of year	224	111	71
Budget authority and outlays, net:			
Mandatory:			
4090 Budget authority, gross	3,004	3,009	3,048
Outlays, gross:			
4100 Outlays from new mandatory authority	2,809	2,813	2,873
4101 Outlays from mandatory balances	222	113	40
4110 Outlays, gross (total)	3,031	2,926	2,913
Offsets against gross budget authority and outlays:			
Offsetting collections (collected) from:			
4120 Federal sources	–2,764	–2,765	–2,798
4123 Non-Federal sources	–1		
4130 Offsets against gross budget authority and outlays (total)	–2,765	–2,765	–2,798
4160 Budget authority, net (mandatory)	239	244	250
4170 Outlays, net (mandatory)	266	161	115
4180 Budget authority, net (total)	239	244	250
4190 Outlays, net (total)	266	161	115

Federal Employees' Compensation Act benefits.—The Federal Employees' Compensation Act (FECA) program provides monetary and medical benefits to Federal workers who sustain work-related injury or disease. Not all benefits are paid by the program, since the first 45 days of disability are usually covered by keeping injured workers in pay status with their employing agencies (the continuation-of-pay period). A workers' compensation case is created following the receipt of an injury report or claim for occupational disease. In 2023, the FECA program projects to create 100,000 cases for Federal workers or their survivors; 15,400 Federal employees are projected to submit initial wage-loss claims; and 37,000 are projected to receive long-term wage replacement benefits for job-related injuries, diseases, or deaths. Most of the costs of this account are charged back to the beneficiaries' employing agencies.

FEDERAL EMPLOYEES' COMPENSATION WORKLOAD

	2021 actual	2022 proj.	2023 proj.
Initial Wage-Loss Claims Received	15,982	15,600	15,400
Number of Compensation and Medical Payments Processed (by Chargeback Year)	6,902,085	7,400,000	7,000,000
Cases Created	96,457	100,000	100,000
Periodic Roll Payment Cases - Long-term Disability	35,334	37,000	37,000

Longshore and Harbor Workers' Compensation Act benefits.—Under the Longshore and Harbor Workers' Compensation Act, as amended, the Federal Government pays from direct appropriations one-half of the increased benefits provided by the amendments for persons on the rolls prior to 1972. The remainder is provided from the Special Workers' Compensation Fund, which is financed by private employers, and is assessed at the beginning of each calendar year for their proportionate share of these payments.

Object Classification (in millions of dollars)

Identification code 016–1521–0–1–600	2021 actual	2022 est.	2023 est.
42.0 Direct obligations: Insurance claims and indemnities	239	244	250

Office of Workers' Compensation Programs—Continued
Federal Funds—Continued

SPECIAL BENEFITS—Continued
Object Classification—Continued

Identification code 016–1521–0–1–600	2021 actual	2022 est.	2023 est.
99.0 Reimbursable obligations	2,814	2,569	2,623
99.9 Total new obligations, unexpired accounts	3,053	2,813	2,873

Employment Summary

Identification code 016–1521–0–1–600	2021 actual	2022 est.	2023 est.
2001 Reimbursable civilian full-time equivalent employment	130	143	143

ENERGY EMPLOYEES OCCUPATIONAL ILLNESS COMPENSATION FUND

Program and Financing (in millions of dollars)

Identification code 016–1523–0–1–053	2021 actual	2022 est.	2023 est.
Obligations by program activity:			
0001 Part B benefits and all medical	1,279	1,414	1,498
0002 Part E benefits	443	375	380
0003 RECA DOJ benefits	13	12	12
0900 Total new obligations, unexpired accounts (object class 42.0)	1,735	1,801	1,890
Budgetary resources:			
Budget authority:			
Appropriations, mandatory:			
1200 Appropriation	1,735	1,801	1,890
1900 Budget authority (total)	1,735	1,801	1,890
1930 Total budgetary resources available	1,735	1,801	1,890
Change in obligated balance:			
Unpaid obligations:			
3000 Unpaid obligations, brought forward, Oct 1	27	36	28
3010 New obligations, unexpired accounts	1,735	1,801	1,890
3020 Outlays (gross)	–1,726	–1,809	–1,896
3050 Unpaid obligations, end of year	36	28	22
Memorandum (non-add) entries:			
3100 Obligated balance, start of year	27	36	28
3200 Obligated balance, end of year	36	28	22
Budget authority and outlays, net:			
Mandatory:			
4090 Budget authority, gross	1,735	1,801	1,890
Outlays, gross:			
4100 Outlays from new mandatory authority	1,699	1,801	1,890
4101 Outlays from mandatory balances	27	8	6
4110 Outlays, gross (total)	1,726	1,809	1,896
4180 Budget authority, net (total)	1,735	1,801	1,890
4190 Outlays, net (total)	1,726	1,809	1,896

Energy Employees Occupational Illness Compensation Act of 2000 (EEOICPA) benefits.—The Department of Labor is delegated responsibility to adjudicate and administer claims for benefits under the Energy Employees Occupational Illness Compensation Program Act of 2000 (EEOICPA). In July 2001, the program began accepting claims from employees or survivors of employees of the Department of Energy (DOE) and of private companies under contract with DOE who suffer from a radiation-related cancer, beryllium-related disease, or chronic silicosis as a result of their work in producing or testing nuclear weapons. The Act authorizes a lump-sum payment of $150,000 and reimbursement of medical expenses. This program is EEOICPA Part B.

The Ronald Reagan National Defense Authorization Act of 2005 (P.L. 108–767) amended EEOICPA, giving DOL responsibility for a new program (Part E) to pay workers' compensation benefits to DOE contractors and their families for illness and death arising from toxic exposures in DOE's nuclear weapons complex. This law also provides compensation for uranium workers covered under section 5 of the Radiation Exposure Compensation Act. Benefit payments under Part E began in 2005.

EEOICPA Workload Summary

Part B

	2021 actual	2022 proj.	2023 proj.
Initial Claims Received (Part B)	3,035	4,153	3,887
Consequential Condition Claims Received (Part B and E)	17,695	13,149	18,500
Threads - Medical Authorizations (Part B and E)	32,324	48,559	39,000

Part E

	2021 actual	2022 proj.	2023 proj.
Initial Claims Received (Part E)	3,895	4,360	4,225

ADMINISTRATIVE EXPENSES, ENERGY EMPLOYEES OCCUPATIONAL ILLNESS COMPENSATION FUND

For necessary expenses to administer the Energy Employees Occupational Illness Compensation Program Act, $64,564,000, to remain available until expended: Provided, That the Secretary may require that any person filing a claim for benefits under the Act provide as part of such claim such identifying information (including Social Security account number) as may be prescribed.

Note.—A full-year 2022 appropriation for this account was not enacted at the time the Budget was prepared; therefore, the Budget assumes this account is operating under the Continuing Appropriations Act, 2022 (Division A of Public Law 117–43, as amended). The amounts included for 2022 reflect the annualized level provided by the continuing resolution.

Program and Financing (in millions of dollars)

Identification code 016–1524–0–1–053	2021 actual	2022 est.	2023 est.
Obligations by program activity:			
0002 Energy Part B	59	58	59
0004 Energy Part E	73	74	75
0900 Total new obligations, unexpired accounts	132	132	134
Budgetary resources:			
Unobligated balance:			
1000 Unobligated balance brought forward, Oct 1	2	2	1
1021 Recoveries of prior year unpaid obligations	2		
1070 Unobligated balance (total)	4	2	1
Budget authority:			
Appropriations, mandatory:			
1200 Appropriation (Part B)	63	63	65
1200 Appropriation (Part E)	79	80	81
1230 Appropriations and/or unobligated balance of appropriations permanently reduced	–12	–12	–12
1260 Appropriations, mandatory (total)	130	131	134
1930 Total budgetary resources available	134	133	135
Memorandum (non-add) entries:			
1941 Unexpired unobligated balance, end of year	2	1	1
Change in obligated balance:			
Unpaid obligations:			
3000 Unpaid obligations, brought forward, Oct 1	28	28	23
3010 New obligations, unexpired accounts	132	132	134
3020 Outlays (gross)	–130	–137	–137
3040 Recoveries of prior year unpaid obligations, unexpired	–2		
3050 Unpaid obligations, end of year	28	23	20
Memorandum (non-add) entries:			
3100 Obligated balance, start of year	28	28	23
3200 Obligated balance, end of year	28	23	20
Budget authority and outlays, net:			
Mandatory:			
4090 Budget authority, gross	130	131	134
Outlays, gross:			
4100 Outlays from new mandatory authority	100	131	134
4101 Outlays from mandatory balances	30	6	3
4110 Outlays, gross (total)	130	137	137
4180 Budget authority, net (total)	130	131	134
4190 Outlays, net (total)	130	137	137

Energy Employees Occupational Illness Compensation Program Act of 2000 (EEOICPA) administration.—Under Executive Order 13179 the Secretary of Labor is assigned primary responsibility for administering the EEOICPA program, while other responsibilities have been delegated to the Departments of Health and Human Services (HHS), Energy (DOE), and Justice (DOJ). The Office of Workers' Compensation Programs (OWCP) in the Department of Labor (DOL) is responsible for claims adjudication, and award and payment of compensation and medical benefits. DOL's Office of the Solicitor provides legal support and represents the Department in claimant appeals of OWCP decisions. HHS is responsible for developing individual dose reconstructions to estimate occupational radiation exposure, and developing regulations to guide DOL's determination of whether an individual's cancer was caused by radiation exposure at a DOE or atomic weapons facility. DOE is responsible for providing exposure histories at employment facilities covered under the Act, and other employment information. DOJ assists claimants who have been awarded compensation under the Radiation Exposure Compensation Act to file for additional compensation, including medical benefits, under EEOICPA.

The Ronald Reagan National Defense Authorization Act of 2005 (P.L. 108–767) amended EEOICPA, giving DOL responsibility for a new program Part E, to pay workers' compensation benefits to DOE contractors and their families for illness and death arising from toxic exposures in DOE's nuclear weapons complex. This law also provides compensation for uranium workers covered by the Radiation Exposure Compensation Act.

The Carl Levin and Howard P. "Buck" McKeon National Defense Authorization Act of 2015 (P.L. 113–291) amended EEOICPA to include Section 3687, creating the Advisory Board on Toxic Substances and Worker Health to advise the Secretary of Labor (as delegated by Executive Order 13699) with respect to technical aspects of the EEOICPA program. The Advisory Board is charged with advising the Secretary on four statutorily-specific technical issues related to EEOICPA: DOL's site exposure matrices; medical guidance for claims examiners; evidentiary requirements for claims under subtitle B related to lung disease; and the work of industrial hygienists and staff physicians and consulting physicians to ensure quality, objectivity, and consistency.

Object Classification (in millions of dollars)

Identification code 016–1524–0–1–053		2021 actual	2022 est.	2023 est.
	Direct obligations:			
	Personnel compensation:			
11.1	Full-time permanent	44	45	46
11.5	Other personnel compensation	1	1	1
11.9	Total personnel compensation	45	46	47
12.1	Civilian personnel benefits	15	16	17
21.0	Travel and transportation of persons		1	1
23.1	Rental payments to GSA	5	5	5
23.3	Communications, utilities, and miscellaneous charges		1	1
25.2	Other services from non-Federal sources	26	21	21
25.3	Other goods and services from Federal sources	35	26	26
25.7	Operation and maintenance of equipment	6	16	16
99.9	Total new obligations, unexpired accounts	132	132	134

Employment Summary

Identification code 016–1524–0–1–053	2021 actual	2022 est.	2023 est.
1001 Direct civilian full-time equivalent employment	398	404	404

SPECIAL BENEFITS FOR DISABLED COAL MINERS

For carrying out title IV of the Federal Mine Safety and Health Act of 1977, as amended by Public Law 107–275, $36,031,000, to remain available until expended.

For making after July 31 of the current fiscal year, benefit payments to individuals under title IV of such Act, for costs incurred in the current fiscal year, such amounts as may be necessary.

For making benefit payments under title IV for the first quarter of fiscal year 2024, $10,250,000, to remain available until expended.

Note.—A full-year 2022 appropriation for this account was not enacted at the time the Budget was prepared; therefore, the Budget assumes this account is operating under the Continuing Appropriations Act, 2022 (Division A of Public Law 117–43, as amended). The amounts included for 2022 reflect the annualized level provided by the continuing resolution.

Program and Financing (in millions of dollars)

Identification code 016–0169–0–1–601		2021 actual	2022 est.	2023 est.
	Obligations by program activity:			
0001	Benefits	50	42	42
0002	Administration	5	5	5
0900	Total new obligations, unexpired accounts	55	47	47
	Budgetary resources:			
	Unobligated balance:			
1000	Unobligated balance brought forward, Oct 1	13	13	13
	Budget authority:			
	Appropriations, mandatory:			
1200	Appropriation	41	33	36
	Advance appropriations, mandatory:			
1270	Advance appropriation	14	14	11
1900	Budget authority (total)	55	47	47
1930	Total budgetary resources available	68	60	60
	Memorandum (non-add) entries:			
1941	Unexpired unobligated balance, end of year	13	13	13
	Change in obligated balance:			
	Unpaid obligations:			
3000	Unpaid obligations, brought forward, Oct 1	6	5	4
3010	New obligations, unexpired accounts	55	47	47
3020	Outlays (gross)	–56	–48	–48
3050	Unpaid obligations, end of year	5	4	3
	Memorandum (non-add) entries:			
3100	Obligated balance, start of year	6	5	4
3200	Obligated balance, end of year	5	4	3
	Budget authority and outlays, net:			
	Mandatory:			
4090	Budget authority, gross	55	47	47
	Outlays, gross:			
4100	Outlays from new mandatory authority	51	47	47
4101	Outlays from mandatory balances	5	1	1
4110	Outlays, gross (total)	56	48	48
4180	Budget authority, net (total)	55	47	47
4190	Outlays, net (total)	56	48	48

Title IV of the Federal Mine Safety and Health Act authorizes monthly benefits to coal miners disabled due to coal workers' pneumoconiosis (black lung), and to their widows and certain other dependents. Part B of the Act assigned the processing and paying of claims filed between December 30, 1969 (when the program originated) and June 30, 1973 to the Social Security Administration (SSA). P.L. 107–275 transferred Part B claims processing and payment operations from SSA to the Department of Labor's Office of Workers' Compensation Programs. This change was implemented on October 1, 2003.

	2021 actual	2022 proj.	2023 proj.
Beneficiaries	5,912	5,326	4,827
Benefit Payments ($ in 000s)	$50,055	$48,465	$44,925

Object Classification (in millions of dollars)

Identification code 016–0169–0–1–601		2021 actual	2022 est.	2023 est.
	Direct obligations:			
11.1	Personnel compensation: Full-time permanent	1	1	1
12.1	Civilian personnel benefits	1	1	1
25.3	Other goods and services from Federal sources	2	2	2
25.7	Operation and maintenance of equipment	1	1	1
42.0	Insurance claims and indemnities	50	42	42
99.9	Total new obligations, unexpired accounts	55	47	47

Employment Summary

Identification code 016–0169–0–1–601	2021 actual	2022 est.	2023 est.
1001 Direct civilian full-time equivalent employment	13	13	13

PANAMA CANAL COMMISSION COMPENSATION FUND

Special and Trust Fund Receipts (in millions of dollars)

Identification code 016–5155–0–2–602		2021 actual	2022 est.	2023 est.
0100	Balance, start of year			
	Receipts:			
	Current law:			
1140	Interest on Investments, Panama Canal Commission		1	1
2000	Total: Balances and receipts		1	1
	Appropriations:			
	Current law:			
2101	Panama Canal Commission Compensation Fund		–1	–1
5099	Balance, end of year			

Program and Financing (in millions of dollars)

Identification code 016–5155–0–2–602		2021 actual	2022 est.	2023 est.
	Obligations by program activity:			
0001	Benefits	4	4	4
0900	Total new obligations, unexpired accounts (object class 42.0)	4	4	4
	Budgetary resources:			
	Unobligated balance:			
1000	Unobligated balance brought forward, Oct 1	22	18	15
	Budget authority:			
	Appropriations, mandatory:			
1201	Appropriation (special or trust fund)		1	1
1930	Total budgetary resources available	22	19	16
	Memorandum (non-add) entries:			
1941	Unexpired unobligated balance, end of year	18	15	12
	Change in obligated balance:			
	Unpaid obligations:			
3010	New obligations, unexpired accounts	4	4	4
3020	Outlays (gross)	–4	–4	–4
	Budget authority and outlays, net:			
	Mandatory:			
4090	Budget authority, gross		1	1
	Outlays, gross:			
4100	Outlays from new mandatory authority		1	1
4101	Outlays from mandatory balances	4	3	3
4110	Outlays, gross (total)	4	4	4
4180	Budget authority, net (total)		1	1
4190	Outlays, net (total)	4	4	4
	Memorandum (non-add) entries:			
5000	Total investments, SOY: Federal securities: Par value	22	18	15
5001	Total investments, EOY: Federal securities: Par value	18	15	12

This fund was established to provide for the accumulation of funds to meet the Panama Canal Commission's obligations to defray costs of workers' compensation which will accrue pursuant to the Federal Employees' Compensation Act (FECA). On December 31, 1999, the Commission was dissolved as set forth in the Panama Canal Treaty of 1977; however, the liability of the Commission for payments beyond that date did not end with its termination. The establishment of this fund, into which funds were deposited on a regular basis by the Commission, was in conjunction with the transfer of the administration of the FECA program from the Commission to the Department of Labor, effective January 1, 1989.

Trust Funds

BLACK LUNG DISABILITY TRUST FUND

(INCLUDING TRANSFER OF FUNDS)

Such sums as may be necessary from the Black Lung Disability Trust Fund (the "Fund"), to remain available until expended, for payment of all benefits authorized by section 9501(d)(1), (2), (6), and (7) of the Internal Revenue Code of 1986; and repayment of, and payment of interest on advances, as authorized by section 9501(d)(4) of that Act. In addition, the following amounts may be expended from the Fund for fiscal year 2023 for expenses of operation and administration of the Black Lung Benefits program, as authorized by section 9501(d)(5): not to exceed $42,194,000 for transfer to the Office of Workers' Compensation Programs, "Salaries and Expenses"; not to exceed $38,407,000 for transfer to Departmental Management, "Salaries and Expenses"; not to exceed $353,000 for transfer to Departmental Management, "Office of Inspector General"; and not to exceed $356,000 for payments into miscellaneous receipts for the expenses of the Department of the Treasury.

Note.—A full-year 2022 appropriation for this account was not enacted at the time the Budget was prepared; therefore, the Budget assumes this account is operating under the Continuing Appropriations Act, 2022 (Division A of Public Law 117–43, as amended). The amounts included for 2022 reflect the annualized level provided by the continuing resolution.

Special and Trust Fund Receipts (in millions of dollars)

Identification code 016–8144–0–7–601		2021 actual	2022 est.	2023 est.
0100	Balance, start of year	72	89	94
	Receipts:			
	Current law:			
1110	Transfer from General Fund, Black Lung Benefits Revenue Act Taxes	286	207	151
1130	Miscellaneous Interest, Black Lung Disability Trust Fund	2	2	2
1199	Total current law receipts	288	209	153
1999	Total receipts	288	209	153
2000	Total: Balances and receipts	360	298	247
	Appropriations:			
	Current law:			
2101	Black Lung Disability Trust Fund	–288	–209	–153
2103	Black Lung Disability Trust Fund	–2		
2132	Black Lung Disability Trust Fund	4	5	5
2135	Black Lung Disability Trust Fund	15		
2199	Total current law appropriations	–271	–204	–148
2999	Total appropriations	–271	–204	–148
5099	Balance, end of year	89	94	99

Program and Financing (in millions of dollars)

Identification code 016–8144–0–7–601		2021 actual	2022 est.	2023 est.
	Obligations by program activity:			
0001	Disabled coal miners benefits	126	175	185
0002	Administrative expenses	70	75	77
0003	Interest on zero coupon bonds	90	103	116
0004	Interest on short term advances	4	2	12
0900	Total new obligations, unexpired accounts	290	355	390
	Budgetary resources:			
	Budget authority:			
	Appropriations, mandatory:			
1201	Appropriation (special or trust fund)	288	209	153
1203	Appropriation (previously unavailable)(special or trust)	2		
1232	Appropriations and/or unobligated balance of appropriations temporarily reduced	–4	–5	–5
1235	Appropriations precluded from obligation (special or trust)	–15		
1260	Appropriations, mandatory (total)	271	204	148
	Borrowing authority, mandatory:			
1400	Borrowing authority [combined]	2,462	2,579	2,945
1422	Borrowing authority applied to repay debt [Advances]	–2,323	–2,311	–2,579
1422	Borrowing authority applied to repay debt [Repayment of Treasury Bonds]	–120	–117	–124
1440	Borrowing authority, mandatory (total)	19	151	242
1900	Budget authority (total)	290	355	390
1930	Total budgetary resources available	290	355	390
	Change in obligated balance:			
	Unpaid obligations:			
3000	Unpaid obligations, brought forward, Oct 1	14	13	1
3010	New obligations, unexpired accounts	290	355	390
3020	Outlays (gross)	–291	–367	–390
3050	Unpaid obligations, end of year	13	1	1
	Memorandum (non-add) entries:			
3100	Obligated balance, start of year	14	13	1
3200	Obligated balance, end of year	13	1	1

DEPARTMENT OF LABOR

Office of Workers' Compensation Programs—Continued
Trust Funds—Continued

781

		2021 actual	2022 est.	2023 est.
	Budget authority and outlays, net:			
	Mandatory:			
4090	Budget authority, gross	290	355	390
	Outlays, gross:			
4100	Outlays from new mandatory authority	277	355	390
4101	Outlays from mandatory balances	14	12	
4110	Outlays, gross (total)	291	367	390
4180	Budget authority, net (total)	290	355	390
4190	Outlays, net (total)	291	367	390
	Memorandum (non-add) entries:			
5080	Outstanding debt, SOY	−4,752	−4,620	−4,771
5081	Outstanding debt, EOY	−4,620	−4,771	−5,013
5082	Borrowing	−2,311	−2,579	−2,945

The Black Lung Disability Trust Fund (BLDTF) consists of all monies collected from the coal mine industry under the provisions of the Black Lung Benefits Revenue Act of 1981, as amended by the Consolidated Omnibus Budget Reconciliation Act of 1985, in the form of an excise tax on coal mined and used domestically. These monies are used to pay compensation, medical, and survivor benefits to eligible miners and their survivors, where mine employment terminated prior to 1970 or where no mine operator can be assigned liability. In addition, the BLDTF pays all administrative costs incurred in the operation of Part C of the Black Lung program. The fund is administered jointly by the Secretaries of Labor, Treasury, and Health and Human Services. Because excise tax receipts were insufficient to cover the BLDTF's expenses, the fund borrowed monies necessary to meet the shortfall from the U.S. Treasury, subject to repayment with interest. This led to the fund accumulating a large amount of debt. The Emergency Economic Stabilization Act of 2008, enacted on October 3, 2008, authorized restructuring of the Black Lung Disability Trust Fund (BLDTF) debt by (1) extending the current coal excise tax rates of $1.10 per ton on underground-mined coal and $0.55 per ton on surface-mined coal until December 31, 2018; (2) providing a one-time appropriation for the BLDTF to repay the market value of parts of the outstanding repayable advances and accrued interest; and (3) refinancing the remainder of the outstanding debt through the issuance of zero-coupon bonds, to be retired using the BLDTF's annual operating surplus until all of its remaining obligations have been paid. Due to a decline in coal production and other factors, however, the Trust Fund's debt has continued to grow.

Note.— Between January 1, 2019 and December 31, 2019, the coal excise tax rates on underground-mined coal were $0.50 per ton or 2 percent of the sales price (whichever is lower) and $0.25 per ton or 2 percent of the sales price (whichever is lower) on surface-mined coal. Congress restored the higher 2018 tax rates on underground-mined coal of $1.10 per ton or 2 percent of the sales price (whichever is lower) and $0.55 per ton or 2 percent of the sales price (whichever is lower) on surface-mined coal from January 1, 2020 to December 31, 2021 in the Further Consolidated Appropriations Act, 2020 and the Consolidated Appropriations Act, 2021. Tax rates again reverted to the lower 2019 levels effective January 1, 2022.

BLACK LUNG DISABILITY TRUST FUND WORKLOAD

	2021 actual	2022 proj.	2023 proj.
Number of Claims Received	5,552	6,500	6,000
Number of Trust Fund Beneficiaries	11,401	11,074	10,000
Number of Beneficiaries Paid by Responsible Operators	5,946	6,178	6,400

Status of Funds (in millions of dollars)

Identification code 016–8144–0–7–601	2021 actual	2022 est.	2023 est.
	Unexpended balance, start of year:			
0100	Balance, start of year	−4,353	−4,356	−4,514
0999	Total balance, start of year	−4,353	−4,356	−4,514
	Cash income during the year:			
	Current law:			
	Receipts:			
1110	Transfer from General Fund, Black Lung Benefits Revenue Act Taxes	286	207	151
1150	Miscellaneous Interest, Black Lung Disability Trust Fund	2	2	2
1199	Income under present law	288	209	153
1999	Total cash income	288	209	153
	Cash outgo during year:			
	Current law:			
2100	Black Lung Disability Trust Fund [Budget Acct]	−291	−367	−390
2199	Outgo under current law	−291	−367	−390
2999	Total cash outgo (−)	−291	−367	−390
	Surplus or deficit:			
3110	Excluding interest	−5	−160	−239
3120	Interest	2	2	2
3199	Subtotal, surplus or deficit	−3	−158	−237
3999	Total change in fund balance	−3	−158	−237
	Unexpended balance, end of year:			
4100	Uninvested balance (net), end of year	−4,356	−4,514	−4,751
4999	Total balance, end of year	−4,356	−4,514	−4,751

Object Classification (in millions of dollars)

Identification code 016–8144–0–7–601	2021 actual	2022 est.	2023 est.
	Direct obligations:			
25.3	Other goods and services from Federal sources	70	75	77
42.0	Insurance claims and indemnities	130	177	197
43.0	Interest and dividends	90	103	116
99.9	Total new obligations, unexpired accounts	290	355	390

SPECIAL WORKERS' COMPENSATION EXPENSES

Special and Trust Fund Receipts (in millions of dollars)

Identification code 016–9971–0–7–601	2021 actual	2022 est.	2023 est.
0100	Balance, start of year			5
	Receipts:			
	Current law:			
1110	Longshoremen's and Harbor Workers Compensation Act, Receipts, Special Workers'	84	97	97
1110	Workmen's Compensation Act within District of Columbia, Receipts, Special Workers'	5	6	6
1140	Interest, Special Worker's Compensation Expenses		1	1
1199	Total current law receipts	89	104	104
1999	Total receipts	89	104	104
2000	Total: Balances and receipts	89	104	109
	Appropriations:			
	Current law:			
2101	Special Workers' Compensation Expenses	−2	−2	−2
2101	Special Workers' Compensation Expenses	−87	−97	−97
2199	Total current law appropriations	−89	−99	−99
2999	Total appropriations	−89	−99	−99
5099	Balance, end of year		5	10

Program and Financing (in millions of dollars)

Identification code 016–9971–0–7–601	2021 actual	2022 est.	2023 est.
	Obligations by program activity:			
0001	Longshore and Harbor Workers' Compensation Act, as amended	95	97	97
0002	District of Columbia Compensation Act	6	6	6
0900	Total new obligations, unexpired accounts	101	103	103
	Budgetary resources:			
	Unobligated balance:			
1000	Unobligated balance brought forward, Oct 1	66	54	50
	Budget authority:			
	Appropriations, discretionary:			
1101	Appropriation (special or trust)	2	2	2
	Appropriations, mandatory:			
1201	Appropriation (special or trust fund)	87	97	97
1900	Budget authority (total)	89	99	99
1930	Total budgetary resources available	155	153	149

Office of Workers' Compensation Programs—Continued
Trust Funds—Continued

SPECIAL WORKERS' COMPENSATION EXPENSES—Continued
Program and Financing—Continued

Identification code 016–9971–0–7–601	2021 actual	2022 est.	2023 est.
Memorandum (non-add) entries:			
1941 Unexpired unobligated balance, end of year	54	50	46
Change in obligated balance:			
Unpaid obligations:			
3000 Unpaid obligations, brought forward, Oct 1	....	....	4
3010 New obligations, unexpired accounts	101	103	103
3020 Outlays (gross)	–101	–99	–99
3050 Unpaid obligations, end of year	....	4	8
Memorandum (non-add) entries:			
3100 Obligated balance, start of year	....	....	4
3200 Obligated balance, end of year	....	4	8
Budget authority and outlays, net:			
Discretionary:			
4000 Budget authority, gross	2	2	2
Outlays, gross:			
4010 Outlays from new discretionary authority	2	2	2
Mandatory:			
4090 Budget authority, gross	87	97	97
Outlays, gross:			
4100 Outlays from new mandatory authority	87	97	97
4101 Outlays from mandatory balances	12	....	....
4110 Outlays, gross (total)	99	97	97
4180 Budget authority, net (total)	89	99	99
4190 Outlays, net (total)	101	99	99
Memorandum (non-add) entries:			
5000 Total investments, SOY: Federal securities: Par value	47	46	52
5001 Total investments, EOY: Federal securities: Par value	46	52	48

The trust fund consists of amounts received from employers for the death of an employee where no person is entitled to compensation for such death, for fines and penalty payments, and—pursuant to an annual assessment of the industry—for the general expenses of the fund under the Longshore and Harbor Workers' Compensation Act (LHWCA), as amended.

The trust fund is available for payments of additional compensation for second injuries. When a second injury is combined with a previous disability and results in increased permanent partial disability, permanent total disability, or death, the employer's liability for benefits is limited to a specified period of compensation payments, after which the fund provides continuing compensation benefits. In addition, the fund pays one-half of the increased benefits provided under the LHWCA for persons on the rolls prior to 1972. Maintenance payments are made to disabled employees undergoing vocational rehabilitation to enable them to return to remunerative occupations, and the costs of necessary rehabilitation services not otherwise available to disabled workers are defrayed. Payments are made in cases where other circumstances preclude payment by an employer and to provide medical, surgical, and other treatment in disability cases where there has been a default by the insolvency of an uninsured employer.

Object Classification (in millions of dollars)

Identification code 016–9971–0–7–601	2021 actual	2022 est.	2023 est.
Direct obligations:			
25.3 Other goods and services from Federal sources	2	2	2
42.0 Insurance claims and indemnities	99	101	101
99.9 Total new obligations, unexpired accounts	101	103	103

WAGE AND HOUR DIVISION
Federal Funds

SALARIES AND EXPENSES

For necessary expenses for the Wage and Hour Division, including reimbursement to State, Federal, and local agencies and their employees for inspection services rendered, $307,678,000.

Note.—A full-year 2022 appropriation for this account was not enacted at the time the Budget was prepared; therefore, the Budget assumes this account is operating under the Continuing Appropriations Act, 2022 (Division A of Public Law 117–43, as amended). The amounts included for 2022 reflect the annualized level provided by the continuing resolution.

Program and Financing (in millions of dollars)

Identification code 016–0143–0–1–505	2021 actual	2022 est.	2023 est.
Obligations by program activity:			
0001 Wage and Hour	246	246	308
0002 American Rescue Plan Act	8	13	....
0799 Total direct obligations	254	259	308
0801 Salaries and Expenses (Reimbursable)	4	3	3
0900 Total new obligations, unexpired accounts	258	262	311
Budgetary resources:			
Unobligated balance:			
1000 Unobligated balance brought forward, Oct 1	....	13	....
Budget authority:			
Appropriations, discretionary:			
1100 Appropriation	246	246	308
Appropriations, mandatory:			
1200 Appropriation	21	....	....
Spending authority from offsetting collections, discretionary:			
1700 Collected	4	3	3
1900 Budget authority (total)	271	249	311
1930 Total budgetary resources available	271	262	311
Memorandum (non-add) entries:			
1941 Unexpired unobligated balance, end of year	13	....	....
Change in obligated balance:			
Unpaid obligations:			
3000 Unpaid obligations, brought forward, Oct 1	21	18	25
3010 New obligations, unexpired accounts	258	262	311
3011 Obligations ("upward adjustments"), expired accounts	1	....	....
3020 Outlays (gross)	–260	–255	–306
3041 Recoveries of prior year unpaid obligations, expired	–2	....	....
3050 Unpaid obligations, end of year	18	25	30
Uncollected payments:			
3060 Uncollected pymts, Fed sources, brought forward, Oct 1	–2	....	....
3071 Change in uncollected pymts, Fed sources, expired	2	....	....
Memorandum (non-add) entries:			
3100 Obligated balance, start of year	19	18	25
3200 Obligated balance, end of year	18	25	30
Budget authority and outlays, net:			
Discretionary:			
4000 Budget authority, gross	250	249	311
Outlays, gross:			
4010 Outlays from new discretionary authority	235	229	286
4011 Outlays from discretionary balances	18	19	20
4020 Outlays, gross (total)	253	248	306
Offsets against gross budget authority and outlays:			
Offsetting collections (collected) from:			
4030 Federal sources:	–3	....	....
4033 Non-Federal sources	–3	–3	–3
4040 Offsets against gross budget authority and outlays (total)	–6	–3	–3
Additional offsets against gross budget authority only:			
4052 Offsetting collections credited to expired accounts	2	....	....
4060 Additional offsets against budget authority only (total)	2	....	....
4070 Budget authority, net (discretionary)	246	246	308
4080 Outlays, net (discretionary)	247	245	303
Mandatory:			
4090 Budget authority, gross	21	....	....
Outlays, gross:			
4100 Outlays from new mandatory authority	7	....	....
4101 Outlays from mandatory balances	....	7	....
4110 Outlays, gross (total)	7	7	....
4180 Budget authority, net (total)	267	246	308
4190 Outlays, net (total)	254	252	303

The Wage and Hour Division enforces the minimum wage, overtime, child labor, and other employment standards under the Fair Labor Standards Act (FLSA), the Migrant and Seasonal Agricultural Worker Protection Act (MSPA), the Family and Medical Leave Act (FMLA), certain provisions of the Immigration and Nationality Act (INA), the wage garnishment provisions in Title III of the Consumer Credit Protection Act (CCPA), and the

Employee Polygraph Protection Act (EPPA). The Division also determines prevailing wages and enforces employment standards under various Government contract wage standards, including the Davis-Bacon and Related Acts (DBRA) and the McNamara-O'Hara Service Contract Act (SCA). Collectively, these labor standards cover most private, state, and local government employment. They protect over 148 million workers in more than 10.2 million establishments throughout the United States and its territories.

Object Classification (in millions of dollars)

Identification code 016–0143–0–1–505		2021 actual	2022 est.	2023 est.
	Direct obligations:			
	Personnel compensation:			
11.1	Full-time permanent	125	132	162
11.3	Other than full-time permanent	1	1	1
11.5	Other personnel compensation	3	3	3
11.9	Total personnel compensation	129	136	166
12.1	Civilian personnel benefits	49	53	67
21.0	Travel and transportation of persons	1	1	2
23.1	Rental payments to GSA	13	13	14
23.3	Communications, utilities, and miscellaneous charges	2	2	2
24.0	Printing and reproduction		1	
25.1	Advisory and assistance services	3	3	3
25.2	Other services from non-Federal sources	1	1	1
25.3	Other goods and services from Federal sources	44	41	41
25.7	Operation and maintenance of equipment	8	4	7
26.0	Supplies and materials	1	1	2
31.0	Equipment	3	3	3
99.0	Direct obligations	254	259	308
99.0	Reimbursable obligations	4	3	3
99.9	Total new obligations, unexpired accounts	258	262	311

Employment Summary

Identification code 016–0143–0–1–505	2021 actual	2022 est.	2023 est.
1001 Direct civilian full-time equivalent employment	1,343	1,380	1,556
2001 Reimbursable civilian full-time equivalent employment	1		

H-1 B AND L FRAUD PREVENTION AND DETECTION

Program and Financing (in millions of dollars)

Identification code 016–5393–0–2–505		2021 actual	2022 est.	2023 est.
	Obligations by program activity:			
0001	H-1 B and L Fraud Prevention and Detection	36	48	50
	Budgetary resources:			
	Unobligated balance:			
1000	Unobligated balance brought forward, Oct 1	6	10	10
	Budget authority:			
	Appropriations, mandatory:			
1201	Appropriation (special or trust fund)	40	49	50
1203	Appropriation (previously unavailable)(special or trust)	2	2	3
1232	Appropriations and/or unobligated balance of appropriations temporarily reduced	–2	–3	–3
1260	Appropriations, mandatory (total)	40	48	50
1930	Total budgetary resources available	46	58	60
	Memorandum (non-add) entries:			
1941	Unexpired unobligated balance, end of year	10	10	10
	Change in obligated balance:			
	Unpaid obligations:			
3000	Unpaid obligations, brought forward, Oct 1	4	1	1
3010	New obligations, unexpired accounts	36	48	50
3020	Outlays (gross)	–39	–48	–48
3050	Unpaid obligations, end of year	1	1	3
	Memorandum (non-add) entries:			
3100	Obligated balance, start of year	4	1	1
3200	Obligated balance, end of year	1	1	3
	Budget authority and outlays, net:			
	Mandatory:			
4090	Budget authority, gross	40	48	50
	Outlays, gross:			
4100	Outlays from new mandatory authority		37	48
4101	Outlays from mandatory balances	39	11	
4110	Outlays, gross (total)	39	48	48
4180	Budget authority, net (total)	40	48	50
4190	Outlays, net (total)	39	48	48

The Wage and Hour Division has traditionally had responsibility for enforcing certain worker protections provisions of the Immigration and Nationality Act, specifically the H-2A and H-1B temporary non-immigrant foreign worker programs. Pursuant to an Interagency Agreement (IAA) between the U.S. Department of Homeland Security (DHS) and the U.S. Department of Labor (DOL) and section 214(c)(14)(B) of the Immigration and Nationality Act (INA), 8 U.S.C. 1184(c)(14)(B), DOL and WHD have been delegated the enforcement authority located at section 214(c)(14)(A)(i) of the INA, 8 U.S.C. 1184(c)(14)(A)(i) for enforcing the H-2B temporary non-immigrant foreign worker program. Under section 524 of H.R. 3288, the Secretary of Labor may use one-third of the H-1B and L Fraud Protection and Detection fee account for enforcement of these temporary worker program provisions and for related enforcement activities.

Object Classification (in millions of dollars)

Identification code 016–5393–0–2–505		2021 actual	2022 est.	2023 est.
	Direct obligations:			
	Personnel compensation:			
11.1	Full-time permanent	15	21	21
11.5	Other personnel compensation		1	1
11.9	Total personnel compensation	15	22	22
12.1	Civilian personnel benefits	6	7	7
21.0	Travel and transportation of persons		1	1
25.3	Other goods and services from Federal sources	15	18	20
99.9	Total new obligations, unexpired accounts	36	48	50

Employment Summary

Identification code 016–5393–0–2–505	2021 actual	2022 est.	2023 est.
1001 Direct civilian full-time equivalent employment	153	170	170

OFFICE OF FEDERAL CONTRACT COMPLIANCE PROGRAMS

Federal Funds

SALARIES AND EXPENSES

For necessary expenses for the Office of Federal Contract Compliance Programs, $147,051,000.

Note.—A full-year 2022 appropriation for this account was not enacted at the time the Budget was prepared; therefore, the Budget assumes this account is operating under the Continuing Appropriations Act, 2022 (Division A of Public Law 117–43, as amended). The amounts included for 2022 reflect the annualized level provided by the continuing resolution.

Program and Financing (in millions of dollars)

Identification code 016–0148–0–1–505		2021 actual	2022 est.	2023 est.
	Obligations by program activity:			
0002	Federal contractor EEO standards enforcement	106	106	147
	Budgetary resources:			
	Budget authority:			
	Appropriations, discretionary:			
1100	Appropriation	106	106	147
1930	Total budgetary resources available	106	106	147
	Change in obligated balance:			
	Unpaid obligations:			
3000	Unpaid obligations, brought forward, Oct 1	18	18	18
3010	New obligations, unexpired accounts	106	106	147
3020	Outlays (gross)	–106	–106	–145
3050	Unpaid obligations, end of year	18	18	20

Office of Federal Contract Compliance Programs—Continued
Federal Funds—Continued

SALARIES AND EXPENSES—Continued

Program and Financing—Continued

Identification code 016–0148–0–1–505	2021 actual	2022 est.	2023 est.
Memorandum (non-add) entries:			
3100 Obligated balance, start of year	18	18	18
3200 Obligated balance, end of year	18	18	20
Budget authority and outlays, net:			
Discretionary:			
4000 Budget authority, gross	106	106	147
Outlays, gross:			
4010 Outlays from new discretionary authority	91	96	133
4011 Outlays from discretionary balances	15	10	12
4020 Outlays, gross (total)	106	106	145
4180 Budget authority, net (total)	106	106	147
4190 Outlays, net (total)	106	106	145

The Office of Federal Contract Compliance Programs (OFCCP) enforces, for the benefit of job seekers and wage earners, the affirmative action and equal employment opportunity obligations required of those who do business with the Federal government. OFCCP administers and enforces three equal employment opportunity laws: Executive Order 11246, as amended (Executive Order); Section 503 of the Rehabilitation Act of 1973, as amended, 29 U.S.C. 793 (Section 503); and the Vietnam Era Veterans Readjustment Assistance Act of 1974, as amended, 38 U.S.C. 4212 (VEVRAA).[1] Collectively, these laws, as amended, make it unlawful for contractors and subcontractors doing business with the federal government to discriminate in employment because of race, color, religion, sex, sexual orientation, gender identity, national origin, disability, or status as a protected veteran. In addition, contractors and subcontractors are prohibited from discriminating against applicants or employees because they inquire about, discuss, or disclose their compensation or that of others, subject to certain limitations, and may not retaliate against applicants or employees for engaging in protected activities. OFCCP conducts compliance evaluations and complaint investigations of federal contractors' and subcontractors' personnel policies and procedures. OFCCP also offers compliance assistance to federal contractors and subcontractors to help them understand the regulatory requirements and review process. The 2023 Budget proposes to enable OFCCP to ensure it has the increased capacity to: 1) support OFCCP's increased enforcement responsibility over the growing number of contractors receiving Infrastructure Investment and Jobs Act (IIJA) investments; 2) strengthen its development and resolution of systemic discrimination cases, and 3) engage in effective cross-regional collaboration.

[1] Executive Order 11246, Sept. 24, 1965, 30 FR 12319, 12935, 3 CFR, 1964–1965, Comp., p. 339, as amended; Section 503 of the Rehabilitation Act of 1973, as amended, 29 U.S.C. 793, (Section 503); and the Vietnam Era Veterans Readjustment Assistance Act of 1974, as amended, 38 U.S.C. 4212.

Object Classification (in millions of dollars)

Identification code 016–0148–0–1–505	2021 actual	2022 est.	2023 est.
Direct obligations:			
Personnel compensation:			
11.1 Full-time permanent	46	50	81
11.5 Other personnel compensation	1	1	1
11.9 Total personnel compensation	47	51	82
12.1 Civilian personnel benefits	18	19	28
23.1 Rental payments to GSA	6	6	6
25.2 Other services from non-Federal sources	1	2	2
25.3 Other goods and services from Federal sources	22	18	19
25.7 Operation and maintenance of equipment	11	8	8
26.0 Supplies and materials	....	1	1
31.0 Equipment	1	1	1
99.9 Total new obligations, unexpired accounts	106	106	147

Employment Summary

Identification code 016–0148–0–1–505	2021 actual	2022 est.	2023 est.
1001 Direct civilian full-time equivalent employment	422	420	628

OFFICE OF LABOR MANAGEMENT STANDARDS

Federal Funds

SALARIES AND EXPENSES

For necessary expenses for the Office of Labor-Management Standards, $49,951,000.

Note.—A full-year 2022 appropriation for this account was not enacted at the time the Budget was prepared; therefore, the Budget assumes this account is operating under the Continuing Appropriations Act, 2022 (Division A of Public Law 117–43, as amended). The amounts included for 2022 reflect the annualized level provided by the continuing resolution.

Program and Financing (in millions of dollars)

Identification code 016–0150–0–1–505	2021 actual	2022 est.	2023 est.
Obligations by program activity:			
0002 Labor-management standards	44	44	50
Budgetary resources:			
Budget authority:			
Appropriations, discretionary:			
1100 Appropriation	44	44	50
1900 Budget authority (total)	44	44	50
1930 Total budgetary resources available	44	44	50
Change in obligated balance:			
Unpaid obligations:			
3000 Unpaid obligations, brought forward, Oct 1	4	3	4
3010 New obligations, unexpired accounts	44	44	50
3020 Outlays (gross)	–45	–43	–49
3050 Unpaid obligations, end of year	3	4	5
Memorandum (non-add) entries:			
3100 Obligated balance, start of year	4	3	4
3200 Obligated balance, end of year	3	4	5
Budget authority and outlays, net:			
Discretionary:			
4000 Budget authority, gross	44	44	50
Outlays, gross:			
4010 Outlays from new discretionary authority	42	40	45
4011 Outlays from discretionary balances	3	3	4
4020 Outlays, gross (total)	45	43	49
4180 Budget authority, net (total)	44	44	50
4190 Outlays, net (total)	45	43	49

The Office of Labor-Management Standards (OLMS) administers the Labor-Management Reporting and Disclosure Act (LMRDA) and related laws. The LMRDA was enacted to protect union members by ensuring that unions have the transparency, democracy, and financial integrity members need to make informed decisions about their membership in a union as well as its operations and to ensure that members and employees who are engaged in organizing activities know the sources of their employers' messages urging them not to organize. These laws were enacted to strengthen labor unions by protecting union members from individuals, organizations, and influences that do not function in their best interests. While the vast majority of America's labor unions and their leaders operate for the benefit of the hard working people who comprise their membership, OLMS is tasked with protecting the union members by administering the LMRDA. OLMS also administers employee protections under various federally sponsored transportation programs that require fair and equitable protective arrangements for mass transit employees when federal funds are used to acquire, improve, or operate a transit system.

The FY 2023 funding level provides an additional $2,173,000 to restore OLMS' staffing level to provide unionized workers with the protections to which they are entitled under the LMRDA. Additionally, the FY 2023 funding level provides $1,000,000 to support review of additional Infrastructure Investment and Jobs Act-related Federal Transit Administration grant applications.

Object Classification (in millions of dollars)

Identification code 016–0150–0–1–505		2021 actual	2022 est.	2023 est.
	Direct obligations:			
	Personnel compensation:			
11.1	Full-time permanent	21	21	26
11.5	Other personnel compensation	1	1	1
11.9	Total personnel compensation	22	22	27
12.1	Civilian personnel benefits	9	9	10
21.0	Travel and transportation of persons	....	1	1
23.1	Rental payments to GSA	3	3	3
25.2	Other services from non-Federal sources	....	....	1
25.3	Other goods and services from Federal sources	10	7	8
25.7	Operation and maintenance of equipment	....	2	....
99.9	Total new obligations, unexpired accounts	44	44	50

Employment Summary

Identification code 016–0150–0–1–505	2021 actual	2022 est.	2023 est.
1001 Direct civilian full-time equivalent employment	189	187	204

OCCUPATIONAL SAFETY AND HEALTH ADMINISTRATION

Federal Funds

SALARIES AND EXPENSES

For necessary expenses for the Occupational Safety and Health Administration, $701,405,000, including not to exceed $120,075,000 which shall be the maximum amount available for grants to States under section 23(g) of the Occupational Safety and Health Act (the "Act"), which grants shall be no less than 50 percent of the costs of State occupational safety and health programs required to be incurred under plans approved by the Secretary under section 18 of the Act; and, in addition, notwithstanding 31 U.S.C. 3302, the Occupational Safety and Health Administration may retain up to $499,000 per fiscal year of training institute course tuition and fees, otherwise authorized by law to be collected, and may utilize such sums for occupational safety and health training and education: Provided, That notwithstanding 31 U.S.C. 3302, the Secretary is authorized, during the fiscal year ending September 30, 2023, to collect and retain fees for services provided to Nationally Recognized Testing Laboratories, and may utilize such sums, in accordance with the provisions of 29 U.S.C. 9a, to administer national and international laboratory recognition programs that ensure the safety of equipment and products used by workers in the workplace: Provided further, That none of the funds appropriated under this paragraph shall be obligated or expended to prescribe, issue, administer, or enforce any standard, rule, regulation, or order under the Act which is applicable to any person who is engaged in a farming operation which does not maintain a temporary labor camp and employs 10 or fewer employees: Provided further, That no funds appropriated under this paragraph shall be obligated or expended to administer or enforce any standard, rule, regulation, or order under the Act with respect to any employer of 10 or fewer employees who is included within a category having a Days Away, Restricted, or Transferred ("DART") occupational injury and illness rate, at the most precise industrial classification code for which such data are published, less than the national average rate as such rates are most recently published by the Secretary, acting through the Bureau of Labor Statistics, in accordance with section 24 of the Act, except—

(1) to provide, as authorized by the Act, consultation, technical assistance, educational and training services, and to conduct surveys and studies;

(2) to conduct an inspection or investigation in response to an employee complaint, to issue a citation for violations found during such inspection, and to assess a penalty for violations which are not corrected within a reasonable abatement period and for any willful violations found;

(3) to take any action authorized by the Act with respect to imminent dangers;

(4) to take any action authorized by the Act with respect to health hazards;

(5) to take any action authorized by the Act with respect to a report of an employment accident which is fatal to one or more employees or which results in hospitalization of two or more employees, and to take any action pursuant to such investigation authorized by the Act; and

(6) to take any action authorized by the Act with respect to complaints of discrimination against employees for exercising rights under the Act:

Provided further, That the foregoing proviso shall not apply to any person who is engaged in a farming operation which does not maintain a temporary labor camp and employs 10 or fewer employees: Provided further, That $13,787,000 shall be available for Susan Harwood training grants: Provided further, That not less than $3,500,000 shall be for Voluntary Protection Programs.

Note.—A full-year 2022 appropriation for this account was not enacted at the time the Budget was prepared; therefore, the Budget assumes this account is operating under the Continuing Appropriations Act, 2022 (Division A of Public Law 117–43, as amended). The amounts included for 2022 reflect the annualized level provided by the continuing resolution.

Program and Financing (in millions of dollars)

Identification code 016–0400–0–1–554		2021 actual	2022 est.	2023 est.
	Obligations by program activity:			
0001	Safety and health standards	18	18	29
0002	Federal enforcement	229	229	277
0003	Whistleblower protection	19	19	26
0004	State programs	110	110	120
0005	Technical support	24	24	27
0006	Federal compliance assistance	75	75	92
0007	State consultation grants	62	62	64
0008	Training grants	12	12	14
0009	Safety and health statistics	33	33	42
0010	Executive direction and administration	9	10	10
0011	American Rescue Plan Act	36	43	22
0799	Total direct obligations	627	635	723
0801	Salaries and Expenses (Reimbursable)	2	3	3
0900	Total new obligations, unexpired accounts	629	638	726
	Budgetary resources:			
	Unobligated balance:			
1000	Unobligated balance brought forward, Oct 1	2	65	22
	Budget authority:			
	Appropriations, discretionary:			
1100	Appropriation	592	592	701
1120	Appropriations transferred to DM Salaries and Expenses [016–0165]	–1	....	....
1160	Appropriation, discretionary (total)	591	592	701
	Appropriations, mandatory:			
1200	Appropriation	100	....	....
	Spending authority from offsetting collections, discretionary:			
1700	Collected	2	3	3
1900	Budget authority (total)	693	595	704
1930	Total budgetary resources available	695	660	726
	Memorandum (non-add) entries:			
1940	Unobligated balance expiring	–1	....	....
1941	Unexpired unobligated balance, end of year	65	22	....
	Change in obligated balance:			
	Unpaid obligations:			
3000	Unpaid obligations, brought forward, Oct 1	77	115	138
3010	New obligations, unexpired accounts	629	638	726
3011	Obligations ("upward adjustments"), expired accounts	2	....	....
3020	Outlays (gross)	–589	–615	–714
3041	Recoveries of prior year unpaid obligations, expired	–4	....	....
3050	Unpaid obligations, end of year	115	138	150
	Memorandum (non-add) entries:			
3100	Obligated balance, start of year	77	115	138
3200	Obligated balance, end of year	115	138	150
	Budget authority and outlays, net:			
	Discretionary:			
4000	Budget authority, gross	593	595	704
	Outlays, gross:			
4010	Outlays from new discretionary authority	509	518	613
4011	Outlays from discretionary balances	65	73	77
4020	Outlays, gross (total)	574	591	690
	Offsets against gross budget authority and outlays:			
	Offsetting collections (collected) from:			
4033	Non-Federal sources	–2	–3	–3
4040	Offsets against gross budget authority and outlays (total)	–2	–3	–3
	Mandatory:			
4090	Budget authority, gross	100	....	....
	Outlays, gross:			
4100	Outlays from new mandatory authority	15	....	....
4101	Outlays from mandatory balances	....	24	24
4110	Outlays, gross (total)	15	24	24

SALARIES AND EXPENSES—Continued
Program and Financing—Continued

Identification code 016–0400–0–1–554	2021 actual	2022 est.	2023 est.
4180 Budget authority, net (total)	691	592	701
4190 Outlays, net (total)	587	612	711

Safety and Health Standards.—This activity provides for the protection of worker safety and health through the development, promulgation, review, and evaluation of occupational safety and health standards and guidance, as specified under the Occupational Safety and Health Act of 1970 (OSH Act). Before any standard is proposed or promulgated, a determination is made that: (1) a significant risk of serious injury or health impairment exists; (2) the standard will reduce this risk; (3) the standard is economically and technologically feasible; and (4) the standard is cost effective when compared with alternative regulatory proposals providing equal levels of protection. This activity also ensures, through the Small Business Regulatory Enforcement Fairness Act of 1996 (SBREFA) process, that small business concerns are considered in the process of developing standards.

Federal Enforcement.—This activity provides for the protection of employees through the enforcement of workplace standards promulgated under the OSH Act, through the physical inspection of worksites, and by providing guidance on how to comply with the requirements of OSHA standards. OSHA's enforcement strategy ranges from a selective targeting of inspections and related compliance activities to a focus on specific high-hazard industries and worksites. Enforcement is prioritized by the investigation of imminent danger situations and employee complaints, investigation of fatal and catastrophic accidents, programmed inspections of firms with injury and illness rates that are above the national average, and special emphasis inspections for serious safety and health hazards.

Whistleblower Programs.—This activity provides for the enforcement of 25 whistleblower protection statutes, including Section 11(c) of the OSH Act, which prohibits any person from discharging or in any manner retaliating against any employee because the employee has exercised rights under the Act, including complaining to OSHA and seeking an OSHA inspection, participating in an OSHA inspection, and participating or testifying in any proceeding related to an OSHA inspection. In addition to the OSH Act, this activity includes administration of 24 other whistleblower protection statutes that protect employees who report violations of various airline, commercial motor carrier, consumer product, environmental, financial reform, food safety, health care reform, nuclear, pipeline, public transportation agency, railroad, maritime, automotive manufacturing, and securities, tax, antitrust, and anti-money laundering laws.

State Programs.—This activity supports states that assume responsibility for administering occupational safety and health programs under State Plans approved by the Secretary. Under section 23 of the OSH Act, grants matching up to 50 percent of total program costs are made to States that meet the Act's criteria for establishing and implementing State programs that are at least as effective as the Federal OSHA program. State programs, like Federal OSHA, provide a mix of enforcement, outreach, training, and compliance assistance activities. There are 28 approved State Plans.

Technical Support.—This activity provides support for OSHA's emergency response activities, including responses to oil spills, hurricanes, tornados, and other natural or manmade disasters. This activity also provides specialized technical expertise and advice in support of a wide range of program areas, including construction, standards setting, variance determinations, compliance assistance, and enforcement. Areas of expertise include laboratory accreditation, industrial hygiene, occupational medicine, chemical analysis, equipment calibration, safety engineering, environmental impact statements, technical and scientific databases, computer-based outreach products, and emergency preparedness.

Federal Compliance Assistance.—This activity supports a broad range of training, outreach, and cooperative programs that provide compliance assistance for employers and employees in protecting workers' safety and health, with particular emphasis on high-hazard industries, small business, and other hard-to-reach workers. OSHA works with employer and employee stakeholder groups to share compliance assistance information, resources, and tools, and to plan, coordinate, and participate in meetings, conferences, training events, and outreach activities in support of the agency's key initiatives, including enforcement and rulemaking activities, outreach campaigns, and other priority initiatives. OSHA also works with employers and employees through cooperative programs, such as the Voluntary Protection Programs to recognize employers with exemplary safety and health programs, and Alliances and Strategic Partnerships, which commit organizations to proactively collaborate with OSHA. This activity also provides assistance to federal agencies in implementing and improving their job safety and health programs. Occupational safety and health training is provided at the OSHA Training Institute and affiliated Education Centers throughout the country. Compliance and technical assistance materials are prepared and disseminated to the public through various means, including online.

State Compliance Assistance: Consultation Grants.—This activity supports OSHA's On-Site Consultation Program, which offers no-cost and confidential occupational safety and health services to small- and medium-sized businesses in all 50 states, the District of Columbia, and several U.S. territories, with priority given to high-hazard worksites. On-Site Consultation services are separate from enforcement and do not result in penalties and citations. Consultants from state agencies or universities work with employers to identify workplace hazards, provide advice for compliance with OSHA standards, and assist in establishing and improving safety and health programs. Designated state agencies or universities enter into cooperative agreements that provide a 90 percent federal funding match.

Training Grants.—This activity supports safety and health grants to organizations that provide face-to-face training, education, and technical assistance; and develop educational materials for employers and employees. These grants address education needs for workers with limited access to occupational safety health training, including young workers, temporary, minority, low literacy, domestic, limited English speaking, or other hard-to-reach workers; and specific high-risk topics and industries identified by the agency.

Safety and Health Statistics.—This activity supports the agency's information technology infrastructure, management of information, OSHA's webpage and web-based compliance assistance services, and the statistical basis for OSHA's programs and field operations. These services are provided through an integrated data network and statistical analysis and review. OSHA administers and maintains the recordkeeping system that serves as the foundation for the BLS survey on occupational injuries and illnesses and provides guidance on recordkeeping requirements to both the public and private sectors.

Executive Direction and Administration.—This activity supports overall leadership, direction, and support for agency operations. This includes developing strategic and agency priorities, coordination of policy, planning and evaluation, audit, management support, legislative liaison, interagency affairs, federal agency liaison, administrative services, and budgeting and financial control.

PROGRAM STATISTICS

	2021 actual	2022 est.	2023 est.
Inspections:			
Federal inspections	24,355	31,400	33,790
State program inspections	30,872	30,872	32,772
Whistleblower cases	3,099	3,100	4,500
Consultation Visits	17,607	21,945	23,782

Object Classification (in millions of dollars)

Identification code 016–0400–0–1–554	2021 actual	2022 est.	2023 est.
Direct obligations:			
Personnel compensation:			
11.1 Full-time permanent	188	222	252
11.5 Other personnel compensation	9	5	5
11.9 Total personnel compensation	197	227	257

DEPARTMENT OF LABOR

		2021 actual	2022 est.	2023 est.
12.1	Civilian personnel benefits	71	83	93
21.0	Travel and transportation of persons	3	7	6
23.1	Rental payments to GSA	23	20	20
23.3	Communications, utilities, and miscellaneous charges	2	3	3
24.0	Printing and reproduction	1	1	1
25.1	Advisory and assistance services	2	1	1
25.2	Other services from non-Federal sources	10	12	25
25.3	Other goods and services from Federal sources	99	72	82
25.7	Operation and maintenance of equipment	10	14	22
26.0	Supplies and materials	2	4	4
31.0	Equipment	5	4	7
41.0	Grants, subsidies, and contributions	202	187	202
99.0	Direct obligations	627	635	723
99.0	Reimbursable obligations	2	3	3
99.9	Total new obligations, unexpired accounts	629	638	726

Employment Summary

Identification code 016–0400–0–1–554	2021 actual	2022 est.	2023 est.
1001 Direct civilian full-time equivalent employment	1,833	2,016	2,346
2001 Reimbursable civilian full-time equivalent employment	4	4	4

MINE SAFETY AND HEALTH ADMINISTRATION
Federal Funds

SALARIES AND EXPENSES

For necessary expenses for the Mine Safety and Health Administration, $423,449,000, including purchase and bestowal of certificates and trophies in connection with mine rescue and first-aid work, and the hire of passenger motor vehicles, including up to $2,000,000 for mine rescue and recovery activities and not less than $10,537,000 for State assistance grants: Provided, That notwithstanding 31 U.S.C. 3302, not to exceed $750,000 may be collected by the National Mine Health and Safety Academy for room, board, tuition, and the sale of training materials, otherwise authorized by law to be collected, to be available for mine safety and health education and training activities: Provided further, That notwithstanding 31 U.S.C. 3302, the Mine Safety and Health Administration is authorized to collect and retain up to $2,499,000 from fees collected for the approval and certification of equipment, materials, and explosives for use in mines, and may utilize such sums for such activities: Provided further, That the Secretary is authorized to accept lands, buildings, equipment, and other contributions from public and private sources and to prosecute projects in cooperation with other agencies, Federal, State, or private: Provided further, That the Mine Safety and Health Administration is authorized to promote health and safety education and training in the mining community through cooperative programs with States, industry, and safety associations: Provided further, That the Secretary is authorized to recognize the Joseph A. Holmes Safety Association as a principal safety association and, notwithstanding any other provision of law, may provide funds and, with or without reimbursement, personnel, including service of Mine Safety and Health Administration officials as officers in local chapters or in the national organization: Provided further, That any funds available to the Department of Labor may be used, with the approval of the Secretary, to provide for the costs of mine rescue and survival operations in the event of a major disaster.

Note.—A full-year 2022 appropriation for this account was not enacted at the time the Budget was prepared; therefore, the Budget assumes this account is operating under the Continuing Appropriations Act, 2022 (Division A of Public Law 117–43, as amended). The amounts included for 2022 reflect the annualized level provided by the continuing resolution.

Program and Financing (in millions of dollars)

Identification code 016–1200–0–1–554	2021 actual	2022 est.	2023 est.
Obligations by program activity:			
0003 Standards development	5	6	8
0004 Assessments	8	8	8
0005 Educational policy and development	39	39	40
0006 Technical support	35	35	37
0007 Program administration	16	16	17
0008 Program evaluation & information resources	19	19	19
0009 Mine Safety and Health Enforcement	257	257	294
0010 American Rescue Plan Act	2	6	5
0799 Total direct obligations	381	386	428
0801 Salaries and Expenses (Reimbursable)	1	3	3
0900 Total new obligations, unexpired accounts	382	389	431

		2021 actual	2022 est.	2023 est.
Budgetary resources:				
Unobligated balance:				
1000	Unobligated balance brought forward, Oct 1		11	5
Budget authority:				
Appropriations, discretionary:				
1100	Appropriation	380	380	423
Appropriations, mandatory:				
1200	Appropriation	13		
Spending authority from offsetting collections, discretionary:				
1700	Collected	1	3	3
1900	Budget authority (total)	394	383	426
1930	Total budgetary resources available	394	394	431
Memorandum (non-add) entries:				
1940	Unobligated balance expiring	–1		
1941	Unexpired unobligated balance, end of year	11	5	
Change in obligated balance:				
Unpaid obligations:				
3000	Unpaid obligations, brought forward, Oct 1	54	45	39
3010	New obligations, unexpired accounts	382	389	431
3011	Obligations ("upward adjustments"), expired accounts	1		
3020	Outlays (gross)	–388	–395	–428
3041	Recoveries of prior year unpaid obligations, expired	–4		
3050	Unpaid obligations, end of year	45	39	42
Memorandum (non-add) entries:				
3100	Obligated balance, start of year	54	45	39
3200	Obligated balance, end of year	45	39	42
Budget authority and outlays, net:				
Discretionary:				
4000	Budget authority, gross	381	383	426
Outlays, gross:				
4010	Outlays from new discretionary authority	342	349	388
4011	Outlays from discretionary balances	45	40	35
4020	Outlays, gross (total)	387	389	423
Offsets against gross budget authority and outlays:				
Offsetting collections (collected) from:				
4033	Non-Federal sources	–1	–3	–3
Mandatory:				
4090	Budget authority, gross	13		
Outlays, gross:				
4100	Outlays from new mandatory authority	1		
4101	Outlays from mandatory balances		6	5
4110	Outlays, gross (total)	1	6	5
4180	Budget authority, net (total)	393	380	423
4190	Outlays, net (total)	387	392	425

Enforcement.—The enforcement strategy in 2023 will be an integrated approach toward the prevention of mining accidents, injuries, and occupational illnesses. This includes inspection of mines and other activities as mandated by the Federal Mine Safety and Health Act of 1977 (Mine Act), as amended by the Mine Improvement and New Emergency Response Act of 2006 (MINER Act), special emphasis initiatives that focus on persistent safety and health hazards, promulgation of federal mine safety and health standards, investigation of serious accidents, and on-site education and training. The desired outcome of these enforcement efforts is to prevent death, disease, and injury from mining and promote safe and healthful workplaces for the Nation's miners.

Office of Standards, Regulations, and Variances.—This activity develops standards and regulations for the mining industry that protect the safety and health of miners.

Office of Assessments.—This activity assesses and collects civil monetary penalties for violations of safety and health standards and manages MSHA's accountability, special enforcement, and investigation functions.

Educational Policy and Development.—This activity develops and coordinates MSHA's mine safety and health education and training policies, and provides classroom instruction at the National Mine Health and Safety Academy for MSHA personnel, other governmental personnel, and the mining industry.

Technical Support.—This activity applies engineering and scientific expertise through field and laboratory forensic investigations to resolve technical problems associated with implementing the Mine Act and the MINER Act. Technical Support administers a fee program to approve equipment, materials, and explosives for use in mines and performs field

Mine Safety and Health Administration—Continued
Federal Funds—Continued

SALARIES AND EXPENSES—Continued

and laboratory audits of equipment previously approved by MSHA. It also collects and analyzes data relative to the cause, frequency, and circumstances of mine accidents.

Program Evaluation and Information Resources (PEIR).—This activity provides program evaluation and information technology resource management services for the agency.

Program Administration.—This activity performs general administrative functions and is responsible for meeting performance requirements and developing MSHA's performance plan and Annual Performance Report.

PROGRAM STATISTICS

	2021 Actual	2022 Est.	2023 Est.
Enforcement per 200,000 hours worked by employees:			
Fatality Rates			
All-MSHA fatality rates	0.0153	0.0091	0.0091
Coal Mines	0.0207	0.0129	0.0129
Metal/non-metal mines	0.0138	0.0078	0.0078
Regulations promulgated	0	1	2
Assessments:			
Violations assessed	75,040	75,600	79,500
Educational Policy and Development:			
Course days	750	612	790
Technical Support:			
Equipment approvals	244	300	300
Laboratory samples analyzed	87,545	97,000	161,000

Object Classification (in millions of dollars)

Identification code 016–1200–0–1–554		2021 actual	2022 est.	2023 est.
	Direct obligations:			
	Personnel compensation:			
11.1	Full-time permanent	154	160	193
11.5	Other personnel compensation	5	3	3
11.9	Total personnel compensation	159	163	196
12.1	Civilian personnel benefits	71	72	86
21.0	Travel and transportation of persons	6	8	9
22.0	Transportation of things	6	6	6
23.1	Rental payments to GSA	17	18	18
23.3	Communications, utilities, and miscellaneous charges	6	4	4
25.1	Advisory and assistance services	1	1	1
25.2	Other services from non-Federal sources	4	5	4
25.3	Other goods and services from Federal sources	84	72	74
25.4	Operation and maintenance of facilities	1	1	1
25.7	Operation and maintenance of equipment	1	7	7
26.0	Supplies and materials	4	6	5
31.0	Equipment	5	5	4
32.0	Land and structures	4	6	1
41.0	Grants, subsidies, and contributions	12	12	12
99.0	Direct obligations	381	386	428
99.0	Reimbursable obligations	1	3	3
99.9	Total new obligations, unexpired accounts	382	389	431

Employment Summary

Identification code 016–1200–0–1–554		2021 actual	2022 est.	2023 est.
1001	Direct civilian full-time equivalent employment	1,663	1,686	1,857

BUREAU OF LABOR STATISTICS

Federal Funds

SALARIES AND EXPENSES

For necessary expenses for the Bureau of Labor Statistics, including advances or reimbursements to State, Federal, and local agencies and their employees for services rendered, $673,744,000, together with not to exceed $68,000,000 which may be expended from the Employment Security Administration account in the Unemployment Trust Fund.

Within this amount, $15,410,000, for costs associated with the physical move of the Bureau of Labor Statistics' headquarters, including replication of space, furniture, fixtures, equipment, and related costs, shall remain available until September 30, 2026.

Note.—A full-year 2022 appropriation for this account was not enacted at the time the Budget was prepared; therefore, the Budget assumes this account is operating under the Continuing Appropriations Act, 2022 (Division A of Public Law 117–43, as amended). The amounts included for 2022 reflect the annualized level provided by the continuing resolution.

Program and Financing (in millions of dollars)

Identification code 016–0200–0–1–505		2021 actual	2022 est.	2023 est.
	Obligations by program activity:			
0001	Labor force statistics	290	290	330
0002	Prices and cost of living	220	220	252
0003	Compensation and working conditions	84	84	93
0004	Productivity and technology	11	12	13
0006	Executive direction and staff services	36	36	39
0007	Headquarters Relocation	2	51	15
0799	Total direct obligations	643	693	742
0801	Salaries and Expenses (Reimbursable)	36	43	44
0900	Total new obligations, unexpired accounts	679	736	786
	Budgetary resources:			
	Unobligated balance:			
1000	Unobligated balance brought forward, Oct 1	27	38	....
	Budget authority:			
	Appropriations, discretionary:			
1100	Appropriation	587	587	674
	Spending authority from offsetting collections, discretionary:			
1700	Collected	104	111	112
1900	Budget authority (total)	691	698	786
1930	Total budgetary resources available	718	736	786
	Memorandum (non-add) entries:			
1940	Unobligated balance expiring	–1	....	....
1941	Unexpired unobligated balance, end of year	38	....	....
	Change in obligated balance:			
	Unpaid obligations:			
3000	Unpaid obligations, brought forward, Oct 1	119	120	126
3010	New obligations, unexpired accounts	679	736	786
3011	Obligations ("upward adjustments"), expired accounts	2	....	....
3020	Outlays (gross)	–669	–730	–773
3041	Recoveries of prior year unpaid obligations, expired	–11	....	....
3050	Unpaid obligations, end of year	120	126	139
	Memorandum (non-add) entries:			
3100	Obligated balance, start of year	119	120	126
3200	Obligated balance, end of year	120	126	139
	Budget authority and outlays, net:			
	Discretionary:			
4000	Budget authority, gross	691	698	786
	Outlays, gross:			
4010	Outlays from new discretionary authority	571	616	692
4011	Outlays from discretionary balances	98	114	81
4020	Outlays, gross (total)	669	730	773
	Offsets against gross budget authority and outlays:			
	Offsetting collections (collected) from:			
4030	Federal sources	–103	–110	–111
4033	Non-Federal sources	–1	–1	–1
4040	Offsets against gross budget authority and outlays (total)	–104	–111	–112
4070	Budget authority, net (discretionary)	587	587	674
4080	Outlays, net (discretionary)	565	619	661
4180	Budget authority, net (total)	587	587	674
4190	Outlays, net (total)	565	619	661

Labor Force Statistics.—Publishes monthly estimates of the labor force, employment, unemployment, and earnings for the nation, states, and local areas. Makes studies of the labor force. Publishes data on employment and wages, by industry. Provides economic projections, including changes in the level and structure of the economy, as well as employment projections by industry and by occupational category.

	2021 act.	2022 est.	2023 est.
Labor Force Statistics (selected items):			
Employment and wages for NAICS industries (quarterly series)	3,600,000	3,600,000	3,600,000
Employment and unemployment estimates for States and local areas (monthly and annual series)	108,600	109,400	109,400
Occupational Employment and Wage Statistics (annual series)	131,596	130,000	131,000
Industry projections	205	194	194
Detailed occupations covered in the Occupational Outlook Handbook	561	561	620

Prices and Cost of Living.—Publishes the Consumer Price Index (CPI), the Producer Price Index, U.S. Import and Export Price Indexes, estimates of consumers' expenditures, and studies of price change.

	2021 act.	2022 est.	2023 est.
Consumer Price Indexes published (monthly)	8,410	8,400	8,400
Producer Price Indexes published (monthly)	11,052	10,800	10,700
U.S. Import and Export Price Indexes published (monthly)	1,045	970	970

Compensation and Working Conditions.—Publishes data on employee compensation, including information on wages, salaries, and employer-provided benefits, by occupation for major labor markets and industries. Publishes information on work stoppages. Compiles annual information to estimate the number and incidence rate of work-related injuries, illnesses, and fatalities.

	2021 act.	2022 est.	2023 est.
Compensation and working conditions (major items):			
Employment Cost Index: number of establishments	11,400	11,400	16,000
Occupational safety and health: number of establishments	232,435	230,372	230,000

Productivity and Technology.—Publishes data on labor and total factor productivity trends for major sectors of the economy and individual industries, as well as data on hours worked, labor compensation, and unit labor costs. Analyzes trends in order to examine the factors underlying changes in productivity to understand the relationships between productivity, wages, prices, profits, and employment, to compare trends in efficiency across industries, and to examine the effects of technological improvements.

	2021 act.	2022 est.	2023 est.
Studies, articles, and special reports	17	17	17
Series updated	4,620	4,572	4,572

Executive Direction and Staff Services.—Provides agency-wide policy and management direction, including all centralized program support services in the administrative, publications, information technology, field operations, and statistical methods research areas necessary to produce and release statistical and research output in a reliable, secure, timely, and effective manner.

Headquarters Relocation.—Reflects the funding required for BLS to relocate its National Office Headquarters to the Suitland Federal Center. The current lease for the BLS national office in Washington, DC, at the Postal Square Building expires in May 2022. Funding appropriated to this activity is available to obligate for up to five years.

Object Classification (in millions of dollars)

Identification code 016–0200–0–1–505		2021 actual	2022 est.	2023 est.
	Direct obligations:			
	Personnel compensation:			
11.1	Full-time permanent	190	201	220
11.3	Other than full-time permanent	13	13	14
11.5	Other personnel compensation	6	6	7
11.9	Total personnel compensation	209	220	241
12.1	Civilian personnel benefits	74	81	89
21.0	Travel and transportation of persons		1	3
23.1	Rental payments to GSA	38	40	43
23.3	Communications, utilities, and miscellaneous charges	3	2	4
24.0	Printing and reproduction	1	1	1
25.2	Other services from non-Federal sources	9	6	12
25.3	Other goods and services from Federal sources	139	200	172
25.5	Research and development contracts	17	13	24
25.7	Operation and maintenance of equipment	71	38	61
26.0	Supplies and materials		1	1
31.0	Equipment	5	10	10
41.0	Grants, subsidies, and contributions	77	80	81
99.0	Direct obligations	643	693	742
99.0	Reimbursable obligations	36	43	44
99.9	Total new obligations, unexpired accounts	679	736	786

Employment Summary

Identification code 016–0200–0–1–505	2021 actual	2022 est.	2023 est.
1001 Direct civilian full-time equivalent employment	1,945	1,965	2,094
2001 Reimbursable civilian full-time equivalent employment	163	170	170

DEPARTMENTAL MANAGEMENT

Federal Funds

SALARIES AND EXPENSES

(INCLUDING TRANSFER OF FUNDS)

For necessary expenses for Departmental Management, including the hire of passenger motor vehicles and supporting charging or fueling infrastructure for zero emission passenger motor vehicles, $491,796,000, together with not to exceed $308,000, which may be expended from the Employment Security Administration account in the Unemployment Trust Fund: Provided, That $91,325,000 for the Bureau of International Labor Affairs shall be available for obligation through December 31, 2023: Provided further, That funds available to the Bureau of International Labor Affairs may be used to administer or operate international labor activities, bilateral and multilateral technical assistance, and microfinance programs, by or through contracts, grants, subgrants and other arrangements: Provided further, That not more than $60,825,000 shall be for programs to combat exploitative child labor internationally and not less than $30,500,000 shall be used to implement model programs that address worker rights issues through technical assistance in countries with which the United States has free trade agreements or trade preference programs: Provided further, That the Secretary of Labor may waive the application of section 505 of this Act to awards made from funds available to the Bureau of International Labor Affairs if the Secretary determines that the waiver is necessary to protect human health, safety or welfare: Provided futher, That $11,540,000 shall be used for program evaluation and shall be available for obligation through September 30, 2024: Provided further, That funds available for program evaluation may be used to administer grants for the purpose of evaluation: Provided further, That grants made for the purpose of evaluation shall be awarded through fair and open competition: Provided further, That funds available for program evaluation may be transferred to any other appropriate account in the Department for such purpose: Provided further, That the Committees on Appropriations of the House of Representatives and the Senate are notified at least 15 days in advance of any transfer: Provided further, That the funds available to the Women's Bureau may be used for grants to serve and promote the interests of women in the workforce: Provided further, That of the amounts made available to the Women's Bureau, not less than $1,794,000 shall be used for grants authorized by the Women in Apprenticeship and Nontraditional Occupations Act.

Note.—A full-year 2022 appropriation for this account was not enacted at the time the Budget was prepared; therefore, the Budget assumes this account is operating under the Continuing Appropriations Act, 2022 (Division A of Public Law 117–43, as amended). The amounts included for 2022 reflect the annualized level provided by the continuing resolution.

Program and Financing (in millions of dollars)

Identification code 016–0165–0–1–505		2021 actual	2022 est.	2023 est.
	Obligations by program activity:			
0001	Program direction and support	30	30	42
0002	Legal services	133	144	187
0003	International labor affairs	144	262	129
0004	Administration and management	29	28	45
0005	Adjudication	59	62	73
0007	Women's bureau	15	15	25
0008	Civil rights	7	7	12
0009	Chief Financial Officer	6	6	6
0011	Departmental Program Evaluation	10	31	11
0012	Legal services - American Rescue Plan	8	3	7
0192	Total Direct Program - Subtotal	441	588	537
0799	Total direct obligations	441	588	537
0801	Reimbursable - SOL	11	13	14
0804	Reimbursable - OASAM	10	12	12
0899	Total reimbursable obligations	21	25	26
0900	Total new obligations, unexpired accounts	462	613	563
	Budgetary resources:			
	Unobligated balance:			
1000	Unobligated balance brought forward, Oct 1	269	239	49
1011	Unobligated balance transfer from ETA-TES to DPE [016–0174]		2	
1011	Unobligated balance transfer from ETA-OJC to DPE [016–0181]	1	2	

Departmental Management—Continued
Federal Funds—Continued

SALARIES AND EXPENSES—Continued

Program and Financing—Continued

Identification code 016–0165–0–1–505		2021 actual	2022 est.	2023 est.
1011	Unobligated balance transfer from SUIESO to DPE [016–0179]	....	5	....
1070	Unobligated balance (total)	270	248	49
	Budget authority:			
	Appropriations, discretionary:			
1100	Appropriation (Regular)	349	349	492
1106	Reappropriation	....	....	3
1120	Appropriations transferred to IT WCF [016–4601]	....	....	–3
1121	Appropriations transferred from OSHA to OASAM [016–0400]	1	....	....
1160	Appropriation, discretionary (total)	350	349	492
	Advance appropriations, discretionary:			
1173	Advance appropriations transferred from ETA-TES Advances to DPE [016–0174]	1	5	....
	Appropriations, mandatory:			
1200	Appropriation	28	....	....
	Spending authority from offsetting collections, discretionary:			
1700	Collected	52	60	65
1701	Change in uncollected payments, Federal sources	2	....	....
1750	Spending auth from offsetting collections, disc (total)	54	60	65
1900	Budget authority (total)	433	414	557
1930	Total budgetary resources available	703	662	606
	Memorandum (non-add) entries:			
1940	Unobligated balance expiring	–2	....	....
1941	Unexpired unobligated balance, end of year	239	49	43
	Change in obligated balance:			
	Unpaid obligations:			
3000	Unpaid obligations, brought forward, Oct 1	238	263	421
3010	New obligations, unexpired accounts	462	613	563
3011	Obligations ("upward adjustments"), expired accounts	3	....	....
3020	Outlays (gross)	–435	–455	–553
3041	Recoveries of prior year unpaid obligations, expired	–5	....	....
3050	Unpaid obligations, end of year	263	421	431
	Uncollected payments:			
3060	Uncollected pymts, Fed sources, brought forward, Oct 1	–16	–14	–14
3070	Change in uncollected pymts, Fed sources, unexpired	–2	....	....
3071	Change in uncollected pymts, Fed sources, expired	4	....	....
3090	Uncollected pymts, Fed sources, end of year	–14	–14	–14
	Memorandum (non-add) entries:			
3100	Obligated balance, start of year	222	249	407
3200	Obligated balance, end of year	249	407	417
	Budget authority and outlays, net:			
	Discretionary:			
4000	Budget authority, gross	405	414	557
	Outlays, gross:			
4010	Outlays from new discretionary authority	296	294	395
4011	Outlays from discretionary balances	130	148	156
4020	Outlays, gross (total)	426	442	551
	Offsets against gross budget authority and outlays:			
	Offsetting collections (collected) from:			
4030	Federal sources	–56	–60	–65
4040	Offsets against gross budget authority and outlays (total)	–56	–60	–65
	Additional offsets against gross budget authority only:			
4050	Change in uncollected pymts, Fed sources, unexpired	–2	....	....
4052	Offsetting collections credited to expired accounts	4	....	....
4060	Additional offsets against budget authority only (total)	2	....	....
4070	Budget authority, net (discretionary)	351	354	492
4080	Outlays, net (discretionary)	370	382	486
	Mandatory:			
4090	Budget authority, gross	28	....	....
	Outlays, gross:			
4100	Outlays from new mandatory authority	9	....	....
4101	Outlays from mandatory balances	....	13	2
4110	Outlays, gross (total)	9	13	2
4180	Budget authority, net (total)	379	354	492
4190	Outlays, net (total)	379	395	488

Program Direction and Support.—The Program Direction and Support (PDS) activity provides leadership and direction for the various DOL agencies. As part of its responsibilities, the PDS activity oversees a program of analysis and general research on issues affecting America's workforce, and also evaluates the effectiveness of Departmental programs. The PDS activity includes funding for the following organizations: Office of the Secretary; Office of the Deputy Secretary; Office of the Assistant Secretary for Policy; Office of Congressional and Intergovernmental Affairs; Office of Public Affairs; Office of Public Liaison; and the Centers for Faith and Opportunity Initiatives.

Legal Services.—The Office of the Solicitor (SOL) provides the Secretary of Labor and departmental program officials with the legal services required to accomplish the Department's mission. SOL litigates worker protection enforcement and other cases in Federal and other tribunals, including bankruptcy courts and various administrative forums throughout the nation. SOL has direct civil litigation authority in most programs, but there are occasions where SOL works hand-in-hand with DOJ; and SOL plays a significant role in the development of many criminal investigations referred to DOJ. SOL's legal services are significant to the Department's rulemaking efforts, both in the development and then the defense of rules. SOL provides legal advice to the Department's agencies, including orders, written interpretations, opinions and legislation, as well as legal services to Departmental management with respect to issues like appropriations, procurement, data privacy, FOIA, ethics, and employment law. SOL also supports the Department's enforcement efforts by providing legal advice on individual investigations of labor violations.

International Labor Affairs.—The Bureau of International Labor Affairs (ILAB) safeguards dignity at work, both at home and abroad, by strengthening global labor standards; enforcing labor commitments among trading partners; promoting racial and gender equity; and combating international child labor, forced labor, and human trafficking. ILAB combines monitoring and enforcement of labor provisions in U.S. trade agreements and preference programs, bilateral and multilateral engagement, research, and technical cooperation to carry out the international responsibilities of the Department of Labor.

Administration and Management.—Exercises leadership in all departmental administrative and management programs and services and ensures efficient and effective operation of Departmental programs; provides policy guidance on matters of personnel management, information resource management and procurement; and provides for consistent and constructive internal labor-management relations throughout the Department.

Adjudication.—Renders timely decisions on appeals of claims filed before four different components, which include the Office of Administrative Law Judges, the Administrative Review Board, the Benefits Review Board, and the Employees' Compensation Appeals Board. The Office of Administrative Law Judges also serves as the tribunal of first instance.

Women's Bureau.—Serves as the only Federal agency mandated by Congress to work exclusively on issues that affect women in the workplace and to represent the needs of wage-earning women in the public policy process. The Women's Bureau deploys its research, statistics, advocacy and grantmaking capacity to advising the Secretary, the Administration, and sister DOL agencies on policy and regulatory issues facing working women.

Civil Rights.—Ensures compliance with certain Federal civil rights statutes and Executive Orders, and their implementing regulations, including Titles VI and VII of the Civil Rights Act of 1964, Sections 504 and 508 of the Rehabilitation Act of 1973, Title II of the Americans with Disabilities Act of 1990, , and Section 188 of the Workforce Innovation and Opportunity Act. These laws apply to and protect Department of Labor (DOL) employees, DOL applicants for employment, and individuals who engage the Nation's workforce programs or otherwise interact with DOL-supported programs and activities.

Chief Financial Officer.—Created as a result of the CFO Act of 1990, provides financial management leadership and direction to all DOL program agencies on financial matters arising from legislative and regulatory mandates such as the CFO Act, GMRA, FFMIA, FMFIA, Clinger-Cohen, The Reports Consolidation Act, IPIA, Treasury Financial Manual guidance and OMB Circulars.

Program Evaluation.—The Office of the Chief Evaluation Officer is charged with coordinating and overseeing rigorous evaluations of the Department of Labor's programs, ensuring high standards in evaluations undertaken and funded by the Department, and in leading implementation of the Department's evidence-building agenda. Through its development and dissemination of rigorous scientific knowledge, the office builds evaluation capacity and expertise to ensure that evaluation and research findings are available and accessible for policy and program decision-makers in a timely and user-friendly way.

Object Classification (in millions of dollars)

Identification code 016–0165–0–1–505		2021 actual	2022 est.	2023 est.
	Direct obligations:			
	Personnel compensation:			
11.1	Full-time permanent	161	176	223
11.3	Other than full-time permanent	3	1	2
11.5	Other personnel compensation	4	3	4
11.9	Total personnel compensation	168	180	229
12.1	Civilian personnel benefits	56	60	73
13.0	Benefits for former personnel	1		
21.0	Travel and transportation of persons		1	2
22.0	Transportation of things		1	1
23.1	Rental payments to GSA	19	20	20
23.3	Communications, utilities, and miscellaneous charges	1	1	1
25.1	Advisory and assistance services	13	31	20
25.2	Other services from non-Federal sources	8	7	15
25.3	Other goods and services from Federal sources	60	55	71
25.4	Operation and maintenance of facilities			1
25.7	Operation and maintenance of equipment	1	2	9
26.0	Supplies and materials	2	1	2
31.0	Equipment	1		
41.0	Grants, subsidies, and contributions	111	229	93
99.0	Direct obligations	441	588	537
99.0	Reimbursable obligations	21	25	26
99.9	Total new obligations, unexpired accounts	462	613	563

Employment Summary

Identification code 016–0165–0–1–505	2021 actual	2022 est.	2023 est.
1001 Direct civilian full-time equivalent employment	1,251	1,272	1,554
2001 Reimbursable civilian full-time equivalent employment	55	36	36

SALARIES AND EXPENSES

(Legislative proposal, subject to PAYGO)

The FY 2023 Budget proposes to provide the Department with $275,000,000 over 10 years, in mandatory funding to EBSA and SOL, to increase capacity for the agency to perform audits related to mental health and substance abuse (including investigating reimbursement rates as Non-Quantitative Treatment Limitations) and take action against non-compliant actors. These enhanced oversight and compliance efforts would increase the number of large group market health plans and issuers that are complying with the mental health parity requirements under the Mental Health Parity and Addiction Equity Act.

OFFICE OF DISABILITY EMPLOYMENT POLICY

SALARIES AND EXPENSES

For necessary expenses for the Office of Disability Employment Policy to provide leadership, develop policy and initiatives, and award grants furthering the objective of eliminating barriers to the training and employment of people with disabilities, $58,566,000, of which not less than $9,000,000 shall be for research and demonstration projects related to testing effective ways to promote greater labor force participation of people with disabilities: Provided, That the Secretary may transfer amounts made available under this heading for research and demonstration projects to the "State Unemployment Insurance and Employment Service Operations" account for such purposes.

Note.—A full-year 2022 appropriation for this account was not enacted at the time the Budget was prepared; therefore, the Budget assumes this account is operating under the Continuing Appropriations Act, 2022 (Division A of Public Law 117–43, as amended). The amounts included for 2022 reflect the annualized level provided by the continuing resolution.

Program and Financing (in millions of dollars)

Identification code 016–0166–0–1–505		2021 actual	2022 est.	2023 est.
	Obligations by program activity:			
0001	Office of Disability Employment Policy	39	39	59
0810	Reimbursable program activity	54		
0900	Total new obligations, unexpired accounts	93	39	59
	Budgetary resources:			
	Budget authority:			
	Appropriations, discretionary:			
1100	Appropriation	39	39	59
	Spending authority from offsetting collections, discretionary:			
1700	Collected	54		
1900	Budget authority (total)	93	39	59
1930	Total budgetary resources available	93	39	59
	Change in obligated balance:			
	Unpaid obligations:			
3000	Unpaid obligations, brought forward, Oct 1	45	97	58
3010	New obligations, unexpired accounts	93	39	59
3020	Outlays (gross)	–39	–78	–48
3041	Recoveries of prior year unpaid obligations, expired	–2		
3050	Unpaid obligations, end of year	97	58	69
	Memorandum (non-add) entries:			
3100	Obligated balance, start of year	45	97	58
3200	Obligated balance, end of year	97	58	69
	Budget authority and outlays, net:			
	Discretionary:			
4000	Budget authority, gross	93	39	59
	Outlays, gross:			
4010	Outlays from new discretionary authority	15	13	19
4011	Outlays from discretionary balances	24	65	29
4020	Outlays, gross (total)	39	78	48
	Offsets against gross budget authority and outlays:			
	Offsetting collections (collected) from:			
4030	Federal sources	–54		
4040	Offsets against gross budget authority and outlays (total)	–54		
4180	Budget authority, net (total)	39	39	59
4190	Outlays, net (total)	–15	78	48

Office of Disability Employment Policy.—This agency provides national leadership in developing policy to eliminate barriers to employment faced by people with disabilities. ODEP works within the Department of Labor and in collaboration with other Federal, state and local agencies, private-sector employers, and employer associations to develop and disseminate evidence-based policy strategies and effective practices. ODEP also assists agencies and employers in adopting evidence-based policies and practices. The goal of these efforts is to increase employment opportunities for and the workforce participation rate of people with disabilities.

Object Classification (in millions of dollars)

Identification code 016–0166–0–1–505		2021 actual	2022 est.	2023 est.
	Direct obligations:			
11.1	Personnel compensation: Full-time permanent	7	8	8
12.1	Civilian personnel benefits	3	3	3
23.1	Rental payments to GSA	1	1	1
25.1	Advisory and assistance services	15	13	19
25.3	Other goods and services from Federal sources	3	2	3
25.4	Operation and maintenance of facilities	1		2
41.0	Grants, subsidies, and contributions	9	12	23
99.0	Direct obligations	39	39	59
99.0	Reimbursable obligations	54		
99.9	Total new obligations, unexpired accounts	93	39	59

Employment Summary

Identification code 016–0166–0–1–505	2021 actual	2022 est.	2023 est.
1001 Direct civilian full-time equivalent employment	52	56	58

OFFICE OF INSPECTOR GENERAL

For salaries and expenses of the Office of Inspector General in carrying out the provisions of the Inspector General Act of 1978, $102,024,000, together with not to exceed $5,841,000 which may be expended from the Employment Security Administration account in the Unemployment Trust Fund.

Note.—A full-year 2022 appropriation for this account was not enacted at the time the Budget was prepared; therefore, the Budget assumes this account is operating under the Continuing Appropriations Act, 2022 (Division A of Public Law 117–43, as amended). The amounts included for 2022 reflect the annualized level provided by the continuing resolution.

Program and Financing (in millions of dollars)

Identification code 016–0106–0–1–505		2021 actual	2022 est.	2023 est.
	Obligations by program activity:			
0001	Program and Trust Funds	91	91	108
0002	OIG American Rescue Plan	1	12	1
0003	CARES Act	10	....	....
0900	Total new obligations, unexpired accounts	102	103	109
	Budgetary resources:			
	Unobligated balance:			
1000	Unobligated balance brought forward, Oct 1	25	26	14
	Budget authority:			
	Appropriations, discretionary:			
1100	Appropriation	85	85	102
	Appropriations, mandatory:			
1200	Appropriation	13	....	....
	Spending authority from offsetting collections, discretionary:			
1700	Collected	6	6	6
1900	Budget authority (total)	104	91	108
1930	Total budgetary resources available	129	117	122
	Memorandum (non-add) entries:			
1940	Unobligated balance expiring	–1	....	....
1941	Unexpired unobligated balance, end of year	26	14	13
	Change in obligated balance:			
	Unpaid obligations:			
3000	Unpaid obligations, brought forward, Oct 1	14	21	32
3010	New obligations, unexpired accounts	102	103	109
3011	Obligations ("upward adjustments"), expired accounts	1	....	....
3020	Outlays (gross)	–94	–92	–107
3041	Recoveries of prior year unpaid obligations, expired	–2	....	....
3050	Unpaid obligations, end of year	21	32	34
	Memorandum (non-add) entries:			
3100	Obligated balance, start of year	14	21	32
3200	Obligated balance, end of year	21	32	34
	Budget authority and outlays, net:			
	Discretionary:			
4000	Budget authority, gross	91	91	108
	Outlays, gross:			
4010	Outlays from new discretionary authority	77	77	92
4011	Outlays from discretionary balances	17	14	14
4020	Outlays, gross (total)	94	91	106
	Offsets against gross budget authority and outlays:			
	Offsetting collections (collected) from:			
4030	Federal sources	–6	–6	–6
	Mandatory:			
4090	Budget authority, gross	13	....	....
	Outlays, gross:			
4101	Outlays from mandatory balances	....	1	1
4180	Budget authority, net (total)	98	85	102
4190	Outlays, net (total)	88	86	101

The Office of Inspector General (OIG) conducts audits, investigations, and evaluations that improve the effectiveness, efficiency, and economy of departmental programs and operations. It addresses DOL program fraud and labor racketeering in the American workplace, provides technical assistance to DOL program agencies, and advice to the Secretary and the Congress on how to attain the highest possible program performance. The Office of Audit performs audits of the Department's financial statements, programs, activities, and systems to determine whether information is reliable, controls are effective, and resources are safeguarded. It also ensures funds are expended in a manner consistent with laws and regulations, and with achieving the desired program results. The Office of Investigations-Labor Racketeering and Fraud conducts investigations to detect and deter fraud, waste, and abuse in departmental programs. It also identifies and reduces labor racketeering and corruption in employee benefit plans, labor management relations, and internal union affairs.

	2021 actual	2022 est.	2023 est.
Number of Audits	33	36	36
Number of Investigations Completed	161	310	310

Object Classification (in millions of dollars)

Identification code 016–0106–0–1–505		2021 actual	2022 est.	2023 est.
	Direct obligations:			
	Personnel compensation:			
11.1	Full-time permanent	46	47	49
11.5	Other personnel compensation	2	1	2
11.9	Total personnel compensation	48	48	51
12.1	Civilian personnel benefits	19	22	24
21.0	Travel and transportation of persons	3	1	1
23.1	Rental payments to GSA	5	5	5
25.1	Advisory and assistance services	11	9	10
25.2	Other services from non-Federal sources	2	5	5
25.3	Other goods and services from Federal sources	10	10	10
31.0	Equipment	4	3	3
99.9	Total new obligations, unexpired accounts	102	103	109

Employment Summary

Identification code 016–0106–0–1–505		2021 actual	2022 est.	2023 est.
1001	Direct civilian full-time equivalent employment	314	363	376

VETERANS' EMPLOYMENT AND TRAINING

Not to exceed $268,468,000 may be derived from the Employment Security Administration account in the Unemployment Trust Fund to carry out the provisions of chapters 41, 42, and 43 of title 38, United States Code, of which—

(1) $180,000,000 is for Jobs for Veterans State grants under 38 U.S.C. 4102A(b)(5) to support disabled veterans' outreach program specialists under section 4103A of such title and local veterans' employment representatives under section 4104(b) of such title, and for the expenses described in section 4102A(b)(5)(C), which shall be available for expenditure by the States through September 30, 2025, and not to exceed 3 percent for the necessary Federal expenditures for data systems and contract support to allow for the tracking of participant and performance information: Provided, That, in addition, such funds may be used to support such specialists and representatives in the provision of services to transitioning members of the Armed Forces who have participated in the Transition Assistance Program and have been identified as in need of intensive services, to members of the Armed Forces who are wounded, ill, or injured and receiving treatment in military treatment facilities or warrior transition units, to the spouses or other family caregivers of such wounded, ill, or injured members, and to Gold Star spouses;

(2) $31,379,000 is for carrying out the Transition Assistance Program under 38 U.S.C. 4113 and 10 U.S.C. 1144;

(3) $53,675,000 is for Federal administration of chapters 41, 42, and 43 of title 38, and sections 2021, 2021A and 2023 of title 38, United States Code: Provided, That, up to $500,000 may be used to carry out the Hire VETS Act (division O of Public Law 115–31); and

(4) $3,414,000 is for the National Veterans' Employment and Training Services Institute under 38 U.S.C. 4109:

Provided, That the Secretary may reallocate among the appropriations provided under paragraphs (1) through (4) above an amount not to exceed 3 percent of the appropriation from which such reallocation is made.

In addition, from the General Fund of the Treasury, $62,500,000 is for carrying out programs to assist homeless veterans and veterans at risk of homelessness who are transitioning from certain institutions under sections 2021, 2021A, and 2023 of title 38, United States Code: Provided, That notwithstanding subsections (c)(3) and (d) of section 2023, the Secretary may award grants through September 30, 2023, to provide services under such section: Provided further, That services provided under sections 2021 or under 2021A may include, in addition to services to homeless veterans described in section 2002(a)(1), services to veterans who were homeless at some point within the 60 days prior to program entry or veterans who are at risk of homelessness within the next 60 days, and that services provided under section 2023 may include, in addition to services to the individuals described in subsection

DEPARTMENT OF LABOR

Departmental Management—Continued
Federal Funds—Continued

(e) of such section, services to veterans recently released from incarceration who are at risk of homelessness: Provided further, That notwithstanding paragraph (3) under this heading, funds appropriated in this paragraph may be used for data systems and contract support to allow for the tracking of participant and performance information: Provided further, That notwithstanding sections 2021(e)(2) and 2021A(f)(2) of title 38, United States Code, such funds shall be available for expenditure pursuant to 31 U.S.C. 1553.

In addition, fees may be assessed and deposited in the HIRE Vets Medallion Award Fund pursuant to section 5(b) of the HIRE Vets Act, and such amounts shall be available to the Secretary to carry out the HIRE Vets Medallion Award Program, as authorized by such Act, and shall remain available until expended: Provided, That such sums shall be in addition to any other funds available for such purposes, including funds available under paragraph (3) of this heading: Provided further, That section 2(d) of division O of the Consolidated Appropriations Act, 2017 (Public Law 115–31; 38 U.S.C. 4100 note) shall not apply.

Note.—A full-year 2022 appropriation for this account was not enacted at the time the Budget was prepared; therefore, the Budget assumes this account is operating under the Continuing Appropriations Act, 2022 (Division A of Public Law 117–43, as amended). The amounts included for 2022 reflect the annualized level provided by the continuing resolution.

Program and Financing (in millions of dollars)

Identification code 016–0164–0–1–702		2021 actual	2022 est.	2023 est.
	Obligations by program activity:			
0003	Jobs for Veterans State grants	177	180	180
0004	Transition Assistance Program	31	31	31
0005	Federal Management	47	44	54
0006	National Veterans' Training Institute	3	3	3
0007	Homeless veterans program	58	58	63
0900	Total new obligations, unexpired accounts	316	316	331
	Budgetary resources:			
	Budget authority:			
	Appropriations, discretionary:			
1100	Appropriation	58	58	63
	Spending authority from offsetting collections, discretionary:			
1700	Collected	258	258	268
1900	Budget authority (total)	316	316	331
1930	Total budgetary resources available	316	316	331
	Change in obligated balance:			
	Unpaid obligations:			
3000	Unpaid obligations, brought forward, Oct 1	167	189	124
3010	New obligations, unexpired accounts	316	316	331
3011	Obligations ("upward adjustments"), expired accounts	1		
3020	Outlays (gross)	–281	–381	–326
3041	Recoveries of prior year unpaid obligations, expired	–14		
3050	Unpaid obligations, end of year	189	124	129
	Memorandum (non-add) entries:			
3100	Obligated balance, start of year	167	189	124
3200	Obligated balance, end of year	189	124	129
	Budget authority and outlays, net:			
	Discretionary:			
4000	Budget authority, gross	316	316	331
	Outlays, gross:			
4010	Outlays from new discretionary authority	151	215	224
4011	Outlays from discretionary balances	130	166	102
4020	Outlays, gross (total)	281	381	326
	Offsets against gross budget authority and outlays:			
	Offsetting collections (collected) from:			
4030	Federal sources	–258	–258	–268
4040	Offsets against gross budget authority and outlays (total)	–258	–258	–268
4180	Budget authority, net (total)	58	58	63
4190	Outlays, net (total)	23	123	58

Jobs for Veterans State grants.—The Jobs for Veterans Act (JVA) of 2002 provides the foundation for this budget activity. The JVA requires the Veterans' Employment and Training Service (VETS) to act on behalf of the Secretary in the promulgation of policies and regulations that ensure maximum employment and training opportunities for veterans and priority of service for veterans (38 U.S.C. 4215) within the state workforce delivery system for employment and training programs funded in whole or in part by the U.S. Department of Labor. Under the JVA, grants are allocated to the states according to the statutory formula to support Disabled Veterans' Outreach Program (DVOP) specialists and Local Veterans' Employment Representative (LVERs) staff.

DVOP specialists (38 U.S.C. 4103A) provide intensive services to meet the employment needs of eligible veterans. DVOP specialists place maximum emphasis on assisting veterans with significant barriers to employment. LVER staff (38 U.S.C. 4104) conduct outreach to employers, employer associations, and business groups to promote the advantages of hiring veterans. LVERs also facilitate employment, training, and placement services provided to veterans under the applicable state employment service delivery system, including American Job Centers by educating all workforce partner staff on current employment initiatives and programs for veterans. In addition, each LVER provides reports to the manager of the state employment service delivery system and to the state Director for Veterans Employment and Training (38 U.S.C. 4103) regarding the state's compliance with Federal law and regulations with respect to special services and priorities for eligible veterans.

Transition Assistance Program (TAP).—(10 U.S.C. 1144, 38 U.S.C. 4113) This program provides employment workshops for separating service members and their spouses to prepare these individuals for entry into the civilian workforce and job market. Its primary goal is to facilitate the transition from military to civilian employment. VETS coordinates with Federal agencies including the Departments of Defense, Veterans Affairs, Education and Homeland Security, and also the Small Business Administration and the Office of Personnel Management to provide transition services to military service members separating from active duty. The 2019 National Defense Authorization Act instructed responsible agencies to improve TAP and directed DOL to deliver a mandatory one-day employment planning workshop for all transitioning service members, as well as optional days of instruction on general employment preparation and Vocational Training for transitioning service members interested in apprenticeship opportunities and technical careers. VETS also serves veterans and veteran spouses through the Off Base Transition Training pilot at selected states, to furthur serve and support underserved populations in locations away from active duty installations.

National Veterans' Training Institute (NVTI).—NVTI develops and supplies competency-based training to Federal and state providers of services to veterans (38 U.S.C. 4109). NVTI is administered through a contract and supported by dedicated funds. NVTI ensures that these service providers receive a comprehensive foundation and ongoing staff development so they can effectively assist job-seeking veterans.

Homeless Veterans' Reintegration Program (HVRP).—HVRP (38 U.S.C. 2021, 2021A and 2023) provides grants to states or other public entities, as well as to non-profits, including faith-based organizations. Grantees operate employment programs to assist homeless veterans reintegrate into meaningful employment and stimulate the development of effective service delivery systems that will address the complex problems facing homeless veterans. VETS partners with the U.S. Departments of Veterans Affairs and Housing and Urban Development to promote multi-agency-funded programs that integrate the different services needed by homeless veterans.

Federal management.—VETS' Federal management budget activity supports the Federal administration of 38 U.S.C. 41, 42, and 43. This allows VETS to carry out programs and develop policies to provide employment and training opportunities designed to meet the needs of veterans (38 U.S.C. 4102–4115). This activity provides for the salary and benefits, travel, and training for all VETS' current staff in the national office, six regional offices, and offices in each state, the District of Columbia, and Puerto Rico. In addition, this activity provides for outreach and engagement with Federal, state, and local governments; private sector employers and trade associations; institutions of higher learning; non-profit organizations; and Veteran Service Organizations to help service members, returning veterans, and families reintegrate into the workforce.

It also enables VETS to discharge its responsibilities to administer, interpret, and enforce the Uniformed Services Employment and Reemployment Rights Act of 1994 (USERRA), 38 U.S.C. 4301–4335, by providing tech-

VETERANS' EMPLOYMENT AND TRAINING—Continued

nical assistance and investigating complaints received from veterans and service members who believe their employment and reemployment rights were violated. This budget activity enables VETS to investigate complaints received from veterans who claim a violation of their veterans' preference rights in Federal hiring pursuant to the Veterans' Employment Opportunities Act of 1998 (VEOA), 5 U.S.C. 3330a. VETS' Federal Contractor Program (VETS-4212) is also supported under this activity, pursuant to 38 U.S.C. 4212. These responsibilities involve the administration of a system whereby Federal contractors submit reports setting forth their affirmative action efforts to hire and retain eligible veterans.

Resources under the Federal management activity are also used to evaluate the job training and employment assistance services provided to veterans under the Jobs for Veterans State Grants (38 U.S.C. 4102A(b)(5)), and the Homeless Veterans Reintegration (38 U.S.C. 2021). VETS personnel provide technical assistance to grantees to ensure they meet negotiated and mandated performance goals and other grant provisions.

Federal management supports the oversight and development of policies for TAP (10 U.S.C. 1144 and 38 U.S.C. 4113). Through outreach and education efforts, such as job fairs, VETS staff raise the awareness of employers about the benefits of hiring veterans. The activities of the Advisory Committee for Veterans Employment, Training, and Employer Outreach (38 U.S.C. 4110) also are supported through this budget activity. In addition, through fee collection, the federal management activity fund administrative processes associated with the Honoring Investments in Recruiting and Employing American Military Veterans Act of 2017 (HIRE VETS Act or the Act).

Object Classification (in millions of dollars)

Identification code 016–0164–0–1–702		2021 actual	2022 est.	2023 est.
	Direct obligations:			
	Personnel compensation:			
11.1	Full-time permanent	24	25	31
11.5	Other personnel compensation	1		
11.9	Total personnel compensation	25	25	31
12.1	Civilian personnel benefits	8	9	11
21.0	Travel and transportation of persons		1	1
23.1	Rental payments to GSA	1	1	1
25.2	Other services from non-Federal sources	41	39	38
25.3	Other goods and services from Federal sources	12	9	12
25.7	Operation and maintenance of equipment	3		
41.0	Grants, subsidies, and contributions	225	232	237
99.0	Direct obligations	315	316	331
99.0	Reimbursable obligations	1		
99.9	Total new obligations, unexpired accounts	316	316	331

Employment Summary

Identification code 016–0164–0–1–702	2021 actual	2022 est.	2023 est.
1001 Direct civilian full-time equivalent employment	225	233	261

IT MODERNIZATION

For necessary expenses for Department of Labor centralized infrastructure technology investment activities related to support systems and modernization, $47,969,000, which shall be available through September 30, 2024.

Note.—A full-year 2022 appropriation for this account was not enacted at the time the Budget was prepared; therefore, the Budget assumes this account is operating under the Continuing Appropriations Act, 2022 (Division A of Public Law 117–43, as amended). The amounts included for 2022 reflect the annualized level provided by the continuing resolution.

Program and Financing (in millions of dollars)

Identification code 016–0162–0–1–505		2021 actual	2022 est.	2023 est.
	Obligations by program activity:			
0001	Departmental Support Systems	6	5	16
0002	IT Infrastructure Modernization	22	24	32
0100	Direct program activities, subtotal	28	29	48
0900	Total new obligations, unexpired accounts	28	29	48
	Budgetary resources:			
	Unobligated balance:			
1000	Unobligated balance brought forward, Oct 1	3	2	
	Budget authority:			
	Appropriations, discretionary:			
1100	Appropriation	27	27	48
1930	Total budgetary resources available	30	29	48
	Memorandum (non-add) entries:			
1941	Unexpired unobligated balance, end of year	2		
	Change in obligated balance:			
	Unpaid obligations:			
3000	Unpaid obligations, brought forward, Oct 1	17	13	23
3010	New obligations, unexpired accounts	28	29	48
3020	Outlays (gross)	–32	–19	–35
3050	Unpaid obligations, end of year	13	23	36
	Memorandum (non-add) entries:			
3100	Obligated balance, start of year	17	13	23
3200	Obligated balance, end of year	13	23	36
	Budget authority and outlays, net:			
	Discretionary:			
4000	Budget authority, gross	27	27	48
	Outlays, gross:			
4010	Outlays from new discretionary authority	16	11	19
4011	Outlays from discretionary balances	16	8	16
4020	Outlays, gross (total)	32	19	35
4180	Budget authority, net (total)	27	27	48
4190	Outlays, net (total)	32	19	35

Departmental Support Systems.—This activity represents a permanent, centralized IT investment fund for the Department of Labor managed by the Chief Information Officer. The fund supports enterprise-wide IT security enhancements that facilitate a centrally managed IT environment with increased risk mitigation parameters to protect the integrity of DOL data and network availability. These efforts are achieved through several new and ongoing projects mandated by executive and congressional directives.

IT Infrastructure Modernization.—This Chief Information Officer-managed activity funds the unified IT infrastructure, which is centrally managed and provides all agencies with general purpose business productivity tools, is a shared environment for common data sources, and the underlying IT services to support it.

Object Classification (in millions of dollars)

Identification code 016–0162–0–1–505		2021 actual	2022 est.	2023 est.
	Direct obligations:			
11.1	Personnel compensation: Full-time permanent			2
12.1	Civilian personnel benefits			1
25.1	Advisory and assistance services	1		6
25.3	Other goods and services from Federal sources	1	1	1
25.7	Operation and maintenance of equipment	20	22	33
31.0	Equipment	6	6	5
99.9	Total new obligations, unexpired accounts	28	29	48

Employment Summary

Identification code 016–0162–0–1–505	2021 actual	2022 est.	2023 est.
1001 Direct civilian full-time equivalent employment			15

WORKING CAPITAL FUND

Program and Financing (in millions of dollars)

Identification code 016–4601–0–4–505		2021 actual	2022 est.	2023 est.
	Obligations by program activity:			
0801	Financial and administrative services (includes Core Financial)	161	223	178
0802	Field services	20	21	23

DEPARTMENT OF LABOR

Departmental Management—Continued
Federal Funds—Continued

0804	Human resources services	58	61	73
0805	Telecommunications	26	26	26
0806	Non-DOL Reimbursables		2	2
0808	Information technology services	271	386	408
0900	Total new obligations, unexpired accounts	536	719	710
	Budgetary resources:			
	Unobligated balance:			
1000	Unobligated balance brought forward, Oct 1	55	98	25
1011	Unobligated balance transfer from other acct [047–0616]		10	
1012	Unobligated balance transfers between expired and unexpired accounts	2		
1021	Recoveries of prior year unpaid obligations	13	10	10
1033	Recoveries of prior year paid obligations	1		
1070	Unobligated balance (total)	71	118	35
	Budget authority:			
	Appropriations, discretionary:			
1121	Appropriations transferred from other acct [016–0174]			24
1121	Appropriations transferred from other acct [016–0181]			9
1121	Appropriations transferred from other acct [016–0165]			3
1160	Appropriation, discretionary (total)			36
	Spending authority from offsetting collections, discretionary:			
1700	Collected	571	626	644
1701	Change in uncollected payments, Federal sources	–8		
1750	Spending auth from offsetting collections, disc (total)	563	626	644
1900	Budget authority (total)	563	626	680
1930	Total budgetary resources available	634	744	715
	Memorandum (non-add) entries:			
1941	Unexpired unobligated balance, end of year	98	25	5
	Change in obligated balance:			
	Unpaid obligations:			
3000	Unpaid obligations, brought forward, Oct 1	123	144	289
3010	New obligations, unexpired accounts	536	719	710
3020	Outlays (gross)	–502	–564	–670
3040	Recoveries of prior year unpaid obligations, unexpired	–13	–10	–10
3050	Unpaid obligations, end of year	144	289	319
	Uncollected payments:			
3060	Uncollected pymts, Fed sources, brought forward, Oct 1	–8		
3070	Change in uncollected pymts, Fed sources, unexpired	8		
	Memorandum (non-add) entries:			
3100	Obligated balance, start of year	115	144	289
3200	Obligated balance, end of year	144	289	319
	Budget authority and outlays, net:			
	Discretionary:			
4000	Budget authority, gross	563	626	680
	Outlays, gross:			
4010	Outlays from new discretionary authority		507	554
4011	Outlays from discretionary balances	502	57	116
4020	Outlays, gross (total)	502	564	670
	Offsets against gross budget authority and outlays:			
	Offsetting collections (collected) from:			
4030	Federal sources	–571	–626	–644
4033	Non-Federal sources	–1		
4040	Offsets against gross budget authority and outlays (total)	–572	–626	–644
	Additional offsets against gross budget authority only:			
4050	Change in uncollected pymts, Fed sources, unexpired	8		
4053	Recoveries of prior year paid obligations, unexpired accounts	1		
4060	Additional offsets against budget authority only (total)	9		
4070	Budget authority, net (discretionary)			36
4080	Outlays, net (discretionary)	–70	–62	26
4180	Budget authority, net (total)			36
4190	Outlays, net (total)	–70	–62	26

Financial and Administrative Services.—Provides a program of centralized services at both the national and regional levels supporting financial systems on a Department-wide basis, financial services primarily for DOL national office staff, cost determination activities, maintenance of departmental host computer systems, procurement and contract services, safety and health services, maintenance and operation of the Frances Perkins Building and general administrative support in the following areas: space, property and supplies, printing and reproduction, and energy management. In addition, support is provided for the operation and maintenance of the New Core Financial Management System.

Information Technology Operations. The Information Technology (IT) Operations budget funds the operations and maintenance of the Department's centralized data center and network infrastructure; agency computer systems; cloud computing environment; and additional IT services including email, remote access, file storage, and security operations. The IT Operations budget activity funds all staffing for DOL-wide IT services while the Agency Applications budget activity funds staff who work directly on agency-specific applications.

Telecommunications.—Provides resources for the Enterprise Infrastructure Solutions telecommunications model.

Agency Applications.— The Agency Applications budget activity provides resources for programmatic IT spending. This includes operations and maintenance spending for over 100 mission support applications, as well as development, modernization, and enhancement investments.

Field Services.—Provides a range of administrative and technical services to all agencies of the Department located in its regional and field offices, including space management, financial services, security and emergency management.

Human Resources Services.—Provides leadership, guidance, and technical expertise in all areas related to the management of the Department's human resources, including recruitment, development, and retention of staff, and leadership in labor-management cooperation. This activity's focus is on a strategic planning process that will result in sustained leadership and assistance to DOL agencies in recruiting, developing and retaining a high quality, diverse workforce that effectively meets the changing mission requirements and program priorities of the Department.

Non-DOL Reimbursements.—Provides for services rendered to any entity or person for use of Departmental facilities and services, including associated utilities and security services and support for regional consolidated administrative support unit activities. The income received from non-DOL agencies and organizations funds in full the costs of all services provided. This income is credited to and merged with other income received by the Working Capital Fund.

Financing.—The Working Capital Fund is funded by the agencies and organizations for which centralized services are performed at rates that return in full all expenses of operation, including reserves for accrued annual leave.

Object Classification (in millions of dollars)

Identification code 016–4601–0–4–505	2021 actual	2022 est.	2023 est.
Reimbursable obligations:			
Personnel compensation:			
11.1 Full-time permanent	128	130	143
11.5 Other personnel compensation	4	5	5
11.9 Total personnel compensation	132	135	148
12.1 Civilian personnel benefits	49	50	54
21.0 Travel and transportation of persons	1	2	2
23.1 Rental payments to GSA	11	11	11
23.3 Communications, utilities, and miscellaneous charges	34	29	29
25.1 Advisory and assistance services	65	130	94
25.2 Other services from non-Federal sources	28	48	48
25.3 Other goods and services from Federal sources	18	22	23
25.4 Operation and maintenance of facilities	8	6	6
25.7 Operation and maintenance of equipment	162	268	277
26.0 Supplies and materials	1	3	3
31.0 Equipment	27	15	15
99.9 Total new obligations, unexpired accounts	536	719	710

Employment Summary

Identification code 016–4601–0–4–505	2021 actual	2022 est.	2023 est.
2001 Reimbursable civilian full-time equivalent employment	1,062	1,131	1,192

GENERAL FUND RECEIPT ACCOUNTS

(in millions of dollars)

		2021 actual	2022 est.	2023 est.
Offsetting receipts from the public:				
016–143500	General Fund Proprietary Interest Receipts, not Otherwise Classified	1	1	1
016–322000	All Other General Fund Proprietary Receipts Including Budget Clearing Accounts	9	17	18
016–322000	All Other General Fund Proprietary Receipts Including Budget Clearing Accounts: Legislative proposal, subject to PAYGO			–4
General Fund Offsetting receipts from the public		10	18	15
Intragovernmental payments:				
016–388500	Undistributed Intragovernmental Payments and Receivables from Cancelled Accounts	2		
General Fund Intragovernmental payments		2		

GENERAL PROVISIONS

SEC. 101. None of the funds appropriated by this Act for the Job Corps shall be used to pay the salary and bonuses of an individual, either as direct costs or any proration as an indirect cost, at a rate in excess of Executive Level II.

(TRANSFER OF FUNDS)

SEC. 102. Not to exceed 1 percent of any discretionary funds (pursuant to the Balanced Budget and Emergency Deficit Control Act of 1985) which are appropriated for the current fiscal year for the Department of Labor in this Act may be transferred between a program, project, or activity, but no such program, project, or activity shall be increased by more than 3 percent by any such transfer: Provided, That the transfer authority granted by this section shall not be used to create any new program or to fund any project or activity for which no funds are provided in this Act: Provided further, That the Committees on Appropriations of the House of Representatives and the Senate are notified at least 15 days in advance of any transfer.

SEC. 103. In accordance with Executive Order 13126, none of the funds appropriated or otherwise made available pursuant to this Act shall be obligated or expended for the procurement of goods mined, produced, manufactured, or harvested or services rendered, in whole or in part, by forced or indentured child labor in industries and host countries already identified by the United States Department of Labor prior to enactment of this Act.

SEC. 104. Except as otherwise provided in this section, none of the funds made available to the Department of Labor for grants under section 414(c) of the American Competitiveness and Workforce Improvement Act of 1998 (29 U.S.C. 2916a) may be used for any purpose other than competitive grants for training individuals who are older than 16 years of age and are not currently enrolled in school within a local educational agency in the occupations and industries for which employers are using H-1B visas to hire foreign workers, and the related activities necessary to support such training.

SEC. 105. None of the funds made available by this Act under the heading "Employment and Training Administration" shall be used by a recipient or subrecipient of such funds to pay the salary and bonuses of an individual, either as direct costs or indirect costs, at a rate in excess of Executive Level II. This limitation shall not apply to vendors providing goods and services as defined in Office of Management and Budget Circular A-133. Where States are recipients of such funds, States may establish a lower limit for salaries and bonuses of those receiving salaries and bonuses from subrecipients of such funds, taking into account factors including the relative cost-of-living in the State, the compensation levels for comparable State or local government employees, and the size of the organizations that administer Federal programs involved including Employment and Training Administration programs.

(TRANSFER OF FUNDS)

SEC. 106. (a) Notwithstanding section 102, the Secretary may transfer funds made available to the Employment and Training Administration by this Act, either directly or through a set-aside, for technical assistance services to grantees to "Program Administration" when it is determined that those services will be more efficiently performed by Federal employees: Provided, That this section shall not apply to section 171 of the WIOA.

(b) Notwithstanding section 102, the Secretary may transfer not more than 0.5 percent of each discretionary appropriation made available to the Employment and Training Administration by this Act to "Program Administration" in order to carry out program integrity activities that lead to a reduction in improper payments or prevent the unauthorized use of funds in any of the programs or activities that are funded under any such discretionary appropriations: Provided, That notwithstanding section 102 and the preceding proviso, the Secretary may transfer not more than 0.5 percent of funds made available in paragraphs (1) and (2) of the "Office of Job Corps" account to paragraph (3) of such account to carry out program integrity activities that lead to a reduction in improper payments or prevent the unauthorized use of funds in the Job Corps program: Provided further, That funds transferred under this subsection shall be available to the Secretary to carry out program integrity activities directly or through grants, cooperative agreements, contracts and other arrangements with States and other appropriate entities: Provided further, That funds transferred under the authority provided by this subsection shall be available for obligation through September 30, 2024.

(TRANSFER OF FUNDS)

SEC. 107. (a) The Secretary may reserve not more than 0.75 percent from each appropriation made available in this Act identified in subsection (b) in order to carry out evaluations of any of the programs or activities that are funded under such accounts. Any funds reserved under this section shall be transferred to "Departmental Management" for use by the Office of the Chief Evaluation Officer within the Department of Labor, and shall be available for obligation through September 30, 2024: Provided, That such funds shall only be available if the Chief Evaluation Officer of the Department of Labor submits a plan to the Committees on Appropriations of the House of Representatives and the Senate describing the evaluations to be carried out 15 days in advance of any transfer.

(b) The accounts referred to in subsection (a) are: "Training and Employment Services", "Job Corps", "Community Service Employment for Older Americans", "State Unemployment Insurance and Employment Service Operations", "Employee Benefits Security Administration", "Office of Workers' Compensation Programs", "Wage and Hour Division", "Office of Federal Contract Compliance Programs", "Office of Labor Management Standards", "Occupational Safety and Health Administration", "Mine Safety and Health Administration", "Office of Disability Employment Policy", funding made available to the "Bureau of International Labor Affairs" and "Women's Bureau" within the "Departmental Management, Salaries and Expenses" account, and "Veterans' Employment and Training".

SEC. 108. (a) FLEXIBILITY WITH RESPECT TO THE CROSSING OF H-2B NONIMMIGRANTS WORKING IN THE SEAFOOD INDUSTRY.—

(1) IN GENERAL.—Subject to paragraph (2), if a petition for H-2B nonimmigrants filed by an employer in the seafood industry is granted, the employer may bring the nonimmigrants described in the petition into the United States at any time during the 120-day period beginning on the start date for which the employer is seeking the services of the nonimmigrants without filing another petition.

(2) REQUIREMENTS FOR CROSSINGS AFTER 90TH DAY.—An employer in the seafood industry may not bring H-2B nonimmigrants into the United States after the date that is 90 days after the start date for which the employer is seeking the services of the nonimmigrants unless the employer—

(A) completes a new assessment of the local labor market by—

(i) listing job orders in local newspapers on 2 separate Sundays; and

(ii) posting the job opportunity on the appropriate Department of Labor Electronic Job Registry and at the employer's place of employment; and

(B) offers the job to an equally or better qualified United States worker who—

(i) applies for the job; and

(ii) will be available at the time and place of need.

(3) EXEMPTION FROM RULES WITH RESPECT TO STAGGERING.—The Secretary of Labor shall not consider an employer in the seafood industry who brings H-2B nonimmigrants into the United States during the 120-day period specified in paragraph (1) to be staggering the date of need in violation of section 655.20(d) of title 20, Code of Federal Regulations, or any other applicable provision of law.

(b) H-2B NONIMMIGRANTS DEFINED.—In this section, the term "H-2B nonimmigrants" means aliens admitted to the United States pursuant to section 101(a)(15)(H)(ii)(B) of the Immigration and Nationality Act (8 U.S.C. 1101(a)(15)(H)(ii)(B)).

SEC. 109. Notwithstanding any other provision of law, the Secretary may furnish through grants, cooperative agreements, contracts, and other arrangements, up to $2,000,000 of excess personal property, at a value determined by the Secretary, to apprenticeship programs for the purpose of training apprentices in those programs.

SEC. 110. (a) The Act entitled "An Act to create a Department of Labor", approved March 4, 1913 (37 Stat. 736, chapter 141) shall be applied as if the following text is part of such Act:

"(a) IN GENERAL.—The Secretary of Labor is authorized to employ law enforcement officers or special agents to—

"(1) provide protection for the Secretary of Labor during the workday of the Secretary and during any activity that is preliminary or postliminary to the performance of official duties by the Secretary;

"(2) provide protection, incidental to the protection provided to the Secretary, to a member of the immediate family of the Secretary who is participating in an activity or event relating to the official duties of the Secretary;

"(3) provide continuous protection to the Secretary (including during periods not described in paragraph (1)) and to the members of the immediate family of the Secretary if there is a significant and articulable threat of physical harm, in accordance with guidelines established by the Secretary; and

"(4) provide protection to the Deputy Secretary of Labor in the performance of official duties at a public event outside of the United States if there is a significant and articulable threat of physical harm and protective services are not provided as part of an official U.S. visit.

"(b) AUTHORITIES.—The Secretary of Labor may authorize a law enforcement officer or special agent employed under subsection (a), for the purpose of performing the duties authorized under subsection (a), to—

"(1) carry firearms;

"(2) make arrests without a warrant for any offense against the United States committed in the presence of such officer or special agent;

"(3) perform protective intelligence work, including identifying and mitigating potential threats and conducting advance work to review security matters relating to sites and events;

"(4) coordinate with local law enforcement agencies; and

"(5) initiate criminal and other investigations into potential threats to the security of the Secretary, in coordination with the Inspector General of the Department of Labor.

"(c) COMPLIANCE WITH GUIDELINES.—A law enforcement officer or special agent employed under subsection (a) shall exercise any authority provided under this section in accordance with any—

"(1) guidelines issued by the Attorney General; and

"(2) guidelines prescribed by the Secretary of Labor.".

(b) This section shall be effective on the date of enactment of this Act.

SEC. 111. The Secretary is authorized to dispose of or divest, by any means the Secretary determines appropriate, including an agreement or partnership to construct a new Job Corps center, all or a portion of the real property on which the Treasure Island Job Corps Center is situated. Any sale or other disposition will not be subject to any requirement of any Federal law or regulation relating to the disposition of Federal real property, including but not limited to subchapter III of chapter 5 of title 40 of the United States Code and subchapter V of chapter 119 of title 42 of the United States Code. The net proceeds of such a sale shall be transferred to the Secretary, which shall be available until expended to carry out the Job Corps Program on Treasure Island.

SEC. 112. None of the funds made available by this Act may be used to—

(1) alter or terminate the Interagency Agreement between the United States Department of Labor and the United States Department of Agriculture; or

(2) close any of the Civilian Conservation Centers, except if such closure is necessary to prevent the endangerment of the health and safety of the students, the capacity of the program is retained, and the requirements of section 159(j) of the WIOA are met.

SEC. 113. The Office of Workers' Compensation Programs' treatment suites and any program information prepared by the Office of Workers' Compensation Programs for treatment suites shall be exempt from disclosure under section 552(b)(3) of title 5, United States Code.

SEC. 114. Notwithstanding the Federal Assets Sale and Transfer Act of 2016 (Public Law 114-287), the proceeds from the sale of any Job Corps facility under such Act shall be transferred to the Secretary pursuant to section 158(g) of the WIOA.

SEC. 115. Notwithstanding any other provision of law, not to exceed $36,000,000 of the unobligated balances available to the Secretary of Labor in fiscal year 2023 may be transferred to the Department's Working Capital Fund for the acquisition of capital equipment, the improvement and implementation of Department financial management, information technology, infrastructure technology investment activities related to support systems and modernization, and other support systems necessary for the delivery of financial, administrative, and information technology services of primary benefit to the agencies and programs of the Department of Labor: Provided, That any funds so transferred shall remain available for obligation for five fiscal years after the fiscal year of such transfer: Provided further, That no funds may be transferred pursuant to this section unless the Chief Information Officer of the Department of Labor submits a plan, approved by the Office of Management Budget, to the Committees on Appropriations of the House of Representatives and the Senate describing the amounts to be transferred by account; the planned use of funds, including descriptions of projects; project status, including any scheduled delays and cost overruns; financial expenditures; planned activities; and expected benefits: Provided further, That the transfer authority provided in this section shall be in addition to any other transfer authority provided by law.

SEC. 116. Funds made available to the Employment and Training Administration by this Act, either directly or through a set-aside, to provide technical assistance services to grantees may also be used by the Employment and Training Administration to assist in the establishment and operation of workforce development technical assistance centers, through grants, contracts, or cooperative agreements, to provide technical assistance relating to any of the activities administered by the Employment and Training Administration.

TITLE V—GENERAL PROVISIONS

(TRANSFER OF FUNDS)

SEC. 501. The Secretaries of Labor, Health and Human Services, and Education are authorized to transfer unexpended balances of prior appropriations to accounts corresponding to current appropriations provided in this Act. Such transferred balances shall be used for the same purpose, and for the same periods of time, for which they were originally appropriated.

SEC. 502. No part of any appropriation contained in this Act shall remain available for obligation beyond the current fiscal year unless expressly so provided herein.

SEC. 503. (a) No part of any appropriation contained in this Act or transferred pursuant to section 4002 of Public Law 111-148 shall be used, other than for normal and recognized executive-legislative relationships, for publicity or propaganda purposes, for the preparation, distribution, or use of any kit, pamphlet, booklet, publication, electronic communication, radio, television, or video presentation designed to support or defeat the enactment of legislation before the Congress or any State or local legislature or legislative body, except in presentation to the Congress or any State or local legislature itself, or designed to support or defeat any proposed or pending regulation, administrative action, or order issued by the executive branch of any State or local government, except in presentation to the executive branch of any State or local government itself.

(b) No part of any appropriation contained in this Act or transferred pursuant to section 4002 of Public Law 111-148 shall be used to pay the salary or expenses of any grant or contract recipient, or agent acting for such recipient, related to any activity designed to influence the enactment of legislation, appropriations, regulation, administrative action, or Executive order proposed or pending before the Congress or any State government, State legislature or local legislature or legislative body, other than for normal and recognized executive-legislative and State-local relationships for presentation to any State or local legislature or legislative body itself, or participation by an agency or officer of a State, local or tribal government in policymaking and administrative processes within the executive branch of that government.

(c) The prohibitions in subsections (a) and (b) shall include any activity to advocate or promote any proposed, pending or future Federal, State or local tax increase, or any proposed, pending, or future requirement or restriction on any legal consumer product, including its sale or marketing, including but not limited to the advocacy or promotion of gun control.

SEC. 504. The Secretaries of Labor and Education are authorized to make available not to exceed $28,000 and $20,000, respectively, from funds available for salaries and expenses under titles I and III, respectively, for official reception and representation expenses; the Director of the Federal Mediation and Conciliation Service is authorized to make available for official reception and representation expenses not to exceed $5,000 from the funds available for "Federal Mediation and Conciliation Service, Salaries and Expenses"; and the Chairman of the National Mediation Board is authorized to make available for official reception and representation expenses not to exceed $5,000 from funds available for "National Mediation Board, Salaries and Expenses".

SEC. 505. When issuing statements, press releases, requests for proposals, bid solicitations and other documents describing projects or programs funded in whole or in part with Federal money, all grantees receiving Federal funds included in this Act, including but not limited to State and local governments and recipients of Federal research grants, shall clearly state—

(1) the percentage of the total costs of the program or project which will be financed with Federal money;

(2) the dollar amount of Federal funds for the project or program; and

(3) percentage and dollar amount of the total costs of the project or program that will be financed by non-governmental sources.

SEC. 506. (a) None of the funds made available in this Act may be made available to a Federal agency or program, or to a State or local government, if such agency, program, or government subjects any institutional or individual health care entity to discrimination on the basis that the health care entity does not provide, pay for, provide coverage of, or refer for abortions.

(b) In this section, the term "health care entity" includes an individual physician or other health care professional, a hospital, a provider-sponsored organization, a health maintenance organization, a health insurance plan, or any other kind of health care facility, organization, or plan.

SEC. 507. (a) None of the funds made available in this Act may be used for—

(1) the creation of a human embryo or embryos for research purposes; or

(2) research in which a human embryo or embryos are destroyed, discarded, or knowingly subjected to risk of injury or death greater than that allowed for research on fetuses in utero under 45 CFR 46.204(b) and section 498(b) of the Public Health Service Act (42 U.S.C. 289g(b)).

(b) For purposes of this section, the term "human embryo or embryos" includes any organism, not protected as a human subject under 45 CFR 46 as of the date of the enactment of this Act, that is derived by fertilization, parthenogenesis, cloning, or any other means from one or more human gametes or human diploid cells.

SEC. 508. (a) None of the funds made available in this Act may be used for any activity that promotes the legalization of any drug or other substance included in schedule I of the schedules of controlled substances established under section 202 of the Controlled Substances Act except for normal and recognized executive-congressional communications.

(b) The limitation in subsection (a) shall not apply when there is significant medical evidence of a therapeutic advantage to the use of such drug or other substance or that federally sponsored clinical trials are being conducted to determine therapeutic advantage.

SEC. 509. None of the funds made available in this Act may be used to promulgate or adopt any final standard under section 1173(b) of the Social Security Act providing for, or providing for the assignment of, a unique health identifier for an individual (except in an individual's capacity as an employer or a health care provider), until legislation is enacted specifically approving the standard.

SEC. 510. None of the funds made available in this Act may be obligated or expended to enter into or renew a contract with an entity if—

(1) such entity is otherwise a contractor with the United States and is subject to the requirement in 38 U.S.C. 4212(d) regarding submission of an annual report to the Secretary of Labor concerning employment of certain veterans; and

(2) such entity has not submitted a report as required by that section for the most recent year for which such requirement was applicable to such entity.

SEC. 511. None of the funds made available by this Act to carry out the Library Services and Technology Act may be made available to any library covered by paragraph (1) of section 224(f) of such Act, as amended by the Children's Internet Protection Act, unless such library has made the certifications required by paragraph (4) of such section.

SEC. 512. (a) None of the funds made available in this Act may be used to request that a candidate for appointment to a Federal scientific advisory committee disclose the political affiliation or voting history of the candidate or the position that the candidate holds with respect to political issues not directly related to and necessary for the work of the committee involved.

(b) None of the funds made available in this Act may be used to disseminate information that is deliberately false or misleading.

SEC. 513. None of the funds appropriated in this Act shall be expended or obligated by the Commissioner of Social Security, for purposes of administering Social Security benefit payments under title II of the Social Security Act, to process any claim for credit for a quarter of coverage based on work performed under a social security account number that is not the claimant's number and the performance of such work under such number has formed the basis for a conviction of the claimant of a violation of section 208(a)(6) or (7) of the Social Security Act.

SEC. 514. None of the funds appropriated by this Act may be used by the Commissioner of Social Security or the Social Security Administration to pay the compensation of employees of the Social Security Administration to administer Social Security benefit payments, under any agreement between the United States and Mexico establishing totalization arrangements between the social security system established by title II of the Social Security Act and the social security system of Mexico, which would not otherwise be payable but for such agreement.

SEC. 515. (a) None of the funds made available in this Act may be used to maintain or establish a computer network unless such network blocks the viewing, downloading, and exchanging of pornography.

(b) Nothing in subsection (a) shall limit the use of funds necessary for any Federal, State, tribal, or local law enforcement agency or any other entity carrying out criminal investigations, prosecution, or adjudication activities.

SEC. 516. None of the funds made available under this or any other Act, or any prior Appropriations Act, may be provided to the Association of Community Organizations for Reform Now (ACORN), or any of its affiliates, subsidiaries, allied organizations, or successors.

SEC. 517. (a) Federal agencies may use Federal discretionary funds that are made available in this Act to carry out up to 10 Performance Partnership Pilots. Such Pilots shall be governed by the provisions of section 526 of division H of Public Law 113–76, except that in carrying out such Pilots section 526 shall be applied by substituting "Fiscal Year 2023" for "Fiscal Year 2014" in the title of subsection (b) and by substituting "September 30, 2027" for "September 30, 2018" each place it appears: Provided, That such pilots shall include communities that have been disproportionately impacted by the COVID-19 pandemic.

(b) In addition, Federal agencies may use Federal discretionary funds that are made available in this Act to participate in Performance Partnership Pilots that are being carried out pursuant to the authority provided by section 526 of division H of Public Law 113–76, section 524 of division G of Public Law 113–235, section 525 of division H of Public Law 114–113, section 525 of division H of Public Law 115–31, section 525 of division H of Public Law 115–141, and section 524 of division A of Public Law 116–94.

(c) Pilot sites selected under authorities in this Act and prior appropriations Acts may be granted by relevant agencies up to an additional 5 years to operate under such authorities.

SEC. 518. Evaluation Funding Flexibility

(a) This section applies to:

(1) the Office of the Assistant Secretary for Planning and Evaluation within the Office of the Secretary and the Administration for Children and Families in the Department of Health and Human Services; and

(2) the Chief Evaluation Office and the statistical-related cooperative and interagency agreements and contracting activities of the Bureau of Labor Statistics in the Department of Labor.

(b) Amounts made available under this Act that are either appropriated, allocated, advanced on a reimburseable basis, or transferred to the functions and organizations identified in subsection (a) for research, evaluation, or statistical purposes shall be available for obligation through September 30, 2027: Provided, That when an office referenced in subsection (a) receives research and evaluation funding from multiple appropriations, such office may use a single Treasury account for such activities, with funding advanced on a reimbursable basis.

(c) Amounts referenced in subsection (b) that are unexpended at the time of completion of a contract, grant, or cooperative agreement may be deobligated and shall immediately become available and may be reobligated in that fiscal year or the subsequent fiscal year for the research, evaluation, or statistical purposes for which such amounts are available.

SEC. 519. Of amounts deposited in the Child Enrollment Contingency Fund under section 2104(n)(2) of the Social Security Act and the income derived from investment of those funds pursuant to section 2104(n)(2)(C) of that Act, $19,860,000,000 shall not be available for obligation in this fiscal year.

(CANCELLATION)

SEC. 520. Of the unobligated balances made available for purposes of carrying out section 2105(a)(3) of the Social Security Act, $6,017,000,000 shall not be available for obligation in this fiscal year.

SEC. 521. Of the unobligated balances made available by section 2104(f) of the Social Security Act that are no longer available for the purposes described in such section, $114,474,000 are hereby permanently cancelled.

SEC. 522. Of the unobligated balances made available by section 301(b)(3) of Public Law 114–10, $1,185,000,000 are hereby permanently cancelled.

SEC. 523. Of the unobligated balances made available by section 3002(b)(2) of Public Law 115–120, $4,999,000,000 are hereby permanently cancelled.

DEPARTMENT OF STATE AND OTHER INTERNATIONAL PROGRAMS

The Department of State, the U.S. Agency for International Development (USAID), and other international programs advance the interests and security of the American people by using diplomatic and development tools to address global challenges and advance a free, peaceful, and prosperous world. The Presidents 2023 Budget for State, USAID, and other international programs strengthens American power and influence by working with allies and partners to solve global challenges including through the launch of the President's Build Back Better World Initiative. These investments will position the United States to compete with China, and any other nation, from a position of strength.

ADMINISTRATION OF FOREIGN AFFAIRS

Federal Funds

H&L FRAUD PREVENTION AND DETECTION FEE

Program and Financing (in millions of dollars)

Identification code 019–5515–0–2–153	2021 actual	2022 est.	2023 est.
Obligations by program activity:			
0001 Direct program activity	155	50	50
0900 Total new obligations, unexpired accounts (object class 41.0)	155	50	50
Budgetary resources:			
Unobligated balance:			
1000 Unobligated balance brought forward, Oct 1	126	21	16
1021 Recoveries of prior year unpaid obligations	10		
1070 Unobligated balance (total)	136	21	16
Budget authority:			
Appropriations, mandatory:			
1201 Appropriation (special or trust fund)	40	45	45
1203 Appropriation (previously unavailable)(special or trust)	3	3	3
1232 Appropriations and/or unobligated balance of appropriations temporarily reduced	–3	–3	–3
1260 Appropriations, mandatory (total)	40	45	45
1900 Budget authority (total)	40	45	45
1930 Total budgetary resources available	176	66	61
Memorandum (non-add) entries:			
1941 Unexpired unobligated balance, end of year	21	16	11
Change in obligated balance:			
Unpaid obligations:			
3000 Unpaid obligations, brought forward, Oct 1	41	65	46
3010 New obligations, unexpired accounts	155	50	50
3020 Outlays (gross)	–121	–69	–66
3040 Recoveries of prior year unpaid obligations, unexpired	–10		
3050 Unpaid obligations, end of year	65	46	30
Memorandum (non-add) entries:			
3100 Obligated balance, start of year	41	65	46
3200 Obligated balance, end of year	65	46	30
Budget authority and outlays, net:			
Mandatory:			
4090 Budget authority, gross	40	45	45
Outlays, gross:			
4100 Outlays from new mandatory authority	39	27	27
4101 Outlays from mandatory balances	82	42	39
4110 Outlays, gross (total)	121	69	66
4180 Budget authority, net (total)	40	45	45
4190 Outlays, net (total)	121	69	66

DIPLOMATIC PROGRAMS

For necessary expenses of the Department of State and the Foreign Service not otherwise provided for, $9,637,796,000, to remain available until September 30, 2024, of which up to $3,813,707,000 may remain available until expended for Worldwide Security Protection: Provided, That funds made available under this heading shall be allocated in accordance with paragraphs (1) through (4) as follows:

(1) HUMAN RESOURCES.—For necessary expenses for training, human resources management, and salaries, including employment without regard to civil service and classification laws of persons on a temporary basis (not to exceed $700,000), as authorized by section 801 of the United States Information and Educational Exchange Act of 1948 (62 Stat. 11; Chapter 36), $3,441,076,000, of which up to $684,767,000 is for Worldwide Security Protection.

(2) OVERSEAS PROGRAMS.—For necessary expenses for the regional bureaus of the Department of State and overseas activities as authorized by law, $1,934,833,000.

(3) DIPLOMATIC POLICY AND SUPPORT.—For necessary expenses for the functional bureaus of the Department of State, including representation to certain international organizations in which the United States participates pursuant to treaties ratified pursuant to the advice and consent of the Senate or specific Acts of Congress, general administration, and arms control, nonproliferation, and disarmament activities as authorized, $1,104,829,000.

(4) SECURITY PROGRAMS.—For necessary expenses for security activities, $3,157,058,000, of which up to $3,128,940,000 is for Worldwide Security Protection.

(5) FEES AND PAYMENTS COLLECTED.—In addition to amounts otherwise made available under this heading—

(A) as authorized by section 810 of the United States Information and Educational Exchange Act, not to exceed $5,000,000, to remain available until expended, may be credited to this appropriation from fees or other payments received from English teaching, library, motion pictures, and publication programs and from fees from educational advising and counseling and exchange visitor programs; and

(B) not to exceed $15,000, which shall be derived from reimbursements, surcharges, and fees for use of Blair House facilities.

(6) TRANSFER OF FUNDS, REPROGRAMMING, AND OTHER MATTERS.—

(A) Notwithstanding any other provision of this Act, funds may be reprogrammed within and between paragraphs (1) through (4) under this heading subject to section 7015 of this Act.

(B) Of the amount made available under this heading for Worldwide Security Protection, not to exceed $50,000,000 may be transferred to, and merged with, funds made available by this Act under the heading "Emergencies in the Diplomatic and Consular Service", to be available only for emergency evacuations and rewards, as authorized: Provided, That the exercise of the authority provided by this subparagraph shall be subject to prior notification to the Committees on Appropriations.

(C) Funds appropriated under this heading are available for acquisition by exchange or purchase of passenger motor vehicles, including zero emission passenger motor vehicles and supporting charging and fueling infrastructure, as authorized by law and, pursuant to section 1108(g) of title 31, United States Code, for the field examination of programs and activities in the United States funded from any account contained in this title.

(D) In fiscal year 2023, the Secretary of State is authorized to charge fees for goods and services related to the National Museum of American Diplomacy, including for visitor and outreach services, programs and conference activities, museum shop, and food services: Provided, That fees collected shall be credited to this account as a recovery of costs of operating the National Museum of American Diplomacy and shall remain available until expended.

(E) Funds appropriated under this heading in this Act and prior acts making appropriations for the Department of State, foreign operations, and related programs are available to provide payments pursuant to section 901(i)(2) of title IX of division J of the Further Consolidated Appropriations Act, 2020 (22 U.S.C. 2680b(i)(2)), as amended.

Note.—A full-year 2022 appropriation for this account was not enacted at the time the Budget was prepared; therefore, the Budget assumes this account is operating under the Continuing Appropriations Act, 2022 (Division A of Public Law 117–43, as amended). The amounts included for 2022 reflect the annualized level provided by the continuing resolution.

DIPLOMATIC PROGRAMS

【*For an additional amount for "Diplomatic Programs", $44,300,000, to remain available until expended, for support for Operation Allies Welcome and related efforts by the Department of State, including additional relocations of individuals at risk as a result of the situation in Afghanistan and related expenses, and to reimburse the account under this heading in prior Acts making appropriations for the Department of State, foreign operations, and related programs for obligations previously incurred.*】 (*Additional Afghanistan Supplemental Appropriations Act, 2022.*)

Administration of Foreign Affairs—Continued
Federal Funds—Continued

DIPLOMATIC PROGRAMS—Continued

Program and Financing (in millions of dollars)

Identification code 019–0113–0–1–153	2021 actual	2022 est.	2023 est.
Obligations by program activity:			
0001 Human Resources	2,458	2,409	2,433
0002 Overseas Programs	1,433	1,419	1,433
0003 Overseas Programs - Public Diplomacy	452	447	452
0005 Diplomatic Policy and Support	1,186	1,174	1,186
0006 Security	37	37	37
0007 Security - Worldwide Security Protection	1,696	1,679	1,696
0008 Overseas Contingency Operations	2,802	2,774	2,802
0799 Total direct obligations	10,064	9,939	10,039
0801 Diplomatic and Consular Programs (Reimbursable)	1,301	1,220	1,253
0900 Total new obligations, unexpired accounts	11,365	11,159	11,292
Budgetary resources:			
Unobligated balance:			
1000 Unobligated balance brought forward, Oct 1	2,019	1,307	692
1010 Unobligated balance transfer to other accts [019–5713]	–219		
1011 Unobligated balance transfer from other acct [019–0524]	99		
1012 Unobligated balance transfers between expired and unexpired accounts	317		
1021 Recoveries of prior year unpaid obligations	310		
1033 Recoveries of prior year paid obligations	4		
1070 Unobligated balance (total)	2,530	1,307	692
Budget authority:			
Appropriations, discretionary:			
1100 Appropriation	6,944	6,988	9,638
1100 Appropriation - OCO	2,226	2,226	
1120 Appropriations transferred to other acct [019–0522]	–150		
1131 Unobligated balance of appropriations permanently reduced	–360		
1160 Appropriation, discretionary (total)	8,660	9,214	9,638
Appropriations, mandatory:			
1200 Appropriation	204		
Spending authority from offsetting collections, discretionary:			
1700 Collected	1,476	1,330	1,288
1701 Change in uncollected payments, Federal sources	2		
1750 Spending auth from offsetting collections, disc (total)	1,478	1,330	1,288
1900 Budget authority (total)	10,342	10,544	10,926
1930 Total budgetary resources available	12,872	11,851	11,618
Memorandum (non-add) entries:			
1940 Unobligated balance expiring	–200		
1941 Unexpired unobligated balance, end of year	1,307	692	326
Change in obligated balance:			
Unpaid obligations:			
3000 Unpaid obligations, brought forward, Oct 1	4,506	4,527	5,208
3010 New obligations, unexpired accounts	11,365	11,159	11,292
3011 Obligations ("upward adjustments"), expired accounts	163		
3020 Outlays (gross)	–10,917	–10,478	–10,488
3040 Recoveries of prior year unpaid obligations, unexpired	–310		
3041 Recoveries of prior year unpaid obligations, expired	–280		
3050 Unpaid obligations, end of year	4,527	5,208	6,012
Uncollected payments:			
3060 Uncollected pymts, Fed sources, brought forward, Oct 1	–24	–12	–12
3070 Change in uncollected pymts, Fed sources, unexpired	–2		
3071 Change in uncollected pymts, Fed sources, expired	14		
3090 Uncollected pymts, Fed sources, end of year	–12	–12	–12
Memorandum (non-add) entries:			
3100 Obligated balance, start of year	4,482	4,515	5,196
3200 Obligated balance, end of year	4,515	5,196	6,000
Budget authority and outlays, net:			
Discretionary:			
4000 Budget authority, gross	10,138	10,544	10,926
Outlays, gross:			
4010 Outlays from new discretionary authority	7,442	6,953	7,389
4011 Outlays from discretionary balances	3,446	3,484	3,059
4020 Outlays, gross (total)	10,888	10,437	10,448
Offsets against gross budget authority and outlays:			
Offsetting collections (collected) from:			
4030 Federal sources	–1,089	–1,146	–1,103
4033 Non-Federal sources	–425	–184	–185
4040 Offsets against gross budget authority and outlays (total)	–1,514	–1,330	–1,288
Additional offsets against gross budget authority only:			
4050 Change in uncollected pymts, Fed sources, unexpired	–2		
4052 Offsetting collections credited to expired accounts	34		
4053 Recoveries of prior year paid obligations, unexpired accounts	4		
4060 Additional offsets against budget authority only (total)	36		
4070 Budget authority, net (discretionary)	8,660	9,214	9,638
4080 Outlays, net (discretionary)	9,374	9,107	9,160
Mandatory:			
4090 Budget authority, gross	204		
Outlays, gross:			
4100 Outlays from new mandatory authority	29		
4101 Outlays from mandatory balances		41	40
4110 Outlays, gross (total)	29	41	40
4180 Budget authority, net (total)	8,864	9,214	9,638
4190 Outlays, net (total)	9,403	9,148	9,200

Diplomatic Programs (DP) is financed by this appropriation, fees for services, and reimbursements from other agencies (including for administrative and other services provided by the Department of State). As in previous years, two-year funding is requested for this account, except for funds requested for Worldwide Security Protection (WSP), which are to remain available until expended. DP is the Department of State's primary operating account and funds a broad range of activities from policy setting, planning and design, to implementation and operations and maintenance. The 2023 request includes base funding for the State Department operations in Iraq, Pakistan, and other High Threat Posts (HTP) as well as the remaining overhead costs associated with the suspension of operations in Afghanistan.

Funds are requested in the following categories:

Human Resources.—This category supports American salaries at overseas and domestic United States diplomatic missions, including Department of State employees carrying out security protection activities. Professional development and training is a continuous process by which the Department ensures that its professionals have the skills, experience and judgment to fulfill its functions at all levels. Training programs are designed to provide employees with the specific functional area and language skills needed for the conduct of foreign relations in the Department and abroad. This activity also supports the management, recruitment, and performance evaluation of Foreign and Civil Service employees (including efforts to attract a diverse applicant pool) and locally employed staff.

Overseas Programs.—This category provides funding for the operational programs of all the regional bureaus of the Department of State, which are responsible for managing United States foreign policy through bilateral and multilateral relationships. Funds made available for 2023 will support 276 United States embassies, consulates, and other diplomatic posts worldwide. Resources for this activity are used to provide for: the political and economic reporting and analysis of interests to the United States; the representation of U.S. diplomatic and national interests to countries abroad; and the bilateral and multilateral negotiation of U.S. foreign policy objectives, including the hosting of and participation in various international conferences, meetings, and other multilateral activities in the United States and abroad. This activity also encompasses medical programs for the Department of State, the Foreign Service and other U.S. Government departments and agencies overseas. Centralized funding for travel and transportation of effects associated with the assignment, transfer, home leave and separation of the Department's personnel and dependents is also included in this activity.

Diplomatic Policy and Support.—This category supports the operational programs of the functional bureaus of the Department of State, which includes providing overall policy direction, coordination, and program management among United States missions abroad in pursuit of regional and global foreign policy objectives, including the hosting of various international conferences and meetings in the United States and abroad. Funds to support the work of the Global Engagement Center (GEC) are also included in this category. The GEC's mission is to direct, lead, synchronize, integrate, and coordinate efforts of the Federal Government to recognize, understand, expose, and counter foreign state and foreign non-state propaganda and disinformation efforts aimed at undermining or influencing the policies, security, or stability of the United States, United States allies, and partner nations. Resources also fund the management of U.S. participation in arms control, nonproliferation, and disarmament negotiations and other verification and compliance activities, in addition to funds otherwise available for such purposes. The information management activity in DP includes resources that are used for the creation, collection, processing, use, storage, and disposition of information required for the formulation and execution of foreign policy and for the conduct of daily business. Components of the information management activity include: telecommunications, information security, information system services, pouch, mail and publishing services for both unclassified and classified information. These activities include domestic and overseas execution of Department programs, such as budget and financial management, contracting and procurement, domestic facilities and vehicles, and rental payments to GSA.

Security Programs.—This category provides for the operation of security programs, including for Worldwide Security Protection (WSP) and the Bureau of Diplomatic Security (DS), to protect diplomatic personnel, overseas diplomatic missions, residences, domestic facilities and information. The salaries paid to Department employees who carry out the security protection function worldwide are included in the Human Resources program activity. This activity identifies resources that are used in meeting security and counterterrorism responsibilities, both foreign and domestic. Programs covered in this activity include but are not limited to: security operations; engineering services, which are related to the technical defense of U.S. Government personnel and establishments abroad against electronic and physical attack; homeland security related activities; protection of Department personnel and foreign dignitaries; and physical security operations.

Object Classification (in millions of dollars)

Identification code 019–0113–0–1–153		2021 actual	2022 est.	2023 est.
	Direct obligations:			
	Personnel compensation:			
11.1	Full-time permanent	2,123	2,250	2,376
11.3	Other than full-time permanent	50	52	54
11.5	Other personnel compensation	80	83	87
11.8	Special personal services payments	1	1	1
11.9	Total personnel compensation	2,254	2,386	2,518
12.1	Civilian personnel benefits	940	959	988
13.0	Benefits for former personnel	4	4	4
21.0	Travel and transportation of persons	159	154	157
22.0	Transportation of things	22	21	22
23.1	Rental payments to GSA	377	366	373
23.3	Communications, utilities, and miscellaneous charges	124	120	123
24.0	Printing and reproduction	40	39	40
25.1	Advisory and assistance services	1,435	1,392	1,420
25.2	Other services from non-Federal sources	7	7	7
25.3	Other goods and services from Federal sources	111	108	110
25.3	Purchases of goods and services from Government accounts (ICASS)	3,967	3,778	3,658
25.4	Operation and maintenance of facilities	56	54	56
25.6	Medical care	6	6	6
25.7	Operation and maintenance of equipment	372	361	368
26.0	Supplies and materials	126	122	125
31.0	Equipment	27	26	27
41.0	Grants, subsidies, and contributions	35	34	35
42.0	Insurance claims and indemnities	2	2	2
99.0	Direct obligations	10,064	9,939	10,039
99.0	Reimbursable obligations	1,301	1,220	1,253
99.9	Total new obligations, unexpired accounts	11,365	11,159	11,292

Employment Summary

Identification code 019–0113–0–1–153	2021 actual	2022 est.	2023 est.
1001 Direct civilian full-time equivalent employment	15,157	15,494	16,061
2001 Reimbursable civilian full-time equivalent employment	155	155	155

CONSULAR AND BORDER SECURITY PROGRAMS

Note.—A full-year 2022 appropriation for this account was not enacted at the time the Budget was prepared; therefore, the Budget assumes this account is operating under the Continuing Appropriations Act, 2022 (Division A of Public Law 117–43, as amended). The amounts included for 2022 reflect the annualized level provided by the continuing resolution.

Special and Trust Fund Receipts (in millions of dollars)

Identification code 019–5713–0–2–153		2021 actual	2022 est.	2023 est.
0100	Balance, start of year			
	Receipts:			
	Current law:			
1130	Expedited Passport Fees, Consular and Border Security Programs		433	454
1130	Passport Security Surcharge, Consular and Border Security Programs	819	1,405	1,549
1130	Western Hemisphere Travel Surcharge, Consular and Border Security Programs	348	447	482
1130	Machine-Readable Visa Fee, Consular and Border Security Programs	826	1,390	2,413
1130	Machine-Readable Visa Fee, Consular and Border Security Programs			11
1130	Immigrant Visa Security Surcharge, Consular and Border Security Programs	60	56	57
1130	Affidavit of Support Fee, Consular and Border Security Programs	40	36	37
1130	Diversity Immigrant Lottery Fee, Consular and Border Security Programs	7	9	16
1199	Total current law receipts	2,100	3,776	5,019
1999	Total receipts	2,100	3,776	5,019
2000	Total: Balances and receipts	2,100	3,776	5,019
	Appropriations:			
	Current law:			
2101	Consular and Border Security Programs	–2,100	–3,776	–5,019
5099	Balance, end of year			

Program and Financing (in millions of dollars)

Identification code 019–5713–0–2–153		2021 actual	2022 est.	2023 est.
	Obligations by program activity:			
0001	Consular and Border Security Programs (Direct)	2,669	3,925	3,795
0801	Reimbursable program activity	243		
0900	Total new obligations, unexpired accounts	2,912	3,925	3,795
	Budgetary resources:			
	Unobligated balance:			
1000	Unobligated balance brought forward, Oct 1	857	689	840
1011	Unobligated balance transfer from other acct [019–0113]	219		
1021	Recoveries of prior year unpaid obligations	55		
1033	Recoveries of prior year paid obligations	38		
1070	Unobligated balance (total)	1,169	689	840
	Budget authority:			
	Appropriations, discretionary:			
1100	Appropriation (Annual Appropriation)	300	300	
1101	Appropriation (special or trust)	2,100	3,776	5,019
1160	Appropriation, discretionary (total)	2,400	4,076	5,019
	Spending authority from offsetting collections, discretionary:			
1700	Collected	33		
1900	Budget authority (total)	2,433	4,076	5,019
1930	Total budgetary resources available	3,602	4,765	5,859
	Memorandum (non-add) entries:			
1940	Unobligated balance expiring	–1		
1941	Unexpired unobligated balance, end of year	689	840	2,064
	Special and non-revolving trust funds:			
1951	Unobligated balance expiring	1		
1952	Expired unobligated balance, start of year		1	1
1953	Expired unobligated balance, end of year		1	1
	Change in obligated balance:			
	Unpaid obligations:			
3000	Unpaid obligations, brought forward, Oct 1	1,146	936	924
3010	New obligations, unexpired accounts	2,912	3,925	3,795
3020	Outlays (gross)	–3,067	–3,937	–4,672
3040	Recoveries of prior year unpaid obligations, unexpired	–55		
3050	Unpaid obligations, end of year	936	924	47
	Memorandum (non-add) entries:			
3100	Obligated balance, start of year	1,146	936	924

CONSULAR AND BORDER SECURITY PROGRAMS—Continued

Program and Financing—Continued

Identification code 019–5713–0–2–153		2021 actual	2022 est.	2023 est.
3200	Obligated balance, end of year	936	924	47
	Budget authority and outlays, net:			
	Discretionary:			
4000	Budget authority, gross	2,433	4,076	5,019
	Outlays, gross:			
4010	Outlays from new discretionary authority	2,003	3,108	3,750
4011	Outlays from discretionary balances	1,064	829	922
4020	Outlays, gross (total)	3,067	3,937	4,672
	Offsets against gross budget authority and outlays:			
	Offsetting collections (collected) from:			
4030	Federal sources	–69	....	....
4033	Non-Federal sources	–2	....	....
4040	Offsets against gross budget authority and outlays (total)	–71	....	....
	Additional offsets against gross budget authority only:			
4053	Recoveries of prior year paid obligations, unexpired accounts	38	....	....
4070	Budget authority, net (discretionary)	2,400	4,076	5,019
4080	Outlays, net (discretionary)	2,996	3,937	4,672
4180	Budget authority, net (total)	2,400	4,076	5,019
4190	Outlays, net (total)	2,996	3,937	4,672

The Consular and Border Security Programs account (CBSP) uses revenue from consular fees and surcharges to fund programs and activities, consistent with applicable statutory authorities. These fees and surcharges include Machine Readable Visa (MRV) fees, Western Hemisphere Travel Initiative (WHTI) surcharges, Passport Security surcharges, Immigrant Visa Security surcharges, Diversity Visa Lottery fees, H and L Visa Fraud Prevention and Detection Fees, Affidavit of Support fees, use of J Waiver Fees starting in FY 2021, and full use of Expedited Passport Fees (EPF) starting in FY 2022. In FY 2017 and prior years, these fees were credited in the Diplomatic and Consular Programs account as spending authority from offsetting collections. The Consolidated Appropriations Act of FY 2017 enacted a new standalone account to display fee-funded consular programs independent of the larger Diplomatic Programs (formerly Diplomatic and Consular Programs) account that began in FY 2019. This change enables the Department to provide greater transparency and accountability in financial reporting on these fees and surcharges, facilitate budget estimates for these fees and surcharges, and more easily make the information available to users of budget information and other stakeholders.

Section 7025(i)(1) of the general provisions provides a permanent extension of the Western Hemisphere Travel Initiative Surcharge. Section 7062 provides for the recovery of costs of consular services not otherwise subject to visa fees and surcharges retained by the Department. Section 7063 provides legislative language expanding the authorities of the Border Crossing Card and Passport Security Surcharge. Finally, Section 7052 provides the ability to use the Fraud Prevention and Detection fees for the costs of providing consular services.

These consular fees and surcharges support an array of activities that are vital to ensuring strong U.S border security, including routine and emergency services for U.S. citizens overseas; the issuance of secure passports to U.S. citizens at 29 passport facilities and a partner network of more than 8,000 passport acceptance facilities domestically; the adjudication of visa applications; the prevention and detection of fraud involving visas and passports; and the Department's consular systems. Together with the Department of Homeland Security, the Department of Justice, the Intelligence Community, Department of the Treasury, and the law enforcement community, the Department has built a layered visa and border security screening system that rests on training, technological advances, biometric innovations and expanded data sharing.

Object Classification (in millions of dollars)

Identification code 019–5713–0–2–153		2021 actual	2022 est.	2023 est.
11.1	Direct obligations: Personnel compensation: Full-time permanent	551	552	554
11.9	Total personnel compensation	551	552	554
12.1	Civilian personnel benefits	137	138	139
23.3	Communications, utilities, and miscellaneous charges	1,981	3,235	3,102
99.0	Direct obligations	2,669	3,925	3,795
99.0	Reimbursable obligations	243	....	....
99.9	Total new obligations, unexpired accounts	2,912	3,925	3,795

Employment Summary

Identification code 019–5713–0–2–153	2021 actual	2022 est.	2023 est.
1001 Direct civilian full-time equivalent employment	4,169	4,169	4,169

SUDAN CLAIMS

Program and Financing (in millions of dollars)

Identification code 019–1158–0–1–153		2021 actual	2022 est.	2023 est.
	Obligations by program activity:			
0001	Direct program activity	....	150	....
0900	Total new obligations, unexpired accounts (object class 41.0)	....	150	....
	Budgetary resources:			
	Unobligated balance:			
1000	Unobligated balance brought forward, Oct 1	....	150	....
	Budget authority:			
	Appropriations, discretionary:			
1100	Appropriation	150	....	....
1930	Total budgetary resources available	150	150	....
	Memorandum (non-add) entries:			
1941	Unexpired unobligated balance, end of year	150	....	....
	Change in obligated balance:			
	Unpaid obligations:			
3010	New obligations, unexpired accounts	....	150	....
3020	Outlays (gross)	....	–150	....
	Budget authority and outlays, net:			
	Discretionary:			
4000	Budget authority, gross	150	....	....
	Outlays, gross:			
4011	Outlays from discretionary balances	....	150	....
4180	Budget authority, net (total)	150	....	....
4190	Outlays, net (total)	....	150	....

No funds are requested for this account in FY 2023.

INTERNATIONAL INFORMATION PROGRAMS

Program and Financing (in millions of dollars)

Identification code 019–0201–0–1–154		2021 actual	2022 est.	2023 est.
	Budgetary resources:			
	Unobligated balance:			
1000	Unobligated balance brought forward, Oct 1	1	1	1
1930	Total budgetary resources available	1	1	1
	Memorandum (non-add) entries:			
1941	Unexpired unobligated balance, end of year	1	1	1
4180	Budget authority, net (total)	....	....	....
4190	Outlays, net (total)	....	....	....

The appropriation for overseas information and cultural programs previously provided to the U.S. Information Agency and designed to inform and influence foreign audiences has been administered by the Department of State and funded from Diplomatic Programs and other accounts within the Department of State since 2000, except those activities as are associated with international broadcasting functions which are funded from the U.S.

DEPARTMENT OF STATE AND OTHER INTERNATIONAL PROGRAMS

Agency for Global Media account. This schedule reflects the spend-out of prior year funds. As of FY 2020, the Bureau of International and Information Programs has merged with the Bureau of Public Affairs to create the Bureau of Global Public Affairs.

CONFLICT STABILIZATION OPERATIONS

Program and Financing (in millions of dollars)

Identification code 019–0121–0–1–153		2021 actual	2022 est.	2023 est.
	Change in obligated balance:			
	Unpaid obligations:			
3000	Unpaid obligations, brought forward, Oct 1	8	2	
3020	Outlays (gross)	–6	–2	
3050	Unpaid obligations, end of year	2		
	Memorandum (non-add) entries:			
3100	Obligated balance, start of year	8	2	
3200	Obligated balance, end of year	2		
	Budget authority and outlays, net:			
	Discretionary:			
	Outlays, gross:			
4011	Outlays from discretionary balances	6	2	
4180	Budget authority, net (total)			
4190	Outlays, net (total)	6	2	

For FY 2023, Conflict Stabilization Operations funding is requested under the Diplomatic Programs account. This schedule reflects a spend-out of prior year funds.

CAPITAL INVESTMENT FUND

For necessary expenses of the Capital Investment Fund, as authorized, $470,180,000, to remain available until expended.

Note.—A full-year 2022 appropriation for this account was not enacted at the time the Budget was prepared; therefore, the Budget assumes this account is operating under the Continuing Appropriations Act, 2022 (Division A of Public Law 117–43, as amended). The amounts included for 2022 reflect the annualized level provided by the continuing resolution.

Program and Financing (in millions of dollars)

Identification code 019–0120–0–1–153		2021 actual	2022 est.	2023 est.
	Obligations by program activity:			
0001	Capital Investment Fund	246	253	470
	Budgetary resources:			
	Unobligated balance:			
1000	Unobligated balance brought forward, Oct 1	1	6	3
1021	Recoveries of prior year unpaid obligations	1		
1070	Unobligated balance (total)	2	6	3
	Budget authority:			
	Appropriations, discretionary:			
1100	Appropriation	250	250	470
1930	Total budgetary resources available	252	256	473
	Memorandum (non-add) entries:			
1941	Unexpired unobligated balance, end of year	6	3	3
	Change in obligated balance:			
	Unpaid obligations:			
3000	Unpaid obligations, brought forward, Oct 1	33	138	181
3010	New obligations, unexpired accounts	246	253	470
3020	Outlays (gross)	–140	–210	–365
3040	Recoveries of prior year unpaid obligations, unexpired	–1		
3050	Unpaid obligations, end of year	138	181	286
	Memorandum (non-add) entries:			
3100	Obligated balance, start of year	33	138	181
3200	Obligated balance, end of year	138	181	286
	Budget authority and outlays, net:			
	Discretionary:			
4000	Budget authority, gross	250	250	470
	Outlays, gross:			
4010	Outlays from new discretionary authority	110	125	235
4011	Outlays from discretionary balances	30	85	130
4020	Outlays, gross (total)	140	210	365
4180	Budget authority, net (total)	250	250	470
4190	Outlays, net (total)	140	210	365

The Capital Investment Fund provides for the procurement of information technology and other related capital investments for the Department of State. It is designed to ensure the efficient management, coordination, operation, and utilization of such resources across the enterprise. The fund is used to make investments that improve the Department's cybersecurity posture and operational performance in a continually evolving technological environment.

Object Classification (in millions of dollars)

Identification code 019–0120–0–1–153		2021 actual	2022 est.	2023 est.
	Direct obligations:			
25.2	Other services from non-Federal sources	219	225	418
31.0	Equipment	27	28	52
99.9	Total new obligations, unexpired accounts	246	253	470

OFFICE OF INSPECTOR GENERAL

For necessary expenses of the Office of Inspector General, $133,700,000, to remain available until September 30, 2024, of which $38,600,000 is for the Special Inspector General for Afghanistan Reconstruction (SIGAR) for reconstruction oversight: Provided, That funds appropriated under this heading are made available notwithstanding section 209(a)(1) of the Foreign Service Act of 1980 (22 U.S.C. 3929(a)(1)), as it relates to post inspections: Provided further, That, notwithstanding any other provision of law, any employee of SIGAR who completes at least 12 months of continuous service after the date of enactment of this Act, or who is employed on the date on which SIGAR terminates, whichever occurs first, shall acquire competitive status for appointment to any position in the competitive service for which the employee possesses the required qualifications.

Note.—A full-year 2022 appropriation for this account was not enacted at the time the Budget was prepared; therefore, the Budget assumes this account is operating under the Continuing Appropriations Act, 2022 (Division A of Public Law 117–43, as amended). The amounts included for 2022 reflect the annualized level provided by the continuing resolution.

Program and Financing (in millions of dollars)

Identification code 019–0529–0–1–153		2021 actual	2022 est.	2023 est.
	Obligations by program activity:			
0002	Office of the Inspector General (Direct)	68	69	69
0005	Office of the Inspector General	17	17	18
0006	Office of the Inspector General (SIGAR) - OCO	55	55	55
0799	Total direct obligations	140	141	142
0801	Office of the Inspector General (Reimbursable)		1	1
0900	Total new obligations, unexpired accounts	140	142	143
	Budgetary resources:			
	Unobligated balance:			
1000	Unobligated balance brought forward, Oct 1	6	10	15
	Budget authority:			
	Appropriations, discretionary:			
1100	Appropriation - Office of the Inspector General (base)	91	91	134
1100	Appropriation - SIGAR (OCO)	55	55	
1160	Appropriation, discretionary (total)	146	146	134
	Spending authority from offsetting collections, discretionary:			
1700	Collected		1	1
1900	Budget authority (total)	146	147	135
1930	Total budgetary resources available	152	157	150
	Memorandum (non-add) entries:			
1940	Unobligated balance expiring	–2		
1941	Unexpired unobligated balance, end of year	10	15	7
	Change in obligated balance:			
	Unpaid obligations:			
3000	Unpaid obligations, brought forward, Oct 1	67	66	65
3010	New obligations, unexpired accounts	140	142	143
3011	Obligations ("upward adjustments"), expired accounts	1		
3020	Outlays (gross)	–134	–143	–157
3041	Recoveries of prior year unpaid obligations, expired	–8		
3050	Unpaid obligations, end of year	66	65	51

OFFICE OF INSPECTOR GENERAL—Continued
Program and Financing—Continued

Identification code 019–0529–0–1–153		2021 actual	2022 est.	2023 est.
	Memorandum (non-add) entries:			
3100	Obligated balance, start of year	67	66	65
3200	Obligated balance, end of year	66	65	51
	Budget authority and outlays, net:			
	Discretionary:			
4000	Budget authority, gross	146	147	135
	Outlays, gross:			
4010	Outlays from new discretionary authority	87	113	101
4011	Outlays from discretionary balances	47	30	56
4020	Outlays, gross (total)	134	143	157
	Offsets against gross budget authority and outlays:			
	Offsetting collections (collected) from:			
4030	Federal sources		–1	–1
4180	Budget authority, net (total)	146	146	134
4190	Outlays, net (total)	134	142	156

This appropriation provides for the conduct or supervision of all audits, investigations, and inspections of the Department's programs and operations as mandated by the Inspector General Act of 1978, as amended, and the Foreign Service Act of 1980, as amended. The objectives of the Office of the Inspector General are to: improve the economy, efficiency, and effectiveness of the Department's operations; detect and prevent fraud, waste, abuse, and mismanagement; and evaluate independently the formulation, applicability, and implementation of security standards at all U.S. diplomatic and consular posts. The Office also assesses the implementation of U.S. foreign policy, primarily through its inspection of all overseas posts and domestic offices on a cyclical basis. The State Department's Inspector General also serves as Inspector General of the U.S. Agency for Global Media and has partial oversight of Department of State-managed foreign assistance resources, as mandated by law. In addition, this appropriation funds the Office of the Special Inspector General for Afghanistan Reconstruction (SIGAR). SIGAR provides independent oversight of programs and operations funded with amounts made available for the reconstruction of Afghanistan. SIGAR performs this oversight through audits, field inspections and investigations of potential waste, fraud and abuse in coordination with, and receiving the cooperation of, the Inspectors General of the Department of State, Department of Defense and the United States Agency for International Development.

Object Classification (in millions of dollars)

Identification code 019–0529–0–1–153		2021 actual	2022 est.	2023 est.
	Direct obligations:			
	Personnel compensation:			
11.1	Full-time permanent	41	42	43
11.5	Other personnel compensation	5	5	6
11.9	Total personnel compensation	46	47	49
12.1	Civilian personnel benefits	15	15	15
21.0	Travel and transportation of persons	2	2	2
23.3	Communications, utilities, and miscellaneous charges	3	3	3
24.0	Printing and reproduction	3	3	3
25.2	Other services from non-Federal sources	20	20	20
26.0	Supplies and materials	2	2	2
31.0	Equipment	4	4	4
41.0	Grants, subsidies, and contributions	45	45	44
99.0	Direct obligations	140	141	142
99.0	Reimbursable obligations		1	1
99.9	Total new obligations, unexpired accounts	140	142	143

Employment Summary

Identification code 019–0529–0–1–153	2021 actual	2022 est.	2023 est.
1001 Direct civilian full-time equivalent employment	299	299	329

EDUCATIONAL AND CULTURAL EXCHANGE PROGRAMS

For necessary expenses of educational and cultural exchange programs, as authorized, $741,300,000, to remain available until expended: Provided, That fees or other payments received from, or in connection with, English teaching, educational advising and counseling programs, and exchange visitor programs as authorized may be credited to this account, to remain available until expended: Provided further, That funds made available under this heading may be used to carry out the activities of the Cultural Antiquities Task Force and not to exceed $1,000,000 may be used to make grants for such purposes.

Note.—A full-year 2022 appropriation for this account was not enacted at the time the Budget was prepared; therefore, the Budget assumes this account is operating under the Continuing Appropriations Act, 2022 (Division A of Public Law 117–43, as amended). The amounts included for 2022 reflect the annualized level provided by the continuing resolution.

Program and Financing (in millions of dollars)

Identification code 019–0209–0–1–154		2021 actual	2022 est.	2023 est.
	Obligations by program activity:			
0001	Educational and Cultural Exchange Programs (Direct)	806	780	780
0100	Subtotal, Direct Obligations	806	780	780
0880	Educational and Cultural Exchange Programs (Reimbursable)	13	8	8
0900	Total new obligations, unexpired accounts	819	788	788
	Budgetary resources:			
	Unobligated balance:			
1000	Unobligated balance brought forward, Oct 1	116	77	45
1001	Discretionary unobligated balance brought fwd, Oct 1	115		
1011	Unobligated balance transfer from other acct [072–1037]	11		
1021	Recoveries of prior year unpaid obligations	14	8	8
1070	Unobligated balance (total)	141	85	53
	Budget authority:			
	Appropriations, discretionary:			
1100	Appropriation	740	740	741
	Spending authority from offsetting collections, discretionary:			
1700	Collected	15	8	8
1900	Budget authority (total)	755	748	749
1930	Total budgetary resources available	896	833	802
	Memorandum (non-add) entries:			
1941	Unexpired unobligated balance, end of year	77	45	14
	Change in obligated balance:			
	Unpaid obligations:			
3000	Unpaid obligations, brought forward, Oct 1	857	1,096	1,022
3010	New obligations, unexpired accounts	819	788	788
3020	Outlays (gross)	–557	–854	–756
3040	Recoveries of prior year unpaid obligations, unexpired	–14	–8	–8
3041	Recoveries of prior year unpaid obligations, expired	–9		
3050	Unpaid obligations, end of year	1,096	1,022	1,046
	Memorandum (non-add) entries:			
3100	Obligated balance, start of year	857	1,096	1,022
3200	Obligated balance, end of year	1,096	1,022	1,046
	Budget authority and outlays, net:			
	Discretionary:			
4000	Budget authority, gross	755	748	749
	Outlays, gross:			
4010	Outlays from new discretionary authority	228	230	230
4011	Outlays from discretionary balances	329	624	526
4020	Outlays, gross (total)	557	854	756
	Offsets against gross budget authority and outlays:			
	Offsetting collections (collected) from:			
4030	Federal sources	–6	–4	–4
4033	Non-Federal sources	–9	–4	–4
4040	Offsets against gross budget authority and outlays (total)	–15	–8	–8
4070	Budget authority, net (discretionary)	740	740	741
4080	Outlays, net (discretionary)	542	846	748
4180	Budget authority, net (total)	740	740	741
4190	Outlays, net (total)	542	846	748

This appropriation provides funding to the Bureau of Educational and Cultural Affairs (ECA) for international exchange programs authorized by the Mutual Educational and Cultural Exchange Act of 1961, as amended, to support U.S. foreign, economic, security policy objectives and to advance U.S. influence overseas. These goals are addressed by building increased

DEPARTMENT OF STATE AND OTHER INTERNATIONAL PROGRAMS

Administration of Foreign Affairs—Continued
Federal Funds—Continued

805

mutual understanding through international exchange and professional development activities. Programs under this appropriation include:

Academic Programs.—Includes the J. William Fulbright Educational Exchange Program, which provides U.S. and foreign students, teachers, scholars, and administrators the opportunity to pursue degrees, teach, and conduct research in foreign and U.S. universities. Academic Programs also include English language programming and educational advising services. English language programs help train and develop foreign teachers of English, send Americans overseas to teach English and train instructors, teach English to disadvantaged students, and provide language learning materials and resources. In addition, educational advising programming supports outreach to foreign students across the world to assist in the process of applying to U.S. universities. Additional academic programs such as the Benjamin A. Gilman International Scholarship Program provide opportunities for American participants with financial needs to study abroad, and the American Spaces Program supports more than 600 open-access cultural centers that freely share American books, movies, and programs that demonstrate American values with foreign audiences in more than 140 countries to connect the world with the United States.

Professional/Cultural Exchanges.—Includes exchanges linking U.S. and foreign participants in multiple fields directly tied to U.S. foreign policy goals. The International Visitor Leadership Program brings thousands of foreign leaders to the United States for intensive short-term professional exchanges to meet and confer with their American counterparts, gaining first-hand knowledge about U.S. society, culture and democratic values. The Citizen Exchanges Program participants partner with an extensive network of organizations and experts from across the United States to conduct professional fellowships as well as arts, sports, and high school exchange programs focused on current and future leaders. The Citizen Exchanges Program also includes the TechCamp Program, which leverages cutting-edge communications and private sector expertise to build networks of influential activists around the world to advance shared policies to include countering disinformation, supporting good governance, and mitigating violent extremism.

Youth Leadership Initiatives.—Includes programs targeting young private, public, and civil sector leaders in Africa, Southeast Asia, and the Americas.

Program and Performance.—Includes the U.S. Speakers Program that connects professional foreign audiences with American experts on topics of strategic importance to the United States and collaborates with U.S. embassies and consulates around the world to develop and implement customized programs. Funds also support opportunities for ECA program alumni to build on participant experiences and maximize the return on investment in people-to-people connections by turning exchange experiences into enduring relationships that are part of a growing network of active alumni associations across the globe, as well as on-going evidence-based program performance measurements and independent evaluations to strengthen ECA's ability to monitor, evaluate, learn, and innovate.

Exchanges Support.—Includes all domestic staff, overseas Regional Language Officers, and operational support costs managed by ECA, and provides government-wide exchanges coordination.

Object Classification (in millions of dollars)

Identification code 019–0209–0–1–154		2021 actual	2022 est.	2023 est.
	Direct obligations:			
11.1	Personnel compensation: Full-time permanent	46	48	50
12.1	Civilian personnel benefits	13	13	13
21.0	Travel and transportation of persons	29	20	20
23.3	Communications, utilities, and miscellaneous charges	2	2	2
25.2	Other services from non-Federal sources	45	30	30
26.0	Supplies and materials	1	1	1
41.0	Grants, subsidies, and contributions	670	666	664
99.0	Direct obligations	806	780	780
99.0	Reimbursable obligations	13	8	8
99.9	Total new obligations, unexpired accounts	819	788	788

Employment Summary

Identification code 019–0209–0–1–154	2021 actual	2022 est.	2023 est.
1001 Direct civilian full-time equivalent employment	455	455	455

EMBASSY SECURITY, CONSTRUCTION, AND MAINTENANCE

For necessary expenses for carrying out the Foreign Service Buildings Act of 1926 (22 U.S.C. 292 et seq.), preserving, maintaining, repairing, and planning for real property that are owned or leased by the Department of State, and renovating, in addition to funds otherwise available, the Harry S Truman Building, $902,615,000, to remain available until expended, of which not to exceed $25,000 may be used for overseas representation expenses as authorized: Provided, That none of the funds appropriated in this paragraph shall be available for acquisition of furniture, furnishings, or generators for other departments and agencies of the United States Government.

In addition, for the costs of worldwide security upgrades, acquisition, and construction as authorized, $1,055,206,000, to remain available until expended.

Note.—A full-year 2022 appropriation for this account was not enacted at the time the Budget was prepared; therefore, the Budget assumes this account is operating under the Continuing Appropriations Act, 2022 (Division A of Public Law 117–43, as amended). The amounts included for 2022 reflect the annualized level provided by the continuing resolution.

Program and Financing (in millions of dollars)

Identification code 019–0535–0–1–153		2021 actual	2022 est.	2023 est.
	Obligations by program activity:			
0001	Capital Security Construction	1,035	803	759
0002	Compound Security	117	55	52
0003	Repair and Construction	108	360	341
0004	Operations	784	919	869
0005	Supplemental Appropriations	17	42	40
0006	OCO	81	837	791
0100	Total direct program	2,142	3,016	2,852
0799	Total direct obligations	2,142	3,016	2,852
0801	Asset Management		105	102
0802	Leaseholds and Functional Programs	206	351	332
0803	Capital Security Cost Sharing	1,056	869	822
0804	Other Reimbursements	24	12	11
0899	Total reimbursable obligations	1,286	1,337	1,267
0900	Total new obligations, unexpired accounts	3,428	4,353	4,119
	Budgetary resources:			
	Unobligated balance:			
1000	Unobligated balance brought forward, Oct 1	9,127	9,869	9,246
1021	Recoveries of prior year unpaid obligations	296	299	299
1033	Recoveries of prior year paid obligations	25		
1070	Unobligated balance (total)	9,448	10,168	9,545
	Budget authority:			
	Appropriations, discretionary:			
1100	Appropriation	1,950	1,126	1,958
1100	Appropriation - OCO		824	
1160	Appropriation, discretionary (total)	1,950	1,950	1,958
	Spending authority from offsetting collections, discretionary:			
1700	Offsetting collections (cash) - Capital Security Cost Sharing	1,633	1,188	1,264
1700	Offsetting collections (cash) - Other Collections	300	293	290
1701	Change in uncollected payments, Federal sources	–34		
1750	Spending auth from offsetting collections, disc (total)	1,899	1,481	1,554
1900	Budget authority (total)	3,849	3,431	3,512
1930	Total budgetary resources available	13,297	13,599	13,057
	Memorandum (non-add) entries:			
1941	Unexpired unobligated balance, end of year	9,869	9,246	8,938
	Change in obligated balance:			
	Unpaid obligations:			
3000	Unpaid obligations, brought forward, Oct 1	6,359	6,225	6,888
3010	New obligations, unexpired accounts	3,428	4,353	4,119
3020	Outlays (gross)	–3,266	–3,391	–3,600
3040	Recoveries of prior year unpaid obligations, unexpired	–296	–299	–299
3050	Unpaid obligations, end of year	6,225	6,888	7,108
	Uncollected payments:			
3060	Uncollected pymts, Fed sources, brought forward, Oct 1	–37	–3	–3

EMBASSY SECURITY, CONSTRUCTION, AND MAINTENANCE—Continued

Program and Financing—Continued

Identification code 019–0535–0–1–153		2021 actual	2022 est.	2023 est.
3070	Change in uncollected pymts, Fed sources, unexpired	34	....	....
3090	Uncollected pymts, Fed sources, end of year	–3	–3	–3
	Memorandum (non-add) entries:			
3100	Obligated balance, start of year	6,322	6,222	6,885
3200	Obligated balance, end of year	6,222	6,885	7,105
	Budget authority and outlays, net:			
	Discretionary:			
4000	Budget authority, gross	3,849	3,431	3,512
	Outlays, gross:			
4010	Outlays from new discretionary authority	1,323	1,140	1,246
4011	Outlays from discretionary balances	1,943	2,251	2,354
4020	Outlays, gross (total)	3,266	3,391	3,600
	Offsets against gross budget authority and outlays:			
	Offsetting collections (collected) from:			
4030	Federal sources	–1,490	–1,481	–1,554
4033	Non-Federal sources	–468	....	....
4040	Offsets against gross budget authority and outlays (total)	–1,958	–1,481	–1,554
	Additional offsets against gross budget authority only:			
4050	Change in uncollected pymts, Fed sources, unexpired	34	....	....
4053	Recoveries of prior year paid obligations, unexpired accounts	25	....	....
4060	Additional offsets against budget authority only (total)	59	....	....
4070	Budget authority, net (discretionary)	1,950	1,950	1,958
4080	Outlays, net (discretionary)	1,308	1,910	2,046
4180	Budget authority, net (total)	1,950	1,950	1,958
4190	Outlays, net (total)	1,308	1,910	2,046

Under the direction of the Secretary of State, the overall mission of the Bureau of Overseas Buildings Operations (OBO) is to provide U.S. diplomatic and consular missions abroad with safe, secure, and functional facilities that support the foreign policy objectives of the United States. Specific program functions include: providing guidance to posts, the regional bureaus and other foreign affairs agencies on the renovation, construction and operations of facilities; providing expert space and facilities planning; managing and overseeing the design, construction, and renovation of mission facilities; incorporating security features into overseas and domestic facilities; and ensuring the security of facilities during construction or renovation. In addition, OBO is responsible for establishing standards and policies for overseas housing, developing, in conjunction with posts, effective maintenance programs for post facilities, and monitoring and reporting the inventory of maintenance and backlog requirements. OBO also ensures the safety of the building occupants through the development of fire/life safety and accessibility compliance programs.

In 2023, the Department will manage the nineteenth year of the Capital Security Cost Sharing (CSCS) Program. This program has two main goals: accelerating the construction of new safe, secure and functional embassy and consulate compounds, and providing an incentive for all United States Government agencies to right-size their presence overseas through the use of cost-sharing. The $2.2 billion program is consistent with the Benghazi Accountability Review Board's recommended funding level for the construction of new secure facilities overseas. The 2023 request continues the Maintenance Cost Sharing (MCS) Program to provide critically needed renovation, construction and repair of overseas facilities, to provide adequate working conditions for multi-agency staffs, and protect the U.S. taxpayer investment. Both programs are funded within a combined CSCS-MCS program in FY 2023. Funding sources include ESCM appropriations, interagency contributions, and consular fee revenues.

The objective of the Asset Management Program is to obtain the best use of diplomatic and consular properties overseas through sale of surplus or underutilized properties and reinvestment of the proceeds in properties that provide a greater return to the U.S. Government and/or improve the safety of mission personnel. In lieu of appropriated resources, OBO uses asset sales proceeds for long-term capital investment to minimize the growth of U.S. Government leasehold requirements (through property acquisition) or to address a high-priority need for new construction or fit-out of leased space.

This appropriation also provides for capital expenditures necessary to preserve, maintain, repair, and plan for buildings owned or leased by the Department of State overseas.

Object Classification (in millions of dollars)

Identification code 019–0535–0–1–153		2021 actual	2022 est.	2023 est.
	Direct obligations:			
	Personnel compensation:			
11.1	Full-time permanent	83	90	95
11.3	Other than full-time permanent	37	40	42
11.5	Other personnel compensation	3	3	3
11.9	Total personnel compensation	123	133	140
12.1	Civilian personnel benefits	51	57	63
21.0	Travel and transportation of persons	23	32	30
22.0	Transportation of objects	6	9	9
23.2	Rental payments to other entities	20	28	26
23.3	Communications, utilities, and miscellaneous charges	278	391	370
25.2	Other services from non-Federal sources	244	344	325
25.4	Operation and maintenance of facilities	275	387	366
26.0	Supplies and materials	42	59	56
31.0	Equipment	50	70	66
32.0	Land and structures	980	1,435	1,334
41.0	Grants, subsidies, and contributions	50	71	67
99.0	Direct obligations	2,142	3,016	2,852
99.0	Reimbursable obligations	1,286	1,337	1,267
99.9	Total new obligations, unexpired accounts	3,428	4,353	4,119

Employment Summary

Identification code 019–0535–0–1–153	2021 actual	2022 est.	2023 est.
1001 Direct civilian full-time equivalent employment	1,034	1,034	1,034

REPRESENTATION EXPENSES

For representation expenses as authorized, $7,415,000.

Note.—A full-year 2022 appropriation for this account was not enacted at the time the Budget was prepared; therefore, the Budget assumes this account is operating under the Continuing Appropriations Act, 2022 (Division A of Public Law 117–43, as amended). The amounts included for 2022 reflect the annualized level provided by the continuing resolution.

Program and Financing (in millions of dollars)

Identification code 019–0545–0–1–153		2021 actual	2022 est.	2023 est.
	Obligations by program activity:			
0001	Representation Expenses	6	7	7
0900	Total new obligations, unexpired accounts (object class 26.0)	6	7	7
	Budgetary resources:			
	Budget authority:			
	Appropriations, discretionary:			
1100	Appropriation	8	7	7
1900	Budget authority (total)	8	7	7
1930	Total budgetary resources available	8	7	7
	Memorandum (non-add) entries:			
1940	Unobligated balance expiring	–2	....	....
	Change in obligated balance:			
	Unpaid obligations:			
3000	Unpaid obligations, brought forward, Oct 1	2	2	1
3010	New obligations, unexpired accounts	6	7	7
3020	Outlays (gross)	–5	–8	–7
3041	Recoveries of prior year unpaid obligations, expired	–1	....	....
3050	Unpaid obligations, end of year	2	1	1
	Memorandum (non-add) entries:			
3100	Obligated balance, start of year	2	2	1
3200	Obligated balance, end of year	2	1	1
	Budget authority and outlays, net:			
	Discretionary:			
4000	Budget authority, gross	8	7	7

DEPARTMENT OF STATE AND OTHER INTERNATIONAL PROGRAMS

Administration of Foreign Affairs—Continued
Federal Funds—Continued

807

		2021 actual	2022 est.	2023 est.
	Outlays, gross:			
4010	Outlays from new discretionary authority	4	6	6
4011	Outlays from discretionary balances	1	2	1
4020	Outlays, gross (total)	5	8	7
4180	Budget authority, net (total)	8	7	7
4190	Outlays, net (total)	5	8	7

Funds are used to reimburse State Department employees posted overseas, in whole or in part, for certain costs incurred related to carrying out official representation functions.

PROTECTION OF FOREIGN MISSIONS AND OFFICIALS

For necessary expenses, not otherwise provided, to enable the Secretary of State to provide for extraordinary protective services, as authorized, $30,890,000, to remain available until September 30, 2024.

Note.—A full-year 2022 appropriation for this account was not enacted at the time the Budget was prepared; therefore, the Budget assumes this account is operating under the Continuing Appropriations Act, 2022 (Division A of Public Law 117–43, as amended). The amounts included for 2022 reflect the annualized level provided by the continuing resolution.

Program and Financing (in millions of dollars)

Identification code 019–0520–0–1–153		2021 actual	2022 est.	2023 est.
	Obligations by program activity:			
0001	Missions and officials to United Nations	34	34	34
0002	Missions and officials in United States	4	4	4
0900	Total new obligations, unexpired accounts (object class 25.2)	38	38	38
	Budgetary resources:			
	Unobligated balance:			
1000	Unobligated balance brought forward, Oct 1	15	19	12
1021	Recoveries of prior year unpaid obligations	11		
1070	Unobligated balance (total)	26	19	12
	Budget authority:			
	Appropriations, discretionary:			
1100	Appropriation	31	31	31
1930	Total budgetary resources available	57	50	43
	Memorandum (non-add) entries:			
1941	Unexpired unobligated balance, end of year	19	12	5
	Change in obligated balance:			
	Unpaid obligations:			
3000	Unpaid obligations, brought forward, Oct 1	21	34	34
3010	New obligations, unexpired accounts	38	38	38
3020	Outlays (gross)	–14	–38	–37
3040	Recoveries of prior year unpaid obligations, unexpired	–11		
3050	Unpaid obligations, end of year	34	34	35
	Memorandum (non-add) entries:			
3100	Obligated balance, start of year	21	34	34
3200	Obligated balance, end of year	34	34	35
	Budget authority and outlays, net:			
	Discretionary:			
4000	Budget authority, gross	31	31	31
	Outlays, gross:			
4010	Outlays from new discretionary authority	1	9	9
4011	Outlays from discretionary balances	13	29	28
4020	Outlays, gross (total)	14	38	37
4180	Budget authority, net (total)	31	31	31
4190	Outlays, net (total)	14	38	37

This appropriation provides for extraordinary protection of: 1) foreign missions and officials, including those accredited to the United Nations and other international organizations, and visiting foreign dignitaries (under certain circumstances) in New York; and 2) international organizations, foreign missions and officials, and visiting foreign dignitaries (under certain circumstances) throughout the United States. Funds may be used to reimburse state or local law enforcement authorities, contracts for private security firm services, or reimburse Federal agencies for extraordinary protective services. The Department is requesting continued authority to transfer expired balances from the Diplomatic Programs account to this account in order to reduce accumulated arrears to state or local law enforcement entities.

EMERGENCIES IN THE DIPLOMATIC AND CONSULAR SERVICE

For necessary expenses to enable the Secretary of State to meet unforeseen emergencies arising in the Diplomatic and Consular Service, as authorized, $8,885,000, to remain available until expended, of which not to exceed $1,000,000 may be transferred to, and merged with, funds appropriated by this Act under the heading "Repatriation Loans Program Account": Provided, That funds transferred pursuant to the eleventh proviso under the heading "Diplomatic and Consular Programs" in the Department of State, Foreign Operations, and Related Programs Appropriations Act, 2008 (title I of division J of Public Law 110–161) in this and prior fiscal years may be used for expenses of rewards programs.

Note.—A full-year 2022 appropriation for this account was not enacted at the time the Budget was prepared; therefore, the Budget assumes this account is operating under the Continuing Appropriations Act, 2022 (Division A of Public Law 117–43, as amended). The amounts included for 2022 reflect the annualized level provided by the continuing resolution.

EMERGENCIES IN THE DIPLOMATIC AND CONSULAR SERVICE

[*For an additional amount for "Emergencies in the Diplomatic and Consular Service", $276,900,000, to remain available until expended, for support for Operation Allies Welcome and related efforts by the Department of State, including additional relocations of individuals at risk as a result of the situation in Afghanistan and related expenses, and to reimburse the account under this heading in prior acts making appropriations for the Department of State, foreign operations, and related programs for obligations previously incurred.*] *(Afghanistan Supplemental Appropriations Act, 2022.)*

EMERGENCIES IN THE DIPLOMATIC AND CONSULAR SERVICE

[*For an additional amount for "Emergencies in the Diplomatic and Consular Service", $36,000,000, to remain available until expended, for support for Operation Allies Welcome and related efforts by the Department of State, including additional relocations of individuals at risk as a result of the situation in Afghanistan and related expenses, and to reimburse the account under this heading in prior Acts making appropriations for the Department of State, foreign operations, and related programs for obligations previously incurred.*] *(Additional Afghanistan Supplemental Appropriations Act, 2022.)*

Program and Financing (in millions of dollars)

Identification code 019–0522–0–1–153		2021 actual	2022 est.	2023 est.
	Obligations by program activity:			
0001	Emergencies in the Diplomatic and Consular Service	162	323	23
0700	Direct program activities, subtotal	162	323	23
	Budgetary resources:			
	Unobligated balance:			
1000	Unobligated balance brought forward, Oct 1	275	351	351
1012	Unobligated balance transfers between expired and unexpired accounts	34		
1021	Recoveries of prior year unpaid obligations	14	2	2
1033	Recoveries of prior year paid obligations	30		
1070	Unobligated balance (total)	353	353	353
	Budget authority:			
	Appropriations, discretionary:			
1100	Appropriation	8	321	9
1121	Appropriations transferred from other acct [019–0113]	150		
1160	Appropriation, discretionary (total)	158	321	9
	Spending authority from offsetting collections, discretionary:			
1700	Collected	2		
1900	Budget authority (total)	160	321	9
1930	Total budgetary resources available	513	674	362
	Memorandum (non-add) entries:			
1941	Unexpired unobligated balance, end of year	351	351	339
	Change in obligated balance:			
	Unpaid obligations:			
3000	Unpaid obligations, brought forward, Oct 1	53	74	24
3010	New obligations, unexpired accounts	162	323	23
3020	Outlays (gross)	–127	–371	–22
3040	Recoveries of prior year unpaid obligations, unexpired	–14	–2	–2
3050	Unpaid obligations, end of year	74	24	23
	Memorandum (non-add) entries:			
3100	Obligated balance, start of year	53	74	24

Administration of Foreign Affairs—Continued
Federal Funds—Continued

EMERGENCIES IN THE DIPLOMATIC AND CONSULAR SERVICE—Continued

Program and Financing—Continued

Identification code 019–0522–0–1–153	2021 actual	2022 est.	2023 est.
3200 Obligated balance, end of year	74	24	23
Budget authority and outlays, net:			
Discretionary:			
4000 Budget authority, gross	160	321	9
Outlays, gross:			
4010 Outlays from new discretionary authority	63	319	6
4011 Outlays from discretionary balances	64	52	16
4020 Outlays, gross (total)	127	371	22
Offsets against gross budget authority and outlays:			
Offsetting collections (collected) from:			
4030 Federal sources	–12		
4033 Non-Federal sources	–20		
4040 Offsets against gross budget authority and outlays (total)	–32		
Additional offsets against gross budget authority only:			
4053 Recoveries of prior year paid obligations, unexpired accounts	30		
4070 Budget authority, net (discretionary)	158	321	9
4080 Outlays, net (discretionary)	95	371	22
4180 Budget authority, net (total)	158	321	9
4190 Outlays, net (total)	95	371	22

These funds are used primarily for purposes authorized by section 4 of the State Department Basic Authorities Act of 1956, as amended (22 U.S.C. 2671), for rewards authorized by section 36 of that Act, as amended (22 U.S.C. 2708), and for purposes authorized by section 804(3) of the United States Information and Educational Exchange Act of 1948, as amended (22 U.S.C. 1474(3)).

Object Classification (in millions of dollars)

Identification code 019–0522–0–1–153	2021 actual	2022 est.	2023 est.
Direct obligations:			
21.0 Travel and transportation of persons	152	313	14
25.2 Other services from non-Federal sources	10	10	9
99.9 Total new obligations, unexpired accounts	162	323	23

BUYING POWER MAINTENANCE

Program and Financing (in millions of dollars)

Identification code 019–0524–0–1–153	2021 actual	2022 est.	2023 est.
Budgetary resources:			
Unobligated balance:			
1000 Unobligated balance brought forward, Oct 1	12	99	99
1010 Unobligated balance transfer to other accts [019–0113]	–99		
1012 Unobligated balance transfers between expired and unexpired accounts	186		
1070 Unobligated balance (total)	99	99	99
1930 Total budgetary resources available	99	99	99
Memorandum (non-add) entries:			
1941 Unexpired unobligated balance, end of year	99	99	99
4180 Budget authority, net (total)			
4190 Outlays, net (total)			

This account is available to offset adverse exchange rate and overseas wage and price fluctuations unanticipated in the budget as authorized by section 24(b) of the State Department Basic Authorities Act of 1956 (22 U.S.C 2696(b)).

PAYMENT TO THE AMERICAN INSTITUTE IN TAIWAN

For necessary expenses to carry out the Taiwan Relations Act (Public Law 96–8), $32,583,000.

Note.—A full-year 2022 appropriation for this account was not enacted at the time the Budget was prepared; therefore, the Budget assumes this account is operating under the Continuing Appropriations Act, 2022 (Division A of Public Law 117–43, as amended). The amounts included for 2022 reflect the annualized level provided by the continuing resolution.

Program and Financing (in millions of dollars)

Identification code 019–0523–0–1–153	2021 actual	2022 est.	2023 est.
Obligations by program activity:			
0001 Payment to the American Institute in Taiwan (Direct)	32	32	33
0100 Direct program activities, subtotal	32	32	33
0801 Reimbursable program activity	5	2	2
0809 Reimbursable program activities, subtotal	5	2	2
0900 Total new obligations, unexpired accounts	37	34	35
Budgetary resources:			
Budget authority:			
Appropriations, discretionary:			
1100 Appropriation	32	32	33
Spending authority from offsetting collections, discretionary:			
1700 Collected	5	2	2
1900 Budget authority (total)	37	34	35
1930 Total budgetary resources available	37	34	35
Change in obligated balance:			
Unpaid obligations:			
3000 Unpaid obligations, brought forward, Oct 1	38	33	23
3010 New obligations, unexpired accounts	37	34	35
3020 Outlays (gross)	–35	–44	–45
3041 Recoveries of prior year unpaid obligations, expired	–7		
3050 Unpaid obligations, end of year	33	23	13
Memorandum (non-add) entries:			
3100 Obligated balance, start of year	38	33	23
3200 Obligated balance, end of year	33	23	13
Budget authority and outlays, net:			
Discretionary:			
4000 Budget authority, gross	37	34	35
Outlays, gross:			
4010 Outlays from new discretionary authority	26	23	24
4011 Outlays from discretionary balances	9	21	21
4020 Outlays, gross (total)	35	44	45
Offsets against gross budget authority and outlays:			
Offsetting collections (collected) from:			
4030 Federal sources	–5	–2	–2
4033 Non-Federal sources	–1		
4040 Offsets against gross budget authority and outlays (total)	–6	–2	–2
Additional offsets against gross budget authority only:			
4052 Offsetting collections credited to expired accounts	1		
4070 Budget authority, net (discretionary)	32	32	33
4080 Outlays, net (discretionary)	29	42	43
4180 Budget authority, net (total)	32	32	33
4190 Outlays, net (total)	29	42	43

The Taiwan Relations Act (Public Law 96–8) requires programs with respect to Taiwan to be carried out by or through the American Institute in Taiwan (AIT). AIT supports U.S. interests by promoting U.S. exports, economic and commercial services, and cultural and information exchange; facilitating military sales; providing consular related services for Americans and the people of Taiwan; and on behalf of the Department of State and various U.S. Government agencies, carrying out liaison with Taiwan's counterpart organizations.

The Department contracts with AIT to conduct commercial, cultural, and other relations with the people of Taiwan. Consular related expenses for AIT are funded with fee revenue from the Consular and Border Security Program.

Object Classification (in millions of dollars)

Identification code 019–0523–0–1–153	2021 actual	2022 est.	2023 est.
Direct obligations:			
11.8 Personnel compensation: Special personal services payments	14	15	16
12.1 Civilian personnel benefits	7	7	7
23.2 Rental payments to others	11	10	10
99.0 Direct obligations	32	32	33

		2021 actual	2022 est.	2023 est.
99.0	Reimbursable obligations	5	2	2
99.9	Total new obligations, unexpired accounts	37	34	35

PAYMENT TO THE FOREIGN SERVICE RETIREMENT AND DISABILITY FUND

For payment to the Foreign Service Retirement and Disability Fund, as authorized, $158,900,000.

Note.—A full-year 2022 appropriation for this account was not enacted at the time the Budget was prepared; therefore, the Budget assumes this account is operating under the Continuing Appropriations Act, 2022 (Division A of Public Law 117–43, as amended). The amounts included for 2022 reflect the annualized level provided by the continuing resolution.

Program and Financing (in millions of dollars)

Identification code 019–0540–0–1–153		2021 actual	2022 est.	2023 est.
	Obligations by program activity:			
0001	Payment to Foreign Service Retirement and Disability Fund	481	456	457
0900	Total new obligations, unexpired accounts (object class 42.0)	481	456	457
	Budgetary resources:			
	Budget authority:			
	Appropriations, mandatory:			
1200	Appropriation	481	456	457
1930	Total budgetary resources available	481	456	457
	Change in obligated balance:			
	Unpaid obligations:			
3010	New obligations, unexpired accounts	481	456	457
3020	Outlays (gross)	–481	–456	–457
	Budget authority and outlays, net:			
	Mandatory:			
4090	Budget authority, gross	481	456	457
	Outlays, gross:			
4100	Outlays from new mandatory authority	481	456	457
4180	Budget authority, net (total)	481	456	457
4190	Outlays, net (total)	481	456	457

The current appropriation finances any unfunded liability created by new or liberalized benefits, new groups of beneficiaries, and salary increases. The 2023 permanent appropriation provides a supplemental payment to the fund for disbursements attributable to the Foreign Service Pension System; and unfunded interest along with liability from military service for the Foreign Service Retirement and Disability System. In addition, the appropriation also finances the annual balance of the Foreign Service normal cost not met by employee and employer contributions. The amount of the appropriation is determined by the annual evaluation of the Fund balance derived from current statistical actuarial data, which includes inflationary cost-of-living adjustments.

FOREIGN SERVICE NATIONAL DEFINED CONTRIBUTIONS RETIREMENT FUND

Special and Trust Fund Receipts (in millions of dollars)

Identification code 019–5497–0–2–602		2021 actual	2022 est.	2023 est.
0100	Balance, start of year			1
	Receipts:			
	Current law:			
1140	Employing Agency Contributions, Foreign Service National Defined Contributions Retirement Fund	19	19	20
1140	Interest on Investments, Foreign Service National Defined Contributions Retirement Fund		1	1
1140	Employee Contributions, Foreign Service National Defined Contributions Retirement Fund, State	5	5	5
1199	Total current law receipts	24	25	26
1999	Total receipts	24	25	26
2000	Total: Balances and receipts	24	25	27

		2021 actual	2022 est.	2023 est.
	Appropriations:			
	Current law:			
2101	Foreign Service National Defined Contributions Retirement Fund	–24	–24	–25
5099	Balance, end of year		1	2

Program and Financing (in millions of dollars)

Identification code 019–5497–0–2–602		2021 actual	2022 est.	2023 est.
	Obligations by program activity:			
0001	Retiree payments	13	14	15
0900	Total new obligations, unexpired accounts (object class 42.0)	13	14	15
	Budgetary resources:			
	Unobligated balance:			
1000	Unobligated balance brought forward, Oct 1	35	46	56
	Budget authority:			
	Appropriations, mandatory:			
1201	Appropriation (special or trust fund)	24	24	25
1930	Total budgetary resources available	59	70	81
	Memorandum (non-add) entries:			
1941	Unexpired unobligated balance, end of year	46	56	66
	Change in obligated balance:			
	Unpaid obligations:			
3000	Unpaid obligations, brought forward, Oct 1			8
3010	New obligations, unexpired accounts	13	14	15
3020	Outlays (gross)	–13	–6	–12
3050	Unpaid obligations, end of year		8	11
	Memorandum (non-add) entries:			
3100	Obligated balance, start of year			8
3200	Obligated balance, end of year		8	11
	Budget authority and outlays, net:			
	Mandatory:			
4090	Budget authority, gross	24	24	25
	Outlays, gross:			
4100	Outlays from new mandatory authority	13	6	6
4101	Outlays from mandatory balances			6
4110	Outlays, gross (total)	13	6	12
4180	Budget authority, net (total)	24	24	25
4190	Outlays, net (total)	13	6	12
	Memorandum (non-add) entries:			
5000	Total investments, SOY: Federal securities: Par value	33	44	49
5001	Total investments, EOY: Federal securities: Par value	44	49	56

The Foreign Service National Defined Contributions Fund (FSNDCF) is an after-employment benefit plan for Locally Employed Staff (LE Staff) working for the Department of State and other Foreign Affairs agencies. The purpose of the fund is to accumulate and distribute U.S. Government (USG)-funded contributions for end-of-service benefits for LE Staff in countries where U.S. missions have determined that participation in the local social security system (LSSS) is not in the public interest of the USG. The Department determines which countries are eligible to participate in the fund. Upon separation, payments under this Plan shall be made consistent with the host country law, including any court order affecting payments to participants, unless decided otherwise by the Department.

WORKING CAPITAL FUND

Program and Financing (in millions of dollars)

Identification code 019–4519–0–4–153		2021 actual	2022 est.	2023 est.
	Obligations by program activity:			
0801	Working Capital Fund Programs	753	735	1,072
0802	HR/Post Assignment Travel	350	365	381
0803	Medical Programs	39	80	60
0804	IT Desktop	85	68	70
0805	Aviation Programs	315	338	184
0806	Office of Foreign Missions	20	29	35
0807	Special Issuance Passports	27	33	33
0812	International cooperative administrative support services (ICASS)	3,957	3,967	3,912

WORKING CAPITAL FUND—Continued
Program and Financing—Continued

Identification code 019–4519–0–4–153	2021 actual	2022 est.	2023 est.
0900 Total new obligations, unexpired accounts	5,546	5,615	5,747
Budgetary resources:			
Unobligated balance:			
1000 Unobligated balance brought forward, Oct 1	1,034	1,105	1,176
1021 Recoveries of prior year unpaid obligations	362	300	300
1033 Recoveries of prior year paid obligations	37		
1070 Unobligated balance (total)	1,433	1,405	1,476
Budget authority:			
Spending authority from offsetting collections, discretionary:			
1700 Collected	5,251	5,386	5,504
1701 Change in uncollected payments, Federal sources	–33		
1750 Spending auth from offsetting collections, disc (total)	5,218	5,386	5,504
1930 Total budgetary resources available	6,651	6,791	6,980
Memorandum (non-add) entries:			
1941 Unexpired unobligated balance, end of year	1,105	1,176	1,233
Change in obligated balance:			
Unpaid obligations:			
3000 Unpaid obligations, brought forward, Oct 1	2,058	2,124	2,188
3010 New obligations, unexpired accounts	5,546	5,615	5,747
3020 Outlays (gross)	–5,118	–5,251	–5,390
3040 Recoveries of prior year unpaid obligations, unexpired	–362	–300	–300
3050 Unpaid obligations, end of year	2,124	2,188	2,245
Uncollected payments:			
3060 Uncollected pymts, Fed sources, brought forward, Oct 1	–119	–86	–86
3070 Change in uncollected pymts, Fed sources, unexpired	33		
3090 Uncollected pymts, Fed sources, end of year	–86	–86	–86
Memorandum (non-add) entries:			
3100 Obligated balance, start of year	1,939	2,038	2,102
3200 Obligated balance, end of year	2,038	2,102	2,159
Budget authority and outlays, net:			
Discretionary:			
4000 Budget authority, gross	5,218	5,386	5,504
Outlays, gross:			
4010 Outlays from new discretionary authority	3,784	3,770	3,853
4011 Outlays from discretionary balances	1,334	1,481	1,537
4020 Outlays, gross (total)	5,118	5,251	5,390
Offsets against gross budget authority and outlays:			
Offsetting collections (collected) from:			
4030 Federal sources	–5,221	–5,310	–5,427
4033 Non-Federal sources	–67	–76	–77
4040 Offsets against gross budget authority and outlays (total)	–5,288	–5,386	–5,504
Additional offsets against gross budget authority only:			
4050 Change in uncollected pymts, Fed sources, unexpired	33		
4053 Recoveries of prior year paid obligations, unexpired accounts	37		
4060 Additional offsets against budget authority only (total)	70		
4080 Outlays, net (discretionary)	–170	–135	–114
4180 Budget authority, net (total)			
4190 Outlays, net (total)	–170	–135	–114

This fund, which is available without fiscal year limitations and is authorized by sections 13 and 23 of the State Department Basic Authorities Act of 1956 (22 U.S.C. 2684), finances on a reimbursable basis certain administrative services, such as printing and reproduction, editorial material, motor pool, operations and dispatch agencies operations, inter-agency cooperative administrative support services, acquisition services, information technology support, medical services, aviation services, special issuance passport services, and expenses of carrying out the Foreign Missions Act, including any acquisitions of property under the authority of the Foreign Missions Act. In FY 2023 the Department plans to add a new service center for Real Property Management.

The International Cooperative Administrative Support Services (ICASS) program was fully implemented in 1998 using the Working Capital Fund. ICASS allows more decision-making and managerial participation by all participating agencies, more equitable cost distribution, and incentives for efficient provision of services. Under ICASS, each agency represented at an overseas post chooses the services it wishes to receive and pays a proportional share of the cost of those services. Working through inter-agency councils at each overseas post, all agencies have a say in determining post administrative budgets and defining service standards, as well as reviewing costs and vendor performance.

Object Classification (in millions of dollars)

Identification code 019–4519–0–4–153	2021 actual	2022 est.	2023 est.
Reimbursable obligations:			
Personnel compensation:			
11.1 Full-time permanent	302	320	333
11.3 Other than full-time permanent	100	104	106
11.5 Other personnel compensation	10	11	11
11.9 Total personnel compensation	412	435	450
12.1 Civilian personnel benefits	490	500	500
21.0 Travel and transportation of persons	107	110	110
22.0 Transportation of things	380	390	382
23.2 Rental payments to others	420	400	410
25.2 Other services from non-Federal sources	3,195	3,220	3,353
26.0 Supplies and materials	250	260	252
31.0 Equipment	232	240	235
41.0 Grants, subsidies, and contributions	60	60	55
99.9 Total new obligations, unexpired accounts	5,546	5,615	5,747

Employment Summary

Identification code 019–4519–0–4–153	2021 actual	2022 est.	2023 est.
2001 Reimbursable civilian full-time equivalent employment	2,782	2,782	2,782

REPATRIATION LOANS PROGRAM ACCOUNT

For the cost of direct loans, $1,300,000, as authorized: Provided, That such costs, including the cost of modifying such loans, shall be as defined in section 502 of the Congressional Budget Act of 1974: Provided further, That such funds are available to subsidize gross obligations for the principal amount of direct loans not to exceed $4,753,048.

Note.—A full-year 2022 appropriation for this account was not enacted at the time the Budget was prepared; therefore, the Budget assumes this account is operating under the Continuing Appropriations Act, 2022 (Division A of Public Law 117–43, as amended). The amounts included for 2022 reflect the annualized level provided by the continuing resolution.

Program and Financing (in millions of dollars)

Identification code 019–0601–0–1–153	2021 actual	2022 est.	2023 est.
Obligations by program activity:			
Credit program obligations:			
0701 Direct loan subsidy	3	1	1
0709 Administrative expenses		2	
0900 Total new obligations, unexpired accounts (object class 41.0)	3	3	1
Budgetary resources:			
Budget authority:			
Appropriations, discretionary:			
1100 Appropriation	3	3	1
1930 Total budgetary resources available	3	3	1
Change in obligated balance:			
Unpaid obligations:			
3010 New obligations, unexpired accounts	3	3	1
3020 Outlays (gross)	–3	–3	–1
Budget authority and outlays, net:			
Discretionary:			
4000 Budget authority, gross	3	3	1
Outlays, gross:			
4010 Outlays from new discretionary authority	3	3	1
4180 Budget authority, net (total)	3	3	1
4190 Outlays, net (total)	3	3	1

DEPARTMENT OF STATE AND OTHER INTERNATIONAL PROGRAMS

Summary of Loan Levels, Subsidy Budget Authority and Outlays by Program (in millions of dollars)

Identification code 019–0601–0–1–153		2021 actual	2022 est.	2023 est.
	Direct loan levels supportable by subsidy budget authority:			
115001	Repatriation Loans	3	3	3
	Direct loan subsidy (in percent):			
132001	Repatriation Loans	55.45	46.58	48.39
132999	Weighted average subsidy rate	55.45	46.58	48.39
	Direct loan subsidy budget authority:			
133001	Repatriation Loans	2	1	1
	Direct loan subsidy outlays:			
134001	Repatriation Loans	2	1	1
	Direct loan reestimates:			
135001	Repatriation Loans	–1	–3	

As required by the Federal Credit Reform Act of 1990, this account records the subsidy costs associated with direct loans for this program. The subsidy amounts are estimated on a net present value basis. Administrative expenses for the program are funded with fee revenue from the Consular and Border Security Programs.

REPATRIATION LOANS FINANCING ACCOUNT

Program and Financing (in millions of dollars)

Identification code 019–4107–0–3–153		2021 actual	2022 est.	2023 est.
	Obligations by program activity:			
	Credit program obligations:			
0710	Direct loan obligations	4	2	2
0742	Downward reestimates paid to receipt accounts	1	3	
0900	Total new obligations, unexpired accounts	5	5	2
	Budgetary resources:			
	Unobligated balance:			
1000	Unobligated balance brought forward, Oct 1	1	1	
1023	Unobligated balances applied to repay debt	–1		
1070	Unobligated balance (total)		1	
	Financing authority:			
	Borrowing authority, mandatory:			
1400	Borrowing authority	2	1	1
	Spending authority from offsetting collections, mandatory:			
1800	Collected	6	3	3
1825	Spending authority from offsetting collections applied to repay debt	–2		
1850	Spending auth from offsetting collections, mand (total)	4	3	3
1900	Budget authority (total)	6	4	4
1930	Total budgetary resources available	6	5	4
	Memorandum (non-add) entries:			
1941	Unexpired unobligated balance, end of year	1		2
	Change in obligated balance:			
	Unpaid obligations:			
3000	Unpaid obligations, brought forward, Oct 1	2	4	6
3010	New obligations, unexpired accounts	5	5	2
3020	Outlays (gross)	–3	–3	–3
3050	Unpaid obligations, end of year	4	6	5
	Memorandum (non-add) entries:			
3100	Obligated balance, start of year	2	4	6
3200	Obligated balance, end of year	4	6	5
	Financing authority and disbursements, net:			
	Mandatory:			
4090	Budget authority, gross	6	4	4
	Financing disbursements:			
4110	Outlays, gross (total)	3	3	3
	Offsets against gross financing authority and disbursements:			
	Offsetting collections (collected) from:			
4120	Payments from program account	–3	–2	–2
4123	Non-Federal sources	–3	–1	–1
4130	Offsets against gross budget authority and outlays (total)	–6	–3	–3
4160	Budget authority, net (mandatory)		1	1
4170	Outlays, net (mandatory)	–3		
4180	Budget authority, net (total)		1	1
4190	Outlays, net (total)	–3		

Administration of Foreign Affairs—Continued
Trust Funds
811

Status of Direct Loans (in millions of dollars)

Identification code 019–4107–0–3–153		2021 actual	2022 est.	2023 est.
	Position with respect to appropriations act limitation on obligations:			
1111	Direct loan obligations from current-year authority	4	2	2
1150	Total direct loan obligations	4	2	2
	Cumulative balance of direct loans outstanding:			
1210	Outstanding, start of year	5	6	7
1231	Disbursements: Direct loan disbursements	2	2	2
1251	Repayments: Repayments and prepayments	–1	–1	–1
1290	Outstanding, end of year	6	7	8

Balance Sheet (in millions of dollars)

Identification code 019–4107–0–3–153		2020 actual	2021 actual
	ASSETS:		
1101	Federal assets: Fund balances with Treasury	5	5
	Net value of assets related to post-1991 direct loans receivable:		
1401	Direct loans receivable, gross	6	6
1405	Allowance for subsidy cost (-)	–2	–2
1499	Net present value of assets related to direct loans	4	4
1999	Total assets	9	9
	LIABILITIES:		
	Federal liabilities:		
2103	Debt	3	4
2104	Resources payable to Treasury		
2105	Other	1	4
2201	Non-Federal liabilities: Accounts payable	5	1
2999	Total liabilities	9	9
	NET POSITION:		
3300	Cumulative results of operations		
4999	Total liabilities and net position	9	9

Trust Funds

FOREIGN SERVICE RETIREMENT AND DISABILITY FUND

Special and Trust Fund Receipts (in millions of dollars)

Identification code 019–8186–0–7–602		2021 actual	2022 est.	2023 est.
0100	Balance, start of year	19,981	20,347	20,630
	Receipts:			
	Current law:			
1110	Deductions from Employees Salaries, Foreign Service Retirement and Disability Fund	40	37	38
1140	Interest on Investments, Foreign Service Retirement and Disability Fund	480	458	413
1140	Employing Agency Contributions, Foreign Service Retirement and Disability Fund	384	386	394
1140	Receipts from Civil Service Retirement and Disability Fund, Foreign Service Retirement and Disability Fund	2	1	1
1140	Federal Contributions, Foreign Service Retirement and Disability Fund	481	456	457
1199	Total current law receipts	1,387	1,338	1,303
1999	Total receipts	1,387	1,338	1,303
2000	Total: Balances and receipts	21,368	21,685	21,933
	Appropriations:			
	Current law:			
2101	Foreign Service Retirement and Disability Fund	–1,387	–1,055	–1,060
2135	Foreign Service Retirement and Disability Fund	367		
2199	Total current law appropriations	–1,020	–1,055	–1,060
2999	Total appropriations	–1,020	–1,055	–1,060
5098	Rounding adjustment	–1		
5099	Balance, end of year	20,347	20,630	20,873

Administration of Foreign Affairs—Continued
Trust Funds—Continued

FOREIGN SERVICE RETIREMENT AND DISABILITY FUND—Continued

Program and Financing (in millions of dollars)

Identification code 019–8186–0–7–602	2021 actual	2022 est.	2023 est.
Obligations by program activity:			
0001 Payments to beneficiaries	1,020	1,055	1,060
0900 Total new obligations, unexpired accounts (object class 42.0)	1,020	1,055	1,060
Budgetary resources:			
Budget authority:			
Appropriations, mandatory:			
1201 Appropriation (special or trust fund)	1,387	1,055	1,060
1235 Appropriations precluded from obligation (special or trust)	–367		
1260 Appropriations, mandatory (total)	1,020	1,055	1,060
1930 Total budgetary resources available	1,020	1,055	1,060
Change in obligated balance:			
Unpaid obligations:			
3000 Unpaid obligations, brought forward, Oct 1		1	
3010 New obligations, unexpired accounts	1,020	1,055	1,060
3020 Outlays (gross)	–1,019	–1,056	–1,060
3050 Unpaid obligations, end of year	1		
Memorandum (non-add) entries:			
3100 Obligated balance, start of year		1	
3200 Obligated balance, end of year	1		
Budget authority and outlays, net:			
Mandatory:			
4090 Budget authority, gross	1,020	1,055	1,060
Outlays, gross:			
4100 Outlays from new mandatory authority	1,014	1,055	1,060
4101 Outlays from mandatory balances	5	1	
4110 Outlays, gross (total)	1,019	1,056	1,060
4180 Budget authority, net (total)	1,020	1,055	1,060
4190 Outlays, net (total)	1,019	1,056	1,060
Memorandum (non-add) entries:			
5000 Total investments, SOY: Federal securities: Par value	19,981	20,347	20,720
5001 Total investments, EOY: Federal securities: Par value	20,347	20,720	21,093

The Foreign Service Retirement and Disability Fund (FSRDF) was established in 1924 to provide pensions to retired and disabled members of the Foreign Service. The FSRDF's revenues consist of contributions from active participants and their U.S. Government agency employers; appropriations; and interest on investments. Monthly annuity payments are made to eligible retired employees or their survivors. The FSRDF includes the operations of two separate retirement systems—the Foreign Service Retirement and Disability System (FSRDS) and the Foreign Service Pension System (FSPS). This appropriation provides mandatory funding for the Foreign Service Retirement and Disability Fund (FSRDF) as prescribed in the Foreign Service Act of 1980 as authorized in Section(s) 821 and 822.

Status of Funds (in millions of dollars)

Identification code 019–8186–0–7–602	2021 actual	2022 est.	2023 est.
Unexpended balance, start of year:			
0100 Balance, start of year	19,981	20,347	20,629
0999 Total balance, start of year	19,981	20,347	20,629
Cash income during the year:			
Current law:			
Receipts:			
1110 Deductions from Employees Salaries, Foreign Service Retirement and Disability Fund	40	37	38
1150 Interest on Investments, Foreign Service Retirement and Disability Fund	480	458	413
1160 Employing Agency Contributions, Foreign Service Retirement and Disability Fund	384	386	394
1160 Receipts from Civil Service Retirement and Disability Fund, Foreign Service Retirement and Disability Fund	2	1	1
1160 Federal Contributions, Foreign Service Retirement and Disability Fund	481	456	457
1199 Income under present law	1,387	1,338	1,303
1999 Total cash income	1,387	1,338	1,303
Cash outgo during year:			
Current law:			
2100 Foreign Service Retirement and Disability Fund [Budget Acct]	–1,019	–1,056	–1,060
2199 Outgo under current law	–1,019	–1,056	–1,060
2999 Total cash outgo (–)	–1,019	–1,056	–1,060
Surplus or deficit:			
3110 Excluding interest	–112	–176	–170
3120 Interest	480	458	413
3199 Subtotal, surplus or deficit	368	282	243
3298 Reconciliation adjustment	–2		
3299 Total adjustments	–2		
3999 Total change in fund balance	366	282	243
Unexpended balance, end of year:			
4100 Uninvested balance (net), end of year		–91	–221
4200 Foreign Service Retirement and Disability Fund	20,347	20,720	21,093
4999 Total balance, end of year	20,347	20,629	20,872

FOREIGN SERVICE NATIONAL SEPARATION LIABILITY TRUST FUND

Special and Trust Fund Receipts (in millions of dollars)

Identification code 019–8340–0–7–602	2021 actual	2022 est.	2023 est.
0100 Balance, start of year			2
Receipts:			
Current law:			
1140 Foreign Service National Separation Liability Trust Fund	33	35	35
2000 Total: Balances and receipts	33	35	37
Appropriations:			
Current law:			
2101 Foreign Service National Separation Liability Trust Fund	–33	–33	–33
5099 Balance, end of year		2	4

Program and Financing (in millions of dollars)

Identification code 019–8340–0–7–602	2021 actual	2022 est.	2023 est.
Obligations by program activity:			
0001 Payments to Beneficiaries - Locally Engaged Staff	41	40	42
0900 Total new obligations, unexpired accounts (object class 42.0)	41	40	42
Budgetary resources:			
Unobligated balance:			
1000 Unobligated balance brought forward, Oct 1	366	360	353
1021 Recoveries of prior year unpaid obligations	2		
1070 Unobligated balance (total)	368	360	353
Budget authority:			
Appropriations, mandatory:			
1201 Appropriation (special or trust fund)	33	33	33
1930 Total budgetary resources available	401	393	386
Memorandum (non-add) entries:			
1941 Unexpired unobligated balance, end of year	360	353	344
Change in obligated balance:			
Unpaid obligations:			
3000 Unpaid obligations, brought forward, Oct 1	8	7	4
3010 New obligations, unexpired accounts	41	40	42
3020 Outlays (gross)	–40	–43	–33
3040 Recoveries of prior year unpaid obligations, unexpired	–2		
3050 Unpaid obligations, end of year	7	4	13
Memorandum (non-add) entries:			
3100 Obligated balance, start of year	8	7	4
3200 Obligated balance, end of year	7	4	13
Budget authority and outlays, net:			
Mandatory:			
4090 Budget authority, gross	33	33	33
Outlays, gross:			
4100 Outlays from new mandatory authority	3	33	33
4101 Outlays from mandatory balances	37	10	
4110 Outlays, gross (total)	40	43	33
4180 Budget authority, net (total)	33	33	33

DEPARTMENT OF STATE AND OTHER INTERNATIONAL PROGRAMS

International Organizations and Conferences
Federal Funds — 813

		2021 actual	2022 est.	2023 est.
4190	Outlays, net (total)	40	43	33

This fund is maintained to pay accrued separation liability payments for eligible Foreign Service National (FSN), FSN Personal Service Contractors (PSC), and FSN Personal Service Agreements (PSA) employees of the Department of State in those countries in which such pay is legally authorized. The fund, as authorized by section 151 of Public Law 102–138 (22 U.S.C. 4012a), is maintained by annual government contributions from the Department's Diplomatic Programs (DP) account (including Program Direct, Public Diplomacy and Worldwide Security Protection resources), Consular Affairs (CA) Consular and Border Security Program (CBSP) fees, the International Narcotics Control and Law Enforcement (INCLE) account, and International Cooperative Administrative Support Services (ICASS) working capital fund that includes both State's DP and other agencies shares. Eligible local staff include former United States Agency for International Development (USAID) ICASS employees who were consolidated into the Department. The Department of State funds and manages its own FSNSLTF separate and apart from any separation pay that may be provided by other agencies to non-State Locally Employed Staff (LE Staff).

MISCELLANEOUS TRUST FUNDS

Special and Trust Fund Receipts (in millions of dollars)

Identification code 019–9971–0–7–153	2021 actual	2022 est.	2023 est.
0100 Balance, start of year			3
Receipts:			
Current law:			
1130 Contributions, Educational and Cultural Exchange, USIA		1	1
1130 Unconditional Gift Fund	11	11	11
1130 Deposits, Conditional Gift Fund	3	3	3
1140 Earnings on Investments, Unconditional Gift Fund		1	1
1140 Interest, Miscellaneous Trust Funds, USIA		1	1
1199 Total current law receipts	14	17	17
1999 Total receipts	14	17	17
2000 Total: Balances and receipts	14	17	20
Appropriations:			
Current law:			
2101 Miscellaneous Trust Funds	–14	–14	–14
5099 Balance, end of year		3	6

Program and Financing (in millions of dollars)

Identification code 019–9971–0–7–153	2021 actual	2022 est.	2023 est.
Obligations by program activity:			
0001 Conditional gift fund	14	20	20
0900 Total new obligations, unexpired accounts (object class 33.0)	14	20	20
Budgetary resources:			
Unobligated balance:			
1000 Unobligated balance brought forward, Oct 1	46	47	41
1021 Recoveries of prior year unpaid obligations	1		
1070 Unobligated balance (total)	47	47	41
Budget authority:			
Appropriations, mandatory:			
1201 Appropriation (special or trust fund)	14	14	14
1930 Total budgetary resources available	61	61	55
Memorandum (non-add) entries:			
1941 Unexpired unobligated balance, end of year	47	41	35
Change in obligated balance:			
Unpaid obligations:			
3000 Unpaid obligations, brought forward, Oct 1	44	33	39
3010 New obligations, unexpired accounts	14	20	20
3020 Outlays (gross)	–24	–14	–19
3040 Recoveries of prior year unpaid obligations, unexpired	–1		
3050 Unpaid obligations, end of year	33	39	40
Memorandum (non-add) entries:			
3100 Obligated balance, start of year	44	33	39
3200 Obligated balance, end of year	33	39	40
Budget authority and outlays, net:			
Mandatory:			
4090 Budget authority, gross	14	14	14
Outlays, gross:			
4100 Outlays from new mandatory authority	4	7	7
4101 Outlays from mandatory balances	20	7	12
4110 Outlays, gross (total)	24	14	19
4180 Budget authority, net (total)	14	14	14
4190 Outlays, net (total)	24	14	19
Memorandum (non-add) entries:			
5000 Total investments, SOY: Federal securities: Par value	23	26	26
5001 Total investments, EOY: Federal securities: Par value	26	26	26

Gift funds.—The Department has authority to accept gifts for use in carrying out the Department's functions, pursuant to statutes including section 25 of the State Department Basic Authorities Act (22 U.S.C. 2697). Among other purposes, funds are used to renovate, furnish, and maintain the Department's diplomatic reception rooms and embassy properties overseas.

INTERNATIONAL ORGANIZATIONS AND CONFERENCES

Federal Funds

CONTRIBUTIONS TO INTERNATIONAL ORGANIZATIONS

For necessary expenses, not otherwise provided for, to meet annual obligations of membership in international multilateral organizations, pursuant to treaties ratified pursuant to the advice and consent of the Senate, conventions, or specific Acts of Congress, $1,658,239,000, to remain available until September 30, 2024.

Note.—A full-year 2022 appropriation for this account was not enacted at the time the Budget was prepared; therefore, the Budget assumes this account is operating under the Continuing Appropriations Act, 2022 (Division A of Public Law 117-43, as amended). The amounts included for 2022 reflect the annualized level provided by the continuing resolution.

Program and Financing (in millions of dollars)

Identification code 019–1126–0–1–153	2021 actual	2022 est.	2023 est.
Obligations by program activity:			
0001 Contributions to International Organizations	1,410	1,410	1,658
0002 Contributions to International Organizations - OCO	192	96	
0900 Total new obligations, unexpired accounts (object class 41.0)	1,602	1,506	1,658
Budgetary resources:			
Unobligated balance:			
1000 Unobligated balance brought forward, Oct 1	102	6	6
Budget authority:			
Appropriations, discretionary:			
1100 Appropriation	1,410	1,410	1,658
1100 Appropriation - OCO	96	96	
1160 Appropriation, discretionary (total)	1,506	1,506	1,658
1930 Total budgetary resources available	1,608	1,512	1,664
Memorandum (non-add) entries:			
1941 Unexpired unobligated balance, end of year	6	6	6
Change in obligated balance:			
Unpaid obligations:			
3000 Unpaid obligations, brought forward, Oct 1	253	90	155
3010 New obligations, unexpired accounts	1,602	1,506	1,658
3020 Outlays (gross)	–1,745	–1,441	–1,611
3041 Recoveries of prior year unpaid obligations, expired	–20		
3050 Unpaid obligations, end of year	90	155	202
Memorandum (non-add) entries:			
3100 Obligated balance, start of year	253	90	155
3200 Obligated balance, end of year	90	155	202
Budget authority and outlays, net:			
Discretionary:			
4000 Budget authority, gross	1,506	1,506	1,658
Outlays, gross:			
4010 Outlays from new discretionary authority	1,488	1,360	1,492
4011 Outlays from discretionary balances	257	81	119
4020 Outlays, gross (total)	1,745	1,441	1,611
4180 Budget authority, net (total)	1,506	1,506	1,658

CONTRIBUTIONS TO INTERNATIONAL ORGANIZATIONS—Continued
Program and Financing—Continued

Identification code 019–1126–0–1–153	2021 actual	2022 est.	2023 est.
4190 Outlays, net (total)	1,745	1,441	1,611

As a member of the United Nations (UN) and other international organizations, the United States contributes an assessed share to meet annual obligations to these organizations, net of certain withholdings. The appropriation enables continued support to and influence with organizations that serve important U.S. interests.

CONTRIBUTIONS FOR INTERNATIONAL PEACEKEEPING ACTIVITIES

For necessary expenses to pay assessed and other expenses of international peacekeeping activities directed to the maintenance or restoration of international peace and security, $2,327,235,000, to remain available until September 30, 2024: Provided, That such funds may be made available above the amount authorized in section 404(b)(2) of the Foreign Relations Authorization Act, Fiscal Years 1994 and 1995, as amended (22 U.S.C. 287e note).

Note.—A full-year 2022 appropriation for this account was not enacted at the time the Budget was prepared; therefore, the Budget assumes this account is operating under the Continuing Appropriations Act, 2022 (Division A of Public Law 117–43, as amended). The amounts included for 2022 reflect the annualized level provided by the continuing resolution.

Program and Financing (in millions of dollars)

Identification code 019–1124–0–1–153		2021 actual	2022 est.	2023 est.
	Obligations by program activity:			
0020	Contributions for International Peacekeeping Activities (Direct)	2,104	1,456	2,327
0900	Total new obligations, unexpired accounts (object class 41.0)	2,104	1,456	2,327
	Budgetary resources:			
	Unobligated balance:			
1000	Unobligated balance brought forward, Oct 1	740		
	Budget authority:			
	Appropriations, discretionary:			
1100	Appropriation	750	750	2,327
1100	Appropriation [OCO]	706	706	
1160	Appropriation, discretionary (total)	1,456	1,456	2,327
1930	Total budgetary resources available	2,196	1,456	2,327
	Memorandum (non-add) entries:			
1940	Unobligated balance expiring	–92		
	Change in obligated balance:			
	Unpaid obligations:			
3000	Unpaid obligations, brought forward, Oct 1		723	334
3010	New obligations, unexpired accounts	2,104	1,456	2,327
3020	Outlays (gross)	–1,381	–1,845	–2,312
3050	Unpaid obligations, end of year	723	334	349
	Memorandum (non-add) entries:			
3100	Obligated balance, start of year		723	334
3200	Obligated balance, end of year	723	334	349
	Budget authority and outlays, net:			
	Discretionary:			
4000	Budget authority, gross	1,456	1,456	2,327
	Outlays, gross:			
4010	Outlays from new discretionary authority	641	1,316	1,978
4011	Outlays from discretionary balances	740	529	334
4020	Outlays, gross (total)	1,381	1,845	2,312
4180	Budget authority, net (total)	1,456	1,456	2,327
4190	Outlays, net (total)	1,381	1,845	2,312

This appropriation provides funds for the United States' contributions toward the expenses associated with United Nations (UN) peacekeeping operations for which costs are distributed among UN members based on a scale of assessments. The purpose of this appropriation is to ensure continued support of UN peacekeeping activities that serve U.S. interests in promoting international security, stability, and democracy. The request includes funding to pay our contributions on time and in full as well as resources for payment of cap-related UN peacekeeping arrears including those accumulated in the past five years.

INTERNATIONAL COMMISSIONS
Federal Funds

INTERNATIONAL COMMISSIONS

For necessary expenses, not otherwise provided for, to meet obligations of the United States arising under treaties, or specific Acts of Congress, as follows:

INTERNATIONAL BOUNDARY AND WATER COMMISSION, UNITED STATES AND MEXICO

For necessary expenses for the United States Section of the International Boundary and Water Commission, United States and Mexico, and to comply with laws applicable to the United States Section, including not to exceed $6,000 for representation expenses; as follows:

SALARIES AND EXPENSES

For salaries and expenses, not otherwise provided for, $59,935,000, of which $8,990,250 may remain available until September 30, 2024.

Note.—A full-year 2022 appropriation for this account was not enacted at the time the Budget was prepared; therefore, the Budget assumes this account is operating under the Continuing Appropriations Act, 2022 (Division A of Public Law 117–43, as amended). The amounts included for 2022 reflect the annualized level provided by the continuing resolution.

Program and Financing (in millions of dollars)

Identification code 019–1069–0–1–301		2021 actual	2022 est.	2023 est.
	Obligations by program activity:			
0001	International Boundary and Water Commission - Salaries and Expenses	49	50	53
0801	Salaries and Expenses, IBWC (Reimbursable)	11	8	8
0900	Total new obligations, unexpired accounts	60	58	61
	Budgetary resources:			
	Unobligated balance:			
1000	Unobligated balance brought forward, Oct 1		1	
	Budget authority:			
	Appropriations, discretionary:			
1100	Appropriation	50	50	60
	Spending authority from offsetting collections, discretionary:			
1700	Collected	8	7	7
1701	Change in uncollected payments, Federal sources	3		
1750	Spending auth from offsetting collections, disc (total)	11	7	7
1900	Budget authority (total)	61	57	67
1930	Total budgetary resources available	61	58	67
	Memorandum (non-add) entries:			
1941	Unexpired unobligated balance, end of year	1		6
	Change in obligated balance:			
	Unpaid obligations:			
3000	Unpaid obligations, brought forward, Oct 1	15	22	13
3010	New obligations, unexpired accounts	60	58	61
3011	Obligations ("upward adjustments"), expired accounts	1		
3020	Outlays (gross)	–52	–67	–69
3041	Recoveries of prior year unpaid obligations, expired	–2		
3050	Unpaid obligations, end of year	22	13	5
	Uncollected payments:			
3060	Uncollected pymts, Fed sources, brought forward, Oct 1	–3	–3	–3
3070	Change in uncollected pymts, Fed sources, unexpired	–3		
3071	Change in uncollected pymts, Fed sources, expired	3		
3090	Uncollected pymts, Fed sources, end of year	–3	–3	–3
	Memorandum (non-add) entries:			
3100	Obligated balance, start of year	12	19	10
3200	Obligated balance, end of year	19	10	2
	Budget authority and outlays, net:			
	Discretionary:			
4000	Budget authority, gross	61	57	67
	Outlays, gross:			
4010	Outlays from new discretionary authority	40	49	58
4011	Outlays from discretionary balances	12	18	11
4020	Outlays, gross (total)	52	67	69
	Offsets against gross budget authority and outlays:			
	Offsetting collections (collected) from:			
4030	Federal sources	–5	–7	–7

4033	Non-Federal sources	–5		
4040	Offsets against gross budget authority and outlays (total)	–10	–7	–7
	Additional offsets against gross budget authority only:			
4050	Change in uncollected pymts, Fed sources, unexpired	–3		
4052	Offsetting collections credited to expired accounts	2		
4060	Additional offsets against budget authority only (total)	–1		
4070	Budget authority, net (discretionary)	50	50	60
4080	Outlays, net (discretionary)	42	60	62
4180	Budget authority, net (total)	50	50	60
4190	Outlays, net (total)	42	60	62

Pursuant to treaties between the United States and Mexico and U.S. law, the U.S. Section of the International Boundary and Water Commission (IBWC) is charged with the identification and resolution of current and anticipated boundary and water problems arising along the almost 2,000-mile common border, including the southern borders of Texas, New Mexico, Arizona, and California. Administration, Engineering, and Operations and Maintenance activities are also funded by the Salaries and Expenses appropriation.

Administration.—Resources provide for negotiations and supervision of joint projects with Mexico to resolve international boundary, water, and environmental problems; overall control of the operation of the U.S. section of the Commission; formulation of operating policies and procedures; and financial management and administrative services to carry out international obligations of the United States, pursuant to treaty and congressional authorization.

Engineering.—Resources provide for technical engineering guidance and supervision of planning, construction, operation and maintenance, and environmental monitoring and compliance of international projects; studies relating to international problems of a continuing nature; and preliminary surveys and investigations to determine the need for and feasibility of projects for the resolution of international problems arising along the boundary.

Operation and Maintenance (O&M).—This activity finances the measurement and determination of the national ownership of boundary waters and the distribution thereof, as well as the U.S. part of the operations and maintenance of sanitation facilities, river channel and levee projects, flood control dams and hydroelectric power, gauging stations, water quality control projects and boundary demarcation, monuments, and markers. Reimbursements are received from Mexico for O&M costs of the South Bay and Nogales International Wastewater Treatment Plants as well as from the City of Nogales for O&M costs at Nogales. Other reimbursements are received from the Western Area Power Administration, U.S. Department of Energy, for O&M and capital costs of hydroelectric generation at Falcon and Amistad International Dams.

Object Classification (in millions of dollars)

Identification code 019–1069–0–1–301		2021 actual	2022 est.	2023 est.
	Direct obligations:			
11.1	Personnel compensation: Full-time permanent	19	20	22
12.1	Civilian personnel benefits	6	6	6
22.0	Transportation of things	1	1	1
23.2	Rental payments to others	4	4	4
25.2	Other services from non-Federal sources	16	16	17
26.0	Supplies and materials	2	2	2
41.0	Grants, subsidies, and contributions	1	1	1
99.0	Direct obligations	49	50	53
99.0	Reimbursable obligations	11	8	8
99.9	Total new obligations, unexpired accounts	60	58	61

Employment Summary

Identification code 019–1069–0–1–301		2021 actual	2022 est.	2023 est.
1001	Direct civilian full-time equivalent employment	253	253	253

Construction

For detailed plan preparation and construction of authorized projects, $41,800,000, to remain available until expended, as authorized: Provided, That of the funds appropriated under this heading in this Act and prior Acts making appropriations for the Department of State, foreign operations, and related programs for the United States Section, up to $5,000,000 may be transferred to, and merged with, funds appropriated under the heading "Salaries and Expenses" to carry out the purposes of the United States Section, which shall be subject to prior notification to, and the regular notification procedures of, the Committees on Appropriations: Provided further, That such transfer authority is in addition to any other transfer authority provided in this Act.

Note.—A full-year 2022 appropriation for this account was not enacted at the time the Budget was prepared; therefore, the Budget assumes this account is operating under the Continuing Appropriations Act, 2022 (Division A of Public Law 117–43, as amended). The amounts included for 2022 reflect the annualized level provided by the continuing resolution.

Program and Financing (in millions of dollars)

Identification code 019–1078–0–1–301		2021 actual	2022 est.	2023 est.
	Obligations by program activity:			
0003	International Boundary and Water Commission - Construction	24	49	44
0100	Construction, IBWC (Direct)	24	49	44
0801	Construction, IBWC (Reimbursable)		3	3
0900	Total new obligations, unexpired accounts	24	52	47
	Budgetary resources:			
	Unobligated balance:			
1000	Unobligated balance brought forward, Oct 1	142	168	168
1021	Recoveries of prior year unpaid obligations	1		
1070	Unobligated balance (total)	143	168	168
	Budget authority:			
	Appropriations, discretionary:			
1100	Appropriation	49	49	42
	Spending authority from offsetting collections, discretionary:			
1700	Collected		3	3
1900	Budget authority (total)	49	52	45
1930	Total budgetary resources available	192	220	213
	Memorandum (non-add) entries:			
1941	Unexpired unobligated balance, end of year	168	168	166
	Change in obligated balance:			
	Unpaid obligations:			
3000	Unpaid obligations, brought forward, Oct 1	14	25	3
3010	New obligations, unexpired accounts	24	52	47
3020	Outlays (gross)	–12	–74	–47
3040	Recoveries of prior year unpaid obligations, unexpired	–1		
3050	Unpaid obligations, end of year	25	3	3
	Memorandum (non-add) entries:			
3100	Obligated balance, start of year	14	25	3
3200	Obligated balance, end of year	25	3	3
	Budget authority and outlays, net:			
	Discretionary:			
4000	Budget authority, gross	49	52	45
	Outlays, gross:			
4010	Outlays from new discretionary authority	2	52	45
4011	Outlays from discretionary balances	10	22	2
4020	Outlays, gross (total)	12	74	47
	Offsets against gross budget authority and outlays:			
	Offsetting collections (collected) from:			
4033	Non-Federal sources		–3	–3
4040	Offsets against gross budget authority and outlays (total)		–3	–3
4180	Budget authority, net (total)	49	49	42
4190	Outlays, net (total)	12	71	44

Construction.—This fund provides for the construction of projects to resolve current and anticipated international problems of water supply, water quality, sewage treatment, flood damage reduction, and management, security, and operation of facilities and infrastructure, pursuant to the treaties and international agreements with Mexico. Projects are normally constructed jointly with Mexico. This account also receives reimbursement for such projects.

816　International Commissions—Continued
Federal Funds—Continued

THE BUDGET FOR FISCAL YEAR 2023

CONSTRUCTION—Continued

Object Classification (in millions of dollars)

Identification code 019–1078–0–1–301	2021 actual	2022 est.	2023 est.
	Direct obligations:			
25.2	Other services from non-Federal sources	2	4	4
32.0	Land and structures	22	45	40
99.0	Direct obligations	24	49	44
99.0	Reimbursable obligations	....	3	3
99.9	Total new obligations, unexpired accounts	24	52	47

AMERICAN SECTIONS, INTERNATIONAL COMMISSIONS

For necessary expenses, not otherwise provided, for the International Joint Commission and the International Boundary Commission, United States and Canada, as authorized by treaties between the United States and Canada or Great Britain, $13,204,000: Provided, That of the amount provided under this heading for the International Joint Commission, up to $1,250,000 may remain available until September 30, 2024, and up to $9,000 may be made available for representation expenses: Provided further, That of the amount provided under this heading for the International Boundary Commission, up to $1,000 may be made available for representation expenses.

Note.—A full-year 2022 appropriation for this account was not enacted at the time the Budget was prepared; therefore, the Budget assumes this account is operating under the Continuing Appropriations Act, 2022 (Division A of Public Law 117–43, as amended). The amounts included for 2022 reflect the annualized level provided by the continuing resolution.

Program and Financing (in millions of dollars)

Identification code 019–1082–0–1–301	2021 actual	2022 est.	2023 est.
	Obligations by program activity:			
0001	American Sections, International Commissions (Direct)	14	15	13
	Budgetary resources:			
	Budget authority:			
	Appropriations, discretionary:			
1100	Appropriation	15	15	13
1930	Total budgetary resources available	15	15	13
	Memorandum (non-add) entries:			
1940	Unobligated balance expiring	–1	....	....
	Change in obligated balance:			
	Unpaid obligations:			
3000	Unpaid obligations, brought forward, Oct 1	9	8	7
3010	New obligations, unexpired accounts	14	15	13
3020	Outlays (gross)	–15	–16	–14
3050	Unpaid obligations, end of year	8	7	6
	Memorandum (non-add) entries:			
3100	Obligated balance, start of year	9	8	7
3200	Obligated balance, end of year	8	7	6
	Budget authority and outlays, net:			
	Discretionary:			
4000	Budget authority, gross	15	15	13
	Outlays, gross:			
4010	Outlays from new discretionary authority	9	10	9
4011	Outlays from discretionary balances	6	6	5
4020	Outlays, gross (total)	15	16	14
4180	Budget authority, net (total)	15	15	13
4190	Outlays, net (total)	15	16	14

These funds are used for payment of the U.S. share of the expenses of:

International Boundary Commission (IBC).—The Commission, in accordance with existing treaties, maintains the integrity of a well-delineated boundary between the United States and Canada by: surveying, inspecting, and clearing the boundary; repairing or replacing monuments; regulating construction crossing the boundary; and serving as the official U.S. Government source for boundary-specific positional and cartographic data.

International Joint Commission (IJC).—Pursuant to the Boundary Waters Treaty of 1909 and related treaties and agreements, the Commission approves, regulates, and monitors structures in boundary waters and transboundary streams, apportions waters between the United States and Canada in selected rivers, and investigates matters referred to it by the United States and Canada that principally include transboundary environmental issues.

Border Environment Cooperation Commission (BECC).—The Commission was integrated within the North American Development Bank (NADB) on November 10, 2017. No appropriation is being requested for BECC in FY 2023.

Object Classification (in millions of dollars)

Identification code 019–1082–0–1–301	2021 actual	2022 est.	2023 est.
11.1	Direct obligations: Personnel compensation: Full-time permanent	2	2	2
11.9	Total personnel compensation	2	2	2
25.2	Other services from non-Federal sources	12	13	11
99.9	Total new obligations, unexpired accounts	14	15	13

Employment Summary

Identification code 019–1082–0–1–301	2021 actual	2022 est.	2023 est.
1001	Direct civilian full-time equivalent employment	27	27	27

INTERNATIONAL FISHERIES COMMISSIONS

For necessary expenses for international fisheries commissions, not otherwise provided for, as authorized by law, $53,766,000: Provided, That the United States share of such expenses may be advanced to the respective commissions pursuant to section 3324 of title 31, United States Code.

Note.—A full-year 2022 appropriation for this account was not enacted at the time the Budget was prepared; therefore, the Budget assumes this account is operating under the Continuing Appropriations Act, 2022 (Division A of Public Law 117–43, as amended). The amounts included for 2022 reflect the annualized level provided by the continuing resolution.

Program and Financing (in millions of dollars)

Identification code 019–1087–0–1–302	2021 actual	2022 est.	2023 est.
	Obligations by program activity:			
0002	International Fisheries Commissions	2	2	2
0006	Great Lakes Fishery Commission	47	47	38
0008	Inter-Pacific Halibut Commission	5	5	5
0009	Pacific Salmon Commission	6	6	6
0010	Other Commissions and Marine Science Organizations	3	3	3
0900	Total new obligations, unexpired accounts (object class 41.0)	63	63	54
	Budgetary resources:			
	Budget authority:			
	Appropriations, discretionary:			
1100	Appropriation	63	63	54
1930	Total budgetary resources available	63	63	54
	Change in obligated balance:			
	Unpaid obligations:			
3000	Unpaid obligations, brought forward, Oct 1	....	1	1
3010	New obligations, unexpired accounts	63	63	54
3020	Outlays (gross)	–62	–63	–54
3050	Unpaid obligations, end of year	1	1	1
	Memorandum (non-add) entries:			
3100	Obligated balance, start of year	....	1	1
3200	Obligated balance, end of year	1	1	1
	Budget authority and outlays, net:			
	Discretionary:			
4000	Budget authority, gross	63	63	54
	Outlays, gross:			
4010	Outlays from new discretionary authority	62	62	53
4011	Outlays from discretionary balances	....	1	1
4020	Outlays, gross (total)	62	63	54
4180	Budget authority, net (total)	63	63	54
4190	Outlays, net (total)	62	63	54

This appropriation provides the United States' treaty mandated assessments and expenses to 19 international commissions and organizations including three bilateral commissions (the Great Lakes Fisheries Commission, the International Pacific Halibut Commission, and the Pacific Salmon Commission), nine multilateral bodies, two marine science organizations, one whaling commission, the Arctic Council and the Antarctic Treaty Secretariat, as well as funding regional sea turtle and shark conservation, and travel expenses of non-government U.S. commissioners and their advisors. These commissions and organizations coordinate scientific studies of shared fish stocks and other living marine resources and their habitats and establish common management measures to be implemented by member governments based on their results. Many also oversee the allocation of fishing rights to their members. In addition, the Great Lakes Fishery Commission carries out a program to eradicate the invasive, parasitic sea lamprey. The marine science organizations coordinate international research on valuable fisheries, oceanography, and marine ecosystems and the results are publicly disseminated and used to advise member governments on fisheries and marine science policy.

OTHER

Federal Funds

GLOBAL HIV/AIDS INITIATIVE

Program and Financing (in millions of dollars)

Identification code 019–1030–0–1–151	2021 actual	2022 est.	2023 est.
Obligations by program activity:			
0001 Global HIV/AIDs Initiative	2	4	4
0900 Total new obligations, unexpired accounts (object class 41.0)	2	4	4
Budgetary resources:			
Unobligated balance:			
1000 Unobligated balance brought forward, Oct 1	6	5	3
1021 Recoveries of prior year unpaid obligations	1	2	2
1070 Unobligated balance (total)	7	7	5
1930 Total budgetary resources available	7	7	5
Memorandum (non-add) entries:			
1941 Unexpired unobligated balance, end of year	5	3	1
Change in obligated balance:			
Unpaid obligations:			
3000 Unpaid obligations, brought forward, Oct 1	7	5	4
3010 New obligations, unexpired accounts	2	4	4
3020 Outlays (gross)	–3	–3	
3040 Recoveries of prior year unpaid obligations, unexpired	–1	–2	–2
3050 Unpaid obligations, end of year	5	4	6
Memorandum (non-add) entries:			
3100 Obligated balance, start of year	7	5	4
3200 Obligated balance, end of year	5	4	6
Budget authority and outlays, net:			
Discretionary:			
Outlays, gross:			
4011 Outlays from discretionary balances	3	3	
4180 Budget authority, net (total)			
4190 Outlays, net (total)	3	3	

The first phase of the President's Emergency Plan for AIDS Relief (PEPFAR), from 2004 to 2008, was the largest ever global public health initiative by a single country to fight the HIV/AIDS epidemic. Funding was appropriated in the Global HIV/AIDS Initiative account for this purpose through 2007. Beginning in 2008, funds were appropriated in the Global Health and Child Survival (now Global Health Programs) account, and will continue to be requested in that account.

FUNDS APPROPRIATED TO THE PRESIDENT

For necessary expenses to enable the President to carry out the provisions of the Foreign Assistance Act of 1961, and for other purposes, as follows:

GLOBAL HEALTH PROGRAMS

For necessary expenses to carry out the provisions of chapters 1 and 10 of part I of the Foreign Assistance Act of 1961, for global health activities, in addition to funds otherwise available for such purposes, $3,956,000,000, to remain available until September 30, 2024, and which shall be apportioned directly to the United States Agency for International Development: Provided, That this amount shall be made available for training, equipment, and technical assistance to build the capacity of public health institutions and organizations in developing countries, and for such activities as: (1) child survival and maternal health programs; (2) immunization and oral rehydration programs; (3) other health, nutrition, water and sanitation programs which directly address the needs of mothers and children, and related education programs; (4) assistance for children displaced or orphaned by causes other than AIDS; (5) programs for the prevention, treatment, control of, and research on HIV/AIDS, tuberculosis, polio, malaria, and other infectious diseases including neglected tropical diseases, and for assistance to communities severely affected by HIV/AIDS, including children infected or affected by AIDS; (6) disaster preparedness training for health crises; (7) programs to prevent, prepare for, and respond to, unanticipated and emerging global health threats, including zoonotic diseases; and (8) family planning/reproductive health: Provided further, That funds appropriated under this paragraph may be made available for a United States contribution to The GAVI Alliance: Provided further, That none of the funds made available in this Act nor any unobligated balances from prior appropriations Acts may be made available to any organization or program which, as determined by the President of the United States, supports or participates in the management of a program of coercive abortion or involuntary sterilization: Provided further, That any determination made under the previous proviso must be made not later than 6 months after the date of enactment of this Act, and must be accompanied by the evidence and criteria utilized to make the determination: Provided further, That none of the funds made available under this Act may be used to pay for the performance of abortion as a method of family planning or to motivate or coerce any person to practice abortions: Provided further, That nothing in this paragraph shall be construed to alter any existing statutory prohibitions against abortion under section 104 of the Foreign Assistance Act of 1961: Provided further, That none of the funds made available under this Act may be used to lobby for or against abortion: Provided further, That in order to reduce reliance on abortion in developing nations, funds shall be available only to voluntary family planning projects which offer, either directly or through referral to, or information about access to, a broad range of family planning methods and services, and that any such voluntary family planning project shall meet the following requirements: (1) service providers or referral agents in the project shall not implement or be subject to quotas, or other numerical targets, of total number of births, number of family planning acceptors, or acceptors of a particular method of family planning (this provision shall not be construed to include the use of quantitative estimates or indicators for budgeting and planning purposes); (2) the project shall not include payment of incentives, bribes, gratuities, or financial reward to: (A) an individual in exchange for becoming a family planning acceptor; or (B) program personnel for achieving a numerical target or quota of total number of births, number of family planning acceptors, or acceptors of a particular method of family planning; (3) the project shall not deny any right or benefit, including the right of access to participate in any program of general welfare or the right of access to health care, as a consequence of any individual's decision not to accept family planning services; (4) the project shall provide family planning acceptors comprehensible information on the health benefits and risks of the method chosen, including those conditions that might render the use of the method inadvisable and those adverse side effects known to be consequent to the use of the method; and (5) the project shall ensure that experimental contraceptive drugs and devices and medical procedures are provided only in the context of a scientific study in which participants are advised of potential risks and benefits; and, not less than 60 days after the date on which the USAID Administrator determines that there has been a violation of the requirements contained in paragraph (1), (2), (3), or (5) of this proviso, or a pattern or practice of violations of the requirements contained in paragraph (4) of this proviso, the Administrator shall submit to the Committees on Appropriations a report containing a description of such violation and the corrective action taken by the Agency: Provided further, That in awarding grants for natural family planning under section 104 of the Foreign Assistance Act of 1961 no applicant shall be discriminated against because of such applicant's religious or conscientious commitment to offer only natural family planning; and, additionally, all such applicants shall comply with the requirements of the previous proviso: Provided further, That for purposes of this or any other Act authorizing or appropriating funds for the Department of State, foreign operations, and related programs, the term "motivate", as it relates to family planning assistance, shall not be construed to prohibit the provision, consistent with local law, of information or counseling about all pregnancy options: Provided further, That information provided about the use of condoms as part of

GLOBAL HEALTH PROGRAMS—Continued

projects or activities that are funded from amounts appropriated by this Act shall be medically accurate and shall include the public health benefits and failure rates of such use.

In addition, for necessary expenses to carry out the provisions of the Foreign Assistance Act of 1961 for the prevention, treatment, and control of, and research on, HIV/AIDS, and for global pandemic preparedness, including for an international financing mechanism for such purposes, which may be made available as contributions, $6,620,000,000, to remain available until September 30, 2027: Provided, That funds appropriated under this paragraph may be made available, notwithstanding any other provision of law, except for the United States Leadership Against HIV/AIDS, Tuberculosis, and Malaria Act of 2003 (Public Law 108–25), as amended, for a United States contribution to the Global Fund to Fight AIDS, Tuberculosis and Malaria (Global Fund): Provided further, That the amount of such contribution should be $2,000,000,000: Provided further, That up to 5 percent of the aggregate amount of funds made available to the Global Fund in fiscal year 2023 may be made available to USAID for technical assistance related to the activities of the Global Fund, subject to the regular notification procedures of the Committees on Appropriations: Provided further, That of the funds appropriated under this paragraph, up to $20,000,000 may be made available, in addition to amounts otherwise available for such purposes, for administrative expenses of the Office of the United States Global AIDS Coordinator.

In addition, for necessary expenses to carry out the Foreign Assistance Act of 1961, for a Health Resilience Fund for global health activities in challenging environments and countries in crisis, in addition to funds otherwise available for such purposes, $10,000,000, which shall be apportioned directly to United States Agency for International Development and shall remain available until expended: Provided, That funds appropriated under this paragraph may be made available, notwithstanding any other provision of law, except for provisions under this heading and the United States Leadership Against HIV/AIDS, Tuberculosis, and Malaria Act of 2003 (Public Law 108–25), as amended: Provided further, That such funds may support activities relating to health service delivery, health workforce, health information systems, access to essential medicines, health systems financing, and governance: Provided further, That funds made available under the headings "Global Health Programs" and "Economic Support Fund" in this Act or prior Acts may be transferred to, and merged with, funds made available for the Health Resilience Fund.

Note.—A full-year 2022 appropriation for this account was not enacted at the time the Budget was prepared; therefore, the Budget assumes this account is operating under the Continuing Appropriations Act, 2022 (Division A of Public Law 117–43, as amended). The amounts included for 2022 reflect the annualized level provided by the continuing resolution.

Program and Financing (in millions of dollars)

Identification code 019–1031–0–1–151	2021 actual	2022 est.	2023 est.
Obligations by program activity:			
0001 Direct Global Health program activity	10,367	11,600	11,600
0002 Administrative Expenses	11	15	15
0799 Total direct obligations	10,378	11,615	11,615
0801 Reimbursable program activity - WCF	811	520	520
0900 Total new obligations, unexpired accounts	11,189	12,135	12,135
Budgetary resources:			
Unobligated balance:			
1000 Unobligated balance brought forward, Oct 1	7,587	9,724	6,790
1010 Unobligated balance transfer to other accts [077–0110]	–1		
1012 Unobligated balance transfers between expired and unexpired accounts	23		
1021 Recoveries of prior year unpaid obligations	110		
1033 Recoveries of prior year paid obligations	7		
1070 Unobligated balance (total)	7,726	9,724	6,790
Budget authority:			
Appropriations, discretionary:			
1100 Appropriation	9,196	9,196	10,576
1100 Appropriation - Title IX Emergency Funds	4,000		
1121 Appropriations transferred from other acct [019–1005]	2		
1160 Appropriation, discretionary (total)	13,198	9,196	10,576
Spending authority from offsetting collections, discretionary:			
1700 Collected		5	5
1900 Budget authority (total)	13,198	9,201	10,581
1930 Total budgetary resources available	20,924	18,925	17,371
Memorandum (non-add) entries:			
1940 Unobligated balance expiring	–11		
1941 Unexpired unobligated balance, end of year	9,724	6,790	5,236
Change in obligated balance:			
Unpaid obligations:			
3000 Unpaid obligations, brought forward, Oct 1	9,274	7,138	11,165
3010 New obligations, unexpired accounts	11,189	12,135	12,135
3011 Obligations ("upward adjustments"), expired accounts	24		
3020 Outlays (gross)	–13,155	–8,108	–8,249
3040 Recoveries of prior year unpaid obligations, unexpired	–110		
3041 Recoveries of prior year unpaid obligations, expired	–84		
3050 Unpaid obligations, end of year	7,138	11,165	15,051
Memorandum (non-add) entries:			
3100 Obligated balance, start of year	9,274	7,138	11,165
3200 Obligated balance, end of year	7,138	11,165	15,051
Budget authority and outlays, net:			
Discretionary:			
4000 Budget authority, gross	13,198	9,201	10,581
Outlays, gross:			
4010 Outlays from new discretionary authority	4,428	859	1,048
4011 Outlays from discretionary balances	8,727	7,249	7,201
4020 Outlays, gross (total)	13,155	8,108	8,249
Offsets against gross budget authority and outlays:			
Offsetting collections (collected) from:			
4030 Federal sources		–5	–5
4033 Non-Federal sources	–12		
4040 Offsets against gross budget authority and outlays (total)	–12	–5	–5
Additional offsets against gross budget authority only:			
4052 Offsetting collections credited to expired accounts	5		
4053 Recoveries of prior year paid obligations, unexpired accounts	7		
4060 Additional offsets against budget authority only (total)	12		
4070 Budget authority, net (discretionary)	13,198	9,196	10,576
4080 Outlays, net (discretionary)	13,143	8,103	8,244
4180 Budget authority, net (total)	13,198	9,196	10,576
4190 Outlays, net (total)	13,143	8,103	8,244

Summary of Budget Authority and Outlays (in millions of dollars)

	2021 actual	2022 est.	2023 est.
Enacted/requested:			
Budget Authority	13,198	9,196	10,576
Outlays	13,143	8,103	8,244
Legislative proposal, subject to PAYGO:			
Budget Authority			6,500
Outlays			2,275
Total:			
Budget Authority	13,198	9,196	17,076
Outlays	13,143	8,103	10,519

The Global Health Programs account funds health-related foreign assistance for the Department of State (DOS) and the U.S. Agency for International Development (USAID). Global health programs seek to improve health outcomes by increasing impact through strategic integration and coordination; strengthening and leveraging multilateral institutions; encouraging country ownership and investing in country-led plans; building sustainability through health systems strengthening; improving metrics, monitoring and evaluation; and promoting research, development and innovation.

Global Health Programs-State.—The Global Health Programs (GHP-State) account supports the goal of controlling the HIV/AIDS epidemic through the President's Emergency Plan for AIDS Relief (PEPFAR). The 2023 Budget requests $6,620.0 million in the GHP-State account for global HIV programming. PEPFAR is led and coordinated by the Office of the Global AIDS Coordinator (S/GAC) in DOS, which draws upon the expertise and experience of other U.S. government partners including USAID, the Department of Health and Human Services, the Department of Defense, and the Peace Corps to align resources, activities, and expertise at the country level in the fight against global AIDS. Programs work through expanded partnerships to build capacity for efficient, effective, innovative, country-led, and sustainable services, and to create a supportive and enabling policy environment for combating HIV/AIDS, including as part of the broader USG and country-level health and development approach. In addition, S/GAC supports strong monitoring evaluation and accountability systems to set benchmarks for outcomes and programmatic efficiencies

DEPARTMENT OF STATE AND OTHER INTERNATIONAL PROGRAMS

through regularly assessed planning and reporting processes to ensure goals are being met. PEPFAR programs support strategic, scientifically sound investments to rapidly scale up core HIV/AIDS prevention, care, and treatment interventions within the context of strengthened health systems, particularly in terms of human resources in nations with severe health worker shortages and lack of service delivery capacity. PEPFAR integrates its efforts with important programs in other areas of global health as well as other areas of development, including the areas of education, gender equity, and economic development. A contribution of $2,000.0 million to the Global Fund to Fight AIDS, Tuberculosis and Malaria is included in GHP-State for the seventh replenishment, with the United States offering to match $1 for every $2 contributed by other donors. $45 million is requested for a United States contribution to the United Nations Joint Program on HIV/AIDS (UNAIDS) in support of the Sustainable Development Goal 3 to end AIDS by 2030 through strategic direction, normative guidance through WHO, civil society advocacy and technical support. The request also includes $250 million and the authority for a new international financing facility to support global health security and pandemic preparedness.

Global Heath Programs-USAID.—The 2023 Budget requests $3,956.0 million in the GHP-USAID account for a comprehensive and integrated approach to prevent child and maternal deaths, combat infectious disease threats, and control the HIV epidemic. This approach strives to maximize impact and to expand its reach by building upon previous investments made through maternal and child health, nutrition, family planning and reproductive health, vulnerable children, tuberculosis, neglected tropical diseases, global health security, the President's Emergency Plan for AIDS Relief, and the President's Malaria Initiative. This approach will continue to save millions of lives while fostering sustainable health care delivery systems that can address the full range of developing country health needs including preparing for, and responding to, the next global disease outbreak or pandemic. USAID, working in partnership with foreign governments, local private sector and non-governmental organizations, and other public-private partnerships, will build capacity, strengthen health systems, and promote sustainable integrated health care for vulnerable populations. The Budget provides $290 million to support a multi-year (2020–2023), $1.16 billion contribution to Gavi, the Vaccine Alliance. It also provides $250 million for contributions to multilateral organizations leading the global COVID response through the Act-Accelerator platform, $90 million to replenish the Emergency Reserve Fund, and $10 million for the Health Resilience Fund for global health activities in challenging environments and countries in crisis.

Object Classification (in millions of dollars)

Identification code 019–1031–0–1–151		2021 actual	2022 est.	2023 est.
	Direct obligations:			
	Personnel compensation:			
11.1	Full-time permanent	6	6	6
11.3	Other than full-time permanent	1	1	1
11.9	Total personnel compensation	7	7	7
12.1	Civilian personnel benefits	6	6	6
21.0	Travel and transportation of persons	3	3	3
23.1	Rental payments to GSA	19	19	19
23.2	Rental payments to others	5	5	5
23.3	Communications, utilities, and miscellaneous charges	2	2	2
25.1	Advisory and assistance services	342	342	342
25.2	Other services from non-Federal sources	3	3	3
25.3	Other goods and services from Federal sources	31	31	31
25.7	Operation and maintenance of equipment	15	15	15
31.0	Equipment	7	7	7
41.0	Grants, subsidies, and contributions	9,938	11,175	11,175
99.0	Direct obligations	10,378	11,615	11,615
99.0	Reimbursable obligations	811	520	520
99.9	Total new obligations, unexpired accounts	11,189	12,135	12,135

Employment Summary

Identification code 019–1031–0–1–151	2021 actual	2022 est.	2023 est.
1001 Direct civilian full-time equivalent employment	51	51	51

GLOBAL HEALTH PROGRAMS

(Legislative proposal, subject to PAYGO)

Program and Financing (in millions of dollars)

Identification code 019–1031–4–1–151		2021 actual	2022 est.	2023 est.
	Obligations by program activity:			
0001	Direct Global Health program activity			2,272
0002	Administrative Expenses			3
0799	Total direct obligations			2,275
0900	Total new obligations, unexpired accounts (object class 41.0)			2,275
	Budgetary resources:			
	Budget authority:			
	Appropriations, mandatory:			
1200	Appropriation			6,500
1930	Total budgetary resources available			6,500
	Memorandum (non-add) entries:			
1941	Unexpired unobligated balance, end of year			4,225
	Change in obligated balance:			
	Unpaid obligations:			
3010	New obligations, unexpired accounts			2,275
3020	Outlays (gross)			–2,275
	Budget authority and outlays, net:			
	Mandatory:			
4090	Budget authority, gross			6,500
	Outlays, gross:			
4100	Outlays from new mandatory authority			2,275
4180	Budget authority, net (total)			6,500
4190	Outlays, net (total)			2,275

The Global Health Programs account funds health-related foreign assistance for the Department of State (DOS) and the U.S. Agency for International Development (USAID). Global health programs seek to improve health outcomes by increasing impact through strategic integration and coordination; strengthening and leveraging multilateral institutions; encouraging country ownership and investing in country-led plans; building sustainability through health systems strengthening; improving metrics, monitoring and evaluation; and promoting research, development and innovation.

The FY 2023 Budget includes $6.5 billion in mandatory funding for State and USAID as part of a larger interagency proposal to make transmformative investments in pandemic and other biolgoical threat preparedness globally . The pandemic preparedness funding will strengthen the global health workforce, support pandemic preparedness R&D, advance global research anddevelopment capacity, and support health security financing to strengthen global capacity to prevent, detect, and respond to future COVID variants and other infectious disease outbreaks.

MIGRATION AND REFUGEE ASSISTANCE

For necessary expenses not otherwise provided for, to enable the Secretary of State to carry out the provisions of section 2(a) and (b) of the Migration and Refugee Assistance Act of 1962, and other activities to meet refugee and migration needs; salaries and expenses of personnel and dependents as authorized by the Foreign Service Act of 1980 (22 U.S.C. 3901 et seq.); allowances as authorized by sections 5921 through 5925 of title 5, United States Code; purchase and hire of passenger motor vehicles; and services as authorized by section 3109 of title 5, United States Code, $3,912,000,000, to remain available until expended, of which $5,000,000 shall be made available for refugees resettling in Israel: Provided, That funds available under this heading may be used to carry out section 5(a)(6) of the Migration and Refugee Assistance Act of 1962 (22 U.S.C. 2605(a)(6)), as amended, without regard to the geographic limitation referenced therein, for employing up to 100 individuals domestically, in addition to any other use of such authority.

MIGRATION AND REFUGEE ASSISTANCE—Continued

Note.—A full-year 2022 appropriation for this account was not enacted at the time the Budget was prepared; therefore, the Budget assumes this account is operating under the Continuing Appropriations Act, 2022 (Division A of Public Law 117–43, as amended). The amounts included for 2022 reflect the annualized level provided by the continuing resolution.

MIGRATION AND REFUGEE ASSISTANCE

⟦For an additional amount for "Migration and Refugee Assistance", $415,000,000, to remain available until expended, to address humanitarian needs in, and to assist refugees from, Afghanistan.⟧ *(Afghanistan Supplemental Appropriations Act, 2022.)*

Program and Financing (in millions of dollars)

Identification code 019–1143–0–1–151		2021 actual	2022 est.	2023 est.
	Obligations by program activity:			
0001	Overseas assistance	3,972	3,603	3,044
0002	U.S. refugee admissions program	334	550	823
0003	Refugees to Israel	5	5	5
0005	Administrative expenses	51	62	70
0799	Total direct obligations	4,362	4,220	3,942
0801	Migration and Refugee Assistance (Reimbursable)	....	....	1
0900	Total new obligations, unexpired accounts	4,362	4,220	3,943
	Budgetary resources:			
	Unobligated balance:			
1000	Unobligated balance brought forward, Oct 1	602	342	....
1001	Discretionary unobligated balance brought fwd, Oct 1	602	....	....
1021	Recoveries of prior year unpaid obligations	70	30	30
1070	Unobligated balance (total)	672	372	30
	Budget authority:			
	Appropriations, discretionary:			
1100	Appropriation	3,532	3,847	3,912
	Appropriations, mandatory:			
1200	Appropriation	500	....	....
	Spending authority from offsetting collections, discretionary:			
1700	Collected	....	1	1
1900	Budget authority (total)	4,032	3,848	3,913
1930	Total budgetary resources available	4,704	4,220	3,943
	Memorandum (non-add) entries:			
1941	Unexpired unobligated balance, end of year	342	....	....
	Change in obligated balance:			
	Unpaid obligations:			
3000	Unpaid obligations, brought forward, Oct 1	1,495	1,522	1,331
3010	New obligations, unexpired accounts	4,362	4,220	3,943
3020	Outlays (gross)	–4,265	–4,381	–3,984
3040	Recoveries of prior year unpaid obligations, unexpired	–70	–30	–30
3050	Unpaid obligations, end of year	1,522	1,331	1,260
	Memorandum (non-add) entries:			
3100	Obligated balance, start of year	1,495	1,522	1,331
3200	Obligated balance, end of year	1,522	1,331	1,260
	Budget authority and outlays, net:			
	Discretionary:			
4000	Budget authority, gross	3,532	3,848	3,913
	Outlays, gross:			
4010	Outlays from new discretionary authority	2,643	3,021	3,072
4011	Outlays from discretionary balances	1,290	1,360	912
4020	Outlays, gross (total)	3,933	4,381	3,984
	Offsets against gross budget authority and outlays:			
	Offsetting collections (collected) from:			
4030	Federal sources	....	–1	–1
	Mandatory:			
4090	Budget authority, gross	500	....	....
	Outlays, gross:			
4100	Outlays from new mandatory authority	332	....	....
4180	Budget authority, net (total)	4,032	3,847	3,912
4190	Outlays, net (total)	4,265	4,380	3,983

Overseas Assistance.—The majority of the Migration and Refugee Assistance (MRA) account addresses the protection and assistance needs of refugees, conflict victims, stateless persons, and vulnerable migrants worldwide. Funds primarily support the programs of international organizations, including the United Nations High Commissioner for Refugees (UNHCR), the International Committee of the Red Cross (ICRC), the United Nations Relief and Works Agency for Palestine Refugees in the Near East (UNRWA), and the International Organization for Migration (IOM), as well as non-governmental organizations (NGOs).

Humanitarian Migrants to Israel.—These funds assist humanitarian migrants resettling in Israel.

U.S. Refugee Admissions.—MRA funds overseas processing, transportation, and initial placement for refugees and certain other categories of special immigrants resettling in the United States. These activities are carried out primarily by NGO partners and the International Organization for Migration (IOM).

Administrative Expenses.—These funds finance the salaries and operating expenses for the Bureau of Population, Refugees, and Migration in Washington, D.C. and overseas. (Note: Funds for the salaries and support costs of the positions dedicated to international population policy and coordination are requested under the Department of State's Diplomatic and Consular Programs appropriation.)

In FY 2023, the MRA account will support ongoing as well as new needs.

Object Classification (in millions of dollars)

Identification code 019–1143–0–1–151		2021 actual	2022 est.	2023 est.
	Direct obligations:			
11.1	Personnel compensation: Full-time permanent	23	23	33
12.1	Civilian personnel benefits	9	9	12
21.0	Travel and transportation of persons	1	1	3
23.3	Communications, utilities, and miscellaneous charges	2	2	2
25.2	Other services from non-Federal sources	50	50	54
41.0	Grants, subsidies, and contributions	4,277	4,135	3,838
99.0	Direct obligations	4,362	4,220	3,942
99.0	Reimbursable obligations	....	....	1
99.9	Total new obligations, unexpired accounts	4,362	4,220	3,943

Employment Summary

Identification code 019–1143–0–1–151	2021 actual	2022 est.	2023 est.
1001 Direct civilian full-time equivalent employment	175	220	277

UNITED STATES EMERGENCY REFUGEE AND MIGRATION ASSISTANCE FUND

For necessary expenses to carry out the provisions of section 2(c) of the Migration and Refugee Assistance Act of 1962 (22 U.S.C. 2601(c)), $100,000,000, to remain available until expended.

Note.—A full-year 2022 appropriation for this account was not enacted at the time the Budget was prepared; therefore, the Budget assumes this account is operating under the Continuing Appropriations Act, 2022 (Division A of Public Law 117–43, as amended). The amounts included for 2022 reflect the annualized level provided by the continuing resolution.

UNITED STATES EMERGENCY REFUGEE AND MIGRATION ASSISTANCE FUND

⟦For an additional amount for "United States Emergency Refugee and Migration Assistance Fund", $1,076,100,000, to remain available until expended, notwithstanding section 2(c)(2) of the Migration and Refugee Assistance Act of 1962 (22 U.S.C. 2601(c)(2)), of which $976,100,000 is for support for Operation Allies Welcome and related efforts by the Department of State, including additional relocations of individuals at risk as a result of the situation in Afghanistan and related expenses, and $100,000,000 is to respond to other unexpected and urgent humanitarian emergencies.⟧ *(Afghanistan Supplemental Appropriations Act, 2022.)*

UNITED STATES EMERGENCY REFUGEE AND MIGRATION ASSISTANCE FUND

⟦For an additional amount for "United States Emergency Refugee and Migration Assistance Fund", $1,200,000,000, to remain available until expended, notwithstanding section 2(c)(2) of the Migration and Refugee Assistance Act of 1962 (22 U.S.C. 2601(c)(2)), for support for Operation Allies Welcome and related efforts by the Department of State, including additional relocations of individuals at risk as a result of the situation in Afghanistan and related expenses.⟧ *(Additional Afghanistan Supplemental Appropriations Act, 2022.)*

DEPARTMENT OF STATE AND OTHER INTERNATIONAL PROGRAMS

Program and Financing (in millions of dollars)

Identification code 011–0040–0–1–151		2021 actual	2022 est.	2023 est.
	Obligations by program activity:			
0001	United States Emergency Refugee and Migration Assistance Fund (Direct)	591	2,276	109
0900	Total new obligations, unexpired accounts (object class 41.0)	591	2,276	109
	Budgetary resources:			
	Unobligated balance:			
1000	Unobligated balance brought forward, Oct 1	100	9	9
	Budget authority:			
	Appropriations, discretionary:			
1100	Appropriation	500	2,276	100
1930	Total budgetary resources available	600	2,285	109
	Memorandum (non-add) entries:			
1941	Unexpired unobligated balance, end of year		9	9
	Change in obligated balance:			
	Unpaid obligations:			
3000	Unpaid obligations, brought forward, Oct 1		544	228
3010	New obligations, unexpired accounts	591	2,276	109
3020	Outlays (gross)	–47	–2,592	–308
3050	Unpaid obligations, end of year	544	228	29
	Memorandum (non-add) entries:			
3100	Obligated balance, start of year		544	228
3200	Obligated balance, end of year	544	228	29
	Budget authority and outlays, net:			
	Discretionary:			
4000	Budget authority, gross	500	2,276	100
	Outlays, gross:			
4010	Outlays from new discretionary authority	45	2,048	80
4011	Outlays from discretionary balances	2	544	228
4020	Outlays, gross (total)	47	2,592	308
4180	Budget authority, net (total)	500	2,276	100
4190	Outlays, net (total)	47	2,592	308

The Emergency Refugee and Migration Assistance Fund enables the President to provide humanitarian assistance for unexpected and urgent refugee and migration needs.

COMPLEX CRISES FUND

For necessary expenses to carry out the provisions of section 509(b) of the Global Fragility Act of 2019 (title V of division J of Public Law 116–94), $40,000,000, to remain available until expended: Provided, That notwithstanding the percentage in paragraph (4)(B) of such section, up to ten percent of the funds appropriated under this heading may be used for administrative expenses, in addition to funds otherwise available for such purposes: Provided further, That funds appropriated under this heading may be made available notwithstanding any other provision of law.

(CANCELLATION)

Of the unobligated balances available under the heading "Complex Crises Fund" from prior Acts making appropriations for the Department of State, foreign operations, and related programs, $10,000,000 are hereby permanently cancelled.

Note.—A full-year 2022 appropriation for this account was not enacted at the time the Budget was prepared; therefore, the Budget assumes this account is operating under the Continuing Appropriations Act, 2022 (Division A of Public Law 117–43, as amended). The amounts included for 2022 reflect the annualized level provided by the continuing resolution.

Program and Financing (in millions of dollars)

Identification code 072–1015–0–1–151		2021 actual	2022 est.	2023 est.
	Obligations by program activity:			
0001	Complex Crises Fund (Direct)	45	35	45
0900	Total new obligations, unexpired accounts (object class 41.0)	45	35	45
	Budgetary resources:			
	Unobligated balance:			
1000	Unobligated balance brought forward, Oct 1	51	36	31
	Budget authority:			
	Appropriations, discretionary:			
1100	Appropriation	30	30	40

Other—Continued
Federal Funds—Continued

1131	Unobligated balance of appropriations permanently reduced			–10
1160	Appropriation, discretionary (total)	30	30	30
1930	Total budgetary resources available	81	66	61
	Memorandum (non-add) entries:			
1941	Unexpired unobligated balance, end of year	36	31	16
	Change in obligated balance:			
	Unpaid obligations:			
3000	Unpaid obligations, brought forward, Oct 1	28	52	49
3010	New obligations, unexpired accounts	45	35	45
3020	Outlays (gross)	–20	–38	–31
3041	Recoveries of prior year unpaid obligations, expired	–1		
3050	Unpaid obligations, end of year	52	49	63
	Memorandum (non-add) entries:			
3100	Obligated balance, start of year	28	52	49
3200	Obligated balance, end of year	52	49	63
	Budget authority and outlays, net:			
	Discretionary:			
4000	Budget authority, gross	30	30	30
	Outlays, gross:			
4010	Outlays from new discretionary authority	6	8	
4011	Outlays from discretionary balances	14	30	31
4020	Outlays, gross (total)	20	38	31
4180	Budget authority, net (total)	30	30	30
4190	Outlays, net (total)	20	38	31

The Complex Crises Fund (CCF) account supports programs to prevent or respond to emerging or unforeseen complex crises overseas. USAID deploys CCF when there is an unanticipated and overwhelming urgent need or window of opportunity where a U.S. Government response will help stem the rise of violent conflict and instability or advance the consolidation of peace and democracy. CCF funding allows the U.S. Government to respond to rapidly changing, complex crises that include a combination of humanitarian, political, and security dimensions and contributes to overarching U.S. foreign policy or national security goals.

DEPARTMENT OF STATE

INTERNATIONAL NARCOTICS CONTROL AND LAW ENFORCEMENT

For necessary expenses to carry out section 481 of the Foreign Assistance Act of 1961, $1,466,000,000, to remain available until September 30, 2024: Provided, That the Department of State may use the authority of section 608 of the Foreign Assistance Act of 1961, without regard to its restrictions, to receive excess property from an agency of the United States Government for the purpose of providing such property to a foreign country or international organization under chapter 8 of part I of such Act: Provided further, That section 482(b) of the Foreign Assistance Act of 1961 shall not apply to funds appropriated under this heading: Provided further, That funds made available under this heading for Program Development and Support may be made available notwithstanding pre-obligation requirements contained in this Act, except for the notification requirements of section 7015.

Note.—A full-year 2022 appropriation for this account was not enacted at the time the Budget was prepared; therefore, the Budget assumes this account is operating under the Continuing Appropriations Act, 2022 (Division A of Public Law 117–43, as amended). The amounts included for 2022 reflect the annualized level provided by the continuing resolution.

Program and Financing (in millions of dollars)

Identification code 019–1022–0–1–151		2021 actual	2022 est.	2023 est.
	Obligations by program activity:			
0001	Counterdrug and Anti-Crime Programs	1,444	1,498	1,485
0801	International Narcotics Control and Law Enforcement (Reimbursable)	20	6	6
0900	Total new obligations, unexpired accounts	1,464	1,504	1,491
	Budgetary resources:			
	Unobligated balance:			
1000	Unobligated balance brought forward, Oct 1	1,292	1,271	1,151
1010	Unobligated balance transfer to other accts [072–1037]	–27		
1010	Unobligated balance transfer to other accts [011–1021]	–4		
1012	Unobligated balance transfers between expired and unexpired accounts	123	45	45

DEPARTMENT OF STATE—Continued
Program and Financing—Continued

Identification code 019–1022–0–1–151		2021 actual	2022 est.	2023 est.
1021	Recoveries of prior year unpaid obligations	4	3	3
1070	Unobligated balance (total)	1,388	1,319	1,199
	Budget authority:			
	Appropriations, discretionary:			
1100	Appropriation (regular)	1,386	1,386	1,466
1131	Unobligated balance of appropriations permanently reduced	−50	−50	
1160	Appropriation, discretionary (total)	1,336	1,336	1,466
	Spending authority from offsetting collections, discretionary:			
1700	Collected	27		
1900	Budget authority (total)	1,363	1,336	1,466
1930	Total budgetary resources available	2,751	2,655	2,665
	Memorandum (non-add) entries:			
1940	Unobligated balance expiring	−16		
1941	Unexpired unobligated balance, end of year	1,271	1,151	1,174
	Change in obligated balance:			
	Unpaid obligations:			
3000	Unpaid obligations, brought forward, Oct 1	3,702	3,764	3,416
3010	New obligations, unexpired accounts	1,464	1,504	1,491
3011	Obligations ("upward adjustments"), expired accounts	7		
3020	Outlays (gross)	−1,274	−1,849	−1,914
3040	Recoveries of prior year unpaid obligations, unexpired	−4	−3	−3
3041	Recoveries of prior year unpaid obligations, expired	−131		
3050	Unpaid obligations, end of year	3,764	3,416	2,990
	Uncollected payments:			
3060	Uncollected pymts, Fed sources, brought forward, Oct 1	−3		
3071	Change in uncollected pymts, Fed sources, expired	3		
	Memorandum (non-add) entries:			
3100	Obligated balance, start of year	3,699	3,764	3,416
3200	Obligated balance, end of year	3,764	3,416	2,990
	Budget authority and outlays, net:			
	Discretionary:			
4000	Budget authority, gross	1,363	1,336	1,466
	Outlays, gross:			
4010	Outlays from new discretionary authority	94	134	147
4011	Outlays from discretionary balances	1,180	1,715	1,767
4020	Outlays, gross (total)	1,274	1,849	1,914
	Offsets against gross budget authority and outlays:			
	Offsetting collections (collected) from:			
4030	Federal sources	−24		
4033	Non-Federal sources	−7		
4040	Offsets against gross budget authority and outlays (total)	−31		
	Additional offsets against gross budget authority only:			
4052	Offsetting collections credited to expired accounts	4		
4060	Additional offsets against budget authority only (total)	4		
4070	Budget authority, net (discretionary)	1,336	1,336	1,466
4080	Outlays, net (discretionary)	1,243	1,849	1,914
4180	Budget authority, net (total)	1,336	1,336	1,466
4190	Outlays, net (total)	1,243	1,849	1,914

International Narcotics Control and Law Enforcement (INCLE) advances U.S. national security interests by supporting bilateral, regional, and global programs that enable partners and allies to manage and address transnational threats at their source. INCLE programs mitigate security threats posed by all forms of transnational crime, including production and trafficking of narcotics, and strengthen partner countries' criminal justice systems. These programs improve the ability of partner countries to cooperate effectively with U.S. law enforcement, and address the underlying conditions, such as corruption and weak rule of law, that foster state fragility and spur irregular migration to the United States.

Object Classification (in millions of dollars)

Identification code 019–1022–0–1–151		2021 actual	2022 est.	2023 est.
	Direct obligations:			
	Personnel compensation:			
11.1	Full-time permanent	44	45	45
11.3	Other than full-time permanent	11	11	11
11.9	Total personnel compensation	55	56	56
12.1	Civilian personnel benefits	20	18	18
13.0	Benefits for former personnel	5	5	5
21.0	Travel and transportation of persons	64	59	62
22.0	Transportation of things	4	4	4
23.2	Rental payments to others	40	40	40
25.2	Other services from non-Federal sources	428	425	427
26.0	Supplies and materials	16	16	16
31.0	Equipment	32	32	32
41.0	Grants, subsidies, and contributions	780	843	825
99.0	Direct obligations	1,444	1,498	1,485
99.0	Reimbursable obligations	20	6	6
99.9	Total new obligations, unexpired accounts	1,464	1,504	1,491

Employment Summary

Identification code 019–1022–0–1–151	2021 actual	2022 est.	2023 est.
1001 Direct civilian full-time equivalent employment	437	437	437

ANDEAN COUNTERDRUG PROGRAMS

Program and Financing (in millions of dollars)

Identification code 019–1154–0–1–151		2021 actual	2022 est.	2023 est.
	Budgetary resources:			
	Unobligated balance:			
1000	Unobligated balance brought forward, Oct 1	2	2	2
1930	Total budgetary resources available	2	2	2
	Memorandum (non-add) entries:			
1941	Unexpired unobligated balance, end of year	2	2	2
4180	Budget authority, net (total)			
4190	Outlays, net (total)			

This account funded U.S. assistance to Plan Colombia and follow-on activities from 2000 to 2010. These funds supported the Colombian Army's push into southern Colombia in support of the Colombian National Police, enhanced drug interdiction in Colombia and the region, provided for economic development in Colombia and the Andean region, and boosted Colombia's local and national government capacity. Since 2010, funds for these programs are requested and appropriated in the International Narcotics Control and Law Enforcement (INCLE) account.

DEMOCRACY FUND

For necessary expenses to carry out the provisions of the Foreign Assistance Act of 1961 for the promotion of democracy globally, including to carry out the purposes of section 502(b)(3) and (5) of Public Law 98–164 (22 U.S.C. 4411), $190,450,000, to remain available until September 30, 2024, which shall be made available for the Human Rights and Democracy Fund of the Bureau of Democracy, Human Rights, and Labor, Department of State: Provided, That funds appropriated under this heading that are made available to the National Endowment for Democracy and its core institutes are in addition to amounts otherwise available by this Act for such purposes.

For an additional amount for such purposes, $100,250,000, to remain available until September 30, 2024, which shall be made available for the Bureau for Development, Democracy, and Innovation, United States Agency for International Development.

Note.—A full-year 2022 appropriation for this account was not enacted at the time the Budget was prepared; therefore, the Budget assumes this account is operating under the Continuing Appropriations Act, 2022 (Division A of Public Law 117–43, as amended). The amounts included for 2022 reflect the annualized level provided by the continuing resolution.

Program and Financing (in millions of dollars)

Identification code 019–1121–0–1–151		2021 actual	2022 est.	2023 est.
	Obligations by program activity:			
0001	Democracy Fund (Direct)	277	290	290
0900	Total new obligations, unexpired accounts (object class 41.0)	277	290	290

DEPARTMENT OF STATE AND OTHER INTERNATIONAL PROGRAMS

Other—Continued
Federal Funds—Continued

823

		2021 actual	2022 est.	2023 est.
	Budgetary resources:			
	Unobligated balance:			
1000	Unobligated balance brought forward, Oct 1	274	290	291
1012	Unobligated balance transfers between expired and unexpired accounts	2		
1070	Unobligated balance (total)	276	290	291
	Budget authority:			
	Appropriations, discretionary:			
1100	Appropriation	291	291	291
1930	Total budgetary resources available	567	581	582
	Memorandum (non-add) entries:			
1941	Unexpired unobligated balance, end of year	290	291	292
	Change in obligated balance:			
	Unpaid obligations:			
3000	Unpaid obligations, brought forward, Oct 1	403	491	420
3010	New obligations, unexpired accounts	277	290	290
3011	Obligations ("upward adjustments"), expired accounts	2		
3020	Outlays (gross)	−182	−361	−362
3041	Recoveries of prior year unpaid obligations, expired	−9		
3050	Unpaid obligations, end of year	491	420	348
	Memorandum (non-add) entries:			
3100	Obligated balance, start of year	403	491	420
3200	Obligated balance, end of year	491	420	348
	Budget authority and outlays, net:			
	Discretionary:			
4000	Budget authority, gross	291	291	291
	Outlays, gross:			
4010	Outlays from new discretionary authority		96	96
4011	Outlays from discretionary balances	182	265	266
4020	Outlays, gross (total)	182	361	362
4180	Budget authority, net (total)	291	291	291
4190	Outlays, net (total)	182	361	362

This appropriation funds some democracy promotion activities of the Department of State and the U.S. Agency for International Development.

THE ASIA FOUNDATION

For a grant to The Asia Foundation, as authorized by The Asia Foundation Act (22 U.S.C. 4402), $20,000,000, to remain available until expended.

Note.—A full-year 2022 appropriation for this account was not enacted at the time the Budget was prepared; therefore, the Budget assumes this account is operating under the Continuing Appropriations Act, 2022 (Division A of Public Law 117–43, as amended). The amounts included for 2022 reflect the annualized level provided by the continuing resolution.

Program and Financing (in millions of dollars)

Identification code 019–0525–0–1–154		2021 actual	2022 est.	2023 est.
	Obligations by program activity:			
0001	Payment to the Asia Foundation (Direct)	20	20	20
0900	Total new obligations, unexpired accounts (object class 41.0)	20	20	20
	Budgetary resources:			
	Budget authority:			
	Appropriations, discretionary:			
1100	Appropriation	20	20	20
1930	Total budgetary resources available	20	20	20
	Change in obligated balance:			
	Unpaid obligations:			
3000	Unpaid obligations, brought forward, Oct 1	7	9	
3010	New obligations, unexpired accounts	20	20	20
3020	Outlays (gross)	−18	−29	−20
3050	Unpaid obligations, end of year	9		
	Memorandum (non-add) entries:			
3100	Obligated balance, start of year	7	9	
3200	Obligated balance, end of year	9		
	Budget authority and outlays, net:			
	Discretionary:			
4000	Budget authority, gross	20	20	20
	Outlays, gross:			
4010	Outlays from new discretionary authority	11	20	20
4011	Outlays from discretionary balances	7	9	
4020	Outlays, gross (total)	18	29	20
4180	Budget authority, net (total)	20	20	20
4190	Outlays, net (total)	18	29	20

The Asia Foundation (TAF) is a private, nonprofit organization incorporated and headquartered in California. TAF operates programs through 18 country offices to support democratic initiatives, governance and economic reform, rule of law, women's empowerment programs, environment and climate action, and closer U.S.-Asian relations and provides grants to institutions in Asia.

NATIONAL ENDOWMENT FOR DEMOCRACY

For grants made by the Department of State to the National Endowment for Democracy, as authorized by the National Endowment for Democracy Act (22 U.S.C. 4412), $300,000,000, to remain available until expended.

Note.—A full-year 2022 appropriation for this account was not enacted at the time the Budget was prepared; therefore, the Budget assumes this account is operating under the Continuing Appropriations Act, 2022 (Division A of Public Law 117–43, as amended). The amounts included for 2022 reflect the annualized level provided by the continuing resolution.

Program and Financing (in millions of dollars)

Identification code 019–0210–0–1–154		2021 actual	2022 est.	2023 est.
	Obligations by program activity:			
0001	National Endowment for Democracy (Direct)	300	300	300
0900	Total new obligations, unexpired accounts (object class 41.0)	300	300	300
	Budgetary resources:			
	Unobligated balance:			
1000	Unobligated balance brought forward, Oct 1	1	1	1
	Budget authority:			
	Appropriations, discretionary:			
1100	Appropriation	300	300	300
1930	Total budgetary resources available	301	301	301
	Memorandum (non-add) entries:			
1941	Unexpired unobligated balance, end of year	1	1	1
	Change in obligated balance:			
	Unpaid obligations:			
3000	Unpaid obligations, brought forward, Oct 1	249	296	224
3010	New obligations, unexpired accounts	300	300	300
3020	Outlays (gross)	−253	−372	−416
3050	Unpaid obligations, end of year	296	224	108
	Memorandum (non-add) entries:			
3100	Obligated balance, start of year	249	296	224
3200	Obligated balance, end of year	296	224	108
	Budget authority and outlays, net:			
	Discretionary:			
4000	Budget authority, gross	300	300	300
	Outlays, gross:			
4010	Outlays from new discretionary authority	88	207	207
4011	Outlays from discretionary balances	165	165	209
4020	Outlays, gross (total)	253	372	416
4180	Budget authority, net (total)	300	300	300
4190	Outlays, net (total)	253	372	416

The National Endowment for Democracy (NED) is a private, nonprofit corporation established in Washington, D.C. to encourage and strengthen the development of democratic institutions and processes internationally. NED supports democratic initiatives in six regions of the world: Africa, Asia, Central and Eastern Europe, Latin America, the Middle East, and Eurasia.

The National Endowment for Democracy Act (Public Law 98–164), as amended, provides for an annual grant to the Endowment to fulfill the purposes of the Act.

EAST-WEST CENTER

To enable the Secretary of State to provide for carrying out the provisions of the Center for Cultural and Technical Interchange Between East and West Act of 1960,

EAST-WEST CENTER—Continued

by grant to the Center for Cultural and Technical Interchange Between East and West in the State of Hawaii, $19,700,000.

Note.—A full-year 2022 appropriation for this account was not enacted at the time the Budget was prepared; therefore, the Budget assumes this account is operating under the Continuing Appropriations Act, 2022 (Division A of Public Law 117–43, as amended). The amounts included for 2022 reflect the annualized level provided by the continuing resolution.

Program and Financing (in millions of dollars)

Identification code 019–0202–0–1–154		2021 actual	2022 est.	2023 est.
	Obligations by program activity:			
0001	East-West Center (Direct)	20	20	20
0900	Total new obligations, unexpired accounts (object class 41.0)	20	20	20
	Budgetary resources:			
	Budget authority:			
	Appropriations, discretionary:			
1100	Appropriation	20	20	20
1930	Total budgetary resources available	20	20	20
	Change in obligated balance:			
	Unpaid obligations:			
3000	Unpaid obligations, brought forward, Oct 1	2	5	
3010	New obligations, unexpired accounts	20	20	20
3020	Outlays (gross)	–17	–25	–20
3050	Unpaid obligations, end of year	5		
	Memorandum (non-add) entries:			
3100	Obligated balance, start of year	2	5	
3200	Obligated balance, end of year	5		
	Budget authority and outlays, net:			
	Discretionary:			
4000	Budget authority, gross	20	20	20
	Outlays, gross:			
4010	Outlays from new discretionary authority	16	20	20
4011	Outlays from discretionary balances	1	5	
4020	Outlays, gross (total)	17	25	20
4180	Budget authority, net (total)	20	20	20
4190	Outlays, net (total)	17	25	20

The Center for Cultural and Technical Interchange Between East and West (East-West Center) is an educational institution administered by a public, nonprofit educational corporation. The East-West Center promotes U.S. foreign policy interests and people-to-people engagement in the Asia Pacific region through cooperative research, education, and dialogue on critical issues of common interest.

INTERNATIONAL LITIGATION FUND

Special and Trust Fund Receipts (in millions of dollars)

Identification code 019–5177–0–2–153		2021 actual	2022 est.	2023 est.
0100	Balance, start of year			1
	Receipts:			
	Current law:			
1140	Proprietary Receipts, International Litigation Fund		1	1
1140	Federal Payments, International Litigation Fund	4	1	1
1199	Total current law receipts	4	2	2
1999	Total receipts	4	2	2
2000	Total: Balances and receipts	4	2	3
	Appropriations:			
	Current law:			
2101	International Litigation Fund	–4	–1	–1
5099	Balance, end of year		1	2

Program and Financing (in millions of dollars)

Identification code 019–5177–0–2–153		2021 actual	2022 est.	2023 est.
	Obligations by program activity:			
0001	International Litigation Fund	4	4	4
0100	Direct program activities, subtotal	4	4	4
0801	International Litigation Fund		1	1
0809	Reimbursable program activities, subtotal		1	1
0900	Total new obligations, unexpired accounts (object class 25.2)	4	5	5
	Budgetary resources:			
	Unobligated balance:			
1000	Unobligated balance brought forward, Oct 1	12	14	10
1021	Recoveries of prior year unpaid obligations	2		
1070	Unobligated balance (total)	14	14	10
	Budget authority:			
	Appropriations, mandatory:			
1201	Appropriation (special or trust fund)	4	1	1
1900	Budget authority (total)	4	1	1
1930	Total budgetary resources available	18	15	11
	Memorandum (non-add) entries:			
1941	Unexpired unobligated balance, end of year	14	10	6
	Change in obligated balance:			
	Unpaid obligations:			
3000	Unpaid obligations, brought forward, Oct 1	6	4	5
3010	New obligations, unexpired accounts	4	5	5
3020	Outlays (gross)	–4	–4	–2
3040	Recoveries of prior year unpaid obligations, unexpired	–2		
3050	Unpaid obligations, end of year	4	5	8
	Memorandum (non-add) entries:			
3100	Obligated balance, start of year	6	4	5
3200	Obligated balance, end of year	4	5	8
	Budget authority and outlays, net:			
	Mandatory:			
4090	Budget authority, gross	4	1	1
	Outlays, gross:			
4100	Outlays from new mandatory authority		1	1
4101	Outlays from mandatory balances	4	3	1
4110	Outlays, gross (total)	4	4	2
4180	Budget authority, net (total)	4	1	1
4190	Outlays, net (total)	4	4	2

The International Litigation Fund (ILF) is authorized by section 38(d) of the State Department Basic Authorities Act of 1956 (22 U.S.C. 2710(d)) to pay for expenses incurred by the Department of State relative to preparing or prosecuting a proceeding before an international tribunal or a claim by or against a foreign government or other foreign entity. Monies otherwise available for such purposes are authorized to be deposited in ILF. Funds received by the Department from other U.S. Government agencies or from private parties for these purposes are also deposited in ILF.

In addition, section 38(e) authorizes the Secretary to retain 1.5 percent of any amount between $100,000 and $5,000,000, and one percent of any amount over $5,000,000, received per claim under chapter 34 of the Act of February 1896 (22 U.S.C. 2668a; 29 Stat. 32).

INTERNATIONAL CENTER, WASHINGTON, DISTRICT OF COLUMBIA

Not to exceed $1,842,732 shall be derived from fees collected from other executive agencies for lease or use of facilities at the International Center in accordance with section 4 of the International Center Act (Public Law 90–553), and, in addition, as authorized by section 5 of such Act, $743,000, to be derived from the reserve authorized by such section, to be used for the purposes set out in that section.

Note.—A full-year 2022 appropriation for this account was not enacted at the time the Budget was prepared; therefore, the Budget assumes this account is operating under the Continuing Appropriations Act, 2022 (Division A of Public Law 117–43, as amended). The amounts included for 2022 reflect the annualized level provided by the continuing resolution.

Special and Trust Fund Receipts (in millions of dollars)

Identification code 019–5151–0–2–153		2021 actual	2022 est.	2023 est.
0100	Balance, start of year	16	13	11
	Receipts:			
	Current law:			
1130	International Center, Washington, D.C., Sale and Rent of Real Property		1	1
2000	Total: Balances and receipts	16	14	12

DEPARTMENT OF STATE AND OTHER INTERNATIONAL PROGRAMS

		2021 actual	2022 est.	2023 est.
	Appropriations: Current law:			
2101	International Center, Washington, D.C.	–3	–3	–1
5099	Balance, end of year	13	11	11

Program and Financing (in millions of dollars)

Identification code 019–5151–0–2–153		2021 actual	2022 est.	2023 est.
	Obligations by program activity:			
0001	International Center, Washington, D.C. (Direct)	2	3	1
0801	International Center, Washington, D.C. (Reimbursable)	2	2	2
0900	Total new obligations, unexpired accounts	4	5	3
	Budgetary resources: Unobligated balance:			
1000	Unobligated balance brought forward, Oct 1	4	5	5
	Budget authority: Appropriations, discretionary:			
1101	Appropriation (special or trust)	3	3	1
	Spending authority from offsetting collections, discretionary:			
1700	Collected	2	2	2
1900	Budget authority (total)	5	5	3
1930	Total budgetary resources available	9	10	8
	Memorandum (non-add) entries:			
1941	Unexpired unobligated balance, end of year	5	5	5
	Change in obligated balance: Unpaid obligations:			
3000	Unpaid obligations, brought forward, Oct 1	1	2	....
3010	New obligations, unexpired accounts	4	5	3
3020	Outlays (gross)	–3	–7	–3
3050	Unpaid obligations, end of year	2	....	....
	Memorandum (non-add) entries:			
3100	Obligated balance, start of year	1	2	....
3200	Obligated balance, end of year	2	....	....
	Budget authority and outlays, net: Discretionary:			
4000	Budget authority, gross	5	5	3
	Outlays, gross:			
4010	Outlays from new discretionary authority	1	5	3
4011	Outlays from discretionary balances	2	2	....
4020	Outlays, gross (total)	3	7	3
	Offsets against gross budget authority and outlays: Offsetting collections (collected) from:			
4030	Federal sources	–2	–2	–2
4180	Budget authority, net (total)	3	3	1
4190	Outlays, net (total)	1	5	1
	Memorandum (non-add) entries:			
5000	Total investments, SOY: Federal securities: Par value	12	12	12
5001	Total investments, EOY: Federal securities: Par value	12	12	12

These funds provide for the development, lease, or exchange of property owned by the United States at the International Center located in Washington, D.C. to foreign governments or international organizations. Funds also provide for operation of the Federal facility located at the International Center, for maintenance and security of those public improvements that have not been conveyed to a government or international organization, and for surveys and plans related to development of additional areas within the Nation's Capital for chancery and diplomatic purposes.

Object Classification (in millions of dollars)

Identification code 019–5151–0–2–153		2021 actual	2022 est.	2023 est.
32.0	Direct obligations: Land and structures	2	3	1
99.0	Reimbursable obligations	2	2	2
99.9	Total new obligations, unexpired accounts	4	5	3

FISHERMEN'S PROTECTIVE FUND

Program and Financing (in millions of dollars)

Identification code 019–5116–0–2–376		2021 actual	2022 est.	2023 est.
	Budgetary resources: Unobligated balance:			
1000	Unobligated balance brought forward, Oct 1	1	1	1
1930	Total budgetary resources available	1	1	1
	Memorandum (non-add) entries:			
1941	Unexpired unobligated balance, end of year	1	1	1
4180	Budget authority, net (total)	....	....	....
4190	Outlays, net (total)	....	....	....

The Fishermen's Protective Fund provides for reimbursement to owners of vessels for amounts of fines, fees, and other direct charges that were paid by owners to a foreign country to secure the release of their vessels and crews and for other specified charges. No new budget authority is requested in FY 2023.

FISHERMEN'S GUARANTY FUND

Program and Financing (in millions of dollars)

Identification code 019–5121–0–2–376		2021 actual	2022 est.	2023 est.
	Budgetary resources: Unobligated balance:			
1000	Unobligated balance brought forward, Oct 1	3	3	3
1930	Total budgetary resources available	3	3	3
	Memorandum (non-add) entries:			
1941	Unexpired unobligated balance, end of year	3	3	3
4180	Budget authority, net (total)	....	....	....
4190	Outlays, net (total)	....	....	....

This fund provides for payment to vessel owners to compensate for certain financial losses sustained as a result of foreign seizures of U.S. commercial fishing vessels on the basis of claims to jurisdiction not recognized by the United States. No new budget authority is requested for FY 2023.

Trust Funds

EISENHOWER EXCHANGE FELLOWSHIP PROGRAM

For necessary expenses of Eisenhower Exchange Fellowships, Incorporated, as authorized by sections 4 and 5 of the Eisenhower Exchange Fellowship Act of 1990 (20 U.S.C. 5204–5205), all interest and earnings accruing to the Eisenhower Exchange Fellowship Program Trust Fund on or before September 30, 2023, to remain available until expended: Provided, That none of the funds appropriated herein shall be used to pay any salary or other compensation, or to enter into any contract providing for the payment thereof, in excess of the rate authorized by section 5376 of title 5, United States Code; or for purposes which are not in accordance with section 200 of title 2 of the Code of Federal Regulations, including the restrictions on compensation for personal services.

ISRAELI ARAB SCHOLARSHIP PROGRAM

For necessary expenses of the Israeli Arab Scholarship Program, as authorized by section 214 of the Foreign Relations Authorization Act, Fiscal Years 1992 and 1993 (22 U.S.C. 2452 note), all interest and earnings accruing to the Israeli Arab Scholarship Fund on or before September 30, 2023, to remain available until expended.

Note.—A full-year 2022 appropriation for this account was not enacted at the time the Budget was prepared; therefore, the Budget assumes this account is operating under the Continuing Appropriations Act, 2022 (Division A of Public Law 117–43, as amended). The amounts included for 2022 reflect the annualized level provided by the continuing resolution.

Special and Trust Fund Receipts (in millions of dollars)

Identification code 570–8276–0–7–154		2021 actual	2022 est.	2023 est.
0100	Balance, start of year	13	12	12
2000	Total: Balances and receipts	13	12	12

ISRAELI ARAB AND EISENHOWER EXCHANGE FELLOWSHIP PROGRAMS—Continued

Special and Trust Fund Receipts—Continued

Identification code 570–8276–0–7–154	2021 actual	2022 est.	2023 est.
Appropriations:			
Current law:			
2101 Israeli Arab and Eisenhower Exchange Fellowship Programs	–1		
5099 Balance, end of year	12	12	12

Program and Financing (in millions of dollars)

Identification code 570–8276–0–7–154	2021 actual	2022 est.	2023 est.
Budgetary resources:			
Unobligated balance:			
1000 Unobligated balance brought forward, Oct 1	1	2	2
Budget authority:			
Appropriations, discretionary:			
1101 Appropriation (special or trust)	1		
1930 Total budgetary resources available	2	2	2
Memorandum (non-add) entries:			
1941 Unexpired unobligated balance, end of year	2	2	2
Budget authority and outlays, net:			
Discretionary:			
4000 Budget authority, gross	1		
4180 Budget authority, net (total)	1		
4190 Outlays, net (total)			
Memorandum (non-add) entries:			
5000 Total investments, SOY: Federal securities: Par value	12	9	9
5001 Total investments, EOY: Federal securities: Par value	9	9	9

The Eisenhower Exchange Fellowship Trust Fund (EEF Trust Fund) was created in 1992 with an appropriation of $5,000,000. In 1995, an additional payment of $2,500,000 was made to the EEF Trust Fund. This exchange program honors the late president and increases educational opportunities for young leaders in preparation for and enhancement of their professional careers and advancement of peace through international understanding.

The Israeli Arab Scholarship Trust Fund was created in 1992 with an appropriation of $4,978,500 to provide scholarships for Israeli Arab students to attend institutions of higher learning in the United States.

CENTER FOR MIDDLE EASTERN-WESTERN DIALOGUE TRUST FUND

For necessary expenses of the Center for Middle Eastern-Western Dialogue Trust Fund, as authorized by section 633 of the Departments of Commerce, Justice, and State, the Judiciary, and Related Agencies Appropriations Act, 2004 (22 U.S.C. 2078), the total amount of the interest and earnings accruing to such Fund on or before September 30, 2023, to remain available until expended.

Note.—A full-year 2022 appropriation for this account was not enacted at the time the Budget was prepared; therefore, the Budget assumes this account is operating under the Continuing Appropriations Act, 2022 (Division A of Public Law 117–43, as amended). The amounts included for 2022 reflect the annualized level provided by the continuing resolution.

Program and Financing (in millions of dollars)

Identification code 019–8813–0–7–153	2021 actual	2022 est.	2023 est.
Obligations by program activity:			
0001 Center for Middle Eastern-Western Dialogue Trust Fund (Direct)	1	1	1
0900 Total new obligations, unexpired accounts (object class 25.2)	1	1	1
Budgetary resources:			
Unobligated balance:			
1000 Unobligated balance brought forward, Oct 1	12	11	10
1930 Total budgetary resources available	12	11	10
Memorandum (non-add) entries:			
1941 Unexpired unobligated balance, end of year	11	10	9
Change in obligated balance:			
Unpaid obligations:			
3000 Unpaid obligations, brought forward, Oct 1	2	2	2
3010 New obligations, unexpired accounts	1	1	1
3020 Outlays (gross)	–1	–1	–1
3050 Unpaid obligations, end of year	2	2	2
Memorandum (non-add) entries:			
3100 Obligated balance, start of year	2	2	2
3200 Obligated balance, end of year	2	2	2
Budget authority and outlays, net:			
Discretionary:			
Outlays, gross:			
4011 Outlays from discretionary balances	1	1	1
4180 Budget authority, net (total)			
4190 Outlays, net (total)	1	1	1
Memorandum (non-add) entries:			
5000 Total investments, SOY: Federal securities: Par value	11	11	11
5001 Total investments, EOY: Federal securities: Par value	11	11	11

The International Center for Middle Eastern-Western Dialogue (Hollings Center) was created in 2004 to promote dialogue and cross-cultural understanding between the United States and nations of the Middle East, Turkey, Central and North Africa, Southwest and Southeast Asia and other countries with predominantly Muslim populations. The Hollings Center may use the trust fund principal and accrued interest and earnings to support annual operations.

GENERAL FUND RECEIPT ACCOUNTS

(in millions of dollars)

	2021 actual	2022 est.	2023 est.
Governmental receipts:			
020–083000 Immigration, Passport, and Consular Fees	497	552	552
General Fund Governmental receipts	497	552	552
Offsetting receipts from the public:			
019–143500 General Fund Proprietary Interest Receipts, not Otherwise Classified	3	3	3
019–277630 Repatriation Loans, Downward Reestimate of Subsidies	1	3	
019–322000 All Other General Fund Proprietary Receipts Including Budget Clearing Accounts	5	5	5
General Fund Offsetting receipts from the public	9	11	8
Intragovernmental payments:			
019–388500 Undistributed Intragovernmental Payments and Receivables from Cancelled Accounts	174	174	174
General Fund Intragovernmental payments	174	174	174

MILLENNIUM CHALLENGE CORPORATION

Federal Funds

MILLENNIUM CHALLENGE CORPORATION

For necessary expenses to carry out the provisions of the Millennium Challenge Act of 2003 (22 U.S.C. 7701 et seq.) (MCA), $930,000,000, to remain available until expended: Provided, That of the funds appropriated under this heading, up to $130,000,000 may be available for administrative expenses of the Millennium Challenge Corporation: Provided further, That section 605(e) of the MCA (22 U.S.C. 7704(e)) shall apply to funds appropriated under this heading: Provided further, That funds appropriated under this heading may be made available for a Millennium Challenge Compact entered into pursuant to section 609 of the MCA (22 U.S.C. 7708) only if such Compact obligates, or contains a commitment to obligate subject to the availability of funds and the mutual agreement of the parties to the Compact to proceed, the entire amount of the United States Government funding anticipated for the duration of the Compact: Provided further, That of the funds appropriated under this heading, not to exceed $100,000 may be available for representation and entertainment expenses, of which not to exceed $5,000 may be available for entertainment expenses.

Note.—A full-year 2022 appropriation for this account was not enacted at the time the Budget was prepared; therefore, the Budget assumes this account is operating under the Continuing Appropriations Act, 2022 (Division A of Public Law 117–43, as amended). The amounts included for 2022 reflect the annualized level provided by the continuing resolution.

DEPARTMENT OF STATE AND OTHER INTERNATIONAL PROGRAMS

International Security Assistance—Federal Funds — 827

Program and Financing (in millions of dollars)

Identification code 524–2750–0–1–151	2021 actual	2022 est.	2023 est.
Obligations by program activity:			
0001 Compact Assistance	858	1,119	76
0002 Threshold Programs	34	105	25
0003 Due Diligence	73	82	85
0004 Compact Development Funding	13	54	28
0005 Administrative Expenses	115	125	130
0006 USAID Inspector General	4	5	5
0799 Total direct obligations	1,097	1,490	349
0801 Reimbursable program activity		2	2
0900 Total new obligations, unexpired accounts	1,097	1,492	351
Budgetary resources:			
Unobligated balance:			
1000 Unobligated balance brought forward, Oct 1	3,593	3,461	2,891
1021 Recoveries of prior year unpaid obligations	49	10	10
1070 Unobligated balance (total)	3,642	3,471	2,901
Budget authority:			
Appropriations, discretionary:			
1100 Appropriation	912	912	930
Spending authority from offsetting collections, discretionary:			
1700 Collected	4		
1900 Budget authority (total)	916	912	930
1930 Total budgetary resources available	4,558	4,383	3,831
Memorandum (non-add) entries:			
1941 Unexpired unobligated balance, end of year	3,461	2,891	3,480
Change in obligated balance:			
Unpaid obligations:			
3000 Unpaid obligations, brought forward, Oct 1	2,182	2,502	3,219
3010 New obligations, unexpired accounts	1,097	1,492	351
3020 Outlays (gross)	–728	–765	–931
3040 Recoveries of prior year unpaid obligations, unexpired	–49	–10	–10
3050 Unpaid obligations, end of year	2,502	3,219	2,629
Memorandum (non-add) entries:			
3100 Obligated balance, start of year	2,182	2,502	3,219
3200 Obligated balance, end of year	2,502	3,219	2,629
Budget authority and outlays, net:			
Discretionary:			
4000 Budget authority, gross	916	912	930
Outlays, gross:			
4010 Outlays from new discretionary authority	86	120	132
4011 Outlays from discretionary balances	642	645	799
4020 Outlays, gross (total)	728	765	931
Offsets against gross budget authority and outlays:			
Offsetting collections (collected) from:			
4030 Federal sources	–4		
4040 Offsets against gross budget authority and outlays (total)	–4		
4180 Budget authority, net (total)	912	912	930
4190 Outlays, net (total)	724	765	931

Established by the Millennium Challenge Act of 2003, the Millennium Challenge Corporation (MCC) partners with low and low-middle income countries to reduce poverty through economic growth. MCC provides large grants to developing countries that meet rigorous standards for good governance, from fighting corruption to respecting democratic rights, as evaluated by MCCs scorecard. MCC takes a business-like approach, with bedrock commitments to data, accountability, and evidence-based decision making. Since its inception, MCC has signed 38 compacts and 30 threshold program agreements, totaling an investment of $13.9 billion dollars. In addition to providing large grants, MCC works with countries to advance policy and institutional reforms to create the enabling conditions for private sector-led growth. MCC's evidence-based approach leads to compacts that drive partner country ownership, including financial accountability and transparent and fair procurement practices, and measurable development impact to ensure that MCC assistance is used responsibly and effectively. In FY 2023, MCC will build on its rigorous, evidence-based model and will focus on the strategic areas of climate change, inclusion and gender, and catalyzing private investment as well as sustainable infrastructure investments that are aligned with the Build Back Better World (B3W) initiative. Focusing on these priority areas will enable MCC to expand impact and further strengthen its ability to deliver on its mission to reduce poverty through sustainable and inclusive economic growth.

Object Classification (in millions of dollars)

Identification code 524–2750–0–1–151	2021 actual	2022 est.	2023 est.
Direct obligations:			
Personnel compensation:			
11.1 Full-time permanent	40	41	42
11.3 Other than full-time permanent	9	10	10
11.5 Other personnel compensation	1	1	1
11.9 Total personnel compensation	50	52	53
12.1 Civilian personnel benefits	18	18	19
21.0 Travel and transportation of persons	1	3	6
23.2 Rental payments to others	9	10	10
25.1 Advisory and assistance services	11	13	14
25.2 Other services from non-Federal sources	67	90	92
25.3 Other goods and services from Federal sources	13	18	19
25.5 Research and development contracts	14		
25.7 Operation and maintenance of equipment	3	3	3
26.0 Supplies and materials		1	1
31.0 Equipment	1	1	1
41.0 Country Program Assistance	905	1,278	129
41.0 Grants, subsidies, and contributions	5	3	2
99.0 Direct obligations	1,097	1,490	349
99.0 Reimbursable obligations		2	2
99.9 Total new obligations, unexpired accounts	1,097	1,492	351

Employment Summary

Identification code 524–2750–0–1–151	2021 actual	2022 est.	2023 est.
1001 Direct civilian full-time equivalent employment	315	320	324

INTERNATIONAL SECURITY ASSISTANCE

Federal Funds

ECONOMIC SUPPORT FUND

For necessary expenses to carry out the provisions of chapter 4 of part II of the Foreign Assistance Act of 1961, $4,122,463,000, to remain available until September 30, 2024.

Note.—A full-year 2022 appropriation for this account was not enacted at the time the Budget was prepared; therefore, the Budget assumes this account is operating under the Continuing Appropriations Act, 2022 (Division A of Public Law 117–43, as amended). The amounts included for 2022 reflect the annualized level provided by the continuing resolution.

Program and Financing (in millions of dollars)

Identification code 072–1037–0–1–152	2021 actual	2022 est.	2023 est.
Obligations by program activity:			
0001 Economic Support Fund (Direct)	9,940	7,147	6,100
0002 Transfer to DFC Program Account		50	50
0799 Total direct obligations	9,940	7,197	6,150
0801 Economic Support Fund (Reimbursable)	81	40	40
0900 Total new obligations, unexpired accounts	10,021	7,237	6,190
Budgetary resources:			
Unobligated balance:			
1000 Unobligated balance brought forward, Oct 1	2,574	6,913	2,118
1010 Unobligated balance transfer to other accts [019–0209]	–11		
1010 Unobligated balance transfer to other accts [077–0110]	–15		
1010 Unobligated balance transfer to other accts [020–0077]	–25		
1010 Unobligated balance transfer to other accts [020–0073]		–300	
1011 Unobligated balance transfer from other acct [019–1022]	27		
1011 Unobligated balance transfer from other acct [011–1082]	18		
1011 Unobligated balance transfer from other acct [011–1075]	15		
1012 Unobligated balance transfers between expired and unexpired accounts	9		
1021 Recoveries of prior year unpaid obligations	42		
1070 Unobligated balance (total)	2,634	6,613	2,118
Budget authority:			
Appropriations, discretionary:			
1100 Appropriation	3,152	3,152	4,122

828　International Security Assistance—Continued
Federal Funds—Continued

THE BUDGET FOR FISCAL YEAR 2023

ECONOMIC SUPPORT FUND—Continued

Program and Financing—Continued

Identification code 072–1037–0–1–152	2021 actual	2022 est.	2023 est.
1100　Appropriation-Emergency	700		
1120　Appropriations transferred to other accts [020–0077]	–25		
1120　Appropriations transferred to other acct [072–1027]	–30		
1120　Appropriations transferred to other acct [077–0110]		–50	–50
1120　Appropriations transferred to other acct [999–0007]		–285	
1121　Appropriations transferred from other acct [097–0100]	15		
1131　Unobligated balance of appropriations permanently reduced		–75	–75
1160　Appropriation, discretionary (total)	3,737	2,742	4,072
Appropriations, mandatory:			
1200　Appropriation - ARP Act	8,675		
Spending authority from offsetting collections, discretionary:			
1700　Collected	2,014		
1900　Budget authority (total)	14,426	2,742	4,072
1930　Total budgetary resources available	17,060	9,355	6,190
Memorandum (non-add) entries:			
1940　Unobligated balance expiring	–126		
1941　Unexpired unobligated balance, end of year	6,913	2,118	
Change in obligated balance:			
Unpaid obligations:			
3000　Unpaid obligations, brought forward, Oct 1	9,102	13,544	13,224
3010　New obligations, unexpired accounts	10,021	7,237	6,190
3011　Obligations ("upward adjustments"), expired accounts	61		
3020　Outlays (gross)	–5,552	–7,557	–6,350
3040　Recoveries of prior year unpaid obligations, unexpired	–42		
3041　Recoveries of prior year unpaid obligations, expired	–46		
3050　Unpaid obligations, end of year	13,544	13,224	13,064
Uncollected payments:			
3060　Uncollected pymts, Fed sources, brought forward, Oct 1	–4		
3071　Change in uncollected pymts, Fed sources, expired	4		
Memorandum (non-add) entries:			
3100　Obligated balance, start of year	9,098	13,544	13,224
3200　Obligated balance, end of year	13,544	13,224	13,064
Budget authority and outlays, net:			
Discretionary:			
4000　Budget authority, gross	5,751	2,742	4,072
Outlays, gross:			
4010　Outlays from new discretionary authority	625	182	291
4011　Outlays from discretionary balances	3,248	4,773	3,890
4020　Outlays, gross (total)	3,873	4,955	4,181
Offsets against gross budget authority and outlays:			
Offsetting collections (collected) from:			
4030　Federal sources	–2,025		
4033　Non-Federal sources	–35		
4040　Offsets against gross budget authority and outlays (total)	–2,060		
Additional offsets against gross budget authority only:			
4052　Offsetting collections credited to expired accounts	46		
4060　Additional offsets against budget authority only (total)	46		
4070　Budget authority, net (discretionary)	3,737	2,742	4,072
4080　Outlays, net (discretionary)	1,813	4,955	4,181
Mandatory:			
4090　Budget authority, gross	8,675		
Outlays, gross:			
4100　Outlays from new mandatory authority	1,679		
4101　Outlays from mandatory balances		2,602	2,169
4110　Outlays, gross (total)	1,679	2,602	2,169
4180　Budget authority, net (total)	12,412	2,742	4,072
4190　Outlays, net (total)	3,492	7,557	6,350

Programs funded through the Economic Support Fund (ESF) account help foster stable, resilient, prosperous, and inclusive countries of strategic importance to meet their near and long-term political, economic, and development needs. The 2023 Budget prioritizes and focuses resources in regions and on programs that strengthen ties with America's global allies and partners.

Object Classification (in millions of dollars)

Identification code 072–1037–0–1–152	2021 actual	2022 est.	2023 est.
Direct obligations:			
Personnel compensation:			
11.1　Full-time permanent	2	2	2
11.3　Other than full-time permanent	3	3	3
11.9　Total personnel compensation	5	5	5
12.1　Civilian personnel benefits	23	23	23
25.1　Advisory and assistance services	38	38	38
25.3　Other goods and services from Federal sources	2	2	2
41.0　Grants, subsidies, and contributions	9,872	7,129	6,082
99.0　Direct obligations	9,940	7,197	6,150
99.0　Reimbursable obligations	81	40	40
99.9　Total new obligations, unexpired accounts	10,021	7,237	6,190

Employment Summary

Identification code 072–1037–0–1–152	2021 actual	2022 est.	2023 est.
1001　Direct civilian full-time equivalent employment	35	35	35

CENTRAL AMERICA AND CARIBBEAN EMERGENCY DISASTER RECOVERY FUND

Program and Financing (in millions of dollars)

Identification code 072–1096–0–1–151	2021 actual	2022 est.	2023 est.
Budgetary resources:			
Unobligated balance:			
1000　Unobligated balance brought forward, Oct 1	5	5	5
1930　Total budgetary resources available	5	5	5
Memorandum (non-add) entries:			
1941　Unexpired unobligated balance, end of year	5	5	5
4180　Budget authority, net (total)			
4190　Outlays, net (total)			

FOREIGN MILITARY FINANCING PROGRAM

For necessary expenses for grants to enable the President to carry out the provisions of section 23 of the Arms Export Control Act (22 U.S.C. 2763), $6,057,049,000: Provided, That to expedite the provision of assistance to foreign countries and international organizations, the Secretary of State may use the funds appropriated under this heading to procure defense articles and services to enhance the capacity of foreign security forces: Provided further, That funds appropriated under this heading for assistance for Israel may be disbursed within 30 days of enactment of this Act: Provided further, That funds appropriated or otherwise made available under this heading shall be nonrepayable notwithstanding any requirement in section 23 of the Arms Export Control Act: Provided further, That funds made available under this heading shall be obligated upon apportionment in accordance with paragraph (5)(C) of section 1501(a) of title 31, United States Code.

None of the funds made available under this heading shall be available to finance the procurement of defense articles, defense services, or design and construction services that are not sold by the United States Government under the Arms Export Control Act unless the foreign country proposing to make such procurement has first signed an agreement with the United States Government specifying the conditions under which such procurement may be financed with such funds: Provided, That all country and funding level increases in allocations shall be submitted through the regular notification procedures of section 7015 of this Act: Provided further, That funds made available under this heading may be used, notwithstanding any other provision of law, for demining, the clearance of unexploded ordnance, and related activities, and may include activities implemented through nongovernmental and international organizations: Provided further, That countries for which Foreign Military Financing was justified in the congressional budget justification for the current fiscal year, or for which such funds could be made available under this Act, may utilize funds made available under this heading for procurement of defense articles, defense services, or design and construction services that are not sold by the United States Government under the Arms Export Control Act: Provided further, That funds appropriated under this heading shall be expended at the minimum rate necessary to make timely payment for defense articles and services: Provided further, That not more than $70,000,000 of the funds appropriated under this heading may

DEPARTMENT OF STATE AND OTHER INTERNATIONAL PROGRAMS

be obligated for necessary expenses, including the purchase of passenger motor vehicles for replacement only for use outside of the United States, for the general costs of administering military assistance and sales, except that this limitation may be exceeded only through the regular notification procedures of the Committees on Appropriations: Provided further, That of the funds made available under this heading for general costs of administering military assistance and sales, not to exceed $4,000 may be available for entertainment expenses and not to exceed $130,000 may be available for representation expenses: Provided further, That not more than $1,253,810,229 of funds realized pursuant to section 21(e)(1)(A) of the Arms Export Control Act (22 U.S.C. 2761(e)(1)(A)) may be obligated for expenses incurred by the Department of Defense during fiscal year 2022 pursuant to section 43(b) of the Arms Export Control Act (22 U.S.C. 2792(b)), except that this limitation may be exceeded only through the regular notification procedures of the Committees on Appropriations.

Note.—A full-year 2022 appropriation for this account was not enacted at the time the Budget was prepared; therefore, the Budget assumes this account is operating under the Continuing Appropriations Act, 2022 (Division A of Public Law 117–43, as amended). The amounts included for 2022 reflect the annualized level provided by the continuing resolution.

Program and Financing (in millions of dollars)

Identification code 011–1082–0–1–152		2021 actual	2022 est.	2023 est.
	Obligations by program activity:			
0001	Country grants	6,284	6,012	6,012
0009	Administrative Expenses	70	70	70
0192	Total Direct Obligations	6,354	6,082	6,082
0799	Total direct obligations	6,354	6,082	6,082
0900	Total new obligations, unexpired accounts (object class 41.0)	6,354	6,082	6,082
	Budgetary resources:			
	Unobligated balance:			
1000	Unobligated balance brought forward, Oct 1	1,663	1,647	1,716
1010	Unobligated balance transfer to other accts [072–1037]	–18		
1012	Unobligated balance transfers between expired and unexpired accounts	212		
1033	Recoveries of prior year paid obligations	1		
1070	Unobligated balance (total)	1,858	1,647	1,716
	Budget authority:			
	Appropriations, discretionary:			
1100	Appropriation	6,176	6,176	6,057
1131	Unobligated balance of appropriations permanently reduced	–25	–25	
1160	Appropriation, discretionary (total)	6,151	6,151	6,057
1900	Budget authority (total)	6,151	6,151	6,057
1930	Total budgetary resources available	8,009	7,798	7,773
	Memorandum (non-add) entries:			
1940	Unobligated balance expiring	–8		
1941	Unexpired unobligated balance, end of year	1,647	1,716	1,691
	Change in obligated balance:			
	Unpaid obligations:			
3000	Unpaid obligations, brought forward, Oct 1	5,244	6,407	4,853
3010	New obligations, unexpired accounts	6,354	6,082	6,082
3011	Obligations ("upward adjustments"), expired accounts	92		
3020	Outlays (gross)	–5,069	–7,636	–6,844
3041	Recoveries of prior year unpaid obligations, expired	–214		
3050	Unpaid obligations, end of year	6,407	4,853	4,091
	Memorandum (non-add) entries:			
3100	Obligated balance, start of year	5,244	6,407	4,853
3200	Obligated balance, end of year	6,407	4,853	4,091
	Budget authority and outlays, net:			
	Discretionary:			
4000	Budget authority, gross	6,151	6,151	6,057
	Outlays, gross:			
4010	Outlays from new discretionary authority	3,356	3,453	3,522
4011	Outlays from discretionary balances	1,713	4,183	3,322
4020	Outlays, gross (total)	5,069	7,636	6,844
	Offsets against gross budget authority and outlays:			
	Offsetting collections (collected) from:			
4030	Federal sources	–1		
4033	Non-Federal sources	–32		
4040	Offsets against gross budget authority and outlays (total)	–33		
	Additional offsets against gross budget authority only:			
4052	Offsetting collections credited to expired accounts	32		
4053	Recoveries of prior year paid obligations, unexpired accounts	1		
4060	Additional offsets against budget authority only (total)	33		
4070	Budget authority, net (discretionary)	6,151	6,151	6,057
4080	Outlays, net (discretionary)	5,036	7,636	6,844
4180	Budget authority, net (total)	6,151	6,151	6,057
4190	Outlays, net (total)	5,036	7,636	6,844

Foreign Military Financing (FMF) funds procure, via grant, loan, or guarantee, U.S. defense articles and services to help friendly and allied countries to defend themselves, contribute to regional and global stability, and contain transnational threats, including terrorism.

PAKISTAN COUNTERINSURGENCY CAPABILITY FUND

Program and Financing (in millions of dollars)

Identification code 011–1083–0–1–152		2021 actual	2022 est.	2023 est.
	Change in obligated balance:			
	Unpaid obligations:			
3000	Unpaid obligations, brought forward, Oct 1	4	4	3
3020	Outlays (gross)		–1	–1
3050	Unpaid obligations, end of year	4	3	2
	Memorandum (non-add) entries:			
3100	Obligated balance, start of year	4	4	3
3200	Obligated balance, end of year	4	3	2
	Budget authority and outlays, net:			
	Discretionary:			
	Outlays, gross:			
4011	Outlays from discretionary balances		1	1
4180	Budget authority, net (total)			
4190	Outlays, net (total)		1	1

The Pakistan Counterinsurgency Capability Fund (PCCF) was designed to build the counterinsurgency capabilities of Pakistan's security forces engaged in operations against militant extremists. Since FY 2012, these needs have been met through other accounts.

INTERNATIONAL MILITARY EDUCATION AND TRAINING

For necessary expenses to carry out the provisions of section 541 of the Foreign Assistance Act of 1961, $112,925,000, to remain available until September 30, 2024: Provided, That the civilian personnel for whom military education and training may be provided under this heading may include civilians who are not members of a government whose participation would contribute to improved civil-military relations, civilian control of the military, or respect for human rights: Provided further, That of the funds appropriated under this heading, up to $3,000,000 may remain available until expended to increase the participation of women in programs and activities funded under this heading: Provided further, That of the funds appropriated under this heading, not to exceed $50,000 may be available for entertainment expenses.

Note.—A full-year 2022 appropriation for this account was not enacted at the time the Budget was prepared; therefore, the Budget assumes this account is operating under the Continuing Appropriations Act, 2022 (Division A of Public Law 117–43, as amended). The amounts included for 2022 reflect the annualized level provided by the continuing resolution.

Program and Financing (in millions of dollars)

Identification code 011–1081–0–1–152		2021 actual	2022 est.	2023 est.
	Obligations by program activity:			
0001	International Military Education and Training (Direct)	123	105	105
0900	Total new obligations, unexpired accounts (object class 41.0)	123	105	105
	Budgetary resources:			
	Unobligated balance:			
1000	Unobligated balance brought forward, Oct 1	33	12	20
1012	Unobligated balance transfers between expired and unexpired accounts	12		
1021	Recoveries of prior year unpaid obligations	1		
1070	Unobligated balance (total)	46	12	20

INTERNATIONAL MILITARY EDUCATION AND TRAINING—Continued
Program and Financing—Continued

Identification code 011–1081–0–1–152		2021 actual	2022 est.	2023 est.
	Budget authority:			
	Appropriations, discretionary:			
1100	Appropriation	113	113	113
1900	Budget authority (total)	113	113	113
1930	Total budgetary resources available	159	125	133
	Memorandum (non-add) entries:			
1940	Unobligated balance expiring	–24		
1941	Unexpired unobligated balance, end of year	12	20	28
	Change in obligated balance:			
	Unpaid obligations:			
3000	Unpaid obligations, brought forward, Oct 1	125	143	98
3010	New obligations, unexpired accounts	123	105	105
3011	Obligations ("upward adjustments"), expired accounts	18		
3020	Outlays (gross)	–88	–150	–125
3040	Recoveries of prior year unpaid obligations, unexpired	–1		
3041	Recoveries of prior year unpaid obligations, expired	–34		
3050	Unpaid obligations, end of year	143	98	78
	Memorandum (non-add) entries:			
3100	Obligated balance, start of year	125	143	98
3200	Obligated balance, end of year	143	98	78
	Budget authority and outlays, net:			
	Discretionary:			
4000	Budget authority, gross	113	113	113
	Outlays, gross:			
4010	Outlays from new discretionary authority	27	45	45
4011	Outlays from discretionary balances	61	105	80
4020	Outlays, gross (total)	88	150	125
	Offsets against gross budget authority and outlays:			
	Offsetting collections (collected) from:			
4033	Non-Federal sources	–5		
4040	Offsets against gross budget authority and outlays (total)	–5		
	Additional offsets against gross budget authority only:			
4052	Offsetting collections credited to expired accounts	5		
4070	Budget authority, net (discretionary)	113	113	113
4080	Outlays, net (discretionary)	83	150	125
4180	Budget authority, net (total)	113	113	113
4190	Outlays, net (total)	83	150	125

International Military Education and Training (IMET) assistance provides grants for foreign military and civilian personnel to attend military education and training provided by the United States Government either at United States military schools or by trainers in country. In addition to helping these countries professionalize their militaries, this program also exposes foreign students to American democratic values, particularly respect for civilian control of the military and for internationally recognized standards of individual and human rights.

PEACEKEEPING OPERATIONS

For necessary expenses to carry out the provisions of section 551 of the Foreign Assistance Act of 1961, $463,559,000, of which $330,000,000 shall remain available until September 30, 2024: Provided, That funds appropriated under this heading may be used, notwithstanding section 660 of the Foreign Assistance Act of 1961, to provide assistance to enhance the capacity of foreign civilian security forces, including gendarmes, to participate in peacekeeping operations: Provided further, That of the funds appropriated under this heading, not less than $24,000,000 may be made available for a United States contribution to the Multinational Force and Observers mission in the Sinai: Provided further, That funds appropriated under this heading may be made available to pay assessed expenses of international peacekeeping activities in Somalia under the same terms and conditions, as applicable, as funds appropriated by this Act under the heading "Contributions for International Peacekeeping Activities".

Note.—A full-year 2022 appropriation for this account was not enacted at the time the Budget was prepared; therefore, the Budget assumes this account is operating under the Continuing Appropriations Act, 2022 (Division A of Public Law 117–43, as amended). The amounts included for 2022 reflect the annualized level provided by the continuing resolution.

Program and Financing (in millions of dollars)

Identification code 072–1032–0–1–152		2021 actual	2022 est.	2023 est.
	Obligations by program activity:			
0001	Peacekeeping Operations (Direct)	498	401	400
0900	Total new obligations, unexpired accounts (object class 41.0)	498	401	400
	Budgetary resources:			
	Unobligated balance:			
1000	Unobligated balance brought forward, Oct 1	269	215	215
1012	Unobligated balance transfers between expired and unexpired accounts	40		
1070	Unobligated balance (total)	309	215	215
	Budget authority:			
	Appropriations, discretionary:			
1100	Appropriation	441	441	464
1131	Unobligated balance of appropriations permanently reduced	–40	–40	
1160	Appropriation, discretionary (total)	401	401	464
	Spending authority from offsetting collections, discretionary:			
1700	Collected	3		
1900	Budget authority (total)	404	401	464
1930	Total budgetary resources available	713	616	679
	Memorandum (non-add) entries:			
1941	Unexpired unobligated balance, end of year	215	215	279
	Change in obligated balance:			
	Unpaid obligations:			
3000	Unpaid obligations, brought forward, Oct 1	360	356	264
3010	New obligations, unexpired accounts	498	401	400
3011	Obligations ("upward adjustments"), expired accounts	5		
3020	Outlays (gross)	–474	–493	–589
3041	Recoveries of prior year unpaid obligations, expired	–33		
3050	Unpaid obligations, end of year	356	264	75
	Memorandum (non-add) entries:			
3100	Obligated balance, start of year	360	356	264
3200	Obligated balance, end of year	356	264	75
	Budget authority and outlays, net:			
	Discretionary:			
4000	Budget authority, gross	404	401	464
	Outlays, gross:			
4010	Outlays from new discretionary authority	159	251	320
4011	Outlays from discretionary balances	315	242	269
4020	Outlays, gross (total)	474	493	589
	Offsets against gross budget authority and outlays:			
	Offsetting collections (collected) from:			
4030	Federal sources	–19		
4033	Non-Federal sources	–3		
4040	Offsets against gross budget authority and outlays (total)	–22		
	Additional offsets against gross budget authority only:			
4052	Offsetting collections credited to expired accounts	19		
4070	Budget authority, net (discretionary)	401	401	464
4080	Outlays, net (discretionary)	452	493	589
4180	Budget authority, net (total)	401	401	464
4190	Outlays, net (total)	452	493	589

This account funds U.S. assistance to international efforts to monitor and maintain peace around the world, and provides funds to other programs carried out in furtherance of the national security interests of the United States. In 2023, support is planned for programs in Africa, the Multinational Force and Observers Mission in the Sinai, the Global Peace Operations Initiative, the Global Defense Reform Program, the Trans-Sahara Counterterrorism Partnership, and other activities.

NONPROLIFERATION, ANTI-TERRORISM, DEMINING AND RELATED PROGRAMS

For necessary expenses for nonproliferation, anti-terrorism, demining and related programs and activities, $900,247,000, to remain available until September 30, 2024, to carry out the provisions of chapter 8 of part II of the Foreign Assistance Act of 1961 for anti-terrorism assistance, chapter 9 of part II of the Foreign Assistance Act of 1961, section 504 of the FREEDOM Support Act (22 U.S.C. 5854), section 23 of the Arms Export Control Act (22 U.S.C. 2763), or the Foreign Assistance Act of 1961 for demining activities, the clearance of unexploded ordnance, the

DEPARTMENT OF STATE AND OTHER INTERNATIONAL PROGRAMS

destruction of small arms, and related activities, notwithstanding any other provision of law, including activities implemented through nongovernmental and international organizations, and section 301 of the Foreign Assistance Act of 1961 for a United States contribution to the Comprehensive Nuclear Test Ban Treaty Preparatory Commission, notwithstanding section 1279E of the National Defense Authorization Act for Fiscal Year 2018 (Public Law 115–91), and for a voluntary contribution to the International Atomic Energy Agency (IAEA): Provided, That funds made available under this heading for the Nonproliferation and Disarmament Fund shall be made available, notwithstanding any other provision of law, to promote bilateral and multilateral activities relating to nonproliferation, disarmament, and weapons destruction, and shall remain available until expended: Provided further, That such funds may also be used for such countries other than the Independent States of the former Soviet Union and international organizations when it is in the national security interest of the United States to do so: Provided further, That funds made available for conventional weapons destruction programs, including demining and related activities, in addition to funds otherwise available for such purposes, may be used for administrative expenses related to the operation and management of such programs and activities: Provided further, That funds made available under this heading for Export Control and Related Border Security, Global Threat Reduction, and countering Weapons of Mass Destruction Terrorism shall be made available notwithstanding any other provision of law.

(CANCELLATION)

Of the unobligated balances available under the heading "Nonproliferation, Antiterrorism, Demining and Related Programs" from prior Acts making appropriations for the Department of State, foreign operations, and related programs, $40,000,000 are hereby permanently cancelled.

Note.—A full-year 2022 appropriation for this account was not enacted at the time the Budget was prepared; therefore, the Budget assumes this account is operating under the Continuing Appropriations Act, 2022 (Division A of Public Law 117–43, as amended). The amounts included for 2022 reflect the annualized level provided by the continuing resolution.

Program and Financing (in millions of dollars)

Identification code 011–1075–0–1–152	2021 actual	2022 est.	2023 est.
Obligations by program activity:			
0001 Nonproliferation, Antiterrorism, Demining, and Related Programs (Direct)	963	920	920
0801 Nonproliferation, Antiterrorism, Demining, and Related Programs (Reimbursable)	48	30	30
0900 Total new obligations, unexpired accounts	1,011	950	950
Budgetary resources:			
Unobligated balance:			
1000 Unobligated balance brought forward, Oct 1	972	967	936
1010 Unobligated balance transfer to other accts [072–1037]	–15		
1012 Unobligated balance transfers between expired and unexpired accounts	105		
1021 Recoveries of prior year unpaid obligations	2		
1033 Recoveries of prior year paid obligations	2		
1070 Unobligated balance (total)	1,066	967	936
Budget authority:			
Appropriations, discretionary:			
1100 Appropriation	889	889	900
1131 Unobligated balance of appropriations permanently reduced			–40
1160 Appropriation, discretionary (total)	889	889	860
Spending authority from offsetting collections, discretionary:			
1700 Collected	48	30	30
1900 Budget authority (total)	937	919	890
1930 Total budgetary resources available	2,003	1,886	1,826
Memorandum (non-add) entries:			
1940 Unobligated balance expiring	–25		
1941 Unexpired unobligated balance, end of year	967	936	876
Change in obligated balance:			
Unpaid obligations:			
3000 Unpaid obligations, brought forward, Oct 1	1,165	1,286	1,204
3010 New obligations, unexpired accounts	1,011	950	950
3011 Obligations ("upward adjustments"), expired accounts	7		
3020 Outlays (gross)	–815	–1,032	–1,051
3040 Recoveries of prior year unpaid obligations, unexpired	–2		
3041 Recoveries of prior year unpaid obligations, expired	–80		
3050 Unpaid obligations, end of year	1,286	1,204	1,103
Memorandum (non-add) entries:			
3100 Obligated balance, start of year	1,165	1,286	1,204
3200 Obligated balance, end of year	1,286	1,204	1,103

		2021 actual	2022 est.	2023 est.
Budget authority and outlays, net:				
Discretionary:				
4000	Budget authority, gross	937	919	890
Outlays, gross:				
4010	Outlays from new discretionary authority	139	386	390
4011	Outlays from discretionary balances	676	646	661
4020	Outlays, gross (total)	815	1,032	1,051
Offsets against gross budget authority and outlays:				
Offsetting collections (collected) from:				
4030	Federal sources	–38	–30	–30
4033	Non-Federal sources	–17		
4040	Offsets against gross budget authority and outlays (total)	–55	–30	–30
Additional offsets against gross budget authority only:				
4052	Offsetting collections credited to expired accounts	5		
4053	Recoveries of prior year paid obligations, unexpired accounts	2		
4060	Additional offsets against budget authority only (total)	7		
4070	Budget authority, net (discretionary)	889	889	860
4080	Outlays, net (discretionary)	760	1,002	1,021
4180	Budget authority, net (total)	889	889	860
4190	Outlays, net (total)	760	1,002	1,021

This account provides assistance for nonproliferation, demining, antiterrorism, export control assistance, and other related activities. It also funds contributions to certain organizations supporting nonproliferation activities. In addition, notwithstanding authorities are requested for funds made available for the United States contribution to the Comprehensive Nuclear Test Ban Treaty Preparatory Commission, Export Control and Related Border Security, Global Threat Reduction, and countering Weapons of Mass Destruction Terrorism programs.

Object Classification (in millions of dollars)

Identification code 011–1075–0–1–152	2021 actual	2022 est.	2023 est.
Direct obligations:			
21.0 Travel and transportation of persons	15	15	15
25.2 Other services from non-Federal sources	375	375	375
31.0 Equipment	150	150	150
41.0 Grants, subsidies, and contributions	423	380	380
99.0 Direct obligations	963	920	920
99.0 Reimbursable obligations	48	30	30
99.9 Total new obligations, unexpired accounts	1,011	950	950

GLOBAL SECURITY CONTINGENCY FUND

Program and Financing (in millions of dollars)

Identification code 011–1041–0–1–152	2021 actual	2022 est.	2023 est.
Obligations by program activity:			
0001 Global Security Contingency Fund (Direct)	3	7	7
0900 Total new obligations, unexpired accounts (object class 41.0)	3	7	7
Budgetary resources:			
Unobligated balance:			
1000 Unobligated balance brought forward, Oct 1	29	26	19
1930 Total budgetary resources available	29	26	19
Memorandum (non-add) entries:			
1941 Unexpired unobligated balance, end of year	26	19	12
Change in obligated balance:			
Unpaid obligations:			
3000 Unpaid obligations, brought forward, Oct 1	7	6	10
3010 New obligations, unexpired accounts	3	7	7
3020 Outlays (gross)	–4	–3	–3
3050 Unpaid obligations, end of year	6	10	14
Memorandum (non-add) entries:			
3100 Obligated balance, start of year	7	6	10
3200 Obligated balance, end of year	6	10	14

GLOBAL SECURITY CONTINGENCY FUND—Continued
Program and Financing—Continued

Identification code 011–1041–0–1–152	2021 actual	2022 est.	2023 est.
Budget authority and outlays, net:			
Discretionary:			
Outlays, gross:			
4011 Outlays from discretionary balances	4	3	3
4180 Budget authority, net (total)	....	....	....
4190 Outlays, net (total)	4	3	3

The Global Security Contingency Fund (GSCF) permits the Department of State and the Department of Defense to combine resources and expertise to address emergent challenges and opportunities. The GSCF can be used to provide military and other security sector assistance to enhance a country's national-level military or other security forces' capabilities to conduct border and maritime security, internal defense, and counterterrorism operations, or to participate in or support military, stability, or peace support operations, consistent with U.S. foreign policy and national security interests. The GSCF can also be used to provide assistance to the justice sector (including law enforcement and prisons), rule of law programs, and stabilization efforts in cases where civilian providers are challenged in their ability to operate. Assistance programs under this account are collaboratively developed by the Department of State and the Department of Defense. The fund allows direct contributions from each Department to be transferred into the fund for implementation by the most appropriate agency in a given situation, be it State, Defense, the U.S. Agency for International Development, or others. No direct funding is requested in 2023.

FOREIGN MILITARY FINANCING LOAN PROGRAM ACCOUNT
Summary of Loan Levels, Subsidy Budget Authority and Outlays by Program (in millions of dollars)

Identification code 011–1085–0–1–152	2021 actual	2022 est.	2023 est.
Direct loan levels supportable by subsidy budget authority:			
115001 FMF Direct Loan Program	....	4,000	4,000
Direct loan subsidy (in percent):			
132001 FMF Direct Loan Program	....	0.00	0.00
Direct loan reestimates:			
135001 FMF Direct Loan Program	–607	–184	....
Guaranteed loan levels supportable by subsidy budget authority:			
215001 FMF Guaranteed Loan Program	....	4,000	4,000
Guaranteed loan subsidy (in percent):			
232001 FMF Guaranteed Loan Program	....	0.00	0.00

Foreign Military Financing (FMF) direct and guaranteed loans finance sales of defense articles, defense services, and design and construction services to foreign countries and international organizations. The FMF Loan Program Account was established pursuant to the Federal Credit Reform Act (FCRA) of 1990, as amended, to provide the funds necessary to support the cost of FMF direct loans and guarantees. Expenditures from this account finance the subsidy cost of direct loan disbursements and loan guarantees committed, and are transferred to the respective FMF Financing Account.

FOREIGN MILITARY FINANCING DIRECT LOAN FINANCING ACCOUNT
Program and Financing (in millions of dollars)

Identification code 011–4122–0–3–152	2021 actual	2022 est.	2023 est.
Obligations by program activity:			
Credit program obligations:			
0710 Direct loan obligations	....	4,000	4,000
0713 Payment of interest to Treasury	37	68	252
0742 Downward reestimates paid to receipt accounts	557	166	....
0743 Interest on downward reestimates	50	18	....
0900 Total new obligations, unexpired accounts	644	4,252	4,252

	2021 actual	2022 est.	2023 est.
Budgetary resources:			
Unobligated balance:			
1000 Unobligated balance brought forward, Oct 1	33	56	....
Financing authority:			
Borrowing authority, mandatory:			
1400 Borrowing authority	607	4,000	4,000
Spending authority from offsetting collections, mandatory:			
1800 Collected	810	901	901
1825 Spending authority from offsetting collections applied to repay debt	–750	–705	–649
1850 Spending auth from offsetting collections, mand (total)	60	196	252
1900 Budget authority (total)	667	4,196	4,252
1930 Total budgetary resources available	700	4,252	4,252
Memorandum (non-add) entries:			
1941 Unexpired unobligated balance, end of year	56	....	....
Change in obligated balance:			
Unpaid obligations:			
3000 Unpaid obligations, brought forward, Oct 1	....	....	252
3010 New obligations, unexpired accounts	644	4,252	4,252
3020 Outlays (gross)	–644	–4,000	–4,000
3050 Unpaid obligations, end of year	....	252	504
Memorandum (non-add) entries:			
3100 Obligated balance, start of year	....	....	252
3200 Obligated balance, end of year	....	252	504
Financing authority and disbursements, net:			
Discretionary:			
4020 Outlays, gross (total)	....	3,979	3,979
Mandatory:			
4090 Budget authority, gross	667	4,196	4,252
Financing disbursements:			
4110 Outlays, gross (total)	644	21	21
Offsets against gross financing authority and disbursements:			
Offsetting collections (collected) from:			
4122 Interest on uninvested funds	–1	....	....
4123 Non-Federal sources	–809	–901	–901
4130 Offsets against gross budget authority and outlays (total)	–810	–901	–901
4160 Budget authority, net (mandatory)	–143	3,295	3,351
4170 Outlays, net (mandatory)	–166	–880	–880
4180 Budget authority, net (total)	–143	3,295	3,351
4190 Outlays, net (total)	–166	3,099	3,099

Status of Direct Loans (in millions of dollars)

Identification code 011–4122–0–3–152	2021 actual	2022 est.	2023 est.
Position with respect to appropriations act limitation on obligations:			
1111 Direct loan obligations from current-year authority	....	4,000	4,000
1150 Total direct loan obligations	....	4,000	4,000
Cumulative balance of direct loans outstanding:			
1210 Outstanding, start of year	2,581	1,948	5,043
1231 Disbursements: Direct loan disbursements	....	4,000	4,000
1251 Repayments: Repayments and prepayments	–633	–901	–901
1263 Write-offs for default: Direct loans	....	–4	–4
1290 Outstanding, end of year	1,948	5,043	8,138

As required by the Federal Credit Reform Act (FCRA) of 1990, the Foreign Military Financing (FMF) Direct Loan Financing Account is a non-budgetary account that records all cash flows to and from the Government resulting from FMF direct loans obligated in 1992 and beyond. Amounts in this account are a means of financing and are not included in budget totals. The FY 2023 Budget includes a request for an FMF direct loan program for NATO and Major Non-NATO allies to complement traditional FMF grant assistance.

Balance Sheet (in millions of dollars)

Identification code 011–4122–0–3–152	2020 actual	2021 actual
ASSETS:		
1101 Federal assets: Fund balances with Treasury	33	56
Net value of assets related to post-1991 direct loans receivable:		
1401 Direct loans receivable, gross	2,581	1,948
1405 Allowance for subsidy cost (-)	–857	–391
1499 Net present value of assets related to direct loans	1,724	1,557
1999 Total assets	1,757	1,613

DEPARTMENT OF STATE AND OTHER INTERNATIONAL PROGRAMS

International Security Assistance—Continued
Federal Funds—Continued   **833**

	LIABILITIES:		
	Federal liabilities:		
2103	Debt	1,757	1,613
2104	Resources payable to Treasury	....	....
2999	Total liabilities	1,757	1,613
	NET POSITION:		
3300	Cumulative results of operations	....	....
4999	Total liabilities and net position	1,757	1,613

FOREIGN MILITARY FINANCING GUARANTEED LOAN FINANCING ACCOUNT

Program and Financing (in millions of dollars)

Identification code 011–4386–0–3–152	2021 actual	2022 est.	2023 est.
Obligations by program activity:			
Credit program obligations:			
0711 Default claim payments on principal	....	3	3
0713 Payment of interest to Treasury	....	1	1
0900 Total new obligations, unexpired accounts	....	4	4
Budgetary resources:			
Unobligated balance:			
1000 Unobligated balance brought forward, Oct 1	....	....	146
Financing authority:			
Spending authority from offsetting collections, mandatory:			
1800 Collected	....	150	150
1900 Budget authority (total)	....	150	150
1930 Total budgetary resources available	....	150	296
Memorandum (non-add) entries:			
1941 Unexpired unobligated balance, end of year	....	146	292
Change in obligated balance:			
Unpaid obligations:			
3000 Unpaid obligations, brought forward, Oct 1	....	....	4
3010 New obligations, unexpired accounts	....	4	4
3050 Unpaid obligations, end of year	....	4	8
Memorandum (non-add) entries:			
3100 Obligated balance, start of year	....	....	4
3200 Obligated balance, end of year	....	4	8
Financing authority and disbursements, net:			
Mandatory:			
4090 Budget authority, gross	....	150	150
Offsets against gross financing authority and disbursements:			
Offsetting collections (collected) from:			
4123 Non-Federal sources	....	–150	–150
4180 Budget authority, net (total)	....	....	....
4190 Outlays, net (total)	....	–150	–150

Status of Guaranteed Loans (in millions of dollars)

Identification code 011–4386–0–3–152	2021 actual	2022 est.	2023 est.
Position with respect to appropriations act limitation on commitments:			
2111 Guaranteed loan commitments from current-year authority	....	4,000	4,000
2150 Total guaranteed loan commitments	....	4,000	4,000
2199 Guaranteed amount of guaranteed loan commitments	....	3,200	3,200
Cumulative balance of guaranteed loans outstanding:			
2210 Outstanding, start of year	....	....	3,783
2231 Disbursements of new guaranteed loans	....	4,000	4,000
2251 Repayments and prepayments	....	–213	–213
2263 Adjustments: Terminations for default that result in claim payments	....	–4	–4
2290 Outstanding, end of year	....	3,783	7,566
Memorandum:			
2299 Guaranteed amount of guaranteed loans outstanding, end of year	....	3,026	3,026

As required by the Federal Credit Reform Act (FCRA) of 1990, the Foreign Military Financing (FMF) Guaranteed Loan Financing Account is a non-budgetary account that will record all cash flows to and from the Government resulting from FMF loan guarantees committed. Amounts in this account are a means of financing and are not included in the budget totals. The FY 2023 Budget includes a request for an FMF loan guarantee program for NATO and Major Non-NATO allies to complement traditional FMF grant assistance.

FOREIGN MILITARY LOAN LIQUIDATING ACCOUNT

Program and Financing (in millions of dollars)

Identification code 011–4121–0–3–152	2021 actual	2022 est.	2023 est.
Budgetary resources:			
Budget authority:			
Spending authority from offsetting collections, mandatory:			
1800 Offsetting collections (cash) from country loans	68	18	18
1820 Capital transfer of spending authority from offsetting collections to general fund	–68	–18	–18
Budget authority and outlays, net:			
Mandatory:			
Offsets against gross budget authority and outlays:			
Offsetting collections (collected) from:			
4120 Federal sources	–67	....	....
4123 Non-Federal sources	–1	–18	–18
4130 Offsets against gross budget authority and outlays (total)	–68	–18	–18
4160 Budget authority, net (mandatory)	–68	–18	–18
4170 Outlays, net (mandatory)	–68	–18	–18
4180 Budget authority, net (total)	–68	–18	–18
4190 Outlays, net (total)	–68	–18	–18

Status of Direct Loans (in millions of dollars)

Identification code 011–4121–0–3–152	2021 actual	2022 est.	2023 est.
Cumulative balance of direct loans outstanding:			
1210 Outstanding, start of year	311	220	202
1251 Repayments: Repayments and prepayments from country	–1	–18	–18
1264 Other adjustments, net (+ or -)	–90	....	....
1290 Outstanding, end of year	220	202	184

The Foreign Military Loan Liquidating Account records all cash flows to and from the Government resulting from direct loans obligated and loan guarantees for foreign military financing committed prior to 1992. This account is shown on a cash basis and reflects the transactions resulting from loans provided to finance sales of defense articles, defense services, and design and construction services to foreign countries and international organizations. No new loan disbursements are made from this account. Certain collections made into this account are made available for default claim payments. The Federal Credit Reform Act (FCRA) provides permanent indefinite authority to cover obligations for default payments if the liquidating account funds are otherwise insufficient. All new foreign military financing credit activity in 1992 and after (including modifications of direct loans or loan guarantees that resulted from obligations or commitments in any year) is recorded in corresponding program and financing accounts.

Balance Sheet (in millions of dollars)

Identification code 011–4121–0–3–152	2020 actual	2021 actual
ASSETS:		
1601 Direct loans, gross	311	220
1602 Interest receivable	2,353	1,734
1603 Allowance for estimated uncollectible loans and interest (-)	–1,981	–1,504
1699 Value of assets related to direct loans	683	450
1999 Total assets	683	450
LIABILITIES:		
Federal liabilities:		
2102 Accrued Interest Payable to FFB	....	....
2103 Debt - Principal owed to FFB	....	....
2104 Resources payable to Treasury	683	450
2999 Total liabilities	683	450
NET POSITION:		
3300 Cumulative results of operations	....	....

International Security Assistance—Continued
Federal Funds—Continued

FOREIGN MILITARY LOAN LIQUIDATING ACCOUNT—Continued

Balance Sheet—Continued

Identification code 011–4121–0–3–152	2020 actual	2021 actual
4999 Total liabilities and net position	683	450

MILITARY DEBT REDUCTION FINANCING ACCOUNT

Program and Financing (in millions of dollars)

Identification code 011–4174–0–3–152	2021 actual	2022 est.	2023 est.
Obligations by program activity:			
Credit program obligations:			
0713 Payment of interest to Treasury	....	1	....
0744 Adjusting payments to liquidating accounts	68	....	....
0900 Total new obligations, unexpired accounts	68	1	....
Budgetary resources:			
Financing authority:			
Borrowing authority, mandatory:			
1400 Borrowing authority	39	1	....
Spending authority from offsetting collections, mandatory:			
1800 Collected	29	....	....
1900 Budget authority (total)	68	1	....
1930 Total budgetary resources available	68	1	....
Change in obligated balance:			
Unpaid obligations:			
3000 Unpaid obligations, brought forward, Oct 1	....	....	1
3010 New obligations, unexpired accounts	68	1	....
3020 Outlays (gross)	–68	....	....
3050 Unpaid obligations, end of year	....	1	1
Memorandum (non-add) entries:			
3100 Obligated balance, start of year	....	....	1
3200 Obligated balance, end of year	....	1	1
Financing authority and disbursements, net:			
Mandatory:			
4090 Budget authority, gross	68	1	....
Financing disbursements:			
4110 Outlays, gross (total)	68	....	....
Offsets against gross financing authority and disbursements:			
Offsetting collections (collected) from:			
4120 Federal sources	–28	....	....
4122 Interest on uninvested funds	–1	....	....
4130 Offsets against gross budget authority and outlays (total)	–29	....	....
4160 Budget authority, net (mandatory)	39	1	....
4170 Outlays, net (mandatory)	39	....	....
4180 Budget authority, net (total)	39	1	....
4190 Outlays, net (total)	39	....	....

Status of Direct Loans (in millions of dollars)

Identification code 011–4174–0–3–152	2021 actual	2022 est.	2023 est.
Cumulative balance of direct loans outstanding:			
1210 Outstanding, start of year	191	259	259
1233 Disbursements: Purchase of loans assets from a liquidating account	68	....	....
1290 Outstanding, end of year	259	259	259

As required by the Federal Credit Reform Act of 1990, the Military Debt Reduction Financing (MDRF) Account is a non-budgetary financing account that records all cash flows to and from the Government resulting from restructuring foreign military loans. The amounts in this account are a means of financing and are not included in budget totals. It is an account established for the debt relief of certain countries as established by Public Law 103–87, Foreign Operations, Export Financing, and Related Programs Appropriations Act, 1994, Section 11, Special Debt Relief for the Poorest, Most Heavily Indebted Countries. The MDRF buys a portfolio of loans from the Foreign Military Loan Liquidating Account, thus transferring the loans from the Liquidating Account to the MDRF Account.

Balance Sheet (in millions of dollars)

Identification code 011–4174–0–3–152	2020 actual	2021 actual
ASSETS:		
1101 Federal assets: Fund balances with Treasury	....	....
Net value of assets related to post-1991 direct loans receivable:		
1401 Direct loans receivable, gross	191	259
1402 Interest receivable	55	....
1405 Allowance for subsidy cost (-)	–234	–220
1499 Net present value of assets related to direct loans	12	39
1999 Total assets	12	39
LIABILITIES:		
2103 Federal liabilities: Debt	12	39
NET POSITION:		
3300 Cumulative results of operations	....	....
4999 Total liabilities and net position	12	39

MULTILATERAL ASSISTANCE

Federal Funds

CONTRIBUTION TO THE CLEAN TECHNOLOGY FUND

For contribution to the Clean Technology Fund, $550,000,000, to remain available until expended, of which not to exceed $520,000,000 shall be available to cover the costs, as defined in section 502 of the Congressional Budget Act of 1974, of direct loans issued to the Clean Technology Fund.

Note.—A full-year 2022 appropriation for this account was not enacted at the time the Budget was prepared; therefore, the Budget assumes this account is operating under the Continuing Appropriations Act, 2022 (Division A of Public Law 117–43, as amended). The amounts included for 2022 reflect the annualized level provided by the continuing resolution.

Program and Financing (in millions of dollars)

Identification code 020–0080–0–1–151	2021 actual	2022 est.	2023 est.
Obligations by program activity:			
0001 Grants	....	....	30
Credit program obligations:			
0701 Direct loan subsidy	....	....	520
0900 Total new obligations, unexpired accounts (object class 41.0)	....	....	550
Budgetary resources:			
Budget authority:			
Appropriations, discretionary:			
1100 Appropriation	....	....	550
1930 Total budgetary resources available	....	....	550
Change in obligated balance:			
Unpaid obligations:			
3010 New obligations, unexpired accounts	....	....	550
3020 Outlays (gross)	....	....	–126
3050 Unpaid obligations, end of year	....	....	424
Memorandum (non-add) entries:			
3200 Obligated balance, end of year	....	....	424
Budget authority and outlays, net:			
Discretionary:			
4000 Budget authority, gross	....	....	550
Outlays, gross:			
4010 Outlays from new discretionary authority	....	....	126
4180 Budget authority, net (total)	....	....	550
4190 Outlays, net (total)	....	....	126

Summary of Loan Levels, Subsidy Budget Authority and Outlays by Program (in millions of dollars)

Identification code 020–0080–0–1–151	2021 actual	2022 est.	2023 est.
Direct loan levels supportable by subsidy budget authority:			
115001 Clean Technology Fund Direct Loans	....	....	3,220
Direct loan subsidy (in percent):			
132001 Clean Technology Fund Direct Loans	....	....	16.15
132999 Weighted average subsidy rate	0.00	0.00	16.15
Direct loan subsidy budget authority:			
133001 Clean Technology Fund Direct Loans	....	....	520

	Direct loan subsidy outlays:			
134001	Clean Technology Fund Direct Loans			119

Climate Investment Funds

The Climate Investment Funds (CIFs), comprised of the Clean Technology Fund (CTF) and the Strategic Climate Fund (SCF), were created in 2008 to integrate concessional climate finance into MDB operations. The CIFs provide concessional financing to MDB projects or stand-alone projects and have supported investments in clean technology, energy access, land use, sustainable forestry, and climate resilience. As the need for climate finance has grown, donor and recipient governments agree that the CIFs play an important and targeted role to further "green" MDB operations and to incentivize climate investments that are complementary but not duplicative to other climate finance sources.

From 2008 to 2020, the CTF invested over $5.3 billion in helping emerging markets scale up deployment of clean and energy efficient technologies. During this period, the SCF invested over $2.2 billion in renewable energy solutions, sustainable forestry, and climate resilient planning. The CIFs have paid particular attention to lower income countries and the inclusion of indigenous and other marginalized groups in planning stages and as beneficiaries. The CIFs have mobilized over $60 billion in co-financing since 2008.

The CTF is accepting new contributions, including to the newly launched Accelerating Coal Transition (ACT) Investment Program, which the Administration believes could have significant near-term impact and be highly catalytic in supporting developing countries' transitions away from coal. President Biden announced U.S. support for the ACT program at the G7 Summit in June 2021.

The 2023 Budget requests $550 million for the Clean Technology Fund, of which up to $520 million will cover the subsidy cost of a loan and at least $30 million of which will be in the form of a grant contribution. The loan will scale up this program to support countries seeking to transition from coal-based energy to clean fuel sources.

CLEAN TECHNOLOGY FUND LOANS FINANCING ACCOUNT

Program and Financing (in millions of dollars)

Identification code 011–4618–0–3–151		2021 actual	2022 est.	2023 est.
	Obligations by program activity:			
	Credit program obligations:			
0710	Direct loan obligations			3,220
0713	Payment of interest to Treasury			1
0900	Total new obligations, unexpired accounts			3,221
	Budgetary resources:			
	Financing authority:			
	Borrowing authority, mandatory:			
1400	Borrowing authority			3,101
	Spending authority from offsetting collections, mandatory:			
1800	Collected			120
1900	Budget authority (total)			3,221
1930	Total budgetary resources available			3,221
	Change in obligated balance:			
	Unpaid obligations:			
3010	New obligations, unexpired accounts			3,221
3020	Outlays (gross)			–738
3050	Unpaid obligations, end of year			2,483
	Memorandum (non-add) entries:			
3200	Obligated balance, end of year			2,483
	Financing authority and disbursements, net:			
	Mandatory:			
4090	Budget authority, gross			3,221
	Financing disbursements:			
4110	Outlays, gross (total)			738
	Offsets against gross financing authority and disbursements:			
	Offsetting collections (collected) from:			
4120	Federal sources			–119
4123	Non-Federal sources			–1
4130	Offsets against gross budget authority and outlays (total)			–120
4160	Budget authority, net (mandatory)			3,101
4170	Outlays, net (mandatory)			618
4180	Budget authority, net (total)			3,101
4190	Outlays, net (total)			618

Status of Direct Loans (in millions of dollars)

Identification code 011–4618–0–3–151		2021 actual	2022 est.	2023 est.
	Position with respect to appropriations act limitation on obligations:			
1111	Direct loan obligations from current-year authority			3,220
1150	Total direct loan obligations			3,220
	Cumulative balance of direct loans outstanding:			
1231	Disbursements: Direct loan disbursements			738
1290	Outstanding, end of year			738

As required by the Federal Credit Reform Act of 1990, as amended, this non-budgetary account records all cash flows to and from the Government resulting from direct loans and other investments obligated by the Clean Technology Fund (CTF), including modifications of those direct loans. The amounts in this account are a means of financing and are not included in the budget totals. The 2023 Budget includes a request for a direct loan program for the CTF.

GLOBAL AGRICULTURE AND FOOD SECURITY PROGRAM

The Global Agriculture and Food Security Program (GAFSP) is a multi-donor trust fund called for by G-20 leaders in 2009 to fund projects that support the agricultural investment plans of poor countries. No new funding is requested in 2023.

CONTRIBUTION TO THE GREEN CLIMATE FUND

For contribution to the Green Climate Fund by the Secretary of the Treasury, $1,600,000,000, to remain available until expended.

Note.—A full-year 2022 appropriation for this account was not enacted at the time the Budget was prepared; therefore, the Budget assumes this account is operating under the Continuing Appropriations Act, 2022 (Division A of Public Law 117–43, as amended). The amounts included for 2022 reflect the annualized level provided by the continuing resolution.

Program and Financing (in millions of dollars)

Identification code 011–0095–0–1–151		2021 actual	2022 est.	2023 est.
	Obligations by program activity:			
0001	Direct program activity			1,600
0900	Total new obligations, unexpired accounts (object class 41.0)			1,600
	Budgetary resources:			
	Budget authority:			
	Appropriations, discretionary:			
1100	Appropriation			1,600
1930	Total budgetary resources available			1,600
	Change in obligated balance:			
	Unpaid obligations:			
3010	New obligations, unexpired accounts			1,600
3020	Outlays (gross)			–1,600
	Budget authority and outlays, net:			
	Discretionary:			
4000	Budget authority, gross			1,600
	Outlays, gross:			
4010	Outlays from new discretionary authority			1,600
4180	Budget authority, net (total)			1,600
4190	Outlays, net (total)			1,600

Multilateral Assistance—Continued
Federal Funds—Continued

CONTRIBUTION TO THE GREEN CLIMATE FUND—Continued

Green Climate Fund

The Green Climate Fund (GCF) is the world's largest multilateral climate fund, established in 2010 to foster climate-resilient and low-emissions development. The GCF advances its mission by using a range of financial instruments to support projects and programs that promise the greatest impact in reducing greenhouse gas emissions and building climate resilience in developing countries. It also seeks to mobilize private sector capital and foster stronger policy environments that better address the challenges of a changing climate.

The GCF funds activities across a variety of sectors, including transport, water and other infrastructure, energy generation and efficiency, and land use, including agriculture and forestry. As of October 2021, the GCF has approved 190 projects, using $10.0 billion in funding and attracting $27.1 billion in co-financing. Through these investments, the GCF will support development that is sustainable, resilient, and resource-efficient, and that minimizes the potential negative impacts of climate change on citizens' health and well-being. The 2023 Budget includes $1,600 million for the GCF.

CONTRIBUTION TO THE GLOBAL ENVIRONMENT FACILITY

For payment to the International Bank for Reconstruction and Development as trustee for the Global Environment Facility by the Secretary of the Treasury, $150,200,000, to remain available until expended.

CONTRIBUTION TO THE INTERNATIONAL BANK FOR RECONSTRUCTION AND DEVELOPMENT

For payment to the International Bank for Reconstruction and Development by the Secretary of the Treasury for the United States share of the paid-in portion of the increases in capital stock, $206,500,000, to remain available until expended.

LIMITATION ON CALLABLE CAPITAL SUBSCRIPTIONS

The United States Governor of the International Bank for Reconstruction and Development may subscribe without fiscal year limitation to the callable capital portion of the United States share of increases in capital stock in an amount not to exceed $1,421,275,728.70.

Note.—A full-year 2022 appropriation for this account was not enacted at the time the Budget was prepared; therefore, the Budget assumes this account is operating under the Continuing Appropriations Act, 2022 (Division A of Public Law 117–43, as amended). The amounts included for 2022 reflect the annualized level provided by the continuing resolution.

Program and Financing (in millions of dollars)

Identification code 020–0077–0–1–151		2021 actual	2022 est.	2023 est.
	Obligations by program activity:			
0001	Global Environment Facility	140	140	150
0002	International Bank for Reconstruction and Development	243	220	207
0799	Total direct obligations	383	360	357
0801	International Bank for Reconstruction and Development	2		
0809	Reimbursable program activities, subtotal	2		
0900	Total new obligations, unexpired accounts	385	360	357
	Budgetary resources:			
	Unobligated balance:			
1000	Unobligated balance brought forward, Oct 1	7,665	7,677	7,664
1011	Unobligated balance transfer from other acct [072–1037]	25		
1070	Unobligated balance (total)	7,690	7,677	7,664
	Budget authority:			
	Appropriations, discretionary:			
1100	Appropriation	347	347	357
1121	Appropriations transferred from other acct [072–1037]	25		
1160	Appropriation, discretionary (total)	372	347	357
	Spending authority from offsetting collections, discretionary:			
1700	Collected	2		
1701	Change in uncollected payments, Federal sources	–2		
1900	Budget authority (total)	372	347	357
1930	Total budgetary resources available	8,062	8,024	8,021
	Memorandum (non-add) entries:			
1941	Unexpired unobligated balance, end of year	7,677	7,664	7,664
	Change in obligated balance:			
	Unpaid obligations:			
3000	Unpaid obligations, brought forward, Oct 1	27	1	1
3010	New obligations, unexpired accounts	385	360	357
3020	Outlays (gross)	–411	–360	–357
3050	Unpaid obligations, end of year	1	1	1
	Uncollected payments:			
3060	Uncollected pymts, Fed sources, brought forward, Oct 1	–2		
3070	Change in uncollected pymts, Fed sources, unexpired	2		
	Memorandum (non-add) entries:			
3100	Obligated balance, start of year	25	1	1
3200	Obligated balance, end of year	1	1	1
	Budget authority and outlays, net:			
	Discretionary:			
4000	Budget authority, gross	372	347	357
	Outlays, gross:			
4010	Outlays from new discretionary authority	359	347	357
4011	Outlays from discretionary balances	52	13	
4020	Outlays, gross (total)	411	360	357
	Offsets against gross budget authority and outlays:			
	Offsetting collections (collected) from:			
4030	Federal sources	–2		
	Additional offsets against gross budget authority only:			
4050	Change in uncollected pymts, Fed sources, unexpired	2		
4070	Budget authority, net (discretionary)	372	347	357
4080	Outlays, net (discretionary)	409	360	357
4180	Budget authority, net (total)	372	347	357
4190	Outlays, net (total)	409	360	357

International Bank for Reconstruction and Development

The 2023 Budget requests $206.5 million towards the fourth of up to six installments under the current International Bank for Reconstruction and Development's (IBRD) capital increase.

IBRD is the arm of the World Bank that provides financing to creditworthy lower middle and middle-income countries to promote inclusive economic growth and reduce poverty. These countries—home to over 70 percent of the world's poor—rely on the IBRD for financial resources and strategic advice to meet their development needs. Working across a range of sectors, including governance, agriculture, sustainable infrastructure, health and nutrition, and education, the IBRD supports long-term human and social development needs which private creditors generally do not finance. During its 2021 fiscal year (July 1, 2020 to June 30, 2021), the IBRD approved $30.5 billion in loans and technical assistance. Latin America and the Caribbean received the largest portion of the IBRD's lending at $9.5 billion (31 percent), followed by the East Asia and Pacific region at $6.8 billion (22 percent) and the Europe and Central Asia region (15 percent). Since the beginning of the COVID-19 pandemic, IBRD lending has focused on helping countries address the health and economic impacts of the pandemic. In the April 2020 to November 2021 period, approximately 63 percent of IBRD's commitments ($31.3 billion out of $50 billion total) were for COVID-19 response. IBRD has financed COVID-19 response efforts under four strategic pillars: (1) saving lives by addressing the acute impacts of the pandemic, including financing of vaccines; (2) protecting the poor and vulnerable; (3) ensuring sustainable business growth and job creation; and (4) strengthening policies, institutions, and investments to rebuild better. In FY 2021, IBRD approved over $7.3 billion in infrastructure financing (24 percent of total approvals) comprised of $2.4 billion in energy, $773 million in information and communications technologies, $2.3 billion in transportation, and $1.9 billion in water infrastructure.

The United States is and will remain the largest shareholder in the IBRD, and the United States is the only country with veto power over amendments to the Articles of Agreement. The United States share of total voting power will be 15.9 percent after all countries subscribe to their shares under the 2018 capital increase. The next largest countries are Japan, whose share will be 6.8 percent, followed by China, with a 5.5 percent share.

Global Environment Facility

The Global Environment Facility (GEF) is one of the largest dedicated funders of projects to improve the global environment. Since its inception, the GEF has provided $15.6 billion in funding towards projects, including $4 billion during the GEF seventh replenishment (GEF-7). The GEF benefits the U.S. economy and environment by addressing many global environmental problems that affect our domestic health, safety, and prosperity, such as by supporting climate change mitigation, combatting wildlife trafficking, reducing harmful pollution, and conserving fish stocks outside U.S. waters. The FY 2023 Budget requests $150.2 million for the Global Environment Facility (GEF), in support of GEF programs during the GEF eighth replenishment (GEF-8) period (July 1, 2022 through June 30, 2026), including for the first installment of the GEF-8 replenishment.

International Finance Corporation

The International Finance Corporation (IFC) is the private sector arm of the World Bank Group. Established in 1956, it promotes private sector development in developing countries by making loans and equity investments in private sector projects, mobilizing private capital alongside its own resources, and providing advisory and technical assistance services. In its 2021 fiscal year, the IFC made $12.5 billion in long-term investment commitments from its own resources ("own account") and mobilized an additional $10.8 billion from other sources for 313 projects in 71 countries. IFC made 25 percent of its long-term, own account commitments to the poorest and most fragile countries (those eligible for funding from the World Bank's IDA) in 2021, up from a baseline of 21 percent in 2018. IFC aims to increase this share to 40 percent by 2030. IFC also made $8.2 billion in short-term investment commitments in 2021. IFC made long-term commitments across the globe in 2021. The largest recipient regions were East Asia and Pacific at $2.8 billion (23 percent), Latin America and Caribbean at $2.8 billion (22 percent), Sub-Saharan Africa at $2.4 billion (20 percent), and Europe and Central Asia at $2.0 billion (16 percent). The top sectors for IFC long-term investment in 2021 were financial markets at $5.9 billion (47 percent), health and education at $1.3 billion (11 percent), and infrastructure at $1.6 billion (13 percent). IFC spent $244 million on advisory services in 2021, with sub-Saharan Africa receiving $77 million (32 percent). The Administration is not requesting funding for the IFC in 2023.

Object Classification (in millions of dollars)

Identification code 020–0077–0–1–151		2021 actual	2022 est.	2023 est.
33.0	Direct obligations: Investments and loans	383	360	357
99.0	Reimbursable obligations	2		
99.9	Total new obligations, unexpired accounts	385	360	357

CONTRIBUTION TO THE INTERNATIONAL DEVELOPMENT ASSOCIATION

For payment to the International Development Association by the Secretary of the Treasury, $1,430,256,000, to remain available until expended.

Note.—A full-year 2022 appropriation for this account was not enacted at the time the Budget was prepared; therefore, the Budget assumes this account is operating under the Continuing Appropriations Act, 2022 (Division A of Public Law 117–43, as amended). The amounts included for 2022 reflect the annualized level provided by the continuing resolution.

Program and Financing (in millions of dollars)

Identification code 020–0073–0–1–151		2021 actual	2022 est.	2023 est.
	Obligations by program activity:			
0001	International Development Association	1,001	1,301	1,430
0900	Total new obligations, unexpired accounts (object class 33.0)	1,001	1,301	1,430
	Budgetary resources:			
	Unobligated balance:			
1011	Unobligated balance transfer from other acct [072–1037]		300	
	Budget authority:			
	Appropriations, discretionary:			
1100	Appropriation - IDA	1,001	1,001	1,430
1930	Total budgetary resources available	1,001	1,301	1,430
	Change in obligated balance:			
	Unpaid obligations:			
3010	New obligations, unexpired accounts	1,001	1,301	1,430
3020	Outlays (gross)	–1,001	–1,301	–1,430
	Budget authority and outlays, net:			
	Discretionary:			
4000	Budget authority, gross	1,001	1,001	1,430
	Outlays, gross:			
4010	Outlays from new discretionary authority	1,001	1,001	1,430
4011	Outlays from discretionary balances		300	
4020	Outlays, gross (total)	1,001	1,301	1,430
4180	Budget authority, net (total)	1,001	1,001	1,430
4190	Outlays, net (total)	1,001	1,301	1,430

International Development Association

The 2023 Budget requests $1,430.3 million for the International Development Association (IDA) in support of IDA programs over the twentieth replenishment period (IDA 20, FY 2023-FY 2025.) It includes support for the final installment of the IDA-19 replenishment and the first of three installments to IDA-20.

IDA is the arm of the World Bank Group that supports poverty reduction and development in the world's 74 poorest countries. IDA works across a wide range of sectors including education, health, clean water and sanitation, environment, infrastructure, agriculture, and governance. Because countries receiving IDA financing are too poor to attract sufficient capital to support their significant development needs, they depend on concessional finance—low or no interest loans and grants—to create jobs, build critical infrastructure, improve governance and public service delivery, increase agricultural productivity, increase access to energy, improve job creation and the business environment, and invest in the health and education of future generations. IDA's goal is to help countries reduce poverty and achieve higher levels of growth and institutional capacity. Over time, IDA's support helps countries finance their development needs through domestic revenues and borrowing at non-concessional rates, including through international markets. During the World Bank's 2021 fiscal year (July 1, 2020, to June 30, 2021), IDA supported projects totaling $36 billion, of which, $25 billion (70 percent) went to countries in Sub-Saharan Africa. Countries in the South Asia region received the second largest amount at $7 billion (20 percent). Since the beginning of the COVID-19 pandemic, IDA financing has focused on helping countries address the health and economic impacts of the pandemic. In the April 2020-November 2021 period, nearly one-half of IDA commitments ($27.1 billion out of $56.9 billion total) were for COVID-19 response. IDA has financed COVID-19 response efforts under four strategic pillars: (1) saving lives by addressing the acute impacts of the pandemic, including financing of vaccines; (2) protecting the poor and vulnerable; (3) ensuring sustainable business growth and job creation; and (4) strengthening policies, institutions, and investments to rebuild better. In FY 2021, IDA also committed nearly $9.7 billion (27 percent of total approvals) in infrastructure-related financing, consisting of $3.8 billion in energy, $1.2 billion in information and communication technologies, $2.4 billion in transportation, and $2.4 billion in water infrastructure. As of January 2022, the United States holds the largest percent of total votes in IDA at 9.9 percent, followed by Japan at 8.3 percent and the United Kingdom at 6.7 percent. Voting power distribution fluctuates slightly with each IDA replenishment.

Multilateral Debt Relief Initiative

Launched in 2006 at the urging of the United States, the Multilateral Debt Relief Initiative (MDRI) provides 100 percent cancellation of eligible debt to the concessional financing windows of the World Bank and the African Development Bank. Countries receive MDRI benefits after completing the reforms under the Heavily Indebted Poor Countries (HIPC) Initiative and

CONTRIBUTION TO THE INTERNATIONAL DEVELOPMENT ASSOCIATION—Continued

demonstrating a track record of improved economic policy performance. The purpose of this debt reduction is to free up more resources in well-performing low-income countries for poverty-reducing expenditures in areas such as health, education, and rural development. In accordance with MDRI rules, donors compensate IDA for the cancelled debt on a dollar-for-dollar basis according to the payment schedules of the original loans. IDA calculates donors' MDRI commitments at the start of each three-year replenishment cycle according to a burden-sharing percentage. Each donor's commitments to MDRI at IDA must be met within the three-year replenishment period to avoid a negative impact on IDA's financial capacity. The U.S. share of the cost of MDRI under IDA-19 is $878.8 million. No funding is requested for IDA MDRI in 2023.

CONTRIBUTION TO MULTILATERAL INVESTMENT GUARANTEE AGENCY

Program and Financing (in millions of dollars)

Identification code 020–0084–0–1–151	2021 actual	2022 est.	2023 est.
Change in obligated balance:			
Unpaid obligations:			
3000 Unpaid obligations, brought forward, Oct 1	22	22	22
3050 Unpaid obligations, end of year	22	22	22
Memorandum (non-add) entries:			
3100 Obligated balance, start of year	22	22	22
3200 Obligated balance, end of year	22	22	22
4180 Budget authority, net (total)			
4190 Outlays, net (total)			

The Multilateral Investment Guarantee Agency (MIGA) is a member of the World Bank Group designed to encourage the flow of foreign private investment to and among developing countries by issuing guarantees against non-commercial risks and carrying out investment promotion activities. No funding is requested for MIGA in 2023.

CONTRIBUTION TO THE INTER-AMERICAN DEVELOPMENT BANK

Program and Financing (in millions of dollars)

Identification code 020–0072–0–1–151	2021 actual	2022 est.	2023 est.
Budgetary resources:			
Unobligated balance:			
1000 Unobligated balance brought forward, Oct 1	3,798	3,798	3,798
1930 Total budgetary resources available	3,798	3,798	3,798
Memorandum (non-add) entries:			
1941 Unexpired unobligated balance, end of year	3,798	3,798	3,798
4180 Budget authority, net (total)			
4190 Outlays, net (total)			

Inter-American Development Bank

The Inter-American Development Bank (IDB) is the largest source of development financing for 26 countries in Latin America and the Caribbean, a strategically significant and economically important region for the United States where roughly 144 million people live in poverty. In 2021, the IDB approved 103 projects totaling $14.5 billion in financing. The IDB works in a range of sectors, and in 2020 committed roughly half (51 percent) of its funding to support fiscal sustainability, competitiveness, and access to credit. The other half is split between social sector programs (36 percent) and infrastructure and the environment (14 percent). The United States is the largest shareholder in the IDB, with 30 percent of total shareholding, enabling the United States to wield significant influence over major decisions about the direction of the IDB. No new funding is requested for the IDB in 2023.

Inter-American Investment Corporation (IDB Invest)

The Inter-American Investment Corporation (IIC), colloquially known as IDB Invest, is a member of the Inter-American Development Bank Group established in 1984. IDB Invest promotes development of the private sector in Latin America and the Caribbean. It is a legally autonomous entity whose resources and management are separate from those of the IDB itself. In 2017, the IIC implemented organizational and operational reforms stemming from the 2016 consolidation of the IDB's private sector financing activities into the IIC. As a result of this consolidation, all of the IDB Group's private sector lending activities, including small- and medium-sized enterprises and financing for private infrastructure and corporate entities (with the exception of small-scale innovation focused work being done by IDB lab), are now funded by IDB Invest. In 2021, IDB Invest committed $6.3 billion in short- and long-term financing from its own resources and mobilized an additional $3.0 billion. This includes over $1.3 billion committed to the infrastructure and energy sectors, comprising 21 percent of approvals. No funding is requested for the IIC in 2023.

CONTRIBUTION TO THE ASIAN DEVELOPMENT FUND

For payment to the Asian Development Bank's Asian Development Fund by the Secretary of the Treasury, $43,610,000, to remain available until expended.

Note.—A full-year 2022 appropriation for this account was not enacted at the time the Budget was prepared; therefore, the Budget assumes this account is operating under the Continuing Appropriations Act, 2022 (Division A of Public Law 117–43, as amended). The amounts included for 2022 reflect the annualized level provided by the continuing resolution.

Program and Financing (in millions of dollars)

Identification code 020–0076–0–1–151	2021 actual	2022 est.	2023 est.
Obligations by program activity:			
0002 Asian Development Fund	47	47	44
0900 Total new obligations, unexpired accounts (object class 33.0)	47	47	44
Budgetary resources:			
Unobligated balance:			
1000 Unobligated balance brought forward, Oct 1	748	748	748
Budget authority:			
Appropriations, discretionary:			
1100 Appropriation - Fund	47	47	44
1930 Total budgetary resources available	795	795	792
Memorandum (non-add) entries:			
1941 Unexpired unobligated balance, end of year	748	748	748
Change in obligated balance:			
Unpaid obligations:			
3010 New obligations, unexpired accounts	47	47	44
3020 Outlays (gross)	–47	–47	–44
Budget authority and outlays, net:			
Discretionary:			
4000 Budget authority, gross	47	47	44
Outlays, gross:			
4010 Outlays from new discretionary authority	47	47	44
4180 Budget authority, net (total)	47	47	44
4190 Outlays, net (total)	47	47	44

Asian Development Bank

The Asian Development Bank (AsDB) promotes broad-based sustainable economic growth and development, poverty alleviation, and regional cooperation and integration in the Asia-Pacific region. It has two main financing windows: 1) the Asian Development Bank's Ordinary Capital Resources (OCR), which provides "hard loans" at market-linked rates and "soft loans" to eligible countries at concessional rates; and 2) the Asian Development Fund (AsDF), which provides grants to the region's poorest countries that are at moderate or high risk of debt distress. Prior to January 2017, when AsDF's equity and lending operations were merged with AsDB's OCR, the AsDF also provided concessional loans which it no longer provides.

The AsDB provides long-term loans at market-based rates to 23 middle-income Asian countries that utilize such resources to finance their national economies, build critical infrastructure, and support inclusive growth. AsDB also supports private sector development with technical assistance, loans, guarantees, and direct equity investments in viable private sector projects with strong development impacts. In 2021, AsDB committed $22.8 billion from its own resources, including grants issued by the Asian Development Fund, for projects and mobilized another $12.9 billion in co-financing from official and commercial sources. Through its lending, equity investments, trade finance, and technical assistance, AsDB supports investments in critical infrastructure, the expansion of private enterprise, and sustainable economic growth. Typically, the majority of AsDB assistance is for investments in energy, transportation, agriculture and natural resources, public sector management, water supply, municipal infrastructure, finance, and education. In 2021, the AsDB directed a total of $13.5 billion, or 59 percent of its financing, toward addressing the impact of the COVID-19 pandemic and broadened its operations to include more health interventions. In 2020, the AsDB invested approximately $9.3 billion in infrastructure, or about 30 percent of total commitments that year. AsDB is financed through capital contributions from donors, income earned on its loan and investment portfolios, and bond issuances. No funding is requested for AsDB in 2023.

Asian Development Fund

The 2023 Budget requests $43.6 million in support of Asian Development Fund (AsDF) programs over the twelfth replenishment (AsDF-13; FY 2022-FY 2025), including towards AsDF-13.

AsDF currently provides grants to 17 of the poorest countries in Asia and the Pacific that face moderate or high risk of debt distress. It focuses on supporting inclusive, sustainable economic growth, as well as regional cooperation and integration. AsDF projects support water, energy, transportation, financial sector deepening, agriculture, and health. In 2020 and 2021, AsDF focused considerable funding on COVID-19 response. AsDF also invests in cross-cutting activities, such as connecting entrepreneurial training with financing for small and medium-sized enterprises. In 2021, AsDF committed a total of $320 million in grants for AsDF-eligible countries, of which $123 million was targeted at COVID-19 response. As a result of the merger of AsDF's lending assets into AsDB's OCR on January 1, 2017, AsDF now provides only grants. In recent years, the United States has focused attention within AsDF on countries where support aligns with U.S. strategic interests, including support for the Pacific island countries.

CONTRIBUTION TO THE AFRICAN DEVELOPMENT FUND

For payment to the African Development Fund by the Secretary of the Treasury, $171,300,000, to remain available until expended.

CONTRIBUTION TO THE AFRICAN DEVELOPMENT BANK

For payment to the African Development Bank by the Secretary of the Treasury for the United States share of the paid-in portion of the increases in capital stock, $54,648,752, to remain available until expended.

LIMITATION ON CALLABLE CAPITAL SUBSCRIPTIONS

The United States Governor of the African Development Bank may subscribe without fiscal year limitation to the callable capital portion of the United States share of increases in capital stock in an amount not to exceed $856,174,624.

Note.—A full-year 2022 appropriation for this account was not enacted at the time the Budget was prepared; therefore, the Budget assumes this account is operating under the Continuing Appropriations Act, 2022 (Division A of Public Law 117–43, as amended). The amounts included for 2022 reflect the annualized level provided by the continuing resolution.

Program and Financing (in millions of dollars)

Identification code 020–0082–0–1–151	2021 actual	2022 est.	2023 est.
Obligations by program activity:			
0001 Bank	55	55	55
0002 Fund	171	171	171
0900 Total new obligations, unexpired accounts (object class 33.0)	226	226	226
Budgetary resources:			
Budget authority:			
Appropriations, discretionary:			
1100 Appropriation - Bank	226	55	55
1100 Appropriation - Fund		171	171
1160 Appropriation, discretionary (total)	226	226	226
1930 Total budgetary resources available	226	226	226
Change in obligated balance:			
Unpaid obligations:			
3010 New obligations, unexpired accounts	226	226	226
3020 Outlays (gross)	–226	–226	–226
Budget authority and outlays, net:			
Discretionary:			
4000 Budget authority, gross	226	226	226
Outlays, gross:			
4010 Outlays from new discretionary authority	226	226	226
4180 Budget authority, net (total)	226	226	226
4190 Outlays, net (total)	226	226	226

The African Development Bank Group includes: 1) the African Development Bank (AfDB), which lends at market-linked rates to middle-income African countries and Africa's private-sector; and 2) the African Development Fund (AfDF), which provides grants and concessional loans to the poorest African countries. The AfDF account includes a portion of the U.S. commitment to the Multilateral Debt Relief Initiative (MDRI). In 2021, approximately 43 percent of AfDB and AfDF project approvals were in the infrastructure sector, comprised of investments in transportation, power, water and sanitation, environment, and urban development.

African Development Bank

The 2023 Budget requests $54.6 million for the third of eight equal installments for the AfDB's Seventh General Capital Increase (GCI-VII). The AfDB provides public sector financing at market-linked rates to 20 middle-income African countries and provides loans, equity investments, lines of credit, and guarantees to support private sector investments in all 54 African member countries. In 2021, the AfDB approved $3.4 billion in financing. 2021 lending activities focused on helping countries provide effective public health and economic recovery responses through the AfDB's COVID-19 Response Facility. From April 2020 to December 2021, the AfDB window committed over $2.6 billion for COVID-19 response to middle-income countries in Africa. These loans have supported activities such as increasing testing capacity and personal protective equipment stocks, social protection projects that emphasize preserving jobs and food access, and country-specific reforms to enhance competitiveness for post-COVID-19 economic recovery. Other key lending areas included energy and transportation infrastructure, agriculture, and governance. The United States will remain the largest non-regional shareholder of the AfDB and the second-largest shareholder after Nigeria. The United States' shareholding will remain unchanged at 6.4 percent after all countries subscribe to their shares under GCI-VII.

African Development Fund

The 2023 Budget requests $171.3 million in support of AfDF programs over the fifteenth replenishment (AfDF-15; FY 2021-FY 2023), including towards a third installment to AfDF-15.

The AfDF is the AfDB Group's concessional lending window and traditionally one of the largest official financiers of infrastructure in Sub-Saharan Africa, providing grants and highly concessional loans to the poorest countries in Africa. Some AfDF recipient countries are becoming frontier emerging markets and growing U.S. trading partners. Some other AfDF recipient countries, however, remain fragile and are trapped in conflict and poverty. Most AfDF countries are highly vulnerable to both internal and external shocks. In 2021, the AfDF provided approximately $2.4 billion in financing, technical assistance, and capacity-building activities to eligible countries. Of this amount, the AfDF committed nearly $1.5 billion in COVID-19 related support. The AfDF also sets aside special funding for regional projects and fragile and transitioning states. In total, approximately half of its resources continue to be directed to fragile states.

CONTRIBUTION TO THE AFRICAN DEVELOPMENT BANK—Continued

Multilateral Debt Relief Initiative

Launched in 2006 at the urging of the United States, the Multilateral Debt Relief Initiative (MDRI) provides 100 percent cancellation of eligible debt to the concessional financing windows of the World Bank and the AfDB. Eligible countries receive MDRI benefits after completing the reforms under the HIPC Initiative and demonstrating a track record of improved economic policy performance. The purpose of this debt reduction is to free up more resources in well-performing low-income countries for poverty-reducing expenditures in areas such as health, education, and rural development. In accordance with MDRI rules, donors compensate AfDF for cancelled debt on a dollar-for-dollar basis according to the payment schedules of the original loans. Similar to IDA, AfDF calculates donors' MDRI commitments at the start of each three-year replenishment cycle according to a burden-sharing percentage. Donor commitments must be met within the three-year replenishment period to avoid a negative impact on the AfDF's commitment capacity. The U.S. share of the cost of MDRI under AfDF-15 (FY 2021-FY 2023) is $68.0 million. No funding is requested for AfDF MDRI in 2023.

CONTRIBUTION TO THE EUROPEAN BANK FOR RECONSTRUCTION AND DEVELOPMENT

Program and Financing (in millions of dollars)

Identification code 020–0088–0–1–151		2021 actual	2022 est.	2023 est.
	Obligations by program activity:			
0801	Reimbursable program activity	7	6	
0900	Total new obligations, unexpired accounts (object class 33.0)	7	6	
	Budgetary resources:			
	Unobligated balance:			
1000	Unobligated balance brought forward, Oct 1		7	
	Budget authority:			
	Spending authority from offsetting collections, discretionary:			
1700	Collected		6	
1930	Total budgetary resources available	7	6	
	Change in obligated balance:			
	Unpaid obligations:			
3010	New obligations, unexpired accounts	7	6	
3020	Outlays (gross)	–7	–6	
	Budget authority and outlays, net:			
	Discretionary:			
4000	Budget authority, gross		6	
	Outlays, gross:			
4010	Outlays from new discretionary authority		6	
4011	Outlays from discretionary balances	7		
4020	Outlays, gross (total)	7	6	
	Offsets against gross budget authority and outlays:			
	Offsetting collections (collected) from:			
4030	Federal sources		–6	
4180	Budget authority, net (total)			
4190	Outlays, net (total)	7		

Created in 1990, the European Bank for Reconstruction and Development (EBRD) supports market-oriented economic reform and democratic pluralism, predominately through private-sector lending and investments. Its original field of operation in the countries of Central and Eastern Europe and the former Soviet Union was expanded in 2012 to aid in the transitions of key countries in the Middle East and North Africa. No funding is requested for the EBRD in 2023.

CONTRIBUTION TO THE NORTH AMERICAN DEVELOPMENT BANK

The North American Development Bank (NADB) finances infrastructure projects that help preserve, protect, and enhance the environment of the U.S.-Mexico border region in order to advance the well-being of people in both the United States and Mexico. NADB provides funding for projects to benefit communities on both sides of the border. Eligible projects must be located within 100 kilometers (around 62 miles) of the border on the U.S. side and 300 kilometers (around 186 miles) on the Mexican side. NADB provides loans and grants to both private sponsors and to municipalities and public utilities. Under its charter the United States and Mexico contribute equally to NADB's capital. No funding is requested for NADB in 2023.

CONTRIBUTION TO ENTERPRISE FOR THE AMERICAS MULTILATERAL INVESTMENT FUND

The Multilateral Investment Fund (MIF), colloquially known as IDB Lab and administered by the Inter-American Development Bank, provides grants, loans and equity investments to support private-sector development in Latin America and the Caribbean, with a focus on creating opportunities for poor and vulnerable populations. Grants and loans are used for technical assistance to identify innovative markets, products and business processes, investments in human capital, and business infrastructure and development. No funding is requested for the MIF in 2023.

CONTRIBUTION TO THE INTERNATIONAL FUND FOR AGRICULTURAL DEVELOPMENT

For payment to the International Fund for Agricultural Development by the Secretary of the Treasury, $43,000,000, to remain available until expended.

Note.—A full-year 2022 appropriation for this account was not enacted at the time the Budget was prepared; therefore, the Budget assumes this account is operating under the Continuing Appropriations Act, 2022 (Division A of Public Law 117–43, as amended). The amounts included for 2022 reflect the annualized level provided by the continuing resolution.

Program and Financing (in millions of dollars)

Identification code 020–1039–0–1–151		2021 actual	2022 est.	2023 est.
	Obligations by program activity:			
0001	Contributions to the International Fund for Agricultural Develop (Direct)	33	33	43
0900	Total new obligations, unexpired accounts (object class 33.0)	33	33	43
	Budgetary resources:			
	Budget authority:			
	Appropriations, discretionary:			
1100	Appropriation	33	33	43
1930	Total budgetary resources available	33	33	43
	Change in obligated balance:			
	Unpaid obligations:			
3010	New obligations, unexpired accounts	33	33	43
3020	Outlays (gross)	–33	–33	–43
	Budget authority and outlays, net:			
	Discretionary:			
4000	Budget authority, gross	33	33	43
	Outlays, gross:			
4010	Outlays from new discretionary authority	33	33	43
4180	Budget authority, net (total)	33	33	43
4190	Outlays, net (total)	33	33	43

The International Fund for Agricultural Development (IFAD) was established in 1977 as an international financial institution and specialized U.N. agency focused on promoting rural agricultural development and food security in developing countries. IFAD's mandate is to help rural, small-scale producers and subsistence farmers increase their agricultural productivity, incomes, and access to markets as well as to promote job creation and rural economic growth in developing countries, including conflict-affected and fragile areas. In 2021, IFAD approved $1.07 billion in new projects and grants. IFAD focuses its operations on low-income countries (LICs) and lower middle-income countries (LMICs) with 46 percent of programming going toward LICs and 42 percent of programming going toward LMICs. IFAD targets its assistance to poor and vulnerable rural populations in these countries. Its portfolio is primarily oriented towards sub-Saharan Africa (about 56 percent) and the Asia and Pacific region (about 32 percent).

The following sectors accounted for most of IFAD's portfolio in 2021: access to markets (29 percent), production sectors (28 percent), and policy and institutions (13 percent). Treasury requests $43 million to support IFAD programming during IFAD's twelfth replenishment period (2022–2024), including for a second of three installment payments.

INTERNATIONAL AFFAIRS TECHNICAL ASSISTANCE

For necessary expenses to carry out the provisions of section 129 of the Foreign Assistance Act of 1961, $38,000,000, to remain available until expended: Provided, That amounts made available under this heading may be made available to contract for services as described in section 129(d)(3)(A) of the Foreign Assistance Act of 1961, without regard to the location in which such services are performed.

Note.—A full-year 2022 appropriation for this account was not enacted at the time the Budget was prepared; therefore, the Budget assumes this account is operating under the Continuing Appropriations Act, 2022 (Division A of Public Law 117–43, as amended). The amounts included for 2022 reflect the annualized level provided by the continuing resolution.

Program and Financing (in millions of dollars)

Identification code 020–1045–0–1–151		2021 actual	2022 est.	2023 est.
Obligations by program activity:				
0001	International Affairs Technical Assistance Program (Direct)	34	34	34
0801	International Affairs Technical Assistance Program (Reimbursable)	11	11	11
0900	Total new obligations, unexpired accounts	45	45	45
Budgetary resources:				
	Unobligated balance:			
1000	Unobligated balance brought forward, Oct 1	45	48	60
1021	Recoveries of prior year unpaid obligations	9	4	4
1070	Unobligated balance (total)	54	52	64
	Budget authority:			
	Appropriations, discretionary:			
1100	Appropriation	33	33	38
	Spending authority from offsetting collections, discretionary:			
1700	Collected	7	20	20
1900	Budget authority (total)	40	53	58
1930	Total budgetary resources available	94	105	122
	Memorandum (non-add) entries:			
1940	Unobligated balance expiring	–1		
1941	Unexpired unobligated balance, end of year	48	60	77
Change in obligated balance:				
	Unpaid obligations:			
3000	Unpaid obligations, brought forward, Oct 1	31	33	20
3010	New obligations, unexpired accounts	45	45	45
3011	Obligations ("upward adjustments"), expired accounts	6		
3020	Outlays (gross)	–36	–54	–54
3040	Recoveries of prior year unpaid obligations, unexpired	–9	–4	–4
3041	Recoveries of prior year unpaid obligations, expired	–4		
3050	Unpaid obligations, end of year	33	20	7
	Memorandum (non-add) entries:			
3100	Obligated balance, start of year	31	33	20
3200	Obligated balance, end of year	33	20	7
Budget authority and outlays, net:				
	Discretionary:			
4000	Budget authority, gross	40	53	58
	Outlays, gross:			
4010	Outlays from new discretionary authority		3	4
4011	Outlays from discretionary balances	36	51	50
4020	Outlays, gross (total)	36	54	54
	Offsets against gross budget authority and outlays:			
	Offsetting collections (collected) from:			
4030	Federal sources	–7	–20	–20
4040	Offsets against gross budget authority and outlays (total)	–7	–20	–20
4180	Budget authority, net (total)	33	33	38
4190	Outlays, net (total)	29	34	34

International Affairs Technical Assistance Program

Pursuant to the Office of Technical Assistance's (OTA) authorizing statute, OTA provides technical assistance to facilitate the implementation of policy, management, and administrative reforms in the areas of revenue, budget, government debt, banking and financial institutions, and economic crime-fighting in developing and transitional countries. This assistance supports U.S. foreign policy and national security objectives.

The 2023 Budget includes $38 million to fund full-time resident technical assistance advisors, intermittent advisors, program-related administrative costs, and enhanced program and project monitoring and evaluation. The appropriation will support technical assistance programs in Asia, the Middle East, Africa, Latin America, the Caribbean, and Europe. It will enable the provision of technical assistance to developing and transition countries to strengthen the capacity of finance ministries, central banks, and other government institutions to manage public finances and oversee the financial sector. Technical assistance projects support efficient revenue collection, well-planned and executed budgets, judicious debt management, sound banking systems, and strong controls to combat corruption and economic crimes, including terrorist financing. The appropriation will also support Treasury's work to strengthen the financial underpinnings for infrastructure development. OTA will continue to coordinate its activities with the Department of State, USAID, and other relevant U.S. Government agencies as well as international financial institutions and other bilateral donors when determining where its technical assistance program can have the greatest positive impact.

Object Classification (in millions of dollars)

Identification code 020–1045–0–1–151		2021 actual	2022 est.	2023 est.
11.1	Direct obligations: Personnel compensation: Full-time permanent	2	2	2
11.9	Total personnel compensation	2	2	2
12.1	Civilian personnel benefits	1	1	1
21.0	Travel and transportation of persons	1	1	1
23.2	Rental payments to others	4	4	4
25.1	Advisory and assistance services	18	18	18
25.2	Other services from non-Federal sources	9	9	9
99.0	Direct obligations	35	35	35
99.0	Reimbursable obligations	10	10	10
99.9	Total new obligations, unexpired accounts	45	45	45

Employment Summary

Identification code 020–1045–0–1–151		2021 actual	2022 est.	2023 est.
1001	Direct civilian full-time equivalent employment	10	10	10

FUNDS APPROPRIATED TO THE PRESIDENT

INTERNATIONAL ORGANIZATIONS AND PROGRAMS

For necessary expenses to carry out the provisions of section 301 of the Foreign Assistance Act of 1961 and section 2 of the United Nations Environment Program Participation Act of 1973, $457,200,000: Provided, That section 307(a) of the Foreign Assistance Act of 1961 shall not apply to contributions to the United Nations Democracy Fund.

Note.—A full-year 2022 appropriation for this account was not enacted at the time the Budget was prepared; therefore, the Budget assumes this account is operating under the Continuing Appropriations Act, 2022 (Division A of Public Law 117–43, as amended). The amounts included for 2022 reflect the annualized level provided by the continuing resolution.

Program and Financing (in millions of dollars)

Identification code 019–1005–0–1–151		2021 actual	2022 est.	2023 est.
Obligations by program activity:				
0001	International Organizations and Programs (Direct)	386	968	457
0900	Total new obligations, unexpired accounts (object class 41.0)	386	968	457
Budgetary resources:				
	Unobligated balance:			
1000	Unobligated balance brought forward, Oct 1		580	
	Budget authority:			
	Appropriations, discretionary:			
1100	Appropriation	388	388	457

FUNDS APPROPRIATED TO THE PRESIDENT—Continued

Program and Financing—Continued

Identification code 019–1005–0–1–151		2021 actual	2022 est.	2023 est.
1120	Appropriations transferred to other accts [019–1031]	–2	....	....
1160	Appropriation, discretionary (total)	386	388	457
	Appropriations, mandatory:			
1200	Appropriation - ARP Act	580	....	....
1900	Budget authority (total)	966	388	457
1930	Total budgetary resources available	966	968	457
	Memorandum (non-add) entries:			
1941	Unexpired unobligated balance, end of year	580	....	....
	Change in obligated balance:			
	Unpaid obligations:			
3000	Unpaid obligations, brought forward, Oct 1	6	8	....
3010	New obligations, unexpired accounts	386	968	457
3011	Obligations ("upward adjustments"), expired accounts	2	....	....
3020	Outlays (gross)	–384	–976	–457
3041	Recoveries of prior year unpaid obligations, expired	–2	....	....
3050	Unpaid obligations, end of year	8	....	....
	Memorandum (non-add) entries:			
3100	Obligated balance, start of year	6	8	....
3200	Obligated balance, end of year	8	....	....
	Budget authority and outlays, net:			
	Discretionary:			
4000	Budget authority, gross	386	388	457
	Outlays, gross:			
4010	Outlays from new discretionary authority	380	388	457
4011	Outlays from discretionary balances	4	8	....
4020	Outlays, gross (total)	384	396	457
	Mandatory:			
4090	Budget authority, gross	580	....	....
	Outlays, gross:			
4101	Outlays from mandatory balances	....	580	....
4180	Budget authority, net (total)	966	388	457
4190	Outlays, net (total)	384	976	457

In addition to its assessed payments, the United States contributes to voluntary funds of many UN-affiliated and other international organizations and programs involved in a wide range of sustainable development, humanitarian, scientific, environmental and security activities. Through such contributions, the United States can multiply the influence and effectiveness of its own assistance and provide support for international programs that are capable of attracting additional resources from other donors, leveraging those contributions to advance U.S. strategic goals.

DEBT RESTRUCTURING

For "Bilateral Economic Assistance—Department of the Treasury—Debt Restructuring" there is appropriated $52,000,000, to remain available until expended, for the costs, as defined in section 502 of the Congressional Budget Act of 1974, of modifying loans and loan guarantees for, or credits extended to, such countries as the President may determine, including the cost of selling, reducing, or canceling amounts owed to the United States pursuant to the Paris Club debt restructurings or the "Common Framework for Debt Treatments beyond the Debt Service Suspension Initiative" (DSSI), and for reducing interest rates paid by any country eligible for the DSSI: Provided, That such amounts may be used notwithstanding any other provision of law.

TROPICAL FOREST AND CORAL REEF CONSERVATION ACT

For the costs, as defined in section 502 of the Congressional Budget Act of 1974, of modifying loans and loan guarantees, as the President may determine, for which funds have been appropriated or otherwise made available for programs within the International Affairs Budget Function 150, including the cost of selling, reducing, or canceling amounts owed to the United States as a result of concessional loans made or credits extended to eligible countries, pursuant to part V of the Foreign Assistance Act of 1961, $15,000,000, to remain available until expended.

Note.—A full-year 2022 appropriation for this account was not enacted at the time the Budget was prepared; therefore, the Budget assumes this account is operating under the Continuing Appropriations Act, 2022 (Division A of Public Law 117–43, as amended). The amounts included for 2022 reflect the annualized level provided by the continuing resolution.

Program and Financing (in millions of dollars)

Identification code 020–0091–0–1–151		2021 actual	2022 est.	2023 est.
	Obligations by program activity:			
0103	Tropical Forest Conservation Initiative	15	15	15
0104	Debt Relief and Restructuring	120	151	12
0191	Direct program activities, subtotal	135	166	27
0900	Total new obligations, unexpired accounts (object class 41.0)	135	166	27
	Budgetary resources:			
	Unobligated balance:			
1000	Unobligated balance brought forward, Oct 1	16	205	243
	Budget authority:			
	Appropriations, discretionary:			
1100	Appropriation	324	204	67
1930	Total budgetary resources available	340	409	310
	Memorandum (non-add) entries:			
1941	Unexpired unobligated balance, end of year	205	243	283
	Change in obligated balance:			
	Unpaid obligations:			
3000	Unpaid obligations, brought forward, Oct 1	76	177	159
3010	New obligations, unexpired accounts	135	166	27
3020	Outlays (gross)	–34	–184	–47
3050	Unpaid obligations, end of year	177	159	139
	Memorandum (non-add) entries:			
3100	Obligated balance, start of year	76	177	159
3200	Obligated balance, end of year	177	159	139
	Budget authority and outlays, net:			
	Discretionary:			
4000	Budget authority, gross	324	204	67
	Outlays, gross:			
4010	Outlays from new discretionary authority	....	73	24
4011	Outlays from discretionary balances	34	111	23
4020	Outlays, gross (total)	34	184	47
4180	Budget authority, net (total)	324	204	67
4190	Outlays, net (total)	34	184	47

Summary of Loan Levels, Subsidy Budget Authority and Outlays by Program (in millions of dollars)

Identification code 020–0091–0–1–151		2021 actual	2022 est.	2023 est.
	Direct loan subsidy outlays:			
134003	Department of Agriculture	5	15	....
134004	Defense Security Cooperation Agency	29	....	....
134999	Total subsidy outlays	34	15	....

Debt Relief and Debt Restructuring

Debt relief and restructuring are fundamental to helping countries stabilize their economies, restart economic growth, and alleviate poverty and instability. Restructuring debt, including with principal haircuts, also allows beneficiary countries to increase poverty reduction expenditures in areas such as health, education, and rural development. The United States regularly provides debt restructuring through the Paris Club, in coordination with other bilateral lenders. However, since the COVID-19 pandemic begam debt burdens for low-income countries have substantially increased. In response, with strong U.S. leadership and support, the G20 and Paris Club developed the Debt Service Suspension Initiative (DSSI) and the G20 Common Framework for Debt Treatments beyond DSSI (Common Framework) as central pillars of the international policy response to the COVID-19 pandemic. The DSSI has provided official bilateral debt service suspension to low-income countries, allowing them to focus on responding to immediate health, economic, and social spending needs related to COVID-19. Recognizing that many countries may need more comprehensive debt treatment to address unsustainable debt and heightened liquidity needs, the G20 and Paris Club in November 2020 also endorsed the Common Framework, which aims to facilitate timely and orderly treatments within the context of an IMF program, and fosters fair burden sharing among all official bilateral creditors and comparable treatment from private creditors.

The Tropical Forest and Coral Reef Conservation Act contributes to achieving U.S. Government policy priorities of conserving tropical forests and coral reefs by enabling eligible countries to redirect debt payments to a local conservation fund dedicated to those objectives.

The 2023 Budget requests $67 million for Treasury's Debt Restructuring account to pay for the cost of the United States' bilateral debt restructuring and debt relief funding. Of this, $52 million is for interest rate reductions on debt service deferrals under the DSSI and debt treatments through the Common Framework and Paris Club, and $15 million is for debt treatments to support conservation maintenance and restoration of tropical forests and coral reef ecosystems under the Tropical Forest and Coral Reef Conservation Act.

AGENCY FOR INTERNATIONAL DEVELOPMENT

Federal Funds

DEVELOPMENT ASSISTANCE

For necessary expenses to carry out the provisions of sections 103, 105, 106, 214, and sections 251 through 255, and chapter 10 of part I of the Foreign Assistance Act of 1961, $4,769,787,000, to remain available until September 30, 2024: Provided, That in addition to funds otherwise available for such purposes, up to $30,000,000 of the funds appropriated under this heading and allocated to the USAID Development Innovation Ventures program may be made available for the purposes of chapter 1 of part I of the Foreign Assistance Act of 1961.

Note.—A full-year 2022 appropriation for this account was not enacted at the time the Budget was prepared; therefore, the Budget assumes this account is operating under the Continuing Appropriations Act, 2022 (Division A of Public Law 117–43, as amended). The amounts included for 2022 reflect the annualized level provided by the continuing resolution.

Program and Financing (in millions of dollars)

Identification code 072–1021–0–1–151		2021 actual	2022 est.	2023 est.
	Obligations by program activity:			
0001	Development Assistance Program (Direct)	3,409	3,650	3,550
	Budgetary resources:			
	Unobligated balance:			
1000	Unobligated balance brought forward, Oct 1	3,502	3,611	3,460
1010	Unobligated balance transfer to other accts [077–0110]	–10	–1	–1
1011	Unobligated balance transfer from other acct [019–1022]	4		
1021	Recoveries of prior year unpaid obligations	21		
1070	Unobligated balance (total)	3,517	3,610	3,459
	Budget authority:			
	Appropriations, discretionary:			
1100	Appropriation	3,500	3,500	4,770
	Spending authority from offsetting collections, discretionary:			
1700	Collected	3		
1900	Budget authority (total)	3,503	3,500	4,770
1930	Total budgetary resources available	7,020	7,110	8,229
	Memorandum (non-add) entries:			
1941	Unexpired unobligated balance, end of year	3,611	3,460	4,679
	Change in obligated balance:			
	Unpaid obligations:			
3000	Unpaid obligations, brought forward, Oct 1	5,350	6,234	6,994
3010	New obligations, unexpired accounts	3,409	3,650	3,550
3011	Obligations ("upward adjustments"), expired accounts	2		
3020	Outlays (gross)	–2,498	–2,890	–3,382
3040	Recoveries of prior year unpaid obligations, unexpired	–21		
3041	Recoveries of prior year unpaid obligations, expired	–8		
3050	Unpaid obligations, end of year	6,234	6,994	7,162
	Uncollected payments:			
3060	Uncollected pymts, Fed sources, brought forward, Oct 1	–1	–1	–1
3090	Uncollected pymts, Fed sources, end of year	–1	–1	–1
	Memorandum (non-add) entries:			
3100	Obligated balance, start of year	5,349	6,233	6,993
3200	Obligated balance, end of year	6,233	6,993	7,161
	Budget authority and outlays, net:			
	Discretionary:			
4000	Budget authority, gross	3,503	3,500	4,770
	Outlays, gross:			
4010	Outlays from new discretionary authority		350	477
4011	Outlays from discretionary balances	2,498	2,540	2,905
4020	Outlays, gross (total)	2,498	2,890	3,382
	Offsets against gross budget authority and outlays:			
	Offsetting collections (collected) from:			
4030	Federal sources	–3		
4040	Offsets against gross budget authority and outlays (total)	–3		
4180	Budget authority, net (total)	3,500	3,500	4,770
4190	Outlays, net (total)	2,495	2,890	3,382

Development Assistance Programs. —The Development Assistance (DA) account invests in partnerships that support countries' development plans, by supporting and implementing solutions to overcome their development challenges, working to end extreme poverty, and promoting resilient, democratic societies around the world. The U.S. Agency for International Development (USAID) invests in programs that mitigate the impacts of changing climate, advance basic and higher education, respond to the short- and long-term impacts of the COVID-19 pandemic, and create avenues for sustainable and inclusive economic growth. . Resources include increased funding to advance global democracy programming, further gender and racial equity, address the root causes of migration, and combat poverty and food insecurity.

Object Classification (in millions of dollars)

Identification code 072–1021–0–1–151		2021 actual	2022 est.	2023 est.
	Direct obligations:			
	Personnel compensation:			
11.1	Full-time permanent	31	31	31
11.3	Other than full-time permanent	9	9	9
11.8	Special personal services payments	1	1	1
11.9	Total personnel compensation	41	41	41
12.1	Civilian personnel benefits	8	8	8
23.1	Rental payments to GSA	7	7	7
23.3	Communications, utilities, and miscellaneous charges	3	3	3
25.1	Advisory and assistance services	106	106	106
25.3	Other goods and services from Federal sources	4	4	4
31.0	Equipment	1	1	1
41.0	Grants, subsidies, and contributions	3,239	3,480	3,380
99.9	Total new obligations, unexpired accounts	3,409	3,650	3,550

Employment Summary

Identification code 072–1021–0–1–151	2021 actual	2022 est.	2023 est.
1001 Direct civilian full-time equivalent employment	250	250	250

CHILD SURVIVAL AND HEALTH PROGRAMS

Program and Financing (in millions of dollars)

Identification code 072–1095–0–1–151		2021 actual	2022 est.	2023 est.
	Obligations by program activity:			
0001	Child Survival and Health Programs (Direct)		2	2
0900	Total new obligations, unexpired accounts (object class 41.0)		2	2
	Budgetary resources:			
	Unobligated balance:			
1000	Unobligated balance brought forward, Oct 1	38	38	36
1930	Total budgetary resources available	38	38	36
	Memorandum (non-add) entries:			
1941	Unexpired unobligated balance, end of year	38	36	34
	Change in obligated balance:			
	Unpaid obligations:			
3000	Unpaid obligations, brought forward, Oct 1	4	4	1
3010	New obligations, unexpired accounts		2	2
3020	Outlays (gross)		–5	–3
3050	Unpaid obligations, end of year	4	1	
	Uncollected payments:			
3060	Uncollected pymts, Fed sources, brought forward, Oct 1	–5	–5	–5
3090	Uncollected pymts, Fed sources, end of year	–5	–5	–5
	Memorandum (non-add) entries:			
3100	Obligated balance, start of year	–1	–1	–4

Agency for International Development—Continued
Federal Funds—Continued

CHILD SURVIVAL AND HEALTH PROGRAMS—Continued

Program and Financing—Continued

Identification code 072–1095–0–1–151	2021 actual	2022 est.	2023 est.
3200 Obligated balance, end of year	–1	–4	–5
Budget authority and outlays, net:			
Discretionary:			
Outlays, gross:			
4011 Outlays from discretionary balances		5	3
4180 Budget authority, net (total)			
4190 Outlays, net (total)		5	3

Prior to 2008, funds were appropriated to the Child Survival and Health Programs account to support activities that address family planning/reproductive health; child survival and maternal health, including activities directed at vulnerable children and the primary causes of morbidity and mortality, polio, micronutrients and iodine deficiency; preventing and treating infectious diseases such as malaria and tuberculosis; and reducing HIV transmission and the impact of the HIV/AIDS pandemic in developing countries. Additional funding for HIV/AIDS was appropriated in the Global HIV/AIDS Initiative account for this purpose through 2007. Beginning in 2008, funds for these activities were appropriated in the Global Health and Child Survival (now Global Health Programs) account, and will continue to be requested in that account.

HIV/AIDS WORKING CAPITAL FUND

Program and Financing (in millions of dollars)

Identification code 072–1033–0–1–151	2021 actual	2022 est.	2023 est.
Obligations by program activity:			
0801 HIV/AIDS Working Capital Fund (Reimbursable)	767	500	400
0900 Total new obligations, unexpired accounts (object class 41.0)	767	500	400
Budgetary resources:			
Unobligated balance:			
1000 Unobligated balance brought forward, Oct 1	541	251	151
Budget authority:			
Spending authority from offsetting collections, discretionary:			
1700 Collected	582	400	400
1701 Change in uncollected payments, Federal sources	–105		
1750 Spending auth from offsetting collections, disc (total)	477	400	400
1930 Total budgetary resources available	1,018	651	551
Memorandum (non-add) entries:			
1941 Unexpired unobligated balance, end of year	251	151	151
Change in obligated balance:			
Unpaid obligations:			
3000 Unpaid obligations, brought forward, Oct 1	618	810	700
3010 New obligations, unexpired accounts	767	500	400
3020 Outlays (gross)	–575	–610	–520
3050 Unpaid obligations, end of year	810	700	580
Uncollected payments:			
3060 Uncollected pymts, Fed sources, brought forward, Oct 1	–105		
3070 Change in uncollected pymts, Fed sources, unexpired	105		
Memorandum (non-add) entries:			
3100 Obligated balance, start of year	513	810	700
3200 Obligated balance, end of year	810	700	580
Budget authority and outlays, net:			
Discretionary:			
4000 Budget authority, gross	477	400	400
Outlays, gross:			
4010 Outlays from new discretionary authority	34	260	260
4011 Outlays from discretionary balances	541	350	260
4020 Outlays, gross (total)	575	610	520
Offsets against gross budget authority and outlays:			
Offsetting collections (collected) from:			
4030 Federal sources	–582	–400	–400
4040 Offsets against gross budget authority and outlays (total)	–582	–400	–400
Additional offsets against gross budget authority only:			
4050 Change in uncollected pymts, Fed sources, unexpired	105		
4060 Additional offsets against budget authority only (total)	105		
4080 Outlays, net (discretionary)	–7	210	120
4180 Budget authority, net (total)			
4190 Outlays, net (total)	–7	210	120

The HIV/AIDS Working Capital Fund (WCF) was established to assist in providing a safe, secure, reliable, and sustainable supply chain of pharmaceuticals and other products needed to provide care to and treatment for persons with HIV/AIDS and related infections. These include anti-retroviral drugs; other pharmaceuticals and medical items; laboratory and other supplies for performing tests; other medical supplies needed for the operation of HIV/AIDS treatment and care centers, including products needed in programs for the prevention of mother-to-child transmission; pharmaceuticals and health commodities needed for the provision of palliative care; and laboratory and clinical equipment, equipment needed for the transportation and care of HIV/AIDS supplies, and other equipment and technical assistance needed to provide prevention, care and treatment of HIV/AIDS described above. Funds in the WCF may also be made available for pharmaceuticals and other products for other global health activities.

DEVELOPMENT FUND FOR AFRICA

Program and Financing (in millions of dollars)

Identification code 072–1014–0–1–151	2021 actual	2022 est.	2023 est.
Obligations by program activity:			
0001 Development Fund for Africa (Direct)		1	1
0900 Total new obligations, unexpired accounts (object class 41.0)		1	1
Budgetary resources:			
Unobligated balance:			
1000 Unobligated balance brought forward, Oct 1	3	3	2
1930 Total budgetary resources available	3	3	2
Memorandum (non-add) entries:			
1941 Unexpired unobligated balance, end of year	3	2	1
Change in obligated balance:			
Unpaid obligations:			
3000 Unpaid obligations, brought forward, Oct 1	3	3	2
3010 New obligations, unexpired accounts		1	1
3020 Outlays (gross)		–2	–1
3050 Unpaid obligations, end of year	3	2	2
Memorandum (non-add) entries:			
3100 Obligated balance, start of year	3	3	2
3200 Obligated balance, end of year	3	2	2
Budget authority and outlays, net:			
Discretionary:			
Outlays, gross:			
4011 Outlays from discretionary balances		2	1
4180 Budget authority, net (total)			
4190 Outlays, net (total)		2	1

For 2023, assistance to Africa is requested in other assistance accounts.

ASSISTANCE FOR EUROPE, EURASIA AND CENTRAL ASIA

For necessary expenses to carry out the provisions of the Foreign Assistance Act of 1961, the FREEDOM Support Act (Public Law 102–511), and the Support for Eastern European Democracy (SEED) Act of 1989 (Public Law 101–179), $984,429,000, to remain available until September 30, 2024, which shall be available, notwithstanding any other provision of law, except section 7033 of this Act, for assistance and related programs for countries identified in section 3 of the FREEDOM Support Act (22 U.S.C. 5801) and section 3(c) of the SEED Act of 1989 (22 U.S.C. 5402), in addition to funds otherwise available for such purposes: Provided, That funds appropriated by this Act under the headings "Global Health Programs", "Economic Support Fund", and "International Narcotics Control and Law Enforcement" that are made available for assistance for such countries shall be administered in accordance with the responsibilities of the coordinator designated pursuant to

DEPARTMENT OF STATE AND OTHER INTERNATIONAL PROGRAMS

Agency for International Development—Continued
Federal Funds—Continued

845

section 102 of the FREEDOM Support Act and section 601 of the SEED Act of 1989: Provided further, That funds appropriated under this heading shall be considered to be economic assistance under the Foreign Assistance Act of 1961 for purposes of making available the administrative authorities contained in that Act for the use of economic assistance: Provided further, That funds appropriated under this heading may be made available for contributions to multilateral initiatives to counter hybrid threats.

Note.—A full-year 2022 appropriation for this account was not enacted at the time the Budget was prepared; therefore, the Budget assumes this account is operating under the Continuing Appropriations Act, 2022 (Division A of Public Law 117–43, as amended). The amounts included for 2022 reflect the annualized level provided by the continuing resolution.

Program and Financing (in millions of dollars)

Identification code 072–0306–0–1–151	2021 actual	2022 est.	2023 est.
Obligations by program activity:			
0001 Assistance for Europe, Eurasia and Central Asia (Direct)	778	820	800
Budgetary resources:			
Unobligated balance:			
1000 Unobligated balance brought forward, Oct 1	799	791	741
1010 Unobligated balance transfer to other accts [089–0319]	–6		
1010 Unobligated balance transfer to other accts [011–1001]	–2		
1010 Unobligated balance transfer to other accts [077–0110]	–5		
1012 Unobligated balance transfers between expired and unexpired accounts		8	
1021 Recoveries of prior year unpaid obligations	2		
1070 Unobligated balance (total)	796	791	741
Budget authority:			
Appropriations, discretionary:			
1100 Appropriation	770	770	984
Spending authority from offsetting collections, discretionary:			
1700 Collected	3		
1900 Budget authority (total)	773	770	984
1930 Total budgetary resources available	1,569	1,561	1,725
Memorandum (non-add) entries:			
1941 Unexpired unobligated balance, end of year	791	741	925
Change in obligated balance:			
Unpaid obligations:			
3000 Unpaid obligations, brought forward, Oct 1	1,237	1,356	1,427
3010 New obligations, unexpired accounts	778	820	800
3011 Obligations ("upward adjustments"), expired accounts	7		
3020 Outlays (gross)	–641	–749	–943
3040 Recoveries of prior year unpaid obligations, unexpired	–2		
3041 Recoveries of prior year unpaid obligations, expired	–23		
3050 Unpaid obligations, end of year	1,356	1,427	1,284
Memorandum (non-add) entries:			
3100 Obligated balance, start of year	1,237	1,356	1,427
3200 Obligated balance, end of year	1,356	1,427	1,284
Budget authority and outlays, net:			
Discretionary:			
4000 Budget authority, gross	773	770	984
Outlays, gross:			
4010 Outlays from new discretionary authority		38	49
4011 Outlays from discretionary balances	641	711	894
4020 Outlays, gross (total)	641	749	943
Offsets against gross budget authority and outlays:			
Offsetting collections (collected) from:			
4030 Federal sources	–3		
4033 Non-Federal sources	–1		
4040 Offsets against gross budget authority and outlays (total)	–4		
Additional offsets against gross budget authority only:			
4052 Offsetting collections credited to expired accounts	1		
4070 Budget authority, net (discretionary)	770	770	984
4080 Outlays, net (discretionary)	637	749	943
4180 Budget authority, net (total)	770	770	984
4190 Outlays, net (total)	637	749	943

The purpose of the Assistance for Europe, Eurasia and Central Asia (AEECA) account is to support programs to foster the democratic and economic transitions of the countries of Southeastern Europe and the independent states that emerged from the dissolution of the Soviet Union, as well as related efforts to address social sector reform and combat transnational threats in these countries.

Object Classification (in millions of dollars)

Identification code 072–0306–0–1–151	2021 actual	2022 est.	2023 est.
Direct obligations:			
21.0 Travel and transportation of persons	1	1	1
25.1 Advisory and assistance services	2	2	2
25.3 Other goods and services from Federal sources	3	3	3
26.0 Supplies and materials	1	1	1
41.0 Grants, subsidies, and contributions	771	813	793
99.9 Total new obligations, unexpired accounts	778	820	800

ASSISTANCE FOR EASTERN EUROPE AND THE BALTIC STATES

Program and Financing (in millions of dollars)

Identification code 072–1010–0–1–151	2021 actual	2022 est.	2023 est.
Budgetary resources:			
Unobligated balance:			
1000 Unobligated balance brought forward, Oct 1	1	1	1
1930 Total budgetary resources available	1	1	1
Memorandum (non-add) entries:			
1941 Unexpired unobligated balance, end of year	1	1	1
Change in obligated balance:			
Unpaid obligations:			
3000 Unpaid obligations, brought forward, Oct 1	3	3	2
3020 Outlays (gross)		–1	–1
3050 Unpaid obligations, end of year	3	2	1
Memorandum (non-add) entries:			
3100 Obligated balance, start of year	3	3	2
3200 Obligated balance, end of year	3	2	1
Budget authority and outlays, net:			
Discretionary:			
Outlays, gross:			
4011 Outlays from discretionary balances		1	1
4180 Budget authority, net (total)			
4190 Outlays, net (total)		1	1

This account provided funds for assistance programs that fostered the democratic and economic transitions of Eastern Europe and the Baltic states as well as related efforts to address social sector reform and combat transnational threats. Beginning in 2009, funds for these activities have been appropriated and requested in other assistance accounts.

ASSISTANCE FOR THE INDEPENDENT STATES OF THE FORMER SOVIET UNION

Program and Financing (in millions of dollars)

Identification code 072–1093–0–1–151	2021 actual	2022 est.	2023 est.
Obligations by program activity:			
0001 Assistance for the Independent States of the Former Soviet Union (Direct)		1	1
0900 Total new obligations, unexpired accounts (object class 41.0)		1	1
Budgetary resources:			
Unobligated balance:			
1000 Unobligated balance brought forward, Oct 1	3	5	4
1021 Recoveries of prior year unpaid obligations	2		
1070 Unobligated balance (total)	5	5	4
1930 Total budgetary resources available	5	5	4
Memorandum (non-add) entries:			
1941 Unexpired unobligated balance, end of year	5	4	3
Change in obligated balance:			
Unpaid obligations:			
3000 Unpaid obligations, brought forward, Oct 1	6	3	3
3010 New obligations, unexpired accounts		1	1
3020 Outlays (gross)	–1	–1	–1
3040 Recoveries of prior year unpaid obligations, unexpired	–2		
3050 Unpaid obligations, end of year	3	3	3

Agency for International Development—Continued
Federal Funds—Continued

ASSISTANCE FOR THE INDEPENDENT STATES OF THE FORMER SOVIET UNION—Continued

Program and Financing—Continued

Identification code 072–1093–0–1–151		2021 actual	2022 est.	2023 est.
	Memorandum (non-add) entries:			
3100	Obligated balance, start of year	6	3	3
3200	Obligated balance, end of year	3	3	3
	Budget authority and outlays, net:			
	Discretionary:			
	Outlays, gross:			
4011	Outlays from discretionary balances	1	1	1
4180	Budget authority, net (total)	....	....	....
4190	Outlays, net (total)	1	1	1

This account provided funds for assistance programs that fostered the democratic and economic transitions of the independent states that emerged from the former Soviet Union, as well as related efforts to address social sector reform and combat transnational threats. Beginning in 2009, funds for these activities have been appropriated and requested in other assistance accounts.

INTERNATIONAL DISASTER ASSISTANCE

For necessary expenses to carry out the provisions of section 491 of the Foreign Assistance Act of 1961 for international disaster relief, rehabilitation, and reconstruction assistance, $4,699,362,000, to remain available until expended.

Note.—A full-year 2022 appropriation for this account was not enacted at the time the Budget was prepared; therefore, the Budget assumes this account is operating under the Continuing Appropriations Act, 2022 (Division A of Public Law 117–43, as amended). The amounts included for 2022 reflect the annualized level provided by the continuing resolution.

INTERNATIONAL DISASTER ASSISTANCE

[*For an additional amount for "International Disaster Assistance", $400,000,000, to remain available until expended, to address humanitarian needs in Afghanistan and the region impacted by the situation in Afghanistan.*] *(Afghanistan Supplemental Appropriations Act, 2022.)*

Program and Financing (in millions of dollars)

Identification code 072–1035–0–1–151		2021 actual	2022 est.	2023 est.
	Obligations by program activity:			
0001	International Disaster Assistance (Direct)	4,429	4,600	4,600
	Budgetary resources:			
	Unobligated balance:			
1000	Unobligated balance brought forward, Oct 1	1,421	1,488	1,685
1010	Unobligated balance transfer to other accts [070–0702]	–8	....	....
1021	Recoveries of prior year unpaid obligations	109	....	....
1070	Unobligated balance (total)	1,522	1,488	1,685
	Budget authority:			
	Appropriations, discretionary:			
1100	Appropriation	4,395	4,395	4,699
1100	Appropriation	....	400	....
1160	Appropriation, discretionary (total)	4,395	4,795	4,699
	Spending authority from offsetting collections, discretionary:			
1700	Collected	1	2	....
1701	Change in uncollected payments, Federal sources	–1	....	....
1750	Spending auth from offsetting collections, disc (total)	....	2	....
1900	Budget authority (total)	4,395	4,797	4,699
1930	Total budgetary resources available	5,917	6,285	6,384
	Memorandum (non-add) entries:			
1941	Unexpired unobligated balance, end of year	1,488	1,685	1,784
	Change in obligated balance:			
	Unpaid obligations:			
3000	Unpaid obligations, brought forward, Oct 1	5,335	4,351	6,256
3010	New obligations, unexpired accounts	4,429	4,600	4,600
3020	Outlays (gross)	–5,304	–2,695	–2,838
3040	Recoveries of prior year unpaid obligations, unexpired	–109	....	....
3050	Unpaid obligations, end of year	4,351	6,256	8,018
	Uncollected payments:			
3060	Uncollected pymts, Fed sources, brought forward, Oct 1	–1	....	....
3070	Change in uncollected pymts, Fed sources, unexpired	1	....	....
	Memorandum (non-add) entries:			
3100	Obligated balance, start of year	5,334	4,351	6,256
3200	Obligated balance, end of year	4,351	6,256	8,018
	Budget authority and outlays, net:			
	Discretionary:			
4000	Budget authority, gross	4,395	4,797	4,699
	Outlays, gross:			
4010	Outlays from new discretionary authority	1,078	961	940
4011	Outlays from discretionary balances	4,226	1,734	1,898
4020	Outlays, gross (total)	5,304	2,695	2,838
	Offsets against gross budget authority and outlays:			
	Offsetting collections (collected) from:			
4030	Federal sources	–1	–2	....
	Additional offsets against gross budget authority only:			
4050	Change in uncollected pymts, Fed sources, unexpired	1	....	....
4070	Budget authority, net (discretionary)	4,395	4,795	4,699
4080	Outlays, net (discretionary)	5,303	2,693	2,838
4180	Budget authority, net (total)	4,395	4,795	4,699
4190	Outlays, net (total)	5,303	2,693	2,838

The IDA account provides funds to save lives, reduce human suffering, and mitigate and prepare for natural and complex emergencies overseas. Specifically, these funds provide for the management of humanitarian assistance, rehabilitation, disaster risk reduction, transition to development assistance programs, as well as emergency food interventions. Humanitarian relief interventions include, but are not limited to, shelter, emergency health and nutrition, as well as the provision of safe drinking water. Emergency food responses include interventions such as local and regional purchase of food near crises, the provision of U.S. commodities, food vouchers, or cash transfers and complementary activities that support the relief, recovery and resilience of populations affected by food crises. IDA programs target the most vulnerable populations who are affected by disasters and complex crises, including those who are internally displaced and refugees.

Object Classification (in millions of dollars)

Identification code 072–1035–0–1–151		2021 actual	2022 est.	2023 est.
	Direct obligations:			
12.1	Civilian personnel benefits	64	64	64
21.0	Travel and transportation of persons	7	7	7
23.1	Rental payments to GSA	1	1	1
23.2	Rental payments to others	2	2	2
23.3	Communications, utilities, and miscellaneous charges	1	1	1
25.1	Advisory and assistance services	38	38	38
25.3	Other goods and services from Federal sources	12	....	....
41.0	Grants, subsidies, and contributions	4,304	4,487	4,487
99.9	Total new obligations, unexpired accounts	4,429	4,600	4,600

Employment Summary

Identification code 072–1035–0–1–151	2021 actual	2022 est.	2023 est.
1001 Direct civilian full-time equivalent employment	2	2	2

FUNDS APPROPRIATED TO THE PRESIDENT

OPERATING EXPENSES

For necessary expenses to carry out the provisions of section 667 of the Foreign Assistance Act of 1961, $1,743,350,000, to remain available until September 30, 2024: Provided, That contracts or agreements entered into with funds appropriated under this heading may entail commitments for the expenditure of such funds through the following fiscal year: Provided further, That the authority of sections 610 and 109 of the Foreign Assistance Act of 1961 may be exercised by the Secretary of State to transfer funds appropriated to carry out chapter 1 of part I of such Act to "Operating Expenses" in accordance with the provisions of those sections: Provided further, That of the funds appropriated or made available under this heading, not to exceed $250,000 may be available for representation and entertainment expenses, of which not to exceed $5,000 may be available for entertainment expenses, and not to exceed $100,500 shall be for official residence expenses, for USAID during the current fiscal year.

DEPARTMENT OF STATE AND OTHER INTERNATIONAL PROGRAMS

Note.—A full-year 2022 appropriation for this account was not enacted at the time the Budget was prepared; therefore, the Budget assumes this account is operating under the Continuing Appropriations Act, 2022 (Division A of Public Law 117–43, as amended). The amounts included for 2022 reflect the annualized level provided by the continuing resolution.

Program and Financing (in millions of dollars)

Identification code 072–1000–0–1–151		2021 actual	2022 est.	2023 est.
	Obligations by program activity:			
0001	Operating Expenses of the Agency for International Development (Direct)	1,469	1,531	1,741
0002	Foreign national separation fund	2	2	2
0799	Total direct obligations	1,471	1,533	1,743
0801	Operating Expenses of the Agency for International Development (Reimbursable)	59	59	59
0900	Total new obligations, unexpired accounts	1,530	1,592	1,802
	Budgetary resources:			
	Unobligated balance:			
1000	Unobligated balance brought forward, Oct 1	165	156	
1012	Unobligated balance transfers between expired and unexpired accounts	41		
1021	Recoveries of prior year unpaid obligations	6		
1070	Unobligated balance (total)	212	156	
	Budget authority:			
	Appropriations, discretionary:			
1100	Appropriation	1,378	1,378	1,743
	Appropriations, mandatory:			
1200	Appropriation	41		
	Spending authority from offsetting collections, discretionary:			
1700	Collected	50	58	59
1701	Change in uncollected payments, Federal sources	8		
1750	Spending auth from offsetting collections, disc (total)	58	58	59
1900	Budget authority (total)	1,477	1,436	1,802
1930	Total budgetary resources available	1,689	1,592	1,802
	Memorandum (non-add) entries:			
1940	Unobligated balance expiring	–3		
1941	Unexpired unobligated balance, end of year	156		
	Change in obligated balance:			
	Unpaid obligations:			
3000	Unpaid obligations, brought forward, Oct 1	782	775	944
3010	New obligations, unexpired accounts	1,530	1,592	1,802
3011	Obligations ("upward adjustments"), expired accounts	45		
3020	Outlays (gross)	–1,502	–1,423	–1,667
3040	Recoveries of prior year unpaid obligations, unexpired	–6		
3041	Recoveries of prior year unpaid obligations, expired	–74		
3050	Unpaid obligations, end of year	775	944	1,079
	Uncollected payments:			
3060	Uncollected pymts, Fed sources, brought forward, Oct 1	–17	–16	–16
3070	Change in uncollected pymts, Fed sources, unexpired	–8		
3071	Change in uncollected pymts, Fed sources, expired	9		
3090	Uncollected pymts, Fed sources, end of year	–16	–16	–16
	Memorandum (non-add) entries:			
3100	Obligated balance, start of year	765	759	928
3200	Obligated balance, end of year	759	928	1,063
	Budget authority and outlays, net:			
	Discretionary:			
4000	Budget authority, gross	1,436	1,436	1,802
	Outlays, gross:			
4010	Outlays from new discretionary authority	850	950	1,187
4011	Outlays from discretionary balances	652	473	480
4020	Outlays, gross (total)	1,502	1,423	1,667
	Offsets against gross budget authority and outlays:			
	Offsetting collections (collected) from:			
4030	Federal sources	–58	–58	–59
4033	Non-Federal sources	–41		
4040	Offsets against gross budget authority and outlays (total)	–99	–58	–59
	Additional offsets against gross budget authority only:			
4050	Change in uncollected pymts, Fed sources, unexpired	–8		
4052	Offsetting collections credited to expired accounts	49		
4060	Additional offsets against budget authority only (total)	41		
4070	Budget authority, net (discretionary)	1,378	1,378	1,743
4080	Outlays, net (discretionary)	1,403	1,365	1,608
	Mandatory:			
4090	Budget authority, gross	41		
4180	Budget authority, net (total)	1,419	1,378	1,743
4190	Outlays, net (total)	1,403	1,365	1,608

This account supports the cost of managing U.S. Agency for International Development (USAID) programs, including salaries and other expenses of direct-hire personnel as well as costs associated with physical security of Agency personnel. USAID currently maintains resident staff in more than 70 foreign countries as well as a headquarters in Washington, D.C., which supports field programs and manages regional and worldwide activities.

Object Classification (in millions of dollars)

Identification code 072–1000–0–1–151		2021 actual	2022 est.	2023 est.
	Direct obligations:			
	Personnel compensation:			
11.1	Full-time permanent	465	488	551
11.3	Other than full-time permanent	75	78	82
11.5	Other personnel compensation	40	42	47
11.9	Total personnel compensation	580	608	680
12.1	Civilian personnel benefits	206	214	245
21.0	Travel and transportation of persons	49	50	55
22.0	Transportation of things	26	27	29
23.1	Rental payments to GSA	31	40	65
23.2	Rental payments to others	46	48	58
23.3	Communications, utilities, and miscellaneous charges	14	14	16
24.0	Printing and reproduction		1	1
25.1	Advisory and assistance services	236	236	250
25.2	Other services from non-Federal sources	46	48	55
25.3	Other goods and services from Federal sources	141	150	181
25.4	Operation and maintenance of facilities	6	6	8
25.6	Medical care	1	1	1
25.7	Operation and maintenance of equipment	3	3	5
26.0	Supplies and materials	6	7	8
31.0	Equipment	37	37	40
32.0	Land and structures	42	42	45
42.0	Insurance claims and indemnities	1	1	1
99.0	Direct obligations	1,471	1,533	1,743
99.0	Reimbursable obligations	57	57	57
99.5	Adjustment for rounding	2	2	2
99.9	Total new obligations, unexpired accounts	1,530	1,592	1,802

Employment Summary

Identification code 072–1000–0–1–151		2021 actual	2022 est.	2023 est.
1001	Direct civilian full-time equivalent employment	3,241	3,300	3,548
2001	Reimbursable civilian full-time equivalent employment	5	5	5

CAPITAL INVESTMENT FUND

For necessary expenses for overseas construction and related costs, and for the procurement and enhancement of information technology and related capital investments, pursuant to section 667 of the Foreign Assistance Act of 1961, $289,100,000, to remain available until expended: Provided, That this amount is in addition to funds otherwise available for such purposes.

Note.—A full-year 2022 appropriation for this account was not enacted at the time the Budget was prepared; therefore, the Budget assumes this account is operating under the Continuing Appropriations Act, 2022 (Division A of Public Law 117–43, as amended). The amounts included for 2022 reflect the annualized level provided by the continuing resolution.

Program and Financing (in millions of dollars)

Identification code 072–0300–0–1–151		2021 actual	2022 est.	2023 est.
	Obligations by program activity:			
0001	IT/New Construction	259	262	289
	Budgetary resources:			
	Unobligated balance:			
1000	Unobligated balance brought forward, Oct 1	3	4	
1021	Recoveries of prior year unpaid obligations	2		
1070	Unobligated balance (total)	5	4	
	Budget authority:			
	Appropriations, discretionary:			
1100	Appropriation - IT/New Construction	258	258	289
1930	Total budgetary resources available	263	262	289

CAPITAL INVESTMENT FUND—Continued
Program and Financing—Continued

Identification code 072–0300–0–1–151	2021 actual	2022 est.	2023 est.
	Memorandum (non-add) entries:			
1941	Unexpired unobligated balance, end of year	4		
	Change in obligated balance:			
	Unpaid obligations:			
3000	Unpaid obligations, brought forward, Oct 1	26	12	16
3010	New obligations, unexpired accounts	259	262	289
3020	Outlays (gross)	–271	–258	–288
3040	Recoveries of prior year unpaid obligations, unexpired	–2		
3050	Unpaid obligations, end of year	12	16	17
	Memorandum (non-add) entries:			
3100	Obligated balance, start of year	26	12	16
3200	Obligated balance, end of year	12	16	17
	Budget authority and outlays, net:			
	Discretionary:			
4000	Budget authority, gross	258	258	289
	Outlays, gross:			
4010	Outlays from new discretionary authority	254	245	275
4011	Outlays from discretionary balances	17	13	13
4020	Outlays, gross (total)	271	258	288
4180	Budget authority, net (total)	258	258	289
4190	Outlays, net (total)	271	258	288

$289.1 million is requested in base funding for this account, which funds capital information technology (IT) investments for USAID, maintenance of USAID-owned properties, and USAID's contribution to the Capital Security Cost Sharing (CSCS) Program. Funds from the Capital Investment Fund will only be made available after USAID has demonstrated a successful business case for its IT investments.

The Administration also requests funds for maintenance of USAID-owned properties and USAID's per capita contribution to the CSCS Program administered by the Department of State Overseas Building Operations. The CSCS program is designed to accelerate the construction of secure, safe, functional facilities for all U.S. Government personnel overseas.

Object Classification (in millions of dollars)

Identification code 072–0300–0–1–151	2021 actual	2022 est.	2023 est.
	Direct obligations:			
25.1	Advisory and assistance services	11	26	89
25.4	Operation and maintenance of facilities		11	10
32.0	Land and structures	248	225	190
99.0	Direct obligations	259	262	289
99.9	Total new obligations, unexpired accounts	259	262	289

TRANSITION INITIATIVES

For necessary expenses for international disaster rehabilitation and reconstruction assistance administered by the Office of Transition Initiatives, United States Agency for International Development, pursuant to section 491 of the Foreign Assistance Act of 1961, and to support transition to democracy and long-term development of countries in crisis, $102,000,000, to remain available until expended: Provided, That such support may include assistance to develop, strengthen, or preserve democratic institutions and processes, revitalize basic infrastructure, and foster the peaceful resolution of conflict: Provided further, That the USAID Administrator shall submit a report to the Committees on Appropriations at least 5 days prior to beginning a new program of assistance: Provided further, That if the Secretary of State determines that it is important to the national interest of the United States to provide transition assistance in excess of the amount appropriated under this heading, up to $15,000,000 of the funds appropriated by this Act to carry out the provisions of part I of the Foreign Assistance Act of 1961 may be used for purposes of this heading and under the authorities applicable to funds appropriated under this heading.

Note.—A full-year 2022 appropriation for this account was not enacted at the time the Budget was prepared; therefore, the Budget assumes this account is operating under the Continuing Appropriations Act, 2022 (Division A of Public Law 117–43, as amended). The amounts included for 2022 reflect the annualized level provided by the continuing resolution.

Program and Financing (in millions of dollars)

Identification code 072–1027–0–1–151	2021 actual	2022 est.	2023 est.
	Obligations by program activity:			
0001	Transition Initiatives (Direct)	139	95	95
	Budgetary resources:			
	Unobligated balance:			
1000	Unobligated balance brought forward, Oct 1	23	14	11
1021	Recoveries of prior year unpaid obligations	8		
1070	Unobligated balance (total)	31	14	11
	Budget authority:			
	Appropriations, discretionary:			
1100	Appropriation	92	92	102
1121	Appropriations transferred from other acct [072–1037]	30		
1160	Appropriation, discretionary (total)	122	92	102
1930	Total budgetary resources available	153	106	113
	Memorandum (non-add) entries:			
1941	Unexpired unobligated balance, end of year	14	11	18
	Change in obligated balance:			
	Unpaid obligations:			
3000	Unpaid obligations, brought forward, Oct 1	122	140	134
3010	New obligations, unexpired accounts	139	95	95
3020	Outlays (gross)	–113	–101	–98
3040	Recoveries of prior year unpaid obligations, unexpired	–8		
3050	Unpaid obligations, end of year	140	134	131
	Memorandum (non-add) entries:			
3100	Obligated balance, start of year	122	140	134
3200	Obligated balance, end of year	140	134	131
	Budget authority and outlays, net:			
	Discretionary:			
4000	Budget authority, gross	122	92	102
	Outlays, gross:			
4010	Outlays from new discretionary authority	30	23	26
4011	Outlays from discretionary balances	83	78	72
4020	Outlays, gross (total)	113	101	98
4180	Budget authority, net (total)	122	92	102
4190	Outlays, net (total)	113	101	98

The Transition Initiatives (TI) account addresses opportunities and challenges facing conflict-prone countries and those countries making the transition from the initial crisis stage of a complex emergency to sustainable development and democracy. Programs are focused on advancing peace and stability, including promoting the responsiveness of central governments to local needs, increasing civic participation, raising awareness of national issues through media, addressing the underlying causes of instability, and supporting conflict resolution measures. Recent country examples where TI funds were used include , Columbia, Ethiopia, Libya and Ukraine. TI funding has provided core operational funds for the Office of Transition Initiatives within the U.S. Agency for International Development (USAID) Bureau for Conflict Prevention and Stabilization.

Object Classification (in millions of dollars)

Identification code 072–1027–0–1–151	2021 actual	2022 est.	2023 est.
	Direct obligations:			
12.1	Civilian personnel benefits	3		
21.0	Travel and transportation of persons	2		
23.1	Rental payments to GSA	1		
23.2	Rental payments to others	1		
25.3	Other goods and services from Federal sources	3		
41.0	Grants, subsidies, and contributions	129	95	95
99.9	Total new obligations, unexpired accounts	139	95	95

DEPARTMENT OF STATE AND OTHER INTERNATIONAL PROGRAMS

Employment Summary

Identification code 072–1027–0–1–151	2021 actual	2022 est.	2023 est.
1001 Direct civilian full-time equivalent employment	2		

UKRAINE LOAN GUARANTEES PROGRAM ACCOUNT

Summary of Loan Levels, Subsidy Budget Authority and Outlays by Program (in millions of dollars)

Identification code 072–0402–0–1–151	2021 actual	2022 est.	2023 est.
Guaranteed loan reestimates:			
235001 Ukraine Loan Guarantees	–651	–267	

CONFLICT STABILIZATION OPERATIONS

Program and Financing (in millions of dollars)

Identification code 072–0305–0–1–151	2021 actual	2022 est.	2023 est.
Budgetary resources:			
Unobligated balance:			
1000 Unobligated balance brought forward, Oct 1	1	1	1
1930 Total budgetary resources available	1	1	1
Memorandum (non-add) entries:			
1941 Unexpired unobligated balance, end of year	1	1	1
4180 Budget authority, net (total)			
4190 Outlays, net (total)			

OFFICE OF INSPECTOR GENERAL

For necessary expenses to carry out the provisions of section 667 of the Foreign Assistance Act of 1961, $80,500,000, to remain available until September 30, 2024, for the Office of Inspector General of the United States Agency for International Development.

Note.—A full-year 2022 appropriation for this account was not enacted at the time the Budget was prepared; therefore, the Budget assumes this account is operating under the Continuing Appropriations Act, 2022 (Division A of Public Law 117–43, as amended). The amounts included for 2022 reflect the annualized level provided by the continuing resolution.

Program and Financing (in millions of dollars)

Identification code 072–1007–0–1–151	2021 actual	2022 est.	2023 est.
Obligations by program activity:			
0001 Operating Expenses, Office of Inspector General (Direct)	76	76	81
0801 Operating Expenses, Office of Inspector General (Reimbursable)	4	5	5
0900 Total new obligations, unexpired accounts	80	81	86
Budgetary resources:			
Unobligated balance:			
1000 Unobligated balance brought forward, Oct 1	9	9	10
1021 Recoveries of prior year unpaid obligations		1	1
1070 Unobligated balance (total)	9	10	11
Budget authority:			
Appropriations, discretionary:			
1100 Appropriation	76	76	81
Spending authority from offsetting collections, discretionary:			
1700 Collected	3	5	5
1701 Change in uncollected payments, Federal sources	2		
1750 Spending auth from offsetting collections, disc (total)	5	5	5
1900 Budget authority (total)	81	81	86
1930 Total budgetary resources available	90	91	97
Memorandum (non-add) entries:			
1940 Unobligated balance expiring	–1		
1941 Unexpired unobligated balance, end of year	9	10	11
Change in obligated balance:			
Unpaid obligations:			
3000 Unpaid obligations, brought forward, Oct 1	53	46	15
3010 New obligations, unexpired accounts	80	81	86
3011 Obligations ("upward adjustments"), expired accounts	1		
3020 Outlays (gross)	–83	–111	–85
3040 Recoveries of prior year unpaid obligations, unexpired		–1	–1
3041 Recoveries of prior year unpaid obligations, expired	–5		
3050 Unpaid obligations, end of year	46	15	15
Uncollected payments:			
3060 Uncollected pymts, Fed sources, brought forward, Oct 1	–4	–5	–5
3070 Change in uncollected pymts, Fed sources, unexpired	–2		
3071 Change in uncollected pymts, Fed sources, expired	1		
3090 Uncollected pymts, Fed sources, end of year	–5	–5	–5
Memorandum (non-add) entries:			
3100 Obligated balance, start of year	49	41	10
3200 Obligated balance, end of year	41	10	10
Budget authority and outlays, net:			
Discretionary:			
4000 Budget authority, gross	81	81	86
Outlays, gross:			
4010 Outlays from new discretionary authority	45	66	70
4011 Outlays from discretionary balances	38	45	15
4020 Outlays, gross (total)	83	111	85
Offsets against gross budget authority and outlays:			
Offsetting collections (collected) from:			
4030 Federal sources	–3	–5	–5
4040 Offsets against gross budget authority and outlays (total)	–3	–5	–5
Additional offsets against gross budget authority only:			
4050 Change in uncollected pymts, Fed sources, unexpired	–2		
4060 Additional offsets against budget authority only (total)	–2		
4070 Budget authority, net (discretionary)	76	76	81
4080 Outlays, net (discretionary)	80	106	80
4180 Budget authority, net (total)	76	76	81
4190 Outlays, net (total)	80	106	80

The funds cover the costs of operations of the Office of the Inspector General, U.S. Agency for International Development, and include salaries, expenses, and support costs of the Inspector General's personnel.

Object Classification (in millions of dollars)

Identification code 072–1007–0–1–151	2021 actual	2022 est.	2023 est.
Direct obligations:			
Personnel compensation:			
11.1 Full-time permanent	26	26	29
11.3 Other than full-time permanent	3	3	3
11.9 Total personnel compensation	29	29	32
12.1 Civilian personnel benefits	18	18	19
21.0 Travel and transportation of persons	1	1	1
22.0 Transportation of things	1	1	1
23.1 Rental payments to GSA	3	3	3
23.2 Rental payments to others	1	1	1
25.1 Advisory and assistance services	7	7	8
25.2 Other services from non-Federal sources	2	2	2
25.3 Other goods and services from Federal sources	8	8	8
25.7 Operation and maintenance of equipment	2	2	2
31.0 Equipment	4	4	4
99.0 Direct obligations	76	76	81
99.0 Reimbursable obligations	4	5	5
99.9 Total new obligations, unexpired accounts	80	81	86

Employment Summary

Identification code 072–1007–0–1–151	2021 actual	2022 est.	2023 est.
1001 Direct civilian full-time equivalent employment	221	229	235
2001 Reimbursable civilian full-time equivalent employment	8		

PROPERTY MANAGEMENT FUND

Program and Financing (in millions of dollars)

Identification code 072–4175–0–3–151	2021 actual	2022 est.	2023 est.
Obligations by program activity:			
0801 Property Management Fund (Reimbursable)	6	16	

Agency for International Development—Continued
Federal Funds—Continued

PROPERTY MANAGEMENT FUND—Continued

Program and Financing—Continued

Identification code 072–4175–0–3–151	2021 actual	2022 est.	2023 est.
0900 Total new obligations, unexpired accounts (object class 25.4)	6	16	....
Budgetary resources:			
Unobligated balance:			
1000 Unobligated balance brought forward, Oct 1	21	16	....
Budget authority:			
Spending authority from offsetting collections, mandatory:			
1800 Collected	1	....	....
1930 Total budgetary resources available	22	16	....
Memorandum (non-add) entries:			
1941 Unexpired unobligated balance, end of year	16	....	....
Change in obligated balance:			
Unpaid obligations:			
3000 Unpaid obligations, brought forward, Oct 1	5	6	16
3010 New obligations, unexpired accounts	6	16	....
3020 Outlays (gross)	–5	–6	....
3050 Unpaid obligations, end of year	6	16	16
Memorandum (non-add) entries:			
3100 Obligated balance, start of year	5	6	16
3200 Obligated balance, end of year	6	16	16
Budget authority and outlays, net:			
Mandatory:			
4090 Budget authority, gross	1	....	....
Outlays, gross:			
4100 Outlays from new mandatory authority	1	....	....
4101 Outlays from mandatory balances	4	6	....
4110 Outlays, gross (total)	5	6	....
Offsets against gross budget authority and outlays:			
Offsetting collections (collected) from:			
4123 Non-Federal sources	–1	....	....
4180 Budget authority, net (total)	....	....	....
4190 Outlays, net (total)	4	6	....

This Fund, as authorized by Public Law 101–513, is maintained for the deposit of proceeds from the sale of overseas property acquired by the U.S. Agency for International Development (USAID). The proceeds are available to construct or otherwise acquire outside the United States: 1) essential living quarters, office space, and necessary supporting facilities for use of USAID personnel; and 2) schools (including dormitories and boarding facilities) and hospitals for use of USAID and other U.S. Government personnel and their dependents. In addition, the proceeds may be used to equip, staff, operate, and maintain such schools and hospitals.

UKRAINE LOAN GUARANTEES FINANCING ACCOUNT

Program and Financing (in millions of dollars)

Identification code 072–4345–0–3–151	2021 actual	2022 est.	2023 est.
Obligations by program activity:			
Credit program obligations:			
0742 Downward reestimates paid to receipt accounts	555	227	....
0743 Interest on downward reestimates	96	39	....
0900 Total new obligations, unexpired accounts	651	266	....
Budgetary resources:			
Unobligated balance:			
1000 Unobligated balance brought forward, Oct 1	910	266	28
Financing authority:			
Spending authority from offsetting collections, mandatory:			
1800 Collected	7	28	28
1930 Total budgetary resources available	917	294	56
Memorandum (non-add) entries:			
1941 Unexpired unobligated balance, end of year	266	28	56
Change in obligated balance:			
Unpaid obligations:			
3000 Unpaid obligations, brought forward, Oct 1	....	....	266
3010 New obligations, unexpired accounts	651	266	....
3020 Outlays (gross)	–651	....	....
3050 Unpaid obligations, end of year	....	266	266
Memorandum (non-add) entries:			
3100 Obligated balance, start of year	....	....	266
3200 Obligated balance, end of year	....	266	266
Financing authority and disbursements, net:			
Mandatory:			
4090 Budget authority, gross	7	28	28
Financing disbursements:			
4110 Outlays, gross (total)	651	....	....
Offsets against gross financing authority and disbursements:			
Offsetting collections (collected) from:			
4122 Interest on uninvested funds	–7	–28	–28
4180 Budget authority, net (total)	....	....	....
4190 Outlays, net (total)	644	–28	–28

Status of Guaranteed Loans (in millions of dollars)

Identification code 072–4345–0–3–151	2021 actual	2022 est.	2023 est.
Position with respect to appropriations act limitation on commitments:			
2111 Guaranteed loan commitments from current-year authority	....	....	....
2121 Limitation available from carry-forward	....	....	....
2143 Uncommitted limitation carried forward	....	....	....
2150 Total guaranteed loan commitments	....	....	....
2199 Guaranteed amount of guaranteed loan commitments	....	....	....
Cumulative balance of guaranteed loans outstanding:			
2210 Outstanding, start of year	1,000	....	....
2231 Disbursements of new guaranteed loans	....	....	....
2251 Repayments and prepayments	–1,000	....	....
2290 Outstanding, end of year	....	....	....
Memorandum:			
2299 Guaranteed amount of guaranteed loans outstanding, end of year	....	....	....

Balance Sheet (in millions of dollars)

Identification code 072–4345–0–3–151	2020 actual	2021 actual
ASSETS:		
Federal assets:		
1101 Fund balances with Treasury	910	267
Investments in U.S. securities:		
1106 Receivables, net	....	....
1999 Total assets	910	267
LIABILITIES:		
2105 Federal liabilities: Other	650	267
2204 Non-Federal liabilities: Liabilities for loan guarantees	260	....
2999 Total liabilities	910	267
NET POSITION:		
3300 Cumulative results of operations	....	....
4999 Total liabilities and net position	910	267

WORKING CAPITAL FUND

Program and Financing (in millions of dollars)

Identification code 072–4513–0–4–151	2021 actual	2022 est.	2023 est.
Obligations by program activity:			
0801 Working Capital Fund (Reimbursable)	24	24	24
Budgetary resources:			
Unobligated balance:			
1000 Unobligated balance brought forward, Oct 1	22	25	25
1021 Recoveries of prior year unpaid obligations	1	....	....
1070 Unobligated balance (total)	23	25	25
Budget authority:			
Spending authority from offsetting collections, discretionary:			
1700 Collected	29	24	24
1701 Change in uncollected payments, Federal sources	–3	....	....
1750 Spending auth from offsetting collections, disc (total)	26	24	24
1930 Total budgetary resources available	49	49	49

DEPARTMENT OF STATE AND OTHER INTERNATIONAL PROGRAMS

Agency for International Development—Continued
Federal Funds—Continued

851

	Memorandum (non-add) entries:	2021 actual	2022 est.	2023 est.
1941	Unexpired unobligated balance, end of year	25	25	25
	Change in obligated balance:			
	Unpaid obligations:			
3000	Unpaid obligations, brought forward, Oct 1	9	15	1
3010	New obligations, unexpired accounts	24	24	24
3020	Outlays (gross)	–17	–38	–24
3040	Recoveries of prior year unpaid obligations, unexpired	–1		
3050	Unpaid obligations, end of year	15	1	1
	Uncollected payments:			
3060	Uncollected pymts, Fed sources, brought forward, Oct 1	–23	–20	–20
3070	Change in uncollected pymts, Fed sources, unexpired	3		
3090	Uncollected pymts, Fed sources, end of year	–20	–20	–20
	Memorandum (non-add) entries:			
3100	Obligated balance, start of year	–14	–5	–19
3200	Obligated balance, end of year	–5	–19	–19
	Budget authority and outlays, net:			
	Discretionary:			
4000	Budget authority, gross	26	24	24
	Outlays, gross:			
4010	Outlays from new discretionary authority	10	24	24
4011	Outlays from discretionary balances	7	14	
4020	Outlays, gross (total)	17	38	24
	Offsets against gross budget authority and outlays:			
	Offsetting collections (collected) from:			
4030	Federal sources	–29	–24	–24
4040	Offsets against gross budget authority and outlays (total)	–29	–24	–24
	Additional offsets against gross budget authority only:			
4050	Change in uncollected pymts, Fed sources, unexpired	3		
4080	Outlays, net (discretionary)	–12	14	
4180	Budget authority, net (total)			
4190	Outlays, net (total)	–12	14	

The Fund, authorized by section 635(m) of the Foreign Assistance Act of 1961, finances on a reimbursable basis the costs associated with providing administrative support to other agencies under the International Cooperative Administrative Support Services (ICASS) program overseas. Under ICASS, each agency pays a proportional share of the cost of those services they have agreed to receive. Working through inter-agency councils at post, all agencies have a say in determining which services the USAID mission will provide, defining service standards, reviewing costs, and determining funding levels. The Fund is also used for deposit of rebates from the use of Federal credit cards, the deposits then being made available for start-up costs at new ICASS service-provider missions and technical support to missions currently providing services.

Object Classification (in millions of dollars)

Identification code 072–4513–0–4–151	2021 actual	2022 est.	2023 est.
Reimbursable obligations:			
Personnel compensation:			
11.3 Other than full-time permanent	4	4	4
11.5 Other personnel compensation	1	1	1
11.9 Total personnel compensation	5	5	5
12.1 Civilian personnel benefits	1	1	1
23.2 Rental payments to others	1	1	1
23.3 Communications, utilities, and miscellaneous charges	2	2	2
25.1 Advisory and assistance services	7	7	7
25.2 Other services from non-Federal sources	1	1	1
25.3 Other goods and services from Federal sources	1	1	1
25.4 Operation and maintenance of facilities	1	1	1
26.0 Supplies and materials	1	1	1
31.0 Equipment	2	2	2
32.0 Land and structures	1	1	1
99.0 Reimbursable obligations	23	23	23
99.5 Adjustment for rounding	1	1	1
99.9 Total new obligations, unexpired accounts	24	24	24

LOAN GUARANTEES TO ISRAEL PROGRAM ACCOUNT

Program and Financing (in millions of dollars)

Identification code 072–0301–0–1–151	2021 actual	2022 est.	2023 est.
Obligations by program activity:			
Credit program obligations:			
0707 Reestimates of loan guarantee subsidy	4		
0708 Interest on reestimates of loan guarantee subsidy	13		
0900 Total new obligations, unexpired accounts (object class 41.0)	17		
Budgetary resources:			
Budget authority:			
Appropriations, mandatory:			
1200 Appropriation	17		
1930 Total budgetary resources available	17		
Change in obligated balance:			
Unpaid obligations:			
3010 New obligations, unexpired accounts	17		
3020 Outlays (gross)	–17		
Budget authority and outlays, net:			
Mandatory:			
4090 Budget authority, gross	17		
Outlays, gross:			
4100 Outlays from new mandatory authority	17		
4180 Budget authority, net (total)	17		
4190 Outlays, net (total)	17		

Summary of Loan Levels, Subsidy Budget Authority and Outlays by Program (in millions of dollars)

Identification code 072–0301–0–1–151	2021 actual	2022 est.	2023 est.
Guaranteed loan levels supportable by subsidy budget authority:			
215001 Loan Guarantees to Israel		500	500
Guaranteed loan subsidy (in percent):			
232001 Loan Guarantees to Israel		0.00	0.00
Guaranteed loan reestimates:			
235001 Loan Guarantees to Israel	–107	–122	

LOAN GUARANTEES TO ISRAEL FINANCING ACCOUNT

Program and Financing (in millions of dollars)

Identification code 072–4119–0–3–151	2021 actual	2022 est.	2023 est.
Obligations by program activity:			
Credit program obligations:			
0742 Downward reestimates paid to receipt accounts	27	26	
0743 Interest on downward reestimates	98	96	
0900 Total new obligations, unexpired accounts	125	122	
Budgetary resources:			
Unobligated balance:			
1000 Unobligated balance brought forward, Oct 1	1,083	1,033	1,040
Financing authority:			
Spending authority from offsetting collections, mandatory:			
1800 Collected	75	129	129
1930 Total budgetary resources available	1,158	1,162	1,169
Memorandum (non-add) entries:			
1941 Unexpired unobligated balance, end of year	1,033	1,040	1,169
Change in obligated balance:			
Unpaid obligations:			
3000 Unpaid obligations, brought forward, Oct 1		1	123
3010 New obligations, unexpired accounts	125	122	
3020 Outlays (gross)	–124		
3050 Unpaid obligations, end of year	1	123	123
Memorandum (non-add) entries:			
3100 Obligated balance, start of year		1	123
3200 Obligated balance, end of year	1	123	123
Financing authority and disbursements, net:			
Mandatory:			
4090 Budget authority, gross	75	129	129
Financing disbursements:			
4110 Outlays, gross (total)	124		

852　Agency for International Development—Continued
Federal Funds—Continued

THE BUDGET FOR FISCAL YEAR 2023

LOAN GUARANTEES TO ISRAEL FINANCING ACCOUNT—Continued

Program and Financing—Continued

Identification code 072–4119–0–3–151	2021 actual	2022 est.	2023 est.
Offsets against gross financing authority and disbursements: Offsetting collections (collected) from:			
4120　Federal sources (Upward reestimate of subsidy)	–17	....	....
4122　Interest on uninvested funds	–58	–80	–80
4123　Non-Federal sources - Fees	....	–49	–49
4130　Offsets against gross budget authority and outlays (total)	–75	–129	–129
4170　Outlays, net (mandatory)	49	–129	–129
4180　Budget authority, net (total)	....	....	....
4190　Outlays, net (total)	49	–129	–129

Status of Guaranteed Loans (in millions of dollars)

Identification code 072–4119–0–3–151	2021 actual	2022 est.	2023 est.
Position with respect to appropriations act limitation on commitments:			
2121　Limitation available from carry-forward	3,814	3,314	3,314
2143　Uncommitted limitation carried forward	–3,814	–2,814	–2,814
2150　Total guaranteed loan commitments	....	500	500
2199　Guaranteed amount of guaranteed loan commitments	....	....	....
Cumulative balance of guaranteed loans outstanding:			
2210　Outstanding, start of year	8,699	8,397	8,051
2231　Disbursements of new guaranteed loans	500	500	500
2251　Repayments and prepayments	–802	–846	–846
2264　Adjustments: Other adjustments, net	....	....	....
2290　Outstanding, end of year	8,397	8,051	7,705
Memorandum:			
2299　Guaranteed amount of guaranteed loans outstanding, end of year	8,397	8,051	7,705

Balance Sheet (in millions of dollars)

Identification code 072–4119–0–3–151	2020 actual	2021 actual
ASSETS:		
Federal assets:		
1101　Fund balances with Treasury	1,083	1,034
Investments in U.S. securities:		
1106　Receivables, net	17	....
1999　Total assets	1,100	1,034
LIABILITIES:		
2105　Federal liabilities: Other	124	122
2204　Non-Federal liabilities: Liabilities for loan guarantees	976	912
2999　Total liabilities	1,100	1,034
NET POSITION:		
3300　Cumulative results of operations	....	....
4999　Total upward reestimate subsidy BA [72–0301]	1,100	1,034

MENA LOAN GUARANTEE PROGRAM ACCOUNT

Summary of Loan Levels, Subsidy Budget Authority and Outlays by Program (in millions of dollars)

Identification code 072–0409–0–1–151	2021 actual	2022 est.	2023 est.
Guaranteed loan reestimates:			
235001　Loan Guarantees to Tunisia	–109	–185	....
235002　Loan Guarantees to Jordan	–12	–273	....
235003　Loan Guarantees to Iraq	–4	–5	....
235999　Total guaranteed loan reestimates	–125	–463	....

MENA LOAN GUARANTEE FINANCING ACCOUNT

Program and Financing (in millions of dollars)

Identification code 072–4493–0–3–151	2021 actual	2022 est.	2023 est.
Obligations by program activity:			
Credit program obligations:			
0742　Downward reestimates paid to receipt accounts	102	392	....
0743　Interest on downward reestimates	23	72	....
0900　Total new obligations, unexpired accounts	125	464	....
Budgetary resources:			
Unobligated balance:			
1000　Unobligated balance brought forward, Oct 1	1,175	1,075	650
Financing authority:			
Spending authority from offsetting collections, mandatory:			
1800　Collected	25	39	39
1930　Total budgetary resources available	1,200	1,114	689
Memorandum (non-add) entries:			
1941　Unexpired unobligated balance, end of year	1,075	650	689
Change in obligated balance:			
Unpaid obligations:			
3000　Unpaid obligations, brought forward, Oct 1	....	....	464
3010　New obligations, unexpired accounts	125	464	....
3020　Outlays (gross)	–125	....	....
3050　Unpaid obligations, end of year	....	464	464
Memorandum (non-add) entries:			
3100　Obligated balance, start of year	....	....	464
3200　Obligated balance, end of year	....	464	464
Financing authority and disbursements, net:			
Mandatory:			
4090　Budget authority, gross	25	39	39
Financing disbursements:			
4110　Outlays, gross (total)	125	....	....
Offsets against gross financing authority and disbursements:			
Offsetting collections (collected) from:			
4122　Interest on uninvested funds	–25	–39	–39
4180　Budget authority, net (total)	....	....	....
4190　Outlays, net (total)	100	–39	–39

Status of Guaranteed Loans (in millions of dollars)

Identification code 072–4493–0–3–151	2021 actual	2022 est.	2023 est.
Position with respect to appropriations act limitation on commitments:			
2111　Guaranteed loan commitments from current-year authority	....	....	....
2121　Limitation available from carry-forward	....	....	....
2143　Uncommitted limitation carried forward	....	....	....
2150　Total guaranteed loan commitments	....	....	....
Cumulative balance of guaranteed loans outstanding:			
2210　Outstanding, start of year	4,750	2,500	500
2231　Disbursements of new guaranteed loans	....	....	....
2251　Repayments and prepayments	–2,250	–2,000	–300
2264　Adjustments: Other adjustments, net	....	....	....
2290　Outstanding, end of year	2,500	500	200
Memorandum:			
2299　Guaranteed amount of guaranteed loans outstanding, end of year	2,500	500	200

Balance Sheet (in millions of dollars)

Identification code 072–4493–0–3–151	2020 actual	2021 actual
ASSETS:		
Federal assets:		
1101　Fund balances with Treasury	1,175	1,075
Investments in U.S. securities:		
1104　Adjustment GTAS	....	....
1106　Receivables, net (subsidy from program fund)	....	....
1999　Total assets	1,175	1,075
LIABILITIES:		
2105　Federal liabilities: Other	125	464
Non-Federal liabilities:		
2204　Liabilities for loan guarantees	1,050	611
2205　Lease liabilities, net	....	....
2207　Other Liabilities without related budgetary obligations	....	....

		2999	Total liabilities	1,175	1,075
			NET POSITION:		
		3300	Cumulative results of operations	....	....
		4999	Total liabilities and net position	1,175	1,075

		Memorandum:			
		2299	Guaranteed amount of guaranteed loans outstanding, end of year	....	....	....

DEVELOPMENT CREDIT AUTHORITY PROGRAM ACCOUNT

Program and Financing (in millions of dollars)

Identification code 072–1264–0–1–151		2021 actual	2022 est.	2023 est.
	Budgetary resources:			
	Unobligated balance:			
1010	Unobligated balance transfer to other accts [077–4483]	–1	....	....
1021	Recoveries of prior year unpaid obligations	1	....	....
	Change in obligated balance:			
	Unpaid obligations:			
3000	Unpaid obligations, brought forward, Oct 1	82	....	....
3020	Outlays (gross)	–11	....	....
3030	Unpaid obligations transferred to other accts [077–0110]	–70	....	....
3040	Recoveries of prior year unpaid obligations, unexpired	–1	....	....
	Memorandum (non-add) entries:			
3100	Obligated balance, start of year	82	....	....
	Budget authority and outlays, net:			
	Discretionary:			
	Outlays, gross:			
4011	Outlays from discretionary balances	11	....	....
4180	Budget authority, net (total)	....	....	....
4190	Outlays, net (total)	11	....	....

As required by the Federal Credit Reform Act of 1990, this account recorded, for the Development Credit Authority (DCA), the subsidy costs associated with direct loans obligated and loan guarantees committed in 1992 and beyond (including modifications of direct loans or loan guarantees that resulted from obligations or commitments in any year), as well as administrative expenses of this program and legacy USAID credit programs. The subsidy amounts are estimated on a net present value basis; the administrative expenses are estimated on a cash basis.

In 2020, per the modernizations and other reforms included in the Better Utilization of Investments Leading to Development Act of 2018, DCA was consolidated with other development finance functions, such as the Overseas Private Investment Corporation, into the new U.S. International Development Finance Corporation (DFC). All future DCA activities are presented in the DFC accounts.

DEVELOPMENT CREDIT AUTHORITY GUARANTEED LOAN FINANCING ACCOUNT

Status of Guaranteed Loans (in millions of dollars)

Identification code 072–4266–0–3–151		2021 actual	2022 est.	2023 est.
	Position with respect to appropriations act limitation on commitments:			
2111	Guaranteed loan commitments from current-year authority	....	....	....
2121	Limitation available from carry-forward	....	....	....
2142	Uncommitted loan guarantee limitation	....	....	....
2143	Uncommitted limitation carried forward	....	....	....
2150	Total guaranteed loan commitments	....	....	....
2199	Guaranteed amount of guaranteed loan commitments	....	....	....
	Cumulative balance of guaranteed loans outstanding:			
2210	Outstanding, start of year	382	....	....
2231	Disbursements of new guaranteed loans	....	....	....
2251	Repayments and prepayments	....	....	....
	Adjustments:			
2263	Terminations for default that result in claim payments	....	....	....
2264	Other adjustments, net	–382	....	....
2290	Outstanding, end of year	....	....	....

ECONOMIC ASSISTANCE LOANS LIQUIDATING ACCOUNT

This account consolidates direct loan activity from legacy credit programs funded under various accounts, including the Economic Support Fund, Functional Development Assistance Program, and the Development Loan Fund. In FY 2020, this account was transferred to the new U.S. International Development Finance Corporation.

Trust Funds

FOREIGN SERVICE NATIONAL SEPARATION LIABILITY TRUST FUND

Special and Trust Fund Receipts (in millions of dollars)

Identification code 072–8342–0–7–602		2021 actual	2022 est.	2023 est.
0100	Balance, start of year	....	....	....
	Receipts:			
	Current law:			
1140	Foreign Service National Separation Liability Trust Fund	9	9	9
2000	Total: Balances and receipts	9	9	9
	Appropriations:			
	Current law:			
2101	Foreign Service National Separation Liability Trust Fund	–9	–9	–9
5099	Balance, end of year	....	....	....

Program and Financing (in millions of dollars)

Identification code 072–8342–0–7–602		2021 actual	2022 est.	2023 est.
	Obligations by program activity:			
0001	Foreign Service National Separation Liability Trust Fund (Direct)	8	8	8
0900	Total new obligations, unexpired accounts (object class 13.0)	8	8	8
	Budgetary resources:			
	Unobligated balance:			
1000	Unobligated balance brought forward, Oct 1	10	15	16
1021	Recoveries of prior year unpaid obligations	4	....	....
1070	Unobligated balance (total)	14	15	16
	Budget authority:			
	Appropriations, mandatory:			
1201	Appropriation (special or trust fund)	9	9	9
1900	Budget authority (total)	9	9	9
1930	Total budgetary resources available	23	24	25
	Memorandum (non-add) entries:			
1941	Unexpired unobligated balance, end of year	15	16	17
	Change in obligated balance:			
	Unpaid obligations:			
3000	Unpaid obligations, brought forward, Oct 1	49	49	44
3010	New obligations, unexpired accounts	8	8	8
3020	Outlays (gross)	–4	–13	–4
3040	Recoveries of prior year unpaid obligations, unexpired	–4	....	....
3050	Unpaid obligations, end of year	49	44	48
	Memorandum (non-add) entries:			
3100	Obligated balance, start of year	49	49	44
3200	Obligated balance, end of year	49	44	48
	Budget authority and outlays, net:			
	Mandatory:			
4090	Budget authority, gross	9	9	9
	Outlays, gross:			
4101	Outlays from mandatory balances	4	13	4
4180	Budget authority, net (total)	9	9	9
4190	Outlays, net (total)	4	13	4

This Fund is maintained to pay separation costs for Foreign Service National employees of the U.S. Agency for International Development in those countries in which such pay is legally required. The Fund, as author-

Agency for International Development—Continued
Trust Funds—Continued

FOREIGN SERVICE NATIONAL SEPARATION LIABILITY TRUST FUND—Continued

ized by Public Law 102–138, is maintained by annual Government contributions which are appropriated in several Agency accounts.

MISCELLANEOUS TRUST FUNDS, AID

Special and Trust Fund Receipts (in millions of dollars)

Identification code 072–9971–0–7–151		2021 actual	2022 est.	2023 est.
0100	Balance, start of year			105
	Receipts:				
	Current law:				
1130	Gifts and Donations, Agency for International Development	41	45	45
1130	Miscellaneous Trust Funds, AID	2,002	160	160
1199	Total current law receipts	2,043	205	205
1999	Total receipts	2,043	205	205
2000	Total: Balances and receipts	2,043	205	310
	Appropriations:				
	Current law:				
2101	Miscellaneous Trust Funds, AID	–2,043	–100	–100
5099	Balance, end of year		105	210

Program and Financing (in millions of dollars)

Identification code 072–9971–0–7–151		2021 actual	2022 est.	2023 est.
	Obligations by program activity:				
0001	Miscellaneous Trust Funds, AID (Direct)	2,050	100	100
0900	Total new obligations, unexpired accounts (object class 41.0)	2,050	100	100
	Budgetary resources:				
	Unobligated balance:				
1000	Unobligated balance brought forward, Oct 1	45	39	39
1021	Recoveries of prior year unpaid obligations	1	....	....
1070	Unobligated balance (total)	46	39	39
	Budget authority:				
	Appropriations, mandatory:				
1201	Appropriation (special or trust fund)	2,043	100	100
1900	Budget authority (total)	2,043	100	100
1930	Total budgetary resources available	2,089	139	139
	Memorandum (non-add) entries:				
1941	Unexpired unobligated balance, end of year	39	39	39
	Change in obligated balance:				
	Unpaid obligations:				
3000	Unpaid obligations, brought forward, Oct 1	81	52	70
3010	New obligations, unexpired accounts	2,050	100	100
3020	Outlays (gross)	–2,078	–82	–67
3040	Recoveries of prior year unpaid obligations, unexpired	–1	....	....
3050	Unpaid obligations, end of year	52	70	103
	Memorandum (non-add) entries:				
3100	Obligated balance, start of year	81	52	70
3200	Obligated balance, end of year	52	70	103
	Budget authority and outlays, net:				
	Mandatory:				
4090	Budget authority, gross	2,043	100	100
	Outlays, gross:				
4100	Outlays from new mandatory authority	2,014	50	50
4101	Outlays from mandatory balances	64	32	17
4110	Outlays, gross (total)	2,078	82	67
4180	Budget authority, net (total)	2,043	100	100
4190	Outlays, net (total)	2,078	82	67

The Miscellaneous Trust Funds account includes gifts and donations that the U.S. Agency for International Development (USAID) receives from other governments, non-governmental organizations, or private citizens. USAID has authority to spend these gifts and donations for development purposes under Section 635(d) of the Foreign Assistance Act.

OVERSEAS PRIVATE INVESTMENT CORPORATION
Federal Funds

OVERSEAS PRIVATE INVESTMENT CORPORATION NONCREDIT ACCOUNT

Program and Financing (in millions of dollars)

Identification code 071–4184–0–3–151		2021 actual	2022 est.	2023 est.
	Budgetary resources:				
	Unobligated balance:				
1000	Unobligated balance brought forward, Oct 1	2	....	....
1010	Unobligated balance transfer to other accts [077–4483]	–2	....	....
	Change in obligated balance:				
	Unpaid obligations:				
3000	Unpaid obligations, brought forward, Oct 1	5	....	....
3020	Outlays (gross)	–1	....	....
3030	Unpaid obligations transferred to other accts [077–4483]	–4	....	....
	Memorandum (non-add) entries:				
3100	Obligated balance, start of year	5	....	....
	Budget authority and outlays, net:				
	Discretionary:				
	Outlays, gross:				
4011	Outlays from discretionary balances	1	....	....
4180	Budget authority, net (total)	....	....	....
4190	Outlays, net (total)	1	....	....

On October 5, 2018, President Donald J. Trump signed into law the Better Utilization of Investments Leading to Development Act of 2018 (The BUILD Act). The BUILD Act consolidates, modernizes and reforms the U.S. Government's development finance capabilities—primarily the Overseas Private Investment Corporation (OPIC) and the Development Credit Authority (DCA) of the U.S. Agency for International Development (USAID)—into a new agency: the United States International Development Finance Corporation (DFC), which launched on January 2, 2020. DFC continues to finalize the transfer process of OPIC accounts to DFC accounts. Upon completion, all future OPIC activity will be presented in the DFC accounts.

OPIC encouraged the participation of United States private sector capital and skills in the economic and social development of developing countries and emerging market economies. Its primary noncredit program was political risk insurance against losses due to expropriation, inconvertibility, and damage due to political violence.

OVERSEAS PRIVATE INVESTMENT CORPORATION PROGRAM ACCOUNT

Program and Financing (in millions of dollars)

Identification code 071–0100–0–1–151		2021 actual	2022 est.	2023 est.
	Budgetary resources:				
	Unobligated balance:				
1000	Unobligated balance brought forward, Oct 1	4	....	....
1010	Unobligated balance transfer to other accts [077–0110]	–4	....	....
	Change in obligated balance:				
	Unpaid obligations:				
3000	Unpaid obligations, brought forward, Oct 1	60	29	....
3020	Outlays (gross)	–15	....	....
3030	Unpaid obligations transferred to other accts [077–0110]	–12	–29	....
3041	Recoveries of prior year unpaid obligations, expired	–4	....	....
3050	Unpaid obligations, end of year	29	....	....
	Memorandum (non-add) entries:				
3100	Obligated balance, start of year	60	29	....
3200	Obligated balance, end of year	29	....	....
	Budget authority and outlays, net:				
	Discretionary:				
	Outlays, gross:				
4011	Outlays from discretionary balances	3	....	....
	Mandatory:				
	Outlays, gross:				
4101	Outlays from mandatory balances	12	....	....
4180	Budget authority, net (total)	....	....	....

DEPARTMENT OF STATE AND OTHER INTERNATIONAL PROGRAMS

		2021 actual	2022 est.	2023 est.
4190	Outlays, net (total)	15		

Summary of Loan Levels, Subsidy Budget Authority and Outlays by Program (in millions of dollars)

Identification code 071–0100–0–1–151	2021 actual	2022 est.	2023 est.
Direct loan subsidy outlays:			
134001 OPIC Direct Loans	4		
134999 Total subsidy outlays	4		
Guaranteed loan subsidy outlays:			
234001 OPIC Loan Guarantees	10		
234999 Total subsidy outlays	10		

On October 5, 2018 President Donald J. Trump signed into law the Better Utilization of Investments Leading to Development Act of 2018 (The BUILD Act). The BUILD Act consolidates, modernizes and reforms the U.S. Government's development finance capabilities—primarily the Overseas Private Investment Corporation (OPIC) and the Development Credit Authority (DCA) of the U.S. Agency for International Development (USAID)—into a new agency: the United States International Development Finance Corporation (DFC), which launched on January 2, 2020. DFC continues to finalize the transfer process of OPIC accounts to DFC accounts. Upon completion, all future OPIC activity will be presented in the DFC accounts.

OPIC encouraged the participation of United States private sector capital and skills in the economic and social development of developing countries and emerging market economies. Its credit program provided investment financing through loans and guaranteed loans. As required by the Federal Credit Reform Act of 1990, the Program Account records the subsidy costs associated with the direct loans obligated and loan guarantees committed in 1992 and beyond (including modifications of direct loans or loan guarantees that resulted from obligations or commitments in any year), as well as administrative expenses of this program. The subsidy amounts are estimated on a present value basis; the administrative expenses are estimated on a cash basis.

OVERSEAS PRIVATE INVESTMENT CORPORATION GUARANTEED LOAN FINANCING ACCOUNT

Status of Guaranteed Loans (in millions of dollars)

Identification code 071–4075–0–3–151	2021 actual	2022 est.	2023 est.
Position with respect to appropriations act limitation on commitments:			
2111 Guaranteed loan commitments from current-year authority			
2150 Total guaranteed loan commitments			
2199 Guaranteed amount of guaranteed loan commitments			
Cumulative balance of guaranteed loans outstanding:			
2210 Outstanding, start of year	6,951		
2231 Disbursements of new guaranteed loans			
2251 Repayments and prepayments			
Adjustments:			
2261 Terminations for default that result in loans receivable			
2264 Other adjustments, net	–6,951		
2290 Outstanding, end of year			
Memorandum:			
2299 Guaranteed amount of guaranteed loans outstanding, end of year			
Addendum:			
Cumulative balance of defaulted guaranteed loans that result in loans receivable:			
2310 Outstanding, start of year			
2331 Disbursements for guaranteed loan claims			
2351 Repayments of loans receivable			
2361 Write-offs of loans receivable			
2364 Other adjustments, net			

		2021 actual	2022 est.	2023 est.
2390	Outstanding, end of year			

TRADE AND DEVELOPMENT AGENCY

Federal Funds

TRADE AND DEVELOPMENT AGENCY

For necessary expenses to carry out the provisions of section 661 of the Foreign Assistance Act of 1961, $98,000,000, to remain available until September 30, 2024, of which not more than $21,000,000 may be used for administrative expenses: Provided, That of the funds appropriated under this heading, not more than $5,000 may be available for representation and entertainment expenses.

Note.—A full-year 2022 appropriation for this account was not enacted at the time the Budget was prepared; therefore, the Budget assumes this account is operating under the Continuing Appropriations Act, 2022 (Division A of Public Law 117–43, as amended). The amounts included for 2022 reflect the annualized level provided by the continuing resolution.

Program and Financing (in millions of dollars)

Identification code 011–1001–0–1–151	2021 actual	2022 est.	2023 est.
Obligations by program activity:			
0001 Feasibility studies, technical assistance, and other activities	87	61	77
0002 Operating expenses		18	21
0100 Direct program activities, subtotal	87	79	98
0799 Total direct obligations	87	79	98
0801 Trade and Development Agency (Reimbursable)		10	10
0900 Total new obligations, unexpired accounts	87	89	108
Budgetary resources:			
Unobligated balance:			
1000 Unobligated balance brought forward, Oct 1	42	39	35
1011 Unobligated balance transfer from other acct [072–0306]	2		
1021 Recoveries of prior year unpaid obligations		2	2
1070 Unobligated balance (total)	44	41	37
Budget authority:			
Appropriations, discretionary:			
1100 Appropriation	80	80	98
Spending authority from offsetting collections, discretionary:			
1700 Collected	5	3	
1701 Change in uncollected payments, Federal sources	–2		
1750 Spending auth from offsetting collections, disc (total)	3	3	
1900 Budget authority (total)	83	83	98
1930 Total budgetary resources available	127	124	135
Memorandum (non-add) entries:			
1940 Unobligated balance expiring	–1		
1941 Unexpired unobligated balance, end of year	39	35	27
Change in obligated balance:			
Unpaid obligations:			
3000 Unpaid obligations, brought forward, Oct 1	163	167	102
3010 New obligations, unexpired accounts	87	89	108
3011 Obligations ("upward adjustments"), expired accounts	2		
3020 Outlays (gross)	–62	–152	–85
3040 Recoveries of prior year unpaid obligations, unexpired		–2	–2
3041 Recoveries of prior year unpaid obligations, expired	–23		
3050 Unpaid obligations, end of year	167	102	123
Uncollected payments:			
3060 Uncollected pymts, Fed sources, brought forward, Oct 1	–34	–29	–29
3070 Change in uncollected pymts, Fed sources, unexpired	2		
3071 Change in uncollected pymts, Fed sources, expired	3		
3090 Uncollected pymts, Fed sources, end of year	–29	–29	–29
Memorandum (non-add) entries:			
3100 Obligated balance, start of year	129	138	73
3200 Obligated balance, end of year	138	73	94
Budget authority and outlays, net:			
Discretionary:			
4000 Budget authority, gross	83	83	98
Outlays, gross:			
4010 Outlays from new discretionary authority	13	25	28
4011 Outlays from discretionary balances	49	127	57
4020 Outlays, gross (total)	62	152	85

TRADE AND DEVELOPMENT AGENCY—Continued
Program and Financing—Continued

Identification code 011–1001–0–1–151		2021 actual	2022 est.	2023 est.
	Offsets against gross budget authority and outlays:			
	Offsetting collections (collected) from:			
4030	Federal sources	–8	–3	
4040	Offsets against gross budget authority and outlays (total)	–8	–3	
	Additional offsets against gross budget authority only:			
4050	Change in uncollected pymts, Fed sources, unexpired	2		
4052	Offsetting collections credited to expired accounts	3		
4060	Additional offsets against budget authority only (total)	5		
4070	Budget authority, net (discretionary)	80	80	98
4080	Outlays, net (discretionary)	54	149	85
4180	Budget authority, net (total)	80	80	98
4190	Outlays, net (total)	54	149	85

The FY 2023 request for the U.S. Trade and Development Agency (USTDA) of $98 million will strengthen the Agency's ability to help U.S. companies create jobs through the export of U.S. goods and services for priority development projects in emerging economies. USTDA links U.S. businesses to export opportunities by funding project preparation activities, pilot projects and reverse trade missions that create sustainable infrastructure and foster economic growth in its partner countries. In carrying out its mission, USTDA prioritizes activities where there is a high likelihood for the export of U.S. goods and services that can match the development needs of the Agency's overseas partners.

Object Classification (in millions of dollars)

Identification code 011–1001–0–1–151		2021 actual	2022 est.	2023 est.
	Direct obligations:			
	Personnel compensation:			
11.1	Full-time permanent	7	6	8
11.3	Other than full-time permanent	2	2	2
11.9	Total personnel compensation	9	8	10
12.1	Civilian personnel benefits	3	2	2
23.1	Rental payments to GSA	2	2	2
25.1	Advisory and assistance services		4	4
25.3	Other goods and services from Federal sources		2	3
41.0	Grants, subsidies, and contributions	73	61	77
99.0	Direct obligations	87	79	98
99.0	Reimbursable obligations		10	10
99.9	Total new obligations, unexpired accounts	87	89	108

Employment Summary

Identification code 011–1001–0–1–151		2021 actual	2022 est.	2023 est.
1001	Direct civilian full-time equivalent employment	65	65	68

UNITED STATES INTERNATIONAL DEVELOPMENT FINANCE CORPORATION

Federal Funds

U.S. INTERNATIONAL DEVELOPMENT FINANCE CORPORATION INSURANCE OF DEBT PROGRAM ACCOUNT

Summary of Loan Levels, Subsidy Budget Authority and Outlays by Program (in millions of dollars)

Identification code 077–0410–0–1–151		2021 actual	2022 est.	2023 est.
	Guaranteed loan levels supportable by subsidy budget authority:			
215001	Insurance of Debt	425		
	Guaranteed loan subsidy (in percent):			
232001	Insurance of Debt	–1.00		
232999	Weighted average subsidy rate	–1.00	0.00	0.00

	Guaranteed loan subsidy budget authority:			
233001	Insurance of Debt		–4	

CORPORATE CAPITAL ACCOUNT

The United States International Development Finance Corporation (the Corporation) is authorized to make such expenditures and commitments within the limits of funds and borrowing authority available to the Corporation, and in accordance with the law, and to make such expenditures and commitments without regard to fiscal year limitations, as provided by section 9104 of title 31, United States Code, as may be necessary in carrying out the programs for the current fiscal year for the Corporation: *Provided,* That for necessary expenses of the activities described in subsections (b), (c), (e), (f), and (g) of section 1421 of the BUILD Act of 2018 (division F of Public Law 115–254) and for administrative expenses to carry out authorized activities and project-specific transaction costs described in section 1434(d) of such Act, $1,000,000,000: *Provided further,* That of the amount provided—

(1) $220,000,000 shall remain available until September 30, 2025, for administrative expenses to carry out authorized activities (including an amount for official reception and representation expenses which shall not exceed $25,000) and project-specific transaction costs as described in section 1434(k) of such Act, of which $1,000,000 shall remain available until September 30, 2027;

(2) $780,000,000 shall remain available until September 30, 2025, for the activities described in subsections (b), (c), (e), (f), and (g) of section 1421 of the BUILD Act of 2018, except such amounts obligated in a fiscal year for activities described in section 1421(c) of such Act shall remain available for disbursement for the term of the underlying project: *Provided further,* That if the term of the project extends longer than 10 fiscal years, the Chief Executive Officer of the Corporation shall inform the appropriate congressional committees prior to the obligation or disbursement of funds, as applicable: *Provided further,* That amounts made available under this paragraph may be paid to the "United States International Development Finance Corporation—Program Account" for programs authorized by subsections (b), (e), (f), and (g) of section 1421 of the BUILD Act of 2018:

Provided further, That funds may only be obligated pursuant to section 1421(g) of the BUILD Act of 2018 subject to prior notification to the appropriate congressional committees and the regular notification procedures of the Committees on Appropriations: *Provided further,* That in fiscal year 2023, collections of amounts described in section 1434(h) of the BUILD Act of 2018 shall be credited as offsetting collections to this appropriation: *Provided further,* That such collections collected in fiscal year 2023 in excess of $1,000,000,000 shall be credited to this account and shall be available in future fiscal years only to the extent provided in advance in appropriations Acts: *Provided further,* That in fiscal year 2023, if such collections are less than $1,000,000,000, receipts collected pursuant to the BUILD Act of 2018 and the Federal Credit Reform Act of 1990, in an amount equal to such shortfall, shall be credited as offsetting collections to this appropriation: *Provided further,* That funds appropriated or otherwise made available under this heading may not be used to provide any type of assistance that is otherwise prohibited by any other provision of law or to provide assistance to any foreign country that is otherwise prohibited by any other provision of law: *Provided further,* That the sums herein appropriated from the General Fund shall be reduced on a dollar-for-dollar basis by the offsetting collections described under this heading so as to result in a final fiscal year appropriation from the General Fund estimated at $550,000,000.

Note.—A full-year 2022 appropriation for this account was not enacted at the time the Budget was prepared; therefore, the Budget assumes this account is operating under the Continuing Appropriations Act, 2022 (Division A of Public Law 117–43, as amended). The amounts included for 2022 reflect the annualized level provided by the continuing resolution.

Program and Financing (in millions of dollars)

Identification code 077–4483–0–3–151		2021 actual	2022 est.	2023 est.
	Obligations by program activity:			
0001	Administrative Expenses	129	164	220
0002	Program - Equity	224	500	660
0004	Program - Positive Subsidy & TA	60	108	120
0005	Project Specific Costs		22	20
0799	Total direct obligations	413	794	1,020
0801	Reimbursable program activity (IAAs)	6	4	5
0900	Total new obligations, unexpired accounts	419	798	1,025

DEPARTMENT OF STATE AND OTHER INTERNATIONAL PROGRAMS

United States International Development Finance Corporation—Continued
Federal Funds—Continued

857

		2021 actual	2022 est.	2023 est.
	Budgetary resources:			
	Unobligated balance:			
1000	Unobligated balance brought forward, Oct 1	6,186	6,429	6,247
1011	Unobligated balance transfer from other acct [071–4184]	2		
1011	Unobligated balance transfer from other acct [072–1264]	1		
1012	Unobligated balance transfers between expired and unexpired accounts	10		
1021	Recoveries of prior year unpaid obligations	34	1	1
1070	Unobligated balance (total)	6,233	6,430	6,248
	Budget authority:			
	Appropriations, discretionary:			
1100	Appropriation -(reduced by offsetting collections)	128	176	550
	Spending authority from offsetting collections, discretionary:			
1700	Collected - Treasury Interest	131	123	122
1700	Collected - Negative Subsidy To This Acct (NSR)	287	243	301
1700	Collected - DFC Deal Fees	21	25	26
1700	Collected - IAA reimbursables	11	10	10
1700	Collected - Equity Fees	2	2	2
1700	Collected - Unidentified	8		
1701	Change in uncollected payments, Federal sources	−11		
1750	Spending auth from offsetting collections, disc (total)	449	403	461
	Spending authority from offsetting collections, mandatory:			
1800	Collected - Insurance Premiums	19	17	26
1800	Collected - OPIC Portfolio - Fees	20	19	19
1850	Spending auth from offsetting collections, mand (total)	39	36	45
1900	Budget authority (total)	616	615	1,056
1930	Total budgetary resources available	6,849	7,045	7,304
	Memorandum (non-add) entries:			
1940	Unobligated balance expiring	−1		
1941	Unexpired unobligated balance, end of year	6,429	6,247	6,279
	Change in obligated balance:			
	Unpaid obligations:			
3000	Unpaid obligations, brought forward, Oct 1	225	337	446
3010	New obligations, unexpired accounts	419	798	1,025
3020	Outlays (gross)	−277	−688	−874
3031	Unpaid obligations transferred from other accts [071–4184]	4		
3040	Recoveries of prior year unpaid obligations, unexpired	−34	−1	−1
3050	Unpaid obligations, end of year	337	446	596
	Uncollected payments:			
3060	Uncollected pymts, Fed sources, brought forward, Oct 1	−48	−37	−37
3070	Change in uncollected pymts, Fed sources, unexpired	11		
3090	Uncollected pymts, Fed sources, end of year	−37	−37	−37
	Memorandum (non-add) entries:			
3100	Obligated balance, start of year	177	300	409
3200	Obligated balance, end of year	300	409	559
	Budget authority and outlays, net:			
	Discretionary:			
4000	Budget authority, gross	577	579	1,011
	Outlays, gross:			
4010	Outlays from new discretionary authority	147	488	736
4011	Outlays from discretionary balances	130	158	124
4020	Outlays, gross (total)	277	646	860
	Offsets against gross budget authority and outlays:			
	Offsetting collections (collected) from:			
4030	Federal sources	−298	−253	−311
4031	Interest on Treasury securities	−131	−123	−122
4033	Non-Federal sources - DFC Deal Fees	−21	−25	−26
4033	Non-Federal sources - Equity Fees	−2	−2	−2
4033	Non-Federal sources - Unidentified	−8		
4040	Offsets against gross budget authority and outlays (total)	−460	−403	−461
	Additional offsets against gross budget authority only:			
4050	Change in uncollected pymts, Fed sources, unexpired	11		
4070	Budget authority, net (discretionary)	128	176	550
4080	Outlays, net (discretionary)	−183	243	399
	Mandatory:			
4090	Budget authority, gross	39	36	45
	Outlays, gross:			
4100	Outlays from new mandatory authority		14	14
4101	Outlays from mandatory balances		28	
4110	Outlays, gross (total)		42	14
	Offsets against gross budget authority and outlays:			
	Offsetting collections (collected) from:			
4123	Non-Federal sources	−39	−36	−45
4180	Budget authority, net (total)	128	176	550
4190	Outlays, net (total)	−222	249	368

		2021 actual	2022 est.	2023 est.
	Memorandum (non-add) entries:			
5000	Total investments, SOY: Federal securities: Par value	6,165	6,128	6,272
5001	Total investments, EOY: Federal securities: Par value	6,128	6,272	6,326

All the United States International Development Finance Corporation (DFC) administrative, insurance and program (including subsidy, equity, and technical assistance) activities are presented in the DFC Corporate Capital Account. Upon receipt of funding, DFC transfers program funding that supports debt activities and technical assistance to the Program Account.

Object Classification (in millions of dollars)

Identification code 077–4483–0–3–151		2021 actual	2022 est.	2023 est.
	Direct obligations:			
11.1	Personnel compensation: Full-time permanent	54	72	96
12.1	Civilian personnel benefits	18	24	32
21.0	Travel and transportation of persons	1	5	10
23.2	Rental payments to others	10	12	12
23.3	Communications, utilities, and miscellaneous charges	1	1	3
25.1	Advisory and assistance services	34	26	35
25.1	Advisory and assistance services [Project Specific Costs]		22	20
25.2	Other services from non-Federal sources	1	1	1
25.4	Operation and maintenance of facilities	1		
25.7	Operation and maintenance of equipment	7	20	23
26.0	Supplies and materials	2	3	8
41.0	Equity	224	500	660
41.0	Grants, subsidies, and technical assistance	60	108	120
99.0	Direct obligations	413	794	1,020
25.2	Reimbursable obligations: Other services from non-Federal sources	6	4	5
99.0	Reimbursable obligations	6	4	5
99.9	Total new obligations, unexpired accounts	419	798	1,025

Employment Summary

Identification code 077–4483–0–3–151	2021 actual	2022 est.	2023 est.
1001 Direct civilian full-time equivalent employment	342	440	600

PROGRAM ACCOUNT

Amounts paid from "United States International Development Finance Corporation—Corporate Capital Account" (CCA) shall remain available until September 30, 2025: Provided, That amounts transferred to this account pursuant to section 1434(j) of the BUILD Act of 2018 (division F of Public Law 115–254) shall be merged with and available for the same time period and purposes as provided herein: Provided further, That amounts paid to this account from CCA or transferred to this account pursuant to section 1434(j) of the BUILD Act of 2018 (division F of Public Law 115–254) shall be available for the costs of direct and guaranteed loans provided by the Corporation pursuant to section 1421(b) of such Act: Provided further, That such costs, including the cost of modifying such loans, shall be as defined in section 502 of the Congressional Budget Act of 1974: Provided further, That such amounts obligated in a fiscal year shall remain available for disbursement for the following 8 fiscal years: Provided further, That the total loan principal or guaranteed principal amount shall not exceed $10,000,000,000.

Note.—A full-year 2022 appropriation for this account was not enacted at the time the Budget was prepared; therefore, the Budget assumes this account is operating under the Continuing Appropriations Act, 2022 (Division A of Public Law 117–43, as amended). The amounts included for 2022 reflect the annualized level provided by the continuing resolution.

Program and Financing (in millions of dollars)

Identification code 077–0110–0–1–151		2021 actual	2022 est.	2023 est.
	Obligations by program activity:			
	Credit program obligations:			
0701	Direct loan subsidy	36	73	81
0702	Loan guarantee subsidy	27	11	23
0703	Subsidy for modifications of direct loans	4		
0705	Reestimates of direct loan subsidy	145	191	
0706	Interest on reestimates of direct loan subsidy	25	17	
0707	Reestimates of loan guarantee subsidy	258	286	
0708	Interest on reestimates of loan guarantee subsidy	32	54	

United States International Development Finance Corporation—Continued
Federal Funds—Continued

PROGRAM ACCOUNT—Continued

Program and Financing—Continued

Identification code 077–0110–0–1–151	2021 actual	2022 est.	2023 est.
0715 Technical assistance	12	20	15
0900 Total new obligations, unexpired accounts (object class 41.0)	539	652	119
Budgetary resources:			
Unobligated balance:			
1000 Unobligated balance brought forward, Oct 1	12	45	42
1011 Unobligated balance transfer from other acct [072–1021]	10	1	1
1011 Unobligated balance transfer from other acct [019–1031]	1		
1011 Unobligated balance transfer from other acct [072–1037]	15		
1011 Unobligated balance transfer from other acct [072–0306]	5		
1011 Unobligated balance transfer from other acct [071–0100]	4		
1012 Unobligated balance transfers between expired and unexpired accounts	10		
1021 Recoveries of prior year unpaid obligations	7		
1070 Unobligated balance (total)	64	46	43
Budget authority:			
Appropriations, discretionary:			
1121 Appropriations transferred from other acct [072–1037]		50	50
Appropriations, mandatory:			
1200 Appropriation - re-estimates	460	548	
Spending authority from offsetting collections, discretionary:			
1700 Collected - DFC CCA	60	50	120
1900 Budget authority (total)	520	648	170
1930 Total budgetary resources available	584	694	213
Memorandum (non-add) entries:			
1941 Unexpired unobligated balance, end of year	45	42	94
Change in obligated balance:			
Unpaid obligations:			
3000 Unpaid obligations, brought forward, Oct 1	20	147	156
3010 New obligations, unexpired accounts	539	652	119
3020 Outlays (gross)	–487	–672	–116
3031 Unpaid obligations transferred from other accts [071–0100]	12	29	
3031 Unpaid obligations transferred from other accts [072–1264]	70		
3040 Recoveries of prior year unpaid obligations, unexpired	–7		
3050 Unpaid obligations, end of year	147	156	159
Memorandum (non-add) entries:			
3100 Obligated balance, start of year	20	147	156
3200 Obligated balance, end of year	147	156	159
Budget authority and outlays, net:			
Discretionary:			
4000 Budget authority, gross	60	100	170
Outlays, gross:			
4010 Outlays from new discretionary authority	12	64	84
4011 Outlays from discretionary balances	15	60	32
4020 Outlays, gross (total)	27	124	116
Offsets against gross budget authority and outlays:			
Offsetting collections (collected) from:			
4030 Federal sources: 72–1037 ESF	–60	–50	
4030 Federal sources: 77–4483 Corporate Capital Account			–120
4040 Offsets against gross budget authority and outlays (total)	–60	–50	–120
4070 Budget authority, net (discretionary)		50	50
4080 Outlays, net (discretionary)	–33	74	–4
Mandatory:			
4090 Budget authority, gross	460	548	
Outlays, gross:			
4100 Outlays from new mandatory authority		548	
4101 Outlays from mandatory balances	460		
4110 Outlays, gross (total)	460	548	
4180 Budget authority, net (total)	460	598	50
4190 Outlays, net (total)	427	622	–4

Summary of Loan Levels, Subsidy Budget Authority and Outlays by Program (in millions of dollars)

Identification code 077–0110–0–1–151	2021 actual	2022 est.	2023 est.
Direct loan levels supportable by subsidy budget authority:			
115001 Direct Loans	2,886	2,277	2,050
115003 Direct Loan Investment Funds	174	255	500
115004 Direct Loans in Foreign Currencies	119	535	575
115005 Hybrid Participation Notes	15		
115999 Total direct loan levels	3,194	3,067	3,125
Direct loan subsidy (in percent):			
132001 Direct Loans	–7.87	–8.06	–9.21
132003 Direct Loan Investment Funds	–11.54	–3.25	–9.13
132004 Direct Loans in Foreign Currencies	8.65	10.00	10.00
132005 Hybrid Participation Notes	0.19		
132999 Weighted average subsidy rate	–7.42	–4.51	–5.66
Direct loan subsidy budget authority:			
133001 Direct Loans	–227	–184	–189
133003 Direct Loan Investment Funds	–20	–8	–46
133004 Direct Loans in Foreign Currencies	10	54	58
133999 Total subsidy budget authority	–237	–138	–177
Direct loan subsidy outlays:			
134001 Direct Loans	–239	–121	–164
134003 Direct Loan Investment Funds	–4	–15	–27
134004 Direct Loans in Foreign Currencies	10	15	30
134999 Total subsidy outlays	–233	–121	–161
Direct loan reestimates:			
135001 Direct Loans	75	43	
135002 NIS Direct Loans		–1	
135003 Direct Loan Investment Funds	–1	–8	
135999 Total direct loan reestimates	74	34	
Guaranteed loan levels supportable by subsidy budget authority:			
215001 USAID Mission-led Guarantees	288	13	300
215002 Loan Guarantees	705	520	700
215006 Limited Arbitral Award Coverage	425	400	300
215999 Total loan guarantee levels	1,418	933	1,300
Guaranteed loan subsidy (in percent):			
232001 USAID Mission-led Guarantees	5.09	5.37	5.92
232002 Loan Guarantees	–1.82	–3.93	–8.20
232006 Limited Arbitral Award Coverage	–1.00	–3.69	–3.69
232999 Weighted average subsidy rate	–.17	–3.70	–3.90
Guaranteed loan subsidy budget authority:			
233001 USAID Mission-led Guarantees	15	1	18
233002 Loan Guarantees	–13	–20	–57
233006 Limited Arbitral Award Coverage	–4	–15	–11
233999 Total subsidy budget authority	–2	–34	–50
Guaranteed loan subsidy outlays:			
234001 USAID Mission-led Guarantees	2	29	21
234002 Loan Guarantees	–110	–46	–50
234003 Guaranteed Loan Investment Funds	–9	–20	–16
234006 Limited Arbitral Award Coverage		–13	–13
234999 Total subsidy outlays	–117	–50	–58
Guaranteed loan reestimates:			
235001 USAID Mission-led Guarantees	–9	–13	
235002 Loan Guarantees	45	164	
235003 Guaranteed Loan Investment Funds	16	–20	
235004 Non-Honoring of Sovereign Guarantees	–3	1	
235005 NIS Guaranteed Loans		3	
235999 Total guaranteed loan reestimates	49	135	

As required by the Federal Credit Reform Act of 1990, the Program Account records the subsidy costs associated with the direct loans obligated and loan guarantees committed in 1992 and beyond (including modifications and cost re-estimates of direct loans or loan guarantees that resulted from obligations or commitments in any year). The subsidy amounts are estimated on a present value basis.

UNITED STATES INTERNATIONAL DEVELOPMENT FINANCE CORPORATION

INSPECTOR GENERAL

For necessary expenses of the Office of Inspector General in carrying out the provisions of the Inspector General Act of 1978 (5 U.S.C. App.), $5,133,000, to remain available until September 30, 2024.

Note.—A full-year 2022 appropriation for this account was not enacted at the time the Budget was prepared; therefore, the Budget assumes this account is operating under the Continuing Appropriations Act, 2022 (Division A of Public Law 117–43, as amended). The amounts included for 2022 reflect the annualized level provided by the continuing resolution.

Program and Financing (in millions of dollars)

Identification code 077–0111–0–1–151	2021 actual	2022 est.	2023 est.
Obligations by program activity:			
0001 Office of the Inspector General	2	3	6

DEPARTMENT OF STATE AND OTHER INTERNATIONAL PROGRAMS

United States International Development Finance Corporation—Continued
Federal Funds—Continued

859

		2021 actual	2022 est.	2023 est.
	Budgetary resources:			
	Unobligated balance:			
1000	Unobligated balance brought forward, Oct 1	2	2	1
	Budget authority:			
	Appropriations, discretionary:			
1100	Appropriation	2	2	5
1900	Budget authority (total)	2	2	5
1930	Total budgetary resources available	4	4	6
	Memorandum (non-add) entries:			
1941	Unexpired unobligated balance, end of year	2	1	....
	Change in obligated balance:			
	Unpaid obligations:			
3010	New obligations, unexpired accounts	2	3	6
3020	Outlays (gross)	−2	−3	−5
3050	Unpaid obligations, end of year	....	....	1
	Memorandum (non-add) entries:			
3200	Obligated balance, end of year	....	....	1
	Budget authority and outlays, net:			
	Discretionary:			
4000	Budget authority, gross	2	2	5
	Outlays, gross:			
4010	Outlays from new discretionary authority	....	2	5
4011	Outlays from discretionary balances	2	1	....
4020	Outlays, gross (total)	2	3	5
4180	Budget authority, net (total)	2	2	5
4190	Outlays, net (total)	2	3	5

The DFC mission to partner with the private sector to finance solutions to the most critical challenges facing the developing world today while also advancing U.S. foreign policy priorities requires an effective OIG to ensure American taxpayer dollars are protected. The OIG does this by providing independent oversight of DFC programs and operations in accordance with the Inspector General Act of 1978, as amended. OIG audits, investigations, inspections, and evaluations prevent and detect waste, fraud, abuse, and mismanagement; provide advice and assistance to agency management, the DFC Board of Directors, and Congress; and promote efficiency, effectiveness and economy in DFC programs and operations.

The President's Budget requests $5.133 million for the independent Inspector General function to be funded from the General Fund. This will allow OIG to independently oversee DFC through audits and investigations, and identify improvements to the management and execution of DFC's operations and programs.

Object Classification (in millions of dollars)

Identification code 077–0111–0–1–151	2021 actual	2022 est.	2023 est.
Direct obligations:			
11.1 Personnel compensation: Full-time permanent	....	1	1
12.1 Civilian personnel benefits	....	1	1
25.1 Advisory and assistance services	2	1	4
99.9 Total new obligations, unexpired accounts	2	3	6

Employment Summary

Identification code 077–0111–0–1–151	2021 actual	2022 est.	2023 est.
1001 Direct civilian full-time equivalent employment	2	9	9

UNITED STATES INTERNATIONAL DEVELOPMENT FINANCE CORPORATION GUARANTEED LOAN FINANCING ACCOUNT

Program and Financing (in millions of dollars)

Identification code 077–4485–0–3–151	2021 actual	2022 est.	2023 est.
Obligations by program activity:			
Credit program obligations:			
0711 Default claim payments on principal	264	264	206
0713 Payment of interest to Treasury	29	35	38
0740 Negative subsidy obligations	25	46	74
0742 Downward reestimates paid to receipt accounts	199	171	....
0743 Interest on downward reestimates	42	34	....
0900 Total new obligations, unexpired accounts	559	550	318
Budgetary resources:			
Unobligated balance:			
1000 Unobligated balance brought forward, Oct 1	387	866	2,046
1021 Recoveries of prior year unpaid obligations	141	134	134
1023 Unobligated balances applied to repay debt	−137	−167	−167
1024 Unobligated balance of borrowing authority withdrawn	−141	....	....
1070 Unobligated balance (total)	250	833	2,013
Financing authority:			
Borrowing authority, mandatory:			
1400 Borrowing authority	653	1,210	1,210
Spending authority from offsetting collections, mandatory:			
1800 Collected	638	697	349
1801 Change in uncollected payments, Federal sources	1	60	60
1825 Spending authority from offsetting collections applied to repay debt	−117	−204	−204
1850 Spending auth from offsetting collections, mand (total)	522	553	205
1900 Budget authority (total)	1,175	1,763	1,415
1930 Total budgetary resources available	1,425	2,596	3,428
Memorandum (non-add) entries:			
1941 Unexpired unobligated balance, end of year	866	2,046	3,110
Change in obligated balance:			
Unpaid obligations:			
3000 Unpaid obligations, brought forward, Oct 1	512	293	69
3010 New obligations, unexpired accounts	559	550	318
3020 Outlays (gross)	−637	−640	−253
3040 Recoveries of prior year unpaid obligations, unexpired	−141	−134	−134
3050 Unpaid obligations, end of year	293	69	....
Uncollected payments:			
3060 Uncollected pymts, Fed sources, brought forward, Oct 1	−20	−21	−81
3070 Change in uncollected pymts, Fed sources, unexpired	−1	−60	−60
3090 Uncollected pymts, Fed sources, end of year	−21	−81	−141
Memorandum (non-add) entries:			
3100 Obligated balance, start of year	492	272	−12
3200 Obligated balance, end of year	272	−12	−141
Financing authority and disbursements, net:			
Mandatory:			
4090 Budget authority, gross	1,175	1,763	1,415
Financing disbursements:			
4110 Outlays, gross (total)	637	640	253
Offsets against gross financing authority and disbursements:			
Offsetting collections (collected) from:			
4120 Federal sources - subsidy payments from program account	−317	−382	−32
4122 Interest on uninvested funds	−13	−15	−17
4123 Claims recoveries - DCA	−308	−300	−300
4130 Offsets against gross budget authority and outlays (total)	−638	−697	−349
Additional offsets against financing authority only (total):			
4140 Change in uncollected pymts, Fed sources, unexpired	−1	−60	−60
4160 Budget authority, net (mandatory)	536	1,006	1,006
4170 Outlays, net (mandatory)	−1	−57	−96
4180 Budget authority, net (total)	536	1,006	1,006
4190 Outlays, net (total)	−1	−57	−96

Status of Guaranteed Loans (in millions of dollars)

Identification code 077–4485–0–3–151	2021 actual	2022 est.	2023 est.
Position with respect to appropriations act limitation on commitments:			
2111 Guaranteed loan commitments from current-year authority	1,418	933	1,300
2121 Limitation available from carry-forward	....	....	....
2150 Total guaranteed loan commitments	1,418	933	1,300
2199 Guaranteed amount of guaranteed loan commitments	359	900	900
Cumulative balance of guaranteed loans outstanding:			
2210 Outstanding, start of year	8,531	21,001	23,389
2231 Disbursements of new guaranteed loans	640	27	27
2231 Disbursements of new guaranteed loans	12,094	2,625	2,625
2251 Repayments and prepayments	....	....	....
Adjustments:			
2261 Terminations for default that result in loans receivable	−264	−264	−264
2263 Terminations for default that result in claim payments	....	....	....
2264 Other adjustments, net	....	....	....
2290 Outstanding, end of year	21,001	23,389	25,777

UNITED STATES INTERNATIONAL DEVELOPMENT FINANCE CORPORATION GUARANTEED LOAN FINANCING ACCOUNT—Continued

Status of Guaranteed Loans—Continued

Identification code 077–4485–0–3–151	2021 actual	2022 est.	2023 est.
Memorandum:			
2299 Guaranteed amount of guaranteed loans outstanding, end of year		15	15
2299 Guaranteed amount of guaranteed loans outstanding, end of year	10,977	11,007	11,007
Addendum:			
Cumulative balance of defaulted guaranteed loans that result in loans receivable:			
2310 Outstanding, start of year	300	300	300
2310 Outstanding, start of year	366	578	586
2331 Disbursements for guaranteed loan claims	264	206	206
2351 Repayments of loans receivable	–92	–179	–179
2361 Write-offs of loans receivable	–260	–19	–19
2364 Other adjustments, net	....	....	....
2390 Outstanding, end of year	578	586	594

As required by the Federal Credit Reform Act of 1990, this non-budgetary account records all cash flows to and from the Government resulting from loans guaranteed in 1992 and beyond. The amounts in this account are a means of financing and are not included in the budget totals.

Balance Sheet (in millions of dollars)

Identification code 077–4485–0–3–151	2020 actual	2021 actual
ASSETS:		
Federal assets:		
1101 Fund balances with Treasury	540	846
Investments in U.S. securities:		
1106 Receivables, net	292	340
1206 Non-Federal assets: Receivables, net	83	99
Net value of assets related to post-1991 acquired defaulted guaranteed loans receivable:		
1501 Defaulted guaranteed loans receivable, gross	366	578
1502 Interest receivable	18	26
1505 Allowance for subsidy cost (–)	–263	–354
1599 Net present value of assets related to defaulted guaranteed loans	121	250
1901 Other Federal assets: Other assets	....	....
1999 Total assets	1,036	1,535
LIABILITIES:		
Federal liabilities:		
2103 Debt	934	1,239
2104 Resources payable to Treasury	....	....
2105 Other	242	204
Non-Federal liabilities:		
2204 Liabilities for loan guarantees	–149	84
2207 Other	1	1
2999 Total liabilities	1,028	1,528
NET POSITION:		
3300 Cumulative results of operations	8	7
4999 Total liabilities and net position	1,036	1,535

UNITED STATES INTERNATIONAL DEVELOPMENT FINANCE CORPORATION DIRECT LOAN FINANCING ACCOUNT

Program and Financing (in millions of dollars)

Identification code 077–4484–0–3–151	2021 actual	2022 est.	2023 est.
Obligations by program activity:			
Credit program obligations:			
0710 Direct loan obligations	3,194	3,067	3,125
0713 Payment of interest to Treasury	127	250	124
0740 Negative subsidy obligations	273	212	258
0742 Downward reestimates paid to receipt accounts	86	112	....
0743 Interest on downward reestimates	10	62	....
0900 Total new obligations, unexpired accounts	3,690	3,703	3,507

	2021 actual	2022 est.	2023 est.
Budgetary resources:			
Unobligated balance:			
1000 Unobligated balance brought forward, Oct 1	18	254	2,643
1021 Recoveries of prior year unpaid obligations	196	....	....
1023 Unobligated balances applied to repay debt	–18	....	....
1024 Unobligated balance of borrowing authority withdrawn	–195	....	....
1070 Unobligated balance (total)	1	254	2,643
Financing authority:			
Borrowing authority, mandatory:			
1400 Borrowing authority	3,752	5,450	3,650
Spending authority from offsetting collections, mandatory:			
1800 Collected	907	952	767
1801 Change in uncollected payments, Federal sources	24	90	80
1825 Spending authority from offsetting collections applied to repay debt	–740	–400	–551
1850 Spending auth from offsetting collections, mand (total)	191	642	296
1900 Budget authority (total)	3,943	6,092	3,946
1930 Total budgetary resources available	3,944	6,346	6,589
Memorandum (non-add) entries:			
1941 Unexpired unobligated balance, end of year	254	2,643	3,082
Change in obligated balance:			
Unpaid obligations:			
3000 Unpaid obligations, brought forward, Oct 1	4,837	4,785	3,388
3010 New obligations, unexpired accounts	3,690	3,703	3,507
3020 Outlays (gross)	–3,546	–5,100	–4,850
3040 Recoveries of prior year unpaid obligations, unexpired	–196	....	....
3050 Unpaid obligations, end of year	4,785	3,388	2,045
Uncollected payments:			
3060 Uncollected pymts, Fed sources, brought forward, Oct 1	–22	–46	–136
3070 Change in uncollected pymts, Fed sources, unexpired	–24	–90	–80
3090 Uncollected pymts, Fed sources, end of year	–46	–136	–216
Memorandum (non-add) entries:			
3100 Obligated balance, start of year	4,815	4,739	3,252
3200 Obligated balance, end of year	4,739	3,252	1,829
Financing authority and disbursements, net:			
Mandatory:			
4090 Budget authority, gross	3,943	6,092	3,946
Financing disbursements:			
4110 Outlays, gross (total)	3,546	5,100	4,850
Offsets against gross financing authority and disbursements:			
Offsetting collections (collected) from:			
4120 Federal sources, credit subsidy	–195	–237	–50
4122 Interest on uninvested funds	–37	–40	–42
4123 Repayments of principal	–675	–500	–500
4123 Interest and fees received on loans	....	–175	–175
4130 Offsets against gross budget authority and outlays (total)	–907	–952	–767
Additional offsets against financing authority only (total):			
4140 Change in uncollected pymts, Fed sources, unexpired	–24	–90	–80
4160 Budget authority, net (mandatory)	3,012	5,050	3,099
4170 Outlays, net (mandatory)	2,639	4,148	4,083
4180 Budget authority, net (total)	3,012	5,050	3,099
4190 Outlays, net (total)	2,639	4,148	4,083

Status of Direct Loans (in millions of dollars)

Identification code 077–4484–0–3–151	2021 actual	2022 est.	2023 est.
Position with respect to appropriations act limitation on obligations:			
1111 Direct loan obligations from current-year authority	3,194	3,067	3,125
1150 Total direct loan obligations	3,194	3,067	3,125
Cumulative balance of direct loans outstanding:			
1210 Outstanding, start of year	3,659	6,196	8,975
1231 Disbursements: Direct loan disbursements	3,140	3,240	3,340
1251 Repayments: Repayments and prepayments	–499	–333	–333
1263 Write-offs for default: Direct loans	–104	–128	–128
1290 Outstanding, end of year	6,196	8,975	11,854

As required by the Federal Credit Reform Act of 1990, this non-budgetary account records all cash flows to and from the Government resulting from direct loans obligated in 1992 and beyond. The amounts in this account are a means of financing and are not included in the budget totals.

Balance Sheet (in millions of dollars)

Identification code 077–4484–0–3–151		2020 actual	2021 actual
	ASSETS:		
	Federal assets:		
1101	Fund balances with Treasury	151	253
	Investments in U.S. securities:		
1106	Receivables, net	170	
1206	Non-Federal assets: Receivables, net		210
	Net value of assets related to post-1991 direct loans receivable:		
1401	Direct loans receivable, gross	3,659	6,196
1402	Interest receivable	97	84
1405	Allowance for subsidy cost (-)	–238	–84
1499	Net present value of assets related to direct loans	3,518	6,196
1999	Total assets	3,839	6,659
	LIABILITIES:		
	Federal liabilities:		
2103	Debt	3,744	6,485
2105	Other	95	174
2999	Total liabilities	3,839	6,659
	NET POSITION:		
3300	Cumulative results of operations		
4999	Total liabilities and net position	3,839	6,659

U.S. INTERNATIONAL DEVELOPMENT FINANCE CORPORATION INSURANCE OF DEBT FINANCING ACCOUNT

Program and Financing (in millions of dollars)

Identification code 077–4389–0–3–151		2021 actual	2022 est.	2023 est.
	Obligations by program activity:			
	Credit program obligations:			
0740	Negative subsidy obligations	4		
0900	Total new obligations, unexpired accounts	4		
	Budgetary resources:			
	Financing authority:			
	Borrowing authority, mandatory:			
1400	Borrowing authority	4		
1930	Total budgetary resources available	4		
	Change in obligated balance:			
	Unpaid obligations:			
3000	Unpaid obligations, brought forward, Oct 1		4	4
3010	New obligations, unexpired accounts	4		
3050	Unpaid obligations, end of year	4	4	4
	Memorandum (non-add) entries:			
3100	Obligated balance, start of year		4	4
3200	Obligated balance, end of year	4	4	4
	Financing authority and disbursements, net:			
	Mandatory:			
4090	Budget authority, gross	4		
4180	Budget authority, net (total)	4		
4190	Outlays, net (total)			

Status of Guaranteed Loans (in millions of dollars)

Identification code 077–4389–0–3–151		2021 actual	2022 est.	2023 est.
	Position with respect to appropriations act limitation on commitments:			
2111	Guaranteed loan commitments from current-year authority	425		
2150	Total guaranteed loan commitments	425		

URBAN AND ENVIRONMENTAL CREDIT PROGRAM ACCOUNT

Program and Financing (in millions of dollars)

Identification code 077–0401–0–1–151		2021 actual	2022 est.	2023 est.
	Obligations by program activity:			
	Credit program obligations:			
0708	Interest on reestimates of loan guarantee subsidy		34	
0900	Total new obligations, unexpired accounts (object class 41.0)		34	
	Budgetary resources:			
	Unobligated balance:			
1000	Unobligated balance brought forward, Oct 1	2	2	2
	Budget authority:			
	Appropriations, mandatory:			
1200	Appropriation - Reestimates		34	
1930	Total budgetary resources available	2	36	2
	Memorandum (non-add) entries:			
1941	Unexpired unobligated balance, end of year	2	2	2
	Change in obligated balance:			
	Unpaid obligations:			
3010	New obligations, unexpired accounts		34	
3020	Outlays (gross)		–34	
	Budget authority and outlays, net:			
	Mandatory:			
4090	Budget authority, gross		34	
	Outlays, gross:			
4100	Outlays from new mandatory authority		34	
4180	Budget authority, net (total)		34	
4190	Outlays, net (total)		34	

Summary of Loan Levels, Subsidy Budget Authority and Outlays by Program (in millions of dollars)

Identification code 077–0401–0–1–151		2021 actual	2022 est.	2023 est.
	Guaranteed loan reestimates:			
235001	DFC Urban and Environmental Loan Guarantees	–4	–2	

As required by the Federal Credit Reform Act of 1990, this account records, for this program, that supports Urban and Environmental Credit, the subsidy costs associated with loan guarantees committed in 1992 and beyond. The subsidy amounts are estimated on a net present value basis.

URBAN AND ENVIRONMENTAL CREDIT GUARANTEED LOAN FINANCING ACCOUNT

Program and Financing (in millions of dollars)

Identification code 077–4344–0–3–151		2021 actual	2022 est.	2023 est.
	Obligations by program activity:			
0001	Direct program activity	6		
	Credit program obligations:			
0711	Default claim payments on principal		5	5
0712	Default claim payments on interest		1	1
0742	Downward reestimates paid to receipt accounts	1	36	
0743	Interest on downward reestimates	3		
0791	Direct program activities, subtotal	4	42	6
0900	Total new obligations, unexpired accounts	10	42	6
	Budgetary resources:			
	Unobligated balance:			
1000	Unobligated balance brought forward, Oct 1	32	26	59
	Financing authority:			
	Appropriations, mandatory:			
1200	Appropriation [Reestimates]		36	
	Spending authority from offsetting collections, mandatory:			
1800	Collected	4	39	5
1900	Budget authority (total)	4	75	5
1930	Total budgetary resources available	36	101	64
	Memorandum (non-add) entries:			
1941	Unexpired unobligated balance, end of year	26	59	58
	Change in obligated balance:			
	Unpaid obligations:			
3000	Unpaid obligations, brought forward, Oct 1	1	2	38
3010	New obligations, unexpired accounts	10	42	6

URBAN AND ENVIRONMENTAL CREDIT GUARANTEED LOAN FINANCING ACCOUNT—Continued

Program and Financing—Continued

Identification code 077–4344–0–3–151		2021 actual	2022 est.	2023 est.
3020	Outlays (gross)	−9	−6	−6
3050	Unpaid obligations, end of year	2	38	38
	Memorandum (non-add) entries:			
3100	Obligated balance, start of year	1	2	38
3200	Obligated balance, end of year	2	38	38
	Financing authority and disbursements, net:			
	Mandatory:			
4090	Budget authority, gross	4	75	5
	Financing disbursements:			
4110	Outlays, gross (total)	9	6	6
	Offsets against gross financing authority and disbursements:			
	Offsetting collections (collected) from:			
4120	Federal sources	....	−34	....
4122	Interest on uninvested funds	−2	−2	−2
4123	Non-Federal sources	−2	−3	−3
4130	Offsets against gross budget authority and outlays (total)	−4	−39	−5
4160	Budget authority, net (mandatory)	....	36	....
4170	Outlays, net (mandatory)	5	−33	1
4180	Budget authority, net (total)	....	36	....
4190	Outlays, net (total)	5	−33	1

Status of Guaranteed Loans (in millions of dollars)

Identification code 077–4344–0–3–151		2021 actual	2022 est.	2023 est.
	Position with respect to appropriations act limitation on commitments:			
2111	Guaranteed loan commitments from current-year authority	....	....	....
2150	Total guaranteed loan commitments	....	....	....
	Cumulative balance of guaranteed loans outstanding:			
2210	Outstanding, start of year	56	112	168
2251	Repayments and prepayments	−8	−8	−8
	Adjustments:			
2263	Terminations for default that result in claim payments	−5	−5	−5
2264	Other adjustments, net	69	69	69
2290	Outstanding, end of year	112	168	224
	Memorandum:			
2299	Guaranteed amount of guaranteed loans outstanding, end of year	56	56	56
	Addendum:			
	Cumulative balance of defaulted guaranteed loans that result in loans receivable:			
2310	Outstanding, start of year	....	78	78
2364	Other adjustments, net	78	....	....
2390	Outstanding, end of year	78	78	78

This account is a non-budgetary account that records all of the cash flows resulting from post–1991 direct loans or loan guarantees that have been made under the U.S. Agency for International Development's (USAID's) urban and environment guaranty program.

Balance Sheet (in millions of dollars)

Identification code 077–4344–0–3–151		2020 actual	2021 actual
	ASSETS:		
	Federal assets:		
1101	Fund balances with Treasury	33	28
	Investments in U.S. securities:		
1106	Receivables, net	....	34
	Non-Federal assets:		
1206	Receivables, net	4	4
1207	Advances and prepayments	1	3
	Net value of assets related to post-1991 acquired defaulted guaranteed loans receivable:		
1501	Defaulted guaranteed loans receivable, gross	77	78
1502	Interest receivable	54	57
1599	Net present value of assets related to defaulted guaranteed loans	131	135
1999	Total assets	169	204
	LIABILITIES:		
	Federal liabilities:		
2101	Accounts payable	....	....
2105	Other	4	36
2204	Non-Federal liabilities: Liabilities for loan guarantees	164	167
2999	Total liabilities	168	203
	NET POSITION:		
3300	Cumulative results of operations	1	1
4999	Total liabilities and net position	169	204

MICROENTERPRISE AND SMALL ENTERPRISE DEVELOPMENT PROGRAM ACCOUNT

Program and Financing (in millions of dollars)

Identification code 077–0400–0–1–151		2021 actual	2022 est.	2023 est.
	Budgetary resources:			
	Unobligated balance:			
1000	Unobligated balance brought forward, Oct 1	3	3	3
1930	Total budgetary resources available	3	3	3
	Memorandum (non-add) entries:			
1941	Unexpired unobligated balance, end of year	3	3	3
4180	Budget authority, net (total)	....	....	....
4190	Outlays, net (total)	....	....	....

As required by the Federal Credit Reform Act of 1990, this account records, for this program, that supports Microenterprise and Small Enterprise Development, the subsidy costs associated with loan guarantees committed in 1992 and beyond. The subsidy amounts are estimated on a net present value basis.

MICROENTERPRISE AND SMALL ENTERPRISE DEVELOPMENT GUARANTEED LOAN FINANCING ACCOUNT

This account is a non-budgetary account that records all of the cash flows resulting from post–1991 direct loans or loan guarantees that have been made under the U.S. Agency for International Development's (USAID's) microenterprise and small enterprise guaranty program.

DEBT REDUCTION FINANCING ACCOUNT

Program and Financing (in millions of dollars)

Identification code 077–4137–0–3–151		2021 actual	2022 est.	2023 est.
	Obligations by program activity:			
	Credit program obligations:			
0713	Payment of interest to Treasury	....	16	16
0900	Total new obligations, unexpired accounts	....	16	16
	Budgetary resources:			
	Unobligated balance:			
1000	Unobligated balance brought forward, Oct 1	181	171	190
1022	Capital transfer of unobligated balances to general fund	−20	....	....
1070	Unobligated balance (total)	161	171	190
	Financing authority:			
	Spending authority from offsetting collections, mandatory:			
1800	Collected	10	9	9
1800	Collected	....	26	26
1850	Spending auth from offsetting collections, mand (total)	10	35	35
1930	Total budgetary resources available	171	206	225
	Memorandum (non-add) entries:			
1941	Unexpired unobligated balance, end of year	171	190	209
	Change in obligated balance:			
	Unpaid obligations:			
3010	New obligations, unexpired accounts	....	16	16
3020	Outlays (gross)	....	−16	−16
	Financing authority and disbursements, net:			
	Mandatory:			
4090	Budget authority, gross	10	35	35

DEPARTMENT OF STATE AND OTHER INTERNATIONAL PROGRAMS

United States International Development Finance Corporation—Continued
Federal Funds—Continued

863

		2021 actual	2022 est.	2023 est.
	Financing disbursements:			
4110	Outlays, gross (total)	....	16	16
	Offsets against gross financing authority and disbursements:			
	Offsetting collections (collected) from:			
4122	Interest on uninvested funds	–10	–15	–15
4123	Non-Federal sources Loan Repayment Principal	....	–12	–12
4123	Non-Federal sources Loan Repayment Interest	....	–8	–8
4130	Offsets against gross budget authority and outlays (total)	–10	–35	–35
4170	Outlays, net (mandatory)	–10	–19	–19
4180	Budget authority, net (total)	....	....	....
4190	Outlays, net (total)	–10	–19	–19

Status of Direct Loans (in millions of dollars)

Identification code 077–4137–0–3–151	2021 actual	2022 est.	2023 est.
Cumulative balance of direct loans outstanding:			
1210 Outstanding, start of year	656	656	644
1251 Repayments: Repayments and prepayments	....	–12	–12
1290 Outstanding, end of year	656	644	632

This account is a non-budgetary account that records all of the cash flows resulting from post–1991 direct loans or loan guarantees that have been reduced pursuant to programs such as the Heavily Indebted Poor Countries (HIPC) Initiative, and the Multilateral Debt Relief Initiative (MDRI), as well as through the Paris Club.

Balance Sheet (in millions of dollars)

Identification code 077–4137–0–3–151	2020 actual	2021 actual
ASSETS:		
1101 Federal assets: Fund balances with Treasury	181	171
1206 Non-Federal assets: Receivables, net	6	....
Net value of assets related to post-1991 direct loans receivable:		
1401 Direct loans receivable, gross	656	656
1402 Interest receivable	15	39
1405 Allowance for subsidy cost (-)	–838	–865
1499 Net present value of assets related to direct loans	–167	–170
1999 Total assets	20	1
LIABILITIES:		
2105 Federal liabilities: Other	....	....
2207 Non-Federal liabilities: Other	....	....
2999 Total liabilities	....	....
NET POSITION:		
3300 Cumulative results of operations	20	1
4999 Total liabilities and net position	20	1

HOUSING AND OTHER CREDIT GUARANTY PROGRAMS LIQUIDATING ACCOUNT

Program and Financing (in millions of dollars)

Identification code 077–4340–0–3–151	2021 actual	2022 est.	2023 est.
Obligations by program activity:			
Credit program obligations:			
0711 Default claim payments on principal	3	5	5
0712 Default claim payments on interest	1	3	3
0900 Total new obligations, unexpired accounts (object class 33.0)	4	8	8
Budgetary resources:			
Unobligated balance:			
1000 Unobligated balance brought forward, Oct 1	6	....	....
1022 Capital transfer of unobligated balances to general fund	–6	....	....
Budget authority:			
Appropriations, mandatory:			
1200 Appropriation	4	8	8
Spending authority from offsetting collections, mandatory:			
1800 Collected	3	9	9
1820 Capital transfer of spending authority from offsetting collections to general fund	–3	–9	–9
1900 Budget authority (total)	4	8	8
1930 Total budgetary resources available	4	8	8

		2021 actual	2022 est.	2023 est.
	Change in obligated balance:			
	Unpaid obligations:			
3000	Unpaid obligations, brought forward, Oct 1	....	....	5
3010	New obligations, unexpired accounts	4	8	8
3020	Outlays (gross)	–4	–3	–2
3050	Unpaid obligations, end of year	....	5	11
	Memorandum (non-add) entries:			
3100	Obligated balance, start of year	....	....	5
3200	Obligated balance, end of year	....	5	11
	Budget authority and outlays, net:			
	Mandatory:			
4090	Budget authority, gross	4	8	8
	Outlays, gross:			
4100	Outlays from new mandatory authority	....	3	2
4101	Outlays from mandatory balances	4	....	....
4110	Outlays, gross (total)	4	3	2
	Offsets against gross budget authority and outlays:			
	Offsetting collections (collected) from:			
4123	Non-Federal sources	–3	–9	–9
4180	Budget authority, net (total)	1	–1	–1
4190	Outlays, net (total)	1	–6	–7

Status of Guaranteed Loans (in millions of dollars)

Identification code 077–4340–0–3–151	2021 actual	2022 est.	2023 est.
Cumulative balance of guaranteed loans outstanding:			
2210 Outstanding, start of year	97	192	283
2251 Repayments and prepayments	–25	–25	–25
Adjustments:			
2261 Terminations for default that result in loans receivable	–4	–8	–8
2264 Other adjustments, net	124	124	124
2290 Outstanding, end of year	192	283	374
Memorandum:			
2299 Guaranteed amount of guaranteed loans outstanding, end of year	93	93	93
Addendum:			
Cumulative balance of defaulted guaranteed loans that result in loans receivable:			
2310 Outstanding, start of year	....	83	299
2310 Outstanding, start of year	218	83	299
2331 Disbursements for guaranteed loan claims	3	4	4
2351 Repayments of loans receivable	–2	–12	–12
2364 Other adjustments, net	–136	224	224
2364 Other adjustments, net	....	....	....
2390 Outstanding, end of year	83	299	515

This is a budget account that records all cash flows to and from the Government resulting from pre–1992 loan guarantee commitments from the U.S. Agency for International Development's (USAID's) legacy housing and urban and environment guaranty programs (unless they were modified and transferred to a financing account).

Balance Sheet (in millions of dollars)

Identification code 077–4340–0–3–151	2020 actual	2021 actual
ASSETS:		
1101 Federal assets: Fund balances with Treasury	7	1
1207 Non-Federal assets: Advances and prepayments	....	1
1701 Defaulted guaranteed loans, gross	85	83
1702 Interest receivable	12	14
1703 Allowance for estimated uncollectible loans and interest (-)	–41	–41
1704 Defaulted guaranteed loans and interest receivable, net	56	56
1705 Accounts receivable from foreclosed property	1	1
1799 Value of assets related to loan guarantees	57	57
1999 Total assets	64	59
LIABILITIES:		
2105 Federal liabilities: Other	....	65
Non-Federal liabilities:		
2204 Liabilities for loan guarantees	–2	–5
2207 Other	61	....
2999 Total liabilities	59	60
NET POSITION:		
3300 Cumulative results of operations	5	–1

HOUSING AND OTHER CREDIT GUARANTY PROGRAMS LIQUIDATING ACCOUNT—Continued

Balance Sheet—Continued

Identification code 077–4340–0–3–151	2020 actual	2021 actual
4999 Total liabilities and net position	64	59

ECONOMIC ASSISTANCE LOANS LIQUIDATING ACCOUNT

Program and Financing (in millions of dollars)

Identification code 077–4103–0–3–151	2021 actual	2022 est.	2023 est.
Budgetary resources:			
Unobligated balance:			
1000 Unobligated balance brought forward, Oct 1	229	7	....
1022 Capital transfer of unobligated balances to general fund	–229	–7	....
Budget authority:			
Spending authority from offsetting collections, mandatory:			
1800 Collected	209	230	230
1820 Capital transfer of spending authority from offsetting collections to general fund	–202	–230	–230
1850 Spending auth from offsetting collections, mand (total)	7	....	....
1930 Total budgetary resources available	7	....	....
Memorandum (non-add) entries:			
1941 Unexpired unobligated balance, end of year	7	....	....
Budget authority and outlays, net:			
Mandatory:			
4090 Budget authority, gross	7	....	....
Offsets against gross budget authority and outlays:			
Offsetting collections (collected) from:			
4123 Non-Federal sources	–209	–230	–230
4180 Budget authority, net (total)	–202	–230	–230
4190 Outlays, net (total)	–209	–230	–230

Status of Direct Loans (in millions of dollars)

Identification code 077–4103–0–3–151	2021 actual	2022 est.	2023 est.
Cumulative balance of direct loans outstanding:			
1210 Outstanding, start of year	593	394	394
1251 Repayments: Repayments and prepayments	–200	–190	–190
1264 Other adjustments, net (+ or -)	1	190	190
1290 Outstanding, end of year	394	394	394

This account consolidates direct loan activity from legacy credit programs funded under various accounts, including the Economic Support Fund, Functional Development Assistance Program, and the Development Loan Fund.

Balance Sheet (in millions of dollars)

Identification code 077–4103–0–3–151	2020 actual	2021 actual
ASSETS:		
1101 Federal assets: Fund balances with Treasury	229	7
1206 Non-Federal assets: Receivables, net	6	....
1601 Direct loans, gross	593	394
1602 Interest receivable	384	403
1603 Allowance for estimated uncollectible loans and interest (-)	–536	–536
1604 Direct loans and interest receivable, net	441	261
1605 Accounts receivable from foreclosed property	....	....
1699 Value of assets related to direct loans	441	261
1999 Total assets	676	268
LIABILITIES:		
2105 Federal liabilities: Other	596	596
2207 Non-Federal liabilities: Other	....	....
2999 Total liabilities	596	596
NET POSITION:		
3300 Cumulative results of operations	80	–328
4999 Total liabilities and net position	676	268

PEACE CORPS
Federal Funds
PEACE CORPS
(INCLUDING TRANSFER OF FUNDS)

For necessary expenses to carry out the provisions of the Peace Corps Act (22 U.S.C. 2501 et seq.), including the purchase of not to exceed five passenger motor vehicles for administrative purposes for use outside of the United States, $430,500,000, of which $7,300,000 is for the Office of Inspector General, to remain available until September 30, 2024: Provided, That the Director of the Peace Corps may transfer to the Foreign Currency Fluctuations Account, as authorized by section 16 of the Peace Corps Act (22 U.S.C. 2515), an amount not to exceed $5,000,000: Provided further, That funds transferred pursuant to the previous proviso may not be derived from amounts made available for Peace Corps overseas operations: Provided further, That of the funds appropriated under this heading, not to exceed $104,000 may be available for representation expenses, of which not to exceed $4,000 may be made available for entertainment expenses: Provided further, That in addition to the requirements under section 7015(a) of this Act, the Peace Corps shall notify the Committees on Appropriations prior to any decision to open, close, or suspend a domestic or overseas office or a country program unless there is a substantial risk to volunteers or other Peace Corps personnel: Provided further, That none of the funds appropriated under this heading shall be used to pay for abortions: Provided further, That notwithstanding the previous proviso, section 614 of division E of Public Law 113–76 shall apply to funds appropriated under this heading.

(CANCELLATION)

Of the unobligated balances available under the heading "Peace Corps" from prior Acts making appropriations for the Department of State, foreign operations, and related programs, $15,000,000 are hereby permanently cancelled: Provided, That no amounts may be cancelled from amounts that were designated by the Congress as an emergency requirement pursuant to a concurrent resolution on the budget or the Balanced Budget and Emergency Deficit Control Act of 1985, as amended.

Note.—A full-year 2022 appropriation for this account was not enacted at the time the Budget was prepared; therefore, the Budget assumes this account is operating under the Continuing Appropriations Act, 2022 (Division A of Public Law 117–43, as amended). The amounts included for 2022 reflect the annualized level provided by the continuing resolution.

Program and Financing (in millions of dollars)

Identification code 011–0100–0–1–151	2021 actual	2022 est.	2023 est.
Obligations by program activity:			
0001 Direct program activity - Peace Corps	369	403	454
0002 Direct program activity - Peace Corps Inspector General	....	6	7
0799 Total direct obligations	369	409	461
0801 Peace Corps (Reimbursable)	6	6	6
0900 Total new obligations, unexpired accounts	375	415	467
Budgetary resources:			
Unobligated balance:			
1000 Unobligated balance brought forward, Oct 1	85	110	101
1020 Adjustment of unobligated bal brought forward, Oct 1	–5	....	....
1021 Recoveries of prior year unpaid obligations	17	10	10
1070 Unobligated balance (total)	97	120	111
Budget authority:			
Appropriations, discretionary:			
1100 Appropriation	411	411	431
1131 Unobligated balance of appropriations permanently reduced	–30	–30	–15
1160 Appropriation, discretionary (total)	381	381	416
Spending authority from offsetting collections, discretionary:			
1700 Collected	3	15	7
1701 Change in uncollected payments, Federal sources	4	....	....
1750 Spending auth from offsetting collections, disc (total)	7	15	7
1900 Budget authority (total)	388	396	423
1930 Total budgetary resources available	485	516	534
Memorandum (non-add) entries:			
1941 Unexpired unobligated balance, end of year	110	101	67

Change in obligated balance:

		2021 actual	2022 est.	2023 est.
	Unpaid obligations:			
3000	Unpaid obligations, brought forward, Oct 1	115	111	123
3010	New obligations, unexpired accounts	375	415	467
3011	Obligations ("upward adjustments"), expired accounts	4		
3020	Outlays (gross)	–357	–391	–414
3040	Recoveries of prior year unpaid obligations, unexpired	–17	–10	–10
3041	Recoveries of prior year unpaid obligations, expired	–9	–2	–2
3050	Unpaid obligations, end of year	111	123	164
	Uncollected payments:			
3060	Uncollected pymts, Fed sources, brought forward, Oct 1	–5	–4	–4
3061	Adjustments to uncollected pymts, Fed sources, brought forward, Oct 1	5		
3070	Change in uncollected pymts, Fed sources, unexpired	–4		
3090	Uncollected pymts, Fed sources, end of year	–4	–4	–4
	Memorandum (non-add) entries:			
3100	Obligated balance, start of year	115	107	119
3200	Obligated balance, end of year	107	119	160
	Budget authority and outlays, net:			
	Discretionary:			
4000	Budget authority, gross	388	396	423
	Outlays, gross:			
4010	Outlays from new discretionary authority	225	277	296
4011	Outlays from discretionary balances	132	114	118
4020	Outlays, gross (total)	357	391	414
	Offsets against gross budget authority and outlays:			
	Offsetting collections (collected) from:			
4030	Federal sources	–2	–14	–6
4033	Non-Federal sources	–1	–1	–1
4040	Offsets against gross budget authority and outlays (total)	–3	–15	–7
	Additional offsets against gross budget authority only:			
4050	Change in uncollected pymts, Fed sources, unexpired	–4		
4060	Additional offsets against budget authority only (total)	–4		
4070	Budget authority, net (discretionary)	381	381	416
4080	Outlays, net (discretionary)	354	376	407
4180	Budget authority, net (total)	381	381	416
4190	Outlays, net (total)	354	376	407

The Peace Corps will provide direct and indirect support to Americans serving as Volunteers in approximately 60 countries worldwide in 2023, including the necessary safety and security provisions for Volunteers, trainees, and staff. The 2023 Budget supports recruitment, screening, and placement of Peace Corps trainees. The Peace Corps enters a country upon invitation of the host country government. The Volunteers directly respond to the host country needs by helping fill the trained manpower needs of developing countries and encourage self-sustaining development of skilled manpower. The Peace Corps also promotes mutual understanding between the peoples of the developing world and the United States and focuses the attention of the American people on the benefits of community service. Peace Corps Volunteers work primarily in the areas of agriculture, community economic development, education, environment, health and HIV/AIDS, and youth in development.

The Peace Corps Office of Inspector General provides independent oversight in accordance with the Inspector General Act of 1978, as amended. Through audits, evaluations and investigations the office prevents and detects waste, fraud, abuse and mismanagement; provides advice and assistance to agency management; and promotes efficiency, effectiveness and economy in agency programs and operations.

Object Classification (in millions of dollars)

Identification code 011–0100–0–1–151		2021 actual	2022 est.	2023 est.
	Direct obligations:			
	Personnel compensation:			
11.1	Full-time permanent	88	92	100
11.3	Other than full-time permanent	15	16	21
11.5	Other personnel compensation	1	1	1
11.9	Total personnel compensation	104	109	122
12.1	Civilian personnel benefits	51	60	85
21.0	Travel and transportation of persons	5	20	21
22.0	Transportation of things	3	3	3
23.1	Rental payments to GSA	10	11	11
23.2	Rental payments to others	16	17	17
23.3	Communications, utilities, and miscellaneous charges	8	8	8
25.1	Advisory and assistance services	28	29	19
25.2	Other services from non-Federal sources	77	81	98
25.3	Other goods and services from Federal sources	11	12	14
25.4	Operation and maintenance of facilities	3	3	2
25.6	Medical care	27	30	33
25.7	Operation and maintenance of equipment	9	9	9
26.0	Supplies and materials	3	7	10
31.0	Equipment	10	6	6
32.0	Land and structures	4	4	3
99.0	Direct obligations	369	409	461
99.0	Reimbursable obligations	6	6	6
99.9	Total new obligations, unexpired accounts	375	415	467

Employment Summary

Identification code 011–0100–0–1–151	2021 actual	2022 est.	2023 est.
1001 Direct civilian full-time equivalent employment	953	997	1,039
2001 Reimbursable civilian full-time equivalent employment	15	13	13

FOREIGN CURRENCY FLUCTUATIONS

Program and Financing (in millions of dollars)

Identification code 011–0101–0–1–151	2021 actual	2022 est.	2023 est.
Budgetary resources:			
Unobligated balance:			
1000 Unobligated balance brought forward, Oct 1	5	5	5
1930 Total budgetary resources available	5	5	5
Memorandum (non-add) entries:			
1941 Unexpired unobligated balance, end of year	5	5	5
4180 Budget authority, net (total)			
4190 Outlays, net (total)			

This account transfers funds to the operating expense account for the Peace Corps to finance upward adjustments of recorded obligations because of foreign currency fluctuations. Transfers are made as needed to meet disbursement requirements in excess of funds otherwise available for obligation adjustment. Net gains resulting from favorable exchange rates are returned to this account and are available for subsequent transfer when needed. The account is replenished through the utilization of a special transfer authority that allows the Peace Corps to withdraw unobligated balances from the operating expenses account from prior years as long as the authorized limit of $5 million is not exceeded at the time of the transfer.

HOST COUNTRY RESIDENT CONTRACTORS SEPARATION LIABILITY FUND

Special and Trust Fund Receipts (in millions of dollars)

Identification code 011–5395–0–2–151	2021 actual	2022 est.	2023 est.
0100 Balance, start of year			3
Receipts:			
Current law:			
1140 Agency Contributions, Host Country Resident Contractors Separation Liability Fund	9	3	3
2000 Total: Balances and receipts	9	3	6
Appropriations:			
Current law:			
2101 Host Country Resident Contractors Separation Liability Fund	–9		
5099 Balance, end of year		3	6

Program and Financing (in millions of dollars)

Identification code 011–5395–0–2–151	2021 actual	2022 est.	2023 est.
Obligations by program activity:			
0801 Host Country Resident Contractors Separation Liability Fund (Reimbursable)	9	2	2
0900 Total new obligations, unexpired accounts (object class 25.2)	9	2	2

Host Country Resident Contractors Separation Liability Fund—Continued

Program and Financing—Continued

Identification code 011–5395–0–2–151	2021 actual	2022 est.	2023 est.
Budgetary resources:			
Unobligated balance:			
1021 Recoveries of prior year unpaid obligations		2	2
Budget authority:			
Appropriations, mandatory:			
1201 Appropriation (special or trust fund)	9		
1930 Total budgetary resources available	9	2	2
Change in obligated balance:			
Unpaid obligations:			
3000 Unpaid obligations, brought forward, Oct 1	34	37	
3010 New obligations, unexpired accounts	9	2	2
3020 Outlays (gross)	–6	–37	
3040 Recoveries of prior year unpaid obligations, unexpired		–2	–2
3050 Unpaid obligations, end of year	37		
Memorandum (non-add) entries:			
3100 Obligated balance, start of year	34	37	
3200 Obligated balance, end of year	37		
Budget authority and outlays, net:			
Mandatory:			
4090 Budget authority, gross	9		
Outlays, gross:			
4101 Outlays from mandatory balances	6	37	
4180 Budget authority, net (total)	9		
4190 Outlays, net (total)	6	37	

This fund is maintained to pay separation costs for Host Country Resident Personal Services Contractors of the Peace Corps in those countries in which such pay is legally authorized. The fund will be maintained by annual government contributions which are appropriated in the Peace Corps' operating account.

Trust Funds

PEACE CORPS MISCELLANEOUS TRUST FUND

Special and Trust Fund Receipts (in millions of dollars)

Identification code 011–9972–0–7–151	2021 actual	2022 est.	2023 est.
0100 Balance, start of year			3
Receipts:			
Current law:			
1130 Miscellaneous Trust Funds, Peace Corps	1	3	3
2000 Total: Balances and receipts	1	3	6
Appropriations:			
Current law:			
2101 Peace Corps Miscellaneous Trust Fund	–1		
5099 Balance, end of year		3	6

Program and Financing (in millions of dollars)

Identification code 011–9972–0–7–151	2021 actual	2022 est.	2023 est.
Obligations by program activity:			
0881 Peace Corps Miscellaneous Trust Fund (Reimbursable)		2	2
0900 Total new obligations, unexpired accounts (object class 25.2)		2	2
Budgetary resources:			
Unobligated balance:			
1000 Unobligated balance brought forward, Oct 1	3	4	4
Budget authority:			
Appropriations, mandatory:			
1201 Appropriation (special or trust fund)	1		
Spending authority from offsetting collections, discretionary:			
1700 Collected		2	2
1900 Budget authority (total)	1	2	2
1930 Total budgetary resources available	4	6	6
Memorandum (non-add) entries:			
1941 Unexpired unobligated balance, end of year	4	4	4

Change in obligated balance:

Unpaid obligations:			
3000 Unpaid obligations, brought forward, Oct 1	2	2	
3010 New obligations, unexpired accounts		2	2
3020 Outlays (gross)		–4	–2
3050 Unpaid obligations, end of year	2		
Memorandum (non-add) entries:			
3100 Obligated balance, start of year	2	2	
3200 Obligated balance, end of year	2		
Budget authority and outlays, net:			
Discretionary:			
4000 Budget authority, gross		2	2
Outlays, gross:			
4010 Outlays from new discretionary authority		2	2
4011 Outlays from discretionary balances		2	
4020 Outlays, gross (total)		4	2
Offsets against gross budget authority and outlays:			
Offsetting collections (collected) from:			
4033 Non-Federal sources		–2	–2
Mandatory:			
4090 Budget authority, gross	1		
4180 Budget authority, net (total)	1		
4190 Outlays, net (total)		2	

Miscellaneous contributions received by gift, devise, or bequest, that are used for the furtherance of the program, as authorized by 22 U.S.C. 2509(a)(4) (75 Stat. 612, as amended). Trust funds also include a fund to pay separation costs for Foreign Service National employees of the Peace Corps in those countries in which such pay is legally authorized. The fund, as authorized by Section 151 of Public Law 102–138, is maintained by annual Government contributions which are appropriated in the Peace Corps salaries and expenses account.

INTER-AMERICAN FOUNDATION

Federal Funds

INTER-AMERICAN FOUNDATION

For necessary expenses to carry out the functions of the Inter-American Foundation in accordance with the provisions of section 401 of the Foreign Assistance Act of 1969, $38,000,000, to remain available until September 30, 2024: Provided, That of the funds appropriated under this heading, not to exceed $2,000 may be available for representation expenses.

Note.—A full-year 2022 appropriation for this account was not enacted at the time the Budget was prepared; therefore, the Budget assumes this account is operating under the Continuing Appropriations Act, 2022 (Division A of Public Law 117–43, as amended). The amounts included for 2022 reflect the annualized level provided by the continuing resolution.

Special and Trust Fund Receipts (in millions of dollars)

Identification code 164–3100–0–1–151	2021 actual	2022 est.	2023 est.
0100 Balance, start of year			
Receipts:			
Current law:			
1130 Gifts and Contributions, Inter-American Foundation			1
2000 Total: Balances and receipts			1
5099 Balance, end of year			1

Program and Financing (in millions of dollars)

Identification code 164–3100–0–1–151	2021 actual	2022 est.	2023 est.
Obligations by program activity:			
0001 Development grants	30	19	20
0003 Program Implementation Expenses	8	11	10
0005 Administrative Expenses	7	10	8
0799 Total direct obligations	45	40	38
0801 Development Grants (SPTF)	1	1	1
0805 USAID ESC ECAR Partnership		1	
0899 Total reimbursable obligations	1	2	1
0900 Total new obligations, unexpired accounts	46	42	39

DEPARTMENT OF STATE AND OTHER INTERNATIONAL PROGRAMS

African Development Foundation
Federal Funds 867

		2021 actual	2022 est.	2023 est.
	Budgetary resources:			
	Unobligated balance:			
1000	Unobligated balance brought forward, Oct 1	18	11	9
1021	Recoveries of prior year unpaid obligations	1	2	2
1070	Unobligated balance (total)	19	13	11
	Budget authority:			
	Appropriations, discretionary:			
1100	Appropriation	38	38	38
1900	Budget authority (total)	38	38	38
1930	Total budgetary resources available	57	51	49
	Memorandum (non-add) entries:			
1941	Unexpired unobligated balance, end of year	11	9	10
	Change in obligated balance:			
	Unpaid obligations:			
3000	Unpaid obligations, brought forward, Oct 1	39	48	58
3010	New obligations, unexpired accounts	46	42	39
3020	Outlays (gross)	–36	–29	–36
3040	Recoveries of prior year unpaid obligations, unexpired	–1	–2	–2
3041	Recoveries of prior year unpaid obligations, expired		–1	–1
3050	Unpaid obligations, end of year	48	58	58
	Uncollected payments:			
3060	Uncollected pymts, Fed sources, brought forward, Oct 1	–1	–1	–1
3090	Uncollected pymts, Fed sources, end of year	–1	–1	–1
	Memorandum (non-add) entries:			
3100	Obligated balance, start of year	38	47	57
3200	Obligated balance, end of year	47	57	57
	Budget authority and outlays, net:			
	Discretionary:			
4000	Budget authority, gross	38	38	38
	Outlays, gross:			
4010	Outlays from new discretionary authority	13	14	14
4011	Outlays from discretionary balances	23	15	22
4020	Outlays, gross (total)	36	29	36
4180	Budget authority, net (total)	38	38	38
4190	Outlays, net (total)	36	29	36
	Memorandum (non-add) entries:			
5010	Total investments, SOY: non-Fed securities: Market value		1	
5011	Total investments, EOY: non-Fed securities: Market value	1		

The Inter-American Foundation (IAF) invests directly in community-designed and community-led development across Latin America and the Caribbean to create more prosperous, peaceful, and democratic communities. The agency provides small grants to local leaders, innovators, and entrepreneurs working to address their communities' needs and seize development opportunities. IAF works to address critical issues in the region and advance the inclusion of historically marginalized populations, including women, youth, Indigenous peoples, African descendants, LGBTQI+, and persons with disabilities, in economic and civic life. The IAF's deep ties and more than half a century of expertise working with civil society complement the efforts of other U.S. foreign assistance agencies and advance the strategic, economic, and security interests of the United States.

Object Classification (in millions of dollars)

Identification code 164–3100–0–1–151		2021 actual	2022 est.	2023 est.
	Direct obligations:			
11.1	Personnel compensation: Full-time permanent	5	6	7
12.1	Civilian personnel benefits	2	2	2
23.2	Rental payments to others		1	
25.1	Advisory and assistance services	5	7	7
25.3	Other goods and services from Federal sources	2	2	2
41.0	Grants, subsidies, and contributions	30	21	20
99.0	Direct obligations	44	39	38
99.0	Reimbursable obligations	1	2	1
99.5	Adjustment for discretionary rounding	1	1	
99.9	Total new obligations, unexpired accounts	46	42	39

Employment Summary

Identification code 164–3100–0–1–151	2021 actual	2022 est.	2023 est.
1001 Direct civilian full-time equivalent employment	48	52	52

AFRICAN DEVELOPMENT FOUNDATION
Federal Funds

UNITED STATES AFRICAN DEVELOPMENT FOUNDATION

For necessary expenses to carry out the African Development Foundation Act (title V of Public Law 96–533; 22 U.S.C. 290h et seq.), $33,000,000, to remain available until September 30, 2024, of which not to exceed $2,000 may be available for representation expenses: Provided, That funds made available to grantees may be invested pending expenditure for project purposes when authorized by the Board of Directors of the United States African Development Foundation (USADF): Provided further, That interest earned shall be used only for the purposes for which the grant was made: Provided further, That notwithstanding section 505(a)(2) of the African Development Foundation Act (22 U.S.C. 290h–3(a)(2)), in exceptional circumstances the Board of Directors of the USADF may waive the $250,000 limitation contained in that section with respect to a project and a project may exceed the limitation by up to 10 percent if the increase is due solely to foreign currency fluctuation: Provided further, That the USADF shall submit a report to the appropriate congressional committees after each time such waiver authority is exercised: Provided further, That the USADF may make rent or lease payments in advance from appropriations available for such purpose for offices, buildings, grounds, and quarters in Africa as may be necessary to carry out its functions: Provided further, That the USADF may maintain bank accounts outside the United States Treasury and retain any interest earned on such accounts, in furtherance of the purposes of the African Development Foundation Act: Provided further, That the USADF may not withdraw any appropriation from the Treasury prior to the need of spending such funds for program purposes.

Note.—A full-year 2022 appropriation for this account was not enacted at the time the Budget was prepared; therefore, the Budget assumes this account is operating under the Continuing Appropriations Act, 2022 (Division A of Public Law 117–43, as amended). The amounts included for 2022 reflect the annualized level provided by the continuing resolution.

Program and Financing (in millions of dollars)

Identification code 166–0700–0–1–151		2021 actual	2022 est.	2023 est.
	Obligations by program activity:			
0001	Administrative expenses	7	7	7
0002	Development grants	21	21	21
0004	Other program costs	6	5	5
0799	Total direct obligations	34	33	33
0802	Development Grants	4		
0899	Total reimbursable obligations	4		
0900	Total new obligations, unexpired accounts	38	33	33
	Budgetary resources:			
	Unobligated balance:			
1000	Unobligated balance brought forward, Oct 1	5	2	3
1021	Recoveries of prior year unpaid obligations	2	1	1
1070	Unobligated balance (total)	7	3	4
	Budget authority:			
	Appropriations, discretionary:			
1100	Appropriation	33	33	33
	Spending authority from offsetting collections, discretionary:			
1700	Collected	1		
1701	Change in uncollected payments, Federal sources	–1		
1900	Budget authority (total)	33	33	33
1930	Total budgetary resources available	40	36	37
	Memorandum (non-add) entries:			
1941	Unexpired unobligated balance, end of year	2	3	4
	Change in obligated balance:			
	Unpaid obligations:			
3000	Unpaid obligations, brought forward, Oct 1	31	31	30
3010	New obligations, unexpired accounts	38	33	33
3011	Obligations ("upward adjustments"), expired accounts	1		
3020	Outlays (gross)	–35	–33	–38
3040	Recoveries of prior year unpaid obligations, unexpired	–2	–1	–1
3041	Recoveries of prior year unpaid obligations, expired	–2		

UNITED STATES AFRICAN DEVELOPMENT FOUNDATION—Continued
Program and Financing—Continued

Identification code 166–0700–0–1–151	2021 actual	2022 est.	2023 est.
3050 Unpaid obligations, end of year	31	30	24
Uncollected payments:			
3060 Uncollected pymts, Fed sources, brought forward, Oct 1	–1	....	....
3070 Change in uncollected pymts, Fed sources, unexpired	1	....	....
Memorandum (non-add) entries:			
3100 Obligated balance, start of year	30	31	30
3200 Obligated balance, end of year	31	30	24
Budget authority and outlays, net:			
Discretionary:			
4000 Budget authority, gross	33	33	33
Outlays, gross:			
4010 Outlays from new discretionary authority	18	16	16
4011 Outlays from discretionary balances	17	17	22
4020 Outlays, gross (total)	35	33	38
Offsets against gross budget authority and outlays:			
Offsetting collections (collected) from:			
4030 Federal sources	–1	....	....
Additional offsets against gross budget authority only:			
4050 Change in uncollected pymts, Fed sources, unexpired	1	....	....
4070 Budget authority, net (discretionary)	33	33	33
4080 Outlays, net (discretionary)	34	33	38
4180 Budget authority, net (total)	33	33	33
4190 Outlays, net (total)	34	33	38

The United States African Development Foundation (USADF) is a Federally funded public corporation that promotes economic development among marginalized populations in Sub-Saharan Africa. The agency provides small grants to increase food security, power local communities and enterprises through clean energy solutions, and provide entrepreneurial opportunities and improved income potential for Africa's women and youth. USADF furthers U.S. priorities in these areas to ensure critical development initiatives enacted by Congress, such as the Global Food Security Act, Electrify Africa Act, and the African Growth and Opportunities Act, extend to rural populations.

Object Classification (in millions of dollars)

Identification code 166–0700–0–1–151	2021 actual	2022 est.	2023 est.
Direct obligations:			
Personnel compensation:			
11.1 Full-time permanent	3	3	3
11.3 Other than full-time permanent	2	2	2
11.9 Total personnel compensation	5	5	5
12.1 Civilian personnel benefits	1	1	1
21.0 Travel and transportation of persons	....	1	1
23.2 Rental payments to others	1	1	1
25.1 Other administrative costs	....	2	2
25.2 Other services from non-Federal sources	4	1	1
25.3 Other goods and services from Federal sources	2	....	....
41.0 Development grants	21	22	22
99.0 Direct obligations	34	33	33
99.0 Reimbursable obligations	4	....	....
99.9 Total new obligations, unexpired accounts	38	33	33

Employment Summary

Identification code 166–0700–0–1–151	2021 actual	2022 est.	2023 est.
1001 Direct civilian full-time equivalent employment	32	31	32

Trust Funds
GIFTS AND DONATIONS, AFRICAN DEVELOPMENT FOUNDATION

Special and Trust Fund Receipts (in millions of dollars)

Identification code 166–8239–0–7–151	2021 actual	2022 est.	2023 est.
0100 Balance, start of year	....	....	....
Receipts:			
Current law:			
1130 Gifts and Donations, African Development Foundation	6	7	7
2000 Total: Balances and receipts	6	7	7
Appropriations:			
Current law:			
2101 Gifts and Donations, African Development Foundation	–6	–7	–7
5099 Balance, end of year	....	....	....

Program and Financing (in millions of dollars)

Identification code 166–8239–0–7–151	2021 actual	2022 est.	2023 est.
Obligations by program activity:			
0001 Project Grants	6	7	7
0900 Total new obligations, unexpired accounts (object class 41.0)	6	7	7
Budgetary resources:			
Unobligated balance:			
1000 Unobligated balance brought forward, Oct 1	5	5	5
Budget authority:			
Appropriations, mandatory:			
1201 Appropriation (special or trust fund)	6	7	7
1900 Budget authority (total)	6	7	7
1930 Total budgetary resources available	11	12	12
Memorandum (non-add) entries:			
1941 Unexpired unobligated balance, end of year	5	5	5
Change in obligated balance:			
Unpaid obligations:			
3000 Unpaid obligations, brought forward, Oct 1	4	7	7
3010 New obligations, unexpired accounts	6	7	7
3020 Outlays (gross)	–3	–7	–9
3050 Unpaid obligations, end of year	7	7	5
Memorandum (non-add) entries:			
3100 Obligated balance, start of year	4	7	7
3200 Obligated balance, end of year	7	7	5
Budget authority and outlays, net:			
Mandatory:			
4090 Budget authority, gross	6	7	7
Outlays, gross:			
4100 Outlays from new mandatory authority	1	4	4
4101 Outlays from mandatory balances	2	3	5
4110 Outlays, gross (total)	3	7	9
4180 Budget authority, net (total)	6	7	7
4190 Outlays, net (total)	3	7	9

USADF has the authority to accept contributions from any legitimate source, such as foreign governments, private businesses, foundations, non-governmental organizations, international donors, and other strategic partners committed to promoting grassroots-based economic growth and development in Africa. These funds are used in coordination with appropriated amounts to further expand the reach and impact of USADF's programs.

INTERNATIONAL MONETARY PROGRAMS
Federal Funds
UNITED STATES QUOTA, INTERNATIONAL MONETARY FUND

Program and Financing (in millions of dollars)

Identification code 020–0003–0–1–155	2021 actual	2022 est.	2023 est.
4180 Budget authority, net (total)	....	....	....
4190 Outlays, net (total)	....	....	....
Memorandum (non-add) entries:			
5112 IMF quota reserve tranche	32,963	22,955	22,955
5113 IMF quota letter of credit	85,066	90,033	90,033

The United States is a member of the International Monetary Fund (IMF) through its quota subscription to the IMF, denominated in Special Drawing Rights (SDRs). An IMF member's quota subscription determines the

DEPARTMENT OF STATE AND OTHER INTERNATIONAL PROGRAMS

International Monetary Programs—Continued
Federal Funds—Continued

maximum amount of financial resources that the member must commit to the IMF. Under reforms to IMF quotas decided in 2010 and implemented by the IMF in early 2016 after Congress passed the necessary legislation, the U.S. quota at the IMF increased by SDR 40,871,800,000 (approximately $58 billion using the current exchange rate) and is presently SDR 82,994,200,000 (approximately $115 billion using the current exchange rate). Quotas are the IMF's first line of financial resources and the main metric used by the IMF to determine members' voting shares and access to IMF financing.

The use of U.S. quota resources at the IMF constitutes an exchange of monetary assets and does not result in budget outlays. When the United States transfers dollars or other reserve assets to the IMF under the U.S. quota subscription, the United States receives an equal, offsetting, and interest-bearing claim on the IMF, which is reflected as an increase in U.S. international monetary reserves. The U.S. reserve position in the IMF is readily available to meet a U.S. balance-of-payments financing need.

See the "Loans to International Monetary Fund" account for additional information about the 2020 IMF agreement.

LOANS TO INTERNATIONAL MONETARY FUND

Program and Financing (in millions of dollars)

Identification code 020–0074–0–1–155	2021 actual	2022 est.	2023 est.
4180 Budget authority, net (total)			
4190 Outlays, net (total)			
Memorandum (non-add) entries:			
5114 New Arrangements to Borrow (Increase)	40,619		
5116 New Arrangements to Borrow	79,467	79,394	79,394

In January 1997, the Executive Board of the IMF approved the creation of the New Arrangements to Borrow (NAB), which is a standing arrangement among certain IMF members to supplement the IMF's quota resources as needed to forestall or cope with an impairment of the international monetary system or to deal with an exceptional situation that poses a threat to the stability of the system. The NAB became effective on November 17, 1998. It is now the second line of defense for IMF resources after a prior arrangement, the General Arrangements to Borrow (GAB), lapsed on December 25, 2018. The amounts authorized for the GAB were also authorized to be used for the NAB.

In 2019, the United States joined other key countries and IMF leadership in advancing a package of actions to maintain the overall level of IMF resources in conjunction with reforms to IMF governance and lending. As part of this package, the IMF and NAB participants agreed to double the size of the NAB, while the IMF reduced its bilateral borrowing agreements by a similar amount. Congress authorized Treasury to double the size of the United States' NAB participation in the 2020 Coronavirus Aid, Relief, and Economic Security (CARES) Act. The new NAB reforms, which include our increased participation, took effect at the IMF in January 2021 and remains in effect until the end of 2025.

A total of 40 countries and institutions participate in the NAB for a total of SDR 361 billion (about $515 billion), of which the current U.S. share is approximately SDR 56 billion (about $80 billion). The NAB is currently not activated, meaning that at present the IMF is relying on quota resources for current financing.

With respect to this account, resources provided by the United States under the NAB constitute an exchange of monetary assets and do not result in any budgetary outlays because such transactions result in an equivalent increase in U.S. international reserve assets in the form of an equal, offsetting, interest-bearing claim on the IMF. (See the *Analytical Perspectives* for additional information.)

CONTRIBUTIONS TO IMF FACILITIES AND TRUST FUNDS

For contribution to the Poverty Reduction and Growth Trust (PRGT) or to the proposed Resilience and Sustainability Trust Fund (RST) of the International Monetary Fund (IMF) by the Secretary of the Treasury, $20,000,000, to remain available until September 30, 2031: Provided, That these funds shall be available to cover the cost, as defined in section 502 of the Congressional Budget Act of 1974, of loans made by the Secretary of the Treasury to the PRGT or the RST of the IMF: Provided further, That these funds shall be available to subsidize gross obligations for the principal amount of direct loans not to exceed $21,000,000,000 in the aggregate, and the Secretary of the Treasury is authorized to make such loans: Provided further, That the Exchange Stabilization Fund (ESF) and the financing account corresponding to transactions with the IMF are authorized to enter into such transactions as necessary to effectuate loans from resources held in the ESF to the PRGT or RST of the IMF.

Note.—A full-year 2022 appropriation for this account was not enacted at the time the Budget was prepared; therefore, the Budget assumes this account is operating under the Continuing Appropriations Act, 2022 (Division A of Public Law 117–43, as amended). The amounts included for 2022 reflect the annualized level provided by the continuing resolution.

Program and Financing (in millions of dollars)

Identification code 011–1752–0–1–155	2021 actual	2022 est.	2023 est.
Obligations by program activity:			
Credit program obligations:			
0701 Direct loan subsidy			4
0701 Direct loan subsidy			7
0791 Direct program activities, subtotal			11
0900 Total new obligations, unexpired accounts (object class 41.0)			11
Budgetary resources:			
Budget authority:			
Appropriations, discretionary:			
1100 Appropriation			20
1900 Budget authority (total)			20
1930 Total budgetary resources available			20
Memorandum (non-add) entries:			
1941 Unexpired unobligated balance, end of year			9
Change in obligated balance:			
Unpaid obligations:			
3010 New obligations, unexpired accounts			11
3020 Outlays (gross)			−3
3050 Unpaid obligations, end of year			8
Memorandum (non-add) entries:			
3200 Obligated balance, end of year			8
Budget authority and outlays, net:			
Discretionary:			
4000 Budget authority, gross			20
Outlays, gross:			
4010 Outlays from new discretionary authority			3
4180 Budget authority, net (total)			20
4190 Outlays, net (total)			3

Summary of Loan Levels, Subsidy Budget Authority and Outlays by Program (in millions of dollars)

Identification code 011–1752–0–1–155	2021 actual	2022 est.	2023 est.
Direct loan levels supportable by subsidy budget authority:			
115001 Loans to Poverty Reduction and Growth Trust			6,000
115002 Loans to Resilience and Sustainability Trust			8,000
115999 Total direct loan levels			14,000
Direct loan subsidy (in percent):			
132001 Loans to Poverty Reduction and Growth Trust			0.07
132002 Loans to Resilience and Sustainability Trust			0.09
132999 Weighted average subsidy rate			0.08
Direct loan subsidy budget authority:			
133001 Loans to Poverty Reduction and Growth Trust			4
133002 Loans to Resilience and Sustainability Trust			7
133999 Total subsidy budget authority			11
Direct loan subsidy outlays:			
134001 Loans to Poverty Reduction and Growth Trust			1
134002 Loans to Resilience and Sustainability Trust			1
134999 Total subsidy outlays			2

International Monetary Programs—Continued
Federal Funds—Continued

CONTRIBUTIONS TO IMF FACILITIES AND TRUST FUNDS—Continued

Contributions to IMF Facilities and Trust Funds

The International Monetary Fund (IMF) maintains several facilities, many in the form of trust funds, to provide assistance to the world's poorest countries. The Poverty Reduction and Growth Trust (PRGT) is the IMFs concessional lending facility for low-income countries (LICs). Through the PRGT, the IMF makes subsidized loans (currently at zero percent interest) to the world's poorest countries in the context of longer-term economic adjustment programs. During the COVID-19 pandemic crisis, the PRGT has provided essential resources to help LICs—which generally lack reliable access to global capital markets and some of which are facing acute balance of payment stresses—respond to the pandemic and prevent economic collapse. Since the start of the pandemic, the IMF has lent about $170 billion to countries in need. Of this amount, the PRGT provided about $18.2 billion in concessional financing to about 55 poor countries, roughly a fivefold increase in annual lending from the PRGT's pre-pandemic average. A U.S. contribution to the PRGT would help sustain the PRGT with the resources it needs to continue to help countries respond to and recover from the pandemic and mitigate economic scarring, and it would particularly benefit the most vulnerable populations in these countries.

The United States, the IMF, and the rest of the international community are also exploring ways for major economies to provide additional support through the IMF to vulnerable countries in need. The United States has led the design of a proposed new IMF trust fund, the Resilience and Sustainability Trust (RST), which will provide affordable, long-term financing alongside a regular IMF program for countries facing current or potential balance of payments gaps resulting from reforms taken to enhance pandemic preparedness or mitigate climate change. By providing affordable, longer-term financing alongside regular IMF programs, RST lending will benefit from IMF lending safeguards, including strong governance requirements on borrowers, and will be overseen and approved by the IMFs Executive Board. Treasury expects that the IMFs Executive Board will establish the RST in 2022. A U.S. contribution to the RST would help establish the fund with the resources it needs to begin lending to vulnerable countries. The United States has played a leading role in championing the RST.

The 2023 Budget requests a total of $20 million to enable the United States to make a contribution to IMF facilities and trust funds by covering the subsidy cost of lending from Treasury's Exchange Stabilization Fund to the PRGT and the RST.

CONTRIBUTIONS TO IMF FACILITIES AND TRUST FUNDS FINANCING ACCOUNT

Program and Financing (in millions of dollars)

Identification code 011–4617–0–-155		2021 actual	2022 est.	2023 est.
	Obligations by program activity:			
	Credit program obligations:			
0710	Direct loan obligations			14,000
0713	Payment of interest to Treasury			6
0900	Total new obligations, unexpired accounts			14,006
	Budgetary resources:			
	Financing authority:			
	Borrowing authority, mandatory:			
1400	Borrowing authority			13,998
	Spending authority from offsetting collections, mandatory:			
1800	Collected			8
1900	Budget authority (total)			14,006
1930	Total budgetary resources available			14,006
	Change in obligated balance:			
	Unpaid obligations:			
3010	New obligations, unexpired accounts			14,006
3020	Outlays (gross)			–2,000
3050	Unpaid obligations, end of year			12,006
	Memorandum (non-add) entries:			
3200	Obligated balance, end of year			12,006
	Financing authority and disbursements, net:			
	Mandatory:			
4090	Budget authority, gross			14,006
	Financing disbursements:			
4110	Outlays, gross (total)			2,000
	Offsets against gross financing authority and disbursements:			
	Offsetting collections (collected) from:			
4120	Federal sources			–2
4123	Non-Federal sources			–6
4130	Offsets against gross budget authority and outlays (total)			–8
4160	Budget authority, net (mandatory)			13,998
4170	Outlays, net (mandatory)			1,992
4180	Budget authority, net (total)			13,998
4190	Outlays, net (total)			1,992

Status of Direct Loans (in millions of dollars)

Identification code 011–4617–0–-155	2021 actual	2022 est.	2023 est.
Position with respect to appropriations act limitation on obligations:			
1111 Direct loan obligations from current-year authority			14,000
1150 Total direct loan obligations			14,000
Cumulative balance of direct loans outstanding:			
1231 Disbursements: Direct loan disbursements			2,000
1290 Outstanding, end of year			2,000

As required by the Federal Credit Reform Act of 1990, as amended, this non-budgetary account records all cash flows to and from the Government resulting from direct loans and other investments obligated by the Secretary of the Treasury to the International Monetary Fund's (IMF) Poverty Reduction and Growth Trust (PRGT) or Resilience and Sustainability Trust (RST), including modifications of those direct loans. The amounts in this account are a means of financing and are not included in the budget totals. The 2023 Budget includes the request first made in the President's 2022 Budget for authorization of a direct loan to the PRGT and the RST.

MILITARY SALES PROGRAM

Federal Funds

SPECIAL DEFENSE ACQUISITION FUND

Program and Financing (in millions of dollars)

Identification code 011–4116–0–3–155		2021 actual	2022 est.	2023 est.
	Obligations by program activity:			
0801	Special Defense Acquisition Fund (Reimbursable)	217	169	112
0900	Total new obligations, unexpired accounts (object class 25.3)	217	169	112
	Budgetary resources:			
	Unobligated balance:			
1000	Unobligated balance brought forward, Oct 1	235	330	314
1001	Discretionary unobligated balance brought fwd, Oct 1	235		
1012	Unobligated balance transfers between expired and unexpired accounts	26		
1021	Recoveries of prior year unpaid obligations	7		
1033	Recoveries of prior year paid obligations	171		
1070	Unobligated balance (total)	439	330	314
	Budget authority:			
	Spending authority from offsetting collections, discretionary:			
1700	Collected	113	153	150
1900	Budget authority (total)	113	153	150
1930	Total budgetary resources available	552	483	464
	Memorandum (non-add) entries:			
1940	Unobligated balance expiring	–5		
1941	Unexpired unobligated balance, end of year	330	314	352
	Change in obligated balance:			
	Unpaid obligations:			
3000	Unpaid obligations, brought forward, Oct 1	128	252	252
3010	New obligations, unexpired accounts	217	169	112
3011	Obligations ("upward adjustments"), expired accounts	105		

DEPARTMENT OF STATE AND OTHER INTERNATIONAL PROGRAMS

Military Sales Program—Continued
Trust Funds

		2021 actual	2022 est.	2023 est.
3020	Outlays (gross)	−176	−169	−219
3040	Recoveries of prior year unpaid obligations, unexpired	−7		
3041	Recoveries of prior year unpaid obligations, expired	−15		
3050	Unpaid obligations, end of year	252	252	145
	Memorandum (non-add) entries:			
3100	Obligated balance, start of year	128	252	252
3200	Obligated balance, end of year	252	252	145
	Budget authority and outlays, net:			
	Discretionary:			
4000	Budget authority, gross	113	153	150
	Outlays, gross:			
4010	Outlays from new discretionary authority		115	112
4011	Outlays from discretionary balances	176	54	107
4020	Outlays, gross (total)	176	169	219
	Offsets against gross budget authority and outlays:			
	Offsetting collections (collected) from:			
4030	Federal sources	−113	−153	−150
4033	Non-Federal sources	−171		
4040	Offsets against gross budget authority and outlays (total)	−284	−153	−150
	Additional offsets against gross budget authority only:			
4053	Recoveries of prior year paid obligations, unexpired accounts	171		
4060	Additional offsets against budget authority only (total)	171		
4080	Outlays, net (discretionary)	−108	16	69
4180	Budget authority, net (total)			
4190	Outlays, net (total)	−108	16	69

The Special Defense Acquisition Fund (SDAF) helps expedite the procurement of defense articles for provision to foreign nations and international organizations. The 2023 request reflects $900 million in new SDAF obligation authority, to be funded by a combination of offsetting collections and previous SDAF procurements, referred to as SDAF reimbursements. In 2023, offsetting collections will be derived from the FMS sales of stock as well as other receipts consistent with section 51(b) of the Arms Export Control Act. The 2023 request will support advance purchases of high-demand equipment that has long procurement lead times, which is often the main limiting factor in our ability to provide coalition partners with critical equipment to make them operationally effective in a timely manner. Improving the mechanism for supporting U.S. partners is a high priority for both the Departments of State and Defense.

Trust Funds

FOREIGN MILITARY SALES TRUST FUND

Special and Trust Fund Receipts (in millions of dollars)

Identification code 011–8242–0–7–155	2021 actual	2022 est.	2023 est.
0100 Balance, start of year	5,690	79	4,959
0198 Reconciliation adjustment	8		
0199 Balance, start of year	5,698	79	4,959
Receipts:			
Current law:			
1130 Deposits, Advances, Foreign Military Sales Trust Fund	35,898	51,460	49,947
2000 Total: Balances and receipts	41,596	51,539	54,906
Appropriations:			
Current law:			
2101 Foreign Military Sales Trust Fund	−35,898	−46,980	−47,048
2103 Foreign Military Sales Trust Fund	−5,620	−8	−8
2132 Foreign Military Sales Trust Fund	1	8	8
2135 Foreign Military Sales Trust Fund		400	400
2199 Total current law appropriations	−41,517	−46,580	−46,648
2999 Total appropriations	−41,517	−46,580	−46,648
5099 Balance, end of year	79	4,959	8,258

Program and Financing (in millions of dollars)

Identification code 011–8242–0–7–155	2021 actual	2022 est.	2023 est.
Obligations by program activity:			
0003 Aircraft	16,559	19,042	19,337
0004 Missiles	8,404	4,722	4,802
0005 Communication Equipment	1,213	731	731
0006 Maintenance and Support Equipment	1,140	8,035	8,120
0007 Special Activities/R&D	1,434	5,040	5,100
0008 Tactical/Support/Combat Vehicles	845	6,766	6,856
0009 Ammunition	5,740	1,548	1,558
0010 Supplies & Supply Operations	477	498	498
0011 Construction	334	1,160	1,170
0012 Weapons	80	1,767	1,775
0013 Training	478	1,597	1,605
0014 Ships	73	498	498
0015 Administration	1,137	1,186	1,254
0900 Total new obligations, unexpired accounts	37,914	52,590	53,304
Budgetary resources:			
Unobligated balance:			
1000 Unobligated balance brought forward, Oct 1	171,749	176,266	176,362
1020 Adjustment of unobligated bal brought forward, Oct 1	−8		
1021 Recoveries of prior year unpaid obligations	2,414		
1033 Recoveries of prior year paid obligations	20		
1070 Unobligated balance (total)	174,175	176,266	176,362
Budget authority:			
Appropriations, mandatory:			
1201 Appropriation (special or trust fund)	35,898	46,980	47,048
1203 Appropriation (previously unavailable)(special or trust)	5,620	8	8
1232 Appropriations and/or unobligated balance of appropriations temporarily reduced	−1	−8	−8
1235 Appropriations precluded from obligation (special or trust)		−400	−400
1238 Appropriations applied to liquidate contract authority	−35,898	−45,394	−45,394
1260 Appropriations, mandatory (total)	5,619	1,186	1,254
Contract authority, mandatory:			
1600 Contract authority	34,386	51,500	51,500
1900 Budget authority (total)	40,005	52,686	52,754
1930 Total budgetary resources available	214,180	228,952	229,116
Memorandum (non-add) entries:			
1941 Unexpired unobligated balance, end of year	176,266	176,362	175,812
Change in obligated balance:			
Unpaid obligations:			
3000 Unpaid obligations, brought forward, Oct 1	50,800	51,846	57,586
3010 New obligations, unexpired accounts	37,914	52,590	53,304
3020 Outlays (gross)	−34,454	−46,850	−47,184
3040 Recoveries of prior year unpaid obligations, unexpired	−2,414		
3050 Unpaid obligations, end of year	51,846	57,586	63,706
Memorandum (non-add) entries:			
3100 Obligated balance, start of year	50,800	51,846	57,586
3200 Obligated balance, end of year	51,846	57,586	63,706
Budget authority and outlays, net:			
Mandatory:			
4090 Budget authority, gross	40,005	52,686	52,754
Outlays, gross:			
4100 Outlays from new mandatory authority	1,209	19,336	18,924
4101 Outlays from mandatory balances	33,245	27,514	28,260
4110 Outlays, gross (total)	34,454	46,850	47,184
Offsets against gross budget authority and outlays:			
Offsetting collections (collected) from:			
4123 Non-Federal sources	−20		
Additional offsets against gross budget authority only:			
4143 Recoveries of prior year paid obligations, unexpired accounts	20		
4160 Budget authority, net (mandatory)	40,005	52,686	52,754
4170 Outlays, net (mandatory)	34,434	46,850	47,184
4180 Budget authority, net (total)	40,005	52,686	52,754
4190 Outlays, net (total)	34,434	46,850	47,184
Memorandum (non-add) entries:			
5050 Unobligated balance, SOY: Contract authority	142,563	139,997	140,363
5051 Unobligated balance, EOY: Contract authority	139,997	140,363	140,349
5052 Obligated balance, SOY: Contract authority	50,800	51,846	57,586
5053 Obligated balance, EOY: Contract authority	51,846	57,586	63,706

The Foreign Military Sales Trust Fund facilitates government-to-government sales of defense articles, defense services, and design and construction services. Estimates of sales used in this budget are in millions of dollars:

ESTIMATES OF NEW SALES

	2021 Actual	2022.	2023 Est.
Estimates of new orders (sales)	$34,800	$51,500	$51,500

Foreign Military Sales Trust Fund—Continued

Object Classification (in millions of dollars)

Identification code 011–8242–0–7–155		2021 actual	2022 est.	2023 est.
	Direct obligations:			
11.1	Personnel compensation: Full-time permanent	....	521	551
25.2	Other services from non-Federal sources	37,914	52,069	52,753
99.9	Total new obligations, unexpired accounts	37,914	52,590	53,304

Federal Funds

UKRAINE LOAN GUARANTEE PROGRAM ACCOUNT

Program and Financing (in millions of dollars)

Identification code 999–0007–0–1–151		2021 actual	2022 est.	2023 est.
	Obligations by program activity:			
	Credit program obligations:			
0702	Loan guarantee subsidy	....	285	....
0900	Total new obligations, unexpired accounts (object class 41.0)	....	285	....
	Budgetary resources:			
	Budget authority:			
	Appropriations, discretionary:			
1121	Appropriations transferred from other acct [072–1037]	....	285	....
1930	Total budgetary resources available	....	285	....
	Change in obligated balance:			
	Unpaid obligations:			
3010	New obligations, unexpired accounts	....	285	....
3020	Outlays (gross)	....	–285	....
	Budget authority and outlays, net:			
	Discretionary:			
4000	Budget authority, gross	....	285	....
	Outlays, gross:			
4010	Outlays from new discretionary authority	....	285	....
4180	Budget authority, net (total)	....	285	....
4190	Outlays, net (total)	....	285	....

Summary of Loan Levels, Subsidy Budget Authority and Outlays by Program (in millions of dollars)

Identification code 999–0007–0–1–151		2021 actual	2022 est.	2023 est.
	Guaranteed loan levels supportable by subsidy budget authority:			
215001	Ukraine Sovereign Loan Guarantee		1,000	
	Guaranteed loan subsidy budget authority:			
233001	Ukraine Sovereign Loan Guarantee		285	

Ukraine Loan Guarantee Program Account

The United States is reaffirming our strong commitment to the Ukrainian people by joining with allies and partners to mobilize robust international support for Ukraine. The account reflects the Administration's commitment to provide a sovereign loan guarantee to Ukraine of up to $1 billion in fiscal year 2022 to foster macroeconomic stability and continued engagement with the International Monetary Fund (IMF).

UKRAINE LOAN GUARANTEE FINANCING ACCOUNT

Status of Guaranteed Loans (in millions of dollars)

Identification code 999–4404–0–3–151		2021 actual	2022 est.	2023 est.
	Position with respect to appropriations act limitation on commitments:			
2111	Guaranteed loan commitments from current-year authority	....	1,000	....
2150	Total guaranteed loan commitments	....	1,000	....

GENERAL FUND RECEIPT ACCOUNTS

(in millions of dollars)

		2021 actual	2022 est.	2023 est.
Offsetting receipts from the public:				
011–272430	Foreign Military Financing, Downward Reestimates of Subsidies	607	184	....
011–388044	All Other General Fund Proprietary Receipts Including Budget Clearing Accounts	1		
072–143500	General Fund Proprietary Interest Receipts, not Otherwise Classified	1	1	1
072–267630	Downward Reestimates, MENA Loan Guarantee Program	125	464	....
072–272530	Loan Guarantees to Israel, Downward Reestimates of Subsidies	124	122	....
072–273130	Ukraine Loan Guarantees Program, Downward Reestimates	651	267	....
072–322000	All Other General Fund Proprietary Receipts Including Budget Clearing Accounts	14	....	
077–268730	Urban and Environmental Credit Program, Downward Reestimates of Subsidies	4	36	....
077–268930	United States International Development Finance Corporation Loans, Downward Reestimates of Subsidy	337	379	....
General Fund Offsetting receipts from the public		1,864	1,453	1
Intragovernmental payments:				
072–388500	Undistributed Intragovernmental Payments and Receivables from Cancelled Accounts	2	....	....
General Fund Intragovernmental payments		2	....	....

GENERAL PROVISIONS

ALLOWANCES AND DIFFERENTIALS

SEC. 7001. *Funds appropriated under title I of this Act shall be available, except as otherwise provided, for allowances and differentials as authorized by subchapter 59 of title 5, United States Code; for services as authorized by section 3109 of such title and for hire of passenger transportation pursuant to section 1343(b) of title 31, United States Code.*

CONSULTING SERVICES

SEC. 7002. *The expenditure of any appropriation under title I of this Act for any consulting service through procurement contract, pursuant to section 3109 of title 5, United States Code, shall be limited to those contracts where such expenditures are a matter of public record and available for public inspection, except where otherwise provided under existing law, or under existing Executive order issued pursuant to existing law.*

DIPLOMATIC FACILITIES

SEC. 7003. *(a) CAPITAL SECURITY COST SHARING EXCEPTION.—Notwithstanding paragraph (2) of section 604(e) of the Secure Embassy Construction and Counterterrorism Act of 1999 (title VI of division A of H.R. 3427, as enacted into law by section 1000(a)(7) of Public Law 106–113 and contained in appendix G of that Act), as amended by section 111 of the Department of State Authorities Act, Fiscal Year 2017 (Public Law 114–323), a project to construct a facility of the United States may include office space or other accommodations for members of the United States Marine Corps.*

(b) NEW DIPLOMATIC FACILITIES.—For the purposes of calculating the fiscal year 2023 costs of providing new United States diplomatic facilities in accordance with section 604(e) of the Secure Embassy Construction and Counterterrorism Act of 1999 (22 U.S.C. 4865 note), the Secretary of State, in consultation with the Director of the Office of Management and Budget, shall determine the annual program level and agency shares in a manner that is proportional to the contribution of the Department of State for this purpose.

(c) SOFT TARGETS.—Funds appropriated by this Act under the heading "Embassy Security, Construction, and Maintenance" may be made available for security upgrades to soft targets, including schools, recreational facilities, and residences used by United States diplomatic personnel and their dependents.

PERSONNEL ACTIONS

SEC. 7004. *Any costs incurred by a department or agency funded under title I of this Act resulting from personnel actions taken in response to funding reductions included in this Act shall be absorbed within the total budgetary resources available under title I to such department or agency: Provided, That the authority to transfer funds between appropriations accounts as may be necessary to carry out this section is provided in addition to authorities included elsewhere in this Act.*

PROHIBITION ON PUBLICITY OR PROPAGANDA

SEC. 7005. No part of any appropriation contained in this Act shall be used for publicity or propaganda purposes within the United States not authorized before enactment of this Act by Congress: *Provided*, That up to $25,000 may be made available to carry out the provisions of section 316 of the International Security and Development Cooperation Act of 1980 (Public Law 96–533; 22 U.S.C. 2151a note).

PROHIBITION AGAINST DIRECT FUNDING FOR CERTAIN COUNTRIES

SEC. 7006. None of the funds appropriated or otherwise made available pursuant to titles III through VI of this Act shall be obligated or expended to finance directly any assistance or reparations for the governments of Cuba, North Korea, Iran, or Syria: *Provided*, That for purposes of this section, the prohibition on obligations or expenditures shall include direct loans, credits, insurance, and guarantees of the Export-Import Bank or its agents.

COUPS D'ETAT

SEC. 7007. None of the funds appropriated or otherwise made available pursuant to titles III through VI of this Act shall be obligated to finance directly any assistance to the government of any country whose duly elected head of government is deposed by military coup d'etat or decree or, after the date of enactment of this Act, a coup d'etat or decree in which the military plays a decisive role: *Provided*, That assistance may be resumed to such government if the Secretary of State certifies and reports to the appropriate congressional committees that subsequent to the termination of assistance a democratically elected government has taken office or that provision of assistance is in the national interest of the United States: *Provided further*, That the provisions of this section shall not apply to assistance to promote democratic elections or public participation in democratic processes: *Provided further*, That funds made available pursuant to the previous provisos shall be subject to the regular notification procedures of the Committees on Appropriations.

TRANSFER OF FUNDS AUTHORITY

SEC. 7008. (a) DEPARTMENT OF STATE AND UNITED STATES AGENCY FOR GLOBAL MEDIA.—

(1) DEPARTMENT OF STATE.—

(A) IN GENERAL.—Not to exceed the greater of 5 percent or $2,000,000 of any appropriations for the Department of State under title I of this Act or under title I of prior Acts may be transferred between, and merged with, such appropriations, but no such appropriation, except as otherwise specifically provided, shall be increased by more than 10 percent by any such transfers.

(B) EMBASSY SECURITY.—Funds appropriated under the headings "Diplomatic Programs", including for Worldwide Security Protection, "Embassy Security, Construction, and Maintenance", and "Emergencies in the Diplomatic and Consular Service" in this Act may be transferred to, and merged with, funds appropriated under such headings if the Secretary of State determines and reports to the Committees on Appropriations that to do so is necessary to implement the recommendations of the Benghazi Accountability Review Board, for emergency evacuations, or to prevent or respond to security situations and requirements, subject to the regular notification procedures of, such Committees: *Provided*, That such transfer authority is in addition to any transfer authority otherwise available in this Act and under any other provision of law.

(2) UNITED STATES AGENCY FOR GLOBAL MEDIA.—Not to exceed 5 percent of any appropriation made available for the current fiscal year for the United States Agency for Global Media under title I of this Act may be transferred between, and merged with, such appropriations, but no such appropriation, except as otherwise specifically provided, shall be increased by more than 10 percent by any such transfers.

(3) TREATMENT AS REPROGRAMMING.—Any transfer pursuant to this subsection shall be treated as a reprogramming of funds under section 7012 of this Act and shall not be available for obligation or expenditure except in compliance with the procedures set forth in that section.

(b) AVAILABILITY OF FUNDS FOR THE DEVELOPMENT FINANCE CORPORATION.—

(1) Funds appropriated by this Act and prior Acts making appropriations for the Department of State, foreign operations, and related programs and transferred to the United States Development Finance Corporation pursuant to section 1434(j) of the BUILD Act of 2018 (division F of Public Law 115–254) shall be paid to the United States International Development Finance Corporation Program Account.

(2) Funds appropriated under the heading "Economic Support Fund" directed to implement the Nita M. Lowey Middle East Partnership for Peace Act by application of section 7019 of the Department of State, Foreign Operations, and Related Programs Appropriations Act, 2021 (Fiscal Year 2021 Act) shall be excluded from the limitation on transfers pursuant to section 1434(j) of the BUILD Act of 2018 (division F of Public Law 112–54) contained in section 7009(c) of the Fiscal Year 2021 Act.

(3) Whenever, in coordination, the Chief Executive Officer of the Millennium Challenge Corporation determines that it is in furtherance of the purposes of Millennium Challenge Act of 2003 (title VI of division D of Public Law 108–199, as amended), and the Chief Executive Officer of the United States International Development Finance Corporation determines that it is in furtherance of the purposes of the BUILD Act of 2018 (division F of Public Law 115–254), funds appropriated under the heading Millennium Challenge Corporation in this or prior Acts may be transferred to and merged with amounts under the heading United States International Development Finance Corporation—Program Account: *Provided*, That, when so transferred and merged, such funds shall be available for the costs of loans and guaranties provided by the United States International Development Finance Corporation pursuant to section 1421(b) of the BUILD Act and shall be subject to the limitations provided in the second, third, and fifth provisos under the heading United States International Development Finance Corporation—Program Account found in Public Law 116–260: *Provided further*, That such funds shall not be available for administrative expenses of the United States International Development Finance Corporation: *Provided further*, That the exercise of such authority shall be subject to the regular notification procedures of the Committees on Appropriations: *Provided further*, That the transfer authority provided in this section is in addition to any other transfer authority provided by law.

(c) AUDIT OF INTER-AGENCY TRANSFERS OF FUNDS.—Any agreement for the transfer or allocation of funds appropriated by this Act or prior Acts making appropriations for the Department of State, foreign operations, and related programs entered into between the Department of State or USAID and another agency of the United States Government under the authority of section 632(a) of the Foreign Assistance Act of 1961, or any comparable provision of law, shall expressly provide that the Inspector General (IG) for the agency receiving the transfer or allocation of such funds, or other entity with audit responsibility if the receiving agency does not have an IG, shall perform periodic program and financial audits of the use of such funds and report to the Department of State or USAID, as appropriate, upon completion of such audits: *Provided*, That such audits shall be transmitted to the Committees on Appropriations by the Department of State or USAID, as appropriate: *Provided further*, That funds transferred under such authority may be made available for the cost of such audits.

(d) ADDITIONAL TRANSFER AUTHORITY.—

(1) Funds appropriated by this Act under the headings "Transition Initiatives", "Economic Support Fund", "Development Assistance", "Assistance for Europe, Eurasia, and Central Asia", "Democracy Fund", "International Narcotics Control and Law Enforcement", "Nonproliferation, Anti-terrorism, Demining, and Related Programs", "Peacekeeping Operations", and "Foreign Military Financing Program" may be transferred to, and merged with, funds appropriated by this Act under such headings.

(2) Funds appropriated by this Act under the headings "Transition Initiatives", "Economic Support Fund", "Development Assistance", "Assistance for Europe, Eurasia, and Central Asia", "Democracy Fund", "International Narcotics Control and Law Enforcement", "Nonproliferation, Anti-terrorism, Demining, and Related Programs", "Peacekeeping Operations", and "Foreign Military Financing Program" may be transferred to, and merged with, funds appropriated by this Act under the headings "International Disaster Assistance" and "Migration and Refugee Assistance".

(3) The authority provided in subsections (d)(1) and (d)(2) may be used to transfer up to $400,000,000 from the funds appropriated by this Act and may be exercised only if the Secretary of State determines that such transfer is needed to address unexpected contingencies, man-made or natural disasters, or other urgent needs.

(4) The authority provided by this subsection shall be subject to the regular notification procedures of the Committees on Appropriations: *Provided*, That such transfer authority is in addition to any transfer authority otherwise available under any other provision of law, including section 610 of the Foreign Assistance Act of 1961, which may be exercised by the Secretary of State for the purposes of this Act.

PROHIBITION AND LIMITATION ON CERTAIN EXPENSES

SEC. 7009. (a) FIRST-CLASS TRAVEL.—None of the funds made available by this Act may be used for first-class travel by employees of United States Government departments and agencies funded by this Act in contravention of section 301–10.122 through 301–10.124 of title 41, Code of Federal Regulations.

(b) COMPUTER NETWORKS.—None of the funds made available by this Act for the operating expenses of any United States Government department or agency may be used to establish or maintain a computer network for use by such department or agency unless such network has filters designed to block access to sexually explicit websites: *Provided*, That nothing in this subsection shall limit the use of funds necessary for any Federal, State, tribal, or local law enforcement agency, or any other entity carrying out the following activities: criminal investigations, prosecutions, and adjudications; administrative discipline; and the monitoring of such websites undertaken as part of official business.

(c) LIMITATIONS ON ENTERTAINMENT EXPENSES.—None of the funds appropriated or otherwise made available by this Act under the headings "International Military Education and Training" or "Foreign Military Financing Program" for Informational Program activities or under the headings "Global Health Programs", "Development Assistance", "Economic Support Fund", and "Assistance for Europe, Eurasia and Central Asia" may be obligated or expended to pay for—

(1) alcoholic beverages; or

(2) entertainment expenses for activities that are substantially of a recreational character, including entrance fees at sporting events, theatrical and musical productions, and amusement parks.

AVAILABILITY OF FUNDS

SEC. 7010. No part of any appropriation contained in this Act shall remain available for obligation after the expiration of the current fiscal year unless expressly so provided by this Act: Provided, That funds appropriated for the purposes of chapters 1 and 8 of part I, sections 661 and 667, chapters 4, 5, 6, 8, and 9 of part II of the Foreign Assistance Act of 1961, section 23 of the Arms Export Control Act (22 U.S.C. 2763), and funds made available for "United States International Development Finance Corporation" and under the heading "Assistance for Europe, Eurasia and Central Asia" shall remain available for an additional 4 years from the date on which the availability of such funds would otherwise have expired, if such funds are initially obligated before the expiration of their respective periods of availability contained in this Act: Provided further, That notwithstanding any other provision of this Act, any funds made available for the purposes of chapter 1 of part I and chapter 4 of part II of the Foreign Assistance Act of 1961 which are allocated or obligated for cash disbursements in order to address balance of payments or economic policy reform objectives, shall remain available for an additional 4 years from the date on which the availability of such funds would otherwise have expired, if such funds are initially allocated or obligated before the expiration of their respective periods of availability contained in this Act: Provided further, That the authorities of this section shall be deemed to apply to funds appropriated under sections 10003, 10004, and 10005 of the American Rescue Plan Act of 2021 (Public Law 117–2), including to such funds obligated prior to the enactment of this Act.

RESERVATIONS OF FUNDS

SEC. 7011. (a) REPROGRAMMING.—Funds appropriated under titles III through VI of this Act which are specifically designated may be reprogrammed for other programs within the same account notwithstanding the designation if compliance with the designation is made impossible by operation of any provision of this or any other Act or by a significant change in circumstances as determined by the Secretary of State: Provided, That any such reprogramming shall be subject to the regular notification procedures of the Committees on Appropriations: Provided further, That assistance that is reprogrammed pursuant to this subsection shall be made available under the same terms and conditions as originally provided.

(b) EXTENSION OF AVAILABILITY.—In addition to the authority contained in subsection (a), the original period of availability of funds appropriated by this Act and administered by the Department of State or the United States Agency for International Development that are specifically designated for particular programs or activities by this or any other Act may be extended for an additional fiscal year if the Secretary of State or the USAID Administrator, as appropriate, determines and reports promptly to the Committees on Appropriations that the termination of assistance to a country or a significant change in circumstances makes it unlikely that such designated funds can be obligated during the original period of availability: Provided, That such designated funds that continue to be available for an additional fiscal year shall be obligated only for the purpose of such designation.

(c) OTHER ACTS.—Ceilings and specifically designated funding levels contained in this Act shall not be applicable to funds or authorities appropriated or otherwise made available by any subsequent Act unless such Act specifically so directs: Provided, That specifically designated funding levels or minimum funding requirements contained in any other Act shall not be applicable to funds appropriated by this Act.

NOTIFICATION REQUIREMENTS

SEC. 7012. (a) NOTIFICATION OF CHANGES IN PROGRAMS, PROJECTS, AND ACTIVITIES.—None of the funds made available in titles I, II, and VI, and under the headings "Peace Corps" and "Millennium Challenge Corporation", of this Act or prior Acts making appropriations for the Department of State, foreign operations, and related programs to the departments and agencies funded by this Act that remain available for obligation in fiscal year 2023, or provided from any accounts in the Treasury of the United States derived by the collection of fees or of currency reflows or other offsetting collections, or made available by transfer, to the departments and agencies funded by this Act, shall be available for obligation to—

(1) create new programs;

(2) eliminate a program, project, or activity;

(3) close, open, or reopen a mission or post;

(4) create, close, reorganize, or rename bureaus, centers, or offices; or

(5) contract out or privatize any functions or activities presently performed by Federal employees;

unless the Committees on Appropriations are notified 15 days in advance of such obligation.

(b) NOTIFICATION OF REPROGRAMMING OF FUNDS.—None of the funds provided under titles I, II, and VI of this Act or prior Acts making appropriations for the Department of State, foreign operations, and related programs, to the departments and agencies funded under such titles that remain available for obligation in fiscal year 2023, or provided from any accounts in the Treasury of the United States derived by the collection of fees available to the department and agency funded under title I of this Act, shall be available for obligation for programs, projects, or activities through a reprogramming of funds in excess of $2,000,000 or 10 percent, whichever is less, that—

(1) augments or changes existing programs, projects, or activities;

(2) reduces by 10 percent funding for any existing program, project, or activity, or numbers of personnel by 10 percent as approved by Congress; or

(3) results from any general savings, including savings from a reduction in personnel, which would result in a change in existing programs, projects, or activities as approved by Congress;

unless the Committees on Appropriations are notified 15 days in advance of such reprogramming of funds.

(c) NOTIFICATION REQUIREMENT.—None of the funds made available by this Act under the headings "Global Health Programs", "Development Assistance", "International Organizations and Programs", "Trade and Development Agency", "International Narcotics Control and Law Enforcement", "Economic Support Fund", "Democracy Fund", "Assistance for Europe, Eurasia and Central Asia", "Peacekeeping Operations", "Nonproliferation, Anti-terrorism, Demining and Related Programs", "Millennium Challenge Corporation", "Foreign Military Financing Program", "International Military Education and Training", "United States International Development Finance Corporation", and "Peace Corps", shall be available for obligation for programs, projects, activities, type of materiel assistance, countries, or other operations not justified or in excess of the amount justified to the Committees on Appropriations for obligation under any of these specific headings unless the Committees on Appropriations are notified 15 days in advance of such obligation: Provided, That the President shall not enter into any commitment of funds appropriated for the purposes of section 23 of the Arms Export Control Act for the provision of major defense equipment, other than conventional ammunition, or other major defense items defined to be aircraft, ships, missiles, or combat vehicles, not previously justified to Congress or 20 percent in excess of the quantities justified to Congress unless the Committees on Appropriations are notified 15 days in advance of such commitment: Provided further, That requirements of this subsection or any similar provision of this or any other Act shall not apply to any reprogramming for a program, project, or activity for which funds are appropriated under titles III through VI of this Act of less than 10 percent of the amount previously justified to Congress for obligation for such program, project, or activity for the current fiscal year.

(d) WAIVER.—The requirements of this section or any similar provision of this Act or any other Act, including any prior Act requiring notification in accordance with the regular notification procedures of the Committees on Appropriations, may be waived if failure to do so would pose a substantial risk to human health or welfare: Provided, That in case of any such waiver, notification to the Committees on Appropriations shall be provided as early as practicable, but in no event later than 3 days after taking the action to which such notification requirement was applicable, in the context of the circumstances necessitating such waiver: Provided further, That any notification provided pursuant to such a waiver shall contain an explanation of the emergency circumstances.

DOCUMENT REQUESTS, RECORDS MANAGEMENT, AND RELATED CYBERSECURITY PROTECTIONS

SEC. 7013.

DOCUMENT REQUESTS.—None of the funds appropriated or made available pursuant to titles III through VI of this Act shall be available to a nongovernmental organization, including any contractor, which fails to provide upon timely request any document, file, or record necessary to the auditing requirements of the Department of State and the United States Agency for International Development.

PROHIBITION ON FUNDING FOR ABORTIONS AND INVOLUNTARY STERILIZATION

SEC. 7014. None of the funds made available to carry out part I of the Foreign Assistance Act of 1961, as amended, may be used to pay for the performance of abortions as a method of family planning or to motivate or coerce any person to practice abortions. None of the funds made available to carry out part I of the Foreign Assistance Act of 1961, as amended, may be used to pay for the performance of involuntary sterilization as a method of family planning or to coerce or provide any financial incentive to any person to undergo sterilizations. None of the funds made available to carry out part I of the Foreign Assistance Act of 1961, as amended, may be used to pay for any biomedical research which relates in whole or in part, to methods of, or the performance of, abortions or involuntary sterilization as a means of family planning. None of the funds made available to carry out part I of the Foreign Assistance Act of 1961, as amended, may be obligated or expended for any country or organization if the President certifies that the use of these funds by any such country or organization would violate any of the above provisions related to abortions and involuntary sterilizations.

AUTHORIZATION REQUIREMENTS

SEC. 7015. Funds appropriated by this Act, except funds appropriated under the heading "Trade and Development Agency", may be obligated and expended notwithstanding section 10 of Public Law 91–672 (22 U.S.C. 2412), section 15 of the State Department Basic Authorities Act of 1956 (22 U.S.C. 2680), section 313 of the Foreign Relations Authorization Act, Fiscal Years 1994 and 1995 (22 U.S.C. 6212), and section 504(a)(1) of the National Security Act of 1947 (50 U.S.C. 3094(a)(1)).

DEFINITION OF PROGRAM, PROJECT, AND ACTIVITY

SEC. 7016. For the purpose of titles II through VI of this Act "program, project, and activity" shall be defined at the appropriations Act account level and shall include all appropriations and authorizations Acts funding directives, ceilings, and limitations with the exception that for the "Economic Support Fund", "Assistance for Europe, Eurasia and Central Asia", and "Foreign Military Financing Program" accounts, "program, project, and activity" shall also be considered to include country, regional, and central program level funding within each such account, and for the development assistance accounts of the United States Agency for International Development, "program, project, and activity" shall also be considered to include central, country, regional, and program level funding, either as—

(1) justified to Congress; or

(2) allocated by the Executive Branch in accordance with the report required by section 653(a) of the Foreign Assistance Act of 1961.

AUTHORITIES FOR THE PEACE CORPS, INTER-AMERICAN FOUNDATION, AND UNITED STATES AFRICAN DEVELOPMENT FOUNDATION

SEC. 7017. Unless expressly provided to the contrary, provisions of this or any other Act, including provisions contained in prior Acts authorizing or making appropriations for the Department of State, foreign operations, and related programs, shall not be construed to prohibit activities authorized by or conducted under the Peace Corps Act, the Inter-American Foundation Act, or the African Development Foundation Act: Provided, That prior to conducting activities in a country for which assistance is prohibited, the agency shall notify the Committees on Appropriations and report to such Committees within 15 days of taking such action.

COMMERCE, TRADE AND SURPLUS COMMODITIES

SEC. 7018. (a) WORLD MARKETS.—None of the funds appropriated or made available pursuant to titles III through VI of this Act for direct assistance and none of the funds otherwise made available to the Export-Import Bank and the United States International Development Finance Corporation shall be obligated or expended to finance any loan, any assistance, or any other financial commitments for establishing or expanding production of any commodity for export by any country other than the United States, if the commodity is likely to be in surplus on world markets at the time the resulting productive capacity is expected to become operative and if the assistance will cause substantial injury to United States producers of the same, similar, or competing commodity: Provided, That such prohibition shall not apply to the Export-Import Bank if in the judgment of its Board of Directors the benefits to industry and employment in the United States are likely to outweigh the injury to United States producers of the same, similar, or competing commodity, and the Chairman of the Board so notifies the Committees on Appropriations: Provided further, That this subsection shall not prohibit—

(1) activities in a country that is eligible for assistance from the International Development Association, is not eligible for assistance from the International Bank for Reconstruction and Development, and does not export on a consistent basis the agricultural commodity with respect to which assistance is furnished; or

(2) activities in a country the President determines is recovering from widespread conflict, a humanitarian crisis, or a complex emergency.

(b) EXPORTS.—None of the funds appropriated by this or any other Act to carry out chapter 1 of part I of the Foreign Assistance Act of 1961 shall be available for any testing or breeding feasibility study, variety improvement or introduction, consultancy, publication, conference, or training in connection with the growth or production in a foreign country of an agricultural commodity for export which would compete with a similar commodity grown or produced in the United States: Provided, That this subsection shall not prohibit—

(1) activities designed to increase food security in developing countries where such activities will not have a significant impact on the export of agricultural commodities of the United States;

(2) research activities intended primarily to benefit United States producers;

(3) activities in a country that is eligible for assistance from the International Development Association, is not eligible for assistance from the International Bank for Reconstruction and Development, and does not export on a consistent basis the agricultural commodity with respect to which assistance is furnished; or

(4) activities in a country the President determines is recovering from widespread conflict, a humanitarian crisis, or a complex emergency.

ELIGIBILITY FOR ASSISTANCE

SEC. 7019. (a) ASSISTANCE THROUGH NONGOVERNMENTAL ORGANIZATIONS.—Restrictions contained in this or any other Act with respect to assistance for a country shall not be construed to restrict assistance in support of programs of nongovernmental organizations from funds appropriated by this Act to carry out the provisions of chapters 1, 10, 11, and 12 of part I and chapter 4 of part II of the Foreign Assistance Act of 1961 and from funds appropriated under the heading "Assistance for Europe, Eurasia and Central Asia": Provided, That nothing in this subsection shall be construed to alter any existing statutory prohibitions against abortion or involuntary sterilizations contained in this or any other Act.

(b) PUBLIC LAW 480.—During fiscal year 2023, restrictions contained in this or any other Act with respect to assistance for a country shall not be construed to restrict assistance under the Food for Peace Act (Public Law 83–480; 7 U.S.C. 1721 et seq.).

SEC. 7020. (a) EXTENSION OF PROCUREMENT AUTHORITY.—Section 7077 of the Department of State, Foreign Operations, and Related Programs Appropriations Act, 2012 (division I of Public Law 112–74) shall continue in effect during fiscal year 2023.

INSECURE COMMUNICATIONS NETWORKS

SEC. 7021. Funds appropriated by this Act may be made available for programs designed to enable a more prosperous and secure cyberspace, including through the Digital Connectivity and Cybersecurity Partnership, such as to—

(1) advance the adoption of secure, next-generation communications networks and services, including 5G, and cybersecurity policies, in countries receiving assistance under this Act and prior Acts making appropriations for the Department of State, foreign operations, and related programs;

(2) counter the establishment of insecure communications networks and services, including 5G, promoted by the People's Republic of China and other state-backed enterprises that are subject to undue or extrajudicial control by their country of origin; and

(3) provide policy and technical training on deploying open, interoperable, reliable, and secure networks to information communication technology professionals in countries receiving assistance under this Act, as appropriate:

Provided, That such funds, including funds under the "Economic Support Fund" heading, may be used to strengthen civilian cybersecurity capacity activities including participation of foreign military personnel in non-military activities, notwithstanding any other provision of law, following consultation with the Committees on Appropriations.

FINANCIAL MANAGEMENT AND BUDGET TRANSPARENCY

SEC. 7022. (a) FOREIGN ASSISTANCE WEBSITE.—Funds appropriated by this Act, including funds made available for any agency, may be made available to support the provision of additional information on United States Government foreign assistance on the "ForeignAssistance.gov" website: Provided, That all Federal agencies funded under this Act shall provide such information on foreign assistance, upon request and in a timely manner, to the Department of State and USAID.

DEMOCRACY PROGRAMS

SEC. 7023. (a) AUTHORITIES.—

AVAILABILITY.—Funds made available by this Act for democracy programs may be made available notwithstanding any other provision of law, and with regard to the National Endowment for Democracy (NED), any regulation.

(b) DEFINITION OF DEMOCRACY PROGRAMS.—For purposes of funds appropriated by this Act, the term "democracy programs" means programs that support good governance, credible and competitive elections, freedom of expression, association, assembly, and religion, human rights, labor rights, independent media, and the rule of law, and that otherwise strengthen the capacity of democratic political parties, governments, nongovernmental organizations and institutions, and citizens to support the development of democratic states and institutions that are responsive and accountable to citizens.

(c) RESTRICTION ON PRIOR APPROVAL.—With respect to the provision of assistance for democracy programs in this Act, the Secretary of State should oppose, through appropriate means, efforts by foreign governments to dictate the nature of United States assistance for civil society, the selection of individuals or entities to implement such programs, or the selection of recipients or beneficiaries of those programs.

INTERNATIONAL RELIGIOUS FREEDOM

SEC. 7024.

Funds appropriated by this Act and prior Acts making appropriations for the Department of State, foreign operations, and related programs under the heading "Economic Support Fund" may be made available notwithstanding any other provision of law for assistance for ethnic and religious minorities in Iraq and Syria.

SPECIAL PROVISIONS

SEC. 7025. (a) VICTIMS OF WAR, DISPLACED CHILDREN, AND DISPLACED BURMESE.—Funds appropriated in title III of this Act that are made available for assistance for Afghanistan, Burma, Iraq, Sudan, Lebanon, Pakistan, victims of war, victims of torture and trauma, displaced children, displaced Burmese, and to combat trafficking in persons and assist victims of such trafficking, may be made available notwithstanding any other provision of law.

(b) WORLD FOOD PROGRAMME.—Funds managed by the Bureau for Humanitarian Assistance, United States Agency for International Development, from this or any other Act, may be made available as a general contribution to the World Food Programme, notwithstanding any other provision of law.

(c) DIRECTIVES AND AUTHORITIES.—

(1) RESEARCH AND TRAINING.—Funds appropriated by this Act under the heading "Assistance for Europe, Eurasia and Central Asia" may be made available to carry out the Program for Research and Training on Eastern Europe and the Independent States of the Former Soviet Union as authorized by the Soviet-Eastern European Research and Training Act of 1983 (22 U.S.C. 4501 et seq.).

(2) GENOCIDE VICTIMS MEMORIAL SITES.—Funds appropriated by this Act and prior Acts making appropriations for the Department of State, foreign operations, and related programs under the headings "Economic Support Fund" and "Assistance for Europe, Eurasia and Central Asia" may be made available as contributions to establish and maintain memorial sites of genocide, subject to the regular notification procedures of the Committees on Appropriations.

(3) PRIVATE SECTOR PARTNERSHIPS.—Of the funds appropriated by this Act under the headings "Development Assistance" and "Economic Support Fund" that are made available for private sector partnerships, up to $50,000,000 may remain available until September 30, 2025.

(4) ADDITIONAL AUTHORITIES.—Of the amounts made available by title I of this Act under the heading "Diplomatic Programs", up to $500,000 may be made available for grants pursuant to section 504 of the Foreign Relations Authorization Act, Fiscal Year 1979 (22 U.S.C. 2656d), including to facilitate collaboration with indigenous communities.

(5) INNOVATION.—The USAID Administrator may use funds appropriated by this Act under title III to make innovation incentive awards: Provided, That for purposes of this paragraph the term "innovation incentive award" means the provision of funding on a competitive basis that (A) encourages and rewards the development of solutions for a particular, well-defined problem related to the alleviation of poverty; or (B) helps identify and promote a broad range of ideas and practices facilitating further development of an idea or practice by third parties in accordance with the terms and conditions of section 7034(e)(4) of the Department of State, Foreign Operations, and Related Programs Appropriations Act, 2019 (division F of Public Law 116–6): Provided further, That each individual award may not exceed $100,000: Provided further, That no more than 15 such awards may be made during fiscal year 2023.

(6) CLARIFICATION.—Section 104A(g) of the Foreign Assistance Act of 1961 (22 U.S.C. 2151b–2(g)) is amended by inserting "section 104(c), section 104B, section 104C," after "in support of activities described in".

(d) PARTNER VETTING.—Funds appropriated by this Act or in titles I through IV of prior Acts making appropriations for the Department of State, foreign operations, and related programs may be used by the Secretary of State and the USAID Administrator, as appropriate, to support the continued implementation of partner vetting: Provided further, That the Secretary and the Administrator may restrict the award of, terminate, or cancel contracts, grants, or cooperative agreements or require an awardee to restrict the award of, terminate, or cancel a sub-award based on information in connection with a partner vetting program.

(e) CONTINGENCIES.—During fiscal year 2023, the President may use up to $200,000,000 under the authority of section 451 of the Foreign Assistance Act of 1961, notwithstanding any other provision of law.

(f) TRANSFER OF FUNDS FOR EXTRAORDINARY PROTECTION.—The Secretary of State may transfer to, and merge with, funds under the heading "Protection of Foreign Missions and Officials" unobligated balances of expired funds appropriated under the heading "Diplomatic Programs" for fiscal year 2023, at no later than the end of the fifth fiscal year after the last fiscal year for which such funds are available for the purposes for which appropriated: Provided, That not more than $50,000,000 may be transferred.

(g) AUTHORITY.—Funds made available by this Act under the heading "Economic Support Fund" to counter extremism may be made available notwithstanding any other provision of law restricting assistance to foreign countries.

(h) REPORTS REPEALED.—Section 111(a) of Public Law 111–195; section 4 of Public Law 107–243; sections 51(a)(2) and 404(e) of Public Law 84–885; section 804(b) of Public Law 101–246; section 1012(c) of Public Law 103–337; sections 549, 620C(c), 655, and 656 of Public Law 87–195; section 8 of Public Law 107–245; section 181 of Public Law 102–138; section 527(f) of Public Law 103–236; section 12(a)–(b) of Public Law 108–19; section 702 of Public Law 107–228; section 570(d) of Public Law 104–208; section 5103(f) of Public Law 111–13; Section 4 of Public Law 79–264 (22 U.S.C. 287b(a)); section 118(f) of the Foreign Assistance Act of 1961 (22 U.S.C. 2151p–1(f)); and section 6502(b) of Public Law 117–81 are hereby repealed. Section 136 of the Foreign Assistance Act of 1961 (22 U.S.C. 2152h) is amended in subsections (e)(1)(B)(ii) and (e)(2)(B)(ii) by striking "and revision, not less frequently than once every 5 years," and in subsection (j)(1) by striking ", October 1, 2022, and October 1, 2027,"; section 110(b)(l) of the Trafficking Victims Protection Act of 2000 (22 U.S.C. 7107(b)(l)) is amended by striking "June 1" and inserting "June 30".

(i) EXTENSION OF AUTHORITIES.—

(1) PASSPORT FEES.—Section 1(b) of the Passport Act of June 4, 1920 (22 U.S.C. 214(b)) is amended by striking paragraph (2) and re-designating paragraph (3) as paragraph (2).

(2) INCENTIVES FOR CRITICAL POSTS.—The authority contained in section 1115(d) of the Supplemental Appropriations Act, 2009 (Public Law 111–32) shall remain in effect through September 30, 2023.

(3) USAID CIVIL SERVICE ANNUITANT WAIVER.—Section 625(j)(1) of the Foreign Assistance Act of 1961 (22 U.S.C. 2385(j)(1)) shall be applied by substituting "September 30, 2023" for "October 1, 2010" in subparagraph (B).

(4) OVERSEAS PAY COMPARABILITY AND LIMITATION.—

The authority provided by section 1113 of the Supplemental Appropriations Act, 2009 (Public Law 111–32) shall remain in effect through September 30, 2023.

(5) CATEGORICAL ELIGIBILITY.—The Foreign Operations, Export Financing, and Related Programs Appropriations Act, 1990 (Public Law 101–167) is amended—

(A) in section 599D (8 U.S.C. 1157 note)—

(i) in subsection (b)(3), by striking "and 2021" and inserting "2021, 2022, and 2023"; and

(ii) in subsection (e), by striking "2021" each place it appears and inserting "2023"; and

(B) in section 599E(b)(2) (8 U.S.C. 1255 note), by striking "2021" and inserting "2023".

(6) INSPECTOR GENERAL ANNUITANT WAIVER.—The authorities provided in section 1015(b) of the Supplemental Appropriations Act, 2010 (Public Law 111–212) shall remain in effect through September 30, 2023, and may be used to facilitate the assignment of persons for oversight of programs in Syria, South Sudan, Yemen, Somalia, and Venezuela.

(7) ACCOUNTABILITY REVIEW BOARDS.—The authority provided by section 301(a)(3) of the Omnibus Diplomatic Security and Antiterrorism Act of 1986 (22 U.S.C. 4831(a)(3)) shall be in effect for facilities in Afghanistan, Iraq, Pakistan, Somalia, Libya, Syria, and Yemen through September 30, 2023, except that the notification and reporting requirements contained in such section shall include the Committees on Appropriations.

(8) SPECIAL INSPECTOR GENERAL FOR AFGHANISTAN RECONSTRUCTION COMPETITIVE STATUS.—Notwithstanding any other provision of law, any employee of the Special Inspector General for Afghanistan Reconstruction (SIGAR) who completes at least 12 months of continuous service after enactment of this Act or who is employed on the date on which SIGAR terminates, whichever occurs first, shall acquire competitive status for appointment to any position in the competitive service for which the employee possesses the required qualifications.

(9) TRANSFER OF BALANCES.—Section 7081(h) of the Department of State, Foreign Operations, and Related Programs Appropriations Act, 2017 (division J of Public Law 115–31) shall continue in effect during fiscal year 2023.

(10) DEPARTMENT OF STATE INSPECTOR GENERAL WAIVER AUTHORITY.—The Inspector General of the Department of State may waive the provisions of subsections (a) through (d) of section 824 of the Foreign Service Act of 1980 (22 U.S.C. 4064) on a case-by-case basis for an annuitant reemployed by the Inspector General on a temporary basis, subject to the same constraints and in the same manner by which the Secretary of State may exercise such waiver authority pursuant to subsection (g) of such section.

(11) SPECIALIZED AGENCY WAIVER AND TRANSFER AUTHORITY.—The President may waive section 414 of Public Law 101–246 and section 410 of Public Law 103–236 on a case-by-case basis, if the President determines and certifies in writing to the Speaker of the House of Representatives, the President Pro Tempore of the Senate, and the Committees on Appropriations that to do so is important to the national interest of the United States.

(12) Section 9(2) of the United Nations Participation Act of 1945 (22 U.S.C. 287e–1(2)) is amended by striking "30" and inserting "41".

(j) HIV/AIDS WORKING CAPITAL FUND.—Funds available in the HIV/AIDS Working Capital Fund established pursuant to section 525(b)(1) of the Foreign Operations, Export Financing, and Related Programs Appropriations Act, 2005 (Public Law 108–447) may be made available for pharmaceuticals and other products for other global health activities to the same extent as HIV/AIDS pharmaceuticals and other products, subject to the terms and conditions in such section: *Provided,* That the authority in section 525(b)(5) of the Foreign Operations, Export Financing, and Related Programs Appropriation Act, 2005 (Public Law 108–447) shall be exercised by the Assistant Administrator for Global Health, USAID, with respect to funds deposited for such non-HIV/AIDS pharmaceuticals and other products, and shall be subject to the regular notification procedures of the Committees on Appropriations: *Provided further,* That the Secretary of State shall include in the congressional budget justification an accounting of budgetary resources, disbursements, balances, and reimbursements related to such fund.

(k) LOANS, CONSULTATION, AND NOTIFICATION.—

(1) LOAN GUARANTEES AND ENTERPRISE FUNDS.—Funds appropriated under the headings "Economic Support Fund" and "Assistance for Europe, Eurasia and Central Asia" by this Act and prior Acts making appropriations for the Department of State, foreign operations, and related programs including balances that were previously designated by the Congress for Overseas Contingency Operations/Global War on Terrorism pursuant to section 251(b)(2)(A)(ii) of the Balanced Budget and Emergency Deficit Control Act of 1985, and funds provided as a gift pursuant to section 635(d) of the Foreign Assistance Act of 1961 that are used for the purposes of this subsection, may be made available for the cost of loan guarantees, including the cost of modifying such guarantees, as defined in section 502 of the Congressional Budget Act of 1974, which are authorized to be provided: *Provided,* That these funds are available to subsidize gross obligations for the total loan principal, any part of which is to be guaranteed: *Provided further,* That the Government of the United States may charge fees for loan guarantees authorized under this paragraph, which shall be collected from borrowers or third parties on behalf of such borrowers in accordance with section 502(7) of the Congressional Budget Act of 1974: *Provided further,* That amounts made available under this paragraph for the costs of such guarantees shall not be considered assistance for the purposes of provisions of law limiting assistance to a country.

(2) FOREIGN MILITARY FINANCING DIRECT LOANS.—During fiscal year 2023, direct loans under section 23 of the Arms Export Control Act may be made available for North Atlantic Treaty Organization (NATO) or Major Non-NATO Allies, notwithstanding section 23(c)(1) of the Arms Export Control Act, gross obligations for the principal amounts of which shall not exceed $4,000,000,000: *Provided,* That funds appropriated under the heading "Foreign Military Financing Program" in this Act and prior Acts making appropriations for the Department of State, foreign operations, and related programs including balances that were previously designated by the Congress for Overseas Contingency Operation/Global War on Terrorism pursuant to section 251(b)(2)(A)(ii) of the Balanced Budget and Emergency Deficit Control Act of 1985, may be made available for the costs, as defined in section 502 of the Congressional Budget Act of 1974, of such loans: *Provided further,* That such costs, including the cost of modifying such loans, shall be as defined in section 502 of the Congressional Budget Act of 1974 and may include the costs of selling, reducing, or cancelling any amounts owed to the United States or any agency of the United States: *Provided further,* That the Government of the United States may charge fees for such loans, which shall be collected from borrowers in accordance with section 502(7) of the Congressional Budget Act of 1974: *Provided further,* That no funds made available to the North Atlantic Treaty Organization (NATO) or major non-NATO allies by this or any other appropriations Act for this fiscal year or prior fiscal years may be used for payment of any fees associated with such loans: *Provided further,* That such loans shall be repaid in not more than 12 years, including a grace period of up to one year on repayment of principal: *Provided further,* That notwithstanding section 23(c)(1) of the Arms Export Control Act, interest for such loans may be charged at a rate determined by the Secretary of State, except that such rate may not be less than the prevailing interest rate on marketable Treasury securities of similar maturity: *Provided further,* That amounts made available under this paragraph for such costs shall not be considered assistance for the purposes of provisions of law limiting assistance to a country.

(3) FOREIGN MILITARY FINANCING LOAN GUARANTEES.—Funds appropriated under the heading "Foreign Military Financing Program" in this Act and prior Acts making appropriations for the Department of State, foreign operations, and related programs including balances that were previously designated by the Congress for Overseas Contingency Operations/Global War on Terrorism pursuant to section 251(b)(2)(A)(ii) of the Balanced Budget and Emergency Deficit Control Act of 1985, may be made available, notwithstanding the third proviso under such heading, for the costs of loan guarantees under section 24 of the Arms Export Control Act for North Atlantic Treaty Organization (NATO) or Major Non-NATO Allies, which are authorized to be provided: *Provided,* That such funds are available to subsidize gross obligations for the principal amount of commercial loans, and total loan principal, any part of which is to be guaranteed, not to exceed $4,000,000,000: *Provided further,* That no loan guarantee with respect to any one borrower may exceed 80 percent of the loan principal: *Provided further,* That any loan guaranteed under this paragraph may not be subordinated to another debt contracted by the borrower or to any other claims against the borrower in the case of default: *Provided further,* That repayment in United States dollars of any loan guaranteed under this paragraph shall be required within a period not to exceed 12 years after the loan agreement is signed: *Provided further,* That the Government of the United States may charge fees for such loan guarantees, as may be determined, notwithstanding section 24 of the Arms Export Control Act, which shall be collected from borrowers or third parties on behalf of such borrowers in accordance with section 502(7) of the Congressional Budget Act of 1974: *Provided further,* That amounts made available under this paragraph for the costs of such guarantees shall not be considered assistance for the purposes of provisions of law limiting assistance to a country.

(l) DEFINITIONS.—

(1) APPROPRIATE CONGRESSIONAL COMMITTEES.—Unless otherwise defined in this Act, for purposes of this Act the term "appropriate congressional committees" means the Committees on Appropriations and Foreign Relations of the Senate and the Committees on Appropriations and Foreign Affairs of the House of Representatives.

(2) FUNDS APPROPRIATED BY THIS ACT AND PRIOR ACTS.—Unless otherwise defined in this Act, for purposes of this Act the term "funds appropriated by this Act and prior Acts making appropriations for the Department of State, foreign operations, and related programs" means funds that remain available for obligation, and have not expired.

(3) INTERNATIONAL FINANCIAL INSTITUTIONS.—In this Act "international financial institutions" means the International Bank for Reconstruction and Development, the International Development Association, the International Finance Corporation, the Inter-American Development Bank, the International Monetary Fund, the International Fund for Agricultural Development, the Asian Development Bank, the Asian Development Fund, the Inter-American Investment Corporation, the North American Development Bank, the European Bank for Reconstruction and Development, the African Development Bank, the African Development Fund, and the Multilateral Investment Guarantee Agency.

(4) SUCCESSOR OPERATING UNIT.—Any reference to a particular USAID operating unit or office in this or prior Acts making appropriations for the Department of State, foreign operations, and related programs shall be deemed to include any successor operating unit or office performing the same or similar functions.

(5) USAID.—In this Act, the term "USAID" means the United States Agency for International Development.

(6) NOTWITHSTANDING.—Any provision in this Act authorizing assistance to be made available "notwithstanding any other provision of law" or "notwithstanding" certain provisions of law shall be deemed to apply to such assistance made available from funds appropriated under section 10003 of the American Rescue Plan Act of 2021 (Public Law 117–2): *Provided,* That the authorities of section 491 of the Foreign Assistance Act of 1961 shall be applicable to such funds used for international disaster relief, rehabilitation, and reconstruction.

LAW ENFORCEMENT AND SECURITY

SEC. 7026. (a) ASSISTANCE.—

(1) COMMUNITY-BASED POLICE ASSISTANCE.—Funds made available under titles III and IV of this Act to carry out the provisions of chapter 1 of part I and chapters 4 and 6 of part II of the Foreign Assistance Act of 1961, may be used, notwithstanding section 660 of that Act, to enhance the effectiveness and accountability of civilian police authority through training and technical assistance in human rights, the rule of law, anti-corruption, strategic planning, and through assistance to foster civilian police roles that support democratic governance, including assistance for programs to prevent conflict, respond to disasters, address gender-based violence, and foster improved police relations with the communities they serve.

(2) GLOBAL SECURITY CONTINGENCY FUND.—Notwithstanding any other provision of this Act, funds appropriated by this Act under the headings "Peacekeeping Operations", "Foreign Military Financing Program", and "International Narcotics and Law Enforcement" may be transferred to, and merged with, funds previously made available under the heading "Global Security Contingency Fund".

(3) INTERNATIONAL PRISON CONDITIONS.—Funds appropriated by this Act may be made available for assistance to eliminate inhumane conditions in foreign prisons and other detention facilities, notwithstanding section 660 of the Foreign Assistance Act of 1961.

(b) AUTHORITIES.—

(1) RECONSTITUTING CIVILIAN POLICE AUTHORITY.—In providing assistance with funds appropriated by this Act under section 660(b)(6) of the Foreign Assistance Act of 1961, support for a nation emerging from instability may be deemed to mean support for regional, district, municipal, or other sub-national entity emerging from instability, as well as a nation emerging from instability.

(2) DISARMAMENT, DEMOBILIZATION, AND REINTEGRATION.—Section 7034(d) of the Department of State, Foreign Operations, and Related Programs Appropriations Act, 2015 (division J of Public Law 113–235) shall continue in effect during fiscal year 2023.

(3) EXTENSION OF WAR RESERVES STOCKPILE AUTHORITY.—

(A) Section 12001(d) of the Department of Defense Appropriations Act, 2005 (Public Law 108–287; 118 Stat. 1011) is amended by striking "of this section" and all that follows through the period at the end and inserting "of this section after September 30, 2025.".

(B) Section 514(b)(2)(A) of the Foreign Assistance Act of 1961 (22 U.S.C. 2321h(b)(2)(A)) is amended by striking "and 2024" and inserting "2024 and 2025".

(4) COMMERCIAL LEASING OF DEFENSE ARTICLES.—Notwithstanding any other provision of law, and subject to the regular notification procedures of the Committees on Appropriations, the authority of section 23(a) of the Arms Export Control Act (22 U.S.C. 2763) may be used to provide financing to Israel, Egypt, the North Atlantic Treaty Organization (NATO), and major non-NATO allies for the procurement by leasing (including leasing with an option to purchase) of defense articles from United States commercial suppliers, not including Major Defense Equipment (other than helicopters and other types of aircraft having possible civilian application), if the President determines that there are compelling foreign policy or national security reasons for those defense articles being provided by commercial lease rather than by government-to-government sale under such Act.

(5) SPECIAL DEFENSE ACQUISITION FUND.—Not to exceed $900,000,000 may be obligated pursuant to section 51(c)(2) of the Arms Export Control Act (22 U.S.C. 2795(c)(2)) for the purposes of the Special Defense Acquisition Fund (the Fund), to remain available for obligation until September 30, 2025: Provided, That the provision of defense articles and defense services to foreign countries or international organizations from the Fund shall be subject to the concurrence of the Secretary of State.

(c) LIMITATIONS.—

(1) CHILD SOLDIERS.—Funds appropriated by this Act should not be used to support any military training or operations that include child soldiers.

(2) LANDMINES AND CLUSTER MUNITIONS.—

(A) LANDMINES.—Notwithstanding any other provision of law, demining equipment available to the United States Agency for International Development and the Department of State and used in support of the clearance of landmines and unexploded ordnance for humanitarian purposes may be disposed of on a grant basis in foreign countries, subject to such terms and conditions as the Secretary of State may prescribe.

(B) CLUSTER MUNITIONS.—No military assistance shall be furnished for cluster munitions, no defense export license for cluster munitions may be issued, and no cluster munitions or cluster munitions technology shall be sold or transferred, unless—

(i) the submunitions of the cluster munitions, after arming, do not result in more than 1 percent unexploded ordnance across the range of intended operational environments, and the agreement applicable to the assistance, transfer, or sale of such cluster munitions or cluster munitions technology specifies that the cluster munitions will only be used against clearly defined military targets and will not be used where civilians are known to be present or in areas normally inhabited by civilians; or

(ii) such assistance, license, sale, or transfer is for the purpose of demilitarizing or permanently disposing of such cluster munitions.

(3) CROWD CONTROL ITEMS.—Funds appropriated by this Act should not be used for tear gas, small arms, light weapons, ammunition, or other items for crowd control purposes for foreign security forces that use excessive force to repress peaceful expression, association, or assembly in countries that the Secretary of State determines are undemocratic or are undergoing democratic transitions.

(d) Section 503(a)(3) of Public Law 87–195 (22 U.S.C. 2311(a)(3)) is amended after "the Coast Guard" by inserting "and the reserve components of the Army, Navy, Air Force, or Marines Corps who are ordered to active duty pursuant to chapter 1209 of title 10, United States Code, and at the request of the Secretary of State".

(e) IMET Ineligibility. Section 546(b) of the Foreign Assistance Act of 1961 (22 U.S.C. 2347e(b)) is amended by striking "and Spain" and inserting "Spain, Saudi Arabia, United Arab Emirates, and Qatar".

ARAB LEAGUE BOYCOTT OF ISRAEL

SEC. 7027. It is the sense of the Congress that—

(1) the Arab League boycott of Israel, and the secondary boycott of American firms that have commercial ties with Israel, is an impediment to peace in the region and to United States investment and trade in the Middle East and North Africa;

(2) the Arab League boycott, which was regrettably reinstated in 1997, should be immediately and publicly terminated, and the Central Office for the Boycott of Israel immediately disbanded;

(3) all Arab League states should normalize relations with their neighbor Israel;

(4) the President and the Secretary of State should continue to vigorously oppose the Arab League boycott of Israel and find concrete steps to demonstrate that opposition by, for example, taking into consideration the participation of any recipient country in the boycott when determining to sell weapons to said country; and

(5) the President should report to Congress annually on specific steps being taken by the United States to encourage Arab League states to normalize their relations with Israel to bring about the termination of the Arab League boycott of Israel, including those to encourage allies and trading partners of the United States to enact laws prohibiting businesses from complying with the boycott and penalizing businesses that do comply.

MIDDLE EAST AND NORTH AFRICA

SEC. 7028. (a) EGYPT.—

(1) CERTIFICATION AND REPORT.—Funds appropriated by this Act that are available for assistance for Egypt may be made available notwithstanding any other provision of law restricting assistance for Egypt, except for this subsection and section 620M of the Foreign Assistance Act of 1961, and may only be made available for assistance for the Government of Egypt if the Secretary of State certifies and reports to the Committees on Appropriations that such government is—

(A) sustaining the strategic relationship with the United States; and

(B) meeting its obligations under the 1979 Egypt-Israel Peace Treaty.

(2) FOREIGN MILITARY FINANCING PROGRAM.—

Of the funds appropriated by this Act under the heading "Foreign Military Financing Program", $1,300,000,000, to remain available until September 30, 2024, may be made available for assistance for Egypt: Provided, That such funds may be transferred to an interest bearing account in the Federal Reserve Bank of New York.

(b) IRAQ.—

Funds appropriated under titles III and IV of this Act may be made available for assistance for Iraq.

(c) LEBANON.—

ASSISTANCE.—Funds appropriated by this Act may be made available for assistance for Lebanon notwithstanding any other provision of law.

(d) SYRIA.—

(1) NON-LETHAL ASSISTANCE.— Funds appropriated by titles III and IV of this Act may be made available, notwithstanding any other provision of law, for non-lethal stabilization assistance for Syria.

(2) The President may exercise the authority of sections 552(c) and 610 of the Foreign Assistance Act of 1961 to provide assistance for Syria, notwithstanding any other provision of law and without regard to the percentage and dollar limitations in such sections.

(e) WEST BANK AND GAZA.—

(1) The President may waive the provisions of section 1003(1), (2), and (3) of Public Law 100–204 if the President determines and certifies in writing to the Speaker of the House of Representatives, the President pro tempore of the Senate, and the Committees on Appropriations that it is important to the national security interests of the United States or the conduct of diplomacy.

(2) PERIOD OF APPLICATION OF THE WAIVER. Any waiver pursuant to paragraph (1) shall be effective for no more than a period of 6 months at a time.

(f) JORDAN - Of the funds appropriated by this Act under the heading "Economic Support Fund" for Jordan, up to $250,000,000 shall remain available until September 30, 2026, and may be made available for assistance for Jordan if negotiated benchmarks towards reforms are met: Provided, That such funds may be made available for other purposes of the Economic Support Fund, subject to the regular notification procedures of the Committees on Appropriations.

AFRICA

SEC. 7029. (a) CENTRAL AFRICAN REPUBLIC.— Funds appropriated by this Act under the heading "Economic Support Fund" may be made available for a contribution to the Special Criminal Court in Central African Republic.

(b) DEMOCRATIC REPUBLIC OF THE CONGO.— Funds appropriated by this Act under the headings "Peacekeeping Operations" and "International Military Education and Training" that are made available for assistance for the Democratic Republic of the Congo may be made available notwithstanding any other provision of law, except section 620M of the Foreign Assistance Act of 1961.

(c) SUDAN.—

ASSISTANCE.—Funds appropriated by this Act and prior Acts making appropriations for the Department of State, foreign operations, and related programs may be made available for assistance for Sudan notwithstanding any other provision of law.

EAST ASIA AND THE PACIFIC

SEC. 7030. (a) BURMA.—Funds appropriated by this Act and prior Acts making appropriations for the Department of State, foreign operations, and related programs may be made available for assistance for Burma notwithstanding any other provision of law, and may also be made available for ethnic groups and civil society in Burma to help sustain ceasefire agreements and further prospects for reconciliation and peace, which may include support to representatives of ethnic armed groups for this purpose under the headings "Economic Support Fund" and "Development Assistance".

(b)

COUNTERING PRC MALIGN INFLUENCE FUND.—Funds appropriated by this Act under the headings "Development Assistance", "Economic Support Fund", "International Narcotics Control and Law Enforcement", "Peacekeeping Operations", "Nonproliferation, Anti-terrorism, Demining and Related Programs", and "Foreign Military Financing Program", may be made available for a Countering PRC Malign Influence Fund to counter the malign influence of the Government of the People's Republic of China and the Chinese Communist Party and entities acting on their behalf globally notwithstanding any other provision of law: Provided, That such funds appropriated under such headings may be transferred to, and merged with, funds appropriated under such headings: Provided further, That such transfer authority is in addition to any other transfer authority provided by this Act or any other Act, and is subject to the regular notification procedures of the Committees on Appropriations.

(c) NORTH KOREA.—Funds appropriated under the heading "Economic Support Fund" may be made available for programs to support initiatives relating to North Korea that are in the national interest of the United States, notwithstanding any other provision of law.

(d) PEOPLE'S REPUBLIC OF CHINA.—

(1) CLARIFICATION.—Funds appropriated by this Act and prior Acts making appropriations for the Department of State, foreign operations, and related programs that are made available for programs in the People's Republic of China may be used to counter the impact of Chinese influence and investments in the Greater Mekong Subregion, following notification to the Committees on Appropriations.

(2) Notwithstanding any other provision of law, funds appropriated by this Act may be made available for activities with the People's Republic of China designed to leverage assistance programs and improve aid effectiveness.

(e) TIBET.—

PROGRAMS FOR TIBETAN COMMUNITIES.—

(A) Notwithstanding any other provision of law, funds appropriated by this Act under the heading "Economic Support Fund" may be made available to nongovernmental organizations to support activities which preserve cultural traditions and promote sustainable development, education, and environmental conservation in Tibetan communities in the Tibet Autonomous Region and in other Tibetan communities in China.

(f) VIETNAM.—Funds appropriated under titles III and IV of this Act may be made available for assistance for Vietnam, notwithstanding any other provision of law, for activities related to the remediation of dioxin contaminated sites in Vietnam and may be made available for assistance for the Government of Vietnam, including the military, for such purposes.

(g) Funds appropriated under the heading "Economic Support Fund" may be made available for the Association of Southeast Asian Nations, the ASEAN Regional Forum, the Mekong-U.S. Partnership, and APEC programs that include countries or governments otherwise ineligible for United States assistance, notwithstanding any other provision of law.

SOUTH AND CENTRAL ASIA

SEC. 7031. (a) AFGHANISTAN.—

(1) FUNDING AND LIMITATIONS.—Funds appropriated by this Act under the headings "Economic Support Fund" and "International Narcotics Control and Law Enforcement" that are made available for assistance for Afghanistan may be made available notwithstanding any other provision of law.

(2) AFGHAN WOMEN.—

Funds appropriated by this Act and prior Acts making appropriations for the Department of State, foreign operations, and related programs under the heading "Economic Support Fund" may be made available for an endowment pursuant to paragraph (3)(A)(iv) of this subsection for a not-for-profit institution of higher education that is accessible to both women and men in a coeducational environment: Provided, That such endowment may be established in partnership with a United States-based American higher education institution that will serve on its board of trustees.

(3) AUTHORITIES.—

(A) Funds appropriated by this Act under titles III through VI that are made available for assistance for Afghanistan may be made available—

(i) for reconciliation programs and disarmament, demobilization, and reintegration activities for former combatants who have renounced violence;

(ii) for an endowment to empower women and girls;

(iii) for an endowment for higher education; and

(iv) as a United States contribution, including to a multi-donor trust fund for Afghanistan.

(B) Funds appropriated or otherwise made available by this and prior Acts for assistance for Afghanistan, including balances that were previously designated by the Congress for Overseas Contingency Operations/Global War on Terrorism pursuant to section 251(b)(2)(A)(ii) of the Balanced Budget and Emergency Deficit Control Act of 1985, as amended, may be made available as a United States contribution to other multi-donor trust funds.

(C) Section 1102(c) of the Supplemental Appropriations Act, 2009 (Public Law 111–32) shall continue in effect during fiscal year 2023 as if part of this Act.

(4) None of the funds appropriated in titles III and IV of this Act and made available for assistance for Afghanistan may be made available for direct assistance to the Taliban unless the Secretary of State certifies that to do so is in the national interest of the United States.

(b) PAKISTAN.—Funds appropriated under titles III and IV of this Act may be made available for assistance for Pakistan notwithstanding any other provision of law.

(c) REGIONAL PROGRAMS.—Funds appropriated by this Act may be provided, notwithstanding any other provision of law, for cross border stabilization and development programs between Afghanistan and Pakistan, or between either country and the Central Asian countries.

LATIN AMERICA AND THE CARIBBEAN

SEC. 7032. (a) COLOMBIA.—Funds appropriated by this Act and made available to the Department of State for assistance for the Government of Colombia may be used to support a unified campaign against narcotics trafficking, organizations designated as Foreign Terrorist Organizations, and other criminal or illegal armed groups, and to take actions to protect human health and welfare in emergency circumstances, including undertaking rescue operations: Provided, That the first, second, and third provisos of paragraph (1) of section 7045(a) of the Department of State, Foreign Operations, and Related Programs Appropriations Act, 2012 (division I of Public Law 112–74) shall continue in effect during fiscal year 2023 and shall apply to funds appropriated by this Act and made available for assistance for Colombia as if included in this Act.

(b) HAITI.—

HAITIAN COAST GUARD.—The Government of Haiti shall be eligible to purchase defense articles and services under the Arms Export Control Act (22 U.S.C. 2751 et seq.) for the Coast Guard.

(c) VENEZUELA.—Funds appropriated in Titles III and IV of this Act may be made available, notwithstanding any other provision of law, for assistance to support a democratic transition in Venezuela and respond to needs in the region related to such transition or the crisis in Venezuela.

(d) Of the funds provided for Central America, not less than $47,600,000 may be made available for assistance for El Salvador, Guatemala, and Honduras for programs that support locally led development in such countries and may remain available until September 30, 2028: Provided, That up to 15 percent of the funds made available to carry out this subsection may be used by the United States Agency for International Development for administrative and oversight expenses.

EUROPE AND EURASIA

SEC. 7033.

SECTION 907 OF THE FREEDOM SUPPORT ACT.—Section 907 of the FREEDOM Support Act (22 U.S.C. 5812 note) shall not apply to—

(a) activities to support democracy or assistance under title V of the FREEDOM Support Act (22 U.S.C. 5851 et seq.) and section 1424 of the Defense Against Weapons of Mass Destruction Act of 1996 (50 U.S.C. 2333) or non-proliferation assistance;

(b) any assistance provided by the Trade and Development Agency under section 661 of the Foreign Assistance Act of 1961;

(c) any activity carried out by a member of the United States and Foreign Commercial Service while acting within his or her official capacity;

(d) any insurance, reinsurance, guarantee, or other assistance provided by the United States International Development Finance Corporation as authorized by the BUILD Act of 2018 (division F of Public Law 115–254);

(e) any financing provided under the Export-Import Bank Act of 1945 (Public Law 79–173); or

(f) humanitarian assistance.

COUNTERING RUSSIAN INFLUENCE AND AGGRESSION

SEC. 7034. (a) LIMITATION.—None of the funds appropriated by this Act may be made available for assistance for the central Government of the Russian Federation.

(b) ANNEXATION OF CRIMEA.—

(1) None of the funds appropriated by this Act may be made available for assistance for the central government of a country that the Secretary of State determines and reports to the Committees on Appropriations has taken affirmative steps intended to support or be supportive of the Russian Federation annexation of Crimea or other territory in Ukraine: Provided, That except as otherwise provided in subsection (a), the Secretary may waive the restriction on assistance required by this paragraph if the Secretary determines and reports to such Committees that to do so is in the national interest of the United States, and includes a justification for such interest.

(2) LIMITATION.—None of the funds appropriated by this Act may be made available for—

(A) the facilitation, financing, or guarantee of United States Government investments in Crimea or other territory in Ukraine under the control of Russian-backed separatists, if such activity includes the participation of Russian Government officials, or other Russian-owned or controlled financial entities; or

(B) assistance for Crimea or other territory in Ukraine under the control of Russian-backed separatists, if such assistance includes the participation of Russian Government officials, or other Russian-owned or controlled financial entities.

(3) INTERNATIONAL FINANCIAL INSTITUTIONS.—The Secretary of the Treasury should instruct the United States executive directors of each international financial institution to use the voice and vote of the United States to oppose any assistance by such institution (including any loan, credit, or guarantee) for any program that violates the sovereignty or territorial integrity of Ukraine.

(4) DURATION.—The requirements and limitations of this subsection shall cease to be in effect if the Secretary of State determines and reports to the Committees on Appropriations that the Government of Ukraine has reestablished sovereignty over Crimea and other territory in Ukraine under the control of Russian-backed separatists.

(c) OCCUPATION OF THE GEORGIAN TERRITORIES OF ABKHAZIA AND TSKHINVALI REGION / SOUTH OSSETIA.—

(1) PROHIBITION.—None of the funds appropriated by this Act may be made available for assistance for the central government of a country that the Secretary of State determines and reports to the Committees on Appropriations has recognized the independence of, or has established diplomatic relations with, the Russian-occupied Georgian territories of Abkhazia and Tskhinvali Region/South Ossetia: Provided, That the Secretary shall publish on the Department of State website a list of any such central governments in a timely manner: Provided further, That the Secretary may waive the restriction on assistance required by this paragraph if the Secretary determines and reports to the Committees on Appropriations that to do so is in the national interest of the United States, and includes a justification for such interest.

(2) LIMITATION.—None of the funds appropriated by this Act may be made available to support the Russian occupation of the Georgian territories of Abkhazia and Tskhinvali Region/South Ossetia.

(3) INTERNATIONAL FINANCIAL INSITUTIONS.—The Secretary of the Treasury should instruct the United States executive directors of each international financial institution to use the voice and vote of the United States to oppose any assistance by such institution (including any loan, credit, or guarantee) for any program that violates the sovereignty and territorial integrity of Georgia.

(d) COUNTERING RUSSIAN INFLUENCE FUND.—

ASSISTANCE.—Funds appropriated by this Act under the headings "Assistance for Europe, Eurasia and Central Asia", "International Narcotics Control and Law Enforcement", "International Military Education and Training", and "Foreign Military Financing Program", not less than $290,000,000 may be made available to carry out the purposes of the Countering Russian Influence Fund, as authorized by section 254 of the Countering Russian Influence in Europe and Eurasia Act of 2017 (Public Law 115–44; 22 U.S.C. 9543) and notwithstanding the country limitation in subsection (b) of such section, and programs to enhance the capacity of law enforcement and security forces in countries in Europe, Eurasia, and Central Asia and strengthen security cooperation between such countries and the United States and the North Atlantic Treaty Organization, as appropriate.

(e) DEMOCRACY PROGRAMS.—Funds appropriated by this Act shall be made available to support democracy programs in the Russian Federation, including to promote Internet freedom: Provided, That not later than 90 days after enactment of this Act, the Secretary of State, in consultation with the Administrator of the United States Agency for International Development, shall submit to the appropriate congressional committees a comprehensive, multiyear strategy for the promotion of democracy in such countries.

UNITED NATIONS

SEC. 7035. (a) SEXUAL EXPLOITATION AND ABUSE IN PEACEKEEPING OPERATIONS.—The Secretary of State should withhold assistance to any unit of the security forces of a foreign country if the Secretary has credible information that such unit has engaged in sexual exploitation or abuse, including while serving in a United Nations peacekeeping operation, until the Secretary determines that the government of such country is taking effective steps to hold the responsible members of such unit accountable and to prevent future incidents: Provided, That the Secretary shall promptly notify the government of each country subject to any withholding of assistance pursuant to this paragraph, and shall notify the appropriate congressional committees of such withholding not later than 10 days after a determination to withhold such assistance is made: Provided further, That the Secretary shall, to the maximum extent practicable, assist such government in bringing the responsible members of such unit to justice.

(b) ADDITIONAL AVAILABILITY.—Funds appropriated by this Act which are returned or not made available due to section 307(a) of the Foreign Assistance Act of 1961 (22 U.S.C. 2227(a)), shall remain available for obligation until September 30, 2023: Provided, That the requirement to withhold funds for programs in Burma under section 307(a) of the Foreign Assistance Act of 1961 shall not apply to funds appropriated by this Act.

WAR CRIMES TRIBUNALS

SEC. 7036.

If the President determines that doing so will contribute to a just resolution of charges regarding genocide or other violations of international humanitarian law, the President may direct a drawdown pursuant to section 552(c) of the Foreign Assistance Act of 1961 of up to $30,000,000 of commodities and services for the United Nations War Crimes Tribunal established with regard to the former Yugoslavia by the United Nations Security Council or such other tribunals or commissions as the Council may establish or authorize to deal with such violations, without regard to the ceiling limitation contained in paragraph (2) thereof: Provided, That the determination required under this section shall be in lieu of any determinations otherwise required under section 552(c).

GLOBAL INTERNET FREEDOM

SEC. 7037. (a) FUNDING.— Of the funds made available for obligation during fiscal year 2023 under the headings "International Broadcasting Operations", "Economic Support Fund", "Democracy Fund", and "Assistance for Europe, Eurasia and Central Asia," not less than $70,000,000 shall be made available for programs to promote Internet freedom globally, notwithstanding any other provision of law: Provided, That such programs shall be prioritized for countries whose governments restrict freedom of expression on the Internet, and that are important to the national interest of the United States: Provided further, That funds made available pursuant to this section shall be matched, to the maximum extent practicable, by sources other than the United States Government, including from the private sector.

(b) REQUIREMENTS—

(1) DEPARTMENT OF STATE AND UNITED STATES AGENCY FOR INTERNATIONAL DEVELOPMENT.—Funds appropriated by this Act under the headings "Economic Support Fund", "Democracy Fund", and "Assistance for Europe, Eurasia and Central Asia" that are made available pursuant to subsection (a) shall be:

(A) coordinated with other democracy programs funded by this Act under such headings, and shall be incorporated into country assistance and democracy promotion strategies, as appropriate;

(B) for programs to implement the May 2011, International Strategy for Cyberspace, the Department of State International Cyberspace Policy Strategy required by section 402 of the Cybersecurity Act of 2015 (division N of Public Law 114–113), and the comprehensive strategy to promote Internet freedom and access to information in Iran, as required by section 414 of the Iran Threat Reduction and Syria Human Rights Act of 2012 (22 U.S.C. 8754);

(C) made available for programs that support the efforts of civil society to counter the development of repressive Internet-related laws and regulations, including countering threats to Internet freedom at international organizations; to combat violence against bloggers and other users; and to enhance digital security training and capacity building for democracy activists;

(D) made available for research of key threats to Internet freedom; the continued development of technologies that provide or enhance access to the Internet, including circumvention tools that bypass Internet blocking, filtering, and other censorship techniques used by authoritarian governments; and maintenance of the technological advantage of the United States Government over such censorship techniques: Provided, That the Secretary of State, in consultation with the United States Agency for Global Media Chief Executive Officer (USAGM CEO) and the President of the Open Technology Fund (OTF), shall coordinate any such research and development programs with other relevant United States Government departments and agencies in order to share information, technologies, and best practices, and to assess the effectiveness of such technologies; and

(E) made available only after the Assistant Secretary for Democracy, Human Rights, and Labor, Department of State, concurs that such funds are allocated consistent with -

(i) the strategies referenced in subparagraph (B) of this paragraph;

(ii) best practices regarding security for, and oversight of, Internet freedom programs; and

(iii) sufficient resources and support for the development and maintenance of anticensorship technology and tools.

(2) UNITED STATES AGENCY FOR GLOBAL MEDIA.—Funds appropriated by this Act under the heading International Broadcasting Operations that are made available pursuant to subsection (a) shall be—

(A) made available only for open-source tools and techniques to securely develop and distribute USAGM digital content, facilitate audience access to such content on websites that are censored, coordinate the distribution of USAGM digital content to targeted regional audiences, and to promote and distribute such tools and techniques, including digital security techniques;

(B) coordinated by the USAGM CEO, in consultation with the OTF President, with programs funded by this Act under the heading International Broadcasting Operations, and shall be incorporated into country broadcasting strategies, as appropriate;

(C) coordinated by the USAGM CEO, in consultation with the OTF President, to solicit project proposals through an open, transparent, and competitive application process, seek input from technical and subject matter experts to select proposals, and support Internet circumvention tools and techniques for audiences in countries that are strategic priorities for the OTF and in a manner consistent with the United States Government Internet freedom strategy; and

(D) made available for the research and development of new tools or techniques authorized in subparagraph (A) only after the USAGM CEO, in consultation with the Secretary of State, the OTF President, and other relevant United States Government departments and agencies, evaluates the risks and benefits of such new tools or techniques, and establishes safeguards to minimize the use of such new tools or techniques for illicit purposes.

(c) COORDINATION AND SPEND PLANS.—After consultation among the relevant Agency heads to coordinate and de-conflict planned activities, but not later than 90 days after enactment of this Act, the Secretary of State and the USAGM CEO, in consultation with the OTF President, shall submit to the Committees on Appropriations spend plans for funds made available by this Act for programs to promote Internet freedom globally, which shall include a description of safeguards established by relevant agencies to ensure that such programs are not used for illicit purposes: Provided, That the Department of State spend plan shall include funding for all such programs for all relevant Department of State and the United States Agency for International Development offices and bureaus.

(d) SECURITY AUDITS.—Funds made available pursuant to this section to promote Internet freedom globally may only be made available to support open source technologies that undergo comprehensive security audits consistent with the requirements of the Bureau of Democracy, Human Rights, and Labor, Department of State to ensure that such technology is secure and has not been compromised in a manner detrimental to the interest of the United States or to individuals and organizations benefiting from programs supported by such funds: Provided, That the security auditing procedures used by such Bureau shall be reviewed and updated periodically to reflect current industry security standards.

(e) SURGE.—Of the funds appropriated by this Act under the heading "Economic Support Fund", up to $2,500,000 may be made available to surge Internet freedom programs in closed societies if the Secretary of State determines and reports to the appropriate congressional committees that such use of funds is in the national interest: Provided, That such funds are in addition to amounts made available for such purposes: Provided further, That such funds may be transferred to, and merged with, funds appropriated by this Act under the heading "International Broadcasting Operations", for Internet freedom programs in closed societies, subject to the regular notification procedures following consultation with the Committees on Appropriations.

TORTURE AND OTHER CRUEL, INHUMAN, OR DEGRADING TREATMENT OR PUNISHMENT

SEC. 7038. (a) LIMITATION.—None of the funds made available by this Act may be used to support or justify the use of torture and other cruel, inhuman, or degrading treatment or punishment by any official or contract employee of the United States Government.

(b) ASSISTANCE.—Funds appropriated under titles III and IV of this Act may be made available, notwithstanding section 660 of the Foreign Assistance Act of 1961, for assistance to eliminate torture and other cruel, inhuman, or degrading treatment or punishment by foreign police, military or other security forces in countries receiving assistance from funds appropriated by this Act.

AIRCRAFT TRANSFER, COORDINATION, AND USE

SEC. 7039. (a) TRANSFER AUTHORITY.—Notwithstanding any other provision of law or regulation, aircraft, and equipment procured with funds appropriated by this Act and prior Acts making appropriations for the Department of State, foreign operations, and related programs under the headings "Diplomatic Programs", "International Narcotics Control and Law Enforcement", "Andean Counterdrug Initiative", and "Andean Counterdrug Programs" may be used for any other program and in any region: Provided, That such authority shall apply to equipment procured with funds appropriated under the heading "Pakistan Counterinsurgency Capability Fund" in prior Acts.

(b) AIRCRAFT COORDINATION.—

(1) AUTHORITY.—The uses of aircraft purchased or leased by the Department of State and the United States Agency for International Development with funds made available in this Act or prior Acts making appropriations for the Department of State, foreign operations, and related programs should be coordinated under the authority of the appropriate Chief of Mission: Provided, That such aircraft may be used to transport, on a reimbursable or non-reimbursable basis, Federal and non-Federal personnel supporting Department of State and USAID programs and activities: Provided further, That official travel for other agencies for other purposes may be supported on a reimbursable basis, or without reimbursement when traveling on a space available basis: Provided further, That funds received by the Department of State in connection with the use of aircraft owned, leased, or chartered by the Department of State may be credited to the Working Capital Fund of the Department and shall be available for expenses related to the purchase, lease, maintenance, chartering, or operation of such aircraft.

(2) SCOPE.—The requirement and authorities of this subsection shall only apply to aircraft, the primary purpose of which is the transportation of personnel.

(c) AIRCRAFT OPERATIONS AND MAINTENANCE.—To the maximum extent practicable, the costs of operations and maintenance, including fuel, of aircraft funded by this Act shall be borne by the recipient.

PARKING FINES AND REAL PROPERTY TAXES OWED BY FOREIGN GOVERNMENTS

SEC. 7040. The terms and conditions of section 7055 of the Department of State, Foreign Operations, and Related Programs Appropriations Act, 2010 (division F of Public Law 111–117) shall apply to this Act: Provided, That the date "September 30, 2009" in subsection (f)(2)(B) of such section shall be deemed to be "September 30, 2022".

INTERNATIONAL MONETARY FUND

SEC. 7041. (a) EXTENSIONS.—The terms and conditions of sections 7086(b) (1) and (2) and 7090(a) of the Department of State, Foreign Operations, and Related Programs Appropriations Act, 2010 (division F of Public Law 111–117) shall apply to this Act.

(b) REPAYMENT.—The Secretary of the Treasury shall instruct the United States Executive Director of the International Monetary Fund (IMF) to seek to ensure that any loan will be repaid to the IMF before other private or multilateral creditors.

EXTRADITION

SEC. 7042. (a) LIMITATION.—None of the funds appropriated in this Act may be used to provide assistance (other than funds provided under the headings "Development Assistance", "International Disaster Assistance", "Complex Crises Fund", "International Narcotics Control and Law Enforcement", "Migration and Refugee Assistance", "United States Emergency Refugee and Migration Assistance Fund", and "Nonproliferation, Anti-terrorism, Demining and Related Assistance") for the central government of a country which has notified the Department of State of its refusal to extradite to the United States any individual indicted for a criminal offense for which the maximum penalty is life imprisonment without the possibility of parole or for killing a law enforcement officer, as specified in a United States extradition request.

(b) CLARIFICATION.—Subsection (a) shall only apply to the central government of a country with which the United States maintains diplomatic relations and with which the United States has an extradition treaty and the government of that country is in violation of the terms and conditions of the treaty.

(c) WAIVER.—The Secretary of State may waive the restriction in subsection (a) on a case-by-case basis if the Secretary certifies to the Committees on Appropriations that such waiver is important to the national interest of the United States.

IMPACT ON JOBS IN THE UNITED STATES

SEC. 7043. None of the funds appropriated or otherwise made available under titles III through VI of this Act may be obligated or expended to provide—

(1) any financial incentive to a business enterprise currently located in the United States for the purpose of inducing such an enterprise to relocate outside the United States if such incentive or inducement is likely to reduce the number of employees of such business enterprise in the United States because United States production is being replaced by such enterprise outside the United States;

(2) assistance for any program, project, or activity that contributes to the violation of internationally recognized workers' rights, as defined in section 507(4) of the Trade Act of 1974, of workers in the recipient country, including any designated zone or area in that country: Provided, That the application of section 507(4)(D) and (E) of such Act (19 U.S.C. 2467(4)(D) and (E)) should be commensurate with the level of development of the recipient country and sector, and shall not preclude assistance for the informal sector in such country, micro and small-scale enterprise, and smallholder agriculture; or

(3) any assistance to an entity outside the United States if such assistance is for the purpose of directly relocating or transferring jobs from the United States to other countries and adversely impacts the labor force in the United States.

GLOBAL HEALTH ACTIVITIES

SEC. 7044. (a) IN GENERAL.—Funds appropriated by titles III and IV of this Act that are made available for global health programs including activities relating to research on, and the prevention, treatment and control of, HIV/AIDS may be made available notwithstanding any other provision of law except for provisions under the heading "Global Health Programs" and the United States Leadership Against HIV/AIDS, Tuberculosis, and Malaria Act of 2003 (117 Stat. 711; 22 U.S.C. 7601 et seq.), as amended: Provided, That of the funds appropriated under "Global Health Programs" under title III of this Act, not less than $572,000,000 may be made available for family planning/reproductive health, including in areas where population growth threatens biodiversity or endangered species.

(b) INFECTIOUS DISEASE OUTBREAKS.—

(1) EXTRAORDINARY MEASURES.—If the Secretary of State determines and reports to the Committees on Appropriations that an international infectious disease outbreak is sustained, severe, and is spreading internationally, or that it is in the national interest to respond to a Public Health Emergency of International Concern, funds appropriated by this Act under the headings "Global Health Programs", "Development Assistance", "International Disaster Assistance", "Complex Crises Fund", "Economic Support Fund", "Democracy Fund", "Assistance for Europe, Eurasia and Central Asia", "Migration and Refugee Assistance", and "Millennium Challenge Corporation" may be made available to combat such infectious disease or public health emergency, and may be transferred to, and merged with, funds appropriated under such headings for the purposes of this paragraph.

(2) EMERGENCY RESERVE FUND.—Funds made available under the heading "Global Health Programs" may be made available for the Emergency Reserve Fund established pursuant to section 7058(c)(1) of the Department of State, Foreign Operations, and Related Programs Appropriations Act, 2017 (division J of Public Law 115–31): Provided, That such funds shall be made available under the same terms and conditions of such section.

GENDER EQUALITY

SEC. 7045. (a) WOMEN'S EMPOWERMENT.—

(1) GENDER EQUALITY.—Funds appropriated by this Act may be made available notwithstanding any other provision of law to promote gender equality including by such activities as raising the status, increasing the economic participation, increasing opportunity for leadership positions, increasing the role in peace and security, and protecting the rights of women and girls worldwide.

(2) WOMEN'S ECONOMIC EMPOWERMENT.—Funds appropriated by this Act may be made available to implement the Women's Entrepreneurship and Economic Empowerment Act of 2018 (Public Law 115–428).

(3) GENDER EQUITY AND EQUALITY ACTION FUND.—Funds appropriated under title III of this Act may be made available for the Gender Equity and Equality Action Fund.

(b) WOMEN'S LEADERSHIP.—Funds appropriated by this Act may be made available for programs specifically designed to increase leadership opportunities for women in countries where women and girls suffer discrimination due to law, policy, or practice, by strengthening protections for women's political status, expanding women's participation in political parties and elections, and increasing women's opportunities for leadership positions in the public and private sectors at the local, provincial, and national levels.

(c) GENDER-BASED VIOLENCE.—

(1) Funds appropriated under titles III and IV of this Act should be made available to implement a multi-year strategy to prevent and respond to gender-based violence in countries where it is common in conflict and non-conflict settings.

(2) Funds appropriated under titles III and IV of this Act that are available to train foreign police, judicial, and military personnel, including for international peacekeeping operations, may address, where appropriate, prevention and response to gender-based violence and trafficking in persons, and may promote the integration of women into the police and other security forces.

(d) WOMEN, PEACE, AND SECURITY.—Funds appropriated by this Act under the headings "Development Assistance", "Economic Support Fund", "Assistance for Europe, Eurasia and Central Asia", and "International Narcotics Control and Law Enforcement", should be made available to support a multi-year strategy to expand, and improve coordination of, United States Government efforts to empower women as equal partners in conflict prevention, peace building, transitional processes, and reconstruction efforts in countries affected by conflict or in political transition, and to ensure the equitable provision of relief and recovery assistance to women and girls.

(e) WOMEN AND GIRLS AT RISK FROM EXTREMISM AND CONFLICT.—Funds appropriated by this Act under the heading "Economic Support Fund" should be made available to support women and girls who are at risk from extremism and conflict, and for the activities described in section 7059(e)(1) of the Department of State, Foreign Operations, and Related Programs Appropriations Act, 2018 (division K of Public Law 115–141).

SECTOR ALLOCATIONS

SEC. 7046. (a) BASIC EDUCATION AND HIGHER EDUCATION.—

(1) BASIC EDUCATION.—Funds appropriated under title III of this Act may be made available for assistance for Nita M. Lowey Basic Education Fund notwithstanding any other provision of law: Provided, That if the USAID Administrator determines that any unobligated balances of funds specifically designated for assistance for basic education in prior Acts making appropriations for the Department of State, foreign operations, and related programs are in excess of the absorptive capacity of recipient countries, such funds may be made available for other programs authorized under chapter 1 of part I of the Foreign Assistance Act of 1961, notwithstanding such funding designation.

(2) HIGHER EDUCATION.—Funds appropriated by title III of this Act may be made available for assistance for higher education notwithstanding any other provision of law.

(b) ENVIRONMENT PROGRAMS.—

(1)

(A) Funds appropriated by this Act to carry out the provisions of sections 103 through 106, and chapter 4 of part II, of the Foreign Assistance Act of 1961 may be used, notwithstanding any other provision of law, to support environment programs.

(B) Funds provided by this Act may be made available for United States contribution to multilateral environmental funds and facilities to support adaptation and mitigation programs.

(c) FOOD SECURITY AND AGRICULTURAL DEVELOPMENT.—Funds appropriated by this Act may be made available for food security and agricultural development programs notwithstanding any other provision of law, and for a contribution as authorized by section 3202 of the Food, Conservation, and Energy Act of 2008 (Public Law 110–246), as amended by section 3310 of the Agriculture Improvement Act of 2018 (Public Law 115–334).

(d) RECONCILIATION PROGRAMS.—Funds appropriated by this Act may be made available to support people-to-people reconciliation programs which bring together individuals of different ethnic, religious, and political backgrounds from areas of civil strife and war notwithstanding any other provision of law.

DEPARTMENT OF STATE MANAGEMENT

SEC. 7047. (a) WORKING CAPITAL FUND.—Funds appropriated by this Act or otherwise made available to the Department of State for payments to the Working Capital Fund may be used for service centers not included in the Congressional Budget Justification, Department of State, Foreign Operations, and Related Programs, Fiscal Year 2023 subject to the regular notification procedures of the Committees on Appropriations.

(b) CERTIFICATION.—

(1) COMPLIANCE.—Not later than 45 days after the initial obligation of funds appropriated under titles III and IV of this Act that are made available to a Department of State bureau or office with responsibility for the management and oversight of such funds, the Secretary of State shall certify and report to the Committees on Appropriations, on an individual bureau or office basis, that such bureau or office is in compliance with Department and Federal financial and grants management policies, procedures, and regulations, as applicable.

(2) CONSIDERATIONS.—When making a certification required by paragraph (1), the Secretary of State shall consider the capacity of a bureau or office to—

(A) account for the obligated funds at the country and program level, as appropriate;

(B) identify risks and develop mitigation and monitoring plans;

(C) establish performance measures and indicators;

(D) review activities and performance; and

(E) assess final results and reconcile finances.

(3) PLAN.—If the Secretary of State is unable to make a certification required by paragraph (1), the Secretary shall submit a plan and timeline detailing the steps to be taken to bring such bureau or office into compliance.

UNITED STATES AGENCY FOR INTERNATIONAL DEVELOPMENT MANAGEMENT

SEC. 7048. (a) AUTHORITY.—Up to $125,000,000 of the funds made available in title III of this Act pursuant to or to carry out the provisions of part I of the Foreign Assistance Act of 1961, including funds appropriated under the heading "Assistance for Europe, Eurasia and Central Asia", may be used by the United States Agency for International Development to hire and employ individuals in the United States and overseas on a limited appointment basis pursuant to the authority of sections 308 and 309 of the Foreign Service Act of 1980 (22 U.S.C. 3948 and 3949).

(b) RESTRICTION.—The authority to hire individuals contained in subsection (a) shall expire on September 30, 2024.

(c) PROGRAM ACCOUNT CHARGED.—The account charged for the cost of an individual hired and employed under the authority of this section shall be the account to which the responsibilities of such individual primarily relate: Provided, That funds made available to carry out this section may be transferred to, and merged with, funds appropriated by this Act in title II under the heading "Operating Expenses".

(d) FOREIGN SERVICE LIMITED EXTENSIONS.—Individuals hired and employed by USAID, with funds made available in this Act or prior Acts making appropriations for the Department of State, foreign operations, and related programs, pursuant to the authority of section 309 of the Foreign Service Act of 1980 (22 U.S.C. 3949), may be extended for a period of up to 4 years notwithstanding the limitation set forth in such section.

(e) DISASTER SURGE CAPACITY.—Funds appropriated under title III of this Act to carry out part I of the Foreign Assistance Act of 1961, including funds appropriated under the heading "Assistance for Europe, Eurasia and Central Asia", may be used, in addition to funds otherwise available for such purposes, for the cost (including the support costs) of individuals detailed to or employed by USAID whose primary responsibility is to carry out programs in response to natural disasters, or man-made disasters .

(f) PERSONAL SERVICES CONTRACTORS.—Funds appropriated by this Act to carry out chapter 1 of part I, chapter 4 of part II, and section 667 of the Foreign Assistance Act of 1961, and title II of the Food for Peace Act (Public Law 83–480; 7 U.S.C. 1721 et seq.), may be used by USAID to employ up to 40 personal services contractors in the United States, notwithstanding any other provision of law, for the purpose of providing direct, interim support for new or expanded overseas programs and activities managed by the agency until permanent direct hire personnel are hired and trained: Provided, That not more than 15 of such contractors shall be assigned to any bureau or office: Provided further, That such funds appropriated to carry out title II of the Food for Peace Act (Public Law 83–480; 7 U.S.C. 1721 et seq.), may be made available only for personal services contractors assigned to the Bureau for Humanitarian Assistance.

(g) SMALL BUSINESS.—In entering into multiple award indefinite-quantity contracts with funds appropriated by this Act, USAID may provide an exception to the fair opportunity process for placing task orders under such contracts when the order is placed with any category of small or small disadvantaged business.

(h) SENIOR FOREIGN SERVICE LIMITED APPOINTMENTS.—Individuals hired pursuant to the authority provided by section 7059(o) of the Department of State, Foreign Operations, and Related Programs Appropriations Act, 2010 (division F of Public Law 111–117) may be assigned to or support programs in Afghanistan or Pakistan with funds made available in this Act and prior Acts making appropriations for the Department of State, foreign operations, and related programs.

(i) CRISIS OPERATIONS STAFFING.—Up to $86,000,000 of the funds made available in title III of this Act pursuant to or to carry out the provisions of part I of the Foreign Assistance Act of 1961 and section 509(b) of the Global Fragility Act of 2019 (title V of division J of Public Law 116–94) may be made available for the United States Agency for International Development to appoint and employ personnel in the Excepted Service to perform functions related to the purpose for which the funds were appropriated: Provided, That such funds shall be available in addition to funds otherwise made available for such purposes and may remain attributed to any minimum funding requirement for which they were originally made available: Provided further, That USAID shall coordinate with OPM on implementation of this provision.

STABILIZATION AND DEVELOPMENT IN REGIONS IMPACTED BY EXTREMISM AND CONFLICT

SEC. 7049. (a) PREVENTION AND STABILIZATION FUND.—

FUNDS AND TRANSFER AUTHORITY.—Funds appropriated by this Act under the headings "Economic Support Fund", "International Narcotics Control and Law Enforcement", "Nonproliferation, Anti-terrorism, Demining and Related Programs", "Peacekeeping Operations", and "Foreign Military Financing Program", may be made available for the purposes of the Prevention and Stabilization Fund, as authorized by, and for the purposes enumerated in, section 509(a) of the Global Fragility Act of 2019 (title V of division J of Public Law 116–94): Provided, That such funds appropriated under such headings may be transferred to, and merged with, funds appropriated under such headings: Provided further, That such transfer authority is in addition to any other transfer authority provided by this Act or any other Act.

(b) GLOBAL FRAGILITY ACT IMPLEMENTATION.—Funds appropriated by this Act may be made available to implement the Global Fragility Act of 2019 (title V of division J of Public Law 116–94).

(c) GLOBAL COMMUNITY ENGAGEMENT AND RESILIENCE FUND.—Funds appropriated by this Act and prior Acts making appropriations for the Department of State, foreign operations, and related programs under the heading "Economic Support Fund" may be made available to the Global Community Engagement and Resilience Fund (GCERF), including as a contribution.

DISABILITY PROGRAMS

SEC. 7050. (a) ASSISTANCE.—Funds appropriated by this Act under the heading "Development Assistance" may be made available for programs and activities administered by the United States Agency for International Development to address the needs and protect and promote the rights of people with disabilities in developing countries, including initiatives that focus on independent living, economic self-sufficiency, advocacy, education, employment, transportation, sports, political and electoral participation, and integration of individuals with disabilities, including for the cost of translation.

(b) MANAGEMENT, OVERSIGHT, AND TECHNICAL SUPPORT.—Of the funds made available pursuant to this section, 5 percent may be used by USAID for management, oversight, and technical support.

DEBT-FOR-DEVELOPMENT

SEC. 7051. *In order to enhance the continued participation of nongovernmental organizations in economic assistance activities under the Foreign Assistance Act of 1961, including endowments, debt-for-development and debt-for-nature exchanges, a nongovernmental organization which is a grantee or contractor of the United States Agency for International Development may place in interest bearing accounts funds made available under this Act or prior Acts or local currencies which accrue to that organization as a result of economic assistance provided under title III of this Act and, subject to the regular notification procedures of the Committees on Appropriations, any interest earned on such investment shall be used for the purpose for which the assistance was provided to that organization.*

EXTENSION OF CONSULAR FEES AND RELATED AUTHORITIES

SEC. 7052. *(a) Section 1(b)(1) of the Passport Act of June 4, 1920 (22 U.S.C. 214(b)(1)) shall be applied through fiscal year 2023 by substituting "the costs of providing consular services" for "such costs".*

(b) Section 21009 of the Emergency Appropriations for Coronavirus Health Response and Agency Operations (division B of Public Law 116–136; 134 Stat. 592) shall be applied during fiscal year 2023 by substituting "2020, 2021, 2022, and 2023" for "2020 and 2021".

(c) Discretionary amounts made available to the Department of State under the heading "Administration of Foreign Affairs" of this Act, and discretionary unobligated balances under such heading from prior Acts making appropriations for the Department of State, foreign operations, and related programs including balances that were previously designated by the Congress for Overseas Contingency Operations/Global War on Terrorism pursuant to section 251(b)(2)(A)(ii) of the Balanced Budget and Emergency Deficit Control Act of 1985, may be transferred to the Consular and Border Security Programs account if the Secretary of State determines and reports to the Committees on Appropriations that to do so is necessary to sustain consular operations: Provided, That such transfer authority is in addition to any transfer authority otherwise available in this Act and under any other provision of law.

(d) In addition to the uses permitted pursuant to section 286(v)(2)(A) of the Immigration and Nationality Act (8 U.S.C. 1356(v)(2)(A)), for fiscal year 2023, the Secretary of State may also use fees deposited into the Fraud Prevention and Detection Account for the costs of providing consular services.

PROTECTIVE SERVICES

SEC. 7053. *Of the funds appropriated under the heading "Diplomatic Programs" by this Act and prior Acts making appropriations for the Department of State, foreign operations, and related programs, except for funds designated by the Congress as an emergency requirement pursuant to a concurrent resolution on the budget or the Balanced Budget and Emergency Deficit Control Act of 1985, up to $30,000,000 may be made available to provide protective services to former or retired senior Department of State officials or employees that the Secretary of State, in consultation with the Director of National Intelligence, determines and reports to congressional leadership and the appropriate congressional committees, face a serious and credible threat from a foreign power or the agent of a foreign power arising from duties performed by such official or employee while employed by the Department: Provided, That such determination shall include a justification for the provision of protective services by the Department, including the identification of the specific nature of the threat and the anticipated duration of such services provided, which may be submitted in classified form, if necessary: Provided further, That such protective services shall be consistent with other such services performed by the Bureau of Diplomatic Security under 22 U.S.C. 2709 for Department officials, and shall be made available for an initial period of not more than 180 days, which may be extended for additional consecutive periods of 90 days upon a subsequent determination by the Secretary that the specific threat persists: Provided further, That not later than 45 days after enactment of this Act and quarterly thereafter, the Secretary shall submit a report to congressional leadership and the appropriate congressional committees detailing the number of individuals receiving protective services and the amount of funds expended for such services on a case-by-case basis, which may be submitted in classified form, if necessary: Provided further, That for purposes of this section a former or retired senior Department of State official or employee means a person that served in the Department at the Assistant Secretary, Special Representative, or Senior Advisor level, or in a comparable or more senior position, and has separated from service at the Department: Provided further, That funds made available pursuant to this section are in addition to amounts otherwise made available for such purposes: Provided further, That the Department of State is authorized to make more than $30,000,000 available to provide protective services pursuant to this section, subject to the regular notification procedures of the Committees on Appropriations.*

AUTHORITY TO ISSUE ADMINISTRATIVE SUBPOENAS

SEC. 7054. *The Secretary of State may use on the authority in section 3486(a)(1)(A)(iii) of title 18, United States Code, in relevant part, and this authority shall be available also for investigations of offenses under section 878 of title 18, United States Code, or a threat against a person, foreign mission or international organization authorized to receive protection by special agents of the Department of State and the Foreign Service or an offense under chapter 75 of title 18, United States Code: Provided, That when exercising such authority, imminence of threat, if applicable, shall be determined by the Director of the Diplomatic Security Service.*

CONSULAR NOTIFICATION COMPLIANCE

SEC. 7055. *(a)* PETITION FOR REVIEW.—

(1) JURISDICTION.—*Notwithstanding any other provision of law, a Federal court shall have jurisdiction to review the merits of a petition claiming violation of Article 36(1)(b) or (c) of the Vienna Convention on Consular Relations, done at Vienna April 24, 1963, or a comparable provision of a bilateral international agreement addressing consular notification and access, filed by an individual convicted and sentenced to death by any Federal or State court before the date of enactment of this Act.*

(2) STANDARD.—*To obtain relief, an individual described in paragraph (1) must make a showing of actual prejudice to the criminal conviction or sentence as a result of the violation: Provided, That the court may conduct an evidentiary hearing if necessary to supplement the record and, upon a finding of actual prejudice, shall order a new trial or sentencing proceeding.*

(3) LIMITATIONS.—

(A) INITIAL SHOWING.—*To qualify for review under this subsection, a petition must make an initial showing that*

(i) a violation of Article 36(1)(b) or (c) of the Vienna Convention on Consular Relations, done at Vienna April 24, 1963, or a comparable provision of a bilateral international agreement addressing consular notification and access, occurred with respect to the individual described in paragraph (1); and

(ii) if such violation had not occurred, the consulate would have provided assistance to the individual.

(B) EFFECT OF PRIOR ADJUDICATION.—*A petition for review under this subsection shall not be granted if the claimed violation described in paragraph (1) has previously been adjudicated on the merits by a Federal or State court of competent jurisdiction in a proceeding in which no Federal or State procedural bars were raised with respect to such violation and in which the court provided review equivalent to the review provided in this subsection, unless the adjudication of the claim resulted in a decision that was based on an unreasonable determination of the facts in light of the evidence presented in the prior Federal or State court proceeding.*

(C) FILING DEADLINE.—*A petition for review under this subsection shall be filed within 1 year of the later of*

(i) the date of enactment of this Act;

(ii) the date on which the Federal or State court judgment against the individual described in paragraph (1) became final by the conclusion of direct review or the expiration of the time for seeking such review; or

(iii) the date on which the impediment to filing a petition created by Federal or State action in violation of the Constitution or laws of the United States is removed, if the individual described in paragraph (1) was prevented from filing by such Federal or State action.

(D) TOLLING.—*The time during which a properly filed application for State post-conviction or other collateral review with respect to the pertinent judgment or claim is pending shall not be counted toward the 1-year period of limitation.*

(E) TIME LIMIT FOR REVIEW.—*A Federal court shall give priority to a petition for review filed under this subsection over all noncapital matters: Provided, That with respect to a petition for review filed under this subsection and claiming only a violation described in paragraph (1), a Federal court shall render a final determination and enter a final judgment not later than one year after the date on which the petition is filed.*

(4) HABEAS PETITION.—*A petition for review under this subsection shall be part of the first Federal habeas corpus application or motion for Federal collateral relief under chapter 153 of title 28, United States Code, filed by an individual, except that if an individual filed a Federal habeas corpus application or motion for Federal collateral relief before the date of enactment of this Act or if such application is required to be filed before the date that is 1 year after the date of enactment of this Act, such petition for review under this subsection shall be filed not later than 1 year after the enactment date or within the period prescribed by paragraph (3)(C)(iii), whichever is later: Provided, That no petition filed in conformity with the requirements of the preceding sentence shall be considered a second or successive habeas corpus application or subjected to*

any bars to relief based on preenactment proceedings other than as specified in paragraph (2).

(5) REFERRAL TO MAGISTRATE.—A Federal court acting under this subsection may refer the petition for review to a Federal magistrate for proposed findings and recommendations pursuant to 28 U.S.C. 636(b)(1)(B).

(6) APPEAL.—

(A) IN GENERAL.—A final order on a petition for review under paragraph (1) shall be subject to review on appeal by the court of appeals for the circuit in which the proceeding is held.

(B) APPEAL BY PETITIONER.—An individual described in paragraph (1) may appeal a final order on a petition for review under paragraph (1) only if a district or circuit judge issues a certificate of appealability: Provided, That a district or circuit court judge shall issue or deny a certificate of appealability not later than 30 days after an application for a certificate of appealability is filed: Provided further, That a district judge or circuit judge may issue a certificate of appealability under this subparagraph if the individual has made a substantial showing of actual prejudice to the criminal conviction or sentence of the individual as a result of a violation described in paragraph (1).

(b) VIOLATION.—

(1) IN GENERAL.—An individual not covered by subsection (a) who is arrested, detained, or held for trial on a charge that would expose the individual to a capital sentence if convicted may raise a claim of a violation of Article 36(1)(b) or (c) of the Vienna Convention on Consular Relations, done at Vienna April 24, 1963, or of a comparable provision of a bilateral international agreement addressing consular notification and access, at a reasonable time after the individual becomes aware of the violation, before the court with jurisdiction over the charge: Provided, That, upon a finding of such a violation (A) the consulate of the foreign state of which the individual is a national shall be notified immediately by the detaining authority, and consular access to the individual shall be afforded in accordance with the provisions of the Vienna Convention on Consular Relations, done at Vienna April 24, 1963, or the comparable provisions of a bilateral international agreement addressing consular notification and access; and (B) the court (i) shall postpone any proceedings to the extent the court determines necessary to allow for adequate opportunity for consular access and assistance; and (ii) may enter necessary orders to facilitate consular access and assistance.

(2) EVIDENTIARY HEARINGS.—The court may conduct evidentiary hearings if necessary to resolve factual issues.

(3) RULE OF CONSTRUCTION.—Nothing in this subsection shall be construed to create any additional remedy.

(c) DEFINITIONS.—In this section the term "State" means any State of the United States, the District of Columbia, the Commonwealth of Puerto Rico, and any territory or possession of the United States.

(d) APPLICABILITY.—The provisions of this section shall apply during the current fiscal year.

ACQUISITION AND ASSISTANCE WORKING CAPITAL FUND

SEC. 7056. (a) The Administrator of the United States Agency for International Development (the Administrator) is authorized to establish a Working Capital Fund (in this section referred to as the "Fund").

(b) Funds deposited in the Fund in this and subsequent fiscal years shall be available without fiscal year limitation and used, in addition to other funds available for such purposes, for administrative costs resulting from agency acquisition and assistance operations, the administration of this Fund, and administrative contingencies designated by the Administrator: Provided, That such expenses may include (1) personnel and nonpersonnel services; (2) training; (3) supplies; and (4) other administrative costs related to acquisition and assistance operations.

(c) There may be deposited during any fiscal year in the Fund up to 1 percent of the total value of obligations entered into by the United States Agency for International Development (USAID) from appropriations available in this Act or subsequent appropriations Acts to USAID and any appropriation made available in this Act or subsequent appropriations Acts for the purpose of providing capital: Provided, That receipts from the disposal of, or repayments for the loss or damage to, property held in the Fund, rebates, reimbursements, refunds and other credits applicable to the operation of the Fund may be deposited into the Fund.

(d) At the close of each fiscal year the Administrator shall transfer to the general fund of the Treasury amounts in excess of $100,000,000, and such other amounts as the Administrator determines to be in excess of the needs of the Fund.

INFORMATION TECHNOLOGY WORKING CAPITAL FUND

SEC. 7057. Up to 5 percent or $30,000,000, whichever is less, of funds appropriated by this Act under each of the headings "Operating Expenses", "Global Health Programs", "Economic Support Fund", "Development Assistance", "Assistance for Europe, Eurasia and Central Asia" and "International Disaster Assistance", may be transferred to the USAID Information Technology Working Capital Fund (IT WCF) established pursuant to the Modernizing Government Technology (MGT) Act: Provided, That funds transferred to the IT WCF shall remain available for three fiscal years for the purposes described in such Act.

U.S. PARTICIPATION IN INTERNATIONAL FAIRS AND EXPOSITIONS

SEC. 7058. Notwithstanding section 204 of the Admiral James W. Nance and Meg Donovan Foreign Relations Authorization Act, Fiscal Years 2000 and 2001 (22 U.S.C. 2452b), amounts available under title I of this Act or prior Acts may be made available for United States participation in international fairs and expositions abroad, including for construction and operation of United States pavilions or other major exhibits.

REPEAL OF HELMS AMENDMENT CONCERNING DIPLOMATIC FACILITIES

SEC. 7059. Section 305 of Public Law 100–459 is repealed.

REPORT REFORM

SEC. 7060. Notwithstanding any other provision of law, any provision of law enacted before or after the date of enactment of this section that requires submission of a report to Congress or its committees at regular periodic intervals (including annually, semi-annually, biennially, quarterly or after other stated periods) pertaining to matters within the purview of, or prepared primarily by, the Department of State shall cease to be effective three years after the date of enactment of the provision of law requiring such report and after the Secretary has identified and included in a notification to Congress any such provision of law requiring the report and a statement that the reporting requirement is terminated under this sunset legislative provision.

DEFENSE TRADE CONTROLS REGISTRATION FEES

SEC. 7061. Section 45 of the State Department Basic Authorities Act of 1956 (22 U.S.C. 2717) is amended as follows:

(a) in the first sentence, by inserting "defense trade control" after "100 percent of the"; striking "the Office of Defense Trade Controls of"; and inserting after "incurred for" the following: "management, licensing, compliance, and policy activities in the defense trade controls function, including";

(b) in subpart (1), by striking "contract personnel to assist in";

(c) in subpart (2), by striking the "and" after "computer equipment and related software;";

(d) in subpart (3), by striking the period "." after "defense trade export controls" and inserting a ";";

(e) by adding a new subpart (4) to read as follows: "the facilitation of defense trade policy development and implementation, review of commodity jurisdiction determinations, public outreach to industry and foreign parties, and analysis of scientific and technological developments as they relate to the exercise of defense trade control authorities; and"; and

(f) by adding a new subpart (5) to read as follows: "(5) contract personnel to assist in such activities."

CONSULAR AND BORDER SECURITY PROGRAMS VISA SERVICES COST RECOVERY PROPOSAL

SEC. 7062. Section 103 of Public Law 107–173 (8 U.S.C. 1713) is amended as follows:

(a) in subsection (b), inserting "or surcharge" after "machine-readable visa fee";

(b) inserting at the end of subsection (b): "The amount of the machine-readable visa fee or surcharge may also account for the cost of other consular services not otherwise subject to a fee or surcharge retained by the Department of State."; and

(c) in subsection (d), inserting "or surcharges" after "amounts collected as fees".

CONSULAR AND BORDER SECURITY PROGRAMS

SEC. 7063. (a) BORDER CROSSING CARD FEE FOR MINORS.—Section 410(a)(1)(A) of the Department of State and Related Agencies Appropriations Act, 1999 (title IV of Public Law 105–277) is amended by striking "a fee of $13" and inserting "a fee equal to one half the fee that would otherwise apply for processing a machine readable combined border crossing identification card and non-immigrant visa".

(b) PASSPORT AND IMMIGRANT VISA SECURITY SURCHARGES.—

(1) The fourth paragraph under the heading "Diplomatic and Consular Programs" in title IV of division B of Public Law 108–447 (8 U.S.C. 1714) is amended by inserting "and the consular protection of U.S. citizens and their interests overseas" after "in support of enhanced border security";

(2) Section 6 of Public Law 109–472 (8 U.S.C. 1714 note) is amended by inserting "and the consular protection of U.S. citizens and their interests overseas" after "in support of enhanced border security" each place it appears.

INTERNSHIPS

SEC. 7066. The Department of State may offer compensated internships, and select, appoint, employ individuals for not more than 52 weeks, under an excepted service, and remove any such compensated intern without regard to the provisions of law governing appointments in the excepted service, notwithstanding any other provision of law: Provided, That the Department shall consult with OPM on implementation of this authority, including on the number of individuals to be hired annually hereunder.

DIPLOMATIC RECEPTION ROOMS

SEC. 7067. *The Secretary of State is authorized to sell goods and services and to use the proceeds of such sales for administration and related support of the reception area consistent with section 41(a) of the State Department Basic Authorities Act of 1956 (22 U.S.C. 2713(a)): Provided, That amounts collected pursuant to this authority may be deposited into an account in the Treasury, to remain available until expended.*

ASIAN DEVELOPMENT FUND TWELFTH REPLENISHMENT

SEC. 7068. *The Asian Development Bank Act, Public Law 89–369, as amended, (22 U.S.C 285 et seq.), is further amended by adding at the end thereof the following new section: "Sec. 37. Twelfth replenishment.*

(a) The United States Governor of the Bank is authorized to contribute, on behalf of the United States, $177,440,000 to the twelfth replenishment of the resources of the Fund, subject to obtaining the necessary appropriations.

(b) In order to pay for the United States contribution provided for in subsection (a), there are authorized to be appropriated, without fiscal year limitation, $177,440,000 for payment by the Secretary of the Treasury."

EXEMPTION OF THE INTERNATIONAL DEVELOPMENT ASSOCIATION SECURITIES FROM SECURITIES AND EXCHANGE COMMISSION (SEC) REGULATION

SEC. 7069. *(a) EXEMPTION FROM SECURITIES LAWS; REPORTS TO SECURITIES AND EXCHANGE COMMISSION—Any securities issued by the Association (including any guaranty by the Association, whether or not limited in scope) and any securities guaranteed by the Association as to both principal and interest shall be deemed to be exempted securities within the meaning of section 3(a)(2) of the Securities Act of 1933 (15 U.S.C. 77c(a)(2)) and section 3(a)(12) of the Securities Exchange Act of 1934 (15 U.S.C. 78c(a)(12)): Provided, That the Association shall file with the Securities and Exchange Commission such annual and other reports with regard to such securities as the Commission shall determine to be appropriate in view of the special character of the Association and its operations and necessary in the public interest or for the protection of investors.*

(b) AUTHORITY OF SECURITIES AND EXCHANGE COMMISSION TO SUSPEND EXEMPTION; REPORTS TO CONGRESS—The Securities and Exchange Commission, acting in consultation with the National Advisory Council on International Monetary and Financial Policies, is authorized to suspend the provisions of subsection (a) of this section at any time as to any or all securities issued or guaranteed by the Association during the period of such suspension: Provided, That the Commission shall include in its annual reports to the Congress such information as it shall deem advisable with regard to the operations and effect of this section.

EXPORT-IMPORT BANK DEFAULT RATES AND LENDING CAP FREEZE

SEC. 7070. *(a) Section 6(a)(3) of the Export-Import Bank Act of 1945 (12 U.S.C. 635e(a)(3)) shall be applied through September 30, 2023, by substituting "4 percent" for "2 percent" in each place it appears.*

(b) Section 8(g) of the Export-Import Bank Act of 1945 (12 U.S.C. 635g(g)) shall be applied through September 30, 2023, by substituting "4 percent" for "2 percent" in each place it appears.

GLOBAL ENGAGEMENT CENTER

SEC. 7071. *Section 1287(j) of the National Defense Authorization Act for Fiscal Year 2017 (22 U.S.C. 2656 note) is amended by striking "the date that is 8 years after the date of the enactment of this Act" and inserting "December 31, 2027".*

FOREIGN ASSISTANCE ACT 506(A) DRAWDOWN AUTHORITY

SEC. 7072. *For fiscal year 2023, section 506 of the Foreign Assistance Act of 1961 (22 U.S.C. 2318) shall be applied (1) in subsection (a)(1), by substituting $200,000,000 for $100,000,000; (2) in subsection (a)(2)(B), by substituting $400,000,000 for $200,000,000; and (3) in subsections (a)(2)(B)(i), by substituting $150,000,000 for $75,000,000.*

BUILD BACK BETTER WORLD

SEC. 7073. *Of the funds appropriated under title III of this Act, up to $350,000,000 may be made available for a Build Back Better World (B3W) Fund, notwithstanding any other provision of law, for assistance, including through contributions, to address climate, health and health security, digital connectivity, and gender equity, in addition to amounts otherwise made available for such purposes: Provided, That funds made available for the B3W Fund may be transferred to, and merged with, funds appropriated under title III of this Act: Provided further, That such funds which are specifically designated may be made available for the purposes of the B3W Fund notwithstanding the designation.*

MANAGEMENT OF INTERNATIONAL TRANSBOUNDARY WATER POLLUTION

SEC. 7074. *(a) DEFINITIONS.—In this section:*

(1) ADMINISTRATOR.—The term "Administrator" means the Administrator of the Environmental Protection Agency.

(2) COMMISSION.—The term "Commission" means the United States section of the International Boundary and Water Commission.

(3) COVERED FUNDS.—The term "covered funds" means amounts made available to the Administrator under the heading "Environmental Protection Agency-State and Tribal Assistance Grants" under title IX of the United States-Mexico Canada Agreement Implementation Act (Public Law 116–113) and any other relevant funds.

(4) TREATMENT WORKS.—The term "treatment works" has the meaning given that term in section 212 of the Federal Water Pollution Control Act (33 U.S.C. 1292).

(b) TRANSFER OF FUNDS.—The Administrator is authorized to transfer covered funds, by entering into an interagency agreement or by awarding a grant, to the Commission, with concurrence of the Commissioner, to support the construction of treatment works, which will be owned and operated by the Commission.

(c) USE OF FUNDS.—The Commission is authorized to use funds received under this section to plan, study, design, and construct treatment works and carry out any related activities, including construction management and payment for general and administrative overhead, that

(1) protect residents within the U.S.-Mexico border region from pollution resulting from

(A) transboundary flows of wastewater, stormwater or other international transboundary water flows originating in Mexico; and

(B) any inadequacies or breakdowns of treatment works in Mexico; and

(2) provide treatment of such flows in compliance with local, State, and Federal law.

(d) OPERATION AND MAINTENANCE.—The Commission shall operate and maintain new treatment works in accordance with future appropriations.

(e) CONSULTATION AND COORDINATION.—The Commission shall consult and coordinate with the Administrator in carrying out any project using funds received under this section.

(f) APPLICATION OF OTHER REQUIREMENTS.—The requirements of sections 513 and 608 of the Federal Water Pollution Control Act (33 U.S.C. 1372, 1388) shall apply to the construction of any treatment works in the United States for which the Commission receives funds under this section.

(g) SAVINGS PROVISION.—Nothing in this section shall be construed to modify, amend, repeal or otherwise limit the authority of the International Boundary and Water Commission in accordance with the treaty relating to the utilization of the waters of the Colorado and Tijuana Rivers and of the Rio Grande (Rio Bravo) from Fort Quitman, Texas, to the Gulf of Mexico, and supplementary protocol, signed at Washington February 3, 1944 (59 Stat. 1219), between the United States and Mexico.

FUNDING FOR COMPACTS WITH LOW-TO-MIDDLE INCOME COUNTRIES

SEC. 7075. *Section 606 of the Millennium Challenge Act of 2003 (22 U.S.C. 7705) is amended by striking subsection (b)(3).*

UPDATING MILLENNIUM CHALLENGE CORPORATION ANNUAL REPORT REQUIREMENTS

SEC. 7076. *Section 613 of the Millennium Challenge Act of 2003 (22 U.S.C. 7712) is amended by striking subsection (a); and inserting:*

"(a) Report. No later than the third Friday in December of each year, the Chief Executive Officer shall submit to Congress a report on the assistance provided under section 605 of this title during the prior fiscal year."

GENERAL PROVISIONS—THIS TITLE

[SEC. 2401. During fiscal years 2022 and 2023, notwithstanding any applicable restrictions on the ability of the Department of State and the United States Agency for International Development to enter into personal services contracts, including section 704 of the Financial Services and General Government Appropriations Act, 2021 (division E of Public Law 116–260) as continued by section 101 of division A of this Act (and any successor provision in a subsequently enacted appropriations Act), the authorities of section 2(c) of the State Department Basic Authorities Act of 1956 (22 U.S.C. 2669(c)), section 636(a)(3) of the Foreign Assistance Act of 1961 (22 U.S.C. 2396(a)(3)), and section 5(a)(6) of the Migration and Refugee Assistance Act of 1962 (22 U.S.C. 2605(a)(6)) may be exercised, without regard to the geographic limitations referenced therein, particularly to enter into, extend, and maintain contracts with individuals who have served as locally employed staff of the United States mission in Afghanistan.]

[SEC. 2402. The Secretary of State, in consultation with the Administrator of the United States Agency for International Development, shall submit to the Committees on Appropriations, not later than 45 days after the date of enactment of this Act, a report on the proposed uses of funds appropriated by this title under the headings "Emergencies in the Diplomatic and Consular Service" and "United States Emergency

Refugee and Migration Assistance Fund", by program, project, and activity, for which the obligation of funds is anticipated: *Provided*, That such report shall be updated (including any changes in proposed uses from the initial plan) and submitted to the Committees on Appropriations every 45 days until September 30, 2023.]

[SEC. 2403. Not later than 45 days after the date of enactment of this Act, the Secretary of State, in consultation with the Secretary of Homeland Security and the heads of other relevant Federal agencies, shall submit to the Committees on Appropriations a report on the status of the Priority 2 (P-2) designation granting United States Refugee Admissions Program (USRAP) access for certain at risk Afghan nationals and their eligible family members that was announced by the Department of State on August 2, 2021: *Provided*, That such report shall include the approximate number of Afghan nationals and their eligible family members who have been referred to the program, the number of Afghan nationals who have contacted a Resettlement Support Center to begin processing of their P-2 referral, the estimated time for processing such applications, an assessment of the obstacles facing P-2 eligible individuals seeking to leave Afghanistan, and a plan for augmenting personnel needed for refugee processing or humanitarian parole: *Provided further*, That such report shall be submitted in unclassified form, but may be accompanied by a classified annex.]

[SEC. 2404. None of the funds appropriated in this title and made available for assistance for Afghanistan may be made available for direct assistance to the Taliban.] *(Afghanistan Supplemental Appropriations Act, 2022.)*

[SEC. 1401. The Secretary of State shall include in the reports required by section 2402 of title IV of the Afghanistan Supplemental Appropriations Act, 2022 (division C of Public Law 117–43) the proposed uses of funds appropriated under this title.] *(Additional Afghanistan Supplemental Appropriations Act, 2022.)*

DEPARTMENT OF TRANSPORTATION

OFFICE OF THE SECRETARY

Federal Funds

GENERAL FUND PAYMENT TO NATIONAL SURFACE TRANSPORTATION AND INNOVATIVE FINANCE BUREAU HIGHWAY TRUST FUND ACCOUNT, UPWARD REESTIMATES

Program and Financing (in millions of dollars)

Identification code 069–0149–0–1–401	2021 actual	2022 est.	2023 est.
Obligations by program activity:			
0001 General Fund Payment to NSTIFB	380	206	
0900 Total new obligations, unexpired accounts (object class 43.0)	380	206	
Budgetary resources:			
Budget authority:			
Appropriations, mandatory:			
1200 Appropriation		380	206
1930 Total budgetary resources available		380	206
Change in obligated balance:			
Unpaid obligations:			
3010 New obligations, unexpired accounts		380	206
3020 Outlays (gross)		–380	–206
Budget authority and outlays, net:			
Mandatory:			
4090 Budget authority, gross		380	206
Outlays, gross:			
4100 Outlays from new mandatory authority		380	206
4180 Budget authority, net (total)		380	206
4190 Outlays, net (total)		380	206

RESEARCH AND TECHNOLOGY

For necessary expenses related to the Office of the Assistant Secretary for Research and Technology, $48,147,000, of which $33,718,000 shall remain available until expended: Provided, That there may be credited to this appropriation, to be available until expended, funds received from States, counties, municipalities, other public authorities, and private sources for expenses incurred for training: Provided further, That any reference in law, regulation, judicial proceedings, or elsewhere to the Research and Innovative Technology Administration shall continue to be deemed to be a reference to the Office of the Assistant Secretary for Research and Technology of the Department of Transportation.

Note.—A full-year 2022 appropriation for this account was not enacted at the time the Budget was prepared; therefore, the Budget assumes this account is operating under the Continuing Appropriations Act, 2022 (Division A of Public Law 117–43, as amended). The amounts included for 2022 reflect the annualized level provided by the continuing resolution.

Program and Financing (in millions of dollars)

Identification code 069–1730–0–1–407	2021 actual	2022 est.	2023 est.
Obligations by program activity:			
0001 Salaries and administrative expenses	6	9	14
0002 Highly Automated Systems Safety Center of Excellence		5	5
0003 Research development & technology coordination	9	15	26
0004 Advanced Research Projects - Infrastructure			3
0007 Transportation Safety Institute	10	15	15
0100 Direct program by activities, subtotal	25	44	63
0799 Total direct obligations	25	44	63
0802 Transportation Safety Institute	2	5	5
0809 Reimbursable program activities, subtotal	2	5	5
0900 Total new obligations, unexpired accounts	27	49	68
Budgetary resources:			
Unobligated balance:			
1000 Unobligated balance brought forward, Oct 1	20	29	23
Budget authority:			
Appropriations, discretionary:			
1100 Appropriation	23	23	48
Spending authority from offsetting collections, discretionary:			
1700 Collected	13	20	20
1900 Budget authority (total)	36	43	68
1930 Total budgetary resources available	56	72	91
Memorandum (non-add) entries:			
1941 Unexpired unobligated balance, end of year	29	23	23
Change in obligated balance:			
Unpaid obligations:			
3000 Unpaid obligations, brought forward, Oct 1	32	32	40
3010 New obligations, unexpired accounts	27	49	68
3020 Outlays (gross)	–27	–41	–52
3050 Unpaid obligations, end of year	32	40	56
Uncollected payments:			
3060 Uncollected pymts, Fed sources, brought forward, Oct 1	–3	–3	–3
3090 Uncollected pymts, Fed sources, end of year	–3	–3	–3
Memorandum (non-add) entries:			
3100 Obligated balance, start of year	29	29	37
3200 Obligated balance, end of year	29	37	53
Budget authority and outlays, net:			
Discretionary:			
4000 Budget authority, gross	36	43	68
Outlays, gross:			
4010 Outlays from new discretionary authority	6	29	39
4011 Outlays from discretionary balances	21	12	13
4020 Outlays, gross (total)	27	41	52
Offsets against gross budget authority and outlays:			
Offsetting collections (collected) from:			
4030 Federal sources	–11	–15	–15
4033 Non-Federal sources	–2	–5	–5
4040 Offsets against gross budget authority and outlays (total)	–13	–20	–20
4070 Budget authority, net (discretionary)	23	23	48
4080 Outlays, net (discretionary)	14	21	32
4180 Budget authority, net (total)	23	23	48
4190 Outlays, net (total)	14	21	32

This appropriation is responsible for coordinating, facilitating, reviewing and ensuring the non-duplication of the Department of Transportation's (DOT) research, development, and technology portfolio, as well as enhancing the data collection and statistical analysis programs to support data-driven decision-making and evidence building. The Office of the Assistant Secretary for Research and Technology is also responsible for civil Positioning, Navigation, and Timing (PNT) and DOT Spectrum Management, the Highly Automated Systems Safety Center of Excellence, and the Climate Change Center.

This appropriation oversees and provides direction to the following programs and activities:

The Bureau of Transportation Statistics (BTS) manages and shares statistical knowledge and information on the Nation's transportation systems, including statistics on freight movement, geospatial transportation information, and transportation economics. BTS is funded by an allocation from the Federal Highway Administration's Federal-Aid Highways account.

The University Transportation Centers (UTC) advance U.S. technology and expertise in many transportation-related disciplines through grants for transportation education, research, and technology transfer at university-based centers of excellence. The UTC Program funding is provided to the Office of the Assistant Secretary for Research and Technology through an allocation from the Federal Highway Administration.

The John A. Volpe National Transportation Systems Center (Cambridge, MA) provides technical expertise in research, analysis, engineering, technology deployment, and other technical knowledge to DOT and non-DOT customers on specific transportation system projects or issues on a fee-for-service basis.

The Transportation Safety Institute (Oklahoma City, OK) develops and delivers safety, security, and environmental training, products, and services for both the public and private sector on a fee-for-service and tuition basis.

Office of the Secretary—Continued
Federal Funds—Continued

RESEARCH AND TECHNOLOGY—Continued

Object Classification (in millions of dollars)

Identification code 069–1730–0–1–407		2021 actual	2022 est.	2023 est.
	Direct obligations:			
11.1	Personnel compensation: Full-time permanent	6	6	8
12.1	Civilian personnel benefits	2	2	2
23.1	Rental payments to GSA	1	1	1
25.1	Advisory and assistance services	2	2	5
25.3	Other goods and services from Federal sources	10	32	46
26.0	Supplies and materials	1	1	1
41.0	Grants, subsidies, and contributions	3	....	....
99.0	Direct obligations	25	44	63
99.0	Reimbursable obligations	2	5	5
99.9	Total new obligations, unexpired accounts	27	49	68

Employment Summary

Identification code 069–1730–0–1–407		2021 actual	2022 est.	2023 est.
1001	Direct civilian full-time equivalent employment	23	29	55
2001	Reimbursable civilian full-time equivalent employment	32	32	32
3001	Allocation account civilian full-time equivalent employment	65	80	80

SALARIES AND EXPENSES

For necessary expenses of the Office of the Secretary, $184,419,000, to remain available until September 30, 2024: Provided, That not to exceed $70,000 shall be for allocation within the Department for official reception and representation expenses as the Secretary may determine: Provided further, That notwithstanding any other provision of law, there may be credited to this appropriation up to $2,500,000 in funds received in user fees.

Note.—A full-year 2022 appropriation for this account was not enacted at the time the Budget was prepared; therefore, the Budget assumes this account is operating under the Continuing Appropriations Act, 2022 (Division A of Public Law 117–43, as amended). The amounts included for 2022 reflect the annualized level provided by the continuing resolution.

Program and Financing (in millions of dollars)

Identification code 069–0102–0–1–407		2021 actual	2022 est.	2023 est.
	Obligations by program activity:			
0001	General administration	123	127	186
0002	SCASDP Program	16	1	1
0003	CAREs	4	....	....
0100	Subtotal Direct Obligations	143	128	187
0799	Total direct obligations	143	128	187
0801	Salaries and Expenses (Reimbursable)	8	19	19
0900	Total new obligations, unexpired accounts	151	147	206
	Budgetary resources:			
	Unobligated balance:			
1000	Unobligated balance brought forward, Oct 1	33	29	28
	Budget authority:			
	Appropriations, discretionary:			
1100	Appropriation	126	126	184
	Spending authority from offsetting collections, discretionary:			
1700	Collected	26	20	20
1900	Budget authority (total)	152	146	204
1930	Total budgetary resources available	185	175	232
	Memorandum (non-add) entries:			
1940	Unobligated balance expiring	–5	....	....
1941	Unexpired unobligated balance, end of year	29	28	26
	Change in obligated balance:			
	Unpaid obligations:			
3000	Unpaid obligations, brought forward, Oct 1	41	60	29
3010	New obligations, unexpired accounts	151	147	206
3011	Obligations ("upward adjustments"), expired accounts	1	....	....
3020	Outlays (gross)	–131	–178	–194
3041	Recoveries of prior year unpaid obligations, expired	–2	....	....
3050	Unpaid obligations, end of year	60	29	41
	Memorandum (non-add) entries:			
3100	Obligated balance, start of year	41	60	29
3200	Obligated balance, end of year	60	29	41
	Budget authority and outlays, net:			
	Discretionary:			
4000	Budget authority, gross	152	146	204
	Outlays, gross:			
4010	Outlays from new discretionary authority	117	121	168
4011	Outlays from discretionary balances	14	57	26
4020	Outlays, gross (total)	131	178	194
	Offsets against gross budget authority and outlays:			
	Offsetting collections (collected) from:			
4030	Federal sources	–26	–19	–19
4033	Non-Federal sources	–1	–1	–1
4040	Offsets against gross budget authority and outlays (total)	–27	–20	–20
	Additional offsets against gross budget authority only:			
4052	Offsetting collections credited to expired accounts	1	....	....
4060	Additional offsets against budget authority only (total)	1	....	....
4070	Budget authority, net (discretionary)	126	126	184
4080	Outlays, net (discretionary)	104	158	174
4180	Budget authority, net (total)	126	126	184
4190	Outlays, net (total)	104	158	174

The Office of the Secretary is responsible for the overall planning, coordination, and administration of the Department's programs. Funding supports the Secretary, Deputy Secretary, Under Secretary for Policy, Secretarial Officers, and their immediate staffs, who provide Federal transportation policy development and guidance, institutional and public liaison activities. It also funds Departmental legal, procurement, budget and finance, human resources, and other administrative functions.

Object Classification (in millions of dollars)

Identification code 069–0102–0–1–407		2021 actual	2022 est.	2023 est.
	Direct obligations:			
	Personnel compensation:			
11.1	Full-time permanent	51	66	80
11.3	Other than full-time permanent	4	2	3
11.5	Other personnel compensation	2	2	3
11.9	Total personnel compensation	57	70	86
12.1	Civilian personnel benefits	19	22	23
21.0	Travel and transportation of persons	....	1	1
23.1	Rental payments to GSA	7	8	9
25.1	Advisory and assistance services	6	2	2
25.2	Other services from non-Federal sources	3	4	4
25.3	Other goods and services from Federal sources	32	20	59
31.0	Equipment	1	1	3
41.0	Grants, subsidies, and contributions	18	....	....
99.0	Direct obligations	143	128	187
99.0	Reimbursable obligations	8	19	19
99.9	Total new obligations, unexpired accounts	151	147	206

Employment Summary

Identification code 069–0102–0–1–407		2021 actual	2022 est.	2023 est.
1001	Direct civilian full-time equivalent employment	397	457	547
2001	Reimbursable civilian full-time equivalent employment	25	31	32

NATIONAL SURFACE TRANSPORTATION AND INNOVATIVE FINANCE BUREAU

For necessary expenses of the National Surface Transportation and Innovative Finance Bureau as authorized by 49 U.S.C. 116, $3,850,000, to remain available until expended: Provided, That the Secretary may collect and spend fees, as authorized by title 23, United States Code, to cover the costs of services of expert firms, including counsel, in the field of municipal and project finance to assist in the underwriting and servicing of Federal credit instruments and all or a portion of the costs to the Federal Government of servicing such credit instruments: Provided further, That such fees are available until expended to pay for such costs: Provided further, That such amounts are in addition to other amounts made available for such purposes and are not subject to any obligation limitation or the limitation on administrative expenses under section 608 of title 23, United States Code.

Note.—A full-year 2022 appropriation for this account was not enacted at the time the Budget was prepared; therefore, the Budget assumes this account is operating under the Continuing Appropriations Act, 2022 (Division A of Public Law 117–43, as amended). The amounts included for 2022 reflect the annualized level provided by the continuing resolution.

DEPARTMENT OF TRANSPORTATION

Office of the Secretary—Continued
Federal Funds—Continued

Program and Financing (in millions of dollars)

Identification code 069–0170–0–1–401	2021 actual	2022 est.	2023 est.
Obligations by program activity:			
0001 General Administration - Bureau	4	4	4
0003 TIFIA Revenue Fee		3	3
0900 Total new obligations, unexpired accounts	4	7	7
Budgetary resources:			
Unobligated balance:			
1000 Unobligated balance brought forward, Oct 1	7	11	13
Budget authority:			
Appropriations, discretionary:			
1100 Appropriation	5	5	4
Spending authority from offsetting collections, discretionary:			
1700 Collected	2	3	3
Spending authority from offsetting collections, mandatory:			
1800 Collected	1	1	
1900 Budget authority (total)	8	9	7
1930 Total budgetary resources available	15	20	20
Memorandum (non-add) entries:			
1941 Unexpired unobligated balance, end of year	11	13	13
Change in obligated balance:			
Unpaid obligations:			
3000 Unpaid obligations, brought forward, Oct 1	1	2	
3010 New obligations, unexpired accounts	4	7	7
3020 Outlays (gross)	–3	–9	–7
3050 Unpaid obligations, end of year	2		
Memorandum (non-add) entries:			
3100 Obligated balance, start of year	1	2	
3200 Obligated balance, end of year	2		
Budget authority and outlays, net:			
Discretionary:			
4000 Budget authority, gross	7	8	7
Outlays, gross:			
4010 Outlays from new discretionary authority	3	7	7
4011 Outlays from discretionary balances		2	
4020 Outlays, gross (total)	3	9	7
Offsets against gross budget authority and outlays:			
Offsetting collections (collected) from:			
4033 Non-Federal sources	–2	–3	–3
Mandatory:			
4090 Budget authority, gross	1	1	
Offsets against gross budget authority and outlays:			
Offsetting collections (collected) from:			
4123 Non-Federal sources	–1	–1	
4180 Budget authority, net (total)	5	5	4
4190 Outlays, net (total)		5	4

This appropriation supports the administrative expenses of the National Surface Transportation and Innovative Finance Bureau (known as the Build America Bureau). The Bureau fulfills a number of responsibilities, including providing assistance and communicating best practices and financing and funding opportunities to entities eligible under DOT infrastructure finance programs; administering the application process for DOT infrastructure finance programs, private activity bonds under 26 U.S.C. 142(m), and the Rural and Tribal Assistance Pilot Program; reducing uncertainty and delays related to environmental reviews and permitting, as well as project delivery and procurement risks, and costs for projects financed by the DOT infrastructure finance programs; increasing transparency and the public availability of information regarding projects financed by DOT infrastructure finance programs; and promoting best practices in procurement. The fees in this account cover the costs of services of expert firms in the field of municipal and project finance to assist in the underwriting and servicing of Federal credit instruments.

Object Classification (in millions of dollars)

Identification code 069–0170–0–1–401	2021 actual	2022 est.	2023 est.
Direct obligations:			
11.1 Personnel compensation: Full-time permanent	1	1	1
12.1 Civilian personnel benefits	1	1	1
23.1 Rental payments to GSA		3	3
25.1 Advisory and assistance services	2	2	2
99.0 Direct obligations	4	7	7
99.9 Total new obligations, unexpired accounts	4	7	7

Employment Summary

Identification code 069–0170–0–1–401	2021 actual	2022 est.	2023 est.
1001 Direct civilian full-time equivalent employment	11	16	16

TIGER TIFIA DIRECT LOAN FINANCING ACCOUNT, RECOVERY ACT

Program and Financing (in millions of dollars)

Identification code 069–4347–0–3–401	2021 actual	2022 est.	2023 est.
Obligations by program activity:			
Credit program obligations:			
0713 Payment of interest to Treasury	2	2	
0900 Total new obligations, unexpired accounts	2	2	
Budgetary resources:			
Financing authority:			
Spending authority from offsetting collections, mandatory:			
1800 Collected	2	2	
1900 Budget authority (total)	2	2	
1930 Total budgetary resources available	2	2	
Change in obligated balance:			
Unpaid obligations:			
3010 New obligations, unexpired accounts	2	2	
3020 Outlays (gross)	–2	–2	
Financing authority and disbursements, net:			
Mandatory:			
4090 Budget authority, gross	2	2	
Financing disbursements:			
4110 Outlays, gross (total)	2	2	
Offsets against gross financing authority and disbursements:			
Offsetting collections (collected) from:			
4123 Non-Federal sources	–2	–2	
4180 Budget authority, net (total)			
4190 Outlays, net (total)			

Status of Direct Loans (in millions of dollars)

Identification code 069–4347–0–3–401	2021 actual	2022 est.	2023 est.
Cumulative balance of direct loans outstanding:			
1210 Outstanding, start of year		61	61
1261 Adjustments: Capitalized interest	1		
1264 Other adjustments, net (+ or -)	60		
1290 Outstanding, end of year	61	61	61

Balance Sheet (in millions of dollars)

Identification code 069–4347–0–3–401	2020 actual	2021 actual
ASSETS:		
Federal assets:		
1101 Fund balances with Treasury		
Investments in U.S. securities:		
1106 Receivables, net		
Net value of assets related to post-1991 direct loans receivable:		
1401 Direct loans receivable, gross		61
1405 Allowance for subsidy cost (-)		1
1499 Net present value of assets related to direct loans		62
1999 Total assets		62
LIABILITIES:		
Federal liabilities:		
2103 Debt		62
2105 Other		
2999 Total liabilities		62
NET POSITION:		
3100 Unexpended appropriations		
3300 Cumulative results of operations		
3999 Total net position		

Office of the Secretary—Continued
Federal Funds—Continued

TIGER TIFIA DIRECT LOAN FINANCING ACCOUNT, RECOVERY ACT—Continued

Balance Sheet—Continued

Identification code 069–4347–0–3–401	2020 actual	2021 actual
4999 Total liabilities and net position		62

THRIVING COMMUNITIES

(INCLUDING TRANSFER OF FUNDS)

For necessary expenses to provide technical assistance and capacity building to improve equity and foster thriving communities through transportation infrastructure improvements, $110,737,000, to remain available until September 30, 2025: Provided, That the Secretary may enter into cooperative agreements to provide such technical assistance and capacity building: Provided further, That the Secretary may transfer amounts made available under this heading among the Office of the Secretary and the operating administrations of the Department.

Note.—A full-year 2022 appropriation for this account was not enacted at the time the Budget was prepared; therefore, the Budget assumes this account is operating under the Continuing Appropriations Act, 2022 (Division A of Public Law 117–43, as amended). The amounts included for 2022 reflect the annualized level provided by the continuing resolution.

Program and Financing (in millions of dollars)

Identification code 069–0162–0–1–401	2021 actual	2022 est.	2023 est.
Obligations by program activity:			
0001 Thriving Communities			100
0002 Administrative			11
0900 Total new obligations, unexpired accounts			111
Budgetary resources:			
Budget authority:			
Appropriations, discretionary:			
1100 Appropriation			111
1930 Total budgetary resources available			111
Change in obligated balance:			
Unpaid obligations:			
3010 New obligations, unexpired accounts			111
3050 Unpaid obligations, end of year			111
Memorandum (non-add) entries:			
3200 Obligated balance, end of year			111
Budget authority and outlays, net:			
Discretionary:			
4000 Budget authority, gross			111
4180 Budget authority, net (total)			111
4190 Outlays, net (total)			

The Thriving Communities program will advance transformative investment in underserved and overburdened communities by providing technical assistance using a coordinated place-based approach that strengthens local capacity to develop and execute infrastructure projects.

Object Classification (in millions of dollars)

Identification code 069–0162–0–1–401	2021 actual	2022 est.	2023 est.
Direct obligations:			
11.1 Personnel compensation: Full-time permanent			1
25.2 Other services from non-Federal sources			10
41.0 Grants, subsidies, and contributions			100
99.9 Total new obligations, unexpired accounts			111

Employment Summary

Identification code 069–0162–0–1–401	2021 actual	2022 est.	2023 est.
1001 Direct civilian full-time equivalent employment			7

NATIONAL INFRASTRUCTURE INVESTMENTS

(INCLUDING TRANSFER OF FUNDS)

For necessary expenses to carry out sections 6701 and 6702 of title 49, United States Code, $1,500,000,000 to remain available until expended: Provided, That the Secretary shall apply to projects under this heading the Federal requirements that the Secretary determines are appropriate based on the purpose of the program established under those sections and the Federal requirements applicable to comparable projects supported by other Department of Transportation financial assistance programs, including domestic preference requirements, contracting opportunities for small and disadvantaged businesses, and labor practices: Provided further, That the Secretary may retain up to 2 percent of the amounts made available under this heading, and may transfer portions of such amounts to the Administrators of the Federal Aviation Administration, the Federal Highway Administration, the Federal Transit Administration, the Federal Railroad Administration and the Maritime Administration to fund the award and oversight of grants and credit assistance made under the National Infrastructure Investments program.

Note.—A full-year 2022 appropriation for this account was not enacted at the time the Budget was prepared; therefore, the Budget assumes this account is operating under the Continuing Appropriations Act, 2022 (Division A of Public Law 117–43, as amended). The amounts included for 2022 reflect the annualized level provided by the continuing resolution.

NATIONAL INFRASTRUCTURE INVESTMENTS

[For an additional amount for "National Infrastructure Investments", $12,500,000,000, to remain available until expended, for necessary expenses to carry out chapter 67 of title 49, United States Code, of which $5,000,000,000 shall be to carry out section 6701 of such title and $7,500,000,000 shall be to carry out section 6702 of such title: Provided, That of the amount made available under this heading in this Act to carry out section 6701 of title 49, United States Code, $1,000,000,000, to remain available until expended, shall be made available for fiscal year 2022, $1,000,000,000, to remain available until expended, shall be made available for fiscal year 2023, $1,000,000,000, to remain available until expended, shall be made available for fiscal year 2024, $1,000,000,000, to remain available until expended, shall be made available for fiscal year 2025, and $1,000,000,000, to remain available until expended, shall be made available for fiscal year 2026: Provided further, That, of the amount made available under this heading in this Act to carry out section 6702 of title 49, United States Code, $1,500,000,000, to remain available until September 30, 2026, shall be made available for fiscal year 2022, $1,500,000,000, to remain until September 30, 2027, shall be made available for fiscal year 2023, $1,500,000,000, to remain available until September 30, 2028, shall be made available for fiscal year 2024, $1,500,000,000, to remain available until September 30, 2029, shall be made available for fiscal year 2025, and $1,500,000,000, to remain available September 30, 2030, shall be made available for fiscal year 2026: Provided further, That such amount is designated by the Congress as being for an emergency requirement pursuant to section 4112(a) of H. Con. Res. 71 (115th Congress), the concurrent resolution on the budget for fiscal year 2018, and pursuant to section 251(b) of the Balanced Budget and Emergency Deficit Control Act of 1985.] (Infrastructure Investments and Jobs Appropriations Act.)

Program and Financing (in millions of dollars)

Identification code 069–0143–0–1–401	2021 actual	2022 est.	2023 est.
Obligations by program activity:			
0001 National Infrastructure Investments Grants	545	1,965	2,027
0002 Award & Oversight	12	14	14
0900 Total new obligations, unexpired accounts	557	1,979	2,041
Budgetary resources:			
Unobligated balance:			
1000 Unobligated balance brought forward, Oct 1	1,852	2,295	3,791
Budget authority:			
Appropriations, discretionary:			
1100 Appropriation	1,399	1,000	1,500
1100 Appropriation		2,500	
1120 Appropriations transferred to other acct [069–1732]		–25	
1131 Unobligated balance of appropriations permanently reduced	–399		
1160 Appropriation, discretionary (total)	1,000	3,475	1,500
Advance appropriations, discretionary:			
1170 Advance appropriation			2,500
1172 Advance appropriations transferred to other accounts [069–1732]			–25
1180 Advanced appropriation, discretionary (total)			2,475
1900 Budget authority (total)	1,000	3,475	3,975
1930 Total budgetary resources available	2,852	5,770	7,766

DEPARTMENT OF TRANSPORTATION

Office of the Secretary—Continued
Federal Funds—Continued
893

		2021 actual	2022 est.	2023 est.
	Memorandum (non-add) entries:			
1941	Unexpired unobligated balance, end of year	2,295	3,791	5,725
	Change in obligated balance:			
	Unpaid obligations:			
3000	Unpaid obligations, brought forward, Oct 1	2,171	1,981	2,803
3010	New obligations, unexpired accounts	557	1,979	2,041
3020	Outlays (gross)	–704	–1,157	–1,201
3041	Recoveries of prior year unpaid obligations, expired	–43		
3050	Unpaid obligations, end of year	1,981	2,803	3,643
	Memorandum (non-add) entries:			
3100	Obligated balance, start of year	2,171	1,981	2,803
3200	Obligated balance, end of year	1,981	2,803	3,643
	Budget authority and outlays, net:			
	Discretionary:			
4000	Budget authority, gross	1,000	3,475	3,975
	Outlays, gross:			
4011	Outlays from discretionary balances	704	1,157	1,201
	Offsets against gross budget authority and outlays:			
	Offsetting collections (collected) from:			
4030	Federal sources	–1		
	Additional offsets against gross budget authority only:			
4052	Offsetting collections credited to expired accounts	1		
4070	Budget authority, net (discretionary)	1,000	3,475	3,975
4080	Outlays, net (discretionary)	703	1,157	1,201
4180	Budget authority, net (total)	1,000	3,475	3,975
4190	Outlays, net (total)	703	1,157	1,201

The National Infrastructure Investments grant programs provide awards on a competitive basis for surface transportation infrastructure projects. Under this heading the Local and Regional Project Assistance program, known as the Rebuilding American Infrastructure with Sustainability and Equity program, authorized under 49 U.S.C. 6702, provides competitive grants for highway, transit, rail, and other projects that will have a significant local or regional impact and improve transportation infrastructure. Also under this heading the National Infrastructure Project Assistance program, authorized under 49 U.S.C. 6701, provides competitive grants for large-scale highway, transit, intercity passenger rail, freight, and other projects likely to generate national or regional benefits.

Object Classification (in millions of dollars)

Identification code 069–0143–0–1–401	2021 actual	2022 est.	2023 est.
Direct obligations:			
Personnel compensation:			
11.1 Full-time permanent	1	1	1
11.1 Full-time permanent - Allocation	2	2	2
11.9 Total personnel compensation	3	3	3
25.2 Other services from Federal sources	5	5	5
25.2 Other services from non-Federal sources - Allocation	5	6	6
41.0 Grants, subsidies, and contributions - Allocation	545	1,965	2,027
99.0 Direct obligations	558	1,979	2,041
99.5 Adjustment for rounding	–1		
99.9 Total new obligations, unexpired accounts	557	1,979	2,041

Employment Summary

Identification code 069–0143–0–1–401	2021 actual	2022 est.	2023 est.
1001 Direct civilian full-time equivalent employment	5	7	7

ELECTRIC VEHICLE FLEET
(INCLUDING TRANSFER OF FUNDS)

For necessary expenses for the Department's transition to the General Services Administration's leased vehicle fleet, and for the purchase of zero emission passenger motor vehicles and supporting charging or fueling infrastructure, $16,000,000, to remain available until expended: Provided, That such amounts are in addition to any other amounts available for such purposes: Provided further, That amounts made available under this heading may be transferred to other accounts of the Department of Transportation for the purposes of this heading.

Note.—A full-year 2022 appropriation for this account was not enacted at the time the Budget was prepared; therefore, the Budget assumes this account is operating under the Continuing Appropriations Act, 2022 (Division A of Public Law 117–43, as amended). The amounts included for 2022 reflect the annualized level provided by the continuing resolution.

Program and Financing (in millions of dollars)

Identification code 069–0161–0–1–401	2021 actual	2022 est.	2023 est.
Obligations by program activity:			
0001 Electric Vehicle Fleet			16
Budgetary resources:			
Budget authority:			
Appropriations, discretionary:			
1100 Appropriation			16
1930 Total budgetary resources available			16
Change in obligated balance:			
Unpaid obligations:			
3010 New obligations, unexpired accounts			16
3020 Outlays (gross)			–11
3050 Unpaid obligations, end of year			5
Memorandum (non-add) entries:			
3200 Obligated balance, end of year			5
Budget authority and outlays, net:			
Discretionary:			
4000 Budget authority, gross			16
Outlays, gross:			
4010 Outlays from new discretionary authority			11
4180 Budget authority, net (total)			16
4190 Outlays, net (total)			11

This appropriation supports the Administration's goal of transitioning to a fully Zero Emission Vehicle (ZEV) Federal fleet. These funds will be used for the acquisition and deployment of vehicles which are battery electric, plug-in electric hybrid, and hydrogen fuel cell vehicles. Funding will also be used to acquire the necessary vehicle charging and refueling infrastructure. These acquisitions are a significant step towards eliminating tailpipe emissions of greenhouse gases (GHG) from the Department's fleet and aligning the Department's fleet operations with the goal of achieving a fully ZEV federal fleet.

Object Classification (in millions of dollars)

Identification code 069–0161–0–1–401	2021 actual	2022 est.	2023 est.
Direct obligations:			
25.3 Other goods and services from Federal sources			13
31.0 Equipment			3
99.9 Total new obligations, unexpired accounts			16

TRANSPORTATION DEMONSTRATION PROGRAM

Note.—A full-year 2022 appropriation for this account was not enacted at the time the Budget was prepared; therefore, the Budget assumes this account is operating under the Continuing Appropriations Act, 2022 (Division A of Public Law 117–43, as amended). The amounts included for 2022 reflect the annualized level provided by the continuing resolution.

Program and Financing (in millions of dollars)

Identification code 069–1731–0–1–400	2021 actual	2022 est.	2023 est.
Obligations by program activity:			
0001 Transportation Demonstration Grants		100	
0900 Total new obligations, unexpired accounts (object class 41.0)		100	
Budgetary resources:			
Unobligated balance:			
1000 Unobligated balance brought forward, Oct 1		100	100
Budget authority:			
Appropriations, discretionary:			
1100 Appropriation	100	100	
1930 Total budgetary resources available	100	200	100

Office of the Secretary—Continued
Federal Funds—Continued

TRANSPORTATION DEMONSTRATION PROGRAM—Continued

Program and Financing—Continued

Identification code 069–1731–0–1–400	2021 actual	2022 est.	2023 est.
Memorandum (non-add) entries:			
1941 Unexpired unobligated balance, end of year	100	100	100
Change in obligated balance:			
Unpaid obligations:			
3000 Unpaid obligations, brought forward, Oct 1			92
3010 New obligations, unexpired accounts		100	
3020 Outlays (gross)		–8	–28
3050 Unpaid obligations, end of year		92	64
Memorandum (non-add) entries:			
3100 Obligated balance, start of year			92
3200 Obligated balance, end of year		92	64
Budget authority and outlays, net:			
Discretionary:			
4000 Budget authority, gross		100	
Outlays, gross:			
4011 Outlays from discretionary balances		8	28
4180 Budget authority, net (total)	100	100	
4190 Outlays, net (total)		8	28

The Transportation Demonstration Program provides grants to expand intermodal and multimodal freight and cargo transportation infrastructure, including airport development under chapter 471 of title 49, United States Code. No funding is requested in 2023.

ASSET CONCESSIONS AND INNOVATIVE FINANCE ASSISTANCE

Program and Financing (in millions of dollars)

Identification code 069–1736–0–1–401	2021 actual	2022 est.	2023 est.
Obligations by program activity:			
0001 Asset Concessions		20	20
0900 Total new obligations, unexpired accounts (object class 41.0)		20	20
Budgetary resources:			
Budget authority:			
Appropriations, mandatory:			
1200 Appropriation		20	20
1900 Budget authority (total)		20	20
1930 Total budgetary resources available		20	20
Change in obligated balance:			
Unpaid obligations:			
3000 Unpaid obligations, brought forward, Oct 1			2
3010 New obligations, unexpired accounts		20	20
3020 Outlays (gross)		–18	–20
3050 Unpaid obligations, end of year		2	2
Memorandum (non-add) entries:			
3100 Obligated balance, start of year			2
3200 Obligated balance, end of year		2	2
Budget authority and outlays, net:			
Mandatory:			
4090 Budget authority, gross		20	20
Outlays, gross:			
4100 Outlays from new mandatory authority		18	18
4101 Outlays from mandatory balances			2
4110 Outlays, gross (total)		18	20
4180 Budget authority, net (total)		20	20
4190 Outlays, net (total)		18	20

The Asset Concessions and Innovative Finance Assistance program facilitates access to expert services for, and provides grants to State, local, and Tribal governments and other entities to enhance their technical capacity to evaluate public-private partnerships in which the private sector partner could assume a greater role in project planning, development, financing, construction, maintenance and operation, including by assisting eligible entities in entering into asset concessions.

SAFE STREETS AND ROADS FOR ALL GRANTS

[For an additional amount for "Safe Streets and Roads for All Grants", $5,000,000,000, to remain available until expended, for competitive grants, as authorized under section 24112 of division B of this Act: *Provided*, That $1,000,000,000, to remain available until expended, shall be made available for fiscal year 2022, $1,000,000,000, to remain available until expended, shall be made available for fiscal year 2023, $1,000,000,000, to remain available until expended, shall be made available for fiscal year 2024, $1,000,000,000, to remain available until expended, shall be made available for fiscal year 2025, and $1,000,000,000, to remain available until expended, shall be made available for fiscal year 2026: *Provided further*, That the Secretary shall issue a notice of funding opportunity not later than 180 days after each date upon which funds are made available under the preceding proviso: *Provided further*, That the Secretary shall make awards not later than 270 days after issuing the notices of funding opportunity required under the preceding proviso: *Provided further*, That such amount is designated by the Congress as being for an emergency requirement pursuant to section 4112(a) of H. Con. Res. 71 (115th Congress), the concurrent resolution on the budget for fiscal year 2018, and to section 251(b) of the Balanced Budget and Emergency Deficit Control Act of 1985.] *(Infrastructure Investments and Jobs Appropriations Act.)*

Program and Financing (in millions of dollars)

Identification code 069–1735–0–1–401	2021 actual	2022 est.	2023 est.
Obligations by program activity:			
0001 Grants		249	998
0002 Award and Oversight		1	2
0900 Total new obligations, unexpired accounts		250	1,000
Budgetary resources:			
Unobligated balance:			
1000 Unobligated balance brought forward, Oct 1			750
Budget authority:			
Appropriations, discretionary:			
1100 Appropriation		1,000	
Advance appropriations, discretionary:			
1170 Advance appropriation			1,000
1900 Budget authority (total)		1,000	1,000
1930 Total budgetary resources available		1,000	1,750
Memorandum (non-add) entries:			
1941 Unexpired unobligated balance, end of year		750	750
Change in obligated balance:			
Unpaid obligations:			
3000 Unpaid obligations, brought forward, Oct 1			240
3010 New obligations, unexpired accounts		250	1,000
3020 Outlays (gross)		–10	–220
3050 Unpaid obligations, end of year		240	1,020
Memorandum (non-add) entries:			
3100 Obligated balance, start of year			240
3200 Obligated balance, end of year		240	1,020
Budget authority and outlays, net:			
Discretionary:			
4000 Budget authority, gross		1,000	1,000
Outlays, gross:			
4010 Outlays from new discretionary authority		10	10
4011 Outlays from discretionary balances			210
4020 Outlays, gross (total)		10	220
4180 Budget authority, net (total)		1,000	1,000
4190 Outlays, net (total)		10	220

The Safe Streets and Roads for All grant program provides grants, on a competitive basis, to regional, local, and Tribal governments to prevent transportation-related fatalities and serious injuries on our Nations roadways. This program funds the development of comprehensive safety action plans to support Vision Zero or Toward Zero Deaths. The funding also allows recipients to conduct planning, design, and development activities for projects and strategies or to carry out projects and strategies identified in a comprehensive safety action plan.

DEPARTMENT OF TRANSPORTATION

Office of the Secretary—Continued
Federal Funds—Continued

Object Classification (in millions of dollars)

Identification code 069–1735–0–1–401	2021 actual	2022 est.	2023 est.
Direct obligations:			
11.1 Personnel compensation: Full-time permanent		1	1
41.0 Grants, subsidies, and contributions		249	999
99.9 Total new obligations, unexpired accounts		250	1,000

Employment Summary

Identification code 069–1735–0–1–401	2021 actual	2022 est.	2023 est.
1001 Direct civilian full-time equivalent employment		3	10

STRENGTHENING MOBILITY AND REVOLUTIONIZING TRANSPORTATION GRANT PROGRAM

[For an additional amount for "Strengthening Mobility and Revolutionizing Transportation Grant Program", $500,000,000, to remain available until expended, as authorized by section 25005 of division B of this Act: *Provided*, That $100,000,000, to remain available until expended, shall be made available for fiscal year 2022, $100,000,000, to remain available until expended, shall be made available for fiscal year 2023, $100,000,000, to remain available until expended, shall be made available for fiscal year 2024, $100,000,000, to remain available until expended, shall be made available for fiscal year 2025, and $100,000,000, to remain available until expended, shall be made available for fiscal year 2026: *Provided further*, That such amount is designated by the Congress as being for an emergency requirement pursuant to section 4112(a) of H. Con. Res. 71 (115th Congress), the concurrent resolution on the budget for fiscal year 2018, and to section 251(b) of the Balanced Budget and Emergency Deficit Control Act of 1985.] *(Infrastructure Investments and Jobs Appropriations Act.)*

Program and Financing (in millions of dollars)

Identification code 069–1734–0–1–407	2021 actual	2022 est.	2023 est.
Obligations by program activity:			
0001 Strengthening Mobility and Revolutionizing Transportation Grant		40	99
0900 Total new obligations, unexpired accounts (object class 41.0)		40	99
Budgetary resources:			
Unobligated balance:			
1000 Unobligated balance brought forward, Oct 1			59
Budget authority:			
Appropriations, discretionary:			
1100 Appropriation		100	
1120 Appropriations transferred to other acct [069–1732]		–1	
1160 Appropriation, discretionary (total)		99	
Advance appropriations, discretionary:			
1170 Advance appropriation			100
1172 Advance appropriations transferred to other accounts [069–1732]			–1
1180 Advanced appropriation, discretionary (total)			99
1900 Budget authority (total)		99	99
1930 Total budgetary resources available		99	158
Memorandum (non-add) entries:			
1941 Unexpired unobligated balance, end of year		59	59
Change in obligated balance:			
Unpaid obligations:			
3000 Unpaid obligations, brought forward, Oct 1			40
3010 New obligations, unexpired accounts		40	99
3020 Outlays (gross)			–9
3050 Unpaid obligations, end of year		40	130
Memorandum (non-add) entries:			
3100 Obligated balance, start of year			40
3200 Obligated balance, end of year		40	130
Budget authority and outlays, net:			
Discretionary:			
4000 Budget authority, gross		99	99
Outlays, gross:			
4011 Outlays from discretionary balances			9
4180 Budget authority, net (total)		99	99
4190 Outlays, net (total)			9

The Strengthening Mobility and Revolutionizing Transportation (SMART) Grant Program will harness technology, analytics, and innovation to improve transportation safety and efficiency. The SMART program aims to achieve safety, climate, and equity goals by supporting demonstration projects focused on advanced smart city or community technologies and systems in a variety of communities.

NATIONAL CULVERT REMOVAL, REPLACEMENT, AND RESTORATION GRANTS

[For an additional amount for "National Culvert Removal, Replacement, and Restoration Grants", $1,000,000,000, to remain available until expended, as authorized by section 6203 of title 49, United States Code: *Provided*, That $200,000,000, to remain available until expended, shall be made available for fiscal year 2022, $200,000,000, to remain available until expended, shall be made available for fiscal year 2023, $200,000,000, to remain available until expended, shall be made available for fiscal year 2024, $200,000,000, to remain available until expended, shall be made available for fiscal year 2025, and $200,000,000, to remain available until expended, shall be made available for fiscal year 2026: *Provided further*, That such amount is designated by the Congress as being for an emergency requirement pursuant to section 4112(a) of H. Con. Res. 71 (115th Congress), the concurrent resolution on the budget for fiscal year 2018, and to section 251(b) of the Balanced Budget and Emergency Deficit Control Act of 1985.] *(Infrastructure Investments and Jobs Appropriations Act.)*

Program and Financing (in millions of dollars)

Identification code 069–1733–0–1–401	2021 actual	2022 est.	2023 est.
Obligations by program activity:			
0001 National Culvert Removal, Replacement, and Restoration Grants		39	197
0002 Award & Oversight		1	1
0900 Total new obligations, unexpired accounts		40	198
Budgetary resources:			
Unobligated balance:			
1000 Unobligated balance brought forward, Oct 1			158
Budget authority:			
Appropriations, discretionary:			
1100 Appropriation		200	
1120 Appropriations transferred to other acct [069–1732]		–2	
1160 Appropriation, discretionary (total)		198	
Advance appropriations, discretionary:			
1170 Advance appropriation			200
1172 Advance appropriations transferred to other accounts [069–1732]			–2
1180 Advanced appropriation, discretionary (total)			198
1900 Budget authority (total)		198	198
1930 Total budgetary resources available		198	356
Memorandum (non-add) entries:			
1941 Unexpired unobligated balance, end of year		158	158
Change in obligated balance:			
Unpaid obligations:			
3000 Unpaid obligations, brought forward, Oct 1			40
3010 New obligations, unexpired accounts		40	198
3020 Outlays (gross)			–6
3050 Unpaid obligations, end of year		40	232
Memorandum (non-add) entries:			
3100 Obligated balance, start of year			40
3200 Obligated balance, end of year		40	232
Budget authority and outlays, net:			
Discretionary:			
4000 Budget authority, gross		198	198
Outlays, gross:			
4011 Outlays from discretionary balances			6
4180 Budget authority, net (total)		198	198
4190 Outlays, net (total)			6

The National Culvert Removal, Replacement, and Restoration Grant Program provides competitive grants to States, local governments, and Tribal governments for projects for the replacement, removal, and repair

NATIONAL CULVERT REMOVAL, REPLACEMENT, AND RESTORATION GRANTS—Continued

of culverts or weirs that meaningfully improve or restore fish passage for anadromous fish.

Object Classification (in millions of dollars)

Identification code 069–1733–0–1–401		2021 actual	2022 est.	2023 est.
	Direct obligations:			
11.1	Personnel compensation: Full-time permanent - Allocation	....	1	1
41.0	Grants, subsidies, and contributions - Allocation	....	39	197
99.9	Total new obligations, unexpired accounts	....	40	198

OFFICE OF MULTIMODAL FREIGHT INFRASTRUCTURE AND POLICY

For necessary expenses for the Office of Multimodal Freight Infrastructure and Policy, as authorized by section 118 of title 49, United States Code, $2,000,000, to remain available until expended: Provided, That such amounts may be transferred to and merged with appropriations made available under the heading "Office of the Secretary—Salaries and Expenses": Provided further, That upon a determination that that all or part of the funds transferred from this appropriation are no longer necessary for the purposes for which they were initially transferred, such amounts may be transferred back to this appropriation.

Program and Financing (in millions of dollars)

Identification code 069–1732–0–1–407		2021 actual	2022 est.	2023 est.
	Obligations by program activity:			
0001	Administration of Discretionary Grant Programs (NII, SMART, RAISE, INFRA)	....	28	28
0002	Multimodal Freight Infrastructure Policy	....	....	2
0900	Total new obligations, unexpired accounts	....	28	30
	Budgetary resources:			
	Budget authority:			
	Appropriations, discretionary:			
1100	Appropriation	....	....	2
1121	Appropriations transferred from other acct [069–0143]	....	25	....
1121	Appropriations transferred from other acct [069–1733]	....	2	....
1121	Appropriations transferred from other acct [069–1734]	....	1	....
1160	Appropriation, discretionary (total)	....	28	2
	Advance appropriations, discretionary:			
1173	Advance appropriations transferred from other accounts [069–1733]	....	....	2
1173	Advance appropriations transferred from other accounts [069–1734]	....	....	1
1173	Advance appropriations transferred from other accounts [069–0143]	....	....	25
1180	Advanced appropriation, discretionary (total)	....	....	28
1900	Budget authority (total)	....	28	30
1930	Total budgetary resources available	....	28	30
	Change in obligated balance:			
	Unpaid obligations:			
3000	Unpaid obligations, brought forward, Oct 1	....	....	3
3010	New obligations, unexpired accounts	....	28	30
3020	Outlays (gross)	....	–25	–30
3050	Unpaid obligations, end of year	....	3	3
	Memorandum (non-add) entries:			
3100	Obligated balance, start of year	....	....	3
3200	Obligated balance, end of year	....	3	3
	Budget authority and outlays, net:			
	Discretionary:			
4000	Budget authority, gross	....	28	30
	Outlays, gross:			
4010	Outlays from new discretionary authority	....	25	27
4011	Outlays from discretionary balances	....	....	3
4020	Outlays, gross (total)	....	25	30
4180	Budget authority, net (total)	....	28	30
4190	Outlays, net (total)	....	25	30

The Office of Multimodal Freight Infrastructure and Policy (MFIP) is authorized under 49 U.S.C. 118. MFIP administers and oversees certain multimodal freight grant programs, carries out national multimodal freight policy, promotes and facilitates the sharing of information between the private and public sectors with respect to freight issues, conducts and coordinates research on improving multimodal freight mobility, assists cities and States in developing freight mobility and supply chain expertise, and coordinates with other Federal departments and agencies to support the seamless movement of freight across and within different modes of transportation.

Object Classification (in millions of dollars)

Identification code 069–1732–0–1–407		2021 actual	2022 est.	2023 est.
	Direct obligations:			
11.1	Personnel compensation: Full-time permanent	....	2	5
12.1	Civilian personnel benefits	....	1	2
25.1	Advisory and assistance services	....	25	23
99.9	Total new obligations, unexpired accounts	....	28	30

Employment Summary

Identification code 069–1732–0–1–407		2021 actual	2022 est.	2023 est.
1001	Direct civilian full-time equivalent employment	....	13	40

TIFIA HIGHWAY TRUST FUND DIRECT LOAN FINANCING ACCOUNT

Program and Financing (in millions of dollars)

Identification code 069–4123–0–3–401		2021 actual	2022 est.	2023 est.
	Obligations by program activity:			
	Credit program obligations:			
0710	Direct loan obligations	8,959	10,987	10,987
0713	Payment of interest to Treasury	484	700	700
0740	Negative subsidy obligations	71	133	....
0742	Downward reestimates paid to receipt accounts	358	977	....
0743	Interest on downward reestimates	30	85	....
0900	Total new obligations, unexpired accounts	9,902	12,882	11,687
	Budgetary resources:			
	Unobligated balance:			
1000	Unobligated balance brought forward, Oct 1	72	666	....
1021	Recoveries of prior year unpaid obligations	5,921	....	....
1023	Unobligated balances applied to repay debt	–70	....	....
1024	Unobligated balance of borrowing authority withdrawn	–5,743	....	....
1070	Unobligated balance (total)	180	666	....
	Financing authority:			
	Appropriations, mandatory:			
1200	Appropriation	1	....	....
1236	Appropriations applied to repay debt	–1	....	....
	Borrowing authority, mandatory:			
1400	Borrowing authority	9,629	10,881	11,286
	Spending authority from offsetting collections, mandatory:			
1800	Collected	4,098	1,500	566
1801	Change in uncollected payments, Federal sources	–218	–15	–15
1820	Capital transfer of spending authority from offsetting collections to general fund	–33	....	....
1825	Spending authority from offsetting collections applied to repay debt	–3,088	–150	–150
1850	Spending auth from offsetting collections, mand (total)	759	1,335	401
1900	Budget authority (total)	10,388	12,216	11,687
1930	Total budgetary resources available	10,568	12,882	11,687
	Memorandum (non-add) entries:			
1941	Unexpired unobligated balance, end of year	666	....	....
	Change in obligated balance:			
	Unpaid obligations:			
3000	Unpaid obligations, brought forward, Oct 1	8,780	10,532	19,871
3010	New obligations, unexpired accounts	9,902	12,882	11,687
3020	Outlays (gross)	–2,229	–3,543	–3,543
3040	Recoveries of prior year unpaid obligations, unexpired	–5,921	....	....
3050	Unpaid obligations, end of year	10,532	19,871	28,015
	Uncollected payments:			
3060	Uncollected pymts, Fed sources, brought forward, Oct 1	–250	–32	–17
3070	Change in uncollected pymts, Fed sources, unexpired	218	15	15

DEPARTMENT OF TRANSPORTATION

3090	Uncollected pymts, Fed sources, end of year	−32	−17	−2
	Memorandum (non-add) entries:			
3100	Obligated balance, start of year	8,530	10,500	19,854
3200	Obligated balance, end of year	10,500	19,854	28,013
	Financing authority and disbursements, net:			
	Mandatory:			
4090	Budget authority, gross	10,388	12,216	11,687
	Financing disbursements:			
4110	Outlays, gross (total)	2,229	3,543	3,543
	Offsets against gross financing authority and disbursements:			
	Offsetting collections (collected) from:			
4120	Federal sources: subsidy from program account	−1,052	−273	−35
4122	Interest on uninvested funds	−69	−70	−80
4123	Non-Federal sources - Interest payments	−2,977	−261	−200
4123	Non-Federal sources - Principal payments		−896	−251
4130	Offsets against gross budget authority and outlays (total)	−4,098	−1,500	−566
	Additional offsets against financing authority only (total):			
4140	Change in uncollected pymts, Fed sources, unexpired	218	15	15
4160	Budget authority, net (mandatory)	6,508	10,731	11,136
4170	Outlays, net (mandatory)	−1,869	2,043	2,977
4180	Budget authority, net (total)	6,508	10,731	11,136
4190	Outlays, net (total)	−1,869	2,043	2,977

Status of Direct Loans (in millions of dollars)

Identification code 069–4123–0–3–401	2021 actual	2022 est.	2023 est.
Position with respect to appropriations act limitation on obligations:			
1111 Direct loan obligations from current-year authority	8,959	10,987	10,987
1150 Total direct loan obligations	8,959	10,987	10,987
Cumulative balance of direct loans outstanding:			
1210 Outstanding, start of year	14,233	13,089	17,082
1231 Disbursements: Direct loan disbursements	1,051	3,543	3,543
1251 Repayments: Repayments and prepayments	−2,444	−150	−150
1261 Adjustments: Capitalized interest	249	600	600
1290 Outstanding, end of year	13,089	17,082	21,075

This non-budgetary financing account records all cash flows to and from the Government resulting from the Transportation Infrastructure Finance and Innovation Act Highway Trust Fund Program Account (program account). The amounts in this account are a means of financing and are not included in the budget totals. For 2023, cash flows are based on contract authority and obligation limitation equal to the baseline in the program account.

Balance Sheet (in millions of dollars)

Identification code 069–4123–0–3–401	2020 actual	2021 actual
ASSETS:		
Federal assets:		
1101 Fund balances with Treasury	70	665
Investments in U.S. securities:		
1106 Receivables, net	380	206
Net value of assets related to post-1991 direct loans receivable:		
1401 Direct loans receivable, gross	14,233	13,089
1402 Interest receivable		
1404 Foreclosed property	167	167
1405 Allowance for subsidy cost (-)	217	372
1499 Net present value of assets related to direct loans	14,617	13,628
1999 Total assets	15,067	14,499
LIABILITIES:		
Federal liabilities:		
2103 Debt	14,679	13,436
2105 Other	388	1,063
2999 Total liabilities	15,067	14,499
NET POSITION:		
3300 Cumulative results of operations		
4999 Total liabilities and net position	15,067	14,499

WORKING CAPITAL FUND, VOLPE NATIONAL TRANSPORTATION SYSTEMS CENTER

For necessary expenses of the Volpe National Transportation Systems Center, as authorized in section 328 of title 49, United States Code, $4,500,000, to remain available until expended.

Program and Financing (in millions of dollars)

Identification code 069–4522–0–4–407	2021 actual	2022 est.	2023 est.
Obligations by program activity:			
0001 New Building			5
0801 Working Capital Fund, Volpe National Transportation Systems Cent (Reimbursable)	227	345	345
0900 Total new obligations, unexpired accounts	227	345	350
Budgetary resources:			
Unobligated balance:			
1000 Unobligated balance brought forward, Oct 1	180	141	141
1021 Recoveries of prior year unpaid obligations	5		
1070 Unobligated balance (total)	185	141	141
Budget authority:			
Appropriations, discretionary:			
1100 Appropriation			5
Spending authority from offsetting collections, discretionary:			
1700 Collected	202	345	345
1701 Change in uncollected payments, Federal sources	−19		
1750 Spending auth from offsetting collections, disc (total)	183	345	345
1900 Budget authority (total)	183	345	350
1930 Total budgetary resources available	368	486	491
Memorandum (non-add) entries:			
1941 Unexpired unobligated balance, end of year	141	141	141
Change in obligated balance:			
Unpaid obligations:			
3000 Unpaid obligations, brought forward, Oct 1	138	137	344
3010 New obligations, unexpired accounts	227	345	350
3020 Outlays (gross)	−223	−138	−350
3040 Recoveries of prior year unpaid obligations, unexpired	−5		
3050 Unpaid obligations, end of year	137	344	344
Uncollected payments:			
3060 Uncollected pymts, Fed sources, brought forward, Oct 1	−88	−69	−69
3070 Change in uncollected pymts, Fed sources, unexpired	19		
3090 Uncollected pymts, Fed sources, end of year	−69	−69	−69
Memorandum (non-add) entries:			
3100 Obligated balance, start of year	50	68	275
3200 Obligated balance, end of year	68	275	275
Budget authority and outlays, net:			
Discretionary:			
4000 Budget authority, gross	183	345	350
Outlays, gross:			
4010 Outlays from new discretionary authority	37	138	142
4011 Outlays from discretionary balances	186		208
4020 Outlays, gross (total)	223	138	350
Offsets against gross budget authority and outlays:			
Offsetting collections (collected) from:			
4030 Federal sources	−195	−345	−345
4033 Non-Federal sources	−7		
4040 Offsets against gross budget authority and outlays (total)	−202	−345	−345
Additional offsets against gross budget authority only:			
4050 Change in uncollected pymts, Fed sources, unexpired	19		
4070 Budget authority, net (discretionary)			5
4080 Outlays, net (discretionary)	21	−207	5
4180 Budget authority, net (total)			5
4190 Outlays, net (total)	21	−207	5

The Working Capital Fund finances multidisciplinary research, evaluation, analytical, and related activities undertaken at the Volpe Transportation Systems Center (Volpe Center) in Cambridge, MA. The fund is financed through negotiated agreements with other offices within the Office of the Secretary, Departmental operating administrations, other governmental elements, and non-governmental entities using the Center's capabilities. These agreements also define the activities undertaken at the Volpe Center.

WORKING CAPITAL FUND, VOLPE NATIONAL TRANSPORTATION SYSTEMS CENTER—Continued

Object Classification (in millions of dollars)

Identification code 069–4522–0–4–407		2021 actual	2022 est.	2023 est.
25.2	Direct obligations: Other services from non-Federal sources			5
	Reimbursable obligations:			
	Personnel compensation:			
11.1	Full-time permanent	62	62	62
11.3	Other than full-time permanent	4	5	5
11.5	Other personnel compensation	1		
11.9	Total personnel compensation	67	67	67
12.1	Civilian personnel benefits	23	24	24
21.0	Travel and transportation of persons		5	5
23.3	Communications, utilities, and miscellaneous charges	2	3	3
25.1	Advisory and assistance services	90	110	110
25.2	Other services from non-Federal sources	2	3	3
25.3	Other goods and services from Federal sources	9	6	6
25.4	Operation and maintenance of facilities	6	5	5
25.5	Research and development contracts	1	90	90
25.7	Operation and maintenance of equipment	7	9	9
25.8	Subsistence and support of persons		1	1
26.0	Supplies and materials	1	1	1
31.0	Equipment	4	10	10
32.0	Land and structures	1	1	1
44.0	Refunds	14	10	10
99.0	Reimbursable obligations	227	345	345
99.9	Total new obligations, unexpired accounts	227	345	350

Employment Summary

Identification code 069–4522–0–4–407	2021 actual	2022 est.	2023 est.
2001 Reimbursable civilian full-time equivalent employment	545	570	570

TIFIA GENERAL FUND PROGRAM ACCOUNT

Program and Financing (in millions of dollars)

Identification code 069–0542–0–1–401		2021 actual	2022 est.	2023 est.
	Obligations by program activity:			
	Credit program obligations:			
0705	Reestimates of direct loan subsidy	1		
0706	Interest on reestimates of direct loan subsidy	4		
0900	Total new obligations, unexpired accounts (object class 41.0)	5		
	Budgetary resources:			
	Budget authority:			
	Appropriations, mandatory:			
1200	Appropriation	5		
1900	Budget authority (total)	5		
1930	Total budgetary resources available	5		
	Change in obligated balance:			
	Unpaid obligations:			
3000	Unpaid obligations, brought forward, Oct 1			1
3010	New obligations, unexpired accounts	5		
3020	Outlays (gross)	–4	–1	
3050	Unpaid obligations, end of year	1		
	Memorandum (non-add) entries:			
3100	Obligated balance, start of year			1
3200	Obligated balance, end of year	1		
	Budget authority and outlays, net:			
	Mandatory:			
4090	Budget authority, gross	5		
	Outlays, gross:			
4100	Outlays from new mandatory authority	4		
4101	Outlays from mandatory balances		1	
4110	Outlays, gross (total)	4	1	
4180	Budget authority, net (total)	5		
4190	Outlays, net (total)	4	1	

Summary of Loan Levels, Subsidy Budget Authority and Outlays by Program (in millions of dollars)

Identification code 069–0542–0–1–401	2021 actual	2022 est.	2023 est.
Direct loan reestimates:			
135001 TIFIA TIGER Direct Loans	2	–1	

The Office of the Secretary of Transportation (OST) received appropriations totaling $1,127 million for the Transportation Investment Generating Economic Recovery (TIGER) discretionary grants as part of the 2010 and 2011 Department of Transportation (DOT) appropriations acts. The appropriations authorized DOT to pay subsidy and administrative costs, not to exceed $300 million, of projects eligible for Federal credit assistance under Chapter 6 of Title 23 United States Code. In 2012, $45 million was provided for TIGER discretionary grants as part of the 2012 DOT appropriation act to pay subsidy and administrative costs under the Transportation Infrastructure Finance and Innovation Act program.

TIFIA GENERAL FUND DIRECT LOAN FINANCING ACCOUNT

Program and Financing (in millions of dollars)

Identification code 069–4348–0–3–401		2021 actual	2022 est.	2023 est.
	Obligations by program activity:			
	Credit program obligations:			
0713	Payment of interest to Treasury	13	14	14
0742	Downward reestimates paid to receipt accounts	1	1	
0743	Interest on downward reestimates	1		
0900	Total new obligations, unexpired accounts	15	15	14
	Budgetary resources:			
	Unobligated balance:			
1000	Unobligated balance brought forward, Oct 1	2		
1023	Unobligated balances applied to repay debt	–2		
	Financing authority:			
	Borrowing authority, mandatory:			
1400	Borrowing authority	2	2	2
	Spending authority from offsetting collections, mandatory:			
1800	Collected	22	51	16
1825	Spending authority from offsetting collections applied to repay debt	–9	–38	–4
1850	Spending auth from offsetting collections, mand (total)	13	13	12
1900	Budget authority (total)	15	15	14
1930	Total budgetary resources available	15	15	14
	Change in obligated balance:			
	Unpaid obligations:			
3000	Unpaid obligations, brought forward, Oct 1			
3010	New obligations, unexpired accounts	15	15	14
3020	Outlays (gross)	–15	–14	–14
3050	Unpaid obligations, end of year		1	1
	Memorandum (non-add) entries:			
3100	Obligated balance, start of year			1
3200	Obligated balance, end of year		1	1
	Financing authority and disbursements, net:			
	Mandatory:			
4090	Budget authority, gross	15	15	14
	Financing disbursements:			
4110	Outlays, gross (total)	15	14	14
	Offsets against gross financing authority and disbursements:			
	Offsetting collections (collected) from:			
4120	Federal sources	–4		
4122	Interest on uninvested funds	–1	–1	–1
4123	Non-Federal sources - Interest payments	–17	–13	–11
4123	Non-Federal sources - Principal payments		–37	–4
4130	Offsets against gross budget authority and outlays (total)	–22	–51	–16
4160	Budget authority, net (mandatory)	–7	–36	–2
4170	Outlays, net (mandatory)	–7	–37	–2
4180	Budget authority, net (total)	–7	–36	–2
4190	Outlays, net (total)	–7	–37	–2

DEPARTMENT OF TRANSPORTATION

Office of the Secretary—Continued
Federal Funds—Continued

Status of Direct Loans (in millions of dollars)

Identification code 069–4348–0–3–401	2021 actual	2022 est.	2023 est.
Cumulative balance of direct loans outstanding:			
1210 Outstanding, start of year	445	442	438
1251 Repayments: Repayments and prepayments	–3	–4	–4
1290 Outstanding, end of year	442	438	434

This is the financing account for the Transportation Infrastructure Finance and Innovation Act (TIFIA) General Fund Program Account. This nonbudgetary account records all cash flows to and from the Government resulting from TIFIA credit assistance provided under this program.

Balance Sheet (in millions of dollars)

Identification code 069–4348–0–3–401	2020 actual	2021 actual
ASSETS:		
Federal assets:		
1101 Fund balances with Treasury	2	
Investments in U.S. securities:		
1106 Receivables, net	4	
Net value of assets related to post-1991 direct loans receivable:		
1401 Direct loans receivable, gross	445	442
1405 Allowance for subsidy cost (-)	–35	–35
1499 Net present value of assets related to direct loans	410	407
1999 Total assets	416	407
LIABILITIES:		
Federal liabilities:		
2103 Debt	414	406
2105 Other	2	1
2999 Total liabilities	416	407
NET POSITION:		
3300 Cumulative results of operations		
4999 Total liabilities and net position	416	407

FINANCIAL MANAGEMENT CAPITAL

For necessary expenses for upgrading and enhancing the Department of Transportation's financial systems and re-engineering business processes, $5,000,000, to remain available through September 30, 2024.

Note.—A full-year 2022 appropriation for this account was not enacted at the time the Budget was prepared; therefore, the Budget assumes this account is operating under the Continuing Appropriations Act, 2022 (Division A of Public Law 117–43, as amended). The amounts included for 2022 reflect the annualized level provided by the continuing resolution.

Program and Financing (in millions of dollars)

Identification code 069–0116–0–1–407	2021 actual	2022 est.	2023 est.
Obligations by program activity:			
0001 Financial management capital	3	3	5
Budgetary resources:			
Unobligated balance:			
1000 Unobligated balance brought forward, Oct 1	3	2	1
Budget authority:			
Appropriations, discretionary:			
1100 Appropriation	2	2	5
1930 Total budgetary resources available	5	4	6
Memorandum (non-add) entries:			
1941 Unexpired unobligated balance, end of year	2	1	1
Change in obligated balance:			
Unpaid obligations:			
3000 Unpaid obligations, brought forward, Oct 1	1	2	3
3010 New obligations, unexpired accounts	3	3	5
3020 Outlays (gross)	–2	–2	–3
3050 Unpaid obligations, end of year	2	3	5
Memorandum (non-add) entries:			
3100 Obligated balance, start of year	1	2	3
3200 Obligated balance, end of year	2	3	5
Budget authority and outlays, net:			
Discretionary:			
4000 Budget authority, gross	2	2	5
Outlays, gross:			
4010 Outlays from new discretionary authority			1
4011 Outlays from discretionary balances	2	2	2
4020 Outlays, gross (total)	2	2	3
4180 Budget authority, net (total)	2	2	5
4190 Outlays, net (total)	2	2	3

This appropriation provides funds to support projects that modernize the Department's financial systems and business processes to comply with key financial management initiatives. These funds will assist the Department in increasing data quality, ensuring compliance with financial standards and reporting, strengthening capabilities to provide oversight over the Department's risk and controls, execution of DATA Act requirements, and other critical needs that may arise.

Object Classification (in millions of dollars)

Identification code 069–0116–0–1–407	2021 actual	2022 est.	2023 est.
Direct obligations:			
25.1 Advisory and assistance services	1	1	2
25.3 Other goods and services from Federal sources	2	2	3
99.9 Total new obligations, unexpired accounts	3	3	5

CYBER SECURITY INITIATIVES

For necessary expenses for cyber security initiatives, including necessary upgrades to network and information technology infrastructure, improvement of identity management and authentication capabilities, securing and protecting data, implementation of Federal cyber security initiatives, implementation of enhanced security controls on agency computers and mobile devices, and related purposes, $48,100,000, to remain available until September 30, 2024.

Note.—A full-year 2022 appropriation for this account was not enacted at the time the Budget was prepared; therefore, the Budget assumes this account is operating under the Continuing Appropriations Act, 2022 (Division A of Public Law 117–43, as amended). The amounts included for 2022 reflect the annualized level provided by the continuing resolution.

Program and Financing (in millions of dollars)

Identification code 069–0159–0–1–407	2021 actual	2022 est.	2023 est.
Obligations by program activity:			
0001 Cyber Security Initiatives (Direct)	9	31	25
0100 Direct program activities, subtotal	9	31	25
Budgetary resources:			
Unobligated balance:			
1000 Unobligated balance brought forward, Oct 1	7	20	11
Budget authority:			
Appropriations, discretionary:			
1100 Appropriation	22	22	48
1930 Total budgetary resources available	29	42	59
Memorandum (non-add) entries:			
1941 Unexpired unobligated balance, end of year	20	11	34
Change in obligated balance:			
Unpaid obligations:			
3000 Unpaid obligations, brought forward, Oct 1	8	5	17
3010 New obligations, unexpired accounts	9	31	25
3020 Outlays (gross)	–12	–19	–26
3050 Unpaid obligations, end of year	5	17	16
Memorandum (non-add) entries:			
3100 Obligated balance, start of year	8	5	17
3200 Obligated balance, end of year	5	17	16
Budget authority and outlays, net:			
Discretionary:			
4000 Budget authority, gross	22	22	48
Outlays, gross:			
4010 Outlays from new discretionary authority		3	7
4011 Outlays from discretionary balances	12	16	19
4020 Outlays, gross (total)	12	19	26
4180 Budget authority, net (total)	22	22	48
4190 Outlays, net (total)	12	19	26

899

CYBER SECURITY INITIATIVES—Continued

This appropriation will fund cyber security initiatives, including necessary upgrades to the wide area network and information technology infrastructure. The funding will support key program enhancements, infrastructure improvements, and contractual resources to enhance the security of the Department of Transportation network, and reduce the risk of security breaches.

Object Classification (in millions of dollars)

Identification code 069–0159–0–1–407		2021 actual	2022 est.	2023 est.
	Direct obligations:			
25.1	Advisory and assistance services	1	10	5
25.3	Other goods and services from Federal sources	....	3	3
25.7	Operation and maintenance of equipment	3	13	14
31.0	Equipment	5	5	3
99.9	Total new obligations, unexpired accounts	9	31	25

OFFICE OF CIVIL RIGHTS

For necessary expenses of the Office of Civil Rights, $20,555,000, to remain available until September 30, 2024.

Note.—A full-year 2022 appropriation for this account was not enacted at the time the Budget was prepared; therefore, the Budget assumes this account is operating under the Continuing Appropriations Act, 2022 (Division A of Public Law 117–43, as amended). The amounts included for 2022 reflect the annualized level provided by the continuing resolution.

Program and Financing (in millions of dollars)

Identification code 069–0118–0–1–407		2021 actual	2022 est.	2023 est.
	Obligations by program activity:			
0001	Office of Civil Rights	9	10	21
	Budgetary resources:			
	Unobligated balance:			
1000	Unobligated balance brought forward, Oct 1	....	1	1
	Budget authority:			
	Appropriations, discretionary:			
1100	Appropriation	10	10	21
1930	Total budgetary resources available	10	11	22
	Memorandum (non-add) entries:			
1941	Unexpired unobligated balance, end of year	1	1	1
	Change in obligated balance:			
	Unpaid obligations:			
3000	Unpaid obligations, brought forward, Oct 1	4	4	2
3010	New obligations, unexpired accounts	9	10	21
3020	Outlays (gross)	–9	–12	–18
3050	Unpaid obligations, end of year	4	2	5
	Memorandum (non-add) entries:			
3100	Obligated balance, start of year	4	4	2
3200	Obligated balance, end of year	4	2	5
	Budget authority and outlays, net:			
	Discretionary:			
4000	Budget authority, gross	10	10	21
	Outlays, gross:			
4010	Outlays from new discretionary authority	7	8	16
4011	Outlays from discretionary balances	2	4	2
4020	Outlays, gross (total)	9	12	18
4180	Budget authority, net (total)	10	10	21
4190	Outlays, net (total)	9	12	18

The Departmental Office of Civil Rights (DOCR) plays a central leadership role in ensuring that the Department fulfills its goals of advancing equity and opportunity for all individuals and communities throughout its internal and external programs. DOCR provides oversight, guidance, and expertise on civil rights policy, programming, and enforcement for the Office of the Secretary, the Deputy Secretary, and Departmental Executives Management on measures designed to promote equity, diversity, and inclusion in its activities and its workforce.

Object Classification (in millions of dollars)

Identification code 069–0118–0–1–407		2021 actual	2022 est.	2023 est.
	Direct obligations:			
11.1	Personnel compensation: Full-time permanent	4	5	8
12.1	Civilian personnel benefits	1	1	2
25.1	Advisory and assistance services	2	2	....
25.2	Other services from non-Federal sources	....	....	2
25.3	Other goods and services from Federal sources	2	2	9
99.9	Total new obligations, unexpired accounts	9	10	21

Employment Summary

Identification code 069–0118–0–1–407	2021 actual	2022 est.	2023 est.
1001 Direct civilian full-time equivalent employment	31	45	61

SMALL AND DISADVANTAGED BUSINESS UTILIZATION AND OUTREACH

For necessary expenses for small and disadvantaged business utilization and outreach activities, $7,094,000, to remain available until September 30, 2024: Provided, That notwithstanding section 332 of title 49, United States Code, such amounts may be used for business opportunities related to any mode of transportation: Provided further, That appropriations made available under this heading shall be available for any purpose consistent with prior year appropriations that were made available under the heading "Office of the Secretary—Minority Business Resource Center Program".

Note.—A full-year 2022 appropriation for this account was not enacted at the time the Budget was prepared; therefore, the Budget assumes this account is operating under the Continuing Appropriations Act, 2022 (Division A of Public Law 117–43, as amended). The amounts included for 2022 reflect the annualized level provided by the continuing resolution.

Program and Financing (in millions of dollars)

Identification code 069–0119–0–1–407		2021 actual	2022 est.	2023 est.
	Obligations by program activity:			
0001	Minority business outreach	5	5	7
	Budgetary resources:			
	Unobligated balance:			
1000	Unobligated balance brought forward, Oct 1	4	4	4
	Budget authority:			
	Appropriations, discretionary:			
1100	Appropriation	5	5	7
1930	Total budgetary resources available	9	9	11
	Memorandum (non-add) entries:			
1941	Unexpired unobligated balance, end of year	4	4	4
	Change in obligated balance:			
	Unpaid obligations:			
3000	Unpaid obligations, brought forward, Oct 1	2	2	2
3010	New obligations, unexpired accounts	5	5	7
3020	Outlays (gross)	–5	–5	–6
3050	Unpaid obligations, end of year	2	2	3
	Memorandum (non-add) entries:			
3100	Obligated balance, start of year	2	2	2
3200	Obligated balance, end of year	2	2	3
	Budget authority and outlays, net:			
	Discretionary:			
4000	Budget authority, gross	5	5	7
	Outlays, gross:			
4010	Outlays from new discretionary authority	2	2	3
4011	Outlays from discretionary balances	3	3	3
4020	Outlays, gross (total)	5	5	6
4180	Budget authority, net (total)	5	5	7
4190	Outlays, net (total)	5	5	6

This appropriation includes funding for the Office of Small and Disadvantaged Business Utilization to ensure that: 1) the small and disadvantaged business policies and programs of the Secretary of Transportation are developed and implemented throughout the Department in a fair, efficient, and effective manner; and 2) effective outreach activities are in place to assist small businesses owned and controlled by socially and economically disadvantaged individuals, small businesses owned and controlled by women, small businesses owned and controlled by service disabled-veterans, Native American small business concerns, and qualified Historically Underutilized Business Zone (HUB Zone) small businesses concerned with securing Department of Transportation contracting and subcontracting opportunities.

Object Classification (in millions of dollars)

Identification code 069–0119–0–1–407	2021 actual	2022 est.	2023 est.
Direct obligations:			
11.1 Personnel compensation: Full-time permanent	1	1	2
41.0 Grants, subsidies, and contributions	4	4	5
99.9 Total new obligations, unexpired accounts	5	5	7

Employment Summary

Identification code 069–0119–0–1–407	2021 actual	2022 est.	2023 est.
1001 Direct civilian full-time equivalent employment	10	13	14

AVIATION MANUFACTURING JOBS PROTECTION PROGRAM

Program and Financing (in millions of dollars)

Identification code 069–0110–0–1–402	2021 actual	2022 est.	2023 est.
Obligations by program activity:			
0001 Aviation Manufacturing Payroll	404	291	
0002 Administrative Funding	9	13	
0900 Total new obligations, unexpired accounts	413	304	
Budgetary resources:			
Unobligated balance:			
1000 Unobligated balance brought forward, Oct 1		2,587	2,283
Budget authority:			
Appropriations, mandatory:			
1200 Appropriation	3,000		
1930 Total budgetary resources available	3,000	2,587	2,283
Memorandum (non-add) entries:			
1941 Unexpired unobligated balance, end of year	2,587	2,283	2,283
Change in obligated balance:			
Unpaid obligations:			
3000 Unpaid obligations, brought forward, Oct 1		225	14
3010 New obligations, unexpired accounts	413	304	
3020 Outlays (gross)	–188	–515	–12
3050 Unpaid obligations, end of year	225	14	2
Memorandum (non-add) entries:			
3100 Obligated balance, start of year		225	14
3200 Obligated balance, end of year	225	14	2
Budget authority and outlays, net:			
Mandatory:			
4090 Budget authority, gross	3,000		
Outlays, gross:			
4100 Outlays from new mandatory authority	188		
4101 Outlays from mandatory balances		515	12
4110 Outlays, gross (total)	188	515	12
4180 Budget authority, net (total)	3,000		
4190 Outlays, net (total)	188	515	12

The Aviation Manufacturing Jobs Protection (AMJP) Program is a program created in March 2021, under the American Rescue Plan Act. The AMJP Program provides funding to eligible businesses, to pay up to half of their compensation costs for certain categories of employees, for up to six months. In return, businesses have to make several legal commitments, including a commitment not to conduct involuntarily layoffs, furloughs, or reductions in pay or benefits for the covered employees. The statute established a six-month timeframe for the Department to make awards. No funds are requested for this account in 2023.

Object Classification (in millions of dollars)

Identification code 069–0110–0–1–402	2021 actual	2022 est.	2023 est.
Direct obligations:			
25.3 Other goods and services from Federal sources	9	13	
41.0 Grants, subsidies, and contributions	404	291	
99.9 Total new obligations, unexpired accounts	413	304	

TRANSPORTATION PLANNING, RESEARCH, AND DEVELOPMENT

(INCLUDING TRANSFER OF FUNDS)

For necessary expenses for conducting transportation planning, research, systems development, development activities, and making grants, $19,648,000, to remain available until expended: Provided, That of such amount, not less than $7,136,000 shall be for necessary expenses of the Interagency Infrastructure Permitting Improvement Center (IIPIC): Provided further, That there may be transferred to this appropriation, to remain available until expended, amounts transferred from other Federal agencies for expenses incurred under this heading for IIPIC activities not related to transportation infrastructure: Provided further, That the tools and analysis developed by the IIPIC shall be available to other Federal agencies for the permitting and review of major infrastructure projects not related to transportation only to the extent that other Federal agencies provide funding to the Department in accordance with the preceding proviso.

Note.—A full-year 2022 appropriation for this account was not enacted at the time the Budget was prepared; therefore, the Budget assumes this account is operating under the Continuing Appropriations Act, 2022 (Division A of Public Law 117–43, as amended). The amounts included for 2022 reflect the annualized level provided by the continuing resolution.

Program and Financing (in millions of dollars)

Identification code 069–0142–0–1–407	2021 actual	2022 est.	2023 est.
Obligations by program activity:			
0001 Transportation policy and planning	10	13	19
0003 Interagency Infrastructure Permitting Improvement Center (IIPIC)	2	2	7
0004 Automated Vehicles	3	6	
0005 Non-Traditional and Emerging Transportation Technology (NETT) Council		2	
0100 Total direct program	15	23	26
0799 Total direct obligations	15	23	26
0801 Transportation Planning, Research, and Development (Reimbursable)	3	1	1
0900 Total new obligations, unexpired accounts	18	24	27
Budgetary resources:			
Unobligated balance:			
1000 Unobligated balance brought forward, Oct 1	23	21	7
1021 Recoveries of prior year unpaid obligations	6		
1070 Unobligated balance (total)	29	21	7
Budget authority:			
Appropriations, discretionary:			
1100 Appropriation	9	9	20
Spending authority from offsetting collections, discretionary:			
1700 Collected	1	1	
1900 Budget authority (total)	10	10	20
1930 Total budgetary resources available	39	31	27
Memorandum (non-add) entries:			
1941 Unexpired unobligated balance, end of year	21	7	
Change in obligated balance:			
Unpaid obligations:			
3000 Unpaid obligations, brought forward, Oct 1	12	5	19
3010 New obligations, unexpired accounts	18	24	27
3020 Outlays (gross)	–19	–10	–14
3040 Recoveries of prior year unpaid obligations, unexpired	–6		
3050 Unpaid obligations, end of year	5	19	32
Uncollected payments:			
3060 Uncollected pymts, Fed sources, brought forward, Oct 1	–4	–4	–4
3090 Uncollected pymts, Fed sources, end of year	–4	–4	–4
Memorandum (non-add) entries:			
3100 Obligated balance, start of year	8	1	15
3200 Obligated balance, end of year	1	15	28

Office of the Secretary—Continued
Federal Funds—Continued

TRANSPORTATION PLANNING, RESEARCH, AND DEVELOPMENT—Continued

Program and Financing—Continued

Identification code 069–0142–0–1–407	2021 actual	2022 est.	2023 est.
Budget authority and outlays, net:			
Discretionary:			
4000 Budget authority, gross	10	10	20
Outlays, gross:			
4010 Outlays from new discretionary authority	....	4	8
4011 Outlays from discretionary balances	19	6	6
4020 Outlays, gross (total)	19	10	14
Offsets against gross budget authority and outlays:			
Offsetting collections (collected) from:			
4030 Federal sources	–1	–1	....
4040 Offsets against gross budget authority and outlays (total)	–1	–1	....
4180 Budget authority, net (total)	9	9	20
4190 Outlays, net (total)	18	9	14

This appropriation funds research and initiatives concerned with planning, analysis, and information development needed to support the Secretary's responsibilities in the formulation of National transportation policies and the coordination of National-level transportation planning. Funding also supports Departmental leadership in areas such as safety, climate, equity, economic impacts, aviation policy, and international transportation issues. The program activities include contracts with other Federal agencies, educational institutions, non-profit research organizations, and private firms. This appropriation also funds the Interagency Infrastructure Permitting Improvement Center, including an online database Permitting Dashboard, to support permitting/environmental review reforms to improve interagency coordination, and make the process for Federal approval for major infrastructure projects more efficient.

Object Classification (in millions of dollars)

Identification code 069–0142–0–1–407	2021 actual	2022 est.	2023 est.
Direct obligations:			
11.1 Personnel compensation: Full-time permanent	6	6	8
12.1 Civilian personnel benefits	2	2	2
25.1 Advisory and assistance services	2	2	2
25.2 Other services from non-Federal sources	....	....	8
25.3 Other goods and services from Federal sources	5	13	4
99.0 Direct obligations	15	23	24
99.0 Reimbursable obligations	3	1	3
99.9 Total new obligations, unexpired accounts	18	24	27

Employment Summary

Identification code 069–0142–0–1–407	2021 actual	2022 est.	2023 est.
1001 Direct civilian full-time equivalent employment	37	39	50

ESSENTIAL AIR SERVICE AND RURAL AIRPORT IMPROVEMENT FUND

Program and Financing (in millions of dollars)

Identification code 069–5423–0–2–402	2021 actual	2022 est.	2023 est.
Obligations by program activity:			
0001 Essential air service and rural airport improvement	195	79	85
Budgetary resources:			
Unobligated balance:			
1000 Unobligated balance brought forward, Oct 1	99	1	....
1011 Unobligated balance transfer from other acct [069–5422]	14	5	....
1020 Adjustment of unobligated bal brought forward, Oct 1	–3	....	....
1021 Recoveries of prior year unpaid obligations	22	....	....
1070 Unobligated balance (total)	132	6	....
Budget authority:			
Appropriations, mandatory:			
1200 Appropriation	23	....	....
1201 Appropriation (special or trust fund)	7	2	4
1221 Appropriations transferred from other acct [069–5422]	36	75	86
1232 Appropriations and/or unobligated balance of appropriations temporarily reduced	–2	–4	–5
1260 Appropriations, mandatory (total)	64	73	85
1900 Budget authority (total)	64	73	85
1930 Total budgetary resources available	196	79	85
Memorandum (non-add) entries:			
1941 Unexpired unobligated balance, end of year	1	....	....
Change in obligated balance:			
Unpaid obligations:			
3000 Unpaid obligations, brought forward, Oct 1	54	29	61
3010 New obligations, unexpired accounts	195	79	85
3020 Outlays (gross)	–198	–47	–110
3040 Recoveries of prior year unpaid obligations, unexpired	–22	....	....
3050 Unpaid obligations, end of year	29	61	36
Memorandum (non-add) entries:			
3100 Obligated balance, start of year	54	29	61
3200 Obligated balance, end of year	29	61	36
Budget authority and outlays, net:			
Mandatory:			
4090 Budget authority, gross	64	73	85
Outlays, gross:			
4100 Outlays from new mandatory authority	64	42	49
4101 Outlays from mandatory balances	134	5	61
4110 Outlays, gross (total)	198	47	110
4180 Budget authority, net (total)	64	73	85
4190 Outlays, net (total)	198	47	110
Memorandum (non-add) entries:			
5090 Unexpired unavailable balance, SOY: Offsetting collections	1	....	....
5092 Unexpired unavailable balance, EOY: Offsetting collections	1	....	....

The Federal Aviation Reauthorization Act of 1996 (P.L. 104–264) authorized the collection of user fees for services provided by the Federal Aviation Administration (FAA) to aircraft that neither take off nor land in the United States, commonly known as overflight fees. The Act permanently appropriated the first $50 million of such fees for the Essential Air Service (EAS) program and rural airport improvements. In addition, the FAA Modernization and Reauthorization Act (P.L. 112–95) requires that, in any fiscal year, overflight fees collected in excess of $50 million will be available to carry out the EAS program.

Object Classification (in millions of dollars)

Identification code 069–5423–0–2–402	2021 actual	2022 est.	2023 est.
Direct obligations:			
11.1 Personnel compensation: Full-time permanent	2	2	2
12.1 Civilian personnel benefits	1	1	1
25.1 Advisory and assistance services	1	1	1
41.0 Grants, subsidies, and contributions	191	75	81
99.9 Total new obligations, unexpired accounts	195	79	85

Employment Summary

Identification code 069–5423–0–2–402	2021 actual	2022 est.	2023 est.
1001 Direct civilian full-time equivalent employment	12	14	14

WORKING CAPITAL FUND

Note.—A full-year 2022 appropriation for this account was not enacted at the time the Budget was prepared; therefore, the Budget assumes this account is operating under the Continuing Appropriations Act, 2022 (Division A of Public Law 117–43, as amended). The amounts included for 2022 reflect the annualized level provided by the continuing resolution.

Program and Financing (in millions of dollars)

Identification code 069–4520–0–4–407	2021 actual	2022 est.	2023 est.
Obligations by program activity:			
0801 DOT service center activities	294	396	505
0802 Non-DOT service center activities	92	307	259
0900 Total new obligations, unexpired accounts	386	703	764

DEPARTMENT OF TRANSPORTATION

Office of the Secretary—Continued
Federal Funds—Continued

903

		2021 actual	2022 est.	2023 est.
	Budgetary resources:			
	Unobligated balance:			
1000	Unobligated balance brought forward, Oct 1	88	105	28
1021	Recoveries of prior year unpaid obligations	28		
1070	Unobligated balance (total)	116	105	28
	Budget authority:			
	Spending authority from offsetting collections, discretionary:			
1700	Collected	373	626	764
1701	Change in uncollected payments, Federal sources	2		
1750	Spending auth from offsetting collections, disc (total)	375	626	764
1930	Total budgetary resources available	491	731	792
	Memorandum (non-add) entries:			
1941	Unexpired unobligated balance, end of year	105	28	28
	Change in obligated balance:			
	Unpaid obligations:			
3000	Unpaid obligations, brought forward, Oct 1	136	123	187
3010	New obligations, unexpired accounts	386	703	764
3020	Outlays (gross)	–371	–639	–753
3040	Recoveries of prior year unpaid obligations, unexpired	–28		
3050	Unpaid obligations, end of year	123	187	198
	Uncollected payments:			
3060	Uncollected pymts, Fed sources, brought forward, Oct 1	–21	–23	–23
3070	Change in uncollected pymts, Fed sources, unexpired	–2		
3090	Uncollected pymts, Fed sources, end of year	–23	–23	–23
	Memorandum (non-add) entries:			
3100	Obligated balance, start of year	115	100	164
3200	Obligated balance, end of year	100	164	175
	Budget authority and outlays, net:			
	Discretionary:			
4000	Budget authority, gross	375	626	764
	Outlays, gross:			
4010	Outlays from new discretionary authority	260	545	665
4011	Outlays from discretionary balances	111	94	88
4020	Outlays, gross (total)	371	639	753
	Offsets against gross budget authority and outlays:			
	Offsetting collections (collected) from:			
4030	Federal sources	–371	–626	–764
4033	Non-Federal sources	–2		
4040	Offsets against gross budget authority and outlays (total)	–373	–626	–764
	Additional offsets against gross budget authority only:			
4050	Change in uncollected pymts, Fed sources, unexpired	–2		
4080	Outlays, net (discretionary)	–2	13	–11
4180	Budget authority, net (total)			
4190	Outlays, net (total)	–2	13	–11

The Working Capital Fund finances common administrative services and other services that are centrally performed in the interest of economy and efficiency. The fund is financed through agreements with the Department of Transportation Operating Administrations (OAs) and other customers. In 2023, the Working Capital Fund will obligate millions across the Department, to include the Department's implementation of a shared services environment for commodity information technology (IT) investments. The IT shared services initiative will modernize IT across the Department and improve mission delivery by consolidating separate, overlapping, and duplicative processes and functions. In 2023, the Department will continue consolidating commodity IT services across OAs. As a key part of this effort, the Office of the Chief Information Officer will focus on investment-level commodity IT as well as IT Security and Compliance activities. Utilizing shared services will enable the Department to improve cybersecurity, increase efficiencies, and improve transparency in IT spending.

Object Classification (in millions of dollars)

Identification code 069–4520–0–4–407		2021 actual	2022 est.	2023 est.
	Reimbursable obligations:			
	Personnel compensation:			
11.1	Full-time permanent	31	43	45
11.3	Other than full-time permanent	1	1	1
11.9	Total personnel compensation	32	44	46
12.1	Civilian personnel benefits	11	15	17
13.0	Benefits for former personnel	1	2	2
22.0	Transportation of things	1	1	1
23.1	Rental payments to GSA	11	11	66
23.3	Communications, utilities, and miscellaneous charges	10	10	11
25.2	Other services from non-Federal sources	114	186	184
25.3	Other goods and services from Federal sources	46	51	59
25.4	Operation and maintenance of facilities	1		
25.7	Operation and maintenance of equipment	44	29	71
26.0	Supplies and materials	74	302	257
31.0	Equipment	22	52	50
44.0	Refunds	19		
99.9	Total new obligations, unexpired accounts	386	703	764

Employment Summary

Identification code 069–4520–0–4–407	2021 actual	2022 est.	2023 est.
2001 Reimbursable civilian full-time equivalent employment	255	291	299

RAILROAD REHABILITATION AND IMPROVEMENT FINANCING PROGRAM

The Secretary is authorized to issue direct loans and loan guarantees pursuant to chapter 224 of title 49, United States Code, such authority shall exist as long as any such direct loan or loan guarantee is outstanding.

Note.—A full-year 2022 appropriation for this account was not enacted at the time the Budget was prepared; therefore, the Budget assumes this account is operating under the Continuing Appropriations Act, 2022 (Division A of Public Law 117–43, as amended). The amounts included for 2022 reflect the annualized level provided by the continuing resolution.

Program and Financing (in millions of dollars)

Identification code 069–0750–0–1–401		2021 actual	2022 est.	2023 est.
	Obligations by program activity:			
	Credit program obligations:			
0705	Reestimates of direct loan subsidy	45		
0706	Interest on reestimates of direct loan subsidy	24		
0791	Direct program activities, subtotal	69		
0900	Total new obligations, unexpired accounts	69		
	Budgetary resources:			
	Unobligated balance:			
1000	Unobligated balance brought forward, Oct 1	26	26	26
	Budget authority:			
	Appropriations, mandatory:			
1200	Appropriation	69		
1900	Budget authority (total)	69		
1930	Total budgetary resources available	95	26	26
	Memorandum (non-add) entries:			
1941	Unexpired unobligated balance, end of year	26	26	26
	Change in obligated balance:			
	Unpaid obligations:			
3010	New obligations, unexpired accounts	69		
3020	Outlays (gross)	–69		
	Budget authority and outlays, net:			
	Mandatory:			
4090	Budget authority, gross	69		
	Outlays, gross:			
4100	Outlays from new mandatory authority	69		
4180	Budget authority, net (total)	69		
4190	Outlays, net (total)	69		

Summary of Loan Levels, Subsidy Budget Authority and Outlays by Program (in millions of dollars)

Identification code 069–0750–0–1–401		2021 actual	2022 est.	2023 est.
	Direct loan levels supportable by subsidy budget authority:			
115001	Railroad Rehabilitation and Improvement Financing Direct Loans	908	600	600
	Direct loan subsidy (in percent):			
132001	Railroad Rehabilitation and Improvement Financing Direct Loans	–1.61	–1.71	–.79
132999	Weighted average subsidy rate	–1.61	–1.71	–.79
	Direct loan subsidy budget authority:			
133001	Railroad Rehabilitation and Improvement Financing Direct Loans	–15	–10	–5
	Direct loan reestimates:			
135001	Railroad Rehabilitation and Improvement Financing Direct Loans	57	–96	

Office of the Secretary—Continued
Federal Funds—Continued

RAILROAD REHABILITATION AND IMPROVEMENT FINANCING PROGRAM—Continued

The Railroad Rehabilitation and Improvement Program, authorized under chapter 224 of title 49, provides loans and loan guarantees to: 1) acquire, improve, or rehabilitate intermodal or rail equipment or facilities, including track, components of track, bridges, yards, buildings, or shops; 2) refinance debt; 3) develop and establish new intermodal or railroad facilities; 4) reimburse related planning and design expenses; and 5) to finance certain economic development related to passenger rail stations.

Object Classification (in millions of dollars)

Identification code 069–0750–0–1–401		2021 actual	2022 est.	2023 est.
	Direct obligations:			
33.0	Investments and loans	45		
43.0	Interest and dividends	24		
99.9	Total new obligations, unexpired accounts	69		

RAILROAD REHABILITATION AND IMPROVEMENT DIRECT LOAN FINANCING ACCOUNT

Program and Financing (in millions of dollars)

Identification code 069–4420–0–3–401		2021 actual	2022 est.	2023 est.
	Obligations by program activity:			
	Credit program obligations:			
0710	Direct loan obligations	908	600	600
0713	Payment of interest to Treasury	47	38	38
0740	Negative subsidy obligations	15	10	5
0742	Downward reestimates paid to receipt accounts	11	76	
0743	Interest on downward reestimates	1	20	
0900	Total new obligations, unexpired accounts	982	744	643
	Budgetary resources:			
	Unobligated balance:			
1000	Unobligated balance brought forward, Oct 1	90	193	84
1021	Recoveries of prior year unpaid obligations	1,188		
1024	Unobligated balance of borrowing authority withdrawn	–1,188		
1070	Unobligated balance (total)	90	193	84
	Financing authority:			
	Borrowing authority, mandatory:			
1400	Borrowing authority	935	600	600
	Spending authority from offsetting collections, mandatory:			
1800	Offsetting collections (interest on uninvested funds)	816	3	3
1800	Offsetting collections (principal-borrowers)		35	60
1800	Offsetting collections (interest-borrowers)		8	27
1800	Collected		10	10
1825	Spending authority from offsetting collections applied to repay debt	–666	–21	–62
1850	Spending auth from offsetting collections, mand (total)	150	35	38
1900	Budget authority (total)	1,085	635	638
1930	Total budgetary resources available	1,175	828	722
	Memorandum (non-add) entries:			
1941	Unexpired unobligated balance, end of year	193	84	79
	Change in obligated balance:			
	Unpaid obligations:			
3000	Unpaid obligations, brought forward, Oct 1	3,936	3,671	3,388
3010	New obligations, unexpired accounts	982	744	643
3020	Outlays (gross)	–59	–1,027	–1,027
3040	Recoveries of prior year unpaid obligations, unexpired	–1,188		
3050	Unpaid obligations, end of year	3,671	3,388	3,004
	Memorandum (non-add) entries:			
3100	Obligated balance, start of year	3,936	3,671	3,388
3200	Obligated balance, end of year	3,671	3,388	3,004
	Financing authority and disbursements, net:			
	Mandatory:			
4090	Budget authority, gross	1,085	635	638
	Financing disbursements:			
4110	Outlays, gross (total)	59	1,027	1,027
	Offsets against gross financing authority and disbursements:			
	Offsetting collections (collected) from:			
4120	Federal sources	–69		
4122	Interest on uninvested funds	–4	–3	–3
4123	Credit Risk Premium	–743	–10	–10
4123	Principal Repayment		–35	–60
4123	Interest Repayment		–8	–27
4130	Offsets against gross budget authority and outlays (total)	–816	–56	–100
4160	Budget authority, net (mandatory)	269	579	538
4170	Outlays, net (mandatory)	–757	971	927
4180	Budget authority, net (total)	269	579	538
4190	Outlays, net (total)	–757	971	927

Status of Direct Loans (in millions of dollars)

Identification code 069–4420–0–3–401		2021 actual	2022 est.	2023 est.
	Position with respect to appropriations act limitation on obligations:			
1111	Direct loan obligations from current-year authority	908	600	600
1150	Total direct loan obligations	908	600	600
	Cumulative balance of direct loans outstanding:			
1210	Outstanding, start of year	1,444	760	1,322
1231	Disbursements: Direct loan disbursements		598	598
1251	Repayments: Repayments and prepayments	–684	–35	–60
1263	Write-offs for default: Direct loans		–1	–1
1290	Outstanding, end of year	760	1,322	1,859

As required by the Federal Credit Reform Act of 1990, this non-budgetary financing account records all cash flows to and from the Government resulting from the Railroad Rehabilitation and Improvement Financing Program Account. The amounts in this account are a means of financing and are not included in the budget totals.

Balance Sheet (in millions of dollars)

Identification code 069–4420–0–3–401		2020 actual	2021 actual
	ASSETS:		
	Federal assets:		
1101	Fund balances with Treasury	90	194
	Investments in U.S. securities:		
1106	Receivables, net	53	
	Net value of assets related to post-1991 direct loans receivable:		
1401	Direct loans receivable, gross	1,444	760
1405	Allowance for subsidy cost (-)	–172	–109
1499	Net present value of assets related to direct loans	1,272	651
1999	Total assets	1,415	845
	LIABILITIES:		
	Federal liabilities:		
2103	Debt	1,403	749
2105	Other	12	96
2999	Total liabilities	1,415	845
	NET POSITION:		
3300	Cumulative results of operations		
4999	Total liabilities and net position	1,415	845

Trust Funds

TIFIA HIGHWAY TRUST FUND PROGRAM ACCOUNT

Special and Trust Fund Receipts (in millions of dollars)

Identification code 069–8634–0–7–401		2021 actual	2022 est.	2023 est.
0100	Balance, start of year	80		
0198	Adjustment for split account with Highway Trust Fund	–80		
0199	Balance, start of year			
	Receipts:			
	Current law:			
1140	Payment From The General Fund, National Surface Transportation and Innovative Finance Bureau Highway Trust Fund Account, Upward Reestimates	380	207	
2000	Total: Balances and receipts	380	207	
	Appropriations:			
	Current law:			
2101	TIFIA Highway Trust Fund Program Account	–380	–207	
5099	Balance, end of year			

DEPARTMENT OF TRANSPORTATION

Office of the Secretary—Continued
Trust Funds—Continued

Program and Financing (in millions of dollars)

Identification code 069–8634–0–7–401	2021 actual	2022 est.	2023 est.
Obligations by program activity:			
0001 TIFIA Revenue Fee	2	2	
0091 Direct program activities, subtotal	2	2	
Credit program obligations:			
0701 Direct loan subsidy	8	61	19
0703 Subsidy for modifications of direct loans	625	465	
0705 Reestimates of direct loan subsidy	258	172	
0706 Interest on reestimates of direct loan subsidy	122	35	
0709 Administrative expenses	8	8	10
0715 Fee Assistance for Small Projects		2	2
0791 Direct program activities, subtotal	1,021	743	31
0900 Total new obligations, unexpired accounts	1,023	745	31
Budgetary resources:			
Unobligated balance:			
1000 Unobligated balance brought forward, Oct 1	26	396	392
1001 Discretionary unobligated balance brought fwd, Oct 1	15		
1013 Unobligated balance of contract authority transferred to or from other accounts [069–8083]	826	534	35
1021 Recoveries of prior year unpaid obligations	178		
1070 Unobligated balance (total)	1,030	930	427
Budget authority:			
Appropriations, discretionary:			
1121 Appropriations transferred from other acct [069–8083]	846	481	9
1138 Appropriations applied to liquidate contract authority	–846	–481	–9
Appropriations, mandatory:			
1201 Appropriation (special or trust fund)	380	207	
Contract authority, mandatory:			
1611 Contract authority transferred from other accounts [069–8083]	9		
1900 Budget authority (total)	389	207	
1930 Total budgetary resources available	1,419	1,137	427
Memorandum (non-add) entries:			
1941 Unexpired unobligated balance, end of year	396	392	396
Change in obligated balance:			
Unpaid obligations:			
3000 Unpaid obligations, brought forward, Oct 1	260	42	34
3010 New obligations, unexpired accounts	1,023	745	31
3020 Outlays (gross)	–1,063	–753	–43
3040 Recoveries of prior year unpaid obligations, unexpired	–178		
3050 Unpaid obligations, end of year	42	34	22
Memorandum (non-add) entries:			
3100 Obligated balance, start of year	260	42	34
3200 Obligated balance, end of year	42	34	22
Budget authority and outlays, net:			
Discretionary:			
Outlays, gross:			
4010 Outlays from new discretionary authority		481	3
4011 Outlays from discretionary balances	683	65	40
4020 Outlays, gross (total)	683	546	43
Mandatory:			
4090 Budget authority, gross	389	207	
Outlays, gross:			
4100 Outlays from new mandatory authority	380	207	
4180 Budget authority, net (total)	389	207	
4190 Outlays, net (total)	1,063	753	43
Memorandum (non-add) entries:			
5050 Unobligated balance, SOY: Contract authority			19
5051 Unobligated balance, EOY: Contract authority		19	57
5052 Obligated balance, SOY: Contract authority	11		34
5053 Obligated balance, EOY: Contract authority		34	22
5061 Limitation on obligations (Transportation Trust Funds)	121	534	35

Summary of Loan Levels, Subsidy Budget Authority and Outlays by Program (in millions of dollars)

Identification code 069–8634–0–7–401	2021 actual	2022 est.	2023 est.
Direct loan levels supportable by subsidy budget authority:			
115002 TIFIA Direct Loans	8,959	10,987	10,987
115999 Total direct loan levels	8,959	10,987	10,987
Direct loan subsidy (in percent):			
132002 TIFIA Direct Loans	–.71	–1.21	0.17
132999 Weighted average subsidy rate	–.71	–1.21	0.17
Direct loan subsidy budget authority:			
133002 TIFIA Direct Loans	–63	–72	19
133999 Total subsidy budget authority	–63	–72	19
Direct loan subsidy outlays:			
134002 TIFIA Direct Loans	669	67	35
134999 Total subsidy outlays	669	67	35
Direct loan reestimates:			
135002 TIFIA Direct Loans	–8	–857	
135999 Total direct loan reestimates	–8	–857	
Administrative expense data:			
3510 Budget authority	7	7	7
3590 Outlays from new authority	7	7	7

This is the program account for the Transportation Infrastructure Finance and Innovation Act (TIFIA) program that receives funding from the Highway Trust Fund. The TIFIA program provides credit assistance for eligible transportation projects of regional and national significance.

Object Classification (in millions of dollars)

Identification code 069–8634–0–7–401	2021 actual	2022 est.	2023 est.
Direct obligations:			
11.1 Personnel compensation: Full-time permanent	4	4	5
12.1 Civilian personnel benefits	1	1	1
25.1 Advisory and assistance services	3	5	4
25.3 Other goods and services from Federal sources	2	2	2
33.0 Investments and loans	380	207	
41.0 Grants, subsidies, and contributions	633	526	19
99.9 Total new obligations, unexpired accounts	1,023	745	31

Employment Summary

Identification code 069–8634–0–7–401	2021 actual	2022 est.	2023 est.
1001 Direct civilian full-time equivalent employment	23	23	33

PAYMENTS TO AIR CARRIERS

(AIRPORT AND AIRWAY TRUST FUND)

In addition to funds made available from any other source to carry out the essential air service program under sections 41731 through 41742 of title 49, United States Code, $368,727,000, to be derived from the Airport and Airway Trust Fund, to remain available until expended: Provided, That in determining between or among carriers competing to provide service to a community, the Secretary may consider the relative subsidy requirements of the carriers: Provided further, That basic essential air service minimum requirements shall not include the 15-passenger capacity requirement under section 41732(b)(3) of title 49, United States Code: Provided further, That amounts authorized to be distributed for the essential air service program under section 41742(b) of title 49, United States Code, shall be made available immediately from amounts otherwise provided to the Administrator of the Federal Aviation Administration: Provided further, That the Administrator may reimburse such amounts from fees credited to the account established under section 45303 of title 49, United States Code.

Note.—A full-year 2022 appropriation for this account was not enacted at the time the Budget was prepared; therefore, the Budget assumes this account is operating under the Continuing Appropriations Act, 2022 (Division A of Public Law 117–43, as amended). The amounts included for 2022 reflect the annualized level provided by the continuing resolution.

Program and Financing (in millions of dollars)

Identification code 069–8304–0–7–402	2021 actual	2022 est.	2023 est.
Obligations by program activity:			
0001 Payments to air carriers	159	248	370
0900 Total new obligations, unexpired accounts (object class 41.0)	159	248	370
Budgetary resources:			
Unobligated balance:			
1000 Unobligated balance brought forward, Oct 1	3	1	1
1021 Recoveries of prior year unpaid obligations	15		
1070 Unobligated balance (total)	18	1	1

Office of the Secretary—Continued
Trust Funds—Continued

PAYMENTS TO AIR CARRIERS—Continued

Program and Financing—Continued

Identification code 069–8304–0–7–402	2021 actual	2022 est.	2023 est.
Budget authority:			
Appropriations, discretionary:			
1101 Appropriation (special or trust)	142	248	369
1930 Total budgetary resources available	160	249	370
Memorandum (non-add) entries:			
1941 Unexpired unobligated balance, end of year	1	1	
Change in obligated balance:			
Unpaid obligations:			
3000 Unpaid obligations, brought forward, Oct 1	18	19	98
3010 New obligations, unexpired accounts	159	248	370
3020 Outlays (gross)	–143	–169	–320
3040 Recoveries of prior year unpaid obligations, unexpired	–15		
3050 Unpaid obligations, end of year	19	98	148
Memorandum (non-add) entries:			
3100 Obligated balance, start of year	18	19	98
3200 Obligated balance, end of year	19	98	148
Budget authority and outlays, net:			
Discretionary:			
4000 Budget authority, gross	142	248	369
Outlays, gross:			
4010 Outlays from new discretionary authority	123	149	221
4011 Outlays from discretionary balances	20	20	99
4020 Outlays, gross (total)	143	169	320
4180 Budget authority, net (total)	142	248	369
4190 Outlays, net (total)	143	169	320

Through 1997, the Essential Air Service (EAS) program was funded from the Airport and Airway Trust Fund. Starting in 1998, the Federal Aviation Administration reauthorization funded it as a mandatory program supported by overflight fees under the EAS and Rural Airport Improvement Fund. In addition to mandatory funding supported by overflight fees, direct appropriations from the Airport and Airway Trust Fund to Payments to Air Carriers have been enacted every year beginning in 2002 to meet the needs of the Essential Air Service program.

ADMINISTRATIVE PROVISIONS

SEC. 101. None of the funds made available by this Act to the Department of Transportation may be obligated for the Office of the Secretary of Transportation to approve assessments or reimbursable agreements pertaining to funds appropriated to the operating administrations in this Act, except for activities underway on the date of enactment of this Act, unless such assessments or agreements have completed the normal reprogramming process for congressional notification.

SEC. 102. The Secretary shall post on the web site of the Department of Transportation a schedule of all meetings of the Council on Credit and Finance, including the agenda for each meeting, and require the Council on Credit and Finance to record the decisions and actions of each meeting.

SEC. 103. In addition to authority provided by section 327 of title 49, United States Code, the Department's Working Capital Fund is authorized to provide partial or full payments in advance and accept subsequent reimbursements from all Federal agencies from available funds for transit benefit distribution services that are necessary to carry out the Federal transit pass transportation fringe benefit program under Executive Order No. 13150 and section 3049 of SAFETEA-LU (5 U.S.C. 7905 note): Provided, That the Department shall maintain a reasonable operating reserve in the Working Capital Fund, to be expended in advance to provide uninterrupted transit benefits to Government employees: Provided further, That such reserve shall not exceed 1 month of benefits payable and may be used only for the purpose of providing for the continuation of transit benefits: Provided further, That the Working Capital Fund shall be fully reimbursed by each customer agency from available funds for the actual cost of the transit benefit.

SEC. 104. Receipts collected in the Department's Working Capital Fund, as authorized by section 327 of title 49, United States Code, for unused transit and van pool benefits, in an amount not to exceed 10 percent of fiscal year 2022 collections, shall be available until expended in the Department's Working Capital Fund to provide contractual services in support of section 199A of this Act: Provided, That obligations in fiscal year 2023 of such collections shall not exceed $1,000,000.

SEC. 105. None of the funds in this Act may be obligated or expended for retention or senior executive bonuses for an employee of the Department of Transportation without the prior written approval of the Assistant Secretary for Administration.

SEC. 106. In addition to authority provided by section 327 of title 49, United States Code, the Department's Administrative Working Capital Fund is hereby authorized to transfer information technology equipment, software, and systems from Departmental sources or other entities and collect and maintain a reserve at rates which will return full cost of transferred assets.

SEC. 107. None of the funds provided in this Act to the Department of Transportation may be used to provide credit assistance unless not less than 3 days before any application approval to provide credit assistance under sections 603 and 604 of title 23, United States Code, the Secretary provides notification in writing to the following committees: the House and Senate Committees on Appropriations; the Committee on Environment and Public Works and the Committee on Banking, Housing and Urban Affairs of the Senate; and the Committee on Transportation and Infrastructure of the House of Representatives: Provided, That such notification shall include, but not be limited to, the name of the project sponsor; a description of the project; whether credit assistance will be provided as a direct loan, loan guarantee, or line of credit; and the amount of credit assistance.

SEC. 108. Section 312 of title 49, United States Code, is repealed.

SEC. 109. (a) Amounts made available to the Secretary of Transportation or the Department of Transportation's Operating Administrations in this Act for the costs of award, administration, or oversight of financial assistance under the programs identified in subsection (c) may be transferred to the account identified in section 801 of division J of Public Law 117–58, to remain available until expended, for necessary expenses of award, administration, or oversight of any financial assistance programs in the Department of Transportation.

(b) Amounts transferred under the authority in this section are available in addition to amounts otherwise available for such purposes.

(c) The programs from which funds made available under this Act may be transferred under subsection (a) are:

(1) the national infrastructure project assistance program under section 6701 of title 49, United States Code;

(2) the local and regional project assistance program under section 6702 of title 49, United States Code; and

(3) any other financial assistance program that is funded under this Act and administered from the Office of the Secretary.

SEC. 110. Sec. 801 of division J of Public Law 117–58 is amended to read as follows: "Sec. 801. (a) Amounts made available to the Secretary of Transportation or the Department of Transportation's Operating Administrations in this title in this Act and in section 117 of title 23, United States Code, for fiscal years 2022 through 2026 for the costs of award, administration, or oversight of financial assistance under the programs administered by the Office of the Secretary may be transferred to an Operational Support account, to remain available until expended, for necessary expenses of (1) coordinating the implementation of any division of this Act, or (2) the award, administration, or oversight of any financial assistance programs funded under this title in this Act or divisions A, B, C, or G of this Act: Provided, That amounts transferred pursuant to this subsection are available in addition to amounts otherwise available for such purposes: Provided further, That one-half of one percent of the amounts transferred pursuant to this subsection in each of fiscal years 2022 through 2026 shall be transferred to the Office of Inspector General of the Department of Transportation for oversight of funding provided to the Department of Transportation in this title in this Act: Provided further, That the amount provided by this section is designated by the Congress as being for an emergency requirement pursuant to section 4112(a) of H. Con. Res. 71 (115th Congress), the concurrent resolution on the budget for fiscal year 2018, and to section 251(b) of the Balanced Budget and Emergency Deficit Control Act of 1985. (b) In addition to programs identified in section 118(d) of title 49, United States Code, the Office of the Secretary shall administer, with support from the Department's Operating Administrations, the following financial assistance programs—(1) the national infrastructure projects program under section 6701 of title 49, United States Code; (2) the local and regional projects program under section 6702 of title 49, United States Code; (3) the strengthening mobility and revolutionizing transportation grant program under section 25005 of division B of this Act; (4) the nationally significant freight and highways projects under section 117 of title 23, United States Code; (5) the national culvert removal, replacement, and restoration grant program under section 6703 of title 49, United States Code; and (6) other discretionary financial assistance programs that the Secretary determines should be administered by the Office of the Secretary, subject to prior notification of the House and Senate Committees on Appropriations.".

DEPARTMENT OF TRANSPORTATION

Federal Aviation Administration
Federal Funds 907

ADMINISTRATIVE PROVISIONS—OFFICE OF THE SECRETARY OF TRANSPORTATION

[(INCLUDING TRANSFER OF FUNDS)]

[SEC. 801. (a) Amounts made available to the Secretary of Transportation or the Department of Transportation's Operating Administrations in this title in this Act and in section 117 of title 23, United States Code, for fiscal years 2022 through 2026 for the costs of award, administration, or oversight of financial assistance under the programs administered by the Office of Multimodal Infrastructure and Freight may be transferred to an "Office of Multimodal Infrastructure and Freight" account, to remain available until expended, for the necessary expenses of award, administration, or oversight of any discretionary financial assistance programs funded under this title in this Act or division A of this Act: *Provided*, That one-half of one percent of the amounts transferred pursuant to the authority in this section in each of fiscal years 2022 through 2026 shall be transferred to the Office of Inspector General of the Department of Transportation for oversight of funding provided to the Department of Transportation in this title in this Act: *Provided further*, That the amount provided by this section is designated by the Congress as being for an emergency requirement pursuant to section 4112(a) of H. Con. Res. 71 (115th Congress), the concurrent resolution on the budget for fiscal year 2018, and to section 251(b) of the Balanced Budget and Emergency Deficit Control Act of 1985.

(b) In addition to programs identified in section 118(d) of title 49, United States Code, the Office of Multimodal Infrastructure and Freight shall administer, with support from the Department's Operating Administrations, the following financial assistance programs—

(1) the national infrastructure projects program under section 6701 of title 49, United States Code;

(2) the local and regional projects program under section 6702 of title 49, United States Code;

(3) the strengthening mobility and revolutionizing transportation grant program under section 25005 of division B of this Act;

(4) the nationally significant freight and highways projects under section 117 of title 23, United States Code;

(5) the national culvert removal, replacement, and restoration grant program under section 6203 of title 49, United States Code; and

(6) other discretionary financial assistance programs that the Secretary determines should be administered by the Office of Multimodal Infrastructure and Freight, subject to the approval of the House and Senate Committees on Appropriations as required under section 405 of Division L of the Consolidated Appropriations Act, 2021.]

(Infrastructure Investments and Jobs Appropriations Act.)

FEDERAL AVIATION ADMINISTRATION

Federal Funds

OPERATIONS

(AIRPORT AND AIRWAY TRUST FUND)

For necessary expenses of the Federal Aviation Administration, not otherwise provided for, including operations and research activities related to commercial space transportation, administrative expenses for research and development, establishment of air navigation facilities, the operation (including leasing) and maintenance of aircraft, subsidizing the cost of aeronautical charts and maps sold to the public, the lease or purchase of passenger motor vehicles for replacement only, $11,933,821,000, to remain available until September 30, 2024, of which $9,933,821,000 shall be derived from the Airport and Airway Trust Fund: *Provided*, That not later than 60 days after the submission of the budget request, the Administrator of the Federal Aviation Administration shall transmit to Congress an annual update to the report submitted to Congress in December 2004 pursuant to section 221 of the Vision 100-Century of Aviation Reauthorization Act (49 U.S.C. 40101 note): *Provided further*, That not later than 60 days after the submission of the budget request, the Administrator shall transmit to Congress a companion report that describes a comprehensive strategy for staffing, hiring, and training flight standards and aircraft certification staff in a format similar to the one utilized for the controller staffing plan, including stated attrition estimates and numerical hiring goals by fiscal year: *Provided further*, That funds may be used to enter into a grant agreement with a nonprofit standard-setting organization to assist in the development of aviation safety standards: *Provided further*, That none of the funds made available by this Act shall be available for new applicants for the second career training program: *Provided further*, That there may be credited to this appropriation, as offsetting collections, funds received from States, counties, municipalities, foreign authorities, other public authorities, and private sources for expenses incurred in the provision of agency services, including receipts for the maintenance and operation of air navigation facilities, and for issuance, renewal or modification of certificates, including airman, aircraft, and repair station certificates, or for tests related thereto, or for processing major repair or alteration forms.

Note.—A full-year 2022 appropriation for this account was not enacted at the time the Budget was prepared; therefore, the Budget assumes this account is operating under the Continuing Appropriations Act, 2022 (Division A of Public Law 117–43, as amended). The amounts included for 2022 reflect the annualized level provided by the continuing resolution.

Program and Financing (in millions of dollars)

Identification code 069–1301–0–1–402		2021 actual	2022 est.	2023 est.
	Obligations by program activity:			
0001	Air Traffic Organization (ATO)	8,257	8,230	8,770
0002	NextGen	65	65	....
0003	Finance & Management	842	843	917
0004	Aviation Safety	1,494	1,508	1,599
0005	Commercial Space Transportation	27	30	41
0006	Security & Hazardous Materials Safety	125	129	156
0007	Staff Offices	268	268	301
0008	2017/2018 Hurricanes & CARES Act	16	....	....
0010	Research and Development	....	....	56
0011	Integration and Engagement	....	....	35
0100	Direct Program Activities Subtotal	11,094	11,073	11,875
0799	Total direct obligations	11,094	11,073	11,875
0801	Operations (Reimbursable)	147	143	145
0900	Total new obligations, unexpired accounts	11,241	11,216	12,020
	Budgetary resources:			
	Unobligated balance:			
1000	Unobligated balance brought forward, Oct 1	167	153	124
1021	Recoveries of prior year unpaid obligations	89	....	....
1070	Unobligated balance (total)	256	153	124
	Budget authority:			
	Appropriations, discretionary:			
1100	Appropriation	483	483	2,000
	Spending authority from offsetting collections, discretionary:			
1700	Collected	10,400	10,861	10,086
1701	Change in uncollected payments, Federal sources	266	–157	33
1750	Spending auth from offsetting collections, disc (total)	10,666	10,704	10,119
1900	Budget authority (total)	11,149	11,187	12,119
1930	Total budgetary resources available	11,405	11,340	12,243
	Memorandum (non-add) entries:			
1940	Unobligated balance expiring	–11	....	....
1941	Unexpired unobligated balance, end of year	153	124	223
	Change in obligated balance:			
	Unpaid obligations:			
3000	Unpaid obligations, brought forward, Oct 1	1,772	1,842	1,392
3010	New obligations, unexpired accounts	11,241	11,216	12,020
3011	Obligations ("upward adjustments"), expired accounts	40	....	....
3020	Outlays (gross)	–11,092	–11,666	–12,203
3040	Recoveries of prior year unpaid obligations, unexpired	–89	....	....
3041	Recoveries of prior year unpaid obligations, expired	–30	....	....
3050	Unpaid obligations, end of year	1,842	1,392	1,209
	Uncollected payments:			
3060	Uncollected pymts, Fed sources, brought forward, Oct 1	–877	–1,128	–971
3070	Change in uncollected pymts, Fed sources, unexpired	–266	157	–33
3071	Change in uncollected pymts, Fed sources, expired	15	....	....
3090	Uncollected pymts, Fed sources, end of year	–1,128	–971	–1,004
	Memorandum (non-add) entries:			
3100	Obligated balance, start of year	895	714	421
3200	Obligated balance, end of year	714	421	205
	Budget authority and outlays, net:			
	Discretionary:			
4000	Budget authority, gross	11,149	11,187	12,119
	Outlays, gross:			
4010	Outlays from new discretionary authority	9,426	9,867	10,687
4011	Outlays from discretionary balances	1,666	1,799	1,516
4020	Outlays, gross (total)	11,092	11,666	12,203
	Offsets against gross budget authority and outlays:			
	Offsetting collections (collected) from:			
4030	Federal sources	–10,395	–10,825	–10,050
4033	Non-Federal sources	–22	–35	–35
4034	Offsetting governmental collections	–2	–1	–1
4040	Offsets against gross budget authority and outlays (total)	–10,419	–10,861	–10,086
	Additional offsets against gross budget authority only:			
4050	Change in uncollected pymts, Fed sources, unexpired	–266	157	–33

OPERATIONS—Continued

Program and Financing—Continued

Identification code 069–1301–0–1–402	2021 actual	2022 est.	2023 est.
4052 Offsetting collections credited to expired accounts	19		
4060 Additional offsets against budget authority only (total)	–247	157	–33
4070 Budget authority, net (discretionary)	483	483	2,000
4080 Outlays, net (discretionary)	673	805	2,117
4180 Budget authority, net (total)	483	483	2,000
4190 Outlays, net (total)	673	805	2,117

The 2023 Budget requests $11.934 billion for Federal Aviation Administration (FAA) operations. These funds will be used to continue to promote aviation safety and efficiency. The Budget provides funding for the Air Traffic Organization (ATO) which is responsible for managing the air traffic control system. As a performance-based organization, the ATO is designed to provide cost-effective, efficient, and, above all, safe air traffic services. The Budget also funds the Aviation Safety Organization which ensures the safe operation of the airlines and certifies new aviation products. In addition, the request also funds regulation of the commercial space transportation industry, as well as FAA policy oversight and overall management functions.

Object Classification (in millions of dollars)

Identification code 069–1301–0–1–402	2021 actual	2022 est.	2023 est.
Direct obligations:			
Personnel compensation:			
11.1 Full-time permanent	4,922	5,039	5,277
11.3 Other than full-time permanent	34	35	39
11.5 Other personnel compensation	466	579	601
11.9 Total personnel compensation	5,422	5,653	5,917
12.1 Civilian personnel benefits	2,316	2,447	2,551
13.0 Benefits for former personnel	8	3	3
21.0 Travel and transportation of persons	48	80	82
22.0 Transportation of things	23	26	20
23.1 Rental payments to GSA	127	129	147
23.2 Rental payments to others	55	55	56
23.3 Communications, utilities, and miscellaneous charges	388	398	396
24.0 Printing and reproduction	3	3	3
25.1 Advisory and assistance services	790	710	893
25.2 Other services from non-Federal sources	1,734	1,382	1,594
26.0 Supplies and materials	120	118	120
31.0 Equipment	55	64	88
32.0 Land and structures	3	3	3
41.0 Grants, subsidies, and contributions		1	1
42.0 Insurance claims and indemnities	2	1	1
99.0 Direct obligations	11,094	11,073	11,875
99.0 Reimbursable obligations	147	143	145
99.9 Total new obligations, unexpired accounts	11,241	11,216	12,020

Employment Summary

Identification code 069–1301–0–1–402	2021 actual	2022 est.	2023 est.
1001 Direct civilian full-time equivalent employment	39,259	39,331	39,891
2001 Reimbursable civilian full-time equivalent employment	212	212	196

EMERGENCY FAA EMPLOYEE LEAVE FUND

Program and Financing (in millions of dollars)

Identification code 069–2816–0–1–402	2021 actual	2022 est.	2023 est.
Obligations by program activity:			
0001 Emergency FAA Employee Fund	1	8	
Budgetary resources:			
Unobligated balance:			
1000 Unobligated balance brought forward, Oct 1		8	
Budget authority:			
Appropriations, mandatory:			
1200 Appropriation	9		
1930 Total budgetary resources available	9	8	
Memorandum (non-add) entries:			
1941 Unexpired unobligated balance, end of year	8		
Change in obligated balance:			
Unpaid obligations:			
3010 New obligations, unexpired accounts	1	8	
3020 Outlays (gross)	–1	–8	
Budget authority and outlays, net:			
Mandatory:			
4090 Budget authority, gross	9		
Outlays, gross:			
4100 Outlays from new mandatory authority	1		
4101 Outlays from mandatory balances		8	
4110 Outlays, gross (total)	1	8	
4180 Budget authority, net (total)	9		
4190 Outlays, net (total)	1	8	

The American Rescue Plan Act of 2021 (P.L. 117–2) established the Emergency FAA Employee Leave Fund and appropriated $9 million, which shall be deposited into the Fund and remain available through September 30, 2022. The Fund is for the use of paid leave for FAA employees who are unable to work due to reasons related to the COVID-19 pandemic.

Object Classification (in millions of dollars)

Identification code 069–2816–0–1–402	2021 actual	2022 est.	2023 est.
Direct obligations:			
11.1 Personnel compensation: Full-time permanent	1	7	
12.1 Civilian personnel benefits		1	
99.9 Total new obligations, unexpired accounts	1	8	

FACILITIES AND EQUIPMENT

[For an additional amount for "Facilities and Equipment", $100,000,000, to remain available until September 30, 2024, for necessary expenses related to the consequences of Hurricane Ida.] *(Disaster Relief Supplemental Appropriations Act, 2022.)*

FACILITIES AND EQUIPMENT

[For an additional amount for "Facilities and Equipment", $5,000,000,000, to remain available until expended: *Provided*, That $1,000,000,000, to remain available until expended, shall be made available for fiscal year 2022, $1,000,000,000, to remain available until expended, shall be made available for fiscal year 2023, $1,000,000,000, to remain available until expended, shall be made available for fiscal year 2024, $1,000,000,000, to remain available until expended, shall be made available for fiscal year 2025, and $1,000,000,000, to remain available until expended, shall be made available for fiscal year 2026: *Provided further*, That amounts made available under this heading in this Act shall be derived from the general fund of the Treasury: *Provided further*, That funds provided under this heading in this Act shall be for: (1) replacing terminal and en route air traffic control facilities; (2) improving air route traffic control center and combined control facility buildings; (3) improving air traffic control en route radar facilities; (4) improving air traffic control tower and terminal radar approach control facilities; (5) national airspace system facilities OSHA and environmental standards compliance; (6) landing and navigational aids; (7) fuel storage tank replacement and management; (8) unstaffed infrastructure sustainment; (9) real property disposition; (10) electrical power system sustain and support; (11) energy maintenance and compliance; (12) hazardous materials management and environmental cleanup; (13) facility security risk management; (14) mobile asset management program; and (15) administrative expenses, including salaries and expenses, administration, and oversight: *Provided further*, That not less than $200,000,000 of the funds made available under this heading in this Act shall be for air traffic control towers that are owned by the Federal Aviation Administration and staffed through the contract tower program: *Provided further*, That not later than 90 days after the date of enactment of this Act, the Secretary of Transportation shall submit to the House and Senate Committees on Appropriations a detailed spend plan, including a list of project locations of air traffic control towers and contract towers, to be funded for fiscal year 2022: *Provided further*, That for each fiscal year through 2026, as part of the annual budget submission of the President under section 1105(a) of title 31, United States Code, the Secretary of Transportation shall submit a detailed spend plan for funding that will be made available under this heading in the upcoming fiscal year, including a list of projects for replacing facilities that are owned by the Federal Aviation Administration, including air traffic control towers that are staffed through the contract tower program: *Provided further,* That such amount is designated by the Congress as being for an emergency requirement pursuant to section 4112(a) of H. Con. Res. 71 (115th Congress), the concurrent resolution on the budget for fiscal year 2018, and to section 251(b) of the Balanced Budget and Emergency Deficit Control Act of 1985.] *(Infrastructure Investments and Jobs Appropriations Act.)*

Program and Financing (in millions of dollars)

Identification code 069–1308–0–1–402		2021 actual	2022 est.	2023 est.
	Obligations by program activity:			
0001	Infrastructure Investment and Jobs Act, F&E	....	452	702
0002	Hurricane Ida	....	10	50
0900	Total new obligations, unexpired accounts	....	462	752
	Budgetary resources:			
	Unobligated balance:			
1000	Unobligated balance brought forward, Oct 1	....	....	638
	Budget authority:			
	Appropriations, discretionary:			
1100	Appropriation	....	1,100	....
	Advance appropriations, discretionary:			
1170	Advance appropriation	....	....	1,000
1900	Budget authority (total)	....	1,100	1,000
1930	Total budgetary resources available	....	1,100	1,638
	Memorandum (non-add) entries:			
1941	Unexpired unobligated balance, end of year	....	638	886
	Change in obligated balance:			
	Unpaid obligations:			
3000	Unpaid obligations, brought forward, Oct 1	....	....	392
3010	New obligations, unexpired accounts	....	462	752
3020	Outlays (gross)	....	–70	–365
3050	Unpaid obligations, end of year	....	392	779
	Memorandum (non-add) entries:			
3100	Obligated balance, start of year	....	....	392
3200	Obligated balance, end of year	....	392	779
	Budget authority and outlays, net:			
	Discretionary:			
4000	Budget authority, gross	....	1,100	1,000
	Outlays, gross:			
4010	Outlays from new discretionary authority	....	70	93
4011	Outlays from discretionary balances	....	....	272
4020	Outlays, gross (total)	....	70	365
4180	Budget authority, net (total)	....	1,100	1,000
4190	Outlays, net (total)	....	70	365

The Infrastructure Investment and Jobs Act (P.L. 117–58) appropriated $5 billion for Facilities & Equipment in annual installments of $1 billion from 2022 to 2026. This funding supports the improvement of existing and construction of new air traffic control infrastructure. The Extending Government Funding and Delivering Emergency Assistance Act (P.L. 117–43) appropriated $100 million for necessary expenses related to the consequences of Hurricane Ida.

Object Classification (in millions of dollars)

Identification code 069–1308–0–1–402		2021 actual	2022 est.	2023 est.
	Direct obligations:			
11.1	Personnel compensation: Full-time permanent	....	10	21
12.1	Civilian personnel benefits	....	4	8
21.0	Travel and transportation of persons	....	8	16
22.0	Transportation of things	....	2	2
23.1	Rental payments to GSA	....	1	1
25.1	Advisory and assistance services	....	265	379
25.2	Other services from non-Federal sources	....	21	35
25.4	Operation and maintenance of facilities	....	32	94
25.7	Operation and maintenance of equipment	....	2	4
26.0	Supplies and materials	....	6	7
31.0	Equipment	....	72	86
32.0	Land and structures	....	34	76
33.0	Investments and loans	....	5	23
99.9	Total new obligations, unexpired accounts	....	462	752

Employment Summary

Identification code 069–1308–0–1–402	2021 actual	2022 est.	2023 est.
1001 Direct civilian full-time equivalent employment	....	70	170

RELIEF FOR AIRPORTS

Program and Financing (in millions of dollars)

Identification code 069–2815–0–1–402		2021 actual	2022 est.	2023 est.
	Obligations by program activity:			
0001	Direct program activity	4,341	3,659	....
0900	Total new obligations, unexpired accounts (object class 41.0)	4,341	3,659	....
	Budgetary resources:			
	Unobligated balance:			
1000	Unobligated balance brought forward, Oct 1	....	3,659	....
	Budget authority:			
	Appropriations, mandatory:			
1200	Appropriation	8,000	....	....
1930	Total budgetary resources available	8,000	3,659	....
	Memorandum (non-add) entries:			
1941	Unexpired unobligated balance, end of year	3,659	....	....
	Change in obligated balance:			
	Unpaid obligations:			
3000	Unpaid obligations, brought forward, Oct 1	....	4,008	3,427
3010	New obligations, unexpired accounts	4,341	3,659	....
3020	Outlays (gross)	–333	–4,240	–2,160
3050	Unpaid obligations, end of year	4,008	3,427	1,267
	Memorandum (non-add) entries:			
3100	Obligated balance, start of year	....	4,008	3,427
3200	Obligated balance, end of year	4,008	3,427	1,267
	Budget authority and outlays, net:			
	Mandatory:			
4090	Budget authority, gross	8,000	....	....
	Outlays, gross:			
4100	Outlays from new mandatory authority	333	....	....
4101	Outlays from mandatory balances	....	4,240	2,160
4110	Outlays, gross (total)	333	4,240	2,160
4180	Budget authority, net (total)	8,000	....	....
4190	Outlays, net (total)	333	4,240	2,160

The American Rescue Plan Act of 2021 (P.L. 117–2) appropriated $8 billion, to remain available until September 30, 2024, for assistance to sponsors of airports, to be made available to prevent, prepare for, and respond to coronavirus.

Employment Summary

Identification code 069–2815–0–1–402	2021 actual	2022 est.	2023 est.
1001 Direct civilian full-time equivalent employment	4	3	3

PAYMENT TO GRANTS-IN-AID FOR AIRPORTS

Program and Financing (in millions of dollars)

Identification code 069–2813–0–1–402		2021 actual	2022 est.	2023 est.
	Obligations by program activity:			
0001	Direct program activity	2,400	400	....
0900	Total new obligations, unexpired accounts (object class 94.0)	2,400	400	....
	Budgetary resources:			
	Budget authority:			
	Appropriations, discretionary:			
1100	Appropriation	2,400	400	....
1930	Total budgetary resources available	2,400	400	....

PAYMENT TO GRANTS-IN-AID FOR AIRPORTS—Continued

Program and Financing—Continued

Identification code 069–2813–0–1–402	2021 actual	2022 est.	2023 est.
Change in obligated balance:			
Unpaid obligations:			
3010 New obligations, unexpired accounts		2,400	400
3020 Outlays (gross)		–2,400	–400
Budget authority and outlays, net:			
Discretionary:			
4000 Budget authority, gross		2,400	400
Outlays, gross:			
4010 Outlays from new discretionary authority		2,400	400
4180 Budget authority, net (total)		2,400	400
4190 Outlays, net (total)		2,400	400

The regular appropriations acts for 2020 and 2021 each provided $400 million of supplemental funding for Grants-in-Aid for Airports. Funds are appropriated from the General Fund of the U.S. Treasury. Discretionary grants are being awarded to qualified airports, with up to 0.5 percent of the funds provided applied to the administrative costs of awarding grants under the program. In addition, the CARES Act provided $10 billion in 2020 and the Coronavirus Response and Relief Supplemental Appropriations Act of 2021 provided $2 billion, both from the General Fund of the U.S. Treasury, to help airports prevent, prepare for, and respond to coronavirus.

PAYMENT TO THE AIRPORT AND AIRWAY TRUST FUND

Program and Financing (in millions of dollars)

Identification code 069–0250–0–1–402	2021 actual	2022 est.	2023 est.
Obligations by program activity:			
0001 Direct program activity	14,000		
0900 Total new obligations, unexpired accounts (object class 94.0)	14,000		
Budgetary resources:			
Budget authority:			
Appropriations, mandatory:			
1200 Appropriation	14,000		
1930 Total budgetary resources available	14,000		
Change in obligated balance:			
Unpaid obligations:			
3010 New obligations, unexpired accounts	14,000		
3020 Outlays (gross)	–14,000		
Budget authority and outlays, net:			
Mandatory:			
4090 Budget authority, gross	14,000		
Outlays, gross:			
4100 Outlays from new mandatory authority	14,000		
4180 Budget authority, net (total)	14,000		
4190 Outlays, net (total)	14,000		

AIRPORT TERMINAL PROGRAM

[(INCLUDING TRANSFER OF FUNDS)]

[For an additional amount for "Airport Terminal Program", $5,000,000,000, to remain available until September 30, 2030, for the Secretary of Transportation to provide competitive grants for airport terminal development projects that address the aging infrastructure of the nation's airports: *Provided*, That $1,000,000,000, to remain available until September 30, 2026, shall be made available for fiscal year 2022, $1,000,000,000, to remain available until September 30, 2027, shall be made available for fiscal year 2023, $1,000,000,000, to remain available until September 30, 2028, shall be made available for fiscal year 2024, $1,000,000,000, to remain available until September 30, 2029, shall be made available for fiscal year 2025, and $1,000,000,000, to remain available until September 30, 2030, shall be made available for fiscal year 2026: *Provided further*, That amounts made available under this heading in this Act shall be derived from the general fund of the Treasury: *Provided further*, That the Secretary shall issue a notice of funding opportunity not later than 60 days after the date of enactment of this Act: *Provided further*, That of the funds made available under this heading in this Act, not more than 55 percent shall be for large hub airports, not more than 15 percent shall be for medium hub airports, not more than 20 percent shall be for small hub airports, and not less than 10 percent shall be for nonhub and nonprimary airports: *Provided further*, That in awarding grants for terminal development projects from funds made available under this heading in this Act, the Secretary may consider projects that qualify as "terminal development" (including multimodal terminal development), as that term is defined in 49 U.S.C. 47102(28), projects for on-airport rail access projects as set forth in Passenger Facility Charge (PFC) Update 75–21, and projects for relocating, reconstructing, repairing, or improving an airport-owned air traffic control tower: *Provided further*, That in awarding grants for terminal development projects from funds made available under this heading in this Act, the Secretary shall give consideration to projects that increase capacity and passenger access; projects that replace aging infrastructure; projects that achieve compliance with the Americans with Disabilities Act and expand accessibility for persons with disabilities; projects that improve airport access for historically disadvantaged populations; projects that improve energy efficiency, including upgrading environmental systems, upgrading plant facilities, and achieving Leadership in Energy and Environmental Design (LEED) accreditation standards; projects that improve airfield safety through terminal relocation; and projects that encourage actual and potential competition: *Provided further*, That the Federal share of the cost of a project carried out from funds made available under this heading in this Act shall be 80 percent for large and medium hub airports and 95 percent for small hub, nonhub, and nonprimary airports: *Provided further*, That a grant made from funds made available under this heading in this Act shall be treated as having been made pursuant to the Secretary's authority under section 47104(a) of title 49, United States Code: *Provided further*, That the Secretary may provide grants from funds made available under this heading in this Act for a project at any airport that is eligible to receive a grant from the discretionary fund under section 47115(a) of title 49, United States Code: *Provided further*, That in making awards from funds made available under this heading in this Act, the Secretary shall provide a preference to projects that achieve a complete development objective, even if awards for the project must be phased, and the Secretary shall prioritize projects that have received partial awards: *Provided further*, That up to 3 percent of the amounts made available under this heading in this Act in each fiscal year shall be for personnel, contracting and other costs to administer and oversee grants, of which $1,000,000 in each fiscal year shall be transferred to the Office of Inspector General of the Department of Transportation for oversight of funding provided to the Department of Transportation in this title in this Act: *Provided further*, That such amount is designated by the Congress as being for an emergency requirement pursuant to section 4112(a) of H. Con. Res. 71 (115th Congress), the concurrent resolution on the budget for fiscal year 2018, and to section 251(b) of the Balanced Budget and Emergency Deficit Control Act of 1985.] *(Infrastructure Investments and Jobs Appropriations Act.)*

Program and Financing (in millions of dollars)

Identification code 069–1337–0–1–402	2021 actual	2022 est.	2023 est.
Obligations by program activity:			
0001 Airport Terminal Program		999	999
Budgetary resources:			
Budget authority:			
Appropriations, discretionary:			
1100 Appropriation		1,000	
1120 Appropriations transferred to other acct [069–0130]		–1	
1160 Appropriation, discretionary (total)		999	
Advance appropriations, discretionary:			
1170 Advance appropriation			1,000
1172 Advance appropriations transferred to other accounts [069–0130]			–1
1180 Advanced appropriation, discretionary (total)			999
1900 Budget authority (total)		999	999
1930 Total budgetary resources available		999	999
Change in obligated balance:			
Unpaid obligations:			
3000 Unpaid obligations, brought forward, Oct 1			959
3010 New obligations, unexpired accounts		999	999
3020 Outlays (gross)		–40	–639
3050 Unpaid obligations, end of year		959	1,319

DEPARTMENT OF TRANSPORTATION

Federal Aviation Administration—Continued
Federal Funds—Continued

911

		2021 actual	2022 est.	2023 est.
	Memorandum (non-add) entries:			
3100	Obligated balance, start of year			959
3200	Obligated balance, end of year		959	1,319
	Budget authority and outlays, net:			
	Discretionary:			
4000	Budget authority, gross		999	999
	Outlays, gross:			
4010	Outlays from new discretionary authority		40	110
4011	Outlays from discretionary balances			529
4020	Outlays, gross (total)		40	639
4180	Budget authority, net (total)		999	999
4190	Outlays, net (total)		40	639

The Infrastructure Investment and Jobs Act (P.L. 117–58) appropriated $5 billion for the Airport Terminal Program, in annual $1 billion installments from 2022 to 2026, for the Secretary of Transportation to provide competitive grants for airport terminal development projects that address the aging infrastructure of the nation's airports.

Object Classification (in millions of dollars)

Identification code 069–1337–0–1–402	2021 actual	2022 est.	2023 est.
11.1 Direct obligations: Personnel compensation: Full-time permanent		1	4
11.9 Total personnel compensation		1	4
12.1 Civilian personnel benefits			2
25.2 Other services from non-Federal sources		1	1
41.0 Grants, subsidies, and contributions		997	992
99.9 Total new obligations, unexpired accounts		999	999

Employment Summary

Identification code 069–1337–0–1–402	2021 actual	2022 est.	2023 est.
1001 Direct civilian full-time equivalent employment		11	31

AIRPORT INFRASTRUCTURE GRANTS

[(INCLUDING TRANSFER OF FUNDS)]

[For an additional amount for "Airport Infrastructure Grants", $15,000,000,000, to remain available until September 30, 2030: *Provided*, That $3,000,000,000, to remain available until September 30, 2026, shall be made available for fiscal year 2022, $3,000,000,000, to remain available until September 30, 2027, shall be made available for fiscal year 2023, $3,000,000,000, to remain available until September 30, 2028, shall be made available for fiscal year 2024, $3,000,000,000, to remain available until September 30, 2029, shall be made available for fiscal year 2025, and $3,000,000,000, to remain available until September 30, 2030, shall be made available for fiscal year 2026: *Provided further*, That amounts made available under this heading in this Act shall be derived from the general fund of the Treasury: *Provided further*, That amounts made available under this heading in this Act shall be made available to sponsors of any airport eligible to receive grants under section 47115 of title 49, United States Code, for airport-related projects defined under section 40117(a)(3) of title 49, United States Code: *Provided further*, That of the funds made available under this heading in this Act, in each of fiscal years 2022 through 2026—]

[(1) Not more than $2,480,000,000 shall be available for primary airports as defined in section 47102(16) of title 49, United States Code, and certain cargo airports: *Provided*, That such funds shall not be subject to the reduced apportionments of section 47114(f) of title 49, United States Code: *Provided further*, That such funds shall first be apportioned as set forth in sections 47114(c)(1)(A), 47114(c)(1)(C)(i), 47114(c)(1)(C)(ii), 47114(c)(2)(A), 47114(c)(2)(B), and 47114(c)(2)(E), 47114(c)(1)(J) of title 49, United States Code: *Provided further*, That there shall be no maximum apportionment limit: *Provided further*, That any remaining funds after such apportionment shall be distributed to all sponsors of primary airports (as defined in section 47102(16) of title 49, United States Code) based on each such airport's passenger enplanements compared to total passenger enplanements of all airports defined in section 47102(16) of title 49, United States Code, for calendar year 2019 in fiscal years 2022 and 2023 and thereafter for the most recent calendar year enplanements upon which the Secretary has apportioned funds pursuant to section 47114(c) of title 49, United States Code;]

[(2) Not more than $500,000,000 shall be for general aviation and commercial service airports that are not primary airports as defined in paragraphs (7), (8), and (16) of section 47102 of title 49, United States Code: *Provided*, That the Secretary of Transportation shall apportion the remaining funds to each non-primary airport based on the categories published in the most current National Plan of Integrated Airport Systems, reflecting the percentage of the aggregate published eligible development costs for each such category, and then dividing the allocated funds evenly among the eligible airports in each category, rounding up to the nearest thousand dollars: *Provided further*, That any remaining funds under this paragraph in this Act shall be distributed as described in paragraph (3) in this proviso under this heading in this Act; and]

[(3) $20,000,000 for the Secretary of Transportation to make competitive grants to sponsors of airports participating in the contract tower program and the contract tower cost share program under section 47124 of title 49, United States Code to: (1) sustain, construct, repair, improve, rehabilitate, modernize, replace or relocate nonapproach control towers; (2) acquire and install air traffic control, communications, and related equipment to be used in those towers; and (3) construct a remote tower certified by the Federal Aviation Administration, including acquisition and installation of air traffic control, communications, or related equipment: *Provided*, That the Federal Aviation Administration shall give priority consideration to projects that enhance aviation safety and improve air traffic efficiency: *Provided further*, That the Federal share of the costs for which a grant is made under this paragraph shall be 100 percent:]

[*Provided further*, That any funds made available in a given fiscal year that remain unobligated at the end of the fourth fiscal year after which they were first made available for obligation shall be made available in the fifth fiscal year after which they were first made available for obligation to the Secretary for competitive grants: *Provided further*, That of the amounts made available to the Secretary for competitive grants under the preceding proviso, the Secretary shall first provide up to $100,000,000, as described in paragraph (3) of the fourth proviso, and any remaining unobligated balances in excess of that amount shall be available to the Secretary for competitive grants otherwise eligible under the third proviso that reduce airport emissions, reduce noise impact to the surrounding community, reduce dependence on the electrical grid, or provide general benefits to the surrounding community: *Provided further*, That none of the amounts made available under this heading in this Act may be used to pay for airport debt service: *Provided further*, That a grant made from funds made available under this heading in this Act shall be treated as having been made pursuant to the Secretary's authority under section 47104(a) of title 49, United States Code: *Provided further*, That up to 3 percent of the amounts made available under this heading in this Act in each of fiscal years 2022 through 2026 shall be for personnel, contracting, and other costs to administer and oversee grants, of which $1,000,000 in each fiscal year shall be transferred to the Office of Inspector General of the Department of Transportation for oversight of funding provided to the Department of Transportation in this title in this Act: *Provided further*, That the Federal share of the costs of a project under paragraphs (1) and (2) of the fourth proviso under this heading shall be the percent for which a project for airport development would be eligible under section 47109 of title 49, United States Code: *Provided further*, That obligations of funds under this heading in this Act shall not be subject to any limitations on obligations provided in any Act making annual appropriations: *Provided further*, That such amount is designated by the Congress as being for an emergency requirement pursuant to section 4112(a) of H. Con. Res. 71 (115th Congress), the concurrent resolution on the budget for fiscal year 2018, and to section 251(b) of the Balanced Budget and Emergency Deficit Control Act of 1985.] *(Infrastructure Investments and Jobs Appropriations Act.)*

Program and Financing (in millions of dollars)

Identification code 069–1338–0–1–402	2021 actual	2022 est.	2023 est.
Obligations by program activity:			
0001 Airports Infrastructure Grants		2,999	2,999
Budgetary resources:			
Budget authority:			
Appropriations, discretionary:			
1100 Appropriation		3,000	
1120 Appropriations transferred to other acct [069–0130]		–1	
1160 Appropriation, discretionary (total)		2,999	
Advance appropriations, discretionary:			
1170 Advance appropriation			3,000
1172 Advance appropriations transferred to other accounts [069–0130]			–1
1180 Advanced appropriation, discretionary (total)			2,999
1900 Budget authority (total)		2,999	2,999

912 Federal Aviation Administration—Continued
Federal Funds—Continued

AIRPORT INFRASTRUCTURE GRANTS—Continued

Program and Financing—Continued

Identification code 069–1338–0–1–402	2021 actual	2022 est.	2023 est.
1930 Total budgetary resources available		2,999	2,999
Change in obligated balance:			
Unpaid obligations:			
3000 Unpaid obligations, brought forward, Oct 1			2,879
3010 New obligations, unexpired accounts		2,999	2,999
3020 Outlays (gross)		–120	–1,919
3050 Unpaid obligations, end of year		2,879	3,959
Memorandum (non-add) entries:			
3100 Obligated balance, start of year			2,879
3200 Obligated balance, end of year		2,879	3,959
Budget authority and outlays, net:			
Discretionary:			
4000 Budget authority, gross		2,999	2,999
Outlays, gross:			
4010 Outlays from new discretionary authority		120	330
4011 Outlays from discretionary balances			1,589
4020 Outlays, gross (total)		120	1,919
4180 Budget authority, net (total)		2,999	2,999
4190 Outlays, net (total)		120	1,919

The Infrastructure Investment and Jobs Act (P.L. 117–58) appropriated $15 billion, in annual installments of $3 billion from 2022 to 2026, for airport projects that increase safety and expand capacity.

Object Classification (in millions of dollars)

Identification code 069–1338–0–1–402	2021 actual	2022 est.	2023 est.
11.1 Direct obligations: Personnel compensation: Full-time permanent		3	12
11.9 Total personnel compensation		3	12
12.1 Civilian personnel benefits		2	6
21.0 Travel and transportation of persons		2	2
25.2 Other services from non-Federal sources		3	3
41.0 Grants, subsidies, and contributions		2,989	2,976
99.9 Total new obligations, unexpired accounts		2,999	2,999

Employment Summary

Identification code 069–1338–0–1–402	2021 actual	2022 est.	2023 est.
1001 Direct civilian full-time equivalent employment		30	87

AVIATION USER FEES

Special and Trust Fund Receipts (in millions of dollars)

Identification code 069–5422–0–2–402	2021 actual	2022 est.	2023 est.
0100 Balance, start of year	7	2	4
0198 Reconciliation adjustment	–3		
0199 Balance, start of year	4	2	4
Receipts:			
Current law:			
1110 Aviation User Fees, Overflight Fees	36	75	86
1130 Property Disposal or Lease Proceeds, Aviation User Fee	9		
1199 Total current law receipts	45	75	86
1999 Total receipts	45	75	86
2000 Total: Balances and receipts	49	77	90
Appropriations:			
Current law:			
2101 Essential Air Service and Rural Airport Improvement Fund	–7	–2	–4
2101 Aviation User Fees	–45	–75	–86
2132 Essential Air Service and Rural Airport Improvement Fund	2	4	5
2199 Total current law appropriations	–50	–73	–85
2999 Total appropriations	–50	–73	–85

5098 Reconciliation adjustment	3		
5099 Balance, end of year	2	4	5

Program and Financing (in millions of dollars)

Identification code 069–5422–0–2–402	2021 actual	2022 est.	2023 est.
Obligations by program activity:			
0001 Land Proceeds	1		
0100 Direct program activities, subtotal	1		
0900 Total new obligations, unexpired accounts (object class 25.2)	1		
Budgetary resources:			
Unobligated balance:			
1000 Unobligated balance brought forward, Oct 1	21	15	10
1010 Unobligated balance transfer to other accts [069–5423]	–14	–5	
1070 Unobligated balance (total)	7	10	10
Budget authority:			
Appropriations, mandatory:			
1201 Appropriation (special or trust fund)	45	75	86
1220 Appropriations transferred to other accts [069–5423]	–36	–75	–86
1260 Appropriations, mandatory (total)	9		
1900 Budget authority (total)	9		
1930 Total budgetary resources available	16	10	10
Memorandum (non-add) entries:			
1941 Unexpired unobligated balance, end of year	15	10	10
Change in obligated balance:			
Unpaid obligations:			
3000 Unpaid obligations, brought forward, Oct 1	2	1	
3010 New obligations, unexpired accounts	1		
3020 Outlays (gross)	–2	–1	
3050 Unpaid obligations, end of year	1		
Memorandum (non-add) entries:			
3100 Obligated balance, start of year	2	1	
3200 Obligated balance, end of year	1		
Budget authority and outlays, net:			
Mandatory:			
4090 Budget authority, gross	9		
Outlays, gross:			
4101 Outlays from mandatory balances	2	1	
4180 Budget authority, net (total)	9		
4190 Outlays, net (total)	2	1	

The Federal Aviation Reauthorization Act of 1996 (P.L. 104–264) authorized the collection of user fees for air traffic control and related services provided by the Federal Aviation Administration to aircraft that neither take off nor land in the United States, commonly known as overflight fees. The Budget estimates that $86.2 million in overflight fees will be collected in 2023.

AVIATION INSURANCE REVOLVING FUND

Program and Financing (in millions of dollars)

Identification code 069–4120–0–3–402	2021 actual	2022 est.	2023 est.
Obligations by program activity:			
0801 Program Administration	1	2	2
0802 Insurance Claims	3	2	2
0900 Total new obligations, unexpired accounts	4	4	4
Budgetary resources:			
Unobligated balance:			
1000 Unobligated balance brought forward, Oct 1	2,300	2,315	2,345
Budget authority:			
Spending authority from offsetting collections, mandatory:			
1800 Collected	19	34	25
1900 Budget authority (total)	19	34	25
1930 Total budgetary resources available	2,319	2,349	2,370
Memorandum (non-add) entries:			
1941 Unexpired unobligated balance, end of year	2,315	2,345	2,366

DEPARTMENT OF TRANSPORTATION　　　Federal Aviation Administration—Continued
Federal Funds—Continued　　913

		2021 actual	2022 est.	2023 est.
	Change in obligated balance:			
	Unpaid obligations:			
3000	Unpaid obligations, brought forward, Oct 1	2	2	2
3010	New obligations, unexpired accounts	4	4	4
3020	Outlays (gross)	–4	–4	–2
3050	Unpaid obligations, end of year	2	2	4
	Memorandum (non-add) entries:			
3100	Obligated balance, start of year	2	2	2
3200	Obligated balance, end of year	2	2	4
	Budget authority and outlays, net:			
	Mandatory:			
4090	Budget authority, gross	19	34	25
	Outlays, gross:			
4100	Outlays from new mandatory authority	3	2	2
4101	Outlays from mandatory balances	1	2	
4110	Outlays, gross (total)	4	4	2
	Offsets against gross budget authority and outlays:			
	Offsetting collections (collected) from:			
4120	Federal sources		–2	–2
4121	Interest on Federal securities	–19	–32	–23
4130	Offsets against gross budget authority and outlays (total)	–19	–34	–25
4170	Outlays, net (mandatory)	–15	–30	–23
4180	Budget authority, net (total)			
4190	Outlays, net (total)	–15	–30	–23
	Memorandum (non-add) entries:			
5000	Total investments, SOY: Federal securities: Par value	2,302	2,217	2,313
5001	Total investments, EOY: Federal securities: Par value	2,217	2,313	2,330

The fund provides direct support for the aviation insurance program (chapter 443 of title 49, U.S. Code). In December 2014, the Congress sunset part of the aviation insurance program. Specifically, the Congress returned U.S. air carriers to the commercial aviation market for all of their war risk insurance coverage by ending the FAA's authority to provide war risk insurance for a premium. Pursuant to 49 U.S.C. 44305, the FAA may provide insurance without premium at the request of the Secretary of Defense, or the head of a department, agency, or instrumentality designated by the President, when the Secretary of Defense, or the designated head, agrees to indemnify the Secretary of Transportation against all losses covered by the insurance. The "non-premium" aviation insurance program was authorized through September 30, 2023 in the National Defense Authorization Act for 2020.

Object Classification (in millions of dollars)

Identification code 069–4120–0–3–402		2021 actual	2022 est.	2023 est.
	Reimbursable obligations:			
11.1	Personnel compensation: Full-time permanent		1	1
25.2	Other services from non-Federal sources	1	1	1
42.0	Projected Insurance claims and indemnities	3	2	2
99.9	Total new obligations, unexpired accounts	4	4	4

Employment Summary

Identification code 069–4120–0–3–402	2021 actual	2022 est.	2023 est.
2001　Reimbursable civilian full-time equivalent employment	2	4	4

ADMINISTRATIVE SERVICES FRANCHISE FUND

Program and Financing (in millions of dollars)

Identification code 069–4562–0–4–402		2021 actual	2022 est.	2023 est.
	Obligations by program activity:			
0801	Accounting Services	39	50	52
0804	Information Services	110	143	129
0806	Multi Media	11	3	3
0807	FLLI (formerly CMEL/Training)	6	9	9
0808	International Training	2	2	2
0810	Logistics	287	292	294
0811	Aircraft Maintenance	61	57	62
0812	Acquisition	5	5	6
0900	Total new obligations, unexpired accounts	521	561	557
	Budgetary resources:			
	Unobligated balance:			
1000	Unobligated balance brought forward, Oct 1	230	213	235
1021	Recoveries of prior year unpaid obligations	34	36	36
1070	Unobligated balance (total)	264	249	271
	Budget authority:			
	Spending authority from offsetting collections, discretionary:			
1700	Collected	470	547	542
1930	Total budgetary resources available	734	796	813
	Memorandum (non-add) entries:			
1941	Unexpired unobligated balance, end of year	213	235	256
	Change in obligated balance:			
	Unpaid obligations:			
3000	Unpaid obligations, brought forward, Oct 1	170	186	89
3010	New obligations, unexpired accounts	521	561	557
3020	Outlays (gross)	–471	–622	–578
3040	Recoveries of prior year unpaid obligations, unexpired	–34	–36	–36
3050	Unpaid obligations, end of year	186	89	32
	Memorandum (non-add) entries:			
3100	Obligated balance, start of year	170	186	89
3200	Obligated balance, end of year	186	89	32
	Budget authority and outlays, net:			
	Discretionary:			
4000	Budget authority, gross	470	547	542
	Outlays, gross:			
4010	Outlays from new discretionary authority	362	372	369
4011	Outlays from discretionary balances	109	250	209
4020	Outlays, gross (total)	471	622	578
	Offsets against gross budget authority and outlays:			
	Offsetting collections (collected) from:			
4030	Federal sources	–404	–545	–540
4033	Non-Federal sources	–66	–2	–2
4040	Offsets against gross budget authority and outlays (total)	–470	–547	–542
4080	Outlays, net (discretionary)	1	75	36
4180	Budget authority, net (total)			
4190	Outlays, net (total)	1	75	36

In 1997, the Federal Aviation Administration (FAA) established a franchise fund to finance operations where the costs for goods and services provided are charged to the users on a fee-for-service basis. The fund improves organizational efficiency and provides better support to FAA's internal and external customers. The activities included in this franchise fund are: training, accounting, travel, duplicating services, multi-media services, information technology, material management (logistics), and aircraft maintenance.

Object Classification (in millions of dollars)

Identification code 069–4562–0–4–402		2021 actual	2022 est.	2023 est.
	Reimbursable obligations:			
	Personnel compensation:			
11.1	Full-time permanent	119	132	136
11.3	Other than full-time permanent	1	1	1
11.5	Other personnel compensation	5	5	5
11.9	Total personnel compensation	125	138	142
12.1	Civilian personnel benefits	49	52	53
21.0	Travel and transportation of persons	4	8	8
22.0	Transportation of things	8	6	6
23.2	Rental payments to others	3	3	4
23.3	Communications, utilities, and miscellaneous charges	13	11	14
25.1	Advisory and assistance services	63	71	60
25.2	Other services from non-Federal sources	59	73	57
25.3	Other goods and services from Federal sources	15	17	14
25.4	Operation and maintenance of facilities	6	5	6
25.7	Operation and maintenance of equipment	71	59	68
26.0	Supplies and materials	76	108	114
31.0	Equipment	5	4	4
32.0	Land and structures	2	2	2
44.0	Refunds	22	4	5
99.9	Total new obligations, unexpired accounts	521	561	557

914 Federal Aviation Administration—Continued
Federal Funds—Continued

THE BUDGET FOR FISCAL YEAR 2023

ADMINISTRATIVE SERVICES FRANCHISE FUND—Continued

Employment Summary

Identification code 069–4562–0–4–402	2021 actual	2022 est.	2023 est.
2001 Reimbursable civilian full-time equivalent employment	1,367	1,416	1,416

Trust Funds
AIRPORT AND AIRWAY TRUST FUND

Program and Financing (in millions of dollars)

Identification code 069–8103–0–7–402	2021 actual	2022 est.	2023 est.
4180 Budget authority, net (total)			
4190 Outlays, net (total)			
Memorandum (non-add) entries:			
5000 Total investments, SOY: Federal securities: Par value	7,900	15,902	13,020
5001 Total investments, EOY: Federal securities: Par value	15,902	13,020	10,892

Section 9502 of Title 26, U.S. Code provides for amounts equivalent to the funds received in the Treasury for the passenger ticket tax, and certain other taxes paid by airport and airway users, to be transferred to the Airport and Airway Trust Fund. In turn, appropriations are authorized from this fund to meet obligations for airport improvement grants; Federal Aviation Administration facilities and equipment; research, operations, and payment to air carriers; and for the Bureau of Transportation Statistics Office of Airline Information.

Status of Funds (in millions of dollars)

Identification code 069–8103–0–7–402	2021 actual	2022 est.	2023 est.
Unexpended balance, start of year:			
0100 Balance, start of year	8,971	14,796	12,298
0999 Total balance, start of year	8,971	14,796	12,298
Cash income during the year:			
Current law:			
Receipts:			
1110 Excise Taxes, Airport and Airway Trust Fund	8,184	14,369	17,642
1130 Grants-in-aid for Airports (Airport and Airway Trust Fund)	1	2	2
1130 Facilities and Equipment (Airport and Airway Trust Fund)	28	30	30
1150 Interest, Airport and Airway Trust Fund			
1150 Interest, Airport and Airway Trust Fund	268	222	169
1160 General Fund Payment, Airport and Airway Trust Fund	14,000		
1160 Facilities and Equipment (Airport and Airway Trust Fund)	43	36	36
1160 Research, Engineering and Development (Airport and Airway Trust Fund)	8	9	9
1199 Income under present law	22,532	14,668	17,888
1999 Total cash income	22,532	14,668	17,888
Cash outgo during year:			
Current law:			
2100 Payments to Air Carriers [Budget Acct]	–143	–169	–320
2100 Trust Fund Share of FAA Activities (Airport and Airway Trust Fund) [Budget Acct]	–10,272	–10,699	–9,981
2100 Grants-in-aid for Airports (Airport and Airway Trust Fund) [Budget Acct]	–8,837	–6,187	–5,379
2100 Facilities and Equipment (Airport and Airway Trust Fund) [Budget Acct]	–2,832	–2,917	–3,154
2100 Research, Engineering and Development (Airport and Airway Trust Fund) [Budget Acct]	–167	–258	–286
2198 Grants-in-aid for Airports adjustment	5,544	3,064	1,547
2199 Outgo under current law	–16,707	–17,166	–17,573
2999 Total cash outgo (–)	–16,707	–17,166	–17,573
Surplus or deficit:			
3110 Excluding interest	5,557	–2,720	146
3120 Interest	268	222	169
3199 Subtotal, surplus or deficit	5,825	–2,498	315
3999 Total change in fund balance	5,825	–2,498	315
Unexpended balance, end of year:			
4100 Uninvested balance (net), end of year	–1,106	–722	1,721
4200 Airport and Airway Trust Fund	15,902	13,020	10,892
4999 Total balance, end of year	14,796	12,298	12,613

GRANTS-IN-AID FOR AIRPORTS
(LIQUIDATION OF CONTRACT AUTHORIZATION)
(LIMITATION ON OBLIGATIONS)
(AIRPORT AND AIRWAY TRUST FUND)

For liquidation of obligations incurred for grants-in-aid for airport planning and development, and noise compatibility planning and programs as authorized under subchapter I of chapter 471 and subchapter I of chapter 475 of title 49, United States Code, and under other law authorizing such obligations; for procurement, installation, and commissioning of runway incursion prevention devices and systems at airports of such title; for grants authorized under section 41743 of title 49, United States Code; and for inspection activities and administration of airport safety programs, including those related to airport operating certificates under section 44706 of title 49, United States Code, $3,350,000,000, to be derived from the Airport and Airway Trust Fund and to remain available until expended: Provided, That none of the amounts made available under this heading shall be available for the planning or execution of programs the obligations for which are in excess of $3,350,000,000, in fiscal year 2023, notwithstanding section 47117(g) of title 49, United States Code: Provided further, That none of the amounts made available under this heading shall be available for the replacement of baggage conveyor systems, reconfiguration of terminal baggage areas, or other airport improvements that are necessary to install bulk explosive detection systems: Provided further, That notwithstanding any other provision of law, of amounts limited under this heading, not more than $137,372,000 shall be available for administration, not less than $15,000,000 shall be available for the Airport Cooperative Research Program, and not less than $40,828,000 shall be available for Airport Technology Research.

GRANTS-IN-AID FOR AIRPORTS

Note.—A full-year 2022 appropriation for this account was not enacted at the time the Budget was prepared; therefore, the Budget assumes this account is operating under the Continuing Appropriations Act, 2022 (Division A of Public Law 117–43, as amended). The amounts included for 2022 reflect the annualized level provided by the continuing resolution.

Special and Trust Fund Receipts (in millions of dollars)

Identification code 069–8106–0–7–402	2021 actual	2022 est.	2023 est.
0100 Balance, start of year			
Receipts:			
Current law:			
1140 General Fund Payment, Grants-in-Aid for Airports	2,400	400	
2000 Total: Balances and receipts	2,400	400	
Appropriations:			
Current law:			
2101 Grants-in-aid for Airports (Airport and Airway Trust Fund)	–2,400	–400	
5099 Balance, end of year			

Program and Financing (in millions of dollars)

Identification code 069–8106–0–7–402	2021 actual	2022 est.	2023 est.
Obligations by program activity:			
0001 Grants-in-aid for airports	3,301	3,165	3,157
0002 Personnel and related expenses	119	119	137
0003 Airport technology research	41	41	41
0005 Small community air service	10	10	
0006 Airport Cooperative Research	15	15	15
0007 Grants - General Fund Appropriation	390	258	226
0008 Administrative Expenses - General Fund Appropriation			1
0009 Coronavirus Aid, Relief, and Economic Security Act, P.L. 116–136	512	30	
0010 Coronavirus Response and Relief Supplemental Appropriations (CRRSA) Act - Grants Program	1,996		
0011 Coronavirus Response and Relief Supplemental Appropriations (CRRSA) Act - SCASDP Program	4		
0100 Total direct program	6,388	3,638	3,577
0799 Total direct obligations	6,388	3,638	3,577
0801 Grants-in-aid for Airports (Airport and Airway Trust Fund) (Reimbursable)	1	2	2

DEPARTMENT OF TRANSPORTATION

		2021 actual	2022 est.	2023 est.
0900	Total new obligations, unexpired accounts	6,389	3,640	3,579
	Budgetary resources:			
	Unobligated balance:			
1000	Unobligated balance brought forward, Oct 1	1,125	706	818
1001	Discretionary unobligated balance brought fwd, Oct 1	1,107		
1021	Recoveries of prior year unpaid obligations	219		
1033	Recoveries of prior year paid obligations	1		
1070	Unobligated balance (total)	1,345	706	818
	Budget authority:			
	Appropriations, discretionary:			
1101	Appropriation (special or trust)	3,350	3,350	3,350
1101	Appropriation (special or trust)	2,400	400	
1138	Appropriations applied to liquidate contract authority	–3,350	–3,350	–3,350
1160	Appropriation, discretionary (total)	2,400	400	
	Contract authority, mandatory:			
1600	Contract authority (Reauthorization)	3,350	3,350	3,350
	Spending authority from offsetting collections, discretionary:			
1700	Collected		2	2
1900	Budget authority (total)	5,750	3,752	3,352
1930	Total budgetary resources available	7,095	4,458	4,170
	Memorandum (non-add) entries:			
1941	Unexpired unobligated balance, end of year	706	818	591
	Special and non-revolving trust funds:			
1952	Expired unobligated balance, start of year		2	2
1953	Expired unobligated balance, end of year	2	2	2
	Change in obligated balance:			
	Unpaid obligations:			
3000	Unpaid obligations, brought forward, Oct 1	13,001	10,332	7,785
3010	New obligations, unexpired accounts	6,389	3,640	3,579
3020	Outlays (gross)	–8,837	–6,187	–5,379
3040	Recoveries of prior year unpaid obligations, unexpired	–219		
3041	Recoveries of prior year unpaid obligations, expired	–2		
3050	Unpaid obligations, end of year	10,332	7,785	5,985
	Memorandum (non-add) entries:			
3100	Obligated balance, start of year	13,001	10,332	7,785
3200	Obligated balance, end of year	10,332	7,785	5,985
	Budget authority and outlays, net:			
	Discretionary:			
4000	Budget authority, gross	2,400	402	2
	Outlays, gross:			
4010	Outlays from new discretionary authority	1,091	501	468
4011	Outlays from discretionary balances	7,746	5,686	4,911
4020	Outlays, gross (total)	8,837	6,187	5,379
	Offsets against gross budget authority and outlays:			
	Offsetting collections (collected) from:			
4033	Non-Federal sources	–1	–2	–2
4040	Offsets against gross budget authority and outlays (total)	–1	–2	–2
	Additional offsets against gross budget authority only:			
4053	Recoveries of prior year paid obligations, unexpired accounts	1		
4070	Budget authority, net (discretionary)	2,400	400	
4080	Outlays, net (discretionary)	8,836	6,185	5,377
	Mandatory:			
4090	Budget authority, gross	3,350	3,350	3,350
4180	Budget authority, net (total)	5,750	3,750	3,350
4190	Outlays, net (total)	8,836	6,185	5,377
	Memorandum (non-add) entries:			
5052	Obligated balance, SOY: Contract authority	4,164	4,164	4,164
5053	Obligated balance, EOY: Contract authority	4,164	4,164	4,164
5061	Limitation on obligations (Transportation Trust Funds)	3,350	3,350	3,350

Subchapter I of chapter 471, title 49, U.S. Code provides for airport improvement grants, including those emphasizing capacity development, safety, and security needs; and chapter 475 of title 49 provides for grants for aircraft noise compatibility planning and programs.

Object Classification (in millions of dollars)

Identification code 069–8106–0–7–402		2021 actual	2022 est.	2023 est.
	Direct obligations:			
	Personnel compensation:			
11.1	Full-time permanent	76	77	78
11.3	Other than full-time permanent	1	1	1
11.5	Other personnel compensation	2	2	2
11.9	Total personnel compensation	79	80	81
12.1	Civilian personnel benefits	28	29	29
21.0	Travel and transportation of persons	1	1	1
23.2	Rental payments to others	1	1	1
25.1	Advisory and assistance services	39	37	37
25.2	Other services from non-Federal sources	1	1	1
25.3	Other goods and services from Federal sources	19	19	19
25.7	Operation and maintenance of equipment	9	9	9
26.0	Supplies and materials	1	1	1
31.0	Equipment	1	1	1
41.0	Grants, subsidies, and contributions	6,195	3,445	3,384
94.0	Financial transfers	14	14	14
99.0	Direct obligations	6,388	3,638	3,578
99.0	Reimbursable obligations	1	2	1
99.9	Total new obligations, unexpired accounts	6,389	3,640	3,579

Employment Summary

Identification code 069–8106–0–7–402	2021 actual	2022 est.	2023 est.
1001 Direct civilian full-time equivalent employment	591	611	637
1001 Direct civilian full-time equivalent employment	4	1	1
2001 Reimbursable civilian full-time equivalent employment	6	4	2

FACILITIES AND EQUIPMENT

(AIRPORT AND AIRWAY TRUST FUND)

For necessary expenses, not otherwise provided for, for acquisition, establishment, technical support services, improvement by contract or purchase, and hire of national airspace systems and experimental facilities and equipment, as authorized under part A of subtitle VII of title 49, United States Code, including initial acquisition of necessary sites by lease or grant; engineering and service testing, including construction of test facilities and acquisition of necessary sites by lease or grant; construction and furnishing of quarters and related accommodations for officers and employees of the Federal Aviation Administration stationed at remote localities where such accommodations are not available; and the purchase, lease, or transfer of aircraft from funds available under this heading, including aircraft for aviation regulation and certification; to be derived from the Airport and Airway Trust Fund, $3,015,000,000, of which $570,000,000 shall remain available until September 30, 2024, and $2,445,000,000 shall remain available until September 30, 2025: Provided, That there may be credited to this appropriation funds received from States, counties, municipalities, other public authorities, and private sources, for expenses incurred in the establishment, improvement, and modernization of national airspace systems: Provided further, That not later than 60 days after submission of the budget request, the Secretary shall transmit to the Congress an investment plan for the Federal Aviation Administration which includes funding for each budget line item for fiscal years 2024 through 2028, with total funding for each year of the plan constrained to the funding targets for those years as estimated and approved by the Office of Management and Budget.

Note.—A full-year 2022 appropriation for this account was not enacted at the time the Budget was prepared; therefore, the Budget assumes this account is operating under the Continuing Appropriations Act, 2022 (Division A of Public Law 117–43, as amended). The amounts included for 2022 reflect the annualized level provided by the continuing resolution.

Program and Financing (in millions of dollars)

Identification code 069–8107–0–7–402		2021 actual	2022 est.	2023 est.
	Obligations by program activity:			
0001	Engineering, development, test and evaluation	206	189	187
0002	Procurement and modernization of air traffic control (ATC) facilities and equipment	1,751	1,834	1,816
0003	Procurement and modernization of non-ATC facilities and equipment	212	197	195
0004	Mission support	298	238	235
0005	Personnel and related expenses	532	574	555
0007	Spectrum Efficient National Surveillance Radar (SENSR)	2		
0008	2017 Hurricanes / 2018 Supplemental	7	8	6
0100	Subtotal, direct program	3,008	3,040	2,994
0799	Total direct obligations	3,008	3,040	2,994
0801	Facilities and Equipment (Airport and Airway Trust Fund) (Reimbursable)	116	92	92
0900	Total new obligations, unexpired accounts	3,124	3,132	3,086

FACILITIES AND EQUIPMENT—Continued
Program and Financing—Continued

Identification code 069–8107–0–7–402	2021 actual	2022 est.	2023 est.
Budgetary resources:			
Unobligated balance:			
1000 Unobligated balance brought forward, Oct 1	2,154	2,206	2,155
1001 Discretionary unobligated balance brought fwd, Oct 1	2,152		
1021 Recoveries of prior year unpaid obligations	106		
1070 Unobligated balance (total)	2,260	2,206	2,155
Budget authority:			
Appropriations, discretionary:			
1101 Appropriation (special or trust)	3,015	3,015	3,015
Spending authority from offsetting collections, discretionary:			
1700 Collected	56	66	66
1701 Change in uncollected payments, Federal sources	4		
1750 Spending auth from offsetting collections, disc (total)	60	66	66
1900 Budget authority (total)	3,075	3,081	3,081
1930 Total budgetary resources available	5,335	5,287	5,236
Memorandum (non-add) entries:			
1940 Unobligated balance expiring	–5		
1941 Unexpired unobligated balance, end of year	2,206	2,155	2,150
Special and non-revolving trust funds:			
1950 Other balances withdrawn and returned to unappropriated receipts	30		
1951 Unobligated balance expiring	5		
1952 Expired unobligated balance, start of year	87	86	86
1953 Expired unobligated balance, end of year	81	86	86
1954 Unobligated balance canceling	30		
Change in obligated balance:			
Unpaid obligations:			
3000 Unpaid obligations, brought forward, Oct 1	2,208	2,370	2,585
3010 New obligations, unexpired accounts	3,124	3,132	3,086
3011 Obligations ("upward adjustments"), expired accounts	1		
3020 Outlays (gross)	–2,832	–2,917	–3,154
3040 Recoveries of prior year unpaid obligations, unexpired	–106		
3041 Recoveries of prior year unpaid obligations, expired	–25		
3050 Unpaid obligations, end of year	2,370	2,585	2,517
Uncollected payments:			
3060 Uncollected pymts, Fed sources, brought forward, Oct 1	–55	–46	–46
3061 Adjustments to uncollected pymts, Fed sources, brought forward, Oct 1	–1		
3070 Change in uncollected pymts, Fed sources, unexpired	–4		
3071 Change in uncollected pymts, Fed sources, expired	14		
3090 Uncollected pymts, Fed sources, end of year	–46	–46	–46
Memorandum (non-add) entries:			
3100 Obligated balance, start of year	2,152	2,324	2,539
3200 Obligated balance, end of year	2,324	2,539	2,471
Budget authority and outlays, net:			
Discretionary:			
4000 Budget authority, gross	3,075	3,081	3,081
Outlays, gross:			
4010 Outlays from new discretionary authority	925	1,015	1,033
4011 Outlays from discretionary balances	1,900	1,902	2,121
4020 Outlays, gross (total)	2,825	2,917	3,154
Offsets against gross budget authority and outlays:			
Offsetting collections (collected) from:			
4030 Federal sources	–43	–36	–36
4033 Non-Federal sources	–28	–30	–30
4040 Offsets against gross budget authority and outlays (total)	–71	–66	–66
Additional offsets against gross budget authority only:			
4050 Change in uncollected pymts, Fed sources, unexpired	–4		
4052 Offsetting collections credited to expired accounts	15		
4060 Additional offsets against budget authority only (total)	11		
4070 Budget authority, net (discretionary)	3,015	3,015	3,015
4080 Outlays, net (discretionary)	2,754	2,851	3,088
Mandatory:			
Outlays, gross:			
4101 Outlays from mandatory balances	7		
4180 Budget authority, net (total)	3,015	3,015	3,015
4190 Outlays, net (total)	2,761	2,851	3,088
Memorandum (non-add) entries:			
5090 Unexpired unavailable balance, SOY: Offsetting collections	3	3	3
5092 Unexpired unavailable balance, EOY: Offsetting collections	3	3	3

Funding in this account provides for the deployment of communications, navigation, surveillance, and related capabilities within the National Airspace System (NAS). This includes funding for several activities of the Next Generation Air Transportation System, a joint effort between the Department of Transportation, the National Aeronautics and Space Administration, and the Departments of Defense, Homeland Security, and Commerce to improve the safety, capacity, security, and environmental performance of the NAS. The funding request supports the Federal Aviation Administration's comprehensive plan for modernizing, maintaining, and improving air traffic control and airway facilities services.

Object Classification (in millions of dollars)

Identification code 069–8107–0–7–402	2021 actual	2022 est.	2023 est.
Direct obligations:			
Personnel compensation:			
11.1 Full-time permanent	361	369	383
11.3 Other than full-time permanent	2	2	1
11.5 Other personnel compensation	8	8	7
11.9 Total personnel compensation	371	379	391
12.1 Civilian personnel benefits	130	137	143
21.0 Travel and transportation of persons	17	41	11
22.0 Transportation of things	3	2	2
23.2 Rental payments to others	44	39	39
23.3 Communications, utilities, and miscellaneous charges	96	45	45
25.1 Advisory and assistance services	1,702	1,708	1,690
25.2 Other services from non-Federal sources	168	125	119
25.3 Other goods and services from Federal sources	12	43	42
25.4 Operation and maintenance of facilities	79	83	80
25.5 Research and development contracts	13	1	1
25.7 Operation and maintenance of equipment	84	63	62
25.8 Subsistence and support of persons		1	1
26.0 Supplies and materials	15	31	30
31.0 Equipment	194	202	198
32.0 Land and structures	77	137	137
41.0 Grants, subsidies, and contributions		3	3
43.0 Interest and dividends	3		
99.0 Direct obligations	3,008	3,040	2,994
99.0 Reimbursable obligations	116	92	92
99.9 Total new obligations, unexpired accounts	3,124	3,132	3,086

Employment Summary

Identification code 069–8107–0–7–402	2021 actual	2022 est.	2023 est.
1001 Direct civilian full-time equivalent employment	2,815	2,815	2,815
2001 Reimbursable civilian full-time equivalent employment	50	50	53

RESEARCH, ENGINEERING, AND DEVELOPMENT
(AIRPORT AND AIRWAY TRUST FUND)

For necessary expenses, not otherwise provided for, for research, engineering, and development, as authorized under part A of subtitle VII of title 49, United States Code, including construction of experimental facilities and acquisition of necessary sites by lease or grant, $260,500,000, to be derived from the Airport and Airway Trust Fund and to remain available until September 30, 2025: Provided, That there may be credited to this appropriation as offsetting collections, funds received from States, counties, municipalities, other public authorities, and private sources, which shall be available for expenses incurred for research, engineering, and development.

Note.—A full-year 2022 appropriation for this account was not enacted at the time the Budget was prepared; therefore, the Budget assumes this account is operating under the Continuing Appropriations Act, 2022 (Division A of Public Law 117–43, as amended). The amounts included for 2022 reflect the annualized level provided by the continuing resolution.

Program and Financing (in millions of dollars)

Identification code 069–8108–0–7–402	2021 actual	2022 est.	2023 est.
Obligations by program activity:			
0011 Improve aviation safety	94	29	
0012 Improve Efficiency	3		
0013 Reduce environmental impact of aviation	26	3	
0014 Improve the efficiency of mission support	1	10	
0015 Research, Engineering & Development	95	205	234

DEPARTMENT OF TRANSPORTATION

ADMINISTRATIVE PROVISIONS—FEDERAL AVIATION ADMINISTRATION 917

		2021 actual	2022 est.	2023 est.
0100	Subtotal, direct program	219	247	234
0799	Total direct obligations	219	247	234
0801	Research, Engineering and Development (Airport and Airway Trust (Reimbursable)	11	11	11
0900	Total new obligations, unexpired accounts	230	258	245
	Budgetary resources:			
	Unobligated balance:			
1000	Unobligated balance brought forward, Oct 1	171	149	98
1021	Recoveries of prior year unpaid obligations	2		
1070	Unobligated balance (total)	173	149	98
	Budget authority:			
	Appropriations, discretionary:			
1101	Appropriation (special or trust)	198	198	261
	Spending authority from offsetting collections, discretionary:			
1700	Collected	7	9	9
1701	Change in uncollected payments, Federal sources	1		
1750	Spending auth from offsetting collections, disc (total)	8	9	9
1900	Budget authority (total)	206	207	270
1930	Total budgetary resources available	379	356	368
	Memorandum (non-add) entries:			
1941	Unexpired unobligated balance, end of year	149	98	123
	Special and non-revolving trust funds:			
1950	Other balances withdrawn and returned to unappropriated receipts	2		
1952	Expired unobligated balance, start of year	6	5	5
1953	Expired unobligated balance, end of year	5	5	5
1954	Unobligated balance canceling	2		
	Change in obligated balance:			
	Unpaid obligations:			
3000	Unpaid obligations, brought forward, Oct 1	166	225	225
3010	New obligations, unexpired accounts	230	258	245
3011	Obligations ("upward adjustments"), expired accounts	1		
3020	Outlays (gross)	−167	−258	−286
3040	Recoveries of prior year unpaid obligations, unexpired	−2		
3041	Recoveries of prior year unpaid obligations, expired	−3		
3050	Unpaid obligations, end of year	225	225	184
	Uncollected payments:			
3060	Uncollected pymts, Fed sources, brought forward, Oct 1	−9	−9	−9
3070	Change in uncollected pymts, Fed sources, unexpired	−1		
3071	Change in uncollected pymts, Fed sources, expired	1		
3090	Uncollected pymts, Fed sources, end of year	−9	−9	−9
	Memorandum (non-add) entries:			
3100	Obligated balance, start of year	157	216	216
3200	Obligated balance, end of year	216	216	175
	Budget authority and outlays, net:			
	Discretionary:			
4000	Budget authority, gross	206	207	270
	Outlays, gross:			
4010	Outlays from new discretionary authority	46	96	124
4011	Outlays from discretionary balances	121	162	162
4020	Outlays, gross (total)	167	258	286
	Offsets against gross budget authority and outlays:			
	Offsetting collections (collected) from:			
4030	Federal sources	−8	−9	−9
4040	Offsets against gross budget authority and outlays (total)	−8	−9	−9
	Additional offsets against gross budget authority only:			
4050	Change in uncollected pymts, Fed sources, unexpired	−1		
4052	Offsetting collections credited to expired accounts	1		
4070	Budget authority, net (discretionary)	198	198	261
4080	Outlays, net (discretionary)	159	249	277
4180	Budget authority, net (total)	198	198	261
4190	Outlays, net (total)	159	249	277

This account provides funding to conduct research, engineering, and development to improve the national airspace system's capacity and safety, as well as the ability to meet environmental needs. The request includes funding for several research and development activities of the Next Generation Air Transportation System (NextGen), as well as activities related to unmanned aircraft systems.

Object Classification (in millions of dollars)

Identification code 069–8108–0–7–402	2021 actual	2022 est.	2023 est.
Direct obligations:			
11.1 Personnel compensation: Full-time permanent	27	32	34
12.1 Civilian personnel benefits	9	11	12
21.0 Travel and transportation of persons		1	1
25.1 Advisory and assistance services	34	38	34
25.2 Other services from non-Federal sources	62	69	64
25.3 Other goods and services from Federal sources	9	10	10
25.4 Operation and maintenance of facilities	1	1	1
25.5 Research and development contracts	11	12	11
26.0 Supplies and materials	1	1	1
31.0 Equipment	2	2	2
41.0 Grants, subsidies, and contributions	63	70	64
99.0 Direct obligations	219	247	234
99.0 Reimbursable obligations	11	11	11
99.9 Total new obligations, unexpired accounts	230	258	245

Employment Summary

Identification code 069–8108–0–7–402	2021 actual	2022 est.	2023 est.
1001 Direct civilian full-time equivalent employment	196	217	227

TRUST FUND SHARE OF FAA ACTIVITIES (AIRPORT AND AIRWAY TRUST FUND)

Program and Financing (in millions of dollars)

Identification code 069–8104–0–7–402	2021 actual	2022 est.	2023 est.
Obligations by program activity:			
0001 Payment to Operations	10,519	10,519	9,934
0900 Total new obligations, unexpired accounts (object class 94.0)	10,519	10,519	9,934
Budgetary resources:			
Budget authority:			
Appropriations, discretionary:			
1101 Appropriation (special or trust)	10,519	10,519	9,934
1930 Total budgetary resources available	10,519	10,519	9,934
Change in obligated balance:			
Unpaid obligations:			
3000 Unpaid obligations, brought forward, Oct 1	775	1,022	842
3010 New obligations, unexpired accounts	10,519	10,519	9,934
3020 Outlays (gross)	−10,272	−10,699	−9,981
3050 Unpaid obligations, end of year	1,022	842	795
Memorandum (non-add) entries:			
3100 Obligated balance, start of year	775	1,022	842
3200 Obligated balance, end of year	1,022	842	795
Budget authority and outlays, net:			
Discretionary:			
4000 Budget authority, gross	10,519	10,519	9,934
Outlays, gross:			
4010 Outlays from new discretionary authority	9,500	9,677	9,139
4011 Outlays from discretionary balances	772	1,022	842
4020 Outlays, gross (total)	10,272	10,699	9,981
4180 Budget authority, net (total)	10,519	10,519	9,934
4190 Outlays, net (total)	10,272	10,699	9,981

The 2023 Budget proposes $11.934 billion for Federal Aviation Administration Operations, of which $9.934 billion would be provided from the Airport and Airway Trust Fund.

ADMINISTRATIVE PROVISIONS—FEDERAL AVIATION ADMINISTRATION

SEC. 110. *The Administrator of the Federal Aviation Administration may reimburse amounts made available to satisfy section 41742(a)(1) of title 49, United States Code, from fees credited under section 45303 of title 49, United States Code, and any amount remaining in such account at the close of any fiscal year may be made available to satisfy section 41742(a)(1) of title 49, United States Code, for the subsequent fiscal year.*

ADMINISTRATIVE PROVISIONS—FEDERAL AVIATION ADMINISTRATION—Continued

SEC. 111. *Amounts collected under section 40113(e) of title 49, United States Code, shall be credited to the appropriation current at the time of collection, to be merged with and available for the same purposes as such appropriation.*

SEC. 112. *None of the funds made available by this Act shall be available for paying premium pay under subsection 5546(a) of title 5, United States Code, to any Federal Aviation Administration employee unless such employee actually performed work during the time corresponding to such premium pay.*

SEC. 113. *None of the funds made available by this Act may be obligated or expended for an employee of the Federal Aviation Administration to purchase a store gift card or gift certificate through use of a Government-issued credit card.*

SEC. 114. *Notwithstanding any other transfer restriction under this Act, not to exceed 10 percent of any appropriation made available for the current fiscal year for the Federal Aviation Administration by this Act or provided by previous appropriations Acts may be transferred between such appropriations for the Federal Aviation Administration, but no such appropriation, except as otherwise specifically provided, shall be increased by more than 10 percent by any such transfer: Provided, That funds transferred under this section shall be treated as a reprogramming of funds under section 404 of this Act and shall not be available for obligation unless the Committees on Appropriations of the Senate and House of Representatives are notified 15 days in advance of such transfer: Provided further, That any transfer from an amount made available for obligation as discretionary grants-in-aid for airports pursuant to section 47117(f) of title 49, United States Code shall be deemed as obligated for grants-in-aid for airports under part B of subtitle VII of title 49, United States Code, for the purposes of complying with the limitation on incurring obligations in this appropriations Act or any other appropriations Act under the heading "Grants-in-Aid for Airports".*

SEC. 115. *The Federal Aviation Administration Administrative Services Franchise Fund may be reimbursed after performance or paid in advance from funds available to the Federal Aviation Administration and other Federal agencies for which the Fund performs services.*

FEDERAL HIGHWAY ADMINISTRATION

The 2023 Budget requests $58.8 billion in obligation limitation for the Federal Highway Administration's (FHWA) Federal-aid Highways program. This funding, when combined with supplemental appropriations provided by the Infrastructure Investment and Jobs Act, will provide the needed funding to: significantly improve the condition and performance of our national highway infrastructure; make roads and bridges safe for all users; provide equitable travel for all people; address the climate change challenge; and spur innovation.

Federal Funds

MISCELLANEOUS APPROPRIATIONS

Program and Financing (in millions of dollars)

Identification code 069–9911–0–1–401		2021 actual	2022 est.	2023 est.
	Obligations by program activity:			
0004	Miscellaneous Appropriations	7	7	7
0900	Total new obligations, unexpired accounts (object class 41.0)	7	7	7
	Budgetary resources:			
	Unobligated balance:			
1000	Unobligated balance brought forward, Oct 1	96	91	84
1001	Discretionary unobligated balance brought fwd, Oct 1	96		
1021	Recoveries of prior year unpaid obligations	2		
1070	Unobligated balance (total)	98	91	84
1930	Total budgetary resources available	98	91	84
	Memorandum (non-add) entries:			
1941	Unexpired unobligated balance, end of year	91	84	77
	Change in obligated balance:			
	Unpaid obligations:			
3000	Unpaid obligations, brought forward, Oct 1	27	18	15
3010	New obligations, unexpired accounts	7	7	7
3020	Outlays (gross)	–14	–10	–9
3040	Recoveries of prior year unpaid obligations, unexpired	–2		
3050	Unpaid obligations, end of year	18	15	13
	Memorandum (non-add) entries:			
3100	Obligated balance, start of year	27	18	15
3200	Obligated balance, end of year	18	15	13
	Budget authority and outlays, net:			
	Discretionary:			
	Outlays, gross:			
4011	Outlays from discretionary balances	14	10	9
4180	Budget authority, net (total)			
4190	Outlays, net (total)	14	10	9
	Memorandum (non-add) entries:			
5103	Unexpired unavailable balance, SOY: Fulfilled purpose	1	1	
5104	Unexpired unavailable balance, EOY: Fulfilled purpose	1		

This consolidated schedule shows obligations and outlays of amounts appropriated from the General Fund for miscellaneous programs. The schedule reflects a $19.9 million rescission enacted in the Department of Transportation Appropriations Act, 2020 (Public Law 116–94). No appropriations are requested for 2023.

EMERGENCY RELIEF PROGRAM

⟦*For an additional amount for the "Emergency Relief Program" as authorized under section 125 of title 23, United States Code, $2,600,000,000, to remain available until expended.*⟧ *(Disaster Relief Supplemental Appropriations Act, 2022.)*

Program and Financing (in millions of dollars)

Identification code 069–0500–0–1–401		2021 actual	2022 est.	2023 est.
	Obligations by program activity:			
0001	Emergency Relief Program (Direct)	625	1,509	1,091
0900	Total new obligations, unexpired accounts (object class 41.0)	625	1,509	1,091
	Budgetary resources:			
	Unobligated balance:			
1000	Unobligated balance brought forward, Oct 1	1,360	838	1,929
1021	Recoveries of prior year unpaid obligations	103		
1070	Unobligated balance (total)	1,463	838	1,929
	Budget authority:			
	Appropriations, discretionary:			
1100	Appropriation		2,600	
1930	Total budgetary resources available	1,463	3,438	1,929
	Memorandum (non-add) entries:			
1941	Unexpired unobligated balance, end of year	838	1,929	838
	Change in obligated balance:			
	Unpaid obligations:			
3000	Unpaid obligations, brought forward, Oct 1	1,096	983	1,207
3010	New obligations, unexpired accounts	625	1,509	1,091
3020	Outlays (gross)	–635	–1,285	–1,315
3040	Recoveries of prior year unpaid obligations, unexpired	–103		
3050	Unpaid obligations, end of year	983	1,207	983
	Memorandum (non-add) entries:			
3100	Obligated balance, start of year	1,096	983	1,207
3200	Obligated balance, end of year	983	1,207	983
	Budget authority and outlays, net:			
	Discretionary:			
4000	Budget authority, gross		2,600	
	Outlays, gross:			
4010	Outlays from new discretionary authority		702	
4011	Outlays from discretionary balances	635	583	1,315
4020	Outlays, gross (total)	635	1,285	1,315
4180	Budget authority, net (total)		2,600	
4190	Outlays, net (total)	635	1,285	1,315

This account includes General Fund discretionary resources appropriated as needed for FHWA's Emergency Relief program, as authorized under 23 U.S.C. 125. In 2012, $1.7 billion was enacted to remain available until expended; in 2013, $2.0 billion was enacted to remain available until expended; in 2017, $1.5 billion was enacted to remain available until expended; in 2018, $1.4 billion was enacted to remain available until expended; in 2019, $1.7 billion was enacted to remain available until expended; and in 2023, $2.6 billion was enacted to remain available until expended, all for necessary expenses for repairing or reconstructing highways seriously damaged as a result of major disasters declared pursuant to the Robert T. Stafford Disaster Relief and Emergency Assistance Act (42 U.S.C. 5121 et seq.). These appropriations have been provided to supplement the $100 million authorized annually out of the Highway Trust Fund under 23 U.S.C. 125 for the Emergency Relief program and included in the Federal-Aid Highways account.

No further appropriations are requested for this account in 2023.

APPALACHIAN DEVELOPMENT HIGHWAY SYSTEM

Program and Financing (in millions of dollars)

Identification code 069–0640–0–1–401		2021 actual	2022 est.	2023 est.
Obligations by program activity:				
0001	Appalachian Development Highway System	10	7	4
0900	Total new obligations, unexpired accounts (object class 41.0)	10	7	4
Budgetary resources:				
Unobligated balance:				
1000	Unobligated balance brought forward, Oct 1	12	12	5
1021	Recoveries of prior year unpaid obligations	10		
1070	Unobligated balance (total)	22	12	5
1930	Total budgetary resources available	22	12	5
Memorandum (non-add) entries:				
1941	Unexpired unobligated balance, end of year	12	5	1
Change in obligated balance:				
Unpaid obligations:				
3000	Unpaid obligations, brought forward, Oct 1	30	18	16
3010	New obligations, unexpired accounts	10	7	4
3020	Outlays (gross)	–12	–9	–7
3040	Recoveries of prior year unpaid obligations, unexpired	–10		
3050	Unpaid obligations, end of year	18	16	13
Memorandum (non-add) entries:				
3100	Obligated balance, start of year	30	18	16
3200	Obligated balance, end of year	18	16	13
Budget authority and outlays, net:				
Discretionary:				
Outlays, gross:				
4011	Outlays from discretionary balances	12	9	7
4180	Budget authority, net (total)			
4190	Outlays, net (total)	12	9	7

Funding for this program is used for constructing and improving corridors of the Appalachian Development Highway System. The Infrastructure Investment Jobs Act provides supplemental appropriations for the Appalachian Development Highway System in each year from 2022 through 2026 through the Highway Infrastructure Programs.

No funding is requested for 2023 in this account.

STATE INFRASTRUCTURE BANKS

Program and Financing (in millions of dollars)

Identification code 069–0549–0–1–401		2021 actual	2022 est.	2023 est.
Budgetary resources:				
Unobligated balance:				
1000	Unobligated balance brought forward, Oct 1	1	1	1
1930	Total budgetary resources available	1	1	1
Memorandum (non-add) entries:				
1941	Unexpired unobligated balance, end of year	1	1	1
4180	Budget authority, net (total)			
4190	Outlays, net (total)			

In 1997, FHWA received an appropriation from the General Fund for the State Infrastructure Banks (SIBs) program.

All of the funds have been provided to the States to capitalize the infrastructure banks. Because the funding was provided as grants, and not loans, FHWA will not receive reimbursements of amounts expended for the SIBs program. No new budgetary resources are requested in 2023.

PAYMENT TO THE HIGHWAY TRUST FUND

Program and Financing (in millions of dollars)

Identification code 069–0534–0–1–401		2021 actual	2022 est.	2023 est.
Obligations by program activity:				
0001	Payment to the highway trust fund	13,600	118,000	
0900	Total new obligations, unexpired accounts (object class 94.0)	13,600	118,000	
Budgetary resources:				
Budget authority:				
Appropriations, mandatory:				
1200	Appropriation	13,600	118,000	
1930	Total budgetary resources available	13,600	118,000	
Change in obligated balance:				
Unpaid obligations:				
3010	New obligations, unexpired accounts	13,600	118,000	
3020	Outlays (gross)	–13,600	–118,000	
Budget authority and outlays, net:				
Mandatory:				
4090	Budget authority, gross	13,600	118,000	
Outlays, gross:				
4100	Outlays from new mandatory authority	13,600	118,000	
4180	Budget authority, net (total)	13,600	118,000	
4190	Outlays, net (total)	13,600	118,000	

HIGHWAY INFRASTRUCTURE PROGRAMS

Note.—A full-year 2022 appropriation for this account was not enacted at the time the Budget was prepared; therefore, the Budget assumes this account is operating under the Continuing Appropriations Act, 2022 (Division A of Public Law 117–43, as amended). The amounts included for 2022 reflect the annualized level provided by the continuing resolution.

HIGHWAY INFRASTRUCTURE PROGRAM

[(INCLUDING TRANSFER OF FUNDS)]

[For an additional amount for "Highway Infrastructure Programs", $47,272,000,000, to remain available until expended except as otherwise provided under this heading: *Provided*, That of the amount provided under this heading in this Act, $9,454,400,000, to remain available until September 30, 2025, shall be made available for fiscal year 2022, $9,454,400,000, to remain available until September 30, 2026, shall be made available for fiscal year 2023, $9,454,400,000, to remain available until September 30, 2027, shall be made available for fiscal year 2024, $9,454,400,000, to remain available until September 30, 2028, shall be made available for fiscal year 2025, and $9,454,400,000, to remain available until September 30, 2029, shall be made available for fiscal year 2026: *Provided further*, That the funds made available under this heading in this Act shall be derived from the general fund of the Treasury, shall be in addition to any other amounts made available for such purpose, and shall not affect the distribution or amount of funds provided in any Act making annual appropriations: *Provided further*, That, except for funds provided in paragraph (1) under this heading in this Act, up to 1.5 percent of the amounts made available under this heading in this Act in each of fiscal years 2022 through 2026 shall be for operations and administrations of the Federal Highway Administration, of which $1,000,000 in each fiscal year shall be transferred to the Office of the Inspector General of the Department of Transportation for oversight of funding provided to the Department of Transportation in this title in this Act: *Provided further*, That the amounts made available in the preceding proviso may be combined with the funds made available in paragraph (1) under this heading in this Act for the same purposes in the same account: *Provided further*, That the funds made available under this heading in this Act shall not be subject to any limitation on obligations for Federal-aid highways or highway safety construction programs set forth in any Act making annual appropriations: *Provided further*, That, of the amount provided under this heading in this Act, the following amounts shall be for the following purposes in equal amounts for each of fiscal years 2022 through 2026—]

[(1) $27,500,000,000 shall be for a bridge replacement, rehabilitation, preservation, protection, and construction program: *Provided further*, That, except as oth-

HIGHWAY INFRASTRUCTURE PROGRAMS—Continued

erwise provided under this paragraph in this Act, the funds made available under this paragraph in this Act shall be administered as if apportioned under chapter 1 of title 23, United States Code: *Provided further*, That a project funded with funds made available under this paragraph in this Act shall be treated as a project on a Federal-aid highway: *Provided further*, That, of the funds made available under this paragraph in this Act for a fiscal year, 3 percent shall be set aside to carry out section 202(d) of title 23, United States Code: *Provided further*, That funds set aside under the preceding proviso to carry out section 202(d) of such title shall be in addition to funds otherwise made available to carry out such section and shall be administered as if made available under such section: *Provided further*, That for funds set aside under the third proviso of this paragraph in this Act to carry out section 202(d) of title 23, United States Code, the Federal share of the costs shall be 100 percent: *Provided further*, That, for the purposes of funds made available under this paragraph in this Act: (1) the term State has the meaning given such term in section 101 of title 23, United States Code; (2) the term off-system bridge means a highway bridge located on a public road, other than a bridge on a Federal-aid highway; and (3) the term Federal-aid highway means a public highway eligible for assistance under chapter 1 of title 23, United States Code, other than a highway functionally classified as a local road or rural minor collector: *Provided further*, That up to one-half of one percent of the amounts made available under this paragraph in this Act in each fiscal year shall be for the administration and operations of the Federal Highway Administration: *Provided further*, That, after setting aside funds under the third proviso of this paragraph in this Act the Secretary shall distribute the remaining funds made available under this paragraph in this Act among States as follows—]

[(A) 75 percent by the proportion that the total cost of replacing all bridges classified in poor condition in such State bears to the sum of the total cost to replace all bridges classified in poor condition in all States; and]

[(B) 25 percent by the proportion that the total cost of rehabilitating all bridges classified in fair condition in such State bears to the sum of the total cost to rehabilitate all bridges classified in fair condition in all States:]

[*Provided further*, That the amounts calculated under the preceding proviso shall be adjusted such that each State receives, for each of fiscal years 2022 through 2026, no less than $45,000,000 under such proviso: *Provided further*, That for purposes of the preceding 2 provisos, the Secretary shall determine replacement and rehabilitation costs based on the average unit costs of bridges from 2016 through 2020, as submitted by States to the Federal Highway Administration, as required by section 144(b)(5) of title 23, United States Code: *Provided further*, That for purposes of determining the distribution of funds to States under this paragraph in this Act, the Secretary shall calculate the total deck area of bridges classified as in poor or fair condition based on the National Bridge Inventory as of December 31, 2020: *Provided further*, That, subject to the following proviso, funds made available under this paragraph in this Act that are distributed to States shall be used for highway bridge replacement, rehabilitation, preservation, protection, or construction projects on public roads: *Provided further*, That of the funds made available under this paragraph in this Act that are distributed to a State, 15 percent shall be set aside for use on off-system bridges for the same purposes as described in the preceding proviso: *Provided further*, That, except as provided in the following proviso, for funds made available under this paragraph in this Act that are distributed to States, the Federal share shall be determined in accordance with section 120 of title 23, United States Code: *Provided further*, That for funds made available under this paragraph in this Act that are distributed to States and used on an off-system bridge that is owned by a county, town, township, city, municipality or other local agency, or federally-recognized Tribe the Federal share shall be 100 percent;]

[(2) $5,000,000,000, to remain available until expended for amounts made available for each of fiscal years 2022 through 2026, shall be to carry out a National Electric Vehicle Formula Program (referred to in this paragraph in this Act as the "Program") to provide funding to States to strategically deploy electric vehicle charging infrastructure and to establish an interconnected network to facilitate data collection, access, and reliability: *Provided*, That funds made available under this paragraph in this Act shall be used for: (1) the acquisition and installation of electric vehicle charging infrastructure to serve as a catalyst for the deployment of such infrastructure and to connect it to a network to facilitate data collection, access, and reliability; (2) proper operation and maintenance of electric vehicle charging infrastructure; and (3) data sharing about electric vehicle charging infrastructure to ensure the long-term success of investments made under this paragraph in this Act: *Provided further*, That for each of fiscal years 2022 through 2026, the Secretary shall distribute among the States the funds made available under this paragraph in this Act so that each State receives an amount equal to the proportion that the total base apportionment or allocation determined for the State under subsection (c) of section 104 or under section 165 of title 23, United States Code, bears to the total base apportionments or allocations for all States under subsection (c) of section 104 and section 165 of title 23, United States Code: *Provided further*, That the Federal share payable for the cost of a project funded under this paragraph in this Act shall be 80 percent: *Provided further*, That the Secretary shall establish a deadline by which a State shall provide a plan to the Secretary, in such form and such manner that the Secretary requires (to be made available on the Department's website), describing how such State intends to use funds distributed to the State under this paragraph in this Act to carry out the Program for each fiscal year in which funds are made available: *Provided further*, That, not later than 120 days after the deadline established in the preceding proviso, the Secretary shall make publicly available on the Department's website and submit to the House Committee on Transportation and Infrastructure, the Senate Committee on Environment and Public Works, and the House and Senate Committees on Appropriations, a report summarizing each plan submitted by a State to the Department of Transportation and an assessment of how such plans make progress towards the establishment of a national network of electric vehicle charging infrastructure: *Provided further*, That if a State fails to submit the plan required under the fourth proviso of this paragraph in this Act to the Secretary by the date specified in such proviso, or if the Secretary determines a State has not taken action to carry out its plan, the Secretary may withhold or withdraw, as applicable, funds made available under this paragraph in this Act for the fiscal year from the State and award such funds on a competitive basis to local jurisdictions within the State for use on projects that meet the eligibility requirements under this paragraph in this Act: *Provided further*, That, prior to the Secretary making a determination that a State has not taken actions to carry out its plan, the Secretary shall notify the State, consult with the State, and identify actions that can be taken to rectify concerns, and provide at least 90 days for the State to rectify concerns and take action to carry out its plan: *Provided further*, That the Secretary shall provide notice to a State on the intent to withhold or withdraw funds not less than 60 days before withholding or withdrawing any funds, during which time the States shall have an opportunity to appeal a decision to withhold or withdraw funds directly to the Secretary: *Provided further*, That if the Secretary determines that any funds withheld or withdrawn from a State under the preceding proviso cannot be fully awarded to local jurisdictions within the State under the preceding proviso in a manner consistent with the purpose of this paragraph in this Act, any such funds remaining shall be distributed among other States (except States for which funds for that fiscal year have been withheld or withdrawn under the preceding proviso) in the same manner as funds distributed for that fiscal year under the second proviso under this paragraph in this Act, except that the ratio shall be adjusted to exclude States for which funds for that fiscal year have been withheld or withdrawn under the preceding proviso: *Provided further*, That funds distributed under the preceding proviso shall only be available to carry out this paragraph in this Act: *Provided further*, That funds made available under this paragraph in this Act may be used to contract with a private entity for acquisition and installation of publicly accessible electric vehicle charging infrastructure and the private entity may pay the non-Federal share of the cost of a project funded under this paragraph: *Provided further*, That funds made available under this paragraph in this Act shall be for projects directly related to the charging of a vehicle and only for electric vehicle charging infrastructure that is open to the general public or to authorized commercial motor vehicle operators from more than one company: *Provided further*, That any electric vehicle charging infrastructure acquired or installed with funds made available under this paragraph in this Act shall be located along a designated alternative fuel corridor: *Provided further*, That no later than 90 days after the date of enactment of this Act, the Secretary of Transportation, in coordination with the Secretary of Energy, shall develop guidance for States and localities to strategically deploy electric vehicle charging infrastructure, consistent with this paragraph in this Act: *Provided further*, That the Secretary of Transportation, in coordination with the Secretary of Energy, shall consider the following in developing the guidance described in the preceding proviso: (1) the distance between publicly available electric vehicle charging infrastructure; (2) connections to the electric grid, including electric distribution upgrades; vehicle-to-grid integration, including smart charge management or other protocols that can minimize impacts to the grid; alignment with electric distribution interconnection processes, and plans for the use of renewable energy sources to power charging and energy storage; (3) the proximity of existing off-highway travel centers, fuel retailers, and small businesses to electric vehicle charging infrastructure acquired or funded under this paragraph in this Act; (4) the need for publicly available electric vehicle charging infrastructure in rural corridors and underserved or disadvantaged communities; (5) the long-term operation and maintenance of publicly available electric vehicle charging infrastructure to avoid stranded assets and protect the investment of public funds in that infrastructure; (6) existing private, national, State, local, Tribal, and territorial government electric vehicle charging infrastructure programs and incentives; (7) fostering enhanced, coordinated, public-private or private investment in electric vehicle charging infrastructure; (8) meeting current and anticipated market demands for electric vehicle charging infrastructure, including with regard to power levels and charging speed, and minimizing the time to charge current and anticipated vehicles; and (9) any other factors, as determined by the Secretary: *Provided further,* That if a State determines, and the Secretary certifies, that the designated alternative fuel corridors in the States are fully built out, then the State may use funds provided under this paragraph for electric vehicle charging infrastructure on any public road or in other publically accessible locations, such as parking facilities at public buildings, public schools, and public parks, or in publically accessible parking facilities owned or managed by a private entity: *Provided further,* That subject to the minimum standards and requirements established under the following proviso, funds made available under this paragraph in this Act may be used for: (1) the acquisition or installation of electric vehicle charging infrastructure; (2) operating assistance for costs allocable to operating and maintaining electric vehicle charging infrastructure acquired or installed under this paragraph in this Act, for a period not to exceed five years; (3) the acquisition or installation of traffic control devices located in the right-of-way to provide directional information to electric vehicle charging infrastructure acquired, installed, or operated under this paragraph in this Act; (4) on-premises signs to provide information about electric vehicle charging infrastructure acquired, installed, or operated under this paragraph in this Act; (5) development phase activities relating to the acquisition or installation of electric vehicle charging infrastructure, as determined by the Secretary; or (6) mapping and analysis activities to evaluate, in an area in the United States designated by the eligible entity, the locations of current and future electric vehicle owners, to forecast commuting and travel patterns of electric vehicles and the quantity of electricity required to serve electric vehicle charging stations, to estimate the concentrations of electric vehicle charging stations to meet the needs of current and future electric vehicle drivers, to estimate future needs for electric vehicle charging stations to support the adoption and use of electric vehicles in shared mobility solutions, such as micro-transit and transportation network companies, and to develop an analytical model to allow a city, county, or other political subdivision of a State or a local agency to compare and evaluate different adoption and use scenarios for electric vehicles and electric vehicle charging stations: *Provided further,* That not later than 180 days after the date of enactment of this Act, the Secretary of Transportation, in coordination with the Secretary of Energy and in consultation with relevant stakeholders, shall, as appropriate, develop minimum standards and requirements related to: (1) the installation, operation, or maintenance by qualified technicians of electric vehicle charging infrastructure under this paragraph in this Act; (2) the interoperability of electric vehicle charging infrastructure under this paragraph in this Act; (3) any traffic control device or on-premises sign acquired, installed, or operated under this paragraph in this Act; (4) any data requested by the Secretary related to a project funded under this paragraph in this Act, including the format and schedule for the submission of such data; (5) network connectivity of electric vehicle charging infrastructure; and (6) information on publicly available electric vehicle charging infrastructure locations, pricing, real-time availability, and accessibility through mapping applications: *Provided further,* That not later than 1 year after the date of enactment of this Act, the Secretary shall designate national electric vehicle charging corridors that identify the near- and long-term need for, and the location of, electric vehicle charging infrastructure to support freight and goods movement at strategic locations along major national highways, the National Highway Freight Network established under section 167 of title 23, United States Code, and goods movement locations including ports, intermodal centers, and warehousing locations: *Provided further,* That the report issued under section 151(e) of title 23, United States Code, shall include a description of efforts to achieve strategic deployment of electric vehicle charging infrastructure in electric vehicle charging corridors, including progress on the implementation of the Program under this paragraph in this Act: *Provided further,* That, for fiscal year 2022, before distributing funds made available under this paragraph in this Act to States, the Secretary shall set aside from funds made available under this paragraph in this Act to carry out this paragraph in this Act not more than $300,000,000, which may be transferred to the Joint Office described in the twenty-fourth proviso of this paragraph in this Act, to establish such Joint Office and carry out its duties under this paragraph in this Act: *Provided further,* That, for each of fiscal years 2022 through 2026, after setting aside funds under the preceding proviso, and before distributing funds made available under this paragraph in this Act to States, the Secretary shall set aside from funds made available under this paragraph in this Act for such fiscal year to carry out this paragraph in this Act 10 percent for grants to States or localities that require additional assistance to strategically deploy electric vehicle charging infrastructure: *Provided further,* That not later than 1 year after the date of enactment of this Act, the Secretary shall establish a grant program to administer to States or localities the amounts set aside under the preceding proviso: *Provided further,* That, except as otherwise specified under this paragraph in this Act, funds made available under this paragraph in this Act, other than funds transferred under the nineteenth proviso of this paragraph in this Act to the Joint Office, shall be administered as if apportioned under chapter 1 of title 23, United States Code: *Provided further,* That funds made available under this paragraph in this Act shall not be transferable under section 126 of title 23, United States Code: *Provided further,* That there is established a Joint Office of Energy and Transportation (referred to in this paragraph in this Act as the "Joint Office") in the Department of Transportation and the Department of Energy to study, plan, coordinate, and implement issues of joint concern between the two agencies, which shall include: (1) technical assistance related to the deployment, operation, and maintenance of zero emission vehicle charging and refueling infrastructure, renewable energy generation, vehicle-to-grid integration, including microgrids, and related programs and policies; (2) data sharing of installation, maintenance, and utilization in order to continue to inform the network build out of zero emission vehicle charging and refueling infrastructure; (3) performance of a national and regionalized study of zero emission vehicle charging and refueling infrastructure needs and deployment factors, to support grants for community resilience and electric vehicle integration; (4) development and deployment of training and certification programs; (5) establishment and implementation of a program to promote renewable energy generation, storage, and grid integration, including microgrids, in transportation rights-of-way; (6) studying, planning, and funding for high-voltage distributed current infrastructure in the rights-of way of the Interstate System and for constructing high-voltage and or medium-voltage transmission pilots in the rights-of-way of the Interstate System; (7) research, strategies, and actions under the Departments' statutory authorities to reduce transportation-related emissions and mitigate the effects of climate change; (8) development of a streamlined utility accommodations policy for high-voltage and medium-voltage transmission in the transportation right-of-way; and (9) any other issues that the Secretary of Transportation and the Secretary of Energy identify as issues of joint interest: *Provided further,* That the Joint Office of Energy and Transportation shall establish and maintain a public database, accessible on both Department of Transportation and Department of Energy websites, that includes: (1) information maintained on the Alternative Fuel Data Center by the Office of Energy Efficiency and Renewable Energy of the Department of Energy with respect to the locations of electric vehicle charging stations; (2) potential locations for electric vehicle charging stations identified by eligible entities through the program; and (3) the ability to sort generated results by various characteristics with respect to electric vehicle charging stations, including location, in terms of the State, city, or county; status (operational, under construction, or planned); and charging type, in terms of Level 2 charging equipment or Direct Current Fast Charging Equipment: *Provided further,* That the Secretary of Transportation and the Secretary of Energy shall cooperatively administer the Joint Office consistent with this paragraph in this Act: *Provided further,* That the Secretary of Transportation and the Secretary of Energy may transfer funds between the Department of Transportation and the Department of Energy from funds provided under this paragraph in this Act to establish the Joint Office and to carry out its duties under this paragraph in this Act and any such funds or portions thereof transferred to the Joint Office may be transferred back to and merged with this account: *Provided further,* That the Secretary of Transportation and the Secretary of Energy shall notify the House and Senate Committees on Appropriations not less than 15 days prior to transferring any funds under the previous proviso: *Provided further,* That for the purposes of funds made available under this paragraph in this Act: (1) the term State has the meaning given such term in section 101 of title 23, United States Code; and (2) the term Federal-aid highway means a public highway eligible for assistance under chapter 1 of title 23, United States Code, other than a highway functionally classified as a local road or rural minor collector: *Provided further,* That, of the funds made available in this division or division A of this Act for the Federal lands transportation program under section 203 of title 23, United States Code, not less than $7,000,000 shall be made available for each Federal agency otherwise eligible to compete for amounts made available under that section for each of fiscal years 2022 through 2026;]

[(3) $3,200,000,000 shall be to carry out the Nationally Significant Freight and Highway Projects program under section 117 of title 23, United States Code;]

[(4) $9,235,000,000 shall be to carry out the Bridge Investment Program under section 124 of title 23, United States Code: *Provided,* That, of the funds made available under this paragraph in this Act for a fiscal year, $20,000,000 shall be set aside to carry out section 202(d) of title 23, United States Code: *Provided further,* That, of the funds made available under this paragraph in this Act for a fiscal year, $20,000,000 shall be set aside to provide grants for planning, feasibility analysis, and revenue forecasting associated with the development of a project that would subsequently be eligible to apply for assistance under this paragraph:

HIGHWAY INFRASTRUCTURE PROGRAMS—Continued

Provided further, That funds set aside under the first proviso of this paragraph in this Act to carry out section 202(d) of such title shall be in addition to funds otherwise made available to carry out such section and shall be administered as if made available under such section: *Provided further*, That for funds set aside under the first proviso of this paragraph in this Act to carry out section 202(d) of title 23, United States Code, the Federal share of the costs shall be 100 percent;]

[(5) $150,000,000 shall be to carry out the Reduction of Truck Emissions at Port Facilities Program under section 11402 of division A of this Act: *Provided*, That, except as otherwise provided in section 11402 of division A of this Act, the funds made available under this paragraph in this Act shall be administered as if apportioned under chapter 1 of title 23, United States Code;]

[(6) $95,000,000, to remain available until expended for amounts made available for each of fiscal years 2022 through 2026, shall be to carry out the University Transportation Centers Program under section 5505 of title 49, United States Code;]

[(7) $500,000,000, to remain available until expended for amounts made available for each of fiscal years 2022 through 2026, shall be to carry out the Reconnecting Communities Pilot Program (referred to under this paragraph in this Act as the "pilot program") under section 11509 of division A of this Act, of which $100,000,000 shall be for planning grants under section 11509(c) of division A of this Act and of which $400,000,000 shall be available for capital construction grants under section 11509(d) of division A of this Act: *Provided*, That of the amounts made available under this paragraph in this Act for section 11509(c) of division A of this Act, the Secretary may use not more than $15,000,000 during the period of fiscal years 2022 through 2026 to provide technical assistance under section 11509(c)(3) of division A of this Act: *Provided further*, That, except as otherwise provided in section 11509 of division A of this Act, amounts made available under this paragraph in this Act shall be administered as if made available under chapter 1 of title 23, United States Code;]

[(8) $342,000,000, to remain available until expended for amounts made available for each of fiscal years 2022 through 2026, shall be to carry out the Construction of Ferry Boats and Ferry Terminal Facilities program under section 147 of title 23, United States Code: *Provided*, That amounts made available under this paragraph in this Act shall be administered as if made available under section 147 of title 23, United States Code; and]

[(9) $1,250,000,000, to remain available until expended for amounts made available for each of fiscal years 2022 through 2026, shall be for construction of the Appalachian Development Highway System as authorized under section 1069(y) of Public Law 102–240: *Provided*, That, for the purposes of funds made available under this paragraph in this Act for construction of the Appalachian Development Highway System, the term "Appalachian State" means a State that contains 1 or more counties (including any political subdivision located within the area) in the Appalachian region, as defined in section 14102(a) of title 40, United States Code: *Provided further*, That a project carried out with funds made available under this paragraph in this Act for construction of the Appalachian Development Highway System shall be made available for obligation in the same manner as if apportioned under chapter 1 of title 23, United States Code, except that: (1) the Federal share of the cost of any project carried out with those amounts shall be determined in accordance with section 14501 of title 40, United States Code; and (2) the amounts shall be available to construct highways and access roads under section 14501 of title 40, United States Code: *Provided further*, That, subject to the following two provisos, in consultation with the Appalachian Regional Commission, the funds made available under this paragraph in this Act for construction of the Appalachian Development Highway System shall be apportioned to Appalachian States according to the percentages derived from the 2021 Appalachian Development Highway System Cost-to-Complete Estimate, dated March 2021, and confirmed as each Appalachian State's relative share of the estimated remaining need to complete the Appalachian Development Highway System, adjusted to exclude those corridors that such States have no current plans to complete, as reported in the 2013 Appalachian Development Highway System Completion Report, unless those States have modified and assigned a higher priority for completion of an Appalachian Development Highway System corridor, as reported in the 2020 Appalachian Development Highway System Future Outlook: *Provided further*, That the Secretary shall adjust apportionments made under the third proviso in this paragraph in this Act so that no Appalachian State shall be apportioned an amount in excess of 30 percent of the amount made available for construction of the Appalachian Development Highway System under this heading: *Provided further*, That the Secretary shall adjust apportionments made under the third proviso in this paragraph in this Act so that: (1) each State shall be apportioned an amount not less than $10,000,000 for each of fiscal years 2022 through 2026; and (2) notwithstanding paragraph (1) of this proviso, a State shall not receive an apportionment that exceeds the remaining funds needed to complete the Appalachian development highway corridor or corridors in the State, as identified in the latest available cost to complete estimate for the system prepared by the Appalachian Regional Commission: *Provided further*, That the Federal share of the cost of any project carried out with funds made available under this paragraph in this Act shall be up to 100 percent, as determined by the State: *Provided further*, That such amount is designated by the Congress as being for an emergency requirement pursuant to section 4112(a) of H. Con. Res. 71 (115th Congress), the concurrent resolution on the budget for fiscal year 2018, and to section 251(b) of the Balanced Budget and Emergency Deficit Control Act of 1985.] *(Infrastructure Investments and Jobs Appropriations Act.)*

Program and Financing (in millions of dollars)

Identification code 069–0548–0–1–401	2021 actual	2022 est.	2023 est.
Obligations by program activity:			
0001 Highway infrastructure programs	7,012	10,431	10,522
Budgetary resources:			
Unobligated balance:			
1000 Unobligated balance brought forward, Oct 1	4,581	9,652	10,674
1010 Unobligated balance transfer to other accts [069–2812]	–2		
1021 Recoveries of prior year unpaid obligations	89		
1070 Unobligated balance (total)	4,668	9,652	10,674
Budget authority:			
Appropriations, discretionary:			
1100 Appropriation	12,000	11,454	
1120 Appropriations transferred to other acct [069–0130]		–1	
1160 Appropriation, discretionary (total)	12,000	11,453	
Advance appropriations, discretionary:			
1170 Advance appropriation			9,454
1172 Advance appropriations transferred to other accounts [069–0130]			–1
1180 Advanced appropriation, discretionary (total)			9,453
1900 Budget authority (total)	12,000	11,453	9,453
1930 Total budgetary resources available	16,668	21,105	20,127
Memorandum (non-add) entries:			
1940 Unobligated balance expiring	–4		
1941 Unexpired unobligated balance, end of year	9,652	10,674	9,605
Change in obligated balance:			
Unpaid obligations:			
3000 Unpaid obligations, brought forward, Oct 1	1,621	5,325	11,731
3010 New obligations, unexpired accounts	7,012	10,431	10,522
3020 Outlays (gross)	–3,219	–4,025	–7,074
3040 Recoveries of prior year unpaid obligations, unexpired	–89		
3050 Unpaid obligations, end of year	5,325	11,731	15,179
Memorandum (non-add) entries:			
3100 Obligated balance, start of year	1,621	5,325	11,731
3200 Obligated balance, end of year	5,325	11,731	15,179
Budget authority and outlays, net:			
Discretionary:			
4000 Budget authority, gross	12,000	11,453	9,453
Outlays, gross:			
4010 Outlays from new discretionary authority	1,971	1,030	850
4011 Outlays from discretionary balances	1,248	2,995	6,224
4020 Outlays, gross (total)	3,219	4,025	7,074
4180 Budget authority, net (total)	12,000	11,453	9,453
4190 Outlays, net (total)	3,219	4,025	7,074

In 2010, the Congress appropriated $650 million for the restoration, repair, and construction of highway infrastructure, and other activities eligible under paragraph (b) of section 133 of title 23, United States Code. The Congress has appropriated additional General Fund amounts in recent years including: $2.5 billion in 2018; $3.3 billion in 2019; $2.2 billion in 2020; and $12 billion in 2021 which includes $10 billion through the Coronavirus Response and Relief Supplemental Appropriations Act, 2021. No appropriations are requested for this account in 2023.

The Infrastructure Investment Jobs Act provided supplemental appropriations from the General Fund for the Highway Infrastructure Programs in the amount of $9.5 billion annually for 2022 through 2026 for the following programs:

The Bridge Replacement, Rehabilitation, Preservation, Protection, and Construction Program ($5.5 billion) will provide formula funds to States for bridge replacement, rehabilitation, preservation, protection, or construction projects on public roads.

The National Electric Vehicle Formula Program ($1.0 billion) will provide funding to States to strategically deploy electric vehicle charging infrastructure and to establish an interconnected network to facilitate data collection, access, and reliability.

The Nationally Significant Freight and Highway Projects (known as the Infrastructure for Rebuilding America Program) ($640 million) will advance nationally significant freight and highway projects to improve the safety, efficiency and reliability of the movement of freight and people. This program receives additional funds through the Highway Trust Fund as part of the Federal-aid Highways Program.

The Bridge Investment Program ($1.8 billion) will assist eligible entities in rehabilitating or replacing bridges, including culverts, with the goal of improving the safety efficiency, and reliability of the movement of people and freight over bridges. This program receives additional funds through the Highway Trust Fund as part of the Federal-aid Highways Program.

The Reduction of Truck Emissions at Port Facilities Program ($30 million) will fund competitive grants for eligible projects that reduce port-related emissions from idling trucks, including through the advancement of port electrification, improvements in efficiency, and other emerging technologies and strategies. This program receives additional funds through the Highway Trust Fund as part of the Federal-aid Highways Program.

The University Transportation Centers Program ($19 million) is administered by the Department of Transportation's Office of the Assistant Secretary for Research and Technology. This program receives additional funds through the Highway Trust Fund as part of the Federal-aid Highways Program.

The Reconnecting Communities Pilot Program ($100 million) will award planning and capital construction grants to assess the feasibility and impacts of removing, or retrofitting existing transportation facilities that create barriers to mobility, or to carry out projects that remove, retrofit, or replace an eligible facility. This program receives additional funds through the Highway Trust Fund as part of the Federal-aid Highways Program.

The Construction of Ferry Boats and Ferry Terminal Facilities Program ($68 million) will addresses mobility and access in urban and rural areas by providing valuable assistance to help States and other entities replace or acquire new ferry boats; replace propulsion systems with newer cleaner and more energy-efficient power plants; update navigational control systems; construct new terminals; improve access for the disabled; and replace and construct new docking facilities. This program receives additional funds through the Highway Trust Fund as part of the Federal-aid Highways Program.

The Appalachian Development Highway System Program ($250 million) will distribute funds by formula to States with one or more counties in the Appalachian Region for construction of the Appalachian Development Highway System.

Object Classification (in millions of dollars)

Identification code 069–0548–0–1–401		2021 actual	2022 est.	2023 est.
	Direct obligations:			
25.2	Other services from non-Federal sources	27	40	41
25.3	Other goods and services from Federal sources	1	1	1
41.0	Grants, subsidies, and contributions	6,984	10,390	10,480
99.9	Total new obligations, unexpired accounts	7,012	10,431	10,522

Trust Funds

RIGHT-OF-WAY REVOLVING FUND LIQUIDATING ACCOUNT

Program and Financing (in millions of dollars)

Identification code 069–8402–0–8–401		2021 actual	2022 est.	2023 est.
	Change in obligated balance:			
	Unpaid obligations:			
3000	Unpaid obligations, brought forward, Oct 1	4	4	
3020	Outlays (gross)		–4	
3050	Unpaid obligations, end of year	4		
	Memorandum (non-add) entries:			
3100	Obligated balance, start of year	4	4	
3200	Obligated balance, end of year	4		
	Budget authority and outlays, net:			
	Mandatory:			
	Outlays, gross:			
4101	Outlays from mandatory balances		4	
4180	Budget authority, net (total)			
4190	Outlays, net (total)		4	

The Federal-Aid Highway Act of 1968 authorized the establishment of a right-of-way revolving fund. This fund was used to make cash advances to States for the purpose of purchasing right-of-way parcels in advance of highway construction and thereby preventing the inflation of land prices from significantly increasing construction costs. The purchase of right-of-way is an eligible expense of the Federal-Aid Highway program.

This program was terminated by the Transportation Equity Act for the 21st Century of 1998, but will continue to be shown for reporting purposes as loan balances remain outstanding. No new budgetary resources are requested in 2023.

HIGHWAY TRUST FUND

Program and Financing (in millions of dollars)

Identification code 069–8102–0–7–401		2021 actual	2022 est.	2023 est.
4180	Budget authority, net (total)			
4190	Outlays, net (total)			
	Memorandum (non-add) entries:			
5000	Total investments, SOY: Federal securities: Par value	12,081	12,043	106,443
5001	Total investments, EOY: Federal securities: Par value	12,043	106,443	82,843

The Highway Revenue Act of 1956, as amended, provides for the transfer from the General Fund to the Highway Trust Fund of revenue from the motor fuel tax, and certain other taxes paid by highway users. The Secretary of the Treasury estimates the amounts to be transferred. In turn, appropriations are authorized from this fund to meet expenditures for Federal-aid highways and other programs as specified by law. Per the Cash Management Improvement Act of 1990, this account reflects the net of State interest liability and adjusted Federal interest liability payments to or from States.

The following is the status of Highway Trust Fund.

Cash balances.—The Status of Funds table begins with the unexpended balance on a "cash basis" at the start of the year. The table shows the amount of cash invested in Federal securities at par value and the amount of cash on hand (i.e., uninvested balance). Next, the table provides the amounts of cash income and cash outlays during each year to show the cash balance at the end of each year.

Revenues.—The Budget presentation includes estimated receipts from existing Highway Trust Fund excise taxes, which would continue to be deposited into the Highway and Mass Transit Accounts of the Highway Trust Fund in the same manner as current law.

General Fund transfers. In 2022, the Infrastructure Investment Jobs Act transferred from the General Fund $90 billion to the Highway Account of the Highway Trust Fund and $28 billion to the Mass Transit Account of the Highway Trust Fund.

HIGHWAY TRUST FUND—Continued
Status of Funds (in millions of dollars)

Identification code 069–8102–0–7–401		2021 actual	2022 est.	2023 est.
	Unexpended balance, start of year:			
0100	Balance, start of year	17,829	21,049	124,210
0298	Reconciliation adjustment	–116		
0298	Split account Adjs w/ Motor Carrier Safety Operations and Programs & TIFIA Highway Trust Fund Program Account	–82		
0999	Total balance, start of year	17,631	21,049	124,210
	Cash income during the year:			
	Current law:			
	Receipts:			
1110	Highway Trust Fund, Deposits (Highway Account)	38,038	37,887	38,324
1110	Highway Trust Fund, Deposits (Mass Transit Account)	5,426	5,246	5,205
1120	Motor Carrier Safety Operations and Programs	68		
1130	Federal-aid Highways	92		
1150	CMIA Interest, Highway Trust Fund (highway Account)	1	1	1
1150	Earnings on Investments, Highway Trust Fund	10	181	688
1160	Payment from the General Fund, Highway Trust Fund (Mass Transit)	3,200	28,000	
1160	Payment from the General Fund, Highway Trust Fund (Highway)	10,400	90,000	
1160	Federal-aid Highways	367	400	400
1160	Operations and Research (Highway Trust Fund)	3	5	5
1199	Income under present law	57,605	161,720	44,623
1999	Total cash income	57,605	161,720	44,623
	Cash outgo during year:			
	Current law:			
2100	TIFIA Highway Trust Fund Program Account [Budget Acct]	–1,063	–753	–43
2100	Federal-aid Highways [Budget Acct]		–2,992	–4,543
2100	Federal-aid Highways [Budget Acct]	–44,078	–44,146	–48,756
2100	Right-of-way Revolving Fund Liquidating Account [Budget Acct]		–4	
2100	Miscellaneous Highway Trust Funds [Budget Acct]	–7	–9	–8
2100	Motor Carrier Safety Grants [Budget Acct]		–11	–38
2100	Motor Carrier Safety Grants [Budget Acct]	–332	–400	–448
2100	Motor Carrier Safety Operations and Programs [Budget Acct]		–24	–5
2100	Motor Carrier Safety Operations and Programs [Budget Acct]	–303	–346	–396
2100	Operations and Research (Highway Trust Fund) [Budget Acct]		–18	–14
2100	Operations and Research (Highway Trust Fund) [Budget Acct]	–151	–188	–199
2100	Highway Traffic Safety Grants [Budget Acct]		–36	–92
2100	Highway Traffic Safety Grants [Budget Acct]	–693	–830	–797
2100	Discretionary Grants (Highway Trust Fund, Mass Transit Account) [Budget Acct]		–15	
2100	Transit Formula Grants [Budget Acct]		–192	–256
2100	Transit Formula Grants [Budget Acct]	–7,962	–8,842	–10,123
2198	Split account Adjs w/ Motor Carrier Safety Operations and Programs & TIFIA Highway Trust Fund Program Account	403	247	38
2199	Outgo under current law	–54,186	–58,559	–65,680
2999	Total cash outgo (–)	–54,186	–58,559	–65,680
	Surplus or deficit:			
3110	Excluding interest	3,408	102,979	–21,746
3120	Interest	11	182	689
3199	Subtotal, surplus or deficit	3,419	103,161	–21,057
3230	TIFIA Highway Trust Fund Program Account	846	481	9
3230	Federal-aid Highways	–846	–481	–9
3230	Federal-aid Highways	115		
3230	Federal-aid Highways	–1,200	–1,300	–1,300
3230	Federal-aid Highways		–27	
3230	Federal-aid Highways	–105	–99	
3230	Highway Traffic Safety Grants		27	
3230	Highway Traffic Safety Grants	105	99	
3230	Transit Formula Grants	1,200	1,300	1,300
3230	Transit Formula Grants	–115		
3298	Reconciliation adjustment	–93		
3298	Split account Adjs w/ Motor Carrier Safety Operations and Programs & TIFIA Highway Trust Fund Program Account	92		
3299	Total adjustments	–1		
3999	Total change in fund balance	3,418	103,161	–21,057
	Unexpended balance, end of year:			
4100	Uninvested balance (net), end of year	9,006	17,767	20,310
4200	Highway Trust Fund	12,043	106,443	82,843
4999	Total balance, end of year	21,049	124,210	103,153

FEDERAL-AID HIGHWAYS

LIMITATION ON ADMINISTRATIVE EXPENSES

(HIGHWAY TRUST FUND)

(INCLUDING TRANSFER OF FUNDS)

Not to exceed $476,783,991 together with advances and reimbursements received by the Federal Highway Administration, shall be obligated for necessary expenses for administration and operation of the Federal Highway Administration or transferred to the Appalachian Regional Commission for administrative activities associated with the Appalachian Development Highway System.

(LIMITATION ON OBLIGATIONS)

(HIGHWAY TRUST FUND)

Funds available for the implementation or execution of authorized Federal-aid highway and highway safety construction programs shall not exceed total obligations of $58,764,510,674 for fiscal year 2023: Provided, That the limitation on obligations under this heading shall only apply to contract authority authorized from the Highway Trust Fund (other than the Mass Transit Account), unless otherwise specified in law.

(LIQUIDATION OF CONTRACT AUTHORIZATION)

(HIGHWAY TRUST FUND)

For the payment of obligations incurred in carrying out authorized Federal-aid highway and highway safety construction programs, $59,461,387,674 derived from the Highway Trust Fund (other than the Mass Transit Account), to remain available until expended.

Note.—A full-year 2022 appropriation for this account was not enacted at the time the Budget was prepared; therefore, the Budget assumes this account is operating under the Continuing Appropriations Act, 2022 (Division A of Public Law 117–43, as amended). The amounts included for 2022 reflect the annualized level provided by the continuing resolution.

Program and Financing (in millions of dollars)

Identification code 069–8083–0–7–401		2021 actual	2022 est.	2023 est.
	Obligations by program activity:			
0010	Surface transportation block grant program	13,602	14,201	16,984
0014	National highway performance program	19,811	20,893	25,399
0015	Congestion mitigation and air quality improvement program	1,074	1,093	1,306
0016	Highway safety improvement program	3,309	3,999	4,782
0017	Metropolitan planning program	323	254	303
0019	National highway freight program	1,086	1,144	1,368
0020	Nationally significant freight and highway projects	889	918	1,100
0024	Federal lands and tribal programs	982	1,032	1,242
0029	Research, technology and education program	301	326	401
0032	Administration - LAE	466	477	475
0033	Administration - ARC	2	2	2
0040	PROTECT formula program			1,431
0041	Carbon reduction program			1,258
0042	Bridge investment program			640
0043	Charging and fueling infrastructure grants			400
0044	Rural surface transportation grant program			350
0045	PROTECT discretionary program			250
0058	Other programs	2,243	1,122	561
0091	Programs subject to obligation limitation	44,088	45,461	58,252
0211	Exempt Programs	504	807	793
0500	Total direct program	44,592	46,268	59,045
0799	Total direct obligations	44,592	46,268	59,045
0801	Federal-aid Highways (Reimbursable)	774	400	400
0900	Total new obligations, unexpired accounts	45,366	46,668	59,445
	Budgetary resources:			
	Unobligated balance:			
1000	Unobligated balance brought forward, Oct 1	22,516	22,248	32,190
1001	Discretionary unobligated balance brought fwd, Oct 1	691		
1013	Unobligated balance of contract authority transferred to or from other accounts [069–8350]	–344		
1013	Unobligated balance of contract authority transferred to or from other accounts [069–8634]	–826	–534	–35
1025	Unobligated balance of contract authority withdrawn	–547		
1070	Unobligated balance (total)	20,799	21,714	32,155

DEPARTMENT OF TRANSPORTATION

Federal Highway Administration—Continued
Trust Funds—Continued

		2021 actual	2022 est.	2023 est.
	Budget authority:			
	Appropriations, discretionary:			
1101	Appropriation (special or trust)	47,104	47,104	59,461
1120	Appropriations transferred to other accts [069–8350]	–1,200	–1,300	–1,300
1120	Appropriations transferred to other accts [069–8020]	–105	–99	
1120	Appropriations transferred to other acct [069–8634]	–846	–481	–9
1121	Appropriations transferred from other acct [069–8350]	115		
1138	Appropriations applied to liquidate contract authority	–45,068	–45,224	–58,152
	Contract authority, mandatory:			
1600	Contract authority	47,104	58,212	59,504
1610	Transferred to other accounts [069–8350]	–927	–1,300	–1,300
1610	Transferred to other accounts [069–8020]	–105	–126	
1610	Contract authority transferred to other accounts [069–8634]	–9		
1611	Transferred from other accounts [069–8350]	79		
1621	Contract authority temporarily reduced	–42	–42	–42
1640	Contract authority, mandatory (total)	46,100	56,744	58,162
	Spending authority from offsetting collections, discretionary:			
1700	Collected	459	400	400
1701	Change in uncollected payments, Federal sources	256		
1750	Spending auth from offsetting collections, disc (total)	715	400	400
1900	Budget authority (total)	46,815	57,144	58,562
1930	Total budgetary resources available	67,614	78,858	90,717
	Memorandum (non-add) entries:			
1941	Unexpired unobligated balance, end of year	22,248	32,190	31,272
	Change in obligated balance:			
	Unpaid obligations:			
3000	Unpaid obligations, brought forward, Oct 1	61,244	62,532	65,054
3010	New obligations, unexpired accounts	45,366	46,668	59,445
3020	Outlays (gross)	–44,078	–44,146	–48,756
3050	Unpaid obligations, end of year	62,532	65,054	75,743
	Uncollected payments:			
3060	Uncollected pymts, Fed sources, brought forward, Oct 1	–659	–915	–915
3070	Change in uncollected pymts, Fed sources, unexpired	–256		
3090	Uncollected pymts, Fed sources, end of year	–915	–915	–915
	Memorandum (non-add) entries:			
3100	Obligated balance, start of year	60,585	61,617	64,139
3200	Obligated balance, end of year	61,617	64,139	74,828
	Budget authority and outlays, net:			
	Discretionary:			
4000	Budget authority, gross	715	400	400
	Outlays, gross:			
4010	Outlays from new discretionary authority	12,034	12,397	15,907
4011	Outlays from discretionary balances	31,444	31,103	32,105
4020	Outlays, gross (total)	43,478	43,500	48,012
	Offsets against gross budget authority and outlays:			
	Offsetting collections (collected) from:			
4030	Federal sources	–367	–400	–400
4033	Non-Federal sources	–92		
4040	Offsets against gross budget authority and outlays (total)	–459	–400	–400
	Additional offsets against gross budget authority only:			
4050	Change in uncollected pymts, Fed sources, unexpired	–256		
4080	Outlays, net (discretionary)	43,019	43,100	47,612
	Mandatory:			
4090	Budget authority, gross	46,100	56,744	58,162
	Outlays, gross:			
4100	Outlays from new mandatory authority	196	188	188
4101	Outlays from mandatory balances	404	458	556
4110	Outlays, gross (total)	600	646	744
4180	Budget authority, net (total)	46,100	56,744	58,162
4190	Outlays, net (total)	43,619	43,746	48,356
	Memorandum (non-add) entries:			
5050	Unobligated balance, SOY: Contract authority			1,356
5051	Unobligated balance, EOY: Contract authority		1,356	
5052	Obligated balance, SOY: Contract authority	56,109	55,424	65,054
5053	Obligated balance, EOY: Contract authority	55,424	65,054	66,385
5061	Limitation on obligations (Transportation Trust Funds)	45,403	44,432	57,430
5099	Unexpired unavailable balance, SOY: Contract authority	347	389	431
5100	Unexpired unavailable balance, EOY: Contract authority	389	431	473

Summary of Budget Authority and Outlays (in millions of dollars)

	2021 actual	2022 est.	2023 est.
Enacted/requested:			
Budget Authority	46,100	56,744	58,162
Outlays	43,619	43,746	48,356
Amounts included in the adjusted baseline:			
Outlays		2,992	4,543
Total:			
Budget Authority	46,100	56,744	58,162
Outlays	43,619	46,738	52,899

The Federal-aid Highways (FAH) program is designed to aid in the development, operations, and management of an intermodal transportation system. All programs included within the FAH program are financed from the Highway Account of the Highway Trust Fund, and most are distributed via apportionments and allocations to States. Liquidating cash appropriations provide the authority for outlays resulting from obligations of contract authority. The Infrastructure Investment and Jobs Act authorized funding for the FAH program in fiscal years 2022 through 2026. This includes $59.5 billion in 2023.

Object Classification (in millions of dollars)

Identification code 069–8083–0–7–401	2021 actual	2022 est.	2023 est.
Direct obligations:			
Personnel compensation:			
11.1 Full-time permanent	282	290	310
11.3 Other than full-time permanent	2	2	2
11.5 Other personnel compensation	30	30	30
11.9 Total personnel compensation	314	322	342
12.1 Civilian personnel benefits	113	115	120
21.0 Travel and transportation of persons	8	15	15
22.0 Transportation of things	1	2	2
23.1 Rental payments to GSA	25	25	26
23.2 Rental payments to others	1	1	1
23.3 Communications, utilities, and miscellaneous charges	1	1	1
25.1 Advisory and assistance services	92	92	92
25.2 Other services from non-Federal sources	475	475	475
25.3 Other goods and services from Federal sources	196	196	196
25.4 Operation and maintenance of facilities	27	27	27
25.7 Operation and maintenance of equipment	65	65	65
26.0 Supplies and materials	3	7	7
31.0 Equipment	5	19	19
32.0 Land and structures	20	20	20
41.0 Grants, subsidies, and contributions	43,246	44,886	57,637
99.0 Direct obligations	44,592	46,268	59,045
99.0 Reimbursable obligations	774	400	400
99.9 Total new obligations, unexpired accounts	45,366	46,668	59,445

Employment Summary

Identification code 069–8083–0–7–401	2021 actual	2022 est.	2023 est.
1001 Direct civilian full-time equivalent employment	2,626	2,641	2,706
2001 Reimbursable civilian full-time equivalent employment	54	54	54
3001 Allocation account civilian full-time equivalent employment	4	4	4

FEDERAL-AID HIGHWAYS

(Amounts included in the adjusted baseline)

Program and Financing (in millions of dollars)

Identification code 069–8083–7–7–401	2021 actual	2022 est.	2023 est.
Obligations by program activity:			
0010 Surface transportation block grant program		2,212	
0014 National highway performance program		3,265	
0015 Congestion mitigation and air quality improvement program		169	
0016 Highway safety improvement program		619	
0017 Metropolitan planning program		39	
0019 National highway freight program		177	
0020 Nationally significant freight and highway projects		142	
0024 Federal lands and tribal programs		160	
0029 Research, technology and education program		50	
0032 Administration - LAE		–12	
0040 PROTECT formula program		1,403	
0041 Carbon reduction program		1,234	
0042 Bridge investment program		600	
0043 Charging and fueling infrastructure grants		300	
0044 Rural surface transportation grant program		300	
0045 PROTECT discretionary program		250	
0058 Other programs		174	
0091 Programs subject to obligation limitation		11,082	
0500 Total direct program		11,082	

925

Federal Highway Administration—Continued
Trust Funds—Continued

FEDERAL-AID HIGHWAYS—Continued
Program and Financing—Continued

Identification code 069–8083–7–7–401	2021 actual	2022 est.	2023 est.
0799 Total direct obligations	....	11,082	....
0900 Total new obligations, unexpired accounts (object class 41.0)	....	11,082	....
Budgetary resources:			
Unobligated balance:			
1000 Unobligated balance brought forward, Oct 1	....	....	–11,082
Budget authority:			
Appropriations, discretionary:			
1101 Appropriation (special or trust)	....	11,108	....
1120 Appropriations transferred to other acct [069–8020]	....	–27	....
1138 Appropriations applied to liquidate contract authority	....	–11,081	....
1930 Total budgetary resources available	....	....	–11,082
Memorandum (non-add) entries:			
1941 Unexpired unobligated balance, end of year	....	–11,082	–11,082
Change in obligated balance:			
Unpaid obligations:			
3000 Unpaid obligations, brought forward, Oct 1	....	....	8,090
3010 New obligations, unexpired accounts	....	11,082	....
3020 Outlays (gross)	....	–2,992	–4,543
3050 Unpaid obligations, end of year	....	8,090	3,547
Memorandum (non-add) entries:			
3100 Obligated balance, start of year	....	....	8,090
3200 Obligated balance, end of year	....	8,090	3,547
Budget authority and outlays, net:			
Discretionary:			
Outlays, gross:			
4010 Outlays from new discretionary authority	....	2,992	....
4011 Outlays from discretionary balances	....	....	4,543
4020 Outlays, gross (total)	....	2,992	4,543
4180 Budget authority, net (total)	....	....	....
4190 Outlays, net (total)	....	2,992	4,543
Memorandum (non-add) entries:			
5052 Obligated balance, SOY: Contract authority	....	....	–11,081
5053 Obligated balance, EOY: Contract authority	....	–11,081	–11,081
5061 Limitation on obligations (Transportation Trust Funds)	....	11,081	....

MISCELLANEOUS TRUST FUNDS

Special and Trust Fund Receipts (in millions of dollars)

Identification code 069–9971–0–7–999	2021 actual	2022 est.	2023 est.
0100 Balance, start of year	....	....	....
Receipts:			
Current law:			
1130 Advances from State Cooperating Agencies and Foreign Governments, FHA Miscellaneous Trust	2	2	2
1130 Advances for Highway Research Program, Miscellaneous Trust	1	1	1
1199 Total current law receipts	3	3	3
1999 Total receipts	3	3	3
2000 Total: Balances and receipts	3	3	3
Appropriations:			
Current law:			
2101 Miscellaneous Trust Funds	–3	–3	–3
5099 Balance, end of year	....	....	....

Program and Financing (in millions of dollars)

Identification code 069–9971–0–7–999	2021 actual	2022 est.	2023 est.
Obligations by program activity:			
0001 Advances from State cooperating agencies 69-X-8054	103	10	9
Budgetary resources:			
Unobligated balance:			
1000 Unobligated balance brought forward, Oct 1	119	24	17
1021 Recoveries of prior year unpaid obligations	5	....	....
1070 Unobligated balance (total)	124	24	17
Budget authority:			
Appropriations, mandatory:			
1201 Appropriation (special or trust fund)	3	3	3
1930 Total budgetary resources available	127	27	20
Memorandum (non-add) entries:			
1941 Unexpired unobligated balance, end of year	24	17	11
Change in obligated balance:			
Unpaid obligations:			
3000 Unpaid obligations, brought forward, Oct 1	34	24	21
3010 New obligations, unexpired accounts	103	10	9
3020 Outlays (gross)	–108	–13	–12
3040 Recoveries of prior year unpaid obligations, unexpired	–5	....	....
3050 Unpaid obligations, end of year	24	21	18
Memorandum (non-add) entries:			
3100 Obligated balance, start of year	34	24	21
3200 Obligated balance, end of year	24	21	18
Budget authority and outlays, net:			
Mandatory:			
4090 Budget authority, gross	3	3	3
Outlays, gross:			
4100 Outlays from new mandatory authority	....	2	2
4101 Outlays from mandatory balances	108	11	10
4110 Outlays, gross (total)	108	13	12
4180 Budget authority, net (total)	3	3	3
4190 Outlays, net (total)	108	13	12

The Miscellaneous Trust Funds account reflects work performed by the Federal Highway Administration (FHWA) on behalf of other entities.

Advances from State cooperating agencies and foreign governments.—Contributions are received from other entities in connection with cooperative engineering, survey, maintenance, and construction projects.

Contributions for highway research programs.—Contributions are received from various sources in support of FHWA transportation research programs. The funds are used primarily in support of pooled-funds projects.

The Budget estimates that $3 million of new authority will be available from non-FHWA sources in 2023.

Object Classification (in millions of dollars)

Identification code 069–9971–0–7–999	2021 actual	2022 est.	2023 est.
Direct obligations:			
25.3 Other goods and services from Federal sources	10	10	9
44.0 Refunds	93	....	....
99.9 Total new obligations, unexpired accounts	103	10	9

MISCELLANEOUS HIGHWAY TRUST FUNDS

Program and Financing (in millions of dollars)

Identification code 069–9972–0–7–401	2021 actual	2022 est.	2023 est.
Obligations by program activity:			
0027 Obligations by program activity Miscellaneous highway projects	7	6	6
0100 Direct program activities, subtotal	7	6	6
0900 Total new obligations, unexpired accounts (object class 41.0)	7	6	6
Budgetary resources:			
Unobligated balance:			
1000 Unobligated balance brought forward, Oct 1	48	43	37
1021 Recoveries of prior year unpaid obligations	2	....	....
1070 Unobligated balance (total)	50	43	37
1930 Total budgetary resources available	50	43	37
Memorandum (non-add) entries:			
1941 Unexpired unobligated balance, end of year	43	37	31
Change in obligated balance:			
Unpaid obligations:			
3000 Unpaid obligations, brought forward, Oct 1	30	28	25

3010	New obligations, unexpired accounts	7	6	6
3020	Outlays (gross)	−7	−9	−8
3040	Recoveries of prior year unpaid obligations, unexpired	−2		
3050	Unpaid obligations, end of year	28	25	23
	Memorandum (non-add) entries:			
3100	Obligated balance, start of year	30	28	25
3200	Obligated balance, end of year	28	25	23

Budget authority and outlays, net:
Discretionary:
Outlays, gross:

4011	Outlays from discretionary balances	7	9	8
4180	Budget authority, net (total)			
4190	Outlays, net (total)	7	9	8

Memorandum (non-add) entries:

5103	Unexpired unavailable balance, SOY: Fulfilled purpose	1	1	
5104	Unexpired unavailable balance, EOY: Fulfilled purpose	1		

This account contains miscellaneous appropriations from the Highway Trust Fund. No appropriations are requested for 2023.

ADMINISTRATIVE PROVISIONS—FEDERAL HIGHWAY ADMINISTRATION

SEC. 120. (a) For fiscal year 2023, the Secretary of Transportation shall—
(1) not distribute from the obligation limitation for Federal-aid highways—
(A) amounts authorized for administrative expenses and programs by section 104(a) of title 23, United States Code; and
(B) amounts authorized for the Bureau of Transportation Statistics;
(2) not distribute an amount from the obligation limitation for Federal-aid highways that is equal to the unobligated balance of amounts—
(A) made available from the Highway Trust Fund (other than the Mass Transit Account) for Federal-aid highway and highway safety construction programs for previous fiscal years the funds for which are allocated by the Secretary (or apportioned by the Secretary under sections 202 or 204 of title 23, United States Code); and
(B) for which obligation limitation was provided in a previous fiscal year;
(3) determine the proportion that—
(A) the obligation limitation for Federal-aid highways, less the aggregate of amounts not distributed under paragraphs (1) and (2) of this subsection; bears to
(B) the total of the sums authorized to be appropriated for the Federal-aid highway and highway safety construction programs (other than sums authorized to be appropriated for provisions of law described in paragraphs (1) through (11) of subsection (b) and sums authorized to be appropriated for section 119 of title 23, United States Code, equal to the amount referred to in subsection (b)(12) for such fiscal year), less the aggregate of the amounts not distributed under paragraphs (1) and (2) of this subsection;
(4) distribute the obligation limitation for Federal-aid highways, less the aggregate amounts not distributed under paragraphs (1) and (2), for each of the programs (other than programs to which paragraph (1) applies) that are allocated by the Secretary under authorized Federal-aid highway and highway safety construction programs, or apportioned by the Secretary under sections 202 or 204 of title 23, United States Code, by multiplying—
(A) the proportion determined under paragraph (3); by
(B) the amounts authorized to be appropriated for each such program for such fiscal year; and
(5) distribute the obligation limitation for Federal-aid highways, less the aggregate amounts not distributed under paragraphs (1) and (2) and the amounts distributed under paragraph (4), for Federal-aid highway and highway safety construction programs that are apportioned by the Secretary under title 23, United States Code (other than the amounts apportioned for the National Highway Performance Program in section 119 of title 23, United States Code, that are exempt from the limitation under subsection (b)(12) and the amounts apportioned under sections 202 and 204 of that title) in the proportion that—
(A) amounts authorized to be appropriated for the programs that are apportioned under title 23, United States Code, to each State for such fiscal year; bears to
(B) the total of the amounts authorized to be appropriated for the programs that are apportioned under title 23, United States Code, to all States for such fiscal year.
(b) EXCEPTIONS FROM OBLIGATION LIMITATION.—The obligation limitation for Federal-aid highways shall not apply to obligations under or for—

(1) section 125 of title 23, United States Code;
(2) section 147 of the Surface Transportation Assistance Act of 1978 (23 U.S.C. 144 note; 92 Stat. 2714);
(3) section 9 of the Federal-Aid Highway Act of 1981 (95 Stat. 1701);
(4) subsections (b) and (j) of section 131 of the Surface Transportation Assistance Act of 1982 (96 Stat. 2119);
(5) subsections (b) and (c) of section 149 of the Surface Transportation and Uniform Relocation Assistance Act of 1987 (101 Stat. 198);
(6) sections 1103 through 1108 of the Intermodal Surface Transportation Efficiency Act of 1991 (105 Stat. 2027);
(7) section 157 of title 23, United States Code (as in effect on June 8, 1998);
(8) section 105 of title 23, United States Code (as in effect for fiscal years 1998 through 2004, but only in an amount equal to $639,000,000 for each of those fiscal years);
(9) Federal-aid highway programs for which obligation authority was made available under the Transportation Equity Act for the 21st Century (112 Stat. 107) or subsequent Acts for multiple years or to remain available until expended, but only to the extent that the obligation authority has not lapsed or been used;
(10) section 105 of title 23, United States Code (as in effect for fiscal years 2005 through 2012, but only in an amount equal to $639,000,000 for each of those fiscal years);
(11) section 1603 of SAFETEA-LU (23 U.S.C. 118 note; 119 Stat. 1248), to the extent that funds obligated in accordance with that section were not subject to a limitation on obligations at the time at which the funds were initially made available for obligation; and
(12) section 119 of title 23, United States Code (but, for each of fiscal years 2013 through 2022, only in an amount equal to $639,000,000).
(c) REDISTRIBUTION OF UNUSED OBLIGATION AUTHORITY.—Notwithstanding subsection (a), the Secretary shall, after August 1 of such fiscal year—
(1) revise a distribution of the obligation limitation made available under subsection (a) if an amount distributed cannot be obligated during that fiscal year; and
(2) redistribute sufficient amounts to those States able to obligate amounts in addition to those previously distributed during that fiscal year, giving priority to those States having large unobligated balances of funds apportioned under sections 144 (as in effect on the day before the date of enactment of Public Law 112–141) and 104 of title 23, United States Code.
(d) APPLICABILITY OF OBLIGATION LIMITATIONS TO TRANSPORTATION RESEARCH PROGRAMS.—
(1) IN GENERAL.—Except as provided in paragraph (2), the obligation limitation for Federal-aid highways shall apply to contract authority for transportation research programs carried out under—
(A) chapter 5 of title 23, United States Code; and
(B) the current or prior surface transportation authorization acts.
(2) EXCEPTION.—Obligation authority made available under paragraph (1) shall—
(A) remain available for a period of 4 fiscal years; and
(B) be in addition to the amount of any limitation imposed on obligations for Federal-aid highway and highway safety construction programs for future fiscal years.
(e) REDISTRIBUTION OF CERTAIN AUTHORIZED FUNDS.—
(1) IN GENERAL.—Not later than 30 days after the date of distribution of obligation limitation under subsection (a), the Secretary shall distribute to the States any funds (excluding funds authorized for the program under section 202 of title 23, United States Code) that—
(A) are authorized to be appropriated for such fiscal year for Federal-aid highway programs; and
(B) the Secretary determines will not be allocated to the States (or will not be apportioned to the States under section 204 of title 23, United States Code), and will not be available for obligation, for such fiscal year because of the imposition of any obligation limitation for such fiscal year.
(2) RATIO.—Funds shall be distributed under paragraph (1) in the same proportion as the distribution of obligation authority under subsection (a)(5).
(3) AVAILABILITY.—Funds distributed to each State under paragraph (1) shall be available for any purpose described in section 133(b) of title 23, United States Code.
SEC. 121. Notwithstanding 31 U.S.C. 3302, funds received by the Bureau of Transportation Statistics from the sale of data products, for necessary expenses incurred pursuant to chapter 63 of title 49, United States Code, may be credited to the Federal-aid highways account for the purpose of reimbursing the Bureau for such expenses.

SEC. 122. *Not less than 15 days prior to waiving, under his or her statutory authority, any Buy America requirement for Federal-aid highways projects, the Secretary of Transportation shall make an informal public notice and comment opportunity on the intent to issue such waiver and the reasons therefor.*

SEC. 123. *None of the funds made available in this Act may be used to make a grant for a project under section 117 of title 23, United States Code, unless the Secretary, at least 60 days before making a grant under that section, provides written notification to the House and Senate Committees on Appropriations of the proposed grant, including an evaluation and justification for the project and the amount of the proposed grant award.*

SEC. 124. *(a) A State or territory, as defined in section 165 of title 23, United States Code, may use for any project eligible under section 133(b) of title 23 or section 165 of title 23 and located within the boundary of the State or territory any earmarked amount, and any associated obligation limitation: Provided, That the Department of Transportation for the State or territory for which the earmarked amount was originally designated or directed notifies the Secretary of its intent to use its authority under this section and submits an annual report to the Secretary identifying the projects to which the funding would be applied. Notwithstanding the original period of availability of funds to be obligated under this section, such funds and associated obligation limitation shall remain available for obligation for a period of 3 fiscal years after the fiscal year in which the Secretary is notified. The Federal share of the cost of a project carried out with funds made available under this section shall be the same as associated with the earmark.*

(b) In this section, the term "earmarked amount" means—

(1) congressionally directed spending, as defined in rule XLIV of the Standing Rules of the Senate, identified in a prior law, report, or joint explanatory statement, which was authorized to be appropriated or appropriated more than 10 fiscal years prior to the current fiscal year, and administered by the Federal Highway Administration; or

(2) a congressional earmark, as defined in rule XXI of the Rules of the House of Representatives, identified in a prior law, report, or joint explanatory statement, which was authorized to be appropriated or appropriated more than 10 fiscal years prior to the current fiscal year, and administered by the Federal Highway Administration.

(c) The authority under subsection (a) may be exercised only for those projects or activities that have obligated less than 10 percent of the amount made available for obligation as of October 1 of the current fiscal year, and shall be applied to projects within the same general geographic area within 25 miles for which the funding was designated, except that a State or territory may apply such authority to unexpended balances of funds from projects or activities the State or territory certifies have been closed and for which payments have been made under a final voucher.

(d) The Secretary shall submit consolidated reports of the information provided by the States and territories annually to the House and Senate Committees on Appropriations.

FEDERAL MOTOR CARRIER SAFETY ADMINISTRATION

The Federal Motor Carrier Safety Administration (FMCSA) was established within the Department of Transportation by the Motor Carrier Safety Improvement Act of 1999 (P.L. 106–159). Prior to this legislation, motor carrier safety responsibilities were under the jurisdiction of the Federal Highway Administration.

FMCSA's mission is to promote safe commercial motor vehicle operation, and reduce truck and bus crashes. The Agency accomplishes this mission by reducing fatalities and property losses associated with commercial motor vehicles through education, regulation, enforcement, research, and innovative technology, thereby achieving a safer and more secure transportation environment. FMCSA is also responsible for enforcing Federal motor carrier safety and hazardous materials regulations for all commercial vehicles entering the United States along its southern and northern borders.

Federal Funds

MOTOR CARRIER SAFETY GRANTS

[For an additional amount for "Motor Carrier Safety Grants", $622,500,000, to remain available until September 30, 2029, to carry out sections 31102, 31103, 31104, and 31313 of title 49, United States Code, in addition to amounts otherwise provided for such purpose: *Provided*, That $124,500,000, to remain available until September 30, 2025, shall be made available for fiscal year 2022, $124,500,000, to remain available until September 30, 2026, shall be made available for fiscal year 2023, $124,500,000, to remain available until September 30, 2027, shall be made available for fiscal year 2024, $124,500,000, to remain available until September 30, 2028, shall be made available for fiscal year 2025, and $124,500,000, to remain available until September 30, 2029, shall be made available for fiscal year 2026: *Provided further*, That, of the amounts provided under this heading in this Act, the following amounts shall be available for the following purposes in equal amounts for each of fiscal years 2022 through 2026—]

[(1) up to $400,000,000 shall be for the motor carrier safety assistance program;]

[(2) up to $80,000,000 shall be for the commercial driver's license program implementation program;]

[(3) up to $132,500,000 shall be for the high priority activities program; and]

[(4) up to $10,000,000 shall be for commercial motor vehicle operators grants:]

[*Provided further*, That amounts made available under this heading in this Act shall be derived from the general fund of the Treasury, shall be in addition to any other amounts made available for such purpose, and shall not affect the distribution or amount of funds provided in any Act making annual appropriations: *Provided further*, That obligations of funds under this heading in this Act shall not be subject to any limitations on obligations provided in any Act making annual appropriations: *Provided further*, That up to 1.5 percent of the amounts made available under this heading in this Act in each fiscal year shall be for oversight and administration: *Provided further*, That such amount is designated by the Congress as being for an emergency requirement pursuant to section 4112(a) of H. Con. Res. 71 (115th Congress), the concurrent resolution on the budget for fiscal year 2018, and pursuant to section 251(b) of the Balanced Budget and Emergency Deficit Control Act of 1985.] *(Infrastructure Investments and Jobs Appropriations Act.)*

Program and Financing (in millions of dollars)

Identification code 069–2817–0–1–401	2021 actual	2022 est.	2023 est.
Obligations by program activity:			
0001 Motor Carrier Safety Assistance Program		80	80
0002 Commercial Driver's License (CDL) Program Implementation Grants		16	16
0003 High Priority Activities Program		27	27
0004 Commercial Motor Vehicle Operator (CMV) Grant		2	2
0900 Total new obligations, unexpired accounts		125	125
Budgetary resources:			
Budget authority:			
Appropriations, discretionary:			
1100 Appropriation		125	
Advance appropriations, discretionary:			
1170 Advance appropriation			125
1900 Budget authority (total)		125	125
1930 Total budgetary resources available		125	125
Change in obligated balance:			
Unpaid obligations:			
3000 Unpaid obligations, brought forward, Oct 1			106
3010 New obligations, unexpired accounts		125	125
3020 Outlays (gross)		–19	–81
3050 Unpaid obligations, end of year		106	150
Memorandum (non-add) entries:			
3100 Obligated balance, start of year			106
3200 Obligated balance, end of year		106	150
Budget authority and outlays, net:			
Discretionary:			
4000 Budget authority, gross		125	125
Outlays, gross:			
4010 Outlays from new discretionary authority		19	19
4011 Outlays from discretionary balances			62
4020 Outlays, gross (total)		19	81
4180 Budget authority, net (total)		125	125
4190 Outlays, net (total)		19	81

Motor Carrier Safety Grants provide funding to eligible States so they may conduct compliance reviews, identify and apprehend traffic violators, conduct roadside inspections, and support safety audits on new entrant carriers. FMCSA also supports States by conducting training for State agency personnel to accomplish motor carrier safety objectives. In addition, FMCSA reviews State commercial driver's license (CDL) oversight activities to prevent unqualified drivers from being issued CDLs, and actively

DEPARTMENT OF TRANSPORTATION

Federal Motor Carrier Safety Administration—Continued
Trust Funds — 929

engages with industry and other stakeholders through Innovative Technology programs to improve the safety and productivity of commercial vehicles and drivers.

Object Classification (in millions of dollars)

Identification code 069–2817–0–1–401	2021 actual	2022 est.	2023 est.
Direct obligations:			
21.0 Travel and transportation of persons		2	2
41.0 Grants, subsidies, and contributions		123	123
99.9 Total new obligations, unexpired accounts		125	125

MOTOR CARRIER SAFETY OPERATIONS AND PROGRAM

[For an additional amount for "Motor Carrier Safety Operations and Program", $50,000,000, to remain available until September 30, 2029, to carry out motor carrier safety operations and programs pursuant to section 31110 of title 49, United States Code, in addition to amounts otherwise provided for such purpose: *Provided*, That $10,000,000, to remain available until September 30, 2025, shall be made available for fiscal year 2022, $10,000,000, to remain available until September 30, 2026, shall be made available for fiscal year 2023, $10,000,000, to remain available until September 30, 2027, shall be made available for fiscal year 2024, $10,000,000, to remain available until September 30, 2028, shall be made available for fiscal year 2025, and $10,000,000, to remain available until September 30, 2029, shall be made available for fiscal year 2026: *Provided further*, That amounts made available under this heading in this Act shall be derived from the general fund of the Treasury, shall be in addition to any other amounts made available for such purpose, and shall not affect the distribution or amount of funds provided in any Act making annual appropriations: *Provided further*, That obligations of funds under this heading in this Act shall not be subject to any limitations on obligations provided in any Act making annual appropriations: *Provided further*, That such amount is designated by the Congress as being for an emergency requirement pursuant to section 4112(a) of H. Con. Res. 71 (115th Congress), the concurrent resolution on the budget for fiscal year 2018, and pursuant to section 251(b) of the Balanced Budget and Emergency Deficit Control Act of 1985.] *(Infrastructure Investments and Jobs Appropriations Act.)*

Program and Financing (in millions of dollars)

Identification code 069–2818–0–1–401	2021 actual	2022 est.	2023 est.
Obligations by program activity:			
0001 Operating Expenses		10	10
Budgetary resources:			
Budget authority:			
Appropriations, discretionary:			
1100 Appropriation		10	
Advance appropriations, discretionary:			
1170 Advance appropriation			10
1900 Budget authority (total)		10	10
1930 Total budgetary resources available		10	10
Change in obligated balance:			
Unpaid obligations:			
3000 Unpaid obligations, brought forward, Oct 1			3
3010 New obligations, unexpired accounts		10	10
3020 Outlays (gross)		–7	–9
3050 Unpaid obligations, end of year		3	4
Memorandum (non-add) entries:			
3100 Obligated balance, start of year			3
3200 Obligated balance, end of year		3	4
Budget authority and outlays, net:			
Discretionary:			
4000 Budget authority, gross		10	10
Outlays, gross:			
4010 Outlays from new discretionary authority		7	7
4011 Outlays from discretionary balances			2
4020 Outlays, gross (total)		7	9
4180 Budget authority, net (total)		10	10
4190 Outlays, net (total)		7	9

The Operations and Programs account provides the necessary resources to support program and administrative activities for motor carrier safety. The Federal Motor Carrier Safety Administration (FMCSA) will continue to improve safety and reduce severe and fatal commercial motor vehicles crashes by requiring operators to maintain standards to remain in the industry, and by removing high-risk carriers, vehicles, drivers, and service providers from operation. Funding supports Nation-wide motor carrier safety and consumer enforcement efforts, including the continuation of the Compliance, Safety and Accountability Program; regulation and enforcement of movers of household goods; and Federal safety enforcement activities at the borders to ensure that foreign-domiciled carriers entering the U.S. are in compliance with FMSCA regulations. Resources are also provided to fund regulatory development and implementation; investment in research and technology with a focus on research regarding highly automated vehicles and related technology; information technology and information management; safety outreach; and education.

Object Classification (in millions of dollars)

Identification code 069–2818–0–1–401	2021 actual	2022 est.	2023 est.
Direct obligations:			
21.0 Travel and transportation of persons		2	2
25.2 Other services from non-Federal sources		8	8
99.9 Total new obligations, unexpired accounts		10	10

Trust Funds

MOTOR CARRIER SAFETY

Program and Financing (in millions of dollars)

Identification code 069–8055–0–7–401	2021 actual	2022 est.	2023 est.
4180 Budget authority, net (total)			
4190 Outlays, net (total)			
Memorandum (non-add) entries:			
5054 Fund balance in excess of liquidating requirements, SOY: Contract authority	41	41	41
5055 Fund balance in excess of liquidating requirements, EOY: Contract authority	41	41	41

Activities have not been funded in this account since 2005. This schedule shows the obligations and outlays of funding made available for this program in fiscal years prior to 2006.

NATIONAL MOTOR CARRIER SAFETY PROGRAM

Program and Financing (in millions of dollars)

Identification code 069–8048–0–7–401	2021 actual	2022 est.	2023 est.
Budgetary resources:			
Unobligated balance:			
1000 Unobligated balance brought forward, Oct 1	10	10	10
1930 Total budgetary resources available	10	10	10
Memorandum (non-add) entries:			
1941 Unexpired unobligated balance, end of year	10	10	10
Change in obligated balance:			
Unpaid obligations:			
3000 Unpaid obligations, brought forward, Oct 1	2	2	2
3050 Unpaid obligations, end of year	2	2	2
Memorandum (non-add) entries:			
3100 Obligated balance, start of year	2	2	2
3200 Obligated balance, end of year	2	2	2
4180 Budget authority, net (total)			
4190 Outlays, net (total)			
Memorandum (non-add) entries:			
5050 Unobligated balance, SOY: Contract authority	3	3	3
5051 Unobligated balance, EOY: Contract authority	3	3	3
5052 Obligated balance, SOY: Contract authority	2	2	2

NATIONAL MOTOR CARRIER SAFETY PROGRAM—Continued

Program and Financing—Continued

Identification code 069–8048–0–7–401	2021 actual	2022 est.	2023 est.
5053 Obligated balance, EOY: Contract authority	2	2	2

No funding is requested for this account in 2023.

MOTOR CARRIER SAFETY GRANTS

(LIQUIDATION OF CONTRACT AUTHORIZATION)

(LIMITATION ON OBLIGATIONS)

(HIGHWAY TRUST FUND)

(INCLUDING TRANSFERS OF FUNDS)

For payment of obligations incurred in carrying out sections 31102, 31103, 31104, and 31313 of title 49, United States Code, $506,150,000 to be derived from the Highway Trust Fund (other than the Mass Transit Account) and to remain available until expended: Provided, That funds available for the implementation or execution of motor carrier safety programs shall not exceed total obligations of $506,150,000 in fiscal year 2023 for "Motor Carrier Safety Grants" provided under this heading: Provided further, That of the sums appropriated under this heading:

(1) $398,500,000 shall be available for the motor carrier safety assistance program;

(2) $42,650,000 shall be available for the commercial driver's license program implementation program;

(3) $58,800,000 shall be available for the high priority activities program;

(4) $1,200,000 shall be available for the commercial motor vehicle operators grant program; and

(5) $5,000,000 shall be available for the commercial motor vehicle enforcement training and support grant program.

Note.—A full-year 2022 appropriation for this account was not enacted at the time the Budget was prepared; therefore, the Budget assumes this account is operating under the Continuing Appropriations Act, 2022 (Division A of Public Law 117–43, as amended). The amounts included for 2022 reflect the annualized level provided by the continuing resolution.

Program and Financing (in millions of dollars)

Identification code 069–8158–0–7–401		2021 actual	2022 est.	2023 est.
	Obligations by program activity:			
0001	Motor Carrier Safety Assistance Program	309	309	398
0004	Commercial Driver's License (CDL) Program Implementation Grants	29	33	43
0007	High Priority Activities Program	46	46	59
0009	Commercial Motor Vehicle Operator (CMV) Grant	2	2	1
0010	Border Maintenance & Modernization	1	....	....
0012	Large Truck Crash Causal Factors Study (LTCCFS)	....	30	....
0013	CMV Enforcement Training & Support	....	....	5
0900	Total new obligations, unexpired accounts	387	420	506
	Budgetary resources:			
	Unobligated balance:			
1000	Unobligated balance brought forward, Oct 1	120	131	207
1021	Recoveries of prior year unpaid obligations	10	....	....
1070	Unobligated balance (total)	130	131	207
	Budget authority:			
	Appropriations, discretionary:			
1101	Appropriation (special or trust)	420	420	506
1138	Portion applied to liquidate contract authority, Motor Carrier Safety Grants	–420	–420	–506
	Contract authority, mandatory:			
1600	Contract authority, Motor Carrier Safety Grants	388	496	506
1900	Budget authority (total)	388	496	506
1930	Total budgetary resources available	518	627	713
	Memorandum (non-add) entries:			
1941	Unexpired unobligated balance, end of year	131	207	207
	Change in obligated balance:			
	Unpaid obligations:			
3000	Unpaid obligations, brought forward, Oct 1	676	721	741
3010	New obligations, unexpired accounts	387	420	506
3020	Outlays (gross)	–332	–400	–448
3040	Recoveries of prior year unpaid obligations, unexpired	–10	....	....
3050	Unpaid obligations, end of year	721	741	799
	Memorandum (non-add) entries:			
3100	Obligated balance, start of year	676	721	741
3200	Obligated balance, end of year	721	741	799
	Budget authority and outlays, net:			
	Discretionary:			
	Outlays, gross:			
4010	Outlays from new discretionary authority	21	63	76
4011	Outlays from discretionary balances	311	337	372
4020	Outlays, gross (total)	332	400	448
	Mandatory:			
4090	Budget authority, gross	388	496	506
4180	Budget authority, net (total)	388	496	506
4190	Outlays, net (total)	332	400	448
	Memorandum (non-add) entries:			
5054	Fund balance in excess of liquidating requirements, SOY: Contract authority	218	250	174
5055	Fund balance in excess of liquidating requirements, EOY: Contract authority	250	174	174
5061	Limitation on obligations (Transportation Trust Funds)	420	420	506

Summary of Budget Authority and Outlays (in millions of dollars)

	2021 actual	2022 est.	2023 est.
Enacted/requested:			
Budget Authority	388	496	506
Outlays	332	400	448
Amounts included in the adjusted baseline:			
Outlays	....	11	38
Total:			
Budget Authority	388	496	506
Outlays	332	411	486

Motor Carrier Safety Grants provide funding to eligible States so they may conduct compliance reviews, identify and apprehend traffic violators, conduct roadside inspections, and support safety audits on new entrant carriers. FMCSA also supports States by conducting training for State agency personnel to accomplish motor carrier safety objectives. In addition, FMCSA reviews State commercial driver's license (CDL) oversight activities to prevent unqualified drivers from being issued CDLs, and actively engages with industry and other stakeholders through Innovative Technology programs to improve the safety and productivity of commercial vehicles and drivers.

Object Classification (in millions of dollars)

Identification code 069–8158–0–7–401		2021 actual	2022 est.	2023 est.
	Direct obligations:			
25.2	Other services from non-Federal sources	1	1	1
25.3	Other goods and services from Federal sources	6	6	6
41.0	Grants, subsidies, and contributions	380	413	499
99.9	Total new obligations, unexpired accounts	387	420	506

MOTOR CARRIER SAFETY GRANTS

(Amounts included in the adjusted baseline)

Program and Financing (in millions of dollars)

Identification code 069–8158–7–7–401		2021 actual	2022 est.	2023 est.
	Obligations by program activity:			
0001	Motor Carrier Safety Assistance Program	....	81	....
0004	Commercial Driver's License (CDL) Program Implementation Grants	....	9	....
0007	High Priority Activities Program	....	12	....
0009	Commercial Motor Vehicle Operator (CMV) Grant	....	–1	....
0012	Large Truck Crash Causal Factors Study (LTCCFS)	....	–30	....
0013	CMV Enforcement Training & Support	....	5	....
0900	Total new obligations, unexpired accounts (object class 41.0)	....	76	....
	Budgetary resources:			
	Unobligated balance:			
1000	Unobligated balance brought forward, Oct 1	....	....	–76
	Budget authority:			
	Appropriations, discretionary:			
1101	Appropriation (special or trust)	....	76	....

DEPARTMENT OF TRANSPORTATION

Federal Motor Carrier Safety Administration—Continued
Trust Funds—Continued

931

		2021 actual	2022 est.	2023 est.
1138	Portion applied to liquidate contract authority, Motor Carrier Safety Grants		–76	
1930	Total budgetary resources available			–76
	Memorandum (non-add) entries:			
1941	Unexpired unobligated balance, end of year		–76	–76
	Change in obligated balance:			
	Unpaid obligations:			
3000	Unpaid obligations, brought forward, Oct 1			65
3010	New obligations, unexpired accounts		76	
3020	Outlays (gross)		–11	–38
3050	Unpaid obligations, end of year		65	27
	Memorandum (non-add) entries:			
3100	Obligated balance, start of year			65
3200	Obligated balance, end of year		65	27
	Budget authority and outlays, net:			
	Discretionary:			
	Outlays, gross:			
4010	Outlays from new discretionary authority		11	
4011	Outlays from discretionary balances			38
4020	Outlays, gross (total)		11	38
4180	Budget authority, net (total)			
4190	Outlays, net (total)		11	38
	Memorandum (non-add) entries:			
5052	Obligated balance, SOY: Contract authority			–76
5053	Obligated balance, EOY: Contract authority		–76	–76
5061	Limitation on obligations (Transportation Trust Funds)		76	

MOTOR CARRIER SAFETY OPERATIONS AND PROGRAMS

(LIQUIDATION OF CONTRACT AUTHORIZATION)
(LIMITATION ON OBLIGATIONS)
(HIGHWAY TRUST FUND)
(INCLUDING TRANSFERS OF FUNDS)

For payment of obligations incurred in the implementation, execution and administration of motor carrier safety operations and programs pursuant to section 31110 of title 49, United States Code, $367,500,000, to be derived from the Highway Trust Fund (other than the Mass Transit Account), together with advances and reimbursements received by the Federal Motor Carrier Safety Administration, the sum of which shall remain available until expended: Provided, That funds available for implementation, execution, or administration of motor carrier safety operations and programs authorized under title 49, United States Code, shall not exceed total obligations of $367,500,000, for "Motor Carrier Safety Operations and Programs" for fiscal year 2023, of which not less than $63,098,000, to remain available for obligation until September 30, 2025, is for development, modernization, enhancement, and continued operation and maintenance of information technology and information management, and of which $14,073,000, to remain available for obligation until September 30, 2025, is for the research and technology program.

Note.—A full-year 2022 appropriation for this account was not enacted at the time the Budget was prepared; therefore, the Budget assumes this account is operating under the Continuing Appropriations Act, 2022 (Division A of Public Law 117–43, as amended). The amounts included for 2022 reflect the annualized level provided by the continuing resolution.

Special and Trust Fund Receipts (in millions of dollars)

Identification code 069–8159–0–7–401	2021 actual	2022 est.	2023 est.
0100 Balance, start of year			
Receipts:			
Current law:			
1110 Licensing and Insuring Fees, Motor Carrier Safety Operations and Programs		30	30
1110 Drug and Alcohol Clearinghouse Fees, Motor Carrier Safety Operations and Programs		10	10
1199 Total current law receipts		40	40
1999 Total receipts		40	40
2000 Total: Balances and receipts		40	40
Appropriations:			
Current law:			
2101 Motor Carrier Safety Operations and Programs		–40	–40
5099 Balance, end of year			

Program and Financing (in millions of dollars)

Identification code 069–8159–0–7–401	2021 actual	2022 est.	2023 est.
Obligations by program activity:			
0001 Operating Expenses	234	244	291
0002 Research and Technology	13	9	14
0003 Information Management	46	75	63
0007 Licensing & Insuring Fees	23	30	30
0010 Drug and Alcohol Clearinghouse Fees	5	10	10
0100 Direct program activities, subtotal	321	368	408
0900 Total new obligations, unexpired accounts	321	368	408
Budgetary resources:			
Unobligated balance:			
1000 Unobligated balance brought forward, Oct 1	106	145	177
1021 Recoveries of prior year unpaid obligations	8		
1070 Unobligated balance (total)	114	145	177
Budget authority:			
Appropriations, discretionary:			
1101 Appropriation (special or trust)	318	328	368
1138 Appropriations applied to liquidate contract authority	–318	–328	–368
Appropriations, mandatory:			
1201 Appropriation (special or trust fund)		40	40
1232 Appropriations and/or unobligated balance of appropriations temporarily reduced		–2	–2
1260 Appropriations, mandatory (total)		38	38
Contract authority, mandatory:			
1600 Contract authority	288	360	368
Spending authority from offsetting collections, mandatory:			
1800 Collected	68		
1802 Offsetting collections (previously unavailable)		2	
1823 New and/or unobligated balance of spending authority from offsetting collections temporarily reduced	–4		
1850 Spending auth from offsetting collections, mand (total)	64	2	
1900 Budget authority (total)	352	400	406
1930 Total budgetary resources available	466	545	583
Memorandum (non-add) entries:			
1941 Unexpired unobligated balance, end of year	145	177	175
Change in obligated balance:			
Unpaid obligations:			
3000 Unpaid obligations, brought forward, Oct 1	78	88	110
3010 New obligations, unexpired accounts	321	368	408
3020 Outlays (gross)	–303	–346	–396
3040 Recoveries of prior year unpaid obligations, unexpired	–8		
3050 Unpaid obligations, end of year	88	110	122
Memorandum (non-add) entries:			
3100 Obligated balance, start of year	78	88	110
3200 Obligated balance, end of year	88	110	122
Budget authority and outlays, net:			
Discretionary:			
Outlays, gross:			
4010 Outlays from new discretionary authority	242	246	276
4011 Outlays from discretionary balances	40	51	82
4020 Outlays, gross (total)	282	297	358
Mandatory:			
4090 Budget authority, gross	352	400	406
Outlays, gross:			
4100 Outlays from new mandatory authority	15	49	38
4101 Outlays from mandatory balances	6		
4110 Outlays, gross (total)	21	49	38
Offsets against gross budget authority and outlays:			
Offsetting collections (collected) from:			
4124 Offsetting governmental collections	–68		
4180 Budget authority, net (total)	284	400	406
4190 Outlays, net (total)	235	346	396
Memorandum (non-add) entries:			
5054 Fund balance in excess of liquidating requirements, SOY: Contract authority	16	46	14
5055 Fund balance in excess of liquidating requirements, EOY: Contract authority	46	14	14
5061 Limitation on obligations (Transportation Trust Funds)	328	328	368
5090 Unexpired unavailable balance, SOY: Offsetting collections		4	2
5092 Unexpired unavailable balance, EOY: Offsetting collections	4	2	2

Federal Motor Carrier Safety Administration—Continued
Trust Funds—Continued

MOTOR CARRIER SAFETY OPERATIONS AND PROGRAMS—Continued

Summary of Budget Authority and Outlays (in millions of dollars)

	2021 actual	2022 est.	2023 est.
Enacted/requested:			
Budget Authority	284	400	406
Outlays	235	346	396
Amounts included in the adjusted baseline:			
Outlays		24	5
Total:			
Budget Authority	284	400	406
Outlays	235	370	401

The Operations and Programs account provides the necessary resources to support program and administrative activities for motor carrier safety. The Federal Motor Carrier Safety Administration (FMCSA) will continue to improve safety and reduce severe and fatal commercial motor vehicles crashes by requiring operators to maintain standards to remain in the industry, and by removing high-risk carriers, vehicles, drivers, and service providers from operation. Funding supports Nation-wide motor carrier safety and consumer enforcement efforts, including the continuation of the Compliance, Safety and Accountability Program; regulation and enforcement of movers of household goods; and Federal safety enforcement activities at the borders to ensure that foreign-domiciled carriers entering the U.S. are in compliance with FMSCA regulations. Resources are also provided to fund regulatory development and implementation; investment in research and technology with a focus on research regarding highly automated vehicles and related technology; information technology and information management; safety outreach; and education.

Object Classification (in millions of dollars)

Identification code 069–8159–0–7–401	2021 actual	2022 est.	2023 est.
Direct obligations:			
Personnel compensation:			
11.1 Full-time permanent	115	116	136
11.3 Other than full-time permanent	4	4	4
11.9 Total personnel compensation	119	120	140
12.1 Civilian personnel benefits	45	46	55
21.0 Travel and transportation of persons	2	2	2
23.1 Rental payments to GSA	16	16	15
25.2 Other services from non-Federal sources	126	171	168
25.5 Research and development contracts	12	12	27
26.0 Supplies and materials	1	1	1
99.9 Total new obligations, unexpired accounts	321	368	408

Employment Summary

Identification code 069–8159–0–7–401	2021 actual	2022 est.	2023 est.
1001 Direct civilian full-time equivalent employment	1,115	1,186	1,285

MOTOR CARRIER SAFETY OPERATIONS AND PROGRAMS

(Amounts included in the adjusted baseline)

Program and Financing (in millions of dollars)

Identification code 069–8159–7–7–401	2021 actual	2022 est.	2023 est.
Obligations by program activity:			
0001 Operating Expenses		60	
0002 Research and Technology		5	
0003 Information Management		–33	
0100 Direct program activities, subtotal		32	
0900 Total new obligations, unexpired accounts		32	
Budgetary resources:			
Unobligated balance:			
1000 Unobligated balance brought forward, Oct 1			–32
Budget authority:			
Appropriations, discretionary:			
1101 Appropriation (special or trust)		32	
1138 Appropriations applied to liquidate contract authority		–32	
1930 Total budgetary resources available			–32
Memorandum (non-add) entries:			
1941 Unexpired unobligated balance, end of year		–32	–32
Change in obligated balance:			
Unpaid obligations:			
3000 Unpaid obligations, brought forward, Oct 1			8
3010 New obligations, unexpired accounts		32	
3020 Outlays (gross)		–24	–5
3050 Unpaid obligations, end of year		8	3
Memorandum (non-add) entries:			
3100 Obligated balance, start of year			8
3200 Obligated balance, end of year		8	3
Budget authority and outlays, net:			
Discretionary:			
Outlays, gross:			
4010 Outlays from new discretionary authority		24	
4011 Outlays from discretionary balances			5
4020 Outlays, gross (total)		24	5
4180 Budget authority, net (total)			
4190 Outlays, net (total)		24	5
Memorandum (non-add) entries:			
5054 Fund balance in excess of liquidating requirements, SOY: Contract authority			32
5055 Fund balance in excess of liquidating requirements, EOY: Contract authority		32	32
5061 Limitation on obligations (Transportation Trust Funds)		32	

Object Classification (in millions of dollars)

Identification code 069–8159–7–7–401	2021 actual	2022 est.	2023 est.
11.1 Direct obligations: Personnel compensation: Full-time permanent		3	
11.9 Total personnel compensation		3	
12.1 Civilian personnel benefits		1	
25.2 Other services from non-Federal sources		28	
99.9 Total new obligations, unexpired accounts		32	

Employment Summary

Identification code 069–8159–7–7–401	2021 actual	2022 est.	2023 est.
1001 Direct civilian full-time equivalent employment		23	

NATIONAL HIGHWAY TRAFFIC SAFETY ADMINISTRATION

The National Highway Traffic Safety Administration (NHTSA) is responsible for motor vehicle safety, highway safety behavioral programs, motor vehicle information, and automobile fuel economy programs. NHTSA is charged with reducing traffic crashes and deaths and injuries resulting from traffic crashes; establishing safety standards for motor vehicles and motor vehicle equipment; carrying out needed safety research and development; and the operation of the National Driver Register.

Federal Funds

CONSUMER ASSISTANCE TO RECYCLE AND SAVE PROGRAM

Program and Financing (in millions of dollars)

Identification code 069–0654–0–1–376	2021 actual	2022 est.	2023 est.
Budgetary resources:			
Unobligated balance:			
1000 Unobligated balance brought forward, Oct 1	20	20	20
1930 Total budgetary resources available	20	20	20
Memorandum (non-add) entries:			
1941 Unexpired unobligated balance, end of year	20	20	20
4180 Budget authority, net (total)			
4190 Outlays, net (total)			

The schedule above shows the remaining activity associated with the completed Consumer Assistance to Recycle and Save (Cash for Clunkers) program. No new funds are requested for this program in 2023.

OPERATIONS AND RESEARCH

For expenses necessary to discharge the functions of the Secretary, with respect to traffic and highway safety authorized under chapter 301 and part C of subtitle VI of title 49, United States Code, $272,650,000, of which $60,000,000 shall remain available through September 30, 2024.

Note.—A full-year 2022 appropriation for this account was not enacted at the time the Budget was prepared; therefore, the Budget assumes this account is operating under the Continuing Appropriations Act, 2022 (Division A of Public Law 117–43, as amended). The amounts included for 2022 reflect the annualized level provided by the continuing resolution.

Program and Financing (in millions of dollars)

Identification code 069–0650–0–1–401	2021 actual	2022 est.	2023 est.
Obligations by program activity:			
0001 Motor Vehicle Safety	200	194	273
0002 Section 142	15	17	
0003 Vehicle Safety Programs - Transfer from 0670		70	70
0004 Administrative Expenses - Transfer from 0669		5	5
0799 Total direct obligations	215	286	348
0801 Reimbursable program activity	2	2	2
0900 Total new obligations, unexpired accounts	217	288	350
Budgetary resources:			
Unobligated balance:			
1000 Unobligated balance brought forward, Oct 1	24	20	20
1033 Recoveries of prior year paid obligations	1		
1070 Unobligated balance (total)	25	20	20
Budget authority:			
Appropriations, discretionary:			
1100 Appropriation	211	211	273
1121 Appropriations transferred from other acct [069–0669]		5	
1121 Appropriations transferred from other acct [069–0670]		70	
1160 Appropriation, discretionary (total)	211	286	273
Advance appropriations, discretionary:			
1173 Advance appropriations transferred from other accounts [069–0669]			5
1173 Advance appropriations transferred from other accounts [069–0670]			70
1180 Advanced appropriation, discretionary (total)			75
Spending authority from offsetting collections, discretionary:			
1700 Collected	2	2	2
1900 Budget authority (total)	213	288	350
1930 Total budgetary resources available	238	308	370
Memorandum (non-add) entries:			
1940 Unobligated balance expiring	–1		
1941 Unexpired unobligated balance, end of year	20	20	20
Change in obligated balance:			
Unpaid obligations:			
3000 Unpaid obligations, brought forward, Oct 1	171	171	232
3010 New obligations, unexpired accounts	217	288	350
3020 Outlays (gross)	–214	–227	–344
3041 Recoveries of prior year unpaid obligations, expired	–3		
3050 Unpaid obligations, end of year	171	232	238
Memorandum (non-add) entries:			
3100 Obligated balance, start of year	171	171	232
3200 Obligated balance, end of year	171	232	238
Budget authority and outlays, net:			
Discretionary:			
4000 Budget authority, gross	213	288	350
Outlays, gross:			
4010 Outlays from new discretionary authority	101	142	184
4011 Outlays from discretionary balances	113	85	160
4020 Outlays, gross (total)	214	227	344
Offsets against gross budget authority and outlays:			
Offsetting collections (collected) from:			
4030 Federal sources	–2	–2	–2
4033 Non-Federal sources	–1		
4040 Offsets against gross budget authority and outlays (total)	–3	–2	–2
Additional offsets against gross budget authority only:			
4053 Recoveries of prior year paid obligations, unexpired accounts	1		
4060 Additional offsets against budget authority only (total)	1		
4070 Budget authority, net (discretionary)	211	286	348
4080 Outlays, net (discretionary)	211	225	342
4180 Budget authority, net (total)	211	286	348
4190 Outlays, net (total)	211	225	342

The Vehicle Safety programs support activities to reduce highway fatalities, prevent injuries, and reduce their associated economic toll by developing, setting, and enforcing Federal Motor Vehicle Safety Standards and rooting out safety-related defects in motor vehicles and motor vehicle equipment. These programs also set and enforce fuel economy standards for motor vehicles. These activities play a key role in advancing the President's Agenda on climate and energy policy and has significant societal and economic impacts. The National Highway Traffic Safety Administration's (NHTSA)s efforts to develop and set new fuel economy standards are guided by the best science and protected by governed processes that ensure the integrity of Federal decision-making. NHTSA supports research into cutting-edge technologies, including complex safety-critical electronic control systems, vehicle cybersecurity, and new and emerging Automated Driving System technologies. Additional research areas include biomechanics, heavy vehicles safety technologies, and vehicle safety issues related to fuel efficiency and alternative fuels. The Operation and Research program supports a broad range of initiatives, including the development of rulemaking and safety standards, such as the motor vehicle fuel economy standards, harmonization efforts with international partners, and modernizing the New Car Assessment Program. This funding also supports compliance programs for motor vehicle safety and fuel economy standards, investigations of safety-related motor vehicle defects, enforcement of Federal odometer law, and oversight of safety recalls. NHTSA also leverages this funding to collect and analyze crash data to identify safety trends and develop countermeasures.

Object Classification (in millions of dollars)

Identification code 069–0650–0–1–401	2021 actual	2022 est.	2023 est.
Direct obligations:			
Personnel compensation:			
11.1 Full-time permanent	47	50	59
11.1 Full-time permanent		1	1
11.1 Full-time permanent		1	3
11.5 Other personnel compensation	1	1	2
11.9 Total personnel compensation	48	53	65
12.1 Civilian personnel benefits	16	18	26
12.1 Civilian personnel benefits			1
12.1 Civilian personnel benefits			1
23.1 Rental payments to GSA	5	5	5
25.1 Advisory and assistance services	73	73	73
25.2 Other services from non-Federal sources	6	6	6
25.3 Other goods and services from Federal sources	23	24	54
25.5 Research and development contracts	29	92	102
25.7 Operation and maintenance of equipment	3	3	3
26.0 Supplies and materials	1	1	1
31.0 Equipment	8	8	8
41.0 Grants, subsidies, and contributions	3	3	3
99.0 Direct obligations	215	286	348
99.0 Reimbursable obligations	2	2	2
99.9 Total new obligations, unexpired accounts	217	288	350

Employment Summary

Identification code 069–0650–0–1–401	2021 actual	2022 est.	2023 est.
1001 Direct civilian full-time equivalent employment	353	357	428
1001 Direct civilian full-time equivalent employment		3	10
1001 Direct civilian full-time equivalent employment		5	18

SUPPLEMENTAL HIGHWAY TRAFFIC SAFETY PROGRAMS

[For an additional amount for "Supplemental Highway Traffic Safety Programs", $310,000,000, to remain available until September 30, 2029, to carry out sections 402 and 405 of title 23, United States Code, and section 24101(a)(5) of division B of this Act: *Provided*, That $62,000,000, to remain available until September 30, 2025, shall be made available for fiscal year 2022, $62,000,000, to remain available until September 30, 2026, shall be made available for fiscal year 2023, $62,000,000, to remain available until September 30, 2027, shall be made available for fiscal year 2024, $62,000,000, to remain available until September 30, 2028, shall be made available for fiscal year 2025, and $62,000,000 to remain available until September 30, 2029, shall be made available for fiscal year 2026: *Provided further*, That amounts made available under this heading in this Act shall be derived from the general fund of the Treasury: *Provided further*, That obligations of funds under this heading in this Act shall not be subject to any limitations on obligations provided in any Act making annual appropriations: *Provided further*, That, of the amounts provided under this heading in this Act, the following amounts shall be for the following purposes in equal amounts for each of fiscal years 2022 through 2026:]

[(1) $100,000,000 shall be for highway safety programs under section 402 of title 23, United States Code;]

[(2) $110,000,000 shall be for national priority safety programs under section 405 of title 23, United States Code; and]

[(3) $100,000,000 shall be for administrative expenses under section 24101(a)(5) of division B of this Act:]

[*Provided further*, That such amount is designated by the Congress as being for an emergency requirement pursuant to section 4112(a) of H. Con. Res. 71 (115th Congress), the concurrent resolution on the budget for fiscal year 2018, and pursuant to section 251(b) of the Balanced Budget and Emergency Deficit Control Act of 1985.] *(Infrastructure Investments and Jobs Appropriations Act.)*

Program and Financing (in millions of dollars)

Identification code 069–0671–0–1–401		2021 actual	2022 est.	2023 est.
	Obligations by program activity:			
0001	Sec. 402 - Highway Safety Programs		20	20
0002	Sec. 405 - National Priority Safety Programs		22	22
0003	Administrative Expenses		20	20
0900	Total new obligations, unexpired accounts		62	62
	Budgetary resources:			
	Budget authority:			
	Appropriations, discretionary:			
1100	Appropriation		62	
	Advance appropriations, discretionary:			
1170	Advance appropriation			62
1900	Budget authority (total)		62	62
1930	Total budgetary resources available		62	62
	Change in obligated balance:			
	Unpaid obligations:			
3000	Unpaid obligations, brought forward, Oct 1			50
3010	New obligations, unexpired accounts		62	62
3020	Outlays (gross)		–12	–42
3050	Unpaid obligations, end of year		50	70
	Memorandum (non-add) entries:			
3100	Obligated balance, start of year			50
3200	Obligated balance, end of year		50	70
	Budget authority and outlays, net:			
	Discretionary:			
4000	Budget authority, gross		62	62
	Outlays, gross:			
4010	Outlays from new discretionary authority		12	12
4011	Outlays from discretionary balances			30
4020	Outlays, gross (total)		12	42
4180	Budget authority, net (total)		62	62
4190	Outlays, net (total)		12	42

Supplemental Highway Traffic Safety Grants funding will support additional grants to States for activities related to highway traffic safety. The Infrastructure Investment and Jobs Act provides additional funding for the State and Community Safety Grants Program (Section 402), National Priority Safety Programs (Section 405), and grants administration.

Object Classification (in millions of dollars)

Identification code 069–0671–0–1–401		2021 actual	2022 est.	2023 est.
	Direct obligations:			
25.2	Other services from non-Federal sources		20	20
41.0	Grants, subsidies, and contributions		42	42
99.9	Total new obligations, unexpired accounts		62	62

NEXT GENERATION 911 IMPLEMENTATION GRANTS

Program and Financing (in millions of dollars)

Identification code 069–0661–0–1–407		2021 actual	2022 est.	2023 est.
	Obligations by program activity:			
0001	Grants	2		
0002	Administration		2	
0900	Total new obligations, unexpired accounts (object class 25.2)	2	2	
	Budgetary resources:			
	Unobligated balance:			
1000	Unobligated balance brought forward, Oct 1	2	2	
1033	Recoveries of prior year paid obligations	2		
1070	Unobligated balance (total)	4	2	
1930	Total budgetary resources available	4	2	
	Memorandum (non-add) entries:			
1941	Unexpired unobligated balance, end of year		2	
	Change in obligated balance:			
	Unpaid obligations:			
3000	Unpaid obligations, brought forward, Oct 1	101	72	17
3010	New obligations, unexpired accounts	2	2	
3020	Outlays (gross)	–31	–57	–10
3050	Unpaid obligations, end of year	72	17	7
	Memorandum (non-add) entries:			
3100	Obligated balance, start of year	101	72	17
3200	Obligated balance, end of year	72	17	7
	Budget authority and outlays, net:			
	Mandatory:			
	Outlays, gross:			
4101	Outlays from mandatory balances	31	57	10
	Offsets against gross budget authority and outlays:			
	Offsetting collections (collected) from:			
4123	Non-Federal sources	–2		
	Additional offsets against gross budget authority only:			
4143	Recoveries of prior year paid obligations, unexpired accounts	2		
4170	Outlays, net (mandatory)	29	57	10
4180	Budget authority, net (total)			
4190	Outlays, net (total)	29	57	10

The 911 Grant Program was authorized by the Next Generation 911 Advancement Act of 2012, which allows eligible entities to utilize funds to implement and operate 911 services, and to train public safety personnel. The program helps 911 call centers upgrade to Next Generation 911 (NG911) capabilities, such as providing digital and network capabilities and implementing advanced mapping systems that will make it easier to identify a 911 caller's location. NG911 also helps 911 call centers manage call overloads and funds for training costs directly related to NG911 implementation. The program is funded by the Public Safety Trust Fund. The authority to expend these funds expires on September 30, 2022. The schedule above shows the remaining activity associated with the completed grant program. No new funds are requested for this program in 2023.

CRASH DATA

[(INCLUDING TRANSFER OF FUNDS)]

[For an additional amount for "Crash Data", $750,000,000, to remain available until September 30, 2029, to carry out section 24108 of division B of this Act: *Provided*, That $150,000,000, to remain available until September 30, 2025, shall be made available for fiscal year 2022, $150,000,000, to remain available until

DEPARTMENT OF TRANSPORTATION

National Highway Traffic Safety Administration—Continued
Federal Funds—Continued   935

September 30, 2026, shall be made available for fiscal year 2023, $150,000,000, to remain available until September 30, 2027, shall be made available for fiscal year 2024, $150,000,000, to remain available until September 30, 2028, shall be made available for fiscal year 2025, and $150,000,000, to remain available until September 30, 2029, shall be made available for fiscal year 2026: *Provided further*, That up to 3 percent of the amounts made available under this heading in this Act in each of fiscal years 2022 through 2026 shall be for salaries and expenses, administration, and oversight, and shall be transferred and merged with the appropriations under the heading "Operations and Research": *Provided further*, That not later than 90 days after the date of enactment of this Act, the Secretary of Transportation shall submit to the House and Senate Committees on Appropriations a funding allocation plan for fiscal year 2022: *Provided further*, That for each fiscal year through 2026, as part of the annual budget submission of the President under section 1105(a) of title 31, United States Code, the Secretary of Transportation shall submit a funding allocation plan for funding that will be made available under this heading in the upcoming fiscal year: *Provided further*, That such amount is designated by the Congress as being for an emergency requirement pursuant to section 4112(a) of H. Con. Res. 71 (115th Congress), the concurrent resolution on the budget for fiscal year 2018, and pursuant to section 251(b) of the Balanced Budget and Emergency Deficit Control Act of 1985.] *(Infrastructure Investments and Jobs Appropriations Act.)*

Program and Financing (in millions of dollars)

Identification code 069–0669–0–1–401	2021 actual	2022 est.	2023 est.
Obligations by program activity:			
0001 Crash Data Program		145	145
Budgetary resources:			
Budget authority:			
Appropriations, discretionary:			
1100 Appropriation		150	
1120 Appropriations transferred to other acct [069–0650]		–5	
1160 Appropriation, discretionary (total)		145	
Advance appropriations, discretionary:			
1170 Advance appropriation			150
1172 Advance appropriations transferred to other accounts [069–0650]			–5
1180 Advanced appropriation, discretionary (total)			145
1900 Budget authority (total)		145	145
1930 Total budgetary resources available		145	145
Change in obligated balance:			
Unpaid obligations:			
3000 Unpaid obligations, brought forward, Oct 1			80
3010 New obligations, unexpired accounts		145	145
3020 Outlays (gross)		–65	–126
3050 Unpaid obligations, end of year		80	99
Memorandum (non-add) entries:			
3100 Obligated balance, start of year			80
3200 Obligated balance, end of year		80	99
Budget authority and outlays, net:			
Discretionary:			
4000 Budget authority, gross		145	145
Outlays, gross:			
4010 Outlays from new discretionary authority		65	65
4011 Outlays from discretionary balances			61
4020 Outlays, gross (total)		65	126
4180 Budget authority, net (total)		145	145
4190 Outlays, net (total)		65	126

Several new initiatives in the Infrastructure Investment and Jobs Act (IIJA) will expand, improve, and enhance NHTSAs crash data program. The funding supports revision of NHTSAs crash data programs to collect information on personal conveyances (scooters, bicycles, etc.) in crashes, update the Model Minimum Uniform Crash Criteria (MMUCC), collect additional data elements related to vulnerable road users, and coordinate with the Centers for Disease Control and Prevention on an implementation plan for States to produce a national database of pedestrian injuries and fatalities. This will allow the agency to identify, analyze, and develop strategies to reduce these crashes. The Crash Investigation Sample System (CISS) will be transformed by increasing the number of sites and adding more researchers which will expand the scope of the study to include all crash types and increase the number of cases. This will enable the agency to make more timely and accurate assessments of automated driving in real-world crash scenarios. While many States are interested in participating in electronic data transfer, and several pilot States are already transferring data successfully, some States crash data systems are not advanced enough to enable full electronic data transfer. Additional IIJA funding will support a grant program for States to upgrade and standardize their crash data systems to enable electronic collection, intra-State sharing, and transfer to NHTSA; all of which would increase the accuracy, timeliness, and accessibility of the data for all users.

Object Classification (in millions of dollars)

Identification code 069–0669–0–1–401	2021 actual	2022 est.	2023 est.
Direct obligations:			
25.2 Other services from non-Federal sources		80	80
41.0 Grants, subsidies, and contributions		65	65
99.9 Total new obligations, unexpired accounts		145	145

VEHICLE SAFETY AND BEHAVIORAL RESEARCH PROGRAMS

[(INCLUDING TRANSFER OF FUNDS)]

[For an additional amount for "Vehicle Safety and Behavioral Research Programs", $548,500,000, to remain available until September 30, 2029, to carry out the provisions of section 403 of title 23, United States Code, including behavioral research on Automated Systems and Advanced Driver Assistance Systems and improving consumer responses to safety recalls, and chapter 303 of title 49, United States Code, in addition to amounts otherwise provided for such purpose: *Provided*, That $109,700,000, to remain available until September 30, 2025, shall be made available for fiscal year 2022, $109,700,000, to remain available until September 30, 2026, shall be made available for fiscal year 2023, $109,700,000, to remain available until September 30, 2027, shall be made available for fiscal year 2024, $109,700,000, to remain available until September 30, 2028, shall be made available for fiscal year 2025, and $109,700,000 to remain available until September 30, 2029, shall be made available for fiscal year 2026: *Provided further*, That amounts made available under this heading in this Act shall be derived from the general fund of the Treasury: *Provided further*, That obligations of funds under this heading in this Act shall not be subject to any limitations on obligations provided in any Act making annual appropriations: *Provided further*, That of the amounts made available under this heading in this Act, up to $350,000,000 may be transferred to "Operations and Research" to carry out traffic and highway safety authorized under chapter 301 and part C of subtitle VI of title 49, United States Code: *Provided further*, That not later than 90 days after the date of enactment of this Act, the Secretary of Transportation shall submit to the House and Senate Committees on Appropriations a funding allocation for fiscal year 2022: *Provided further*, That for each fiscal year through 2026, as part of the annual budget submission of the President under section 1105(a) of title 31, United States Code, the Secretary of Transportation shall submit a funding allocation for funding that will be made available under this heading in the upcoming fiscal year: *Provided further*, That such amount is designated by the Congress as being for an emergency requirement pursuant to section 4112(a) of H. Con. Res. 71 (115th Congress), the concurrent resolution on the budget for fiscal year 2018, and pursuant to section 251(b) of the Balanced Budget and Emergency Deficit Control Act of 1985.] *(Infrastructure Investments and Jobs Appropriations Act.)*

Program and Financing (in millions of dollars)

Identification code 069–0670–0–1–401	2021 actual	2022 est.	2023 est.
Obligations by program activity:			
0001 Behavioral Research Programs		40	40
0900 Total new obligations, unexpired accounts (object class 25.2)		40	40
Budgetary resources:			
Budget authority:			
Appropriations, discretionary:			
1100 Appropriation		110	
1120 Appropriations transferred to other acct [069–0650]		–70	
1160 Appropriation, discretionary (total)		40	

VEHICLE SAFETY AND BEHAVIORAL RESEARCH PROGRAMS—Continued
Program and Financing—Continued

Identification code 069–0670–0–1–401	2021 actual	2022 est.	2023 est.
Advance appropriations, discretionary:			
1170 Advance appropriation			110
1172 Advance appropriations transferred to other accounts [069–0650]			–70
1180 Advanced appropriation, discretionary (total)			40
1900 Budget authority (total)		40	40
1930 Total budgetary resources available		40	40
Change in obligated balance:			
Unpaid obligations:			
3000 Unpaid obligations, brought forward, Oct 1			22
3010 New obligations, unexpired accounts		40	40
3020 Outlays (gross)		–18	–35
3050 Unpaid obligations, end of year		22	27
Memorandum (non-add) entries:			
3100 Obligated balance, start of year			22
3200 Obligated balance, end of year		22	27
Budget authority and outlays, net:			
Discretionary:			
4000 Budget authority, gross		40	40
Outlays, gross:			
4010 Outlays from new discretionary authority		18	18
4011 Outlays from discretionary balances			17
4020 Outlays, gross (total)		18	35
4180 Budget authority, net (total)		40	40
4190 Outlays, net (total)		18	35

Vehicle Safety and Behavioral Research funding will support increased behavioral safety program efforts including research, communication, evaluation, and national leadership activities. These projects will provide data, analysis, and other insights to inform strategies to combat the risky driving behaviors that have increased during the pandemic and to implement a Safe System Approach. This funding supports data collection on alcohol and drug use, research to develop passive alcohol detection technology, as well as emergency medical services data collection and analysis. The funding will also support state grants to develop and implement processes for informing vehicle owners and lessees of the open recalls. Further, the program will support public education and awareness campaigns such as the risks of speeding, protecting pupil transportation safety and child passenger safety.

Funding also supports additional vehicle safety research, particularly in the critical areas of vehicle electronics and cybersecurity, and automated driving systems. Cutting-edge technologies, including complex safety-critical electronic control systems, vehicle cybersecurity, and new and emerging Automated Driving System technologies will also be evaluated. Additional research areas include biomechanics, heavy vehicles safety technologies, and vehicle safety issues related to fuel efficiency and alternative fuels. NHTSA's research advances vehicle and road user safety by informing the development of regulations and safety standards.

Trust Funds

OPERATIONS AND RESEARCH

(LIQUIDATION OF CONTRACT AUTHORIZATION)

(LIMITATION ON OBLIGATIONS)

(HIGHWAY TRUST FUND)

For payment of obligations incurred in carrying out the provisions of 23 U.S.C. 403, including behavioral research on Automated Driving Systems and Advanced Driver Assistance Systems and improving consumer responses to safety recalls, section 25024 of the Infrastructure Investment and Jobs Act (Public Law 117–58), and chapter 303 of title 49, United States Code, $197,000,000, to be derived from the Highway Trust Fund (other than the Mass Transit Account) and to remain available until expended: Provided, That none of the funds in this Act shall be available for the planning or execution of programs the total obligations for which, in fiscal year 2023, are in excess of $197,000,000: Provided further, That of the sums appropriated under this heading—

(1) $190,000,000 shall be for programs authorized under 23 U.S.C. 403, including behavioral research on Automated Driving Systems and Advanced Driver Assistance Systems and improving consumer responses to safety recalls, and section 4011 of the Fixing America's Surface Transportation Act (Public Law 114–94); and

(2) $7,000,000 shall be for the National Driver Register authorized under chapter 303 of title 49, United States Code:

Provided further, That within the $197,000,000 obligation limitation for operations and research, $57,500,000 shall remain available until September 30, 2024, and shall be in addition to the amount of any limitation imposed on obligations for future years: Provided further, That amounts for behavioral research on Automated Driving Systems and Advanced Driver Assistance Systems and improving consumer responses to safety recalls are in addition to any other funds provided for those purposes for fiscal year 2023 in this Act.

Note.—A full-year 2022 appropriation for this account was not enacted at the time the Budget was prepared; therefore, the Budget assumes this account is operating under the Continuing Appropriations Act, 2022 (Division A of Public Law 117–43, as amended). The amounts included for 2022 reflect the annualized level provided by the continuing resolution.

Program and Financing (in millions of dollars)

Identification code 069–8016–0–7–401	2021 actual	2022 est.	2023 est.
Obligations by program activity:			
0001 Sec. 403 - Highway Safety Research & Development	147	150	190
0002 National Driver Register	5	5	7
0100 Total Direct Obligations	152	155	197
0799 Total direct obligations	152	155	197
0801 Operations and Research (Transportation Trust Fund) (Reimbursable)	6	5	5
0900 Total new obligations, unexpired accounts	158	160	202
Budgetary resources:			
Unobligated balance:			
1000 Unobligated balance brought forward, Oct 1	25	28	66
1001 Discretionary unobligated balance brought fwd, Oct 1	10		
1021 Recoveries of prior year unpaid obligations	3		
1070 Unobligated balance (total)	28	28	66
Budget authority:			
Appropriations, discretionary:			
1101 Appropriation (special or trust)	155	155	197
1138 Appropriations applied to liquidate contract authority	–155	–155	–197
Contract authority, mandatory:			
1600 Contract authority	155	193	197
Spending authority from offsetting collections, discretionary:			
1700 Collected	3	5	5
1900 Budget authority (total)	158	198	202
1930 Total budgetary resources available	186	226	268
Memorandum (non-add) entries:			
1941 Unexpired unobligated balance, end of year	28	66	66
Change in obligated balance:			
Unpaid obligations:			
3000 Unpaid obligations, brought forward, Oct 1	150	154	126
3010 New obligations, unexpired accounts	158	160	202
3020 Outlays (gross)	–151	–188	–199
3040 Recoveries of prior year unpaid obligations, unexpired	–3		
3050 Unpaid obligations, end of year	154	126	129
Memorandum (non-add) entries:			
3100 Obligated balance, start of year	150	154	126
3200 Obligated balance, end of year	154	126	129
Budget authority and outlays, net:			
Discretionary:			
4000 Budget authority, gross	3	5	5
Outlays, gross:			
4010 Outlays from new discretionary authority	74	76	96
4011 Outlays from discretionary balances	77	112	103
4020 Outlays, gross (total)	151	188	199
Offsets against gross budget authority and outlays:			
Offsetting collections (collected) from:			
4030 Federal sources	–3	–5	–5
4040 Offsets against gross budget authority and outlays (total)	–3	–5	–5
Mandatory:			
4090 Budget authority, gross	155	193	197
4180 Budget authority, net (total)	155	193	197

		2021 actual	2022 est.	2023 est.
4190	Outlays, net (total)	148	183	194
	Memorandum (non-add) entries:			
5054	Fund balance in excess of liquidating requirements, SOY:			
	Contract authority	46	47	9
5055	Fund balance in excess of liquidating requirements, EOY:			
	Contract authority	47	9	9
5061	Limitation on obligations (Transportation Trust Funds)	155	155	197

Summary of Budget Authority and Outlays (in millions of dollars)

	2021 actual	2022 est.	2023 est.
Enacted/requested:			
Budget Authority	155	193	197
Outlays	148	183	194
Amounts included in the adjusted baseline:			
Outlays		18	14
Total:			
Budget Authority	155	193	197
Outlays	148	201	208

The Highway Safety Research and Development programs support research, demonstrations, evaluation, technical assistance, and national leadership activities for behavioral safety programs conducted by State and local governments, as well as various safety associations and organizations. These programs are designed to provide our State and local partners with the latest tools to combat impaired, distracted, and drowsy driving while encouraging occupant protection, pedestrian and bicycle safety, and development of best practices for emergency medical and trauma care systems as part of a comprehensive highway and traffic safety system. This funding supports the National Driver Register's Problem Driver Pointer System, which helps to identify drivers who have been suspended for or convicted of serious traffic offenses, such as driving under the influence of alcohol or other drugs. Finally, this funding will allow NHTSA to improve its vital data collection and analysis, which drives all of the agency's safety activities.

Object Classification (in millions of dollars)

Identification code 069–8016–0–7–401		2021 actual	2022 est.	2023 est.
	Direct obligations:			
	Personnel compensation:			
11.1	Full-time permanent	22	26	30
11.1	Full-time permanent		1	1
11.5	Other personnel compensation	1	1	1
11.9	Total personnel compensation	23	28	32
12.1	Civilian personnel benefits	8	7	14
12.1	Civilian personnel benefits			1
23.1	Rental payments to GSA	3	2	2
25.1	Advisory and assistance services	75	75	101
25.2	Other services from non-Federal sources	1	1	1
25.3	Other goods and services from Federal sources	19	19	19
41.0	Grants, subsidies, and contributions	23	23	27
99.0	Direct obligations	152	155	197
99.0	Reimbursable obligations	6	5	5
99.9	Total new obligations, unexpired accounts	158	160	202

Employment Summary

Identification code 069–8016–0–7–401	2021 actual	2022 est.	2023 est.
1001 Direct civilian full-time equivalent employment	171	166	221
1001 Direct civilian full-time equivalent employment		9	11

OPERATIONS AND RESEARCH (HIGHWAY TRUST FUND)

(Amounts included in the adjusted baseline)

Program and Financing (in millions of dollars)

Identification code 069–8016–7–7–401		2021 actual	2022 est.	2023 est.
	Obligations by program activity:			
0001	Sec. 403 - Highway Safety Research & Development		36	
0002	National Driver Register		2	
0100	Total Direct Obligations		38	
0799	Total direct obligations		38	
0900	Total new obligations, unexpired accounts		38	
	Budgetary resources:			
	Unobligated balance:			
1000	Unobligated balance brought forward, Oct 1			–38
	Budget authority:			
	Appropriations, discretionary:			
1101	Appropriation (special or trust)		38	
1138	Appropriations applied to liquidate contract authority		–38	
1930	Total budgetary resources available			–38
	Memorandum (non-add) entries:			
1941	Unexpired unobligated balance, end of year		–38	–38
	Change in obligated balance:			
	Unpaid obligations:			
3000	Unpaid obligations, brought forward, Oct 1			20
3010	New obligations, unexpired accounts		38	
3020	Outlays (gross)		–18	–14
3050	Unpaid obligations, end of year		20	6
	Memorandum (non-add) entries:			
3100	Obligated balance, start of year			20
3200	Obligated balance, end of year		20	6
	Budget authority and outlays, net:			
	Discretionary:			
	Outlays, gross:			
4010	Outlays from new discretionary authority		18	
4011	Outlays from discretionary balances			14
4020	Outlays, gross (total)		18	14
4180	Budget authority, net (total)			
4190	Outlays, net (total)		18	14
	Memorandum (non-add) entries:			
5061	Limitation on obligations (Transportation Trust Funds)		38	

Object Classification (in millions of dollars)

Identification code 069–8016–7–7–401		2021 actual	2022 est.	2023 est.
11.1	Direct obligations: Personnel compensation: Full-time permanent		2	
11.9	Total personnel compensation		2	
25.1	Advisory and assistance services		29	
25.3	Other goods and services from Federal sources		2	
41.0	Grants, subsidies, and contributions		5	
99.0	Direct obligations		38	
99.9	Total new obligations, unexpired accounts		38	

Employment Summary

Identification code 069–8016–7–7–401	2021 actual	2022 est.	2023 est.
1001 Direct civilian full-time equivalent employment		15	
1001 Direct civilian full-time equivalent employment		1	

HIGHWAY TRAFFIC SAFETY GRANTS

(LIQUIDATION OF CONTRACT AUTHORIZATION)

(LIMITATION ON OBLIGATIONS)

(HIGHWAY TRUST FUND)

For payment of obligations incurred in carrying out provisions of 23 U.S.C. 402, 404, and 405, and grant administrative expenses under chapter 4 of title 23, United States Code, to remain available until expended, $795,220,000, to be derived from the Highway Trust Fund (other than the Mass Transit Account): Provided, That none of the funds in this Act shall be available for the planning or execution of programs for which the total obligations in fiscal year 2023 are in excess of $795,220,000 for programs authorized under 23 U.S.C. 402, 404, and 405, and grant administrative expenses under chapter 4 of title 23, United States Code: Provided further, That of the sums appropriated under this heading—

HIGHWAY TRAFFIC SAFETY GRANTS—Continued

(1) $370,990,000 shall be for "Highway Safety Programs" under 23 U.S.C. 402;

(2) $346,500,000 shall be for "National Priority Safety Programs" under 23 U.S.C. 405;

(3) $38,300,000 shall be for the "High Visibility Enforcement Program" under 23 U.S.C. 404; and

(4) $39,520,000 shall be for grant administrative expenses under chapter 4 of title 23, United States Code:

Provided further, That none of these funds shall be used for construction, rehabilitation, or remodeling costs, or for office furnishings and fixtures for State, local or private buildings or structures: Provided further, That not to exceed $500,000 of the funds made available for "National Priority Safety Programs" under 23 U.S.C. 405 for "Impaired Driving Countermeasures" (as described in subsection (d) of that section) shall be available for technical assistance to the States: Provided further, That with respect to the "Transfers" provision under 23 U.S.C. 405(a)(8), any amounts transferred to increase the amounts made available under section 402 shall include the obligation authority for such amounts: Provided further, That the Administrator shall notify the House and Senate Committees on Appropriations of any exercise of the authority granted under the previous proviso or under 23 U.S.C. 405(a)(8) within 5 days.

Note.—A full-year 2022 appropriation for this account was not enacted at the time the Budget was prepared; therefore, the Budget assumes this account is operating under the Continuing Appropriations Act, 2022 (Division A of Public Law 117–43, as amended). The amounts included for 2022 reflect the annualized level provided by the continuing resolution.

Program and Financing (in millions of dollars)

Identification code 069–8020–0–7–401		2021 actual	2022 est.	2023 est.
	Obligations by program activity:			
0001	Sec. 402 - Highway Safety Programs	293	280	371
0002	Sec. 404 - High-visibility Enforcement Program	31	31	38
0003	Sec. 405 - National Priority Safety Programs	272	285	347
0004	Administrative Expenses	26	27	39
0005	Sec. 154 / Sec. 164 Transfer from FHWA	105	99	....
0900	Total new obligations, unexpired accounts	727	722	795
	Budgetary resources:			
	Unobligated balance:			
1000	Unobligated balance brought forward, Oct 1	178	182	361
1021	Recoveries of prior year unpaid obligations	3	1	1
1070	Unobligated balance (total)	181	183	362
	Budget authority:			
	Appropriations, discretionary:			
1101	Appropriation (special or trust)	623	623	795
1121	Appropriations transferred from other acct [069–8083]	105	99	....
1138	Appropriations applied to liquidate contract authority	–728	–722	–795
	Contract authority, mandatory:			
1600	Contract authority	623	774	795
1611	Contract authority transferred from other accounts [069–8083]	105	126	....
1640	Contract authority, mandatory (total)	728	900	795
1900	Budget authority (total)	728	900	795
1930	Total budgetary resources available	909	1,083	1,157
	Memorandum (non-add) entries:			
1941	Unexpired unobligated balance, end of year	182	361	362
	Change in obligated balance:			
	Unpaid obligations:			
3000	Unpaid obligations, brought forward, Oct 1	1,016	1,047	938
3010	New obligations, unexpired accounts	727	722	795
3020	Outlays (gross)	–693	–830	–797
3040	Recoveries of prior year unpaid obligations, unexpired	–3	–1	–1
3050	Unpaid obligations, end of year	1,047	938	935
	Memorandum (non-add) entries:			
3100	Obligated balance, start of year	1,016	1,047	938
3200	Obligated balance, end of year	1,047	938	935
	Budget authority and outlays, net:			
	Discretionary:			
	Outlays, gross:			
4010	Outlays from new discretionary authority	101	133	158
4011	Outlays from discretionary balances	592	697	639
4020	Outlays, gross (total)	693	830	797
	Mandatory:			
4090	Budget authority, gross	728	900	795
4180	Budget authority, net (total)	728	900	795
4190	Outlays, net (total)	693	830	797
	Memorandum (non-add) entries:			
5052	Obligated balance, SOY: Contract authority			100
5053	Obligated balance, EOY: Contract authority		100	100
5054	Fund balance in excess of liquidating requirements, SOY: Contract authority	78	78	
5055	Fund balance in excess of liquidating requirements, EOY: Contract authority	78		
5061	Limitation on obligations (Transportation Trust Funds)	728	722	795

Summary of Budget Authority and Outlays (in millions of dollars)

	2021 actual	2022 est.	2023 est.
Enacted/requested:			
Budget Authority	728	900	795
Outlays	693	830	797
Amounts included in the adjusted baseline:			
Outlays		36	92
Total:			
Budget Authority	728	900	795
Outlays	693	866	889

NHTSA provides grants to States for activities related to highway traffic safety. The State and Community Safety Grants Program (Section 402) supports multi-faceted State highway safety programs designed to reduce traffic crashes and the resulting deaths, injuries, and property damage. The Agency will continue to implement the use of performance measures and data-driven targets as a condition of approval in these programs and to ensure efficient and effective use of funds. NHTSA also will use dedicated funds from the program to support high visibility enforcement campaigns that promote the use of seat belts and the reduction of impaired and distracted driving. The National Priority Safety Programs (Section 405) allow the Agency to make grant awards to States to address national priorities, such as impaired driving, occupant protection, distracted driving, nonmotorized safety, among others.

Object Classification (in millions of dollars)

Identification code 069–8020–0–7–401		2021 actual	2022 est.	2023 est.
	Direct obligations:			
11.1	Personnel compensation: Full-time permanent	10	12	13
12.1	Civilian personnel benefits	4	5	6
23.1	Rental payments to GSA	1	1	1
25.1	Advisory and assistance services	41	40	51
25.2	Other services from non-Federal sources	1	1	1
25.3	Other goods and services from Federal sources	5	5	5
41.0	Grants, subsidies, and contributions	665	658	718
99.9	Total new obligations, unexpired accounts	727	722	795

Employment Summary

Identification code 069–8020–0–7–401	2021 actual	2022 est.	2023 est.
1001 Direct civilian full-time equivalent employment	82	88	96

HIGHWAY TRAFFIC SAFETY GRANTS

(Amounts included in the adjusted baseline)

Program and Financing (in millions of dollars)

Identification code 069–8020–7–7–401		2021 actual	2022 est.	2023 est.
	Obligations by program activity:			
0001	Sec. 402 - Highway Safety Programs		83	
0002	Sec. 404 - High-visibility Enforcement Program		5	
0003	Sec. 405 - National Priority Safety Programs		52	
0004	Administrative Expenses		11	
0005	Sec. 154 / Sec. 164 Transfer from FHWA		27	
0900	Total new obligations, unexpired accounts		178	
	Budgetary resources:			
	Unobligated balance:			
1000	Unobligated balance brought forward, Oct 1			–178

		2021 actual	2022 est.	2023 est.
	Budget authority:			
	Appropriations, discretionary:			
1101	Appropriation (special or trust)		151	
1121	Appropriations transferred from other acct [069–8083]		27	
1138	Appropriations applied to liquidate contract authority		–178	
1930	Total budgetary resources available			–178
	Memorandum (non-add) entries:			
1941	Unexpired unobligated balance, end of year		–178	–178
	Change in obligated balance:			
	Unpaid obligations:			
3000	Unpaid obligations, brought forward, Oct 1			142
3010	New obligations, unexpired accounts		178	
3020	Outlays (gross)		–36	–92
3050	Unpaid obligations, end of year		142	50
	Memorandum (non-add) entries:			
3100	Obligated balance, start of year			142
3200	Obligated balance, end of year		142	50
	Budget authority and outlays, net:			
	Discretionary:			
	Outlays, gross:			
4010	Outlays from new discretionary authority		36	
4011	Outlays from discretionary balances			92
4020	Outlays, gross (total)		36	92
4180	Budget authority, net (total)			
4190	Outlays, net (total)		36	92
	Memorandum (non-add) entries:			
5052	Obligated balance, SOY: Contract authority			–100
5053	Obligated balance, EOY: Contract authority		–100	–100
5054	Fund balance in excess of liquidating requirements, SOY: Contract authority			78
5055	Fund balance in excess of liquidating requirements, EOY: Contract authority		78	78
5061	Limitation on obligations (Transportation Trust Funds)		178	

Object Classification (in millions of dollars)

Identification code 069–8020–7–7–401	2021 actual	2022 est.	2023 est.
Direct obligations:			
25.2 Other services from non-Federal sources		17	
41.0 Grants, subsidies, and contributions		161	
99.9 Total new obligations, unexpired accounts		178	

Employment Summary

Identification code 069–8020–7–7–401	2021 actual	2022 est.	2023 est.
1001 Direct civilian full-time equivalent employment		2	

ADMINISTRATIVE PROVISIONS

SEC. 140. An additional $130,000 shall be made available to the National Highway Traffic Safety Administration, out of the amount limited for section 402 of title 23, United States Code, to pay for travel and related expenses for State management reviews and to pay for core competency development training and related expenses for highway safety staff.

SEC. 141. The limitations on obligations for the programs of the National Highway Traffic Safety Administration set in this Act shall not apply to obligations for which obligation authority was made available in previous public laws but only to the extent that the obligation authority has not lapsed or been used.

SEC. 142. None of the funds in this Act or any other Act shall be used to enforce the requirements of section 405(a)(9) of title 23, United States Code.

FEDERAL RAILROAD ADMINISTRATION

The Federal Railroad Administration (FRA) oversees the safety of the U.S. railroad industry by carrying out a robust regulatory enforcement and technical assistance program. FRA also administers a broad portfolio of grants aimed at improving safety and the condition of the Nations rail infrastructure, while enhancing the operating performance of both intercity passenger and freight rail service. Finally, these railroad safety and investment programs are supported by research and development, through which FRA advances technology innovations and new practices to improve rail safety and efficiency.

Federal Funds

SAFETY AND OPERATIONS

For necessary expenses of the Federal Railroad Administration, not otherwise provided for, $254,426,000, of which $25,000,000 shall remain available until expended.

Note.—A full-year 2022 appropriation for this account was not enacted at the time the Budget was prepared; therefore, the Budget assumes this account is operating under the Continuing Appropriations Act, 2022 (Division A of Public Law 117–43, as amended). The amounts included for 2022 reflect the annualized level provided by the continuing resolution.

Program and Financing (in millions of dollars)

Identification code 069–0700–0–1–401	2021 actual	2022 est.	2023 est.
Obligations by program activity:			
0001 Safety and Operations	222	234	253
0006 Alaska railroad liabilities	1	1	1
0100 Total direct program	223	235	254
0799 Total direct obligations	223	235	254
0801 Reimbursable services	1		
0900 Total new obligations, unexpired accounts	224	235	254
Budgetary resources:			
Unobligated balance:			
1000 Unobligated balance brought forward, Oct 1	28	42	42
1021 Recoveries of prior year unpaid obligations	4		
1070 Unobligated balance (total)	32	42	42
Budget authority:			
Appropriations, discretionary:			
1100 Appropriation	235	235	254
1900 Budget authority (total)	235	235	254
1930 Total budgetary resources available	267	277	296
Memorandum (non-add) entries:			
1940 Unobligated balance expiring	–1		
1941 Unexpired unobligated balance, end of year	42	42	42
Change in obligated balance:			
Unpaid obligations:			
3000 Unpaid obligations, brought forward, Oct 1	101	103	56
3010 New obligations, unexpired accounts	224	235	254
3011 Obligations ("upward adjustments"), expired accounts	1		
3020 Outlays (gross)	–225	–282	–256
3031 Unpaid obligations transferred from other accts [070–0413]	10		
3040 Recoveries of prior year unpaid obligations, unexpired	–4		
3041 Recoveries of prior year unpaid obligations, expired	–4		
3050 Unpaid obligations, end of year	103	56	54
Memorandum (non-add) entries:			
3100 Obligated balance, start of year	101	103	56
3200 Obligated balance, end of year	103	56	54
Budget authority and outlays, net:			
Discretionary:			
4000 Budget authority, gross	235	235	254
Outlays, gross:			
4010 Outlays from new discretionary authority	173	188	203
4011 Outlays from discretionary balances	52	94	53
4020 Outlays, gross (total)	225	282	256
4180 Budget authority, net (total)	235	235	254
4190 Outlays, net (total)	225	282	256

Funds requested in the Safety and Operations account support the Federal Railroad Administration's (FRA) personnel and administrative expenses, the cost of rail safety inspectors, and other program activities including contracts. Resources are also provided to fund information management, technology, safety education, and outreach.

940   Federal Railroad Administration—Continued
Federal Funds—Continued

THE BUDGET FOR FISCAL YEAR 2023

SAFETY AND OPERATIONS—Continued

Object Classification (in millions of dollars)

Identification code 069–0700–0–1–401	2021 actual	2022 est.	2023 est.
Direct obligations:			
Personnel compensation:			
11.1 Full-time permanent	98	104	113
11.3 Other than full-time permanent	1	1	1
11.5 Other personnel compensation	3	3	3
11.9 Total personnel compensation	102	108	117
12.1 Civilian personnel benefits	38	40	45
21.0 Travel and transportation of persons	7	10	11
23.1 Rental payments to GSA	5	3	5
23.3 Communications, utilities, and miscellaneous charges	1	1	
24.0 Printing and reproduction	1	1	1
25.1 Advisory and assistance services	46	52	49
25.3 Other goods and services from Federal sources	21	18	23
25.4 Operation and maintenance of facilities	1	1	1
25.7 Operation and maintenance of equipment			1
26.0 Supplies and materials			1
41.0 Grants, subsidies, and contributions	1	1	
99.0 Direct obligations	223	235	254
99.0 Reimbursable obligations	1		
99.9 Total new obligations, unexpired accounts	224	235	254

Employment Summary

Identification code 069–0700–0–1–401	2021 actual	2022 est.	2023 est.
1001 Direct civilian full-time equivalent employment	857	856	915

RAILROAD SAFETY GRANTS

Program and Financing (in millions of dollars)

Identification code 069–0702–0–1–401	2021 actual	2022 est.	2023 est.
Obligations by program activity:			
0001 Rail Safety Grants	....	1	....
0900 Total new obligations, unexpired accounts (object class 41.0)	....	1	....
Budgetary resources:			
Unobligated balance:			
1000 Unobligated balance brought forward, Oct 1	5	6	5
1021 Recoveries of prior year unpaid obligations	1	....	....
1070 Unobligated balance (total)	6	6	5
1930 Total budgetary resources available	6	6	5
Memorandum (non-add) entries:			
1941 Unexpired unobligated balance, end of year	6	5	5
Change in obligated balance:			
Unpaid obligations:			
3000 Unpaid obligations, brought forward, Oct 1	23	16	3
3010 New obligations, unexpired accounts	....	1	....
3020 Outlays (gross)	–6	–14	–3
3040 Recoveries of prior year unpaid obligations, unexpired	–1	....	....
3050 Unpaid obligations, end of year	16	3	....
Memorandum (non-add) entries:			
3100 Obligated balance, start of year	23	16	3
3200 Obligated balance, end of year	16	3	....
Budget authority and outlays, net:			
Discretionary:			
Outlays, gross:			
4011 Outlays from discretionary balances	6	14	3
4180 Budget authority, net (total)	....	....	....
4190 Outlays, net (total)	6	14	3

In 2016, $50 million was appropriated under the Railroad Safety Grants heading to be equally distributed to Railroad Safety Infrastructure Improvement Grants and Railroad Safety Technology Grants. The Fixing America's Surface Transportation (FAST) Act of 2015 (P.L. 114–94) repealed the Railroad Safety Infrastructure Improvement Grants program and did not authorize new funding for the Railroad Safety Technology Grants program. No new funds are requested for this account for 2023.

RAILROAD RESEARCH AND DEVELOPMENT

For necessary expenses for railroad research and development, $58,000,000, to remain available until expended: Provided, that of the amounts provided under this heading, up to $3,000,000 shall be available pursuant to section 20108(d) of title 49, United States Code, for the construction, alteration, and repair of buildings and improvements at the Transportation Technology Center.

Note.—A full-year 2022 appropriation for this account was not enacted at the time the Budget was prepared; therefore, the Budget assumes this account is operating under the Continuing Appropriations Act, 2022 (Division A of Public Law 117–43, as amended). The amounts included for 2022 reflect the annualized level provided by the continuing resolution.

Program and Financing (in millions of dollars)

Identification code 069–0745–0–1–401	2021 actual	2022 est.	2023 est.
Obligations by program activity:			
0001 Railroad system issues	7	9	20
0002 Human factors	6	6	7
0011 Planning	....	1	....
0012 Track Program	13	11	12
0013 Rolling Stock Program	10	12	10
0014 Train Control and Communication	8	8	9
0100 Total direct program	44	47	58
0799 Total direct obligations	44	47	58
0900 Total new obligations, unexpired accounts	44	47	58
Budgetary resources:			
Unobligated balance:			
1000 Unobligated balance brought forward, Oct 1	10	9	3
1021 Recoveries of prior year unpaid obligations	2	....	....
1070 Unobligated balance (total)	12	9	3
Budget authority:			
Appropriations, discretionary:			
1100 Appropriation	41	41	58
1900 Budget authority (total)	41	41	58
1930 Total budgetary resources available	53	50	61
Memorandum (non-add) entries:			
1941 Unexpired unobligated balance, end of year	9	3	3
Change in obligated balance:			
Unpaid obligations:			
3000 Unpaid obligations, brought forward, Oct 1	61	64	67
3010 New obligations, unexpired accounts	44	47	58
3020 Outlays (gross)	–39	–44	–52
3040 Recoveries of prior year unpaid obligations, unexpired	–2	....	....
3050 Unpaid obligations, end of year	64	67	73
Memorandum (non-add) entries:			
3100 Obligated balance, start of year	61	64	67
3200 Obligated balance, end of year	64	67	73
Budget authority and outlays, net:			
Discretionary:			
4000 Budget authority, gross	41	41	58
Outlays, gross:			
4010 Outlays from new discretionary authority	12	10	14
4011 Outlays from discretionary balances	27	34	38
4020 Outlays, gross (total)	39	44	52
4180 Budget authority, net (total)	41	41	58
4190 Outlays, net (total)	39	44	52

Funding requested in the Railroad Research and Development Program is focused on improving railroad safety. It provides scientific and engineering support for the Federal Railroad Administration's rail safety enforcement and rulemaking efforts. It also identifies and develops emerging technologies for the rail industry to adopt voluntarily. The outcomes of the research and development reduce accidents and incidents. In addition to improving safety, the program contributes significantly towards activities to achieve and maintain a state of good repair, promote job creation and economic growth, and improve energy efficiency and reduce emissions of rail transportation.

DEPARTMENT OF TRANSPORTATION

Federal Railroad Administration—Continued
Federal Funds—Continued

941

The program focuses on the following areas of research:

Track Program.—Reducing derailments due to track related causes.

Rolling Stock Program.—Reducing derailments due to equipment failures, to minimize the consequences of derailments, and to minimize hazardous material releases.

Train Control and Communication.—Reducing train to train collisions and train collisions with objects on the line and at grade crossings.

Human Factors Program.—Reducing accidents caused by human error.

Railroad System Issues Program.—Prioritizing Research and Development projects on the basis of relevance to safety risk reduction and other DOT goals, energy and emissions research, and workforce development.

Object Classification (in millions of dollars)

Identification code 069–0745–0–1–401		2021 actual	2022 est.	2023 est.
	Direct obligations:			
25.1	Advisory and assistance services	2	1	4
25.4	Operation and maintenance of facilities	1	1	3
25.5	Research and development contracts	38	43	48
41.0	Grants, subsidies, and contributions	3	2	3
99.0	Direct obligations	44	47	58
99.9	Total new obligations, unexpired accounts	44	47	58

RESTORATION AND ENHANCEMENT

For necessary expenses related to Restoration and Enhancement Grants, as authorized by section 22908 of title 49, United States Code, $50,000,000, to remain available until expended: Provided, That amounts made available under this heading in previous fiscal years are subject to section 22908 of title 49, United States Code, as in effect on the effective date of the Infrastructure Investment and Jobs Act (Public Law 117–58): Provided further, That the limitation in subsection 22908(e)(2) of title 49, United States Code, shall not apply to amounts made available in this or any prior Act for grants under 22908 of title 49: Provided further, That the Secretary may withhold up to 1 percent of the funds provided under this heading to fund the costs of award and project management oversight of grants carried out under title 49, United States Code.

Note.—A full-year 2022 appropriation for this account was not enacted at the time the Budget was prepared; therefore, the Budget assumes this account is operating under the Continuing Appropriations Act, 2022 (Division A of Public Law 117–43, as amended). The amounts included for 2022 reflect the annualized level provided by the continuing resolution.

Program and Financing (in millions of dollars)

Identification code 069–0127–0–1–401		2021 actual	2022 est.	2023 est.
	Obligations by program activity:			
0001	R&E Grants		5	15
0900	Total new obligations, unexpired accounts (object class 41.0)		5	15
	Budgetary resources:			
	Unobligated balance:			
1000	Unobligated balance brought forward, Oct 1	32	37	37
	Budget authority:			
	Appropriations, discretionary:			
1100	Appropriation	5	5	50
1930	Total budgetary resources available	37	42	87
	Memorandum (non-add) entries:			
1941	Unexpired unobligated balance, end of year	37	37	72
	Change in obligated balance:			
	Unpaid obligations:			
3000	Unpaid obligations, brought forward, Oct 1			5
3010	New obligations, unexpired accounts		5	15
3020	Outlays (gross)			–1
3050	Unpaid obligations, end of year		5	19
	Memorandum (non-add) entries:			
3100	Obligated balance, start of year			5
3200	Obligated balance, end of year		5	19
	Budget authority and outlays, net:			
	Discretionary:			
4000	Budget authority, gross		5	5	50
	Outlays, gross:			
4011	Outlays from discretionary balances			1
4180	Budget authority, net (total)	5	5	50
4190	Outlays, net (total)			1

Restoration and Enhancement Grants provide operating assistance to initiate, restore, or enhance intercity passenger rail transportation. The program limits assistance to six years per route.. Eligible recipients include States (including interstate compacts); local governments; Amtrak or other rail carriers that provide intercity passenger rail service; federally recognized Indian Tribes; and any rail carrier in partnership with another eligible public-sector applicant.

MAGNETIC LEVITATION TECHNOLOGY DEPLOYMENT PROGRAM

Note.—A full-year 2022 appropriation for this account was not enacted at the time the Budget was prepared; therefore, the Budget assumes this account is operating under the Continuing Appropriations Act, 2022 (Division A of Public Law 117–43, as amended). The amounts included for 2022 reflect the annualized level provided by the continuing resolution.

Program and Financing (in millions of dollars)

Identification code 069–0129–0–1–401		2021 actual	2022 est.	2023 est.
	Obligations by program activity:			
0001	Magnetic Levitation Technology Deployment Grants			10
0900	Total new obligations, unexpired accounts (object class 41.0)			10
	Budgetary resources:			
	Unobligated balance:			
1000	Unobligated balance brought forward, Oct 1	12	14	16
	Budget authority:			
	Appropriations, discretionary:			
1100	Appropriation	2	2	
1930	Total budgetary resources available	14	16	16
	Memorandum (non-add) entries:			
1941	Unexpired unobligated balance, end of year	14	16	6
	Change in obligated balance:			
	Unpaid obligations:			
3010	New obligations, unexpired accounts			10
3050	Unpaid obligations, end of year			10
	Memorandum (non-add) entries:			
3200	Obligated balance, end of year			10
	Budget authority and outlays, net:			
	Discretionary:			
4000	Budget authority, gross	2	2	
4180	Budget authority, net (total)	2	2	
4190	Outlays, net (total)			

The Magnetic Levitation Technology Deployment Program provides grants to states to fund eligible capital costs and preconstruction planning activities that support the deployment of magnetic levitation (maglev) transportation projects. No new funds are requested for this account for 2023.

GRANTS TO THE NATIONAL RAILROAD PASSENGER CORPORATION

Program and Financing (in millions of dollars)

Identification code 069–0704–0–1–401		2021 actual	2022 est.	2023 est.
	Obligations by program activity:			
0007	Capital And Debt Grant Sandy Mitigation		32	
0900	Total new obligations, unexpired accounts (object class 41.0)		32	
	Budgetary resources:			
	Unobligated balance:			
1000	Unobligated balance brought forward, Oct 1	32	32	
1930	Total budgetary resources available	32	32	
	Memorandum (non-add) entries:			
1941	Unexpired unobligated balance, end of year	32		

GRANTS TO THE NATIONAL RAILROAD PASSENGER CORPORATION—Continued

Program and Financing—Continued

Identification code 069–0704–0–1–401	2021 actual	2022 est.	2023 est.
Change in obligated balance:			
Unpaid obligations:			
3000 Unpaid obligations, brought forward, Oct 1	13	13	37
3010 New obligations, unexpired accounts		32	
3020 Outlays (gross)		–8	–13
3050 Unpaid obligations, end of year	13	37	24
Memorandum (non-add) entries:			
3100 Obligated balance, start of year	13	13	37
3200 Obligated balance, end of year	13	37	24
Budget authority and outlays, net:			
Discretionary:			
Outlays, gross:			
4011 Outlays from discretionary balances		8	13
4180 Budget authority, net (total)			
4190 Outlays, net (total)		8	13

The National Railroad Passenger Corporation (Amtrak) was established in 1970 through the Rail Passenger Service Act. Amtrak is operated and managed as a for-profit corporation. Amtrak is not an agency or instrument of the U.S. Government, although, since the railroad's creation FRA has provided annual grants for operating, capital and debt service costs.

Prior to 2006, FRA received annual appropriations in this account for grants to Amtrak. Since then, several one-time appropriations or funding transfers have been directed to this account, including $1.3 billion in funds under the American Recovery and Reinvestment Act of 2009; $112 million from the Disaster Relief Appropriations Act of 2013 (P.L. 113–2) for recovery efforts from super storm Sandy; $185 million transfer from the Federal Transit Administration for the Hudson Yards disaster resiliency project in New York City; and a $13 million transfer from the Federal Transit Administration for the Metropolitan Transportation Authority/Long Island Rail Road's River to River Rail Resiliency project in New York City. No new funds are requested for this account for 2023.

CAPITAL AND DEBT SERVICE GRANTS TO THE NATIONAL RAILROAD PASSENGER CORPORATION

Program and Financing (in millions of dollars)

Identification code 069–0125–0–1–401	2021 actual	2022 est.	2023 est.
Budgetary resources:			
Unobligated balance:			
1000 Unobligated balance brought forward, Oct 1	10		
Budget authority:			
Appropriations, discretionary:			
1131 Unobligated balance of appropriations permanently reduced	–10		
Change in obligated balance:			
Unpaid obligations:			
3000 Unpaid obligations, brought forward, Oct 1	1	1	
3020 Outlays (gross)		–1	
3050 Unpaid obligations, end of year	1		
Memorandum (non-add) entries:			
3100 Obligated balance, start of year	1	1	
3200 Obligated balance, end of year	1		
Budget authority and outlays, net:			
Discretionary:			
4000 Budget authority, gross	–10		
Outlays, gross:			
4011 Outlays from discretionary balances		1	
4180 Budget authority, net (total)	–10		
4190 Outlays, net (total)		1	

From 2006 to 2016, the Federal Railroad Administration received appropriations to this account to make grants to the National Railroad Passenger Corporation (Amtrak) for capital investments and debt service assistance.

The FAST Act authorized two new appropriations accounts for Amtrak—Northeast Corridor grants and National Network grants—which first received funding in 2017. No new funds are requested for this account for 2023.

NATIONAL NETWORK GRANTS TO THE NATIONAL RAILROAD PASSENGER CORPORATION

To enable the Secretary of Transportation to make grants to the National Railroad Passenger Corporation for activities associated with the National Network as authorized by section 22101(b) of division B of the Infrastructure Investment and Jobs Act (Public Law 117–58), $1,800,000,000, to remain available until expended: Provided, That Amtrak may use up to $100,000,000 of the funds provided under this heading in this Act for corridor development activities authorized by section 22101(h) of division B of the Infrastructure Investment and Jobs Act (Public Law 117–58).

Note.—A full-year 2022 appropriation for this account was not enacted at the time the Budget was prepared; therefore, the Budget assumes this account is operating under the Continuing Appropriations Act, 2022 (Division A of Public Law 117–43, as amended). The amounts included for 2022 reflect the annualized level provided by the continuing resolution.

NATIONAL NETWORK GRANTS TO THE NATIONAL RAILROAD PASSENGER CORPORATION

[(INCLUDING TRANSFER OF FUNDS)]

[For an additional amount for "National Network Grants to the National Railroad Passenger Corporation", $16,000,000,000, to remain available until expended, for activities associated with the National Network, as authorized by section 22101(b) of division B of this Act: *Provided*, That $3,200,000,000, to remain available until expended, shall be made available for fiscal year 2022, $3,200,000,000, to remain available until expended, shall be made available for fiscal year 2023, $3,200,000,000, to remain available until expended, shall be made available for fiscal year 2024, $3,200,000,000, to remain available until expended, shall be made available for fiscal year 2025, and $3,200,000,000, to remain available until expended, shall be made available for fiscal year 2026: *Provided further*, That amounts made available under this heading in this Act shall be made available for capital projects for the purpose of eliminating Amtrak's deferred maintenance backlog of rolling stock, facilities, stations and infrastructure, including—]

[(1) acquiring new passenger rolling stock to replace obsolete passenger equipment used in Amtrak's long-distance and state-supported services, and associated rehabilitation, upgrade, or expansion of facilities used to maintain and store such equipment;]

[(2) bringing Amtrak-served stations to full compliance with the Americans with Disabilities Act;]

[(3) eliminating the backlog of deferred capital work on Amtrak-owned railroad assets not located on the Northeast Corridor; and]

[(4) projects to eliminate the backlog of obsolete assets associated with Amtrak's national rail passenger transportation system, such as systems for reservations, security, training centers, and technology:]

[*Provided further*, That not later than 180 days after the date of enactment of this Act, the Secretary of Transportation shall submit to the House and Senate Committees on Appropriations a detailed spend plan, including a list of project locations under the preceding proviso to be funded for fiscal year 2022: *Provided further*, That for each fiscal year through 2026, as part of the annual budget submission of the President under section 1105(a) of title 31, United States Code, the Secretary of Transportation shall submit a detailed spend plan for that fiscal year, including a list of project locations under the third proviso: *Provided further*, That of the amounts made available under this heading in this Act, and in addition to amounts made available for similar purposes under this heading in prior Acts, Amtrak shall use such amounts as necessary for the replacement of single-level passenger cars and associated rehabilitation, upgrade, and expansion of facilities used to maintain and store such passenger cars, and such amounts shall be for its direct costs and in lieu of payments from States for such purposes, notwithstanding section 209 of the Passenger Rail Investment and Improvement Act of 2008 (Public Law 110–432), as amended: *Provided further*, That amounts made available under this heading in this Act shall be in addition to other amounts made available for such purposes, including to enable the Secretary of Transportation to make or amend existing grants to Amtrak for activities associated with the National Network, as authorized by section 22101(b) of division B of this Act: *Provided further*, That in addition to the oversight funds authorized under section 22101(c) of division B of this Act, the Secretary may retain up to $3,000,000 of the funds made available under this heading in this Act for each fiscal year for the State-Supported Route Committee established under section 24712(a) of title 49, United States Code: *Provided further*, That of

DEPARTMENT OF TRANSPORTATION

the funds made available under this heading in this Act, the Secretary may retain up to $3,000,000 for each fiscal year for interstate rail compact grants, as authorized by section 22910 of title 49, United States Code: *Provided further*, That of the funds made available under this heading in this Act, not less than $50,000,000 for each fiscal year shall be used to make grants, as authorized under section 22908 of title 49 United States Code consistent with the requirements of that section: *Provided further*, That of the amounts made available under this heading in this Act, such sums as are necessary, shall be available for purposes authorized in section 22214 of division B of this Act: *Provided further*, That amounts made available under this heading in this Act may be transferred to and merged with amounts made available under the heading "Northeast Corridor Grants to the National Railroad Passenger Corporation" in this Act for the purposes authorized under that heading: *Provided further*, That such amount is designated by the Congress as being for an emergency requirement pursuant to section 4112(a) of H. Con. Res. 71 (115th Congress), the concurrent resolution on the budget for fiscal year 2018, and to section 251(b) of the Balanced Budget and Emergency Deficit Control Act of 1985.] *(Infrastructure Investments and Jobs Appropriations Act.)*

Program and Financing (in millions of dollars)

Identification code 069–1775–0–1–401	2021 actual	2022 est.	2023 est.
Obligations by program activity:			
0001 Grants for National Network	1,953	1,223	1,788
0002 Management Oversight	7	7	2
0003 State Supported Route Committee		2	3
0004 Americans with Disabilities Act (ADA)	67	67	
0009 Grants for National Network (COVID)	344		
0010 Oversight for National Network (COVID)	1	1	
0011 Grants for National Network (IIJA Supp)		3,128	3,128
0013 State Supported Route Committee (IIJA Supp)		3	3
0014 Amtrak Restoration and Enhancement Grants (IIJA Supp)		50	50
0015 Interstate Rail Compact Grants ((IIJA Supp)		3	3
0900 Total new obligations, unexpired accounts	2,372	4,484	4,977
Budgetary resources:			
Unobligated balance:			
1000 Unobligated balance brought forward, Oct 1	5	8	8
1001 Discretionary unobligated balance brought fwd, Oct 1	5	8	
Budget authority:			
Appropriations, discretionary:			
1100 Appropriation	1,645	4,500	1,800
1120 Appropriations transferred to other acct [069–0759]		–16	–9
1160 Appropriation, discretionary (total)	1,645	4,484	1,791
Advance appropriations, discretionary:			
1170 Advance appropriation [Discretionary, IIJA of 2021, Appropriations Committee]			3,200
1172 Advance appropriations transferred to other accounts [069–0759]			–16
1180 Advanced appropriation, discretionary (total)			3,184
Appropriations, mandatory:			
1200 Appropriation	730		
1900 Budget authority (total)	2,375	4,484	4,975
1930 Total budgetary resources available	2,380	4,492	4,983
Memorandum (non-add) entries:			
1941 Unexpired unobligated balance, end of year	8	8	6
Change in obligated balance:			
Unpaid obligations:			
3000 Unpaid obligations, brought forward, Oct 1	11	9	16
3010 New obligations, unexpired accounts	2,372	4,484	4,977
3020 Outlays (gross)	–2,374	–4,477	–4,974
3050 Unpaid obligations, end of year	9	16	19
Memorandum (non-add) entries:			
3100 Obligated balance, start of year	11	9	16
3200 Obligated balance, end of year	9	16	19
Budget authority and outlays, net:			
Discretionary:			
4000 Budget authority, gross	1,645	4,484	4,975
Outlays, gross:			
4010 Outlays from new discretionary authority	1,638	4,476	4,964
4011 Outlays from discretionary balances	7	1	10
4020 Outlays, gross (total)	1,645	4,477	4,974
Mandatory:			
4090 Budget authority, gross	730		
Outlays, gross:			
4100 Outlays from new mandatory authority	729		
4180 Budget authority, net (total)	2,375	4,484	4,975

Federal Railroad Administration—Continued
Federal Funds—Continued

4190 Outlays, net (total)	2,374	4,477	4,974

The Fixing America's Surface Transportation Act authorized two new appropriations accounts for the National Railroad Passenger Corporation (Amtrak)—Northeast Corridor Grants and National Network Grants. Funds for the National Network Grants to the National Railroad Passenger Corporation account provide capital, operating, and debt service funding for Amtrak activities related to the National Network, which includes Amtrak's State-Supported services, Long Distance services, and other Amtrak costs not allocated to the Northeast Corridor. Amtrak began receiving its annual appropriations from the Congress under this account structure in 2017.

Object Classification (in millions of dollars)

Identification code 069–1775–0–1–401	2021 actual	2022 est.	2023 est.
Direct obligations:			
11.1 Personnel compensation: Full-time permanent	2	2	
12.1 Civilian personnel benefits	1	1	
25.1 Advisory and assistance services	4	4	2
25.7 Operation and maintenance of equipment	1		
41.0 Grants, subsidies, and contributions	2,364	4,477	4,975
99.9 Total new obligations, unexpired accounts	2,372	4,484	4,977

Employment Summary

Identification code 069–1775–0–1–401	2021 actual	2022 est.	2023 est.
1001 Direct civilian full-time equivalent employment	15	13	

NORTHEAST CORRIDOR GRANTS TO THE NATIONAL RAILROAD PASSENGER CORPORATION

To enable the Secretary of Transportation to make grants to the National Railroad Passenger Corporation for activities associated with the Northeast Corridor as authorized by section 22101(a) of division B of the Infrastructure Investment and Jobs Act (Public Law 117–58), $1,200,000,000, to remain available until expended: Provided, That the Secretary may retain up to one-half of 1 percent of the funds provided under both this heading and the "National Network Grants to the National Railroad Passenger Corporation" heading to fund the costs of project management and oversight of activities authorized by section 22101(c) of division B of the Infrastructure Investment and Jobs Act (Public Law 117–58): Provided further, That notwithstanding paragraphs (2) and (3) of section 24319(e) of title 49, United States Code, the Secretary shall make payments to Amtrak on a reimbursable basis for activities funded by grants under both this heading in this Act and the "National Network Grants to the National Railroad Passenger Corporation" heading in this Act that are defined in clauses (ii) through (v) of section 24319(c)(2)(C) and in section 24319(c)(2)(D): Provided further, That the Secretary may use an otherwise allowable approach to the payment method for the operations, services, programs, projects, and other activities identified in the previous proviso if the Secretary and Amtrak agree that a different payment method is necessary to successfully implement and report on an operation, service, program, project, or other activity.

Note.—A full-year 2022 appropriation for this account was not enacted at the time the Budget was prepared; therefore, the Budget assumes this account is operating under the Continuing Appropriations Act, 2022 (Division A of Public Law 117–43, as amended). The amounts included for 2022 reflect the annualized level provided by the continuing resolution.

NORTHEAST CORRIDOR GRANTS TO THE NATIONAL RAILROAD PASSENGER CORPORATION

[(INCLUDING TRANSFER OF FUNDS)]

[For an additional amount for "Northeast Corridor Grants to the National Railroad Passenger Corporation", $6,000,000,000, to remain available until expended, for activities associated with the Northeast Corridor, as authorized by section 22101(a) of division B of this Act: *Provided*, That $1,200,000,000, to remain available until expended, shall be made available for fiscal year 2022, $1,200,000,000, to remain available until expended, shall be made available for fiscal year 2023, $1,200,000,000, to remain available until expended, shall be made available for fiscal year 2024, $1,200,000,000, to remain available until expended, shall be made available for fiscal year 2025, and $1,200,000,000, to remain available until expended, shall be made available for fiscal year 2026: *Provided further*, That the amounts made available under this heading in this Act shall be made available for capital projects for the purpose of eliminating the backlog of obsolete assets and Amtrak's

NORTHEAST CORRIDOR GRANTS TO THE NATIONAL RAILROAD PASSENGER CORPORATION—Continued

deferred maintenance backlog of rolling stock, facilities, stations, and infrastructure: *Provided further,* That amounts made available under this heading in this Act shall be made available for the following capital projects—]

[(1) acquiring new passenger rolling stock for the replacement of single-level passenger cars used in Amtrak's Northeast Corridor services, and associated rehabilitation, upgrade, and expansion of facilities used to maintain and store such equipment;]

[(2) bringing Amtrak-served stations to full compliance with the Americans with Disabilities Act;]

[(3) eliminating the backlog of deferred capital work on sole-benefit Amtrak-owned assets located on the Northeast Corridor; or]

[(4) carrying out Northeast Corridor capital renewal backlog projects:]

[*Provided further,* That not later than 180 days after the date of enactment of this Act, the Secretary of Transportation shall submit to the House and Senate Committees on Appropriations a detailed spend plan, including a list of project locations under the preceding proviso to be funded for fiscal year 2022: *Provided further,* That for each fiscal year through 2026, as part of the annual budget submission of the President under section 1105(a) of title 31, United States Code, the Secretary of Transportation shall submit a detailed spend plan for that fiscal year, including a list of project locations under the third proviso: *Provided further,* That amounts made available under this heading in this Act shall be in addition to other amounts made available for such purposes, including to enable the Secretary of Transportation to make or amend existing grants to Amtrak for activities associated with the Northeast Corridor, as authorized by section 22101(a) of division B of this Act: *Provided further,* That amounts made available under this heading in this Act may be used by Amtrak to fund, in whole or in part, the capital costs of Northeast Corridor capital renewal backlog projects, including the costs of joint public transportation and intercity passenger rail capital projects, notwithstanding the limitations in section 24319(g) and section 24905(c) of title 49, United States Code: *Provided further,* That notwithstanding section 24911(f) of title 49, United States Code, amounts made available under this heading in this Act may be used as non-Federal share for Northeast Corridor projects selected for award under such section after the date of enactment of this Act: *Provided further,* That the Secretary may retain up to one half of 1 percent of the amounts made available under both this heading in this Act and the "National Network Grants to the National Railroad Passenger Corporation" heading in this Act to fund the costs of oversight of Amtrak, as authorized by section 22101(c) of division B of this Act: *Provided further,* That in addition to the oversight funds authorized under section 22101(c) of division B of this Act, the Secretary may retain up to $5,000,000 of the funds made available under this heading in this Act for each fiscal year for the Northeast Corridor Commission established under section 24905 of title 49, United States Code, to facilitate a coordinated and efficient delivery of projects carried out under this heading in this Act: *Provided further,* That amounts made available under this heading in this Act may be transferred to and merged with amounts made available under the heading "National Network Grants to the National Railroad Passenger Corporation" in this Act for the purposes authorized under that heading: *Provided further,* That such amount is designated by the Congress as being for an emergency requirement pursuant to section 4112(a) of H. Con. Res. 71 (115th Congress), the concurrent resolution on the budget for fiscal year 2018, and to section 251(b) of the Balanced Budget and Emergency Deficit Control Act of 1985.] *(Infrastructure Investments and Jobs Appropriations Act.)*

Program and Financing (in millions of dollars)

Identification code 069–1774–0–1–401		2021 actual	2022 est.	2023 est.
	Obligations by program activity:			
0001	Grants for Northeast Corridor	1,654	689	1,185
0002	Management Oversight	2	2	3
0003	Northeast Corridor Commission	10	5	6
0004	Americans with Disabilities Act (ADA)	7	8	....
0009	Grants for Northeast Corridor (COVID)	654	....	....
0010	Oversight for Northeast Corridor (COVID)	1	1	....
0011	Grants for Northeast Corridor (IIJA SUPP)	....	1,189	1,189
0013	Northeast Corridor Commission (IIJA SUPP)	....	5	5
0900	Total new obligations, unexpired accounts	2,328	1,899	2,388
	Budgetary resources:			
	Unobligated balance:			
1000	Unobligated balance brought forward, Oct 1	15	12	7
1001	Discretionary unobligated balance brought fwd, Oct 1	15		
	Budget authority:			
	Appropriations, discretionary:			
1100	Appropriation	1,355	1,900	1,200
1120	Appropriations transferred to other acct [069–0759]	....	–6	–6
1160	Appropriation, discretionary (total)	1,355	1,894	1,194
	Advance appropriations, discretionary:			
1170	Advance appropriation [Discretionary, IIJA of 2021, Appropriations Committee]	....	....	1,200
1172	Advance appropriations transferred to other accounts [069–0759]	....	....	–6
1180	Advanced appropriation, discretionary (total)	....	....	1,194
	Appropriations, mandatory:			
1200	Appropriation	970	....	....
1900	Budget authority (total)	2,325	1,894	2,388
1930	Total budgetary resources available	2,340	1,906	2,395
	Memorandum (non-add) entries:			
1941	Unexpired unobligated balance, end of year	12	7	7
	Change in obligated balance:			
	Unpaid obligations:			
3000	Unpaid obligations, brought forward, Oct 1	5	9	23
3010	New obligations, unexpired accounts	2,328	1,899	2,388
3020	Outlays (gross)	–2,324	–1,885	–2,379
3050	Unpaid obligations, end of year	9	23	32
	Memorandum (non-add) entries:			
3100	Obligated balance, start of year	5	9	23
3200	Obligated balance, end of year	9	23	32
	Budget authority and outlays, net:			
	Discretionary:			
4000	Budget authority, gross	1,355	1,894	2,388
	Outlays, gross:			
4010	Outlays from new discretionary authority	1,348	1,881	2,367
4011	Outlays from discretionary balances	7	4	12
4020	Outlays, gross (total)	1,355	1,885	2,379
	Mandatory:			
4090	Budget authority, gross	970	....	....
	Outlays, gross:			
4100	Outlays from new mandatory authority	969	....	....
4180	Budget authority, net (total)	2,325	1,894	2,388
4190	Outlays, net (total)	2,324	1,885	2,379

The Fixing America's Surface Transportation Act authorized two new appropriations accounts for the National Railroad Passenger Corporation (Amtrak)—Northeast Corridor Grants and National Network Grants. Funds for the Northeast Corridor Grants to the National Railroad Passenger Corporation account provide capital, operating, and debt service funding for Amtrak activities related to the Northeast Corridor. Amtrak began receiving its annual appropriations from Congress under this account structure in 2017.

Object Classification (in millions of dollars)

Identification code 069–1774–0–1–401		2021 actual	2022 est.	2023 est.
	Direct obligations:			
25.1	Advisory and assistance services	3	3	3
41.0	Grants, subsidies, and contributions	2,325	1,896	2,385
99.9	Total new obligations, unexpired accounts	2,328	1,899	2,388

INTERCITY PASSENGER RAIL GRANT PROGRAM

Program and Financing (in millions of dollars)

Identification code 069–0715–0–1–401		2021 actual	2022 est.	2023 est.
	Budgetary resources:			
	Unobligated balance:			
1000	Unobligated balance brought forward, Oct 1	10	....	....
	Budget authority:			
	Appropriations, discretionary:			
1131	Unobligated balance of appropriations permanently reduced	–10		
	Change in obligated balance:			
	Unpaid obligations:			
3000	Unpaid obligations, brought forward, Oct 1	10	7	2
3020	Outlays (gross)	–3	–5	–2
3050	Unpaid obligations, end of year	7	2	....

DEPARTMENT OF TRANSPORTATION

Federal Railroad Administration—Continued
Federal Funds—Continued
945

		2021 actual	2022 est.	2023 est.
	Memorandum (non-add) entries:			
3100	Obligated balance, start of year	10	7	2
3200	Obligated balance, end of year	7	2	
	Budget authority and outlays, net:			
	Discretionary:			
4000	Budget authority, gross	–10		
	Outlays, gross:			
4011	Outlays from discretionary balances	3	5	2
4180	Budget authority, net (total)	–10		
4190	Outlays, net (total)	3	5	2

This competitive grant program encourages State participation in passenger rail service. Under this program, a State or States may apply for grants for up to 50 percent of the cost of capital investments necessary to support improved intercity passenger rail service that either requires no operating subsidy or for which the State or States agree to provide any needed operating subsidy. To qualify for funding, States must include intercity passenger rail service as an integral part of statewide transportation planning as required under 23 U.S.C. 135. Additionally, the specific project must be on the Statewide Transportation Improvement Plan at the time of application. No new funds are requested for this account for 2023.

CAPITAL ASSISTANCE FOR HIGH SPEED RAIL CORRIDORS AND INTERCITY PASSENGER RAIL SERVICE

Program and Financing (in millions of dollars)

Identification code 069–0719–0–1–401		2021 actual	2022 est.	2023 est.
	Obligations by program activity:			
0003	Capital Assistance High-Speed Rail Corridors and IPR Service Grants	928		
0004	Capital Assistance High-Speed Rail Corridors and IPR Service Oversight	1		
0900	Total new obligations, unexpired accounts	929		
	Budgetary resources:			
	Unobligated balance:			
1000	Unobligated balance brought forward, Oct 1	992	67	67
1021	Recoveries of prior year unpaid obligations	4		
1070	Unobligated balance (total)	996	67	67
1930	Total budgetary resources available	996	67	67
	Memorandum (non-add) entries:			
1941	Unexpired unobligated balance, end of year	67	67	67
	Change in obligated balance:			
	Unpaid obligations:			
3000	Unpaid obligations, brought forward, Oct 1	302	1,215	1,174
3010	New obligations, unexpired accounts	929		
3020	Outlays (gross)	–12	–41	–56
3040	Recoveries of prior year unpaid obligations, unexpired	–4		
3050	Unpaid obligations, end of year	1,215	1,174	1,118
	Memorandum (non-add) entries:			
3100	Obligated balance, start of year	302	1,215	1,174
3200	Obligated balance, end of year	1,215	1,174	1,118
	Budget authority and outlays, net:			
	Discretionary:			
	Outlays, gross:			
4011	Outlays from discretionary balances	12	41	56
4180	Budget authority, net (total)			
4190	Outlays, net (total)	12	41	56

Through this program, FRA provides capital grants to States to invest and improve intercity passenger rail service, including the development of new high-speed rail capacity. This account received $8 billion provided by the American Recovery and Reinvestment Act of 2009 and an additional $2.1 billion provided in 2010. No new funds are requested for this account for 2023.

Object Classification (in millions of dollars)

Identification code 069–0719–0–1–401		2021 actual	2022 est.	2023 est.
	Direct obligations:			
25.1	Advisory and assistance services	1		
41.0	Grants, subsidies, and contributions	928		
99.9	Total new obligations, unexpired accounts	929		

NEXT GENERATION HIGH-SPEED RAIL

Program and Financing (in millions of dollars)

Identification code 069–0722–0–1–401		2021 actual	2022 est.	2023 est.
	Budgetary resources:			
	Unobligated balance:			
1000	Unobligated balance brought forward, Oct 1	3		
	Budget authority:			
	Appropriations, discretionary:			
1131	Unobligated balance of appropriations permanently reduced	–3		
	Change in obligated balance:			
	Unpaid obligations:			
3000	Unpaid obligations, brought forward, Oct 1	1	1	
3020	Outlays (gross)		–1	
3050	Unpaid obligations, end of year	1		
	Memorandum (non-add) entries:			
3100	Obligated balance, start of year	1	1	
3200	Obligated balance, end of year	1		
	Budget authority and outlays, net:			
	Discretionary:			
4000	Budget authority, gross	–3		
	Outlays, gross:			
4011	Outlays from discretionary balances		1	
4180	Budget authority, net (total)	–3		
4190	Outlays, net (total)		1	

The Next Generation High-Speed Rail Program funds research, development, technology demonstration programs, and the planning and analysis required to evaluate high speed rail technology proposals. No new funds are requested for this account for 2023.

NORTHEAST CORRIDOR IMPROVEMENT PROGRAM

Program and Financing (in millions of dollars)

Identification code 069–0123–0–1–401		2021 actual	2022 est.	2023 est.
	Change in obligated balance:			
	Unpaid obligations:			
3000	Unpaid obligations, brought forward, Oct 1	17	12	3
3020	Outlays (gross)	–5	–9	–3
3050	Unpaid obligations, end of year	12	3	
	Memorandum (non-add) entries:			
3100	Obligated balance, start of year	17	12	3
3200	Obligated balance, end of year	12	3	
	Budget authority and outlays, net:			
	Discretionary:			
	Outlays, gross:			
4011	Outlays from discretionary balances	5	9	3
4180	Budget authority, net (total)			
4190	Outlays, net (total)	5	9	3

Prior to 2001, this program provided funds to continue the upgrade of passenger rail service in the corridor between Washington, District of Columbia, and Boston, Massachusetts. For 2016, $19 million was provided for grants to Amtrak for shared use infrastructure on the Northeast Corridor identified in the Northeast Corridor Infrastructure and Operations Advisory

NORTHEAST CORRIDOR IMPROVEMENT PROGRAM—Continued

Commission's five-year capital plan. No new funds are requested for this account for 2023.

RAIL LINE RELOCATION AND IMPROVEMENT PROGRAM

Program and Financing (in millions of dollars)

Identification code 069–0716–0–1–401		2021 actual	2022 est.	2023 est.
	Budgetary resources:			
	Unobligated balance:			
1000	Unobligated balance brought forward, Oct 1	14	3	
1021	Recoveries of prior year unpaid obligations	2		
1070	Unobligated balance (total)	16	3	
	Budget authority:			
	Appropriations, discretionary:			
1131	Unobligated balance of appropriations permanently reduced	–13	–3	
1930	Total budgetary resources available	3		
	Memorandum (non-add) entries:			
1941	Unexpired unobligated balance, end of year	3		
	Change in obligated balance:			
	Unpaid obligations:			
3000	Unpaid obligations, brought forward, Oct 1	2		
3040	Recoveries of prior year unpaid obligations, unexpired	–2		
	Memorandum (non-add) entries:			
3100	Obligated balance, start of year	2		
	Budget authority and outlays, net:			
	Discretionary:			
4000	Budget authority, gross	–13	–3	
4180	Budget authority, net (total)	–13	–3	
4190	Outlays, net (total)			

The Rail Line Relocation and Improvement program provides Federal assistance to States for relocating or making necessary improvements to local rail lines. The program was repealed by the Fixing America's Surface Transportation (FAST) Act; however, the project eligibilities are included under the Consolidated Rail Infrastructure and Safety Improvements program. No new funds are requested for this account for 2023.

RAIL SAFETY TECHNOLOGY PROGRAM

Program and Financing (in millions of dollars)

Identification code 069–0701–0–1–401		2021 actual	2022 est.	2023 est.
	Budgetary resources:			
	Unobligated balance:			
1000	Unobligated balance brought forward, Oct 1	1		
	Budget authority:			
	Appropriations, discretionary:			
1131	Unobligated balance of appropriations permanently reduced	–1		
	Change in obligated balance:			
	Unpaid obligations:			
3000	Unpaid obligations, brought forward, Oct 1	1	1	
3020	Outlays (gross)		–1	
3050	Unpaid obligations, end of year	1		
	Memorandum (non-add) entries:			
3100	Obligated balance, start of year	1	1	
3200	Obligated balance, end of year	1		
	Budget authority and outlays, net:			
	Discretionary:			
4000	Budget authority, gross	–1		
	Outlays, gross:			
4011	Outlays from discretionary balances			1
4180	Budget authority, net (total)	–1		
4190	Outlays, net (total)			1

The Railroad Safety Technology Program is a competitive grant program for the deployment of train control technologies to passenger and freight rail carriers, railroad suppliers, and State and local governments. No new funds are requested for this account for 2023.

FEDERAL-STATE PARTNERSHIP FOR INTERCITY PASSENGER RAIL GRANTS

For necessary expenses related to Federal-State Partnership for Intercity Passenger Rail Grants, as authorized by section 24911 of title 49, United States Code, $555,000,000, to remain available until expended: Provided, That for projects benefitting underserved communities, as determined by the Secretary, the Federal share of total project costs may exceed 80 percent but shall not exceed 90 percent, notwithstanding section 24911(f)(2) of title 49, United States Code: Provided further, That the Secretary may withhold up to 2 percent of the amount provided under this heading for the costs of award and project management oversight of grants carried out under title 49, United States Code.

Note.—A full-year 2022 appropriation for this account was not enacted at the time the Budget was prepared; therefore, the Budget assumes this account is operating under the Continuing Appropriations Act, 2022 (Division A of Public Law 117–43, as amended). The amounts included for 2022 reflect the annualized level provided by the continuing resolution.

FEDERAL-STATE PARTNERSHIP FOR INTERCITY PASSENGER RAIL GRANTS

[*For an additional amount for "Federal-State Partnership for Intercity Passenger Rail Grants", $36,000,000,000, to remain available until expended, for grants, as authorized section 24911 of title 49, United States Code: Provided, That $7,200,000,000, to remain available until expended, shall be made available for fiscal year 2022, $7,200,000,000, to remain available until expended, shall be made available for fiscal year 2023, $7,200,000,000, to remain available until expended, shall be made available for fiscal year 2024, $7,200,000,000, to remain available until expended, shall be made available for fiscal year 2025, and $7,200,000,000, to remain available until expended, shall be made available for fiscal year 2026: Provided further, That, notwithstanding subsection 24911(d)(3) of title 49, United States Code, not more than $24,000,000,000 of the amounts made available under this heading in this Act for fiscal years 2022 through 2026 shall be for projects for the Northeast Corridor: Provided further, That amounts made available under the heading "Northeast Corridor Grants to the National Railroad Passenger Corporation" in this Act may be used as non-Federal share for Northeast Corridor projects selected for award under section 24911 of title 49, United States Code, after the date of enactment of this Act, notwithstanding subsection 24911(f) of such title: Provided further, That the Secretary may withhold up to 2 percent of the amount provided under this heading in this Act in each fiscal year for the costs of award and project management oversight of grants carried out under section 24911 of title 49, United States Code: Provided further, That such amount is designated by the Congress as being for an emergency requirement pursuant to section 4112(a) of H. Con. Res. 71 (115th Congress), the concurrent resolution on the budget for fiscal year 2018, and to section 251(b) of the Balanced Budget and Emergency Deficit Control Act of 1985.*] *(Infrastructure Investments and Jobs Appropriations Act.)*

Program and Financing (in millions of dollars)

Identification code 069–2810–0–1–401		2021 actual	2022 est.	2023 est.
	Obligations by program activity:			
0001	Fed-State SOGR Grants	80	590	167
0002	Fed-State SOGR Oversight	4	1	1
0900	Total new obligations, unexpired accounts	84	591	168
	Budgetary resources:			
	Unobligated balance:			
1000	Unobligated balance brought forward, Oct 1	806	922	7,587
	Budget authority:			
	Appropriations, discretionary:			
1100	Appropriation	200	7,400	555
1120	Appropriations transferred to other acct [069–0759]		–144	–11
1160	Appropriation, discretionary (total)	200	7,256	544
	Advance appropriations, discretionary:			
1170	Advance appropriation			7,200
1172	Advance appropriations transferred to other accounts [069–0759]			–144
1180	Advanced appropriation, discretionary (total)			7,056
1900	Budget authority (total)	200	7,256	7,600
1930	Total budgetary resources available	1,006	8,178	15,187
	Memorandum (non-add) entries:			
1941	Unexpired unobligated balance, end of year	922	7,587	15,019

DEPARTMENT OF TRANSPORTATION

Federal Railroad Administration—Continued
Federal Funds—Continued

Change in obligated balance:
Unpaid obligations:

		2021 actual	2022 est.	2023 est.
3000	Unpaid obligations, brought forward, Oct 1	68	150	701
3010	New obligations, unexpired accounts	84	591	168
3020	Outlays (gross)	−2	−40	−188
3050	Unpaid obligations, end of year	150	701	681
	Memorandum (non-add) entries:			
3100	Obligated balance, start of year	68	150	701
3200	Obligated balance, end of year	150	701	681
	Budget authority and outlays, net:			
	Discretionary:			
4000	Budget authority, gross	200	7,256	7,600
	Outlays, gross:			
4011	Outlays from discretionary balances	2	40	188
4180	Budget authority, net (total)	200	7,256	7,600
4190	Outlays, net (total)	2	40	188

The Federal-State Partnership for Intercity Passenger Rail program is intended to reduce the state of good repair backlog, improve performance, or expand or establish new intercity passenger rail service. Eligible activities include capital projects to meet the program purpose, as well as planning, environmental studies, and final design of such projects. Eligible recipients include states (including interstate compacts), local governments, Amtrak, and federally recognized Indian Tribes. The program was originally authorized in 2015 by the Fixing America's Surface Transportation Act and was modified in 2021 by the Infrastructure Investment and Jobs Act.

Object Classification (in millions of dollars)

Identification code 069–2810–0–1–401		2021 actual	2022 est.	2023 est.
	Direct obligations:			
25.1	Advisory and assistance services	4	1	1
41.0	Grants, subsidies, and contributions	80	590	167
99.9	Total new obligations, unexpired accounts	84	591	168

CONSOLIDATED RAIL INFRASTRUCTURE AND SAFETY IMPROVEMENTS

For necessary expenses related to Consolidated Rail Infrastructure and Safety Improvements Grants, as authorized by section 22907 of title 49, United States Code, $500,000,000, to remain available until expended: Provided, That for eligible projects under section 22907(c)(11) of title 49, United States Code, eligible recipients under section 22907(b) of title 49, United States Code, shall include any State, county, municipal, local, and regional law enforcement agency: Provided further, That for amounts available under this heading, the Secretary may award a grant without regard to the requirement in section 22905(c)(1) of title 49, United States Code: Provided further, That for projects benefitting underserved communities, as determined by the Secretary, section 22907(e)(1)(A) of title 49, United States Code, shall not apply and the Federal share of total project costs may exceed 80 percent but shall not exceed 90 percent, notwithstanding section 22907(h)(2) of such title: Provided further, That the Secretary may retain up to $5,000,0000 of the amount provided under this heading to establish a National Railroad Institute to develop and conduct training and education programs for both public and private sector railroad and railroad-related industry employees (including the railroad manufacturing, supply, and consulting fields): Provided further, That the Secretary may withhold up to 2 percent of the amount provided under this heading for the costs of award and project management oversight of grants carried out under title 49, United States Code.

Note.—A full-year 2022 appropriation for this account was not enacted at the time the Budget was prepared; therefore, the Budget assumes this account is operating under the Continuing Appropriations Act, 2022 (Division A of Public Law 117–43, as amended). The amounts included for 2022 reflect the annualized level provided by the continuing resolution.

CONSOLIDATED RAIL INFRASTRUCTURE AND SAFETY IMPROVEMENTS

[For an additional amount for "Consolidated Rail Infrastructure and Safety Improvements", $5,000,000,000, to remain available until expended, for competitive grants, as authorized under section 22907 of title 49, United States Code: *Provided*, That $1,000,000,000, to remain available until expended, shall be made available for fiscal year 2022, $1,000,000,000, to remain available until expended, shall be made available for fiscal year 2023, $1,000,000,000, to remain available until expended, shall be made available for fiscal year 2024, $1,000,000,000, to remain available until expended, shall be made available for fiscal year 2025, and $1,000,000,000, to remain available until expended, shall be made available for fiscal year 2026: *Provided further*, That the Secretary may withhold up to 2 percent of the amounts provided under this heading in this Act in each fiscal year for the costs of award and project management oversight of grants carried out under section 22907 of title 49, United States Code: *Provided further*, That such amount is designated by the Congress as being for an emergency requirement pursuant to section 4112(a) of H. Con. Res. 71 (115th Congress), the concurrent resolution on the budget for fiscal year 2018, and to section 251(b) of the Balanced Budget and Emergency Deficit Control Act of 1985.] *(Infrastructure Investments and Jobs Appropriations Act.)*

Program and Financing (in millions of dollars)

Identification code 069–2811–0–1–401		2021 actual	2022 est.	2023 est.
	Obligations by program activity:			
0001	CRISI Grants	176	513	128
0002	CRISI Oversight	7	1	1
0003	CRISI Initiation or Restoration IPR Grants			17
0004	CRISI Special Transportation Circumstances	13	5	
0005	CRISI Positive Train Control	12	11	
0006	CRISI Acquisitions for New IPR Services			45
0900	Total new obligations, unexpired accounts	208	530	191
	Budgetary resources:			
	Unobligated balance:			
1000	Unobligated balance brought forward, Oct 1	885	1,055	1,880
1021	Recoveries of prior year unpaid obligations	3		
1070	Unobligated balance (total)	888	1,055	1,880
	Budget authority:			
	Appropriations, discretionary:			
1100	Appropriation	375	1,375	500
1120	Appropriations transferred to other acct [069–0759]		−20	−10
1160	Appropriation, discretionary (total)	375	1,355	490
	Advance appropriations, discretionary:			
1170	Advance appropriation			1,000
1172	Advance appropriations transferred to other accounts [069–0759]			−20
1180	Advanced appropriation, discretionary (total)			980
1900	Budget authority (total)	375	1,355	1,470
1930	Total budgetary resources available	1,263	2,410	3,350
	Memorandum (non-add) entries:			
1941	Unexpired unobligated balance, end of year	1,055	1,880	3,159
	Change in obligated balance:			
	Unpaid obligations:			
3000	Unpaid obligations, brought forward, Oct 1	198	339	662
3010	New obligations, unexpired accounts	208	530	191
3020	Outlays (gross)	−64	−207	−224
3040	Recoveries of prior year unpaid obligations, unexpired	−3		
3050	Unpaid obligations, end of year	339	662	629
	Memorandum (non-add) entries:			
3100	Obligated balance, start of year	198	339	662
3200	Obligated balance, end of year	339	662	629
	Budget authority and outlays, net:			
	Discretionary:			
4000	Budget authority, gross	375	1,355	1,470
	Outlays, gross:			
4011	Outlays from discretionary balances	64	207	224
4180	Budget authority, net (total)	375	1,355	1,470
4190	Outlays, net (total)	64	207	224

Consolidated Rail Infrastructure and Safety Improvements are intended to improve the safety, efficiency, and reliability of passenger and freight rail systems. Eligible activities include a wide range of freight and passenger rail capital, safety technology deployment, planning, environmental analyses, research, workforce development and training projects. Eligible recipients include States (including interstate compacts); local governments; Class II and Class III railroads and associations that represent such entities; Amtrak and other intercity passenger rail operators; rail carriers and equipment manufacturers that partner with an eligible public-sector applicant; federally recognized Indian Tribes; the Transportation Research Board; University Transportation Centers; and non-profit rail labor organizations. The 2023 request includes several changes to enhance the program, including bolstering workforce development capacity and reducing the non-

CONSOLIDATED RAIL INFRASTRUCTURE AND SAFETY IMPROVEMENTS—Continued

Federal contribution requirement for CRISI projects benefitting underserved communities, among other improvements.

Object Classification (in millions of dollars)

Identification code 069–2811–0–1–401		2021 actual	2022 est.	2023 est.
	Direct obligations:			
25.1	Advisory and assistance services	7	1	1
41.0	Grants, subsidies, and contributions	201	529	190
99.9	Total new obligations, unexpired accounts	208	530	191

RAILROAD CROSSING ELIMINATION PROGRAM

For necessary expenses related to Railroad Crossing Elimination Grants, as authorized by section 22909 of title 49, United States Code, $245,000,000, to remain available until expended: Provided, That for projects benefitting underserved communities, as determined by the Secretary, the Federal share of total project costs may exceed 80 percent but shall not exceed 90 percent, notwithstanding section 22909(g) of title 49, United States Code: Provided further, That up to $1,000,000 shall be available for highway-rail grade crossing safety information and education programs authorized in section 22104(c) of division B of the Infrastructure Investment and Jobs Act (Public Law 117–58), and that eligible recipients for such funds shall include non-profit organizations: Provided further, That the Secretary may withhold up to 2 percent of the amount provided under this heading for the costs of award and project management oversight of grants carried out under title 49, United States Code.

RAILROAD CROSSING ELIMINATION PROGRAM

[*For an additional amount for "Railroad Crossing Elimination Program", $3,000,000,000, to remain available until expended, for competitive grants, as authorized under section 22909 of title 49, United States Code: Provided, That $600,000,000, to remain available until expended, shall be made available for fiscal year 2022, $600,000,000, to remain available until expended, shall be made available for fiscal year 2023, $600,000,000, to remain available until expended, shall be made available for fiscal year 2024, $600,000,000, to remain available until expended, shall be made available for fiscal year 2025, and $600,000,000, to remain available until expended, shall be made available for fiscal year 2026: Provided further, That the Secretary may withhold up to 2 percent of the amounts provided under this heading in this Act for the costs of award and project management oversight of grants carried out under section 22909 of title 49, United States Code: Provided further, That such amount is designated by the Congress as being for an emergency requirement pursuant to section 4112(a) of H. Con. Res. 71 (115th Congress), the concurrent resolution on the budget for fiscal year 2018, and to section 251(b) of the Balanced Budget and Emergency Deficit Control Act of 1985.*] *(Infrastructure Investments and Jobs Appropriations Act.)*

Program and Financing (in millions of dollars)

Identification code 069–0760–0–1–401		2021 actual	2022 est.	2023 est.
	Budgetary resources:			
	Unobligated balance:			
1000	Unobligated balance brought forward, Oct 1			588
	Budget authority:			
	Appropriations, discretionary:			
1100	Appropriation		600	245
1120	Appropriations transferred to other acct [069–0759]		–12	–5
1160	Appropriation, discretionary (total)		588	240
	Advance appropriations, discretionary:			
1170	Advance appropriation			600
1172	Advance appropriations transferred to other accounts [069–0759]			–12
1180	Advanced appropriation, discretionary (total)			588
1900	Budget authority (total)		588	828
1930	Total budgetary resources available		588	1,416
	Memorandum (non-add) entries:			
1941	Unexpired unobligated balance, end of year		588	1,416
	Budget authority and outlays, net:			
	Discretionary:			
4000	Budget authority, gross		588	828
4180	Budget authority, net (total)		588	828
4190	Outlays, net (total)			

The Railroad Crossing Elimination Program was authorized by the Infrastructure Investment and Jobs Act to award grants for highway-rail and pathway-rail grade crossing projects to improve safety and the mobility of people and goods. Eligible projects include grade separations and closures, track relocation, and improvements to or installation of protection devices, as well as planning, environmental review, and design of such projects.

FINANCIAL ASSISTANCE OVERSIGHT AND TECHNICAL ASSISTANCE

Program and Financing (in millions of dollars)

Identification code 069–0759–0–1–401		2021 actual	2022 est.	2023 est.
	Obligations by program activity:			
0001	Oversight		15	39
	Budgetary resources:			
	Unobligated balance:			
1000	Unobligated balance brought forward, Oct 1			183
	Budget authority:			
	Appropriations, discretionary:			
1121	Appropriations transferred from other acct [069–0760]		12	5
1121	Appropriations transferred from other acct [069–1774]		6	6
1121	Appropriations transferred from other acct [069–1775]		16	9
1121	Appropriations transferred from other acct [069–2810]		144	11
1121	Appropriations transferred from other acct [069–2811]		20	10
1160	Appropriation, discretionary (total)		198	41
	Advance appropriations, discretionary:			
1173	Advance appropriations transferred from other accounts [069–0760]			12
1173	Advance appropriations transferred from other accounts [069–1774]			6
1173	Advance appropriations transferred from other accounts [069–1775]			16
1173	Advance appropriations transferred from other accounts [069–2810]			144
1173	Advance appropriations transferred from other accounts [069–2811]			20
1180	Advanced appropriation, discretionary (total)			198
1900	Budget authority (total)		198	239
1930	Total budgetary resources available		198	422
	Memorandum (non-add) entries:			
1941	Unexpired unobligated balance, end of year		183	383
	Change in obligated balance:			
	Unpaid obligations:			
3000	Unpaid obligations, brought forward, Oct 1			3
3010	New obligations, unexpired accounts		15	39
3020	Outlays (gross)		–12	–30
3050	Unpaid obligations, end of year		3	12
	Memorandum (non-add) entries:			
3100	Obligated balance, start of year			3
3200	Obligated balance, end of year		3	12
	Budget authority and outlays, net:			
	Discretionary:			
4000	Budget authority, gross		198	239
	Outlays, gross:			
4010	Outlays from new discretionary authority		12	14
4011	Outlays from discretionary balances			16
4020	Outlays, gross (total)		12	30
4180	Budget authority, net (total)		198	239
4190	Outlays, net (total)		12	30

This account may receive funds transferred from programs authorized by the Infrastructure Investment and Jobs Act that support the award, administration, project management oversight, and technical assistance for financial assistance programs administered by the Federal Railroad Administration.

Object Classification (in millions of dollars)

Identification code 069–0759–0–1–401		2021 actual	2022 est.	2023 est.
	Direct obligations:			
11.1	Personnel compensation: Full-time permanent		3	12

12.1	Civilian personnel benefits		1	5
21.0	Travel and transportation of persons			1
25.1	Advisory and assistance services		8	18
31.0	Equipment		3	3
99.9	Total new obligations, unexpired accounts		15	39

Employment Summary

Identification code 069–0759–0–1–401	2021 actual	2022 est.	2023 est.
1001 Direct civilian full-time equivalent employment		24	91

ADMINISTRATIVE PROVISIONS—FEDERAL RAILROAD ADMINISTRATION

SEC. 150. *None of the funds made available to the National Railroad Passenger Corporation may be used to fund any overtime costs in excess of $35,000 for any individual employee: Provided, That the President of Amtrak may waive the cap set in the preceding proviso for specific employees when the President of Amtrak determines such a cap poses a risk to the safety and operational efficiency of the system: Provided further, That the President of Amtrak shall report to the House and Senate Committees on Appropriations no later than 60 days after the date of enactment of this Act, a summary of all overtime payments incurred by Amtrak for 2022 and the 3 prior calendar years: Provided further, That such summary shall include the total number of employees that received waivers and the total overtime payments Amtrak paid to employees receiving waivers for each month for 2022 and for the 3 prior calendar years.*

SEC. 151. *Amounts made available in this and prior Acts to the Secretary or Federal Railroad Administration for the costs of award, administration, and project management oversight of financial assistance which are administered by the Federal Railroad Administration may be transferred to the Federal Railroad Administration's "Financial Assistance Oversight and Technical Assistance" account for necessary expenses to support the award, administration, project management oversight, and technical assistance of financial assistance administered by the Federal Railroad Administration, in the same manner as appropriated in this and such prior Acts: Provided, That this section shall not apply to amounts that were previously designated by the Congress as an emergency requirement pursuant to a concurrent resolution on the budget or section 251(b)(2)(A)(i) of the Balanced Budget and Emergency Deficit Control Act of 1985.*

ADMINISTRATIVE PROVISIONS—FEDERAL RAILROAD ADMINISTRATION

[(INCLUDING TRANSFER OF FUNDS)]

[SEC. 802. Amounts made available to the Secretary of Transportation or to the Federal Railroad Administration in this title in this Act for the costs of award, administration, and project management oversight of financial assistance under the programs that are administered by the Federal Railroad Administration may be transferred to a "Financial Assistance Oversight and Technical Assistance" account, to remain available until expended, for the necessary expenses to support the award, administration, project management oversight, and technical assistance of programs administered by the Federal Railroad Administration under this Act: *Provided*, That one-quarter of one percent of the amounts transferred pursuant to the authority in this section in each of fiscal years 2022 through 2026 shall be transferred to the Office of Inspector General of the Department of Transportation for oversight of funding provided to the Department of Transportation in this title in this Act: *Provided further*, That one-quarter of one percent of the amounts transferred pursuant to the authority in this section in each of fiscal years 2022 through 2026 shall be transferred to the National Railroad Passenger Corporation Office of Inspector General for oversight of funding provided to the National Railroad Passenger Corporation in this title in this Act.] *(Infrastructure Investments and Jobs Appropriations Act.)*

FEDERAL TRANSIT ADMINISTRATION

The 2023 Budget request of $16.9 billion will provide grant funding to State and local governments, public and private transit operators, and other recipients to enhance public transportation across the United States. Additionally, the Infrastructure Investment and Jobs Act provides $4.25 billion in supplemental advance appropriations for FTA, bringing total budgetary resources to $21.1 billion. The Federal Transit Administration's (FTA) grant programs fund and oversee the construction of new public transit and the purchase and maintenance of transit vehicles and equipment, subsidize public transit operations, support regional transportation planning efforts, and improve technology and service methods critical to the delivery of public transportation.

Federal Funds

ADMINISTRATIVE EXPENSES

Note.—A full-year 2022 appropriation for this account was not enacted at the time the Budget was prepared; therefore, the Budget assumes this account is operating under the Continuing Appropriations Act, 2022 (Division A of Public Law 117–43, as amended). The amounts included for 2022 reflect the annualized level provided by the continuing resolution.

Program and Financing (in millions of dollars)

Identification code 069–1120–0–1–401	2021 actual	2022 est.	2023 est.
Obligations by program activity:			
0001 Administrative expenses	123	117	
0002 Transit Safety Oversight		4	
0003 Transit Asset Management		1	
0900 Total new obligations, unexpired accounts	123	122	
Budgetary resources:			
Unobligated balance:			
1000 Unobligated balance brought forward, Oct 1	3	1	
Budget authority:			
Appropriations, discretionary:			
1100 Appropriation	121	121	
1930 Total budgetary resources available	124	122	
Memorandum (non-add) entries:			
1941 Unexpired unobligated balance, end of year	1		
Change in obligated balance:			
Unpaid obligations:			
3000 Unpaid obligations, brought forward, Oct 1	13	19	6
3010 New obligations, unexpired accounts	123	122	
3011 Obligations ("upward adjustments"), expired accounts	1		
3020 Outlays (gross)	–117	–135	–6
3041 Recoveries of prior year unpaid obligations, expired	–1		
3050 Unpaid obligations, end of year	19	6	
Memorandum (non-add) entries:			
3100 Obligated balance, start of year	13	19	6
3200 Obligated balance, end of year	19	6	
Budget authority and outlays, net:			
Discretionary:			
4000 Budget authority, gross	121	121	
Outlays, gross:			
4010 Outlays from new discretionary authority	106	115	
4011 Outlays from discretionary balances	11	20	6
4020 Outlays, gross (total)	117	135	6
Offsets against gross budget authority and outlays:			
Offsetting collections (collected) from:			
4033 Non-Federal sources	–1		
4040 Offsets against gross budget authority and outlays (total)	–1		
Additional offsets against gross budget authority only:			
4052 Offsetting collections credited to expired accounts	1		
4070 Budget authority, net (discretionary)	121	121	
4080 Outlays, net (discretionary)	116	135	6
4180 Budget authority, net (total)	121	121	
4190 Outlays, net (total)	116	135	6

As authorized under Infrastructure Investment and Jobs Act, beginning in 2023 FTA's administrative expenses activities are moved to the Transit Formula Grants Account.

Object Classification (in millions of dollars)

Identification code 069–1120–0–1–401	2021 actual	2022 est.	2023 est.
11.1 Direct obligations: Personnel compensation: Full-time permanent	65		
11.9 Total personnel compensation	65		
12.1 Civilian personnel benefits	24		

950　**Federal Transit Administration**—Continued
　　Federal Funds—Continued

THE BUDGET FOR FISCAL YEAR 2023

ADMINISTRATIVE EXPENSES—Continued

Object Classification—Continued

Identification code 069–1120–0–1–401	2021 actual	2022 est.	2023 est.
23.1　Rental payments to GSA	8	8	
23.3　Communications, utilities, and miscellaneous charges	1	1	
25.2　Other services from non-Federal sources	2	2	
25.3　Other goods and services from Federal sources	23	111	
99.9　Total new obligations, unexpired accounts	123	122	

Employment Summary

Identification code 069–1120–0–1–401	2021 actual	2022 est.	2023 est.
1001　Direct civilian full-time equivalent employment	507		

JOB ACCESS AND REVERSE COMMUTE GRANTS

Program and Financing (in millions of dollars)

Identification code 069–1125–0–1–401	2021 actual	2022 est.	2023 est.
Change in obligated balance:			
Unpaid obligations:			
3000　Unpaid obligations, brought forward, Oct 1	1	1	
3020　Outlays (gross)		–1	
3050　Unpaid obligations, end of year	1		
Memorandum (non-add) entries:			
3100　Obligated balance, start of year	1	1	
3200　Obligated balance, end of year	1		
Budget authority and outlays, net:			
Discretionary:			
Outlays, gross:			
4011　Outlays from discretionary balances		1	
4180　Budget authority, net (total)			
4190　Outlays, net (total)		1	

For 2023, no resources are requested for this account.

GRANTS TO THE WASHINGTON METROPOLITAN AREA TRANSIT AUTHORITY

For grants to the Washington Metropolitan Area Transit Authority as authorized under section 601 of division B of the Passenger Rail Investment and Improvement Act of 2008 (Public Law 110–432), $150,000,000, to remain available until expended: Provided, That the Secretary of Transportation shall approve grants for capital and preventive maintenance expenditures for the Washington Metropolitan Area Transit Authority only after receiving and reviewing a request for each specific project: Provided further, That the Secretary shall determine that the Washington Metropolitan Area Transit Authority has placed the highest priority on those investments that will improve the safety of the system before approving such grants.

Note.—A full-year 2022 appropriation for this account was not enacted at the time the Budget was prepared; therefore, the Budget assumes this account is operating under the Continuing Appropriations Act, 2022 (Division A of Public Law 117–43, as amended). The amounts included for 2022 reflect the annualized level provided by the continuing resolution.

Program and Financing (in millions of dollars)

Identification code 069–1128–0–1–401	2021 actual	2022 est.	2023 est.
Obligations by program activity:			
0001　Washington Metropolitan Area Transit Authority	149	149	149
0002　Oversight		1	1
0900　Total new obligations, unexpired accounts	149	150	150
Budgetary resources:			
Unobligated balance:			
1000　Unobligated balance brought forward, Oct 1	6	7	7
Budget authority:			
Appropriations, discretionary:			
1100　Appropriation	150	150	150
1930　Total budgetary resources available	156	157	157
Memorandum (non-add) entries:			
1941　Unexpired unobligated balance, end of year	7	7	7
Change in obligated balance:			
Unpaid obligations:			
3000　Unpaid obligations, brought forward, Oct 1	126	145	159
3010　New obligations, unexpired accounts	149	150	150
3020　Outlays (gross)	–130	–136	–138
3050　Unpaid obligations, end of year	145	159	171
Memorandum (non-add) entries:			
3100　Obligated balance, start of year	126	145	159
3200　Obligated balance, end of year	145	159	171
Budget authority and outlays, net:			
Discretionary:			
4000　Budget authority, gross	150	150	150
Outlays, gross:			
4010　Outlays from new discretionary authority	42	42	42
4011　Outlays from discretionary balances	88	94	96
4020　Outlays, gross (total)	130	136	138
4180　Budget authority, net (total)	150	150	150
4190　Outlays, net (total)	130	136	138

This program provides grants to the Washington Metropolitan Area Transit Authority (WMATA) for capital investment and asset rehabilitation activities. The 2023 budget requests $150 million for capital projects to help return the existing system to a state of good repair and to improve the safety and reliability of service throughout the WMATA system. This funding will support WMATA in addressing ongoing safety deficiencies and improve the reliability of service throughout the Metrorail system.

Object Classification (in millions of dollars)

Identification code 069–1128–0–1–401	2021 actual	2022 est.	2023 est.
Direct obligations:			
25.2　Other services from non-Federal sources		1	1
41.0　Grants, subsidies, and contributions	149	149	149
99.9　Total new obligations, unexpired accounts	149	150	150

FORMULA GRANTS

Program and Financing (in millions of dollars)

Identification code 069–1129–0–1–401	2021 actual	2022 est.	2023 est.
Obligations by program activity:			
0004　Other Programs		6	
0900　Total new obligations, unexpired accounts (object class 41.0)		6	
Budgetary resources:			
Unobligated balance:			
1000　Unobligated balance brought forward, Oct 1	10	8	
Budget authority:			
Appropriations, discretionary:			
1131　Unobligated balance of appropriations permanently reduced		–2	
Spending authority from offsetting collections, discretionary:			
1722　Unobligated balance of spending authority from offsetting collections permanently reduced	–2		
1900　Budget authority (total)	–2	–2	
1930　Total budgetary resources available	8	6	
Memorandum (non-add) entries:			
1941　Unexpired unobligated balance, end of year	8		
Change in obligated balance:			
Unpaid obligations:			
3000　Unpaid obligations, brought forward, Oct 1	26	17	14
3010　New obligations, unexpired accounts		6	
3020　Outlays (gross)	–9	–9	–9
3050　Unpaid obligations, end of year	17	14	5
Uncollected payments:			
3060　Uncollected pymts, Fed sources, brought forward, Oct 1	–2	–2	–2
3090　Uncollected pymts, Fed sources, end of year	–2	–2	–2
Memorandum (non-add) entries:			
3100　Obligated balance, start of year	24	15	12

DEPARTMENT OF TRANSPORTATION

3200	Obligated balance, end of year	15	12	3
	Budget authority and outlays, net:			
	Discretionary:			
4000	Budget authority, gross	−2	−2	
	Outlays, gross:			
4011	Outlays from discretionary balances	9	9	9
4180	Budget authority, net (total)	−2	−2	
4190	Outlays, net (total)	9	9	9

For 2023, no resources are requested for this account.

CAPITAL INVESTMENT GRANTS

For necessary expenses to carry out fixed guideway capital investment grants under section 5309 of title 49, United States Code, and section 3005(b) of the Fixing America's Surface Transportation Act (Public Law 114–94), $2,850,000,000, to remain available until expended.

Note.—A full-year 2022 appropriation for this account was not enacted at the time the Budget was prepared; therefore, the Budget assumes this account is operating under the Continuing Appropriations Act, 2022 (Division A of Public Law 117–43, as amended). The amounts included for 2022 reflect the annualized level provided by the continuing resolution.

CAPITAL INVESTMENT GRANTS

[(INCLUDING TRANSFER OF FUNDS)]

[For an additional amount for "Capital Investment Grants", $8,000,000,000, to remain available until expended: *Provided*, That $1,600,000,000, to remain available until expended, shall be made available for fiscal year 2022, $1,600,000,000, to remain available until expended, shall be made available for fiscal year 2023, $1,600,000,000, to remain available until expended, shall be made available for fiscal year 2024, $1,600,000,000, to remain available until expended, shall be made available for fiscal year 2025, and $1,600,000,000, to remain available until expended, shall be made available for fiscal year 2026: *Provided further*, That not more than 55 percent of the funds made available under this heading in this Act in each fiscal year may be available for projects authorized under section 5309(d) of title 49, United States Code: *Provided further*, That not more than 20 percent of the funds made available under this heading in this Act in each fiscal year may be available for projects authorized under section 5309(e) of title 49, United States Code: *Provided further*, That not more than 15 percent of the funds made available under this heading in this Act in each fiscal year may be available for projects authorized under section 5309(h) of title 49, United States Code: *Provided further*, That not more than 10 percent of the funds made available under this heading in this Act in each fiscal year may be available for projects authorized under section 3005(b) of the Fixing America's Surface Transportation Act: *Provided further*, That the Secretary may adjust the percentage limitations in any of the preceding four provisos by up to 5 percent in each fiscal year for which funds are made available under this heading in this Act only when there are unobligated carry over balances from funds provided for section 5309(d), section 5309(e), or section 5309(h) of title 49, United States Code, or section 3005(b) of the Fixing America's Transportation Act that are equal to or greater than amounts provided under this heading in this Act: *Provided further*, That for each fiscal year through 2026, as part of the annual budget submission of the President under section 1105(a) of title 31, United States Code, the Secretary of Transportation shall submit a list of potential projects eligible for the funds made available under this heading in this Act for that fiscal year, including project locations and proposed funding amounts consistent with the projects Full Funding Grant Agreement annual funding profile where applicable: *Provided further*, That funds allocated to any project during fiscal years 2015 or 2017 pursuant to section 5309 of title 49, United States Code, shall remain allocated to that project through fiscal year 2023: *Provided further*, That such amount is designated by the Congress as being for an emergency requirement pursuant to section 4112(a) of H. Con. Res. 71 (115th Congress), the concurrent resolution on the budget for fiscal year 2018, and to section 251(b) of the Balanced Budget and Emergency Deficit Control Act of 1985.] *(Infrastructure Investments and Jobs Appropriations Act.)*

Program and Financing (in millions of dollars)

Identification code 069–1134–0–1–401		2021 actual	2022 est.	2023 est.
	Obligations by program activity:			
0001	Capital Investment Grant	3,296	1,994	2,822
0003	Oversight	17	20	28
0005	Capital Investment Grants - IIJA		1,600	1,600
0799	Total direct obligations	3,313	3,614	4,450

Federal Transit Administration—Continued
Federal Funds—Continued

951

		2021 actual	2022 est.	2023 est.
0900	Total new obligations, unexpired accounts	3,313	3,614	4,450
	Budgetary resources:			
	Unobligated balance:			
1000	Unobligated balance brought forward, Oct 1	3,514	2,309	2,309
1021	Recoveries of prior year unpaid obligations	91		
1033	Recoveries of prior year paid obligations	3		
1070	Unobligated balance (total)	3,608	2,309	2,309
	Budget authority:			
	Appropriations, discretionary:			
1100	Appropriation	2,014	3,614	2,850
	Advance appropriations, discretionary:			
1170	Advance appropriation			1,600
1900	Budget authority (total)	2,014	3,614	4,450
1930	Total budgetary resources available	5,622	5,923	6,759
	Memorandum (non-add) entries:			
1941	Unexpired unobligated balance, end of year	2,309	2,309	2,309
	Change in obligated balance:			
	Unpaid obligations:			
3000	Unpaid obligations, brought forward, Oct 1	3,106	4,428	5,124
3010	New obligations, unexpired accounts	3,313	3,614	4,450
3020	Outlays (gross)	−1,900	−2,918	−2,778
3040	Recoveries of prior year unpaid obligations, unexpired	−91		
3050	Unpaid obligations, end of year	4,428	5,124	6,796
	Memorandum (non-add) entries:			
3100	Obligated balance, start of year	3,106	4,428	5,124
3200	Obligated balance, end of year	4,428	5,124	6,796
	Budget authority and outlays, net:			
	Discretionary:			
4000	Budget authority, gross	2,014	3,614	4,450
	Outlays, gross:			
4010	Outlays from new discretionary authority	361	542	668
4011	Outlays from discretionary balances	1,539	2,376	2,110
4020	Outlays, gross (total)	1,900	2,918	2,778
	Offsets against gross budget authority and outlays:			
	Offsetting collections (collected) from:			
4033	Non-Federal sources:	−3		
4040	Offsets against gross budget authority and outlays (total)	−3		
	Additional offsets against gross budget authority only:			
4053	Recoveries of prior year paid obligations, unexpired accounts	3		
4070	Budget authority, net (discretionary)	2,014	3,614	4,450
4080	Outlays, net (discretionary)	1,897	2,918	2,778
4180	Budget authority, net (total)	2,014	3,614	4,450
4190	Outlays, net (total)	1,897	2,918	2,778

The Capital Investment Grants (CIG) program supports the construction of new fixed guideway systems or extensions to fixed guideways including, corridor-based bus rapid transit systems and core capacity improvement projects. These projects include heavy rail, light rail, commuter rail, bus rapid transit, and streetcar systems. This account also received an additional advance appropriation of $1.6 billion from the Infrastructure Investment Jobs Act bringing the total available for this account to $4.5 billion in 2023.

Object Classification (in millions of dollars)

Identification code 069–1134–0–1–401		2021 actual	2022 est.	2023 est.
	Direct obligations:			
25.2	Other services from non-Federal sources	17	20	28
41.0	Grants, subsidies, and contributions	3,296	3,594	4,422
99.0	Direct obligations	3,313	3,614	4,450
99.9	Total new obligations, unexpired accounts	3,313	3,614	4,450

TRANSIT RESEARCH

For necessary expenses to carry out section 5312 of title 49, United States Code, $30,000,000, to remain available until expended: Provided, That such amounts are in addition to any other amounts made available for such purposes and shall not be subject to any limitation on obligations for transit programs set forth in this or any other Act.

Federal Transit Administration—Continued
Federal Funds—Continued

TRANSIT RESEARCH—Continued

Note.—A full-year 2022 appropriation for this account was not enacted at the time the Budget was prepared; therefore, the Budget assumes this account is operating under the Continuing Appropriations Act, 2022 (Division A of Public Law 117–43, as amended). The amounts included for 2022 reflect the annualized level provided by the continuing resolution.

Program and Financing (in millions of dollars)

Identification code 069–1137–0–1–401	2021 actual	2022 est.	2023 est.
Obligations by program activity:			
0001 Direct Obligations	1	1	8
0900 Total new obligations, unexpired accounts (object class 25.2)	1	1	8
Budgetary resources:			
Unobligated balance:			
1000 Unobligated balance brought forward, Oct 1	9	9	8
1021 Recoveries of prior year unpaid obligations	1		
1070 Unobligated balance (total)	10	9	8
Budget authority:			
Appropriations, discretionary:			
1100 Appropriation			30
1900 Budget authority (total)			30
1930 Total budgetary resources available	10	9	38
Memorandum (non-add) entries:			
1941 Unexpired unobligated balance, end of year	9	8	30
Change in obligated balance:			
Unpaid obligations:			
3000 Unpaid obligations, brought forward, Oct 1	18	11	5
3010 New obligations, unexpired accounts	1	1	8
3020 Outlays (gross)	–7	–7	–10
3040 Recoveries of prior year unpaid obligations, unexpired	–1		
3050 Unpaid obligations, end of year	11	5	3
Uncollected payments:			
3060 Uncollected pymts, Fed sources, brought forward, Oct 1	–6	–6	–6
3090 Uncollected pymts, Fed sources, end of year	–6	–6	–6
Memorandum (non-add) entries:			
3100 Obligated balance, start of year	12	5	–1
3200 Obligated balance, end of year	5	–1	–3
Budget authority and outlays, net:			
Discretionary:			
4000 Budget authority, gross			30
Outlays, gross:			
4010 Outlays from new discretionary authority			8
4011 Outlays from discretionary balances	7	7	2
4020 Outlays, gross (total)	7	7	10
4180 Budget authority, net (total)			30
4190 Outlays, net (total)	7	7	10

Transit Research will provide funding to support research, demonstration and deployment projects that will leverage new mobility trends in a post-COVID world, accelerate the adoption of zero-emission buses in public transportation, and advance transit safety innovation research. The 2023 Budget requests $30 million.

PUBLIC TRANSPORTATION EMERGENCY RELIEF PROGRAM

Program and Financing (in millions of dollars)

Identification code 069–1140–0–1–401	2021 actual	2022 est.	2023 est.
Obligations by program activity:			
0001 2013 Hurricane Sandy Emergency Supplemental (P.L. 113–2)	45	92	
0003 2013 Hurricane Sandy Emergency Supp (P.L. 113–2 Administration and Oversight)	5	5	4
0004 2018 Hurricanes Harvey, Irma, and Maria	20	29	50
0005 2018 Hurricanes Harvey, Irma, and Maria (Admin and Oversight)	1	1	
0006 FY 2019 Public Transportation Emergency Relief	1	5	4
0799 Total direct obligations	72	132	58
0900 Total new obligations, unexpired accounts	72	132	58
Budgetary resources:			
Unobligated balance:			
1000 Unobligated balance brought forward, Oct 1	413	350	218
1021 Recoveries of prior year unpaid obligations	9		
1070 Unobligated balance (total)	422	350	218
1930 Total budgetary resources available	422	350	218
Memorandum (non-add) entries:			
1941 Unexpired unobligated balance, end of year	350	218	160
Change in obligated balance:			
Unpaid obligations:			
3000 Unpaid obligations, brought forward, Oct 1	6,016	5,205	4,552
3010 New obligations, unexpired accounts	72	132	58
3020 Outlays (gross)	–874	–785	–780
3040 Recoveries of prior year unpaid obligations, unexpired	–9		
3050 Unpaid obligations, end of year	5,205	4,552	3,830
Uncollected payments:			
3060 Uncollected pymts, Fed sources, brought forward, Oct 1	–5	–5	–5
3090 Uncollected pymts, Fed sources, end of year	–5	–5	–5
Memorandum (non-add) entries:			
3100 Obligated balance, start of year	6,011	5,200	4,547
3200 Obligated balance, end of year	5,200	4,547	3,825
Budget authority and outlays, net:			
Discretionary:			
Outlays, gross:			
4011 Outlays from discretionary balances	874	785	780
4180 Budget authority, net (total)			
4190 Outlays, net (total)	874	785	780

The Public Transportation Emergency Relief Program helps transit agencies restore needed transportation services immediately following disaster events. Both capital and operating costs are eligible for funding following an emergency; however, this program does not replace the Federal Emergency Management Agency's capital assistance program. FTA administers the $10.9 billion supplemental appropriation (adjusted to $10.2 billion after sequestration and the transfer of funds to the Office of the Inspector General and the Federal Railroad Administration) provided by the Disaster Relief Appropriations Act, 2013 (Public Law 113–2) following Hurricane Sandy through this account. The Bipartisan Budget Account of 2018 (Public Law 115–123) also provided $330 million for eligible capital and operating costs for areas affected by Hurricanes Harvey, Irma, and Maria. The Additional Supplemental Appropriations for Disaster Relief Act, 2019 (Public Law 116–20) also provided $10.5 million for transit systems affected by major declared disasters occurring in calendar year 2018.

For 2023, no resources are requested for this account.

Object Classification (in millions of dollars)

Identification code 069–1140–0–1–401	2021 actual	2022 est.	2023 est.
11.1 Direct obligations: Personnel compensation: Full-time permanent	4	4	3
11.9 Total personnel compensation	4	4	3
12.1 Civilian personnel benefits	1	1	1
41.0 Grants, subsidies, and contributions	67	127	54
99.0 Direct obligations	72	132	58
99.9 Total new obligations, unexpired accounts	72	132	58

Employment Summary

Identification code 069–1140–0–1–401	2021 actual	2022 est.	2023 est.
1001 Direct civilian full-time equivalent employment	27	29	28

TECHNICAL ASSISTANCE AND TRAINING

For necessary expenses to carry out section 5314 of title 49, United States Code, $8,000,000, to remain available until September 30, 2024: Provided, That the assistance provided under this heading does not duplicate the activities of section 5311(b) or section 5312 of title 49, United States Code: Provided further, That such amounts

DEPARTMENT OF TRANSPORTATION

Federal Transit Administration—Continued
Federal Funds—Continued

953

are in addition to any other amounts made available for such purposes and shall not be subject to any limitation on obligations set forth in this or any other Act.

Note.—A full-year 2022 appropriation for this account was not enacted at the time the Budget was prepared; therefore, the Budget assumes this account is operating under the Continuing Appropriations Act, 2022 (Division A of Public Law 117–43, as amended). The amounts included for 2022 reflect the annualized level provided by the continuing resolution.

Program and Financing (in millions of dollars)

Identification code 069–1142–0–1–401	2021 actual	2022 est.	2023 est.
Obligations by program activity:			
0001 Technical Assistance and Standards Development	7	8	8
0900 Total new obligations, unexpired accounts (object class 41.0)	7	8	8
Budgetary resources:			
Unobligated balance:			
1000 Unobligated balance brought forward, Oct 1	4	5	5
Budget authority:			
Appropriations, discretionary:			
1100 Appropriation	8	8	8
1930 Total budgetary resources available	12	13	13
Memorandum (non-add) entries:			
1941 Unexpired unobligated balance, end of year	5	5	5
Change in obligated balance:			
Unpaid obligations:			
3000 Unpaid obligations, brought forward, Oct 1	7	9	10
3010 New obligations, unexpired accounts	7	8	8
3020 Outlays (gross)	–5	–7	–7
3050 Unpaid obligations, end of year	9	10	11
Memorandum (non-add) entries:			
3100 Obligated balance, start of year	7	9	10
3200 Obligated balance, end of year	9	10	11
Budget authority and outlays, net:			
Discretionary:			
4000 Budget authority, gross	8	8	8
Outlays, gross:			
4010 Outlays from new discretionary authority		1	1
4011 Outlays from discretionary balances	5	6	6
4020 Outlays, gross (total)	5	7	7
4180 Budget authority, net (total)	8	8	8
4190 Outlays, net (total)	5	7	7

The Budget requests $8 million for technical assistance and training activities. These funds will increase the capacity and capabilities of States and transit agencies to attract and retain the next generation of the transit workforce, effectively implement transit programs and meet Federal requirements, and transform transit to meet the mobility, equity, climate and safety challenges facing communities and the Nation.

TRANSIT INFRASTRUCTURE GRANTS

For necessary expenses for Zero Emission System Transformation Planning grants, Climate Resilience and Adaptation grants, and Integrated Smart Mobility grants, $200,000,000, to remain available until expended: Provided, That of the sums provided under this heading—

(1) $50,000,000 shall be available for competitive Zero Emission System Transformation Planning grants to eligible entities for planning related to conversion of recipients' transit bus fleet to zero emission buses, and other related planning expenses: Provided, That eligible entities are eligible recipients under section 5339(c) of title 49, United States Code: Provided further, That the Federal share for projects funded under this paragraph shall not exceed 80 percent of the net project cost;

(2) $100,000,000 shall be available for competitive Climate Resilience and Adaptation grants to eligible entities for capital projects that improve the resilience of transit assets related to climate hazards by protecting transit infrastructure, including stations, tunnels, and tracks, from flooding, extreme temperatures, and other climate-related hazards: Provided, That eligible entities are designated recipients, local governmental authorities, States, and Indian Tribes: Provided further, That an eligible subrecipient is any entity eligible to be a recipient: Provided further, That the Federal share for projects funded under this paragraph shall not exceed 80 percent of the net project cost; and

(3) $50,000,000 shall be available for no more than five competitive Integrated Smart Mobility grants to eligible entities for planning and capital projects that support the adoption of innovative approaches to mobility that will improve safety, accessibility, and equity in access to community services and economic opportunities, including first and last mile options such as optimizing transit route planning and using integrated travel planning and payment systems: Provided, That eligible entities are designated recipients, local governmental authorities, States, and Indian Tribes: Provided further, That an eligible subrecipient is any entity eligible to be a recipient: Provided further, That the Federal share for projects funded under this paragraph shall not exceed 80 percent of the net project cost:

Provided further, That the amounts made available under this heading shall be derived from the general fund: Provided further, That the amounts made available under this heading shall not be subject to any limitation on obligations for transit programs set forth in this or any other Act: Provided further, That notwithstanding any other provision of law, 1 percent of the funds provided for grants under this heading shall be available for administrative expenses and ongoing program management oversight as authorized under sections 5334 and 5338(c)(2) of title 49, United States Code, and shall be in addition to any other appropriations available for such purpose: Provided further, That unless otherwise specified, applicable requirements under chapter 53 of title 49, United States Code, shall apply to the amounts made available under this heading.

Note.—A full-year 2022 appropriation for this account was not enacted at the time the Budget was prepared; therefore, the Budget assumes this account is operating under the Continuing Appropriations Act, 2022 (Division A of Public Law 117–43, as amended). The amounts included for 2022 reflect the annualized level provided by the continuing resolution.

TRANSIT INFRASTRUCTURE GRANTS

[(INCLUDING TRANSFER OF FUNDS)]

[For an additional amount for "Transit Infrastructure Grants", $10,250,000,000, to remain available until expended: *Provided*, That $2,050,000,000, to remain available until expended, shall be made available for fiscal year 2022, $2,050,000,000, to remain available until expended, shall be made available for fiscal year 2023, $2,050,000,000, to remain available until expended, shall be made available for fiscal year 2024, $2,050,000,000, to remain available until expended, shall be made available for fiscal year 2025, and $2,050,000,000, to remain available until expended, shall be made available for fiscal year 2026: *Provided further*, That the funds made available under this heading in this Act shall be derived from the general fund of the Treasury, shall be in addition to any other amounts made available for such purpose, and shall not affect the distribution of funds provided in any Act making annual appropriations: *Provided further*, That the funds made available under this heading in this Act shall not be subject to any limitation on obligations for the Federal Public Transportation Assistance Program set forth in any Act making annual appropriations: *Provided further*, That, of the amount provided under this heading in this Act, the following amounts shall be for the following purposes in equal amounts for each of fiscal years 2022 through 2026—]

[(1) $4,750,000,000 shall be to carry out the state of good repair grants under section 5337(c) and (d) of title 49, United States Code;]

[(2) $5,250,000,000 shall be to carry out the low or no emission grants under section 5339(c) of title 49, United States Code; and]

[(3) $250,000,000 shall be to carry out the formula grants for the enhanced mobility of seniors and individuals with disabilities as authorized under section 5310 of title 49, United States Code:]

[*Provided further*, That not more than two percent of the funds made available under this heading in this Act shall be available for administrative and oversight expenses as authorized under section 5334 and section 5338(c) of title 49, United States Code, and shall be in addition to any other appropriations for such purpose: *Provided further*, That one-half of one percent of the amounts in the preceding proviso shall be transferred to the Office of Inspector General of the Department of Transportation for oversight of funding provided to the Department of Transportation in this title in this Act: *Provided further*, That such amount is designated by the Congress as being for an emergency requirement pursuant to section 4112(a) of H. Con. Res. 71 (115th Congress), the concurrent resolution on the budget for fiscal year 2018, and to section 251(b) of the Balanced Budget and Emergency Deficit Control Act of 1985.] *(Infrastructure Investments and Jobs Appropriations Act.)*

Program and Financing (in millions of dollars)

Identification code 069–2812–0–1–401	2021 actual	2022 est.	2023 est.
Obligations by program activity:			
0001 Bus & Bus Facilities- competitive	263	263	473
0002 State of Good Repair	372	372	342
0003 Bus Testing Facility			1
0004 Low or NO Emission Bus Testing			1
0005 High Density State	110	110	77
0007 Positive Train Control	2	2	1
0008 Rural Formula Grants	36	36	22

954 Federal Transit Administration—Continued
Federal Funds—Continued

THE BUDGET FOR FISCAL YEAR 2023

TRANSIT INFRASTRUCTURE GRANTS—Continued

Program and Financing—Continued

Identification code 069–2812–0–1–401	2021 actual	2022 est.	2023 est.
0009 Bus & Bus Facility Formula	145	145	....
0010 Competitive Persistent Poverty	6	6	9
0011 Research	1	1	1
0012 CARES Act, 2020	1,296	351	9
0013 CRRSA Act, 2021	7,262	6,718	2
0014 Passenger Ferry Boat	....	4	4
0016 ARP Act, 2021	7,779	22,200	482
0017 IIJA Act, 2021	....	....	20
0900 Total new obligations, unexpired accounts	17,272	30,208	1,444
Budgetary resources:			
Unobligated balance:			
1000 Unobligated balance brought forward, Oct 1	2,785	30,606	2,964
1001 Discretionary unobligated balance brought fwd, Oct 1	2,785	....	....
1011 Unobligated balance transfer from other acct [069–0548]	2	....	....
1021 Recoveries of prior year unpaid obligations	114	....	....
1070 Unobligated balance (total)	2,901	30,606	2,964
Budget authority:			
Appropriations, discretionary:			
1100 Appropriation	14,516	2,566	200
Advance appropriations, discretionary:			
1170 Advance appropriation	....	....	2,050
Appropriations, mandatory:			
1200 Appropriation	30,461	....	....
1900 Budget authority (total)	44,977	2,566	2,250
1930 Total budgetary resources available	47,878	33,172	5,214
Memorandum (non-add) entries:			
1941 Unexpired unobligated balance, end of year	30,606	2,964	3,770
Change in obligated balance:			
Unpaid obligations:			
3000 Unpaid obligations, brought forward, Oct 1	12,087	15,874	24,825
3010 New obligations, unexpired accounts	17,272	30,208	1,444
3020 Outlays (gross)	–13,371	–21,257	–12,100
3040 Recoveries of prior year unpaid obligations, unexpired	–114	....	....
3050 Unpaid obligations, end of year	15,874	24,825	14,169
Memorandum (non-add) entries:			
3100 Obligated balance, start of year	12,087	15,874	24,825
3200 Obligated balance, end of year	15,874	24,825	14,169
Budget authority and outlays, net:			
Discretionary:			
4000 Budget authority, gross	14,516	2,566	2,250
Outlays, gross:			
4010 Outlays from new discretionary authority	3,771	25	22
4011 Outlays from discretionary balances	8,794	9,370	3,774
4020 Outlays, gross (total)	12,565	9,395	3,796
Mandatory:			
4090 Budget authority, gross	30,461	....	....
Outlays, gross:			
4100 Outlays from new mandatory authority	806	....	....
4101 Outlays from mandatory balances	....	11,862	8,304
4110 Outlays, gross (total)	806	11,862	8,304
4180 Budget authority, net (total)	44,977	2,566	2,250
4190 Outlays, net (total)	13,371	21,257	12,100

The 2023 Budget requests $200 million for Transit Infrastructure Grants to fund competitively-selected projects. This request includes $100 million for the Climate Resilience and Adaptation Grants to improve resilience of transit assets to climate-related hazards; $50 million for the Integrated Smart Mobility Grants to fund up to five pilot projects that adopt innovative approaches to mobility that will improve safety, accessibility, and equity; and $50 million for the Zero Emission System Transformation Planning Grants to support agencies' planning for transition to zero emission buses and associated infrastructure. This Account also received an additional advance appropriation of $2.1 billion from the Infrastructure Investment Jobs Act ($950 million for State of Good Repair formula funding; $1.1 billion for Low or No Emission Grants; and $50 million for Enhanced Mobility of Seniors and Individuals with Disabilities grants) bringing the total available for this account to $2.3 billion in 2023.

Object Classification (in millions of dollars)

Identification code 069–2812–0–1–401	2021 actual	2022 est.	2023 est.
Direct obligations:			
11.1 Personnel compensation: Full-time permanent	2	4	13
12.1 Civilian personnel benefits	1	2	5
25.2 Other services from non-Federal sources	1	35	23
41.0 Grants, subsidies, and contributions	17,268	30,167	1,403
99.9 Total new obligations, unexpired accounts	17,272	30,208	1,444

Employment Summary

Identification code 069–2812–0–1–401	2021 actual	2022 est.	2023 est.
1001 Direct civilian full-time equivalent employment	16	89	161

FERRY SERVICE FOR RURAL COMMUNITIES

〖(INCLUDING TRANSFER OF FUNDS)〗

〖For competitive grants to States for eligible essential ferry service as authorized under section 71103 of division G of this Act, $1,000,000,000, to remain available until expended: *Provided*, That $200,000,000, to remain available until expended, shall be made available for fiscal year 2022, $200,000,000, to remain available until expended, shall be made available for fiscal year 2023, $200,000,000, to remain available until expended, shall be made available for fiscal year 2024, $200,000,000, to remain available until expended, shall be made available for fiscal year 2025, and $200,000,000, to remain available until expended, shall be made available for fiscal year 2026: *Provided further*, That amounts made available under this heading in this Act shall be derived from the general fund of the Treasury: *Provided further*, That amounts made available under this heading in this Act shall not be subject to any limitation on obligations for the Federal Public Transportation Assistance Program set forth in any Act making annual appropriations: *Provided further*, That not more than two percent of the funds made available under this heading in this Act shall be available for administrative and oversight expenses as authorized under section 5334 and section 5338(c) of title 49, United States Code, and shall be in addition to any other appropriations for such purpose: *Provided further*, That one-half of one percent of the amounts in the preceding proviso shall be transferred to the Office of Inspector General of the Department of Transportation for oversight of funding provided to the Department of Transportation in this title in this Act: *Provided further*, That such amount is designated by the Congress as being for an emergency requirement pursuant to section 4112(a) of H. Con. Res. 71 (115th Congress), the concurrent resolution on the budget for fiscal year 2018, and to section 251(b) of the Balanced Budget and Emergency Deficit Control Act of 1985.〗 *(Infrastructure Investments and Jobs Appropriations Act.)*

Program and Financing (in millions of dollars)

Identification code 069–1146–0–1–403	2021 actual	2022 est.	2023 est.
Obligations by program activity:			
0001 Direct program activity	....	200	200
Budgetary resources:			
Budget authority:			
Appropriations, discretionary:			
1100 Appropriation	....	200	....
Advance appropriations, discretionary:			
1170 Advance appropriation	....	....	200
1900 Budget authority (total)	....	200	200
1930 Total budgetary resources available	....	200	200
Change in obligated balance:			
Unpaid obligations:			
3000 Unpaid obligations, brought forward, Oct 1	....	....	200
3010 New obligations, unexpired accounts	....	200	200
3020 Outlays (gross)	....	....	–40
3050 Unpaid obligations, end of year	....	200	360
Memorandum (non-add) entries:			
3100 Obligated balance, start of year	....	....	200
3200 Obligated balance, end of year	....	200	360
Budget authority and outlays, net:			
Discretionary:			
4000 Budget authority, gross	....	200	200

DEPARTMENT OF TRANSPORTATION

		2021 actual	2022 est.	2023 est.
	Outlays, gross:			
4010	Outlays from new discretionary authority			20
4011	Outlays from discretionary balances			20
4020	Outlays, gross (total)			40
4180	Budget authority, net (total)		200	200
4190	Outlays, net (total)			40

The Ferry Service for Rural Communities program received advance appropriations of $200 million in 2023 as enacted in the Infrastructure Investment Jobs Act. The program supports basic essential ferry services to rural areas.

For 2023, no additional resources are requested for this account.

Object Classification (in millions of dollars)

Identification code 069–1146–0–1–403		2021 actual	2022 est.	2023 est.
	Direct obligations:			
25.2	Other services from non-Federal sources		4	4
41.0	Grants, subsidies, and contributions		196	196
99.9	Total new obligations, unexpired accounts		200	200

ELECTRIC OR LOW-EMITTING FERRY PROGRAM

[(INCLUDING TRANSFER OF FUNDS)]

[For competitive grants for electric or low-emitting ferry pilot program grants as authorized under section 71102 of division G of this Act, $250,000,000, to remain available until expended: *Provided*, That $50,000,000, to remain available until expended, shall be made available for fiscal year 2022, $50,000,000, to remain available until expended, shall be made available for fiscal year 2023, $50,000,000, to remain available until expended, shall be made available for fiscal year 2024, $50,000,000, to remain available until expended, shall be made available for fiscal year 2025, and $50,000,000, to remain available until expended, shall be made available for fiscal year 2026: *Provided further*, That amounts made available under this heading in this Act shall be derived from the general fund of the Treasury: *Provided further*, That the amounts made available under this heading in this Act shall not be subject to any limitation on obligations for transit programs set forth in any Act making annual appropriations: *Provided further*, That not more than two percent of the funds made available under this heading in this Act shall be available for administrative and oversight expenses as authorized under section 5334 and section 5338(c) of title 49, United States Code, and shall be in addition to any other appropriations for such purpose: *Provided further*, That one-half of one percent of the of the amounts in the preceding proviso shall be transferred to the Office of Inspector General of the Department of Transportation for oversight of funding provided to the Department of Transportation in this title in this Act: *Provided further*, That such amount is designated by the Congress as being for an emergency requirement pursuant to section 4112(a) of H. Con. Res. 71 (115th Congress), the concurrent resolution on the budget for fiscal year 2018, and to section 251(b) of the Balanced Budget and Emergency Deficit Control Act of 1985.] *(Infrastructure Investments and Jobs Appropriations Act.)*

Program and Financing (in millions of dollars)

Identification code 069–1144–0–1–403		2021 actual	2022 est.	2023 est.
	Obligations by program activity:			
0001	Electric or Low-Emitting Ferry Program		50	50
	Budgetary resources:			
	Budget authority:			
	Appropriations, discretionary:			
1100	Appropriation		50	
	Advance appropriations, discretionary:			
1170	Advance appropriation			50
1900	Budget authority (total)		50	50
1930	Total budgetary resources available		50	50
	Change in obligated balance:			
	Unpaid obligations:			
3000	Unpaid obligations, brought forward, Oct 1			50
3010	New obligations, unexpired accounts		50	50
3020	Outlays (gross)			–10
3050	Unpaid obligations, end of year		50	90

		2021 actual	2022 est.	2023 est.
	Memorandum (non-add) entries:			
3100	Obligated balance, start of year			50
3200	Obligated balance, end of year		50	90
	Budget authority and outlays, net:			
	Discretionary:			
4000	Budget authority, gross		50	50
	Outlays, gross:			
4010	Outlays from new discretionary authority			5
4011	Outlays from discretionary balances			5
4020	Outlays, gross (total)			10
4180	Budget authority, net (total)		50	50
4190	Outlays, net (total)			10

The Electric or Low-Emitting Ferry program received advance appropriations of $50 million in 2023 enacted in the Infrastructure Investment Jobs Act. The program supports the purchase of electric or low-emitting ferries and the electrification of or other reduction of emissions from existing ferries.

For 2023, no additional resources are requested for this account.

Object Classification (in millions of dollars)

Identification code 069–1144–0–1–403		2021 actual	2022 est.	2023 est.
	Direct obligations:			
25.3	Other goods and services from Federal sources		1	1
41.0	Grants, subsidies, and contributions		49	49
99.9	Total new obligations, unexpired accounts		50	50

ALL STATIONS ACCESSIBILITY PROGRAM

[(INCLUDING TRANSFER OF FUNDS)]

[For an additional amount for "All Stations Accessibility Program", $1,750,000,000, to remain available until expended, for the Secretary of Transportation to make competitive grants to assist eligible entities in financing capital projects to upgrade the accessibility of legacy rail fixed guideway public transportation systems for persons with disabilities, including those who use wheelchairs, by increasing the number of existing (as of the date of enactment of this Act) stations or facilities for passenger use that meet or exceed the new construction standards of title II of the Americans with Disabilities Act of 1990 (42 U.S.C. 12131 et seq.): *Provided*, That $350,000,000, to remain available until expended, shall be made available for fiscal year 2022, $350,000,000, to remain available until expended, shall be made available for fiscal year 2023, $350,000,000, to remain available until expended, shall be made available for fiscal year 2024, $350,000,000, to remain available until expended, shall be made available for fiscal year 2025, and $350,000,000, to remain available until expended, shall be made available for fiscal year 2026: *Provided further*, That the funds made available under this heading in this Act shall be derived from the general fund of the Treasury: *Provided further*, That eligible entities under this heading in this Act shall include a State or local government authority: *Provided further*, That an eligible entity may use a grant awarded under this heading in this Act: (1) for a project to repair, improve, modify, retrofit, or relocate infrastructure of stations or facilities for passenger use, including load-bearing members that are an essential part of the structural frame; or (2) to develop or modify a plan for pursuing public transportation accessibility projects, assessments of accessibility, or assessments of planned modifications to stations or facilities for passenger use: *Provided further*, That eligible entities are encouraged to consult with appropriate stakeholders and the surrounding community to ensure accessibility for individuals with disabilities, including accessibility for individuals with physical disabilities, including those who use wheelchairs, accessibility for individuals with sensory disabilities, and accessibility for individuals with intellectual or developmental disabilities: *Provided further*, That all projects shall at least meet the new construction standards of title II of the Americans with Disabilities Act of 1990: *Provided further*, That eligible costs for a project funded with a grant awarded under this heading in this Act shall be limited to the costs associated with carrying out the purpose described in the preceding proviso: *Provided further*, That an eligible entity may not use a grant awarded under this heading in this Act to upgrade a station or facility for passenger use that is accessible to and usable by individuals with disabilities, including individuals who use wheelchairs, consistent with current (as of the date of the upgrade) new construction standards under title II of the Americans with

ALL STATIONS ACCESSIBILITY PROGRAM—Continued

Disabilities Act of 1990 (42 U.S.C. 12131 et seq.): *Provided further*, That a grant for a project made with amounts made available under this heading in this Act shall be for 80 percent of the net project cost: *Provided further*, That the total Federal financial assistance available under chapter 53 of title 49, United States Code, for an eligible entity that receives a grant awarded under this heading in this Act may not exceed 80 percent: *Provided further*, That the recipient of a grant made with amounts made available under this heading in this Act may provide additional local matching amounts: *Provided further*, That not more than two percent of the funds made available under this heading in this Act shall be available for administrative and oversight expenses as authorized under section 5334 and section 5338(c) of title 49, United States Code, and shall be in addition to any other appropriations for such purpose: *Provided further*, That one-half of one percent of the of the amounts in the preceding proviso shall be transferred to the Office of Inspector General of the Department of Transportation for oversight of funding provided to the Department of Transportation in this title in this Act: *Provided further*, That such amount is designated by the Congress as being for an emergency requirement pursuant to section 4112(a) of H. Con. Res. 71 (115th Congress), the concurrent resolution on the budget for fiscal year 2018, and to section 251(b) of the Balanced Budget and Emergency Deficit Control Act of 1985.] *(Infrastructure Investments and Jobs Appropriations Act.)*

Program and Financing (in millions of dollars)

Identification code 069–1145–0–1–402	2021 actual	2022 est.	2023 est.
Obligations by program activity:			
0001 All Stations Accessibility Program		350	350
Budgetary resources:			
Budget authority:			
Appropriations, discretionary:			
1100 Appropriation		350	
Advance appropriations, discretionary:			
1170 Advance appropriation			350
1900 Budget authority (total)		350	350
1930 Total budgetary resources available		350	350
Change in obligated balance:			
Unpaid obligations:			
3000 Unpaid obligations, brought forward, Oct 1			350
3010 New obligations, unexpired accounts		350	350
3020 Outlays (gross)			–70
3050 Unpaid obligations, end of year		350	630
Memorandum (non-add) entries:			
3100 Obligated balance, start of year			350
3200 Obligated balance, end of year		350	630
Budget authority and outlays, net:			
Discretionary:			
4000 Budget authority, gross		350	350
Outlays, gross:			
4010 Outlays from new discretionary authority			35
4011 Outlays from discretionary balances			35
4020 Outlays, gross (total)			70
4180 Budget authority, net (total)		350	350
4190 Outlays, net (total)			70

The All Stations Accessibility Program received advance appropriations of $350 million in 2023 as enacted in the Infrastructure Investment Jobs Act. The program provides competitive grants for capital projects that will upgrade the accessibility of legacy rail fixed guideway public transportation systems for persons with disabilities, including those who use wheelchairs. For 2023, no additional resources are requested for this account.

Object Classification (in millions of dollars)

Identification code 069–1145–0–1–402	2021 actual	2022 est.	2023 est.
Direct obligations:			
25.2 Other services from non-Federal sources		7	7
41.0 Grants, subsidies, and contributions		343	343
99.9 Total new obligations, unexpired accounts		350	350

Trust Funds

DISCRETIONARY GRANTS (HIGHWAY TRUST FUND, MASS TRANSIT ACCOUNT)

Program and Financing (in millions of dollars)

Identification code 069–8191–0–7–401	2021 actual	2022 est.	2023 est.
Obligations by program activity:			
0001 Discretionary grants		15	
0900 Total new obligations, unexpired accounts (object class 41.0)		15	
Budgetary resources:			
Unobligated balance:			
1000 Unobligated balance brought forward, Oct 1	15	15	
1930 Total budgetary resources available	15	15	
Memorandum (non-add) entries:			
1941 Unexpired unobligated balance, end of year	15		
Change in obligated balance:			
Unpaid obligations:			
3010 New obligations, unexpired accounts		15	
3020 Outlays (gross)		–15	
Budget authority and outlays, net:			
Discretionary:			
Outlays, gross:			
4011 Outlays from discretionary balances		15	
4180 Budget authority, net (total)			
4190 Outlays, net (total)		15	
Memorandum (non-add) entries:			
5054 Fund balance in excess of liquidating requirements, SOY: Contract authority	38	38	38
5055 Fund balance in excess of liquidating requirements, EOY: Contract authority	38	38	38

For 2023, no resources are requested for this account.

TRANSIT FORMULA GRANTS

(LIQUIDATION OF CONTRACT AUTHORIZATION)

(LIMITATION ON OBLIGATIONS)

(HIGHWAY TRUST FUND)

For payment of obligations incurred in the Federal Public Transportation Assistance Program in this account, and for payment of obligations incurred in carrying out the provisions of 49 U.S.C. 5305, 5307, 5310, 5311, 5312, 5314, 5318, 5329(e)(6), 5334, 5335, 5337, 5339, and 5340, section 20005(b) of Public Law 112–141, and section 3006(b) of Public Law 114–94, $13,634,000,000, to be derived from the Mass Transit Account of the Highway Trust Fund and to remain available until expended: *Provided*, That funds available for the implementation or execution of programs authorized under 49 U.S.C. 5305, 5307, 5310, 5311, 5312, 5314, 5318, 5329(e)(6), 5334, 5335, 5337, 5339, and 5340, section 20005(b) of Public Law 112–141, and section 3006(b) of Public Law 114–94, shall not exceed total obligations of $13,634,000,000 in fiscal year 2023.

Note.—A full-year 2022 appropriation for this account was not enacted at the time the Budget was prepared; therefore, the Budget assumes this account is operating under the Continuing Appropriations Act, 2022 (Division A of Public Law 117–43, as amended). The amounts included for 2022 reflect the annualized level provided by the continuing resolution.

Program and Financing (in millions of dollars)

Identification code 069–8350–0–7–401	2021 actual	2022 est.	2023 est.
Obligations by program activity:			
0001 Urbanized area programs	5,974	6,000	7,398
0003 Bus and bus facility grants- Competitive	359	400	224
0006 Planning Programs	82	90	127
0010 Seniors and persons with disabilities	257	300	419
0011 Non-urbanized area programs	652	700	573
0013 National Transit Database	4	4	4
0014 Oversight	94	115	81
0015 Transit Oriented Development	25	10	3
0016 Bus and Bus Facilities Formula Grants	376	400	416
0017 Bus Testing Facility	3	5	6
0019 State of Good Repair Grants	2,858	3,000	2,798
0020 Public Transportation Innovation (Research)	41	31	31
0021 Technical Assistance and Workforce Development	12	12	7

DEPARTMENT OF TRANSPORTATION

Federal Transit Administration—Continued
Trust Funds—Continued

		2021 actual	2022 est.	2023 est.
0023	Pilot Program for Enhanced Mobility	2	2	
0024	FY 2018 Automated Driving Systems Grants			7
0025	Administrative Expenses		121	130
0900	Total new obligations, unexpired accounts	10,739	11,190	12,224
	Budgetary resources:			
	Unobligated balance:			
1000	Unobligated balance brought forward, Oct 1	11,464	12,404	15,869
1013	Unobligated balance of contract authority transferred to or from other accounts [069–8083]	344		
1021	Recoveries of prior year unpaid obligations	337		
1070	Unobligated balance (total)	12,145	12,404	15,869
	Budget authority:			
	Appropriations, discretionary:			
1101	Appropriation (special or trust)	10,800	10,800	10,800
1120	Appropriations transferred to other acct [069–8083]	–115		
1121	Appropriations transferred from other acct [069–8083]	1,200	1,300	1,300
1138	Appropriations applied to liquidate contract authority	–11,885	–12,100	–12,100
	Contract authority, mandatory:			
1600	Contract authority	10,150	13,355	13,634
1610	Contract authority transferred to other accounts [069–8083]	–79		
1611	Contract authority transferred from other accounts [069–8083]	927	1,300	1,300
1640	Contract authority, mandatory (total)	10,998	14,655	14,934
1900	Budget authority (total)	10,998	14,655	14,934
1930	Total budgetary resources available	23,143	27,059	30,803
	Memorandum (non-add) entries:			
1941	Unexpired unobligated balance, end of year	12,404	15,869	18,579
	Change in obligated balance:			
	Unpaid obligations:			
3000	Unpaid obligations, brought forward, Oct 1	20,734	23,174	25,522
3010	New obligations, unexpired accounts	10,739	11,190	12,224
3020	Outlays (gross)	–7,962	–8,842	–10,123
3040	Recoveries of prior year unpaid obligations, unexpired	–337		
3050	Unpaid obligations, end of year	23,174	25,522	27,623
	Memorandum (non-add) entries:			
3100	Obligated balance, start of year	20,734	23,174	25,522
3200	Obligated balance, end of year	23,174	25,522	27,623
	Budget authority and outlays, net:			
	Discretionary:			
	Outlays, gross:			
4010	Outlays from new discretionary authority	699	830	1,039
4011	Outlays from discretionary balances	7,263	8,012	9,084
4020	Outlays, gross (total)	7,962	8,842	10,123
	Mandatory:			
4090	Budget authority, gross	10,998	14,655	14,934
4180	Budget authority, net (total)	10,998	14,655	14,934
4190	Outlays, net (total)	7,962	8,842	10,123
	Memorandum (non-add) entries:			
5052	Obligated balance, SOY: Contract authority	3,338	2,795	5,350
5053	Obligated balance, EOY: Contract authority	2,795	5,350	8,184
5061	Limitation on obligations (Transportation Trust Funds)	11,450	11,450	14,934

Summary of Budget Authority and Outlays (in millions of dollars)

	2021 actual	2022 est.	2023 est.
Enacted/requested:			
Budget Authority	10,998	14,655	14,934
Outlays	7,962	8,842	10,123
Amounts included in the adjusted baseline:			
Outlays		192	256
Total:			
Budget Authority	10,998	14,655	14,934
Outlays	7,962	9,034	10,379

The 2023 Budget request includes $13.6 billion for existing core transit programs, including State and Metropolitan Planning Formula Grants, Urbanized Area Formula Grants, Railcar Replacement Grants, Rural Area Formula Grants, State of Good Repair Formula Grants, Grants for Buses and Bus Facilities, Enhanced Mobility of Seniors and Individuals with Disabilities, State Safety Oversight, Public Transportation Innovation, Technical Assistance and Workforce Development, Bus Testing, the National Transit Database, and Administrative Expenses under the Mass Transit Account of the Highway Trust Fund. These programs support formula and competitive grants, contracts, and cooperative agreements with transit agencies, State departments of transportation, academia, and the private sector. This account also includes support for grant management, project development, technical assistance, program and safety oversight, and core operations.

Object Classification (in millions of dollars)

Identification code 069–8350–0–7–401	2021 actual	2022 est.	2023 est.
Direct obligations:			
11.1 Personnel compensation: Full-time permanent	4	69	75
12.1 Civilian personnel benefits	2	26	27
25.2 Other services from non-Federal sources	92	141	145
41.0 Grants, subsidies, and contributions	10,641	10,954	11,977
99.9 Total new obligations, unexpired accounts	10,739	11,190	12,224

Employment Summary

Identification code 069–8350–0–7–401	2021 actual	2022 est.	2023 est.
1001 Direct civilian full-time equivalent employment	35	551	551

TRANSIT FORMULA GRANTS

(Amounts included in the adjusted baseline)

Program and Financing (in millions of dollars)

Identification code 069–8350–7–7–401	2021 actual	2022 est.	2023 est.
Obligations by program activity:			
0001 Urbanized area programs		877	
0003 Bus and bus facility grants- Competitive		58	
0006 Planning Programs		13	
0010 Seniors and persons with disabilities		44	
0011 Non-urbanized area programs		102	
0013 National Transit Database		1	
0015 Transit Oriented Development		1	
0016 Bus and Bus Facilities Formula Grants		58	
0017 Bus Testing Facility		1	
0019 State of Good Repair Grants		439	
0020 Public Transportation Innovation (Research)		5	
0021 Technical Assistance and Workforce Development		2	
0900 Total new obligations, unexpired accounts (object class 41.0)		1,601	
Budgetary resources:			
Unobligated balance:			
1000 Unobligated balance brought forward, Oct 1			–1,601
Budget authority:			
Appropriations, discretionary:			
1101 Appropriation (special or trust)		3,205	
1138 Appropriations applied to liquidate contract authority		–3,205	
1930 Total budgetary resources available			–1,601
Memorandum (non-add) entries:			
1941 Unexpired unobligated balance, end of year		–1,601	–1,601
Change in obligated balance:			
Unpaid obligations:			
3000 Unpaid obligations, brought forward, Oct 1			1,409
3010 New obligations, unexpired accounts		1,601	
3020 Outlays (gross)		–192	–256
3050 Unpaid obligations, end of year		1,409	1,153
Memorandum (non-add) entries:			
3100 Obligated balance, start of year			1,409
3200 Obligated balance, end of year		1,409	1,153
Budget authority and outlays, net:			
Discretionary:			
Outlays, gross:			
4010 Outlays from new discretionary authority		192	
4011 Outlays from discretionary balances			256
4020 Outlays, gross (total)		192	256
4180 Budget authority, net (total)			
4190 Outlays, net (total)		192	256
Memorandum (non-add) entries:			
5052 Obligated balance, SOY: Contract authority			–3,205
5053 Obligated balance, EOY: Contract authority		–3,205	–3,205

TRANSIT FORMULA GRANTS—Continued
Program and Financing—Continued

Identification code 069–8350–7–7–401	2021 actual	2022 est.	2023 est.
5061 Limitation on obligations (Transportation Trust Funds)	....	3,205	....

ADMINISTRATIVE PROVISIONS—FEDERAL TRANSIT ADMINISTRATION

SEC. 160. The limitations on obligations for the programs of the Federal Transit Administration shall not apply to any authority under 49 U.S.C. 5338, previously made available for obligation, or to any other authority previously made available for obligation.

SEC. 161. Notwithstanding any other provision of law, funds appropriated or limited by this Act under the heading "Capital Investment Grants" of the Federal Transit Administration for projects specified in this Act or identified in the explanatory statement or reports accompanying this Act not obligated by September 30, 2026, and other recoveries, shall be directed to projects eligible to use the funds for the purposes for which they were originally provided.

SEC. 162. Notwithstanding any other provision of law, any funds appropriated before October 1, 2022, under any section of chapter 53 of title 49, United States Code, that remain available for expenditure, may be transferred to and administered under the most recent appropriation heading for any such section.

SEC. 163. None of the funds made available by this Act or any other Act shall be used to adjust apportionments or withhold funds from apportionments pursuant to section 9503(e)(4) of the Internal Revenue Code of 1986 (26 U.S.C. 9503(e)(4)).

GREAT LAKES ST. LAWRENCE SEAWAY DEVELOPMENT CORPORATION

Federal Funds

GREAT LAKES ST. LAWRENCE SEAWAY DEVELOPMENT CORPORATION

The Great Lakes St. Lawrence Seaway Development Corporation is hereby authorized to make such expenditures, within the limits of funds and borrowing authority available to the Corporation, and in accord with law, and to make such contracts and commitments without regard to fiscal year limitations, as provided by section 9104 of title 31, United States Code, as may be necessary in carrying out the programs set forth in the Corporation's budget for the current fiscal year.

Note.—A full-year 2022 appropriation for this account was not enacted at the time the Budget was prepared; therefore, the Budget assumes this account is operating under the Continuing Appropriations Act, 2022 (Division A of Public Law 117–43, as amended). The amounts included for 2022 reflect the annualized level provided by the continuing resolution.

Program and Financing (in millions of dollars)

Identification code 069–4089–0–3–403	2021 actual	2022 est.	2023 est.
Obligations by program activity:			
0001 Direct program activity: Operations and maintenance	33	23	24
0002 Direct program activity: Replacements and improvements	....	15	15
0799 Total direct obligations	33	38	39
0801 Operations and maintenance	....	1	1
0899 Total reimbursable obligations	....	1	1
0900 Total new obligations, unexpired accounts	33	39	40
Budgetary resources:			
Unobligated balance:			
1000 Unobligated balance brought forward, Oct 1	37	44	44
1021 Recoveries of prior year unpaid obligations	1	....	....
1070 Unobligated balance (total)	38	44	44
Budget authority:			
Spending authority from offsetting collections, mandatory:			
1800 Collected	39	39	40
1930 Total budgetary resources available	77	83	84
Memorandum (non-add) entries:			
1941 Unexpired unobligated balance, end of year	44	44	44
Change in obligated balance:			
Unpaid obligations:			
3000 Unpaid obligations, brought forward, Oct 1	17	12	8
3010 New obligations, unexpired accounts	33	39	40
3020 Outlays (gross)	–37	–43	–40
3040 Recoveries of prior year unpaid obligations, unexpired	–1	....	....
3050 Unpaid obligations, end of year	12	8	8
Memorandum (non-add) entries:			
3100 Obligated balance, start of year	17	12	8
3200 Obligated balance, end of year	12	8	8
Budget authority and outlays, net:			
Mandatory:			
4090 Budget authority, gross	39	39	40
Outlays, gross:			
4100 Outlays from new mandatory authority	24	31	32
4101 Outlays from mandatory balances	13	12	8
4110 Outlays, gross (total)	37	43	40
Offsets against gross budget authority and outlays:			
Offsetting collections (collected) from:			
4120 Federal sources	–38	–38	–39
4123 Non-Federal sources	–1	–1	–1
4130 Offsets against gross budget authority and outlays (total)	–39	–39	–40
4170 Outlays, net (mandatory)	–2	4	....
4180 Budget authority, net (total)	....	....	....
4190 Outlays, net (total)	–2	4	....

The Great Lakes St. Lawrence Seaway Development Corporation (GLS) is a wholly-owned U.S. Government corporation responsible for the operation, maintenance, and development of the U.S. portion of the St. Lawrence Seaway between Montreal and mid-Lake Erie. The GLS is also responsible for regional trade and economic development. The St. Lawrence Seaway is a binational waterway and lock transportation system for the efficient and economic movement of commercial cargoes to and from the Great Lakes region of North America. The GLS works with its Canadian counterpart agency (the St. Lawrence Seaway Management Corporation) to ensure the safety and reliability of the locks and waterway and the uninterrupted flow of maritime commerce through the system.

Appropriations from the Harbor Maintenance Trust Fund, and revenues from other non-Federal sources, are used to finance operational and capital infrastructure needs for the U.S. portion of the St. Lawrence Seaway.

Object Classification (in millions of dollars)

Identification code 069–4089–0–3–403	2021 actual	2022 est.	2023 est.
Direct obligations:			
11.1 Personnel compensation: Full-time permanent	12	12	13
12.1 Civilian personnel benefits	4	5	5
25.1 Advisory and assistance services	1	....	....
25.2 Other services from non-Federal sources	4	4	4
25.3 Other goods and services from Federal sources	2	2	2
26.0 Supplies and materials	1	1	1
31.0 Equipment	1	3	3
32.0 Land and structures	8	11	11
99.0 Direct obligations	33	38	39
25.3 Reimbursable obligations: Other goods and services from Federal sources	....	1	1
99.0 Reimbursable obligations	....	1	1
99.9 Total new obligations, unexpired accounts	33	39	40

Employment Summary

Identification code 069–4089–0–3–403	2021 actual	2022 est.	2023 est.
1001 Direct civilian full-time equivalent employment	124	143	143

Trust Funds

OPERATIONS AND MAINTENANCE

(HARBOR MAINTENANCE TRUST FUND)

For necessary expenses to conduct the operations, maintenance, and capital infrastructure activities on portions of the Great Lakes St. Lawrence Seaway owned, operated, and maintained by the Great Lakes St. Lawrence Seaway Development Corporation, $38,500,000, to be derived from the Harbor Maintenance Trust Fund, pursuant to section 210 of the Water Resources Development Act of 1986 (33 U.S.C.

2238): *Provided,* That of the amounts made available under this heading, not less than $14,800,000 shall be for the Seaway infrastructure program and not more than $1,000,000 shall be for the operations and maintenance of the Seaway International Bridge.

Note.—A full-year 2022 appropriation for this account was not enacted at the time the Budget was prepared; therefore, the Budget assumes this account is operating under the Continuing Appropriations Act, 2022 (Division A of Public Law 117–43, as amended). The amounts included for 2022 reflect the annualized level provided by the continuing resolution.

Program and Financing (in millions of dollars)

Identification code 069–8003–0–7–403		2021 actual	2022 est.	2023 est.
	Obligations by program activity:			
0001	Operations and maintenance	38	38	39
0900	Total new obligations, unexpired accounts (object class 25.3)	38	38	39
	Budgetary resources:			
	Budget authority:			
	Appropriations, discretionary:			
1101	Appropriation (special or trust)	38	38	39
1930	Total budgetary resources available	38	38	39
	Change in obligated balance:			
	Unpaid obligations:			
3010	New obligations, unexpired accounts	38	38	39
3020	Outlays (gross)	–38	–38	–39
	Budget authority and outlays, net:			
	Discretionary:			
4000	Budget authority, gross	38	38	39
	Outlays, gross:			
4010	Outlays from new discretionary authority	38	38	39
4180	Budget authority, net (total)	38	38	39
4190	Outlays, net (total)	38	38	39

The Water Resources Development Act of 1986 (P.L. 99–662) authorizes use of the Harbor Maintenance Trust Fund as an appropriation source for the Great Lakes St. Lawrence Seaway Development Corporation's operating and capital infrastructure programs.

PIPELINE AND HAZARDOUS MATERIALS SAFETY ADMINISTRATION

The 2023 Budget request will provide $539 million to protect people and the environment by advancing the safe transportation of energy products and other hazardous materials that are essential to our daily lives. The Pipeline And Hazardous Materials Safety Administration (PHMSA) establishes national policy; sets and enforces safety standards; provides grants for the repair and replacement of ageing pipelines, state safety inspections and safety training; conducts research; and prepares the public and first responders to reduce consequences, should an incident occur.

Federal Funds

OPERATIONAL EXPENSES

For necessary operational expenses of the Pipeline and Hazardous Materials Safety Administration, $30,150,000, of which $4,500,000 shall remain available until September 30, 2025.

Note.—A full-year 2022 appropriation for this account was not enacted at the time the Budget was prepared; therefore, the Budget assumes this account is operating under the Continuing Appropriations Act, 2022 (Division A of Public Law 117–43, as amended). The amounts included for 2022 reflect the annualized level provided by the continuing resolution.

Program and Financing (in millions of dollars)

Identification code 069–1400–0–1–407		2021 actual	2022 est.	2023 est.
	Obligations by program activity:			
0001	Operations	24	24	25
0002	Grants	2	5	5
0799	Total direct obligations	26	29	30
0900	Total new obligations, unexpired accounts	26	29	30
	Budgetary resources:			
	Unobligated balance:			
1000	Unobligated balance brought forward, Oct 1		3	3
	Budget authority:			
	Appropriations, discretionary:			
1100	Appropriation	29	29	30
1930	Total budgetary resources available	29	32	33
	Memorandum (non-add) entries:			
1941	Unexpired unobligated balance, end of year	3	3	3
	Change in obligated balance:			
	Unpaid obligations:			
3000	Unpaid obligations, brought forward, Oct 1	8	11	9
3010	New obligations, unexpired accounts	26	29	30
3020	Outlays (gross)	–23	–31	–32
3050	Unpaid obligations, end of year	11	9	7
	Memorandum (non-add) entries:			
3100	Obligated balance, start of year	8	11	9
3200	Obligated balance, end of year	11	9	7
	Budget authority and outlays, net:			
	Discretionary:			
4000	Budget authority, gross	29	29	30
	Outlays, gross:			
4010	Outlays from new discretionary authority	17	20	20
4011	Outlays from discretionary balances	6	11	12
4020	Outlays, gross (total)	23	31	32
4180	Budget authority, net (total)	29	29	30
4190	Outlays, net (total)	23	31	32

The success of the Pipeline and Hazardous Materials Safety Administration (PHMSA) safety programs is dependent on effective support organizations that hire staff, acquire goods and services, develop and sustain information technology, write complex regulations, and support enforcement actions, among others. PHMSA provides support through the Offices of the Administrator, Deputy Administrator, Executive Director/Chief Safety Officer; Planning and Analytics; Chief Counsel; Governmental, International and Public Affairs; Chief Financial Officer, Budget and Finance, Acquisition and Information Technology Services; Associate Administrator for Administration, Administrative Services, Human Resources; and Civil Rights.

Object Classification (in millions of dollars)

Identification code 069–1400–0–1–407		2021 actual	2022 est.	2023 est.
	Direct obligations:			
	Personnel compensation:			
11.1	Full-time permanent	9	9	10
11.3	Other than full-time permanent	1	1	
11.9	Total personnel compensation	10	10	10
12.1	Civilian personnel benefits	3	4	4
23.1	Rental payments to GSA	1	1	1
25.1	Advisory and assistance services	5	3	5
25.3	Other goods and services from Federal sources	2	2	2
25.7	Operation and maintenance of equipment	3	4	3
31.0	Equipment	1		
41.0	Grants, subsidies, and contributions	2	5	5
99.0	Direct obligations	27	29	30
99.5	Adjustment for rounding	–1		
99.9	Total new obligations, unexpired accounts	26	29	30

Employment Summary

Identification code 069–1400–0–1–407	2021 actual	2022 est.	2023 est.
1001 Direct civilian full-time equivalent employment	64	68	69

HAZARDOUS MATERIALS SAFETY

For expenses necessary to discharge the hazardous materials safety functions of the Pipeline and Hazardous Materials Safety Administration, $74,211,000, to remain available until September 30, 2025: Provided, That up to $800,000 in fees collected

HAZARDOUS MATERIALS SAFETY—Continued

under 49 U.S.C. 5108(g) shall be deposited in the general fund of the Treasury as offsetting receipts: *Provided further*, *That there may be credited to this appropriation, to be available until expended, funds received from States, counties, municipalities, other public authorities, and private sources for expenses incurred for training, for reports publication and dissemination, and for travel expenses incurred in performance of hazardous materials exemptions and approvals functions.*

Note.—A full-year 2022 appropriation for this account was not enacted at the time the Budget was prepared; therefore, the Budget assumes this account is operating under the Continuing Appropriations Act, 2022 (Division A of Public Law 117–43, as amended). The amounts included for 2022 reflect the annualized level provided by the continuing resolution.

Program and Financing (in millions of dollars)

Identification code 069–1401–0–1–407	2021 actual	2022 est.	2023 est.
Obligations by program activity:			
0001 Operations	48	53	65
0002 Research and development	8	5	8
0003 Grants	1	4	1
0799 Total direct obligations	57	62	74
0801 Reimbursable program	1	1	1
0900 Total new obligations, unexpired accounts	58	63	75
Budgetary resources:			
Unobligated balance:			
1000 Unobligated balance brought forward, Oct 1	6	11	11
Budget authority:			
Appropriations, discretionary:			
1100 Appropriation	62	62	74
Spending authority from offsetting collections, discretionary:			
1700 Collected	1	1	1
1900 Budget authority (total)	63	63	75
1930 Total budgetary resources available	69	74	86
Memorandum (non-add) entries:			
1941 Unexpired unobligated balance, end of year	11	11	11
Change in obligated balance:			
Unpaid obligations:			
3000 Unpaid obligations, brought forward, Oct 1	25	24	16
3010 New obligations, unexpired accounts	58	63	75
3020 Outlays (gross)	–59	–71	–79
3050 Unpaid obligations, end of year	24	16	12
Memorandum (non-add) entries:			
3100 Obligated balance, start of year	25	24	16
3200 Obligated balance, end of year	24	16	12
Budget authority and outlays, net:			
Discretionary:			
4000 Budget authority, gross	63	63	75
Outlays, gross:			
4010 Outlays from new discretionary authority	44	43	51
4011 Outlays from discretionary balances	15	28	28
4020 Outlays, gross (total)	59	71	79
Offsets against gross budget authority and outlays:			
Offsetting collections (collected) from:			
4030 Federal sources	–1	–1	–1
4040 Offsets against gross budget authority and outlays (total)	–1	–1	–1
4180 Budget authority, net (total)	62	62	74
4190 Outlays, net (total)	58	70	78

PHMSA's Hazardous Materials Safety program is responsible for the oversight of the safe transportation of hazardous materials. The program relies on comprehensive risk management to establish policy, standards and regulations for classifying, packaging, hazard communication, handling, training and transporting hazardous materials via air, highway, rail and vessel. The program uses inspection, enforcement, outreach and incident analysis in efforts to reduce incidents, minimize fatalities and injuries, mitigate the consequences of incidents that occur, train and prepare first responders and enhance safety.

Object Classification (in millions of dollars)

Identification code 069–1401–0–1–407	2021 actual	2022 est.	2023 est.
Direct obligations:			
Personnel compensation:			
11.1 Full-time permanent	23	24	28
11.5 Other personnel compensation	1	1	1
11.9 Total personnel compensation	24	25	29
12.1 Civilian personnel benefits	8	9	10
21.0 Travel and transportation of persons	1	1	2
23.1 Rental payments to GSA	2	2	3
25.1 Advisory and assistance services	8	9	13
25.3 Other goods and services from Federal sources	7	6	8
25.5 Research and development contracts	1	5	8
25.7 Operation and maintenance of equipment	5	....	....
41.0 Grants, subsidies, and contributions	1	4	1
99.0 Direct obligations	57	61	74
99.0 Reimbursable obligations	1	1	1
99.5 Adjustment for rounding	....	1	....
99.9 Total new obligations, unexpired accounts	58	63	75

Employment Summary

Identification code 069–1401–0–1–407	2021 actual	2022 est.	2023 est.
1001 Direct civilian full-time equivalent employment	188	203	219

NATURAL GAS DISTRIBUTION INFRASTRUCTURE SAFETY AND MODERNIZATION GRANT PROGRAM

〔(INCLUDING TRANSFER OF FUNDS)〕

〔For an additional amount for "Natural Gas Distribution Infrastructure Safety and Modernization Grant Program", $1,000,000,000, to remain available until expended for the Secretary of Transportation to make competitive grants for the modernization of natural gas distribution pipelines: *Provided*, That $200,000,000, to remain available until September 30, 2032, shall be made available for fiscal year 2022, $200,000,000, to remain available until September 30, 2033, shall be made available for fiscal year 2023, $200,000,000, to remain available until September 30, 2034, shall be made available for fiscal year 2024, $200,000,000, to remain available until September 30, 2035, shall be made available for fiscal year 2025, and $200,000,000, to remain available until September 30, 2036, shall be made available for fiscal year 2026: *Provided further*, That grants from funds made available under this heading in this Act shall be available to a municipality or community owned utility (not including for-profit entities) to repair, rehabilitate, or replace its natural gas distribution pipeline system or portions thereof or to acquire equipment to (1) reduce incidents and fatalities and (2) avoid economic losses: *Provided further*, That in making grants from funds made available under this heading in this Act, the Secretary shall establish procedures for awarding grants that take into consideration the following: (1) the risk profile of the existing pipeline system operated by the applicant, including the presence of pipe prone to leakage; (2) the potential of the project for creating jobs; (3) the potential for benefiting disadvantaged rural and urban communities; and (4) economic impact or growth: *Provided further*, That the Secretary shall not award more than 12.5 percent of the funds available under this heading to a single municipality or community-owned utility: *Provided further*, That the Secretary shall issue a notice of funding opportunity not later than 180 days after each date upon which funds are made available under the first proviso: *Provided further*, That the Secretary shall make awards not later than 270 days after issuing the notices of funding opportunity required under the preceding proviso: *Provided further*, That not more than 2 percent of the amounts made available in each fiscal year shall be available to pay the administrative costs of carrying out the grant program under this heading in this Act: *Provided further*, That one-half of one percent of the amounts transferred pursuant to the authority in this section in each of fiscal years 2022 through 2026 shall be transferred to the Office of Inspector General of the Department of Transportation for oversight of funding provided to the Department of Transportation in this Act: *Provided further*, That such amount is designated by the Congress as being for an emergency requirement pursuant to section 4112(a) of H. Con. Res. 71 (115th Congress), the concurrent resolution on the budget for fiscal year 2018, and to section 251(b) of the Balanced Budget and Emergency Deficit Control Act of 1985.〕 *(Infrastructure Investments and Jobs Appropriations Act.)*

Program and Financing (in millions of dollars)

Identification code 069–1402–0–1–407	2021 actual	2022 est.	2023 est.
Obligations by program activity:			
0001 Operations	....	4	4
0002 Grants	....	196	196

		2021 actual	2022 est.	2023 est.
0900	Total new obligations, unexpired accounts		200	200
	Budgetary resources:			
	Budget authority:			
	Appropriations, discretionary:			
1100	Appropriation		200	
	Advance appropriations, discretionary:			
1170	Advance appropriation			200
1900	Budget authority (total)		200	200
1930	Total budgetary resources available		200	200
	Change in obligated balance:			
	Unpaid obligations:			
3000	Unpaid obligations, brought forward, Oct 1			199
3010	New obligations, unexpired accounts		200	200
3020	Outlays (gross)		–1	–80
3050	Unpaid obligations, end of year		199	319
	Memorandum (non-add) entries:			
3100	Obligated balance, start of year			199
3200	Obligated balance, end of year		199	319
	Budget authority and outlays, net:			
	Discretionary:			
4000	Budget authority, gross		200	200
	Outlays, gross:			
4010	Outlays from new discretionary authority		1	40
4011	Outlays from discretionary balances			40
4020	Outlays, gross (total)		1	80
4180	Budget authority, net (total)		200	200
4190	Outlays, net (total)		1	80

The Infrastructure Investment and Jobs Act (IIJA) of 2021 provided funding for the Natural Gas Distribution Infrastructure Safety and Modernization Grant Program. Grant funds are made available to a municipality or community owned utility (not including for-profit entities) to repair, rehabilitate, or replace its natural gas distribution pipeline system or portions thereof or to acquire equipment to (1) reduce incidents and fatalities and (2) avoid economic losses. With the replacement of legacy gas distribution pipelines, these systems will operate more safely, reduce methane emissions, and will serve as the building blocks of the infrastructure to transport fuels of the future.

Object Classification (in millions of dollars)

Identification code 069–1402–0–1–407	2021 actual	2022 est.	2023 est.
Direct obligations:			
11.1 Personnel compensation: Full-time permanent			1
21.0 Travel and transportation of persons		1	1
25.1 Advisory and assistance services		3	2
41.0 Grants, subsidies, and contributions		196	196
99.9 Total new obligations, unexpired accounts		200	200

Employment Summary

Identification code 069–1402–0–1–407	2021 actual	2022 est.	2023 est.
1001 Direct civilian full-time equivalent employment		4	8

PIPELINE SAFETY

(PIPELINE SAFETY FUND)

(OIL SPILL LIABILITY TRUST FUND)

For expenses necessary to carry out a pipeline safety program, as authorized by 49 U.S.C. 60107, and to discharge the pipeline program responsibilities of the Oil Pollution Act of 1990, $187,800,000, to remain available until September 30, 2025, of which $29,000,000 shall be derived from the Oil Spill Liability Trust Fund; of which $151,400,000 shall be derived from the Pipeline Safety Fund; of which $400,000 shall be derived from the fees collected under 49 U.S.C. 60303 and deposited in the Liquified Natural Gas Siting Account for compliance reviews of liquefied natural gas facilities; and of which $7,000,000 shall be derived from fees collected under 49 U.S.C. 60302 and deposited in the Underground Natural Gas Storage Facility Safety Account for the purpose of carrying out 49 U.S.C. 60141.

Note.—A full-year 2022 appropriation for this account was not enacted at the time the Budget was prepared; therefore, the Budget assumes this account is operating under the Continuing Appropriations Act, 2022 (Division A of Public Law 117–43, as amended). The amounts included for 2022 reflect the annualized level provided by the continuing resolution.

Special and Trust Fund Receipts (in millions of dollars)

Identification code 069–5172–0–2–407	2021 actual	2022 est.	2023 est.
0100 Balance, start of year	50	51	51
Receipts:			
Current law:			
1120 Pipeline Safety Fund	137	137	151
1120 Underground Natural Gas Storage Facility Safety	8	8	7
1199 Total current law receipts	145	145	158
1999 Total receipts	145	145	158
2000 Total: Balances and receipts	195	196	209
Appropriations:			
Current law:			
2101 Pipeline Safety	–145	–145	–159
Special and trust fund receipts returned:			
3010 Pipeline Safety	2		
3010 Pipeline Safety	2		
5098 Reconciliation adjustment	–3		
5099 Balance, end of year	51	51	50

Program and Financing (in millions of dollars)

Identification code 069–5172–0–2–407	2021 actual	2022 est.	2023 est.
Obligations by program activity:			
0001 Operations	91	114	107
0002 Research and development	15	32	15
0003 Grants	73	71	66
0799 Total direct obligations	179	217	188
0801 Reimbursable program		1	1
0900 Total new obligations, unexpired accounts	179	218	189
Budgetary resources:			
Unobligated balance:			
1000 Unobligated balance brought forward, Oct 1	44	50	1
1021 Recoveries of prior year unpaid obligations	17		
1070 Unobligated balance (total)	61	50	1
Budget authority:			
Appropriations, discretionary:			
1101 Appropriation (special or trust)	145	145	159
Spending authority from offsetting collections, discretionary:			
1700 Collected	26	24	30
1701 Change in uncollected payments, Federal sources	–3		
1750 Spending auth from offsetting collections, disc (total)	23	24	30
1900 Budget authority (total)	168	169	189
1930 Total budgetary resources available	229	219	190
Memorandum (non-add) entries:			
1941 Unexpired unobligated balance, end of year	50	1	1
Special and non-revolving trust funds:			
1950 Other balances withdrawn and returned to unappropriated receipts	2		
1952 Expired unobligated balance, start of year	3	7	7
1953 Expired unobligated balance, end of year	7	7	7
1954 Unobligated balance canceling	2		
Change in obligated balance:			
Unpaid obligations:			
3000 Unpaid obligations, brought forward, Oct 1	138	126	139
3010 New obligations, unexpired accounts	179	218	189
3011 Obligations ("upward adjustments"), expired accounts	2		
3020 Outlays (gross)	–170	–205	–205
3040 Recoveries of prior year unpaid obligations, unexpired	–17		
3041 Recoveries of prior year unpaid obligations, expired	–6		
3050 Unpaid obligations, end of year	126	139	123
Uncollected payments:			
3060 Uncollected pymts, Fed sources, brought forward, Oct 1	–18	–15	–15
3070 Change in uncollected pymts, Fed sources, unexpired	3		
3090 Uncollected pymts, Fed sources, end of year	–15	–15	–15
Memorandum (non-add) entries:			
3100 Obligated balance, start of year	120	111	124
3200 Obligated balance, end of year	111	124	108

PIPELINE SAFETY—Continued
Program and Financing—Continued

Identification code 069–5172–0–2–407	2021 actual	2022 est.	2023 est.
Budget authority and outlays, net:			
Discretionary:			
4000 Budget authority, gross	168	169	189
Outlays, gross:			
4010 Outlays from new discretionary authority	47	83	93
4011 Outlays from discretionary balances	123	122	112
4020 Outlays, gross (total)	170	205	205
Offsets against gross budget authority and outlays:			
Offsetting collections (collected) from:			
4030 Federal sources	–26	–24	–30
4033 Non-Federal sources	–2		
4040 Offsets against gross budget authority and outlays (total)	–28	–24	–30
Additional offsets against gross budget authority only:			
4050 Change in uncollected pymts, Fed sources, unexpired	3		
4052 Offsetting collections credited to expired accounts	2		
4060 Additional offsets against budget authority only (total)	5		
4070 Budget authority, net (discretionary)	145	145	159
4080 Outlays, net (discretionary)	142	181	175
4180 Budget authority, net (total)	145	145	159
4190 Outlays, net (total)	142	181	175

PHMSA oversees the safe transportation of energy products and hazardous materials through pipelines. PHMSA's Pipeline Safety program regulates an expansive network of more than 2.8 million miles of gas and hazardous liquid pipelines within the United States, as well as facilities that liquefy natural gas and store natural gas underground. PHMSA establishes and enforces pipeline safety standards and conducts safety inspections in collaboration with State partners to monitor the construction and operating safety of pipelines. The Pipeline Safety program is funded by fees collected from pipeline and underground natural gas storage facility operators, as well as an annual allocation from the Oil Spill Liability Trust Fund.

Object Classification (in millions of dollars)

Identification code 069–5172–0–2–407	2021 actual	2022 est.	2023 est.
Direct obligations:			
Personnel compensation:			
11.1 Full-time permanent	37	39	45
11.5 Other personnel compensation	1	1	1
11.9 Total personnel compensation	38	40	46
12.1 Civilian personnel benefits	14	15	17
21.0 Travel and transportation	1	3	4
23.1 Rental payments to GSA	4	4	4
25.1 Advisory and assistance services	15	22	24
25.3 Other goods and services from Federal sources	8	11	9
25.5 Research and development contracts	15	32	15
25.7 Operation and maintenance of equipment	14	17	2
26.0 Supplies and materials			1
31.0 Equipment		1	
41.0 Grants, subsidies, and contributions	71	71	66
99.0 Direct obligations	180	216	188
99.0 Reimbursable obligations		1	1
99.5 Adjustment for rounding	–1	1	
99.9 Total new obligations, unexpired accounts	179	218	189

Employment Summary

Identification code 069–5172–0–2–407	2021 actual	2022 est.	2023 est.
1001 Direct civilian full-time equivalent employment	304	316	338

EMERGENCY PREPAREDNESS GRANTS

Note.—A full-year 2022 appropriation for this account was not enacted at the time the Budget was prepared; therefore, the Budget assumes this account is operating under the Continuing Appropriations Act, 2022 (Division A of Public Law 117–43, as amended). The amounts included for 2022 reflect the annualized level provided by the continuing resolution.

Special and Trust Fund Receipts (in millions of dollars)

Identification code 069–5282–0–2–407	2021 actual	2022 est.	2023 est.
0100 Balance, start of year	1	1	3
Receipts:			
Current law:			
1130 Hazardous Materials Transportation Registration, Filing, and Permit Fees, Emergency Preparedness Grants	27	29	47
2000 Total: Balances and receipts	28	30	50
Appropriations:			
Current law:			
2101 Emergency Preparedness Grants	–29	–29	–47
2132 Emergency Preparedness Grants	2	2	2
2199 Total current law appropriations	–27	–27	–45
2999 Total appropriations	–27	–27	–45
5099 Balance, end of year	1	3	5

Program and Financing (in millions of dollars)

Identification code 069–5282–0–2–407	2021 actual	2022 est.	2023 est.
Obligations by program activity:			
0001 Operations	1	1	1
0002 Emergency Preparedness Grants	22	22	39
0003 Competitive Training Grants	3	4	5
0004 Supplemental Training Grants	1	1	2
0005 ALERT Grants	2	1	
0900 Total new obligations, unexpired accounts	29	29	47
Budgetary resources:			
Unobligated balance:			
1000 Unobligated balance brought forward, Oct 1	13	17	16
1021 Recoveries of prior year unpaid obligations	5		
1070 Unobligated balance (total)	18	17	16
Budget authority:			
Appropriations, discretionary:			
1100 Appropriation		1	
Appropriations, mandatory:			
1200 Appropriation	1		
1201 Appropriation (special or trust fund)	29	29	47
1232 Appropriations and/or unobligated balance of appropriations temporarily reduced	–2	–2	–2
1260 Appropriations, mandatory (total)	28	27	45
1900 Budget authority (total)	28	28	45
1930 Total budgetary resources available	46	45	61
Memorandum (non-add) entries:			
1941 Unexpired unobligated balance, end of year	17	16	14
Change in obligated balance:			
Unpaid obligations:			
3000 Unpaid obligations, brought forward, Oct 1	53	56	44
3010 New obligations, unexpired accounts	29	29	47
3020 Outlays (gross)	–21	–41	–47
3040 Recoveries of prior year unpaid obligations, unexpired	–5		
3050 Unpaid obligations, end of year	56	44	44
Memorandum (non-add) entries:			
3100 Obligated balance, start of year	53	56	44
3200 Obligated balance, end of year	56	44	44
Budget authority and outlays, net:			
Discretionary:			
4000 Budget authority, gross		1	
Mandatory:			
4090 Budget authority, gross	28	27	45
Outlays, gross:			
4100 Outlays from new mandatory authority		9	15
4101 Outlays from mandatory balances	21	32	32
4110 Outlays, gross (total)	21	41	47
4180 Budget authority, net (total)	28	28	45
4190 Outlays, net (total)	21	41	47

PHMSA operates a national registration program for shippers and carriers of hazardous materials and collects a fee from each registrant. The fees collected are used for emergency preparedness planning and training grants; publication and distribution of the Emergency Response Guidebook; development of training curriculum guidelines for emergency responders and

DEPARTMENT OF TRANSPORTATION

technical assistance to States, political subdivisions, and Federally-recognized tribes; and administrative costs for these programs.

Object Classification (in millions of dollars)

Identification code 069–5282–0–2–407	2021 actual	2022 est.	2023 est.
Direct obligations:			
25.3 Other goods and services from Federal sources	1	1	1
41.0 Grants, subsidies, and contributions	28	28	46
99.0 Direct obligations	29	29	47
99.9 Total new obligations, unexpired accounts	29	29	47

Trust Funds
TRUST FUND SHARE OF PIPELINE SAFETY

Program and Financing (in millions of dollars)

Identification code 069–8121–0–7–407	2021 actual	2022 est.	2023 est.
Obligations by program activity:			
0001 Trust fund share of pipeline safety	23	23	29
0900 Total new obligations, unexpired accounts (object class 94.0)	23	23	29
Budgetary resources:			
Budget authority:			
Appropriations, discretionary:			
1101 Appropriation (special or trust)	23	23	29
1930 Total budgetary resources available	23	23	29
Change in obligated balance:			
Unpaid obligations:			
3000 Unpaid obligations, brought forward, Oct 1	18	15	19
3010 New obligations, unexpired accounts	23	23	29
3020 Outlays (gross)	–26	–19	–32
3050 Unpaid obligations, end of year	15	19	16
Memorandum (non-add) entries:			
3100 Obligated balance, start of year	18	15	19
3200 Obligated balance, end of year	15	19	16
Budget authority and outlays, net:			
Discretionary:			
4000 Budget authority, gross	23	23	29
Outlays, gross:			
4010 Outlays from new discretionary authority	11	11	14
4011 Outlays from discretionary balances	15	8	18
4020 Outlays, gross (total)	26	19	32
4180 Budget authority, net (total)	23	23	29
4190 Outlays, net (total)	26	19	32

PHMSA has multiple responsibilities to inspect, investigate failures, regulate, and research hazardous liquid pipelines. In addition, PHMSA collects and reviews oil spill response plans prepared under the Oil Pollution Act of 1990. Operators that store, handle, or transport oil are required to develop response plans to minimize the environmental impact of oil spills and improve incident response. PHMSA reviews these plans to make sure that they are submitted on time, updated regularly, and that they comply with regulations. PHMSA improves oil spill preparedness and incident response through data analysis, inspections, exercises, spill monitoring, pipeline mapping in areas unusually sensitive to environmental damage, and by advancing technologies to detect and prevent leaks from hazardous liquid pipelines. These activities are funded in part by the Oil Spill Liability Trust Fund.

ADMINISTRATIVE PROVISIONS

SEC. 180. The matter under the heading "Department of Transportation—Pipeline and Hazardous Materials Safety Administration—Natural Gas Distribution Infrastructure Safety and Modernization Grant Program" in title VIII of division J of Public Law 117–58 is amended in the eighth proviso by striking "transferred pursuant to the authority in this section in each of fiscal years 2022 through 2026" and inserting "referred to in the preceding proviso".

SEC. 181. Section 5108(g)(2)(A) of title 49, United States Code, is amended by striking "$3,000" and inserting "$15,000".

SEC. 182. Notwithstanding section 5116(h)(4) of title 49, United States Code, not more than 4 percent of the amounts made available from the account established under section 5116 of such title shall be available to pay administrative costs of carrying out sections 5116, 5107(e), and 5108(g)(2) of such title.

OFFICE OF INSPECTOR GENERAL

Federal Funds

SALARIES AND EXPENSES

For necessary expenses of the Office of Inspector General to carry out the provisions of the Inspector General Act of 1978, as amended, $108,073,000: Provided, That the Inspector General shall have all necessary authority, in carrying out the duties specified in the Inspector General Act, as amended (5 U.S.C. App.), to investigate allegations of fraud, including false statements to the government (18 U.S.C. 1001), by any person or entity that is subject to regulation by the Department of Transportation.

Note.—A full-year 2022 appropriation for this account was not enacted at the time the Budget was prepared; therefore, the Budget assumes this account is operating under the Continuing Appropriations Act, 2022 (Division A of Public Law 117–43, as amended). The amounts included for 2022 reflect the annualized level provided by the continuing resolution.

Program and Financing (in millions of dollars)

Identification code 069–0130–0–1–407	2021 actual	2022 est.	2023 est.
Obligations by program activity:			
0101 General administration	98	98	108
0103 Disaster Relief and Oversight FY 2013	1	1	1
0104 Coronavirus Aid, Relief, and Economic Security Act	1	1	1
0105 Infrastructure and Investment Jobs Act 2021			1
0900 Total new obligations, unexpired accounts	100	100	111
Budgetary resources:			
Unobligated balance:			
1000 Unobligated balance brought forward, Oct 1	8	6	7
Budget authority:			
Appropriations, discretionary:			
1100 Appropriation	98	98	108
1121 Appropriations transferred from other acct [069–1338]		1	
1121 Appropriations transferred from other acct [069–1337]		1	
1121 Appropriations transferred from other acct [069–0548]		1	
1160 Appropriation, discretionary (total)	98	101	108
Advance appropriations, discretionary:			
1173 Advance appropriations transferred from other accounts [069–1338]			1
1173 Advance appropriations transferred from other accounts [069–1337]			1
1173 Advance appropriations transferred from other accounts [069–0548]			1
1180 Advanced appropriation, discretionary (total)			3
1900 Budget authority (total)	98	101	111
1930 Total budgetary resources available	106	107	118
Memorandum (non-add) entries:			
1941 Unexpired unobligated balance, end of year	6	7	7
Change in obligated balance:			
Unpaid obligations:			
3000 Unpaid obligations, brought forward, Oct 1	10	14	13
3010 New obligations, unexpired accounts	100	100	111
3020 Outlays (gross)	–95	–101	–109
3041 Recoveries of prior year unpaid obligations, expired	–1		
3050 Unpaid obligations, end of year	14	13	15
Memorandum (non-add) entries:			
3100 Obligated balance, start of year	10	14	13
3200 Obligated balance, end of year	14	13	15
Budget authority and outlays, net:			
Discretionary:			
4000 Budget authority, gross	98	101	111
Outlays, gross:			
4010 Outlays from new discretionary authority	87	88	98
4011 Outlays from discretionary balances	8	13	11
4020 Outlays, gross (total)	95	101	109

SALARIES AND EXPENSES—Continued
Program and Financing—Continued

Identification code 069–0130–0–1–407	2021 actual	2022 est.	2023 est.
4180 Budget authority, net (total)	98	101	111
4190 Outlays, net (total)	95	101	109

The Department of Transportation (DOT) Inspector General conducts independent audits, investigations, and evaluations to promote economy, efficiency, and effectiveness in the management and administration of DOT programs and operations, including contracts, grants, and financial management; and to prevent and detect fraud, waste, abuse, and mismanagement in such activities. This appropriation provides funds to enable the Office of the Inspector General to perform these oversight responsibilities in accordance with the Inspector General Act of 1978, as amended (5 U.S.C. App.).

Object Classification (in millions of dollars)

Identification code 069–0130–0–1–407		2021 actual	2022 est.	2023 est.
	Direct obligations:			
	Personnel compensation:			
11.1	Full-time permanent	48	49	54
11.3	Other than full-time permanent	1	1	1
11.5	Other personnel compensation	4	4	4
11.9	Total personnel compensation	53	54	59
12.1	Civilian personnel benefits	21	23	26
21.0	Travel and transportation of persons	1	1	2
23.1	Rental payments to GSA	5	5	5
23.3	Communications, utilities, and miscellaneous charges	1	1	1
25.2	Other services from non-Federal sources	5	4	4
25.3	Other goods and services from Federal sources	7	8	9
25.7	Operation and maintenance of equipment	2	2	2
31.0	Equipment	2	1	2
32.0	Land and structures	1		
99.0	Direct obligations	98	99	110
99.5	Adjustment for rounding	2	1	1
99.9	Total new obligations, unexpired accounts	100	100	111

Employment Summary

Identification code 069–0130–0–1–407	2021 actual	2022 est.	2023 est.
1001 Direct civilian full-time equivalent employment	389	393	425

MARITIME ADMINISTRATION
Federal Funds

OPERATIONS AND TRAINING

For necessary expenses of operations and training activities authorized by law, $192,000,000: Provided, That of the amounts made available under this heading—

(1) $87,848,000, to remain available until September 30, 2024, shall be for the operations of the United States Merchant Marine Academy;

(2) $11,900,000, to remain available until expended, shall be for facilities maintenance and repair, and equipment, at the United States Merchant Marine Academy;

(3) $10,000,000, to remain available until September 30, 2024, shall be for the Maritime Environmental and Technical Assistance program authorized under section 50307 of title 46, United States Code; and

(4) $10,819,000, to remain available until expended, shall be for grants for the America's Marine Highway Program to make grants for the purposes authorized under paragraphs (1) and (3) of section 55601(b) of title 46, United States Code: Provided further, That not to exceed 10 percent of any funds made available for any program, project, or activity under this heading in this Act may be transferred to any other budget activity under this heading: Provided further, That funds transferred pursuant to this section shall be made available for the same purposes and the same time period as the budget activity to which the funds are transferred: Provided further, That no transfer under this section may increase or decrease any program, project, or activity under the heading "Department of Transportation—Maritime Administration—Operations and Training" by more than 10 percent, except that increases for facilities maintenance and repair and equipment at the United States Merchant Marine Academy may exceed 10 percent: Provided further, That any increase or decrease in excess of 10 percent, except as provided for in the previous proviso, shall be treated as a reprogramming of funds under section 405 of this Act and shall not be available for obligation or expenditure except in compliance with the procedures set forth in that section: Provided further, That the Administrator of the Maritime Administration shall transmit to the House and Senate Committees on Appropriations the annual report on sexual assault and sexual harassment at the United States Merchant Marine Academy as required pursuant to section 3510 of the National Defense Authorization Act for Fiscal Year 2017 (46 U.S.C. 51318): Provided further, That available balances under this heading for the Short Sea Transportation Program (now known as the America's Marine Highway Program) from prior year recoveries shall be available to carry out activities authorized under paragraphs (1) and (3) of section 55601(b) of title 46, United States Code.

Note.—A full-year 2022 appropriation for this account was not enacted at the time the Budget was prepared; therefore, the Budget assumes this account is operating under the Continuing Appropriations Act, 2022 (Division A of Public Law 117–43, as amended). The amounts included for 2022 reflect the annualized level provided by the continuing resolution.

OPERATIONS AND TRAINING

[For an additional amount for "Operations and Training", $25,000,000, to remain available until September 30, 2032, for the America's Marine Highway Program to make grants for the purposes authorized under sections 55601(b)(1) and (3) of title 46, United States Code: *Provided*, That such amount is designated by the Congress as being for an emergency requirement pursuant to section 4112(a) of H. Con. Res. 71 (115th Congress), the concurrent resolution on the budget for fiscal year 2018, and to section 251(b) of the Balanced Budget and Emergency Deficit Control Act of 1985.] *(Infrastructure Investments and Jobs Appropriations Act.)*

Program and Financing (in millions of dollars)

Identification code 069–1750–0–1–403		2021 actual	2022 est.	2023 est.
	Obligations by program activity:			
0001	Academy Operations	87	77	87
0002	USMMA Capital Asset Management Program	17	26	63
0008	Maritime Operations	55	56	67
0009	Maritime Environment and Technical Assistance	2	3	3
0010	Short Sea Transportation	6	10	13
0012	Title XI Administrative Expenses	3	3	3
0017	USMMA Collections	1	1	1
0018	America's Marine Highway Grants - IIJA			5
0020	Sealift Contested Environment Evaluation			2
0021	National Defense Reserve Fleet (NDRF) Resiliency			1
0022	TSSM Maritime Training Platform Requirements			1
0100	Subtotal, Direct program	171	176	246
0799	Total direct obligations	171	176	246
0801	Operations and Training (Reimbursable)	1	15	15
0900	Total new obligations, unexpired accounts	172	191	261
	Budgetary resources:			
	Unobligated balance:			
1000	Unobligated balance brought forward, Oct 1	157	150	155
1021	Recoveries of prior year unpaid obligations	1		
1070	Unobligated balance (total)	158	150	155
	Budget authority:			
	Appropriations, discretionary:			
1100	Appropriation	156	156	192
1100	Appropriation- IIJA		25	
1160	Appropriation, discretionary (total)	156	181	192
	Spending authority from offsetting collections, discretionary:			
1700	Collected	8	15	15
1701	Change in uncollected payments, Federal sources	1		
1750	Spending auth from offsetting collections, disc (total)	9	15	15
1900	Budget authority (total)	165	196	207
1930	Total budgetary resources available	323	346	362
	Memorandum (non-add) entries:			
1940	Unobligated balance expiring	–1		
1941	Unexpired unobligated balance, end of year	150	155	101
	Change in obligated balance:			
	Unpaid obligations:			
3000	Unpaid obligations, brought forward, Oct 1	77	79	82
3010	New obligations, unexpired accounts	172	191	261
3020	Outlays (gross)	–168	–188	–194
3040	Recoveries of prior year unpaid obligations, unexpired	–1		
3041	Recoveries of prior year unpaid obligations, expired	–1		

DEPARTMENT OF TRANSPORTATION

		2021 actual	2022 est.	2023 est.
3050	Unpaid obligations, end of year	79	82	149
	Uncollected payments:			
3060	Uncollected pymts, Fed sources, brought forward, Oct 1	−39	−37	−37
3070	Change in uncollected pymts, Fed sources, unexpired	−1		
3071	Change in uncollected pymts, Fed sources, expired	3		
3090	Uncollected pymts, Fed sources, end of year	−37	−37	−37
	Memorandum (non-add) entries:			
3100	Obligated balance, start of year	38	42	45
3200	Obligated balance, end of year	42	45	112
	Budget authority and outlays, net:			
	Discretionary:			
4000	Budget authority, gross	165	196	207
	Outlays, gross:			
4010	Outlays from new discretionary authority	122	138	169
4011	Outlays from discretionary balances	46	50	25
4020	Outlays, gross (total)	168	188	194
	Offsets against gross budget authority and outlays:			
	Offsetting collections (collected) from:			
4030	Federal sources	−7	−15	−15
4033	Non-Federal sources	−2		
4040	Offsets against gross budget authority and outlays (total)	−9	−15	−15
	Additional offsets against gross budget authority only:			
4050	Change in uncollected pymts, Fed sources, unexpired	−1		
4052	Offsetting collections credited to expired accounts	1		
4070	Budget authority, net (discretionary)	156	181	192
4080	Outlays, net (discretionary)	159	173	179
4180	Budget authority, net (total)	156	181	192
4190	Outlays, net (total)	159	173	179

The appropriation for Operations and Training funds the United States Merchant Marine Academy (USMMA) located in Kings Point, New York, as well as headquarters staff to administer and direct Maritime Administration operations and programs including the Maritime Environmental and Technical Assistance program and America's Marine Highway program.

The USMMA, a Federal service academy and accredited institution of higher education, provides instruction to individuals to prepare them for service in the merchant marine. Funding supports traditional operations of the academic institution, midshipmen training at sea, and capital maintenance of the USMMA campus facilities.

Maritime Administration operations includes planning for coordination of U.S. maritime industry activities under emergency conditions; promotion of efficiency, safety, risk mitigation, environmental stewardship, and maritime industry standards; strategic outreach with maritime stakeholders in education and industry; and port and intermodal development oversight to increase capacity and mitigate congestion in freight movements.

Object Classification (in millions of dollars)

Identification code 069–1750–0–1–403		2021 actual	2022 est.	2023 est.
	Direct obligations:			
	Personnel compensation:			
11.1	Full-time permanent	45	47	50
11.3	Other than full-time permanent	8	8	9
11.5	Other personnel compensation	2	2	2
11.9	Total personnel compensation	55	57	61
12.1	Civilian personnel benefits	20	20	21
21.0	Travel and transportation of persons	2	1	1
23.1	Rental payments to GSA	2	2	3
23.3	Communications, utilities, and miscellaneous charges	5	4	5
25.1	Advisory and assistance services	2	2	2
25.2	Other services from non-Federal sources	2	2	2
25.3	Other goods and services from Federal sources	26	24	37
25.4	Operation and maintenance of facilities	14	9	11
25.6	Medical care	4	3	3
25.7	Operation and maintenance of equipment	6	4	5
26.0	Supplies and materials	5	4	5
31.0	Equipment	9	7	8
32.0	Land and structures	13	27	64
41.0	Grants, subsidies, and contributions	6	10	18
99.0	Direct obligations	171	176	246
99.0	Reimbursable obligations	1	15	15
99.9	Total new obligations, unexpired accounts	172	191	261

Maritime Administration—Continued
Federal Funds—Continued

Employment Summary

Identification code 069–1750–0–1–403	2021 actual	2022 est.	2023 est.
1001 Direct civilian full-time equivalent employment	455	458	512
1001 Direct civilian full-time equivalent employment			1
2001 Reimbursable civilian full-time equivalent employment	1	1	1
3001 Allocation account civilian full-time equivalent employment	7	8	8

STATE MARITIME ACADEMY OPERATIONS

For necessary expenses of operations, support, and training activities for State Maritime Academies, $77,700,000: Provided, That of the sums appropriated under this heading—

(1) $30,500,000, to remain available until expended, shall be for maintenance, repair, life extension, insurance, and capacity improvement of National Defense Reserve Fleet training ships, for support of training ship operations at the State Maritime Academies, and for costs associated with training vessel sharing pursuant to 46 U.S.C. 51504(g)(3) for costs associated with mobilizing, operating and demobilizing the vessel, including travel costs for students, faculty and crew, the costs of the general agent, crew costs, fuel, insurance, operational fees, and vessel hire costs, as determined by the Secretary;

(2) $35,000,000, to remain available until expended, shall be for the National Security Multi-Mission Vessel Program, including funds for construction, planning, administration, and design of school ships, and, as determined by the Secretary, necessary expenses to construct infrastructure to berth such ships;

(3) $2,400,000 to remain available through September 30, 2027, shall be for the Student Incentive Program;

(4) $3,800,000 shall remain available until expended, shall be for training ship fuel assistance; and

(5) $6,000,000, to remain available until September 30, 2024, shall be for direct payments for State Maritime Academies.

Note.—A full-year 2022 appropriation for this account was not enacted at the time the Budget was prepared; therefore, the Budget assumes this account is operating under the Continuing Appropriations Act, 2022 (Division A of Public Law 117–43, as amended). The amounts included for 2022 reflect the annualized level provided by the continuing resolution.

Program and Financing (in millions of dollars)

Identification code 069–1712–0–1–403		2021 actual	2022 est.	2023 est.
	Obligations by program activity:			
0001	Student Incentive Program	2	2	2
0002	Direct Payments	6	6	6
0003	Training Ship Fuel Assistance	3	5	4
0004	Training Vessel Sharing	5	5	
0005	Schoolship Maintenance & Repair	26	41	31
0006	Schoolship Replacement - NSMMV	601	426	35
0900	Total new obligations, unexpired accounts	643	485	78
	Budgetary resources:			
	Unobligated balance:			
1000	Unobligated balance brought forward, Oct 1	264	56	4
1021	Recoveries of prior year unpaid obligations	3		
1070	Unobligated balance (total)	267	56	4
	Budget authority:			
	Appropriations, discretionary:			
1100	Appropriation	433	433	78
1930	Total budgetary resources available	700	489	82
	Memorandum (non-add) entries:			
1940	Unobligated balance expiring	−1		
1941	Unexpired unobligated balance, end of year	56	4	4
	Change in obligated balance:			
	Unpaid obligations:			
3000	Unpaid obligations, brought forward, Oct 1	543	791	930
3010	New obligations, unexpired accounts	643	485	78
3020	Outlays (gross)	−392	−346	−291
3040	Recoveries of prior year unpaid obligations, unexpired	−3		
3050	Unpaid obligations, end of year	791	930	717
	Memorandum (non-add) entries:			
3100	Obligated balance, start of year	543	791	930
3200	Obligated balance, end of year	791	930	717
	Budget authority and outlays, net:			
	Discretionary:			
4000	Budget authority, gross	433	433	78

965

Maritime Administration—Continued
Federal Funds—Continued

STATE MARITIME ACADEMY OPERATIONS—Continued
Program and Financing—Continued

Identification code 069–1712–0–1–403	2021 actual	2022 est.	2023 est.
Outlays, gross:			
4010 Outlays from new discretionary authority	135	95	42
4011 Outlays from discretionary balances	257	251	249
4020 Outlays, gross (total)	392	346	291
4180 Budget authority, net (total)	433	433	78
4190 Outlays, net (total)	392	346	291

State Maritime Academy (SMA) Operations provides Federal assistance to the six SMAs, to help educate and train mariners and future leaders to support the U.S. marine transportation system. These graduates promote the commerce of the United States and aid in the national defense by serving in the merchant marine. The SMA Operations request funds student financial assistance, direct assistance to each of the six SMAs, and activities in support of the construction and berthing of new training vessels under the National Security Multi-Mission Vessel Program.

Object Classification (in millions of dollars)

Identification code 069–1712–0–1–403	2021 actual	2022 est.	2023 est.
Direct obligations:			
25.1 Advisory and assistance services	609	10	4
25.2 Other services from non-Federal sources	6	6	6
25.4 Operation and maintenance of facilities	6	9	7
25.7 Operation and maintenance of equipment	12	18	13
26.0 Supplies and materials	5	8	6
31.0 Equipment		426	35
41.0 Grants, subsidies, and contributions	4	7	6
99.0 Direct obligations	642	484	77
99.5 Adjustment for rounding	1	1	1
99.9 Total new obligations, unexpired accounts	643	485	78

ASSISTANCE TO SMALL SHIPYARDS

To make grants to qualified shipyards as authorized under section 54101 of title 46, United States Code, $20,000,000, to remain available until expended.

Note.—A full-year 2022 appropriation for this account was not enacted at the time the Budget was prepared; therefore, the Budget assumes this account is operating under the Continuing Appropriations Act, 2022 (Division A of Public Law 117–43, as amended). The amounts included for 2022 reflect the annualized level provided by the continuing resolution.

Program and Financing (in millions of dollars)

Identification code 069–1770–0–1–403	2021 actual	2022 est.	2023 est.
Obligations by program activity:			
0001 Grants for Capital Improvement for Small Shipyards	20	20	20
0900 Total new obligations, unexpired accounts (object class 41.0)	20	20	20
Budgetary resources:			
Unobligated balance:			
1000 Unobligated balance brought forward, Oct 1	1	1	1
Budget authority:			
Appropriations, discretionary:			
1100 Appropriation	20	20	20
1930 Total budgetary resources available	21	21	21
Memorandum (non-add) entries:			
1941 Unexpired unobligated balance, end of year	1	1	1
Change in obligated balance:			
Unpaid obligations:			
3000 Unpaid obligations, brought forward, Oct 1	24	30	30
3010 New obligations, unexpired accounts	20	20	20
3020 Outlays (gross)	–14	–20	–24
3050 Unpaid obligations, end of year	30	30	26
Memorandum (non-add) entries:			
3100 Obligated balance, start of year	24	30	30
3200 Obligated balance, end of year	30	30	26

	2021 actual	2022 est.	2023 est.
Budget authority and outlays, net:			
Discretionary:			
4000 Budget authority, gross	20	20	20
Outlays, gross:			
4010 Outlays from new discretionary authority	3	17	17
4011 Outlays from discretionary balances	11	3	7
4020 Outlays, gross (total)	14	20	24
4180 Budget authority, net (total)	20	20	20
4190 Outlays, net (total)	14	20	24

The National Defense Authorization Act of 2006 authorized the Maritime Administration to make grants for capital and related improvements at eligible shipyard facilities that will foster efficiency, competitive operations, and quality ship construction, repair, and reconfiguration. Grant funds may also be used for maritime training programs to enhance technical skills and operational productivity in communities whose economies are related to or dependent upon the maritime industry.

The Assistance to Small Shipyard program provides grants to small shipyards for capital improvements and training programs.

Employment Summary

Identification code 069–1770–0–1–403	2021 actual	2022 est.	2023 est.
1001 Direct civilian full-time equivalent employment	1	1	1

SHIP DISPOSAL
(INCLUDING CANCELLATION OF FUNDS)

For necessary expenses related to the disposal of obsolete vessels in the National Defense Reserve Fleet of the Maritime Administration, $6,000,000, to remain available until expended: Provided, That of the unobligated balances from prior year appropriations made available under this heading, $12,000,000 is hereby permanently cancelled.

Note.—A full-year 2022 appropriation for this account was not enacted at the time the Budget was prepared; therefore, the Budget assumes this account is operating under the Continuing Appropriations Act, 2022 (Division A of Public Law 117–43, as amended). The amounts included for 2022 reflect the annualized level provided by the continuing resolution.

Program and Financing (in millions of dollars)

Identification code 069–1768–0–1–403	2021 actual	2022 est.	2023 est.
Obligations by program activity:			
0001 Ship Disposal	1	1	1
0002 N.S. Savannah Protective Storage	1	1	2
0003 NSS Decommissioning	46	38	
0900 Total new obligations, unexpired accounts	48	40	3
Budgetary resources:			
Unobligated balance:			
1000 Unobligated balance brought forward, Oct 1	92	48	12
Budget authority:			
Appropriations, discretionary:			
1100 Appropriation	4	4	6
1131 Unobligated balance of appropriations permanently reduced			–12
1160 Appropriation, discretionary (total)	4	4	–6
1930 Total budgetary resources available	96	52	6
Memorandum (non-add) entries:			
1941 Unexpired unobligated balance, end of year	48	12	3
Change in obligated balance:			
Unpaid obligations:			
3000 Unpaid obligations, brought forward, Oct 1	8	34	49
3010 New obligations, unexpired accounts	48	40	3
3020 Outlays (gross)	–22	–25	–31
3050 Unpaid obligations, end of year	34	49	21
Memorandum (non-add) entries:			
3100 Obligated balance, start of year	8	34	49
3200 Obligated balance, end of year	34	49	21
Budget authority and outlays, net:			
Discretionary:			
4000 Budget authority, gross	4	4	–6

DEPARTMENT OF TRANSPORTATION

Maritime Administration—Continued
Federal Funds—Continued

967

		2021 actual	2022 est.	2023 est.
	Outlays, gross:			
4010	Outlays from new discretionary authority	4	2	3
4011	Outlays from discretionary balances	18	23	28
4020	Outlays, gross (total)	22	25	31
4180	Budget authority, net (total)	4	4	–6
4190	Outlays, net (total)	22	25	31

The Ship Disposal program provides resources to properly dispose of obsolete Government-owned merchant ships maintained by the Maritime Administration in the National Defense Reserve Fleet. The Maritime Administration contracts with domestic shipbreaking firms to dismantle these vessels in accordance with guidelines set forth by the U.S. Environmental Protection Agency. The Ship Disposal program also funds the cost of program administration and maintenance of the Nuclear Ship Savannah in protective storage.

Object Classification (in millions of dollars)

Identification code 069–1768–0–1–403		2021 actual	2022 est.	2023 est.
	Direct obligations:			
11.1	Personnel compensation: Full-time permanent	1	1	1
23.2	Rental payments to others	2	1	1
25.1	Advisory and assistance services	39	34	....
25.2	Other services from non-Federal sources	5	4	1
99.0	Direct obligations	47	40	3
99.5	Adjustment for rounding	1	....	....
99.9	Total new obligations, unexpired accounts	48	40	3

Employment Summary

Identification code 069–1768–0–1–403		2021 actual	2022 est.	2023 est.
1001	Direct civilian full-time equivalent employment	9	13	13

MARITIME SECURITY PROGRAM

(INCLUDING CANCELLATION OF FUNDS)

For necessary expenses to maintain and preserve a U.S.-flag merchant fleet to serve the national security needs of the United States, $318,000,000, to remain available until expended: Provided, That of the unobligated balances from prior year appropriations made available under this heading, $55,000,000 is hereby permanently cancelled.

Note.—A full-year 2022 appropriation for this account was not enacted at the time the Budget was prepared; therefore, the Budget assumes this account is operating under the Continuing Appropriations Act, 2022 (Division A of Public Law 117–43, as amended). The amounts included for 2022 reflect the annualized level provided by the continuing resolution.

Program and Financing (in millions of dollars)

Identification code 069–1711–0–1–054		2021 actual	2022 est.	2023 est.
	Obligations by program activity:			
0001	Maritime Security Program	306	314	318
0900	Total new obligations, unexpired accounts (object class 41.0)	306	314	318
	Budgetary resources:			
	Unobligated balance:			
1000	Unobligated balance brought forward, Oct 1	47	59	59
1021	Recoveries of prior year unpaid obligations	4	....	....
1070	Unobligated balance (total)	51	59	59
	Budget authority:			
	Appropriations, discretionary:			
1100	Appropriation	314	314	318
1131	Unobligated balance of appropriations permanently reduced	....	....	–55
1160	Appropriation, discretionary (total)	314	314	263
1930	Total budgetary resources available	365	373	322
	Memorandum (non-add) entries:			
1941	Unexpired unobligated balance, end of year	59	59	4
	Change in obligated balance:			
	Unpaid obligations:			
3000	Unpaid obligations, brought forward, Oct 1	29	30	26
3010	New obligations, unexpired accounts	306	314	318
3020	Outlays (gross)	–301	–318	–318
3040	Recoveries of prior year unpaid obligations, unexpired	–4	....	....
3050	Unpaid obligations, end of year	30	26	26
	Memorandum (non-add) entries:			
3100	Obligated balance, start of year	29	30	26
3200	Obligated balance, end of year	30	26	26
	Budget authority and outlays, net:			
	Discretionary:			
4000	Budget authority, gross	314	314	263
	Outlays, gross:			
4010	Outlays from new discretionary authority	277	292	296
4011	Outlays from discretionary balances	24	26	22
4020	Outlays, gross (total)	301	318	318
4180	Budget authority, net (total)	314	314	263
4190	Outlays, net (total)	301	318	318

The Maritime Security Program provides direct payments to U.S. flag ship operators engaged in foreign commerce to partially offset the higher operating costs of U.S. registry. The purpose of the program is to establish and sustain a fleet of active ships that are privately owned, commercially viable, and militarily useful to meet national defense and other emergency sealift requirements. Participating operators are required to make their ships and commercial transportation resources available upon request by the Secretary of Defense during times of war or national emergency. Commercial transportation resources include ships, logistics management services, port terminal facilities, and U.S. citizen merchant mariners to crew both commercial and Government-owned merchant ships. The program will also sustain a base of U.S. Merchant Mariners to support national security requirements during times of urgent need.

CABLE SECURITY FLEET

Note.—A full-year 2022 appropriation for this account was not enacted at the time the Budget was prepared; therefore, the Budget assumes this account is operating under the Continuing Appropriations Act, 2022 (Division A of Public Law 117–43, as amended). The amounts included for 2022 reflect the annualized level provided by the continuing resolution.

Program and Financing (in millions of dollars)

Identification code 069–1717–0–1–054		2021 actual	2022 est.	2023 est.
	Obligations by program activity:			
0001	Cable Security Fleet	....	10	....
0900	Total new obligations, unexpired accounts (object class 41.0)	....	10	....
	Budgetary resources:			
	Unobligated balance:			
1000	Unobligated balance brought forward, Oct 1	....	10	10
	Budget authority:			
	Appropriations, discretionary:			
1100	Appropriation	10	10	....
1930	Total budgetary resources available	10	20	10
	Memorandum (non-add) entries:			
1941	Unexpired unobligated balance, end of year	10	10	10
	Change in obligated balance:			
	Unpaid obligations:			
3000	Unpaid obligations, brought forward, Oct 1	....	....	1
3010	New obligations, unexpired accounts	....	10	....
3020	Outlays (gross)	....	–9	–1
3050	Unpaid obligations, end of year	....	1	....
	Memorandum (non-add) entries:			
3100	Obligated balance, start of year	....	....	1
3200	Obligated balance, end of year	....	1	....
	Budget authority and outlays, net:			
	Discretionary:			
4000	Budget authority, gross	10	10	....
	Outlays, gross:			
4010	Outlays from new discretionary authority	....	9	....
4011	Outlays from discretionary balances	....	....	1
4020	Outlays, gross (total)	....	9	1
4180	Budget authority, net (total)	10	10	....

Maritime Administration—Continued
Federal Funds—Continued

CABLE SECURITY FLEET—Continued
Program and Financing—Continued

Identification code 069–1717–0–1–054	2021 actual	2022 est.	2023 est.
4190 Outlays, net (total)		9	1

The Cable Security Fleet Program provides direct payments to U.S. Flagship operators who in turn are required to operate cable repair ships in commercial service providing undersea cable repair services, and to make such vessels available upon request by the Department of Defense (DOD). The program will also sustain a base of U.S. Merchant Mariners to support national security requirements during times of urgent need.

TANKER SECURITY PROGRAM

For Tanker Security Fleet payments, as authorized under section 53406 of title 46, United States Code, $60,000,000, to remain available until expended.

Note.—A full-year 2022 appropriation for this account was not enacted at the time the Budget was prepared; therefore, the Budget assumes this account is operating under the Continuing Appropriations Act, 2022 (Division A of Public Law 117–43, as amended). The amounts included for 2022 reflect the annualized level provided by the continuing resolution.

Program and Financing (in millions of dollars)

Identification code 069–1718–0–1–054	2021 actual	2022 est.	2023 est.
Obligations by program activity:			
0001 Tanker Security Program			60
0900 Total new obligations, unexpired accounts (object class 41.0)			60
Budgetary resources:			
Budget authority:			
Appropriations, discretionary:			
1100 Appropriation			60
1930 Total budgetary resources available			60
Change in obligated balance:			
Unpaid obligations:			
3010 New obligations, unexpired accounts			60
3020 Outlays (gross)			–56
3050 Unpaid obligations, end of year			4
Memorandum (non-add) entries:			
3200 Obligated balance, end of year			4
Budget authority and outlays, net:			
Discretionary:			
4000 Budget authority, gross			60
Outlays, gross:			
4010 Outlays from new discretionary authority			56
4180 Budget authority, net (total)			60
4190 Outlays, net (total)			56

The Tanker Security Program provides direct payments to U.S. Flagship product tankers capable of supporting national economic and Department of Defense (DOD) contingency requirements. The purpose of this program is to provide retainer payments to carriers to support a fleet of militarily-useful, commercially viable product tankers sailing in international trade, as well as assured access to a global network of intermodal facilities. The program will also sustain a base of U.S. Merchant Mariners to support national security requirements during times of urgent need.

READY RESERVE FORCE

Program and Financing (in millions of dollars)

Identification code 069–1710–0–1–054	2021 actual	2022 est.	2023 est.
Obligations by program activity:			
0801 Ready Reserve Force (Reimbursable)	494	726	514
Budgetary resources:			
Unobligated balance:			
1000 Unobligated balance brought forward, Oct 1	44	51	132
1021 Recoveries of prior year unpaid obligations	20		
1070 Unobligated balance (total)	64	51	132
Budget authority:			
Spending authority from offsetting collections, discretionary:			
1700 Collected	419	807	505
1701 Change in uncollected payments, Federal sources	125		
1750 Spending auth from offsetting collections, disc (total)	544	807	505
1930 Total budgetary resources available	608	858	637
Memorandum (non-add) entries:			
1940 Unobligated balance expiring	–63		
1941 Unexpired unobligated balance, end of year	51	132	123
Change in obligated balance:			
Unpaid obligations:			
3000 Unpaid obligations, brought forward, Oct 1	210	225	161
3010 New obligations, unexpired accounts	494	726	514
3020 Outlays (gross)	–454	–790	–565
3040 Recoveries of prior year unpaid obligations, unexpired	–20		
3041 Recoveries of prior year unpaid obligations, expired	–5		
3050 Unpaid obligations, end of year	225	161	110
Uncollected payments:			
3060 Uncollected pymts, Fed sources, brought forward, Oct 1	–116	–174	
3070 Change in uncollected pymts, Fed sources, unexpired	–125		
3071 Change in uncollected pymts, Fed sources, expired	67	174	
3090 Uncollected pymts, Fed sources, end of year	–174		
Memorandum (non-add) entries:			
3100 Obligated balance, start of year	94	51	161
3200 Obligated balance, end of year	51	161	110
Budget authority and outlays, net:			
Discretionary:			
4000 Budget authority, gross	544	807	505
Outlays, gross:			
4010 Outlays from new discretionary authority	292	726	454
4011 Outlays from discretionary balances	162	64	111
4020 Outlays, gross (total)	454	790	565
Offsets against gross budget authority and outlays:			
Offsetting collections (collected) from:			
4030 Federal sources	–474	–807	–505
4040 Offsets against gross budget authority and outlays (total)	–474	–807	–505
Additional offsets against gross budget authority only:			
4050 Change in uncollected pymts, Fed sources, unexpired	–125		
4052 Offsetting collections credited to expired accounts	55		
4060 Additional offsets against budget authority only (total)	–70		
4080 Outlays, net (discretionary)	–20	–17	60
4180 Budget authority, net (total)			
4190 Outlays, net (total)	–20	–17	60

The Ready Reserve Force (RRF) fleet is comprised of Government-owned merchant ships within the National Defense Reserve Fleet that are maintained in an advanced state of surge sealift readiness for the transport of cargo to a given area of operation to satisfy combatant commanders' critical war fighting requirements. Resources for RRF vessel maintenance, activation and operation costs, as well as RRF infrastructure support costs and additional Department of Defense/Navy-sponsored sealift activities and special projects, are provided by reimbursement from the Department of Navy.

Object Classification (in millions of dollars)

Identification code 069–1710–0–1–054	2021 actual	2022 est.	2023 est.
Reimbursable obligations:			
Personnel compensation:			
11.1 Full-time permanent	29	30	29
11.5 Other personnel compensation	2	2	2
11.9 Total personnel compensation	31	32	31
12.1 Civilian personnel benefits	12	12	12
23.1 Rental payments to GSA	2	2	2
23.2 Rental payments to others	22	22	22
23.3 Communications, utilities, and miscellaneous charges	7	7	7
25.1 Advisory and assistance services	8	78	8
25.2 Other services from non-Federal sources	1	1	1
25.3 Other goods and services from Federal sources	9	9	9
25.4 Operation and maintenance of facilities	361	513	382

DEPARTMENT OF TRANSPORTATION

		2021 actual	2022 est.	2023 est.
25.7	Operation and maintenance of equipment	1	1	1
26.0	Supplies and materials	35	45	35
31.0	Equipment	3	3	3
32.0	Land and structures	1	1	1
99.0	Reimbursable obligations	493	726	514
99.5	Adjustment for rounding	1	....	....
99.9	Total new obligations, unexpired accounts	494	726	514

Employment Summary

Identification code 069–1710–0–1–054	2021 actual	2022 est.	2023 est.
2001 Reimbursable civilian full-time equivalent employment	295	295	295

VESSEL OPERATIONS REVOLVING FUND

Program and Financing (in millions of dollars)

Identification code 069–4303–0–3–403		2021 actual	2022 est.	2023 est.
	Obligations by program activity:			
0001	National Defense Reserve Fleet	....	2	2
0002	State Maritime Academies	....	1	1
0003	Preservation of Maritime Heritage Assets	....	1	1
0900	Total new obligations, unexpired accounts	....	4	4
	Budgetary resources:			
	Unobligated balance:			
1000	Unobligated balance brought forward, Oct 1	22	31	31
	Budget authority:			
	Spending authority from offsetting collections, discretionary:			
1700	Collected	9	4	3
1930	Total budgetary resources available	31	35	34
	Memorandum (non-add) entries:			
1941	Unexpired unobligated balance, end of year	31	31	30
	Change in obligated balance:			
	Unpaid obligations:			
3010	New obligations, unexpired accounts	....	4	4
3020	Outlays (gross)	....	–4	–3
3050	Unpaid obligations, end of year	....	....	1
	Memorandum (non-add) entries:			
3200	Obligated balance, end of year	....	....	1
	Budget authority and outlays, net:			
	Discretionary:			
4000	Budget authority, gross	9	4	3
	Outlays, gross:			
4010	Outlays from new discretionary authority	....	4	3
	Offsets against gross budget authority and outlays:			
	Offsetting collections (collected) from:			
4033	Non-Federal sources	–9	–4	–3
4040	Offsets against gross budget authority and outlays (total)	–9	–4	–3
4180	Budget authority, net (total)	....	....	....
4190	Outlays, net (total)	–9	....	....
	Memorandum (non-add) entries:			
5090	Unexpired unavailable balance, SOY: Offsetting collections	1	1	1
5092	Unexpired unavailable balance, EOY: Offsetting collections	1	1	1

This fund is authorized for the receipt of sales proceeds from the disposition of obsolete Government-owned merchant vessels. Collections from this account are authorized for allocation and distribution according to prescribed statutory formulas for use under three maritime-related purpose areas: 1) supporting acquisition, maintenance, repair, reconditioning, or improvement of National Defense Reserve Fleet vessels; 2) supporting state maritime academies and the United States Merchant Marine Academy; and 3) supporting the preservation and presentation to the public of maritime property and assets, including funds for the National Park Service National Maritime Heritage Grant Program.

Maritime Administration—Continued
Federal Funds—Continued 969

Object Classification (in millions of dollars)

Identification code 069–4303–0–3–403		2021 actual	2022 est.	2023 est.
	Direct obligations:			
25.2	Other services from non-Federal sources	....	2	2
25.7	Operation and maintenance of equipment	....	1	1
41.0	Grants, subsidies, and contributions	....	1	1
99.0	Direct obligations	....	4	4
99.9	Total new obligations, unexpired accounts	....	4	4

WAR RISK INSURANCE REVOLVING FUND

Program and Financing (in millions of dollars)

Identification code 069–4302–0–3–403		2021 actual	2022 est.	2023 est.
	Budgetary resources:			
	Unobligated balance:			
1000	Unobligated balance brought forward, Oct 1	50	51	51
	Budget authority:			
	Spending authority from offsetting collections, discretionary:			
1700	Collected	1	....	....
1930	Total budgetary resources available	51	51	51
	Memorandum (non-add) entries:			
1941	Unexpired unobligated balance, end of year	51	51	51
	Budget authority and outlays, net:			
	Discretionary:			
4000	Budget authority, gross	1	....	....
	Offsets against gross budget authority and outlays:			
	Offsetting collections (collected) from:			
4031	Interest on Federal securities	–1	....	....
4180	Budget authority, net (total)	....	....	....
4190	Outlays, net (total)	–1	....	....
	Memorandum (non-add) entries:			
5000	Total investments, SOY: Federal securities: Par value	50	32	51
5001	Total investments, EOY: Federal securities: Par value	32	51	51

The Maritime Administration is authorized to insure against war risk loss or damage to maritime operators until commercial insurance can be obtained on reasonable terms and conditions. This insurance includes war risk hull and disbursements interim insurance, war risk protection and indemnity interim insurance, second seamen's war risk interim insurance, and the war risk cargo insurance standby program.

PORT OF GUAM IMPROVEMENT ENTERPRISE FUND

Program and Financing (in millions of dollars)

Identification code 069–5560–0–2–403		2021 actual	2022 est.	2023 est.
	Obligations by program activity:			
0001	Port of Guam Improvement Enterprise Program	....	2	....
0900	Total new obligations, unexpired accounts (object class 41.0)	....	2	....
	Budgetary resources:			
	Unobligated balance:			
1000	Unobligated balance brought forward, Oct 1	2	2	....
1930	Total budgetary resources available	2	2	....
	Memorandum (non-add) entries:			
1941	Unexpired unobligated balance, end of year	2	....	....
	Change in obligated balance:			
	Unpaid obligations:			
3000	Unpaid obligations, brought forward, Oct 1	1	1	2
3010	New obligations, unexpired accounts	....	2	....
3020	Outlays (gross)	....	–1	....
3050	Unpaid obligations, end of year	1	2	2
	Memorandum (non-add) entries:			
3100	Obligated balance, start of year	1	1	2
3200	Obligated balance, end of year	1	2	2

PORT OF GUAM IMPROVEMENT ENTERPRISE FUND—Continued

Program and Financing—Continued

Identification code 069–5560–0–2–403	2021 actual	2022 est.	2023 est.
Budget authority and outlays, net:			
Discretionary:			
Outlays, gross:			
4011 Outlays from discretionary balances		1	
4180 Budget authority, net (total)			
4190 Outlays, net (total)		1	

MARITIME GUARANTEED LOAN (TITLE XI) PROGRAM ACCOUNT

(INCLUDING TRANSFER OF FUNDS)

For administrative expenses to carry out the guaranteed loan program, $3,000,000, which shall be transferred to and merged with the appropriations for "Maritime Administration—Operations and Training".

Note.—A full-year 2022 appropriation for this account was not enacted at the time the Budget was prepared; therefore, the Budget assumes this account is operating under the Continuing Appropriations Act, 2022 (Division A of Public Law 117–43, as amended). The amounts included for 2022 reflect the annualized level provided by the continuing resolution.

Program and Financing (in millions of dollars)

Identification code 069–1752–0–1–403	2021 actual	2022 est.	2023 est.
Obligations by program activity:			
Credit program obligations:			
0701 Direct loan subsidy			9
0706 Interest on reestimates of direct loan subsidy	4		
0707 Reestimates of loan guarantee subsidy	38		
0708 Interest on reestimates of loan guarantee subsidy	20		
0709 Administrative expenses	3	3	3
0900 Total new obligations, unexpired accounts	65	3	12
Budgetary resources:			
Unobligated balance:			
1000 Unobligated balance brought forward, Oct 1	36	36	36
Budget authority:			
Appropriations, discretionary:			
1100 Appropriation	3	3	3
Appropriations, mandatory:			
1200 Appropriation (LG)	58		
1200 Appropriation (DL)	4		
1260 Appropriations, mandatory (total)	62		
1900 Budget authority (total)	65	3	3
1930 Total budgetary resources available	101	39	39
Memorandum (non-add) entries:			
1941 Unexpired unobligated balance, end of year	36	36	27
Change in obligated balance:			
Unpaid obligations:			
3010 New obligations, unexpired accounts	65	3	12
3020 Outlays (gross)	–65	–3	–3
3050 Unpaid obligations, end of year			9
Memorandum (non-add) entries:			
3200 Obligated balance, end of year			9
Budget authority and outlays, net:			
Discretionary:			
4000 Budget authority, gross	3	3	3
Outlays, gross:			
4010 Outlays from new discretionary authority	3	3	3
Mandatory:			
4090 Budget authority, gross	62		
Outlays, gross:			
4100 Outlays from new mandatory authority	62		
4180 Budget authority, net (total)	65	3	3
4190 Outlays, net (total)	65	3	3

Summary of Loan Levels, Subsidy Budget Authority and Outlays by Program (in millions of dollars)

Identification code 069–1752–0–1–403	2021 actual	2022 est.	2023 est.
Direct loan levels supportable by subsidy budget authority:			
115001 Federal Ship Financing FFB Loan Guarantees		53	239
Direct loan subsidy (in percent):			
132001 Federal Ship Financing FFB Loan Guarantees		–.27	3.73
132999 Weighted average subsidy rate	0.00	–.27	3.73
Direct loan subsidy budget authority:			
133001 Federal Ship Financing FFB Loan Guarantees			9
Direct loan reestimates:			
135001 Federal Ship Financing FFB Loan Guarantees	3		
Guaranteed loan reestimates:			
235014 Federal Ship Financing Loan Guarantees	38	–46	
235999 Total guaranteed loan reestimates	38	–46	
Administrative expense data:			
3510 Budget authority			3
3590 Outlays from new authority			3

The Maritime Guaranteed Loan (Title XI) program provides for a full faith and credit guarantee of debt obligations issued by U.S or foreign ship owners to finance or refinance the construction, reconstruction, or reconditioning of U.S.-flag vessels or eligible export vessels in U.S. shipyards; or for a full faith and credit guarantee of debt obligations issued by U.S. shipyard owners to finance the modernization of shipbuilding technology at shipyards located in the United States.

As required by the Federal Credit Reform Act of 1990, this account also includes the subsidy costs associated with loan guarantee commitments made in 1992 and subsequent years which are estimated on a present value basis.

Funding for the Maritime Guaranteed Loan (Title XI) program will be used for administrative expenses of the program which are paid to the Maritime Administration's Operations and Training account.

Object Classification (in millions of dollars)

Identification code 069–1752–0–1–403	2021 actual	2022 est.	2023 est.
Direct obligations:			
41.0 Grants, subsidies, and contributions	62		9
94.0 Financial transfers	3	3	3
99.9 Total new obligations, unexpired accounts	65	3	12

MARITIME GUARANTEED LOAN (TITLE XI) FFB FINANCING ACCOUNT

Program and Financing (in millions of dollars)

Identification code 069–4494–0–3–403	2021 actual	2022 est.	2023 est.
Obligations by program activity:			
Credit program obligations:			
0710 Direct loan obligations		53	239
0713 Payment of interest to Treasury		1	
0715 Payment of Interest to FFB	4	4	7
0740 Negative subsidy obligations		1	
0742 Downward reestimates paid to receipt accounts	1		
0900 Total new obligations, unexpired accounts	5	59	246
Budgetary resources:			
Unobligated balance:			
1000 Unobligated balance brought forward, Oct 1	8	11	9
Financing authority:			
Borrowing authority, mandatory:			
1400 Borrowing authority - BFS		1	
1400 Borrowing authority - FFB		53	239
1440 Borrowing authority, mandatory (total)		54	239
Spending authority from offsetting collections, mandatory:			
1800 Collected	22	17	17
1825 Spending authority from offsetting collections applied to repay debt	–14	–14	–14
1850 Spending auth from offsetting collections, mand (total)	8	3	3
1900 Budget authority (total)	8	57	242
1930 Total budgetary resources available	16	68	251
Memorandum (non-add) entries:			
1941 Unexpired unobligated balance, end of year	11	9	5

DEPARTMENT OF TRANSPORTATION

Change in obligated balance:
Unpaid obligations:

3000	Unpaid obligations, brought forward, Oct 1	....	....	6
3010	New obligations, unexpired accounts	5	59	246
3020	Outlays (gross)	–5	–53	–239
3050	Unpaid obligations, end of year	....	6	13
	Memorandum (non-add) entries:			
3100	Obligated balance, start of year	....	....	6
3200	Obligated balance, end of year	....	6	13

Financing authority and disbursements, net:
Mandatory:

4090	Budget authority, gross	8	57	242
	Financing disbursements:			
4110	Outlays, gross (total)	5	53	239
	Offsets against gross financing authority and disbursements:			
	Offsetting collections (collected) from:			
4120	Payments from Program Account - Upward Reestimate	–4	....	....
4123	Non-Federal sources	–18	–17	–17
4130	Offsets against gross budget authority and outlays (total)	–22	–17	–17
4160	Budget authority, net (mandatory)	–14	40	225
4170	Outlays, net (mandatory)	–17	36	222
4180	Budget authority, net (total)	–14	40	225
4190	Outlays, net (total)	–17	36	222

Status of Direct Loans (in millions of dollars)

Identification code 069–4494–0–3–403	2021 actual	2022 est.	2023 est.
Position with respect to appropriations act limitation on obligations:			
1111 Direct loan obligations from current-year authority	....	53	239
1150 Total direct loan obligations	....	53	239
Cumulative balance of direct loans outstanding:			
1210 Outstanding, start of year	....	312	350
1231 Disbursements: Direct loan disbursements	....	53	239
1251 Repayments: Repayments and prepayments	–14	–15	–16
1264 Other adjustments, net (+ or -) [Adjustment for Outstanding SOY Bal.]	326	....	....
1290 Outstanding, end of year	312	350	573

As required by the Federal Credit Reform Act of 1990, this non-budgetary account records all cash flows to and from the Government resulting from Maritime Guaranteed Loan (Title XI) program loan guarantee commitments financed by the Federal Financing Bank (FFB), beginning in 2020 for all new loan guarantees. The amounts in this account are a means of financing and are not included in the budget totals.

Balance Sheet (in millions of dollars)

Identification code 069–4494–0–3–403	2020 actual	2021 actual
ASSETS:		
Federal assets:		
1101 Fund balances with Treasury	8	11
Investments in U.S. securities:		
1106 Receivables, net	4	....
Net value of assets related to post-1991 direct loans receivable:		
1401 Direct loans receivable, gross	309	312
1404 Foreclosed property	1	....
1405 Allowance for subsidy cost (-)	....	–16
1499 Net present value of assets related to direct loans	310	296
1999 Total assets	322	307
LIABILITIES:		
2103 Federal liabilities: Debt	326	312
2204 Non-Federal liabilities: Liabilities for loan guarantees	1	....
2999 Total liabilities	327	312
NET POSITION:		
3300 Cumulative results of operations	–5	–5
4999 Total liabilities and net position	322	307

PORT INFRASTRUCTURE DEVELOPMENT PROGRAM

To make grants to improve port facilities as authorized under section 54301 of title 46, United States Code, $230,000,000, to remain available until expended: Provided, That projects eligible for amounts made available under this heading shall be projects for coastal seaports, inland river ports, or Great Lakes ports: Provided further, That the Maritime Administration shall distribute amounts made available under this heading as discretionary grants: Provided further, That for grants awarded under this heading, the Secretary shall prioritize projects that address climate change, environmental justice, and racial equity considerations related to the movement of goods: Provided further, That projects eligible for amounts made available under this heading shall be located—

(1) within the boundary of a port; or

(2) outside the boundary of a port, and directly related to port operations, or to an intermodal connection to a port:

Provided further, That the Federal share of the costs for which an amount is provided under this heading shall be up to 80 percent: Provided further, That for grants awarded under this heading, the minimum grant size shall be $1,000,000: Provided further, That for grant awards of less than $10,000,000, the Secretary shall prioritize ports that handled less than 8,000,000 short tons, as reflected in the Waterborne Commerce of the United States Annual Report issued immediately preceding the date of enactment of this Act: Provided further, That not to exceed 2 percent of the amounts made available under this heading shall be available for necessary costs of grant administration.

Note.—A full-year 2022 appropriation for this account was not enacted at the time the Budget was prepared; therefore, the Budget assumes this account is operating under the Continuing Appropriations Act, 2022 (Division A of Public Law 117–43, as amended). The amounts included for 2022 reflect the annualized level provided by the continuing resolution.

PORT INFRASTRUCTURE DEVELOPMENT PROGRAM

[For an additional amount for "Port Infrastructure Development Program", $2,250,000,000, to remain available until September 30, 2036: *Provided*, That $450,000,000, to remain available until September 30, 2032, shall be made available for fiscal year 2022, $450,000,000, to remain available until September 30, 2033, shall be made available for fiscal year 2023, $450,000,000, to remain available until September 30, 2034, shall be made available for fiscal year 2024, $450,000,000, to remain available until September 30, 2035, shall be made available for fiscal year 2025, and $450,000,000, to remain available until September 30, 2036, shall be made available for fiscal year 2026: *Provided further*, That for the purposes of amounts made available under this heading in this Act and in prior Acts, and in addition to projects already eligible for awards under this heading, eligible projects, as defined under section 50302(c)(3) of title 46, United States Code, shall also include projects that improve the resiliency of ports to address sea-level rise, flooding, extreme weather events, earthquakes, and tsunami inundation, as well as projects that reduce or eliminate port-related criteria pollutant or greenhouse gas emissions, including projects for—]

[(1) Port electrification or electrification master planning;]

[(2) Harbor craft or equipment replacements/retrofits;]

[(3) Development of port or terminal micro-grids;]

[(4) Providing idling reduction infrastructure;]

[(5) Purchase of cargo handling equipment and related infrastructure;]

[(6) Worker training to support electrification technology;]

[(7) Installation of port bunkering facilities from ocean-going vessels for fuels;]

[(8) Electric vehicle charge or hydrogen refueling infrastructure for drayage, and medium or heavy duty trucks and locomotives that service the port and related grid upgrades; or]

[(9) Other related to port activities including charging infrastructure, electric rubber-tired gantry cranes, and anti-idling technologies:]

[*Provided further*, That such amount is designated by the Congress as being for an emergency requirement pursuant to section 4112(a) of H. Con. Res. 71 (115th Congress), the concurrent resolution on the budget for fiscal year 2018, and to section 251(b) of the Balanced Budget and Emergency Deficit Control Act of 1985.] *(Infrastructure Investments and Jobs Appropriations Act.)*

Program and Financing (in millions of dollars)

Identification code 069–1713–0–1–403	2021 actual	2022 est.	2023 est.
Obligations by program activity:			
0001 Discretionary Grants	126	291	225
0002 Targeted Grants	39	52	....
0003 Grant Administration	2	2	2
0004 Discretionary Grants -IIJA	....	....	450
0005 Admin & Oversight Cost - IIJA	....	4	9
0900 Total new obligations, unexpired accounts	167	349	686
Budgetary resources:			
Unobligated balance:			
1000 Unobligated balance brought forward, Oct 1	517	580	911

Maritime Administration—Continued
Federal Funds—Continued

PORT INFRASTRUCTURE DEVELOPMENT PROGRAM—Continued

Program and Financing—Continued

Identification code 069–1713–0–1–403		2021 actual	2022 est.	2023 est.
	Budget authority:			
	Appropriations, discretionary:			
1100	Appropriation	230	230	230
1100	Appropriation	....	450	....
1160	Appropriation, discretionary (total)	230	680	230
	Advance appropriations, discretionary:			
1170	Advance appropriation	....	....	450
1900	Budget authority (total)	230	680	680
1930	Total budgetary resources available	747	1,260	1,591
	Memorandum (non-add) entries:			
1941	Unexpired unobligated balance, end of year	580	911	905
	Change in obligated balance:			
	Unpaid obligations:			
3000	Unpaid obligations, brought forward, Oct 1	....	166	395
3010	New obligations, unexpired accounts	167	349	686
3020	Outlays (gross)	–1	–120	–198
3050	Unpaid obligations, end of year	166	395	883
	Memorandum (non-add) entries:			
3100	Obligated balance, start of year	....	166	395
3200	Obligated balance, end of year	166	395	883
	Budget authority and outlays, net:			
	Discretionary:			
4000	Budget authority, gross	230	680	680
	Outlays, gross:			
4010	Outlays from new discretionary authority	1	9	9
4011	Outlays from discretionary balances	....	111	189
4020	Outlays, gross (total)	1	120	198
4180	Budget authority, net (total)	230	680	680
4190	Outlays, net (total)	1	120	198

The Port Infrastructure Development Program provides grants for coastal seaports, inland river ports, and Great Lakes ports infrastructure to improve the safety, efficiency, or reliability of the movement of goods and to reduce environmental impacts in and around ports.

Object Classification (in millions of dollars)

Identification code 069–1713–0–1–403		2021 actual	2022 est.	2023 est.
	Direct obligations:			
11.1	Personnel compensation: Full-time permanent	1	3	5
12.1	Civilian personnel benefits	....	1	2
25.3	Other goods and services from Federal sources	....	2	4
41.0	Grants, subsidies, and contributions	165	343	675
99.0	Direct obligations	166	349	686
99.5	Adjustment for rounding	1	....	....
99.9	Total new obligations, unexpired accounts	167	349	686

Employment Summary

Identification code 069–1713–0–1–403		2021 actual	2022 est.	2023 est.
1001	Direct civilian full-time equivalent employment	7	8	8
1001	Direct civilian full-time equivalent employment	....	13	34

MARITIME GUARANTEED LOAN (TITLE XI) FINANCING ACCOUNT

Program and Financing (in millions of dollars)

Identification code 069–4304–0–3–999		2021 actual	2022 est.	2023 est.
	Obligations by program activity:			
	Credit program obligations:			
0712	Default claim payments on interest	....	3	3
0713	Payment of interest to Treasury	2	1	1
0715	Default related activity	1	10	10
0742	Downward reestimates paid to receipt accounts	9	31	....
0743	Interest on downward reestimates	11	16	....
0900	Total new obligations, unexpired accounts	23	61	14
	Budgetary resources:			
	Unobligated balance:			
1000	Unobligated balance brought forward, Oct 1	113	132	71
1021	Recoveries of prior year unpaid obligations	1	....	....
1023	Unobligated balances applied to repay debt	–24	....	....
1070	Unobligated balance (total)	90	132	71
	Financing authority:			
	Spending authority from offsetting collections, mandatory:			
1800	Collected	65	....	....
1900	Budget authority (total)	65	....	....
1930	Total budgetary resources available	155	132	71
	Memorandum (non-add) entries:			
1941	Unexpired unobligated balance, end of year	132	71	57
	Change in obligated balance:			
	Unpaid obligations:			
3000	Unpaid obligations, brought forward, Oct 1	1	....	47
3010	New obligations, unexpired accounts	23	61	14
3020	Outlays (gross)	–23	–14	–14
3040	Recoveries of prior year unpaid obligations, unexpired	–1	....	....
3050	Unpaid obligations, end of year	....	47	47
	Memorandum (non-add) entries:			
3100	Obligated balance, start of year	1	....	47
3200	Obligated balance, end of year	....	47	47
	Financing authority and disbursements, net:			
	Mandatory:			
4090	Budget authority, gross	65	....	....
	Financing disbursements:			
4110	Outlays, gross (total)	23	14	14
	Offsets against gross financing authority and disbursements:			
	Offsetting collections (collected) from:			
4120	Payments from program account - Upward Reestimate	–58	....	....
4122	Interest on uninvested funds	–6	....	....
4123	Loan Repayment	–1	....	....
4130	Offsets against gross budget authority and outlays (total)	–65	....	....
4170	Outlays, net (mandatory)	–42	14	14
4180	Budget authority, net (total)	....	....	....
4190	Outlays, net (total)	–42	14	14

Status of Guaranteed Loans (in millions of dollars)

Identification code 069–4304–0–3–999		2021 actual	2022 est.	2023 est.
	Position with respect to appropriations act limitation on commitments:			
2111	Guaranteed loan commitments from current-year authority	....	....	....
2150	Total guaranteed loan commitments	....	....	....
	Cumulative balance of guaranteed loans outstanding:			
2210	Outstanding, start of year	1,324	1,324	1,324
2231	Disbursements of new guaranteed loans	....	....	....
2251	Repayments and prepayments	....	....	....
2262	Adjustments: Terminations for default that result in acquisition of property	....	....	....
2290	Outstanding, end of year	1,324	1,324	1,324
	Memorandum:			
2299	Guaranteed amount of guaranteed loans outstanding, end of year	1,324	1,324	1,324
	Addendum:			
	Cumulative balance of defaulted guaranteed loans that result in loans receivable:			
2310	Outstanding, start of year	204	204	204
2331	Disbursements for guaranteed loan claims	....	....	....
2351	Repayments of loans receivable	....	....	....
2361	Write-offs of loans receivable	....	....	....
2364	Other adjustments, net	....	....	....
2390	Outstanding, end of year	204	204	204

As required by the Federal Credit Reform Act of 1990, this non-budgetary account records all cash flows to and from the Government resulting from Maritime Guaranteed Loan (Title XI) program loan guarantee commitments in 1992 and subsequent years. The amounts in this account are a means of financing and are not included in the budget totals.

DEPARTMENT OF TRANSPORTATION

Balance Sheet (in millions of dollars)

Identification code 069–4304–0–3–999		2020 actual	2021 actual
	ASSETS:		
	Federal assets:		
1101	Fund balances with Treasury	114	114
	Investments in U.S. securities:		
1106	Receivables, net	58	58
	Net value of assets related to post-1991 acquired defaulted guaranteed loans receivable:		
1501	Defaulted guaranteed loans receivable, gross	204	204
1504	Foreclosed property	1	1
1599	Net present value of assets related to defaulted guaranteed loans	205	205
1999	Total assets	377	377
	LIABILITIES:		
	Federal liabilities:		
2103	Debt	126	126
2105	Other	20	20
2204	Non-Federal liabilities: Liabilities for loan guarantees	193	193
2999	Total liabilities	339	339
	NET POSITION:		
3300	Cumulative results of operations	38	38
4999	Total liabilities and net position	377	377

Trust Funds

MISCELLANEOUS TRUST FUNDS, MARITIME ADMINISTRATION

Special and Trust Fund Receipts (in millions of dollars)

Identification code 069–8547–0–7–403		2021 actual	2022 est.	2023 est.
0100	Balance, start of year			
	Receipts:			
	Current law:			
1130	Gifts and Bequests, Maritime Administration, Transportation	1	2	2
2000	Total: Balances and receipts	1	2	2
	Appropriations:			
	Current law:			
2101	Miscellaneous Trust Funds, Maritime Administration	–1	–2	–2
5099	Balance, end of year			

Program and Financing (in millions of dollars)

Identification code 069–8547–0–7–403		2021 actual	2022 est.	2023 est.
	Obligations by program activity:			
0001	Gifts and Bequests		2	2
0100	Total direct program - Subtotal (running)		2	2
	Budgetary resources:			
	Unobligated balance:			
1000	Unobligated balance brought forward, Oct 1	5	6	6
	Budget authority:			
	Appropriations, mandatory:			
1201	Appropriation (special or trust fund) - Gifts and Bequests	1	2	2
1930	Total budgetary resources available	6	8	8
	Memorandum (non-add) entries:			
1941	Unexpired unobligated balance, end of year	6	6	6
	Change in obligated balance:			
	Unpaid obligations:			
3010	New obligations, unexpired accounts		2	2
3020	Outlays (gross)		–2	–2
	Budget authority and outlays, net:			
	Mandatory:			
4090	Budget authority, gross	1	2	2
	Outlays, gross:			
4100	Outlays from new mandatory authority		2	2
4180	Budget authority, net (total)	1	2	2
4190	Outlays, net (total)		2	2

GENERAL PROVISIONS—DEPARTMENT OF TRANSPORTATION

Object Classification (in millions of dollars)

Identification code 069–8547–0–7–403		2021 actual	2022 est.	2023 est.
	Direct obligations:			
21.0	Travel and transportation of persons		1	1
26.0	Supplies and materials		1	1
99.0	Direct obligations		2	2
99.9	Total new obligations, unexpired accounts		2	2

ADMINISTRATIVE PROVISIONS—MARITIME ADMINISTRATION

SEC. 170. *Notwithstanding any other provision of this Act, in addition to any existing authority, the Maritime Administration is authorized to furnish utilities and services and make necessary repairs in connection with any lease, contract, or occupancy involving Government property under control of the Maritime Administration: Provided, That payments received therefor shall be credited to the appropriation charged with the cost thereof and shall remain available until expended: Provided further, That rental payments under any such lease, contract, or occupancy for items other than such utilities, services, or repairs shall be deposited into the Treasury as miscellaneous receipts.*

GENERAL FUND RECEIPT ACCOUNTS

(in millions of dollars)

		2021 actual	2022 est.	2023 est.
Offsetting receipts from the public:				
069–085500	Hazardous Materials Transportation Registration, Filing, and Permit Fees, Administrative Costs	1	1	1
069–143500	General Fund Proprietary Interest Receipts, not Otherwise Classified	2		
069–272830	Maritime (title XI) Loan Program, Downward Reestimates of Subsidies	21	47	
069–276030	Downward Reestimates, Railroad Rehabilitation and Improvement Program	12	96	
069–276810	Transportation Infrastructure Finance and Innovation Program, Negative Subsidies	3		
069–276830	Transportation Infrastructure Finance and Innovation Program, Interest on Downward Reestimates	390	1,064	
069–322000	All Other General Fund Proprietary Receipts Including Budget Clearing Accounts	28		
General Fund Offsetting receipts from the public		457	1,208	1
Intragovernmental payments:				
069–388500	Undistributed Intragovernmental Payments and Receivables from Cancelled Accounts	4		
General Fund Intragovernmental payments		4		

GENERAL PROVISIONS—DEPARTMENT OF TRANSPORTATION

SEC. 190. *(a) During the current fiscal year, applicable appropriations to the Department of Transportation shall be available for maintenance and operation of aircraft; hire of passenger motor vehicles and aircraft; purchase of liability insurance for motor vehicles operating in foreign countries on official department business; and uniforms or allowances therefor, as authorized by sections 5901 and 5902 of title 5, United States Code.*

(b) During the current fiscal year, applicable appropriations to the Department and its operating administrations shall be available for the purchase, maintenance, operation, and deployment of unmanned aircraft systems that advance the missions of the Department of Transportation or an operating administration of the Department of Transportation.

(c) Any unmanned aircraft system purchased, procured, or contracted for by the Department prior to the date of enactment of this Act shall be deemed authorized by Congress as if this provision was in effect when the system was purchased, procured, or contracted for.

SEC. 191. *Appropriations contained in this Act for the Department of Transportation shall be available for services as authorized by section 3109 of title 5, United States Code, but at rates for individuals not to exceed the per diem rate equivalent to the rate for an Executive Level IV.*

SEC. 192. (a) No recipient of amounts made available by this Act shall disseminate personal information (as defined in section 2725(3) of title 18, United States Code) obtained by a State department of motor vehicles in connection with a motor vehicle record as defined in section 2725(1) of title 18, United States Code, except as provided in section 2721 of title 18, United States Code, for a use permitted under section 2721 of title 18, United States Code.

(b) Notwithstanding subsection (a), the Secretary shall not withhold amounts made available by this Act for any grantee if a State is in noncompliance with this provision.

SEC. 193. None of the funds made available by this Act shall be available for salaries and expenses of more than 125 political and Presidential appointees in the Department of Transportation: Provided, That none of the personnel covered by this provision may be assigned on temporary detail outside the Department of Transportation.

SEC. 194. Funds received by the Federal Highway Administration and Federal Railroad Administration from States, counties, municipalities, other public authorities, and private sources for expenses incurred for training may be credited respectively to the Federal Highway Administration's "Federal-Aid Highways" account and to the Federal Railroad Administration's "Safety and Operations" account, except for State rail safety inspectors participating in training pursuant to section 20105 of title 49, United States Code.

SEC. 195. None of the funds made available by this Act to the Department of Transportation may be used to make a loan, loan guarantee, line of credit, letter of intent, federally funded cooperative agreement, full funding grant agreement, or discretionary grant unless the Secretary of Transportation notifies the House and Senate Committees on Appropriations not less than 3 full business days before any project competitively selected to receive any discretionary grant award, letter of intent, loan commitment, loan guarantee commitment, line of credit commitment, federally funded cooperative agreement, or full funding grant agreement is announced by the Department or its operating administrations: Provided, That the Secretary of Transportation shall provide the House and Senate Committees on Appropriations with a comprehensive list of all such loans, loan guarantees, lines of credit, letters of intent, federally funded cooperative agreements, full funding grant agreements, and discretionary grants prior to the notification required under the previous proviso: Provided further, That the Secretary gives concurrent notification to the House and Senate Committees on Appropriations for any "quick release" of funds from the emergency relief program: Provided further, That no notification shall involve funds that are not available for obligation.

SEC. 196. Rebates, refunds, incentive payments, minor fees, and other funds received by the Department of Transportation from travel management centers, charge card programs, the subleasing of building space, and miscellaneous sources are to be credited to appropriations of the Department of Transportation and allocated to elements of the Department of Transportation using fair and equitable criteria and such funds shall be available until expended.

SEC. 197. Notwithstanding any other provision of law, if any funds provided by or limited by this Act are subject to a reprogramming action that requires notice to be provided to the House and Senate Committees on Appropriations, transmission of such reprogramming notice shall be provided solely to the House and Senate Committees on Appropriations: Provided, That the Secretary of Transportation may provide notice to other congressional committees of the action of the House and Senate Committees on Appropriations on such reprogramming.

SEC. 198. Funds appropriated by this Act to the operating administrations may be obligated for the Office of the Secretary for the costs related to assessments or reimbursable agreements only when such amounts are for the costs of goods and services that are purchased to provide a direct benefit to the applicable operating administration or administrations.

SEC. 199. The Secretary of Transportation is authorized to carry out a program that establishes uniform standards for developing and supporting agency transit pass and transit benefits authorized under section 7905 of title 5, United States Code, including distribution of transit benefits by various paper and electronic media.

SEC. 200. The Department of Transportation may use funds provided by this Act, or any other Act, to assist a contract under title 49 U.S.C. or title 23 U.S.C. utilizing geographic, economic, or any other hiring preference not otherwise authorized by law, or to amend a rule, regulation, policy or other measure that forbids a recipient of a Federal Highway Administration or Federal Transit Administration grant from imposing such hiring preference on a contract or construction project with which the Department of Transportation is assisting, only if the grant recipient certifies the following:

(1) that except with respect to apprentices or trainees, a pool of readily available but unemployed individuals possessing the knowledge, skill, and ability to perform the work that the contract requires resides in the jurisdiction;

(2) that the grant recipient will include appropriate provisions in its bid document ensuring that the contractor does not displace any of its existing employees in order to satisfy such hiring preference; and

(3) that any increase in the cost of labor, training, or delays resulting from the use of such hiring preference does not delay or displace any transportation project in the applicable Statewide Transportation Improvement Program or Transportation Improvement Program.

SEC. 201. The Secretary of Transportation shall coordinate with the Secretary of Homeland Security to ensure that best practices for Industrial Control Systems Procurement are up-to-date and shall ensure that systems procured with funds provided under this title were procured using such practices.

GENERAL PROVISIONS—THIS ACT

SEC. 401. None of the funds in this Act shall be used for the planning or execution of any program to pay the expenses of, or otherwise compensate, non-Federal parties intervening in regulatory or adjudicatory proceedings funded in this Act.

SEC. 402. None of the funds appropriated in this Act shall remain available for obligation beyond the current fiscal year, nor may any be transferred to other appropriations, unless expressly so provided herein.

SEC. 403. The expenditure of any appropriation under this Act for any consulting service through a procurement contract pursuant to section 3109 of title 5, United States Code, shall be limited to those contracts where such expenditures are a matter of public record and available for public inspection, except where otherwise provided under existing law, or under existing Executive order issued pursuant to existing law.

SEC. 404. Except as otherwise provided in this Act, none of the funds provided in titles I or III of this Act, provided by previous appropriations Acts to the agencies or entities funded in titles I or III of this Act that remain available for obligation or expenditure in fiscal year 2023, or provided from any accounts in the Treasury derived by the collection of fees and available to the agencies funded by titles I or III of this Act, shall be available for obligation or expenditure through a reprogramming of funds that—

(1) creates a new program;

(2) eliminates a program, project, or activity;

(3) increases funds or personnel for any program, project, or activity for which funds have been denied or restricted by the Congress;

(4) proposes to use funds directed for a specific activity in an appropriations Act for a different purpose;

(5) augments existing programs, projects, or activities in excess of $5,000,000 or 10 percent, whichever is less;

(6) reduces existing programs, projects, or activities by $5,000,000 or 10 percent, whichever is less; or

(7) creates, reorganizes, or restructures a branch, division, office, bureau, board, commission, agency, administration, or department different from the budget justifications submitted to the Committees on Appropriations or the table accompanying the explanatory statement described in section 4 (in the matter preceding division A of this consolidated Act), whichever is more detailed, unless prior notice is transmitted to the House and Senate Committees on Appropriations: Provided, That not later than 60 days after the date of enactment of this Act, each agency funded by this Act shall submit a report to the Committees on Appropriations of the Senate and of the House of Representatives to establish the baseline for application of reprogramming and transfer authorities for the current fiscal year: Provided further, That the report shall include—

(A) a table for each appropriation with a separate column to display the prior year enacted level, the President's budget request, adjustments made by Congress, adjustments due to enacted rescissions, if appropriate, and the fiscal year enacted level;

(B) a delineation in the table for each appropriation and its respective prior year enacted level by object class and program, project, and activity as detailed in this Act, the table accompanying the explanatory statement described in section 4 (in the matter preceding division A of this consolidated Act), accompanying reports of the House and Senate Committee on Appropriations, or in the budget appendix for the respective appropriations, whichever is more detailed, and shall apply to all items for which a dollar amount is specified and to all programs for which new budget (obligational) authority is provided, as well as to discretionary grants and discretionary grant allocations; and

(C) an identification of items of special congressional interest.

SEC. 405. Except as otherwise specifically provided by law, not to exceed 50 percent of unobligated balances remaining available at the end of fiscal year 2023 from appropriations made available for salaries and expenses for fiscal year 2023 in this Act, shall remain available through September 30, 2024, for each such account for the purposes authorized: *Provided,* That a notification shall be submitted to the House and Senate Committees on Appropriations prior to the expenditure of such funds: *Provided further,* That these requests shall be made in compliance with reprogramming guidelines under section 404 of this Act.

SEC. 406. No funds in this Act may be used to support any Federal, State, or local projects that seek to use the power of eminent domain, unless eminent domain is employed only for a public use: *Provided,* That for purposes of this section, public use shall not be construed to include economic development that primarily benefits private entities: *Provided further,* That any use of funds for mass transit, railroad, airport, seaport or highway projects, as well as utility projects which benefit or serve the general public (including energy-related, communication-related, water-related and wastewater-related infrastructure), other structures designated for use by the general public or which have other common-carrier or public-utility functions that serve the general public and are subject to regulation and oversight by the government, and projects for the removal of an immediate threat to public health and safety or brownfields as defined in the Small Business Liability Relief and Brownfields Revitalization Act (Public Law 107–118) shall be considered a public use for purposes of eminent domain.

SEC. 407. No funds appropriated pursuant to this Act may be expended by an entity unless the entity agrees that in expending the assistance the entity will comply with sections 2 through 4 of the Act of March 3, 1933 (41 U.S.C. 8301–8305, popularly known as the "Buy American Act").

SEC. 408. No funds appropriated or otherwise made available under this Act shall be made available to any person or entity that has been convicted of violating the Buy American Act (41 U.S.C. 8301–8305).

SEC. 409. None of the funds made available in this Act may be used for first-class airline accommodations in contravention of sections 301–10.122 and 301–10.123 of title 41, Code of Federal Regulations.

SEC. 410.

(a) None of the funds made available in this Act may be used to maintain or establish a computer network unless such network blocks the viewing, downloading, and exchanging of pornography.

(b) Nothing in subsection (a) shall limit the use of funds necessary for any Federal, State, tribal, or local law enforcement agency or any other entity carrying out criminal investigations, prosecution, or adjudication activities.

SEC. 411. (a) None of the funds made available in this Act may be used to deny an Inspector General funded under this Act timely access to any records, documents, or other materials available to the department or agency over which that Inspector General has responsibilities under the Inspector General Act of 1978 (5 U.S.C. App.), or to prevent or impede that Inspector General's access to such records, documents, or other materials, under any provision of law, except a provision of law that expressly refers to the Inspector General and expressly limits the Inspector General's right of access.

(b) A department or agency covered by this section shall provide its Inspector General with access to all such records, documents, and other materials in a timely manner.

(c) Each Inspector General shall ensure compliance with statutory limitations on disclosure relevant to the information provided by the establishment over which that Inspector General has responsibilities under the Inspector General Act of 1978 (5 U.S.C. App.).

(d) Each Inspector General covered by this section shall report to the Committees on Appropriations of the House of Representatives and the Senate within 5 calendar days any failures to comply with this requirement.

SEC. 412. None of the funds appropriated or otherwise made available by this Act may be used to pay award or incentive fees for contractors whose performance has been judged to be below satisfactory, behind schedule, over budget, or has failed to meet the basic requirements of a contract, unless the Agency determines that any such deviations are due to unforeseeable events, government-driven scope changes, or are not significant within the overall scope of the project and/or program unless such awards or incentive fees are consistent with 16.401(e)(2) of the Federal Acquisition Regulations.

GENERAL PROVISION—DEPARTMENT OF TRANSPORTATION

〖SEC. 803. Any funds transferred to the Office of Inspector General of the Department of Transportation from amounts made available in this division in this Act shall remain available until expended.〗 *(Infrastructure Investments and Jobs Appropriations Act.)*

DEPARTMENT OF THE TREASURY

DEPARTMENTAL OFFICES

Federal Funds

SALARIES AND EXPENSES

For necessary expenses of the Departmental Offices including operation and maintenance of the Treasury Building and Freedman's Bank Building; hire of passenger motor vehicles; maintenance, repairs, and improvements of, and purchase of commercial insurance policies for, real properties leased or owned overseas, when necessary for the performance of official business; executive direction program activities; international affairs and economic policy activities; domestic finance and tax policy activities, including technical assistance to State, local, and territorial entities; and Treasury-wide management policies and programs activities, $293,242,000: Provided, That of the amount appropriated under this heading—

(1) not to exceed $350,000 is for official reception and representation expenses;

(2) not to exceed $258,000 is for unforeseen emergencies of a confidential nature to be allocated and expended under the direction of the Secretary of the Treasury and to be accounted for solely on the Secretary's certificate; and

(3) not to exceed $34,000,000 shall remain available until September 30, 2024, for—

(A) the Treasury-wide Financial Statement Audit and Internal Control Program;

(B) information technology modernization requirements;

(C) the audit, oversight, and administration of the Gulf Coast Restoration Trust Fund;

(D) the development and implementation of programs within the Office of Cybersecurity and Critical Infrastructure Protection, including entering into cooperative agreements;

(E) operations and maintenance of facilities; and

(F) international operations.

Note.—A full-year 2022 appropriation for this account was not enacted at the time the Budget was prepared; therefore, the Budget assumes this account is operating under the Continuing Appropriations Act, 2022 (Division A of Public Law 117–43, as amended). The amounts included for 2022 reflect the annualized level provided by the continuing resolution.

Program and Financing (in millions of dollars)

Identification code 020–0101–0–1–803		2021 actual	2022 est.	2023 est.
	Obligations by program activity:			
0001	Executive Direction	33	36	49
0002	International Affairs and Economic Policy	55	53	71
0003	Domestic Finance and Tax Policy	77	81	101
0005	Treasury-wide Management and Programs	40	40	47
0006	CFIUS	39	38	41
0007	Coronavirus Response Support to SBA	1		
0100	Subtotal, Direct programs	245	248	309
0799	Total direct obligations	245	248	309
0811	Salaries and Expenses (Reimbursable)	9	12	12
0900	Total new obligations, unexpired accounts	254	260	321
	Budgetary resources:			
	Unobligated balance:			
1000	Unobligated balance brought forward, Oct 1	54	34	34
1012	Unobligated balance transfers between expired and unexpired accounts	1		
1021	Recoveries of prior year unpaid obligations	1		
1033	Recoveries of prior year paid obligations	1		
1070	Unobligated balance (total)	57	34	34
	Budget authority:			
	Appropriations, discretionary:			
1100	Appropriation	233	233	293
	Spending authority from offsetting collections, discretionary:			
1700	Collected	7	12	12
1700	Collected	15	15	15
1701	Change in uncollected payments, Federal sources	1		
1750	Spending auth from offsetting collections, disc (total)	23	27	27
1900	Budget authority (total)	256	260	320
1930	Total budgetary resources available	313	294	354
	Memorandum (non-add) entries:			
1940	Unobligated balance expiring	–25		
1941	Unexpired unobligated balance, end of year	34	34	33
	Change in obligated balance:			
	Unpaid obligations:			
3000	Unpaid obligations, brought forward, Oct 1	52	43	37
3010	New obligations, unexpired accounts	254	260	321
3011	Obligations ("upward adjustments"), expired accounts	4		
3020	Outlays (gross)	–255	–266	–313
3040	Recoveries of prior year unpaid obligations, unexpired	–1		
3041	Recoveries of prior year unpaid obligations, expired	–11		
3050	Unpaid obligations, end of year	43	37	45
	Uncollected payments:			
3060	Uncollected pymts, Fed sources, brought forward, Oct 1	–5	–4	–4
3070	Change in uncollected pymts, Fed sources, unexpired	–1		
3071	Change in uncollected pymts, Fed sources, expired	2		
3090	Uncollected pymts, Fed sources, end of year	–4	–4	–4
	Memorandum (non-add) entries:			
3100	Obligated balance, start of year	47	39	33
3200	Obligated balance, end of year	39	33	41
	Budget authority and outlays, net:			
	Discretionary:			
4000	Budget authority, gross	256	260	320
	Outlays, gross:			
4010	Outlays from new discretionary authority	208	228	280
4011	Outlays from discretionary balances	47	38	33
4020	Outlays, gross (total)	255	266	313
	Offsets against gross budget authority and outlays:			
	Offsetting collections (collected) from:			
4030	Federal sources	–23	–27	–27
4033	Non-Federal sources	–3		
4040	Offsets against gross budget authority and outlays (total)	–26	–27	–27
	Additional offsets against gross budget authority only:			
4050	Change in uncollected pymts, Fed sources, unexpired	–1		
4052	Offsetting collections credited to expired accounts	3		
4053	Recoveries of prior year paid obligations, unexpired accounts	1		
4060	Additional offsets against budget authority only (total)	3		
4070	Budget authority, net (discretionary)	233	233	293
4080	Outlays, net (discretionary)	229	239	286
4180	Budget authority, net (total)	233	233	293
4190	Outlays, net (total)	229	239	286

Treasury's mission is to maintain a strong economy by promoting conditions that enable equitable and sustainable economic growth at home and abroad, combating threats to, and protecting the integrity of the financial system, and managing the Government's finances and resources effectively. Departmental Offices, as the headquarters bureau for the Department of the Treasury, provides leadership in economic and financial policy, terrorism and financial intelligence, financial crimes, and general management. The Secretary of the Treasury has the primary role of formulating and managing the domestic and international tax and financial policies of the Federal Government. Through effective management, policies, and leadership, the Treasury Department protects our national security through targeted financial actions, promotes the stability of the Nation's financial markets, and ensures the Government's ability to collect revenue and fund its operations.

Object Classification (in millions of dollars)

Identification code 020–0101–0–1–803		2021 actual	2022 est.	2023 est.
	Direct obligations:			
	Personnel compensation:			
11.1	Full-time permanent	94	104	129
11.3	Other than full-time permanent	3	3	3
11.5	Other personnel compensation	3	4	4
11.8	Special personal services payments	1	1	1
11.9	Total personnel compensation	101	112	137
12.1	Civilian personnel benefits	33	38	47
21.0	Travel and transportation of persons	1	4	4
23.2	Rental payments to others	1	1	1
25.1	Advisory and assistance services	13	14	14
25.2	Other services from non-Federal sources	3	2	3
25.3	Other goods and services from Federal sources	82	72	97
26.0	Supplies and materials	3	3	3

SALARIES AND EXPENSES—Continued

Object Classification—Continued

Identification code 020–0101–0–1–803	2021 actual	2022 est.	2023 est.
31.0 Equipment	3	2	2
32.0 Land and structures	5		
99.0 Direct obligations	245	248	308
99.0 Reimbursable obligations	9	11	10
99.5 Adjustment for rounding		1	3
99.9 Total new obligations, unexpired accounts	254	260	321

Employment Summary

Identification code 020–0101–0–1–803	2021 actual	2022 est.	2023 est.
1001 Direct civilian full-time equivalent employment	672	740	869
2001 Reimbursable civilian full-time equivalent employment	40	41	41

OFFICE OF TERRORISM AND FINANCIAL INTELLIGENCE

SALARIES AND EXPENSES

For the necessary expenses of the Office of Terrorism and Financial Intelligence to safeguard the financial system against illicit use and to combat rogue nations, terrorist facilitators, weapons of mass destruction proliferators, human rights abusers, money launderers, drug kingpins, and other national security threats, $212,059,000, of which not less than $3,000,000 shall be available for addressing human rights violations and corruption, including activities authorized by the Global Magnitsky Human Rights Accountability Act (22 U.S.C. 2656 note): Provided, That of the amounts appropriated under this heading, up to $12,000,000 shall remain available until September 30, 2024.

Note.—A full-year 2022 appropriation for this account was not enacted at the time the Budget was prepared; therefore, the Budget assumes this account is operating under the Continuing Appropriations Act, 2022 (Division A of Public Law 117–43, as amended). The amounts included for 2022 reflect the annualized level provided by the continuing resolution.

Program and Financing (in millions of dollars)

Identification code 020–1804–0–1–803	2021 actual	2022 est.	2023 est.
Obligations by program activity:			
0001 Terrorism and Financial Intelligence	173	175	210
0002 Kleptocracy Asset Recovery Rewards Pilot Program			2
0799 Total direct obligations	173	175	212
0811 Salaries and Expenses (Reimbursable)	8	11	11
0900 Total new obligations, unexpired accounts	181	186	223
Budgetary resources:			
Unobligated balance:			
1000 Unobligated balance brought forward, Oct 1	10	10	10
Budget authority:			
Appropriations, discretionary:			
1100 Appropriation	175	175	212
Spending authority from offsetting collections, discretionary:			
1700 Collected	5	11	11
1701 Change in uncollected payments, Federal sources	3		
1750 Spending auth from offsetting collections, disc (total)	8	11	11
1900 Budget authority (total)	183	186	223
1930 Total budgetary resources available	193	196	233
Memorandum (non-add) entries:			
1940 Unobligated balance expiring	–2		
1941 Unexpired unobligated balance, end of year	10	10	10
Change in obligated balance:			
Unpaid obligations:			
3000 Unpaid obligations, brought forward, Oct 1	62	56	39
3010 New obligations, unexpired accounts	181	186	223
3011 Obligations ("upward adjustments"), expired accounts	3		
3020 Outlays (gross)	–186	–203	–226
3041 Recoveries of prior year unpaid obligations, expired	–4		
3050 Unpaid obligations, end of year	56	39	36
Uncollected payments:			
3060 Uncollected pymts, Fed sources, brought forward, Oct 1	–6	–7	–7
3070 Change in uncollected pymts, Fed sources, unexpired	–3		
3071 Change in uncollected pymts, Fed sources, expired	2		
3090 Uncollected pymts, Fed sources, end of year	–7	–7	–7
Memorandum (non-add) entries:			
3100 Obligated balance, start of year	56	49	32
3200 Obligated balance, end of year	49	32	29
Budget authority and outlays, net:			
Discretionary:			
4000 Budget authority, gross	183	186	223
Outlays, gross:			
4010 Outlays from new discretionary authority	138	154	185
4011 Outlays from discretionary balances	48	49	41
4020 Outlays, gross (total)	186	203	226
Offsets against gross budget authority and outlays:			
Offsetting collections (collected) from:			
4030 Federal sources	–7	–11	–11
Additional offsets against gross budget authority only:			
4050 Change in uncollected pymts, Fed sources, unexpired	–3		
4052 Offsetting collections credited to expired accounts	2		
4060 Additional offsets against budget authority only (total)	–1		
4070 Budget authority, net (discretionary)	175	175	212
4080 Outlays, net (discretionary)	179	192	215
4180 Budget authority, net (total)	175	175	212
4190 Outlays, net (total)	179	192	215

The Office of Terrorism and Financial Intelligence (TFI) safeguards the financial system against illicit use and combats rogue nations, terrorist facilitators, weapons of mass destruction proliferators, human rights abusers, money launderers, drug kingpins, and other national security threats. In addition to the Financial Crimes Enforcement Network (FinCEN) and Treasury Executive Office for Asset Forfeiture (TEOAF), which are shown separately, TFI includes three other components: 1) the Office of Terrorist Financing and Financial Crimes (TFFC), responsible for policy and outreach such as U.S. representation to the Financial Action Task Force (FATF); 2) the Office of Intelligence and Analysis (OIA), the sole intelligence community (IC) component in the Department of the Treasury; and 3) the Office of Foreign Assets Control (OFAC), which administers and enforces economic and trade sanctions.

Object Classification (in millions of dollars)

Identification code 020–1804–0–1–803	2021 actual	2022 est.	2023 est.
Direct obligations:			
Personnel compensation:			
11.1 Full-time permanent	64	72	84
11.5 Other personnel compensation	2	2	3
11.9 Total personnel compensation	66	74	87
12.1 Civilian personnel benefits	23	25	30
21.0 Travel and transportation of persons		1	2
25.1 Advisory and assistance services	13	12	13
25.2 Other services from non-Federal sources	4	4	4
25.3 Other goods and services from Federal sources	45	44	54
25.7 Operation and maintenance of equipment	5	4	8
26.0 Supplies and materials	3	4	4
31.0 Equipment	3	3	5
32.0 Land and structures	10	5	4
91.0 Unvouchered			2
99.0 Direct obligations	172	176	213
99.0 Reimbursable obligations	9	10	10
99.9 Total new obligations, unexpired accounts	181	186	223

Employment Summary

Identification code 020–1804–0–1–803	2021 actual	2022 est.	2023 est.
1001 Direct civilian full-time equivalent employment	524	561	624
2001 Reimbursable civilian full-time equivalent employment	35	41	41

CYBERSECURITY ENHANCEMENT ACCOUNT

For salaries and expenses for enhanced cybersecurity for systems operated by the Department of the Treasury, $215,000,000, to remain available until September 30, 2025: Provided, That such funds shall supplement and not supplant any other amounts made available to the Treasury offices and bureaus for cybersecurity:

DEPARTMENT OF THE TREASURY

Provided further, That of the total amount made available under this heading $9,000,000 shall be available for administrative expenses for the Treasury Chief Information Officer to provide oversight of the investments made under this heading: Provided further, That such funds shall supplement and not supplant any other amounts made available to the Treasury Chief Information Officer.

Note.—A full-year 2022 appropriation for this account was not enacted at the time the Budget was prepared; therefore, the Budget assumes this account is operating under the Continuing Appropriations Act, 2022 (Division A of Public Law 117–43, as amended). The amounts included for 2022 reflect the annualized level provided by the continuing resolution.

Program and Financing (in millions of dollars)

Identification code 020–1855–0–1–808		2021 actual	2022 est.	2023 est.
	Obligations by program activity:			
0001	Cybersecurity Enhancement Account	28	21	122
	Budgetary resources:			
	Unobligated balance:			
1000	Unobligated balance brought forward, Oct 1	27	18	17
1021	Recoveries of prior year unpaid obligations	2	2	2
1070	Unobligated balance (total)	29	20	19
	Budget authority:			
	Appropriations, discretionary:			
1100	Appropriation	18	18	215
1930	Total budgetary resources available	47	38	234
	Memorandum (non-add) entries:			
1940	Unobligated balance expiring	–1		
1941	Unexpired unobligated balance, end of year	18	17	112
	Change in obligated balance:			
	Unpaid obligations:			
3000	Unpaid obligations, brought forward, Oct 1	16	24	18
3010	New obligations, unexpired accounts	28	21	122
3020	Outlays (gross)	–16	–25	–133
3040	Recoveries of prior year unpaid obligations, unexpired	–2	–2	–2
3041	Recoveries of prior year unpaid obligations, expired	–2		
3050	Unpaid obligations, end of year	24	18	5
	Memorandum (non-add) entries:			
3100	Obligated balance, start of year	16	24	18
3200	Obligated balance, end of year	24	18	5
	Budget authority and outlays, net:			
	Discretionary:			
4000	Budget authority, gross	18	18	215
	Outlays, gross:			
4010	Outlays from new discretionary authority		4	122
4011	Outlays from discretionary balances	16	21	11
4020	Outlays, gross (total)	16	25	133
4180	Budget authority, net (total)	18	18	215
4190	Outlays, net (total)	16	25	133

Trillions of dollars are accounted for and processed by the Department of the Treasury's information technology (IT) systems and therefore these systems are a constant target for sophisticated threat actors. The Cybersecurity Enhancement Account (CEA) allows Treasury to more proactively and strategically protect Treasury systems against cybersecurity threats. The account supports enterprise-wide services and capabilities. The CEA budgetary resources will be used to address new cybersecurity requirements outlined in Executive Order 14028— *Improving the Nation's Cybersecurity* — and associated guidance at the enterprise level as well as targeted bureau-specific cyber investments.

Object Classification (in millions of dollars)

Identification code 020–1855–0–1–808		2021 actual	2022 est.	2023 est.
	Direct obligations:			
11.1	Personnel compensation: Full-time permanent		1	2	3
12.1	Civilian personnel benefits			1
23.3	Communications, utilities, and miscellaneous charges		1	7
25.1	Advisory and assistance services	25	11	71
25.2	Other services from non-Federal sources		1	5
25.3	Other goods and services from Federal sources		1	4
25.7	Operation and maintenance of equipment		2	14
31.0	Equipment	2	3	17
99.9	Total new obligations, unexpired accounts	28	21	122

Employment Summary

Identification code 020–1855–0–1–808	2021 actual	2022 est.	2023 est.
1001 Direct civilian full-time equivalent employment	4	10	21

DEPARTMENT-WIDE SYSTEMS AND CAPITAL INVESTMENTS PROGRAMS

(INCLUDING TRANSFER OF FUNDS)

For development and acquisition of automatic data processing equipment, software, and services; for the hire of zero emission passenger motor vehicles and for supporting charging or fueling infrastructure; and for repairs and renovations to buildings owned by the Department of the Treasury, $11,118,000, to remain available until September 30, 2025: Provided, That these funds shall be transferred to accounts and in amounts as necessary to satisfy the requirements of the Department's offices, bureaus, and other organizations: Provided further, That this transfer authority shall be in addition to any other transfer authority provided in this Act: Provided further, That none of the funds appropriated under this heading shall be used to support or supplement "Internal Revenue Service, Operations Support" or "Internal Revenue Service, Business Systems Modernization".

Note.—A full-year 2022 appropriation for this account was not enacted at the time the Budget was prepared; therefore, the Budget assumes this account is operating under the Continuing Appropriations Act, 2022 (Division A of Public Law 117–43, as amended). The amounts included for 2022 reflect the annualized level provided by the continuing resolution.

Program and Financing (in millions of dollars)

Identification code 020–0115–0–1–803		2021 actual	2022 est.	2023 est.
	Obligations by program activity:			
0001	Department-wide Systems and Capital Investments Programs (Direct)	9	9	11
	Budgetary resources:			
	Unobligated balance:			
1000	Unobligated balance brought forward, Oct 1	6	3	
	Budget authority:			
	Appropriations, discretionary:			
1100	Appropriation	6	6	11
1930	Total budgetary resources available	12	9	11
	Memorandum (non-add) entries:			
1941	Unexpired unobligated balance, end of year	3		
	Change in obligated balance:			
	Unpaid obligations:			
3000	Unpaid obligations, brought forward, Oct 1	4	9	9
3010	New obligations, unexpired accounts	9	9	11
3020	Outlays (gross)	–4	–9	–10
3050	Unpaid obligations, end of year	9	9	10
	Memorandum (non-add) entries:			
3100	Obligated balance, start of year	4	9	9
3200	Obligated balance, end of year	9	9	10
	Budget authority and outlays, net:			
	Discretionary:			
4000	Budget authority, gross	6	6	11
	Outlays, gross:			
4010	Outlays from new discretionary authority	2	3	5
4011	Outlays from discretionary balances	2	6	5
4020	Outlays, gross (total)	4	9	10
4180	Budget authority, net (total)	6	6	11
4190	Outlays, net (total)	4	9	10

This account is authorized to be used by Treasury's offices and bureaus to modernize business processes, increase efficiency, and improve infrastructure through technology and capital investments.

Object Classification (in millions of dollars)

Identification code 020–0115–0–1–803		2021 actual	2022 est.	2023 est.
	Direct obligations:			
23.3	Communications, utilities, and miscellaneous charges			5
25.1	Advisory and assistance services		1	
31.0	Equipment	2		
32.0	Land and structures	7	8	6

DEPARTMENT-WIDE SYSTEMS AND CAPITAL INVESTMENTS PROGRAMS—Continued
Object Classification—Continued

Identification code 020–0115–0–1–803	2021 actual	2022 est.	2023 est.
99.9 Total new obligations, unexpired accounts	9	9	11

SALARIES AND EXPENSES

For necessary expenses of the Office of Inspector General in carrying out the provisions of the Inspector General Act of 1978, $43,878,000, including hire of passenger motor vehicles; of which not to exceed $100,000 shall be available for unforeseen emergencies of a confidential nature, to be allocated and expended under the direction of the Inspector General of the Treasury; of which up to $2,800,000 to remain available until September 30, 2024, shall be for audits and investigations conducted pursuant to section 1608 of the Resources and Ecosystems Sustainability, Tourist Opportunities, and Revived Economies of the Gulf Coast States Act of 2012 (33 U.S.C. 1321 note); and of which not to exceed $1,000 shall be available for official reception and representation expenses.

Note.—A full-year 2022 appropriation for this account was not enacted at the time the Budget was prepared; therefore, the Budget assumes this account is operating under the Continuing Appropriations Act, 2022 (Division A of Public Law 117–43, as amended). The amounts included for 2022 reflect the annualized level provided by the continuing resolution.

Program and Financing (in millions of dollars)

Identification code 020–0106–0–1–803		2021 actual	2022 est.	2023 est.
	Obligations by program activity:			
0001	Audits	29	32	33
0002	Investigations	10	11	11
0003	Coronavirus Relief Fund Oversight	8	9	9
0004	Emergency Rental Assistance Oversight		1	1
0005	Homeowner Assistance Oversight		1	1
0799	Total direct obligations	47	54	55
0801	Office of Inspector General (Reimbursable)	9	12	12
0900	Total new obligations, unexpired accounts	56	66	67
	Budgetary resources:			
	Unobligated balance:			
1000	Unobligated balance brought forward, Oct 1	35	41	29
1012	Unobligated balance transfers between expired and unexpired accounts	1	1	1
1070	Unobligated balance (total)	36	42	30
	Budget authority:			
	Appropriations, discretionary:			
1100	Appropriation	41	41	44
1100	Appropriation (Consolidated Appropriations Act, 2021)	7		
1160	Appropriation, discretionary (total)	48	41	44
	Appropriations, mandatory:			
1221	Appropriations transferred from other acct [020–0124]	3		
1221	Appropriations transferred from other acct [020–0150]	3		
1260	Appropriations, mandatory (total)	6		
	Spending authority from offsetting collections, discretionary:			
1700	Collected	4	12	12
1701	Change in uncollected payments, Federal sources	6		
1750	Spending auth from offsetting collections, disc (total)	10	12	12
1900	Budget authority (total)	64	53	56
1930	Total budgetary resources available	100	95	86
	Memorandum (non-add) entries:			
1940	Unobligated balance expiring	–3		
1941	Unexpired unobligated balance, end of year	41	29	19
	Change in obligated balance:			
	Unpaid obligations:			
3000	Unpaid obligations, brought forward, Oct 1	12	16	13
3010	New obligations, unexpired accounts	56	66	67
3011	Obligations ("upward adjustments"), expired accounts	5		
3020	Outlays (gross)	–53	–69	–67
3041	Recoveries of prior year unpaid obligations, expired	–4		
3050	Unpaid obligations, end of year	16	13	13
	Uncollected payments:			
3060	Uncollected pymts, Fed sources, brought forward, Oct 1	–5	–6	–6
3070	Change in uncollected pymts, Fed sources, unexpired	–6		
3071	Change in uncollected pymts, Fed sources, expired	5		
3090	Uncollected pymts, Fed sources, end of year	–6	–6	–6
	Memorandum (non-add) entries:			
3100	Obligated balance, start of year	7	10	7
3200	Obligated balance, end of year	10	7	7
	Budget authority and outlays, net:			
	Discretionary:			
4000	Budget authority, gross	58	53	56
	Outlays, gross:			
4010	Outlays from new discretionary authority	40	39	42
4011	Outlays from discretionary balances	13	28	23
4020	Outlays, gross (total)	53	67	65
	Offsets against gross budget authority and outlays:			
	Offsetting collections (collected) from:			
4030	Federal sources	–9	–12	–12
	Additional offsets against gross budget authority only:			
4050	Change in uncollected pymts, Fed sources, unexpired	–6		
4052	Offsetting collections credited to expired accounts	5		
4060	Additional offsets against budget authority only (total)	–1		
4070	Budget authority, net (discretionary)	48	41	44
4080	Outlays, net (discretionary)	44	55	53
	Mandatory:			
4090	Budget authority, gross	6		
	Outlays, gross:			
4101	Outlays from mandatory balances		2	2
4180	Budget authority, net (total)	54	41	44
4190	Outlays, net (total)	44	57	55

The Office of Inspector General (OIG) conducts audits and investigations designed to promote integrity, efficiency, and effectiveness in programs and operations within the Department and across the OIG's jurisdiction, as well as to keep the Secretary and the Congress fully informed of problems and deficiencies in the administration of such programs and operations. The OIG conducts audits and investigations of Treasury programs and operations except those under jurisdictional oversight of the Treasury Inspector General for Tax Administration, the Special Inspector General for the Troubled Asset Relief Program, and the Special Inspector General for Pandemic Recovery. In addition, the Treasury Inspector General functions as Chair of the Council of Inspectors General on Financial Oversight. The Resources and Ecosystems Sustainability, Tourist Opportunities, and Revived Economies of the Gulf Coast States Act tasked the OIG with oversight of all projects, programs, and operations of the Gulf Coast Restoration Trust Fund (Trust Fund), which extends to the Gulf Coast Ecosystem Restoration Council.

The Budget request for the OIG will be used to fund audit, investigative, and mission support activities to meet the requirements of the Inspector General Act, as well as other statutes relating to: 1) cyber threats; 2) Bank Secrecy Act, anti-money laundering, and anti-terrorist financing enforcement; 3) spending transparency and improper payments; and 4) administration of the Trust Fund. Specific mandates include audits of the Department's financial statements, compliance with FISMA, and actions in implementing cybersecurity information sharing. In its oversight of the Office of the Comptroller of the Currency, OIG conducts material loss reviews of failed national banks and trusts insured by the Federal Deposit Insurance Corporation. With resources available after mandated requirements are met, the OIG will conduct audits and reviews of the Department's highest risk programs and operations. The OIG will also respond to stakeholder requests.

The Office of Audit expects to complete 100 percent of statutory audits by the required deadline and to complete 82 audit products in 2023, as well as provide oversight, on a reimbursable basis, of the Small Business Lending Fund.

In 2023, the Office of Investigations will continue to investigate all reports of fraud, waste, abuse, and criminal activity affecting Treasury programs and operations. It will also continue proactive efforts to detect, investigate, and deter electronic crimes and other threats to Treasury's physical and IT critical infrastructure, and will continue current efforts to aggressively investigate, close, and refer cases for criminal prosecution, civil litigation, or corrective administrative action in a timely manner.

This account also supports the oversight of COVID response programs, such as the Coronavirus Relief Fund, Emergency Rental Assistance, and the Homeowner Assistance Fund pursuant to the Coronavirus Aid, Relief, and Economic Security (CARES) Act, Division N of the Consolidated Appropriations Act, 2021, and the American Rescue Plan Act of 2021.

Object Classification (in millions of dollars)

Identification code 020–0106–0–1–803		2021 actual	2022 est.	2023 est.
	Direct obligations:			
	Personnel compensation:			
11.1	Full-time permanent	22	27	28
11.5	Other personnel compensation	1	1	1
11.9	Total personnel compensation	23	28	29
12.1	Civilian personnel benefits	9	10	11
21.0	Travel and transportation of persons		1	1
23.1	Rental payments to GSA		4	4
23.3	Communications, utilities, and miscellaneous charges		1	1
25.1	Advisory and assistance services	1		
25.2	Other services from non-Federal sources	4	2	2
25.3	Other goods and services from Federal sources	8	7	7
31.0	Equipment	1		
99.0	Direct obligations	46	53	55
99.0	Reimbursable obligations	9	12	12
99.5	Adjustment for rounding	1	1	
99.9	Total new obligations, unexpired accounts	56	66	67

Employment Summary

Identification code 020–0106–0–1–803	2021 actual	2022 est.	2023 est.
1001 Direct civilian full-time equivalent employment	189	190	190

COMMITTEE ON FOREIGN INVESTMENT IN THE UNITED STATES FUND

(INCLUDING TRANSFER OF FUNDS)

For necessary expenses of the Committee on Foreign Investment in the United States, $20,000,000, to remain available until expended: Provided, That the chairperson of the Committee may transfer such amounts to any department or agency represented on the Committee (including the Department of the Treasury) subject to advance notification to the Committees on Appropriations of the House of Representatives and the Senate: Provided further, That amounts so transferred shall remain available until expended for expenses of implementing section 721 of the Defense Production Act of 1950, as amended (50 U.S.C. 4565), and shall be available in addition to any other funds available to any department or agency: Provided further, That fees authorized by section 721(p) of such Act shall be credited to this appropriation as offsetting collections: Provided further, That the total amount appropriated under this heading from the general fund shall be reduced as such offsetting collections are received during fiscal year 2023, so as to result in a total appropriation from the general fund estimated at not more than $0.

Note.—A full-year 2022 appropriation for this account was not enacted at the time the Budget was prepared; therefore, the Budget assumes this account is operating under the Continuing Appropriations Act, 2022 (Division A of Public Law 117–43, as amended). The amounts included for 2022 reflect the annualized level provided by the continuing resolution.

Program and Financing (in millions of dollars)

Identification code 020–0165–0–1–803		2021 actual	2022 est.	2023 est.
	Obligations by program activity:			
0001	Transfer to Departmental Offices	15	15	15
0002	Transfer to Member Agencies	1	5	5
0900	Total new obligations, unexpired accounts (object class 94.0)	16	20	20
	Budgetary resources:			
	Unobligated balance:			
1000	Unobligated balance brought forward, Oct 1	5	12	12
	Budget authority:			
	Spending authority from offsetting collections, discretionary:			
1700	Collected	23	20	20
1930	Total budgetary resources available	28	32	32
	Memorandum (non-add) entries:			
1941	Unexpired unobligated balance, end of year	12	12	12
	Change in obligated balance:			
	Unpaid obligations:			
3000	Unpaid obligations, brought forward, Oct 1		1	
3010	New obligations, unexpired accounts	16	20	20
3020	Outlays (gross)	–15	–21	–20
3050	Unpaid obligations, end of year	1		
	Memorandum (non-add) entries:			
3100	Obligated balance, start of year		1	
3200	Obligated balance, end of year	1		
	Budget authority and outlays, net:			
	Discretionary:			
4000	Budget authority, gross	23	20	20
	Outlays, gross:			
4010	Outlays from new discretionary authority	15	20	20
4011	Outlays from discretionary balances		1	
4020	Outlays, gross (total)	15	21	20
	Offsets against gross budget authority and outlays:			
	Offsetting collections (collected) from:			
4033	Non-Federal sources	–23	–20	–20
4180	Budget authority, net (total)			
4190	Outlays, net (total)	–8	1	

The Committee on Foreign Investment in the United States (CFIUS) is an interagency committee, chaired by the Secretary of the Treasury, authorized to review certain transactions involving foreign investment in the United States and certain real estate transactions by foreign persons in order to determine the effect of such transactions on the national security of the United States. The Foreign Investment Risk Review Modernization Act of 2018 established the CFIUS Fund. This account funds investments necessary to the functioning of CFIUS and allows the transfer of a portion of such funds to CFIUS agencies to address emerging needs.

TREASURY INSPECTOR GENERAL FOR TAX ADMINISTRATION

SALARIES AND EXPENSES

For necessary expenses of the Treasury Inspector General for Tax Administration in carrying out the Inspector General Act of 1978, as amended, including purchase and hire of passenger motor vehicles (31 U.S.C. 1343(b)); and services authorized by 5 U.S.C. 3109, at such rates as may be determined by the Inspector General for Tax Administration; $182,409,000, of which $5,000,000 shall remain available until September 30, 2024; of which not to exceed $6,000,000 shall be available for official travel expenses; of which not to exceed $500,000 shall be available for unforeseen emergencies of a confidential nature, to be allocated and expended under the direction of the Inspector General for Tax Administration; and of which not to exceed $1,500 shall be available for official reception and representation expenses.

Note.—A full-year 2022 appropriation for this account was not enacted at the time the Budget was prepared; therefore, the Budget assumes this account is operating under the Continuing Appropriations Act, 2022 (Division A of Public Law 117–43, as amended). The amounts included for 2022 reflect the annualized level provided by the continuing resolution.

Program and Financing (in millions of dollars)

Identification code 020–0119–0–1–803		2021 actual	2022 est.	2023 est.
	Obligations by program activity:			
0001	Audit	65	65	67
0002	Investigations	109	110	115
0799	Total direct obligations	174	175	182
0801	Treasury Inspector General for Tax Administration (Reimbursable)	1	1	1
0900	Total new obligations, unexpired accounts	175	176	183
	Budgetary resources:			
	Unobligated balance:			
1000	Unobligated balance brought forward, Oct 1	4	7	2
	Budget authority:			
	Appropriations, discretionary:			
1100	Appropriation	170	170	182
	Appropriations, mandatory:			
1200	Appropriation [ARP]	8		
	Spending authority from offsetting collections, discretionary:			
1700	Collected	1	1	1
1900	Budget authority (total)	179	171	183
1930	Total budgetary resources available	183	178	185
	Memorandum (non-add) entries:			
1940	Unobligated balance expiring	–1		
1941	Unexpired unobligated balance, end of year	7	2	2

TREASURY INSPECTOR GENERAL FOR TAX ADMINISTRATION—Continued
Program and Financing—Continued

Identification code 020–0119–0–1–803	2021 actual	2022 est.	2023 est.
Change in obligated balance:			
Unpaid obligations:			
3000 Unpaid obligations, brought forward, Oct 1	19	19	14
3010 New obligations, unexpired accounts	175	176	183
3011 Obligations ("upward adjustments"), expired accounts	9		
3020 Outlays (gross)	–175	–181	–182
3041 Recoveries of prior year unpaid obligations, expired	–9		
3050 Unpaid obligations, end of year	19	14	15
Memorandum (non-add) entries:			
3100 Obligated balance, start of year	19	19	14
3200 Obligated balance, end of year	19	14	15
Budget authority and outlays, net:			
Discretionary:			
4000 Budget authority, gross	171	171	183
Outlays, gross:			
4010 Outlays from new discretionary authority	157	157	168
4011 Outlays from discretionary balances	16	18	14
4020 Outlays, gross (total)	173	175	182
Offsets against gross budget authority and outlays:			
Offsetting collections (collected) from:			
4030 Federal sources	–1	–1	–1
Mandatory:			
4090 Budget authority, gross	8		
Outlays, gross:			
4100 Outlays from new mandatory authority	2		
4101 Outlays from mandatory balances		6	
4110 Outlays, gross (total)	2	6	
4180 Budget authority, net (total)	178	170	182
4190 Outlays, net (total)	174	180	181

The Treasury Inspector General for Tax Administration (TIGTA), an independent office within the Department of the Treasury, was established by Congress under the Internal Revenue Service (IRS) Restructuring and Reform Act of 1998 (RRA 98). It provides oversight of IRS activities by conducting independent audits, investigations, and inspections and evaluations necessary to prevent and detect waste, fraud, and abuse in IRS programs and operations. TIGTA also identifies and recommends strategies to address IRS management challenges and implement the Department's priorities.

TIGTA's Office of Audit focuses on the major management and performance challenges confronting the IRS by prioritizing statutory audit coverage and audit work in high-risk tax administration areas. Statutory coverage includes audits mandated by RRA 98 and other statutory authorities involving computer security, taxpayer rights and privacy issues. Through its audit programs, TIGTA promotes efficiency and effectiveness in the administration of internal revenue laws. TIGTA is dedicated to the prevention and detection of fraud, waste, and abuse affecting tax administration.

TIGTA's Office of Investigations (OI) concentrates on three areas: 1) employee integrity; 2) employee and infrastructure security; and 3) external attempts to corrupt tax administration. OI's performance model uses a ratio of those investigations that have the greatest impact on IRS' operations and/or the protection of Federal tax administration to the total number of investigations conducted. Investigations in these areas protect IRS personnel, data, and facilities, as well as the public's confidence in the tax system.

TIGTA's Office of Inspections and Evaluations (I&E) identifies opportunities for improvements in IRS and TIGTA programs by performing inspections and evaluations that report timely, useful, and reliable information to decisionmakers and stakeholders. The oversight activities of I&E include inspecting the compliance of the IRS with established system controls and operating procedures, as well as evaluating the Agency's operations for high-risk systemic inefficiencies.

This account also supports the oversight of Economic Impact Payments and other fast and direct relief pursuant to Division N of the Consolidated Appropriations Act, 2021, and the American Rescue Plan Act of 2021.

Object Classification (in millions of dollars)

Identification code 020–0119–0–1–803	2021 actual	2022 est.	2023 est.
Direct obligations:			
Personnel compensation:			
11.1 Full-time permanent	88	87	94
11.1 Full-time permanent - ARPA Fund	1	4	
11.5 Other personnel compensation	9	9	9
11.9 Total personnel compensation	98	100	103
12.1 Civilian personnel benefits	42	42	46
12.1 Civilian personnel benefits - ARPA Fund	1	2	
21.0 Travel and transportation of persons	1	1	3
23.1 Rental payments to GSA	9	8	8
23.3 Communications, utilities, and miscellaneous charges	1	1	1
25.1 Advisory and assistance services	2	2	2
25.2 Other services from non-Federal sources	1	1	1
25.3 Other goods and services from Federal sources	11	11	12
25.7 Operation and maintenance of equipment	2	2	2
26.0 Supplies and materials	1	1	1
31.0 Equipment	5	4	3
99.0 Direct obligations	174	175	182
99.0 Reimbursable obligations		1	1
99.5 Adjustment for rounding	1		
99.9 Total new obligations, unexpired accounts	175	176	183

Employment Summary

Identification code 020–0119–0–1–803	2021 actual	2022 est.	2023 est.
1001 Direct civilian full-time equivalent employment	739	760	760
2001 Reimbursable civilian full-time equivalent employment	2	2	2

TERRORISM INSURANCE PROGRAM

Program and Financing (in millions of dollars)

Identification code 020–0123–0–1–376	2021 actual	2022 est.	2023 est.
Obligations by program activity:			
0001 Base Administrative Expenses	3	6	5
0003 Projected Payments to Insurers		24	74
0900 Total new obligations, unexpired accounts	3	30	79
Budgetary resources:			
Unobligated balance:			
1000 Unobligated balance brought forward, Oct 1		1	1
1021 Recoveries of prior year unpaid obligations	1		
1070 Unobligated balance (total)	1	1	1
Budget authority:			
Appropriations, mandatory:			
1200 Appropriation	3	30	79
1930 Total budgetary resources available	4	31	80
Memorandum (non-add) entries:			
1941 Unexpired unobligated balance, end of year	1	1	1
Change in obligated balance:			
Unpaid obligations:			
3000 Unpaid obligations, brought forward, Oct 1	1		8
3010 New obligations, unexpired accounts	3	30	79
3020 Outlays (gross)	–3	–22	–67
3040 Recoveries of prior year unpaid obligations, unexpired	–1		
3050 Unpaid obligations, end of year		8	20
Memorandum (non-add) entries:			
3100 Obligated balance, start of year	1		8
3200 Obligated balance, end of year		8	20
Budget authority and outlays, net:			
Mandatory:			
4090 Budget authority, gross	3	30	79
Outlays, gross:			
4100 Outlays from new mandatory authority	2	22	59
4101 Outlays from mandatory balances	1		8
4110 Outlays, gross (total)	3	22	67
4180 Budget authority, net (total)	3	30	79
4190 Outlays, net (total)	3	22	67

The Terrorism Risk Insurance Program Reauthorization Act of 2019 (P.L. 116–94) reauthorized and revised the program established by the Terrorism Risk Insurance Act of 2002 (TRIA) (P.L. 107–297). The 2019 Act extended the Terrorism Risk Insurance Program (TRIP) for seven years, through December 31, 2027. The Budget baseline includes the estimated Federal cost of providing payments in connection with terrorism risk insurance losses. There have been no prior payments under the Program. While the Budget does not forecast any specific payment triggering events, the Budget includes estimates representing the weighted average of payments over a full range of possible scenarios, most of which include no notional payment triggering events and some of which include notional triggering events of varying magnitude. Relying upon this methodology, the Budget baseline projects net spending associated with the current reauthorization of $497 million over the 2023–2032 period. Mechanisms in TRIA result in Treasury's relative share of any covered losses decreasing over time as premiums in the insurance market increase. The budget estimate reflects this projected decrease in Treasury's share.

Object Classification (in millions of dollars)

Identification code 020–0123–0–1–376		2021 actual	2022 est.	2023 est.
	Direct obligations:			
11.1	Personnel compensation: Full-time permanent	1	2	2
25.1	Advisory and assistance services	1	4	3
25.3	Other goods and services from Federal sources	1	....	....
42.0	Insurance claims and indemnities	....	24	74
99.0	Direct obligations	3	30	79
99.9	Total new obligations, unexpired accounts	3	30	79

Employment Summary

Identification code 020–0123–0–1–376	2021 actual	2022 est.	2023 est.
1001 Direct civilian full-time equivalent employment	7	8	10

TREASURY FORFEITURE FUND

Special and Trust Fund Receipts (in millions of dollars)

Identification code 020–5697–0–2–751		2021 actual	2022 est.	2023 est.
0100	Balance, start of year	30	45	32
	Receipts:			
	Current law:			
1110	Forfeited Cash and Proceeds from Sale of Forfeited Property, Treasury Forfeiture Fund	784	562	573
1140	Earnings on Investments, Treasury Forfeiture Fund	2	5	5
1199	Total current law receipts	786	567	578
1999	Total receipts	786	567	578
2000	Total: Balances and receipts	816	612	610
	Appropriations:			
	Current law:			
2101	Treasury Forfeiture Fund	–786	–567	–578
2103	Treasury Forfeiture Fund	–30	–45	–32
2132	Treasury Forfeiture Fund	45	32	33
2199	Total current law appropriations	–771	–580	–577
2999	Total appropriations	–771	–580	–577
5099	Balance, end of year	45	32	33

Program and Financing (in millions of dollars)

Identification code 020–5697–0–2–751		2021 actual	2022 est.	2023 est.
	Obligations by program activity:			
0001	Mandatory	624	453	462
0002	Strategic Support	360	98	100
0003	Secretary's Enforcement Fund	15	35	35
0900	Total new obligations, unexpired accounts	999	586	597

		2021 actual	2022 est.	2023 est.
	Budgetary resources:			
	Unobligated balance:			
1000	Unobligated balance brought forward, Oct 1	691	877	808
1021	Recoveries of prior year unpaid obligations	34	12	12
1033	Recoveries of prior year paid obligations	455	....	....
1070	Unobligated balance (total)	1,180	889	820
	Budget authority:			
	Appropriations, discretionary:			
1130	Appropriations permanently reduced		–75	
	Appropriations, mandatory:			
1201	Appropriation (special or trust fund)	786	567	578
1203	Appropriation (previously unavailable)(special or trust)	30	45	32
1230	Appropriations and/or unobligated balance of appropriations permanently reduced	–75		
1232	Appropriations and/or unobligated balance of appropriations temporarily reduced	–45	–32	–33
1260	Appropriations, mandatory (total)	696	580	577
1900	Budget authority (total)	696	505	577
1930	Total budgetary resources available	1,876	1,394	1,397
	Memorandum (non-add) entries:			
1941	Unexpired unobligated balance, end of year	877	808	800
	Change in obligated balance:			
	Unpaid obligations:			
3000	Unpaid obligations, brought forward, Oct 1	531	863	928
3010	New obligations, unexpired accounts	999	586	597
3020	Outlays (gross)	–633	–509	–535
3040	Recoveries of prior year unpaid obligations, unexpired	–34	–12	–12
3050	Unpaid obligations, end of year	863	928	978
	Memorandum (non-add) entries:			
3100	Obligated balance, start of year	531	863	928
3200	Obligated balance, end of year	863	928	978
	Budget authority and outlays, net:			
	Discretionary:			
4000	Budget authority, gross		–75	
	Outlays, gross:			
4010	Outlays from new discretionary authority		–8	
4011	Outlays from discretionary balances			–19
4020	Outlays, gross (total)		–8	–19
	Mandatory:			
4090	Budget authority, gross	696	580	577
	Outlays, gross:			
4100	Outlays from new mandatory authority		29	28
4101	Outlays from mandatory balances	633	488	526
4110	Outlays, gross (total)	633	517	554
	Offsets against gross budget authority and outlays:			
	Offsetting collections (collected) from:			
4120	Federal sources	–455		
	Additional offsets against gross budget authority only:			
4143	Recoveries of prior year paid obligations, unexpired accounts	455		
4160	Budget authority, net (mandatory)	696	580	577
4170	Outlays, net (mandatory)	178	517	554
4180	Budget authority, net (total)	696	505	577
4190	Outlays, net (total)	178	509	535
	Memorandum (non-add) entries:			
5000	Total investments, SOY: Federal securities: Par value	1,218	1,825	2,008
5001	Total investments, EOY: Federal securities: Par value	1,825	2,008	2,029

The mission of the Treasury Forfeiture Fund (Fund) is to affirmatively influence the consistent and strategic use of asset forfeiture by law enforcement bureaus that participate in the Fund to disrupt and dismantle criminal enterprises. The Fund supports Federal, State, and local law enforcement's use of asset forfeiture to disrupt and deter criminal activity. Proceeds from non-tax forfeitures made by participating bureaus of the Department of the Treasury and the Department of Homeland Security are deposited into the Fund. Such proceeds are available to pay or reimburse certain costs and expenses related to seizures and forfeitures that occur pursuant to laws enforced by the bureaus and other expenses authorized by 31 U.S.C. 9705. Forfeiture proceeds can also be used to fund Federal law enforcement-related activities based on requests from Federal agencies and evaluation by the Secretary of the Treasury.

TREASURY FORFEITURE FUND—Continued

Object Classification (in millions of dollars)

Identification code 020–5697–0–2–751	2021 actual	2022 est.	2023 est.
Direct obligations:			
25.2 Other services from non-Federal sources	67	16	15
25.3 Other goods and services from Federal sources	233	295	302
41.0 Grants, subsidies, and contributions	132	158	161
44.0 Refunds	192	88	89
94.0 Financial transfers	375	29	30
99.9 Total new obligations, unexpired accounts	999	586	597

FINANCIAL RESEARCH FUND

Special and Trust Fund Receipts (in millions of dollars)

Identification code 020–5590–0–2–376	2021 actual	2022 est.	2023 est.
0100 Balance, start of year	4	4	5
Receipts:			
Current law:			
1110 Fees and Assessments, Financial Research Fund	69	93	94
2000 Total: Balances and receipts	73	97	99
Appropriations:			
Current law:			
2101 Financial Research Fund	–69	–93	–94
2103 Financial Research Fund	–4	–4	–5
2132 Financial Research Fund	4	5	5
2199 Total current law appropriations	–69	–92	–94
2999 Total appropriations	–69	–92	–94
5099 Balance, end of year	4	5	5

Program and Financing (in millions of dollars)

Identification code 020–5590–0–2–376	2021 actual	2022 est.	2023 est.
Obligations by program activity:			
0002 FSOC	5	8	8
0003 FDIC Payments	4	3	5
0091 FSOC subtotal	9	11	13
0101 OFR	71	78	88
0900 Total new obligations, unexpired accounts	80	89	101
Budgetary resources:			
Unobligated balance:			
1000 Unobligated balance brought forward, Oct 1	62	52	59
1021 Recoveries of prior year unpaid obligations	1	4	4
1070 Unobligated balance (total)	63	56	63
Budget authority:			
Appropriations, mandatory:			
1201 Appropriation (special or trust fund)	69	93	94
1203 Appropriation (previously unavailable)(special or trust)	4	4	5
1232 Appropriations and/or unobligated balance of appropriations temporarily reduced	–4	–5	–5
1260 Appropriations, mandatory (total)	69	92	94
1930 Total budgetary resources available	132	148	157
Memorandum (non-add) entries:			
1941 Unexpired unobligated balance, end of year	52	59	56
Change in obligated balance:			
Unpaid obligations:			
3000 Unpaid obligations, brought forward, Oct 1	27	34	23
3010 New obligations, unexpired accounts	80	89	101
3020 Outlays (gross)	–72	–96	–95
3040 Recoveries of prior year unpaid obligations, unexpired	–1	–4	–4
3050 Unpaid obligations, end of year	34	23	25
Memorandum (non-add) entries:			
3100 Obligated balance, start of year	27	34	23
3200 Obligated balance, end of year	34	23	25
Budget authority and outlays, net:			
Mandatory:			
4090 Budget authority, gross	69	92	94
Outlays, gross:			
4100 Outlays from new mandatory authority	59	18	24
4101 Outlays from mandatory balances	13	78	71
4110 Outlays, gross (total)	72	96	95
4180 Budget authority, net (total)	69	92	94
4190 Outlays, net (total)	72	96	95
Memorandum (non-add) entries:			
5000 Total investments, SOY: Federal securities: Par value	84	80	59
5001 Total investments, EOY: Federal securities: Par value	80	59	57

The Office of Financial Research (OFR) and the Financial Stability Oversight Council (Council), whose expenses are paid for out of the Financial Research Fund, were established under the Dodd-Frank Wall Street Reform and Consumer Protection Act (the Act) (P.L. 111–203).

The OFR was established to serve the Council, its member agencies, and other stakeholders by improving the quality, transparency, and accessibility of financial data and information, by conducting and sponsoring research related to financial stability, and by promoting best practices in risk management. The OFR is an office within the Department of the Treasury.

The Council is comprised of 10 voting members, including the heads of all Federal financial regulators, and five non-voting members. The Secretary of the Treasury serves as Chairperson of the Council. The Council's purpose is to identify risks to the financial stability of the United States, promote market discipline, and respond to emerging threats to the stability of the U.S. financial system.

As required under Section 210(n)(10) of the Act, the Council's expenses also include reimbursement of certain reasonable expenses incurred by the Federal Deposit Insurance Corporation in implementing Orderly Liquidation Authority, provided by Title II of the Act.

Since July 2012, OFR and the Council have been funded through assessments on certain bank holding companies and nonbank financial companies supervised by the Board of Governors. Expenses of the Council are considered expenses of, and are paid by, the OFR. Projected fees and assessments are estimates and may change.

Object Classification (in millions of dollars)

Identification code 020–5590–0–2–376	2021 actual	2022 est.	2023 est.
Direct obligations:			
Personnel compensation:			
11.1 Full-time permanent	23	30	35
11.5 Other personnel compensation	1	1	1
11.9 Total personnel compensation	24	31	36
12.1 Civilian personnel benefits	9	11	13
25.1 Advisory and assistance services	23	24	26
25.3 Other goods and services from Federal sources	7	6	6
25.7 Operation and maintenance of equipment	7	7	7
26.0 Supplies and materials	9	9	9
31.0 Equipment	1	1	1
41.0 Grants, subsidies, and contributions	....	....	2
99.0 Direct obligations	80	89	100
99.5 Adjustment for rounding	....	....	1
99.9 Total new obligations, unexpired accounts	80	89	101

Employment Summary

Identification code 020–5590–0–2–376	2021 actual	2022 est.	2023 est.
1001 Direct civilian full-time equivalent employment	125	166	190

PRESIDENTIAL ELECTION CAMPAIGN FUND

Special and Trust Fund Receipts (in millions of dollars)

Identification code 020–5081–0–2–808	2021 actual	2022 est.	2023 est.
0100 Balance, start of year	1	1	26

DEPARTMENT OF THE TREASURY

Departmental Offices—Continued
Federal Funds—Continued 985

		2021 actual	2022 est.	2023 est.
	Receipts:			
	Current law:			
1110	Presidential Election Campaign Fund	24	50	50
2000	Total: Balances and receipts	25	51	76
	Appropriations:			
	Current law:			
2101	Presidential Election Campaign Fund	−24	−25	−25
2103	Presidential Election Campaign Fund	−1	−1	−1
2132	Presidential Election Campaign Fund	1	1	1
2199	Total current law appropriations	−24	−25	−25
2999	Total appropriations	−24	−25	−25
5099	Balance, end of year	1	26	51

Program and Financing (in millions of dollars)

Identification code 020–5081–0–2–808		2021 actual	2022 est.	2023 est.
	Obligations by program activity:			
0001	Presidential Election Campaigns	....	....	41
0900	Total new obligations, unexpired accounts (object class 41.0)	....	....	41
	Budgetary resources:			
	Unobligated balance:			
1000	Unobligated balance brought forward, Oct 1	377	401	426
	Budget authority:			
	Appropriations, mandatory:			
1201	Appropriation (special or trust fund)	24	25	25
1203	Appropriation (Sequestration pop-up, Authorizing Committee)	1	1	1
1232	Appropriations and/or unobligated balance of appropriations temporarily reduced	−1	−1	−1
1260	Appropriations, mandatory (total)	24	25	25
1930	Total budgetary resources available	401	426	451
	Memorandum (non-add) entries:			
1941	Unexpired unobligated balance, end of year	401	426	410
	Change in obligated balance:			
	Unpaid obligations:			
3010	New obligations, unexpired accounts	....	....	41
3020	Outlays (gross)	....	....	−41
	Budget authority and outlays, net:			
	Mandatory:			
4090	Budget authority, gross	24	25	25
	Outlays, gross:			
4101	Outlays from mandatory balances	....	....	41
4180	Budget authority, net (total)	24	25	25
4190	Outlays, net (total)	....	....	41

Individual Federal income tax returns include an optional Federal income tax designation of $3 that an individual may elect to be paid to the Presidential Election Campaign Fund (PECF). The Department of the Treasury collects the income tax designations and makes distributions from the PECF to qualified presidential candidates. Amounts not made available to and used by qualified candidates are transferred to the 10-Year Pediatric Research Initiative Fund, which was established in 2014 by the Gabriella Miller Kids First Research Act.

The Federal Election Commission administers the public funding program, determines which candidates are eligible, the amount to which they are entitled, and audits their use of the funds.

Amounts previously transferred were intended to cover the years between elections and no funds will be transferred for FY 2022 and FY 2023.

TREASURY FRANCHISE FUND

Program and Financing (in millions of dollars)

Identification code 020–4560–0–4–803		2021 actual	2022 est.	2023 est.
	Obligations by program activity:			
0802	Financial Management Administrative Support Service	224	214	211
0804	Information Technology Services	231	215	221
0806	Shared Services Program	359	314	327
0808	Centralized Treasury Administrative Services	130	138	160
0900	Total new obligations, unexpired accounts	944	881	919
	Budgetary resources:			
	Unobligated balance:			
1000	Unobligated balance brought forward, Oct 1	168	124	137
1021	Recoveries of prior year unpaid obligations	13	13	13
1033	Recoveries of prior year paid obligations	1	....	....
1070	Unobligated balance (total)	182	137	150
	Budget authority:			
	Spending authority from offsetting collections, discretionary:			
1700	Collected	880	881	919
1701	Change in uncollected payments, Federal sources	6	....	....
1750	Spending auth from offsetting collections, disc (total)	886	881	919
1930	Total budgetary resources available	1,068	1,018	1,069
	Memorandum (non-add) entries:			
1941	Unexpired unobligated balance, end of year	124	137	150
	Change in obligated balance:			
	Unpaid obligations:			
3000	Unpaid obligations, brought forward, Oct 1	245	303	288
3010	New obligations, unexpired accounts	944	881	919
3020	Outlays (gross)	−873	−883	−1,065
3040	Recoveries of prior year unpaid obligations, unexpired	−13	−13	−13
3050	Unpaid obligations, end of year	303	288	129
	Uncollected payments:			
3060	Uncollected pymts, Fed sources, brought forward, Oct 1	−26	−32	−32
3070	Change in uncollected pymts, Fed sources, unexpired	−6	....	....
3090	Uncollected pymts, Fed sources, end of year	−32	−32	−32
	Memorandum (non-add) entries:			
3100	Obligated balance, start of year	219	271	256
3200	Obligated balance, end of year	271	256	97
	Budget authority and outlays, net:			
	Discretionary:			
4000	Budget authority, gross	886	881	919
	Outlays, gross:			
4010	Outlays from new discretionary authority	717	758	790
4011	Outlays from discretionary balances	156	125	275
4020	Outlays, gross (total)	873	883	1,065
	Offsets against gross budget authority and outlays:			
	Offsetting collections (collected) from:			
4030	Federal sources	−881	−881	−919
	Additional offsets against gross budget authority only:			
4050	Change in uncollected pymts, Fed sources, unexpired	−6	....	....
4053	Recoveries of prior year paid obligations, unexpired accounts	1	....	....
4060	Additional offsets against budget authority only (total)	−5	....	....
4080	Outlays, net (discretionary)	−8	2	146
4180	Budget authority, net (total)	....	....	....
4190	Outlays, net (total)	−8	2	146

The Treasury Franchise Fund (the Fund) was established by P.L. 104–208, made permanent by P.L. 108–447, and codified as 31 U.S.C. 322, note. The Fund is revolving in nature and provides financial management, procurement, travel, human resources, and information technology services through its four business lines: the Administrative Resource Center (ARC) Administrative Services, ARC Information Technology Services, Treasury Shared Services Programs (TSSP), and Centralized Treasury Administrative Services (CTAS). Services are provided to Federal customers on a reimbursable, fee-for-service basis.

Object Classification (in millions of dollars)

Identification code 020–4560–0–4–803		2021 actual	2022 est.	2023 est.
	Reimbursable obligations:			
	Personnel compensation:			
11.1	Full-time permanent	187	189	193
11.3	Other than full-time permanent	1	1	1
11.5	Other personnel compensation	8	6	6
11.9	Total personnel compensation	196	196	200
12.1	Civilian personnel benefits	72	72	77
23.1	Rental payments to GSA	36	33	34
23.3	Communications, utilities, and miscellaneous charges	82	88	92
25.1	Advisory and assistance services	224	129	141
25.2	Other services from non-Federal sources	40	32	40
25.3	Other goods and services from Federal sources	154	147	160
25.4	Operation and maintenance of facilities	1	2	5
25.7	Operation and maintenance of equipment	87	127	114

Departmental Offices—Continued
Federal Funds—Continued

TREASURY FRANCHISE FUND—Continued

Object Classification—Continued

Identification code 020–4560–0–4–803	2021 actual	2022 est.	2023 est.
26.0 Supplies and materials	3	3	3
31.0 Equipment	44	50	52
32.0 Land and structures	4	1	1
99.0 Reimbursable obligations	943	880	919
99.5 Adjustment for rounding	1	1	....
99.9 Total new obligations, unexpired accounts	944	881	919

Employment Summary

Identification code 020–4560–0–4–803	2021 actual	2022 est.	2023 est.
2001 Reimbursable civilian full-time equivalent employment	2,036	2,232	2,209

EXCHANGE STABILIZATION FUND

Program and Financing (in millions of dollars)

Identification code 020–4444–0–3–155	2021 actual	2022 est.	2023 est.
Obligations by program activity:			
0001 Exchange Stabilization Fund (Direct)	114,139	....	....
0900 Total new obligations, unexpired accounts (object class 25.2)	114,139	....	....
Budgetary resources:			
Unobligated balance:			
1000 Unobligated balance brought forward, Oct 1	21,102	40,566	40,616
1021 Recoveries of prior year unpaid obligations	10,520	....	....
1026 Adjustment for change in allocation of trust fund limitation or foreign exchange valuation	111,428	....	....
1070 Unobligated balance (total)	143,050	40,566	40,616
Budget authority:			
Spending authority from offsetting collections, mandatory:			
1800 Collected	11,655	50	353
1930 Total budgetary resources available	154,705	40,616	40,969
Memorandum (non-add) entries:			
1941 Unexpired unobligated balance, end of year	40,566	40,616	40,969
Change in obligated balance:			
Unpaid obligations:			
3000 Unpaid obligations, brought forward, Oct 1	63,417	167,036	167,036
3010 New obligations, unexpired accounts	114,139	....	....
3040 Recoveries of prior year unpaid obligations, unexpired	–10,520	....	....
3050 Unpaid obligations, end of year	167,036	167,036	167,036
Memorandum (non-add) entries:			
3100 Obligated balance, start of year	63,417	167,036	167,036
3200 Obligated balance, end of year	167,036	167,036	167,036
Budget authority and outlays, net:			
Mandatory:			
4090 Budget authority, gross	11,655	50	353
Offsets against gross budget authority and outlays:			
Offsetting collections (collected) from:			
4121 Interest on Federal securities	–7	–43	–346
4123 Non-Federal sources	–11,648	–7	–7
4130 Offsets against gross budget authority and outlays (total)	–11,655	–50	–353
4170 Outlays, net (mandatory)	–11,655	–50	–353
4180 Budget authority, net (total)	....	....	....
4190 Outlays, net (total)	–11,655	–50	–353
Memorandum (non-add) entries:			
5000 Total investments, SOY: Federal securities: Par value	11,170	22,837	22,880
5001 Total investments, EOY: Federal securities: Par value	22,837	22,880	23,226
5010 Total investments, SOY: non-Fed securities: Market value	47	....	....

Under the law governing the Exchange Stabilization Fund (ESF), section 10 of the Gold Reserve Act of 1934, as amended, codified at 31 U.S.C. 5302, the Secretary of the Treasury, with the approval of the President, is authorized to deal in gold, foreign exchange, and other instruments of credit and securities, as the Secretary considers necessary, consistent with U.S. obligations in the International Monetary Fund regarding orderly exchange arrangements and a stable system of exchange rates. All earnings and interest accruing to the ESF are available for the purposes thereof. U.S. holdings of Special Drawing Rights (SDRs) are credited to the account of, and administered as part of the fund. By law, the fund is not available to pay administrative expenses.

Since 1934, the principal sources of the fund's income have been earnings on investments held by the fund, including interest earned on fund holdings of U.S. Government securities. In the wake of the COVID-19 pandemic, Treasury used funds in the ESF to invest and provide other support to the Commercial Paper Funding Facility (CPFF) and the Money Market Mutual Fund Liquidity Facility (MMLF) established by the Federal Reserve to enhance liquidity and support the flow of credit to households, and businesses. The investments in these two Federal Reserve facilities were unwound in accordance with their terms in 2021, and the ESF received interest and other earnings from these transactions.

The amounts reflected in 2022 estimates entail only projected net interest earnings on ESF assets. The estimates are subject to considerable variance, depending on changes in the amount and composition of assets and the interest rates applied to investments. In addition, these estimates make no attempt to forecast gains or losses on SDR valuation or foreign currency valuation.

Balance Sheet (in millions of dollars)

Identification code 020–4444–0–3–155	2020 actual	2021 actual
ASSETS:		
Federal assets:		
Investments in U.S. securities:		
1102 Treasury securities, par	11,170	22,837
1106 Receivables, net	....	....
1201 Non-Federal assets: Foreign Currency Investments	33,341	20,945
1801 Other Federal assets: Special Drawing Rights	51,733	163,874
1999 Total assets	96,244	207,656
LIABILITIES:		
2207 Non-Federal liabilities: Other	54,917	167,036
NET POSITION:		
3100 Unexpended appropriations	200	200
3300 Cumulative results of operations	41,127	40,420
3999 Total net position	41,327	40,620
4999 Total liabilities and net position	96,244	207,656

ECONOMIC STABILIZATION PROGRAM ACCOUNT

Program and Financing (in millions of dollars)

Identification code 020–1889–0–1–376	2021 actual	2022 est.	2023 est.
Obligations by program activity:			
0001 Administrative Expenses	20	5	36
0002 Congressional Oversight Commission	2	....	....
0091 Direct program activities, subtotal	22	5	36
Credit program obligations:			
0701 Direct loan subsidy	9	....	....
0703 Subsidy for modifications of direct loans	8	....	....
0705 Reestimates of direct loan subsidy	309	....	....
0706 Interest on reestimates of direct loan subsidy	597	3	....
0791 Direct program activities, subtotal	923	3	....
0900 Total new obligations, unexpired accounts	945	8	36
Budgetary resources:			
Unobligated balance:			
1000 Unobligated balance brought forward, Oct 1	468,136	1,591	220
1021 Recoveries of prior year unpaid obligations	12,290	....	....
1070 Unobligated balance (total)	480,426	1,591	220
Budget authority:			
Appropriations, mandatory:			
1200 Appropriation	906	3	....
1230 Appropriations and/or unobligated balance of appropriations permanently reduced	–478,796	–1,366	....
1260 Appropriations, mandatory (total)	–477,890	–1,363	....

DEPARTMENT OF THE TREASURY

		2021 actual	2022 est.	2023 est.
1900	Budget authority (total)	−477,890	−1,363	
1930	Total budgetary resources available	2,536	228	220
	Memorandum (non-add) entries:			
1941	Unexpired unobligated balance, end of year	1,591	220	184
	Change in obligated balance:			
	Unpaid obligations:			
3000	Unpaid obligations, brought forward, Oct 1	12,508	13	8
3010	New obligations, unexpired accounts	945	8	36
3020	Outlays (gross)	−1,150	−13	−39
3040	Recoveries of prior year unpaid obligations, unexpired	−12,290		
3050	Unpaid obligations, end of year	13	8	5
	Memorandum (non-add) entries:			
3100	Obligated balance, start of year	12,508	13	8
3200	Obligated balance, end of year	13	8	5
	Budget authority and outlays, net:			
	Mandatory:			
4090	Budget authority, gross	−477,890	−1,363	
	Outlays, gross:			
4101	Outlays from mandatory balances	1,150	13	39
4180	Budget authority, net (total)	−477,890	−1,363	
4190	Outlays, net (total)	1,150	13	39

Summary of Loan Levels, Subsidy Budget Authority and Outlays by Program (in millions of dollars)

Identification code 020–1889–0–1–376		2021 actual	2022 est.	2023 est.
	Direct loan levels supportable by subsidy budget authority:			
115005	Businesses Critical to National Security	36		
115007	Passenger Carriers, Small	325		
115008	MRO and Ticketing Agencies	40		
115009	Cargo Carriers	2		
115999	Total direct loan levels	403		
	Direct loan subsidy (in percent):			
132005	Businesses Critical to National Security	4.70		
132007	Passenger Carriers, Small	1.11		
132008	MRO and Ticketing Agencies	8.62		
132009	Cargo Carriers	7.75		
132999	Weighted average subsidy rate	2.21		
	Direct loan subsidy budget authority:			
133005	Businesses Critical to National Security	2		
133007	Passenger Carriers, Small	4		
133008	MRO and Ticketing Agencies	3		
133999	Total subsidy budget authority	9		
	Direct loan subsidy outlays:			
134002	13(3) Main Street Lending Program	8		
134005	Businesses Critical to National Security	209		
134007	Passenger Carriers, Small	4		
134008	MRO and Ticketing Agencies	3		
134999	Total subsidy outlays	224		
	Direct loan reestimates:			
135001	13(3) Municipal Liquidity Facility	454	−218	
135002	13(3) Main Street Lending Program	−13,367	−3,252	
135003	13(3) Term Asset-Backed Securities Loan Facility	96	−98	
135004	13(3) Corporate Credit Facilities	−269	−451	
135005	Businesses Critical to National Security	−47	−231	
135006	Passenger Carriers, Large	9	−157	
135007	Passenger Carriers, Small		−1	
135008	MRO and Ticketing Agencies		−3	
135999	Total direct loan reestimates	−13,124	−4,411	
	Administrative expense data:			
3580	Outlays from balances	15	5	36

The CARES Act (P.L. 116–136) authorized the Department of the Treasury to make up to $500 billion in loans and other investments in support of and to provide liquidity to eligible businesses, nonprofits, states, and municipalities impacted by the COVID-19 pandemic. This included investments in facilities established by the Board of Governors of the Federal Reserve System pursuant to Section 13(3) of the Federal Reserve Act to provide liquidity to the financial system. The CARES Act also authorized Treasury to use up to $46 billion of these funds to make loans to passenger and cargo air carriers, certain other aviation businesses, and businesses critical to maintaining national security. As required by the Federal Credit Reform Act of 1990, as amended, this account records the subsidy costs associated with these loans and investments, which are estimated on a present value basis. The Consolidated Appropriations Act, 2021 (P.L. 116–260) Sec. 1003 rescinded $478.8 billion in budget authority from this program in 2021 and the Infrastructure Investment and Jobs Act (PL 117–58) Sec. 90007 further rescinded $1.4 billion in 2022.

Starting in 2023, obligations, outlays and staffing include administrative activities for programs authorized by Sec. 9901 of the American Rescue Plan, consistent with Sec. 123 of the Treasury Administrative Provisions.

Object Classification (in millions of dollars)

Identification code 020–1889–0–1–376		2021 actual	2022 est.	2023 est.
	Direct obligations:			
	Personnel compensation:			
11.1	Full-time permanent	2	1	8
11.8	Special personal services payments	2		
11.9	Total personnel compensation	4	1	8
12.1	Civilian personnel benefits	1		2
25.1	Advisory and assistance services	13		11
25.3	Other goods and services from Federal sources	4	4	15
41.0	Grants, subsidies, and contributions	923	3	
99.0	Direct obligations	945	8	36
99.9	Total new obligations, unexpired accounts	945	8	36

Employment Summary

Identification code 020–1889–0–1–376		2021 actual	2022 est.	2023 est.
1001	Direct civilian full-time equivalent employment	11	5	64

ECONOMIC STABILIZATION DIRECT LOAN FINANCING ACCOUNT

Program and Financing (in millions of dollars)

Identification code 020–4447–0–3–376		2021 actual	2022 est.	2023 est.
	Obligations by program activity:			
	Credit program obligations:			
0710	Direct loan obligations	403		
0713	Payment of interest to Treasury	607	198	195
0741	Modification savings		155	
0742	Downward reestimates paid to receipt accounts	14,024	4,341	
0743	Interest on downward reestimates	6	74	
0900	Total new obligations, unexpired accounts	15,040	4,768	195
	Budgetary resources:			
	Unobligated balance:			
1000	Unobligated balance brought forward, Oct 1		379	
1021	Recoveries of prior year unpaid obligations	105,580		
1024	Unobligated balance of borrowing authority withdrawn	−93,291		
1070	Unobligated balance (total)	12,289	379	
	Financing authority:			
	Borrowing authority, mandatory:			
1400	Borrowing authority	14,714	3,775	112
1424	Capital transfers of borrowing authority to general fund	−1		
1440	Borrowing authority, mandatory (total)	14,713	3,775	112
	Spending authority from offsetting collections, mandatory:			
1800	Collected	78,980	5,753	83
1801	Change in uncollected payments, Federal sources	−12,497		
1825	Spending authority from offsetting collections applied to repay debt	−78,066	−5,139	
1850	Spending auth from offsetting collections, mand (total)	−11,583	614	83
1900	Budget authority (total)	3,130	4,389	195
1930	Total budgetary resources available	15,419	4,768	195
	Memorandum (non-add) entries:			
1941	Unexpired unobligated balance, end of year	379		
	Change in obligated balance:			
	Unpaid obligations:			
3000	Unpaid obligations, brought forward, Oct 1	106,035		
3010	New obligations, unexpired accounts	15,040	4,768	195
3020	Outlays (gross)	−15,495	−4,768	−195
3040	Recoveries of prior year unpaid obligations, unexpired	−105,580		
	Uncollected payments:			
3060	Uncollected pymts, Fed sources, brought forward, Oct 1	−12,497		

ECONOMIC STABILIZATION DIRECT LOAN FINANCING ACCOUNT—Continued

Program and Financing—Continued

Identification code 020–4447–0–3–376	2021 actual	2022 est.	2023 est.
3070 Change in uncollected pymts, Fed sources, unexpired	12,497		
Memorandum (non-add) entries:			
3100 Obligated balance, start of year	93,538		
Financing authority and disbursements, net:			
Mandatory:			
4090 Budget authority, gross	3,130	4,389	195
Financing disbursements:			
4110 Outlays, gross (total)	15,495	4,768	195
Offsets against gross financing authority and disbursements:			
Offsetting collections (collected) from:			
4120 Federal sources	–1,131	–3	
4122 Interest on uninvested funds	–130	–12	–3
4123 Non-Federal sources	–77,719	–5,738	–80
4130 Offsets against gross budget authority and outlays (total)	–78,980	–5,753	–83
Additional offsets against financing authority only (total):			
4140 Change in uncollected pymts, Fed sources, unexpired	12,497		
4160 Budget authority, net (mandatory)	–63,353	–1,364	112
4170 Outlays, net (mandatory)	–63,485	–985	112
4180 Budget authority, net (total)	–63,353	–1,364	112
4190 Outlays, net (total)	–63,485	–985	112

Status of Direct Loans (in millions of dollars)

Identification code 020–4447–0–3–376	2021 actual	2022 est.	2023 est.
Position with respect to appropriations act limitation on obligations:			
1111 Direct loan obligations from current-year authority	403		
1150 Total direct loan obligations	403		
Cumulative balance of direct loans outstanding:			
1210 Outstanding, start of year	104,320	27,544	22,382
1231 Disbursements: Direct loan disbursements	858		
1251 Repayments: Repayments and prepayments	–77,634	–5,162	–80
1290 Outstanding, end of year	27,544	22,382	22,302

As authorized by the Coronavirus Aid, Relief, and Economic Security Act (P.L. 116–136) and required by the Federal Credit Reform Act of 1990, as amended, this non-budgetary account records all cash flows to and from the Government resulting from direct loans and other investments obligated in FY 2020 and FY 2021, including modifications of those direct loans. The amounts in this account are a means of financing and are not included in the Budget totals.

Balance Sheet (in millions of dollars)

Identification code 020–4447–0–3–376	2020 actual	2021 actual
ASSETS:		
Federal assets:		
1101 Fund balances with Treasury		380
Investments in U.S. securities:		
1106 Receivables, net	458	
Non-Federal assets:		
1201 Investments in non-Federal securities, net	97,899	25,578
1206 Receivables, net		462
Net value of assets related to post-1991 direct loans receivable:		
1401 Direct loans receivable, gross	1,821	1,147
1402 Interest receivable	2	7
1405 Allowance for subsidy cost (-)	–243	158
1499 Net present value of assets related to direct loans	1,580	1,312
1999 Total assets	99,937	27,732
LIABILITIES:		
Federal liabilities:		
2103 Debt	87,102	23,998
2105 Other	12,835	3,734
2205 Non-Federal liabilities: Lease liabilities, net		
2999 Total liabilities	99,937	27,732
NET POSITION:		
3300 Cumulative results of operations		
3300 Cumulative results of operations		
3300 Cumulative results of operations		
3300 Cumulative results of operations		
3300 Cumulative results of operations		
3300 Cumulative results of operations		
3999 Total net position		
4999 Total liabilities and net position	99,937	27,732

AIR CARRIER WORKER SUPPORT

Program and Financing (in millions of dollars)

Identification code 020–1894–0–1–402	2021 actual	2022 est.	2023 est.
Obligations by program activity:			
0001 Administrative Expenses	15	7	7
0002 Passenger Air Carrier Worker Relief	28,582	4	
0003 Cargo Air Carrier Worker Relief	5		
0004 Air Carrier Contractor Worker Relief	2,244	2	
0900 Total new obligations, unexpired accounts	30,846	13	7
Budgetary resources:			
Unobligated balance:			
1000 Unobligated balance brought forward, Oct 1	3,794	3,993	903
1021 Recoveries of prior year unpaid obligations	34	31	
1033 Recoveries of prior year paid obligations	11	92	
1070 Unobligated balance (total)	3,839	4,116	903
Budget authority:			
Appropriations, mandatory:			
1200 Appropriation	31,000		
1230 Appropriations and/or unobligated balance of appropriations permanently reduced		–3,200	
1260 Appropriations, mandatory (total)	31,000	–3,200	
1930 Total budgetary resources available	34,839	916	903
Memorandum (non-add) entries:			
1941 Unexpired unobligated balance, end of year	3,993	903	896
Change in obligated balance:			
Unpaid obligations:			
3000 Unpaid obligations, brought forward, Oct 1	65	110	
3010 New obligations, unexpired accounts	30,846	13	7
3020 Outlays (gross)	–30,767	–92	–7
3040 Recoveries of prior year unpaid obligations, unexpired	–34	–31	
3050 Unpaid obligations, end of year	110		
Memorandum (non-add) entries:			
3100 Obligated balance, start of year	65	110	
3200 Obligated balance, end of year	110		
Budget authority and outlays, net:			
Mandatory:			
4090 Budget authority, gross	31,000	–3,200	
Outlays, gross:			
4100 Outlays from new mandatory authority	30,260		
4101 Outlays from mandatory balances	507	92	7
4110 Outlays, gross (total)	30,767	92	7
Offsets against gross budget authority and outlays:			
Offsetting collections (collected) from:			
4123 Non-Federal sources	–11	–92	
Additional offsets against gross budget authority only:			
4143 Recoveries of prior year paid obligations, unexpired accounts	11	92	
4160 Budget authority, net (mandatory)	31,000	–3,200	
4170 Outlays, net (mandatory)	30,756		7
4180 Budget authority, net (total)	31,000	–3,200	
4190 Outlays, net (total)	30,756		7

The Coronavirus Aid, Relief, and Economic Security Act (P.L. 116–136) Section 4112 (CARES Act), Consolidated Appropriations Act, 2021 (P.L. 116–260) Division N Section 402, and the American Rescue Plan Act of 2021 (P.L. 117–2) Section 7301 each authorized the Secretary of the Treasury to provide financial assistance to the aviation industry for the continued payment of employee wages, salaries, and benefits. The CARES Act provided for financial assistance to passenger air carriers, cargo air carriers, and airline contractors. The two subsequent laws provided for additional financial assistance only for passenger air carriers and airline contractors. The Infrastructure Investment and Jobs Act (P.L. 117–58) Section 90007 rescinded $3 billion from CARES Act Section 4120 budget

DEPARTMENT OF THE TREASURY

Departmental Offices—Continued
Federal Funds—Continued

989

authority, which corresponded with a lack of demand for the program among cargo airlines, as well as $200 million from the P.L. 116–260 Division N Sec. 411 budget authority.

Starting in 2023, obligations and outlays also reflect amounts provided for the administration of the Emergency Rental Assistance program and programs authorized by Sec. 9901 of the American Rescue Plan, consistent with Sec. 123 of the Treasury Administrative Provisions.

Object Classification (in millions of dollars)

Identification code 020–1894–0–1–402		2021 actual	2022 est.	2023 est.
	Direct obligations:			
	Personnel compensation:			
11.1	Full-time permanent	2	1	....
11.8	Special personal services payments	1	....	....
11.9	Total personnel compensation	3	1	....
12.1	Civilian personnel benefits	1	....	....
25.1	Advisory and assistance services	6	2	4
25.3	Other goods and services from Federal sources	5	4	3
41.0	Grants, subsidies, and contributions	30,831	6	....
99.0	Direct obligations	30,846	13	7
99.9	Total new obligations, unexpired accounts	30,846	13	7

Employment Summary

Identification code 020–1894–0–1–402	2021 actual	2022 est.	2023 est.
1001 Direct civilian full-time equivalent employment	14	5	1

TRANSPORTATION SERVICES ECONOMIC RELIEF

Program and Financing (in millions of dollars)

Identification code 020–0156–0–1–401		2021 actual	2022 est.	2023 est.
	Obligations by program activity:			
0002	Administrative Costs	4	9	6
0003	Passenger Vessel Companies	279	80	....
0004	Motor Coach Companies	721	318	....
0005	School Bus Companies	290	285	....
0006	Pilotage Companies	1	1	....
0900	Total new obligations, unexpired accounts	1,295	693	6
	Budgetary resources:			
	Unobligated balance:			
1000	Unobligated balance brought forward, Oct 1	....	705	19
1021	Recoveries of prior year unpaid obligations	....	7	....
1070	Unobligated balance (total)	....	712	19
	Budget authority:			
	Appropriations, mandatory:			
1200	Appropriation	2,000	....	....
1930	Total budgetary resources available	2,000	712	19
	Memorandum (non-add) entries:			
1941	Unexpired unobligated balance, end of year	705	19	13
	Change in obligated balance:			
	Unpaid obligations:			
3000	Unpaid obligations, brought forward, Oct 1	....	1	2
3010	New obligations, unexpired accounts	1,295	693	6
3020	Outlays (gross)	–1,294	–685	–8
3040	Recoveries of prior year unpaid obligations, unexpired	....	–7	....
3050	Unpaid obligations, end of year	1	2	....
	Memorandum (non-add) entries:			
3100	Obligated balance, start of year	....	1	2
3200	Obligated balance, end of year	1	2	....
	Budget authority and outlays, net:			
	Mandatory:			
4090	Budget authority, gross	2,000	....	....
	Outlays, gross:			
4100	Outlays from new mandatory authority	1,294	....	....
4101	Outlays from mandatory balances	....	685	8
4110	Outlays, gross (total)	1,294	685	8
4180	Budget authority, net (total)	2,000	....	....
4190	Outlays, net (total)	1,294	685	8

The Consolidated Appropriations Act, 2021 (P.L. 116–260) Section 421 authorized the Secretary of the Treasury, in consultation with the Secretary of Transportation, to make grants available to eligible providers of transportation services that suffered revenue loss due to the coronavirus pandemic. Eligible companies provided charter, local, commuter, school, and tour bus services. Eligible small passenger vessels (as defined in 46 U.S.C 85, 116, and 2101) and the pilotage industry were also included.

Object Classification (in millions of dollars)

Identification code 020–0156–0–1–401		2021 actual	2022 est.	2023 est.
	Direct obligations:			
11.1	Personnel compensation: Full-time permanent	....	2	1
25.1	Advisory and assistance services	2	5	4
25.3	Other goods and services from Federal sources	2	2	1
41.0	Grants, subsidies, and contributions	1,291	684	....
99.9	Total new obligations, unexpired accounts	1,295	693	6

Employment Summary

Identification code 020–0156–0–1–401	2021 actual	2022 est.	2023 est.
1001 Direct civilian full-time equivalent employment	2	11	4

CORONAVIRUS RELIEF FUND

Program and Financing (in millions of dollars)

Identification code 020–1892–0–1–806		2021 actual	2022 est.	2023 est.
	Obligations by program activity:			
0004	States and DC (ARP)	154,140	41,160	....
0005	Territories (ARP)	4,500	....	....
0006	Tribal Governments (ARP)	19,957	44	....
0007	Local – Metro Cities (ARP)	22,506	23,063	....
0008	Local – Counties (ARP)	32,284	32,816	....
0009	Local – Nonentitlement Units (ARP)	9,546	9,984	....
0012	Administrative Expenses	16	28	4
0013	State Capital Projects	....	9,800	....
0014	Territories Capital Projects	....	100	....
0015	Tribal Government Capital Projects	....	100	....
0016	Local Assistance	....	750	750
0017	Tribal Consistency	....	250	250
0900	Total new obligations, unexpired accounts	242,949	118,095	1,004
	Budgetary resources:			
	Unobligated balance:			
1000	Unobligated balance brought forward, Oct 1	....	119,101	1,006
	Budget authority:			
	Appropriations, mandatory:			
1200	Appropriation [State Local Tribes etc.]	350,000	....	....
1200	Appropriation [Admin]	50	....	....
1200	Appropriation [Capital Projects]	10,000	....	....
1200	Appropriation [Local Assistance and Tribal Consistency]	2,000	....	....
1260	Appropriations, mandatory (total)	362,050	....	....
1930	Total budgetary resources available	362,050	119,101	1,006
	Memorandum (non-add) entries:			
1941	Unexpired unobligated balance, end of year	119,101	1,006	2
	Change in obligated balance:			
	Unpaid obligations:			
3000	Unpaid obligations, brought forward, Oct 1	534	23	8,441
3010	New obligations, unexpired accounts	242,949	118,095	1,004
3011	Obligations ("upward adjustments"), expired accounts	1	....	....
3020	Outlays (gross)	–243,460	–109,677	–3,523
3041	Recoveries of prior year unpaid obligations, expired	–1	....	....
3050	Unpaid obligations, end of year	23	8,441	5,922
	Memorandum (non-add) entries:			
3100	Obligated balance, start of year	534	23	8,441
3200	Obligated balance, end of year	23	8,441	5,922

CORONAVIRUS RELIEF FUND—Continued
Program and Financing—Continued

Identification code 020–1892–0–1–806	2021 actual	2022 est.	2023 est.
Budget authority and outlays, net:			
Mandatory:			
4090 Budget authority, gross	362,050		
Outlays, gross:			
4100 Outlays from new mandatory authority	242,944		
4101 Outlays from mandatory balances	516	109,677	3,523
4110 Outlays, gross (total)	243,460	109,677	3,523
4180 Budget authority, net (total)	362,050		
4190 Outlays, net (total)	243,460	109,677	3,523

The Coronavirus Aid, Relief, and Economic Security Act (P.L. 116–136) Section 5001, as amended by the Consolidated Appropriations Act, 2021 (P.L. 116–260) Section 1001, and the American Rescue Plan Act of 2021 (P.L. 117–2) Section 9901 (ARP) amended the Social Security Act (42 U.S.C. 301 et seq.) to authorize the Secretary of the Treasury to make payments to states, territories, tribal governments, and units of local government to assist with expenditures related to, as well as to mitigate the fiscal effects stemming from, the coronavirus pandemic.

In addition, the ARP established a Coronavirus Capital Projects Fund and a Local Assistance and Tribal Consistency Fund. The Coronavirus Capital Projects Fund provides payments to states, territories, and tribal governments to carry out critical capital projects, including broadband infrastructure, directly enabling work, education, and health monitoring, including remote options, in response to the coronavirus pandemic. The Local Assistance and Tribal Consistency Fund provides payments to eligible revenue sharing counties and eligible tribal governments for any governmental purpose other than lobbying activity.

Starting in 2023, obligations, outlays, and staffing associated with the administration of programs authorized by Sec. 9901 of the American Rescue Plan are reflected in the Economic Stabilization Program and the Air Carrier Worker Support accounts, consistent with Sec. 123 of the Treasury Administrative Provisions.

Object Classification (in millions of dollars)

Identification code 020–1892–0–1–806	2021 actual	2022 est.	2023 est.
Direct obligations:			
Personnel compensation:			
11.1 Full-time permanent	1	7	
11.8 Special personal services payments	2		
11.9 Total personnel compensation	3	7	
12.1 Civilian personnel benefits		2	
25.1 Advisory and assistance services	5	8	2
25.3 Other goods and services from Federal sources	8	10	2
41.0 Grants, subsidies, and contributions	242,933	118,066	1,000
99.0 Direct obligations	242,949	118,093	1,004
99.5 Adjustment for rounding		2	
99.9 Total new obligations, unexpired accounts	242,949	118,095	1,004

Employment Summary

Identification code 020–1892–0–1–806	2021 actual	2022 est.	2023 est.
1001 Direct civilian full-time equivalent employment	7	61	

EMERGENCY RENTAL ASSISTANCE
Program and Financing (in millions of dollars)

Identification code 020–0150–0–1–604	2021 actual	2022 est.	2023 est.
Obligations by program activity:			
0001 Payments to Territories (CAA21)	400		
0002 Payments to Tribes and Hawaiian Homeland (CAA21)	800	200	
0003 Payments to States (CAA21)	23,785	5,054	
0004 Administrative Costs	13	14	11
0005 States and Other Entities (ARP)	7,308	11,404	
0006 Territories (ARP)	148	157	
0007 Payments to High-need Grantees (ARP)	1,004	1,496	
0900 Total new obligations, unexpired accounts	33,458	18,325	11
Budgetary resources:			
Unobligated balance:			
1000 Unobligated balance brought forward, Oct 1		13,083	12
1012 Unobligated balance transfers between expired and unexpired accounts		5,254	
1070 Unobligated balance (total)		18,337	12
Budget authority:			
Appropriations, mandatory:			
1200 Appropriation	46,550		
1220 Appropriations transferred to other acct [020–0106]	–3		
1260 Appropriations, mandatory (total)	46,547		
1930 Total budgetary resources available	46,547	18,337	12
Memorandum (non-add) entries:			
1940 Unobligated balance expiring	–6		
1941 Unexpired unobligated balance, end of year	13,083	12	1
Change in obligated balance:			
Unpaid obligations:			
3000 Unpaid obligations, brought forward, Oct 1		146	1
3010 New obligations, unexpired accounts	33,458	18,325	11
3020 Outlays (gross)	–33,312	–18,470	–10
3050 Unpaid obligations, end of year	146	1	2
Memorandum (non-add) entries:			
3100 Obligated balance, start of year		146	1
3200 Obligated balance, end of year	146	1	2
Budget authority and outlays, net:			
Mandatory:			
4090 Budget authority, gross	46,547		
Outlays, gross:			
4100 Outlays from new mandatory authority	33,312		
4101 Outlays from mandatory balances		18,470	10
4110 Outlays, gross (total)	33,312	18,470	10
4180 Budget authority, net (total)	46,547		
4190 Outlays, net (total)	33,312	18,470	10

The Consolidated Appropriations Act, 2021 (P.L. 116–260) Division N Section 501 established the Emergency Rental Assistance program to provide grants to states, territories, tribes, localities, and other eligible entities to provide financial assistance and housing stability services to eligible households. These services may include the payment of rent, rental arrears, and utilities and home energy costs for a specified period of time. The American Rescue Plan Act of 2021 (P.L. 117–2) Section 3201 provided for additional assistance and expanded housing stability services, in addition to allocating a subset of the funds specifically for high-need grantees in FY 2022 and FY 2023.

Starting in 2023, obligations and outlays associated with the administration of the Emergency Rental Assistance program are reflected in the Air Carrier Worker Support account, consistent with Sec. 123 of the Treasury Administrative Provisions.

Object Classification (in millions of dollars)

Identification code 020–0150–0–1–604	2021 actual	2022 est.	2023 est.
Direct obligations:			
Personnel compensation:			
11.1 Full-time permanent		3	3
11.8 Special personal services payments	2		
11.9 Total personnel compensation	2	3	3
12.1 Civilian personnel benefits		1	1
25.1 Advisory and assistance services	3	4	1
25.3 Other goods and services from Federal sources	8	6	6
41.0 Grants, subsidies, and contributions	33,445	18,311	
99.9 Total new obligations, unexpired accounts	33,458	18,325	11

DEPARTMENT OF THE TREASURY

Departmental Offices—Continued
Federal Funds—Continued

Employment Summary

Identification code 020–0150–0–1–604	2021 actual	2022 est.	2023 est.
1001 Direct civilian full-time equivalent employment	3	20	21

HOMEOWNER ASSISTANCE FUND

Program and Financing (in millions of dollars)

Identification code 020–0124–0–1–604	2021 actual	2022 est.	2023 est.
Obligations by program activity:			
0001 Payments to Territories	....	3	27
0002 Payments to Tribes	32	466	....
0003 Payments to States	931	8,460	....
0004 Administrative Costs	4	12	12
0900 Total new obligations, unexpired accounts	970	8,965	12
Budgetary resources:			
Unobligated balance:			
1000 Unobligated balance brought forward, Oct 1	....	8,988	23
Budget authority:			
Appropriations, mandatory:			
1200 Appropriation	9,961	....	....
1220 Appropriations transferred to other acct [020–0106]	–3	....	....
1260 Appropriations, mandatory (total)	9,958	....	....
1930 Total budgetary resources available	9,958	8,988	23
Memorandum (non-add) entries:			
1941 Unexpired unobligated balance, end of year	8,988	23	11
Change in obligated balance:			
Unpaid obligations:			
3000 Unpaid obligations, brought forward, Oct 1	....	2	....
3010 New obligations, unexpired accounts	970	8,965	12
3020 Outlays (gross)	–968	–8,967	–12
3050 Unpaid obligations, end of year	2	....	....
Memorandum (non-add) entries:			
3100 Obligated balance, start of year	....	2	....
3200 Obligated balance, end of year	2	....	....
Budget authority and outlays, net:			
Mandatory:			
4090 Budget authority, gross	9,958	....	....
Outlays, gross:			
4100 Outlays from new mandatory authority	968	....	....
4101 Outlays from mandatory balances	....	8,967	12
4110 Outlays, gross (total)	968	8,967	12
4180 Budget authority, net (total)	9,958	....	....
4190 Outlays, net (total)	968	8,967	12

The American Rescue Plan Act of 2021 (P.L. 117–2) Section 3206 established the Homeowner Assistance Fund to mitigate financial hardships associated with the coronavirus pandemic by providing funds to states, territories, tribes, and other eligible entities in order to prevent homeowner mortgage delinquencies, defaults, foreclosures, loss of utilities or home energy services, displacements, and post-foreclosure evictions.

Object Classification (in millions of dollars)

Identification code 020–0124–0–1–604	2021 actual	2022 est.	2023 est.
Direct obligations:			
11.1 Personnel compensation: Full-time permanent	....	4	4
12.1 Civilian personnel benefits	....	1	1
25.1 Advisory and assistance services	1	3	3
25.3 Other goods and services from Federal sources	2	4	5
41.0 Grants, subsidies, and contributions	965	8,953	....
99.0 Direct obligations	968	8,965	13
99.5 Adjustment for rounding	2	....	–1
99.9 Total new obligations, unexpired accounts	970	8,965	12

Employment Summary

Identification code 020–0124–0–1–604	2021 actual	2022 est.	2023 est.
1001 Direct civilian full-time equivalent employment	2	27	26

STATE SMALL BUSINESS CREDIT INITIATIVE

Program and Financing (in millions of dollars)

Identification code 020–0142–0–1–376	2021 actual	2022 est.	2023 est.
Obligations by program activity:			
0001 SSBCI Program	....	7,800	....
0002 Secretary's Priorities	....	1,500	....
0003 Tribal Governments	....	500	....
0004 Administrative Expenses	6	23	27
0900 Total new obligations, unexpired accounts	6	9,823	27
Budgetary resources:			
Unobligated balance:			
1000 Unobligated balance brought forward, Oct 1	....	9,994	171
Budget authority:			
Appropriations, mandatory:			
1200 Appropriation	10,000	....	....
1900 Budget authority (total)	10,000	....	....
1930 Total budgetary resources available	10,000	9,994	171
Memorandum (non-add) entries:			
1941 Unexpired unobligated balance, end of year	9,994	171	144
Change in obligated balance:			
Unpaid obligations:			
3000 Unpaid obligations, brought forward, Oct 1	1	5	6,900
3010 New obligations, unexpired accounts	6	9,823	27
3020 Outlays (gross)	–2	–2,928	–1,327
3050 Unpaid obligations, end of year	5	6,900	5,600
Memorandum (non-add) entries:			
3100 Obligated balance, start of year	1	5	6,900
3200 Obligated balance, end of year	5	6,900	5,600
Budget authority and outlays, net:			
Mandatory:			
4090 Budget authority, gross	10,000	....	....
Outlays, gross:			
4100 Outlays from new mandatory authority	2	....	....
4101 Outlays from mandatory balances	....	2,928	1,327
4110 Outlays, gross (total)	2	2,928	1,327
4180 Budget authority, net (total)	10,000	....	....
4190 Outlays, net (total)	2	2,928	1,327

The American Rescue Plan Act of 2021 (P.L. 117–2) Section 3301, amends the State Small Business Credit Initiative Act of 2010 (12 U.S.C. 4701 et seq.) and provides additional funding for the State Small Business Credit Initiative (SSBCI) that was originally established in the Small Business Jobs Act of 2010 (P.L. 111–240). SSBCI funds eligible state, territorial and tribal government programs through September 29, 2030, which provide support to investment and credit programs for small businesses, with particular emphasis on business enterprises owned and controlled by socially and economically disadvantaged individuals. Additionally, SSBCI funds technical assistance for small businesses applying for Federal and State support programs.

Object Classification (in millions of dollars)

Identification code 020–0142–0–1–376	2021 actual	2022 est.	2023 est.
Direct obligations:			
11.1 Personnel compensation: Full-time permanent	....	6	6
12.1 Civilian personnel benefits	....	2	2
25.1 Advisory and assistance services	....	10	13
25.3 Other goods and services from Federal sources	5	5	5
41.0 Grants, subsidies, and contributions	....	9,800	....
99.0 Direct obligations	5	9,823	26
99.5 Adjustment for rounding	1	....	1
99.9 Total new obligations, unexpired accounts	6	9,823	27

STATE SMALL BUSINESS CREDIT INITIATIVE—Continued

Employment Summary

Identification code 020–0142–0–1–376	2021 actual	2022 est.	2023 est.
1001 Direct civilian full-time equivalent employment	3	37	39

SPECIAL INSPECTOR GENERAL FOR PANDEMIC RECOVERY

SALARIES AND EXPENSES

For necessary expenses of the Office of the Special Inspector General for Pandemic Recovery in carrying out section 4018 of the Coronavirus Aid, Relief, and Economic Security Act of 2020 (Public Law 116–136), in addition to amounts otherwise available for such purpose, $25,000,000, to remain available until September 30, 2025.

Program and Financing (in millions of dollars)

Identification code 020–1893–0–1–376	2021 actual	2022 est.	2023 est.
Obligations by program activity:			
0001 Special Inspector General for Pandemic Recovery	11	13	25
Budgetary resources:			
Unobligated balance:			
1000 Unobligated balance brought forward, Oct 1	24	13	
Budget authority:			
Appropriations, discretionary:			
1100 Appropriation			25
1900 Budget authority (total)			25
1930 Total budgetary resources available	24	13	25
Memorandum (non-add) entries:			
1941 Unexpired unobligated balance, end of year	13		
Change in obligated balance:			
Unpaid obligations:			
3000 Unpaid obligations, brought forward, Oct 1	1	1	1
3010 New obligations, unexpired accounts	11	13	25
3020 Outlays (gross)	–11	–13	–23
3050 Unpaid obligations, end of year	1	1	3
Memorandum (non-add) entries:			
3100 Obligated balance, start of year	1	1	1
3200 Obligated balance, end of year	1	1	3
Budget authority and outlays, net:			
Discretionary:			
4000 Budget authority, gross			25
Outlays, gross:			
4010 Outlays from new discretionary authority			23
Mandatory:			
Outlays, gross:			
4101 Outlays from mandatory balances	11	13	
4180 Budget authority, net (total)			25
4190 Outlays, net (total)	11	13	23

The Special Inspector General for Pandemic Recovery (SIGPR) was established by Section 4018 of the Coronavirus Aid, Relief, and Economic Security (CARES) Act.

SIGPR has the duty to conduct, supervise, and coordinate audits, evaluations, and investigations of the making, purchase, management, and sale of loans, loan guarantees, and other investments made by the Secretary of the Treasury under programs established by the Secretary, as authorized by Section 4018(c) of the CARES Act, and the management by the Secretary of programs, as authorized by Section 4018(c) of the CARES Act.

By express incorporation, SIGPR also has the duties, responsibilities, powers, and authorities granted inspectors general under the Inspector General Act of 1978, including broad subpoena authority.

The role and mission of SIGPR is to safeguard the peoples' tax dollars appropriated by Congress through the CARES Act. SIGPR strives to ensure that the American taxpayer gets the best return on investment by efficiently rooting out fraud, waste, and abuse. In carrying out its mission, SIGPR's goal is to treat everyone with respect, to operate with the utmost integrity, and to be fair, objective, and independent.

The CARES Act provided an initial appropriation of $25 million to SIGPR derived from amounts made available under section 4027. The Budget proposes appropriations language to provide SIGPR $25 million in appropriated funds to carry out section 4018 of the CARES Act. This funding is critical in ensuring that SIGPR's audit and investigative services have the necessary resources to identify waste, fraud, and abuse, protect the integrity of CARES Act funds, and aid in the conviction of perpetrators of unlawful activity, while collecting renumeration for the U.S. Treasury.

Object Classification (in millions of dollars)

Identification code 020–1893–0–1–376	2021 actual	2022 est.	2023 est.
Direct obligations:			
11.1 Personnel compensation: Full-time permanent	6	8	12
12.1 Civilian personnel benefits	1	2	3
23.1 Rental payments to GSA	1	1	1
25.3 Other goods and services from Federal sources	4	2	6
99.0 Direct obligations	12	13	22
99.5 Adjustment for rounding	–1		3
99.9 Total new obligations, unexpired accounts	11	13	25

Employment Summary

Identification code 020–1893–0–1–376	2021 actual	2022 est.	2023 est.
1001 Direct civilian full-time equivalent employment	35	38	66

COMMUNITY DEVELOPMENT FINANCIAL INSTITUTIONS FUND PROGRAM ACCOUNT

To carry out the Riegle Community Development and Regulatory Improvement Act of 1994 (subtitle A of title I of Public Law 103–325), including services authorized by section 3109 of title 5, United States Code, but at rates for individuals not to exceed the per diem rate equivalent to the rate for EX-III, $331,420,000. Of the amount appropriated under this heading—

(1) not less than $217,383,000, notwithstanding section 108(e) of Public Law 103–325 (12 U.S.C. 4707(e)) with regard to Small and/or Emerging Community Development Financial Institutions Assistance awards, is available until September 30, 2024, for financial assistance and technical assistance under subparagraphs (A) and (B) of section 108(a)(1), respectively, of Public Law 103–325 (12 U.S.C. 4707(a)(1)(A) and (B)), of which up to $1,600,000 may be available for training and outreach under section 109 of Public Law 103–325 (12 U.S.C. 4708), of which up to $3,153,750 may be used for the cost of direct loans, of which up to $6,000,000, notwithstanding subsection (d) of section 108 of Public Law 103–325 (12 U.S.C. 4707 (d)), may be available to provide financial assistance, technical assistance, training, and outreach to community development financial institutions to expand investments that benefit individuals with disabilities, and of which not less than $2,000,000 shall be for the Economic Mobility Corps to be operated in conjunction with the Corporation for National and Community Service, pursuant to 42 U.S.C. 12571: Provided, That the cost of direct and guaranteed loans, including the cost of modifying such loans, shall be as defined in section 502 of the Congressional Budget Act of 1974: Provided further, That these funds are available to subsidize gross obligations for the principal amount of direct loans not to exceed $25,000,000: Provided further, That of the funds provided under this paragraph, excluding those made to community development financial institutions to expand investments that benefit individuals with disabilities and those made to community development financial institutions that serve populations living in persistent poverty counties, the CDFI Fund shall prioritize Financial Assistance awards to organizations that invest and lend in high-poverty areas: Provided further, That for purposes of this section, the term "high-poverty area" means any census tract with a poverty rate of at least 20 percent as measured by the 2011–2015 5-year data series available from the American Community Survey of the Bureau of the Census for all States and Puerto Rico or with a poverty rate of at least 20 percent as measured by the 2010 Island areas Decennial Census data for any territory or possession of the United States;

(2) not less than $21,500,000, notwithstanding section 108(e) of Public Law 103–325 (12 U.S.C. 4707(e)), is available until September 30, 2024, for financial assistance, technical assistance, training, and outreach programs designed to benefit Native American, Native Hawaiian, and Alaska Native communities and provided primarily through qualified community development lender organizations with experience and expertise in community development banking and lending in

Indian country, Native American organizations, Tribes and Tribal organizations, and other suitable providers;

(3) not less than $26,000,000 is available until September 30, 2024, for the Bank Enterprise Award program;

(4) not less than $23,000,000, notwithstanding subsections (d) and (e) of section 108 of Public Law 103–325 (12 U.S.C. 4707(d) and (e)), is available until September 30, 2024, for a Healthy Food Financing Initiative to provide financial assistance, technical assistance, training, and outreach to community development financial institutions for the purpose of offering affordable financing and technical assistance to expand the availability of healthy food options in distressed communities;

(5) not less than $8,500,000 is available until September 30, 2024, to provide grants for loan loss reserve funds and to provide technical assistance for small dollar loan programs under section 122 of Public Law 103–325 (12 U.S.C. 4719): Provided, That sections 108(d) and 122(b)(2) of such Public Law shall not apply to the provision of such grants and technical assistance;

(6) up to $35,037,000 is available until September 30, 2023, for administrative expenses, including administration of CDFI Fund programs and the New Markets Tax Credit Program, of which not less than $1,000,000 is for the development of tools to better assess and inform CDFI investment performance and CDFI Fund program impacts, and up to $300,000 is for administrative expenses to carry out the direct loan program; and

(7) during fiscal year 2023, none of the funds available under this heading are available for the cost, as defined in section 502 of the Congressional Budget Act of 1974, of commitments to guarantee bonds and notes under section 114A of the Riegle Community Development and Regulatory Improvement Act of 1994 (12 U.S.C. 4713a): Provided, That commitments to guarantee bonds and notes under such section 114A shall not exceed $500,000,000: Provided further, That such section 114A shall remain in effect until December 31, 2023: Provided further, That of the funds awarded under this heading, except those provided for the Economic Mobility Corps, not less than 10 percent shall be used for awards that support investments that serve populations living in persistent poverty counties: Provided further, That for the purposes of this paragraph and paragraph (1), the term "persistent poverty counties" means any county, including county equivalent areas in Puerto Rico, that has had 20 percent or more of its population living in poverty over the past 30 years, as measured by the 1990 and 2000 decennial censuses and the 2011–2015 5-year data series available from the American Community Survey of the Bureau of the Census or any other territory or possession of the United States that has had 20 percent or more of its population living in poverty over the past 30 years, as measured by the 1990, 2000 and 2010 Island Areas Decennial Censuses, or equivalent data, of the Bureau of the Census.

Note.—A full-year 2022 appropriation for this account was not enacted at the time the Budget was prepared; therefore, the Budget assumes this account is operating under the Continuing Appropriations Act, 2022 (Division A of Public Law 117–43, as amended). The amounts included for 2022 reflect the annualized level provided by the continuing resolution.

Program and Financing (in millions of dollars)

Identification code 020–1881–0–1–451	2021 actual	2022 est.	2023 est.
Obligations by program activity:			
0009 General Administrative Expenses	30	29	35
0012 Financial Assistance	22	312	215
0013 Small Dollar Loan Program	11	12	8
0014 Native American/Hawaiian Program	3	30	22
0015 Economic Mobility Corps	2	4	2
0026 Healthy Food Initiative	....	45	23
0028 Bank Enterprise Award	....	26	52
0050 No Year Account	....	3	1
0091 Direct program activities, subtotal	68	461	358
Credit program obligations:			
0701 Direct loan subsidy	....	3	2
0705 Reestimates of direct loan subsidy	1	1	....
0706 Interest on reestimates of direct loan subsidy	14	17	....
0791 Direct program activities, subtotal	15	21	2
0900 Total new obligations, unexpired accounts	83	482	360
Budgetary resources:			
Unobligated balance:			
1000 Unobligated balance brought forward, Oct 1	14	218	28
1001 Discretionary unobligated balance brought fwd, Oct 1	12	....	....
1021 Recoveries of prior year unpaid obligations	....	1	1
1070 Unobligated balance (total)	14	219	29
Budget authority:			
Appropriations, discretionary:			
1100 Appropriation	270	270	331
Appropriations, mandatory:			
1200 Appropriation	16	18	1
Spending authority from offsetting collections, discretionary:			
1700 Collected	....	2	....
Spending authority from offsetting collections, mandatory:			
1800 Collected	1	1	....
1900 Budget authority (total)	287	291	332
1930 Total budgetary resources available	301	510	361
Memorandum (non-add) entries:			
1941 Unexpired unobligated balance, end of year	218	28	1
Change in obligated balance:			
Unpaid obligations:			
3000 Unpaid obligations, brought forward, Oct 1	267	75	284
3010 New obligations, unexpired accounts	83	482	360
3020 Outlays (gross)	–274	–272	–279
3040 Recoveries of prior year unpaid obligations, unexpired	....	–1	–1
3041 Recoveries of prior year unpaid obligations, expired	–1	....	....
3050 Unpaid obligations, end of year	75	284	364
Memorandum (non-add) entries:			
3100 Obligated balance, start of year	267	75	284
3200 Obligated balance, end of year	75	284	364
Budget authority and outlays, net:			
Discretionary:			
4000 Budget authority, gross	270	272	331
Outlays, gross:			
4010 Outlays from new discretionary authority	21	25	27
4011 Outlays from discretionary balances	237	229	250
4020 Outlays, gross (total)	258	254	277
Offsets against gross budget authority and outlays:			
Offsetting collections (collected) from:			
4033 Non-Federal sources	....	–2	....
4040 Offsets against gross budget authority and outlays (total)	....	–2	....
Mandatory:			
4090 Budget authority, gross	17	19	1
Outlays, gross:			
4100 Outlays from new mandatory authority	16	18	1
4101 Outlays from mandatory balances	....	....	1
4110 Outlays, gross (total)	16	18	2
Offsets against gross budget authority and outlays:			
Offsetting collections (collected) from:			
4123 Non-Federal sources	–1	–1	....
4180 Budget authority, net (total)	286	288	332
4190 Outlays, net (total)	273	269	279
Memorandum (non-add) entries:			
5010 Total investments, SOY: non-Fed securities: Market value	16	47	47
5011 Total investments, EOY: non-Fed securities: Market value	47	47	47

Summary of Loan Levels, Subsidy Budget Authority and Outlays by Program (in millions of dollars)

Identification code 020–1881–0–1–451	2021 actual	2022 est.	2023 est.
Direct loan levels supportable by subsidy budget authority:			
115001 Community Development Financial Institutions Prog Fin Assist.	....	25	25
115002 Bond Guarantee Program	100	500	500
115999 Total direct loan levels	100	525	525
Direct loan subsidy (in percent):			
132001 Community Development Financial Institutions Prog Fin Assist.	....	12.61	9.08
132002 Bond Guarantee Program	–4.62	0.00	0.00
132999 Weighted average subsidy rate	–4.62	0.60	0.43
Direct loan subsidy budget authority:			
133001 Community Development Financial Institutions Prog Fin Assist.	....	3	2
133002 Bond Guarantee Program	–5	....	....
133999 Total subsidy budget authority	–5	3	2
Direct loan subsidy outlays:			
134002 Bond Guarantee Program	–3	....	....
134999 Total subsidy outlays	–3	....	....
Direct loan reestimates:			
135001 Community Development Financial Institutions Prog Fin Assist.	2	–2	....
135002 Bond Guarantee Program	4	4	....

COMMUNITY DEVELOPMENT FINANCIAL INSTITUTIONS FUND PROGRAM ACCOUNT—Continued

Summary of Loan Levels, Subsidy Budget Authority and Outlays by Program—Continued

Identification code 020–1881–0–1–451	2021 actual	2022 est.	2023 est.
135999 Total direct loan reestimates	6	2	....

The Community Development Financial Institutions (CDFI) Fund promotes economic and community development through investment in and assistance to CDFIs (including community development banks, credit unions, loan funds, and venture capital funds) to expand the availability of financial services and affordable credit for underserved populations and communities. The 2023 Budget provides funding for the CDFI Program, the Healthy Food Financing Initiative, the Native American CDFI Assistance Program, the Bank Enterprise Award Program, the AmeriCorps CDFI Economic Mobility Corps, and the Small Dollar Loan Program.

The CDFI Fund's Bond Guarantee Program (BGP) was originally authorized in the Small Business Jobs Act of 2010 (P.L. 111–240) for a period of four years to provide a source of long-term capital in low-income and underserved communities. The Budget proposes an annual commitment authority of $500 million.

Object Classification (in millions of dollars)

Identification code 020–1881–0–1–451	2021 actual	2022 est.	2023 est.
Direct obligations:			
11.1 Personnel compensation: Full-time permanent	9	10	12
12.1 Civilian personnel benefits	3	4	4
25.1 Advisory and assistance services	5	2	4
25.3 Other goods and services from Federal sources	8	12	10
25.7 Operation and maintenance of equipment	....	3	4
31.0 Equipment	5	6	4
41.0 Grants, subsidies, and contributions	53	446	322
99.0 Direct obligations	83	483	360
99.5 Adjustment for rounding	....	–1	....
99.9 Total new obligations, unexpired accounts	83	482	360

Employment Summary

Identification code 020–1881–0–1–451	2021 actual	2022 est.	2023 est.
1001 Direct civilian full-time equivalent employment	67	82	89

COMMUNITY DEVELOPMENT FINANCIAL INSTITUTIONS FUND DIRECT LOAN FINANCING ACCOUNT

Program and Financing (in millions of dollars)

Identification code 020–4088–0–3–451	2021 actual	2022 est.	2023 est.
Obligations by program activity:			
Credit program obligations:			
0710 Direct loan obligations	100	525	525
0713 Payment of interest to Treasury	3	3	3
0715 Payments of interest to FFB	34	34	40
0740 Negative subsidy obligations	5	....	....
0742 Downward reestimates paid to receipt accounts	9	16	....
0743 Interest on downward reestimates	....	1	....
0900 Total new obligations, unexpired accounts	151	579	568
Budgetary resources:			
Unobligated balance:			
1000 Unobligated balance brought forward, Oct 1	2	2	2
1021 Recoveries of prior year unpaid obligations	27	....	....
1023 Unobligated balances applied to repay debt	–2	–2	–2
1024 Unobligated balance of borrowing authority withdrawn	–27	....	....
Financing authority:			
Borrowing authority, mandatory:			
1400 Borrowing authority	117	525	525
Spending authority from offsetting collections, mandatory:			
1800 Collected	95	105	103
1825 Spending authority from offsetting collections applied to repay debt	–59	–49	–58
1850 Spending auth from offsetting collections, mand (total)	36	56	45
1900 Budget authority (total)	153	581	570
1930 Total budgetary resources available	153	581	570
Memorandum (non-add) entries:			
1941 Unexpired unobligated balance, end of year	2	2	2
Change in obligated balance:			
Unpaid obligations:			
3000 Unpaid obligations, brought forward, Oct 1	423	402	784
3010 New obligations, unexpired accounts	151	579	568
3020 Outlays (gross)	–145	–197	–290
3040 Recoveries of prior year unpaid obligations, unexpired	–27	....	....
3050 Unpaid obligations, end of year	402	784	1,062
Memorandum (non-add) entries:			
3100 Obligated balance, start of year	423	402	784
3200 Obligated balance, end of year	402	784	1,062
Financing authority and disbursements, net:			
Mandatory:			
4090 Budget authority, gross	153	581	570
Financing disbursements:			
4110 Outlays, gross (total)	145	197	290
Offsets against gross financing authority and disbursements:			
Offsetting collections (collected) from:			
4120 Federal sources	–16	–18	....
4122 Interest on uninvested funds	–3	–3	–3
4123 Non-Federal sources - Interest repayments	–76	–35	–42
4123 Non-Federal sources - Principal Repayments	....	–49	–58
4130 Offsets against gross budget authority and outlays (total)	–95	–105	–103
4160 Budget authority, net (mandatory)	58	476	467
4170 Outlays, net (mandatory)	50	92	187
4180 Budget authority, net (total)	58	476	467
4190 Outlays, net (total)	50	92	187

Status of Direct Loans (in millions of dollars)

Identification code 020–4088–0–3–451	2021 actual	2022 est.	2023 est.
Position with respect to appropriations act limitation on obligations:			
1111 Direct loan obligations from current-year authority	100	525	525
1150 Total direct loan obligations	100	525	525
Cumulative balance of direct loans outstanding:			
1210 Outstanding, start of year	1,213	1,265	1,412
1231 Disbursements: Direct loan disbursements	95	197	290
1251 Repayments: Repayments and prepayments	–42	–49	–58
1263 Write-offs for default: Direct loans	–1	–1	–1
1290 Outstanding, end of year	1,265	1,412	1,643

Balance Sheet (in millions of dollars)

Identification code 020–4088–0–3–451	2020 actual	2021 actual
ASSETS:		
Federal assets:		
1101 Fund balances with Treasury	2	2
Investments in U.S. securities:		
1106 Receivables, net	19	20
Net value of assets related to post-1991 direct loans receivable:		
1401 Direct loans receivable, gross	1,213	1,265
1402 Interest receivable	....	1
1405 Allowance for subsidy cost (-)	35	40
1499 Net present value of assets related to direct loans	1,248	1,306
1801 Other Federal assets: Cash and other monetary assets	....	....
1999 Total assets	1,269	1,328
LIABILITIES:		
Federal liabilities:		
2103 Debt	1,257	1,308
2105 Other Liabilities without Related Budgetary Offset	12	20
2999 Total liabilities	1,269	1,328
NET POSITION:		
3300 Cumulative results of operations	....	....
4999 Total liabilities and net position	1,269	1,328

COMMUNITY DEVELOPMENT FINANCIAL INSTITUTIONS FUND PROGRAM, EMERGENCY SUPPORT

Program and Financing (in millions of dollars)

Identification code 020–0160–0–1–451	2021 actual	2022 est.	2023 est.
Obligations by program activity:			
0001 CDFI Grants Economic Impact Rapid Response	1,248		
0002 CDFI Grants Economic Impact Underserved Communities			1,739
0003 Administrative		3	3
0900 Total new obligations, unexpired accounts	1,248	3	1,742
Budgetary resources:			
Unobligated balance:			
1000 Unobligated balance brought forward, Oct 1		1,750	1,747
Budget authority:			
Appropriations, mandatory:			
1200 Appropriation	3,000		
1930 Total budgetary resources available	3,000	1,750	1,747
Memorandum (non-add) entries:			
1940 Unobligated balance expiring	–2		
1941 Unexpired unobligated balance, end of year	1,750	1,747	5
Change in obligated balance:			
Unpaid obligations:			
3000 Unpaid obligations, brought forward, Oct 1		163	33
3010 New obligations, unexpired accounts	1,248	3	1,742
3020 Outlays (gross)	–1,085	–133	–905
3050 Unpaid obligations, end of year	163	33	870
Memorandum (non-add) entries:			
3100 Obligated balance, start of year		163	33
3200 Obligated balance, end of year	163	33	870
Budget authority and outlays, net:			
Mandatory:			
4090 Budget authority, gross	3,000		
Outlays, gross:			
4100 Outlays from new mandatory authority	1,085		
4101 Outlays from mandatory balances		133	905
4110 Outlays, gross (total)	1,085	133	905
4180 Budget authority, net (total)	3,000		
4190 Outlays, net (total)	1,085	133	905

The Consolidated Appropriations Act, 2021 (P. L. 116–260) provided $3 billion to deliver immediate assistance to CDFIs in communities impacted by the COVID-19 pandemic. In the spring of 2021, the CDFI Fund awarded $1.25 billion of these funds through its newly established CDFI Rapid Response Program (CDFI RRP), which was designed to quickly deploy capital to CDFIs through a streamlined application and review process.

The CDFI Fund will begin the process of making $1.75 billion in grant funds available to CDFIs to expand their lending, grant making, or investment activity in low- or moderate-income minority communities and to minorities that have significant unmet capital or financial service needs.

Object Classification (in millions of dollars)

Identification code 020–0160–0–1–451	2021 actual	2022 est.	2023 est.
Direct obligations:			
11.1 Personnel compensation: Full-time permanent		1	1
12.1 Civilian personnel benefits		1	1
25.3 Other goods and services from Federal sources		1	1
41.0 Grants, subsidies, and contributions	1,248		1,739
99.9 Total new obligations, unexpired accounts	1,248	3	1,742

Employment Summary

Identification code 020–0160–0–1–451	2021 actual	2022 est.	2023 est.
1001 Direct civilian full-time equivalent employment	3	12	12

EMERGENCY CAPITAL INVESTMENT FUND

Program and Financing (in millions of dollars)

Identification code 020–0161–0–1–451	2021 actual	2022 est.	2023 est.
Obligations by program activity:			
0001 Administrative Costs	24	36	15
0002 Preferred Stock Investments		4,816	
0003 Debt Purchases		3,931	
0900 Total new obligations, unexpired accounts	24	8,783	15
Budgetary resources:			
Unobligated balance:			
1000 Unobligated balance brought forward, Oct 1		8,976	193
Budget authority:			
Appropriations, mandatory:			
1200 Appropriation	9,000		
1930 Total budgetary resources available	9,000	8,976	193
Memorandum (non-add) entries:			
1941 Unexpired unobligated balance, end of year	8,976	193	178
Change in obligated balance:			
Unpaid obligations:			
3000 Unpaid obligations, brought forward, Oct 1		19	18
3010 New obligations, unexpired accounts	24	8,783	15
3020 Outlays (gross)	–5	–8,784	–15
3050 Unpaid obligations, end of year	19	18	18
Memorandum (non-add) entries:			
3100 Obligated balance, start of year		19	18
3200 Obligated balance, end of year	19	18	18
Budget authority and outlays, net:			
Mandatory:			
4090 Budget authority, gross	9,000		
Outlays, gross:			
4100 Outlays from new mandatory authority	5		
4101 Outlays from mandatory balances		8,784	15
4110 Outlays, gross (total)	5	8,784	15
4180 Budget authority, net (total)	9,000		
4190 Outlays, net (total)	5	8,784	15

The Emergency Capital Investment Program (ECIP) invests in either perpetual preferred equity or subordinated debt (with a maturity of fifteen or thirty years) issued by financial institutions consistent with ECIP's terms. Institutions eligible to participate must be: 1) Community Development Financial Institutions or Minority Depository Institutions; 2) insured depository institutions, bank or savings and loan holding companies, or federally insured credit unions; and 3) supportive of low-and middle-income communities. Dividend yields or interest paid on ECIP securities decrease when institutions reach lending goals established at the time of their participation. Division N, Section 522 of the Consolidated Appropriations Act, 2021 (P.L. 116–260) established ECIP by amending the Community Development Banking and Financial Institutions Act of 1994 (12 U.S.C. 4701 et seq.) and provided $9 billion for the program. Treasury issued an interim final rule for ECIP on March 9, 2021, and on March 22, 2021, the Board of Governors of the Federal Reserve System (FRB), Federal Deposit Insurance Corporation (FDIC) and the Office of the Comptroller of the Currency (OCC) jointly issued an interim final rule for securities issued under ECIP, providing that preferred stock issued qualifies as additional tier 1 capital and subordinated debt qualifies as tier 2 capital under the FRB/FDIC/OCC capital rule. The ECIP application period closed on September 1, 2021 and preliminary recipients were announced in December 2021.

Object Classification (in millions of dollars)

Identification code 020–0161–0–1–451	2021 actual	2022 est.	2023 est.
Direct obligations:			
11.1 Personnel compensation: Full-time permanent		3	3
12.1 Civilian personnel benefits		1	1
25.1 Advisory and assistance services	13	27	8
25.2 Other services from non-Federal sources	8		
25.3 Other goods and services from Federal sources	2	4	3
41.0 Grants, subsidies, and contributions		8,747	
99.0 Direct obligations	23	8,782	15

Departmental Offices—Continued
Federal Funds—Continued

EMERGENCY CAPITAL INVESTMENT FUND—Continued

Object Classification—Continued

Identification code 020–0161–0–1–451	2021 actual	2022 est.	2023 est.
99.5 Adjustment for rounding		1	1	....
99.9 Total new obligations, unexpired accounts	24	8,783	15

Employment Summary

Identification code 020–0161–0–1–451	2021 actual	2022 est.	2023 est.
1001 Direct civilian full-time equivalent employment	....	27	23

COMMUNITY FINANCIAL DEVELOPMENT INSTITUTIONS AFFORDABLE HOUSING SUPPLY FUND

(Legislative proposal, subject to PAYGO)

Program and Financing (in millions of dollars)

Identification code 020–1898–4–1–604	2021 actual	2022 est.	2023 est.
Obligations by program activity:			
0001 Direct program activity	....	....	500
0900 Total new obligations, unexpired accounts (object class 41.0)	....	....	500
Budgetary resources:			
Budget authority:			
Appropriations, mandatory:			
1200 Appropriation	....	....	5,000
1930 Total budgetary resources available	....	....	5,000
Memorandum (non-add) entries:			
1941 Unexpired unobligated balance, end of year	....	....	4,500
Change in obligated balance:			
Unpaid obligations:			
3010 New obligations, unexpired accounts	....	....	500
3020 Outlays (gross)	....	....	–500
Budget authority and outlays, net:			
Mandatory:			
4090 Budget authority, gross	....	....	5,000
Outlays, gross:			
4100 Outlays from new mandatory authority	....	....	500
4180 Budget authority, net (total)	....	....	5,000
4190 Outlays, net (total)	....	....	500

The CDFI Affordable Housing Supply Fund expands lending in disadvantaged communities and increases the affordable housing supply. The 2023 Budget proposes $5 billion in long-term mandatory funding to support lending by eligible CDFIs to finance new construction and substantial rehabilitation that creates net new units of affordable rental and for sale housing.

OFFICE OF FINANCIAL STABILITY

Program and Financing (in millions of dollars)

Identification code 020–0128–0–1–376	2021 actual	2022 est.	2023 est.
Obligations by program activity:			
0001 Office of Financial Stability (Direct)	36	38	34
Budgetary resources:			
Unobligated balance:			
1000 Unobligated balance brought forward, Oct 1	....	1	1
Budget authority:			
Appropriations, mandatory:			
1200 Appropriation	41	38	34
1930 Total budgetary resources available	41	39	35
Memorandum (non-add) entries:			
1940 Unobligated balance expiring	–4	....	....
1941 Unexpired unobligated balance, end of year	1	1	1
Change in obligated balance:			
Unpaid obligations:			
3000 Unpaid obligations, brought forward, Oct 1	30	19	24
3010 New obligations, unexpired accounts	36	38	34
3020 Outlays (gross)	–31	–33	–30
3041 Recoveries of prior year unpaid obligations, expired	–16	....	....
3050 Unpaid obligations, end of year	19	24	28
Memorandum (non-add) entries:			
3100 Obligated balance, start of year	30	19	24
3200 Obligated balance, end of year	19	24	28
Budget authority and outlays, net:			
Mandatory:			
4090 Budget authority, gross	41	38	34
Outlays, gross:			
4100 Outlays from new mandatory authority	23	25	17
4101 Outlays from mandatory balances	8	8	13
4110 Outlays, gross (total)	31	33	30
4180 Budget authority, net (total)	41	38	34
4190 Outlays, net (total)	31	33	30

The Emergency Economic Stabilization Act of 2008 (EESA) (P.L. 110–343) authorized the establishment of the Troubled Asset Relief Program (TARP) and the Office of Financial Stability (OFS) to purchase and insure certain types of troubled assets for the purpose of providing stability to and preventing disruption in the economy and financial system and protecting taxpayers. The Act gave the Secretary of the Treasury broad and flexible authority to purchase and insure mortgages and other troubled assets, as well as inject capital by taking limited equity positions, as needed to stabilize the financial markets. This account provides for the administrative costs of OFS, which oversees and manages TARP.

Object Classification (in millions of dollars)

Identification code 020–0128–0–1–376	2021 actual	2022 est.	2023 est.
Direct obligations:			
11.1 Personnel compensation: Full-time permanent	1	1	1
25.1 Advisory and assistance services	3	3	3
25.2 Other services from non-Federal sources	22	28	24
25.3 Other goods and services from Federal sources	5	5	5
41.0 Grants, subsidies, and contributions	4	....	....
99.0 Direct obligations	35	37	33
99.5 Adjustment for rounding	1	1	1
99.9 Total new obligations, unexpired accounts	36	38	34

Employment Summary

Identification code 020–0128–0–1–376	2021 actual	2022 est.	2023 est.
1001 Direct civilian full-time equivalent employment	10	10	8

TROUBLED ASSET RELIEF PROGRAM ACCOUNT

Summary of Loan Levels, Subsidy Budget Authority and Outlays by Program (in millions of dollars)

Identification code 020–0132–0–1–376	2021 actual	2022 est.	2023 est.
Direct loan reestimates:			
135001 Automotive Industry Financing Program	....	–3	....
135999 Total direct loan reestimates	....	–3	....

As authorized by the Emergency Economic Stabilization Act of 2008 (EESA) (P.L. 110–343) and required by the Federal Credit Reform Act of 1990, as amended, this account records the subsidy costs associated with Troubled Asset Relief Program (TARP) direct loans obligated and loan guarantees including modifications of direct loans or loan guarantees that resulted from obligations or commitments in any year. The subsidy amounts are estimated on a present value basis using a risk-adjusted discount rate, as required by EESA.

DEPARTMENT OF THE TREASURY

Departmental Offices—Continued
Federal Funds—Continued

997

The authority to make new financial commitments via TARP expired on October 3, 2010, under the terms of EESA. However, Treasury can continue to execute commitments entered into before October 3, 2010.

TROUBLED ASSET RELIEF PROGRAM DIRECT LOAN FINANCING ACCOUNT

Program and Financing (in millions of dollars)

Identification code 020–4277–0–3–376	2021 actual	2022 est.	2023 est.
Obligations by program activity:			
Credit program obligations:			
0742 Downward reestimates paid to receipt accounts	....	2	....
0743 Interest on downward reestimates	....	1	....
0900 Total new obligations, unexpired accounts	....	3	....
Budgetary resources:			
Unobligated balance:			
1000 Unobligated balance brought forward, Oct 1	....	3	....
Financing authority:			
Spending authority from offsetting collections, mandatory:			
1800 Collected	3	....	....
1900 Budget authority (total)	3	....	....
1930 Total budgetary resources available	3	3	....
Memorandum (non-add) entries:			
1941 Unexpired unobligated balance, end of year	3	....	....
Change in obligated balance:			
Unpaid obligations:			
3000 Unpaid obligations, brought forward, Oct 1	....	....	3
3010 New obligations, unexpired accounts	....	3	....
3050 Unpaid obligations, end of year	....	3	3
Memorandum (non-add) entries:			
3100 Obligated balance, start of year	....	....	3
3200 Obligated balance, end of year	....	3	3
Financing authority and disbursements, net:			
Mandatory:			
4090 Budget authority, gross	3	....	....
Offsets against gross financing authority and disbursements:			
Offsetting collections (collected) from:			
4123 Principal	–3	....	....
4180 Budget authority, net (total)	....	....	....
4190 Outlays, net (total)	–3	....	....

As authorized by the Emergency Economic Stabilization Act of 2008 (P.L. 110–343) and required by the Federal Credit Reform Act of 1990, as amended, this non-budgetary account records all cash flows to and from the Government resulting from direct loans obligated in 2008 and beyond including modifications of direct loans that resulted from obligations in any year. The amounts in this account are a means of financing and are not included in the budget totals.

Balance Sheet (in millions of dollars)

Identification code 020–4277–0–3–376	2020 actual	2021 actual
ASSETS:		
1101 Federal assets: Fund balances with Treasury	13	3
Net value of assets related to post-1991 direct loans receivable:		
1401 Direct loans receivable, gross	....	....
1401 Direct loans receivable, gross	....	....
1405 Allowance for subsidy cost (–)	....	....
1405 Allowance for subsidy cost (–)	....	....
1499 Net present value of assets related to direct loans	....	....
1999 Total assets	13	3
LIABILITIES:		
Federal liabilities:		
2104 Resources payable to Treasury	13	....
2105 Other	....	3
2999 Total upward reestimate subsidy BA [20–0132]	13	3
NET POSITION:		
3300 Cumulative results of operations	....	....

4999 Total liabilities and net position	13	3

TROUBLED ASSET RELIEF PROGRAM EQUITY PURCHASE PROGRAM

Program and Financing (in millions of dollars)

Identification code 020–0134–0–1–376	2021 actual	2022 est.	2023 est.
Obligations by program activity:			
Credit program obligations:			
0705 Reestimates of direct loan subsidy	2	4	....
0706 Interest on reestimates of direct loan subsidy	3	8	....
0900 Total new obligations, unexpired accounts (object class 41.0)	5	12	....
Budgetary resources:			
Budget authority:			
Appropriations, mandatory:			
1200 Appropriation	5	12	....
1930 Total budgetary resources available	5	12	....
Change in obligated balance:			
Unpaid obligations:			
3010 New obligations, unexpired accounts	5	12	....
3020 Outlays (gross)	–5	–12	....
Budget authority and outlays, net:			
Mandatory:			
4090 Budget authority, gross	5	12	....
Outlays, gross:			
4100 Outlays from new mandatory authority	5	12	....
4180 Budget authority, net (total)	5	12	....
4190 Outlays, net (total)	5	12	....

Summary of Loan Levels, Subsidy Budget Authority and Outlays by Program (in millions of dollars)

Identification code 020–0134–0–1–376	2021 actual	2022 est.	2023 est.
Direct loan reestimates:			
135001 Capital Purchase Program	–3	12	....
135006 Community Development Capital Initiative	5	....	....
135999 Total direct loan reestimates	2	12	....

As authorized by the Emergency Economic Stabilization Act of 2008 (EESA) (P.L. 110–343) and required by the Federal Credit Reform Act of 1990, as amended, this account records the subsidy costs associated with TARP equity purchase obligations (including modifications of equity purchases that resulted from obligations in any year). The subsidy amounts are estimated on a present value basis using a risk-adjusted discount rate, as required by EESA.

The authority to make new financial commitments via TARP expired on October 3, 2010, under the terms of EESA. However, Treasury can continue to execute commitments entered into before October 3, 2010.

TROUBLED ASSET RELIEF PROGRAM EQUITY PURCHASE FINANCING ACCOUNT

Program and Financing (in millions of dollars)

Identification code 020–4278–0–3–376	2021 actual	2022 est.	2023 est.
Obligations by program activity:			
Credit program obligations:			
0713 Payment of interest to Treasury	1	1	....
0742 Downward reestimates paid to receipt accounts	1	....	....
0743 Interest on downward reestimates	2	....	....
0900 Total new obligations, unexpired accounts	4	1	....
Budgetary resources:			
Unobligated balance:			
1000 Unobligated balance brought forward, Oct 1	4	1	13
1023 Unobligated balances applied to repay debt	–3	....	–1
1070 Unobligated balance (total)	1	1	12

TROUBLED ASSET RELIEF PROGRAM EQUITY PURCHASE FINANCING ACCOUNT—Continued

Program and Financing—Continued

Identification code 020–4278–0–3–376		2021 actual	2022 est.	2023 est.
	Financing authority:			
	Borrowing authority, mandatory:			
1400	Borrowing authority	3	....	....
	Spending authority from offsetting collections, mandatory:			
1800	Collected	6	13	1
1825	Spending authority from offsetting collections applied to repay debt	–5	....	....
1850	Spending auth from offsetting collections, mand (total)	1	13	1
1900	Budget authority (total)	4	13	1
1930	Total budgetary resources available	5	14	13
	Memorandum (non-add) entries:			
1941	Unexpired unobligated balance, end of year	1	13	13
	Change in obligated balance:			
	Unpaid obligations:			
3000	Unpaid obligations, brought forward, Oct 1	....	....	1
3010	New obligations, unexpired accounts	4	1	....
3020	Outlays (gross)	–4	....	....
3050	Unpaid obligations, end of year	....	1	1
	Memorandum (non-add) entries:			
3100	Obligated balance, start of year	....	....	1
3200	Obligated balance, end of year	....	1	1
	Financing authority and disbursements, net:			
	Mandatory:			
4090	Budget authority, gross	4	13	1
	Financing disbursements:			
4110	Outlays, gross (total)	4	....	....
	Offsets against gross financing authority and disbursements:			
	Offsetting collections (collected) from:			
4120	Federal sources	–5	–13	....
4123	Dividends	–1	....	....
4123	Redemption	....	....	–1
4130	Offsets against gross budget authority and outlays (total)	–6	–13	–1
4160	Budget authority, net (mandatory)	–2	....	....
4170	Outlays, net (mandatory)	–2	–13	–1
4180	Budget authority, net (total)	–2	....	....
4190	Outlays, net (total)	–2	–13	–1

Status of Direct Loans (in millions of dollars)

Identification code 020–4278–0–3–376		2021 actual	2022 est.	2023 est.
	Cumulative balance of direct loans outstanding:			
1210	Outstanding, start of year	23	13	13
1251	Repayments: Repayments and prepayments	–1	....	–1
1263	Write-offs for default: Direct loans	–4	....	....
1264	Other adjustments, net (+ or –)	–5	....	....
1290	Outstanding, end of year	13	13	12

As authorized by the Emergency Economic Stabilization Act of 2008 (P.L. 110–343) and required by the Federal Credit Reform Act of 1990, as amended, this non-budgetary account records all cash flows to and from the Government resulting from equity purchases obligated in 2008 and beyond including modifications of equity purchases that resulted from obligations in any year. The amounts in this account are a means of financing and are not included in the budget totals.

Balance Sheet (in millions of dollars)

Identification code 020–4278–0–3–376		2020 actual	2021 actual
	ASSETS:		
	Federal assets:		
1101	Fund balances with Treasury	4	1
	Investments in U.S. securities:		
1106	Receivables, net	....	12
	Non-Federal assets:		
1201	Investments in non-Federal securities, net	....	....
1206	Receivables, net	2	....
	Net value of assets related to post-1991 direct loans receivable:		
1401	Direct loans receivable, gross	23	13
1405	Allowance for subsidy cost (–)	–7	–9
1499	Net present value of assets related to direct loans	16	4
1999	Total assets	22	17
	LIABILITIES:		
	Federal liabilities:		
2103	Debt	22	17
2105	Other	....	....
2999	Total liabilities	22	17
	NET POSITION:		
3300	Cumulative results of operations	....	....
4999	Total liabilities and net position	22	17

TROUBLED ASSET RELIEF PROGRAM, HOUSING PROGRAMS

Program and Financing (in millions of dollars)

Identification code 020–0136–0–1–604		2021 actual	2022 est.	2023 est.
	Budgetary resources:			
	Unobligated balance:			
1000	Unobligated balance brought forward, Oct 1	91	91	91
1031	Other balances not available	–114	....	....
1033	Recoveries of prior year paid obligations	114	....	....
1070	Unobligated balance (total)	91	91	91
1930	Total budgetary resources available	91	91	91
	Memorandum (non-add) entries:			
1941	Unexpired unobligated balance, end of year	91	91	91
	Change in obligated balance:			
	Unpaid obligations:			
3000	Unpaid obligations, brought forward, Oct 1	1,693	1,214	706
3020	Outlays (gross)	–479	–508	–456
3050	Unpaid obligations, end of year	1,214	706	250
	Memorandum (non-add) entries:			
3100	Obligated balance, start of year	1,693	1,214	706
3200	Obligated balance, end of year	1,214	706	250
	Budget authority and outlays, net:			
	Mandatory:			
	Outlays, gross:			
4101	Outlays from mandatory balances	479	508	456
	Offsets against gross budget authority and outlays:			
	Offsetting collections (collected) from:			
4123	Non-Federal sources	–114	....	....
	Additional offsets against gross budget authority only:			
4143	Recoveries of prior year paid obligations, unexpired accounts	114	....	....
4170	Outlays, net (mandatory)	365	508	456
4180	Budget authority, net (total)	....	....	....
4190	Outlays, net (total)	365	508	456
	Memorandum (non-add) entries:			
5103	Unexpired unavailable balance, SOY: Fulfilled purpose	13,069	13,183	12,509
5104	Unexpired unavailable balance, EOY: Fulfilled purpose	13,183	12,509	12,509

Summary of Loan Levels, Subsidy Budget Authority and Outlays by Program (in millions of dollars)

Identification code 020–0136–0–1–604		2021 actual	2022 est.	2023 est.
	Guaranteed loan reestimates:			
235001	FHA Refi Letter of Credit	–1	–1	....

Treasury's Home Affordable Modification Program (HAMP) offered mortgage modifications to homeowners at risk of foreclosure under the authority of sections 101 and 109 of the Emergency Economic Stabilization Act of 2008, as amended (EESA) (P.L. 110–343). HAMP closed to new applications on December 30, 2016, but incentive payments continue to be made on modifications entered into on or before December 1, 2017. Additionally, the Hardest Hit Fund has allocated $9.6 billion under EESA to State housing finance agencies in 18 States and the District of Columbia for foreclosure prevention programs. Funds under EESA also support a Federal Housing Administration (FHA) refinance program that helps homeowners refinance into a new FHA-insured loan if their existing mortgage holders agree to write down principal.

TROUBLED ASSET RELIEF PROGRAM, HOUSING PROGRAMS, LETTER OF CREDIT FINANCING ACCOUNT

Program and Financing (in millions of dollars)

Identification code 020–4329–0–3–371		2021 actual	2022 est.	2023 est.
	Obligations by program activity:			
	Credit program obligations:			
0742	Downward reestimates paid to receipt accounts	1	1	
0900	Total new obligations, unexpired accounts	1	1	
	Budgetary resources:			
	Unobligated balance:			
1000	Unobligated balance brought forward, Oct 1		2	1
1930	Total budgetary resources available		2	1
	Memorandum (non-add) entries:			
1941	Unexpired unobligated balance, end of year	1		
	Change in obligated balance:			
	Unpaid obligations:			
3000	Unpaid obligations, brought forward, Oct 1			1
3010	New obligations, unexpired accounts	1	1	
3020	Outlays (gross)	–1		
3050	Unpaid obligations, end of year		1	1
	Memorandum (non-add) entries:			
3100	Obligated balance, start of year			1
3200	Obligated balance, end of year		1	1
	Financing authority and disbursements, net:			
	Mandatory:			
	Financing disbursements:			
4110	Outlays, gross (total)	1		
4180	Budget authority, net (total)			
4190	Outlays, net (total)	1		

Status of Guaranteed Loans (in millions of dollars)

Identification code 020–4329–0–3–371		2021 actual	2022 est.	2023 est.
	Position with respect to appropriations act limitation on commitments:			
2111	Guaranteed loan commitments from current-year authority			
2150	Total guaranteed loan commitments			
	Cumulative balance of guaranteed loans outstanding:			
2210	Outstanding, start of year	135	111	111
2251	Repayments and prepayments	–23		
2263	Adjustments: Terminations for default that result in claim payments	–1		
2290	Outstanding, end of year	111	111	111
	Memorandum:			
2299	Guaranteed amount of guaranteed loans outstanding, end of year	55	45	45

Balance Sheet (in millions of dollars)

Identification code 020–4329–0–3–371		2020 actual	2021 actual
	ASSETS:		
1101	Federal assets: Fund balances with Treasury	3	1
1999	Total assets	3	1
	LIABILITIES:		
	Federal liabilities:		
2104	Resources payable to Treasury	2	
2105	Other		1
2204	Non-Federal liabilities: Liabilities for loan guarantees	1	
2999	Total liabilities	3	1
	NET POSITION:		
3300	Cumulative results of operations		

4999	Total liabilities and net position	3	1

SPECIAL INSPECTOR GENERAL FOR THE TROUBLED ASSET RELIEF PROGRAM

SALARIES AND EXPENSES

For necessary expenses of the Office of the Special Inspector General in carrying out the provisions of the Emergency Economic Stabilization Act of 2008 (Public Law 110–343), $9,000,000.

Note.—A full-year 2022 appropriation for this account was not enacted at the time the Budget was prepared; therefore, the Budget assumes this account is operating under the Continuing Appropriations Act, 2022 (Division A of Public Law 117–43, as amended). The amounts included for 2022 reflect the annualized level provided by the continuing resolution.

Program and Financing (in millions of dollars)

Identification code 020–0133–0–1–376		2021 actual	2022 est.	2023 est.
	Obligations by program activity:			
0001	Special Inspector General for the Troubled Asset Relief Program (Direct)	21	19	17
	Budgetary resources:			
	Unobligated balance:			
1000	Unobligated balance brought forward, Oct 1	15	13	13
	Budget authority:			
	Appropriations, discretionary:			
1100	Appropriation	19	19	9
1900	Budget authority (total)	19	19	9
1930	Total budgetary resources available	34	32	22
	Memorandum (non-add) entries:			
1941	Unexpired unobligated balance, end of year	13	13	5
	Change in obligated balance:			
	Unpaid obligations:			
3000	Unpaid obligations, brought forward, Oct 1	4	4	3
3010	New obligations, unexpired accounts	21	19	17
3011	Obligations ("upward adjustments"), expired accounts	1		
3020	Outlays (gross)	–21	–20	–19
3041	Recoveries of prior year unpaid obligations, expired	–1		
3050	Unpaid obligations, end of year	4	3	1
	Memorandum (non-add) entries:			
3100	Obligated balance, start of year	4	4	3
3200	Obligated balance, end of year	4	3	1
	Budget authority and outlays, net:			
	Discretionary:			
4000	Budget authority, gross	19	19	9
	Outlays, gross:			
4010	Outlays from new discretionary authority	18	15	7
4011	Outlays from discretionary balances	1	5	12
4020	Outlays, gross (total)	19	20	19
	Mandatory:			
	Outlays, gross:			
4101	Outlays from mandatory balances	2		
4180	Budget authority, net (total)	19	19	9
4190	Outlays, net (total)	21	20	19

The mission of the Office of the Special Inspector General for the Troubled Asset Relief Program (SIGTARP) is to prevent and detect fraud, waste, and abuse in the more than $442 billion in funds and programs from the Emergency Economic Stabilization Act of 2008 (EESA) (P.L. 110–343) and $2 billion in funds from the Consolidated Appropriations Act of 2016, and to promote economy, efficiency, effectiveness, and accountability in these economic stability programs. SIGTARP received an initial appropriation of $50 million in permanent, indefinite budget authority in EESA. The Public-Private Investment Program Improvement and Oversight Act of 2009 (12 U.S.C. 5231a) provided $15 million in supplemental funding. Since 2010, SIGTARP has received annual appropriations to fund its operations. The FY 2023 Budget requests $9 million, a reduction of 47 percent from the FY 2022 level of $17 million.

Departmental Offices—Continued
Federal Funds—Continued

SPECIAL INSPECTOR GENERAL FOR THE TROUBLED ASSET RELIEF PROGRAM—Continued

Object Classification (in millions of dollars)

Identification code 020–0133–0–1–376		2021 actual	2022 est.	2023 est.
	Direct obligations:			
	Personnel compensation:			
11.1	Full-time permanent	8	8	4
11.3	Other than full-time permanent	3	3	2
11.5	Other personnel compensation	1	2	1
11.9	Total personnel compensation	12	13	7
12.1	Civilian personnel benefits	3	2	2
23.1	Rental payments to GSA	1	1	1
25.3	Other goods and services from Federal sources	6	3	7
99.0	Direct obligations	22	19	17
99.5	Adjustment for rounding	–1		
99.9	Total new obligations, unexpired accounts	21	19	17

Employment Summary

Identification code 020–0133–0–1–376	2021 actual	2022 est.	2023 est.
1001 Direct civilian full-time equivalent employment	70	68	45

SMALL BUSINESS LENDING FUND PROGRAM ACCOUNT

Program and Financing (in millions of dollars)

Identification code 020–0141–0–1–376		2021 actual	2022 est.	2023 est.
	Obligations by program activity:			
	Credit program obligations:			
0709	Administrative expenses	2	2	2
0900	Total new obligations, unexpired accounts	2	2	2
	Budgetary resources:			
	Budget authority:			
	Appropriations, mandatory:			
1200	Appropriation	2	2	2
1930	Total budgetary resources available	2	2	2
	Change in obligated balance:			
	Unpaid obligations:			
3000	Unpaid obligations, brought forward, Oct 1	8	9	6
3010	New obligations, unexpired accounts	2	2	2
3020	Outlays (gross)	–1	–5	–4
3050	Unpaid obligations, end of year	9	6	4
	Memorandum (non-add) entries:			
3100	Obligated balance, start of year	8	9	6
3200	Obligated balance, end of year	9	6	4
	Budget authority and outlays, net:			
	Mandatory:			
4090	Budget authority, gross	2	2	2
	Outlays, gross:			
4100	Outlays from new mandatory authority	1	2	2
4101	Outlays from mandatory balances		3	2
4110	Outlays, gross (total)	1	5	4
4180	Budget authority, net (total)	2	2	2
4190	Outlays, net (total)	1	5	4

Summary of Loan Levels, Subsidy Budget Authority and Outlays by Program (in millions of dollars)

Identification code 020–0141–0–1–376	2021 actual	2022 est.	2023 est.
Direct loan reestimates:			
135001 Small Business Lending Fund Investments	–1	–5	
Administrative expense data:			
3510 Budget authority	2	2	2
3580 Outlays from balances		3	2
3590 Outlays from new authority	1	2	2

The Small Business Lending Fund (SBLF) was established by the Small Business Jobs Act of 2010 (P.L. 111–240) and is a dedicated investment fund that encourages lending to small businesses by providing capital to qualified community banks and community development loan funds (CDLFs). In total, the SBLF provided $4.0 billion to 281 community banks and 51 CDLFs in 2011. As of December 1, 2021, 327 institutions with aggregate investments of $3.95 billion have fully redeemed their SBLF investments and exited the program. For institutions that still participate in the program, CDLF securities matured by 2021. As of September 30, 2021, only one CDLF security remained outstanding, to a CDLF in bankruptcy. Community bank participants were generally expected to end their participation in 2021, although because Treasury holds perpetual preferred shares in these banks, they are not required to redeem. As of September 30, 2021, two operating bank participants remained in the program and have yet to decide when to purchase their outstanding perpetual preferred shares from Treasury. A third participant that has remained outstanding is in bankruptcy.

Object Classification (in millions of dollars)

Identification code 020–0141–0–1–376		2021 actual	2022 est.	2023 est.
25.3	Direct obligations: Other goods and services from Federal sources	1	1	1
99.0	Direct obligations	1	1	1
99.5	Adjustment for rounding	1	1	1
99.9	Total new obligations, unexpired accounts	2	2	2

Employment Summary

Identification code 020–0141–0–1–376	2021 actual	2022 est.	2023 est.
1001 Direct civilian full-time equivalent employment	2	2	2

SMALL BUSINESS LENDING FUND FINANCING ACCOUNT

Program and Financing (in millions of dollars)

Identification code 020–4349–0–3–376		2021 actual	2022 est.	2023 est.
	Obligations by program activity:			
	Credit program obligations:			
0713	Payment of interest to Treasury	1	1	
0742	Downward reestimates paid to receipt accounts	1	4	
0743	Interest on downward reestimates		1	
0900	Total new obligations, unexpired accounts	2	6	
	Budgetary resources:			
	Unobligated balance:			
1000	Unobligated balance brought forward, Oct 1	2	2	3
1023	Unobligated balances applied to repay debt	–2	–2	
1070	Unobligated balance (total)			3
	Financing authority:			
	Borrowing authority, mandatory:			
1400	Borrowing authority	1	1	
	Spending authority from offsetting collections, mandatory:			
1800	Collected	15	8	6
1825	Spending authority from offsetting collections applied to repay debt	–12		
1850	Spending auth from offsetting collections, mand (total)	3	8	6
1900	Budget authority (total)	4	9	6
1930	Total budgetary resources available	4	9	9
	Memorandum (non-add) entries:			
1941	Unexpired unobligated balance, end of year	2	3	9
	Change in obligated balance:			
	Unpaid obligations:			
3000	Unpaid obligations, brought forward, Oct 1			6
3010	New obligations, unexpired accounts	2	6	
3020	Outlays (gross)	–2		
3050	Unpaid obligations, end of year		6	6
	Memorandum (non-add) entries:			
3100	Obligated balance, start of year			6
3200	Obligated balance, end of year		6	6

DEPARTMENT OF THE TREASURY

Departmental Offices—Continued
Federal Funds—Continued   1001

	Financing authority and disbursements, net: Mandatory:	2021 actual	2022 est.	2023 est.
4090	Budget authority, gross	4	9	6
	Financing disbursements:			
4110	Outlays, gross (total)	2		
	Offsets against gross financing authority and disbursements: Offsetting collections (collected) from:			
4123	Non-Federal sources - Principal	–11	–5	–4
4123	Non-Federal sources - Dividends	–4	–3	–2
4130	Offsets against gross budget authority and outlays (total)	–15	–8	–6
4160	Budget authority, net (mandatory)	–11	1	
4170	Outlays, net (mandatory)	–13	–8	–6
4180	Budget authority, net (total)	–11	1	
4190	Outlays, net (total)	–13	–8	–6

Status of Direct Loans (in millions of dollars)

Identification code 020–4349–0–3–376		2021 actual	2022 est.	2023 est.
	Cumulative balance of direct loans outstanding:			
1210	Outstanding, start of year	81	70	65
1251	Repayments: Repayments and prepayments	–11	–5	–4
1290	Outstanding, end of year	70	65	61

Balance Sheet (in millions of dollars)

Identification code 020–4349–0–3–376		2020 actual	2021 actual
	ASSETS: Federal assets:		
1101	Fund balances with Treasury	2	3
	Investments in U.S. securities:		
1106	Receivables, net		
	Net value of assets related to post-1991 direct loans receivable:		
1401	Direct loans receivable, gross	81	70
1405	Allowance for subsidy cost (-)	–36	–39
1499	Net present value of assets related to direct loans	45	31
1999	Total assets	47	34
	LIABILITIES:		
2103	Federal liabilities: Debt	47	34
	NET POSITION:		
3300	Cumulative results of operations		
4999	Total liabilities and net position	47	34

SOCIAL IMPACT DEMONSTRATION PROJECTS

Program and Financing (in millions of dollars)

Identification code 020–0146–0–1–506		2021 actual	2022 est.	2023 est.
	Obligations by program activity:			
0001	Administrative Costs	1	2	2
0002	Social Impact Demonstration Projects	8	39	37
0900	Total new obligations, unexpired accounts	9	41	39
	Budgetary resources: Unobligated balance:			
1000	Unobligated balance brought forward, Oct 1	97	88	47
1930	Total budgetary resources available	97	88	47
	Memorandum (non-add) entries:			
1941	Unexpired unobligated balance, end of year	88	47	8
	Change in obligated balance: Unpaid obligations:			
3000	Unpaid obligations, brought forward, Oct 1		8	41
3010	New obligations, unexpired accounts	9	41	39
3020	Outlays (gross)	–1	–8	–13
3050	Unpaid obligations, end of year	8	41	67
	Memorandum (non-add) entries:			
3100	Obligated balance, start of year		8	41
3200	Obligated balance, end of year	8	41	67
	Budget authority and outlays, net: Mandatory:			
	Outlays, gross:			
4101	Outlays from mandatory balances	1	8	13
4180	Budget authority, net (total)			
4190	Outlays, net (total)	1	8	13

The Social Impact Partnerships to Pay for Results Act (SIPPRA) was included as part of the Bipartisan Budget Act of 2018 (P.L. 115–123). SIPPRA created a ten-year $100 million fund to support social impact partnership projects by State and local governments to support new and innovative ways to solve entrenched social problems. The program funds social programs at the State or local level that achieve demonstrable, measurable, and scalable results, by making payment of funds contingent on positive outcomes.

Object Classification (in millions of dollars)

Identification code 020–0146–0–1–506		2021 actual	2022 est.	2023 est.
	Direct obligations:			
11.1	Personnel compensation: Full-time permanent		1	1
25.1	Advisory and assistance services		1	11
41.0	Grants, subsidies, and contributions	8	39	27
99.0	Direct obligations	8	41	39
99.5	Adjustment for rounding	1		
99.9	Total new obligations, unexpired accounts	9	41	39

Employment Summary

Identification code 020–0146–0–1–506		2021 actual	2022 est.	2023 est.
1001	Direct civilian full-time equivalent employment	1	5	5

GSE PREFERRED STOCK PURCHASE AGREEMENTS

Program and Financing (in millions of dollars)

Identification code 020–0125–0–1–371		2021 actual	2022 est.	2023 est.
	Budgetary resources: Unobligated balance:			
1000	Unobligated balance brought forward, Oct 1	254,051	254,051	254,051
1930	Total budgetary resources available	254,051	254,051	254,051
	Memorandum (non-add) entries:			
1941	Unexpired unobligated balance, end of year	254,051	254,051	254,051
4180	Budget authority, net (total)			
4190	Outlays, net (total)			

In 2008, under temporary authority granted by section 1117 of the Housing and Economic Recovery Act of 2008 (P.L. 110–289), Treasury entered into agreements with Fannie Mae and Freddie Mac (the GSEs) to purchase senior preferred stock of each GSE and to provide up to $100 billion when needed to ensure that each company maintains a positive net worth. In May 2009, Treasury increased the Senior Preferred Stock Purchase Agreement (PSPA) funding commitment caps to $200 billion for each GSE, and in December 2009 Treasury modified the funding commitment caps in the PSPAs to be the greater of $200 billion or $200 billion plus cumulative net worth deficits experienced during 2010–2012, less any surplus remaining as of December 31, 2012. Based on the financial results reported by each GSE as of December 31, 2012, and under the terms of the PSPAs, the combined cumulative funding commitment cap for Fannie Mae and Freddie Mac was set at $445.5 billion. Treasury's authority to purchase obligations or other securities of the GSEs or to increase the funding commitment expired on December 31, 2009. Under the PSPAs, Treasury has maintained the solvency of the GSEs by providing $191.5 billion of investment to the GSEs. For additional discussion of the GSEs, please see the *Analytical Perspectives* volume of the Budget.

Departmental Offices—Continued
Federal Funds—Continued

GSE MORTGAGE-BACKED SECURITIES PURCHASE PROGRAM ACCOUNT

Program and Financing (in millions of dollars)

Identification code 020–0126–0–1–371	2021 actual	2022 est.	2023 est.
Obligations by program activity:			
0010 Financial Agent Services	1	1	1
0900 Total new obligations, unexpired accounts (object class 25.2)	1	1	1
Budgetary resources:			
Budget authority:			
Appropriations, mandatory:			
1221 Appropriations transferred from other acct [020–1802]	1	1	1
1930 Total budgetary resources available	1	1	1
Change in obligated balance:			
Unpaid obligations:			
3010 New obligations, unexpired accounts	1	1	1
3020 Outlays (gross)	–1	–1	–1
Budget authority and outlays, net:			
Mandatory:			
4090 Budget authority, gross	1	1	1
Outlays, gross:			
4100 Outlays from new mandatory authority	1	1	1
4180 Budget authority, net (total)	1	1	1
4190 Outlays, net (total)	1	1	1

Summary of Loan Levels, Subsidy Budget Authority and Outlays by Program (in millions of dollars)

Identification code 020–0126–0–1–371	2021 actual	2022 est.	2023 est.
Direct loan reestimates:			
135002 New Issue Bond Program SF	–122	–90	
135003 New Issue Bond Program MF	–51	–50	
135999 Total direct loan reestimates	–173	–140	

The authority for the three programs displayed in this account: Fannie Mae and Freddie Mac's mortgage-backed securities purchase program, which purchased and then liquidated mortgage backed securities; the Temporary Credit and Liquidity Program, which provided liquidity to State housing financing agencies (HFAs); and the New Issue Bond Program, which purchased securities backed by new HFA housing bonds was provided in section 1117 of the Housing and Economic Recovery Act of 2008 (P.L. 110–289). As required by the Federal Credit Reform Act of 1990 as amended, this account records the subsidy costs associated with these programs, which are treated as direct loans for budget execution. The subsidy amounts are estimated on a present value basis.

STATE HFA DIRECT LOAN FINANCING ACCOUNT

Program and Financing (in millions of dollars)

Identification code 020–4298–0–3–371	2021 actual	2022 est.	2023 est.
Obligations by program activity:			
Credit program obligations:			
0713 Payment of interest to Treasury	79	61	61
0742 Downward reestimates paid to receipt accounts	114	88	
0743 Interest on downward reestimates	59	52	
0900 Total new obligations, unexpired accounts	252	201	61
Budgetary resources:			
Unobligated balance:			
1000 Unobligated balance brought forward, Oct 1	137	54	
1023 Unobligated balances applied to repay debt	–137		
1070 Unobligated balance (total)		54	
Financing authority:			
Borrowing authority, mandatory:			
1400 Borrowing authority	173	147	57
Spending authority from offsetting collections, mandatory:			
1800 Collected	1,196	85	83
1825 Spending authority from offsetting collections applied to repay debt	–1,063	–85	–21
1850 Spending auth from offsetting collections, mand (total)	133		62
1900 Budget authority (total)	306	147	119
1930 Total budgetary resources available	306	201	119
Memorandum (non-add) entries:			
1941 Unexpired unobligated balance, end of year	54		58
Change in obligated balance:			
Unpaid obligations:			
3000 Unpaid obligations, brought forward, Oct 1			51
3010 New obligations, unexpired accounts	252	201	61
3020 Outlays (gross)	–252	–150	–61
3050 Unpaid obligations, end of year		51	51
Memorandum (non-add) entries:			
3100 Obligated balance, start of year			51
3200 Obligated balance, end of year		51	51
Financing authority and disbursements, net:			
Mandatory:			
4090 Budget authority, gross	306	147	119
Financing disbursements:			
4110 Outlays, gross (total)	252	150	61
Offsets against gross financing authority and disbursements:			
Offsetting collections (collected) from:			
4122 Interest on uninvested funds	–12	–4	–4
4123 Non-Federal sources - Interest	–61	–45	–44
4123 Non-Federal sources - Principal	–1,123	–36	–35
4130 Offsets against gross budget authority and outlays (total)	–1,196	–85	–83
4160 Budget authority, net (mandatory)	–890	62	36
4170 Outlays, net (mandatory)	–944	65	–22
4180 Budget authority, net (total)	–890	62	36
4190 Outlays, net (total)	–944	65	–22

Status of Direct Loans (in millions of dollars)

Identification code 020–4298–0–3–371	2021 actual	2022 est.	2023 est.
Cumulative balance of direct loans outstanding:			
1210 Outstanding, start of year	2,789	1,667	1,630
1251 Repayments: Repayments and prepayments	–1,122	–37	–35
1290 Outstanding, end of year	1,667	1,630	1,595

Balance Sheet (in millions of dollars)

Identification code 020–4298–0–3–371	2020 actual	2021 actual
ASSETS:		
1101 Federal assets: Fund balances with Treasury	137	54
Net value of assets related to post-1991 direct loans receivable:		
1401 Direct loans receivable, gross	2,789	1,667
1405 Allowance for subsidy cost (-)	–396	–249
1499 Net present value of assets related to direct loans	2,393	1,418
1999 Total assets	2,530	1,472
LIABILITIES:		
Federal liabilities:		
2103 Debt	2,357	1,331
2105 Other	173	141
2999 Total liabilities	2,530	1,472
NET POSITION:		
3300 Cumulative results of operations		
4999 Total liabilities and net position	2,530	1,472

Trust Funds

CAPITAL MAGNET FUND, COMMUNITY DEVELOPMENT FINANCIAL INSTITUTIONS

Special and Trust Fund Receipts (in millions of dollars)

Identification code 020–8524–0–7–451	2021 actual	2022 est.	2023 est.
0100 Balance, start of year	10	22	21
Receipts:			
Current law:			
1130 Affordable Housing Allocation, Capital Magnet Fund	383	367	212
2000 Total: Balances and receipts	393	389	233

DEPARTMENT OF THE TREASURY

	Appropriations: Current law:	2021 actual	2022 est.	2023 est.
2101	Capital Magnet Fund, Community Development Financial Institutions	−383	−367	−212
2103	Capital Magnet Fund, Community Development Financial Institutions	−10	−22	−21
2132	Capital Magnet Fund, Community Development Financial Institutions	22	21	12
2199	Total current law appropriations	−371	−368	−221
2999	Total appropriations	−371	−368	−221
5099	Balance, end of year	22	21	12

Program and Financing (in millions of dollars)

Identification code 020–8524–0–7–451		2021 actual	2022 est.	2023 est.
	Obligations by program activity:			
0001	CDFI Allocations	175	380	364
0002	CMF Administration	2	3	3
0900	Total new obligations, unexpired accounts	177	383	367
	Budgetary resources:			
	Unobligated balance:			
1000	Unobligated balance brought forward, Oct 1	173	367	352
	Budget authority:			
	Appropriations, mandatory:			
1201	Appropriation (special or trust fund)	383	367	212
1203	Appropriation (previously unavailable)(special or trust)	10	22	21
1232	Appropriations and/or unobligated balance of appropriations temporarily reduced	−22	−21	−12
1260	Appropriations, mandatory (total)	371	368	221
1930	Total budgetary resources available	544	735	573
	Memorandum (non-add) entries:			
1941	Unexpired unobligated balance, end of year	367	352	206
	Change in obligated balance:			
	Unpaid obligations:			
3000	Unpaid obligations, brought forward, Oct 1	8	13	74
3010	New obligations, unexpired accounts	177	383	367
3020	Outlays (gross)	−172	−322	−353
3050	Unpaid obligations, end of year	13	74	88
	Memorandum (non-add) entries:			
3100	Obligated balance, start of year	8	13	74
3200	Obligated balance, end of year	13	74	88
	Budget authority and outlays, net:			
	Mandatory:			
4090	Budget authority, gross	371	368	221
	Outlays, gross:			
4100	Outlays from new mandatory authority	167		
4101	Outlays from mandatory balances	5	322	353
4110	Outlays, gross (total)	172	322	353
4180	Budget authority, net (total)	371	368	221
4190	Outlays, net (total)	172	322	353

Established by the Housing and Economic Recovery Act of 2008 (HERA) (P.L. 110–289), the Capital Magnet Fund (CMF) awards grants to CDFIs and qualified non-profit housing organizations to finance affordable housing activities, as well as related economic development activities and community service facilities. Organizations that receive Capital Magnet Fund awards are required to produce housing and community development investments at least ten times the size of the award amount. Funding is provided by the Government-Sponsored Enterprises, Fannie Mae and Freddie Mac, which are required to set aside an amount equal to 4.2 basis points of each dollar of the unpaid principal balance of their total new business purchases and to allocate and transfer those funds to CMF and the Housing Trust Fund.

Object Classification (in millions of dollars)

Identification code 020–8524–0–7–451		2021 actual	2022 est.	2023 est.
	Direct obligations:			
11.1	Personnel compensation: Full-time permanent	1	1	2
31.0	Equipment	1	2	1
41.0	Grants, subsidies, and contributions	175	380	364

Financial Crimes Enforcement Network
Federal Funds

		2021 actual	2022 est.	2023 est.
99.9	Total new obligations, unexpired accounts	177	383	367

Employment Summary

Identification code 020–8524–0–7–451	2021 actual	2022 est.	2023 est.
1001 Direct civilian full-time equivalent employment	4	6	9

GIFTS AND BEQUESTS

Program and Financing (in millions of dollars)

Identification code 020–8790–0–7–803		2021 actual	2022 est.	2023 est.
	Budgetary resources:			
	Unobligated balance:			
1000	Unobligated balance brought forward, Oct 1	2	2	2
1930	Total budgetary resources available	2	2	2
	Memorandum (non-add) entries:			
1941	Unexpired unobligated balance, end of year	2	2	2
4180	Budget authority, net (total)			
4190	Outlays, net (total)			
	Memorandum (non-add) entries:			
5000	Total investments, SOY: Federal securities: Par value	1	1	1
5001	Total investments, EOY: Federal securities: Par value	1	1	1

This account was established pursuant to 31 U.S.C. 321 to receive gifts and bequests to the Department. These funds support the restoration of the Treasury building and historical collection of art, furniture, and artifacts owned by the Department. The fund is also used as an endowment for Treasury's restored rooms.

FINANCIAL CRIMES ENFORCEMENT NETWORK
Federal Funds

SALARIES AND EXPENSES

For necessary expenses of the Financial Crimes Enforcement Network, including hire of passenger motor vehicles; travel and training expenses of non-Federal and foreign government personnel to attend meetings and training concerned with domestic and foreign financial intelligence activities, law enforcement, and financial regulation; services authorized by 5 U.S.C. 3109; not to exceed $45,000 for official reception and representation expenses; and for assistance to Federal law enforcement agencies, with or without reimbursement, $210,330,000, of which not to exceed $94,600,000 shall remain available until September 30, 2025 for information technology and to implement Division F of the William M. (Mac) Thornberry National Defense Authorization Act for Fiscal Year 2021 (Public Law 116–283).

Note.—A full-year 2022 appropriation for this account was not enacted at the time the Budget was prepared; therefore, the Budget assumes this account is operating under the Continuing Appropriations Act, 2022 (Division A of Public Law 117–43, as amended). The amounts included for 2022 reflect the annualized level provided by the continuing resolution.

Program and Financing (in millions of dollars)

Identification code 020–0173–0–1–751		2021 actual	2022 est.	2023 est.
	Obligations by program activity:			
0001	BSA administration and Analysis	143	167	216
0801	Reimbursable program activity	2	4	4
0900	Total new obligations, unexpired accounts	145	171	220
	Budgetary resources:			
	Unobligated balance:			
1000	Unobligated balance brought forward, Oct 1	29	20	3
	Budget authority:			
	Appropriations, discretionary:			
1100	Appropriation	127	127	210
	Spending authority from offsetting collections, discretionary:			
1700	Collected	1	27	10
1701	Change in uncollected payments, Federal sources	8		
1750	Spending auth from offsetting collections, disc (total)	9	27	10
1900	Budget authority (total)	136	154	220
1930	Total budgetary resources available	165	174	223

Financial Crimes Enforcement Network—Continued
Federal Funds—Continued

SALARIES AND EXPENSES—Continued

Program and Financing—Continued

Identification code 020–0173–0–1–751	2021 actual	2022 est.	2023 est.
Memorandum (non-add) entries:			
1941 Unexpired unobligated balance, end of year	20	3	3
Change in obligated balance:			
Unpaid obligations:			
3000 Unpaid obligations, brought forward, Oct 1	58	62	81
3010 New obligations, unexpired accounts	145	171	220
3020 Outlays (gross)	–138	–152	–143
3041 Recoveries of prior year unpaid obligations, expired	–3		
3050 Unpaid obligations, end of year	62	81	158
Uncollected payments:			
3060 Uncollected pymts, Fed sources, brought forward, Oct 1	–1	–8	–8
3070 Change in uncollected pymts, Fed sources, unexpired	–8		
3071 Change in uncollected pymts, Fed sources, expired	1		
3090 Uncollected pymts, Fed sources, end of year	–8	–8	–8
Memorandum (non-add) entries:			
3100 Obligated balance, start of year	57	54	73
3200 Obligated balance, end of year	54	73	150
Budget authority and outlays, net:			
Discretionary:			
4000 Budget authority, gross	136	154	220
Outlays, gross:			
4010 Outlays from new discretionary authority	78	104	101
4011 Outlays from discretionary balances	60	48	42
4020 Outlays, gross (total)	138	152	143
Offsets against gross budget authority and outlays:			
Offsetting collections (collected) from:			
4030 Federal sources	–2	–27	–10
Additional offsets against gross budget authority only:			
4050 Change in uncollected pymts, Fed sources, unexpired	–8		
4052 Offsetting collections credited to expired accounts	1		
4060 Additional offsets against budget authority only (total)	–7		
4070 Budget authority, net (discretionary)	127	127	210
4080 Outlays, net (discretionary)	136	125	133
4180 Budget authority, net (total)	127	127	210
4190 Outlays, net (total)	136	125	133

The Federal Crimes Enforcement Network (FinCEN) is the primary Federal regulator for the Bank Secrecy Act (BSA) and is responsible for the regulations and implementation of the non-public database of ownership and/or effective control of firms (i.e. beneficial ownership) pursuant to the Corporate Transparency Act (CTA). In this role, FinCEN safeguards the financial system from illicit use, combats money laundering, and promotes national security through the strategic use of financial authorities and the collection, analysis, and dissemination of financial intelligence. FinCEN carries out its mission by: 1) developing and issuing regulations under the BSA; 2) enforcing compliance with the BSA in partnership with regulatory partners and law enforcement, including responsibilities under the Anti-Money Laundering Act; 3) receiving and maintaining certain types of beneficial ownership and financial transaction data; 4) analyzing and disseminating financial intelligence for law enforcement purposes; and 5) serving as the U.S. Financial Intelligence Unit (FIU) and maintaining a network of information sharing with over 150 FIU partner countries.

Object Classification (in millions of dollars)

Identification code 020–0173–0–1–751	2021 actual	2022 est.	2023 est.
Direct obligations:			
Personnel compensation:			
11.1 Full-time permanent	37	41	66
11.5 Other personnel compensation	1	1	1
11.9 Total personnel compensation	38	42	67
12.1 Civilian personnel benefits	12	14	22
21.0 Travel and transportation of persons	1		1
23.1 Rental payments to GSA	5	4	4
23.2 Rental payments to others			1
23.3 Communications, utilities, and miscellaneous charges	3	3	3
25.1 Advisory and assistance services	2	4	8
25.2 Other services from non-Federal sources	54	74	68
25.3 Other goods and services from Federal sources	12	14	21
25.7 Operation and maintenance of equipment	8	9	9
26.0 Supplies and materials			2
31.0 Equipment	8	4	10
99.0 Direct obligations	143	168	216
99.0 Reimbursable obligations	2	4	4
99.5 Adjustment for rounding		–1	
99.9 Total new obligations, unexpired accounts	145	171	220

Employment Summary

Identification code 020–0173–0–1–751	2021 actual	2022 est.	2023 est.
1001 Direct civilian full-time equivalent employment	269	285	420
2001 Reimbursable civilian full-time equivalent employment	2	3	3

FISCAL SERVICE

Federal Funds

SALARIES AND EXPENSES

For necessary expenses of operations of the Bureau of the Fiscal Service, $372,485,000; of which not to exceed $8,000,000, to remain available until September 30, 2025, is for information systems modernization initiatives; and of which $5,000 shall be available for official reception and representation expenses.

In addition, $165,000, to be derived from the Oil Spill Liability Trust Fund to reimburse administrative and personnel expenses for financial management of the Fund, as authorized by section 1012 of Public Law 101–380.

Note.—A full-year 2022 appropriation for this account was not enacted at the time the Budget was prepared; therefore, the Budget assumes this account is operating under the Continuing Appropriations Act, 2022 (Division A of Public Law 117–43, as amended). The amounts included for 2022 reflect the annualized level provided by the continuing resolution.

Special and Trust Fund Receipts (in millions of dollars)

Identification code 020–0520–0–1–803	2021 actual	2022 est.	2023 est.
0100 Balance, start of year	3		
0198 Reconciliation adjustment	–3		
0199 Balance, start of year			
2000 Total: Balances and receipts			
5099 Balance, end of year			

Program and Financing (in millions of dollars)

Identification code 020–0520–0–1–803	2021 actual	2022 est.	2023 est.
Obligations by program activity:			
0001 Collections	41	44	48
0005 Accounting and Reporting	97	97	98
0006 Payments	145	144	132
0007 Retail Securities Services	62	66	68
0009 Wholesale Securities Services	24	25	26
0010 Matured Unreedeemed Debt	5	26	19
0799 Total direct obligations	374	402	391
0801 Salaries and Expenses (Reimbursable)	225	209	185
0900 Total new obligations, unexpired accounts	599	611	576
Budgetary resources:			
Unobligated balance:			
1000 Unobligated balance brought forward, Oct 1	121	74	43
1001 Discretionary unobligated balance brought fwd, Oct 1	121		
1010 Unobligated balance transfer to other accts [020–5445]	–49		
1012 Unobligated balance transfers between expired and unexpired accounts	1		
1021 Recoveries of prior year unpaid obligations	1		
1033 Recoveries of prior year paid obligations	3		
1070 Unobligated balance (total)	77	74	43
Budget authority:			
Appropriations, discretionary:			
1100 Appropriation	371	371	372
Appropriations, mandatory:			
1200 Appropriation—American Rescue Plan	23		
Spending authority from offsetting collections, discretionary:			
1700 Collected	228	209	185

DEPARTMENT OF THE TREASURY

Fiscal Service—Continued
Federal Funds—Continued

1005

		2021 actual	2022 est.	2023 est.
1701	Change in uncollected payments, Federal sources	−25		
1750	Spending auth from offsetting collections, disc (total)	203	209	185
1900	Budget authority (total)	597	580	557
1930	Total budgetary resources available	674	654	600
	Memorandum (non-add) entries:			
1940	Unobligated balance expiring	−1		
1941	Unexpired unobligated balance, end of year	74	43	24
	Change in obligated balance:			
	Unpaid obligations:			
3000	Unpaid obligations, brought forward, Oct 1	65	69	83
3010	New obligations, unexpired accounts	599	611	576
3011	Obligations ("upward adjustments"), expired accounts	3		
3020	Outlays (gross)	−592	−597	−569
3040	Recoveries of prior year unpaid obligations, unexpired	−1		
3041	Recoveries of prior year unpaid obligations, expired	−5		
3050	Unpaid obligations, end of year	69	83	90
	Uncollected payments:			
3060	Uncollected pymts, Fed sources, brought forward, Oct 1	−43	−10	−10
3070	Change in uncollected pymts, Fed sources, unexpired	25		
3071	Change in uncollected pymts, Fed sources, expired	8		
3090	Uncollected pymts, Fed sources, end of year	−10	−10	−10
	Memorandum (non-add) entries:			
3100	Obligated balance, start of year	22	59	73
3200	Obligated balance, end of year	59	73	80
	Budget authority and outlays, net:			
	Discretionary:			
4000	Budget authority, gross	574	580	557
	Outlays, gross:			
4010	Outlays from new discretionary authority	520	519	495
4011	Outlays from discretionary balances	69	74	74
4020	Outlays, gross (total)	589	593	569
	Offsets against gross budget authority and outlays:			
	Offsetting collections (collected) from:			
4030	Federal sources	−239	−209	−185
4040	Offsets against gross budget authority and outlays (total)	−239	−209	−185
	Additional offsets against gross budget authority only:			
4050	Change in uncollected pymts, Fed sources, unexpired	25		
4052	Offsetting collections credited to expired accounts	8		
4053	Recoveries of prior year paid obligations, unexpired accounts	3		
4060	Additional offsets against budget authority only (total)	36		
4070	Budget authority, net (discretionary)	371	371	372
4080	Outlays, net (discretionary)	350	384	384
	Mandatory:			
4090	Budget authority, gross	23		
	Outlays, gross:			
4100	Outlays from new mandatory authority	2		
4101	Outlays from mandatory balances	1	4	
4110	Outlays, gross (total)	3	4	
4180	Budget authority, net (total)	394	371	372
4190	Outlays, net (total)	353	388	384

The mission of the Fiscal Service is to promote the financial integrity and operational efficiency of the U.S. Government through exceptional accounting, financing, collections, payments, and shared services. The Fiscal Service engages in efforts to streamline the Government's audit processes, and to reduce intra-governmental accounting differences that stand in the way of a clean audit opinion on the Financial Report of the U.S. Government.

The Budget ensures the viability of the Government's National Financial Critical Infrastructure (NFCI) that finances Federal operations, collects revenue, disburses payments, and reports on the Government's financial position. Included in the Budget are resources to improve the accuracy and availability of financial information, implement new, innovative financial practices, strengthen the resiliency of our infrastructure, and enhance the customer value and experience. Because of Fiscal Service's central role in Government-wide financial operations, the Budget supports Treasury's leadership in transforming Federal financial management to become more efficient, more accurate and deliver better service to citizens.

Object Classification (in millions of dollars)

Identification code 020–0520–0–1–803	2021 actual	2022 est.	2023 est.
Direct obligations:			
Personnel compensation:			
11.1 Full-time permanent	157	158	165
11.5 Other personnel compensation	7	5	5
11.9 Total personnel compensation	164	163	170
12.1 Civilian personnel benefits	60	64	67
21.0 Travel and transportation of persons		1	1
23.1 Rental payments to GSA	21	22	24
23.3 Communications, utilities, and miscellaneous charges	9	11	12
25.1 Advisory and assistance services	25	14	14
25.2 Other services from non-Federal sources	23	44	35
25.3 Other goods and services from Federal sources	48	65	61
25.4 Operation and maintenance of facilities	2	2	2
25.7 Operation and maintenance of equipment	4	3	3
26.0 Supplies and materials	7	11	2
31.0 Equipment	10	2	
32.0 Land and structures	1		
99.0 Direct obligations	374	402	391
99.0 Reimbursable obligations	225	209	185
99.9 Total new obligations, unexpired accounts	599	611	576

Employment Summary

Identification code 020–0520–0–1–803	2021 actual	2022 est.	2023 est.
1001 Direct civilian full-time equivalent employment	1,590	1,559	1,561
2001 Reimbursable civilian full-time equivalent employment	15	9	9

DEBT COLLECTION FUND

Special and Trust Fund Receipts (in millions of dollars)

Identification code 020–5445–0–2–803	2021 actual	2022 est.	2023 est.
0100 Balance, start of year		1	1
0198 Reconciliation adjustment	2		
0199 Balance, start of year	2	1	1
Receipts:			
Current law:			
1130 Non Federal Fee, Debt Collection Fund	121	153	163
1140 Federal Fee, Debt Collection Fund	27	34	36
1199 Total current law receipts	148	187	199
Proposed:			
1230 Non Federal Fee, Debt Collection Fund			22
1999 Total receipts	148	187	221
2000 Total: Balances and receipts	150	188	222
Appropriations:			
Current law:			
2101 Debt Collection Fund	−148	−187	−199
2103 Debt Collection Fund	−2	−1	−1
2132 Debt Collection Fund	1	1	1
2199 Total current law appropriations	−149	−187	−199
Proposed:			
2201 Debt Collection Fund			−22
2999 Total appropriations	−149	−187	−221
5099 Balance, end of year	1	1	1

Program and Financing (in millions of dollars)

Identification code 020–5445–0–2–803	2021 actual	2022 est.	2023 est.
Obligations by program activity:			
0001 Direct program activity	166	187	199
Budgetary resources:			
Unobligated balance:			
1000 Unobligated balance brought forward, Oct 1	101	146	146
1011 Unobligated balance transfer from other acct [020–0520]	49		
1012 Unobligated balance transfers between expired and unexpired accounts	10		
1021 Recoveries of prior year unpaid obligations	3		

Fiscal Service—Continued
Federal Funds—Continued

DEBT COLLECTION FUND—Continued

Program and Financing—Continued

Identification code 020–5445–0–2–803	2021 actual	2022 est.	2023 est.
1070 Unobligated balance (total)	163	146	146
Budget authority:			
Appropriations, mandatory:			
1201 Appropriation (special or trust fund)	148	187	199
1203 Appropriation (previously unavailable)(special or trust)	2	1	1
1232 Appropriations and/or unobligated balance of appropriations temporarily reduced	–1	–1	–1
1260 Appropriations, mandatory (total)	149	187	199
1930 Total budgetary resources available	312	333	345
Memorandum (non-add) entries:			
1941 Unexpired unobligated balance, end of year	146	146	146
Special and non-revolving trust funds:			
1952 Expired unobligated balance, start of year	10		
Change in obligated balance:			
Unpaid obligations:			
3000 Unpaid obligations, brought forward, Oct 1	18	11	11
3010 New obligations, unexpired accounts	166	187	199
3020 Outlays (gross)	–170	–187	–192
3040 Recoveries of prior year unpaid obligations, unexpired	–3		
3050 Unpaid obligations, end of year	11	11	18
Memorandum (non-add) entries:			
3100 Obligated balance, start of year	18	11	11
3200 Obligated balance, end of year	11	11	18
Budget authority and outlays, net:			
Mandatory:			
4090 Budget authority, gross	149	187	199
Outlays, gross:			
4100 Outlays from new mandatory authority		68	73
4101 Outlays from mandatory balances	170	119	119
4110 Outlays, gross (total)	170	187	192
4180 Budget authority, net (total)	149	187	199
4190 Outlays, net (total)	170	187	192

Summary of Budget Authority and Outlays (in millions of dollars)

	2021 actual	2022 est.	2023 est.
Enacted/requested:			
Budget Authority	149	187	199
Outlays	170	187	192
Legislative proposal, subject to PAYGO:			
Budget Authority			22
Outlays			22
Total:			
Budget Authority	149	187	221
Outlays	170	187	214

The Debt Collection Fund was authorized in the Debt Collection Improvement Act of 1996 to hold debt collection fee revenue available to cover costs associated with the implementation and operation for such activities, including centralized debt collections services Government-wide, managing the Government's delinquent debt portfolio, and collecting delinquent debts owed to the United States. Delinquent debts are collected in several ways, including offsetting Federal payments, sending demand letters to debtors, entering into payment agreements, withholding wages administratively, referring debts to the Department of Justice for action, reporting credit to bureaus, and contracting for services of private collection agencies.

Object Classification (in millions of dollars)

Identification code 020–5445–0–2–803	2021 actual	2022 est.	2023 est.
Direct obligations:			
Personnel compensation:			
11.1 Full-time permanent	33	32	36
11.5 Other personnel compensation	1	1	1
11.9 Total personnel compensation	34	33	37
12.1 Civilian personnel benefits	13	12	13
21.0 Travel and transportation of persons			1
23.1 Rental payments to GSA	4	4	4
23.3 Communications, utilities, and miscellaneous charges	2	4	5
25.1 Advisory and assistance services	29	38	44
25.2 Other services from non-Federal sources	3	3	3
25.3 Other goods and services from Federal sources	79	92	91
25.7 Operation and maintenance of equipment	1	1	1
31.0 Equipment	1		
99.9 Total new obligations, unexpired accounts	166	187	199

Employment Summary

Identification code 020–5445–0–2–803	2021 actual	2022 est.	2023 est.
1001 Direct civilian full-time equivalent employment	332	307	335

DEBT COLLECTION FUND

(Legislative proposal, subject to PAYGO)

Program and Financing (in millions of dollars)

Identification code 020–5445–4–2–803	2021 actual	2022 est.	2023 est.
Obligations by program activity:			
0001 Direct program activity			22
0900 Total new obligations, unexpired accounts (object class 25.3)			22
Budgetary resources:			
Budget authority:			
Appropriations, mandatory:			
1201 Appropriation (special or trust fund)			22
1930 Total budgetary resources available			22
Change in obligated balance:			
Unpaid obligations:			
3010 New obligations, unexpired accounts			22
3020 Outlays (gross)			–22
Budget authority and outlays, net:			
Mandatory:			
4090 Budget authority, gross			22
Outlays, gross:			
4100 Outlays from new mandatory authority			22
4180 Budget authority, net (total)			22
4190 Outlays, net (total)			22

The Budget proposes legislation to allow Fiscal Service to recover its costs of collecting delinquent tax debt directly from levy collections, rather than from IRS direct appropriation. This would reduce administrative and overhead costs for both Fiscal Service and the IRS.

REIMBURSEMENTS TO FEDERAL RESERVE BANKS

Program and Financing (in millions of dollars)

Identification code 020–0562–0–1–803	2021 actual	2022 est.	2023 est.
Obligations by program activity:			
0001 Reimbursements to Federal Reserve Banks (Direct)	158	183	188
0900 Total new obligations, unexpired accounts (object class 25.2)	158	183	188
Budgetary resources:			
Unobligated balance:			
1021 Recoveries of prior year unpaid obligations	1		
Budget authority:			
Appropriations, mandatory:			
1200 Appropriation	157	183	188
1930 Total budgetary resources available	158	183	188
Change in obligated balance:			
Unpaid obligations:			
3000 Unpaid obligations, brought forward, Oct 1	41	46	47
3010 New obligations, unexpired accounts	158	183	188
3020 Outlays (gross)	–152	–182	–187
3040 Recoveries of prior year unpaid obligations, unexpired	–1		
3050 Unpaid obligations, end of year	46	47	48
Memorandum (non-add) entries:			
3100 Obligated balance, start of year	41	46	47
3200 Obligated balance, end of year	46	47	48

DEPARTMENT OF THE TREASURY

Fiscal Service—Continued
Federal Funds—Continued 1007

		2021 actual	2022 est.	2023 est.
	Budget authority and outlays, net:			
	Mandatory:			
4090	Budget authority, gross	157	183	188
	Outlays, gross:			
4100	Outlays from new mandatory authority	111	137	141
4101	Outlays from mandatory balances	41	45	46
4110	Outlays, gross (total)	152	182	187
4180	Budget authority, net (total)	157	183	188
4190	Outlays, net (total)	152	182	187

This Fund was established by the Treasury, Postal Service, and General Government Appropriations Act of 1991 (P.L. 101–509, 104 Stat. 1389, 1394) as a permanent, indefinite appropriation to reimburse the Federal Reserve Banks for acting as fiscal agents of the Federal Government in support of financing the public debt.

PAYMENT TO THE RESOLUTION FUNDING CORPORATION

Program and Financing (in millions of dollars)

Identification code 020–1851–0–1–908		2021 actual	2022 est.	2023 est.
	Obligations by program activity:			
0001	Payment to the Resolution Funding Corporation (Direct)	1,367	920	920
0900	Total new obligations, unexpired accounts (object class 41.0)	1,367	920	920
	Budgetary resources:			
	Budget authority:			
	Appropriations, mandatory:			
1200	Appropriation	1,367	920	920
1930	Total budgetary resources available	1,367	920	920
	Change in obligated balance:			
	Unpaid obligations:			
3010	New obligations, unexpired accounts	1,367	920	920
3020	Outlays (gross)	–1,367	–920	–920
	Budget authority and outlays, net:			
	Mandatory:			
4090	Budget authority, gross	1,367	920	920
	Outlays, gross:			
4100	Outlays from new mandatory authority	1,367	920	920
4180	Budget authority, net (total)	1,367	920	920
4190	Outlays, net (total)	1,367	920	920

The Financial Institutions Reform, Recovery, and Enforcement Act of 1989 (the Act) authorized and appropriated to the Secretary of the Treasury such sums as may be necessary to cover interest payments on obligations issued by the Resolution Funding Corporation (REFCORP). REFCORP was established under the Act to raise $31.2 billion for the Resolution Trust Corporation (RTC) in order to resolve savings institution insolvencies. Bonds issued had a 30 year maturity with the last bond maturing in 2030.

Sources of payment for interest due on REFCORP obligations have included REFCORP investment income, proceeds from the sale of assets or warrants acquired by the RTC, and contributions by the Federal Home Loan Banks. Indefinite, mandatory funds appropriated to the Treasury are primarily used to meet any shortfall.

HOPE RESERVE FUND

Program and Financing (in millions of dollars)

Identification code 020–5581–0–2–371		2021 actual	2022 est.	2023 est.
	Budgetary resources:			
	Unobligated balance:			
1000	Unobligated balance brought forward, Oct 1	86	86	86
1930	Total budgetary resources available	86	86	86
	Memorandum (non-add) entries:			
1941	Unexpired unobligated balance, end of year	86	86	86
4180	Budget authority, net (total)	....	....	....
4190	Outlays, net (total)	....	....	....

The HOPE Reserve Fund was authorized by section 1337(e) of the Housing and Economic Recovery Act of 2008 (HERA, P.L. 110–289), which directed the account be funded from assessments on Fannie Mae and Freddie Mac.

FEDERAL RESERVE BANK REIMBURSEMENT FUND

Program and Financing (in millions of dollars)

Identification code 020–1884–0–1–803		2021 actual	2022 est.	2023 est.
	Obligations by program activity:			
0001	Federal Reserve Bank services	681	665	685
0900	Total new obligations, unexpired accounts (object class 25.2)	681	665	685
	Budgetary resources:			
	Unobligated balance:			
1021	Recoveries of prior year unpaid obligations	61	....	....
	Budget authority:			
	Appropriations, mandatory:			
1200	Appropriation	620	665	685
1930	Total budgetary resources available	681	665	685
	Change in obligated balance:			
	Unpaid obligations:			
3000	Unpaid obligations, brought forward, Oct 1	161	185	171
3010	New obligations, unexpired accounts	681	665	685
3020	Outlays (gross)	–596	–679	–685
3040	Recoveries of prior year unpaid obligations, unexpired	–61	....	....
3050	Unpaid obligations, end of year	185	171	171
	Memorandum (non-add) entries:			
3100	Obligated balance, start of year	161	185	171
3200	Obligated balance, end of year	185	171	171
	Budget authority and outlays, net:			
	Mandatory:			
4090	Budget authority, gross	620	665	685
	Outlays, gross:			
4100	Outlays from new mandatory authority	435	499	514
4101	Outlays from mandatory balances	161	180	171
4110	Outlays, gross (total)	596	679	685
4180	Budget authority, net (total)	620	665	685
4190	Outlays, net (total)	596	679	685

This Fund was established by the Treasury and General Government Appropriations Act, 1998, Title I (P.L. 105–61, 111 Stat. 1276) as a permanent, indefinite appropriation to reimburse Federal Reserve Banks for services provided, when directed by the Secretary of the Treasury in accordance with 12 U.S.C. 391, in their capacity as depositaries and fiscal agents for the United States.

PAYMENT OF GOVERNMENT LOSSES IN SHIPMENT

Program and Financing (in millions of dollars)

Identification code 020–1710–0–1–803		2021 actual	2022 est.	2023 est.
	Obligations by program activity:			
0001	Payment of Government Losses in Shipment (Direct)	....	2	2
0900	Total new obligations, unexpired accounts (object class 42.0)	....	2	2
	Budgetary resources:			
	Budget authority:			
	Appropriations, mandatory:			
1200	Appropriation	....	2	2
1930	Total budgetary resources available	....	2	2
	Change in obligated balance:			
	Unpaid obligations:			
3000	Unpaid obligations, brought forward, Oct 1	....	....	1
3010	New obligations, unexpired accounts	....	2	2
3020	Outlays (gross)	....	–1	–1
3050	Unpaid obligations, end of year	....	1	2

1008   **Fiscal Service**—Continued
Federal Funds—Continued

THE BUDGET FOR FISCAL YEAR 2023

PAYMENT OF GOVERNMENT LOSSES IN SHIPMENT—Continued

Program and Financing—Continued

Identification code 020–1710–0–1–803	2021 actual	2022 est.	2023 est.
	Memorandum (non-add) entries:			
3100	Obligated balance, start of year	....	....	1
3200	Obligated balance, end of year	....	1	2
	Budget authority and outlays, net:			
	Mandatory:			
4090	Budget authority, gross	....	2	2
	Outlays, gross:			
4100	Outlays from new mandatory authority	....	1	1
4180	Budget authority, net (total)	....	2	2
4190	Outlays, net (total)	....	1	1

This account was created as self-insurance to cover losses in shipment of Government property such as coins, currency, securities, certain losses incurred by the Postal Service, and losses in connection with the redemption of savings bonds. Approximately 1,000 claims are paid annually.

FINANCIAL AGENT SERVICES

Program and Financing (in millions of dollars)

Identification code 020–1802–0–1–803	2021 actual	2022 est.	2023 est.
	Obligations by program activity:			
0001	Financial agent services	940	1,015	1,011
0900	Total new obligations, unexpired accounts (object class 25.2)	940	1,015	1,011
	Budgetary resources:			
	Unobligated balance:			
1000	Unobligated balance brought forward, Oct 1	....	....	15
1021	Recoveries of prior year unpaid obligations	31	15	....
1070	Unobligated balance (total)	31	15	15
	Budget authority:			
	Appropriations, mandatory:			
1200	Appropriation	910	1,016	1,012
1220	Appropriations transferred to other accts [020–0126]	–1	–1	–1
1260	Appropriations, mandatory (total)	909	1,015	1,011
1930	Total budgetary resources available	940	1,030	1,026
	Memorandum (non-add) entries:			
1941	Unexpired unobligated balance, end of year	....	15	15
	Change in obligated balance:			
	Unpaid obligations:			
3000	Unpaid obligations, brought forward, Oct 1	103	81	76
3010	New obligations, unexpired accounts	940	1,015	1,011
3020	Outlays (gross)	–931	–1,005	–1,011
3040	Recoveries of prior year unpaid obligations, unexpired	–31	–15	....
3050	Unpaid obligations, end of year	81	76	76
	Memorandum (non-add) entries:			
3100	Obligated balance, start of year	103	81	76
3200	Obligated balance, end of year	81	76	76
	Budget authority and outlays, net:			
	Mandatory:			
4090	Budget authority, gross	909	1,015	1,011
	Outlays, gross:			
4100	Outlays from new mandatory authority	828	924	920
4101	Outlays from mandatory balances	103	81	91
4110	Outlays, gross (total)	931	1,005	1,011
4180	Budget authority, net (total)	909	1,015	1,011
4190	Outlays, net (total)	931	1,005	1,011

This permanent, indefinite appropriation was established to reimburse financial institutions for the services they provide as depositaries and financial agents of the Federal Government. The services include the acceptance and processing of deposits of public money, as well as services essential to the disbursement of, and accounting for, public monies. The services provided are authorized under numerous statutes including, but not limited to, 12 U.S.C. 90 and 265. This permanent, indefinite appropriation is authorized by P.L. 108–100, the Check Clearing for the 21st Century Act, and permanently appropriated by P.L. 108–199, the Consolidated Appropriations Act of 2004. Additionally, financial agent administrative and financial analysis costs for the Government Sponsored Enterprise Mortgage Backed Securities Purchase Program and State Housing Finance Agency program are reimbursed from this account.

INTEREST ON UNINVESTED FUNDS

Program and Financing (in millions of dollars)

Identification code 020–1860–0–1–908	2021 actual	2022 est.	2023 est.
	Obligations by program activity:			
0001	Interest of uninvested funds	2	9	9
0900	Total new obligations, unexpired accounts (object class 43.0)	2	9	9
	Budgetary resources:			
	Budget authority:			
	Appropriations, mandatory:			
1200	Appropriation	2	9	9
1930	Total budgetary resources available	2	9	9
	Change in obligated balance:			
	Unpaid obligations:			
3000	Unpaid obligations, brought forward, Oct 1	98	93	62
3010	New obligations, unexpired accounts	2	9	9
3020	Outlays (gross)	–7	–40	–40
3050	Unpaid obligations, end of year	93	62	31
	Memorandum (non-add) entries:			
3100	Obligated balance, start of year	98	93	62
3200	Obligated balance, end of year	93	62	31
	Budget authority and outlays, net:			
	Mandatory:			
4090	Budget authority, gross	2	9	9
	Outlays, gross:			
4100	Outlays from new mandatory authority	....	9	9
4101	Outlays from mandatory balances	7	31	31
4110	Outlays, gross (total)	7	40	40
4180	Budget authority, net (total)	2	9	9
4190	Outlays, net (total)	7	40	40

This account was established for the purpose of paying interest on certain uninvested funds placed in trust in the Treasury in accordance with various statutes (31 U.S.C. 1321; 2 U.S.C. 158 (P.L. 94–289); 20 U.S.C. 74a (P.L. 94–418) and 101; 24 U.S.C. 46 (P.L. 94–290) and 69 Stat. 533).

FEDERAL INTEREST LIABILITIES TO STATES

Program and Financing (in millions of dollars)

Identification code 020–1877–0–1–908	2021 actual	2022 est.	2023 est.
	Obligations by program activity:			
0001	Federal interest liabilities to States	1	1	1
0900	Total new obligations, unexpired accounts (object class 25.2)	1	1	1
	Budgetary resources:			
	Budget authority:			
	Appropriations, mandatory:			
1200	Appropriation	....	1	1
	Spending authority from offsetting collections, mandatory:			
1800	Collected	1	....	....
1900	Budget authority (total)	1	1	1
1930	Total budgetary resources available	1	1	1
	Change in obligated balance:			
	Unpaid obligations:			
3010	New obligations, unexpired accounts	1	1	1
3020	Outlays (gross)	–1	–1	–1
	Budget authority and outlays, net:			
	Mandatory:			
4090	Budget authority, gross	1	1	1

DEPARTMENT OF THE TREASURY

Fiscal Service—Continued
Federal Funds—Continued

1009

		2021 actual	2022 est.	2023 est.
	Outlays, gross:			
4100	Outlays from new mandatory authority	1	1	1
	Offsets against gross budget authority and outlays:			
	Offsetting collections (collected) from:			
4120	Federal sources	−1	....	....
4180	Budget authority, net (total)	....	1	1
4190	Outlays, net (total)	....	1	1

Pursuant to the Cash Management Improvement Act (P.L. 101–453, 104 Stat. 1058) as amended (P.L. 102–589, 106 Stat. 5133), and Treasury regulations codified at 31 CFR Part 205, under certain circumstances, interest is paid when Federal funds are not transferred to States in a timely manner.

INTEREST PAID TO CREDIT FINANCING ACCOUNTS

Program and Financing (in millions of dollars)

Identification code 020–1880–0–1–908	2021 actual	2022 est.	2023 est.
Obligations by program activity:			
0001 Interest paid to credit financing accounts	12,762	10,813	13,320
0900 Total new obligations, unexpired accounts (object class 43.0)	12,762	10,813	13,320
Budgetary resources:			
Budget authority:			
Appropriations, mandatory:			
1200 Appropriation	12,762	10,813	13,320
1930 Total budgetary resources available	12,762	10,813	13,320
Change in obligated balance:			
Unpaid obligations:			
3010 New obligations, unexpired accounts	12,762	10,813	13,320
3020 Outlays (gross)	−12,762	−10,813	−13,320
Budget authority and outlays, net:			
Mandatory:			
4090 Budget authority, gross	12,762	10,813	13,320
Outlays, gross:			
4100 Outlays from new mandatory authority	12,762	10,813	13,320
4180 Budget authority, net (total)	12,762	10,813	13,320
4190 Outlays, net (total)	12,762	10,813	13,320

This account pays interest on the invested balances of guaranteed and direct loan financing accounts. For guaranteed loan financing accounts, balances result when the accounts receive up-front payments and fees to be held in reserve to make payments on defaults. Direct loan financing accounts normally borrow from Treasury to disburse loans and receive interest and principal payments and other payments from borrowers. Because direct loan financing accounts generally repay borrowing from Treasury at the end of the year, they can build up balances of payments received during the year. Interest on invested balances is paid to the financing accounts from the general fund of the Treasury, in accordance with section 505(c) of the Federal Credit Reform Act of 1990.

CLAIMS, JUDGMENTS, AND RELIEF ACTS

Program and Financing (in millions of dollars)

Identification code 020–1895–0–1–808	2021 actual	2022 est.	2023 est.
Obligations by program activity:			
0001 Claims for damages	2	13	2
0003 Claims for contract disputes	223	240	240
0091 Total claims adjudicated administratively	225	253	242
0101 Judgments, Court of Claims	7,435	1,000	1,300
0102 Judgments, U.S. courts	820	1,205	1,205
0191 Total court judgments	8,255	2,205	2,505
0900 Total new obligations, unexpired accounts (object class 42.0)	8,480	2,458	2,747
Budgetary resources:			
Budget authority:			
Appropriations, mandatory:			
1200 Appropriation	8,480	2,458	2,747
1930 Total budgetary resources available	8,480	2,458	2,747
Change in obligated balance:			
Unpaid obligations:			
3000 Unpaid obligations, brought forward, Oct 1	25	315	....
3010 New obligations, unexpired accounts	8,480	2,458	2,747
3020 Outlays (gross)	−8,190	−2,773	−2,747
3050 Unpaid obligations, end of year	315	....	....
Memorandum (non-add) entries:			
3100 Obligated balance, start of year	25	315	....
3200 Obligated balance, end of year	315	....	....
Budget authority and outlays, net:			
Mandatory:			
4090 Budget authority, gross	8,480	2,458	2,747
Outlays, gross:			
4100 Outlays from new mandatory authority	8,165	2,458	2,747
4101 Outlays from mandatory balances	25	315	....
4110 Outlays, gross (total)	8,190	2,773	2,747
4180 Budget authority, net (total)	8,480	2,458	2,747
4190 Outlays, net (total)	8,190	2,773	2,747

Funds are made available for cases in which the Federal Government is found by courts to be liable for payment of claims and interest for damages not chargeable to appropriations of individual agencies, and for payment of private and public relief acts. Public Law 95–26 authorized a permanent, indefinite appropriation to pay certain judgments from the general fund of the Treasury.

RESTITUTION OF FORGONE INTEREST

Program and Financing (in millions of dollars)

Identification code 020–1875–0–1–908	2021 actual	2022 est.	2023 est.
Obligations by program activity:			
0001 Restitution of Forgone Interest (Direct)	....	1,135	....
0900 Total new obligations, unexpired accounts (object class 43.0)	....	1,135	....
Budgetary resources:			
Budget authority:			
Appropriations, mandatory:			
1200 Appropriation	....	1,135	....
1930 Total budgetary resources available	....	1,135	....
Change in obligated balance:			
Unpaid obligations:			
3010 New obligations, unexpired accounts	....	1,135	....
3020 Outlays (gross)	....	−1,135	....
Budget authority and outlays, net:			
Mandatory:			
4090 Budget authority, gross	....	1,135	....
Outlays, gross:			
4100 Outlays from new mandatory authority	....	1,135	....
4180 Budget authority, net (total)	....	1,135	....
4190 Outlays, net (total)	....	1,135	....

This account provides funds for the payment of interest on investments in Treasury securities that the Secretary of the Treasury has suspended or redeemed. The Secretary is permitted to take such action when Treasury is constrained by the statutory debt limit and must take extraordinary measures to avoid defaulting. Treasury is required to restore all due interest and principal to the respective investments.

GUAM WORLD WAR II CLAIMS FUND

Program and Financing (in millions of dollars)

Identification code 020–5680–0–2–806	2021 actual	2022 est.	2023 est.
Obligations by program activity:			
0001 Direct program activity	7	2	2

Fiscal Service—Continued
Federal Funds—Continued

GUAM WORLD WAR II CLAIMS FUND—Continued
Program and Financing—Continued

Identification code 020–5680–0–2–806	2021 actual	2022 est.	2023 est.
0900 Total new obligations, unexpired accounts (object class 42.0)	7	2	2
Budgetary resources:			
Unobligated balance:			
1000 Unobligated balance brought forward, Oct 1	15	10	8
1020 Adjustment of unobligated bal brought forward, Oct 1	2		
1070 Unobligated balance (total)	17	10	8
1930 Total budgetary resources available	17	10	8
Memorandum (non-add) entries:			
1941 Unexpired unobligated balance, end of year	10	8	6
Change in obligated balance:			
Unpaid obligations:			
3000 Unpaid obligations, brought forward, Oct 1		3	3
3010 New obligations, unexpired accounts	7	2	2
3020 Outlays (gross)	–4	–2	–2
3050 Unpaid obligations, end of year	3	3	3
Memorandum (non-add) entries:			
3100 Obligated balance, start of year		3	3
3200 Obligated balance, end of year	3	3	3
Budget authority and outlays, net:			
Mandatory:			
Outlays, gross:			
4101 Outlays from mandatory balances	4	2	2
4180 Budget authority, net (total)			
4190 Outlays, net (total)	4	2	2

This fund was established by the Guam World War II Loyalty Recognition Act of 2016. It requires the establishment of the "Claims Fund", a special fund for the payment of claims submitted by compensable Guam victims and survivors of compensable Guam decedents. Duties, taxes, and fees collected from Guam in excess of 2014 baseline tax collections for the territory will be deposited annually into the Claims Fund. Funding will be used to compensate residents of Guam for damages resulting from the Imperial Japanese military's occupation of Guam during World War II.

CONTINUED DUMPING AND SUBSIDY OFFSET

Special and Trust Fund Receipts (in millions of dollars)

Identification code 020–5688–0–2–376	2021 actual	2022 est.	2023 est.
0100 Balance, start of year	3		
Receipts:			
Current law:			
1110 Antidumping and Countervailing Duties, Continued Dumping and Subsidy Offset	1	10	9
2000 Total: Balances and receipts	4	10	9
Appropriations:			
Current law:			
2101 Continued Dumping and Subsidy Offset	–1	–10	–9
2103 Continued Dumping and Subsidy Offset	–3	–1	–1
2132 Continued Dumping and Subsidy Offset		1	1
2199 Total current law appropriations	–4	–10	–9
2999 Total appropriations	–4	–10	–9
5099 Balance, end of year			

Program and Financing (in millions of dollars)

Identification code 020–5688–0–2–376	2021 actual	2022 est.	2023 est.
Obligations by program activity:			
0001 Continued dumping and subsidy offset	58	1	10
0900 Total new obligations, unexpired accounts (object class 41.0)	58	1	10
Budgetary resources:			
Unobligated balance:			
1000 Unobligated balance brought forward, Oct 1	158	104	113
Budget authority:			
Appropriations, mandatory:			
1201 Appropriation (special or trust fund)	1	10	9
1203 Appropriation (previously unavailable)(special or trust)	3	1	1
1232 Appropriations and/or unobligated balance of appropriations temporarily reduced		–1	–1
1260 Appropriations, mandatory (total)	4	10	9
1930 Total budgetary resources available	162	114	122
Memorandum (non-add) entries:			
1941 Unexpired unobligated balance, end of year	104	113	112
Change in obligated balance:			
Unpaid obligations:			
3010 New obligations, unexpired accounts	58	1	10
3020 Outlays (gross)	–58	–1	–10
Budget authority and outlays, net:			
Mandatory:			
4090 Budget authority, gross	4	10	9
Outlays, gross:			
4101 Outlays from mandatory balances	58	1	10
4180 Budget authority, net (total)	4	10	9
4190 Outlays, net (total)	58	1	10

U.S. Customs and Border Protection, Department of Homeland Security, collects duties assessed pursuant to a countervailing duty order, an anti-dumping duty order, or a finding under the Antidumping Act of 1921. Under a provision enacted in 2000 CBP, through the Treasury, distributes certain of these duties to affected domestic producers. These distributions provide an additional subsidy to producers that already gain protection from the increased import prices, including tariffs. The authority to distribute assessments on entries made after October 1, 2007, has been repealed. Assessments on entries made before October 1, 2007, will be disbursed as if the authority had not been repealed. Assessments collected on eligible entries are to be disbursed within 60 days of the end of the fiscal year in which they were collected.

CHECK FORGERY INSURANCE FUND

Program and Financing (in millions of dollars)

Identification code 020–4109–0–3–803	2021 actual	2022 est.	2023 est.
Obligations by program activity:			
0801 Check Forgery Insurance Fund (Reimbursable)	22	1	1
0900 Total new obligations, unexpired accounts (object class 42.0)	22	1	1
Budgetary resources:			
Unobligated balance:			
1000 Unobligated balance brought forward, Oct 1	5	4	4
Budget authority:			
Spending authority from offsetting collections, mandatory:			
1800 Collected	21	1	1
1900 Budget authority (total)	21	1	1
1930 Total budgetary resources available	26	5	5
Memorandum (non-add) entries:			
1941 Unexpired unobligated balance, end of year	4	4	4
Change in obligated balance:			
Unpaid obligations:			
3010 New obligations, unexpired accounts	22	1	1
3020 Outlays (gross)	–22	–1	–1
Budget authority and outlays, net:			
Mandatory:			
4090 Budget authority, gross	21	1	1
Outlays, gross:			
4100 Outlays from new mandatory authority	17	1	1
4101 Outlays from mandatory balances	5		
4110 Outlays, gross (total)	22	1	1
Offsets against gross budget authority and outlays:			
Offsetting collections (collected) from:			
4123 Non-Federal sources	–21	–1	–1
4180 Budget authority, net (total)			
4190 Outlays, net (total)	1		

This Fund was established as a permanent, indefinite appropriation in order to maintain adequate funding of the Check Forgery Insurance Fund. The Fund facilitates timely payments for replacement Treasury checks necessitated due to a claim of forgery. The Fund recoups disbursements through reclamations made against banks negotiating forged checks.

To reduce hardships sustained by payees of Government checks that have been stolen and forged, settlement is made in advance of the receipt of funds from the endorsers of the checks. If the U.S. Treasury is unable to recover funds through reclamation procedures, the Fund sustains the loss.

Public Law 108–447 expanded the use of the Fund to include payments made via electronic funds transfer. A technical correction to the Fund's statutes to ensure and clarify that the Fund can be utilized as a funding source for relief of administrative disbursing errors was enacted by P.L. 110–161, Division D, section 119.

Trust Funds

CHEYENNE RIVER SIOUX TRIBE TERRESTRIAL WILDLIFE HABITAT RESTORATION TRUST FUND

Special and Trust Fund Receipts (in millions of dollars)

Identification code 020–8209–0–7–306	2021 actual	2022 est.	2023 est.
0100 Balance, start of year	60	60	60
Receipts:			
Current law:			
1140 Earnings on Investments, Cheyenne River Sioux Tribe Terrestrial Wildlife Habitat Restoration Trust Fund	1	1	1
2000 Total: Balances and receipts	61	61	61
Appropriations:			
Current law:			
2101 Cheyenne River Sioux Tribe Terrestrial Wildlife Habitat Restoration Trust Fund	–1	–1	–1
5099 Balance, end of year	60	60	60

Program and Financing (in millions of dollars)

Identification code 020–8209–0–7–306	2021 actual	2022 est.	2023 est.
Obligations by program activity:			
0001 Cheyenne River Sioux Tribe Terrestrial Wildlife Habitat Restorat (Direct)	1	1	1
0900 Total new obligations, unexpired accounts (object class 43.0)	1	1	1
Budgetary resources:			
Unobligated balance:			
1000 Unobligated balance brought forward, Oct 1	1	1	1
Budget authority:			
Appropriations, mandatory:			
1201 Appropriation (special or trust fund)	1	1	1
1930 Total budgetary resources available	2	2	2
Memorandum (non-add) entries:			
1941 Unexpired unobligated balance, end of year	1	1	1
Change in obligated balance:			
Unpaid obligations:			
3010 New obligations, unexpired accounts	1	1	1
3020 Outlays (gross)	–1	–1	
3050 Unpaid obligations, end of year			1
Memorandum (non-add) entries:			
3200 Obligated balance, end of year			1
Budget authority and outlays, net:			
Mandatory:			
4090 Budget authority, gross	1	1	1
Outlays, gross:			
4101 Outlays from mandatory balances	1	1	
4180 Budget authority, net (total)	1	1	1
4190 Outlays, net (total)	1	1	
Memorandum (non-add) entries:			
5000 Total investments, SOY: Federal securities: Par value	61	61	61
5001 Total investments, EOY: Federal securities: Par value	61	61	61

The Water Resources Development Act of 1999 (P.L. 106–53) established trust funds to provide resources for the restoration of terrestrial wildlife habitat lost from flooding related to the Big Bend and Oahe Dam projects along the Missouri River, as part of the Flood Control Act of 1944.

The funds received annual General Fund appropriations beginning in FY 1999 until they became fully capitalized in FY 2010. Once fully capitalized, the interest earnings accumulated from the inception of the funds and all future earnings are available to pay for terrestrial wildlife restoration projects per the Restoration Plans of the beneficiaries of the trusts, the Cheyenne River Sioux Tribe Terrestrial Wildlife Restoration Trust Fund and the Lower Brule Sioux Tribe Terrestrial Wildlife Restoration Trust Fund.

GULF COAST RESTORATION TRUST FUND

Special and Trust Fund Receipts (in millions of dollars)

Identification code 020–8625–0–7–452	2021 actual	2022 est.	2023 est.
0100 Balance, start of year	20	17	29
Receipts:			
Current law:			
1110 Administrative and Civil Penalties, Gulf Coast Restoration Trust Fund	303	304	303
1140 Earnings on Investments, Gulf Coast Restoration Trust Fund	11	16	17
1199 Total current law receipts	314	320	320
1999 Total receipts	314	320	320
2000 Total: Balances and receipts	334	337	349
Appropriations:			
Current law:			
2101 Gulf Coast Restoration Trust Fund	–315	–308	–309
2103 Gulf Coast Restoration Trust Fund	–20	–18	–18
2132 Gulf Coast Restoration Trust Fund	18	18	18
2199 Total current law appropriations	–317	–308	–309
2999 Total appropriations	–317	–308	–309
5099 Balance, end of year	17	29	40

Program and Financing (in millions of dollars)

Identification code 020–8625–0–7–452	2021 actual	2022 est.	2023 est.
Obligations by program activity:			
0001 Direct Component	40	66	65
0002 Comprehensive Plan Component	150	48	57
0003 Oil Spill Restoration Impact Component	127	49	75
0004 NOAA RESTORE Act Science Program	6	6	8
0005 Centers of Excellence Research Grants		3	3
0900 Total new obligations, unexpired accounts	323	172	208
Budgetary resources:			
Unobligated balance:			
1000 Unobligated balance brought forward, Oct 1	1,080	1,075	1,218
1021 Recoveries of prior year unpaid obligations	1	7	
1070 Unobligated balance (total)	1,081	1,082	1,218
Budget authority:			
Appropriations, mandatory:			
1201 Appropriation (special or trust fund)	315	308	309
1203 Appropriation (previously unavailable)(special or trust)	20	18	18
1232 Appropriations and/or unobligated balance of appropriations temporarily reduced	–18	–18	–18
1260 Appropriations, mandatory (total)	317	308	309
1900 Budget authority (total)	317	308	309
1930 Total budgetary resources available	1,398	1,390	1,527
Memorandum (non-add) entries:			
1941 Unexpired unobligated balance, end of year	1,075	1,218	1,319
Change in obligated balance:			
Unpaid obligations:			
3000 Unpaid obligations, brought forward, Oct 1	570	748	727
3010 New obligations, unexpired accounts	323	172	208
3020 Outlays (gross)	–144	–186	–231
3040 Recoveries of prior year unpaid obligations, unexpired	–1	–7	
3050 Unpaid obligations, end of year	748	727	704

Gulf Coast Restoration Trust Fund—Continued

Program and Financing—Continued

Identification code 020–8625–0–7–452	2021 actual	2022 est.	2023 est.
Memorandum (non-add) entries:			
3100 Obligated balance, start of year	570	748	727
3200 Obligated balance, end of year	748	727	704
Budget authority and outlays, net:			
Mandatory:			
4090 Budget authority, gross	317	308	309
Outlays, gross:			
4101 Outlays from mandatory balances	144	186	231
4180 Budget authority, net (total)	317	308	309
4190 Outlays, net (total)	144	186	231
Memorandum (non-add) entries:			
5000 Total investments, SOY: Federal securities: Par value	1,681	1,843	1,965
5001 Total investments, EOY: Federal securities: Par value	1,843	1,965	2,043

This fund was established by the Resources and Ecosystems Sustainability, Tourist Opportunities, and Revived Economies of the Gulf Coast States Act of 2012 (RESTORE Act). It will receive 80 percent of the civil and administrative penalties collected after July 6, 2012, from parties responsible for the *Deepwater Horizon* oil spill. Funding will be used by Federal, State, and local governments for activities to restore and protect the ecosystems and economy of the Gulf Coast region, research and monitoring, and related oversight and management responsibilities. The current estimates represent known settlement amounts; additional funds may become available through future court judgments or settlements.

Object Classification (in millions of dollars)

Identification code 020–8625–0–7–452	2021 actual	2022 est.	2023 est.
Direct obligations:			
41.0 Grants, subsidies, and contributions	46	68	68
94.0 Financial transfers	277	104	140
99.9 Total new obligations, unexpired accounts	323	172	208

FEDERAL FINANCING BANK

Federal Funds

FEDERAL FINANCING BANK

Program and Financing (in millions of dollars)

Identification code 020–4521–0–4–803	2021 actual	2022 est.	2023 est.
Obligations by program activity:			
0801 Administrative Expenses	10	12	13
0802 Interest on borrowings from Treasury	1,810	2,045	2,168
0803 Interest on borrowings from CRSDF	192	157	123
0900 Total new obligations, unexpired accounts	2,012	2,214	2,304
Budgetary resources:			
Unobligated balance:			
1000 Unobligated balance brought forward, Oct 1	3,760	3,654	3,880
1023 Unobligated balances applied to repay debt	–1,209	–1,208	–1,208
1046 Adjustment for change in net principal	911	1,088	515
1070 Unobligated balance (total)	3,462	3,534	3,187
Budget authority:			
Spending authority from offsetting collections, mandatory:			
1800 Collected	2,204	2,560	2,595
1930 Total budgetary resources available	5,666	6,094	5,782
Memorandum (non-add) entries:			
1941 Unexpired unobligated balance, end of year	3,654	3,880	3,478
Change in obligated balance:			
Unpaid obligations:			
3010 New obligations, unexpired accounts	2,012	2,214	2,304
3020 Outlays (gross)	–2,012	–2,214	–2,304
Budget authority and outlays, net:			
Mandatory:			
4090 Budget authority, gross	2,204	2,560	2,595
Outlays, gross:			
4100 Outlays from new mandatory authority	2,012	2,214	2,304
Offsets against gross budget authority and outlays:			
Offsetting collections (collected) from:			
4120 Federal sources	–2,204	–2,560	–2,595
4180 Budget authority, net (total)	....	....	....
4190 Outlays, net (total)	–192	–346	–291

The Federal Financing Bank (FFB) was created in 1973 to reduce the costs of certain Federal and federally-assisted borrowing and to ensure the coordination of such borrowing from the public in a manner least disruptive to private financial markets and institutions. With the implementation of the Federal Credit Reform Act of 1990 agencies finance such loan programs through direct loan financing accounts that borrow directly from the Treasury. The FFB finances these Federal direct loans to the public which are fully guaranteed by a Federal agency. FFB loans are also used to finance activities of the U.S. Postal Service.

Lending by the FFB may take one of three forms, depending on the authorizing statutes pertaining to a particular agency or program; 1) the FFB may purchase agency financial assets; 2) the FFB may acquire debt securities that the agency is otherwise authorized to issue and 3) the FFB may provide direct loans on behalf of a Federal agency by disbursing loans directly to private borrowers and receiving repayments from the private borrower guaranteed by the agency. Because the law requires that transactions by the FFB be treated as a means of financing agency obligations, the budgetary effect of the third type of transaction is reflected in the Budget in the following sequence: a loan by the FFB to the agency, a loan by the agency to a private borrower, a repayment by a private borrower to the agency, and a repayment by the agency to the FFB.

In 2021, FFB's net inflows were $59 million. In addition to its authority to borrow from the Treasury (Fiscal Service), the FFB has the statutory authority to borrow up to $15 billion from other sources. Any such borrowing is exempt from the statutory ceiling on Federal debt. The FFB used this authority most recently in October 2015.

The following tables show (1) the annual net lending by the FFB by agency and program and the amount outstanding at the end of each year and (2) principal repayments from the borrower in excess of principal repaid to the Fiscal Service each year.

NET LENDING AND LOANS OUTSTANDING, END OF YEAR

(in millions of dollars)

	2021 actual	2022 est.	2023 est.
A. Department of Agriculture:			
1. Rural Utilities Service:			
Lending, net	2,089	4,525	5,134
Loans outstanding	48,742	53,267	58,401
B. Department of Education:			
1. Historically black colleges and universities:			
Lending, net	–1,341	183	218
Loans outstanding	160	343	561
C. Department of Energy:			
1. Title 17 innovative technology loans:			
Lending, net	754	183	218
Loans outstanding	15,175	15,358	15,576
2. Advanced technology vehicles manufacturing loans:			
Lending, net	–591	–39	4,192
Loans outstanding	437	397	4,589
D. Department of Housing and Urban Development:			
1. Multifamily Risk Share Program:			
Lending, net	266	–97	–104
Loans outstanding	2,630	2,533	2,429
E. Department of Transportation:			
1. MARAD Title XI:			
Lending, net	–14	....	–14
Loans outstanding	312	312	298
F. Department of the Treasury:			
1. CDFI Fund Bond Guarantee Program:			
Lending, net	53	124	211
Loans outstanding	1,208	1,332	1,543
G. Department of Veterans Affairs:			
1. Transitional housing for homeless veterans:			
Lending, net	....	....	....
Loans outstanding	4	4	4

DEPARTMENT OF THE TREASURY

	2021 actual	2022 est.	2023 est.
H. General Services Administration:			
1. Federal buildings fund:			
Lending, net	......	......	......
Loans outstanding	......	......	......
I. International Assistance Programs:			
1. Foreign military sales credit:			
Lending, net	......	......	......
Loans outstanding	......	......	......
J. Postal Service:			
1. Postal Service fund:			
Lending, net	–3,000	–1,000	......
Loans outstanding	11,000	10,000	10,000
Total lending:			
Lending, net	–1,784	3,879	9,855
Loans outstanding	79,667	83,546	93,401

PRINCIPAL REPAYMENTS, END OF YEAR

	2021 actual	2022 est.	2023 est.
Agency or Guaranteed Principal Received:			
A. Department of Education:			
1. Historically black colleges and universities	520	......	......
B. National Credit Union Administration:			
1. Central liquidity facility	......	......	......
C. Department of Agriculture:			
1. Rural Utilities Service	916	1,210	585
D. Postal Service:			
1. Postal Service fund	3,000	1,000	......
E. Department of Veterans Affairs:			
1. Transitional housing for homeless veterans	......	......	......
Total Agency or Guaranteed Principal Received	4,436	2,210	585
Principal Repaid to the Fiscal Service:			
A. Department of Education:			
1. Historically black colleges and universities	376	......	......
B. National Credit Union Administration:			
1. Central Liquidity Facility	......	......	......
C. Department of Agriculture:			
1. Rural Utilities Service	149	122	71
D. Postal Service:			
1. Postal Service fund	3,000	1,000	......
E. Department of Veterans Affairs:			
1. Transitional housing for homeless veterans	......	......	......
Total Agency or Guaranteed Principal Repaid	3,525	1,122	71
Agency or guaranteed principal received in excess of principal repaid to the Fiscal Service			
A. Department of Education:			
1. Historically black colleges and universities	144	......	......
B. National Credit Union Administration:			
1. Central Liquidity Facility	......	......	......
C. Department of Agriculture:			
1. Rural Utilities Service	767	1,088	515
D. Postal Service:			
1. Postal Service fund	......	......	......
E. Department of Veterans Affairs:			
1. Transitional housing for homeless veterans	......	......	......
Total Agency or guaranteed principal received in excess of principal repaid to the Fiscal Service	911	1,088	515

Object Classification (in millions of dollars)

Identification code 020–4521–0–4–803	2021 actual	2022 est.	2023 est.
Reimbursable obligations:			
25.2 Other services from non-Federal sources	10	12	13
43.0 Interest and dividends	2,002	2,202	2,291
99.9 Total new obligations, unexpired accounts	2,012	2,214	2,304

ALCOHOL AND TOBACCO TAX AND TRADE BUREAU

Federal Funds

SALARIES AND EXPENSES

For necessary expenses of carrying out section 1111 of the Homeland Security Act of 2002, including hire of passenger motor vehicles, $150,863,000; of which $5,000,000 shall remain available until September 30, 2024; of which not to exceed $6,000 shall be available for official reception and representation expenses; and of which not to exceed $50,000 shall be available for cooperative research and development programs for laboratory services; and provision of laboratory assistance to State and local agencies with or without reimbursement.

Note.—A full-year 2022 appropriation for this account was not enacted at the time the Budget was prepared; therefore, the Budget assumes this account is operating under the Continuing Appropriations Act, 2022 (Division A of Public Law 117–43, as amended). The amounts included for 2022 reflect the annualized level provided by the continuing resolution.

Program and Financing (in millions of dollars)

Identification code 020–1008–0–1–803		2021 actual	2022 est.	2023 est.
	Obligations by program activity:			
0001	Protect the Public	71	67	75
0002	Collect revenue	54	58	76
0192	Total direct program	125	125	151
0799	Total direct obligations	125	125	151
0801	Protect the Public	3	3	3
0802	Collect Revenue	4	5	5
0899	Total reimbursable obligations	7	8	8
0900	Total new obligations, unexpired accounts	132	133	159
	Budgetary resources:			
	Unobligated balance:			
1000	Unobligated balance brought forward, Oct 1	4	4	3
	Budget authority:			
	Appropriations, discretionary:			
1100	Appropriation	124	124	151
	Spending authority from offsetting collections, discretionary:			
1700	Collected	5	8	8
1701	Change in uncollected payments, Federal sources	3	......	......
1750	Spending auth from offsetting collections, disc (total)	8	8	8
1900	Budget authority (total)	132	132	159
1930	Total budgetary resources available	136	136	162
	Memorandum (non-add) entries:			
1941	Unexpired unobligated balance, end of year	4	3	3
	Change in obligated balance:			
	Unpaid obligations:			
3000	Unpaid obligations, brought forward, Oct 1	27	31	19
3010	New obligations, unexpired accounts	132	133	159
3011	Obligations ("upward adjustments"), expired accounts	2	......	......
3020	Outlays (gross)	–128	–145	–153
3041	Recoveries of prior year unpaid obligations, expired	–2	......	......
3050	Unpaid obligations, end of year	31	19	25
	Uncollected payments:			
3060	Uncollected pymts, Fed sources, brought forward, Oct 1	–3	–3	–3
3070	Change in uncollected pymts, Fed sources, unexpired	–3	......	......
3071	Change in uncollected pymts, Fed sources, expired	3	......	......
3090	Uncollected pymts, Fed sources, end of year	–3	–3	–3
	Memorandum (non-add) entries:			
3100	Obligated balance, start of year	24	28	16
3200	Obligated balance, end of year	28	16	22
	Budget authority and outlays, net:			
	Discretionary:			
4000	Budget authority, gross	132	132	159
	Outlays, gross:			
4010	Outlays from new discretionary authority	99	110	132
4011	Outlays from discretionary balances	29	35	21
4020	Outlays, gross (total)	128	145	153
	Offsets against gross budget authority and outlays:			
	Offsetting collections (collected) from:			
4030	Federal sources	–4	–4	–4
4033	Non-Federal sources	–4	–4	–4
4040	Offsets against gross budget authority and outlays (total)	–8	–8	–8
	Additional offsets against gross budget authority only:			
4050	Change in uncollected pymts, Fed sources, unexpired	–3	......	......
4052	Offsetting collections credited to expired accounts	3	......	......
4070	Budget authority, net (discretionary)	124	124	151
4080	Outlays, net (discretionary)	120	137	145
4180	Budget authority, net (total)	124	124	151
4190	Outlays, net (total)	120	137	145

The Alcohol and Tobacco Tax and Trade Bureau (TTB) enforces various Federal laws and regulations relating to alcohol and tobacco. TTB collects excise taxes and seeks to eliminate or prevent tax evasion and other criminal conduct, prevent consumer deception relating to alcohol beverages, and ensure that regulated alcohol and tobacco products comply with various Federal commodity, product integrity, and distribution requirements.

Alcohol and Tobacco Tax and Trade Bureau—Continued
Federal Funds—Continued

SALARIES AND EXPENSES—Continued

Object Classification (in millions of dollars)

Identification code 020–1008–0–1–803	2021 actual	2022 est.	2023 est.
Direct obligations:			
Personnel compensation:			
11.1 Full-time permanent	53	56	64
11.5 Other personnel compensation	1	1	2
11.9 Total personnel compensation	54	57	66
12.1 Civilian personnel benefits	20	21	24
21.0 Travel and transportation of persons	....	2	2
23.1 Rental payments to GSA	4	4	5
23.3 Communications, utilities, and miscellaneous charges	1	1	1
25.1 Advisory and assistance services	9	9	20
25.2 Other services from non-Federal sources	14	15	17
25.3 Other goods and services from Federal sources	9	9	10
25.7 Operation and maintenance of equipment	3	3	3
31.0 Equipment	8	4	3
99.0 Direct obligations	122	125	151
99.0 Reimbursable obligations	6	8	8
99.5 Adjustment for rounding	4	....	....
99.9 Total new obligations, unexpired accounts	132	133	159

Employment Summary

Identification code 020–1008–0–1–803	2021 actual	2022 est.	2023 est.
1001 Direct civilian full-time equivalent employment	487	508	548
2001 Reimbursable civilian full-time equivalent employment	14	12	12

INTERNAL REVENUE COLLECTIONS FOR PUERTO RICO

Special and Trust Fund Receipts (in millions of dollars)

Identification code 020–5737–0–2–806	2021 actual	2022 est.	2023 est.
0100 Balance, start of year	....	....	....
Receipts:			
Current law:			
1110 Deposits, Internal Revenue Collections for Puerto Rico	520	524	451
2000 Total: Balances and receipts	520	524	451
Appropriations:			
Current law:			
2101 Internal Revenue Collections for Puerto Rico	–520	–524	–451
5099 Balance, end of year	....	....	....

Program and Financing (in millions of dollars)

Identification code 020–5737–0–2–806	2021 actual	2022 est.	2023 est.
Obligations by program activity:			
0001 Internal revenue collections for Puerto Rico	520	524	451
0900 Total new obligations, unexpired accounts (object class 41.0)	520	524	451
Budgetary resources:			
Budget authority:			
Appropriations, mandatory:			
1201 Appropriation (special or trust fund)	520	524	451
1930 Total budgetary resources available	520	524	451
Change in obligated balance:			
Unpaid obligations:			
3010 New obligations, unexpired accounts	520	524	451
3020 Outlays (gross)	–520	–524	–451
Budget authority and outlays, net:			
Mandatory:			
4090 Budget authority, gross	520	524	451
Outlays, gross:			
4100 Outlays from new mandatory authority	520	524	451
4180 Budget authority, net (total)	520	524	451
4190 Outlays, net (total)	520	524	451

Excise taxes collected under the Internal Revenue laws of the United States on articles produced in Puerto Rico and transported to the United States are covered-over (paid) to Puerto Rico (26 U.S.C. 7652(a)). Excise taxes collected on articles produced in the U.S. Virgin Islands and transported to the United States are covered-over to the U.S. Virgin Islands. (26 U.S.C. 7652(b)). Excise taxes collected on rum imported from everywhere other than Puerto Rico or the U.S. Virgin Islands are also covered-over to the treasuries of Puerto Rico and the U.S. Virgin Islands under a formula set forth in 27 CFR 26.31.

BUREAU OF ENGRAVING AND PRINTING

Federal Funds

BUREAU OF ENGRAVING AND PRINTING FUND

Program and Financing (in millions of dollars)

Identification code 020–4502–0–4–803	2021 actual	2022 est.	2023 est.
Obligations by program activity:			
0801 Currency program	1,213	1,067	1,140
0803 Other programs	2	3	3
0804 DC Replacement Facility	34	12	897
0900 Total new obligations, unexpired accounts	1,249	1,082	2,040
Budgetary resources:			
Unobligated balance:			
1000 Unobligated balance brought forward, Oct 1	748	603	1,919
1021 Recoveries of prior year unpaid obligations	6	6	4
1070 Unobligated balance (total)	754	609	1,923
Budget authority:			
Spending authority from offsetting collections, discretionary:			
1700 Collected (YCO)	891	1,070	1,140
1701 Change in uncollected payments, Federal sources (YCO)	207	....	....
1701 Change in uncollected payments, Federal sources (DCF)	....	1,322	....
1750 Spending auth from offsetting collections, disc (total)	1,098	2,392	1,140
1930 Total budgetary resources available	1,852	3,001	3,063
Memorandum (non-add) entries:			
1941 Unexpired unobligated balance, end of year	603	1,919	1,023
Change in obligated balance:			
Unpaid obligations:			
3000 Unpaid obligations, brought forward, Oct 1	534	816	781
3010 New obligations, unexpired accounts	1,249	1,082	2,040
3020 Outlays (gross)	–961	–1,111	–1,432
3040 Recoveries of prior year unpaid obligations, unexpired	–6	–6	–4
3050 Unpaid obligations, end of year	816	781	1,385
Uncollected payments:			
3060 Uncollected pymts, Fed sources, brought forward, Oct 1	–1,109	–1,316	–2,638
3070 Change in uncollected pymts, Fed sources, unexpired	–207	–1,322	....
3090 Uncollected pymts, Fed sources, end of year	–1,316	–2,638	–2,638
Memorandum (non-add) entries:			
3100 Obligated balance, start of year	–575	–500	–1,857
3200 Obligated balance, end of year	–500	–1,857	–1,253
Budget authority and outlays, net:			
Discretionary:			
4000 Budget authority, gross	1,098	2,392	1,140
Outlays, gross:			
4010 Outlays from new discretionary authority	735	828	855
4011 Outlays from discretionary balances	226	283	577
4020 Outlays, gross (total)	961	1,111	1,432
Offsets against gross budget authority and outlays:			
Offsetting collections (collected) from:			
4030 Federal sources	....	–267	–484
4033 Non-Federal sources	–891	–803	–656
4040 Offsets against gross budget authority and outlays (total)	–891	–1,070	–1,140
Additional offsets against gross budget authority only:			
4050 Change in uncollected pymts, Fed sources, unexpired	–207	–1,322	....
4080 Outlays, net (discretionary)	70	41	292
4180 Budget authority, net (total)	....	....	....
4190 Outlays, net (total)	70	41	292

The Bureau of Engraving and Printing (BEP) produces and delivers U.S. currency notes for the Federal Reserve System ordered by the Board of

Governors of the Federal Reserve and other security products for the Federal Government. BEP began printing currency in 1862 and operates on the basis of authority conferred upon the Secretary of the Treasury by 31 U.S.C. 321(a) (4) to engrave and print currency and other security documents. Operations are financed through a revolving fund established in 1950 in accordance with Public Law 81–656. The fund is reimbursed for direct and indirect costs of operations, including administrative expenses, through product sales. In 1977, Public Law 95–81 authorized BEP to include an amount sufficient to fund capital investment and to meet working capital requirements in the prices charged for products, eliminating the need for appropriations from Congress. In 2019, Public Law 116–6 authorized the use of the revolving fund for acquisition of necessary land for, and construction of, a replacement currency production facility.

The Bureau has three strategic goals: to safely and timely deliver quality products to stakeholders in a cost-effective and environmentally responsible manner; to create innovative designs, processes, and products that exceed stakeholders' expectations and to achieve overall excellence by balanced investment in people, processes, facilities, and technology. Other activities at BEP include engraving plates and dies; manufacturing inks used to print security products; purchasing materials, supplies, equipment; and storing and delivering products in accordance with customer requirements. In addition, BEP provides technical assistance, advice, and production services to other Federal agencies in the development of security documents that require counterfeit deterrent features due to their innate value or other characteristics. BEP supports the Treasury goals to Boost U.S. Economic Growth and Achieve Operational Excellence.

BEP's 2023 priorities include: (1) meeting the needs of the Nation for currency; (2) designing the next family of notes to include security feature development and currency design/development; (3) modernizing facilities, including the new DC Production Facility and Western Currency Facility Expansion; and (4) retooling manufacturing processes with state-of-the-art intaglio printing presses, electronic inspection systems, and finishing equipment. In 2022, the Federal Reserve Board (Board) established a minimum quantity of 6.876 billion notes with a ceiling up to 9.654 billion notes.

Object Classification (in millions of dollars)

Identification code 020–4502–0–4–803		2021 actual	2022 est.	2023 est.
	Reimbursable obligations:			
	Personnel compensation:			
11.1	Full-time permanent	169	190	195
11.5	Other personnel compensation	45	39	43
11.9	Total personnel compensation	214	229	238
12.1	Civilian personnel benefits	76	84	86
21.0	Travel and transportation of persons		1	1
22.0	Transportation of things	1	1	1
23.1	Rental payments to GSA	4	3	3
23.2	Rental payments to others	1	1	1
23.3	Communications, utilities, and miscellaneous charges	18	19	19
25.1	Advisory and assistance services	30	31	34
25.2	Other services from non-Federal sources	171	198	205
25.3	Other goods and services from Federal sources	34	35	915
25.4	Operation and maintenance of facilities	1	1	1
25.5	Research and development contracts	3	4	3
26.0	Supplies and materials	579	351	394
31.0	Equipment	84	124	139
32.0	Land and structures	33		
99.0	Reimbursable obligations	1,249	1,082	2,040
99.9	Total new obligations, unexpired accounts	1,249	1,082	2,040

Employment Summary

Identification code 020–4502–0–4–803	2021 actual	2022 est.	2023 est.
2001 Reimbursable civilian full-time equivalent employment	1,821	1,863	1,863

UNITED STATES MINT

Federal Funds

UNITED STATES MINT PUBLIC ENTERPRISE FUND

Pursuant to section 5136 of title 31, United States Code, the United States Mint is provided funding through the United States Mint Public Enterprise Fund for costs associated with the production of circulating coins, numismatic coins, and protective services, including both operating expenses and capital investments: Provided, That the aggregate amount of new liabilities and obligations incurred during fiscal year 2023 under such section 5136 for circulating coinage and protective service capital investments of the United States Mint shall not exceed $50,000,000.

Note.—A full-year 2022 appropriation for this account was not enacted at the time the Budget was prepared; therefore, the Budget assumes this account is operating under the Continuing Appropriations Act, 2022 (Division A of Public Law 117–43, as amended). The amounts included for 2022 reflect the annualized level provided by the continuing resolution.

Program and Financing (in millions of dollars)

Identification code 020–4159–0–3–803		2021 actual	2022 est.	2023 est.
	Obligations by program activity:			
0806	Total Operating	4,970	3,341	3,327
0807	Circulating and Protection Capital	50	50	50
0808	Numismatic Capital	10	20	20
0900	Total new obligations, unexpired accounts	5,030	3,411	3,397
	Budgetary resources:			
	Unobligated balance:			
1000	Unobligated balance brought forward, Oct 1	599	886	906
1021	Recoveries of prior year unpaid obligations	20	20	20
1070	Unobligated balance (total)	619	906	926
	Budget authority:			
	Spending authority from offsetting collections, discretionary:			
1700	Collected	5,297	3,411	3,397
1930	Total budgetary resources available	5,916	4,317	4,323
	Memorandum (non-add) entries:			
1941	Unexpired unobligated balance, end of year	886	906	926
	Change in obligated balance:			
	Unpaid obligations:			
3000	Unpaid obligations, brought forward, Oct 1	440	635	238
3010	New obligations, unexpired accounts	5,030	3,411	3,397
3020	Outlays (gross)	–4,815	–3,788	–3,400
3040	Recoveries of prior year unpaid obligations, unexpired	–20	–20	–20
3050	Unpaid obligations, end of year	635	238	215
	Memorandum (non-add) entries:			
3100	Obligated balance, start of year	440	635	238
3200	Obligated balance, end of year	635	238	215
	Budget authority and outlays, net:			
	Discretionary:			
4000	Budget authority, gross	5,297	3,411	3,397
	Outlays, gross:			
4010	Outlays from new discretionary authority	4,723	2,729	2,718
4011	Outlays from discretionary balances	92	1,059	682
4020	Outlays, gross (total)	4,815	3,788	3,400
	Offsets against gross budget authority and outlays:			
	Offsetting collections (collected) from:			
4033	Non-Federal sources	–5,297	–3,411	–3,397
4040	Offsets against gross budget authority and outlays (total)	–5,297	–3,411	–3,397
4180	Budget authority, net (total)			
4190	Outlays, net (total)	–482	377	3

The United States Mint mints and issues circulating coins, produces and distributes numismatic items, and provides security and asset protection. Since 1996, the Mint's operations have been funded through the Public Enterprise Fund (PEF) established by section 522 of Public Law 104–52 (31 U.S.C. 5136). The operations of the Mint are divided into two major components, circulating coinage and numismatic products. Finances for the two components are accounted for separately; Receipts from circulating coinage operations are not used to fund numismatic operations and receipts from numismatic operations are not used to fund circulating coinage operations. The Mint generates revenue through the issuance of circulating coins to the Federal Reserve Banks (FRBs) and the sale of numismatic products to the public and bullion coins to authorized purchasers. The Mint

UNITED STATES MINT PUBLIC ENTERPRISE FUND—Continued

submits annual audited financial statements to the Secretary of the Treasury and to the Congress in support of the operations of the PEF. In 2021, the Mint transferred $140 million to the General Fund.

Circulating Coinage.— This activity funds the minting and issuance of circulating coins to the FRBs in amounts that the Secretary of the Treasury determines are necessary to meet the needs of the United States. The 2023 Budget reflects production volumes that correspond to expected demand and raw materials costs, which are driven by commodity prices and volumes. The Mint receives funds from the Federal Reserve equal to the face value of the circulating coins shipped to the FRB. The Mint is credited with the full cost of producing and distributing the coins that are put into circulation, including the depreciation of manufacturing facilities and equipment. The difference between the face value of the coins and the full cost of producing the coins is called seigniorage, which is a means of financing the deficit and transferred periodically to the General Fund. The annual appropriations bill includes a statutory cap on Mint expenditures on circulating and protection capital investments. The cap for 2023 is $50 million.

Numismatic Items.— This activity funds the manufacturing of numismatic items, which include collectible coins and sets, medals, bullion coins, and other products for sale to collectors and other members of the public who desire high-quality or investment-grade versions of the Nation's coinage. These products include annual proof and uncirculated sets; investment-grade silver and gold bullion coins; uncirculated silver and gold coins; proof silver, gold, platinum and palladium coins; and commemorative coins and medals that are authorized to commemorate events, individuals, places, or other subjects. Prices for numismatic products are based on the estimated product cost plus a reasonable margin to assure that the numismatic program operates at no net cost to the taxpayer. Similarly, bullion coins are priced based on the market price of the precious metals plus a premium to cover manufacturing, marketing, and distribution costs. Making numismatic products accessible, available, and affordable to Americans who choose to purchase them is the highest priority of the Mint's numismatic operations.

Object Classification (in millions of dollars)

Identification code 020–4159–0–3–803		2021 actual	2022 est.	2023 est.
	Reimbursable obligations:			
	Personnel compensation:			
11.1	Full-time permanent	142	170	180
11.5	Other personnel compensation	18	16	16
11.9	Total personnel compensation	160	186	196
12.1	Civilian personnel benefits	59	56	57
13.0	Benefits for former personnel		1	1
21.0	Travel and transportation of persons		3	3
22.0	Transportation of things	42	34	34
23.1	Rental payments to GSA	1		
23.2	Rental payments to others	16	14	14
23.3	Communications, utilities, and miscellaneous charges	14	19	19
24.0	Printing and reproduction	1	3	3
25.1	Advisory and assistance services	55	53	53
25.2	Other services from non-Federal sources	20	21	22
25.3	Other goods and services from Federal sources	22	21	22
25.4	Operation and maintenance of facilities	9	9	10
25.5	Research and development contracts		1	1
25.6	Medical care	1	1	1
25.7	Operation and maintenance of equipment	9	7	7
26.0	Supplies and materials	4,560	2,909	2,880
31.0	Equipment	42	60	61
32.0	Land and structures	19	13	13
99.0	Reimbursable obligations	5,030	3,411	3,397
99.9	Total new obligations, unexpired accounts	5,030	3,411	3,397

Employment Summary

Identification code 020–4159–0–3–803	2021 actual	2022 est.	2023 est.
2001 Reimbursable civilian full-time equivalent employment	1,566	1,705	1,705

INTERNAL REVENUE SERVICE

The Internal Revenue Service (IRS) collects the revenue that funds the Government and administers the Nation's tax laws. During 2021, the IRS processed 269 million tax forms and collected $4.1 trillion in taxes (gross receipts before tax refunds), totaling 96 percent of Federal Government receipts. The IRS taxpayer service program assists millions of taxpayers in understanding and meeting their tax obligations. The IRS tax enforcement and compliance program deters taxpayers inclined to evade their responsibilities while pursuing those who violate tax laws.

The 2023 Budget provides $14.1 billion for the IRS to administer the tax code and implement key strategic priorities.

Taxpayer Service Account.— The Budget includes funding for Taxpayer Services that will allow the IRS to continue delivering services to taxpayers using a variety of in-person, telephone, and web-based methods. These tools help taxpayers understand their obligations, correctly file their returns, and pay taxes due in a timely manner with as little burden as possible. In fiscal year 2021, the IRS processed more than 155 million individual tax returns and issued more than 112 million federal tax refunds totaling more than $320.8 billion.

Enforcement Account.— The Enforcement account funds activities that protect revenue by identifying fraud and preventing issuance of questionable refunds including those related to identity theft; increase compliance by addressing offshore tax evasion; strengthen examination and collection programs, including return preparer; and address compliance issues in the tax-exempt sector. During 2021, the IRS achieved 2,766 criminal convictions with a conviction rate of 89.4 percent.

Operations Support Account.— The Budget includes funding for the overall planning, direction, operations and critical infrastructure activities, including the IT and cybersecurity that keep tax systems running and protect taxpayer data, the financial management activities that ensure effective stewardship of the Nation's revenues, and the physical infrastructure of IRS facilities. For example, in 2021, the IRS reduced the percentage of aged hardware within the IT environment from 16 percent at the end of 2020 to 9.3 percent through refreshing employee workstations, upgrading aged server operating systems and related aged hardware, and phasing out old equipment.

Business Systems Modernization Account.— IRS modernization efforts focus on building and deploying advanced information technology systems, processes, and tools to improve efficiency and enhance productivity. Modernizing is necessary to maintain the integrity of the Nation's voluntary tax system and collect trillions of dollars in tax revenue. With improved online services, taxpayers will be able to receive notifications, check their account balance, set up payment plans, and connect with an IRS representative through a single, online session. Other projects will help the IRS manage its caseload, increase productivity of its workforce, and ensure the security of taxpayer information.

Federal Funds

TAXPAYER SERVICES

For necessary expenses of the Internal Revenue Service to provide taxpayer services, including pre-filing assistance and education, filing and account services, taxpayer advocacy services, associated support costs, and other services as authorized by 5 U.S.C. 3109, at such rates as may be determined by the Commissioner, $3,684,593,000; of which not to exceed $100,000,000 shall remain available until September 30, 2024; of which not less than $11,000,000 shall be for the Tax Counseling for the Elderly Program; of which not less than $26,000,000 shall be available for low-income taxpayer clinic grants, including grants to individual clinics of up

DEPARTMENT OF THE TREASURY

Internal Revenue Service—Continued
Federal Funds—Continued

1017

to $200,000; of which not less than $30,000,000, to remain available until September 30, 2024, shall be available for the Community Volunteer Income Tax Assistance Matching Grants Program for tax return preparation assistance; and of which not less than $235,000,000 shall be available for operating expenses of the Taxpayer Advocate Service: Provided, That of the amounts made available for the Taxpayer Advocate Service, not less than $5,500,000 shall be for identity theft and refund fraud casework.

Note.—A full-year 2022 appropriation for this account was not enacted at the time the Budget was prepared; therefore, the Budget assumes this account is operating under the Continuing Appropriations Act, 2022 (Division A of Public Law 117–43, as amended). The amounts included for 2022 reflect the annualized level provided by the continuing resolution.

Program and Financing (in millions of dollars)

Identification code 020–0912–0–1–803		2021 actual	2022 est.	2023 est.
	Obligations by program activity:			
0001	Pre-filing taxpayer assistance and education	674	691	867
0002	Filing and account services	2,535	2,428	2,901
0100	Subtotal, direct programs	3,209	3,119	3,768
0799	Total direct obligations	3,209	3,119	3,768
0801	Taxpayer Services (Reimbursable)	39	45	47
0900	Total new obligations, unexpired accounts	3,248	3,164	3,815
	Budgetary resources:			
	Unobligated balance:			
1000	Unobligated balance brought forward, Oct 1	176	280	8
1011	Unobligated balance transfer from other acct [020–5432]	63	30	30
1011	Unobligated balance transfer from other acct [020–0913]	4		
1012	Unobligated balance transfers between expired and unexpired accounts	11		
1020	Adjustment of unobligated bal brought forward, Oct 1		–3	
1021	Recoveries of prior year unpaid obligations	22	7	7
1070	Unobligated balance (total)	276	314	45
	Budget authority:			
	Appropriations, discretionary:			
1100	Appropriation	2,556	2,556	3,685
1100	Appropriation [PL 116–260 Div. N — EIP #2]	178		
1121	Appropriations transferred from other acct [020–0913]	50	208	
1121	Appropriations transferred from other acct [020–5432]	2	49	49
1160	Appropriation, discretionary (total)	2,786	2,813	3,734
	Appropriations, mandatory:			
1200	Appropriation [ARP Child Tax Credit]	206		
1200	Appropriation [ARP EIP #3]	216		
1260	Appropriations, mandatory (total)	422		
	Spending authority from offsetting collections, discretionary:			
1700	Collected	42	45	47
1701	Change in uncollected payments, Federal sources	4		
1750	Spending auth from offsetting collections, disc (total)	46	45	47
1900	Budget authority (total)	3,254	2,858	3,781
1930	Total budgetary resources available	3,530	3,172	3,826
	Memorandum (non-add) entries:			
1940	Unobligated balance expiring	–2		
1941	Unexpired unobligated balance, end of year	280	8	11
	Change in obligated balance:			
	Unpaid obligations:			
3000	Unpaid obligations, brought forward, Oct 1	308	295	278
3010	New obligations, unexpired accounts	3,248	3,164	3,815
3011	Obligations ("upward adjustments"), expired accounts	42		
3020	Outlays (gross)	–3,256	–3,156	–3,697
3040	Recoveries of prior year unpaid obligations, unexpired	–22	–7	–7
3041	Recoveries of prior year unpaid obligations, expired	–25	–18	–18
3050	Unpaid obligations, end of year	295	278	371
	Uncollected payments:			
3060	Uncollected pymts, Fed sources, brought forward, Oct 1	–20	–4	–4
3070	Change in uncollected pymts, Fed sources, unexpired	–4		
3071	Change in uncollected pymts, Fed sources, expired	20		
3090	Uncollected pymts, Fed sources, end of year	–4	–4	–4
	Memorandum (non-add) entries:			
3100	Obligated balance, start of year	288	291	274
3200	Obligated balance, end of year	291	274	367
	Budget authority and outlays, net:			
	Discretionary:			
4000	Budget authority, gross	2,832	2,858	3,781
	Outlays, gross:			
4010	Outlays from new discretionary authority	2,579	2,621	3,464
4011	Outlays from discretionary balances	541	264	221
4020	Outlays, gross (total)	3,120	2,885	3,685
	Offsets against gross budget authority and outlays:			
	Offsetting collections (collected) from:			
4030	Federal sources	–66	–58	–60
4033	Non-Federal sources	–38	–22	–22
4040	Offsets against gross budget authority and outlays (total)	–104	–80	–82
	Additional offsets against gross budget authority only:			
4050	Change in uncollected pymts, Fed sources, unexpired	–4		
4052	Offsetting collections credited to expired accounts	62	35	35
4060	Additional offsets against budget authority only (total)	58	35	35
4070	Budget authority, net (discretionary)	2,786	2,813	3,734
4080	Outlays, net (discretionary)	3,016	2,805	3,603
	Mandatory:			
4090	Budget authority, gross	422		
	Outlays, gross:			
4100	Outlays from new mandatory authority	136		
4101	Outlays from mandatory balances		271	12
4110	Outlays, gross (total)	136	271	12
4180	Budget authority, net (total)	3,208	2,813	3,734
4190	Outlays, net (total)	3,152	3,076	3,615

This account primarily funds staffing for the processing of tax returns and related documents, and assistance for taxpayers in filing returns and paying taxes in a timely manner. It also supports a number of other activities, including forms, publications, and taxpayer advocacy services.

The 2023 Budget proposes changes to IRS appropriation language that allow the IRS to move certain support activities from the Operations Support appropriation to charge the full cost of mission activities to the Taxpayer Services and Enforcement appropriations. In the 2023 Budget, the IRS proposes to move $266 million in rent and $33 million in CFO expenses to Taxpayer Services from Operations Support.

Object Classification (in millions of dollars)

Identification code 020–0912–0–1–803		2021 actual	2022 est.	2023 est.
	Direct obligations:			
	Personnel compensation:			
11.1	Full-time permanent	1,748	1,714	2,069
11.3	Other than full-time permanent	55	63	70
11.5	Other personnel compensation	230	172	167
11.8	Special personal services payments		11	10
11.9	Total personnel compensation	2,033	1,960	2,316
12.1	Civilian personnel benefits	745	745	794
13.0	Benefits for former personnel	17	13	14
21.0	Travel and transportation of persons		6	11
22.0	Transportation of things	1	1	1
23.1	Rental payments to GSA			266
23.3	Communications, utilities, and miscellaneous charges	1	1	1
24.0	Printing and reproduction	9	10	11
25.1	Advisory and assistance services	171	211	142
25.2	Other services from non-Federal sources	106	42	50
25.3	Other goods and services from Federal sources	68	71	80
25.6	Medical care			15
26.0	Supplies and materials	4	4	4
41.0	Grants, subsidies, and contributions	54	54	63
42.0	Insurance claims and indemnities		1	
99.0	Direct obligations	3,209	3,119	3,768
99.0	Reimbursable obligations	39	45	47
99.9	Total new obligations, unexpired accounts	3,248	3,164	3,815

Employment Summary

Identification code 020–0912–0–1–803		2021 actual	2022 est.	2023 est.
1001	Direct civilian full-time equivalent employment	31,440	33,707	33,961
1001	Direct civilian full-time equivalent employment	71	71	71
2001	Reimbursable civilian full-time equivalent employment	514	429	450

ENFORCEMENT

For necessary expenses for tax enforcement activities of the Internal Revenue Service to determine and collect owed taxes, to provide legal and litigation support,

ENFORCEMENT—Continued

to conduct criminal investigations, to enforce criminal statutes related to violations of internal revenue laws and other financial crimes, to purchase and hire passenger motor vehicles (31 U.S.C. 1343(b)), associated support costs, and to provide other services as authorized by 5 U.S.C. 3109, at such rates as may be determined by the Commissioner, $6,272,313,000; of which not to exceed $250,000,000 shall remain available until September 30, 2024; of which not less than $60,257,000 shall be for the Interagency Crime and Drug Enforcement program; and of which not to exceed $21,000,000 shall be for investigative technology for the Criminal Investigation Division: Provided, That the amount made available for investigative technology for the Criminal Investigation Division shall be in addition to amounts made available for the Criminal Investigation Division under the "Operations Support" heading.

Note.—A full-year 2022 appropriation for this account was not enacted at the time the Budget was prepared; therefore, the Budget assumes this account is operating under the Continuing Appropriations Act, 2022 (Division A of Public Law 117–43, as amended). The amounts included for 2022 reflect the annualized level provided by the continuing resolution.

Program and Financing (in millions of dollars)

Identification code 020–0913–0–1–999		2021 actual	2022 est.	2023 est.
	Obligations by program activity:			
0001	Investigations	681	708	852
0002	Exam and Collections	4,187	4,351	5,230
0003	Regulatory	159	201	205
0100	Subtotal, Direct program	5,027	5,260	6,287
0799	Total direct obligations	5,027	5,260	6,287
0801	Enforcement (Reimbursable)	43	57	60
0900	Total new obligations, unexpired accounts	5,070	5,317	6,347
	Budgetary resources:			
	Unobligated balance:			
1000	Unobligated balance brought forward, Oct 1	276	252	11
1001	Discretionary unobligated balance brought fwd, Oct 1	273		
1010	Unobligated balance transfer to other accts [020–0912]	–4		
1010	Unobligated balance transfer to other accts [020–0919]	–16		
1012	Unobligated balance transfers between expired and unexpired accounts	1		
1021	Recoveries of prior year unpaid obligations	1	1	2
1033	Recoveries of prior year paid obligations	3	4	3
1070	Unobligated balance (total)	261	257	16
	Budget authority:			
	Appropriations, discretionary:			
1100	Appropriation	5,212	5,212	6,272
1100	Appropriation (PL 116–260 Div. N — EIP #2)	58		
1120	Appropriations transferred to other acct [020–0919]	–216		
1120	Appropriations transferred to other acct [020–0912]	–50	–208	
1160	Appropriation, discretionary (total)	5,004	5,004	6,272
	Spending authority from offsetting collections, discretionary:			
1700	Collected	24	29	31
1701	Change in uncollected payments, Federal sources	43	38	40
1750	Spending auth from offsetting collections, disc (total)	67	67	71
1900	Budget authority (total)	5,071	5,071	6,343
1930	Total budgetary resources available	5,332	5,328	6,359
	Memorandum (non-add) entries:			
1940	Unobligated balance expiring	–10		
1941	Unexpired unobligated balance, end of year	252	11	12
	Change in obligated balance:			
	Unpaid obligations:			
3000	Unpaid obligations, brought forward, Oct 1	500	590	613
3010	New obligations, unexpired accounts	5,070	5,317	6,347
3011	Obligations ("upward adjustments"), expired accounts	31		
3020	Outlays (gross)	–4,984	–5,273	–6,214
3040	Recoveries of prior year unpaid obligations, unexpired	–1	–1	–2
3041	Recoveries of prior year unpaid obligations, expired	–26	–20	–20
3050	Unpaid obligations, end of year	590	613	724
	Uncollected payments:			
3060	Uncollected pymts, Fed sources, brought forward, Oct 1	–32	–45	–83
3070	Change in uncollected pymts, Fed sources, unexpired	–43	–38	–40
3071	Change in uncollected pymts, Fed sources, expired	30		
3090	Uncollected pymts, Fed sources, end of year	–45	–83	–123
	Memorandum (non-add) entries:			
3100	Obligated balance, start of year	468	545	530
3200	Obligated balance, end of year	545	530	601
	Budget authority and outlays, net:			
	Discretionary:			
4000	Budget authority, gross	5,071	5,071	6,343
	Outlays, gross:			
4010	Outlays from new discretionary authority	4,413	4,651	5,823
4011	Outlays from discretionary balances	570	622	391
4020	Outlays, gross (total)	4,983	5,273	6,214
	Offsets against gross budget authority and outlays:			
	Offsetting collections (collected) from:			
4030	Federal sources	–56	–60	–61
4033	Non-Federal sources	–13	–17	–17
4040	Offsets against gross budget authority and outlays (total)	–69	–77	–78
	Additional offsets against gross budget authority only:			
4050	Change in uncollected pymts, Fed sources, unexpired	–43	–38	–40
4052	Offsetting collections credited to expired accounts	42	44	44
4053	Recoveries of prior year paid obligations, unexpired accounts	3	4	3
4060	Additional offsets against budget authority only (total)	2	10	7
4070	Budget authority, net (discretionary)	5,004	5,004	6,272
4080	Outlays, net (discretionary)	4,914	5,196	6,136
	Mandatory:			
	Outlays, gross:			
4101	Outlays from mandatory balances	1		
4180	Budget authority, net (total)	5,004	5,004	6,272
4190	Outlays, net (total)	4,915	5,196	6,136

This account primarily funds staffing for: the examination of tax returns, both domestic and international; the administrative and judicial settlement of taxpayer appeals of examination findings; technical rulings; monitoring employee pension plans; determining qualifications of organizations seeking tax-exempt status; examining the tax returns of exempt organizations; enforcing statutes relating to detection and investigation of criminal violations of the internal revenue laws and other financial crimes; identifying underreporting of tax obligations; securing unfiled tax returns; and collecting unpaid accounts.

The 2023 Budget proposes changes to IRS appropriation language that allow the IRS to move certain support activities from the Operations Support appropriation to charge the full cost of mission activities to the Taxpayer Services and Enforcement appropriations. In the 2023 Budget, the IRS proposes to move $369 million in rent and $42 million in CFO expenses to Enforcement from Operations Support.

Object Classification (in millions of dollars)

Identification code 020–0913–0–1–999		2021 actual	2022 est.	2023 est.
	Direct obligations:			
	Personnel compensation:			
11.1	Full-time permanent	3,162	3,216	3,653
11.3	Other than full-time permanent	25	22	23
11.5	Other personnel compensation	153	142	163
11.8	Special personal services payments	49	36	39
11.9	Total personnel compensation	3,389	3,416	3,878
12.1	Civilian personnel benefits	1,312	1,370	1,574
21.0	Travel and transportation of persons	8	58	119
22.0	Transportation of things	9	9	21
23.1	Rental payments to GSA			369
23.3	Communications, utilities, and miscellaneous charges	5	6	6
24.0	Printing and reproduction	2	3	7
25.1	Advisory and assistance services	171	243	124
25.2	Other services from non-Federal sources	28	43	76
25.3	Other goods and services from Federal sources	42	54	42
25.6	Medical care			9
25.7	Operation and maintenance of equipment	2	2	8
26.0	Supplies and materials	24	29	24
31.0	Equipment	25	10	16
32.0	Land and structures	1		2
42.0	Insurance claims and indemnities	2	1	12
91.0	Unvouchered	7	16	
99.0	Direct obligations	5,027	5,260	6,287
99.0	Reimbursable obligations	43	57	60
99.9	Total new obligations, unexpired accounts	5,070	5,317	6,347

Employment Summary

Identification code 020–0913–0–1–999	2021 actual	2022 est.	2023 est.
1001 Direct civilian full-time equivalent employment	35,060	34,118	38,831
2001 Reimbursable civilian full-time equivalent employment	101	80	84

OPERATIONS SUPPORT

For necessary expenses to operate the Internal Revenue Service, including headquarters; the hire of passenger motor vehicles (31 U.S.C. 1343(b)); the operations of the Internal Revenue Service Oversight Board; and other services as authorized by 5 U.S.C. 3109, at such rates as may be determined by the Commissioner; $3,833,734,000; of which not to exceed $275,000,000 shall remain available until September 30, 2024; of which not to exceed $10,000,000 shall remain available until expended for acquisition of equipment and construction, repair and renovation of facilities; of which not to exceed $1,000,000 shall remain available until September 30, 2025, for research; and of which not to exceed $20,000 shall be for official reception and representation expenses: Provided, That not later than 30 days after the end of each quarter, the Internal Revenue Service shall submit a report to the Committees on Appropriations of the House of Representatives and the Senate and the Comptroller General of the United States detailing major information technology investments in the Internal Revenue Service Integrated Modernization Business Plan portfolio, including detailed, plain language summaries on the status of plans, costs, and results; prior results and actual expenditures of the prior quarter; upcoming deliverables and costs for the fiscal year; risks and mitigation strategies associated with ongoing work; reasons for any cost or schedule variances; and total expenditures by fiscal year: Provided further, That the Internal Revenue Service shall include, in its budget justification for fiscal year 2024, a summary of cost and schedule performance information for its major information technology systems.

Note.—A full-year 2022 appropriation for this account was not enacted at the time the Budget was prepared; therefore, the Budget assumes this account is operating under the Continuing Appropriations Act, 2022 (Division A of Public Law 117–43, as amended). The amounts included for 2022 reflect the annualized level provided by the continuing resolution.

Program and Financing (in millions of dollars)

Identification code 020–0919–0–1–803		2021 actual	2022 est.	2023 est.
Obligations by program activity:				
0002	Infrastructure	917	900	406
0003	Shared Services and Support	1,377	1,160	1,126
0004	Information Services	2,823	2,701	2,778
0100	Subtotal, direct programs	5,117	4,761	4,310
0799	Total direct obligations	5,117	4,761	4,310
0801	Operations Support (Reimbursable)	55	55	58
0900	Total new obligations, unexpired accounts	5,172	4,816	4,368
Budgetary resources:				
	Unobligated balance:			
1000	Unobligated balance brought forward, Oct 1	163	841	361
1011	Unobligated balance transfer from other acct [020–5432]	178	156	80
1011	Unobligated balance transfer from other acct [020–0913]	16		
1012	Unobligated balance transfers between expired and unexpired accounts	4		
1020	Adjustment of unobligated bal brought forward, Oct 1		3	
1021	Recoveries of prior year unpaid obligations	22	15	15
1070	Unobligated balance (total)	383	1,015	456
	Budget authority:			
	Appropriations, discretionary:			
1100	Appropriation	3,928	3,928	3,834
1100	Appropriation [PL 116–260 Div. N — EIP #2]	273		
1121	Appropriations transferred from other acct [020–5432]	226	179	181
1121	Appropriations transferred from other acct [020–0913]	216		
1160	Appropriation, discretionary (total)	4,643	4,107	4,015
	Appropriations, mandatory:			
1200	Appropriation [ARP Child Tax Credit]	191		
1200	Appropriation [ARP EIP #3]	249		
1200	Appropriation [ARP Modernization]	500		
1260	Appropriations, mandatory (total)	940		
	Spending authority from offsetting collections, discretionary:			
1700	Collected	49	55	58
1701	Change in uncollected payments, Federal sources	6		
1750	Spending auth from offsetting collections, disc (total)	55	55	58
1900	Budget authority (total)	5,638	4,162	4,073
1930	Total budgetary resources available	6,021	5,177	4,529
	Memorandum (non-add) entries:			
1940	Unobligated balance expiring	–8		
1941	Unexpired unobligated balance, end of year	841	361	161
Change in obligated balance:				
	Unpaid obligations:			
3000	Unpaid obligations, brought forward, Oct 1	1,140	1,394	1,195
3010	New obligations, unexpired accounts	5,172	4,816	4,368
3011	Obligations ("upward adjustments"), expired accounts	20		
3020	Outlays (gross)	–4,852	–4,944	–4,431
3040	Recoveries of prior year unpaid obligations, unexpired	–22	–15	–15
3041	Recoveries of prior year unpaid obligations, expired	–64	–56	–56
3050	Unpaid obligations, end of year	1,394	1,195	1,061
	Uncollected payments:			
3060	Uncollected pymts, Fed sources, brought forward, Oct 1	–15	–6	–6
3070	Change in uncollected pymts, Fed sources, unexpired	–6		
3071	Change in uncollected pymts, Fed sources, expired	15		
3090	Uncollected pymts, Fed sources, end of year	–6	–6	–6
	Memorandum (non-add) entries:			
3100	Obligated balance, start of year	1,125	1,388	1,189
3200	Obligated balance, end of year	1,388	1,189	1,055
Budget authority and outlays, net:				
	Discretionary:			
4000	Budget authority, gross	4,698	4,162	4,073
	Outlays, gross:			
4010	Outlays from new discretionary authority	3,607	3,225	3,155
4011	Outlays from discretionary balances	1,117	1,210	1,020
4020	Outlays, gross (total)	4,724	4,435	4,175
	Offsets against gross budget authority and outlays:			
	Offsetting collections (collected) from:			
4030	Federal sources	–60	–61	–64
4033	Non-Federal sources	–14	–10	–10
4040	Offsets against gross budget authority and outlays (total)	–74	–71	–74
	Additional offsets against gross budget authority only:			
4050	Change in uncollected pymts, Fed sources, unexpired	–6		
4052	Offsetting collections credited to expired accounts	25	16	16
4060	Additional offsets against budget authority only (total)	19	16	16
4070	Budget authority, net (discretionary)	4,643	4,107	4,015
4080	Outlays, net (discretionary)	4,650	4,364	4,101
	Mandatory:			
4090	Budget authority, gross	940		
	Outlays, gross:			
4100	Outlays from new mandatory authority	128		
4101	Outlays from mandatory balances		509	256
4110	Outlays, gross (total)	128	509	256
4180	Budget authority, net (total)	5,583	4,107	4,015
4190	Outlays, net (total)	4,778	4,873	4,357

This account provides resources for overall planning, direction, operations, and critical infrastructure activities for the IRS. These activities include IT and cybersecurity that keep tax systems running and protect taxpayer data, the financial management activities that ensure effective stewardship of the nation's revenues, and the physical infrastructure that help IRS employees serve customers in office, campus, and Taxpayer Assistance Center sites. Telecommunications, human resource, and communications infrastructure are also critical components of this appropriation and are vital to maintaining adequate levels of customer service and the post-filing processes necessary for the tax system to properly function.

The 2023 Budget proposes changes to IRS appropriation language that allow the IRS to move certain support activities from the Operations Support appropriation to charge the full cost of mission activities to the Taxpayer Services and Enforcement appropriations. In the 2023 Budget, the IRS proposes to move $635 million in rent and $75 million in CFO expenses from Operations Support to Taxpayer Services and Enforcement.

Object Classification (in millions of dollars)

Identification code 020–0919–0–1–803		2021 actual	2022 est.	2023 est.
	Direct obligations:			
	Personnel compensation:			
11.1	Full-time permanent	1,304	1,478	1,395
11.3	Other than full-time permanent	6	5	5

Internal Revenue Service—Continued
Federal Funds—Continued

OPERATIONS SUPPORT—Continued
Object Classification—Continued

Identification code 020–0919–0–1–803		2021 actual	2022 est.	2023 est.
11.5	Other personnel compensation	33	44	43
11.8	Special personal services payments	....	1	1
11.9	Total personnel compensation	1,343	1,528	1,444
12.1	Civilian personnel benefits	483	538	523
21.0	Travel and transportation of persons	2	9	12
22.0	Transportation of things	13	14	16
23.1	Rental payments to GSA	580	609	....
23.2	Rental payments to others	5	....	....
23.3	Communications, utilities, and miscellaneous charges	558	309	339
24.0	Printing and reproduction	59	33	22
25.1	Advisory and assistance services	1,191	938	1,031
25.2	Other services from non-Federal sources	42	26	50
25.3	Other goods and services from Federal sources	71	65	69
25.4	Operation and maintenance of facilities	195	203	224
25.6	Medical care	15	14	20
25.7	Operation and maintenance of equipment	71	44	54
26.0	Supplies and materials	7	6	7
31.0	Equipment	422	396	420
32.0	Land and structures	60	28	78
42.0	Insurance claims and indemnities	....	1	1
99.0	Direct obligations	5,117	4,761	4,310
99.0	Reimbursable obligations	55	55	58
99.9	Total new obligations, unexpired accounts	5,172	4,816	4,368

Employment Summary

Identification code 020–0919–0–1–803		2021 actual	2022 est.	2023 est.
1001	Direct civilian full-time equivalent employment	11,775	12,092	11,564
1001	Direct civilian full-time equivalent employment	10	15	....
2001	Reimbursable civilian full-time equivalent employment	79	76	80

BUSINESS SYSTEMS MODERNIZATION

For necessary expenses of the Internal Revenue Service's business systems modernization program, $310,027,000, to remain available until September 30, 2025, for the capital asset acquisition of information technology systems, including management and related contractual costs of said acquisitions, including related Internal Revenue Service labor costs, and contractual costs associated with operations authorized by 5 U.S.C. 3109: Provided, That not later than 30 days after the end of each quarter, the Internal Revenue Service shall submit a report to the Committees on Appropriations of the House of Representatives and the Senate and the Comptroller General of the United States detailing major information technology investments in the Internal Revenue Service Integrated Modernization Business Plan portfolio, including detailed, plain language summaries on the status of plans, costs, and results; prior results and actual expenditures of the prior quarter; upcoming deliverables and costs for the fiscal year; risks and mitigation strategies associated with ongoing work; reasons for any cost or schedule variances; and total expenditures by fiscal year.

Note.—A full-year 2022 appropriation for this account was not enacted at the time the Budget was prepared; therefore, the Budget assumes this account is operating under the Continuing Appropriations Act, 2022 (Division A of Public Law 117–43, as amended). The amounts included for 2022 reflect the annualized level provided by the continuing resolution.

Program and Financing (in millions of dollars)

Identification code 020–0921–0–1–803		2021 actual	2022 est.	2023 est.
	Obligations by program activity:			
0001	Business Systems Modernization	348	462	512
	Budgetary resources:			
	Unobligated balance:			
1000	Unobligated balance brought forward, Oct 1	30	437	204
1001	Discretionary unobligated balance brought fwd, Oct 1	30	....	....
1010	Unobligated balance transfer to other accts [020–5432]	–1	....	....
1021	Recoveries of prior year unpaid obligations	4	6	3
1070	Unobligated balance (total)	33	443	207
	Budget authority:			
	Appropriations, discretionary:			
1100	Appropriation	223	223	310
1121	Appropriations transferred from other acct [020–5432]	29	....	....
1160	Appropriation, discretionary (total)	252	223	310
	Appropriations, mandatory:			
1200	Appropriation [ARP IT Modernization]	500	....	....
1900	Budget authority (total)	752	223	310
1930	Total budgetary resources available	785	666	517
	Memorandum (non-add) entries:			
1941	Unexpired unobligated balance, end of year	437	204	5
	Change in obligated balance:			
	Unpaid obligations:			
3000	Unpaid obligations, brought forward, Oct 1	161	201	256
3010	New obligations, unexpired accounts	348	462	512
3020	Outlays (gross)	–302	–399	–425
3040	Recoveries of prior year unpaid obligations, unexpired	–4	–6	–3
3041	Recoveries of prior year unpaid obligations, expired	–2	–2	–2
3050	Unpaid obligations, end of year	201	256	338
	Memorandum (non-add) entries:			
3100	Obligated balance, start of year	161	201	256
3200	Obligated balance, end of year	201	256	338
	Budget authority and outlays, net:			
	Discretionary:			
4000	Budget authority, gross	252	223	310
	Outlays, gross:			
4010	Outlays from new discretionary authority	137	88	122
4011	Outlays from discretionary balances	151	86	78
4020	Outlays, gross (total)	288	174	200
	Mandatory:			
4090	Budget authority, gross	500	....	....
	Outlays, gross:			
4100	Outlays from new mandatory authority	14	....	....
4101	Outlays from mandatory balances	....	225	225
4110	Outlays, gross (total)	14	225	225
4180	Budget authority, net (total)	752	223	310
4190	Outlays, net (total)	302	399	425

This account provides resources for the planning and capital asset acquisition of information technology to modernize key tax administration systems based on the IRS's multi-year plan to transform the taxpayer experience and modernize the core tax processing systems while enhancing information technology and taxpayer protections. It provides funding to support the Customer Account Data Engine (CADE2); cybersecurity; IT infrastructure; the Enterprise Case Management system; and taxpayers' online experience and secure digital communications and capabilities.

Object Classification (in millions of dollars)

Identification code 020–0921–0–1–803		2021 actual	2022 est.	2023 est.
	Direct obligations:			
	Personnel compensation:			
11.1	Full-time permanent	42	45	62
11.5	Other personnel compensation	1	1	1
11.9	Total personnel compensation	43	46	63
12.1	Civilian personnel benefits	15	16	21
21.0	Travel and transportation of persons	....	1	1
25.1	Advisory and assistance services	243	274	327
25.2	Other services from non-Federal sources	22	61	43
25.7	Operation and maintenance of equipment	....	....	1
31.0	Equipment	25	64	56
99.0	Direct obligations	348	462	512
99.9	Total new obligations, unexpired accounts	348	462	512

Employment Summary

Identification code 020–0921–0–1–803		2021 actual	2022 est.	2023 est.
1001	Direct civilian full-time equivalent employment	305	324	412

BUILD AMERICA BOND PAYMENTS, RECOVERY ACT

Program and Financing (in millions of dollars)

Identification code 020–0935–0–1–806	2021 actual	2022 est.	2023 est.
Obligations by program activity:			
0001 Build America Bond Payments, Recovery Act (Direct)	3,012	2,614	2,587
0900 Total new obligations, unexpired accounts (object class 41.0)	3,012	2,614	2,587
Budgetary resources:			
Budget authority:			
Appropriations, mandatory:			
1200 Appropriation	3,199	2,772	2,743
1230 Appropriations and/or unobligated balance of appropriations permanently reduced	–187	–158	–156
1260 Appropriations, mandatory (total)	3,012	2,614	2,587
1930 Total budgetary resources available	3,012	2,614	2,587
Change in obligated balance:			
Unpaid obligations:			
3010 New obligations, unexpired accounts	3,012	2,614	2,587
3020 Outlays (gross)	–3,012	–2,614	–2,587
Budget authority and outlays, net:			
Mandatory:			
4090 Budget authority, gross	3,012	2,614	2,587
Outlays, gross:			
4100 Outlays from new mandatory authority	3,012	2,614	2,587
4180 Budget authority, net (total)	3,012	2,614	2,587
4190 Outlays, net (total)	3,012	2,614	2,587

The American Recovery and Reinvestment Act of 2009 (P.L. 111–5), section 1531, allows State and local governments to issue Build America Bonds through December 31, 2010. These tax credit bonds, which include Recovery Zone Bonds, differ from tax-exempt governmental obligation bonds in two principal ways: 1) interest paid on tax credit bonds is taxable; and 2) a portion of the interest paid on tax credit bonds takes the form of a Federal tax credit. The bond issuer may elect to receive a direct payment in the amount of the tax credit for obligations issued before January 1, 2011. This account reflects the continuing interest payments over time.

PAYMENT WHERE EARNED INCOME CREDIT EXCEEDS LIABILITY FOR TAX

Program and Financing (in millions of dollars)

Identification code 020–0906–0–1–609	2021 actual	2022 est.	2023 est.
Obligations by program activity:			
0001 Payment Where Earned Income Credit Exceeds Liability for Tax (Direct)	60,757	67,719	56,321
0002 Payment where Earned Income Tax Credit Exceeds Liability for Tax Territories	....	734	749
0900 Total new obligations, unexpired accounts (object class 41.0)	60,757	68,453	57,070
Budgetary resources:			
Budget authority:			
Appropriations, mandatory:			
1200 Appropriation	60,757	68,453	57,070
1930 Total budgetary resources available	60,757	68,453	57,070
Change in obligated balance:			
Unpaid obligations:			
3010 New obligations, unexpired accounts	60,757	68,453	57,070
3020 Outlays (gross)	–60,757	–68,453	–57,070
Budget authority and outlays, net:			
Mandatory:			
4090 Budget authority, gross	60,757	68,453	57,070
Outlays, gross:			
4100 Outlays from new mandatory authority	60,757	68,453	57,070
4180 Budget authority, net (total)	60,757	68,453	57,070
4190 Outlays, net (total)	60,757	68,453	57,070

Summary of Budget Authority and Outlays (in millions of dollars)

	2021 actual	2022 est.	2023 est.
Enacted/requested:			
Budget Authority	60,757	68,453	57,070
Outlays	60,757	68,453	57,070
Legislative proposal, subject to PAYGO:			
Budget Authority			65
Outlays			65
Total:			
Budget Authority	60,757	68,453	57,135
Outlays	60,757	68,453	57,135

The Earned Income Tax Credit (EITC) was enacted by the Tax Reduction Act of 1975 (P.L. 94–12) and made permanent by the Revenue Act of 1978 (P.L. 95–600). The amount of EITC a taxpayer may receive depends on, among other factors, the number of qualifying children the taxpayer has. The amount of EITC a taxpayer may receive initially increases as the taxpayer earns more income, then remains constant over a range of income, and then decreases as income increases further. The credit phases out based on the greater of (1) earned income and (2) adjusted gross income. As provided by law, there are instances where the EITC exceeds the amount of tax liability owed through the individual income tax system, resulting in a potential refund to the taxpayer.

Sections 9621 through 9626 of the American Rescue Plan Act of 2021, (P.L. 117–2) (American Rescue Plan) modified the EITC. For Tax Year 2021 only, the American Rescue Plan, generally, (i) reduced from 25 to 19 the general minimum age to claim the EITC with no qualifying children (Childless EITC); (ii) eliminated the upper-age limit for the Childless EITC; (iii) increased the credit amount and the phaseout percentages for the Childless EITC; and (iv) allowed individuals to use their earned income from Tax Year 2019 instead of their earned income from Tax Year 2021, if earned income from Tax Year 2021 is less, for purposes of calculating the EITC for Tax Year 2021. The American Rescue Plan also permanently modified the rules, beginning in 2021, regarding (i) children who fail to meet certain identification requirements, (ii) separated spouses, (iii) the disqualified investment income test, and (iv) the application of the EITC to the U.S. territories.

PAYMENT WHERE EARNED INCOME CREDIT EXCEEDS LIABILITY FOR TAX

(Legislative proposal, subject to PAYGO)

Program and Financing (in millions of dollars)

Identification code 020–0906–4–1–609	2021 actual	2022 est.	2023 est.
Obligations by program activity:			
0001 Payment Where Earned Income Credit Exceeds Liability for Tax (Direct)			65
0900 Total new obligations, unexpired accounts (object class 41.0)			65
Budgetary resources:			
Budget authority:			
Appropriations, mandatory:			
1200 Appropriation			65
1930 Total budgetary resources available			65
Change in obligated balance:			
Unpaid obligations:			
3010 New obligations, unexpired accounts			65
3020 Outlays (gross)			–65
Budget authority and outlays, net:			
Mandatory:			
4090 Budget authority, gross			65
Outlays, gross:			
4100 Outlays from new mandatory authority			65
4180 Budget authority, net (total)			65
4190 Outlays, net (total)			65

The Budget proposes the following that have an impact on EITC: increase the amount of the tax penalties that apply to paid tax return preparers for willful, reckless, or unreasonable understatements, and other forms of

PAYMENT WHERE EARNED INCOME CREDIT EXCEEDS LIABILITY FOR TAX—Continued

noncompliance; establish new penalties for the appropriation of Preparer Tax Identification Numbers and Electronic Filing Identification Numbers and for failing to disclose the use of a paid tax return preparer, increases the time period during which the penalty may be assessed to six years for a failure to furnish the preparer's identifying number, and provide the Secretary of the Treasury with explicit authority to regulate all paid preparers of Federal tax returns; permanently exclude certain discharged student loan amounts from gross income; and various health reforms.

U.S. CORONAVIRUS PAYMENTS

Program and Financing (in millions of dollars)

Identification code 020–0905–0–1–609		2021 actual	2022 est.	2023 est.
	Obligations by program activity:			
0001	Economic Impact Payments	431		
0002	Economic Impact Payments, Territories	2		
0003	Economic Impact Payments, 2nd	140,385		
0004	Economic Impact Payments, Territories 2nd	984	15	
0005	Recovery Rebate Credit	23,403	1,198	
0006	Economic Impact Payments, 3rd	400,188	3,102	
0007	Economic Impact Payments, Territories 3rd	4,115	25	
0008	Recovery Rebate Credit, 3rd		2,264	24
0900	Total new obligations, unexpired accounts (object class 41.0)	569,508	6,604	24
	Budgetary resources:			
	Budget authority:			
	Appropriations, mandatory:			
1200	Appropriation [CARES Act]	433		
1200	Appropriation [CAA]	141,369	15	
1200	Appropriation [Recovery Rebates (CARES Act and CAA)]	23,403	1,198	
1200	Appropriation [ARP]	404,303	5,391	24
1260	Appropriations, mandatory (total)	569,508	6,604	24
1930	Total budgetary resources available	569,508	6,604	24
	Change in obligated balance:			
	Unpaid obligations:			
3010	New obligations, unexpired accounts	569,508	6,604	24
3020	Outlays (gross)	–569,508	–6,604	–24
	Budget authority and outlays, net:			
	Mandatory:			
4090	Budget authority, gross	569,508	6,604	24
	Outlays, gross:			
4100	Outlays from new mandatory authority	569,508	6,604	24
4180	Budget authority, net (total)	569,508	6,604	24
4190	Outlays, net (total)	569,508	6,604	24

This account includes the 2020 and 2021 recovery rebate credits, including the advance Economic Impact Payments of those credits, enacted in Section 2201(a) of the Coronavirus Aid, Relief, and Economic Security Act (CARES Act) (P.L. 116–136), Section 272(a) of the COVID-related Tax Relief Act of 2020, enacted in Subtitle B of Title II of Division N of the Consolidated Appropriations Act, 2021 (P.L. 116–260), and Section 9601(a) of the American Rescue Plan Act of 2021 (P.L. 117–2).

PAYMENT WHERE CHILD TAX CREDIT EXCEEDS LIABILITY FOR TAX

Program and Financing (in millions of dollars)

Identification code 020–0922–0–1–609		2021 actual	2022 est.	2023 est.
	Obligations by program activity:			
0001	Payment Where Child Tax Credit Exceeds Liability for Tax (Direct)	32,755	51,407	28,816
0002	Payment Where Child Tax Credit Exceeds Liability for Tax Territory Payment	59	192	248
0003	Payment for the Advanced Child Tax Credit	45,950	46,902	
0004	Payment for the Advanced Child Tax Credit (Territory Payment)	195		
0900	Total new obligations, unexpired accounts (object class 41.0)	78,959	98,501	29,064
	Budgetary resources:			
	Budget authority:			
	Appropriations, mandatory:			
1200	Appropriation	78,959	98,501	29,064
1930	Total budgetary resources available	78,959	98,501	29,064
	Change in obligated balance:			
	Unpaid obligations:			
3010	New obligations, unexpired accounts	78,959	98,501	29,064
3020	Outlays (gross)	–78,959	–98,501	–29,064
	Budget authority and outlays, net:			
	Mandatory:			
4090	Budget authority, gross	78,959	98,501	29,064
	Outlays, gross:			
4100	Outlays from new mandatory authority	78,959	98,501	29,064
4180	Budget authority, net (total)	78,959	98,501	29,064
4190	Outlays, net (total)	78,959	98,501	29,064

Summary of Budget Authority and Outlays (in millions of dollars)

	2021 actual	2022 est.	2023 est.
Enacted/requested:			
Budget Authority	78,959	98,501	29,064
Outlays	78,959	98,501	29,064
Legislative proposal, subject to PAYGO:			
Budget Authority			48
Outlays			48
Total:			
Budget Authority	78,959	98,501	29,112
Outlays	78,959	98,501	29,112

The Child Tax Credit (CTC) was enacted by the Taxpayer Relief Act of 1997 (P.L. 105–34). The Tax Cuts and Jobs Act (P.L. 115–97) (TCJA) increased the credit to $2,000 per qualifying child under age 17 for tax years 2018–2025. The CTC phases out for higher-income taxpayers. Taxpayers with insufficient tax liability to claim the entire CTC may receive up to $1,400 in a refundable credit, known as the Additional Child Tax Credit (ACTC). TCJA also provided that, in order to receive the CTC and/or ACTC, a taxpayer must include a Social Security number for each qualifying child for whom the credit is claimed on the tax return.

Sections 9611 and 9612 of the American Rescue Plan Act of 2021 (P.L. 117–2) (American Rescue Plan) amended the Internal Revenue Code (Code) to modify the CTC generally for 2021 only. Section 9611 of the American Rescue Plan amended Section 24 of the Code to make the entire amount of the CTC refundable and extended the CTC to cover qualifying children 17 years old and younger. The legislation also increased the amount of the CTC from $2,000 to $3,600 for qualifying children under age 6, and $3,000 for other qualifying children under age 18. The amount of this increase in the CTC (that is, $1,600 in the case of qualifying children under age 6 and $1,000 in the case of other qualifying children under age 18) is reduced by $50 for each $1,000 (or fraction thereof) by which the taxpayer's modified adjusted gross income exceeds certain thresholds. These thresholds are (i) $150,000 for joint filers and surviving spouses, (ii) $112,500 for heads of household, and (iii) $75,000 in all other cases. In addition, the American Rescue Plan amended the Code to require advance payments of the CTC to be made periodically throughout 2021, beginning after July 1, based on the taxpayer's 2020 or 2019 tax returns, in an aggregate amount equal to 50 percent of the estimated amount of the taxpayer's refundable CTC. Section 9612 of the American Rescue Plan amended Section 24 of the Code to remove the requirement for bona fide residents of Puerto Rico to have three qualifying children to claim the CTC. For 2021 and years thereafter, bona fide residents of Puerto Rico need only one qualifying child to claim the CTC. In addition, section 9612 of the American Rescue Plan amended Section 24 of the Code to provide that certain residents of American Samoa, the Commonwealth of the Northern Mariana Islands, Guam, or the U.S. Virgin Islands, may have been eligible to receive from their territory tax agency advance Child Tax Credit payments under the expanded, refundable CTC for 2021.

DEPARTMENT OF THE TREASURY

PAYMENT WHERE CHILD TAX CREDIT EXCEEDS LIABILITY FOR TAX

(Legislative proposal, subject to PAYGO)

Program and Financing (in millions of dollars)

Identification code 020–0922–4–1–609	2021 actual	2022 est.	2023 est.
Obligations by program activity:			
0001 Payment Where Child Tax Credit Exceeds Liability for Tax (Direct)			48
0900 Total new obligations, unexpired accounts (object class 41.0)			48
Budgetary resources:			
Budget authority:			
Appropriations, mandatory:			
1200 Appropriation			48
1930 Total budgetary resources available			48
Change in obligated balance:			
Unpaid obligations:			
3010 New obligations, unexpired accounts			48
3020 Outlays (gross)			–48
Budget authority and outlays, net:			
Mandatory:			
4090 Budget authority, gross			48
Outlays, gross:			
4100 Outlays from new mandatory authority			48
4180 Budget authority, net (total)			48
4190 Outlays, net (total)			48

The Budget proposes the following that have an impact on CTC: increase the amount of the tax penalties that apply to paid tax return preparers for willful, reckless, or unreasonable understatements, and other forms of noncompliance; establish new penalties for the appropriation of Preparer Tax Identification Numbers and Electronic Filing Identification Numbers and for failing to disclose the use of a paid tax return preparer, increases the time period during which the penalty may be assessed to six years for a failure to furnish the preparer's identifying number, and provide the Secretary of the Treasury with explicit authority to regulate all paid preparers of Federal tax returns; permanently exclude certain discharged student loan amounts from gross income; and various health reforms.

PAYMENT WHERE HEALTH COVERAGE TAX CREDIT EXCEEDS LIABILITY FOR TAX

Program and Financing (in millions of dollars)

Identification code 020–0923–0–1–551	2021 actual	2022 est.	2023 est.
Obligations by program activity:			
0001 Payment Where Health Coverage Tax Credit Exceeds Liability for T (Direct)		23	20
0900 Total new obligations, unexpired accounts (object class 41.0)		23	20
Budgetary resources:			
Budget authority:			
Appropriations, mandatory:			
1200 Appropriation		23	20
1930 Total budgetary resources available		23	20
Change in obligated balance:			
Unpaid obligations:			
3010 New obligations, unexpired accounts		23	20
3020 Outlays (gross)		–23	–20
Budget authority and outlays, net:			
Mandatory:			
4090 Budget authority, gross		23	20
Outlays, gross:			
4100 Outlays from new mandatory authority		23	20
4180 Budget authority, net (total)		23	20
4190 Outlays, net (total)		23	20

The Health Coverage Tax Credit (HCTC) is a refundable tax credit that pays 72.5% of qualified health insurance premiums for eligible individuals and their families (as provided in IRC 35(a)). Those eligible include certain recipients of Trade Adjustment Assistance (TAA) and beneficiaries of the Pension Benefit Guaranty Corporation who are aged 55 through 64. Individuals cannot claim both HCTC and a premium tax credit for the same coverage. The credit can be paid in advance. The HCTC was created in the Trade Act of 2002 (P.L. 107–210), subsequently extended, temporarily eliminated in 2014 (P.L. 112–40, section 241), then later reinstated through December 31, 2019 (P.L. 114–27, section 407). The Further Consolidated Appropriations Act, 2020 (P.L. 116–94, section 146) extended the credit through December 31, 2020, and the Consolidated Appropriations Act, 2021 (P.L. 116–260, section 134) extended the credit though December 31, 2021.

U.S. CORONAVIRUS REFUNDABLE CREDITS

Program and Financing (in millions of dollars)

Identification code 020–0936–0–1–609	2021 actual	2022 est.	2023 est.
Obligations by program activity:			
0001 Paid Family and Sick Leave Credits	689	750	
0003 Employee Retention Credit	9,280	7,800	20
0005 COBRA Credits	174	450	
0900 Total new obligations, unexpired accounts (object class 41.0)	10,143	9,000	20
Budgetary resources:			
Budget authority:			
Appropriations, mandatory:			
1200 Appropriation	10,143	9,000	20
1930 Total budgetary resources available	10,143	9,000	20
Change in obligated balance:			
Unpaid obligations:			
3010 New obligations, unexpired accounts	10,143	9,000	20
3020 Outlays (gross)	–10,143	–9,000	–20
Budget authority and outlays, net:			
Mandatory:			
4090 Budget authority, gross	10,143	9,000	20
Outlays, gross:			
4100 Outlays from new mandatory authority	10,143	9,000	20
4180 Budget authority, net (total)	10,143	9,000	20
4190 Outlays, net (total)	10,143	9,000	20

Employee Retention Credit.—Section 2301 of the Coronavirus Aid, Relief, and Economic Security Act (CARES Act, P.L. 116–136) created the employee retention credit, a refundable tax credit against certain employment taxes equal to 50 percent of the qualified wages certain businesses and tax-exempt employers pay to employees (up to $10,000 per employee) after March 12, 2020, and before January 1, 2021. Eligible employers could get immediate access to the credit by reducing employment tax deposits they were otherwise required to make and by requesting an advance of the credit.

Section 206 of the Taxpayer Certainty and Disaster Tax Relief Act of 2020, enacted as Division EE of the Consolidated Appropriations Act, 2021 (P.L. 116–260) amended and made technical changes to section 2301 of the CARES Act retroactive to the section 2301's original effective date including permitting an employer that received a Paycheck Protection Program (PPP) loan to be eligible to claim an employee retention credit under section 2301, provided the wages reported in support of the forgiveness of the PPP loan are not the same wages for which the credit is claimed.

Section 207 of the Taxpayer Certainty and Disaster Tax Relief Act of 2020 extended the employee retention credit to qualified wages paid after December 31, 2020 and before July 1, 2021; increased the maximum credit amount that may be claimed per employee (making it equal to 70 percent of $10,000 of qualified wages paid to an employee per calendar quarter); limited eligibility for and amount of the credit advance; and expanded the category of employers that may be entitled to claim the credit, among other technical amendments.

U.S. Coronavirus Refundable Credits—Continued

Section 9651 of the American Rescue Plan (ARP) Act of 2021 (P.L. 117–2) enacted section 3134 of the Internal Revenue Code of 1986, which extended the availability of the employee retention credit to wages paid after June 30, 2021, and before January 1, 2022. Section 3134 generally maintained the structure of the employee retention credit as provided under section 2301 of the CARES Act, as amended, with certain changes.

Employers in a U.S. Territory that otherwise qualify for the employee retention credit can claim the credit. Payments of wages by employers in U.S. Territories are wages within the meaning of section 3121(a) and therefore employers eligible to claim the credit include employers in the U.S. Territories that pay qualified wages and otherwise meet the requirements for the credit.

Section 80604 of the Infrastructure Investment and Jobs Act of 2021 (P.L. 117–58) amended section 3134 of the Internal Revenue Code to provide that the employee retention credit under section 3134 shall apply only to wages paid after June 30, 2021, and before October 1, 2021 (or, in the case of wages paid by an eligible employer which is a recovery startup business, January 1, 2022).

Paid Leave Credits.—Sections 7001 and 7003 of Division G of the Families First Coronavirus Response Act (FFCRA, P.L. 116–127) created refundable tax credits against certain employment taxes for small and midsize employers to reimburse them for the cost of providing required paid sick and family leave wages to their employees for leave related to COVID-19 as set forth under Division E, the Emergency Paid Sick Leave Act (EPSLA) and Division C, the Emergency Family and Medical Leave Expansion Act (Expanded FMLA) of the FFCRA. Sections 7002 and 7004 of the FFCRA created similar credits for certain self-employed persons in similar COVID-related circumstances. An employer is eligible for credits for qualified sick leave wages up to $511 per day and $5,110 in the aggregate (for up to 10 days of leave) and up to $200 per day and $10,000 in the aggregate (for up to 10 weeks of leave) for qualifying COVID-related leave reasons. Eligible employers could get immediate access to the credit by reducing employment tax deposits they are otherwise required to make and by requesting an advance of the credit. The requirement to provide leave under the EPSLA and Expanded FMLA expired on December 31, 2020, but the credits for paid leave that otherwise would have satisfied the requirements under the EPSLA and Expanded FMLA were later extended through September 30, 2021.

Sections 286, 287 and 288 of the COVID-related Tax Relief Act of 2020, enacted under Division N of the Consolidated Appropriations Act, 2021 (P.L. 116–260) extended the credits for periods of leave from January 1, 2021, through March 31, 2021, and made certain technical improvements to the FFCRA credit provisions.

Section 9641 of the ARP enacted sections 3131, 3132, and 3133 of the Internal Revenue Code to extend the credits through the period from April 1, 2021 through September 30, 2021; expand the category of employers eligible for the credit; reset the limitations on the amount of qualified wages that may be taken into account for purposes of the credits (and increased the aggregate cap for paid family leave wages from $10,000 to $12,000); expand the category of qualifying reasons for paid leave wages eligible for the credits (including leave to receive and recover from a COVID-19 vaccine), and make other technical amendments. (Sections 9642 and 9643 of the ARP amended and extended the equivalent tax credits for certain self-employed individuals for April 1, 2021, through September 30, 2021.)

Employers in a U.S. Territory that otherwise qualify for the paid leave credits can claim the credit. Payments of wages by employers in U.S. Territories are wages within the meaning of section 3121(a) and therefore employers eligible to claim the credit include employers in the U.S. Territories that pay qualified wages and otherwise meet the requirements for the credit.

COBRA Credit.—Section 9501 of the ARP required certain employers to offer free Consolidated Omnibus Budget Reconciliation Act (COBRA) coverage to certain qualified individuals for periods of coverage from April 1, 2021 through September 30, 2021. The ARP provided tax credits to employers to offset the cost of the COBRA coverage. The ARP provision subsidized 100 percent of COBRA premiums for six months for individuals who lost employment involuntarily or had reduced hours.

Payment Where Small Business Health Insurance Tax Credit Exceeds Liability for Tax

Program and Financing (in millions of dollars)

Identification code 020–0951–0–1–551		2021 actual	2022 est.	2023 est.
	Change in obligated balance:			
	Unpaid obligations:			
3000	Unpaid obligations, brought forward, Oct 1	1	1	1
3050	Unpaid obligations, end of year	1	1	1
	Memorandum (non-add) entries:			
3100	Obligated balance, start of year	1	1	1
3200	Obligated balance, end of year	1	1	1
4180	Budget authority, net (total)			
4190	Outlays, net (total)			

The Patient Protection and Affordable Care Act (P.L. 111–148), section 1421, allows certain small employers (including small tax-exempt employers) to claim a credit when they pay at least half of the health care premiums for single health insurance coverage for their employees. Small employers can claim the credit for 2010 through 2013 and after that for the first two consecutive years of having coverage purchased through the small business health options program. Generally, employers that have no more than 25 full-time equivalent employees and pay wages averaging less than $50,000 per employee per year may qualify for the credit.

This account includes state innovation waiver pass-through payments in lieu of the Small Business Health Insurance Tax Credit to qualifying states under section 1332(a)(3) of the PPACA.

Payment Where Certain Tax Credits Exceed Liability for Corporate Tax

Program and Financing (in millions of dollars)

Identification code 020–0931–0–1–376		2021 actual	2022 est.	2023 est.
	Obligations by program activity:			
0001	Payment Where Certain Tax Credits Exceed Liability for Corporate (Direct)	190		
0002	Credit for Prior Year Minimum Tax Liability of Corporations	8,970	1,294	10
0900	Total new obligations, unexpired accounts (object class 41.0)	9,160	1,294	10
	Budgetary resources:			
	Budget authority:			
	Appropriations, mandatory:			
1200	Appropriation	9,160	1,294	10
1930	Total budgetary resources available	9,160	1,294	10
	Change in obligated balance:			
	Unpaid obligations:			
3010	New obligations, unexpired accounts	9,160	1,294	10
3020	Outlays (gross)	–9,160	–1,294	–10
	Budget authority and outlays, net:			
	Mandatory:			
4090	Budget authority, gross	9,160	1,294	10
	Outlays, gross:			
4100	Outlays from new mandatory authority	9,160	1,294	10
4180	Budget authority, net (total)	9,160	1,294	10
4190	Outlays, net (total)	9,160	1,294	10

This account shows the outlays for the provision that allows certain businesses to accelerate the recognition of a portion of certain other credits in lieu of taking bonus depreciation. The Housing and Economic Recovery Act of 2008 (P.L. 110–289), section 3081, amended section 168(k) of the Internal Revenue Code (Code) to allow certain businesses to accelerate the recognition of a portion of their unused pre–2006 alternative minimum tax

(AMT) or research and development (R&D) credits in lieu of taking bonus depreciation. The portion of the unused credit that can be accelerated under this provision is capped at the lesser of $30 million or 6 percent of eligible AMT and R&D credits. The accelerated credit amount is refundable. The American Recovery and Reinvestment Act of 2009 (P.L. 111–5), section 1201(b), extended this temporary benefit through 2009. The Tax Relief, Unemployment Insurance Reauthorization, and Job Creation Act of 2010 (P.L. 111–312), section 401(c), extended this temporary benefit through the end of 2012, but only with respect to AMT credits. The American Taxpayer Relief Act of 2012 (P.L. 112–240), section 331(c), extended this temporary benefit through 2013 only with respect to AMT credits. The Tax Increase Prevention Act, Title I—Certain Expiring Provisions (P.L. 113–295), section 125(c), extended this temporary benefit through 2014 only with respect to AMT credits. The Protecting Americans from Tax Hikes (PATH) Act of 2015 (P.L. 114–113), extended this provision through 2015 only with respect to AMT credits. The PATH Act also extended and modified this provision for 2016 through 2019 only with respect to AMT credits.

The Tax Cuts and Jobs Act (P.L. 115–97) (TCJA) repealed the corporate alternative minimum tax. To conform to this repeal, the election to accelerate AMT credits in lieu of taking bonus depreciation was repealed, effective for property placed in service after September 27, 2017. Further, the TCJA amended the AMT credit limitation in section 53 of the Code to allow unused AMT credits to fully offset the regular federal income tax liability for any taxable year beginning after 2017. The TCJA also added section 53(e) to the Code to treat unused AMT credits as refundable for any taxable year beginning after 2017 and before 2022 in an amount equal to 50 percent (100 percent in the case of taxable years beginning in 2021) of the excess of the unused AMT credit as of the beginning of the taxable year over the amount of the credit allowable for the year against regular federal income tax liability. The Coronavirus Aid, Relief, and Economic Security Act (P.L. 116–136) (CARES Act) retroactively amended section 53(e) of the Code to allow unused AMT credits to be fully refunded in tax years beginning in 2018 or 2019. The refundable corporate minimum tax credit claimed under sections 53 and 168(k)(4) of the Code as in effect for taxable years beginning before Jan. 1, 2018, is not direct spending under the Balanced Budget and Deficit Control Act, as amended, and thus is not subject to sequestration.

CHILD AND DEPENDENT CARE TAX CREDIT

Program and Financing (in millions of dollars)

Identification code 020–0943–0–1–609		2021 actual	2022 est.	2023 est.
Obligations by program activity:				
0001	Payment Where CDCTC Exceeds Liability for Tax (Direct)	....	7,577	50
0002	Payment Where CDCTC Exceeds Liability for Tax (Territory Pymt)	....	53	....
0900	Total new obligations, unexpired accounts (object class 41.0)	....	7,630	50
Budgetary resources:				
	Budget authority:			
	Appropriations, mandatory:			
1200	Appropriation	....	7,630	50
1930	Total budgetary resources available	....	7,630	50
Change in obligated balance:				
	Unpaid obligations:			
3010	New obligations, unexpired accounts	....	7,630	50
3020	Outlays (gross)	....	–7,630	–50
Budget authority and outlays, net:				
	Mandatory:			
4090	Budget authority, gross	....	7,630	50
	Outlays, gross:			
4100	Outlays from new mandatory authority	....	7,630	50
4180	Budget authority, net (total)	....	7,630	50
4190	Outlays, net (total)	....	7,630	50

Section 9631(a) of the American Rescue Plan Act of 2021 (P.L. 117–2) (American Rescue Plan) amended Section 21 of the Internal Revenue Code (Code) to provide special rules for the Child and Dependent Care Tax Credit (CDCTC) solely for Tax Year 2021. Specifically, the American Rescue Plan made the CDCTC fully refundable. In addition, the maximum credit rate of the CDCTC increased from 35 percent to 50 percent. The amount of expenses that are eligible for the CDCTC was increased from $3,000 to $8,000 for one qualifying dependent (from $6,000 to $16,000 for two or more qualifying dependents). The American Rescue Plan increased the phase-out threshold of the CDCTC from $15,000 of AGI to $125,000. The credit rate is phased down, but not below 20 percent, by 1 percentage point for each $2,000 (or fraction thereof) by which the taxpayer's adjusted gross income (AGI) exceeds this threshold. The American Rescue Plan further phased down the credit rate of 20 percent by 1 percentage point for each $2,000 (or fraction thereof) by which the taxpayer's AGI exceeds $400,000. Section 9631(b) of the American Rescue Plan amended Section 21 of the Code to authorize payments to U.S. territories with mirror code tax systems and to U.S. territories with non-mirror code tax systems.

Section 9632(a) of the American Rescue Plan Act amended Section 129(a)(2) of the Code to increase, for Tax Year 2021 only, the maximum amount of employer-provided dependent care assistance that may be excluded from gross income. This increase doubles the generally applicable amounts that is, $5,000 (or $2,500 in the case of a married individual filing a separate return) such that an eligible employee for Tax Year 2021 can receive an exclusion of $10,500 (or $5,250 in the case of a married individual filing a separate return).

PAYMENT WHERE AMERICAN OPPORTUNITY CREDIT EXCEEDS LIABILITY FOR TAX

Program and Financing (in millions of dollars)

Identification code 020–0932–0–1–502		2021 actual	2022 est.	2023 est.
Obligations by program activity:				
0001	Payment Where American Opportunity Credit Exceeds Liability for (Direct)	3,967	3,250	3,105
0900	Total new obligations, unexpired accounts (object class 41.0)	3,967	3,250	3,105
Budgetary resources:				
	Budget authority:			
	Appropriations, mandatory:			
1200	Appropriation	3,967	3,250	3,105
1930	Total budgetary resources available	3,967	3,250	3,105
Change in obligated balance:				
	Unpaid obligations:			
3010	New obligations, unexpired accounts	3,967	3,250	3,105
3020	Outlays (gross)	–3,967	–3,250	–3,105
Budget authority and outlays, net:				
	Mandatory:			
4090	Budget authority, gross	3,967	3,250	3,105
	Outlays, gross:			
4100	Outlays from new mandatory authority	3,967	3,250	3,105
4180	Budget authority, net (total)	3,967	3,250	3,105
4190	Outlays, net (total)	3,967	3,250	3,105

Summary of Budget Authority and Outlays (in millions of dollars)

	2021 actual	2022 est.	2023 est.
Enacted/requested:			
Budget Authority	3,967	3,250	3,105
Outlays	3,967	3,250	3,105
Legislative proposal, subject to PAYGO:			
Budget Authority			3
Outlays			3
Total:			
Budget Authority	3,967	3,250	3,108
Outlays	3,967	3,250	3,108

The American Opportunity Tax Credit (AOTC) was enacted by the American Recovery and Reinvestment Act of 2009 (Public Law 111–5),

Internal Revenue Service—Continued
Federal Funds—Continued

PAYMENT WHERE AMERICAN OPPORTUNITY CREDIT EXCEEDS LIABILITY FOR TAX—Continued

was extended temporarily by Public Laws 111–312 and 112–240, and was made permanent by Public Law 114–113. A taxpayer may claim an AOTC of 100 percent of the first $2,000 of qualified tuition, fees, and course materials paid by the taxpayer for each eligible student or dependent and 25 percent of the next $2,000 of these qualifying expenses. Up to 40 percent of the otherwise eligible credit is refundable. The AOTC may be claimed only for the first four years of post-secondary education per student. The AOTC phases out for higher income taxpayers as the taxpayer's income increases.

PAYMENT WHERE AMERICAN OPPORTUNITY CREDIT EXCEEDS LIABILITY FOR TAX
(Legislative proposal, subject to PAYGO)

Program and Financing (in millions of dollars)

Identification code 020–0932–4–1–502	2021 actual	2022 est.	2023 est.
Obligations by program activity:			
0001 Payment Where American Opportunity Credit Exceeds Liability for (Direct)	....	....	3
0900 Total new obligations, unexpired accounts (object class 41.0)	....	....	3
Budgetary resources:			
Budget authority:			
Appropriations, mandatory:			
1200 Appropriation			3
1930 Total budgetary resources available			3
Change in obligated balance:			
Unpaid obligations:			
3010 New obligations, unexpired accounts			3
3020 Outlays (gross)			–3
Budget authority and outlays, net:			
Mandatory:			
4090 Budget authority, gross			3
Outlays, gross:			
4100 Outlays from new mandatory authority			3
4180 Budget authority, net (total)			3
4190 Outlays, net (total)			3

The Budget proposes to improve access and coverage for behavioral health. This proposal impacts the American Opportunity Tax Credit.

PAYMENT TO ISSUER OF QUALIFIED ENERGY CONSERVATION BONDS

Program and Financing (in millions of dollars)

Identification code 020–0948–0–1–272	2021 actual	2022 est.	2023 est.
Obligations by program activity:			
0001 Payment to Issuer of Qualified Energy Conservation Bonds (Direct)	43	35	35
0900 Total new obligations, unexpired accounts (object class 41.0)	43	35	35
Budgetary resources:			
Budget authority:			
Appropriations, mandatory:			
1200 Appropriation	46	37	37
1230 Appropriations and/or unobligated balance of appropriations permanently reduced	–3	–2	–2
1260 Appropriations, mandatory (total)	43	35	35
1930 Total budgetary resources available	43	35	35
Change in obligated balance:			
Unpaid obligations:			
3010 New obligations, unexpired accounts	43	35	35
3020 Outlays (gross)	–43	–35	–35
Budget authority and outlays, net:			
Mandatory:			
4090 Budget authority, gross	43	35	35
Outlays, gross:			
4100 Outlays from new mandatory authority	43	35	35
4180 Budget authority, net (total)	43	35	35
4190 Outlays, net (total)	43	35	35

The Emergency Economic Stabilization Act of 2008 (P.L. 110–343), section 301, created Qualified Energy Conservation Bonds; and the American Recovery and Reinvestment Act of 2009 (P.L. 111–5), section 1112, increased the limitation on issuance of qualified energy conservation bonds from $800 million to $3.2 billion.

The Hiring Incentives to Restore Employment Act (P.L. 111–147), section 301, amended section 6431 of the Internal Revenue Code of 1986 by allowing issuers of Qualified Energy Conservation Bonds to irrevocably elect to issue the bonds as specified tax credit bonds with a direct-pay subsidy. The issuer of such qualifying bonds receives a direct interest payment subsidy from the Federal Government. Bondholders receive a taxable interest payment from the issuer in lieu of a tax credit.

PAYMENT TO ISSUER OF NEW CLEAN RENEWABLE ENERGY BONDS

Program and Financing (in millions of dollars)

Identification code 020–0947–0–1–271	2021 actual	2022 est.	2023 est.
Obligations by program activity:			
0001 Payment to Issuer of New Clean Renewable Energy Bonds (Direct)	57	41	40
0900 Total new obligations, unexpired accounts (object class 41.0)	57	41	40
Budgetary resources:			
Budget authority:			
Appropriations, mandatory:			
1200 Appropriation	60	43	42
1230 Appropriations and/or unobligated balance of appropriations permanently reduced	–3	–2	–2
1260 Appropriations, mandatory (total)	57	41	40
1930 Total budgetary resources available	57	41	40
Change in obligated balance:			
Unpaid obligations:			
3010 New obligations, unexpired accounts	57	41	40
3020 Outlays (gross)	–57	–41	–40
Budget authority and outlays, net:			
Mandatory:			
4090 Budget authority, gross	57	41	40
Outlays, gross:			
4100 Outlays from new mandatory authority	57	41	40
4180 Budget authority, net (total)	57	41	40
4190 Outlays, net (total)	57	41	40

The Emergency Economic Stabilization Act of 2008 (P.L. 110–343), section 107, created New Clean Renewable Energy Bonds, and the American Recovery and Reinvestment Act of 2009 (P.L. 111–5), section 1111, increased the limitation on issuance of New Clean Renewable Energy Bonds to a total limitation of $2.4 billion.

The Hiring Incentives to Restore Employment Act (P.L. 111–147), section 301, amended section 6431 of the Internal Revenue Code of 1986 by adding a new subsection (f) allowing issuers of New Clean Renewable Energy Bonds to irrevocably elect to issue the bonds as specified tax credit bonds with a direct-pay subsidy. The issuer of such qualifying bonds receives a direct interest payment subsidy from the Federal Government. Bondholders receive a taxable interest payment from the issuer in lieu of a tax credit.

DEPARTMENT OF THE TREASURY

PAYMENT TO ISSUER OF QUALIFIED SCHOOL CONSTRUCTION BONDS

Program and Financing (in millions of dollars)

Identification code 020–0946–0–1–501	2021 actual	2022 est.	2023 est.
Obligations by program activity:			
0001 Payment to Issuer of Qualified School Construction Bonds (Direct)	797	563	559
0900 Total new obligations, unexpired accounts (object class 41.0)	797	563	559
Budgetary resources:			
Budget authority:			
Appropriations, mandatory:			
1200 Appropriation	846	597	593
1230 Appropriations and/or unobligated balance of appropriations permanently reduced	–49	–34	–34
1260 Appropriations, mandatory (total)	797	563	559
1930 Total budgetary resources available	797	563	559
Change in obligated balance:			
Unpaid obligations:			
3010 New obligations, unexpired accounts	797	563	559
3020 Outlays (gross)	–797	–563	–559
Budget authority and outlays, net:			
Mandatory:			
4090 Budget authority, gross	797	563	559
Outlays, gross:			
4100 Outlays from new mandatory authority	797	563	559
4180 Budget authority, net (total)	797	563	559
4190 Outlays, net (total)	797	563	559

The American Recovery and Reinvestment Act of 2009 (P.L. 111–5), section 1521, created Qualified School Construction Bonds with a calendar year limitation of $11 billion for 2009 and 2010, and zero after 2010.

The Hiring Incentives to Restore Employment Act (P.L. 111–147), section 301, amended section 6431 of the Internal Revenue Code of 1986 by adding a new subsection (f) allowing issuers of Qualified School Construction Bonds to irrevocably elect to issue the bonds as specified tax credit bonds with a direct-pay subsidy. The issuer of such qualifying bonds receives a direct interest payment subsidy from the Federal Government. Bondholders receive a taxable interest payment from the issuer in lieu of a tax credit.

PAYMENT TO ISSUER OF QUALIFIED ZONE ACADEMY BONDS

Program and Financing (in millions of dollars)

Identification code 020–0945–0–1–501	2021 actual	2022 est.	2023 est.
Obligations by program activity:			
0001 Payment to Issuer of Qualified Zone Academy Bonds (Direct)	54	40	40
0900 Total new obligations, unexpired accounts (object class 41.0)	54	40	40
Budgetary resources:			
Budget authority:			
Appropriations, mandatory:			
1200 Appropriation	57	42	42
1230 Appropriations and/or unobligated balance of appropriations permanently reduced	–3	–2	–2
1260 Appropriations, mandatory (total)	54	40	40
1930 Total budgetary resources available	54	40	40
Change in obligated balance:			
Unpaid obligations:			
3010 New obligations, unexpired accounts	54	40	40
3020 Outlays (gross)	–54	–40	–40
Budget authority and outlays, net:			
Mandatory:			
4090 Budget authority, gross	54	40	40
Outlays, gross:			
4100 Outlays from new mandatory authority	54	40	40
4180 Budget authority, net (total)	54	40	40
4190 Outlays, net (total)	54	40	40

The American Recovery and Reinvestment Act of 2009 (P.L. 111–5), section 1522, extended and expanded the calendar year limitation for Qualified Zone Academy Bonds to $1.4 billion for 2009 and 2010. The Tax Relief, Unemployment Insurance Reauthorization, and Job Creation Act of 2010 (P.L. 111–312), section 758, extended the Qualified Zone Academy Bonds for 2011 and reduced the calendar year limitation to $400 million. The American Taxpayer Relief Act of 2012 (P.L. 112–240), section 310, extended the calendar year limitation of $400 million through tax year 2013 (a two-year extension). The Tax Increase Prevention Act, Title I—Certain Expiring Provisions (P.L. 113–295), section 120, extended the calendar year limitation of $400 million through tax year 2014 (a one-year extension). The Protecting Americans from Tax Hikes Act of 2015 (P.L. 114–113), extended the calendar year limitation of $400 million through tax year 2016 (a two-year extension).

The Hiring Incentives to Restore Employment Act (P.L. 111–147), section 301, amended section 6431 of the Internal Revenue Code of 1986 by adding a new subsection (f) allowing issuers of Qualified Zone Academy Bonds to irrevocably elect to issue the bonds as specified tax credit bonds with a direct-pay subsidy. The issuer of such qualifying bonds receives a direct interest payment subsidy from the Federal Government. Bondholders receive a taxable interest payment from the issuer in lieu of a tax credit.

The Tax Relief, Unemployment Insurance Reauthorization and Job Creation Act of 2010 (P.L. 111–312) amended section 6431(f)(3)(A)(iii) to provide that direct pay treatment for Qualified Zone Academy Bonds is not available for Qualified Zone Academy Bond allocations from the 2011 national limitation or any carry forward of the 2011 allocation.

PAYMENT TO UNITED STATES VIRGIN ISLANDS AND PUERTO RICO FOR DISASTER TAX RELIEF

Program and Financing (in millions of dollars)

Identification code 020–0159–0–1–609	2021 actual	2022 est.	2023 est.
Obligations by program activity:			
0001 Payments to Puerto Rico		51	
0900 Total new obligations, unexpired accounts (object class 41.0)		51	
Budgetary resources:			
Budget authority:			
Appropriations, mandatory:			
1200 Appropriation		51	
1930 Total budgetary resources available		51	
Change in obligated balance:			
Unpaid obligations:			
3010 New obligations, unexpired accounts		51	
3020 Outlays (gross)		–51	
Budget authority and outlays, net:			
Mandatory:			
4090 Budget authority, gross		51	
Outlays, gross:			
4100 Outlays from new mandatory authority		51	
4180 Budget authority, net (total)		51	
4190 Outlays, net (total)		51	

The Disaster Tax Relief and Airport and Airway Extension Act of 2017 (P.L. 115–63) amended the Internal Revenue Code to allow various tax credits, deductions, and modifications to existing rules for individuals and businesses affected by Hurricanes Harvey, Irma, and Maria. Section 504(d) provided that the Department of the Treasury pay: (1) to the U.S. Virgin Islands amounts equal to the loss in revenues to the U.S. Virgin Islands by reason of the provisions of this title, and (2) to the Commonwealth of Puerto Rico amounts equal to the aggregate benefits that would have been provided to residents of Puerto Rico by reason of the provisions of this title if a mirror code tax system had been in effect in Puerto Rico.

REFUNDING INTERNAL REVENUE COLLECTIONS, INTEREST

Program and Financing (in millions of dollars)

Identification code 020–0904–0–1–908		2021 actual	2022 est.	2023 est.
	Obligations by program activity:			
0001	Refunding Internal Revenue Collections, Interest (Direct)	3,033	3,022	2,169
0900	Total new obligations, unexpired accounts (object class 43.0)	3,033	3,022	2,169
	Budgetary resources:			
	Budget authority:			
	Appropriations, mandatory:			
1200	Appropriation	3,033	3,022	2,169
1930	Total budgetary resources available	3,033	3,022	2,169
	Change in obligated balance:			
	Unpaid obligations:			
3010	New obligations, unexpired accounts	3,033	3,022	2,169
3020	Outlays (gross)	–3,033	–3,022	–2,169
	Budget authority and outlays, net:			
	Mandatory:			
4090	Budget authority, gross	3,033	3,022	2,169
	Outlays, gross:			
4100	Outlays from new mandatory authority	3,033	3,022	2,169
4180	Budget authority, net (total)	3,033	3,022	2,169
4190	Outlays, net (total)	3,033	3,022	2,169

Under certain circumstances, as provided in 26 U.S.C. 6611, interest is paid on Internal Revenue collections that must be refunded. The Tax Equity and Fiscal Responsibility Act of 1982 (P.L. 97–248) provides for daily compounding of interest. Under the Tax Reform Act of 1986 (P.L. 99–514), interest paid on Internal Revenue collections will equal the Federal short-term rate plus three percentage points (two percentage points in the case of a corporation), with such rate to be adjusted quarterly.

REFUNDABLE PREMIUM TAX CREDIT

Program and Financing (in millions of dollars)

Identification code 020–0949–0–1–551		2021 actual	2022 est.	2023 est.
	Obligations by program activity:			
0001	Premium assistance tax credit	59,948	52,099	37,150
0003	Basic Health Program	7,031	8,392	6,760
0004	State Innovation Waivers	1,742	2,181	1,803
0900	Total new obligations, unexpired accounts (object class 41.0)	68,721	62,672	45,713
	Budgetary resources:			
	Unobligated balance:			
1033	Recoveries of prior year paid obligations	3,641		
1037	Unobligated balance of appropriations withdrawn	–3,641		
	Budget authority:			
	Appropriations, mandatory:			
1200	Appropriation	68,721	62,672	45,713
1900	Budget authority (total)	68,721	62,672	45,713
1930	Total budgetary resources available	68,721	62,672	45,713
	Change in obligated balance:			
	Unpaid obligations:			
3000	Unpaid obligations, brought forward, Oct 1	1,611	2,057	2,057
3010	New obligations, unexpired accounts	68,721	62,672	45,713
3020	Outlays (gross)	–68,275	–62,672	–45,713
3050	Unpaid obligations, end of year	2,057	2,057	2,057
	Memorandum (non-add) entries:			
3100	Obligated balance, start of year	1,611	2,057	2,057
3200	Obligated balance, end of year	2,057	2,057	2,057
	Budget authority and outlays, net:			
	Mandatory:			
4090	Budget authority, gross	68,721	62,672	45,713
	Outlays, gross:			
4100	Outlays from new mandatory authority	67,009	60,615	43,941
4101	Outlays from mandatory balances	1,266	2,057	1,772
4110	Outlays, gross (total)	68,275	62,672	45,713
	Offsets against gross budget authority and outlays:			
	Offsetting collections (collected) from:			
4123	Non-Federal sources	–3,641		
	Additional offsets against gross budget authority only:			
4143	Recoveries of prior year paid obligations, unexpired accounts	3,641		
4160	Budget authority, net (mandatory)	68,721	62,672	45,713
4170	Outlays, net (mandatory)	64,634	62,672	45,713
4180	Budget authority, net (total)	68,721	62,672	45,713
4190	Outlays, net (total)	64,634	62,672	45,713

Summary of Budget Authority and Outlays (in millions of dollars)

	2021 actual	2022 est.	2023 est.
Enacted/requested:			
Budget Authority	68,721	62,672	45,713
Outlays	64,634	62,672	45,713
Legislative proposal, subject to PAYGO:			
Budget Authority			522
Outlays			522
Total:			
Budget Authority	68,721	62,672	46,235
Outlays	64,634	62,672	46,235

The Patient Protection and Affordable Care Act (PPACA) of 2010 (P.L. 111–148) established the Premium Tax Credit. This credit is an advanceable, refundable tax credit designed to help eligible individuals and families with low or moderate income afford health insurance purchased through a Health Insurance Exchange, beginning in 2014. The credit can be paid in advance to the taxpayer's insurance company to lower the monthly premiums, or it can be claimed when a taxpayer files their income tax return for the year. If the credit is paid in advance, the taxpayer must reconcile the advance credit payments with the actual credit computed on the tax return and repay any excess advance credit payments, subject to certain caps.

The American Rescue Plan Act of 2021 (P.L. 117–2) increased the Premium Tax Credit in three ways. For 2021 and 2022, the legislation increased the Premium Tax Credit for currently eligible individuals and families, providing access to free plans for those earning 100 to 150 percent of the Federal poverty level, and expanded eligibility to newly include individuals and families with income above 400 percent of the federal poverty level. The legislation also expanded eligibility in 2021 to individuals who receive unemployment insurance for any week in 2021. The legislation also eliminated the requirement for individuals to repay any excess advance payments of the Premium Tax Credit for 2020.

This account includes state innovation waiver pass-through payments in lieu of the Premium Tax Credit to qualifying states under section 1332(a)(3) of the PPACA, as well as payments to states under the Basic Health Program established under section 1331 of PPACA.

REFUNDABLE PREMIUM TAX CREDIT

(Legislative proposal, subject to PAYGO)

Program and Financing (in millions of dollars)

Identification code 020–0949–4–1–551		2021 actual	2022 est.	2023 est.
	Obligations by program activity:			
0001	Premium assistance tax credit			512
0003	Basic Health Program			10
0900	Total new obligations, unexpired accounts (object class 41.0)			522
	Budgetary resources:			
	Budget authority:			
	Appropriations, mandatory:			
1200	Appropriation			522
1900	Budget authority (total)			522
1930	Total budgetary resources available			522
	Change in obligated balance:			
	Unpaid obligations:			
3010	New obligations, unexpired accounts			522
3020	Outlays (gross)			–522

DEPARTMENT OF THE TREASURY

Budget authority and outlays, net:
Mandatory:

4090	Budget authority, gross			522
	Outlays, gross:			
4100	Outlays from new mandatory authority			522
4180	Budget authority, net (total)			522
4190	Outlays, net (total)			522

The proposals build on existing consumer protections and improve access to behavioral health services by doing the following: requiring coverage of mental health and substance use disorder benefits for all plans and issuers; requiring coverage of three behavioral health visits and three primary care visits without cost-sharing; limiting utilization management controls for behavioral health; amending MHPAEA to authorize the Secretaries to regulate behavioral health network adequacy for all plans and issuers; and creating a new standard for parity in behavioral health based on comparative analysis of reimbursement rates.

IRS MISCELLANEOUS RETAINED FEES

Special and Trust Fund Receipts (in millions of dollars)

Identification code 020–5432–0–2–803		2021 actual	2022 est.	2023 est.
0100	Balance, start of year			
	Receipts:			
	Current law:			
1110	Enrolled Agent Fee Increase, IRS Miscellaneous Retained Fees	8	8	12
1110	Tax Preparer Registration Fees, IRS Miscellaneous Retained Fees	16	16	16
1130	New Installment Agreements, IRS Miscellaneous Retained Fees	124	124	124
1130	Restructured Installment Agreements, IRS Miscellaneous Retained Fees	73	73	73
1130	General User Fees, IRS Miscellaneous Retained Fees	166	128	122
1130	Photocopying and Historical Conservation Easement Fees, IRS Miscellaneous Retained Fees	6	4	3
1199	Total current law receipts	393	353	350
1999	Total receipts	393	353	350
2000	Total: Balances and receipts	393	353	350
	Appropriations:			
	Current law:			
2101	IRS Miscellaneous Retained Fees	–393	–353	–350
5099	Balance, end of year			

Program and Financing (in millions of dollars)

Identification code 020–5432–0–2–803		2021 actual	2022 est.	2023 est.
	Obligations by program activity:			
0001	IRS Miscellaneous Retained Fees (Direct)	3	3	3
0900	Total new obligations, unexpired accounts (object class 44.0)	3	3	3
	Budgetary resources:			
	Unobligated balance:			
1000	Unobligated balance brought forward, Oct 1	395	288	224
1010	Unobligated balance transfer to other accts [020–0919]	–178	–156	–80
1010	Unobligated balance transfer to other accts [020–0912]	–63	–30	–30
1011	Unobligated balance transfer from other acct [020–0921]	1		
1070	Unobligated balance (total)	155	102	114
	Budget authority:			
	Appropriations, discretionary:			
1120	Appropriations transferred to other accts [020–0919]	–226	–179	–181
1120	Appropriations transferred to other accts [020–0921]	–29		
1120	Appropriations transferred to other accts [020–0912]	–2	–49	–49
1160	Appropriation, discretionary (total)	–257	–228	–230
	Appropriations, mandatory:			
1201	Appropriation (special or trust fund)	393	353	350
1900	Budget authority (total)	136	125	120
1930	Total budgetary resources available	291	227	234
	Memorandum (non-add) entries:			
1941	Unexpired unobligated balance, end of year	288	224	231

Change in obligated balance:
Unpaid obligations:

3010	New obligations, unexpired accounts	3	3	3
3020	Outlays (gross)	–3	–3	–3
	Budget authority and outlays, net:			
	Discretionary:			
4000	Budget authority, gross	–257	–228	–230
	Mandatory:			
4090	Budget authority, gross	393	353	350
	Outlays, gross:			
4101	Outlays from mandatory balances	3	3	3
4180	Budget authority, net (total)	136	125	120
4190	Outlays, net (total)	3	3	3

As provided by law (26 U.S.C. 7801), the Secretary of the Treasury may establish new fees or raise existing fees for services provided by the IRS to recover the value of the service provided, where such fees are authorized by another law, and may spend the new or increased fee receipts to supplement appropriations made available to the IRS appropriations accounts. Funds in this account are transferred to other IRS appropriations accounts for expenditure.

GIFTS TO THE UNITED STATES FOR REDUCTION OF THE PUBLIC DEBT

Special and Trust Fund Receipts (in millions of dollars)

Identification code 020–5080–0–2–808		2021 actual	2022 est.	2023 est.
0100	Balance, start of year			
	Receipts:			
	Current law:			
1130	Gifts to the United States for Reduction of the Public Debt	1	3	3
2000	Total: Balances and receipts	1	3	3
	Appropriations:			
	Current law:			
2101	Gifts to the United States for Reduction of the Public Debt	–1	–3	–3
5099	Balance, end of year			

Program and Financing (in millions of dollars)

Identification code 020–5080–0–2–808		2021 actual	2022 est.	2023 est.
	Budgetary resources:			
	Budget authority:			
	Appropriations, mandatory:			
1201	Appropriation (special or trust fund)	1	3	3
1236	Appropriations applied to repay debt	–1	–3	–3
4180	Budget authority, net (total)			
4190	Outlays, net (total)			

As provided by law (31 U.S.C. 3113), the Secretary of the Treasury is authorized to accept conditional gifts to the United States for the purpose of reducing the public debt.

PRIVATE COLLECTION AGENT PROGRAM

Special and Trust Fund Receipts (in millions of dollars)

Identification code 020–5510–0–2–803		2021 actual	2022 est.	2023 est.
0100	Balance, start of year	9	13	8
	Receipts:			
	Current law:			
1110	Private Collection Agent Program	221	145	171
2000	Total: Balances and receipts	230	158	179
	Appropriations:			
	Current law:			
2101	Private Collection Agent Program	–221	–145	–171
2103	Private Collection Agent Program	–9	–13	–8
2132	Private Collection Agent Program	13	8	10
2199	Total current law appropriations	–217	–150	–169

PRIVATE COLLECTION AGENT PROGRAM—Continued
Special and Trust Fund Receipts—Continued

Identification code 020–5510–0–2–803	2021 actual	2022 est.	2023 est.
2999 Total appropriations	–217	–150	–169
5099 Balance, end of year	13	8	10

Program and Financing (in millions of dollars)

Identification code 020–5510–0–2–803	2021 actual	2022 est.	2023 est.
Obligations by program activity:			
0002 Payments to Private Collection Agencies	87	46	55
0003 Special Compliance Personnel Program	51	71	91
0900 Total new obligations, unexpired accounts	138	117	146
Budgetary resources:			
Unobligated balance:			
1000 Unobligated balance brought forward, Oct 1	104	183	216
Budget authority:			
Appropriations, mandatory:			
1201 Appropriation (special or trust fund)	221	145	171
1203 Appropriation (previously unavailable)(special or trust)	9	13	8
1232 Appropriations and/or unobligated balance of appropriations temporarily reduced	–13	–8	–10
1260 Appropriations, mandatory (total)	217	150	169
1930 Total budgetary resources available	321	333	385
Memorandum (non-add) entries:			
1941 Unexpired unobligated balance, end of year	183	216	239
Change in obligated balance:			
Unpaid obligations:			
3000 Unpaid obligations, brought forward, Oct 1	10	8	12
3010 New obligations, unexpired accounts	138	117	146
3020 Outlays (gross)	–140	–113	–129
3050 Unpaid obligations, end of year	8	12	29
Memorandum (non-add) entries:			
3100 Obligated balance, start of year	10	8	12
3200 Obligated balance, end of year	8	12	29
Budget authority and outlays, net:			
Mandatory:			
4090 Budget authority, gross	217	150	169
Outlays, gross:			
4100 Outlays from new mandatory authority	123	71	123
4101 Outlays from mandatory balances	17	42	6
4110 Outlays, gross (total)	140	113	129
4180 Budget authority, net (total)	217	150	169
4190 Outlays, net (total)	140	113	129

This account reflects the funds that the IRS is allowed to retain and expend for qualified tax collection contracts with private collection agents and the special compliance personnel program. The American Jobs Creation Act of 2004 (P.L. 108–357) allowed the IRS to use private collection contractors to supplement its own collection staff efforts to ensure that all taxpayers pay what they owe. The statute authorized the Treasury to retain and use an amount not in excess of 25 percent of the amount collected under any qualified tax collection contract for payments to private collection agents, and an amount not in excess of 25 percent of the amount collected for enforcement activities of the IRS (26 U.S.C. 6306). The IRS used this authority to contract with several private debt collection agencies starting in 2006. In March 2009, the IRS allowed its private debt collection contracts to expire, thereby administratively terminating the program in accordance with Omnibus Appropriations Act, 2009 Administrative Provisions — Internal Revenue Service, Section 106 (P.L. 111–8). This provision stated that none of the funds made available in this Act maybe used to enter into, renew, extend, administer, implement, enforce, or provide oversight of any qualified tax collection contract as defined in section 6306 of the Internal Revenue Code of 1986.

Section 32102(a) of the Fixing America's Surface Transportation Act of 2015 (P.L. 114–94), amended section 6306 of the Internal Revenue Code (IRC) and requires the Secretary of the Treasury to enter into one or more qualified tax collection contracts for the collection of all outstanding inactive tax receivables. These agreements are applicable to tax receivables as identified by the Secretary after December 4, 2015. Section 6306 of the IRC prohibits the payment of fees for all services in excess of 25 percent of the amount collected under a tax collection contract for payments to private collection agents. In addition, up to 25 percent of the amount collected may be used to fund the special compliance personnel program account under section 6307.

Inactive tax receivables, as redefined by the Taxpayer First Act (P.L. 116–25), are defined as any tax receivable: 1) removed from the active inventory for lack of resources or inability to locate the taxpayer; 2) for which more than two years has passed since assessment and no IRS employee has been assigned to collect the receivable; or 3) for which a receivable has been assigned for collection but more than 365 days have passed without interaction with the taxpayer or a third party for purposes of furthering the collection. Tax receivables are defined as any outstanding assessment that the IRS includes in potentially collectible inventory. The Taxpayer First Act also made certain receivables of individual taxpayers ineligible for collection, including taxpayers whose income substantially consists of disability insurance benefits or supplemental security income benefits or whose adjusted gross income does not exceed 200 percent of the applicable federal poverty level.

Object Classification (in millions of dollars)

Identification code 020–5510–0–2–803	2021 actual	2022 est.	2023 est.
Direct obligations:			
Personnel compensation:			
11.1 Full-time permanent	18	29	36
11.5 Other personnel compensation	1	3	4
11.9 Total personnel compensation	19	32	40
12.1 Civilian personnel benefits	7	11	14
23.1 Rental payments to GSA	20	25	34
23.3 Communications, utilities, and miscellaneous charges	1	1	1
25.1 Advisory and assistance services	90	48	57
25.3 Other goods and services from Federal sources	1		
99.0 Direct obligations	138	117	146
99.9 Total new obligations, unexpired accounts	138	117	146

Employment Summary

Identification code 020–5510–0–2–803	2021 actual	2022 est.	2023 est.
1001 Direct civilian full-time equivalent employment	334	460	821

INFORMANT PAYMENTS
Special and Trust Fund Receipts (in millions of dollars)

Identification code 020–5433–0–2–803	2021 actual	2022 est.	2023 est.
0100 Balance, start of year			5
Receipts:			
Current law:			
1140 Underpayment and Fraud Collection	26	85	85
2000 Total: Balances and receipts	26	85	90
Appropriations:			
Current law:			
2101 Informant Payments	–26	–85	–85
2132 Informant Payments		5	5
2199 Total current law appropriations	–26	–80	–80
2999 Total appropriations	–26	–80	–80
5099 Balance, end of year		5	10

Program and Financing (in millions of dollars)

Identification code 020–5433–0–2–803	2021 actual	2022 est.	2023 est.
Obligations by program activity:			
0001 Informant Payments	26	80	80
0900 Total new obligations, unexpired accounts (object class 91.0)	26	80	80
Budgetary resources:			
Budget authority:			
Appropriations, mandatory:			
1201 Appropriation (special or trust fund)	26	85	85
1232 Appropriations and/or unobligated balance of appropriations temporarily reduced		–5	–5
1260 Appropriations, mandatory (total)	26	80	80
1930 Total budgetary resources available	26	80	80
Change in obligated balance:			
Unpaid obligations:			
3010 New obligations, unexpired accounts	26	80	80
3020 Outlays (gross)	–26	–80	–80
Budget authority and outlays, net:			
Mandatory:			
4090 Budget authority, gross	26	80	80
Outlays, gross:			
4100 Outlays from new mandatory authority	26	80	80
4180 Budget authority, net (total)	26	80	80
4190 Outlays, net (total)	26	80	80

As provided by law (26 U.S.C. 7623), the Secretary of the Treasury may make payments to individuals who provide information that leads to the collection of Internal Revenue taxes. The Taxpayer Bill of Rights of 1996 (P.L. 104–168) provides for payments of such sums to individuals from the proceeds of amounts collected by reason of the information provided, and any amount collected shall be available for such payments. This information must lead to the detection of underpayments of taxes, or detection and bringing to trial and punishment of persons guilty of violating the Internal Revenue laws. This provision was further amended by the Tax Relief and Health Care Act of 2006 (P.L. 109–432) to provide for mandatory payments in certain circumstances and to encourage use of the program. A reward payment typically ranges between 15 and 30 percent of the collected proceeds for cases where the amount of collected proceeds exceeds $2 million. Lower payments are allowed in certain circumstances, including cases in which information is provided that was already available from another source. Section 41108 of the Bipartisan Budget Act of 2018 (P.L. 115–123) expanded the definition of proceeds to include proceeds arising from the laws for which the Internal Revenue Service is authorized to administer, enforce, or investigate. Section 41108 further provides that the expanded definition of proceeds shall be used to determine eligibility for a mandatory award under section 7623(b)(5) and states that the amount of proceeds are to be determined without regard to whether such proceeds are available to the Secretary.

FEDERAL TAX LIEN REVOLVING FUND

Program and Financing (in millions of dollars)

Identification code 020–4413–0–3–803	2021 actual	2022 est.	2023 est.
Obligations by program activity:			
0001 Federal Tax Lien Revolving Fund	1	3	3
0900 Total new obligations, unexpired accounts (object class 32.0)	1	3	3
Budgetary resources:			
Unobligated balance:			
1000 Unobligated balance brought forward, Oct 1	7	7	7
Budget authority:			
Spending authority from offsetting collections, mandatory:			
1800 Collected	1	3	3
1930 Total budgetary resources available	8	10	10
Memorandum (non-add) entries:			
1941 Unexpired unobligated balance, end of year	7	7	7
Change in obligated balance:			
Unpaid obligations:			
3010 New obligations, unexpired accounts	1	3	3
3020 Outlays (gross)	–1	–3	–3
Budget authority and outlays, net:			
Mandatory:			
4090 Budget authority, gross	1	3	3
Outlays, gross:			
4101 Outlays from mandatory balances	1	3	3
Offsets against gross budget authority and outlays:			
Offsetting collections (collected) from:			
4123 Non-Federal sources	–1	–3	–3
4180 Budget authority, net (total)			
4190 Outlays, net (total)			

This revolving fund was established pursuant to section 112(a) of the Federal Tax Lien Act of 1966, to serve as the source of financing the redemption of real property by the United States. During the process of collecting unpaid taxes, the Government may place a tax lien on real estate in order to protect the Government's interest and this account provides the resources to administer the program.

PAYMENT WHERE ADOPTION CREDIT EXCEEDS LIABILITY FOR TAX
(Legislative proposal, subject to PAYGO)

The Budget proposes to make the adoption credit fully refundable. In addition, taxpayers with unused carryforward amounts from eligible expenses from earlier adoptions would be able to claim the full amount of any unused carryforward on their 2023 tax return. The proposal would also allow families who enter into a guardianship relationship with a child that meets certain requirements to claim a refundable credit for the expenses related to establishing the guardianship relationship.

INTERNAL REVENUE SERVICE OVERSIGHT BOARD

The Internal Revenue Service Restructuring and Reform Act of 1998 (P.L. 105–206) directs the IRS Oversight Board to provide an annual budget request for the IRS. The Oversight Board's request shall be submitted to the President by the Secretary without revision, and the President shall submit the request, without revision, to Congress together with the President's Budget request for the IRS. The Board did not make a recommendation for 2023 as it currently lacks a quorum. The Board will reconvene once it has enough Senate-confirmed members to make a quorum.

ADMINISTRATIVE PROVISIONS—INTERNAL REVENUE SERVICE
(INCLUDING TRANSFER OF FUNDS)

SEC. 101. Not to exceed 4 percent of the appropriation made available in this Act to the Internal Revenue Service under the "Enforcement" heading, and not to exceed 5 percent of any other appropriation made available in this Act to the Internal Revenue Service, may be transferred to any other Internal Revenue Service appropriation upon advance notice to the Committees on Appropriations of the House of Representatives and the Senate: Provided, That an additional 2 percent of the appropriation made available in this Act to the Internal Revenue Service under the "Enforcement"heading may be transferred to the appropriation made available in this Act to the Internal Revenue Service under the "Taxpayer Services" heading upon advance notice to the Committees on Appropriations of the House of Representatives and the Senate.

SEC. 102. The Internal Revenue Service shall maintain an employee training program, which shall include the following topics: taxpayers' rights, dealing courteously with taxpayers, cross-cultural relations, ethics, and the impartial application of tax law.

SEC. 103. The Internal Revenue Service shall institute and enforce policies and procedures that will safeguard the confidentiality of taxpayer information and protect taxpayers against identity theft.

SEC. 104. *Funds made available by this or any other Act to the Internal Revenue Service shall be available for improved facilities and increased staffing to provide sufficient and effective 1–800 help line service for taxpayers. The Commissioner shall continue to make improvements to the Internal Revenue Service 1–800 help line service a priority and allocate resources necessary to enhance the response time to taxpayer communications, particularly with regard to victims of tax-related crimes.*

SEC. 105. *The Internal Revenue Service shall issue a notice of confirmation of any address change relating to an employer making employment tax payments, and such notice shall be sent to both the employer's former and new address and an officer or employee of the Internal Revenue Service shall give special consideration to an offer-in-compromise from a taxpayer who has been the victim of fraud by a third party payroll tax preparer.*

SEC. 106. *None of the funds made available under this Act may be used by the Internal Revenue Service to target citizens of the United States for exercising any right guaranteed under the First Amendment to the Constitution of the United States.*

SEC. 107. *None of the funds made available in this Act may be used by the Internal Revenue Service to target groups for regulatory scrutiny based on their ideological beliefs.*

SEC. 108. *None of funds made available by this Act to the Internal Revenue Service shall be obligated or expended on conferences that do not adhere to the procedures, verification processes, documentation requirements, and policies issued by the Chief Financial Officer, Human Capital Office, and Agency-Wide Shared Services as a result of the recommendations in the report published on May 31, 2013, by the Treasury Inspector General for Tax Administration entitled "Review of the August 2010 Small Business/Self-Employed Division's Conference in Anaheim, California" (Reference Number 2013–10–037).*

SEC. 109. *None of the funds made available in this Act to the Internal Revenue Service may be obligated or expended—*

(1) to make a payment to any employee under a bonus, award, or recognition program; or

(2) under any hiring or personnel selection process with respect to re-hiring a former employee;

unless such program or process takes into account the conduct and Federal tax compliance of such employee or former employee.

SEC. 110. *None of the funds made available by this Act may be used in contravention of section 6103 of the Internal Revenue Code of 1986 (relating to confidentiality and disclosure of returns and return information).*

SEC. 111. *Notwithstanding any Congressional notification requirements for a reprogramming of funds in this Act, funds provided in this Act for the Internal Revenue Service shall be available for obligation and expenditure through a reprogramming of funds that augments or reduces existing programs, projects, or activities by up to $10,000,000 without prior Congressional notification of such action.*

COMPTROLLER OF THE CURRENCY

Trust Funds

ASSESSMENT FUNDS

Program and Financing (in millions of dollars)

Identification code 020–8413–0–8–373	2021 actual	2022 est.	2023 est.
Obligations by program activity:			
0881 Bank Supervision	1,112	1,217	1,225
Budgetary resources:			
Unobligated balance:			
1000 Unobligated balance brought forward, Oct 1	1,656	1,718	1,692
1021 Recoveries of prior year unpaid obligations	8		
1070 Unobligated balance (total)	1,664	1,718	1,692
Budget authority:			
Spending authority from offsetting collections, mandatory:			
1800 Collected	1,167	1,191	1,191
1801 Change in uncollected payments, Federal sources	–1		
1850 Spending auth from offsetting collections, mand (total)	1,166	1,191	1,191
1930 Total budgetary resources available	2,830	2,909	2,883
Memorandum (non-add) entries:			
1941 Unexpired unobligated balance, end of year	1,718	1,692	1,658
Change in obligated balance:			
Unpaid obligations:			
3000 Unpaid obligations, brought forward, Oct 1	328	380	416
3010 New obligations, unexpired accounts	1,112	1,217	1,225
3020 Outlays (gross)	–1,052	–1,181	–1,188
3040 Recoveries of prior year unpaid obligations, unexpired	–8		
3050 Unpaid obligations, end of year	380	416	453
Uncollected payments:			
3060 Uncollected pymts, Fed sources, brought forward, Oct 1	–9	–8	–8
3070 Change in uncollected pymts, Fed sources, unexpired	1		
3090 Uncollected pymts, Fed sources, end of year	–8	–8	–8
Memorandum (non-add) entries:			
3100 Obligated balance, start of year	319	372	408
3200 Obligated balance, end of year	372	408	445
Budget authority and outlays, net:			
Mandatory:			
4090 Budget authority, gross	1,166	1,191	1,191
Outlays, gross:			
4100 Outlays from new mandatory authority	354	402	404
4101 Outlays from mandatory balances	698	779	784
4110 Outlays, gross (total)	1,052	1,181	1,188
Offsets against gross budget authority and outlays:			
Offsetting collections (collected) from:			
4120 Federal sources	–19	–14	–14
4121 Interest on Federal securities	–17	–18	–18
4123 Non-Federal sources	–1,131	–1,159	–1,159
4130 Offsets against gross budget authority and outlays (total)	–1,167	–1,191	–1,191
Additional offsets against gross budget authority only:			
4140 Change in uncollected pymts, Fed sources, unexpired	1		
4170 Outlays, net (mandatory)	–115	–10	–3
4180 Budget authority, net (total)			
4190 Outlays, net (total)	–115	–10	–3
Memorandum (non-add) entries:			
5000 Total investments, SOY: Federal securities: Par value	1,983	2,090	2,114
5001 Total investments, EOY: Federal securities: Par value	2,090	2,114	2,139
5010 Total investments, SOY: non-Fed securities: Market value	5	5	5
5011 Total investments, EOY: non-Fed securities: Market value	5	5	5

The Office of the Comptroller of the Currency (OCC) was created by Congress to charter national banks; oversee a nationwide system of banking institutions; and ensure national banks are safe and sound, competitive and profitable, and capable of serving in the best possible manner the banking needs of their customers. The National Currency Act of 1863 (12 U.S.C. 1 et seq., 12 Stat. 665), rewritten and reenacted as the National Bank Act of 1864, provided for the chartering and supervising functions of the OCC. Income of the OCC is derived principally from assessments paid by national banks and interest on investments in U.S. Government securities. The OCC receives no appropriated funds from Congress.

As of September 30, 2021, the OCC supervised 797 national bank charters, 52 Federal branches of foreign banks, and 269 Federal savings associations. In total, the OCC supervises approximately $14.9 trillion in financial institution assets.

As of September 30, 2021, the net position of the OCC was $1,642.5 million. The OCC allocates a significant portion of the net position to its financial reserves to cover undelivered orders and capital investments. Financial reserves are integral to the effective stewardship of the OCCs resources, and the OCC has a disciplined process for reviewing its reserve balances and allocating funds appropriately to support its ability to accomplish the agency's mission. The OCCs financial reserves are available to reduce the impact on the OCCs operations in the event of a significant fluctuation in revenues or expenses. In 2018, the OCC established a new receivership contingency fund of $86.6 million within its financial reserves to facilitate the conduct of receiverships of uninsured federal branches or agencies of a foreign banking organization. In 2017, the OCC established a contingency of $100 million within its reserves to act as receiver of those national trust banks which are not FDIC-insured.

Object Classification (in millions of dollars)

Identification code 020–8413–0–8–373	2021 actual	2022 est.	2023 est.
Reimbursable obligations:			
Personnel compensation:			
11.1 Full-time permanent	550	580	586
11.3 Other than full-time permanent	4	3	3

DEPARTMENT OF THE TREASURY

		2021 actual	2022 est.	2023 est.
11.5	Other personnel compensation	4	4	4
11.9	Total personnel compensation	558	587	593
12.1	Civilian personnel benefits	260	267	269
21.0	Travel and transportation of persons	5	23	23
22.0	Transportation of things	3	3	3
23.2	Rental payments to others	66	66	66
23.3	Communications, utilities, and miscellaneous charges	23	16	16
25.1	Advisory and assistance services	26	40	40
25.2	Other services from non-Federal sources	31	36	36
25.3	Other goods and services from Federal sources	9	9	9
25.4	Operation and maintenance of facilities	6	8	8
25.7	Operation and maintenance of equipment	77	108	108
26.0	Supplies and materials	5	7	7
31.0	Equipment	29	36	36
32.0	Land and structures	13	10	10
42.0	Insurance claims and indemnities	1	1	1
99.0	Reimbursable obligations	1,112	1,217	1,225
99.9	Total new obligations, unexpired accounts	1,112	1,217	1,225

Employment Summary

Identification code 020–8413–0–8–373	2021 actual	2022 est.	2023 est.
2001 Reimbursable civilian full-time equivalent employment	3,491	3,555	3,555

INTEREST ON THE PUBLIC DEBT

Federal Funds

INTEREST ON TREASURY DEBT SECURITIES (GROSS)

Program and Financing (in millions of dollars)

Identification code 020–0550–0–1–901	2021 actual	2022 est.	2023 est.
Obligations by program activity:			
0001 Interest on Treasury Debt Securities	562,388	561,817	576,776
0900 Total new obligations, unexpired accounts (object class 43.0)	562,388	561,817	576,776
Budgetary resources:			
Budget authority:			
Appropriations, mandatory:			
1200 Appropriation	562,388	561,817	576,776
1930 Total budgetary resources available	562,388	561,817	576,776
Change in obligated balance:			
Unpaid obligations:			
3010 New obligations, unexpired accounts	562,388	561,817	576,776
3020 Outlays (gross)	–562,388	–561,817	–576,776
Budget authority and outlays, net:			
Mandatory:			
4090 Budget authority, gross	562,388	561,817	576,776
Outlays, gross:			
4100 Outlays from new mandatory authority	562,388	561,817	576,776
4180 Budget authority, net (total)	562,388	561,817	576,776
4190 Outlays, net (total)	562,388	561,817	576,776

Such amounts are appropriated as may be necessary to pay the interest each year on the public debt (31 U.S.C. 1305, 3123). Interest on Government account series securities is generally calculated on a cash basis. Interest is generally calculated on an accrual basis for all other types of securities.

INTEREST ON TREASURY DEBT SECURITIES (GROSS)

(Legislative proposal, not subject to PAYGO)

Program and Financing (in millions of dollars)

Identification code 020–0550–2–1–901	2021 actual	2022 est.	2023 est.
4180 Budget authority, net (total)			–5
4190 Outlays, net (total)			–5

GENERAL FUND RECEIPT ACCOUNTS

(in millions of dollars)

		2021 actual	2022 est.	2023 est.
Governmental receipts:				
010–086400	Filing Fees, P.L. 109–171, Title X	39	39	39
020–015800	Transportation Fuels Tax	–6,036	–4,692	–2,427
020–015800	Transportation Fuels Tax: Legislative proposal, subject to PAYGO			5
020–065000	Deposit of Earnings, Federal Reserve System	100,054	107,749	75,625
020–085000	Registration, Filing, and Transaction Fees	4	4	4
020–086900	Fees for Legal and Judicial Services, not Otherwise Classified	34	34	34
020–089100	Miscellaneous Fees for Regulatory and Judicial Services, not Otherwise Classified	629	615	615
020–101000	Fines, Penalties, and Forfeitures, Agricultural Laws	3	3	3
020–104000	Fines, Penalties, and Forfeitures, Customs, Commerce, and Antitrust Laws	649	3,115	3,115
020–105000	Fines, Penalties, and Forfeitures, Narcotic Prohibition and Alcohol Laws	10	34	34
020–106000	Forfeitures of Unclaimed Money and Property	34	24	24
020–108000	Fines, Penalties, and Forfeitures, Federal Coal Mine Health and Safety Laws	34	40	40
020–109600	Penalties on Employers Who Do not Offer Health Coverage or Delay Eligibility for New Employees		170	217
020–241100	User Fees for IRS	3	3	3
020–249200	Premiums, Terrorism Risk Insurance Program			38
020–309400	Recovery from Airport and Airway Trust Fund for Refunds of Taxes	13	18	19
020–309500	Recovery from Leaking Underground Storage Tank Trust Fund for Refunds of Taxes, EPA	7	6	6
020–309990	Refunds of Moneys Erroneously Received and Recovered (20X1807)	–17	–17	–17
021–103000	Fines, Penalties, and Forfeitures, Immigration and Labor Laws	172	184	184
050–085015	Registration, Filing, and Transaction Fees, SEC	783	825	846
220–109900	Fines, Penalties, and Forfeitures, not Otherwise Classified	5,588	4,514	4,674
901–011050	Individual Income Taxes	2,044,132	2,257,051	2,305,216
901–011050	Individual Income Taxes: Legislative proposal, not subject to PAYGO			–21
901–011050	Individual Income Taxes: Legislative proposal, subject to PAYGO		6,124	39,794
999–011100	Corporation Income and Excess Profits Taxes	371,831	382,560	411,806
999–011100	Corporation Income and Excess Profits Taxes: Legislative proposal, not subject to PAYGO			–7
999–011100	Corporation Income and Excess Profits Taxes: Legislative proposal, subject to PAYGO			89,113
901–015250	Other Federal Fund Excise Taxes	–320	1,843	1,918
901–015250	Other Federal Fund Excise Taxes: Legislative proposal, subject to PAYGO			16
999–015300	Estate and Gift Taxes	27,140	25,742	24,802
999–015300	Estate and Gift Taxes: Legislative proposal, subject to PAYGO			625
901–015500	Tobacco Excise Tax	12,136	11,549	11,732
901–015600	Alcohol Excise Tax	10,274	10,598	10,751
901–015700	Telephone Excise Tax	321	235	191
901–015913	Fee on Health Insurance Providers	206		
901–015914	Tax on Indoor Tanning Services	70	64	59
901–015915	Excise Tax on Medical Device Manufacturers	–3		
901–031050	Other Federal Fund Customs Duties	52,558	62,832	35,701
General Fund Governmental receipts		2,620,348	2,871,266	3,014,777
Offsetting receipts from the public:				
020–129900	Gifts to the United States, not Otherwise Classified	3	3	3
020–143500	General Fund Proprietary Interest Receipts, not Otherwise Classified	2	2	2
020–145000	Interest Payments from States, Cash Management Improvement	25	32	32
020–146310	Interest on Quota in International Monetary Fund	22	22	22
020–146320	Interest on Loans to International Monetary Fund	1	1	1
020–149900	Interest Received from Credit Financing Accounts	47,401	51,726	45,903
020–168200	Gain by Exchange on Foreign Currency Denominated Public Debt Securities	8		
020–248500	GSE Fees Pursuant to P.L. 112–78 Sec. 401	4,930	5,606	5,906
020–267710	Community Development Financial Institutions Fund, Negative Subsidies	3		
020–269130	Economic Stabilization, Downward Reestimates of Subsidies	14,030	4,415	
020–276330	Community Development Financial Institutions Fund, Downward Re-estimate of Subsidies	10	17	
020–278430	Small Business Lending Fund Direct Loans, Downward Reestimates of Subsidies	1	5	
020–279030	GSE Mortgage-backed Securities Direct Loans, Downward Reestimates of Subsidies	173	140	
020–279230	Troubled Asset Relief Program, Downward Reestimates of Subsidies	4	4	
020–289700	Proceeds, Air Carrier Equity Related Transactions	220	145	145

General Fund Receipt Accounts—Continued

		2021 actual	2022 est.	2023 est.
020–322000	All Other General Fund Proprietary Receipts	571	485	485
020–387500	Budget Clearing Account (suspense)	–466		
086–289100	Proceeds, Grants for Emergency Mortgage Relief Derived from Emergency Homeowners' Relief Fund	2	2	2
	General Fund Offsetting receipts from the public	66,940	62,605	52,501
Intragovernmental payments:				
020–133800	Interest on Loans to the Presidio	2	2	2
020–135100	Interest on Loans to BPA	147	149	151
020–136000	Interest on Loans to Western Area Power Administration	2	3	7
020–136300	Interest on Loans for College Housing and Academic Facilities Loans, Education	1	1	1
020–140100	Interest on Loans to Commodity Credit Corporation	13	49	104
020–141500	Interest on Loans to Federal Deposit Insurance Corporation		9	51
020–141800	Interest on Loans to Federal Financing Bank	1,810	2,045	2,168
020–143300	Interest on Loans to National Flood Insurance Fund, DHS	357	289	322
020–149500	Interest Payments on Repayable Advances to the Black Lung Disability Trust Fund	95	105	128
020–149700	Payment of Interest on Advances to the Railroad Retirement Board	100	92	109
020–150110	Interest on Loans or Advances to the Extended Unemployment Compensation Account	117	210	150
020–150120	Interest on Loans and Repayable Advances to the Federal Unemployment Account	981	810	520
020–241600	Charges for Administrative Expenses of Social Security Act As Amended	770	854	890
020–310100	Recoveries from Federal Agencies for Settlement of Claims for Contract Disputes	55	55	55
020–311200	Reimbursement from Federal Agencies for Payments Made As a Result of Discriminatory Conduct	56	56	56
020–388500	Undistributed Intragovernmental Payments and Receivables from Cancelled Accounts	659		
	General Fund Intragovernmental payments	5,165	4,729	4,714

ADMINISTRATIVE PROVISIONS—DEPARTMENT OF THE TREASURY

(INCLUDING TRANSFERS OF FUNDS)

SEC. 111. Appropriations to the Department of the Treasury in this Act shall be available for uniforms or allowances therefor, as authorized by law (5 U.S.C. 5901), including maintenance, repairs, and cleaning; purchase of insurance for official motor vehicles operated in foreign countries; purchase of motor vehicles without regard to the general purchase price limitations for vehicles purchased and used overseas for the current fiscal year; entering into contracts with the Department of State for the furnishing of health and medical services to employees and their dependents serving in foreign countries; and services authorized by 5 U.S.C. 3109.

SEC. 112. Not to exceed 2 percent of any appropriations in this title made available under the headings "Departmental Offices—Salaries and Expenses", "Office of Inspector General", "Special Inspector General for the Troubled Asset Relief Program", "Financial Crimes Enforcement Network", "Bureau of the Fiscal Service", and "Alcohol and Tobacco Tax and Trade Bureau" may be transferred between such appropriations upon the advance notification of the Committees on Appropriations of the House of Representatives and the Senate: Provided, That no transfer under this section may increase or decrease any such appropriation by more than 2 percent.

SEC. 113. Not to exceed 2 percent of any appropriation made available in this Act to the Internal Revenue Service may be transferred to the Treasury Inspector General for Tax Administration's appropriation upon the advance notification of the Committees on Appropriations of the House of Representatives and the Senate: Provided, That no transfer may increase or decrease any such appropriation by more than 2 percent.

SEC. 114. None of the funds appropriated in this Act or otherwise available to the Department of the Treasury or the Bureau of Engraving and Printing may be used to redesign the $1 Federal Reserve note.

SEC. 115. The Secretary of the Treasury may transfer funds from the "Bureau of the Fiscal Service—Salaries and Expenses" to the Debt Collection Fund as necessary to cover the costs of debt collection: Provided, That such amounts shall be reimbursed to such salaries and expenses account from debt collections received in the Debt Collection Fund.

SEC. 116. None of the funds appropriated or otherwise made available by this or any other Act may be used by the United States Mint to construct or operate any museum without the prior notification of the Committees on Appropriations of the House of Representatives and the Senate, the House Committee on Financial Services, and the Senate Committee on Banking, Housing, and Urban Affairs.

SEC. 117. None of the funds appropriated or otherwise made available by this or any other Act or source to the Department of the Treasury, the Bureau of Engraving and Printing, and the United States Mint, individually or collectively, may be used to consolidate any or all functions of the Bureau of Engraving and Printing and the United States Mint without the prior notification of the House Committee on Financial Services; the Senate Committee on Banking, Housing, and Urban Affairs; and the Committees on Appropriations of the House of Representatives and the Senate.

SEC. 118. Funds appropriated by this Act, or made available by the transfer of funds in this Act, for the Department of the Treasury's intelligence or intelligence related activities are deemed to be specifically authorized by the Congress for purposes of section 504 of the National Security Act of 1947 (50 U.S.C. 414) during fiscal year 2023 until the enactment of the Intelligence Authorization Act for Fiscal Year 2023.

SEC. 119. Not to exceed $5,000 shall be made available from the Bureau of Engraving and Printing's Industrial Revolving Fund for necessary official reception and representation expenses.

SEC. 120. Within 45 days after the date of enactment of this Act, the Secretary of the Treasury shall submit an itemized report to the Committees on Appropriations of the House of Representatives and the Senate on the amount of total funds charged to each office by the Franchise Fund including the amount charged for each service provided by the Franchise Fund to each office, a detailed description of the services, a detailed explanation of how each charge for each service is calculated, and a description of the role customers have in governing in the Franchise Fund.

SEC. 121. During fiscal year 2023—

(1) none of the funds made available in this or any other Act may be used by the Department of the Treasury, including the Internal Revenue Service, to issue, revise, or finalize any regulation, revenue ruling, or other guidance not limited to a particular taxpayer relating to the standard which is used to determine whether an organization is operated exclusively for the promotion of social welfare for purposes of section 501(c)(4) of the Internal Revenue Code of 1986 (including the proposed regulations published at 78 Fed. Reg. 71535 (November 29, 2013)); and

(2) the standard and definitions as in effect on January 1, 2010, which are used to make such determinations shall apply after the date of the enactment of this Act for purposes of determining status under section 501(c)(4) of such Code of organizations created on, before, or after such date.

SEC. 122. (a) Not later than 60 days after the end of each quarter, the Office of Financial Research shall submit reports on their activities to the Committees on Appropriations of the House of Representatives and the Senate, the Committee on Financial Services of the House of Representatives and the Senate Committee on Banking, Housing, and Urban Affairs.

(b) The reports required under subsection (a) shall include—

(1) the obligations made during the previous quarter by object class, office, and activity;

(2) the estimated obligations for the remainder of the fiscal year by object class, office, and activity;

(3) the number of full-time equivalents within each office during the previous quarter;

(4) the estimated number of full-time equivalents within each office for the remainder of the fiscal year; and

(5) actions taken to achieve the goals, objectives, and performance measures of each office.

(c) At the request of any such Committees specified in subsection (a), the Office of Financial Research shall make officials available to testify on the contents of the reports required under subsection (a).

SEC. 123. Notwithstanding any other provision of law, the unobligated balances from amounts made available to the Secretary of the Treasury for administrative expenses pursuant to sections 4003(f) and 4112(b) of the Coronavirus Aid, Relief, and Economic Security Act (Public Law 116–136); section 421(f)(2) of Division N of the Consolidated Appropriations Act, 2021 (Public Law 116–260); sections 3201(a)(2)(B), 3206(d)(1)(A), and 7301(b)(5) of the American Rescue Plan Act of 2021 (Public Law 117–2); and section 602(a)(2) of the Social Security Act, as added by section 9901 of the American Rescue Plan Act of 2021 (Public Law 117–2), shall be available for any administrative expenses determined by the Secretary of the Treasury to be necessary to respond to the coronavirus, including but not limited to expenses necessary to implement any provision of the Coronavirus Aid, Relief, and Economic Security Act (Public Law 116–136), Division N of the Consolidated Appropriations Act, 2021 (Public Law 116–260), the American Rescue Plan Act (Public Law 117–2), or title VI of the Social Security Act: Provided, That such unobligated balances shall be available in addition to any other appropriations provided for such purposes.

SEC. 124. Section 121 of the Emergency Economic Stabilization Act of 2008 (12 U.S.C. 5231) is amended in subsection (e)(1)(B)(ii) by striking "subparagraph" and all that follows through the period at the end and inserting "subparagraph, the Special Inspector General may not make any appointment that exceeds 18 months or that extends beyond the date on which the Special Inspector General terminates under subsection (k).".

SEC. 125. Not to exceed 5 percent of any appropriation made available in this Act for the Department of the Treasury may be transferred to the Department's information technology system modernization and working capital fund (IT WCF), as authorized by section 1077(b)(1) of title X of division A of the National Defense Authorization Act for Fiscal Year 2018, for the purposes specified in section 1077(b)(3) of such Act, upon the prior notification of the Committees on Appropriations of the House of Representatives and the Senate: Provided, That amounts transferred to the IT WCF under this section shall remain available for obligation through September 30, 2026.

TITLE VI—GENERAL PROVISIONS

SEC. 601. None of the funds in this Act shall be used for the planning or execution of any program to pay the expenses of, or otherwise compensate, non-Federal parties intervening in regulatory or adjudicatory proceedings funded in this Act.

SEC. 602. None of the funds appropriated in this Act shall remain available for obligation beyond the current fiscal year, nor may any be transferred to other appropriations, unless expressly so provided herein.

SEC. 603. The expenditure of any appropriation under this Act for any consulting service through procurement contract pursuant to 5 U.S.C. 3109 shall be limited to those contracts where such expenditures are a matter of public record and available for public inspection, except where otherwise provided under existing law, or under existing Executive order issued pursuant to existing law.

SEC. 604. None of the funds made available by this Act shall be available for any activity or for paying the salary of any Government employee where funding an activity or paying a salary to a Government employee would result in a decision, determination, rule, regulation, or policy that would prohibit the enforcement of section 307 of the Tariff Act of 1930 (19 U.S.C. 1307).

SEC. 605. No funds appropriated pursuant to this Act may be expended by an entity unless the entity agrees that in expending the assistance the entity will comply with chapter 83 of title 41, United States Code.

SEC. 606. No funds appropriated or otherwise made available under this Act shall be made available to any person or entity that has been convicted of violating chapter 83 of title 41, United States Code.

SEC. 607. Except as otherwise provided in this Act, none of the funds provided in this Act, provided by previous appropriations Acts to the agencies or entities funded in this Act that remain available for obligation or expenditure in fiscal year 2023, or provided from any accounts in the Treasury derived by the collection of fees and available to the agencies funded by this Act, shall be available for obligation or expenditure through a reprogramming of funds that: (1) creates a new program; (2) eliminates a program, project, or activity; (3) increases funds or personnel for any program, project, or activity for which funds have been denied or restricted by the Congress; (4) proposes to use funds directed for a specific activity by the Committee on Appropriations of either the House of Representatives or the Senate for a different purpose; (5) augments existing programs, projects, or activities in excess of $5,000,000 or 10 percent, whichever is less; (6) reduces existing programs, projects, or activities by $5,000,000 or 10 percent, whichever is less; or (7) creates or reorganizes offices, programs, or activities unless advance notification is provided to the Committees on Appropriations of the House of Representatives and the Senate: Provided, That prior to any significant reorganization, restructuring, relocation, or closing of offices, programs, or activities, each agency or entity funded in this Act shall notify the Committees on Appropriations of the House of Representatives and the Senate: Provided further, That not later than 60 days after the date of enactment of this Act, each agency funded by this Act shall submit a report to the Committees on Appropriations of the House of Representatives and the Senate to establish the baseline for application of reprogramming and transfer authorities for the current fiscal year: Provided further, That at a minimum the report shall include: (1) a table for each appropriation, detailing both full-time employee equivalents and budget authority, with separate columns to display the prior year enacted level, the President's budget request, adjustments made by Congress, adjustments due to enacted rescissions, if appropriate, and the fiscal year enacted level; (2) a delineation in the table for each appropriation and its respective prior year enacted level by object class and program, project, and activity as detailed in this Act, in the accompanying report, or in the budget appendix for the respective appropriation, whichever is more detailed, and which shall apply to all items for which a dollar amount is specified and to all programs for which new budget authority is provided, as well as to discretionary grants and discretionary grant allocations; and (3) an identification of items of special congressional interest.

SEC. 608. Except as otherwise specifically provided by law, not to exceed 50 percent of unobligated balances remaining available at the end of fiscal year 2023 from appropriations made available for salaries and expenses for fiscal year 2023 in this Act, shall remain available through September 30, 2024, for each such account for the purposes authorized: Provided, That notice thereof shall be provided to the Committees on Appropriations of the House of Representatives and the Senate prior to the expenditure of such funds.

SEC. 609. (a) None of the funds made available in this Act may be used by the Executive Office of the President to request—

(1) any official background investigation report on any individual from the Federal Bureau of Investigation; or

(2) a determination with respect to the treatment of an organization as described in section 501(c) of the Internal Revenue Code of 1986 and exempt from taxation under section 501(a) of such Code from the Department of the Treasury or the Internal Revenue Service.

(b) Subsection (a) shall not apply—

(1) in the case of an official background investigation report, if such individual has given express written consent for such request not more than 6 months prior to the date of such request and during the same presidential administration; or

(2) if such request is required due to extraordinary circumstances involving national security.

SEC. 610. The cost accounting standards promulgated under chapter 15 of title 41, United States Code shall not apply with respect to a contract under the Federal Employees Health Benefits Program established under chapter 89 of title 5, United States Code.

SEC. 611. For the purpose of resolving litigation and implementing any settlement agreements regarding the nonforeign area cost-of-living allowance program, the Office of Personnel Management may accept and utilize (without regard to any restriction on unanticipated travel expenses imposed in an Appropriations Act) funds made available to the Office of Personnel Management pursuant to court approval.

SEC. 612. No funds appropriated by this Act shall be available to pay for an abortion, or the administrative expenses in connection with any health plan under the Federal employees health benefits program which provides any benefits or coverage for abortions.

SEC. 613. The provision of section 612 shall not apply where the life of the mother would be endangered if the fetus were carried to term, or the pregnancy is the result of an act of rape or incest.

SEC. 614. In order to promote Government access to commercial information technology, the restriction on purchasing nondomestic articles, materials, and supplies set forth in chapter 83 of title 41, United States Code (popularly known as the Buy American Act), shall not apply to the acquisition by the Federal Government of information technology (as defined in section 11101 of title 40, United States Code), that is a commercial item (as defined in section 103 of title 41, United States Code).

SEC. 615. Notwithstanding section 1353 of title 31, United States Code, no officer or employee of any regulatory agency or commission funded by this Act may accept on behalf of that agency, nor may such agency or commission accept, payment or reimbursement from a non-Federal entity for travel, subsistence, or related expenses for the purpose of enabling an officer or employee to attend and participate in any meeting or similar function relating to the official duties of the officer or employee when the entity offering payment or reimbursement is a person or entity subject to regulation by such agency or commission, or represents a person or entity subject to regulation by such agency or commission, unless the person or entity is an organization described in section 501(c)(3) of the Internal Revenue Code of 1986 and exempt from tax under section 501(a) of such Code.

SEC. 616. (a)(1) Notwithstanding any other provision of law, an Executive agency covered by this Act otherwise authorized to enter into contracts for either leases or the construction or alteration of real property for office, meeting, storage, or other space must consult with the General Services Administration before issuing a solicitation for offers of new leases or construction contracts, and in the case of succeeding leases, before entering into negotiations with the current lessor.

(2) Any such agency with authority to enter into an emergency lease may do so during any period declared by the President to require emergency leasing authority with respect to such agency.

(b) For purposes of this section, the term "Executive agency covered by this Act" means any Executive agency provided funds by this Act, but does not include the General Services Administration or the United States Postal Service.

SEC. 617. (a) There are appropriated for the following activities the amounts required under current law:
   (1) Compensation of the President (3 U.S.C. 102).
   (2) Payments to—
      (A) the Judicial Officers' Retirement Fund (28 U.S.C. 377(o));
      (B) the Judicial Survivors' Annuities Fund (28 U.S.C. 376(c)); and
      (C) the United States Court of Federal Claims Judges' Retirement Fund (28 U.S.C. 178(l)).
   (3) Payment of Government contributions—
      (A) with respect to the health benefits of retired employees, as authorized by chapter 89 of title 5, United States Code, and the Retired Federal Employees Health Benefits Act (74 Stat. 849); and
      (B) with respect to the life insurance benefits for employees retiring after December 31, 1989 (5 U.S.C. ch. 87).
   (4) Payment to finance the unfunded liability of new and increased annuity benefits under the Civil Service Retirement and Disability Fund (5 U.S.C. 8348).
   (5) Payment of annuities authorized to be paid from the Civil Service Retirement and Disability Fund by statutory provisions other than subchapter III of chapter 83 or chapter 84 of title 5, United States Code.
   (b) Nothing in this section may be construed to exempt any amount appropriated by this section from any otherwise applicable limitation on the use of funds contained in this Act.

SEC. 618. None of the funds made available in this Act may be used by the Federal Trade Commission to complete the draft report entitled "Interagency Working Group on Food Marketed to Children: Preliminary Proposed Nutrition Principles to Guide Industry Self-Regulatory Efforts" unless the Interagency Working Group on Food Marketed to Children complies with Executive Order No. 13563.

SEC. 619. (a) The head of each executive branch agency funded by this Act shall ensure that the Chief Information Officer of the agency has the authority to participate in decisions regarding the budget planning process related to information technology.
   (b) Amounts appropriated for any executive branch agency funded by this Act that are available for information technology shall be allocated within the agency, consistent with the provisions of appropriations Acts and budget guidelines and recommendations from the Director of the Office of Management and Budget, in such manner as specified by, or approved by, the Chief Information Officer of the agency in consultation with the Chief Financial Officer of the agency and budget officials.

SEC. 620. None of the funds made available in this Act may be used by a governmental entity to require the disclosure by a provider of electronic communication service to the public or remote computing service of the contents of a wire or electronic communication that is in electronic storage with the provider (as such terms are defined in sections 2510 and 2711 of title 18, United States Code) in a manner that violates the Fourth Amendment to the Constitution of the United States.

SEC. 621. No funds provided in this Act shall be used to deny an Inspector General funded under this Act timely access to any records, documents, or other materials available to the department or agency over which that Inspector General has responsibilities under the Inspector General Act of 1978, or to prevent or impede that Inspector General's access to such records, documents, or other materials, under any provision of law, except a provision of law that expressly refers to the Inspector General and expressly limits the Inspector General's right of access. A department or agency covered by this section shall provide its Inspector General with access to all such records, documents, and other materials in a timely manner. Each Inspector General shall ensure compliance with statutory limitations on disclosure relevant to the information provided by the establishment over which that Inspector General has responsibilities under the Inspector General Act of 1978. Each Inspector General covered by this section shall report to the Committees on Appropriations of the House of Representatives and the Senate within 5 calendar days any failures to comply with this requirement.

SEC. 622. (a) None of the funds made available in this Act may be used to maintain or establish a computer network unless such network blocks the viewing, downloading, and exchanging of pornography.
   (b) Nothing in subsection (a) shall limit the use of funds necessary for any Federal, State, tribal, or local law enforcement agency or any other entity carrying out criminal investigations, prosecution, adjudication activities, or other law enforcement- or victim assistance-related activity.

SEC. 623. None of the funds appropriated or other-wise made available by this Act may be used to pay award or incentive fees for contractors whose performance has been judged to be below satisfactory, behind schedule, over budget, or has failed to meet the basic requirements of a contract, unless the Agency determines that any such deviations are due to unforeseeable events, government-driven scope changes, or are not significant within the overall scope of the project and/or program and unless such awards or incentive fees are consistent with 16.401(e)(2) of the Federal Acquisition Regulation.

SEC. 624. None of the funds made available by this Act may be used for first-class or business-class travel by the employees of executive branch agencies funded by this Act in contravention of sections 301–10.122 through 301–10.125 of title 41, Code of Federal Regulations.

SEC. 625. In addition to any amounts appropriated or otherwise made available for expenses related to enhancements to www.oversight.gov, $850,000, to remain available until expended, shall be provided for an additional amount for such purpose to the Inspectors General Council Fund established pursuant to section 11(c)(3)(B) of the Inspector General Act of 1978 (5 U.S.C. App.): Provided, That these amounts shall be in addition to any amounts or any authority available to the Council of the Inspectors General on Integrity and Efficiency under section 11 of the Inspector General Act of 1978 (5 U.S.C. App.).

SEC. 626. None of the funds made available by this Act may be obligated on contracts in excess of $5,000 for public relations, as that term is defined in Office and Management and Budget Circular A-87 (revised May 10, 2004), unless advance notice of such an obligation is transmitted to the Committees on Appropriations of the House of Representatives and the Senate.

SEC. 627. When issuing statements, press releases, requests for proposals, bid solicitations and other documents describing projects or programs funded in whole or in part with Federal money, all grantees receiving Federal funds included in this act, shall clearly state—
   (1) the percentage of the total costs of the program or project which will be financed with Federal money;
   (2) the dollar amount of Federal funds for the project or program; and
   (3) percentage and dollar amount of the total costs of the project or program that will be financed by non-governmental sources.

SEC. 628. Notwithstanding section 708 of this Act, funds made available to the Commodity Futures Trading Commission and the Securities and Exchange Commission by this or any other Act may be used for the interagency funding and sponsorship of a joint advisory committee to advise on emerging regulatory issues.

SEC. 629. Title 44, United States Code, is amended as follows—
   (a) in subsection (a)(2) of section 2107, by striking "the head of such agency has certified in writing to the Archivist" and inserting "the Archivist determines, after consulting with the head of such agency,";
   (b) in subsection (d) of section 2904, by striking the first instance of "digital or electronic";
   (c) in subsection (e) of section 3303a, by striking "the written consent of" and inserting "advance notice to"; and
   (d) in section 3308, by striking "empower" and inserting "direct".

SEC. 630. Section 644 of the Treasury and General Government Appropriations Act, 2003 (division J of Public Law 108–7) is repealed.

DEPARTMENT OF VETERANS AFFAIRS

VETERANS HEALTH ADMINISTRATION
Federal Funds
MEDICAL SERVICES

For necessary expenses for furnishing, as authorized by law, inpatient and outpatient care and treatment to beneficiaries of the Department of Veterans Affairs and veterans described in section 1705(a) of title 38, United States Code, including care and treatment in facilities not under the jurisdiction of the Department, and including medical supplies and equipment, bioengineering services, food services, and salaries and expenses of healthcare employees hired under title 38, United States Code, assistance and support services for caregivers as authorized by section 1720G of title 38, United States Code, loan repayments authorized by section 604 of the Caregivers and Veterans Omnibus Health Services Act of 2010 (Public Law 111–163; 124 Stat. 1174; 38 U.S.C. 7681 note), monthly assistance allowances authorized by section 322(d) of title 38, United States Code, grants authorized by section 521A of title 38, United States Code, and administrative expenses necessary to carry out sections 322(d) and 521A of title 38, United States Code, and hospital care and medical services authorized by section 1787 of title 38, United States Code; $261,000,000, which shall remain available until September 30, 2024, and shall be in addition to funds previously appropriated under this heading that became available on October 1, 2022; and, in addition, $74,004,000,000, plus reimbursements, shall become available on October 1, 2023, and shall remain available until September 30, 2024: Provided, That, of the amount made available on October 1, 2023, under this heading, $2,000,000,000 shall remain available until September 30, 2025: Provided further, That, notwithstanding any other provision of law, the Secretary of Veterans Affairs shall establish a priority for the provision of medical treatment for veterans who have service-connected disabilities, lower income, or have special needs: Provided further, That, notwithstanding any other provision of law, the Secretary of Veterans Affairs shall give priority funding for the provision of basic medical benefits to veterans in enrollment priority groups 1 through 6: Provided further, That, notwithstanding any other provision of law, the Secretary of Veterans Affairs may authorize the dispensing of prescription drugs from Veterans Health Administration facilities to enrolled veterans with privately written prescriptions based on requirements established by the Secretary: Provided further, That the implementation of the program described in the previous proviso shall incur no additional cost to the Department of Veterans Affairs: Provided further, That the Secretary of Veterans Affairs shall ensure that sufficient amounts appropriated under this heading for medical supplies and equipment are available for the acquisition of prosthetics designed specifically for female veterans.

Note.—A full-year 2022 appropriation for this account was not enacted at the time the Budget was prepared; therefore, the Budget assumes this account is operating under the Continuing Appropriations Act, 2022 (Division A of Public Law 117–43, as amended). The amounts included for 2022 reflect the annualized level provided by the continuing resolution.

Special and Trust Fund Receipts (in millions of dollars)

Identification code 036–0160–0–1–703		2021 actual	2022 est.	2023 est.
0100	Balance, start of year	219	274	274
	Receipts:			
	Current law:			
1130	Pharmaceutical Co-payments, MCCF	207	323	331
1130	Medical Care Collections Fund, Third Party Prescription Claims	145	152	154
1130	Enhanced-use Lease Proceeds, MCCF	1	1	1
1130	Fee Basis 3rd Party MCCF	577	693	771
1130	Fee Basis First Party Collections, Medical Care Collections Fund	16	20	21
1130	First Party Collections, MCCF	48	154	158
1130	Third Party Collections, MCCF	2,111	2,548	2,434
1130	Parking Fees, MCCF	4	2	2
1130	Compensated Work Therapy, MCCF	35	27	36
1130	MCCF, Long-term Care Copayments		1	1
1140	Payments from Compensation and Pension, MCCF	2	1	1
1199	Total current law receipts	3,146	3,922	3,910
1999	Total receipts	3,146	3,922	3,910
2000	Total: Balances and receipts	3,365	4,196	4,184
	Appropriations:			
	Current law:			
2101	Medical Care Collections Fund	–3,091	–3,922	–3,910
5099	Balance, end of year	274	274	274

Program and Financing (in millions of dollars)

Identification code 036–0160–0–1–703		2021 actual	2022 est.	2023 est.
	Obligations by program activity:			
0001	Outpatient care	21,204	22,399	29,606
0002	Inpatient care	9,323	9,145	9,831
0004	Mental health care	8,320	7,472	8,528
0005	Long-term care	4,280	4,265	4,546
0006	Pharmacy	8,987	9,769	10,688
0007	Prosthetics care	3,474	3,756	4,070
0008	Dental care	766	806	934
0009	Rehabilitation	785	816	887
0010	Homeless Grants	1,079	906	970
0011	Readjustment Counseling	229	266	277
0012	Caregivers (Title I) P.L. 111–163	863	1,339	1,813
0013	Prior-Year Recoveries	374		
0014	CHAMPVA	396	436	476
0015	Outpatient care (ARP P.L. 117–2, Section 8007)		628	
0091	Total operating expenses	60,080	62,003	72,626
0101	Outpatient care	1,201	1,322	1,488
0102	Inpatient care	477	495	559
0103	Mental health care	85	88	99
0104	Long-term care	167	173	195
0105	Pharmacy	64	66	75
0107	Dental care	53	55	62
0108	Rehabilitation	28	29	33
0109	Readjustment Counseling	5		5
0113	Prior-Year Recoveries	68		
0191	Total Capital Investment	2,148	2,228	2,516
0799	Total direct obligations	62,228	64,231	75,142
0801	Medical Services (Reimbursable)	104	133	133
0900	Total new obligations, unexpired accounts	62,332	64,364	75,275
	Budgetary resources:			
	Unobligated balance:			
1000	Unobligated balance brought forward, Oct 1	12,485	3,836	1,669
1001	Discretionary unobligated balance brought fwd, Oct 1	12,460		
1010	Unobligated balance transfer to other accts [036–0140]	–5,400		
1010	Unobligated balance transfer to other accts [036–0152]	–105		
1010	Unobligated balance transfer to other accts [036–0162]	–140		
1010	Unobligated balance transfer to other accts [036–0169]	–10		
1021	Recoveries of prior year unpaid obligations	339		
1033	Recoveries of prior year paid obligations	103		
1070	Unobligated balance (total)	7,272	3,836	1,669
	Budget authority:			
	Appropriations, discretionary:			
1100	Appropriation	497	497	261
1120	Appropriations transferred to other acct [036–0140]	–100		
1120	Appropriations transferred to other acct [036–0151]	–338		
1120	Appropriations transferred to other acct [036–1122]	–1		
1120	Appropriations transferred to other acct [036–0129]	–12		
1120	Appropriations transferred to other acct [036–4014]	–140		
1120	Appropriations transferred to other acct [036–0167]	–45		
1121	Appropriations transferred from other acct [036–5287]	2,514	3,192	3,103
1131	Unobligated balance of appropriations permanently reduced	–100	–100	
1160	Appropriation, discretionary (total)	2,275	3,589	3,364
	Advance appropriations, discretionary:			
1170	Advance appropriation	56,158	58,897	70,323
1172	Advance appropriations transferred to other accounts [036–0165]	–15	–15	–15
1172	Advance appropriations transferred to other accounts [036–0169]	–216	–204	–190
1172	Advance appropriations transferred to other accounts [036–0151]		–178	
1172	Advance appropriations transferred to other accounts [036–1122]		–6	
1172	Advance appropriations transferred to other accounts [036–0167]		–10	
1180	Advanced appropriation, discretionary (total)	55,927	58,484	70,118
	Appropriations, mandatory:			
1200	Appropriation [P.L. 117–2, Section 8007]	628		
	Spending authority from offsetting collections, discretionary:			
1700	Collected	126	111	111
1701	Change in uncollected payments, Federal sources	7	13	13
1750	Spending auth from offsetting collections, disc (total)	133	124	124
1900	Budget authority (total)	58,963	62,197	73,606

MEDICAL SERVICES—Continued
Program and Financing—Continued

Identification code 036–0160–0–1–703	2021 actual	2022 est.	2023 est.
1930 Total budgetary resources available	66,235	66,033	75,275
Memorandum (non-add) entries:			
1940 Unobligated balance expiring	–67		
1941 Unexpired unobligated balance, end of year	3,836	1,669	
Change in obligated balance:			
Unpaid obligations:			
3000 Unpaid obligations, brought forward, Oct 1	7,542	8,866	11,295
3010 New obligations, unexpired accounts	62,332	64,364	75,275
3011 Obligations ("upward adjustments"), expired accounts	927		
3020 Outlays (gross)	–60,959	–61,935	–73,170
3040 Recoveries of prior year unpaid obligations, unexpired	–339		
3041 Recoveries of prior year unpaid obligations, expired	–637		
3050 Unpaid obligations, end of year	8,866	11,295	13,400
Uncollected payments:			
3060 Uncollected pymts, Fed sources, brought forward, Oct 1	–15	–20	–33
3070 Change in uncollected pymts, Fed sources, unexpired	–7	–13	–13
3071 Change in uncollected pymts, Fed sources, expired	2		
3090 Uncollected pymts, Fed sources, end of year	–20	–33	–46
Memorandum (non-add) entries:			
3100 Obligated balance, start of year	7,527	8,846	11,262
3200 Obligated balance, end of year	8,846	11,262	13,354
Budget authority and outlays, net:			
Discretionary:			
4000 Budget authority, gross	58,335	62,197	73,606
Outlays, gross:			
4010 Outlays from new discretionary authority	48,873	53,959	64,154
4011 Outlays from discretionary balances	12,082	7,407	8,955
4020 Outlays, gross (total)	60,955	61,366	73,109
Offsets against gross budget authority and outlays:			
Offsetting collections (collected) from:			
4030 Federal sources	–194	–42	–42
4033 Non-Federal sources	–387	–69	–69
4040 Offsets against gross budget authority and outlays (total)	–581	–111	–111
Additional offsets against gross budget authority only:			
4050 Change in uncollected pymts, Fed sources, unexpired	–7	–13	–13
4052 Offsetting collections credited to expired accounts	352		
4053 Recoveries of prior year paid obligations, unexpired accounts	103		
4060 Additional offsets against budget authority only (total)	448	–13	–13
4070 Budget authority, net (discretionary)	58,202	62,073	73,482
4080 Outlays, net (discretionary)	60,374	61,255	72,998
Mandatory:			
4090 Budget authority, gross	628		
Outlays, gross:			
4101 Outlays from mandatory balances	4	569	61
4180 Budget authority, net (total)	58,830	62,073	73,482
4190 Outlays, net (total)	60,378	61,824	73,059

Medical Care.— In 2023, the Administration requests an additional $7.5 billion over the 2023 advance appropriation of $111.3 billion for the Department of Veterans Affairs (VA) Medical Care programs, consisting of four appropriations: Medical Services, Medical Community Care, Medical Support and Compliance, and Medical Facilities. Each year, VA updates its budget estimates to incorporate the most recent data on healthcare utilization rates, actual program experience, and other factors, such as economic trends in unemployment and inflation. As a result of these updates, the adjusted budget estimates more accurately reflect the projected medical demands of veterans enrolled in the VA healthcare system.

In 2023, the Budget makes robust investments in VA Medical Care programs, including: $2.7 billion for veterans' homelessness programs and $13.9 billion for veterans' mental health care services, including $497 million for veteran suicide prevention initiatives. The Budget also includes $663 million for VA's Opioid Prevention and Treatment programs, including programs in support of the Jason Simcakoski Memorial and Promise Act.

For 2024, the Budget requests $128.1 billion in advance appropriations for VA Medical Care. This request for advance appropriations fulfills the Administration's commitment to provide reliable and timely resources to support the delivery of accessible and high-quality medical services for veterans.

With the resources requested for 2023 and 2024, VA will provide the highest quality healthcare services for veterans. VA estimates it will treat 7.3 million patients in 2023 and 7.4 million patients in 2024. Operation Enduring Freedom, Operation Iraqi Freedom, and Operation New Dawn (OEF/OIF/OND) veterans are expected to be 1.3 million in 2023 and 1.4 million in 2024.

Medical Care Collections Fund (MCCF).—VA estimates collections of $3.9 billion in 2023 and $4.0 billion in 2024. VA has the authority to collect inpatient and outpatient co-payments, medication co-payments, and nursing home co-payments; authority for certain income verification; authority to recover third-party insurance payments from veterans for nonservice-connected conditions; and authority to collect revenue from enhanced use leases. These collections also include those collected from the Compensated Work Therapy Program, Compensation and Living Expenses Program, and the Parking Program.

Medical Services.—For Medical Services, the Budget reflects the 2023 advance appropriation request of $70.3 billion and an annual appropriation request of $261 million; and the 2024 advance appropriation request of $74.0 billion. This appropriation provides for the component of VA's comprehensive, integrated healthcare delivery system that addresses the needs of eligible veterans and beneficiaries in VA facilities.

WORKLOAD

Estimated obligations and workload for seven categories of healthcare services are shown below: outpatient care, inpatient care, mental healthcare, long term services and supports, prosthetics care, dental care, and rehabilitation care. In addition, estimated obligations and workload are also shown for six programs: CHAMPVA and other dependent programs, readjustment counseling, Caregivers, pharmacy, the Camp Lejeune Family Member, and State Homes. Estimated obligations and workload reflect care in total provided through the Medical Services and Medical Community Care appropriations, as applicable.

Ambulatory Care (Outpatient care).—Obligations for 2023 are estimated to be $42,987 million for Medical Services and Medical Community Care for this health service category, which includes funding for ambulatory care in VA facilities and in the community.

Estimated operating levels are:

Number of Outpatient Visits	2021 actual	2022 est.	2023 est.
VA	92,150,762	99,667,382	107,751,153
Community Care	32,998,210	36,225,736	39,079,400
Total	125,148,972	135,893,118	146,830,553

Inpatient care.—Obligations for 2023 are estimated to be $19.112 million for Medical Services and Medical Community Care.

Estimated operating levels are:

Number of Patients Treated, Inpatient	2021 actual	2022 est.	2023 est.
Acute Hospital, Medicine	315,834	320,329	324,734
Acute Hospital, Neurology	3,231	3,743	3,422
Acute Hospital, Surgery	70,620	83,805	82,100
Acute Hospital (Community Care)	537,633	567,132	590,731
Subacute (Intermediate)	1,259	1,108	958
Total	928,577	976,117	1,001,945

Mental health care.—Obligations for 2023 are estimated to be $8,907 million for Medical Services and Medical Community Care for the inpatient, residential, and outpatient care of veterans with conditions related to mental illness, including alcohol and other substance use disorders. Mental health services and operations ensure the availability of a range of services, from treatment of a variety of common mental health conditions in primary care to more intensive interventions in specialty mental health programs for more severe and persisting mental health conditions. Specialty services such as evidence-based psychotherapies, intensive outpatient programs, residential rehabilitation treatment, and inpatient care are available to meet the range of veterans' needs.

DEPARTMENT OF VETERANS AFFAIRS

Estimated operating levels are:

Average Daily Census	2021 actual	2022 est.	2023 est.
Acute Psychiatry	1,742	2,032	1,986
Acute Psychiatry (Community Care)	1,168	1,311	1,382
Residential Recovery Programs	2,670	3,341	3,039
Total	5,580	6,684	6,407

Long term services and supports (LTSS).—Obligations for 2023 are estimated to be $8,167 million for Medical Services and Medical Community Care for the care of veteran residents in VA- and community-operated long-term care programs. VA offers a spectrum of geriatric and extended care services to veterans enrolled in its healthcare system. The spectrum of long-term care services includes non-institutional and institutional services. All VA medical centers provide home- and community-based long-term care programs. The patient-focused approach supports veterans who wish to live safely at home in their own communities for as long as possible.

Estimated operating levels are:

LTSS Facility-Based Services: Average Daily Census	2021 actual	2022 est.	2023 est.
VA Community Living Center (Nursing Home)	6,684	8,302	7,902
Community Nursing Home	9,928	11,612	12,205
Total	16,612	19,914	20,107

LTSS Home & Community-Based Services: Number of Visits/Procedures	2021 actual	2022 est.	2023 est.
Community Adult Day Health Care	290,468	252,688	222,463
Community Residential Care	36,719	51,722	60,724
Home Hospice Care	577,064	603,858	616,786
Home Respite Care	21,803	23,482	24,751
Home Telehealth	766,817	742,355	730,124
Home-Based Primary Care	1,222,310	1,471,052	1,719,793
Homemaker/Home Health Aide Programs	10,456,956	11,464,836	12,472,715
Purchased Skilled Home Care	99,904	105,958	109,590
Spinal Cord Injury Home Care	15,105	17,163	18,246
State Adult Day Health Care	8,613	8,815	9,010
VA Adult Day Health Care	3,272	3,000	3,000
Total	13,499,031	14,744,927	15,987,202

Prosthetics care.—Obligations in Medical Services for 2023 are estimated to be $4,070 million for veterans. Prosthetic and Sensory Aids Service is an integrated delivery system designed to provide medically prescribed prosthetic and sensory aids, medical devices, assistive aids, repairs and services to eligible disabled veterans to maximize their independence and enhance their quality of life. This includes, but is not limited to, artificial limbs, hearing aids, and home oxygen; items that improve accessibility such as ramps and vehicle modifications, wheelchairs and mobility aids; and devices surgically placed in the veteran, such as stents.

Dental care.—Obligations for 2023 are estimated to be $1,597 million for Medical Services and Medical Community Care for the treatment of veterans who require dental care. Dental care services are provided to eligible veterans with a "medical condition negatively impacted by poor dentition." These patients may include poorly controlled diabetic patients, patients with head or neck cancer, organ transplant patients, and others. Veterans with a 100-percent service-connected disability are eligible for comprehensive dental care as needed. In addition, homeless veterans enrolled in certain residential treatment programs are also eligible for dental treatment.

Estimated operating levels are:

Number of Procedures	2021 actual	2022 est.	2023 est.
VA	4,190,000	5,397,000	5,586,000
Community Care	1,240,000	1,430,000	1,619,000
Total	5,430,000	6,827,000	7,205,000

Rehabilitation.—Obligations for 2023 are estimated to be $920 million for Medical Services for the provision of rehabilitative care, including Blind Rehabilitation and Spinal Cord Injury programs. These services include inpatient and outpatient blind and vision rehabilitation programs, adjustment to blindness counseling, patient and family education, and assistive technology. The mission of Spinal Cord Injury and Disorders (SCI/D) services is to promote the health, independence, quality of life and productivity of individuals with spinal cord injury and disorders through efficient delivery of acute rehabilitation, psychological, social, vocational, medical and surgical care, professional training, as well as patient and family education.

Estimated operating levels are:

Average Daily Census	2021 actual	2022 est.	2023 est.
Rehabilitative Medicine	810	1,114	1,109
Blind Rehabilitation	38	146	155
Spinal Cord Injury	568	728	722
Total	1,416	1,988	1,986

Civilian Health and Medical Program of the Department of Veterans Affairs (CHAMPVA) and other Dependent Programs.—Obligations for 2023 are estimated to be $1,995 million for Medical Services and Medical Community Care for pharmacy and medical service personnel for CHAMPVA and other dependent programs.

Estimated operating levels are:

Number of Unique Patients	2021 actual	2022 est.	2023 est.
CHAMPVA In-house Treatment Initiative (CITI)	13,019	10,967	9,902
CHAMPVA (excluding CITI)	426,690	443,653	447,798
Foreign Medical Program (medical only)	4,929	5,010	5,210
Foreign Compensation & Pension Exams	122	20	5
Spina Bifida Health Care Benefits Program	871	863	858
Total	445,631	460,513	463,773

Readjustment Counseling.—Obligations in Medical Services for 2023 are estimated to $283 million. This program provides readjustment counseling services at VA Vet Centers. Vet Centers are community-based counseling centers that provide a wide range of social and psychological services to include: professional readjustment counseling to veterans who have served in a combat zone, military sexual trauma counseling, bereavement counseling for families who experience an active duty death, substance abuse assessments and referral, medical referral, Veterans Benefits Administration (VBA) benefits explanation and referral, and employment counseling. Services are also extended to the family members of eligible veterans for issues related to military service and the readjustment of those veterans.

Estimated operating levels are:

Number of Visits	2021 actual	2022 est.	2023 est.
Total	1,490,000	1,522,000	1,553,000

Caregivers Programs.—Obligations in Medical Services for 2023 are estimated to be $1,813 million. The Caregivers and Veterans Omnibus Health Services Act of 2010 (P.L. 111–163), authorized VA to provide assistance and support services for Caregivers of eligible veterans. The Program of Comprehensive Assistance for Family Caregivers provides a wide range of services for primary caregivers to include: a monthly personal caregiver stipend, respite care, access to mental health services, beneficiary travel, and healthcare benefits through the existing CHAMPVA program.

Estimated operating levels are:

	2021 actual	2022 est.	2023 est.
Caregiver Stipend (dollars in millions)	$624	$844	$1,409
Participants in the Program of Comprehensive Assistance for Family Caregivers	34,678	45,101	59,113

Pharmacy.—Obligations in the Medical Services account for 2023 are estimated to be $10,763 million for pharmacy costs. VA's use of medication therapies is a fundamental underpinning of how VA delivers healthcare today. VA's primary focus is on diagnosis and treatment in an ambulatory environment and home environment basis with institutional care as the modality of last resort.

Estimated operating levels are:

Number of 30-day Prescriptions (in millions)	2021 actual	2022 est.	2023 est.
Total	303	309	313

Camp Lejeune Family Member Program.—Obligations in Medical Community Care for 2023 are estimated to be $3.8 million for the Camp Lejeune Family Member program. The Honoring America's Veterans and Caring for Camp Lejeune Families Act of 2012 (P.L. 112–154) extended eligibility for VA hospital care and medical services to certain veterans who were stationed at Camp Lejeune, North Carolina, for at least 30 days between 1957 and 1987. Family members of such veterans who resided, or were in utero, at Camp Lejeune for at least 30 days during that period are eligible for reimbursement of hospital care and medical services for 15 specified illnesses and conditions, and VA is the payer of last resort.

MEDICAL SERVICES—Continued

State Home Programs.—Obligations in Medical Community Care for 2023 are estimated to be $1,504 million for State Home Programs. State Veterans Homes are facilities approved by VA that a State has established primarily for the care of veterans disabled by age, disease, or otherwise, who, because of such disability, are incapable of earning a living. VA pays a per diem to States for the care of eligible veterans, but the per diem rates are different for each of the three levels of care offered: Nursing Home Care, Domiciliary Care, or Adult Day Health Care (ADHC).

Patients Treated	2021 actual	2022 est.	2023 est.
State Home Nursing	22,485	26,118	27,481
State Home Domiciliary	3,311	3,095	2,932
Average Daily Census (ADHC)	65	102	110

Object Classification (in millions of dollars)

Identification code 036–0160–0–1–703		2021 actual	2022 est.	2023 est.
	Direct obligations:			
	Personnel compensation:			
11.1	Full-time permanent	23,967	24,751	27,139
11.3	Other than full-time permanent	518	535	586
11.5	Other personnel compensation	2,757	2,847	3,122
11.9	Total personnel compensation	27,242	28,133	30,847
12.1	Civilian personnel benefits	9,681	10,170	11,295
13.0	Benefits for former personnel	13	19	19
21.0	Travel & Transportation of Persons	1,405	1,464	1,615
22.0	Transportation of things	27	30	31
23.2	Rent, Communications & Utilities	637	690	733
24.0	Printing and reproduction	13	14	14
25.2	Other contractual services	5,910	5,744	11,983
25.2	Other contractual services (ARP P.L. 117–2, Section 8007)		628	
26.0	Supplies & Materials	13,615	14,194	14,727
31.0	Equipment	2,079	2,227	2,515
32.0	Land and structures	1	1	1
41.0	Grants, Subsidies & Contributions	1,153	906	1,351
42.0	Insurance claims and indemnities	9	11	11
44.0	Prior-year Recoveries	443		
99.0	Direct obligations	62,228	64,231	75,142
99.0	Reimbursable obligations	104	133	133
99.9	Total new obligations, unexpired accounts	62,332	64,364	75,275

Employment Summary

Identification code 036–0160–0–1–703		2021 actual	2022 est.	2023 est.
1001	Direct civilian full-time equivalent employment	267,761	268,213	282,398
2001	Reimbursable civilian full-time equivalent employment	391	391	391

MEDICAL SERVICES

(Legislative proposal, not subject to PAYGO)

Contingent upon the enactment of legislation establishing a Department of Veterans Affairs Public Health Service Joint Scholarship Program in chapter 76 of title 38, United States Code, the Secretary of Veterans Affairs may carry out such program from within amounts appropriated under this heading, including amounts previously appropriated under this heading that became available on October 1, 2022.

In addition, contingent upon the enactment of authorizing legislation, the Secretary of Veterans Affairs may reimburse qualifying veterans for certain adoption expenses from within amounts appropriated under this heading, including amounts previously appropriated under this heading that became available on October 1, 2022.

MEDICAL COMMUNITY CARE

For necessary expenses for furnishing health care to individuals pursuant to chapter 17 of title 38, United States Code, at non-Department facilities, $4,300,000,000, which shall remain available until September 30, 2024, and shall be in addition to funds previously appropriated under this heading that became available on October 1, 2022; and, in addition, $33,000,000,000, plus reimbursements, shall become available on October 1, 2023, and shall remain available until September 30, 2025.

Note.—A full-year 2022 appropriation for this account was not enacted at the time the Budget was prepared; therefore, the Budget assumes this account is operating under the Continuing Appropriations Act, 2022 (Division A of Public Law 117–43, as amended). The amounts included for 2022 reflect the annualized level provided by the continuing resolution.

Program and Financing (in millions of dollars)

Identification code 036–0140–0–1–703		2021 actual	2022 est.	2023 est.
	Obligations by program activity:			
0001	Ambulatory	9,411	6,850	11,601
0002	Dental Care	434	686	602
0003	Inpatient Care	6,968	8,578	8,722
0004	LTSS: Facility Based Services	1,189	1,253	1,385
0005	LTSS: Home & Community Based Services	1,543	1,881	2,041
0006	Mental Health Care	280	317	279
0007	CHAMPVA & Other Dependent Programs	1,599	1,457	1,519
0008	State Home Programs	1,551	1,456	1,504
0009	Camp Lejeune, Veterans Families	4	3	4
0010	Network Development and Maintenance	405	1,234	1,249
0013	Prior Year Recoveries	90		
0014	Urgent Care	56	266	291
0900	Total new obligations, unexpired accounts	23,530	23,981	29,197
	Budgetary resources:			
	Unobligated balance:			
1000	Unobligated balance brought forward, Oct 1	425	1,855	72
1001	Discretionary unobligated balance brought fwd, Oct 1	425	1,783	
1011	Unobligated balance transfer from other acct [036–0160]	5,400		
1021	Recoveries of prior year unpaid obligations	55		
1033	Recoveries of prior year paid obligations	35		
1070	Unobligated balance (total)	5,915	1,855	72
	Budget authority:			
	Appropriations, discretionary:			
1100	Appropriation	1,381	1,381	4,300
1121	Appropriations transferred from other acct [036–5287]	564	713	791
1121	Appropriations transferred from other acct [036–0160]	100		
1160	Appropriation, discretionary (total)	2,045	2,094	5,091
	Advance appropriations, discretionary:			
1170	Advance appropriation	17,131	20,148	24,157
1172	Advance appropriations transferred to other accounts [036–0169]	–28	–44	–51
1180	Advanced appropriation, discretionary (total)	17,103	20,104	24,106
	Appropriations, mandatory:			
1200	Appropriation [P.L. 117–2, Section 8004]	250		
1200	Appropriation [P.L. 117–2, Section 8007]	72		
1260	Appropriations, mandatory (total)	322		
1900	Budget authority (total)	19,470	22,198	29,197
1930	Total budgetary resources available	25,385	24,053	29,269
	Memorandum (non-add) entries:			
1941	Unexpired unobligated balance, end of year	1,855	72	72
	Change in obligated balance:			
	Unpaid obligations:			
3000	Unpaid obligations, brought forward, Oct 1	9,525	261	6,218
3001	Adjustments to unpaid obligations, brought forward, Oct 1	–9,303		
3010	New obligations, unexpired accounts	23,530	23,981	29,197
3011	Obligations ("upward adjustments"), expired accounts	63		
3020	Outlays (gross)	–23,469	–18,024	–26,185
3040	Recoveries of prior year unpaid obligations, unexpired	–55		
3041	Recoveries of prior year unpaid obligations, expired	–30		
3050	Unpaid obligations, end of year	261	6,218	9,230
	Memorandum (non-add) entries:			
3100	Obligated balance, start of year	222	261	6,218
3200	Obligated balance, end of year	261	6,218	9,230
	Budget authority and outlays, net:			
	Discretionary:			
4000	Budget authority, gross	19,148	22,198	29,197
	Outlays, gross:			
4010	Outlays from new discretionary authority	17,116	16,649	21,898
4011	Outlays from discretionary balances	6,103	1,310	4,281
4020	Outlays, gross (total)	23,219	17,959	26,179
	Offsets against gross budget authority and outlays:			
	Offsetting collections (collected) from:			
4030	Federal sources	–11		
4033	Non-Federal sources	–57		
4040	Offsets against gross budget authority and outlays (total)	–68		
	Additional offsets against gross budget authority only:			
4052	Offsetting collections credited to expired accounts	33		
4053	Recoveries of prior year paid obligations, unexpired accounts	35		
4060	Additional offsets against budget authority only (total)	68		

DEPARTMENT OF VETERANS AFFAIRS

Veterans Health Administration—Continued
Federal Funds—Continued

1041

		2021 actual	2022 est.	2023 est.
4070	Budget authority, net (discretionary)	19,148	22,198	29,197
4080	Outlays, net (discretionary)	23,151	17,959	26,179
	Mandatory:			
4090	Budget authority, gross	322		
	Outlays, gross:			
4100	Outlays from new mandatory authority	250		
4101	Outlays from mandatory balances		65	6
4110	Outlays, gross (total)	250	65	6
4180	Budget authority, net (total)	19,470	22,198	29,197
4190	Outlays, net (total)	23,401	18,024	26,185

The Medical Community Care appropriation provides funding for community care services to eligible veterans and other beneficiaries, which has been an essential part of the Department of Veterans Affairs (VA) healthcare system for decades.

The Budget reflects the following discretionary appropriation funding: the 2023 advance appropriation request of $24.2 billion, together with an annual appropriation request of $4.3 billion; and the 2024 advance appropriation request of $33.0 billion.

The 2024 request for advance appropriation fulfills the Administration's commitment to provide reliable and timely resources to support the delivery of accessible and high-quality medical services for veterans.

Section 8004 of the American Rescue Plan Act of 2021 (P.L. 117–2) provided $250 million in 2021 for a one-time only obligation and expenditure to existing State extended care facilities for veterans in proportion to each State's share of the total resident capacity in such facilities as of the date of enactment of this Act. Capacity includes only veterans on whose behalf the Department pays a per diem payment pursuant to section 1741 or 1745 of title 38, United States Code. The period of availability is from the date of the enactment of the Act, March 11, 2021, through September 30, 2022. VA obligated $104 million in 2021 and plans to obligate the remaining $396 million in 2022.

Object Classification (in millions of dollars)

Identification code 036–0140–0–1–703		2021 actual	2022 est.	2023 est.
	Direct obligations:			
21.0	Travel and transportation of persons	12		
25.2	Other Contractual Services	21,495	22,112	27,267
26.0	Supplies and materials	381	413	426
41.0	State Homes	1,301	1,456	1,504
41.0	State Homes: ARP	250		
42.0	Insurance claims and indemnities	1		
44.0	Prior Year Recoveries	90		
99.9	Total new obligations, unexpired accounts	23,530	23,981	29,197

MEDICAL SUPPORT AND COMPLIANCE

For necessary expenses in the administration of the medical, hospital, nursing home, domiciliary, construction, supply, and research activities, as authorized by law; administrative expenses in support of capital policy activities; and administrative and legal expenses of the Department for collecting and recovering amounts owed the Department as authorized under chapter 17 of title 38, United States Code, and the Federal Medical Care Recovery Act (42 U.S.C. 2651 et seq.), $1,400,000,000, which shall remain available until September 30, 2024, and shall be in addition to funds previously appropriated under this heading that became available on October 1, 2022; and, in addition, $12,300,000,000, plus reimbursements, shall become available on October 1, 2023, and shall remain available until September 30, 2024: Provided, That, of the amount made available on October 1, 2023, under this heading, $500,000,000 shall remain available until September 30, 2025.

Note.—A full-year 2022 appropriation for this account was not enacted at the time the Budget was prepared; therefore, the Budget assumes this account is operating under the Continuing Appropriations Act, 2022 (Division A of Public Law 117–43, as amended). The amounts included for 2022 reflect the annualized level provided by the continuing resolution.

Program and Financing (in millions of dollars)

Identification code 036–0152–0–1–703		2021 actual	2022 est.	2023 est.
	Obligations by program activity:			
0001	VAMCs & Other Field Activities	4,387	4,263	5,980
0002	VISN Headquarters	876	915	949
0016	Community Care	987	1,054	1,089
0020	Prior Year Recoveries	2		
0021	Clinical Services	89	170	274
0022	Operations	154	190	251
0023	Patient Care Services	141	208	317
0024	Quality and Patient Safety	126	132	206
0025	Support Services	440	676	689
0027	Discovery, Education and Affiliate Networks	54	56	127
0028	Human Capital Management	208	212	340
0029	Health Informatics	136	141	179
0030	All Other Support and Program Offices	519	550	773
0091	Total operating expenses	8,119	8,567	11,174
0101	VAMCs & Other Field Activities	38	39	41
0102	VISN Headquarters	2	2	2
0118	Operations	2	2	3
0191	Total Capital Investment	42	43	46
0293	Total direct program	8,161	8,610	11,220
0799	Total direct obligations	8,161	8,610	11,220
0801	Medical Support and Compliance (Reimbursable)	55	63	63
0900	Total new obligations, unexpired accounts	8,216	8,673	11,283
	Budgetary resources:			
	Unobligated balance:			
1000	Unobligated balance brought forward, Oct 1	284	159	191
1001	Discretionary unobligated balance brought fwd, Oct 1	271		
1011	Unobligated balance transfer from other acct [036–0160]	105		
1021	Recoveries of prior year unpaid obligations	2		
1070	Unobligated balance (total)	391	159	191
	Budget authority:			
	Appropriations, discretionary:			
1100	Appropriation	300	300	1,400
1131	Unobligated balance of appropriations permanently reduced [Rescission P.L. 116–94]	–15	–15	
1160	Appropriation, discretionary (total)	285	285	1,400
	Advance appropriations, discretionary:			
1170	Advance appropriation	7,914	8,403	9,673
1172	Advance appropriations transferred to other accounts [036–0169]	–30	–31	–30
1180	Advanced appropriation, discretionary (total)	7,884	8,372	9,643
	Spending authority from offsetting collections, discretionary:			
1700	Collected	58	48	50
1701	Change in uncollected payments, Federal sources	5		
1750	Spending auth from offsetting collections, disc (total)	63	48	50
1900	Budget authority (total)	8,232	8,705	11,093
1930	Total budgetary resources available	8,623	8,864	11,284
	Memorandum (non-add) entries:			
1940	Unobligated balance expiring	–248		
1941	Unexpired unobligated balance, end of year	159	191	1
	Change in obligated balance:			
	Unpaid obligations:			
3000	Unpaid obligations, brought forward, Oct 1	1,249	1,485	1,589
3010	New obligations, unexpired accounts	8,216	8,673	11,283
3011	Obligations ("upward adjustments"), expired accounts	89		
3020	Outlays (gross)	–7,953	–8,569	–9,962
3040	Recoveries of prior year unpaid obligations, unexpired	–2		
3041	Recoveries of prior year unpaid obligations, expired	–114		
3050	Unpaid obligations, end of year	1,485	1,589	2,910
	Uncollected payments:			
3060	Uncollected pymts, Fed sources, brought forward, Oct 1	–1	–5	–5
3070	Change in uncollected pymts, Fed sources, unexpired	–5		
3071	Change in uncollected pymts, Fed sources, expired	1		
3090	Uncollected pymts, Fed sources, end of year	–5	–5	–5
	Memorandum (non-add) entries:			
3100	Obligated balance, start of year	1,248	1,480	1,584
3200	Obligated balance, end of year	1,480	1,584	2,905
	Budget authority and outlays, net:			
	Discretionary:			
4000	Budget authority, gross	8,232	8,705	11,093
	Outlays, gross:			
4010	Outlays from new discretionary authority	6,609	7,717	8,837
4011	Outlays from discretionary balances	1,341	850	1,123
4020	Outlays, gross (total)	7,950	8,567	9,960
	Offsets against gross budget authority and outlays:			
	Offsetting collections (collected) from:			
4030	Federal sources	–84	–19	–20
4033	Non-Federal sources	–26	–29	–30

MEDICAL SUPPORT AND COMPLIANCE—Continued
Program and Financing—Continued

Identification code 036–0152–0–1–703	2021 actual	2022 est.	2023 est.
4040 Offsets against gross budget authority and outlays (total)	–110	–48	–50
Additional offsets against gross budget authority only:			
4050 Change in uncollected pymts, Fed sources, unexpired	–5		
4052 Offsetting collections credited to expired accounts	52		
4060 Additional offsets against budget authority only (total)	47		
4070 Budget authority, net (discretionary)	8,169	8,657	11,043
4080 Outlays, net (discretionary)	7,840	8,519	9,910
Mandatory:			
Outlays, gross:			
4101 Outlays from mandatory balances	3	2	2
4180 Budget authority, net (total)	8,169	8,657	11,043
4190 Outlays, net (total)	7,843	8,521	9,912

Medical Support and Compliance finances the expenses of management, security, and administration of the Department of Veterans Affairs (VA) healthcare system through the operation of VA medical centers, other facilities, Veterans Integrated Service Network offices and facility director offices, chief of staff operations, quality of care oversight, legal services, billing and coding activities, procurement, financial management, and human resource management.

For Medical Support and Compliance, the Budget reflects the following discretionary appropriation funding: the 2023 advance appropriation request of $9.7 billion, together with an annual appropriation request of $1.4 billion; and the 2024 advance appropriation request of $12.3 billion.

The 2024 advance appropriation request continues the Administration's commitment to provide reliable and timely resources to support the delivery of accessible and high-quality medical services for veterans.

Object Classification (in millions of dollars)

Identification code 036–0152–0–1–703	2021 actual	2022 est.	2023 est.
Direct obligations:			
Personnel compensation:			
11.1 Full-time permanent	3,943	4,422	5,406
11.3 Other than full-time permanent	85	95	116
11.5 Other personnel compensation	456	511	624
11.9 Total personnel compensation	4,484	5,028	6,146
12.1 Civilian personnel benefits	1,696	1,892	2,286
13.0 Benefits for former personnel	3	3	3
21.0 Travel & Transportation of Persons	17	34	69
22.0 Transportation of things	17	21	25
23.3 Communications, utilities, and miscellaneous charges	128	148	168
24.0 Printing and reproduction	22	30	38
25.2 Other contractual services	1,632	1,284	2,309
26.0 Medical supplies and materials	102	106	110
31.0 Equipment	41	44	46
32.0 Land and structures	1		
42.0 Insurance claims and indemnities	16	20	20
44.0 Prior-Year Recoveries	2		
99.0 Direct obligations	8,161	8,610	11,220
99.0 Reimbursable obligations	55	63	63
99.9 Total new obligations, unexpired accounts	8,216	8,673	11,283

Employment Summary

Identification code 036–0152–0–1–703	2021 actual	2022 est.	2023 est.
1001 Direct civilian full-time equivalent employment	56,839	58,182	67,010
2001 Reimbursable civilian full-time equivalent employment	365	365	365

DOD-VA HEALTH CARE SHARING INCENTIVE FUND

Program and Financing (in millions of dollars)

Identification code 036–0165–0–1–703	2021 actual	2022 est.	2023 est.
Obligations by program activity:			
0001 DOD-VA health care sharing incentive fund	21	21	21
0002 Capital Investment	3	3	3
0900 Total new obligations, unexpired accounts	24	24	24
Budgetary resources:			
Unobligated balance:			
1000 Unobligated balance brought forward, Oct 1	81	89	95
1021 Recoveries of prior year unpaid obligations	2		
1070 Unobligated balance (total)	83	89	95
Budget authority:			
Appropriations, discretionary:			
1121 Appropriations transferred from other acct [097–0130]	15	15	15
Advance appropriations, discretionary:			
1173 Advance appropriations transferred from other accounts [036–0160]	15	15	15
1900 Budget authority (total)	30	30	30
1930 Total budgetary resources available	113	119	125
Memorandum (non-add) entries:			
1941 Unexpired unobligated balance, end of year	89	95	101
Change in obligated balance:			
Unpaid obligations:			
3000 Unpaid obligations, brought forward, Oct 1	21	25	32
3010 New obligations, unexpired accounts	24	24	24
3020 Outlays (gross)	–18	–17	–31
3040 Recoveries of prior year unpaid obligations, unexpired	–2		
3050 Unpaid obligations, end of year	25	32	25
Memorandum (non-add) entries:			
3100 Obligated balance, start of year	21	25	32
3200 Obligated balance, end of year	25	32	25
Budget authority and outlays, net:			
Discretionary:			
4000 Budget authority, gross	30	30	30
Outlays, gross:			
4011 Outlays from discretionary balances	18	17	31
4180 Budget authority, net (total)	30	30	30
4190 Outlays, net (total)	18	17	31

The purpose of the Department of Defense-Veterans Affairs Health Care Sharing Incentive Fund, often referred to as the Joint Incentive Fund (JIF), is to enable the Departments to carry out a program to identify and provide incentives to implement creative sharing initiatives at the facility, intra-regional and nationwide levels. The JIF promotes collaboration and new approaches to problem solving to enable the Departments to improve the coordination of health care services. The Departments have established the fund and developed processes and criteria to solicit and select projects. Section 721 of the National Defense Authorization Act for Fiscal Year 2003, Public Law 107–314, established the fund and requires the Departments to establish a joint incentive program. In 2023, each Secretary shall contribute a minimum of $15 million to the fund after the appropriation is enacted.

Object Classification (in millions of dollars)

Identification code 036–0165–0–1–703	2021 actual	2022 est.	2023 est.
Direct obligations:			
11.1 Personnel compensation: Full-time permanent	3	3	3
25.1 Advisory and assistance services	16	18	18
31.0 Equipment	3	3	3
44.0 Prior Year Recoveries	2		
99.9 Total new obligations, unexpired accounts	24	24	24

Employment Summary

Identification code 036–0165–0–1–703	2021 actual	2022 est.	2023 est.
1001 Direct civilian full-time equivalent employment	29	29	29

MEDICAL FACILITIES

For necessary expenses for the maintenance and operation of hospitals, nursing homes, domiciliary facilities, and other necessary facilities of the Veterans Health Administration; for administrative expenses in support of planning, design, project management, real property acquisition and disposition, construction, and renovation of any facility under the jurisdiction or for the use of the Department; for oversight, engineering, and architectural activities not charged to project costs; for repairing, altering, improving, or providing facilities in the several hospitals and homes under the jurisdiction of the Department, not otherwise provided for, either by contract or by the hire of temporary employees and purchase of materials; for leases of facilities; and for laundry services; $1,500,000,000, which shall remain available until September 30, 2024, and shall be in addition to funds previously appropriated under this heading that became available on October 1, 2022; and, in addition, $8,800,000,000, plus reimbursements, shall become available on October 1, 2023, and shall remain available until September 30, 2024: Provided, That, of the amount made available on October 1, 2023, under this heading, $1,000,000,000 shall remain available until September 30, 2025.

Note.—A full-year 2022 appropriation for this account was not enacted at the time the Budget was prepared; therefore, the Budget assumes this account is operating under the Continuing Appropriations Act, 2022 (Division A of Public Law 117–43, as amended). The amounts included for 2022 reflect the annualized level provided by the continuing resolution.

Program and Financing (in millions of dollars)

Identification code 036–0162–0–1–703		2021 actual	2022 est.	2023 est.
	Obligations by program activity:			
0002	Engineering & Environmental Management Services	740	841	837
0003	Engineering Service	1,037	1,178	1,174
0004	Grounds Maintenance & Fire Protection	112	128	127
0005	Leases	818	956	1,154
0007	Non-Recurring Maintenance	45		
0008	Operating Equipment Maintenance & Repair	326	370	369
0009	Other Facilities Operation Support	42	48	48
0011	Plant Operation	825	938	935
0012	Recurring Maintenance & Repair	562	638	636
0013	Textile Care Processing & Management	163	186	185
0014	Transportation	209	237	236
0023	Prior-Year Recoveries	55		
0091	Total operating expenses	4,934	5,520	5,701
0102	Engineering & Environmental Management Services	52	81	81
0103	Engineering Service	18	28	29
0104	Grounds Maintenance & Fire Protection	8	12	12
0105	Leases	221	344	346
0106	Non-Recurring Maintenance	1,987	882	2,505
0107	Operating Equipment Maintenance & Repair	19	29	30
0108	Other Facilities Operation Support	48	75	75
0109	Plant Operation	23	36	36
0110	Recurring Maintenance & Repair	40	62	62
0111	Textile Care Processing & Management	31	49	49
0122	Transportation	5	8	8
0191	Total capital investment	2,452	1,606	3,233
0799	Total direct obligations	7,386	7,126	8,934
0801	Medical Facilities (Reimbursable)	18	25	25
0900	Total new obligations, unexpired accounts	7,404	7,151	8,959
	Budgetary resources:			
	Unobligated balance:			
1000	Unobligated balance brought forward, Oct 1	1,332	687	353
1001	Discretionary unobligated balance brought fwd, Oct 1	1,301		
1011	Unobligated balance transfer from other acct [036–0160]	140		
1021	Recoveries of prior year unpaid obligations	55		5
1070	Unobligated balance (total)	1,527	687	358
	Budget authority:			
	Appropriations, discretionary:			
1100	Appropriation	150	150	1,500
	Advance appropriations, discretionary:			
1170	Advance appropriation	6,433	6,735	7,134
1172	Advance appropriations transferred to other accounts [036–0169]	–40	–93	–50
1180	Advanced appropriation, discretionary (total)	6,393	6,642	7,084
	Spending authority from offsetting collections, discretionary:			
1700	Collected	24	25	25
1701	Change in uncollected payments, Federal sources	1		
1750	Spending auth from offsetting collections, disc (total)	25	25	25
1900	Budget authority (total)	6,568	6,817	8,609
1930	Total budgetary resources available	8,095	7,504	8,967
	Memorandum (non-add) entries:			
1940	Unobligated balance expiring	–4		
1941	Unexpired unobligated balance, end of year	687	353	8
	Change in obligated balance:			
	Unpaid obligations:			
3000	Unpaid obligations, brought forward, Oct 1	4,429	4,879	5,332
3010	New obligations, unexpired accounts	7,404	7,151	8,959
3011	Obligations ("upward adjustments"), expired accounts	219		
3020	Outlays (gross)	–6,863	–6,698	–7,941
3040	Recoveries of prior year unpaid obligations, unexpired	–55		–5
3041	Recoveries of prior year unpaid obligations, expired	–255		
3050	Unpaid obligations, end of year	4,879	5,332	6,345
	Uncollected payments:			
3060	Uncollected pymts, Fed sources, brought forward, Oct 1		–1	–1
3070	Change in uncollected pymts, Fed sources, unexpired	–1		
3090	Uncollected pymts, Fed sources, end of year	–1	–1	–1
	Memorandum (non-add) entries:			
3100	Obligated balance, start of year	4,429	4,878	5,331
3200	Obligated balance, end of year	4,878	5,331	6,344
	Budget authority and outlays, net:			
	Discretionary:			
4000	Budget authority, gross	6,568	6,817	8,609
	Outlays, gross:			
4010	Outlays from new discretionary authority	4,105	5,178	5,626
4011	Outlays from discretionary balances	2,741	1,485	2,315
4020	Outlays, gross (total)	6,846	6,663	7,941
	Offsets against gross budget authority and outlays:			
	Offsetting collections (collected) from:			
4030	Federal sources	–44	–11	–15
4033	Non-Federal sources	–48	–14	–10
4040	Offsets against gross budget authority and outlays (total)	–92	–25	–25
	Additional offsets against gross budget authority only:			
4050	Change in uncollected pymts, Fed sources, unexpired	–1		
4052	Offsetting collections credited to expired accounts	68		
4060	Additional offsets against budget authority only (total)	67		
4070	Budget authority, net (discretionary)	6,543	6,792	8,584
4080	Outlays, net (discretionary)	6,754	6,638	7,916
	Mandatory:			
	Outlays, gross:			
4101	Outlays from mandatory balances	17	35	
4180	Budget authority, net (total)	6,543	6,792	8,584
4190	Outlays, net (total)	6,771	6,673	7,916

Medical Facilities provides for the operations and maintenance of the capital infrastructure required to provide healthcare to the Nation's veterans. These costs include utilities, engineering, capital planning, leases, laundry services, grounds maintenance, trash removal, housekeeping, fire protection, pest management, facility repair and maintenance, and property disposition and acquisition.

For Medical Facilities, the Budget reflects the following discretionary appropriation funding: the 2023 advance appropriation request of $7.1 billion, together with an annual appropriation request of $1.5 billion; and the 2024 advance appropriation request of $8.8 billion.

The 2024 advance appropriation request fulfills the Administration's commitment to provide reliable and timely resources to support the delivery of accessible and high-quality medical services for veterans.

Object Classification (in millions of dollars)

Identification code 036–0162–0–1–703		2021 actual	2022 est.	2023 est.
	Direct obligations:			
	Personnel compensation:			
11.1	Full-time permanent	1,357	1,455	1,690
11.3	Other than full-time permanent	29	31	36
11.5	Other personnel compensation	157	169	196
11.9	Total personnel compensation	1,543	1,655	1,922
12.1	Civilian personnel benefits	589	630	739
13.0	Benefits for former personnel	1	3	3
21.0	Travel & Transportation of Persons	46	48	50
22.0	Transportation of things	18	19	20
23.2	Rent, Communications & Utilities	1,377	1,828	1,796
25.2	Other Contractual Services	901	773	583
26.0	Supplies & Materials	400	562	585
31.0	Equipment	148	134	160
32.0	Lands & Structures	2,306	1,472	3,073
42.0	Insurance claims and indemnities	2	2	3
44.0	Prior Year Recoveries	55		
99.0	Direct obligations	7,386	7,126	8,934
99.0	Reimbursable obligations	18	25	25
99.9	Total new obligations, unexpired accounts	7,404	7,151	8,959

MEDICAL FACILITIES—Continued
Employment Summary

Identification code 036–0162–0–1–703	2021 actual	2022 est.	2023 est.
1001 Direct civilian full-time equivalent employment	25,530	25,396	28,354
2001 Reimbursable civilian full-time equivalent employment	273	273	273

VETERANS MEDICAL CARE AND HEALTH FUND

Program and Financing (in millions of dollars)

Identification code 036–0173–0–1–703	2021 actual	2022 est.	2023 est.
Obligations by program activity:			
0001 Medical Services	....	3,208	726
0002 Medical Support and Compliance	....	634	345
0003 Medical Facilities	....	408	392
0004 Community Care	....	1,901	2,099
0005 Research	7	2	....
0006 Office of Information Technology	....	513	529
0091 Direct program activities, subtotal	7	6,666	4,091
0101 Medical Services	....	1,746	....
0103 Medical Facilities	....	1,773	....
0106 Office of Information Technology	....	98	101
0191 Direct program activities, subtotal	....	3,617	101
0900 Total new obligations, unexpired accounts	7	10,283	4,192
Budgetary resources:			
Unobligated balance:			
1000 Unobligated balance brought forward, Oct 1	....	14,475	4,192
Budget authority:			
Appropriations, mandatory:			
1200 Appropriation	14,482	....	....
1930 Total budgetary resources available	14,482	14,475	4,192
Memorandum (non-add) entries:			
1941 Unexpired unobligated balance, end of year	14,475	4,192	....
Change in obligated balance:			
Unpaid obligations:			
3000 Unpaid obligations, brought forward, Oct 1	....	3	4,613
3010 New obligations, unexpired accounts	7	10,283	4,192
3020 Outlays (gross)	–4	–5,673	–7,026
3050 Unpaid obligations, end of year	3	4,613	1,779
Memorandum (non-add) entries:			
3100 Obligated balance, start of year	....	3	4,613
3200 Obligated balance, end of year	3	4,613	1,779
Budget authority and outlays, net:			
Mandatory:			
4090 Budget authority, gross	14,482	....	....
Outlays, gross:			
4100 Outlays from new mandatory authority	4	....	....
4101 Outlays from mandatory balances	....	5,673	7,026
4110 Outlays, gross (total)	4	5,673	7,026
4180 Budget authority, net (total)	14,482	....	....
4190 Outlays, net (total)	4	5,673	7,026

Section 8002 of the American Rescue Plan Act of 2021 (Public Law 117–2) provided $14.482 billion in 2021 to remain available until September 30, 2023 for allocation under chapters 17, 20, 73, and 81 of title 38, United States Code, of which not more than $4 billion shall be available pursuant to section 1703 of title 38, United States Code for healthcare furnished through the Veterans Community Care program. The Veterans Medical Care and Health Fund was established to execute section 8002 of the American Rescue Plan Act, and the Budget displays estimated allocations by categories of activity funded by section 8002. Final funding allocations among categories may change based on execution and in response to workload demand requirements.

Object Classification (in millions of dollars)

Identification code 036–0173–0–1–703	2021 actual	2022 est.	2023 est.
11.1 Direct obligations: Personnel compensation: Full-time permanent	....	2	1	....
11.9 Total personnel compensation	2	1	....
23.3 Communications, utilities, and miscellaneous charges	....	543	139
25.2 Other Contractual Services	3	5,300	3,952
26.0 Supplies and materials	1	400	....
31.0 Equipment	1	1,844	101
32.0 Land and structures	....	1,773	....
41.0 Grants, subsidies, and contributions	....	422	....
99.9 Total new obligations, unexpired accounts	7	10,283	4,192

Employment Summary

Identification code 036–0173–0–1–703	2021 actual	2022 est.	2023 est.
1001 Direct civilian full-time equivalent employment	40	8	....

MEDICAL AND PROSTHETIC RESEARCH

For necessary expenses in carrying out programs of medical and prosthetic research and development as authorized by chapter 73 of title 38, United States Code, $916,000,000, plus reimbursements, shall remain available until September 30, 2024: Provided, That the Secretary of Veterans Affairs shall ensure that sufficient amounts appropriated under this heading are available for prosthetic research specifically for female veterans, and for toxic exposure research.

Note.—A full-year 2022 appropriation for this account was not enacted at the time the Budget was prepared; therefore, the Budget assumes this account is operating under the Continuing Appropriations Act, 2022 (Division A of Public Law 117–43, as amended). The amounts included for 2022 reflect the annualized level provided by the continuing resolution.

Program and Financing (in millions of dollars)

Identification code 036–0161–0–1–703	2021 actual	2022 est.	2023 est.
Obligations by program activity:			
0001 Bio-medical laboratory science research	348	322	355
0002 Rehabilitation research	114	104	116
0003 Health services research	135	125	138
0004 Clinical science research	297	274	303
0091 Total operating expenses	894	825	912
0799 Total direct obligations	894	825	912
0801 Medical and Prosthetic Research (Reimbursable)	40	61	61
0900 Total new obligations, unexpired accounts	934	886	973
Budgetary resources:			
Unobligated balance:			
1000 Unobligated balance brought forward, Oct 1	159	115	123
1021 Recoveries of prior year unpaid obligations	52	52	90
1070 Unobligated balance (total)	211	167	213
Budget authority:			
Appropriations, discretionary:			
1100 Appropriation	815	815	916
1131 Unobligated balance of appropriations permanently reduced	–20	–20	....
1160 Appropriation, discretionary (total)	795	795	916
Spending authority from offsetting collections, discretionary:			
1700 Collected	45	47	61
1701 Change in uncollected payments, Federal sources	–2	....	....
1750 Spending auth from offsetting collections, disc (total)	43	47	61
1900 Budget authority (total)	838	842	977
1930 Total budgetary resources available	1,049	1,009	1,190
Memorandum (non-add) entries:			
1941 Unexpired unobligated balance, end of year	115	123	217
Change in obligated balance:			
Unpaid obligations:			
3000 Unpaid obligations, brought forward, Oct 1	343	400	301
3010 New obligations, unexpired accounts	934	886	973
3011 Obligations ("upward adjustments"), expired accounts	3	....	....
3020 Outlays (gross)	–814	–933	–892
3040 Recoveries of prior year unpaid obligations, unexpired	–52	–52	–90

DEPARTMENT OF VETERANS AFFAIRS

Veterans Health Administration—Continued
Federal Funds—Continued

1045

3041	Recoveries of prior year unpaid obligations, expired	−14		
3050	Unpaid obligations, end of year	400	301	292
	Uncollected payments:			
3060	Uncollected pymts, Fed sources, brought forward, Oct 1	−2		
3070	Change in uncollected pymts, Fed sources, unexpired	2		
	Memorandum (non-add) entries:			
3100	Obligated balance, start of year	341	400	301
3200	Obligated balance, end of year	400	301	292
	Budget authority and outlays, net:			
	Discretionary:			
4000	Budget authority, gross	838	842	977
	Outlays, gross:			
4010	Outlays from new discretionary authority	429	598	693
4011	Outlays from discretionary balances	385	335	199
4020	Outlays, gross (total)	814	933	892
	Offsets against gross budget authority and outlays:			
	Offsetting collections (collected) from:			
4030	Federal sources	−25	−47	−45
4033	Non-Federal sources	−22		−16
4040	Offsets against gross budget authority and outlays (total)	−47	−47	−61
	Additional offsets against gross budget authority only:			
4050	Change in uncollected pymts, Fed sources, unexpired	2		
4052	Offsetting collections credited to expired accounts	2		
4060	Additional offsets against budget authority only (total)	4		
4070	Budget authority, net (discretionary)	795	795	916
4080	Outlays, net (discretionary)	767	886	831
4180	Budget authority, net (total)	795	795	916
4190	Outlays, net (total)	767	886	831

For 2023, the total budgetary resources of over $2.3 billion is comprised of $916 million in direct appropriations, $778.6 million in medical care support such as physicians' pay, utilities and other overhead, $540 million in Federal grants and other non-Federal resources, and $61 million in reimbursements. The Department of Veterans Affairs (VA) research program will support 4,523 full time equivalents through direct appropriations and reimbursable resources. These combined resources will support approximately 2,697 research projects.

This account is an intramural research program with outstanding success leading to critical clinical achievements that improve the health and quality of life for veterans and the Nation. As a health research program focused exclusively on the needs of veterans, VA research continues to play a vital role in the care and rehabilitation of our men and women who have served in uniform. Building on more than 90 years of discovery and innovation engaging veterans as research volunteers, VA research has a proud track record of transforming VA healthcare by bringing new evidence-based treatments and technologies into everyday clinical care. The 2023 request builds upon the historic investment from the 2022 request to continue to increase funding to advance the Department's research missions in military toxic exposures, traumatic brain injury, cancer and precision oncology, and mental health. This request supports our six-cross cutting clinical priorities: suicide prevention; pain management and opioid use; traumatic brain injury (TBI), posttraumatic stress disorder (PTSD); Gulf War illness and military toxic exposures; and cancer, with a focus on precision oncology.

SUMMARY OF PROGRAM RESOURCES

[in millions of dollars]

	2021 Actual	2022 Est.	2023 Est.
Medical and Prosthetic Research Appropriation[1]	795	882	916
American Rescue Plan Act (P.L. 117–2, Section 8002) (Mandatory)[2]	9	30	0
Medical Care Support[3]	668	750	779
Other Federal and Non-Federal Resources	532	540	540
Reimbursements	81	61	61
Total Program Resources	2,085	2,263	2,296

[1] The appropriation amounts for 2021 are net of a rescission of $20 million from P.L. 116–260 and align with Congressional scoring. (Public Law Section 117–2, Section 8002).

[2] In 2022, VA plans to reallocate $30 million of the funding provided in Section 8002 of the American Rescue Plan Act for Research, which will be executed out of the Veterans Medical Care and Health Fund. Final 2022 funding allocations among categories may change in response to workload demand requirements throughout 2022.

[3] Medical Care Support includes funding from the Medical Services, Medical Support and Compliance, and Medical Facilities appropriations to support Research.

	2021 actual	2022 est.	2023 est.
FTE (includes Direct and Reimbursable)	4,175	4,292	4,523

Object Classification (in millions of dollars)

Identification code 036–0161–0–1–703	2021 actual	2022 est.	2023 est.
11.1 Direct obligations: Personnel compensation: Full-time permanent	340	314	347
11.9 Total personnel compensation	340	314	347
12.1 Civilian personnel benefits	135	125	139
23.3 Communications, utilities, and miscellaneous charges	10	9	10
24.0 Printing and reproduction	1	1	1
25.2 Other services from non-Federal sources	324	298	333
26.0 Supplies and materials	56	52	54
31.0 Equipment	28	26	28
99.0 Direct obligations	894	825	912
99.0 Reimbursable obligations	40	61	61
99.9 Total new obligations, unexpired accounts	934	886	973

Employment Summary

Identification code 036–0161–0–1–703	2021 actual	2022 est.	2023 est.
1001 Direct civilian full-time equivalent employment	3,997	4,146	4,410
2001 Reimbursable civilian full-time equivalent employment	138	138	113

JOINT DEPARTMENT OF DEFENSE-DEPARTMENT OF VETERANS AFFAIRS MEDICAL FACILITY DEMONSTRATION FUND

Program and Financing (in millions of dollars)

Identification code 036–0169–0–1–703	2021 actual	2022 est.	2023 est.
Obligations by program activity:			
0001 Joint DOD-VA Medical Facility Demonstration Fund (Direct)	489	532	514
0801 Joint DOD-VA Medical Facility Demonstration Fund (Reimbursable)	12	13	13
0900 Total new obligations, unexpired accounts	501	545	527
Budgetary resources:			
Unobligated balance:			
1000 Unobligated balance brought forward, Oct 1	7		2
1011 Unobligated balance transfer from other acct [036–0160]	10		
1070 Unobligated balance (total)	17		2
Budget authority:			
Appropriations, discretionary:			
1121 Appropriations transferred from other acct [036–0167]	8	8	8
1121 Appropriations transferred from other acct [097–0130]	137	137	168
1121 Appropriations transferred from other acct [036–5287]	13	17	16
1160 Appropriation, discretionary (total)	158	162	192
Advance appropriations, discretionary:			
1173 Advance appropriations transferred from other accounts [036–0160]	216	204	190
1173 Advance appropriations transferred from other accounts [036–0140]	28	44	51
1173 Advance appropriations transferred from other accounts [036–0152]	30	31	30
1173 Advance appropriations transferred from other accounts [036–0162]	40	93	50
1180 Advanced appropriation, discretionary (total)	314	372	321
Spending authority from offsetting collections, discretionary:			
1700 Collected	12	13	13
1900 Budget authority (total)	484	547	526
1930 Total budgetary resources available	501	547	528
Memorandum (non-add) entries:			
1941 Unexpired unobligated balance, end of year		2	1

JOINT DEPARTMENT OF DEFENSE-DEPARTMENT OF VETERANS AFFAIRS MEDICAL FACILITY DEMONSTRATION FUND—Continued

Program and Financing—Continued

Identification code 036–0169–0–1–703	2021 actual	2022 est.	2023 est.
Change in obligated balance:			
Unpaid obligations:			
3000 Unpaid obligations, brought forward, Oct 1	56	65	59
3010 New obligations, unexpired accounts	501	545	527
3011 Obligations ("upward adjustments"), expired accounts	31		
3020 Outlays (gross)	–505	–551	–526
3041 Recoveries of prior year unpaid obligations, expired	–18		
3050 Unpaid obligations, end of year	65	59	60
Memorandum (non-add) entries:			
3100 Obligated balance, start of year	56	65	59
3200 Obligated balance, end of year	65	59	60
Budget authority and outlays, net:			
Discretionary:			
4000 Budget authority, gross	484	547	526
Outlays, gross:			
4010 Outlays from new discretionary authority	425	493	474
4011 Outlays from discretionary balances	80	58	52
4020 Outlays, gross (total)	505	551	526
Offsets against gross budget authority and outlays:			
Offsetting collections (collected) from:			
4030 Federal sources	–13	–12	–12
4033 Non-Federal sources	–6	–1	–1
4040 Offsets against gross budget authority and outlays (total)	–19	–13	–13
Additional offsets against gross budget authority only:			
4052 Offsetting collections credited to expired accounts	7		
4070 Budget authority, net (discretionary)	472	534	513
4080 Outlays, net (discretionary)	486	538	513
4180 Budget authority, net (total)	472	534	513
4190 Outlays, net (total)	486	538	513

The Department of Veterans Affairs (VA) and the Department of Defense (DOD) will each contribute funding to the Joint Department of Defense-Department of Veterans Affairs Medical Facility Demonstration Fund, established by section 1704 of Public Law 111–84, the National Defense Authorization Act for Fiscal Year 2010. This funding will support the continuing operations of the Captain James A. Lovell Federal Health Care Center (FHCC), which opened on December 20, 2010. In 2023, VA expects to transfer funds from the Medical Services, Medical Community Care, Medical Support and Compliance, Medical Facilities, and Information Technology Systems accounts, while DOD expects to transfer funds from the Defense Health Program account.

Object Classification (in millions of dollars)

Identification code 036–0169–0–1–703	2021 actual	2022 est.	2023 est.
Direct obligations:			
Personnel compensation:			
11.1 Full-time permanent	170	175	184
11.3 Other than full-time permanent	4	4	4
11.5 Other personnel compensation	20	21	22
11.9 Total personnel compensation	194	200	210
12.1 Civilian personnel benefits	73	76	79
21.0 Travel and transportation of persons	3	3	3
23.3 Communications, utilities, and miscellaneous charges	8	9	9
25.1 Advisory and assistance services	119	148	103
26.0 Supplies and materials	71	74	77
31.0 Equipment	10	10	11
32.0 Land and structures	10	11	21
41.0 Grants, subsidies, and contributions	1	1	1
99.0 Direct obligations	489	532	514
99.0 Reimbursable obligations	12	13	13
99.9 Total new obligations, unexpired accounts	501	545	527

Employment Summary

Identification code 036–0169–0–1–703	2021 actual	2022 est.	2023 est.
1001 Direct civilian full-time equivalent employment	2,275	2,275	2,324

MEDICAL CARE COLLECTIONS FUND

Program and Financing (in millions of dollars)

Identification code 036–5287–0–2–703	2021 actual	2022 est.	2023 est.
Obligations by program activity:			
0001 Refunds	244	56	
0900 Total new obligations, unexpired accounts (object class 44.0)	244	56	
Budgetary resources:			
Unobligated balance:			
1000 Unobligated balance brought forward, Oct 1		56	
Budget authority:			
Appropriations, discretionary:			
1101 Appropriation (special or trust)	3,091	3,922	3,910
1120 Appropriations transferred to other accts [036–0160]	–2,514	–3,192	–3,103
1120 Appropriations transferred to other accts [036–0169]	–13	–17	–16
1120 Appropriations transferred to other acct [036–0140]	–564	–713	–791
Appropriations, mandatory:			
1200 Appropriation	300		
1900 Budget authority (total)	300		
1930 Total budgetary resources available	300	56	
Memorandum (non-add) entries:			
1941 Unexpired unobligated balance, end of year	56		
Change in obligated balance:			
Unpaid obligations:			
3010 New obligations, unexpired accounts	244	56	
3020 Outlays (gross)	–244	–56	
Budget authority and outlays, net:			
Mandatory:			
4090 Budget authority, gross	300		
Outlays, gross:			
4100 Outlays from new mandatory authority	244		
4101 Outlays from mandatory balances		56	
4110 Outlays, gross (total)	244	56	
4180 Budget authority, net (total)	300		
4190 Outlays, net (total)	244	56	

The Department of Veterans Affairs has the authority to collect co-payments, which are deposited into the Medical Care Collections Fund (MCCF) account. As allowed by the provisions of the appropriations Act, these receipts are transferred to Medical Services, Medical Community Care, and the Joint Department of Defense-Department of Veterans Affairs Medical Facility Demonstration Fund (Joint Demonstration Fund) where they remain available until expended for the purposes of the account. In 2023, VA anticipates collecting $3.9 billion in the MCCF account, which will be transferred to Medical Services, Medical Community Care, and the Joint Demonstration Fund to provide healthcare to veterans. These collections consist of co-payments from veterans for inpatient, outpatient, and nursing home care, and prescribed medications; third-party insurance payments from veterans for nonservice-connected conditions; and collections from enhanced-use leases, the Compensated Work Therapy Program, Compensation and Living Expensed Program, and the Parking Program.

Section 8007 of the American Rescue Plan Act of 2021 directed the Department of Veterans Affairs to provide for any copayment or other cost sharing with respect to healthcare, and reimburse any veteran who paid a copayment or other cost sharing related to healthcare, during the period beginning on April 6, 2020, and ending on September 30, 2021. The Department was appropriated $1 billion, to remain available until expended, to carry out this section. Of that amount, VA estimated $300 million would be executed from the MCCF account and used to reimburse veterans who paid a copayment or other cost sharing during the specified period. VA obligated $244 million for this purpose in 2021.

DEPARTMENT OF VETERANS AFFAIRS

Veterans Health Administration—Continued
Federal Funds—Continued 1047

The remaining $700 million will be used to supplement VA Medical Centers for lost collections revenue and will be executed from the Medical Services and Medical Community Care accounts.

CANTEEN SERVICE REVOLVING FUND

Program and Financing (in millions of dollars)

Identification code 036–4014–0–3–705		2021 actual	2022 est.	2023 est.
	Obligations by program activity:			
0801	Reimbursable operating expenses	375	252	260
0810	Reimbursable capital investment: Sales program: Purchase of equipment and leasehold	3	2	2
0899	Total reimbursable obligations	378	254	262
0900	Total new obligations, unexpired accounts	378	254	262
	Budgetary resources:			
	Unobligated balance:			
1000	Unobligated balance brought forward, Oct 1	....	112	108
1021	Recoveries of prior year unpaid obligations	....	2	....
1070	Unobligated balance (total)	....	114	108
	Budget authority:			
	Appropriations, mandatory:			
1221	Appropriations transferred from other acct [036–0160]	140	....	....
	Spending authority from offsetting collections, mandatory:			
1800	Collected	349	248	248
1801	Change in uncollected payments, Federal sources	1	....	....
1850	Spending auth from offsetting collections, mand (total)	350	248	248
1900	Budget authority (total)	490	248	248
1930	Total budgetary resources available	490	362	356
	Memorandum (non-add) entries:			
1941	Unexpired unobligated balance, end of year	112	108	94
	Change in obligated balance:			
	Unpaid obligations:			
3000	Unpaid obligations, brought forward, Oct 1	17	47	24
3010	New obligations, unexpired accounts	378	254	262
3020	Outlays (gross)	–348	–275	–261
3040	Recoveries of prior year unpaid obligations, unexpired	....	–2	....
3050	Unpaid obligations, end of year	47	24	25
	Uncollected payments:			
3060	Uncollected pymts, Fed sources, brought forward, Oct 1	–1	–2	–2
3070	Change in uncollected pymts, Fed sources, unexpired	–1	....	....
3090	Uncollected pymts, Fed sources, end of year	–2	–2	–2
	Memorandum (non-add) entries:			
3100	Obligated balance, start of year	16	45	22
3200	Obligated balance, end of year	45	22	23
	Budget authority and outlays, net:			
	Mandatory:			
4090	Budget authority, gross	490	248	248
	Outlays, gross:			
4100	Outlays from new mandatory authority	331	243	243
4101	Outlays from mandatory balances	17	32	18
4110	Outlays, gross (total)	348	275	261
	Offsets against gross budget authority and outlays:			
	Offsetting collections (collected) from:			
4123	Non-Federal sources	–349	–248	–248
	Additional offsets against gross budget authority only:			
4140	Change in uncollected pymts, Fed sources, unexpired	–1	....	....
4160	Budget authority, net (mandatory)	140	....	....
4170	Outlays, net (mandatory)	–1	27	13
4180	Budget authority, net (total)	140	....	....
4190	Outlays, net (total)	–1	27	13

The Veterans Canteen Service was established to furnish, at reasonable prices, meals, merchandise, and services necessary for the comfort and well-being of veterans in Department of Veterans Affairs medical facilities. In 2023, operations will be financed from current revenues.

Object Classification (in millions of dollars)

Identification code 036–4014–0–3–705		2021 actual	2022 est.	2023 est.
11.1	Reimbursable obligations: Personnel compensation: Full-time permanent	84	57	58
11.9	Total personnel compensation	84	57	58
12.1	Civilian personnel benefits	45	30	31
21.0	Travel and transportation of persons	1	1	1
22.0	Transportation of things	3	2	2
25.2	Other services from non-Federal sources	17	11	12
26.0	Supplies and materials	225	151	156
31.0	Equipment	3	2	2
99.0	Reimbursable obligations	378	254	262
99.9	Total new obligations, unexpired accounts	378	254	262

Employment Summary

Identification code 036–4014–0–3–705	2021 actual	2022 est.	2023 est.
2001 Reimbursable civilian full-time equivalent employment	2,267	2,250	2,318

VETERANS CHOICE FUND

Program and Financing (in millions of dollars)

Identification code 036–0172–0–1–703		2021 actual	2022 est.	2023 est.
	Obligations by program activity:			
0001	Veterans Choice Fund - Administrative	2	....	....
0002	Veterans Choice Fund - Program	23	....	....
0006	MCC (0140) Expenditure Transfers	....	15	266
0091	Direct program activities, subtotal	25	15	266
0900	Total new obligations, unexpired accounts (object class 25.2)	25	15	266
	Budgetary resources:			
	Unobligated balance:			
1000	Unobligated balance brought forward, Oct 1	–248	281	266
1020	Adjustment of unobligated bal brought forward, Oct 1	398	....	....
1021	Recoveries of prior year unpaid obligations	21	....	....
1033	Recoveries of prior year paid obligations	135	....	....
1070	Unobligated balance (total)	306	281	266
1930	Total budgetary resources available	306	281	266
	Memorandum (non-add) entries:			
1941	Unexpired unobligated balance, end of year	281	266	....
	Change in obligated balance:			
	Unpaid obligations:			
3000	Unpaid obligations, brought forward, Oct 1	453	....	....
3001	Adjustments to unpaid obligations, brought forward, Oct 1	–398	....	....
3010	New obligations, unexpired accounts	25	15	266
3020	Outlays (gross)	–59	–15	–118
3040	Recoveries of prior year unpaid obligations, unexpired	–21	....	....
3050	Unpaid obligations, end of year	....	....	148
	Memorandum (non-add) entries:			
3100	Obligated balance, start of year	55	....	....
3200	Obligated balance, end of year	....	....	148
	Budget authority and outlays, net:			
	Mandatory:			
	Outlays, gross:			
4101	Outlays from mandatory balances	59	15	118
	Offsets against gross budget authority and outlays:			
	Offsetting collections (collected) from:			
4120	Federal sources	–135	....	....
	Additional offsets against gross budget authority only:			
4143	Recoveries of prior year paid obligations, unexpired accounts	135	....	....
4170	Outlays, net (mandatory)	–76	15	118
4180	Budget authority, net (total)	....	....	....
4190	Outlays, net (total)	–76	15	118

The Veterans Access, Choice, and Accountability Act of 2014 ("Veterans Choice Act"), Public Law 113–146, provided $10 billion in mandatory funding to establish a temporary program ("Veterans Choice Program")

VETERANS CHOICE FUND—Continued

improving veterans' access to health care by allowing eligible veterans who met certain wait time or distance standards to use eligible healthcare providers outside the Department of Veterans Affairs (VA) system. The law directed that this funding be deposited in the Veterans Choice Fund. In July 2015, the Congress passed Public Law 114–41, the Surface Transportation and Veterans Health Care Choice Improvement Act of 2015, which gave VA temporary authority, ending October 1, 2015, to use a certain level of Veterans Choice Fund dollars for pharmaceutical expenses related to treatment of Hepatitis C and for Care in the Community.

Public Law 115–26 amended the Veterans Choice Act to eliminate the original August 7, 2017, sunset date for the Veterans Choice Program and allowed the program to operate until all of the funds in the Veterans Choice Fund were expended.

Public Law 115–46, the VA Choice and Quality Employment Act of 2017, provided $2.1 billion in mandatory funding for the Veterans Choice Fund, to remain available until expended. In 2018, Public Law 115–96 provided $2.1 billion more in mandatory funding, to remain available until expended; and Public Law 115–182, the MISSION Act, provided an additional $5.2 billion in mandatory funding, to remain available without fiscal year limitation. The MISSION Act provided VA with flexibility, beginning on March 1, 2019, to use Veterans Choice Fund dollars for community care. In addition, the MISSION Act sunset the Choice Program in June 2019 and established the new Veterans Community Care Program. The Further Consolidated Appropriations Act, 2020 (Public Law 116–94) transferred $615 million from the 2020 start of year unobligated balances in the Veterans Choice Fund account to the Medical Community Care account.

EMERGENCY DEPARTMENT OF VETERANS AFFAIRS EMPLOYEE LEAVE FUND

Program and Financing (in millions of dollars)

Identification code 036–0131–0–1–703		2021 actual	2022 est.	2023 est.
	Obligations by program activity:			
0001	Employee reimbursement		18	
0900	Total new obligations, unexpired accounts (object class 44.0)		18	
	Budgetary resources:			
	Unobligated balance:			
1000	Unobligated balance brought forward, Oct 1			62
	Budget authority:			
	Appropriations, mandatory:			
1200	Appropriation [P.L. 117–2, Section 8008]		80	
1930	Total budgetary resources available		80	62
	Memorandum (non-add) entries:			
1940	Unobligated balance expiring			–62
1941	Unexpired unobligated balance, end of year		62	
	Change in obligated balance:			
	Unpaid obligations:			
3010	New obligations, unexpired accounts		18	
3020	Outlays (gross)		–18	
	Budget authority and outlays, net:			
	Mandatory:			
4090	Budget authority, gross		80	
	Outlays, gross:			
4100	Outlays from new mandatory authority		18	
4180	Budget authority, net (total)		80	
4190	Outlays, net (total)		18	

Section 8008 of the American Rescue Plan Act of 2021 (P.L. 117–2) provided $80 million to establish the Emergency Department of Veterans Affairs Employee Leave Fund. The law directed that the funds be available for payment to the Department for the use of paid leave by any employee appointed under chapter 74 of title 38, United States Code who is unable to work due to certain circumstances resulting from the COVID-19 pandemic. The authorization for the paid leave under Section 8008 is from the date of enactment of the Act, March 11, 2021, through September 30, 2021. The period of availability for Section 8008 funding is from the date of enactment of the Act, March 11, 2021, through September 20, 2022.

Trust Funds

GENERAL POST FUND, NATIONAL HOMES

Special and Trust Fund Receipts (in millions of dollars)

Identification code 036–8180–0–7–705		2021 actual	2022 est.	2023 est.
0100	Balance, start of year		1	3
	Receipts:			
	Current law:			
1130	General Post Fund, National Homes, Deposits	20	20	20
1140	General Post Fund, National Homes, Interest on Investments	1	3	3
1199	Total current law receipts	21	23	23
1999	Total receipts	21	23	23
2000	Total: Balances and receipts	21	24	26
	Appropriations:			
	Current law:			
2101	General Post Fund, National Homes	–20	–21	–21
5099	Balance, end of year	1	3	5

Program and Financing (in millions of dollars)

Identification code 036–8180–0–7–705		2021 actual	2022 est.	2023 est.
	Obligations by program activity:			
0001	Religious, recreational, and entertainment activities	14	15	16
0003	Therapeutic residence maintenance	1	1	1
0900	Total new obligations, unexpired accounts	15	16	17
	Budgetary resources:			
	Unobligated balance:			
1000	Unobligated balance brought forward, Oct 1	121	127	134
1021	Recoveries of prior year unpaid obligations	1	2	1
1070	Unobligated balance (total)	122	129	135
	Budget authority:			
	Appropriations, mandatory:			
1201	Appropriation (special or trust fund)	20	21	21
1930	Total budgetary resources available	142	150	156
	Memorandum (non-add) entries:			
1941	Unexpired unobligated balance, end of year	127	134	139
	Change in obligated balance:			
	Unpaid obligations:			
3000	Unpaid obligations, brought forward, Oct 1	3	3	1
3010	New obligations, unexpired accounts	15	16	17
3020	Outlays (gross)	–14	–16	–17
3040	Recoveries of prior year unpaid obligations, unexpired	–1	–2	–1
3050	Unpaid obligations, end of year	3	1	
	Memorandum (non-add) entries:			
3100	Obligated balance, start of year	3	3	1
3200	Obligated balance, end of year	3	1	
	Budget authority and outlays, net:			
	Mandatory:			
4090	Budget authority, gross	20	21	21
	Outlays, gross:			
4100	Outlays from new mandatory authority		16	17
4101	Outlays from mandatory balances	14		
4110	Outlays, gross (total)	14	16	17
4180	Budget authority, net (total)	20	21	21
4190	Outlays, net (total)	14	16	17
	Memorandum (non-add) entries:			
5000	Total investments, SOY: Federal securities: Par value	112	90	90
5001	Total investments, EOY: Federal securities: Par value	90	90	90

This fund consists of gifts, bequests, and proceeds from the sale of property left in the care of the facilities by former beneficiaries; patients' fund balances; and proceeds from the sale of effects of beneficiaries who die leaving no heirs or without having otherwise disposed of their estate.

DEPARTMENT OF VETERANS AFFAIRS

Such funds are used to promote the comfort and welfare of veterans at hospitals, nursing homes, and domiciliaries where no general appropriation is available. Public Law 102–54 authorizes compensation work therapy and therapeutic transitional housing and loan programs to be funded from the General Post Fund (38 U.S.C. chapters 83 and 85).

Object Classification (in millions of dollars)

Identification code 036–8180–0–7–705		2021 actual	2022 est.	2023 est.
	Direct obligations:			
21.0	Travel and transportation of persons	1		
23.3	Communications, utilities, and miscellaneous charges	1	1	1
25.2	Other services from non-Federal sources	3	5	4
26.0	Supplies and materials	9	9	11
31.0	Equipment	1	1	1
99.9	Total new obligations, unexpired accounts	15	16	17

BENEFITS PROGRAMS

Federal Funds

COMPENSATION AND PENSIONS

(INCLUDING TRANSFER OF FUNDS)

For the payment of compensation benefits to or on behalf of veterans and a pilot program for disability examinations as authorized by section 107 and chapters 11, 13, 18, 51, 53, 55, and 61 of title 38, United States Code; pension benefits to or on behalf of veterans as authorized by chapters 15, 51, 53, 55, and 61 of title 38, United States Code; and burial benefits, the Reinstated Entitlement Program for Survivors, emergency and other officers' retirement pay, adjusted-service credits and certificates, payment of premiums due on commercial life insurance policies guaranteed under the provisions of title IV of the Servicemembers Civil Relief Act (50 U.S.C. App. 541 et seq.) and for other benefits as authorized by sections 107, 1312, 1977, and 2106, and chapters 23, 51, 53, 55, and 61 of title 38, United States Code, $146,778,136,000, which shall become available on October 1, 2023, to remain available until expended: Provided, That not to exceed $21,423,000 of the amount made available for fiscal year 2024 under this heading shall be reimbursed to "General Operating Expenses, Veterans Benefits Administration", and "Information Technology Systems" for necessary expenses in implementing the provisions of chapters 51, 53, and 55 of title 38, United States Code, the funding source for which is specifically provided as the "Compensation and Pensions" appropriation: Provided further, That such sums as may be earned on an actual qualifying patient basis, shall be reimbursed to "Medical Care Collections Fund" to augment the funding of individual medical facilities for nursing home care provided to pensioners as authorized.

Note.—A full-year 2022 appropriation for this account was not enacted at the time the Budget was prepared; therefore, the Budget assumes this account is operating under the Continuing Appropriations Act, 2022 (Division A of Public Law 117–43, as amended). The amounts included for 2022 reflect the annualized level provided by the continuing resolution.

Program and Financing (in millions of dollars)

Identification code 036–0102–0–1–701		2021 actual	2022 est.	2023 est.
	Obligations by program activity:			
0101	Veterans	101,806	116,246	128,751
0102	Survivors	7,987	9,881	8,939
0191	Compensation sub-total	109,793	126,127	137,690
0200	Other compensation expenses	109,793	126,127	137,690
0201	Chapter 18	22	23	24
0202	Clothing allowance	118	129	140
0203	Misc assistance (EAJ, SAFD)	43	48	53
0204	Medical exam pilot program	2,226	3,051	3,505
0205	OBRA payment to VBA and IT	3	8	8
0291	Total other compensation expenses	2,412	3,259	3,730
0293	Total compensation	112,205	129,386	141,420
0302	Veterans	2,607	2,509	2,302
0303	Survivors	1,466	1,310	1,235
0391	Pensions sub total	4,073	3,819	3,537
0401	Reimbursements to GOE, IT and VHA	12	13	13
0492	Total pensions	4,085	3,832	3,550
0502	Burial allowance	18	43	60
0503	Burial plots	43	45	49
0504	Service-connected deaths	90	140	149
0505	Burial flags	23	23	24
0506	Headstones and markers	86	92	93
0508	Graveliners	5	3	3
0509	Pre-Place Crypts	41	31	34
0591	Total burial program	306	377	412
0900	Total new obligations, unexpired accounts (object class 42.0)	116,596	133,595	145,382
	Budgetary resources:			
	Unobligated balance:			
1000	Unobligated balance brought forward, Oct 1	645	8,798	5,431
1021	Recoveries of prior year unpaid obligations	24		
1033	Recoveries of prior year paid obligations	368		
1070	Unobligated balance (total)	1,037	8,798	5,431
	Budget authority:			
	Appropriations, mandatory:			
1200	Appropriation	6,110		
	Advance appropriations, mandatory:			
1270	Advance appropriation	118,247	130,228	152,017
1900	Budget authority (total)	124,357	130,228	152,017
1930	Total budgetary resources available	125,394	139,026	157,448
	Memorandum (non-add) entries:			
1941	Unexpired unobligated balance, end of year	8,798	5,431	12,066
	Change in obligated balance:			
	Unpaid obligations:			
3000	Unpaid obligations, brought forward, Oct 1	9,299	9,362	365
3010	New obligations, unexpired accounts	116,596	133,595	145,382
3011	Obligations ("upward adjustments"), expired accounts	86		
3020	Outlays (gross)	−116,595	−142,592	−144,047
3040	Recoveries of prior year unpaid obligations, unexpired	−24		
3050	Unpaid obligations, end of year	9,362	365	1,700
	Memorandum (non-add) entries:			
3100	Obligated balance, start of year	9,299	9,362	365
3200	Obligated balance, end of year	9,362	365	1,700
	Budget authority and outlays, net:			
	Mandatory:			
4090	Budget authority, gross	124,357	130,228	152,017
	Outlays, gross:			
4100	Outlays from new mandatory authority	107,494	124,432	138,251
4101	Outlays from mandatory balances	9,101	18,160	5,796
4110	Outlays, gross (total)	116,595	142,592	144,047
	Offsets against gross budget authority and outlays:			
	Offsetting collections (collected) from:			
4123	Non-Federal sources	−368		
	Additional offsets against gross budget authority only:			
4143	Recoveries of prior year paid obligations, unexpired accounts	368		
4160	Budget authority, net (mandatory)	124,357	130,228	152,017
4170	Outlays, net (mandatory)	116,227	142,592	144,047
4180	Budget authority, net (total)	124,357	130,228	152,017
4190	Outlays, net (total)	116,227	142,592	144,047

WORKLOAD

	2021 actual	2022 est.	2023 est.
Compensation Completed Claims:			
Rating	1,399,049	1,694,569	1,811,609
Not-Rating Claims	2,678,778	2,784,652	2,834,814
Pension Completed Claims:			
Rating	123,881	119,098	123,479
Non-Rating Claims	346,132	271,948	298,230

For 2024, the Budget requests $146,778,136,000 in advance appropriation for Compensation and Pensions. This request satisfies the requirement created by the Consolidated and Further Continuing Appropriations Act, 2015 (P.L. 113–235) and prevents our Nation's veterans from being adversely affected by budget delays.

This appropriation provides for the payment of compensation, pension, and burial benefits to veterans and survivors.

Compensation is paid to veterans for disabilities incurred in or aggravated during active military service. Dependency and Indemnity Compensation is paid to survivors of servicepersons or veterans whose death occurred while on active duty or as a result of service-connected disabilities. Compensation and vocational rehabilitation is provided to the children of Vietnam veterans who were born with certain birth defects. The Secretary may

COMPENSATION AND PENSIONS—Continued

pay a clothing allowance to each veteran who uses a prescribed medication for a service-connected skin condition or wears a prosthetic or orthopedic appliance (including a wheelchair) which, in the judgment of the Secretary, tends to damage or tear the clothing of such veteran.

Miscellaneous benefits provided for are:

(a) payments for claims made pursuant to the provision of the World War Adjusted Compensation Act of 1924, as amended;

(b) a special allowance (38 U.S.C. 1312) to dependents of certain veterans who died after December 31, 1956, but who were not fully and currently insured under the Social Security Act; and

(c) payments authorized by the Equal Access to Justice Act.

The appropriation also provides for a program to allow the Department of Veterans Affairs (VA) to perform income matches for certain compensation recipients.

In accordance with Public Law 97–377, the Reinstated Entitlement Program for Survivors (REPS) program restores Social Security benefits to certain surviving spouses or children of veterans who died of service-connected causes.

Legislation is proposed to provide a cost-of-living adjustment comparable to the annual Social Security increase to recipients of disability compensation, dependency and indemnity compensation, and clothing allowances. The increase, effective with payments made on January 1, 2023, is expected to be 4.3 percent.

AVERAGE NUMBER OF COMPENSATION CASES AND PAYMENTS

	2021 actual	2022 est.	2023 est.
Veterans:			
Cases	5,150,221	5,324,457	5,538,958
Average payment per case, per year	$19,784	$21,832	$23,245
Total obligations (in millions)	$101,892	$116,246	$128,751
Survivors:			
Cases	453,342	467,244	482,949
Average payment per case, per year	$17,619	$21,147	$18,510
Total obligations (in millions)	$7,987	$9,881	$8,939
Chapter 18:			
Children	1,118	1,108	1,098
Average payment per case, per year	$19,505	$20,656	$21,544
Total obligations (in millions)	$22	$23	$24
Clothing allowance:			
Number of veterans	141,010	145,504	151,258
Average payment per case, per year	$840	$890	$928
Total obligations (in millions)	$118	$129	$140
Special Allowance for Dependents:			
Cases	16	15	14
Average benefit	$2,760	$2,923	$3,049
Total obligations (in millions)	$0	$0	$0
Equal Access to Justice Act:			
Cases	7,245	7,626	8,007
Average benefit	$5,941	$6,291	$6,562
Total obligations (in millions)	$43	$48	$53
REPS:			
Cases	1	1	1
Average benefit	$14,232	$18,734	$19,540
Total obligations (in millions)	$0	$0	$0

Pension benefits may be paid to veterans or their survivors. A veteran's entitlement is based on active duty service of a specific length (normally 90 days or more) during a designated war period, disabilities considered permanent and total, and countable income below established levels. There is no disability requirement for survivor cases or veterans age 65 or older. Income support is provided at established benefit levels.

An automatic annual cost-of-living increase comparable to the annual social security increase is provided for those pensioners in the improved program and to parents receiving dependency and indemnity compensation. The increase, effective with payments made on January 1, 2023, is expected to be 4.3 percent.

AVERAGE NUMBER OF PENSION CASES AND PAYMENTS

	2021 actual	2022 est.	2023 est.
Veterans:			
Cases	204,562	184,320	162,377
Average payment per case, per year	$12,745	$13,610	$14,173
Total obligations (in millions)	$2,607	$2,509	$2,301
Survivors:			
Cases	146,680	125,983	114,250
Average payment per case, per year	$9,994	$10,401	$10,805
Total obligations (in millions)	$1,466	$1,310	$1,235

Burial benefits in 2022 provide for: (a) the payment of an allowance of $828 toward burial and funeral expenses; (b) the payment of $828 for a plot allowance where an eligible veteran is not buried in a national cemetery or other cemetery under the jurisdiction of the United States; (c) the payment of a burial allowance of up to $2,000 when a veteran dies as a result of a service-connected disability; (d) furnishing a flag to drape the casket of each deceased veteran entitled thereto; (e) furnishing a headstone or marker for the grave of a veteran and, in certain cases, eligible dependents; and (f) authority to provide outer burial receptacles in the National Cemetery Administration.

NUMBER OF BURIAL BENEFITS

	2021 actual	2022 est.	2023 est.
Burial allowance	43,888	30,097	30,503
Burial allowances for deaths in Dept. facility	1,146	15,833	16,046
Burial plot	53,697	54,766	55,503
Service-connected deaths	49,390	52,125	53,974
Burial flags	473,490	450,848	450,848
Headstones and markers	350,032	332,501	337,312
Graveliners	9,128	8,671	8,796
Preplaced crypts	64,955	61,702	69,062
Caskets and Urns	287	273	277
Urns and Plaques	0	0	1,247

COMPENSATION AND PENSIONS

(Legislative proposal, subject to PAYGO)

Modernizing VA's Records Management Program: This proposal would amend Title 38, United States Code, by creating a new section 5707 to codify the Veterans Benefits Administration's procedures with respect to imaged source paper files, input records, reports, or other documents under the Records Control Schedule required by Title 44, United States Code. In 2023, there is no cost associated with this proposal.

READJUSTMENT BENEFITS

For the payment of readjustment and rehabilitation benefits to or on behalf of veterans as authorized by chapters 21, 30, 31, 33, 34, 35, 36, 39, 41, 51, 53, 55, and 61 of title 38, United States Code, $8,452,500,000, which shall become available on October 1, 2023, to remain available until expended: Provided, That expenses for rehabilitation program services and assistance which the Secretary is authorized to provide under subsection (a) of section 3104 of title 38, United States Code, other than under paragraphs (1), (2), (5), and (11) of that subsection, shall be charged to this account.

Note.—A full-year 2022 appropriation for this account was not enacted at the time the Budget was prepared; therefore, the Budget assumes this account is operating under the Continuing Appropriations Act, 2022 (Division A of Public Law 117–43, as amended). The amounts included for 2022 reflect the annualized level provided by the continuing resolution.

Program and Financing (in millions of dollars)

Identification code 036–0137–0–1–702	2021 actual	2022 est.	2023 est.
Obligations by program activity:			
0101 Sons and daughters	915	990	1,106
0102 Spouses	204	222	249
0191 Total education and training	1,119	1,212	1,355
0201 Vocational rehabilitation training	828	946	996
0202 Subsistence allowance	591	718	722
0203 Automobiles and adaptive equipment	106	110	114
0204 Housing Grants	132	170	173
0291 Total special assistance to disabled veterans	1,657	1,944	2,005
0301 Work study	29	30	33
0302 Payments to States	24	26	27
0303 All-volunteer assistance: Basic benefits and all other	9,292	8,471	8,923
0305 Tuition Assistance	3	2	2
0306 Licensing and Certification	2	3	3
0307 Veterans Rapid Retraining Assistance Program	32	319	35
0308 Reporting Fees	14	14	14
0310 Contract Counseling	2	6	6
0391 Total All-volunteer assistance and other	9,398	8,871	9,043
0799 Total direct obligations	12,174	12,027	12,403
0802 Veterans and servicepersons supplementary benefits	5	5	4

DEPARTMENT OF VETERANS AFFAIRS

Benefits Programs—Continued
Federal Funds—Continued

		2021 actual	2022 est.	2023 est.
0803	Chapter 1606 reservists benefits	72	71	72
0804	Chapter 1606 reservists supplementary benefits	26	25	26
0807	Chapter 33 DoD Reimbursements	52	52	52
0899	Total reimbursable obligations	155	153	154
0900	Total new obligations, unexpired accounts	12,329	12,180	12,557
	Budgetary resources:			
	Unobligated balance:			
1000	Unobligated balance brought forward, Oct 1	4,467	5,394	8,314
1021	Recoveries of prior year unpaid obligations	8		
1033	Recoveries of prior year paid obligations	128		
1070	Unobligated balance (total)	4,603	5,394	8,314
	Budget authority:			
	Appropriations, mandatory:			
1200	Appropriation	386		
	Advance appropriations, mandatory:			
1270	Advance appropriation	12,579	14,947	8,907
	Spending authority from offsetting collections, mandatory:			
1800	Collected	155	153	154
1900	Budget authority (total)	13,120	15,100	9,061
1930	Total budgetary resources available	17,723	20,494	17,375
	Memorandum (non-add) entries:			
1941	Unexpired unobligated balance, end of year	5,394	8,314	4,818
	Change in obligated balance:			
	Unpaid obligations:			
3000	Unpaid obligations, brought forward, Oct 1	766	738	138
3010	New obligations, unexpired accounts	12,329	12,180	12,557
3020	Outlays (gross)	–12,349	–12,780	–12,456
3040	Recoveries of prior year unpaid obligations, unexpired	–8		
3050	Unpaid obligations, end of year	738	138	239
	Uncollected payments:			
3060	Uncollected pymts, Fed sources, brought forward, Oct 1	–1	–1	–1
3090	Uncollected pymts, Fed sources, end of year	–1	–1	–1
	Memorandum (non-add) entries:			
3100	Obligated balance, start of year	765	737	137
3200	Obligated balance, end of year	737	137	238
	Budget authority and outlays, net:			
	Mandatory:			
4090	Budget authority, gross	13,120	15,100	9,061
	Outlays, gross:			
4100	Outlays from new mandatory authority	7,115	6,647	4,004
4101	Outlays from mandatory balances	5,234	6,133	8,452
4110	Outlays, gross (total)	12,349	12,780	12,456
	Offsets against gross budget authority and outlays:			
	Offsetting collections (collected) from:			
4120	Federal sources	–155	–153	–154
4123	Non-Federal sources	–128		
4130	Offsets against gross budget authority and outlays (total)	–283	–153	–154
	Additional offsets against gross budget authority only:			
4143	Recoveries of prior year paid obligations, unexpired accounts	128		
4160	Budget authority, net (mandatory)	12,965	14,947	8,907
4170	Outlays, net (mandatory)	12,066	12,627	12,302
4180	Budget authority, net (total)	12,965	14,947	8,907
4190	Outlays, net (total)	12,066	12,627	12,302

Summary of Budget Authority and Outlays (in millions of dollars)

	2021 actual	2022 est.	2023 est.
Enacted/requested:			
Budget Authority	12,965	14,947	8,907
Outlays	12,066	12,627	12,302
Legislative proposal, subject to PAYGO:			
Budget Authority			2
Outlays			2
Total:			
Budget Authority	12,965	14,947	8,909
Outlays	12,066	12,627	12,304

WORKLOAD—Veteran Readiness and Employment

	2021 actual	2022 est.	2023 est.
Evaluation and planning	71,951	72,692	73,455
Rehabilitation services	110,659	111,799	112,973
Employment services status	29,440	29,743	30,056
Vocational/educational counseling	2,923	3,069	3,223

WORKLOAD—Education

	2021 actual	2022 est.	2023 est.
Original claims	317,891	302,701	292,143
Adjustments/supplemental claims	3,129,136	3,060,564	2,970,470

For 2024, the Budget requests $8,452,500,000 in advance appropriation for Readjustment Benefits. This request satisfies the requirement created by the Consolidated and Further Continuing Appropriations Act, 2015 (P.L. 113–235) and prevents our Nation's veterans from being adversely affected by budget delays.

This appropriation finances educational assistance allowances for certain servicemembers, veterans, and for eligible dependents of those: (a) veterans who died from service-connected causes or have a total and permanent rated service-connected disability; and (b) servicemembers who were captured or missing in action. In addition, certain disabled veterans are provided with vocational rehabilitation, specially adapted housing grants, and automobile grants with the associated approved adaptive equipment. Voluntary contributions by eligible servicemembers and matching contributions provided by the Department of Defense are included in the Post-Vietnam Era Veterans Education Account.

The Post–9/11 GI Bill (Chapter 33).—P.L. 110–252 greatly expanded education benefits beginning on August 1, 2009. Based on length of active duty service and training rate, trainees may be entitled to benefits including: tuition and fees, housing allowance, books and supplies stipend, kickers, and Yellow Ribbon matching payments. Certain active duty members of the Armed Forces may transfer benefits to a spouse or children.

Survivors and Dependents Educational Assistance (Chapter 35).—Benefits are provided to children and spouses of veterans who died of a service-connected disability or whose service-connected disability is rated permanent and total. In addition, dependents of servicemembers missing in action or interred by a hostile foreign government for more than 90 days are also eligible. The table below provides a comparison of trainees and costs for the Dependents Educational Assistance.

All volunteer force educational assistance (Montgomery GI Bill).—P.L. 98–525, enacted October 19, 1984, established two new educational programs: an assistance program for veterans who enter active duty during the period beginning July 1, 1985; and an assistance program for certain members of the Selected Reserve. The Readjustment Benefit appropriation pays the basic benefit allowance for veterans, except for certain Post-Vietnam Era Veterans Education participants who transferred to the Montgomery GI Bill program. Supplementary educational assistance, Post-Vietnam Era Veterans Education converters, and reservists are financed by payments from the Department of Defense. Due to P.L. 116–315, the Montgomery GI Bill will be phased out starting in 2030.

Veteran Employment Through Technology Education Courses (VET TEC).—P.L. 115–48 established a high technology pilot program to provide eligible veterans who are entitled to educational assistance under chapter 30, 32, 33, 34, or 35 of title 38, United States Code, or chapter 1606 or 1607 of title 10, United States Code, with the opportunity to enroll in high technology programs of education that VA determines provide training and skills sought by employers in a relevant field or industry.

Veteran Rapid Retraining Assistance Program (VRRAP).—P.L. 117–2 established the VRRAP program and appropriated $386 million for benefits payments. P.L. 117–16 made further improvements to the program. VRRAP provides an eligible veteran with up to 12 months of tuition and fees and a monthly housing allowance based on Post–9/11 GI Bill rates, to be used towards training in a covered program of education that leads to a high-demand job. Covered programs include associate degrees, non-college degrees, and certificate programs. The Department of Labor determines what is considered a high-demand job for VRRAP. To be eligible for this program, individuals must be:

- At least 22 years of age and less than 67 years of age,
- Unemployed due to COVID-19 pandemic,
- Not eligible for GI Bill or VR&E benefits,
- Not enrolled in a Federal or State jobs program,

Readjustment Benefits—Continued

-Not receiving VA disability compensation because a veteran is unable to work, and

-Not receiving unemployment compensation, including enhanced benefits under the CARES Act.

The following table shows a caseload and cost comparison for these beneficiaries under existing legislation.

CASELOAD AND AVERAGE COST DATA

	2021 actual	2022 est.	2023 est.
Chapter 33:			
Number of trainees	610,009	562,246	564,972
Average cost per trainee	$14,985	$14,772	$15,532
Total cost (in millions)	$9,141	$8,305	$8,775
Chapter 35 Sons and Daughters:			
Number of trainees	131,941	140,795	150,271
Average cost per trainee (in dollars)	$6,933	$7,032	$7,354
Total cost (in millions)	$915	$990	$1,105
Chapter 35 Wives and Widow(ers):			
Number of trainees	35,626	38,265	41,122
Average cost per trainee (in dollars)	$5,719	$5,800	$6,067
Total cost (in millions)	$204	$222	$249
Chapter 30:			
Number of trainees	21,356	21,001	19,542
Average cost per trainee	$7,939	$7,952	$8,151
Total cost (in millions)	$170	$167	$159
Chapter 1606:			
Number of trainees	37,071	35,618	34,210
Average cost per trainee	$2,620	$2,665	$2,812
Total cost (in millions)	$97	$95	$96
Veteran Employment Through Technology Education Courses (VET TEC):			
Number of trainees	2,658	3,653	2,938
Average cost per trainee	$14,300	$14,801	$15,319
Total cost (in millions)	$38	$54	$45
Veteran Rapid Retraining Assistance Program (VRRAP)			
Number of trainees	2,079	10,131	6,661
Average cost per trainee	$15,417	$31,444	$5,308
Total cost (in millions)	$32	$319	$35

Veteran Readiness and Employment (VR&E, Chapter 31).—VR&E provides servicemembers and veterans with service-connected disabilities receive the assistance necessary to help them prepare for, obtain, and maintain suitable employment. Comprehensive assessments may include interest and aptitude testing as well as specialized assessments such as functional capacity examinations. During the training phase of the program, eligible servicemembers and veterans are provided assistance for necessary training such as tuition, fees, books and supplies at colleges, technical schools and other training programs. A veteran enrolled in training receives a monthly subsistence allowance. Eligible veterans may also receive specialized or adaptive equipment to help them overcome a disability or enable them to compete with non-disabled individuals. At the completion of training, veterans are provided with employment and placement services, including supplies and equipment needed to enter employment, adaptive equipment and workplace accommodations, incentives to employers to reimburse them for hiring and training veterans with disabilities, and two final months of subsistence allowance.

CASELOAD AND AVERAGE COST DATA

	2021 actual	2022 est.	2023 est.
Chapter 31:			
Rehabilitation, Evaluation, Planning and Service cases	33,229	33,588	36,208
Number of trainees	91,915	99,856	101,750
Average cost per trainee (in dollars)	$15,439	$16,663	$16,884
Total cost (in millions)	$1,419	$1,664	$1,718

Specially Adapted Housing Grants.—Specially adapted housing grants are provided to certain severely disabled veterans. In 2022, the maximum grant amount is $101,754. Veterans who suffer service-connected blindness or who have lost the use of both upper extremities can receive up to $20,387.

Specially Adapted Housing Assistive Technology Grants.—Under the Veterans Benefits Act of 2010 (P.L. 111–275), VA may provide grants of up to $200,000 per fiscal year to individuals or entities for the development of specially adapted housing assistive technologies, and an additional $1 million is authorized each fiscal year for such grants.

Automobile Grants and Adaptive Equipment.—Certain disabled veterans are provided with automobile grants with the associated approved adaptive equipment. An allowance is provided to certain service-disabled veterans and servicemembers toward the purchase price of an automobile. The maximum allowance increased to $22,355.72 in 2022 and will continue to increase based on the CPI-U. Adaptive equipment and the maintenance and replacement of such equipment is also provided.

CASELOAD AND AVERAGE COST DATA

	2021 actual	2022 est.	2023 est.
Housing grants:			
Number of housing grants	2,938	3,727	3,755
Average cost per grant	$44,997	$45,579	$45,972
Total cost (in millions)	$132	$170	$173
Number of housing technology grants	4	7	0
Average cost per grant	$199,815	$200,000	$0
Total cost (in millions)	$0.8	$1.4	$0
Automobiles or other conveyances:			
Number of conveyances	1,239	1,239	1,239
Average benefit	$21,029	$21,436	$21,852
Obligations (in millions)	$26	$27	$27
Adaptive equipment (including maintenance, repair, and installation for automobiles):			
Number of items	3,535	3,535	3,535
Average benefit	$22,668	$23,648	$24,670
Obligations (in millions)	$80	$84	$87

Tuition Assistance.—Public Law 106–398, enacted October 30, 2000, allows the military services to pay up to 100 percent of tuition and expenses charged by a school for servicemembers. If a service department pays less than 100 percent, a servicemember eligible for the Montgomery GI Bill Active-duty (MGIB) or the Post–9/11 GI Bill (Chapter 33) can elect to receive VA benefits for all or a portion of the remaining expenses. Public Law 108–454 established a program that provides availability of education benefits for payment for national admissions exams and national exams for credit at institutions of higher education.

The National Exams.—The benefit allows VA to reimburse for the fee charged for national tests for admission to institutions of higher learning and national tests providing an opportunity for course credit at institutions of higher learning.

Licensing and Certification Test Payments.—Under Public Law 106–419, veterans and other eligible persons may receive up to $2,000 to pay fees required for civilian occupational licensing and certification examinations needed to enter, maintain, or advance in employment in a vocation or profession, effective March 1, 2001.

Work-Study.—Certain veterans, reservists, and dependents pursuing a program of rehabilitation, education or training, who are enrolled as full-time students, can work up to 250 hours per semester, receiving the Federal ($7.25 as of July 24, 2009) or State minimum wage rate, whichever is higher.

Payments to States.—State approving agencies are reimbursed for the costs of inspecting, approving, and supervising programs of education and training offered by educational institutions and training establishments in which veterans, dependents, and reservists are enrolled or are about to enter.

Reporting Fees.—Reporting fees are paid to education and training institutions to help defray the costs of certifying education enrollment for veterans enrolled in training during a calendar year.

Object Classification (in millions of dollars)

Identification code 036–0137–0–1–702		2021 actual	2022 est.	2023 est.
41.0	Direct obligations: Grants, subsidies, and contributions	12,174	12,027	12,403
99.0	Reimbursable obligations	155	153	154
99.9	Total new obligations, unexpired accounts	12,329	12,180	12,557

DEPARTMENT OF VETERANS AFFAIRS

Benefits Programs—Continued
Federal Funds—Continued

1053

READJUSTMENT BENEFITS

(Legislative proposal, subject to PAYGO)

Program and Financing (in millions of dollars)

Identification code 036–0137–4–1–702		2021 actual	2022 est.	2023 est.
	Obligations by program activity:			
0204	Housing Grants	....	....	1
0205	Housing Technology Grants	....	....	1
0291	Total special assistance to disabled veterans	....	....	2
0799	Total direct obligations	....	....	2
0900	Total new obligations, unexpired accounts (object class 41.0)	....	....	2
	Budgetary resources:			
	Budget authority:			
	Appropriations, mandatory:			
1200	Appropriation	....	....	2
1900	Budget authority (total)	....	....	2
1930	Total budgetary resources available	....	....	2
	Change in obligated balance:			
	Unpaid obligations:			
3010	New obligations, unexpired accounts	....	....	2
3020	Outlays (gross)	....	....	–2
	Budget authority and outlays, net:			
	Mandatory:			
4090	Budget authority, gross	....	....	2
	Outlays, gross:			
4100	Outlays from new mandatory authority	....	....	2
4180	Budget authority, net (total)	....	....	2
4190	Outlays, net (total)	....	....	2

Extension of Authority for the Specially Adapted Housing (SAH) Assistive Technology Grant Program: This proposal would extend the authority of the Secretary of the Department of Veterans Affairs (VA) to award SAH Assistive Technology (SAHAT) grants and administer the program through September 30, 2027. Section 203 of Public Law (P.L.) 111–275 (Veterans Benefits Act of 2010), codified at 38 U.S.C. 2108, established the SAHAT grant program with a sunset date of September 30, 2016. Congress has since extended the sunset date four times. Most recently, Congress extended the program authority, via section 5201 of Public Law 116–159, through September 30, 2022. In 2023, the cost of this proposal is estimated to be $1 million.

Extension of Authority for the Specially Adapted Housing (SAH) Temporary Residence Adaptation (TRA) Grant: This proposal would extend the authority of the Secretary of Veterans Affairs (VA) to award SAH TRA grants through September 30, 2032. Section 101 of the Veterans Housing Opportunity and Benefits Improvement Act of 2006, codified at 38 U.S.C. 2102A, established the TRA grant with a sunset date of five years from enactment. Public Law 109–233, section 101, 120 Stat. 397 (2006). Congress has since extended the sunset date two times. Most recently, Congress extended the program authority, via section 205 of the Honoring Americas Veterans and Caring for Camp Lejeune Families Act of 2012, through December 31, 2022. Public Law 112–154, section 205, 126 Stat. 1165 (2012). In 2023, the cost of this proposal is estimated to be $810 thousand.

VETERANS INSURANCE AND INDEMNITIES

For military and naval insurance, national service life insurance, servicemen's indemnities, service-disabled veterans insurance, and veterans mortgage life insurance as authorized by chapters 19 and 21 of title 38, United States Code, $121,126,000, which shall become available on October 1, 2023, to remain available until expended.

Note.—A full-year 2022 appropriation for this account was not enacted at the time the Budget was prepared; therefore, the Budget assumes this account is operating under the Continuing Appropriations Act, 2022 (Division A of Public Law 117–43, as amended). The amounts included for 2022 reflect the annualized level provided by the continuing resolution.

Program and Financing (in millions of dollars)

Identification code 036–0120–0–1–701		2021 actual	2022 est.	2023 est.
	Obligations by program activity:			
0011	VMLI Death Claims	34	40	38
0012	Payment to Service-Disabled Veterans Insurance	103	107	78
0100	Total direct expenses	137	147	116
0900	Total new obligations, unexpired accounts	137	147	116
	Budgetary resources:			
	Unobligated balance:			
1000	Unobligated balance brought forward, Oct 1	3	3	....
	Budget authority:			
	Appropriations, mandatory:			
1200	Appropriation	2	....	....
	Advance appropriations, mandatory:			
1270	Advance appropriation	129	137	110
	Spending authority from offsetting collections, mandatory:			
1800	Collected	6	7	6
1900	Budget authority (total)	137	144	116
1930	Total budgetary resources available	140	147	116
	Memorandum (non-add) entries:			
1941	Unexpired unobligated balance, end of year	3	....	....
	Change in obligated balance:			
	Unpaid obligations:			
3000	Unpaid obligations, brought forward, Oct 1	7	8	1
3010	New obligations, unexpired accounts	137	147	116
3020	Outlays (gross)	–136	–154	–116
3050	Unpaid obligations, end of year	8	1	1
	Memorandum (non-add) entries:			
3100	Obligated balance, start of year	7	8	1
3200	Obligated balance, end of year	8	1	1
	Budget authority and outlays, net:			
	Mandatory:			
4090	Budget authority, gross	137	144	116
	Outlays, gross:			
4100	Outlays from new mandatory authority	127	144	116
4101	Outlays from mandatory balances	9	10	....
4110	Outlays, gross (total)	136	154	116
	Offsets against gross budget authority and outlays:			
	Offsetting collections (collected) from:			
4123	Non-Federal sources	–6	–7	–6
4180	Budget authority, net (total)	131	137	110
4190	Outlays, net (total)	130	147	110

WORKLOAD

	2021 actual	2022 est.	2023 est.
Policy service actions	565,257	572,560	743,180
Collections	206,358	201,800	169,400
Disability claims	22,671	37,740	259,300
Insurance awards	105,298	103,190	107,770

For 2024, the Budget requests $121,126,000 in advance appropriation for Veterans Insurance and Indemnities (VI&I). This request satisfies the requirement created by the Consolidated and Further Continuing Appropriations Act, 2015 (P.L. 113–235) and prevents our Nation's veterans from being adversely affected by budget delays.

Note.—Department of Veterans Affairs insurance policy loans are not an extension of Federal credit. Credit schedules previously shown for this account have been discontinued.

The insurance business line administers six life insurance programs, including two trust funds, two public enterprise funds, a trust revolving fund, and Veterans' Mortgage Life Insurance (VMLI); and supervises four additional programs for the benefit of servicemembers, veterans, and their beneficiaries through contracts with a commercial company. All programs are operated on a commercial basis, to the extent possible, consistent with all applicable statutes. The insurance appropriation is the supplemental funding mechanism for the following Government life insurance activities: National Service Life Insurance (NSLI); Service-Disabled Veterans Insurance Fund (S-DVI); and VMLI.

National Service Life Insurance (NSLI).—Payments are made to the NSLI fund for certain World War II veterans for: (a) extra hazards of service; (b) gratuitous insurance granted to certain persons unable to apply for

VETERANS INSURANCE AND INDEMNITIES—Continued

NSLI; and (c) death claims on policies under the waiver of a premium while the insured was on active duty.

Payment to Service-Disabled Veterans Insurance Fund (S-DVI).—Payments are made to the S-DVI fund to supplement the premiums and other receipts of the fund in amounts necessary to pay claims on insurance policies issued to veterans with service-connected disabilities.

Veterans' Mortgage Life Insurance (VMLI).—Payments are made to mortgage holders under this program, which provides mortgage protection life insurance to veterans who have received a grant for specially adapted housing due to severe disabilities. The trend in the number and amount of insurance policies in force appears in the following table.

POLICIES AND INSURANCE IN FORCE

VMLI Policies	2021 actual	2022 est.	2023 est.
Number of Policies	2,479	2,500	2,540
Amount of Insurance (dollars in millions)	$353	$373	$382

Object Classification (in millions of dollars)

Identification code 036–0120–0–1–701		2021 actual	2022 est.	2023 est.
42.0	Direct obligations: Insurance claims and indemnities	135	143	113
99.0	Reimbursable obligations	2	4	3
99.9	Total new obligations, unexpired accounts	137	147	116

FILIPINO VETERANS EQUITY COMPENSATION FUND

Program and Financing (in millions of dollars)

Identification code 036–1121–0–1–701		2021 actual	2022 est.	2023 est.
	Budgetary resources:			
	Unobligated balance:			
1000	Unobligated balance brought forward, Oct 1	56	56	56
1930	Total budgetary resources available	56	56	56
	Memorandum (non-add) entries:			
1941	Unexpired unobligated balance, end of year	56	56	56
4180	Budget authority, net (total)			
4190	Outlays, net (total)			

The Filipino Veterans Equity Compensation Fund was established under the Consolidated Security, Disaster Assistance, and Continuing Appropriations Act of 2009 (P.L. 110–329), to make payments to eligible persons who served in the Philippines during World War II. Payments were subsequently authorized by the Congress in the American Recovery and Reinvestment Act of 2009 (P.L. 111–5). Original funding of $198,000,000 was supplemented by a transfer of $67,000,000 authorized by Public Law 111–212 that remains available until expended. Payments to citizens of the United States are $15,000. Payments to non-U.S. citizens are $9,000.

GENERAL OPERATING EXPENSES, VETERANS BENEFITS ADMINISTRATION

For necessary operating expenses of the Veterans Benefits Administration, not otherwise provided for, including hire of passenger motor vehicles, reimbursement of the General Services Administration for security guard services, and reimbursement of the Department of Defense for the cost of overseas employee mail, $3,863,000,000: Provided, That expenses for services and assistance authorized under paragraphs (1), (2), (5), and (11) of section 3104(a) of title 38, United States Code, that the Secretary of Veterans Affairs determines are necessary to enable entitled veterans: (1) to the maximum extent feasible, to become employable and to obtain and maintain suitable employment; or (2) to achieve maximum independence in daily living, shall be charged to this account: Provided further, That, of the funds made available under this heading, not to exceed 10 percent shall remain available until September 30, 2024.

Note.—A full-year 2022 appropriation for this account was not enacted at the time the Budget was prepared; therefore, the Budget assumes this account is operating under the Continuing Appropriations Act, 2022 (Division A of Public Law 117–43, as amended). The amounts included for 2022 reflect the annualized level provided by the continuing resolution.

Program and Financing (in millions of dollars)

Identification code 036–0151–0–1–705		2021 actual	2022 est.	2023 est.
	Obligations by program activity:			
0010	Compensation and pensions	2,677	2,582	3,036
0011	Education	451	267	352
0012	VRE	275	334	294
0013	Insurance	2	2	2
0014	Housing	25	39	42
0015	Transition and Economic Development	111	118	137
0799	Total direct obligations	3,541	3,342	3,863
0801	Compensation and pensions	2,224	3,064	3,521
0802	Education	1	2	
0804	Insurance	31	43	45
0805	Housing	144	146	171
0806	Transition and Economic Development	1		
0807	VRE	1	2	2
0899	Total reimbursable obligations	2,402	3,257	3,739
0900	Total new obligations, unexpired accounts	5,943	6,599	7,602
	Budgetary resources:			
	Unobligated balance:			
1000	Unobligated balance brought forward, Oct 1	14	282	547
1012	Unobligated balance transfers between expired and unexpired accounts	74		
1070	Unobligated balance (total)	88	282	547
	Budget authority:			
	Appropriations, discretionary:			
1100	Appropriation	3,180	3,180	3,863
1121	Appropriations transferred from other acct [036–0160]	338		
1131	Unobligated balance of appropriations permanently reduced	–16	–16	
1160	Appropriation, discretionary (total)	3,502	3,164	3,863
	Advance appropriations, discretionary:			
1173	Advance appropriations transferred from other accounts [036–0160]		178	
	Appropriations, mandatory:			
1200	Appropriation [P.L. 117–2, Section 8001]	262		
	Spending authority from offsetting collections, discretionary:			
1700	Collected	2,243	3,522	3,739
1701	Change in uncollected payments, Federal sources	217		
1750	Spending auth from offsetting collections, disc (total)	2,460	3,522	3,739
1900	Budget authority (total)	6,224	6,864	7,602
1930	Total budgetary resources available	6,312	7,146	8,149
	Memorandum (non-add) entries:			
1940	Unobligated balance expiring	–87		
1941	Unexpired unobligated balance, end of year	282	547	547
	Change in obligated balance:			
	Unpaid obligations:			
3000	Unpaid obligations, brought forward, Oct 1	1,532	2,130	509
3010	New obligations, unexpired accounts	5,943	6,599	7,602
3011	Obligations ("upward adjustments"), expired accounts	58		
3020	Outlays (gross)	–5,296	–8,220	–7,727
3041	Recoveries of prior year unpaid obligations, expired	–107		
3050	Unpaid obligations, end of year	2,130	509	384
	Uncollected payments:			
3060	Uncollected pymts, Fed sources, brought forward, Oct 1		–217	–217
3070	Change in uncollected pymts, Fed sources, unexpired	–217		
3090	Uncollected pymts, Fed sources, end of year	–217	–217	–217
	Memorandum (non-add) entries:			
3100	Obligated balance, start of year	1,532	1,913	292
3200	Obligated balance, end of year	1,913	292	167
	Budget authority and outlays, net:			
	Discretionary:			
4000	Budget authority, gross	5,962	6,864	7,602
	Outlays, gross:			
4010	Outlays from new discretionary authority	4,107	5,881	6,868
4011	Outlays from discretionary balances	1,189	2,081	856
4020	Outlays, gross (total)	5,296	7,962	7,724
	Offsets against gross budget authority and outlays:			
	Offsetting collections (collected) from:			
4030	Federal sources	–2,259	–3,522	–3,739
4033	Non-Federal sources	–2		
4040	Offsets against gross budget authority and outlays (total)	–2,261	–3,522	–3,739
	Additional offsets against gross budget authority only:			
4050	Change in uncollected pymts, Fed sources, unexpired	–217		

		2021 actual	2022 est.	2023 est.
4052	Offsetting collections credited to expired accounts	18		
4060	Additional offsets against budget authority only (total)	−199		
4070	Budget authority, net (discretionary)	3,502	3,342	3,863
4080	Outlays, net (discretionary)	3,035	4,440	3,985
	Mandatory:			
4090	Budget authority, gross	262		
	Outlays, gross:			
4101	Outlays from mandatory balances		258	3
4180	Budget authority, net (total)	3,764	3,342	3,863
4190	Outlays, net (total)	3,035	4,698	3,988

General Operating Expenses, Veterans Benefits Administration.—This appropriation provides for the Department's top management direction and administrative support, including fiscal, personnel, and legal services, as well as for the administration of veteran benefits. The total cost of administering veterans insurance programs is funded through direct appropriations to this account and through reimbursements from the insurance trust fund.

Note.—Reflects FTE treated as reimbursements in all years and the effects of Credit Reform, per Public Law 101–508.

Object Classification (in millions of dollars)

Identification code 036–0151–0–1–705		2021 actual	2022 est.	2023 est.
	Direct obligations:			
	Personnel compensation:			
11.1	Full-time permanent	1,735	1,780	1,844
11.5	Other personnel compensation	657	658	672
11.9	Total personnel compensation	2,392	2,438	2,516
12.1	Civilian personnel benefits	568	436	480
13.0	Benefits for former personnel	1	1	1
21.0	Travel and transportation of persons	28	5	35
22.0	Transportation of things	2	2	2
23.1	Rent	144	144	154
23.2	Rental payments to others	21	21	21
23.3	Communications, utilities, and miscellaneous charges	17	17	17
24.0	Printing and reproduction	3	3	3
25.2	Other services from non-Federal sources	332	242	601
26.0	Supplies and materials	7	7	7
31.0	Equipment	25	25	25
42.0	Insurance claims and indemnities	1	1	1
99.0	Direct obligations	3,541	3,342	3,863
99.0	Reimbursable obligations	2,402	3,257	3,739
99.9	Total new obligations, unexpired accounts	5,943	6,599	7,602

Employment Summary

Identification code 036–0151–0–1–705		2021 actual	2022 est.	2023 est.
1001	Direct civilian full-time equivalent employment	23,504	23,900	25,164
2001	Reimbursable civilian full-time equivalent employment	1,135	1,392	1,317

SERVICE-DISABLED VETERANS INSURANCE FUND

Program and Financing (in millions of dollars)

Identification code 036–4012–0–3–701		2021 actual	2022 est.	2023 est.
	Obligations by program activity:			
0801	Capital investment	25	30	30
0802	Death claims	134	133	135
0803	All other	29	7	7
0804	Payments to GOE and IT	6	36	31
0900	Total new obligations, unexpired accounts	194	206	203
	Budgetary resources:			
	Unobligated balance:			
1000	Unobligated balance brought forward, Oct 1	50	59	61
	Budget authority:			
	Spending authority from offsetting collections, mandatory:			
1800	Collected	203	208	176
1930	Total budgetary resources available	253	267	237
	Memorandum (non-add) entries:			
1941	Unexpired unobligated balance, end of year	59	61	34
	Change in obligated balance:			
	Unpaid obligations:			
3000	Unpaid obligations, brought forward, Oct 1	32	38	46
3010	New obligations, unexpired accounts	194	206	203
3020	Outlays (gross)	−188	−198	−203
3050	Unpaid obligations, end of year	38	46	46
	Memorandum (non-add) entries:			
3100	Obligated balance, start of year	32	38	46
3200	Obligated balance, end of year	38	46	46
	Budget authority and outlays, net:			
	Mandatory:			
4090	Budget authority, gross	203	208	176
	Outlays, gross:			
4100	Outlays from new mandatory authority	100	162	176
4101	Outlays from mandatory balances	88	36	27
4110	Outlays, gross (total)	188	198	203
	Offsets against gross budget authority and outlays:			
	Offsetting collections (collected) from:			
4120	Federal sources	−103	−107	−78
4123	Non-Federal sources	−100	−5	−5
4123	Non-Federal sources		−71	−68
4123	Non-Federal sources		−25	−25
4130	Offsets against gross budget authority and outlays (total)	−203	−208	−176
4170	Outlays, net (mandatory)	−15	−10	27
4180	Budget authority, net (total)			
4190	Outlays, net (total)	−15	−10	27

The Insurance Act of 1951 established the Service-Disabled Veterans Insurance (S-DVI) program for veterans with service-connected disabilities. S-DVI will remain open to new policy issuances through December 31, 2022, for veterans who separated from the service on or after April 25, 1951. This fund finances the payment of claims on existing life insurance policies and remains open for new issues at standard rates to veterans having service-connected disabilities.

OPERATING COSTS

Death claims.—Represents payments to designated beneficiaries.

All other.—Represents payments to policyholders who surrender their policies for their cash value and hold endowment policies which have matured.

Capital investment.—A policyholder may borrow up to 94 percent of the value of his or her policy.

Administration.—Represents the administrative costs of claims processing and account maintenance.

The trend in the number and amount of policies in force is indicated in the following table.

POLICIES AND INSURANCE IN FORCE

	2021 actual	2022 est.	2023 est.
Number of policies (EOY)	276,060	280,955	270,667
Insurance in force (dollars in millions) (EOY)	$2,907	$2,973	$2,862

Financing.—Operations are financed from premiums and other receipts. Additional funds are received by transfer from the Veterans Insurance and Indemnities appropriation, instead of direct appropriations to this fund.

Operating results and financial condition.—Since premium and other receipts are insufficient to cover operations, the fund continues to project liabilities in excess of assets. The deficit is expected to reach an estimated $1,576 million by September 30, 2022. The expected deficit is financed by additional funds from the above-mentioned Veterans Insurance and Indemnities appropriations.

Object Classification (in millions of dollars)

Identification code 036–4012–0–3–701		2021 actual	2022 est.	2023 est.
	Reimbursable obligations:			
33.0	Investments and loans	24	30	30
42.0	Insurance claims and indemnities	170	176	173
99.9	Total new obligations, unexpired accounts	194	206	203

Benefits Programs—Continued
Federal Funds—Continued

VETERANS REOPENED INSURANCE FUND

Program and Financing (in millions of dollars)

Identification code 036–4010–0–3–701	2021 actual	2022 est.	2023 est.
Obligations by program activity:			
0801 Death claims	10	7	6
0802 Dividends	1	1	....
0803 All other	4	3	2
0900 Total new obligations, unexpired accounts	15	11	8
Budgetary resources:			
Unobligated balance:			
1000 Unobligated balance brought forward, Oct 1	50	38	29
Budget authority:			
Spending authority from offsetting collections, mandatory:			
1800 Collected	3	2	2
1930 Total budgetary resources available	53	40	31
Memorandum (non-add) entries:			
1941 Unexpired unobligated balance, end of year	38	29	23
Change in obligated balance:			
Unpaid obligations:			
3000 Unpaid obligations, brought forward, Oct 1	17	13	12
3010 New obligations, unexpired accounts	15	11	8
3020 Outlays (gross)	–19	–12	–11
3050 Unpaid obligations, end of year	13	12	9
Uncollected payments:			
3060 Uncollected pymts, Fed sources, brought forward, Oct 1	–1	–1	–1
3090 Uncollected pymts, Fed sources, end of year	–1	–1	–1
Memorandum (non-add) entries:			
3100 Obligated balance, start of year	16	12	11
3200 Obligated balance, end of year	12	11	8
Budget authority and outlays, net:			
Mandatory:			
4090 Budget authority, gross	3	2	2
Outlays, gross:			
4100 Outlays from new mandatory authority	3	2	2
4101 Outlays from mandatory balances	16	10	9
4110 Outlays, gross (total)	19	12	11
Offsets against gross budget authority and outlays:			
Offsetting collections (collected) from:			
4121 Interest on Federal securities	–2	–2	–1
4123 Non-Federal sources	–1	....	–1
4130 Offsets against gross budget authority and outlays (total)	–3	–2	–2
4170 Outlays, net (mandatory)	16	10	9
4180 Budget authority, net (total)	....	....	....
4190 Outlays, net (total)	16	10	9
Memorandum (non-add) entries:			
5000 Total investments, SOY: Federal securities: Par value	66	49	39
5001 Total investments, EOY: Federal securities: Par value	49	39	30

Note.—Department of Veterans Affairs insurance policy loans are not an extension of Federal credit. Credit schedules previously shown for this account have been discontinued.

The Veterans' Reopened Insurance Fund pays claims and administrative costs on participating life insurance policies issued during the period May 1, 1965, through May 2, 1966, under three life insurance programs: 1) service-disabled standard insurance; 2) service-disabled rated insurance; and 3) nonservice-disabled insurance availing disabled World War II and Korean conflict veterans an opportunity to acquire life insurance coverage who were no longer eligible for other government insurance.

Budget program:

Death claims.—Represents payments to designated beneficiaries.

Dividends.—Policyholders participate in the distribution of annual dividends.

All other.—This represents resources for the administrative costs of processing claims and maintaining the accounts, and to those policyholders who: (a) surrender their policies for cash value; (b) hold endowment policies which have matured; and (c) have purchased total disability income coverage and subsequently become disabled.

Policy loans made.—A policyholder may borrow up to 94 percent of the cash value of his policy at an interest rate adjusted to reflect private sector borrowing costs.

The following table reflects the decrease in the number of policies and the amount of insurance in force:

POLICIES AND INSURANCE IN FORCE

	2021 actual	2022 est.	2023 est.
Number of policies	3,647	2,797	2,121
Insurance in force (dollars in millions)	$37	$51	$38

Financing.—Operations are financed from premiums collected from policyholders and interest on investments. Excess earnings of the fund are distributed to the policyholders in the form of an annual dividend.

Object Classification (in millions of dollars)

Identification code 036–4010–0–3–701	2021 actual	2022 est.	2023 est.
Reimbursable obligations:			
42.0 Insurance claims and indemnities	14	10	7
43.0 Interest and dividends	1	1	1
99.9 Total new obligations, unexpired accounts	15	11	8

SERVICEMEMBERS' GROUP LIFE INSURANCE FUND

Program and Financing (in millions of dollars)

Identification code 036–4009–0–3–701	2021 actual	2022 est.	2023 est.
Obligations by program activity:			
0801 Premium payments	213	660	660
0802 Payments to carrier	1	....	....
0803 Payment to GOE	2	3	3
0900 Total new obligations, unexpired accounts (object class 41.0)	216	663	663
Budgetary resources:			
Unobligated balance:			
1000 Unobligated balance brought forward, Oct 1	1,264	2,532	3,165
Budget authority:			
Spending authority from offsetting collections, mandatory:			
1800 Collected	1,477	1,296	1,209
1801 Change in uncollected payments, Federal sources	7	....	....
1850 Spending auth from offsetting collections, mand (total)	1,484	1,296	1,209
1930 Total budgetary resources available	2,748	3,828	4,374
Memorandum (non-add) entries:			
1941 Unexpired unobligated balance, end of year	2,532	3,165	3,711
Change in obligated balance:			
Unpaid obligations:			
3010 New obligations, unexpired accounts	216	663	663
3020 Outlays (gross)	–216	–663	–663
Uncollected payments:			
3060 Uncollected pymts, Fed sources, brought forward, Oct 1	–2	–9	–9
3070 Change in uncollected pymts, Fed sources, unexpired	–7	....	....
3090 Uncollected pymts, Fed sources, end of year	–9	–9	–9
Memorandum (non-add) entries:			
3100 Obligated balance, start of year	–2	–9	–9
3200 Obligated balance, end of year	–9	–9	–9
Budget authority and outlays, net:			
Mandatory:			
4090 Budget authority, gross	1,484	1,296	1,209
Outlays, gross:			
4100 Outlays from new mandatory authority	216	663	663
Offsets against gross budget authority and outlays:			
Offsetting collections (collected) from:			
4121 Interest on Federal securities	–13	–33	–46
4123 Non-Federal sources	–1,464	–663	–663
4124 Offsetting governmental collections	....	–600	–500
4130 Offsets against gross budget authority and outlays (total)	–1,477	–1,296	–1,209
Additional offsets against gross budget authority only:			
4140 Change in uncollected pymts, Fed sources, unexpired	–7	....	....
4170 Outlays, net (mandatory)	–1,261	–633	–546
4180 Budget authority, net (total)	....	....	....
4190 Outlays, net (total)	–1,261	–633	–546

DEPARTMENT OF VETERANS AFFAIRS

Benefits Programs—Continued
Federal Funds—Continued

1057

	Memorandum (non-add) entries:			
5000	Total investments, SOY: Federal securities: Par value	1,262	2,523	3,165
5001	Total investments, EOY: Federal securities: Par value	2,523	3,165	3,711

This fund finances the payment of group life insurance premiums to private insurance companies under the Servicemembers' Group Life Insurance (SGLI) Act of 1965, as amended. SGLI is a program for servicemembers on active duty, ready reservists, members of the National Guard, members of the Commissioned Corps of the National Oceanic and Atmospheric Administration and the Public Health Service, cadets and midshipmen of the four service academies, and members of the Reserve Officer Training Corps. SGLI coverage is available in $50,000 increments up to the maximum of $400,000. Veterans' Group Life Insurance (VGLI) is a program of post-separation insurance which allows servicemembers to convert their SGLI coverage to renewable term insurance. Family Servicemembers' Group Life Insurance (FSGLI) is a program extended to the spouses and dependent children of members insured under the SGLI program. FSGLI provides up to a maximum of $100,000 of insurance coverage for spouses, not to exceed the amount of SGLI the insured member has in force, and $10,000 of free coverage for dependent children. Spousal coverage is issued in increments of $10,000.

The Servicemembers' Group Life Insurance Traumatic Injury Protection Program (TSGLI) became effective December 1, 2005. TSGLI provides for payment between $25,000 and $100,000 (depending on the type of injury) to any member of the uniformed services covered by SGLI who sustains a traumatic injury that results in certain serious losses.

VETERANS AFFAIRS LIFE INSURANCE

Program and Financing (in millions of dollars)

Identification code 036–4379–0–3–705	2021 actual	2022 est.	2023 est.
Obligations by program activity:			
0801 Death Claims			7
0805 Payment to Insurance account			7
0900 Total new obligations, unexpired accounts			14
Budgetary resources:			
Budget authority:			
Spending authority from offsetting collections, mandatory:			
1800 Collected			232
1930 Total budgetary resources available			232
Memorandum (non-add) entries:			
1941 Unexpired unobligated balance, end of year			218
Change in obligated balance:			
Unpaid obligations:			
3010 New obligations, unexpired accounts			14
3020 Outlays (gross)			–14
Budget authority and outlays, net:			
Mandatory:			
4090 Budget authority, gross			232
Outlays, gross:			
4100 Outlays from new mandatory authority			14
Offsets against gross budget authority and outlays:			
Offsetting collections (collected) from:			
4120 Federal sources			–232
4180 Budget authority, net (total)			....
4190 Outlays, net (total)			–218

Veterans Affairs Life Insurance (VALI) was established under Public Law 116–315 and is effective starting January 1, 2023, replacing the Servicemembers-Disabled Veterans Insurance (S-DVI) program. The program provides guaranteed whole life insurance coverage to participants and expands eligibility to all S-DVI Veterans under age 81 without medical underwriting. Insurance coverage ranges from $10,000 to $40,000 and provides financial assurance to beneficiaries. This program is designed to be self-supporting.

Object Classification (in millions of dollars)

Identification code 036–4379–0–3–705	2021 actual	2022 est.	2023 est.
Reimbursable obligations:			
33.0 Investments and loans			11
42.0 Insurance claims and indemnities			3
99.9 Total new obligations, unexpired accounts			14

VETERANS HOUSING BENEFIT PROGRAM FUND

For the cost of direct and guaranteed loans, such sums as may be necessary to carry out the program, as authorized by subchapters I through III of chapter 37 of title 38, United States Code: Provided, That such costs, including the cost of modifying such loans, shall be as defined in section 502 of the Congressional Budget Act of 1974: Provided further, That, during fiscal year 2023, within the resources available, not to exceed $500,000 in gross obligations for direct loans are authorized for specially adapted housing loans.

In addition, for administrative expenses to carry out the direct and guaranteed loan programs, $282,361,131.

Note.—A full-year 2022 appropriation for this account was not enacted at the time the Budget was prepared; therefore, the Budget assumes this account is operating under the Continuing Appropriations Act, 2022 (Division A of Public Law 117–43, as amended). The amounts included for 2022 reflect the annualized level provided by the continuing resolution.

Program and Financing (in millions of dollars)

Identification code 036–1119–0–1–704	2021 actual	2022 est.	2023 est.
Obligations by program activity:			
Credit program obligations:			
0701 Direct loan subsidy			3
0702 Loan guarantee subsidy			246
0704 Subsidy for modifications of loan guarantees	68		
0705 Reestimates of direct loan subsidy	5	16	
0706 Interest on reestimates of direct loan subsidy	5	8	
0707 Reestimates of loan guarantee subsidy	544	1,860	
0708 Interest on reestimates of loan guarantee subsidy	45	23	
0709 Administrative expenses	204	204	282
0900 Total new obligations, unexpired accounts	871	2,111	531
Budgetary resources:			
Budget authority:			
Appropriations, discretionary:			
1100 Appropriation	204	204	282
Appropriations, mandatory:			
1200 Appropriation	599	1,907	249
1200 Appropriation	68		
1260 Appropriations, mandatory (total)	667	1,907	249
1900 Budget authority (total)	871	2,111	531
1930 Total budgetary resources available	871	2,111	531
Change in obligated balance:			
Unpaid obligations:			
3000 Unpaid obligations, brought forward, Oct 1	44	187	
3010 New obligations, unexpired accounts	871	2,111	531
3020 Outlays (gross)	–728	–2,298	–531
3050 Unpaid obligations, end of year	187		
Memorandum (non-add) entries:			
3100 Obligated balance, start of year	44	187	
3200 Obligated balance, end of year	187		
Budget authority and outlays, net:			
Discretionary:			
4000 Budget authority, gross	204	204	282
Outlays, gross:			
4010 Outlays from new discretionary authority	20	204	282
4011 Outlays from discretionary balances	41	187	
4020 Outlays, gross (total)	61	391	282
Mandatory:			
4090 Budget authority, gross	667	1,907	249
Outlays, gross:			
4100 Outlays from new mandatory authority	667	1,907	249
4180 Budget authority, net (total)	871	2,111	531
4190 Outlays, net (total)	728	2,298	531

VETERANS HOUSING BENEFIT PROGRAM FUND—Continued

Summary of Loan Levels, Subsidy Budget Authority and Outlays by Program (in millions of dollars)

Identification code 036–1119–0–1–704		2021 actual	2022 est.	2023 est.
	Direct loan levels supportable by subsidy budget authority:			
115001	Acquired Direct Loans	....	28	33
115004	Vendee Direct Loans	5	168	179
115999	Total direct loan levels	5	196	212
	Direct loan subsidy (in percent):			
132001	Acquired Direct Loans	....	–1.91	7.62
132004	Vendee Direct Loans	–22.54	–27.09	–26.29
132999	Weighted average subsidy rate	–22.54	–23.49	–21.01
	Direct loan subsidy budget authority:			
133001	Acquired Direct Loans	....	–1	3
133004	Vendee Direct Loans	–2	–45	–47
133999	Total subsidy budget authority	–2	–46	–44
	Direct loan subsidy outlays:			
134001	Acquired Direct Loans	....	....	3
134004	Vendee Direct Loans	–2	–45	–47
134005	Acquired and Vendee Loan Reestimates	1	....	....
134999	Total subsidy outlays	–1	–45	–44
	Direct loan reestimates:			
135001	Acquired Direct Loans	4	....	....
135004	Vendee Direct Loans	–27	16	....
135005	Acquired and Vendee Loan Reestimates	–23	....	....
135999	Total direct loan reestimates	–46	16	....
	Guaranteed loan levels supportable by subsidy budget authority:			
215001	Housing Guaranteed Loans	422,798	305,293	314,709
215999	Total loan guarantee levels	422,798	305,293	314,709
	Guaranteed loan subsidy (in percent):			
232001	Housing Guaranteed Loans	–.50	–.08	0.08
232999	Weighted average subsidy rate	–.50	–.08	0.08
	Guaranteed loan subsidy budget authority:			
233001	Housing Guaranteed Loans	–2,114	–236	246
233999	Total subsidy budget authority	–2,114	–236	246
	Guaranteed loan subsidy outlays:			
234001	Housing Guaranteed Loans	–2,046	–236	246
234002	Guaranteed Loan Sale Securities—Vendee	8	....	....
234999	Total subsidy outlays	–2,038	–236	246
	Guaranteed loan reestimates:			
235001	Housing Guaranteed Loans	–1,298	1,555	....
235002	Guaranteed Loan Sale Securities—Vendee	–80	–2	....
235999	Total guaranteed loan reestimates	–1,378	1,553	....
	Administrative expense data:			
3510	Budget authority	204	204	282
3590	Outlays from new authority	18	204	281

Veterans Affairs (VA) Housing Program Account.—The housing program helps eligible veterans, active duty personnel, surviving spouses, and members of the Reserves and National Guard purchase, retain, and adapt homes in recognition of their service to the Nation. When a borrower purchases a home, the program operates by substituting the Federal Government's guaranty for a down payment that might otherwise be required.

Under 38 U.S.C. 3703, the guaranty amount for a borrower with full entitlement (first-time users of the program or users whose entitlement is fully restored) is as follows:

(a) 50 percent for loans of $45,000 or less;

(b) $22,500 for loans greater than $45,000, but no more than $56,250;

(c) the lesser of $36,000 or 40 percent of the loan amount for loans greater than $56,250, but not more than $144,000; or

(d) 25 percent of the loan amount for loans of $144,001 or greater.

This appropriation provides for the corporate leadership and operational support to VA's Housing business line. The Housing Program facilitates the extension of private capital, on more liberal terms than generally available to nonveterans, to assist veterans and servicemembers in obtaining housing credit, and assist veterans in retaining their homes during periods of temporary economic difficulty through intensive supplemental mortgage loan servicing.

Guaranteed transitional housing loans for homeless veterans.—Established as a pilot project by the Veterans Benefits Improvement Act of 1998 (Public Law 105–368), this program does not require any new loan subsidy funding. The program has originated no new loans since 2009. The program was canceled in 2012. The existing loan will continue to be serviced within the program's financing account.

WORKLOAD

[in thousands]

	2021 actual	2022 est.	2023 est.
Construction and valuation	700	680	650
Loan processing	556	548	506
Loan service and claims	162	120	109

Object Classification (in millions of dollars)

Identification code 036–1119–0–1–704		2021 actual	2022 est.	2023 est.
	Direct obligations:			
25.2	Other services from non-Federal sources	204	204	282
41.0	Grants, subsidies, and contributions	667	1,907	249
99.9	Total new obligations, unexpired accounts	871	2,111	531

HOUSING DIRECT LOAN FINANCING ACCOUNT

Program and Financing (in millions of dollars)

Identification code 036–4127–0–3–704		2021 actual	2022 est.	2023 est.
	Obligations by program activity:			
0004	Property management/other expense	3	....	1
0091	Direct program activities, subtotal	3	....	1
	Credit program obligations:			
0710	Direct loan obligations	5	196	212
0713	Payment of interest to Treasury	19	28	31
0740	Negative subsidy obligations	2	46	47
0742	Downward reestimates paid to receipt accounts	36	3	....
0743	Interest on downward reestimates	18	5	....
0791	Direct program activities, subtotal	80	278	290
0900	Total new obligations, unexpired accounts	83	278	291
	Budgetary resources:			
	Unobligated balance:			
1000	Unobligated balance brought forward, Oct 1	92	66	1
1023	Unobligated balances applied to repay debt	–66	–66	....
1070	Unobligated balance (total)	26	....	1
	Financing authority:			
	Borrowing authority, mandatory:			
1400	Borrowing authority	124	279	288
1422	Borrowing authority applied to repay debt	–1	....	....
1440	Borrowing authority, mandatory (total)	123	279	288
	Spending authority from offsetting collections, mandatory:			
1800	Collected	89	54	40
1825	Spending authority from offsetting collections applied to repay debt	–89	–54	–37
1850	Spending auth from offsetting collections, mand (total)	....	....	3
1900	Budget authority (total)	123	279	291
1930	Total budgetary resources available	149	279	292
	Memorandum (non-add) entries:			
1941	Unexpired unobligated balance, end of year	66	1	1
	Change in obligated balance:			
	Unpaid obligations:			
3000	Unpaid obligations, brought forward, Oct 1	5	1	3
3010	New obligations, unexpired accounts	83	278	291
3020	Outlays (gross)	–87	–276	–290
3050	Unpaid obligations, end of year	1	3	4
	Memorandum (non-add) entries:			
3100	Obligated balance, start of year	5	1	3
3200	Obligated balance, end of year	1	3	4
	Financing authority and disbursements, net:			
	Mandatory:			
4090	Budget authority, gross	123	279	291

DEPARTMENT OF VETERANS AFFAIRS

Benefits Programs—Continued
Federal Funds—Continued

1059

		2021 actual	2022 est.	2023 est.
	Financing disbursements:			
4110	Outlays, gross (total)	87	276	290
	Offsets against gross financing authority and disbursements:			
	Offsetting collections (collected) from:			
4120	Federal sources: Payments from program account	–10	–24	–3
4122	Interest on uninvested funds	–5		
4123	Interest and principal received on loans	–71	–26	–32
4123	Fees		–4	–4
4123	Cash sale of properties	–1		–1
4123	Other	–2		
4130	Offsets against gross budget authority and outlays (total)	–89	–54	–40
4160	Budget authority, net (mandatory)	34	225	251
4170	Outlays, net (mandatory)	–2	222	250
4180	Budget authority, net (total)	34	225	251
4190	Outlays, net (total)	–2	222	250

Status of Direct Loans (in millions of dollars)

Identification code 036–4127–0–3–704		2021 actual	2022 est.	2023 est.
	Position with respect to appropriations act limitation on obligations:			
1111	Direct loan obligations from current-year authority	5	196	212
1150	Total direct loan obligations	5	196	212
	Cumulative balance of direct loans outstanding:			
1210	Outstanding, start of year	347	292	477
1231	Disbursements: Direct loan disbursements	5	196	212
1251	Repayments: Repayments and prepayments	–59	–10	–11
1263	Write-offs for default: Direct loans	–1	–1	–1
1290	Outstanding, end of year	292	477	677

Balance Sheet (in millions of dollars)

Identification code 036–4127–0–3–704		2020 actual	2021 actual
	ASSETS:		
	Federal assets:		
1101	Fund balances with Treasury	97	67
	Investments in U.S. securities:		
1106	Receivables, net	9	43
1206	Non-Federal assets: Receivables, net	5	5
	Net value of assets related to post-1991 direct loans receivable:		
1401	Direct loans receivable, gross	347	292
1402	Interest receivable	16	14
1404	Foreclosed property	1	1
1405	Allowance for subsidy cost (-)	49	68
1499	Net present value of assets related to direct loans	413	375
1901	Other Federal assets: Other assets		
1999	Total assets	524	490
	LIABILITIES:		
	Federal liabilities:		
2101	Accounts payable	18	16
2103	Debt	503	471
2105	Other	3	3
	Non-Federal liabilities:		
2201	Accounts payable		
2207	Other		
2999	Total liabilities	524	490
	NET POSITION:		
3300	Cumulative results of operations		
4999	Total liabilities and net position	524	490

HOUSING GUARANTEED LOAN FINANCING ACCOUNT

Program and Financing (in millions of dollars)

Identification code 036–4129–0–3–704		2021 actual	2022 est.	2023 est.
	Obligations by program activity:			
0002	Losses on defaulted loans	262	4,433	1,378
0005	Payment to trustee reserve	1		
0009	Property sales expense	24	103	112
0010	Property management expense	46	92	97
0011	Property improvement expense		3	3
0012	Loans acquired		33	39
0013	Refunds	132	278	300
0091	Direct program activities, subtotal	465	4,942	1,929
	Credit program obligations:			
0711	Default claim payments on principal	140	1,398	1,518
0713	Payment of interest to Treasury	11		
0740	Negative subsidy obligations	2,114	236	
0742	Downward reestimates paid to receipt accounts	1,703	286	
0743	Interest on downward reestimates	264	42	
0791	Direct program activities, subtotal	4,232	1,962	1,518
0900	Total new obligations, unexpired accounts	4,697	6,904	3,447
	Budgetary resources:			
	Unobligated balance:			
1000	Unobligated balance brought forward, Oct 1	8,005	7,659	6,870
1022	Capital transfer of unobligated balances to general fund	–2		
1033	Recoveries of prior year paid obligations	6		
1070	Unobligated balance (total)	8,009	7,659	6,870
	Financing authority:			
	Appropriations, mandatory:			
1200	Appropriation	3		
	Borrowing authority, mandatory:			
1400	Borrowing authority	539	236	
	Spending authority from offsetting collections, mandatory:			
1800	Collected	4,347	6,115	4,953
1801	Change in uncollected payments, Federal sources	–3		
1825	Spending authority from offsetting collections applied to repay debt	–539	–236	
1850	Spending auth from offsetting collections, mand (total)	3,805	5,879	4,953
1900	Budget authority (total)	4,347	6,115	4,953
1930	Total budgetary resources available	12,356	13,774	11,823
	Memorandum (non-add) entries:			
1941	Unexpired unobligated balance, end of year	7,659	6,870	8,376
	Change in obligated balance:			
	Unpaid obligations:			
3000	Unpaid obligations, brought forward, Oct 1	137	117	132
3010	New obligations, unexpired accounts	4,697	6,904	3,447
3020	Outlays (gross)	–4,717	–6,889	–3,505
3050	Unpaid obligations, end of year	117	132	74
	Uncollected payments:			
3060	Uncollected pymts, Fed sources, brought forward, Oct 1	–4	–1	–1
3070	Change in uncollected pymts, Fed sources, unexpired	3		
3090	Uncollected pymts, Fed sources, end of year	–1	–1	–1
	Memorandum (non-add) entries:			
3100	Obligated balance, start of year	133	116	131
3200	Obligated balance, end of year	116	131	73
	Financing authority and disbursements, net:			
	Mandatory:			
4090	Budget authority, gross	4,347	6,115	4,953
	Financing disbursements:			
4110	Outlays, gross (total)	4,717	6,889	3,505
	Offsets against gross financing authority and disbursements:			
	Offsetting collections (collected) from:			
4120	Payments from program account	–657	–1,881	–246
4120	Recoveries from DLFA	–8	–203	–223
4122	Interest on uninvested funds	–144	–184	–198
4123	Funding fees	–3,211	–2,328	–2,289
4123	Cash sale of properties	–320	–1,180	–1,283
4123	Redemption of Properties/Other income and receivables	–13	–339	–714
4130	Offsets against gross budget authority and outlays (total)	–4,353	–6,115	–4,953
	Additional offsets against financing authority only (total):			
4140	Change in uncollected pymts, Fed sources, unexpired	3		
4143	Recoveries of prior year paid obligations, unexpired accounts	6		
4150	Additional offsets against budget authority only (total)	9		
4160	Budget authority, net (mandatory)	3		
4170	Outlays, net (mandatory)	364	774	–1,448
4180	Budget authority, net (total)	3		
4190	Outlays, net (total)	364	774	–1,448

Status of Guaranteed Loans (in millions of dollars)

Identification code 036–4129–0–3–704		2021 actual	2022 est.	2023 est.
	Position with respect to appropriations act limitation on commitments:			
2111	Guaranteed loan commitments from current-year authority	422,798	305,293	314,709
2150	Total guaranteed loan commitments	422,798	305,293	314,709

Benefits Programs—Continued
Federal Funds—Continued

HOUSING GUARANTEED LOAN FINANCING ACCOUNT—Continued

Status of Guaranteed Loans—Continued

Identification code 036–4129–0–3–704	2021 actual	2022 est.	2023 est.
2199 Guaranteed amount of guaranteed loan commitments	116,693	84,261	86,860
Cumulative balance of guaranteed loans outstanding:			
2210 Outstanding, start of year	816,524	862,728	807,616
2231 Disbursements of new guaranteed loans	422,798	305,293	314,709
2251 Repayments and prepayments	–376,192	–354,541	–340,665
Adjustments:			
2262 Terminations for default that result in acquisition of property	–140	–1,398	–1,518
2263 Terminations for default that result in claim payments	–262	–4,466	–1,417
2290 Outstanding, end of year	862,728	807,616	778,725
Memorandum:			
2299 Guaranteed amount of guaranteed loans outstanding, end of year	218,279	204,327	197,013

Balance Sheet (in millions of dollars)

Identification code 036–4129–0–3–704	2020 actual	2021 actual
ASSETS:		
Federal assets:		
1101 Fund balances with Treasury	8,137	7,774
Investments in U.S. securities:		
1106 Receivables, net	615	2,884
1206 Non-Federal assets: Receivables, net	9	7
Net value of assets related to post-1991 acquired defaulted guaranteed loans receivable:		
1504 Accounts receivable from foreclosed property		
1504 Foreclosed property	280	200
1599 Net present value of assets related to defaulted guaranteed loans	280	200
1999 Total assets	9,041	10,865
LIABILITIES:		
Federal liabilities:		
2103 Debt		
2105 Other liabilities	1,787	165
Non-Federal liabilities:		
2201 Accounts payable	137	116
2204 Non-federal liabilities for loan guarantees	7,117	10,584
2999 Total liabilities	9,041	10,865
NET POSITION:		
3300 Cumulative results of operations		
4999 Total liabilities and net position	9,041	10,865

HOUSING LIQUIDATING ACCOUNT

Program and Financing (in millions of dollars)

Identification code 036–4025–0–3–704	2021 actual	2022 est.	2023 est.
Budgetary resources:			
Unobligated balance:			
1000 Unobligated balance brought forward, Oct 1	1	1	
1022 Capital transfer of unobligated balances to general fund	–2	–1	
1033 Recoveries of prior year paid obligations	1		
Budget authority:			
Spending authority from offsetting collections, mandatory:			
1800 Collected	6	4	
1820 Capital transfer of spending authority from offsetting collections to general fund	–5	–4	
1850 Spending auth from offsetting collections, mand (total)	1		
1930 Total budgetary resources available	1		
Memorandum (non-add) entries:			
1941 Unexpired unobligated balance, end of year	1		
Change in obligated balance:			
Unpaid obligations:			
3000 Unpaid obligations, brought forward, Oct 1	1		
3020 Outlays (gross)	–1		
Memorandum (non-add) entries:			
3100 Obligated balance, start of year	1		

Identification code 036–4025–0–3–704	2021 actual	2022 est.	2023 est.
Budget authority and outlays, net:			
Mandatory:			
4090 Budget authority, gross	1		
Outlays, gross:			
4101 Outlays from mandatory balances	1		
Offsets against gross budget authority and outlays:			
Offsetting collections (collected) from:			
4123 Sale of homes, cash	–1		
4123 Interest collection on Veteran liability debts	–3	–2	
4123 Principal collection on Veteran liability debts	–3	–2	
4130 Offsets against gross budget authority and outlays (total)	–7	–4	
Additional offsets against gross budget authority only:			
4143 Recoveries of prior year paid obligations, unexpired accounts	1		
4160 Budget authority, net (mandatory)	–5	–4	
4170 Outlays, net (mandatory)	–6	–4	
4180 Budget authority, net (total)	–5	–4	
4190 Outlays, net (total)	–6	–4	
Memorandum (non-add) entries:			
5010 Total investments, SOY: non-Fed securities: Market value	140	140	140
5011 Total investments, EOY: non-Fed securities: Market value	140	140	

Status of Direct Loans (in millions of dollars)

Identification code 036–4025–0–3–704	2021 actual	2022 est.	2023 est.
Cumulative balance of direct loans outstanding:	*		
1210 Outstanding, start of year	37	37	33
1251 Repayments: Repayments and prepayments		–4	
1290 Outstanding, end of year	37	33	33

Status of Guaranteed Loans (in millions of dollars)

Identification code 036–4025–0–3–704	2021 actual	2022 est.	2023 est.
Cumulative balance of guaranteed loans outstanding:			
2210 Outstanding, start of year	3		
2251 Repayments and prepayments	–3		
2262 Adjustments: Terminations for default that result in acquisition of property			
2290 Outstanding, end of year			
Memorandum:			
2299 Guaranteed amount of guaranteed loans outstanding, end of year			
Addendum:			
Cumulative balance of defaulted guaranteed loans that result in loans receivable:			
2310 Outstanding, start of year	1	1	
2331 Disbursements for guaranteed loan claims			
2351 Repayments of loans receivable			
2364 Other adjustments, net		–1	
2390 Outstanding, end of year	1		

Balance Sheet (in millions of dollars)

Identification code 036–4025–0–3–704	2020 actual	2021 actual
ASSETS:		
1101 Federal assets: Fund balances with Treasury	2	2
Non-Federal assets:		
1201 Investments in non-Federal securities, net	106	106
1206 Receivables, net	1	1
1601 Direct loans, gross	37	37
1602 Interest receivable	31	31
1603 Allowance for estimated uncollectible loans and interest (-)	–31	–31
1604 Direct loans and interest receivable, net	37	37
1605 Accounts receivable from foreclosed property		
1699 Value of assets related to direct loans	37	37
1701 Defaulted guaranteed loans, gross	1	1
1703 Allowance for estimated uncollectible loans and interest (-)		
1704 Defaulted guaranteed loans and interest receivable, net	1	1
1706 Foreclosed property		
1799 Value of assets related to loan guarantees	1	1
1999 Total assets	147	147

DEPARTMENT OF VETERANS AFFAIRS

Benefits Programs—Continued
Federal Funds—Continued

1061

		2021 actual	2022 est.
	LIABILITIES:		
	Non-Federal liabilities:		
2201	Accounts payable	1	1
2204	Liabilities for loan guarantees	146	146
2207	Other Deferred Revenue		
2999	Total liabilities	147	147
	NET POSITION:		
3300	Cumulative results of operations		
4999	Total liabilities and net position	147	147

NATIVE AMERICAN VETERAN HOUSING LOAN PROGRAM ACCOUNT

For administrative expenses to carry out the direct loan program authorized by subchapter V of chapter 37 of title 38, United States Code, $1,186,000.

VOCATIONAL REHABILITATION LOANS PROGRAM ACCOUNT

For the cost of direct loans, $7,171, as authorized by chapter 31 of title 38, United States Code: Provided, That such costs, including the cost of modifying such loans, shall be as defined in section 502 of the Congressional Budget Act of 1974: Provided further, That funds made available under this heading are available to subsidize gross obligations for the principal amount of direct loans not to exceed $942,330.

In addition, for administrative expenses necessary to carry out the direct loan program, $445,698, which may be paid to the appropriation for "General Operating Expenses, Veterans Benefits Administration".

Note.—A full-year 2022 appropriation for this account was not enacted at the time the Budget was prepared; therefore, the Budget assumes this account is operating under the Continuing Appropriations Act, 2022 (Division A of Public Law 117–43, as amended). The amounts included for 2022 reflect the annualized level provided by the continuing resolution.

Program and Financing (in millions of dollars)

Identification code 036–1120–0–1–704		2021 actual	2022 est.	2023 est.
	Obligations by program activity:			
	Credit program obligations:			
0705	Reestimates of direct loan subsidy	1	3	
0706	Interest on reestimates of direct loan subsidy		1	
0709	Administrative expenses	2	2	2
0900	Total new obligations, unexpired accounts (object class 25.2)	3	6	2
	Budgetary resources:			
	Unobligated balance:			
1000	Unobligated balance brought forward, Oct 1	2	2	1
	Budget authority:			
	Appropriations, discretionary:			
1100	Appropriation	2	2	2
	Appropriations, mandatory:			
1200	Appropriation	1	3	
1900	Budget authority (total)	3	5	2
1930	Total budgetary resources available	5	7	3
	Memorandum (non-add) entries:			
1941	Unexpired unobligated balance, end of year	2	1	1
	Change in obligated balance:			
	Unpaid obligations:			
3000	Unpaid obligations, brought forward, Oct 1		1	1
3010	New obligations, unexpired accounts	3	6	2
3020	Outlays (gross)	–2	–6	–2
3050	Unpaid obligations, end of year	1	1	1
	Memorandum (non-add) entries:			
3100	Obligated balance, start of year		1	1
3200	Obligated balance, end of year	1	1	1
	Budget authority and outlays, net:			
	Discretionary:			
4000	Budget authority, gross	2	2	2
	Outlays, gross:			
4010	Outlays from new discretionary authority	1	2	2
4011	Outlays from discretionary balances		1	
4020	Outlays, gross (total)	1	3	2
	Mandatory:			
4090	Budget authority, gross	1	3	
	Outlays, gross:			
4100	Outlays from new mandatory authority	1	3	
4180	Budget authority, net (total)	3	5	2
4190	Outlays, net (total)	2	6	2

Summary of Loan Levels, Subsidy Budget Authority and Outlays by Program (in millions of dollars)

Identification code 036–1120–0–1–704		2021 actual	2022 est.	2023 est.
	Direct loan levels supportable by subsidy budget authority:			
115002	Native American Direct Loans	12	11	11
115003	Vocational Rehabilitation	1	2	1
115999	Total direct loan levels	13	13	12
	Direct loan subsidy (in percent):			
132002	Native American Direct Loans	–20.25	–17.62	–17.15
132003	Vocational Rehabilitation	1.37	0.17	0.76
132999	Weighted average subsidy rate	–18.59	–14.88	–15.66
	Direct loan subsidy budget authority:			
133002	Native American Direct Loans	–3	–2	–2
133999	Total subsidy budget authority	–3	–2	–2
	Direct loan subsidy outlays:			
134002	Native American Direct Loans	–2	–2	–2
134999	Total subsidy outlays	–2	–2	–2
	Direct loan reestimates:			
135002	Native American Direct Loans		3	
135999	Total direct loan reestimates		3	
	Administrative expense data:			
3510	Budget authority	2	2	2
3590	Outlays from new authority	1	2	2

The Native American Veteran Housing Loan program provides direct loans to veterans living on trust lands under 38 U.S.C. chapter 37, section 3761. These loans are available to purchase, construct, or improve homes to be occupied as the veteran's residence. This program began as a pilot in 1993 and was made permanent on June 15, 2006, through Public Law 109–233.

The Vocational Rehabilitation Loan Program provides temporary loans to cover the costs of subsistence, tuition, books, supplies, and equipment in conjunction with service-connected disability benefits provided to veterans participating in the Department of Veterans Affairs' Veteran Readiness and Employment Program as authorized by chapter 31 of title 38, United States Code. Repayment of these loans is made in monthly installments, without interest, through deductions from future payments of compensation, pension, subsistence allowance, educational assistance allowance, or retired pay.

NATIVE AMERICAN DIRECT LOAN FINANCING ACCOUNT

Program and Financing (in millions of dollars)

Identification code 036–4130–0–3–704		2021 actual	2022 est.	2023 est.
	Obligations by program activity:			
	Credit program obligations:			
0710	Direct loan obligations	12	12	12
0713	Payment of interest to Treasury	3	3	3
0740	Negative subsidy obligations	3	2	2
0742	Downward reestimates paid to receipt accounts	1		
0900	Total new obligations, unexpired accounts	19	17	17
	Budgetary resources:			
	Unobligated balance:			
1000	Unobligated balance brought forward, Oct 1	10	14	14
1023	Unobligated balances applied to repay debt	–8		
1070	Unobligated balance (total)	2	14	14
	Financing authority:			
	Borrowing authority, mandatory:			
1400	Borrowing authority	24	14	17
1422	Borrowing authority applied to repay debt	–2		
1440	Borrowing authority, mandatory (total)	22	14	17
	Spending authority from offsetting collections, mandatory:			
1800	Collected	16	11	8
1825	Spending authority from offsetting collections applied to repay debt	–7	–8	–8
1850	Spending auth from offsetting collections, mand (total)	9	3	
1900	Budget authority (total)	31	17	17
1930	Total budgetary resources available	33	31	31

Benefits Programs—Continued
Federal Funds—Continued

NATIVE AMERICAN DIRECT LOAN FINANCING ACCOUNT—Continued

Program and Financing—Continued

Identification code 036–4130–0–3–704	2021 actual	2022 est.	2023 est.
Memorandum (non-add) entries:			
1941 Unexpired unobligated balance, end of year	14	14	14
Change in obligated balance:			
Unpaid obligations:			
3000 Unpaid obligations, brought forward, Oct 1	2	2	....
3010 New obligations, unexpired accounts	19	17	17
3020 Outlays (gross)	–19	–19	–17
3050 Unpaid obligations, end of year	2	....	....
Memorandum (non-add) entries:			
3100 Obligated balance, start of year	2	2	....
3200 Obligated balance, end of year	2	....	....
Financing authority and disbursements, net:			
Mandatory:			
4090 Budget authority, gross	31	17	17
Financing disbursements:			
4110 Outlays, gross (total)	19	19	17
Offsets against gross financing authority and disbursements:			
Offsetting collections (collected) from:			
4120 Federal sources	–1	–3	....
4122 Interest on uninvested funds	–1	....	....
4123 Non-federal sources - Repayments and prepayments of principal	–11	–5	–5
4123 Non-Federal sources - Interest received on loans	–3	–3	–3
4130 Offsets against gross budget authority and outlays (total)	–16	–11	–8
4160 Budget authority, net (mandatory)	15	6	9
4170 Outlays, net (mandatory)	3	8	9
4180 Budget authority, net (total)	15	6	9
4190 Outlays, net (total)	3	8	9

Status of Direct Loans (in millions of dollars)

Identification code 036–4130–0–3–704	2021 actual	2022 est.	2023 est.
Position with respect to appropriations act limitation on obligations:			
1111 Direct loan obligations from current-year authority	12	12	12
1150 Total direct loan obligations	12	12	12
Cumulative balance of direct loans outstanding:			
1210 Outstanding, start of year	65	67	76
1231 Disbursements: Direct loan disbursements	13	14	11
1251 Repayments: Repayments and prepayments	–11	–5	–5
1290 Outstanding, end of year	67	76	82

Balance Sheet (in millions of dollars)

Identification code 036–4130–0–3–704	2020 actual	2021 actual
ASSETS:		
Federal assets:		
1101 Fund balances with Treasury	12	15
Investments in U.S. securities:		
1106 Receivables, net	....	....
Net value of assets related to post-1991 direct loans receivable:		
1401 Direct loans receivable, gross	65	67
1402 Interest receivable	2	2
1405 Other assets	2	2
1499 Net present value of assets related to direct loans	69	71
1999 Total assets	81	86
LIABILITIES:		
Federal liabilities:		
2103 Federal liabilities debt	81	86
2105 Other liabilities	....	....
2999 Total liabilities	81	86
NET POSITION:		
3300 Cumulative results of operations	....	....
4999 Total liabilities and net position	81	86

TRANSITIONAL HOUSING DIRECT LOAN FINANCING ACCOUNT

Program and Financing (in millions of dollars)

Identification code 036–4258–0–3–704	2021 actual	2022 est.	2023 est.
Obligations by program activity:			
0001 Direct program activity	....	1	1
0900 Total new obligations, unexpired accounts	....	1	1
Budgetary resources:			
Unobligated balance:			
1000 Unobligated balance brought forward, Oct 1	4	4	4
Financing authority:			
Spending authority from offsetting collections, mandatory:			
1800 Collected	....	1	1
1930 Total budgetary resources available	4	5	5
Memorandum (non-add) entries:			
1941 Unexpired unobligated balance, end of year	4	4	4
Change in obligated balance:			
Unpaid obligations:			
3010 New obligations, unexpired accounts	....	1	1
3020 Outlays (gross)	....	–1	–1
Financing authority and disbursements, net:			
Mandatory:			
4090 Budget authority, gross	....	....	....
Financing disbursements:			
4110 Outlays, gross (total)	....	1	1
Offsets against gross financing authority and disbursements:			
Offsetting collections (collected) from:			
4123 Non-Federal sources	....	–1	–1
4180 Budget authority, net (total)	....	....	....
4190 Outlays, net (total)	....	....	....

Status of Direct Loans (in millions of dollars)

Identification code 036–4258–0–3–704	2021 actual	2022 est.	2023 est.
Position with respect to appropriations act limitation on obligations:			
1121 Limitation available from carry-forward	95	95	95
1143 Unobligated limitation carried forward	–95	–95	–95
Cumulative balance of direct loans outstanding:			
1210 Outstanding, start of year	4	4	4
1290 Outstanding, end of year	4	4	4

Balance Sheet (in millions of dollars)

Identification code 036–4258–0–3–704	2020 actual	2021 actual
ASSETS:		
1101 Federal assets: Fund balances with Treasury	5	4
1401 Net value of assets related to post-1991 direct loans receivable:	4	4
Direct loans receivable, gross		
1999 Total assets	9	8
LIABILITIES:		
Federal liabilities:		
2103 Debt	5	4
2105 Loan Guaranty/Other Liabilities	4	4
2999 Total liabilities	9	8
4999 Total liabilities and net position	9	8

VOCATIONAL REHABILITATION DIRECT LOAN FINANCING ACCOUNT

Program and Financing (in millions of dollars)

Identification code 036–4112–0–3–702	2021 actual	2022 est.	2023 est.
Obligations by program activity:			
Credit program obligations:			
0710 Direct loan obligations	1	2	1
0900 Total new obligations, unexpired accounts	1	2	1
Budgetary resources:			
Unobligated balance:			
1000 Unobligated balance brought forward, Oct 1	1	....	1

DEPARTMENT OF VETERANS AFFAIRS

Benefits Programs—Continued
Trust Funds

1063

		2021 actual	2022 est.	2023 est.
1023	Unobligated balances applied to repay debt	−1		
1070	Unobligated balance (total)			1
	Financing authority:			
	Borrowing authority, mandatory:			
1400	Authority to borrow (indefinite)	2	2	1
1422	Borrowing authority applied to repay debt	−1		
1440	Borrowing authority, mandatory (total)	1	2	1
	Spending authority from offsetting collections, mandatory:			
1800	Collected	1	2	1
1825	Spending authority from offsetting collections applied to repay debt	−1	−1	−1
1850	Spending auth from offsetting collections, mand (total)		1	
1900	Budget authority (total)	1	3	1
1930	Total budgetary resources available	1	3	2
	Memorandum (non-add) entries:			
1941	Unexpired unobligated balance, end of year		1	1
	Change in obligated balance:			
	Unpaid obligations:			
3010	New obligations, unexpired accounts	1	2	1
3020	Outlays (gross)	−1	−2	−1
	Financing authority and disbursements, net:			
	Mandatory:			
4090	Budget authority, gross	1	3	1
	Financing disbursements:			
4110	Outlays, gross (total)	1	2	1
	Offsets against gross financing authority and disbursements:			
	Offsetting collections (collected) from:			
4123	Repayments and prepayments of principal	−1	−2	−1
4180	Budget authority, net (total)		1	
4190	Outlays, net (total)			

Status of Direct Loans (in millions of dollars)

Identification code 036–4112–0–3–702	2021 actual	2022 est.	2023 est.
Position with respect to appropriations act limitation on obligations:			
1111 Direct loan obligations from current-year authority	1	2	1
1150 Total direct loan obligations	1	2	1
Cumulative balance of direct loans outstanding:			
1210 Outstanding, start of year	1	1	1
1231 Disbursements: Direct loan disbursements	1	2	1
1251 Repayments: Repayments and prepayments	−1	−2	−1
1290 Outstanding, end of year	1	1	1

Balance Sheet (in millions of dollars)

Identification code 036–4112–0–3–702	2020 actual	2021 actual
ASSETS:		
Federal assets:		
Investments in U.S. securities:		
1104 Investments US Securities		
1401 Net value of assets related to post-1991 direct loans receivable:		
Direct loans receivable, gross	1	1
1999 Total assets	1	1
LIABILITIES:		
2103 Federal liabilities: Debt	1	1
4999 Total liabilities and net position	1	1

Trust Funds

POST-VIETNAM ERA VETERANS EDUCATION ACCOUNT

Program and Financing (in millions of dollars)

Identification code 036–8133–0–7–702	2021 actual	2022 est.	2023 est.
Obligations by program activity:			
0001 Disenrollments	1	1	1
0900 Total new obligations, unexpired accounts (object class 44.0)	1	1	1
Budgetary resources:			
Unobligated balance:			
1000 Unobligated balance brought forward, Oct 1	62	61	60
1930 Total budgetary resources available	62	61	60

		2021 actual	2022 est.	2023 est.
	Memorandum (non-add) entries:			
1941	Unexpired unobligated balance, end of year	61	60	59
	Change in obligated balance:			
	Unpaid obligations:			
3000	Unpaid obligations, brought forward, Oct 1	1	1	1
3010	New obligations, unexpired accounts	1	1	1
3020	Outlays (gross)	−1	−1	−1
3050	Unpaid obligations, end of year	1	1	1
	Memorandum (non-add) entries:			
3100	Obligated balance, start of year	1	1	1
3200	Obligated balance, end of year	1	1	1
	Budget authority and outlays, net:			
	Mandatory:			
	Outlays, gross:			
4101	Outlays from mandatory balances	1	1	1
4180	Budget authority, net (total)			
4190	Outlays, net (total)	1	1	1

The Post-Vietnam Era Veterans' Educational Assistance Program was established under Public Law 94–502, Veterans' Education and Employment Assistance Act, 1976. This program consists of voluntary contributions by eligible servicemembers and matching contributions provided by the Department of Defense and provides educational assistance payments to participants who entered the service after December 31, 1976. Chapter 32, title 38, U.S.C. Section 901 is a non-contributory program with educational assistance provided by the Department of Defense. Public Law 99–576, enacted October 28, 1986, closed the program permanently for new enrollments effective March 31, 1987. The estimated activity in the fund follows:

CONTRIBUTIONS, PARTICIPANTS, DISENROLLMENTS, REFUNDS AND TRAINEES

	2021 actual	2022 est.	2023 est.
Total program obligations (in thousands)	$756	$1,444	$1,430
Number of disenrollments	831	1,060	1,049
Total refunds (in thousands)	$756	$1,444	$1,430
Average Refund	$910	$1,363	$1,363
Total trainees	0	0	0
Total trainee cost (in thousands)	$0	$0	$0
Average trainee cost	$0	$0	$0
Section 901 trainees	0	0	0
Total Section 901 trainee cost (in thousands)	$0	$0	$0
Average Section 901 trainee cost	$0	$0	$0

NATIONAL SERVICE LIFE INSURANCE FUND

Special and Trust Fund Receipts (in millions of dollars)

Identification code 036–8132–0–7–701	2021 actual	2022 est.	2023 est.
0100 Balance, start of year	1,461	1,094	788
Receipts:			
Current law:			
1130 NSLI Fund, Premium and Other Receipts	24	32	23
1140 NSLI Fund, Interest	61	49	32
1199 Total current law receipts	85	81	55
1999 Total receipts	85	81	55
2000 Total: Balances and receipts	1,546	1,175	843
Appropriations:			
Current law:			
2101 National Service Life Insurance Fund	−85	−80	−55
2103 National Service Life Insurance Fund	−366	−307	−244
2199 Total current law appropriations	−451	−387	−299
2999 Total appropriations	−451	−387	−299
5098 Rounding adjustment	−1		
5099 Balance, end of year	1,094	788	544

Program and Financing (in millions of dollars)

Identification code 036–8132–0–7–701	2021 actual	2022 est.	2023 est.
Obligations by program activity:			
0001 Death claims	298	247	181
0002 Disability claims	1	1	1
0003 Matured endowments	99	97	86

NATIONAL SERVICE LIFE INSURANCE FUND—Continued
Program and Financing—Continued

Identification code 036–8132–0–7–701	2021 actual	2022 est.	2023 est.
0004 Cash surrenders	14	13	9
0005 Dividends	19	12	9
0006 Interest paid on dividend credits and deposits	8	6	4
0007 Payment to general operating expenses	10	8	6
0091 Total operating expenses	449	384	296
0201 Capital investment: Policy loans	2	3	2
0799 Total direct obligations	451	387	298
0801 Death claims	14	19	16
0803 Matured endowments	5	7	7
0804 Cash surrenders	1	1	1
0805 Dividends	1	1	1
0806 Interest paid on dividend credits and deposits	....	1	....
0807 Payment to general operating expenses	1	1	1
0899 Total reimbursable obligations	22	30	26
0900 Total new obligations, unexpired accounts	473	417	324
Budgetary resources:			
Unobligated balance:			
1021 Recoveries of prior year unpaid obligations	1	....	....
Budget authority:			
Appropriations, mandatory:			
1201 Appropriation (special or trust fund)	85	80	55
1203 Appropriation (previously unavailable)(special or trust)	366	307	244
1260 Appropriations, mandatory (total)	451	387	299
Spending authority from offsetting collections, mandatory:			
1800 Collected	21	30	26
1900 Budget authority (total)	472	417	325
1930 Total budgetary resources available	473	417	325
Memorandum (non-add) entries:			
1941 Unexpired unobligated balance, end of year	....	....	1
Change in obligated balance:			
Unpaid obligations:			
3000 Unpaid obligations, brought forward, Oct 1	492	395	307
3010 New obligations, unexpired accounts	473	417	324
3020 Outlays (gross)	–569	–505	–416
3040 Recoveries of prior year unpaid obligations, unexpired	–1	....	....
3050 Unpaid obligations, end of year	395	307	215
Memorandum (non-add) entries:			
3100 Obligated balance, start of year	492	395	307
3200 Obligated balance, end of year	395	307	215
Budget authority and outlays, net:			
Mandatory:			
4090 Budget authority, gross	472	417	325
Outlays, gross:			
4100 Outlays from new mandatory authority	106	110	172
4101 Outlays from mandatory balances	463	395	244
4110 Outlays, gross (total)	569	505	416
Offsets against gross budget authority and outlays:			
Offsetting collections (collected) from:			
4123 Non-Federal sources	–21	–30	–26
4180 Budget authority, net (total)	451	387	299
4190 Outlays, net (total)	548	475	390
Memorandum (non-add) entries:			
5000 Total investments, SOY: Federal securities: Par value	1,946	1,476	1,053
5001 Total investments, EOY: Federal securities: Par value	1,476	1,053	718

Note.—Department of Veterans Affairs insurance policy loans are not an extension of Federal credit. Credit schedules previously shown for this account have been discontinued.

The National Service Life Insurance Fund was established in 1940. It is for the World War II servicemembers' and veterans' insurance program. Over 22 million policies were issued under this program. Activity of the fund reflects a declining claim workload. The trend in the number and amount of policies in force is shown as follows:

POLICIES AND INSURANCE IN FORCE

	2021 actual	2022 est.	2023 est.
Number of policies	90,489	65,552	46,234
Insurance in force (dollars in millions)	$1,149	$1,171	$840

This fund is operated on a commercial basis to the extent possible. The income of the fund is derived from premium receipts, interest on investments, and payments which are made to the fund from the Veterans Insurance and Indemnities appropriation.

Assets of the fund, which are largely invested in special interest-bearing Treasury securities and in policy loans, are expected to decrease from an estimated $1,123 million as of September 30, 2022 to $786 million as of September 30, 2023. The actuarial estimate of policy obligations as of September 30, 2023, totals $744 million, leaving a balance of $42 million for contingency reserves.

Status of Funds (in millions of dollars)

Identification code 036–8132–0–7–701	2021 actual	2022 est.	2023 est.
Unexpended balance, start of year:			
0100 Balance, start of year	1,953	1,489	1,095
0999 Total balance, start of year	1,953	1,489	1,095
Cash income during the year:			
Current law:			
Receipts:			
1130 NSLI Fund, Premium and Other Receipts	24	32	23
1130 National Service Life Insurance Fund	21	30	26
1150 NSLI Fund, Interest	61	49	32
1199 Income under present law	106	111	81
1999 Total cash income	106	111	81
Cash outgo during year:			
Current law:			
2100 National Service Life Insurance Fund [Budget Acct]	–569	–505	–416
2199 Outgo under current law	–569	–505	–416
2999 Total cash outgo (-)	–569	–505	–416
Surplus or deficit:			
3110 Excluding interest	–524	–443	–367
3120 Interest	61	49	32
3199 Subtotal, surplus or deficit	–463	–394	–335
3298 Reconciliation adjustment	–1	....	....
3299 Total adjustments	–1	....	....
3999 Total change in fund balance	–464	–394	–335
Unexpended balance, end of year:			
4100 Uninvested balance (net), end of year	13	42	42
4200 National Service Life Insurance Fund	1,476	1,053	718
4999 Total balance, end of year	1,489	1,095	760

Object Classification (in millions of dollars)

Identification code 036–8132–0–7–701	2021 actual	2022 est.	2023 est.
Direct obligations:			
33.0 Investments and loans	2	3	2
42.0 Insurance claims and indemnities	412	358	277
43.0 Interest and dividends	37	26	19
99.0 Direct obligations	451	387	298
99.0 Reimbursable obligations	22	30	26
99.9 Total new obligations, unexpired accounts	473	417	324

UNITED STATES GOVERNMENT LIFE INSURANCE FUND

Special and Trust Fund Receipts (in millions of dollars)

Identification code 036–8150–0–7–701	2021 actual	2022 est.	2023 est.
0100 Balance, start of year	1	1	1
2000 Total: Balances and receipts	1	1	1
5099 Balance, end of year	1	1	1

DEPARTMENT OF VETERANS AFFAIRS

Program and Financing (in millions of dollars)

Identification code 036–8150–0–7–701	2021 actual	2022 est.	2023 est.
Change in obligated balance:			
Unpaid obligations:			
3000 Unpaid obligations, brought forward, Oct 1	1	1	....
3020 Outlays (gross)	....	–1	....
3050 Unpaid obligations, end of year	1	....	....
Memorandum (non-add) entries:			
3100 Obligated balance, start of year	1	1	....
3200 Obligated balance, end of year	1	....	....
Budget authority and outlays, net:			
Mandatory:			
Outlays, gross:			
4101 Outlays from mandatory balances	....	1	....
4180 Budget authority, net (total)	....	....	....
4190 Outlays, net (total)	....	1	....
Memorandum (non-add) entries:			
5000 Total investments, SOY: Federal securities: Par value	2	2	1
5001 Total investments, EOY: Federal securities: Par value	2	1	1

Note.—Department of Veterans Affairs insurance policy loans are not an extension of Federal credit. Credit schedules previously shown for this account have been discontinued.

The United States Government Life Insurance Fund (USGLI) was established in 1919 to receive premiums and pay claims on insurance issued under the provisions of the War Risk Insurance Act. The general decline in the activity of the fund is indicated in the table below. All USGLI program policies have reached the maturity age. However, the program will continue to disburse insurance annuity benefits to beneficiaries.

POLICIES AND INSURANCE IN FORCE

	2021 actual	2022 est.	2023 est.
Number of policies	3	0	0
Insurance in force (dollars in millions)	$.013	$0	$0

The fund is operated on a commercial basis to the extent possible. The income of the fund is derived from interest on investments. Effective January 1, 1983, premiums were discontinued because reserves held in the fund were adequate to meet future liabilities of the program.

Assets of the fund, which are largely invested in interest-bearing securities and policy loans, are estimated to decrease from $1.3 million as of September 30, 2022, to $1.1 million as of September 30, 2023, as an increasing number of policies mature through death or disability. The actuarial evaluation of policy obligations as of September 30, 2023, totals $0.7 million, leaving a balance of $0.4 million for contingency reserves.

Status of Funds (in millions of dollars)

Identification code 036–8150–0–7–701	2021 actual	2022 est.	2023 est.
Unexpended balance, start of year:			
0100 Balance, start of year	2	2	1
0999 Total balance, start of year	2	2	1
Cash outgo during year:			
Current law:			
2100 United States Government Life Insurance Fund [Budget Acct]	....	–1	....
2199 Outgo under current law	....	–1	....
2999 Total cash outgo (-)	....	–1	....
Surplus or deficit:			
3110 Excluding interest	....	–1	....
3199 Subtotal, surplus or deficit	....	–1	....
3999 Total change in fund balance	....	–1	....
Unexpended balance, end of year:			
4100 Uninvested balance (net), end of year	....	....	....
4200 United States Government Life Insurance Fund	2	1	1
4999 Total balance, end of year	2	1	1

VETERANS SPECIAL LIFE INSURANCE FUND

Program and Financing (in millions of dollars)

Identification code 036–8455–0–8–701	2021 actual	2022 est.	2023 est.
Obligations by program activity:			
0801 Death claims	142	131	121
0802 Cash surrenders	9	7	4
0803 Dividends	10	8	8
0804 All other	12	11	10
0805 Payments to insurance account	8	8	6
0806 Capital investment	2	3	3
0900 Total new obligations, unexpired accounts	183	168	152
Budgetary resources:			
Unobligated balance:			
1000 Unobligated balance brought forward, Oct 1	885	766	661
Budget authority:			
Spending authority from offsetting collections, mandatory:			
1800 Collected	66	63	51
1801 Change in uncollected payments, Federal sources	–2	....	....
1850 Spending auth from offsetting collections, mand (total)	64	63	51
1930 Total budgetary resources available	949	829	712
Memorandum (non-add) entries:			
1941 Unexpired unobligated balance, end of year	766	661	560
Change in obligated balance:			
Unpaid obligations:			
3000 Unpaid obligations, brought forward, Oct 1	351	310	266
3010 New obligations, unexpired accounts	183	168	152
3020 Outlays (gross)	–224	–212	–174
3050 Unpaid obligations, end of year	310	266	244
Uncollected payments:			
3060 Uncollected pymts, Fed sources, brought forward, Oct 1	–12	–10	–10
3070 Change in uncollected pymts, Fed sources, unexpired	2	....	....
3090 Uncollected pymts, Fed sources, end of year	–10	–10	–10
Memorandum (non-add) entries:			
3100 Obligated balance, start of year	339	300	256
3200 Obligated balance, end of year	300	256	234
Budget authority and outlays, net:			
Mandatory:			
4090 Budget authority, gross	64	63	51
Outlays, gross:			
4100 Outlays from new mandatory authority	64	63	51
4101 Outlays from mandatory balances	160	149	123
4110 Outlays, gross (total)	224	212	174
Offsets against gross budget authority and outlays:			
Offsetting collections (collected) from:			
4121 Interest on Federal securities	–45	–40	–32
4123 Non–Federal sources	–21	–2	–2
4123 Non–Federal sources	....	–13	–11
4123 Non–Federal sources	....	–8	–6
4130 Offsets against gross budget authority and outlays (total)	–66	–63	–51
Additional offsets against gross budget authority only:			
4140 Change in uncollected pymts, Fed sources, unexpired	2	....	....
4170 Outlays, net (mandatory)	158	149	123
4180 Budget authority, net (total)	....	....	....
4190 Outlays, net (total)	158	149	123
Memorandum (non-add) entries:			
5000 Total investments, SOY: Federal securities: Par value	1,222	1,064	917
5001 Total investments, EOY: Federal securities: Par value	1,064	917	794

Note.—Department of Veterans Affairs insurance policy loans are not an extension of Federal credit. Credit schedules previously shown for this account have been discontinued.

The Veterans' Special Life Insurance Fund finances the payment of claims on life insurance policies issued before January 3, 1957, to veterans who served in the Armed Forces subsequent to April 1, 1951. No new policies can be issued.

Benefit program:

Death claims.—Represents payments to designated beneficiaries.

Cash surrenders.—A policyholder may terminate his or her insurance by cashing in the policy for its cash value.

VETERANS SPECIAL LIFE INSURANCE FUND—Continued

Dividends.—Policyholders participate in the distribution of annual dividends.

All other.—Classified in this category are payments to policyholders who: (a) hold endowment policies which have matured; (b) have purchased total disability income coverage and subsequently become disabled; and (c) are paid interest on dividend credits and deposits.

The following table reflects the decrease in the number of policies and the amounts of insurance in force:

POLICIES AND INSURANCE IN FORCE

	2021 actual	2022 est.	2023 est.
Number of policies	59,612	50,717	42,147
Insurance in force (dollars in millions)	$896	$775	$645

Financing.—Payments from this fund are financed primarily from premium receipts and interest on investments.

Object Classification (in millions of dollars)

Identification code 036–8455–0–8–701		2021 actual	2022 est.	2023 est.
	Reimbursable obligations:			
33.0	Investments and loans	3	3	3
42.0	Insurance claims and indemnities	159	147	133
43.0	Interest and dividends	21	18	16
99.9	Total new obligations, unexpired accounts	183	168	152

DEPARTMENTAL ADMINISTRATION

Federal Funds

CONSTRUCTION, MAJOR PROJECTS

For constructing, altering, extending, and improving any of the facilities, including parking projects, under the jurisdiction or for the use of the Department of Veterans Affairs, or for any of the purposes set forth in sections 316, 2404, 2406 and chapter 81 of title 38, United States Code, not otherwise provided for, including planning, architectural and engineering services, construction management services, maintenance or guarantee period services costs associated with equipment guarantees provided under the project, services of claims analysts, offsite utility and storm drainage system construction costs, and site acquisition, where the estimated cost of a project is more than the amount set forth in section 8104(a)(3)(A) of title 38, United States Code, or where funds for a project were made available in a previous major project appropriation, $1,447,890,000, of which $731,722,000 shall remain available until September 30, 2027, and of which $716,168,000 shall remain available until expended, of which $1,500,000 shall be available for seismic improvement projects and seismic program management activities, including for projects that would otherwise be funded by the Construction, Minor Projects, Medical Facilities or National Cemetery Administration accounts: Provided, That except for advance planning activities, including needs assessments which may or may not lead to capital investments, and other capital asset management related activities, including portfolio development and management activities, and planning, cost estimating, and design for major medical facility projects and major medical facility leases and investment strategy studies funded through the advance planning fund and the planning and design activities funded through the design fund, staffing expenses, and funds provided for the purchase, security, and maintenance of land for the National Cemetery Administration and the Veterans Health Administration through the land acquisition line items, none of the funds made available under this heading shall be used for any project that has not been notified to Congress through the budgetary process or that has not been approved by the Congress through statute, joint resolution, or in the explanatory statement accompanying such Act and presented to the President at the time of enrollment: Provided further, That such sums as may be necessary shall be available to reimburse the "General Administration" account for payment of salaries and expenses of all Office of Construction and Facilities Management employees to support the full range of capital infrastructure services provided, including minor construction and leasing services: Provided further, That funds made available under this heading for fiscal year 2023, for each approved project shall be obligated: (1) by the awarding of a construction documents contract by September 30, 2023; and (2) by the awarding of a construction contract by September 30, 2024: Provided further, That the Secretary of Veterans Affairs shall promptly submit to the Committees on Appropriations of both Houses of Congress a written report on any approved major construction project for which obligations are not incurred within the time limitations established above: Provided further, That notwithstanding the requirements of section 8104(a) of title 38, United States Code, amounts made available under this heading for seismic improvement projects and seismic program management activities shall be available for the completion of both new and existing seismic projects of the Department.

Note.—A full-year 2022 appropriation for this account was not enacted at the time the Budget was prepared; therefore, the Budget assumes this account is operating under the Continuing Appropriations Act, 2022 (Division A of Public Law 117–43, as amended). The amounts included for 2022 reflect the annualized level provided by the continuing resolution.

Program and Financing (in millions of dollars)

Identification code 036–0110–0–1–703		2021 actual	2022 est.	2023 est.
	Obligations by program activity:			
0001	Medical programs	1,074	1,766	1,707
0002	National cemeteries	163	84	241
0005	Staff offices	4	12	11
0799	Total direct obligations	1,241	1,862	1,959
0900	Total new obligations, unexpired accounts	1,241	1,862	1,959
	Budgetary resources:			
	Unobligated balance:			
1000	Unobligated balance brought forward, Oct 1	2,683	3,015	2,456
1021	Recoveries of prior year unpaid obligations	107		
1033	Recoveries of prior year paid obligations	166		
1070	Unobligated balance (total)	2,956	3,015	2,456
	Budget authority:			
	Appropriations, discretionary:			
1100	Appropriation	1,316	1,316	1,448
1900	Budget authority (total)	1,316	1,316	1,448
1930	Total budgetary resources available	4,272	4,331	3,904
	Memorandum (non-add) entries:			
1940	Unobligated balance expiring	–16	–13	
1941	Unexpired unobligated balance, end of year	3,015	2,456	1,945
	Change in obligated balance:			
	Unpaid obligations:			
3000	Unpaid obligations, brought forward, Oct 1	806	881	1,381
3010	New obligations, unexpired accounts	1,241	1,862	1,959
3011	Obligations ("upward adjustments"), expired accounts	1	5	7
3020	Outlays (gross)	–1,043	–1,367	–1,355
3040	Recoveries of prior year unpaid obligations, unexpired	–107		
3041	Recoveries of prior year unpaid obligations, expired	–17		
3050	Unpaid obligations, end of year	881	1,381	1,992
	Memorandum (non-add) entries:			
3100	Obligated balance, start of year	806	881	1,381
3200	Obligated balance, end of year	881	1,381	1,992
	Budget authority and outlays, net:			
	Discretionary:			
4000	Budget authority, gross	1,316	1,316	1,448
	Outlays, gross:			
4010	Outlays from new discretionary authority	485	508	558
4011	Outlays from discretionary balances	558	859	797
4020	Outlays, gross (total)	1,043	1,367	1,355
	Offsets against gross budget authority and outlays:			
	Offsetting collections (collected) from:			
4030	Federal sources	–166		
4040	Offsets against gross budget authority and outlays (total)	–166		
	Additional offsets against gross budget authority only:			
4053	Recoveries of prior year paid obligations, unexpired accounts	166		
4060	Additional offsets against budget authority only (total)	166		
4070	Budget authority, net (discretionary)	1,316	1,316	1,448
4080	Outlays, net (discretionary)	877	1,367	1,355
4180	Budget authority, net (total)	1,316	1,316	1,448
4190	Outlays, net (total)	877	1,367	1,355

The Construction, Major Projects appropriation funds construction projects currently costing more than $20 million. Funding is requested for four on-going projects in Louisville, KY; Alameda, CA; Livermore, CA; and El Paso, TX. In addition, three national cemetery expansion projects in Elmira, NY; Albuquerque, NM; and St. Louis, MO will be funded. Funds are also requested for major construction line item requirements, including salaries and associated expenses for staff for the Office of Construction

DEPARTMENT OF VETERANS AFFAIRS

and Facilities Management, to support advance planning and design activities, and for, seismic corrections.

Object Classification (in millions of dollars)

Identification code 036–0110–0–1–703		2021 actual	2022 est.	2023 est.
	Direct obligations:			
21.0	Travel and transportation of persons	1	2	2
25.2	Other services from non-Federal sources	57	86	91
25.3	Other goods and services from Federal sources	90	135	142
32.0	Land and structures	1,093	1,639	1,724
99.0	Direct obligations	1,241	1,862	1,959
99.9	Total new obligations, unexpired accounts	1,241	1,862	1,959

CONSTRUCTION, MINOR PROJECTS

For constructing, altering, extending, and improving any of the facilities, including parking projects, under the jurisdiction or for the use of the Department of Veterans Affairs, including planning and assessments of needs which may lead to capital investments, architectural and engineering services, maintenance or guarantee period services costs associated with equipment guarantees provided under the project, services of claims analysts, offsite utility and storm drainage system construction costs, and site acquisition, or for any of the purposes set forth in sections 316, 2404, 2406 and chapter 81 of title 38, United States Code, not otherwise provided for, where the estimated cost of a project is equal to or less than the amount set forth in section 8104(a)(3)(A) of title 38, United States Code, $626,110,000, of which $563,499,000 shall remain available until September 30, 2027, and of which $62,611,000 shall remain available until expended, along with unobligated balances of previous "Construction, Minor Projects" appropriations which are hereby made available for any project where the estimated cost is equal to or less than the amount set forth in such section: Provided, That funds made available under this heading shall be for: (1) repairs to any of the nonmedical facilities under the jurisdiction or for the use of the Department which are necessary because of loss or damage caused by any natural disaster or catastrophe; and (2) temporary measures necessary to prevent or to minimize further loss by such causes.

Note.—A full-year 2022 appropriation for this account was not enacted at the time the Budget was prepared; therefore, the Budget assumes this account is operating under the Continuing Appropriations Act, 2022 (Division A of Public Law 117-43, as amended). The amounts included for 2022 reflect the annualized level provided by the continuing resolution.

Program and Financing (in millions of dollars)

Identification code 036–0111–0–1–703		2021 actual	2022 est.	2023 est.
	Obligations by program activity:			
0001	Medical programs	518	264	323
0002	National cemeteries	92	92	163
0003	Regional offices	66	46	60
0004	Staff offices	45	40	78
0005	Choice Act, P.L. 113–146, Sec. 801	3	....	....
0900	Total new obligations, unexpired accounts	724	442	624
	Budgetary resources:			
	Unobligated balance:			
1000	Unobligated balance brought forward, Oct 1	708	383	285
1001	Discretionary unobligated balance brought fwd, Oct 1	704		
1021	Recoveries of prior year unpaid obligations	58		
1070	Unobligated balance (total)	766	383	285
	Budget authority:			
	Appropriations, discretionary:			
1100	Appropriation	390	390	626
1131	Unobligated balance of appropriations permanently reduced	–36	–36	....
1160	Appropriation, discretionary (total)	354	354	626
1900	Budget authority (total)	354	354	626
1930	Total budgetary resources available	1,120	737	911
	Memorandum (non-add) entries:			
1940	Unobligated balance expiring	–13	–10	
1941	Unexpired unobligated balance, end of year	383	285	287
	Change in obligated balance:			
	Unpaid obligations:			
3000	Unpaid obligations, brought forward, Oct 1	1,147	1,154	1,112
3010	New obligations, unexpired accounts	724	442	624
3011	Obligations ("upward adjustments"), expired accounts	20	5	4
3020	Outlays (gross)	–659	–489	–644
3040	Recoveries of prior year unpaid obligations, unexpired	–58		
3041	Recoveries of prior year unpaid obligations, expired	–20		
3050	Unpaid obligations, end of year	1,154	1,112	1,096
	Memorandum (non-add) entries:			
3100	Obligated balance, start of year	1,147	1,154	1,112
3200	Obligated balance, end of year	1,154	1,112	1,096
	Budget authority and outlays, net:			
	Discretionary:			
4000	Budget authority, gross	354	354	626
	Outlays, gross:			
4010	Outlays from new discretionary authority	35	71	117
4011	Outlays from discretionary balances	616	237	304
4020	Outlays, gross (total)	651	308	421
	Offsets against gross budget authority and outlays:			
	Offsetting collections (collected) from:			
4030	Federal sources	–6		
4040	Offsets against gross budget authority and outlays (total)	–6		
	Additional offsets against gross budget authority only:			
4052	Offsetting collections credited to expired accounts	6		
4060	Additional offsets against budget authority only (total)	6		
4070	Budget authority, net (discretionary)	354	354	626
4080	Outlays, net (discretionary)	645	308	421
	Mandatory:			
	Outlays, gross:			
4101	Outlays from mandatory balances	8	181	223
4180	Budget authority, net (total)	354	354	626
4190	Outlays, net (total)	653	489	644

The Construction, Minor Projects appropriation funds construction projects costing equal to or less than $20 million. This account is used to improve the infrastructure of medical facilities and other Department-owned facilities to reduce the risk to patient life and safety, correct code deficiencies, and improve national cemeteries and regional and staff offices.

Object Classification (in millions of dollars)

Identification code 036–0111–0–1–703		2021 actual	2022 est.	2023 est.
	Direct obligations:			
25.2	Other services from non-Federal sources	8	8	8
25.3	Other goods and services from Federal sources	29	29	29
32.0	Land and structures	687	405	587
99.9	Total new obligations, unexpired accounts	724	442	624

GRANTS FOR CONSTRUCTION OF STATE EXTENDED CARE FACILITIES

For grants to assist States to acquire or construct State nursing home and domiciliary facilities and to remodel, modify, or alter existing hospital, nursing home, and domiciliary facilities in State homes, for furnishing care to veterans as authorized by sections 8131 through 8137 of title 38, United States Code, $150,000,000, to remain available until expended.

Note.—A full-year 2022 appropriation for this account was not enacted at the time the Budget was prepared; therefore, the Budget assumes this account is operating under the Continuing Appropriations Act, 2022 (Division A of Public Law 117-43, as amended). The amounts included for 2022 reflect the annualized level provided by the continuing resolution.

Program and Financing (in millions of dollars)

Identification code 036–0181–0–1–703		2021 actual	2022 est.	2023 est.
	Obligations by program activity:			
0001	Grants for construction of state extended care facilities	298	398	398
0900	Total new obligations, unexpired accounts (object class 41.0)	298	398	398
	Budgetary resources:			
	Unobligated balance:			
1000	Unobligated balance brought forward, Oct 1	266	566	298
1001	Discretionary unobligated balance brought fwd, Oct 1	266	171	
1021	Recoveries of prior year unpaid obligations	8	40	150
1070	Unobligated balance (total)	274	606	448

GRANTS FOR CONSTRUCTION OF STATE EXTENDED CARE FACILITIES—Continued

Program and Financing—Continued

Identification code 036–0181–0–1–703		2021 actual	2022 est.	2023 est.
	Budget authority:			
	Appropriations, discretionary:			
1100	Appropriation	90	90	150
	Appropriations, mandatory:			
1200	Appropriation	500		
1900	Budget authority (total)	590	90	150
1930	Total budgetary resources available	864	696	598
	Memorandum (non-add) entries:			
1941	Unexpired unobligated balance, end of year	566	298	200
	Change in obligated balance:			
	Unpaid obligations:			
3000	Unpaid obligations, brought forward, Oct 1	687	671	942
3010	New obligations, unexpired accounts	298	398	398
3020	Outlays (gross)	–306	–87	–302
3040	Recoveries of prior year unpaid obligations, unexpired	–8	–40	–150
3050	Unpaid obligations, end of year	671	942	888
	Memorandum (non-add) entries:			
3100	Obligated balance, start of year	687	671	942
3200	Obligated balance, end of year	671	942	888
	Budget authority and outlays, net:			
	Discretionary:			
4000	Budget authority, gross	90	90	150
	Outlays, gross:			
4010	Outlays from new discretionary authority		2	3
4011	Outlays from discretionary balances	306	17	105
4020	Outlays, gross (total)	306	19	108
	Mandatory:			
4090	Budget authority, gross	500		
	Outlays, gross:			
4101	Outlays from mandatory balances		68	194
4180	Budget authority, net (total)	590	90	150
4190	Outlays, net (total)	306	87	302

The Grants for Construction of State Extended Care Facilities program is authorized by sections 8131 through 8137 of title 38, United States Code. It is a shared program between States and the Department of Veterans Affairs (VA), whereby VA provides no more than 65 percent of the funding for new construction of State home facilities, furnishing of domiciliary or nursing home care to veterans, and expansion, remodeling, or alteration of existing State home facilities. The State is responsible for providing the remaining 35 percent of funding.

Section 8004 of the American Rescue Plan Act of 2021 (Public Law 117–2) provided $500 million in 2021 to remain available until expended, for allocation under section 8131 through 8137 of title 38, United States Code. VA obligated $104 million in 2021 and plans to obligate the remaining $396 million in 2022.

GRANTS FOR CONSTRUCTION OF VETERANS CEMETERIES

For grants to assist States and tribal organizations in establishing, expanding, or improving veterans cemeteries as authorized by section 2408 of title 38, United States Code, $50,000,000, to remain available until expended.

Note.—A full-year 2022 appropriation for this account was not enacted at the time the Budget was prepared; therefore, the Budget assumes this account is operating under the Continuing Appropriations Act, 2022 (Division A of Public Law 117–43, as amended). The amounts included for 2022 reflect the annualized level provided by the continuing resolution.

Program and Financing (in millions of dollars)

Identification code 036–0183–0–1–705		2021 actual	2022 est.	2023 est.
	Obligations by program activity:			
0001	Grants for construction of state veterans cemeteries	52	49	54
0900	Total new obligations, unexpired accounts (object class 41.0)	52	49	54
	Budgetary resources:			
	Unobligated balance:			
1000	Unobligated balance brought forward, Oct 1	7	3	
1021	Recoveries of prior year unpaid obligations	3	1	4
1070	Unobligated balance (total)	10	4	4
	Budget authority:			
	Appropriations, discretionary:			
1100	Appropriation	45	45	50
1930	Total budgetary resources available	55	49	54
	Memorandum (non-add) entries:			
1941	Unexpired unobligated balance, end of year	3		
	Change in obligated balance:			
	Unpaid obligations:			
3000	Unpaid obligations, brought forward, Oct 1	90	94	53
3010	New obligations, unexpired accounts	52	49	54
3020	Outlays (gross)	–45	–89	–43
3040	Recoveries of prior year unpaid obligations, unexpired	–3	–1	–4
3050	Unpaid obligations, end of year	94	53	60
	Memorandum (non-add) entries:			
3100	Obligated balance, start of year	90	94	53
3200	Obligated balance, end of year	94	53	60
	Budget authority and outlays, net:			
	Discretionary:			
4000	Budget authority, gross	45	45	50
	Outlays, gross:			
4010	Outlays from new discretionary authority		20	22
4011	Outlays from discretionary balances	45	69	21
4020	Outlays, gross (total)	45	89	43
4180	Budget authority, net (total)	45	45	50
4190	Outlays, net (total)	45	89	43

GENERAL ADMINISTRATION

(INCLUDING TRANSFER OF FUNDS)

For necessary operating expenses of the Department of Veterans Affairs, not otherwise provided for, including administrative expenses in support of Department-wide capital planning, management and policy activities, uniforms, or allowances therefor; not to exceed $25,000 for official reception and representation expenses; hire of passenger motor vehicles; and reimbursement of the General Services Administration for security guard services, $435,000,000, of which not to exceed 10 percent shall remain available until September 30, 2024: Provided, That funds provided under this heading may be transferred to "General Operating Expenses, Veterans Benefits Administration".

Note.—A full-year 2022 appropriation for this account was not enacted at the time the Budget was prepared; therefore, the Budget assumes this account is operating under the Continuing Appropriations Act, 2022 (Division A of Public Law 117–43, as amended). The amounts included for 2022 reflect the annualized level provided by the continuing resolution.

Program and Financing (in millions of dollars)

Identification code 036–0142–0–1–705		2021 actual	2022 est.	2023 est.
	Obligations by program activity:			
0014	General administration	372	366	435
0806	General administration, reimbursable program	393	395	447
0900	Total new obligations, unexpired accounts	765	761	882
	Budgetary resources:			
	Unobligated balance:			
1000	Unobligated balance brought forward, Oct 1	9	10	
1012	Unobligated balance transfers between expired and unexpired accounts	23	2	
1070	Unobligated balance (total)	32	12	
	Budget authority:			
	Appropriations, discretionary:			
1100	Appropriation	366	366	435
1131	Unobligated balance of appropriations permanently reduced	–12	–12	
1160	Appropriation, discretionary (total)	354	354	435
	Spending authority from offsetting collections, discretionary:			
1700	Collected	393	395	447
1900	Budget authority (total)	747	749	882
1930	Total budgetary resources available	779	761	882
	Memorandum (non-add) entries:			
1940	Unobligated balance expiring	–4		
1941	Unexpired unobligated balance, end of year	10		

DEPARTMENT OF VETERANS AFFAIRS

Departmental Administration—Continued
Federal Funds—Continued

1069

	Change in obligated balance:	2021 actual	2022 est.	2023 est.
	Unpaid obligations:			
3000	Unpaid obligations, brought forward, Oct 1	220	247	103
3010	New obligations, unexpired accounts	765	761	882
3011	Obligations ("upward adjustments"), expired accounts	10		
3020	Outlays (gross)	−731	−905	−854
3041	Recoveries of prior year unpaid obligations, expired	−17		
3050	Unpaid obligations, end of year	247	103	131
	Uncollected payments:			
3060	Uncollected pymts, Fed sources, brought forward, Oct 1	−10	−9	−9
3071	Change in uncollected pymts, Fed sources, expired	1		
3090	Uncollected pymts, Fed sources, end of year	−9	−9	−9
	Memorandum (non-add) entries:			
3100	Obligated balance, start of year	210	238	94
3200	Obligated balance, end of year	238	94	122
	Budget authority and outlays, net:			
	Discretionary:			
4000	Budget authority, gross	747	749	882
	Outlays, gross:			
4010	Outlays from new discretionary authority	558	664	777
4011	Outlays from discretionary balances	173	241	77
4020	Outlays, gross (total)	731	905	854
	Offsets against gross budget authority and outlays:			
	Offsetting collections (collected) from:			
4030	Federal sources	−393	−395	−447
4033	Non-Federal sources	−3		
4040	Offsets against gross budget authority and outlays (total)	−396	−395	−447
	Additional offsets against gross budget authority only:			
4052	Offsetting collections credited to expired accounts	3		
4060	Additional offsets against budget authority only (total)	3		
4070	Budget authority, net (discretionary)	354	354	435
4080	Outlays, net (discretionary)	335	510	407
4180	Budget authority, net (total)	354	354	435
4190	Outlays, net (total)	335	510	407

General Administration.—Includes departmental executive direction, departmental support offices, the Office of General Counsel, and the Office of Accountability and Whistleblower Protection. Also included in this account is the Pershing Hall Revolving Fund which operates and manages Pershing Hall, an asset of the United States, located in Paris, France. All operating expenses for Pershing Hall are borne by the revolving fund and all receipts generated by the operation of Pershing Hall are deposited in the revolving fund.

Object Classification (in millions of dollars)

Identification code 036–0142–0–1–705	2021 actual	2022 est.	2023 est.
Direct obligations:			
Personnel compensation:			
11.1 Full-time permanent	208	210	243
11.5 Other personnel compensation	4	4	15
11.9 Total personnel compensation	212	214	258
12.1 Civilian personnel benefits	75	77	91
21.0 Travel and transportation of persons	1	2	3
23.1 Rent	18	16	21
23.2 Rental payments to others	4	4	
23.3 Communications, utilities, and miscellaneous charges			3
25.2 Other services from non-Federal sources	60	51	57
26.0 Supplies and materials	1	1	1
41.0 Grants, subsidies, and contributions	1	1	1
99.0 Direct obligations	372	366	435
99.0 Reimbursable obligations	393	395	447
99.9 Total new obligations, unexpired accounts	765	761	882

Employment Summary

Identification code 036–0142–0–1–705	2021 actual	2022 est.	2023 est.
1001 Direct civilian full-time equivalent employment	1,671	1,633	1,856
2001 Reimbursable civilian full-time equivalent employment	1,097	1,162	1,596

ASSET INFRASTRUCTURE REVIEW COMMISSION

For carrying out the VA Asset and Infrastructure Review Act of 2018 (subtitle A of title II of Public Law 115–182), $5,000,000, to remain available until September 30, 2024: Provided, That amounts made available under the headings "Construction, Major Projects", "Construction, Minor Projects", "Medical Facilities", and "General Administration" in this Act or prior Acts that remain available for obligation in fiscal year 2023 may be transferred to and merged with the amounts made available under this heading: Provided further, That in advance of any such transfer, the Secretary of Veterans Affairs shall notify the Committees on Appropriations of both Houses of Congress of the amount and purpose of the transfer: Provided further, That the transfer authority provided under this heading is in addition to any other transfer authority provided by law.

Note.—A full-year 2022 appropriation for this account was not enacted at the time the Budget was prepared; therefore, the Budget assumes this account is operating under the Continuing Appropriations Act, 2022 (Division A of Public Law 117–43, as amended). The amounts included for 2022 reflect the annualized level provided by the continuing resolution.

Program and Financing (in millions of dollars)

Identification code 036–1130–0–1–705	2021 actual	2022 est.	2023 est.
Obligations by program activity:			
0014 Direct program activity			5
Budgetary resources:			
Budget authority:			
Appropriations, discretionary:			
1100 Appropriation			5
1930 Total budgetary resources available			5
Change in obligated balance:			
Unpaid obligations:			
3010 New obligations, unexpired accounts			5
3020 Outlays (gross)			−4
3050 Unpaid obligations, end of year			1
Memorandum (non-add) entries:			
3200 Obligated balance, end of year			1
Budget authority and outlays, net:			
Discretionary:			
4000 Budget authority, gross			5
Outlays, gross:			
4010 Outlays from new discretionary authority			4
4180 Budget authority, net (total)			5
4190 Outlays, net (total)			4

VA MISSION Act of 2018 (P.L. 115–182), Title II, section 202 established an independent commission, the "Asset and Infrastructure Review Commission" (the Commission) with members appointed by the President with the consent of the Senate. The Commission shall meet only during calendar years 2022 and 2023, and those meetings shall be open to the public. The Commission will review recommendations made by the Secretary of the Department of Veterans Affairs (VA) to modernize or realign Veterans Health Administration (VHA) facilities, including leased facilities, on the basis of criteria published in the Federal Register in accordance with Title II. The Commission shall, no later than January 31, 2023, transmit to the President a report containing the Commissions findings and conclusions based on a review and analysis of the recommendations made by the Secretary, together with the Commissions recommendations, for modernizations and realignments of VHA facilities. The Budget request for this account provides funding for support staff to conduct in-depth field hearings and receive input from Veterans, Veterans Service Organizations, local VA providers, local governments, and the public.

Object Classification (in millions of dollars)

Identification code 036–1130–0–1–705	2021 actual	2022 est.	2023 est.
11.1 Direct obligations: Personnel compensation: Full-time permanent			2
11.9 Total personnel compensation			2
12.1 Civilian personnel benefits			1
21.0 Travel and transportation of persons			1
25.2 Other services from non-Federal sources			1

ASSET INFRASTRUCTURE REVIEW COMMISSION—Continued

Object Classification—Continued

Identification code 036–1130–0–1–705	2021 actual	2022 est.	2023 est.
99.9 Total new obligations, unexpired accounts			5

Employment Summary

Identification code 036–1130–0–1–705	2021 actual	2022 est.	2023 est.
1001 Direct civilian full-time equivalent employment			20

BOARD OF VETERANS APPEALS

For necessary operating expenses of the Board of Veterans Appeals, $285,000,000, of which not to exceed 10 percent shall remain available until September 30, 2024.

Note.—A full-year 2022 appropriation for this account was not enacted at the time the Budget was prepared; therefore, the Budget assumes this account is operating under the Continuing Appropriations Act, 2022 (Division A of Public Law 117–43, as amended). The amounts included for 2022 reflect the annualized level provided by the continuing resolution.

Program and Financing (in millions of dollars)

Identification code 036–1122–0–1–705	2021 actual	2022 est.	2023 est.
Obligations by program activity:			
0014 Board of Veterans' Appeals	202	209	288
Budgetary resources:			
Unobligated balance:			
1000 Unobligated balance brought forward, Oct 1		9	3
1012 Unobligated balance transfers between expired and unexpired accounts	5	1	
1070 Unobligated balance (total)	5	10	3
Budget authority:			
Appropriations, discretionary:			
1100 Appropriation	196	196	285
1121 Appropriations transferred from other acct [036–0160]	1		
1160 Appropriation, discretionary (total)	197	196	285
Advance appropriations, discretionary:			
1173 Advance appropriations transferred from other accounts [036–0160]		6	
Appropriations, mandatory:			
1200 Appropriation	10		
1900 Budget authority (total)	207	202	285
1930 Total budgetary resources available	212	212	288
Memorandum (non-add) entries:			
1940 Unobligated balance expiring	–1		
1941 Unexpired unobligated balance, end of year	9	3	
Change in obligated balance:			
Unpaid obligations:			
3000 Unpaid obligations, brought forward, Oct 1	12	14	38
3010 New obligations, unexpired accounts	202	209	288
3020 Outlays (gross)	–199	–185	–275
3041 Recoveries of prior year unpaid obligations, expired	–1		
3050 Unpaid obligations, end of year	14	38	51
Memorandum (non-add) entries:			
3100 Obligated balance, start of year	12	14	38
3200 Obligated balance, end of year	14	38	51
Budget authority and outlays, net:			
Discretionary:			
4000 Budget authority, gross	197	202	285
Outlays, gross:			
4010 Outlays from new discretionary authority	182	171	241
4011 Outlays from discretionary balances	16	14	31
4020 Outlays, gross (total)	198	185	272
Mandatory:			
4090 Budget authority, gross	10		
Outlays, gross:			
4100 Outlays from new mandatory authority	1		
4101 Outlays from mandatory balances			3
4110 Outlays, gross (total)	1		3
4180 Budget authority, net (total)	207	202	285
4190 Outlays, net (total)	199	185	275

The mission of the Board of Veterans' Appeals (Board or BVA), as set forth in 38 U.S.C. 7101(a) is to conduct hearings and consider appeals for benefits and services properly before the Board in a timely manner. The Board's goal is to issue quality decisions in compliance with the requirements of the law, including the precedential decisions of the United States Court of Appeals for Veterans Claims and other federal courts. The Board makes final decisions on behalf of the Secretary on appeals from decisions of the agencies of original jurisdiction with the Department of Veterans Affairs offices. The Board reviews all appeals for entitlement to veterans' benefits, including claims for service connection, increased disability ratings, total disability ratings, pension, insurance benefits, educational benefits, home loan guaranties, vocational rehabilitation, dependency and indemnity compensation, memorial benefits, and healthcare delivery to include a program of comprehensive assistance for family caregivers. The Veterans Appeals Improvement and Modernization Act of 2017, enacted on August 23, 2017, became effective on February 19, 2019. This law reformed the current appeals process and replaced it with a new, simpler process that uses easy to understand language and gives veterans choice and control of their appeal.

Object Classification (in millions of dollars)

Identification code 036–1122–0–1–705	2021 actual	2022 est.	2023 est.
Direct obligations:			
Personnel compensation:			
11.1 Full-time permanent	136	139	181
11.5 Other personnel compensation	2	2	12
11.9 Total personnel compensation	138	141	193
12.1 Civilian personnel benefits	47	48	66
23.2 Rental payments to others	8	10	10
23.3 Communications, utilities, and miscellaneous charges	7	7	10
25.2 Other services from non-Federal sources	2	3	8
31.0 Equipment			1
99.9 Total new obligations, unexpired accounts	202	209	288

Employment Summary

Identification code 036–1122–0–1–705	2021 actual	2022 est.	2023 est.
1001 Direct civilian full-time equivalent employment	1,182	1,169	1,532

OFFICE OF INSPECTOR GENERAL

For necessary expenses of the Office of Inspector General, to include information technology, in carrying out the provisions of the Inspector General Act of 1978 (5 U.S.C. App.), $273,000,000, of which not to exceed 10 percent shall remain available until September 30, 2024.

Note.—A full-year 2022 appropriation for this account was not enacted at the time the Budget was prepared; therefore, the Budget assumes this account is operating under the Continuing Appropriations Act, 2022 (Division A of Public Law 117–43, as amended). The amounts included for 2022 reflect the annualized level provided by the continuing resolution.

Program and Financing (in millions of dollars)

Identification code 036–0170–0–1–705	2021 actual	2022 est.	2023 est.
Obligations by program activity:			
0101 Office of Inspector General (Direct)	229	250	276
0192 Total direct program	229	250	276
Budgetary resources:			
Unobligated balance:			
1000 Unobligated balance brought forward, Oct 1	2	22	3
1012 Unobligated balance transfers between expired and unexpired accounts	14	3	
1070 Unobligated balance (total)	16	25	3
Budget authority:			
Appropriations, discretionary:			
1100 Appropriation	228	228	273
Appropriations, mandatory:			
1200 Appropriation	10		
1900 Budget authority (total)	238	228	273

DEPARTMENT OF VETERANS AFFAIRS

Departmental Administration—Continued
Federal Funds—Continued

1071

		2021 actual	2022 est.	2023 est.
1930	Total budgetary resources available	254	253	276
	Memorandum (non-add) entries:			
1940	Unobligated balance expiring	−3		
1941	Unexpired unobligated balance, end of year	22	3	
	Change in obligated balance:			
	Unpaid obligations:			
3000	Unpaid obligations, brought forward, Oct 1	26	28	90
3010	New obligations, unexpired accounts	229	250	276
3011	Obligations ("upward adjustments"), expired accounts	2		
3020	Outlays (gross)	−224	−188	−261
3041	Recoveries of prior year unpaid obligations, expired	−5		
3050	Unpaid obligations, end of year	28	90	105
	Memorandum (non-add) entries:			
3100	Obligated balance, start of year	26	28	90
3200	Obligated balance, end of year	28	90	105
	Budget authority and outlays, net:			
	Discretionary:			
4000	Budget authority, gross	228	228	273
	Outlays, gross:			
4010	Outlays from new discretionary authority	192	170	204
4011	Outlays from discretionary balances	32	18	56
4020	Outlays, gross (total)	224	188	260
	Mandatory:			
4090	Budget authority, gross	10		
	Outlays, gross:			
4101	Outlays from mandatory balances			1
4180	Budget authority, net (total)	238	228	273
4190	Outlays, net (total)	224	188	261

This appropriation provides for carrying out the independent oversight responsibilities of the Inspector General Act of 1978. This oversight includes Department of Veterans Affairs (VA)-wide audit, investigation, health care inspection, and management support functions to identify and report weaknesses and deficiencies that create conditions for actual or potential fraud and other criminal activity, mismanagement, and waste in VA programs and operations. The audit function plans and conducts internal programmatic and financial audits and evaluations of all facets of VA operations. The health care inspection function performs legislatively mandated medical care quality assurance reviews and oversight of VA health care programs. The investigative function performs criminal and administrative investigations of improper and illegal activities involving VA operations, personnel, beneficiaries, and other parties.

Object Classification (in millions of dollars)

Identification code 036–0170–0–1–705		2021 actual	2022 est.	2023 est.
	Direct obligations:			
	Personnel compensation:			
11.1	Full-time permanent	128	141	153
11.5	Other personnel compensation	10	10	11
11.9	Total personnel compensation	138	151	164
12.1	Civilian personnel benefits	55	60	65
21.0	Employee Travel	2	3	7
23.1	Rental payments to GSA	7	8	14
23.2	Rental payments to others	4		
23.3	Communications, utilities, and miscellaneous charges	1	6	
25.2	Other services from non-Federal sources	18	20	21
26.0	Supplies and materials	1		
31.0	Equipment	3	2	5
99.0	Direct obligations	229	250	276
99.9	Total new obligations, unexpired accounts	229	250	276

Employment Summary

Identification code 036–0170–0–1–705	2021 actual	2022 est.	2023 est.
1001 Direct civilian full-time equivalent employment	1,032	1,100	1,135

INFORMATION TECHNOLOGY SYSTEMS

(INCLUDING TRANSFER OF FUNDS)

For necessary expenses for information technology systems and telecommunications support, including developmental information systems and operational information systems; for pay and associated costs; and for the capital asset acquisition of information technology systems, including management and related contractual costs of said acquisitions, including contractual costs associated with operations authorized by section 3109 of title 5, United States Code, $5,782,000,000, plus reimbursements: Provided, That $1,494,230,000 shall be for pay and associated costs, of which not to exceed 3 percent shall remain available until September 30, 2024: Provided further, That $4,145,678,000 shall be for operations and maintenance, of which not to exceed 5 percent shall remain available until September 30, 2024: Provided further, That $142,092,000 shall be for information technology systems development, and shall remain available until September 30, 2024: Provided further, That amounts made available for salaries and expenses, operations and maintenance, and information technology systems development may be transferred among the three subaccounts after the Secretary of Veterans Affairs submits notice thereof to the Committees on Appropriations of both Houses of Congress : Provided further, That amounts made available for the "Information Technology Systems" account for development may be transferred among projects or to newly defined projects: Provided further, That no project may be increased or decreased by more than $3,000,000 of cost prior to submitting notice thereof to the Committees on Appropriations of both Houses of Congress .

Note.—A full-year 2022 appropriation for this account was not enacted at the time the Budget was prepared; therefore, the Budget assumes this account is operating under the Continuing Appropriations Act, 2022 (Division A of Public Law 117–43, as amended). The amounts included for 2022 reflect the annualized level provided by the continuing resolution.

Program and Financing (in millions of dollars)

Identification code 036–0167–0–1–705		2021 actual	2022 est.	2023 est.
	Obligations by program activity:			
0001	Development	515	471	142
0002	Operations and maintenance	3,293	3,228	4,142
0003	Administrative and salaries	1,231	1,217	1,490
0004	P.L. 113–146, Sec. 801 – IT Support	2	1	
0005	P.L. 116–136, CARES Act – Dev	57		
0006	P.L. 116–136, CARES Act – OM	890		
0007	P.L. 116–136, CARES Act – Pay	124		
0008	P.L. 117–2, ARP, Section 8003		100	
0799	Total direct obligations	6,112	5,017	5,774
0804	IT Systems, Reimbursable obligations	118	108	126
0900	Total new obligations, unexpired accounts	6,230	5,125	5,900
	Budgetary resources:			
	Unobligated balance:			
1000	Unobligated balance brought forward, Oct 1	1,184	141	
1001	Discretionary unobligated balance brought fwd, Oct 1	1,182		
1021	Recoveries of prior year unpaid obligations	58		
1070	Unobligated balance (total)	1,242	141	
	Budget authority:			
	Appropriations, discretionary:			
1100	Appropriation	4,912	4,912	5,782
1120	Appropriations transferred to other accts [036–0169]	−8	−8	−8
1121	Appropriations transferred from other acct [036–0160]	45		
1131	Unobligated balance of appropriations permanently reduced	−38	−38	
1160	Appropriation, discretionary (total)	4,911	4,866	5,774
	Advance appropriations, discretionary:			
1173	Advance appropriations transferred from other accounts [036–0160]		10	
	Appropriations, mandatory:			
1200	Appropriation [P.L. 117–2 Section 8003]		100	
	Spending authority from offsetting collections, discretionary:			
1700	Collected	40	108	126
1701	Change in uncollected payments, Federal sources	78		
1750	Spending auth from offsetting collections, disc (total)	118	108	126
1900	Budget authority (total)	5,129	4,984	5,900
1930	Total budgetary resources available	6,371	5,125	5,900
	Memorandum (non-add) entries:			
1941	Unexpired unobligated balance, end of year	141		
	Change in obligated balance:			
	Unpaid obligations:			
3000	Unpaid obligations, brought forward, Oct 1	2,203	2,748	1,345
3010	New obligations, unexpired accounts	6,230	5,125	5,900

Departmental Administration—Continued
Federal Funds—Continued

INFORMATION TECHNOLOGY SYSTEMS—Continued

Program and Financing—Continued

Identification code 036–0167–0–1–705	2021 actual	2022 est.	2023 est.
3011 Obligations ("upward adjustments"), expired accounts	13	....	....
3020 Outlays (gross)	–5,577	–6,528	–5,845
3040 Recoveries of prior year unpaid obligations, unexpired	–58	....	....
3041 Recoveries of prior year unpaid obligations, expired	–63	....	....
3050 Unpaid obligations, end of year	2,748	1,345	1,400
Uncollected payments:			
3060 Uncollected pymts, Fed sources, brought forward, Oct 1	–52	–82	–82
3070 Change in uncollected pymts, Fed sources, unexpired	–78	....	....
3071 Change in uncollected pymts, Fed sources, expired	48	....	....
3090 Uncollected pymts, Fed sources, end of year	–82	–82	–82
Memorandum (non-add) entries:			
3100 Obligated balance, start of year	2,151	2,666	1,263
3200 Obligated balance, end of year	2,666	1,263	1,318
Budget authority and outlays, net:			
Discretionary:			
4000 Budget authority, gross	5,029	4,984	5,900
Outlays, gross:			
4010 Outlays from new discretionary authority	3,055	4,011	4,745
4011 Outlays from discretionary balances	2,522	2,427	1,090
4020 Outlays, gross (total)	5,577	6,438	5,835
Offsets against gross budget authority and outlays:			
Offsetting collections (collected) from:			
4030 Federal sources	–91	–108	–126
4033 Non-Federal sources	–4	....	....
4040 Offsets against gross budget authority and outlays (total)	–95	–108	–126
Additional offsets against gross budget authority only:			
4050 Change in uncollected pymts, Fed sources, unexpired	–78	....	....
4052 Offsetting collections credited to expired accounts	55	....	....
4060 Additional offsets against budget authority only (total)	–23	....	....
4070 Budget authority, net (discretionary)	4,911	4,876	5,774
4080 Outlays, net (discretionary)	5,482	6,330	5,709
Mandatory:			
4090 Budget authority, gross	100	....	....
Outlays, gross:			
4101 Outlays from mandatory balances	....	90	10
4180 Budget authority, net (total)	5,011	4,876	5,774
4190 Outlays, net (total)	5,482	6,420	5,719

The Information Technology (IT) Systems appropriation funds IT services such as systems development and performance, operations and maintenance, information security, and customer support. This appropriation enables the effective and efficient delivery of services to the Nation's largest healthcare network, as well as the veterans benefits and corporate business lines within the Department of Veterans Affairs (VA).

Development.—The Office of Information & Technology invests in projects designed to improve the delivery of VA services and benefits for veterans and their families. This account also supports improvements in the Community Care Program, modernizations to veterans benefits and appeals processing, as well as the divestiture of legacy IT systems.

Operations and Maintenance.—The Office of Information & Technology purchases, maintains, manages, and supports all the computer, phone, telecommunication, and data systems equipment and infrastructure for all VA facilities.

Object Classification (in millions of dollars)

Identification code 036–0167–0–1–705	2021 actual	2022 est.	2023 est.
Direct obligations:			
Personnel compensation:			
11.1 Full-time permanent	780	880	935
11.1 Full-time permanent - CARES Act, P.L. 116–136	75	....	....
11.9 Total personnel compensation	855	880	935
12.1 Civilian personnel benefits	306	379	402
12.1 Civilian personnel benefits - CARES Act, P.L. 116–136	30	....	....
21.0 Travel and transportation of persons	1	13	16
23.3 Communications, utilities, and miscellaneous charges	1,099	888	1,089
23.3 Communications, utilities, and miscellaneous charges - CARES Act, P.L. 116–136	5	....	....
25.2 Other services from non-Federal sources	2,352	2,450	2,957
25.2 Other services from non-Federal -Choice Act, P.L. 113–146, Sec. 801	2	1	....
25.2 Other services from non-Federal sources - CARES Act, P.L. 116–136	740	....	....
25.2 Other services from non-Federal sources - ARP, P.L. 117–2, Section 8003	....	100	....
26.0 Supplies and materials	2	19	23
31.0 Equipment	499	286	352
31.0 Equipment - CARES Act, P.L. 116–136	221	....	....
42.0 Insurance claims and indemnities	....	1	....
99.0 Direct obligations	6,112	5,017	5,774
99.0 Reimbursable obligations	118	108	126
99.9 Total new obligations, unexpired accounts	6,230	5,125	5,900

Employment Summary

Identification code 036–0167–0–1–705	2021 actual	2022 est.	2023 est.
1001 Direct civilian full-time equivalent employment	8,121	8,668	8,918
2001 Reimbursable civilian full-time equivalent employment	65	78	75

VETERANS ELECTRONIC HEALTH RECORD

For activities related to implementation, preparation, development, interface, management, rollout, and maintenance of a Veterans Electronic Health Record system, including contractual costs associated with operations authorized by section 3109 of title 5, United States Code, and salaries and expenses of employees hired under titles 5 and 38, United States Code, $1,759,000,000, to remain available until September 30, 2025: Provided, That the Secretary of Veterans Affairs shall submit to the Committees on Appropriations of both Houses of Congress quarterly reports detailing obligations, expenditures, and deployment implementation by facility, including any changes from the deployment plan or schedule: Provided further, That the funds provided in this account shall only be available to the Office of the Deputy Secretary, to be administered by that Office.

Note.—A full-year 2022 appropriation for this account was not enacted at the time the Budget was prepared; therefore, the Budget assumes this account is operating under the Continuing Appropriations Act, 2022 (Division A of Public Law 117–43, as amended). The amounts included for 2022 reflect the annualized level provided by the continuing resolution.

Program and Financing (in millions of dollars)

Identification code 036–1123–0–1–703	2021 actual	2022 est.	2023 est.
Obligations by program activity:			
0001 EHR Contract	673	1,949	1,119
0002 PMO Support	213	330	199
0003 Infrastructure Readiness	1,075	1,048	441
0900 Total new obligations, unexpired accounts	1,961	3,327	1,759
Budgetary resources:			
Unobligated balance:			
1000 Unobligated balance brought forward, Oct 1	24	720	....
1021 Recoveries of prior year unpaid obligations	31	....	....
1033 Recoveries of prior year paid obligations	19	....	....
1070 Unobligated balance (total)	74	720	....
Budget authority:			
Appropriations, discretionary:			
1100 Appropriation	2,627	2,627	1,759
1131 Unobligated balance of appropriations permanently reduced	–20	–20	....
1160 Appropriation, discretionary (total)	2,607	2,607	1,759
1930 Total budgetary resources available	2,681	3,327	1,759
Memorandum (non-add) entries:			
1941 Unexpired unobligated balance, end of year	720	....	....
Change in obligated balance:			
Unpaid obligations:			
3000 Unpaid obligations, brought forward, Oct 1	1,652	2,242	2,076
3010 New obligations, unexpired accounts	1,961	3,327	1,759
3011 Obligations ("upward adjustments"), expired accounts	2	....	....
3020 Outlays (gross)	–1,342	–3,493	–2,200
3040 Recoveries of prior year unpaid obligations, unexpired	–31	....	....
3050 Unpaid obligations, end of year	2,242	2,076	1,635
Memorandum (non-add) entries:			
3100 Obligated balance, start of year	1,652	2,242	2,076

DEPARTMENT OF VETERANS AFFAIRS

Departmental Administration—Continued
Federal Funds—Continued

		2021 actual	2022 est.	2023 est.
3200	Obligated balance, end of year	2,242	2,076	1,635
	Budget authority and outlays, net:			
	Discretionary:			
4000	Budget authority, gross	2,607	2,607	1,759
	Outlays, gross:			
4010	Outlays from new discretionary authority	373	1,251	844
4011	Outlays from discretionary balances	969	2,242	1,356
4020	Outlays, gross (total)	1,342	3,493	2,200
	Offsets against gross budget authority and outlays:			
	Offsetting collections (collected) from:			
4030	Federal sources	–2		
4033	Non-Federal sources	–20		
4040	Offsets against gross budget authority and outlays (total)	–22		
	Additional offsets against gross budget authority only:			
4052	Offsetting collections credited to expired accounts	3		
4053	Recoveries of prior year paid obligations, unexpired accounts	19		
4060	Additional offsets against budget authority only (total)	22		
4070	Budget authority, net (discretionary)	2,607	2,607	1,759
4080	Outlays, net (discretionary)	1,320	3,493	2,200
4180	Budget authority, net (total)	2,607	2,607	1,759
4190	Outlays, net (total)	1,320	3,493	2,200

The Veterans Electronic Health Care Record appropriation funds necessary expenses related to the development and deployment of a new Veterans Electronic Health Record (EHR) system. This new EHR will allow the Department of Veterans Affairs (VA) to move toward a single common health record that has full integration between the Department of Defense and VA, as well as community providers. From the veteran perspective, the new system will provide a single, accurate, lifetime health record while improving patient care and safety.

Object Classification (in millions of dollars)

Identification code 036–1123–0–1–703	2021 actual	2022 est.	2023 est.
Direct obligations:			
11.1 Personnel compensation: Full-time permanent	23	29	29
12.1 Civilian personnel benefits	8	10	10
21.0 Travel and transportation of persons	1	2	1
23.1 Rental payments to GSA	4	4	
23.3 Communications, utilities, and miscellaneous charges	51	67	34
25.2 Other services from non-Federal sources	1,513	2,811	1,488
25.3 Other goods and services from Federal sources (FTE to VHA)	14	30	13
25.3 Other goods and services from Federal sources	95	117	78
31.0 Equipment	252	257	106
99.0 Direct obligations	1,961	3,327	1,759
99.9 Total new obligations, unexpired accounts	1,961	3,327	1,759

Employment Summary

Identification code 036–1123–0–1–703	2021 actual	2022 est.	2023 est.
1001 Direct civilian full-time equivalent employment	175	222	227

NATIONAL CEMETERY ADMINISTRATION

For necessary expenses of the National Cemetery Administration for operations and maintenance, not otherwise provided for, including uniforms or allowances therefor; cemeterial expenses as authorized by law; purchase of one passenger motor vehicle for use in cemeterial operations; hire of passenger motor vehicles; and repair, alteration or improvement of facilities under the jurisdiction of the National Cemetery Administration, $430,000,000 of which not to exceed 10 percent shall remain available until September 30, 2024.

Note.—A full-year 2022 appropriation for this account was not enacted at the time the Budget was prepared; therefore, the Budget assumes this account is operating under the Continuing Appropriations Act, 2022 (Division A of Public Law 117–43, as amended). The amounts included for 2022 reflect the annualized level provided by the continuing resolution.

Program and Financing (in millions of dollars)

Identification code 036–0129–0–1–705	2021 actual	2022 est.	2023 est.
Obligations by program activity:			
0201 Operations and maintenance	368	354	433
Budgetary resources:			
Unobligated balance:			
1000 Unobligated balance brought forward, Oct 1	2	6	4
1012 Unobligated balance transfers between expired and unexpired accounts	8		
1070 Unobligated balance (total)	10	6	4
Budget authority:			
Appropriations, discretionary:			
1100 Appropriation	352	352	430
1121 Appropriations transferred from other acct [036–0160]	12		
1160 Appropriation, discretionary (total)	364	352	430
Spending authority from offsetting collections, discretionary:			
1700 Collected	2		
1900 Budget authority (total)	366	352	430
1930 Total budgetary resources available	376	358	434
Memorandum (non-add) entries:			
1940 Unobligated balance expiring	–2		
1941 Unexpired unobligated balance, end of year	6	4	1
Change in obligated balance:			
Unpaid obligations:			
3000 Unpaid obligations, brought forward, Oct 1	72	96	63
3010 New obligations, unexpired accounts	368	354	433
3011 Obligations ("upward adjustments"), expired accounts	3		
3020 Outlays (gross)	–339	–387	–412
3041 Recoveries of prior year unpaid obligations, expired	–8		
3050 Unpaid obligations, end of year	96	63	84
Memorandum (non-add) entries:			
3100 Obligated balance, start of year	72	96	63
3200 Obligated balance, end of year	96	63	84
Budget authority and outlays, net:			
Discretionary:			
4000 Budget authority, gross	366	352	430
Outlays, gross:			
4010 Outlays from new discretionary authority	274	297	363
4011 Outlays from discretionary balances	64	90	49
4020 Outlays, gross (total)	338	387	412
Offsets against gross budget authority and outlays:			
Offsetting collections (collected) from:			
4030 Federal sources	–2		
4040 Offsets against gross budget authority and outlays (total)	–2		
Mandatory:			
Outlays, gross:			
4101 Outlays from mandatory balances	1		
4180 Budget authority, net (total)	364	352	430
4190 Outlays, net (total)	337	387	412

The mission of the National Cemetery Administration is to honor veterans with final resting places in national shrines and with lasting tributes that commemorate their service to our Nation. The National Cemetery Administration's vision is to serve all veterans and their families with the utmost dignity, respect, and compassion. Every national cemetery will be a place that inspires visitors to understand and appreciate the service and sacrifice of our Nation's veterans. There are a number of related programs managed by the National Cemetery Administration including: 1) burying eligible veterans and their family members in national cemeteries and maintaining the graves and their environs as national shrines; 2) administering grants to States and Tribal organizations in establishing, expanding, improving, or operating veterans cemeteries; 3) providing headstones and markers for the graves of eligible veterans; 4) providing medallions commemorating the veterans' service that may be affixed to the privately purchased headstones or markers for veterans interred in private cemeteries; 5) providing presidential memorial certificates to family and friends of deceased veterans, recognizing the veterans' contribution and service to the Nation; 6) providing graveliners or partial reimbursement for a privately purchased outer burial receptacle for each new grave in open national cemeteries administered by the National Cemetery Administration; 7) providing reim-

NATIONAL CEMETERY ADMINISTRATION—Continued

bursement for caskets and urns for veterans' remains when there are no next of kin and insufficient resources; and 8) recording First Notice of Veteran Deaths into the Department of Veterans Affairs electronic files to ensure timely termination of benefits and next-of-kin notification of possible entitlement to survivor benefits.

The National Cemetery Administration also reflects budget information for the National Cemetery Gift Fund and the National Cemetery Administration Facilities Operation Fund. Through the Gift Fund, the Secretary is authorized to accept gifts and bequests which are made for the purpose of beautifying national cemeteries or are determined to be beneficial to such cemeteries.

Object Classification (in millions of dollars)

Identification code 036–0129–0–1–705		2021 actual	2022 est.	2023 est.
	Direct obligations:			
	Personnel compensation:			
11.1	Full-time permanent	139	146	165
11.5	Other personnel compensation	5	4	4
11.9	Total personnel compensation	144	150	169
12.1	Civilian personnel benefits	58	58	64
21.0	Travel and transportation of persons	3	3	3
22.0	Transportation of things	3	2	2
23.1	Rent	3	3	3
23.3	Communications, utilities, and miscellaneous charges	13	13	14
24.0	Printing and reproduction	2	2	2
25.2	Other services from non-Federal sources	104	91	129
26.0	Supplies and materials	14	13	18
31.0	Equipment	19	16	26
32.0	Land and structures	5	3	3
99.9	Total new obligations, unexpired accounts	368	354	433

Employment Summary

Identification code 036–0129–0–1–705		2021 actual	2022 est.	2023 est.
1001	Direct civilian full-time equivalent employment	2,078	2,151	2,281

SUPPLY FUND

Program and Financing (in millions of dollars)

Identification code 036–4537–0–4–705		2021 actual	2022 est.	2023 est.
	Obligations by program activity:			
0801	Reimbursable program-Merchandizing	1,000	1,669	1,662
0802	Reimbursable program-Operations	350	431	438
0900	Total new obligations, unexpired accounts	1,350	2,100	2,100
	Budgetary resources:			
	Unobligated balance:			
1000	Unobligated balance brought forward, Oct 1	430	456	456
1021	Recoveries of prior year unpaid obligations	94		
1070	Unobligated balance (total)	524	456	456
	Budget authority:			
	Spending authority from offsetting collections, mandatory:			
1800	Collected	1,249	2,100	2,100
1801	Change in uncollected payments, Federal sources	33		
1850	Spending auth from offsetting collections, mand (total)	1,282	2,100	2,100
1930	Total budgetary resources available	1,806	2,556	2,556
	Memorandum (non-add) entries:			
1941	Unexpired unobligated balance, end of year	456	456	456
	Change in obligated balance:			
	Unpaid obligations:			
3000	Unpaid obligations, brought forward, Oct 1	947	903	608
3010	New obligations, unexpired accounts	1,350	2,100	2,100
3020	Outlays (gross)	–1,300	–2,395	–2,143
3040	Recoveries of prior year unpaid obligations, unexpired	–94		
3050	Unpaid obligations, end of year	903	608	565
	Uncollected payments:			
3060	Uncollected pymts, Fed sources, brought forward, Oct 1	–1,044	–1,077	–1,077
3070	Change in uncollected pymts, Fed sources, unexpired	–33		
3090	Uncollected pymts, Fed sources, end of year	–1,077	–1,077	–1,077
	Memorandum (non-add) entries:			
3100	Obligated balance, start of year	–97	–174	–469
3200	Obligated balance, end of year	–174	–469	–512
	Budget authority and outlays, net:			
	Mandatory:			
4090	Budget authority, gross	1,282	2,100	2,100
	Outlays, gross:			
4100	Outlays from new mandatory authority		1,995	1,995
4101	Outlays from mandatory balances	1,300	400	148
4110	Outlays, gross (total)	1,300	2,395	2,143
	Offsets against gross budget authority and outlays:			
	Offsetting collections (collected) from:			
4120	Federal sources	–1,110	–2,100	–2,100
4123	Non-Federal sources	–139		
4130	Offsets against gross budget authority and outlays (total)	–1,249	–2,100	–2,100
	Additional offsets against gross budget authority only:			
4140	Change in uncollected pymts, Fed sources, unexpired	–33		
4170	Outlays, net (mandatory)	51	295	43
4180	Budget authority, net (total)			
4190	Outlays, net (total)	51	295	43

Under the provisions of 38 U.S.C. 8121, the Supply Fund is responsible for the operation and maintenance of a supply system for the Department of Veterans Affairs (VA). In this capacity, it provides policy and oversight to VA's acquisition and logistics programs, and provides best value acquisition of goods and services through its National Acquisition Center, Denver Acquisition and Logistics Center, Service and Distribution Center, Technology Acquisition Center and Strategic Acquisition Center. Operating as an intra-governmental revolving fund without fiscal year limitations, the Supply Fund is financed by revenue from fees on acquisitions of supplies, equipment, and services for both VA and other Government agency customers.

Object Classification (in millions of dollars)

Identification code 036–4537–0–4–705		2021 actual	2022 est.	2023 est.
	Reimbursable obligations:			
11.1	Personnel compensation: Full-time permanent	109	130	136
12.1	Civilian personnel benefits	40	48	50
21.0	Travel and transportation of persons		11	13
23.1	Rental payments to GSA	7	7	7
23.3	Communications, utilities, and miscellaneous charges	28	24	26
24.0	Printing and reproduction	10	1	1
25.2	Other services from non-Federal sources	280	201	197
26.0	Supplies and materials	523	713	705
31.0	Equipment	353	965	965
99.9	Total new obligations, unexpired accounts	1,350	2,100	2,100

Employment Summary

Identification code 036–4537–0–4–705		2021 actual	2022 est.	2023 est.
2001	Reimbursable civilian full-time equivalent employment	1,002	1,300	1,273

FRANCHISE FUND

Program and Financing (in millions of dollars)

Identification code 036–4539–0–4–705		2021 actual	2022 est.	2023 est.
	Obligations by program activity:			
0801	Franchise Fund (Reimbursable)	1,359	1,716	1,719
	Budgetary resources:			
	Unobligated balance:			
1000	Unobligated balance brought forward, Oct 1	178	265	265
1021	Recoveries of prior year unpaid obligations	129		
1070	Unobligated balance (total)	307	265	265
	Budget authority:			
	Spending authority from offsetting collections, discretionary:			
1700	Collected	1,223	1,716	1,719

		2021 actual	2022 est.	2023 est.
1701	Change in uncollected payments, Federal sources	94		
1750	Spending auth from offsetting collections, disc (total)	1,317	1,716	1,719
1930	Total budgetary resources available	1,624	1,981	1,984
	Memorandum (non-add) entries:			
1941	Unexpired unobligated balance, end of year	265	265	265
	Change in obligated balance:			
	Unpaid obligations:			
3000	Unpaid obligations, brought forward, Oct 1	440	473	497
3010	New obligations, unexpired accounts	1,359	1,716	1,719
3020	Outlays (gross)	−1,197	−1,692	−1,695
3040	Recoveries of prior year unpaid obligations, unexpired	−129		
3050	Unpaid obligations, end of year	473	497	521
	Uncollected payments:			
3060	Uncollected pymts, Fed sources, brought forward, Oct 1	−231	−325	−325
3070	Change in uncollected pymts, Fed sources, unexpired	−94		
3090	Uncollected pymts, Fed sources, end of year	−325	−325	−325
	Memorandum (non-add) entries:			
3100	Obligated balance, start of year	209	148	172
3200	Obligated balance, end of year	148	172	196
	Budget authority and outlays, net:			
	Discretionary:			
4000	Budget authority, gross	1,317	1,716	1,719
	Outlays, gross:			
4010	Outlays from new discretionary authority	580	1,287	1,289
4011	Outlays from discretionary balances	617	405	406
4020	Outlays, gross (total)	1,197	1,692	1,695
	Offsets against gross budget authority and outlays:			
	Offsetting collections (collected) from:			
4030	Federal sources	−1,223	−1,716	−1,719
	Additional offsets against gross budget authority only:			
4050	Change in uncollected pymts, Fed sources, unexpired	−94		
4080	Outlays, net (discretionary)	−26	−24	−24
4180	Budget authority, net (total)			
4190	Outlays, net (total)	−26	−24	−24

The Department of Veterans Affairs (VA) Franchise Fund was established under the authority of the Government Management Reform Act of 1994 and the VA and Housing and Urban Development and Independent Agencies Act of 1997. VA was selected by the Office of Management and Budget in 1996 as one of the six executive branch agencies to establish a franchise fund pilot program. Created as a revolving fund, the VA Franchise Fund began providing common administrative support services to the VA and other Government agencies in 1997 on a fee-for-service basis. In 2006, under the Military Quality of Life and Veterans Affairs Appropriations Act (Public Law 109–114), permanent status was conferred upon the VA Franchise Fund. The Franchise Fund concept is intended to increase competition for Government administrative services, resulting in lower costs and higher quality.

Object Classification (in millions of dollars)

Identification code 036–4539–0–4–705		2021 actual	2022 est.	2023 est.
	Reimbursable obligations:			
11.1	Personnel compensation: Full-time permanent	167	240	246
12.1	Civilian personnel benefits	63	78	81
21.0	Travel and transportation of persons	1	5	5
23.1	Rental payments to GSA	9	11	10
23.3	Communications, utilities, and miscellaneous charges	124	166	170
24.0	Printing and reproduction	10	13	13
25.2	Other services from non-Federal sources	854	1,098	1,111
26.0	Supplies and materials	1	7	7
31.0	Equipment	130	98	76
99.9	Total new obligations, unexpired accounts	1,359	1,716	1,719

Employment Summary

Identification code 036–4539–0–4–705	2021 actual	2022 est.	2023 est.
2001 Reimbursable civilian full-time equivalent employment	1,875	2,436	2,461

RECURRING EXPENSES TRANSFORMATIONAL FUND

Program and Financing (in millions of dollars)

Identification code 036–1124–0–1–705		2021 actual	2022 est.	2023 est.
	Obligations by program activity:			
0001	RETF - Information Technology		718	
0002	RETF - Nonrecurring Maintenance		150	
0003	RETF - Major Construction			805
0004	RETF - Minor Construction			163
0900	Total new obligations, unexpired accounts (object class 25.2)		868	968
	Budgetary resources:			
	Unobligated balance:			
1000	Unobligated balance brought forward, Oct 1		868	968
1012	Unobligated balance transfers between expired and unexpired accounts	868	968	700
1070	Unobligated balance (total)	868	1,836	1,668
1930	Total budgetary resources available	868	1,836	1,668
	Memorandum (non-add) entries:			
1941	Unexpired unobligated balance, end of year	868	968	700
	Change in obligated balance:			
	Unpaid obligations:			
3000	Unpaid obligations, brought forward, Oct 1			538
3010	New obligations, unexpired accounts		868	968
3020	Outlays (gross)		−330	−1,092
3050	Unpaid obligations, end of year		538	414
	Memorandum (non-add) entries:			
3100	Obligated balance, start of year			538
3200	Obligated balance, end of year		538	414
	Budget authority and outlays, net:			
	Discretionary:			
	Outlays, gross:			
4011	Outlays from discretionary balances		330	1,092
4180	Budget authority, net (total)			
4190	Outlays, net (total)		330	1,092

The Consolidated Appropriations Act of 2016 (Public Law 114–113) authorized the Recurring Expenses Transformational Fund (Transformational Fund). Unobligated balances of expired discretionary funds appropriated in 2016 or any succeeding fiscal year from the General Fund of the Treasury to the Department of Veterans Affairs may be transferred to the Transformational Fund at the end of the fifth fiscal year after the last fiscal year for which such funds are available for the purposes for which appropriated. Balances available in the Transformational Fund shall be available until expended for facilities infrastructure improvements, including nonrecurring maintenance, at existing hospitals and clinics of the Veterans Health Administration, and for information technology systems improvements and sustainment.

The 2023 Budget anticipates a transfer of $968 million in unobligated balances into the Transformational Fund at the end of 2022, of which $805 million will be obligated in 2023 for three Major Construction projects in Portland, OR; Canandaigua, NY; and Ft. Harrison, MT and $163 million will be obligated for Minor Construction projects that improve Veterans Health Administrations facilities infrastructure.

ADMINISTRATIVE PROVISIONS

(INCLUDING TRANSFER OF FUNDS)

SEC. 201. *Any appropriation for fiscal year 2023 for "Compensation and Pensions", "Readjustment Benefits", and "Veterans Insurance and Indemnities" may be transferred as necessary to any other of the mentioned appropriations: Provided, That, before any such transfer may take place, the Secretary of Veterans Affairs shall submit notice thereof to the Committees on Appropriations of both Houses of Congress.*

(INCLUDING TRANSFER OF FUNDS)

SEC. 202. *Amounts made available for the Department of Veterans Affairs for fiscal year 2023, in this or any other Act, under the "Medical Services", "Medical Community Care", "Medical Support and Compliance", and "Medical Facilities" accounts may be transferred among the accounts: Provided, That before any such* transfer may take place, the Secretary of Veterans Affairs shall submit notice thereof to the Committees on Appropriations of both Houses of Congress.

SEC. 203. Appropriations available in this title for salaries and expenses shall be available for services authorized by section 3109 of title 5, United States Code; hire of passenger motor vehicles; lease of a facility or land or both; and uniforms or allowances therefore, as authorized by sections 5901 through 5902 of title 5, United States Code.

SEC. 204. No appropriations in this title (except the appropriations for "Construction, Major Projects", and "Construction, Minor Projects") shall be available for the purchase of any site for or toward the construction of any new hospital or home.

SEC. 205. No appropriations in this title shall be available for hospitalization or examination of any persons (except beneficiaries entitled to such hospitalization or examination under the laws providing such benefits to veterans, and persons receiving such treatment under sections 7901 through 7904 of title 5, United States Code, or the Robert T. Stafford Disaster Relief and Emergency Assistance Act (42 U.S.C. 5121 et seq.)), unless reimbursement of the cost of such hospitalization or examination is made to the "Medical Services" account at such rates as may be fixed by the Secretary of Veterans Affairs.

SEC. 206. Appropriations available in this title for "Compensation and Pensions", "Readjustment Benefits", and "Veterans Insurance and Indemnities" shall be available for payment of prior year accrued obligations required to be recorded by law against the corresponding prior year accounts within the last quarter of fiscal year 2022.

SEC. 207. Appropriations available in this title shall be available to pay prior year obligations of corresponding prior year appropriations accounts resulting from sections 3328(a), 3334, and 3712(a) of title 31, United States Code, except that if such obligations are from trust fund accounts they shall be payable only from "Compensation and Pensions".

(INCLUDING TRANSFER OF FUNDS)

SEC. 208. Notwithstanding any other provision of law, during fiscal year 2023, the Secretary of Veterans Affairs shall, from the National Service Life Insurance Fund under section 1920 of title 38, United States Code, the Veterans' Special Life Insurance Fund under section 1923 of title 38, United States Code, and the United States Government Life Insurance Fund under section 1955 of title 38, United States Code, reimburse the "General Operating Expenses, Veterans Benefits Administration" and "Information Technology Systems" accounts for the cost of administration of the insurance programs financed through those accounts: Provided, That reimbursement shall be made only from the surplus earnings accumulated in such an insurance program during fiscal year 2023 that are available for dividends in that program after claims have been paid and actuarially determined reserves have been set aside: Provided further, That if the cost of administration of such an insurance program exceeds the amount of surplus earnings accumulated in that program, reimbursement shall be made only to the extent of such surplus earnings: Provided further, That the Secretary shall determine the cost of administration for fiscal year 2023 which is properly allocable to the provision of each such insurance program and to the provision of any total disability income insurance included in that insurance program.

SEC. 209. Amounts deducted from enhanced-use lease proceeds to reimburse an account for expenses incurred by that account during a prior fiscal year for providing enhanced-use lease services shall be available until expended.

(INCLUDING TRANSFER OF FUNDS)

SEC. 210. Funds available in this title or funds for salaries and other administrative expenses shall also be available to reimburse the Office of Resolution Management, Diversity and Inclusion, the Office of Employment Discrimination Complaint Adjudication, and the Alternative Dispute Resolution function within the Office of Human Resources and Administration for all services provided at rates which will recover actual costs but not to exceed $86,481,000 for the Office of Resolution Management, Diversity and Inclusion, $6,812,000 for the Office of Employment Discrimination Complaint Adjudication, and $4,576,000 for the Alternative Dispute Resolution function within the Office of Human Resources and Administration: Provided, That payments may be made in advance for services to be furnished based on estimated costs: Provided further, That amounts received shall be credited to the "General Administration" and "Information Technology Systems" accounts for use by the office that provided the service.

SEC. 211. No funds of the Department of Veterans Affairs shall be available for hospital care, nursing home care, or medical services provided to any person under chapter 17 of title 38, United States Code, for a non-service-connected disability described in section 1729(a)(2) of such title, unless that person has disclosed to the Secretary of Veterans Affairs, in such form as the Secretary may require, current, accurate third-party reimbursement information for purposes of section 1729 of such title: Provided, That the Secretary may recover, in the same manner as any other debt due the United States, the reasonable charges for such care or services from any person who does not make such disclosure as required: Provided further,

That any amounts so recovered for care or services provided in a prior fiscal year may be obligated by the Secretary during the fiscal year in which amounts are received.

(INCLUDING TRANSFER OF FUNDS)

SEC. 212. Notwithstanding any other provision of law, proceeds or revenues derived from enhanced-use leasing activities (including disposal) may be deposited into the "Construction, Major Projects" and "Construction, Minor Projects" accounts and be used for construction (including site acquisition and disposition), alterations, and improvements of any medical facility under the jurisdiction or for the use of the Department of Veterans Affairs. Such sums as realized are in addition to the amount provided for in "Construction, Major Projects" and "Construction, Minor Projects".

SEC. 213. Amounts made available under "Medical Services" are available—
(1) for furnishing recreational facilities, supplies, and equipment; and
(2) for funeral expenses, burial expenses, and other expenses incidental to funerals and burials for beneficiaries receiving care in the Department.

(INCLUDING TRANSFER OF FUNDS)

SEC. 214. Such sums as may be deposited in the Medical Care Collections Fund pursuant to section 1729A of title 38, United States Code, may be transferred to the "Medical Services" and "Medical Community Care" accounts to remain available until expended for the purposes of these accounts.

SEC. 215. The Secretary of Veterans Affairs may enter into agreements with Federally Qualified Health Centers in the State of Alaska and Indian tribes and tribal organizations which are party to the Alaska Native Health Compact with the Indian Health Service, to provide healthcare, including behavioral health and dental care, to veterans in rural Alaska. The Secretary shall require participating veterans and facilities to comply with all appropriate rules and regulations, as established by the Secretary. The term "rural Alaska" shall mean those lands which are not within the boundaries of the municipality of Anchorage or the Fairbanks North Star Borough.

(INCLUDING TRANSFER OF FUNDS)

SEC. 216. Such sums as may be deposited to the Department of Veterans Affairs Capital Asset Fund pursuant to section 8118 of title 38, United States Code, may be transferred to the "Construction, Major Projects" and "Construction, Minor Projects" accounts, to remain available until expended for the purposes of these accounts.

SEC. 217. Not later than 30 days after the end of each fiscal quarter, the Secretary of Veterans Affairs shall submit to the Committees on Appropriations of both Houses of Congress a report on the financial status of the Department of Veterans Affairs for the preceding quarter: Provided, That, at a minimum, the report shall include the direction contained in the paragraph entitled "Quarterly reporting", under the heading "General Administration" in the joint explanatory statement accompanying Public Law 114–223.

(INCLUDING TRANSFER OF FUNDS)

SEC. 218. Amounts made available under the "Medical Services", "Medical Community Care", "Medical Support and Compliance", "Medical Facilities", "General Operating Expenses, Veterans Benefits Administration", "Board of Veterans Appeals", "General Administration", and "National Cemetery Administration" accounts for fiscal year 2023 may be transferred to or from the "Information Technology Systems" account: Provided, That such transfers may not result in a more than 10 percent aggregate increase in the total amount made available by this Act for the "Information Technology Systems" account: Provided further, That, before a transfer may take place, the Secretary of Veterans Affairs shall submit notice thereof to the Committees on Appropriations of both Houses of Congress.

(INCLUDING TRANSFER OF FUNDS)

SEC. 219. Of the amounts appropriated to the Department of Veterans Affairs for fiscal year 2023 for "Medical Services", "Medical Community Care", "Medical Support and Compliance", "Medical Facilities", "Construction, Minor Projects", and "Information Technology Systems", up to $330,140,000, plus reimbursements, may be transferred to the Joint Department of Defense—Department of Veterans Affairs Medical Facility Demonstration Fund, established by section 1704 of the National Defense Authorization Act for Fiscal Year 2010 (Public Law 111–84; 123 Stat. 2571) and may be used for operation of the facilities designated as combined Federal medical facilities as described by section 706 of the Duncan Hunter National Defense Authorization Act for Fiscal Year 2009 (Public Law 110–417; 122 Stat. 4500): Provided, That additional funds may be transferred from accounts designated in this section to the Joint Department of Defense—Department of Veterans Affairs Medical Facility Demonstration Fund upon written notification by the Secretary of Veterans Affairs to the Committees on Appropriations of both Houses of Congress: Provided further, That section 220 of title II of division J of Public Law 116–260 is repealed.

(INCLUDING TRANSFER OF FUNDS)

SEC. 220. Of the amounts appropriated to the Department of Veterans Affairs which become available on October 1, 2023, for "Medical Services", "Medical

Community Care", "Medical Support and Compliance", and "Medical Facilities", up to $314,825,000, plus reimbursements, may be transferred to the Joint Department of Defense—Department of Veterans Affairs Medical Facility Demonstration Fund, established by section 1704 of the National Defense Authorization Act for Fiscal Year 2010 (Public Law 111–84; 123 Stat. 2571) and may be used for operation of the facilities designated as combined Federal medical facilities as described by section 706 of the Duncan Hunter National Defense Authorization Act for Fiscal Year 2009 (Public Law 110–417; 122 Stat. 4500): Provided, That additional funds may be transferred from accounts designated in this section to the Joint Department of Defense—Department of Veterans Affairs Medical Facility Demonstration Fund upon written notification by the Secretary of Veterans Affairs to the Committees on Appropriations of both Houses of Congress.

(INCLUDING TRANSFER OF FUNDS)

SEC. 221. Such sums as may be deposited to the Medical Care Collections Fund pursuant to section 1729A of title 38, United States Code, for healthcare provided at facilities designated as combined Federal medical facilities as described by section 706 of the Duncan Hunter National Defense Authorization Act for Fiscal Year 2009 (Public Law 110–417; 122 Stat. 4500) shall also be available: (1) for transfer to the Joint Department of Defense—Department of Veterans Affairs Medical Facility Demonstration Fund, established by section 1704 of the National Defense Authorization Act for Fiscal Year 2010 (Public Law 111–84; 123 Stat. 3571); and (2) for operations of the facilities designated as combined Federal medical facilities as described by section 706 of the Duncan Hunter National Defense Authorization Act for Fiscal Year 2009 (Public Law 110–417; 122 Stat. 4500): Provided, That, notwithstanding section 1704(b)(3) of the National Defense Authorization Act for Fiscal Year 2010 (Public Law 111–84; 123 Stat. 2573), amounts transferred to the Joint Department of Defense—Department of Veterans Affairs Medical Facility Demonstration Fund shall remain available until expended.

(INCLUDING TRANSFER OF FUNDS)

SEC. 222. Of the amounts available in this title for "Medical Services", "Medical Community Care", "Medical Support and Compliance", and "Medical Facilities", a minimum of $15,000,000 shall be transferred to the DOD-VA Health Care Sharing Incentive Fund, as authorized by section 8111(d) of title 38, United States Code, to remain available until expended, for any purpose authorized by section 8111 of title 38, United States Code.

(INCLUDING TRANSFER OF FUNDS)

SEC. 223. The Secretary of Veterans Affairs, upon determination that such action is necessary to address needs of the Veterans Health Administration, may transfer to the "Medical Services" account any discretionary appropriations made available for fiscal year 2023 in this title (except appropriations made to the "General Operating Expenses, Veterans Benefits Administration" account) or any discretionary unobligated balances within the Department of Veterans Affairs, including those appropriated for fiscal year 2023, that were provided in advance by appropriations Acts: Provided, That transfers shall be made only with the approval of the Office of Management and Budget: Provided further, That the transfer authority provided in this section is in addition to any other transfer authority provided by law: Provided further, That no amounts may be transferred from amounts that were designated by Congress as an emergency requirement pursuant to a concurrent resolution on the budget or the Balanced Budget and Emergency Deficit Control Act of 1985: Provided further, That such authority to transfer may not be used unless for higher priority items, based on emergent healthcare requirements, than those for which originally appropriated and in no case where the item for which funds are requested has been denied by Congress: Provided further, That, upon determination that all or part of the funds transferred from an appropriation are not necessary, such amounts may be transferred back to that appropriation and shall be available for the same purposes as originally appropriated: Provided further, That before a transfer may take place, the Secretary of Veterans Affairs shall submit notice thereof to the Committees on Appropriations of both Houses of Congress.

(INCLUDING TRANSFER OF FUNDS)

SEC. 224. Amounts made available for the Department of Veterans Affairs for fiscal year 2023, under the "Board of Veterans Appeals" and the "General Operating Expenses, Veterans Benefits Administration" accounts may be transferred between such accounts: Provided, That before a transfer may take place, the Secretary of Veterans Affairs shall submit notice thereof to the Committees on Appropriations of both Houses of Congress.

SEC. 225. The Secretary of Veterans Affairs may not reprogram funds among major construction projects or programs if such instance of reprogramming will exceed $7,000,000, unless the Secretary of Veterans Affairs submits notice thereof to the Committees on Appropriations of both Houses of Congress.

SEC. 226. None of the funds appropriated or otherwise made available by this Act or any other Act for the Department of Veterans Affairs may be used in a manner that is inconsistent with: (1) section 842 of the Transportation, Treasury, Housing and Urban Development, the Judiciary, the District of Columbia, and Independent Agencies Appropriations Act, 2006 (Public Law 109–115; 119 Stat. 2506); or (2) section 8110(a)(5) of title 38, United States Code.

SEC. 227. Section 842 of Public Law 109–115 shall not apply to conversion of an activity or function of the Veterans Health Administration, Veterans Benefits Administration, or National Cemetery Administration to contractor performance by a business concern that is at least 51 percent owned by one or more Indian tribes as defined in section 5304(e) of title 25, United States Code, or one or more Native Hawaiian Organizations as defined in section 637(a)(15) of title 15, United States Code.

SEC. 228. (a) Except as provided in subsection (b), the Secretary of Veterans Affairs, in consultation with the Secretary of Defense and the Secretary of Labor, shall discontinue using Social Security account numbers to identify individuals in all information systems of the Department of Veterans Affairs as follows:

(1) For all veterans submitting to the Secretary of Veterans Affairs new claims for benefits under laws administered by the Secretary, not later than March 23, 2023.

(2) For all individuals not described in paragraph (1), not later than March 23, 2026.

(b) The Secretary of Veterans Affairs may use a Social Security account number to identify an individual in an information system of the Department of Veterans Affairs if and only if the use of such number is required to obtain information the Secretary requires from an information system that is not under the jurisdiction of the Secretary.

(c) The matter in subsections (a) and (b) shall supersede section 238 of Public Law 116–94.

SEC. 229. Of the funds provided to the Department of Veterans Affairs for each of fiscal year 2023 and fiscal year 2024 for "Medical Services", funds may be used in each year to carry out and expand the child care program authorized by section 205 of Public Law 111–163, notwithstanding subsection (e) of such section.

SEC. 230. (a) No funds provided in this Act shall be used to deny an Inspector General funded under this Act timely access to any records, documents, or other materials available to the department or agency over which that Inspector General has responsibilities under the Inspector General Act of 1978, or to prevent or impede that Inspector General's access to such records, documents, or other materials, under any provision of law, except a provision of law that expressly refers to the Inspector General and expressly limits the Inspector General's right of access.

(b) A department or agency covered by this section shall provide its Inspector General access to all records, documents, and other materials in a timely manner.

(c) Each Inspector General shall ensure compliance with statutory limitations on disclosure relevant to the information provided by the establishment over which that Inspector General has responsibilities under the Inspector General Act of 1978.

(d) Each Inspector General covered by this section shall report to the Committee on Appropriations of the Senate and the Committee on Appropriations of the House of Representatives within 5 calendar days of any failure by any department or agency covered by this section to comply with this requirement.

SEC. 231. For funds provided to the Department of Veterans Affairs for each of fiscal year 2023 and 2024, section 248 of division A of Public Law 114–223 shall apply.

SEC. 232. (a) None of the funds appropriated or otherwise made available by this Act may be used to conduct research commencing on or after October 1, 2019, that uses any canine, feline, or non-human primate unless the Secretary of Veterans Affairs approves such research specifically and in writing pursuant to subsection (b).

(b)

(1) The Secretary of Veterans Affairs may approve the conduct of research commencing on or after October 1, 2019, using canines, felines, or non-human primates if the Secretary determines that—

(A) the scientific objectives of the research can only be met by using such canines, felines, or non-human primates;

(B) such scientific objectives are directly related to an illness or injury that is combat-related; and

(C) the research is consistent with the revised Department of Veterans Affairs canine research policy document dated December 15, 2017, including any subsequent revisions to such document.

(2) The Secretary may not delegate the authority under this subsection.

(c) If the Secretary approves any new research pursuant to subsection (b), not later than 30 days before the commencement of such research, the Secretary shall submit to the Committees on Appropriations of the Senate and House of Representatives a report describing—

(1) the nature of the research to be conducted using canines, felines, or non-human primates;

(2) the date on which the Secretary approved the research;

(3) the justification for the determination of the Secretary that the scientific objectives of such research could only be met using canines, felines, or non-human primates;

(4) the frequency and duration of such research; and

(5) the protocols in place to ensure the necessity, safety, and efficacy of the research; and

(d) Not later than 180 days after the date of the enactment of this Act, and biannually thereafter, the Secretary shall submit to such Committees a report describing—

(1) any research being conducted by the Department of Veterans Affairs using canines, felines, or non-human primates as of the date of the submittal of the report;

(2) the circumstances under which such research was conducted using canines, felines, or non-human primates;

(3) the justification for using canines, felines, or non-human primates to conduct such research; and

(4) the protocols in place to ensure the necessity, safety, and efficacy of such research.

(e) Not later than December 31, 2022, the Secretary shall submit to such Committees an updated plan under which the Secretary will eliminate or reduce the research conducted using canines, felines, or non-human primates by not later than 5 years after the date of enactment of Public Law 116–94.

SEC. 233. Amounts made available for the "Veterans Health Administration, Medical Community Care" account in this or any other Act for fiscal years 2023 and 2024 may be used for expenses that would otherwise be payable from the Veterans Choice Fund established by section 802 of the Veterans Access, Choice, and Accountability Act, as amended (38 U.S.C. 1701 note).

SEC. 234. Obligations and expenditures applicable to the "Medical Services" account in fiscal years 2017 through 2019 for aid to state homes (as authorized by section 1741 of title 38, United States Code) shall remain in the "Medical Community Care" account for such fiscal years.

GENERAL FUND RECEIPT ACCOUNTS

(in millions of dollars)

		2021 actual	2022 est.	2023 est.
Offsetting receipts from the public:				
036–143500	General Fund Proprietary Interest Receipts, not Otherwise Classified	1	6	7
036–247300	Contributions from Military Personnel, Veteran's Educational Assistance Act of 1984	132	122	34
036–273330	Housing Downward Reestimates	2,022	337	
036–275110	Native American Veteran Housing Loans, Negative Subsidies	2	2	2
036–275130	Native American Direct Loans, Downward Reestimate of Subsidies	1		
036–275510	Housing Negative Subsidies	2,115	282	47
036–322000	All Other General Fund Proprietary Receipts Including Budget Clearing Accounts	44	53	54
General Fund Offsetting receipts from the public		4,317	802	144
Intragovernmental payments:				
036–388500	Undistributed Intragovernmental Payments and Receivables from Cancelled Accounts	8	7	8
General Fund Intragovernmental payments		8	7	8

GENERAL PROVISIONS

SEC. 501. No part of any appropriation contained in this Act shall remain available for obligation beyond the current fiscal year unless expressly so provided herein.

SEC. 502. None of the funds made available in this Act may be used for any program, project, or activity, when it is made known to the Federal entity or official to which the funds are made available that the program, project, or activity is not in compliance with any Federal law relating to risk assessment, the protection of private property rights, or unfunded mandates.

SEC. 503. Unless stated otherwise, all reports and notifications required by this Act shall be submitted to the Subcommittee on Military Construction and Veterans Affairs, and Related Agencies of the Committee on Appropriations of the House of Representatives and the Subcommittee on Military Construction and Veterans Affairs, and Related Agencies of the Committee on Appropriations of the Senate.

SEC. 504. None of the funds made available in this Act may be transferred to any department, agency, or instrumentality of the United States Government except pursuant to a transfer made by, or transfer authority provided in, this or any other appropriations Act.

SEC. 505. None of the funds made available in this Act may be used for a project or program named for an individual serving as a Member, Delegate, or Resident Commissioner of the United States House of Representatives.

SEC. 506. (a) None of the funds made available in this Act may be used to maintain or establish a computer network unless such network blocks the viewing, downloading, and exchanging of pornography.

(b) Nothing in subsection (a) shall limit the use of funds necessary for any Federal, State, tribal, or local law enforcement agency or any other entity carrying out criminal investigations, prosecution, or adjudication activities.

SEC. 507. None of the funds made available in this Act may be used by an agency of the executive branch to pay for first-class travel by an employee of the agency in contravention of sections 301–10.122 through 301–10.124 of title 41, Code of Federal Regulations.

SEC. 508. None of the funds made available in this Act may be used to execute a contract for goods or services, including construction services, where the contractor has not complied with Executive Order No. 12989.

CORPS OF ENGINEERS—CIVIL WORKS

The following appropriations shall be expended under the direction of the Secretary of the Army and the supervision of the Chief of Engineers for authorized civil functions of the Department of the Army pertaining to commercial navigation, flood and storm damage reduction, aquatic ecosystem restoration, and related efforts.

Federal Funds

OFFICE OF THE ASSISTANT SECRETARY OF THE ARMY FOR CIVIL WORKS

For the Office of the Assistant Secretary of the Army for Civil Works, $5,000,000, to remain available until September 30, 2024.

Note.—A full-year 2022 appropriation for this account was not enacted at the time the Budget was prepared; therefore, the Budget assumes this account is operating under the Continuing Appropriations Act, 2022 (Division A of Public Law 117–43, as amended). The amounts included for 2022 reflect the annualized level provided by the continuing resolution.

Program and Financing (in millions of dollars)

Identification code 096–3132–0–1–301		2021 actual	2022 est.	2023 est.
	Obligations by program activity:			
0001	Office of Assistant Secretary of the Army (Civil Works)	5	5	5
0900	Total new obligations, unexpired accounts (object class 25.3)	5	5	5
	Budgetary resources:			
	Unobligated balance:			
1021	Recoveries of prior year unpaid obligations	1	1	1
	Budget authority:			
	Appropriations, discretionary:			
1100	Appropriation	5	5	5
1131	Unobligated balance of appropriations permanently reduced	–1	–1	
1160	Appropriation, discretionary (total)	4	4	5
1930	Total budgetary resources available	5	5	6
	Memorandum (non-add) entries:			
1941	Unexpired unobligated balance, end of year			1
	Change in obligated balance:			
	Unpaid obligations:			
3000	Unpaid obligations, brought forward, Oct 1	5	4	3
3010	New obligations, unexpired accounts	5	5	5
3020	Outlays (gross)	–4	–5	–6
3040	Recoveries of prior year unpaid obligations, unexpired	–1	–1	–1
3041	Recoveries of prior year unpaid obligations, expired	–1		
3050	Unpaid obligations, end of year	4	3	1
	Memorandum (non-add) entries:			
3100	Obligated balance, start of year	5	4	3
3200	Obligated balance, end of year	4	3	1
	Budget authority and outlays, net:			
	Discretionary:			
4000	Budget authority, gross	4	4	5
	Outlays, gross:			
4010	Outlays from new discretionary authority	1	4	5
4011	Outlays from discretionary balances	3	1	1
4020	Outlays, gross (total)	4	5	6
4180	Budget authority, net (total)	4	4	5
4190	Outlays, net (total)	4	5	6

This appropriation funds strategic planning for and overall supervision of the Army's civil works program.

WATER INFRASTRUCTURE FINANCE AND INNOVATION PROGRAM ACCOUNT

For administrative expenses to carry out the direct and guaranteed loan programs authorized by the Water Infrastructure Finance and Innovation Act of 2014, notwithstanding subsections (b)(2) and (c) of section 5033 of such Act, $10,000,000, to remain available until September 30, 2024: Provided, That such amounts shall only be used for administrative expenses of projects funded with amounts provided under this heading in the Consolidated Appropriations Act, 2021 (Public Law 116–260) or the Infrastructure Investment and Jobs Act (Public Law 117–58).

Note.—A full-year 2022 appropriation for this account was not enacted at the time the Budget was prepared; therefore, the Budget assumes this account is operating under the Continuing Appropriations Act, 2022 (Division A of Public Law 117–43, as amended). The amounts included for 2022 reflect the annualized level provided by the continuing resolution.

WATER INFRASTRUCTURE FINANCE AND INNOVATION PROGRAM ACCOUNT

[For an additional amount for "Water Infrastructure Finance and Innovation Program Account", $75,000,000, to remain available until expended: Provided, That of the amounts provided under this heading in this Act, $64,000,000 shall be for the cost of direct loans and for the cost of guaranteed loans, for safety projects to maintain, upgrade, and repair dams identified in the National Inventory of Dams with a primary owner type of state, local government, public utility, or private: Provided further, That no project may be funded with amounts provided under this heading for a dam that is identified as jointly owned in the National Inventory of Dams and where one of those joint owners is the Federal Government: Provided further, That of the amounts provided under this heading in this Act $11,000,000 shall be for administrative expenses to carry out the direct and guaranteed loan programs, notwithstanding section 5033 of the Water Infrastructure Finance and Innovation Act of 2014: Provided further, That such amount is designated by the Congress as being for an emergency requirement pursuant to section 4112(a) of H. Con. Res. 71 (115th Congress), the concurrent resolution on the budget for fiscal year 2018, and to section 251(b) of the Balanced Budget and Emergency Deficit Control Act of 1985.] (Infrastructure Investments and Jobs Appropriations Act.)

Program and Financing (in millions of dollars)

Identification code 096–3139–0–1–301		2021 actual	2022 est.	2023 est.
	Obligations by program activity:			
	Credit program obligations:			
0709	Administrative expenses	1	1	1
0900	Total new obligations, unexpired accounts (object class 41.0)	1	1	1
	Budgetary resources:			
	Unobligated balance:			
1000	Unobligated balance brought forward, Oct 1		13	101
	Budget authority:			
	Appropriations, discretionary:			
1100	Appropriation		89	10
	Advance appropriations, discretionary:			
1170	Advance appropriation	14		
1900	Budget authority (total)	14	89	10
1930	Total budgetary resources available	14	102	111
	Memorandum (non-add) entries:			
1941	Unexpired unobligated balance, end of year	13	101	110
	Change in obligated balance:			
	Unpaid obligations:			
3000	Unpaid obligations, brought forward, Oct 1		1	1
3010	New obligations, unexpired accounts	1	1	1
3020	Outlays (gross)		–1	–1
3050	Unpaid obligations, end of year	1	1	1
	Memorandum (non-add) entries:			
3100	Obligated balance, start of year		1	1
3200	Obligated balance, end of year	1	1	1
	Budget authority and outlays, net:			
	Discretionary:			
4000	Budget authority, gross	14	89	10
	Outlays, gross:			
4011	Outlays from discretionary balances		1	1
4180	Budget authority, net (total)	14	89	10
4190	Outlays, net (total)		1	1

Summary of Loan Levels, Subsidy Budget Authority and Outlays by Program (in millions of dollars)

Identification code 096–3139–0–1–301		2021 actual	2022 est.	2023 est.
	Administrative expense data:			
3510	Budget authority	14	89	10

A new federal credit program for dam safety at non-federal dams is being established with funds first appropriated in FY 2021. The Army Corps is currently working on regulations to implement this program. The 2023

WATER INFRASTRUCTURE FINANCE AND INNOVATION PROGRAM ACCOUNT—Continued

Budget proposes $10 million for administrative expenses related to non-federal dam safety projects for this program.

CONSTRUCTION

For expenses necessary for the construction of commercial navigation, flood and storm damage reduction, and aquatic ecosystem restoration projects, and related efforts; and for studies, design work, and plans and specifications of such projects, and related efforts, $1,221,288,000, to remain available until expended.

Note.—A full-year 2022 appropriation for this account was not enacted at the time the Budget was prepared; therefore, the Budget assumes this account is operating under the Continuing Appropriations Act, 2022 (Division A of Public Law 117–43, as amended). The amounts included for 2022 reflect the annualized level provided by the continuing resolution.

CONSTRUCTION

[For an additional amount for "Construction" for necessary expenses, $3,000,000,000, to remain available until expended, to construct flood and storm damage reduction, including shore protection, projects that are currently authorized or that are authorized after the date of enactment of this Act, and flood and storm damage reduction, including shore protection, projects that have signed Chief's Reports as of the date of enactment of this Act or that are studied using funds provided under the heading "Investigations" if the Secretary determines such projects to be technically feasible, economically justified, and environmentally acceptable: Provided, That of such amount, $1,500,000,000 shall be available for such projects in States with a major disaster declared due to Hurricane Ida pursuant to the Robert T. Stafford Disaster Relief and Emergency Assistance Act (42 U.S.C. 5121 et seq.) in fiscal year 2021: Provided further, That the provisions of section 902 of the Water Resources Development Act of 1986 shall not apply to the construction of projects, including initial construction or periodic nourishment, completed using funding under this heading in this Act: Provided further, That the completion of ongoing construction projects receiving funding provided under this heading in this Act shall be at full Federal expense with respect to such funds: Provided further, That for any projects using funding provided under this heading in this Act, the non-Federal cash contribution for projects other than ongoing construction projects shall be financed in accordance with the provisions of section 103(k) of Public Law 99–662 over a period of 30 years from the date of completion of the project or separable element: Provided further, That up to $65,000,000 of the amounts made available under this heading in this Act shall be used for continuing authorities projects to reduce the risk of flooding and storm damage: Provided further, That any projects using funding appropriated under this heading in this Act shall be initiated only after non-Federal interests have entered into binding agreements with the Secretary requiring, where applicable, the non-Federal interests to pay 100 percent of the operation, maintenance, repair, replacement, and rehabilitation costs of the project and to hold and save the United States free from damages due to the construction or operation and maintenance of the project, except for damages due to the fault or negligence of the United States or its contractors: Provided further, That of the amounts made available under this heading in this Act, such sums as are necessary to cover the Federal share of construction costs for facilities under the Dredged Material Disposal Facilities Program shall be derived from the general fund of the Treasury: Provided further, That the Assistant Secretary of the Army for Civil Works shall provide a monthly report directly to the Committees on Appropriations of the House of Representatives and the Senate detailing the allocation and obligation of these funds, beginning not later than 60 days after the date of enactment of this Act.] (Disaster Relief Supplemental Appropriations Act, 2022.)

CONSTRUCTION

[For an additional amount for "Construction", $11,615,000,000, to remain available until expended: Provided, That the Secretary may initiate additional new construction starts with funds provided under this heading in this Act: Provided further, That the limitation concerning total project costs in section 902 of the Water Resources Development Act of 1986 (Public Law 99–662; 33 U.S.C. 2280), as amended, shall not apply to any project completed using funds provided under this heading in this Act: Provided further, That of the amount provided under this heading in this Act, such sums as are necessary to cover the Federal share of construction costs for facilities under the Dredged Material Disposal Facilities program shall be derived from the general fund of the Treasury: Provided further, That of the amount provided under this heading in this Act, $1,500,000,000 shall be for major rehabilitation, construction, and related activities for rivers and harbors, of which not more than $250,000,000 shall be to undertake work at harbors defined by section 2006 of the Water Resources Development Act of 2007 (Public Law 110–114, 33 U.S.C. 2242), as amended, and not more than $250,000,000 may be for projects determined to require repair in the report prepared pursuant to section 1104 of the Water Infrastructure Improvements for the Nation Act (Public Law 114–322): Provided further, That of the amount provided under this heading in this Act, $200,000,000 shall be for water-related environmental infrastructure assistance: Provided further, That of the amount provided under this heading in this Act, $2,500,000,000 shall be for construction, replacement, rehabilitation, and expansion of inland waterways projects: Provided further, That section 102(a) of the Water Resources Development Act of 1986 (Public Law 99–662; 33 U.S.C. 2212(a)) and section 109 of the Water Resources Development Act of 2020 (Public Law 116–260; 134 Stat. 2624) shall not apply to the extent that such projects are carried out using funds provided in the preceding proviso: Provided further, That in using such funds referred to in the preceding proviso, the Secretary shall give priority to projects included in the Capital Investment Strategy of the Corps of Engineers: Provided further, That of the amount provided under this heading in this Act, $465,000,000 shall be used by the Secretary of the Army, acting through the Chief of Engineers, to undertake work authorized to be carried out in accordance with section 14, as amended, of the Flood Control Act of 1946 (33 U.S.C. 701r), section 103, as amended, of the River and Harbor Act of 1962 (Public Law 87–874), section 107, as amended, of the River and Harbor Act 1960 (Public Law 86–645), section 204 of the Water Resources Development Act of 1992 (33 U.S.C. 2326), section 205 of the Flood Control Act of 1948 (33 U.S.C. 701s), section 206 of the Water Resources Development Act of 1996 (Public Law 104–303; 33 U.S.C. 2330), section 1135 of the Water Resources Development Act of 1986 (Public Law 99–662; 33 U.S.C. 2309a), or section 165(a) of division AA of the Consolidated Appropriations Act, 2021 (Public Law 116–260), notwithstanding the project number or program cost limitations set forth in those sections: Provided further, That of the amounts in the preceding proviso, $115,000,000, shall be used under the aquatic ecosystem restoration program under section 206 of the Water Resources Development Act of 1996 (33 U.S.C. 2330) to restore fish and wildlife passage by removing in-stream barriers and provide technical assistance to non-Federal interests carrying out such activities, at full Federal expense and notwithstanding the individual project cost limitation set forth in that section: Provided further, That the amounts provided in the preceding proviso shall not be construed to provide any new authority to remove, breach, or otherwise alter the operations of a Federal hydropower dam, and do not limit the Secretary of the Army, acting through the Chief of Engineers, from allotting additional funds from amounts provided under this heading in this Act for other purposes allowed under section 206 of the Water Resources Development Act of 1996 (33 U.S.C. 2330): Provided further, That of the amount provided under this heading in this Act, $1,900,000,000 shall be for aquatic ecosystem restoration projects, of which not less than $1,000,000,000 shall be for multi-purpose projects or multi-purpose programs that include aquatic ecosystem restoration as a purpose: Provided further, That of the amount provided under this heading in this Act, $2,550,000,000 shall be for coastal storm risk management, hurricane and storm damage reduction projects, and related activities targeting States that have been impacted by federally declared disasters over the last six years, which may include projects authorized by section 116 of Public Law 111–85, of which not less than $1,000,000,000 shall be for multi-purpose projects or multi-purpose programs that include flood risk management benefits as a purpose: Provided further, That of the amount provided in the preceding proviso, $200,000,000 shall be for shore protection projects: Provided further, That of the funds in the preceding proviso, $100,000,000, to remain available until expended, shall be made available for fiscal year 2022, $50,000,000, to remain available until expended, shall be made available for fiscal year 2023, and $50,000,000, to remain available until expended, shall be made available for fiscal year 2024: Provided further, That of the amount provided under this heading in this Act, $2,500,000,000 shall be for inland flood risk management projects, of which not less than $750,000,000 shall be for multi-purpose projects or multi-purpose programs that include flood risk management as a purpose: Provided further, That in selecting projects under the previous proviso, the Secretary of the Army shall prioritize projects with overriding life-safety benefits: Provided further, That of the funds in the proviso preceding the preceding proviso, the Secretary of the Army shall, to the maximum extent practicable, prioritize projects in the work plan that directly benefit economically disadvantaged communities, and may take into consideration prioritizing projects that benefit areas in which the percentage of people that live in poverty or identify as belonging to a minority group is greater than the average such percentage in the United States, based on data from the Bureau of the Census: Provided further, That not later than 60 days after the date of enactment of this Act, the Chief of Engineers shall submit to the House and Senate Committees on Appropriations a detailed spend plan for the funds provided under this heading in this Act for each fiscal year, including a list of project locations and new construction projects selected to be initiated: Provided further, That beginning not later than 120 days after the enactment of this Act, the Chief of Engineers shall provide a monthly report to the Committees on Appropriations of the House of Representatives and the Senate detailing the allocation and obligation of these funds, including new construction projects selected to be initiated using funds provided under this heading in this Act: *Provided further,* That such amount is designated by the Congress as being for an emergency requirement pursuant to section 4112(a) of H. Con. Res. 71 (115th Congress), the concurrent resolution on the budget for fiscal year 2018, and to section 251(b) of the Balanced Budget and Emergency Deficit Control Act of 1985.] *(Infrastructure Investments and Jobs Appropriations Act.)*

Program and Financing (in millions of dollars)

Identification code 096–3122–0–1–301		2021 actual	2022 est.	2023 est.
	Obligations by program activity:			
0001	Commercial Navigation	765	624	522
0002	Flood Risk Management	1,771	1,355	1,135
0003	Aquatic Ecosystem Restoration	545	341	285
0005	Multipurpose and Other Programs	113	80	67
0100	Direct program subtotal	3,194	2,400	2,009
0799	Total direct obligations	3,194	2,400	2,009
0801	Department of Homeland Security	378	1,202	1,015
0802	Department of Veteran Affairs	1,297	692	782
0803	Environmental Protection Agency	150	143	145
0804	National Aeronautics and Space Administration	15	25	25
0805	Department of Energy	51	74	62
0806	Other Federal Agencies	120	131	131
0807	Non-Federal Agencies	62	204	134
0808	Intra-Corps	100	139	137
0899	Total reimbursable obligations	2,173	2,610	2,431
0900	Total new obligations, unexpired accounts	5,367	5,010	4,440
	Budgetary resources:			
	Unobligated balance:			
1000	Unobligated balance brought forward, Oct 1	24,256	22,176	36,577
1021	Recoveries of prior year unpaid obligations	94		
1033	Recoveries of prior year paid obligations	1		
1042	Adjustment for change in allocation (general fund portion)		–74	
1043	Adjustment for change in allocation (offsetting collection/collected portion)	74		
1070	Unobligated balance (total)	24,351	22,176	36,577
	Budget authority:			
	Appropriations, discretionary:			
1100	Appropriation	2,652	17,030	1,221
	Advance appropriations, discretionary:			
1170	Advance appropriation			50
	Spending authority from offsetting collections, discretionary:			
1700	Collected (Inland Waterways Trust Fund)	25	64	
1700	Collected (Inland Waterways Trust Fund FY2020)	8		
1700	Collected (Inland Waterways Trust Fund FY2019)	5		
1700	Collected (Harbor Maintenance Trust Fund)	80		
1700	Collected (Harbor Maintenance Trust Fund FY2020)	95		
1700	Collected (Harbor Maintenance Trust Fund FY2019)	24		
1700	Collected (Construction)	1,737	2,317	2,273
1701	Change in uncollected payments, Federal sources	–1,434		
1750	Spending auth from offsetting collections, disc (total)	540	2,381	2,273
1900	Budget authority (total)	3,192	19,411	3,544
1930	Total budgetary resources available	27,543	41,587	40,121
	Memorandum (non-add) entries:			
1941	Unexpired unobligated balance, end of year	22,176	36,577	35,681
	Change in obligated balance:			
	Unpaid obligations:			
3000	Unpaid obligations, brought forward, Oct 1	7,502	8,282	8,511
3010	New obligations, unexpired accounts	5,367	5,010	4,440
3020	Outlays (gross)	–4,493	–4,781	–4,170
3040	Recoveries of prior year unpaid obligations, unexpired	–94		
3050	Unpaid obligations, end of year	8,282	8,511	8,781
	Uncollected payments:			
3060	Uncollected pymts, Fed sources, brought forward, Oct 1	–5,329	–3,895	–3,895
3070	Change in uncollected pymts, Fed sources, unexpired	1,434		
3090	Uncollected pymts, Fed sources, end of year	–3,895	–3,895	–3,895
	Memorandum (non-add) entries:			
3100	Obligated balance, start of year	2,173	4,387	4,616
3200	Obligated balance, end of year	4,387	4,616	4,886
	Budget authority and outlays, net:			
	Discretionary:			
4000	Budget authority, gross	3,192	19,411	3,544
	Outlays, gross:			
4010	Outlays from new discretionary authority		998	460
4011	Outlays from discretionary balances	4,493	3,783	3,710
4020	Outlays, gross (total)	4,493	4,781	4,170
	Offsets against gross budget authority and outlays:			
	Offsetting collections (collected) from:			
4030	Federal sources	–2,005	–2,381	–2,273
4033	Non-Federal sources	–44		
4040	Offsets against gross budget authority and outlays (total)	–2,049	–2,381	–2,273
	Additional offsets against gross budget authority only:			
4050	Change in uncollected pymts, Fed sources, unexpired	1,434		
4053	Recoveries of prior year paid obligations, unexpired accounts	1		
4055	Adjustment for change in allocation (offsetting collection portion)	74		
4060	Additional offsets against budget authority only (total)	1,509		
4070	Budget authority, net (discretionary)	2,652	17,030	1,271
4080	Outlays, net (discretionary)	2,444	2,400	1,897
4180	Budget authority, net (total)	2,652	17,030	1,271
4190	Outlays, net (total)	2,444	2,400	1,897

This appropriation funds the construction, replacement, rehabilitation, and expansion of water resources projects whose principal purpose is to provide commercial navigation, flood and storm damage reduction, or aquatic ecosystem restoration benefits to the Nation, and related efforts.

This account allocates funds on a performance basis to high-performing projects. The Budget funds those investments within the three main mission areas of the Corps civil works program—commercial navigation, flood and storm damage reduction, and aquatic ecosystem restoration—as well as related efforts that provide the best economic, environmental, and public safety returns to the Nation. In developing the Budget, consideration was given to advancing three key objectives including: 1) increasing infrastructure and ecosystem resilience to climate change and decreasing climate risk for communities based on the best available science; and 2) promoting environmental justice in disadvantaged communities in line with Justice40 and creating good paying jobs that promote a chance to join a union.

This account includes $392.7 million for work under the Comprehensive Everglades Restoration Plan (CERP), which represents approximately 32.2 percent of the total amount in this account and approximately 6.0 percent of the total amount in the civil works program. Funding CERP at this level would not have a significant impact on the overall civil works program in 2023. Construction account funding for CERP in future years will depend on the availability of funds, so the impact of such future funding on the overall civil works program cannot be determined at this time. Funding for the Department of the Interior (DOI) includes an additional $12.0 million for work under CERP. This account also includes approximately $14.3 million for other ecosystem restoration work by the Corps in South Florida, including the Everglades ecosystem. Funding for DOI includes $59.2 million for such non-CERP work. The Budget for the two agencies includes a total of $478.2 million for ecosystem restoration work in South Florida, of which $404.7 million is for CERP and $73.4 million is for non-CERP work (P.L. 106–541 section 601).

This appropriation also funds the Corps continuing authorities programs, which involve the planning, design, and construction of smaller projects that do not require specific authorizing legislation.

Object Classification (in millions of dollars)

Identification code 096–3122–0–1–301		2021 actual	2022 est.	2023 est.
	Direct obligations:			
	Personnel compensation:			
11.1	Full-time permanent	387	345	360
11.3	Other than full-time permanent	6	6	6
11.5	Other personnel compensation	15	13	14
11.8	Special personal services payments	21	22	21
11.9	Total personnel compensation	429	386	401
12.1	Civilian personnel benefits	74	65	68
21.0	Travel and transportation of persons	5	4	3
23.2	Rental payments to others	1		
25.1	Advisory and assistance services	36	13	10
25.2	Other services from non-Federal sources	157	121	96
25.3	Purchase of goods and services from Government accounts	72	55	43
25.4	Operation and maintenance of facilities	4	5	4

CONSTRUCTION—Continued

Object Classification—Continued

Identification code 096–3122–0–1–301	2021 actual	2022 est.	2023 est.
26.0 Supplies and materials	1	1	1
31.0 Equipment	1	1	1
32.0 Land and structures	2,412	1,747	1,380
41.0 Grants, subsidies, and contributions	2	2	2
99.0 Direct obligations	3,194	2,400	2,009
99.0 Reimbursable obligations	2,173	2,610	2,431
99.9 Total new obligations, unexpired accounts	5,367	5,010	4,440

Employment Summary

Identification code 096–3122–0–1–301	2021 actual	2022 est.	2023 est.
1001 Direct civilian full-time equivalent employment	3,239	3,002	3,002
2001 Reimbursable civilian full-time equivalent employment	1,547	1,600	1,600

OPERATION AND MAINTENANCE

For expenses necessary for the operation, maintenance, and care of existing commercial navigation, flood and storm damage reduction, and aquatic ecosystem restoration projects, and related efforts; providing security for infrastructure owned or operated by the Corps, including administrative buildings and laboratories; maintaining harbor channels provided by a State, municipality, or other public agency that serve essential navigation needs of general commerce, where authorized by law; surveying and charting northern and northwestern lakes and connecting waters; clearing and straightening channels; and removing obstructions to navigation, $2,599,047,000, to remain available until expended; of which such sums as become available from the special account for the Corps of Engineers established by the Land and Water Conservation Fund Act of 1965 shall be derived from that account for resource protection, research, interpretation, and maintenance activities related to resource protection in the areas managed by the Army Corps of Engineers at which outdoor recreation is available; and of which such sums as become available from fees collected under section 217 of Public Law 104–303 shall be used to cover the cost of operation and maintenance of the dredged material disposal facilities for which such fees have been collected.

Note.—A full-year 2022 appropriation for this account was not enacted at the time the Budget was prepared; therefore, the Budget assumes this account is operating under the Continuing Appropriations Act, 2022 (Division A of Public Law 117–43, as amended). The amounts included for 2022 reflect the annualized level provided by the continuing resolution.

OPERATION AND MAINTENANCE

[For an additional amount for "Operation and Maintenance" for necessary expenses to dredge Federal navigation projects in response to, and repair damages to Corps of Engineers Federal projects caused by, natural disasters, $887,000,000, to remain available until expended, of which such sums as are necessary to cover the Federal share of eligible operation and maintenance costs for coastal harbors and channels, and for inland harbors shall be derived from the general fund of the Treasury: *Provided*, That the Assistant Secretary of the Army for Civil Works shall provide a monthly report directly to the Committees on Appropriations of the House of Representatives and the Senate detailing the allocation and obligation of these funds, beginning not later than 60 days after the date of enactment of this Act.] *(Disaster Relief Supplemental Appropriations Act, 2022.)*

OPERATION AND MAINTENANCE

(INCLUDING TRANSFER OF FUNDS)

[For an additional amount for "Operations and Maintenance", $4,000,000,000, to remain available until expended: *Provided*, That $2,000,000,000, to remain available until expended, shall be made available for fiscal year 2022, $1,000,000,000, to remain available until expended, shall be made available for fiscal year 2023, $1,000,000,000, to remain available until expended, shall be made available for fiscal year 2024: *Provided further*, That of the amount provided under this heading in this Act for fiscal year 2022, $626,000,000, which shall be obligated within 90 days of enactment of this Act, shall be used for necessary expenses to dredge Federal navigation projects in response to, and repair damages to Corps of Engineers Federal projects caused by, natural disasters: *Provided further*, That of the amount provided under this heading in this Act, $40,000,000 shall be to carry out Soil Moisture and Snowpack Monitoring activities, as authorized in section 4003(a) of the Water Resources Reform and Development Act of 2014, as amended:

Provided further, That not later than 60 days after the date of enactment of this Act, the Chief of Engineers shall submit to the House and Senate Committees on Appropriations a detailed spend plan for fiscal year 2022, including a list of project locations, other than for the amount for natural disasters identified in the second proviso: *Provided further*, That for fiscal years 2023 and 2024, as part of the annual budget submission of the President under section 1105(a) of title 31, United States Code, the Chief of Engineers shall submit a detailed spend plan for that fiscal year, including a list of project locations: *Provided further*, That of the amount provided under this heading in this Act, such sums as are necessary to cover the Federal share of eligible operation and maintenance costs for coastal harbors and channels, and for inland harbors shall be derived from the general fund of the Treasury: *Provided further*, That up to three percent of the amounts made available under this heading in this Act for any fiscal year may be transferred to "Regulatory Program" or "Expenses" to carry out activities funded by those accounts: *Provided further*, That the Committees on Appropriations of the Senate and the House of Representatives shall be notified at least 30 days in advance of any transfer made pursuant to the preceding proviso: *Provided further*, That such amount is designated by the Congress as being for an emergency requirement pursuant to section 4112(a) of H. Con. Res. 71 (115th Congress), the concurrent resolution on the budget for fiscal year 2018, and to section 251(b) of the Balanced Budget and Emergency Deficit Control Act of 1985.] *(Infrastructure Investments and Jobs Appropriations Act.)*

Program and Financing (in millions of dollars)

Identification code 096–3123–0–1–301	2021 actual	2022 est.	2023 est.
Obligations by program activity:			
0001 Commercial Navigation	2,040	2,143	2,152
0002 Flood Risk Management	266	263	266
0003 Aquatic Ecosystem Restoration	41	32	35
0004 Hydropower	....	4	3
0005 Multipurpose and Other Programs	1,769	1,772	1,798
0006 Emergency Management	10	9	11
0799 Total direct obligations	4,126	4,223	4,265
0801 Department of Homeland Security	51	287	380
0802 Department of Veteran Affairs	5	3	3
0804 National Aeronautics and Space Administration	....	1	1
0805 Department of Energy	7	7	7
0806 Other Federal Agencies	22	14	15
0807 Non-Federal Agencies	71	42	37
0808 Intra-Corps	40	135	118
0899 Total reimbursable obligations	196	489	561
0900 Total new obligations, unexpired accounts	4,322	4,712	4,826
Budgetary resources:			
Unobligated balance:			
1000 Unobligated balance brought forward, Oct 1	2,103	1,324	4,007
1021 Recoveries of prior year unpaid obligations	127	....	....
1033 Recoveries of prior year paid obligations	1	....	....
1042 Adjustment for change in allocation (general fund portion)	–590	....	....
1043 Adjustment for change in allocation (offsetting collection/collected portion)	590	....	....
1070 Unobligated balance (total)	2,231	1,324	4,007
Budget authority:			
Appropriations, discretionary:			
1100 Appropriation	2,927	5,131	2,553
1121 Appropriations transferred from other acct [096–5383]	42	49	46
1160 Appropriation, discretionary (total)	2,969	5,180	2,599
Advance appropriations, discretionary:			
1170 Advance appropriation	....	....	1,000
Spending authority from offsetting collections, discretionary:			
1700 Collected (Harbor Maintenance Trust Fund)	557	1,557	....
1700 Collected (Operation and Maintenance)	....	658	658
1700 Collected (Harbor Maintenance Trust Fund FY20)	406	....	....
1700 Collected (Harbor Maintenance Trust Fund FY19 Supplemental)	109	....	....
1700 Collected (Harbor Maintenance Trust Fund FY19)	12	....	....
1701 Change in uncollected payments, Federal sources	–638	....	....
1750 Spending auth from offsetting collections, disc (total)	446	2,215	658
1900 Budget authority (total)	3,415	7,395	4,257
1930 Total budgetary resources available	5,646	8,719	8,264
Memorandum (non-add) entries:			
1941 Unexpired unobligated balance, end of year	1,324	4,007	3,438
Change in obligated balance:			
Unpaid obligations:			
3000 Unpaid obligations, brought forward, Oct 1	2,477	2,329	2,226

		2021 actual	2022 est.	2023 est.
3010	New obligations, unexpired accounts	4,322	4,712	4,826
3020	Outlays (gross)	−4,343	−4,815	−3,222
3040	Recoveries of prior year unpaid obligations, unexpired	−127		
3050	Unpaid obligations, end of year	2,329	2,226	3,830
	Uncollected payments:			
3060	Uncollected pymts, Fed sources, brought forward, Oct 1	−762	−124	−124
3070	Change in uncollected pymts, Fed sources, unexpired	638		
3090	Uncollected pymts, Fed sources, end of year	−124	−124	−124
	Memorandum (non-add) entries:			
3100	Obligated balance, start of year	1,715	2,205	2,102
3200	Obligated balance, end of year	2,205	2,102	3,706
	Budget authority and outlays, net:			
	Discretionary:			
4000	Budget authority, gross	3,415	7,395	4,257
	Outlays, gross:			
4010	Outlays from new discretionary authority	999	2,690	1,874
4011	Outlays from discretionary balances	3,344	2,125	1,348
4020	Outlays, gross (total)	4,343	4,815	3,222
	Offsets against gross budget authority and outlays:			
	Offsetting collections (collected) from:			
4030	Federal sources:	−1,600	−2,215	−658
4033	Non-Federal sources:	−75		
4040	Offsets against gross budget authority and outlays (total)	−1,675	−2,215	−658
	Additional offsets against gross budget authority only:			
4050	Change in uncollected pymts, Fed sources, unexpired	638		
4053	Recoveries of prior year paid obligations, unexpired accounts	1		
4055	Adjustment for change in allocation (offsetting collection portion)	590		
4060	Additional offsets against budget authority only (total)	1,229		
4070	Budget authority, net (discretionary)	2,969	5,180	3,599
4080	Outlays, net (discretionary)	2,668	2,600	2,564
4180	Budget authority, net (total)	2,969	5,180	3,599
4190	Outlays, net (total)	2,668	2,600	2,564

This appropriation funds inspection, operation, maintenance, and related activities for water resources projects operated and maintained by the Corps. These projects include navigation channels, navigation locks and dams, structures to reduce the risk of flood and storm damage (e.g., levees), and multi-purpose projects, as authorized in River and Harbor, Flood Control, and Water Resources Development Acts and other laws. Key infrastructure that is of central importance to the Nation and the continued safety of the public is given the highest priority for funding in this account.

This appropriation funds all of the costs associated with protecting Corps facilities from potential security threats. It also funds the national emergency preparedness program under Executive Order 11490.

In developing the Budget, consideration was given to advancing two key objectives including: 1) increasing infrastructure and ecosystem resilience to climate change and decreasing climate risk for communities based on the best available science; and 2) promoting environmental justice in disadvantaged communities in line with Justice40 and creating good paying jobs that provide the free and fair chance to join a union and collectively bargain.

Object Classification (in millions of dollars)

Identification code 096–3123–0–1–301		2021 actual	2022 est.	2023 est.
	Direct obligations:			
	Personnel compensation:			
11.1	Full-time permanent	1,077	1,043	1,059
11.3	Other than full-time permanent	9	9	9
11.5	Other personnel compensation	60	59	59
11.8	Special personal services payments	8	8	8
11.9	Total personnel compensation	1,154	1,119	1,135
12.1	Civilian personnel benefits	233	221	226
21.0	Travel and transportation of persons	30	31	30
22.0	Transportation of things	1	1	1
23.2	Rental payments to others	3	2	2
23.3	Communications, utilities, and miscellaneous charges	37	36	36
25.1	Advisory and assistance services	15	16	17
25.2	Other services from non-Federal sources	431	364	370
25.3	Other goods and services from Federal sources	518	559	559
25.4	Operation and maintenance of facilities	351	362	360
25.7	Operation and maintenance of equipment	6	6	6
26.0	Supplies and materials	75	68	70
31.0	Equipment	19	26	23
32.0	Land and structures	1,253	1,412	1,430
99.0	Direct obligations	4,126	4,223	4,265
99.0	Reimbursable obligations	196	489	561
99.9	Total new obligations, unexpired accounts	4,322	4,712	4,826

Employment Summary

Identification code 096–3123–0–1–301	2021 actual	2022 est.	2023 est.
1001 Direct civilian full-time equivalent employment	12,489	12,300	12,300
2001 Reimbursable civilian full-time equivalent employment	266	300	300

SPECIAL RECREATION USER FEE

Special and Trust Fund Receipts (in millions of dollars)

Identification code 096–5383–0–2–301		2021 actual	2022 est.	2023 est.
0100	Balance, start of year	42	69	72
	Receipts:			
	Current law:			
1130	Special Recreation Use Fees, Corps of Engineers	67	51	51
1130	User Fees, Fund for Non-Federal Use of Disposal Facilities	2	1	1
1199	Total current law receipts	69	52	52
1999	Total receipts	69	52	52
2000	Total: Balances and receipts	111	121	124
	Appropriations:			
	Current law:			
2101	Special Recreation User Fee	−42	−49	−46
5099	Balance, end of year	69	72	78

Program and Financing (in millions of dollars)

Identification code 096–5383–0–2–301		2021 actual	2022 est.	2023 est.
	Budgetary resources:			
	Budget authority:			
	Appropriations, discretionary:			
1101	Appropriation (special or trust)	42	49	46
1120	Appropriations transferred to other accts [096–3123]	−42	−49	−46
4180	Budget authority, net (total)			
4190	Outlays, net (total)			

Pursuant to the requirements of 16 U.S.C. 460d–3, the Corps deposits certain recreation use fees collected at Corps projects into this account. Types of fees include daily user fees, camping fees, recreational fees, annual pass fees, and other permit type fees. Pursuant to appropriations acts, funding in the Operation and Maintenance appropriation is derived in part from this account for resource protection, research, interpretation, and maintenance activities related to resource protection at Corps projects where outdoor recreation is available.

MISSISSIPPI RIVER AND TRIBUTARIES

For expenses necessary for flood damage reduction projects and related efforts in the Mississippi River alluvial valley below Cape Girardeau, Missouri, as authorized by law, $225,000,000, to remain available until expended.

Note.—A full-year 2022 appropriation for this account was not enacted at the time the Budget was prepared; therefore, the Budget assumes this account is operating under the Continuing Appropriations Act, 2022 (Division A of Public Law 117–43, as amended). The amounts included for 2022 reflect the annualized level provided by the continuing resolution.

MISSISSIPPI RIVER AND TRIBUTARIES

[For an additional amount for "Mississippi River and Tributaries" for necessary expenses to address emergency situations at Corps of Engineers projects, and to construct, and rehabilitate and repair damages to Corps of Engineers projects, caused by natural disasters, $868,000,000, to remain available until expended: *Provided*, That of the amounts made available under this heading in this Act, such sums as are necessary to cover the Federal share of eligible operation and maintenance costs for coastal harbors and channels, and for inland harbors shall be derived from the gen-

Corps of Engineers—Civil Works—Continued
Federal Funds—Continued

MISSISSIPPI RIVER AND TRIBUTARIES—Continued

eral fund of the Treasury: *Provided further*, That of the amounts made available under this heading in this Act, $500,000,000 shall be available to construct flood and storm damage reduction projects that are currently authorized or that are authorized after the date of enactment of this Act in States with a major disaster declared due to Hurricane Ida pursuant to the Robert T. Stafford Disaster Relief and Emergency Assistance Act (42 U.S.C. 5121 et seq.) in fiscal year 2021: *Provided further*, That the provisions of section 902 of the Water Resources Development Act of 1986 shall not apply to the construction of projects, including initial construction or periodic nourishment, completed using funding under this heading in this Act: *Provided further*, That to the extent that ongoing construction projects are constructed using funding provided under this heading in this Act, such construction shall be at full Federal expense: *Provided further*, That for any projects using funding provided under this heading in this Act, the non-Federal cash contribution for projects other than ongoing construction projects shall be financed in accordance with the provisions of section 103(k) of Public Law 99–662 over a period of 30 years from the date of completion of the project or separable element: *Provided further*, That any projects using funding appropriated under this heading in this Act shall be initiated only after non-Federal interests have entered into binding agreements with the Secretary requiring, where applicable, the non-Federal interests to pay 100 percent of the operation, maintenance, repair, replacement, and rehabilitation costs of the project and to hold and save the United States free from damages due to the construction or operation and maintenance of the project, except for damages due to the fault or negligence of the United States or its contractors: *Provided further*, That the Assistant Secretary of the Army for Civil Works shall provide a monthly report directly to the Committees on Appropriations of the House of Representatives and the Senate detailing the allocation and obligation of these funds, beginning not later than 60 days after the date of enactment of this Act.] *(Disaster Relief Supplemental Appropriations Act, 2022.)*

MISSISSIPPI RIVER AND TRIBUTARIES

[For an additional amount for "Mississippi River and Tributaries", $808,000,000, to remain available until expended: *Provided*, That of the amount provided under this heading in this Act, $258,000,000, which shall be obligated within 90 days of enactment of this Act, shall be used for necessary expenses to address emergency situations at Corps of Engineers Federal projects caused by natural disasters: *Provided further*, That the Secretary may initiate additional new construction starts with funds provided under this heading in this Act: *Provided further*, That the limitation concerning total project costs in section 902 of the Water Resources Development Act of 1986 (Public Law 99–662; 33 U.S.C. 2280), as amended, shall not apply to any project receiving funds provided under this heading in this Act: *Provided further*, That not later than 60 days after the date of enactment of this Act, the Chief of Engineers shall submit to the House and Senate Committees on Appropriations a detailed spend plan for fiscal year 2022, including a list of project locations and construction projects selected to be initiated: *Provided further*, That of the amount provided under this heading in this Act, such sums as are necessary to cover the Federal share of eligible operation and maintenance costs for inland harbors shall be derived from the general fund of the Treasury: *Provided further*, That beginning not later than 120 days after the enactment of this Act, the Chief of Engineers shall provide a monthly report to the Committees on Appropriations of the House of Representatives and the Senate detailing the allocation and obligation of these funds, including construction projects selected to be initiated using funds provided under this heading in this Act: *Provided further*, That such amount is designated by the Congress as being for an emergency requirement pursuant to section 4112(a) of H. Con. Res. 71 (115th Congress), the concurrent resolution on the budget for fiscal year 2018, and to section 251(b) of the Balanced Budget and Emergency Deficit Control Act of 1985.] *(Infrastructure Investments and Jobs Appropriations Act.)*

Program and Financing (in millions of dollars)

Identification code 096–3112–0–1–301	2021 actual	2022 est.	2023 est.
Obligations by program activity:			
0001 Commercial Navigation	50	56	58
0002 Flood Risk Management	471	453	441
0005 Multipurpose and Other Programs	105	109	106
0799 Total direct obligations	626	618	605
0808 Intra-Corps	2	53	41
0900 Total new obligations, unexpired accounts	628	671	646
Budgetary resources:			
Unobligated balance:			
1000 Unobligated balance brought forward, Oct 1	945	711	2,154
1021 Recoveries of prior year unpaid obligations	12		
1033 Recoveries of prior year paid obligations	1		
1070 Unobligated balance (total)	958	711	2,154
Budget authority:			
Appropriations, discretionary:			
1100 Appropriation	375	2,051	225
Spending authority from offsetting collections, discretionary:			
1700 Collected (Non-Harbor Maintenance Trust Fund)	2	58	39
1700 Collected (Harbor Maintenance Trust Fund)	5	5	5
1701 Change in uncollected payments, Federal sources	–1		
1750 Spending auth from offsetting collections, disc (total)	6	63	44
1900 Budget authority (total)	381	2,114	269
1930 Total budgetary resources available	1,339	2,825	2,423
Memorandum (non-add) entries:			
1941 Unexpired unobligated balance, end of year	711	2,154	1,777
Change in obligated balance:			
Unpaid obligations:			
3000 Unpaid obligations, brought forward, Oct 1	588	484	509
3010 New obligations, unexpired accounts	628	671	646
3020 Outlays (gross)	–720	–646	–583
3040 Recoveries of prior year unpaid obligations, unexpired	–12		
3050 Unpaid obligations, end of year	484	509	572
Uncollected payments:			
3060 Uncollected pymts, Fed sources, brought forward, Oct 1	–2	–1	–1
3070 Change in uncollected pymts, Fed sources, unexpired	1		
3090 Uncollected pymts, Fed sources, end of year	–1	–1	–1
Memorandum (non-add) entries:			
3100 Obligated balance, start of year	586	483	508
3200 Obligated balance, end of year	483	508	571
Budget authority and outlays, net:			
Discretionary:			
4000 Budget authority, gross	381	2,114	269
Outlays, gross:			
4010 Outlays from new discretionary authority		308	122
4011 Outlays from discretionary balances	720	338	461
4020 Outlays, gross (total)	720	646	583
Offsets against gross budget authority and outlays:			
Offsetting collections (collected) from:			
4030 Federal sources	–6	–63	–44
4033 Non-Federal sources	–2		
4040 Offsets against gross budget authority and outlays (total)	–8	–63	–44
Additional offsets against gross budget authority only:			
4050 Change in uncollected pymts, Fed sources, unexpired	1		
4053 Recoveries of prior year paid obligations, unexpired accounts	1		
4060 Additional offsets against budget authority only (total)	2		
4070 Budget authority, net (discretionary)	375	2,051	225
4080 Outlays, net (discretionary)	712	583	539
4180 Budget authority, net (total)	375	2,051	225
4190 Outlays, net (total)	712	583	539

This appropriation funds planning, design, construction, and operation and maintenance activities associated with projects to reduce the risk of flood damage in the lower Mississippi River alluvial valley below Cape Girardeau, Missouri.

Object Classification (in millions of dollars)

Identification code 096–3112–0–1–301	2021 actual	2022 est.	2023 est.
Direct obligations:			
Personnel compensation:			
11.1 Full-time permanent	90	88	90
11.3 Other than full-time permanent	2	2	2
11.5 Other personnel compensation	6	8	7
11.9 Total personnel compensation	98	98	99
12.1 Civilian personnel benefits	21	20	21
21.0 Travel and transportation of persons	4	4	4
23.3 Communications, utilities, and miscellaneous	3	5	4
25.2 Other services from non-Federal sources	21	20	20
25.3 Purchase goods & svcs. fm Government	150	158	138
25.4 Operation and maintenance of facilities	20	24	24
25.7 Operation and maintenance of equipment	3	1	2
26.0 Supplies and materials	7	9	9
31.0 Equipment	1	1	1
32.0 Land and structures	298	278	283
99.0 Direct obligations	626	618	605

CORPS OF ENGINEERS—CIVIL WORKS

		2021 actual	2022 est.	2023 est.
99.0	Reimbursable obligations	2	53	41
99.9	Total new obligations, unexpired accounts	628	671	646

Employment Summary

Identification code 096–3112–0–1–301	2021 actual	2022 est.	2023 est.
1001 Direct civilian full-time equivalent employment	1,300	1,300	1,300
2001 Reimbursable civilian full-time equivalent employment	3	3	3

FLOOD CONTROL AND COASTAL EMERGENCIES

For expenses necessary to prepare for flood, hurricane, and other natural disasters and support emergency operations, repairs, and other activities in response to such disasters as authorized by law, $35,000,000, to remain available until expended.

Note.—A full-year 2022 appropriation for this account was not enacted at the time the Budget was prepared; therefore, the Budget assumes this account is operating under the Continuing Appropriations Act, 2022 (Division A of Public Law 117–43, as amended). The amounts included for 2022 reflect the annualized level provided by the continuing resolution.

FLOOD CONTROL AND COASTAL EMERGENCIES

[For an additional amount for "Flood Control and Coastal Emergencies", as authorized by section 5 of the Act of August 18, 1941 (33 U.S.C. 701n), for necessary expenses to prepare for flood, hurricane and other natural disasters and support emergency operations, repairs, and other activities in response to such disasters, as authorized by law, $826,000,000, to remain available until expended: *Provided*, That funding utilized for authorized shore protection projects shall restore such projects to the full project profile at full Federal expense: *Provided further*, That the Assistant Secretary of the Army for Civil Works shall provide a monthly report directly to the Committees on Appropriations of the House of Representatives and the Senate detailing the allocation and obligation of these funds, beginning not later than 60 days after the date of enactment of this Act.] *(Disaster Relief Supplemental Appropriations Act, 2022.)*

FLOOD CONTROL AND COASTAL EMERGENCIES

[For an additional amount for "Flood Control and Coastal Emergencies", $251,000,000, to remain available until expended: *Provided*, That funding provided under this heading in this Act and utilized for authorized shore protection projects shall restore such projects to the full project profile at full Federal expense: *Provided further*, That such amount is designated by the Congress as being for an emergency requirement pursuant to section 4112(a) of H. Con. Res. 71 (115th Congress), the concurrent resolution on the budget for fiscal year 2018, and to section 251(b) of the Balanced Budget and Emergency Deficit Control Act of 1985.] *(Infrastructure Investments and Jobs Appropriations Act.)*

Program and Financing (in millions of dollars)

Identification code 096–3125–0–1–301		2021 actual	2022 est.	2023 est.
	Obligations by program activity:			
0006	Emergency Management	643	680	693
0801	Department of Homeland Security	197	267	188
0806	Other Federal Agencies	1		
0807	Non-Federal Agencies		3	1
0808	Intra-Corps	17	52	29
0899	Total reimbursable obligations	215	322	218
0900	Total new obligations, unexpired accounts	858	1,002	911
	Budgetary resources:			
	Unobligated balance:			
1000	Unobligated balance brought forward, Oct 1	1,838	1,126	2,417
1021	Recoveries of prior year unpaid obligations	62		
1070	Unobligated balance (total)	1,900	1,126	2,417
	Budget authority:			
	Appropriations, discretionary:			
1100	Appropriation	35	1,112	35
	Spending authority from offsetting collections, discretionary:			
1700	Collected	168	1,181	492
1701	Change in uncollected payments, Federal sources	–119		
1750	Spending auth from offsetting collections, disc (total)	49	1,181	492
1900	Budget authority (total)	84	2,293	527
1930	Total budgetary resources available	1,984	3,419	2,944
	Memorandum (non-add) entries:			
1941	Unexpired unobligated balance, end of year	1,126	2,417	2,033

	Change in obligated balance:			
	Unpaid obligations:			
3000	Unpaid obligations, brought forward, Oct 1	869	860	708
3010	New obligations, unexpired accounts	858	1,002	911
3020	Outlays (gross)	–805	–1,154	–894
3040	Recoveries of prior year unpaid obligations, unexpired	–62		
3050	Unpaid obligations, end of year	860	708	725
	Uncollected payments:			
3060	Uncollected pymts, Fed sources, brought forward, Oct 1	–640	–521	–521
3070	Change in uncollected pymts, Fed sources, unexpired	119		
3090	Uncollected pymts, Fed sources, end of year	–521	–521	–521
	Memorandum (non-add) entries:			
3100	Obligated balance, start of year	229	339	187
3200	Obligated balance, end of year	339	187	204
	Budget authority and outlays, net:			
	Discretionary:			
4000	Budget authority, gross	84	2,293	527
	Outlays, gross:			
4010	Outlays from new discretionary authority		505	181
4011	Outlays from discretionary balances	805	649	713
4020	Outlays, gross (total)	805	1,154	894
	Offsets against gross budget authority and outlays:			
	Offsetting collections (collected) from:			
4030	Federal sources	–167	–1,181	–492
4033	Non-Federal sources	–1		
4040	Offsets against gross budget authority and outlays (total)	–168	–1,181	–492
	Additional offsets against gross budget authority only:			
4050	Change in uncollected pymts, Fed sources, unexpired	119		
4060	Additional offsets against budget authority only (total)	119		
4070	Budget authority, net (discretionary)	35	1,112	35
4080	Outlays, net (discretionary)	637	–27	402
4180	Budget authority, net (total)	35	1,112	35
4190	Outlays, net (total)	637	–27	402

This appropriation funds the planning, training, exercises, and other preparedness measures that help the Corps respond to floods, hurricanes, and other natural disasters, and support emergency operations in response to such natural disasters, including advance measures, flood fighting, providing potable water, and the repair of certain damaged flood and storm damage reduction projects. The funding in the Budget is for preparedness and training activities.

Object Classification (in millions of dollars)

Identification code 096–3125–0–1–301		2021 actual	2022 est.	2023 est.
	Direct obligations:			
	Personnel compensation:			
11.1	Full-time permanent	65	72	72
11.3	Other than full-time permanent	1	2	2
11.5	Other personnel compensation	4	6	5
11.9	Total personnel compensation	70	80	79
12.1	Civilian personnel benefits	14	15	15
21.0	Travel and transportation of persons	2	3	3
25.1	Advisory and assistance services	2	8	7
25.2	Other services from non-Federal sources	49	24	32
25.3	Other goods and services from Federal sources	10	15	15
25.4	Operation and maintenance of facilities	1	7	7
26.0	Supplies and materials	1	2	1
32.0	Land and structures	494	525	533
99.0	Direct obligations	643	679	692
99.0	Reimbursable obligations	215	323	219
99.9	Total new obligations, unexpired accounts	858	1,002	911

Employment Summary

Identification code 096–3125–0–1–301	2021 actual	2022 est.	2023 est.
1001 Direct civilian full-time equivalent employment	750	650	650
2001 Reimbursable civilian full-time equivalent employment	82	82	82

INVESTIGATIONS

For expenses necessary for the collection and study of basic information pertaining to the development, management, restoration, and protection of water resources; for studies, design work, and plans and specifications of proposed commercial navigation, flood and storm damage reduction, and aquatic ecosystem restoration projects, and related efforts prior to construction; for restudy of authorized projects and related efforts; and for miscellaneous investigations, $105,910,000, to remain available until expended.

Note.—A full-year 2022 appropriation for this account was not enacted at the time the Budget was prepared; therefore, the Budget assumes this account is operating under the Continuing Appropriations Act, 2022 (Division A of Public Law 117–43, as amended). The amounts included for 2022 reflect the annualized level provided by the continuing resolution.

INVESTIGATIONS

[For an additional amount for "Investigations" for necessary expenses related to the completion, or initiation and completion, of flood and storm damage reduction, including shore protection, studies that are currently authorized or that are authorized after the date of enactment of this Act, to reduce risk from future floods and hurricanes, at full Federal expense, $100,000,000, to remain available until expended: *Provided*, That funds made available under this heading in this Act shall be for high-priority studies of projects in States with a major disaster declared due to Hurricane Ida pursuant to the Robert T. Stafford Disaster Relief and Emergency Assistance Act (42 U.S.C. 5121 et seq.) in fiscal year 2021: *Provided further*, That the Assistant Secretary of the Army for Civil Works shall provide a monthly report directly to the Committees on Appropriations of the House of Representatives and the Senate detailing the allocation and obligation of these funds, including new studies selected to be initiated using funds provided under this heading in this Act, beginning not later than 60 days after the date of enactment of this Act.] *(Disaster Relief Supplemental Appropriations Act, 2022.)*

INVESTIGATIONS

[For an additional amount for "Investigations", $150,000,000, to remain available until expended: *Provided*, That of the amount provided under this heading in this Act, $30,000,000 shall be used by the Secretary of the Army, acting through the Chief of Engineers, to undertake work authorized to be carried out in accordance with section 22 of the Water Resources Development Act of 1974 (Public Law 93–251; 42 U.S.C. 1962d–16), as amended: *Provided further*, That of the amount provided under this heading in this Act, $45,000,000 shall be used by the Secretary of the Army, acting through the Chief of Engineers, to undertake work authorized to be carried out in accordance with section 206 of the 1960 Flood Control Act (Public Law 86–645), as amended: *Provided further*, That of the amount provided under this heading in this Act, $75,000,000 shall be used for necessary expenses related to the completion, or initiation and completion, of studies which are authorized prior to the date of enactment of this Act, of which $30,000,000, to become available on October 1, 2022, shall be used by the Secretary of the Army, acting through the Chief of Engineers, to complete, or to initiate and complete, studies carried out in accordance with section 118 of division AA of the Consolidated Appropriations Act, 2021 (Public Law 116–260), except that the limitation on the number of studies authorized to be carried out under section 118(b) and section 118(c) shall not apply: *Provided further*, That not later than 60 days after the date of enactment of this Act, the Chief of Engineers shall submit to the House and Senate Committees on Appropriations a detailed spend plan for the funds identified for fiscal year 2022 in the preceding proviso, including a list of project locations and new studies selected to be initiated: *Provided further*, That not later than 60 days after the date of enactment of this Act, the Chief of Engineers shall provide a briefing to the House and Senate Committees on Appropriations on an implementation plan, including a schedule for solicitation of projects and expenditure of funds, for the funding provided for fiscal year 2023 to undertake work authorized to be carried out in accordance with section 118 of division AA of the Consolidated Appropriations Act, 2021 (Public Law 116–260): *Provided further*, That for fiscal year 2023, as part of the annual budget submission of the President under section 1105(a) of title 31, United States Code, the Chief of Engineers shall submit a detailed spend plan for that fiscal year, including a list of project locations for the funding provided to undertake work authorized to be carried out in accordance with section 118 of division AA of the Consolidated Appropriations Act, 2021 (Public Law 116–260): *Provided further*, That beginning not later than 120 days after the enactment of this Act, the Chief of Engineers shall provide a monthly report to the Committees on Appropriations of the House of Representatives and the Senate detailing the allocation and obligation of the funds provided under this heading in this Act, including new studies selected to be initiated using funds provided under this heading: *Provided further*, That such amount is designated by the Congress as being for an emergency requirement pursuant to section 4112(a) of H. Con. Res. 71 (115th Congress), the concurrent resolution on the budget for fiscal year 2018, and to section 251(b) of the Balanced Budget and Emergency Deficit Control Act of 1985.] *(Infrastructure Investments and Jobs Appropriations Act.)*

Program and Financing (in millions of dollars)

Identification code 096–3121–0–1–301		2021 actual	2022 est.	2023 est.
	Obligations by program activity:			
0001	Commercial Navigation	40	31	33
0002	Flood Risk Management	94	79	85
0003	Aquatic Ecosystem Restoration	15	15	16
0005	Multipurpose and Other Programs	23	17	18
0799	Total direct obligations	172	142	152
0801	Department of Homeland Security	18	11	18
0802	Department of Veteran Affairs	1		
0804	National Aeronautics and Space Administration	1	1	1
0806	Other Federal Agencies	6	10	8
0807	Non-Federal Agencies	9	8	8
0808	Intra-Corps	4	10	8
0899	Total reimbursable obligations	39	40	43
0900	Total new obligations, unexpired accounts	211	182	195
	Budgetary resources:			
	Unobligated balance:			
1000	Unobligated balance brought forward, Oct 1	281	266	498
1021	Recoveries of prior year unpaid obligations	2		
1070	Unobligated balance (total)	283	266	498
	Budget authority:			
	Appropriations, discretionary:			
1100	Appropriation	153	373	106
	Advance appropriations, discretionary:			
1170	Advance appropriation			30
	Spending authority from offsetting collections, discretionary:			
1700	Collected	42	41	37
1701	Change in uncollected payments, Federal sources	–1		
1750	Spending auth from offsetting collections, disc (total)	41	41	37
1900	Budget authority (total)	194	414	173
1930	Total budgetary resources available	477	680	671
	Memorandum (non-add) entries:			
1941	Unexpired unobligated balance, end of year	266	498	476
	Change in obligated balance:			
	Unpaid obligations:			
3000	Unpaid obligations, brought forward, Oct 1	79	88	79
3010	New obligations, unexpired accounts	211	182	195
3020	Outlays (gross)	–200	–191	–170
3040	Recoveries of prior year unpaid obligations, unexpired	–2		
3050	Unpaid obligations, end of year	88	79	104
	Uncollected payments:			
3060	Uncollected pymts, Fed sources, brought forward, Oct 1	–54	–53	–53
3070	Change in uncollected pymts, Fed sources, unexpired	1		
3090	Uncollected pymts, Fed sources, end of year	–53	–53	–53
	Memorandum (non-add) entries:			
3100	Obligated balance, start of year	25	35	26
3200	Obligated balance, end of year	35	26	51
	Budget authority and outlays, net:			
	Discretionary:			
4000	Budget authority, gross	194	414	173
	Outlays, gross:			
4010	Outlays from new discretionary authority		79	58
4011	Outlays from discretionary balances	200	112	112
4020	Outlays, gross (total)	200	191	170
	Offsets against gross budget authority and outlays:			
	Offsetting collections (collected) from:			
4030	Federal sources	–31	–41	–37
4033	Non-Federal sources	–11		
4040	Offsets against gross budget authority and outlays (total)	–42	–41	–37
	Additional offsets against gross budget authority only:			
4050	Change in uncollected pymts, Fed sources, unexpired	1		
4060	Additional offsets against budget authority only (total)	1		
4070	Budget authority, net (discretionary)	153	373	136
4080	Outlays, net (discretionary)	158	150	133
4180	Budget authority, net (total)	153	373	136
4190	Outlays, net (total)	158	150	133

This appropriation funds studies to determine the engineering feasibility, economic and environmental return to the Nation, and public safety impacts of potential solutions to water and related land resources problems; preconstruction engineering and design; and related data collection, interagency coordination, and research. In developing the Budget, consideration was given to advancing two key objectives including: 1) increasing infrastructure and ecosystem resilience to climate change and decreasing climate risk for communities based on the best available science; and 2) promoting environmental justice in disadvantaged communities in line with Justice40 and creating good paying jobs that provide the free and fair chance to join a union and collectively bargain.

Object Classification (in millions of dollars)

Identification code 096–3121–0–1–301		2021 actual	2022 est.	2023 est.
	Direct obligations:			
	Personnel compensation:			
11.1	Full-time permanent	97	97	98
11.3	Other than full-time permanent	3	4	4
11.5	Other personnel compensation	2	1	1
11.8	Special personal services payments		2	4
11.9	Total personnel compensation	102	104	107
12.1	Civilian personnel benefits	19	17	17
21.0	Travel and transportation of persons	1	1	1
25.1	Advisory and assistance services	6	2	3
25.2	Other services from non-Federal sources	12	4	5
25.3	Purchase of goods and services from Government accounts	8	6	8
25.4	Operation and maintenance of facilities	5	2	3
26.0	Supplies and materials	1		
31.0	Equipment	1	1	
32.0	Land and structures	17	5	8
99.0	Direct obligations	172	142	152
99.0	Reimbursable obligations	39	40	43
99.9	Total new obligations, unexpired accounts	211	182	195

Employment Summary

Identification code 096–3121–0–1–301	2021 actual	2022 est.	2023 est.
1001 Direct civilian full-time equivalent employment	803	800	800

REGULATORY PROGRAM

For expenses necessary for administration of laws pertaining to regulation of navigable waters and wetlands, $210,000,000, to remain available until September 30, 2024.

Note.—A full-year 2022 appropriation for this account was not enacted at the time the Budget was prepared; therefore, the Budget assumes this account is operating under the Continuing Appropriations Act, 2022 (Division A of Public Law 117–43, as amended). The amounts included for 2022 reflect the annualized level provided by the continuing resolution.

REGULATORY PROGRAM

[For an additional amount for "Regulatory Program", $160,000,000, to remain available until September 30, 2026: *Provided*, That such amount is designated by the Congress as being for an emergency requirement pursuant to section 4112(a) of H. Con. Res. 71 (115th Congress), the concurrent resolution on the budget for fiscal year 2018, and to section 251(b) of the Balanced Budget and Emergency Deficit Control Act of 1985.] *(Infrastructure Investments and Jobs Appropriations Act.)*

Program and Financing (in millions of dollars)

Identification code 096–3126–0–1–301		2021 actual	2022 est.	2023 est.
	Obligations by program activity:			
0008	Regulatory	204	206	207
0192	Total direct obligations	204	206	207
0806	Other Federal Agencies	1	1	1
0807	Non-Federal Agencies	14	13	13
0899	Total reimbursable obligations	15	14	14
0900	Total new obligations, unexpired accounts	219	220	221
	Budgetary resources:			
	Unobligated balance:			
1000	Unobligated balance brought forward, Oct 1	17	20	182
	Budget authority:			
	Appropriations, discretionary:			
1100	Appropriation	210	370	210
	Spending authority from offsetting collections, discretionary:			
1700	Collected	16	12	15
1900	Budget authority (total)	226	382	225
1930	Total budgetary resources available	243	402	407
	Memorandum (non-add) entries:			
1940	Unobligated balance expiring	–4		
1941	Unexpired unobligated balance, end of year	20	182	186
	Change in obligated balance:			
	Unpaid obligations:			
3000	Unpaid obligations, brought forward, Oct 1	7	7	25
3010	New obligations, unexpired accounts	219	220	221
3011	Obligations ("upward adjustments"), expired accounts	2		
3020	Outlays (gross)	–221	–202	–205
3050	Unpaid obligations, end of year	7	25	41
	Memorandum (non-add) entries:			
3100	Obligated balance, start of year	7	7	25
3200	Obligated balance, end of year	7	25	41
	Budget authority and outlays, net:			
	Discretionary:			
4000	Budget authority, gross	226	382	225
	Outlays, gross:			
4010	Outlays from new discretionary authority	200	198	199
4011	Outlays from discretionary balances	21	4	6
4020	Outlays, gross (total)	221	202	205
	Offsets against gross budget authority and outlays:			
	Offsetting collections (collected) from:			
4030	Federal sources	–1	–1	–1
4033	Non-Federal sources	–15	–11	–14
4040	Offsets against gross budget authority and outlays (total)	–16	–12	–15
4070	Budget authority, net (discretionary)	210	370	210
4080	Outlays, net (discretionary)	205	190	190
4180	Budget authority, net (total)	210	370	210
4190	Outlays, net (total)	205	190	190

This appropriation provides funds to administer the laws and regulations pertaining to activities affecting U.S. waters, including wetlands, in accordance with the Rivers and Harbors Appropriation Act of 1899, the Clean Water Act of 1972, and the Marine Protection, Research and Sanctuaries Act of 1972.

The requested funds are needed to review and process permit applications, ensure compliance on permitted sites, and protect important aquatic resources.

Object Classification (in millions of dollars)

Identification code 096–3126–0–1–301		2021 actual	2022 est.	2023 est.
	Direct obligations:			
	Personnel compensation:			
11.1	Full-time permanent	159	160	161
11.3	Other than full-time permanent	2	2	2
11.5	Other personnel compensation	1	1	1
11.9	Total personnel compensation	162	163	164
12.1	Civilian personnel benefits	34	34	34
21.0	Travel and transportation of persons	2	2	2
25.2	Other services from non-Federal sources	1	1	1
25.3	Purchase goods & svcs. fm Government accts.	5	6	6
99.0	Direct obligations	204	206	207
99.0	Reimbursable obligations	15	14	14
99.9	Total new obligations, unexpired accounts	219	220	221

Employment Summary

Identification code 096–3126–0–1–301	2021 actual	2022 est.	2023 est.
1001 Direct civilian full-time equivalent employment	1,361	1,400	1,400

FORMERLY UTILIZED SITES REMEDIAL ACTION PROGRAM

For expenses necessary to clean up contamination from sites in the United States resulting from work performed as part of the Nation's early atomic energy program, $250,000,000, to remain available until expended.

Note.—A full-year 2022 appropriation for this account was not enacted at the time the Budget was prepared; therefore, the Budget assumes this account is operating under the Continuing Appropriations Act, 2022 (Division A of Public Law 117–43, as amended). The amounts included for 2022 reflect the annualized level provided by the continuing resolution.

Program and Financing (in millions of dollars)

Identification code 096–3130–0–1–053		2021 actual	2022 est.	2023 est.
	Obligations by program activity:			
0007	Formerly Utilized Site Remedial Action Program	230	184	194
0808	Intra-Corps	1	6	5
0899	Total reimbursable obligations	1	6	5
0900	Total new obligations, unexpired accounts	231	190	199
	Budgetary resources:			
	Unobligated balance:			
1000	Unobligated balance brought forward, Oct 1	38	60	129
1021	Recoveries of prior year unpaid obligations	3		
1070	Unobligated balance (total)	41	60	129
	Budget authority:			
	Appropriations, discretionary:			
1100	Appropriation	250	250	250
	Spending authority from offsetting collections, discretionary:			
1700	Collected	5	9	7
1701	Change in uncollected payments, Federal sources	–5		
1750	Spending auth from offsetting collections, disc (total)		9	7
1900	Budget authority (total)	250	259	257
1930	Total budgetary resources available	291	319	386
	Memorandum (non-add) entries:			
1941	Unexpired unobligated balance, end of year	60	129	187
	Change in obligated balance:			
	Unpaid obligations:			
3000	Unpaid obligations, brought forward, Oct 1	154	209	89
3010	New obligations, unexpired accounts	231	190	199
3020	Outlays (gross)	–173	–310	–223
3040	Recoveries of prior year unpaid obligations, unexpired	–3		
3050	Unpaid obligations, end of year	209	89	65
	Uncollected payments:			
3060	Uncollected pymts, Fed sources, brought forward, Oct 1	–7	–2	–2
3070	Change in uncollected pymts, Fed sources, unexpired	5		
3090	Uncollected pymts, Fed sources, end of year	–2	–2	–2
	Memorandum (non-add) entries:			
3100	Obligated balance, start of year	147	207	87
3200	Obligated balance, end of year	207	87	63
	Budget authority and outlays, net:			
	Discretionary:			
4000	Budget authority, gross	250	259	257
	Outlays, gross:			
4010	Outlays from new discretionary authority		140	138
4011	Outlays from discretionary balances	173	170	85
4020	Outlays, gross (total)	173	310	223
	Offsets against gross budget authority and outlays:			
	Offsetting collections (collected) from:			
4030	Federal sources	–5	–9	–7
4040	Offsets against gross budget authority and outlays (total)	–5	–9	–7
	Additional offsets against gross budget authority only:			
4050	Change in uncollected pymts, Fed sources, unexpired	5		
4070	Budget authority, net (discretionary)	250	250	250
4080	Outlays, net (discretionary)	168	301	216
4180	Budget authority, net (total)	250	250	250
4190	Outlays, net (total)	168	301	216

The Budget funds the clean-up of certain low-level radioactive materials and mixed wastes, located mostly at sites contaminated as a result of the Nation's early efforts to develop atomic weapons.

Object Classification (in millions of dollars)

Identification code 096–3130–0–1–053		2021 actual	2022 est.	2023 est.
11.1	Direct obligations: Personnel compensation: Full-time permanent	17	16	17
11.9	Total personnel compensation	17	16	17
12.1	Civilian personnel benefits	4	3	3
25.1	Advisory and assistance services	32	12	15
25.2	Other services from non-Federal sources	87	65	64
25.3	Other goods and services from Federal sources	7	13	10
32.0	Land and structures	83	75	85
99.0	Direct obligations	230	184	194
99.0	Reimbursable obligations	1	6	5
99.9	Total new obligations, unexpired accounts	231	190	199

Employment Summary

Identification code 096–3130–0–1–053		2021 actual	2022 est.	2023 est.
1001	Direct civilian full-time equivalent employment	112	112	112

EXPENSES

For expenses necessary for the supervision and general administration of the civil works program in the headquarters of the Corps of Engineers and the offices of the Division Engineers; and for costs of management and operation of the Humphreys Engineer Center Support Activity, the Institute for Water Resources, the United States Army Engineer Research and Development Center, and the United States Army Corps of Engineers Finance Center allocable to the civil works program, $200,000,000, to remain available until September 30, 2024, of which not to exceed $5,000 may be used for official reception and representation purposes and only during the current fiscal year: Provided, That no part of any other appropriation provided in this title shall be available to fund the civil works activities of the Office of the Chief of Engineers or the civil works executive direction and management activities of the division offices: Provided further, That any Flood Control and Coastal Emergencies appropriation may be used to fund the supervision and general administration of emergency operations, repairs, and other activities in response to any flood, hurricane, or other natural disaster.

Note.—A full-year 2022 appropriation for this account was not enacted at the time the Budget was prepared; therefore, the Budget assumes this account is operating under the Continuing Appropriations Act, 2022 (Division A of Public Law 117–43, as amended). The amounts included for 2022 reflect the annualized level provided by the continuing resolution.

EXPENSES

⟦*For an additional amount for "Expenses" for necessary expenses to administer and oversee the obligation and expenditure of amounts provided in this Act for the Corps of Engineers, $30,000,000, to remain available until expended: Provided, That the Assistant Secretary of the Army for Civil Works shall provide a monthly report directly to the Committees on Appropriations of the House of Representatives and the Senate detailing the allocation and obligation of these funds, beginning not later than 60 days after the date of enactment of this Act.*⟧ *(Disaster Relief Supplemental Appropriations Act, 2022.)*

EXPENSES

⟦*For an additional amount for "Expenses", $40,000,000, to remain available until expended: Provided, That such amount is designated by the Congress as being for an emergency requirement pursuant to section 4112(a) of H. Con. Res. 71 (115th Congress), the concurrent resolution on the budget for fiscal year 2018, and to section 251(b) of the Balanced Budget and Emergency Deficit Control Act of 1985.*⟧ *(Infrastructure Investments and Jobs Appropriations Act.)*

Program and Financing (in millions of dollars)

Identification code 096–3124–0–1–301		2021 actual	2022 est.	2023 est.
	Obligations by program activity:			
0009	Executive Direction and Management	220	194	201
0010	Support Activities	1	19	16
0799	Total direct obligations	221	213	217
0808	Intra-Corps		2	1
0899	Total reimbursable obligations		2	1

CORPS OF ENGINEERS—CIVIL WORKS

		2021 actual	2022 est.	2023 est.
0900	Total new obligations, unexpired accounts	221	215	218
	Budgetary resources:			
	Unobligated balance:			
1000	Unobligated balance brought forward, Oct 1	29	16	84
1021	Recoveries of prior year unpaid obligations	3		
1070	Unobligated balance (total)	32	16	84
	Budget authority:			
	Appropriations, discretionary:			
1100	Appropriation	206	276	200
	Spending authority from offsetting collections, discretionary:			
1700	Collected	1	7	3
1701	Change in uncollected payments, Federal sources	1		
1750	Spending auth from offsetting collections, disc (total)	2	7	3
1900	Budget authority (total)	208	283	203
1930	Total budgetary resources available	240	299	287
	Memorandum (non-add) entries:			
1940	Unobligated balance expiring	−3		
1941	Unexpired unobligated balance, end of year	16	84	69
	Change in obligated balance:			
	Unpaid obligations:			
3000	Unpaid obligations, brought forward, Oct 1	18	17	20
3010	New obligations, unexpired accounts	221	215	218
3020	Outlays (gross)	−217	−212	−204
3040	Recoveries of prior year unpaid obligations, unexpired	−3		
3041	Recoveries of prior year unpaid obligations, expired	−2		
3050	Unpaid obligations, end of year	17	20	34
	Uncollected payments:			
3060	Uncollected pymts, Fed sources, brought forward, Oct 1	−1	−2	−2
3070	Change in uncollected pymts, Fed sources, unexpired	−1		
3090	Uncollected pymts, Fed sources, end of year	−2	−2	−2
	Memorandum (non-add) entries:			
3100	Obligated balance, start of year	17	15	18
3200	Obligated balance, end of year	15	18	32
	Budget authority and outlays, net:			
	Discretionary:			
4000	Budget authority, gross	208	283	203
	Outlays, gross:			
4010	Outlays from new discretionary authority	196	212	182
4011	Outlays from discretionary balances	21		22
4020	Outlays, gross (total)	217	212	204
	Offsets against gross budget authority and outlays:			
	Offsetting collections (collected) from:			
4030	Federal sources	−1	−7	−3
	Additional offsets against gross budget authority only:			
4050	Change in uncollected pymts, Fed sources, unexpired	−1		
4060	Additional offsets against budget authority only (total)	−1		
4070	Budget authority, net (discretionary)	206	276	200
4080	Outlays, net (discretionary)	216	205	201
4180	Budget authority, net (total)	206	276	200
4190	Outlays, net (total)	216	205	201

This appropriation funds the command and control, policy and guidance, program management, national and regional coordination, and quality assurance for the civil works program. These activities are carried out by Corps headquarters and eight division offices:

Corps Headquarters.—This office provides executive direction and management for the civil works program.

Division Offices.—Eight of the nine Corps division offices provide quality assurance for and supervise work of the 38 district offices that have civil works responsibilities. This appropriation also funds certain costs allocable to the civil works program of these Corps-wide support facilities:

Institute for Water Resources.—This institute performs studies and analyses on a wide range of water resources issues and develops project planning techniques.

Engineer Research and Development Center.—This center operates seven labs and conducts research and development for the Corps and other agencies.

Finance Center.—This center supports all Corps finance and accounting activities.

Humphreys Engineer Center.—This field operating activity of the Corps provides day-to-day operational support services to the Corps.

Object Classification (in millions of dollars)

Identification code 096–3124–0–1–301		2021 actual	2022 est.	2023 est.
	Direct obligations:			
	Personnel compensation:			
11.1	Full-time permanent	120	117	119
11.3	Other than full-time permanent	1	1	1
11.5	Other personnel compensation	4	2	3
11.8	Special personal services payments		5	3
11.9	Total personnel compensation	125	125	126
12.1	Civilian personnel benefits	38	36	37
21.0	Travel and transportation of persons	2	4	3
23.1	Rental payments to GSA	3	3	3
23.2	Rental payments to others	2	1	1
25.1	Advisory and assistance services	2	2	2
25.2	Other services from non-Federal sources	2	2	3
25.3	Other goods and services from Federal sources	40	36	37
25.4	Operation and maintenance of facilities	6	2	3
31.0	Equipment		1	1
32.0	Land and structures	1	1	1
99.0	Direct obligations	221	213	217
99.0	Reimbursable obligations		2	1
99.9	Total new obligations, unexpired accounts	221	215	218

Employment Summary

Identification code 096–3124–0–1–301	2021 actual	2022 est.	2023 est.
1001 Direct civilian full-time equivalent employment	907	895	895
2001 Reimbursable civilian full-time equivalent employment	49	50	50

WASHINGTON AQUEDUCT

The Washington Aqueduct supplies drinking water to customers in four jurisdictions: the District of Columbia; Arlington County, Virginia; the City of Falls Church, Virginia; and part of Fairfax County, Virginia. Although the Aqueduct is owned and operated by the Corps (40 U.S.C. 9501 et seq.), the customers finance the operation, maintenance, and certain capital improvements of Aqueduct facilities. The Aqueduct's customers also pay in advance the full cost of those capital improvements.

PERMANENT APPROPRIATIONS

Special and Trust Fund Receipts (in millions of dollars)

Identification code 096–9921–0–2–999		2021 actual	2022 est.	2023 est.
0100	Balance, start of year	36	39	42
0198	Rounding adjustment	−2		
0199	Balance, start of year	34	39	42
	Receipts:			
	Current law:			
1110	Licenses under Federal Power Act, Improvements of Navigable Waters, Maintenance and Operation of Dams, Etc.	11	10	10
1130	Receipts from Leases of Lands Acquired for Flood Control, Navigation, and Allied Purposes	16	14	14
1199	Total current law receipts	27	24	24
1999	Total receipts	27	24	24
2000	Total: Balances and receipts	61	63	66
	Appropriations:			
	Current law:			
2101	Permanent Appropriations	−23	−21	−25
2103	Permanent Appropriations	−1	−1	−1
2132	Permanent Appropriations	1	1	1
2199	Total current law appropriations	−23	−21	−25
2999	Total appropriations	−23	−21	−25
5098	Reconciliation adjustment	1		
5099	Balance, end of year	39	42	41

Corps of Engineers—Civil Works—Continued
Federal Funds—Continued

PERMANENT APPROPRIATIONS—Continued

Program and Financing (in millions of dollars)

Identification code 096–9921–0–2–999		2021 actual	2022 est.	2023 est.
	Obligations by program activity:			
0002	Maintenance and operation of dams and other improvements of navigable waters	21	25	24
	Budgetary resources:			
	Unobligated balance:			
1000	Unobligated balance brought forward, Oct 1	30	33	29
1021	Recoveries of prior year unpaid obligations	1		
1070	Unobligated balance (total)	31	33	29
	Budget authority:			
	Appropriations, mandatory:			
1201	Appropriation (special or trust fund)	23	21	25
1203	Appropriation (previously unavailable)(special or trust)	1	1	1
1232	Appropriations and/or unobligated balance of appropriations temporarily reduced	–1	–1	–1
1260	Appropriations, mandatory (total)	23	21	25
1930	Total budgetary resources available	54	54	54
	Memorandum (non-add) entries:			
1941	Unexpired unobligated balance, end of year	33	29	30
	Change in obligated balance:			
	Unpaid obligations:			
3000	Unpaid obligations, brought forward, Oct 1	11	5	9
3010	New obligations, unexpired accounts	21	25	24
3020	Outlays (gross)	–26	–21	–23
3040	Recoveries of prior year unpaid obligations, unexpired	–1		
3050	Unpaid obligations, end of year	5	9	10
	Memorandum (non-add) entries:			
3100	Obligated balance, start of year	11	5	9
3200	Obligated balance, end of year	5	9	10
	Budget authority and outlays, net:			
	Mandatory:			
4090	Budget authority, gross	23	21	25
	Outlays, gross:			
4100	Outlays from new mandatory authority		21	23
4101	Outlays from mandatory balances	26		
4110	Outlays, gross (total)	26	21	23
4180	Budget authority, net (total)	23	21	25
4190	Outlays, net (total)	26	21	23

This account covers three permanent appropriations:

Hydraulic mining debris reservoir.—The Corps uses fees collected from the Yuba County Water Agency to help maintain the Englebright Dam, Yuba River, California project. (33 U.S.C. 683)

Maintenance and operation of dams and other improvements of navigable waters.—The Corps uses its share of certain fees levied by the Federal Energy Regulatory Commission (on the private use of Federal property, including facilities and land; private construction and operation of water management and appurtenant facilities; and private benefit from headwater improvement by others) for construction, operation, and maintenance of Federal water management facilities. (16 U.S.C. 810(a))

Payments to States.— The Corps pays to States three-fourths of the rent received from the leasing of lands acquired for flood control, navigation, and allied purposes, including the development of hydroelectric power. (33 U.S.C. 701c–3)

Object Classification (in millions of dollars)

Identification code 096–9921–0–2–999		2021 actual	2022 est.	2023 est.
	Direct obligations:			
11.1	Personnel compensation: Full-time permanent	2	2	2
25.3	Other goods and services from Federal sources	13	13	14
25.4	Operation and maintenance of facilities	4	3	4
32.0	Land and structures	2	7	4
99.9	Total new obligations, unexpired accounts	21	25	24

Employment Summary

Identification code 096–9921–0–2–999		2021 actual	2022 est.	2023 est.
1001	Direct civilian full-time equivalent employment	30	25	25

REVOLVING FUND

Program and Financing (in millions of dollars)

Identification code 096–4902–0–4–301		2021 actual	2022 est.	2023 est.
	Obligations by program activity:			
0803	Intra-Corps	10,034	9,503	9,697
0809	Reimbursable program activities, subtotal	10,034	9,503	9,697
	Budgetary resources:			
	Unobligated balance:			
1000	Unobligated balance brought forward, Oct 1	1,018	987	919
1021	Recoveries of prior year unpaid obligations	146		
1033	Recoveries of prior year paid obligations	1	1	1
1070	Unobligated balance (total)	1,165	988	920
	Budget authority:			
	Spending authority from offsetting collections, mandatory:			
1800	Collected	9,846	9,432	9,608
1801	Change in uncollected payments, Federal sources	11	3	4
1823	New and/or unobligated balance of spending authority from offsetting collections temporarily reduced	–1	–1	–1
1850	Spending auth from offsetting collections, mand (total)	9,856	9,434	9,611
1900	Budget authority (total)	9,856	9,434	9,611
1930	Total budgetary resources available	11,021	10,422	10,531
	Memorandum (non-add) entries:			
1941	Unexpired unobligated balance, end of year	987	919	834
	Change in obligated balance:			
	Unpaid obligations:			
3000	Unpaid obligations, brought forward, Oct 1	1,209	1,310	1,506
3010	New obligations, unexpired accounts	10,034	9,503	9,697
3020	Outlays (gross)	–9,787	–9,307	–9,473
3040	Recoveries of prior year unpaid obligations, unexpired	–146		
3050	Unpaid obligations, end of year	1,310	1,506	1,730
	Uncollected payments:			
3060	Uncollected pymts, Fed sources, brought forward, Oct 1	–82	–93	–96
3070	Change in uncollected pymts, Fed sources, unexpired	–11	–3	–4
3090	Uncollected pymts, Fed sources, end of year	–93	–96	–100
	Memorandum (non-add) entries:			
3100	Obligated balance, start of year	1,127	1,217	1,410
3200	Obligated balance, end of year	1,217	1,410	1,630
	Budget authority and outlays, net:			
	Mandatory:			
4090	Budget authority, gross	9,856	9,434	9,611
	Outlays, gross:			
4100	Outlays from new mandatory authority	7,560	7,258	7,379
4101	Outlays from mandatory balances	2,227	2,049	2,094
4110	Outlays, gross (total)	9,787	9,307	9,473
	Offsets against gross budget authority and outlays:			
	Offsetting collections (collected) from:			
4120	Federal sources	–9,847	–9,410	–9,586
4123	Non-Federal sources		–23	–23
4130	Offsets against gross budget authority and outlays (total)	–9,847	–9,433	–9,609
	Additional offsets against gross budget authority only:			
4140	Change in uncollected pymts, Fed sources, unexpired	–11	–3	–4
4143	Recoveries of prior year paid obligations, unexpired accounts	1	1	1
4150	Additional offsets against budget authority only (total)	–10	–2	–3
4160	Budget authority, net (mandatory)	–1	–1	–1
4170	Outlays, net (mandatory)	–60	–126	–136
4180	Budget authority, net (total)	–1	–1	–1
4190	Outlays, net (total)	–60	–126	–136
	Memorandum (non-add) entries:			
5090	Unexpired unavailable balance, SOY: Offsetting collections	13	14	15
5092	Unexpired unavailable balance, EOY: Offsetting collections	14	15	16

This revolving fund provides for the acquisition, operation, and maintenance of plant and equipment used by the civil works program and for temporary financing of services chargeable to the civil works program. The fund also initially finances Corps district office operating expenses, which the districts later reimburse with project-specific funds. In addition, payments are made into the fund when other agencies or entities use plant and equipment acquired by the fund.

Object Classification (in millions of dollars)

Identification code 096–4902–0–4–301	2021 actual	2022 est.	2023 est.
Reimbursable obligations:			
21.0 Travel and transportation of persons	88	94	90
22.0 Transportation of things	15	15	15
23.1 Rental payments to GSA	286	263	276
23.2 Rental payments to others	53	40	45
23.3 Communications, utilities, and miscellaneous charges	124	106	114
24.0 Printing and reproduction	....	1	1
25.1 Advisory and assistance services	53	46	51
25.2 Other services from non-Federal sources	437	2,849	1,272
25.3 Other goods and services from Federal sources	8,512	5,635	7,362
25.4 Operation and maintenance of facilities	124	116	122
25.7 Operation and maintenance of equipment	94	88	97
26.0 Supplies and materials	110	112	113
31.0 Equipment	59	55	56
32.0 Land and structures	79	83	83
99.9 Total new obligations, unexpired accounts	10,034	9,503	9,697

INTERAGENCY AMERICA THE BEAUTIFUL PASS REVENUES

Special and Trust Fund Receipts (in millions of dollars)

Identification code 096–5570–0–2–303	2021 actual	2022 est.	2023 est.
0100 Balance, start of year	....	....	....
Receipts:			
Current law:			
1130 Fees, Interagency America the Beautiful Pass Revenues	1	1	1
2000 Total: Balances and receipts	1	1	1
Appropriations:			
Current law:			
2101 Interagency America the Beautiful Pass Revenues	–1	–1	–1
5099 Balance, end of year	....	....	....

Program and Financing (in millions of dollars)

Identification code 096–5570–0–2–303	2021 actual	2022 est.	2023 est.
Obligations by program activity:			
0001 Interagency America the Beautiful Pass Revenues	1	1	1
0900 Total new obligations, unexpired accounts (object class 25.4)	1	1	1
Budgetary resources:			
Unobligated balance:			
1000 Unobligated balance brought forward, Oct 1	4	4	4
Budget authority:			
Appropriations, mandatory:			
1201 Appropriation (special or trust fund)	1	1	1
1930 Total budgetary resources available	5	5	5
Memorandum (non-add) entries:			
1941 Unexpired unobligated balance, end of year	4	4	4
Change in obligated balance:			
Unpaid obligations:			
3010 New obligations, unexpired accounts	1	1	1
3020 Outlays (gross)	–1	–1	–1
Budget authority and outlays, net:			
Mandatory:			
4090 Budget authority, gross	1	1	1
Outlays, gross:			
4100 Outlays from new mandatory authority	....	1	1
4101 Outlays from mandatory balances	1	....	....
4110 Outlays, gross (total)	1	1	1
4180 Budget authority, net (total)	1	1	1
4190 Outlays, net (total)	1	1	1

Funds in this account are collected from the sale of interagency America the Beautiful National Parks and Federal Recreational Lands Passes as authorized in the Water Resources Reform and Development Act of 2014 (P.L. 113–121, section 1048). The Corps sells and distributes the passes to the public at over 200 Corps locations and deposits the funds into this account. The funds are expended as allowed by the Federal Lands Recreation Enhancement Act at the locations where they are collected.

SPECIAL USE PERMIT FEES

Special and Trust Fund Receipts (in millions of dollars)

Identification code 096–5607–0–2–303	2021 actual	2022 est.	2023 est.
0100 Balance, start of year	....	....	....
Receipts:			
Current law:			
1130 Fees, Special Use Permit Fees	....	1	1
2000 Total: Balances and receipts	....	1	1
Appropriations:			
Current law:			
2101 Special Use Permit Fees	....	–1	....
5099 Balance, end of year	....	....	1

Program and Financing (in millions of dollars)

Identification code 096–5607–0–2–303	2021 actual	2022 est.	2023 est.
Obligations by program activity:			
0001 Recreational Resources	1	1	1
0900 Total new obligations, unexpired accounts (object class 25.4)	1	1	1
Budgetary resources:			
Unobligated balance:			
1000 Unobligated balance brought forward, Oct 1	2	1	1
Budget authority:			
Appropriations, mandatory:			
1201 Appropriation (special or trust fund)	....	1	....
1930 Total budgetary resources available	2	2	1
Memorandum (non-add) entries:			
1941 Unexpired unobligated balance, end of year	1	1	....
Change in obligated balance:			
Unpaid obligations:			
3010 New obligations, unexpired accounts	1	1	1
3020 Outlays (gross)	–1	–1	....
3050 Unpaid obligations, end of year	....	....	1
Memorandum (non-add) entries:			
3200 Obligated balance, end of year	....	....	1
Budget authority and outlays, net:			
Mandatory:			
4090 Budget authority, gross	....	1	....
Outlays, gross:			
4100 Outlays from new mandatory authority	....	1	....
4101 Outlays from mandatory balances	1	....	....
4110 Outlays, gross (total)	1	1	....
4180 Budget authority, net (total)	....	1	....
4190 Outlays, net (total)	1	1	....

Funds in this account are collected from the issuance of special use permits for activities, events, facility use, and other specialized recreation uses, as authorized in the Water Resources Reform and Development Act of 2014 (P.L. 113–121, section 1047(a)). These funds are expended on labor, vehicle costs, materials, supplies, utilities, and other costs associated with administering the special permits and carrying out related operation and maintenance activities at the site where the fees are collected.

Corps of Engineers—Civil Works—Continued
Trust Funds

Trust Funds

HARBOR MAINTENANCE TRUST FUND

For expenses necessary to perform work authorized by law to be financed from the Harbor Maintenance Trust Fund, and to be derived from such fund, $1,726,000,000 to remain available until expended; of which $22,345,000 shall be used to cover the Federal share of construction costs for dredged material disposal facilities; of which $1,698,340,000 shall be used to cover the Federal share of eligible operation and maintenance costs for coastal harbors and channels and inland harbors; and of which $5,315,000 shall be used to cover the Federal share of eligible operation and maintenance costs for inland harbors on the lower Mississippi River.

Note.—A full-year 2022 appropriation for this account was not enacted at the time the Budget was prepared; therefore, the Budget assumes this account is operating under the Continuing Appropriations Act, 2022 (Division A of Public Law 117–43, as amended). The amounts included for 2022 reflect the annualized level provided by the continuing resolution.

Special and Trust Fund Receipts (in millions of dollars)

Identification code 096–8863–0–7–301		2021 actual	2022 est.	2023 est.
0100	Balance, start of year	9,146	9,250	9,407
	Receipts:			
	Current law:			
1110	User Fees, Harbor Maintenance Trust Fund	1,557	1,718	1,760
1140	Earnings on Investments, Harbor Maintenance Trust Fund	60	106	111
1199	Total current law receipts	1,617	1,824	1,871
1999	Total receipts	1,617	1,824	1,871
2000	Total: Balances and receipts	10,763	11,074	11,278
	Appropriations:			
	Current law:			
2101	Operations and Maintenance	–38	–38	–39
2101	Operations and Support	–3	–3	–3
2101	Harbor Maintenance Trust Fund	–880	–1,557	–1,698
2101	Harbor Maintenance Trust Fund	–16	–64	–23
2101	Harbor Maintenance Trust Fund	–5	–5	–5
2199	Total current law appropriations	–942	–1,667	–1,768
2999	Total appropriations	–942	–1,667	–1,768
5098	Change in allocation adjustment	–652		
5098	Reconciliation adjustment	81		
5099	Balance, end of year	9,250	9,407	9,510

Program and Financing (in millions of dollars)

Identification code 096–8863–0–7–301		2021 actual	2022 est.	2023 est.
	Obligations by program activity:			
0001	Commercial navigation	1,553	1,626	1,626
	Budgetary resources:			
	Unobligated balance:			
1045	Adjustment for change in allocation (O&M FY 2020)	406		
1045	Adjustment for change in allocation (Construction FY 2020)	49		
1045	Adjustment for change in allocation (O&M FY 2019)	76		
1045	Adjustment for change in allocation (Construction FY 2019)	12		
1045	Adjustment for change in allocation (O&M Supplemental FY 2019)	109		
1070	Unobligated balance (total)	652		
	Budget authority:			
	Appropriations, discretionary:			
1101	Appropriation (O&M)	880	1,557	1,698
1101	Appropriation (Construction)	16	64	23
1101	Appropriation (MR&T)	5	5	5
1160	Appropriation, discretionary (total)	901	1,626	1,726
1930	Total budgetary resources available	1,553	1,626	1,726
	Memorandum (non-add) entries:			
1941	Unexpired unobligated balance, end of year			100
	Change in obligated balance:			
	Unpaid obligations:			
3000	Unpaid obligations, brought forward, Oct 1			650
3010	New obligations, unexpired accounts	1,553	1,626	1,626
3020	Outlays (gross)	–1,553	–976	–1,361
3050	Unpaid obligations, end of year		650	915
	Memorandum (non-add) entries:			
3100	Obligated balance, start of year			650
3200	Obligated balance, end of year		650	915
	Budget authority and outlays, net:			
	Discretionary:			
4000	Budget authority, gross	901	1,626	1,726
	Outlays, gross:			
4010	Outlays from new discretionary authority	901	976	1,036
4011	Outlays from discretionary balances	652		325
4020	Outlays, gross (total)	1,553	976	1,361
4180	Budget authority, net (total)	901	1,626	1,726
4190	Outlays, net (total)	1,553	976	1,361
	Memorandum (non-add) entries:			
5000	Total investments, SOY: Federal securities: Par value	9,060	9,124	9,250
5001	Total investments, EOY: Federal securities: Par value	9,124	9,250	9,406

The Harbor Maintenance Trust Fund is authorized under the Harbor Maintenance Revenue Act of 1986 (P.L. 99–662, Title XIV), as amended. Under current law, revenue is derived from a 0.125 percent ad valorem tax imposed upon commercial users of specified U.S. ports, Saint Lawrence Seaway tolls, and investment interest. The Budget proposes to execute these appropriations within the Harbor Maintenance Trust Fund rather than to transfer and execute them in the Construction, Operation and Maintenance, and Mississippi River and Tributaries accounts.

The Harbor Maintenance Revenue Act authorizes expenditures from this fund to finance up to 100 percent of eligible Corps harbor operation and maintenance costs, including the operation and maintenance of Great Lakes navigation projects. The fund fully finances eligible operation and maintenance costs of the Saint Lawrence Seaway Development Corporation. The Water Resources Development Act of 1996 (P.L. 104–303, section 201) authorizes the fund to pay the Federal share of the costs for the construction of dredged material disposal facilities that are necessary for the operation and maintenance of coastal or inland harbors, the dredging and disposal of contaminated sediments that are in or affect the operation and maintenance of Federal navigation channels, the mitigation of impacts resulting from Federal navigation operation and maintenance activities, and the operation and maintenance of dredged material disposal facilities.

The North American Free Trade Agreement Implementation Act (26 U.S.C. 9505(c)(3)) authorizes the fund to pay all expenses of administration incurred by the Department of the Treasury, the Corps, and the Department of Commerce related to the administration of the harbor maintenance tax (under 26 U.S.C. 4461 et seq.), but not in excess of $5 million for any fiscal year.

In 1998, the U.S. Supreme Court excluded all U.S. exports from the harbor maintenance tax. The Court found that the tax violated Article I, section 9, clause 5 of the constitution because the value of the cargo, which is the basis for calculating this tax, does not fairly match the use of port services and facilities by exporters.

The proposed appropriations language for eligible operation and maintenance costs for inland harbors on the lower Mississippi River is intended to only apply to: Helena Harbor, Phillips County, AR; Baton Rouge Harbor, Devil Swamp, LA; Greenville Harbor, MS; Vicksburg Harbor, MS; and Memphis Harbor, McKellar Lake, Memphis, TN.

Object Classification (in millions of dollars)

Identification code 096–8863–0–7–301		2021 actual	2022 est.	2023 est.
	Direct obligations:			
94.0	Financial transfers (Operation and Maintenance)	1,470	1,557	1,557
94.0	Financial transfers (Construction)	78	64	64
94.0	Financial transfers (MR&T)	5	5	5
99.9	Total new obligations, unexpired accounts	1,553	1,626	1,626

CORPS OF ENGINEERS—CIVIL WORKS

INLAND WATERWAYS TRUST FUND

For expenses necessary to cover 35 percent of the costs of construction, replacement, rehabilitation, and expansion of inland waterways projects, except as otherwise specifically provided by law, $13,755,000, which shall be derived from the Inland Waterways Trust Fund and remain available until expended.

Note.—A full-year 2022 appropriation for this account was not enacted at the time the Budget was prepared; therefore, the Budget assumes this account is operating under the Continuing Appropriations Act, 2022 (Division A of Public Law 117–43, as amended). The amounts included for 2022 reflect the annualized level provided by the continuing resolution.

Special and Trust Fund Receipts (in millions of dollars)

Identification code 096–8861–0–7–301	2021 actual	2022 est.	2023 est.
0100 Balance, start of year	131	222	212
Receipts:			
Current law:			
1110 Transfer from General Fund, Inland Waterways Revenue Act Taxes	128	102	99
1140 Interest and Profits on Investments in Public Debt Securities, Inland Waterways Trust Fund	....	1	1
1199 Total current law receipts	128	103	100
1999 Total receipts	128	103	100
2000 Total: Balances and receipts	259	325	312
Appropriations:			
Current law:			
2101 Inland Waterways Trust Fund	–25	–113	–14
5098 Change in allocation adjustment	–12	....	....
5099 Balance, end of year	222	212	298

Program and Financing (in millions of dollars)

Identification code 096–8861–0–7–301	2021 actual	2022 est.	2023 est.
Obligations by program activity:			
0001 Inland Waterways Trust Fund	38	46	45
Budgetary resources:			
Unobligated balance:			
1000 Unobligated balance brought forward, Oct 1	....	....	67
1045 Adjustment for change in allocation (trust fund portion)	13	....	....
1070 Unobligated balance (total)	13	....	67
Budget authority:			
Appropriations, discretionary:			
1101 Appropriation (Construction)	25	113	14
1930 Total budgetary resources available	38	113	81
Memorandum (non-add) entries:			
1941 Unexpired unobligated balance, end of year	....	67	36
Change in obligated balance:			
Unpaid obligations:			
3000 Unpaid obligations, brought forward, Oct 1	....	....	6
3010 New obligations, unexpired accounts	38	46	45
3020 Outlays (gross)	–38	–40	–33
3050 Unpaid obligations, end of year	....	6	18
Memorandum (non-add) entries:			
3100 Obligated balance, start of year	....	....	6
3200 Obligated balance, end of year	....	6	18
Budget authority and outlays, net:			
Discretionary:			
4000 Budget authority, gross	25	113	14
Outlays, gross:			
4010 Outlays from new discretionary authority	25	40	5
4011 Outlays from discretionary balances	13	....	28
4020 Outlays, gross (total)	38	40	33
4180 Budget authority, net (total)	25	113	14
4190 Outlays, net (total)	38	40	33
Memorandum (non-add) entries:			
5000 Total investments, SOY: Federal securities: Par value	113	210	250
5001 Total investments, EOY: Federal securities: Par value	210	250	295

The Inland Waterways Trust Fund is authorized under the Inland Waterways Revenue Act of 1978 (P.L. 95–502), as amended by the Water Resources Development Act (WRDA) of 1986 (P.L. 99–662). The fund is used to pay one-half of the costs associated with the construction, replacement, rehabilitation, and expansion of Federal inland waterways projects, except as otherwise specifically provided for in law. Section 109 of WRDA 2020 (Division AA of P.L. 116–260) specifically provides that for a project for navigation receiving a construction appropriation during fiscal years 2021 through 2031, 35 percent of the costs of construction of the project shall be paid from the fund until such construction of the project is complete. Under current law, revenue is derived from an excise tax imposed on diesel fuel for commercial vessels on most of the inland waterways, plus investment interest. The Budget proposes to execute these appropriations within the Inland Waterways Trust Fund rather than to transfer and execute them in the Construction account.

Object Classification (in millions of dollars)

Identification code 096–8861–0–7–301	2021 actual	2022 est.	2023 est.
Direct obligations:			
25.2 Other services from non-Federal sources	35	42	40
32.0 Land and structures	3	4	5
99.9 Total new obligations, unexpired accounts	38	46	45

RIVERS AND HARBORS CONTRIBUTED FUNDS

Special and Trust Fund Receipts (in millions of dollars)

Identification code 096–8862–0–7–301	2021 actual	2022 est.	2023 est.
0100 Balance, start of year	10	9	9
Receipts:			
Current law:			
1130 Contributions, Rivers and Harbors, Other Than Port and Harbor User Fees	739	601	601
2000 Total: Balances and receipts	749	610	610
Appropriations:			
Current law:			
2101 Rivers and Harbors Contributed Funds	–739	–601	–601
2103 Rivers and Harbors Contributed Funds	–10	–9	–9
2132 Rivers and Harbors Contributed Funds	9	9	9
2199 Total current law appropriations	–740	–601	–601
2999 Total appropriations	–740	–601	–601
5099 Balance, end of year	9	9	9

Program and Financing (in millions of dollars)

Identification code 096–8862–0–7–301	2021 actual	2022 est.	2023 est.
Obligations by program activity:			
0001 Commercial Navigation	165	163	148
0002 Flood Risk Management	282	213	226
0003 Aquatic Ecosystem Restoration	21	15	16
0004 Hydropower	12	24	22
0005 Multipurpose and Other Programs	214	153	182
0006 Emergency Management	9	3	5
0007 Direct program activities	....	2	4
0799 Total direct obligations	703	573	603
0900 Total new obligations, unexpired accounts	703	573	603
Budgetary resources:			
Unobligated balance:			
1000 Unobligated balance brought forward, Oct 1	1,320	1,412	1,440
1021 Recoveries of prior year unpaid obligations	36	....	....
1033 Recoveries of prior year paid obligations	19	....	....
1070 Unobligated balance (total)	1,375	1,412	1,440
Budget authority:			
Appropriations, mandatory:			
1201 Appropriation (special or trust fund)	739	601	601
1203 Appropriation (previously unavailable)(special or trust)	10	9	9
1232 Appropriations and/or unobligated balance of appropriations temporarily reduced	–9	–9	–9
1260 Appropriations, mandatory (total)	740	601	601
1900 Budget authority (total)	740	601	601
1930 Total budgetary resources available	2,115	2,013	2,041

1093

RIVERS AND HARBORS CONTRIBUTED FUNDS—Continued
Program and Financing—Continued

Identification code 096–8862–0–7–301		2021 actual	2022 est.	2023 est.
	Memorandum (non-add) entries:			
1941	Unexpired unobligated balance, end of year	1,412	1,440	1,438
	Change in obligated balance:			
	Unpaid obligations:			
3000	Unpaid obligations, brought forward, Oct 1	584	765	904
3010	New obligations, unexpired accounts	703	573	603
3020	Outlays (gross)	–486	–434	–418
3040	Recoveries of prior year unpaid obligations, unexpired	–36	....	....
3050	Unpaid obligations, end of year	765	904	1,089
	Memorandum (non-add) entries:			
3100	Obligated balance, start of year	584	765	904
3200	Obligated balance, end of year	765	904	1,089
	Budget authority and outlays, net:			
	Mandatory:			
4090	Budget authority, gross	740	601	601
	Outlays, gross:			
4100	Outlays from new mandatory authority	....	120	120
4101	Outlays from mandatory balances	486	314	298
4110	Outlays, gross (total)	486	434	418
	Offsets against gross budget authority and outlays:			
	Offsetting collections (collected) from:			
4123	Non-Federal sources	–19	....	....
	Additional offsets against gross budget authority only:			
4143	Recoveries of prior year paid obligations, unexpired accounts	19	....	....
4160	Budget authority, net (mandatory)	740	601	601
4170	Outlays, net (mandatory)	467	434	418
4180	Budget authority, net (total)	740	601	601
4190	Outlays, net (total)	467	434	418

The funds in this account are provided by non-Federal interests to cover some or all of the costs for the study, design, construction, and operation and maintenance of water resources projects. These funds include amounts for the authorized non-Federal share of the costs, amounts in excess of the authorized non-Federal share that are provided voluntarily as contributed or advanced funds, and amounts for certain work carried out in connection with a project with 100 percent non-Federal funding.

Object Classification (in millions of dollars)

Identification code 096–8862–0–7–301		2021 actual	2022 est.	2023 est.
	Direct obligations:			
	Personnel compensation:			
11.1	Full-time permanent	69	70	73
11.3	Other than full-time permanent	1	2	2
11.5	Other personnel compensation	3	3	3
11.9	Total personnel compensation	73	75	78
12.1	Civilian personnel benefits	14	13	14
21.0	Travel and transportation of persons	1	1	1
25.1	Advisory and assistance services	11	5	7
25.2	Other services from non-Federal sources	41	36	38
25.3	Other goods and services from Federal sources	20	26	26
25.4	Operation and maintenance of facilities	19	18	18
31.0	Equipment	1	2	2
32.0	Land and structures	523	397	419
99.0	Direct obligations	703	573	603
99.9	Total new obligations, unexpired accounts	703	573	603

Employment Summary

Identification code 096–8862–0–7–301		2021 actual	2022 est.	2023 est.
1001	Direct civilian full-time equivalent employment	522	550	550

COASTAL WETLANDS RESTORATION TRUST FUND
Program and Financing (in millions of dollars)

Identification code 096–8333–0–7–301		2021 actual	2022 est.	2023 est.
	Obligations by program activity:			
0001	Coastal Wetlands Restoration Trust Fund	65	87	101
	Budgetary resources:			
	Unobligated balance:			
1000	Unobligated balance brought forward, Oct 1	334	375	378
1021	Recoveries of prior year unpaid obligations	12	....	....
1070	Unobligated balance (total)	346	375	378
	Budget authority:			
	Appropriations, mandatory:			
1203	Appropriation (previously unavailable)(special or trust)	5	5	5
1221	Appropriations transferred from other acct [014–8151]	94	90	90
1232	Appropriations and/or unobligated balance of appropriations temporarily reduced	–5	–5	–5
1260	Appropriations, mandatory (total)	94	90	90
1930	Total budgetary resources available	440	465	468
	Memorandum (non-add) entries:			
1941	Unexpired unobligated balance, end of year	375	378	367
	Change in obligated balance:			
	Unpaid obligations:			
3000	Unpaid obligations, brought forward, Oct 1	203	192	204
3010	New obligations, unexpired accounts	65	87	101
3020	Outlays (gross)	–64	–75	–72
3040	Recoveries of prior year unpaid obligations, unexpired	–12	....	....
3050	Unpaid obligations, end of year	192	204	233
	Memorandum (non-add) entries:			
3100	Obligated balance, start of year	203	192	204
3200	Obligated balance, end of year	192	204	233
	Budget authority and outlays, net:			
	Mandatory:			
4090	Budget authority, gross	94	90	90
	Outlays, gross:			
4100	Outlays from new mandatory authority	....	22	22
4101	Outlays from mandatory balances	64	53	50
4110	Outlays, gross (total)	64	75	72
4180	Budget authority, net (total)	94	90	90
4190	Outlays, net (total)	64	75	72

The Coastal Wetlands Planning, Protection and Restoration Act (P.L. 101–646, Title III), as amended, directs the Secretary of the Interior to distribute to the Coastal Wetlands Restoration Trust Fund a portion of the amounts appropriated each fiscal year from the Sport Fish Restoration Account. The Louisiana Coastal Wetlands Conservation and Restoration Task Force, which is an interagency task force consisting of the Corps, Environmental Protection Agency, Fish and Wildlife Service, Natural Resources Conservation Service, National Marine Fisheries Service, and the State of Louisiana, uses these funds to plan, set priorities, and carry out projects for the creation, protection, and restoration of coastal wetlands in the State of Louisiana.

Object Classification (in millions of dollars)

Identification code 096–8333–0–7–301		2021 actual	2022 est.	2023 est.
	Direct obligations:			
11.1	Personnel compensation: Full-time permanent	1	1	1
25.2	Other services from non-Federal sources	40	40	49
25.3	Other goods and services from Federal sources	24	46	51
99.9	Total new obligations, unexpired accounts	65	87	101

Employment Summary

Identification code 096–8333–0–7–301		2021 actual	2022 est.	2023 est.
1001	Direct civilian full-time equivalent employment	7	7	7

SOUTH DAKOTA TERRESTRIAL WILDLIFE HABITAT RESTORATION TRUST FUND

Special and Trust Fund Receipts (in millions of dollars)

Identification code 096–8217–0–7–306	2021 actual	2022 est.	2023 est.
0100 Balance, start of year	110	110	110
Receipts:			
Current law:			
1140 Earnings on Investments, South Dakota Terrestrial Wildlife Habitat Restoration Trust Fund	2	2	2
2000 Total: Balances and receipts	112	112	112
Appropriations:			
Current law:			
2101 South Dakota Terrestrial Wildlife Habitat Restoration Trust Fund	–2	–2	–2
5099 Balance, end of year	110	110	110

Program and Financing (in millions of dollars)

Identification code 096–8217–0–7–306	2021 actual	2022 est.	2023 est.
Obligations by program activity:			
0001 Wildlife Habitat Restoration	1	1	1
0900 Total new obligations, unexpired accounts (object class 25.2)	1	1	1
Budgetary resources:			
Unobligated balance:			
1000 Unobligated balance brought forward, Oct 1	5	6	7
Budget authority:			
Appropriations, mandatory:			
1201 Appropriation (special or trust fund)	2	2	2
1930 Total budgetary resources available	7	8	9
Memorandum (non-add) entries:			
1941 Unexpired unobligated balance, end of year	6	7	8
Change in obligated balance:			
Unpaid obligations:			
3010 New obligations, unexpired accounts	1	1	1
3020 Outlays (gross)	–1	–1	–1
Budget authority and outlays, net:			
Mandatory:			
4090 Budget authority, gross	2	2	2
Outlays, gross:			
4100 Outlays from new mandatory authority		1	1
4101 Outlays from mandatory balances	1		
4110 Outlays, gross (total)	1	1	1
4180 Budget authority, net (total)	2	2	2
4190 Outlays, net (total)	1	1	1
Memorandum (non-add) entries:			
5000 Total investments, SOY: Federal securities: Par value	116	117	118
5001 Total investments, EOY: Federal securities: Par value	117	118	119

This fund, authorized by the Water Resources Development Act of 1999 (P.L. 106–53), supports wildlife habitat restoration efforts undertaken by the State of South Dakota. The establishment of this fund satisfies the Federal obligation under the Fish and Wildlife Coordination Act (16 U.S.C. 1661 et seq.) to mitigate for the loss of habitat due to flooding from the Oahe and Big Bend projects, which the Corps constructed under the Pick-Sloan Missouri River Basin program.

GENERAL FUND RECEIPT ACCOUNTS

(in millions of dollars)

	2021 actual	2022 est.	2023 est.
Offsetting receipts from the public:			
096–143500 General Fund Proprietary Interest Receipts, not Otherwise Classified	21	20	20
096–322000 All Other General Fund Proprietary Receipts Including Budget Clearing Accounts	523	163	163
General Fund Offsetting receipts from the public	544	183	183
Intragovernmental payments:			
096–388500 Undistributed Intragovernmental Payments and Receivables from Cancelled Accounts		–1	–1
General Fund Intragovernmental payments		–1	–1

GENERAL PROVISIONS—CORPS OF ENGINEERS—CIVIL

(INCLUDING TRANSFER OF FUNDS)

SEC. 101. (a) None of the funds provided in title I of this Act shall be available for obligation or expenditure through a reprogramming of funds that:

(1) creates or initiates a new program, project, or activity;

(2) eliminates a program, project, or activity;

(3) increases funds or personnel for any program, project, or activity for which funds have been denied or restricted by this Act, unless notice has been transmitted to the Committees on Appropriations of both Houses of Congress;

(4) proposes to use funds directed for a specific activity for a different purpose, unless notice has been transmitted to the Committees on Appropriations of both Houses of Congress;

(5) augments or reduces existing programs, projects, or activities in excess of the amounts contained in paragraphs (6) through (10), unless notice has been transmitted to the Committees on Appropriations of both Houses of Congress;

(6) INVESTIGATIONS.—For a base level over $100,000, reprogramming of 25 percent of the base amount up to a limit of $150,000 per project, study or activity is allowed: Provided, That for a base level less than $100,000, the reprogramming limit is $25,000: Provided further, That up to $25,000 may be reprogrammed into any continuing study or activity that did not receive an appropriation for existing obligations and concomitant administrative expenses;

(7) CONSTRUCTION.—For a base level over $2,000,000, reprogramming of 15 percent of the base amount up to a limit of $3,000,000 per project, study or activity is allowed: Provided, That for a base level less than $2,000,000, the reprogramming limit is $300,000: Provided further, That up to $3,000,000 may be reprogrammed for settled contractor claims, changed conditions, or real estate deficiency judgments: Provided further, That up to $300,000 may be reprogrammed into any continuing study or activity that did not receive an appropriation for existing obligations and concomitant administrative expenses;

(8) OPERATION AND MAINTENANCE.—Unlimited reprogramming authority is granted for the Corps to be able to respond to emergencies: Provided, That the Chief of Engineers shall notify the Committees on Appropriations of both Houses of Congress of these emergency actions as soon thereafter as practicable: Provided further, That for a base level over $1,000,000, reprogramming of 15 percent of the base amount up to a limit of $5,000,000 per project, study, or activity is allowed: Provided further, That for a base level less than $1,000,000, the reprogramming limit is $150,000: Provided further, That $150,000 may be reprogrammed into any continuing study or activity that did not receive an appropriation;

(9) MISSISSIPPI RIVER AND TRIBUTARIES.—The reprogramming guidelines in paragraphs (6), (7), and (8) shall apply to the Investigations, Construction, and Operation and Maintenance portions of the Mississippi River and Tributaries Account, respectively; and

(10) FORMERLY UTILIZED SITES REMEDIAL ACTION PROGRAM.—Reprogramming of up to 15 percent of the base of the receiving project is permitted.

(b) DE MINIMUS REPROGRAMMINGS.—In no case should a reprogramming for less than $50,000 be submitted to the Committees on Appropriations of both Houses of Congress.

(c) CONTINUING AUTHORITIES PROGRAM.—Subsection (a)(1) shall not apply to any project or activity funded under the continuing authorities program.

(d) Not later than 60 days after the date of enactment of this Act, the Secretary shall submit a report to the Committees on Appropriations of both Houses of Congress to establish the baseline for application of reprogramming and transfer authorities for the current fiscal year which shall include:

(1) A table for each appropriation with a separate column to display the President's budget request, adjustments made by Congress, adjustments due to enacted rescissions, if applicable, and the fiscal year enacted level; and

(2) A delineation in the table for each appropriation both by object class and program, project and activity as detailed in the budget appendix for the respective appropriations.

SEC. 102. None of the funds made available in this title may be used to award or modify any contract that commits funds beyond the amounts appropriated for that program, project, or activity that remain unobligated, except that such amounts may include any funds that have been made available through reprogramming pursuant to section 101.

SEC. 103. *The Secretary of the Army may transfer to the Fish and Wildlife Service, and the Fish and Wildlife Service may accept and expend, such funds as the Secretary of the Army and the Director of the Fish and Wildlife Service determine, through consultation, are appropriate, from the funds provided in this title under the heading "Operation and Maintenance" to mitigate for fisheries lost due to Corps of Engineers projects.*

GENERAL PROVISIONS—CORPS OF ENGINEERS

⟦SEC. 300. For projects that are carried out with funds under this heading, the Secretary of the Army and the Director of the Office of Management and Budget shall consider other factors in addition to the benefit-cost ratio when determining the economic benefits of projects that benefit disadvantaged communities.⟧ *(Infrastructure Investments and Jobs Appropriations Act.)*

OTHER DEFENSE—CIVIL PROGRAMS

MILITARY RETIREMENT
Federal Funds
PAYMENT TO MILITARY RETIREMENT FUND

Program and Financing (in millions of dollars)

Identification code 097–0040–0–1–054	2021 actual	2022 est.	2023 est.
Obligations by program activity:			
0001 Direct program activity	98,106	114,463	120,357
0900 Total new obligations, unexpired accounts (object class 13.0)	98,106	114,463	120,357
Budgetary resources:			
Budget authority:			
Appropriations, mandatory:			
1200 Appropriation	98,106	114,463	120,357
1930 Total budgetary resources available	98,106	114,463	120,357
Change in obligated balance:			
Unpaid obligations:			
3010 New obligations, unexpired accounts	98,106	114,463	120,357
3020 Outlays (gross)	–98,106	–114,463	–120,357
Budget authority and outlays, net:			
Mandatory:			
4090 Budget authority, gross	98,106	114,463	120,357
Outlays, gross:			
4100 Outlays from new mandatory authority	98,106	114,463	120,357
4180 Budget authority, net (total)	98,106	114,463	120,357
4190 Outlays, net (total)	98,106	114,463	120,357

The 2022 payment to the Military Retirement Fund includes funds for the amortization of the unfunded liability for all retirement benefits earned by military personnel for service prior to 1985. The amortization schedule for the unfunded liability is determined by the Department of Defense Retirement Board of Actuaries. Included in the unfunded liability are the consolidated requirements of the military departments to cover retired officers and enlisted personnel of the Army, Navy, Marine Corps, and Air Force; retainer pay of enlisted personnel of the Fleet Reserve of the Navy and Marine Corps; and survivors' benefits.

The 2004 National Defense Authorization Act (P.L. 108–136) created additional benefits for certain retirees who receive disability compensation from the Department of Veterans Affairs and moved the responsibility for payments under the Combat-Related Special Compensation program to the Military Retirement Fund. Any additional funding requirements for retirees with service prior to 1985 will be included in this payment.

The 2016 National Defense Authorization Act (P.L. 114–92) enacted substantial changes to the current military retirement system. The new retirement system, which took effect January 1, 2018, is a blend of several components, including a defined retired pay benefit, a defined contribution to the Thrift Savings Plan, and a bonus (continuation pay) paid to the member to maintain Service retention requirements. Currently serving members will remain grandfathered under the legacy retirement system.

Trust Funds
MILITARY RETIREMENT FUND

Special and Trust Fund Receipts (in millions of dollars)

Identification code 097–8097–0–7–602	2021 actual	2022 est.	2023 est.
0100 Balance, start of year	892,953	1,008,978	1,142,051
Receipts:			
Current law:			
1140 Employing Agency Contributions, Military Retirement Fund	25,236	25,639	28,189
1140 Earnings on Investments, Military Retirement Fund	45,976	48,724	40,384
1140 Federal Contributions, Military Retirement Fund	98,106	114,463	120,357
1140 Federal Contributions (concurrent Receipt Accruals), Military Retirement Fund	9,845	10,569	10,897
1199 Total current law receipts	179,163	199,395	199,827
1999 Total receipts	179,163	199,395	199,827
2000 Total: Balances and receipts	1,072,116	1,208,373	1,341,878
Appropriations:			
Current law:			
2101 Military Retirement Fund	–178,576	–199,397	–200,813
2135 Military Retirement Fund	115,439	133,075	129,004
2199 Total current law appropriations	–63,137	–66,322	–71,809
2999 Total appropriations	–63,137	–66,322	–71,809
5098 Rounding adjustment	–1		
5099 Balance, end of year	1,008,978	1,142,051	1,270,069

Program and Financing (in millions of dollars)

Identification code 097–8097–0–7–602	2021 actual	2022 est.	2023 est.
Obligations by program activity:			
0001 Nondisability	55,208	57,954	62,572
0002 Temporary disability	479	111	121
0003 Permanent disability	1,869	1,933	2,098
0004 Fleet reserve	1,732	1,818	1,963
0005 Survivors' benefits	3,849	4,506	5,055
0900 Total new obligations, unexpired accounts (object class 42.0)	63,137	66,322	71,809
Budgetary resources:			
Budget authority:			
Appropriations, mandatory:			
1201 Appropriation (special or trust fund)	178,576	199,397	200,813
1235 Appropriations precluded from obligation (special or trust)	–115,439	–133,075	–129,004
1260 Appropriations, mandatory (total)	63,137	66,322	71,809
1930 Total budgetary resources available	63,137	66,322	71,809
Change in obligated balance:			
Unpaid obligations:			
3000 Unpaid obligations, brought forward, Oct 1	5,118	5,201	5,069
3010 New obligations, unexpired accounts	63,137	66,322	71,809
3020 Outlays (gross)	–63,054	–66,454	–71,550
3050 Unpaid obligations, end of year	5,201	5,069	5,328
Memorandum (non-add) entries:			
3100 Obligated balance, start of year	5,118	5,201	5,069
3200 Obligated balance, end of year	5,201	5,069	5,328
Budget authority and outlays, net:			
Mandatory:			
4090 Budget authority, gross	63,137	66,322	71,809
Outlays, gross:			
4100 Outlays from new mandatory authority	57,936	61,253	66,481
4101 Outlays from mandatory balances	5,118	5,201	5,069
4110 Outlays, gross (total)	63,054	66,454	71,550
4180 Budget authority, net (total)	63,137	66,322	71,809
4190 Outlays, net (total)	63,054	66,454	71,550
Memorandum (non-add) entries:			
5000 Total investments, SOY: Federal securities: Par value	916,264	1,032,000	1,147,493
5001 Total investments, EOY: Federal securities: Par value	1,032,000	1,147,493	1,276,757

Public Law 98–94 provided for accrual funding of the military retirement system and for the establishment of a Department of Defense Military Retirement Fund in 1985. The fund has three sources of income. The first is payments from the military personnel accounts, which cover the accruing costs of the future retirement benefits being earned by today's service members. The second source is interest on investments of the fund. The third source is made up of two payments from the general fund of the Treasury. The first Treasury payment covers a portion of the accrued unfunded liability for all the retirees and current members who had earned benefits before the accrual funding system was set up. The second Treasury payment covers the liability for concurrent receipt of military retired pay and disability compensation paid by the Department of Veterans Affairs. This benefit was added in the 2004 National Defense Authorization Act.

MILITARY RETIREMENT FUND—Continued

The 2016 National Defense Authorization Act (P.L. 114–92) enacted substantial changes to the current military retirement system. The new retirement system, which took effect January 1, 2018 is a blend of several components, including a defined retired pay benefit, a defined contribution to the Thrift Savings Plan, and a bonus (continuation pay) paid to the member to maintain Service retention requirements. Currently serving members will remain grandfathered under the legacy retirement system.

The status of the fund is as follows:

Status of Funds (in millions of dollars)

Identification code 097–8097–0–7–602		2021 actual	2022 est.	2023 est.
	Unexpended balance, start of year:			
0100	Balance, start of year	898,071	1,014,180	1,147,121
0999	Total balance, start of year	898,071	1,014,180	1,147,121
	Cash income during the year:			
	Current law:			
	Receipts:			
1150	Earnings on Investments, Military Retirement Fund	45,976	48,724	40,384
1160	Employing Agency Contributions, Military Retirement Fund	25,236	25,639	28,189
1160	Federal Contributions, Military Retirement Fund	98,106	114,463	120,357
1160	Federal Contributions (concurrent Receipt Accruals), Military Retirement Fund	9,845	10,569	10,897
1199	Income under present law	179,163	199,395	199,827
1999	Total cash income	179,163	199,395	199,827
	Cash outgo during year:			
	Current law:			
2100	Military Retirement Fund [Budget Acct]	–63,054	–66,454	–71,550
2199	Outgo under current law	–63,054	–66,454	–71,550
2999	Total cash outgo (-)	–63,054	–66,454	–71,550
	Surplus or deficit:			
3110	Excluding interest	70,133	84,217	87,893
3120	Interest	45,976	48,724	40,384
3199	Subtotal, surplus or deficit	116,109	132,941	128,277
3999	Total change in fund balance	116,109	132,941	128,277
	Unexpended balance, end of year:			
4100	Uninvested balance (net), end of year	–17,820	–372	–1,359
4200	Military Retirement Fund	1,032,000	1,147,493	1,276,757
4999	Total balance, end of year	1,014,180	1,147,121	1,275,398

RETIREE HEALTH CARE

Federal Funds

PAYMENT TO DEPARTMENT OF DEFENSE MEDICARE-ELIGIBLE RETIREE HEALTH CARE FUND

Program and Financing (in millions of dollars)

Identification code 097–0850–0–1–054		2021 actual	2022 est.	2023 est.
	Obligations by program activity:			
0001	Direct program activity	6,983	7,503	7,409
0900	Total new obligations, unexpired accounts (object class 13.0)	6,983	7,503	7,409
	Budgetary resources:			
	Budget authority:			
	Appropriations, mandatory:			
1200	Appropriation	6,983	7,503	7,409
1900	Budget authority (total)	6,983	7,503	7,409
1930	Total budgetary resources available	6,983	7,503	7,409
	Change in obligated balance:			
	Unpaid obligations:			
3010	New obligations, unexpired accounts	6,983	7,503	7,409
3020	Outlays (gross)	–6,983	–7,503	–7,409
	Budget authority and outlays, net:			
	Mandatory:			
4090	Budget authority, gross	6,983	7,503	7,409
	Outlays, gross:			
4100	Outlays from new mandatory authority	6,983	7,503	7,409
4180	Budget authority, net (total)	6,983	7,503	7,409
4190	Outlays, net (total)	6,983	7,503	7,409

DEPARTMENT OF DEFENSE MEDICARE-ELIGIBLE RETIREE HEALTH CARE FUND

Special and Trust Fund Receipts (in millions of dollars)

Identification code 097–5472–0–2–551		2021 actual	2022 est.	2023 est.
0100	Balance, start of year	263,690	284,820	304,748
	Receipts:			
	Current law:			
1140	Non-DoD Employing Agency Contributions, DoD Medicare-Eligible Retiree Health Care Fund	246	278	293
1140	Earnings on Investments, DoD Medicare-Eligible Retiree Health Care Fund	16,580	14,211	12,124
1140	Federal Contributions, DoD Medicare-Eligible Retiree Health Care Fund	6,983	7,503	7,409
1140	Department of Defense Contributions, DoD Medicare-Eligible Retiree Health Care Fund	8,376	9,336	9,743
1199	Total current law receipts	32,185	31,328	29,569
	Proposed:			
1240	Earnings on Investments, DoD Medicare-Eligible Retiree Health Care Fund	....	....	–4
1999	Total receipts	32,185	31,328	29,565
2000	Total: Balances and receipts	295,875	316,148	334,313
	Appropriations:			
	Current law:			
2101	Department of Defense Medicare-Eligible Retiree Health Care Fund	–32,009	–31,870	–29,685
2135	Department of Defense Medicare-Eligible Retiree Health Care Fund	20,954	20,470	17,080
2199	Total current law appropriations	–11,055	–11,400	–12,605
2999	Total appropriations	–11,055	–11,400	–12,605
5099	Balance, end of year	284,820	304,748	321,708

Program and Financing (in millions of dollars)

Identification code 097–5472–0–2–551		2021 actual	2022 est.	2023 est.
	Obligations by program activity:			
0001	Direct program activity	11,055	11,400	12,605
0900	Total new obligations, unexpired accounts (object class 13.0)	11,055	11,400	12,605
	Budgetary resources:			
	Budget authority:			
	Appropriations, mandatory:			
1201	Appropriation (special or trust fund)	32,009	31,870	29,685
1235	Appropriations precluded from obligation (special or trust)	–20,954	–20,470	–17,080
1260	Appropriations, mandatory (total)	11,055	11,400	12,605
1930	Total budgetary resources available	11,055	11,400	12,605
	Change in obligated balance:			
	Unpaid obligations:			
3000	Unpaid obligations, brought forward, Oct 1	495	354	456
3010	New obligations, unexpired accounts	11,055	11,400	12,605
3020	Outlays (gross)	–11,196	–11,298	–12,557
3050	Unpaid obligations, end of year	354	456	504
	Memorandum (non-add) entries:			
3100	Obligated balance, start of year	495	354	456
3200	Obligated balance, end of year	354	456	504
	Budget authority and outlays, net:			
	Mandatory:			
4090	Budget authority, gross	11,055	11,400	12,605
	Outlays, gross:			
4100	Outlays from new mandatory authority	10,701	10,944	12,101
4101	Outlays from mandatory balances	495	354	456
4110	Outlays, gross (total)	11,196	11,298	12,557
4180	Budget authority, net (total)	11,055	11,400	12,605
4190	Outlays, net (total)	11,196	11,298	12,557

OTHER DEFENSE—CIVIL PROGRAMS

Educational Benefits Trust Funds 1099

		2021 actual	2022 est.	2023 est.
	Memorandum (non-add) entries:			
5000	Total investments, SOY: Federal securities: Par value	268,894	289,738	305,543
5001	Total investments, EOY: Federal securities: Par value	289,738	305,543	322,623

Public Law 106–398 provides for accrual funding for health care to Medicare-eligible retirees. The statute establishes an accrual health care fund which has three sources of funding. The first is contributions from employing agencies, which cover the liability for future benefits accruing to current service members. The second is an annual payment from the general fund of the Treasury on the accrued unfunded liability, and the third source is income from the investment of fund balances.

Status of Funds (in millions of dollars)

Identification code 097–5472–0–2–551		2021 actual	2022 est.	2023 est.
	Unexpended balance, start of year:			
0100	Balance, start of year	264,188	285,173	305,203
0298	Reconciliation adjustment	–3		
0999	Total balance, start of year	264,185	285,173	305,203
	Cash income during the year:			
	Current law:			
	Receipts:			
1150	Earnings on Investments, DoD Medicare-Eligible Retiree Health Care Fund	16,580	14,211	12,124
1160	Non-DoD Employing Agency Contributions, DoD Medicare-Eligible Retiree Health Care Fund	246	278	293
1160	Federal Contributions, DoD Medicare-Eligible Retiree Health Care Fund	6,983	7,503	7,409
1160	Department of Defense Contributions, DoD Medicare-Eligible Retiree Health Care Fund	8,376	9,336	9,743
1199	Income under present law	32,185	31,328	29,569
	Proposed:			
1250	Earnings on Investments, DoD Medicare-Eligible Retiree Health Care Fund			–4
	Offsetting governmental receipts:			
1260	Federal Contributions, DoD Medicare-Eligible Retiree Health Care Fund			
1260	Department of Defense Contributions, DoD Medicare-Eligible Retiree Health Care Fund			
1299	Income proposed			–4
1999	Total cash income	32,185	31,328	29,565
	Cash outgo during year:			
	Current law:			
2100	Department of Defense Medicare-Eligible Retiree Health Care Fund [Budget Acct]	–11,196	–11,298	–12,557
2199	Outgo under current law	–11,196	–11,298	–12,557
2999	Total cash outgo (-)	–11,196	–11,298	–12,557
	Surplus or deficit:			
3110	Excluding interest	4,409	5,819	4,888
3120	Interest	16,580	14,211	12,120
3199	Subtotal, surplus or deficit	20,989	20,030	17,008
3298	Reconciliation adjustment	–1		
3299	Total adjustments	–1		
3999	Total change in fund balance	20,988	20,030	17,008
	Unexpended balance, end of year:			
4100	Uninvested balance (net), end of year	–4,565	–340	–412
4200	Department of Defense Medicare-Eligible Retiree Health Care Fund	289,738	305,543	322,623
4999	Total balance, end of year	285,173	305,203	322,211

EDUCATIONAL BENEFITS

Trust Funds

EDUCATION BENEFITS FUND

Special and Trust Fund Receipts (in millions of dollars)

Identification code 097–8098–0–7–702		2021 actual	2022 est.	2023 est.
0100	Balance, start of year	1,045	1,006	978

		2021 actual	2022 est.	2023 est.
	Receipts:			
	Current law:			
1140	Employing Agency Contributions, Education Benefits Fund	69	86	38
1140	Interest on Investments, Education Benefits Fund	47	27	14
1199	Total current law receipts	116	113	52
1999	Total receipts	116	113	52
2000	Total: Balances and receipts	1,161	1,119	1,030
	Appropriations:			
	Current law:			
2101	Education Benefits Fund	–116	–113	–52
2103	Education Benefits Fund	–126	–28	–97
2135	Education Benefits Fund	88		
2199	Total current law appropriations	–154	–141	–149
2999	Total appropriations	–154	–141	–149
5098	Rounding adjustment	–1		
5099	Balance, end of year	1,006	978	881

Program and Financing (in millions of dollars)

Identification code 097–8098–0–7–702		2021 actual	2022 est.	2023 est.
	Obligations by program activity:			
0001	Active duty program	42	39	41
0002	Selected Reserve program	112	102	108
0900	Total new obligations, unexpired accounts (object class 13.0)	154	141	149
	Budgetary resources:			
	Budget authority:			
	Appropriations, mandatory:			
1201	Appropriation (special or trust fund)	116	113	52
1203	Appropriation (previously unavailable)(special or trust)	126	28	97
1235	Appropriations precluded from obligation (special or trust)	–88		
1260	Appropriations, mandatory (total)	154	141	149
1930	Total budgetary resources available	154	141	149
	Change in obligated balance:			
	Unpaid obligations:			
3000	Unpaid obligations, brought forward, Oct 1	1		
3010	New obligations, unexpired accounts	154	141	149
3020	Outlays (gross)	–155	–141	–149
	Memorandum (non-add) entries:			
3100	Obligated balance, start of year	1		
	Budget authority and outlays, net:			
	Mandatory:			
4090	Budget authority, gross	154	141	149
	Outlays, gross:			
4100	Outlays from new mandatory authority		141	149
4101	Outlays from mandatory balances	155		
4110	Outlays, gross (total)	155	141	149
4180	Budget authority, net (total)	154	141	149
4190	Outlays, net (total)	155	141	149
	Memorandum (non-add) entries:			
5000	Total investments, SOY: Federal securities: Par value	1,050	1,009	981
5001	Total investments, EOY: Federal securities: Par value	1,009	981	884

The 1985 Department of Defense Authorization Act, Public Law 98–525, as amended by Public Laws 100–48 and 108–375, and the Post 9/11 Veterans Educational Assistance Improvements Act of 2010, Public Law 111–377, provide for the accrual funding of certain education benefits for active duty military personnel under the authority of Chapters 30 and 33, Title 38 U.S.C., and to selected Reserve personnel under the authority of Chapters 1606 and 1607, Title 10 U.S.C. Chapter 1607 was sunset by Public Law 114–92, although the statute allows members who were receiving Chapter 1607 benefits before the statute was enacted to continue to receive these education benefits through November 2019. The fund is financed through actuarially determined Government contributions from the Department of Defense military personnel appropriations and interest on investments. Funds are transferred to the Department of Veterans Affairs

EDUCATION BENEFITS FUND—Continued

to make benefit payments to eligible personnel. The status of the fund is as follows:

Status of Funds (in millions of dollars)

Identification code 097–8098–0–7–702		2021 actual	2022 est.	2023 est.
	Unexpended balance, start of year:			
0100	Balance, start of year	1,045	1,007	979
0999	Total balance, start of year	1,045	1,007	979
	Cash income during the year:			
	Current law:			
	Receipts:			
1150	Interest on Investments, Education Benefits Fund	47	27	14
1160	Employing Agency Contributions, Education Benefits Fund	69	86	38
1199	Income under present law	116	113	52
1999	Total cash income	116	113	52
	Cash outgo during year:			
	Current law:			
2100	Education Benefits Fund [Budget Acct]	–155	–141	–149
2199	Outgo under current law	–155	–141	–149
2999	Total cash outgo (–)	–155	–141	–149
	Surplus or deficit:			
3110	Excluding interest	–86	–55	–111
3120	Interest	47	27	14
3199	Subtotal, surplus or deficit	–39	–28	–97
3298	Reconciliation adjustment	1		
3299	Total adjustments	1		
3999	Total change in fund balance	–38	–28	–97
	Unexpended balance, end of year:			
4100	Uninvested balance (net), end of year	–2	–2	–2
4200	Education Benefits Fund	1,009	981	884
4999	Total balance, end of year	1,007	979	882

AMERICAN BATTLE MONUMENTS COMMISSION

Federal Funds

SALARIES AND EXPENSES

For necessary expenses, not otherwise provided for, of the American Battle Monuments Commission, including the acquisition of land or interest in land in foreign countries; purchases and repair of uniforms for caretakers of national cemeteries and monuments outside of the United States and its territories and possessions; rent of office and garage space in foreign countries; purchase (one-for-one replacement basis only) and hire of passenger motor vehicles; not to exceed $15,000 for official reception and representation expenses; and insurance of official motor vehicles in foreign countries, when required by law of such countries, $86,800,000, to remain available until expended.

Note.—A full-year 2022 appropriation for this account was not enacted at the time the Budget was prepared; therefore, the Budget assumes this account is operating under the Continuing Appropriations Act, 2022 (Division A of Public Law 117–43, as amended). The amounts included for 2022 reflect the annualized level provided by the continuing resolution.

Program and Financing (in millions of dollars)

Identification code 074–0100–0–1–705		2021 actual	2022 est.	2023 est.
	Obligations by program activity:			
0001	Administration	43	35	35
0002	Cemetery operations	61	50	52
0900	Total new obligations, unexpired accounts	104	85	87
	Budgetary resources:			
	Unobligated balance:			
1000	Unobligated balance brought forward, Oct 1	58	40	40
1010	Unobligated balance transfer to other accts [074–0101]	–1		
1011	Unobligated balance transfer from other acct [074–0101]	1		
1021	Recoveries of prior year unpaid obligations	2		
1070	Unobligated balance (total)	60	40	40
	Budget authority:			
	Appropriations, discretionary:			
1100	Appropriation	84	85	87
1930	Total budgetary resources available	144	125	127
	Memorandum (non-add) entries:			
1941	Unexpired unobligated balance, end of year	40	40	40
	Change in obligated balance:			
	Unpaid obligations:			
3000	Unpaid obligations, brought forward, Oct 1	34	45	45
3010	New obligations, unexpired accounts	104	85	87
3020	Outlays (gross)	–91	–85	–87
3040	Recoveries of prior year unpaid obligations, unexpired	–2		
3050	Unpaid obligations, end of year	45	45	45
	Memorandum (non-add) entries:			
3100	Obligated balance, start of year	34	45	45
3200	Obligated balance, end of year	45	45	45
	Budget authority and outlays, net:			
	Discretionary:			
4000	Budget authority, gross	84	85	87
	Outlays, gross:			
4010	Outlays from new discretionary authority	69	51	52
4011	Outlays from discretionary balances	22	34	35
4020	Outlays, gross (total)	91	85	87
4180	Budget authority, net (total)	84	85	87
4190	Outlays, net (total)	91	85	87

The American Battle Monuments Commission is responsible for: the maintenance and construction of U.S. monuments and memorials commemorating the achievements in battle of our Armed Forces since 1917; controlling erection of monuments and markers by U.S. citizens and organizations in foreign countries; and the design, construction, and maintenance of permanent military cemetery memorials in foreign countries. The Commission requests 465 full-time equivalent (FTE) civilian employees to manage and support the annual investment in maintenance, infrastructure, and interpretive projects.

Object Classification (in millions of dollars)

Identification code 074–0100–0–1–705		2021 actual	2022 est.	2023 est.
	Direct obligations:			
	Personnel compensation:			
11.1	Full-time permanent	24	25	26
11.3	Other than full-time permanent	1	1	1
11.5	Other personnel compensation	1	1	1
11.9	Total personnel compensation	26	27	28
12.1	Civilian personnel benefits	15	12	12
21.0	Travel and transportation of persons	1	1	1
22.0	Transportation of things	1	1	1
23.1	Rental payments to GSA	1	1	1
23.3	Communications, utilities, and miscellaneous charges	6	5	5
25.1	Advisory and assistance services	8	6	7
25.2	Other services from non-Federal sources	2	2	2
25.3	Other goods and services from Federal sources	13	13	13
25.4	Operation and maintenance of facilities	10	8	9
26.0	Supplies and materials	4	4	4
31.0	Equipment	3	2	2
32.0	Land and structures	14	3	2
99.9	Total new obligations, unexpired accounts	104	85	87

Employment Summary

Identification code 074–0100–0–1–705		2021 actual	2022 est.	2023 est.
1001	Direct civilian full-time equivalent employment	473	447	465

FOREIGN CURRENCY FLUCTUATIONS ACCOUNT

For necessary expenses, not otherwise provided for, of the American Battle Monuments Commission, such sums as may be necessary, to remain available until expended, for purposes authorized by section 2109 of title 36, United States Code.

Note.—A full-year 2022 appropriation for this account was not enacted at the time the Budget was prepared; therefore, the Budget assumes this account is operating under the Continuing Appropriations Act, 2022 (Division A of Public Law 117–43, as amended). The amounts included for 2022 reflect the annualized level provided by the continuing resolution.

OTHER DEFENSE—CIVIL PROGRAMS

Program and Financing (in millions of dollars)

Identification code 074–0101–0–1–705	2021 actual	2022 est.	2023 est.
Budgetary resources:			
Unobligated balance:			
1000 Unobligated balance brought forward, Oct 1	20	20	20
1010 Unobligated balance transfer to other accts [074–0101]	–1		
1011 Unobligated balance transfer from other acct [074–0101]	1		
1070 Unobligated balance (total)	20	20	20
1930 Total budgetary resources available	20	20	20
Memorandum (non-add) entries:			
1941 Unexpired unobligated balance, end of year	20	20	20
4180 Budget authority, net (total)			
4190 Outlays, net (total)			

The agency has a currency fluctuation account that insulates its appropriation's buying power from changes in exchange rates. Under "such sums as may be necessary" language, the Commission will reprogram prior year available funds to address exchange rate imbalances in 2021. The Commission will continue to estimate and report its Foreign Currency Fluctuations Account requirements.

Trust Funds
CONTRIBUTIONS

Special and Trust Fund Receipts (in millions of dollars)

Identification code 074–8569–0–7–705	2021 actual	2022 est.	2023 est.
0100 Balance, start of year			1
Receipts:			
Current law:			
1130 Contributions, American Battle Monuments Commission		1	1
1140 Earnings on Investments, American Battle Monuments Commission		1	1
1199 Total current law receipts		2	2
1999 Total receipts		2	2
2000 Total: Balances and receipts		2	3
Appropriations:			
Current law:			
2101 Contributions		–1	–1
5099 Balance, end of year		1	2

Program and Financing (in millions of dollars)

Identification code 074–8569–0–7–705	2021 actual	2022 est.	2023 est.
Obligations by program activity:			
0004 World War II Memorial	1	2	1
0900 Total new obligations, unexpired accounts (object class 25.4)	1	2	1
Budgetary resources:			
Unobligated balance:			
1000 Unobligated balance brought forward, Oct 1	2	1	
Budget authority:			
Appropriations, mandatory:			
1201 Appropriation (special or trust fund)		1	1
1930 Total budgetary resources available	2	2	1
Memorandum (non-add) entries:			
1941 Unexpired unobligated balance, end of year	1		
Change in obligated balance:			
Unpaid obligations:			
3000 Unpaid obligations, brought forward, Oct 1	1	1	2
3010 New obligations, unexpired accounts	1	2	1
3020 Outlays (gross)	–1	–1	
3050 Unpaid obligations, end of year	1	2	3
Memorandum (non-add) entries:			
3100 Obligated balance, start of year	1	1	2
3200 Obligated balance, end of year	1	2	3
Budget authority and outlays, net:			
Mandatory:			
4090 Budget authority, gross		1	1

Outlays, gross:			
4101 Outlays from mandatory balances	1	1	
4180 Budget authority, net (total)		1	1
4190 Outlays, net (total)	1	1	

Repair of non-Federal war memorials.—When requested to do so and upon receipt of the necessary funds, the Commission arranges for and oversees the repair of war memorials to U.S. Forces erected in foreign countries by American citizens, States, municipalities, or associations.

ARMED FORCES RETIREMENT HOME
Federal Funds
GENERAL FUND PAYMENT, ARMED FORCES RETIREMENT HOME

Program and Financing (in millions of dollars)

Identification code 084–0100–0–1–701	2021 actual	2022 est.	2023 est.
Obligations by program activity:			
0001 General fund payment	22	22	102
0900 Total new obligations, unexpired accounts (object class 94.0)	22	22	102
Budgetary resources:			
Budget authority:			
Appropriations, discretionary:			
1100 Appropriation	22	22	102
1930 Total budgetary resources available	22	22	102
Change in obligated balance:			
Unpaid obligations:			
3010 New obligations, unexpired accounts	22	22	102
3020 Outlays (gross)	–22	–22	–102
Budget authority and outlays, net:			
Discretionary:			
4000 Budget authority, gross	22	22	102
Outlays, gross:			
4010 Outlays from new discretionary authority	22	22	102
4180 Budget authority, net (total)	22	22	102
4190 Outlays, net (total)	22	22	102

Trust Funds
ARMED FORCES RETIREMENT HOME TRUST FUND

For expenses necessary for the Armed Forces Retirement Home to operate and maintain the Armed Forces Retirement Home—Washington, District of Columbia, and the Armed Forces Retirement Home—Gulfport, Mississippi, to be paid from funds available in the Armed Forces Retirement Home Trust Fund, $75,360,000, to remain available until September 30, 2024, of which $7,300,000 shall remain available until expended for construction and renovation of the physical plants at the Armed Forces Retirement Home—Washington, District of Columbia, and the Armed Forces Retirement Home—Gulfport, Mississippi: Provided, That of the amounts made available under this heading from funds available in the Armed Forces Retirement Home Trust Fund, $25,000,000 shall be paid from the general fund of the Treasury to the Trust Fund.

ARMED FORCES RETIREMENT HOME MAJOR CONSTRUCTION

For an additional amount for necessary expenses related to design, planning, and construction for renovation of the Sheridan Building at the Armed Forces Retirement Home—Washington, $77,000,000, to remain available until expended, shall be paid from the general fund of the Treasury to the Armed Forces Retirement Home Trust Fund.

Note.—A full-year 2022 appropriation for this account was not enacted at the time the Budget was prepared; therefore, the Budget assumes this account is operating under the Continuing Appropriations Act, 2022 (Division A of Public Law 117–43, as amended). The amounts included for 2022 reflect the annualized level provided by the continuing resolution.

Special and Trust Fund Receipts (in millions of dollars)

Identification code 084–8522–0–7–701	2021 actual	2022 est.	2023 est.
0100 Balance, start of year	40	40	41
0198 Rounding adjustment	2		

ARMED FORCES RETIREMENT HOME TRUST FUND—Continued

Special and Trust Fund Receipts—Continued

Identification code 084–8522–0–7–701	2021 actual	2022 est.	2023 est.
0199 Balance, start of year	42	40	41
Receipts:			
Current law:			
1110 Deductions, Armed Forces Retirement Home	7	7	22
1110 Fines and Forfeitures, Armed Forces Retirement Home	20	20	20
1130 Other Receipts, Armed Forces Retirement Home	14	15	16
1130 Gifts, Armed Forces Retirement Home	1	1	1
1130 Property Sales/Leases, Armed Forces Retirement Home	3	5	6
1140 Interest from Investments, Armed Forces Retirement Home	....	....	1
1140 General Fund Payment to the Armed Forces Retirement Home	22	22	102
1199 Total current law receipts	67	70	168
1999 Total receipts	67	70	168
2000 Total: Balances and receipts	109	110	209
Appropriations:			
Current law:			
2101 Armed Forces Retirement Home Trust Fund	–75	–75	–152
Special and trust fund receipts returned:			
3010 Armed Forces Retirement Home Trust Fund	7	6	4
5098 Reconciliation adjustment	–1	....	....
5099 Balance, end of year	40	41	61

Program and Financing (in millions of dollars)

Identification code 084–8522–0–7–701	2021 actual	2022 est.	2023 est.
Obligations by program activity:			
0001 Operations and maintenance	63	66	68
0002 Construction	2	9	84
0900 Total new obligations, unexpired accounts	65	75	152
Budgetary resources:			
Unobligated balance:			
1000 Unobligated balance brought forward, Oct 1	35	37	30
1021 Recoveries of prior year unpaid obligations	....	1	1
1030 Other balances withdrawn to special or trust funds	–7	–6	–4
1070 Unobligated balance (total)	28	32	27
Budget authority:			
Appropriations, discretionary:			
1101 Appropriation (special or trust)	75	75	152
1930 Total budgetary resources available	103	107	179
Memorandum (non-add) entries:			
1940 Unobligated balance expiring	–1	–2	–2
1941 Unexpired unobligated balance, end of year	37	30	25
Special and non-revolving trust funds:			
1950 Other balances withdrawn and returned to unappropriated receipts	7	6	4
1951 Unobligated balance expiring	1	2	2
1952 Expired unobligated balance, start of year	7	9	11
1953 Expired unobligated balance, end of year	8	9	11
Change in obligated balance:			
Unpaid obligations:			
3000 Unpaid obligations, brought forward, Oct 1	16	15	17
3010 New obligations, unexpired accounts	65	75	152
3011 Obligations ("upward adjustments"), expired accounts	1	....	....
3020 Outlays (gross)	–66	–72	–111
3040 Recoveries of prior year unpaid obligations, unexpired	....	–1	–1
3041 Recoveries of prior year unpaid obligations, expired	–1	....	....
3050 Unpaid obligations, end of year	15	17	57
Memorandum (non-add) entries:			
3100 Obligated balance, start of year	16	15	17
3200 Obligated balance, end of year	15	17	57
Budget authority and outlays, net:			
Discretionary:			
4000 Budget authority, gross	75	75	152
Outlays, gross:			
4010 Outlays from new discretionary authority	51	59	98
4011 Outlays from discretionary balances	15	13	13
4020 Outlays, gross (total)	66	72	111
4180 Budget authority, net (total)	75	75	152
4190 Outlays, net (total)	66	72	111
Memorandum (non-add) entries:			
5000 Total investments, SOY: Federal securities: Par value	93	95	97
5001 Total investments, EOY: Federal securities: Par value	95	97	99

Public Law 101–510 created an Armed Forces Retirement Home (AFRH) Trust Fund to finance the AFRH—Gulfport and the AFRH—Washington Homes. The Homes are financed by appropriations drawn from the Trust Fund. AFRH provides residences and related services for certain retired and former members of the Armed Forces and the Coast Guard. The members receiving domiciliary and hospital care are:

	2021 actual	2022 est.	2023 est.
Domiciliary care	495	545	598
Hospital care	120	132	145
Totals	615	677	743

Both AFRH facilities (Gulfport, MS and Washington, DC) are accredited in all areas by The Joint Commission (TJC) and Commission on Accreditation of Rehabilitation Facilities (CARF). AFRH is accredited with TJC for the wellness clinics (Ambulatory Care) and nursing care (Assisted Living, Memory Support, Long Term Care, and Independent Living Plus (Home Health Care)). For FY 2021, AFRH earned its 17th consecutive unmodified financial audit opinion with no weaknesses or deficiencies identified in the management letter. From March 2020 to March 2021, access at both AFRH campuses was restricted due to the COVID-19 pandemic. As a result, resident activities and new resident admissions were curtailed. In March 2021 the campuses began a pilot plan for phased reopening to safely restore activities, visitation, and new admissions. In November 2019, AFRH selected a development team for the 80-acre master planned parcel on the Washington campus with the goal of executing a lease agreement in FY 2020. The master plan authorizes 4.3 million square feet of mixed-use development (residential, commercial, retail, hotel) under a ground lease for AFRH to receive long-term revenue from previously underutilized property. In July 2020, AFRH executed a memorandum of understanding with the National Capital Planning Commission and the District of Columbia Office of Planning laying out the zoning process for private redevelopment on AFRH's federally-owned land. AFRH continues to work with the development team, National Capital Planning Commission, and the District of Columbia on Master Plan refinements, tax increment financing, zoning map and text amendments, traffic mitigation, environmental impacts and utilities planning.

Object Classification (in millions of dollars)

Identification code 084–8522–0–7–701	2021 actual	2022 est.	2023 est.
Direct obligations:			
Personnel compensation:			
11.1 Full-time permanent	18	20	21
11.5 Other personnel compensation	2	2	2
11.9 Total personnel compensation	20	22	23
12.1 Civilian personnel benefits	8	9	9
21.0 Travel and transportation of persons	....	1	....
23.3 Communications, utilities, and miscellaneous charges	4	3	4
25.1 Advisory and assistance services	1	1	1
25.2 Other services from non-Federal sources	2	3	4
25.3 Other goods and services from Federal sources	5	5	5
25.4 Operation and maintenance of facilities	6	6	6
25.6 Medical care	3	3	3
25.7 Operation and maintenance of equipment	3	3	3
25.8 Subsistence and support of persons	9	9	9
26.0 Supplies and materials	1	1	1
31.0 Equipment	1	....	....
32.0 Land and structures	2	9	84
99.9 Total new obligations, unexpired accounts	65	75	152

OTHER DEFENSE—CIVIL PROGRAMS
                                                                                                                                                         Cemeterial Expenses
                                                                                                                                                            Federal Funds   1103

Employment Summary

Identification code 084–8522–0–7–701	2021 actual	2022 est.	2023 est.
1001 Direct civilian full-time equivalent employment	279	363	363

CEMETERIAL EXPENSES
Federal Funds

SALARIES AND EXPENSES

For necessary expenses for maintenance, operation, and improvement of Arlington National Cemetery and Soldiers' and Airmen's Home National Cemetery, including the purchase or lease of passenger motor vehicles for replacement on a one-for-one basis only, and not to exceed $2,000 for official reception and representation expenses, $93,400,000, of which not to exceed $15,000,000 shall remain available until September 30, 2025. In addition, such sums as may be necessary for parking maintenance, repairs and replacement, to be derived from the "Lease of Department of Defense Real Property for Defense Agencies" account.

Note.—A full-year 2022 appropriation for this account was not enacted at the time the Budget was prepared; therefore, the Budget assumes this account is operating under the Continuing Appropriations Act, 2022 (Division A of Public Law 117–43, as amended). The amounts included for 2022 reflect the annualized level provided by the continuing resolution.

Program and Financing (in millions of dollars)

Identification code 021–1805–0–1–705	2021 actual	2022 est.	2023 est.
Obligations by program activity:			
0008 Salaries and Expenses	82	78	93
0020 Undistributed	....	–5	....
0900 Total new obligations, unexpired accounts	82	73	93
Budgetary resources:			
Unobligated balance:			
1000 Unobligated balance brought forward, Oct 1	7	8	17
1021 Recoveries of prior year unpaid obligations	1	....	....
1070 Unobligated balance (total)	8	8	17
Budget authority:			
Appropriations, discretionary:			
1100 Appropriation	82	82	93
1900 Budget authority (total)	82	82	93
1930 Total budgetary resources available	90	90	110
Memorandum (non-add) entries:			
1941 Unexpired unobligated balance, end of year	8	17	17
Change in obligated balance:			
Unpaid obligations:			
3000 Unpaid obligations, brought forward, Oct 1	56	55	40
3010 New obligations, unexpired accounts	82	73	93
3011 Obligations ("upward adjustments"), expired accounts	2	....	....
3020 Outlays (gross)	–82	–88	–102
3040 Recoveries of prior year unpaid obligations, unexpired	–1	....	....
3041 Recoveries of prior year unpaid obligations, expired	–2	....	....
3050 Unpaid obligations, end of year	55	40	31
Memorandum (non-add) entries:			
3100 Obligated balance, start of year	56	55	40
3200 Obligated balance, end of year	55	40	31
Budget authority and outlays, net:			
Discretionary:			
4000 Budget authority, gross	82	82	93
Outlays, gross:			
4010 Outlays from new discretionary authority	43	57	65
4011 Outlays from discretionary balances	39	31	37
4020 Outlays, gross (total)	82	88	102
Offsets against gross budget authority and outlays:			
Offsetting collections (collected) from:			
4033 Non-Federal sources	–1	....	....
4040 Offsets against gross budget authority and outlays (total)	–1	....	....
Additional offsets against gross budget authority only:			
4052 Offsetting collections credited to expired accounts	1	....	....
4060 Additional offsets against budget authority only (total)	1	....	....
4070 Budget authority, net (discretionary)	82	82	93
4080 Outlays, net (discretionary)	81	88	102
4180 Budget authority, net (total)	82	82	93
4190 Outlays, net (total)	81	88	102

Operation and Maintenance.—Funding supports day-to-day operations of Arlington National Cemetery (ANC), including planning and execution for more than 7,000 interments and inurnments annually, as well as routine repairs made to facilities, contracted services, and horticultural work at Arlington National Cemetery and the Soldiers' and Airmen's Home National Cemetery.

Construction.—A ten-year capital investment plan has been developed to manage all construction, major rehabilitation, major maintenance, automation and study efforts. Funding supports long-term planning and capital investments made in construction of facilities, land improvements, and other major infrastructure sustainment, restoration, and maintenance.

Sustainment, Restoration and Modernization (SRM).—Funding supports ANC's infrastructure to include the renovation, sustainment, and maintenance of ANC facilities, infrastructure, and roadways.

Object Classification (in millions of dollars)

Identification code 021–1805–0–1–705	2021 actual	2022 est.	2023 est.
Direct obligations:			
Personnel compensation:			
11.1 Full-time permanent	17	17	20
11.5 Other personnel compensation	1	1	1
11.9 Total personnel compensation	18	18	21
12.1 Civilian personnel benefits	6	7	7
23.3 Communications, utilities, and miscellaneous charges	1	1	3
25.2 Other services from non-Federal sources	34	28	38
26.0 Supplies and materials	1	1	1
31.0 Equipment	1	....	....
32.0 Land and structures	21	23	23
92.0 Undistributed	....	–5	....
99.9 Total new obligations, unexpired accounts	82	73	93

Employment Summary

Identification code 021–1805–0–1–705	2021 actual	2022 est.	2023 est.
1001 Direct civilian full-time equivalent employment	197	201	219

CONSTRUCTION

For necessary expenses for planning and design and construction at Arlington National Cemetery and Soldiers' and Airmen's Home National Cemetery, $62,500,000, to remain available until expended, of which $2,500,000 shall be for study, planning and design, and architect and engineering services for Memorial Avenue improvements project at Arlington National Cemetery; and $60,000,000 shall be for planning and design and construction associated with the Southern Expansion project.

Note.—A full-year 2022 appropriation for this account was not enacted at the time the Budget was prepared; therefore, the Budget assumes this account is operating under the Continuing Appropriations Act, 2022 (Division A of Public Law 117–43, as amended). The amounts included for 2022 reflect the annualized level provided by the continuing resolution.

Program and Financing (in millions of dollars)

Identification code 021–1809–0–1–705	2021 actual	2022 est.	2023 est.
Obligations by program activity:			
0001 Major Construction	66	89	60
0003 Planning and Design	3	....	2
0900 Total new obligations, unexpired accounts (object class 32.0)	69	89	62
Budgetary resources:			
Unobligated balance:			
1000 Unobligated balance brought forward, Oct 1	176	107	19
Budget authority:			
Appropriations, discretionary:			
1100 Appropriation	....	1	63
1930 Total budgetary resources available	176	108	82
Memorandum (non-add) entries:			
1941 Unexpired unobligated balance, end of year	107	19	20

CONSTRUCTION—Continued
Program and Financing—Continued

Identification code 021–1809–0–1–705	2021 actual	2022 est.	2023 est.
Change in obligated balance:			
Unpaid obligations:			
3000 Unpaid obligations, brought forward, Oct 1	14	8	92
3010 New obligations, unexpired accounts	69	89	62
3020 Outlays (gross)	–75	–5	–3
3050 Unpaid obligations, end of year	8	92	151
Memorandum (non-add) entries:			
3100 Obligated balance, start of year	14	8	92
3200 Obligated balance, end of year	8	92	151
Budget authority and outlays, net:			
Discretionary:			
4000 Budget authority, gross	....	1	63
Outlays, gross:			
4011 Outlays from discretionary balances	75	5	3
4180 Budget authority, net (total)	....	1	63
4190 Outlays, net (total)	75	5	3

NATIONAL MILITARY CEMETERIES CONCESSIONS, ARMY

Special and Trust Fund Receipts (in millions of dollars)

Identification code 021–5602–0–2–705	2021 actual	2022 est.	2023 est.
0100 Balance, start of year	1	1	2
Receipts:			
Current law:			
1130 Concessions Fees, Army National Military Cemeteries	....	1	1
2000 Total: Balances and receipts	1	2	3
5099 Balance, end of year	1	2	3

Program and Financing (in millions of dollars)

Identification code 021–5602–0–2–705	2021 actual	2022 est.	2023 est.
Obligations by program activity:			
0010 Direct program activity	....	1	....
0900 Total new obligations, unexpired accounts (object class 25.1)	....	1	....
Budgetary resources:			
Unobligated balance:			
1000 Unobligated balance brought forward, Oct 1	1	1	1
Budget authority:			
Spending authority from offsetting collections, discretionary:			
1700 Collected	1	....	....
1900 Budget authority (total)	1	....	....
1930 Total budgetary resources available	2	1	1
Memorandum (non-add) entries:			
1941 Unexpired unobligated balance, end of year	1	1	1
Change in obligated balance:			
Unpaid obligations:			
3000 Unpaid obligations, brought forward, Oct 1	....	....	1
3010 New obligations, unexpired accounts	1	....	....
3020 Outlays (gross)	....	–1	....
3050 Unpaid obligations, end of year	....	1	....
Memorandum (non-add) entries:			
3100 Obligated balance, start of year	....	....	1
3200 Obligated balance, end of year	....	1	....
Budget authority and outlays, net:			
Discretionary:			
4000 Budget authority, gross	1	....	....
Outlays, gross:			
4011 Outlays from discretionary balances	....	1	....
Offsets against gross budget authority and outlays:			
Offsetting collections (collected) from:			
4033 Non-Federal sources	–1	....	....
4180 Budget authority, net (total)	....	....	....
4190 Outlays, net (total)	....	1	....

ADMINISTRATIVE PROVISION

SEC. 301. *Amounts deposited into the special account established under 10 U.S.C. 7727 are appropriated and shall be available until expended to support activities at the Army National Military Cemeteries.*

FOREST AND WILDLIFE CONSERVATION, MILITARY RESERVATIONS

Federal Funds

WILDLIFE CONSERVATION

Special and Trust Fund Receipts (in millions of dollars)

Identification code 097–5095–0–2–303	2021 actual	2022 est.	2023 est.
0100 Balance, start of year	....	....	....
Receipts:			
Current law:			
1130 Sales of Hunting and Fishing Permits, Military Reservations	14	3	3
2000 Total: Balances and receipts	14	3	3
Appropriations:			
Current law:			
2101 Wildlife Conservation	–14	–3	–3
5099 Balance, end of year	....	....	....

Program and Financing (in millions of dollars)

Identification code 097–5095–0–2–303	2021 actual	2022 est.	2023 est.
Obligations by program activity:			
0001 Department of the Army	3	2	2
Budgetary resources:			
Unobligated balance:			
1000 Unobligated balance brought forward, Oct 1	24	36	37
1001 Discretionary unobligated balance brought fwd, Oct 1	2	....	....
1021 Recoveries of prior year unpaid obligations	1	....	....
1070 Unobligated balance (total)	25	36	37
Budget authority:			
Appropriations, mandatory:			
1201 Appropriation (special or trust fund)	14	3	3
1900 Budget authority (total)	14	3	3
1930 Total budgetary resources available	39	39	40
Memorandum (non-add) entries:			
1941 Unexpired unobligated balance, end of year	36	37	38
Change in obligated balance:			
Unpaid obligations:			
3000 Unpaid obligations, brought forward, Oct 1	38	19	8
3010 New obligations, unexpired accounts	3	2	2
3020 Outlays (gross)	–21	–13	–10
3040 Recoveries of prior year unpaid obligations, unexpired	–1	....	....
3050 Unpaid obligations, end of year	19	8	....
Memorandum (non-add) entries:			
3100 Obligated balance, start of year	38	19	8
3200 Obligated balance, end of year	19	8	....
Budget authority and outlays, net:			
Mandatory:			
4090 Budget authority, gross	14	3	3
Outlays, gross:			
4100 Outlays from new mandatory authority	....	2	2
4101 Outlays from mandatory balances	21	11	8
4110 Outlays, gross (total)	21	13	10
4180 Budget authority, net (total)	14	3	3
4190 Outlays, net (total)	21	13	10

These appropriations provide for development and conservation of fish and wildlife and recreational facilities on military installations. Proceeds from the sale of fishing and hunting permits are used for these programs

OTHER DEFENSE—CIVIL PROGRAMS

at Army, Navy, Marine Corps, and Air Force installations charging such user fees. These programs are carried out through cooperative plans agreed upon by the local representatives of the Secretary of Defense, the Secretary of the Interior, and the appropriate agency of the State in which the installation is located.

Object Classification (in millions of dollars)

Identification code 097–5095–0–2–303	2021 actual	2022 est.	2023 est.
Direct obligations:			
26.0 Supplies and materials	2	2	2
32.0 Land and structures	1		
99.9 Total new obligations, unexpired accounts	3	2	2

SELECTIVE SERVICE SYSTEM

Federal Funds

SALARIES AND EXPENSES

For necessary expenses of the Selective Service System, including expenses of attendance at meetings and of training for uniformed personnel assigned to the Selective Service System, as authorized by 5 U.S.C. 4101–4118 for civilian employees; hire of passenger motor vehicles; services as authorized by 5 U.S.C. 3109; and not to exceed $750 for official reception and representation expenses; $29,700,000: Provided, That during the current fiscal year, the President may exempt this appropriation from the provisions of 31 U.S.C. 1341, whenever the President deems such action to be necessary in the interest of national defense: Provided further, That none of the funds appropriated by this Act may be expended for or in connection with the induction of any person into the Armed Forces of the United States.

Note.—A full-year 2022 appropriation for this account was not enacted at the time the Budget was prepared; therefore, the Budget assumes this account is operating under the Continuing Appropriations Act, 2022 (Division A of Public Law 117–43, as amended). The amounts included for 2022 reflect the annualized level provided by the continuing resolution.

Program and Financing (in millions of dollars)

Identification code 090–0400–0–1–054	2021 actual	2022 est.	2023 est.
Obligations by program activity:			
0001 Selective Service System	26	26	30
Budgetary resources:			
Unobligated balance:			
1000 Unobligated balance brought forward, Oct 1		1	2
Budget authority:			
Appropriations, discretionary:			
1100 Appropriation	26	26	30
Spending authority from offsetting collections, discretionary:			
1700 Collected	1	1	1
1900 Budget authority (total)	27	27	31
1930 Total budgetary resources available	27	28	33
Memorandum (non-add) entries:			
1941 Unexpired unobligated balance, end of year	1	2	3
Change in obligated balance:			
Unpaid obligations:			
3000 Unpaid obligations, brought forward, Oct 1	8	7	5
3010 New obligations, unexpired accounts	26	26	30
3011 Obligations ("upward adjustments"), expired accounts	1		
3020 Outlays (gross)	–26	–28	–31
3041 Recoveries of prior year unpaid obligations, expired	–2		
3050 Unpaid obligations, end of year	7	5	4
Memorandum (non-add) entries:			
3100 Obligated balance, start of year	8	7	5
3200 Obligated balance, end of year	7	5	4
Budget authority and outlays, net:			
Discretionary:			
4000 Budget authority, gross	27	27	31
Outlays, gross:			
4010 Outlays from new discretionary authority	20	22	25
4011 Outlays from discretionary balances	6	6	6
4020 Outlays, gross (total)	26	28	31
Offsets against gross budget authority and outlays:			
Offsetting collections (collected) from:			
4030 Federal sources	–1	–1	–1
4180 Budget authority, net (total)	26	26	30
4190 Outlays, net (total)	25	27	30

The Selective Service System (SSS) registers young men when they reach age 18 and maintains an active database of over 92 million registrant records. The agency stands poised to deliver personnel to the Department of Defense (DoD) when directed by Congress and the President. In the event of a national emergency and call for conscription, the agency would mobilize, conduct the lottery process, issue induction notices, and transport the first draftees to military entrance processing stations. The law also requires the agency to manage a program for conscientious objectors in lieu of military service that contributes to the maintenance of the national health, safety, and interest of the United States.

While SSS continues to strengthen its national security partnership with the Armed Services, the agency pursues strong outreach initiatives and social media presence to inform men and their influencers of the importance of registration to achieve the most fair and equitable draft. The agency's critical national security capabilities provide young men with the opportunity to fulfill their civic duty and to serve their country if called.

The agency's strategy to modernize all operations to 21st century standards has enabled SSS to complete its mission from virtually anywhere and at anytime during this challenging period through state-of-the-art secure, agile, and redundant IT solutions. The agency strives to continually improve corebusiness processes through best-in-class customer service, information technology and cyber services delivery, and continuous risk management. Our next generation of cloud-based solutions will deliver cost-efficient and secure data and agile applications to meet the agency's mission, while delivering robust security, higher bandwidth, and sustained services in support of more efficient and accurate registration processing and mobilization readiness.

Object Classification (in millions of dollars)

Identification code 090–0400–0–1–054	2021 actual	2022 est.	2023 est.
Direct obligations:			
Personnel compensation:			
11.1 Full-time permanent	11	11	13
11.8 Special personal services payments	2	2	2
11.9 Total personnel compensation	13	13	15
12.1 Civilian personnel benefits	3	3	4
23.1 Rental payments to GSA	1	1	1
23.3 Communications, utilities, and miscellaneous charges	8	8	8
25.2 Other services from non-Federal sources	1	1	2
99.9 Total new obligations, unexpired accounts	26	26	30

Employment Summary

Identification code 090–0400–0–1–054	2021 actual	2022 est.	2023 est.
1001 Direct civilian full-time equivalent employment	117	121	122

ENVIRONMENTAL PROTECTION AGENCY

Federal Funds

OFFICE OF INSPECTOR GENERAL

For necessary expenses of the Office of Inspector General in carrying out the provisions of the Inspector General Act of 1978, $55,865,000, to remain available until September 30, 2024.

Note.—A full-year 2022 appropriation for this account was not enacted at the time the Budget was prepared; therefore, the Budget assumes this account is operating under the Continuing Appropriations Act, 2022 (Division A of Public Law 117–43, as amended). The amounts included for 2022 reflect the annualized level provided by the continuing resolution.

Program and Financing (in millions of dollars)

Identification code 068–0112–0–1–304		2021 actual	2022 est.	2023 est.
	Obligations by program activity:			
0003	Rule of Law and Process	41	102	99
0799	Total direct obligations	41	102	99
0801	Reimbursable from Superfund Trust Fund	12	12	12
0900	Total new obligations, unexpired accounts	53	114	111
	Budgetary resources:			
	Unobligated balance:			
1000	Unobligated balance brought forward, Oct 1	4	5	13
1021	Recoveries of prior year unpaid obligations		1	1
1070	Unobligated balance (total)	4	6	14
	Budget authority:			
	Appropriations, discretionary:			
1100	Appropriation	44	44	56
1121	Appropriations transferred from other acct [068–0108]		2	
1121	Appropriations transferred from other acct [068–0103]		45	
1160	Appropriation, discretionary (total)	44	91	56
	Advance appropriations, discretionary:			
1173	Advance appropriations transferred from other accounts [068–0103]			47
1173	Advance appropriations transferred from other accounts [068–0108]			2
1180	Advanced appropriation, discretionary (total)			49
	Spending authority from offsetting collections, discretionary:			
1700	Collected	12	30	12
1701	Change in uncollected payments, Federal sources	–1		
1750	Spending auth from offsetting collections, disc (total)	11	30	12
1900	Budget authority (total)	55	121	117
1930	Total budgetary resources available	59	127	131
	Memorandum (non-add) entries:			
1940	Unobligated balance expiring	–1		
1941	Unexpired unobligated balance, end of year	5	13	20
	Change in obligated balance:			
	Unpaid obligations:			
3000	Unpaid obligations, brought forward, Oct 1	3	3	7
3010	New obligations, unexpired accounts	53	114	111
3020	Outlays (gross)	–53	–109	–110
3040	Recoveries of prior year unpaid obligations, unexpired		–1	–1
3050	Unpaid obligations, end of year	3	7	7
	Uncollected payments:			
3060	Uncollected pymts, Fed sources, brought forward, Oct 1	–3	–2	–2
3070	Change in uncollected pymts, Fed sources, unexpired	1		
3090	Uncollected pymts, Fed sources, end of year	–2	–2	–2
	Memorandum (non-add) entries:			
3100	Obligated balance, start of year		1	5
3200	Obligated balance, end of year	1	5	5
	Budget authority and outlays, net:			
	Discretionary:			
4000	Budget authority, gross	55	121	117
	Outlays, gross:			
4010	Outlays from new discretionary authority	47	103	102
4011	Outlays from discretionary balances	6	6	8
4020	Outlays, gross (total)	53	109	110
	Offsets against gross budget authority and outlays:			
	Offsetting collections (collected) from:			
4030	Federal sources	–12	–30	–12
	Additional offsets against gross budget authority only:			
4050	Change in uncollected pymts, Fed sources, unexpired	1		
4070	Budget authority, net (discretionary)	44	91	105
4080	Outlays, net (discretionary)	41	79	98
4180	Budget authority, net (total)	44	91	105
4190	Outlays, net (total)	41	79	98

This appropriation supports the Environmental Protection Agency's (EPA) core programs by providing funds for independent Office of Inspector General (OIG) audit, evaluation, and investigative products and advisory services. These products and services consistently provide significant positive monetary return on investment and contribute substantially to risk reduction, improved environmental quality and human health, as well as improved business practices, operational efficiency, and accountability. Specifically, the OIG performs contract audits and investigations that focus on costs claimed by contractors and assess the effectiveness of contract management. Assistance agreement audits and investigations evaluate the award, administration, and costs of assistance agreements. Program audits, evaluations, and investigations determine the extent to which the desired results or benefits envisioned by the Administration and the Congress are being achieved, and identify activities that could undermine the integrity, efficiency, and effectiveness of EPA programs. Financial statement audits review financial systems and statements to ensure that adequate controls are in place and EPA's accounting information is timely, accurate, reliable and useful, and complies with applicable laws and regulations. Efficiency, risk assessment, and program performance audits review the economy, efficiency, and effectiveness of operations by examining EPA's structure and processes for achieving environmental goals, including assessing risk, setting priorities, developing implementation strategies, and measuring performance. Information resource management audits review EPA information technology and systems to test the integrity of data and systems controls, as well as compliance with a variety of Federal information security laws and requirements. Investigations prevent, detect, and seek prosecution for criminal activity and serious misconduct in EPA programs and operations. Major areas of investigative focus include: financial fraud; infrastructure/terrorist threat; program integrity; employee integrity; cybercrimes; and theft of intellectual or sensitive data. In addition, the EPA Inspector General serves as the IG for the U.S. Chemical Safety and Hazard Investigation Board, providing the full range of audit, evaluation, and investigative services specified by the Inspector General Act, as amended. Additional funds for audit, evaluation, and investigative activities associated with the Hazardous Substance Superfund are appropriated under that account and transferred to the Inspector General account.

Object Classification (in millions of dollars)

Identification code 068–0112–0–1–304		2021 actual	2022 est.	2023 est.
	Direct obligations:			
	Personnel compensation:			
11.1	Full-time permanent	27	62	60
11.5	Other personnel compensation	2	5	5
11.9	Total personnel compensation	29	67	65
12.1	Civilian personnel benefits	10	24	23
25.1	Advisory and assistance services	2	9	9
25.7	Operation and maintenance of equipment		2	2
99.0	Direct obligations	41	102	99
99.0	Reimbursable obligations	12	12	12
99.9	Total new obligations, unexpired accounts	53	114	111

Employment Summary

Identification code 068–0112–0–1–304	2021 actual	2022 est.	2023 est.
1001 Direct civilian full-time equivalent employment	206	433	433
1101 Direct military average strength employment	1	1	1
2001 Reimbursable civilian full-time equivalent employment	54	54	54

SCIENCE AND TECHNOLOGY

For science and technology, including research and development activities, which shall include research and development activities under the Comprehensive Environmental Response, Compensation, and Liability Act of 1980; necessary expenses for personnel and related costs, for executive oversight of regional laboratories, and travel expenses; procurement of laboratory equipment and supplies; hire, maintenance, and operation of aircraft; and other operating expenses in support of research and development, $863,155,000, to remain available until September 30, 2024.

Note.—A full-year 2022 appropriation for this account was not enacted at the time the Budget was prepared; therefore, the Budget assumes this account is operating under the Continuing Appropriations Act, 2022 (Division A of Public Law 117–43, as amended). The amounts included for 2022 reflect the annualized level provided by the continuing resolution.

Program and Financing (in millions of dollars)

Identification code 068–0107–0–1–304		2021 actual	2022 est.	2023 est.
	Obligations by program activity:			
0001	Core Mission	182	182	207
0003	Rule of Law and Process	575	575	656
0799	Total direct obligations	757	757	863
0801	Reimbursements from Superfund Trust Fund	34	31	31
0802	Other Reimbursements	4	4	4
0899	Total reimbursable obligations	38	35	35
0900	Total new obligations, unexpired accounts	795	792	898
	Budgetary resources:			
	Unobligated balance:			
1000	Unobligated balance brought forward, Oct 1	125	115	101
1021	Recoveries of prior year unpaid obligations	19	30	30
1070	Unobligated balance (total)	144	145	131
	Budget authority:			
	Appropriations, discretionary:			
1100	Appropriation	729	729	863
	Spending authority from offsetting collections, discretionary:			
1700	Collected	31	19	19
1701	Change in uncollected payments, Federal sources	8		
1750	Spending auth from offsetting collections, disc (total)	39	19	19
1900	Budget authority (total)	768	748	882
1930	Total budgetary resources available	912	893	1,013
	Memorandum (non-add) entries:			
1940	Unobligated balance expiring	–2		
1941	Unexpired unobligated balance, end of year	115	101	115
	Change in obligated balance:			
	Unpaid obligations:			
3000	Unpaid obligations, brought forward, Oct 1	307	315	325
3010	New obligations, unexpired accounts	795	792	898
3011	Obligations ("upward adjustments"), expired accounts	1		
3020	Outlays (gross)	–766	–752	–829
3040	Recoveries of prior year unpaid obligations, unexpired	–19	–30	–30
3041	Recoveries of prior year unpaid obligations, expired	–3		
3050	Unpaid obligations, end of year	315	325	364
	Uncollected payments:			
3060	Uncollected pymts, Fed sources, brought forward, Oct 1	–31	–37	–37
3070	Change in uncollected pymts, Fed sources, unexpired	–8		
3071	Change in uncollected pymts, Fed sources, expired	2		
3090	Uncollected pymts, Fed sources, end of year	–37	–37	–37
	Memorandum (non-add) entries:			
3100	Obligated balance, start of year	276	278	288
3200	Obligated balance, end of year	278	288	327
	Budget authority and outlays, net:			
	Discretionary:			
4000	Budget authority, gross	768	748	882
	Outlays, gross:			
4010	Outlays from new discretionary authority	479	448	523
4011	Outlays from discretionary balances	287	304	306
4020	Outlays, gross (total)	766	752	829
	Offsets against gross budget authority and outlays:			
	Offsetting collections (collected) from:			
4030	Federal sources	–28	–19	–19
4033	Non-Federal sources	–5		
4040	Offsets against gross budget authority and outlays (total)	–33	–19	–19
	Additional offsets against gross budget authority only:			
4050	Change in uncollected pymts, Fed sources, unexpired	–8		
4052	Offsetting collections credited to expired accounts	2		
4060	Additional offsets against budget authority only (total)	–6		
4070	Budget authority, net (discretionary)	729	729	863
4080	Outlays, net (discretionary)	733	733	810
4180	Budget authority, net (total)	729	729	863
4190	Outlays, net (total)	733	733	810

This appropriation finances salary, travel, science, technology, environmental monitoring, research, and development activities including laboratory and center supplies, certain operating expenses (including activities under the Working Capital Fund), contracts, grants, intergovernmental agreements, and purchases of scientific equipment. In addition, the Administrator will employ persons in the Office of Research and Development (ORD) under the authority provided in 42 U.S.C. 209. The Budget proposes to increase ORD's appointment ceiling under this authority and extend the authority to the Office of Chemical Safety and Pollution Prevention. Furthermore, the Budget proposes to extend student contractor hiring authority for the Office of Chemical Safety and Pollution Prevention and the Office of Water through 2027. These activities prioritize robust science and strengthen the Environmental Protection Agency's (EPA) research and scientific analysis to inform EPA policy and regulatory development actions to ensure good stewardship and positive environmental outcomes. Specifically in 2023, EPA will place emphasis on the following:

The Air, Climate, and Energy (ACE) research program will conduct a range of science and technology activities to develop and implement strategies to improve air quality and take action on climate change. These include: research to inform the review of the national ambient air quality standards to improve understanding of ozone, particulate matter, lead, sulfur dioxide, carbon monoxide, and nitrogen dioxide; system research and life cycle analysis to understand the production, operation, and impacts of energy systems on health and the environment; research on the generation, fate, transport, and chemical transformation of air emissions to identify individual and population health risks to inform clean air management decisions; research on the impacts of climate change on human health and the environment; development and evaluation of new approaches for monitoring levels of air pollutants (including air toxics); development of tools to provide technical assistance to State and local governments and Tribes to use in developing clean air plans to achieve air quality standards; and the production of information, decision support tools, and adaptation strategies to enable stakeholders to account for climate change when making decisions. EPA will continue to implement the renewable fuels provisions of the Energy Policy Act of 2005 (P.L. 109–58) and the Energy Independence and Security Act of 2007 (P.L. 110–140), and will develop, implement, and ensure compliance with regulatory programs that will significantly reduce emissions from highway and non-road sources.

The Safe and Sustainable Water Resources (SSWR) research program conducts research to meet the science needs in EPA's water program, including: evaluating groups of contaminants for the protection of human health and the environment; developing innovative tools, technologies, and strategies for managing water resources (including stormwater); and supporting a systems approach for protecting and restoring aquatic systems. The systems approach includes: research to inform setting water quality criteria; establishing measures to assess and manage watersheds; and developing effective source control and management methods, especially for urban uses. A major component of the research program is working to support EPA's Drinking Water Strategy. Within the SSWR program, research will assess, develop, and compile scientifically rigorous tools and models that will be used by the Agency, States, Tribes, and municipalities to address issues such as lead in drinking water and excess nutrient loading.

The Sustainable and Healthy Communities (SHC) research program, including Superfund research, implements system-based research to develop a new generation of smart technologies to address environmental conditions in a community. Superfund research costs are appropriated to the Hazardous Substance Superfund Trust Fund appropriation and transferred to this account to allow for proper accounting. The SHC research program develops decision support tools to enable communities' decision makers to solve complex human health and environmental problems. The program will identify health risks and stressors, especially those that disproportionately impact vulnerable populations such as children and the elderly. The decision support tools support critical policy, regulatory, and non-regulatory needs related to contaminated site remediation, children's health protection, waste management, and our economy's reliance on quality ecosystem goods and services. These tools account for the interrelationships between social, economic, health, ecological, and environmental factors with the aim to minimize unintended consequences that can result from decisions about land use, transportation, and solid waste management, as well as promote more robust and efficient infrastructure.

The Health and Environmental Risk Assessment (HERA) research program develops assessments and scientific products that are used extensively by EPA's Program and Regional offices, and other parties, to estimate the potential risk to public health from exposure to environmental contaminants, to develop regulatory standards, and to manage environmental clean-ups. This includes EPA's All Ages Lead Model which predicts lead concentration in body tissues and organs for a hypothetical individual, based on a simulated lifetime of lead exposure. The HERA research program provides the scientific foundation for Agency actions to protect public health and the environment.

The Homeland Security Research Program (HSRP) will continue to support research efforts on evaluating chemical, biological, and radiological (CBR) analytical methods. The HSRP will conduct research on decontamination and methods to manage potential public health consequences and develop methods to protect water infrastructures and assess threats and consequences. In 2023, decontamination research will continue to address existing scientific knowledge gaps in responding to and recovering from wide-area CBR attacks on urban centers and public areas. Water Infrastructure Protection Research will focus on developing and testing decontamination approaches for water infrastructure and on treating CBR contaminated water caused by terrorist attacks, natural disasters, and/or accidents. Research on real-time distribution system models and methods to isolate and treat contaminated water, clean distribution systems, redirect water, and return water systems to service quickly and affordably is in progress. EPA also will continue to support water sector-specific agency responsibilities to protect the Nation's critical water infrastructure.

EPA's Chemical Safety for Sustainability (CSS) research program is designed to strengthen the Agency's ability to evaluate and predict the potential environmental and human health impacts from use of manufactured chemicals throughout their lifecycle. The CSS program supports the development and application of improved and new computational systems; models of pathways and tissues; rapid cost-efficient exposure models; and user-friendly web-based tools for analysis and decision support. The CSS program will continue to develop approaches for using toxicity and exposure data to inform screening and prioritization of the over 40,000 chemicals currently on the TSCA Active List, and will continue to inform the Agency's implementation of key environmental regulations and to address contaminants of emerging concern, such as Per- and Polyfluoroalkyl Substances (PFAS). As it relates to the Science and Technology account and the overall mission of EPA, the protection of human health includes: ensuring the availability of appropriate analytical methods for detecting pesticide residues in food and feed; ensuring suitability for monitoring pesticide residues; and enforcing tolerances. The program accomplishes this by developing and validating multi-residue pesticide analytical methods for food, feed, and water for use by other Federal and State laboratories and EPA's programs and regions. Laboratories further support the estimation of human health risks from pesticide use by operating the National Pesticide Standard Repository (NPSR).

EPA's Forensics Support program provides expert scientific and technical support for criminal and civil environmental enforcement cases, as well as technical support for the Agency's compliance efforts. EPA's National Enforcement Investigations Center (NEIC) is an environmental forensic center accredited for both laboratory and field sampling operations that generate environmental data for law enforcement purposes. It is fully accredited under International Standards Organization 17025, the main standard used by testing and calibration laboratories, as recommended by the National Academy of Sciences (see Strengthening Forensic Science in the United States: A Path Forward, National Academy of Sciences, 2009). The NEIC maintains a sophisticated chemistry laboratory and a corps of highly trained inspectors and scientists with expertise across media. The NEIC works closely with EPA's Criminal Investigation Division to provide technical support (e.g., sampling, analysis, consultation, and testimony) to criminal investigations. The NEIC also works closely with EPA's Program and Regional Offices to provide technical support, consultation, on-site inspection, investigation, and case resolution services in support of the Agency's Civil Enforcement program.

EPA's internal operations programs provide centralized management services to ensure that EPA is fulfilling its mission. The office and the functions it performs is: Office of Mission Support (facilities infrastructure and operations and information technology/data management).

Object Classification (in millions of dollars)

Identification code 068–0107–0–1–304		2021 actual	2022 est.	2023 est.
	Direct obligations:			
	Personnel compensation:			
11.1	Full-time permanent	239	239	272
11.3	Other than full-time permanent	13	13	15
11.5	Other personnel compensation	6	6	7
11.7	Military personnel	1	1	1
11.9	Total personnel compensation	259	259	295
12.1	Civilian personnel benefits	93	93	105
22.0	Transportation of things	1	1	1
23.1	Rental payments to GSA	30	30	34
23.2	Rental payments to others	1	1	1
23.3	Communications, utilities, and miscellaneous charges	11	11	13
24.0	Printing and reproduction	1	1	1
25.1	Advisory and assistance services	65	65	74
25.2	Other services from non-Federal sources	68	68	78
25.3	Other goods and services from Federal sources	42	42	48
25.4	Operation and maintenance of facilities	34	34	39
25.5	Research and development contracts	59	59	67
25.7	Operation and maintenance of equipment	8	8	9
26.0	Supplies and materials	12	12	14
31.0	Equipment	19	19	22
41.0	Grants, subsidies, and contributions	53	53	61
99.0	Direct obligations	756	756	862
99.0	Reimbursable obligations	39	36	36
99.9	Total new obligations, unexpired accounts	795	792	898

Employment Summary

Identification code 068–0107–0–1–304	2021 actual	2022 est.	2023 est.
1001 Direct civilian full-time equivalent employment	1,995	1,995	1,995
1101 Direct military average strength employment	10	10	10
2001 Reimbursable civilian full-time equivalent employment	68	68	68

ENVIRONMENTAL PROGRAMS AND MANAGEMENT

For environmental programs and management, including necessary expenses not otherwise provided for, for personnel and related costs and travel expenses; hire and purchase of passenger motor vehicles, including zero emission passenger motor vehicles; hire, maintenance, and operation of aircraft; purchase of reprints; library memberships in societies or associations which issue publications to members only or at a price to members lower than to subscribers who are not members; administrative costs of the brownfields program under the Small Business Liability Relief and Brownfields Revitalization Act of 2002; implementation of a coal combustion residual permit program under section 2301 of the Water and Waste Act of 2016; and not to exceed $9,000 for official reception and representation expenses, $3,796,280,000, to remain available until September 30, 2024: Provided, That of the funds included under this heading, $578,336,000 shall be for Geographic Programs specified in the explanatory statement: Provided further, That of the funds included under this heading, the Chemical Risk Review and Reduction program

ENVIRONMENTAL PROGRAMS AND MANAGEMENT—Continued

project shall be allocated for this fiscal year, excluding the amount of any fees appropriated, not less than the amount of appropriations for that program project for fiscal year 2014: Provided further, That of the funds included under this heading, $140,000,000, to remain available until expended, shall be for environmental justice implementation grants, of which $50,000,000 shall be for competitive grants to reduce the disproportionate health impacts of environmental pollution in the environmental justice community; $25,000,000 shall be for an Environmental Justice Community Grant Program for grants to nonprofits to reduce the disproportionate health impacts of environmental pollution in the environmental justice community; $25,000,000 shall be for an Environmental Justice State Grant Program for grants to states to create or support state environmental justice programs; $25,000,000 shall be for a Tribal Environmental Justice Grant Program for grants to tribes or intertribal consortia to support tribal work to eliminate disproportionately adverse human health or environmental effects on environmental justice communities in Tribal and indigenous communities; and $15,000,000 shall be for a competitive Community-based Participatory Research Grant Program for grants to institutions of higher education to develop partnerships with community-based organizations to improve the health outcomes of residents and workers in environmental justice communities: Provided further, That up to 5% of the funds provided by the previous proviso may be reserved for salaries, expenses, and administration: Provided further, That of the funds included under this heading, $10,000,000, to remain available until expended, shall be for an Environmental Justice Training Program for grants to nonprofits for multi-media or single media activities to increase the capacity of residents of underserved communities to identify and address disproportionately adverse human health or environmental effects of pollution: Provided further, That up to 5% of the funds provided by the previous proviso may be reserved for salaries, expenses, and administration.

Note.—A full-year 2022 appropriation for this account was not enacted at the time the Budget was prepared; therefore, the Budget assumes this account is operating under the Continuing Appropriations Act, 2022 (Division A of Public Law 117–43, as amended). The amounts included for 2022 reflect the annualized level provided by the continuing resolution.

ENVIRONMENTAL PROGRAMS AND MANAGEMENT

[(INCLUDING TRANSFERS OF FUNDS)]

[For an additional amount for "Environmental Programs and Management", $1,959,000,000, which shall be allocated as follows:]

[(1) $1,717,000,000, to remain available until expended, for Geographic Programs as specified in the explanatory statement described in section 4 of the matter preceding division A of Public Law 116—260: *Provided*, That $343,400,000, to remain available until expended, shall be made available for fiscal year 2022, $343,400,000, to remain available until expended, shall be made available for fiscal year 2023, $343,400,000, to remain available until expended, shall be made available for fiscal year 2024, $343,400,000, to remain available until expended, shall be made available for fiscal year 2025, and $343,400,000, to remain available until expended, shall be made available for fiscal year 2026: *Provided further*, That of the funds made available in this paragraph in this Act, the following amounts shall be for the following purposes in equal amounts for each of fiscal years 2022 through 2026—]

[(A)$1,000,000,000 shall be for Great Lakes Restoration Initiative;]
[(B)$238,000,000 shall be for Chesapeake Bay;]
[(C)$24,000,000 shall be for San Francisco Bay;]
[(D)$89,000,000 shall be for Puget Sound;]
[(E)$106,000,000 shall be for Long Island Sound;]
[(F)$53,000,000 shall be for Gulf of Mexico;]
[(G)$16,000,000 shall be for South Florida;]
[(H)$40,000,000 shall be for Lake Champlain;]
[(I)$53,000,000 shall be for Lake Pontchartrain;]
[(J)$15,000,000 shall be for Southern New England Estuaries;]
[(K)$79,000,000 shall be for Columbia River Basin; and]
[(L)$4,000,000 shall be for other geographic activities which includes Pacific Northwest:]

[*Provided further*, That the Administrator may waive or reduce the required non-Federal share for amounts made available under this paragraph in this Act for the purposes described in the preceding proviso;]

[(2) $132,000,000, to remain available until expended, for the National Estuary Program grants under section 320(g)(2) of the Federal Water Pollution Control Act, notwithstanding the funding limitation in section 320(i)(2)(B) of the Act: *Provided*, That $26,400,000, to remain available until expended, shall be made available for fiscal year 2022, $26,400,000, to remain available until expended, shall be made available for fiscal year 2023, $26,400,000, to remain available until expended, shall be made available for fiscal year 2024, $26,400,000, to remain available until expended, shall be made available for fiscal year 2025, and $26,400,000, to remain available until expended, shall be made available for fiscal year 2026: *Provided further*, That the Administrator may waive or reduce the required non-Federal share for amounts made available under this paragraph in this Act: *Provided further*, That up to three percent of the amounts made available under this paragraph in this Act shall be for salaries, expenses, and administration;]

[(3) $60,000,000, to remain available until expended, for actions under the Gulf Hypoxia Action Plan: *Provided*, That $12,000,000, to remain available until expended, shall be made available for fiscal year 2022, $12,000,000, to remain available until expended, shall be made available for fiscal year 2023, $12,000,000, to remain available until expended, shall be made available for fiscal year 2024, $12,000,000, to remain available until expended, shall be made available for fiscal year 2025, and $12,000,000, to remain available until expended, shall be made available for fiscal year 2026: *Provided further*, That funds shall be provided annually to the twelve states serving as members of the Mississippi River/Gulf of Mexico Watershed Nutrient Task Force (Arkansas, Iowa, Illinois, Indiana, Kentucky, Louisiana, Minnesota, Missouri, Mississippi, Ohio, Tennessee, and Wisconsin) in equal amounts for each state for the period of fiscal year 2022 to fiscal year 2026: *Provided further*, That up to three percent of the amounts made available under this paragraph in this Act shall be for salaries, expenses, and administration;]

[(4) $25,000,000, to remain available until expended, to support permitting of Class VI wells as authorized under section 40306 of division D of this Act, to be carried out by Drinking Water Programs: *Provided*, That $5,000,000, to remain available until expended, shall be made available for fiscal year 2022, $5,000,000, to remain available until expended, shall be made available for fiscal year 2023, $5,000,000, to remain available until expended, shall be made available for fiscal year 2024, $5,000,000, to remain available until expended, shall be made available for fiscal year 2025, and $5,000,000, to remain available until expended, shall be made available for fiscal year 2026;]

[(5) $10,000,000, to remain available until September 30, 2026, for developing battery recycling best practices, as authorized under section 70401(b) of division G of this Act, to be carried out by the Resource Conservation and Recovery Act program;]

[(6) $15,000,000, to remain available until September 30, 2026, for developing voluntary battery labeling guidelines, as authorized under section 70401(c) of division G of this Act, to be carried out by the Resource Conservation and Recovery Act program;]

[*Provided*, That funds provided for the purposes described in paragraphs (1), (2), and (3) under this heading in this Act may be transferred to the United States Fish and Wildlife Service and the National Marine Fisheries Service for the costs of carrying out their responsibilities under the Endangered Species Act of 1973 (16 U.S.C. 1531 et seq.) to consult and conference, as required by section 7 of such Act, in connection with Geographic programs, the National Estuary Program, and the Gulf Hypoxia Action Plan: *Provided further*, That amounts provided under this heading in this Act shall be in addition to amounts otherwise available for such purposes: *Provided further*, That one-half of one percent of the amounts made available under this heading in this Act in each of fiscal years 2022 through 2026 shall be transferred to the Office of Inspector General of the Environmental Protection Agency for oversight of funding provided to the Environmental Protection Agency in this title in this Act: *Provided further*, That such amount is designated by the Congress as being for an emergency requirement pursuant to section 4112(a) of H. Con. Res. 71 (115th Congress), the concurrent resolution on the budget for fiscal year 2018, and to section 251(b) of the Balanced Budget and Emergency Deficit Control Act of 1985.] *(Infrastructure Investments and Jobs Appropriations Act.)*

Program and Financing (in millions of dollars)

Identification code 068–0108–0–1–304	2021 actual	2022 est.	2023 est.
Obligations by program activity:			
0001 Core Mission	1,667	1,644	2,183
0002 Cooperative Federalism	233	228	303
0003 Rule of Law and Process	940	929	1,233
0799 Total direct obligations	2,840	2,801	3,719
0801 Environmental Programs and Management (Reimbursable)	70	50	50
0900 Total new obligations, unexpired accounts	2,910	2,851	3,769
Budgetary resources:			
Unobligated balance:			
1000 Unobligated balance brought forward, Oct 1	268	308	820
1021 Recoveries of prior year unpaid obligations	39	70	70
1070 Unobligated balance (total)	307	378	890

ENVIRONMENTAL PROTECTION AGENCY

	Budget authority:			
	Appropriations, discretionary:			
1100	Appropriation	2,762	3,173	3,796
1120	Appropriations transferred to other acct [068–0112]		–2	
1121	Appropriations transferred from other acct [068–5664]	29	7	
1160	Appropriation, discretionary (total)	2,791	3,178	3,796
	Advance appropriations, discretionary:			
1170	Advance appropriation			387
1172	Advance appropriations transferred to other accounts [068–0112]			–2
1180	Advanced appropriation, discretionary (total)			385
	Appropriations, mandatory:			
1200	Appropriation [American Rescue Plan P.L. 117–2]	46		
	Spending authority from offsetting collections, discretionary:			
1700	Collected [Offsetting Collections]	62	115	117
1701	Change in uncollected payments, Federal sources	59		
1750	Spending auth from offsetting collections, disc (total)	121	115	117
1900	Budget authority (total)	2,958	3,293	4,298
1930	Total budgetary resources available	3,265	3,671	5,188
	Memorandum (non-add) entries:			
1940	Unobligated balance expiring	–47		
1941	Unexpired unobligated balance, end of year	308	820	1,419
	Change in obligated balance:			
	Unpaid obligations:			
3000	Unpaid obligations, brought forward, Oct 1	1,469	1,641	1,456
3010	New obligations, unexpired accounts	2,910	2,851	3,769
3011	Obligations ("upward adjustments"), expired accounts	11		
3020	Outlays (gross)	–2,686	–2,966	–3,716
3040	Recoveries of prior year unpaid obligations, unexpired	–39	–70	–70
3041	Recoveries of prior year unpaid obligations, expired	–24		
3050	Unpaid obligations, end of year	1,641	1,456	1,439
	Uncollected payments:			
3060	Uncollected pymts, Fed sources, brought forward, Oct 1	–231	–126	–126
3070	Change in uncollected pymts, Fed sources, unexpired	–59		
3071	Change in uncollected pymts, Fed sources, expired	164		
3090	Uncollected pymts, Fed sources, end of year	–126	–126	–126
	Memorandum (non-add) entries:			
3100	Obligated balance, start of year	1,238	1,515	1,330
3200	Obligated balance, end of year	1,515	1,330	1,313
	Budget authority and outlays, net:			
	Discretionary:			
4000	Budget authority, gross	2,912	3,293	4,298
	Outlays, gross:			
4010	Outlays from new discretionary authority	1,812	1,894	2,551
4011	Outlays from discretionary balances	871	1,060	1,150
4020	Outlays, gross (total)	2,683	2,954	3,701
	Offsets against gross budget authority and outlays:			
	Offsetting collections (collected) from:			
4030	Federal sources	–58	–60	–61
4033	Non-Federal sources	–21	–55	–56
4040	Offsets against gross budget authority and outlays (total)	–79	–115	–117
	Additional offsets against gross budget authority only:			
4050	Change in uncollected pymts, Fed sources, unexpired	–59		
4052	Offsetting collections credited to expired accounts	17		
4060	Additional offsets against budget authority only (total)	–42		
4070	Budget authority, net (discretionary)	2,791	3,178	4,181
4080	Outlays, net (discretionary)	2,604	2,839	3,584
	Mandatory:			
4090	Budget authority, gross	46		
	Outlays, gross:			
4100	Outlays from new mandatory authority	3		
4101	Outlays from mandatory balances		12	15
4110	Outlays, gross (total)	3	12	15
4180	Budget authority, net (total)	2,837	3,178	4,181
4190	Outlays, net (total)	2,607	2,851	3,599

This appropriation includes funds for salaries, travel, contracts, grants, and cooperative agreements for pollution abatement, control, and compliance activities and administrative activities of the operating programs, including activities under the Working Capital Fund. This appropriation supports core agency programs implementing environmental statutes.

To protect and improve air quality, the Environmental Protection Agency (EPA) applies a variety of approaches and tools. These include: developing and implementing strategies to attain ambient air quality standards for the six criteria pollutants; reducing regional haze through regional approaches where significant transport of pollutants occurs; and developing control measures for sources that are appropriately regulated at the Federal level. EPA develops and issues national technology-based and risk-based standards using a sector-based approach to reduce the quantity of toxic air pollutants emitted from industrial and manufacturing processes, as well as from urban sources. The Acid Rain program will continue its market-based approach to achieving reduced emissions of sulfur dioxide, primarily from electric utilities. The market-based approach also will be used in other programs, where permitted under the Clean Air Act, to reduce emissions of air pollutants. EPA will work with States and sources to implement the Greenhouse Gas Reporting Rule to obtain high quality data in a cost-effective manner. In addition, EPA will develop and use public information and training to reduce public exposure to radiation. EPA will focus its domestic efforts to ensure that ozone-depleting substance production and import caps under the Montreal Protocol and Clean Air Act continue to be met.

EPA works to protect and restore our waters to ensure that drinking water is safe, and that aquatic ecosystems sustain fish, plants and wildlife, as well as support economic, recreational, and subsistence activities. EPA will focus on core statutory requirements and water infrastructure. EPA will support the following Clean Water Act program components: water quality criteria, standards and technology; National Pollutant Discharge Elimination System (NPDES); water monitoring; Total Maximum Daily Loads (TMDLs); watershed management; water infrastructure and grants management; core wetlands programs and Clean Water Act section 106 program management. EPA also will work with States and Tribes to reduce risks to drinking water contaminants, for example, through proposed revisions to the Lead and Copper Rule. In addition, EPA will continue work with States to transition to the next generation management and reporting tool, the Safe Drinking Water Information System (SDWIS) Prime used by the majority of state drinking water programs. The new SDWIS Prime management and reporting tool will provide improvements in program efficiency and data quality, greater public access to drinking water data, facilitation of electronic reporting, reductions in reporting burdens on laboratories and water utilities, reductions in data management burdens, and ultimately reduction in public health risk.

EPA's programs work to preserve land by ensuring proper management of waste under multiple environmental statutes. EPA will continue to assist States in putting in place and maintaining permits at facilities that treat, store, or dispose of hazardous waste. Although States are the primary implementers of the Corrective Action program, which requires facilities managing hazardous waste to clean up past releases, EPA directly implements the program in six States and provides technical support and oversight for State activities. EPA also works with Tribes to maintain tribal underground storage tank (UST) programs. EPA also supports the operations and management of the Brownfields program, including training and technical support to assist communities to address issues associated with redevelopment or reuse of properties that may be complicated by the presence of contamination. EPA works with State, local, and tribal partners to help protect the public and the environment from releases of hazardous substances from chemical handling facilities by helping them develop area-wide emergency response and contingency plans. EPA conducts audits and inspections of those facilities handling more than a threshold quantity of certain extremely hazardous chemicals and that are required to implement a Risk Management Program to prevent releases.

In collaboration with our tribal government partners, EPA works to strengthen human health and environmental protection in Indian Country. EPA works to ensure that its environmental protection programs are implemented in Indian Country either by EPA or by the Tribes. EPA will continue the direct implementation assessment to better understand EPA direct implementation responsibilities and activities on a program-by-program basis in Indian Country. Also, EPA provides resources and technical assistance for federally recognized Tribes to create and maintain effective environmental programs by collaborating with Tribes to develop long-term EPA-Tribal Environmental Plans (ETEP) for all federally recognized Tribes.

ENVIRONMENTAL PROGRAMS AND MANAGEMENT—Continued

To ensure that food will be free from unsafe levels of pesticide residues, EPA applies strict health-based standards in establishing and reevaluating tolerances for residues in food or animal feed. EPA also works to expedite the registration of reduced risk pesticides when possible, and to ensure that older pesticides meet current health and environmental standards. To respond to emerging health issues, EPA develops methods to evaluate the efficacy of products intended to combat public health pests. EPA intends to reduce potential human and environmental risks from commercial and residential exposure to pesticides through programs that focus on farm worker protection, pollinator health and protection, endangered species protection, environmental stewardship, and integrated pest management. EPA's toxics program will continue to make substantial progress in protecting public health and the environment from potentially harmful industrial chemicals by assessing the safety of new and existing chemicals, reducing gaps in the availability of chemical data, strengthening management of chemical information, and providing easier and more complete public access to non-confidential chemical data. EPA will conduct existing chemical prioritization and evaluations under the provisions of the Toxic Substances Control Act (TSCA) as amended by the Frank R. Lautenberg Chemical Safety for the Twenty-First Century Act, and address any unreasonable risks identified through such evaluations.

EPA will engage both bilaterally and through multilateral institutions to improve international cooperation to prevent and address the transboundary movement of pollution and coordinate with other nations to protect the environment and human health.

Combined with public demand for information, unprecedented changes in information technology are altering the way EPA, States, and Tribes collect, manage, analyze, use, secure, and provide access to quality environmental information. EPA is working with the States and Tribes to strengthen our information quality, leverage information maintained by other government organizations, and develop new tools that provide the public with simultaneous access to multiple data sets, allowing users to understand local, tribal, State, regional, and national environmental conditions. Key to achieving information quality will be the further development of the National Environmental Information Exchange Network, which is primarily an affiliation between EPA and the States and Tribes. EPA will continue to reduce reporting burdens, improve data quality, and accelerate data publications by accelerating the replacement of paper-based submissions with electronic reporting under the Toxic Release Inventory and other programs.

EPA works in partnership with State and tribal agencies to enforce and build compliance with Federal environmental laws passed by the Congress that ensure our communities have clean air, water, and land. EPA will enforce environmental laws to correct noncompliance and promote cleanup of contaminated sites. To improve compliance with environmental laws, EPA works to provide easy access to tools that help regulated entities, Federal agencies, and the public understand these laws and find efficient, cost-effective means for putting them into practice. EPA's enforcement program targets inspections and other compliance monitoring activities according to the degree of health and environmental risk. The program collaborates with the Department of Justice, States, local government agencies, and tribal governments to ensure consistent and fair enforcement of all environmental laws and regulations. The program seeks to aggressively pursue violations that threaten communities, ensure a level economic playing field by ensuring that violators do not realize an economic benefit from noncompliance, and deter future violations. The Civil Enforcement program develops, litigates, and settles administrative and civil judicial cases against serious violators of environmental laws. The Criminal Enforcement program enforces the nation's environmental laws through targeted investigations of criminal conduct, committed by individual and corporate defendants, that threatens public health and the environment. Bringing criminal cases sends a strong deterrence message to potential violators, enhances aggregate compliance with laws and regulations and protects our communities. To maximize compliance, the Agency will refocus efforts towards areas with significant noncompliance issues and where enforcement can address the most substantial impacts to human health and the environment.

The Budget identifies environmental justice priority areas that aim to expand EPA's work to ensure environmental justice in underserved communities and cumulative impacts of environmental pollution. It includes proposed authorization language to carry out new environmental justice grants aimed at reducing the disproportionate health impacts of environmental pollution and to establish an Environmental Justice Training Program charged with increasing the capacity of residents of underserved communities to identify and address disproportionately adverse human health or environmental effects.

EPA's internal operations programs provide centralized management services and leadership to ensure that EPA is fulfilling its mission. The offices and the functions they perform within the Environmental Programs and Management appropriation are: the Office of the Administrator (civil rights/Title VII compliance; congressional, intergovernmental and external relations; Science Advisory Board; children's health; Small Business Ombudsman; Small Minority Business Assistance; Environmental Justice; NEPA Implementation; and regulatory and economic management and analysis work); the Office of the Chief Financial Officer (strategic planning, annual planning, and budgeting, financial services, financial management, analysis, and accountability); the Office of General Counsel (FOIA management, civil rights/Title VI compliance, alternate dispute resolution, and legal advice); and the Office of Mission Support (facilities, infrastructure and operations; acquisition management; human resources management services; grants and interagency agreements; suspension and debarment; administrative law exchange network; information security; and information technology/data management). Since these centralized services provide support across EPA, many of these programs are funded across EPA's appropriations.

Object Classification (in millions of dollars)

Identification code 068–0108–0–1–304		2021 actual	2022 est.	2023 est.
	Direct obligations:			
	Personnel compensation:			
11.1	Full-time permanent	1,041	1,040	1,385
11.3	Other than full-time permanent	29	34	45
11.5	Other personnel compensation	30	28	37
11.7	Military personnel	5	5	5
11.9	Total personnel compensation	1,105	1,107	1,472
12.1	Civilian personnel benefits	392	379	503
13.0	Benefits for former personnel	4	4	5
21.0	Travel and transportation of persons	4	10	14
22.0	Transportation of things		1	1
23.1	Rental payments to GSA	145	161	214
23.2	Rental payments to others	2	3	4
23.3	Communications, utilities, and miscellaneous charges	5	4	4
24.0	Printing and reproduction	5	4	5
25.1	Advisory and assistance services	203	164	218
25.2	Other services from non-Federal sources	302	287	380
25.3	Other goods and services from Federal sources	323	325	432
25.4	Operation and maintenance of facilities	13	9	12
25.7	Operation and maintenance of equipment	3	19	25
26.0	Supplies and materials	4	4	5
31.0	Equipment	10	6	8
41.0	Grants, subsidies, and contributions	318	313	415
42.0	Insurance claims and indemnities	2	1	1
99.0	Direct obligations	2,840	2,801	3,719
99.0	Reimbursable obligations	70	50	50
99.9	Total new obligations, unexpired accounts	2,910	2,851	3,769

Employment Summary

Identification code 068–0108–0–1–304	2021 actual	2022 est.	2023 est.
1001 Direct civilian full-time equivalent employment	8,458	8,458	10,228
1101 Direct military average strength employment	33	33	33

ENVIRONMENTAL PROTECTION AGENCY

| 2001 | Reimbursable civilian full-time equivalent employment | 52 | 52 | 52 |

BUILDINGS AND FACILITIES

For construction, repair, improvement, extension, alteration, and purchase of fixed equipment or facilities of, or for use by, the Environmental Protection Agency, $80,570,000, to remain available until expended.

Note.—A full-year 2022 appropriation for this account was not enacted at the time the Budget was prepared; therefore, the Budget assumes this account is operating under the Continuing Appropriations Act, 2022 (Division A of Public Law 117–43, as amended). The amounts included for 2022 reflect the annualized level provided by the continuing resolution.

Program and Financing (in millions of dollars)

Identification code 068–0110–0–1–304	2021 actual	2022 est.	2023 est.
Obligations by program activity:			
0003 Rule of Law and Process	43	31	75
Budgetary resources:			
Unobligated balance:			
1000 Unobligated balance brought forward, Oct 1	15	12	21
1021 Recoveries of prior year unpaid obligations	6	6	6
1070 Unobligated balance (total)	21	18	27
Budget authority:			
Appropriations, discretionary:			
1100 Appropriation	34	34	81
1930 Total budgetary resources available	55	52	108
Memorandum (non-add) entries:			
1941 Unexpired unobligated balance, end of year	12	21	33
Change in obligated balance:			
Unpaid obligations:			
3000 Unpaid obligations, brought forward, Oct 1	57	56	45
3010 New obligations, unexpired accounts	43	31	75
3020 Outlays (gross)	–38	–36	–44
3040 Recoveries of prior year unpaid obligations, unexpired	–6	–6	–6
3050 Unpaid obligations, end of year	56	45	70
Memorandum (non-add) entries:			
3100 Obligated balance, start of year	57	56	45
3200 Obligated balance, end of year	56	45	70
Budget authority and outlays, net:			
Discretionary:			
4000 Budget authority, gross	34	34	81
Outlays, gross:			
4010 Outlays from new discretionary authority	1	6	14
4011 Outlays from discretionary balances	37	30	30
4020 Outlays, gross (total)	38	36	44
4180 Budget authority, net (total)	34	34	81
4190 Outlays, net (total)	38	36	44

This appropriation provides for the construction, repair, improvement, extension, alteration, and purchase of fixed equipment or facilities of, or for use by the Environmental Protection Agency (EPA). This appropriation supports providing centralized management services to ensure that EPA is fulfilling its mission. EPA's management infrastructure will set and implement quality standards for effective internal management and fiscal responsibility. The facilities funded by this account will provide quality work environments and laboratories that address employee safety and security and pollution prevention. The appropriation would also include costs associated with climate resiliency and sustainability for Agency facilities, and costs associated with a growing workforce.

Object Classification (in millions of dollars)

Identification code 068–0110–0–1–304	2021 actual	2022 est.	2023 est.
Direct obligations:			
25.3 Other goods and services from Federal sources		7	16
32.0 Land and structures	43	24	59
99.9 Total new obligations, unexpired accounts	43	31	75

STATE AND TRIBAL ASSISTANCE GRANTS

For environmental programs and infrastructure assistance, including capitalization grants for State revolving funds and performance partnership grants, $5,729,143,000, to remain available until expended, of which—

(1) $1,638,847,000 shall be for making capitalization grants for the Clean Water State Revolving Funds under title VI of the Federal Water Pollution Control Act; and of which $1,126,095,000 shall be for making capitalization grants for the Drinking Water State Revolving Funds under section 1452 of the Safe Drinking Water Act: Provided, That for fiscal year 2023, to the extent there are sufficient eligible project applications and projects are consistent with State Intended Use Plans, not less than 10 percent of the funds made available under this title to each State for Clean Water State Revolving Fund capitalization grants shall be used by the State for projects to address green infrastructure, water or energy efficiency improvements, or other environmentally innovative activities: Provided further, That the Administrator is authorized to use any remaining funds made available under section 608(f) of title VI of the Federal Water Pollution Control Act (33 U.S.C. 1388), in addition to amounts otherwise available, after necessary funds are used to carry out the management and oversight of section 608, up to $1,500,000 for conducting the Clean Watersheds Needs Survey: Provided further, That for fiscal year 2023, funds made available under this title to each State for Drinking Water State Revolving Fund capitalization grants may, at the discretion of each State, be used for projects to address green infrastructure, water or energy efficiency improvements, or other environmentally innovative activities: Provided further, that the Administrator is authorized to use any remaining funds made available under section 1452(4)(F) of the Safe Drinking Water Act, in addition to amounts otherwise available, after necessary funds are used to carry out the management and oversight of section 1452(4), up to $1,500,000 for conducting the Drinking Water Needs Survey: Provided further, That notwithstanding section 603(d)(7) of the Federal Water Pollution Control Act, the limitation on the amounts in a State water pollution control revolving fund that may be used by a State to administer the fund shall not apply to amounts included as principal in loans made by such fund in fiscal year 2023 and prior years where such amounts represent costs of administering the fund to the extent that such amounts are or were deemed reasonable by the Administrator, accounted for separately from other assets in the fund, and used for eligible purposes of the fund, including administration: Provided further, That for fiscal year 2023, notwithstanding the provisions of subsections (g)(1), (h), and (l) of section 201 of the Federal Water Pollution Control Act, grants made under title II of such Act for American Samoa, Guam, the Commonwealth of the Northern Marianas, the United States Virgin Islands, and the District of Columbia may also be made for the purpose of providing assistance: (1) solely for facility plans, design activities, or plans, specifications, and estimates for any proposed project for the construction of treatment works; and (2) for the construction, repair, or replacement of privately owned treatment works serving one or more principal residences or small commercial establishments: Provided further, That for fiscal year 2023, notwithstanding the provisions of such subsections (g)(1), (h), and (l) of section 201 and section 518(c) of the Federal Water Pollution Control Act, funds reserved by the Administrator for grants under section 518(c) of the Federal Water Pollution Control Act may also be used to provide assistance: (1) solely for facility plans, design activities, or plans, specifications, and estimates for any proposed project for the construction of treatment works; and (2) for the construction, repair, or replacement of privately owned treatment works serving one or more principal residences or small commercial establishments: Provided further, That for fiscal year 2023, notwithstanding any provision of the Federal Water Pollution Control Act and regulations issued pursuant thereof, up to a total of $2,000,000 of the funds reserved by the Administrator for grants under section 518(c) of such Act may also be used for grants for training, technical assistance, and educational programs relating to the operation and management of the treatment works specified in section 518(c) of such Act: Provided further, That for fiscal year 2022, funds reserved under section 518(c) of such Act shall be available for grants only to Indian tribes, as defined in section 518(h) of such Act and former Indian reservations in Oklahoma (as determined by the Secretary of the Interior) and Native Villages as defined in Public Law 92–203: Provided further, That for fiscal year 2023, notwithstanding the limitation on amounts in section 518(c) of the Federal Water Pollution Control Act, up to a total of 2 percent of the funds appropriated, or $30,000,000, whichever is greater, and notwithstanding the limitation on amounts in section 1452(i) of the Safe Drinking Water Act, up to a total of 2 percent of the funds appropriated, or $20,000,000, whichever is greater, for State Revolving Funds under such Acts may be reserved by the Administrator for grants under section 518(c) and section 1452(i) of such Acts: Provided further, That for fiscal year 2023, notwithstanding the amounts specified in section 205(c) of the Federal Water Pollution Control Act, up to 1.5 percent of the aggregate funds appropriated for the Clean Water

STATE AND TRIBAL ASSISTANCE GRANTS—Continued

State Revolving Fund program under the Act less any sums reserved under section 518(c) of the Act, may be reserved by the Administrator for grants made under title II of the Federal Water Pollution Control Act for American Samoa, Guam, the Commonwealth of the Northern Marianas, and United States Virgin Islands: Provided further, That for fiscal year 2023, notwithstanding the limitations on amounts specified in section 1452(j) of the Safe Drinking Water Act, up to 1.5 percent of the funds appropriated for the Drinking Water State Revolving Fund programs under the Safe Drinking Water Act may be reserved by the Administrator for grants made under section 1452(j) of the Safe Drinking Water Act: Provided further, That 10 percent of the funds made available under this title to each State for Clean Water State Revolving Fund capitalization grants and 14 percent of the funds made available under this title to each State for Drinking Water State Revolving Fund capitalization grants shall be used by the State to provide additional subsidy to eligible recipients in the form of forgiveness of principal, negative interest loans, or grants (or any combination of these), and shall be so used by the State only where such funds are provided as initial financing for an eligible recipient or to buy, refinance, or restructure the debt obligations of eligible recipients only where such debt was incurred on or after the date of enactment of this Act, or where such debt was incurred prior to the date of enactment of this Act if the State, with concurrence from the Administrator, determines that such funds could be used to help address a threat to public health from heightened exposure to lead in drinking water or if a Federal or State emergency declaration has been issued due to a threat to public health from heightened exposure to lead in a municipal drinking water supply before the date of enactment of this Act: Provided further, That in a State in which such an emergency declaration has been issued, the State may use more than 14 percent of the funds made available under this title to the State for Drinking Water State Revolving Fund capitalization grants to provide additional subsidy to eligible recipients: Provided further, That notwithstanding section 1452(o) of the Safe Drinking Water Act (42 U.S.C. 300j–12(o)), for fiscal years 2023–2027, the Administrator shall reserve $12,000,000 of amounts made available for making capitalization grants for the Drinking Water State Revolving Funds to pay the costs of monitoring for unregulated contaminants under section 1445(a)(2)(C) of such Act;

(2) $30,000,000 shall be for architectural, engineering, planning, design, construction and related activities in connection with the construction of high priority water and wastewater facilities in the area of the United States-Mexico Border, after consultation with the appropriate border commission: Provided, That no funds provided by this appropriations Act to address the water, wastewater and other critical infrastructure needs of the colonias in the United States along the United States-Mexico border shall be made available to a county or municipal government unless that government has established an enforceable local ordinance, or other zoning rule, which prevents in that jurisdiction the development or construction of any additional colonia areas, or the development within an existing colonia the construction of any new home, business, or other structure which lacks water, wastewater, or other necessary infrastructure;

(3) $40,000,000 shall be for grants to the State of Alaska to address drinking water and wastewater infrastructure needs of rural and Alaska Native Villages: Provided, That of these funds: (A) the State of Alaska shall provide a match of 25 percent; (B) no more than 5 percent of the funds may be used for administrative and overhead expenses; and (C) the State of Alaska shall make awards consistent with the Statewide priority list established in conjunction with the Agency and the U.S. Department of Agriculture for all water, sewer, waste disposal, and similar projects carried out by the State of Alaska that are funded under section 221 of the Federal Water Pollution Control Act (33 U.S.C. 1301) or the Consolidated Farm and Rural Development Act (7 U.S.C. 1921 et seq.) which shall allocate not less than 25 percent of the funds provided for projects in regional hub communities;

(4) $130,982,000 shall be to carry out section 104(k) of the Comprehensive Environmental Response, Compensation, and Liability Act of 1980 (CERCLA), including grants, interagency agreements, and associated program support costs;

(5) $150,000,000 shall be for grants under title VII, subtitle G of the Energy Policy Act of 2005;

(6) $59,000,000 shall be for targeted airshed grants in accordance with the terms and conditions in the explanatory statement described in section 4 (in the matter preceding division A of this consolidated Act);

(7) $4,000,000 shall be to carry out the water quality program authorized in section 5004(d) of the Water Infrastructure Improvements for the Nation Act (Public Law 114–322);

(8) $80,002,000 shall be for grants under subsections (a) through (j) of section 1459A of the Safe Drinking Water Act (42 U.S.C. 300j–19a);

(9) $36,500,000 shall be for grants under section 1464(d) of the Safe Drinking Water Act (42 U.S.C. 300j–24(d));

(10) $182,002,000 shall be for grants under section 1459B of the Safe Drinking Water Act (42 U.S.C. 300j–19b);

(11) $25,000,000 shall be for grants under section 1459A(l) of the Safe Drinking Water Act (42 U.S.C. 300j–19a(l));

(12) $18,000,000 shall be for grants under section 104(b)(8) of the Federal Water Pollution Control Act (33 U.S.C. 1254(b)(8));

(13) $280,000,000 shall be for grants under section 221 of the Federal Water Pollution Control Act (33 U.S.C. 1301);

(14) $17,711,000 shall be for grants under section 4304(b) of the America's Water Infrastructure Act of 2018 (Public Law 115–270);

(15) $1,311,004,000 shall be for grants, including associated program support costs, to States, federally recognized tribes, interstate agencies, tribal consortia, and air pollution control agencies for multi-media or single media pollution prevention, control and abatement, and related activities, including activities pursuant to the provisions set forth under this heading in Public Law 104–134, and for making grants under section 103 of the Clean Air Act for particulate matter monitoring and data collection activities subject to terms and conditions specified by the Administrator, and under section 2301 of the Water and Waste Act of 2016 to assist States in developing and implementing programs for control of coal combustion residuals, of which: $46,954,000 shall be for carrying out section 128 of CERCLA; $15,000,000 shall be for Environmental Information Exchange Network grants, including associated program support costs; $1,505,000 shall be for grants to States under section 2007(f)(2) of the Solid Waste Disposal Act, which shall be in addition to funds appropriated under the heading "Leaking Underground Storage Tank Trust Fund Program" to carry out the provisions of the Solid Waste Disposal Act specified in section 9508(c) of the Internal Revenue Code other than section 9003(h) of the Solid Waste Disposal Act; $18,500,000 of the funds available for grants under section 106 of the Federal Water Pollution Control Act shall be for State participation in national- and State-level statistical surveys of water resources and enhancements to State monitoring programs; $10,200,000 shall be for multipurpose grants, including interagency agreements, in accordance with the terms and conditions described in the explanatory statement described in section 4 (in the matter preceding division A of this consolidated Act);

(16) $10,000,000 shall be for carrying out section 302(a) of the Save Our Seas 2.0 Act (Public Law 116–224), including up to two percent of this amount for the Environmental Protection Agency's administrative costs: Provided, That notwithstanding section 302(a) of such Act, the Administrator may also provide grants pursuant to such authority to intertribal consortia, consistent with the requirements in 40 C.F.R. 35.504(a), to former Indian reservations in Oklahoma (as determined by the Secretary of the Interior), and Alaskan Native Villages as defined in Public Law 92–203;

(17) $50,000,000 shall be for grants under section 1442(b) of the Safe Drinking Water Act (42 U.S.C. 300j–1(b)), of which $15,000,000 shall be for emergency situations affecting small public water systems;

(18) $5,000,000 shall be for grants under section 1454(c) of the Safe Drinking Water Act (42 U.S.C. 300j–14(c));

(19) $20,000,000 shall be for grants under section 1459A(m) of the Safe Drinking Water Act (42 U.S.C. 300j–19a(m));

(20) $50,000,000 shall be for grants under section 1459A(n) of the Safe Drinking Water Act (42 U.S.C. 300j–19a(n));

(21) $50,000,000 shall be for grants under section 1459E of the Safe Drinking Water Act (42 U.S.C. 300j–19f);

(22) $50,000,000 shall be for grants under section 1459F of the Safe Drinking Water Act (42 U.S.C. 300j–19g);

(23) $50,000,000 shall be for carrying out section 2001 of the America's Water Infrastructure Act of 2018 (Public Law 115–270, 42 U.S.C. 300j–3c note); Provided, that the Administrator may award grants and enter into contracts with tribes, intertribal consortia, public or private agencies, institutions, organizations, and individuals, without regard to section 3324(a) and (b) of title 31 and section 6101 of title 41, United States Code, and enter into interagency agreements as appropriate;

(24) $10,000,000 shall be for grants under section 1459G(b) of the Safe Drinking Water Act (42 U.S.C. 300j–19h(b));

(25) $75,000,000, in addition to amounts otherwise available, shall be for grants under sections 104(b)(3), 104(b)(8), and 104(g) of the Federal Water Pollution Control Act (33 U.S.C. 1254(b)(3), 1254(b)(8) and 1254(g));

(26) $20,000,000 shall be for grants under section 222 of the Federal Water Pollution Control Act (33 U.S.C. 1302);

(27) $25,000,000 shall be for grants under section 223 of the Federal Water Pollution Control Act (33 U.S.C. 1302a);

(28) $10,000,000 shall be for grants under section 224 of the Federal Water Pollution Control Act (33 U.S.C. 1302b);

(29) $50,000,000 shall be for grants under section 226 of the Federal Water Pollution Control Act (33 U.S.C. 1302d);

(30) $40,000,000 shall be for grants under section 227 of the Federal Water Pollution Control Act (33 U.S.C. 1302e);

(31) $15,000,000 shall be for grants under section 50213 of the Infrastructure Investment and Jobs Act (42 U.S.C. 10361 note; Public Law 117–58);

(32) $5,000,000 shall be for grants under section 50217(b) of the Infrastructure Investment and Jobs Act (33 U.S.C. 1302f(b); Public Law 117–58);

(33) $10,000,000 shall be for grants under section 50217(c) of the Infrastructure Investment and Jobs Act (33 U.S.C. 1302f(c); Public Law 117–58);

(34) $25,000,000 shall be for grants under section 220 of the Federal Water Pollution Control Act (33 U.S.C. 1300);

(35) $5,000,000 shall be for grants under section 124 of the Federal Water Pollution Control Act (33 U.S.C. 1276); and

(36) $25,000,000, in addition to amounts otherwise available, shall be for competitive grants to meet cybersecurity infrastructure needs within the water sector.

Provided, That up to 5 percent of the funds appropriated under this heading in each of paragraphs (17) through (35) may be reserved for salaries, expenses, and administration, and may be transferred to the Environmental Programs and Management account or the Science and Technology account as needed.

Note.—A full-year 2022 appropriation for this account was not enacted at the time the Budget was prepared; therefore, the Budget assumes this account is operating under the Continuing Appropriations Act, 2022 (Division A of Public Law 117–43, as amended). The amounts included for 2022 reflect the annualized level provided by the continuing resolution.

STATE AND TRIBAL ASSISTANCE GRANTS

[(INCLUDING TRANSFERS OF FUNDS)]

[For an additional amount for "State and Tribal Assistance Grants", $55,426,000,000, to remain available until expended: *Provided*, That amounts made available under this heading in this Act shall be allocated as follows:]

[(1) $11,713,000,000 for capitalization grants for the Clean Water State Revolving Funds under title VI of the Federal Water Pollution Control Act: *Provided*, That $1,902,000,000, to remain available until expended, shall be made available for fiscal year 2022, $2,202,000,000, to remain available until expended, shall be made available for fiscal year 2023, $2,403,000,000, to remain available until expended, shall be made available for fiscal year 2024, $2,603,000,000, to remain available until expended, shall be made available for fiscal year 2025, and $2,603,000,000, to remain available until expended, shall be made available for fiscal year 2026: *Provided further*, That for the funds provided under this paragraph in this Act in fiscal year 2022 and fiscal year 2023, the State shall deposit in the State loan fund from State moneys an amount equal to at least 10 percent of the total amount of the grant to be made to the State, notwithstanding sections 602(b)(2), 602(b)(3) or 202 of the Federal Water Pollution Control Act: *Provided further*, That for the funds made available under this paragraph in this Act, forty-nine percent of the funds made available to each State for Clean Water State Revolving Fund capitalization grants shall be used by the State to provide subsidy to eligible recipients in the form of assistance agreements with 100 percent forgiveness of principal or grants (or any combination of these), notwithstanding section 603(i)(3)(B) of the Federal Water Pollution Control Act (33 U.S.C. 1383): *Provided further*, That up to three percent of the amounts made available under this paragraph in this Act in fiscal year 2022 and up to two percent in each of fiscal years 2023 through 2026 shall be for salaries, expenses, and administration: *Provided further*, That not less than 80 percent of the amounts the Administrator uses in each fiscal year for salaries, expenses, and administration from amounts made available under this paragraph in this Act for such purposes shall be used for purposes other than hiring full-time employees: *Provided further*, That 0.35 percent of the amounts made available under this paragraph in this Act in each of fiscal years 2022 through 2026 shall be transferred to the Office of Inspector General of the Environmental Protection Agency for oversight of funding provided to the Environmental Protection Agency in this title in this Act;]

[(2) $11,713,000,000 for capitalization grants for the Drinking Water State Revolving Funds under section 1452 of the Safe Drinking Water Act: *Provided*, That $1,902,000,000, to remain available until expended, shall be made available for fiscal year 2022, $2,202,000,000, to remain available until expended, shall be made available for fiscal year 2023, $2,403,000,000, to remain available until expended, shall be made available for fiscal year 2024, $2,603,000,000, to remain available until expended, shall be made available for fiscal year 2025, and $2,603,000,000, to remain available until expended, shall be made available for fiscal year 2026: *Provided further*, That for the funds provided under this paragraph in this Act in fiscal year 2022 and fiscal year 2023, the State shall deposit in the State loan fund from State moneys an amount equal to at least 10 percent of the total amount of the grant to be made to the State, notwithstanding section 1452(e) of the Safe Drinking Water Act: *Provided further*, That for the funds made available under this paragraph in this Act, forty-nine percent of the funds made available to each State for Drinking Water State Revolving Fund capitalization grants shall be used by the State to provide subsidy to eligible recipients in the form of assistance agreements with 100 percent forgiveness of principal or grants (or any combination of these), notwithstanding section 1452(d)(2) of the Safe Drinking Water Act (42 U.S.C. 300j—12): *Provided further*, That up to three percent of the amounts made available under this paragraph in this Act in fiscal year 2022 and up to two percent in each of fiscal years 2023 through 2026 shall be for salaries, expenses, and administration: *Provided further*, That not less than 80 percent of the amounts the Administrator uses in each fiscal year for salaries, expenses, and administration from amounts made available under this paragraph in this Act for such purposes shall be used for purposes other than hiring full-time employees: *Provided further*, That 0.35 percent of the amounts made available under this paragraph in this Act in each of fiscal years 2022 through 2026 shall be transferred to the Office of Inspector General of the Environmental Protection Agency for oversight of funding provided to the Environmental Protection Agency in this title in this Act;]

[(3) $15,000,000,000 for capitalization grants for the Drinking Water State Revolving Funds under section 1452 of the Safe Drinking Water Act: *Provided*, That $3,000,000,000, to remain available until expended, shall be made available for fiscal year 2022, $3,000,000,000, to remain available until expended, shall be made available for fiscal year 2023, $3,000,000,000, to remain available until expended, shall be made available for fiscal year 2024, $3,000,000,000, to remain available until expended, shall be made available for fiscal year 2025, and $3,000,000,000, to remain available until expended, shall be made available for fiscal year 2026: *Provided further*, That the funds provided under this paragraph in this Act shall be for lead service line replacement projects and associated activities directly connected to the identification, planning, design, and replacement of lead service lines: *Provided further*, That for the funds made available under this paragraph in this Act, forty-nine percent of the funds made available to each State for Drinking Water State Revolving Fund capitalization grants shall be used by the State to provide subsidy to eligible recipients in the form of assistance agreements with 100 percent forgiveness of principal or grants (or any combination of these), notwithstanding section 1452(d)(2) of the Safe Drinking Water Act (42 U.S.C. 300j—12): *Provided further*, That the funds provided under this paragraph in this Act shall not be subject to the matching or cost share requirements of section 1452(e) of the Safe Drinking Water Act: *Provided further*, That up to three percent of the amounts made available under this paragraph in this Act in fiscal year 2022 and up to two percent in each of fiscal years 2023 through 2026 shall be for salaries, expenses, and administration: *Provided further*, That one-half of one percent of the amounts made available under this paragraph in this Act in each of fiscal years 2022 through 2026 shall be transferred to the Office of Inspector General of the Environmental Protection Agency for oversight of funding provided to the Environmental Protection Agency in this title in this Act;]

[(4) $1,000,000,000 for capitalization grants for the Clean Water State Revolving Funds under title VI of the Federal Water Pollution Control Act: *Provided*, That $100,000,000, to remain available until expended, shall be made available for fiscal year 2022, $225,000,000, to remain available until expended, shall be made available for fiscal year 2023, $225,000,000, to remain available until expended, shall be made available for fiscal year 2024, $225,000,000, to remain available until expended, shall be made available for fiscal year 2025, and $225,000,000, to remain available until expended, shall be made available for fiscal year 2026: *Provided further*, That funds provided under this paragraph in this Act shall be for eligible uses under section 603(c) of the Federal Water Pollution Control Act that address emerging contaminants: *Provided further*, That funds provided under this paragraph in this Act shall not be subject to the matching or cost share requirements of sections 602(b)(2), 602(b)(3), or 202 of the Federal Water Pollution Control Act: *Provided further*, That funds provided under this paragraph in this Act deposited into the state revolving fund shall be provided to eligible recipients as assistance agreements with 100 percent principal forgiveness or as grants (or a combination of these): *Provided further*, That up to three percent of the amounts made available under this paragraph in this Act in fiscal year 2022 and up to two percent in each of fiscal years 2023 through 2026 shall be for salaries, expenses, and administration: *Provided further*, That one-half of one percent of the amounts made available under this paragraph in this Act in each of fiscal years 2022 through 2026 shall be transferred to the Office of Inspector General of the Environmental Protection Agency for oversight of funding provided to the Environmental Protection Agency in this title in this Act;]

[(5) $4,000,000,000 for capitalization grants for the Drinking Water State Revolving Funds under section 1452 of the Safe Drinking Water Act: *Provided*, That $800,000,000, to remain available until expended, shall be made available for fiscal year 2022, $800,000,000, to remain available until expended, shall be made

STATE AND TRIBAL ASSISTANCE GRANTS—Continued

available for fiscal year 2023, $800,000,000, to remain available until expended, shall be made available for fiscal year 2024, $800,000,000, to remain available until expended, shall be made available for fiscal year 2025, and $800,000,000, to remain available until expended, shall be made available for fiscal year 2026: *Provided further*, That funds provided under this paragraph in this Act shall be to address emerging contaminants in drinking water with a focus on perfluoroalkyl and polyfluoroalkyl substances through capitalization grants under section 1452(t) of the Safe Drinking Water Act for the purposes described in section 1452(a)(2)(G) of such Act: *Provided further*, That funds provided under this paragraph in this Act deposited into the State revolving fund shall be provided to eligible recipients as loans with 100 percent principal forgiveness or as grants (or a combination of these): *Provided further*, That funds provided under this paragraph in this Act shall not be subject to the matching or cost share requirements of section 1452(e) of the Safe Drinking Water Act: *Provided further*, That up to three percent of the amounts made available under this paragraph in this Act in fiscal year 2022 and up to two percent in each of fiscal years 2023 through 2026 shall be for salaries, expenses, and administration: *Provided further*, That one-half of one percent of the amounts made available under this paragraph in this Act in each of fiscal years 2022 through 2026 shall be transferred to the Office of Inspector General of the Environmental Protection Agency for oversight of funding provided to the Environmental Protection Agency in this title in this Act;]

[(6) $5,000,000,000 for grants for addressing emerging contaminants under subsections (a) through (j) of section 1459A of the Safe Drinking Water Act (42 U.S.C. 300j—19a): *Provided*, That $1,000,000,000, to remain available until expended, shall be made available for fiscal year 2022, $1,000,000,000, to remain available until expended, shall be made available for fiscal year 2023, $1,000,000,000, to remain available until expended, shall be made available for fiscal year 2024, $1,000,000,000, to remain available until expended, shall be made available for fiscal year 2025, and $1,000,000,000, to remain available until expended, shall be made available for fiscal year 2026: *Provided further*, That funds provided to States under this paragraph may be used for projects that address emerging contaminants supporting a community described in section 1459A, subsection (c)(2), of the Safe Drinking Water Act, notwithstanding the definition of underserved communities in section 1459A, subsection (a)(2), of the Safe Drinking Water Act: *Provided further*, That funds provided under this paragraph in this Act shall not be subject to the matching or cost share requirements of section 1459A of the Safe Drinking Water Act: *Provided further*, That up to three percent of the amounts made available under this paragraph in this Act in each of fiscal years 2022 through 2026 shall be for salaries, expenses, and administration: *Provided further*, That one-half of one percent of the amounts made available under this paragraph in this Act in each of fiscal years 2022 through 2026 shall be transferred to the Office of Inspector General of the Environmental Protection Agency for oversight of funding provided to the Environmental Protection Agency in this title in this Act;]

[(7) $50,000,000, to remain available until expended, to award Underground Injection Control grants, as authorized under section 40306 of division D of this Act, and for activities to support states' efforts to develop programs leading to primacy: *Provided*, That up to three percent of the amounts made available under this paragraph in this Act shall be for salaries, expenses, and administration: *Provided further*, That one-half of one percent of the amounts made available under this paragraph in this Act shall be transferred to the Office of Inspector General of the Environmental Protection Agency for oversight of funding provided to the Environmental Protection Agency in this title in this Act;]

[(8) $1,500,000,000 for brownfields activities: *Provided*, That $300,000,000, to remain available until expended, shall be made available for fiscal year 2022, $300,000,000, to remain available until expended, shall be made available for fiscal year 2023, $300,000,000, to remain available until expended, shall be made available for fiscal year 2024, $300,000,000, to remain available until expended, shall be made available for fiscal year 2025, and $300,000,000, to remain available until expended, shall be made available for fiscal year 2026: *Provided further*, That of the amounts made available in this paragraph in this Act, the following amounts shall be for the following purposes, in equal amounts for each of fiscal years 2022 through 2026—]

[(A) $1,200,000,000 shall be to carry out Brownfields projects authorized by section 104(k) of the Comprehensive Environmental Response, Compensation, and Liability Act of 1980 (CERCLA), including grants, interagency agreements and associated program support costs, of which up to $600,000,000, notwithstanding funding limitations in such sections of such Act, may be for—]

[(i) grants under section 104(k)(3)(A)(ii) of CERCLA to remediate brownfields sites in amounts not to exceed $5,000,000 per grant;]

[(ii) multipurpose grants under section 104(k)(4)(B)(i) of CERCLA in amounts not to exceed $10,000,000 per grant;]

[(iii) grants under sections 104(k)(2)(B) and 104(k)(5)(A)(i) of CERCLA for site characterization and assessment activities on a community-wide or site-by-site basis in amounts not to exceed $10,000,000 per grant and without further limitation on the amount that may be expended for any individual brownfield site;]

[(iv) grants under sections 104(k)(3)(A)(i) and 104(k)(5)(A)(ii) of CERCLA for capitalization of revolving loan funds in amounts not to exceed $10,000,000 per grant; and]

[(v) grants under section 104(k)(7) of CERCLA for job training in amounts not to exceed $1,000,000 per grant; and]

[(B) $300,000,000 shall be to carry out section 128 of the Comprehensive Environmental Response, Compensation, and Liability Act of 1980:]

[*Provided further*, That funds provided under this paragraph in this Act shall not be subject to cost share requirements under section 104(k)(10)(B)(iii) of the Comprehensive Environmental Response, Compensation, and Liability Act of 1980: *Provided further*, That the Administrator of the Environmental Protection Agency shall annually report to Congress on the status of funded projects: *Provided further*, That up to three percent of the amounts made available under this paragraph in this Act in each of fiscal years 2022 through 2026 shall be for salaries, expenses, and administration: *Provided further*, That one-half of one percent of the amounts made available under this paragraph in this Act in each of fiscal years 2022 through 2026 shall be transferred to the Office of Inspector General of the Environmental Protection Agency for oversight of funding provided to the Environmental Protection Agency in this title in this Act;]

[(9) $100,000,000 for all costs for carrying out section 6605 of the Pollution Prevention Act: *Provided*, That $20,000,000, to remain available until expended, shall be made available for fiscal year 2022, $20,000,000, to remain available until expended, shall be made available for fiscal year 2023, $20,000,000, to remain available until expended, shall be made available for fiscal year 2024, $20,000,000, to remain available until expended, shall be made available for fiscal year 2025, and $20,000,000, to remain available until expended, shall be made available for fiscal year 2026: *Provided further*, That funds provided under this paragraph in this Act shall not be subject to cost share requirements under section 6605(c) of the Pollution Prevention Act: *Provided further*, That one-half of one percent of the amounts made available under this paragraph in this Act in each of fiscal years 2022 through 2026 shall be transferred to the Office of Inspector General of the Environmental Protection Agency for oversight of funding provided to the Environmental Protection Agency in this title in this Act;]

[(10) $275,000,000 for grants under section 302(a) of the Save Our Seas 2.0 Act (Public Law 116—224): *Provided*, That $55,000,000, to remain available until expended, shall be made available for fiscal year 2022, $55,000,000, to remain available until expended, shall be made available for fiscal year 2023, $55,000,000, to remain available until expended, shall be made available for fiscal year 2024, $55,000,000, to remain available until expended, shall be made available for fiscal year 2025, and $55,000,000, to remain available until expended, shall be made available for fiscal year 2026: *Provided further*, That notwithstanding section 302(a) of such Act, the Administrator may also provide grants pursuant to such authority to tribes, intertribal consortia consistent with the requirements in 40 CFR 35.504(a), former Indian reservations in Oklahoma (as determined by the Secretary of the Interior), and Alaskan Native Villages as defined in Public Law 92—203: *Provided further*, That up to three percent of the amounts made available under this paragraph in this Act in each of fiscal years 2022 through 2026 shall be for salaries, expenses, and administration: *Provided further*, That one-half of one percent of the amounts made available under this paragraph in this Act in each of fiscal years 2022 through 2026 shall be transferred to the Office of Inspector General of the Environmental Protection Agency for oversight of funding provided to the Environmental Protection Agency in this title in this Act;]

[(11) $75,000,000 to award grants focused on improving material recycling, recovery, management, and reduction, as authorized under section 70402 of division G of this Act: *Provided*, That $15,000,000, to remain available until expended, shall be made available for fiscal year 2022, $15,000,000, to remain available until expended, shall be made available for fiscal year 2023, $15,000,000, to remain available until expended, shall be made available for fiscal year 2024, $15,000,000, to remain available until expended, shall be made available for fiscal year 2025, and $15,000,000, to remain available until expended, shall be made available for fiscal year 2026: *Provided further*, That up to three percent of the amounts made available under this paragraph in this Act in each of fiscal years 2022 through 2026 shall be for salaries, expenses, and administration: *Provided further*, That one-half of one percent of the amounts made available under this paragraph in this Act in each of fiscal years 2022 through 2026 shall be transferred to the Office of

ENVIRONMENTAL PROTECTION AGENCY

Inspector General of the Environmental Protection Agency for oversight of funding provided to the Environmental Protection Agency in this title in this Act;]

[(12) $5,000,000,000 for the Clean School Bus Program as authorized under section 741 of the Energy Policy Act of 2005 (42 U.S.C. 16091), as amended by section 71101 of division G of this Act: *Provided*, That $1,000,000,000, to remain available until expended, shall be made available for fiscal year 2022, $1,000,000,000, to remain available until expended, shall be made available for fiscal year 2023, $1,000,000,000, to remain available until expended, shall be made available for fiscal year 2024, $1,000,000,000, to remain available until expended, shall be made available for fiscal year 2025, and $1,000,000,000, to remain available until expended, shall be made available for fiscal year 2026: *Provided further*, That of the funds provided, $500,000,000 shall be provided annually for zero-emission school buses, as defined in section 741(a)(8) of the Energy Policy Act of 2005 (42 U.S.C. 16091(a)(8)), as amended by section 71101 of division G of this Act, and $500,000,000 shall be provided annually for clean school buses and zero-emission school buses, as defined in section 741(a)(3) of the Energy Policy Act of 2005 (42 U.S.C. 16091(a)(3)), as amended by section 71101 of division G of this Act: *Provided further*, That up to three percent of the amounts made available under this paragraph in this Act in each of fiscal years 2022 through 2026 shall be for salaries, expenses, and administration: *Provided further*, That up to one-half of one percent of the of the amounts made available under this heading in this Act in each of fiscal years 2022 through 2026 shall be transferred to the Office of Inspector General of the Environmental Protection Agency for oversight of funding provided to the Environmental Protection Agency in this title in this Act: *Provided further*, That if there are unobligated funds in any of fiscal years 2022 through 2026 after the Administrator of the Environmental Protection Agency issues awards for that fiscal year, States may compete for those funds, notwithstanding the 10 percent limitation under section 741(b)(7)(B) of the Energy Policy Act of 2005 (42 U.S.C. 16091(b)(7)(B)), as amended by section 71101 of division G of this Act:]

[*Provided further*, That amounts provided under this heading in this Act shall be in addition to amounts otherwise available for such purposes: *Provided further*, That such amount is designated by the Congress as being for an emergency requirement pursuant to section 4112(a) of H. Con. Res. 71 (115th Congress), the concurrent resolution on the budget for fiscal year 2018, and to section 251(b) of the Balanced Budget and Emergency Deficit Control Act of 1985.] *(Infrastructure Investments and Jobs Appropriations Act.)*

Program and Financing (in millions of dollars)

Identification code 068–0103–0–1–304		2021 actual	2022 est.	2023 est.
	Obligations by program activity:			
0001	Core Mission	4,442	9,866	9,882
0002	Cooperative Federalism	105	225	225
0003	Rule of Law and Process	10	20	20
0900	Total new obligations, unexpired accounts	4,557	10,111	10,127
	Budgetary resources:			
	Unobligated balance:			
1000	Unobligated balance brought forward, Oct 1	1,045	917	5,291
1001	Discretionary unobligated balance brought fwd, Oct 1	1,045		
1021	Recoveries of prior year unpaid obligations	88	100	100
1070	Unobligated balance (total)	1,133	1,017	5,391
	Budget authority:			
	Appropriations, discretionary:			
1100	Appropriation	4,314	14,458	5,729
1120	Appropriations transferred to other acct [068–0112]		–45	
1131	Unobligated balance permanently reduced (balances cancelled)	–28	–28	
1160	Appropriation, discretionary (total)	4,286	14,385	5,729
	Advance appropriations, discretionary:			
1170	Advance appropriation			10,819
1172	Advance appropriations transferred to other accounts [068–0112]			–47
1180	Advanced appropriation, discretionary (total)			10,772
	Appropriations, mandatory:			
1200	Appropriation	55		
1900	Budget authority (total)	4,341	14,385	16,501
1930	Total budgetary resources available	5,474	15,402	21,892
	Memorandum (non-add) entries:			
1941	Unexpired unobligated balance, end of year	917	5,291	11,765
	Change in obligated balance:			
	Unpaid obligations:			
3000	Unpaid obligations, brought forward, Oct 1	6,456	7,211	13,529
3010	New obligations, unexpired accounts	4,557	10,111	10,127
3020	Outlays (gross)	–3,714	–3,693	–8,289
3040	Recoveries of prior year unpaid obligations, unexpired	–88	–100	–100
3050	Unpaid obligations, end of year	7,211	13,529	15,267
	Memorandum (non-add) entries:			
3100	Obligated balance, start of year	6,456	7,211	13,529
3200	Obligated balance, end of year	7,211	13,529	15,267
	Budget authority and outlays, net:			
	Discretionary:			
4000	Budget authority, gross	4,286	14,385	16,501
	Outlays, gross:			
4010	Outlays from new discretionary authority	517	963	1,148
4011	Outlays from discretionary balances	3,197	2,717	7,129
4020	Outlays, gross (total)	3,714	3,680	8,277
	Mandatory:			
4090	Budget authority, gross	55		
	Outlays, gross:			
4101	Outlays from mandatory balances		13	12
4180	Budget authority, net (total)	4,341	14,385	16,501
4190	Outlays, net (total)	3,714	3,693	8,289

This appropriation supports core Environmental Protection Agency (EPA) programs through grants to States, Tribes and U.S. districts and Territories. Funding is provided to assist State and tribal partners in implementing their environmental programs to protect human health and the environment. EPA is using common elements for State and tribal grant agreements, including Performance Partnership Grants.

The EPA will provide financial and technical assistance to assist States and Tribes in the development and management of their clean air plans and support solutions that address their local air quality management needs. EPA also will provide funds to States and Tribes using section 105 authority of the Clean Air Act to operate and maintain air monitoring networks to obtain data on emissions of criteria pollutants and air toxics. EPA has funded State and local fine particulate monitoring using the requirements of section 103 of the Clean Air Act, as authorized in annual appropriation bills. EPA also is committed to transitioning funding for fine particulate monitoring into the funding authorized by section 105 of the Clean Air Act. Section 103 provides full funding for pilot programs, demonstrations, research, and other one-time activities, whereas section 105 requires States and local agencies to provide matching funds of at least 40 percent of the amount required for the entire continuing State or local clean air program. Using funds provided by EPA under Clean Air Act sections 103 and 105, States and Tribes will prepare State Implementation Plans and Tribal Implementation Plans to achieve the National Ambient Air Quality Standards, implement monitoring requirements, and support the National Air Toxics Trends Stations monitoring network. Additionally, States may utilize funding to support States' collection, review, and use of greenhouse gas (GHG) emissions data and permitting of large sources of GHG's. EPA also will implement the Diesel Emissions Reduction Act Grant Program by providing funding through grants and rebates to continue to reduce diesel emissions in priority areas and areas of highly concentrated diesel pollution.

EPA also will support its partnerships with States, Tribes, and U.S. Territories through water grants and Performance Partnership grants to carry out core statutory requirements of the Clean Water Act and the Safe Drinking Water Act. Funding supports work to reduce human exposure to contaminants in drinking water, fish and shellfish, and recreational waters and to protect and restore watersheds and aquatic ecosystems. Funding is provided through the Drinking Water State Revolving Fund (SRF) for States and Tribes to make low interest loans to public water systems to upgrade drinking water infrastructure to help them provide safe drinking water. In addition, Clean Water SRF funding provides low interest loans to communities and includes a set-aside for Tribes and U.S. Territories to construct wastewater treatment infrastructure, in addition to other projects that enhance water quality. In sum, the Federal Government has invested over $72 billion in grants to help capitalize the SRFs. With the required State match, additional State contributions, and funds from program leveraging, funds made available for loans total over $200 billion since their inception. EPA will continue to work with its partners to enhance the

STATE AND TRIBAL ASSISTANCE GRANTS—Continued

capacity of communities, States, and private investors to plan and finance drinking water and wastewater infrastructure improvements.

Direct grants also are provided to help address the significant water and wastewater infrastructure needs of Alaska Native Villages. EPA has implemented a management plan that optimizes the pace of the program. EPA will continue to strengthen State core water quality protection and water enforcement programs.

The Budget proposes funds for the America's Water Infrastructure Act and Water Infrastructure Improvements for the Nation Act grant programs that will assist in lead testing in schools, reducing lead in drinking water, increasing resiliency at drinking water systems, sewer overflow control, and water infrastructure workforce investment. These resources would complement State and local drinking water and wastewater infrastructure investments as well as funding provided through other Federal channels.

The Budget proposes funds for several new grants authorized by the Drinking Water Infrastructure Act of 2021 (DWWIA). The Budget proposes funds for several new grants authorized by the Drinking Water Infrastructure Act of 2021 (DWWIA). DWWIA takes important steps towards providing everyone in this country with access to clean, safe, and affordable water. It authorizes increased funding for new and existing drinking water, wastewater, and stormwater programs that will help to provide critical resources to communities across the country. While much more needs to be done, including acting upon President Biden's ambitious proposals for addressing our water infrastructure problems, DWWIA makes important contributions to the tremendous task of fixing our failing infrastructure.

Consistent with the Biden-Harris Lead Pipe and Paint Action Plan, the Budget includes a lead pipe inventory of existing funding that tracks Administration-wide investments in lead pipe replacement. This crosscut can be found in the Supplemental Materials of the Analytical Perspectives published by the Office of Management and Budget.

EPA's Brownfields program supports land revitalization by providing grants to States, Tribes, and local communities to assess and clean up real property which may be complicated by the presence or potential presence of a hazardous substance, pollutant, or contaminant. EPA Brownfields assessment and clean-up projects assist local communities in paving the way for the productive reuse of contaminated properties and abandoned sites.

Hazardous and non-hazardous wastes on the land can migrate to the air, groundwater, and surface water, contaminating drinking water supplies, causing acute illnesses or chronic diseases, and threatening healthy ecosystems in urban, rural, and suburban areas. Under the Resource Conservation and Recovery Act of 1976, as amended, EPA provides grants to States to strengthen their ability to implement hazardous waste programs. When appropriate, EPA also may provide financial and technical assistance to eligible tribal governments and inter-tribal consortia to conduct hazardous waste work in Indian Country. The Budget proposes resources for carrying out section 302(a) of the Save our Seas 2.0 Act.

In addition, EPA provides grants to assist States, Tribes, and other partners with worker safety activities, protection of endangered species and water sources, and promotion of environmental stewardship. To protect, sustain or restore the health of people, communities and ecosystems, EPA focuses on the geographic areas with human and ecological communities at most risk. EPA is working to protect, sustain, and restore the health of natural habitats and ecosystems by identifying and evaluating problem areas, developing tools, and improving community capacity to address problems.

Under Federal environmental statutes, EPA is responsible for protecting human health and the environment in Indian Country. EPA works with over 560 federally recognized Tribes located across the United States to improve environmental and human health outcomes. Indian Country totals more than 70 million acres, with reservations ranging from less than 10 acres to more than 14 million acres. EPA will provide funding to build and enhance the capacity of Tribes to address environmental and public health challenges in Indian Country, including lack of access to safe drinking water, sanitation, adequate waste facilities, and other environmental safeguards taken for granted elsewhere.

EPA will provide funding to States, U.S. Territories, Tribes, and inter-tribal consortia to help them develop their information management and technology capabilities. The purpose of this support is two-fold: to assist the Agency in providing ready access to real-time environmental information; and to allow States and Tribes to better integrate and share their environmental information.

To promote compliance with laws intended to protect human health and the environment, EPA will continue to award State and tribal grants to assist in the implementation of compliance and enforcement provisions of environmental laws. EPA provides funding to States and Tribes for compliance assurance activities including inspections and enforcement case support activities. EPA programs will provide Pesticide Program State and Tribal Assistance Grants that support pesticide product and user compliance with provisions of the Federal Insecticide, Fungicide, and Rodenticide Act (FIFRA) through cooperative agreements with States and Tribes. The cooperative agreements support State and tribal compliance and enforcement activities under FIFRA.

Toxic Substance Compliance Grants are provided to States and Tribes to prevent or eliminate unreasonable risks to human health or the environment and to ensure compliance with toxic substance regulations. The grants support inspection programs associated with the Asbestos Hazard Emergency Response Act (AHERA), lead-based paint (402(a), 406(b), and the Renovation, Repair and Painting rule [RRP]), and polychlorinated biphenyls (PCBs). The compliance monitoring activities conducted by the States will be a cooperative endeavor addressing the priorities of the Federal Toxic Substances Control Act program and State toxics program issues.

Object Classification (in millions of dollars)

Identification code 068–0103–0–1–304		2021 actual	2022 est.	2023 est.
	Direct obligations:			
11.1	Personnel compensation: Full-time permanent	1	45	17
25.1	Advisory and assistance services	2	7	2
25.2	Other services from non-Federal sources	20	59	20
25.3	Other goods and services from Federal sources	103	152	103
41.0	Grants, subsidies, and contributions	4,431	9,848	9,985
99.9	Total new obligations, unexpired accounts	4,557	10,111	10,127

Employment Summary

Identification code 068–0103–0–1–304	2021 actual	2022 est.	2023 est.
1001 Direct civilian full-time equivalent employment	8	359	134

WATER INFRASTRUCTURE FINANCE AND INNOVATION PROGRAM ACCOUNT

For the cost of direct loans and for the cost of guaranteed loans, as authorized by the Water Infrastructure Finance and Innovation Act of 2014, $72,108,000, to remain available until expended: Provided, That such costs, including the cost of modifying such loans, shall be as defined in section 502 of the Congressional Budget Act of 1974: Provided further, That these funds are available to subsidize gross obligations for the principal amount of direct loans, including capitalized interest, and total loan principal, including capitalized interest, any part of which is to be guaranteed, not to exceed $12,500,000,000: Provided further, That of the funds made available under this heading, $5,000,000 shall be used solely for the cost of direct loans and for the cost of guaranteed loans for projects described in section 5026(9) of the Water Infrastructure Finance and Innovation Act of 2014 to State infrastructure financing authorities, as authorized by section 5033(e) of such Act: Provided further, That the use of direct loans or loan guarantee authority under this heading for direct loans or commitments to guarantee loans for any project shall be in accordance with the criteria published in the Federal Register on June 30, 2020 (85 FR 39189) pursuant to the fourth proviso under the heading "Water Infrastructure Finance and Innovation Program Account" in division D of the Further Consolidated Appropriations Act, 2020 (Public Law 116–94): Provided further, That none of the direct loans or loan guarantee authority made available under this heading shall be available for any project unless the Administrator and the Director of the Office of

ENVIRONMENTAL PROTECTION AGENCY

Management and Budget have certified in advance in writing that the direct loan or loan guarantee, as applicable, and the project comply with the criteria referenced in the previous proviso: Provided further, That, for the purposes of carrying out the Congressional Budget Act of 1974, the Director of the Congressional Budget Office may request, and the Administrator shall promptly provide, documentation and information relating to a project identified in a Letter of Interest submitted to the Administrator pursuant to a Notice of Funding Availability for applications for credit assistance under the Water Infrastructure Finance and Innovation Act Program, including with respect to a project that was initiated or completed before the date of enactment of this Act.

In addition, fees authorized to be collected pursuant to sections 5029 and 5030 of the Water Infrastructure Finance and Innovation Act of 2014 shall be deposited in this account, to remain available until expended.

In addition, for administrative expenses to carry out the direct and guaranteed loan programs, notwithstanding section 5033 of the Water Infrastructure Finance and Innovation Act of 2014, $8,236,000, to remain available until September 30, 2024.

Note.—A full-year 2022 appropriation for this account was not enacted at the time the Budget was prepared; therefore, the Budget assumes this account is operating under the Continuing Appropriations Act, 2022 (Division A of Public Law 117–43, as amended). The amounts included for 2022 reflect the annualized level provided by the continuing resolution.

Program and Financing (in millions of dollars)

Identification code 068–0254–0–1–301	2021 actual	2022 est.	2023 est.
Obligations by program activity:			
Credit program obligations:			
0701 Direct loan subsidy	51	60	72
0705 Reestimates of direct loan subsidy	23	115	
0706 Interest on reestimates of direct loan subsidy	1	7	
0709 Administrative expenses	6	6	8
0900 Total new obligations, unexpired accounts	81	188	80
Budgetary resources:			
Unobligated balance:			
1000 Unobligated balance brought forward, Oct 1	149	143	177
1020 Adjustment of unobligated bal brought forward, Oct 1		24	
1021 Recoveries of prior year unpaid obligations	1		
1070 Unobligated balance (total)	150	167	177
Budget authority:			
Appropriations, discretionary:			
1100 Appropriation	65	66	80
Appropriations, mandatory:			
1200 Appropriation		122	
Spending authority from offsetting collections, discretionary:			
1700 Collected	9	10	10
1900 Budget authority (total)	74	198	90
1930 Total budgetary resources available	224	365	267
Memorandum (non-add) entries:			
1941 Unexpired unobligated balance, end of year	143	177	187
Change in obligated balance:			
Unpaid obligations:			
3000 Unpaid obligations, brought forward, Oct 1	59	101	62
3010 New obligations, unexpired accounts	81	188	80
3020 Outlays (gross)	–38	–227	–63
3040 Recoveries of prior year unpaid obligations, unexpired	–1		
3050 Unpaid obligations, end of year	101	62	79
Memorandum (non-add) entries:			
3100 Obligated balance, start of year	59	101	62
3200 Obligated balance, end of year	101	62	79
Budget authority and outlays, net:			
Discretionary:			
4000 Budget authority, gross	74	76	90
Outlays, gross:			
4010 Outlays from new discretionary authority	30	28	32
4011 Outlays from discretionary balances	8	19	31
4020 Outlays, gross (total)	38	47	63
Offsets against gross budget authority and outlays:			
Offsetting collections (collected) from:			
4033 Non-Federal sources	–9	–10	–10
4040 Offsets against gross budget authority and outlays (total)	–9	–10	–10
Mandatory:			
4090 Budget authority, gross		122	
Outlays, gross:			
4100 Outlays from new mandatory authority		122	
4101 Outlays from mandatory balances		58	
4110 Outlays, gross (total)		180	
4180 Budget authority, net (total)	65	188	80
4190 Outlays, net (total)	29	217	53

Summary of Loan Levels, Subsidy Budget Authority and Outlays by Program (in millions of dollars)

Identification code 068–0254–0–1–301	2021 actual	2022 est.	2023 est.
Direct loan levels supportable by subsidy budget authority:			
115002 Water Infrastructure Direct Loans	5,459	5,550	7,143
Direct loan subsidy (in percent):			
132002 Water Infrastructure Direct Loans	0.83	1.07	1.01
132999 Weighted average subsidy rate	0.83	1.07	1.01
Direct loan subsidy budget authority:			
133002 Water Infrastructure Direct Loans	51	59	72
Direct loan subsidy outlays:			
134002 Water Infrastructure Direct Loans	3	33	48
Direct loan reestimates:			
135002 Water Infrastructure Direct Loans	24	121	
Administrative expense data:			
3510 Budget authority	6	8	8
3580 Outlays from balances	3		2
3590 Outlays from new authority	5	8	4

This appropriation supports all activities necessary for the implementation of the Water Infrastructure Finance and Innovation program established by the Water Resources Reform and Development Act of 2014, Title V, Subtitle C. The program will provide low-interest Federal loans or loan guarantees to eligible entities for a wide range of nationally and regionally significant water and wastewater projects. Eligible assistance recipients include corporations, partnerships, government entities, and State Revolving Fund (SRF) programs, among others. Eligible projects include, among others: Clean and Drinking Water State Revolving Fund eligible projects; projects for enhanced energy efficiency at drinking water and wastewater facilities; brackish or seawater desalination, aquifer recharge, water recycling; acquisition of property if it is integral to the project or will mitigate the environmental impact of a project; bundled SRF projects under one application; and a combination of projects secured by a common security pledge. Of the total $80 million request to implement the Water Infrastructure Finance and Innovation Act (WIFIA) program, $8 million is for the Environmental Protection Agency's (EPA) management and operation of the program, including contract support and associated payroll. The WIFIA program will be administered by EPA's Office of Water.

Object Classification (in millions of dollars)

Identification code 068–0254–0–1–301	2021 actual	2022 est.	2023 est.
Direct obligations:			
11.1 Personnel compensation: Full-time permanent	6	6	6
12.1 Civilian personnel benefits	2	2	2
25.1 Advisory and assistance services	8	8	8
25.2 Other services from non-Federal sources	2	2	2
41.0 Grants, subsidies, and contributions	63	170	62
99.9 Total new obligations, unexpired accounts	81	188	80

Employment Summary

Identification code 068–0254–0–1–301	2021 actual	2022 est.	2023 est.
1001 Direct civilian full-time equivalent employment	37	37	37

WATER INFRASTRUCTURE FINANCE AND INNOVATION DIRECT LOAN FINANCING ACCOUNT

Program and Financing (in millions of dollars)

Identification code 068–4372–0–3–301	2021 actual	2022 est.	2023 est.
Obligations by program activity:			
Credit program obligations:			
0710 Direct loan obligations	5,459	5,550	7,143
0713 Payment of interest to Treasury	23	32	33

WATER INFRASTRUCTURE FINANCE AND INNOVATION DIRECT LOAN FINANCING ACCOUNT—Continued

Program and Financing—Continued

Identification code 068–4372–0–3–301		2021 actual	2022 est.	2023 est.
0742	Downward reestimates paid to receipt accounts	....	1	....
0900	Total new obligations, unexpired accounts	5,482	5,583	7,176
	Budgetary resources:			
	Unobligated balance:			
1000	Unobligated balance brought forward, Oct 1	615	....	....
1020	Adjustment of unobligated bal brought forward, Oct 1	–615	....	....
	Financing authority:			
	Borrowing authority, mandatory:			
1400	Borrowing authority	5,387	5,550	7,143
	Spending authority from offsetting collections, mandatory:			
1800	Collected	51	200	235
1801	Change in uncollected payments, Federal sources	44	....	....
1825	Spending authority from offsetting collections applied to repay debt	....	–167	–202
1850	Spending auth from offsetting collections, mand (total)	95	33	33
1900	Budget authority (total)	5,482	5,583	7,176
1930	Total budgetary resources available	5,482	5,583	7,176
	Change in obligated balance:			
	Unpaid obligations:			
3000	Unpaid obligations, brought forward, Oct 1	6,323	11,480	13,384
3001	Adjustments to unpaid obligations, brought forward, Oct 1	221	128	....
3010	New obligations, unexpired accounts	5,482	5,583	7,176
3020	Outlays (gross)	–546	–3,807	–5,296
3050	Unpaid obligations, end of year	11,480	13,384	15,264
	Uncollected payments:			
3060	Uncollected pymts, Fed sources, brought forward, Oct 1	....	–90	–90
3061	Adjustments to uncollected pymts, Fed sources, brought forward, Oct 1	–46	....	....
3070	Change in uncollected pymts, Fed sources, unexpired	–44	....	....
3090	Uncollected pymts, Fed sources, end of year	–90	–90	–90
	Memorandum (non-add) entries:			
3100	Obligated balance, start of year	6,498	11,518	13,294
3200	Obligated balance, end of year	11,390	13,294	15,174
	Financing authority and disbursements, net:			
	Mandatory:			
4090	Budget authority, gross	5,482	5,583	7,176
	Financing disbursements:			
4110	Outlays, gross (total)	546	3,807	5,296
	Offsets against gross financing authority and disbursements:			
	Offsetting collections (collected) from:			
4120	Federal sources	–26	–155	–48
4122	Interest on uninvested funds	–11	–10	....
4123	Non-Federal sources (Interest)	–14	–5	....
4123	Non-Federal sources (Principal)	....	–30	–187
4130	Offsets against gross budget authority and outlays (total)	–51	–200	–235
	Additional offsets against financing authority only (total):			
4140	Change in uncollected pymts, Fed sources, unexpired	–44	....	....
4160	Budget authority, net (mandatory)	5,387	5,383	6,941
4170	Outlays, net (mandatory)	495	3,607	5,061
4180	Budget authority, net (total)	5,387	5,383	6,941
4190	Outlays, net (total)	495	3,607	5,061

Status of Direct Loans (in millions of dollars)

Identification code 068–4372–0–3–301		2021 actual	2022 est.	2023 est.
	Position with respect to appropriations act limitation on obligations:			
1111	Direct loan obligations from current-year authority	5,459	5,550	7,143
1150	Total direct loan obligations	5,459	5,550	7,143
	Cumulative balance of direct loans outstanding:			
1210	Outstanding, start of year	221	735	4,512
1231	Disbursements: Direct loan disbursements	523	3,807	5,296
1251	Repayments: Repayments and prepayments	–9	–30	–187
1290	Outstanding, end of year	735	4,512	9,621

Balance Sheet (in millions of dollars)

Identification code 068–4372–0–3–301		2020 actual	2021 actual
	ASSETS:		
	Federal assets:		
1101	Fund balances with Treasury	....	31
	Investments in U.S. securities:		
1106	Receivables, net	24	122
	Net value of assets related to post-1991 direct loans receivable:		
1401	Direct loans receivable, gross	221	735
1402	Interest receivable	....	1
1405	Allowance for subsidy cost (-)	–25	–149
1499	Net present value of assets related to direct loans	196	587
1999	Total assets	220	740
	LIABILITIES:		
	Federal liabilities:		
2101	Accounts payable	....	....
2103	Debt	220	747
2999	Total liabilities	220	747
	NET POSITION:		
3300	Cumulative results of operations	....	–7
4999	Total liabilities and net position	220	740

PAYMENT TO THE HAZARDOUS SUBSTANCE SUPERFUND

Program and Financing (in millions of dollars)

Identification code 068–0250–0–1–304		2021 actual	2022 est.	2023 est.
	Obligations by program activity:			
0001	Payment to the hazardous substance superfund	1,153	4,649	1,542
0900	Total new obligations, unexpired accounts (object class 94.0)	1,153	4,649	1,542
	Budgetary resources:			
	Budget authority:			
	Appropriations, discretionary:			
1100	Appropriation	1,153	4,649	1,542
1930	Total budgetary resources available	1,153	4,649	1,542
	Change in obligated balance:			
	Unpaid obligations:			
3010	New obligations, unexpired accounts	1,153	4,649	1,542
3020	Outlays (gross)	–1,153	–4,649	–1,542
	Budget authority and outlays, net:			
	Discretionary:			
4000	Budget authority, gross	1,153	4,649	1,542
	Outlays, gross:			
4010	Outlays from new discretionary authority	1,153	4,649	1,542
4180	Budget authority, net (total)	1,153	4,649	1,542
4190	Outlays, net (total)	1,153	4,649	1,542

The Comprehensive Environmental Response, Compensation, and Liability Act of 1980, as amended, authorizes appropriations from the general fund to finance activities conducted through the Hazardous Substance Superfund. The Administration proposes to continue the payment from the general fund in 2023 in amounts necessary to reach the full appropriated amount for carrying out CERCLA. In addition, Superfund excise tax revenues are expected to be collected in 2022 and available for use in 2023. The Biden-Harris Administration looks forward to working with Congress to change the Superfund excise tax outlays from discretionary to mandatory.

ENVIRONMENTAL SERVICES

Special and Trust Fund Receipts (in millions of dollars)

Identification code 068–5295–0–2–304		2021 actual	2022 est.	2023 est.
0100	Balance, start of year	518	546	572
	Receipts:			
	Current law:			
1120	Environmental Services	28	26	26

ENVIRONMENTAL PROTECTION AGENCY

		2021 actual	2022 est.	2023 est.
2000	Total: Balances and receipts	546	572	598
5099	Balance, end of year	546	572	598

The Environmental Services special fund was established for the deposit of fee receipts associated with environmental programs that may, by statute, be deposited into the fund.

TSCA SERVICE FEE FUND

Special and Trust Fund Receipts (in millions of dollars)

Identification code 068–5664–0–2–304		2021 actual	2022 est.	2023 est.
0100	Balance, start of year			
	Receipts:			
	Current law:			
1130	User Fees, TSCA Service Fee Fund	29	7	6
2000	Total: Balances and receipts	29	7	6
	Appropriations:			
	Current law:			
2101	TSCA Service Fee Fund	–29	–7	–5
5099	Balance, end of year			1

Program and Financing (in millions of dollars)

Identification code 068–5664–0–2–304		2021 actual	2022 est.	2023 est.
	Budgetary resources:			
	Budget authority:			
	Appropriations, discretionary:			
1101	Appropriation (special or trust)	29	7	5
1120	Appropriations transferred to other acct [068–0108]	–29	–7	
1160	Appropriation, discretionary (total)			5
1930	Total budgetary resources available			5
	Memorandum (non-add) entries:			
1941	Unexpired unobligated balance, end of year			5
	Budget authority and outlays, net:			
	Discretionary:			
4000	Budget authority, gross			5
4180	Budget authority, net (total)			5
4190	Outlays, net (total)			

TSCA Service Fees are authorized by section 26 of the Toxic Substances Control Act, as amended by Public Law 114–182, the Frank R. Lautenberg Chemical Safety for the 21st Century Act. Fees deposited in this account are paid by chemical manufacturers (including importers) and, in limited circumstances, processors who are required to: submit test data (TSCA section 4); submit notification of or information related to intent to manufacture a new chemical or significant new use of a chemical (TSCA section 5); manufacture a chemical substance that is subject to a risk evaluation (TSCA section 6); or request that the Environmental Protection Agency (EPA) conduct a risk evaluation on an existing chemical (TSCA section 6), subject to the agency's approval of the request. TSCA Service Fees are estimated to offset 25 percent of the costs to administer sections 4, 5, and 6 of the law as well as collecting, processing, reviewing, and protecting information about chemical substances from disclosure as appropriate under TSCA section 14. The statute requires that fees for manufacturer-requested risk evaluations offset 50 or 100 percent of the costs of those evaluations. EPA finalized a rule for the collection of TSCA fees on September 27, 2018. The final rule became effective in October 2018.

PESTICIDE REGISTRATION FUND

Special and Trust Fund Receipts (in millions of dollars)

Identification code 068–5374–0–2–304		2021 actual	2022 est.	2023 est.
0100	Balance, start of year	1	1	1

Environmental Protection Agency—Continued
Federal Funds—Continued

1121

		2021 actual	2022 est.	2023 est.
	Receipts:			
	Current law:			
1130	Registration Service Fees, Pesticide Registration Fund	20	20	20
2000	Total: Balances and receipts	21	21	21
	Appropriations:			
	Current law:			
2101	Pesticide Registration Fund	–20	–20	–20
5099	Balance, end of year	1	1	1

Program and Financing (in millions of dollars)

Identification code 068–5374–0–2–304		2021 actual	2022 est.	2023 est.
	Obligations by program activity:			
0001	Core Mission	21	21	21
	Budgetary resources:			
	Unobligated balance:			
1000	Unobligated balance brought forward, Oct 1	9	9	9
1021	Recoveries of prior year unpaid obligations	1	1	1
1070	Unobligated balance (total)	10	10	10
	Budget authority:			
	Appropriations, discretionary:			
1101	Appropriation (special or trust)	20	20	20
1930	Total budgetary resources available	30	30	30
	Memorandum (non-add) entries:			
1941	Unexpired unobligated balance, end of year	9	9	9
	Change in obligated balance:			
	Unpaid obligations:			
3000	Unpaid obligations, brought forward, Oct 1	7	7	7
3010	New obligations, unexpired accounts	21	21	21
3020	Outlays (gross)	–20	–20	–20
3040	Recoveries of prior year unpaid obligations, unexpired	–1	–1	–1
3050	Unpaid obligations, end of year	7	7	7
	Memorandum (non-add) entries:			
3100	Obligated balance, start of year	7	7	7
3200	Obligated balance, end of year	7	7	7
	Budget authority and outlays, net:			
	Discretionary:			
4000	Budget authority, gross	20	20	20
	Outlays, gross:			
4010	Outlays from new discretionary authority	15	12	12
4011	Outlays from discretionary balances	5	8	8
4020	Outlays, gross (total)	20	20	20
4180	Budget authority, net (total)	20	20	20
4190	Outlays, net (total)	20	20	20

Fees deposited in this account are paid by industry to partially offset the costs associated with reviewing all applications for which registration service fees have been paid, including for associated establishment of tolerances for pesticides to be used in or on food and animal feed; and to partially fund the enhancement of scientific and regulatory activities relating to worker protection, to partially fund partnership grants, and to partially fund the pesticide safety education program. These Pesticide Registration Service fees are authorized by section 33 of the Federal Insecticide, Fungicide, and Rodenticide Act, as amended by Public Law 116–8, the Pesticide Registration Improvement Extension Act of 2018.

Object Classification (in millions of dollars)

Identification code 068–5374–0–2–304		2021 actual	2022 est.	2023 est.
	Direct obligations:			
	Personnel compensation:			
11.1	Full-time permanent	8	8	8
11.3	Other than full-time permanent	1	1	1
11.9	Total personnel compensation	9	9	9
12.1	Civilian personnel benefits	3	3	3
25.1	Advisory and assistance services	1	1	1
25.2	Other services from non-Federal sources	6	6	6
41.0	Grants, subsidies, and contributions	2	2	2
99.9	Total new obligations, unexpired accounts	21	21	21

Environmental Protection Agency—Continued
Federal Funds—Continued

PESTICIDE REGISTRATION FUND—Continued

Employment Summary

Identification code 068–5374–0–2–304	2021 actual	2022 est.	2023 est.
1001 Direct civilian full-time equivalent employment	70	70	70

REREGISTRATION AND EXPEDITED PROCESSING REVOLVING FUND

Program and Financing (in millions of dollars)

Identification code 068–4310–0–3–304	2021 actual	2022 est.	2023 est.
Obligations by program activity:			
0801 Core Mission	49	48	38
0803 Rule of Law and Process	1	1	1
0900 Total new obligations, unexpired accounts	50	49	39
Budgetary resources:			
Unobligated balance:			
1000 Unobligated balance brought forward, Oct 1	42	26	10
1021 Recoveries of prior year unpaid obligations	2	1	9
1070 Unobligated balance (total)	44	27	19
Budget authority:			
Spending authority from offsetting collections, mandatory:			
1800 Collected	32	32	31
1802 Offsetting collections (previously unavailable)	2	2	2
1823 New and/or unobligated balance of spending authority from offsetting collections temporarily reduced	–2	–2	–2
1850 Spending auth from offsetting collections, mand (total)	32	32	31
1900 Budget authority (total)	32	32	31
1930 Total budgetary resources available	76	59	50
Memorandum (non-add) entries:			
1941 Unexpired unobligated balance, end of year	26	10	11
Change in obligated balance:			
Unpaid obligations:			
3000 Unpaid obligations, brought forward, Oct 1	8	10	25
3010 New obligations, unexpired accounts	50	49	39
3020 Outlays (gross)	–46	–33	–34
3040 Recoveries of prior year unpaid obligations, unexpired	–2	–1	–9
3050 Unpaid obligations, end of year	10	25	21
Memorandum (non-add) entries:			
3100 Obligated balance, start of year	8	10	25
3200 Obligated balance, end of year	10	25	21
Budget authority and outlays, net:			
Mandatory:			
4090 Budget authority, gross	32	32	31
Outlays, gross:			
4100 Outlays from new mandatory authority	32	21	21
4101 Outlays from mandatory balances	14	12	13
4110 Outlays, gross (total)	46	33	34
Offsets against gross budget authority and outlays:			
Offsetting collections (collected) from:			
4121 Interest on Federal securities		–1	
4123 Non-Federal sources	–32	–31	–31
4130 Offsets against gross budget authority and outlays (total)	–32	–32	–31
4170 Outlays, net (mandatory)	14	1	3
4180 Budget authority, net (total)			
4190 Outlays, net (total)	14	1	3
Memorandum (non-add) entries:			
5090 Unexpired unavailable balance, SOY: Offsetting collections	2	2	2
5092 Unexpired unavailable balance, EOY: Offsetting collections	2	2	2

Summary of Budget Authority and Outlays (in millions of dollars)

	2021 actual	2022 est.	2023 est.
Enacted/requested:			
Outlays	14	1	3
Legislative proposal, subject to PAYGO:			
Outlays			2
Total:			
Outlays	14	1	5

Pesticide maintenance fees are paid by industry to partially offset the costs of pesticide reregistration and expedited processing of certain registration applications; to partially offset the costs of registration review; to review and evaluate inert ingredients; to support enhancements to the Good Laboratory Practices program inspections and audits; and to support efficacy guideline development and rulemaking. This fee is authorized in section 4(i) of the Federal Insecticide, Fungicide, and Rodenticide Act, as amended by Public Law 116–8, the Pesticide Registration Improvement Extension Act of 2018.

Object Classification (in millions of dollars)

Identification code 068–4310–0–3–304	2021 actual	2022 est.	2023 est.
Reimbursable obligations:			
Personnel compensation:			
11.1 Full-time permanent	21	21	18
11.3 Other than full-time permanent	1	1	1
11.9 Total personnel compensation	22	22	19
12.1 Civilian personnel benefits	8	8	6
23.1 Rental payments to GSA	1	1	1
25.1 Advisory and assistance services	6	6	4
25.2 Other services from non-Federal sources	12	11	9
25.3 Other goods and services from Federal sources	1	1	
99.9 Total new obligations, unexpired accounts	50	49	39

Employment Summary

Identification code 068–4310–0–3–304	2021 actual	2022 est.	2023 est.
1001 Direct civilian full-time equivalent employment	186	186	186

REREGISTRATION AND EXPEDITED PROCESSING REVOLVING FUND

(Legislative proposal, subject to PAYGO)

Program and Financing (in millions of dollars)

Identification code 068–4310–4–3–304	2021 actual	2022 est.	2023 est.
Obligations by program activity:			
0801 Core Mission			11
Memorandum (non-add) entries:			
1941 Unexpired unobligated balance, end of year			–11
Change in obligated balance:			
Unpaid obligations:			
3010 New obligations, unexpired accounts			11
3020 Outlays (gross)			–2
3050 Unpaid obligations, end of year			9
Memorandum (non-add) entries:			
3200 Obligated balance, end of year			9
Budget authority and outlays, net:			
Mandatory:			
Outlays, gross:			
4101 Outlays from mandatory balances			2
4180 Budget authority, net (total)			
4190 Outlays, net (total)			2

Fee Spending Restrictions. Current statutory language in the Federal Insecticide, Fungicide, and Rodenticide Act (FIFRA) restricts the activities that Environmental Protection Agency can fund from collections deposited in the Reregistration and Expedited Processing Revolving Fund. The Budget proposes language to clarify the Agency's authority to utilize resources in the Fund to review existing pesticide registrations for their compliance with current FIFRA standards, ensuring market access for pesticide registrants. Specifically, fees collected would be available for the following pesticide regulatory activities: processing and review of submissions made under FIFRA, data submitted in association with a current registration, information submitted pursuant to section 6(a)(2), processing and review of additional uses registered by States under section 24(c), applications for emergency exemptions, and notifications; laboratory support; administrative and systems support; development of policy and guidance; rulemaking

ENVIRONMENTAL PROTECTION AGENCY

support; information collection activities; and the portions of salaries related to work in these areas.

Object Classification (in millions of dollars)

Identification code 068–4310–4–3–304		2021 actual	2022 est.	2023 est.
11.1	Reimbursable obligations: Personnel compensation: Full-time permanent			5
11.9	Total personnel compensation			5
12.1	Civilian personnel benefits			2
25.1	Advisory and assistance services			1
25.2	Other services from non-Federal sources			3
99.9	Total new obligations, unexpired accounts			11

Employment Summary

Identification code 068–4310–4–3–304		2021 actual	2022 est.	2023 est.
1001	Direct civilian full-time equivalent employment			66

HAZARDOUS WASTE ELECTRONIC MANIFEST SYSTEM FUND

Note.—A full-year 2022 appropriation for this account was not enacted at the time the Budget was prepared; therefore, the Budget assumes this account is operating under the Continuing Appropriations Act, 2022 (Division A of Public Law 117–43, as amended). The amounts included for 2022 reflect the annualized level provided by the continuing resolution.

Program and Financing (in millions of dollars)

Identification code 068–4330–0–3–304		2021 actual	2022 est.	2023 est.
	Obligations by program activity:			
0001	Core Mission	22	24	24
0799	Total direct obligations	22	24	24
	Budgetary resources:			
	Unobligated balance:			
1000	Unobligated balance brought forward, Oct 1	6	9	13
	Budget authority:			
	Spending authority from offsetting collections, discretionary:			
1700	Collected	25	28	27
1900	Budget authority (total)	25	28	27
1930	Total budgetary resources available	31	37	40
	Memorandum (non-add) entries:			
1941	Unexpired unobligated balance, end of year	9	13	16
	Change in obligated balance:			
	Unpaid obligations:			
3000	Unpaid obligations, brought forward, Oct 1	5	10	27
3010	New obligations, unexpired accounts	22	24	24
3020	Outlays (gross)	–17	–7	–11
3050	Unpaid obligations, end of year	10	27	40
	Memorandum (non-add) entries:			
3100	Obligated balance, start of year	5	10	27
3200	Obligated balance, end of year	10	27	40
	Budget authority and outlays, net:			
	Discretionary:			
4000	Budget authority, gross	25	28	27
	Outlays, gross:			
4010	Outlays from new discretionary authority	13	6	5
4011	Outlays from discretionary balances	4	1	6
4020	Outlays, gross (total)	17	7	11
	Offsets against gross budget authority and outlays:			
	Offsetting collections (collected) from:			
4033	Non-Federal sources	–25	–28	–27
4180	Budget authority, net (total)			
4190	Outlays, net (total)	–8	–21	–16

In accordance with section 3024 of the Solid Waste Disposal Act (42 U.S.C. 6939g(c)), the Administrator of the Environmental Protection Agency is authorized to collect and obligate e-Manifest user fees. In 2023, EPA will continue to operate the e-Manifest system established by the Hazardous Waste Electronic Manifest Establishment Act (Public Law 112–195). Based upon authority to collect and spend e-Manifest fees provided by the Congress in annual appropriations bills, the Agency anticipates collecting and depositing approximately $26.6 million in e-Manifest user fees into the Hazardous Waste Electronic Manifest System Fund. Fees deposited in this account will fully support the e-Manifest program, including operation of the system, necessary program expenses, and future development costs.

Object Classification (in millions of dollars)

Identification code 068–4330–0–3–304		2021 actual	2022 est.	2023 est.
	Direct obligations:			
11.1	Personnel compensation: Full-time permanent	1	1	1
12.1	Civilian personnel benefits	1	1	1
25.1	Advisory and assistance services	8	8	8
25.2	Other services from non-Federal sources	10	12	12
25.3	Other goods and services from Federal sources	2	2	2
99.0	Direct obligations	22	24	24
99.9	Total new obligations, unexpired accounts	22	24	24

Employment Summary

Identification code 068–4330–0–3–304		2021 actual	2022 est.	2023 est.
1001	Direct civilian full-time equivalent employment	11	11	11

DAMAGE ASSESSMENT AND RESTORATION REVOLVING FUND

Program and Financing (in millions of dollars)

Identification code 068–4365–0–3–306		2021 actual	2022 est.	2023 est.
	Obligations by program activity:			
0001	Core Mission	1	1	1
0900	Total new obligations, unexpired accounts (object class 11.1)	1	1	1
	Budgetary resources:			
	Unobligated balance:			
1000	Unobligated balance brought forward, Oct 1	2	2	3
	Budget authority:			
	Appropriations, mandatory:			
1221	Appropriations transferred from other acct [014–1618]	1	2	2
1900	Budget authority (total)	1	2	2
1930	Total budgetary resources available	3	4	5
	Memorandum (non-add) entries:			
1941	Unexpired unobligated balance, end of year	2	3	4
	Change in obligated balance:			
	Unpaid obligations:			
3010	New obligations, unexpired accounts	1	1	1
3020	Outlays (gross)	–1	–1	
3050	Unpaid obligations, end of year			1
	Memorandum (non-add) entries:			
3200	Obligated balance, end of year			1
	Budget authority and outlays, net:			
	Mandatory:			
4090	Budget authority, gross	1	2	2
	Outlays, gross:			
4100	Outlays from new mandatory authority	1		
4101	Outlays from mandatory balances		1	
4110	Outlays, gross (total)	1	1	
4180	Budget authority, net (total)	1	2	2
4190	Outlays, net (total)	1	1	

These funds pay for the Environmental Protection Agency's (EPA) assessment and restoration activities resulting from the Deepwater Horizon Oil Spill in conjunction with injury to, destruction of, or loss of the use of natural resources, including their supporting ecosystems. EPA was designated as a trustee for Natural Resource Damage Assessment (NRDA) under Executive Order 13626, and this fund was established under the authority of section 1006(f) (33 U.S.C. 2706(f)) of the Oil Pollution Act of 1990.

Environmental Protection Agency—Continued
Federal Funds—Continued

DAMAGE ASSESSMENT AND RESTORATION REVOLVING FUND—Continued

Employment Summary

Identification code 068–4365–0–3–306	2021 actual	2022 est.	2023 est.
2001 Reimbursable civilian full-time equivalent employment	4	4	4

WORKING CAPITAL FUND

Program and Financing (in millions of dollars)

Identification code 068–4565–0–4–304		2021 actual	2022 est.	2023 est.
	Obligations by program activity:			
0801	ETSD Operations	265	275	288
0802	Postage	1	1	2
0804	eRelocation	27	37	40
0805	COOP	1	1	1
0806	Background Investigations	7	10	12
0808	Legal Services	5	6	8
0810	Cincy VoIP	2	3	4
0811	Regional IT	7	8	10
0812	Enterprise HR	6	7	9
0813	Agency wide Contracts	3	4	6
0814	Budget Formulation	2	3	5
0815	Financial and Administrative Service	20	24	29
0900	Total new obligations, unexpired accounts	346	379	414
	Budgetary resources:			
	Unobligated balance:			
1000	Unobligated balance brought forward, Oct 1	72	71	81
1021	Recoveries of prior year unpaid obligations	13	10	10
1070	Unobligated balance (total)	85	81	91
	Budget authority:			
	Spending authority from offsetting collections, discretionary:			
1700	Collected	323	379	414
1701	Change in uncollected payments, Federal sources	9		
1750	Spending auth from offsetting collections, disc (total)	332	379	414
1930	Total budgetary resources available	417	460	505
	Memorandum (non-add) entries:			
1941	Unexpired unobligated balance, end of year	71	81	91
	Change in obligated balance:			
	Unpaid obligations:			
3000	Unpaid obligations, brought forward, Oct 1	153	185	204
3010	New obligations, unexpired accounts	346	379	414
3020	Outlays (gross)	–301	–350	–386
3040	Recoveries of prior year unpaid obligations, unexpired	–13	–10	–10
3050	Unpaid obligations, end of year	185	204	222
	Uncollected payments:			
3060	Uncollected pymts, Fed sources, brought forward, Oct 1	–138	–147	–147
3070	Change in uncollected pymts, Fed sources, unexpired	–9		
3090	Uncollected pymts, Fed sources, end of year	–147	–147	–147
	Memorandum (non-add) entries:			
3100	Obligated balance, start of year	15	38	57
3200	Obligated balance, end of year	38	57	75
	Budget authority and outlays, net:			
	Discretionary:			
4000	Budget authority, gross	332	379	414
	Outlays, gross:			
4010	Outlays from new discretionary authority	188	265	290
4011	Outlays from discretionary balances	113	85	96
4020	Outlays, gross (total)	301	350	386
	Offsets against gross budget authority and outlays:			
	Offsetting collections (collected) from:			
4030	Federal sources	–323	–379	–414
4040	Offsets against gross budget authority and outlays (total)	–323	–379	–414
	Additional offsets against gross budget authority only:			
4050	Change in uncollected pymts, Fed sources, unexpired	–9		
4080	Outlays, net (discretionary)	–22	–29	–28
4180	Budget authority, net (total)			
4190	Outlays, net (total)	–22	–29	–28

The Environmental Protection Agency (EPA) received authority to establish a Working Capital Fund (WCF) and was designated a pilot franchise fund under Public Law 103–356, the Government Management and Reform Act of 1994. EPA received permanent authority for the WCF in Public Law 105–65, as part of an effort to increase competition for governmental administrative services. The Modernizing Government Technology (MGT) Act (Public Law 115–91) provided additional authority for information technology development activities in agency working capital funds. EPA's WCF became operational in 1997 and funds the following main activities: information technology services, agency postage costs, Cincinnati voice services background investigations, and enterprise human resources IT services managed by the Office of Mission Support; financial and administrative systems, employee relocations, and a budget formulation system managed by the Office of the Chief Financial Officer; the Agency's Continuity of Operations (COOP) site managed by the Office of Land and Emergency Management; legal services managed by the Office of General Counsel; regional information technology service and support managed by EPA Region 8; and multimedia and agency servicing contracts managed by the Office of the Administrator. The 2023 amount reflects only base resources and may change during the year in accordance with programmatic needs.

Object Classification (in millions of dollars)

Identification code 068–4565–0–4–304		2021 actual	2022 est.	2023 est.
	Reimbursable obligations:			
	Personnel compensation:			
11.1	Full-time permanent	26	36	46
11.5	Other personnel compensation	1	1	1
11.9	Total personnel compensation	27	37	47
12.1	Civilian personnel benefits	31	41	46
23.1	Rental payments to GSA	2	3	5
23.3	Communications, utilities, and miscellaneous charges	6	7	7
25.1	Advisory and assistance services	16	17	18
25.2	Other services from non-Federal sources	66	70	73
25.3	Other goods and services from Federal sources	173	175	180
25.7	Operation and maintenance of equipment	12	14	15
26.0	Supplies and materials	1	2	4
31.0	Equipment	12	13	19
99.9	Total new obligations, unexpired accounts	346	379	414

Employment Summary

Identification code 068–4565–0–4–304	2021 actual	2022 est.	2023 est.
2001 Reimbursable civilian full-time equivalent employment	218	252	285

Trust Funds

HAZARDOUS SUBSTANCE SUPERFUND

(INCLUDING TRANSFERS OF FUNDS)

For necessary expenses to carry out the Comprehensive Environmental Response, Compensation, and Liability Act of 1980 (CERCLA), including sections 111(c)(3), (c)(5), (c)(6), and (e)(4) (42 U.S.C. 9611), and hire, maintenance, and operation of aircraft, $1,154,168,000, to remain available until expended, consisting of such sums as are available in and not already appropriated from the Trust Fund on September 30, 2022, as authorized by section 517(a) of the Superfund Amendments and Reauthorization Act of 1986 (SARA) and up to $1,154,168,000 as a payment from general revenues to the Hazardous Substance Superfund for purposes as authorized by section 517(b) of SARA: Provided, That funds appropriated under this heading may be allocated to other Federal agencies in accordance with section 111(a) of CERCLA: Provided further, That of the funds appropriated under this heading, $12,062,000 shall be paid to the "Office of Inspector General" appropriation to remain available until September 30, 2024, and $31,368,000 shall be paid to the "Science and Technology" appropriation, to remain available until September 30, 2024: Provided further, That of the amounts provided under this heading for Superfund—Enforcement, up to eleven percent shall be transferred to "Department of Justice—Legal Activities—Salaries and Expenses—General Legal Activities" and shall remain available until expended for expenses of CERCLA-related activities conducted by the Environment and Natural Resources Division on behalf of the Environmental Protection Agency.

Note.—A full-year 2022 appropriation for this account was not enacted at the time the Budget was prepared; therefore, the Budget assumes this account is operating under the Continuing

ENVIRONMENTAL PROTECTION AGENCY

Appropriations Act, 2022 (Division A of Public Law 117–43, as amended). The amounts included for 2022 reflect the annualized level provided by the continuing resolution.

HAZARDOUS SUBSTANCE SUPERFUND

[(INCLUDING TRANSFERS OF FUNDS)]

[For an additional amount for "Hazardous Substance Superfund", $3,500,000,000, to remain available until expended, consisting of such sums as are available in the Trust Fund on September 30, 2021, as authorized by section 517(a) of the Superfund Amendments and Reauthorization Act of 1986 (SARA) and up to $3,500,000,000 as a payment from general revenues to the Hazardous Substance Superfund for purposes as authorized by section 517(b) of SARA, for all costs associated with Superfund: Remedial activities: *Provided*, That in providing technical and project implementation assistance for amounts made available under this heading in this Act, the Administrator shall consider the unique needs of Tribal communities with contaminated sites where the potentially responsible parties cannot pay or cannot be identified, but shall not alter the process for prioritizing site cleanups: *Provided further*, That amounts provided under this heading in this Act shall be in addition to amounts otherwise available for such purposes: *Provided further*, That amounts provided under this heading in this Act shall not be subject to cost share requirements under section 104(c)(3) of the Comprehensive Environmental Response, Compensation, and Liability Act of 1980 (CERCLA) (42 U.S.C. 9604(c)(3)): *Provided further*, That the Administrator of the Environmental Protection Agency shall annually report to Congress on the status of funded projects: *Provided further*, That one-half of one percent of the amounts made available under this heading in this Act in each of fiscal years 2022 through 2026 shall be transferred to the Office of Inspector General of the Environmental Protection Agency for oversight of funding provided to the Environmental Protection Agency in this title in this Act: *Provided further*, That such amount is designated by the Congress as being for an emergency requirement pursuant to section 4112(a) of H. Con. Res. 71 (115th Congress), the concurrent resolution on the budget for fiscal year 2018, and to section 251(b) of the Balanced Budget and Emergency Deficit Control Act of 1985.] *(Infrastructure Investments and Jobs Appropriations Act.)*

Special and Trust Fund Receipts (in millions of dollars)

Identification code 068–8145–0–7–304		2021 actual	2022 est.	2023 est.
0100	Balance, start of year	75	85	458
	Receipts:			
	Current law:			
1110	Excise Taxes, Hazardous Substance Superfund	....	388	1,574
1110	Fines and Penalties, and Miscellaneous, Hazardous Substance Superfund	2	4	4
1130	Recoveries, Hazardous Substance Superfund	44	36	36
1130	Future Clean Up Cost Settlements, Hazardous Substance Superfund Trust Fund	206	350	350
1140	Interest and Profits on Investments, Hazardous Substance Superfund	65	84	86
1140	Interest and Profits on Investments, Hazardous Substance Superfund	12	16	16
1140	Interfund Transactions, Hazardous Substance Superfund	....	3,443	....
1140	Interfund Transactions, Hazardous Substance Superfund	1,153	1,206	1,542
1199	Total current law receipts	1,482	5,527	3,608
	Proposed:			
1210	Excise Taxes, Hazardous Substance Superfund	....	....	85
1999	Total receipts	1,482	5,527	3,693
2000	Total: Balances and receipts	1,557	5,612	4,151
	Appropriations:			
	Current law:			
2101	Hazardous Substance Superfund	–1,163	–4,645	–1,093
2101	Hazardous Substance Superfund	–12	–12	–12
2101	Hazardous Substance Superfund	–31	–31	–31
2101	Hazardous Substance Superfund	....	....	–388
2101	Hazardous Substance Superfund	....	–18	....
2101	Hazardous Substance Superfund	....	....	–18
2101	Hazardous Substance Superfund	–270	–350	–350
2101	Hazardous Substance Superfund	....	–100	–102
2103	Hazardous Substance Superfund	....	–4	–6
2132	Hazardous Substance Superfund	4	6	6
2199	Total current law appropriations	–1,472	–5,154	–1,994
2999	Total appropriations	–1,472	–5,154	–1,994
5099	Balance, end of year	85	458	2,157

Program and Financing (in millions of dollars)

Identification code 068–8145–0–7–304		2021 actual	2022 est.	2023 est.
	Obligations by program activity:			
0001	Core Mission	937	1,997	1,936
0002	Cooperative Federalism	3	5	5
0003	Rule of Law and Process	392	903	1,040
0004	Enforcement Transfer to DOJ	....	....	18
0100	Subtotal direct program	1,332	2,905	2,999
0799	Total direct obligations	1,332	2,905	2,999
0801	Hazardous Substance Superfund (Reimbursable)	364	295	295
0900	Total new obligations, unexpired accounts	1,696	3,200	3,294
	Budgetary resources:			
	Unobligated balance:			
1000	Unobligated balance brought forward, Oct 1	3,604	3,555	5,775
1001	Discretionary unobligated balance brought fwd, Oct 1	188	....	....
1021	Recoveries of prior year unpaid obligations	137	200	200
1033	Recoveries of prior year paid obligations	14	....	....
1070	Unobligated balance (total)	3,755	3,755	5,975
	Budget authority:			
	Appropriations, discretionary:			
1101	Appropriation (special or trust)	1,163	4,645	1,093
1101	Appropriation (special or trust fund) IG Transfer	12	12	12
1101	Appropriation (special or trust fund) S&T Transfer	31	31	31
1101	Appropriation (special or trust) Excise Tax	....	....	388
1101	Appropriation (special or trust) IIJA IG Transfer	....	18	....
1101	Appropriation (special or trust) Transfer to DOJ	....	....	18
1160	Appropriation, discretionary (total)	1,206	4,706	1,542
	Appropriations, mandatory:			
1201	Appropriation [Special Account Collections]	270	350	350
1201	Appropriation [Special Account Interest]	....	100	102
1203	Appropriation (previously unavailable)(special or trust)	....	4	6
1232	Appropriations temporarily reduced - Sequester	–4	–6	–6
1260	Appropriations, mandatory (total)	266	448	452
	Spending authority from offsetting collections, discretionary:			
1700	Collected	10	66	66
1701	Change in uncollected payments, Federal sources	14	....	....
1750	Spending auth from offsetting collections, disc (total)	24	66	66
1900	Budget authority (total)	1,496	5,220	2,060
1930	Total budgetary resources available	5,251	8,975	8,035
	Memorandum (non-add) entries:			
1941	Unexpired unobligated balance, end of year	3,555	5,775	4,741
	Change in obligated balance:			
	Unpaid obligations:			
3000	Unpaid obligations, brought forward, Oct 1	1,414	1,568	2,999
3010	New obligations, unexpired accounts	1,696	3,200	3,294
3020	Outlays (gross)	–1,405	–1,569	–2,610
3040	Recoveries of prior year unpaid obligations, unexpired	–137	–200	–200
3050	Unpaid obligations, end of year	1,568	2,999	3,483
	Uncollected payments:			
3060	Uncollected pymts, Fed sources, brought forward, Oct 1	–8	–22	–22
3070	Change in uncollected pymts, Fed sources, unexpired	–14	....	....
3090	Uncollected pymts, Fed sources, end of year	–22	–22	–22
	Memorandum (non-add) entries:			
3100	Obligated balance, start of year	1,406	1,546	2,977
3200	Obligated balance, end of year	1,546	2,977	3,461
	Budget authority and outlays, net:			
	Discretionary:			
4000	Budget authority, gross	1,230	4,772	1,608
	Outlays, gross:			
4010	Outlays from new discretionary authority	566	387	430
4011	Outlays from discretionary balances	512	817	1,803
4020	Outlays, gross (total)	1,078	1,204	2,233
	Offsets against gross budget authority and outlays:			
	Offsetting collections (collected) from:			
4030	Federal sources	–1	–16	–16
4033	Non-Federal sources	–23	–50	–50
4040	Offsets against gross budget authority and outlays (total)	–24	–66	–66
	Additional offsets against gross budget authority only:			
4050	Change in uncollected pymts, Fed sources, unexpired	–14	....	....
4053	Recoveries of prior year paid obligations, unexpired accounts	14	....	....
4070	Budget authority, net (discretionary)	1,206	4,706	1,542
4080	Outlays, net (discretionary)	1,054	1,138	2,167

Environmental Protection Agency—Continued
Trust Funds—Continued

HAZARDOUS SUBSTANCE SUPERFUND—Continued
Program and Financing—Continued

Identification code 068–8145–0–7–304		2021 actual	2022 est.	2023 est.
	Mandatory:			
4090	Budget authority, gross	266	448	452
	Outlays, gross:			
4100	Outlays from new mandatory authority	71	117	119
4101	Outlays from mandatory balances	256	248	258
4110	Outlays, gross (total)	327	365	377
4180	Budget authority, net (total)	1,472	5,154	1,994
4190	Outlays, net (total)	1,381	1,503	2,544
	Memorandum (non-add) entries:			
5000	Total investments, SOY: Federal securities: Par value	4,933	5,048	7,246
5001	Total investments, EOY: Federal securities: Par value	5,048	7,246	3,806

This appropriation provides funds for the implementation of the Comprehensive Environmental Response, Compensation and Liability Act of 1980, as amended (CERCLA). This appropriation supports core Environmental Protection Agency (EPA) programs.

To preserve and restore land and to protect human health and the environment, EPA reduces the risks posed by releases of hazardous substances, pollutants, and contaminants, and protects against unacceptable exposure by cleaning up contaminated sites and restoring ground water to beneficial use. EPA applies the most effective and scientifically sound methods to address the risks associated with the presence of hazardous substances, pollutants, and contaminants, improve response capabilities, and maximize the effectiveness of response and cleanup actions. Cleanup and response activity at contaminated sites addresses environmental concerns, such as the removal of contaminated soil and treatment of contaminated groundwater, to reduce human exposures to hazardous substances, pollutants, and contaminants, and to provide long-term human health protection. EPA works to ensure that all releases of hazardous substances, pollutants, and contaminants into the environment are appropriately addressed by responding to incidents and providing technical support. To prepare for and respond to incidents of national significance, EPA includes among its efforts improving decontamination readiness. EPA conducts research to improve methods and models and to accelerate scientifically defensible and cost-effective decisions for cleanup at complex contaminated sites in accordance with CERCLA. EPA also works to maximize responsible parties' participation in site cleanups and pursue greater recovery of EPA's cleanup costs.

EPA protects communities and helps return contaminated properties to productive use by ensuring that responsible parties pay for and/or conduct cleanups. The enforcement program recovers Federal cleanup funds from responsible parties to save taxpayer dollars. The goal is to maximize the participation of liable and viable parties in performing and paying for cleanups in both the remedial and removal programs. EPA investigates and refers for prosecution criminal and civil violations of CERCLA.

EPA's internal operations programs provide centralized management services to ensure that EPA is fulfilling its mission. The offices and the functions they perform within the Superfund appropriation are: the Office of the Administrator (environmental justice); the Office of Chief Financial Officer (strategic planning, annual planning and budgeting, financial services, and financial management, analysis, and accountability); the Office of General Counsel (alternate dispute resolution and legal advice); and the Office of Mission Support (facilities infrastructure and operations; acquisition management; human resources management services; grant and interagency agreement management; suspension and debarment; exchange network; information security; and information technology/data management) Because these centralized services provide support across EPA, the internal operations programs are funded across EPA's appropriations.

Status of Funds (in millions of dollars)

Identification code 068–8145–0–7–304		2021 actual	2022 est.	2023 est.
	Unexpended balance, start of year:			
0100	Balance, start of year	5,085	5,186	9,210
0999	Total balance, start of year	5,085	5,186	9,210
	Cash income during the year:			
	Current law:			
	Receipts:			
1110	Excise Taxes, Hazardous Substance Superfund		388	1,574
1110	Fines and Penalties, and Miscellaneous, Hazardous Substance Superfund	2	4	4
1130	Hazardous Substance Superfund	23	50	50
1130	Recoveries, Hazardous Substance Superfund	44	36	36
1130	Future Clean Up Cost Settlements, Hazardous Substance Superfund Trust Fund	206	350	350
1150	Interest and Profits on Investments, Hazardous Substance Superfund	65	84	86
1150	Interest and Profits on Investments, Hazardous Substance Superfund	12	16	16
1160	Hazardous Substance Superfund	1	16	16
1160	Interfund Transactions, Hazardous Substance Superfund	1,153	1,206	1,542
1160	Interfund Transactions, Hazardous Substance Superfund		3,443	
1199	Income under present law	1,506	5,593	3,674
	Proposed:			
1210	Excise Taxes, Hazardous Substance Superfund			85
1299	Income proposed			85
1999	Total cash income	1,506	5,593	3,759
	Cash outgo during year:			
	Current law:			
2100	Hazardous Substance Superfund [Budget Acct]	–1,405	–1,569	–2,610
2199	Outgo under current law	–1,405	–1,569	–2,610
2999	Total cash outgo (–)	–1,405	–1,569	–2,610
	Surplus or deficit:			
3110	Excluding interest	24	3,924	1,047
3120	Interest	77	100	102
3199	Subtotal, surplus or deficit	101	4,024	1,149
3999	Total change in fund balance	101	4,024	1,149
	Unexpended balance, end of year:			
4100	Uninvested balance (net), end of year	138	1,964	6,553
4200	Hazardous Substance Superfund	5,048	7,246	3,806
4999	Total balance, end of year	5,186	9,210	10,359

Object Classification (in millions of dollars)

Identification code 068–8145–0–7–304		2021 actual	2022 est.	2023 est.
	Direct obligations:			
	Personnel compensation:			
11.1	Full-time permanent	299	342	342
11.3	Other than full-time permanent	5	6	6
11.5	Other personnel compensation	9	12	12
11.9	Total personnel compensation	313	360	360
12.1	Civilian personnel benefits	113	126	126
13.0	Benefits for former personnel	1	1	1
21.0	Travel and transportation of persons	4	7	14
23.1	Rental payments to GSA	40	106	109
23.2	Rental payments to others	1	2	2
23.3	Communications, utilities, and miscellaneous charges	3	5	5
25.1	Advisory and assistance services	71	113	116
25.2	Other services from non-Federal sources	490	1,516	1,569
25.3	Other goods and services	203	461	477
25.4	Operation and maintenance of facilities	6	16	16
25.7	Operation and maintenance of equipment	5	18	19
26.0	Supplies and materials	3	7	4
31.0	Equipment	10	18	9
41.0	Grants, subsidies, and contributions	63	135	140
42.0	Insurance claims and indemnities	6	14	14
94.0	Financial transfers			18
99.0	Direct obligations	1,332	2,905	2,999
99.0	Reimbursable obligations	364	295	295
99.9	Total new obligations, unexpired accounts	1,696	3,200	3,294

ENVIRONMENTAL PROTECTION AGENCY

Employment Summary

Identification code 068–8145–0–7–304	2021 actual	2022 est.	2023 est.
1001 Direct civilian full-time equivalent employment	2,419	2,744	2,744
1101 Direct military average strength employment	5	5	5
2001 Reimbursable civilian full-time equivalent employment	98	98	98

LEAKING UNDERGROUND STORAGE TANK TRUST FUND PROGRAM

For necessary expenses to carry out leaking underground storage tank cleanup activities authorized by subtitle I of the Solid Waste Disposal Act, $93,814,000, to remain available until expended, of which $67,145,000 shall be for carrying out leaking underground storage tank cleanup activities authorized by section 9003(h) of the Solid Waste Disposal Act; $26,669,000 shall be for carrying out the other provisions of the Solid Waste Disposal Act specified in section 9508(c) of the Internal Revenue Code: Provided, That the Administrator is authorized to use appropriations made available under this heading to implement section 9013 of the Solid Waste Disposal Act to provide financial assistance to federally recognized Indian tribes for the development and implementation of programs to manage underground storage tanks.

Note.—A full-year 2022 appropriation for this account was not enacted at the time the Budget was prepared; therefore, the Budget assumes this account is operating under the Continuing Appropriations Act, 2022 (Division A of Public Law 117–43, as amended). The amounts included for 2022 reflect the annualized level provided by the continuing resolution.

Special and Trust Fund Receipts (in millions of dollars)

Identification code 068–8153–0–7–999	2021 actual	2022 est.	2023 est.
0100 Balance, start of year	827	977	1,080
Receipts:			
Current law:			
1110 Transfer from the General Fund Amounts Equivalent to Taxes, Leaking Underground Storage Tank Trust Fund	242	194	193
1140 Earnings on Investments, Leaking Underground Storage Tank Trust Fund	....	1	1
1199 Total current law receipts	242	195	194
1999 Total receipts	242	195	194
2000 Total: Balances and receipts	1,069	1,172	1,274
Appropriations:			
Current law:			
2101 Leaking Underground Storage Tank Trust Fund	–92	–92	–94
5099 Balance, end of year	977	1,080	1,180

Program and Financing (in millions of dollars)

Identification code 068–8153–0–7–999	2021 actual	2022 est.	2023 est.
Obligations by program activity:			
0001 Core Mission	90	90	91
0003 Rule of Law and Process	3	3	3
0900 Total new obligations, unexpired accounts	93	93	94
Budgetary resources:			
Unobligated balance:			
1000 Unobligated balance brought forward, Oct 1	5	7	9
1021 Recoveries of prior year unpaid obligations	3	3	3
1070 Unobligated balance (total)	8	10	12
Budget authority:			
Appropriations, discretionary:			
1101 Appropriation (special or trust)	92	92	94
1900 Budget authority (total)	92	92	94
1930 Total budgetary resources available	100	102	106
Memorandum (non-add) entries:			
1941 Unexpired unobligated balance, end of year	7	9	12
Change in obligated balance:			
Unpaid obligations:			
3000 Unpaid obligations, brought forward, Oct 1	91	97	98
3010 New obligations, unexpired accounts	93	93	94
3020 Outlays (gross)	–84	–89	–91
3040 Recoveries of prior year unpaid obligations, unexpired	–3	–3	–3
3050 Unpaid obligations, end of year	97	98	98
Memorandum (non-add) entries:			
3100 Obligated balance, start of year	91	97	98
3200 Obligated balance, end of year	97	98	98
Budget authority and outlays, net:			
Discretionary:			
4000 Budget authority, gross	92	92	94
Outlays, gross:			
4010 Outlays from new discretionary authority	19	28	29
4011 Outlays from discretionary balances	65	61	62
4020 Outlays, gross (total)	84	89	91
4180 Budget authority, net (total)	92	92	94
4190 Outlays, net (total)	84	89	91
Memorandum (non-add) entries:			
5000 Total investments, SOY: Federal securities: Par value	895	1,037	1,190
5001 Total investments, EOY: Federal securities: Par value	1,037	1,190	1,340

The Leaking Underground Storage Tank (LUST) Trust Fund, authorized by the Superfund Amendments and Reauthorization Act of 1986, as amended by the Omnibus Budget Reconciliation Act of 1990, the Taxpayer Relief Act of 1997, the Energy Policy Act (EPAct) of 2005, the Moving Ahead for Progress in the 21st Century Act (MAP-21), and the Fixing America's Surface Transportation Act (FAST Act), provides funds for preventing and responding to releases from underground storage tanks. The Trust Fund is financed by a 0.1 cent per gallon tax on motor fuels through September 30, 2022.

LUST funds are allocated to States through cooperative agreements to clean up sites posing the greatest threat to human health and the environment as authorized under section 9003(h) of the Solid Waste Disposal Act of 1965, as amended, and also to implement the activities authorized by Title XV, Subtitle B of EPAct. Funds also are used for grants to non-state entities under section 8001 of the Resource Conservation and Recovery Act of 1976, as amended. Federally recognized Tribes receive grant funding under Public Law 105–276. The Environmental Protection Agency (EPA) supports oversight, clean-up, and enforcement programs which are implemented by the States. LUST Trust Fund dollars can be used for state-led clean-ups and for State oversight of responsible party clean-ups. The LUST program promotes effective responses to releases from federally regulated underground storage tanks containing petroleum by enhancing State, local, and tribal enforcement and response capability. This appropriation supports core agency programs.

To protect the Nation's groundwater and drinking water from petroleum releases from Underground Storage Tanks (UST), EPA provides compliance assistance tools, technical assistance and training to promote and enforce UST systems compliance and clean-ups. EPA also focuses its LUST research efforts on assessing sites and evaluating the implications of alternative remediation technologies, policies, and management actions to assess and cleanup leaks at fueling stations.

EPA's internal operations programs provide centralized management services to ensure that EPA is fulfilling its mission. The offices and the functions they perform are: Office of Mission Support (facilities infrastructure and operations, and acquisition management); and the Office of Chief Financial Officer (strategic planning; annual planning and budgeting; financial services; and financial management, analysis, and accountability).

Status of Funds (in millions of dollars)

Identification code 068–8153–0–7–999	2021 actual	2022 est.	2023 est.
Unexpended balance, start of year:			
0100 Balance, start of year	923	1,081	1,187
0999 Total balance, start of year	923	1,081	1,187
Cash income during the year:			
Current law:			
Receipts:			
1110 Transfer from the General Fund Amounts Equivalent to Taxes, Leaking Underground Storage Tank Trust Fund	242	194	193
1150 Earnings on Investments, Leaking Underground Storage Tank Trust Fund	....	1	1
1199 Income under present law	242	195	194
1999 Total cash income	242	195	194

Environmental Protection Agency—Continued
Trust Funds—Continued

LEAKING UNDERGROUND STORAGE TANK TRUST FUND PROGRAM—Continued

Status of Funds—Continued

Identification code 068–8153–0–7–999		2021 actual	2022 est.	2023 est.
	Cash outgo during year:			
	Current law:			
2100	Leaking Underground Storage Tank Trust Fund [Budget Acct]	–84	–89	–91
2199	Outgo under current law	–84	–89	–91
2999	Total cash outgo (–)	–84	–89	–91
	Surplus or deficit:			
3110	Excluding interest	158	105	102
3120	Interest	....	1	1
3199	Subtotal, surplus or deficit	158	106	103
3999	Total change in fund balance	158	106	103
	Unexpended balance, end of year:			
4100	Uninvested balance (net), end of year	44	–3	–50
4200	Leaking Underground Storage Tank Trust Fund	1,037	1,190	1,340
4999	Total balance, end of year	1,081	1,187	1,290

Object Classification (in millions of dollars)

Identification code 068–8153–0–7–999		2021 actual	2022 est.	2023 est.
	Direct obligations:			
11.1	Personnel compensation: Full-time permanent	5	5	5
12.1	Civilian personnel benefits	2	2	2
23.1	Rental payments to GSA	1	1	1
25.1	Advisory and assistance services	1	1	1
25.2	Other services from non-Federal sources	1	1	1
25.3	Other goods and services from Federal sources	1	1	1
41.0	Grants, subsidies, and contributions	82	82	83
99.9	Total new obligations, unexpired accounts	93	93	94

Employment Summary

Identification code 068–8153–0–7–999		2021 actual	2022 est.	2023 est.
1001	Direct civilian full-time equivalent employment	43	43	47

INLAND OIL SPILL PROGRAMS

For expenses necessary to carry out the Environmental Protection Agency's responsibilities under the Oil Pollution Act of 1990, including hire, maintenance, and operation of aircraft, $26,502,000, to be derived from the Oil Spill Liability trust fund, to remain available until expended.

Note.—A full-year 2022 appropriation for this account was not enacted at the time the Budget was prepared; therefore, the Budget assumes this account is operating under the Continuing Appropriations Act, 2022 (Division A of Public Law 117–43, as amended). The amounts included for 2022 reflect the annualized level provided by the continuing resolution.

Program and Financing (in millions of dollars)

Identification code 068–8221–0–7–304		2021 actual	2022 est.	2023 est.
	Obligations by program activity:			
0001	Core Mission	15	15	22
0003	Rule of Law and Process	4	5	5
0100	Direct Program	19	20	27
0799	Total direct obligations	19	20	27
0801	Inland Oil Spill Programs (Reimbursable)	18	18	18
0900	Total new obligations, unexpired accounts	37	38	45
	Budgetary resources:			
	Unobligated balance:			
1000	Unobligated balance brought forward, Oct 1	48	53	50
1021	Recoveries of prior year unpaid obligations	3	3	3
1070	Unobligated balance (total)	51	56	53
	Budget authority:			
	Appropriations, discretionary:			
1101	Appropriation (special or trust)	20	20	27
	Spending authority from offsetting collections, discretionary:			
1700	Collected [Offsetting Collections]	23	12	12
1701	Change in uncollected payments, Federal sources	–4	....	....
1750	Spending auth from offsetting collections, disc (total)	19	12	12
1900	Budget authority (total)	39	32	39
1930	Total budgetary resources available	90	88	92
	Memorandum (non-add) entries:			
1941	Unexpired unobligated balance, end of year	53	50	47
	Change in obligated balance:			
	Unpaid obligations:			
3000	Unpaid obligations, brought forward, Oct 1	18	23	29
3010	New obligations, unexpired accounts	37	38	45
3020	Outlays (gross)	–29	–29	–38
3040	Recoveries of prior year unpaid obligations, unexpired	–3	–3	–3
3050	Unpaid obligations, end of year	23	29	33
	Uncollected payments:			
3060	Uncollected pymts, Fed sources, brought forward, Oct 1	–54	–50	–50
3070	Change in uncollected pymts, Fed sources, unexpired	4	....	....
3090	Uncollected pymts, Fed sources, end of year	–50	–50	–50
	Memorandum (non-add) entries:			
3100	Obligated balance, start of year	–36	–27	–21
3200	Obligated balance, end of year	–27	–21	–17
	Budget authority and outlays, net:			
	Discretionary:			
4000	Budget authority, gross	39	32	39
	Outlays, gross:			
4010	Outlays from new discretionary authority	19	21	25
4011	Outlays from discretionary balances	10	8	13
4020	Outlays, gross (total)	29	29	38
	Offsets against gross budget authority and outlays:			
	Offsetting collections (collected) from:			
4030	Federal sources	–23	–12	–12
4040	Offsets against gross budget authority and outlays (total)	–23	–12	–12
	Additional offsets against gross budget authority only:			
4050	Change in uncollected pymts, Fed sources, unexpired	4	....	....
4070	Budget authority, net (discretionary)	20	20	27
4080	Outlays, net (discretionary)	6	17	26
4180	Budget authority, net (total)	20	20	27
4190	Outlays, net (total)	6	17	26

This appropriation provides for the Environmental Protection Agency's (EPA) responsibilities for prevention, preparedness, response, and enforcement activities authorized under the Federal Water Pollution Control Act, as amended by the Oil Pollution Act of 1990 (OPA). This appropriation supports core Agency programs.

EPA's Oil Spill program protects U.S. waters by preventing, preparing for, responding to, and monitoring oil discharges. Under the regulatory framework established by the Spill Prevention, Control, and Countermeasure (SPCC) and Federal Response Plan (FRP) regulations, EPA conducts oil spill prevention, preparedness, inspection, and enforcement activities associated with more than 600,000 non-transportation-related oil storage facilities. The National Oil and Hazardous Substances Pollution Contingency Plan (NCP) identifies EPA's jurisdiction over inland oil spills and sets forth the framework for response. EPA accesses the Oil Spill Liability Trust Fund, administered by the U.S. Coast Guard, to obtain reimbursement for site-specific spill response activities. More than 30,000 oil and hazardous substance discharges occur in the United States every year, with a significant portion of these discharges occurring in the inland zone over which EPA has jurisdiction.

EPA develops and manages the regulations and protocols under Subpart J of the NCP which require manufacturers of various oil spill response products to test their products prior to listing on a Product Schedule. The Product Schedule identifies those oil spill remediation agents, such as dispersants and surface washing agents, which could be authorized for use by an On-Scene Coordinator (OSC) on an oil discharge. Product testing ensures their effectiveness and provides toxicity information used by OSCs and Regional Response Teams in making informed decisions regarding the use of certain products in response to specific spills. EPA focuses its oil spill research efforts on human health impacts, ecological effects, and shoreline and coastal impacts from oil discharges and use of dispersants and other chemical agents, as well as spill remediation alternatives and innovative technology development and evaluation, including green technologies. Spill response is a priority for the Agency, and EPA has been instrumental in providing guidance for various response technologies. A key factor in providing guidance on spill response technologies is developing a firm understanding of the science behind spill behavior in the environment.

Appropriated funds for the Inland Oil Spill Programs support work designed to prevent oil spills using civil enforcement and compliance assistance approaches, as well as to prepare for and respond to any oil discharges affecting the inland waters of the United States. Pursuant to Clean Water Act section 311 (Oil Spill and Hazardous Substances Liability) requirements, EPA's Civil Enforcement program develops policies; issues administrative clean-up and removal orders and orders protecting public health; pursues administrative remedies and/or refers civil judicial actions to the Department of Justice; assesses civil penalties for discharges into the environment or violations of administrative orders or oil pollution prevention regulations; assists regulated entities in understanding their legal requirements under the Clean Water Act; and assists in the recovery of clean-up costs expended by the Government.

EPA's internal operations programs provide centralized management services to ensure that EPA is fulfilling is mission. The office and function is Office of Mission Support (facilities infrastructure and operations).

Object Classification (in millions of dollars)

Identification code 068–8221–0–7–304		2021 actual	2022 est.	2023 est.
	Direct obligations:			
	Personnel compensation:			
11.1	Full-time permanent	10	11	13
11.5	Other personnel compensation	1		
11.9	Total personnel compensation	11	11	13
12.1	Civilian personnel benefits	3	3	5
23.1	Rental payments to GSA	1	1	2
25.1	Advisory and assistance services	1	2	3
25.2	Other services from non-Federal sources	3	3	4
99.0	Direct obligations	19	20	27
99.0	Reimbursable obligations	18	18	18
99.9	Total new obligations, unexpired accounts	37	38	45

Employment Summary

Identification code 068–8221–0–7–304	2021 actual	2022 est.	2023 est.
1001 Direct civilian full-time equivalent employment	72	72	94
2001 Reimbursable civilian full-time equivalent employment	5	5	5

GENERAL FUND RECEIPT ACCOUNTS

(in millions of dollars)

		2021 actual	2022 est.	2023 est.
Offsetting receipts from the public:				
068–143500	General Fund Proprietary Interest Receipts, not Otherwise Classified	1	1	1
068–268330	Water Infrastructure Finance and Innovation Downward Reestimate Receipt Account		1	
068–322000	All Other General Fund Proprietary Receipts Including Budget Clearing Accounts	–25	1	1
068–322900	Cellulosic Biofuel Waiver Credits, Renewal Fuel Program	2	1	1
General Fund Offsetting receipts from the public		–22	4	3
Intragovernmental payments:				
068–388500	Undistributed Intragovernmental Payments and Receivables from Cancelled Accounts	24		
General Fund Intragovernmental payments		24		

ADMINISTRATIVE PROVISIONS—ENVIRONMENTAL PROTECTION AGENCY

(INCLUDING TRANSFERS OF FUNDS)

For fiscal year 2023, notwithstanding 31 U.S.C. 6303(1) and 6305(1), the Administrator of the Environmental Protection Agency, in carrying out the Agency's function to implement directly Federal environmental programs required or authorized by law in the absence of an acceptable tribal program, may award cooperative agreements to federally recognized Indian tribes or Intertribal consortia, if authorized by their member tribes, to assist the Administrator in implementing Federal environmental programs for Indian tribes required or authorized by law, except that no such cooperative agreements may be awarded from funds designated for State financial assistance agreements.

The Administrator of the Environmental Protection Agency is authorized to collect and obligate pesticide registration service fees in accordance with section 33 of the Federal Insecticide, Fungicide, and Rodenticide Act (7 U.S.C. 136w–8): Provided, That such fees collected shall remain available until expended.

Notwithstanding section 33(d)(2) of the Federal Insecticide, Fungicide, and Rodenticide Act (FIFRA) (7 U.S.C. 136w–8(d)(2)), the Administrator of the Environmental Protection Agency may assess fees under section 33 of FIFRA (7 U.S.C. 136w–8) for fiscal year 2023.

Notwithstanding any other provision of law, in addition to the activities specified in section 33 of Federal Insecticide, Fungicide, and Rodenticide Act (FIFRA) (7 U.S.C. 136w–8), fees collected in this and prior fiscal years under such section shall be available for the following activities as they relate to pesticide licensing: processing and review of data submitted in association with a registration, information submitted pursuant to section 6(a)(2) of FIFRA (7 U.S.C. 136d(a)(2)), supplemental distributor labels, transfers of registration and data compensation rights, additional uses registered by states under section 24(c) of FIFRA (7 U.S.C. 136v(c)), data compensation petitions, reviews of minor amendments, and notifications; review of applications for emergency exemptions under section 18 of FIFRA (7 U.S.C. 136p) and ensuing data collection activities; laboratory support and audits; administrative support; risk communication activities; development of policy and guidance; rulemaking support; information collection activities; and the portions of salaries related to work in these areas.

The Administrator is authorized to transfer up to $340,110,000 of the funds appropriated for the Great Lakes Restoration Initiative under the heading "Environmental Programs and Management" to the head of any Federal department or agency, with the concurrence of such head, to carry out activities that would support the Great Lakes Restoration Initiative and Great Lakes Water Quality Agreement programs, projects, or activities; to enter into an interagency agreement with the head of such Federal department or agency to carry out these activities; and to make grants to governmental entities, nonprofit organizations, institutions, and individuals for planning, research, monitoring, outreach, and implementation in furtherance of the Great Lakes Restoration Initiative and the Great Lakes Water Quality Agreement.

The Science and Technology, Environmental Programs and Management, Office of Inspector General, Hazardous Substance Superfund, and Leaking Underground Storage Tank Trust Fund Program Accounts, are available for the construction, alteration, repair, rehabilitation, and renovation of facilities, provided that the cost does not exceed $350,000 per project.

The Administrator of the Environmental Protection Agency is authorized to collect and obligate fees in accordance with section 3024 of the Solid Waste Disposal Act (42 U.S.C. 6939g) for fiscal year 2023: Provided, That such fees collected shall remain available expended.

The Administrator of the Environmental Protection Agency is authorized to collect and obligate fees in accordance with section 26(b) of the Toxic Substances Control Act (15 U.S.C. 2625(b)) for fiscal year 2023: Provided, That such fees collected shall remain available until expended.

For fiscal year 2023, and notwithstanding section 518(f) of the Federal Water Pollution Control Act (33 U.S.C. 1377(f)), the Administrator is authorized to use the amounts appropriated for any fiscal year under section 319 of the Act to make grants to Indian tribes pursuant to sections 319(h) and 518(e) of that Act.

The Administrator is authorized to use the amounts appropriated under the heading "Environmental Programs and Management" for fiscal year 2023 to provide grants to implement the Southeastern New England Watershed Restoration Program.

Notwithstanding the limitations on amounts in section 320(i)(2)(B) of the Federal Water Pollution Control Act, not less than $1,500,000 of the funds made available under this title for the National Estuary Program shall be for making competitive awards described in section 320(g)(4).

For fiscal years 2023 through 2027, the Office of Chemical Safety and Pollution Prevention and the Office of Water may, using funds appropriated under the headings "Environmental Programs and Management" and "Science and Technology", contract directly with individuals or indirectly with institutions or nonprofit organizations, *without regard to 41 U.S.C. 5, for the temporary or intermittent personal services of students or recent graduates, who shall be considered employees for the purposes of chapters 57 and 81 of title 5, United States Code, relating to compensation for travel and work injuries, and chapter 171 of title 28, United States Code, relating to tort claims, but shall not be considered to be Federal employees for any other purpose: Provided, That amounts used for this purpose by the Office of Chemical Safety and Pollution Prevention and the Office of Water collectively may not exceed $2,000,000 per year.*

The appropriation provided by 42 U.S.C. 9622(b)(3) is available for the hire, maintenance, and operation of aircraft.

The Environmental Protection Agency Working Capital Fund, 42 U.S.C. 4370e, is available for expenses and equipment necessary for modernization and development of information technology of, or for use by, the Environmental Protection Agency.

The Administrator may, after consultation with the Office of Personnel Management, employ up to seventy-five persons at any one time in the Office of Research and Development and twenty-five persons at any one time in the Office of Chemical Safety and Pollution under the authority provided in 42 U.S.C. 209, through fiscal year 2025.

GENERAL PROVISIONS—ENVIRONMENTAL PROTECTION AGENCY

[(INCLUDING TRANSFERS OF FUNDS)]

[SEC. 611. Funds made available to the Environmental Protection Agency by this Act for salaries, expenses, and administration purposes may be transferred to the "Environmental Programs and Management" account or the "Science and Technology" account as needed for such purposes.]

[SEC. 612. Not later than 90 days after the date of enactment of this Act, the Administrator of the Environmental Protection Agency shall submit to the House and Senate Committees on Appropriations a detailed spend plan for the funds provided to the Environmental Protection Agency in this title for fiscal year 2022, and for each fiscal year through 2026, as part of the annual budget submission of the President under section 1105(a) of title 31, United States Code, the Administrator of the Environmental Protection Agency shall submit a detailed spend plan for the funds provided to the Environmental Protection Agency in this title for that fiscal year.]

[SEC. 613. For this fiscal year and each fiscal year thereafter, such sums as are available in the Hazardous Substance Superfund established under section 9507 of the Internal Revenue Code of 1986 at the end of the preceding fiscal year from taxes received in the Treasury under subsection (b)(1) of such section shall be available, without further appropriation, to be used to carry out the Comprehensive Environmental Response, Compensation, and Liability Act of 1980 (42 U.S.C. 9601 et seq.).]

[SEC. 614. (a) DRINKING WATER.—There is authorized to be appropriated to carry out the purposes of section 1452 of the Safe Drinking Water Act (42 U.S.C. 300j–12), in addition to amounts otherwise authorized to be appropriated for those purposes, an additional $1,126,000,000 for each of fiscal years 2022 through 2026.

(b) CLEAN WATER.—There is authorized to be appropriated to carry out the purposes of title VI of the Federal Water Pollution Control Act (33 U.S.C. 1381 et seq.), in addition to amounts otherwise authorized to be appropriated for those purposes, an additional $1,639,000,000 for each of fiscal years 2022 through 2026.]

(Infrastructure Investments and Jobs Appropriations Act.)

EXECUTIVE OFFICE OF THE PRESIDENT

THE WHITE HOUSE
Federal Funds

SALARIES AND EXPENSES

For necessary expenses for the White House as authorized by law, including not to exceed $3,850,000 for services as authorized by 5 U.S.C. 3109 and 3 U.S.C. 105; subsistence expenses as authorized by 3 U.S.C. 105, which shall be expended and accounted for as provided in that section; hire of passenger motor vehicles, and travel (not to exceed $100,000 to be expended and accounted for as provided by 3 U.S.C. 103); and not to exceed $19,000 pursuant to 3 U.S.C. 105(d)(4), to be available for allocation within the Executive Office of the President; and for necessary expenses of the Office of Policy Development, including services as authorized by 5 U.S.C. 3109 and 3 U.S.C. 107, $77,681,000.

Note.—A full-year 2022 appropriation for this account was not enacted at the time the Budget was prepared; therefore, the Budget assumes this account is operating under the Continuing Appropriations Act, 2022 (Division A of Public Law 117–43, as amended). The amounts included for 2022 reflect the annualized level provided by the continuing resolution.

Program and Financing (in millions of dollars)

Identification code 011–0209–0–1–802	2021 actual	2022 est.	2023 est.
Obligations by program activity:			
0001 Salaries and expenses	71	60	78
0801 The White House (Reimbursable)	1	3	3
0900 Total new obligations, unexpired accounts	72	63	81
Budgetary resources:			
Budget authority:			
Appropriations, discretionary:			
1100 Appropriation	55	60	78
1121 Appropriations transferred from other acct [011–0108]	3		
1160 Appropriation, discretionary (total)	58	60	78
Appropriations, mandatory:			
1200 Appropriation	13		
Spending authority from offsetting collections, discretionary:			
1700 Collected	1	3	3
1900 Budget authority (total)	72	63	81
1930 Total budgetary resources available	72	63	81
Change in obligated balance:			
Unpaid obligations:			
3000 Unpaid obligations, brought forward, Oct 1	8	15	4
3010 New obligations, unexpired accounts	72	63	81
3011 Obligations ("upward adjustments"), expired accounts	3		
3020 Outlays (gross)	–65	–74	–80
3041 Recoveries of prior year unpaid obligations, expired	–3		
3050 Unpaid obligations, end of year	15	4	5
Memorandum (non-add) entries:			
3100 Obligated balance, start of year	8	15	4
3200 Obligated balance, end of year	15	4	5
Budget authority and outlays, net:			
Discretionary:			
4000 Budget authority, gross	59	63	81
Outlays, gross:			
4010 Outlays from new discretionary authority	54	60	77
4011 Outlays from discretionary balances	6	14	3
4020 Outlays, gross (total)	60	74	80
Offsets against gross budget authority and outlays:			
Offsetting collections (collected) from:			
4030 Federal sources	–2	–3	–3
Additional offsets against gross budget authority only:			
4052 Offsetting collections credited to expired accounts	1		
4070 Budget authority, net (discretionary)	58	60	78
4080 Outlays, net (discretionary)	58	71	77
Mandatory:			
4090 Budget authority, gross	13		
Outlays, gross:			
4100 Outlays from new mandatory authority	5		
4180 Budget authority, net (total)	71	60	78
4190 Outlays, net (total)	63	71	77

These funds provide the President with staff assistance and provide administrative services for the direct support of the President, to include support for the offices and councils in the White House as directed by the President.

Object Classification (in millions of dollars)

Identification code 011–0209–0–1–802	2021 actual	2022 est.	2023 est.
Direct obligations:			
11.1 Personnel compensation: Full-time permanent	43	39	47
12.1 Civilian personnel benefits	14	13	17
21.0 Travel and transportation of persons	1	1	3
23.3 Communications, utilities, and miscellaneous charges		1	1
24.0 Printing and reproduction		1	1
25.2 Other services from non-Federal sources	11	4	8
26.0 Supplies and materials	1	1	1
99.0 Direct obligations	70	60	78
99.0 Reimbursable obligations	1	3	3
99.5 Adjustment for rounding	1		
99.9 Total new obligations, unexpired accounts	72	63	81

Employment Summary

Identification code 011–0209–0–1–802	2021 actual	2022 est.	2023 est.
1001 Direct civilian full-time equivalent employment	432	462	486

EXECUTIVE RESIDENCE AT THE WHITE HOUSE
Federal Funds

OPERATING EXPENSES

For necessary expenses of the Executive Residence at the White House, $15,609,000, to be expended and accounted for as provided by 3 U.S.C. 105, 109, 110, and 112–114.

REIMBURSABLE EXPENSES

For the reimbursable expenses of the Executive Residence at the White House, such sums as may be necessary: Provided, That all reimbursable operating expenses of the Executive Residence shall be made in accordance with the provisions of this paragraph: Provided further, That, notwithstanding any other provision of law, such amount for reimbursable operating expenses shall be the exclusive authority of the Executive Residence to incur obligations and to receive offsetting collections, for such expenses: Provided further, That the Executive Residence shall require each person sponsoring a reimbursable political event to pay in advance an amount equal to the estimated cost of the event, and all such advance payments shall be credited to this account and remain available until expended: Provided further, That the Executive Residence shall require the national committee of the political party of the President to maintain on deposit $25,000, to be separately accounted for and available for expenses relating to reimbursable political events sponsored by such committee during such fiscal year: Provided further, That the Executive Residence shall ensure that a written notice of any amount owed for a reimbursable operating expense under this paragraph is submitted to the person owing such amount within 60 days after such expense is incurred, and that such amount is collected within 30 days after the submission of such notice: Provided further, That the Executive Residence shall charge interest and assess penalties and other charges on any such amount that is not reimbursed within such 30 days, in accordance with the interest and penalty provisions applicable to an outstanding debt on a United States Government claim under 31 U.S.C. 3717: Provided further, That each such amount that is reimbursed, and any accompanying interest and charges, shall be deposited in the Treasury as miscellaneous receipts: Provided further, That the Executive Residence shall prepare and submit to the Committees on Appropriations, by not later than 90 days after the end of the fiscal year covered by this Act, a report setting forth the reimbursable operating expenses of the Executive Residence during the preceding fiscal year, including the total amount of such expenses, the amount of such total that consists of reimbursable official and ceremonial events, the amount of such total that consists of reimbursable political events, and the portion of each such amount that has been reimbursed as of the date of the report: Provided further, That the Executive Residence shall maintain a system for the tracking of expenses related to reimbursable events within the Executive Residence that includes a standard for the classification of any such expense as political or nonpolitical: Provided further, That no provision of this paragraph may be construed to exempt

Executive Residence at the White House—Continued
Federal Funds—Continued

OPERATING EXPENSES—Continued

the Executive Residence from any other applicable requirement of subchapter I or II of chapter 37 of title 31, United States Code.

Note.—A full-year 2022 appropriation for this account was not enacted at the time the Budget was prepared; therefore, the Budget assumes this account is operating under the Continuing Appropriations Act, 2022 (Division A of Public Law 117–43, as amended). The amounts included for 2022 reflect the annualized level provided by the continuing resolution.

Program and Financing (in millions of dollars)

Identification code 011–0210–0–1–802	2021 actual	2022 est.	2023 est.
Obligations by program activity:			
0001 Operating Expenses (Direct)	14	14	16
0831 Operating Expenses (Reimbursable)	3	5	7
0900 Total new obligations, unexpired accounts	17	19	23
Budgetary resources:			
Budget authority:			
Appropriations, discretionary:			
1100 Appropriation	14	14	16
Spending authority from offsetting collections, discretionary:			
1700 Collected	3	5	7
1701 Change in uncollected payments, Federal sources	2		
1750 Spending auth from offsetting collections, disc (total)	5	5	7
1900 Budget authority (total)	19	19	23
1930 Total budgetary resources available	19	19	23
Memorandum (non-add) entries:			
1940 Unobligated balance expiring	–2		
Change in obligated balance:			
Unpaid obligations:			
3000 Unpaid obligations, brought forward, Oct 1	4	4	4
3010 New obligations, unexpired accounts	17	19	23
3011 Obligations ("upward adjustments"), expired accounts	1		
3020 Outlays (gross)	–17	–19	–22
3041 Recoveries of prior year unpaid obligations, expired	–1		
3050 Unpaid obligations, end of year	4	4	5
Uncollected payments:			
3060 Uncollected pymts, Fed sources, brought forward, Oct 1	–6	–4	–4
3070 Change in uncollected pymts, Fed sources, unexpired	–2		
3071 Change in uncollected pymts, Fed sources, expired	4		
3090 Uncollected pymts, Fed sources, end of year	–4	–4	–4
Memorandum (non-add) entries:			
3100 Obligated balance, start of year	–2		
3200 Obligated balance, end of year			1
Budget authority and outlays, net:			
Discretionary:			
4000 Budget authority, gross	19	19	23
Outlays, gross:			
4010 Outlays from new discretionary authority	14	15	19
4011 Outlays from discretionary balances	3	4	3
4020 Outlays, gross (total)	17	19	22
Offsets against gross budget authority and outlays:			
Offsetting collections (collected) from:			
4030 Federal sources	–3	–3	–5
4033 Non-Federal sources	–2	–2	–2
4040 Offsets against gross budget authority and outlays (total)	–5	–5	–7
Additional offsets against gross budget authority only:			
4050 Change in uncollected pymts, Fed sources, unexpired	–2		
4052 Offsetting collections credited to expired accounts	2		
4070 Budget authority, net (discretionary)	14	14	16
4080 Outlays, net (discretionary)	12	14	15
4180 Budget authority, net (total)	14	14	16
4190 Outlays, net (total)	12	14	15

These funds provide for the care, maintenance, and operation of the Executive Residence.

Object Classification (in millions of dollars)

Identification code 011–0210–0–1–802	2021 actual	2022 est.	2023 est.
Direct obligations:			
11.1 Personnel compensation: Full-time permanent	8	8	9
12.1 Civilian personnel benefits	3	3	4
23.3 Communications, utilities, and miscellaneous charges	1	1	1
25.2 Other services from non-Federal sources	1	1	1
26.0 Supplies and materials	1	1	1
99.0 Direct obligations	14	14	16
99.0 Reimbursable obligations	3	5	7
99.9 Total new obligations, unexpired accounts	17	19	23

Employment Summary

Identification code 011–0210–0–1–802	2021 actual	2022 est.	2023 est.
1001 Direct civilian full-time equivalent employment	83	89	98

WHITE HOUSE REPAIR AND RESTORATION

For the repair, alteration, and improvement of the Executive Residence at the White House pursuant to 3 U.S.C. 105(d), $2,500,000, to remain available until expended, for required maintenance, resolution of safety and health issues, and continued preventative maintenance.

Note.—A full-year 2022 appropriation for this account was not enacted at the time the Budget was prepared; therefore, the Budget assumes this account is operating under the Continuing Appropriations Act, 2022 (Division A of Public Law 117–43, as amended). The amounts included for 2022 reflect the annualized level provided by the continuing resolution.

Program and Financing (in millions of dollars)

Identification code 011–0109–0–1–802	2021 actual	2022 est.	2023 est.
Obligations by program activity:			
0001 White House Repair and Restoration (Direct)	2	3	3
0900 Total new obligations, unexpired accounts (object class 25.2)	2	3	3
Budgetary resources:			
Unobligated balance:			
1000 Unobligated balance brought forward, Oct 1	3	4	4
Budget authority:			
Appropriations, discretionary:			
1100 Appropriation	3	3	3
1930 Total budgetary resources available	6	7	7
Memorandum (non-add) entries:			
1941 Unexpired unobligated balance, end of year	4	4	4
Change in obligated balance:			
Unpaid obligations:			
3010 New obligations, unexpired accounts	2	3	3
3020 Outlays (gross)	–2	–3	–3
Budget authority and outlays, net:			
Discretionary:			
4000 Budget authority, gross	3	3	3
Outlays, gross:			
4010 Outlays from new discretionary authority		3	3
4011 Outlays from discretionary balances	2		
4020 Outlays, gross (total)	2	3	3
4180 Budget authority, net (total)	3	3	3
4190 Outlays, net (total)	2	3	3

These funds provide for the repair, alteration, and improvement of the Executive Residence at the White House.

SPECIAL ASSISTANCE TO THE PRESIDENT AND THE OFFICIAL RESIDENCE OF THE VICE PRESIDENT

Federal Funds

SALARIES AND EXPENSES

SPECIAL ASSISTANCE TO THE PRESIDENT

For necessary expenses to enable the Vice President to provide assistance to the President in connection with specially assigned functions; services as authorized by 5 U.S.C. 3109 and 3 U.S.C. 106, including subsistence expenses as authorized by 3 U.S.C. 106, which shall be expended and accounted for as provided in that section; and hire of passenger motor vehicles, $6,076,000.

OPERATING EXPENSES

(INCLUDING TRANSFER OF FUNDS)

For the care, operation, refurnishing, improvement, and to the extent not otherwise provided for, heating and lighting, including electric power and fixtures, of the official residence of the Vice President; the hire of passenger motor vehicles; and not to exceed $90,000 pursuant to 3 U.S.C. 106(b)(2), $321,000: Provided, That advances, repayments, or transfers from this appropriation may be made to any department or agency for expenses of carrying out such activities.

Note.—A full-year 2022 appropriation for this account was not enacted at the time the Budget was prepared; therefore, the Budget assumes this account is operating under the Continuing Appropriations Act, 2022 (Division A of Public Law 117–43, as amended). The amounts included for 2022 reflect the annualized level provided by the continuing resolution.

Program and Financing (in millions of dollars)

Identification code 011–1454–0–1–802	2021 actual	2022 est.	2023 est.
Obligations by program activity:			
0001 Special Assistance to the President and the Official Residence O (Direct)	4	5	6
0801 Special Assistance to the President and the Official Residence O (Reimbursable)	1	1	1
0900 Total new obligations, unexpired accounts	5	6	7
Budgetary resources:			
Unobligated balance:			
1000 Unobligated balance brought forward, Oct 1		1	1
Budget authority:			
Appropriations, discretionary:			
1100 Appropriation	5	5	6
Spending authority from offsetting collections, discretionary:			
1700 Collected	1	1	1
1900 Budget authority (total)	6	6	7
1930 Total budgetary resources available	6	7	8
Memorandum (non-add) entries:			
1941 Unexpired unobligated balance, end of year	1	1	1
Change in obligated balance:			
Unpaid obligations:			
3000 Unpaid obligations, brought forward, Oct 1	1		
3010 New obligations, unexpired accounts	5	6	7
3020 Outlays (gross)	–6	–6	–7
Memorandum (non-add) entries:			
3100 Obligated balance, start of year	1		
Budget authority and outlays, net:			
Discretionary:			
4000 Budget authority, gross	6	6	7
Outlays, gross:			
4010 Outlays from new discretionary authority	5	6	7
4011 Outlays from discretionary balances	1		
4020 Outlays, gross (total)	6	6	7
Offsets against gross budget authority and outlays:			
Offsetting collections (collected) from:			
4030 Federal sources	–1	–1	–1
4180 Budget authority, net (total)	5	5	6
4190 Outlays, net (total)	5	5	6

These funds are used by the Vice President to carry out responsibilities assigned to the Vice President by the President and by various statutes. These funds also provide for the care and operation of the Vice President's official residence.

Object Classification (in millions of dollars)

Identification code 011–1454–0–1–802	2021 actual	2022 est.	2023 est.
Direct obligations:			
11.1 Personnel compensation: Full-time permanent	3	3	3
12.1 Civilian personnel benefits	1	1	1
21.0 Travel and transportation of persons			1
25.2 Other services from non-Federal sources			1
99.0 Direct obligations	4	4	6
99.0 Reimbursable obligations		1	1
99.5 Adjustment for rounding	1	1	
99.9 Total new obligations, unexpired accounts	5	6	7

Employment Summary

Identification code 011–1454–0–1–802	2021 actual	2022 est.	2023 est.
1001 Direct civilian full-time equivalent employment	21	23	27

COUNCIL OF ECONOMIC ADVISERS

Federal Funds

SALARIES AND EXPENSES

For necessary expenses of the Council of Economic Advisers in carrying out its functions under the Employment Act of 1946 (15 U.S.C. 1021 et seq.), $4,903,000.

Note.—A full-year 2022 appropriation for this account was not enacted at the time the Budget was prepared; therefore, the Budget assumes this account is operating under the Continuing Appropriations Act, 2022 (Division A of Public Law 117–43, as amended). The amounts included for 2022 reflect the annualized level provided by the continuing resolution.

Program and Financing (in millions of dollars)

Identification code 011–1900–0–1–802	2021 actual	2022 est.	2023 est.
Obligations by program activity:			
0001 Salaries and Expenses (Direct)	3	4	5
Budgetary resources:			
Budget authority:			
Appropriations, discretionary:			
1100 Appropriation	4	4	5
1930 Total budgetary resources available	4	4	5
Memorandum (non-add) entries:			
1940 Unobligated balance expiring	–1		
Change in obligated balance:			
Unpaid obligations:			
3000 Unpaid obligations, brought forward, Oct 1	1		
3010 New obligations, unexpired accounts	3	4	5
3020 Outlays (gross)	–4	–4	–5
Memorandum (non-add) entries:			
3100 Obligated balance, start of year	1		
Budget authority and outlays, net:			
Discretionary:			
4000 Budget authority, gross	4	4	5
Outlays, gross:			
4010 Outlays from new discretionary authority	3	3	4
4011 Outlays from discretionary balances	1	1	1
4020 Outlays, gross (total)	4	4	5
4180 Budget authority, net (total)	4	4	5
4190 Outlays, net (total)	4	4	5

The Council of Economic Advisers analyzes the national economy and its various segments, advises the President on economic developments, recommends policies for economic growth and stability, appraises economic programs and policies of the Federal Government, and assists in preparation of the annual Economic Report of the President to the Congress.

Object Classification (in millions of dollars)

Identification code 011–1900–0–1–802	2021 actual	2022 est.	2023 est.
Direct obligations:			
11.1 Personnel compensation: Full-time permanent	2	3	3
12.1 Civilian personnel benefits	1	1	1
99.0 Direct obligations	3	4	4
99.5 Adjustment for rounding			1
99.9 Total new obligations, unexpired accounts	3	4	5

Employment Summary

Identification code 011–1900–0–1–802	2021 actual	2022 est.	2023 est.
1001 Direct civilian full-time equivalent employment	20	28	28

COUNCIL ON ENVIRONMENTAL QUALITY AND OFFICE OF ENVIRONMENTAL QUALITY

Federal Funds

COUNCIL ON ENVIRONMENTAL QUALITY AND OFFICE OF ENVIRONMENTAL QUALITY

For necessary expenses to continue functions assigned to the Council on Environmental Quality and Office of Environmental Quality pursuant to the National Environmental Policy Act of 1969, the Environmental Quality Improvement Act of 1970, and Reorganization Plan No. 1 of 1977, and not to exceed $750 for official reception and representation expenses, $4,360,000: Provided, That notwithstanding section 202 of the National Environmental Policy Act of 1970, the Council shall consist of one member, appointed by the President, by and with the advice and consent of the Senate, serving as chairman and exercising all powers, functions, and duties of the Council.

Note.—A full-year 2022 appropriation for this account was not enacted at the time the Budget was prepared; therefore, the Budget assumes this account is operating under the Continuing Appropriations Act, 2022 (Division A of Public Law 117–43, as amended). The amounts included for 2022 reflect the annualized level provided by the continuing resolution.

Program and Financing (in millions of dollars)

Identification code 011–1453–0–1–802		2021 actual	2022 est.	2023 est.
	Obligations by program activity:			
0001	Council on Environmental Quality and Office of Environmental Quality	3	4	4
	Budgetary resources:			
	Unobligated balance:			
1000	Unobligated balance brought forward, Oct 1		1	1
	Budget authority:			
	Appropriations, discretionary:			
1100	Appropriation	4	4	4
1930	Total budgetary resources available	4	5	5
	Memorandum (non-add) entries:			
1941	Unexpired unobligated balance, end of year	1	1	1
	Change in obligated balance:			
	Unpaid obligations:			
3000	Unpaid obligations, brought forward, Oct 1			1
3010	New obligations, unexpired accounts	3	4	4
3020	Outlays (gross)	–3	–3	–4
3050	Unpaid obligations, end of year		1	1
	Memorandum (non-add) entries:			
3100	Obligated balance, start of year			1
3200	Obligated balance, end of year		1	1
	Budget authority and outlays, net:			
	Discretionary:			
4000	Budget authority, gross	4	4	4
	Outlays, gross:			
4010	Outlays from new discretionary authority	3	3	3
4011	Outlays from discretionary balances			1
4020	Outlays, gross (total)	3	3	4
4180	Budget authority, net (total)	4	4	4
4190	Outlays, net (total)	3	3	4

This appropriation provides funds for the Council on Environmental Quality and the Office of Environmental Quality to serve as the focal point for environmental policy development within the Administration and conduct compliance oversight activities under the National Environmental Policy Act (NEPA).

Object Classification (in millions of dollars)

Identification code 011–1453–0–1–802		2021 actual	2022 est.	2023 est.
	Direct obligations:			
11.1	Personnel compensation: Full-time permanent	2	2	3
12.1	Civilian personnel benefits	1	1	1
99.0	Direct obligations	3	3	4
99.5	Adjustment for rounding		1	
99.9	Total new obligations, unexpired accounts	3	4	4

Employment Summary

Identification code 011–1453–0–1–802		2021 actual	2022 est.	2023 est.
1001	Direct civilian full-time equivalent employment	14	17	22

MANAGEMENT FUND, OFFICE OF ENVIRONMENTAL QUALITY

Program and Financing (in millions of dollars)

Identification code 011–3963–0–1–802		2021 actual	2022 est.	2023 est.
	Obligations by program activity:			
0801	Management Fund, Office of Environmental Quality (Reimbursable)		1	3
0809	Reimbursable program activities, subtotal		1	3
0900	Total new obligations, unexpired accounts (object class 25.2)		1	3
	Budgetary resources:			
	Budget authority:			
	Spending authority from offsetting collections, discretionary:			
1700	Collected		1	3
1930	Total budgetary resources available		1	3
	Change in obligated balance:			
	Unpaid obligations:			
3010	New obligations, unexpired accounts		1	3
3020	Outlays (gross)		–1	–3
	Budget authority and outlays, net:			
	Discretionary:			
4000	Budget authority, gross		1	3
	Outlays, gross:			
4010	Outlays from new discretionary authority		1	3
	Offsets against gross budget authority and outlays:			
	Offsetting collections (collected) from:			
4030	Federal sources		–1	–3
4180	Budget authority, net (total)			
4190	Outlays, net (total)			

The Office of Environmental Quality Management Fund finances study contracts that are jointly sponsored by the Office of Environmental Quality and one or more other Federal agencies. The Management Fund also finances Federal interagency environmental projects (including task forces) in which the Office participates.

NATIONAL SECURITY COUNCIL AND HOMELAND SECURITY COUNCIL

Federal Funds

SALARIES AND EXPENSES

For necessary expenses of the National Security Council and the Homeland Security Council, including services as authorized by 5 U.S.C. 3109, $13,901,000, of which not to exceed $10,000 shall be available for official reception and representation expenses.

Note.—A full-year 2022 appropriation for this account was not enacted at the time the Budget was prepared; therefore, the Budget assumes this account is operating under the Continuing Appropriations Act, 2022 (Division A of Public Law 117–43, as amended). The amounts included for 2022 reflect the annualized level provided by the continuing resolution.

Program and Financing (in millions of dollars)

Identification code 011–2000–0–1–802		2021 actual	2022 est.	2023 est.
	Obligations by program activity:			
0001	National Security Council	12	12	14
0801	Salaries and Expenses (Reimbursable)		1	1
0900	Total new obligations, unexpired accounts	12	13	15
	Budgetary resources:			
	Budget authority:			
	Appropriations, discretionary:			
1100	Appropriation	12	12	14

EXECUTIVE OFFICE OF THE PRESIDENT

Office of the National Cyber Director
Federal Funds   1135

		2021 actual	2022 est.	2023 est.
	Spending authority from offsetting collections, discretionary:			
1700	Collected		1	1
1701	Change in uncollected payments, Federal sources	1		
1750	Spending auth from offsetting collections, disc (total)	1	1	1
1900	Budget authority (total)	13	13	15
1930	Total budgetary resources available	13	13	15
	Memorandum (non-add) entries:			
1940	Unobligated balance expiring	–1		
	Change in obligated balance:			
	Unpaid obligations:			
3000	Unpaid obligations, brought forward, Oct 1	3	2	1
3010	New obligations, unexpired accounts	12	13	15
3011	Obligations ("upward adjustments"), expired accounts	1		
3020	Outlays (gross)	–13	–14	–15
3041	Recoveries of prior year unpaid obligations, expired	–1		
3050	Unpaid obligations, end of year	2	1	1
	Uncollected payments:			
3060	Uncollected pymts, Fed sources, brought forward, Oct 1	–1	–2	–2
3070	Change in uncollected pymts, Fed sources, unexpired	–1		
3090	Uncollected pymts, Fed sources, end of year	–2	–2	–2
	Memorandum (non-add) entries:			
3100	Obligated balance, start of year	2		–1
3200	Obligated balance, end of year		–1	–1
	Budget authority and outlays, net:			
	Discretionary:			
4000	Budget authority, gross	13	13	15
	Outlays, gross:			
4010	Outlays from new discretionary authority	11	12	14
4011	Outlays from discretionary balances	2	2	1
4020	Outlays, gross (total)	13	14	15
	Offsets against gross budget authority and outlays:			
	Offsetting collections (collected) from:			
4030	Federal sources		–1	–1
4040	Offsets against gross budget authority and outlays (total)		–1	–1
	Additional offsets against gross budget authority only:			
4050	Change in uncollected pymts, Fed sources, unexpired	–1		
4060	Additional offsets against budget authority only (total)	–1		
4070	Budget authority, net (discretionary)	12	12	14
4080	Outlays, net (discretionary)	13	13	14
4180	Budget authority, net (total)	12	12	14
4190	Outlays, net (total)	13	13	14

The National Security Council and Homeland Security Council advise the President on the integration of domestic, foreign, and military policies relating to national security.

Object Classification (in millions of dollars)

Identification code 011–2000–0–1–802	2021 actual	2022 est.	2023 est.
Direct obligations:			
11.1 Personnel compensation: Full-time permanent	8	7	8
12.1 Civilian personnel benefits	2	2	3
21.0 Travel and transportation of persons	1	1	1
99.0 Direct obligations	11	10	12
99.0 Reimbursable obligations		1	1
99.5 Adjustment for rounding	1	2	2
99.9 Total new obligations, unexpired accounts	12	13	15

Employment Summary

Identification code 011–2000–0–1–802	2021 actual	2022 est.	2023 est.
1001 Direct civilian full-time equivalent employment	61	69	73

OFFICE OF THE NATIONAL CYBER DIRECTOR

Federal Funds

SALARIES AND EXPENSES

For necessary expenses of the Office of the National Cyber Director in carrying out the purposes of section 1752 of the National Defense Authorization Act for Fiscal Year 2021 (Public Law 116–283), $21,926,000, of which not to exceed $5,000 shall be available for official reception and representation expenses.

Note.—A full-year 2022 appropriation for this account was not enacted at the time the Budget was prepared; therefore, the Budget assumes this account is operating under the Continuing Appropriations Act, 2022 (Division A of Public Law 117–43, as amended). The amounts included for 2022 reflect the annualized level provided by the continuing resolution.

SALARIES AND EXPENSES

For an additional amount for "Office of the National Cyber Director", $21,000,000, to remain available until September 30, 2022, to carry out the purposes of section 1752 of the National Defense Authorization Act for Fiscal Year 2021 (Public Law 116–283): *Provided*, That such amount is designated by the Congress as being for an emergency requirement pursuant to section 4112(a) of H. Con. Res. 71 (115th Congress), the concurrent resolution on the budget for fiscal year 2018, and to section 251(b) of the Balanced Budget and Emergency Deficit Control Act of 1985. *(Infrastructure Investments and Jobs Appropriations Act.)*

Program and Financing (in millions of dollars)

Identification code 011–1800–0–1–802	2021 actual	2022 est.	2023 est.
Obligations by program activity:			
0001 Salaries and Expenses		21	22
Budgetary resources:			
Budget authority:			
Appropriations, discretionary:			
1100 Appropriation		21	22
1930 Total budgetary resources available		21	22
Change in obligated balance:			
Unpaid obligations:			
3000 Unpaid obligations, brought forward, Oct 1			6
3010 New obligations, unexpired accounts		21	22
3020 Outlays (gross)		–15	–26
3050 Unpaid obligations, end of year		6	2
Memorandum (non-add) entries:			
3100 Obligated balance, start of year			6
3200 Obligated balance, end of year		6	2
Budget authority and outlays, net:			
Discretionary:			
4000 Budget authority, gross		21	22
Outlays, gross:			
4010 Outlays from new discretionary authority		15	22
4011 Outlays from discretionary balances			4
4020 Outlays, gross (total)		15	26
4180 Budget authority, net (total)		21	22
4190 Outlays, net (total)		15	26

The National Cyber Director was created in the National Defense Authorization Act of 2021. The National Cyber Director advises the President on cybersecurity and related emerging technology issues and leads national level coordination of cybersecurity strategy and policy, including Executive Branch development of an integrated national cybersecurity strategy.

Object Classification (in millions of dollars)

Identification code 011–1800–0–1–802	2021 actual	2022 est.	2023 est.
Direct obligations:			
11.1 Personnel compensation: Full-time permanent		10	11
12.1 Civilian personnel benefits		4	4
23.1 Rental payments to GSA		3	3
25.3 Other goods and services from Federal sources		3	3
26.0 Supplies and materials		1	1
99.9 Total new obligations, unexpired accounts		21	22

Employment Summary

Identification code 011–1800–0–1–802	2021 actual	2022 est.	2023 est.
1001 Direct civilian full-time equivalent employment		75	77

OFFICE OF ADMINISTRATION
Federal Funds
SALARIES AND EXPENSES

For necessary expenses of the Office of Administration, including services as authorized by 5 U.S.C. 3109 and 3 U.S.C. 107, and hire of passenger motor vehicles, $115,463,000, of which not to exceed $12,800,000 shall remain available until expended for continued modernization of information resources within the Executive Office of the President.

Note.—A full-year 2022 appropriation for this account was not enacted at the time the Budget was prepared; therefore, the Budget assumes this account is operating under the Continuing Appropriations Act, 2022 (Division A of Public Law 117–43, as amended). The amounts included for 2022 reflect the annualized level provided by the continuing resolution.

Program and Financing (in millions of dollars)

Identification code 011–0038–0–1–802		2021 actual	2022 est.	2023 est.
	Obligations by program activity:			
0001	Salaries & Expenses	88	87	102
0013	Capital Investment Plan	8	13	13
0100	Direct program activities, subtotal	96	100	115
0799	Total direct obligations	96	100	115
0880	Salaries and Expenses (Reimbursable)	4	5	7
0900	Total new obligations, unexpired accounts	100	105	122
	Budgetary resources:			
	Unobligated balance:			
1000	Unobligated balance brought forward, Oct 1	22	26	26
	Budget authority:			
	Appropriations, discretionary:			
1100	Appropriation	100	100	115
	Spending authority from offsetting collections, discretionary:			
1700	Collected	4	5	7
1900	Budget authority (total)	104	105	122
1930	Total budgetary resources available	126	131	148
	Memorandum (non-add) entries:			
1941	Unexpired unobligated balance, end of year	26	26	26
	Change in obligated balance:			
	Unpaid obligations:			
3000	Unpaid obligations, brought forward, Oct 1	24	23	23
3010	New obligations, unexpired accounts	100	105	122
3011	Obligations ("upward adjustments"), expired accounts	2		
3020	Outlays (gross)	–100	–105	–117
3041	Recoveries of prior year unpaid obligations, expired	–3		
3050	Unpaid obligations, end of year	23	23	28
	Uncollected payments:			
3060	Uncollected pymts, Fed sources, brought forward, Oct 1	–2	–2	–2
3090	Uncollected pymts, Fed sources, end of year	–2	–2	–2
	Memorandum (non-add) entries:			
3100	Obligated balance, start of year	22	21	21
3200	Obligated balance, end of year	21	21	26
	Budget authority and outlays, net:			
	Discretionary:			
4000	Budget authority, gross	104	105	122
	Outlays, gross:			
4010	Outlays from new discretionary authority	77	79	92
4011	Outlays from discretionary balances	23	26	25
4020	Outlays, gross (total)	100	105	117
	Offsets against gross budget authority and outlays:			
	Offsetting collections (collected) from:			
4030	Federal sources	–4	–5	–7
4180	Budget authority, net (total)	100	100	115
4190	Outlays, net (total)	96	100	110

The Office of Administration's mission is to provide a full array of customer-based administrative services to all entities of the Executive Office of the President. These services, defined by Executive Order 12028 of 1977, include financial, personnel, library, information management systems, security and emergency preparedness, and general office administrative services.

Object Classification (in millions of dollars)

Identification code 011–0038–0–1–802		2021 actual	2022 est.	2023 est.
	Direct obligations:			
11.1	Personnel compensation: Full-time permanent	29	30	32
12.1	Civilian personnel benefits	10	11	13
23.1	Rental payments to GSA	19	20	20
25.2	Other services from non-Federal sources	33	34	43
26.0	Supplies and materials	2	2	2
31.0	Equipment	2	2	4
32.0	Land and structures	1		
99.0	Direct obligations	96	99	114
99.0	Reimbursable obligations	4	5	7
99.5	Adjustment for rounding		1	1
99.9	Total new obligations, unexpired accounts	100	105	122

Employment Summary

Identification code 011–0038–0–1–802		2021 actual	2022 est.	2023 est.
1001	Direct civilian full-time equivalent employment	235	245	245

PRESIDENTIAL TRANSITION ADMINISTRATIVE SUPPORT

Program and Financing (in millions of dollars)

Identification code 011–0108–0–1–802		2021 actual	2022 est.	2023 est.
	Obligations by program activity:			
0001	Administrative support	5		
	Budgetary resources:			
	Budget authority:			
	Appropriations, discretionary:			
1100	Appropriation	8		
1120	Appropriations transferred to other acct [011–0110]	–3		
1160	Appropriation, discretionary (total)	5		
1930	Total budgetary resources available	5		
	Change in obligated balance:			
	Unpaid obligations:			
3000	Unpaid obligations, brought forward, Oct 1		1	
3010	New obligations, unexpired accounts	5		
3020	Outlays (gross)	–4	–1	
3050	Unpaid obligations, end of year	1		
	Memorandum (non-add) entries:			
3100	Obligated balance, start of year		1	
3200	Obligated balance, end of year	1		
	Budget authority and outlays, net:			
	Discretionary:			
4000	Budget authority, gross	5		
	Outlays, gross:			
4010	Outlays from new discretionary authority	4		
4011	Outlays from discretionary balances		1	
4020	Outlays, gross (total)	4	1	
4180	Budget authority, net (total)	5		
4190	Outlays, net (total)	4	1	

Object Classification (in millions of dollars)

Identification code 011–0108–0–1–802		2021 actual	2022 est.	2023 est.
	Direct obligations:			
25.2	Other services from non-Federal sources	2		
31.0	Equipment	2		
99.0	Direct obligations	4		
99.5	Adjustment for rounding	1		
99.9	Total new obligations, unexpired accounts	5		

OFFICE OF MANAGEMENT AND BUDGET
Federal Funds
SALARIES AND EXPENSES

For necessary expenses of the Office of Management and Budget, including hire of passenger motor vehicles and services as authorized by 5 U.S.C. 3109, to carry out the provisions of chapter 35 of title 44, United States Code, and to prepare and submit the budget of the United States Government, in accordance with section 1105(a) of title 31, United States Code, $128,035,000, of which not to exceed $3,000 shall be available for official representation expenses.

Note.—A full-year 2022 appropriation for this account was not enacted at the time the Budget was prepared; therefore, the Budget assumes this account is operating under the Continuing Appropriations Act, 2022 (Division A of Public Law 117–43, as amended). The amounts included for 2022 reflect the annualized level provided by the continuing resolution.

Program and Financing (in millions of dollars)

Identification code 011–0300–0–1–802	2021 actual	2022 est.	2023 est.
Obligations by program activity:			
0001 National Security Programs	12	11	14
0002 Transportation, Homeland Security, Justice, and Services Programs	7	7	8
0003 Housing, Treasury, and Commerce Programs	5	5	6
0005 Climate, Energy, Environment, and Science Programs	11	11	13
0006 Health Programs	9	9	10
0007 Education, Income Maintenance, and Labor Programs	7	6	8
0008 Office of Federal Financial Management	4	4	5
0009 Information and Regulatory Affairs	12	12	15
0010 Office of Federal Procurement Policy	4	4	4
0011 OMB-wide Offices	36	38	45
0100 Direct program activities, subtotal	107	107	128
0799 Total direct obligations	107	107	128
0801 Reimbursable Program Activities	1	4	
0900 Total new obligations, unexpired accounts	108	111	128
Budgetary resources:			
Budget authority:			
Appropriations, discretionary:			
1100 Appropriation	107	107	128
Spending authority from offsetting collections, discretionary:			
1700 Collected	1	4	
1900 Budget authority (total)	108	111	128
1930 Total budgetary resources available	108	111	128
Change in obligated balance:			
Unpaid obligations:			
3000 Unpaid obligations, brought forward, Oct 1	11	11	10
3010 New obligations, unexpired accounts	108	111	128
3011 Obligations ("upward adjustments"), expired accounts	4		
3020 Outlays (gross)	–107	–112	–126
3041 Recoveries of prior year unpaid obligations, expired	–5		
3050 Unpaid obligations, end of year	11	10	12
Uncollected payments:			
3060 Uncollected pymts, Fed sources, brought forward, Oct 1	–2	–2	–2
3090 Uncollected pymts, Fed sources, end of year	–2	–2	–2
Memorandum (non-add) entries:			
3100 Obligated balance, start of year	9	9	8
3200 Obligated balance, end of year	9	8	10
Budget authority and outlays, net:			
Discretionary:			
4000 Budget authority, gross	108	111	128
Outlays, gross:			
4010 Outlays from new discretionary authority	98	102	117
4011 Outlays from discretionary balances	9	10	9
4020 Outlays, gross (total)	107	112	126
Offsets against gross budget authority and outlays:			
Offsetting collections (collected) from:			
4030 Federal sources	–1	–4	
4180 Budget authority, net (total)	107	107	128
4190 Outlays, net (total)	106	108	126

The Office of Management and Budget (OMB) assists the President in the discharge of budgetary, management, and other executive responsibilities.

National Security Programs; Transportation, Homeland Security, Justice, and Services Programs; Housing, Treasury, and Commerce Programs; Climate, Energy, Environment, and Science Programs; Health Programs; and Education, Income Maintenance, and Labor Programs.—These offices examine Federal agency programs, budget requests, and management activities, analyze legislation, apportion appropriations, study proposed changes in agency functions, and conduct special studies aimed at establishing goals and objectives that would result in long- and short-range improvements in the agencies' financial, administrative, and operational management.

Financial Management.—The OMB Office of Federal Financial Management develops and provides direction on the implementation of financial management policies and systems. This office also supports the effective and transparent use of Federal financial resources by improving the quality, utility, and transparency of financial information, and protecting against waste, fraud and abuse in the Federal government.

Information and Regulatory Affairs.—The OMB Office of Information and Regulatory Affairs reviews and coordinates agency proposals to implement or revise Federal regulations and information collection requirements. In addition, it analyses, develops, coordinates, and maintains information resources management and statistical policies and practices.

Procurement Policy.—The OMB Office of Federal Procurement Policy provides overall direction of Government-wide procurement policies, regulations, and procedures for executive agencies.

OMB-wide Offices.—These offices provide executive direction and coordination for all OMB activities. This includes the Director's Office; the Deputy Director, the Deputy Director for Management and the Executive Associate Director; Communications; General Counsel; Legislative Affairs; Economic Policy; Management and Operations Division; the Legislative Reference Division; the Budget Review Division; and the Performance and Personnel Management. In addition, these offices provide overall leadership for OMB's activities; develop instructions and procedures on a wide range of management, legislative, legal, economic, budgetary, administrative, and IT-related issues; coordinate OMB review of agency activities; and prepare the President's Budget documents.

Object Classification (in millions of dollars)

Identification code 011–0300–0–1–802	2021 actual	2022 est.	2023 est.
Direct obligations:			
11.1 Personnel compensation: Full-time permanent	68	68	79
12.1 Civilian personnel benefits	23	24	29
23.1 Rental payments to GSA	7	7	7
25.2 Other services from non-Federal sources	8	6	11
26.0 Supplies and materials	1	1	1
31.0 Equipment		1	1
99.0 Direct obligations	107	107	128
99.0 Reimbursable obligations	1	4	
99.9 Total new obligations, unexpired accounts	108	111	128

Employment Summary

Identification code 011–0300–0–1–802	2021 actual	2022 est.	2023 est.
1001 Direct civilian full-time equivalent employment	469	451	516

OFFICE OF NATIONAL DRUG CONTROL POLICY
Federal Funds
SALARIES AND EXPENSES

For necessary expenses of the Office of National Drug Control Policy; for research activities pursuant to the Office of National Drug Control Policy Reauthorization Act of 1998, as amended; not to exceed $10,000 for official reception and representation expenses; and for participation in joint projects or in the provision of services on matters of mutual interest with nonprofit, research, or public organizations or agencies, with or without reimbursement, $22,340,000: Provided, That the Office

Office of National Drug Control Policy—Continued
Federal Funds—Continued

SALARIES AND EXPENSES—Continued

is authorized to accept, hold, administer, and utilize gifts, both real and personal, public and private, without fiscal year limitation, for the purpose of aiding or facilitating the work of the Office.

Note.—A full-year 2022 appropriation for this account was not enacted at the time the Budget was prepared; therefore, the Budget assumes this account is operating under the Continuing Appropriations Act, 2022 (Division A of Public Law 117–43, as amended). The amounts included for 2022 reflect the annualized level provided by the continuing resolution.

Program and Financing (in millions of dollars)

Identification code 011–1457–0–1–802		2021 actual	2022 est.	2023 est.
	Obligations by program activity:			
0001	Operations	18	18	22
0801	Reimbursable program activity	3		
0900	Total new obligations, unexpired accounts	21	18	22
	Budgetary resources:			
	Budget authority:			
	Appropriations, discretionary:			
1100	Appropriation	18	18	22
	Spending authority from offsetting collections, discretionary:			
1700	Collected	3		
1900	Budget authority (total)	21	18	22
1930	Total budgetary resources available	21	18	22
	Change in obligated balance:			
	Unpaid obligations:			
3000	Unpaid obligations, brought forward, Oct 1	9	10	5
3010	New obligations, unexpired accounts	21	18	22
3011	Obligations ("upward adjustments"), expired accounts	1		
3020	Outlays (gross)	–20	–23	–22
3041	Recoveries of prior year unpaid obligations, expired	–1		
3050	Unpaid obligations, end of year	10	5	5
	Memorandum (non-add) entries:			
3100	Obligated balance, start of year	9	10	5
3200	Obligated balance, end of year	10	5	5
	Budget authority and outlays, net:			
	Discretionary:			
4000	Budget authority, gross	21	18	22
	Outlays, gross:			
4010	Outlays from new discretionary authority	15	14	18
4011	Outlays from discretionary balances	5	9	4
4020	Outlays, gross (total)	20	23	22
	Offsets against gross budget authority and outlays:			
	Offsetting collections (collected) from:			
4030	Federal sources	–3		
4180	Budget authority, net (total)	18	18	22
4190	Outlays, net (total)	17	23	22

The Office of National Drug Control Policy (ONDCP), pursuant to the Office of National Drug Control Policy Reauthorization Act of 1998, as amended, is charged with developing policies, objectives, and priorities for the National Drug Control Program. This account provides funding for personnel compensation, travel, rent, and other basic operations of the Office.

Object Classification (in millions of dollars)

Identification code 011–1457–0–1–802		2021 actual	2022 est.	2023 est.
	Direct obligations:			
11.1	Personnel compensation: Full-time permanent	9	11	12
12.1	Civilian personnel benefits	3	3	5
23.1	Rental payments to GSA	3	3	3
25.2	Other services from non-Federal sources	1		1
25.3	Other goods and services from Federal sources	2	1	1
99.0	Direct obligations	18	18	22
99.0	Reimbursable obligations	3		
99.9	Total new obligations, unexpired accounts	21	18	22

Employment Summary

Identification code 011–1457–0–1–802	2021 actual	2022 est.	2023 est.
1001 Direct civilian full-time equivalent employment	57	65	74

OFFICE OF SCIENCE AND TECHNOLOGY POLICY
Federal Funds

OFFICE OF SCIENCE AND TECHNOLOGY POLICY

For necessary expenses of the Office of Science and Technology Policy, in carrying out the purposes of the National Science and Technology Policy, Organization, and Priorities Act of 1976 (42 U.S.C. 6601 et seq.), hire of passenger motor vehicles, and services as authorized by section 3109 of title 5, United States Code, not to exceed $2,250 for official reception and representation expenses, and rental of conference rooms in the District of Columbia, $7,965,000.

Note.—A full-year 2022 appropriation for this account was not enacted at the time the Budget was prepared; therefore, the Budget assumes this account is operating under the Continuing Appropriations Act, 2022 (Division A of Public Law 117–43, as amended). The amounts included for 2022 reflect the annualized level provided by the continuing resolution.

Program and Financing (in millions of dollars)

Identification code 011–2600–0–1–802		2021 actual	2022 est.	2023 est.
	Obligations by program activity:			
0001	Office of Science and Technology Policy	5	6	8
	Budgetary resources:			
	Unobligated balance:			
1000	Unobligated balance brought forward, Oct 1		1	1
	Budget authority:			
	Appropriations, discretionary:			
1100	Appropriation	6	6	8
1930	Total budgetary resources available	6	7	9
	Memorandum (non-add) entries:			
1941	Unexpired unobligated balance, end of year	1	1	1
	Change in obligated balance:			
	Unpaid obligations:			
3000	Unpaid obligations, brought forward, Oct 1	1	1	1
3010	New obligations, unexpired accounts	5	6	8
3020	Outlays (gross)	–5	–6	–7
3050	Unpaid obligations, end of year	1	1	2
	Memorandum (non-add) entries:			
3100	Obligated balance, start of year	1	1	1
3200	Obligated balance, end of year	1	1	2
	Budget authority and outlays, net:			
	Discretionary:			
4000	Budget authority, gross	6	6	8
	Outlays, gross:			
4010	Outlays from new discretionary authority	4	5	6
4011	Outlays from discretionary balances	1	1	1
4020	Outlays, gross (total)	5	6	7
4180	Budget authority, net (total)	6	6	8
4190	Outlays, net (total)	5	6	7

The Office of Science and Technology Policy (OSTP) provides advice to the President concerning policies in science and technology and on the use of science and technology in addressing important national problems. The OSTP operations include support to other Executive Office of the President organizations on issues with science and technology considerations; with the Office of Management and Budget, review and analysis of and recommendations on research and development budgets for all Federal agencies; coordination of research and development programs of the Federal Government; coordination of the implementation of a number of important international science and technology agreements; and other activities necessary to carry out the duties, functions, and activities described in Public Law 94–282, the National Science and Technology Policy, Organization, and Priorities Act of 1976. OSTP also provides support for the National Science and Technology Council.

EXECUTIVE OFFICE OF THE PRESIDENT

Office of the United States Trade Representative
Federal Funds 1139

Object Classification (in millions of dollars)

Identification code 011–2600–0–1–802	2021 actual	2022 est.	2023 est.
Direct obligations:			
11.1 Personnel compensation: Full-time permanent	3	4	5
12.1 Civilian personnel benefits	1	1	2
25.2 Other services from non-Federal sources	1	1	1
99.0 Direct obligations	5	6	8
99.9 Total new obligations, unexpired accounts	5	6	8

Employment Summary

Identification code 011–2600–0–1–802	2021 actual	2022 est.	2023 est.
1001 Direct civilian full-time equivalent employment	22	33	46

NATIONAL SPACE COUNCIL

Federal Funds

NATIONAL SPACE COUNCIL

For necessary expenses of the National Space Council, in carrying out the purposes of title V of Public Law 100–685 and Executive Order No. 13803, hire of passenger motor vehicles, and services as authorized by section 3109 of title 5, United States Code, not to exceed $2,250 for official reception and representation expenses, $1,965,000: Provided, That notwithstanding any other provision of law, the National Space Council may accept personnel support from Federal agencies, departments, and offices, and such Federal agencies, departments, and offices may detail staff without reimbursement to the National Space Council for purposes provided herein.

Note.—A full-year 2022 appropriation for this account was not enacted at the time the Budget was prepared; therefore, the Budget assumes this account is operating under the Continuing Appropriations Act, 2022 (Division A of Public Law 117–43, as amended). The amounts included for 2022 reflect the annualized level provided by the continuing resolution.

Program and Financing (in millions of dollars)

Identification code 011–0048–0–1–802	2021 actual	2022 est.	2023 est.
Obligations by program activity:			
0001 National Space Council	2	2	2
Budgetary resources:			
Budget authority:			
Appropriations, discretionary:			
1100 Appropriation	2	2	2
1930 Total budgetary resources available	2	2	2
Change in obligated balance:			
Unpaid obligations:			
3000 Unpaid obligations, brought forward, Oct 1		2	
3010 New obligations, unexpired accounts	2	2	2
3020 Outlays (gross)		–4	–2
3050 Unpaid obligations, end of year	2		
Memorandum (non-add) entries:			
3100 Obligated balance, start of year		2	
3200 Obligated balance, end of year	2		
Budget authority and outlays, net:			
Discretionary:			
4000 Budget authority, gross	2	2	2
Outlays, gross:			
4010 Outlays from new discretionary authority		2	2
4011 Outlays from discretionary balances		2	
4020 Outlays, gross (total)		4	2
4180 Budget authority, net (total)	2	2	2
4190 Outlays, net (total)		4	2

The National Space Council provides advice and assistance to the President on national space policy and strategy. The President has directed it to review United States Government space policy, including long-range goals, and develop a strategy for national space activities; develop recommendations for the President on space policy and space-related issues; monitor and coordinate implementation of the objectives of the President's national space policy by executive departments and agencies; and foster close coordination, cooperation, and technology and information exchange among the civil, national security, and commercial space sectors, and facilitate resolution of differences concerning major space and space-related policy issues.

Object Classification (in millions of dollars)

Identification code 011–0048–0–1–802	2021 actual	2022 est.	2023 est.
Direct obligations:			
11.1 Personnel compensation: Full-time permanent		1	1
25.2 Other services from non-Federal sources	1		
99.0 Direct obligations	1	1	1
99.5 Adjustment for rounding	1	1	1
99.9 Total new obligations, unexpired accounts	2	2	2

Employment Summary

Identification code 011–0048–0–1–802	2021 actual	2022 est.	2023 est.
1001 Direct civilian full-time equivalent employment	2	7	7

OFFICE OF THE UNITED STATES TRADE REPRESENTATIVE

Federal Funds

SALARIES AND EXPENSES

For necessary expenses of the Office of the United States Trade Representative, including the hire of passenger motor vehicles and the employment of experts and consultants as authorized by section 3109 of title 5, United States Code, $61,540,000, of which $1,000,000 shall remain available until expended: Provided, That of the total amount made available under this heading, not to exceed $124,000 shall be available for official reception and representation expenses.

Note.—A full-year 2022 appropriation for this account was not enacted at the time the Budget was prepared; therefore, the Budget assumes this account is operating under the Continuing Appropriations Act, 2022 (Division A of Public Law 117–43, as amended). The amounts included for 2022 reflect the annualized level provided by the continuing resolution.

Program and Financing (in millions of dollars)

Identification code 011–0400–0–1–999	2021 actual	2022 est.	2023 est.
Obligations by program activity:			
0001 Office of the United States Trade Representative	65	60	67
0801 Office of the United States Trade Representative (Reimbursable)		1	1
0900 Total new obligations, unexpired accounts	65	61	68
Budgetary resources:			
Unobligated balance:			
1000 Unobligated balance brought forward, Oct 1	47	37	32
1033 Recoveries of prior year paid obligations	1		
1070 Unobligated balance (total)	48	37	32
Budget authority:			
Appropriations, discretionary:			
1100 Appropriation	55	55	62
Spending authority from offsetting collections, discretionary:			
1700 Collected		1	1
1701 Change in uncollected payments, Federal sources	1		
1750 Spending auth from offsetting collections, disc (total)	1	1	1
1900 Budget authority (total)	56	56	63
1930 Total budgetary resources available	104	93	95
Memorandum (non-add) entries:			
1940 Unobligated balance expiring	–2		
1941 Unexpired unobligated balance, end of year	37	32	27
Change in obligated balance:			
Unpaid obligations:			
3000 Unpaid obligations, brought forward, Oct 1	10	19	19
3010 New obligations, unexpired accounts	65	61	68
3011 Obligations ("upward adjustments"), expired accounts	3		
3020 Outlays (gross)	–56	–61	–76
3041 Recoveries of prior year unpaid obligations, expired	–3		
3050 Unpaid obligations, end of year	19	19	11

Office of the United States Trade Representative—Continued
Federal Funds—Continued

SALARIES AND EXPENSES—Continued

Program and Financing—Continued

Identification code 011–0400–0–1–999	2021 actual	2022 est.	2023 est.
Uncollected payments:			
3060 Uncollected pymts, Fed sources, brought forward, Oct 1	–1	–2	–2
3070 Change in uncollected pymts, Fed sources, unexpired	–1	....	....
3090 Uncollected pymts, Fed sources, end of year	–2	–2	–2
Memorandum (non-add) entries:			
3100 Obligated balance, start of year	9	17	17
3200 Obligated balance, end of year	17	17	9
Budget authority and outlays, net:			
Discretionary:			
4000 Budget authority, gross	56	56	63
Outlays, gross:			
4010 Outlays from new discretionary authority	47	51	58
4011 Outlays from discretionary balances	9	10	18
4020 Outlays, gross (total)	56	61	76
Offsets against gross budget authority and outlays:			
Offsetting collections (collected) from:			
4030 Federal sources	–1	–1	–1
4040 Offsets against gross budget authority and outlays (total)	–1	–1	–1
Additional offsets against gross budget authority only:			
4050 Change in uncollected pymts, Fed sources, unexpired	–1	....	....
4053 Recoveries of prior year paid obligations, unexpired accounts	1	....	....
4070 Budget authority, net (discretionary)	55	55	62
4080 Outlays, net (discretionary)	55	60	75
4180 Budget authority, net (total)	55	55	62
4190 Outlays, net (total)	55	60	75

The Office of the United States Trade Representative (USTR) is responsible for developing and coordinating America's trade policy, leading trade negotiations with other nations, and enforcing compliance with our trade agreements and U.S. trade laws. USTR also coordinates with other Federal agencies in developing trade policy and advising the President on trade matters.

USTR provides trade policy leadership and negotiating expertise in its major areas of responsibility, including industrial, textile, agricultural, and services trade policy; bilateral, regional, and multilateral trade and investment issues; trade-related intellectual property protection, labor and environmental issues; all matters within the World Trade Organization; and direct investment matters dealt with by international institutions such as the Organization for Economic Cooperation and Development and the United Nations Conference on Trade Development. USTR is organized to accomodate sectoral, regional, and functional policy perspectives, which are integrated into the decision-making process and coordinated externally with the Congress, other government agencies, the private sector, and foreign entities.

Object Classification (in millions of dollars)

Identification code 011–0400–0–1–999	2021 actual	2022 est.	2023 est.
Direct obligations:			
11.1 Personnel compensation: Full-time permanent	34	37	40
12.1 Civilian personnel benefits	13	14	14
21.0 Travel and transportation of persons	....	2	3
23.2 Rental payments to others	1	....	1
23.3 Communications, utilities, and miscellaneous charges	....	1	1
25.2 Other services from non-Federal sources	16	6	7
99.0 Direct obligations	64	60	65
99.0 Reimbursable obligations	....	1	1
99.5 Adjustment for rounding	1	....	2
99.9 Total new obligations, unexpired accounts	65	61	68

Employment Summary

Identification code 011–0400–0–1–999	2021 actual	2022 est.	2023 est.
1001 Direct civilian full-time equivalent employment	209	238	247

GENERAL FUND PAYMENT TO THE TRADE ENFORCEMENT TRUST FUND

Program and Financing (in millions of dollars)

Identification code 011–1750–0–1–376	2021 actual	2022 est.	2023 est.
Obligations by program activity:			
0001 Payment to Trade Enforcement Trust Fund	14	15	15
0900 Total new obligations, unexpired accounts (object class 94.0)	14	15	15
Budgetary resources:			
Budget authority:			
Appropriations, mandatory:			
1200 Appropriation	15	15	15
1930 Total budgetary resources available	15	15	15
Memorandum (non-add) entries:			
1940 Unobligated balance expiring	–1	....	....
Change in obligated balance:			
Unpaid obligations:			
3010 New obligations, unexpired accounts	14	15	15
3020 Outlays (gross)	–14	–15	–15
Budget authority and outlays, net:			
Mandatory:			
4090 Budget authority, gross	15	15	15
Outlays, gross:			
4100 Outlays from new mandatory authority	14	15	15
4180 Budget authority, net (total)	15	15	15
4190 Outlays, net (total)	14	15	15

The Trade Facilitation and Trade Enforcement Act of 2015 provides $15 million in mandatory funding annually from the general fund to finance the Trade Enforcement Trust Fund, which has an overall maximum ceiling of $30 million.

Trust Funds

TRADE ENFORCEMENT TRUST FUND

(INCLUDING TRANSFER OF FUNDS)

For activities of the United States Trade Representative authorized by section 611 of the Trade Facilitation and Trade Enforcement Act of 2015 (19 U.S.C. 4405), including transfers, $15,000,000, to be derived from the Trade Enforcement Trust Fund: Provided, That any transfer pursuant to subsection (d)(1) of such section shall be treated as a reprogramming under section 505 of this Act.

Note.—A full-year 2022 appropriation for this account was not enacted at the time the Budget was prepared; therefore, the Budget assumes this account is operating under the Continuing Appropriations Act, 2022 (Division A of Public Law 117–43, as amended). The amounts included for 2022 reflect the annualized level provided by the continuing resolution.

Special and Trust Fund Receipts (in millions of dollars)

Identification code 011–8581–0–7–376	2021 actual	2022 est.	2023 est.
0100 Balance, start of year	15	14	14
Receipts:			
Current law:			
1140 General Fund Payment, Trade Enforcement Trust Fund	14	15	15
2000 Total: Balances and receipts	29	29	29
Appropriations:			
Current law:			
2101 Trade Enforcement Trust Fund	–15	–15	–15
5099 Balance, end of year	14	14	14

EXECUTIVE OFFICE OF THE PRESIDENT

Program and Financing (in millions of dollars)

Identification code 011–8581–0–7–376		2021 actual	2022 est.	2023 est.
	Obligations by program activity:			
0001	Trade Enforcement	22	19	17
	Budgetary resources:			
	Unobligated balance:			
1000	Unobligated balance brought forward, Oct 1	37	29	25
	Budget authority:			
	Appropriations, discretionary:			
1101	Appropriation (special or trust)	15	15	15
1930	Total budgetary resources available	52	44	40
	Memorandum (non-add) entries:			
1940	Unobligated balance expiring	–1		
1941	Unexpired unobligated balance, end of year	29	25	23
	Special and non-revolving trust funds:			
1951	Unobligated balance expiring	1		
1952	Expired unobligated balance, start of year	8	9	9
1953	Expired unobligated balance, end of year	8	9	9
	Change in obligated balance:			
	Unpaid obligations:			
3000	Unpaid obligations, brought forward, Oct 1	8	14	12
3010	New obligations, unexpired accounts	22	19	17
3020	Outlays (gross)	–16	–21	–21
3050	Unpaid obligations, end of year	14	12	8
	Memorandum (non-add) entries:			
3100	Obligated balance, start of year	8	14	12
3200	Obligated balance, end of year	14	12	8
	Budget authority and outlays, net:			
	Discretionary:			
4000	Budget authority, gross	15	15	15
	Outlays, gross:			
4010	Outlays from new discretionary authority	9	14	14
4011	Outlays from discretionary balances	7	7	7
4020	Outlays, gross (total)	16	21	21
4180	Budget authority, net (total)	15	15	15
4190	Outlays, net (total)	16	21	21

The Trade Enforcement Trust Fund was established to receive transfers from the general fund that may be expended, only as provided by appropriations Acts. The Budget requests that $15 million be derived from this Fund in 2022.

Object Classification (in millions of dollars)

Identification code 011–8581–0–7–376		2021 actual	2022 est.	2023 est.
	Direct obligations:			
11.1	Personnel compensation: Full-time permanent	6	6	6
12.1	Civilian personnel benefits	2	2	2
23.1	Rental payments to GSA	1	1	1
25.1	Advisory and assistance services	2	2	2
25.2	Other services from non-Federal sources	4	7	5
25.3	Other goods and services from Federal sources	7		
99.0	Direct obligations	22	18	16
99.5	Adjustment for rounding		1	1
99.9	Total new obligations, unexpired accounts	22	19	17

Employment Summary

Identification code 011–8581–0–7–376	2021 actual	2022 est.	2023 est.
1001 Direct civilian full-time equivalent employment	38	38	38

UNANTICIPATED NEEDS

Federal Funds

UNANTICIPATED NEEDS

For expenses necessary to enable the President to meet unanticipated needs, in furtherance of the national interest, security, or defense which may arise at home or abroad during the current fiscal year, as authorized by 3 U.S.C. 108, $1,000,000, to remain available until September 30, 2024.

Note.—A full-year 2022 appropriation for this account was not enacted at the time the Budget was prepared; therefore, the Budget assumes this account is operating under the Continuing Appropriations Act, 2022 (Division A of Public Law 117–43, as amended). The amounts included for 2022 reflect the annualized level provided by the continuing resolution.

Program and Financing (in millions of dollars)

Identification code 011–0037–0–1–802		2021 actual	2022 est.	2023 est.
	Obligations by program activity:			
0001	Direct program activity	1	1	1
0900	Total new obligations, unexpired accounts (object class 25.3)	1	1	1
	Budgetary resources:			
	Unobligated balance:			
1000	Unobligated balance brought forward, Oct 1	1	1	
1021	Recoveries of prior year unpaid obligations			1
1070	Unobligated balance (total)	1	1	1
	Budget authority:			
	Appropriations, discretionary:			
1100	Appropriation	1	1	1
1930	Total budgetary resources available	2	2	2
	Memorandum (non-add) entries:			
1940	Unobligated balance expiring		–1	–1
1941	Unexpired unobligated balance, end of year	1	1	1
	Change in obligated balance:			
	Unpaid obligations:			
3000	Unpaid obligations, brought forward, Oct 1			1
3010	New obligations, unexpired accounts	1	1	1
3020	Outlays (gross)	–1		
3040	Recoveries of prior year unpaid obligations, unexpired			–1
3050	Unpaid obligations, end of year		1	1
	Memorandum (non-add) entries:			
3100	Obligated balance, start of year			1
3200	Obligated balance, end of year		1	1
	Budget authority and outlays, net:			
	Discretionary:			
4000	Budget authority, gross	1	1	1
	Outlays, gross:			
4011	Outlays from discretionary balances	1		
4180	Budget authority, net (total)	1	1	1
4190	Outlays, net (total)	1		

This account represents amounts appropriated to the President to meet unanticipated needs in furtherance of national interest, security, or defense.

INTELLECTUAL PROPERTY ENFORCEMENT COORDINATOR

For necessary expenses of the Office of the Intellectual Property Enforcement Coordinator, as authorized by title III of the Prioritizing Resources and Organization for Intellectual Property Act of 2008 (Public Law 110–403), including services authorized by 5 U.S.C. 3109, $1,902,000.

Note.—A full-year 2022 appropriation for this account was not enacted at the time the Budget was prepared; therefore, the Budget assumes this account is operating under the Continuing Appropriations Act, 2022 (Division A of Public Law 117–43, as amended). The amounts included for 2022 reflect the annualized level provided by the continuing resolution.

Program and Financing (in millions of dollars)

Identification code 011–1751–0–1–802		2021 actual	2022 est.	2023 est.
	Obligations by program activity:			
0001	Intellectual Property Enforcement Coordinator	1	2	2
0900	Total new obligations, unexpired accounts	1	2	2
	Budgetary resources:			
	Budget authority:			
	Appropriations, discretionary:			
1100	Appropriation	2	2	2
1930	Total budgetary resources available	2	2	2
	Memorandum (non-add) entries:			
1940	Unobligated balance expiring	–1		
	Change in obligated balance:			
	Unpaid obligations:			
3010	New obligations, unexpired accounts	1	2	2

INTELLECTUAL PROPERTY ENFORCEMENT COORDINATOR—Continued

Program and Financing—Continued

Identification code 011–1751–0–1–802	2021 actual	2022 est.	2023 est.
3020 Outlays (gross)	–1	–2	–2
Budget authority and outlays, net:			
Discretionary:			
4000 Budget authority, gross	2	2	2
Outlays, gross:			
4010 Outlays from new discretionary authority	1	2	2
4180 Budget authority, net (total)	2	2	2
4190 Outlays, net (total)	1	2	2

The Office of the U.S. Intellectual Property Enforcement Coordinator is focused on promoting and protecting our great competitive advantage: the Nation's innovative economy. The Office coordinates and develops the United States' overall intellectual property policy and strategy, to promote innovation and creativity, and to ensure effective intellectual property protection and enforcement domestically and abroad.

Object Classification (in millions of dollars)

Identification code 011–1751–0–1–802	2021 actual	2022 est.	2023 est.
11.1 Direct obligations: Personnel compensation: Full-time permanent	....	1	1
99.5 Adjustment for rounding	1	1	1
99.9 Total new obligations, unexpired accounts	1	2	2

Employment Summary

Identification code 011–1751–0–1–802	2021 actual	2022 est.	2023 est.
1001 Direct civilian full-time equivalent employment	3	7	7

INFORMATION TECHNOLOGY OVERSIGHT AND REFORM

(INCLUDING TRANSFER OF FUNDS)

For necessary expenses for the furtherance of integrated, efficient, secure, and effective uses of information technology in the Federal Government, $13,700,000, to remain available until expended: Provided, That the Director of the Office of Management and Budget may transfer these funds to one or more other agencies to carry out projects to meet these purposes.

Note.—A full-year 2022 appropriation for this account was not enacted at the time the Budget was prepared; therefore, the Budget assumes this account is operating under the Continuing Appropriations Act, 2022 (Division A of Public Law 117–43, as amended). The amounts included for 2022 reflect the annualized level provided by the continuing resolution.

Program and Financing (in millions of dollars)

Identification code 011–0036–0–1–802	2021 actual	2022 est.	2023 est.
Obligations by program activity:			
0001 Oversight, Cybersecurity and Program Management	8	12	14
0002 U.S. Digital Service	5	....	....
0003 U.S. Digital Service — ARP	12	59	64
0799 Total direct obligations	25	71	78
0801 Reimbursable program activity	13	12	12
0900 Total new obligations, unexpired accounts	38	83	90
Budgetary resources:			
Unobligated balance:			
1000 Unobligated balance brought forward, Oct 1	39	223	155
1021 Recoveries of prior year unpaid obligations	1	....	....
1070 Unobligated balance (total)	40	223	155
Budget authority:			
Appropriations, discretionary:			
1100 Appropriation	13	12	14
Appropriations, mandatory:			
1200 Appropriation	200	....	....
Spending authority from offsetting collections, discretionary:			
1700 Collected	12	3	3
1900 Budget authority (total)	225	15	17
1930 Total budgetary resources available	265	238	172
Memorandum (non-add) entries:			
1940 Unobligated balance expiring	–4	....	....
1941 Unexpired unobligated balance, end of year	223	155	82
Change in obligated balance:			
Unpaid obligations:			
3000 Unpaid obligations, brought forward, Oct 1	3	3	16
3010 New obligations, unexpired accounts	38	83	90
3020 Outlays (gross)	–37	–70	–79
3040 Recoveries of prior year unpaid obligations, unexpired	–1	....	....
3050 Unpaid obligations, end of year	3	16	27
Uncollected payments:			
3060 Uncollected pymts, Fed sources, brought forward, Oct 1	–26	–26	–26
3090 Uncollected pymts, Fed sources, end of year	–26	–26	–26
Memorandum (non-add) entries:			
3100 Obligated balance, start of year	–23	–23	–10
3200 Obligated balance, end of year	–23	–10	1
Budget authority and outlays, net:			
Discretionary:			
4000 Budget authority, gross	25	15	17
Outlays, gross:			
4010 Outlays from new discretionary authority	20	9	9
4011 Outlays from discretionary balances	6	9	6
4020 Outlays, gross (total)	26	18	15
Offsets against gross budget authority and outlays:			
Offsetting collections (collected) from:			
4030 Federal sources	–12	–3	–3
4040 Offsets against gross budget authority and outlays (total)	–12	–3	–3
Mandatory:			
4090 Budget authority, gross	200	....	....
Outlays, gross:			
4100 Outlays from new mandatory authority	11	....	....
4101 Outlays from mandatory balances	....	52	64
4110 Outlays, gross (total)	11	52	64
4180 Budget authority, net (total)	213	12	14
4190 Outlays, net (total)	25	67	76

Information Technology Oversight and Reform (ITOR) funding provides the Government with a resource base controlled by the Director of the Office of Management and Budget (OMB) to support activities and tools that enhance the efficiency, effectiveness, and security of Federal investments in information technology (IT). ITOR supports Government-wide efforts to modernize out-of-date and inefficient IT, secure Federal IT systems and the agency data within, increase transparency in IT spending, and improve the governance of IT projects and services.

Information Technology Oversight and Analysis.—Under the direction of the Federal Chief Information Officer (CIO), the Office of the Federal CIO (OFCIO) will continue engaging with agency CIOs to refine the guidance and tools supporting effective management of the large investment by Federal agencies in information technology. Additionally, ITOR funds will support policy analysis and development efforts to support innovative approaches to IT management, leveraging modern solutions to IT problems faced by all organizations, through reliance on cloud-based and shared solutions where appropriate. OMB will continue to ensure effective implementation by agencies of the Federal Information Technology Acquisition Reform Act (FITARA), as directed in OMB guidance.

Cybersecurity.—ITOR funding for cybersecurity will continue to enable OMB to expand its data-driven, risk-based oversight of agency and government-wide cybersecurity programs. It will ensure OMB continues the issuance and implementation of Federal policies consistent with emerging technologies and evolving cyber threats. OMB will expand its work with the FASC and its implementation, the sharing of supply chain risk information, and the exercise of its authorities to recommend issuances of removal and exclusion orders to address supply chain security risks within agencies. OFCIO will continue to develop and enhance strategies to protect Federal information assets, acting in cooperation with the Office of the National Cyber Director, National Security Council staff, the Department of Homeland Security, the National Institute for Standards and Technology, the Congress, and Federal agency Chief Information Officers and Chief Information Security Officers.

United States Digital Service (USDS).—USDS deploys small, responsive teams of engineers, service designers, product managers, and procurement experts to work with and empower civil servants. These multi-disciplinary teams bring best practices and new approaches to rapidly respond to technology emergencies and modernize systems for long-term stability and customer experience. USDS received $200 million in the American Rescue Plan (ARP) that supports relief implementation projects, improves service delivery, and provides system stability through recovery. USDS is executing high-impact projects across the Federal Government that make services more straightforward and sustainable, making it easier for the public, including families, small businesses, and Veterans, to get the services they need.

Object Classification (in millions of dollars)

Identification code 011–0036–0–1–802		2021 actual	2022 est.	2023 est.
	Direct obligations:			
11.1	Personnel compensation: Full-time permanent	17	39	42
12.1	Civilian personnel benefits	6	21	23
25.3	Other goods and services from Federal sources	2	11	13
99.0	Direct obligations	25	71	78
99.0	Reimbursable obligations	13	12	12
99.9	Total new obligations, unexpired accounts	38	83	90

Employment Summary

Identification code 011–0036–0–1–802		2021 actual	2022 est.	2023 est.
1001	Direct civilian full-time equivalent employment	110	278	303
2001	Reimbursable civilian full-time equivalent employment	54	39	39

SPECTRUM RELOCATION FUND

Special and Trust Fund Receipts (in millions of dollars)

Identification code 011–5512–0–2–376		2021 actual	2022 est.	2023 est.
0100	Balance, start of year	7,454	11,460	33,158
	Receipts:			
	Current law:			
1130	Spectrum Relocation Receipts	4,466	22,418	
2000	Total: Balances and receipts	11,920	33,878	33,158
	Appropriations:			
	Current law:			
2103	Spectrum Relocation Fund	–512	–758	–784
2132	Spectrum Relocation Fund	25	38	39
2199	Total current law appropriations	–487	–720	–745
2999	Total appropriations	–487	–720	–745
4030	Spectrum Relocation Fund	27		
5099	Balance, end of year	11,460	33,158	32,413

Program and Financing (in millions of dollars)

Identification code 011–5512–0–2–376		2021 actual	2022 est.	2023 est.
	Budgetary resources:			
	Unobligated balance:			
1011	Unobligated balance transfer from other acct [070–0530]	12		
1011	Unobligated balance transfer from other acct [015–0700]	15		
1035	Unobligated balance precluded from obligation (limitation on obligations)(special and trust)	–27		
	Budget authority:			
	Appropriations, mandatory:			
1203	Appropriation (previously unavailable)(special or trust)	512	758	784
1220	Appropriations transferred to other accts [021–2040]	–11	–39	–30
1220	Appropriations transferred to other accts [021–2031]	–70	–18	–6
1220	Appropriations transferred to other accts [021–2035]	–18	–6	–5
1220	Appropriations transferred to other accts [021–2020]	–9	–8	–16
1220	Appropriations transferred to other accts [017–1319]	–100	–63	–208
1220	Appropriations transferred to other accts [017–1506]	–40	–51	–108
1220	Appropriations transferred to other accts [017–1810]	–30	–37	–84
1220	Appropriations transferred to other accts [017–1109]	–35	–11	–12
1220	Appropriations transferred to other accts [017–1804]	–16	–16	–35
1220	Appropriations transferred to other accts [057–3600]	–46	–30	–48
1220	Appropriations transferred to other accts [057–3010]	–3		
1220	Appropriations transferred to other accts [057–3080]	–1		–1
1220	Appropriations transferred to other accts [057–3400]	–14	–5	–17
1220	Appropriations transferred to other accts [097–0100]	–15	–14	–25
1220	Appropriations transferred to other accts [097–0400]	–61	–99	–71
1220	Appropriations transferred to other accts [015–0200]	–4	–42	–52
1220	Appropriations transferred to other accts [015–0324]		–3	–8
1220	Appropriations transferred to other accts [015–1100]	–11	–8	–8
1220	Appropriations transferred to other acct [099–9032]		–267	
1220	Appropriations transferred to other acct [017–1106]	–3	–3	–11
1232	Appropriations and/or unobligated balance of appropriations temporarily reduced	–25	–38	–39
4180	Budget authority, net (total)			
4190	Outlays, net (total)			

The Spectrum Relocation Fund (SRF), created by the Commercial Spectrum Enhancement Act of 2004, as amended by the Middle Class Tax Relief and Job Creation Act of 2012, reimburses Federal agencies that must relocate or share wireless communications systems in Federal spectrum that has been or will be reallocated to commercial use. Auction receipts associated with the reallocated spectrum are deposited into the SRF to pay eligible pre- and post-auction costs that help efficiently and effectively transition Federal agencies off of the reallocated spectrum or facilitate the sharing of Federal systems with non-Federal systems. The Office of Management and Budget (OMB) administers the SRF in consultation with the National Telecommunications and Information Administration (NTIA) of the Department of Commerce. In 2015, a portion of receipts associated with the Advanced Wireless Services 3 (AWS-3) auction, which reallocates Federal and other spectrum for flexible commercial use, were deposited into the SRF. Funds from the AWS-3 auction are being transferred to agencies with approved transition plans to reimburse them for the costs associated with clearing or sharing the auctioned bands. Transfers were made in 2015, 2016, 2017, 2018, 2019, 2020, and 2021, and will continue in future years. In addition, receipts associated with the Citizens Broadband Radio Service auction were deposited into the SRF, and funds are being transferred to agencies with approved transition plans to reimburse them for the costs associated with sharing the auctioned spectrum. Transfers were made in 2021 and 2022 and will continue in future years. Most funds in the SRF must be returned to the Treasury eight years after they are deposited.

The Spectrum Pipeline Act of 2015, part of the Bipartisan Budget Act of 2015, authorized the transfer to agencies of up to $500 million of SRF balances, and a portion of future deposits into the SRF, to fund advance planning and research projects that are expected to facilitate future spectrum auctions. OMB, NTIA, and the Federal Communications Commission have approved projects totaling $400 million through the end of 2021.

ADMINISTRATIVE PROVISIONS—EXECUTIVE OFFICE OF THE PRESIDENT AND FUNDS APPROPRIATED TO THE PRESIDENT

(INCLUDING TRANSFER OF FUNDS)

SEC. 201. *From funds made available in this Act under the headings "The White House", "Executive Residence at the White House", "White House Repair and Restoration", "Council of Economic Advisers", "National Security Council and Homeland Security Council", "Office of Administration", "Special Assistance to the President", and "Official Residence of the Vice President", the Director of the Office of Management and Budget (or such other officer as the President may designate in writing), may, with advance notice to the Committees on Appropriations of the House of Representatives and the Senate, transfer not to exceed 10 percent of any such appropriation to any other such appropriation, to be merged with and available for the same time and for the same purposes as the appropriation to which transferred: Provided, That the amount of an appropriation shall not be increased by more than 50 percent by such transfers: Provided further, That no amount shall be transferred from "Special Assistance to the President" or "Official Residence of the Vice President" without the approval of the Vice President.*

SEC. 202. *(a) The Office of Administration may carry out a program to provide payments (such as stipends, subsistence allowances, cost reimbursements, or awards) to students, recent graduates, and veterans recently discharged from active duty* who are performing voluntary services in the Executive Office of the President under 5 U.S.C. 3111(b) or comparable authority. Such payments shall not be considered compensation for purposes of 5 U.S.C. 3111(b)(2) and may be paid in advance.

(b) Of the amounts made available to the Office of Administration for salaries and expenses, up to $7,000,000 shall be available to carry out the program, to be allocated as the Director of the Office of Administration considers appropriate.

(c) Amounts available under subsections (a) and (b) are in addition to any other amounts available to a component of the Executive Office of the President for making payments or providing compensation to students, recent graduates, and veterans recently discharged from active duty.

SEC. 203. Section 107(b) of title 3, United States Code, is amended by adding at the end the following new paragraphs:

"(3) In addition to any authority granted under paragraphs (1) and (2) of this subsection, the President (or his designee) is authorized to employ not more than 12 individuals in the Office of Administration in accordance with sections 3131 and 5108 of title 5 and provisions relating thereto. Each such position shall be designated a career reserved position and shall not be subject to section 435(g) of this title. Any individual employed in such a position is not subject to the limitation specified in section 114 of this title.

"(4) Consistent with section 904 of Public Law 95–454 and section 637 of Public Law 107–67, all authorities under this subsection are retained and exercised by the President (or his designee), without the involvement of the Office of Personnel Management.".

GENERAL SERVICES ADMINISTRATION

REAL PROPERTY ACTIVITIES
Federal Funds

FEDERAL BUILDINGS FUND

LIMITATIONS ON AVAILABILITY OF REVENUE

(INCLUDING TRANSFERS OF FUNDS)

Amounts in the Fund, including revenues and collections deposited into the Fund, shall be available for necessary expenses of real property management and related activities not otherwise provided for, including operation, maintenance, and protection of federally owned and leased buildings; rental of buildings in the District of Columbia; restoration of leased premises; moving governmental agencies (including space adjustments and telecommunications relocation expenses) in connection with the assignment, allocation, and transfer of space; contractual services incident to cleaning or servicing buildings, and moving; repair and alteration of federally owned buildings, including grounds, approaches, and appurtenances; care and safeguarding of sites; maintenance, preservation, demolition, and equipment; acquisition of buildings and sites by purchase, condemnation, or as otherwise authorized by law; acquisition of options to purchase buildings and sites; conversion and extension of federally owned buildings; preliminary planning and design of projects by contract or otherwise; construction of new buildings (including equipment for such buildings); and payment of principal, interest, and any other obligations for public buildings acquired by installment purchase and purchase contract; in the aggregate amount of $10,866,978,000, of which—

(1) $408,023,000 shall remain available until expended for construction and acquisition (including funds for sites and expenses, and associated design and construction services): Provided, That amounts identified in the spend plan for construction and acquisition required by section 525 of this division may be exceeded to the extent that savings are effected in other such projects, but not to exceed 10 percent of the amounts included in a transmitted prospectus, if required, unless advance notice is transmitted to the Committees on Appropriations of a greater amount;

(2) $1,751,870,000 shall remain available until expended for repairs and alterations, including associated design and construction services, of which—

(A) $1,188,073,000 is for Major Repairs and Alterations;
(B) $398,797,000 is for Basic Repairs and Alterations; and
(C) $165,000,000 is for Special Emphasis Programs;

Provided, That amounts identified in the spend plan for major repairs and alterations required by section 525 of this division may be exceeded to the extent that savings are effected in other such projects, but not to exceed 10 percent of the amounts included in a transmitted prospectus, if required, unless advance notice is transmitted to the Committees on Appropriations of a greater amount: Provided further, That additional projects for which prospectuses have been transmitted may be funded under this category only if advance notice is transmitted to the Committees on Appropriations: Provided further, That the amounts provided in this or any prior Act for "Repairs and Alterations" may be used to fund costs associated with implementing security improvements to buildings necessary to meet the minimum standards for security in accordance with current law and in compliance with the reprogramming guidelines of the appropriate Committees of the House and Senate: Provided further, That the difference between the funds appropriated and expended on any projects in this or any prior Act, under the heading "Repairs and Alterations", may be transferred to "Basic Repairs and Alterations" or used to fund authorized increases in prospectus projects: Provided further, That the amount provided in this or any prior Act for "Basic Repairs and Alterations" may be used to pay claims against the Government arising from any projects under the heading "Repairs and Alterations" or used to fund authorized increases in prospectus projects;

(3) $5,645,680,000 for rental of space to remain available until expended; and
(4) $2,992,381,000 for building operations to remain available until expended: Provided, That the total amount of funds made available from this Fund to the General Services Administration shall not be available for expenses of any construction, repair, alteration and acquisition project for which a prospectus, if required to be submitted pursuant to 40 U.S.C. 3307, has not been transmitted to the Committees referenced therein, except that necessary funds may be expended for each project for required expenses for the development of a proposed prospectus: Provided further, That funds available in the Federal Buildings Fund may be expended for emergency repairs when advance notice is transmitted to the Committees on Appropriations: Provided further, That amounts necessary to provide reimbursable special services to other agencies under 40 U.S.C. 592(b)(2) and amounts to provide such reimbursable fencing, lighting, guard booths, and other facilities on private or other property not in Government ownership or control as may be appropriate to enable the United States Secret Service to perform its protective functions pursuant to 18 U.S.C. 3056, shall be available from such revenues and collections: Provided further, That revenues and collections and any other sums accruing to this Fund during fiscal year 2023, excluding reimbursements under 40 U.S.C. 592(b)(2), in excess of the aggregate new obligational authority authorized for Real Property Activities of the Federal Buildings Fund in this Act shall remain in the Fund and shall not be available for expenditure except as authorized in appropriations Acts.

Note.—A full-year 2022 appropriation for this account was not enacted at the time the Budget was prepared; therefore, the Budget assumes this account is operating under the Continuing Appropriations Act, 2022 (Division A of Public Law 117–43, as amended). The amounts included for 2022 reflect the annualized level provided by the continuing resolution.

FEDERAL BUILDINGS FUND

〔(INCLUDING TRANSFERS OF FUNDS)〕

〔For an additional amount to be deposited in the "Federal Buildings Fund", $3,418,008,000, to remain available until expended, for construction and acquisition, and repairs and alterations of border stations and land ports of entry, of which no more than $250,000,000 shall be for Program Contingency and Operational Support for necessary expenses for projects funded under this heading, including, moving governmental agencies (including space alterations and adjustments, and telecommunications relocation expenses) in connection with the assignment, allocation and transfer of space, leasing of temporary space, and building operations, of which—〕

〔(1) $2,527,808,000 shall be for projects on the U.S. Customs and Border Protection five-year plan;〕

〔(2) $430,200,000 shall be for projects with completed U.S. Customs and Border Protection/General Services Administration feasibility studies as prioritized in the "American Jobs Plan Project List" submitted to the House and Senate Committees on Appropriations on May 28, 2021; and〕

〔(3) $210,000,000 shall be for land ports of entry (LPOE) infrastructure paving; acquisition of leased LPOEs; and additional Federal Motor Carrier Safety Administration requirements at the Southern Border:〕

〔*Provided*, That the General Services Administration shall submit a plan, by project, regarding the use of funds made available to the Administrator under this heading in this Act to the Committees on Appropriations of the House of Representatives and the Senate within 90 days of enactment of this Act: *Provided further*, That the Administrator of General Services shall notify the Committees on Appropriations of the House of Representatives and the Senate quarterly on the obligations and expenditures of the funds provided under this heading in this Act by account of the Federal Buildings Fund: *Provided further*, That funds made available under this heading in this Act for Federal Buildings Fund activities may be transferred to, and merged with, other accounts within the Federal Buildings Fund only to the extent necessary to meet program requirements for such activities: *Provided further*, That the General Services Administration will provide notice in advance to the Committees on Appropriations of the House of Representatives and the Senate of any proposed transfers: *Provided further*, That funds made available to the Administrator under this heading in this Act shall not be subject to section 3307 of title 40, United States Code: *Provided further*, That amounts made available under this heading in this Act shall be in addition to any other amounts made available for such purposes, including for construction and acquisition or repairs and alterations: *Provided further*, That such amount is designated by the Congress as being for an emergency requirement pursuant to section 4112(a) of H. Con. Res. 71 (115th Congress), the concurrent resolution on the budget for fiscal year 2018, and to section 251(b) of the Balanced Budget and Emergency Deficit Control Act of 1985.〕 (*Infrastructure Investments and Jobs Appropriations Act.*)

Program and Financing (in millions of dollars)

Identification code 047–4542–0–4–804	2021 actual	2022 est.	2023 est.
Obligations by program activity:			
0009 CARES Act	86	60	25
0010 Disaster Recovery	14		
0011 Direct Reimbursable	165		
0012 Infrastructure Investment and Jobs Act		342	169
0799 Total direct obligations	265	402	194
0801 Construction and acquisition of facilities	333	721	734
0802 Repairs and alterations	893	850	839
0809 Reimbursable program activities, subtotal	1,226	1,571	1,573
0810 Rental of space	5,561	5,850	5,645

FEDERAL BUILDINGS FUND—Continued
Program and Financing—Continued

Identification code 047–4542–0–4–804	2021 actual	2022 est.	2023 est.
0811 Building operations	2,576	3,077	3,178
0819 Reimbursable program activities, subtotal	8,137	8,927	8,823
0820 Special services and improvements	1,728	1,181	1,234
0899 Total reimbursable obligations	11,091	11,679	11,630
0900 Total new obligations, unexpired accounts	11,356	12,081	11,824
Budgetary resources:			
Unobligated balance:			
1000 Unobligated balance brought forward, Oct 1	5,215	5,030	7,035
1021 Recoveries of prior year unpaid obligations	112		
1033 Recoveries of prior year paid obligations	3		
1070 Unobligated balance (total)	5,330	5,030	7,035
Budget authority:			
Appropriations, discretionary:			
1100 Appropriation		3,418	
Spending authority from offsetting collections, discretionary:			
1700 Collected	11,933	12,239	11,892
1701 Change in uncollected payments, Federal sources	308		
1702 Offsetting collections (previously unavailable)	7,629	8,814	10,385
1724 Spending authority from offsetting collections precluded from obligation (limitation on obligations)	–8,814	–10,385	–10,076
1750 Spending auth from offsetting collections, disc (total)	11,056	10,668	12,201
1900 Budget authority (total)	11,056	14,086	12,201
1930 Total budgetary resources available	16,386	19,116	19,236
Memorandum (non-add) entries:			
1941 Unexpired unobligated balance, end of year	5,030	7,035	7,412
Change in obligated balance:			
Unpaid obligations:			
3000 Unpaid obligations, brought forward, Oct 1	4,139	4,413	4,648
3010 New obligations, unexpired accounts	11,356	12,081	11,824
3020 Outlays (gross)	–10,970	–11,846	–11,873
3040 Recoveries of prior year unpaid obligations, unexpired	–112		
3050 Unpaid obligations, end of year	4,413	4,648	4,599
Uncollected payments:			
3060 Uncollected pymts, Fed sources, brought forward, Oct 1	–4,469	–4,777	–4,777
3070 Change in uncollected pymts, Fed sources, unexpired	–308		
3090 Uncollected pymts, Fed sources, end of year	–4,777	–4,777	–4,777
Memorandum (non-add) entries:			
3100 Obligated balance, start of year	–330	–364	–129
3200 Obligated balance, end of year	–364	–129	–178
Budget authority and outlays, net:			
Discretionary:			
4000 Budget authority, gross	11,056	14,086	12,201
Outlays, gross:			
4010 Outlays from new discretionary authority	7,858	8,696	9,022
4011 Outlays from discretionary balances	3,112	3,150	2,851
4020 Outlays, gross (total)	10,970	11,846	11,873
Offsets against gross budget authority and outlays:			
Offsetting collections (collected) from:			
4030 Federal sources	–11,876	–12,139	–11,792
4033 Non-Federal sources	–60	–100	–100
4040 Offsets against gross budget authority and outlays (total)	–11,936	–12,239	–11,892
Additional offsets against gross budget authority only:			
4050 Change in uncollected pymts, Fed sources, unexpired	–308		
4053 Recoveries of prior year paid obligations, unexpired accounts	3		
4060 Additional offsets against budget authority only (total)	–305		
4070 Budget authority, net (discretionary)	–1,185	1,847	309
4080 Outlays, net (discretionary)	–966	–393	–19
4180 Budget authority, net (total)	–1,185	1,847	309
4190 Outlays, net (total)	–966	–393	–19
Memorandum (non-add) entries:			
5090 Unexpired unavailable balance, SOY: Offsetting collections	7,629	8,814	10,385
5092 Unexpired unavailable balance, EOY: Offsetting collections	8,814	10,385	10,076

Summary of Budget Authority and Outlays (in millions of dollars)

	2021 actual	2022 est.	2023 est.
Enacted/requested:			
Budget Authority	–1,185	1,847	309
Outlays	–966	–393	–19
Legislative proposal, not subject to PAYGO:			
Budget Authority			69
Outlays			–935
Total:			
Budget Authority	–1,185	1,847	378
Outlays	–966	–393	–954

This revolving fund provides for real property management and related activities, including operation, maintenance, and repair of federally owned buildings, and the construction of Federal buildings, courthouses, and land ports of entry. Expenses of the Federal Buildings Fund (FBF) are financed from rental charges assessed to occupants of General Services Administration (GSA)-controlled space. Rent assessments, by law, approximate commercial rates for comparable space and services. Rental income is augmented by appropriations to the Fund when new construction needs exceed the resources available for investment within the Fund.

The Budget requests $10,867 million in new obligational authority for the FBF, which represents $378 million in net positive net budget request. The Administration's proposal ensures that GSA spends at least at the level of anticipated rent that it collects from Federal departments and agencies in order to provide space and services to those customers.

Historically, the FBF has been permitted to spend at least what it collects from agencies to support leasing from the private sector, as well as maintenance, repairs, major renovations, and new construction to accommodate agency needs in buildings that GSA owns and operates. However, in several recent years, the FBF appropriations were significantly below the anticipated level of rent collections from agencies, denying GSA the ability to pursue an appropriately-sized capital program relative to the size of its portfolio. This year's $378 billion net positive budget request will allow GSA to proceed with important investments in the Federal real property portfolio improving resilience and utilization as well as proactively mitigate cost in leased facilities to deliver the best possible value in real estate management for our partners and across Government.

The following table reports rent and other income to the Fund:
[In millions of dollars]

	2021 act.	2022 est.	2023 est.
Rental Charges	10,357	10,637	10,489
Collections for:			
(a) Special services and improvements	1,884	1,360	1,420
(b) Miscellaneous income			
Total receipts and reimbursements	12,241	11,997	11,909

The following tables report the planned financing for the Fund in 2023:
[In millions of dollars]

2023 Program	Obligations	End of Year Unobligated Balance	Total	New	From Prior Year
1. Construction and Acquisition of Facilities	731	644	1,375	408	967
2. Repairs and Alterations	841	1,549	2,390	1,752	638
3. Installment Acquisition Payments	69	0	69	69	0
4. Construction of Lease Purchase Facilities	0	24	24	0	24
5. Rental of Space	5,646	127	5,773	5,646	127
6. Building Operations*	3,179	(677)	2,502	2,992	(490)
7. International Trade Center	0	13	13	0	13
8. Pennsylvania Avenue Activities	0	31	31	0	31
Total Basic Program	10.466	1,711	12,177	10,867	1,310
Other Programs					
Special Services and Improvements	1,234	2,401	3,635	1,420	2,215
Total Federal Buildings Fund	11,699	4,112	15,812	12,287	3,525

The FBF consists of the following activities:

Construction and Acquisition of Facilities.—This activity provides for the construction or purchase of prospectus-level facilities, prospectus-level additions to existing buildings, and remediation. All costs directly attributable to site acquisition, construction, and the full range of design and construction services, and management and inspection of construction projects are funded under this activity (estimated project cost in thousands).

New Construction Executive Agencies	
Washington, DC DHS Consolidation at St. Elizabeths	379,938
Washington, DC Southeast Federal Center Remediation	7,085
Washington, DC Federal Energy Regulatory Commission Lease Purchase	21,000
Total 2023 Construction and Acquisition of Facilities Program	408,023

FBI headquarters project: The Administration also recognizes the critical need for a new FBI headquarters. The J. Edgar Hoover building can no longer support the long-term mission of the FBI. The Administration has begun a multi-year process of constructing a modern, secure suburban facility from which the FBI can continue its mission to protect the American people.

During the next year, GSA and FBI will work to identify a location to construct a Federally owned, modern and secure facility for at least 7,500 personnel in the suburbs. Over the next year, GSA and FBI will finalize an updated program of requirements for a secure suburban campus, including the final number of personnel, to inform a 2024 Budget request for the new facility. GSA will also begin initial steps to acquire, if necessary, the site for the new suburban location.

Additionally, GSA and FBI will work to identify a Federally-owned location in the District of Columbia to support a presence of approximately 750–1,000 FBI personnel that would support day-to-day FBI engagement with DOJ headquarters, the White House, and Congress. Steps to initiate any necessary site acquisition are dependent upon the final details of the secure campus and will rely upon close collaboration between GSA and FBI. Final action to acquire any site will be dependent upon a prospectus that GSA submits to Congress.

Repairs and Alterations.—This activity provides for repairs and alterations of existing buildings as well as associated design and construction services. Protection of the Government's investment, the health and safety of building occupants, relocation of agencies from leased space, and cost effectiveness are the principle criteria used in establishing priorities. Repairs and alterations to improve space utilization, address life safety issues, and prevent deterioration and damage to buildings, building support systems, and operating equipment are given priority (estimated project costs in thousands).

Nonprospectus (Basic) Repairs and Alterations Program	398,797
Major Repairs and Alterations Projects	
Nationwide Conveying Systems - Various Buildings	63,198
Nationwide Fire Alarm Systems - Various Buildings	81,125
New York, NY Alexander Hamilton U.S. Courthouse	68,497
Philadelphia, PA James A. Byrne U.S. Courthouse	83,955
Boston, MA John J. Moakley U.S. Courthouse	115,354
Atlanta, GA Sam Nunn Atlanta Federal Center	72,015
Butte, MT Mike Mansfield Federal Building and U.S. Courthouse	25,792
Cleveland, OH Carl B. Stokes U.S. Courthouse	55,830
Greenville, SC C.F. Haynesworth Federal Building U.S. Courthouse	59,850
Lakewood, CO Denver Federal Center Infrastructure	47,664
Oklahoma City, OK William J. Holloway, Jr U.S. Courthouse and U.S. Post Office	55,199
San Francisco, CA San Francisco Federal Building	15,687
St. Albans, VT Federal Building U.S. Post Office and Courthouse	17,978
Lakewood, CO Denver Federal Center Building 56	47,663
Seattle, WA Henry M. Jackson Federal Building	33,720
Seattle, WA William K. Nakamura U.S. Courthouse	52,229
New York, NY Daniel Patrick Moynihan U.S. Courthouse	50,440
New York, NY Silvio J. Mollo Federal Building	241,877
Subtotal, Major Repair and Alteration Projects	1,188,073
Major Repair and Alterations Special Emphasis Programs	
Consolidation Activities Program	30,000
Judiciary Capital Security Program	20,000
Fire Protection and Life Safety Program	30,000
Seismic Mitigation Program	10,000
Energy and Water Retrofit and Conservation Measures Program	60,000
Subtotal, Major Repair and Alterations Special Emphasis Program	165,000
Subtotal, Major Repair and Alterations Program	1,353,073
Total FY 2023 Repairs and Alteration Program	1,751,870

*The above chart does not include additional resources such as recoveries, reimbursable, and indefinite authority which when included are sufficient to support obligations.

Rental of Space.—This activity provides for the leasing of privately-owned buildings when federally owned space is not available. This includes space occupied by Federal agencies, including in U.S. Postal Service facilities. GSA provided 176 million square feet of rental space in 2021. GSA expects to provide 171 million square feet of rental space in 2022 and 170 million in 2023.

Building Operations.—The Building Operations program provides services for both federally owned and leased facilities as well as administration and management of all PBS real property programs. Of the total amount requested in support of Building Operations, the Building Services allocation funds services and cost increases for cleaning, utilities, maintenance, and building services; the Salaries and Expenses allocation supports Public Building Service (PBS) personnel costs excluding reimbursable FTE, PBS-specific IT applications and PBSs contribution to the WCF. The following tables provide additional detail regarding the 2022 and 2023 building operations program (estimated obligations in millions).

	2022 Obligations Est.	2023 Obligations Est.
Cleaning	495,602	483,505
Utilities	369,022	389,540
Maintenance	533,147	546,635
Security	70,056	76,142
Other Building Services	140,732	143,263
IT	46,999	60,775
Salaries and Benefits	837,284	875,290
GSA Working Capital Fund Payments	379,435	392,261
Management Support	70,960	83,038
Travel	10,685	10,899
Other Administrative Costs and Funding Sources	(420,561)	(68,967)
Total	2,533,444	2,992,381

Other Programs.—When requested by other Federal agencies, the Public Buildings Service provides, on a reimbursable basis, building services such as tenant alterations, cleaning, utilities, and other operations, which are in excess of those services provided within the standard commercial rental charges.

Object Classification (in millions of dollars)

Identification code 047–4542–0–4–804		2021 actual	2022 est.	2023 est.
	Direct obligations:			
11.1	Personnel compensation: Full-time permanent	10		
12.1	Civilian personnel benefits	3		
23.2	Rental payments to others	20		
25.1	Advisory and assistance services	86		
25.2	Other services from non-Federal sources	3		
25.4	Operation and maintenance of facilities	121	30	5
25.7	Operation and maintenance of equipment	1		
26.0	Supplies and materials	1		
31.0	Equipment	1		
32.0	Land and structures	20	372	189
99.0	Direct obligations	266	402	194
	Reimbursable obligations:			
	Personnel compensation:			
11.1	Full-time permanent	561	641	658
11.3	Other than full-time permanent	5	5	5
11.5	Other personnel compensation	15	17	18
11.9	Total personnel compensation	581	663	681
12.1	Civilian personnel benefits	209	219	247
21.0	Travel and transportation of persons	1	11	11
23.2	Rental payments to others	5,585	5,850	5,646
23.3	Communications, utilities, and miscellaneous charges	375	431	470
25.1	Advisory and assistance services	459	464	458
25.2	Other services from non-Federal sources	73	68	69
25.3	Other goods and services from Federal sources	434	456	462
25.4	Operation and maintenance of facilities	2,115	1,766	1,837
25.7	Operation and maintenance of equipment	8	34	36
26.0	Supplies and materials	6	12	8
31.0	Equipment	74	85	72
32.0	Land and structures	1,139	1,585	1,583
42.0	Insurance claims and indemnities			1
43.0	Interest and dividends	31	34	49
99.0	Reimbursable obligations	11,090	11,678	11,630
99.5	Adjustment for rounding		1	
99.9	Total new obligations, unexpired accounts	11,356	12,081	11,824

Real Property Activities—Continued
Federal Funds—Continued

FEDERAL BUILDINGS FUND—Continued

Employment Summary

Identification code 047–4542–0–4–804	2021 actual	2022 est.	2023 est.
1001 Direct civilian full-time equivalent employment	87		
2001 Reimbursable civilian full-time equivalent employment	5,295	5,553	5,563

FEDERAL BUILDINGS FUND

(Legislative proposal, not subject to PAYGO)

Contingent upon enactment of the Federal Capital Revolving Fund Act of 2022, amounts in the Fund, including revenues and collections deposited into the Fund, shall be available for acquisition installment payments in the amount of $69,024,000, to remain available until expended, for the first annual repayment amounts to the Federal Capital Revolving Fund: Provided, That $49,024,000 shall be for the Public Buildings Service Jacob K. Javits Federal Building in New York, New York: Provided further, That $735,353,000 is approved for a purchase transfer, as defined in the Act, from the Federal Capital Revolving Fund for the Jacob K. Javits Federal Building: Provided further, That $20,000,000 shall be for the Public Buildings Service Kefauver Complex in Nashville, Tennessee: Provided further, That $300,000,000 is approved for a purchase transfer, as defined in the Act, from the Federal Capital Revolving Fund for the Kefauver Complex: Provided further, That such projects, as defined in the Act, shall be considered designated and approved pursuant to such Act, contingent upon the President's subsequent approval and designation as provided in the Act.

Program and Financing (in millions of dollars)

Identification code 047–4542–2–4–804	2021 actual	2022 est.	2023 est.
Obligations by program activity:			
0804 Installment acquisition payments			69
0809 Reimbursable program activities, subtotal			69
0821 FCRF Projects			135
0899 Total reimbursable obligations			204
0900 Total new obligations, unexpired accounts			204
Budgetary resources:			
Budget authority:			
Spending authority from offsetting collections, discretionary:			
1724 Spending authority from offsetting collections precluded from obligation (limitation on obligations)			69
Spending authority from offsetting collections, mandatory:			
1800 Collected			1,035
1900 Budget authority (total)			1,104
1930 Total budgetary resources available			1,104
Memorandum (non-add) entries:			
1941 Unexpired unobligated balance, end of year			900
Change in obligated balance:			
Unpaid obligations:			
3010 New obligations, unexpired accounts			204
3020 Outlays (gross)			–100
3050 Unpaid obligations, end of year			104
Memorandum (non-add) entries:			
3200 Obligated balance, end of year			104
Budget authority and outlays, net:			
Discretionary:			
4000 Budget authority, gross			69
Outlays, gross:			
4010 Outlays from new discretionary authority			69
Mandatory:			
4090 Budget authority, gross			1,035
Outlays, gross:			
4100 Outlays from new mandatory authority			31
Offsets against gross budget authority and outlays:			
Offsetting collections (collected) from:			
4120 Federal sources			–1,035
4180 Budget authority, net (total)			69
4190 Outlays, net (total)			–935
Memorandum (non-add) entries:			
5092 Unexpired unavailable balance, EOY: Offsetting collections			–69

The President's Budget proposes $69,024,000 for the first repayment of fifteen annual repayments associated with the first two projects identified for funding through the Federal Capital Revolving Fund. These repairs and alterations projects involve building system upgrades and investments in critical building infrastructure that will improve the energy efficiency, environmental impact, life safety, and climate resiliency of the buildings being upgraded.

Federal Capital Revolving Fund Projects

Project	Dollars in Thousands
New York, NY, Jacob K. Javits Federal Building	49,024
Nashville, TN, Estes Kefauver Complex	20,000

Object Classification (in millions of dollars)

Identification code 047–4542–2–4–804	2021 actual	2022 est.	2023 est.
Reimbursable obligations:			
32.0 Land and structures			135
94.0 Financial transfers			69
99.0 Reimbursable obligations			204
99.9 Total new obligations, unexpired accounts			204

FEDERAL BUILDINGS FUND, RECOVERY ACT

Program and Financing (in millions of dollars)

Identification code 047–4543–0–4–804	2021 actual	2022 est.	2023 est.
Budgetary resources:			
Unobligated balance:			
1000 Unobligated balance brought forward, Oct 1	1		
1029 Other balances withdrawn to Treasury	–1		
4180 Budget authority, net (total)			
4190 Outlays, net (total)			

This appropriation provided funding for the construction and renovation of Federal buildings, courthouses, and land ports of entry; the conversion of existing General Services Administration facilities to High-Performance Green Buildings; and $4,000,000 for transfer to the Office of Federal High-Performance Green Buildings. Of the available amounts, $5,000,000,000 was available until September 30, 2010 and the remaining amounts were available until September 30, 2011.

FEDERAL CAPITAL REVOLVING FUND

(Legislative proposal, subject to PAYGO)

Program and Financing (in millions of dollars)

Identification code 047–4614–4–4–804	2021 actual	2022 est.	2023 est.
Obligations by program activity:			
0801 Reimbursable program activity			1,035
0900 Total new obligations, unexpired accounts (object class 94.0)			1,035
Budgetary resources:			
Budget authority:			
Appropriations, mandatory:			
1200 Appropriation			5,000
Spending authority from offsetting collections, mandatory:			
1800 Collected			69
1900 Budget authority (total)			5,069
1930 Total budgetary resources available			5,069
Memorandum (non-add) entries:			
1941 Unexpired unobligated balance, end of year			4,034
Change in obligated balance:			
Unpaid obligations:			
3010 New obligations, unexpired accounts			1,035
3020 Outlays (gross)			–1,035
Budget authority and outlays, net:			
Mandatory:			
4090 Budget authority, gross			5,069

GENERAL SERVICES ADMINISTRATION

		2021 actual	2022 est.	2023 est.
	Outlays, gross:			
4100	Outlays from new mandatory authority			1,035
	Offsets against gross budget authority and outlays:			
	Offsetting collections (collected) from:			
4120	Federal sources			−69
4180	Budget authority, net (total)			5,000
4190	Outlays, net (total)			966

The President's Budget reflects $5 billion in funding in support of the Administration proposal to support a new Federal Capital Revolving Fund (FCRF) to finance federally-owned civilian real property projects.

The FCRF will create a mechanism that is similar to a capital budget but operates within the traditional rules used for the Federal budget. Upon approval in an Appropriations Act, the revolving fund will transfer money to agencies to finance large-dollar real property purchases. Executing agencies will then be required to repay the fund in 15 equal annual amounts using discretionary appropriations.

As a result, purchases/construction/renovation of real property assets will no longer compete with annual operating and programmatic expenses for the limited funding available under tight discretionary caps. Instead agencies will pay for real property over time as it is utilized. Repayments will be made from future appropriations, which will incentivize project selection based on highest mission need and return on investment, including future cost avoidance. The repayments will also replenish the revolving fund so that real property can continually be replaced as needed.

ASSET PROCEEDS AND SPACE MANAGEMENT FUND

For carrying out section 16(b) of the Federal Assets Sale and Transfer Act of 2016 (40 U.S.C. 1303 note), $16,000,000, to remain available until expended.

Note.—A full-year 2022 appropriation for this account was not enacted at the time the Budget was prepared; therefore, the Budget assumes this account is operating under the Continuing Appropriations Act, 2022 (Division A of Public Law 117–43, as amended). The amounts included for 2022 reflect the annualized level provided by the continuing resolution.

Program and Financing (in millions of dollars)

Identification code 047–5594–0–2–804		2021 actual	2022 est.	2023 est.
	Obligations by program activity:			
0001	Relocation and Disposal Activities	13	5	16
	Budgetary resources:			
	Unobligated balance:			
1000	Unobligated balance brought forward, Oct 1	30	33	44
	Budget authority:			
	Appropriations, discretionary:			
1100	Appropriation	16	16	16
1930	Total budgetary resources available	46	49	60
	Memorandum (non-add) entries:			
1941	Unexpired unobligated balance, end of year	33	44	44
	Change in obligated balance:			
	Unpaid obligations:			
3000	Unpaid obligations, brought forward, Oct 1		10	
3010	New obligations, unexpired accounts	13	5	16
3020	Outlays (gross)	−3	−15	−12
3050	Unpaid obligations, end of year	10		4
	Memorandum (non-add) entries:			
3100	Obligated balance, start of year		10	
3200	Obligated balance, end of year	10		4
	Budget authority and outlays, net:			
	Discretionary:			
4000	Budget authority, gross	16	16	16
	Outlays, gross:			
4010	Outlays from new discretionary authority	3		
4011	Outlays from discretionary balances		15	12
4020	Outlays, gross (total)	3	15	12
4180	Budget authority, net (total)	16	16	16
4190	Outlays, net (total)	3	15	12

This activity provides for the purposes of carrying out actions pursuant to the Public Buildings Reform Board (PBRB) recommendations for civilian real property. In addition, amounts received from the sale of any civilian real property pursuant to a recommendation of the PBRB are available, as provided in appropriations Acts. The Federal Asset Sales and Transfer Act authorized uses include co-location, redevelopment, reconfiguration of space, disposal, covering costs associated with sales transactions, acquiring land, construction, constructing replacement facilities, conducting advance planning and design as may be required to transfer functions from a Federal asset or property to another Federal civilian property, and other actions recommended by the PBRB for Federal agencies.

Object Classification (in millions of dollars)

Identification code 047–5594–0–2–804		2021 actual	2022 est.	2023 est.
	Direct obligations:			
25.1	Advisory and assistance services	13	4	
94.0	Financial transfers			16
99.0	Direct obligations	13	4	16
99.5	Adjustment for rounding		1	
99.9	Total new obligations, unexpired accounts	13	5	16

REAL PROPERTY RELOCATION

Program and Financing (in millions of dollars)

Identification code 047–0535–0–1–804		2021 actual	2022 est.	2023 est.
	Budgetary resources:			
	Unobligated balance:			
1000	Unobligated balance brought forward, Oct 1	11	11	11
1930	Total budgetary resources available	11	11	11
	Memorandum (non-add) entries:			
1941	Unexpired unobligated balance, end of year	11	11	11
4180	Budget authority, net (total)			
4190	Outlays, net (total)			

This appropriation covers relocation costs involved in moving agencies from valuable underutilized property, targeted for public sale, to facilities determined to be more economically suitable to their needs. Relocation and disposal is considered when the benefit/cost ratio is at least 2:1. The sale of these valuable underutilized properties would provide significant revenue to the Treasury and would far outweigh the relocation costs involved.

No appropriation is requested for this program in 2023. The General Services Administration will solicit relocation proposals from agencies.

DISPOSAL OF SURPLUS REAL AND RELATED PERSONAL PROPERTY

Special and Trust Fund Receipts (in millions of dollars)

Identification code 047–5254–0–2–804		2021 actual	2022 est.	2023 est.
0100	Balance, start of year	77	79	77
	Receipts:			
	Current law:			
1130	Receipts of Rent, Leases and Lease Payments for Government Owned Real Property		3	3
1130	Other Receipts, Surplus Real and Related Personal Property	13	10	8
1130	Transfers of Surplus Real and Related Personal Property Receipts	−12	−6	−6
1199	Total current law receipts	1	7	5
1999	Total receipts	1	7	5
2000	Total: Balances and receipts	78	86	82
	Appropriations:			
	Current law:			
2101	Disposal of Surplus Real and Related Personal Property	−2	−10	−10
2132	Disposal of Surplus Real and Related Personal Property	1	1	1
2199	Total current law appropriations	−1	−9	−9
	Proposed:			
2201	Disposal of Surplus Real and Related Personal Property			−1
2999	Total appropriations	−1	−9	−10

Real Property Activities—Continued
Federal Funds—Continued

DISPOSAL OF SURPLUS REAL AND RELATED PERSONAL PROPERTY—Continued

Special and Trust Fund Receipts—Continued

Identification code 047–5254–0–2–804	2021 actual	2022 est.	2023 est.
Special and trust fund receipts returned:			
3010 Disposal of Surplus Real and Related Personal Property	1	....	....
3010 Disposal of Surplus Real and Related Personal Property	1	....	....
5099 Balance, end of year	79	77	72

Program and Financing (in millions of dollars)

Identification code 047–5254–0–2–804	2021 actual	2022 est.	2023 est.
Obligations by program activity:			
0001 Real Property Utilization and Disposal	....	9	9
Budgetary resources:			
Budget authority:			
Appropriations, mandatory:			
1201 Appropriation (special or trust fund)	2	10	10
1232 Appropriations and/or unobligated balance of appropriations temporarily reduced	–1	–1	–1
1260 Appropriations, mandatory (total)	1	9	9
1930 Total budgetary resources available	1	9	9
Memorandum (non-add) entries:			
1940 Unobligated balance expiring	–1		
Special and non-revolving trust funds:			
1950 Other balances withdrawn and returned to unappropriated receipts	1		
1951 Unobligated balance expiring	1		
1952 Expired unobligated balance, start of year	6	6	6
1953 Expired unobligated balance, end of year	5	6	6
1954 Unobligated balance canceling	1		
Change in obligated balance:			
Unpaid obligations:			
3010 New obligations, unexpired accounts	....	9	9
3020 Outlays (gross)	....	–9	–9
Budget authority and outlays, net:			
Mandatory:			
4090 Budget authority, gross	1	9	9
Outlays, gross:			
4100 Outlays from new mandatory authority	....	8	8
4101 Outlays from mandatory balances	....	1	1
4110 Outlays, gross (total)	....	9	9
4180 Budget authority, net (total)	1	9	9
4190 Outlays, net (total)	....	9	9

Summary of Budget Authority and Outlays (in millions of dollars)

	2021 actual	2022 est.	2023 est.
Enacted/requested:			
Budget Authority	1	9	9
Outlays	....	9	9
Legislative proposal, subject to PAYGO:			
Budget Authority	....	....	1
Outlays	....	....	1
Total:			
Budget Authority	1	9	10
Outlays	....	9	10

This mandatory appropriation provides for the efficient disposal of real property assets that no longer meet the needs of landholding Federal agencies. The following costs are paid through receipts from such disposals each fiscal year: fees of auctioneers, brokers, appraisers, and environmental consultants; surveying costs; costs of advertising; costs of environmental and historical preservation services; highest and best use of property studies; property utilization studies; deed compliance inspections; and other disposal costs. GSA leverages the expertise of auctioneers and brokers familiar with local markets to accelerate the disposal of surplus real property.

Object Classification (in millions of dollars)

Identification code 047–5254–0–2–804	2021 actual	2022 est.	2023 est.
Direct obligations:			
25.1 Advisory and assistance services	....	8	8
25.3 Other goods and services from Federal sources	....	1	1
99.0 Direct obligations	....	9	9
99.9 Total new obligations, unexpired accounts	....	9	9

DISPOSAL OF SURPLUS REAL AND RELATED PERSONAL PROPERTY

(Legislative proposal, subject to PAYGO)

Program and Financing (in millions of dollars)

Identification code 047–5254–4–2–804	2021 actual	2022 est.	2023 est.
Obligations by program activity:			
0001 Real Property Utilization and Disposal	....	....	1
0900 Total new obligations, unexpired accounts (object class 25.1)	....	....	1
Budgetary resources:			
Budget authority:			
Appropriations, mandatory:			
1201 Appropriation (special or trust fund)	....	....	1
1930 Total budgetary resources available	....	....	1
Change in obligated balance:			
Unpaid obligations:			
3010 New obligations, unexpired accounts	....	....	1
3020 Outlays (gross)	....	....	–1
Budget authority and outlays, net:			
Mandatory:			
4090 Budget authority, gross	....	....	1
Outlays, gross:			
4100 Outlays from new mandatory authority	....	....	1
4180 Budget authority, net (total)	....	....	1
4190 Outlays, net (total)	....	....	1

The Administration proposes to provide GSA with broadened authorities related to the disposal of excess property. The expanded authority will allow GSA to assist agencies in identifying and preparing real property prior to the agency declaring a property excess. Currently, agencies do not always complete these types of activities because agencies must fund the activities from limited resources. This expanded authority will help to reduce the Federal footprint by providing the funding required to assess and prepare potential excess properties for disposal, the funds will then be recovered from the proceeds of sale.

SUPPLY AND TECHNOLOGY ACTIVITIES
Federal Funds

EXPENSES OF TRANSPORTATION AUDIT CONTRACTS AND CONTRACT ADMINISTRATION

Special and Trust Fund Receipts (in millions of dollars)

Identification code 047–5250–0–2–804	2021 actual	2022 est.	2023 est.
0100 Balance, start of year	25	28	19
Receipts:			
Current law:			
1130 Recoveries of Transportation Charges	13	7	6
2000 Total: Balances and receipts	38	35	25
Appropriations:			
Current law:			
2101 Expenses of Transportation Audit Contracts and Contract Administration	–13	–17	–12
2132 Expenses of Transportation Audit Contracts and Contract Administration	1	1	1
2199 Total current law appropriations	–12	–16	–11
2999 Total appropriations	–12	–16	–11
Special and trust fund receipts returned:			
3010 Expenses of Transportation Audit Contracts and Contract Administration	3	....	....

GENERAL SERVICES ADMINISTRATION

Supply and Technology Activities—Continued
Federal Funds—Continued

1151

		2021 actual	2022 est.	2023 est.
3010	Expenses of Transportation Audit Contracts and Contract Administration	3		
5098	Reconciliation adjustment	–4		
5099	Balance, end of year	28	19	14

Program and Financing (in millions of dollars)

Identification code 047–5250–0–2–804		2021 actual	2022 est.	2023 est.
	Obligations by program activity:			
0001	Audit contracts and contract administration	10	16	11
	Budgetary resources:			
	Budget authority:			
	Appropriations, mandatory:			
1201	Appropriation (special or trust fund)	13	17	12
1232	Appropriations and/or unobligated balance of appropriations temporarily reduced	–1	–1	–1
1260	Appropriations, mandatory (total)	12	16	11
1930	Total budgetary resources available	12	16	11
	Memorandum (non-add) entries:			
1940	Unobligated balance expiring	–2		
	Special and non-revolving trust funds:			
1950	Other balances withdrawn and returned to unappropriated receipts	3		
1951	Unobligated balance expiring	2		
1952	Expired unobligated balance, start of year	16	16	16
1953	Expired unobligated balance, end of year	14	16	16
1954	Unobligated balance canceling	3		
	Change in obligated balance:			
	Unpaid obligations:			
3000	Unpaid obligations, brought forward, Oct 1	9	7	9
3010	New obligations, unexpired accounts	10	16	11
3011	Obligations ("upward adjustments"), expired accounts	1		
3020	Outlays (gross)	–11	–14	–12
3041	Recoveries of prior year unpaid obligations, expired	–2		
3050	Unpaid obligations, end of year	7	9	8
	Memorandum (non-add) entries:			
3100	Obligated balance, start of year	9	7	9
3200	Obligated balance, end of year	7	9	8
	Budget authority and outlays, net:			
	Mandatory:			
4090	Budget authority, gross	12	16	11
	Outlays, gross:			
4100	Outlays from new mandatory authority	8	11	7
4101	Outlays from mandatory balances	3	3	5
4110	Outlays, gross (total)	11	14	12
4180	Budget authority, net (total)	12	16	11
4190	Outlays, net (total)	11	14	12

This permanent, indefinite appropriation provides for the detection and recovery of overpayments to carriers for Government moves under rate and service agreements established by the U.S. General Services Administration (GSA) or by other Federal agency transportation managers. Program expenses are financed from overcharges collected from transportation service providers (TSPs) as a result of post payment audits examining the validity, propriety, and conformity of charges with the proper rate authority. Funds recovered in excess of expenses are returned to the U.S Department of the Treasury.

Object Classification (in millions of dollars)

Identification code 047–5250–0–2–804		2021 actual	2022 est.	2023 est.
	Direct obligations:			
11.1	Personnel compensation: Full-time permanent	3	4	4
12.1	Civilian personnel benefits	1	1	1
25.1	Advisory and assistance services	6	11	6
99.9	Total new obligations, unexpired accounts	10	16	11

Employment Summary

Identification code 047–5250–0–2–804	2021 actual	2022 est.	2023 est.
1001 Direct civilian full-time equivalent employment	28	32	32

ACQUISITION SERVICES FUND

Program and Financing (in millions of dollars)

Identification code 047–4534–0–4–804		2021 actual	2022 est.	2023 est.
	Obligations by program activity:			
0001	Multiyear 2021–2025 ARP Transferred Funds		27	51
0700	Direct program activities, subtotal		27	51
0850	Assisted Acquisition Services (AAS) - Flow-Thru	14,396	17,287	18,169
0851	Information Technology Category (ITC) - Flow-Thru	1,285	918	265
0852	General Supplies and Services (GSS) - Flow-Thru	1,195	1,199	1,241
0853	Travel, Transportation and Logistics (TTL) - Flow-Thru	3,274	3,432	3,511
0854	Technology Transformation Services (TTS) - Flow Thru	75	59	86
0855	HR Quality Services Management Office (HR QSMO) Flow-Thru	1		
0856	Integrated Award Environment (Total Operating Exp + Reserves)	156	145	138
0857	Acquisition Services Fund - Operating (Total Operating Exp + Reserves)	1,219	1,361	1,394
0899	Total reimbursable obligations	21,601	24,401	24,804
0900	Total new obligations, unexpired accounts	21,601	24,428	24,855
	Budgetary resources:			
	Unobligated balance:			
1000	Unobligated balance brought forward, Oct 1	1,438	2,098	951
1011	Unobligated balance transfer from other acct TMF-ARP [047–0616]		27	51
1020	Adjustment of unobligated bal brought forward, Oct 1	264		
1021	Recoveries of prior year unpaid obligations	1,234	950	950
1022	Capital transfer of unobligated balances to general fund	–3		
1033	Recoveries of prior year paid obligations	8		
1070	Unobligated balance (total)	2,941	3,075	1,952
	Budget authority:			
	Spending authority from offsetting collections, mandatory:			
1800	Collected	19,439	22,304	23,850
1801	Change in uncollected payments, Federal sources	1,319		
1850	Spending auth from offsetting collections, mand (total)	20,758	22,304	23,850
1930	Total budgetary resources available	23,699	25,379	25,802
	Memorandum (non-add) entries:			
1941	Unexpired unobligated balance, end of year	2,098	951	947
	Change in obligated balance:			
	Unpaid obligations:			
3000	Unpaid obligations, brought forward, Oct 1	13,671	14,844	16,456
3001	Adjustments to unpaid obligations, brought forward, Oct 1	–264		
3010	New obligations, unexpired accounts	21,601	24,428	24,855
3020	Outlays (gross)	–18,930	–21,866	–22,922
3040	Recoveries of prior year unpaid obligations, unexpired	–1,234	–950	–950
3050	Unpaid obligations, end of year	14,844	16,456	17,439
	Uncollected payments:			
3060	Uncollected pymts, Fed sources, brought forward, Oct 1	–13,841	–15,160	–15,160
3070	Change in uncollected pymts, Fed sources, unexpired	–1,319		
3090	Uncollected pymts, Fed sources, end of year	–15,160	–15,160	–15,160
	Memorandum (non-add) entries:			
3100	Obligated balance, start of year	–434	–316	1,296
3200	Obligated balance, end of year	–316	1,296	2,279
	Budget authority and outlays, net:			
	Mandatory:			
4090	Budget authority, gross	20,758	22,304	23,850
	Outlays, gross:			
4100	Outlays from new mandatory authority	8,203	8,922	9,540
4101	Outlays from mandatory balances	10,727	12,944	13,382
4110	Outlays, gross (total)	18,930	21,866	22,922
	Offsets against gross budget authority and outlays:			
	Offsetting collections (collected) from:			
4120	Federal sources	–18,411	–22,304	–23,850
4123	Non-Federal sources	–1,036		
4130	Offsets against gross budget authority and outlays (total)	–19,447	–22,304	–23,850

ACQUISITION SERVICES FUND—Continued

Program and Financing—Continued

Identification code 047–4534–0–4–804	2021 actual	2022 est.	2023 est.
Additional offsets against gross budget authority only:			
4140 Change in uncollected pymts, Fed sources, unexpired	–1,319		
4143 Recoveries of prior year paid obligations, unexpired accounts	8		
4150 Additional offsets against budget authority only (total)	–1,311		
4170 Outlays, net (mandatory)	–517	–438	–928
4180 Budget authority, net (total)			
4190 Outlays, net (total)	–517	–438	–928

The Acquisition Services Fund (ASF) is a full cost recovery revolving fund financing a majority of the Federal Acquisition Service's (FAS) operations. FAS also includes organizations that are funded out of the Operating Expense appropriation, the Transportation Audits warrant, and the Federal Citizen Services Fund (FCSF). The ASF provides for the acquisition of information technology (IT) solutions, telecommunications, motor vehicles, supplies, and a wide range of goods and services for Federal agencies. This fund recovers costs through fees charged to Federal agencies for services rendered and commodities provided.

The ASF is authorized by section 321 of title 40, United States Code, which requires the Administrator to establish rates to be charged to agencies receiving services that: 1) recover costs; and 2) provide for the cost and capital requirements of the ASF. The ASF is authorized to retain earnings to cover these costs, such as replacing fleet vehicles maintaining supply inventories adequate for customer needs, and funding anticipated operating needs specified by the Cost and Capital Plan.

The ASF currently funds six business portfolios and one strategic initiative within FAS:

Assisted Acquisition Services (AAS).—Assists agencies in making informed procurement decisions and serves as a center of acquisition excellence for the Federal community. AAS provides acquisition, technical, and project management services related to information technology and professional services at the best value.

Office of General Supplies and Services Categories (GS&S).—Provides partner agencies with general products such as furniture, office supplies, and hardware products. GS&S centralizes acquisitions on behalf of the Government to strategically procure goods and services at reduced costs while ensuring regulatory compliance for partner agency procurements. This portfolio also provides personal property disposal services to partner agencies, which are partially funded by the Operating Expenses appropriation.

Information Technology Category (ITC).—Provides access to a wide range of commercial and custom IT products, hardware, software, telecommunications, and security services and solutions to Federal, state, and local agencies.

Professional Services & Human Capital Categories (PSHC).—Provides Federal agencies with professional and human capital services contract solutions, including payment solutions through the GSA SmartPay program.

Technology Transformation Services (TTS).—Partners with Government agencies to transform the way they build, buy, and share technology by using modern methodologies and technologies to help Federal agencies improve the public's digital experience with the Government. TTS helps agencies make their services more accessible, efficient, and effective with modern applications, platforms, processes, personnel, and software solutions

Travel, Transportation, and Logistics Categories (TTL).—Provides partner agencies with travel, transportation, and relocation services; motor vehicle acquisition; and motor vehicle fleet leasing services.

Integrated Award Environment (IAE).—IAE provides centralized technology to support a modernized Federal award environment. IAE provides a Government-wide service in collaboration with governance groups of interagency experts by providing technology solutions to manage the collection and display of standardized data that is critical to maintaining the integrity of Federal procurement and financial assistance awarding processes and navigating the Federal acquisition lifecycle.

Object Classification (in millions of dollars)

Identification code 047–4534–0–4–804	2021 actual	2022 est.	2023 est.
Direct obligations:			
11.1 Personnel compensation: Full-time permanent		6	9
12.1 Civilian personnel benefits		2	3
25.1 Advisory and assistance services		19	39
99.0 Direct obligations		27	51
Reimbursable obligations:			
Personnel compensation:			
11.1 Full-time permanent	377	449	476
11.3 Other than full-time permanent	33		
11.5 Other personnel compensation	11	10	10
11.9 Total personnel compensation	421	459	486
12.1 Civilian personnel benefits	147	160	170
21.0 Travel and transportation of persons		10	10
22.0 Transportation of things	32	9	9
23.1 Rental payments to GSA	30	29	30
23.3 Communications, utilities, and miscellaneous charges	1,355	1,032	385
24.0 Printing and reproduction	2	2	2
25.1 Advisory and assistance services	15,010	17,869	18,750
25.2 Other services from non-Federal sources	1	5	5
25.3 Other goods and services from Federal sources	318	302	318
25.7 Operation and maintenance of equipment	211	123	136
26.0 Supplies and materials	1,401	1,380	1,477
31.0 Equipment	2,672	3,021	3,026
42.0 Insurance claims and indemnities	1		
99.0 Reimbursable obligations	21,601	24,401	24,804
99.9 Total new obligations, unexpired accounts	21,601	24,428	24,855

Employment Summary

Identification code 047–4534–0–4–804	2021 actual	2022 est.	2023 est.
2001 Reimbursable civilian full-time equivalent employment	3,485	3,803	3,850

TECHNOLOGY MODERNIZATION FUND

For carrying out the purposes of the Technology Modernization Fund, as authorized by section 1078 of subtitle G of title X of the National Defense Authorization Act for Fiscal Year 2018 (Public Law 115–91; 40 U.S.C. 11301 note), $300,000,000, to remain available until expended.

Note.—A full-year 2022 appropriation for this account was not enacted at the time the Budget was prepared; therefore, the Budget assumes this account is operating under the Continuing Appropriations Act, 2022 (Division A of Public Law 117–43, as amended). The amounts included for 2022 reflect the annualized level provided by the continuing resolution.

Program and Financing (in millions of dollars)

Identification code 047–0616–0–1–808	2021 actual	2022 est.	2023 est.
Obligations by program activity:			
0001 IT Modernization and Development	1	534	642
Budgetary resources:			
Unobligated balance:			
1000 Unobligated balance brought forward, Oct 1	87	1,121	517
1001 Discretionary unobligated balance brought fwd, Oct 1	87		
1010 Unobligated balance transfer to other accts GSA WCF ARP [047–4540]		–22	–6
1010 Unobligated balance transfer to other accts USDA [012–4609]	–1		
1010 Unobligated balance transfer to other accts DOL [016–4601]		–10	
1010 Unobligated balance transfer to other accts EEOC [045–0100]		–2	
1010 Unobligated balance transfer to other accts DHS [070–0532]	–6		
1010 Unobligated balance transfer to other accts GSA ASF ARP [047–4534]		–27	–51
1010 Unobligated balance transfer to other accts GSA-FCSF ARP [047–4549]		–10	–5
1010 Unobligated balance transfer to other accts OPM ARP [024–0100]		–6	–4

1010	Unobligated balance transfer to other accts DHS ARP [070–0406]	....	–35	–16
1011	Unobligated balance transfer from other acct GSA [047–4540]	10	....	....
1011	Unobligated balance transfer from other acct DOE [089–0243]	....	1	....
1070	Unobligated balance (total)	90	1,010	435
	Budget authority:			
	Appropriations, discretionary:			
1100	Appropriation	25	25	300
	Appropriations, mandatory:			
1200	Appropriation	1,000	....	....
	Spending authority from offsetting collections, discretionary:			
1700	Collected	7	16	39
1900	Budget authority (total)	1,032	41	339
1930	Total budgetary resources available	1,122	1,051	774
	Memorandum (non-add) entries:			
1941	Unexpired unobligated balance, end of year	1,121	517	132
	Change in obligated balance:			
	Unpaid obligations:			
3000	Unpaid obligations, brought forward, Oct 1	....	....	39
3010	New obligations, unexpired accounts	1	534	642
3020	Outlays (gross)	–1	–495	–417
3050	Unpaid obligations, end of year	....	39	264
	Memorandum (non-add) entries:			
3100	Obligated balance, start of year	....	....	39
3200	Obligated balance, end of year	....	39	264
	Budget authority and outlays, net:			
	Discretionary:			
4000	Budget authority, gross	32	41	339
	Outlays, gross:			
4010	Outlays from new discretionary authority	....	5	9
4011	Outlays from discretionary balances	1	5	5
4020	Outlays, gross (total)	1	10	14
	Offsets against gross budget authority and outlays:			
	Offsetting collections (collected) from:			
4030	Federal sources	–7	–16	–39
	Mandatory:			
4090	Budget authority, gross	1,000	....	....
	Outlays, gross:			
4101	Outlays from mandatory balances	....	485	403
4180	Budget authority, net (total)	1,025	25	300
4190	Outlays, net (total)	–6	479	378

The Federal Government spends approximately $90 billion annually on information technology (IT) systems and even more on IT-related grants to state, local and territorial governments, yet, IT modernization remains challenging. It can be difficult for agencies to fund large, multi-year modernizations or to address urgent cybersecurity needs within their annual IT budget. The Technology Modernization Fund (TMF) is a revolving fund that helps finance Federal agencies' transition from antiquated legacy information technology systems to more effective, secure, and modern IT platforms. It represents a new and smarter model for funding and overseeing IT modernization projects since it a) relies on technical experts to review requests and oversee performance; b) invests money in smaller, incremental amounts based on the value being delivered; c) allows agencies to request money in a way that is better aligned with the fast pace of change in technology, especially around cybersecurity; and d) provides agencies with more flexible repayment terms and incentivizes the development of shared and reusable services across Government.

The National Defense Authorization Act for Fiscal Year 2018 (Public Law 115–91), Subtitle G—Modernizing Government Technology (MGT), Section 1078 established the TMF and Technology Modernization Board (Board). The TMF is administered by the U.S. General Services Administration (GSA) in accordance with recommendations made by the interagency TMF Board established by the MGT Act. The Board is chaired by the Administrator of the Office of Electronic Government and comprises six additional members, delineated in the Act, possessing expertise in IT development, financial management, cybersecurity and privacy, and acquisition. The MGT Act authorizes the TMF to transfer appropriations and collections in the TMF to other agencies as determined by the TMF Board.

The American Rescue Plan Act of 2021 (Public Law 117–2) added an additional $1 billion to the TMF through appropriations.

In accordance with guidance from OMB, the Board rigorously reviews agency modernization proposals and prioritizes projects that support cross-government collaboration via scalable services, address urgent cybersecurity needs, modernize high-priority systems, and improve a citizen's ability to easily access government services via public-facing digital services. To maintain a focus on delivering impact, the Fund will invest in a diverse portfolio of projects having varying levels of repayment flexibility and expects to recover a portion of the funds.

The MGT Act provides the GSA Administrator and OMB Director with the authority to establish and amend the terms of repayment to the TMF. Extending repayment flexibility to agencies gives the Fund the ability to make smart investments and maximize the benefit to the government and public. It allows the Fund to continue investing in projects with (i) the highest probability of success and (ii) the highest value to the public and/or highest impact cybersecurity outcomes, regardless of whether cost savings are expected. Repayment can range from full repayment on investments with direct cost savings, such as replacing a legacy system with one that can be operated and maintained more efficiently, to minimal repayment for proposals that tackle the most urgent cybersecurity and modernization problems facing our government, where cost savings are not easily realized by the proposing agency.

Ultimately, retiring or modernizing vulnerable and inefficient legacy IT systems will make agencies more secure and yield savings in time and budget. Absent immediate action, the cost to operate and maintain legacy systems will continue to grow while cybersecurity vulnerabilities and other risks grow. As a means of addressing these pressing challenges, the TMF is an important step in changing the way the Federal Government manages its IT portfolio.

Prior to 2021, the Board reviewed more than 50 project proposals requesting over $550 million; this resulted in 11 approved projects representing $89 million in active investments. Since the American Rescue Plan (ARP) was enacted, the Board has received over 120 proposals from Federal agencies requesting more the $2.5 billion in funding. The TMF was able to support seven new modernization projects totaling over $311 million within the first few months of receiving ARP funding. New proposals continue to arrive on a rolling basis and additional investment rounds will be announced in 2022.

Object Classification (in millions of dollars)

Identification code 047–0616–0–1–808	2021 actual	2022 est.	2023 est.
Direct obligations:			
11.1 Personnel compensation: Full-time permanent	1	3	4
12.1 Civilian personnel benefits	....	1	1
25.3 Other goods and services from Federal sources	....	1	1
94.0 Financial transfers	....	529	636
99.0 Direct obligations	1	534	642
99.9 Total new obligations, unexpired accounts	1	534	642

Employment Summary

Identification code 047–0616–0–1–808	2021 actual	2022 est.	2023 est.
1001 Direct civilian full-time equivalent employment	2	18	25

GENERAL ACTIVITIES

Federal Funds

GOVERNMENT-WIDE POLICY

For expenses authorized by law, not otherwise provided for, for Government-wide policy and evaluation activities associated with the management of real and personal property assets and certain administrative services; Government-wide policy support responsibilities relating to acquisition, travel, motor vehicles, information technology

GOVERNMENT-WIDE POLICY—Continued

management, and related technology activities; and services as authorized by 5 U.S.C. 3109; $70,354,000, of which $4,000,000 shall remain available until September 30, 2024.

Note.—A full-year 2022 appropriation for this account was not enacted at the time the Budget was prepared; therefore, the Budget assumes this account is operating under the Continuing Appropriations Act, 2022 (Division A of Public Law 117–43, as amended). The amounts included for 2022 reflect the annualized level provided by the continuing resolution.

Program and Financing (in millions of dollars)

Identification code 047–0401–0–1–804		2021 actual	2022 est.	2023 est.
	Obligations by program activity:			
0001	Government-wide policy	64	64	70
0801	Government-wide Policy (Reimbursable)	38	38	38
0900	Total new obligations, unexpired accounts	102	102	108
	Budgetary resources:			
	Unobligated balance:			
1000	Unobligated balance brought forward, Oct 1	24	21	21
	Budget authority:			
	Appropriations, discretionary:			
1100	Appropriation	64	64	70
	Spending authority from offsetting collections, discretionary:			
1700	Collected	33	38	38
1701	Change in uncollected payments, Federal sources	2		
1750	Spending auth from offsetting collections, disc (total)	35	38	38
1900	Budget authority (total)	99	102	108
1930	Total budgetary resources available	123	123	129
	Memorandum (non-add) entries:			
1941	Unexpired unobligated balance, end of year	21	21	21
	Change in obligated balance:			
	Unpaid obligations:			
3000	Unpaid obligations, brought forward, Oct 1	52	47	45
3010	New obligations, unexpired accounts	102	102	108
3020	Outlays (gross)	–106	–104	–107
3041	Recoveries of prior year unpaid obligations, expired	–1		
3050	Unpaid obligations, end of year	47	45	46
	Uncollected payments:			
3060	Uncollected pymts, Fed sources, brought forward, Oct 1	–3	–4	–4
3070	Change in uncollected pymts, Fed sources, unexpired	–2		
3071	Change in uncollected pymts, Fed sources, expired	1		
3090	Uncollected pymts, Fed sources, end of year	–4	–4	–4
	Memorandum (non-add) entries:			
3100	Obligated balance, start of year	49	43	41
3200	Obligated balance, end of year	43	41	42
	Budget authority and outlays, net:			
	Discretionary:			
4000	Budget authority, gross	99	102	108
	Outlays, gross:			
4010	Outlays from new discretionary authority	50	65	70
4011	Outlays from discretionary balances	56	39	37
4020	Outlays, gross (total)	106	104	107
	Offsets against gross budget authority and outlays:			
	Offsetting collections (collected) from:			
4030	Federal sources	–34	–38	–38
	Additional offsets against gross budget authority only:			
4050	Change in uncollected pymts, Fed sources, unexpired	–2		
4052	Offsetting collections credited to expired accounts	1		
4060	Additional offsets against budget authority only (total)	–1		
4070	Budget authority, net (discretionary)	64	64	70
4080	Outlays, net (discretionary)	72	66	69
4180	Budget authority, net (total)	64	64	70
4190	Outlays, net (total)	72	66	69

This appropriation provides for the activities of the Office of Government-wide Policy (OGP). OGP works cooperatively with other agencies to develop and evaluate a wide-ranging set of policies to improve Government operations: acquisition and acquisition workforce career development; real property (including high-performing building policy); personal property; travel, transportation management, motor vehicles, and aircraft; advisory committee management; information technology (IT) and cybersecurity; evaluation practices; and transparency of regulatory information. OGP also collaborates with agencies and other primary government organizations to provide support for the execution of Government-wide priorities and programs. These programs include program management support for Government-wide shared services, cross-agency priority goals in the President's Management Agenda (PMA) and IT programs. OGP identifies and shares policies and best practices to drive savings, efficiency, and effectiveness across the Federal Government.

Object Classification (in millions of dollars)

Identification code 047–0401–0–1–804		2021 actual	2022 est.	2023 est.
	Direct obligations:			
	Personnel compensation:			
11.1	Full-time permanent	19	22	23
11.3	Other than full-time permanent	1		
11.9	Total personnel compensation	20	22	23
12.1	Civilian personnel benefits	7	7	8
23.1	Rental payments to GSA	2	2	2
25.1	Advisory and assistance services	16	16	20
25.3	Other goods and services from Federal sources	19	15	16
99.0	Direct obligations	64	62	69
99.0	Reimbursable obligations	37	38	38
99.5	Adjustment for rounding	1	2	1
99.9	Total new obligations, unexpired accounts	102	102	108

Employment Summary

Identification code 047–0401–0–1–804		2021 actual	2022 est.	2023 est.
1001	Direct civilian full-time equivalent employment	135	161	153
2001	Reimbursable civilian full-time equivalent employment	30	28	28

OPERATING EXPENSES

For expenses authorized by law, not otherwise provided for, for Government-wide activities associated with utilization and donation of surplus personal property; disposal of real property; agency-wide policy direction and management; the hire of zero emission passenger motor vehicles and supporting charging or fueling infrastructure; and services as authorized by 5 U.S.C. 3109; $54,478,000, of which not to exceed $7,500 is for official reception and representation expenses.

Note.—A full-year 2022 appropriation for this account was not enacted at the time the Budget was prepared; therefore, the Budget assumes this account is operating under the Continuing Appropriations Act, 2022 (Division A of Public Law 117–43, as amended). The amounts included for 2022 reflect the annualized level provided by the continuing resolution.

Program and Financing (in millions of dollars)

Identification code 047–0110–0–1–804		2021 actual	2022 est.	2023 est.
	Obligations by program activity:			
0001	Operating Expenses (Direct)	47	52	54
0801	Operating Expenses (Reimbursable)	3	12	12
0900	Total new obligations, unexpired accounts	50	64	66
	Budgetary resources:			
	Unobligated balance:			
1000	Unobligated balance brought forward, Oct 1	4	4	1
	Budget authority:			
	Appropriations, discretionary:			
1100	Appropriation	49	49	54
	Spending authority from offsetting collections, discretionary:			
1700	Collected	3	12	12
1701	Change in uncollected payments, Federal sources	4		
1750	Spending auth from offsetting collections, disc (total)	7	12	12
1900	Budget authority (total)	56	61	66
1930	Total budgetary resources available	60	65	67
	Memorandum (non-add) entries:			
1940	Unobligated balance expiring	–6		
1941	Unexpired unobligated balance, end of year	4	1	1
	Change in obligated balance:			
	Unpaid obligations:			
3000	Unpaid obligations, brought forward, Oct 1	12	11	13
3010	New obligations, unexpired accounts	50	64	66
3020	Outlays (gross)	–50	–62	–65

GENERAL SERVICES ADMINISTRATION

General Activities—Continued
Federal Funds—Continued

		2021 actual	2022 est.	2023 est.
3041	Recoveries of prior year unpaid obligations, expired	–1		
3050	Unpaid obligations, end of year	11	13	14
	Uncollected payments:			
3060	Uncollected pymts, Fed sources, brought forward, Oct 1	–3	–4	–4
3070	Change in uncollected pymts, Fed sources, unexpired	–4		
3071	Change in uncollected pymts, Fed sources, expired	3		
3090	Uncollected pymts, Fed sources, end of year	–4	–4	–4
	Memorandum (non-add) entries:			
3100	Obligated balance, start of year	9	7	9
3200	Obligated balance, end of year	7	9	10
	Budget authority and outlays, net:			
	Discretionary:			
4000	Budget authority, gross	56	61	66
	Outlays, gross:			
4010	Outlays from new discretionary authority	41	53	57
4011	Outlays from discretionary balances	9	9	8
4020	Outlays, gross (total)	50	62	65
	Offsets against gross budget authority and outlays:			
	Offsetting collections (collected) from:			
4030	Federal sources	–3	–12	–12
	Additional offsets against gross budget authority only:			
4050	Change in uncollected pymts, Fed sources, unexpired	–4		
4060	Additional offsets against budget authority only (total)	–4		
4070	Budget authority, net (discretionary)	49	49	54
4080	Outlays, net (discretionary)	47	50	53
4180	Budget authority, net (total)	49	49	54
4190	Outlays, net (total)	47	50	53

The major programs funded by this appropriation include the personal property utilization and donation activities of the Federal Acquisition Service; the real property utilization and disposal activities of the Public Buildings Service; and Executive Management and Administration activities including support of Government-wide mission assurance activities. This appropriation supports a variety of operational activities that are not feasible or appropriate for a user fee arrangement.

Object Classification (in millions of dollars)

Identification code 047–0110–0–1–804		2021 actual	2022 est.	2023 est.
	Direct obligations:			
	Personnel compensation:			
11.1	Full-time permanent	20	26	27
11.3	Other than full-time permanent	2		
11.5	Other personnel compensation	1		
11.9	Total personnel compensation	23	26	27
12.1	Civilian personnel benefits	8	9	9
23.1	Rental payments to GSA	1	1	1
25.1	Advisory and assistance services	7	6	9
25.3	Other goods and services from Federal sources	8	9	7
99.0	Direct obligations	47	51	53
99.0	Reimbursable obligations	3	12	12
99.5	Adjustment for rounding		1	1
99.9	Total new obligations, unexpired accounts	50	64	66

Employment Summary

Identification code 047–0110–0–1–804		2021 actual	2022 est.	2023 est.
1001	Direct civilian full-time equivalent employment	181	215	215
2001	Reimbursable civilian full-time equivalent employment	12	7	7

CIVILIAN BOARD OF CONTRACT APPEALS

For expenses authorized by law, not otherwise provided for, for the activities associated with the Civilian Board of Contract Appeals, $10,352,000, of which $2,000,000 shall remain available until expended.

Note.—A full-year 2022 appropriation for this account was not enacted at the time the Budget was prepared; therefore, the Budget assumes this account is operating under the Continuing Appropriations Act, 2022 (Division A of Public Law 117–43, as amended). The amounts included for 2022 reflect the annualized level provided by the continuing resolution.

Program and Financing (in millions of dollars)

Identification code 047–0610–0–1–804		2021 actual	2022 est.	2023 est.
	Obligations by program activity:			
0001	Direct program activity	9	9	10
	Budgetary resources:			
	Budget authority:			
	Appropriations, discretionary:			
1100	Appropriation	9	9	10
1900	Budget authority (total)	9	9	10
1930	Total budgetary resources available	9	9	10
	Change in obligated balance:			
	Unpaid obligations:			
3000	Unpaid obligations, brought forward, Oct 1	1	1	
3010	New obligations, unexpired accounts	9	9	10
3020	Outlays (gross)	–9	–10	–10
3050	Unpaid obligations, end of year	1		
	Uncollected payments:			
3060	Uncollected pymts, Fed sources, brought forward, Oct 1	–1	–1	–1
3090	Uncollected pymts, Fed sources, end of year	–1	–1	–1
	Memorandum (non-add) entries:			
3100	Obligated balance, start of year			–1
3200	Obligated balance, end of year		–1	–1
	Budget authority and outlays, net:			
	Discretionary:			
4000	Budget authority, gross	9	9	10
	Outlays, gross:			
4010	Outlays from new discretionary authority	8	9	10
4011	Outlays from discretionary balances	1	1	
4020	Outlays, gross (total)	9	10	10
4180	Budget authority, net (total)	9	9	10
4190	Outlays, net (total)	9	10	10

The Civilian Board of Contract Appeals (CBCA) provides the prompt, efficient, and inexpensive resolution of various disputes involving Federal executive branch agencies. The CBCA adjudicates contract disputes under the Contract Disputes Act (CDA) between Government contractors and all civilian executive agencies other than the National Aeronautics and Space Administration (NASA), the United States Postal Service (USPS), the Postal Regulatory Commission (PRC), and the Tennessee Valley Authority (TVA). Resolving CDA disputes can be accomplished by holding a hearing, deciding on the record, or achieving settlement through alternative dispute resolution (ADR). To accomplish this, the CBCA judges will hold a hearing or engage in ADR in the CBCAs offices or they will travel, at the CBCA's expense, to a mutually agreed upon location.

Object Classification (in millions of dollars)

Identification code 047–0610–0–1–804		2021 actual	2022 est.	2023 est.
	Direct obligations:			
11.1	Personnel compensation: Full-time permanent	4	4	5
12.1	Civilian personnel benefits		1	1
21.0	Travel and transportation of persons	1		
23.1	Rental payments to GSA	3	3	3
25.3	Other goods and services from Federal sources			1
99.0	Direct obligations	8	8	10
99.5	Adjustment for rounding	1	1	
99.9	Total new obligations, unexpired accounts	9	9	10

Employment Summary

Identification code 047–0610–0–1–804		2021 actual	2022 est.	2023 est.
1001	Direct civilian full-time equivalent employment	29	41	41

OFFICE OF INSPECTOR GENERAL

For necessary expenses of the Office of Inspector General and services authorized by 5 U.S.C. 3109, $74,583,000: Provided, That not to exceed $3,000,000 shall be

OFFICE OF INSPECTOR GENERAL—Continued

available for information technology enhancements related to implementing cloud services, improving security measures, and providing modern technology case management solutions: Provided further, That not to exceed $50,000 shall be available for payment for information and detection of fraud against the Government, including payment for recovery of stolen Government property: Provided further, That not to exceed $2,500 shall be available for awards to employees of other Federal agencies and private citizens in recognition of efforts and initiatives resulting in enhanced Office of Inspector General effectiveness.

Note.—A full-year 2022 appropriation for this account was not enacted at the time the Budget was prepared; therefore, the Budget assumes this account is operating under the Continuing Appropriations Act, 2022 (Division A of Public Law 117–43, as amended). The amounts included for 2022 reflect the annualized level provided by the continuing resolution.

Program and Financing (in millions of dollars)

Identification code 047–0108–0–1–804		2021 actual	2022 est.	2023 est.
	Obligations by program activity:			
0001	Office of Inspector General (Direct)	67	67	75
0802	Office of Inspector General (Reimbursable)	....	1	1
0900	Total new obligations, unexpired accounts	67	68	76
	Budgetary resources:			
	Unobligated balance:			
1000	Unobligated balance brought forward, Oct 1	4	3	3
	Budget authority:			
	Appropriations, discretionary:			
1100	Appropriation	67	67	75
	Spending authority from offsetting collections, discretionary:			
1700	Collected	....	1	1
1900	Budget authority (total)	67	68	76
1930	Total budgetary resources available	71	71	79
	Memorandum (non-add) entries:			
1940	Unobligated balance expiring	–1	....	....
1941	Unexpired unobligated balance, end of year	3	3	3
	Change in obligated balance:			
	Unpaid obligations:			
3000	Unpaid obligations, brought forward, Oct 1	8	7	9
3010	New obligations, unexpired accounts	67	68	76
3020	Outlays (gross)	–67	–66	–74
3041	Recoveries of prior year unpaid obligations, expired	–1	....	....
3050	Unpaid obligations, end of year	7	9	11
	Memorandum (non-add) entries:			
3100	Obligated balance, start of year	8	7	9
3200	Obligated balance, end of year	7	9	11
	Budget authority and outlays, net:			
	Discretionary:			
4000	Budget authority, gross	67	68	76
	Outlays, gross:			
4010	Outlays from new discretionary authority	61	57	63
4011	Outlays from discretionary balances	6	9	11
4020	Outlays, gross (total)	67	66	74
	Offsets against gross budget authority and outlays:			
	Offsetting collections (collected) from:			
4030	Federal sources	....	–1	–1
4180	Budget authority, net (total)	67	67	75
4190	Outlays, net (total)	67	65	73

This appropriation provides agency-wide audit, investigative, and inspection functions to identify and correct management and administrative deficiencies within the General Services Administration (GSA), including conditions for existing or potential instances of fraud, waste, and mismanagement. This audit function provides internal audit and contract audit services. Contract audits provide professional advice to GSA contracting officials on accounting and financial matters relative to the negotiation, award, administration, repricing, and settlement of contracts. Internal audits review and evaluate all facets of GSA operations and programs, test internal control systems, and develop information to improve operating efficiencies and enhance customer services. The investigative function provides for the detection and investigation of improper and illegal activities involving GSA programs, personnel, and operations. The inspection function supplements traditional audits and investigations by providing systematic and independent assessments of the design, implementation, and/or results of GSA's operations, programs, or policies.

Object Classification (in millions of dollars)

Identification code 047–0108–0–1–804		2021 actual	2022 est.	2023 est.
	Direct obligations:			
	Personnel compensation:			
11.1	Full-time permanent	35	35	38
11.3	Other than full-time permanent	1	....	....
11.5	Other personnel compensation	3	3	3
11.9	Total personnel compensation	39	38	41
12.1	Civilian personnel benefits	15	15	17
21.0	Travel and transportation of persons	1	1	1
23.1	Rental payments to GSA	5	5	5
25.1	Advisory and assistance services	2	2	5
25.3	Other goods and services from Federal sources	3	4	4
25.7	Operation and maintenance of equipment	1	1	1
31.0	Equipment	1	1	1
99.0	Direct obligations	67	67	75
99.5	Adjustment for rounding	....	1	1
99.9	Total new obligations, unexpired accounts	67	68	76

Employment Summary

Identification code 047–0108–0–1–804		2021 actual	2022 est.	2023 est.
1001	Direct civilian full-time equivalent employment	288	278	294
2001	Reimbursable civilian full-time equivalent employment	1	2	3

ALLOWANCES AND OFFICE STAFF FOR FORMER PRESIDENTS

For carrying out the provisions of the Act of August 25, 1958, as amended (3 U.S.C. 102 note), $5,200,000.

Note.—A full-year 2022 appropriation for this account was not enacted at the time the Budget was prepared; therefore, the Budget assumes this account is operating under the Continuing Appropriations Act, 2022 (Division A of Public Law 117–43, as amended). The amounts included for 2022 reflect the annualized level provided by the continuing resolution.

Program and Financing (in millions of dollars)

Identification code 047–0105–0–1–802		2021 actual	2022 est.	2023 est.
	Obligations by program activity:			
0001	Allowances, pensions, and office staff	4	5	5
	Budgetary resources:			
	Budget authority:			
	Appropriations, discretionary:			
1100	Appropriation	4	5	5
1930	Total budgetary resources available	4	5	5
	Change in obligated balance:			
	Unpaid obligations:			
3010	New obligations, unexpired accounts	4	5	5
3020	Outlays (gross)	–4	–5	–5
	Budget authority and outlays, net:			
	Discretionary:			
4000	Budget authority, gross	4	5	5
	Outlays, gross:			
4010	Outlays from new discretionary authority	4	5	5
4180	Budget authority, net (total)	4	5	5
4190	Outlays, net (total)	4	5	5

This appropriation provides pensions, office staff, and related expenses for former Presidents Jimmy Carter, William Clinton, George W. Bush, Barack Obama, and Donald Trump.

Object Classification (in millions of dollars)

Identification code 047–0105–0–1–802		2021 actual	2022 est.	2023 est.
	Direct obligations:			
12.1	Civilian personnel benefits	....	....	1
13.0	Benefits for former Presidents	1	1	1

GENERAL SERVICES ADMINISTRATION

		2021 actual	2022 est.	2023 est.
23.1	Rental payments to GSA	2	2	2
99.0	Direct obligations	3	3	4
99.5	Adjustment for rounding	1	2	1
99.9	Total new obligations, unexpired accounts	4	5	5

EXPENSES, PRESIDENTIAL TRANSITION

Note.—A full-year 2022 appropriation for this account was not enacted at the time the Budget was prepared; therefore, the Budget assumes this account is operating under the Continuing Appropriations Act, 2022 (Division A of Public Law 117–43, as amended). The amounts included for 2022 reflect the annualized level provided by the continuing resolution.

Program and Financing (in millions of dollars)

Identification code 047–0107–0–1–802		2021 actual	2022 est.	2023 est.
	Obligations by program activity:			
0001	Presidential Transition		10	
	Budgetary resources:			
	Budget authority:			
	Appropriations, discretionary:			
1100	Appropriation		10	
1930	Total budgetary resources available		10	
	Change in obligated balance:			
	Unpaid obligations:			
3000	Unpaid obligations, brought forward, Oct 1			1
3010	New obligations, unexpired accounts		10	
3020	Outlays (gross)		–9	–1
3050	Unpaid obligations, end of year		1	
	Memorandum (non-add) entries:			
3100	Obligated balance, start of year			1
3200	Obligated balance, end of year		1	
	Budget authority and outlays, net:			
	Discretionary:			
4000	Budget authority, gross		10	
	Outlays, gross:			
4010	Outlays from new discretionary authority		9	
4011	Outlays from discretionary balances			1
4020	Outlays, gross (total)		9	1
4180	Budget authority, net (total)		10	
4190	Outlays, net (total)		9	1

This appropriation provides for an orderly transfer of Executive leadership in accordance with the Presidential Transition Act of 1963, as amended. These expenses include costs of $1,000,000 provided for briefing and training personnel associated with the incoming administration. New appropriations are generally requested only in Presidential election years.

Object Classification (in millions of dollars)

Identification code 047–0107–0–1–802		2021 actual	2022 est.	2023 est.
	Direct obligations:			
11.8	Personnel compensation: Special personal services payments		1	
21.0	Travel and transportation of persons		1	
25.1	Advisory and assistance services		7	
99.0	Direct obligations		9	
99.5	Adjustment for rounding		1	
99.9	Total new obligations, unexpired accounts		10	

PRE-ELECTION PRESIDENTIAL TRANSITION

Program and Financing (in millions of dollars)

Identification code 047–0603–0–1–802		2021 actual	2022 est.	2023 est.
	Obligations by program activity:			
0001	Pre-Election Transition		3	
0900	Total new obligations, unexpired accounts (object class 25.1)		3	
	Budgetary resources:			
	Unobligated balance:			
1000	Unobligated balance brought forward, Oct 1		6	
1930	Total budgetary resources available		6	
	Memorandum (non-add) entries:			
1940	Unobligated balance expiring		–3	
	Change in obligated balance:			
	Unpaid obligations:			
3000	Unpaid obligations, brought forward, Oct 1		2	1
3010	New obligations, unexpired accounts		3	
3020	Outlays (gross)		–4	–1
3050	Unpaid obligations, end of year		1	
	Memorandum (non-add) entries:			
3100	Obligated balance, start of year		2	1
3200	Obligated balance, end of year		1	
	Budget authority and outlays, net:			
	Discretionary:			
	Outlays, gross:			
4011	Outlays from discretionary balances		4	1
4180	Budget authority, net (total)			
4190	Outlays, net (total)		4	1

In accordance with the Pre-Election Transition Act of 2010, the Pre-Election Presidential Transition appropriation enables GSA to provide suitable office space for Pre-Election transition activities, acquire communication services and information technology equipment, and for printing and supplies associated with the potential transition. New appropriations are generally requested only the year before a Presidential election year.

ELECTRIC VEHICLES FUND

There is appropriated to the General Services Administration $300,000,000, to remain available until expended, for the purchase of zero emission passenger motor vehicles and supporting charging or fueling infrastructure, notwithstanding 42 U.S.C. 13212(c) and in addition to amounts otherwise available for such purposes: Provided, That amounts available under this heading may be transferred to and merged with appropriations at other Federal agencies, at the discretion of the Administrator, for carrying out the purposes under this heading, including for the procurement of charging infrastructure for the U.S. Postal Service.

Note.—A full-year 2022 appropriation for this account was not enacted at the time the Budget was prepared; therefore, the Budget assumes this account is operating under the Continuing Appropriations Act, 2022 (Division A of Public Law 117–43, as amended). The amounts included for 2022 reflect the annualized level provided by the continuing resolution.

Program and Financing (in millions of dollars)

Identification code 047–0623–0–1–804		2021 actual	2022 est.	2023 est.
	Obligations by program activity:			
0001	Financial Transfers			150
0900	Total new obligations, unexpired accounts (object class 94.0)			150
	Budgetary resources:			
	Budget authority:			
	Appropriations, discretionary:			
1100	Appropriation			300
1900	Budget authority (total)			300
1930	Total budgetary resources available			300
	Memorandum (non-add) entries:			
1941	Unexpired unobligated balance, end of year			150
	Change in obligated balance:			
	Unpaid obligations:			
3010	New obligations, unexpired accounts			150
3020	Outlays (gross)			–50
3050	Unpaid obligations, end of year			100
	Memorandum (non-add) entries:			
3200	Obligated balance, end of year			100
	Budget authority and outlays, net:			
	Discretionary:			
4000	Budget authority, gross			300

ELECTRIC VEHICLES FUND—Continued

Program and Financing—Continued

Identification code 047–0623–0–1–804	2021 actual	2022 est.	2023 est.
Outlays, gross:			
4010 Outlays from new discretionary authority	....	....	50
4180 Budget authority, net (total)	....	....	300
4190 Outlays, net (total)	....	....	50

The Electric Vehicles Fund (EVF) enables the General Services Administration (GSA) to support the Administration's goal of electrifying the Federal fleet by providing the mechanism for GSA to procure zero emission vehicles and the associated charging infrastructure on behalf of Federal agencies.

ACQUISITION WORKFORCE TRAINING FUND

Special and Trust Fund Receipts (in millions of dollars)

Identification code 047–5381–0–2–804	2021 actual	2022 est.	2023 est.
0100 Balance, start of year	3	6	6
Receipts:			
Current law:			
1140 Acquisition Workforce Training Fund	14	12	12
2000 Total: Balances and receipts	17	18	18
Appropriations:			
Current law:			
2101 Acquisition Workforce Training Fund	–11	–12	–12
5099 Balance, end of year	6	6	6

Program and Financing (in millions of dollars)

Identification code 047–5381–0–2–804	2021 actual	2022 est.	2023 est.
Obligations by program activity:			
0002 Acquisition Workforce Training	11	12	12
Budgetary resources:			
Unobligated balance:			
1000 Unobligated balance brought forward, Oct 1	16	16	16
Budget authority:			
Appropriations, mandatory:			
1201 Appropriation (special or trust fund)	11	12	12
1930 Total budgetary resources available	27	28	28
Memorandum (non-add) entries:			
1941 Unexpired unobligated balance, end of year	16	16	16
Special and non-revolving trust funds:			
1952 Expired unobligated balance, start of year	1	....	....
Change in obligated balance:			
Unpaid obligations:			
3000 Unpaid obligations, brought forward, Oct 1	9	10	10
3010 New obligations, unexpired accounts	11	12	12
3020 Outlays (gross)	–10	–12	–12
3050 Unpaid obligations, end of year	10	10	10
Memorandum (non-add) entries:			
3100 Obligated balance, start of year	9	10	10
3200 Obligated balance, end of year	10	10	10
Budget authority and outlays, net:			
Mandatory:			
4090 Budget authority, gross	11	12	12
Outlays, gross:			
4100 Outlays from new mandatory authority	....	1	1
4101 Outlays from mandatory balances	10	11	11
4110 Outlays, gross (total)	10	12	12
4180 Budget authority, net (total)	11	12	12
4190 Outlays, net (total)	10	12	12

The Acquisition Workforce Training Fund (AWTF) is a permanent, indefinite appropriation providing a source of funds to train the Federal acquisition workforce. The AWTF is financed through a credit of five percent of the fees collected from non-Department of Defense activities by the General Services Administration (GSA) and other civilian agencies that manage Government-wide Acquisition Contracts (GWACs), Multiple Award Schedules (MAS) contracts entered into by the Administrator of General Services, and other multi-agency contracts. Receipts are available for expenditure in the fiscal year collected, in addition to the two following fiscal years. The AWTF is managed by the Administrator of General Services through GSA's Federal Acquisition Institute (FAI) in consultation with the Office of Federal Procurement Policy, and the FAI Board of Directors.

Object Classification (in millions of dollars)

Identification code 047–5381–0–2–804	2021 actual	2022 est.	2023 est.
Direct obligations:			
11.1 Personnel compensation: Full-time permanent	....	2	2
12.1 Civilian personnel benefits	....	1	1
25.1 Advisory and assistance services	4	5	5
25.3 Other goods and services from Federal sources	7	4	4
99.9 Total new obligations, unexpired accounts	11	12	12

Employment Summary

Identification code 047–5381–0–2–804	2021 actual	2022 est.	2023 est.
1001 Direct civilian full-time equivalent employment	....	12	12

ENVIRONMENTAL REVIEW IMPROVEMENT FUND

Program and Financing (in millions of dollars)

Identification code 047–5640–0–2–808	2021 actual	2022 est.	2023 est.
Budgetary resources:			
Unobligated balance:			
1000 Unobligated balance brought forward, Oct 1	1	....	....
1010 Unobligated balance transfer to other accts [473–5761]	–1	....	....
4180 Budget authority, net (total)	....	....	....
4190 Outlays, net (total)	....	....	....

The appropriations for the Environmental Review Improvement Fund have transferred and merged with a new independent fund in 2020 in accordance with Public Law 116–93.

FEDERAL CITIZEN SERVICES FUND

(INCLUDING TRANSFER OF FUNDS)

For expenses authorized by 40 U.S.C. 323 and 44 U.S.C. 3604; and for expenses authorized by law, not otherwise provided for, in support of interagency projects that enable the Federal Government to enhance its ability to conduct activities electronically, through the development and implementation of innovative uses of information technology; $115,784,000, to be deposited into the Federal Citizen Services Fund: Provided, That the previous amount may be transferred to Federal agencies to carry out the purpose of the Federal Citizen Services Fund: Provided further, That the appropriations, revenues, reimbursements, and collections deposited into the Fund shall be available until expended for necessary expenses of Federal Citizen Services and other activities that enable the Federal Government to enhance its ability to conduct activities electronically: Provided further, That the transfer authorities provided herein shall be in addition to any other transfer authority provided in this Act.

Note.—A full-year 2022 appropriation for this account was not enacted at the time the Budget was prepared; therefore, the Budget assumes this account is operating under the Continuing Appropriations Act, 2022 (Division A of Public Law 117–43, as amended). The amounts included for 2022 reflect the annualized level provided by the continuing resolution.

Program and Financing (in millions of dollars)

Identification code 047–4549–0–4–376	2021 actual	2022 est.	2023 est.
Obligations by program activity:			
0001 Office of Products and Programs	60	81	88
0003 Digital Services	5	4	13
0004 American Rescue Plan	3	60	60
0799 Total direct obligations	68	145	161

GENERAL SERVICES ADMINISTRATION

		2021 actual	2022 est.	2023 est.
0802	Federal Citizen Services Fund (Reimbursable)	4	7	42
0900	Total new obligations, unexpired accounts	72	152	203
	Budgetary resources:			
	Unobligated balance:			
1000	Unobligated balance brought forward, Oct 1	20	158	78
1001	Discretionary unobligated balance brought fwd, Oct 1	20		
1011	Unobligated balance transfer from other acct [047–0616]		10	5
1021	Recoveries of prior year unpaid obligations	3		
1070	Unobligated balance (total)	23	168	83
	Budget authority:			
	Appropriations, discretionary:			
1100	Appropriation	55	55	116
	Appropriations, mandatory:			
1200	Appropriation	150		
	Spending authority from offsetting collections, discretionary:			
1700	Collected	3	7	42
1701	Change in uncollected payments, Federal sources	–1		
1750	Spending auth from offsetting collections, disc (total)	2	7	42
1900	Budget authority (total)	207	62	158
1930	Total budgetary resources available	230	230	241
	Memorandum (non-add) entries:			
1941	Unexpired unobligated balance, end of year	158	78	38
	Change in obligated balance:			
	Unpaid obligations:			
3000	Unpaid obligations, brought forward, Oct 1	33	36	74
3010	New obligations, unexpired accounts	72	152	203
3020	Outlays (gross)	–66	–114	–172
3040	Recoveries of prior year unpaid obligations, unexpired	–3		
3050	Unpaid obligations, end of year	36	74	105
	Uncollected payments:			
3060	Uncollected pymts, Fed sources, brought forward, Oct 1	–4	–3	–3
3070	Change in uncollected pymts, Fed sources, unexpired	1		
3090	Uncollected pymts, Fed sources, end of year	–3	–3	–3
	Memorandum (non-add) entries:			
3100	Obligated balance, start of year	29	33	71
3200	Obligated balance, end of year	33	71	102
	Budget authority and outlays, net:			
	Discretionary:			
4000	Budget authority, gross	57	62	158
	Outlays, gross:			
4010	Outlays from new discretionary authority	37	51	135
4011	Outlays from discretionary balances	29	11	11
4020	Outlays, gross (total)	66	62	146
	Offsets against gross budget authority and outlays:			
	Offsetting collections (collected) from:			
4030	Federal sources	–3	–7	–42
	Additional offsets against gross budget authority only:			
4050	Change in uncollected pymts, Fed sources, unexpired	1		
4070	Budget authority, net (discretionary)	55	55	116
4080	Outlays, net (discretionary)	63	55	104
	Mandatory:			
4090	Budget authority, gross	150		
	Outlays, gross:			
4101	Outlays from mandatory balances		52	26
4180	Budget authority, net (total)	205	55	116
4190	Outlays, net (total)	63	107	130
	Memorandum (non-add) entries:			
5096	Unexpired unavailable balance, SOY: Appropriations	2	2	2
5098	Unexpired unavailable balance, EOY: Appropriations	2	2	2

GSA established the Technology Transformation Service (TTS) in 2016 to design and deliver a digital Government with and for the American people. Empowered by the Federal Citizen Services Fund (FCSF), the TTS enables public access to, and engagement with, the Federal Government. Through the FCSF, TTS makes Government services more accessible, efficient, and effective with modern applications, personnel, and software services.

The FCSF supports public facing services and agency facing programs that drive Government-wide transformation through shared services, platforms and solutions. The programs funded by the FCSF drive transformation by providing technical expertise to agencies to improve their operations and spur the adoption and improvement of digital services. This appropriation furthers the President's Management Agenda by supporting the Executive Order on Transforming Federal Customer Experience and Service Delivery to Rebuild Trust in Government and making investments in shared services to allow High Impact Service Providers to deliver better customer facing services.

The FCSF appropriation provides for the salaries and expenses of staff and programs authorized by 40 U.S.C. 323 and 44 U.S.C. 3604. Reimbursements from Federal agencies pay for the direct costs of the services provided on behalf of the agencies such as contact center services. The FCSF is also authorized to collect user fees from the public and to accept gifts for the purposes of defraying the costs of publishing and distributing consumer information and educational materials and undertaking other consumer information activities. The income from gifts does not have fiscal year limitations.

Object Classification (in millions of dollars)

Identification code 047–4549–0–4–376		2021 actual	2022 est.	2023 est.
	Direct obligations:			
	Personnel compensation:			
11.1	Full-time permanent	8	11	21
11.3	Other than full-time permanent	1	7	5
11.9	Total personnel compensation	9	18	26
12.1	Civilian personnel benefits	3	6	9
23.3	Communications, utilities, and miscellaneous charges		1	1
25.1	Advisory and assistance services	31	67	83
25.3	Other goods and services from Federal sources	23	53	41
31.0	Equipment	2		
99.0	Direct obligations	68	145	160
	Reimbursable obligations:			
11.1	Personnel compensation: Full-time permanent		1	12
12.1	Civilian personnel benefits			4
25.1	Advisory and assistance services	1	3	12
25.3	Other goods and services from Federal sources	3	3	14
99.0	Reimbursable obligations	4	7	42
99.5	Adjustment for rounding			1
99.9	Total new obligations, unexpired accounts	72	152	203

Employment Summary

Identification code 047–4549–0–4–376		2021 actual	2022 est.	2023 est.
1001	Direct civilian full-time equivalent employment	59	130	187
2001	Reimbursable civilian full-time equivalent employment	2	7	84

WORKING CAPITAL FUND

(INCLUDING TRANSFER OF FUNDS)

For the Working Capital Fund of the General Services Administration, $10,900,000, to remain available until expended, for necessary costs incurred by the Administrator to modernize rulemaking systems and to provide support services for Federal rulemaking agencies: Provided, That amounts made available under this heading shall be in addition to any other amounts available for such purposes.

Note.—A full-year 2022 appropriation for this account was not enacted at the time the Budget was prepared; therefore, the Budget assumes this account is operating under the Continuing Appropriations Act, 2022 (Division A of Public Law 117–43, as amended). The amounts included for 2022 reflect the annualized level provided by the continuing resolution.

Program and Financing (in millions of dollars)

Identification code 047–4540–0–4–804		2021 actual	2022 est.	2023 est.
	Obligations by program activity:			
0002	Working Capital Fund (TMF ARP)		22	6
0004	Direct Appropriations			11
0005	COVID-19 Appropriations		1	
0799	Total direct obligations		23	17
0801	Working Capital Fund (Reimbursable)	714	756	785
0900	Total new obligations, unexpired accounts	714	779	802
	Budgetary resources:			
	Unobligated balance:			
1000	Unobligated balance brought forward, Oct 1	121	129	132

WORKING CAPITAL FUND—Continued
Program and Financing—Continued

Identification code 047–4540–0–4–804	2021 actual	2022 est.	2023 est.
1010 Unobligated balance transfer to other accts [047–0616]	–10		
1011 Unobligated balance transfer from other acct [047–0616]		22	6
1021 Recoveries of prior year unpaid obligations	32	20	20
1070 Unobligated balance (total)	143	171	158
Budget authority:			
Appropriations, discretionary:			
1100 Appropriation			11
Spending authority from offsetting collections, discretionary:			
1700 Collected	702	740	768
1701 Change in uncollected payments, Federal sources	–2		
1750 Spending auth from offsetting collections, disc (total)	700	740	768
1900 Budget authority (total)	700	740	779
1930 Total budgetary resources available	843	911	937
Memorandum (non-add) entries:			
1941 Unexpired unobligated balance, end of year	129	132	135
Change in obligated balance:			
Unpaid obligations:			
3000 Unpaid obligations, brought forward, Oct 1	253	239	224
3010 New obligations, unexpired accounts	714	779	802
3020 Outlays (gross)	–696	–774	–769
3040 Recoveries of prior year unpaid obligations, unexpired	–32	–20	–20
3050 Unpaid obligations, end of year	239	224	237
Uncollected payments:			
3060 Uncollected pymts, Fed sources, brought forward, Oct 1	–8	–6	–6
3070 Change in uncollected pymts, Fed sources, unexpired	2		
3090 Uncollected pymts, Fed sources, end of year	–6	–6	–6
Memorandum (non-add) entries:			
3100 Obligated balance, start of year	245	233	218
3200 Obligated balance, end of year	233	218	231
Budget authority and outlays, net:			
Discretionary:			
4000 Budget authority, gross	700	740	779
Outlays, gross:			
4010 Outlays from new discretionary authority	564	555	584
4011 Outlays from discretionary balances	132	219	185
4020 Outlays, gross (total)	696	774	769
Offsets against gross budget authority and outlays:			
Offsetting collections (collected) from:			
4030 Federal sources	–702	–740	–768
4040 Offsets against gross budget authority and outlays (total)	–702	–740	–768
Additional offsets against gross budget authority only:			
4050 Change in uncollected pymts, Fed sources, unexpired	2		
4060 Additional offsets against budget authority only (total)	2		
4070 Budget authority, net (discretionary)			11
4080 Outlays, net (discretionary)	–6	34	1
4180 Budget authority, net (total)			11
4190 Outlays, net (total)	–6	34	1

The Working Capital Fund (WCF) is a revolving fund that finances GSA's administrative services. Examples of these core support services include: IT management; budget and financial management; legal services; human resources; equal employment opportunity services; procurement and contracting oversight; emergency planning and response; and facilities management of GSA-occupied space. This account also funds liaison activities with the U.S. Small Business Administration to ensure that small and disadvantaged businesses receive a fair share of the Agency's business. WCF offices also provide external administrative services such as human resource management for other Federal agencies, including small boards and commissions on a reimbursable basis. GSA's WCF operations are divided into four types of services: Internal Services, External Services, Major Equipment Acquisition & Development, and Direct Appropriations.

Object Classification (in millions of dollars)

Identification code 047–4540–0–4–804	2021 actual	2022 est.	2023 est.
Direct obligations:			
25.1 Advisory and assistance services		12	17
31.0 Equipment		10	
99.0 Direct obligations		22	17
Reimbursable obligations:			
Personnel compensation:			
11.1 Full-time permanent	234	250	266
11.3 Other than full-time permanent	3		
11.5 Other personnel compensation	9	5	5
11.9 Total personnel compensation	246	255	271
12.1 Civilian personnel benefits	96	88	92
13.0 Benefits for former personnel	1		
21.0 Travel and transportation of persons	3	6	6
22.0 Transportation of things	1	1	1
23.1 Rental payments to GSA	17	19	19
23.3 Communications, utilities, and miscellaneous charges	22	24	24
25.1 Advisory and assistance services	222	229	230
25.2 Other services from non-Federal sources	4	3	3
25.3 Other goods and services from Federal sources	39	63	63
25.4 Operation and maintenance of facilities		4	9
26.0 Supplies and materials	1	1	1
31.0 Equipment	59	64	66
42.0 Insurance claims and indemnities	3		
99.0 Reimbursable obligations	714	757	785
99.9 Total new obligations, unexpired accounts	714	779	802

Employment Summary

Identification code 047–4540–0–4–804	2021 actual	2022 est.	2023 est.
2001 Reimbursable civilian full-time equivalent employment	1,937	2,061	2,085

GENERAL FUND RECEIPT ACCOUNTS
(in millions of dollars)

	2021 actual	2022 est.	2023 est.
Offsetting receipts from the public:			
047–322000 All Other General Fund Proprietary Receipts Including Budget Clearing Accounts	35	26	26
047–384000 Real Property Disposal, GSA	–1		
General Fund Offsetting receipts from the public	34	26	26
Intragovernmental payments:			
047–388500 Undistributed Intragovernmental Payments and Receivables from Cancelled Accounts		11	11
General Fund Intragovernmental payments		11	11

ADMINISTRATIVE PROVISIONS—GENERAL SERVICES ADMINISTRATION
(INCLUDING TRANSFER OF FUNDS)

SEC. 520. Funds available to the General Services Administration shall be available for the hire of passenger motor vehicles.

SEC. 521. Funds in the Federal Buildings Fund made available for fiscal year 2023 for Federal Buildings Fund activities may be transferred between such activities only to the extent necessary to meet program requirements: Provided, That notice of any proposed transfers shall be transmitted in advance to the Committees on Appropriations of the House of Representatives and the Senate.

SEC. 522. Except as otherwise provided in this title, any request for United States Courthouse construction transmitted using funds made available by this Act should: (1) meet the design guide standards for construction as established and approved by the General Services Administration, the Judicial Conference of the United States, and the Office of Management and Budget; (2) reflect the priorities of the Judicial Conference of the United States as set out in its approved five-year construction plan; and (3) include a standardized courtroom utilization study of each facility to be constructed, replaced, or expanded.

SEC. 523. None of the funds provided in this Act may be used to increase the amount of occupiable square feet, provide cleaning services, security enhancements, or any other service usually provided through the Federal Buildings Fund, to any agency that does not pay the rate per square foot assessment for space and services as determined by the General Services Administration in consideration of the Public Buildings Amendments Act of 1972 (Public Law 92–313).

SEC. 524. From funds made available under the heading "Federal Buildings Fund, Limitations on Availability of Revenue", claims against the Government of less than

$250,000 arising from direct construction projects and acquisition of buildings may be liquidated from savings effected in other construction projects with prior notification to the Committees on Appropriations of the House of Representatives and the Senate.

SEC. 525. With respect to the Federal Buildings Fund construction and acquisition and major repair and alteration programs, and with respect to E-Government projects funded under the heading "Federal Citizen Services Fund", the Administrator of General Services shall submit a spending plan and explanation for each project to be undertaken to the Committees on Appropriations of the House of Representatives and the Senate not later than 60 days after the date of enactment of this Act.

SEC. 526. Section 3173(d)(1) of title 40, United States Code, is amended by inserting before the period the following: "or for agency-wide acquisition of equipment or systems or the acquisition of services in lieu thereof, as necessary to implement the Act".

SEC. 527. Section 3173(b)(1) of title 40, United States Code, is amended by inserting ", including advance payments," after "Amounts received".

SEC. 528. Section 323 of title 40, United States Code, is amended by adding at the end a new subsection:

"(f) The Administrator may enter into agreements with Federal agencies to provide services through the Fund on a fully reimbursable basis.".

SEC. 529. Notwithstanding section 602 of this Act, amounts made available to the General Services Administration in this title under the headings "Government-wide Policy", "Operating Expenses", and "Office of Inspector General" may be transferred and merged into the working capital fund of the General Services Administration, as authorized by section 3173(d) of title 40, United States Code: Provided, That amounts so transferred shall be available only for the purposes specified in such section.

NATIONAL AERONAUTICS AND SPACE ADMINISTRATION

Federal Funds

SCIENCE

For necessary expenses, not otherwise provided for, in the conduct and support of science research and development activities, including research, development, operations, support, and services; maintenance and repair, facility planning and design; space flight, spacecraft control, and communications activities; program management; personnel and related costs, including uniforms or allowances therefor, as authorized by sections 5901 and 5902 of title 5, United States Code; travel expenses; purchase and hire of passenger motor vehicles; and purchase, lease, charter, maintenance, and operation of mission and administrative aircraft, $7,988,300,000, to remain available until September 30, 2024.

Note.—A full-year 2022 appropriation for this account was not enacted at the time the Budget was prepared; therefore, the Budget assumes this account is operating under the Continuing Appropriations Act, 2022 (Division A of Public Law 117–43, as amended). The amounts included for 2022 reflect the annualized level provided by the continuing resolution.

Program and Financing (in millions of dollars)

Identification code 080–0120–0–1–252		2021 actual	2022 est.	2023 est.
	Obligations by program activity:			
0001	Science	7,099	7,301	7,988
	Budgetary resources:			
	Unobligated balance:			
1000	Unobligated balance brought forward, Oct 1	640	875	932
1021	Recoveries of prior year unpaid obligations	37	57	57
1070	Unobligated balance (total)	677	932	989
	Budget authority:			
	Appropriations, discretionary:			
1100	Appropriation	7,301	7,301	7,988
1120	Appropriations transferred to CECR [080–0130]	–4		
1160	Appropriation, discretionary (total)	7,297	7,301	7,988
1930	Total budgetary resources available	7,974	8,233	8,977
	Memorandum (non-add) entries:			
1941	Unexpired unobligated balance, end of year	875	932	989
	Change in obligated balance:			
	Unpaid obligations:			
3000	Unpaid obligations, brought forward, Oct 1	4,793	5,075	4,952
3010	New obligations, unexpired accounts	7,099	7,301	7,988
3011	Obligations ("upward adjustments"), expired accounts	7		
3020	Outlays (gross)	–6,770	–7,367	–7,395
3040	Recoveries of prior year unpaid obligations, unexpired	–37	–57	–57
3041	Recoveries of prior year unpaid obligations, expired	–17		
3050	Unpaid obligations, end of year	5,075	4,952	5,488
	Memorandum (non-add) entries:			
3100	Obligated balance, start of year	4,793	5,075	4,952
3200	Obligated balance, end of year	5,075	4,952	5,488
	Budget authority and outlays, net:			
	Discretionary:			
4000	Budget authority, gross	7,297	7,301	7,988
	Outlays, gross:			
4010	Outlays from new discretionary authority	2,639	2,993	3,275
4011	Outlays from discretionary balances	4,131	4,374	4,120
4020	Outlays, gross (total)	6,770	7,367	7,395
	Offsets against gross budget authority and outlays:			
	Offsetting collections (collected) from:			
4030	Federal sources	–2		
4033	Non-Federal sources	–1		
4040	Offsets against gross budget authority and outlays (total)	–3		
	Additional offsets against gross budget authority only:			
4052	Offsetting collections credited to expired accounts	3		
4060	Additional offsets against budget authority only (total)	3		
4070	Budget authority, net (discretionary)	7,297	7,301	7,988
4080	Outlays, net (discretionary)	6,767	7,367	7,395
4180	Budget authority, net (total)	7,297	7,301	7,988
4190	Outlays, net (total)	6,767	7,367	7,395

The Science appropriation provides for NASA's science mission, which is comprised of the agency's Earth and space science programs: Earth Science, Planetary Science, Heliophysics, Biological and Physical Sciences, and Astrophysics. These programs, which are managed by the Science Mission Directorate, focus on three interdisciplinary objectives: discovering the secrets of the Universe; searching for life in the Solar System and beyond; and safeguarding and improving life on Earth. These objectives include research concerning the global Earth system; other planets in the solar system and around other stars; the connections among the Sun, Earth, and heliosphere; and the origin and evolution of planetary systems, the galaxy, and the universe, including the origin and distribution of life in the universe. Program objectives are pursued through robotic flight missions, ground-based scientific research and data analysis, and the development of new technologies for future missions. Additionally, the Budget funds within Science a lunar robotic exploration program that will support innovative approaches to achieving human and science exploration goals.

The Science appropriation provides for all of the research, development, operations, salaries and related expenses, and other general and administrative activities required to execute the programs within this account. Costs include labor, travel, and procurement. Performance goals associated with these activities are addressed in NASA's detailed budget request.

Object Classification (in millions of dollars)

Identification code 080–0120–0–1–252		2021 actual	2022 est.	2023 est.
	Direct obligations:			
	Personnel compensation:			
11.1	Full-time permanent	336	348	367
11.3	Other than full-time permanent	8	8	9
11.5	Other personnel compensation	1	1	1
11.9	Total personnel compensation	345	357	377
12.1	Civilian personnel benefits	121	126	132
21.0	Travel and transportation of persons	6	16	21
22.0	Transportation of things	16	16	18
23.2	Rental payments to others	8	8	8
23.3	Communications, utilities, and miscellaneous charges	9	9	10
24.0	Printing and reproduction	1	1	1
25.1	Advisory and assistance services	143	147	161
25.2	Other services from non-Federal sources	211	217	237
25.3	Other goods and services from Federal sources	260	267	293
25.4	Operation and maintenance of facilities	11	11	12
25.5	Research and development contracts	4,860	4,987	5,471
25.7	Operation and maintenance of equipment	66	68	74
26.0	Supplies and materials	29	30	33
31.0	Equipment	120	123	135
32.0	Land and structures	4	4	5
41.0	Grants, subsidies, and contributions	889	914	1,000
99.9	Total new obligations, unexpired accounts	7,099	7,301	7,988

Employment Summary

Identification code 080–0120–0–1–252	2021 actual	2022 est.	2023 est.
1001 Direct civilian full-time equivalent employment	2,410	2,361	2,404

AERONAUTICS

For necessary expenses, not otherwise provided for, in the conduct and support of aeronautics research and development activities, including research, development, operations, support, and services; maintenance and repair, facility planning and design; space flight, spacecraft control, and communications activities; program management; personnel and related costs, including uniforms or allowances therefor, as authorized by sections 5901 and 5902 of title 5, United States Code; travel expenses; purchase and hire of passenger motor vehicles; and purchase, lease, charter, maintenance, and operation of mission and administrative aircraft, $971,500,000, to remain available until September 30, 2024.

Note.—A full-year 2022 appropriation for this account was not enacted at the time the Budget was prepared; therefore, the Budget assumes this account is operating under the Continuing Appropriations Act, 2022 (Division A of Public Law 117–43, as amended). The amounts included for 2022 reflect the annualized level provided by the continuing resolution.

National Aeronautics and Space Administration—Continued
Federal Funds—Continued

AERONAUTICS—Continued

Program and Financing (in millions of dollars)

Identification code 080–0126–0–1–402	2021 actual	2022 est.	2023 est.
Obligations by program activity:			
0001 Aeronautics	845	829	972
Budgetary resources:			
Unobligated balance:			
1000 Unobligated balance brought forward, Oct 1	29	20	32
1021 Recoveries of prior year unpaid obligations	7	12	12
1070 Unobligated balance (total)	36	32	44
Budget authority:			
Appropriations, discretionary:			
1100 Appropriation	829	829	972
1930 Total budgetary resources available	865	861	1,016
Memorandum (non-add) entries:			
1941 Unexpired unobligated balance, end of year	20	32	44
Change in obligated balance:			
Unpaid obligations:			
3000 Unpaid obligations, brought forward, Oct 1	358	430	439
3010 New obligations, unexpired accounts	845	829	972
3020 Outlays (gross)	–763	–808	–873
3040 Recoveries of prior year unpaid obligations, unexpired	–7	–12	–12
3041 Recoveries of prior year unpaid obligations, expired	–3		
3050 Unpaid obligations, end of year	430	439	526
Memorandum (non-add) entries:			
3100 Obligated balance, start of year	358	430	439
3200 Obligated balance, end of year	430	439	526
Budget authority and outlays, net:			
Discretionary:			
4000 Budget authority, gross	829	829	972
Outlays, gross:			
4010 Outlays from new discretionary authority	470	448	525
4011 Outlays from discretionary balances	293	360	348
4020 Outlays, gross (total)	763	808	873
4180 Budget authority, net (total)	829	829	972
4190 Outlays, net (total)	763	808	873

This appropriation provides for the full costs associated with NASA's Aeronautics Research mission, which aims to expand the boundaries of aeronautical knowledge for the benefit of the nation and the broad aeronautics community. The mission is managed by NASA's Aeronautics Research Mission Directorate, and consists of the following integrated research programs: Airspace Operations and Safety, Advanced Air Vehicles, Integrated Aviation Systems, Transformative Aeronautics Concepts, and Aerosciences Evaluation and Test Capabilities. Full costs of these programs include all labor, travel, procurement, test, and fabrication costs associated with the research, development, operations, and other general and administrative activities required to execute the programs. Performance goals associated with these activities are addressed in NASA's detailed budget request.

Object Classification (in millions of dollars)

Identification code 080–0126–0–1–402	2021 actual	2022 est.	2023 est.
Direct obligations:			
Personnel compensation:			
11.1 Full-time permanent	178	181	202
11.3 Other than full-time permanent	6	6	7
11.9 Total personnel compensation	184	187	209
12.1 Civilian personnel benefits	65	66	74
21.0 Travel and transportation of persons	1	7	8
23.3 Communications, utilities, and miscellaneous charges	6	6	7
25.1 Advisory and assistance services	14	14	16
25.2 Other services from non-Federal sources	29	28	33
25.3 Other goods and services from Federal sources	7	7	8
25.4 Operation and maintenance of facilities	56	55	60
25.5 Research and development contracts	355	333	419
25.7 Operation and maintenance of equipment	42	41	43
26.0 Supplies and materials	9	9	10
31.0 Equipment	25	25	29
32.0 Land and structures	5	5	6
41.0 Grants, subsidies, and contributions	47	46	50
99.9 Total new obligations, unexpired accounts	845	829	972

Employment Summary

Identification code 080–0126–0–1–402	2021 actual	2022 est.	2023 est.
1001 Direct civilian full-time equivalent employment	1,404	1,425	1,493

SPACE TECHNOLOGY

For necessary expenses, not otherwise provided for, in the conduct and support of space technology research and development activities, including research, development, operations, support, and services; maintenance and repair, facility planning and design; space flight, spacecraft control, and communications activities; program management; personnel and related costs, including uniforms or allowances therefor, as authorized by sections 5901 and 5902 of title 5, United States Code; travel expenses; purchase and hire of passenger motor vehicles; and purchase, lease, charter, maintenance, and operation of mission and administrative aircraft, $1,437,900,000, to remain available until September 30, 2024.

Note.—A full-year 2022 appropriation for this account was not enacted at the time the Budget was prepared; therefore, the Budget assumes this account is operating under the Continuing Appropriations Act, 2022 (Division A of Public Law 117–43, as amended). The amounts included for 2022 reflect the annualized level provided by the continuing resolution.

Program and Financing (in millions of dollars)

Identification code 080–0131–0–1–252	2021 actual	2022 est.	2023 est.
Obligations by program activity:			
0001 Space Technology	1,174	1,100	1,438
Budgetary resources:			
Unobligated balance:			
1000 Unobligated balance brought forward, Oct 1	81	27	43
1021 Recoveries of prior year unpaid obligations	20	16	30
1070 Unobligated balance (total)	101	43	73
Budget authority:			
Appropriations, discretionary:			
1100 Appropriation	1,100	1,100	1,438
1930 Total budgetary resources available	1,201	1,143	1,511
Memorandum (non-add) entries:			
1941 Unexpired unobligated balance, end of year	27	43	73
Change in obligated balance:			
Unpaid obligations:			
3000 Unpaid obligations, brought forward, Oct 1	723	806	851
3010 New obligations, unexpired accounts	1,174	1,100	1,438
3011 Obligations ("upward adjustments"), expired accounts	1		
3020 Outlays (gross)	–1,068	–1,039	–1,245
3040 Recoveries of prior year unpaid obligations, unexpired	–20	–16	–30
3041 Recoveries of prior year unpaid obligations, expired	–4		
3050 Unpaid obligations, end of year	806	851	1,014
Memorandum (non-add) entries:			
3100 Obligated balance, start of year	723	806	851
3200 Obligated balance, end of year	806	851	1,014
Budget authority and outlays, net:			
Discretionary:			
4000 Budget authority, gross	1,100	1,100	1,438
Outlays, gross:			
4010 Outlays from new discretionary authority	501	473	618
4011 Outlays from discretionary balances	567	566	627
4020 Outlays, gross (total)	1,068	1,039	1,245
Offsets against gross budget authority and outlays:			
Offsetting collections (collected) from:			
4033 Non-Federal sources	–1		
Additional offsets against gross budget authority only:			
4052 Offsetting collections credited to expired accounts	1		
4070 Budget authority, net (discretionary)	1,100	1,100	1,438
4080 Outlays, net (discretionary)	1,067	1,039	1,245
4180 Budget authority, net (total)	1,100	1,100	1,438
4190 Outlays, net (total)	1,067	1,039	1,245

This appropriation provides for the costs associated with research and development in space technologies serving multiple customers within NASA, private industry, academia, and other government agencies. The

NATIONAL AERONAUTICS AND SPACE ADMINISTRATION

full costs provide for all of the research, development, operations, salaries and related expenses, and other general and administrative activities required to execute the programs within this account. Costs include labor, travel, procurement, and those associated with fabrication, tests and flight demonstrations.

The programs within the Space Technology account are dedicated to developing transformative, cross-cutting technologies that support NASA's missions and contribute towards commercial and other government agencies needs. The Space Technology appropriation funds several programs: Small Business Innovative Research (SBIR), Small Business Technology Transfer (STTR), Early Stage Innovation & Partnerships, Technology Maturation, and Technology Demonstrations.

Object Classification (in millions of dollars)

Identification code 080–0131–0–1–252		2021 actual	2022 est.	2023 est.
	Direct obligations:			
	Personnel compensation:			
11.1	Full-time permanent	117	110	125
11.3	Other than full-time permanent	3	3	4
11.9	Total personnel compensation	120	113	129
12.1	Civilian personnel benefits	43	39	46
21.0	Travel and transportation of persons	1	3	19
22.0	Transportation of things	5	5	6
23.2	Rental payments to others	1	1	1
25.1	Advisory and assistance services	56	52	69
25.2	Other services from non-Federal sources	32	30	39
25.3	Other goods and services from Federal sources	46	43	56
25.4	Operation and maintenance of facilities	4	4	5
25.5	Research and development contracts	762	714	940
25.7	Operation and maintenance of equipment	9	8	11
26.0	Supplies and materials	8	7	10
31.0	Equipment	10	9	12
41.0	Grants, subsidies, and contributions	77	72	95
99.9	Total new obligations, unexpired accounts	1,174	1,100	1,438

Employment Summary

Identification code 080–0131–0–1–252	2021 actual	2022 est.	2023 est.
1001 Direct civilian full-time equivalent employment	911	880	921

DEEP SPACE EXPLORATION SYSTEMS

For necessary expenses, not otherwise provided for, in the conduct and support of exploration research and development activities, including research, development, operations, support, and services; maintenance and repair, facility planning and design; space flight, spacecraft control, and communications activities; program management; personnel and related costs, including uniforms or allowances therefor, as authorized by sections 5901 and 5902 of title 5, United States Code; travel expenses; purchase and hire of passenger motor vehicles; and purchase, lease, charter, maintenance, and operation of mission and administrative aircraft, $7,478,283,000, to remain available until September 30, 2024.

Note.—A full-year 2022 appropriation for this account was not enacted at the time the Budget was prepared; therefore, the Budget assumes this account is operating under the Continuing Appropriations Act, 2022 (Division A of Public Law 117–43, as amended). The amounts included for 2022 reflect the annualized level provided by the continuing resolution.

Program and Financing (in millions of dollars)

Identification code 080–0124–0–1–252		2021 actual	2022 est.	2023 est.
	Obligations by program activity:			
0001	Deep Space Exploration Systems	6,589	6,578	7,478
	Budgetary resources:			
	Unobligated balance:			
1000	Unobligated balance brought forward, Oct 1	198	161	294
1011	Unobligated balance transfer from CECR [080–0130]	7		
1021	Recoveries of prior year unpaid obligations	33	133	133
1070	Unobligated balance (total)	238	294	427
	Budget authority:			
	Appropriations, discretionary:			
1100	Appropriation	6,556	6,555	7,478
1120	Appropriations transferred to CECR [080–0130]	–44	–25	
1121	Appropriations transferred from CECR [080–0130]		48	
1160	Appropriation, discretionary (total)	6,512	6,578	7,478
1930	Total budgetary resources available	6,750	6,872	7,905
	Memorandum (non-add) entries:			
1941	Unexpired unobligated balance, end of year	161	294	427
	Change in obligated balance:			
	Unpaid obligations:			
3000	Unpaid obligations, brought forward, Oct 1	2,692	3,015	2,993
3010	New obligations, unexpired accounts	6,589	6,578	7,478
3011	Obligations ("upward adjustments"), expired accounts	3		
3020	Outlays (gross)	–6,231	–6,467	–7,177
3040	Recoveries of prior year unpaid obligations, unexpired	–33	–133	–133
3041	Recoveries of prior year unpaid obligations, expired	–5		
3050	Unpaid obligations, end of year	3,015	2,993	3,161
	Memorandum (non-add) entries:			
3100	Obligated balance, start of year	2,692	3,015	2,993
3200	Obligated balance, end of year	3,015	2,993	3,161
	Budget authority and outlays, net:			
	Discretionary:			
4000	Budget authority, gross	6,512	6,578	7,478
	Outlays, gross:			
4010	Outlays from new discretionary authority	3,691	3,753	4,262
4011	Outlays from discretionary balances	2,540	2,714	2,915
4020	Outlays, gross (total)	6,231	6,467	7,177
	Offsets against gross budget authority and outlays:			
	Offsetting collections (collected) from:			
4033	Non-Federal sources	–2		
	Additional offsets against gross budget authority only:			
4052	Offsetting collections credited to expired accounts	2		
4070	Budget authority, net (discretionary)	6,512	6,578	7,478
4080	Outlays, net (discretionary)	6,229	6,467	7,177
4180	Budget authority, net (total)	6,512	6,578	7,478
4190	Outlays, net (total)	6,229	6,467	7,177

This appropriation provides for costs associated with the development of systems and capabilities required for human exploration of space. The capabilities include launch and crew vehicles for missions beyond low Earth orbit; providing integrated systems to keep astronauts safe, healthy, and functional during deep space missions; and advancing the tools to increase exploration capabilities and reduce the launch mass and cost of deep space missions. The full costs provide for the research, development, operations, salaries and related expenses, and other general and administrative activities required to execute the programs within this account. Costs include labor, travel, procurement, test, and fabrication costs. Major themes within the Deep Space Exploration Systems account include Common Exploration Systems Development, Artemis Campaign Development, Mars Campaign Development, and Human Exploration Requirements & Architecture and Mars. Performance goals associated with these activities are addressed in NASA's detailed budget request.

The Common Exploration Systems Development theme is comprised of NASA's human deep space exploration programs which include the Space Launch System, Orion, and Exploration Ground Systems. The objective of the theme is to design, develop, test, and evaluate the initial vehicles in these programs and any follow-on development projects needed to enhance the vehicles.

The Artemis Campaign Development theme is comprised of the Gateway, Advanced Cislunar and Surface Capabilities, the Human Lander System, and the xEVA and Surface Mobility Program. These programs are developing the systems that will enable humans to live and operate on and near the Moon in the Artemis campaign.

The Mars Campaign Development theme consists of the Exploration Capabilities Program. This program is investigating new technologies that will be needed in a system to carry humans to Mars.

Object Classification (in millions of dollars)

Identification code 080–0124–0–1–252		2021 actual	2022 est.	2023 est.
	Direct obligations:			
	Personnel compensation:			
11.1	Full-time permanent	390	431	355

1166　National Aeronautics and Space Administration—Continued
Federal Funds—Continued

THE BUDGET FOR FISCAL YEAR 2023

DEEP SPACE EXPLORATION SYSTEMS—Continued

Object Classification—Continued

Identification code 080–0124–0–1–252		2021 actual	2022 est.	2023 est.
11.3	Other than full-time permanent	4	4	5
11.5	Other personnel compensation	3	3	3
11.8	Special personal services payments	1	1	1
11.9	Total personnel compensation	398	439	364
12.1	Civilian personnel benefits	143	154	128
21.0	Travel and transportation of persons	3	15	13
23.3	Communications, utilities, and miscellaneous charges	13	13	15
25.1	Advisory and assistance services	394	390	447
25.2	Other services from non-Federal sources	35	35	40
25.3	Other goods and services from Federal sources	23	23	26
25.4	Operation and maintenance of facilities	120	119	136
25.5	Research and development contracts	4,830	4,765	5,594
25.7	Operation and maintenance of equipment	86	85	98
26.0	Supplies and materials	32	32	36
31.0	Equipment	370	367	420
32.0	Land and structures	96	95	109
41.0	Grants, subsidies, and contributions	46	46	52
99.9	Total new obligations, unexpired accounts	6,589	6,578	7,478

Employment Summary

Identification code 080–0124–0–1–252		2021 actual	2022 est.	2023 est.
1001	Direct civilian full-time equivalent employment	2,927	3,212	2,704

SCIENCE, TECHNOLOGY, ENGINEERING, AND MATHEMATICS ENGAGEMENT

For necessary expenses, not otherwise provided for, in the conduct and support of aerospace and aeronautical education research and development activities, including research, development, operations, support, and services; program management; personnel and related costs, including uniforms or allowances therefor, as authorized by sections 5901 and 5902 of title 5, United States Code; travel expenses; purchase and hire of passenger motor vehicles; and purchase, lease, charter, maintenance, and operation of mission and administrative aircraft, $150,100,000, to remain available until September 30, 2024.

Note.—A full-year 2022 appropriation for this account was not enacted at the time the Budget was prepared; therefore, the Budget assumes this account is operating under the Continuing Appropriations Act, 2022 (Division A of Public Law 117–43, as amended). The amounts included for 2022 reflect the annualized level provided by the continuing resolution.

Program and Financing (in millions of dollars)

Identification code 080–0128–0–1–252		2021 actual	2022 est.	2023 est.
	Obligations by program activity:			
0001	STEM Engagement	129	127	150
	Budgetary resources:			
	Unobligated balance:			
1000	Unobligated balance brought forward, Oct 1	10	8	10
1021	Recoveries of prior year unpaid obligations		2	2
1070	Unobligated balance (total)	10	10	12
	Budget authority:			
	Appropriations, discretionary:			
1100	Appropriation	127	127	150
1930	Total budgetary resources available	137	137	162
	Memorandum (non-add) entries:			
1941	Unexpired unobligated balance, end of year	8	10	12
	Change in obligated balance:			
	Unpaid obligations:			
3000	Unpaid obligations, brought forward, Oct 1	161	172	180
3010	New obligations, unexpired accounts	129	127	150
3020	Outlays (gross)	–117	–117	–131
3040	Recoveries of prior year unpaid obligations, unexpired		–2	–2
3041	Recoveries of prior year unpaid obligations, expired	–1		
3050	Unpaid obligations, end of year	172	180	197
	Memorandum (non-add) entries:			
3100	Obligated balance, start of year	161	172	180
3200	Obligated balance, end of year	172	180	197
	Budget authority and outlays, net:			
	Discretionary:			
4000	Budget authority, gross	127	127	150
	Outlays, gross:			
4010	Outlays from new discretionary authority	15	17	20
4011	Outlays from discretionary balances	102	100	111
4020	Outlays, gross (total)	117	117	131
4180	Budget authority, net (total)	127	127	150
4190	Outlays, net (total)	117	117	131

This appropriation provides for costs associated with the Office of Science, Technology, Engineering, and Mathematics (STEM) Engagement. This includes support for the following projects: the Minority University Research and Education Project (MUREP), to broaden participation in engineering and other STEM fields; Space Grant, which funds education and research projects through a national network of university-based consortia; Next Gen STEM, which reaches K-12 students and provides competitive awards for informal educational institutions and sustains a national network of museums and science centers; and the Established Program to Stimulate Competitive Research (EPSCoR), which provides cooperative agreement opportunities designed to establish partnerships between government, higher education, and industry in an effort to build stronger research and development capabilities in 28 eligible EPSCoR jurisdictions. NASA will expand its efforts to broaden diversity and inclusion in STEM, including working with partner organizations to attract and retain underrepresented students in STEM fields and providing greater access to NASA STEM learning opportunities. Performance goals associated with these activities are addressed in NASA's detailed budget request.

Object Classification (in millions of dollars)

Identification code 080–0128–0–1–252		2021 actual	2022 est.	2023 est.
11.1	Direct obligations: Personnel compensation: Full-time permanent	5	6	7
11.9	Total personnel compensation	5	6	7
12.1	Civilian personnel benefits	2	3	3
21.0	Travel and transportation of persons		1	1
25.1	Advisory and assistance services	1	1	1
25.2	Other services from non-Federal sources	4	4	5
25.5	Research and development contracts	8	8	9
25.7	Operation and maintenance of equipment	5	5	6
31.0	Equipment	3	3	3
41.0	Grants, subsidies, and contributions	101	96	115
99.9	Total new obligations, unexpired accounts	129	127	150

Employment Summary

Identification code 080–0128–0–1–252		2021 actual	2022 est.	2023 est.
1001	Direct civilian full-time equivalent employment	41	45	55

SAFETY, SECURITY AND MISSION SERVICES

For necessary expenses, not otherwise provided for, in the conduct and support of science, aeronautics, space technology, exploration, space operations and education research and development activities, including research, development, operations, support, and services; maintenance and repair, facility planning and design; space flight, spacecraft control, and communications activities; program management; personnel and related costs, including uniforms or allowances therefor, as authorized by sections 5901 and 5902 of title 5, United States Code; travel expenses; purchase and hire of zero emission passenger motor vehicles and supporting charging or fueling infrastructure; not to exceed $63,000 for official reception and representation expenses; and purchase, lease, charter, maintenance, and operation of mission and administrative aircraft, $3,208,700,000, to remain available until September 30, 2024.

Note.—A full-year 2022 appropriation for this account was not enacted at the time the Budget was prepared; therefore, the Budget assumes this account is operating under the Continuing Appropriations Act, 2022 (Division A of Public Law 117–43, as amended). The amounts included for 2022 reflect the annualized level provided by the continuing resolution.

Program and Financing (in millions of dollars)

Identification code 080–0122–0–1–252		2021 actual	2022 est.	2023 est.
	Obligations by program activity:			
0001	Safety, Security and Mission Services	3,025	2,937	3,209
0801	Cross Agency Support (Reimbursable)	1,463	1,671	1,458
0900	Total new obligations, unexpired accounts	4,488	4,608	4,667
	Budgetary resources:			
	Unobligated balance:			
1000	Unobligated balance brought forward, Oct 1	941	763	891
1021	Recoveries of prior year unpaid obligations	41	128	48
1070	Unobligated balance (total)	982	891	939
	Budget authority:			
	Appropriations, discretionary:			
1100	Appropriation	2,937	2,937	3,209
	Spending authority from offsetting collections, discretionary:			
1700	Collected	1,342	1,671	1,458
1701	Change in uncollected payments, Federal sources	–10		
1750	Spending auth from offsetting collections, disc (total)	1,332	1,671	1,458
1900	Budget authority (total)	4,269	4,608	4,667
1930	Total budgetary resources available	5,251	5,499	5,606
	Memorandum (non-add) entries:			
1941	Unexpired unobligated balance, end of year	763	891	939
	Change in obligated balance:			
	Unpaid obligations:			
3000	Unpaid obligations, brought forward, Oct 1	2,167	2,075	1,719
3010	New obligations, unexpired accounts	4,488	4,608	4,667
3011	Obligations ("upward adjustments"), expired accounts	8		
3020	Outlays (gross)	–4,534	–4,836	–4,802
3040	Recoveries of prior year unpaid obligations, unexpired	–41	–128	–48
3041	Recoveries of prior year unpaid obligations, expired	–13		
3050	Unpaid obligations, end of year	2,075	1,719	1,536
	Uncollected payments:			
3060	Uncollected pymts, Fed sources, brought forward, Oct 1	–1,867	–1,687	–1,687
3070	Change in uncollected pymts, Fed sources, unexpired	10		
3071	Change in uncollected pymts, Fed sources, expired	170		
3090	Uncollected pymts, Fed sources, end of year	–1,687	–1,687	–1,687
	Memorandum (non-add) entries:			
3100	Obligated balance, start of year	300	388	32
3200	Obligated balance, end of year	388	32	–151
	Budget authority and outlays, net:			
	Discretionary:			
4000	Budget authority, gross	4,269	4,608	4,667
	Outlays, gross:			
4010	Outlays from new discretionary authority	2,582	2,918	3,063
4011	Outlays from discretionary balances	1,952	1,918	1,739
4020	Outlays, gross (total)	4,534	4,836	4,802
	Offsets against gross budget authority and outlays:			
	Offsetting collections (collected) from:			
4030	Federal sources	–1,277	–1,208	–1,208
4033	Non-Federal sources	–232	–463	–250
4040	Offsets against gross budget authority and outlays (total)	–1,509	–1,671	–1,458
	Additional offsets against gross budget authority only:			
4050	Change in uncollected pymts, Fed sources, unexpired	10		
4052	Offsetting collections credited to expired accounts	167		
4060	Additional offsets against budget authority only (total)	177		
4070	Budget authority, net (discretionary)	2,937	2,937	3,209
4080	Outlays, net (discretionary)	3,025	3,165	3,344
4180	Budget authority, net (total)	2,937	2,937	3,209
4190	Outlays, net (total)	3,025	3,165	3,344

Safety, Security, and Mission Services (SSMS) manages agency-wide mission support functions and some of NASA's research facilities. This appropriation provides for the operations and maintenance, salaries and related expenses, and other general and administrative activities that support all NASA's missions. SSMS programs, projects and activities fall under the two Themes described below. Performance goals associated with these activities are addressed in NASA's detailed budget request.

Mission Services and Capabilities (MSaC) delivers enterprise solutions through three programs: Information Technology; Mission Enabling Services; and Infrastructure and Technical Capabilities. These programs meet workforce, infrastructure, information technology and business operations requirements necessary to enable NASA's mission. MSaC ensures that critical Agency operations across all NASA Centers are effective, efficient, safe, and meet statutory, regulatory, and fiduciary responsibilities.

Engineering, Safety, and Operations (ESO) provides for the ongoing management of NASA Headquarters, nine Centers, and component facilities. It funds medical and engineering technical authorities and contributes to the reduction of program risks by ensuring that technical skills and assets are ready and available to meet program and project requirements. ESO ensures that Center practices are technically and scientifically sound and that specialized infrastructure at the Centers is safe and reliable.

Object Classification (in millions of dollars)

Identification code 080–0122–0–1–252		2021 actual	2022 est.	2023 est.
	Direct obligations:			
	Personnel compensation:			
11.1	Full-time permanent	912	944	999
11.3	Other than full-time permanent	22	22	23
11.5	Other personnel compensation	57	55	60
11.9	Total personnel compensation	991	1,021	1,082
12.1	Civilian personnel benefits	331	341	361
13.0	Benefits for former personnel	1	1	1
21.0	Travel and transportation of persons	2	17	13
22.0	Transportation of things	1	1	1
23.1	Rental payments to GSA	34	36	37
23.2	Rental payments to others	1	1	1
23.3	Communications, utilities, and miscellaneous charges	77	75	82
24.0	Printing and reproduction	2	2	2
25.1	Advisory and assistance services	392	382	415
25.2	Other services from non-Federal sources	235	129	196
25.3	Other goods and services from Federal sources	50	49	53
25.4	Operation and maintenance of facilities	235	228	249
25.5	Research and development contracts	171	166	181
25.6	Medical care	8	8	8
25.7	Operation and maintenance of equipment	281	272	299
26.0	Supplies and materials	14	14	15
31.0	Equipment	154	149	163
32.0	Land and structures	28	27	31
41.0	Grants, subsidies, and contributions	17	18	19
99.0	Direct obligations	3,025	2,937	3,209
99.0	Reimbursable obligations	1,463	1,671	1,458
99.9	Total new obligations, unexpired accounts	4,488	4,608	4,667

Employment Summary

Identification code 080–0122–0–1–252		2021 actual	2022 est.	2023 est.
1001	Direct civilian full-time equivalent employment	6,679	7,154	7,054
2001	Reimbursable civilian full-time equivalent employment	25	300	300

CONSTRUCTION AND ENVIRONMENTAL COMPLIANCE AND RESTORATION

For necessary expenses for construction of facilities including repair, rehabilitation, revitalization, and modification of facilities, construction of new facilities and additions to existing facilities, facility planning and design, and restoration, and acquisition or condemnation of real property, as authorized by law, and environmental compliance and restoration, $424,300,000, to remain available until September 30, 2028: Provided, That proceeds from leases deposited into this account shall be available for a period of 5 years to the extent and in amounts as provided in annual appropriations Acts: Provided further, That such proceeds referred to in the preceding proviso shall be available for obligation for fiscal year 2023 in an amount not to exceed $25,000,000: Provided further, That each annual budget request shall include an annual estimate of gross receipts and collections and proposed use of all funds collected pursuant to section 20145 of title 51, United States Code.

Note.—A full-year 2022 appropriation for this account was not enacted at the time the Budget was prepared; therefore, the Budget assumes this account is operating under the Continuing Appropriations Act, 2022 (Division A of Public Law 117–43, as amended). The amounts included for 2022 reflect the annualized level provided by the continuing resolution.

CONSTRUCTION AND ENVIRONMENTAL COMPLIANCE AND RESTORATION

[(INCLUDING TRANSFER OF FUNDS)]

[*For an additional amount for "Construction and Environmental Compliance and Restoration" for repair at National Aeronautics and Space Administration facilities damaged by Hurricanes Zeta and Ida, $321,400,000, to remain available until expen-*

CONSTRUCTION AND ENVIRONMENTAL COMPLIANCE AND RESTORATION—Continued

ded: *Provided*, That up to 15 percent of such amount may be transferred to "Exploration" for necessary expenses related to flight hardware, tooling, production and schedule delays caused by Hurricane Ida: *Provided further*, That except as provided in the preceding proviso, the amounts appropriated under this heading in this Act shall not be available for transfer under any transfer authority provided for the National Aeronautics and Space Administration in an appropriation Act for fiscal year 2022.] *(Disaster Relief Supplemental Appropriations Act, 2022.)*

Program and Financing (in millions of dollars)

Identification code 080–0130–0–1–252		2021 actual	2022 est.	2023 est.
	Obligations by program activity:			
0001	Construction and Environmental Compliance and Restoration (Direct)	426	688	424
0801	Construction and Environmental Compliance and Restoration (Reimbursable)	....	30	30
0900	Total new obligations, unexpired accounts	426	718	454
	Budgetary resources:			
	Unobligated balance:			
1000	Unobligated balance brought forward, Oct 1	288	335	412
1010	Unobligated balance transfer to Exploration [080–0124]	–7	....	....
1021	Recoveries of prior year unpaid obligations	19	87	87
1033	Recoveries of prior year paid obligations	1	....	....
1070	Unobligated balance (total)	301	422	499
	Budget authority:			
	Appropriations, discretionary:			
1100	Appropriation	390	390	424
1100	Appropriation [Disaster Relief Supplemental]	....	321	....
1120	Appropriations transferred to Exploration [080–0124]	....	–48	....
1121	Appropriations transferred from Science [080–0120]	4	....	....
1121	Appropriations transferred from Exploration [080–0124]	44	25	....
1121	Appropriations transferred from Space Operations [080–0115]	1	....	....
1160	Appropriation, discretionary (total)	439	688	424
	Spending authority from offsetting collections, discretionary:			
1700	Collected	21	20	30
1900	Budget authority (total)	460	708	454
1930	Total budgetary resources available	761	1,130	953
	Memorandum (non-add) entries:			
1941	Unexpired unobligated balance, end of year	335	412	499
	Change in obligated balance:			
	Unpaid obligations:			
3000	Unpaid obligations, brought forward, Oct 1	819	826	1,000
3010	New obligations, unexpired accounts	426	718	454
3020	Outlays (gross)	–399	–457	–524
3040	Recoveries of prior year unpaid obligations, unexpired	–19	–87	–87
3041	Recoveries of prior year unpaid obligations, expired	–1	....	....
3050	Unpaid obligations, end of year	826	1,000	843
	Memorandum (non-add) entries:			
3100	Obligated balance, start of year	819	826	1,000
3200	Obligated balance, end of year	826	1,000	843
	Budget authority and outlays, net:			
	Discretionary:			
4000	Budget authority, gross	460	708	454
	Outlays, gross:			
4010	Outlays from new discretionary authority	14	55	29
4011	Outlays from discretionary balances	385	402	495
4020	Outlays, gross (total)	399	457	524
	Offsets against gross budget authority and outlays:			
	Offsetting collections (collected) from:			
4033	Non-Federal sources	–23	–20	–30
4040	Offsets against gross budget authority and outlays (total)	–23	–20	–30
	Additional offsets against gross budget authority only:			
4052	Offsetting collections credited to expired accounts	1	....	....
4053	Recoveries of prior year paid obligations, unexpired accounts	1	....	....
4060	Additional offsets against budget authority only (total)	2	....	....
4070	Budget authority, net (discretionary)	439	688	424
4080	Outlays, net (discretionary)	376	437	494
4180	Budget authority, net (total)	439	688	424
4190	Outlays, net (total)	376	437	494

This appropriation provides for NASA's construction and environmental compliance and restoration activities, and makes available the net proceeds from Enhanced Use Leases, received under the authority of section 20145 of the National Aeronautics and Space Act (51 U.S.C. 20145), for maintenance, capital revitalization, and improvement of real property assets and related personal property at NASA Centers. Performance goals associated with these activities are addressed in NASA's detailed budget request.

Object Classification (in millions of dollars)

Identification code 080–0130–0–1–252		2021 actual	2022 est.	2023 est.
	Direct obligations:			
23.3	Communications, utilities, and miscellaneous charges	2	2	2
25.1	Advisory and assistance services	21	20	21
25.2	Other services from non-Federal sources	68	64	66
25.3	Other goods and services from Federal sources	16	16	16
25.4	Operation and maintenance of facilities	75	292	75
25.5	Research and development contracts	11	11	11
25.7	Operation and maintenance of equipment	3	13	3
26.0	Supplies and materials	....	13	....
31.0	Equipment	1	14	1
32.0	Land and structures	229	243	229
99.0	Direct obligations	426	688	424
99.0	Reimbursable obligations	....	30	30
99.9	Total new obligations, unexpired accounts	426	718	454

SPACE OPERATIONS

For necessary expenses, not otherwise provided for, in the conduct and support of space operations research and development activities, including research, development, operations, support and services; space flight, spacecraft control, and communications activities, including operations, production, and services; maintenance and repair, facility planning and design; program management; personnel and related costs, including uniforms or allowances therefor, as authorized by sections 5901 and 5902 of title 5, United States Code; travel expenses; purchase and hire of passenger motor vehicles; and purchase, lease, charter, maintenance, and operation of mission and administrative aircraft, $4,266,317,000, to remain available until September 30, 2024.

Note.—A full-year 2022 appropriation for this account was not enacted at the time the Budget was prepared; therefore, the Budget assumes this account is operating under the Continuing Appropriations Act, 2022 (Division A of Public Law 117–43, as amended). The amounts included for 2022 reflect the annualized level provided by the continuing resolution.

Program and Financing (in millions of dollars)

Identification code 080–0115–0–1–252		2021 actual	2022 est.	2023 est.
	Obligations by program activity:			
0001	Space Operations	3,922	3,988	4,266
	Budgetary resources:			
	Unobligated balance:			
1000	Unobligated balance brought forward, Oct 1	111	290	494
1021	Recoveries of prior year unpaid obligations	113	204	204
1033	Recoveries of prior year paid obligations	1	....	....
1070	Unobligated balance (total)	225	494	698
	Budget authority:			
	Appropriations, discretionary:			
1100	Appropriation	3,988	3,988	4,266
1120	Appropriations transferred to CECR [080–0130]	–1	....	....
1160	Appropriation, discretionary (total)	3,987	3,988	4,266
1900	Budget authority (total)	3,987	3,988	4,266
1930	Total budgetary resources available	4,212	4,482	4,964
	Memorandum (non-add) entries:			
1941	Unexpired unobligated balance, end of year	290	494	698
	Change in obligated balance:			
	Unpaid obligations:			
3000	Unpaid obligations, brought forward, Oct 1	2,346	2,247	2,116
3010	New obligations, unexpired accounts	3,922	3,988	4,266
3011	Obligations ("upward adjustments"), expired accounts	4	....	....
3020	Outlays (gross)	–3,903	–3,915	–4,143
3040	Recoveries of prior year unpaid obligations, unexpired	–113	–204	–204
3041	Recoveries of prior year unpaid obligations, expired	–9	....	....
3050	Unpaid obligations, end of year	2,247	2,116	2,035

	Memorandum (non-add) entries:			
3100	Obligated balance, start of year	2,346	2,247	2,116
3200	Obligated balance, end of year	2,247	2,116	2,035
	Budget authority and outlays, net:			
	Discretionary:			
4000	Budget authority, gross	3,987	3,988	4,266
	Outlays, gross:			
4010	Outlays from new discretionary authority	2,065	2,273	2,432
4011	Outlays from discretionary balances	1,838	1,642	1,711
4020	Outlays, gross (total)	3,903	3,915	4,143
	Offsets against gross budget authority and outlays:			
	Offsetting collections (collected) from:			
4030	Federal sources	−1		
4033	Non-Federal sources	−1		
4040	Offsets against gross budget authority and outlays (total)	−2		
	Additional offsets against gross budget authority only:			
4052	Offsetting collections credited to expired accounts	1		
4053	Recoveries of prior year paid obligations, unexpired accounts	1		
4060	Additional offsets against budget authority only (total)	2		
4070	Budget authority, net (discretionary)	3,987	3,988	4,266
4080	Outlays, net (discretionary)	3,901	3,915	4,143
4180	Budget authority, net (total)	3,987	3,988	4,266
4190	Outlays, net (total)	3,901	3,915	4,143

This appropriation provides for the full costs associated with human-related Low Earth Orbit (LEO) and spaceflight operations activities of the Agency. The full costs include all labor, travel, procurement, test, and fabrication costs associated with the research, development, operations, and other general and administrative activities conducted by the programs within this account. Major themes within the Space Operations account include the International Space Station, Space Transportation, Space and Flight Support, Commercial LEO Development, and Exploration Operations. Performance goals associated with these activities are addressed in NASA's detailed budget request.

The International Space Station (ISS) is a complex of research laboratories in LEO where America and its international partners, including Russia, Canada, Europe, and Japan, conduct unique scientific and technological investigations in a microgravity environment. The objective of the International Space Station is to support human space exploration and conduct science experiments and technology development activities unique to the on-orbit attributes of the facility.

The Exploration Operations theme is comprised of the Orion Production and Sustainment Program, SLS Production and Sustainment Program, EGS Production and Sustainment Program and the Exploration Operation Program. The objective of the theme is to build, sustain, and launch the SLS/Orion crew transportation system and plan, train, and fly Artemis missions.

The Space Transportation theme is comprised of the Commercial Crew Program and Crew and Cargo Program, which transport U.S. astronauts and cargo safely back and forth to the ISS and, in the future, to other orbital platforms and destinations. Maintaining the ISS requires a fleet of vehicles and launch locations to transport astronauts, science experiments, supplies, maintenance hardware, and propellant to the ISS, and to dispose of waste generated on the ISS. The Commercial Crew Program partners with two U.S. companies, SpaceX and Boeing, to develop and operate safe, reliable, and affordable crew transportation to LEO. The Crew and Cargo Program purchases cargo transportation services to the ISS through contracts with Northrop Grumman, SpaceX, and Sierra Nevada and purchases crew transportation services from Boeing and SpaceX. Payments to develop and test commercial crew vehicles, and for initial Post Certification Missions for each provider are funded by the Commercial Crew Program, whereas subsequent payments for operational commercial crew missions are funded by the Crew and Cargo Program.

Space and Flight Support is comprised of multiple programs that provide ongoing support for a wide range of services required for safe and successful space mission operations. These programs include Space Communications and Navigation, Communications Services Program, Human Research Program, Human Space Flight Operations, Launch Services, and Rocket Propulsion Testing. Services are provided to a wide range of customers including NASA, other U.S. Federal agencies, foreign governments, and industry partners.

Commercial LEO Development supports efforts to expand commercial activities in LEO, with a focus on enabling, developing, and deploying commercial platforms that can be used by NASA and other customers and on supporting the growth of private sector activity in LEO.

Object Classification (in millions of dollars)

Identification code 080–0115–0–1–252		2021 actual	2022 est.	2023 est.
	Direct obligations:			
	Personnel compensation:			
11.1	Full-time permanent	281	292	326
11.3	Other than full-time permanent	3	3	3
11.5	Other personnel compensation	2	2	2
11.9	Total personnel compensation	286	297	331
12.1	Civilian personnel benefits	102	104	116
21.0	Travel and transportation of persons	4	14	16
22.0	Transportation of things	1,580	1,607	1,670
23.2	Rental payments to others	1	1	1
23.3	Communications, utilities, and miscellaneous charges	9	9	10
25.1	Advisory and assistance services	115	117	125
25.2	Other services from non-Federal sources	159	162	173
25.3	Other goods and services from Federal sources	49	50	53
25.4	Operation and maintenance of facilities	31	32	34
25.5	Research and development contracts	1,330	1,336	1,458
25.7	Operation and maintenance of equipment	197	200	214
26.0	Supplies and materials	13	13	14
31.0	Equipment	18	18	20
32.0	Land and structures	7	7	8
41.0	Grants, subsidies, and contributions	21	21	23
99.9	Total new obligations, unexpired accounts	3,922	3,988	4,266

Employment Summary

Identification code 080–0115–0–1–252		2021 actual	2022 est.	2023 est.
1001	Direct civilian full-time equivalent employment	2,046	1,963	2,259

OFFICE OF INSPECTOR GENERAL

For necessary expenses of the Office of Inspector General in carrying out the Inspector General Act of 1978, $48,400,000, to remain available until September 30, 2024.

Note.—A full-year 2022 appropriation for this account was not enacted at the time the Budget was prepared; therefore, the Budget assumes this account is operating under the Continuing Appropriations Act, 2022 (Division A of Public Law 117–43, as amended). The amounts included for 2022 reflect the annualized level provided by the continuing resolution.

Program and Financing (in millions of dollars)

Identification code 080–0109–0–1–252		2021 actual	2022 est.	2023 est.
	Obligations by program activity:			
0001	Office of Inspector General (Direct)	43	44	48
0801	Office of Inspector General (Reimbursable)	1	2	2
0900	Total new obligations, unexpired accounts	44	46	50
	Budgetary resources:			
	Unobligated balance:			
1000	Unobligated balance brought forward, Oct 1	1		
	Budget authority:			
	Appropriations, discretionary:			
1100	Appropriation	44	44	48
	Spending authority from offsetting collections, discretionary:			
1700	Collected	1	2	2
1900	Budget authority (total)	45	46	50
1930	Total budgetary resources available	46	46	50
	Memorandum (non-add) entries:			
1940	Unobligated balance expiring	−2		
	Change in obligated balance:			
	Unpaid obligations:			
3000	Unpaid obligations, brought forward, Oct 1	6	6	6
3010	New obligations, unexpired accounts	44	46	50

National Aeronautics and Space Administration—Continued
Federal Funds—Continued

OFFICE OF INSPECTOR GENERAL—Continued

Program and Financing—Continued

Identification code 080–0109–0–1–252	2021 actual	2022 est.	2023 est.
3020 Outlays (gross)	–43	–46	–50
3041 Recoveries of prior year unpaid obligations, expired	–1		
3050 Unpaid obligations, end of year	6	6	6
Memorandum (non-add) entries:			
3100 Obligated balance, start of year	6	6	6
3200 Obligated balance, end of year	6	6	6
Budget authority and outlays, net:			
Discretionary:			
4000 Budget authority, gross	45	46	50
Outlays, gross:			
4010 Outlays from new discretionary authority	37	40	44
4011 Outlays from discretionary balances	6	6	6
4020 Outlays, gross (total)	43	46	50
Offsets against gross budget authority and outlays:			
Offsetting collections (collected) from:			
4030 Federal sources	–1	–2	–2
4180 Budget authority, net (total)	44	44	48
4190 Outlays, net (total)	42	44	48

This appropriation provides for the operations of the NASA Office of Inspector General. The mission of the Office of Inspector General is to conduct audits and investigations of agency activities to prevent and detect fraud, waste, abuse, and mismanagement. The Inspector General keeps the NASA Administrator and the Congress informed of problems and deficiencies in agency programs and operations.

Object Classification (in millions of dollars)

Identification code 080–0109–0–1–252	2021 actual	2022 est.	2023 est.
Direct obligations:			
Personnel compensation:			
11.1 Full-time permanent	24	24	26
11.3 Other than full-time permanent	1	1	1
11.5 Other personnel compensation	1	1	1
11.9 Total personnel compensation	26	26	28
12.1 Civilian personnel benefits	10	10	11
21.0 Travel and transportation of persons		1	1
25.2 Other services from non-Federal sources	4	4	5
31.0 Equipment	3	3	3
99.0 Direct obligations	43	44	48
99.0 Reimbursable obligations	1	2	2
99.9 Total new obligations, unexpired accounts	44	46	50

Employment Summary

Identification code 080–0109–0–1–252	2021 actual	2022 est.	2023 est.
1001 Direct civilian full-time equivalent employment	171	187	190
2001 Reimbursable civilian full-time equivalent employment	7	7	7

WORKING CAPITAL FUND

Program and Financing (in millions of dollars)

Identification code 080–4546–0–4–252	2021 actual	2022 est.	2023 est.
Obligations by program activity:			
0801 Working Capital Fund (Reimbursable)	500	522	379
Budgetary resources:			
Unobligated balance:			
1000 Unobligated balance brought forward, Oct 1	27	55	56
1021 Recoveries of prior year unpaid obligations	3	6	6
1070 Unobligated balance (total)	30	61	62
Budget authority:			
Spending authority from offsetting collections, discretionary:			
1700 Collected	525	517	384
1930 Total budgetary resources available	555	578	446
Memorandum (non-add) entries:			
1941 Unexpired unobligated balance, end of year	55	56	67
Change in obligated balance:			
Unpaid obligations:			
3000 Unpaid obligations, brought forward, Oct 1	242	249	205
3010 New obligations, unexpired accounts	500	522	379
3020 Outlays (gross)	–490	–560	–438
3040 Recoveries of prior year unpaid obligations, unexpired	–3	–6	–6
3050 Unpaid obligations, end of year	249	205	140
Memorandum (non-add) entries:			
3100 Obligated balance, start of year	242	249	205
3200 Obligated balance, end of year	249	205	140
Budget authority and outlays, net:			
Discretionary:			
4000 Budget authority, gross	525	517	384
Outlays, gross:			
4010 Outlays from new discretionary authority	238	310	230
4011 Outlays from discretionary balances	252	250	208
4020 Outlays, gross (total)	490	560	438
Offsets against gross budget authority and outlays:			
Offsetting collections (collected) from:			
4030 Federal sources	–494	–472	–339
4033 Non-Federal sources	–31	–45	–45
4040 Offsets against gross budget authority and outlays (total)	–525	–517	–384
4080 Outlays, net (discretionary)	–35	43	54
4180 Budget authority, net (total)			
4190 Outlays, net (total)	–35	43	54

The Working Capital Fund provides goods and services on a reimbursable basis. The Fund currently finances four program activities. The first is the Solutions for Enterprise-wide Procurement program, which finances, on an agency-wide basis, scientific and engineering workstation procurement. The second program is the Information Technology Infrastructure Integration Program which consolidates and centralizes management of NASA information technology services in the areas of customer service and ordering, web services and technologies, enterprise business and management applications, integrated network/communications services, end user services, and data center services. The third program, NASA's Shared Services Center, performs selected financial management, human resources, information technology, and procurement services for NASA Headquarters and Centers. The last program, the National Center for Critical Information Processing and Storage, provides Federal customers collocation services with complete redundancy in the electrical distribution system from the national grid to the rack level.

In FY 2023, NASA's existing authority under 51 U.S.C. 30102 would be amended to make the Working Capital Fund available for IT Modernization activities and to transfer amounts from NASA's Safety, Security and Mission Services account into the Working Capital Fund to finance such activities.

Object Classification (in millions of dollars)

Identification code 080–4546–0–4–252	2021 actual	2022 est.	2023 est.
Reimbursable obligations:			
Personnel compensation:			
11.1 Full-time permanent	19	18	18
11.5 Other personnel compensation	1	1	1
11.9 Total personnel compensation	20	19	19
12.1 Civilian personnel benefits	7	6	6
23.2 Rental payments to others	1	1	1
23.3 Communications, utilities, and miscellaneous charges	15	15	10
25.1 Advisory and assistance services	130	178	111
25.2 Other services from non-Federal sources	45	45	30
25.3 Other goods and services from Federal sources	1	1	1
25.4 Operation and maintenance of facilities	22	22	12
25.7 Operation and maintenance of equipment	173	149	123
26.0 Supplies and materials	1	1	1
31.0 Equipment	82	82	62
32.0 Land and structures	3	3	3
99.9 Total new obligations, unexpired accounts	500	522	379

Employment Summary

Identification code 080–4546–0–4–252	2021 actual	2022 est.	2023 est.
2001 Reimbursable civilian full-time equivalent employment	173	169	165

Trust Funds

SCIENCE, SPACE, AND TECHNOLOGY EDUCATION TRUST FUND

Special and Trust Fund Receipts (in millions of dollars)

Identification code 080–8978–0–7–503	2021 actual	2022 est.	2023 est.
0100 Balance, start of year	16	16	16
Receipts:			
Current law:			
1140 Earnings on Investments, Science, Space and Technology Education Trust Fund	1	....	....
2000 Total: Balances and receipts	17	16	16
Appropriations:			
Current law:			
2103 Science, Space, and Technology Education Trust Fund	–1	....	....
Proposed:			
2201 Science, Space, and Technology Education Trust Fund	....	....	–16
2999 Total appropriations	–1	....	–16
5099 Balance, end of year	16	16	....

Program and Financing (in millions of dollars)

Identification code 080–8978–0–7–503	2021 actual	2022 est.	2023 est.
Obligations by program activity:			
0001 Science, Space, and Technology Education Trust Fund	1	....	....
0900 Total new obligations, unexpired accounts (object class 41.0)	1	....	....
Budgetary resources:			
Unobligated balance:			
1000 Unobligated balance brought forward, Oct 1	1	1	1
Budget authority:			
Appropriations, mandatory:			
1203 Appropriation (previously unavailable)(special or trust)	1	....	....
1930 Total budgetary resources available	2	1	1
Memorandum (non-add) entries:			
1941 Unexpired unobligated balance, end of year	1	1	1
Change in obligated balance:			
Unpaid obligations:			
3010 New obligations, unexpired accounts	1	....	....
3020 Outlays (gross)	–1	....	....
Budget authority and outlays, net:			
Mandatory:			
4090 Budget authority, gross	1	....	....
Outlays, gross:			
4101 Outlays from mandatory balances	1	....	....
4180 Budget authority, net (total)	1	....	....
4190 Outlays, net (total)	1	....	....
Memorandum (non-add) entries:			
5000 Total investments, SOY: Federal securities: Par value	15	15	16
5001 Total investments, EOY: Federal securities: Par value	15	16	16

Summary of Budget Authority and Outlays (in millions of dollars)

	2021 actual	2022 est.	2023 est.
Enacted/requested:			
Budget Authority	1	....	....
Outlays	1	....	....
Legislative proposal, subject to PAYGO:			
Budget Authority	....	....	16
Outlays	....	....	16
Total:			
Budget Authority	1	....	16
Outlays	1	....	16

SCIENCE, SPACE, AND TECHNOLOGY EDUCATION TRUST FUND

(Legislative proposal, subject to PAYGO)

Program and Financing (in millions of dollars)

Identification code 080–8978–4–7–503	2021 actual	2022 est.	2023 est.
Obligations by program activity:			
0001 Science, Space, and Technology Education Trust Fund	....	....	16
0900 Total new obligations, unexpired accounts (object class 41.0)	....	....	16
Budgetary resources:			
Budget authority:			
Appropriations, mandatory:			
1201 Appropriation (special or trust fund)	....	....	16
1930 Total budgetary resources available	....	....	16
Change in obligated balance:			
Unpaid obligations:			
3010 New obligations, unexpired accounts	....	....	16
3020 Outlays (gross)	....	....	–16
Budget authority and outlays, net:			
Mandatory:			
4090 Budget authority, gross	....	....	16
Outlays, gross:			
4100 Outlays from new mandatory authority	....	....	16
4180 Budget authority, net (total)	....	....	16
4190 Outlays, net (total)	....	....	16
Memorandum (non-add) entries:			
5001 Total investments, EOY: Federal securities: Par value	....	....	–16

For FY 2023, the Administration will transmit a legislative proposal to provide the remaining balance of the Science, Space, and Technology Education Trust Fund to the Challenger Center for Space Science Education, in combination with repeal of 51 U.S.C. 40901.

ADMINISTRATIVE PROVISIONS

(INCLUDING TRANSFERS OF FUNDS)

Funds for any announced prize otherwise authorized shall remain available, without fiscal year limitation, until a prize is claimed or the offer is withdrawn.

Not to exceed 5 percent of any appropriation made available for the current fiscal year for the National Aeronautics and Space Administration in this Act may be transferred between such appropriations, but no such appropriation, except as otherwise specifically provided, shall be increased by more than 10 percent by any such transfers. Any funds transferred to "Construction and Environmental Compliance and Restoration" for construction activities shall not increase that account by more than 20 percent. Balances so transferred shall be merged with and available for the same purposes and the same time period as the appropriations to which transferred. Any transfer pursuant to this provision shall be treated as a reprogramming of funds under section 504 of this Act and shall not be available for obligation except in compliance with the procedures set forth in that section.

Not to exceed 5 percent of any appropriation provided for the National Aeronautics and Space Administration under previous appropriations Acts that remains available for obligation or expenditure in fiscal year 2023 may be transferred between such appropriations, but no such appropriation, except as otherwise specifically provided, shall be increased by more than 10 percent by any such transfers. Any transfer pursuant to this provision shall retain its original availability and shall be treated as a reprogramming of funds under section 504 of this Act and shall not be available for obligation except in compliance with the procedures set forth in that section.

The spending plan required by this Act shall be provided by the National Aeronautics and Space Administration at the theme and program level. The spending plan, as well as any subsequent change of an amount established in that spending plan that meets the notification requirements of section 504 of this Act, shall be treated as a reprogramming under section 504 of this Act and shall not be available for obligation or expenditure except in compliance with the procedures set forth in that section.

Of the amounts provided for Orion Multi-purpose Crew Vehicle, up to $718,000,000 may be transferred to Space Operations for Orion Production and Operations consistent with direction provided in the explanatory statement accom-

panying this Act. The authority provided by this paragraph is in addition to the authority provided by the second paragraph under this heading.

Not more than 20 percent or $25,000,000, whichever is less, of the amounts made available in the current-year CECR appropriation may be applied to CECR projects funded under previous years' CECR appropriation Acts. Use of current-year funds under this provision shall be treated as a reprogramming of funds under section 504 of this act and shall not be available for obligation except in compliance with the procedures set forth in that section.

Section 30102(b) of title 51, United States Code, is amended by:
  (1) Redesignating existing paragraph (3) to (4); and
  (2) Inserting, after paragraph (2), the following:
    (3) INFORMATION TECHNOLOGY (IT) MODERNIZATION.—The fund shall also be available for the purpose of funding IT Modernization activities, as described in section 1077(b)(3)(A)–(E) of Public Law 115–91, on a non-reimbursable basis.

Not to exceed $18,162,000 made available for the current fiscal year in this Act within "Safety, Security and Mission Services" may be transferred to the Working Capital Fund of the National Aeronautics and Space Administration. Balances so transferred shall be available until expended only for activities described in section 30102(b)(3) of title 51, United States Code, as amended by this Act, and shall remain available until expended. Any transfer pursuant to this provision shall be treated as a reprogramming of funds under section 504 of this Act and shall not be available for obligation except in compliance with the procedures set forth in that section.

GENERAL FUND RECEIPT ACCOUNTS

(in millions of dollars)

	2021 actual	2022 est.	2023 est.
Offsetting receipts from the public:			
080–322000 All Other General Fund Proprietary Receipts Including Budget Clearing Accounts	2	4	4
General Fund Offsetting receipts from the public	2	4	4
Intragovernmental payments:			
080–388500 Undistributed Intragovernmental Payments and Receivables from Cancelled Accounts	2	2	2
General Fund Intragovernmental payments	2	2	2

NATIONAL SCIENCE FOUNDATION

Federal Funds

RESEARCH AND RELATED ACTIVITIES

For necessary expenses in carrying out the National Science Foundation Act of 1950 (42 U.S.C. 1861 et seq.), and Public Law 86–209 (42 U.S.C. 1880 et seq.); services as authorized by section 3109 of title 5, United States Code; maintenance and operation of aircraft and purchase of flight services for research support; acquisition of aircraft; and authorized travel; $8,425,987,000, to remain available until September 30, 2024, of which not to exceed $640,000,000 shall remain available until expended for polar research and operations support, and for reimbursement to other Federal agencies for operational and science support and logistical and other related activities for the United States Antarctic program: Provided, That receipts for scientific support services and materials furnished by the National Research Centers and other National Science Foundation supported research facilities may be credited to this appropriation.

Note.—A full-year 2022 appropriation for this account was not enacted at the time the Budget was prepared; therefore, the Budget assumes this account is operating under the Continuing Appropriations Act, 2022 (Division A of Public Law 117–43, as amended). The amounts included for 2022 reflect the annualized level provided by the continuing resolution.

Program and Financing (in millions of dollars)

Identification code 049–0100–0–1–999		2021 actual	2022 est.	2023 est.
	Obligations by program activity:			
0001	Biological Sciences	819	795	970
0002	Computer and Information Science and Engineering	1,024	936	1,151
0003	Engineering	1,037	769	940
0005	Geosciences	1,005	1,002	1,239
0006	Mathematical and Physical Sciences	1,595	1,418	1,747
0007	Social, Behavioral and Economic Sciences	283	269	330
0008	Integrative Activities	603	424	546
0009	Office of International Science and Engineering	51	63	74
0010	Office of Polar Programs	484	424	547
0011	Technology, Innovation, and Partnerships		725	880
0013	Arctic Research Commission	2	2	2
0091	Direct program activities, subtotal	6,903	6,827	8,426
0401	American Rescue Plan Act (ARP)	196	271	
0799	Total direct obligations	7,099	7,098	8,426
0801	Research and Related Activities (Reimbursable)	83	120	120
0900	Total new obligations, unexpired accounts	7,182	7,218	8,546
	Budgetary resources:			
	Unobligated balance:			
1000	Unobligated balance brought forward, Oct 1	16	308	120
1001	Discretionary unobligated balance brought fwd, Oct 1	16		
1021	Recoveries of prior year unpaid obligations	25		
1070	Unobligated balance (total)	41	308	120
	Budget authority:			
	Appropriations, discretionary:			
1100	Appropriation	6,910	6,910	8,426
1120	Appropriations transferred to other acct [049–0180]	–29		
1160	Appropriation, discretionary (total)	6,881	6,910	8,426
	Appropriations, mandatory:			
1200	Appropriation	467		
	Spending authority from offsetting collections, discretionary:			
1700	Collected	51	120	120
1701	Change in uncollected payments, Federal sources	53		
1750	Spending auth from offsetting collections, disc (total)	104	120	120
1900	Budget authority (total)	7,452	7,030	8,546
1930	Total budgetary resources available	7,493	7,338	8,666
	Memorandum (non-add) entries:			
1940	Unobligated balance expiring	–3		
1941	Unexpired unobligated balance, end of year	308	120	120
	Change in obligated balance:			
	Unpaid obligations:			
3000	Unpaid obligations, brought forward, Oct 1	12,441	13,577	14,179
3010	New obligations, unexpired accounts	7,182	7,218	8,546
3011	Obligations ("upward adjustments"), expired accounts	65		
3020	Outlays (gross)	–6,020	–6,616	–7,118
3040	Recoveries of prior year unpaid obligations, unexpired	–25		
3041	Recoveries of prior year unpaid obligations, expired	–66		
3050	Unpaid obligations, end of year	13,577	14,179	15,607
	Uncollected payments:			
3060	Uncollected pymts, Fed sources, brought forward, Oct 1	–82	–115	–115
3070	Change in uncollected pymts, Fed sources, unexpired	–53		
3071	Change in uncollected pymts, Fed sources, expired	20		
3090	Uncollected pymts, Fed sources, end of year	–115	–115	–115
	Memorandum (non-add) entries:			
3100	Obligated balance, start of year	12,359	13,462	14,064
3200	Obligated balance, end of year	13,462	14,064	15,492
	Budget authority and outlays, net:			
	Discretionary:			
4000	Budget authority, gross	6,985	7,030	8,546
	Outlays, gross:			
4010	Outlays from new discretionary authority	629	1,502	1,805
4011	Outlays from discretionary balances	5,389	4,952	5,215
4020	Outlays, gross (total)	6,018	6,454	7,020
	Offsets against gross budget authority and outlays:			
	Offsetting collections (collected) from:			
4030	Federal sources	–72	–120	–120
4033	Non-Federal sources	–62		
4040	Offsets against gross budget authority and outlays (total)	–134	–120	–120
	Additional offsets against gross budget authority only:			
4050	Change in uncollected pymts, Fed sources, unexpired	–53		
4052	Offsetting collections credited to expired accounts	83		
4060	Additional offsets against budget authority only (total)	30		
4070	Budget authority, net (discretionary)	6,881	6,910	8,426
4080	Outlays, net (discretionary)	5,884	6,334	6,900
	Mandatory:			
4090	Budget authority, gross	467		
	Outlays, gross:			
4100	Outlays from new mandatory authority	2		
4101	Outlays from mandatory balances		162	98
4110	Outlays, gross (total)	2	162	98
4180	Budget authority, net (total)	7,348	6,910	8,426
4190	Outlays, net (total)	5,886	6,496	6,998

The Research and Related Activities appropriation enables the United States to provide leadership and promote progress across the expanding frontiers of scientific and engineering research and education.

The major research program activities of NSF are:

Biological Sciences.—This activity supports understanding how complex living systems function and interact with each other and with non-living systems, which has direct impacts on issues related to the economy, food, human welfare, and the environment. Research in this activity crosses scales from molecules to cells through organisms to ecosystems. This activity's investment portfolio includes projects on understanding the fundamental characteristics of biological energy systems; the changing dynamics of the biosphere; infrastructure and research resources such as databases, research centers, and observatories; and efforts to broaden participation and develop the next generation of biological researchers.

Computer and Information Science and Engineering.—This activity promotes the progress of computing, communication and information science and engineering research and education, and advances the development and use of advanced cyberinfrastructure across the science and engineering research enterprise; promotes understanding of the principles and uses of computing and information technology in society; and contributes to universal, trustworthy, transparent, and affordable participation in a knowledge-based economy.

Engineering.—Research supported by this activity aims to increase and strengthen U.S. engineering capability and create a better tomorrow by driving discovery, inspiring innovation, enriching education and accelerating access.

Geosciences.—This activity is focused on elucidating the many processes that affect the global environment and earth system through research in earth, ocean, atmospheric, and geospace sciences. This activity supports basic research, facilities, and associated infrastructure that enable an understanding of the causes and implications of climate change, as well as disruptive processes such as earthquakes and storms.

Mathematical and Physical Sciences.—Research in this activity is directed at increasing understanding of natural laws and phenomena across

RESEARCH AND RELATED ACTIVITIES—Continued

the astronomical sciences, chemistry, materials sciences, mathematical sciences, and physics. Research support is available in multiple modalities ranging from multi-user facilities and mid-scale instrumentation to individual investigator awards, from sites for undergraduate research experiences to early career faculty development and collaborative and international efforts.

Social, Behavioral, and Economic Sciences.—This activity supports research, education, and infrastructure in the social, behavioral, cognitive, and economic sciences and funds the collection and dissemination of statistics on the science and engineering enterprise.

Office of International Science and Engineering (OISE).—This activity serves as the focal point of international activities at NSF. In addition to strategic funding and co-funding that targets catalytic partnerships and workforce-building international research opportunities, OISE advances NSF's global science leadership through extensive interactions with U.S. and global counterpart agencies and organizations.

Office of Polar Programs.—This activity supports Arctic and Antarctic research and operational science support and other related activities for United States polar research programs, including funding to support Federal agencies' logistical needs in the Arctic and Antarctica, research collaborations, and related activities supported by the United States Antarctic Program.

Integrative Activities.—This activity supports innovative, transdisciplinary team science, advanced research infrastructure, use-inspired research, and emerging national research priorities. Integrative Activities supports jurisdictional and institutional capacity-building programs helping colleges and universities expand their research capacity and improve competitiveness in science and engineering research. Additionally, Integrative Activities funding supports activities that expand NSF's capacity to use evidence for decision making. This activity provides support for a federally funded Research and Development Center, the Science and Technology Policy Institute.

Technology, Innovation, and Partnerships (TIP).—This activity advances critical and emerging technologies addressing societal and economic challenges and opportunities; accelerates the translation of research results from the lab to market and society; and cultivates new education pathways leading to a diverse skilled technical workforce comprising researchers, practitioners, technicians, and entrepreneurs. TIP will accomplish these objectives by catalyzing strategic partnerships that link academia, industry, government, nonprofits, civil society, and communities of practice to cultivate innovation ecosystems throughout the U.S., growing regional economies, creating the jobs of the future, and enhancing the Nation's long-term competitiveness.

The *United States Arctic Research Commission (USARC)* is an independent agency, funded through NSF's appropriations. USARC promotes Arctic research and recommends national Arctic research policies to guide Federal agencies in developing and implementing their research programs in the Arctic region.

Object Classification (in millions of dollars)

Identification code 049–0100–0–1–999		2021 actual	2022 est.	2023 est.
	Direct obligations:			
11.8	Personnel compensation: Special personal services payments	42	42	43
21.0	Travel and transportation of persons	2	2	2
25.1	Advisory and assistance services	144	144	145
25.2	Other services from non-Federal sources	11	11	11
25.3	Other goods and services from Federal sources	145	145	145
25.4	Operation and maintenance of facilities	233	233	283
25.5	Research and development contracts	11	11	11
31.0	Equipment	4	4	4
41.0	Grants, subsidies, and contributions	6,507	6,506	7,782
99.0	Direct obligations	7,099	7,098	8,426
99.0	Reimbursable obligations	83	120	120
99.9	Total new obligations, unexpired accounts	7,182	7,218	8,546

Employment Summary

Identification code 049–0100–0–1–999	2021 actual	2022 est.	2023 est.
1001 Direct civilian full-time equivalent employment	3	3	3

MAJOR RESEARCH EQUIPMENT AND FACILITIES CONSTRUCTION

For necessary expenses for the acquisition, construction, commissioning, and upgrading of major research equipment, facilities, and other such capital assets pursuant to the National Science Foundation Act of 1950 (42 U.S.C. 1861 et seq.), including authorized travel, $187,230,000, to remain available until expended.

Note.—A full-year 2022 appropriation for this account was not enacted at the time the Budget was prepared; therefore, the Budget assumes this account is operating under the Continuing Appropriations Act, 2022 (Division A of Public Law 117–43, as amended). The amounts included for 2022 reflect the annualized level provided by the continuing resolution.

MAJOR RESEARCH EQUIPMENT AND FACILITIES CONSTRUCTION

[For an additional amount for "Major Research Equipment and Facilities Construction" for necessary expenses related to the National Science Foundation Regional Class Research Vessel construction impacted by Hurricane Ida, $25,000,000, to remain available until expended.] *(Disaster Relief Supplemental Appropriations Act, 2022.)*

Program and Financing (in millions of dollars)

Identification code 049–0551–0–1–251		2021 actual	2022 est.	2023 est.
	Obligations by program activity:			
0001	Major Research Equipment and Facilities Construction	161	475	187
0401	American Rescue Plan Act (ARP)	9	51	....
0900	Total new obligations, unexpired accounts	170	526	187
	Budgetary resources:			
	Unobligated balance:			
1000	Unobligated balance brought forward, Oct 1	129	260	....
1001	Discretionary unobligated balance brought fwd, Oct 1	129		
	Budget authority:			
	Appropriations, discretionary:			
1100	Appropriation	241	266	187
	Appropriations, mandatory:			
1200	Appropriation	60		
1900	Budget authority (total)	301	266	187
1930	Total budgetary resources available	430	526	187
	Memorandum (non-add) entries:			
1941	Unexpired unobligated balance, end of year	260		
	Change in obligated balance:			
	Unpaid obligations:			
3000	Unpaid obligations, brought forward, Oct 1	423	440	603
3010	New obligations, unexpired accounts	170	526	187
3020	Outlays (gross)	–153	–363	–276
3050	Unpaid obligations, end of year	440	603	514
	Memorandum (non-add) entries:			
3100	Obligated balance, start of year	423	440	603
3200	Obligated balance, end of year	440	603	514
	Budget authority and outlays, net:			
	Discretionary:			
4000	Budget authority, gross	241	266	187
	Outlays, gross:			
4010	Outlays from new discretionary authority		16	11
4011	Outlays from discretionary balances	145	318	238
4020	Outlays, gross (total)	145	334	249
	Mandatory:			
4090	Budget authority, gross	60		
	Outlays, gross:			
4100	Outlays from new mandatory authority	8		
4101	Outlays from mandatory balances		29	27
4110	Outlays, gross (total)	8	29	27
4180	Budget authority, net (total)	301	266	187
4190	Outlays, net (total)	153	363	276

This appropriation supports the acquisition, construction, and commissioning of unique national research platforms and major research facilities and equipment.

Object Classification (in millions of dollars)

Identification code 049–0551–0–1–251		2021 actual	2022 est.	2023 est.
	Direct obligations:			
25.7	Operation and maintenance of equipment	4	4	4
41.0	Grants, subsidies, and contributions	166	522	183
99.9	Total new obligations, unexpired accounts	170	526	187

AGENCY OPERATIONS AND AWARD MANAGEMENT

For agency operations and award management necessary in carrying out the National Science Foundation Act of 1950 (42 U.S.C. 1861 et seq.); services authorized by section 3109 of title 5, United States Code; hire of passenger motor vehicles; uniforms or allowances therefor, as authorized by sections 5901 and 5902 of title 5, United States Code; rental of conference rooms in the District of Columbia; and reimbursement of the Department of Homeland Security for security guard services; $473,200,000: Provided, That not to exceed $8,280 is for official reception and representation expenses: Provided further, That contracts may be entered into under this heading in fiscal year 2023 for maintenance and operation of facilities and for other services to be provided during the next fiscal year.

Note.—A full-year 2022 appropriation for this account was not enacted at the time the Budget was prepared; therefore, the Budget assumes this account is operating under the Continuing Appropriations Act, 2022 (Division A of Public Law 117–43, as amended). The amounts included for 2022 reflect the annualized level provided by the continuing resolution.

Program and Financing (in millions of dollars)

Identification code 049–0180–0–1–251		2021 actual	2022 est.	2023 est.
	Obligations by program activity:			
0001	Agency Operations and Award Management	385	346	473
0401	American Rescue Plan Act (ARP)	12		
0799	Total direct obligations	397	346	473
0801	Agency Operations and Award Management (Reimbursable)	6	10	10
0900	Total new obligations, unexpired accounts	403	356	483
	Budgetary resources:			
	Unobligated balance:			
1000	Unobligated balance brought forward, Oct 1	9		
1021	Recoveries of prior year unpaid obligations	1		
1070	Unobligated balance (total)	10		
	Budget authority:			
	Appropriations, discretionary:			
1100	Appropriation	346	346	473
1121	Appropriations transferred from other acct [049–0100]	29		
1160	Appropriation, discretionary (total)	375	346	473
	Appropriations, mandatory:			
1200	Appropriation	12		
	Spending authority from offsetting collections, discretionary:			
1700	Collected	5	10	10
1701	Change in uncollected payments, Federal sources	1		
1750	Spending auth from offsetting collections, disc (total)	6	10	10
1900	Budget authority (total)	393	356	483
1930	Total budgetary resources available	403	356	483
	Change in obligated balance:			
	Unpaid obligations:			
3000	Unpaid obligations, brought forward, Oct 1	67	96	66
3010	New obligations, unexpired accounts	403	356	483
3011	Obligations ("upward adjustments"), expired accounts	1		
3020	Outlays (gross)	–371	–386	–461
3040	Recoveries of prior year unpaid obligations, unexpired	–1		
3041	Recoveries of prior year unpaid obligations, expired	–3		
3050	Unpaid obligations, end of year	96	66	88
	Uncollected payments:			
3060	Uncollected pymts, Fed sources, brought forward, Oct 1	–1	–1	–1
3070	Change in uncollected pymts, Fed sources, unexpired	–1		
3071	Change in uncollected pymts, Fed sources, expired	1		
3090	Uncollected pymts, Fed sources, end of year	–1	–1	–1
	Memorandum (non-add) entries:			
3100	Obligated balance, start of year	66	95	65
3200	Obligated balance, end of year	95	65	87
	Budget authority and outlays, net:			
	Discretionary:			
4000	Budget authority, gross	381	356	483
	Outlays, gross:			
4010	Outlays from new discretionary authority	302	294	398
4011	Outlays from discretionary balances	60	89	63
4020	Outlays, gross (total)	362	383	461
	Offsets against gross budget authority and outlays:			
	Offsetting collections (collected) from:			
4030	Federal sources	–6	–10	–10
4033	Non-Federal sources	–1		
4040	Offsets against gross budget authority and outlays (total)	–7	–10	–10
	Additional offsets against gross budget authority only:			
4050	Change in uncollected pymts, Fed sources, unexpired	–1		
4052	Offsetting collections credited to expired accounts	2		
4060	Additional offsets against budget authority only (total)	1		
4070	Budget authority, net (discretionary)	375	346	473
4080	Outlays, net (discretionary)	355	373	451
	Mandatory:			
4090	Budget authority, gross	12		
	Outlays, gross:			
4100	Outlays from new mandatory authority	9		
4101	Outlays from mandatory balances		3	
4110	Outlays, gross (total)	9	3	
4180	Budget authority, net (total)	387	346	473
4190	Outlays, net (total)	364	376	451

This account funds NSF's scientific, professional, and administrative workforce; the physical and technological infrastructure necessary for a productive, safe, and secure work environment; and the essential business operations critical to NSF's administrative processes.

Object Classification (in millions of dollars)

Identification code 049–0180–0–1–251		2021 actual	2022 est.	2023 est.
	Direct obligations:			
	Personnel compensation:			
11.1	Full-time permanent	180	180	225
11.3	Other than full-time permanent	14	14	15
11.5	Other personnel compensation	7	7	7
11.9	Total personnel compensation	201	201	247
12.1	Civilian personnel benefits	65	65	85
22.0	Transportation of things	1	1	1
23.1	Rental payments	40	20	26
23.2	Rental payments to others	1	1	1
23.3	Communications, utilities, and miscellaneous charges			1
25.1	Advisory and assistance services	46	46	57
25.2	Other services from non-Federal sources	28	6	38
25.3	Other goods and services from Federal sources	12	6	14
26.0	Supplies and materials	1		1
31.0	Equipment	2		2
99.0	Direct obligations	397	346	473
99.0	Reimbursable obligations	6	10	10
99.9	Total new obligations, unexpired accounts	403	356	483

Employment Summary

Identification code 049–0180–0–1–251	2021 actual	2022 est.	2023 est.
1001 Direct civilian full-time equivalent employment	1,368	1,368	1,497

OFFICE OF THE NATIONAL SCIENCE BOARD

For necessary expenses (including payment of salaries, authorized travel, hire of passenger motor vehicles, the rental of conference rooms in the District of Columbia, and the employment of experts and consultants under section 3109 of title 5, United States Code) involved in carrying out section 4 of the National Science Foundation Act of 1950 (42 U.S.C. 1863) and Public Law 86–209 (42 U.S.C. 1880 et seq.), $5,090,000: Provided, That not to exceed $2,500 shall be available for official reception and representation expenses.

Note.—A full-year 2022 appropriation for this account was not enacted at the time the Budget was prepared; therefore, the Budget assumes this account is operating under the Continuing Appropriations Act, 2022 (Division A of Public Law 117–43, as amended). The amounts included for 2022 reflect the annualized level provided by the continuing resolution.

NATIONAL SCIENCE FOUNDATION—Continued
Federal Funds—Continued

OFFICE OF THE NATIONAL SCIENCE BOARD—Continued

Program and Financing (in millions of dollars)

Identification code 049–0350–0–1–251		2021 actual	2022 est.	2023 est.
	Obligations by program activity:			
0001	Office of the National Science Board	4	5	5
	Budgetary resources:			
	Budget authority:			
	Appropriations, discretionary:			
1100	Appropriation	5	5	5
1930	Total budgetary resources available	5	5	5
	Memorandum (non-add) entries:			
1940	Unobligated balance expiring	–1		
	Change in obligated balance:			
	Unpaid obligations:			
3000	Unpaid obligations, brought forward, Oct 1	1	1	1
3010	New obligations, unexpired accounts	4	5	5
3020	Outlays (gross)	–4	–5	–5
3050	Unpaid obligations, end of year	1	1	1
	Memorandum (non-add) entries:			
3100	Obligated balance, start of year	1	1	1
3200	Obligated balance, end of year	1	1	1
	Budget authority and outlays, net:			
	Discretionary:			
4000	Budget authority, gross	5	5	5
	Outlays, gross:			
4010	Outlays from new discretionary authority	3	4	4
4011	Outlays from discretionary balances	1	1	1
4020	Outlays, gross (total)	4	5	5
4180	Budget authority, net (total)	5	5	5
4190	Outlays, net (total)	4	5	5

This appropriation supports the National Science Board, which provides policy-making and related responsibilities for NSF and provides guidance on significant national policy issues in science and engineering research and education, as required by law.

Object Classification (in millions of dollars)

Identification code 049–0350–0–1–251		2021 actual	2022 est.	2023 est.
	Direct obligations:			
11.1	Personnel compensation: Full-time permanent	2	2	2
12.1	Civilian personnel benefits	1	1	1
25.1	Advisory and assistance services	1	2	2
99.9	Total new obligations, unexpired accounts	4	5	5

Employment Summary

Identification code 049–0350–0–1–251	2021 actual	2022 est.	2023 est.
1001 Direct civilian full-time equivalent employment	17	17	18

OFFICE OF INSPECTOR GENERAL

For necessary expenses of the Office of Inspector General as authorized by the Inspector General Act of 1978, $23,393,000, of which $400,000 shall remain available until September 30, 2024.

Note.—A full-year 2022 appropriation for this account was not enacted at the time the Budget was prepared; therefore, the Budget assumes this account is operating under the Continuing Appropriations Act, 2022 (Division A of Public Law 117–43, as amended). The amounts included for 2022 reflect the annualized level provided by the continuing resolution.

Program and Financing (in millions of dollars)

Identification code 049–0300–0–1–251		2021 actual	2022 est.	2023 est.
	Obligations by program activity:			
0001	Office of Inspector General	18	18	23
	Budgetary resources:			
	Budget authority:			
	Appropriations, discretionary:			
1100	Appropriation	18	18	23
1900	Budget authority (total)	18	18	23
1930	Total budgetary resources available	18	18	23
	Change in obligated balance:			
	Unpaid obligations:			
3000	Unpaid obligations, brought forward, Oct 1	2	3	3
3010	New obligations, unexpired accounts	18	18	23
3020	Outlays (gross)	–16	–18	–22
3041	Recoveries of prior year unpaid obligations, expired	–1		
3050	Unpaid obligations, end of year	3	3	4
	Memorandum (non-add) entries:			
3100	Obligated balance, start of year	2	3	3
3200	Obligated balance, end of year	3	3	4
	Budget authority and outlays, net:			
	Discretionary:			
4000	Budget authority, gross	18	18	23
	Outlays, gross:			
4010	Outlays from new discretionary authority	15	15	19
4011	Outlays from discretionary balances	1	3	3
4020	Outlays, gross (total)	16	18	22
4180	Budget authority, net (total)	18	18	23
4190	Outlays, net (total)	16	18	22

This appropriation provides agency-wide audit and investigative functions to identify and correct management and administrative deficiencies which create conditions for existing or potential instances of fraud, waste, and mismanagement consistent with the Inspector General Act of 1978, as amended

Object Classification (in millions of dollars)

Identification code 049–0300–0–1–251		2021 actual	2022 est.	2023 est.
	Direct obligations:			
11.1	Personnel compensation: Full-time permanent	10	10	14
12.1	Civilian personnel benefits	5	5	6
25.2	Other services from non-Federal sources	1	1	1
25.3	Other goods and services from Federal sources	2	2	2
99.9	Total new obligations, unexpired accounts	18	18	23

Employment Summary

Identification code 049–0300–0–1–251	2021 actual	2022 est.	2023 est.
1001 Direct civilian full-time equivalent employment	68	79	93

STEM EDUCATION

For necessary expenses in carrying out science, mathematics, and engineering education and human resources programs and activities pursuant to the National Science Foundation Act of 1950 (42 U.S.C. 1861 et seq.), including services as authorized by section 3109 of title 5, United States Code, authorized travel, and rental of conference rooms in the District of Columbia, $1,377,180,000, to remain available until September 30, 2024.

Note.—A full-year 2022 appropriation for this account was not enacted at the time the Budget was prepared; therefore, the Budget assumes this account is operating under the Continuing Appropriations Act, 2022 (Division A of Public Law 117–43, as amended). The amounts included for 2022 reflect the annualized level provided by the continuing resolution.

Program and Financing (in millions of dollars)

Identification code 049–0106–0–1–251		2021 actual	2022 est.	2023 est.
	Obligations by program activity:			
0001	STEM Education (formerly Education and Human Resources)	969	976	1,377
0100	Total Disc obligations	969	976	1,377
0302	S-STEM Scholarships for STEM	95	161	119
0303	ITEST grants for Mathematics, Science, or Engineering enrichment courses	52	75	40
0391	Total Mandatory Obligations (H-1B)	147	236	159

NATIONAL SCIENCE FOUNDATION

		2021 actual	2022 est.	2023 est.
0401	American Rescue Plan Act (ARP)	24	37	
0799	Total direct obligations	1,140	1,249	1,536
0801	Education and Human Resources (Reimbursable)	4	10	10
0900	Total new obligations, unexpired accounts	1,144	1,259	1,546
	Budgetary resources:			
	Unobligated balance:			
1000	Unobligated balance brought forward, Oct 1	129	179	
1001	Discretionary unobligated balance brought fwd, Oct 1	4		
1021	Recoveries of prior year unpaid obligations	8		
1070	Unobligated balance (total)	137	179	
	Budget authority:			
	Appropriations, discretionary:			
1100	Appropriation	968	968	1,377
1130	Appropriations permanently reduced		–60	
1160	Appropriation, discretionary (total)	968	908	1,377
	Appropriations, mandatory:			
1200	Appropriation - American Rescue Plan Act	61		
1201	Appropriation (special or trust fund)	213	162	159
1203	Appropriations (previously unavailable)(special or trust)	9	9	9
1230	Appropriations and/or unobligated balance of appropriations permanently reduced	–60		
1232	Appropriations and/or unobligated balance of appropriations temporarily reduced	–9	–9	–9
1260	Appropriations, mandatory (total)	214	162	159
	Spending authority from offsetting collections, discretionary:			
1700	Collected	3	10	10
1701	Change in uncollected payments, Federal sources	2		
1750	Spending auth from offsetting collections, disc (total)	5	10	10
1900	Budget authority (total)	1,187	1,080	1,546
1930	Total budgetary resources available	1,324	1,259	1,546
	Memorandum (non-add) entries:			
1940	Unobligated balance expiring	–1		
1941	Unexpired unobligated balance, end of year	179		
	Change in obligated balance:			
	Unpaid obligations:			
3000	Unpaid obligations, brought forward, Oct 1	2,684	2,870	2,816
3010	New obligations, unexpired accounts	1,144	1,259	1,546
3011	Obligations ("upward adjustments"), expired accounts	7		
3020	Outlays (gross)	–934	–1,313	–1,446
3040	Recoveries of prior year unpaid obligations, unexpired	–8		
3041	Recoveries of prior year unpaid obligations, expired	–23		
3050	Unpaid obligations, end of year	2,870	2,816	2,916
	Uncollected payments:			
3060	Uncollected pymts, Fed sources, brought forward, Oct 1	–9	–9	–9
3070	Change in uncollected pymts, Fed sources, unexpired	–2		
3071	Change in uncollected pymts, Fed sources, expired	2		
3090	Uncollected pymts, Fed sources, end of year	–9	–9	–9
	Memorandum (non-add) entries:			
3100	Obligated balance, start of year	2,675	2,861	2,807
3200	Obligated balance, end of year	2,861	2,807	2,907
	Budget authority and outlays, net:			
	Discretionary:			
4000	Budget authority, gross	973	918	1,387
	Outlays, gross:			
4010	Outlays from new discretionary authority	29	146	203
4011	Outlays from discretionary balances	783	978	998
4020	Outlays, gross (total)	812	1,124	1,201
	Offsets against gross budget authority and outlays:			
	Offsetting collections (collected) from:			
4030	Federal sources	–5	–10	–10
4033	Non-Federal sources	–6		
4040	Offsets against gross budget authority and outlays (total)	–11	–10	–10
	Additional offsets against gross budget authority only:			
4050	Change in uncollected pymts, Fed sources, unexpired	–2		
4052	Offsetting collections credited to expired accounts	8		
4060	Additional offsets against budget authority only (total)	6		
4070	Budget authority, net (discretionary)	968	908	1,377
4080	Outlays, net (discretionary)	801	1,114	1,191
	Mandatory:			
4090	Budget authority, gross	214	162	159
	Outlays, gross:			
4100	Outlays from new mandatory authority		10	9
4101	Outlays from mandatory balances	122	179	236
4110	Outlays, gross (total)	122	189	245
4180	Budget authority, net (total)	1,182	1,070	1,536
4190	Outlays, net (total)	923	1,303	1,436

The STEM Education (EDU) (formerly Education and Human Resources) appropriation funds and manages a comprehensive set of programs that further NSF's goals of ensuring a diverse, globally competitive U.S. science, technology, engineering, and mathematics (STEM) workforce, as well as a scientifically literate population. To advance those goals, EDU collaborates with other NSF research units and Federal agencies, and promotes public-private partnerships. EDU supports research on STEM teaching and learning to provide the evidence base for improvements in education at all levels in the STEM disciplines. Supporting development and effective implementation of new learning technologies is also a priority. EDU pre-K-12 education-research programs, for example, develop and test new instruction materials for students and teachers, which incorporate the latest advances in teaching, learning, and education technologies. STEM teacher-education opportunities occur throughout the full continuum, from pre-service and in-service, through life-long learning. Research programs at the undergraduate level improve curricula, strengthen laboratory courses, enhance faculty effectiveness, and lead education reforms in STEM disciplines. Advanced technological education programs strengthen student preparation for the high-technology workforce. Support of graduate-level STEM education primarily includes fellowships and traineeships to sustain U.S. leadership in global science and technology. All EDU programs aim to broaden participation of groups underrepresented in STEM fields by, for example, improving infrastructure and academic programs at minority-serving institutions. EDU activities also include programs supported by H-1B non-immigrant visa fees, which provide undergraduate and graduate scholarships in STEM disciplines, improve educational opportunities for students, and provide research opportunities for STEM teachers and students.

Object Classification (in millions of dollars)

Identification code 049–0106–0–1–251		2021 actual	2022 est.	2023 est.
	Direct obligations:			
11.8	Personnel compensation: Special personal services payments	6	6	6
25.1	Advisory and assistance services	26	26	26
25.3	Other goods and services from Federal sources	2	2	2
41.0	Grants, subsidies, and contributions	1,106	1,215	1,502
99.0	Direct obligations	1,140	1,249	1,536
99.0	Reimbursable obligations	4	10	10
99.9	Total new obligations, unexpired accounts	1,144	1,259	1,546

Trust Funds

DONATIONS

Special and Trust Fund Receipts (in millions of dollars)

Identification code 049–8960–0–7–251		2021 actual	2022 est.	2023 est.
0100	Balance, start of year			
	Receipts:			
	Current law:			
1130	Donations, National Science Foundation	32	10	10
2000	Total: Balances and receipts	32	10	10
	Appropriations:			
	Current law:			
2101	Donations	–32	–10	–10
5099	Balance, end of year			

Program and Financing (in millions of dollars)

Identification code 049–8960–0–7–251		2021 actual	2022 est.	2023 est.
	Obligations by program activity:			
0002	Gemini Telescope	11		
0003	International Ocean Drilling	10		

National Science Foundation—Continued
Trust Funds—Continued

DONATIONS—Continued

Program and Financing—Continued

Identification code 049–8960–0–7–251	2021 actual	2022 est.	2023 est.
0005 General Trust Fund	5	48	10
0900 Total new obligations, unexpired accounts (object class 41.0)	26	48	10
Budgetary resources:			
Unobligated balance:			
1000 Unobligated balance brought forward, Oct 1	32	38	
Budget authority:			
Appropriations, mandatory:			
1201 Appropriation (special or trust fund)	32	10	10
1930 Total budgetary resources available	64	48	10
Memorandum (non-add) entries:			
1941 Unexpired unobligated balance, end of year	38		
Change in obligated balance:			
Unpaid obligations:			
3000 Unpaid obligations, brought forward, Oct 1	53	35	48
3010 New obligations, unexpired accounts	26	48	10
3020 Outlays (gross)	–44	–35	–14
3050 Unpaid obligations, end of year	35	48	44
Memorandum (non-add) entries:			
3100 Obligated balance, start of year	53	35	48
3200 Obligated balance, end of year	35	48	44
Budget authority and outlays, net:			
Mandatory:			
4090 Budget authority, gross	32	10	10
Outlays, gross:			
4100 Outlays from new mandatory authority		6	6
4101 Outlays from mandatory balances	44	29	8
4110 Outlays, gross (total)	44	35	14
4180 Budget authority, net (total)	32	10	10
4190 Outlays, net (total)	44	35	14

This account consists of contributions from organizations and individuals to fund various efforts in science, research, and education supported by NSF.

ADMINISTRATIVE PROVISIONS

(INCLUDING TRANSFER OF FUNDS)

Not to exceed 5 percent of any appropriation made available for the current fiscal year for the National Science Foundation in this Act may be transferred between such appropriations, but no such appropriation shall be increased by more than 10 percent by any such transfers. Any transfer pursuant to this paragraph shall be treated as a reprogramming of funds under section 504 of this Act and shall not be available for obligation except in compliance with the procedures set forth in that section.

The Director of the National Science Foundation (NSF) shall notify the Committees on Appropriations of the House of Representatives and the Senate at least 30 days in advance of any planned divestment through transfer, decommissioning, termination, or deconstruction of any NSF-owned facilities or any NSF capital assets (including land, structures, and equipment) valued greater than $2,500,000.

NSF NONRECURRING EXPENSES FUND

There is hereby established in the Treasury of the United States a fund to be known as the nonrecurring expenses fund (the Fund): Provided, That unobligated balances of expired discretionary funds appropriated for this or any succeeding fiscal year from the general fund of the Treasury to the National Science Foundation by this or any other Act may be transferred (not later than the end of the fifth fiscal year after the last fiscal year for which such funds are available for the purposes for which appropriated) into the Fund: Provided further, That amounts deposited in the Fund shall be available until expended, and in addition to such other funds as may be available for such purposes, for information and business technology system modernization and facilities infrastructure improvements, including nonrecurring maintenance, necessary for the operation of the Foundation or its funded research facilities subject to approval by the Office of Management and Budget: Provided further, That amounts in the Fund may be obligated only after the Committees on Appropriations of the House of Representatives and the Senate are notified at least 15 days in advance of the planned use of funds.

GENERAL FUND RECEIPT ACCOUNTS

(in millions of dollars)

	2021 actual	2022 est.	2023 est.
Offsetting receipts from the public:			
049–320000 Collections of Receivables from Canceled Accounts		1	1
049–322000 All Other General Fund Proprietary Receipts Including Budget Clearing Accounts	3	5	5
General Fund Offsetting receipts from the public	3	6	6

OFFICE OF PERSONNEL MANAGEMENT

Federal Funds

SALARIES AND EXPENSES

(INCLUDING TRANSFER OF TRUST FUNDS)

For necessary expenses to carry out functions of the Office of Personnel Management (OPM) pursuant to Reorganization Plan Numbered 2 of 1978 and the Civil Service Reform Act of 1978, including services as authorized by 5 U.S.C. 3109; medical examinations performed for veterans by private physicians on a fee basis; rental of conference rooms in the District of Columbia and elsewhere; hire of passenger motor vehicles; not to exceed $2,500 for official reception and representation expenses; and payment of per diem and/or subsistence allowances to employees where Voting Rights Act activities require an employee to remain overnight at his or her post of duty, $225,262,000: Provided, That of the total amount made available under this heading, $19,373,000 shall remain available until expended, for information technology modernization and Trust Fund Federal Financial System migration or modernization, and shall be in addition to funds otherwise made available for such purposes: Provided further, That of the total amount made available under this heading, $1,381,748 may be made available for strengthening the capacity and capabilities of the acquisition workforce (as defined by the Office of Federal Procurement Policy Act, as amended (41 U.S.C. 4001 et seq.)), including the recruitment, hiring, training, and retention of such workforce and information technology in support of acquisition workforce effectiveness or for management solutions to improve acquisition management; and in addition $190,316,000 for administrative expenses, to be transferred from the appropriate trust funds of OPM without regard to other statutes, including direct procurement of printed materials, for the retirement and insurance programs: Provided further, That the provisions of this appropriation shall not affect the authority to use applicable trust funds as provided by sections 8348(a)(1)(B), 8958(f)(2)(A), 8988(f)(2)(A), and 9004(f)(2)(A) of title 5, United States Code: Provided further, That no part of this appropriation shall be available for salaries and expenses of the Legal Examining Unit of OPM established pursuant to Executive Order No. 9358 of July 1, 1943, or any successor unit of like purpose: Provided further, That the President's Commission on White House Fellows, established by Executive Order No. 11183 of October 3, 1964, may, during fiscal year 2023, accept donations of money, property, and personal services: Provided further, That such donations, including those from prior years, may be used for the development of publicity materials to provide information about the White House Fellows, except that no such donations shall be accepted for travel or reimbursement of travel expenses, or for the salaries of employees of such Commission: Provided further, That not to exceed 5 percent of amounts made available under this heading may be transferred to an information technology working capital fund established for purposes authorized by subtitle G of title X of division A of the National Defense Authorization Act for Fiscal Year 2018 (Public Law 115–91; 40 U.S.C. 11301 note) upon advance notification to the Committees on Appropriations of the House of Representatives and the Senate: Provided further, That amounts transferred to such a fund under the preceding proviso from any organizational category of the Office of Personnel Management shall not exceed 5 percent of the organizational category's budget, as identified in the report required by section 608 of this Act: Provided further, That amounts transferred to such a fund shall remain available for obligation through September 30, 2026.

Note.—A full-year 2022 appropriation for this account was not enacted at the time the Budget was prepared; therefore, the Budget assumes this account is operating under the Continuing Appropriations Act, 2022 (Division A of Public Law 117–43, as amended). The amounts included for 2022 reflect the annualized level provided by the continuing resolution.

Program and Financing (in millions of dollars)

Identification code 024–0100–0–1–805	2021 actual	2022 est.	2023 est.
Obligations by program activity:			
0001 Employee Services	36	32	46
0002 Merit System Audit & Compliance	12	13	17
0003 Office of the Chief Financial Officer	2	10	12
0004 Office of the Chief Information Officer	36	33	63
0005 Executive Services	13	17	26
0009 Administrative Services and Centrally Financed	41	43	47
0010 Human Capital Data Management & Modernization	10	12	14
0100 Total direct program	150	160	225
0799 Total direct obligations	150	160	225
0801 Trust Fund activity	376	170	190
0900 Total new obligations, unexpired accounts	526	330	415

Budgetary resources:			
Unobligated balance:			
1000 Unobligated balance brought forward, Oct 1	18	26	32
1011 Unobligated balance transfer from other acct [047–0616]	....	6	4
1012 Unobligated balance transfers between expired and unexpired accounts	3	....	....
1021 Recoveries of prior year unpaid obligations	3	....	....
1070 Unobligated balance (total)	24	32	36
Budget authority:			
Appropriations, discretionary:			
1100 Appropriation	160	160	225
Spending authority from offsetting collections, discretionary:			
1700 Collected	307	170	190
1701 Change in uncollected payments, Federal sources	73	....	....
1750 Spending auth from offsetting collections, disc (total)	380	170	190
1900 Budget authority (total)	540	330	415
1930 Total budgetary resources available	564	362	451
Memorandum (non-add) entries:			
1940 Unobligated balance expiring	–12	....	....
1941 Unexpired unobligated balance, end of year	26	32	36
Change in obligated balance:			
Unpaid obligations:			
3000 Unpaid obligations, brought forward, Oct 1	167	176	44
3010 New obligations, unexpired accounts	526	330	415
3011 Obligations ("upward adjustments"), expired accounts	4	....	....
3020 Outlays (gross)	–512	–462	–416
3040 Recoveries of prior year unpaid obligations, unexpired	–3	....	....
3041 Recoveries of prior year unpaid obligations, expired	–6	....	....
3050 Unpaid obligations, end of year	176	44	43
Uncollected payments:			
3060 Uncollected pymts, Fed sources, brought forward, Oct 1	–210	–166	–166
3070 Change in uncollected pymts, Fed sources, unexpired	–73	....	....
3071 Change in uncollected pymts, Fed sources, expired	117	....	....
3090 Uncollected pymts, Fed sources, end of year	–166	–166	–166
Memorandum (non-add) entries:			
3100 Obligated balance, start of year	–43	10	–122
3200 Obligated balance, end of year	10	–122	–123
Budget authority and outlays, net:			
Discretionary:			
4000 Budget authority, gross	540	330	415
Outlays, gross:			
4010 Outlays from new discretionary authority	376	309	386
4011 Outlays from discretionary balances	136	153	30
4020 Outlays, gross (total)	512	462	416
Offsets against gross budget authority and outlays:			
Offsetting collections (collected) from:			
4030 Federal sources	–406	–170	–190
4033 Non-Federal sources	–4	....	....
4040 Offsets against gross budget authority and outlays (total)	–410	–170	–190
Additional offsets against gross budget authority only:			
4050 Change in uncollected pymts, Fed sources, unexpired	–73	....	....
4052 Offsetting collections credited to expired accounts	103	....	....
4060 Additional offsets against budget authority only (total)	30	....	....
4070 Budget authority, net (discretionary)	160	160	225
4080 Outlays, net (discretionary)	102	292	226
4180 Budget authority, net (total)	160	160	225
4190 Outlays, net (total)	102	292	226

The Office of Personnel Management's (OPM) mission is to recruit, retain and honor a world-class workforce for the American people. OPM will lead the way in making the Federal Government the model employer by being the model agency in implementing best practices, leading by example, and becoming the change we want to see.

The functions and objectives of OPM's major organizations are:

Employee Services.—Develops human resource (HR) policies for Executive Branch agencies and provides policy direction and leadership in designing, developing, and promulgating Government-wide HR systems and programs for recruitment, staffing, classification, pay, leave, training, performance management and recognition, employee development, management of executive resources, work/life/wellness programs, and labor and employee relations.

1180   Office of Personnel Management—Continued
       Federal Funds—Continued   THE BUDGET FOR FISCAL YEAR 2023

SALARIES AND EXPENSES—Continued

Merit System Accountability and Compliance.—Ensures Federal agency HR programs are effective, efficient, and meet merit system principles and related civil service requirements by working directly with other Federal agency Chief Human Capital Officers, Accountability Program Managers, HR managers and specialists. It improves agency programs that are not in compliance with Federal HR policies and regulation; and improves the effectiveness and efficiency of the agency programs to meet agency mission and objectives.

Retirement Services Program.—Administers the Civil Service Retirement System and the Federal Employees Retirement System, serving Federal retirees and survivors who receive monthly annuity payments. Retirement Services Program will continue to focus on making initial eligibility determinations, adjudicating new retirements, initiating survivor benefit payments, and calculating post retirement changes due to disability and death.

Healthcare & Insurance.—Administers the Federal Employees Health Benefits Program, the Federal Employees' Group Life Insurance Program, the Federal Flexible Spending Account Program, the Federal Long Term Care Insurance Program, and the Federal Employee Dental and Vision Insurance Program. These programs provide a complete suite of insurance benefits for more than eight million Federal employees, retirees, and their families.

Object Classification (in millions of dollars)

Identification code 024–0100–0–1–805		2021 actual	2022 est.	2023 est.
	Direct obligations:			
	Personnel compensation:			
11.1	Full-time permanent	52	66	80
11.3	Other than full-time permanent	....	3	3
11.5	Other personnel compensation	2	....	....
11.9	Total personnel compensation	54	69	83
12.1	Civilian personnel benefits	18	23	29
21.0	Travel and transportation of persons	....	1	1
23.3	Communications, utilities, and miscellaneous charges	39	24	30
25.2	Other services from non-Federal sources	36	43	80
31.0	Equipment	3	....	2
99.0	Direct obligations	150	160	225
99.0	Reimbursable obligations	376	170	190
99.9	Total new obligations, unexpired accounts	526	330	415

Employment Summary

Identification code 024–0100–0–1–805	2021 actual	2022 est.	2023 est.
1001 Direct civilian full-time equivalent employment	656	729	861
2001 Reimbursable civilian full-time equivalent employment	1,087	704	749

OFFICE OF INSPECTOR GENERAL

SALARIES AND EXPENSES

(INCLUDING TRANSFER OF TRUST FUNDS)

For necessary expenses of the Office of Inspector General in carrying out the provisions of the Inspector General Act of 1978, including services as authorized by 5 U.S.C. 3109, hire of passenger motor vehicles, $5,556,000, and in addition, not to exceed $35,163,000 for administrative expenses to audit, investigate, and provide other oversight of the Office of Personnel Management's retirement and insurance programs, to be transferred from the appropriate trust funds of the Office of Personnel Management, as determined by the Inspector General: Provided, That the Inspector General is authorized to rent conference rooms in the District of Columbia and elsewhere.

Note.—A full-year 2022 appropriation for this account was not enacted at the time the Budget was prepared; therefore, the Budget assumes this account is operating under the Continuing Appropriations Act, 2022 (Division A of Public Law 117–43, as amended). The amounts included for 2022 reflect the annualized level provided by the continuing resolution.

Program and Financing (in millions of dollars)

Identification code 024–0400–0–1–805		2021 actual	2022 est.	2023 est.
	Obligations by program activity:			
0001	Program oversight (audits, investigations, etc.)	5	5	6
0801	Office of Inspector General (Reimbursable)	27	27	35
0900	Total new obligations, unexpired accounts	32	32	41
	Budgetary resources:			
	Budget authority:			
	Appropriations, discretionary:			
1100	Appropriation	5	5	6
	Spending authority from offsetting collections, discretionary:			
1700	Collected	27	27	35
1900	Budget authority (total)	32	32	41
1930	Total budgetary resources available	32	32	41
	Change in obligated balance:			
	Unpaid obligations:			
3000	Unpaid obligations, brought forward, Oct 1	3	3	....
3010	New obligations, unexpired accounts	32	32	41
3020	Outlays (gross)	–32	–35	–41
3050	Unpaid obligations, end of year	3	....	....
	Uncollected payments:			
3060	Uncollected pymts, Fed sources, brought forward, Oct 1	–5	–2	–2
3071	Change in uncollected pymts, Fed sources, expired	3	....	....
3090	Uncollected pymts, Fed sources, end of year	–2	–2	–2
	Memorandum (non-add) entries:			
3100	Obligated balance, start of year	–2	1	–2
3200	Obligated balance, end of year	1	–2	–2
	Budget authority and outlays, net:			
	Discretionary:			
4000	Budget authority, gross	32	32	41
	Outlays, gross:			
4010	Outlays from new discretionary authority	28	31	40
4011	Outlays from discretionary balances	4	4	1
4020	Outlays, gross (total)	32	35	41
	Offsets against gross budget authority and outlays:			
	Offsetting collections (collected) from:			
4030	Federal sources	–29	–27	–35
	Additional offsets against gross budget authority only:			
4052	Offsetting collections credited to expired accounts	2	....	....
4060	Additional offsets against budget authority only (total)	2	....	....
4070	Budget authority, net (discretionary)	5	5	6
4080	Outlays, net (discretionary)	3	8	6
4180	Budget authority, net (total)	5	5	6
4190	Outlays, net (total)	3	8	6

This appropriation funds the U.S. Office of Personnel Management (OPM) Office of Inspector General's (OIG) efforts to protect the integrity of OPM's programs and operations. The OPM OIG's audits, investigations, evaluations, and administrative sanctions programs serve to prevent and detect fraud, waste, abuse, and mismanagement. The OPM OIG's Office of Audits conducts audits of OPM programs and operations. The Office of Audits issued 39 audit reports in 2021, with questioned costs totaling over $29 million. The majority of the Office of Audits' work involves the Federal Employees Health Benefits Program (FEHBP), auditing the health insurance carriers that contract with OPM as well as the pharmacy benefit managers these carriers use to administer the pharmacy benefit. In addition, the Office of Audits focuses on other key OPM benefits programs, including the Federal retirement program, the Federal Employees' Group Life Insurance Program, the Federal Employee Dental and Vision Insurance Program, the Federal Long Term Care Insurance Program, and the Federal Flexible Spending Accounts. The OPM OIG also conducts information systems audits that cover general and application controls and security within OPM information systems and programs as well as OPM contractor systems, such as those of FEHBP insurance carriers. One key project is to provide ongoing oversight of OPM's information technology (IT) modernization efforts. The OPM OIG's longstanding expertise in these areas has been recognized and endorsed by the Congress. The OPM OIG's continued oversight of these efforts is essential to the IT security posture of OPM, its systems, and the highly sensitive data contained in these systems. The Office of Audits also conducts audits of OPM revolving fund programs and operations, and the Office of Audits is responsible for the oversight of the OPM financial statement audit, which is conducted by an independent public accounting firm. The OPM OIG's Office of Investigations detects and investigates improper and illegal activities potentially involving OPM programs, personnel, contractors or operations. The Office of Investigations is a statutory law enforcement organization, with its special agents having the authority to carry firearms, issue subpoenas, and to seek and execute both search and arrest warrants. In 2021, the OPM OIG's activities led to 30 arrests, 35 indictments/criminal informations, and 33 criminal convictions, resulting in over $23 million in recoveries to the OPM Trust Funds. In addition, the Office of Investigations partnered with the U.S. Department of Justice (DOJ) and other Federal, state, and local law enforcement agencies to investigate and help prosecute and collect fines, penalties, and forfeitures to the Federal Government totaling over $466 million. Based on the evidence gathered during OPM OIG investigations, the Office of Investigations pursues appropriate remedies, including referrals to the DOJ for criminal prosecutions or civil action, and/or referral to OPM or to the OIGs FEHBP Administrative Sanctions program. The Office of Investigations also investigates allegations of fraud against OPM programs, such as the FEHBP and the Civil Service and Federal Employees Retirement Systems. When appropriate, the Office of Investigations also conducts investigations of OPM internal operations and employee and contractor misconduct. The OPM OIG's Office of Evaluations conducts nationwide studies of OPM programs from a broad, issue-based perspective, as well as evaluations of specific areas of operation and matters of urgent concern. The Office of Evaluations conducts special reviews in response to Congressional requests for studies or information that may require immediate attention and OPM management requests for independent assessments. Evaluators in this office use a variety of methods and techniques to evaluate and assess an OPM operation or concern to develop recommendations for OPM management, the Congress, and the public. In 2021, the Office of Evaluations issued one final evaluation report. Finally, the OPM OIG FEHBP Administrative Sanctions program debars and suspends health care providers whose loss of licensure or conduct may pose a health and safety risk to FEHBP enrollees and their families or a financial threat to the FEHBP. In 2021, the OPM OIG was responsible for 710 suspensions and debarments within the FEHBP. In January 2014, the Congress passed the OPM IG Act (P.L. 11380). This legislation has provided the necessary funding for the OPM OIG to audit, investigate, and provide other oversight of the activities of the OPM revolving fund programs and operations.

Object Classification (in millions of dollars)

Identification code 024–0400–0–1–805		2021 actual	2022 est.	2023 est.
	Direct obligations:			
11.1	Personnel compensation: Full-time permanent	3	3	4
12.1	Civilian personnel benefits	1	1	1
23.3	Communications, utilities, and miscellaneous charges	1	1	1
99.0	Direct obligations	5	5	6
99.0	Reimbursable obligations	27	27	35
99.9	Total new obligations, unexpired accounts	32	32	41

Employment Summary

Identification code 024–0400–0–1–805		2021 actual	2022 est.	2023 est.
1001	Direct civilian full-time equivalent employment	24	24	26
2001	Reimbursable civilian full-time equivalent employment	111	111	168

GOVERNMENT PAYMENT FOR ANNUITANTS, EMPLOYEES HEALTH BENEFITS

Program and Financing (in millions of dollars)

Identification code 024–0206–0–1–551		2021 actual	2022 est.	2023 est.
	Obligations by program activity:			
0001	Government contribution for annuitants benefits (1959 Act)	13,595	14,329	14,570
0002	Government contribution for annuitants benefits (1960 Act)	....	1	1
0900	Total new obligations, unexpired accounts (object class 13.0)	13,595	14,330	14,571
	Budgetary resources:			
	Budget authority:			
	Appropriations, mandatory:			
1200	Appropriation	13,595	14,330	14,571
1930	Total budgetary resources available	13,595	14,330	14,571
	Change in obligated balance:			
	Unpaid obligations:			
3000	Unpaid obligations, brought forward, Oct 1	1,511	1,583	....
3010	New obligations, unexpired accounts	13,595	14,330	14,571
3020	Outlays (gross)	–13,523	–15,913	–14,571
3050	Unpaid obligations, end of year	1,583		
	Memorandum (non-add) entries:			
3100	Obligated balance, start of year	1,511	1,583	
3200	Obligated balance, end of year	1,583		
	Budget authority and outlays, net:			
	Mandatory:			
4090	Budget authority, gross	13,595	14,330	14,571
	Outlays, gross:			
4100	Outlays from new mandatory authority	12,012	14,330	13,373
4101	Outlays from mandatory balances	1,511	1,583	1,198
4110	Outlays, gross (total)	13,523	15,913	14,571
4180	Budget authority, net (total)	13,595	14,330	14,571
4190	Outlays, net (total)	13,523	15,913	14,571

Summary of Budget Authority and Outlays (in millions of dollars)

	2021 actual	2022 est.	2023 est.
Enacted/requested:			
Budget Authority	13,595	14,330	14,571
Outlays	13,523	15,913	14,571
Legislative proposal, subject to PAYGO:			
Budget Authority			77
Outlays			77
Total:			
Budget Authority	13,595	14,330	14,648
Outlays	13,523	15,913	14,648

This appropriation covers: 1) the Government's share of the cost of health insurance for annuitants as defined in sections 8901 and 8906 of title 5, United States Code; 2) the Government's share of the cost of health insurance for annuitants (who were retired when the Federal employees health benefits law became effective), as defined in the Retired Federal Employees Health Benefits Act of 1960; and 3) the Government's contribution for payment of administrative expenses incurred by OPM in administration of the Act. The budget authority for this account recognizes the amounts being remitted by the Postal Service Retiree Health Benefits Fund to finance a portion of United States Postal Service annuitants' health benefit costs.

	2021 actual	2022 est.	2023 est.
FEHB	1,922,043	1,944,202	1,964,991
USPS annuitants (non-add)	419,000	419,000	419,000
REHB	71	59	48
Total, annuitants	1,922,114	1,944,261	1,965,039

GOVERNMENT PAYMENT FOR ANNUITANTS, EMPLOYEES HEALTH BENEFITS

(Legislative proposal, subject to PAYGO)

Program and Financing (in millions of dollars)

Identification code 024–0206–4–1–551		2021 actual	2022 est.	2023 est.
	Obligations by program activity:			
0002	Government contribution for annuitants benefits (1960 Act)	....	....	77

GOVERNMENT PAYMENT FOR ANNUITANTS, EMPLOYEES HEALTH BENEFITS—Continued

Program and Financing—Continued

Identification code 024–0206–4–1–551	2021 actual	2022 est.	2023 est.
0900 Total new obligations, unexpired accounts (object class 13.0)			77
Budgetary resources:			
Budget authority:			
Appropriations, mandatory:			
1200 Appropriation			77
1930 Total budgetary resources available			77
Change in obligated balance:			
Unpaid obligations:			
3010 New obligations, unexpired accounts			77
3020 Outlays (gross)			–77
Budget authority and outlays, net:			
Mandatory:			
4090 Budget authority, gross			77
Outlays, gross:			
4100 Outlays from new mandatory authority			77
4180 Budget authority, net (total)			77
4190 Outlays, net (total)			77

The President's 2023 Budget proposals aims to improve access to behavioral health services by requiring coverage of three primary visits and three behavior health visits without cost-sharing for all Federal Employees Health Benefit Program plans.

GOVERNMENT PAYMENT FOR ANNUITANTS, EMPLOYEE LIFE INSURANCE

Program and Financing (in millions of dollars)

Identification code 024–0500–0–1–602	2021 actual	2022 est.	2023 est.
Obligations by program activity:			
0001 Government Payment for Annuitants, Employee Life Insurance (Direct)	41	40	41
0900 Total new obligations, unexpired accounts (object class 25.2)	41	40	41
Budgetary resources:			
Budget authority:			
Appropriations, mandatory:			
1200 Appropriation	41	40	41
1930 Total budgetary resources available	41	40	41
Change in obligated balance:			
Unpaid obligations:			
3000 Unpaid obligations, brought forward, Oct 1	5	6	6
3010 New obligations, unexpired accounts	41	40	41
3020 Outlays (gross)	–40	–40	–41
3050 Unpaid obligations, end of year	6	6	6
Memorandum (non-add) entries:			
3100 Obligated balance, start of year	5	6	6
3200 Obligated balance, end of year	6	6	6
Budget authority and outlays, net:			
Mandatory:			
4090 Budget authority, gross	41	40	41
Outlays, gross:			
4100 Outlays from new mandatory authority	35	34	36
4101 Outlays from mandatory balances	5	6	5
4110 Outlays, gross (total)	40	40	41
4180 Budget authority, net (total)	41	40	41
4190 Outlays, net (total)	40	40	41

Per Public Law 96–427, Federal Employees' Group Life Insurance Act of 1980, enacted October 10, 1980, this appropriation finances the Government's share of premiums, which is one-third the cost, for Basic life insurance for annuitants retiring after December 31, 1989, and who are less than 65 years old.

PAYMENT TO CIVIL SERVICE RETIREMENT AND DISABILITY FUND

Program and Financing (in millions of dollars)

Identification code 024–0200–0–1–805	2021 actual	2022 est.	2023 est.
Obligations by program activity:			
0002 Payment of Government share of retirement costs	18,786	18,400	18,000
0003 Transfers for interest on unfunded liability and payment of military service annuities	27,154	27,500	28,000
0005 Spouse equity payment	35	35	35
0900 Total new obligations, unexpired accounts	45,975	45,935	46,035
Budgetary resources:			
Budget authority:			
Appropriations, mandatory:			
1200 Appropriation	27,154	27,500	28,000
1200 Appropriation	18,821	18,435	18,035
1260 Appropriations, mandatory (total)	45,975	45,935	46,035
1930 Total budgetary resources available	45,975	45,935	46,035
Change in obligated balance:			
Unpaid obligations:			
3010 New obligations, unexpired accounts	45,975	45,935	46,035
3020 Outlays (gross)	–45,975	–45,935	–46,035
Budget authority and outlays, net:			
Mandatory:			
4090 Budget authority, gross	45,975	45,935	46,035
Outlays, gross:			
4100 Outlays from new mandatory authority	45,975	45,935	46,035
4180 Budget authority, net (total)	45,975	45,935	46,035
4190 Outlays, net (total)	45,975	45,935	46,035

The Payment to the Civil Service Retirement and Disability Fund consists of an appropriation and a permanent indefinite authorization to pay the Government's share of retirement costs. The payment is made directly from the general fund of the U.S. Treasury into the Civil Service Retirement and Disability Fund and is in addition to appropriated funds that will be contributed from agency budgets.

Current Appropriation Payment of Government Share of Retirement Costs.—The Civil Service Retirement Amendments of 1969 provides for an annual appropriation to amortize, over a 30-year period, all increases in Civil Service Retirement System costs resulting from acts of the Congress granting new or liberalized benefits, extensions of coverage, or pay raises, exclusive of the effects of cost-of-living adjustments. The Office of Personnel Management notifies the Secretary of the Treasury each year of such sums as may be necessary to carry out these provisions.

Permanent Indefinite Authorization.—Transfers for interest on static unfunded liability and payment of military service annuities. The Civil Service Retirement Amendments of 1969 also provides permanent, indefinite authorization for the Secretary of the Treasury to transfer, on an annual basis, an amount equal to five percent interest on the Civil Service Retirement and Disability Fund's current statutory unfunded liability, calculated based on static economic assumptions, and annuity disbursements attributable to credit for military service.

Payments for Spouse Equity.—The permanent, indefinite authorization also includes a payment which provides for the Secretary of the Treasury to transfer an amount equal to the annuities granted to eligible former spouses of annuitants who died between September 1978 and May 1985 who did not elect survivor coverage.

Financing.—The unfunded liability of new and increased annuity benefits becoming effective on or after October 20, 1969, and annuities under special Acts to be credited to the Civil Service Retirement and Disability Fund, may be paid out of the Civil Service Retirement and Disability Fund.

Object Classification (in millions of dollars)

Identification code 024–0200–0–1–805	2021 actual	2022 est.	2023 est.
Direct obligations:			
12.1 Civilian personnel benefits	18,821	18,435	18,035

OFFICE OF PERSONNEL MANAGEMENT

Office of Personnel Management—Continued
Federal Funds—Continued   1183

		2021 actual	2022 est.	2023 est.
13.0	Benefits for former personnel	27,154	27,500	28,000
99.9	Total new obligations, unexpired accounts	45,975	45,935	46,035

FLEXIBLE BENEFITS PLAN RESERVE

Program and Financing (in millions of dollars)

Identification code 024–0800–0–1–805		2021 actual	2022 est.	2023 est.
	Obligations by program activity:			
0801	FSA FEDS Risk Reserve	12	11	11
0900	Total new obligations, unexpired accounts (object class 25.6)	12	11	11
	Budgetary resources:			
	Unobligated balance:			
1000	Unobligated balance brought forward, Oct 1	67	58	54
	Budget authority:			
	Spending authority from offsetting collections, mandatory:			
1800	Collected	4	8	21
1823	New and/or unobligated balance of spending authority from offsetting collections temporarily reduced	–1	–1	–1
1850	Spending auth from offsetting collections, mand (total)	3	7	20
1930	Total budgetary resources available	70	65	74
	Memorandum (non-add) entries:			
1941	Unexpired unobligated balance, end of year	58	54	63
	Change in obligated balance:			
	Unpaid obligations:			
3000	Unpaid obligations, brought forward, Oct 1	7	7	7
3010	New obligations, unexpired accounts	12	11	11
3020	Outlays (gross)	–12	–11	–10
3050	Unpaid obligations, end of year	7	7	8
	Memorandum (non-add) entries:			
3100	Obligated balance, start of year	7	7	7
3200	Obligated balance, end of year	7	7	8
	Budget authority and outlays, net:			
	Mandatory:			
4090	Budget authority, gross	3	7	20
	Outlays, gross:			
4100	Outlays from new mandatory authority	3	8	7
4101	Outlays from mandatory balances	9	3	3
4110	Outlays, gross (total)	12	11	10
	Offsets against gross budget authority and outlays:			
	Offsetting collections (collected) from:			
4120	Federal sources	–1	–1	–1
4123	Non-Federal sources	–3	–7	–20
4130	Offsets against gross budget authority and outlays (total)	–4	–8	–21
4160	Budget authority, net (mandatory)	–1	–1	–1
4170	Outlays, net (mandatory)	8	3	–11
4180	Budget authority, net (total)	–1	–1	–1
4190	Outlays, net (total)	8	3	–11
	Memorandum (non-add) entries:			
5090	Unexpired unavailable balance, SOY: Offsetting collections	11	12	13
5092	Unexpired unavailable balance, EOY: Offsetting collections	12	13	14

This account contains reserve resources required under the Office of Personnel Management's (OPM) contract with the administrator of the Flexible Benefits program. This account is funded by payments from Federal agencies based on the participation of their employees in the program and from net forfeitures, as authorized by the National Defense Authorization Act for Fiscal Year 2004 (P.L. 108–136). Account assets are available to indemnify the administrator when benefit payments exceed contributions, for program enhancements, and for OPM's administration of the program. The reserve account may also be used to mitigate Federal agencies' contractual costs for the program when the account balance exceeds that deemed necessary to defray reasonable risk.

POSTAL SERVICE RETIREE HEALTH BENEFITS FUND

Special and Trust Fund Receipts (in millions of dollars)

Identification code 024–5391–0–2–551		2021 actual	2022 est.	2023 est.
0100	Balance, start of year	41,868	38,849	35,579
	Receipts:			
	Current law:			
1140	Postal Service Contributions for Current Workers, Postal Service Retiree Health Benefits Fund	....	4,262	4,471
1140	Postal Service Contributions for Current Workers, Postal Service Retiree Health Benefits Fund	....	–4,262	–4,471
1140	Earnings on Investments, Postal Service Retiree Health Benefits Fund	1,021	910	809
1140	Postal Service Contributions for Benefits Paid to Retirees, Postal Service Retiree Health Benefits Fund	....	–907	–907
1140	Postal Service Contributions for Benefits Paid to Retirees, Postal Service Retiree Health Benefits Fund	....	907	907
1199	Total current law receipts	1,021	910	809
	Proposed:			
1240	Earnings on Investments, Postal Service Retiree Health Benefits Fund	....	....	–1
1999	Total receipts	1,021	910	808
2000	Total: Balances and receipts	42,889	39,759	36,387
	Appropriations:			
	Current law:			
2101	Postal Service Retiree Health Benefits Fund	–1,021	–1,045	–1,101
2103	Postal Service Retiree Health Benefits Fund	–3,019	–3,135	–3,302
2199	Total current law appropriations	–4,040	–4,180	–4,403
	Proposed:			
2201	Postal Service Retiree Health Benefits Fund	....	....	–23
2999	Total appropriations	–4,040	–4,180	–4,426
5099	Balance, end of year	38,849	35,579	31,961

Program and Financing (in millions of dollars)

Identification code 024–5391–0–2–551		2021 actual	2022 est.	2023 est.
	Obligations by program activity:			
0001	Obligations to FEHB Fund	4,040	4,180	4,403
0900	Total new obligations, unexpired accounts (object class 13.0)	4,040	4,180	4,403
	Budgetary resources:			
	Budget authority:			
	Appropriations, mandatory:			
1201	Appropriation (special or trust fund)	1,021	1,045	1,101
1203	Appropriation (previously unavailable)(special or trust)	3,019	3,135	3,302
1260	Appropriations, mandatory (total)	4,040	4,180	4,403
1930	Total budgetary resources available	4,040	4,180	4,403
	Change in obligated balance:			
	Unpaid obligations:			
3010	New obligations, unexpired accounts	4,040	4,180	4,403
3020	Outlays (gross)	–4,040	–4,180	–4,403
	Budget authority and outlays, net:			
	Mandatory:			
4090	Budget authority, gross	4,040	4,180	4,403
	Outlays, gross:			
4100	Outlays from new mandatory authority	....	4,180	4,403
4101	Outlays from mandatory balances	4,040	....	....
4110	Outlays, gross (total)	4,040	4,180	4,403
4180	Budget authority, net (total)	4,040	4,180	4,403
4190	Outlays, net (total)	4,040	4,180	4,403
	Memorandum (non-add) entries:			
5000	Total investments, SOY: Federal securities: Par value	41,868	38,849	35,790
5001	Total investments, EOY: Federal securities: Par value	38,849	35,790	32,196

Summary of Budget Authority and Outlays (in millions of dollars)

	2021 actual	2022 est.	2023 est.
Enacted/requested:			
Budget Authority	4,040	4,180	4,403
Outlays	4,040	4,180	4,403

Office of Personnel Management—Continued
Federal Funds—Continued

POSTAL SERVICE RETIREE HEALTH BENEFITS FUND—Continued
Summary of Budget Authority and Outlays—Continued

	2021 actual	2022 est.	2023 est.
Legislative proposal, subject to PAYGO:			
Budget Authority			23
Outlays			23
Total:			
Budget Authority	4,040	4,180	4,426
Outlays	4,040	4,180	4,426

POSTAL SERVICE RETIREE HEALTH BENEFITS FUND
(Legislative proposal, subject to PAYGO)

Program and Financing (in millions of dollars)

Identification code 024–5391–4–2–551	2021 actual	2022 est.	2023 est.
Obligations by program activity:			
0001 Obligations to FEHB Fund			23
0900 Total new obligations, unexpired accounts (object class 13.0)			23
Budgetary resources:			
Budget authority:			
Appropriations, mandatory:			
1201 Appropriation (special or trust fund)			23
1930 Total budgetary resources available			23
Change in obligated balance:			
Unpaid obligations:			
3010 New obligations, unexpired accounts			23
3020 Outlays (gross)			–23
Budget authority and outlays, net:			
Mandatory:			
4090 Budget authority, gross			23
Outlays, gross:			
4100 Outlays from new mandatory authority			23
4180 Budget authority, net (total)			23
4190 Outlays, net (total)			23
Memorandum (non-add) entries:			
5001 Total investments, EOY: Federal securities: Par value			–23

The President's 2023 Budget proposals aims to improve access to behavioral health services by requiring coverage of three primary visits and three behavior health visits without cost-sharing for all Federal Employees Health Benefit Program plans.

REVOLVING FUND

Program and Financing (in millions of dollars)

Identification code 024–4571–0–4–805	2021 actual	2022 est.	2023 est.
Obligations by program activity:			
0801 Human Resource Solutions	396	334	357
0802 National Background Investigations Bureau (NBIB)	11		
0803 Human Resources Tools & Technology (HRTT)	71	80	84
0804 Enterprise Human Resources Integration	27	39	19
0806 Suitability Executive Agent	6	10	10
0807 Human Resource Line of Business (HRLoB)	2	3	3
0808 Inspector General Activities	1	1	1
0810 Credit Monitoring	61	86	86
0811 National Background Investigations Bureau Transition	2		
0900 Total new obligations, unexpired accounts	577	553	560
Budgetary resources:			
Unobligated balance:			
1000 Unobligated balance brought forward, Oct 1	712	380	384
1010 Unobligated balance transfer to other accts [097–4932]	–58		
1021 Recoveries of prior year unpaid obligations	145		
1070 Unobligated balance (total)	799	380	384
Budget authority:			
Spending authority from offsetting collections, mandatory:			
1800 Collected	476	557	554
1801 Change in uncollected payments, Federal sources	–318		
1850 Spending auth from offsetting collections, mand (total)	158	557	554
1930 Total budgetary resources available	957	937	938
Memorandum (non-add) entries:			
1941 Unexpired unobligated balance, end of year	380	384	378
Change in obligated balance:			
Unpaid obligations:			
3000 Unpaid obligations, brought forward, Oct 1	343	299	295
3010 New obligations, unexpired accounts	577	553	560
3020 Outlays (gross)	–476	–557	–555
3040 Recoveries of prior year unpaid obligations, unexpired	–145		
3050 Unpaid obligations, end of year	299	295	300
Uncollected payments:			
3060 Uncollected pymts, Fed sources, brought forward, Oct 1	–571	–253	–253
3070 Change in uncollected pymts, Fed sources, unexpired	318		
3090 Uncollected pymts, Fed sources, end of year	–253	–253	–253
Memorandum (non-add) entries:			
3100 Obligated balance, start of year	–228	46	42
3200 Obligated balance, end of year	46	42	47
Budget authority and outlays, net:			
Mandatory:			
4090 Budget authority, gross	158	557	554
Outlays, gross:			
4100 Outlays from new mandatory authority	272	262	380
4101 Outlays from mandatory balances	204	295	175
4110 Outlays, gross (total)	476	557	555
Offsets against gross budget authority and outlays:			
Offsetting collections (collected) from:			
4120 Federal sources	–476	–557	–554
Additional offsets against gross budget authority only:			
4140 Change in uncollected pymts, Fed sources, unexpired	318		
4170 Outlays, net (mandatory)			1
4180 Budget authority, net (total)			
4190 Outlays, net (total)			1

Budget Program.—Pursuant to 5 U.S.C. 1304(e)(1), OPM is authorized to use Revolving Funds without fiscal year limitations to conduct background investigations, training, and other personnel management services that OPM is authorized or required to perform on a reimbursable basis. Under this guidance, OPM operates several programs, which are funded by fees or reimbursement payments collected from other agencies and other payments. The following programs are authorized to use Revolving Funds: Suitability Executive Agent, Human Resources Solutions, Enterprise Human Resources Integration, Human Resources Line of Business, Human Resources Solutions Information Technology Program Management Office, and Credit Monitoring and Identity Protection Services.

Operating Results.—In 2021, OPM's Revolving Fund businesses revenue total was $531 million and the expenses total was $540 million which produced a net loss on operations of -$9 million. The cumulative net position of the fund is $246 million.

The OPM IG Act (the Act) (P.L. 113–80).—The Act extends permitted uses of the Revolving Fund to include financing the cost of audits, investigations, and oversight activities of OPM's Office of the Inspector General. The Act limits the amount of revolving fund resources available to the Office of the Inspector General each year to 0.33 percent of the total budgetary authority estimated for the fund in the year.

Object Classification (in millions of dollars)

Identification code 024–4571–0–4–805	2021 actual	2022 est.	2023 est.
Reimbursable obligations:			
Personnel compensation:			
11.1 Full-time permanent	64	84	81
11.5 Other personnel compensation	3	4	3
11.9 Total personnel compensation	67	88	84
12.1 Civilian personnel benefits	31	32	31
21.0 Travel and transportation of persons		5	4
23.1 Rental payments to GSA	8	9	11
23.3 Communications, utilities, and miscellaneous charges	14	15	18
25.2 Other services from non-Federal sources	455	403	410
26.0 Supplies and materials	1	1	1
31.0 Equipment	1		1

OFFICE OF PERSONNEL MANAGEMENT

		2021 actual	2022 est.	2023 est.
99.9	Total new obligations, unexpired accounts	577	553	560

Employment Summary

Identification code 024–4571–0–4–805	2021 actual	2022 est.	2023 est.
2001 Reimbursable civilian full-time equivalent employment	568	705	727

EMERGENCY FEDERAL EMPLOYEE LEAVE FUND

Program and Financing (in millions of dollars)

Identification code 024–0806–0–1–602		2021 actual	2022 est.	2023 est.
	Obligations by program activity:			
0001	Agency Reimbursement	307		
0900	Total new obligations, unexpired accounts (object class 44.0)	307		
	Budgetary resources:			
	Unobligated balance:			
1000	Unobligated balance brought forward, Oct 1		263	263
	Budget authority:			
	Appropriations, mandatory:			
1200	Appropriation	570		
1930	Total budgetary resources available	570	263	263
	Memorandum (non-add) entries:			
1941	Unexpired unobligated balance, end of year	263	263	263
	Change in obligated balance:			
	Unpaid obligations:			
3000	Unpaid obligations, brought forward, Oct 1			7
3010	New obligations, unexpired accounts	307		
3020	Outlays (gross)	–300	–7	
3050	Unpaid obligations, end of year	7		
	Memorandum (non-add) entries:			
3100	Obligated balance, start of year			7
3200	Obligated balance, end of year	7		
	Budget authority and outlays, net:			
	Mandatory:			
4090	Budget authority, gross	570		
	Outlays, gross:			
4100	Outlays from new mandatory authority	300		
4101	Outlays from mandatory balances		7	
4110	Outlays, gross (total)	300	7	
4180	Budget authority, net (total)	570		
4190	Outlays, net (total)	300	7	

The Emergency Federal Employee Leave Fund (Fund) was established by the American Rescue Plan Act of 2021 (P.L. 117–2). The Fund is available to reimburse Federal agencies for the cost of COVID-19 related paid leave granted under section 4001 of the Act during fiscal year 2021, or until the Fund is exhausted if sooner. Once the Fund is exhausted, the leave program created by the Act ceases. The Fund is also available for reasonable expenses incurred by the Office of Personnel Management. Funds remain available during fiscal year 2022 for accounting adjustments and administrative corrections associated with leave that occurred during fiscal year 2021.

Trust Funds

CIVIL SERVICE RETIREMENT AND DISABILITY FUND

Special and Trust Fund Receipts (in millions of dollars)

Identification code 024–8135–0–7–602		2021 actual	2022 est.	2023 est.
0100	Balance, start of year	954,003	977,981	999,247
	Receipts:			
	Current law:			
1110	Employee Contributions, Civil Service Retirement and Disability Fund	4,967	5,713	6,247
1110	District of Columbia Contributions, Civil Service Retirement and Disability Fund	26	31	30
1110	Employee Deposits, Redeposits and Other Contributions, Civil Service Retirement and Disability Fund	574	562	552
1140	Agency Contributions, Civil Service Retirement and Disability Fund			1,059
1140	Agency Contributions, Civil Service Retirement and Disability Fund	37,764	41,556	42,236
1140	Postal Service Agency Contributions, Civil Service Retirement and Disability Fund			111
1140	Postal Service Agency Contributions, Civil Service Retirement and Disability Fund			–4,460
1140	Postal Service Agency Contributions, Civil Service Retirement and Disability Fund	4,060	4,315	4,340
1140	Postal Service Supplemental Contributions, Civil Service Retirement and Disability Fund		1,401	1,401
1140	Postal Service Supplemental Contributions, Civil Service Retirement and Disability Fund		–1,401	–1,401
1140	Postal Service Amortization Payments, Civil Service Retirement and Disability Fund		1,858	1,858
1140	Postal Service Amortization Payments, Civil Service Retirement and Disability Fund		–1,858	–1,858
1140	FFB, TVA, and USPS Interest, Civil Service Retirement and Disability Fund	192	157	123
1140	Treasury Interest, Civil Service Retirement and Disability Fund	22,996	20,939	18,910
1140	General Fund Payment to the Civil Service Retirement and Disability Fund	45,975	45,935	46,035
1140	Re-employed Annuitants Salary Offset, Civil Service Retirement and Disability Fund	38	39	41
1199	Total current law receipts	116,592	119,247	115,224
1999	Total receipts	116,592	119,247	115,224
2000	Total: Balances and receipts	1,070,595	1,097,228	1,114,471
	Appropriations:			
	Current law:			
2101	Civil Service Retirement and Disability Fund	–126	–126	–139
2101	Civil Service Retirement and Disability Fund	–116,467	–119,124	–119,549
2103	Civil Service Retirement and Disability Fund	–3	–3	–3
2132	Civil Service Retirement and Disability Fund	3	3	3
2135	Civil Service Retirement and Disability Fund	23,978	21,269	16,288
2199	Total current law appropriations	–92,615	–97,981	–103,400
2999	Total appropriations	–92,615	–97,981	–103,400
5098	Rounding adjustment	1		
5099	Balance, end of year	977,981	999,247	1,011,071

Program and Financing (in millions of dollars)

Identification code 024–8135–0–7–602		2021 actual	2022 est.	2023 est.
	Obligations by program activity:			
0001	Annuities	91,942	97,448	102,850
0002	Refunds and death claims	476	407	411
0003	Administration - operations	190	119	130
0004	Transfer to MSPB	2	2	2
0005	Administration - OIG	5	5	7
0900	Total new obligations, unexpired accounts	92,615	97,981	103,400
	Budgetary resources:			
	Budget authority:			
	Appropriations, discretionary:			
1101	Appropriation (special or trust)	126	126	139
	Appropriations, mandatory:			
1201	Appropriation (special or trust fund)	116,467	119,124	119,549
1203	Appropriation (previously unavailable)(special or trust)	3	3	3
1232	Appropriations and/or unobligated balance of appropriations temporarily reduced	–3	–3	–3
1235	Appropriations precluded from obligation (special or trust)	–23,978	–21,269	–16,288
1260	Appropriations, mandatory (total)	92,489	97,855	103,261
1900	Budget authority (total)	92,615	97,981	103,400
1930	Total budgetary resources available	92,615	97,981	103,400
	Change in obligated balance:			
	Unpaid obligations:			
3000	Unpaid obligations, brought forward, Oct 1	8,102	8,370	8,895
3010	New obligations, unexpired accounts	92,615	97,981	103,400
3020	Outlays (gross)	–92,347	–97,456	–102,966
3050	Unpaid obligations, end of year	8,370	8,895	9,329
	Memorandum (non-add) entries:			
3100	Obligated balance, start of year	8,102	8,370	8,895
3200	Obligated balance, end of year	8,370	8,895	9,329

Office of Personnel Management—Continued
Trust Funds—Continued

CIVIL SERVICE RETIREMENT AND DISABILITY FUND—Continued
Program and Financing—Continued

Identification code 024–8135–0–7–602		2021 actual	2022 est.	2023 est.
	Budget authority and outlays, net:			
	Discretionary:			
4000	Budget authority, gross	126	126	139
	Outlays, gross:			
4010	Outlays from new discretionary authority	101	126	139
4011	Outlays from discretionary balances	27		
4020	Outlays, gross (total)	128	126	139
	Mandatory:			
4090	Budget authority, gross	92,489	97,855	103,261
	Outlays, gross:			
4100	Outlays from new mandatory authority	84,144	88,960	93,943
4101	Outlays from mandatory balances	8,075	8,370	8,884
4110	Outlays, gross (total)	92,219	97,330	102,827
4180	Budget authority, net (total)	92,615	97,981	103,400
4190	Outlays, net (total)	92,347	97,456	102,966
	Memorandum (non-add) entries:			
5000	Total investments, SOY: Federal securities: Par value	962,083	925,846	1,007,330
5001	Total investments, EOY: Federal securities: Par value	925,846	1,007,330	1,023,632

The Civil Service Retirement and Disability Fund (CSRDF) is the oldest and largest of the four trust funds administered by the Office of Personnel Management. The fund is financed and structured very differently from the other three trust funds. It is characterized by permanent indefinite budget authority. Budget authority is the authority to incur obligations and pay expenses which become available to an agency during any fiscal year. Once approved, permanent budget authority is permanently available for all future years. Indefinite budget authority is used when the precise amount of budget authority required cannot be forecast in advance and must thus be determined at some future point in time (e.g., when actual receipts and expenses become known).

The CSRDF covers two Federal civilian retirement systems: the Civil Service Retirement System (CSRS) established on May 22, 1920, and the Federal Employees Retirement System (FERS) established on June 6, 1986. The Retirement Fund is a single plan even though there are two different benefit tiers and funding methods. CSRS is largely a defined benefit plan, covering Federal employees hired prior to 1984. CSRS participants do not participate in the Social Security system. FERS is a three-tiered pension program that uses Social Security as a base, provides an additional basic benefit, and includes the Thrift Savings Plan (TSP). FERS covers employees hired after 1983 and formerly CSRS-covered employees who elected to join FERS.

The Budget proposes that the United States Patent and Trademark Office (PTO) continue to fund the full retirement benefits cost for PTO's employees covered under CSRS.

Financing.—CSRS has been financed under a statutory funding method passed by the Congress in 1969. This funding method is based on the static economic assumptions of no future inflation, no future General Schedule salary increases, and a 5.0 percent interest rate. Under CSRS, regular employees contribute 7.0 percent of pay. Law enforcement officers, firefighters, and congressional employees contribute an extra 0.5 percent of pay, and members of the Congress an extra 1.0 percent of pay. Non-United States Postal Service (USPS) agencies match the employee contributions. Also under the static funding method for CSRS, the Treasury pays interest on any static unfunded liabilities that are not being financed by USPS. The Treasury also makes payments to amortize, over a 30-year period, any increases in the static unfunded liability due to salary increases for non-USPS (non-Postal) employees that occurred during the year, and pays for the cost of any benefits attributable to military service for both Postal and non-Postal employees that were paid out during the year.

FERS is funded under a dynamic entry age normal funding method. Employees and agencies together contribute the full amount of the dynamic normal cost rate. The normal cost rate is for the defined benefit plan only, and does not include the cost of Social Security or the TSP. FERS regular employees contribute a percentage of salary that is equal to the contribution rate for CSRS employees, 7.0 percent, as set forth above, less the 6.2 percent tax rate under the Old-Age, Survivors and Disability Insurance portion of Social Security.

Effective 2022, there was a change in the normal cost rates for Postal FERS Employee/Employer Contributions and non-Postal FERS Employer Contributions. Under FERS, the dynamic normal cost rates are as follows: For regular FERS non-Postal employees (other than RAE and FRAE), the normal cost rate is 19.2 percent of pay (employee's share, 0.8 percent, and employer's share, 18.4 percent). Regular FERS Postal employees will be 17.0 percent of pay (employee's share, 0.8 percent, and employer's share, 16.2 percent). For FERS RAE non-Postal employees, the normal cost rate will be 19.7 percent of pay (employee's share, 3.1 percent, and employer's share, 16.6 percent). FERS RAE Postal employees will be 17.5 percent of pay (employee's share, 3.1 percent, and employer's share, 14.4 percent). For FERS FRAE non-Postal employees, the normal cost rate will be 21.0 percent of pay (employee's share, 4.4 percent, employer's share, 16.6 percent, and less excess of 1.1 percent to be credited to the assets of the CSRDF). FERS FRAE Postal employees will be 17.8 percent of pay (employee's share, 4.4 percent, and employer's share, 13.4 percent). Under the Postal Accountability and Enhancement Act (P.L. 109435), USPS must make annual amortization payments beginning in 2017 to reduce any unfunded liability (UFL) for its obligations under CSRS. These payments, along with similar amortization payments for UFL in FERS are paid to CSRDF.

	2021 actual	2022 est.	2023 est.
Active employees	2,513,094	2,503,020	2,487,132
Annuitants:			
Employees	2,258,397	2,286,463	2,312,479
Survivors	502,906	502,422	502,790
Total, Annuitants	2,761,303	2,788,885	2,815,269

Status of Funds (in millions of dollars)

Identification code 024–8135–0–7–602		2021 actual	2022 est.	2023 est.
	Unexpended balance, start of year:			
0100	Balance, start of year	962,104	986,351	1,008,142
0298	Reconciliation adjustment	1		
0999	Total balance, start of year	962,105	986,351	1,008,142
	Cash income during the year:			
	Current law:			
	Receipts:			
1110	Employee Contributions, Civil Service Retirement and Disability Fund	4,967	5,713	6,247
1110	District of Columbia Contributions, Civil Service Retirement and Disability Fund	26	31	30
1110	Employee Deposits, Redeposits and Other Contributions, Civil Service Retirement and Disability Fund	574	562	552
1150	FFB, TVA, and USPS Interest, Civil Service Retirement and Disability Fund	192	157	123
1150	Treasury Interest, Civil Service Retirement and Disability Fund	22,996	20,939	18,910
1160	Agency Contributions, Civil Service Retirement and Disability Fund			1,059
1160	Agency Contributions, Civil Service Retirement and Disability Fund	37,764	41,556	42,236
1160	Postal Service Agency Contributions, Civil Service Retirement and Disability Fund	4,060	4,315	4,340
1160	Postal Service Agency Contributions, Civil Service Retirement and Disability Fund			–4,349
1160	Postal Service Supplemental Contributions, Civil Service Retirement and Disability Fund			
1160	Postal Service Amortization Payments, Civil Service Retirement and Disability Fund			
1160	General Fund Payment to the Civil Service Retirement and Disability Fund	45,975	45,935	46,035
1160	Re-employed Annuitants Salary Offset, Civil Service Retirement and Disability Fund	38	39	41
1199	Income under present law	116,592	119,247	115,224
1999	Total cash income	116,592	119,247	115,224
	Cash outgo during year:			
	Current law:			
2100	Civil Service Retirement and Disability Fund [Budget Acct]	–92,347	–97,456	–102,966

OFFICE OF PERSONNEL MANAGEMENT

		2021 actual	2022 est.	2023 est.
2199	Outgo under current law	−92,347	−97,456	−102,966
2999	Total cash outgo (−)	−92,347	−97,456	−102,966
	Surplus or deficit:			
3110	Excluding interest	1,057	695	−6,775
3120	Interest	23,188	21,096	19,033
3199	Subtotal, surplus or deficit	24,245	21,791	12,258
3298	Reconciliation adjustment	1		
3299	Total adjustments	1		
3999	Total change in fund balance	24,246	21,791	12,258
	Unexpended balance, end of year:			
4100	Uninvested balance (net), end of year	60,505	812	−3,232
4200	Civil Service Retirement and Disability Fund	925,846	1,007,330	1,023,632
4999	Total balance, end of year	986,351	1,008,142	1,020,400

Object Classification (in millions of dollars)

Identification code 024–8135–0–7–602	2021 actual	2022 est.	2023 est.
Direct obligations:			
25.2 Other services from non-Federal sources	197	126	139
42.0 Insurance claims and indemnities	91,942	97,448	102,850
44.0 Refunds and death claims	476	407	411
99.9 Total new obligations, unexpired accounts	92,615	97,981	103,400

EMPLOYEES LIFE INSURANCE FUND

Program and Financing (in millions of dollars)

Identification code 024–8424–0–8–602		2021 actual	2022 est.	2023 est.
	Obligations by program activity:			
0801	Insurance Payments	3,958	3,523	3,743
0802	Insurance Payments Pay Raise Impact		14	23
0804	Administration—OPM & OIG	4	4	5
0805	Administration—long term care	1	1	1
0900	Total new obligations, unexpired accounts (object class 25.2)	3,963	3,542	3,772
	Budgetary resources:			
	Unobligated balance:			
1000	Unobligated balance brought forward, Oct 1	47,753	48,570	50,003
	Budget authority:			
	Spending authority from offsetting collections, discretionary:			
1700	Collected	4	4	5
	Spending authority from offsetting collections, mandatory:			
1800	Collected	4,817	4,753	5,040
1801	Change in uncollected payments, Federal sources	−41	218	21
1850	Spending auth from offsetting collections, mand (total)	4,776	4,971	5,061
1900	Budget authority (total)	4,780	4,975	5,066
1930	Total budgetary resources available	52,533	53,545	55,069
	Memorandum (non-add) entries:			
1941	Unexpired unobligated balance, end of year	48,570	50,003	51,297
	Change in obligated balance:			
	Unpaid obligations:			
3000	Unpaid obligations, brought forward, Oct 1	1,120	1,280	1,239
3010	New obligations, unexpired accounts	3,963	3,542	3,772
3020	Outlays (gross)	−3,803	−3,583	−3,679
3050	Unpaid obligations, end of year	1,280	1,239	1,332
	Uncollected payments:			
3060	Uncollected pymts, Fed sources, brought forward, Oct 1	−167	−126	−344
3070	Change in uncollected pymts, Fed sources, unexpired	41	−218	−21
3090	Uncollected pymts, Fed sources, end of year	−126	−344	−365
	Memorandum (non-add) entries:			
3100	Obligated balance, start of year	953	1,154	895
3200	Obligated balance, end of year	1,154	895	967
	Budget authority and outlays, net:			
	Discretionary:			
4000	Budget authority, gross	4	4	5
	Outlays, gross:			
4010	Outlays from new discretionary authority	3	4	5
4011	Outlays from discretionary balances	1		
4020	Outlays, gross (total)	4	4	5
	Mandatory:			
4090	Budget authority, gross	4,776	4,971	5,061
	Outlays, gross:			
4100	Outlays from new mandatory authority	2,690	2,659	2,774
4101	Outlays from mandatory balances	1,109	920	900
4110	Outlays, gross (total)	3,799	3,579	3,674
	Offsets against gross budget authority and outlays:			
	Offsetting collections (collected) from:			
4120	Federal sources	−626	−626	−631
4120	Federal sources with Pay Raise Impact		−11	−35
4121	Interest on Federal securities	−1,009	−662	−703
4123	Non-Federal sources	−3,186	−3,418	−3,557
4123	Non-Federal sources with Pay Raise Impact		−40	−119
4130	Offsets against gross budget authority and outlays (total)	−4,821	−4,757	−5,045
	Additional offsets against gross budget authority only:			
4140	Change in uncollected pymts, Fed sources, unexpired	41	−218	−21
4160	Budget authority, net (mandatory)	−4	−4	−5
4170	Outlays, net (mandatory)	−1,022	−1,178	−1,371
4180	Budget authority, net (total)			
4190	Outlays, net (total)	−1,018	−1,174	−1,366
	Memorandum (non-add) entries:			
5000	Total investments, SOY: Federal securities: Par value	49,129	50,151	51,154
5001	Total investments, EOY: Federal securities: Par value	50,151	51,154	52,177

This fund finances payments to private insurance companies for Federal Employees' Group Life Insurance and expenses of the Office of Personnel Management in administering the program.

The Administration proposes that the United States Patent and Trademark Office (PTO) will continue to fund the accruing costs associated with post-retirement life insurance benefits for PTO's employees.

Budget program.—The status of the Basic (regular and optional) life insurance program on September 30 is as follows:

	2021 actual	2022 est.	2023 est.
Life insurance in force (in billions of dollars):			
On active employees	913.7	990.2	1,073.1
On retired employees	105.9	106.9	107.9
Total	1,019.6	1,097.1	1,181.0
Number of participants (in thousands):	2021 actual	2022 est.	2023 est.
Active employees	2,730	2,744	2,757
Annuitants	1,742	1,744	1,746
Total	4,472	4,488	4,503

Financing.— Non-United States Postal Service employees and all retirees under 65 pay two-thirds of the premium costs for Basic coverage; agencies pay the remaining third. Optional and certain post-retirement Basic coverages are paid entirely by enrollees. The status of the reserves at the end of the year is as follows:

	2021 actual	2022 est.	2023 est.
Held in reserve (in millions of dollars):			
Contingency reserve	780	780	780
Beneficial association program reserve	0	0	0
U.S. Treasury Reserve	47,753	48,672	49,609
Total reserves	48,533	49,452	50,389

EMPLOYEES AND RETIRED EMPLOYEES HEALTH BENEFITS FUNDS

Program and Financing (in millions of dollars)

Identification code 024–9981–0–8–551		2021 actual	2022 est.	2023 est.
	Obligations by program activity:			
0801	Benefit payments	59,712	59,594	62,348
0802	Payments from OPM contingency reserve	127	300	300
0803	Government payment for annuitants (1960 Act)		1	1
0804	Administration (OPM and OIG)	66	69	84
0806	Administration - dental and vision program	8	7	9
0900	Total new obligations, unexpired accounts (object class 25.6)	59,913	59,971	62,742
	Budgetary resources:			
	Unobligated balance:			
1000	Unobligated balance brought forward, Oct 1	26,272	25,184	26,649
	Budget authority:			
	Spending authority from offsetting collections, discretionary:			
1700	Collected	66	69	84
	Spending authority from offsetting collections, mandatory:			
1800	Collected	58,592	61,228	63,438
1801	Change in uncollected payments, Federal sources	167	139	108
1802	Offsetting collections (previously unavailable)		1	1

Office of Personnel Management—Continued
Trust Funds—Continued

EMPLOYEES AND RETIRED EMPLOYEES HEALTH BENEFITS FUNDS—Continued

Program and Financing—Continued

Identification code 024–9981–0–8–551	2021 actual	2022 est.	2023 est.
1823 New and/or unobligated balance of spending authority from offsetting collections temporarily reduced	....	–1	–1
1850 Spending auth from offsetting collections, mand (total)	58,759	61,367	63,546
1900 Budget authority (total)	58,825	61,436	63,630
1930 Total budgetary resources available	85,097	86,620	90,279
Memorandum (non-add) entries:			
1941 Unexpired unobligated balance, end of year	25,184	26,649	27,537
Change in obligated balance:			
Unpaid obligations:			
3000 Unpaid obligations, brought forward, Oct 1	4,505	5,441	5,371
3010 New obligations, unexpired accounts	59,913	59,971	62,742
3020 Outlays (gross)	–58,977	–60,041	–62,739
3050 Unpaid obligations, end of year	5,441	5,371	5,374
Uncollected payments:			
3060 Uncollected pymts, Fed sources, brought forward, Oct 1	–2,682	–2,849	–2,988
3070 Change in uncollected pymts, Fed sources, unexpired	–167	–139	–108
3090 Uncollected pymts, Fed sources, end of year	–2,849	–2,988	–3,096
Memorandum (non-add) entries:			
3100 Obligated balance, start of year	1,823	2,592	2,383
3200 Obligated balance, end of year	2,592	2,383	2,278
Budget authority and outlays, net:			
Discretionary:			
4000 Budget authority, gross	66	69	84
Outlays, gross:			
4010 Outlays from new discretionary authority	51	69	84
4011 Outlays from discretionary balances	15	....	....
4020 Outlays, gross (total)	66	69	84
Mandatory:			
4090 Budget authority, gross	58,759	61,367	63,546
Outlays, gross:			
4100 Outlays from new mandatory authority	54,469	54,085	56,844
4101 Outlays from mandatory balances	4,442	5,887	5,811
4110 Outlays, gross (total)	58,911	59,972	62,655
Offsets against gross budget authority and outlays:			
Offsetting collections (collected) from:			
4120 Federal Sources [OIG]	–40,445	–42,102	–43,382
4121 Interest on Federal securities	–435	–425	–451
4123 Non-Federal sources	–17,778	–18,770	–19,689
4130 Offsets against gross budget authority and outlays (total)	–58,658	–61,297	–63,522
Additional offsets against gross budget authority only:			
4140 Change in uncollected pymts, Fed sources, unexpired	–167	–139	–108
4160 Budget authority, net (mandatory)	–66	–69	–84
4170 Outlays, net (mandatory)	253	–1,325	–867
4180 Budget authority, net (total)	....	....	....
4190 Outlays, net (total)	319	–1,256	–783
Memorandum (non-add) entries:			
5000 Total investments, SOY: Federal securities: Par value	28,331	27,978	31,496
5001 Total investments, EOY: Federal securities: Par value	27,978	31,496	32,475

Summary of Budget Authority and Outlays (in millions of dollars)

	2021 actual	2022 est.	2023 est.
Enacted/requested:			
Outlays	319	–1,256	–783
Legislative proposal, subject to PAYGO:			
Budget Authority	....	....	2
Outlays	....	....	–27
Total:			
Budget Authority	....	....	2
Outlays	319	–1,256	–810

This display combines the Federal Employees Health Benefit (FEHB) fund and the Retired Employees Health Benefits (REHB) fund. The FEHB fund provides for the cost of health benefits for: 1) active employees; 2) employees who retired after June 1960, or their survivors; 3) annuitants transferred from the REHB fund as authorized by Public Law 93–246; and 4) tribal organizations. The REHB fund, created by the Retired Federal Employees Health Benefits Act of 1960, provides for: 1) the cost of health benefits for retired employees and survivors who were enrolled in a Government-sponsored uniform health benefits plan; 2) the contribution to retired employees and survivors who retain or purchase private health insurance; and 3) expenses of OPM in administering the program.

Budget program.—The balance of the FEHB fund is available for payments without fiscal year limitation. Numbers of participants at the end of each fiscal year are as follows:

	2021 actual	2022 est.	2023 est.
Active employees	2,152,082	2,152,082	2,152,082
USPS active employees (non-add)	419,000	419,000	419,000
Annuitants	1,922,043	1,944,202	1,964,991
Tribal Organizations	31,381	31,381	31,381
Total	4,105,506	4,127,665	4,148,454

In determining a biweekly subscription rate to cover program costs, one percent is added for administrative expenses and three percent is added for a contingency reserve held by OPM for each carrier. OPM is authorized to transfer unused administrative reserve funds to the contingency reserve. The REHB fund is available without fiscal year limitation. The amounts contributed by the Government are paid into the fund from annual appropriations. The number of participants at the end of each fiscal year are as follows:

	2021 actual	2022 est.	2023 est.
Uniform plan	25	21	17
Private plans	46	38	31
Total	71	59	48

Financing.—The funds are financed by: 1) withholdings from active employees and annuitants; 2) agency contributions for active employees; 3) Government contributions for annuitants appropriated to OPM; and 4) contributions made by the United States Postal Service in accordance with the provisions of Public Law 101–508.

Funds made available to carriers but not used to pay claims in the current period are carried forward as special reserves for use in subsequent periods. OPM maintains a contingency reserve, funded by employee and Government contributions, which may be used to defray future cost increases or provide increased benefits. OPM makes payments to carriers from this reserve whenever carrier-held reserves fall below levels prescribed by OPM regulations or when carriers can demonstrate good cause such as unexpected claims experience or variations from expected community rates.

The Budget proposes that the United States Patent and Trademark Office continue to fund the accruing costs associated with post-retirement health benefits for its employees.

Status of Funds (in millions of dollars)

Identification code 024–9981–0–8–551	2021 actual	2022 est.	2023 est.
Unexpended balance, start of year:			
0100 Balance, start of year	28,096	27,776	29,032
0999 Total balance, start of year	28,096	27,776	29,032
Cash income during the year:			
Current law:			
Receipts:			
1130 Employees and Retired Employees Health Benefits Funds	17,778	18,770	19,689
1150 Employees and Retired Employees Health Benefits Funds	435	425	451
1160 Employees and Retired Employees Health Benefits Funds	40,445	42,102	43,382
1199 Income under present law	58,658	61,297	63,522
Proposed:			
Offsetting receipts (proprietary):			
1230 Employees and Retired Employees Health Benefits Funds	....	....	105
Offsetting governmental receipts:			
1260 Employees and Retired Employees Health Benefits Funds	....	....	242
1299 Income proposed	....	....	347
1999 Total cash income	58,658	61,297	63,869
Cash outgo during year:			
Current law:			
2100 Employees and Retired Employees Health Benefits Funds [Budget Acct]	–58,977	–60,041	–62,739

		2021 actual	2022 est.	2023 est.
2199	Outgo under current law	–58,977	–60,041	–62,739
	Proposed:			
2200	Employees and Retired Employees Health Benefits Funds	....	....	–320
2299	Outgo under proposed legislation	....	....	–320
2999	Total cash outgo (–)	–58,977	–60,041	–63,059
	Surplus or deficit:			
3110	Excluding interest	–754	831	359
3120	Interest	435	425	451
3199	Subtotal, surplus or deficit	–319	1,256	810
3298	Reconciliation adjustment	–1	....	....
3299	Total adjustments	–1	....	....
3999	Total change in fund balance	–320	1,256	810
	Unexpended balance, end of year:			
4100	Uninvested balance (net), end of year	–202	–2,464	–2,633
4200	Employees and Retired Employees Health Benefits Funds	27,978	31,496	32,475
4999	Total balance, end of year	27,776	29,032	29,842

EMPLOYEES AND RETIRED EMPLOYEES HEALTH BENEFITS FUNDS

(Legislative proposal, subject to PAYGO)

Program and Financing (in millions of dollars)

Identification code 024–9981–4–8–551		2021 actual	2022 est.	2023 est.
	Obligations by program activity:			
0801	Benefit payments	....	....	347
0804	Administration (OPM and OIG)	....	....	2
0900	Total new obligations, unexpired accounts	....	....	349
	Budgetary resources:			
	Budget authority:			
	Spending authority from offsetting collections, mandatory:			
1800	Collected	....	....	349
1930	Total budgetary resources available	....	....	349
	Change in obligated balance:			
	Unpaid obligations:			
3010	New obligations, unexpired accounts	....	....	349
3020	Outlays (gross)	....	....	–320
3050	Unpaid obligations, end of year	....	....	29
	Memorandum (non-add) entries:			
3200	Obligated balance, end of year	....	....	29
	Budget authority and outlays, net:			
	Mandatory:			
4090	Budget authority, gross	....	....	349
	Outlays, gross:			
4100	Outlays from new mandatory authority	....	....	320
	Offsets against gross budget authority and outlays:			
	Offsetting collections (collected) from:			
4120	Federal Sources	....	....	–242
4123	Non-Federal sources	....	....	–105
4130	Offsets against gross budget authority and outlays (total)	....	....	–347
4160	Budget authority, net (mandatory)	....	....	2
4170	Outlays, net (mandatory)	....	....	–27
4180	Budget authority, net (total)	....	....	2
4190	Outlays, net (total)	....	....	–27

The President's 2023 Budget proposals aim to improve the health coverage enrollment process for Tribal employers and their employees by ensuring that all administrative fees paid by Tribal employers are invested in the Tribal Insurance Processing System (TIPS). The Budget also aims to improve access to behavioral health services by requiring coverage of three primary visits and three behavior health visits without cost-sharing for all Federal Employees Health Benefit Program plans.

Object Classification (in millions of dollars)

Identification code 024–9981–4–8–551		2021 actual	2022 est.	2023 est.
	Reimbursable obligations:			
25.2	Other services from non-Federal sources	....	....	2
25.6	Medical care	....	....	347
99.9	Total new obligations, unexpired accounts	....	....	349

GENERAL FUND RECEIPT ACCOUNT

(in millions of dollars)

	2021 actual	2022 est.	2023 est.
Offsetting receipts from the public:			
024–322000 All Other General Fund Proprietary Receipts Including Budget Clearing Accounts	55	2	2
General Fund Offsetting receipts from the public	55	2	2

SMALL BUSINESS ADMINISTRATION

Federal Funds

EMERGENCY EIDL GRANTS

Program and Financing (in millions of dollars)

Identification code 073–0500–0–1–376	2021 actual	2022 est.	2023 est.
Obligations by program activity:			
0001 EIDL Grants	5,751	2,053	
0900 Total new obligations, unexpired accounts (object class 41.0)	5,751	2,053	
Budgetary resources:			
Unobligated balance:			
1000 Unobligated balance brought forward, Oct 1	43	29,294	320
1033 Recoveries of prior year paid obligations	14		
1070 Unobligated balance (total)	57	29,294	320
Budget authority:			
Appropriations, mandatory:			
1200 Appropriation	35,000		
1220 Appropriations transferred to other acct [073–1152]		–10,634	
1220 Appropriations transferred to other acct [073–0100]		–500	
1230 Appropriations and/or unobligated balance of appropriations permanently reduced		–15,787	
1260 Appropriations, mandatory (total)	35,000	–26,921	
1930 Total budgetary resources available	35,057	2,373	320
Memorandum (non-add) entries:			
1940 Unobligated balance expiring	–12		
1941 Unexpired unobligated balance, end of year	29,294	320	320
Change in obligated balance:			
Unpaid obligations:			
3000 Unpaid obligations, brought forward, Oct 1	246	501	501
3010 New obligations, unexpired accounts	5,751	2,053	
3020 Outlays (gross)	–5,496	–2,053	
3050 Unpaid obligations, end of year	501	501	501
Memorandum (non-add) entries:			
3100 Obligated balance, start of year	246	501	501
3200 Obligated balance, end of year	501	501	501
Budget authority and outlays, net:			
Mandatory:			
4090 Budget authority, gross	35,000	–26,921	
Outlays, gross:			
4100 Outlays from new mandatory authority	5,496		
4101 Outlays from mandatory balances		2,053	
4110 Outlays, gross (total)	5,496	2,053	
Offsets against gross budget authority and outlays:			
Offsetting collections (collected) from:			
4123 Non-Federal sources	–14		
Additional offsets against gross budget authority only:			
4143 Recoveries of prior year paid obligations, unexpired accounts	14		
4160 Budget authority, net (mandatory)	35,000	–26,921	
4170 Outlays, net (mandatory)	5,482	2,053	
4180 Budget authority, net (total)	35,000	–26,921	
4190 Outlays, net (total)	5,482	2,053	

Summary of Budget Authority and Outlays (in millions of dollars)

	2021 actual	2022 est.	2023 est.
Enacted/requested:			
Budget Authority	35,000	–26,921	
Outlays	5,482	2,053	
Legislative proposal, subject to PAYGO:			
Budget Authority			–320
Outlays			–320
Total:			
Budget Authority	35,000	–26,921	–320
Outlays	5,482	2,053	–320

EMERGENCY EIDL GRANTS

(Legislative proposal, subject to PAYGO)

Program and Financing (in millions of dollars)

Identification code 073–0500–4–1–376	2021 actual	2022 est.	2023 est.
Budgetary resources:			
Budget authority:			
Appropriations, mandatory:			
1220 Appropriations transferred to other acct [073–0100]			–320
1930 Total budgetary resources available			–320
Memorandum (non-add) entries:			
1941 Unexpired unobligated balance, end of year			–320
Change in obligated balance:			
Unpaid obligations:			
3020 Outlays (gross)			320
3050 Unpaid obligations, end of year			320
Memorandum (non-add) entries:			
3200 Obligated balance, end of year			320
Budget authority and outlays, net:			
Mandatory:			
4090 Budget authority, gross			–320
Outlays, gross:			
4101 Outlays from mandatory balances			–320
4180 Budget authority, net (total)			–320
4190 Outlays, net (total)			–320

The Infrastructure Investment and Jobs Act (P.L. 117–58) authorized SBA to transfer up to $500 million in unobligated balances from Targeted EIDL Advance funds provided in the American Rescue Plan (P.L. 117–2) to SBA Salaries and Expenses for COVID program administrative needs. The Budget requests the ability to transfer up to an additional $320 million from Targeted EIDL balances to continue to fund these necessary activities in 2023. This transfer will support the continued oversight and monitoring needs of SBA's COVID programs, as well as COVID EIDL servicing.

SALARIES AND EXPENSES

For necessary expenses, not otherwise provided for, of the Small Business Administration, including hire of passenger motor vehicles as authorized by sections 1343 and 1344 of title 31, United States Code, and not to exceed $3,500 for official reception and representation expenses, $346,257,000, of which not less than $12,000,000 shall be available for examinations, reviews, and other lender oversight activities: Provided, That the Administrator is authorized to charge fees to cover the cost of publications developed by the Small Business Administration, and certain loan program activities, including fees authorized by section 5(b) of the Small Business Act: Provided further, That, notwithstanding 31 U.S.C. 3302, revenues received from all such activities shall be credited to this account, to remain available until expended, for carrying out these purposes without further appropriations: Provided further, That the Small Business Administration may accept gifts in an amount not to exceed $4,000,000 and may co-sponsor activities, each in accordance with section 132(a) of division K of Public Law 108–447, during fiscal year 2023: Provided further, That $6,100,000 shall be available for the Loan Modernization and Accounting System, to be available until September 30, 2024: Provided further, That $20,000,000 shall be available for the Veteran's Small Business certification program as authorized by sections 36 and 36A of the Small Business Act, to be available until September 30, 2024.

Note.—A full-year 2022 appropriation for this account was not enacted at the time the Budget was prepared; therefore, the Budget assumes this account is operating under the Continuing Appropriations Act, 2022 (Division A of Public Law 117–43, as amended). The amounts included for 2022 reflect the annualized level provided by the continuing resolution.

Program and Financing (in millions of dollars)

Identification code 073–0100–0–1–376	2021 actual	2022 est.	2023 est.
Obligations by program activity:			
0001 Executive direction	86	68	75
0002 Capital Access	726	120	25

Small Business Administration—Continued
Federal Funds—Continued

SALARIES AND EXPENSES—Continued

Program and Financing—Continued

Identification code 073–0100–0–1–376		2021 actual	2022 est.	2023 est.
0003	Gov. Contracting/Bus. Development	32	35	67
0004	Entrepreneurial Development	18	13	11
0005	Chief Operating Office	36	33	32
0006	Office of Chief Information Officer	58	30	42
0007	Regional & district offices	103	6	5
0008	Agency wide costs	62	77	69
0012	Disaster	939	748	426
0013	Investment & Innovation	13	7	3
0014	International Trade	7	7	9
0799	Total direct obligations	2,080	1,144	764
0802	Capital Access	13	266	65
0807	Regional & district offices	1	96	99
0812	Disaster	10	419	177
0813	Investment & Innovation	7	25	29
0899	Total reimbursable obligations	31	806	370
0900	Total new obligations, unexpired accounts	2,111	1,950	1,134
	Budgetary resources:			
	Unobligated balance:			
1000	Unobligated balance brought forward, Oct 1	1,815	871	497
1021	Recoveries of prior year unpaid obligations	16		
1033	Recoveries of prior year paid obligations	1		
1070	Unobligated balance (total)	1,832	871	497
	Budget authority:			
	Appropriations, discretionary:			
1100	Appropriation	270	270	346
1120	Appropriations transferred to other acct [073–1161]	–6		
1121	Appropriations transferred from other acct [073–0500]		500	
1160	Appropriation, discretionary (total)	264	770	346
	Appropriations, mandatory:			
1200	Appropriation	890		
	Spending authority from offsetting collections, discretionary:			
1700	Collected - Disaster Transfer	353	618	177
1700	Collected		188	193
1750	Spending auth from offsetting collections, disc (total)	353	806	370
1900	Budget authority (total)	1,507	1,576	716
1930	Total budgetary resources available	3,339	2,447	1,213
	Memorandum (non-add) entries:			
1940	Unobligated balance expiring	–357		
1941	Unexpired unobligated balance, end of year	871	497	79
	Change in obligated balance:			
	Unpaid obligations:			
3000	Unpaid obligations, brought forward, Oct 1	700	559	655
3010	New obligations, unexpired accounts	2,111	1,950	1,134
3011	Obligations ("upward adjustments"), expired accounts	9		
3020	Outlays (gross)	–2,233	–1,854	–1,235
3040	Recoveries of prior year unpaid obligations, unexpired	–16		
3041	Recoveries of prior year unpaid obligations, expired	–12		
3050	Unpaid obligations, end of year	559	655	554
	Memorandum (non-add) entries:			
3100	Obligated balance, start of year	700	559	655
3200	Obligated balance, end of year	559	655	554
	Budget authority and outlays, net:			
	Discretionary:			
4000	Budget authority, gross	617	1,576	716
	Outlays, gross:			
4010	Outlays from new discretionary authority	349	1,016	486
4011	Outlays from discretionary balances	1,879	588	643
4020	Outlays, gross (total)	2,228	1,604	1,129
	Offsets against gross budget authority and outlays:			
	Offsetting collections (collected) from:			
4030	Federal sources	–329	–779	–339
4033	Non-Federal sources	–25	–27	–31
4040	Offsets against gross budget authority and outlays (total)	–354	–806	–370
	Additional offsets against gross budget authority only:			
4053	Recoveries of prior year paid obligations, unexpired accounts	1		
4060	Additional offsets against budget authority only (total)	1		
4070	Budget authority, net (discretionary)	264	770	346
4080	Outlays, net (discretionary)	1,874	798	759
	Mandatory:			
4090	Budget authority, gross	890		
	Outlays, gross:			
4101	Outlays from mandatory balances	5	250	106
4180	Budget authority, net (total)	1,154	770	346
4190	Outlays, net (total)	1,879	1,048	865

Summary of Budget Authority and Outlays (in millions of dollars)

	2021 actual	2022 est.	2023 est.
Enacted/requested:			
Budget Authority	1,154	770	346
Outlays	1,879	1,048	865
Legislative proposal, subject to PAYGO:			
Budget Authority			320
Outlays			320
Total:			
Budget Authority	1,154	770	666
Outlays	1,879	1,048	1,185

This account funds the administrative expenses of SBA headquarters and field office operations. Appropriations for the administration of the disaster and business loan programs are transferred to and merged with this account. The 2023 Budget provides $6 million in funding for the continued modernization of the loan management accounting systems, which will improve oversight of SBA's more than $835 billion portfolio of loans and loan guarantees. Funding is also requested for core agency activities, including information technology investments and human capital development and enterprise-wide technology modernization initiatives including hardware, software and application standardization, mobile shared services implementation, security vulnerability reduction, and infrastructure upgrades.

Object Classification (in millions of dollars)

Identification code 073–0100–0–1–376		2021 actual	2022 est.	2023 est.
	Direct obligations:			
	Personnel compensation:			
11.1	Full-time permanent	233	45	100
11.3	Other than full-time permanent	368	163	197
11.5	Other personnel compensation	162	104	6
11.8	Special personal services payments	31		
11.9	Total personnel compensation	794	312	303
12.1	Civilian personnel benefits	168	164	124
13.0	Benefits for former personnel	5		
21.0	Travel and transportation of persons	5	1	5
23.1	Rental payments to GSA	47	35	46
23.3	Communications, utilities, and miscellaneous charges	22	8	8
25.1	Advisory and assistance services	8	1	5
25.2	Other services from non-Federal sources	966	572	218
25.3	Other purchases of goods and services from Government accounts (Disaster Administrative Expenses)	35	8	8
25.4	Operation and maintenance of facilities	1		
25.5	Research and development contracts	2	2	3
25.7	Operation and maintenance of equipment	23	37	38
26.0	Supplies and materials	2	2	3
31.0	Equipment		2	3
41.0	Grants, subsidies, and contributions	2		
99.0	Direct obligations	2,080	1,144	764
99.0	Reimbursable obligations	31	806	370
99.9	Total new obligations, unexpired accounts	2,111	1,950	1,134

Employment Summary

Identification code 073–0100–0–1–376		2021 actual	2022 est.	2023 est.
1001	Direct civilian full-time equivalent employment	5,768	8,317	3,242
2001	Reimbursable civilian full-time equivalent employment	78	2,095	2,054

SMALL BUSINESS ADMINISTRATION

SALARIES AND EXPENSES
(Legislative proposal, subject to PAYGO)

Program and Financing (in millions of dollars)

Identification code 073–0100–4–1–376	2021 actual	2022 est.	2023 est.
Obligations by program activity:			
0012 Disaster	....	....	320
0799 Total direct obligations	....	....	320
0900 Total new obligations, unexpired accounts (object class 25.2)	....	....	320
Budgetary resources:			
Budget authority:			
Appropriations, mandatory:			
1221 Appropriations transferred from other acct [073–0500]	....	....	320
1900 Budget authority (total)	....	....	320
1930 Total budgetary resources available	....	....	320
Change in obligated balance:			
Unpaid obligations:			
3010 New obligations, unexpired accounts	....	....	320
3020 Outlays (gross)	....	....	–320
Budget authority and outlays, net:			
Mandatory:			
4090 Budget authority, gross	....	....	320
Outlays, gross:			
4101 Outlays from mandatory balances	....	....	320
4180 Budget authority, net (total)	....	....	320
4190 Outlays, net (total)	....	....	320

The Infrastructure Investment and Jobs Act (P.L. 117–58) authorized SBA to transfer up to $500 million in unobligated balances from Targeted EIDL Advance funds provided in the American Rescue Plan (P.L. 117–2) to SBA Salaries and Expenses for COVID program administrative needs. The Budget requests the ability to transfer up to an additional $320 million from Targeted EIDL balances to continue to fund these necessary activities in 2023. This transfer will support the continued oversight and monitoring needs of SBA's COVID programs, as well as COVID EIDL servicing.

OFFICE OF INSPECTOR GENERAL

For necessary expenses of the Office of Inspector General in carrying out the provisions of the Inspector General Act of 1978, $32,020,000.

Note.—A full-year 2022 appropriation for this account was not enacted at the time the Budget was prepared; therefore, the Budget assumes this account is operating under the Continuing Appropriations Act, 2022 (Division A of Public Law 117–43, as amended). The amounts included for 2022 reflect the annualized level provided by the continuing resolution.

Program and Financing (in millions of dollars)

Identification code 073–0200–0–1–376	2021 actual	2022 est.	2023 est.
Obligations by program activity:			
0001 Audit	11	13	15
0002 Investigations	13	19	21
0003 Management and Operations	3	5	6
0004 Immediate office and Counsel	1	2	2
0900 Total new obligations, unexpired accounts	28	39	44
Budgetary resources:			
Unobligated balance:			
1000 Unobligated balance brought forward, Oct 1	32	52	39
Budget authority:			
Appropriations, discretionary:			
1100 Appropriation	47	22	32
1121 Appropriations transferred from other acct [073–1152]	....	2	2
1131 Unobligated balance of appropriations permanently reduced	–25	....	....
1160 Appropriation, discretionary (total)	22	24	34
Appropriations, mandatory:			
1200 Appropriation	25	....	....
Spending authority from offsetting collections, discretionary:			
1700 Collected	2	2	2
1900 Budget authority (total)	49	26	36
1930 Total budgetary resources available	81	78	75
Memorandum (non-add) entries:			
1940 Unobligated balance expiring	–1	....	....
1941 Unexpired unobligated balance, end of year	52	39	31
Change in obligated balance:			
Unpaid obligations:			
3000 Unpaid obligations, brought forward, Oct 1	3	2	2
3010 New obligations, unexpired accounts	28	39	44
3020 Outlays (gross)	–28	–39	–45
3041 Recoveries of prior year unpaid obligations, expired	–1	....	....
3050 Unpaid obligations, end of year	2	2	1
Memorandum (non-add) entries:			
3100 Obligated balance, start of year	3	2	2
3200 Obligated balance, end of year	2	2	1
Budget authority and outlays, net:			
Discretionary:			
4000 Budget authority, gross	24	26	36
Outlays, gross:			
4010 Outlays from new discretionary authority	20	26	36
4011 Outlays from discretionary balances	8	6	2
4020 Outlays, gross (total)	28	32	38
Offsets against gross budget authority and outlays:			
Offsetting collections (collected) from:			
4030 Federal sources	–2	–2	–2
Mandatory:			
4090 Budget authority, gross	25	....	....
Outlays, gross:			
4101 Outlays from mandatory balances	....	7	7
4180 Budget authority, net (total)	47	24	34
4190 Outlays, net (total)	26	37	43

The 2023 Budget proposes $32.0 million in new budget authority and $1.6 million transferred from the Disaster Loans Program account for a total of $33.6 million for the Office of Inspector General. This appropriation provides funds to promote economy and efficiency in SBA operations and to prevent and detect waste, fraud, and abuse through agency-wide audit, investigative, and related functions.

Object Classification (in millions of dollars)

Identification code 073–0200–0–1–376	2021 actual	2022 est.	2023 est.
Direct obligations:			
11.1 Personnel compensation: Full-time permanent	15	19	14
12.1 Civilian personnel benefits	7	13	21
25.2 Other services	4	5	7
99.0 Direct obligations	26	37	42
99.0 Reimbursable obligations	2	2	2
99.9 Total new obligations, unexpired accounts	28	39	44

Employment Summary

Identification code 073–0200–0–1–376	2021 actual	2022 est.	2023 est.
1001 Direct civilian full-time equivalent employment	131	172	184

OFFICE OF ADVOCACY

For necessary expenses of the Office of Advocacy in carrying out the provisions of title II of Public Law 94–305 (15 U.S.C. 634a et seq.) and the Regulatory Flexibility Act of 1980 (5 U.S.C. 601 et seq.), $10,211,000, to remain available until expended.

Note.—A full-year 2022 appropriation for this account was not enacted at the time the Budget was prepared; therefore, the Budget assumes this account is operating under the Continuing Appropriations Act, 2022 (Division A of Public Law 117–43, as amended). The amounts included for 2022 reflect the annualized level provided by the continuing resolution.

Program and Financing (in millions of dollars)

Identification code 073–0300–0–1–376	2021 actual	2022 est.	2023 est.
Obligations by program activity:			
0001 Office of Advocacy (Direct)	7	9	9

Small Business Administration—Continued
Federal Funds—Continued

OFFICE OF ADVOCACY—Continued
Program and Financing—Continued

Identification code 073–0300–0–1–376		2021 actual	2022 est.	2023 est.
	Budgetary resources:			
	Unobligated balance:			
1000	Unobligated balance brought forward, Oct 1	1	3	3
	Budget authority:			
	Appropriations, discretionary:			
1100	Appropriation	9	9	10
1930	Total budgetary resources available	10	12	13
	Memorandum (non-add) entries:			
1941	Unexpired unobligated balance, end of year	3	3	4
	Change in obligated balance:			
	Unpaid obligations:			
3000	Unpaid obligations, brought forward, Oct 1	1	....	1
3010	New obligations, unexpired accounts	7	9	9
3020	Outlays (gross)	–8	–8	–9
3050	Unpaid obligations, end of year	....	1	1
	Memorandum (non-add) entries:			
3100	Obligated balance, start of year	1	....	1
3200	Obligated balance, end of year	....	1	1
	Budget authority and outlays, net:			
	Discretionary:			
4000	Budget authority, gross	9	9	10
	Outlays, gross:			
4010	Outlays from new discretionary authority	7	8	9
4011	Outlays from discretionary balances	1	....	....
4020	Outlays, gross (total)	8	8	9
4180	Budget authority, net (total)	9	9	10
4190	Outlays, net (total)	8	8	9

The 2023 Budget proposes $10.2 million in new budget authority for the Office of Advocacy to carry out its statutory duties, including those under the Regulatory Flexibility Act. The Office of Advocacy's advice and small business research help the Federal Government take into account the concerns of small businesses when it develops policies and regulations. The Office's regional advocates support regulatory flexibility at the State level, work with the regional Regulatory Fairness Boards established by the Small Business Regulatory Enforcement Fairness Act, and promote the use of Advocacy research and data products in the curricula of universities and other schools in their respective regions.

Object Classification (in millions of dollars)

Identification code 073–0300–0–1–376		2021 actual	2022 est.	2023 est.
	Direct obligations:			
11.1	Personnel compensation: Full-time permanent	5	6	6
12.1	Civilian personnel benefits	1	2	2
25.2	Other services from non-Federal sources	1	1	1
99.9	Total new obligations, unexpired accounts	7	9	9

Employment Summary

Identification code 073–0300–0–1–376		2021 actual	2022 est.	2023 est.
1001	Direct civilian full-time equivalent employment	33	55	55

ENTREPRENEURIAL DEVELOPMENT PROGRAMS

For necessary expenses of programs supporting entrepreneurial and small business development, $318,000,000, to remain available until September 30, 2024: Provided, That $136,000,000 shall be available to fund grants for performance in fiscal year 2023 or fiscal year 2024 as authorized by section 21 of the Small Business Act: Provided further, That $41,000,000 shall be for marketing, management, and technical assistance under section 7(m) of the Small Business Act (15 U.S.C. 636(m)(4)) by intermediaries that make microloans under the microloan program: Provided further, That $19,500,000 shall be available for grants to States to carry out export programs that assist small business concerns authorized under section 22(l) of the Small Business Act (15 U.S.C. 649(l)).

Note.—A full-year 2022 appropriation for this account was not enacted at the time the Budget was prepared; therefore, the Budget assumes this account is operating under the Continuing Appropriations Act, 2022 (Division A of Public Law 117–43, as amended). The amounts included for 2022 reflect the annualized level provided by the continuing resolution.

Program and Financing (in millions of dollars)

Identification code 073–0400–0–1–376		2021 actual	2022 est.	2023 est.
	Obligations by program activity:			
0001	Non-Credit Programs	299	483	335
	Budgetary resources:			
	Unobligated balance:			
1000	Unobligated balance brought forward, Oct 1	39	240	29
1001	Discretionary unobligated balance brought fwd, Oct 1	31	....	....
1021	Recoveries of prior year unpaid obligations	5	....	....
1070	Unobligated balance (total)	44	240	29
	Budget authority:			
	Appropriations, discretionary:			
1100	Appropriation	322	272	318
	Appropriations, mandatory:			
1200	Appropriation	175	....	....
1900	Budget authority (total)	497	272	318
1930	Total budgetary resources available	541	512	347
	Memorandum (non-add) entries:			
1940	Unobligated balance expiring	–2	....	....
1941	Unexpired unobligated balance, end of year	240	29	12
	Change in obligated balance:			
	Unpaid obligations:			
3000	Unpaid obligations, brought forward, Oct 1	476	531	557
3010	New obligations, unexpired accounts	299	483	335
3011	Obligations ("upward adjustments"), expired accounts	9	....	....
3020	Outlays (gross)	–235	–457	–282
3040	Recoveries of prior year unpaid obligations, unexpired	–5	....	....
3041	Recoveries of prior year unpaid obligations, expired	–13	....	....
3050	Unpaid obligations, end of year	531	557	610
	Memorandum (non-add) entries:			
3100	Obligated balance, start of year	476	531	557
3200	Obligated balance, end of year	531	557	610
	Budget authority and outlays, net:			
	Discretionary:			
4000	Budget authority, gross	322	272	318
	Outlays, gross:			
4010	Outlays from new discretionary authority	22	95	111
4011	Outlays from discretionary balances	168	227	153
4020	Outlays, gross (total)	190	322	264
	Mandatory:			
4090	Budget authority, gross	175	....	....
	Outlays, gross:			
4101	Outlays from mandatory balances	45	135	18
4180	Budget authority, net (total)	497	272	318
4190	Outlays, net (total)	235	457	282

This account supports SBA's core counseling, training and technical assistance programs, including Small Business Development Centers (SBDC), SCORE, Women's Business Centers, Veterans' Business Outreach Centers (VBOC), and Microloan technical assistance, as well as various entrepreneurial development programs and initiatives. These include Entrepreneurial Education, a program designed to train and develop small business owners who are poised for growth; the State Trade Expansion Program (STEP), which helps small businesses tap global markets and expand exports; and Veterans Outreach programs like the Boots to Business program, which provides entrepreneurship training to America's veterans transitioning to civilian life. The Budget also supports other efforts, such as the HUBZone Program, Federal and State Technology (FAST) Partnership Program, and other outreach and contracting activities supporting underserved communities and fostering innovation.

Object Classification (in millions of dollars)

Identification code 073–0400–0–1–376		2021 actual	2022 est.	2023 est.
	Direct obligations:			
11.1	Personnel compensation: Full-time permanent	2	2	2
12.1	Civilian personnel benefits	1	1	1
25.1	Advisory and assistance services	2	....	....

SMALL BUSINESS ADMINISTRATION

		2021 actual	2022 est.	2023 est.
25.2	Other services from non-Federal sources	10	80	6
25.3	Other goods and services from Federal sources	1	....	....
41.0	Grants, subsidies, and contributions	283	400	326
99.9	Total new obligations, unexpired accounts	299	483	335

Employment Summary

Identification code 073–0400–0–1–376	2021 actual	2022 est.	2023 est.
1001 Direct civilian full-time equivalent employment	18	25	25

SHUTTERED VENUE OPERATORS

Program and Financing (in millions of dollars)

Identification code 073–0700–0–1–376		2021 actual	2022 est.	2023 est.
	Obligations by program activity:			
0001	Shuttered Venue Grants	9,713	6,537	....
0900	Total new obligations, unexpired accounts (object class 41.0)	9,713	6,537	....
	Budgetary resources:			
	Unobligated balance:			
1000	Unobligated balance brought forward, Oct 1	....	....	6,537
	Budget authority:			
	Appropriations, mandatory:			
1200	Appropriation	16,250	....	....
1930	Total budgetary resources available	16,250	6,537	....
	Memorandum (non-add) entries:			
1941	Unexpired unobligated balance, end of year	....	6,537	....
	Change in obligated balance:			
	Unpaid obligations:			
3000	Unpaid obligations, brought forward, Oct 1	....	17	17
3010	New obligations, unexpired accounts	9,713	6,537	....
3020	Outlays (gross)	–9,696	–6,537	....
3050	Unpaid obligations, end of year	17	17	17
	Memorandum (non-add) entries:			
3100	Obligated balance, start of year	....	17	17
3200	Obligated balance, end of year	17	17	17
	Budget authority and outlays, net:			
	Mandatory:			
4090	Budget authority, gross	16,250	....	....
	Outlays, gross:			
4100	Outlays from new mandatory authority	9,696	....	....
4101	Outlays from mandatory balances	....	6,537	....
4110	Outlays, gross (total)	9,696	6,537	....
4180	Budget authority, net (total)	16,250	....	....
4190	Outlays, net (total)	9,696	6,537	....

The Shuttered Venue Operators Grant (SVOG) Program was established by the Economic Aid to Hard-Hit Small Businesses, Nonprofits, and Venues Act. The SVOG Program provided funds to support the ongoing operations of eligible live venue operators or promoters, theatrical producers, live performing arts organization operators, relevant museum operators, motion picture theater operators, and talent representatives who experienced significant revenue losses due to the effects of the COVID-19 pandemic.

RESTAURANT REVITALIZATION FUND

Program and Financing (in millions of dollars)

Identification code 073–0800–0–1–376		2021 actual	2022 est.	2023 est.
	Obligations by program activity:			
0001	Restaurant Revitalization Grants	28,514	86	....
0900	Total new obligations, unexpired accounts (object class 41.0)	28,514	86	....
	Budgetary resources:			
	Unobligated balance:			
1000	Unobligated balance brought forward, Oct 1	....	86	....
	Budget authority:			
	Appropriations, mandatory:			
1200	Appropriation	28,600	....	....
1930	Total budgetary resources available	28,600	86	....
	Memorandum (non-add) entries:			
1941	Unexpired unobligated balance, end of year	86	....	....
	Change in obligated balance:			
	Unpaid obligations:			
3000	Unpaid obligations, brought forward, Oct 1	....	47	47
3010	New obligations, unexpired accounts	28,514	86	....
3020	Outlays (gross)	–28,467	–86	....
3050	Unpaid obligations, end of year	47	47	47
	Memorandum (non-add) entries:			
3100	Obligated balance, start of year	....	47	47
3200	Obligated balance, end of year	47	47	47
	Budget authority and outlays, net:			
	Mandatory:			
4090	Budget authority, gross	28,600	....	....
	Outlays, gross:			
4100	Outlays from new mandatory authority	28,467	....	....
4101	Outlays from mandatory balances	....	86	....
4110	Outlays, gross (total)	28,467	86	....
4180	Budget authority, net (total)	28,600	....	....
4190	Outlays, net (total)	28,467	86	....

The Restaurant Revitalization Fund (RRF) was established by the American Rescue Plan. The RRF Program provided funds to support certain payroll and non-payroll expenses for eligible entities in the food and beverage service industry who experienced significant revenue losses due to the effects of the COVID-19 pandemic.

INFORMATION TECHNOLOGY SYSTEM MODERNIZATION AND WORKING CAPITAL FUND

Program and Financing (in millions of dollars)

Identification code 073–1161–0–1–376		2021 actual	2022 est.	2023 est.
	Obligations by program activity:			
0001	IT Working Capital Fund	7	5	2
0900	Total new obligations, unexpired accounts (object class 25.2)	7	5	2
	Budgetary resources:			
	Unobligated balance:			
1000	Unobligated balance brought forward, Oct 1	9	8	3
	Budget authority:			
	Appropriations, discretionary:			
1121	Appropriations transferred from other acct [073–0100]	6	....	....
1930	Total budgetary resources available	15	8	3
	Memorandum (non-add) entries:			
1941	Unexpired unobligated balance, end of year	8	3	1
	Change in obligated balance:			
	Unpaid obligations:			
3000	Unpaid obligations, brought forward, Oct 1	3	6	6
3010	New obligations, unexpired accounts	7	5	2
3020	Outlays (gross)	–4	–5	–2
3050	Unpaid obligations, end of year	6	6	6
	Memorandum (non-add) entries:			
3100	Obligated balance, start of year	3	6	6
3200	Obligated balance, end of year	6	6	6
	Budget authority and outlays, net:			
	Discretionary:			
4000	Budget authority, gross	6	....	....
	Outlays, gross:			
4011	Outlays from discretionary balances	4	5	2
4180	Budget authority, net (total)	6	....	....
4190	Outlays, net (total)	4	5	2

The Information Technology Working Capital Fund finances long-term IT modernization projects, including centralized management of systems, equipment, services, and maintenance.

Small Business Administration—Continued
Federal Funds—Continued

SURETY BOND GUARANTEES REVOLVING FUND

Program and Financing (in millions of dollars)

Identification code 073–4156–0–3–376		2021 actual	2022 est.	2023 est.
	Obligations by program activity:			
0801	Reimbursable obligations	15	18	18
0900	Total new obligations, unexpired accounts (object class 42.0)	15	18	18
	Budgetary resources:			
	Unobligated balance:			
1000	Unobligated balance brought forward, Oct 1	103	106	106
	Budget authority:			
	Spending authority from offsetting collections, discretionary:			
1700	Collected	18	18	18
1930	Total budgetary resources available	121	124	124
	Memorandum (non-add) entries:			
1941	Unexpired unobligated balance, end of year	106	106	106
	Change in obligated balance:			
	Unpaid obligations:			
3010	New obligations, unexpired accounts	15	18	18
3020	Outlays (gross)	–15	–18	–18
	Budget authority and outlays, net:			
	Discretionary:			
4000	Budget authority, gross	18	18	18
	Outlays, gross:			
4010	Outlays from new discretionary authority	15	18	18
	Offsets against gross budget authority and outlays:			
	Offsetting collections (collected) from:			
4033	Non-Federal sources	–18	–18	–18
4180	Budget authority, net (total)	....	....	....
4190	Outlays, net (total)	–3	....	....

SBA is authorized to issue bond guarantees to surety companies for construction, service, and supply contracts or work orders, and to reimburse these sureties up to 90 percent of the losses sustained if the contractor defaults. SBA's guarantees provide an incentive for sureties to issue bonds to small contractors who could not otherwise secure them and compete in the contracting industry. It is estimated that there are sufficient funds in reserve to cover the cost of claim defaults in 2023. Therefore, no new appropriated funds are requested in the Budget.

BUSINESS LOANS PROGRAM ACCOUNT
(INCLUDING TRANSFER OF FUNDS)

For the cost of direct loans, $6,000,000, to remain available until expended: Provided, That such costs, including the cost of modifying such loans, shall be as defined in section 502 of the Congressional Budget Act of 1974: Provided further, That subject to section 502 of the Congressional Budget Act of 1974, during fiscal year 2023 commitments to guarantee loans under section 503 of the Small Business Investment Act of 1958 shall not exceed $9,000,000,000: Provided further, That during fiscal year 2023 commitments for general business loans authorized under paragraphs (1) through (35) of section 7(a) of the Small Business Act shall not exceed $35,000,000,000 for a combination of amortizing term loans and the aggregated maximum line of credit provided by revolving loans: Provided further, That during fiscal year 2023 commitments for loans authorized under subparagraph (C) of section 502(7) of the Small Business Investment Act of 1958 (15 U.S.C. 696(7)) shall not exceed $7,500,000,000: Provided further, That during fiscal year 2023 commitments to guarantee loans for debentures under section 303(b) of the Small Business Investment Act of 1958 shall not exceed $5,000,000,000: Provided further, That during fiscal year 2023, guarantees of trust certificates authorized by section 5(g) of the Small Business Act shall not exceed a principal amount of $15,000,000,000. In addition, for administrative expenses to carry out the direct and guaranteed loan programs, $165,300,000, which may be transferred to and merged with the appropriations for Salaries and Expenses.

Note.—A full-year 2022 appropriation for this account was not enacted at the time the Budget was prepared; therefore, the Budget assumes this account is operating under the Continuing Appropriations Act, 2022 (Division A of Public Law 117–43, as amended). The amounts included for 2022 reflect the annualized level provided by the continuing resolution.

Program and Financing (in millions of dollars)

Identification code 073–1154–0–1–376		2021 actual	2022 est.	2023 est.
	Obligations by program activity:			
	Credit program obligations:			
0701	Direct loan subsidy	4	7	9
0702	Loan guarantee subsidy	283,623	....	....
0703	Subsidy for modifications of direct loans	28	....	....
0704	Subsidy for modifications of loan guarantees	7,013	....	....
0705	Reestimates of direct loan subsidy	16	....	....
0706	Interest on reestimates of direct loan subsidy	2	1	....
0707	Reestimates of loan guarantee subsidy	1,998	9,506	....
0708	Interest on reestimates of loan guarantee subsidy	40	44	....
0709	Administrative expenses	160	160	165
0900	Total new obligations, unexpired accounts	292,884	9,718	174
	Budgetary resources:			
	Unobligated balance:			
1000	Unobligated balance brought forward, Oct 1	147,234	7,213	3,364
1001	Discretionary unobligated balance brought fwd, Oct 1	49	69	....
1021	Recoveries of prior year unpaid obligations	1,865	1,000	3
1070	Unobligated balance (total)	149,099	8,213	3,367
	Budget authority:			
	Appropriations, discretionary:			
1100	Appropriation	180	180	171
1100	Appropriation EAA	1,925	....	....
1160	Appropriation, discretionary (total)	2,105	180	171
	Appropriations, mandatory:			
1200	Appropriation	297,255	9,551	....
1230	Appropriations and/or unobligated balance of appropriations permanently reduced	–146,500	–4,862	....
1260	Appropriations, mandatory (total)	150,755	4,689	....
1900	Budget authority (total)	152,860	4,869	171
1930	Total budgetary resources available	301,959	13,082	3,538
	Memorandum (non-add) entries:			
1940	Unobligated balance expiring	–1,862	....	....
1941	Unexpired unobligated balance, end of year	7,213	3,364	3,364
	Change in obligated balance:			
	Unpaid obligations:			
3000	Unpaid obligations, brought forward, Oct 1	6,477	1,189	1
3010	New obligations, unexpired accounts	292,884	9,718	174
3020	Outlays (gross)	–296,307	–9,906	–172
3040	Recoveries of prior year unpaid obligations, unexpired	–1,865	–1,000	–3
3050	Unpaid obligations, end of year	1,189	1	....
	Memorandum (non-add) entries:			
3100	Obligated balance, start of year	6,477	1,189	1
3200	Obligated balance, end of year	1,189	1	....
	Budget authority and outlays, net:			
	Discretionary:			
4000	Budget authority, gross	2,105	180	171
	Outlays, gross:			
4010	Outlays from new discretionary authority	1,003	162	168
4011	Outlays from discretionary balances	23	93	4
4020	Outlays, gross (total)	1,026	255	172
	Offsets against gross budget authority and outlays:			
	Offsetting collections (collected) from:			
4033	Non-Federal sources	–1	....	....
	Additional offsets against gross budget authority only:			
4052	Offsetting collections credited to expired accounts	1	....	....
4070	Budget authority, net (discretionary)	2,105	180	171
4080	Outlays, net (discretionary)	1,025	255	172
	Mandatory:			
4090	Budget authority, gross	150,755	4,689	....
	Outlays, gross:			
4100	Outlays from new mandatory authority	290,035	9,551	....
4101	Outlays from mandatory balances	5,246	100	....
4110	Outlays, gross (total)	295,281	9,651	....
4180	Budget authority, net (total)	152,860	4,869	171
4190	Outlays, net (total)	296,306	9,906	172

Summary of Loan Levels, Subsidy Budget Authority and Outlays by Program (in millions of dollars)

Identification code 073–1154–0–1–376		2021 actual	2022 est.	2023 est.
	Direct loan levels supportable by subsidy budget authority:			
115001	7(m) Direct Microloans	49	110	110
115999	Total direct loan levels	49	110	110

SMALL BUSINESS ADMINISTRATION

	Direct loan subsidy (in percent):			
132001	7(m) Direct Microloans	8.99	6.28	8.18
132999	Weighted average subsidy rate	8.99	6.28	8.18
	Direct loan subsidy budget authority:			
133001	7(m) Direct Microloans	4	7	9
133999	Total subsidy budget authority	4	7	9
	Direct loan subsidy outlays:			
134001	7(m) Direct Microloans	3	6	7
134012	CARES Act S. 1112 Direct Loans	29		
134999	Total subsidy outlays	32	6	7
	Direct loan reestimates:			
135001	7(m) Direct Microloans	18	–7	
135999	Total direct loan reestimates	18	–7	
	Guaranteed loan levels supportable by subsidy budget authority:			
215002	7(a) General Business Loan Guarantees	4,986	30,000	35,000
215004	Section 504 Certified Development Companies Debentures	1,566	7,500	9,000
215006	SBIC Debentures	3,954	4,000	5,000
215010	Secondary Market Guarantee	8,981	13,000	15,000
215027	504 Commercial Real Estate (CRE) Refinance Program	110	7,500	7,500
215039	Paycheck Protection Program (PPP)	271,814		
215040	7(a) General Business—PL 116–260 Part-Year COVID Support	29,903		
215041	Section 504 Debentures—PL 116–260 Part-Year COVID Support	5,907		
215042	504 CRE Refinance—PL 116–260 Part-Year COVID Support	591		
215999	Total loan guarantee levels	327,812	62,000	71,500
	Guaranteed loan subsidy (in percent):			
232002	7(a) General Business Loan Guarantees	0.08	0.00	0.00
232004	Section 504 Certified Development Companies Debentures	0.00	0.00	0.00
232006	SBIC Debentures	0.00	0.00	0.00
232010	Secondary Market Guarantee	0.00	0.00	0.00
232027	504 Commercial Real Estate (CRE) Refinance Program	0.00	0.00	0.00
232039	Paycheck Protection Program (PPP)	103.70		
232040	7(a) General Business—PL 116–260 Part-Year COVID Support	5.40		
232041	Section 504 Debentures—PL 116–260 Part-Year COVID Support	2.04		
232042	504 CRE Refinance—PL 116–260 Part-Year COVID Support	2.12		
232999	Weighted average subsidy rate	86.52	0.00	0.00
	Guaranteed loan subsidy budget authority:			
233002	7(a) General Business Loan Guarantees	4		
233039	Paycheck Protection Program (PPP)	281,871		
233040	7(a) General Business—PL 116–260 Part-Year COVID Support	1,615		
233041	Section 504 Debentures—PL 116–260 Part-Year COVID Support	121		
233042	504 CRE Refinance—PL 116–260 Part-Year COVID Support	13		
233999	Total subsidy budget authority	283,624		
	Guaranteed loan subsidy outlays:			
234002	7(a) General Business Loan Guarantees	24		
234004	Section 504 Certified Development Companies Debentures		3	3
234010	Secondary Market Guarantee	–13		
234014	CARES Act S. 1112 Guaranteed Loans	3,472		
234039	Paycheck Protection Program (PPP)	289,716		
234040	7(a) General Business—PL 116–260 Part-Year COVID Support	794		
234041	Section 504 Debentures—PL 116–260 Part-Year COVID Support	38		
234042	504 CRE Refinance—PL 116–260 Part-Year COVID Support	4		
234999	Total subsidy outlays	294,035	3	3
	Guaranteed loan reestimates:			
235002	7(a) General Business Loan Guarantees	–926	–542	
235003	7(a) General Business Loan Guarantees—STAR	–1		
235004	Section 504 Certified Development Companies Debentures	–157	–205	
235006	SBIC Debentures	5	–280	
235007	SBIC Participating Securities	–53	–47	
235008	SBIC New Market Venture Capital	7	5	
235010	Secondary Market Guarantee	38	–72	
235015	Secondary Market 504 First Mortgage Guarantees—ARRA		3	
235017	7(a) General Business Loan Guarantees—ARRA	–6	5	
235018	Section 504 Certified Development Companies—ARRA	–14	2	
235026	Section 504 Certified Development Companies Debentures—ARRA Ext	–6	2	
235027	504 Commercial Real Estate (CRE) Refinance Program	–80	–62	
235028	7(a) Business Loan Guarantees—ARRA Extension	–21	2	
235039	Paycheck Protection Program (PPP)	–4,029	4,153	
235040	7(a) General Business—PL 116–260 Part-Year COVID Support		–532	
235041	Section 504 Debentures—PL 116–260 Part-Year COVID Support		–38	
235042	504 CRE Refinance—PL 116–260 Part-Year COVID Support		–9	
235999	Total guaranteed loan reestimates	–5,243	2,385	

As required by the Federal Credit Reform Act of 1990, as amended, this account records the subsidy costs associated with the direct loans obligated and loan guarantees committed in 1992 and beyond (including modifications of direct loans or loan guarantees that resulted from obligations or commitments in any year), as well as administrative expenses of the business loan program. The subsidy amounts are estimated on a present value basis; the administrative expenses are estimated on a cash basis.

For 2023, the Budget proposes $171.3 million in new budget authority for the Business Loans Program account. This includes $160.3 million in administrative expenses funding; $5.0 million to help facilitate access to capital to support climate change resiliency and the clean energy economy; and $6.0 million in credit subsidy for the direct Microloan Program to support a program level of $110 million. The 2023 Budget requests no subsidy appropriation for SBA's business loan guarantee programs, the 7(a), 504 Certified Development Company (CDC), 504 Debt Refinancing, and Small Business Investment Company (SBIC) programs. The Budget supports a program level of $35 billion in Section 7(a) loan guarantees that provide general business credit assistance, while waiving upfront fees on SBA Express loans to Veterans. The Budget also proposes a program level of $9 billion for the guaranteed loan program authorized by Section 503 of the Small Business Investment Act of 1958 for long-term, fixed-rate financing and a program level of $7.5 billion for purposes of refinancing existing commercial mortgage and equipment debt authorized by Section 502(7)(C) of the Small Business Investment Act of 1958. The 2023 Budget continues to support innovative financial instruments through the SBA's SBIC program by providing up to $5 billion in long-term guaranteed loans to support venture capital investments in small businesses. In addition, the Budget supports a $15 billion program level for the Secondary Market Guarantee (SMG) program, which allows SBA's fiscal agent to pool the guaranteed portion of 7(a) loans and sell the securities to investors, in turn providing liquidity to participating 7(a) program lenders.

Object Classification (in millions of dollars)

Identification code 073–1154–0–1–376	2021 actual	2022 est.	2023 est.
Direct obligations:			
25.3 Other goods and services from Federal sources	160	160	165
41.0 Grants, subsidies, and contributions	292,724	9,558	9
99.9 Total new obligations, unexpired accounts	292,884	9,718	174

BUSINESS DIRECT LOAN FINANCING ACCOUNT

Program and Financing (in millions of dollars)

Identification code 073–4148–0–3–376	2021 actual	2022 est.	2023 est.
Obligations by program activity:			
Credit program obligations:			
0710 Direct loan obligations	49	110	110
0713 Payment of interest to Treasury	6	7	7
0716 Subsidy Modification	26	1	
0742 Downward reestimates paid to receipt accounts		7	
0743 Interest on downward reestimates		1	
0900 Total new obligations, unexpired accounts	81	126	117
Budgetary resources:			
Unobligated balance:			
1000 Unobligated balance brought forward, Oct 1	2	11	
1021 Recoveries of prior year unpaid obligations	3	9	3
1023 Unobligated balances applied to repay debt		–9	–3
1070 Unobligated balance (total)	5	11	
Financing authority:			
Borrowing authority, mandatory:			
1400 Borrowing authority	44	97	101
Spending authority from offsetting collections, mandatory:			
1800 Collected	89	50	50
1801 Change in uncollected payments, Federal sources	1		

Small Business Administration—Continued
Federal Funds—Continued

BUSINESS DIRECT LOAN FINANCING ACCOUNT—Continued

Program and Financing—Continued

Identification code 073–4148–0–3–376	2021 actual	2022 est.	2023 est.
1825 Spending authority from offsetting collections applied to repay debt	–47	–32	–34
1850 Spending auth from offsetting collections, mand (total)	43	18	16
1900 Budget authority (total)	87	115	117
1930 Total budgetary resources available	92	126	117
Memorandum (non-add) entries:			
1941 Unexpired unobligated balance, end of year	11		
Change in obligated balance:			
Unpaid obligations:			
3000 Unpaid obligations, brought forward, Oct 1	42	50	82
3010 New obligations, unexpired accounts	81	126	117
3020 Outlays (gross)	–70	–85	–104
3040 Recoveries of prior year unpaid obligations, unexpired	–3	–9	–3
3050 Unpaid obligations, end of year	50	82	92
Uncollected payments:			
3060 Uncollected pymts, Fed sources, brought forward, Oct 1	–4	–5	–5
3070 Change in uncollected pymts, Fed sources, unexpired	–1		
3090 Uncollected pymts, Fed sources, end of year	–5	–5	–5
Memorandum (non-add) entries:			
3100 Obligated balance, start of year	38	45	77
3200 Obligated balance, end of year	45	77	87
Financing authority and disbursements, net:			
Mandatory:			
4090 Budget authority, gross	87	115	117
Financing disbursements:			
4110 Outlays, gross (total)	70	85	104
Offsets against gross financing authority and disbursements:			
Offsetting collections (collected) from:			
4120 Federal sources: Subsidy from program account	–32	–7	–7
4120 Upward reestimate	–16		
4120 Interest on reestimate	–2	–1	
4122 Interest on uninvested funds	–2	–2	–2
4123 Repayments of principal, net	–37	–37	–39
4123 Other income		–3	–2
4130 Offsets against gross budget authority and outlays (total)	–89	–50	–50
Additional offsets against financing authority only (total):			
4140 Change in uncollected pymts, Fed sources, unexpired	–1		
4160 Budget authority, net (mandatory)	–3	65	67
4170 Outlays, net (mandatory)	–19	35	54
4180 Budget authority, net (total)	–3	65	67
4190 Outlays, net (total)	–19	35	54

Status of Direct Loans (in millions of dollars)

Identification code 073–4148–0–3–376	2021 actual	2022 est.	2023 est.
Position with respect to appropriations act limitation on obligations:			
1111 Direct loan obligations from current-year authority	49	82	82
1121 Limitation available from carry-forward	22	53	53
1143 Unobligated limitation carried forward (-)	–22	–25	–25
1150 Total direct loan obligations	49	110	110
Cumulative balance of direct loans outstanding:			
1210 Outstanding, start of year	217	219	250
1231 Disbursements: Direct loan disbursements	37	67	98
1251 Repayments: Repayments and prepayments	–35	–36	–40
1290 Outstanding, end of year	219	250	308

Balance Sheet (in millions of dollars)

Identification code 073–4148–0–3–376	2020 actual	2021 actual
ASSETS:		
Federal assets:		
1101 Fund balances with Treasury	34	42
Investments in U.S. securities:		
1106 Receivables, net	14	1
Net value of assets related to post-1991 direct loans receivable:		
1401 Direct loans receivable, gross	217	219
1402 Interest receivable	1	1
1405 Allowance for subsidy cost (-)	–31	–31
1499 Net present value of assets related to direct loans	187	189
1999 Total assets	235	232
LIABILITIES:		
Federal liabilities:		
2103 Debt	234	224
2104 Resources payable to Treasury (Downward Reestimate)	1	
2105 Resources payable to Treasury (Downward Reestaimate)		8
2201 Non-Federal liabilities: Accounts payable		
2999 Total liabilities	235	232
NET POSITION:		
3300 Cumulative results of operations		
4999 Total liabilities and net position	235	232

BUSINESS GUARANTEED LOAN FINANCING ACCOUNT

Program and Financing (in millions of dollars)

Identification code 073–4149–0–3–376	2021 actual	2022 est.	2023 est.
Obligations by program activity:			
Credit program obligations:			
0711 Default claim payments on principal	1,006	10,136	1,802
0712 Default claim payments on interest	48	298	100
0713 Payment of interest to Treasury	67	60	80
0715 Other Expenses	78	62	72
0716 Subsidy Modification	3,496	371	38
0717 PPP Forgiveness	582,693	216,595	389
0718 Fee Reimbursement	98		
0742 Downward reestimates paid to receipt accounts	1,257	5,099	
0743 Interest on downward reestimates	6,023	2,068	
0900 Total new obligations, unexpired accounts	594,766	234,689	2,481
Budgetary resources:			
Unobligated balance:			
1000 Unobligated balance brought forward, Oct 1	525,188	227,414	4,679
1021 Recoveries of prior year unpaid obligations	4		
1023 Unobligated balances applied to repay debt	–157		
1070 Unobligated balance (total)	525,035	227,414	4,679
Financing authority:			
Appropriations, mandatory:			
1200 Appropriation	36		
Borrowing authority, mandatory:			
1400 Borrowing authority	97	356	356
Spending authority from offsetting collections, mandatory:			
1800 Collected	302,314	11,598	2,377
1801 Change in uncollected payments, Federal sources	–5,288		
1820 Capital transfer of spending authority from offsetting collections to general fund	–14		
1850 Spending auth from offsetting collections, mand (total)	297,012	11,598	2,377
1900 Budget authority (total)	297,145	11,954	2,733
1930 Total budgetary resources available	822,180	239,368	7,412
Memorandum (non-add) entries:			
1941 Unexpired unobligated balance, end of year	227,414	4,679	4,931
Change in obligated balance:			
Unpaid obligations:			
3000 Unpaid obligations, brought forward, Oct 1	313	149	1,655
3010 New obligations, unexpired accounts	594,766	234,689	2,481
3020 Outlays (gross)	–594,926	–233,183	–2,347
3040 Recoveries of prior year unpaid obligations, unexpired	–4		
3050 Unpaid obligations, end of year	149	1,655	1,789
Uncollected payments:			
3060 Uncollected pymts, Fed sources, brought forward, Oct 1	–6,475	–1,187	–1,187
3070 Change in uncollected pymts, Fed sources, unexpired	5,288		
3090 Uncollected pymts, Fed sources, end of year	–1,187	–1,187	–1,187
Memorandum (non-add) entries:			
3100 Obligated balance, start of year	–6,162	–1,038	468
3200 Obligated balance, end of year	–1,038	468	602
Financing authority and disbursements, net:			
Mandatory:			
4090 Budget authority, gross	297,145	11,954	2,733
Financing disbursements:			
4110 Outlays, gross (total)	594,926	233,183	2,347
Offsets against gross financing authority and disbursements:			
Offsetting collections (collected) from:			
4120 Subsidy from program account	–294,058	–3	–3
4120 Upward reestimate	–1,998	–9,506	
4120 Interest on reestimate	–40	–44	
4122 Interest on uninvested funds	–4,205	–90	–90

SMALL BUSINESS ADMINISTRATION

		2021 actual	2022 est.	2023 est.
4123	Fees	−1,151	−1,487	−1,748
4123	Principal	−690	−399	−461
4123	Interest	−68	−39	−45
4123	Sale of Foreclosed Property	−8		
4123	Other	−96	−30	−30
4130	Offsets against gross budget authority and outlays (total)	−302,314	−11,598	−2,377
	Additional offsets against financing authority only (total):			
4140	Change in uncollected pymts, Fed sources, unexpired	5,288		
4160	Budget authority, net (mandatory)	119	356	356
4170	Outlays, net (mandatory)	292,612	221,585	−30
4180	Budget authority, net (total)	119	356	356
4190	Outlays, net (total)	292,612	221,585	−30

Status of Guaranteed Loans (in millions of dollars)

Identification code 073–4149–0–3–376		2021 actual	2022 est.	2023 est.
	Position with respect to appropriations act limitation on commitments:			
2111	Guaranteed loan commitments from current-year authority	385,529	62,000	71,500
2121	Limitation available from carry-forward			
2142	Uncommitted loan guarantee limitation	−57,717		
2150	Total guaranteed loan commitments	327,812	62,000	71,500
2199	Guaranteed amount of guaranteed loan commitments	327,812	62,000	71,500
	Cumulative balance of guaranteed loans outstanding:			
2210	Outstanding, start of year	646,028	459,593	196,769
2231	Disbursements of new guaranteed loans	308,926	44,971	52,403
2251	Repayments and prepayments	−494,067	−296,989	−34,809
	Adjustments:			
2261	Terminations for default that result in loans receivable	−1,082	−8,609	−1,599
2263	Terminations for default that result in claim payments	−220	−2,197	−408
2264	Other adjustments, net	8		
2290	Outstanding, end of year	459,593	196,769	212,356
	Memorandum:			
2299	Guaranteed amount of guaranteed loans outstanding, end of year	435,291	186,363	201,124
	Addendum:			
	Cumulative balance of defaulted guaranteed loans that result in loans receivable:			
2310	Outstanding, start of year	3,526	3,403	11,582
2331	Disbursements for guaranteed loan claims	860	10,235	1,901
2351	Repayments of loans receivable	−618	−439	−505
2361	Write-offs of loans receivable	−520	−1,617	−1,598
2364	Other adjustments, net	155		
2390	Outstanding, end of year	3,403	11,582	11,380

Balance Sheet (in millions of dollars)

Identification code 073–4149–0–3–376		2020 actual	2021 actual
	ASSETS:		
	Federal assets:		
1101	Fund balances with Treasury	519,026	226,376
	Investments in U.S. securities:		
1106	Receivables, net	2,611	9,564
1206	Non-Federal assets: Receivables, net	108	67
	Net value of assets related to post-1991 acquired defaulted guaranteed loans receivable:		
1501	Defaulted guaranteed loans receivable, gross	3,526	3,403
1502	Interest receivable		
1504	Foreclosed property	31	27
1505	Allowance for subsidy cost (-)	−2,215	−2,259
1599	Net present value of assets related to defaulted guaranteed loans	1,342	1,171
1999	Total assets	523,087	237,178
	LIABILITIES:		
	Federal liabilities:		
2103	Debt	2,293	2,233
2105	Other	8,058	7,043
	Non-Federal liabilities:		
2201	Accounts payable	24	70
2204	Liabilities for loan guarantees	512,712	227,832
2999	Total liabilities	523,087	237,178
	NET POSITION:		
3300	Cumulative results of operations		
4999	Total liabilities and net position	523,087	237,178

BUSINESS GUARANTEED LOAN FINANCING ACCOUNT

(Legislative proposal, not subject to PAYGO)

Status of Guaranteed Loans (in millions of dollars)

Identification code 073–4149–2–3–376		2021 actual	2022 est.	2023 est.
	Position with respect to appropriations act limitation on commitments:			
2111	Guaranteed loan commitments from current-year authority			
2121	Limitation available from carry-forward			
2142	Uncommitted loan guarantee limitation			
2150	Total guaranteed loan commitments			
2199	Guaranteed amount of guaranteed loan commitments			
	Cumulative balance of guaranteed loans outstanding:			
2210	Outstanding, start of year			
2231	Disbursements of new guaranteed loans			−24
2251	Repayments and prepayments			
	Adjustments:			
2261	Terminations for default that result in loans receivable			
2263	Terminations for default that result in claim payments			
2264	Other adjustments, net			
2290	Outstanding, end of year			−24
	Memorandum:			
2299	Guaranteed amount of guaranteed loans outstanding, end of year			−23
	Addendum:			
	Cumulative balance of defaulted guaranteed loans that result in loans receivable:			
2310	Outstanding, start of year			
2331	Disbursements for guaranteed loan claims			
2351	Repayments of loans receivable			
2361	Write-offs of loans receivable			
2364	Other adjustments, net			
2390	Outstanding, end of year			

BUSINESS LOAN FUND LIQUIDATING ACCOUNT

Program and Financing (in millions of dollars)

Identification code 073–4154–0–3–376		2021 actual	2022 est.	2023 est.
	Budgetary resources:			
	Budget authority:			
	Spending authority from offsetting collections, mandatory:			
1800	Collected	2	3	1
1820	Capital transfer of spending authority from offsetting collections to general fund	−2	−3	−1
	Budget authority and outlays, net:			
	Mandatory:			
	Offsets against gross budget authority and outlays:			
	Offsetting collections (collected) from:			
4123	Non-Federal sources	−2	−3	−1
4180	Budget authority, net (total)	−2	−3	−1
4190	Outlays, net (total)	−2	−3	−1

Status of Direct Loans (in millions of dollars)

Identification code 073–4154–0–3–376		2021 actual	2022 est.	2023 est.
	Cumulative balance of direct loans outstanding:			
1210	Outstanding, start of year	1	7	7
1264	Other adjustments, net (+ or -)	6		
1290	Outstanding, end of year	7	7	7

Status of Guaranteed Loans (in millions of dollars)

Identification code 073–4154–0–3–376		2021 actual	2022 est.	2023 est.
	Cumulative balance of guaranteed loans outstanding:			
2210	Outstanding, start of year			
2251	Repayments and prepayments			
2290	Outstanding, end of year			

Small Business Administration—Continued
Federal Funds—Continued

BUSINESS LOAN FUND LIQUIDATING ACCOUNT—Continued

Status of Guaranteed Loans—Continued

Identification code 073–4154–0–3–376		2021 actual	2022 est.	2023 est.
	Memorandum:			
2299	Guaranteed amount of guaranteed loans outstanding, end of year			
	Addendum:			
	Cumulative balance of defaulted guaranteed loans that result in loans receivable:			
2310	Outstanding, start of year	1	1	1
2331	Disbursements for guaranteed loan claims			
2351	Repayments of loans receivable			
2361	Write-offs of loans receivable	–1		
2364	Other adjustments, net	1		
2390	Outstanding, end of year	1	1	1

Balance Sheet (in millions of dollars)

Identification code 073–4154–0–3–376		2020 actual	2021 actual
	ASSETS:		
1101	Federal assets: Fund balances with Treasury		
1206	Non-Federal assets: Receivables, net		
1601	Direct loans, gross	1	7
1602	Interest receivable		
1603	Allowance for estimated uncollectible loans and interest (-)	–1	–7
1604	Direct loans and interest receivable, net		
1606	Foreclosed property	5	4
1699	Value of assets related to direct loans	5	4
1701	Defaulted guaranteed loans, gross	1	1
1703	Allowance for estimated uncollectible loans and interest (-)		
1799	Value of assets related to loan guarantees	1	1
1801	Other Federal assets: Cash and other monetary assets	10	3
1999	Total assets	16	8
	LIABILITIES:		
	Federal liabilities:		
2102	Interest payable		
2104	Resources payable to Treasury	15	8
2201	Non-Federal liabilities: Accounts payable	1	
2999	Total liabilities	16	8
	NET POSITION:		
3100	Unexpended appropriations		
3300	Cumulative results of operations		
3999	Total net position		
4999	Total liabilities and net position	16	8

DISASTER LOANS PROGRAM ACCOUNT

(INCLUDING TRANSFERS OF FUNDS)

For administrative expenses to carry out the direct loan program authorized by section 7(b) of the Small Business Act, $179,000,000, to be available until expended, of which $1,600,000 is for the Office of Inspector General of the Small Business Administration for audits and reviews of disaster loans and the disaster loan programs and shall be transferred to and merged with the appropriations for the Office of Inspector General; of which $169,000,000 is for direct administrative expenses of loan making and servicing to carry out the direct loan program, which may be transferred to and merged with the appropriations for Salaries and Expenses; and of which $8,400,000 is for indirect administrative expenses for the direct loan program, which may be transferred to and merged with the appropriations for Salaries and Expenses: Provided, That of the funds provided under this heading, $143,000,000 shall be for major disasters declared pursuant to the Robert T. Stafford Disaster Relief and Emergency Assistance Act (42 U.S.C. 5122(2)): Provided further, That the amount for major disasters under this heading is designated by Congress as being for disaster relief pursuant to a concurrent resolution on the budget.

Note.—A full-year 2022 appropriation for this account was not enacted at the time the Budget was prepared; therefore, the Budget assumes this account is operating under the Continuing Appropriations Act, 2022 (Division A of Public Law 117–43, as amended). The amounts included for 2022 reflect the annualized level provided by the continuing resolution.

[DISASTER LOANS PROGRAM ACCOUNT]

[(INCLUDING TRANSFER OF FUNDS)]

[For an additional amount for "Disaster Loans Program Account" for the cost of direct loans authorized by section 7(b) of the Small Business Act, $1,189,100,000, to remain available until expended: *Provided*, That up to $620,000,000 may be transferred to and merged with "Salaries and Expenses" for administrative expenses to carry out the disaster loan program authorized by section 7(b) of the Small Business Act.] *(Disaster Relief Supplemental Appropriations Act, 2022.)*

Program and Financing (in millions of dollars)

Identification code 073–1152–0–1–453		2021 actual	2022 est.	2023 est.
	Obligations by program activity:			
	Credit program obligations:			
0701	Direct loan subsidy	7,180	15,208	191
0703	Subsidy for modifications of direct loans		608	
0705	Reestimates of direct loan subsidy	83	715	
0706	Interest on reestimates of direct loan subsidy	1,496	196	
0709	Administrative expenses	332	687	179
0900	Total new obligations, unexpired accounts	9,091	17,414	370
	Budgetary resources:			
	Unobligated balance:			
1000	Unobligated balance brought forward, Oct 1	25,007	18,302	501
1001	Discretionary unobligated balance brought fwd, Oct 1	25,007		
1021	Recoveries of prior year unpaid obligations	179	213	280
1070	Unobligated balance (total)	25,186	18,515	781
	Budget authority:			
	Appropriations, discretionary:			
1100	Appropriation	25	25	36
1100	Appropriation, disaster relief pursuant Stafford Act	143	143	143
1100	Appropriation, CR Supplemental		1,189	
1120	Appropriations transferred to other acct [073–0200]		–2	–2
1121	Appropriations transferred from other acct [073–0500]		10,634	
1131	Unobligated balance of appropriations permanently reduced		–13,500	
1160	Appropriation, discretionary (total)	168	–1,511	177
	Appropriations, mandatory:			
1200	Appropriation	1,579	911	
1200	Appropriation ARPA	460		
1260	Appropriations, mandatory (total)	2,039	911	
1900	Budget authority (total)	2,207	–600	177
1930	Total budgetary resources available	27,393	17,915	958
	Memorandum (non-add) entries:			
1941	Unexpired unobligated balance, end of year	18,302	501	588
	Change in obligated balance:			
	Unpaid obligations:			
3000	Unpaid obligations, brought forward, Oct 1	1,879	2,329	3,708
3010	New obligations, unexpired accounts	9,091	17,414	370
3020	Outlays (gross)	–8,462	–15,822	–370
3040	Recoveries of prior year unpaid obligations, unexpired	–179	–213	–280
3050	Unpaid obligations, end of year	2,329	3,708	3,428
	Memorandum (non-add) entries:			
3100	Obligated balance, start of year	1,879	2,329	3,708
3200	Obligated balance, end of year	2,329	3,708	3,428
	Budget authority and outlays, net:			
	Discretionary:			
4000	Budget authority, gross	168	–1,511	177
	Outlays, gross:			
4010	Outlays from new discretionary authority	168	11,858	177
4011	Outlays from discretionary balances	6,670	2,638	193
4020	Outlays, gross (total)	6,838	14,496	370
	Mandatory:			
4090	Budget authority, gross	2,039	911	
	Outlays, gross:			
4100	Outlays from new mandatory authority	1,624	911	
4101	Outlays from mandatory balances		415	
4110	Outlays, gross (total)	1,624	1,326	
4180	Budget authority, net (total)	2,207	–600	177
4190	Outlays, net (total)	8,462	15,822	370

SMALL BUSINESS ADMINISTRATION

Summary of Loan Levels, Subsidy Budget Authority and Outlays by Program (in millions of dollars)

Identification code 073–1152–0–1–453		2021 actual	2022 est.	2023 est.
	Direct loan levels supportable by subsidy budget authority:			
115001	Disaster Assistance Loans	1,741	7,300	1,479
115004	COVID Economic Injury Disaster Loans	78,478	124,180	....
115999	Total direct loan levels	80,219	131,480	1,479
	Direct loan subsidy (in percent):			
132001	Disaster Assistance Loans	8.95	8.96	12.91
132004	COVID Economic Injury Disaster Loans	8.95	11.72	....
132999	Weighted average subsidy rate	8.95	11.57	12.91
	Direct loan subsidy budget authority:			
133001	Disaster Assistance Loans	156	654	191
133004	COVID Economic Injury Disaster Loans	7,024	14,554	....
133999	Total subsidy budget authority	7,180	15,208	191
	Direct loan subsidy outlays:			
134001	Disaster Assistance Loans	130	439	191
134004	COVID Economic Injury Disaster Loans	6,540	13,467	....
134999	Total subsidy outlays	6,670	13,906	191
	Direct loan reestimates:			
135001	Disaster Assistance Loans	–669	–196	....
135002	Economic Injury Disaster Loans—Terrorist Attack	....	–1	....
135004	COVID Economic Injury Disaster Loans	–18,236	–3,584	....
135999	Total direct loan reestimates	–18,905	–3,781	....
	Administrative expense data:			
3510	Budget authority	558	618	179
3590	Outlays from new authority	213	618	179

As required by the Federal Credit Reform Act of 1990, as amended, for loans made pursuant to Section 7(b) of the Small Business Act, as amended, this account records the subsidy costs associated with the direct loans obligated in 1992 and beyond (including modifications of direct loans or loan guarantees that resulted from obligations or commitments in any year), as well as administrative expenses of the disaster loan program. The subsidy amounts are estimated on a present value basis; the administrative expenses are estimated on a cash basis.

Disaster loans made pursuant to Section 7(b) of the Small Business Act provide Federal assistance for non-farm, private sector disaster losses. Through the disaster assistance program, SBA helps homeowners, renters, businesses of all sizes, and non-profit organizations pay for the cost of replacing, rebuilding or repairing property damaged by disasters. The program is the only form of SBA financial assistance not limited to small businesses. The program provides subsidized loans for up to 30 years to borrowers who have incurred uninsured physical losses or economic injury as the result of a disaster. This includes Economic Injury Disaster Loans for COVID-19.

The Budget requests $143 million in new budget authority for administrative expenses related to major disasters (pursuant to a determination under section 102(2) of the Robert T. Stafford Disaster Relief and Emergency Assistance Act) and $36 million for administrative expenses related to non-major disasters and disaster mitigation. This includes $5 million to help facilitate access to capital to support climate change resiliency and the clean energy economy.

Object Classification (in millions of dollars)

Identification code 073–1152–0–1–453		2021 actual	2022 est.	2023 est.
	Direct obligations:			
25.3	Other goods and services from Federal sources	332	687	179
41.0	Grants, subsidies, and contributions	8,759	16,727	191
99.9	Total new obligations, unexpired accounts	9,091	17,414	370

DISASTER DIRECT LOAN FINANCING ACCOUNT

Program and Financing (in millions of dollars)

Identification code 073–4150–0–3–453		2021 actual	2022 est.	2023 est.
	Obligations by program activity:			
	Credit program obligations:			
0710	Direct loan obligations	80,219	131,480	1,479
0713	Payment of interest to Treasury	3,963	5,000	400
0715	Other	19	25	25
0742	Downward reestimates paid to receipt accounts	20,476	4,663	....
0743	Interest on downward reestimates	7	29	....
0900	Total new obligations, unexpired accounts	104,684	141,197	1,904
	Budgetary resources:			
	Unobligated balance:			
1000	Unobligated balance brought forward, Oct 1	133	6,734	10,676
1021	Recoveries of prior year unpaid obligations	1,314	1,500	374
1023	Unobligated balances applied to repay debt	–131	....	....
1070	Unobligated balance (total)	1,316	8,234	11,050
	Financing authority:			
	Borrowing authority, mandatory:			
1400	Borrowing authority	93,794	122,471	10,000
	Spending authority from offsetting collections, mandatory:			
1800	Collected	20,402	27,643	32,944
1801	Change in uncollected payments, Federal sources	331	....	....
1820	Capital transfer of spending authority from offsetting collections to general fund	....	–6,475	–965
1825	Spending authority from offsetting collections applied to repay debt	–4,425	....	....
1850	Spending auth from offsetting collections, mand (total)	16,308	21,168	31,979
1900	Budget authority (total)	110,102	143,639	41,979
1930	Total budgetary resources available	111,418	151,873	53,029
	Memorandum (non-add) entries:			
1941	Unexpired unobligated balance, end of year	6,734	10,676	51,125
	Change in obligated balance:			
	Unpaid obligations:			
3000	Unpaid obligations, brought forward, Oct 1	13,877	19,288	54,085
3010	New obligations, unexpired accounts	104,684	141,197	1,904
3020	Outlays (gross)	–97,959	–104,900	–25,526
3040	Recoveries of prior year unpaid obligations, unexpired	–1,314	–1,500	–374
3050	Unpaid obligations, end of year	19,288	54,085	30,089
	Uncollected payments:			
3060	Uncollected pymts, Fed sources, brought forward, Oct 1	–1,879	–2,210	–2,210
3070	Change in uncollected pymts, Fed sources, unexpired	–331	....	....
3090	Uncollected pymts, Fed sources, end of year	–2,210	–2,210	–2,210
	Memorandum (non-add) entries:			
3100	Obligated balance, start of year	11,998	17,078	51,875
3200	Obligated balance, end of year	17,078	51,875	27,879
	Financing authority and disbursements, net:			
	Mandatory:			
4090	Budget authority, gross	110,102	143,639	41,979
	Financing disbursements:			
4110	Outlays, gross (total)	97,959	104,900	25,526
	Offsets against gross financing authority and disbursements:			
	Offsetting collections (collected) from:			
4120	Payments from program account	–6,670	–13,906	–191
4120	Upward reestimate	–82	–715	....
4120	Interest on upward reestimate	–1,496	–196	....
4122	Interest income from Treasury	–1,021	–1,500	–4,000
4123	Repayments of principal, net	–11,133	–11,326	–28,753
4130	Offsets against gross budget authority and outlays (total)	–20,402	–27,643	–32,944
	Additional offsets against financing authority only (total):			
4140	Change in uncollected pymts, Fed sources, unexpired	–331	....	....
4160	Budget authority, net (mandatory)	89,369	115,996	9,035
4170	Outlays, net (mandatory)	77,557	77,257	–7,418
4180	Budget authority, net (total)	89,369	115,996	9,035
4190	Outlays, net (total)	77,557	77,257	–7,418

Status of Direct Loans (in millions of dollars)

Identification code 073–4150–0–3–453		2021 actual	2022 est.	2023 est.
	Position with respect to appropriations act limitation on obligations:			
1111	Direct loan obligations from current-year authority	486	93,792	....
1121	Limitation available from carry-forward	268,028	39,167	1,479
1143	Unobligated limitation carried forward (-)	–188,295	–1,479	....

Small Business Administration—Continued
Federal Funds—Continued

DISASTER DIRECT LOAN FINANCING ACCOUNT—Continued

Status of Direct Loans—Continued

Identification code 073–4150–0–3–453	2021 actual	2022 est.	2023 est.
1150 Total direct loan obligations	80,219	131,480	1,479
Cumulative balance of direct loans outstanding:			
1210 Outstanding, start of year	187,039	256,712	348,652
1231 Disbursements: Direct loan disbursements	74,505	104,900	25,526
1251 Repayments: Repayments and prepayments	–8,972	–11,111	–7,453
1263 Write-offs for default: Direct loans	–38	–1,849	–5,696
1264 Other adjustments, net (+ or -)	4,178		
1290 Outstanding, end of year	256,712	348,652	361,029

Balance Sheet (in millions of dollars)

Identification code 073–4150–0–3–453	2020 actual	2021 actual
ASSETS:		
Federal assets:		
1101 Fund balances with Treasury	11,217	20,212
Investments in U.S. securities:		
1106 Receivables, net	1,578	911
Net value of assets related to post-1991 direct loans receivable:		
1401 Direct loans receivable, gross	187,039	256,712
1402 Interest receivable		
1404 Foreclosed property	4	3
1405 Allowance for subsidy cost (-)	–5,641	–12,634
1499 Net present value of assets related to direct loans	181,402	244,081
1999 Total assets	194,197	265,204
LIABILITIES:		
Federal liabilities:		
2103 Debt	173,646	260,198
2105 Other	20,483	4,692
2201 Non-Federal liabilities: Accounts payable	68	314
2999 Total liabilities	194,197	265,204
NET POSITION:		
3300 Cumulative results of operations		
4999 Total liabilities and net position	194,197	265,204

DISASTER LOAN FUND LIQUIDATING ACCOUNT

Program and Financing (in millions of dollars)

Identification code 073–4153–0–3–453	2021 actual	2022 est.	2023 est.
Budgetary resources:			
Budget authority:			
Spending authority from offsetting collections, mandatory:			
1800 Collected		1	1
1820 Capital transfer of spending authority from offsetting collections to general fund		–1	–1
Budget authority and outlays, net:			
Mandatory:			
Offsets against gross budget authority and outlays:			
Offsetting collections (collected) from:			
4123 Non-Federal sources		–1	–1
4180 Budget authority, net (total)		–1	–1
4190 Outlays, net (total)		–1	–1

Status of Direct Loans (in millions of dollars)

Identification code 073–4153–0–3–453	2021 actual	2022 est.	2023 est.
Cumulative balance of direct loans outstanding:			
1210 Outstanding, start of year	1	1	1
1290 Outstanding, end of year	1	1	1

Balance Sheet (in millions of dollars)

Identification code 073–4153–0–3–453	2020 actual	2021 actual
ASSETS:		
1101 Federal assets: Fund balances with Treasury		
1601 Direct loans, net	1	1
1603 Allowance for estimated uncollectible loans and interest (-)		
1699 Value of assets related to direct loans	1	1
1999 Total assets	1	1
LIABILITIES:		
2104 Federal liabilities: Resources payable to Treasury	1	1
NET POSITION:		
3100 Unexpended appropriations		
4999 Total liabilities and net position	1	1

GENERAL FUND RECEIPT ACCOUNTS

(in millions of dollars)

	2021 actual	2022 est.	2023 est.
Offsetting receipts from the public:			
073–272130 Disaster Loan Program, Downward Reestimates of Subsidies	20,483	4,692	
073–272210 Business Loan Program, Negative Subsidies	24		
073–272230 Business Loan Program, Downward Reestimates of Subsidies	7,280	7,175	
073–322000 All Other General Fund Proprietary Receipts Including Budget Clearing Accounts	50		
General Fund Offsetting receipts from the public	27,837	11,867	
Intragovernmental payments:			
073–388500 Undistributed Intragovernmental Payments	1		
General Fund Intragovernmental payments	1		

ADMINISTRATIVE PROVISIONS—SMALL BUSINESS ADMINISTRATION

(INCLUDING TRANSFERS OF FUNDS)

SEC. 540. *Not to exceed 5 percent of any appropriation made available for the current fiscal year for the Small Business Administration in this Act may be transferred between such appropriations, but no such appropriation shall be increased by more than 10 percent by any such transfers: Provided, That any transfer pursuant to this paragraph shall be treated as a reprogramming of funds under section 608 of this Act and shall not be available for obligation or expenditure except in compliance with the procedures set forth in that section.*

SEC. 541. *Not to exceed 3 percent of any appropriation made available in this Act for the Small Business Administration under the headings "Salaries and Expenses" and "Business Loans Program Account" may be transferred to the Administration's information technology system modernization and working capital fund (IT WCF), as authorized by section 1077(b)(1) of title X of division A of the National Defense Authorization Act for Fiscal Year 2018, for the purposes specified in section 1077(b)(3) of such Act, upon the advance notice to the Committees on Appropriations of the House of Representatives and the Senate: Provided, That amounts transferred to the IT WCF under this section shall remain available for obligation through September 30, 2026.*

SEC. 542. DEVELOPMENT COMPANY LOANS TO SMALL MANUFACTURERS.—*Section 502(2)(A)(iii) of the Small Business Investment Act of 1958 (15 U.S.C. 696(2)(A)(iii)) is amended by striking "$5,500,000" and inserting "$6,500,000".*

SEC. 543. MICROLOAN PROGRAM FUNDING LEVEL CHANGE.—*Section 7(m)(7)(B)(i)(I)(bb) of the Small Business Act (15 U.S.C. 636(m)(7)(B)(i)(I)(bb)) is amended by striking "1/55" and inserting "1/25".*

SEC. 544. CHANGES TO 7(A) SECONDARY MARKET FEE PROVISIONS.—*Section 5(g)(2) of the Small Business Act is amended—*

    (1) by redesignating the current paragraph as subparagraph (A); and

    (2) by adding a new subparagraph (B) to read as follows:

    "(B) With respect to the Administration's guarantee of the payment of the principal of and interest on the trust certificates issued under this subsection, the Administration may assess, collect, and retain an annual fee, in an amount established once annually by the Administration in the Administration's budget request to Congress, not to exceed 0.05 percent per year of the outstanding balance of such trust certificates. The fee shall, at a minimum, offset the cost (as that term is defined in section 502 of the Federal Credit Reform Act of 1990) to the Administration of such guarantee, and any amounts received that exceed the cost of the payment guarantee shall be maintained in accordance with the Federal Credit Reform Act. The fee shall be payable solely by the holders of such trust certificates and shall not be charged to any borrower whose loan is

part of such trust or pool. The Administration may contract with an agent to carry out, on behalf of the Administration, the assessment and collection of this fee. The fee shall be deducted from the amounts otherwise payable to such holders of the trust certificates.".

SEC. 545. REPEAL OF CERTAIN DISASTER AND BUSINESS LOAN PROGRAM AUTHORITIES.—

(a) Section 42 of the Small Business Act (15 U.S.C. 657n) is repealed.

(b) Section 7(c) of the Small Business Act (15 U.S.C. 636(c)) is repealed.

(c) Section 7(a)(31)(H) of the Small Business Act (15 U.S.C. 636(a)(31)(H)) is repealed.

SEC. 546. PERMANENT INCREASE TO THE UNSECURED THRESHOLD ON PHYSICAL DISASTER.—Section 2102(b) of the RISE After Disaster Act of 2015 (Public Law 114–88) is repealed.

SEC. 547. SMALL BUSINESS DEVELOPMENT CENTERS AND WOMENS BUSINESS CENTER PROGRAM EVALUATIONS.—

(a) Section 21(a)(7)(A) of the Small Business Act (15 U.S.C. 648(a)(7)(A)) is amended by—

(1) striking the word "or" at the end of clause (i);

(2) striking the period at the end of clause (ii) and inserting "; or"; and

(3) adding the following new clause:

"(iii) the Administrator considers such a disclosure to be necessary for the purpose of conducting a program evaluation.".

(b) Section 29(n)(1) of the Small Business Act (15 U.S.C. 656(n)(1)) is amended by

(1) striking the word "or" at the end of subparagraph (A);

(2) striking the period at the end of subparagraph (B) and inserting "; or"; and

(3) adding the following new subparagraph:

"(C) the Administrator considers such a disclosure to be necessary for the purpose of conducting a program evaluation.".

SEC. 548. Section 20(g) of the Small Business Act (15 U.S.C. 631 note) is amended—

(1) in the heading, by striking "GENERAL BUSINESS LOANS" and inserting "COMMITMENTS FOR LOANS AND DEBENTURES"; and

(2) in paragraph (1)—

(A) by striking "2019" and inserting "2023";

(B) by striking "section 7(a)" and inserting "paragraphs (1) through (35) of section 7(a) of the Small Business Act, guarantees of debentures under section 303(b) of the Small Business Investment Act of 1958, or loans authorized under section 503 of the Small Business Investment Act of 1958";

(C) by inserting "or debentures" prior to "under this Act"; and

(D) by inserting "or debentures" prior to "for that fiscal year".

SOCIAL SECURITY ADMINISTRATION

Federal Funds

PAYMENT TO LIMITATION ON ADMINISTRATIVE EXPENSES

Program and Financing (in millions of dollars)

Identification code 028–0419–0–1–651	2021 actual	2022 est.	2023 est.
Obligations by program activity:			
0001 Direct program activity	38		
0900 Total new obligations, unexpired accounts (object class 25.3)	38		
Budgetary resources:			
Budget authority:			
Appropriations, discretionary:			
1100 Appropriation	38		
1930 Total budgetary resources available	38		
Change in obligated balance:			
Unpaid obligations:			
3000 Unpaid obligations, brought forward, Oct 1	42	26	
3010 New obligations, unexpired accounts	38		
3020 Outlays (gross)	–54	–26	
3050 Unpaid obligations, end of year	26		
Memorandum (non-add) entries:			
3100 Obligated balance, start of year	42	26	
3200 Obligated balance, end of year	26		
Budget authority and outlays, net:			
Discretionary:			
4000 Budget authority, gross	38		
Outlays, gross:			
4010 Outlays from new discretionary authority	18		
4011 Outlays from discretionary balances	36	26	
4020 Outlays, gross (total)	54	26	
4180 Budget authority, net (total)	38		
4190 Outlays, net (total)	54	26	

PAYMENTS TO SOCIAL SECURITY TRUST FUNDS

For payment to the Federal Old-Age and Survivors Insurance Trust Fund and the Federal Disability Insurance Trust Fund, as provided under sections 201(m) and 1131(b)(2) of the Social Security Act, $11,000,000.

Note.—A full-year 2022 appropriation for this account was not enacted at the time the Budget was prepared; therefore, the Budget assumes this account is operating under the Continuing Appropriations Act, 2022 (Division A of Public Law 117–43, as amended). The amounts included for 2022 reflect the annualized level provided by the continuing resolution.

Program and Financing (in millions of dollars)

Identification code 028–0404–0–1–651	2021 actual	2022 est.	2023 est.
Obligations by program activity:			
0001 Taxation of benefits	34,806	48,518	50,950
0002 Other	4	11	11
0003 Payroll Tax holiday	2		
0900 Total new obligations, unexpired accounts	34,812	48,529	50,961
Budgetary resources:			
Unobligated balance:			
1000 Unobligated balance brought forward, Oct 1	13	13	13
Budget authority:			
Appropriations, mandatory:			
1200 Appropriation	34,819	48,529	50,961
1930 Total budgetary resources available	34,832	48,542	50,974
Memorandum (non-add) entries:			
1940 Unobligated balance expiring	–7		
1941 Unexpired unobligated balance, end of year	13	13	13
Change in obligated balance:			
Unpaid obligations:			
3000 Unpaid obligations, brought forward, Oct 1	1	1	
3010 New obligations, unexpired accounts	34,812	48,529	50,961
3020 Outlays (gross)	–34,812	–48,529	–50,961
3041 Recoveries of prior year unpaid obligations, expired		–1	
3050 Unpaid obligations, end of year	1		
Memorandum (non-add) entries:			
3100 Obligated balance, start of year	1	1	
3200 Obligated balance, end of year	1		
Budget authority and outlays, net:			
Mandatory:			
4090 Budget authority, gross	34,819	48,529	50,961
Outlays, gross:			
4100 Outlays from new mandatory authority	34,811	48,529	50,961
4101 Outlays from mandatory balances	1		
4110 Outlays, gross (total)	34,812	48,529	50,961
4180 Budget authority, net (total)	34,819	48,529	50,961
4190 Outlays, net (total)	34,812	48,529	50,961

This general fund appropriation reimburses the Social Security trust funds annually for 1) pension reform and 2) interest on unnegotiated checks. Amounts appropriated to this account as permanent indefinite authority include receipts from Federal income taxation of Social Security benefits.

Object Classification (in millions of dollars)

Identification code 028–0404–0–1–651	2021 actual	2022 est.	2023 est.
Direct obligations:			
25.2 Other services from non-Federal sources	4	11	11
94.0 Financial transfers	34,806	48,518	50,950
94.0 Financial transfers	2		
99.9 Total new obligations, unexpired accounts	34,812	48,529	50,961

ADMINISTRATIVE COSTS, THE MEDICARE IMPROVEMENTS FOR PATIENTS AND PROVIDERS ACT

Program and Financing (in millions of dollars)

Identification code 028–0415–0–1–571	2021 actual	2022 est.	2023 est.
Budgetary resources:			
Unobligated balance:			
1000 Unobligated balance brought forward, Oct 1	15	15	15
1930 Total budgetary resources available	15	15	15
Memorandum (non-add) entries:			
1941 Unexpired unobligated balance, end of year	15	15	15
Change in obligated balance:			
Unpaid obligations:			
3000 Unpaid obligations, brought forward, Oct 1	12	12	6
3020 Outlays (gross)		–6	–6
3050 Unpaid obligations, end of year	12	6	
Memorandum (non-add) entries:			
3100 Obligated balance, start of year	12	12	6
3200 Obligated balance, end of year	12	6	
Budget authority and outlays, net:			
Mandatory:			
Outlays, gross:			
4101 Outlays from mandatory balances		6	6
4180 Budget authority, net (total)			
4190 Outlays, net (total)		6	6

Public Law 110–275 requires the Social Security Administration to transmit identity and financial data used to determine eligibility and the amount of Extra Help (also known as low-income subsidy) from the application process to the Medicaid State agency to initiate an application for the Medicare Savings Program. As of 2011, new funding for this program comes from a reimbursable agreement with the Centers for Medicare and Medicaid Services and this funding is reflected within the Limitation on Administrative Expenses account.

ADMINISTRATIVE EXPENSES, CHILDREN'S HEALTH INSURANCE PROGRAM

Program and Financing (in millions of dollars)

Identification code 028–0416–0–1–551	2021 actual	2022 est.	2023 est.
Obligations by program activity:			
0001 Administrative Expenses, Children's Health Insurance Program (Direct)	....	1	1
0100 Direct program activities, subtotal	....	1	1
0900 Total new obligations, unexpired accounts (object class 11.1)	....	1	1
Budgetary resources:			
Unobligated balance:			
1000 Unobligated balance brought forward, Oct 1	2	2	1
1930 Total budgetary resources available	2	2	1
Memorandum (non-add) entries:			
1941 Unexpired unobligated balance, end of year	2	1	....
Change in obligated balance:			
Unpaid obligations:			
3010 New obligations, unexpired accounts	....	1	1
3020 Outlays (gross)	....	–1	–1
Budget authority and outlays, net:			
Mandatory:			
Outlays, gross:			
4101 Outlays from mandatory balances	....	1	1
4180 Budget authority, net (total)	....	....	....
4190 Outlays, net (total)	....	1	1

Public Law 111–3 provides assistance for states to insure low-income children who are not eligible for Medicaid whose parent(s) or guardian(s) cannot afford private insurance.

Employment Summary

Identification code 028–0416–0–1–551	2021 actual	2022 est.	2023 est.
1001 Direct civilian full-time equivalent employment	....	10	10

SUPPLEMENTAL SECURITY INCOME PROGRAM

For carrying out titles XI and XVI of the Social Security Act, section 401 of Public Law 92–603, section 212 of Public Law 93–66, as amended, and section 405 of Public Law 95–216, including payment to the Social Security trust funds for administrative expenses incurred pursuant to section 201(g)(1) of the Social Security Act, $48,828,722,000, to remain available until expended: Provided, That any portion of the funds provided to a State in the current fiscal year and not obligated by the State during that year shall be returned to the Treasury: Provided further, That not more than $86,000,000 shall be available for research and demonstrations under sections 1110, 1115, and 1144 of the Social Security Act, and remain available through September 30, 2025.

For making, after June 15 of the current fiscal year, benefit payments to individuals under title XVI of the Social Security Act, for unanticipated costs incurred for the current fiscal year, such sums as may be necessary.

For making benefit payments under title XVI of the Social Security Act for the first quarter of fiscal year 2024, $15,800,000,000, to remain available until expended.

Note.—A full-year 2022 appropriation for this account was not enacted at the time the Budget was prepared; therefore, the Budget assumes this account is operating under the Continuing Appropriations Act, 2022 (Division A of Public Law 117–43, as amended). The amounts included for 2022 reflect the annualized level provided by the continuing resolution.

Program and Financing (in millions of dollars)

Identification code 028–0406–0–1–609	2021 actual	2022 est.	2023 est.
Obligations by program activity:			
0001 Supplemental Security Income Program (Direct)	58,956	64,791	62,977
0002 Program Integrity	1,289	1,110	1,504
0799 Total direct obligations	60,245	65,901	64,481
0801 State supplementation payments	2,441	3,155	3,145
0809 Reimbursable program activities, subtotal	2,441	3,155	3,145
0900 Total new obligations, unexpired accounts	62,686	69,056	67,626
Budgetary resources:			
Unobligated balance:			
1000 Unobligated balance brought forward, Oct 1	5,037	4,851	2,390
1001 Discretionary unobligated balance brought fwd, Oct 1	2,279	....	....
1021 Recoveries of prior year unpaid obligations	11	....	....
1070 Unobligated balance (total)	5,048	4,851	2,390
Budget authority:			
Appropriations, discretionary:			
1100 Appropriation	4,373	4,470	5,073
Appropriations, mandatory:			
1200 Appropriation	35,786	39,328	43,774
Advance appropriations, mandatory:			
1270 Advance appropriation	19,900	19,600	15,600
Spending authority from offsetting collections, mandatory:			
1800 Collected	2,430	3,197	3,144
1900 Budget authority (total)	62,489	66,595	67,591
1930 Total budgetary resources available	67,537	71,446	69,981
Memorandum (non-add) entries:			
1941 Unexpired unobligated balance, end of year	4,851	2,390	2,355
Change in obligated balance:			
Unpaid obligations:			
3000 Unpaid obligations, brought forward, Oct 1	2,984	3,072	2,992
3010 New obligations, unexpired accounts	62,686	69,056	67,626
3020 Outlays (gross)	–62,584	–69,136	–67,529
3040 Recoveries of prior year unpaid obligations, unexpired	–11	....	....
3041 Recoveries of prior year unpaid obligations, expired	–3	....	....
3050 Unpaid obligations, end of year	3,072	2,992	3,089
Memorandum (non-add) entries:			
3100 Obligated balance, start of year	2,984	3,072	2,992
3200 Obligated balance, end of year	3,072	2,992	3,089
Budget authority and outlays, net:			
Discretionary:			
4000 Budget authority, gross	4,373	4,470	5,073
Outlays, gross:			
4010 Outlays from new discretionary authority	1,473	3,556	4,026
4011 Outlays from discretionary balances	3,025	1,094	984
4020 Outlays, gross (total)	4,498	4,650	5,010
Mandatory:			
4090 Budget authority, gross	58,116	62,125	62,518
Outlays, gross:			
4100 Outlays from new mandatory authority	55,320	61,863	62,275
4101 Outlays from mandatory balances	2,766	2,623	244
4110 Outlays, gross (total)	58,086	64,486	62,519
Offsets against gross budget authority and outlays:			
Offsetting collections (collected) from:			
4123 Non-Federal sources	–2,430	–3,197	–3,144
4180 Budget authority, net (total)	60,059	63,398	64,447
4190 Outlays, net (total)	60,154	65,939	64,385

Summary of Budget Authority and Outlays (in millions of dollars)

	2021 actual	2022 est.	2023 est.
Enacted/requested:			
Budget Authority	60,059	63,398	64,447
Outlays	60,154	65,939	64,385
Legislative proposal, not subject to PAYGO:			
Budget Authority			–19
Outlays			–19
Legislative proposal, subject to PAYGO:			
Budget Authority			16
Outlays			16
Total:			
Budget Authority	60,059	63,398	64,444
Outlays	60,154	65,939	64,382

Title XVI of the Social Security Act established a Supplemental Security Income (SSI) program to provide monthly cash benefits as a federally guaranteed minimum income for low-income individuals who are aged, blind, or disabled. A portion of these funds may be used to fund research and demonstration projects.

Object Classification (in millions of dollars)

Identification code 028–0406–0–1–609	2021 actual	2022 est.	2023 est.
Direct obligations:			
25.3 Administrative Expenses	3,033	3,369	3,542

SOCIAL SECURITY ADMINISTRATION

		2021 actual	2022 est.	2023 est.
25.3	Beneficiary Services	103	118	124
25.3	Program Integrity (Base)	225	198	239
25.3	Program Integrity (Cap)	1,064	912	1,265
41.0	Federal benefits	55,717	61,206	59,225
41.0	Research	103	98	86
99.0	Direct obligations	60,245	65,901	64,481
99.0	Reimbursable obligations	2,441	3,155	3,145
99.9	Total new obligations, unexpired accounts	62,686	69,056	67,626

SUPPLEMENTAL SECURITY INCOME PROGRAM

(Legislative proposal, not subject to PAYGO)

Program and Financing (in millions of dollars)

Identification code 028–0406–2–1–609	2021 actual	2022 est.	2023 est.
Obligations by program activity:			
0001 Supplemental Security Income Program (Direct)			–19
0799 Total direct obligations			–19
0900 Total new obligations, unexpired accounts (object class 41.0)			–19
Budgetary resources:			
Budget authority:			
Appropriations, mandatory:			
1200 Appropriation			–19
1900 Budget authority (total)			–19
1930 Total budgetary resources available			–19
Change in obligated balance:			
Unpaid obligations:			
3010 New obligations, unexpired accounts			–19
3020 Outlays (gross)			19
Budget authority and outlays, net:			
Mandatory:			
4090 Budget authority, gross			–19
Outlays, gross:			
4100 Outlays from new mandatory authority			–19
4180 Budget authority, net (total)			–19
4190 Outlays, net (total)			–19

This schedule reflects the non-PAYGO impacts resulting from the proposed allocation adjustment. Please refer to the narrative in the Limitation on Administrative Expenses account for more information.

SUPPLEMENTAL SECURITY INCOME PROGRAM

(Legislative proposal, subject to PAYGO)

Program and Financing (in millions of dollars)

Identification code 028–0406–4–1–609	2021 actual	2022 est.	2023 est.
Obligations by program activity:			
0001 Direct program activity			16
0900 Total new obligations, unexpired accounts (object class 41.0)			16
Budgetary resources:			
Budget authority:			
Appropriations, mandatory:			
1200 Appropriation			16
1930 Total budgetary resources available			16
Change in obligated balance:			
Unpaid obligations:			
3010 New obligations, unexpired accounts			16
3020 Outlays (gross)			–16
Budget authority and outlays, net:			
Mandatory:			
4090 Budget authority, gross			16
Outlays, gross:			
4100 Outlays from new mandatory authority			16
4180 Budget authority, net (total)			16
4190 Outlays, net (total)			16

SPECIAL BENEFITS FOR CERTAIN WORLD WAR II VETERANS

Special and Trust Fund Receipts (in millions of dollars)

Identification code 028–0401–0–1–701	2021 actual	2022 est.	2023 est.
0100 Balance, start of year	3	3	3
2000 Total: Balances and receipts	3	3	3
5099 Balance, end of year	3	3	3

Program and Financing (in millions of dollars)

Identification code 028–0401–0–1–701	2021 actual	2022 est.	2023 est.
Obligations by program activity:			
0001 Special Benefits for Certain World War II Veterans (Direct)	1		
0900 Total new obligations, unexpired accounts (object class 42.0)	1		
Budgetary resources:			
Budget authority:			
Appropriations, mandatory:			
1200 Appropriation	1		
1900 Budget authority (total)	1		
1930 Total budgetary resources available	1		
Change in obligated balance:			
Unpaid obligations:			
3010 New obligations, unexpired accounts	1		
3020 Outlays (gross)	–1		
Budget authority and outlays, net:			
Mandatory:			
4090 Budget authority, gross	1		
Outlays, gross:			
4100 Outlays from new mandatory authority	1		
4180 Budget authority, net (total)	1		
4190 Outlays, net (total)	1		

Public Law 106–169 established a benefit program for certain individuals who are at least 65 years old; were in the United States military forces, including veterans of the Filipino Army and Filipino Scouts, during World War II; and who were eligible for SSI for the month of December 1999. To receive this benefit, these individuals must reside outside the United States and meet other requirements for eligibility.

OFFICE OF INSPECTOR GENERAL

(INCLUDING TRANSFER OF FUNDS)

For expenses necessary for the Office of Inspector General in carrying out the provisions of the Inspector General Act of 1978, $33,000,000, together with not to exceed $84,500,000, to be transferred and expended as authorized by section 201(g)(1) of the Social Security Act from the Federal Old-Age and Survivors Insurance Trust Fund and the Federal Disability Insurance Trust Fund: Provided, That $2,000,000 shall remain available until expended for information technology modernization, including related hardware and software infrastructure and equipment, and for administrative expenses directly associated with information technology modernization.

In addition, an amount not to exceed 3 percent of the total provided in this appropriation may be transferred from the "Limitation on Administrative Expenses", Social Security Administration, to be merged with this account, to be available for the time and purposes for which this account is available: Provided, That notice of such transfers shall be transmitted promptly to the Committees on Appropriations of the House of Representatives and the Senate at least 15 days in advance of any transfer.

Note.—A full-year 2022 appropriation for this account was not enacted at the time the Budget was prepared; therefore, the Budget assumes this account is operating under the Continuing Appropriations Act, 2022 (Division A of Public Law 117-43, as amended). The amounts included for 2022 reflect the annualized level provided by the continuing resolution.

Program and Financing (in millions of dollars)

Identification code 028–0400–0–1–600	2021 actual	2022 est.	2023 est.
Obligations by program activity:			
0001 Office of Inspector General (Direct)	116	117	132

OFFICE OF INSPECTOR GENERAL—Continued

Program and Financing—Continued

Identification code 028–0400–0–1–600	2021 actual	2022 est.	2023 est.
Budgetary resources:			
Unobligated balance:			
1000 Unobligated balance brought forward, Oct 1	1	1	1
Budget authority:			
Appropriations, discretionary:			
1100 Appropriation	30	30	33
Spending authority from offsetting collections, discretionary:			
1700 Collected	77	76	85
1700 Collected	....	11	15
1701 Change in uncollected payments, Federal sources	10	....	....
1750 Spending auth from offsetting collections, disc (total)	87	87	100
1900 Budget authority (total)	117	117	133
1930 Total budgetary resources available	118	118	134
Memorandum (non-add) entries:			
1940 Unobligated balance expiring	–1	....	....
1941 Unexpired unobligated balance, end of year	1	1	2
Change in obligated balance:			
Unpaid obligations:			
3000 Unpaid obligations, brought forward, Oct 1	16	15	14
3010 New obligations, unexpired accounts	116	117	132
3020 Outlays (gross)	–116	–118	–135
3041 Recoveries of prior year unpaid obligations, expired	–1	....	....
3050 Unpaid obligations, end of year	15	14	11
Uncollected payments:			
3060 Uncollected pymts, Fed sources, brought forward, Oct 1	–15	–18	–18
3070 Change in uncollected pymts, Fed sources, unexpired	–10	....	....
3071 Change in uncollected pymts, Fed sources, expired	7	....	....
3090 Uncollected pymts, Fed sources, end of year	–18	–18	–18
Memorandum (non-add) entries:			
3100 Obligated balance, start of year	1	–3	–4
3200 Obligated balance, end of year	–3	–4	–7
Budget authority and outlays, net:			
Discretionary:			
4000 Budget authority, gross	117	117	133
Outlays, gross:			
4010 Outlays from new discretionary authority	103	106	121
4011 Outlays from discretionary balances	13	12	14
4020 Outlays, gross (total)	116	118	135
Offsets against gross budget authority and outlays:			
Offsetting collections (collected) from:			
4030 Federal sources	–83	–87	–100
Additional offsets against gross budget authority only:			
4050 Change in uncollected pymts, Fed sources, unexpired	–10	....	....
4052 Offsetting collections credited to expired accounts	6	....	....
4060 Additional offsets against budget authority only (total)	–4	....	....
4070 Budget authority, net (discretionary)	30	30	33
4080 Outlays, net (discretionary)	33	31	35
4180 Budget authority, net (total)	30	30	33
4190 Outlays, net (total)	33	31	35

The Office of Inspector General conducts independent audits, evaluations, and investigations to identify and prevent fraud, waste, abuse, and mismanagement of Social Security Administration programs and operations.

Object Classification (in millions of dollars)

Identification code 028–0400–0–1–600	2021 actual	2022 est.	2023 est.
Direct obligations:			
11.1 Personnel compensation: Full-time permanent	70	72	80
12.1 Civilian personnel benefits	32	32	36
21.0 Travel and transportation of persons	1	2	3
23.1 Rental payments to GSA	4	4	4
23.3 Communications, utilities, and miscellaneous charges	1	1	1
25.1 Guard Services	....	....	1
25.2 Other services from non-Federal sources	1	1	1
25.3 Other goods and services from Federal sources	1	1	1
25.4 Operation and maintenance of facilities	....	....	2
25.6 Training	....	....	1
25.7 Operation and maintenance of equipment	....	1	....
31.0 Equipment	6	2	3
99.0 Direct obligations	116	117	132
99.9 Total new obligations, unexpired accounts	116	117	132

Employment Summary

Identification code 028–0400–0–1–600	2021 actual	2022 est.	2023 est.
1001 Direct civilian full-time equivalent employment	508	487	532

ADMINISTRATIVE EXPENSES, RECOVERY ACT

Program and Financing (in millions of dollars)

Identification code 028–0417–0–1–651	2021 actual	2022 est.	2023 est.
Change in obligated balance:			
Unpaid obligations:			
3000 Unpaid obligations, brought forward, Oct 1	3	....	....
3020 Outlays (gross)	–3	....	....
Memorandum (non-add) entries:			
3100 Obligated balance, start of year	3	....	....
Budget authority and outlays, net:			
Discretionary:			
Outlays, gross:			
4011 Outlays from discretionary balances	3	....	....
4180 Budget authority, net (total)	....	....	....
4190 Outlays, net (total)	3	....	....

Public Law 111–5 provided funding to process disability and retirement work, to replace the National Computer Center, and to administer $250 economic recovery payments to eligible Social Security and Supplemental Security Income beneficiaries. The funds for administering the $250 economic recovery payments were obligated by the end of the first quarter of 2011, as payments ended on December 31, 2010. All obligations since 2012 are for the replacement of the National Computer Center. SSA received a Presidential Waiver on December 28, 2012, allowing the agency to retain and continue to obligate funds appropriated for expenses of the replacement of the National Computer Center.

STATE SUPPLEMENTAL FEES

Special and Trust Fund Receipts (in millions of dollars)

Identification code 028–5419–0–2–609	2021 actual	2022 est.	2023 est.
0100 Balance, start of year	....	....	....
Receipts:			
Current law:			
1130 State Supplemental Fees, SSI	126	135	140
2000 Total: Balances and receipts	126	135	140
Appropriations:			
Current law:			
2101 State Supplemental Fees	–126	–135	–140
5099 Balance, end of year	....	....	....

Program and Financing (in millions of dollars)

Identification code 028–5419–0–2–609	2021 actual	2022 est.	2023 est.
Obligations by program activity:			
0001 State Supplemental Fees (Direct)	126	135	140
0900 Total new obligations, unexpired accounts (object class 25.3)	126	135	140
Budgetary resources:			
Budget authority:			
Appropriations, discretionary:			
1101 Appropriation (special or trust)	126	135	140
1930 Total budgetary resources available	126	135	140
Change in obligated balance:			
Unpaid obligations:			
3010 New obligations, unexpired accounts	126	135	140
3020 Outlays (gross)	–126	–135	–140

SOCIAL SECURITY ADMINISTRATION

		2021 actual	2022 est.	2023 est.
	Budget authority and outlays, net:			
	Discretionary:			
4000	Budget authority, gross	126	135	140
	Outlays, gross:			
4010	Outlays from new discretionary authority	126	135	140
4180	Budget authority, net (total)	126	135	140
4190	Outlays, net (total)	126	135	140

The Social Security Administration collects a fee from States for costs related to administering Supplemental Security Income State supplementary payments on behalf of States. A portion of these fees is used to fund some of SSA's administrative costs.

Trust Funds

FEDERAL OLD-AGE AND SURVIVORS INSURANCE TRUST FUND

Special and Trust Fund Receipts (in millions of dollars)

Identification code 028–8006–0–7–651	2021 actual	2022 est.	2023 est.
0100 Balance, start of year	2,721,068	2,662,160	2,602,093
Receipts:			
Current law:			
1110 FOASI, Transfers from General Fund (FICA Taxes)	770,275	851,457	896,727
1110 FOASI, Transfers from General Fund (SECA Taxes)	43,759	47,675	48,616
1110 FOASI, Refunds	....	–3,957	–4,474
1130 FOASI, Non-Attorney Fees	....	1	1
1130 FOASI, Attorney Fees	1	1	1
1130 FOASI, Tax Refund Offset	7	7	7
1140 FOASI, Federal Employer Contributions (FICA Taxes)	17,002	17,731	18,364
1140 FOASI, General Fund Payments for Payroll Tax Holiday (PL 111–312)	2	....	....
1140 FOASI, Interest Received by Trust Funds	70,535	64,745	59,358
1140 FOASI, Federal Payments to the FOASI Trust Fund	34,328	46,988	49,373
1199 Total current law receipts	935,909	1,024,648	1,067,973
Proposed:			
1210 FOASI, Transfers from General Fund (FICA Taxes)	....	....	3
1999 Total receipts	935,909	1,024,648	1,067,976
2000 Total: Balances and receipts	3,656,977	3,686,808	3,670,069
Appropriations:			
Current law:			
2101 Federal Old-age and Survivors Insurance Trust Fund	–3,339	–3,178	–3,592
2101 Federal Old-age and Survivors Insurance Trust Fund	–932,576	–1,021,409	–1,064,345
2103 Federal Old-age and Survivors Insurance Trust Fund	–58,972	–60,128	–108,259
2199 Total current law appropriations	–994,887	–1,084,715	–1,176,196
2999 Total appropriations	–994,887	–1,084,715	–1,176,196
Special and trust fund receipts returned:			
3010 Federal Old-age and Survivors Insurance Trust Fund	7	....	....
3098 Federal Old-age and Survivors Insurance Trust Fund	61	....	....
5098 Reconciliation adjustment	2	....	....
5099 Balance, end of year	2,662,160	2,602,093	2,493,873

Program and Financing (in millions of dollars)

Identification code 028–8006–0–7–651	2021 actual	2022 est.	2023 est.
Obligations by program activity:			
0001 Federal Old-age and Survivors Insurance Trust Fund (Direct)	994,976	1,084,776	1,176,232
Budgetary resources:			
Unobligated balance:			
1012 Unobligated balance transfers between expired and unexpired accounts	....	61	36
1021 Recoveries of prior year unpaid obligations	69	....	....
1026 Adjustment for change in allocation of trust fund limitation or foreign exchange valuation	–61	....	....
1030 Other balances withdrawn to special or trust funds	–7	....	....
1033 Recoveries of prior year paid obligations	88	....	....
1070 Unobligated balance (total)	89	61	36
Budget authority:			
Appropriations, discretionary:			
1101 Appropriation (special or trust)	3,339	3,178	3,592
Appropriations, mandatory:			
1201 Appropriation (special or trust fund)	932,576	1,021,409	1,064,345
1203 Appropriation (previously unavailable)(special or trust)	58,972	60,128	108,259
1260 Appropriations, mandatory (total)	991,548	1,081,537	1,172,604
1900 Budget authority (total)	994,887	1,084,715	1,176,196
1930 Total budgetary resources available	994,976	1,084,776	1,176,232
Memorandum (non-add) entries:			
Special and non-revolving trust funds:			
1950 Other balances withdrawn and returned to unappropriated receipts	7	....	....
Change in obligated balance:			
Unpaid obligations:			
3000 Unpaid obligations, brought forward, Oct 1	90,043	93,571	101,694
3010 New obligations, unexpired accounts	994,976	1,084,776	1,176,232
3020 Outlays (gross)	–991,379	–1,076,653	–1,168,526
3040 Recoveries of prior year unpaid obligations, unexpired	–69	....	....
3050 Unpaid obligations, end of year	93,571	101,694	109,400
Memorandum (non-add) entries:			
3100 Obligated balance, start of year	90,043	93,571	101,694
3200 Obligated balance, end of year	93,571	101,694	109,400
Budget authority and outlays, net:			
Discretionary:			
4000 Budget authority, gross	3,339	3,178	3,592
Outlays, gross:			
4010 Outlays from new discretionary authority	2,881	2,588	2,910
4011 Outlays from discretionary balances	508	705	632
4020 Outlays, gross (total)	3,389	3,293	3,542
Mandatory:			
4090 Budget authority, gross	991,548	1,081,537	1,172,604
Outlays, gross:			
4100 Outlays from new mandatory authority	902,272	980,494	1,164,984
4101 Outlays from mandatory balances	85,718	92,866	....
4110 Outlays, gross (total)	987,990	1,073,360	1,164,984
Offsets against gross budget authority and outlays:			
Offsetting collections (collected) from:			
4123 Non-Federal sources	–88	....	....
Additional offsets against gross budget authority only:			
4143 Recoveries of prior year paid obligations, unexpired accounts	88	....	....
4160 Budget authority, net (mandatory)	991,548	1,081,537	1,172,604
4170 Outlays, net (mandatory)	987,902	1,073,360	1,164,984
4180 Budget authority, net (total)	994,887	1,084,715	1,176,196
4190 Outlays, net (total)	991,291	1,076,653	1,168,526
Memorandum (non-add) entries:			
5000 Total investments, SOY: Federal securities: Par value	2,811,213	2,755,785	2,703,733
5001 Total investments, EOY: Federal securities: Par value	2,755,785	2,703,733	2,603,263

The Old-Age and Survivors Insurance (OASI) program provides monthly cash benefits to retired workers and their dependents, and to survivors of deceased workers.

OASI Cash Outgo Detail

(in millions of dollars)

	2021 actual	2022 est.	2023 est.
Benefit Payments	982,657	1,067,494	1,158,897
Payments to the Railroad Board	4,792	5,263	5,473
Administrative Expenses	3,913	3,880	4,145
Beneficiary Services	16	16	11
Prior Year Employment Tax Receipts Refund	–88	0	0
Total Outgo	991,291	1,076,653	1,168,526

Status of Funds (in millions of dollars)

Identification code 028–8006–0–7–651	2021 actual	2022 est.	2023 est.
Unexpended balance, start of year:			
0100 Balance, start of year	2,811,111	2,755,799	2,703,855
0298 Reconciliation adjustment	70	....	....
0999 Total balance, start of year	2,811,181	2,755,799	2,703,855
Cash income during the year:			
Current law:			
Receipts:			
1110 FOASI, Transfers from General Fund (FICA Taxes)	770,275	851,457	896,727
1110 FOASI, Transfers from General Fund (SECA Taxes)	43,759	47,675	48,616
1110 FOASI, Refunds	....	–3,957	–4,474
1130 Federal Old-age and Survivors Insurance Trust Fund	88	....	....
1130 FOASI, Non-Attorney Fees	....	1	1
1130 FOASI, Attorney Fees	1	1	1
1130 FOASI, Tax Refund Offset	7	7	7
1150 FOASI, Interest Received by Trust Funds	70,535	64,745	59,358
1160 FOASI, Federal Employer Contributions (FICA Taxes)	17,002	17,731	18,364

Social Security Administration—Continued
Trust Funds—Continued

FEDERAL OLD-AGE AND SURVIVORS INSURANCE TRUST FUND—Continued

Status of Funds—Continued

Identification code 028–8006–0–7–651		2021 actual	2022 est.	2023 est.
1160	FOASI, General Fund Payments for Payroll Tax Holiday (PL 111–312)	2		
1160	FOASI, Federal Payments to the FOASI Trust Fund	34,328	46,988	49,373
1199	Income under present law	935,997	1,024,648	1,067,973
	Proposed:			
1210	FOASI, Transfers from General Fund (FICA Taxes)			3
1299	Income proposed			3
1999	Total cash income	935,997	1,024,648	1,067,976
	Cash outgo during year:			
	Current law:			
2100	Federal Old-age and Survivors Insurance Trust Fund [Budget Acct]	–991,379	–1,076,653	–1,168,526
2199	Outgo under current law	–991,379	–1,076,653	–1,168,526
2999	Total cash outgo (–)	–991,379	–1,076,653	–1,168,526
	Surplus or deficit:			
3110	Excluding interest	–125,917	–116,750	–159,908
3120	Interest	70,535	64,745	59,358
3199	Subtotal, surplus or deficit	–55,382	–52,005	–100,550
3230	Federal Old-age and Survivors Insurance Trust Fund		61	36
3299	Total adjustments		61	36
3999	Total change in fund balance	–55,382	–51,944	–100,514
	Unexpended balance, end of year:			
4100	Uninvested balance (net), end of year	14	122	78
4200	Federal Old-age and Survivors Insurance Trust Fund	2,755,785	2,703,733	2,603,263
4999	Total balance, end of year	2,755,799	2,703,855	2,603,341

Object Classification (in millions of dollars)

Identification code 028–8006–0–7–651		2021 actual	2022 est.	2023 est.
	Direct obligations:			
25.2	Other services from non-Federal sources [Beneficiary Services]	16	16	11
25.3	Other goods and services from Federal sources [Treasury Payments]	524	587	603
25.3	Other goods and services from Federal sources [RRB]	4,792	5,263	5,473
42.0	Insurance claims and indemnities	986,216	1,075,671	1,166,517
94.0	Financial transfers [OIG]	42	42	47
94.0	Financial transfers [LAE + Line 1050]	3,386	3,197	3,581
99.9	Total new obligations, unexpired accounts	994,976	1,084,776	1,176,232

FEDERAL DISABILITY INSURANCE TRUST FUND

Special and Trust Fund Receipts (in millions of dollars)

Identification code 028–8007–0–7–651		2021 actual	2022 est.	2023 est.
0100	Balance, start of year	74,547	76,508	92,348
	Receipts:			
	Current law:			
1110	FDI, Transfers from General Fund (FICA Taxes)	130,844	144,581	152,274
1110	FDI, Transfers from General Fund (SECA Taxes)	7,445	8,123	8,255
1110	FDI, Refunds		–672	–760
1130	Attorney Fees, Federal Disability Insurance Trust Fund	20	20	22
1140	FDI, Federal Employer Contributions (FICA Taxes)	2,888	3,010	3,118
1140	FDI, Interest Received by Trust Funds	2,718	2,643	2,714
1140	FDI, Federal Payments to the FDI Trust Fund	481	1,539	1,585
1199	Total current law receipts	144,396	159,244	167,208
	Proposed:			
1210	FDI, Transfers from General Fund (FICA Taxes)			1
1999	Total receipts	144,396	159,244	167,209
2000	Total: Balances and receipts	218,943	235,752	259,557
	Appropriations:			
	Current law:			
2101	Federal Disability Insurance Trust Fund	–2,522	–2,555	–2,919
2101	Federal Disability Insurance Trust Fund	–141,879	–156,618	–167,333
2135	Federal Disability Insurance Trust Fund	1,967	15,769	18,800
2199	Total current law appropriations	–142,434	–143,404	–151,452
	Proposed:			
2201	Federal Disability Insurance Trust Fund			53
2999	Total appropriations	–142,434	–143,404	–151,399
	Special and trust fund receipts returned:			
3010	Federal Disability Insurance Trust Fund	6		
3098	Federal Disability Insurance Trust Fund	195		
5098	Reconciliation adjustment	–202		
5099	Balance, end of year	76,508	92,348	108,158

Program and Financing (in millions of dollars)

Identification code 028–8007–0–7–651		2021 actual	2022 est.	2023 est.
	Obligations by program activity:			
0001	Federal Disability Insurance Trust Fund (Direct)	142,452	143,475	151,481
	Budgetary resources:			
	Unobligated balance:			
1012	Unobligated balance transfers between expired and unexpired accounts		71	29
1021	Recoveries of prior year unpaid obligations	201		
1026	Adjustment for change in allocation of trust fund limitation or foreign exchange valuation	–195		
1030	Other balances withdrawn to special or trust funds	–6		
1033	Recoveries of prior year paid obligations	18		
1070	Unobligated balance (total)	18	71	29
	Budget authority:			
	Appropriations, discretionary:			
1101	Appropriation (special or trust)	2,522	2,555	2,919
	Appropriations, mandatory:			
1201	Appropriation (special or trust fund)	141,879	156,618	167,333
1235	Appropriations precluded from obligation (special or trust)	–1,967	–15,769	–18,800
1260	Appropriations, mandatory (total)	139,912	140,849	148,533
1900	Budget authority (total)	142,434	143,404	151,452
1930	Total budgetary resources available	142,452	143,475	151,481
	Memorandum (non-add) entries:			
	Special and non-revolving trust funds:			
1950	Other balances withdrawn and returned to unappropriated receipts	6		
	Change in obligated balance:			
	Unpaid obligations:			
3000	Unpaid obligations, brought forward, Oct 1	22,516	21,353	21,780
3010	New obligations, unexpired accounts	142,452	143,475	151,481
3020	Outlays (gross)	–143,414	–143,048	–150,666
3040	Recoveries of prior year unpaid obligations, unexpired	–201		
3050	Unpaid obligations, end of year	21,353	21,780	22,595
	Memorandum (non-add) entries:			
3100	Obligated balance, start of year	22,516	21,353	21,780
3200	Obligated balance, end of year	21,353	21,780	22,595
	Budget authority and outlays, net:			
	Discretionary:			
4000	Budget authority, gross	2,522	2,555	2,919
	Outlays, gross:			
4010	Outlays from new discretionary authority	2,173	2,080	2,365
4011	Outlays from discretionary balances	266	567	515
4020	Outlays, gross (total)	2,439	2,647	2,880
	Mandatory:			
4090	Budget authority, gross	139,912	140,849	148,533
	Outlays, gross:			
4100	Outlays from new mandatory authority	128,223	119,555	147,786
4101	Outlays from mandatory balances	12,752	20,846	
4110	Outlays, gross (total)	140,975	140,401	147,786
	Offsets against gross budget authority and outlays:			
	Offsetting collections (collected) from:			
4123	Non-Federal sources	–18		
	Additional offsets against gross budget authority only:			
4143	Recoveries of prior year paid obligations, unexpired accounts	18		
4160	Budget authority, net (mandatory)	139,912	140,849	148,533
4170	Outlays, net (mandatory)	140,957	140,401	147,786
4180	Budget authority, net (total)	142,434	143,404	151,452
4190	Outlays, net (total)	143,396	143,048	150,666
	Memorandum (non-add) entries:			
5000	Total investments, SOY: Federal securities: Par value	97,209	98,032	114,330
5001	Total investments, EOY: Federal securities: Par value	98,032	114,330	130,954

SOCIAL SECURITY ADMINISTRATION

Summary of Budget Authority and Outlays (in millions of dollars)

	2021 actual	2022 est.	2023 est.
Enacted/requested:			
Budget Authority	142,434	143,404	151,452
Outlays	143,396	143,048	150,666
Legislative proposal, not subject to PAYGO:			
Budget Authority			–53
Outlays			–53
Total:			
Budget Authority	142,434	143,404	151,399
Outlays	143,396	143,048	150,613

The Disability Insurance (DI) program provides monthly cash benefits for disabled workers who have not yet attained their normal retirement age, and for their dependents.

DI Cash Outgo Detail
(in millions of dollars)

	2021 actual	2022 est.	2023 est.
Benefit Payments	140,591	140,034	147,330
Payments to the Railroad Board	107	94	91
Administrative Expenses	2,532	2,750	2,985
Beneficiary Services	172	163	207
Demonstration Projects	12	7	0
Prior Year Employment Tax Receipts Refund	–18	0	0
Total Outgo	143,396	143,048	150,613

Status of Funds (in millions of dollars)

Identification code 028–8007–0–7–651		2021 actual	2022 est.	2023 est.
	Unexpended balance, start of year:			
0100	Balance, start of year	97,063	98,063	114,330
0999	Total balance, start of year	97,063	98,063	114,330
	Cash income during the year:			
	Current law:			
	Receipts:			
1110	FDI, Transfers from General Fund (FICA Taxes)	130,844	144,581	152,274
1110	FDI, Transfers from General Fund (SECA Taxes)	7,445	8,123	8,255
1110	FDI, Refunds		–672	–760
1130	Federal Disability Insurance Trust Fund	18		
1130	Attorney Fees, Federal Disability Insurance Trust Fund	20	20	22
1150	FDI, Interest Received by Trust Funds	2,718	2,643	2,714
1160	FDI, Federal Employer Contributions (FICA Taxes)	2,888	3,010	3,118
1160	FDI, Federal Payments to the FDI Trust Fund	481	1,539	1,585
1199	Income under present law	144,414	159,244	167,208
	Proposed:			
1210	FDI, Transfers from General Fund (FICA Taxes)			1
1299	Income proposed			1
1999	Total cash income	144,414	159,244	167,209
	Cash outgo during year:			
	Current law:			
2100	Federal Disability Insurance Trust Fund [Budget Acct]	–143,414	–143,048	–150,666
2199	Outgo under current law	–143,414	–143,048	–150,666
	Proposed:			
2200	Federal Disability Insurance Trust Fund			53
2299	Outgo under proposed legislation			53
2999	Total cash outgo (–)	–143,414	–143,048	–150,613
	Surplus or deficit:			
3110	Excluding interest	–1,718	13,553	13,882
3120	Interest	2,718	2,643	2,714
3199	Subtotal, surplus or deficit	1,000	16,196	16,596
3230	Federal Disability Insurance Trust Fund		71	29
3299	Total adjustments		71	29
3999	Total change in fund balance	1,000	16,267	16,625
	Unexpended balance, end of year:			
4100	Uninvested balance (net), end of year	31		1
4200	Federal Disability Insurance Trust Fund	98,032	114,330	130,954
4999	Total balance, end of year	98,063	114,330	130,955

Object Classification (in millions of dollars)

Identification code 028–8007–0–7–651		2021 actual	2022 est.	2023 est.
	Direct obligations:			
25.2	Beneficiary Services (VR & Tickets)	172	163	207
25.3	Other purchases of goods and services from Government accounts (Treasury Admin)	93	103	105
25.3	Other purchases of goods and services from Government accounts (RRB)	107	94	91
25.5	Research and development contracts	4	2	
42.0	Disability insurance benefits	139,536	140,487	148,130
94.0	Financial transfers (OIG)	32	34	38
94.0	Financial transfers (LAE)	2,508	2,592	2,910
99.9	Total new obligations, unexpired accounts	142,452	143,475	151,481

FEDERAL DISABILITY INSURANCE TRUST FUND

(Legislative proposal, not subject to PAYGO)

Program and Financing (in millions of dollars)

Identification code 028–8007–2–7–651		2021 actual	2022 est.	2023 est.
	Obligations by program activity:			
0001	Federal Disability Insurance Trust Fund (Direct)			–53
0900	Total new obligations, unexpired accounts (object class 42.0)			–53
	Budgetary resources:			
	Budget authority:			
	Appropriations, mandatory:			
1201	Appropriation (special or trust fund)			–53
1900	Budget authority (total)			–53
1930	Total budgetary resources available			–53
	Change in obligated balance:			
	Unpaid obligations:			
3010	New obligations, unexpired accounts			–53
3020	Outlays (gross)			53
	Budget authority and outlays, net:			
	Mandatory:			
4090	Budget authority, gross			–53
	Outlays, gross:			
4100	Outlays from new mandatory authority			–53
4180	Budget authority, net (total)			–53
4190	Outlays, net (total)			–53

This schedule reflects the non-PAYGO impacts resulting from the proposed allocation adjustment. Please refer to the narrative in the Limitation on Administrative Expenses account for more information.

LIMITATION ON ADMINISTRATIVE EXPENSES

For necessary expenses, including the hire and purchase of passenger motor vehicles and charging or fueling infrastructure for zero emission passenger motor vehicles, and not to exceed $20,000 for official reception and representation expenses, not more than $14,632,300,000 may be expended, as authorized by section 201(g)(1) of the Social Security Act, from any one or all of the trust funds referred to in such section: Provided, That not less than $2,750,000 shall be for the Social Security Advisory Board: Provided further, That unobligated balances of funds provided under this paragraph at the end of fiscal year 2023 not needed for fiscal year 2023 shall remain available until expended to invest in the Social Security Administration information technology and telecommunications hardware and software infrastructure, including related equipment and non-payroll administrative expenses associated solely with this information technology and telecommunications infrastructure: Provided further, That the Commissioner of Social Security shall notify the Committees on Appropriations of the House of Representatives and the Senate prior to making unobligated balances available under the authority in the previous proviso: Provided further, That reimbursement to the trust funds under this heading for expenditures for official time for employees of the Social Security Administration pursuant to 5 U.S.C. 7131, and for facilities or support services for labor organizations pursuant to policies, regulations, or procedures referred to in section 7135(b) of such title shall be made by the Secretary of the Treasury, with interest, from amounts in the general fund not otherwise appropriated, as soon as possible after such expenditures are made.

1212　Social Security Administration—Continued
Trust Funds—Continued

THE BUDGET FOR FISCAL YEAR 2023

LIMITATION ON ADMINISTRATIVE EXPENSES—Continued

From funds provided under the first paragraph, $1,799,000,000, to remain available through March 31, 2024, is for the costs associated with continuing disability reviews under titles II and XVI of the Social Security Act, including work-related continuing disability reviews to determine whether earnings derived from services demonstrate an individual's ability to engage in substantial gainful activity, for the cost associated with conducting redeterminations of eligibility under title XVI of the Social Security Act, for the cost of co-operative disability investigation units, and for the cost associated with the prosecution of fraud in the programs and operations of the Social Security Administration by Special Assistant United States Attorneys: Provided, That, of such amount, $288,000,000 is provided to meet the terms of a concurrent resolution on the budget, and $1,511,000,000 is additional new budget authority specified for purposes of a concurrent resolution on the budget: Provided further, That, of the additional new budget authority described in the preceding proviso, up to $15,100,000 may be transferred to the "Office of Inspector General", Social Security Administration, for the cost of jointly operated co-operative disability investigation units: Provided further, That such transfer authority is in addition to any other transfer authority provided by law: Provided further, That the Commissioner shall provide to the Congress (at the conclusion of the fiscal year) a report on the obligation and expenditure of these funds, similar to the reports that were required by section 103(d)(2) of Public Law 104–121 for fiscal years 1996 through 2002: Provided further, That none of the funds described in this paragraph shall be available for transfer or reprogramming except as specified in this paragraph.

In addition, $140,000,000 to be derived from administration fees in excess of $5.00 per supplementary payment collected pursuant to section 1616(d) of the Social Security Act or section 212(b)(3) of Public Law 93–66, which shall remain available until expended: Provided, That to the extent that the amounts collected pursuant to such sections in fiscal year 2023 exceed $140,000,000, the amounts shall be available in fiscal year 2024 only to the extent provided in advance in appropriations Acts.

In addition, up to $1,000,000 to be derived from fees collected pursuant to section 303(c) of the Social Security Protection Act, which shall remain available until expended.

Note.—A full-year 2022 appropriation for this account was not enacted at the time the Budget was prepared; therefore, the Budget assumes this account is operating under the Continuing Appropriations Act, 2022 (Division A of Public Law 117–43, as amended). The amounts included for 2022 reflect the annualized level provided by the continuing resolution.

Program and Financing (in millions of dollars)

Identification code 028–8704–0–7–651		2021 actual	2022 est.	2023 est.
	Obligations by program activity:			
0001	LAE Program Direct	11,361	11,261	12,974
0003	National Support Center	3	....	....
0004	IT Modernization	121	45	....
0005	Altmeyer	3	1	....
0007	AIF/ITS	....	226	150
0009	PI Base	273	273	288
0010	PI Adjustment 21/22	1,105	125	....
0012	OHO 20/21	87	....	....
0013	Rebate 20/21	1	....	....
0014	COVID Response 20/21	28	....	....
0015	PI Additional 20/21	241	....	....
0016	OHO 21/22	26	24	....
0017	OIG Transfer 21/22	11	1	....
0018	OHO Hearings Backlog (22/23)	....	50	....
0020	PI Adjustment - 22/23	....	1,191	100
0021	OIG Transfer from PI CAP - 22/23	....	11	....
0022	OIG Transfer from PI CAP (23/24)	....	....	15
0027	PI Additional 23/24	....	....	1,396
0799	Total direct obligations	13,260	13,208	14,923
0801	Reimbursable activity, general	80	70	69
0802	Low Income Subsidy	....	6	6
0809	Reimbursable program activities, subtotal	80	76	75
0899	Total reimbursable obligations	80	76	75
0900	Total new obligations, unexpired accounts	13,340	13,284	14,998
	Budgetary resources:			
	Unobligated balance:			
1000	Unobligated balance brought forward, Oct 1	557	402	232
1001	Discretionary unobligated balance brought fwd, Oct 1	520	365	....
1012	Unobligated balance transfers between expired and unexpired accounts [ITS Transfers]	220	113	150
1021	Recoveries of prior year unpaid obligations [X Year]	17	....	....
1033	Recoveries of prior year paid obligations	4	....	....
1070	Unobligated balance (total)	798	515	382
	Budget authority:			
	Spending authority from offsetting collections, discretionary:			
1700	Collected - LAE Direct	9,234	11,261	12,974
1700	Collected - PI Additional 20/21	241	....	....
1700	Collected - PI Base	273	273	288
1700	Collected - PI Adjustment 21/22	1,105	....	....
1700	Collected - OIG Transfer 20/21	1	....	....
1700	Collected - OHO 20/21	93	....	....
1700	Collected - Rebate 20/21	6	....	....
1700	Collected - COVID Response 20/21	30	....	....
1700	Collected - IT Modernization	151	45	....
1700	Collected - Altmeyer	47	....	....
1700	Collected - AIF/ITS	42	....	....
1700	Collected - Reimbursables	80	70	69
1700	Collected - OIG Transfer 21/22	9	....	....
1700	Collected - NSC	20	....	....
1700	Collected - OIG Transfer 22/23	3	11	....
1700	Collected - PI Adjustment (22/23)	....	1,291	....
1700	Collected - OHO Hearings Backlog (22/23)	....	50	....
1700	Collected - PI Adjustment 23/24	....	....	1,496
1700	Collected - OIG PI Transfer (23/24)	....	....	15
1701	Change in uncollected payments, Federal sources	1,713	....	....
1750	Spending auth from offsetting collections, disc (total)	13,048	13,001	14,842
	Spending authority from offsetting collections, mandatory:			
1800	Collected	....	6	6
1801	Change in uncollected payments, Federal sources	....	–6	–6
1900	Budget authority (total)	13,048	13,001	14,842
1930	Total budgetary resources available	13,846	13,516	15,224
	Memorandum (non-add) entries:			
1940	Unobligated balance expiring	–104	....	....
1941	Unexpired unobligated balance, end of year	402	232	226
	Special and non-revolving trust funds:			
1951	Unobligated balance expiring	104	....	....
1952	Expired unobligated balance, start of year	397	501	501
1953	Expired unobligated balance, end of year	397	501	501
	Change in obligated balance:			
	Unpaid obligations:			
3000	Unpaid obligations, brought forward, Oct 1	3,423	3,267	3,724
3010	New obligations, unexpired accounts	13,340	13,284	14,998
3011	Obligations ("upward adjustments"), expired accounts	104	....	....
3020	Outlays (gross)	–13,346	–12,827	–14,481
3040	Recoveries of prior year unpaid obligations, unexpired	–17	....	....
3041	Recoveries of prior year unpaid obligations, expired	–237	....	....
3050	Unpaid obligations, end of year	3,267	3,724	4,241
	Uncollected payments:			
3060	Uncollected pymts, Fed sources, brought forward, Oct 1	–4,412	–4,081	–4,075
3070	Change in uncollected pymts, Fed sources, unexpired	–1,713	6	6
3071	Change in uncollected pymts, Fed sources, expired	2,044	....	....
3090	Uncollected pymts, Fed sources, end of year	–4,081	–4,075	–4,069
	Memorandum (non-add) entries:			
3100	Obligated balance, start of year	–989	–814	–351
3200	Obligated balance, end of year	–814	–351	172
	Budget authority and outlays, net:			
	Discretionary:			
4000	Budget authority, gross	13,048	13,001	14,842
	Outlays, gross:			
4010	Outlays from new discretionary authority	10,518	10,433	11,928
4011	Outlays from discretionary balances	2,828	2,388	2,553
4020	Outlays, gross (total)	13,346	12,821	14,481
	Offsets against gross budget authority and outlays:			
	Offsetting collections (collected) from:			
4030	Federal sources - LAE Direct	–11,257	–11,261	–12,974
4030	Federal sources - NCC Replacement	–3	....	....
4030	Federal sources - Program Integrity Base	–273	–273	–288
4030	Federal sources - Reimbursable	–80	–70	–69
4030	Federal sources - Program Integrity Allocation Adjustment 21/22	–1,105	....	....
4030	Federal sources - Altmeyer Renovations	–47	....	....
4030	Federal sources - PI Additional 20/21	–241	....	....
4030	Federal sources - OIG Transfer 20/21	–1	....	....
4030	Federal sources - OHO 20/21	–93	....	....
4030	Federal sources - IT Modernization	–151	–45	....
4030	Federal sources - Rebate 20/21	–6	....	....
4030	Federal sources - COVID Response 20/21	–30	....	....
4030	Federal sources - OHO 21/22	–20	....	....
4030	Federal sources - OIG Transfer 21/22	–9	....	....
4030	Federal sources - OIG Transfer 22/23	....	–11	....
4030	Federal sources - OHO 17/18	–19	....	....
4030	Federal sources - OHO 18/19	–2	....	....
4030	Federal sources - OHO Hearings Backlog 22/23	....	–50	....
4030	Federal sources - PI Additional 22/23	....	–1,291	....
4030	Federal sources - PI Additional 23/24	....	....	–1,496

		2021 actual	2022 est.	2023 est.
4030	Federal sources - OIG PI Transfer 23/24	....	....	−15
4033	Non-Federal sources	−128	....	....
4040	Offsets against gross budget authority and outlays (total)	−13,465	−13,001	−14,842
	Additional offsets against gross budget authority only:			
4050	Change in uncollected pymts, Fed sources, unexpired	−1,713	....	....
4052	Offsetting collections credited to expired accounts	2,126	....	....
4053	Recoveries of prior year paid obligations, unexpired accounts	4	....	....
4060	Additional offsets against budget authority only (total)	417	....	....
4080	Outlays, net (discretionary)	−119	−180	−361
	Mandatory:			
	Outlays, gross:			
4101	Outlays from mandatory balances	....	6	....
	Offsets against gross budget authority and outlays:			
	Offsetting collections (collected) from:			
4120	Federal sources	−5	−6	−6
	Additional offsets against gross budget authority only:			
4140	Change in uncollected pymts, Fed sources, unexpired	....	6	6
4142	Offsetting collections credited to expired accounts	5	....	....
4150	Additional offsets against budget authority only (total)	5	6	6
4170	Outlays, net (mandatory)	−5	....	−6
4180	Budget authority, net (total)	....	....	....
4190	Outlays, net (total)	−124	−180	−367

The Limitation on Administrative Expenses (LAE) account provides resources for Social Security to administer the Old-Age and Survivors Insurance (OASI) and Disability Insurance (SSDI) programs, the Supplemental Security Income (SSI) program, the Special Benefits for Certain World War II Veterans program, and certain health insurance functions for the aged and disabled. Public Law 114–10 prohibits displaying, coding, or embedding Social Security numbers on a beneficiary's Medicare card. In order to fund implementation costs to comply with this provision, SSA received $98 million funded incrementally from FY 2015 to FY 2018. The account also includes funding to improve service delivery and advance equity in SSA programs.

The proposed $1.8 billion in discretionary funding in 2023 for dedicated program integrity activities, including a $1.5 billion allocation adjustment, allows SSA to conduct continuing disability reviews and SSI redeterminations to confirm that participants remain eligible to receive benefits, and it supports anti-fraud cooperative disability investigation (CDI) units and Special Assistant U.S. Fraud Attorneys. To continue to support these important anti-fraud activities, the appropriations language provides for SSA to transfer up to $15.1 million to the SSA Office of the Inspector General to fund CDI unit costs.

Object Classification (in millions of dollars)

Identification code 028–8704–0–7–651	2021 actual	2022 est.	2023 est.
Direct obligations:			
Personnel compensation:			
11.1 Full-time permanent	4,969	5,103	5,554
11.3 Other than full-time permanent	91	74	83
11.5 Other personnel compensation	210	93	368
11.8 Special personal services payments	2	2	2
11.9 Total personnel compensation	5,272	5,272	6,007
12.1 Civilian personnel benefits	1,981	2,111	2,310
13.0 Benefits for former personnel	3	3	3
21.0 Travel and transportation of persons	5	3	3
22.0 Transportation of things	10	6	7
23.1 Rental payments to GSA	713	748	751
23.2 Rental payments to others	....	1	....
23.3 Communications, utilities, and miscellaneous charges	417	427	450
24.0 Printing and reproduction	35	21	21
25.1 Advisory and assistance services	119	98	120
25.2 Other services from non-Federal sources	2,704	2,790	3,065
25.3 Other goods and services from Federal sources	456	314	341
25.4 Operation and maintenance of facilities	69	44	44
25.7 Operation and maintenance of equipment	998	989	1,329
26.0 Supplies and materials	30	18	18
31.0 Equipment	229	231	313
32.0 Land and structures	108	69	70
41.0 Grants, subsidies, and contributions	54	34	35
42.0 Insurance claims and indemnities	46	29	29
94.0 Financial transfers	11	....	7
99.0 Direct obligations	13,260	13,208	14,923
99.0 Reimbursable obligations	80	76	75
99.9 Total new obligations, unexpired accounts	13,340	13,284	14,998

Employment Summary

Identification code 028–8704–0–7–651	2021 actual	2022 est.	2023 est.
1001 Direct civilian full-time equivalent employment	59,190	58,040	59,058
2001 Reimbursable civilian full-time equivalent employment	212	358	358

GENERAL FUND RECEIPT ACCOUNTS

(in millions of dollars)

	2021 actual	2022 est.	2023 est.
Offsetting receipts from the public:			
028–241700 SSI, Attorney Fees	7	8	8
028–309600 Recovery of Beneficiary Overpayments from SSI Program	2,236	2,778	2,881
075–241800 Receipts from SSI Administrative Fee	84	89	81
General Fund Offsetting receipts from the public	2,327	2,875	2,970

COMMISSIONER'S BUDGET

As directed by Section 104 of Public Law 103–296, the Social Security Independence and Program Improvements Act of 1994, the Commissioner of Social Security shall prepare an annual budget for SSA, which shall be submitted by the President to the Congress without revision, together with the President's request for SSA. The Commissioner's budget includes $15,550 million for total administrative discretionary resources in 2023. This represents $15,353 million for SSA administrative expenses including State supplemental fees, $79 million in research, and $118 million for the Office of the Inspector General.

OTHER INDEPENDENT AGENCIES

400 YEARS OF AFRICAN-AMERICAN HISTORY COMMISSION

Federal Funds

400 YEARS OF AFRICAN-AMERICAN HISTORY COMMISSION

Program and Financing (in millions of dollars)

Identification code 247–5721–0–2–801	2021 actual	2022 est.	2023 est.
Obligations by program activity:			
0001 Direct program activity	2	3	3
0900 Total new obligations, unexpired accounts (object class 41.0)	2	3	3
Budgetary resources:			
Budget authority:			
Appropriations, discretionary:			
1121 Appropriations transferred from other acct [014–1036]	3	3	3
1900 Budget authority (total)	3	3	3
1930 Total budgetary resources available	3	3	3
Memorandum (non-add) entries:			
1940 Unobligated balance expiring	–1		
Special and non-revolving trust funds:			
1951 Unobligated balance expiring	1		
1952 Expired unobligated balance, start of year		1	1
1953 Expired unobligated balance, end of year		1	1
Change in obligated balance:			
Unpaid obligations:			
3000 Unpaid obligations, brought forward, Oct 1	2	2	2
3010 New obligations, unexpired accounts	2	3	3
3020 Outlays (gross)	–2	–3	–3
3050 Unpaid obligations, end of year	2	2	2
Memorandum (non-add) entries:			
3100 Obligated balance, start of year	2	2	2
3200 Obligated balance, end of year	2	2	2
Budget authority and outlays, net:			
Discretionary:			
4000 Budget authority, gross	3	3	3
Outlays, gross:			
4010 Outlays from new discretionary authority	1	1	1
4011 Outlays from discretionary balances			2
4020 Outlays, gross (total)	1	1	3
Mandatory:			
Outlays, gross:			
4101 Outlays from mandatory balances	1	2	
4180 Budget authority, net (total)	3	3	3
4190 Outlays, net (total)	2	3	3

The Commission was established in the 400 Years of African-American History Commission Act to coordinate the 400th anniversary of the arrival of the first enslaved Africans in the English colonies. The Commission's purpose is to plan, develop, and carry out programs and activities throughout the United States that recognize and highlight the resilience and cultural contributions of Africans and African Americans over 400 years; acknowledge the impact that slavery and laws that enforced racial discrimination had on the United States; encourage civic, patriotic, historical, educational, artistic, religious, and economic organizations to organize and take part in anniversary activities; assist states, localities, and nonprofit organizations to further the commemoration; and coordinate public scholarly research about the arrival of Africans and their contributions to the United States.

ACCESS BOARD

Federal Funds

SALARIES AND EXPENSES

For expenses necessary for the Access Board, as authorized by section 502 of the Rehabilitation Act of 1973 (29 U.S.C. 792), $9,850,000: Provided, That, notwithstanding any other provision of law, there may be credited to this appropriation funds received for publications and training expenses.

Note.—A full-year 2022 appropriation for this account was not enacted at the time the Budget was prepared; therefore, the Budget assumes this account is operating under the Continuing Appropriations Act, 2022 (Division A of Public Law 117–43, as amended). The amounts included for 2022 reflect the annualized level provided by the continuing resolution.

Program and Financing (in millions of dollars)

Identification code 310–3200–0–1–751	2021 actual	2022 est.	2023 est.
Obligations by program activity:			
0001 Salaries and expenses	9	9	10
Budgetary resources:			
Budget authority:			
Appropriations, discretionary:			
1100 Appropriation	9	9	10
1930 Total budgetary resources available	9	9	10
Change in obligated balance:			
Unpaid obligations:			
3000 Unpaid obligations, brought forward, Oct 1	3	3	3
3010 New obligations, unexpired accounts	9	9	10
3020 Outlays (gross)	–9	–9	–10
3050 Unpaid obligations, end of year	3	3	3
Memorandum (non-add) entries:			
3100 Obligated balance, start of year	3	3	3
3200 Obligated balance, end of year	3	3	3
Budget authority and outlays, net:			
Discretionary:			
4000 Budget authority, gross	9	9	10
Outlays, gross:			
4010 Outlays from new discretionary authority	6	6	7
4011 Outlays from discretionary balances	3	3	3
4020 Outlays, gross (total)	9	9	10
4180 Budget authority, net (total)	9	9	10
4190 Outlays, net (total)	9	9	10

The Architectural and Transportation Barriers Compliance Board (Access Board) was established by section 502 of the Rehabilitation Act of 1973. The Access Board is responsible for developing guidelines under the Americans with Disabilities Act, the Architectural Barriers Act, and the Telecommunications Act. These guidelines ensure that buildings and facilities, transportation vehicles, and telecommunications equipment covered by these laws are readily accessible to and usable by people with disabilities. The Board is also responsible for developing standards under section 508 of the Rehabilitation Act for accessible electronic and information technology used by Federal agencies and standards under section 510 of the Rehabilitation Act for accessible medical diagnostic equipment. In addition, the Access Board enforces the Architectural Barriers Act, and provides training and technical assistance on the guidelines and standards it develops.

The Board also has additional responsibilities under the Help America Vote Act. The Board serves on the Board of Advisors and the Technical Guidelines Development Committee, which helps the Election Assistance Commission develop voluntary guidelines and guidance for voting systems, including accessibility for people with disabilities.

Object Classification (in millions of dollars)

Identification code 310–3200–0–1–751	2021 actual	2022 est.	2023 est.
Direct obligations:			
11.1 Personnel compensation: Full-time permanent	4	4	4
12.1 Civilian personnel benefits	1	1	1
23.1 Rental payments to GSA	1	1	1
25.1 Advisory and assistance services	1	1	2
25.3 Other goods and services from Federal sources	1	1	1
25.7 Operation and maintenance of equipment	1	1	1
99.9 Total new obligations, unexpired accounts	9	9	10

1215

Access Board—Continued
Federal Funds—Continued

SALARIES AND EXPENSES—Continued

Employment Summary

Identification code 310–3200–0–1–751	2021 actual	2022 est.	2023 est.
1001 Direct civilian full-time equivalent employment	29	32	32

ADMINISTRATIVE CONFERENCE OF THE UNITED STATES

Federal Funds

SALARIES AND EXPENSES

For necessary expenses of the Administrative Conference of the United States, authorized by 5 U.S.C. 591 et seq., $3,465,000, to remain available until September 30, 2024, of which not to exceed $1,000 is for official reception and representation expenses.

Note.—A full-year 2022 appropriation for this account was not enacted at the time the Budget was prepared; therefore, the Budget assumes this account is operating under the Continuing Appropriations Act, 2022 (Division A of Public Law 117–43, as amended). The amounts included for 2022 reflect the annualized level provided by the continuing resolution.

Program and Financing (in millions of dollars)

Identification code 302–1700–0–1–751	2021 actual	2022 est.	2023 est.
Obligations by program activity:			
0001 Salaries and Expenses (Direct)	3	3	3
Budgetary resources:			
Budget authority:			
Appropriations, discretionary:			
1100 Appropriation	3	3	3
1930 Total budgetary resources available	3	3	3
Change in obligated balance:			
Unpaid obligations:			
3010 New obligations, unexpired accounts	3	3	3
3020 Outlays (gross)	–3	–3	–3
Budget authority and outlays, net:			
Discretionary:			
4000 Budget authority, gross	3	3	3
Outlays, gross:			
4010 Outlays from new discretionary authority	3	2	2
4011 Outlays from discretionary balances		1	1
4020 Outlays, gross (total)	3	3	3
4180 Budget authority, net (total)	3	3	3
4190 Outlays, net (total)	3	3	3

The Administrative Conference of the United States is an independent agency that assists the President, the Congress, the Judicial Conference, and Federal agencies in improving the regulatory and legal process through consensus-driven applied research. The Conference analyzes the administrative law process and, among its many activities, issues formal recommendations for improvements that reduce costs to government agencies, promote effective public participation in the rulemaking process, and reduce unnecessary litigation. The Conference is a public-private partnership comprised of senior government officials and private sector leaders in law, business, and academia.

Object Classification (in millions of dollars)

Identification code 302–1700–0–1–751	2021 actual	2022 est.	2023 est.
Direct obligations:			
11.1 Personnel compensation: Full-time permanent	2	2	2
25.1 Advisory and assistance services	1	1	1
99.0 Direct obligations	3	3	3
99.9 Total new obligations, unexpired accounts	3	3	3

Employment Summary

Identification code 302–1700–0–1–751	2021 actual	2022 est.	2023 est.
1001 Direct civilian full-time equivalent employment	14	14	14

ADVISORY COUNCIL ON HISTORIC PRESERVATION

Federal Funds

SALARIES AND EXPENSES

For necessary expenses of the Advisory Council on Historic Preservation (Public Law 89–665), $8,585,000.

Note.—A full-year 2022 appropriation for this account was not enacted at the time the Budget was prepared; therefore, the Budget assumes this account is operating under the Continuing Appropriations Act, 2022 (Division A of Public Law 117–43, as amended). The amounts included for 2022 reflect the annualized level provided by the continuing resolution.

Program and Financing (in millions of dollars)

Identification code 306–2300–0–1–303	2021 actual	2022 est.	2023 est.
Obligations by program activity:			
0001 Salaries and Expenses (Direct)	7	8	9
0801 Salaries and Expenses (Reimbursable)	2	2	2
0900 Total new obligations, unexpired accounts	9	10	11
Budgetary resources:			
Unobligated balance:			
1000 Unobligated balance brought forward, Oct 1	1		
1001 Discretionary unobligated balance brought fwd, Oct 1	1		
Budget authority:			
Appropriations, discretionary:			
1100 Appropriation	7	8	9
Spending authority from offsetting collections, discretionary:			
1700 Collected	1	1	1
1701 Change in uncollected payments, Federal sources		1	1
1750 Spending auth from offsetting collections, disc (total)	1	2	2
1900 Budget authority (total)	8	10	11
1930 Total budgetary resources available	9	10	11
Change in obligated balance:			
Unpaid obligations:			
3000 Unpaid obligations, brought forward, Oct 1	1	1	
3010 New obligations, unexpired accounts	9	10	11
3020 Outlays (gross)	–9	–11	–11
3050 Unpaid obligations, end of year	1		
Uncollected payments:			
3060 Uncollected pymts, Fed sources, brought forward, Oct 1	–1	–1	–2
3070 Change in uncollected pymts, Fed sources, unexpired		–1	–1
3090 Uncollected pymts, Fed sources, end of year	–1	–2	–3
Memorandum (non-add) entries:			
3100 Obligated balance, start of year			–2
3200 Obligated balance, end of year		–2	–3
Budget authority and outlays, net:			
Discretionary:			
4000 Budget authority, gross	8	10	11
Outlays, gross:			
4010 Outlays from new discretionary authority	7	10	11
4011 Outlays from discretionary balances	2	1	
4020 Outlays, gross (total)	9	11	11
Offsets against gross budget authority and outlays:			
Offsetting collections (collected) from:			
4030 Federal sources	–1	–1	–1
Additional offsets against gross budget authority only:			
4050 Change in uncollected pymts, Fed sources, unexpired		–1	–1
4070 Budget authority, net (discretionary)	7	8	9
4080 Outlays, net (discretionary)	8	10	10
4180 Budget authority, net (total)	7	8	9
4190 Outlays, net (total)	8	10	10

The Council advises the President and the Congress on national historic preservation policy and promotes the preservation, enhancement, and productive use of our Nation's historic resources.

Object Classification (in millions of dollars)

Identification code 306–2300–0–1–303		2021 actual	2022 est.	2023 est.
	Direct obligations:			
11.1	Personnel compensation: Full-time permanent	4	5	6
12.1	Civilian personnel benefits	1	1	1
23.2	Rental payments to others	1	1	1
25.3	Other goods and services from Federal sources	1	1	1
99.0	Direct obligations	7	8	9
99.0	Reimbursable obligations	1	1	1
99.5	Adjustment for rounding	1	1	1
99.9	Total new obligations, unexpired accounts	9	10	11

Employment Summary

Identification code 306–2300–0–1–303		2021 actual	2022 est.	2023 est.
1001	Direct civilian full-time equivalent employment	35	38	39
2001	Reimbursable civilian full-time equivalent employment	7	7	7

ALYCE SPOTTED BEAR AND WALTER SOBOLEFF COMMISSION ON NATIVE CHILDREN

Federal Funds

ALYCE SPOTTED BEAR AND WALTER SOBOLEFF COMMISSION ON NATIVE CHILDREN

Program and Financing (in millions of dollars)

Identification code 545–2987–0–1–506		2021 actual	2022 est.	2023 est.
	Obligations by program activity:			
0001	Direct program activity	1	1	1
0900	Total new obligations, unexpired accounts (object class 25.2)	1	1	1
	Budgetary resources:			
	Unobligated balance:			
1000	Unobligated balance brought forward, Oct 1	1	1	1
	Budget authority:			
	Appropriations, discretionary:			
1100	Appropriation	1	1	
1930	Total budgetary resources available	2	2	1
	Memorandum (non-add) entries:			
1941	Unexpired unobligated balance, end of year	1	1	
	Change in obligated balance:			
	Unpaid obligations:			
3000	Unpaid obligations, brought forward, Oct 1		1	1
3010	New obligations, unexpired accounts	1	1	1
3020	Outlays (gross)		–1	–1
3050	Unpaid obligations, end of year	1	1	1
	Memorandum (non-add) entries:			
3100	Obligated balance, start of year		1	1
3200	Obligated balance, end of year	1	1	1
	Budget authority and outlays, net:			
	Discretionary:			
4000	Budget authority, gross	1	1	
	Outlays, gross:			
4011	Outlays from discretionary balances		1	1
4180	Budget authority, net (total)	1	1	
4190	Outlays, net (total)		1	1

The Alyce Spotted Bear and Walter Soboleff Commission on Native Children was established by Public Law 114–244 to conduct a comprehensive study of Federal, State, local and tribal programs that serve Native children, and to make recommendations on ways those programs can be improved. The Commission receives support from Federal agencies, including the Department of the Interior, and will utilize available resources for its ongoing activities.

APPALACHIAN REGIONAL COMMISSION

Federal Funds

APPALACHIAN REGIONAL COMMISSION

For expenses necessary to carry out the programs authorized by the Appalachian Regional Development Act of 1965, as amended, and for expenses necessary for the Federal Co-Chairman and the Alternate on the Appalachian Regional Commission, for payment of the Federal share of the administrative expenses of the Commission, including services as authorized by 5 U.S.C. 3109, and hire of passenger motor vehicles, $235,000,000, to remain available until expended.

Note.—A full-year 2022 appropriation for this account was not enacted at the time the Budget was prepared; therefore, the Budget assumes this account is operating under the Continuing Appropriations Act, 2022 (Division A of Public Law 117–43, as amended). The amounts included for 2022 reflect the annualized level provided by the continuing resolution.

APPALACHIAN REGIONAL COMMISSION

[For an additional amount for "Appalachian Regional Commission", $1,000,000,000, to remain available until expended, notwithstanding 40 U.S.C. 14704: *Provided*, That of the funds in the preceding proviso, $200,000,000, to remain available until expended, shall be made available for fiscal year 2022, $200,000,000, to remain available until expended, shall be made available for fiscal year 2023, $200,000,000, to remain available until expended, shall be made available for fiscal year 2024, $200,000,000, to remain available until expended, shall be made available for fiscal year 2025, and $200,000,000, to remain available until expended, shall be made available for fiscal year 2026: *Provided further*, That such amount is designated by the Congress as being for an emergency requirement pursuant to section 4112(a) of H. Con. Res. 71 (115th Congress), the concurrent resolution on the budget for fiscal year 2018, and to section 251(b) of the Balanced Budget and Emergency Deficit Control Act of 1985.] *(Infrastructure Investments and Jobs Appropriations Act.)*

Program and Financing (in millions of dollars)

Identification code 309–0200–0–1–452		2021 actual	2022 est.	2023 est.
	Obligations by program activity:			
0102	Area development and technical assistance program	164	354	424
0103	Local development districts program	7	7	9
0191	Total Appalachian regional development programs	171	361	433
0201	Federal co-chairman and staff	1	1	1
0202	Administrative expenses	5	5	8
0203	Programmatic Salaries and Expenses	4	4	5
0291	Total salaries and expenses	10	10	14
0799	Total direct obligations	181	371	447
0801	Reimbursable program activity	3	3	4
0900	Total new obligations, unexpired accounts	184	374	451
	Budgetary resources:			
	Unobligated balance:			
1000	Unobligated balance brought forward, Oct 1	102	121	145
1001	Discretionary unobligated balance brought fwd, Oct 1	101		
1021	Recoveries of prior year unpaid obligations	19	13	13
1070	Unobligated balance (total)	121	134	158
	Budget authority:			
	Appropriations, discretionary:			
1100	Appropriation	180	180	235
1100	Appropriation (IIJA)		200	
1160	Appropriation, discretionary (total)	180	380	235
	Advance appropriations, discretionary:			
1170	Advance appropriation			200
	Spending authority from offsetting collections, discretionary:			
1700	Collected	1	1	1
	Spending authority from offsetting collections, mandatory:			
1800	Collected	3	4	4
1900	Budget authority (total)	184	385	440
1930	Total budgetary resources available	305	519	598
	Memorandum (non-add) entries:			
1941	Unexpired unobligated balance, end of year	121	145	147
	Change in obligated balance:			
	Unpaid obligations:			
3000	Unpaid obligations, brought forward, Oct 1	372	409	520
3010	New obligations, unexpired accounts	184	374	451
3020	Outlays (gross)	–128	–250	–372
3040	Recoveries of prior year unpaid obligations, unexpired	–19	–13	–13
3050	Unpaid obligations, end of year	409	520	586

APPALACHIAN REGIONAL COMMISSION—Continued
Program and Financing—Continued

Identification code 309–0200–0–1–452		2021 actual	2022 est.	2023 est.
	Memorandum (non-add) entries:			
3100	Obligated balance, start of year	372	409	520
3200	Obligated balance, end of year	409	520	586
	Budget authority and outlays, net:			
	Discretionary:			
4000	Budget authority, gross	181	381	436
	Outlays, gross:			
4010	Outlays from new discretionary authority	25	126	144
4011	Outlays from discretionary balances	100	120	224
4020	Outlays, gross (total)	125	246	368
	Offsets against gross budget authority and outlays:			
	Offsetting collections (collected) from:			
4030	Federal sources	–1	–1	–1
4040	Offsets against gross budget authority and outlays (total)	–1	–1	–1
	Mandatory:			
4090	Budget authority, gross	3	4	4
	Outlays, gross:			
4100	Outlays from new mandatory authority	3	4	4
	Offsets against gross budget authority and outlays:			
	Offsetting collections (collected) from:			
4123	Non-Federal sources	–3	–4	–4
4180	Budget authority, net (total)	180	380	435
4190	Outlays, net (total)	124	245	367

The Budget provides $235 million for Appalachian Regional Commission (ARC), which was established as a Federal-State partnership in 1965 to invest in sustainable economic development in the 423-county Appalachian Region. The Commission is comprised of 13 members representing the States in the region and a Federal Co-Chair, who represents the Federal Government. ARC's mission is to help the Appalachian Region plan and coordinate regional investments and target resources to those communities with the greatest needs by innovating, partnering, and investing to build community capacity and strengthening economic growth. ARC's activities include area development, technical assistance, capacity-building, research, and coordination of regional investments and initiatives. In addition, ARC administers the POWER (Partnerships for Opportunity and Workforce and Economic Revitalization) Initiative, a competitive grant program for communities adversely impacted by the declining use of coal to develop economic diversification activities in emerging opportunity sectors.

Object Classification (in millions of dollars)

Identification code 309–0200–0–1–452		2021 actual	2022 est.	2023 est.
	Direct obligations:			
11.1	Personnel compensation: Full-time permanent	1	1	1
25.2	Other services from non-Federal sources	9	9	13
41.0	Grants, subsidies, and contributions	171	361	433
99.0	Direct obligations	181	371	447
99.0	Reimbursable obligations	3	3	4
99.9	Total new obligations, unexpired accounts	184	374	451

Employment Summary

Identification code 309–0200–0–1–452		2021 actual	2022 est.	2023 est.
1001	Direct civilian full-time equivalent employment	5	7	7

BARRY GOLDWATER SCHOLARSHIP AND EXCELLENCE IN EDUCATION FOUNDATION

Trust Funds

BARRY GOLDWATER SCHOLARSHIP AND EXCELLENCE IN EDUCATION FOUNDATION

Special and Trust Fund Receipts (in millions of dollars)

Identification code 313–8281–0–7–502		2021 actual	2022 est.	2023 est.
0100	Balance, start of year	40	40	40
	Receipts:			
	Current law:			
1140	Interest on Investments, Barry Goldwater Scholarship and Excellence in Education Foundation	2	2	2
2000	Total: Balances and receipts	42	42	42
	Appropriations:			
	Current law:			
2101	Barry Goldwater Scholarship and Excellence in Education Foundation	–2	–2	–2
5099	Balance, end of year	40	40	40

Program and Financing (in millions of dollars)

Identification code 313–8281–0–7–502		2021 actual	2022 est.	2023 est.
	Obligations by program activity:			
0001	Barry Goldwater Scholarship and Excellence in Education Foundation	1	2	2
0002	Scholarship Grant Funding	2	2	2
0900	Total new obligations, unexpired accounts	3	4	4
	Budgetary resources:			
	Unobligated balance:			
1000	Unobligated balance brought forward, Oct 1	35	34	32
	Budget authority:			
	Appropriations, mandatory:			
1201	Appropriation (special or trust fund)	2	2	2
1900	Budget authority (total)	2	2	2
1930	Total budgetary resources available	37	36	34
	Memorandum (non-add) entries:			
1941	Unexpired unobligated balance, end of year	34	32	30
	Change in obligated balance:			
	Unpaid obligations:			
3000	Unpaid obligations, brought forward, Oct 1	1	....	2
3010	New obligations, unexpired accounts	3	4	4
3020	Outlays (gross)	–4	–2	–2
3050	Unpaid obligations, end of year	....	2	4
	Memorandum (non-add) entries:			
3100	Obligated balance, start of year	1	....	2
3200	Obligated balance, end of year	....	2	4
	Budget authority and outlays, net:			
	Mandatory:			
4090	Budget authority, gross	2	2	2
	Outlays, gross:			
4100	Outlays from new mandatory authority	2	2	2
4101	Outlays from mandatory balances	2	....	....
4110	Outlays, gross (total)	4	2	2
4180	Budget authority, net (total)	2	2	2
4190	Outlays, net (total)	4	2	2
	Memorandum (non-add) entries:			
5000	Total investments, SOY: Federal securities: Par value	70	30	30
5001	Total investments, EOY: Federal securities: Par value	30	30	30

Public Law 99–661 established the Barry Goldwater Scholarship and Excellence in Education Foundation to operate the scholarship program that is a significant permanent tribute to the late Senator from Arizona. The Foundation awards scholarships to outstanding undergraduate students who intend to pursue research careers in mathematics, the natural sciences and engineering. The Foundation supports between 250 and 500 scholarships annually.

Object Classification (in millions of dollars)

Identification code 313–8281–0–7–502		2021 actual	2022 est.	2023 est.
41.0	Direct obligations: Grants, subsidies, and contributions	1	2	2
99.0	Reimbursable obligations	2	2	2
99.9	Total new obligations, unexpired accounts	3	4	4

Employment Summary

Identification code 313–8281–0–7–502		2021 actual	2022 est.	2023 est.
1001	Direct civilian full-time equivalent employment	2	2	2

BUREAU OF CONSUMER FINANCIAL PROTECTION

Federal Funds

BUREAU OF CONSUMER FINANCIAL PROTECTION FUND

Special and Trust Fund Receipts (in millions of dollars)

Identification code 581–5577–0–2–376		2021 actual	2022 est.	2023 est.
0100	Balance, start of year			39
	Receipts:			
	Current law:			
1110	Transfers from the Federal Reserve Board, Bureau of Consumer Financial Protection Fund	596	692	732
2000	Total: Balances and receipts	596	692	771
	Appropriations:			
	Current law:			
2101	Bureau of Consumer Financial Protection Fund	–596	–692	–732
2103	Bureau of Consumer Financial Protection Fund			–39
2132	Bureau of Consumer Financial Protection Fund		39	42
2199	Total current law appropriations	–596	–653	–729
2999	Total appropriations	–596	–653	–729
5099	Balance, end of year		39	42

Program and Financing (in millions of dollars)

Identification code 581–5577–0–2–376		2021 actual	2022 est.	2023 est.
	Obligations by program activity:			
0001	Consumer Financial Protection Bureau	595	689	729
0100	Direct program activities, subtotal	595	689	729
0808	Reimbursable program activity	3	3	3
0809	Reimbursable program activities, subtotal	3	3	3
0900	Total new obligations, unexpired accounts	598	692	732
	Budgetary resources:			
	Unobligated balance:			
1000	Unobligated balance brought forward, Oct 1	75	105	77
1021	Recoveries of prior year unpaid obligations	29	8	8
1070	Unobligated balance (total)	104	113	85
	Budget authority:			
	Appropriations, mandatory:			
1201	Appropriation (special or trust fund)	596	692	732
1203	Appropriation (previously unavailable)(special or trust)			39
1232	Appropriations and/or unobligated balance of appropriations temporarily reduced		–39	–42
1260	Appropriations, mandatory (total)	596	653	729
	Spending authority from offsetting collections, mandatory:			
1800	Collected	3	3	3
1900	Budget authority (total)	599	656	732
1930	Total budgetary resources available	703	769	817
	Memorandum (non-add) entries:			
1941	Unexpired unobligated balance, end of year	105	77	85
	Change in obligated balance:			
	Unpaid obligations:			
3000	Unpaid obligations, brought forward, Oct 1	198	200	283
3010	New obligations, unexpired accounts	598	692	732
3020	Outlays (gross)	–567	–601	–680
3040	Recoveries of prior year unpaid obligations, unexpired	–29	–8	–8
3050	Unpaid obligations, end of year	200	283	327
	Uncollected payments:			
3060	Uncollected pymts, Fed sources, brought forward, Oct 1	–2	–2	–2
3090	Uncollected pymts, Fed sources, end of year	–2	–2	–2
	Memorandum (non-add) entries:			
3100	Obligated balance, start of year	196	198	281
3200	Obligated balance, end of year	198	281	325
	Budget authority and outlays, net:			
	Mandatory:			
4090	Budget authority, gross	599	656	732
	Outlays, gross:			
4100	Outlays from new mandatory authority	296	374	513
4101	Outlays from mandatory balances	271	227	167
4110	Outlays, gross (total)	567	601	680
	Offsets against gross budget authority and outlays:			
	Offsetting collections (collected) from:			
4120	Federal sources	–3	–3	–3
4180	Budget authority, net (total)	596	653	729
4190	Outlays, net (total)	564	598	677
	Memorandum (non-add) entries:			
5000	Total investments, SOY: Federal securities: Par value	246	283	350
5001	Total investments, EOY: Federal securities: Par value	283	350	402

The Consumer Financial Protection Bureau (CFPB or Bureau) was established under Title X of the Dodd-Frank Wall Street Reform and Consumer Protection Act (the Act) (P.L. 111–203) as an independent bureau in the Federal Reserve System. The Act consolidated authorities previously shared by seven Federal agencies under Federal consumer financial laws into the CFPB and provided the Bureau with additional authorities to conduct rulemaking, supervision, and enforcement. Funding required to support the CFPB's operations is obtained primarily through transfers from the Board of Governors of the Federal Reserve System. Pursuant to the Act, the CFPB is also authorized to collect civil penalties in any judicial or administrative action under Federal consumer financial laws. These amounts are maintained and displayed in a separate account titled "Consumer Financial Civil Penalty Fund."

Object Classification (in millions of dollars)

Identification code 581–5577–0–2–376		2021 actual	2022 est.	2023 est.
	Direct obligations:			
11.1	Personnel compensation: Full-time permanent	247	291	315
12.1	Civilian personnel benefits	103	122	129
13.0	Benefits for former personnel	3		
21.0	Travel and transportation of persons		11	11
23.1	Rental payments to GSA	3	3	4
23.3	Communications, utilities, and miscellaneous charges	10	10	10
24.0	Printing and reproduction	4	5	5
25.1	Advisory and assistance services	137	155	156
25.2	Other services from non-Federal sources	9	9	12
25.3	Other goods and services from Federal sources	47	50	51
25.7	Operation and maintenance of equipment	4	5	5
26.0	Supplies and materials	6	6	6
31.0	Equipment	22	22	25
99.0	Direct obligations	595	689	729
99.0	Reimbursable obligations	3	3	3
99.9	Total new obligations, unexpired accounts	598	692	732

Employment Summary

Identification code 581–5577–0–2–376		2021 actual	2022 est.	2023 est.
1001	Direct civilian full-time equivalent employment	1,557	1,650	1,697

CONSUMER FINANCIAL CIVIL PENALTY FUND

Special and Trust Fund Receipts (in millions of dollars)

Identification code 581–5578–0–2–376		2021 actual	2022 est.	2023 est.
0100	Balance, start of year	2	3	

Bureau of Consumer Financial Protection—Continued
Federal Funds—Continued

CONSUMER FINANCIAL CIVIL PENALTY FUND—Continued

Special and Trust Fund Receipts—Continued

Identification code 581–5578–0–2–376	2021 actual	2022 est.	2023 est.
Receipts:			
Current law:			
1110 Penalties and Fines, Consumer Financial Protection	61	6	
2000 Total: Balances and receipts	63	9	
Appropriations:			
Current law:			
2101 Consumer Financial Civil Penalty Fund	–61	–6	
2103 Consumer Financial Civil Penalty Fund	–2	–3	
2132 Consumer Financial Civil Penalty Fund	3		
2199 Total current law appropriations	–60	–9	
2999 Total appropriations	–60	–9	
5099 Balance, end of year	3		

Program and Financing (in millions of dollars)

Identification code 581–5578–0–2–376	2021 actual	2022 est.	2023 est.
Obligations by program activity:			
0001 Civil Penalty Payments	102	159	127
0900 Total new obligations, unexpired accounts (object class 25.2)	102	159	127
Budgetary resources:			
Unobligated balance:			
1000 Unobligated balance brought forward, Oct 1	821	783	641
1033 Recoveries of prior year paid obligations	4	8	
1070 Unobligated balance (total)	825	791	641
Budget authority:			
Appropriations, mandatory:			
1201 Appropriation (special or trust fund)	61	6	
1203 Appropriation (previously unavailable)(special or trust)	2	3	
1232 Appropriations and/or unobligated balance of appropriations temporarily reduced	–3		
1260 Appropriations, mandatory (total)	60	9	
1930 Total budgetary resources available	885	800	641
Memorandum (non-add) entries:			
1941 Unexpired unobligated balance, end of year	783	641	514
Change in obligated balance:			
Unpaid obligations:			
3000 Unpaid obligations, brought forward, Oct 1	2	4	1
3010 New obligations, unexpired accounts	102	159	127
3020 Outlays (gross)	–100	–162	–127
3050 Unpaid obligations, end of year	4	1	1
Memorandum (non-add) entries:			
3100 Obligated balance, start of year	2	4	1
3200 Obligated balance, end of year	4	1	1
Budget authority and outlays, net:			
Mandatory:			
4090 Budget authority, gross	60	9	
Outlays, gross:			
4100 Outlays from new mandatory authority		3	
4101 Outlays from mandatory balances	100	159	127
4110 Outlays, gross (total)	100	162	127
Offsets against gross budget authority and outlays:			
Offsetting collections (collected) from:			
4123 Non-Federal sources	–4	–8	
Additional offsets against gross budget authority only:			
4143 Recoveries of prior year paid obligations, unexpired accounts	4	8	
4160 Budget authority, net (mandatory)	60	9	
4170 Outlays, net (mandatory)	96	154	127
4180 Budget authority, net (total)	60	9	
4190 Outlays, net (total)	96	154	127

Pursuant to Title X of the Dodd-Frank Wall Street Reform and Consumer Protection Act (the Act) (P.L. 111–203), the Consumer Financial Protection Bureau (CFPB or Bureau) is authorized to collect civil penalties obtained in any judicial or administrative action under Federal consumer financial laws. Per the Act, such funds will be available for payments to the victims of activities for which civil penalties have been imposed under the Federal consumer financial laws. Obligations related to victim compensation are contingent upon identifying the specific victims qualifying for payments. To the extent that such victims cannot be located or such payments are otherwise not practicable, the Bureau may use such funds for the purpose of consumer education and financial literacy programs.

CENTRAL INTELLIGENCE AGENCY

Federal Funds

CENTRAL INTELLIGENCE AGENCY RETIREMENT AND DISABILITY SYSTEM FUND

For payment to the Central Intelligence Agency Retirement and Disability System Fund, to maintain the proper funding level for continuing the operation of the Central Intelligence Agency Retirement and Disability System, $514,000,000.

Note.—A full-year 2022 appropriation for this account was not enacted at the time the Budget was prepared; therefore, the Budget assumes this account is operating under the Continuing Appropriations Act, 2022 (Division A of Public Law 117–43, as amended). The amounts included for 2022 reflect the annualized level provided by the continuing resolution.

Program and Financing (in millions of dollars)

Identification code 056–3400–0–1–054	2021 actual	2022 est.	2023 est.
Obligations by program activity:			
0001 Personnel benefits	514	514	514
0900 Total new obligations, unexpired accounts (object class 13.0)	514	514	514
Budgetary resources:			
Budget authority:			
Appropriations, mandatory:			
1200 Appropriation	514	514	514
1930 Total budgetary resources available	514	514	514
Change in obligated balance:			
Unpaid obligations:			
3010 New obligations, unexpired accounts	514	514	514
3020 Outlays (gross)	–514	–514	–514
Budget authority and outlays, net:			
Mandatory:			
4090 Budget authority, gross	514	514	514
Outlays, gross:			
4100 Outlays from new mandatory authority	514	514	514
4180 Budget authority, net (total)	514	514	514
4190 Outlays, net (total)	514	514	514

Independent actuarial projections show the CIARDS Fund with an unfunded liability of $4.3 billion. To ensure that the Fund remains solvent and authorized payments to beneficiaries continue, the Budget proposes $514 million in 2023. This amount reflects the amortized cost of recapitalizing the CIARDS Fund over twenty years.

CHEMICAL SAFETY AND HAZARD INVESTIGATION BOARD

Federal Funds

SALARIES AND EXPENSES

For necessary expenses in carrying out activities pursuant to section 112(r)(6) of the Clean Air Act, including hire of passenger vehicles, uniforms or allowances therefor, as authorized by 5 U.S.C. 5901–5902, and for services authorized by 5 U.S.C. 3109 but at rates for individuals not to exceed the per diem equivalent to the maximum rate payable for senior level positions under 5 U.S.C. 5376, $14,400,000, of which $300,000 shall remain available until expended: Provided, That the Chemical Safety and Hazard Investigation Board (Board) shall have not more than three career Senior Executive Service positions: Provided further, That notwithstanding any other provision of law, the individual appointed to the position of Inspector General of the Environmental Protection Agency (EPA) shall, by virtue of such appointment, also hold the position of Inspector General of the Board: Provided further, That notwithstanding any other provision of law, the Inspector General of the Board shall utilize personnel of the Office of Inspector General of EPA in performing the *duties of the Inspector General of the Board, and shall not appoint any individuals to positions within the Board.*

Note.—A full-year 2022 appropriation for this account was not enacted at the time the Budget was prepared; therefore, the Budget assumes this account is operating under the Continuing Appropriations Act, 2022 (Division A of Public Law 117–43, as amended). The amounts included for 2022 reflect the annualized level provided by the continuing resolution.

Program and Financing (in millions of dollars)

Identification code 510–3850–0–1–304	2021 actual	2022 est.	2023 est.
Obligations by program activity:			
0001 Salaries and Expenses (Direct)	11	13	14
Budgetary resources:			
Unobligated balance:			
1000 Unobligated balance brought forward, Oct 1	1	1	
Budget authority:			
Appropriations, discretionary:			
1100 Appropriation	12	12	14
1930 Total budgetary resources available	13	13	14
Memorandum (non-add) entries:			
1940 Unobligated balance expiring	–1		
1941 Unexpired unobligated balance, end of year	1		
Change in obligated balance:			
Unpaid obligations:			
3000 Unpaid obligations, brought forward, Oct 1	2	3	3
3010 New obligations, unexpired accounts	11	13	14
3020 Outlays (gross)	–10	–13	–12
3050 Unpaid obligations, end of year	3	3	5
Memorandum (non-add) entries:			
3100 Obligated balance, start of year	2	3	3
3200 Obligated balance, end of year	3	3	5
Budget authority and outlays, net:			
Discretionary:			
4000 Budget authority, gross	12	12	14
Outlays, gross:			
4010 Outlays from new discretionary authority	8	9	10
4011 Outlays from discretionary balances	2	4	2
4020 Outlays, gross (total)	10	13	12
4180 Budget authority, net (total)	12	12	14
4190 Outlays, net (total)	10	13	12

The Chemical Safety and Hazard Investigation Board, as authorized by the Clean Air Act Amendments of 1990, became operational in 1998. It is an independent, non-regulatory agency that promotes chemical safety and accident prevention through investigating chemical accidents; making recommendations for accident prevention; conducting special studies; broadly disseminating its findings to industry and labor organizations; and informing stakeholder discussions on chemical safety and on actions taken by the Environmental Protection Agency, the Department of Labor, and other entities to implement Board recommendations.

Object Classification (in millions of dollars)

Identification code 510–3850–0–1–304	2021 actual	2022 est.	2023 est.
Direct obligations:			
Personnel compensation:			
11.1 Full-time permanent	4	5	6
11.3 Other than full-time permanent		1	1
11.9 Total personnel compensation	4	6	7
12.1 Civilian personnel benefits	2	2	2
23.2 Rental payments to others	1	1	1
25.1 Advisory and assistance services	2	2	2
25.2 Other services from non-Federal sources	1	1	1
25.3 Other goods and services from Federal sources	1	1	1
99.0 Direct obligations	11	13	14
99.9 Total new obligations, unexpired accounts	11	13	14

Employment Summary

Identification code 510–3850–0–1–304	2021 actual	2022 est.	2023 est.
1001 Direct civilian full-time equivalent employment	32	46	63

COMMISSION OF FINE ARTS

Federal Funds

SALARIES AND EXPENSES

For expenses of the Commission of Fine Arts under chapter 91 of title 40, United States Code, $3,661,000: Provided, That the Commission is authorized to charge fees to cover the full costs of its publications, and such fees shall be credited to this account as an offsetting collection, to remain available until expended without further appropriation: Provided further, That the Commission is authorized to accept gifts, including objects, papers, artwork, drawings and artifacts, that pertain to the history and design of the Nation's Capital or the history and activities of the Commission of Fine Arts, for the purpose of artistic display, study, or education: Provided further, That one-tenth of one percent of the funds provided under this heading may be used for official reception and representation expenses.

Note.—A full-year 2022 appropriation for this account was not enacted at the time the Budget was prepared; therefore, the Budget assumes this account is operating under the Continuing Appropriations Act, 2022 (Division A of Public Law 117–43, as amended). The amounts included for 2022 reflect the annualized level provided by the continuing resolution.

Program and Financing (in millions of dollars)

Identification code 323–2600–0–1–451	2021 actual	2022 est.	2023 est.
Obligations by program activity:			
0001 Salaries and Expenses (Direct)	3	3	4
Budgetary resources:			
Budget authority:			
Appropriations, discretionary:			
1100 Appropriation	3	3	4
1930 Total budgetary resources available	3	3	4
Change in obligated balance:			
Unpaid obligations:			
3010 New obligations, unexpired accounts	3	3	4
3020 Outlays (gross)	–3	–3	–4
Budget authority and outlays, net:			
Discretionary:			
4000 Budget authority, gross	3	3	4
Outlays, gross:			
4010 Outlays from new discretionary authority	3	3	4
4180 Budget authority, net (total)	3	3	4
4190 Outlays, net (total)	3	3	4

The Commission advises the President, the Congress, and Department heads on matters of architecture, sculpture, landscape, and other fine arts. Its primary function is to preserve and enhance the appearance of the Nation's Capital.

Object Classification (in millions of dollars)

Identification code 323–2600–0–1–451	2021 actual	2022 est.	2023 est.
Direct obligations:			
11.1 Personnel compensation: Full-time permanent	1	1	2
12.1 Civilian personnel benefits	1	1	1
99.0 Direct obligations	2	2	3
99.5 Adjustment for rounding	1	1	1
99.9 Total new obligations, unexpired accounts	3	3	4

Employment Summary

Identification code 323–2600–0–1–451	2021 actual	2022 est.	2023 est.
1001 Direct civilian full-time equivalent employment	12	12	14

NATIONAL CAPITAL ARTS AND CULTURAL AFFAIRS

For necessary expenses as authorized by Public Law 99–190 (20 U.S.C. 956a), $5,000,000: Provided, That the item relating to "National Capital Arts and Cultural Affairs" in the Department of the Interior and Related Agencies Appropriations Act, 1986, as enacted into law by section 101(d) of Public Law 99–190 (20 U.S.C. 956a), shall be applied in fiscal year 2022 in the second paragraph by inserting ", calendar year 2020 excluded" before the first period: Provided further, That in determining an eligible organization's annual income for calendar years 2022 and 2023, funds or grants received by the eligible organization from any supplemental appropriations Act related to coronavirus or any other law providing appropriations for the purpose of preventing, preparing for, or responding to coronavirus shall be counted as part of the eligible organization's annual income.

Note.—A full-year 2022 appropriation for this account was not enacted at the time the Budget was prepared; therefore, the Budget assumes this account is operating under the Continuing Appropriations Act, 2022 (Division A of Public Law 117–43, as amended). The amounts included for 2022 reflect the annualized level provided by the continuing resolution.

Program and Financing (in millions of dollars)

Identification code 323–2602–0–1–503	2021 actual	2022 est.	2023 est.
Obligations by program activity:			
0001 National Capital Arts and Cultural Affairs (Direct)	5	5	5
0900 Total new obligations, unexpired accounts (object class 25.2)	5	5	5
Budgetary resources:			
Budget authority:			
Appropriations, discretionary:			
1100 Appropriation	5	5	5
1930 Total budgetary resources available	5	5	5
Change in obligated balance:			
Unpaid obligations:			
3010 New obligations, unexpired accounts	5	5	5
3020 Outlays (gross)	–5	–5	–5
Budget authority and outlays, net:			
Discretionary:			
4000 Budget authority, gross	5	5	5
Outlays, gross:			
4010 Outlays from new discretionary authority	5	5	5
4180 Budget authority, net (total)	5	5	5
4190 Outlays, net (total)	5	5	5

The Budget includes $5 million for the National Capital Arts and Cultural Affairs grant program which supports larger artistic and cultural institutions operating in the District of Columbia. The Budget maintains the requirement under current law that grantees have annual income, exclusive of Federal funds, of at least $1 million for each of the three years prior to receipt of a grant. However, in order to partly compensate for the economic impacts of the Covid–19 pandemic on eligible applicants, particularly organizations with smaller annual operating budgets that may not otherwise qualify in 2022, and 2023 due to reduced levels of income resulting from mandatory closures and reduced programing, the Budget proposes to exclude 2020 from the grant eligibility calculation for 2022, and 2023.

COMMISSION ON CIVIL RIGHTS

Federal Funds

SALARIES AND EXPENSES

For necessary expenses of the Commission on Civil Rights, including hire of passenger motor vehicles, $13,850,000: Provided, That none of the funds appropriated in this paragraph may be used to employ any individuals under Schedule C of subpart C of part 213 of title 5 of the Code of Federal Regulations exclusive of one special assistant for each Commissioner: Provided further, That none of the funds appropriated in this paragraph shall be used to reimburse Commissioners for more than 75 billable days, with the exception of the chairperson, who is permitted 125 billable days: Provided further, That the Chair may accept and use any gift or donation to carry out the work of the Commission: Provided further, That none of the funds appropriated in this paragraph shall be used for any activity or expense that is not explicitly authorized by section 3 of the Civil Rights Commission Act of 1983 (42 U.S.C. 1975a): Provided further, That notwithstanding the preceding proviso, $1,500,000 shall be used to separately fund the Commission on the Social Status of Black Men and Boys.

Note.—A full-year 2022 appropriation for this account was not enacted at the time the Budget was prepared; therefore, the Budget assumes this account is operating under the Continuing Appropriations Act, 2022 (Division A of Public Law 117–43, as amended). The amounts included for 2022 reflect the annualized level provided by the continuing resolution.

Program and Financing (in millions of dollars)

Identification code 326–1900–0–1–751	2021 actual	2022 est.	2023 est.
Obligations by program activity:			
0001 Salaries and Expenses (Direct)	12	13	14
Budgetary resources:			
Budget authority:			
Appropriations, discretionary:			
1100 Appropriation	13	13	14
1930 Total budgetary resources available	13	13	14
Memorandum (non-add) entries:			
1940 Unobligated balance expiring	–1		
Change in obligated balance:			
Unpaid obligations:			
3000 Unpaid obligations, brought forward, Oct 1	2	3	
3010 New obligations, unexpired accounts	12	13	14
3020 Outlays (gross)	–11	–16	–14
3050 Unpaid obligations, end of year	3		
Memorandum (non-add) entries:			
3100 Obligated balance, start of year	2	3	
3200 Obligated balance, end of year	3		
Budget authority and outlays, net:			
Discretionary:			
4000 Budget authority, gross	13	13	14
Outlays, gross:			
4010 Outlays from new discretionary authority	10	13	14
4011 Outlays from discretionary balances	1	3	
4020 Outlays, gross (total)	11	16	14
4180 Budget authority, net (total)	13	13	14
4190 Outlays, net (total)	11	16	14

Originally established by the Civil Rights Act of 1957, the U.S. Commission on Civil Rights is an independent, bipartisan, fact-finding Federal agency. Its mission is to inform the development of national civil rights policy and enhance enforcement of Federal civil rights laws. The Commission pursues this mission by studying alleged deprivations of voting rights and alleged discrimination based on race, color, religion, sex, age, disability, or national origin, or in the administration of justice. The Commission plays a vital role in advancing civil rights through objective and comprehensive investigation, research, and analysis on issues of fundamental concern to the Federal government and the public. The Commission also supports a network of Advisory Committees, each composed of a diverse group of citizen volunteers, which conduct civil rights research at the State and U.S. Territory levels. The Commission on the Social Status of Black Men and Boys Act established the Commission on the Social Status of Black Men and Boys (CSSBMB) within the U.S. Commission on Civil Rights Office of the Staff Director. The CSSBMB studies and makes recommendation to address social problems affecting black men and boys, and for other purposes.

Object Classification (in millions of dollars)

Identification code 326–1900–0–1–751	2021 actual	2022 est.	2023 est.
Direct obligations:			
11.1 Personnel compensation: Full-time permanent	5	6	7
12.1 Civilian personnel benefits	2	2	2
23.1 Rental payments to GSA	2	2	1
25.2 Other services from non-Federal sources	2	2	3
25.3 Other goods and services from Federal sources	1	1	1
99.9 Total new obligations, unexpired accounts	12	13	14

COMMISSION ON COMBATING SYNTHETIC OPIOID TRAFFICKING

Federal Funds

SALARIES AND EXPENSES

Program and Financing (in millions of dollars)

Identification code 256–1760–0–1–751	2021 actual	2022 est.	2023 est.
Obligations by program activity:			
0001 Operations		4	
0900 Total new obligations, unexpired accounts (object class 25.3)		4	
Budgetary resources:			
Unobligated balance:			
1000 Unobligated balance brought forward, Oct 1	5	1	1
1930 Total budgetary resources available	5	1	1
Memorandum (non-add) entries:			
1941 Unexpired unobligated balance, end of year	1	1	1
Change in obligated balance:			
Unpaid obligations:			
3000 Unpaid obligations, brought forward, Oct 1			4
3010 New obligations, unexpired accounts		4	
3020 Outlays (gross)			–4
3050 Unpaid obligations, end of year		4	
Memorandum (non-add) entries:			
3100 Obligated balance, start of year			4
3200 Obligated balance, end of year		4	
Budget authority and outlays, net:			
Discretionary:			
Outlays, gross:			
4011 Outlays from discretionary balances			4
4180 Budget authority, net (total)			
4190 Outlays, net (total)			4

The National Defense Authorization Act for Fiscal Year 2020 established the Commission on Combating Synthetic Opioid Trafficking. See Section 7221, Sub. B, Tit. LXXII, Div. F, of P.L. 116–92. The Commission has 15 members, seven representing the Executive Branch and eight Congressional appointees. The Commission authorized the Office of National Drug Control Policy to manage the Commission's funds. One of the Commission's key responsibilities is to develop a consensus on a strategic approach to combating the flow of synthetic opioids into the United States, and thereafter, submit a mandated report to Congress.

COMMITTEE FOR PURCHASE FROM PEOPLE WHO ARE BLIND OR SEVERELY DISABLED

Federal Funds

SALARIES AND EXPENSES

For expenses necessary for the Committee for Purchase From People Who Are Blind or Severely Disabled (referred to in this title as "the Committee") established under section 8502 of title 41, United States Code, $13,124,000: Provided, That in order to authorize any central nonprofit agency designated pursuant to section 8503(c) of title 41, United States Code, to perform requirements of the Committee as prescribed under section 51–3.2 of title 41, Code of Federal Regulations, the Committee shall enter into a written agreement with any such central nonprofit agency: Provided further, That such agreement shall contain such auditing, oversight, and reporting provisions as necessary to implement chapter 85 of title 41, United States Code: Provided further, That such agreement shall include the elements listed under the heading "Committee For Purchase From People Who Are Blind or Severely Disabled—Written Agreement Elements" in the explanatory statement described in section 4 of Public Law 114–113 (in the matter preceding division A of that consolidated Act): Provided further, That any such central nonprofit agency may not charge a fee under section 51–3.5 of title 41, Code of Federal Regulations, prior to executing a written agreement with the Committee: Provided further, That no less than $3,124,000 shall be available for the Office of Inspector General.

Note.—A full-year 2022 appropriation for this account was not enacted at the time the Budget was prepared; therefore, the Budget assumes this account is operating under the Continuing Appropriations Act, 2022 (Division A of Public Law 117–43, as amended). The amounts included for 2022 reflect the annualized level provided by the continuing resolution.

Program and Financing (in millions of dollars)

Identification code 338–2000–0–1–505	2021 actual	2022 est.	2023 est.
Obligations by program activity:			
0001 Salaries and Expenses	10	11	13
Budgetary resources:			
Unobligated balance:			
1000 Unobligated balance brought forward, Oct 1	1	1	1
Budget authority:			
Appropriations, discretionary:			
1100 Appropriation	11	11	13
1930 Total budgetary resources available	12	12	14
Memorandum (non-add) entries:			
1940 Unobligated balance expiring	–1		
1941 Unexpired unobligated balance, end of year	1	1	1
Change in obligated balance:			
Unpaid obligations:			
3000 Unpaid obligations, brought forward, Oct 1	2	3	2
3010 New obligations, unexpired accounts	10	11	13
3020 Outlays (gross)	–9	–12	–12
3050 Unpaid obligations, end of year	3	2	3
Memorandum (non-add) entries:			
3100 Obligated balance, start of year	2	3	2
3200 Obligated balance, end of year	3	2	3
Budget authority and outlays, net:			
Discretionary:			
4000 Budget authority, gross	11	11	13
Outlays, gross:			
4010 Outlays from new discretionary authority	8	9	10
4011 Outlays from discretionary balances	1	3	2
4020 Outlays, gross (total)	9	12	12
4180 Budget authority, net (total)	11	11	13
4190 Outlays, net (total)	9	12	12

The Committee for Purchase From People Who Are Blind or Severely Disabled (operating as the U.S. AbilityOne Commission, hereafter "Commission") administers the AbilityOne Program under the authority of the Javits-Wagner-O'Day Act of 1971, as amended. The principal objective of AbilityOne is to leverage the purchasing power of the Federal Government to provide employment opportunities for people who are blind or have other significant disabilities. The Commission accomplishes its mission by identifying Government procurement requirements that can create employment opportunities for individuals who are blind or have other significant disabilities. Following opportunities for public comment and after due deliberation, the Commission then places such products and service requirements on the AbilityOne Procurement List, requiring Federal departments and agencies to procure the designated products and services from a network of approximately 500 qualified State and private nonprofit agencies (NPAs) employing people who are blind or have other significant disabilities. The long-term vision of AbilityOne is to enable people who are blind or have other significant disabilities to achieve their maximum employment potential. In FY 2021, approximately 40,000 AbilityOne employees earned a combined total of $668,592,334 in wages, with an average hourly wage of $15.22. The AbilityOne Program continues to emphasize providing employment to veterans, with more than 2,500 employed in direct labor positions. More than 1,500 AbilityOne employees moved into competitive or supported employment in FY 2021 after gaining skills and experience on AbilityOne jobs.

Employment Summary

Identification code 326–1900–0–1–751	2021 actual	2022 est.	2023 est.
1001 Direct civilian full-time equivalent employment	45	53	60

SALARIES AND EXPENSES—Continued

While pursuing its core mission to increase employment opportunities for people who are blind or have other significant disabilities, the Commission is dedicated to effective stewardship and program integrity. The Commission continues to strengthen its Procurement List business processes and to enhance its oversight of AbilityOne Program participants. The resources proposed for 2023 will enable the Commission to continue implementing the requirements of the Consolidated Appropriations Act of 2016. These requirements include establishing and staffing the Commission and the Office of Inspector General for the AbilityOne Program. The requirements also include establishing and administering written agreements that govern the Commission's relationship with its designated central nonprofit agencies, evaluating reports and data from such central nonprofit agencies, implementing the recommendations of the 898 Panel to enhance stewardship, modernizing our information technology and maintaining the Commission's compliance and operations capacity to oversee a national program with approximately $4 billion in annual sales of products and services to the Government.

Object Classification (in millions of dollars)

Identification code 338–2000–0–1–505	2021 actual	2022 est.	2023 est.
Direct obligations:			
11.1 Personnel compensation: Full-time permanent	5	6	8
12.1 Civilian personnel benefits	1	1	2
25.1 Advisory and assistance services	3	3	2
99.0 Direct obligations	9	10	12
99.5 Adjustment for rounding	1	1	1
99.9 Total new obligations, unexpired accounts	10	11	13

Employment Summary

Identification code 338–2000–0–1–505	2021 actual	2022 est.	2023 est.
1001 Direct civilian full-time equivalent employment	44	45	57

COMMODITY FUTURES TRADING COMMISSION

Federal Funds

COMMODITY FUTURES TRADING COMMISSION

(INCLUDING TRANSFERS OF FUNDS)

For necessary expenses to carry out the provisions of the Commodity Exchange Act (7 U.S.C. 1 et seq.), including the purchase and hire of passenger motor vehicles, and the rental of space (to include multiple year leases), in the District of Columbia and elsewhere, $249,000,000, including not to exceed $3,000 for official reception and representation expenses, and not to exceed $25,000 for the expenses for consultations and meetings hosted by the Commission with foreign governmental and other regulatory officials, of which not less than $20,000,000 shall remain available until September 30, 2024, and of which not less than $4,567,000 shall be for expenses of the Office of the Inspector General: Provided, That notwithstanding the limitations in 31 U.S.C. 1553, amounts provided under this heading are available for the liquidation of obligations equal to current year payments on leases entered into prior to the date of enactment of this Act: Provided further, That for the purpose of recording and liquidating any lease obligations that should have been recorded and liquidated against accounts closed pursuant to 31 U.S.C. 1552, and consistent with the preceding proviso, such amounts shall be transferred to and recorded in a no-year account in the Treasury, which has been established for the sole purpose of recording adjustments for and liquidating such unpaid obligations.

Note.—A full-year 2022 appropriation for this account was not enacted at the time the Budget was prepared; therefore, the Budget assumes this account is operating under the Continuing Appropriations Act, 2022 (Division A of Public Law 117–43, as amended). The amounts included for 2022 reflect the annualized level provided by the continuing resolution.

Program and Financing (in millions of dollars)

Identification code 339–1400–0–1–376	2021 actual	2022 est.	2023 est.
Obligations by program activity:			
0001 Salaries and Expenses	279	284	226
0003 Inspector General	3	3	5
0004 Relocation Costs (Regional)	11	9	....
0900 Total new obligations, unexpired accounts	293	296	231
0910 Appropriations used to liquidate unpaid lease obligations	24	22	19
0911 Total new obligations, unexpired accounts; and lease payments	317	318	250
Budgetary resources:			
Unobligated balance:			
1000 Unobligated balance brought forward, Oct 1	24	11	....
1021 Recoveries of prior year unpaid obligations	....	3	1
1033 Recoveries of prior year paid obligations	1	....	....
1070 Unobligated balance (total)	25	14	1
Budget authority:			
Appropriations, discretionary:			
1100 Appropriation	304	304	249
1901 Adjustment for new budget authority used to liquidate deficiencies	–24	–22	–19
1930 Total budgetary resources available	305	296	231
Memorandum (non-add) entries:			
1940 Unobligated balance expiring	–1	....	....
1941 Unexpired unobligated balance, end of year	11	....	....
Change in obligated balance:			
Unpaid obligations:			
3000 Unpaid obligations, brought forward, Oct 1	169	153	85
3010 New obligations, unexpired accounts	293	296	231
3011 Obligations ("upward adjustments"), expired accounts	1	1	1
3020 Outlays (gross)	–307	–362	–266
3040 Recoveries of prior year unpaid obligations, unexpired	....	–3	–1
3041 Recoveries of prior year unpaid obligations, expired	–3	....	....
3050 Unpaid obligations, end of year	153	85	50
Memorandum (non-add) entries:			
3100 Obligated balance, start of year	169	153	85
3200 Obligated balance, end of year	153	85	50
Budget authority and outlays, net:			
Discretionary:			
4000 Budget authority, gross	304	304	249
Outlays, gross:			
4010 Outlays from new discretionary authority	230	245	201
4011 Outlays from discretionary balances	77	117	65
4020 Outlays, gross (total)	307	362	266
Offsets against gross budget authority and outlays:			
Offsetting collections (collected) from:			
4033 Non-Federal sources	–2	....	....
Additional offsets against gross budget authority only:			
4052 Offsetting collections credited to expired accounts	1	....	....
4053 Recoveries of prior year paid obligations, unexpired accounts	1	....	....
4060 Additional offsets against budget authority only (total)	2	....	....
4070 Budget authority, net (discretionary)	304	304	249
4080 Outlays, net (discretionary)	305	362	266
4180 Budget authority, net (total)	304	304	249
4190 Outlays, net (total)	305	362	266
Unfunded deficiencies:			
7000 Unfunded deficiency, start of year	–103	–79	–57
Change in deficiency during the year:			
7012 Budgetary resources used to liquidate deficiencies	24	22	19
7020 Unfunded deficiency, end of year	–79	–57	–38

Summary of Budget Authority and Outlays (in millions of dollars)

	2021 actual	2022 est.	2023 est.
Enacted/requested:			
Budget Authority	304	304	249
Outlays	305	362	266
Legislative proposal, not subject to PAYGO:			
Outlays	....	....	–23
Total:			
Budget Authority	304	304	249
Outlays	305	362	243

The mission of the Commodity Futures Trading Commission (CFTC or Commission) is to: foster open, transparent, competitive, and financially sound markets; prevent and deter price manipulation and other disruptions to market integrity; and protect market participants and the public from fraud, exploitation, and abusive practices related to derivatives and other products that are subject to the Commodity Exchange Act (7 U.S.C. 1 et seq.) (CEA). The CEA established a comprehensive regulatory structure to oversee the futures trading complex, commodity options trading, intermediaries, and swap dealer activities.

The Commission's regulatory landscape is continually changing. As a responsible regulator, the CFTC seeks to promote responsible innovation and development that is consistent with its statutory mission to enhance the derivative trading markets. Further, the agency seeks to lower the systemic risk of the futures and swaps markets to the economy and the public.

The markets under the CFTC's regulatory purview are economically significant. In the United States, the markets for futures and options on futures represent trillions of dollars of notional value while the swaps markets represents hundreds of trillions of dollars in notional value.

The Budget proposes legislation authorizing user fees to fund certain Commission activities, as specified by the CFTC, in line with nearly all other Federal financial and banking regulators. Contingent upon enactment of authorizing legislation, the Budget proposes collections of $116 million to offset a portion of the CFTC's annual appropriation, providing total CFTC funding of $365 million in 2023. CFTC fees would be designed in a way that supports market access, liquidity, and the efficiency of the Nation's derivatives markets.

Object Classification (in millions of dollars)

Identification code 339–1400–0–1–376		2021 actual	2022 est.	2023 est.
	Direct obligations:			
	Personnel compensation:			
11.1	Full-time permanent	134	142	116
11.3	Other than full-time permanent	2	2	
11.5	Other personnel compensation	2	1	
11.9	Total personnel compensation	138	145	116
12.1	Civilian personnel benefits	49	51	42
21.0	Travel and transportation of persons			1
23.1	Rental payments to GSA		2	3
23.2	Rental payments to others	3	5	6
23.3	Communications, utilities, and miscellaneous charges	3	3	2
24.0	Printing and reproduction	1	1	1
25.1	Advisory and assistance services	66	60	43
25.2	Other services from non-Federal sources	4	4	3
25.3	Other goods and services from Federal sources	1	1	1
25.4	Operation and maintenance of facilities	1	8	
25.7	Operation and maintenance of equipment	10	8	7
26.0	Supplies and materials	4	2	2
31.0	Equipment	7	6	4
32.0	Land and structures	6		
99.9	Total new obligations, unexpired accounts	293	296	231
01.2	Rental payments to others	24	22	19
09.9	Total obligations, unexpired accounts; and lease payments	317	318	250

Employment Summary

Identification code 339–1400–0–1–376	2021 actual	2022 est.	2023 est.
1001 Direct civilian full-time equivalent employment	677	666	520

COMMODITY FUTURES TRADING COMMISSION
(Legislative proposal, not subject to PAYGO)

Contingent upon the enactment of legislation authorizing the Commodity Futures Trading Commission to collect user fees to fund the Commission's activities, an additional $116,000,000 shall be appropriated from the General Fund of the Treasury, to remain available until expended: Provided, That fees and charges assessed by the Commission shall be credited to this appropriation as offsetting collections: Provided further, That not to exceed $116,000,000 of such offsetting collections shall be available until expended for necessary expenses of this account: Provided further, That the total amount appropriated under this heading from the general fund for fiscal year 2023 shall be reduced as such offsetting fees are received so as to result in a final total fiscal year 2023 appropriation from the general fund estimated at not more than $249,000,000.

Program and Financing (in millions of dollars)

Identification code 339–1400–2–1–376		2021 actual	2022 est.	2023 est.
	Obligations by program activity:			
0001	Salaries and Expenses			116
0911	Total new obligations, unexpired accounts; and lease payments			116
	Budgetary resources:			
	Budget authority:			
	Spending authority from offsetting collections, discretionary:			
1700	Collected			116
1900	Budget authority (total)			116
1930	Total budgetary resources available			116
	Change in obligated balance:			
	Unpaid obligations:			
3010	New obligations, unexpired accounts			116
3020	Outlays (gross)			–93
3050	Unpaid obligations, end of year			23
	Memorandum (non-add) entries:			
3200	Obligated balance, end of year			23
	Budget authority and outlays, net:			
	Discretionary:			
4000	Budget authority, gross			116
	Outlays, gross:			
4010	Outlays from new discretionary authority			93
	Offsets against gross budget authority and outlays:			
	Offsetting collections (collected) from:			
4034	Offsetting governmental collections			–116
4040	Offsets against gross budget authority and outlays (total)			–116
4180	Budget authority, net (total)			
4190	Outlays, net (total)			–23

The Budget proposes legislation authorizing user fees to fund certain Commission activities, as specified by the CFTC, in line with nearly all other Federal financial and banking regulators. Contingent upon enactment of authorizing legislation, the Budget proposes collections of $116 million to offset a portion of the CFTC's annual appropriation, providing total CFTC funding of $365 million in 2023 CFTC fees would be designed in a way that supports market access, liquidity, and the efficiency of the Nation's derivatives markets.

Object Classification (in millions of dollars)

Identification code 339–1400–2–1–376		2021 actual	2022 est.	2023 est.
11.1	Direct obligations: Personnel compensation: Full-time permanent			54
11.9	Total personnel compensation			54
12.1	Civilian personnel benefits			19
21.0	Travel and transportation of persons			1
23.3	Communications, utilities, and miscellaneous charges			1
25.1	Advisory and assistance services			33
25.2	Other services from non-Federal sources			1
25.3	Other goods and services from Federal sources			1
25.7	Operation and maintenance of equipment			3
26.0	Supplies and materials			1
31.0	Equipment			2
99.9	Total new obligations, unexpired accounts			116
09.9	Total obligations, unexpired accounts; and lease payments			116

Employment Summary

Identification code 339–1400–2–1–376	2021 actual	2022 est.	2023 est.
1001 Direct civilian full-time equivalent employment			239

Commodity Futures Trading Commission—Continued
Federal Funds—Continued

EXPENSES, CUSTOMER PROTECTION FUND

Program and Financing (in millions of dollars)

Identification code 339–1534–0–1–376	2021 actual	2022 est.	2023 est.
Obligations by program activity:			
0002 Whistleblower Program	....	1	....
0900 Total new obligations, unexpired accounts (object class 11.1)	....	1	....
Budgetary resources:			
Unobligated balance:			
1000 Unobligated balance brought forward, Oct 1	....	10	9
1010 Unobligated balance transfer to other accts [339–4334]	....	....	–9
1011 Unobligated balance transfer from other acct [339–4334]	10	....	....
1070 Unobligated balance (total)	10	10	....
1930 Total budgetary resources available	10	10	....
Memorandum (non-add) entries:			
1941 Unexpired unobligated balance, end of year	10	9	....
Change in obligated balance:			
Unpaid obligations:			
3010 New obligations, unexpired accounts	....	1	....
3020 Outlays (gross)	....	–1	....
Budget authority and outlays, net:			
Mandatory:			
Outlays, gross:			
4101 Outlays from mandatory balances	....	1	....
4180 Budget authority, net (total)	....	....	....
4190 Outlays, net (total)	....	1	....

In anticipation of large whistleblower awards that could have depleted the Customer Protection Fund, P.L. 117–025 established a separate account in the Treasury for $10 million dollars for obligations related to the administrative and personnel expenses of the Whistleblower Office and the Office of Customer Education and Outreach. The account can only cover these non-award expenses when there are insufficient unobligated balances of the Customer Protection Fund to pay for them. Pursuant to P.L. 117–025, amounts transferred to this account will remain available until October 1, 2022, at which point they will be returned to the Customer Protection Fund.

Employment Summary

Identification code 339–1534–0–1–376	2021 actual	2022 est.	2023 est.
1001 Direct civilian full-time equivalent employment	....	2	....

CUSTOMER PROTECTION FUND

Program and Financing (in millions of dollars)

Identification code 339–4334–0–3–376	2021 actual	2022 est.	2023 est.
Obligations by program activity:			
0001 Customer Education Program	2	3	4
0002 Whistleblower Program	4	3	4
0003 Whistleblower Awards	3	693	25
0900 Total new obligations, unexpired accounts	9	699	33
Budgetary resources:			
Unobligated balance:			
1000 Unobligated balance brought forward, Oct 1	118	101	....
1010 Unobligated balance transfer to other accts [339–1534]	–10	....	....
1011 Unobligated balance transfer from other acct [339–1534]	....	....	9
1021 Recoveries of prior year unpaid obligations	2	....	....
1070 Unobligated balance (total)	110	101	9
Budget authority:			
Spending authority from offsetting collections, mandatory:			
1800 Collected	....	634	33
1823 New and/or unobligated balance of spending authority from offsetting collections temporarily reduced	....	–36	–3
1850 Spending auth from offsetting collections, mand (total)	....	598	30
1930 Total budgetary resources available	110	699	39
Memorandum (non-add) entries:			
1941 Unexpired unobligated balance, end of year	101	....	6
Change in obligated balance:			
Unpaid obligations:			
3000 Unpaid obligations, brought forward, Oct 1	3	1	101
3010 New obligations, unexpired accounts	9	699	33
3020 Outlays (gross)	–9	–599	–30
3040 Recoveries of prior year unpaid obligations, unexpired	–2	....	....
3050 Unpaid obligations, end of year	1	101	104
Memorandum (non-add) entries:			
3100 Obligated balance, start of year	3	1	101
3200 Obligated balance, end of year	1	101	104
Budget authority and outlays, net:			
Mandatory:			
4090 Budget authority, gross	....	598	30
Outlays, gross:			
4100 Outlays from new mandatory authority	....	598	30
4101 Outlays from mandatory balances	9	1	....
4110 Outlays, gross (total)	9	599	30
Offsets against gross budget authority and outlays:			
Offsetting collections (collected) from:			
4121 Interest on Federal securities	....	....	–1
4123 Non-Federal sources	....	–634	–32
4130 Offsets against gross budget authority and outlays (total)	....	–634	–33
4160 Budget authority, net (mandatory)	....	–36	–3
4170 Outlays, net (mandatory)	9	–35	–3
4180 Budget authority, net (total)	....	–36	–3
4190 Outlays, net (total)	9	–35	–3
Memorandum (non-add) entries:			
5000 Total investments, SOY: Federal securities: Par value	117	....	....
5090 Unexpired unavailable balance, SOY: Offsetting collections	1	1	37
5092 Unexpired unavailable balance, EOY: Offsetting collections	1	37	40

Section 748 of the Dodd-Frank Wall Street Reform and Consumer Protection Act (P.L. 111–203) (the Dodd-Frank Act) amended the Commodity Exchange Act (7 U.S.C. 1 et seq.) (CEA) to establish the Customer Protection Fund (Fund). The Fund is used to pay whistleblower awards, finance customer education initiatives, and administer the programs. The Dodd-Frank Act also authorized the Commodity Futures Trading Commission (Commission) to issue rules implementing incentives and protections for whistleblowers and to conduct customer education initiatives designed to help customers protect themselves against fraud and other violations of the CEA.

The Commission deposits monetary sanctions it collects in covered judicial or administrative actions into this revolving fund. The Commission may deposit such sanctions unless the balance in the Fund at the time the sanction is collected exceeds $100 million. The Commission does not deposit restitution awarded to victims into the Fund.

The Commission is required to submit an annual report on the whistleblower award program and customer education initiatives to the Committee on Agriculture, Nutrition, and Forestry of the Senate and the Committee on Agriculture of the House of Representatives. The report includes: a description of the number of whistleblower awards granted, and the types of cases in which these awards were granted, during the preceding fiscal year; the balance in the Fund; the amounts credited to and paid from the Fund; and a complete set of audited financial statements.

Object Classification (in millions of dollars)

Identification code 339–4334–0–3–376	2021 actual	2022 est.	2023 est.
Direct obligations:			
Personnel compensation:			
11.1 Full-time permanent	3	3	5
11.8 Special personal services payments	3	693	25
11.9 Total personnel compensation	6	696	30
12.1 Civilian personnel benefits	1	1	1
25.1 Advisory and assistance services	2	2	2
99.9 Total new obligations, unexpired accounts	9	699	33

Employment Summary

Identification code 339–4334–0–3–376	2021 actual	2022 est.	2023 est.
1001 Direct civilian full-time equivalent employment	15	15	17

CONSUMER PRODUCT SAFETY COMMISSION

Federal Funds

SALARIES AND EXPENSES

For necessary expenses of the Consumer Product Safety Commission, including hire of passenger motor vehicles, services as authorized by 5 U.S.C. 3109, but at rates for individuals not to exceed the per diem rate equivalent to the maximum rate payable under 5 U.S.C. 5376, purchase of nominal awards to recognize non-Federal officials' contributions to Commission activities, and not to exceed $4,000 for official reception and representation expenses, $195,500,000.

Note.—A full-year 2022 appropriation for this account was not enacted at the time the Budget was prepared; therefore, the Budget assumes this account is operating under the Continuing Appropriations Act, 2022 (Division A of Public Law 117–43, as amended). The amounts included for 2022 reflect the annualized level provided by the continuing resolution.

Program and Financing (in millions of dollars)

Identification code 061–0100–0–1–554	2021 actual	2022 est.	2023 est.
Obligations by program activity:			
0001 Consumer Product Safety - Direct	138	162	201
0100 Direct program activities, subtotal	138	162	201
0801 Consumer Product Safety - Reimbursable	4	5	5
0900 Total new obligations, unexpired accounts	142	167	206
Budgetary resources:			
Unobligated balance:			
1000 Unobligated balance brought forward, Oct 1	2	50	23
1001 Discretionary unobligated balance brought fwd, Oct 1	2	2	
Budget authority:			
Appropriations, discretionary:			
1100 Appropriation	135	135	196
Appropriations, mandatory:			
1200 Appropriation	50		
Spending authority from offsetting collections, discretionary:			
1700 Collected	2	5	5
1701 Change in uncollected payments, Federal sources	3		
1750 Spending auth from offsetting collections, disc (total)	5	5	5
1900 Budget authority (total)	190	140	201
1930 Total budgetary resources available	192	190	224
Memorandum (non-add) entries:			
1941 Unexpired unobligated balance, end of year	50	23	18
Change in obligated balance:			
Unpaid obligations:			
3000 Unpaid obligations, brought forward, Oct 1	42	49	45
3010 New obligations, unexpired accounts	142	167	206
3011 Obligations ("upward adjustments"), expired accounts	1	1	1
3020 Outlays (gross)	–135	–171	–212
3041 Recoveries of prior year unpaid obligations, expired	–1	–1	–1
3050 Unpaid obligations, end of year	49	45	39
Uncollected payments:			
3060 Uncollected pymts, Fed sources, brought forward, Oct 1	–2	–3	–3
3070 Change in uncollected pymts, Fed sources, unexpired	–3		
3071 Change in uncollected pymts, Fed sources, expired	2		
3090 Uncollected pymts, Fed sources, end of year	–3	–3	–3
Memorandum (non-add) entries:			
3100 Obligated balance, start of year	40	46	42
3200 Obligated balance, end of year	46	42	36
Budget authority and outlays, net:			
Discretionary:			
4000 Budget authority, gross	140	140	201
Outlays, gross:			
4010 Outlays from new discretionary authority	102	112	161
4011 Outlays from discretionary balances	33	39	40
4020 Outlays, gross (total)	135	151	201
Offsets against gross budget authority and outlays:			
Offsetting collections (collected) from:			
4030 Federal sources	–4	–5	–5
4040 Offsets against gross budget authority and outlays (total)	–4	–5	–5
Additional offsets against gross budget authority only:			
4050 Change in uncollected pymts, Fed sources, unexpired	–3		
4052 Offsetting collections credited to expired accounts	2		
4060 Additional offsets against budget authority only (total)	–1		
4070 Budget authority, net (discretionary)	135	135	196
4080 Outlays, net (discretionary)	131	146	196
Mandatory:			
4090 Budget authority, gross	50		
Outlays, gross:			
4101 Outlays from mandatory balances		20	11
4180 Budget authority, net (total)	185	135	196
4190 Outlays, net (total)	131	166	207

The U.S. Consumer Product Safety Commission (CPSC) is an independent federal regulatory agency, created in 1972 by the Consumer Product Safety Act (CPSA). In addition to the CPSA, as amended by the Consumer Product Safety Improvement Act of 2008 (CPSIA), and Public Law 112–28, the CPSC also administers other laws, including the Federal Hazardous Substances Act, the Flammable Fabrics Act, the Child Safety Protection Act, the Poison Prevention Packaging Act, the Refrigerator Safety Act, the Virginia Graeme Baker (VGB) Pool and Spa Safety Act, and the Children's Gasoline Burn Prevention Act. The 2023 Budget includes a legislative proposal to streamline the mandatory recall requirements in the CPSA to allow CPSC to more quickly and effectively remove hazardous products from the market when needed.

Object Classification (in millions of dollars)

Identification code 061–0100–0–1–554	2021 actual	2022 est.	2023 est.
Direct obligations:			
Personnel compensation:			
11.1 Full-time permanent	59	71	82
11.3 Other than full-time permanent	3	4	5
11.5 Other personnel compensation	1	2	3
11.9 Total personnel compensation	63	77	90
12.1 Civilian personnel benefits	22	27	31
21.0 Travel and transportation of persons			1
23.1 Rental payments to GSA	7	7	7
23.3 Communications, utilities, and miscellaneous charges	3	3	3
25.1 Advisory and assistance services	8	10	16
25.2 Other services from non-Federal sources	20	23	36
25.3 Other goods and services from Federal sources	3	3	4
25.7 Operation and maintenance of equipment	6	6	7
26.0 Supplies and materials	1	1	1
31.0 Equipment	4	4	5
41.0 Grants, subsidies, and contributions	1	1	
99.0 Direct obligations	138	162	201
99.0 Reimbursable obligations	4	5	5
99.9 Total new obligations, unexpired accounts	142	167	206

Employment Summary

Identification code 061–0100–0–1–554	2021 actual	2022 est.	2023 est.
1001 Direct civilian full-time equivalent employment	520	597	672

CORPORATION FOR NATIONAL AND COMMUNITY SERVICE

Federal Funds

OPERATING EXPENSES

For necessary expenses for the Corporation for National and Community Service (referred to in this title as "CNCS") to carry out the Domestic Volunteer Service Act of 1973 (referred to in this title as "1973 Act") and the National and Community Service Act of 1990 (referred to in this title as "1990 Act"), $982,126,000, notwithstanding sections 198B(b)(3), 198S(g), 501(a)(4)(C), and 501(a)(4)(F) of the 1990 Act: Provided, That of the amounts provided under this heading: (1) up to 1 percent

Corporation for National and Community Service—Continued
Federal Funds—Continued

OPERATING EXPENSES—Continued

of program grant funds may be used to defray the costs of conducting grant application reviews, including the use of outside peer reviewers and electronic management of the grants cycle; (2) $19,538,000 shall be available to provide assistance to State commissions on national and community service, under section 126(a) of the 1990 Act and notwithstanding section 501(a)(5)(B) of the 1990 Act; (3) $37,735,000 shall be available to carry out subtitle E of the 1990 Act; and (4) $6,700,000 shall be available for expenses authorized under section 501(a)(4)(F) of the 1990 Act, which, notwithstanding the provisions of section 198P shall be awarded by CNCS on a competitive basis: Provided further, That for the purposes of carrying out the 1990 Act, satisfying the requirements in section 122(c)(1)(D) may include a determination of need by the local community.

Note.—A full-year 2022 appropriation for this account was not enacted at the time the Budget was prepared; therefore, the Budget assumes this account is operating under the Continuing Appropriations Act, 2022 (Division A of Public Law 117–43, as amended). The amounts included for 2022 reflect the annualized level provided by the continuing resolution.

Program and Financing (in millions of dollars)

Identification code 485–2728–0–1–506	2021 actual	2022 est.	2023 est.
Obligations by program activity:			
0001 AmeriCorps*State and National	722	455	557
0002 Foster Grandparent Program	122	118	131
0003 Senior Companion Program	53	53	59
0004 AmeriCorps*VISTA	102	97	106
0006 AmeriCorps*NCCC	35	34	38
0007 Retired Senior Volunteer Program	51	53	55
0008 State Comm. Support Grants	18	19	20
0009 Evaluations	4	4	6
0011 Innovation, Demon., and Assistance	3	3	3
0012 Volunteer Generation Fund	7	7	7
0799 Total direct obligations	1,117	843	982
0801 Operating Expenses (Reimbursable)	1		
0900 Total new obligations, unexpired accounts	1,118	843	982
Budgetary resources:			
Unobligated balance:			
1000 Unobligated balance brought forward, Oct 1	24	521	565
1021 Recoveries of prior year unpaid obligations	2	2	2
1070 Unobligated balance (total)	26	523	567
Budget authority:			
Appropriations, discretionary:			
1100 Appropriation	843	843	982
Appropriations, mandatory:			
1200 Appropriation	770		
Spending authority from offsetting collections, discretionary:			
1700 Collected	7	42	
1701 Change in uncollected payments, Federal sources	5		
1750 Spending auth from offsetting collections, disc (total)	12	42	
1900 Budget authority (total)	1,625	885	982
1930 Total budgetary resources available	1,651	1,408	1,549
Memorandum (non-add) entries:			
1940 Unobligated balance expiring	–12		
1941 Unexpired unobligated balance, end of year	521	565	567
Change in obligated balance:			
Unpaid obligations:			
3000 Unpaid obligations, brought forward, Oct 1	958	1,272	606
3010 New obligations, unexpired accounts	1,118	843	982
3011 Obligations ("upward adjustments"), expired accounts	41		
3020 Outlays (gross)	–768	–1,507	–1,011
3040 Recoveries of prior year unpaid obligations, unexpired	–2	–2	–2
3041 Recoveries of prior year unpaid obligations, expired	–75		
3050 Unpaid obligations, end of year	1,272	606	575
Uncollected payments:			
3060 Uncollected pymts, Fed sources, brought forward, Oct 1	–8	–6	–6
3070 Change in uncollected pymts, Fed sources, unexpired	–5		
3071 Change in uncollected pymts, Fed sources, expired	7		
3090 Uncollected pymts, Fed sources, end of year	–6	–6	–6
Memorandum (non-add) entries:			
3100 Obligated balance, start of year	950	1,266	600
3200 Obligated balance, end of year	1,266	600	569
Budget authority and outlays, net:			
Discretionary:			
4000 Budget authority, gross	855	885	982
Outlays, gross:			
4010 Outlays from new discretionary authority	134	304	305
4011 Outlays from discretionary balances	630	691	537
4020 Outlays, gross (total)	764	995	842
Offsets against gross budget authority and outlays:			
Offsetting collections (collected) from:			
4030 Federal sources	–3	–42	
4033 Non-Federal sources	–4		
4040 Offsets against gross budget authority and outlays (total)	–7	–42	
Additional offsets against gross budget authority only:			
4050 Change in uncollected pymts, Fed sources, unexpired	–5		
4060 Additional offsets against budget authority only (total)	–5		
4070 Budget authority, net (discretionary)	843	843	982
4080 Outlays, net (discretionary)	757	953	842
Mandatory:			
4090 Budget authority, gross	770		
Outlays, gross:			
4100 Outlays from new mandatory authority	4		
4101 Outlays from mandatory balances		512	169
4110 Outlays, gross (total)	4	512	169
4180 Budget authority, net (total)	1,613	843	982
4190 Outlays, net (total)	761	1,465	1,011

The Corporation for National and Community Service (CNCS) provides service opportunities for Americans of all ages through institutions that include: nonprofits, schools, faith-based and other community organizations, and local governments. CNCS is now operating as AmeriCorps, which is a name adopted after extensive consultations with stakeholders to help streamline, align, and strengthen the agency's brand.

AmeriCorps State and National.—With funds channeled through States, Territories, Tribes, and community-based organizations, AmeriCorps grants enable communities to recruit, train, and place AmeriCorps members to serve in the areas of disaster services, economic opportunity, education, environmental stewardship, healthy futures, and veterans and military families, as directed by the Edward M. Kennedy Serve America Act of 2009.

AmeriCorps National Civilian Community Corps.—AmeriCorps NCCC is a ten-month residential national service program for people ages 18 to 24. AmeriCorps NCCC members are deployed to respond to natural disasters and engage in urban and rural development projects across the nation.

AmeriCorps VISTA.—Provides full-time members to community organizations and public agencies working to resolve local poverty-related problems.

State Service Commission Support Grants.—These grants support the operation of State Service Commissions that administer approximately two-thirds of AmeriCorps State and National grant funds.

Retired Senior Volunteer Program.—RSVP grants support volunteers aged 55 and older with service opportunities, including mentoring children and providing independent living services to adults.

Foster Grandparent Program.—Grants provide low-income volunteers age 55 and older with service opportunities to provide one-on-one mentoring and support to at-risk children.

Senior Companion Program.—Grants support low-income volunteers who provide companionship, transportation, help with light chores, and respite to assist seniors and people with disabilities to remain in their own homes.

Innovation, Demonstration, and Assistance.—These initiatives and programs are aimed at incubating new ideas, while expanding proven initiatives that address specific community needs. For example, the Volunteer Generation Fund focuses on strengthening the ability of nonprofits and other organizations to recruit, retain, and manage volunteers.

Evaluation.—This activity supports the design and implementation of research and evaluation studies and facilitates the use of evidence and evaluation by AmeriCorps and national service organizations.

Object Classification (in millions of dollars)

Identification code 485–2728–0–1–506		2021 actual	2022 est.	2023 est.
	Direct obligations:			
	Personnel compensation:			
11.1	Full-time permanent	9	9	9
11.8	Special personal services payments	55	55	55
11.9	Total personnel compensation	64	64	64
12.1	Civilian personnel benefits	3	3	3
21.0	Travel and transportation of persons	4	4	4
23.2	Rental payments to others	8	8	8
25.2	Other services from non-Federal sources	43	43	43
26.0	Supplies and materials	1	1	1
41.0	Grants, subsidies, and contributions	994	719	858
99.0	Direct obligations	1,117	842	981
99.0	Reimbursable obligations	1	1	1
99.9	Total new obligations, unexpired accounts	1,118	843	982

Employment Summary

Identification code 485–2728–0–1–506		2021 actual	2022 est.	2023 est.
1001	Direct civilian full-time equivalent employment	130	130	130

PAYMENT TO THE NATIONAL SERVICE TRUST FUND

Program and Financing (in millions of dollars)

Identification code 485–2726–0–1–506		2021 actual	2022 est.	2023 est.
	Obligations by program activity:			
0001	Payment to National Service Trust Fund	185	333	85
0900	Total new obligations, unexpired accounts (object class 94.0)	185	333	85
	Budgetary resources:			
	Unobligated balance:			
1000	Unobligated balance brought forward, Oct 1		148	
	Budget authority:			
	Appropriations, discretionary:			
1100	Appropriation	185	185	85
	Appropriations, mandatory:			
1200	Appropriation	148		
1900	Budget authority (total)	333	185	85
1930	Total budgetary resources available	333	333	85
	Memorandum (non-add) entries:			
1941	Unexpired unobligated balance, end of year		148	
	Change in obligated balance:			
	Unpaid obligations:			
3010	New obligations, unexpired accounts	185	333	85
3020	Outlays (gross)	–185	–333	–85
	Budget authority and outlays, net:			
	Discretionary:			
4000	Budget authority, gross	185	185	85
	Outlays, gross:			
4010	Outlays from new discretionary authority	185	185	85
	Mandatory:			
4090	Budget authority, gross	148		
	Outlays, gross:			
4101	Outlays from mandatory balances		148	
4180	Budget authority, net (total)	333	185	85
4190	Outlays, net (total)	185	333	85

This general fund appropriation pays the National Service Trust Fund to make educational awards to eligible national service program participants until the awardees use them.

OFFICE OF INSPECTOR GENERAL

For necessary expenses of the Office of Inspector General in carrying out the Inspector General Act of 1978, $8,121,000.

Note.—A full-year 2022 appropriation for this account was not enacted at the time the Budget was prepared; therefore, the Budget assumes this account is operating under the Continuing Appropriations Act, 2022 (Division A of Public Law 117–43, as amended). The amounts included for 2022 reflect the annualized level provided by the continuing resolution.

Program and Financing (in millions of dollars)

Identification code 485–2721–0–1–506		2021 actual	2022 est.	2023 est.
	Obligations by program activity:			
0001	Office of Inspector General	6	7	8
	Budgetary resources:			
	Unobligated balance:			
1000	Unobligated balance brought forward, Oct 1	1	11	10
1001	Discretionary unobligated balance brought fwd, Oct 1	1		
	Budget authority:			
	Appropriations, discretionary:			
1100	Appropriation	7	6	8
	Appropriations, mandatory:			
1200	Appropriation	9		
1900	Budget authority (total)	16	6	8
1930	Total budgetary resources available	17	17	18
	Memorandum (non-add) entries:			
1941	Unexpired unobligated balance, end of year	11	10	10
	Change in obligated balance:			
	Unpaid obligations:			
3000	Unpaid obligations, brought forward, Oct 1	1	2	1
3010	New obligations, unexpired accounts	6	7	8
3020	Outlays (gross)	–5	–8	–6
3050	Unpaid obligations, end of year	2	1	3
	Memorandum (non-add) entries:			
3100	Obligated balance, start of year	1	2	1
3200	Obligated balance, end of year	2	1	3
	Budget authority and outlays, net:			
	Discretionary:			
4000	Budget authority, gross	7	6	8
	Outlays, gross:			
4010	Outlays from new discretionary authority	4	2	3
4011	Outlays from discretionary balances	1	4	3
4020	Outlays, gross (total)	5	6	6
	Mandatory:			
4090	Budget authority, gross	9		
	Outlays, gross:			
4101	Outlays from mandatory balances		2	
4180	Budget authority, net (total)	16	6	8
4190	Outlays, net (total)	5	8	6

The Office of the Inspector General provides an independent assessment of AmeriCorps operations, primarily through audits and investigations, with a goal of preventing fraud, waste, and abuse.

Object Classification (in millions of dollars)

Identification code 485–2721–0–1–506		2021 actual	2022 est.	2023 est.
	Direct obligations:			
11.1	Personnel compensation: Full-time permanent	3	3	3
12.1	Civilian personnel benefits	1	1	1
25.2	Other services from non-Federal sources	2	3	4
99.9	Total new obligations, unexpired accounts	6	7	8

Employment Summary

Identification code 485–2721–0–1–506		2021 actual	2022 est.	2023 est.
1001	Direct civilian full-time equivalent employment	23	23	23

SALARIES AND EXPENSES

For necessary expenses of administration as provided under section 501(a)(5) of the 1990 Act and under section 504(a) of the 1973 Act, including payment of salaries, authorized travel, hire of passenger motor vehicles, the rental of conference rooms in the District of Columbia, the employment of experts and consultants authorized under 5 U.S.C. 3109, and not to exceed $2,500 for official reception and representation expenses, $114,686,000.

Note.—A full-year 2022 appropriation for this account was not enacted at the time the Budget was prepared; therefore, the Budget assumes this account is operating under the Continuing

Corporation for National and Community Service—Continued
Federal Funds—Continued

SALARIES AND EXPENSES—Continued

Appropriations Act, 2022 (Division A of Public Law 117–43, as amended). The amounts included for 2022 reflect the annualized level provided by the continuing resolution.

Program and Financing (in millions of dollars)

Identification code 485–2722–0–1–506		2021 actual	2022 est.	2023 est.
	Obligations by program activity:			
0001	NCSA Salaries & Expenses	90	86	115
	Budgetary resources:			
	Unobligated balance:			
1000	Unobligated balance brought forward, Oct 1	1	70	70
1001	Discretionary unobligated balance brought fwd, Oct 1	1		
	Budget authority:			
	Appropriations, discretionary:			
1100	Appropriation	86	86	115
	Appropriations, mandatory:			
1200	Appropriation	73		
1900	Budget authority (total)	159	86	115
1930	Total budgetary resources available	160	156	185
	Memorandum (non-add) entries:			
1941	Unexpired unobligated balance, end of year	70	70	70
	Change in obligated balance:			
	Unpaid obligations:			
3000	Unpaid obligations, brought forward, Oct 1	26	34	5
3010	New obligations, unexpired accounts	90	86	115
3011	Obligations ("upward adjustments"), expired accounts	1	24	24
3020	Outlays (gross)	–79	–139	–117
3041	Recoveries of prior year unpaid obligations, expired	–4		
3050	Unpaid obligations, end of year	34	5	27
	Memorandum (non-add) entries:			
3100	Obligated balance, start of year	26	34	5
3200	Obligated balance, end of year	34	5	27
	Budget authority and outlays, net:			
	Discretionary:			
4000	Budget authority, gross	86	86	115
	Outlays, gross:			
4010	Outlays from new discretionary authority	62	66	89
4011	Outlays from discretionary balances	17	22	21
4020	Outlays, gross (total)	79	88	110
	Mandatory:			
4090	Budget authority, gross	73		
	Outlays, gross:			
4101	Outlays from mandatory balances		51	7
4180	Budget authority, net (total)	159	86	115
4190	Outlays, net (total)	79	139	117

For necessary expenses of administration, including payment of salaries, authorized travel, hire of passenger motor vehicles, the rental of conference rooms in the District of Columbia, and the employment of experts and consultants.

Object Classification (in millions of dollars)

Identification code 485–2722–0–1–506		2021 actual	2022 est.	2023 est.
11.1	Direct obligations: Personnel compensation: Full-time permanent	40	38	47
11.9	Total personnel compensation	40	38	47
12.1	Civilian personnel benefits	13	14	12
21.0	Travel and transportation of persons	1	1	1
23.1	Rental payments to GSA	9	8	8
23.3	Communications, utilities, and miscellaneous charges	1	2	2
25.2	Other services from non-Federal sources	24	21	44
26.0	Supplies and materials	1	1	1
31.0	Equipment	1	1	
99.9	Total new obligations, unexpired accounts	90	86	115

Employment Summary

Identification code 485–2722–0–1–506	2021 actual	2022 est.	2023 est.
1001 Direct civilian full-time equivalent employment	400	400	475

VISTA ADVANCE PAYMENTS REVOLVING FUND

Program and Financing (in millions of dollars)

Identification code 485–2723–0–1–506		2021 actual	2022 est.	2023 est.
	Obligations by program activity:			
0801	VISTA Advance Payments Revolving Fund (Reimbursable)	8	13	13
0900	Total new obligations, unexpired accounts (object class 41.0)	8	13	13
	Budgetary resources:			
	Unobligated balance:			
1000	Unobligated balance brought forward, Oct 1	3	3	3
	Budget authority:			
	Spending authority from offsetting collections, discretionary:			
1700	Collected	8	13	13
1900	Budget authority (total)	8	13	13
1930	Total budgetary resources available	11	16	16
	Memorandum (non-add) entries:			
1941	Unexpired unobligated balance, end of year	3	3	3
	Change in obligated balance:			
	Unpaid obligations:			
3000	Unpaid obligations, brought forward, Oct 1		1	
3010	New obligations, unexpired accounts	8	13	13
3020	Outlays (gross)	–7	–14	–13
3050	Unpaid obligations, end of year	1		
	Memorandum (non-add) entries:			
3100	Obligated balance, start of year		1	
3200	Obligated balance, end of year	1		
	Budget authority and outlays, net:			
	Discretionary:			
4000	Budget authority, gross	8	13	13
	Outlays, gross:			
4010	Outlays from new discretionary authority		13	13
4011	Outlays from discretionary balances	7	1	
4020	Outlays, gross (total)	7	14	13
	Offsets against gross budget authority and outlays:			
	Offsetting collections (collected) from:			
4033	Non-Federal sources	–8	–13	–13
4180	Budget authority, net (total)			
4190	Outlays, net (total)	–1	1	

This fund was established in 2007 by Public Law 110–05 as the initial source of funding for VISTA member living allowances for which the Corporation is later reimbursed by nonprofit organizations as part of cost share agreements. All VISTA member benefits and services, and the majority of living allowances, are funded in the Operating Expenses account.

Trust Funds

NATIONAL SERVICE TRUST

For expenses of the National Service Trust established under subtitle D of title I of the 1990 Act, $235,000,000, to remain available until expended, of which $150,000,000 shall be derived from the National Service Trust and $85,000,000 shall be derived from the General Fund of the Treasury: Provided, That CNCS may transfer additional funds from the amount provided within "Operating Expenses" allocated to grants under subtitle C of title I of the 1990 Act to the National Service Trust upon determination that such transfer is necessary to support the activities of national service participants and after notice is transmitted to the Committees on Appropriations of the House of Representatives and the Senate: Provided further, That amounts appropriated for or transferred to the National Service Trust may be invested under section 145(b) of the 1990 Act without regard to the requirement to apportion funds under 31 U.S.C. 1513(b).

Special and Trust Fund Receipts (in millions of dollars)

Identification code 485–9972–0–7–506		2021 actual	2022 est.	2023 est.
0100	Balance, start of year	150	150	237
0198	Adjustment for unavailable earnings on interest		82	
0199	Balance, start of year	150	232	237
	Receipts:			
	Current law:			
1140	Interest on Investment, National Service Trust Fund	1	5	6

Identification code				
1140	Payment from the General Fund, National Service Trust Fund		148	
1140	Payment from the General Fund, National Service Trust Fund	185	185	85
1140	Payment from the Operating Expenses, National Service Trust Fund	18		
1199	Total current law receipts	204	338	91
1999	Total receipts	204	338	91
2000	Total: Balances and receipts	354	570	328
	Appropriations:			
	Current law:			
2101	National Service Trust	−203	−185	−235
2101	National Service Trust	−1	−148	
2199	Total current law appropriations	−204	−333	−235
2999	Total appropriations	−204	−333	−235
5099	Balance, end of year	150	237	93

Program and Financing (in millions of dollars)

Identification code 485–9972–0–7–506		2021 actual	2022 est.	2023 est.
	Obligations by program activity:			
0001	Gifts and contributions	99	333	235
0900	Total new obligations, unexpired accounts (object class 25.2)	99	333	235
	Budgetary resources:			
	Unobligated balance:			
1000	Unobligated balance brought forward, Oct 1	366	471	389
1001	Discretionary unobligated balance brought fwd, Oct 1	366		
1020	Adjustment of unobligated bal brought forward, Oct 1		−82	
1070	Unobligated balance (total)	366	389	389
	Budget authority:			
	Appropriations, discretionary:			
1101	Appropriation (special or trust)	203	185	235
	Appropriations, mandatory:			
1201	Appropriation (special or trust fund)	1	148	
1900	Budget authority (total)	204	333	235
1930	Total budgetary resources available	570	722	624
	Memorandum (non-add) entries:			
1941	Unexpired unobligated balance, end of year	471	389	389
	Change in obligated balance:			
	Unpaid obligations:			
3000	Unpaid obligations, brought forward, Oct 1	567	536	382
3010	New obligations, unexpired accounts	99	333	235
3020	Outlays (gross)	−130	−487	−440
3050	Unpaid obligations, end of year	536	382	177
	Memorandum (non-add) entries:			
3100	Obligated balance, start of year	567	536	382
3200	Obligated balance, end of year	536	382	177
	Budget authority and outlays, net:			
	Discretionary:			
4000	Budget authority, gross	203	185	235
	Outlays, gross:			
4010	Outlays from new discretionary authority		185	235
4011	Outlays from discretionary balances	130	264	169
4020	Outlays, gross (total)	130	449	404
	Mandatory:			
4090	Budget authority, gross	1	148	
	Outlays, gross:			
4100	Outlays from new mandatory authority		38	
4101	Outlays from mandatory balances			36
4110	Outlays, gross (total)		38	36
4180	Budget authority, net (total)	204	333	235
4190	Outlays, net (total)	130	487	440
	Memorandum (non-add) entries:			
5000	Total investments, SOY: Federal securities: Par value	186	1,012	185
5001	Total investments, EOY: Federal securities: Par value	1,012	185	235

The National Service Trust Fund account is a consolidation of two trust funds. In one, gifts and contributions from individuals and organizations are deposited for use in furthering program goals. In the other, funds appropriated to make educational awards to eligible national service program participants are maintained until they are used.

ADMINISTRATIVE PROVISIONS

SEC. 401. CNCS shall make any significant changes to program requirements, service delivery or policy only through public notice and comment rulemaking. For fiscal year 2023, during any grant selection process, an officer or employee of CNCS shall not knowingly disclose any covered grant selection information regarding such selection, directly or indirectly, to any person other than an officer or employee of CNCS that is authorized by CNCS to receive such information.

SEC. 402. AmeriCorps programs receiving grants under the National Service Trust program shall meet an overall minimum share requirement of 24 percent for the first 3 years that they receive AmeriCorps funding, and thereafter shall meet the overall minimum share requirement as provided in section 2521.60 of title 45, Code of Federal Regulations, without regard to the operating costs match requirement in section 121(e) or the member support Federal share limitations in section 140 of the 1990 Act, and subject to partial waiver consistent with section 2521.70 of title 45, Code of Federal Regulations.

SEC. 403. Donations made to CNCS under section 196 of the 1990 Act for the purposes of financing programs and operations under titles I and II of the 1973 Act or subtitle B, C, D, or E of title I of the 1990 Act shall be used to supplement and not supplant current programs and operations.

SEC. 404. In addition to the requirements in section 146(a) of the 1990 Act, use of an educational award for the purpose described in section 148(a)(4) shall be limited to individuals who are veterans as defined under section 101 of the Act.

SEC. 405. For the purpose of carrying out section 189D of the 1990 Act—

(1) entities described in paragraph (a) of such section shall be considered "qualified entities" under section 3 of the National Child Protection Act of 1993 ("NCPA");

(2) individuals described in such section shall be considered "volunteers" under section 3 of NCPA; and

(3) State Commissions on National and Community Service established pursuant to section 178 of the 1990 Act, are authorized to receive criminal history record information, consistent with Public Law 92–544.

SEC. 406. Notwithstanding sections 139(b), 146 and 147 of the 1990 Act, an individual who successfully completes a term of service of not less than 1,200 hours during a period of not more than one year may receive a national service education award having a value of 70 percent of the value of a national service education award determined under section 147(a) of the Act.

SEC. 407. Section 148(f)(2)(A)(i) of the 1990 Act shall be applied for this fiscal year by striking "a national service program that receives a grant under subtitle C" and inserting "an approved national service position".

SEC. 408. (a) Section 137(a)(5) of the 1990 Act shall be applied in fiscal year 2023 as if the following were inserted before the period: ", or has submitted a request for administrative relief pursuant to the policy established in the memorandum of the Secretary of Homeland Security dated June 15, 2012, and entitled 'Exercising Discretion with Respect to Individuals Who Came to the United States as Children' (Deferred Action for Childhood Arrivals)".

(b) Section 146(a)(3) of the 1990 Act shall be applied in fiscal year 2023 as if the following were inserted before the period: ", or has submitted a request for administrative relief pursuant to the policy established in the memorandum of the Secretary of Homeland Security dated June 15, 2012, and entitled 'Exercising Discretion with Respect to Individuals Who Came to the United States as Children' (Deferred Action for Childhood Arrivals)".

(c) Notwithstanding sections 141 and 146 of the 1990 Act, or any other provision of law, a participant in a national service program carried out under the authority of the 1973 Act shall be eligible for the national service educational award described in subtitle D of title I of the 1990 Act if the participant—

(1) meets the criteria specified in paragraphs (1) through (4) of subsection (a) of section 137 of the 1990 Act; and

(2) is a citizen or national of the United States or lawful permanent resident alien of the United States, is able to provide evidence from the Department of Homeland Security that he or she is in the United States for other than a temporary purpose with the intention of becoming a citizen or permanent resident, or has submitted a request for administrative relief pursuant to the policy established in the memorandum of the Secretary of Homeland Security dated June 15, 2012, and entitled 'Exercising Discretion with Respect to Individuals Who Came to the United States as Children' (Deferred Action for Childhood Arrivals)".

SEC. 409. An individual in an approved national service position in a program under section 152(a) of the 1990 Act may, upon the approval of the Director of the

National Civilian Community Corps, continue in a term of service for up to 180 days beyond the period otherwise specified in section 153(d), or 90 days beyond the period otherwise specified in section 154(c).

SEC. 410. (a) Notwithstanding sections 139, 147, 153, and 154 of the 1990 Act, the Director of the National Civilian Community Corps may enter into agreements with eligible individuals to participate in a National Civilian Community Corps program for a period of not less than 90 days and not more than 180 days.

(b) An eligible individual who enters into an agreement with the Director under subsection (a) may receive an educational award in an amount that is proportional to the full-time national service educational award authorized under section 147(a) of the 1990 Act, based on the length of service completed.

(c) For purposes of this section, the term "eligible individual" means an individual who is at least 18 years of age and not more than 26 years of age as of the date the term of service commences.

GENERAL FUND RECEIPT ACCOUNT

(in millions of dollars)

	2021 actual	2022 est.	2023 est.
Offsetting receipts from the public:			
485–322055 All Other General Fund Proprietary Receipts Including Budget Clearing Accounts	1	....	....
General Fund Offsetting receipts from the public	1	....	....

CORPORATION FOR PUBLIC BROADCASTING

Federal Funds

CORPORATION FOR PUBLIC BROADCASTING

For payment to the Corporation for Public Broadcasting ("CPB"), as authorized by the Communications Act of 1934, an amount which shall be available within limitations specified by that Act, for the fiscal year 2025, $565,000,000: Provided, That none of the funds made available to CPB by this Act shall be used to pay for receptions, parties, or similar forms of entertainment for Government officials or employees: Provided further, That none of the funds made available to CPB by this Act shall be available or used to aid or support any program or activity from which any person is excluded, or is denied benefits, or is discriminated against, on the basis of race, color, national origin, religion, or sex: Provided further, That none of the funds made available to CPB by this Act shall be used to apply any political test or qualification in selecting, appointing, promoting, or taking any other personnel action with respect to officers, agents, and employees of CPB.

In addition, for the costs associated with replacing and upgrading the public broadcasting interconnection system, including the costs of interconnection facilities and operations under subsections (k)(3)(A)(i)(II) and (k)(3)(A)(iv)(I) of section 396 of the Communications Act of 1934, and for other technologies and services that create infrastructure and efficiencies within the public media system, $60,000,000: Provided, That such amounts shall be in addition to any other funds available for such purposes.

Note.—A full-year 2022 appropriation for this account was not enacted at the time the Budget was prepared; therefore, the Budget assumes this account is operating under the Continuing Appropriations Act, 2022 (Division A of Public Law 117–43, as amended). The amounts included for 2022 reflect the annualized level provided by the continuing resolution.

Program and Financing (in millions of dollars)

Identification code 020–0151–0–1–503		2021 actual	2022 est.	2023 est.
	Obligations by program activity:			
0001	General programming	445	465	475
0002	Interconnection	20	20	60
0003	Fiscal Stabilization	175	....	....
0900	Total new obligations, unexpired accounts (object class 41.0)	640	485	535
	Budgetary resources:			
	Budget authority:			
	Appropriations, discretionary:			
1100	Appropriation	20	20	60
	Advance appropriations, discretionary:			
1170	Advance appropriation - General Programming	445	465	475
	Appropriations, mandatory:			
1200	Appropriation-ARP Fiscal Stabilization	175	....	....
1900	Budget authority (total)	640	485	535
1930	Total budgetary resources available	640	485	535
	Change in obligated balance:			
	Unpaid obligations:			
3010	New obligations, unexpired accounts	640	485	535
3020	Outlays (gross)	–640	–485	–535
	Budget authority and outlays, net:			
	Discretionary:			
4000	Budget authority, gross	465	485	535
	Outlays, gross:			
4010	Outlays from new discretionary authority	465	485	535
	Mandatory:			
4090	Budget authority, gross	175	....	....
	Outlays, gross:			
4100	Outlays from new mandatory authority	175	....	....
4180	Budget authority, net (total)	640	485	535
4190	Outlays, net (total)	640	485	535

The Budget proposes an advance appropriation of $565 million for the Corporation for Public Broadcasting (CPB) for fiscal year 2025. In 1975, Congress first agreed to begin providing CPB with a two-year advance appropriation to support long-range financing planning and to insulate programming decisions. This commitment of future Federal dollars helps leverage investments from other sources and gives producers essential lead time to plan, design, create, and support programming and services. CPB uses funding to provide grants to qualified public television and radio stations to be used at their discretion for purposes related to program production or acquisition, as well as for general operations. CPB also supports the production and acquisition of radio and television programs for national distribution. In addition, CPB assists in the financing of several system-wide activities, including interconnection services and limited technical assistance, research, and planning services to improve systemwide capacity and performance.

COUNCIL OF THE INSPECTORS GENERAL ON INTEGRITY AND EFFICIENCY

Federal Funds

PANDEMIC RESPONSE ACCOUNTABILITY COMMITTEE

Program and Financing (in millions of dollars)

Identification code 542–1654–0–1–808		2021 actual	2022 est.	2023 est.
	Obligations by program activity:			
0001	Direct program activity	16	32	26
0100	Direct program activities, subtotal	16	32	26
	Budgetary resources:			
	Unobligated balance:			
1000	Unobligated balance brought forward, Oct 1	72	96	64
1001	Discretionary unobligated balance brought fwd, Oct 1	72		
	Budget authority:			
	Appropriations, mandatory:			
1200	Appropriation	40	....	....
1900	Budget authority (total)	40	....	....
1930	Total budgetary resources available	112	96	64
	Memorandum (non-add) entries:			
1941	Unexpired unobligated balance, end of year	96	64	38
	Change in obligated balance:			
	Unpaid obligations:			
3000	Unpaid obligations, brought forward, Oct 1	7	7	6
3010	New obligations, unexpired accounts	16	32	26
3020	Outlays (gross)	–16	–33	–27
3050	Unpaid obligations, end of year	7	6	5
	Memorandum (non-add) entries:			
3100	Obligated balance, start of year	7	7	6
3200	Obligated balance, end of year	7	6	5
	Budget authority and outlays, net:			
	Discretionary:			
	Outlays, gross:			
4011	Outlays from discretionary balances	12	21	15

		2021 actual	2022 est.	2023 est.
	Mandatory:			
4090	Budget authority, gross	40		
	Outlays, gross:			
4100	Outlays from new mandatory authority	4		
4101	Outlays from mandatory balances		12	12
4110	Outlays, gross (total)	4	12	12
4180	Budget authority, net (total)	40		
4190	Outlays, net (total)	16	33	27

The Pandemic Response Accountability Committee (PRAC) was established as a committee of the Council of the Inspectors General on Integrity and Efficiency (CIGIE) by the Coronavirus Aid, Relief, and Economic Security (CARES) Act of 2020 (P.L. 116–136). The primary functions of the PRAC are to promote transparency, provide and support the independent oversight of the roughly $5.5 trillion in funds provided by pandemic relief legislation, and provide oversight of the coronavirus response to detect and remediate fraud, waste, and mismanagement in Federal spending.

Object Classification (in millions of dollars)

Identification code 542–1654–0–1–808		2021 actual	2022 est.	2023 est.
	Direct obligations:			
11.3	Personnel compensation: Other than full-time permanent	4	8	10
12.1	Civilian personnel benefits	1	2	2
25.2	Other services from non-Federal sources	11	22	14
99.9	Total new obligations, unexpired accounts	16	32	26

Employment Summary

Identification code 542–1654–0–1–808		2021 actual	2022 est.	2023 est.
1001	Direct civilian full-time equivalent employment	25	65	65

INSPECTORS GENERAL COUNCIL FUND

Program and Financing (in millions of dollars)

Identification code 542–4592–0–4–808		2021 actual	2022 est.	2023 est.
	Obligations by program activity:			
0801	Inspectors General Council Fund (Reimbursable)	10	15	15
	Budgetary resources:			
	Unobligated balance:			
1000	Unobligated balance brought forward, Oct 1	16	19	19
	Budget authority:			
	Appropriations, discretionary:			
1100	Appropriation	1	1	1
	Spending authority from offsetting collections, mandatory:			
1800	Collected	11	14	14
1801	Change in uncollected payments, Federal sources	1		
1850	Spending auth from offsetting collections, mand (total)	12	14	14
1900	Budget authority (total)	13	15	15
1930	Total budgetary resources available	29	34	34
	Memorandum (non-add) entries:			
1941	Unexpired unobligated balance, end of year	19	19	19
	Change in obligated balance:			
	Unpaid obligations:			
3000	Unpaid obligations, brought forward, Oct 1	4	4	3
3010	New obligations, unexpired accounts	10	15	15
3020	Outlays (gross)	–10	–16	–16
3050	Unpaid obligations, end of year	4	3	2
	Uncollected payments:			
3060	Uncollected pymts, Fed sources, brought forward, Oct 1		–1	–1
3070	Change in uncollected pymts, Fed sources, unexpired	–1		
3090	Uncollected pymts, Fed sources, end of year	–1	–1	–1
	Memorandum (non-add) entries:			
3100	Obligated balance, start of year	4	3	2
3200	Obligated balance, end of year	3	2	1
	Budget authority and outlays, net:			
	Discretionary:			
4000	Budget authority, gross	1	1	1
	Outlays, gross:			
4010	Outlays from new discretionary authority	1	1	1
	Mandatory:			
4090	Budget authority, gross	12	14	14
	Outlays, gross:			
4100	Outlays from new mandatory authority	8	11	11
4101	Outlays from mandatory balances	1	4	4
4110	Outlays, gross (total)	9	15	15
	Offsets against gross budget authority and outlays:			
	Offsetting collections (collected) from:			
4120	Federal sources	–11	–14	–14
	Additional offsets against gross budget authority only:			
4140	Change in uncollected pymts, Fed sources, unexpired	–1		
4170	Outlays, net (mandatory)	–2	1	1
4180	Budget authority, net (total)	1	1	1
4190	Outlays, net (total)	–1	2	2

The Inspector General (IG) Reform Act of 2008 (P.L. 110–409) created the Council of the Inspectors General on Integrity and Efficiency (CIGIE) to address program integrity, efficiency, and effectiveness issues that transcend individual Government agencies and to increase the professionalism and effectiveness of IG staff.

Pursuant to Section 7 of the Inspector General Reform Act of 2008, the revolving fund provides resources for CIGIE activities primarily through interagency funding, which includes member contributions and tuition. Additional appropriations are provided for mandated activities such as Oversight.gov. Consistent with prior years, CIGIE plans to collect member contributions for 2023 during the second half of 2022, to be used primarily for the CIGIE Training Institute and operations. Although CIGIE will collect the required member contributions for 2023 from agency IGs in the second half of 2022, the Budget includes funds in individual IG budgets that are dedicated to CIGIE and will be collected in 2023 for use in 2024.

Object Classification (in millions of dollars)

Identification code 542–4592–0–4–808		2021 actual	2022 est.	2023 est.
	Reimbursable obligations:			
	Personnel compensation:			
11.1	Full-time Permanent	3	4	4
11.8	Special personal services payments	1	1	1
11.9	Total personnel compensation	4	5	5
12.1	Civilian personnel benefits	1	1	1
25.1	Advisory and assistance services	2	3	3
25.2	Other services from non-Federal sources		3	3
25.3	Other goods and services from Federal sources	3	3	3
99.9	Total new obligations, unexpired accounts	10	15	15

Employment Summary

Identification code 542–4592–0–4–808		2021 actual	2022 est.	2023 est.
2001	Reimbursable civilian full-time equivalent employment	27	29	29

COURT SERVICES AND OFFENDER SUPERVISION AGENCY FOR THE DISTRICT OF COLUMBIA

Federal Funds

FEDERAL PAYMENT TO THE COURT SERVICES AND OFFENDER SUPERVISION AGENCY FOR THE DISTRICT OF COLUMBIA

For salaries and expenses, including the transfer and hire of motor vehicles, of the Court Services and Offender Supervision Agency for the District of Columbia, as authorized by the National Capital Revitalization and Self-Government Improvement Act of 1997, $281,516,000, of which not to exceed $2,000 is for official reception and representation expenses related to Community Supervision and Pretrial Services Agency programs, and of which not to exceed $25,000 is for dues and assessments relating to the implementation of the Court Services and Offender Supervision Agency Interstate Supervision Act of 2002: Provided, That, of the funds appropriated under this heading, $204,579,000 shall be for necessary expenses of Community Supervision and Sex Offender Registration, to include expenses relating to the supervision of adults subject to protection orders or the provision of services for or related to such persons, of which $7,798,000 shall remain available until

Court Services and Offender Supervision Agency for the District of Columbia—Continued
Federal Funds—Continued

FEDERAL PAYMENT TO THE COURT SERVICES AND OFFENDER SUPERVISION AGENCY FOR THE DISTRICT OF COLUMBIA—Continued

September 30, 2025, for costs associated with relocation under replacement leases for headquarters offices, field offices and related facilities: Provided further, That, of the funds appropriated under this heading, $76,937,000 shall be available to the Pretrial Services Agency, of which $998,000 shall remain available until September 30, 2025, for costs associated with relocation under a replacement lease for headquarters offices, field offices, and related facilities: Provided further, That notwithstanding any other provision of law, all amounts under this heading shall be apportioned quarterly by the Office of Management and Budget and obligated and expended in the same manner as funds appropriated for salaries and expenses of other Federal agencies: Provided further, That amounts under this heading may be used for programmatic incentives for defendants to successfully complete their terms of supervision.

Note.—A full-year 2022 appropriation for this account was not enacted at the time the Budget was prepared; therefore, the Budget assumes this account is operating under the Continuing Appropriations Act, 2022 (Division A of Public Law 117–43, as amended). The amounts included for 2022 reflect the annualized level provided by the continuing resolution.

Program and Financing (in millions of dollars)

Identification code 511–1734–0–1–752	2021 actual	2022 est.	2023 est.
Obligations by program activity:			
0001 Community supervision program	177	179	205
0002 Pretrial Services Agency	66	70	76
0900 Total new obligations, unexpired accounts	243	249	281
Budgetary resources:			
Unobligated balance:			
1000 Unobligated balance brought forward, Oct 1	18	5	1
Budget authority:			
Appropriations, discretionary:			
1100 Appropriation	246	249	282
Spending authority from offsetting collections, discretionary:			
1700 Collected	1		
1900 Budget authority (total)	247	249	282
1930 Total budgetary resources available	265	254	283
Memorandum (non-add) entries:			
1940 Unobligated balance expiring	–17	–4	–1
1941 Unexpired unobligated balance, end of year	5	1	1
Change in obligated balance:			
Unpaid obligations:			
3000 Unpaid obligations, brought forward, Oct 1	90	91	73
3010 New obligations, unexpired accounts	243	249	281
3011 Obligations ("upward adjustments"), expired accounts	2		
3020 Outlays (gross)	–226	–252	–274
3041 Recoveries of prior year unpaid obligations, expired	–18	–15	–11
3050 Unpaid obligations, end of year	91	73	69
Uncollected payments:			
3060 Uncollected pymts, Fed sources, brought forward, Oct 1	–1	–1	–1
3090 Uncollected pymts, Fed sources, end of year	–1	–1	–1
Memorandum (non-add) entries:			
3100 Obligated balance, start of year	89	90	72
3200 Obligated balance, end of year	90	72	68
Budget authority and outlays, net:			
Discretionary:			
4000 Budget authority, gross	247	249	282
Outlays, gross:			
4010 Outlays from new discretionary authority	191	187	212
4011 Outlays from discretionary balances	35	65	62
4020 Outlays, gross (total)	226	252	274
Offsets against gross budget authority and outlays:			
Offsetting collections (collected) from:			
4030 Federal sources	–1		
4033 Non-Federal sources	–1		
4040 Offsets against gross budget authority and outlays (total)	–2		
Additional offsets against gross budget authority only:			
4052 Offsetting collections credited to expired accounts	1		
4070 Budget authority, net (discretionary)	246	249	282
4080 Outlays, net (discretionary)	224	252	274
4180 Budget authority, net (total)	246	249	282
4190 Outlays, net (total)	224	252	274

The National Capital Revitalization and Self-Government Improvement Act of 1997 established the Court Services and Offender Supervision Agency (CSOSA) for the District of Columbia as an independent Federal agency to perform community supervision of D.C. Code offenders. CSOSA assumed the adult probation function from the D.C. Superior Court and the parole supervision function from the D.C. Board of Parole. The Pretrial Services Agency for the District of Columbia, responsible for supervising pretrial defendants, is an independent entity within CSOSA with its own budget and organizational structure. The mission of CSOSA is to increase public safety, prevent crime, reduce recidivism, and support the fair administration of justice in close collaboration with the community.

The CSOSA appropriation supports the Community Supervision Program and the Pretrial Services Agency.

Community Supervision Program.—This activity provides supervision of adult offenders on probation, parole, or supervised release, consistent with a crime prevention strategy that emphasizes public safety and successful reintegration. The Community Supervision Program employs an integrated system of close supervision, drug testing, graduated sanctions, treatment, transitional housing, and other offender support services, including services from community and faith-based collaborations. The Community Supervision Program also develops and provides the courts and the U.S. Parole Commission with critical information for probation, parole, and supervised release decisions.

Pretrial Services Agency.—This activity assists judicial officers in both the D.C. Superior Court and the U.S. District Court for the District of Columbia by formulating release recommendations and providing supervision and treatment services to defendants that reasonably assure that individuals on conditional release return to court and do not engage in criminal activity pending their trial and/or sentencing. The Pretrial Services Agency is responsible for enforcing conditions of release, conducting drug testing, administering graduated sanctions, referring defendants to treatment and other social services, and reporting to the courts defendants' compliance with their conditions of release.

Object Classification (in millions of dollars)

Identification code 511–1734–0–1–752	2021 actual	2022 est.	2023 est.
Direct obligations:			
Personnel compensation:			
11.1 Full-time permanent	111	116	124
11.3 Other than full-time permanent			1
11.5 Other personnel compensation	3	2	4
11.9 Total personnel compensation	114	118	129
12.1 Civilian personnel benefits	53	58	64
21.0 Travel and transportation of persons	1	1	1
23.1 Rental payments to GSA	15	15	17
23.2 Rental payments to others	6	6	6
23.3 Communications, utilities, and miscellaneous charges	3	3	3
25.1 Advisory and assistance services	8	3	4
25.2 Other services from non-Federal sources	28	32	40
25.3 Other goods and services from Federal sources	6	6	6
25.4 Operation and maintenance of facilities		1	1
25.6 Medical care	2	1	1
25.7 Operation and maintenance of equipment	1	2	2
26.0 Supplies and materials	2	2	2
31.0 Equipment	4	1	5
99.0 Direct obligations	243	249	281
99.9 Total new obligations, unexpired accounts	243	249	281

Employment Summary

Identification code 511–1734–0–1–752	2021 actual	2022 est.	2023 est.
1001 Direct civilian full-time equivalent employment	1,033	1,075	1,124

OTHER INDEPENDENT AGENCIES

DEFENSE NUCLEAR FACILITIES SAFETY BOARD

Federal Funds

SALARIES AND EXPENSES

For expenses necessary for the Defense Nuclear Facilities Safety Board in carrying out activities authorized by the Atomic Energy Act of 1954, as amended by Public Law 100–456, section 1441, $41,401,400, to remain available until September 30, 2024, of which not to exceed $1,000 shall be available for official reception and representation expenses.

Note.—A full-year 2022 appropriation for this account was not enacted at the time the Budget was prepared; therefore, the Budget assumes this account is operating under the Continuing Appropriations Act, 2022 (Division A of Public Law 117–43, as amended). The amounts included for 2022 reflect the annualized level provided by the continuing resolution.

Program and Financing (in millions of dollars)

Identification code 347–3900–0–1–999	2021 actual	2022 est.	2023 est.
Obligations by program activity:			
0001 Salaries and Expenses (Direct)	36	37	41
Budgetary resources:			
Unobligated balance:			
1000 Unobligated balance brought forward, Oct 1	13	9	3
1021 Recoveries of prior year unpaid obligations	1		
1070 Unobligated balance (total)	14	9	3
Budget authority:			
Appropriations, discretionary:			
1100 Appropriation	31	31	41
1930 Total budgetary resources available	45	40	44
Memorandum (non-add) entries:			
1941 Unexpired unobligated balance, end of year	9	3	3
Change in obligated balance:			
Unpaid obligations:			
3000 Unpaid obligations, brought forward, Oct 1	4	9	14
3010 New obligations, unexpired accounts	36	37	41
3020 Outlays (gross)	–30	–32	–39
3040 Recoveries of prior year unpaid obligations, unexpired	–1		
3050 Unpaid obligations, end of year	9	14	16
Memorandum (non-add) entries:			
3100 Obligated balance, start of year	4	9	14
3200 Obligated balance, end of year	9	14	16
Budget authority and outlays, net:			
Discretionary:			
4000 Budget authority, gross	31	31	41
Outlays, gross:			
4010 Outlays from new discretionary authority	18	23	31
4011 Outlays from discretionary balances	12	9	8
4020 Outlays, gross (total)	30	32	39
4180 Budget authority, net (total)	31	31	41
4190 Outlays, net (total)	30	32	39

The Defense Nuclear Facilities Safety Board, an independent, non-regulatory agency within the Executive Branch, is responsible for evaluating the content and implementation of the standards relating to the design, construction, operation, and decommissioning of Department of Energy (DOE) defense nuclear facilities. The Board also reviews the design of new DOE defense nuclear facilities and periodically reviews and monitors construction of such facilities to ensure adequate protection of public and worker health and safety. The Board is also responsible for investigating any event or practice at a defense nuclear facility that has or may adversely affect public health and safety. The Board makes specific recommendations to the Secretary of Energy on measures that should be adopted to protect both public and employee health and safety.

Object Classification (in millions of dollars)

Identification code 347–3900–0–1–999	2021 actual	2022 est.	2023 est.
11.1 Direct obligations: Personnel compensation: Full-time permanent	16	18	20
11.9 Total personnel compensation	16	18	20
12.1 Civilian personnel benefits	6	7	7
21.0 Travel and transportation of persons		1	1
23.1 Rental payments to GSA	3	3	3
25.1 Advisory and assistance services	1	1	1
25.2 Other services from non-Federal sources	9	6	7
25.3 Other goods and services from Federal sources	1	1	1
31.0 Equipment			1
99.0 Direct obligations	36	37	41
99.9 Total new obligations, unexpired accounts	36	37	41

Employment Summary

Identification code 347–3900–0–1–999	2021 actual	2022 est.	2023 est.
1001 Direct civilian full-time equivalent employment	103	115	120

DELTA REGIONAL AUTHORITY

Federal Funds

DELTA REGIONAL AUTHORITY

For expenses necessary for the Delta Regional Authority and to carry out its activities, as authorized by the Delta Regional Authority Act of 2000, notwithstanding sections 382F(d), 382M, and 382N of said Act, $30,100,000, to remain available until expended.

Note.—A full-year 2022 appropriation for this account was not enacted at the time the Budget was prepared; therefore, the Budget assumes this account is operating under the Continuing Appropriations Act, 2022 (Division A of Public Law 117–43, as amended). The amounts included for 2022 reflect the annualized level provided by the continuing resolution.

DELTA REGIONAL AUTHORITY

[For an additional amount for "Delta Regional Authority", $150,000,000 to remain available until expended: *Provided*, That such amount is designated by the Congress as being for an emergency requirement pursuant to section 4112(a) of H. Con. Res. 71 (115th Congress), the concurrent resolution on the budget for fiscal year 2018, and to section 251(b) of the Balanced Budget and Emergency Deficit Control Act of 1985.] *(Infrastructure Investments and Jobs Appropriations Act.)*

Program and Financing (in millions of dollars)

Identification code 517–0750–0–1–452	2021 actual	2022 est.	2023 est.
Obligations by program activity:			
0001 Delta Regional Authority (Direct)	4	15	15
0002 Delta Regional Authority - IIJA Activities (Direct)		29	32
0799 Total direct obligations	4	44	47
0801 Delta Regional Authority (Reimbursable)		15	15
0900 Total new obligations, unexpired accounts	4	59	62
Budgetary resources:			
Unobligated balance:			
1000 Unobligated balance brought forward, Oct 1	8	34	156
Budget authority:			
Appropriations, discretionary:			
1100 Appropriation	30	30	30
1100 Appropriation (IIJA)		150	
1160 Appropriation, discretionary (total)	30	180	30
Spending authority from offsetting collections, discretionary:			
1700 Collected		1	1
1900 Budget authority (total)	30	181	31
1930 Total budgetary resources available	38	215	187
Memorandum (non-add) entries:			
1941 Unexpired unobligated balance, end of year	34	156	125
Change in obligated balance:			
Unpaid obligations:			
3000 Unpaid obligations, brought forward, Oct 1	64	44	56
3010 New obligations, unexpired accounts	4	59	62
3020 Outlays (gross)	–24	–47	–51
3050 Unpaid obligations, end of year	44	56	67
Memorandum (non-add) entries:			
3100 Obligated balance, start of year	64	44	56
3200 Obligated balance, end of year	44	56	67
Budget authority and outlays, net:			
Discretionary:			
4000 Budget authority, gross	30	181	31

DELTA REGIONAL AUTHORITY—Continued
Program and Financing—Continued

Identification code 517–0750–0–1–452		2021 actual	2022 est.	2023 est.
	Outlays, gross:			
4010	Outlays from new discretionary authority	2	17	13
4011	Outlays from discretionary balances	22	30	38
4020	Outlays, gross (total)	24	47	51
	Offsets against gross budget authority and outlays:			
	Offsetting collections (collected) from:			
4030	Federal sources		–1	–1
4180	Budget authority, net (total)	30	180	30
4190	Outlays, net (total)	24	46	50

The Budget provides $30.1 million for the Delta Regional Authority (DRA). Established by Congress in 2000, DRA is a Federal-State partnership created to address the economic needs of the eight-state or 252 county/parish Mississippi Delta region. DRA's economic development investments, including regional planning, support the creation and sustainability of strong local and regional economies. Leveraging private and non-profit sectors, DRA's strategic investments support projects in the following categories: basic public infrastructure, transportation infrastructure, business development with an emphasis in entrepreneurship, and workforce development, as well as increasing access to quality healthcare.

Object Classification (in millions of dollars)

Identification code 517–0750–0–1–452		2021 actual	2022 est.	2023 est.
	Direct obligations:			
11.1	Personnel compensation: Full-time permanent	2	2	2
41.0	Grants, subsidies, and contributions	2	42	45
99.0	Direct obligations	4	44	47
99.0	Reimbursable obligations		15	15
99.9	Total new obligations, unexpired accounts	4	59	62

Employment Summary

Identification code 517–0750–0–1–452	2021 actual	2022 est.	2023 est.
1001 Direct civilian full-time equivalent employment	13	14	14

DENALI COMMISSION
Federal Funds

DENALI COMMISSION

For expenses necessary for the Denali Commission including the purchase, construction, and acquisition of plant and capital equipment as necessary and other expenses, $15,100,000, to remain available until expended, notwithstanding the limitations contained in section 306(g) of the Denali Commission Act of 1998: Provided, That funds shall be available for construction projects for which the Denali Commission is the sole or primary funding source in an amount not to exceed 80 percent of total project cost for distressed communities, as defined by section 307 of the Denali Commission Act of 1998 (division C, title III, Public Law 105–277), as amended by section 701 of appendix D, title VII, Public Law 106–113 (113 Stat. 1501A-280), and an amount not to exceed 50 percent for non-distressed communities: Provided further, That notwithstanding any other provision of law regarding payment of a non-Federal share in connection with a grant-in-aid program, amounts under this heading shall be available for the payment of such a non-Federal share for any project for which the Denali Commission is not the sole or primary funding source, provided that such project is consistent with the purposes of the Commission.

Note.—A full-year 2022 appropriation for this account was not enacted at the time the Budget was prepared; therefore, the Budget assumes this account is operating under the Continuing Appropriations Act, 2022 (Division A of Public Law 117–43, as amended). The amounts included for 2022 reflect the annualized level provided by the continuing resolution.

DENALI COMMISSION

[*For an additional amount for "Denali Commission", $75,000,000 to remain available until expended: Provided further, That such amount is designated by the Congress as being for an emergency requirement pursuant to section 4112(a) of H.* Con. Res. 71 (115th Congress), the concurrent resolution on the budget for fiscal year 2018, and to section 251(b) of the Balanced Budget and Emergency Deficit Control Act of 1985.] *(Infrastructure Investments and Jobs Appropriations Act.)*

Program and Financing (in millions of dollars)

Identification code 513–1200–0–1–452		2021 actual	2022 est.	2023 est.
	Obligations by program activity:			
0101	Denali Commission (Direct)	19	18	18
0102	Denali Commission (Shared Services)	4	5	5
0103	Denali Commission (IIJA - Direct)		20	20
0799	Total direct obligations	23	43	43
0900	Total new obligations, unexpired accounts	23	43	43
	Budgetary resources:			
	Unobligated balance:			
1000	Unobligated balance brought forward, Oct 1	1	2	63
1021	Recoveries of prior year unpaid obligations	1	6	10
1070	Unobligated balance (total)	2	8	73
	Budget authority:			
	Appropriations, discretionary:			
1100	Appropriation	15	15	15
1100	Appropriation (Infrastructure Investment and Jobs Act of 2021)		75	
1160	Appropriation, discretionary (total)	15	90	15
	Spending authority from offsetting collections, discretionary:			
1700	Collected	8	8	8
1900	Budget authority (total)	23	98	23
1930	Total budgetary resources available	25	106	96
	Memorandum (non-add) entries:			
1941	Unexpired unobligated balance, end of year	2	63	53
	Change in obligated balance:			
	Unpaid obligations:			
3000	Unpaid obligations, brought forward, Oct 1	50	52	60
3010	New obligations, unexpired accounts	23	43	43
3020	Outlays (gross)	–20	–29	–52
3040	Recoveries of prior year unpaid obligations, unexpired	–1	–6	–10
3050	Unpaid obligations, end of year	52	60	41
	Memorandum (non-add) entries:			
3100	Obligated balance, start of year	50	52	60
3200	Obligated balance, end of year	52	60	41
	Budget authority and outlays, net:			
	Discretionary:			
4000	Budget authority, gross	23	98	23
	Outlays, gross:			
4010	Outlays from new discretionary authority	7	14	10
4011	Outlays from discretionary balances	13	15	42
4020	Outlays, gross (total)	20	29	52
	Offsets against gross budget authority and outlays:			
	Offsetting collections (collected) from:			
4030	Federal sources	–8	–8	–8
4040	Offsets against gross budget authority and outlays (total)	–8	–8	–8
4180	Budget authority, net (total)	15	90	15
4190	Outlays, net (total)	12	21	44

The Budget provides $15.1 million for the Denali Commission. The Denali Commission was established by the Denali Commission Act of 1998 and is composed of seven members including the Federal Co-Chair. Denali's mission is to promote and provide sustainable infrastructure improvement, job training, and other economic development services that improve health, safety, and economic self-sufficiency within rural communities in Alaska and alleviate the long-term economic disparities suffered by Alaska Native communities.

Object Classification (in millions of dollars)

Identification code 513–1200–0–1–452		2021 actual	2022 est.	2023 est.
	Direct obligations:			
11.1	Personnel compensation: Full-time permanent	2	2	2
12.1	Civilian personnel benefits	1	1	1
25.1	Advisory and assistance services	1		
25.3	Other goods and services from Federal sources	1	6	6
41.0	Grants, subsidies, and contributions	18	34	34

OTHER INDEPENDENT AGENCIES

		2021 actual	2022 est.	2023 est.
99.9	Total new obligations, unexpired accounts	23	43	43

Employment Summary

Identification code 513–1200–0–1–452	2021 actual	2022 est.	2023 est.
1001 Direct civilian full-time equivalent employment	13	14	14

GIFTS AND DONATIONS, DENALI COMMISSION

Program and Financing (in millions of dollars)

Identification code 513–5605–0–2–452	2021 actual	2022 est.	2023 est.
Obligations by program activity:			
0101 Denali Commission Non-Federal Funds (Direct)		15	
Budgetary resources:			
Budget authority:			
Spending authority from offsetting collections, discretionary:			
1700 Collected		15	
1930 Total budgetary resources available		15	
Change in obligated balance:			
Unpaid obligations:			
3000 Unpaid obligations, brought forward, Oct 1			10
3010 New obligations, unexpired accounts		15	
3020 Outlays (gross)		–5	–4
3050 Unpaid obligations, end of year		10	6
Memorandum (non-add) entries:			
3100 Obligated balance, start of year			10
3200 Obligated balance, end of year		10	6
Budget authority and outlays, net:			
Discretionary:			
4000 Budget authority, gross		15	
Outlays, gross:			
4010 Outlays from new discretionary authority		5	
4011 Outlays from discretionary balances			4
4020 Outlays, gross (total)		5	4
Offsets against gross budget authority and outlays:			
Offsetting collections (collected) from:			
4033 Non-Federal sources		–15	
4180 Budget authority, net (total)			
4190 Outlays, net (total)		–10	4

The Denali Commission has gift and transfer authorities, as provided in Sections 305(c), 309(i) and 311 of the Denali Commission Act of 1998. The Budget reflects an estimated transfer of $15 million from the State of Alaska for transportation projects made available in 2022.

Object Classification (in millions of dollars)

Identification code 513–5605–0–2–452	2021 actual	2022 est.	2023 est.
Direct obligations:			
25.3 Other goods and services from Federal sources		1	
41.0 Grants, subsidies, and contributions		14	
99.0 Direct obligations		15	
99.9 Total new obligations, unexpired accounts		15	

Trust Funds

DENALI COMMISSION TRUST FUND

Program and Financing (in millions of dollars)

Identification code 513–8056–0–7–452	2021 actual	2022 est.	2023 est.
Obligations by program activity:			
0101 Denali Commission Trust Fund (Direct)	3	4	4
0900 Total new obligations, unexpired accounts (object class 41.0)	3	4	4

		2021 actual	2022 est.	2023 est.
Budgetary resources:				
Unobligated balance:				
1000	Unobligated balance brought forward, Oct 1			1
1021	Recoveries of prior year unpaid obligations		1	1
1070	Unobligated balance (total)		1	2
Budget authority:				
Appropriations, discretionary:				
1101	Appropriation (special or trust)	3	4	4
1930	Total budgetary resources available	3	5	6
Memorandum (non-add) entries:				
1941	Unexpired unobligated balance, end of year		1	2
Change in obligated balance:				
Unpaid obligations:				
3000	Unpaid obligations, brought forward, Oct 1	12	11	8
3010	New obligations, unexpired accounts	3	4	4
3020	Outlays (gross)	–4	–6	–8
3040	Recoveries of prior year unpaid obligations, unexpired		–1	–1
3050	Unpaid obligations, end of year	11	8	3
Memorandum (non-add) entries:				
3100	Obligated balance, start of year	12	11	8
3200	Obligated balance, end of year	11	8	3
Budget authority and outlays, net:				
Discretionary:				
4000	Budget authority, gross	3	4	4
Outlays, gross:				
4010	Outlays from new discretionary authority		1	1
4011	Outlays from discretionary balances	4	5	7
4020	Outlays, gross (total)	4	6	8
4180	Budget authority, net (total)	3	4	4
4190	Outlays, net (total)	4	6	8

The Budget estimates $3.5 million from the Oil Spill Liability Trust Fund for subsequent transfer to the Denali Commission. The Omnibus Consolidated and Emergency Supplemental Appropriations Act of 1999 (P.L. 105–277) established the annual transfer of interest from the investment of the Trans-Alaska Pipeline Liability Fund balance into the Oil Spill Liability Trust Fund for subsequent transfer to the Denali Commission. As required by the Act, the Denali Commission, in consultation with the Coast Guard, developed a program to use these funds to repair or replace bulk fuel storage tanks in Alaska that were not in compliance with Federal law, including the Oil Pollution Act of 1990, or State law.

DISTRICT OF COLUMBIA

DISTRICT OF COLUMBIA COURTS

Federal Funds

FEDERAL PAYMENT TO THE DISTRICT OF COLUMBIA COURTS

For salaries and expenses, including the transfer and hire of motor vehicles, for the District of Columbia Courts, $295,588,000 to be allocated as follows: for the District of Columbia Court of Appeals, $15,055,000, of which not to exceed $2,500 is for official reception and representation expenses; for the Superior Court of the District of Columbia, $140,973,000, of which not to exceed $2,500 is for official reception and representation expenses; for the District of Columbia Court System, $88,290,000, of which not to exceed $2,500 is for official reception and representation expenses; and $51,270,000, to remain available until September 30, 2024, for capital improvements for District of Columbia courthouse facilities: Provided, That funds made available for capital improvements shall be expended consistent with the District of Columbia Courts master plan study and facilities condition assessment: Provided further, That, in addition to the amounts appropriated herein, fees received by the District of Columbia Courts for administering bar examinations and processing District of Columbia bar admissions may be retained and credited to this appropriation, to remain available until expended, for salaries and expenses associated with such activities, notwithstanding section 450 of the District of Columbia Home Rule Act (D.C. Official Code, sec. 1–204.50): Provided further, That notwithstanding any other provision of law, all amounts under this heading shall be apportioned quarterly by the Office of Management and Budget and obligated and expended in the same manner as funds appropriated for salaries and expenses of other Federal agencies: Provided further, That 30 days after providing written notice to the Committees on Appropriations of the House of Representatives and the Senate, the District of Columbia Courts may reallocate not more than $9,000,000 of the

FEDERAL PAYMENT TO THE DISTRICT OF COLUMBIA COURTS—Continued

funds provided under this heading among the items and entities funded under this heading: Provided further, That the Joint Committee on Judicial Administration in the District of Columbia may, by regulation, establish a program substantially similar to the program set forth in subchapter II of chapter 35 of title 5, United States Code, for employees of the District of Columbia Courts.

Note.—A full-year 2022 appropriation for this account was not enacted at the time the Budget was prepared; therefore, the Budget assumes this account is operating under the Continuing Appropriations Act, 2022 (Division A of Public Law 117–43, as amended). The amounts included for 2022 reflect the annualized level provided by the continuing resolution.

Program and Financing (in millions of dollars)

Identification code 349–1712–0–1–806	2021 actual	2022 est.	2023 est.
Obligations by program activity:			
0001 Court of Appeals	14	14	15
0002 Superior Court	126	126	141
0003 Court system	79	79	88
0004 Capital improvements	32	31	40
0900 Total new obligations, unexpired accounts	251	250	284
Budgetary resources:			
Unobligated balance:			
1000 Unobligated balance brought forward, Oct 1	28	28	30
1021 Recoveries of prior year unpaid obligations	1		
1070 Unobligated balance (total)	29	28	30
Budget authority:			
Appropriations, discretionary:			
1100 Appropriation	250	250	296
Spending authority from offsetting collections, discretionary:			
1700 Collected	1	2	2
1900 Budget authority (total)	251	252	298
1930 Total budgetary resources available	280	280	328
Memorandum (non-add) entries:			
1940 Unobligated balance expiring	–1		
1941 Unexpired unobligated balance, end of year	28	30	44
Change in obligated balance:			
Unpaid obligations:			
3000 Unpaid obligations, brought forward, Oct 1	132	110	106
3010 New obligations, unexpired accounts	251	250	284
3011 Obligations ("upward adjustments"), expired accounts	17		
3020 Outlays (gross)	–270	–254	–288
3040 Recoveries of prior year unpaid obligations, unexpired	–1		
3041 Recoveries of prior year unpaid obligations, expired	–19		
3050 Unpaid obligations, end of year	110	106	102
Memorandum (non-add) entries:			
3100 Obligated balance, start of year	132	110	106
3200 Obligated balance, end of year	110	106	102
Budget authority and outlays, net:			
Discretionary:			
4000 Budget authority, gross	251	252	298
Outlays, gross:			
4010 Outlays from new discretionary authority	190	190	224
4011 Outlays from discretionary balances	80	64	64
4020 Outlays, gross (total)	270	254	288
Offsets against gross budget authority and outlays:			
Offsetting collections (collected) from:			
4030 Federal sources		–1	–1
4033 Non-Federal sources	–2	–1	–1
4040 Offsets against gross budget authority and outlays (total)	–2	–2	–2
Additional offsets against gross budget authority only:			
4052 Offsetting collections credited to expired accounts	1		
4070 Budget authority, net (discretionary)	250	250	296
4080 Outlays, net (discretionary)	268	252	286
4180 Budget authority, net (total)	250	250	296
4190 Outlays, net (total)	268	252	286

Under the National Capital Revitalization and Self-Government Improvement Act of 1997, the Federal Government is required to finance the District of Columbia Courts. This payment to the District of Columbia Courts funds the operations of the District of Columbia Court of Appeals, Superior Court, and the Court System, as well as capital improvements.

The Budget provides resources to support the D.C. Courts' core functions. In addition, the Budget provides resources for capital improvements necessary to renovate the historic Recorder of Deeds building, to maintain court facilities in Judiciary Square, and to maintain and update technology. Additional language clarifies the District of Columbia Courts authority to procure vehicles for official business.

By law, the Courts' annual budget includes estimates of the expenditures for the operations of the District of Columbia Courts prepared by the Joint Committee on Judicial Administration in the District of Columbia and the President's recommendation for funding the District of Columbia Courts. The President's recommended level of $295.6 million includes $244.3 million for the District of Columbia Court of Appeals, the Superior Court of the District of Columbia, and the District of Columbia Court System operations and $51.3 million for capital improvements for District courthouse facilities. Under a separate transmittal to the Congress, the District of Columbia Courts are requesting $362.4 million: $244.8 million for operations and $117.6 million for capital improvements.

Object Classification (in millions of dollars)

Identification code 349–1712–0–1–806	2021 actual	2022 est.	2023 est.
Direct obligations:			
Personnel compensation:			
11.1 Full-time permanent	111	112	117
11.3 Other than full-time permanent	9	10	11
11.9 Total personnel compensation	120	122	128
12.1 Civilian personnel benefits	35	36	37
21.0 Travel and transportation of persons	1	1	1
23.2 Rental payments to others	9	10	11
23.3 Communications, utilities, and miscellaneous charges	9	10	12
24.0 Printing and reproduction	3	2	5
25.1 Advisory and assistance services	20	19	19
25.2 Other services from non-Federal sources	26	25	25
25.3 Other goods and services from Federal sources	4	3	6
25.4 Operation and maintenance of facilities	5	5	8
25.6 Medical care	1	1	1
25.7 Operation and maintenance of equipment	5	4	5
26.0 Supplies and materials	3	3	8
31.0 Equipment	5	4	8
32.0 Land and structures	5	5	10
99.0 Direct obligations	251	250	284
99.9 Total new obligations, unexpired accounts	251	250	284

FEDERAL PAYMENT FOR DEFENDER SERVICES IN DISTRICT OF COLUMBIA COURTS

For payments authorized under section 11–2604 and section 11–2605, D.C. Official Code (relating to representation provided under the District of Columbia Criminal Justice Act), payments for counsel appointed in proceedings in the Family Court of the Superior Court of the District of Columbia under chapter 23 of title 16, D.C. Official Code, or pursuant to contractual agreements to provide guardian ad litem representation, training, technical assistance, and such other services as are necessary to improve the quality of guardian ad litem representation, payments for counsel appointed in adoption proceedings under chapter 3 of title 16, D.C. Official Code, and payments authorized under section 21–2060, D.C. Official Code (relating to services provided under the District of Columbia Guardianship, Protective Proceedings, and Durable Power of Attorney Act of 1986), $46,005,000, to remain available until expended: Provided, That funds provided under this heading shall be administered by the Joint Committee on Judicial Administration in the District of Columbia: Provided further, That, notwithstanding any other provision of law, this appropriation shall be apportioned quarterly by the Office of Management and Budget and obligated and expended in the same manner as funds appropriated for expenses of other Federal agencies: Provided further, That of the unobligated balances from prior year appropriations made available under the heading "Federal Payment for Defender Services in District of Columbia Courts", $22,000,000, are hereby permanently cancelled not later than September 30, 2023.

Note.—A full-year 2022 appropriation for this account was not enacted at the time the Budget was prepared; therefore, the Budget assumes this account is operating under the Continuing Appropriations Act, 2022 (Division A of Public Law 117–43, as amended). The amounts included for 2022 reflect the annualized level provided by the continuing resolution.

Program and Financing (in millions of dollars)

Identification code 349–1736–0–1–806		2021 actual	2022 est.	2023 est.
	Obligations by program activity:			
0001	Federal Payment for Defender Services in District of Columbia Co (Direct)	30	52	46
0900	Total new obligations, unexpired accounts (object class 25.2)	30	52	46
	Budgetary resources:			
	Unobligated balance:			
1000	Unobligated balance brought forward, Oct 1	30	46	40
	Budget authority:			
	Appropriations, discretionary:			
1100	Appropriation	46	46	46
1131	Unobligated balance of appropriations permanently reduced			−22
1160	Appropriation, discretionary (total)	46	46	24
1930	Total budgetary resources available	76	92	64
	Memorandum (non-add) entries:			
1941	Unexpired unobligated balance, end of year	46	40	18
	Change in obligated balance:			
	Unpaid obligations:			
3000	Unpaid obligations, brought forward, Oct 1	21	23	23
3010	New obligations, unexpired accounts	30	52	46
3020	Outlays (gross)	−28	−52	−43
3050	Unpaid obligations, end of year	23	23	26
	Memorandum (non-add) entries:			
3100	Obligated balance, start of year	21	23	23
3200	Obligated balance, end of year	23	23	26
	Budget authority and outlays, net:			
	Discretionary:			
4000	Budget authority, gross	46	46	24
	Outlays, gross:			
4010	Outlays from new discretionary authority	28	24	13
4011	Outlays from discretionary balances		28	30
4020	Outlays, gross (total)	28	52	43
4180	Budget authority, net (total)	46	46	24
4190	Outlays, net (total)	28	52	43

Under three Defender Services programs, the District of Columbia Courts appoint and compensate attorneys to represent persons who are financially unable to obtain such representation on their own. The Defender Services programs are the Criminal Justice Act program, which provides court-appointed attorneys to indigent persons who are charged with criminal offenses; the Counsel for Child Abuse and Neglect program, which provides court-appointed attorneys for family proceedings in which child neglect is alleged or where the termination of the parent-child relationship is under consideration and the parent, guardian, or custodian of the child is indigent; and the Guardianship program, which provides for the representation and protection of mentally incapacitated individuals and minors whose parents are deceased. In addition to legal representation, these programs provide indigent persons with services such as transcripts of court proceedings, expert witness testimony, foreign and sign language interpretation, investigations, and genetic testing. The President's recommended funding level for Defender Services is $46.0 million, the same as the Courts' request, and includes a one-time cancellation of $22.0 million in unobligated balances in the account. Further, the Budget includes language permitting the District of Columbia Courts to set the rate of pay for court-appointed attorneys, capped at the rate paid in Federal courts, and for investigative services. The current attorney hourly rate was set in 2009 at $90; for comparison, the current Federal rate is $158 (75% higher). The ability to set a higher rate will increase the Courts' ability to attract qualified attorneys.

DISTRICT OF COLUMBIA CRIME VICTIMS COMPENSATION FUND

Special and Trust Fund Receipts (in millions of dollars)

Identification code 349–5676–0–2–806		2021 actual	2022 est.	2023 est.
0100	Balance, start of year	1	1	1
	Receipts:			
	Current law:			
1110	Fines and Fees, District of Columbia Crime Victims Compensation Fund	5	6	6
2000	Total: Balances and receipts	6	7	7
	Appropriations:			
	Current law:			
2101	District of Columbia Crime Victims Compensation Fund	−5	−6	−6
5099	Balance, end of year	1	1	1

Program and Financing (in millions of dollars)

Identification code 349–5676–0–2–806		2021 actual	2022 est.	2023 est.
	Obligations by program activity:			
0001	Crime Victims Compensation	5	9	9
0900	Total new obligations, unexpired accounts (object class 25.1)	5	9	9
	Budgetary resources:			
	Unobligated balance:			
1000	Unobligated balance brought forward, Oct 1	1	1	1
	Budget authority:			
	Appropriations, mandatory:			
1201	Appropriation (special or trust fund)	5	6	6
	Spending authority from offsetting collections, mandatory:			
1800	Collected		3	3
1900	Budget authority (total)	5	9	9
1930	Total budgetary resources available	6	10	10
	Memorandum (non-add) entries:			
1941	Unexpired unobligated balance, end of year	1	1	1
	Change in obligated balance:			
	Unpaid obligations:			
3000	Unpaid obligations, brought forward, Oct 1	1		
3010	New obligations, unexpired accounts	5	9	9
3020	Outlays (gross)	−6	−9	−9
	Memorandum (non-add) entries:			
3100	Obligated balance, start of year	1		
	Budget authority and outlays, net:			
	Mandatory:			
4090	Budget authority, gross	5	9	9
	Outlays, gross:			
4100	Outlays from new mandatory authority	4	8	8
4101	Outlays from mandatory balances	2	1	1
4110	Outlays, gross (total)	6	9	9
	Offsets against gross budget authority and outlays:			
	Offsetting collections (collected) from:			
4120	Federal sources		−3	−3
4180	Budget authority, net (total)	5	6	6
4190	Outlays, net (total)	6	6	6

The Superior Court of the District of Columbia administers the Crime Victims Compensation Fund, which finances assistance for innocent victims of violent crime, survivors of homicide victims, and dependent family members of homicide victims. The program provides compensation for certain costs related to the crime, such as medical expenses, temporary emergency housing, and funeral expenses. The Fund is financed through assessments imposed in criminal cases, court fines and fees, and a grant from the U.S. Department of Justice. Under the 2002 Supplemental Appropriations Act for Further Recovery From and Response to Terrorist Attacks on the United States (P.L. 107–206), one half of the Fund's unobligated balances at the end of each year are transferred to the District of Columbia Government for outreach activities designed to increase the number of crime victims who apply for compensation.

FEDERAL PAYMENT TO THE DISTRICT OF COLUMBIA JUDICIAL RETIREMENT AND SURVIVORS ANNUITY FUND

Program and Financing (in millions of dollars)

Identification code 020–1713–0–1–752		2021 actual	2022 est.	2023 est.
	Obligations by program activity:			
0001	Payment to Judicial Retirement Fund	19	19	19

1240　District of Columbia—Continued
Federal Funds—Continued

FEDERAL PAYMENT TO THE DISTRICT OF COLUMBIA JUDICIAL RETIREMENT AND SURVIVORS ANNUITY FUND—Continued

Program and Financing—Continued

Identification code 020–1713–0–1–752	2021 actual	2022 est.	2023 est.
0900　Total new obligations, unexpired accounts (object class 13.0)	19	19	19
Budgetary resources:			
Budget authority:			
Appropriations, mandatory:			
1200　Appropriation	19	19	19
1930　Total budgetary resources available	19	19	19
Change in obligated balance:			
Unpaid obligations:			
3010　New obligations, unexpired accounts	19	19	19
3020　Outlays (gross)	–19	–19	–19
Budget authority and outlays, net:			
Mandatory:			
4090　Budget authority, gross	19	19	19
Outlays, gross:			
4100　Outlays from new mandatory authority	19	19	19
4180　Budget authority, net (total)	19	19	19
4190　Outlays, net (total)	19	19	19

The National Capital Revitalization and Self-Government Improvement Act of 1997, as amended, requires the Secretary of the Treasury to make payments at the end of each fiscal year, beginning in 1998, from the General Fund of the Treasury into the District of Columbia Judicial Retirement and Survivors Annuity Fund (Judicial Fund). Annual payments consist of (1) amounts necessary to amortize: the original unfunded liability over 30 years, the net gain or loss (based on experience) over 10 years, and any other changes in actuarial liability over 20 years and (2) amounts necessary to fund the normal cost and administrative expenses for the year. This account receives the annual payments from the General Fund and immediately transfers these amounts into the Judicial Fund.

Trust Funds

DISTRICT OF COLUMBIA JUDICIAL RETIREMENT AND SURVIVORS ANNUITY FUND

Special and Trust Fund Receipts (in millions of dollars)

Identification code 020–8212–0–7–602	2021 actual	2022 est.	2023 est.
0100　Balance, start of year	177	184	192
Receipts:			
Current law:			
1110　Deductions from Employees Salaries, District of Columbia Judicial Retirement and Survivors Annuity Fund	1	1	1
1140　Earnings on Investments, District of Columbia Judicial Retirement and Survivors Annuity Fund	2	4	3
1140　Federal Payments, D.C. Judicial Retirement and Survivors Annuity	19	19	19
1199　Total current law receipts	22	24	23
1999　Total receipts	22	24	23
2000　Total: Balances and receipts	199	208	215
Appropriations:			
Current law:			
2101　District of Columbia Judicial Retirement and Survivors Annuity Fund	–22	–21	–22
2135　District of Columbia Judicial Retirement and Survivors Annuity Fund	7	5	5
2199　Total current law appropriations	–15	–16	–17
2999　Total appropriations	–15	–16	–17
5099　Balance, end of year	184	192	198

Program and Financing (in millions of dollars)

Identification code 020–8212–0–7–602	2021 actual	2022 est.	2023 est.
Obligations by program activity:			
0001　Retirement payments	15	15	16
0002　Administrative Costs	....	1	1
0900　Total new obligations, unexpired accounts	15	16	17
Budgetary resources:			
Budget authority:			
Appropriations, mandatory:			
1201　Appropriation (special or trust fund)	22	21	22
1235　Appropriations precluded from obligation (special or trust)	–7	–5	–5
1260　Appropriations, mandatory (total)	15	16	17
1930　Total budgetary resources available	15	16	17
Change in obligated balance:			
Unpaid obligations:			
3000　Unpaid obligations, brought forward, Oct 1	1	1	1
3010　New obligations, unexpired accounts	15	16	17
3020　Outlays (gross)	–15	–16	–16
3050　Unpaid obligations, end of year	1	1	2
Memorandum (non-add) entries:			
3100　Obligated balance, start of year	1	1	1
3200　Obligated balance, end of year	1	1	2
Budget authority and outlays, net:			
Mandatory:			
4090　Budget authority, gross	15	16	17
Outlays, gross:			
4100　Outlays from new mandatory authority	14	15	16
4101　Outlays from mandatory balances	1	1	....
4110　Outlays, gross (total)	15	16	16
4180　Budget authority, net (total)	15	16	17
4190　Outlays, net (total)	15	16	16
Memorandum (non-add) entries:			
5000　Total investments, SOY: Federal securities: Par value	180	187	194
5001　Total investments, EOY: Federal securities: Par value	187	194	200

The National Capital Revitalization and Self-Government Improvement Act of 1997, as amended (the Act), established the District of Columbia Judicial Retirement and Survivors Annuity Fund to pay retirement and survivor benefits for District of Columbia judges and expenses necessary to administer the Fund or incurred by the Secretary of the Treasury in carrying out responsibilities regarding such benefits. The Judicial Fund consists of amounts contributed by the judges, proceeds of accumulated pension assets transferred from the District of Columbia and liquidated pursuant to the Act, income earned from the investment of the assets in public debt securities, and amounts appropriated to the Fund.

Object Classification (in millions of dollars)

Identification code 020–8212–0–7–602	2021 actual	2022 est.	2023 est.
Direct obligations:			
25.2　Other services from non-Federal sources	....	1	1
42.0　Payments to annuitants	15	15	16
99.9　Total new obligations, unexpired accounts	15	16	17

DISTRICT OF COLUMBIA GENERAL AND SPECIAL PAYMENTS

The District of Columbia receives direct Federal payments for a number of local programs in recognition of the District's unique status as the seat of the Federal Government. These General and Special Payments are separate from and in addition to the District's local budget, which is funded through local revenues.

Federal Funds

FEDERAL PAYMENT FOR RESIDENT TUITION SUPPORT

For a Federal payment to the District of Columbia, to be deposited into a dedicated account, for a nationwide program to be administered by the Mayor, for District of Columbia resident tuition support, $20,000,000, to remain available until expended: Provided, That such funds, including any interest accrued thereon, may be used on behalf of eligible District of Columbia residents to pay an amount based upon the difference between in-State and out-of-State tuition at public institutions of higher education, or to pay up to $2,500 each year at eligible private institutions of higher education: Provided further, That the awarding of such funds may be prioritized on the basis of a resident's academic merit, the income and need of eligible students and such other factors as may be authorized: Provided further, That the District of Columbia government shall maintain a dedicated account for the Resident Tuition Support Program that shall consist of the Federal funds appropriated to the Program in this Act and any subsequent appropriations, any unobligated balances from prior fiscal years, and any interest earned in this or any fiscal year: Provided further, That the account shall be under the control of the District of Columbia Chief Financial Officer, who shall use those funds solely for the purposes of carrying out the Resident Tuition Support Program: Provided further, That the Office of the Chief Financial Officer shall provide a quarterly financial report to the Committees on Appropriations of the House of Representatives and the Senate for these funds showing, by object class, the expenditures made and the purpose therefor.

Note.—A full-year 2022 appropriation for this account was not enacted at the time the Budget was prepared; therefore, the Budget assumes this account is operating under the Continuing Appropriations Act, 2022 (Division A of Public Law 117–43, as amended). The amounts included for 2022 reflect the annualized level provided by the continuing resolution.

Program and Financing (in millions of dollars)

Identification code 020–1736–0–1–502		2021 actual	2022 est.	2023 est.
	Obligations by program activity:			
0001	Federal Payment for Resident Tuition Support (Direct)	40	40	20
0900	Total new obligations, unexpired accounts (object class 41.0)	40	40	20
	Budgetary resources:			
	Budget authority:			
	Appropriations, discretionary:			
1100	Appropriation	40	40	20
1930	Total budgetary resources available	40	40	20
	Change in obligated balance:			
	Unpaid obligations:			
3010	New obligations, unexpired accounts	40	40	20
3020	Outlays (gross)	–40	–40	–20
	Budget authority and outlays, net:			
	Discretionary:			
4000	Budget authority, gross	40	40	20
	Outlays, gross:			
4010	Outlays from new discretionary authority	40	40	20
4180	Budget authority, net (total)	40	40	20
4190	Outlays, net (total)	40	40	20

The D.C. Tuition Assistance Grant program enables students from the District of Columbia to attend eligible public universities and colleges nationwide at in-state tuition rates. The program also provides grants for students to attend private institutions in the D.C. metropolitan area or private Historically Black Colleges and Universities nationwide, as well as public 2-year community colleges. The Budget proposes to increase the annual and lifetime grant limits, which have not been adjusted since the program's creation, to partially address the increasing costs of higher education.

FEDERAL PAYMENT FOR SCHOOL IMPROVEMENT

For a Federal payment for a school improvement program in the District of Columbia, $52,500,000, to remain available until expended, for payments authorized under the Scholarships for Opportunity and Results Act (division C of Public Law 112–10): Provided, That, to the extent that funds are available for opportunity scholarships and following the priorities included in section 3006 of such Act, the Secretary of Education shall make scholarships available to students eligible under section 3013(3) of such Act (Public Law 112–10; 125 Stat. 211) including students who were not offered a scholarship during any previous school year: Provided further, That within funds provided for opportunity scholarships up to $1,750,000 shall be for the activities specified in sections 3007(b) through 3007(d) of the Act and up to $500,000 shall be for the activities specified in section 3009 of the Act.

Note.—A full-year 2022 appropriation for this account was not enacted at the time the Budget was prepared; therefore, the Budget assumes this account is operating under the Continuing Appropriations Act, 2022 (Division A of Public Law 117–43, as amended). The amounts included for 2022 reflect the annualized level provided by the continuing resolution.

Program and Financing (in millions of dollars)

Identification code 020–1817–0–1–501		2021 actual	2022 est.	2023 est.
	Obligations by program activity:			
0001	Opportunity Scholarship Program	18	18	18
0002	D.C. public schools	18	18	18
0003	D.C. public charter schools	17	17	17
0900	Total new obligations, unexpired accounts (object class 41.0)	53	53	53
	Budgetary resources:			
	Budget authority:			
	Appropriations, discretionary:			
1100	Appropriation	53	53	53
1930	Total budgetary resources available	53	53	53
	Change in obligated balance:			
	Unpaid obligations:			
3010	New obligations, unexpired accounts	53	53	53
3020	Outlays (gross)	–53	–53	–53
	Budget authority and outlays, net:			
	Discretionary:			
4000	Budget authority, gross	53	53	53
	Outlays, gross:			
4010	Outlays from new discretionary authority	53	53	53
4180	Budget authority, net (total)	53	53	53
4190	Outlays, net (total)	53	53	53

The Budget provides $52.5 million to support kindergarten through high school education in the District of Columbia, including $17.5 million for D.C. public schools for continued support of the District's efforts to transform its public education system into an innovative and high-achieving system that could be used as a model for urban school district reform across the Nation, $17.5 million for D.C. charter schools to support facilities and other unmet needs, and $17.5 million to support scholarships for low-income students to attend private schools of their choice and program evaluation for the D.C. Opportunity Scholarship program.

FEDERAL SUPPORT FOR ECONOMIC DEVELOPMENT AND MANAGEMENT REFORMS IN THE DISTRICT

FEDERAL PAYMENT TO THE DISTRICT OF COLUMBIA WATER AND SEWER AUTHORITY

For a Federal payment to the District of Columbia Water and Sewer Authority, $8,000,000, to remain available until expended, to continue implementation of the Combined Sewer Overflow Long-Term Plan: Provided, That the District of Columbia Water and Sewer Authority provides a 100 percent match for this payment.

FEDERAL PAYMENT TO THE CRIMINAL JUSTICE COORDINATING COUNCIL

For a Federal payment to the Criminal Justice Coordinating Council, $2,450,000, to remain available until expended, to support initiatives related to the coordination of Federal and local criminal justice resources in the District of Columbia.

FEDERAL PAYMENT FOR JUDICIAL COMMISSIONS

For a Federal payment, to remain available until September 30, 2023, to the Commission on Judicial Disabilities and Tenure, $330,000, and for the Judicial Nomination Commission, $300,000.

FEDERAL PAYMENT FOR THE DISTRICT OF COLUMBIA NATIONAL GUARD

For a Federal payment to the District of Columbia National Guard, $600,000, to remain available until expended, for the Major General David F. Wherley, Jr. District of Columbia National Guard Retention and College Access Program.

FEDERAL PAYMENT FOR TESTING AND TREATMENT OF HIV/AIDS

For a Federal payment to the District of Columbia for the testing of individuals for, and the treatment of individuals with, human immunodeficiency virus and acquired immunodeficiency syndrome in the District of Columbia, $5,000,000.

Note.—A full-year 2022 appropriation for this account was not enacted at the time the Budget was prepared; therefore, the Budget assumes this account is operating under the Continuing Appropriations Act, 2022 (Division A of Public Law 117–43, as amended). The amounts included for 2022 reflect the annualized level provided by the continuing resolution.

FEDERAL SUPPORT FOR ECONOMIC DEVELOPMENT AND MANAGEMENT REFORMS IN THE DISTRICT—Continued

Program and Financing (in millions of dollars)

Identification code 020–1707–0–1–999	2021 actual	2022 est.	2023 est.
Obligations by program activity:			
0001 Water and Sewer Authority	8	8	8
0002 Criminal Justice Coordinating Council	2	2	3
0019 Judicial Commissions and DC National Guard	1	1	1
0025 HIV/AIDS Prevention	4	4	5
0900 Total new obligations, unexpired accounts (object class 41.0)	15	15	17
Budgetary resources:			
Budget authority:			
Appropriations, discretionary:			
1100 Appropriation	15	15	17
1930 Total budgetary resources available	15	15	17
Change in obligated balance:			
Unpaid obligations:			
3010 New obligations, unexpired accounts	15	15	17
3020 Outlays (gross)	–15	–15	–17
Budget authority and outlays, net:			
Discretionary:			
4000 Budget authority, gross	15	15	17
Outlays, gross:			
4010 Outlays from new discretionary authority	15	15	17
4180 Budget authority, net (total)	15	15	17
4190 Outlays, net (total)	15	15	17

The Budget includes $5 million to fund the D.C. Department of Health's continued efforts to prevent the spread of HIV/AIDS in the District. This funding will allow the District to focus on service saturation in areas of combined high risk and high poverty in order to ensure that ward-level counseling and testing, prevention, and treatment services are readily available and fully utilized. Funding will also be used to bolster social marketing and outreach campaigns for these important public health programs. The Budget also includes $8 million for the D.C. Water and Sewer Authority to continue implementation of the Combined Sewer Overflow Long-Term Plan, $2.45 million for the Criminal Justice Coordinating Council, $0.63 million for judicial commissions, and $0.6 million for the D.C. National Guard.

FEDERAL PAYMENT FOR EMERGENCY PLANNING AND SECURITY COSTS IN THE DISTRICT OF COLUMBIA

For a Federal payment of necessary expenses, as determined by the Mayor of the District of Columbia in written consultation with the elected county or city officials of surrounding jurisdictions, $30,000,000, to remain available until expended, for the costs of providing public safety at events related to the presence of the National Capital in the District of Columbia, including support requested by the Director of the United States Secret Service in carrying out protective duties under the direction of the Secretary of Homeland Security, and for the costs of providing support to respond to immediate and specific terrorist threats or attacks in the District of Columbia or surrounding jurisdictions.

Note.—A full-year 2022 appropriation for this account was not enacted at the time the Budget was prepared; therefore, the Budget assumes this account is operating under the Continuing Appropriations Act, 2022 (Division A of Public Law 117–43, as amended). The amounts included for 2022 reflect the annualized level provided by the continuing resolution.

Program and Financing (in millions of dollars)

Identification code 020–1771–0–1–806	2021 actual	2022 est.	2023 est.
Obligations by program activity:			
0001 Emergency Planning Fund	51	17	30
0900 Total new obligations, unexpired accounts (object class 41.0)	51	17	30
Budgetary resources:			
Budget authority:			
Appropriations, discretionary:			
1100 Appropriation	51	17	30
1930 Total budgetary resources available	51	17	30
Change in obligated balance:			
Unpaid obligations:			
3010 New obligations, unexpired accounts	51	17	30
3020 Outlays (gross)	–51	–17	–30
Budget authority and outlays, net:			
Discretionary:			
4000 Budget authority, gross	51	17	30
Outlays, gross:			
4010 Outlays from new discretionary authority	51	17	30
4180 Budget authority, net (total)	51	17	30
4190 Outlays, net (total)	51	17	30

The Budget provides $30 million for emergency planning and security costs related to the presence of the Federal Government in the District of Columbia, including costs associated with providing support requested by the Director of the U.S. Secret Service.

FEDERAL PAYMENT TO THE DISTRICT OF COLUMBIA PENSION FUND

Program and Financing (in millions of dollars)

Identification code 020–1714–0–1–601	2021 actual	2022 est.	2023 est.
Obligations by program activity:			
0001 Payment to Federal Pension Fund	577	549	548
0900 Total new obligations, unexpired accounts (object class 13.0)	577	549	548
Budgetary resources:			
Budget authority:			
Appropriations, mandatory:			
1200 Appropriation	577	549	548
1930 Total budgetary resources available	577	549	548
Change in obligated balance:			
Unpaid obligations:			
3010 New obligations, unexpired accounts	577	549	548
3020 Outlays (gross)	–577	–549	–548
Budget authority and outlays, net:			
Mandatory:			
4090 Budget authority, gross	577	549	548
Outlays, gross:			
4100 Outlays from new mandatory authority	577	549	548
4180 Budget authority, net (total)	577	549	548
4190 Outlays, net (total)	577	549	548

The National Capital Revitalization and Self-Government Improvement Act of 1997, as amended, requires the Secretary of the Treasury to make payments at the end of each fiscal year from the General Fund of the Treasury into the District of Columbia Federal Pension Fund. This account receives the annual payments from the General Fund and immediately transfers these amounts into the District of Columbia Federal Pension Fund. Annual payments consist of (1) amounts necessary to amortize: the original unfunded liability over 30 years, the net gain or loss (based on experience) over 10 years, and any other changes in actuarial liability over 20 years and (2) amounts necessary to fund administrative expenses for the year.

DISTRICT OF COLUMBIA FEDERAL PENSION FUND

Special and Trust Fund Receipts (in millions of dollars)

Identification code 020–5511–0–2–601	2021 actual	2022 est.	2023 est.
0100 Balance, start of year	3,716	3,763	3,784
Receipts:			
Current law:			
1140 Federal Contribution, DC Federal Pension Fund	577	549	548
1140 Earnings on Investments, DC Federal Pension Fund	19	29	38
1199 Total current law receipts	596	578	586
1999 Total receipts	596	578	586
2000 Total: Balances and receipts	4,312	4,341	4,370

OTHER INDEPENDENT AGENCIES

District of Columbia—Continued
Federal Funds—Continued

1243

		2021 actual	2022 est.	2023 est.
	Appropriations:			
	Current law:			
2101	District of Columbia Federal Pension Fund	−595	−573	−569
2103	District of Columbia Federal Pension Fund	−1	−1	−1
2132	District of Columbia Federal Pension Fund	1	1	1
2135	District of Columbia Federal Pension Fund	48	16	19
2199	Total current law appropriations	−547	−557	−550
2999	Total appropriations	−547	−557	−550
5098	Reconciliation adjustment	−2	....	....
5099	Balance, end of year	3,763	3,784	3,820

Program and Financing (in millions of dollars)

Identification code 020–5511–0–2–601	2021 actual	2022 est.	2023 est.
Obligations by program activity:			
0001 Retirement payments	532	531	525
0002 Administrative costs	20	26	25
0799 Total direct obligations	552	557	550
0801 Reimbursable Program - Retirement Payments	267	303	340
0802 Reimbursable Program - Administrative Expenses	3	3	3
0899 Total reimbursable obligations	270	306	343
0900 Total new obligations, unexpired accounts	822	863	893
Budgetary resources:			
Unobligated balance:			
1000 Unobligated balance brought forward, Oct 1	21	22	24
1021 Recoveries of prior year unpaid obligations	4	....	....
1070 Unobligated balance (total)	25	22	24
Budget authority:			
Appropriations, mandatory:			
1201 Appropriation (special or trust fund)	595	573	569
1203 Appropriation (previously unavailable)(special or trust)	1	1	1
1232 Appropriations and/or unobligated balance of appropriations temporarily reduced	−1	−1	−1
1235 Appropriations precluded from obligation (special or trust)	−48	−16	−19
1260 Appropriations, mandatory (total)	547	557	550
Spending authority from offsetting collections, mandatory:			
1800 Collected	272	308	344
1900 Budget authority (total)	819	865	894
1930 Total budgetary resources available	844	887	918
Memorandum (non-add) entries:			
1941 Unexpired unobligated balance, end of year	22	24	25
Change in obligated balance:			
Unpaid obligations:			
3000 Unpaid obligations, brought forward, Oct 1	58	54	55
3010 New obligations, unexpired accounts	822	863	893
3020 Outlays (gross)	−822	−862	−891
3040 Recoveries of prior year unpaid obligations, unexpired	−4	....	....
3050 Unpaid obligations, end of year	54	55	57
Memorandum (non-add) entries:			
3100 Obligated balance, start of year	58	54	55
3200 Obligated balance, end of year	54	55	57
Budget authority and outlays, net:			
Mandatory:			
4090 Budget authority, gross	819	865	894
Outlays, gross:			
4100 Outlays from new mandatory authority	759	815	860
4101 Outlays from mandatory balances	63	47	31
4110 Outlays, gross (total)	822	862	891
Offsets against gross budget authority and outlays:			
Offsetting collections (collected) from:			
4123 Non-Federal sources	−272	−308	−344
4180 Budget authority, net (total)	547	557	550
4190 Outlays, net (total)	550	554	547
Memorandum (non-add) entries:			
5000 Total investments, SOY: Federal securities: Par value	3,815	3,861	3,879
5001 Total investments, EOY: Federal securities: Par value	3,861	3,879	3,913

The National Capital Revitalization and Self-Government Improvement Act of 1997, as amended, established the District of Columbia Federal Pension Fund to pay retirement benefits for District of Columbia firefighters, police officers, and teachers, and to pay any necessary expenses to administer the Fund or expenses incurred by the Secretary of the Treasury in carrying out responsibilities regarding such benefits. The District of Columbia Federal Pension Fund consists of accumulated pension assets transferred from the District of Columbia, income earned from the investment of the assets in public debt securities, and amounts appropriated to the Fund.

Object Classification (in millions of dollars)

Identification code 020–5511–0–2–601	2021 actual	2022 est.	2023 est.
Direct obligations:			
11.1 Personnel compensation: Full-time permanent	3	3	3
12.1 Civilian personnel benefits	1	1	1
25.1 Advisory and assistance services	9	11	10
25.2 Other services from non-Federal sources	6	8	8
25.3 Other goods and services from Federal sources	1	3	3
42.0 Payments to annuitants	532	531	525
99.0 Direct obligations	552	557	550
99.0 Reimbursable obligations	270	306	343
99.9 Total new obligations, unexpired accounts	822	863	893

Employment Summary

Identification code 020–5511–0–2–601	2021 actual	2022 est.	2023 est.
1001 Direct civilian full-time equivalent employment	19	21	22

FEDERAL PAYMENT FOR WATER AND SEWER SERVICES

Program and Financing (in millions of dollars)

Identification code 020–4446–0–3–806	2021 actual	2022 est.	2023 est.
Obligations by program activity:			
0801 Federal Payment for Water and Sewer Services (Reimbursable)	88	91	97
0900 Total new obligations, unexpired accounts (object class 23.3)	88	91	97
Budgetary resources:			
Budget authority:			
Spending authority from offsetting collections, mandatory:			
1800 Collected	88	91	97
1930 Total budgetary resources available	88	91	97
Change in obligated balance:			
Unpaid obligations:			
3010 New obligations, unexpired accounts	88	91	97
3020 Outlays (gross)	−88	−91	−97
Budget authority and outlays, net:			
Mandatory:			
4090 Budget authority, gross	88	91	97
Outlays, gross:			
4100 Outlays from new mandatory authority	88	91	97
Offsets against gross budget authority and outlays:			
Offsetting collections (collected) from:			
4120 Federal sources	−88	−91	−97
4180 Budget authority, net (total)	....	....	....
4190 Outlays, net (total)	....	....	....

The 1990 District of Columbia Appropriations Act established a system "to improve the means by which the District of Columbia (now the District of Columbia Water and Sewer Authority) is paid for water and sanitary sewer services furnished to the Government of the United States or any department, agency, or independent establishment thereof." Each agency is required to pay on a quarterly basis 25 percent of its estimated yearly bill into this account. If an agency fails to pay its obligation on time, the Treasury Department is authorized to pay the full government-wide bill by making up the missed agency payment(s) with a permanent, indefinite appropriation, which must then be reimbursed by the appropriate agency or agencies.

General Fund Receipt Account

(in millions of dollars)

	2021 actual	2022 est.	2023 est.
Offsetting receipts from the public:			
349–322070 All Other General Fund Proprietary Receipts Including Budget Clearing Accounts	....	1	....
General Fund Offsetting receipts from the public	....	1	....

TITLE VIII—GENERAL PROVISIONS—DISTRICT OF COLUMBIA

(INCLUDING TRANSFERS OF FUNDS)

SEC. 801. There are appropriated from the applicable funds of the District of Columbia such sums as may be necessary for making refunds and for the payment of legal settlements or judgments that have been entered against the District of Columbia government.

SEC. 802. None of the Federal funds provided in this Act shall be used for publicity or propaganda purposes or implementation of any policy including boycott designed to support or defeat legislation pending before Congress or any State legislature.

SEC. 803. (a) None of the Federal funds provided under this Act to the agencies funded by this Act, both Federal and District government agencies, that remain available for obligation or expenditure in fiscal year 2023, or provided from any accounts in the Treasury of the United States derived by the collection of fees available to the agencies funded by this Act, shall be available for obligation or expenditures for an agency through a reprogramming of funds which—

(1) creates new programs;

(2) eliminates a program, project, or responsibility center;

(3) establishes or changes allocations specifically denied, limited or increased under this Act;

(4) increases funds or personnel by any means for any program, project, or responsibility center for which funds have been denied or restricted;

(5) re-establishes any program or project previously deferred through reprogramming;

(6) augments any existing program, project, or responsibility center through a reprogramming of funds in excess of $3,000,000 or 10 percent, whichever is less; or

(7) increases by 20 percent or more personnel assigned to a specific program, project or responsibility center, unless prior notice is provided to the Committees on Appropriations of the House of Representatives and the Senate.

(b) The District of Columbia government is authorized to approve and execute reprogramming and transfer requests of local funds under this title through November 7, 2023.

SEC. 804. None of the Federal funds provided in this Act may be used by the District of Columbia to provide for salaries, expenses, or other costs associated with the offices of United States Senator or United States Representative under section 4(d) of the District of Columbia Statehood Constitutional Convention Initiatives of 1979 (D.C. Law 3–171; D.C. Official Code, sec. 1–123).

SEC. 805. Except as otherwise provided in this section, none of the funds made available by this Act or by any other Act may be used to provide any officer or employee of the District of Columbia with an official vehicle unless the officer or employee uses the vehicle only in the performance of the officer's or employee's official duties. For purposes of this section, the term "official duties" does not include travel between the officer's or employee's residence and workplace, except in the case of—

(1) an officer or employee of the Metropolitan Police Department who resides in the District of Columbia or is otherwise designated by the Chief of the Department;

(2) at the discretion of the Fire Chief, an officer or employee of the District of Columbia Fire and Emergency Medical Services Department who resides in the District of Columbia and is on call 24 hours a day;

(3) at the discretion of the Director of the Department of Corrections, an officer or employee of the District of Columbia Department of Corrections who resides in the District of Columbia and is on call 24 hours a day;

(4) at the discretion of the Chief Medical Examiner, an officer or employee of the Office of the Chief Medical Examiner who resides in the District of Columbia and is on call 24 hours a day;

(5) at the discretion of the Director of the Homeland Security and Emergency Management Agency, an officer or employee of the Homeland Security and Emergency Management Agency who resides in the District of Columbia and is on call 24 hours a day;

(6) the Mayor of the District of Columbia; and

(7) the Chairman of the Council of the District of Columbia.

SEC. 806. (a) None of the Federal funds contained in this Act may be used by the District of Columbia Attorney General or any other officer or entity of the District government to provide assistance for any petition drive or civil action which seeks to require Congress to provide for voting representation in Congress for the District of Columbia.

(b) Nothing in this section bars the District of Columbia Attorney General from reviewing or commenting on briefs in private lawsuits, or from consulting with officials of the District government regarding such lawsuits.

SEC. 807. None of the Federal funds contained in this Act may be used to distribute any needle or syringe for the purpose of preventing the spread of blood borne pathogens in any location that has been determined by the local public health or local law enforcement authorities to be inappropriate for such distribution.

SEC. 808. Nothing in this Act may be construed to prevent the Council or Mayor of the District of Columbia from addressing the issue of the provision of contraceptive coverage by health insurance plans, but it is the intent of Congress that any legislation enacted on such issue should include a "conscience clause" which provides exceptions for religious beliefs and moral convictions.

SEC. 809. (a) None of the Federal funds contained in this Act may be used to enact or carry out any law, rule, or regulation to legalize or otherwise reduce penalties associated with the possession, use, or distribution of any schedule I substance under the Controlled Substances Act (21 U.S.C. 801 et seq.) or any tetrahydrocannabinols derivative.

(b) No funds available for obligation or expenditure by the District of Columbia government under any authority may be used to enact any law, rule, or regulation to legalize or otherwise reduce penalties associated with the possession, use, or distribution of any schedule I substance under the Controlled Substances Act (21 U.S.C. 801 et seq.) or any tetrahydrocannabinols derivative for recreational purposes.

SEC. 810. (a) No later than 30 calendar days after the date of the enactment of this Act, the Chief Financial Officer for the District of Columbia shall submit to the appropriate committees of Congress, the Mayor, and the Council of the District of Columbia, a revised appropriated funds operating budget in the format of the budget that the District of Columbia government submitted pursuant to section 442 of the District of Columbia Home Rule Act (D.C. Official Code, sec. 1–204.42), for all agencies of the District of Columbia government for fiscal year 2023 that is in the total amount of the approved appropriation and that realigns all budgeted data for personal services and other-than-personal services, respectively, with anticipated actual expenditures.

(b) This section shall apply only to an agency for which the Chief Financial Officer for the District of Columbia certifies that a reallocation is required to address unanticipated changes in program requirements.

SEC. 811. No later than 30 calendar days after the date of the enactment of this Act, the Chief Financial Officer for the District of Columbia shall submit to the appropriate committees of Congress, the Mayor, and the Council for the District of Columbia, a revised appropriated funds operating budget for the District of Columbia Public Schools that aligns schools budgets to actual enrollment. The revised appropriated funds budget shall be in the format of the budget that the District of Columbia government submitted pursuant to section 442 of the District of Columbia Home Rule Act (D.C. Official Code, sec. 1–204.42).

SEC. 812. (a) Amounts appropriated in this Act as operating funds may be transferred to the District of Columbia's enterprise and capital funds and such amounts, once transferred, shall retain appropriation authority consistent with the provisions of this Act.

(b) The District of Columbia government is authorized to reprogram or transfer for operating expenses any local funds transferred or reprogrammed in this or the four prior fiscal years from operating funds to capital funds, and such amounts, once transferred or reprogrammed, shall retain appropriation authority consistent with the provisions of this Act.

(c) The District of Columbia government may not transfer or reprogram for operating expenses any funds derived from bonds, notes, or other obligations issued for capital projects.

SEC. 813. None of the Federal funds appropriated in this Act shall remain available for obligation beyond the current fiscal year, nor may any be transferred to other appropriations, unless expressly so provided herein.

SEC. 814. Except as otherwise specifically provided by law or under this Act, not to exceed 50 percent of unobligated balances remaining available at the end of fiscal year 2023 from appropriations of Federal funds made available for salaries and expenses for fiscal year 2023 in this Act, shall remain available through September 30, 2024, for each such account for the purposes authorized: Provided, That a notice shall be submitted to the Committees on Appropriations of the House of Representatives and the Senate prior to the expenditure of such funds: Provided further, That these notices shall be made in compliance with reprogramming guidelines outlined in section 803 of this Act.

SEC. 815. (a)

(1) During fiscal year 2024, during a period in which neither a District of Columbia continuing resolution or a regular District of Columbia appropriation bill is in effect, local funds are appropriated in the amount provided for any project or activity for which local funds are provided in the Act referred to in paragraph (2) (subject to any modifications enacted by the District of Columbia as of the beginning of the period during which this subsection is in effect) at the rate set forth by such Act.

(2) The Act referred to in this paragraph is the Act of the Council of the District of Columbia pursuant to which a proposed budget is approved for fiscal year 2024 which (subject to the requirements of the District of Columbia Home Rule Act) will constitute the local portion of the annual budget for the District of Columbia government for fiscal year 2024 for purposes of section 446 of the District of Columbia Home Rule Act (sec. 1–204.46, D.C. Official Code).

(b) Appropriations made by subsection (a) shall cease to be available—

(1) during any period in which a District of Columbia continuing resolution for fiscal year 2024 is in effect; or

(2) upon the enactment into law of the regular District of Columbia appropriation bill for fiscal year 2024.

(c) An appropriation made by subsection (a) is provided under the authority and conditions as provided under this Act and shall be available to the extent and in the manner that would be provided by this Act.

(d) An appropriation made by subsection (a) shall cover all obligations or expenditures incurred for such project or activity during the portion of fiscal year 2024 for which this section applies to such project or activity.

(e) This section shall not apply to a project or activity during any period of fiscal year 2024 if any other provision of law (other than an authorization of appropriations)—

(1) makes an appropriation, makes funds available, or grants authority for such project or activity to continue for such period; or

(2) specifically provides that no appropriation shall be made, no funds shall be made available, or no authority shall be granted for such project or activity to continue for such period.

(f) Nothing in this section shall be construed to affect obligations of the government of the District of Columbia mandated by other law.

SEC. 816. (a) Section 244 of the Revised Statutes of the United States relating to the District of Columbia (sec. 9–1201.03, D.C. Official Code) does not apply with respect to any railroads installed pursuant to the Long Bridge Project.

(b) In this section, the term "Long Bridge Project" means the project carried out by the District of Columbia and the Commonwealth of Virginia to construct a new Long Bridge adjacent to the existing Long Bridge over the Potomac River, including related infrastructure and other related projects, to expand commuter and regional passenger rail service and to provide bike and pedestrian access crossings over the Potomac River.

SEC. 817. Not later than 45 days after the last day of each quarter, each Federal and District government agency appropriated Federal funds in this Act shall submit to the Committees on Appropriations of the House of Representatives and the Senate a quarterly budget report that includes total obligations of the Agency for that quarter for each Federal funds appropriation provided in this Act, by the source year of the appropriation.

SEC. 818. Except as expressly provided otherwise, any reference to "this Act" contained in this title or in title IV shall be treated as referring only to the provisions of this title or of title IV.

SEC. 819. Section 3 of the District of Columbia College Access Act of 1999 (Public Law 106–98; D.C. Official Code, sec. 38–2702), is amended—

(1) in subsection (a)(2)(A), by striking "$10,000" and inserting "$15,000";

(2) in subsection (a)(2)(B), by striking "$50,000" and inserting "$75,000";

(3) in subsection (b)(1)(A), by striking the word "and" at the end;

(4) by redesignating subparagraph (B) of paragraph (1) of subsection (b) as subparagraph (C);

(5) by inserting after subparagraph (A) of paragraph (1) of subsection (b) the following new subparagraph:

"(B) After making reductions under subparagraph (A) of this paragraph, ratably reduce the amount of the tuition and fee payments for students receiving more than $10,000 annually; and"; and

(6) in subsection (b)(1)(C), as so redesignated, by striking "subparagraph (A)" and inserting "subparagraphs (A) and (B)".

SEC. 820. ADJUSTMENTS IN COMPENSATION RATES FOR CERTAIN PERSONNEL.

(a) Attorneys Representing Indigent Defendants.

(1) IN GENERAL. Section 11–2604(a), District of Columbia Official Code, is amended by striking "at a fixed rate of $90 per hour" and inserting "an hourly rate not to exceed the rate payable under section 3006A(d)(1) of title 18, United States Code".

(2) EFFECTIVE DATE. The amendments made by this section shall apply with respect to cases and proceedings initiated on or after the date of the enactment of this Act.

(b) Criminal Justice Investigators.

(1) IN GENERAL. Section 11–2605, District of Columbia Official Code, is amended in subsections (b) and (c) by striking "(or, in the case of investigative services, a fixed rate of $25 per hour)" each place it appears.

(2) EFFECTIVE DATE. The amendments made by this section shall apply with respect to investigative services provided in connection with cases and proceedings initiated on or after the date of the enactment of this Act.

ELECTION ASSISTANCE COMMISSION

Federal Funds

SALARIES AND EXPENSES

(INCLUDING TRANSFER OF FUNDS)

For necessary expenses to carry out the Help America Vote Act of 2002 (Public Law 107–252), $30,087,000, of which $1,500,000 shall be made available to the National Institute of Standards and Technology for election reform activities authorized under the Help America Vote Act of 2002.

Note.—A full-year 2022 appropriation for this account was not enacted at the time the Budget was prepared; therefore, the Budget assumes this account is operating under the Continuing Appropriations Act, 2022 (Division A of Public Law 117–43, as amended). The amounts included for 2022 reflect the annualized level provided by the continuing resolution.

Program and Financing (in millions of dollars)

Identification code 525–1650–0–1–808		2021 actual	2022 est.	2023 est.
	Obligations by program activity:			
0001	Election Assistance Commission	16	16	30
	Budgetary resources:			
	Budget authority:			
	Appropriations, discretionary:			
1100	Appropriation	17	17	30
1120	Appropriations transferred to other accts [013–0500]	–1	–1	
1160	Appropriation, discretionary (total)	16	16	30
1930	Total budgetary resources available	16	16	30
	Change in obligated balance:			
	Unpaid obligations:			
3000	Unpaid obligations, brought forward, Oct 1	5	10	9
3010	New obligations, unexpired accounts	16	16	30
3020	Outlays (gross)	–11	–17	–33
3050	Unpaid obligations, end of year	10	9	6
	Memorandum (non-add) entries:			
3100	Obligated balance, start of year	5	10	9
3200	Obligated balance, end of year	10	9	6
	Budget authority and outlays, net:			
	Discretionary:			
4000	Budget authority, gross	16	16	30
	Outlays, gross:			
4010	Outlays from new discretionary authority	8	13	24
4011	Outlays from discretionary balances	3	4	9
4020	Outlays, gross (total)	11	17	33
4180	Budget authority, net (total)	16	16	30
4190	Outlays, net (total)	11	17	33

The Election Assistance Commission assists State and local election officials by testing and certifying election equipment, sharing best practices to improve the administration of Federal elections, and providing them with information about the voting system standards established by the Help America Vote Act of 2002 (P.L. 107–252). Of the amounts proposed for 2023, $1.5 million shall be made available to the National Institute of Standards and Technology to support the Technical Guidelines Develop-

Election Assistance Commission—Continued
Federal Funds—Continued

SALARIES AND EXPENSES—Continued

ment Committee in developing a comprehensive set of testing guidelines for voting system hardware and software.

Object Classification (in millions of dollars)

Identification code 525–1650–0–1–808		2021 actual	2022 est.	2023 est.
	Direct obligations:			
11.1	Personnel compensation: Full-time permanent	6	5	8
12.1	Civilian personnel benefits	1	3	4
21.0	Travel and transportation of persons			1
23.1	Rental payments to GSA		1	1
25.2	Other services from non-Federal sources	6	5	14
25.3	Other goods and services from Federal sources	3	2	2
99.9	Total new obligations, unexpired accounts	16	16	30

Employment Summary

Identification code 525–1650–0–1–808	2021 actual	2022 est.	2023 est.
1001 Direct civilian full-time equivalent employment	46	56	78

ELECTION INNOVATION GRANTS

For the establishment of a competitive grant program to foster innovation, enhance processes and procedures, and improve the administration of federal elections, $250,000,000, to remain available through September 30, 2024; of which not to exceed 2 percent shall remain available until September 30, 2028, for the administration and oversight of grants awarded under this heading: Provided, That the Election Assistance Commission shall, consistent with the purposes of the Help America Vote Act of 2002 (Public Law 107–252), award grants to States and eligible units of local government on a competitive basis for projects that will have significant national, regional, or local impact in the improvement of the administration of federal elections through innovation, including, but not limited to, election administration; cybersecurity and statistically valid risk-limiting audits; security of election officials and locations; accessibility for voters, including those with disabilities and other specific access needs, and including vote-by-mail, voter education, language proficiency, usability, and voter technology; or other programs to enhance or reliably secure processes and procedures in administering federal elections without meaningfully impairing access: Provided further, That for purposes of this appropriation, the term State has the meaning given such term in section 901 of the Help America Vote Act of 2002 (52 U.S.C. 21141): Provided further, That for purposes of this appropriation, the Commonwealth of the Northern Mariana Islands shall be deemed to be a State: Provided further, That for purposes of this appropriation, an eligible unit of local government is defined as a unit of local government with responsibility for the administration of Federal elections: Provided further, That a grant awarded under this heading shall be for an amount not greater than $10,000,000, and shall be available for obligation by the State or eligible unit of local government through September 30, 2028: Provided further, That not more than 10 percent of the total amount of funds made available under this heading may be awarded to projects in a single State.

Note.—A full-year 2022 appropriation for this account was not enacted at the time the Budget was prepared; therefore, the Budget assumes this account is operating under the Continuing Appropriations Act, 2022 (Division A of Public Law 117–43, as amended). The amounts included for 2022 reflect the annualized level provided by the continuing resolution.

Program and Financing (in millions of dollars)

Identification code 525–1651–0–1–808		2021 actual	2022 est.	2023 est.
	Obligations by program activity:			
0001	Election Innovation Grants			245
0002	Administrative Expenses			2
0100	Direct program activities, subtotal			247
0900	Total new obligations, unexpired accounts			247
	Budgetary resources:			
	Unobligated balance:			
1000	Unobligated balance brought forward, Oct 1	1	2	2
1021	Recoveries of prior year unpaid obligations	1		
1070	Unobligated balance (total)	2	2	2
	Budget authority:			
	Appropriations, discretionary:			
1100	Appropriation			250
1930	Total budgetary resources available	2	2	252
	Memorandum (non-add) entries:			
1941	Unexpired unobligated balance, end of year	2	2	5
	Change in obligated balance:			
	Unpaid obligations:			
3000	Unpaid obligations, brought forward, Oct 1	4	3	
3010	New obligations, unexpired accounts			247
3020	Outlays (gross)		–3	–246
3040	Recoveries of prior year unpaid obligations, unexpired	–1		
3050	Unpaid obligations, end of year	3		1
	Memorandum (non-add) entries:			
3100	Obligated balance, start of year	4	3	
3200	Obligated balance, end of year	3		1
	Budget authority and outlays, net:			
	Discretionary:			
4000	Budget authority, gross			250
	Outlays, gross:			
4010	Outlays from new discretionary authority			246
4011	Outlays from discretionary balances		3	
4020	Outlays, gross (total)		3	246
	Offsets against gross budget authority and outlays:			
	Offsetting collections (collected) from:			
4033	Non-Federal sources	–37		
	Additional offsets against gross budget authority only:			
4052	Offsetting collections credited to expired accounts	37		
4070	Budget authority, net (discretionary)			250
4080	Outlays, net (discretionary)	–37	3	246
4180	Budget authority, net (total)			250
4190	Outlays, net (total)	–37	3	246

Summary of Budget Authority and Outlays (in millions of dollars)

	2021 actual	2022 est.	2023 est.
Enacted/requested:			
Budget Authority			250
Outlays	–37	3	246
Legislative proposal, subject to PAYGO:			
Budget Authority			10,000
Outlays			2,040
Total:			
Budget Authority			10,250
Outlays	–37	3	2,286

The Election Assistance Commission will administer grants under the Election Innovation Grants program. Consistent with the purposes of the Help America Vote Act of 2002, the EAC will award grants to States and eligible units of local government on a competitive basis for projects that will have significant national, regional, or local impact improving the administration of Federal elections. Eligible uses of funding will include capital investment to accelerate modernization of secure voting systems, efforts to expand voter access, including vote-by-mail, voter education, language proficiency, usability, voter technology, and other initiatives to enhance and secure administration of Federal elections that do not meaningfully impair access.

Object Classification (in millions of dollars)

Identification code 525–1651–0–1–808		2021 actual	2022 est.	2023 est.
	Direct obligations:			
11.1	Personnel compensation: Full-time permanent			1
25.3	Other goods and services from Federal sources			1
41.0	Grants, subsidies, and contributions			245
99.0	Direct obligations			247
99.9	Total new obligations, unexpired accounts			247

Employment Summary

Identification code 525–1651–0–1–808	2021 actual	2022 est.	2023 est.
1001 Direct civilian full-time equivalent employment			5

ELECTION SECURITY GRANTS

(Legislative proposal, subject to PAYGO)

Program and Financing (in millions of dollars)

Identification code 525–1651–4–1–808	2021 actual	2022 est.	2023 est.
Obligations by program activity:			
0001 Direct program activity	....	....	2,040
0100 Direct program activities, subtotal	....	....	2,040
0900 Total new obligations, unexpired accounts (object class 41.0)	....	....	2,040
Budgetary resources:			
Budget authority:			
Appropriations, mandatory:			
1200 Appropriation	....	....	10,000
1930 Total budgetary resources available	....	....	10,000
Memorandum (non-add) entries:			
1941 Unexpired unobligated balance, end of year	....	....	7,960
Change in obligated balance:			
Unpaid obligations:			
3010 New obligations, unexpired accounts	....	....	2,040
3020 Outlays (gross)	....	....	–2,040
Budget authority and outlays, net:			
Mandatory:			
4090 Budget authority, gross	....	....	10,000
Outlays, gross:			
4100 Outlays from new mandatory authority	....	....	2,040
4180 Budget authority, net (total)	....	....	10,000
4190 Outlays, net (total)	....	....	2,040

The Budget proposes legislation to support critical state and local election infrastructure, through a significant and sustained Federal investment to improve equitable access and ensure our elections are secure. The legislation will provide $10 billion in 2023, to be expended over ten years, through formula grants administered by the Election Assistance Commission, to enable crucial election-related capital investments such as upgrades to registration databases, voting systems, and physical structures; support recruitment, training, and retention of election workers; improve physical and cyber security; and improve voters' access to reliable elections.

ELECTION DATA COLLECTION GRANTS

Program and Financing (in millions of dollars)

Identification code 525–1652–0–1–808	2021 actual	2022 est.	2023 est.
Budgetary resources:			
Unobligated balance:			
1000 Unobligated balance brought forward, Oct 1	2	2	2
1930 Total budgetary resources available	2	2	2
Memorandum (non-add) entries:			
1941 Unexpired unobligated balance, end of year	2	2	2
4180 Budget authority, net (total)	....	....	....
4190 Outlays, net (total)	....	....	....

EQUAL EMPLOYMENT OPPORTUNITY COMMISSION

Federal Funds

SALARIES AND EXPENSES

For necessary expenses of the Equal Employment Opportunity Commission as authorized by title VII of the Civil Rights Act of 1964, the Age Discrimination in Employment Act of 1967, the Equal Pay Act of 1963, the Americans with Disabilities Act of 1990, section 501 of the Rehabilitation Act of 1973, the Civil Rights Act of 1991, the Genetic Information Nondiscrimination Act (GINA) of 2008 (Public Law 110–233), the ADA Amendments Act of 2008 (Public Law 110–325), and the Lilly Ledbetter Fair Pay Act of 2009 (Public Law 111–2), including services as authorized by section 3109 of title 5, United States Code; hire of passenger motor vehicles as authorized by section 1343(b) of title 31, United States Code; nonmonetary awards to private citizens; and up to $31,500,000 for payments to State and local enforcement agencies for authorized services to the Commission, $464,650,000, of which $60,160,000 shall remain available until September 30, 2024: Provided, That the Commission is authorized to make available for official reception and representation expenses not to exceed $2,250 from available funds: Provided further, That the Commission may take no action to implement any workforce repositioning, restructuring, or reorganization until such time as the Committees on Appropriations of the House of Representatives and the Senate have been notified of such proposals, in accordance with the reprogramming requirements of section 504 of this Act: Provided further, That the Chair may accept and use any gift or donation to carry out the work of the Commission.

Note.—A full-year 2022 appropriation for this account was not enacted at the time the Budget was prepared; therefore, the Budget assumes this account is operating under the Continuing Appropriations Act, 2022 (Division A of Public Law 117–43, as amended). The amounts included for 2022 reflect the annualized level provided by the continuing resolution.

Program and Financing (in millions of dollars)

Identification code 045–0100–0–1–751	2021 actual	2022 est.	2023 est.
Obligations by program activity:			
0001 Private sector	307	312	367
0002 Federal sector	64	60	66
0003 State and local	32	32	32
0900 Total new obligations, unexpired accounts	403	404	465
Budgetary resources:			
Unobligated balance:			
1000 Unobligated balance brought forward, Oct 1	....	....	2
1011 Unobligated balance transfer from other acct [047–0616]	....	2	....
1070 Unobligated balance (total)	....	2	2
Budget authority:			
Appropriations, discretionary:			
1100 Appropriation	404	404	465
Spending authority from offsetting collections, discretionary:			
1700 Collected	1	....	....
1900 Budget authority (total)	405	404	465
1930 Total budgetary resources available	405	406	467
Memorandum (non-add) entries:			
1940 Unobligated balance expiring	–2	....	....
1941 Unexpired unobligated balance, end of year	....	2	2
Change in obligated balance:			
Unpaid obligations:			
3000 Unpaid obligations, brought forward, Oct 1	82	90	58
3010 New obligations, unexpired accounts	403	404	465
3011 Obligations ("upward adjustments"), expired accounts	1	....	....
3020 Outlays (gross)	–392	–436	–458
3041 Recoveries of prior year unpaid obligations, expired	–4	....	....
3050 Unpaid obligations, end of year	90	58	65
Memorandum (non-add) entries:			
3100 Obligated balance, start of year	82	90	58
3200 Obligated balance, end of year	90	58	65
Budget authority and outlays, net:			
Discretionary:			
4000 Budget authority, gross	405	404	465
Outlays, gross:			
4010 Outlays from new discretionary authority	328	351	405
4011 Outlays from discretionary balances	64	85	53
4020 Outlays, gross (total)	392	436	458
Offsets against gross budget authority and outlays:			
Offsetting collections (collected) from:			
4030 Federal sources	–1	....	....
4040 Offsets against gross budget authority and outlays (total)	–1	....	....
4180 Budget authority, net (total)	404	404	465
4190 Outlays, net (total)	391	436	458

The Equal Employment Opportunity Commission (EEOC) is the Federal agency responsible for enforcement of: Title VII of the Civil Rights Act of 1964, as amended; the Age Discrimination in Employment Act of 1967; the Equal Pay Act of 1963; the Americans with Disabilities Act of 1990 (ADA); the Civil Rights Act of 1991; the Genetic Information Non-Discrimination Act of 2008; the ADA Amendments Act of 2008; the Lilly Ledbetter Fair Pay Act of 2009; and in the Federal sector only, section 501 of the Rehabilitation Act of 1973. These Acts prohibit employment discrimination based on race, sex, religion, national origin, age, disability status, or genetic information. EEOC is also responsible for carrying out Executive

Salaries and Expenses—Continued

Order 12067, which promotes coordination and minimizes conflict and duplication among Federal agencies that administer statutes or regulations involving employment discrimination.

TOTAL WORKLOAD

	2021 actual	2022 est.	2023 est.
Private sector enforcement	104,240	112,853	114,875
Federal sector program:			
Hearings	19,307	19,286	18,447
Appeals	7,588	7,834	8,559
Total workload	131,135	139,973	141,881

The 2023 Budget is an opportunity to advance the work the Commission began with the adoption of the Strategic Plan for 2018–2022. The strategic plan outlines a framework for achieving the EEOC's mission to "Prevent and Remedy Unlawful Employment Discrimination and advance equal opportunity for all in the workplace". The plan's strategic objectives include: 1) Combat and prevent employment discrimination through strategic law enforcement; and 2) Prevent employment discrimination and promote inclusive workplaces through education and outreach. The Budget will permit EEOC to improve efficiencies through data resource consolidation, promote knowledge sharing, and foster communication to avoid unnecessary duplication of effort and continue its standards of providing quality service to the public through enforcement and prevention activities. EEOC's enforcement responsibilities are in two areas: The private sector and the Federal sector.

Private Sector.—EEOC addresses equal employment opportunity in several ways. The agency investigates charges alleging employment discrimination; makes findings on the allegations; resolves charges through mediation; negotiates settlement or conciliation; and litigates cases of employment discrimination by enforcing compliance with existing laws and regulations. The priority for agency resources continues to be litigating systemic cases and maintaining a manageable inventory of cases.

PRIVATE SECTOR ENFORCEMENT WORKLOAD PROJECTIONS

Workload/Workflow	2021 actual	2022 est.	2023 est.
Total pending	42,570	42,811	39,289
Total receipts	61,331	69,304	74,848
Net FEPA transfers/deferrals	339	738	738
Total workload	104,240	112,853	114,875
Resolutions:			
Successful mediation	6,644	6,939	6,770
From contract	266	252	252
From staff	6,378	6,687	6,518
Administrative enforcement resolutions	55,543	66,624	72,676
Total resolutions	62,187	73,563	79,446
Pending ending	42,811*	39,289*	35,430

*Pending ending inventory adjusted to reflect activity spanning fiscal years.

State and Local Program.—EEOC contracts with Fair Employment Practices Agencies (FEPAs) that are responsible for addressing employment discrimination within their respective State and local jurisdictions. In addition, the agency works with Tribal Employment Rights Organizations to promote employment opportunities for Native Americans on or near a reservation.

STATE AND LOCAL WORKLOAD PROJECTIONS

Workload	2021 actual	2022 est.	2023 est.
Charges/complaints pending	58,920	44,125	45,163
Charges/complaints received	28,111	36,432	36,432
Total Workload	87,031	80,557	81,595
Charges/complaints resolved	42,906	35,113	35,113
Charges/complaints deferred to EEOC	0	281	281
Charges/complaints pending ending	44,125	45,163	46,201

Federal Sector.—EEOC holds hearings on complaints of discrimination filed in Federal agencies, decides appeals of complaints of discrimination, and engages in activities to prevent or remove discriminatory barriers to employment opportunities in the Federal Government.

FEDERAL SECTOR PROGRAMS HEARINGS WORKLOAD PROJECTIONS

Workload	2021 actual	2022 est.	2023 est.
Hearings pending	11,666	10,225	9,386
Hearings requests received	7,664	9,100	9,100
Hearings requests consolidated after initial processing	(23)	(39)	(39)
Total workload	19,307	19,286	18,447
Hearings resolved	9,082	9,900	10,148
Hearings pending ending	10,225	9,386	8,299

FEDERAL SECTOR PROGRAMS APPEALS WORKLOAD PROJECTIONS

Workload	2021 actual	2022 est.	2023 est.
Appeals pending	3,381	3,416	4,031
Appeals received	4,207	4,418	4,528
Total workload	7,588	7,834	8,559
Appeals resolved	4,172	3,803	3,915
Appeals pending ending	3,416	4,031	4,644

Object Classification (in millions of dollars)

Identification code 045–0100–0–1–751		2021 actual	2022 est.	2023 est.
	Direct obligations:			
	Personnel compensation:			
11.1	Full-time permanent	199	202	231
11.3	Other than full-time permanent	1	2	2
11.5	Other personnel compensation	7	5	5
11.9	Total personnel compensation	207	209	238
12.1	Civilian personnel benefits	73	85	97
21.0	Travel and transportation of persons		2	2
23.1	Rental payments to GSA	32	33	34
23.2	Rental payments to others	1	1	1
23.3	Communications, utilities, and miscellaneous charges	4	4	4
25.1	State and Local Contracts	32	32	32
25.2	Other services from non-Federal sources	39	25	44
25.2	Security services	4	4	4
25.3	Other goods and services from Federal sources	5	5	5
26.0	Supplies and materials	4	3	3
31.0	Equipment	2	1	1
99.9	Total new obligations, unexpired accounts	403	404	465

Employment Summary

Identification code 045–0100–0–1–751		2021 actual	2022 est.	2023 est.
1001	Direct civilian full-time equivalent employment	1,913	2,053	2,131

EEOC EDUCATION, TECHNICAL ASSISTANCE, AND TRAINING REVOLVING FUND

Program and Financing (in millions of dollars)

Identification code 045–4019–0–3–751		2021 actual	2022 est.	2023 est.
	Obligations by program activity:			
0801	EEOC Education, Technical Assistance, and Training Revolving Fun (Reimbursable)	4	5	5
0809	Reimbursable program activities, subtotal	4	5	5
	Budgetary resources:			
	Unobligated balance:			
1000	Unobligated balance brought forward, Oct 1	3	3	2
	Budget authority:			
	Spending authority from offsetting collections, mandatory:			
1800	Collected	4	4	5
1930	Total budgetary resources available	7	7	7
	Memorandum (non-add) entries:			
1941	Unexpired unobligated balance, end of year	3	2	2
	Change in obligated balance:			
	Unpaid obligations:			
3000	Unpaid obligations, brought forward, Oct 1	1	1	2
3010	New obligations, unexpired accounts	4	5	5
3020	Outlays (gross)	–4	–4	–5
3050	Unpaid obligations, end of year	1	2	2
	Memorandum (non-add) entries:			
3100	Obligated balance, start of year	1	1	2
3200	Obligated balance, end of year	1	2	2

OTHER INDEPENDENT AGENCIES

Budget authority and outlays, net:
Mandatory:

		2021 actual	2022 est.	2023 est.
4090	Budget authority, gross		4	4	5
	Outlays, gross:				
4100	Outlays from new mandatory authority			3	4
4101	Outlays from mandatory balances		4	1	1
4110	Outlays, gross (total)		4	4	5
	Offsets against gross budget authority and outlays:				
	Offsetting collections (collected) from:				
4120	Federal sources		−2	−2	−2
4123	Non-Federal sources		−2	−2	−3
4130	Offsets against gross budget authority and outlays (total)		−4	−4	−5
4180	Budget authority, net (total)				
4190	Outlays, net (total)				
	Memorandum (non-add) entries:				
5096	Unexpired unavailable balance, SOY: Appropriations		1	1	1
5098	Unexpired unavailable balance, EOY: Appropriations		1	1	1

The EEOC Education, Technical Assistance, and Training Revolving Fund Act of 1992 created a revolving fund to pay for the cost of providing education, technical assistance and training relating to the laws administered by the EEOC.

Object Classification (in millions of dollars)

Identification code 045–4019–0–3–751	2021 actual	2022 est.	2023 est.
	Reimbursable obligations:			
11.1	Personnel compensation: Full-time permanent	2	2	2
25.2	Other services from non-Federal sources	2	3	3
99.9	Total new obligations, unexpired accounts	4	5	5

Employment Summary

Identification code 045–4019–0–3–751	2021 actual	2022 est.	2023 est.
2001	Reimbursable civilian full-time equivalent employment	14	14	14

EXPORT-IMPORT BANK OF THE UNITED STATES

Federal Funds

INSPECTOR GENERAL

For necessary expenses of the Office of Inspector General in carrying out the provisions of the Inspector General Act of 1978 (5 U.S.C. App.), $6,415,500, of which up to $962,325 may remain available until September 30, 2024.

Note.—A full-year 2022 appropriation for this account was not enacted at the time the Budget was prepared; therefore, the Budget assumes this account is operating under the Continuing Appropriations Act, 2022 (Division A of Public Law 117–43, as amended). The amounts included for 2022 reflect the annualized level provided by the continuing resolution.

Program and Financing (in millions of dollars)

Identification code 083–0105–0–1–155	2021 actual	2022 est.	2023 est.
	Obligations by program activity:			
0009	Administrative Expenses	5	7	6
	Budgetary resources:			
	Unobligated balance:			
1000	Unobligated balance brought forward, Oct 1	1	1	1
	Budget authority:			
	Appropriations, discretionary:			
1100	Appropriation	7	7	6
1930	Total budgetary resources available	8	8	7
	Memorandum (non-add) entries:			
1940	Unobligated balance expiring	−2		
1941	Unexpired unobligated balance, end of year	1	1	1
	Change in obligated balance:			
	Unpaid obligations:			
3000	Unpaid obligations, brought forward, Oct 1	2	3	2
3010	New obligations, unexpired accounts	5	7	6
3020	Outlays (gross)	−4	−8	−6
3050	Unpaid obligations, end of year	3	2	2

Export-Import Bank of the United States—Federal Funds

	Memorandum (non-add) entries:	2021 actual	2022 est.	2023 est.
3100	Obligated balance, start of year	2	3	2
3200	Obligated balance, end of year	3	2	2
	Budget authority and outlays, net:			
	Discretionary:			
4000	Budget authority, gross	7	7	6
	Outlays, gross:			
4010	Outlays from new discretionary authority	3	5	4
4011	Outlays from discretionary balances	1	3	2
4020	Outlays, gross (total)	4	8	6
4180	Budget authority, net (total)	7	7	6
4190	Outlays, net (total)	4	8	6

Object Classification (in millions of dollars)

Identification code 083–0105–0–1–155	2021 actual	2022 est.	2023 est.
	Direct obligations:			
11.1	Personnel compensation: Full-time permanent	3	4	4
12.1	Civilian personnel benefits	1	2	1
25.2	Other services from non-Federal sources	1	1	1
99.9	Total new obligations, unexpired accounts	5	7	6

Employment Summary

Identification code 083–0105–0–1–155	2021 actual	2022 est.	2023 est.
1001	Direct civilian full-time equivalent employment	21	25	25

PROGRAM ACCOUNT

The Export-Import Bank of the United States is authorized to make such expenditures within the limits of funds and borrowing authority available to such corporation, and in accordance with law, and to make such contracts and commitments without regard to fiscal year limitations, as provided by section 9104 of title 31, United States Code, as may be necessary in carrying out the program for the current fiscal year for such corporation: Provided, That none of the funds available during the current fiscal year may be used to make expenditures, contracts, or commitments for the export of nuclear equipment, fuel, or technology to any country, other than a nuclear-weapon state as defined in Article IX of the Treaty on the Non-Proliferation of Nuclear Weapons eligible to receive economic or military assistance under this Act, that has detonated a nuclear explosive after the date of enactment of this Act.

ADMINISTRATIVE EXPENSES

For administrative expenses to carry out the direct and guaranteed loan and insurance programs, including hire of passenger motor vehicles and services as authorized by section 3109 of title 5, United States Code, and not to exceed $30,000 for official reception and representation expenses for members of the Board of Directors, not to exceed $129,800,000, of which up to $19,470,000 may remain available until September 30, 2024: Provided, That the Export-Import Bank (the Bank) may accept, and use, payment or services provided by transaction participants for legal, financial, or technical services in connection with any transaction for which an application for a loan, guarantee or insurance commitment has been made: Provided further, That notwithstanding chapter 51, subchapter III of chapter 53, and section 5373 of title 5, United States Code, the Board of Directors of the Export-Import Bank of the United States may set an employee's rate of basic pay up to the rate for level III of the Executive Schedule, and this authority may be applied to no more than 35 employees at any point in time and shall remain in effect until September 30, 2023: Provided further, That the Bank shall charge fees for necessary expenses (including special services performed on a contract or fee basis, but not including other personal services) in connection with the collection of moneys owed the Bank, repossession or sale of pledged collateral or other assets acquired by the Bank in satisfaction of moneys owed the Bank, or the investigation or appraisal of any property, or the evaluation of the legal, financial, or technical aspects of any transaction for which an application for a loan, guarantee or insurance commitment has been made, or systems infrastructure: Provided further, That in addition to other funds appropriated for administrative expenses, such fees shall be credited to this account for such purposes, to remain available until expended.

PROGRAM BUDGET APPROPRIATIONS

For the cost of direct loans, loan guarantees, insurance, and tied-aid grants as authorized by section 10 of the Export-Import Bank Act of 1945, as amended, not to exceed $25,000,000: Provided, That such costs, including the cost of modifying

EXPORT-IMPORT BANK LOANS PROGRAM ACCOUNT—Continued

such loans, shall be as defined in section 502 of the Congressional Budget Act of 1974: *Provided further,* That such funds shall remain available until September 30, 2038, for the disbursement of direct loans, loan guarantees, insurance and tied-aid grants obligated in fiscal years 2023, 2024, 2025, and 2026.

RECEIPTS COLLECTED

Receipts collected pursuant to the Export-Import Bank Act of 1945 (Public Law 79–173) and the Federal Credit Reform Act of 1990, in an amount not to exceed the amount appropriated herein, shall be credited as offsetting collections to this account: Provided, That the sums herein appropriated from the General Fund shall be reduced on a dollar-for-dollar basis by such offsetting collections so as to result in a final fiscal year appropriation from the General Fund estimated at $0.

Note.—A full-year 2022 appropriation for this account was not enacted at the time the Budget was prepared; therefore, the Budget assumes this account is operating under the Continuing Appropriations Act, 2022 (Division A of Public Law 117–43, as amended). The amounts included for 2022 reflect the annualized level provided by the continuing resolution.

Program and Financing (in millions of dollars)

Identification code 083–0100–0–1–155		2021 actual	2022 est.	2023 est.
	Obligations by program activity:			
	Credit program obligations:			
0705	Reestimates of direct loan subsidy	215	19	
0706	Interest on reestimates of direct loan subsidy	54	7	
0707	Reestimates of loan guarantee subsidy	363	224	
0708	Interest on reestimates of loan guarantee subsidy	81	48	
0709	Administrative expenses	113	110	130
0715	Other	28	30	57
0900	Total new obligations, unexpired accounts	854	438	187
	Budgetary resources:			
	Unobligated balance:			
1000	Unobligated balance brought forward, Oct 1	145	156	156
1021	Recoveries of prior year unpaid obligations	14		
1070	Unobligated balance (total)	159	156	156
	Budget authority:			
	Appropriations, discretionary:			
1100	Appropriation	48		
	Appropriations, mandatory:			
1200	Appropriation	713	298	
	Spending authority from offsetting collections, discretionary:			
1700	Offsetting collections (Admin Expense)	62	110	130
1700	Offsetting collections (Other)	28	30	30
1700	Offsetting collections (Program Budget)			25
1750	Spending auth from offsetting collections, disc (total)	90	140	185
1900	Budget authority (total)	851	438	185
1930	Total budgetary resources available	1,010	594	341
	Memorandum (non-add) entries:			
1941	Unexpired unobligated balance, end of year	156	156	154
	Change in obligated balance:			
	Unpaid obligations:			
3000	Unpaid obligations, brought forward, Oct 1	112	116	55
3010	New obligations, unexpired accounts	854	438	187
3020	Outlays (gross)	–831	–499	–191
3040	Recoveries of prior year unpaid obligations, unexpired	–14		
3041	Recoveries of prior year unpaid obligations, expired	–5		
3050	Unpaid obligations, end of year	116	55	51
	Memorandum (non-add) entries:			
3100	Obligated balance, start of year	112	116	55
3200	Obligated balance, end of year	116	55	51
	Budget authority and outlays, net:			
	Discretionary:			
4000	Budget authority, gross	138	140	185
	Outlays, gross:			
4010	Outlays from new discretionary authority	72	98	130
4011	Outlays from discretionary balances	46	103	61
4020	Outlays, gross (total)	118	201	191
	Offsets against gross budget authority and outlays:			
	Offsetting collections (collected) from:			
4033	Non-Federal sources (Other)	–90	–30	–55
4033	Non-Federal sources (Receipts collected)		–110	–130
4040	Offsets against gross budget authority and outlays (total)	–90	–140	–185
4070	Budget authority, net (discretionary)	48		
4080	Outlays, net (discretionary)	28	61	6
	Mandatory:			
4090	Budget authority, gross	713	298	
	Outlays, gross:			
4100	Outlays from new mandatory authority	713	298	
4180	Budget authority, net (total)	761	298	
4190	Outlays, net (total)	741	359	6

Summary of Loan Levels, Subsidy Budget Authority and Outlays by Program (in millions of dollars)

Identification code 083–0100–0–1–155		2021 actual	2022 est.	2023 est.
	Direct loan levels supportable by subsidy budget authority:			
115001	Direct Loans: Export Financing	70		
115999	Total direct loan levels	70		
	Direct loan subsidy (in percent):			
132001	Direct Loans: Export Financing	–4.94		
132999	Weighted average subsidy rate	–4.94		
	Direct loan subsidy budget authority:			
133001	Direct Loans: Export Financing	–3		
133999	Total subsidy budget authority	–3		
	Direct loan reestimates:			
135001	Direct Loans: Export Financing	269	–160	
135999	Total direct loan reestimates	269	–160	
	Guaranteed loan levels supportable by subsidy budget authority:			
215004	Long Term Guarantees	2,025	6,187	10,850
215005	Medium Term Guarantees	160	136	360
215006	Short Term Insurance	2,232	2,120	2,710
215007	Medium Term Insurance	41	364	15
215008	Working Capital Fund	1,203	773	1,575
215999	Total loan guarantee levels	5,661	9,580	15,510
	Guaranteed loan subsidy (in percent):			
232004	Long Term Guarantees	–4.19	–5.01	–5.43
232005	Medium Term Guarantees	–3.68	–7.14	–3.90
232006	Short Term Insurance	0.00	0.00	0.00
232007	Medium Term Insurance	–3.35	–8.90	–5.67
232008	Working Capital Fund	0.00	0.00	0.00
232999	Weighted average subsidy rate	–1.63	–3.68	–3.89
	Guaranteed loan subsidy budget authority:			
233004	Long Term Guarantees	–85	–310	–589
233005	Medium Term Guarantees	–6	–10	–14
233007	Medium Term Insurance	–1	–32	–1
233999	Total subsidy budget authority	–92	–352	–604
	Guaranteed loan subsidy outlays:			
234004	Long Term Guarantees		–190	–183
234005	Medium Term Guarantees		–7	–14
234007	Medium Term Insurance		–22	–1
234999	Total subsidy outlays		–219	–198
	Guaranteed loan reestimates:			
235004	Long Term Guarantees	360	229	
235005	Medium Term Guarantees	23	11	
235006	Short Term Insurance	7	–6	
235007	Medium Term Insurance	1	–1	
235999	Total guaranteed loan reestimates	391	233	
	Administrative expense data:			
3510	Budget authority	110	110	130

The Export-Import Bank of the United States (EXIM or the Bank) is the official export credit agency of the United States. EXIM is an independent, Federal agency that supports American jobs by facilitating the export of U.S. goods and services. To accomplish its objectives, the Bank's authority and resources are used to: assume commercial and political risks that exporters or private institutions are unwilling or unable to undertake; overcome maturity and other limitations in private sector export financing; assist U.S. exporters to meet officially sponsored foreign export credit competition; and provide leadership and guidance in export financing to the U.S. exporting and banking communities and to foreign borrowers. The Bank provides its export credit support through direct loan, loan guarantee, and insurance programs.

The 2023 Budget estimates that the Bank's export credit support will total $15.5 billion, and operations and programming will be funded entirely by receipts collected from the Bank's users. The Bank estimates it will collect $363.3 million in 2023 in receipts authorized in 2023 and prior years.

Consistent with 31 U.S.C. 1105, these amounts will be used to cover administrative expenses in an amount not to exceed $129.8. Any excess will be deposited in the General Fund of the Treasury. The 2023 Budget requests $25 million in program budget costs.

As required by the Federal Credit Reform Act of 1990, this account records the costs associated with direct loans and direct grants obligated, and loan guarantees and insurance committed in 1992 and beyond, as well as administrative expenses. The credit transactions are estimated on a present value basis; administrative expenses are estimated on a cash basis.

Object Classification (in millions of dollars)

Identification code 083–0100–0–1–155		2021 actual	2022 est.	2023 est.
	Direct obligations:			
11.1	Personnel compensation: Full-time permanent	50	60	64
12.1	Civilian personnel benefits	19	23	23
21.0	Travel and transportation of persons	1	2	2
23.1	Rental payments to GSA	8	8	8
23.3	Communications, utilities, and miscellaneous charges	2	2	2
25.1	Advisory and assistance services	9	9	10
25.2	Other services from non-Federal sources	19	14	20
25.3	Other goods and services from Federal sources	4	2	4
25.7	Operation and maintenance of equipment	25	18	23
26.0	Supplies and materials	3	1	2
31.0	Equipment	1	1	4
41.0	Grants, subsidies, and contributions	713	298	25
99.9	Total new obligations, unexpired accounts	854	438	187

Employment Summary

Identification code 083–0100–0–1–155	2021 actual	2022 est.	2023 est.
1001 Direct civilian full-time equivalent employment	375	425	429

DEBT REDUCTION FINANCING ACCOUNT

Program and Financing (in millions of dollars)

Identification code 083–4028–0–3–155		2021 actual	2022 est.	2023 est.
	Budgetary resources:			
	Unobligated balance:			
1000	Unobligated balance brought forward, Oct 1			23
	Financing authority:			
	Spending authority from offsetting collections, mandatory:			
1800	Offsetting collections (repayments)	26	23	25
1820	Capital transfer of spending authority from offsetting collections to general fund	–26		
1850	Spending auth from offsetting collections, mand (total)		23	25
1930	Total budgetary resources available		23	48
	Memorandum (non-add) entries:			
1941	Unexpired unobligated balance, end of year		23	48
	Financing authority and disbursements, net:			
	Mandatory:			
4090	Budget authority, gross		23	25
	Offsets against gross financing authority and disbursements:			
	Offsetting collections (collected) from:			
4123	Non-Federal sources - Principal	–26	–23	–25
4180	Budget authority, net (total)	–26		
4190	Outlays, net (total)	–26	–23	–25

Status of Direct Loans (in millions of dollars)

Identification code 083–4028–0–3–155		2021 actual	2022 est.	2023 est.
	Cumulative balance of direct loans outstanding:			
1210	Outstanding, start of year	28	20	12
1251	Repayments: Repayments and prepayments	–8	–8	–3
1290	Outstanding, end of year	20	12	9

Balance Sheet (in millions of dollars)

Identification code 083–4028–0–3–155		2020 actual	2021 actual
	ASSETS:		
	Net value of assets related to post-1991 direct loans receivable:		
1401	Direct loans receivable, gross	28	20
1405	Allowance for subsidy cost (-)	–28	–20
1499	Net present value of assets related to direct loans		
	Net value of assets related to post-1991 acquired defaulted guaranteed loans receivable:		
1501	Defaulted guaranteed loans receivable, gross		41
1505	Allowance for subsidy cost (-)		–41
1599	Net present value of assets related to defaulted guaranteed loans		
1701	Net value of assets related to pre-1992 direct loans receivable and acquired defaulted guaranteed loans receivable: Defaulted guaranteed loans, gross		
1999	Total upward reestimate subsidy BA [11–0091]		
	LIABILITIES:		
2204	Non-Federal liabilities: Liabilities for loan guarantees		
	NET POSITION:		
3300	Cumulative results of operations		
4999	Total liabilities and net position		

EXPORT-IMPORT BANK DIRECT LOAN FINANCING ACCOUNT

Program and Financing (in millions of dollars)

Identification code 083–4161–0–3–155		2021 actual	2022 est.	2023 est.
	Obligations by program activity:			
	Credit program obligations:			
0710	Direct loan obligations	70		
0713	Payment of interest to Treasury	406	500	600
0715	Other	15		
0740	Negative subsidy obligations	3		
0742	Downward reestimates paid to receipt accounts		146	
0743	Interest on downward reestimates		40	
0900	Total new obligations, unexpired accounts	494	686	600
	Budgetary resources:			
	Unobligated balance:			
1000	Unobligated balance brought forward, Oct 1	926	1,508	2,907
1021	Recoveries of prior year unpaid obligations	19		
1024	Unobligated balance of borrowing authority withdrawn	–19		
1070	Unobligated balance (total)	926	1,508	2,907
	Financing authority:			
	Borrowing authority, mandatory:			
1400	Borrowing authority	88		
	Spending authority from offsetting collections, mandatory:			
1800	Spending authority from offsetting collections (cash)	2,763	2,085	2,200
1820	Capital transfer of spending authority from offsetting collections to general fund	–35		
1825	Spending authority from offsetting collections applied to repay debt	–1,740		
1850	Spending auth from offsetting collections, mand (total)	988	2,085	2,200
1900	Budget authority (total)	1,076	2,085	2,200
1930	Total budgetary resources available	2,002	3,593	5,107
	Memorandum (non-add) entries:			
1941	Unexpired unobligated balance, end of year	1,508	2,907	4,507
	Change in obligated balance:			
	Unpaid obligations:			
3000	Unpaid obligations, brought forward, Oct 1	6,889	6,940	5,826
3010	New obligations, unexpired accounts	494	686	600
3020	Outlays (gross)	–424	–1,800	–2,000
3040	Recoveries of prior year unpaid obligations, unexpired	–19		
3050	Unpaid obligations, end of year	6,940	5,826	4,426
	Uncollected payments:			
3060	Uncollected pymts, Fed sources, brought forward, Oct 1	–13	–13	–13
3090	Uncollected pymts, Fed sources, end of year	–13	–13	–13
	Memorandum (non-add) entries:			
3100	Obligated balance, start of year	6,876	6,927	5,813
3200	Obligated balance, end of year	6,927	5,813	4,413

EXPORT-IMPORT BANK DIRECT LOAN FINANCING ACCOUNT—Continued

Program and Financing—Continued

Identification code 083–4161–0–3–155	2021 actual	2022 est.	2023 est.
Financing authority and disbursements, net:			
Mandatory:			
4090 Budget authority, gross	1,076	2,085	2,200
Financing disbursements:			
4110 Outlays, gross (total)	424	1,800	2,000
Offsets against gross financing authority and disbursements:			
Offsetting collections (collected) from:			
4120 Federal sources: Upward reestimate	−268	−25	
4122 Interest on uninvested funds	−90	−285	−285
4123 Repayments and prepayments	−2,405	−1,775	−1,915
4130 Offsets against gross budget authority and outlays (total)	−2,763	−2,085	−2,200
4160 Budget authority, net (mandatory)	−1,687		
4170 Outlays, net (mandatory)	−2,339	−285	−200
4180 Budget authority, net (total)	−1,687		
4190 Outlays, net (total)	−2,339	−285	−200

Status of Direct Loans (in millions of dollars)

Identification code 083–4161–0–3–155	2021 actual	2022 est.	2023 est.
Position with respect to appropriations act limitation on obligations:			
1111 Direct loan obligations from current-year authority	70		
1150 Total direct loan obligations	70		
Cumulative balance of direct loans outstanding:			
1210 Outstanding, start of year	12,899	11,096	10,519
1231 Disbursements: Direct loan disbursements	3	949	1,526
1251 Repayments: Repayments and prepayments	−1,806	−1,526	−1,353
1290 Outstanding, end of year	11,096	10,519	10,692

As required by the Federal Credit Reform Act of 1990, this non-budgetary account records all cash flows to and from the Government resulting from direct loans obligated in 1992 and beyond. The amounts in this account are a means of financing and are not included in the budget totals. As required by the Export-Import Bank Act of 1945 (P.L. 79–173, as amended), this account includes reserves amounting to not less than five percent of the aggregate amount of disbursed and outstanding loans, guarantees, and insurance of the Bank.

Balance Sheet (in millions of dollars)

Identification code 083–4161–0–3–155	2020 actual	2021 actual
ASSETS:		
Federal assets:		
1101 Fund balances with Treasury	2,471	3,052
Investments in U.S. securities:		
1106 Receivables, net	268	25
1206 Non-Federal assets: Receivables, net		
Net value of assets related to post-1991 direct loans receivable:		
1401 Direct loans receivable, gross	12,899	11,096
1402 Interest receivable	143	141
1405 Allowance for subsidy cost (−)	−1,168	−1,143
1499 Net present value of assets related to direct loans	11,874	10,094
1901 Other Federal assets: Other assets		
1999 Total assets	14,613	13,171
LIABILITIES:		
Federal liabilities:		
2101 Accounts payable		
2103 Debt	14,882	13,159
2105 Other	1	185
Non-Federal liabilities:		
2201 Accounts payable	3	3
2207 Other		1
2999 Total liabilities	14,886	13,348
NET POSITION:		
3300 Cumulative results of operations	−273	−177
4999 Total liabilities and net position	14,613	13,171

EXPORT-IMPORT BANK GUARANTEED LOAN FINANCING ACCOUNT

Program and Financing (in millions of dollars)

Identification code 083–4162–0–3–155	2021 actual	2022 est.	2023 est.
Obligations by program activity:			
0003 Payment Certificates	1,037		
0004 Other claim expenses	2		
0091 Direct program activities, subtotal	1,039		
Credit program obligations:			
0711 Default claim payments on principal	800	1,000	250
0713 Payment of interest to Treasury	39	15	15
0740 Negative subsidy obligations	92	352	605
0742 Downward reestimates paid to receipt accounts	33	28	
0743 Interest on downward reestimates	21	11	
0791 Direct program activities, subtotal	985	1,406	870
0900 Total new obligations, unexpired accounts	2,024	1,406	870
Budgetary resources:			
Unobligated balance:			
1000 Unobligated balance brought forward, Oct 1	612	226	372
1021 Recoveries of prior year unpaid obligations	19		
1070 Unobligated balance (total)	631	226	372
Financing authority:			
Borrowing authority, mandatory:			
1400 Borrowing authority	866	1,200	750
Spending authority from offsetting collections, mandatory:			
1800 Spending authority from offsetting collections (cash)	767	352	364
1820 Capital transfer of spending authority from offsetting collections to general fund	−14		
1850 Spending auth from offsetting collections, mand (total)	753	352	364
1900 Budget authority (total)	1,619	1,552	1,114
1930 Total budgetary resources available	2,250	1,778	1,486
Memorandum (non-add) entries:			
1941 Unexpired unobligated balance, end of year	226	372	616
Change in obligated balance:			
Unpaid obligations:			
3000 Unpaid obligations, brought forward, Oct 1	65	1,069	2,475
3010 New obligations, unexpired accounts	2,024	1,406	870
3020 Outlays (gross)	−1,001		
3040 Recoveries of prior year unpaid obligations, unexpired	−19		
3050 Unpaid obligations, end of year	1,069	2,475	3,345
Uncollected payments:			
3060 Uncollected pymts, Fed sources, brought forward, Oct 1	−91	−91	−91
3090 Uncollected pymts, Fed sources, end of year	−91	−91	−91
Memorandum (non-add) entries:			
3100 Obligated balance, start of year	−26	978	2,384
3200 Obligated balance, end of year	978	2,384	3,254
Financing authority and disbursements, net:			
Mandatory:			
4090 Budget authority, gross	1,619	1,552	1,114
Financing disbursements:			
4110 Outlays, gross (total)	1,001		
Offsets against gross financing authority and disbursements:			
Offsetting collections (collected) from:			
4120 Federal Sources: Payments from program account	−445	−284	−10
4122 Interest on uninvested funds	−43	−68	−88
4123 Fees, premiums, claim recoveries	−279		−266
4130 Offsets against gross budget authority and outlays (total)	−767	−352	−364
4160 Budget authority, net (mandatory)	852	1,200	750
4170 Outlays, net (mandatory)	234	−352	−364
4180 Budget authority, net (total)	852	1,200	750
4190 Outlays, net (total)	234	−352	−364

Status of Guaranteed Loans (in millions of dollars)

Identification code 083–4162–0–3–155	2021 actual	2022 est.	2023 est.
Position with respect to appropriations act limitation on commitments:			
2111 Guaranteed loan commitments from current-year authority	5,661	9,580	15,510
2121 Limitation available from carry-forward			
2143 Uncommitted limitation carried forward			
2150 Total guaranteed loan commitments	5,661	9,580	15,510
2199 Guaranteed amount of guaranteed loan commitments	5,661	9,580	15,510

OTHER INDEPENDENT AGENCIES

Export-Import Bank of the United States—Continued
Federal Funds—Continued

1253

		2021 actual	2022 est.	2023 est.
	Cumulative balance of guaranteed loans outstanding:			
2210	Outstanding, start of year	24,095	18,800	20,176
2231	Disbursements of new guaranteed loans	2,399	9,171	11,000
2251	Repayments and prepayments	−5,857	−6,795	−6,800
	Adjustments:			
2263	Terminations for default that result in claim payments	−1,837	−1,000	−250
2264	Other adjustments, net			
2290	Outstanding, end of year	18,800	20,176	24,126
	Memorandum:			
2299	Guaranteed amount of guaranteed loans outstanding, end of year	18,800	17,515	16,980
	Addendum:			
	Cumulative balance of defaulted guaranteed loans that result in loans receivable:			
2310	Outstanding, start of year	951	2,251	2,251
2364	Other adjustments, net	1,300		
2390	Outstanding, end of year	2,251	2,251	2,251

As required by the Federal Credit Reform Act of 1990, this non-budgetary account records all cash flows to and from the Government resulting from loan guarantees committed in 1992 and beyond. The amounts in this account are a means of financing and are not included in the budget totals. As required by the Export-Import Bank Act of 1945 (P.L. 79–173, as amended), this account includes reserves amounting to not less than five percent of the aggregate amount of disbursed and outstanding loans, guarantees, and insurance of the Bank.

Balance Sheet (in millions of dollars)

Identification code 083–4162–0–3–155		2020 actual	2021 actual
	ASSETS:		
	Federal assets:		
1101	Fund balances with Treasury	586	1,204
	Investments in U.S. securities:		
1106	Receivables, net	445	273
1206	Non-Federal assets: Receivables, net	23	14
	Net value of assets related to post-1991 acquired defaulted guaranteed loans receivable:		
1501	Loans receivable, gross	951	2,251
1502	Interest receivable	1	4
1504	Foreclosed property	24	328
1505	Allowance for subsidy cost (-)	−632	−980
1599	Net present value of assets related to defaulted guaranteed loans	344	1,603
1999	Total assets	1,398	3,094
	LIABILITIES:		
	Federal liabilities:		
2103	Debt	506	1,372
2105	Other	54	39
	Non-Federal liabilities:		
2201	Accounts payable	4	4
2202	Interest payable		3
2203	Debt	2	960
2204	Liabilities for loan guarantees	814	679
2207	Other	4	23
2999	Total liabilities	1,384	3,080
	NET POSITION:		
3300	Cumulative results of operations	14	14
4999	Total liabilities and net position	1,398	3,094

EXPORT-IMPORT BANK OF THE UNITED STATES LIQUIDATING ACCOUNT

Program and Financing (in millions of dollars)

Identification code 083–4027–0–3–155		2021 actual	2022 est.	2023 est.
	Budgetary resources:			
	Budget authority:			
	Spending authority from offsetting collections, mandatory:			
1800	Collected		1	7
1820	Capital transfer of spending authority from offsetting collections to general fund		−1	−7
	Budget authority and outlays, net:			
	Mandatory:			
	Offsets against gross budget authority and outlays:			
	Offsetting collections (collected) from:			
4123	Non-Federal sources		−1	−7
4180	Budget authority, net (total)		−1	−7
4190	Outlays, net (total)		−1	−7

Status of Direct Loans (in millions of dollars)

Identification code 083–4027–0–3–155		2021 actual	2022 est.	2023 est.
	Cumulative balance of direct loans outstanding:			
1210	Outstanding, start of year	90	90	89
1251	Repayments: Repayments and prepayments		−1	−1
1290	Outstanding, end of year	90	89	88

Status of Guaranteed Loans (in millions of dollars)

Identification code 083–4027–0–3–155		2021 actual	2022 est.	2023 est.
	Addendum:			
	Cumulative balance of defaulted guaranteed loans that result in loans receivable:			
2310	Outstanding, start of year	27	27	26
2351	Repayments of loans receivable		−1	−1
2390	Outstanding, end of year	27	26	25

EXIM's liquidating account records all cash flows to and from the Government resulting from all EXIM direct loans obligated and loan guarantees committed prior to 1992. This account is shown on a cash basis and reflects the transactions resulting from loans provided to finance exports. No new loan disbursements are made from this account. Certain collections made into this account are made available for default claim payments. The Federal Credit Reform Act provides permanent indefinite authority to cover obligations for default payments if the liquidating account funds are otherwise insufficient. All new EXIM credit activity in 1992 and after (including modifications of direct loans or loan guarantees that resulted from obligations or commitments in any year) is recorded in corresponding program and financing accounts.

Balance Sheet (in millions of dollars)

Identification code 083–4027–0–3–155		2020 actual	2021 actual
	ASSETS:		
1206	Non-Federal assets: Receivables, net	2	2
1601	Direct loans, gross	90	90
1602	Interest receivable	47	50
1603	Allowance for estimated uncollectible loans and interest (-)	−135	−138
1699	Value of assets related to direct loans	2	2
1701	Defaulted guaranteed loans, gross	27	27
1702	Interest receivable	5	5
1703	Allowance for estimated uncollectible loans and interest (-)	−24	−24
1799	Value of assets related to loan guarantees	8	8
1999	Total assets	12	12
	LIABILITIES:		
	Non-Federal liabilities:		
2201	Accounts payable		
2203	Debt		
2204	Liabilities for loan guarantees		
2207	Other	1	1
2999	Total liabilities	1	1
	NET POSITION:		
3300	Cumulative results of operations	11	11
3300	Cumulative results of operations		
3999	Total net position	11	11
4999	Total liabilities and net position	12	12

GENERAL FUND RECEIPT ACCOUNTS

(in millions of dollars)

	2021 actual	2022 est.	2023 est.
Offsetting receipts from the public:			
083–272710 Export-Import Bank Loans, Negative Subsidies		228	208
083–272730 Export-Import Bank Loans, Downward Reestimates of Subsidies	54	225	
General Fund Offsetting receipts from the public	54	453	208

FARM CREDIT ADMINISTRATION

Federal Funds

LIMITATION ON ADMINISTRATIVE EXPENSES

Not to exceed $88,500,000 (from assessments collected from farm credit institutions, including the Federal Agricultural Mortgage Corporation) shall be obligated during the current fiscal year for administrative expenses as authorized under 12 U.S.C. 2249: Provided, That this limitation shall not apply to expenses associated with receiverships: Provided further, That the agency may exceed this limitation by up to 10 percent with notification to the Committees on Appropriations of both Houses of Congress: Provided further, That the purposes of section 3.7(b)(2)(A)(i) of the Farm Credit Act of 1971 (12 U.S.C. 2128(b)(2)(A)(i)), the Farm Credit Administration may exempt, an amount in its sole discretion, from the application of the limitation provided in that clause of export loans described in the clause guaranteed or insured in a manner other than described in subclause (II) of the clause.

Note.—A full-year 2022 appropriation for this account was not enacted at the time the Budget was prepared; therefore, the Budget assumes this account is operating under the Continuing Appropriations Act, 2022 (Division A of Public Law 117–43, as amended). The amounts included for 2022 reflect the annualized level provided by the continuing resolution.

Program and Financing (in millions of dollars)

Identification code 352–4131–0–3–351	2021 actual	2022 est.	2023 est.
Obligations by program activity:			
0801 Limitation on Administrative Expenses (Reimbursable)	76	84	89
Budgetary resources:			
Unobligated balance:			
1000 Unobligated balance brought forward, Oct 1	23	23	22
Budget authority:			
Spending authority from offsetting collections, mandatory:			
1800 Collected	76	83	88
1930 Total budgetary resources available	99	106	110
Memorandum (non-add) entries:			
1941 Unexpired unobligated balance, end of year	23	22	21
Change in obligated balance:			
Unpaid obligations:			
3000 Unpaid obligations, brought forward, Oct 1	16	17	11
3010 New obligations, unexpired accounts	76	84	89
3020 Outlays (gross)	–75	–90	–94
3050 Unpaid obligations, end of year	17	11	6
Uncollected payments:			
3060 Uncollected pymts, Fed sources, brought forward, Oct 1	–1	–1	–1
3090 Uncollected pymts, Fed sources, end of year	–1	–1	–1
Memorandum (non-add) entries:			
3100 Obligated balance, start of year	15	16	10
3200 Obligated balance, end of year	16	10	5
Budget authority and outlays, net:			
Mandatory:			
4090 Budget authority, gross	76	83	88
Outlays, gross:			
4100 Outlays from new mandatory authority	68	83	88
4101 Outlays from mandatory balances	7	7	6
4110 Outlays, gross (total)	75	90	94
Offsets against gross budget authority and outlays:			
Offsetting collections (collected) from:			
4123 Non-Federal sources	–76	–83	–88
4180 Budget authority, net (total)			
4190 Outlays, net (total)	–1	7	6

Memorandum (non-add) entries:			
5000 Total investments, SOY: Federal securities: Par value	34	39	31
5001 Total investments, EOY: Federal securities: Par value	39	31	30

The Farm Credit Administration (FCA) is an independent Federal agency that examines and regulates the Farm Credit System (System) for safety and soundness and program compliance. The System is a cooperative agricultural credit system of farm credit banks and associations that lend to farmers, ranchers, and their cooperatives; farm-related businesses; rural homeowners; and rural utilities. FCA also performs the examination and general supervision of Farmer Mac. In addition, FCA will oversee the safety and soundness examinations of the National Consumer Cooperative Bank, which is not a System institution.

As of October 1, 2021, the System was composed of three Farm Credit Banks, one Agricultural Credit Bank, 67associations, six service corporations, the Federal Farm Credit Banks Funding Corporation, and Farmer Mac.

Assessments based upon estimated administrative expenses are collected from institutions in the System, including Farmer Mac, and are available for administrative expenses. Obligations are incurred within fiscal year budgets approved by the FCA Board. Section 6(g)(1) of the Inspector General Act of 1978, as amended, (IG Act) requires an Inspector General (IG) to include specific information in the budget request that the IG submits to its designated Federal entity to which the IG reports. To fulfill the requirement of Section 6(g)(2) of the IG Act as it pertains to FCA, the FCA Board must in turn include this same information in the budget request that the Agency submits to the President.

The information that the IG Act requires to be included is provided below:

The aggregate budget request for the Office of Inspector General (OIG) is $2,078,119.

The amount needed for OIG training is $44,000.

The amount needed to support the Council of the Inspectors General on Integrity and Efficiency is $8,692.

The FCA IG's budget request for 2023 is being submitted unchanged by the FCA Board.

Object Classification (in millions of dollars)

Identification code 352–4131–0–3–351	2021 actual	2022 est.	2023 est.
Reimbursable obligations:			
Personnel compensation:			
11.1 Full-time permanent	48	50	52
11.3 Other than full-time permanent	1	1	1
11.9 Total personnel compensation	49	51	53
12.1 Civilian personnel benefits	19	22	23
21.0 Travel and transportation of persons		3	3
23.3 Communications, utilities, and miscellaneous charges	1	1	1
25.1 Advisory and assistance services	2	2	3
25.2 Other services from non-Federal sources	1	1	1
25.3 Other goods and services from Federal sources	1	1	1
25.7 Operation and maintenance of equipment	1	1	1
26.0 Supplies and materials	1	1	2
31.0 Equipment	1	1	1
99.9 Total new obligations, unexpired accounts	76	84	89

Employment Summary

Identification code 352–4131–0–3–351	2021 actual	2022 est.	2023 est.
2001 Reimbursable civilian full-time equivalent employment	314	334	333

FARM CREDIT SYSTEM INSURANCE CORPORATION

Federal Funds

FARM CREDIT SYSTEM INSURANCE FUND

Program and Financing (in millions of dollars)

Identification code 352–4136–0–3–351	2021 actual	2022 est.	2023 est.
Obligations by program activity:			
0801 Reimbursable program activity	4	5	5
Budgetary resources:			
Unobligated balance:			
1000 Unobligated balance brought forward, Oct 1	5,163	5,385	5,882
1021 Recoveries of prior year unpaid obligations	1		
1070 Unobligated balance (total)	5,164	5,385	5,882
Budget authority:			
Spending authority from offsetting collections, mandatory:			
1800 Collected	219	495	455
1801 Change in uncollected payments, Federal sources	11	7	3
1824 Spending authority from offsetting collections precluded from obligation (limitation on obligations)	–5		
1850 Spending auth from offsetting collections, mand (total)	225	502	458
1930 Total budgetary resources available	5,389	5,887	6,340
Memorandum (non-add) entries:			
1941 Unexpired unobligated balance, end of year	5,385	5,882	6,335
Change in obligated balance:			
Unpaid obligations:			
3000 Unpaid obligations, brought forward, Oct 1	1		
3010 New obligations, unexpired accounts	4	5	5
3020 Outlays (gross)	–4	–5	–5
3040 Recoveries of prior year unpaid obligations, unexpired	–1		
Uncollected payments:			
3060 Uncollected pymts, Fed sources, brought forward, Oct 1	–16	–27	–34
3070 Change in uncollected pymts, Fed sources, unexpired	–11	–7	–3
3090 Uncollected pymts, Fed sources, end of year	–27	–34	–37
Memorandum (non-add) entries:			
3100 Obligated balance, start of year	–15	–27	–34
3200 Obligated balance, end of year	–27	–34	–37
Budget authority and outlays, net:			
Mandatory:			
4090 Budget authority, gross	225	502	458
Outlays, gross:			
4100 Outlays from new mandatory authority	4	5	5
Offsets against gross budget authority and outlays:			
Offsetting collections (collected) from:			
4121 Interest on Federal securities	37	–61	–71
4123 Non-Federal sources	–256	–434	–384
4130 Offsets against gross budget authority and outlays (total)	–219	–495	–455
Additional offsets against gross budget authority only:			
4140 Change in uncollected pymts, Fed sources, unexpired	–11	–7	–3
4160 Budget authority, net (mandatory)	–5		
4170 Outlays, net (mandatory)	–215	–490	–450
4180 Budget authority, net (total)	–5		
4190 Outlays, net (total)	–215	–490	–450
Memorandum (non-add) entries:			
5000 Total investments, SOY: Federal securities: Par value	5,153	5,365	5,855
5001 Total investments, EOY: Federal securities: Par value	5,365	5,855	6,305
5090 Unexpired unavailable balance, SOY: Offsetting collections		5	5
5092 Unexpired unavailable balance, EOY: Offsetting collections	5	5	5

The Farm Credit System Insurance Corporation (Corporation) was established to insure the timely payment of principal and interest on insured System debt obligations purchased by investors. The Corporation is managed by a three-member board of directors that consists of the same individuals as the Farm Credit Administration Board. However, the same member may not serve as a chair of both entities. The Corporation derives its revenues from insurance premiums collected from insured System banks and from the investment income earned on its investment portfolio. Insurance premiums are assessed on System banks based on the level of adjusted insured obligations outstanding at each bank. Congress established a secure base amount of 2 percent of adjusted outstanding insured System obligations, or such other amount determined by the Corporation's board of directors to be actuarially sound to maintain in the Insurance Fund. As of September 30, 2021, the Insurance Fund was $158 million above the 2 percent secure base amount at 2.06 percent. Insurance premium rates are reviewed semiannually. For 2021, the board of directors set premium rates at its January 28, 2021 meeting at 16 basis points on average adjusted insured debt and continued the assessment of the 10 basis point surcharge on the average principal balance outstanding for nonaccrual loans and other-than-temporarily impaired investments. The board of directors again reviewed premiums at its June 17, 2021 meeting and voted to maintain the premium accrual rate on average adjusted insured debt of 16 basis points and continued the assessment of the 10 basis point surcharge on the average principal balance outstanding for nonaccrual loans and other-than-temporarily impaired investments for the remainder of 2021. In January 2022, the Corporation's Board will meet to set insurance premium rates for calendar year 2022. The Corporation has the authority to make refunds of excess Insurance Fund balances.

The Insurance Fund is available for payment of insured System obligations if a System bank defaults on its primary liability. The Insurance Fund is also available to pay the operating costs of the Corporation and to exercise its authority to make loans, borrow, purchase System bank assets or obligations, provide other financial assistance and otherwise act to reduce its exposure to losses.

Object Classification (in millions of dollars)

Identification code 352–4136–0–3–351	2021 actual	2022 est.	2023 est.
Reimbursable obligations:			
11.1 Personnel compensation: Full-time permanent	2	2	2
12.1 Civilian personnel benefits	1	1	1
25.3 Other goods and services from Federal sources	1	2	2
99.0 Reimbursable obligations	4	5	5
99.9 Total new obligations, unexpired accounts	4	5	5

Employment Summary

Identification code 352–4136–0–3–351	2021 actual	2022 est.	2023 est.
2001 Reimbursable civilian full-time equivalent employment	11	12	12

FEDERAL COMMUNICATIONS COMMISSION

Federal Funds

SALARIES AND EXPENSES

For necessary expenses of the Federal Communications Commission, as authorized by law, including uniforms and allowances therefor, as authorized by 5 U.S.C. 5901–5902; not to exceed $4,000 for official reception and representation expenses; purchase and hire of motor vehicles; special counsel fees; and services as authorized by 5 U.S.C. 3109, $390,192,000, to remain available until expended: Provided, That $390,192,000 of offsetting collections shall be assessed and collected pursuant to section 9 of title I of the Communications Act of 1934, shall be retained and used for necessary expenses and shall remain available until expended: Provided further, That the sum herein appropriated shall be reduced as such offsetting collections are received during fiscal year 2023 so as to result in a final fiscal year 2023 appropriation estimated at $0: Provided further, That, notwithstanding 47 U.S.C. 309(j)(8)(B), proceeds from the use of a competitive bidding system that may be retained and made available for obligation shall not exceed $132,231,000 for fiscal year 2023: Provided further, That, of the amount appropriated under this heading, not less than $12,131,000 shall be for the salaries and expenses of the Office of Inspector General.

Note.—A full-year 2022 appropriation for this account was not enacted at the time the Budget was prepared; therefore, the Budget assumes this account is operating under the Continuing Appropriations Act, 2022 (Division A of Public Law 117–43, as amended). The amounts included for 2022 reflect the annualized level provided by the continuing resolution.

1256 Federal Communications Commission—Continued
Federal Funds—Continued

THE BUDGET FOR FISCAL YEAR 2023

SALARIES AND EXPENSES—Continued

Program and Financing (in millions of dollars)

Identification code 027–0100–0–1–376	2021 actual	2022 est.	2023 est.
Obligations by program activity:			
0001 Salaries and Expenses (Direct - Telehealth)	90	166	....
0002 Salaries and Expenses (Direct - Broadband Map)	....	35	30
0799 Total direct obligations	90	201	30
0801 Salaries and Expenses (Offsetting Collections)	512	515	521
0809 Reimbursable program activities, subtotal	512	515	521
0900 Total new obligations, unexpired accounts	602	716	551
Budgetary resources:			
Unobligated balance:			
1000 Unobligated balance brought forward, Oct 1	76	318	115
1021 Recoveries of prior year unpaid obligations	19	....	....
1070 Unobligated balance (total)	95	318	115
Budget authority:			
Appropriations, discretionary:			
1100 Appropriation (Telehealth)	250	....	....
1100 Appropriation (Broadband Map)	65	....	....
1160 Appropriation, discretionary (total)	315	....	....
Spending authority from offsetting collections, discretionary:			
1700 Offsetting collections (Reimbursables)	4	4	4
1700 Offsetting collections (Auctions)	135	135	132
1700 Offsetting collections (Reg Fees)	374	374	390
1701 Change in uncollected payments, Federal sources	1	....	....
1724 Spending authority from offsetting collections precluded from obligation (limitation on obligations)	–4	....	....
1750 Spending auth from offsetting collections, disc (total)	510	513	526
Spending authority from offsetting collections, mandatory:			
1802 Offsetting collections (previously unavailable)	4	....	....
1820 Capital transfer of spending authority from offsetting collections to general fund	–4	....	....
1900 Budget authority (total)	825	513	526
1930 Total budgetary resources available	920	831	641
Memorandum (non-add) entries:			
1941 Unexpired unobligated balance, end of year	318	115	90
Change in obligated balance:			
Unpaid obligations:			
3000 Unpaid obligations, brought forward, Oct 1	300	246	242
3010 New obligations, unexpired accounts	602	716	551
3020 Outlays (gross)	–637	–720	–584
3040 Recoveries of prior year unpaid obligations, unexpired	–19	....	....
3050 Unpaid obligations, end of year	246	242	209
Uncollected payments:			
3060 Uncollected pymts, Fed sources, brought forward, Oct 1	–1	–1	–1
3070 Change in uncollected pymts, Fed sources, unexpired	–1	....	....
3071 Change in uncollected pymts, Fed sources, expired	1	....	....
3090 Uncollected pymts, Fed sources, end of year	–1	–1	–1
Memorandum (non-add) entries:			
3100 Obligated balance, start of year	299	245	241
3200 Obligated balance, end of year	245	241	208
Budget authority and outlays, net:			
Discretionary:			
4000 Budget authority, gross	825	513	526
Outlays, gross:			
4010 Outlays from new discretionary authority	369	441	452
4011 Outlays from discretionary balances	268	279	132
4020 Outlays, gross (total)	637	720	584
Offsets against gross budget authority and outlays:			
Offsetting collections (collected) from:			
4030 Federal sources	–139	–139	–136
4033 Non-Federal sources	–375	–374	–390
4040 Offsets against gross budget authority and outlays (total)	–514	–513	–526
Additional offsets against gross budget authority only:			
4050 Change in uncollected pymts, Fed sources, unexpired	–1	....	....
4052 Offsetting collections credited to expired accounts	1	....	....
4070 Budget authority, net (discretionary)	311	....	....
4080 Outlays, net (discretionary)	123	207	58
4180 Budget authority, net (total)	311	....	....
4190 Outlays, net (total)	123	207	58
Memorandum (non-add) entries:			
5090 Unexpired unavailable balance, SOY: Offsetting collections	17	17	17
5092 Unexpired unavailable balance, EOY: Offsetting collections	17	17	17

The Federal Communications Commission (FCC or Commission) works to ensure that rapid and efficient communications are available across the country at a reasonable cost. In support of this mission, the FCC's strategic goals for 2023 are: Pursue a "100 Percent" Broadband Policy; Promote Equity and Inclusion; Empower Consumers; Enhance Public Safety; Advance America's Global Competitiveness and National Security; and Foster Operational Excellence. The 2023 Budget includes an overall request of $390 million to fund the Commission. Of that amount, the requested funding for the FCC's Inspector General is $12 million. The Commission is also requesting $132 million for the Spectrum Auctions Program for 2023.

Object Classification (in millions of dollars)

Identification code 027–0100–0–1–376	2021 actual	2022 est.	2023 est.
Direct obligations:			
25.2 Other services from non-Federal sources	7	33	20
25.7 Operation and maintenance of equipment	....	2	10
41.0 Grants, subsidies, and contributions	83	166	....
99.0 Direct obligations	90	201	30
99.0 Reimbursable obligations	512	515	521
99.9 Total new obligations, unexpired accounts	602	716	551

Employment Summary

Identification code 027–0100–0–1–376	2021 actual	2022 est.	2023 est.
2001 Reimbursable civilian full-time equivalent employment	1,464	1,472	1,600

UNIVERSAL SERVICE FUND

Special and Trust Fund Receipts (in millions of dollars)

Identification code 027–5183–0–2–376	2021 actual	2022 est.	2023 est.
0100 Balance, start of year	....	....	....
Receipts:			
Current law:			
1110 Universal Service Fund	9,190	8,038	8,179
2000 Total: Balances and receipts	9,190	8,038	8,179
Appropriations:			
Current law:			
2101 Universal Service Fund	–9,190	–8,038	–8,179
5099 Balance, end of year	....	....	....

Program and Financing (in millions of dollars)

Identification code 027–5183–0–2–376	2021 actual	2022 est.	2023 est.
Obligations by program activity:			
0001 Universal service fund	8,592	15,253	14,417
0002 Program support	200	224	232
0900 Total new obligations, unexpired accounts (object class 41.0)	8,792	15,477	14,649
Budgetary resources:			
Unobligated balance:			
1000 Unobligated balance brought forward, Oct 1	–9,715	–8,870	–15,530
1021 Recoveries of prior year unpaid obligations	402	779	696
1033 Recoveries of prior year paid obligations	45	....	....
1070 Unobligated balance (total)	–9,268	–8,091	–14,834
Budget authority:			
Appropriations, mandatory:			
1201 Appropriation (special fund)—Receipts	9,190	8,038	8,179
1900 Budget authority (total)	9,190	8,038	8,179
1930 Total budgetary resources available	–78	–53	–6,655
Memorandum (non-add) entries:			
1941 Unexpired unobligated balance, end of year	–8,870	–15,530	–21,304
Change in obligated balance:			
Unpaid obligations:			
3000 Unpaid obligations, brought forward, Oct 1	15,627	15,275	21,442

		2021 actual	2022 est.	2023 est.
3010	New obligations, unexpired accounts	8,792	15,477	14,649
3020	Outlays (gross)	–8,742	–8,531	–8,290
3040	Recoveries of prior year unpaid obligations, unexpired	–402	–779	–696
3050	Unpaid obligations, end of year	15,275	21,442	27,105
	Memorandum (non-add) entries:			
3100	Obligated balance, start of year	15,627	15,275	21,442
3200	Obligated balance, end of year	15,275	21,442	27,105
	Budget authority and outlays, net:			
	Mandatory:			
4090	Budget authority, gross	9,190	8,038	8,179
	Outlays, gross:			
4100	Outlays from new mandatory authority	4,498	4,037	4,138
4101	Outlays from mandatory balances	4,244	4,494	4,152
4110	Outlays, gross (total)	8,742	8,531	8,290
	Offsets against gross budget authority and outlays:			
	Offsetting collections (collected) from:			
4123	Non-Federal sources	–45		
	Additional offsets against gross budget authority only:			
4143	Recoveries of prior year paid obligations, unexpired accounts	45		
4160	Budget authority, net (mandatory)	9,190	8,038	8,179
4170	Outlays, net (mandatory)	8,697	8,531	8,290
4180	Budget authority, net (total)	9,190	8,038	8,179
4190	Outlays, net (total)	8,697	8,531	8,290

Pursuant to the Communications Act of 1934, as amended by the Telecommunications Act of 1996 (1996 Act), all telecommunications service providers and certain other providers of telecommunications contribute to the Federal Universal Service Fund (USF) based on a percentage of their interstate and international end-user telecommunications revenues. These companies include wireline phone companies, wireless phone companies, paging service companies and certain Voice over Internet Protocol (VoIP) providers. The goals of USF are to increase access to both telecommunications and advanced services, such as high-speed Internet, for all consumers at just, reasonable and affordable rates. The 1996 Act established principles for universal service that specifically focused on increasing access to evolving services for consumers living in rural and insular areas, and for consumers with low incomes. Additional principles called for increased access to high-speed Internet in the nation's schools, libraries and rural health care facilities. The FCC established four programs within the USF to implement the statute. The four programs are: (1) High Cost—ensures consumers in rural, insular, and high cost areas have access to modern communications networks capable of providing voice and broadband service, both fixed and mobile, at rates that are reasonably comparable to those in urban areas; (2) Lifeline (for low-income consumers)—provides a monthly benefit on home or wireless phone and broadband service to eligible households and includes initiatives to expand phone service for residents of Tribal lands; (3) Schools and Libraries (E-rate)—provides funding to schools and libraries to obtain broadband, among other things; and (4) Rural Health Care—provides funding to eligible health care providers for telecommunications and broadband services necessary for the provision of health care. In addition, in 2020 the Commission established the Connected Care Pilot Program, to provide $100 million in funding for select pilot projects covering 85% of the eligible costs of broadband connectivity, network equipment, and information services necessary to provide connected care services to the intended population over a three year period.

TELECOMMUNICATIONS RELAY SERVICES FUND, FEDERAL COMMUNICATIONS COMMISSION

Special and Trust Fund Receipts (in millions of dollars)

Identification code 027–5700–0–2–376	2021 actual	2022 est.	2023 est.
0100 Balance, start of year			
Receipts:			
Current law:			
1110 Contributions for Telecommunications Relay Services, Telecommunications Relay Services Fund	1,562	1,468	1,483
2000 Total: Balances and receipts	1,562	1,468	1,483

	Appropriations:			
	Current law:			
2101	Telecommunications Relay Services Fund, Federal Communications Commission	–1,562	–1,468	–1,483
5099	Balance, end of year			

Program and Financing (in millions of dollars)

Identification code 027–5700–0–2–376	2021 actual	2022 est.	2023 est.
Obligations by program activity:			
0001 Telecommunications Relay Services Fund	1,428	1,430	1,435
0002 Program Support	19	20	20
0900 Total new obligations, unexpired accounts (object class 41.0)	1,447	1,450	1,455
Budgetary resources:			
Unobligated balance:			
1000 Unobligated balance brought forward, Oct 1	346	463	486
1021 Recoveries of prior year unpaid obligations	2	5	5
1070 Unobligated balance (total)	348	468	491
Budget authority:			
Appropriations, mandatory:			
1201 Appropriation (special or trust fund)	1,562	1,468	1,483
1930 Total budgetary resources available	1,910	1,936	1,974
Memorandum (non-add) entries:			
1941 Unexpired unobligated balance, end of year	463	486	519
Change in obligated balance:			
Unpaid obligations:			
3000 Unpaid obligations, brought forward, Oct 1	31	32	119
3010 New obligations, unexpired accounts	1,447	1,450	1,455
3020 Outlays (gross)	–1,444	–1,358	–1,371
3040 Recoveries of prior year unpaid obligations, unexpired	–2	–5	–5
3050 Unpaid obligations, end of year	32	119	198
Memorandum (non-add) entries:			
3100 Obligated balance, start of year	31	32	119
3200 Obligated balance, end of year	32	119	198
Budget authority and outlays, net:			
Mandatory:			
4090 Budget authority, gross	1,562	1,468	1,483
Outlays, gross:			
4100 Outlays from new mandatory authority	1,190	1,154	1,165
4101 Outlays from mandatory balances	254	204	206
4110 Outlays, gross (total)	1,444	1,358	1,371
4180 Budget authority, net (total)	1,562	1,468	1,483
4190 Outlays, net (total)	1,444	1,358	1,371

As part of the Americans with Disabilities Act of 1990 Congress amended the Communications Act of 1934 to direct the Federal Communications Commission "to ensure that interstate and intrastate telecommunications relay services (TRS) are available, to the extent possible and in the most efficient manner, to hearing and speech-impaired individuals in the United States." Section 225 of the Communications Act also directs the Commission to prescribe regulations that "generally provide that costs caused by interstate telecommunications relay services shall be recovered from all subscribers for every interstate service and costs caused by intrastate telecommunications relay service shall be recovered from the intrastate jurisdiction." The shared-funding mechanism requires providers of interstate telecommunications services to contribute to a fund that reimburses TRS providers for the cost of providing interstate TRS. All telecommunications service providers and certain other providers of telecommunications contribute to the TRS Fund based on a percentage of their end-user telecommunications revenues. These companies include, but are not limited to, wireline phone companies, wireless phone companies, paging service companies and certain Voice over Internet Protocol (VoIP) providers.

Federal Communications Commission—Continued
Federal Funds—Continued

SPECTRUM AUCTION PROGRAM ACCOUNT

Program and Financing (in millions of dollars)

Identification code 027–0300–0–1–376	2021 actual	2022 est.	2023 est.
Budgetary resources:			
Unobligated balance:			
1000 Unobligated balance brought forward, Oct 1	3	3	3
1930 Total budgetary resources available	3	3	3
Memorandum (non-add) entries:			
1941 Unexpired unobligated balance, end of year	3	3	3
4180 Budget authority, net (total)			
4190 Outlays, net (total)			

This program provided direct loans for the purpose of purchasing spectrum licenses at the Federal Communications Commission's auctions. The licenses were purchased on an installment basis, which constitutes an extension of credit. The first year of activity for this program was 1996. As required by the Federal Credit Reform Act of 1990, this account records, for this program, the subsidy costs associated with the direct loans obligated in 1992 and beyond (including modifications of direct loans or loan guarantees that resulted from obligations or commitments in any year), as well as administrative expenses of this program. The subsidy amounts are estimated on a present value basis and administrative expenses are estimated on a cash basis. The FCC no longer offers credit terms on purchases through spectrum auctions. Program activity relates to maintenance and close-out of existing loans.

SPECTRUM AUCTION DIRECT LOAN FINANCING ACCOUNT

Balance Sheet (in millions of dollars)

Identification code 027–4133–0–3–376	2020 actual	2021 actual
ASSETS:		
1101 Federal assets: Fund balances with Treasury	3	3
Net value of assets related to post-1991 direct loans receivable:		
1401 Direct loans receivable, gross		
1402 Interest receivable		
1405 Allowance for subsidy cost (-)		
1499 Net present value of assets related to direct loans		
1999 Total assets	3	3
LIABILITIES:		
2105 Federal liabilities: Other	3	3
4999 Total liabilities and net position	3	3

AFFORDABLE CONNECTIVITY FUND

[For an additional amount for the "Affordable Connectivity Fund", $14,200,000,000, to remain available until expended, for the Affordable Connectivity Program, as authorized under section 904(b)(1) of division N of the Consolidated Appropriations Act, 2021 (Public Law 116–260), as amended by section 60502 of division F of this Act: *Provided*, That such amount is designated by the Congress as being for an emergency requirement pursuant to section 4112(a) of H. Con. Res. 71 (115th Congress), the concurrent resolution on the budget for fiscal year 2018, and to section 251(b) of the Balanced Budget and Emergency Deficit Control Act of 1985.] *(Infrastructure Investments and Jobs Appropriations Act.)*

Program and Financing (in millions of dollars)

Identification code 027–1911–0–1–376	2021 actual	2022 est.	2023 est.
Obligations by program activity:			
0001 Direct program activity	908	3,792	3,600
Budgetary resources:			
Unobligated balance:			
1000 Unobligated balance brought forward, Oct 1		2,292	12,700
Budget authority:			
Appropriations, discretionary:			
1100 Appropriation		14,200	
Appropriations, mandatory:			
1200 Appropriation	3,200		
1900 Budget authority (total)	3,200	14,200	
1930 Total budgetary resources available	3,200	16,492	12,700
Memorandum (non-add) entries:			
1941 Unexpired unobligated balance, end of year	2,292	12,700	9,100
Change in obligated balance:			
Unpaid obligations:			
3000 Unpaid obligations, brought forward, Oct 1		335	300
3010 New obligations, unexpired accounts	908	3,792	3,600
3020 Outlays (gross)	–573	–3,827	–3,500
3050 Unpaid obligations, end of year	335	300	400
Memorandum (non-add) entries:			
3100 Obligated balance, start of year		335	300
3200 Obligated balance, end of year	335	300	400
Budget authority and outlays, net:			
Discretionary:			
4000 Budget authority, gross		14,200	
Outlays, gross:			
4010 Outlays from new discretionary authority		1,200	
4011 Outlays from discretionary balances			3,500
4020 Outlays, gross (total)		1,200	3,500
Mandatory:			
4090 Budget authority, gross	3,200		
Outlays, gross:			
4100 Outlays from new mandatory authority	573		
4101 Outlays from mandatory balances		2,627	
4110 Outlays, gross (total)	573	2,627	
4180 Budget authority, net (total)	3,200	14,200	
4190 Outlays, net (total)	573	3,827	3,500

The Emergency Broadband Connectivity Fund was established in the Consolidated Appropriations Act of 2021 in the amount of $3.2 billion, and FCC was directed to establish an Emergency Broadband Benefit Program (EBB Program). Under this program, eligible households may receive a discount off the cost of broadband service and certain connected devices during an emergency period relating to the COVID-19 pandemic, and participating providers can receive a reimbursement for such discounts. Pursuant to the requirements in the Infrastructure Investment and Jobs Act, 2021, the EBB Program was modified and extended to establish the Affordable Connectivity Program, which began accepting new enrollments on December 31, 2021. Congress established the Affordable Connectivity Fund for this program in the amount of $14.2 billion.

Object Classification (in millions of dollars)

Identification code 027–1911–0–1–376	2021 actual	2022 est.	2023 est.
Direct obligations:			
25.2 Other services from non-Federal sources	49		
41.0 Grants, subsidies, and contributions	859	3,792	3,600
99.9 Total new obligations, unexpired accounts	908	3,792	3,600

SECURE AND TRUSTED COMMUNICATIONS NETWORKS ACT REIMBURSEMENT PROGRAM

Program and Financing (in millions of dollars)

Identification code 027–1912–0–1–376	2021 actual	2022 est.	2023 est.
Obligations by program activity:			
0001 Direct program activity	7	1,880	13
Budgetary resources:			
Unobligated balance:			
1000 Unobligated balance brought forward, Oct 1		1,893	13
Budget authority:			
Appropriations, mandatory:			
1200 Appropriation	1,900		
1930 Total budgetary resources available	1,900	1,893	13
Memorandum (non-add) entries:			
1941 Unexpired unobligated balance, end of year	1,893	13	

Change in obligated balance:

		2021 actual	2022 est.	2023 est.
	Unpaid obligations:			
3000	Unpaid obligations, brought forward, Oct 1	....	5	935
3010	New obligations, unexpired accounts	7	1,880	13
3020	Outlays (gross)	−2	−950	−475
3050	Unpaid obligations, end of year	5	935	473
	Memorandum (non-add) entries:			
3100	Obligated balance, start of year	....	5	935
3200	Obligated balance, end of year	5	935	473
	Budget authority and outlays, net:			
	Mandatory:			
4090	Budget authority, gross	1,900	....	....
	Outlays, gross:			
4100	Outlays from new mandatory authority	2	....	....
4101	Outlays from mandatory balances	....	950	475
4110	Outlays, gross (total)	2	950	475
4180	Budget authority, net (total)	1,900	....	....
4190	Outlays, net (total)	2	950	475

The Secure and Trusted Communications Networks Act of 2019 directed the Commission to establish a Reimbursement Program, and as part of the Consolidated Appropriations Act of 2021, $1.9 billion was appropriated to carry out the program. The Reimbursement Program was established to fund the removal, replacement, and disposal of covered communications equipment or services that pose an unacceptable risk to the national security of the United States or the security and safety of U.S. persons from the networks of providers of advanced communications service.

The Reimbursement Program will provide funding allocations to eligible providers based on their estimated costs. Program recipients can then obtain funding disbursements from their allocation upon showing of actual expenses incurred. Program recipients will have one year from the initial disbursement to complete the permanent removal, replacement, and disposal of covered communications equipment or services with the potential for a general and individual extensions of time.

Object Classification (in millions of dollars)

Identification code 027–1912–0–1–376	2021 actual	2022 est.	2023 est.
Direct obligations:			
25.2 Other services from non-Federal sources	7	....	....
41.0 Grants, subsidies, and contributions	....	1,880	13
99.9 Total new obligations, unexpired accounts	7	1,880	13

EMERGENCY CONNECTIVITY FUND FOR EDUCATIONAL CONNECTIONS AND DEVICES

Program and Financing (in millions of dollars)

Identification code 027–1913–0–1–376	2021 actual	2022 est.	2023 est.
Obligations by program activity:			
0001 Direct program activity	1,311	5,861	....
Budgetary resources:			
Unobligated balance:			
1000 Unobligated balance brought forward, Oct 1	....	5,861	....
Budget authority:			
Appropriations, mandatory:			
1200 Appropriation	7,172	....	....
1930 Total budgetary resources available	7,172	5,861	....
Memorandum (non-add) entries:			
1941 Unexpired unobligated balance, end of year	5,861	....	....
Change in obligated balance:			
Unpaid obligations:			
3000 Unpaid obligations, brought forward, Oct 1	....	1,307	553
3010 New obligations, unexpired accounts	1,311	5,861	....
3020 Outlays (gross)	−4	−6,615	−553
3050 Unpaid obligations, end of year	1,307	553	....
Memorandum (non-add) entries:			
3100 Obligated balance, start of year	....	1,307	553
3200 Obligated balance, end of year	1,307	553	....
Budget authority and outlays, net:			
Mandatory:			
4090 Budget authority, gross	7,172	....	....
Outlays, gross:			
4100 Outlays from new mandatory authority	4	....	....
4101 Outlays from mandatory balances	....	6,615	553
4110 Outlays, gross (total)	4	6,615	553
4180 Budget authority, net (total)	7,172	....	....
4190 Outlays, net (total)	4	6,615	553

Congress established a $7.171 billion Emergency Connectivity Fund as part of the American Rescue Plan Act of 2021 to help schools and libraries provide connected devices, such as a laptop, tablet, or similar end-user devices, and broadband connectivity to students, school staff, and library patrons at locations other than a school or library during the COVID-19 emergency period.

Object Classification (in millions of dollars)

Identification code 027–1913–0–1–376	2021 actual	2022 est.	2023 est.
Direct obligations:			
25.2 Other services from non-Federal sources	108	1	....
41.0 Grants, subsidies, and contributions	1,203	5,860	....
99.9 Total new obligations, unexpired accounts	1,311	5,861	....

TV BROADCASTER RELOCATION FUND

Program and Financing (in millions of dollars)

Identification code 027–5610–0–2–376	2021 actual	2022 est.	2023 est.
Obligations by program activity:			
0001 TV Broadcaster Relocation	143	773	....
0900 Total new obligations, unexpired accounts (object class 41.0)	143	773	....
Budgetary resources:			
Unobligated balance:			
1000 Unobligated balance brought forward, Oct 1	707	655	....
1021 Recoveries of prior year unpaid obligations	90	118	....
1033 Recoveries of prior year paid obligations	1	....	....
1070 Unobligated balance (total)	798	773	....
1930 Total budgetary resources available	798	773	....
Memorandum (non-add) entries:			
1941 Unexpired unobligated balance, end of year	655	....	....
Change in obligated balance:			
Unpaid obligations:			
3000 Unpaid obligations, brought forward, Oct 1	700	443	633
3010 New obligations, unexpired accounts	143	773	....
3020 Outlays (gross)	−310	−465	−633
3040 Recoveries of prior year unpaid obligations, unexpired	−90	−118	....
3050 Unpaid obligations, end of year	443	633	....
Memorandum (non-add) entries:			
3100 Obligated balance, start of year	700	443	633
3200 Obligated balance, end of year	443	633	....
Budget authority and outlays, net:			
Mandatory:			
Outlays, gross:			
4101 Outlays from mandatory balances	310	465	633
Offsets against gross budget authority and outlays:			
Offsetting collections (collected) from:			
4123 Non-Federal sources	−1	....	....
Additional offsets against gross budget authority only:			
4143 Recoveries of prior year paid obligations, unexpired accounts	1	....	....
4170 Outlays, net (mandatory)	309	465	633
4180 Budget authority, net (total)	....	....	....

Federal Communications Commission—Continued
Federal Funds—Continued

TV BROADCASTER RELOCATION FUND—Continued
Program and Financing—Continued

Identification code 027–5610–0–2–376	2021 actual	2022 est.	2023 est.
4190 Outlays, net (total)	309	465	633

GENERAL FUND RECEIPT ACCOUNTS
(in millions of dollars)

	2021 actual	2022 est.	2023 est.
Offsetting receipts from the public:			
027–242900 Fees for Services	29	23	23
027–247400 Auction Receipts	....	81,089	....
027–322000 All Other General Fund Proprietary Receipts Including Budget Clearing Accounts	6	3	3
General Fund Offsetting receipts from the public	35	81,115	26

ADMINISTRATIVE PROVISIONS

SEC. 510. *Section 302 of the Universal Service Antideficiency Temporary Suspension Act is amended by striking "December 31, 2021" each place it appears and inserting "December 31, 2024".*

SEC. 511. *None of the funds appropriated by this Act may be used by the Federal Communications Commission to modify, amend, or change its rules or regulations for universal service support payments to implement the February 27, 2004, recommendations of the Federal-State Joint Board on Universal Service regarding single connection or primary line restrictions on universal service support payments.*

FEDERAL DEPOSIT INSURANCE CORPORATION

The Federal Deposit Insurance Corporation (FDIC) was created by the Banking Act of 1933 to provide protection for bank depositors and to foster sound banking practices. The Federal Deposit Insurance Corporation Improvement Act of 1991 generally requires the FDIC to use the least costly method to resolve failed banks and mandates that the FDIC take prompt corrective action against under-capitalized financial institutions. To protect depositors, the FDIC is authorized to promulgate and enforce rules and regulations relating to the supervision of insured institutions and to perform other regulatory and supervisory duties consistent with its responsibilities as an insurer.

The Financial Institutions Reform, Recovery, and Enforcement Act of 1989 or FIRREA (P.L. 101–73) established the Bank Insurance Fund (BIF), the Savings Association Insurance Fund (SAIF), and the Federal Savings and Loan Insurance Corporation (FSLIC) Resolution Fund (FRF). Under the Deposit Insurance Reform Act of 2005, the BIF and SAIF were merged into a new Deposit Insurance Fund (DIF) in 2006.

DEPOSIT INSURANCE
Federal Funds
DEPOSIT INSURANCE FUND

Program and Financing (in millions of dollars)

Identification code 051–4596–0–4–373	2021 actual	2022 est.	2023 est.
Obligations by program activity:			
0002 Insurance	332	399	408
0003 Supervision	947	1,086	1,111
0004 Receivership Management	278	302	309
0005 General and Administrative	249	358	367
0091 Total operating expenses	1,806	2,145	2,195
0101 Resolution Outlays	222	25	11,081
0900 Total new obligations, unexpired accounts	2,028	2,170	13,276
Budgetary resources:			
Unobligated balance:			
1000 Unobligated balance brought forward, Oct 1	110,835	117,396	124,560
Budget authority:			
Spending authority from offsetting collections, discretionary:			
1710 Spending authority from offsetting collections transferred to other accounts [051–4595]	....	–43	–48
Spending authority from offsetting collections, mandatory:			
1800 Collected	8,721	9,241	22,027
1801 Change in uncollected payments, Federal sources	–90	136	21
1810 Spending authority from offsetting collections transferred to other accounts [051–4595]	–42	....	....
1850 Spending auth from offsetting collections, mand (total)	8,589	9,377	22,048
1900 Budget authority (total)	8,589	9,334	22,000
1930 Total budgetary resources available	119,424	126,730	146,560
Memorandum (non-add) entries:			
1941 Unexpired unobligated balance, end of year	117,396	124,560	133,284
Change in obligated balance:			
Unpaid obligations:			
3000 Unpaid obligations, brought forward, Oct 1	132	256	299
3010 New obligations, unexpired accounts	2,028	2,170	13,276
3020 Outlays (gross)	–1,904	–2,127	–13,228
3050 Unpaid obligations, end of year	256	299	347
Uncollected payments:			
3060 Uncollected pymts, Fed sources, brought forward, Oct 1	–2,744	–2,654	–2,790
3070 Change in uncollected pymts, Fed sources, unexpired	90	–136	–21
3090 Uncollected pymts, Fed sources, end of year	–2,654	–2,790	–2,811
Memorandum (non-add) entries:			
3100 Obligated balance, start of year	–2,612	–2,398	–2,491
3200 Obligated balance, end of year	–2,398	–2,491	–2,464
Budget authority and outlays, net:			
Discretionary:			
4000 Budget authority, gross	....	–43	–48
Outlays, gross:			
4010 Outlays from new discretionary authority	....	–43	–48
Mandatory:			
4090 Budget authority, gross	8,589	9,377	22,048
Outlays, gross:			
4101 Outlays from mandatory balances	1,904	2,170	13,276
Offsets against gross budget authority and outlays:			
Offsetting collections (collected) from:			
4121 Interest on Federal securities	–707	–1,351	–2,403
4123 Non-Federal sources	–8,014	–7,890	–19,624
4130 Offsets against gross budget authority and outlays (total)	–8,721	–9,241	–22,027
Additional offsets against gross budget authority only:			
4140 Change in uncollected pymts, Fed sources, unexpired	90	–136	–21
4160 Budget authority, net (mandatory)	–42	....	....
4170 Outlays, net (mandatory)	–6,817	–7,071	–8,751
4180 Budget authority, net (total)	–42	–43	–48
4190 Outlays, net (total)	–6,817	–7,114	–8,799
Memorandum (non-add) entries:			
5000 Total investments, SOY: Federal securities: Par value	108,949	115,527	122,598
5001 Total investments, EOY: Federal securities: Par value	115,527	122,598	131,301

The primary purpose of the Deposit Insurance Fund (DIF) is to insure deposits and protect the depositors of failed banking institutions. Under the Deposit Insurance Reform Act of 2005, the FDIC's Bank Insurance Fund (BIF) and its Savings Association Insurance Fund (SAIF) were merged into the new DIF on March 31, 2006. Through the DIF, the FDIC resolves and recovers funds disbursed from the assets of failed institutions. The FDIC is authorized to charge risk-based premiums on member institutions to restore and maintain adequate fund reserves, defined as a designated percentage of estimated insured deposits set by the FDIC before the beginning of each year. The Dodd-Frank Wall Street Reform and Consumer Protection Act (the Act) (P.L. 111–203), enacted July 21, 2010, increased the minimum DIF reserve ratio (ratio of the DIF balance to total insured deposits) to 1.35 percent, up from 1.15 percent. In addition to raising the minimum reserve ratio, the Act also: 1) eliminated the FDIC's requirement to rebate premiums when the reserve ratio is between 1.35 and 1.5 percent; 2) gave the FDIC discretion to suspend or limit rebates when the DIF reserve ratio is at least 1.5 percent, effectively removing the 1.5 percent cap

OTHER INDEPENDENT AGENCIES

Federal Deposit Insurance Corporation—Continued
Federal Funds 1261

on the DIF; 3) required the FDIC to offset the effect on small insured depository institutions (defined as banks with assets less than $10 billion) when setting assessments to raise the reserve ratio from 1.15 to 1.35 percent; and 4) permanently increased the insured deposit level to $250,000 at banks insured by the FDIC. The FDIC Board has issued a final rule setting a long-term (greater than 10 years) reserve ratio target of 2 percent, with the goal of maintaining a positive fund balance during any future economic crises and maintaining a moderate, steady, long-term assessment rate that provides transparency and predictability to the banking sector.

As of September 30, 2020, the DIF balance stood at $116.4 billion on an accrual basis, measuring expected losses to current balances. This level is equivalent to a reserve ratio of 1.30 percent. Pursuant to the Act, on September 15, 2020, the FDIC adopted a Restoration Plan to restore the DIF reserve ratio to at least the statutory minimum of 1.35 percent within 8 years after, as of June 30, 2020, the DIF reserve ratio fell to 1.30 percent. The decline was a result of strong one-time growth in insured deposits. Projected growth in the DIF balance in the Budget reflects projections of bank failures in line with historical experience and assessment revenue required to increase the reserve ratio over time.

For more information, please see the Credit and Insurance chapter in the *Analytical Perspectives* volume of the Budget.

Object Classification (in millions of dollars)

Identification code 051–4596–0–4–373		2021 actual	2022 est.	2023 est.
	Direct obligations:			
11.1	Personnel compensation: Full-time permanent	889	1,021	1,046
12.1	Civilian personnel benefits	376	365	374
13.0	Benefits for former personnel	7	....	....
21.0	Travel and transportation of persons	1	62	63
23.2	Rental payments to others	42	48	49
23.3	Communications, utilities, and miscellaneous charges	34	53	54
24.0	Printing and reproduction	1	1	1
25.2	Other services from non-Federal sources	381	527	538
26.0	Supplies and materials	4	5	5
31.0	Equipment	57	30	31
32.0	Land and structures	15	33	34
42.0	Resolution Outlays	221	25	11,081
99.0	Direct obligations	2,028	2,170	13,276
99.9	Total new obligations, unexpired accounts	2,028	2,170	13,276

Employment Summary

Identification code 051–4596–0–4–373	2021 actual	2022 est.	2023 est.
1001 Direct civilian full-time equivalent employment	5,777	6,172	6,172

FSLIC RESOLUTION

Federal Funds

FSLIC RESOLUTION FUND

Program and Financing (in millions of dollars)

Identification code 051–4065–0–3–373		2021 actual	2022 est.	2023 est.
	Budgetary resources:			
	Unobligated balance:			
1000	Unobligated balance brought forward, Oct 1	905	905	907
	Budget authority:			
	Spending authority from offsetting collections, mandatory:			
1800	Offsetting collections	....	2	2
1900	Budget authority (total)	....	2	2
1930	Total budgetary resources available	905	907	909
	Memorandum (non-add) entries:			
1941	Unexpired unobligated balance, end of year	905	907	909
	Budget authority and outlays, net:			
	Mandatory:			
4090	Budget authority, gross	....	2	2
	Offsets against gross budget authority and outlays:			
	Offsetting collections (collected) from:			
4121	Interest on Federal securities	....	–1	–1
4123	Non-Federal sources	....	–1	–1
4130	Offsets against gross budget authority and outlays (total)	....	–2	–2
4170	Outlays, net (mandatory)	....	–2	–2
4180	Budget authority, net (total)	....	....	....
4190	Outlays, net (total)	....	–2	–2
	Memorandum (non-add) entries:			
5000	Total investments, SOY: Federal securities: Par value	881	882	883
5001	Total investments, EOY: Federal securities: Par value	882	883	885

The FSLIC Resolution Fund (FRF) is the ultimate successor to FSLIC assets and liabilities from thrift resolutions prior to August 1989. Beginning in August 1989, the Resolution Trust Corporation (RTC) assumed responsibility for the FSLIC's unresolved cases. On December 31, 1995, the RTC was terminated and its assets and liabilities were transferred to FRF.

Funds for FRF operations have come from: 1) income earned on its assets; 2) liquidation proceeds from receiverships; 3) the proceeds of the sale of bonds by the Financing Corporation; and 4) a portion of insurance premiums paid by Savings Association Insurance Fund (SAIF) members prior to 1993. The Financial Institutions Reform, Recovery, and Enforcement Act or FIRREA (P.L. 101–73) authorizes appropriations to make up for any shortfall. Currently, the FRF consists of two distinct pools of assets and liabilities. One is composed of the assets and liabilities of the FSLIC transferred to the FRF (FRF-FSLIC) and the other is composed of the RTC assets and liabilities (FRF-RTC). The assets of one pool are not available to satisfy obligations of the other. The FRF will continue operations until all of its assets are sold or otherwise liquidated and all its liabilities are satisfied. Any funds remaining in the FRF-FSLIC will be paid to the U.S. Treasury. Any remaining funds of the FRF-RTC will be distributed to the Resolution Funding Corporation to pay interest on its bonds.

ORDERLY LIQUIDATION

Federal Funds

ORDERLY LIQUIDATION FUND

Special and Trust Fund Receipts (in millions of dollars)

Identification code 051–5586–0–2–373		2021 actual	2022 est.	2023 est.
0100	Balance, start of year	....	....	....
	Receipts:			
	Current law:			
1110	Risk-Based Assessments, Orderly Liquidation Fund	....	31	616
2000	Total: Balances and receipts	....	31	616
	Appropriations:			
	Current law:			
2101	Orderly Liquidation Fund	....	–31	–616
5099	Balance, end of year	....	....	....

Program and Financing (in millions of dollars)

Identification code 051–5586–0–2–373		2021 actual	2022 est.	2023 est.
	Obligations by program activity:			
0001	Orderly Liquidation	....	1,781	4,285
0002	Administrative Expenses	....	2	5
0003	Interest to Treasury	....	9	51
0900	Total new obligations, unexpired accounts	....	1,792	4,341
	Budgetary resources:			
	Budget authority:			
	Appropriations, mandatory:			
1201	Appropriation (special or trust fund)	....	31	616
1230	Appropriations and/or unobligated balance of appropriations permanently reduced	....	–2	–35
1260	Appropriations, mandatory (total)	....	29	581
	Borrowing authority, mandatory:			
1400	Borrowing authority	....	1,870	3,987
1421	Borrowing authority temporarily reduced	....	–107	–227
1440	Borrowing authority, mandatory (total)	....	1,763	3,760
1900	Budget authority (total)	....	1,792	4,341

Federal Deposit Insurance Corporation—Continued
Federal Funds—Continued

ORDERLY LIQUIDATION FUND—Continued

Program and Financing—Continued

Identification code 051–5586–0–2–373	2021 actual	2022 est.	2023 est.
1930 Total budgetary resources available	....	1,792	4,341
Change in obligated balance:			
Unpaid obligations:			
3010 New obligations, unexpired accounts	....	1,792	4,341
3020 Outlays (gross)	....	–1,792	–4,341
Budget authority and outlays, net:			
Mandatory:			
4090 Budget authority, gross	....	1,792	4,341
Outlays, gross:			
4100 Outlays from new mandatory authority	....	1,792	4,341
4180 Budget authority, net (total)	....	1,792	4,341
4190 Outlays, net (total)	....	1,792	4,341
Memorandum (non-add) entries:			
5080 Outstanding debt, SOY	....	....	–1,870
5081 Outstanding debt, EOY	....	–1,870	–5,857
5082 Borrowing	....	–1,870	–3,987

Title II of the Dodd-Frank Wall Street Reform and Consumer Protection Act (P.L. 111–203) established an Orderly Liquidation Authority (OLA) permitting the appointment of the FDIC as receiver of financial companies whose failure and resolution under otherwise applicable Federal or State law is determined to have serious adverse effects on financial stability in the United States. The Federal Reserve Board and the FDIC, the Securities and Exchange Commission (for brokers or dealers) or the Federal Insurance Office (for insurance companies) must recommend in writing that the Secretary of the Treasury appoint the FDIC as the company's receiver.

The Secretary of the Treasury must then, in consultation with the President, determine whether seven criteria authorizing the appointment of the FDIC as receiver for the failing financial company have been satisfied, including finding that resolution under otherwise applicable law would have serious adverse effects on financial stability in the United States.

Object Classification (in millions of dollars)

Identification code 051–5586–0–2–373	2021 actual	2022 est.	2023 est.
Direct obligations:			
43.0 Admin	....	2	5
43.0 Interest and Dividends	....	9	51
43.0 Orderly Liquidation	....	1,781	4,285
99.9 Total new obligations, unexpired accounts	....	1,792	4,341

FDIC—OFFICE OF INSPECTOR GENERAL

Federal Funds

OFFICE OF THE INSPECTOR GENERAL

For necessary expenses of the Office of Inspector General in carrying out the provisions of the Inspector General Act of 1978, $47,500,000, to be derived from the Deposit Insurance Fund or, only when appropriate, the FSLIC Resolution Fund.

Note.—A full-year 2022 appropriation for this account was not enacted at the time the Budget was prepared; therefore, the Budget assumes this account is operating under the Continuing Appropriations Act, 2022 (Division A of Public Law 117–43, as amended). The amounts included for 2022 reflect the annualized level provided by the continuing resolution.

Program and Financing (in millions of dollars)

Identification code 051–4595–0–4–373	2021 actual	2022 est.	2023 est.
Obligations by program activity:			
0801 Office of the Inspector General (Reimbursable)	42	43	48
Budgetary resources:			
Budget authority:			
Spending authority from offsetting collections, discretionary:			
1711 Transferred from other accounts [051–4596]	42	43	48
1930 Total budgetary resources available	42	43	48
Change in obligated balance:			
Unpaid obligations:			
3010 New obligations, unexpired accounts	42	43	48
3020 Outlays (gross)	–42	–43	–48
Budget authority and outlays, net:			
Discretionary:			
4000 Budget authority, gross	42	43	48
Outlays, gross:			
4010 Outlays from new discretionary authority	42	43	48
4180 Budget authority, net (total)	42	43	48
4190 Outlays, net (total)	42	43	48

The FDIC's Office of Inspector General (FDIC OIG) is an independent unit within the FDIC that conducts audits, evaluations, and investigations of corporate activities. In addition, the OIG assists the FDIC in preventing and detecting fraud, waste, abuse, and mismanagement. The OIG was established by the FDIC Board pursuant to the Inspector General Act amendments of 1988 (P.L. 100–504). The Resolution Trust Corporation Completion Act (P.L. 103–204), enacted December 17, 1993, provided that the FDIC Inspector General be appointed by the President and confirmed by the Senate. The Completion Act thus added the FDIC to the list of establishments whose OIGs have separate appropriation accounts under Section 1105(a) of Title 31, United States Code, thereby safeguarding FDIC OIG's independence. Assessments paid to the Deposit Insurance Fund (DIF) by insured financial institutions, and administered by the FDIC, fully fund FDIC OIG's appropriation. To the extent that FDIC OIG performs work in connection with the FSLIC Resolution Fund (FRF), the cost of such work is derived from the FRF.

Object Classification (in millions of dollars)

Identification code 051–4595–0–4–373	2021 actual	2022 est.	2023 est.
Reimbursable obligations:			
Personnel compensation:			
11.1 Full-time permanent	23	24	26
11.3 Other than full-time permanent	1	1	1
11.9 Total personnel compensation	24	25	27
12.1 Civilian personnel benefits	12	13	15
21.0 Travel and transportation of persons	1	1	2
25.2 Other services from non-Federal sources	2	2	2
31.0 Equipment	3	2	2
99.9 Total new obligations, unexpired accounts	42	43	48

Employment Summary

Identification code 051–4595–0–4–373	2021 actual	2022 est.	2023 est.
2001 Reimbursable civilian full-time equivalent employment	129	135	144

FEDERAL DRUG CONTROL PROGRAMS

Federal Funds

HIGH INTENSITY DRUG TRAFFICKING AREAS PROGRAM

(INCLUDING TRANSFERS OF FUNDS)

For necessary expenses of the Office of National Drug Control Policy's High Intensity Drug Trafficking Areas Program, $293,500,000, to remain available until September 30, 2024, for drug control activities consistent with the approved strategy for each of the designated High Intensity Drug Trafficking Areas ("HIDTAs"), of which not less than 51 percent shall be transferred to State and local entities for drug control activities and shall be obligated not later than 120 days after enactment of this Act: Provided, That up to 49 percent may be transferred to Federal agencies and departments in amounts determined by the Director of the Office of National Drug Control Policy, of which up to $5,800,000 may be used for auditing services and associated activities and up to $3,500,000 shall be for a new Grants Management System for use by the Office of National Drug Control Policy: Provided further, That any unexpended funds obligated prior to fiscal year 2021 may be used for any other approved activities of that HIDTA, subject to reprogramming requirements:

Provided further, That the Director shall notify the Committees on Appropriations of the initial allocation of fiscal year 2023 funding among HIDTAs not later than 45 days after enactment of this Act, and shall notify the Committees of planned uses of discretionary HIDTA funding, as determined in consultation with the HIDTA Directors, not later than 90 days after enactment of this Act: *Provided further,* That upon a determination that all or part of the funds so transferred from this appropriation are not necessary for the purposes provided herein and upon notification to the Committees on Appropriations of the House of Representatives and the Senate, such amounts may be transferred back to this appropriation.

Note.—A full-year 2022 appropriation for this account was not enacted at the time the Budget was prepared; therefore, the Budget assumes this account is operating under the Continuing Appropriations Act, 2022 (Division A of Public Law 117–43, as amended). The amounts included for 2022 reflect the annualized level provided by the continuing resolution.

Program and Financing (in millions of dollars)

Identification code 011–1070–0–1–754	2021 actual	2022 est.	2023 est.
Obligations by program activity:			
0002 Grants and federal transfers	274	287	284
0003 Auditing services and activities	3	3	6
0004 Grants Management System			4
0900 Total new obligations, unexpired accounts	277	290	294
Budgetary resources:			
Unobligated balance:			
1000 Unobligated balance brought forward, Oct 1	6	4	4
1021 Recoveries of prior year unpaid obligations	6		
1070 Unobligated balance (total)	12	4	4
Budget authority:			
Appropriations, discretionary:			
1100 New budget authority (gross), detail	290	290	294
1120 Appropriations transferred to other accts [070–0540]	–2		
1120 Appropriations transferred to other accts [015–1100]	–15		
1120 Appropriations transferred to other accts [015–0200]	–2		
1120 Appropriations transferred to other accts [015–0322]	–1		
1120 Appropriations transferred to other accts [015–0324]	–1		
1160 Appropriation, discretionary (total)	269	290	294
1930 Total budgetary resources available	281	294	298
Memorandum (non-add) entries:			
1941 Unexpired unobligated balance, end of year	4	4	4
Change in obligated balance:			
Unpaid obligations:			
3000 Unpaid obligations, brought forward, Oct 1	301	320	303
3010 New obligations, unexpired accounts	277	290	294
3011 Obligations ("upward adjustments"), expired accounts	4		
3020 Outlays (gross)	–252	–307	–328
3040 Recoveries of prior year unpaid obligations, unexpired	–6		
3041 Recoveries of prior year unpaid obligations, expired	–4		
3050 Unpaid obligations, end of year	320	303	269
Memorandum (non-add) entries:			
3100 Obligated balance, start of year	301	320	303
3200 Obligated balance, end of year	320	303	269
Budget authority and outlays, net:			
Discretionary:			
4000 Budget authority, gross	269	290	294
Outlays, gross:			
4010 Outlays from new discretionary authority	33	72	74
4011 Outlays from discretionary balances	219	235	254
4020 Outlays, gross (total)	252	307	328
4180 Budget authority, net (total)	269	290	294
4190 Outlays, net (total)	252	307	328

The High Intensity Drug Trafficking Areas (HIDTA) program was established by the Anti-Drug Abuse Act of 1988, as amended, to provide assistance to Federal, State, local, and tribal law enforcement entities operating in those areas most adversely affected by drug trafficking. The HIDTA program provides resources to Federal, State, local, and tribal agencies in each HIDTA region to carry out activities that address the specific drug threats of that region. A central feature of the HIDTA program is the discretion granted to HIDTA Executive Boards to design and carry out activities that reflect the specific drug trafficking threats found in each HIDTA region. This discretion ensures that each HIDTA Executive Board can tailor its strategy and initiatives closely to local conditions and can respond quickly to changes in those conditions. Among the types of activities funded by the HIDTA program are: drug enforcement task forces comprised of multiple Federal, State, local, and tribal agencies designed to dismantle and disrupt drug trafficking organizations; multi-agency intelligence centers that provide drug intelligence to HIDTA initiatives and participating agencies; initiatives to establish or improve interoperability of communications and information systems between and among law enforcement agencies; and investments in technology infrastructure.

Object Classification (in millions of dollars)

Identification code 011–1070–0–1–754	2021 actual	2022 est.	2023 est.
Direct obligations:			
25.2 Auditing services and activities	3	3	6
25.3 Other goods and services from Federal sources			4
41.0 Grants and federal transfers	274	287	284
99.9 Total new obligations, unexpired accounts	277	290	294

OTHER FEDERAL DRUG CONTROL PROGRAMS

(INCLUDING TRANSFERS OF FUNDS)

For other drug control activities authorized by the Anti-Drug Abuse Act of 1988 and the Office of National Drug Control Policy Reauthorization Act of 1998, as amended, $134,670,000, to remain available until expended, which shall be available as follows: $106,000,000 for the Drug-Free Communities Program, of which not more than 12 percent may be used for administrative expenses, notwithstanding section 1024(b) of Public Law 100–690, as amended by section 8203(b)(3) of Public Law 115–271, and $2,500,000 shall be made available as directed by section 4 of Public Law 107–82, as amended by section 8204 of Public Law 115–271; $3,000,000 for drug court training and technical assistance; $14,000,000 for anti-doping activities; up to $3,420,000 for the United States membership dues to the World Anti-Doping Agency; $1,250,000 for the Model Acts Program; $5,200,000 for activities authorized by section 103 of Public Law 114–198, of which not more than 12 percent may be used for administrative expenses, notwithstanding subsection (g) of such section; $1,300,000 for policy research; and $500,000 for performance audits and evaluations: Provided, That amounts made available under this heading may be transferred to other Federal departments and agencies to carry out such activities.

Note.—A full-year 2022 appropriation for this account was not enacted at the time the Budget was prepared; therefore, the Budget assumes this account is operating under the Continuing Appropriations Act, 2022 (Division A of Public Law 117–43, as amended). The amounts included for 2022 reflect the annualized level provided by the continuing resolution.

Program and Financing (in millions of dollars)

Identification code 011–1460–0–1–802	2021 actual	2022 est.	2023 est.
Obligations by program activity:			
0002 Drug-Free Communities Program	133	102	106
0003 Drug Court Training & Technical Assistance	4	3	3
0006 Anti-Doping Activities	14	14	14
0007 Section 103 of Public Law 114–198	4	5	5
0008 Model Acts Program	2	1	1
0009 World Anti-Doping Agency Dues	2	3	4
0010 Policy Research			1
0011 Performance Audits and Evaluations			1
0900 Total new obligations, unexpired accounts	159	128	135
Budgetary resources:			
Unobligated balance:			
1000 Unobligated balance brought forward, Oct 1	80	53	53
1021 Recoveries of prior year unpaid obligations	4		
1070 Unobligated balance (total)	84	53	53
Budget authority:			
Appropriations, discretionary:			
1100 New budget authority (gross), detail	128	128	135
1900 Budget authority (total)	128	128	135
1930 Total budgetary resources available	212	181	188
Memorandum (non-add) entries:			
1941 Unexpired unobligated balance, end of year	53	53	53

OTHER FEDERAL DRUG CONTROL PROGRAMS—Continued

Program and Financing—Continued

Identification code 011–1460–0–1–802	2021 actual	2022 est.	2023 est.
Change in obligated balance:			
Unpaid obligations:			
3000 Unpaid obligations, brought forward, Oct 1	20	18	14
3010 New obligations, unexpired accounts	159	128	135
3020 Outlays (gross)	–157	–132	–135
3040 Recoveries of prior year unpaid obligations, unexpired	–4		
3050 Unpaid obligations, end of year	18	14	14
Memorandum (non-add) entries:			
3100 Obligated balance, start of year	20	18	14
3200 Obligated balance, end of year	18	14	14
Budget authority and outlays, net:			
Discretionary:			
4000 Budget authority, gross	128	128	135
Outlays, gross:			
4010 Outlays from new discretionary authority	86	115	122
4011 Outlays from discretionary balances	71	17	13
4020 Outlays, gross (total)	157	132	135
4180 Budget authority, net (total)	128	128	135
4190 Outlays, net (total)	157	132	135

This account is for other drug control activities authorized by the Office of National Drug Control Policy Reauthorization Act of 1998, as amended through Public Law 115–271. The funds appropriated support high-priority drug control programs and may be transferred to drug control agencies. For FY 2023, funds appropriated to this account will be used for the following activities:

Drug Free Communities Support Program.—The Drug Free Communities Support (DFC) Program provides small grants (no more than $125,000 per year for an initial 5-year period) to established local community drug free coalitions. The grants are awarded competitively to community coalitions that organize multiple sectors of a community to focus on local needs as a means for reducing and/or preventing youth substance use. The Budget also proposes to increase the cap on DFC administrative costs from 8 percent to 12 percent due to the significant level of effort required to effectively manage the DFC Program and ensure continued use of evidence-based prevention in all coalitions funded by the DFC Program.

Drug Court Training & Technical Assistance.—This funding is provided to further the development and sustainability of drug courts in the United States through the review and dissemination of science-based methods to overcome barriers to drug court sustainability, provide up-to-date guidance and training to practitioners and inter-disciplinary drug court teams to increase drug court participant retention and completion rates, and provide a state-by-state examination of drug courts.

Anti-Doping Activities.—This funding continues the effort to educate athletes on the dangers of drug use and to eliminate illegal drug use in Olympic and associated sports in the United States.

World Anti-Doping Agency (WADA) Dues.—WADA was established in 1999 as an international independent agency composed and funded equally by the sport movement and governments of the world. Its key activities include scientific research, education, development of anti-doping capacities, and monitoring of the World Anti-Doping Code—the document harmonizing anti-doping policies in all sports and all countries. ONDCP represents the United States before the agency and is responsible for the payment of U.S. dues.

Model Acts Program.—This funding provides resources to: (1) advise states on establishing laws and policies to address illicit drug use issues; and (2) revise such model state drug laws and draft supplementary model state laws to take into consideration changes in illicit drug use issues in the state involved.

Sec. 103 of Public Law 114–198 (Community-based coalition enhancement grants to address local drug crises).—This funding provides grants to eligible entities to implement comprehensive community-wide strategies that address local drug crises and emerging drug abuse issues within the area served by the eligible entity. The Budget also proposes to increase the cap on administrative costs for these grants from 8 percent to 12 percent due to the significant amount of program management and support required for these grants.

Policy Research.—This funding provides resources to conduct short-turnaround contract research projects to address specific issues concerning policy and in support of the National Drug Control Strategy.

Performance Audits and Evaluations.—This funding provides resources to support performance audits and evaluations to examine the efficiency and effectiveness of federal efforts and provides an avenue for corrective action if the goals/objectives of the National Drug Control Strategy: Performance Review System and the National Drug Control Strategy Assessment are not being met.

Object Classification (in millions of dollars)

Identification code 011–1460–0–1–802	2021 actual	2022 est.	2023 est.
Direct obligations:			
25.2 Other services from non-Federal sources	2	3	5
25.3 Other goods and services from Federal sources	12	8	13
41.0 Grants, subsidies, and contributions	23	21	21
94.0 Financial transfers	122	96	96
99.9 Total new obligations, unexpired accounts	159	128	135

Employment Summary

Identification code 011–1460–0–1–802	2021 actual	2022 est.	2023 est.
1001 Direct civilian full-time equivalent employment	2	2	2

FEDERAL ELECTION COMMISSION

Federal Funds

SALARIES AND EXPENSES

For necessary expenses to carry out the provisions of the Federal Election Campaign Act of 1971, $81,674,000, of which not to exceed $5,000 shall be available for reception and representation expenses.

Note.—A full-year 2022 appropriation for this account was not enacted at the time the Budget was prepared; therefore, the Budget assumes this account is operating under the Continuing Appropriations Act, 2022 (Division A of Public Law 117–43, as amended). The amounts included for 2022 reflect the annualized level provided by the continuing resolution.

Program and Financing (in millions of dollars)

Identification code 360–1600–0–1–808	2021 actual	2022 est.	2023 est.
Obligations by program activity:			
0001 Federal Election Commission	71	71	82
Budgetary resources:			
Budget authority:			
Appropriations, discretionary:			
1100 Appropriation	71	71	82
1930 Total budgetary resources available	71	71	82
Change in obligated balance:			
Unpaid obligations:			
3000 Unpaid obligations, brought forward, Oct 1	16	15	6
3010 New obligations, unexpired accounts	71	71	82
3011 Obligations ("upward adjustments"), expired accounts	1		
3020 Outlays (gross)	–72	–80	–81
3041 Recoveries of prior year unpaid obligations, expired	–1		
3050 Unpaid obligations, end of year	15	6	7
Memorandum (non-add) entries:			
3100 Obligated balance, start of year	16	15	6
3200 Obligated balance, end of year	15	6	7
Budget authority and outlays, net:			
Discretionary:			
4000 Budget authority, gross	71	71	82
Outlays, gross:			
4010 Outlays from new discretionary authority	61	65	75

OTHER INDEPENDENT AGENCIES

Federal Financial Institutions Examination Council
Federal Funds 1265

		2021 actual	2022 est.	2023 est.
4011	Outlays from discretionary balances	11	15	6
4020	Outlays, gross (total)	72	80	81
4180	Budget authority, net (total)	71	71	82
4190	Outlays, net (total)	72	80	81

The Federal Election Commission is responsible for facilitating transparency in the Federal election process through public disclosure of campaign finance activity and for encouraging voluntary compliance with the Federal Election Campaign Act by providing information and policy guidance about the Act and Commission regulations to the public, media, political committees, and election officials. The Commission is also responsible for enforcing the Act through audits, investigations, and civil litigation, and for developing the law by administering and interpreting the Act, the Presidential Election Campaign Fund Act, and the Presidential Primary Matching Payment Account Act.

The Commission is authorized to submit, concurrently, budget estimates to the President and the Congress.

Object Classification (in millions of dollars)

Identification code 360–1600–0–1–808		2021 actual	2022 est.	2023 est.
	Direct obligations:			
	Personnel compensation:			
11.1	Full-time permanent	37	38	44
11.3	Other than full-time permanent	1	1	1
11.9	Total personnel compensation	38	39	45
12.1	Civilian personnel benefits	14	14	15
23.1	Rental payments to GSA	5	5	5
23.3	Communications, utilities, and miscellaneous charges	1	1	1
25.2	Other services from non-Federal sources	9	8	12
25.3	Other goods and services from Federal sources	2	2	2
26.0	Supplies and materials	1	1	1
31.0	Equipment	1	1	1
99.9	Total new obligations, unexpired accounts	71	71	82

Employment Summary

Identification code 360–1600–0–1–808	2021 actual	2022 est.	2023 est.
1001 Direct civilian full-time equivalent employment	306	328	347

FEDERAL FINANCIAL INSTITUTIONS EXAMINATION COUNCIL

Federal Funds

FEDERAL FINANCIAL INSTITUTIONS EXAMINATION COUNCIL ACTIVITIES

Special and Trust Fund Receipts (in millions of dollars)

Identification code 362–5547–0–2–376		2021 actual	2022 est.	2023 est.
0100	Balance, start of year			
	Receipts:			
	Current law:			
1110	Assessments, Federal Financial Instutions Examination Council Activities	15	17	17
2000	Total: Balances and receipts	15	17	17
	Appropriations:			
	Current law:			
2101	Federal Financial Institutions Examination Council Activities	–15	–17	–17
5099	Balance, end of year			

Program and Financing (in millions of dollars)

Identification code 362–5547–0–2–376		2021 actual	2022 est.	2023 est.
	Obligations by program activity:			
0801	FFIEC Activities	15	17	17
	Budgetary resources:			
	Budget authority:			
	Appropriations, mandatory:			
1201	Appropriation (special or trust fund)	15	17	17
1900	Budget authority (total)	15	17	17
1930	Total budgetary resources available	15	17	17
	Change in obligated balance:			
	Unpaid obligations:			
3010	New obligations, unexpired accounts	15	17	17
3020	Outlays (gross)	–15	–17	–17
	Budget authority and outlays, net:			
	Mandatory:			
4090	Budget authority, gross	15	17	17
	Outlays, gross:			
4100	Outlays from new mandatory authority	15	17	17
4180	Budget authority, net (total)	15	17	17
4190	Outlays, net (total)	15	17	17

The Federal Financial Institutions Examination Council (the Council) was established in 1979 pursuant to the Financial Institutions Regulatory and Interest Rate Control Act of 1978 (FIRA) (P.L. 95–630). In 1989, pursuant to the Financial Institutions Reform, Recovery, and Enforcement Act of 1989 (FIRREA) (P.L. 101–73), the Appraisal Subcommittee (ASC) was established within the Council. The Council has limited specified responsibilities regarding the ASC.

The Council is a formal interagency body empowered to prescribe uniform principles, standards, and report forms for the Federal examination of financial institutions; to make recommendations to promote uniformity in the supervision of financial institutions; and to conduct examiner training. Council members include a member of the Board of Governors of the Federal Reserve System, the Chairman of the Federal Deposit Insurance Corporation, the Chairman of the National Credit Union Administration, the Comptroller of the Currency, the Director of the Consumer Financial Protection Bureau, and the Chairman of the State Liaison Committee, which is made up of five representatives from state regulatory agencies that supervise financial institutions.

In addition to its responsibilities under FIRA and FIRREA, the Council was given responsibilities by the Housing and Community Development Act of 1980 (P.L. 96–399) and the Economic Growth and Regulatory Paperwork Reduction Act of 1996 (P.L. 104–208).

The Council's resources are provided by its Federal members and other fees and reimbursements.

Object Classification (in millions of dollars)

Identification code 362–5547–0–2–376		2021 actual	2022 est.	2023 est.
	Reimbursable obligations:			
11.8	Personnel compensation: Special personal services payments	4	4	4
25.1	Advisory and assistance services	11	13	13
99.9	Total new obligations, unexpired accounts	15	17	17

FEDERAL FINANCIAL INSTITUTIONS EXAMINATION COUNCIL APPRAISAL
SUBCOMMITTEE

Federal Funds

REGISTRY FEES

Special and Trust Fund Receipts (in millions of dollars)

Identification code 362–5026–0–2–376		2021 actual	2022 est.	2023 est.
0100	Balance, start of year	5	5	5
	Receipts:			
	Current law:			
1110	Registry Fees, Appraisal Subcommittee, Federal Institution Examination Council	8	7	7
1110	Incremental Registry Fees (Dodd-Frank Act) Appraisal Subcommittee	2	2	2

Federal Financial Institutions Examination Council—Continued
Federal Funds—Continued

REGISTRY FEES—Continued

Special and Trust Fund Receipts—Continued

Identification code 362–5026–0–2–376	2021 actual	2022 est.	2023 est.
1199 Total current law receipts	10	9	9
1999 Total receipts	10	9	9
2000 Total: Balances and receipts	15	14	14
Appropriations:			
Current law:			
2101 Registry Fees	–10	–9	–9
2103 Registry Fees		–1	–1
2132 Registry Fees	1	1	1
2199 Total current law appropriations	–9	–9	–9
2999 Total appropriations	–9	–9	–9
5098 Reconciliation adjustment	–1		
5099 Balance, end of year	5	5	5

Program and Financing (in millions of dollars)

Identification code 362–5026–0–2–376	2021 actual	2022 est.	2023 est.
Obligations by program activity:			
0001 Administrative expenses	3	4	4
0002 Grants, subsidies and contributions	1	2	5
0900 Total new obligations, unexpired accounts	4	6	9
Budgetary resources:			
Unobligated balance:			
1000 Unobligated balance brought forward, Oct 1	6	11	14
Budget authority:			
Appropriations, mandatory:			
1201 Appropriation (special or trust fund)	10	9	9
1203 Appropriation (previously unavailable)(special or trust)		1	1
1232 Appropriations and/or unobligated balance of appropriations temporarily reduced	–1	–1	–1
1260 Appropriations, mandatory (total)	9	9	9
1930 Total budgetary resources available	15	20	23
Memorandum (non-add) entries:			
1941 Unexpired unobligated balance, end of year	11	14	14
Change in obligated balance:			
Unpaid obligations:			
3000 Unpaid obligations, brought forward, Oct 1			2
3010 New obligations, unexpired accounts	4	6	9
3020 Outlays (gross)	–4	–4	–5
3050 Unpaid obligations, end of year		2	6
Memorandum (non-add) entries:			
3100 Obligated balance, start of year			2
3200 Obligated balance, end of year		2	6
Budget authority and outlays, net:			
Mandatory:			
4090 Budget authority, gross	9	9	9
Outlays, gross:			
4100 Outlays from new mandatory authority	4	3	4
4101 Outlays from mandatory balances		1	1
4110 Outlays, gross (total)	4	4	5
4180 Budget authority, net (total)	9	9	9
4190 Outlays, net (total)	4	4	5

The Financial Institutions Reform, Recovery, and Enforcement Act of 1989 (P.L. 101–73) established the Appraisal Subcommittee of the Federal Financial Institutions Examination Council (ASC). The ASC is composed of representatives of the Board of Governors of the Federal Reserve System, the Federal Deposit Insurance Corporation, the National Credit Union Administration, the Office of the Comptroller of the Currency, the Department of Housing and Urban Development, the Consumer Financial Protection Bureau, and the Federal Housing Finance Agency.

The ASC is charged with ensuring that real estate appraisals used in federally-related transactions are performed in accordance with uniform standards by appraisers certified and licensed by the states. Its responsibilities include: 1) monitoring the requirements established by the states for the certification and licensing of appraisers and the registration and supervision of the operations and activities of appraisal management companies; 2) monitoring the requirements established by the Federal financial institutions' regulatory agencies regarding appraisal standards for federally-related transactions under their jurisdiction; 3) monitoring and reviewing the practices, procedures, activities, and organization of the Appraisal Foundation; 4) maintaining the National Registry of licensed and certified appraisers and appraisal management companies; 5) transmitting an annual report to Congress no later than June 15 of each year; and 6) making grants to the Appraisal Foundation and state appraiser certifying and licensing agencies.

The ASC's activities, including grants awarded to the Appraisal Foundation, were initially funded from a one-time appropriation of $5 million. These funds were repaid to Treasury in 1998. The ASC is now operating on fee income from 1) appraisal management companies and 2) state-licensed and state-certified real estate appraisers in the National Registry.

Object Classification (in millions of dollars)

Identification code 362–5026–0–2–376	2021 actual	2022 est.	2023 est.
Direct obligations:			
11.1 Personnel compensation: Full-time permanent	3	4	4
41.0 Grants, subsidies, and contributions	1	2	5
99.0 Direct obligations	4	6	9
99.9 Total new obligations, unexpired accounts	4	6	9

Employment Summary

Identification code 362–5026–0–2–376	2021 actual	2022 est.	2023 est.
1001 Direct civilian full-time equivalent employment	14	15	15

FEDERAL HOUSING FINANCE AGENCY

Federal Funds

FEDERAL HOUSING FINANCE AGENCY, ADMINISTRATIVE EXPENSES

Special and Trust Fund Receipts (in millions of dollars)

Identification code 537–5532–0–2–371	2021 actual	2022 est.	2023 est.
0100 Balance, start of year			
Receipts:			
Current law:			
1110 FHFA, Fees on GSEs for Administrative Expenses	335	359	368
2000 Total: Balances and receipts	335	359	368
Appropriations:			
Current law:			
2101 Federal Housing Finance Agency, Administrative Expenses	–335	–359	–368
5099 Balance, end of year			

Program and Financing (in millions of dollars)

Identification code 537–5532–0–2–371	2021 actual	2022 est.	2023 est.
Obligations by program activity:			
0001 Federal Housing Finance Agency, Administrative Expenses (Direct)	314	366	383
0801 Federal Housing Finance Agency, Administrative Expenses (Reimbursable)	2	2	2
0900 Total new obligations, unexpired accounts	316	368	385
Budgetary resources:			
Unobligated balance:			
1000 Unobligated balance brought forward, Oct 1	52	82	81
1021 Recoveries of prior year unpaid obligations	9	5	5
1033 Recoveries of prior year paid obligations		1	1
1070 Unobligated balance (total)	61	88	87

OTHER INDEPENDENT AGENCIES

Federal Housing Finance Agency—Continued
Federal Funds—Continued

1267

		2021 actual	2022 est.	2023 est.
	Budget authority:			
	Appropriations, mandatory:			
1201	Appropriation (special or trust fund)	335	359	368
	Spending authority from offsetting collections, mandatory:			
1800	Collected	2	2	2
1900	Budget authority (total)	337	361	370
1930	Total budgetary resources available	398	449	457
	Memorandum (non-add) entries:			
1941	Unexpired unobligated balance, end of year	82	81	72
	Change in obligated balance:			
	Unpaid obligations:			
3000	Unpaid obligations, brought forward, Oct 1	49	50	50
3010	New obligations, unexpired accounts	316	368	385
3020	Outlays (gross)	−306	−363	−368
3040	Recoveries of prior year unpaid obligations, unexpired	−9	−5	−5
3050	Unpaid obligations, end of year	50	50	62
	Memorandum (non-add) entries:			
3100	Obligated balance, start of year	49	50	50
3200	Obligated balance, end of year	50	50	62
	Budget authority and outlays, net:			
	Mandatory:			
4090	Budget authority, gross	337	361	370
	Outlays, gross:			
4100	Outlays from new mandatory authority	269	319	327
4101	Outlays from mandatory balances	37	44	41
4110	Outlays, gross (total)	306	363	368
	Offsets against gross budget authority and outlays:			
	Offsetting collections (collected) from:			
4120	Federal sources	−2	−3	−3
	Additional offsets against gross budget authority only:			
4143	Recoveries of prior year paid obligations, unexpired accounts	....	1	1
4160	Budget authority, net (mandatory)	335	359	368
4170	Outlays, net (mandatory)	304	360	365
4180	Budget authority, net (total)	335	359	368
4190	Outlays, net (total)	304	360	365
	Memorandum (non-add) entries:			
5000	Total investments, SOY: Federal securities: Par value	98	130	131
5001	Total investments, EOY: Federal securities: Par value	130	131	132

The Federal Housing Finance Agency (FHFA) is the regulator of the housing Government-Sponsored Enterprises (GSEs) which include Fannie Mae, Freddie Mac, and the eleven Federal Home Loan Banks. FHFA was established by the Housing and Economic Recovery Act of 2008 (P.L. 110–289) which amended the Federal Housing Enterprise Safety and Soundness Act of 1992. FHFA receives direct funding for its activities from mandatory assessments on the GSEs.

Object Classification (in millions of dollars)

Identification code 537–5532–0–2–371		2021 actual	2022 est.	2023 est.
	Direct obligations:			
	Personnel compensation:			
11.1	Full-time permanent	120	114	117
11.3	Other than full-time permanent	3	3	3
11.5	Other personnel compensation	7	7	7
11.9	Total personnel compensation	130	124	127
12.1	Civilian personnel benefits	50	77	79
21.0	Travel and transportation of persons	....	2	3
23.2	Rental payments to others	16	19	21
23.3	Communications, utilities, and miscellaneous charges	2	2	2
25.1	Advisory and assistance services	11	9	9
25.2	Other services from non-Federal sources	39	65	66
25.3	Other goods and services from Federal sources	6	6	6
25.7	Operation and maintenance of equipment	3	3	3
26.0	Supplies and materials	3	3	3
31.0	Equipment	7	9	9
32.0	Land and structures	1	....	....
94.0	Financial transfers	46	47	55
99.0	Direct obligations	314	366	383
99.0	Reimbursable obligations	2	2	2
99.9	Total new obligations, unexpired accounts	316	368	385

Employment Summary

Identification code 537–5532–0–2–371	2021 actual	2022 est.	2023 est.
1001 Direct civilian full-time equivalent employment	671	741	764

OFFICE OF INSPECTOR GENERAL

Program and Financing (in millions of dollars)

Identification code 537–5564–0–2–371		2021 actual	2022 est.	2023 est.
	Obligations by program activity:			
0801	Office of Inspector General Reimbursable	48	50	55
	Budgetary resources:			
	Unobligated balance:			
1000	Unobligated balance brought forward, Oct 1	4	3	....
1021	Recoveries of prior year unpaid obligations	1	....	....
1070	Unobligated balance (total)	5	3	....
	Budget authority:			
	Spending authority from offsetting collections, mandatory:			
1800	Collected	46	47	55
1930	Total budgetary resources available	51	50	55
	Memorandum (non-add) entries:			
1941	Unexpired unobligated balance, end of year	3	....	....
	Change in obligated balance:			
	Unpaid obligations:			
3000	Unpaid obligations, brought forward, Oct 1	10	10	12
3010	New obligations, unexpired accounts	48	50	55
3020	Outlays (gross)	−47	−48	−55
3040	Recoveries of prior year unpaid obligations, unexpired	−1	....	....
3050	Unpaid obligations, end of year	10	12	12
	Memorandum (non-add) entries:			
3100	Obligated balance, start of year	10	10	12
3200	Obligated balance, end of year	10	12	12
	Budget authority and outlays, net:			
	Mandatory:			
4090	Budget authority, gross	46	47	55
	Outlays, gross:			
4100	Outlays from new mandatory authority	39	40	47
4101	Outlays from mandatory balances	8	8	8
4110	Outlays, gross (total)	47	48	55
	Offsets against gross budget authority and outlays:			
	Offsetting collections (collected) from:			
4120	Federal sources	−46	−47	−55
4180	Budget authority, net (total)	....	....	....
4190	Outlays, net (total)	1	1	....

The Federal Housing Finance Agency Office of Inspector General (FHFA-OIG), established in the Housing and Economic Recovery Act of 2008, has duties and responsibilities that are intended to facilitate the efficient and effective conduct of FHFA in its capacity as the primary regulator of the housing Government-Sponsored Enterprises (GSEs) and conservator of Fannie Mae and Freddie Mac. The IG is funded through FHFA's direct assessments on the housing GSEs.

Object Classification (in millions of dollars)

Identification code 537–5564–0–2–371		2021 actual	2022 est.	2023 est.
	Reimbursable obligations:			
	Personnel compensation:			
11.1	Full-time permanent	22	22	24
11.3	Other than full-time permanent	1	1	1
11.5	Other personnel compensation	1	1	1
11.9	Total personnel compensation	24	24	26
12.1	Civilian personnel benefits	10	10	11
21.0	Travel and transportation of persons	1	1	1
23.1	Rental payments to GSA	....	....	1
23.3	Communications, utilities, and miscellaneous charges	1	1	1
25.1	Advisory and assistance services	4	5	5
25.3	Other goods and services from Federal sources	6	7	7
25.7	Operation and maintenance of equipment	1	1	1
26.0	Supplies and materials	....	....	....

OFFICE OF INSPECTOR GENERAL—Continued

Object Classification—Continued

Identification code 537–5564–0–2–371	2021 actual	2022 est.	2023 est.
31.0 Equipment	1	1	1
99.9 Total new obligations, unexpired accounts	48	50	55

Employment Summary

Identification code 537–5564–0–2–371	2021 actual	2022 est.	2023 est.
2001 Reimbursable civilian full-time equivalent employment	121	155	155

FEDERAL LABOR RELATIONS AUTHORITY

Federal Funds

SALARIES AND EXPENSES

For necessary expenses to carry out functions of the Federal Labor Relations Authority, pursuant to Reorganization Plan Numbered 2 of 1978, and the Civil Service Reform Act of 1978, including services authorized by 5 U.S.C. 3109, and including hire of experts and consultants, hire of passenger motor vehicles, and including official reception and representation expenses (not to exceed $1,500) and rental of conference rooms in the District of Columbia and elsewhere, $31,762,000: Provided, That public members of the Federal Service Impasses Panel may be paid travel expenses and per diem in lieu of subsistence as authorized by law (5 U.S.C. 5703) for persons employed intermittently in the Government service, and compensation as authorized by 5 U.S.C. 3109: Provided further, That, notwithstanding 31 U.S.C. 3302, funds received from fees charged to non-Federal participants at labor-management relations conferences shall be credited to and merged with this account, to be available without further appropriation for the costs of carrying out these conferences.

Note.—A full-year 2022 appropriation for this account was not enacted at the time the Budget was prepared; therefore, the Budget assumes this account is operating under the Continuing Appropriations Act, 2022 (Division A of Public Law 117–43, as amended). The amounts included for 2022 reflect the annualized level provided by the continuing resolution.

Program and Financing (in millions of dollars)

Identification code 054–0100–0–1–805	2021 actual	2022 est.	2023 est.
Obligations by program activity:			
0001 Authority	17	17	16
0002 Office of the General Counsel	9	9	15
0003 Federal Service Impasses Panel	1	1	1
0900 Total new obligations, unexpired accounts	27	27	32
Budgetary resources:			
Budget authority:			
Appropriations, discretionary:			
1100 Appropriation	27	27	32
1930 Total budgetary resources available	27	27	32
Change in obligated balance:			
Unpaid obligations:			
3000 Unpaid obligations, brought forward, Oct 1	6	4	3
3010 New obligations, unexpired accounts	27	27	32
3011 Obligations ("upward adjustments"), expired accounts	1		
3020 Outlays (gross)	–28	–28	–30
3041 Recoveries of prior year unpaid obligations, expired	–2		
3050 Unpaid obligations, end of year	4	3	5
Memorandum (non-add) entries:			
3100 Obligated balance, start of year	6	4	3
3200 Obligated balance, end of year	4	3	5
Budget authority and outlays, net:			
Discretionary:			
4000 Budget authority, gross	27	27	32
Outlays, gross:			
4010 Outlays from new discretionary authority	24	24	28
4011 Outlays from discretionary balances	4	4	2
4020 Outlays, gross (total)	28	28	30
4180 Budget authority, net (total)	27	27	32
4190 Outlays, net (total)	28	28	30

The Federal Labor Relations Authority (FLRA) is an independent administrative Federal agency created by Title VII of the Civil Service Reform Act of 1978 (the Statute) with a mission to carry out five statutory responsibilities: 1) determining the appropriateness of units for labor organization representation; 2) resolving complaints of unfair labor practices; 3) adjudicating exceptions to arbitrators' awards; 4) adjudicating legal issues relating to duty to bargain; and 5) resolving impasses during negotiations. All work throughout the agency is undertaken to support a single program—to administer and enforce the Statute by determining the respective rights of employees, agencies, and labor organizations in their relations with one another.

FLRA's authority is divided by law and by delegation among a three-member Authority and an Office of General Counsel, appointed by the President and subject to Senate confirmation; and the Federal Service Impasses Panel, which consists of seven part-time members appointed by the President.

FLRA does not initiate cases. Proceedings before FLRA originate from filings arising through the actions of Federal employees, Federal agencies, or Federal labor organizations. Nationwide, FLRA includes five Regional Offices and a Headquarters site in Washington, D.C.

Authority.—The Authority adjudicates appeals filed by either Federal agencies or Federal labor organizations on negotiability issues, exceptions to arbitration awards, appeals of representation decisions, eligibility of labor organizations for national consultation rights, and unfair labor practice complaints.

Office of the General Counsel.—The General Counsel investigates allegations of unfair labor practices and processes representation petitions. In addition, the General Counsel conducts elections concerning the exclusive recognition of labor organizations and certifies the results of elections.

Federal Service Impasses Panel.—The Panel resolves labor negotiation impasses between Federal agencies and labor organizations.

Object Classification (in millions of dollars)

Identification code 054–0100–0–1–805	2021 actual	2022 est.	2023 est.
11.1 Direct obligations: Personnel compensation: Full-time permanent	15	15	20
11.9 Total personnel compensation	15	15	20
12.1 Civilian personnel benefits	5	5	5
23.1 Rental payments to GSA	3	3	3
25.1 Advisory and assistance services	1	1	1
25.2 Other services from non-Federal sources	1	1	1
25.3 Other goods and services from Federal sources	1	1	1
25.7 Operation and maintenance of equipment	1	1	1
99.0 Direct obligations	27	27	32
99.9 Total new obligations, unexpired accounts	27	27	32

Employment Summary

Identification code 054–0100–0–1–805	2021 actual	2022 est.	2023 est.
1001 Direct civilian full-time equivalent employment	111	115	143

FEDERAL MARITIME COMMISSION

Federal Funds

SALARIES AND EXPENSES

For necessary expenses of the Federal Maritime Commission as authorized by section 201(d) of the Merchant Marine Act, 1936, as amended (46 U.S.C. 46107), including services as authorized by section 3109 of title 5, United States Code; hire of passenger motor vehicles as authorized by section 1343(b) of title 31, United States Code; and uniforms or allowances therefore, as authorized by sections 5901 and 5902 of title 5, United States Code, $34,683,500, of which $2,000,000 shall re-

main available until September 30, 2024: Provided, That not to exceed $3,500 shall be for official reception and representation expenses.

Note.—A full-year 2022 appropriation for this account was not enacted at the time the Budget was prepared; therefore, the Budget assumes this account is operating under the Continuing Appropriations Act, 2022 (Division A of Public Law 117-43, as amended). The amounts included for 2022 reflect the annualized level provided by the continuing resolution.

Program and Financing (in millions of dollars)

Identification code 065–0100–0–1–403		2021 actual	2022 est.	2023 est.
	Obligations by program activity:			
0002	Inspector General	1	1	1
0003	Operational and Administrative	29	29	32
0004	Multi-Year Operational and Administrative			2
0900	Total new obligations, unexpired accounts	30	30	35
	Budgetary resources:			
	Budget authority:			
	Appropriations, discretionary:			
1100	Appropriation	30	30	35
1930	Total budgetary resources available	30	30	35
	Change in obligated balance:			
	Unpaid obligations:			
3000	Unpaid obligations, brought forward, Oct 1	6	5	4
3010	New obligations, unexpired accounts	30	30	35
3020	Outlays (gross)	–30	–30	–34
3041	Recoveries of prior year unpaid obligations, expired	–1	–1	
3050	Unpaid obligations, end of year	5	4	5
	Memorandum (non-add) entries:			
3100	Obligated balance, start of year	6	5	4
3200	Obligated balance, end of year	5	4	5
	Budget authority and outlays, net:			
	Discretionary:			
4000	Budget authority, gross	30	30	35
	Outlays, gross:			
4010	Outlays from new discretionary authority	26	26	30
4011	Outlays from discretionary balances	4	4	4
4020	Outlays, gross (total)	30	30	34
4180	Budget authority, net (total)	30	30	35
4190	Outlays, net (total)	30	30	34

The Federal Maritime Commission (FMC or Commission) regulates oceanborne transportation in the foreign commerce of the United States. The Commission administers the Shipping Act of 1984 (1984 Act) as amended; section 19 of the Merchant Marine Act, 1920 (1920 Act); the Foreign Shipping Practices Act of 1988 (FSPA); Sections 2 and 3 of Public Law 89–777; and Section 834 of the Frank LoBiondo Coast Guard Authorization Act of 2018 (LoBiondo Act). The Commission monitors the activities of ocean common carriers, marine terminal operators (MTOs), ports, and ocean transportation intermediaries who operate in U.S. foreign commerce to ensure that they maintain just and reasonable practices.

Ocean Transportation Intermediaries (OTIs).—The Commission issues licenses to qualified OTIs operating in the United States and ensures that U.S. OTIs are bonded or maintain other evidence of financial responsibility.

Passenger Vessel Operators.—The Commission ensures that passenger vessel operators demonstrate adequate financial responsibility to indemnify passengers in the event of nonperformance of voyages or passenger injury or death.

Shipping Act Compliance.—The FMC maintains trade monitoring and enforcement programs designed to assist regulated entities in achieving compliance and to detect and appropriately remedy malpractices and violations of the prohibited acts set forth in section 10 of the 1984 Act; offers a dispute resolution program to resolve disputes impeding the transportation of cargo; reviews competitive activities of common carrier alliances and other agreements among common carriers and/or terminal operators; monitors the laws and practices of foreign governments which could have a discriminatory or otherwise adverse impact on shipping conditions in U.S. trades, and imposes remedial action, as appropriate, pursuant to section 19 of the 1920 Act or FSPA; enforces special regulatory requirements applicable to carriers owned or controlled by foreign governments; processes and reviews agreements, service contracts, and service arrangements pursuant to the 1984 Act for compliance with statutory requirements; and reviews common carriers' privately published tariff systems for accessibility, accuracy, and reasonable terms.

Object Classification (in millions of dollars)

Identification code 065–0100–0–1–403		2021 actual	2022 est.	2023 est.
	Direct obligations:			
11.1	Personnel compensation: Full-time permanent	16	16	21
12.1	Civilian personnel benefits	5	6	8
23.1	Rental payments to GSA	4	4	
23.3	Communications, utilities, and miscellaneous charges			1
25.1	Advisory and assistance services	2	1	1
25.2	Other services from non-Federal sources	1	1	1
25.3	Other goods and services from Federal sources	1	2	2
31.0	Equipment	1		1
99.9	Total new obligations, unexpired accounts	30	30	35

Employment Summary

Identification code 065–0100–0–1–403		2021 actual	2022 est.	2023 est.
1001	Direct civilian full-time equivalent employment	116	121	150

FEDERAL MEDIATION AND CONCILIATION SERVICE

Federal Funds

SALARIES AND EXPENSES

For expenses necessary for the Federal Mediation and Conciliation Service ("Service") to carry out the functions vested in it by the Labor-Management Relations Act, 1947, including hire of passenger motor vehicles; for expenses necessary for the Labor-Management Cooperation Act of 1978; and for expenses necessary for the Service to carry out the functions vested in it by the Civil Service Reform Act, $53,705,000, of which not to exceed $1,000,000 shall remain available through September 30, 2024, for assistance activities authorized by the Labor-Management Cooperation Act of 1978: Provided, That notwithstanding 31 U.S.C. 3302, fees charged, up to full-cost recovery, for special training activities and other conflict resolution services and technical assistance, including those provided to foreign governments and international organizations, and for arbitration services shall be credited to and merged with this account, and shall remain available until expended: Provided further, That fees for arbitration services shall be available only for education, training, and professional development of the agency workforce: Provided further, That the Director of the Service is authorized to accept and use on behalf of the United States gifts of services and real, personal, or other property, including money, without fiscal year limitation, in the aid of any projects or functions within the Director's jurisdiction.

Note.—A full-year 2022 appropriation for this account was not enacted at the time the Budget was prepared; therefore, the Budget assumes this account is operating under the Continuing Appropriations Act, 2022 (Division A of Public Law 117-43, as amended). The amounts included for 2022 reflect the annualized level provided by the continuing resolution.

Program and Financing (in millions of dollars)

Identification code 093–0100–0–1–505		2021 actual	2022 est.	2023 est.
	Obligations by program activity:			
0001	Dispute mediation and preventive mediation, public information, and grants	37	37	40
0002	Arbitration services	1	1	1
0003	Management and administrative support	9	11	12
0004	Labor-Management Grants (separated from line 0001 for FY17)			1
0091	Total direct program	47	49	54
0101	Reimbursables	2	2	3
0900	Total new obligations, unexpired accounts	49	51	57
	Budgetary resources:			
	Unobligated balance:			
1000	Unobligated balance brought forward, Oct 1	4	5	5
	Budget authority:			
	Appropriations, discretionary:			
1100	Appropriation	49	49	54

Federal Mediation and Conciliation Service—Continued
Federal Funds—Continued

SALARIES AND EXPENSES—Continued

Program and Financing—Continued

Identification code 093–0100–0–1–505		2021 actual	2022 est.	2023 est.
	Spending authority from offsetting collections, discretionary:			
1700	Collected	2	2	3
1701	Change in uncollected payments, Federal sources	1	....	....
1750	Spending auth from offsetting collections, disc (total)	3	2	3
1900	Budget authority (total)	52	51	57
1930	Total budgetary resources available	56	56	62
	Memorandum (non-add) entries:			
1940	Unobligated balance expiring	–2	....	....
1941	Unexpired unobligated balance, end of year	5	5	5
	Change in obligated balance:			
	Unpaid obligations:			
3000	Unpaid obligations, brought forward, Oct 1	6	7	4
3010	New obligations, unexpired accounts	49	51	57
3020	Outlays (gross)	–48	–54	–58
3050	Unpaid obligations, end of year	7	4	3
	Uncollected payments:			
3060	Uncollected pymts, Fed sources, brought forward, Oct 1	–1	–2	–2
3070	Change in uncollected pymts, Fed sources, unexpired	–1	....	....
3090	Uncollected pymts, Fed sources, end of year	–2	–2	–2
	Memorandum (non-add) entries:			
3100	Obligated balance, start of year	5	5	2
3200	Obligated balance, end of year	5	2	1
	Budget authority and outlays, net:			
	Discretionary:			
4000	Budget authority, gross	52	51	57
	Outlays, gross:			
4010	Outlays from new discretionary authority	43	47	52
4011	Outlays from discretionary balances	5	7	6
4020	Outlays, gross (total)	48	54	58
	Offsets against gross budget authority and outlays:			
	Offsetting collections (collected) from:			
4030	Federal sources	–1	....	–1
4033	Non-Federal sources	–1	–2	–2
4040	Offsets against gross budget authority and outlays (total)	–2	–2	–3
	Additional offsets against gross budget authority only:			
4050	Change in uncollected pymts, Fed sources, unexpired	–1	....	....
4060	Additional offsets against budget authority only (total)	–1	....	....
4070	Budget authority, net (discretionary)	49	49	54
4080	Outlays, net (discretionary)	46	52	55
4180	Budget authority, net (total)	49	49	54
4190	Outlays, net (total)	46	52	55

The Federal Mediation and Conciliation Service (FMCS) provides assistance to parties in labor disputes in industries affecting commerce through conciliation and mediation.

Dispute Mediation.—FMCS assists labor and management in the mediation and prevention of disputes, other than those involving rail and air transportation, whenever such disputes threaten to cause a substantial interruption of interstate commerce or a major impairment to the national defense. FMCS also makes mediation and conciliation services available to Federal agencies and organizations representing Federal employees in the resolution of negotiation disputes. FMCS provides mandatory mediation and, where necessary, impartial boards of inquiry to assist in resolving labor disputes involving private nonprofit health care institutions. The workload shown below includes assignments in both the private and public sectors. These numbers include collective bargaining and grievance mediation.

DISPUTE MEDIATION WORKLOAD DATA

	2019 actual	2020 actual	2021 actual	2022 est.	2023 est.
Dispute mediation assignments	13,220	11,640	12,477	13,000	13,000
Total active mediations	5,364	4,684	4,657	4,940	4,940

Preventive Mediation, Public Information, and Educational Activities.—Through its preventive mediation program, FMCS initiates and develops labor-management committees, training programs, conferences, and specialized workshops dealing with issues in collective bargaining.

Mediators also participate in education, advocacy and outreach activities such as lectures, seminars, and conferences.

PREVENTIVE MEDIATION WORKLOAD DATA

	2019 actual	2020 actual	2021 actual	2022 est.	2023 est.
Total preventive mediation cases conducted	1,956	1,675	1,284	1,700	1,700

Arbitration Services.—FMCS assists parties in disputes by utilizing the arbitration process for the resolution of disputes arising under or in the negotiation of collective bargaining agreements in the private and public sectors.

ARBITRATION SERVICES WORKLOAD DATA

	2019 actual	2020 actual	2021 actual	2022 est.	2023 est.
Number of panels issued	10,944	10,340	10,544	11,000	11,000
Number of arbitrators appointed	4,342	4,070	4,417	4,771	4,771

Management and Administrative Support.—This activity provides for overall management and administration, policy planning, research and evaluation, and employee development.

Labor-Management Cooperation Project.—The Labor Management Cooperation Act of 1978 (29 U.S.C. 175a) authorizes FMCS to carry out this program of contracts and grants to support the establishment and operation of plant, area, and industry labor-management committees.

Alternative Dispute Resolution (ADR) Projects.—FMCS assists other Federal agencies by providing mediation and technical assistance in the area of ADR. The ADR cases reduce litigation costs and speed Federal processes. FMCS is funded for this work through interagency reimbursable agreements.

ALTERNATIVE DISPUTE RESOLUTION (ADR) WORKLOAD DATA

	2019 actual	2020 actual	2021 actual	2022 est.	2023 est.
Number of ADR Cases	1,212	1,370	1,169	1,600	1,600

Object Classification (in millions of dollars)

Identification code 093–0100–0–1–505		2021 actual	2022 est.	2023 est.
	Direct obligations:			
11.1	Personnel compensation: Full-time permanent	27	27	30
12.1	Civilian personnel benefits	10	10	11
21.0	Travel and transportation of persons	1	1	1
23.1	Rental payments to GSA	4	4	4
23.3	Communications, utilities, and miscellaneous charges	1	1	1
25.2	Other services from non-Federal sources	4	6	6
41.0	Grants, subsidies, and contributions	....	....	1
99.0	Direct obligations	47	49	54
99.0	Reimbursable obligations	2	2	3
99.9	Total new obligations, unexpired accounts	49	51	57

Employment Summary

Identification code 093–0100–0–1–505	2021 actual	2022 est.	2023 est.
1001 Direct civilian full-time equivalent employment	207	207	220
2001 Reimbursable civilian full-time equivalent employment	8	7	7

FEDERAL MINE SAFETY AND HEALTH REVIEW COMMISSION

Federal Funds

SALARIES AND EXPENSES

For expenses necessary for the Federal Mine Safety and Health Review Commission, $18,012,000.

Note.—A full-year 2022 appropriation for this account was not enacted at the time the Budget was prepared; therefore, the Budget assumes this account is operating under the Continuing Appropriations Act, 2022 (Division A of Public Law 117–43, as amended). The amounts included for 2022 reflect the annualized level provided by the continuing resolution.

Program and Financing (in millions of dollars)

Identification code 368–2800–0–1–554	2021 actual	2022 est.	2023 est.
Obligations by program activity:			
0001 Commission review	5	5	5
0002 Administrative law judge determinations	9	10	10
0003 Office of Executive Director	2	2	3
0900 Total new obligations, unexpired accounts	16	17	18
Budgetary resources:			
Budget authority:			
Appropriations, discretionary:			
1100 Appropriation	17	17	18
1900 Budget authority (total)	17	17	18
1930 Total budgetary resources available	17	17	18
Memorandum (non-add) entries:			
1940 Unobligated balance expiring	–1		
Change in obligated balance:			
Unpaid obligations:			
3000 Unpaid obligations, brought forward, Oct 1	3	5	4
3010 New obligations, unexpired accounts	16	17	18
3011 Obligations ("upward adjustments"), expired accounts	1		
3020 Outlays (gross)	–15	–18	–18
3050 Unpaid obligations, end of year	5	4	4
Memorandum (non-add) entries:			
3100 Obligated balance, start of year	3	5	4
3200 Obligated balance, end of year	5	4	4
Budget authority and outlays, net:			
Discretionary:			
4000 Budget authority, gross	17	17	18
Outlays, gross:			
4010 Outlays from new discretionary authority	14	15	15
4011 Outlays from discretionary balances	1	3	3
4020 Outlays, gross (total)	15	18	18
4180 Budget authority, net (total)	17	17	18
4190 Outlays, net (total)	15	18	18

The Federal Mine Safety and Health Review Commission reviews and decides contested enforcement actions of the Secretary of Labor under the Federal Mine Safety and Health Act of 1977, as amended by the Mine Improvement and New Emergency Response Act of 2006. The Commission also adjudicates claims by miners and miners' representatives concerning their rights under law. The Commission holds fact-finding hearings and issues orders affirming, modifying, or vacating the Secretary's enforcement actions.

Object Classification (in millions of dollars)

Identification code 368–2800–0–1–554	2021 actual	2022 est.	2023 est.
Direct obligations:			
11.1 Personnel compensation: Full-time permanent	9	9	10
12.1 Civilian personnel benefits	2	3	3
23.1 Rental payments to GSA	2	2	2
25.2 Other services from non-Federal sources	2	2	2
26.0 Supplies and materials	1	1	1
99.9 Total new obligations, unexpired accounts	16	17	18

Employment Summary

Identification code 368–2800–0–1–554	2021 actual	2022 est.	2023 est.
1001 Direct civilian full-time equivalent employment	60	65	76

FEDERAL PERMITTING IMPROVEMENT STEERING COUNCIL

Federal Funds

ENVIRONMENTAL REVIEW IMPROVEMENT FUND

For necessary expenses of the Environmental Review Improvement Fund established pursuant to 42 U.S.C. 4370m–8(d), $10,262,000, to remain available until expended.

Note.—A full-year 2022 appropriation for this account was not enacted at the time the Budget was prepared; therefore, the Budget assumes this account is operating under the Continuing Appropriations Act, 2022 (Division A of Public Law 117–43, as amended). The amounts included for 2022 reflect the annualized level provided by the continuing resolution.

ENVIRONMENTAL REVIEW IMPROVEMENT FUND

[For an additional amount for the "Environmental Review Improvement Fund", $3,000,000 to remain available until September 30, 2026: *Provided*, That $650,000, to remain available until September 30, 2022, shall be made available for fiscal year 2022, $650,000, to remain available until September 30, 2023, shall be made available for fiscal year 2023, $650,000, to remain available until September 30, 2024, shall be made available for fiscal year 2024, $650,000, to remain available until September 30, 2025, shall be made available for fiscal year 2025, and $400,000, to remain available until September 30, 2026, shall be made available for fiscal year 2026: *Provided further*, That such amount is designated by the Congress as being for an emergency requirement pursuant to section 4112(a) of H. Con. Res. 71 (115th Congress), the concurrent resolution on the budget for fiscal year 2018, and to section 251(b) of the Balanced Budget and Emergency Deficit Control Act of 1985.] *(Infrastructure Investments and Jobs Appropriations Act.)*

Program and Financing (in millions of dollars)

Identification code 473–5761–0–2–808	2021 actual	2022 est.	2023 est.
Obligations by program activity:			
0001 Salaries and expenses	8	14	13
Budgetary resources:			
Unobligated balance:			
1000 Unobligated balance brought forward, Oct 1	3	6	3
1011 Unobligated balance transfer from other acct [047–5640]	1		
1070 Unobligated balance (total)	4	6	3
Budget authority:			
Appropriations, discretionary:			
1100 Appropriation	10	10	10
1100 Appropriation		1	
1160 Appropriation, discretionary (total)	10	11	10
Advance appropriations, discretionary:			
1170 Advance appropriation			1
1900 Budget authority (total)	10	11	11
1930 Total budgetary resources available	14	17	14
Memorandum (non-add) entries:			
1941 Unexpired unobligated balance, end of year	6	3	1
Change in obligated balance:			
Unpaid obligations:			
3000 Unpaid obligations, brought forward, Oct 1	2	2	5
3010 New obligations, unexpired accounts	8	14	13
3020 Outlays (gross)	–8	–11	–12
3050 Unpaid obligations, end of year	2	5	6
Memorandum (non-add) entries:			
3100 Obligated balance, start of year	2	2	5
3200 Obligated balance, end of year	2	5	6
Budget authority and outlays, net:			
Discretionary:			
4000 Budget authority, gross	10	11	11
Outlays, gross:			
4010 Outlays from new discretionary authority	6	7	7
4011 Outlays from discretionary balances	2	4	5
4020 Outlays, gross (total)	8	11	12
4180 Budget authority, net (total)	10	11	11
4190 Outlays, net (total)	8	11	12

This appropriation supports the authorized activities of the Environmental Review Improvement Fund and the Federal Permitting Improvement Steering Council (Permitting Council) established under Title 41 of the Fixing America's Surface Transportation Act (FAST Act) (Public Law

ENVIRONMENTAL REVIEW IMPROVEMENT FUND—Continued

114–94) and made a permanent agency by the Infrastructure Investment and Jobs Act (Public Law 117–58). The Permitting Council leads ongoing Government-wide efforts to improve the transparency, predictability, and outcomes of the Federal environmental review and authorization process for qualifying major infrastructure projects and works with Federal agency partners to implement and oversee adherence to the statutory requirements set forth in Title 41 of the FAST Act (FAST-41). FAST-41 is a voluntary program for large, complex infrastructure projects that maximizes the positive environmental and community outcomes of those projects through coordinated agency action in developing and implementing comprehensive permitting timetables, coordinated establishment of public and tribal outreach strategies, meaningful project sponsor engagement, identification and implementation of best practices, dispute resolution services, and posting and maintaining transparent, publicly accessible permitting timetables on the Federal Permitting Dashboard. Projects receive these benefits without modifying or undermining any underlying Federal statutes or regulations, or the status of any mandatory reviews.

Object Classification (in millions of dollars)

Identification code 473–5761–0–2–808		2021 actual	2022 est.	2023 est.
	Direct obligations:			
	Personnel compensation:			
11.1	Full-time permanent	1	2	3
11.8	Special personal services payments	1	2	2
11.9	Total personnel compensation	2	4	5
12.1	Civilian personnel benefits	1	1	1
25.1	Advisory and assistance services	5	8	5
99.0	Direct obligations	8	13	11
99.5	Adjustment for rounding		1	2
99.9	Total new obligations, unexpired accounts	8	14	13

Employment Summary

Identification code 473–5761–0–2–808	2021 actual	2022 est.	2023 est.
1001 Direct civilian full-time equivalent employment	9	17	25

FEDERAL TRADE COMMISSION

Federal Funds

SALARIES AND EXPENSES

For necessary expenses of the Federal Trade Commission, including uniforms or allowances therefor, as authorized by 5 U.S.C. 5901–5902; services as authorized by 5 U.S.C. 3109; hire of passenger motor vehicles; and not to exceed $2,000 for official reception and representation expenses, $490,000,000, to remain available until expended: Provided, That not to exceed $300,000 shall be available for use to contract with a person or persons for collection services in accordance with the terms of 31 U.S.C. 3718: Provided further, That, notwithstanding any other provision of law, fees collected for premerger notification filings under the Hart-Scott-Rodino Antitrust Improvements Act of 1976 (15 U.S.C. 18a), regardless of the year of collection (and estimated to be $274,500,000 in fiscal year 2023), shall be retained and used for necessary expenses in this appropriation, and shall remain available until expended: Provided further, That, notwithstanding any other provision of law, fees collected to implement and enforce the Telemarketing Sales Rule, promulgated under the Telemarketing and Consumer Fraud and Abuse Prevention Act (15 U.S.C. 6101 et seq.), regardless of the year of collection (and estimated to be $13,000,000 in fiscal year 2023), shall be credited to this account, and be retained and used for necessary expenses in this appropriation, and shall remain available until expended: Provided further, That the sum herein appropriated from the general fund shall be reduced as such offsetting collections are received during fiscal year 2023, so as to result in a final fiscal year 2023 appropriation from the general fund estimated at not more than $202,500,000: Provided further, That none of the funds made available to the Federal Trade Commission may be used to implement subsection (e)(2)(B) of section 43 of the Federal Deposit Insurance Act (12 U.S.C. 1831t).

Note.—A full-year 2022 appropriation for this account was not enacted at the time the Budget was prepared; therefore, the Budget assumes this account is operating under the Continuing Appropriations Act, 2022 (Division A of Public Law 117–43, as amended). The amounts included for 2022 reflect the annualized level provided by the continuing resolution.

Program and Financing (in millions of dollars)

Identification code 029–0100–0–1–376		2021 actual	2022 est.	2023 est.
	Obligations by program activity:			
0001	Protect Consumers	100	213	250
0002	Maintain Competition	87	164	240
0192	Subtotal, direct program	187	377	490
0799	Total direct obligations	187	377	490
0803	Salaries and Expenses (Reimbursable)	165	3	1
0900	Total new obligations, unexpired accounts	352	380	491
	Budgetary resources:			
	Unobligated balance:			
1000	Unobligated balance brought forward, Oct 1	5	45	22
1001	Discretionary unobligated balance brought fwd, Oct 1	5	19	
1021	Recoveries of prior year unpaid obligations	9	3	5
1070	Unobligated balance (total)	14	48	27
	Budget authority:			
	Appropriations, discretionary:			
1100	Appropriation	188	188	240
	Appropriations, mandatory:			
1200	Appropriation	30		
	Spending authority from offsetting collections, discretionary:			
1700	Offsetting collections (cash) - HSR	237	237	237
1700	Offsetting collections (cash) - Do Not Call	13	13	13
1700	Offsetting collections (cash) - Reimb	1	3	1
1701	Change in uncollected payments, Federal sources	1		
1724	Spending authority from offsetting collections precluded from obligation (limitation on obligations)	–87	–87	
1750	Spending auth from offsetting collections, disc (total)	165	166	251
1900	Budget authority (total)	383	354	491
1930	Total budgetary resources available	397	402	518
	Memorandum (non-add) entries:			
1941	Unexpired unobligated balance, end of year	45	22	27
	Change in obligated balance:			
	Unpaid obligations:			
3000	Unpaid obligations, brought forward, Oct 1	77	70	111
3010	New obligations, unexpired accounts	352	380	491
3020	Outlays (gross)	–350	–336	–423
3040	Recoveries of prior year unpaid obligations, unexpired	–9	–3	–5
3050	Unpaid obligations, end of year	70	111	174
	Uncollected payments:			
3060	Uncollected pymts, Fed sources, brought forward, Oct 1	–1	–2	–2
3070	Change in uncollected pymts, Fed sources, unexpired	–1		
3090	Uncollected pymts, Fed sources, end of year	–2	–2	–2
	Memorandum (non-add) entries:			
3100	Obligated balance, start of year	76	68	109
3200	Obligated balance, end of year	68	109	172
	Budget authority and outlays, net:			
	Discretionary:			
4000	Budget authority, gross	353	354	491
	Outlays, gross:			
4010	Outlays from new discretionary authority	283	221	290
4011	Outlays from discretionary balances	64	89	133
4020	Outlays, gross (total)	347	310	423
	Offsets against gross budget authority and outlays:			
	Offsetting collections (collected) from:			
4030	Federal sources	–1	–3	–1
4034	Offsetting governmental collections	–250	–250	–250
4040	Offsets against gross budget authority and outlays (total)	–251	–253	–251
	Additional offsets against gross budget authority only:			
4050	Change in uncollected pymts, Fed sources, unexpired	–1		
4070	Budget authority, net (discretionary)	101	101	240
4080	Outlays, net (discretionary)	96	57	172
	Mandatory:			
4090	Budget authority, gross	30		
	Outlays, gross:			
4100	Outlays from new mandatory authority	3		
4101	Outlays from mandatory balances		26	
4110	Outlays, gross (total)	3	26	
4180	Budget authority, net (total)	131	101	240
4190	Outlays, net (total)	99	83	172

OTHER INDEPENDENT AGENCIES

Memorandum (non-add) entries:

		2021 actual	2022 est.	2023 est.
5090	Unexpired unavailable balance, SOY: Offsetting collections	32	119	206
5092	Unexpired unavailable balance, EOY: Offsetting collections	119	206	206

Summary of Budget Authority and Outlays (in millions of dollars)

	2021 actual	2022 est.	2023 est.
Enacted/requested:			
Budget Authority	131	101	240
Outlays	99	83	172
Legislative proposal, not subject to PAYGO:			
Budget Authority			–38
Outlays			–38
Total:			
Budget Authority	131	101	202
Outlays	99	83	134

The FTC's mission is to protect consumers and competition by preventing anticompetitive, deceptive, and unfair business practices through law enforcement, advocacy, and education without unduly burdening legitimate business activity. The FTC's mission is based on a vision of a vibrant economy characterized by vigorous competition and consumer access to accurate information.

Protect Consumers.—This goal is to prevent fraud, deception, and unfair business practices in the marketplace. The agency works to accomplish this goal through three objectives: 1) Identify and take actions to address deceptive or unfair practices that harm consumers; 2) Provide the public with knowledge and tools to prevent harm to consumers; and 3) Collaborate with domestic and international partners to enhance consumer protection.

Promote Competition.—This goal is to prevent anticompetitive mergers and other anticompetitive business practices in the marketplace. The agency works to accomplish this goal through three objectives: 1) Identify and take actions to address anticompetitive mergers and practices that harm consumers; 2) Engage in effective research and stakeholder outreach to promote competition, advance its understanding, and create awareness of its benefits to consumers; and 3) Collaborate with domestic partners and international partners to preserve and promote competition.

The 2023 Budget includes a program level for the Commission of $490 million, funded by $202.5 million from the General Fund of the U.S. Treasury and offsetting collections from two sources: $274.5 million from fees for Hart-Scott-Rodino Act premerger notification filings as authorized by 15 U.S.C. 18a and $13 million from fees sufficient to implement and enforce the Telemarketing Sales Rule, promulgated under the Telemarketing and Consumer Fraud and Abuse Prevention Act (15 U.S.C. 6101 et seq., as amended).

Object Classification (in millions of dollars)

Identification code 029–0100–0–1–376		2021 actual	2022 est.	2023 est.
	Direct obligations:			
	Personnel compensation:			
11.1	Full-time permanent	1	193	232
11.5	Other personnel compensation	4	5	6
11.8	Special personal services payments	1		
11.9	Total personnel compensation	6	198	238
12.1	Civilian personnel benefits	56	61	76
21.0	Travel and transportation of persons		3	4
23.1	Rental payments to GSA	25	23	35
23.3	Communications, utilities, and miscellaneous charges	5	5	9
24.0	Printing and reproduction	2	2	2
25.1	Advisory and assistance services	73	65	98
25.2	Other services from non-Federal sources	5	4	4
25.4	Operation and maintenance of facilities	2	1	2
25.7	Operation and maintenance of equipment	12	13	16
26.0	Supplies and materials		1	2
31.0	Equipment	1	1	4
99.0	Direct obligations	187	377	490
99.0	Reimbursable obligations	165	3	1
99.9	Total new obligations, unexpired accounts	352	380	491

Employment Summary

Identification code 029–0100–0–1–376	2021 actual	2022 est.	2023 est.
1001 Direct civilian full-time equivalent employment	1,123	1,140	1,440
2001 Reimbursable civilian full-time equivalent employment	4	1	1

SALARIES AND EXPENSES

(Legislative proposal, not subject to PAYGO)

Program and Financing (in millions of dollars)

Identification code 029–0100–2–1–376		2021 actual	2022 est.	2023 est.
	Budgetary resources:			
	Budget authority:			
	Appropriations, discretionary:			
1100	Appropriation			–38
	Spending authority from offsetting collections, discretionary:			
1700	Offsetting collections (cash) - HSR			38
	Budget authority and outlays, net:			
	Discretionary:			
	Offsets against gross budget authority and outlays:			
	Offsetting collections (collected) from:			
4034	Offsetting governmental collections			–38
4040	Offsets against gross budget authority and outlays (total)			–38
4180	Budget authority, net (total)			–38
4190	Outlays, net (total)			–38

GENERAL FUND RECEIPT ACCOUNT

(in millions of dollars)

	2021 actual	2022 est.	2023 est.
Offsetting receipts from the public:			
029–322000 All Other General Fund Proprietary Receipts Including Budget Clearing Accounts	8		
General Fund Offsetting receipts from the public	8		

GULF COAST ECOSYSTEM RESTORATION COUNCIL

Federal Funds

GULF COAST ECOSYSTEM RESTORATION COUNCIL

Program and Financing (in millions of dollars)

Identification code 471–1770–0–1–452		2021 actual	2022 est.	2023 est.
	Obligations by program activity:			
0801	Comprehensive Plan Administrative Expense	2	2	2
0802	Comprehensive Plan Program Expenses	24	63	77
0803	Spill Impact Program and Projects	95	76	89
0900	Total new obligations, unexpired accounts	121	141	168
	Budgetary resources:			
	Unobligated balance:			
1000	Unobligated balance brought forward, Oct 1	204	307	349
1021	Recoveries of prior year unpaid obligations	2		
1070	Unobligated balance (total)	206	307	349
	Budget authority:			
	Spending authority from offsetting collections, mandatory:			
1800	Collected	89	183	183
1801	Change in uncollected payments, Federal sources	133		
1850	Spending auth from offsetting collections, mand (total)	222	183	183
1930	Total budgetary resources available	428	490	532
	Memorandum (non-add) entries:			
1941	Unexpired unobligated balance, end of year	307	349	364
	Change in obligated balance:			
	Unpaid obligations:			
3000	Unpaid obligations, brought forward, Oct 1	318	395	355
3010	New obligations, unexpired accounts	121	141	168

GULF COAST ECOSYSTEM RESTORATION COUNCIL—Continued

Program and Financing—Continued

Identification code 471–1770–0–1–452		2021 actual	2022 est.	2023 est.
3020	Outlays (gross)	–42	–181	–386
3040	Recoveries of prior year unpaid obligations, unexpired	–2	....	....
3050	Unpaid obligations, end of year	395	355	137
	Uncollected payments:			
3060	Uncollected pymts, Fed sources, brought forward, Oct 1	–334	–467	–467
3070	Change in uncollected pymts, Fed sources, unexpired	–133	....	....
3090	Uncollected pymts, Fed sources, end of year	–467	–467	–467
	Memorandum (non-add) entries:			
3100	Obligated balance, start of year	–16	–72	–112
3200	Obligated balance, end of year	–72	–112	–330
	Budget authority and outlays, net:			
	Mandatory:			
4090	Budget authority, gross	222	183	183
	Outlays, gross:			
4100	Outlays from new mandatory authority	6	8	8
4101	Outlays from mandatory balances	36	173	378
4110	Outlays, gross (total)	42	181	386
	Offsets against gross budget authority and outlays:			
	Offsetting collections (collected) from:			
4120	Federal sources	–89	–183	–183
	Additional offsets against gross budget authority only:			
4140	Change in uncollected pymts, Fed sources, unexpired	–133	....	....
4170	Outlays, net (mandatory)	–47	–2	203
4180	Budget authority, net (total)	....	....	....
4190	Outlays, net (total)	–47	–2	203

The Resources and Ecosystems Sustainability, Tourist Opportunities, and Revived Economies of the Gulf Coast States Act of 2012, or the RESTORE Act, dedicates 80 percent of any civil and administrative penalties paid under the Clean Water Act by responsible parties in connection with the Deepwater Horizon oil spill to the Gulf Coast Restoration Trust Fund (the Trust Fund). These funds may be used for ecosystem restoration, economic recovery, and tourism promotion in the Gulf Coast region.

In addition to establishing the Trust Fund, the RESTORE Act established the Gulf Coast Ecosystem Restoration Council (the Council). The Council has oversight over the expenditure of sixty percent of the funds made available from the Trust Fund. Thirty percent will be administered for restoration and protection according to the Comprehensive Plan developed by the Council. The other thirty percent will be allocated to the States under the Spill Impact Component according to a formula established by the Council through a regulation, and spend according to individual State Expenditure Plans to contribute to the overall economic and ecological recovery of the Gulf. The Council includes the Governors of the States of Alabama, Florida, Louisiana, Mississippi and Texas and the Secretaries of the U.S. Departments of Agriculture, Army, Commerce, Homeland Security and the Interior, and the Administrator of the U.S. Environmental Protection Agency.

Object Classification (in millions of dollars)

Identification code 471–1770–0–1–452		2021 actual	2022 est.	2023 est.
	Reimbursable obligations:			
11.1	Personnel compensation: Full-time permanent	3	3	3
12.1	Civilian personnel benefits	1	1	1
25.1	Advisory and assistance services	2	2	2
25.3	Other goods and services from Federal sources	1	1	1
41.0	Grants, subsidies, and contributions	114	134	161
99.9	Total new obligations, unexpired accounts	121	141	168

Employment Summary

Identification code 471–1770–0–1–452		2021 actual	2022 est.	2023 est.
2001	Reimbursable civilian full-time equivalent employment	23	24	25

HARRY S TRUMAN SCHOLARSHIP FOUNDATION

Federal Funds

PAYMENT TO THE HARRY S TRUMAN SCHOLARSHIP MEMORIAL TRUST FUND

SALARIES AND EXPENSES

Note.—A full-year 2022 appropriation for this account was not enacted at the time the Budget was prepared; therefore, the Budget assumes this account is operating under the Continuing Appropriations Act, 2022 (Division A of Public Law 117–43, as amended). The amounts included for 2022 reflect the annualized level provided by the continuing resolution.

Program and Financing (in millions of dollars)

Identification code 372–0950–0–1–502		2021 actual	2022 est.	2023 est.
	Obligations by program activity:			
0001	Payment to the Harry S Truman Scholarship Memorial Trust Fund	2	2	....
0900	Total new obligations, unexpired accounts (object class 94.0)	2	2	....
	Budgetary resources:			
	Budget authority:			
	Appropriations, discretionary:			
1100	Appropriation	2	2	....
1930	Total budgetary resources available	2	2	....
	Change in obligated balance:			
	Unpaid obligations:			
3010	New obligations, unexpired accounts	2	2	....
3020	Outlays (gross)	–2	–2	....
	Budget authority and outlays, net:			
	Discretionary:			
4000	Budget authority, gross	2	2	....
	Outlays, gross:			
4010	Outlays from new discretionary authority	2	2	....
4180	Budget authority, net (total)	2	2	....
4190	Outlays, net (total)	2	2	....

Trust Funds

HARRY S TRUMAN MEMORIAL SCHOLARSHIP TRUST FUND

Special and Trust Fund Receipts (in millions of dollars)

Identification code 372–8296–0–7–502		2021 actual	2022 est.	2023 est.
0100	Balance, start of year	32	32	32
	Receipts:			
	Current law:			
1140	Interest on Investments, Harry S Truman Memorial Scholarship Trust Fund	1	....	....
1140	General Fund Payment, Harry S Truman Scholarship Trust Fund	2	2	....
1199	Total current law receipts	3	2	....
1999	Total receipts	3	2	....
2000	Total: Balances and receipts	35	34	32
	Appropriations:			
	Current law:			
2101	Harry S Truman Memorial Scholarship Trust Fund	–3	–2	....
5099	Balance, end of year	32	32	32

Program and Financing (in millions of dollars)

Identification code 372–8296–0–7–502		2021 actual	2022 est.	2023 est.
	Obligations by program activity:			
0001	Scholarship awards	2	2	2
0002	Program administration	....	1	1
0900	Total new obligations, unexpired accounts	2	3	3
	Budgetary resources:			
	Unobligated balance:			
1000	Unobligated balance brought forward, Oct 1	20	21	20

		2021 actual	2022 est.	2023 est.
	Budget authority:			
	Appropriations, mandatory:			
1201	Appropriation (special or trust fund)	3	2	
1930	Total budgetary resources available	23	23	20
	Memorandum (non-add) entries:			
1941	Unexpired unobligated balance, end of year	21	20	17
	Change in obligated balance:			
	Unpaid obligations:			
3000	Unpaid obligations, brought forward, Oct 1			1
3010	New obligations, unexpired accounts	2	3	3
3020	Outlays (gross)	–2	–2	
3050	Unpaid obligations, end of year		1	4
	Memorandum (non-add) entries:			
3100	Obligated balance, start of year			1
3200	Obligated balance, end of year		1	4
	Budget authority and outlays, net:			
	Mandatory:			
4090	Budget authority, gross	3	2	
	Outlays, gross:			
4100	Outlays from new mandatory authority	2	2	
4180	Budget authority, net (total)	3	2	
4190	Outlays, net (total)	2	2	
	Memorandum (non-add) entries:			
5000	Total investments, SOY: Federal securities: Par value	34	20	20
5001	Total investments, EOY: Federal securities: Par value	20	20	17

Public Law 93–642 established the Harry S Truman Scholarship Foundation to operate the scholarship program that is the permanent Federal memorial to the 33rd President of the United States. Appropriations in 1975 and 1976, totaling $30 million, established the Foundation's trust fund. The funds have been invested by the Secretary of the Treasury in U.S. Treasury securities, and the interest earned on these funds is available for carrying out the activities of the Foundation. For several years, the Foundation has also received appropriations that are deposited in the trust fund and available for obligation. The Budget proposes no new Federal funding for the Foundation in 2023.

The Foundation awards scholarships for qualified students who demonstrate outstanding potential for and interest in careers in public service at the local, State, or Federal level or in the non-profit sector. In its annual competition, the Foundation selects up to 60 new Truman Scholars. The maximum award is $30,000 toward a graduate level degree program.

Scholarship awards.—This activity is comprised of scholarships awarded to cover eligible educational expenses.

Program administration.—This activity covers all costs of operating the program, including annual program announcement, interview and selection of Truman Scholars, calculation and disbursement of scholarship awards, monitoring of student progress, and special services and activities for scholars, including an orientation week for new scholars, a summer education and internship program, and workshops and conferences.

Object Classification (in millions of dollars)

Identification code 372–8296–0–7–502	2021 actual	2022 est.	2023 est.
Direct obligations:			
11.1 Personnel compensation: Full-time permanent	1	1	1
41.0 Grants, subsidies, and contributions	1	1	1
99.0 Direct obligations	2	2	2
99.5 Adjustment for rounding		1	1
99.9 Total new obligations, unexpired accounts	2	3	3

Employment Summary

Identification code 372–8296–0–7–502	2021 actual	2022 est.	2023 est.
1001 Direct civilian full-time equivalent employment	5	5	5

INSTITUTE OF AMERICAN INDIAN AND ALASKA NATIVE CULTURE AND ARTS DEVELOPMENT

Federal Funds

PAYMENT TO THE INSTITUTE

For payment to the Institute of American Indian and Alaska Native Culture and Arts Development, as authorized by part A of title XV of Public Law 99–498 (20 U.S.C. 4411 et seq.), $11,772,000, which shall become available on July 1, 2023, and shall remain available until September 30, 2024.

Note.—A full-year 2022 appropriation for this account was not enacted at the time the Budget was prepared; therefore, the Budget assumes this account is operating under the Continuing Appropriations Act, 2022 (Division A of Public Law 117–43, as amended). The amounts included for 2022 reflect the annualized level provided by the continuing resolution.

Program and Financing (in millions of dollars)

Identification code 373–2900–0–1–502	2021 actual	2022 est.	2023 est.
Obligations by program activity:			
0001 Payment to the Institute	11	11	12
0900 Total new obligations, unexpired accounts (object class 41.0)	11	11	12
Budgetary resources:			
Budget authority:			
Appropriations, discretionary:			
1100 Appropriation	11	11	12
1930 Total budgetary resources available	11	11	12
Change in obligated balance:			
Unpaid obligations:			
3010 New obligations, unexpired accounts	11	11	12
3020 Outlays (gross)	–11	–11	–12
Budget authority and outlays, net:			
Discretionary:			
4000 Budget authority, gross	11	11	12
Outlays, gross:			
4010 Outlays from new discretionary authority	11	11	12
4180 Budget authority, net (total)	11	11	12
4190 Outlays, net (total)	11	11	12

Title XV of Public Law 99–498 established the Institute of American Indian and Alaska Native Culture and Arts Development as an independent non-profit educational institution. The mission of the Institute is to serve as a multi-tribal center of higher education for Native Americans and is dedicated to the study, creative application, preservation and care of Indian arts and culture. The Institute is federally chartered and under the direction and control of a Board of Trustees appointed by the President of the United States.

Payment to the Institute.—This activity supports the operations of the Institute.

INSTITUTE OF MUSEUM AND LIBRARY SERVICES

Federal Funds

OFFICE OF MUSEUM AND LIBRARY SERVICES: GRANTS AND ADMINISTRATION

For carrying out the Museum and Library Services Act of 1996 and the National Museum of African American History and Culture Act, $276,800,000.

Note.—A full-year 2022 appropriation for this account was not enacted at the time the Budget was prepared; therefore, the Budget assumes this account is operating under the Continuing Appropriations Act, 2022 (Division A of Public Law 117–43, as amended). The amounts included for 2022 reflect the annualized level provided by the continuing resolution.

Program and Financing (in millions of dollars)

Identification code 474–0300–0–1–503	2021 actual	2022 est.	2023 est.
Obligations by program activity:			
0001 Assistance for museums	45	41	52
0002 Assistance for libraries	378	197	201
0003 Administration	21	19	24
0004 Assistance for museums, Mandatory		11	
0005 Assistance for libraries, Mandatory		4	

Office of Museum and Library Services: Grants and Administration—Continued
Program and Financing—Continued

Identification code 474–0300–0–1–503	2021 actual	2022 est.	2023 est.
0799 Total direct obligations	444	272	277
0801 Reimbursable program activity	8		
0900 Total new obligations, unexpired accounts	452	272	277
Budgetary resources:			
Unobligated balance:			
1000 Unobligated balance brought forward, Oct 1	6	19	4
1001 Discretionary unobligated balance brought fwd, Oct 1	6		
Budget authority:			
Appropriations, discretionary:			
1100 Appropriation	257	257	277
Appropriations, mandatory:			
1200 Appropriation	200		
Spending authority from offsetting collections, discretionary:			
1700 Collected	8		
1900 Budget authority (total)	465	257	277
1930 Total budgetary resources available	471	276	281
Memorandum (non-add) entries:			
1941 Unexpired unobligated balance, end of year	19	4	4
Change in obligated balance:			
Unpaid obligations:			
3000 Unpaid obligations, brought forward, Oct 1	368	526	277
3010 New obligations, unexpired accounts	452	272	277
3020 Outlays (gross)	–290	–521	–351
3041 Recoveries of prior year unpaid obligations, expired	–4		
3050 Unpaid obligations, end of year	526	277	203
Memorandum (non-add) entries:			
3100 Obligated balance, start of year	368	526	277
3200 Obligated balance, end of year	526	277	203
Budget authority and outlays, net:			
Discretionary:			
4000 Budget authority, gross	265	257	277
Outlays, gross:			
4010 Outlays from new discretionary authority	40	77	83
4011 Outlays from discretionary balances	229	267	268
4020 Outlays, gross (total)	269	344	351
Offsets against gross budget authority and outlays:			
Offsetting collections (collected) from:			
4030 Federal sources	–8		
Mandatory:			
4090 Budget authority, gross	200		
Outlays, gross:			
4100 Outlays from new mandatory authority	21		
4101 Outlays from mandatory balances		177	
4110 Outlays, gross (total)	21	177	
4180 Budget authority, net (total)	457	257	277
4190 Outlays, net (total)	282	521	351

The Institute of Museum and Library Services (IMLS) is the primary source of Federal support for the nation's more than 116,000 libraries and 30,000 museums. Through strategic grantmaking, policy development, research and data collection, and strategic engagement, IMLS supports libraries and museums as community anchors that provide vital learning experiences and broad access to resources, in particular in under-served communities. IMLS provides leadership to help Americans build critical skills such as digital literacy; pursue education and training; access early learning opportunities; and participate in the workforce and civil society. Through its programs of support, including for State Library Administrative Agencies, Native American and Native Alaskan tribes, and Native Hawaiian organizations, IMLS helps ensure that all Americans, wherever located, have access to essential information and educational resources. The Institute's organization, mission, and functions are defined in the Museum and Library Services Act, as amended, Public Law 115–410; the National Museum of African American History and Culture Act, Public Law 108–184; and the National Museum of the American Latino Act, Public Law 116–260, the Consolidated Appropriations Act, 2021.

Object Classification (in millions of dollars)

Identification code 474–0300–0–1–503	2021 actual	2022 est.	2023 est.
Direct obligations:			
11.1 Personnel compensation: Full-time permanent	9	9	11
12.1 Civilian personnel benefits	3	3	4
23.1 Rental payments to GSA	2	2	2
25.2 Other services from non-Federal sources	7	5	7
41.0 Grants, subsidies, and contributions	423	253	253
99.0 Direct obligations	444	272	277
99.0 Reimbursable obligations	8		
99.9 Total new obligations, unexpired accounts	452	272	277

Employment Summary

Identification code 474–0300–0–1–503	2021 actual	2022 est.	2023 est.
1001 Direct civilian full-time equivalent employment	71	73	82

Office of Museum and Library Services: Grants and Administration
(Legislative proposal, not subject to PAYGO)

Contingent upon the enactment of the National Museum of the American Latino Act, the Director shall carry out such Act from within amounts appropriated under this heading.

INTELLIGENCE COMMUNITY MANAGEMENT ACCOUNT

Federal Funds

INTELLIGENCE COMMUNITY MANAGEMENT ACCOUNT

For necessary expenses of the Intelligence Community Management Account, $635,000,000.

Note.—A full-year 2022 appropriation for this account was not enacted at the time the Budget was prepared; therefore, the Budget assumes this account is operating under the Continuing Appropriations Act, 2022 (Division A of Public Law 117–43, as amended). The amounts included for 2022 reflect the annualized level provided by the continuing resolution.

Program and Financing (in millions of dollars)

Identification code 467–0401–0–1–054	2021 actual	2022 est.	2023 est.
Obligations by program activity:			
0001 Intelligence community management	551	634	635
0801 Intelligence Community Management Account (Reimbursable)	9	30	30
0900 Total new obligations, unexpired accounts	560	664	665
Budgetary resources:			
Budget authority:			
Appropriations, discretionary:			
1100 Appropriation	634	634	635
1120 Appropriations transferred to other accts [097–0100]	–29		
1160 Appropriation, discretionary (total)	605	634	635
Spending authority from offsetting collections, discretionary:			
1700 Collected	9	30	30
1900 Budget authority (total)	614	664	665
1930 Total budgetary resources available	614	664	665
Memorandum (non-add) entries:			
1940 Unobligated balance expiring	–54		
Change in obligated balance:			
Unpaid obligations:			
3000 Unpaid obligations, brought forward, Oct 1	162	160	195
3010 New obligations, unexpired accounts	560	664	665
3011 Obligations ("upward adjustments"), expired accounts	7		
3020 Outlays (gross)	–542	–629	–664
3041 Recoveries of prior year unpaid obligations, expired	–27		
3050 Unpaid obligations, end of year	160	195	196
Uncollected payments:			
3060 Uncollected pymts, Fed sources, brought forward, Oct 1	–8		
3071 Change in uncollected pymts, Fed sources, expired	8		
Memorandum (non-add) entries:			
3100 Obligated balance, start of year	154	160	195
3200 Obligated balance, end of year	160	195	196

OTHER INDEPENDENT AGENCIES

International Trade Commission Federal Funds 1277

	Budget authority and outlays, net:	2021 actual	2022 est.	2023 est.
	Discretionary:			
4000	Budget authority, gross	614	664	665
	Outlays, gross:			
4010	Outlays from new discretionary authority	414	506	506
4011	Outlays from discretionary balances	128	123	158
4020	Outlays, gross (total)	542	629	664
	Offsets against gross budget authority and outlays:			
	Offsetting collections (collected) from:			
4030	Federal sources	–17	–30	–30
4040	Offsets against gross budget authority and outlays (total)	–17	–30	–30
	Additional offsets against gross budget authority only:			
4052	Offsetting collections credited to expired accounts	8		
4060	Additional offsets against budget authority only (total)	8		
4070	Budget authority, net (discretionary)	605	634	635
4080	Outlays, net (discretionary)	525	599	634
4180	Budget authority, net (total)	605	634	635
4190	Outlays, net (total)	525	599	634

The Intelligence Community Management Account (ICMA) provides resources that directly support the Director of National Intelligence (DNI) in managing intelligence integration across the Intelligence Community (IC), such as the IC Inspector General, the IC Chief Information Officer, the IC Equal Employment Opportunity Office, the IC Diversity, Equity, and Inclusion Office, the Civil Liberties, Privacy, and Transparency Office and the IC Chief Financial Officer responsible for oversight of the National Intelligence Program annual budget cycle.

The ICMA funds the support functions of the Office of the Director of National Intelligence, including Legislative Affairs, Chief Operating Officer, Strategic Communications, and Military Affairs. ICMA also funds elements of the Policy and Capabilities Directorate which is focused on policy and strategy, acquisitions and procurement, facilities, human capital, domestic engagement, information sharing and data, and science and technology initiatives.

The ICMA also funds select IC elements such as the National Intelligence Council, the President's Daily Briefing Staff, and the National Intelligence University. These elements are the DNI's principal advisory sources in executing their IC-wide management responsibilities and executing their role as advisor to the President. The National Intelligence Council provides analytical support to the DNI and to senior policy makers. The President's Daily Briefing Staff supports the production of the daily intelligence briefing provided to the President and his senior staff. The National Intelligence University is a federal degree-granting institution with a far-reaching mission to educate and prepare intelligence officers to meet current and future challenges to the United States' national security.

Object Classification (in millions of dollars)

Identification code 467–0401–0–1–054		2021 actual	2022 est.	2023 est.
	Direct obligations:			
	Personnel compensation:			
11.1	Full-time permanent	125	134	136
11.5	Other personnel compensation	8	11	11
11.9	Total personnel compensation	133	145	147
12.1	Civilian personnel benefits	33	51	51
21.0	Travel and transportation of persons	3	10	9
22.0	Transportation of things	5	5	4
23.1	Rental payments to GSA	5	1	1
23.3	Communications, utilities, and miscellaneous charges	8	2	3
24.0	Printing and reproduction	3	2	3
25.1	Advisory and assistance services	240	277	283
25.2	Other services from non-Federal sources	30	28	28
25.3	Other goods and services from Federal sources	5	13	22
25.4	Operation and maintenance of facilities	24	23	20
25.5	Research and development contracts	2	2	2
25.6	Medical care	1	2	2
25.7	Operation and maintenance of equipment	48	54	41
26.0	Supplies and materials	1	2	1
31.0	Equipment	5	2	3
32.0	Land and structures	2	15	15
41.0	Grants, subsidies, and contributions	3		
99.0	Direct obligations	551	634	635
99.0	Reimbursable obligations	9	30	30
99.9	Total new obligations, unexpired accounts	560	664	665

Employment Summary

Identification code 467–0401–0–1–054	2021 actual	2022 est.	2023 est.
1001 Direct civilian full-time equivalent employment	811	876	876

INTERNATIONAL TRADE COMMISSION

Federal Funds

SALARIES AND EXPENSES

For necessary expenses of the International Trade Commission, including hire of passenger motor vehicles and services as authorized by section 3109 of title 5, United States Code, and not to exceed $2,250 for official reception and representation expenses, $106,818,000, to remain available until expended.

Note.—A full-year 2022 appropriation for this account was not enacted at the time the Budget was prepared; therefore, the Budget assumes this account is operating under the Continuing Appropriations Act, 2022 (Division A of Public Law 117–43, as amended). The amounts included for 2022 reflect the annualized level provided by the continuing resolution.

Program and Financing (in millions of dollars)

Identification code 034–0100–0–1–153		2021 actual	2022 est.	2023 est.
	Obligations by program activity:			
0001	Research, investigations, and reports	105	103	107
	Budgetary resources:			
	Unobligated balance:			
1021	Recoveries of prior year unpaid obligations	2		
	Budget authority:			
	Appropriations, discretionary:			
1100	Appropriation	103	103	107
1930	Total budgetary resources available	105	103	107
	Change in obligated balance:			
	Unpaid obligations:			
3000	Unpaid obligations, brought forward, Oct 1	20	21	7
3010	New obligations, unexpired accounts	105	103	107
3020	Outlays (gross)	–102	–117	–107
3040	Recoveries of prior year unpaid obligations, unexpired	–2		
3050	Unpaid obligations, end of year	21	7	7
	Memorandum (non-add) entries:			
3100	Obligated balance, start of year	20	21	7
3200	Obligated balance, end of year	21	7	7
	Budget authority and outlays, net:			
	Discretionary:			
4000	Budget authority, gross	103	103	107
	Outlays, gross:			
4010	Outlays from new discretionary authority	85	97	101
4011	Outlays from discretionary balances	17	20	6
4020	Outlays, gross (total)	102	117	107
4180	Budget authority, net (total)	103	103	107
4190	Outlays, net (total)	102	117	107

The U.S. International Trade Commission (Commission) is an independent, nonpartisan Federal agency with specific responsibilities in investigating, adjudicating, and enforcing certain U.S. trade laws, providing relevant and timely analysis to the President and the Congress on trade issues, and maintaining the Harmonized Tariff Schedule of the United States (HTS).

For FY 2023, the Commission requests an appropriation of $122.4 million to support its authorized operations. Pursuant to section 175 of the Trade Act of 1974, the budget estimates for the Commission are transmitted to Congress without revision by the President. The Administration's FY 2023 request for the Commission is $106.8 million, reflected in the Appendix table and appropriations language.

Although the Commission has one program activity set forth in the Budget of the United States, the Commission's Strategic Plan for FY 2022–2026 sets two strategic goals that cover its programmatic responsibilities: first,

SALARIES AND EXPENSES—Continued

to conduct reliable and thorough investigations and, second, to develop sound and informed analyses and determinations. These goals set objectives for the Commission to adhere to as it carries out its three long-standing, statutory mandates. Those mandates are: (1) to investigate and make determinations in proceedings involving imports claimed to injure a domestic industry, violations of U.S. intellectual property rights, or other unfair methods of competition in connection with imported goods; (2) to provide independent analysis and information on tariffs, trade, and competitiveness to the Congress and the President; and (3) to maintain the Harmonized Tariff Schedule of the United States (HTS). The Commission also set a strategic goal to execute and advance organizational excellence. The Commission's objectives under this goal focus on five functional areas—human resources; budget, acquisitions, and finance; information technology; data; and organizational effectiveness.

The Strategic Plan identifies strategic objectives for each strategic goal, strategies to meet these objectives, and specific performance goals. The performance goals provide the basis by which the Commission can assess whether it is making progress toward its strategic objectives.

The Commission makes available its Strategic Plan, Agency Financial Report, Annual Performance Plan, Annual Performance Report, and Budget Justification at *https://www.usitc.gov/budget_planning_and_organization*.

Object Classification (in millions of dollars)

Identification code 034–0100–0–1–153		2021 actual	2022 est.	2023 est.
	Direct obligations:			
	Personnel compensation:			
11.1	Full-time permanent	50	51	53
11.3	Other than full-time permanent	7	7	7
11.5	Other personnel compensation	1	1	1
11.9	Total personnel compensation	58	59	61
12.1	Civilian personnel benefits	20	20	20
23.1	Rental payments to GSA	8	9	11
23.3	Communications, utilities, and miscellaneous charges	1	1	1
25.1	Advisory and assistance services	1	1	1
25.2	Other services from non-Federal sources	1	1	1
25.3	Other goods and services from Federal sources	4	2	2
25.7	Operation and maintenance of equipment	8	7	7
26.0	Supplies and materials	2	1	1
31.0	Equipment	2	2	2
32.0	Land and structures			
99.0	Direct obligations	105	103	107
99.9	Total new obligations, unexpired accounts	105	103	107

Employment Summary

Identification code 034–0100–0–1–153		2021 actual	2022 est.	2023 est.
1001	Direct civilian full-time equivalent employment	411	400	436

JAMES MADISON MEMORIAL FELLOWSHIP FOUNDATION

Trust Funds

JAMES MADISON MEMORIAL FELLOWSHIP TRUST FUND

Special and Trust Fund Receipts (in millions of dollars)

Identification code 381–8282–0–7–502		2021 actual	2022 est.	2023 est.
0100	Balance, start of year			
	Receipts:			
	Current law:			
1140	Earnings on Investments, James Madison Memorial Fellowship Foundation	2	2	2
2000	Total: Balances and receipts	2	2	2
	Appropriations:			
	Current law:			
2101	James Madison Memorial Fellowship Trust Fund	–2	–2	–2
5099	Balance, end of year			

Program and Financing (in millions of dollars)

Identification code 381–8282–0–7–502		2021 actual	2022 est.	2023 est.
	Obligations by program activity:			
0001	Fellowship awards	2	1	1
0002	Program administration		1	1
0900	Total new obligations, unexpired accounts	2	2	2
	Budgetary resources:			
	Unobligated balance:			
1000	Unobligated balance brought forward, Oct 1	39	39	39
	Budget authority:			
	Appropriations, mandatory:			
1201	Appropriation (special or trust fund)	2	2	2
1930	Total budgetary resources available	41	41	41
	Memorandum (non-add) entries:			
1941	Unexpired unobligated balance, end of year	39	39	39
	Change in obligated balance:			
	Unpaid obligations:			
3000	Unpaid obligations, brought forward, Oct 1	1	1	
3010	New obligations, unexpired accounts	2	2	2
3020	Outlays (gross)	–2	–3	–2
3050	Unpaid obligations, end of year	1		
	Memorandum (non-add) entries:			
3100	Obligated balance, start of year	1	1	
3200	Obligated balance, end of year	1		
	Budget authority and outlays, net:			
	Mandatory:			
4090	Budget authority, gross	2	2	2
	Outlays, gross:			
4100	Outlays from new mandatory authority	2	2	2
4101	Outlays from mandatory balances		1	
4110	Outlays, gross (total)	2	3	2
4180	Budget authority, net (total)	2	2	2
4190	Outlays, net (total)	2	3	2
	Memorandum (non-add) entries:			
5000	Total investments, SOY: Federal securities: Par value	37	37	37
5001	Total investments, EOY: Federal securities: Par value	37	37	37

Public Laws 99–500, 101–208, and 102–221 established the James Madison Memorial Fellowship Foundation to operate a fellowship program to encourage graduate study of the framing, principles, and history of the American Constitution. Appropriations of $10 million in 1988 and 1989 established the Foundation's trust fund. The funds have been invested by the Secretary of the Treasury in U.S. Treasury securities, and the interest earned on these funds is available for carrying out the activities of the Foundation. Funds raised from private sources and the surcharges from commemorative coin sales are also placed in the trust fund.

The Foundation is authorized to award graduate fellowships of up to $24,000 to high school teachers of American history, American government, and civics. College seniors and recent college graduates who want to become secondary school teachers of these subjects are also eligible.

Fellowship awards.—This activity is comprised of fellowship awards to cover educational expenses. It also supports the Foundation's annual Summer Institute on the U.S. Constitution, which all current fellows are required to attend. The Institute is an intensive educational experience that will ensure that all fellows know the history of the framing, ratification, and implementation of the U.S. Constitution and the Bill of Rights.

Program administration.—This activity covers the costs of planning, fund-raising, and the operation of the fellowship program.

Object Classification (in millions of dollars)

Identification code 381–8282–0–7–502		2021 actual	2022 est.	2023 est.
41.0	Direct obligations: Grants, subsidies, and contributions	1	1	1
99.5	Adjustment for rounding	1	1	1
99.9	Total new obligations, unexpired accounts	2	2	2

OTHER INDEPENDENT AGENCIES — Legal Services Corporation / Federal Funds — 1279

Employment Summary

Identification code 381–8282–0–7–502	2021 actual	2022 est.	2023 est.
1001 Direct civilian full-time equivalent employment	6	6	6

JAPAN-UNITED STATES FRIENDSHIP COMMISSION

Trust Funds

JAPAN-UNITED STATES FRIENDSHIP TRUST FUND

Special and Trust Fund Receipts (in millions of dollars)

Identification code 382–8025–0–7–154	2021 actual	2022 est.	2023 est.
0100 Balance, start of year	35	35	35
Receipts:			
Current law:			
1140 Interest on Investment in Public Debt Securities, Japan-United States Friendship Commission	2	3	3
2000 Total: Balances and receipts	37	38	38
Appropriations:			
Current law:			
2101 Japan-United States Friendship Trust Fund	–3	–3	–3
5098 Reconciliation adjustment	1		
5099 Balance, end of year	35	35	35

Program and Financing (in millions of dollars)

Identification code 382–8025–0–7–154	2021 actual	2022 est.	2023 est.
Obligations by program activity:			
0001 Grants	2	2	2
0002 Administration	1	1	1
0900 Total new obligations, unexpired accounts	3	3	3
Budgetary resources:			
Budget authority:			
Appropriations, mandatory:			
1201 Appropriation (special or trust fund)	3	3	3
1930 Total budgetary resources available	3	3	3
Change in obligated balance:			
Unpaid obligations:			
3000 Unpaid obligations, brought forward, Oct 1	1	2	3
3010 New obligations, unexpired accounts	3	3	3
3020 Outlays (gross)	–2	–2	–4
3050 Unpaid obligations, end of year	2	3	2
Memorandum (non-add) entries:			
3100 Obligated balance, start of year	1	2	3
3200 Obligated balance, end of year	2	3	2
Budget authority and outlays, net:			
Mandatory:			
4090 Budget authority, gross	3	3	3
Outlays, gross:			
4100 Outlays from new mandatory authority	2	2	2
4101 Outlays from mandatory balances			2
4110 Outlays, gross (total)	2	2	4
4180 Budget authority, net (total)	3	3	3
4190 Outlays, net (total)	2	2	4
Memorandum (non-add) entries:			
5000 Total investments, SOY: Federal securities: Par value	33	36	36
5001 Total investments, EOY: Federal securities: Par value	36	36	36

The Japan-U.S. Friendship Commission was established as an independent Federal Government agency by the United States Congress in 1975 (P.L. 94–118) to strengthen the U.S.-Japan relationship through educational, cultural, and intellectual exchange. It administers a U.S. Government trust fund that originated in connection with the return to the Japanese government of certain U.S. facilities in Okinawa and for postwar U.S. assistance to Japan. The Commission is allowed to make expenditures from the fund in an amount, not to exceed five percent annually of the fund's original principal, to pay Commission expenses and to make grants to support its mission. The Commission is a grant making agency that supports research, education, public affairs and exchange with Japan. Its mission is to support reciprocal people-to-people understanding, and to promote partnerships that advance common interests between Japan and United States.

Object Classification (in millions of dollars)

Identification code 382–8025–0–7–154	2021 actual	2022 est.	2023 est.
41.0 Direct obligations: Grants, subsidies, and contributions	2	2	2
99.5 Adjustment for rounding	1	1	1
99.9 Total new obligations, unexpired accounts	3	3	3

Employment Summary

Identification code 382–8025–0–7–154	2021 actual	2022 est.	2023 est.
1001 Direct civilian full-time equivalent employment	3	3	3

LEGAL SERVICES CORPORATION

Federal Funds

PAYMENT TO THE LEGAL SERVICES CORPORATION

For payment to the Legal Services Corporation to carry out the purposes of the Legal Services Corporation Act of 1974, $700,000,000; of which $656,100,000 is for basic field programs and required independent audits; $5,700,000 is for the Office of Inspector General, of which such amounts as may be necessary may be used to conduct additional audits of recipients; $26,200,000 is for management and grants oversight; $5,000,000 is for client self-help and information technology; $5,000,000 is for a Pro Bono Innovation Fund; and $2,000,000 is for loan repayment assistance: Provided, That the Legal Services Corporation may continue to provide locality pay to officers and employees at a rate no greater than that provided by the Federal Government to Washington, DC-based employees as authorized by section 5304 of title 5, United States Code, notwithstanding section 1005(d) of the Legal Services Corporation Act (42 U.S.C. 2996d(d)): Provided further, That the authorities provided in section 205 of this Act shall be applicable to the Legal Services Corporation: Provided further, That, for the purposes of section 504 of this Act, the Legal Services Corporation shall be considered an agency of the United States Government.

Note.—A full-year 2022 appropriation for this account was not enacted at the time the Budget was prepared; therefore, the Budget assumes this account is operating under the Continuing Appropriations Act, 2022 (Division A of Public Law 117–43, as amended). The amounts included for 2022 reflect the annualized level provided by the continuing resolution.

PAYMENT TO THE LEGAL SERVICES CORPORATION

【*For an additional amount for "Payment to the Legal Services Corporation" to carry out the purposes of the Legal Services Corporation Act by providing for necessary expenses related to the consequences of hurricanes, wildfires, other extreme weather, and earthquakes that occurred during calendar years 2020 and 2021, $40,000,000, to remain available until September 30, 2022: Provided, That none of the funds appropriated in this Act to the Legal Services Corporation shall be expended for any purpose prohibited or limited by, or contrary to any of the provisions of, sections 501, 502, 503, 504, 505, and 506 of Public Law 105–119, and all funds appropriated in this Act to the Legal Services Corporation shall be subject to the same terms and conditions set forth in such sections, except that all references in sections 502 and 503 to 1997 and 1998 shall be deemed to refer instead to 2021 and 2022, respectively, and except that sections 501 and 503 of Public Law 104–134 (referenced by Public Law 105–119) shall not apply to the amount made available under this heading: Provided further, That, for the purposes of this Act, the Legal Services Corporation shall be considered an agency of the United States.*】 *(Disaster Relief Supplemental Appropriations Act, 2022.)*

Program and Financing (in millions of dollars)

Identification code 020–0501–0–1–752	2021 actual	2022 est.	2023 est.
Obligations by program activity:			
0001 Payment to Legal Services Corporation	468	505	700
0900 Total new obligations, unexpired accounts (object class 41.0)	468	505	700

PAYMENT TO THE LEGAL SERVICES CORPORATION—Continued

Program and Financing—Continued

Identification code 020–0501–0–1–752	2021 actual	2022 est.	2023 est.
Budgetary resources:			
Budget authority:			
Appropriations, discretionary:			
1100 Appropriation	465	465	700
1100 Appropriation		40	
1160 Appropriation, discretionary (total)	465	505	700
Spending authority from offsetting collections, discretionary:			
1700 Collected	3		
1900 Budget authority (total)	468	505	700
1930 Total budgetary resources available	468	505	700
Change in obligated balance:			
Unpaid obligations:			
3000 Unpaid obligations, brought forward, Oct 1			40
3010 New obligations, unexpired accounts	468	505	700
3020 Outlays (gross)	–468	–465	–680
3050 Unpaid obligations, end of year		40	60
Memorandum (non-add) entries:			
3100 Obligated balance, start of year			40
3200 Obligated balance, end of year		40	60
Budget authority and outlays, net:			
Discretionary:			
4000 Budget authority, gross	468	505	700
Outlays, gross:			
4010 Outlays from new discretionary authority	468	465	640
4011 Outlays from discretionary balances			40
4020 Outlays, gross (total)	468	465	680
Offsets against gross budget authority and outlays:			
Offsetting collections (collected) from:			
4030 Federal sources	–3		
4180 Budget authority, net (total)	465	505	700
4190 Outlays, net (total)	465	465	680

The Legal Services Corporation (LSC) distributes appropriated funds to local non-profit organizations that provide free civil legal assistance to people living in poverty, according to locally-determined priorities. The Congress chartered the corporation as a private, non-profit entity outside of the Federal Government. Funding for LSC helps ensure that low-income Americans have an opportunity to obtain access to the courts, due process, and fair treatment. LSC operates under rules and requirements set by the LSC Act, 42 U.S.C. 2996–2996l, and by LSC's annual appropriations. The Administrative Provisions would make two changes. First, they would permit LSC recipients to operate with boards of directors that have as few as 33% attorneys without requiring appointment by bar associations and suspend the 60% attorney requirement in the LSC Act. This will greatly improve recipients' ability to have fiscal experts and community representatives on their governing bodies. Second, they would continue to apply the appropriations restrictions on recipients' use of these appropriated funds while permitting recipients to use funds from other sources as intended by those funders.

ADMINISTRATIVE PROVISION—LEGAL SERVICES CORPORATION

None of the funds appropriated in this Act to the Legal Services Corporation shall be expended for any purpose prohibited or limited by, or contrary to any of the provisions of, sections 501, 502, 503, 504, 505, and 506 of Public Law 105–119, and all funds appropriated in this Act to the Legal Services Corporation shall be subject to the same terms and conditions set forth in such sections, except that all references in sections 502 and 503 to 1997 and 1998 shall be deemed to refer instead to 2022 and 2023, respectively.

Section 501 of the Departments of Commerce, Justice, and State, the Judiciary, and Related Agencies Appropriations Act, 1998 (Public Law 105–119) is amended by adding the following new subsection at the end:

"(d) MODIFIED GOVERNING BODY REQUIREMENT.—For purposes of this Act, section 1007(c) of the Legal Services Corporation Act (42 U.S.C. 2996f(c)) shall be applied by substituting "33 percent" for "60 percent".".

Section 502(2) of the Departments of Commerce, Justice, and State, the Judiciary, and Related Agencies Appropriations Act, 1996 (Public Law 104–134) is amended by striking subparagraph (B) in its entirety and replacing it with the following:

"(B) is governed by a board of directors or other governing body, 33 percent of which is comprised of attorneys who are members of the bar of a State, as defined in section 1002(8) of the Legal Services Corporation Act (42 U.S.C. 2996a(8)), in which the legal assistance is to be provided;".

Section 504 of the Departments of Commerce, Justice, and State, the Judiciary, and Related Agencies Appropriations Act, 1996 (Public Law 104–134) is amended in subsection (a) by striking everything before the first paragraph and inserting the following:

"(a) None of the funds appropriated in this Act to the Legal Services Corporation may be used to provide financial assistance to any person or entity (which may be referred to in this section as a recipient) for any expenditure or activity—".

MARINE MAMMAL COMMISSION

Federal Funds

SALARIES AND EXPENSES

For necessary expenses of the Marine Mammal Commission as authorized by title II of the Marine Mammal Protection Act of 1972 (16 U.S.C. 1361 et seq.), $4,500,000.

Note.—A full-year 2022 appropriation for this account was not enacted at the time the Budget was prepared; therefore, the Budget assumes this account is operating under the Continuing Appropriations Act, 2022 (Division A of Public Law 117–43, as amended). The amounts included for 2022 reflect the annualized level provided by the continuing resolution.

Program and Financing (in millions of dollars)

Identification code 387–2200–0–1–302	2021 actual	2022 est.	2023 est.
Obligations by program activity:			
0001 Salaries and expenses	4	4	5
Budgetary resources:			
Budget authority:			
Appropriations, discretionary:			
1100 Appropriation	4	4	5
1930 Total budgetary resources available	4	4	5
Change in obligated balance:			
Unpaid obligations:			
3000 Unpaid obligations, brought forward, Oct 1	1	1	1
3010 New obligations, unexpired accounts	4	4	5
3020 Outlays (gross)	–4	–4	–5
3050 Unpaid obligations, end of year	1	1	1
Memorandum (non-add) entries:			
3100 Obligated balance, start of year	1	1	1
3200 Obligated balance, end of year	1	1	1
Budget authority and outlays, net:			
Discretionary:			
4000 Budget authority, gross	4	4	5
Outlays, gross:			
4010 Outlays from new discretionary authority	3	3	4
4011 Outlays from discretionary balances	1	1	1
4020 Outlays, gross (total)	4	4	5
4180 Budget authority, net (total)	4	4	5
4190 Outlays, net (total)	4	4	5

The Marine Mammal Commission is charged by the Marine Mammal Protection Act of 1972 to further the conservation of marine mammals and their environment. It provides independent, science-based oversight of domestic and international policies and actions of Federal agencies addressing human impacts on marine mammals and their ecosystems.

Object Classification (in millions of dollars)

Identification code 387–2200–0–1–302	2021 actual	2022 est.	2023 est.
Direct obligations:			
11.1 Personnel compensation: Full-time permanent	2	2	2
25.1 Advisory and assistance services	1	1	2
99.0 Direct obligations	3	3	4
99.5 Adjustment for rounding	1	1	1

MERIT SYSTEMS PROTECTION BOARD

Federal Funds

SALARIES AND EXPENSES

(INCLUDING TRANSFER OF FUNDS)

For necessary expenses to carry out functions of the Merit Systems Protection Board pursuant to Reorganization Plan Numbered 2 of 1978, the Civil Service Reform Act of 1978, and the Whistleblower Protection Act of 1989 (5 U.S.C. 5509 note), including services as authorized by 5 U.S.C. 3109, rental of conference rooms in the District of Columbia and elsewhere, hire of passenger motor vehicles, direct procurement of survey printing, and not to exceed $2,000 for official reception and representation expenses, $51,139,000, to remain available until September 30, 2024, and in addition not to exceed $2,345,000, to remain available until September 30, 2024, for administrative expenses to adjudicate retirement appeals to be transferred from the Civil Service Retirement and Disability Fund in amounts determined by the Merit Systems Protection Board.

Note.—A full-year 2022 appropriation for this account was not enacted at the time the Budget was prepared; therefore, the Budget assumes this account is operating under the Continuing Appropriations Act, 2022 (Division A of Public Law 117–43, as amended). The amounts included for 2022 reflect the annualized level provided by the continuing resolution.

Program and Financing (in millions of dollars)

Identification code 389–0100–0–1–805	2021 actual	2022 est.	2023 est.
Obligations by program activity:			
0001 Adjudication	38	38	44
0002 Merit systems studies	3	3	3
0003 Management support	3	3	4
0799 Total direct obligations	44	44	51
0801 Salaries and Expenses (Reimbursable)	2	2	2
0900 Total new obligations, unexpired accounts	46	46	53
Budgetary resources:			
Unobligated balance:			
1000 Unobligated balance brought forward, Oct 1	6	6	6
Budget authority:			
Appropriations, discretionary:			
1100 Appropriation	44	44	51
Spending authority from offsetting collections, discretionary:			
1700 Collected	2	2	2
1900 Budget authority (total)	46	46	53
1930 Total budgetary resources available	52	52	59
Memorandum (non-add) entries:			
1941 Unexpired unobligated balance, end of year	6	6	6
Change in obligated balance:			
Unpaid obligations:			
3000 Unpaid obligations, brought forward, Oct 1	8	8	2
3010 New obligations, unexpired accounts	46	46	53
3020 Outlays (gross)	–46	–52	–53
3050 Unpaid obligations, end of year	8	2	2
Memorandum (non-add) entries:			
3100 Obligated balance, start of year	8	8	2
3200 Obligated balance, end of year	8	2	2
Budget authority and outlays, net:			
Discretionary:			
4000 Budget authority, gross	46	46	53
Outlays, gross:			
4010 Outlays from new discretionary authority	36	42	49
4011 Outlays from discretionary balances	10	10	4
4020 Outlays, gross (total)	46	52	53
Offsets against gross budget authority and outlays:			
Offsetting collections (collected) from:			
4030 Federal sources	–2	–2	–2
4180 Budget authority, net (total)	44	44	51
4190 Outlays, net (total)	44	50	51

The Merit Systems Protection Board (MSPB) is an independent agency in the Executive Branch of the Federal Government that serves as the guardian of Federal merit systems. The Board's mission is to protect Federal merit systems and the rights of individuals within those systems. The MSPB accomplishes its mission by: hearing and deciding employee appeals from agency actions; hearing and deciding cases brought by the Office of Special Counsel involving alleged abuses of the merit systems, and other cases arising under the Board's original jurisdiction; conducting studies of the civil service and other merit systems in the Executive Branch to determine whether they are free from prohibited personnel practices; and providing oversight of the significant actions and regulations of the Office of Personnel Management (OPM) to determine whether they are in accord with merit system principles. The MSPB's inception began in 1883, when the Congress passed the Pendleton Act establishing the Civil Service Commission and a merit-based employment system for the Federal Government. The Pendleton Act grew out of the 19th century reform movement to curtail the excesses of political patronage in Government. As the Commission's responsibilities multiplied, a growing consensus emerged that it could not properly and adequately perform managerial and adjudicatory functions simultaneously. Concern over the inherent conflict of interest in the Commission's role as both rule-maker and judge was a principal motivating factor behind the enactment by the Congress of the Civil Service Reform Act of 1978. The Act replaced the Civil Service Commission with three new independent agencies: OPM, the Federal Labor Relations Authority, and MSPB. MSPB assumed the employee appeals functions of the Commission and was given the new responsibilities to perform merit systems studies and to review the significant actions of OPM.

Object Classification (in millions of dollars)

Identification code 389–0100–0–1–805	2021 actual	2022 est.	2023 est.
Direct obligations:			
11.1 Personnel compensation: Full-time permanent	28	28	32
12.1 Civilian personnel benefits	8	8	10
23.1 Rental payments to GSA	2	3	4
23.3 Communications, utilities, and miscellaneous charges	1	1	1
25.2 Other services from non-Federal sources	2	1	1
25.3 Other goods and services from Federal sources	2	2	2
31.0 Equipment	1	1	1
99.0 Direct obligations	44	44	51
99.0 Reimbursable obligations	2	2	2
99.9 Total new obligations, unexpired accounts	46	46	53

Employment Summary

Identification code 389–0100–0–1–805	2021 actual	2022 est.	2023 est.
1001 Direct civilian full-time equivalent employment	185	220	223
2001 Reimbursable civilian full-time equivalent employment	15	15	12

MILITARY COMPENSATION AND RETIREMENT MODERNIZATION COMMISSION

Federal Funds

MILITARY COMPENSATION AND RETIREMENT MODERNIZATION COMMISSION

Program and Financing (in millions of dollars)

Identification code 479–2994–0–1–054	2021 actual	2022 est.	2023 est.
Change in obligated balance:			
Unpaid obligations:			
3000 Unpaid obligations, brought forward, Oct 1	1	1	
3020 Outlays (gross)		–1	
3050 Unpaid obligations, end of year	1		
Memorandum (non-add) entries:			
3100 Obligated balance, start of year	1	1	

MILITARY COMPENSATION AND RETIREMENT MODERNIZATION COMMISSION—Continued

Program and Financing—Continued

Identification code 479–2994-0-1-054	2021 actual	2022 est.	2023 est.
3200 Obligated balance, end of year		1	
Budget authority and outlays, net:			
Discretionary:			
Outlays, gross:			
4011 Outlays from discretionary balances			1
4180 Budget authority, net (total)			
4190 Outlays, net (total)			1

MORRIS K. UDALL AND STEWART L. UDALL FOUNDATION

Federal Funds

MORRIS K. UDALL AND STEWART L. UDALL TRUST FUND

(INCLUDING TRANSFER OF FUNDS)

For payment to the Morris K. Udall and Stewart L. Udall Trust Fund, pursuant to the Morris K. Udall and Stewart L. Udall Foundation Act (20 U.S.C. 5601 et seq.), $1,800,000, to remain available until expended, of which, notwithstanding sections 8 and 9 of such Act, up to $1,000,000 shall be available to carry out the activities authorized by section 6(7) of Public Law 102–259 and section 817(a) of Public Law 106–568 (20 U.S.C. 5604(7)): Provided, That all current and previous amounts transferred to the Office of Inspector General of the Department of the Interior will remain available until expended for audits and investigations of the Morris K. Udall and Stewart L. Udall Foundation, consistent with the Inspector General Act of 1978 (5 U.S.C. App.), as amended, and for annual independent financial audits of the Morris K. Udall and Stewart L. Udall Foundation pursuant to the Accountability of Tax Dollars Act of 2002 (Public Law 107–289): Provided further, That previous amounts transferred to the Office of Inspector General of the Department of the Interior may be transferred to the Morris K. Udall and Stewart L. Udall Foundation for annual independent financial audits pursuant to the Accountability of Tax Dollars Act of 2002 (Public Law 107–289).

Note.—A full-year 2022 appropriation for this account was not enacted at the time the Budget was prepared; therefore, the Budget assumes this account is operating under the Continuing Appropriations Act, 2022 (Division A of Public Law 117–43, as amended). The amounts included for 2022 reflect the annualized level provided by the continuing resolution.

Program and Financing (in millions of dollars)

Identification code 487–0900–0–1–502	2021 actual	2022 est.	2023 est.
Obligations by program activity:			
0001 Federal payment to Morris K. Udall Scholarship and Excellence in National Environmental Policy Foundation	2	2	2
0900 Total new obligations, unexpired accounts (object class 94.0)	2	2	2
Budgetary resources:			
Budget authority:			
Appropriations, discretionary:			
1100 Appropriation	2	2	2
1930 Total budgetary resources available	2	2	2
Change in obligated balance:			
Unpaid obligations:			
3010 New obligations, unexpired accounts	2	2	2
3020 Outlays (gross)	–2	–2	–2
Budget authority and outlays, net:			
Discretionary:			
4000 Budget authority, gross	2	2	2
Outlays, gross:			
4010 Outlays from new discretionary authority	2	2	2
4180 Budget authority, net (total)	2	2	2
4190 Outlays, net (total)	2	2	2

The Trust Fund is invested in Treasury securities with maturities suitable to the needs of the Fund. Interest earnings from the investments are used to carry out the activities of the Udall Foundation including awarding scholarships, fellowships, and interships; conducting Parks in Focus program activities; and providing funding to, and through, the Udall Center for environmental and public policy research, the activities of the Native Nations Institute, and the Udall Archives.

The Udall Foundation is authorized by 20 U.S.C. 5604(7) to establish training programs for professionals in Native American and Alaska Native health care and public policy;the Udall Foundation provides these programs through the Native Nations Institute.

ENVIRONMENTAL DISPUTE RESOLUTION FUND

For payment to the Environmental Dispute Resolution Fund to carry out activities authorized in the Environmental Policy and Conflict Resolution Act of 1998, $3,943,000, to remain available until expended.

Note.—A full-year 2022 appropriation for this account was not enacted at the time the Budget was prepared; therefore, the Budget assumes this account is operating under the Continuing Appropriations Act, 2022 (Division A of Public Law 117–43, as amended). The amounts included for 2022 reflect the annualized level provided by the continuing resolution.

Program and Financing (in millions of dollars)

Identification code 487–0925–0–1–306	2021 actual	2022 est.	2023 est.
Obligations by program activity:			
0001 Environmental dispute resolution fund	7	8	8
Budgetary resources:			
Unobligated balance:			
1000 Unobligated balance brought forward, Oct 1	10	8	7
1001 Discretionary unobligated balance brought fwd, Oct 1	8	8	
Budget authority:			
Appropriations, discretionary:			
1100 Appropriation	3	3	4
Spending authority from offsetting collections, mandatory:			
1800 Collected	2	4	4
1900 Budget authority (total)	5	7	8
1930 Total budgetary resources available	15	15	15
Memorandum (non-add) entries:			
1941 Unexpired unobligated balance, end of year	8	7	7
Change in obligated balance:			
Unpaid obligations:			
3000 Unpaid obligations, brought forward, Oct 1	1	2	1
3010 New obligations, unexpired accounts	7	8	8
3020 Outlays (gross)	–6	–9	–8
3050 Unpaid obligations, end of year	2	1	1
Memorandum (non-add) entries:			
3100 Obligated balance, start of year	1	2	1
3200 Obligated balance, end of year	2	1	1
Budget authority and outlays, net:			
Discretionary:			
4000 Budget authority, gross	3	3	4
Outlays, gross:			
4010 Outlays from new discretionary authority	3	3	4
Mandatory:			
4090 Budget authority, gross	2	4	4
Outlays, gross:			
4100 Outlays from new mandatory authority	2	4	4
4101 Outlays from mandatory balances	1	2	
4110 Outlays, gross (total)	3	6	4
Offsets against gross budget authority and outlays:			
Offsetting collections (collected) from:			
4120 Federal sources	–2	–3	–3
4123 Non-Federal sources		–1	–1
4130 Offsets against gross budget authority and outlays (total)	–2	–4	–4
4170 Outlays, net (mandatory)	1	2	
4180 Budget authority, net (total)	3	3	4
4190 Outlays, net (total)	4	5	4
Memorandum (non-add) entries:			
5000 Total investments, SOY: Federal securities: Par value	5	2	2
5001 Total investments, EOY: Federal securities: Par value	2	2	2

In 1998, Public Law 105–56 established the U.S. Institute for Environmental Conflict Resolution (U.S. Institute) as a part of the Udall Foundation. The Further Consolidated Appropriations Act, 2020 renamed the U.S. Institute as the John S. McCain III National Center for Environmental Conflict

Resolution (National Center) to honor the legacy of Senator John McCain who was instrumental in the establishment of the Udall Foundation and its programs. The National Center provides impartial collaboration, consensus-building, and conflict resolution services on a wide range of environmental, natural and cultural resources, Tribal, and public lands issues involving the Federal Government. The National Center's work enhances project efficiency, reduces costs, increases government capacity to serve citizens, increases the likelihood of avoiding litigation, and delivers better and more durable outcomes. The National Center's range of services include consultations, assessments, process design, convening, mediation, facilitation, training, stakeholder engagement, and other related collaboration and conflict resolution activities. The National Center specializes in providing assistance with national and regionally important environmental challenges; multiparty high-conflict cases where an impartial Federal convener is needed to broker participation in a collaborative process or conflict resolution effort; collaborative efforts involving Tribes and Native people, including government-to-government consultation between Tribes and Federal agencies; interagency and interdepartmental collaborations; issues involving multiple levels of government (Federal, State, local, Tribal) and the public; issues that require substantive expertise (e.g., National Environmental Policy Act, transportation infrastructure projects, endangered species, cultural resources); and projects that require funding from multiple agencies and/or private organizations.

Object Classification (in millions of dollars)

Identification code 487–0925–0–1–306	2021 actual	2022 est.	2023 est.
11.1 Direct obligations: Personnel compensation: Full-time permanent	3	4	4
99.0 Direct obligations	3	4	4
99.0 Reimbursable obligations	4	4	4
99.9 Total new obligations, unexpired accounts	7	8	8

Employment Summary

Identification code 487–0925–0–1–306	2021 actual	2022 est.	2023 est.
1001 Direct civilian full-time equivalent employment	28	28	29

Trust Funds

MORRIS K. UDALL AND STEWART L. UDALL FOUNDATION

Special and Trust Fund Receipts (in millions of dollars)

Identification code 487–8615–0–7–502	2021 actual	2022 est.	2023 est.
0100 Balance, start of year	51	52	54
Receipts:			
Current law:			
1140 General Fund Payments, Morris K. Udall Scholarship Fund	2	2	2
1140 Interest on Investments, Morris K. Udall Scholarship Fund	2	2	2
1199 Total current law receipts	4	4	4
1999 Total receipts	4	4	4
2000 Total: Balances and receipts	55	56	58
Appropriations:			
Current law:			
2101 Morris K. Udall and Stewart L. Udall Foundation	–3	–2	–2
5099 Balance, end of year	52	54	56

Program and Financing (in millions of dollars)

Identification code 487–8615–0–7–502	2021 actual	2022 est.	2023 est.
Obligations by program activity:			
0001 Morris K. Udall Scholarship and Excellence in National Environmental Policy Foundation	3	2	2
0900 Total new obligations, unexpired accounts (object class 41.0)	3	2	2
Budgetary resources:			
Unobligated balance:			
1000 Unobligated balance brought forward, Oct 1	1	1	1
Budget authority:			
Appropriations, mandatory:			
1201 Appropriation (special or trust fund)	3	2	2
1930 Total budgetary resources available	4	3	3
Memorandum (non-add) entries:			
1941 Unexpired unobligated balance, end of year	1	1	1
Change in obligated balance:			
Unpaid obligations:			
3000 Unpaid obligations, brought forward, Oct 1	1	1	
3010 New obligations, unexpired accounts	3	2	2
3020 Outlays (gross)	–3	–3	–2
3050 Unpaid obligations, end of year	1		
Memorandum (non-add) entries:			
3100 Obligated balance, start of year	1	1	
3200 Obligated balance, end of year	1		
Budget authority and outlays, net:			
Mandatory:			
4090 Budget authority, gross	3	2	2
Outlays, gross:			
4100 Outlays from new mandatory authority	2	2	2
4101 Outlays from mandatory balances	1	1	
4110 Outlays, gross (total)	3	3	2
4180 Budget authority, net (total)	3	2	2
4190 Outlays, net (total)	3	3	2
Memorandum (non-add) entries:			
5000 Total investments, SOY: Federal securities: Par value	49	31	32
5001 Total investments, EOY: Federal securities: Par value	31	32	33

Public Law 102–259 established the Udall Foundation to award scholarships, fellowships, and internships for study related to the environment, and to Native Americans and Alaska Natives in fields related to health care and tribal public policy; connect youth to the Nation's public lands and natural resources through the Stewart L. Udall Parks In Focus Program (Parks in Focus); provide funding to the Udall Center for Studies in Public Policy (Udall Center) at The University of Arizona, including the Native Nations Institute for Leadership, Management, and Policy (NativeNations Institute), to conduct environmental policy research, research on Native American and Alaska Native health care issues and tribal public policy issues, and training; and provide funding through the Udall Center to The University of Arizona Libraries, Special Collections, to serve as the repository for the papers of Morris K. Udall and Stewart L. Udall (Udall Archives).

NATIONAL ARCHIVES AND RECORDS ADMINISTRATION

Federal Funds

OPERATING EXPENSES

For necessary expenses in connection with the administration of the National Archives and Records Administration and archived Federal records and related activities, as provided by law, and for expenses necessary for the review and declassification of documents, the activities of the Public Interest Declassification Board, the operations and maintenance of the electronic records archives, the hire of passenger motor vehicles, and for uniforms or allowances therefor, as authorized by law (5 U.S.C. 5901), including maintenance, repairs, and cleaning, $426,520,000, of which $30,000,000 shall remain available until expended for expenses necessary to enhance the Federal Government's ability to electronically preserve, manage, and store Government records.

Note.—A full-year 2022 appropriation for this account was not enacted at the time the Budget was prepared; therefore, the Budget assumes this account is operating under the Continuing Appropriations Act, 2022 (Division A of Public Law 117–43, as amended). The amounts included for 2022 reflect the annualized level provided by the continuing resolution.

OPERATING EXPENSES—Continued

Program and Financing (in millions of dollars)

Identification code 088–0300–0–1–804		2021 actual	2022 est.	2023 est.
	Obligations by program activity:			
0001	Legislative Archives, Presidential Libraries, and Museum Services	114	112	118
0002	Citizen Services	114	121	128
0003	Agency and Related Services	82	81	91
0004	Facility Operations	54	66	60
0007	Electronic Records Initiative	4	36	30
0799	Total direct obligations	368	416	427
0888	Operating Expenses (Reimbursable)	1	1	1
0900	Total new obligations, unexpired accounts	369	417	428
	Budgetary resources:			
	Unobligated balance:			
1000	Unobligated balance brought forward, Oct 1	35	39	
	Budget authority:			
	Appropriations, discretionary:			
1100	Appropriation	377	377	427
	Spending authority from offsetting collections, discretionary:			
1700	Collected	1	1	1
1900	Budget authority (total)	378	378	428
1930	Total budgetary resources available	413	417	428
	Memorandum (non-add) entries:			
1940	Unobligated balance expiring	–5		
1941	Unexpired unobligated balance, end of year	39		
	Change in obligated balance:			
	Unpaid obligations:			
3000	Unpaid obligations, brought forward, Oct 1	63	62	101
3010	New obligations, unexpired accounts	369	417	428
3011	Obligations ("upward adjustments"), expired accounts	1		
3020	Outlays (gross)	–368	–378	–382
3041	Recoveries of prior year unpaid obligations, expired	–3		
3050	Unpaid obligations, end of year	62	101	147
	Memorandum (non-add) entries:			
3100	Obligated balance, start of year	63	62	101
3200	Obligated balance, end of year	62	101	147
	Budget authority and outlays, net:			
	Discretionary:			
4000	Budget authority, gross	378	378	428
	Outlays, gross:			
4010	Outlays from new discretionary authority	310	284	321
4011	Outlays from discretionary balances	58	94	61
4020	Outlays, gross (total)	368	378	382
	Offsets against gross budget authority and outlays:			
	Offsetting collections (collected) from:			
4030	Federal sources	–1	–1	–1
4040	Offsets against gross budget authority and outlays (total)	–1	–1	–1
4180	Budget authority, net (total)	377	377	427
4190	Outlays, net (total)	367	377	381

This appropriation provides for the operation of the Federal Government's archives and records management activities, the preservation of permanently valuable historical records, and their access and use by the public.

Legislative Archives, Presidential Libraries, and Museum Services.—This activity provides for the Center for Legislative Archives and the Presidential Materials Division, which provide records management services to Congress and the White House; the Presidential Libraries of fifteen former Presidents; and nationwide education, outreach, and exhibits programs, including the National Archives Museum in Washington, DC.

Citizen Services.—This activity provides for public access to and engagement with permanently valuable Federal Government records by the researcher community and the general public at public research rooms, online at www.archives.gov, and through innovative tools and technology to support collaboration with the public.

Agency and Related Services.—This activity provides for the services NARA provides to other Federal agencies, including records management, appropriate declassification of classified national security information, oversight of the classification system and controlled, unclassified information, and improvements to the administration of the Freedom of Information Act by the Office of Government Information Services; the electronic records management activities of the Electronic Records Archives system; and publication of the Federal Register, U.S. Statutes-at-Large, and Presidential Papers.

Facility Operations.—This activity provides for the operations and maintenance of NARA facilities.

Electronic Records Initiative.—This activity provides for expenses necessary to enhance the Federal Government's ability to electronically preserve, manage, and store Government records.

Object Classification (in millions of dollars)

Identification code 088–0300–0–1–804		2021 actual	2022 est.	2023 est.
	Direct obligations:			
	Personnel compensation:			
11.1	Full-time permanent	136	140	164
11.3	Other than full-time permanent	1	1	
11.5	Other personnel compensation	3	3	3
11.9	Total personnel compensation	140	144	167
12.1	Civilian personnel benefits	50	52	55
22.0	Transportation of things		1	1
23.1	Rental payments to GSA	8	9	9
23.2	Rental payments to others	1	2	3
23.3	Communications, utilities, and miscellaneous charges	11	12	14
24.0	Printing and reproduction			1
25.1	Advisory and assistance services	16	8	8
25.2	Other services from non-Federal sources	28	30	27
25.3	Other goods and services from Federal sources	21	30	35
25.4	Operation and maintenance of facilities	35	35	36
25.7	Operation and maintenance of equipment	49	43	44
26.0	Supplies and materials	1	6	4
31.0	Equipment	8	14	22
32.0	Land and structures		30	1
99.0	Direct obligations	368	416	427
99.0	Reimbursable obligations	1	1	1
99.9	Total new obligations, unexpired accounts	369	417	428

Employment Summary

Identification code 088–0300–0–1–804		2021 actual	2022 est.	2023 est.
1001	Direct civilian full-time equivalent employment	1,382	1,439	1,631
2001	Reimbursable civilian full-time equivalent employment	18	22	22

OFFICE OF INSPECTOR GENERAL

For necessary expenses of the Office of Inspector General in carrying out the provisions of the Inspector General Reform Act of 2008 (Public Law 110–409), and the Inspector General Act of 1978 (5 U.S.C. App.), and for the hire of passenger motor vehicles, $5,980,000.

Note.—A full-year 2022 appropriation for this account was not enacted at the time the Budget was prepared; therefore, the Budget assumes this account is operating under the Continuing Appropriations Act, 2022 (Division A of Public Law 117–43, as amended). The amounts included for 2022 reflect the annualized level provided by the continuing resolution.

Program and Financing (in millions of dollars)

Identification code 088–0305–0–1–804		2021 actual	2022 est.	2023 est.
	Obligations by program activity:			
0001	Office of Inspector General	5	5	6
	Budgetary resources:			
	Budget authority:			
	Appropriations, discretionary:			
1100	Appropriation	5	5	6
1930	Total budgetary resources available	5	5	6
	Change in obligated balance:			
	Unpaid obligations:			
3000	Unpaid obligations, brought forward, Oct 1	1	1	1
3010	New obligations, unexpired accounts	5	5	6
3020	Outlays (gross)	–5	–5	–6
3050	Unpaid obligations, end of year	1	1	1

		2021 actual	2022 est.	2023 est.
	Memorandum (non-add) entries:			
3100	Obligated balance, start of year	1	1	1
3200	Obligated balance, end of year	1	1	1
	Budget authority and outlays, net:			
	Discretionary:			
4000	Budget authority, gross	5	5	6
	Outlays, gross:			
4010	Outlays from new discretionary authority	4	4	5
4011	Outlays from discretionary balances	1	1	1
4020	Outlays, gross (total)	5	5	6
4180	Budget authority, net (total)	5	5	6
4190	Outlays, net (total)	5	5	6

The Office of Inspector General (OIG) provides independent audits, investigations, and other services; and serves as an independent, internal advocate to promote economy, efficiency, and effectiveness at NARA. The Inspector General Act of 1978, as amended, established the OIG's independent role and general responsibilities. The OIG investigates misconduct, evaluates NARA's performance, makes recommendations for improvements, and follows up to ensure economical, efficient, and effective operations and compliance with laws, policies, and regulations.

Object Classification (in millions of dollars)

Identification code 088–0305–0–1–804		2021 actual	2022 est.	2023 est.
	Direct obligations:			
11.1	Personnel compensation: Full-time permanent	3	3	3
12.1	Civilian personnel benefits	1	1	1
25.1	Advisory and assistance services	1	1	2
99.9	Total new obligations, unexpired accounts	5	5	6

Employment Summary

Identification code 088–0305–0–1–804	2021 actual	2022 est.	2023 est.
1001 Direct civilian full-time equivalent employment	19	24	24

REPAIRS AND RESTORATION

For the repair, alteration, and improvement of archives facilities, and to provide adequate storage for holdings, $7,500,000, to remain available until expended.

Note.—A full-year 2022 appropriation for this account was not enacted at the time the Budget was prepared; therefore, the Budget assumes this account is operating under the Continuing Appropriations Act, 2022 (Division A of Public Law 117–43, as amended). The amounts included for 2022 reflect the annualized level provided by the continuing resolution.

Program and Financing (in millions of dollars)

Identification code 088–0302–0–1–804		2021 actual	2022 est.	2023 est.
	Obligations by program activity:			
0001	Repairs and Restoration (Direct)	7	14	9
	Budgetary resources:			
	Unobligated balance:			
1000	Unobligated balance brought forward, Oct 1	3	6	2
	Budget authority:			
	Appropriations, discretionary:			
1100	Appropriation	10	10	8
1930	Total budgetary resources available	13	16	10
	Memorandum (non-add) entries:			
1941	Unexpired unobligated balance, end of year	6	2	1
	Change in obligated balance:			
	Unpaid obligations:			
3000	Unpaid obligations, brought forward, Oct 1	7	8	6
3010	New obligations, unexpired accounts	7	14	9
3020	Outlays (gross)	–6	–16	–12
3050	Unpaid obligations, end of year	8	6	3
	Memorandum (non-add) entries:			
3100	Obligated balance, start of year	7	8	6
3200	Obligated balance, end of year	8	6	3

		2021 actual	2022 est.	2023 est.
	Budget authority and outlays, net:			
	Discretionary:			
4000	Budget authority, gross	10	10	8
	Outlays, gross:			
4010	Outlays from new discretionary authority	3	9	7
4011	Outlays from discretionary balances	3	7	5
4020	Outlays, gross (total)	6	16	12
4180	Budget authority, net (total)	10	10	8
4190	Outlays, net (total)	6	16	12

This appropriation provides for the repair, alteration, and improvement of National Archives facilities and Presidential Libraries nationwide. Funding provided allows NARA to maintain a safe environment for public visitors and researchers, NARA employees, and the permanently valuable Federal Government records stored in NARA buildings.

Object Classification (in millions of dollars)

Identification code 088–0302–0–1–804		2021 actual	2022 est.	2023 est.
	Direct obligations:			
25.1	Advisory and assistance services	1		
25.4	Operation and maintenance of facilities	1		
32.0	Land and structures	5	14	9
99.9	Total new obligations, unexpired accounts	7	14	9

NATIONAL HISTORICAL PUBLICATIONS AND RECORDS COMMISSION

GRANTS PROGRAM

For necessary expenses for allocations and grants for historical publications and records as authorized by 44 U.S.C. 2504, $9,500,000, to remain available until expended.

Note.—A full-year 2022 appropriation for this account was not enacted at the time the Budget was prepared; therefore, the Budget assumes this account is operating under the Continuing Appropriations Act, 2022 (Division A of Public Law 117–43, as amended). The amounts included for 2022 reflect the annualized level provided by the continuing resolution.

Program and Financing (in millions of dollars)

Identification code 088–0301–0–1–804		2021 actual	2022 est.	2023 est.
	Obligations by program activity:			
0001	National Historical Publications and Records Commission (Direct)	7	8	10
0900	Total new obligations, unexpired accounts (object class 41.0)	7	8	10
	Budgetary resources:			
	Unobligated balance:			
1000	Unobligated balance brought forward, Oct 1	1	1	
	Budget authority:			
	Appropriations, discretionary:			
1100	Appropriation	7	7	10
1930	Total budgetary resources available	8	8	10
	Memorandum (non-add) entries:			
1941	Unexpired unobligated balance, end of year	1		
	Change in obligated balance:			
	Unpaid obligations:			
3000	Unpaid obligations, brought forward, Oct 1	11	12	10
3010	New obligations, unexpired accounts	7	8	10
3020	Outlays (gross)	–6	–10	–8
3050	Unpaid obligations, end of year	12	10	12
	Memorandum (non-add) entries:			
3100	Obligated balance, start of year	11	12	10
3200	Obligated balance, end of year	12	10	12
	Budget authority and outlays, net:			
	Discretionary:			
4000	Budget authority, gross	7	7	10
	Outlays, gross:			
4010	Outlays from new discretionary authority		1	1
4011	Outlays from discretionary balances	6	9	7
4020	Outlays, gross (total)	6	10	8
4180	Budget authority, net (total)	7	7	10
4190	Outlays, net (total)	6	10	8

NATIONAL HISTORICAL PUBLICATIONS AND RECORDS COMMISSION—Continued

The National Historical Publications and Records Commission (NHPRC) grants program provides for grants to preserve and publish non-Federal records that document American history.

RECORDS CENTER REVOLVING FUND

Program and Financing (in millions of dollars)

Identification code 088–4578–0–4–804	2021 actual	2022 est.	2023 est.
Obligations by program activity:			
0001 Direct program activity	33	17	....
0801 Records Center Revolving Fund (Reimbursable)	161	194	194
0900 Total new obligations, unexpired accounts	194	211	194
Budgetary resources:			
Unobligated balance:			
1000 Unobligated balance brought forward, Oct 1	40	54	51
1021 Recoveries of prior year unpaid obligations	3	4	4
1070 Unobligated balance (total)	43	58	55
Budget authority:			
Appropriations, discretionary:			
1100 Appropriation	50	....	....
Spending authority from offsetting collections, discretionary:			
1700 Collected	184	204	198
1701 Change in uncollected payments, Federal sources	–29	....	....
1750 Spending auth from offsetting collections, disc (total)	155	204	198
1900 Budget authority (total)	205	204	198
1930 Total budgetary resources available	248	262	253
Memorandum (non-add) entries:			
1941 Unexpired unobligated balance, end of year	54	51	59
Change in obligated balance:			
Unpaid obligations:			
3000 Unpaid obligations, brought forward, Oct 1	26	32	35
3010 New obligations, unexpired accounts	194	211	194
3020 Outlays (gross)	–185	–204	–198
3040 Recoveries of prior year unpaid obligations, unexpired	–3	–4	–4
3050 Unpaid obligations, end of year	32	35	27
Uncollected payments:			
3060 Uncollected pymts, Fed sources, brought forward, Oct 1	–55	–26	–26
3070 Change in uncollected pymts, Fed sources, unexpired	29	....	....
3090 Uncollected pymts, Fed sources, end of year	–26	–26	–26
Memorandum (non-add) entries:			
3100 Obligated balance, start of year	–29	6	9
3200 Obligated balance, end of year	6	9	1
Budget authority and outlays, net:			
Discretionary:			
4000 Budget authority, gross	205	204	198
Outlays, gross:			
4010 Outlays from new discretionary authority	170	182	176
4011 Outlays from discretionary balances	15	22	22
4020 Outlays, gross (total)	185	204	198
Offsets against gross budget authority and outlays:			
Offsetting collections (collected) from:			
4030 Federal sources	–183	–202	–195
4033 Non-Federal sources	–1	–2	–3
4040 Offsets against gross budget authority and outlays (total)	–184	–204	–198
Additional offsets against gross budget authority only:			
4050 Change in uncollected pymts, Fed sources, unexpired	29	....	....
4070 Budget authority, net (discretionary)	50	....	....
4080 Outlays, net (discretionary)	1	....	....
4180 Budget authority, net (total)	50	....	....
4190 Outlays, net (total)	1	....	....

This full cost recovery revolving fund provides for the storage and related services that NARA Records Centers provide to Federal agency customers. NARA Federal Records Centers provide low-cost, high-quality storage and related services, including: transfer, reference, re-file, and disposal services for temporary and pre-archival Federal Government records.

Object Classification (in millions of dollars)

Identification code 088–4578–0–4–804	2021 actual	2022 est.	2023 est.
11.1 Direct obligations: Personnel compensation: Full-time permanent	....	4	....
11.9 Total personnel compensation	....	4	....
12.1 Civilian personnel benefits	....	1	....
23.1 Rental payments to GSA	30	6	....
25.1 Advisory and assistance services	....	1	....
25.2 Other services from non-Federal sources	....	4	....
25.7 Operation and maintenance of equipment	....	1	....
31.0 Equipment	3	....	....
99.0 Direct obligations	33	17	....
Reimbursable obligations:			
Personnel compensation:			
11.1 Full-time permanent	67	68	70
11.3 Other than full-time permanent	....	1	1
11.5 Other personnel compensation	4	3	3
11.9 Total personnel compensation	71	72	74
12.1 Civilian personnel benefits	27	26	27
22.0 Transportation of things	1	1	1
23.1 Rental payments to GSA	15	48	48
23.2 Rental payments to others	12	11	12
23.3 Communications, utilities, and miscellaneous charges	4	4	4
25.1 Advisory and assistance services	3	3	2
25.2 Other services from non-Federal sources	5	5	5
25.3 Other goods and services from Federal sources	10	11	10
25.7 Operation and maintenance of equipment	11	10	9
26.0 Supplies and materials	1	1	1
31.0 Equipment	1	2	1
99.0 Reimbursable obligations	161	194	194
99.9 Total new obligations, unexpired accounts	194	211	194

Employment Summary

Identification code 088–4578–0–4–804	2021 actual	2022 est.	2023 est.
2001 Reimbursable civilian full-time equivalent employment	1,234	1,298	1,298

Trust Funds

NATIONAL ARCHIVES GIFT FUND

Special and Trust Fund Receipts (in millions of dollars)

Identification code 088–8127–0–7–804	2021 actual	2022 est.	2023 est.
0100 Balance, start of year	....	....	....
Receipts:			
Current law:			
1130 Gifts and Bequests, National Archives Gift Fund	2	1	1
1130 Interest and Dividends on Non-Federal Securities, National Archives Gift Fund	1	1	1
1130 Realized Gains on Non-Federal Securities, National Archives Gift Fund	....	1	1
1130 Proceeds from Non-Federal Securities not Immediately Reinvested, National Archives Gift Fund	....	1	1
1199 Total current law receipts	3	4	4
1999 Total receipts	3	4	4
2000 Total: Balances and receipts	3	4	4
Appropriations:			
Current law:			
2101 National Archives Gift Fund	–3	–4	–3
5099 Balance, end of year	....	....	1

Program and Financing (in millions of dollars)

Identification code 088–8127–0–7–804	2021 actual	2022 est.	2023 est.
Obligations by program activity:			
0801 National Archives Gift Fund (Reimbursable)	2	4	4
Budgetary resources:			
Unobligated balance:			
1000 Unobligated balance brought forward, Oct 1	5	6	6

OTHER INDEPENDENT AGENCIES

		2021 actual	2022 est.	2023 est.
	Budget authority:			
	Appropriations, mandatory:			
1201	Appropriation (special or trust fund)	3	4	3
1930	Total budgetary resources available	8	10	9
	Memorandum (non-add) entries:			
1941	Unexpired unobligated balance, end of year	6	6	5
	Change in obligated balance:			
	Unpaid obligations:			
3010	New obligations, unexpired accounts	2	4	4
3020	Outlays (gross)	–2	–4	–4
	Budget authority and outlays, net:			
	Mandatory:			
4090	Budget authority, gross	3	4	3
	Outlays, gross:			
4100	Outlays from new mandatory authority	2	3	2
4101	Outlays from mandatory balances		1	2
4110	Outlays, gross (total)	2	4	4
4180	Budget authority, net (total)	3	4	3
4190	Outlays, net (total)	2	4	4
	Memorandum (non-add) entries:			
5000	Total investments, SOY: Federal securities: Par value	5	6	6
5001	Total investments, EOY: Federal securities: Par value	6	6	6
5010	Total investments, SOY: non-Fed securities: Market value	27	27	27
5011	Total investments, EOY: non-Fed securities: Market value	27	27	27

The National Archives Trust Fund Board may accept conditional and unconditional gifts or bequests of money, securities, or other personal property for the benefit of NARA activities. NARA receives endowments from private foundations to offset a portion of the operating costs of Presidential Libraries.

Object Classification (in millions of dollars)

Identification code 088–8127–0–7–804		2021 actual	2022 est.	2023 est.
	Reimbursable obligations:			
25.2	Other services from non-Federal sources		2	2
33.0	Investments and loans	1	1	1
94.0	Financial transfers	1	1	1
99.9	Total new obligations, unexpired accounts	2	4	4

NATIONAL ARCHIVES TRUST FUND

Program and Financing (in millions of dollars)

Identification code 088–8436–0–8–804		2021 actual	2022 est.	2023 est.
	Obligations by program activity:			
0801	Sales	2	3	4
0802	Presidential libraries	8	8	8
0900	Total new obligations, unexpired accounts	10	11	12
	Budgetary resources:			
	Unobligated balance:			
1000	Unobligated balance brought forward, Oct 1	4	2	2
1021	Recoveries of prior year unpaid obligations	1	1	1
1033	Recoveries of prior year paid obligations	3	1	1
1070	Unobligated balance (total)	8	4	4
	Budget authority:			
	Spending authority from offsetting collections, mandatory:			
1800	Collected	4	9	10
1930	Total budgetary resources available	12	13	14
	Memorandum (non-add) entries:			
1941	Unexpired unobligated balance, end of year	2	2	2
	Change in obligated balance:			
	Unpaid obligations:			
3000	Unpaid obligations, brought forward, Oct 1	3	2	2
3010	New obligations, unexpired accounts	10	11	12
3020	Outlays (gross)	–10	–10	–11
3040	Recoveries of prior year unpaid obligations, unexpired	–1	–1	–1
3050	Unpaid obligations, end of year	2	2	2
	Memorandum (non-add) entries:			
3100	Obligated balance, start of year	3	2	2
3200	Obligated balance, end of year	2	2	2
	Budget authority and outlays, net:			
	Mandatory:			
4090	Budget authority, gross	4	9	10
	Outlays, gross:			
4100	Outlays from new mandatory authority	4	7	8
4101	Outlays from mandatory balances	6	3	3
4110	Outlays, gross (total)	10	10	11
	Offsets against gross budget authority and outlays:			
	Offsetting collections (collected) from:			
4120	Federal sources		–1	–1
4123	Non-Federal sources	–7	–9	–10
4130	Offsets against gross budget authority and outlays (total)	–7	–10	–11
	Additional offsets against gross budget authority only:			
4143	Recoveries of prior year paid obligations, unexpired accounts	3	1	1
4170	Outlays, net (mandatory)	3		
4180	Budget authority, net (total)			
4190	Outlays, net (total)	3		
	Memorandum (non-add) entries:			
5000	Total investments, SOY: Federal securities: Par value	6	4	4
5001	Total investments, EOY: Federal securities: Par value	4	4	4
5010	Total investments, SOY: non-Fed securities: Market value	69	82	82
5011	Total investments, EOY: non-Fed securities: Market value	82	82	82

The Archivist of the United States furnishes, for a fee, copies of unrestricted records in the custody of the National Archives (44 U.S.C. 2116). Proceeds from the sale of copies of microfilm publications, reproductions, special works, and other publications, and admission fees to Presidential Library museum rooms are deposited to the National Archives Trust Fund (44 U.S.C. 2112, 2307).

Object Classification (in millions of dollars)

Identification code 088–8436–0–8–804		2021 actual	2022 est.	2023 est.
	Reimbursable obligations:			
11.1	Personnel compensation: Full-time permanent	3	4	4
12.1	Civilian personnel benefits	1	1	1
25.2	Other services from non-Federal sources	2	1	2
25.3	Other goods and services from Federal sources		1	1
26.0	Supplies and materials	1	1	1
33.0	Investments and loans	3	3	3
99.9	Total new obligations, unexpired accounts	10	11	12

Employment Summary

Identification code 088–8436–0–8–804		2021 actual	2022 est.	2023 est.
2001	Reimbursable civilian full-time equivalent employment	51	59	59

NATIONAL CAPITAL PLANNING COMMISSION

Federal Funds

SALARIES AND EXPENSES

For necessary expenses of the National Capital Planning Commission under chapter 87 of title 40, United States Code, including services as authorized by 5 U.S.C. 3109, $8,630,000: Provided, That one-quarter of 1 percent of the funds provided under this heading may be used for official reception and representational expenses associated with hosting international visitors engaged in the planning and physical development of world capitals.

Note.—A full-year 2022 appropriation for this account was not enacted at the time the Budget was prepared; therefore, the Budget assumes this account is operating under the Continuing Appropriations Act, 2022 (Division A of Public Law 117–43, as amended). The amounts included for 2022 reflect the annualized level provided by the continuing resolution.

Program and Financing (in millions of dollars)

Identification code 394–2500–0–1–451		2021 actual	2022 est.	2023 est.
	Obligations by program activity:			
0001	Salaries and expenses	8	8	9

National Capital Planning Commission—Continued
Federal Funds—Continued

SALARIES AND EXPENSES—Continued

Program and Financing—Continued

Identification code 394–2500–0–1–451	2021 actual	2022 est.	2023 est.
Budgetary resources:			
Budget authority:			
Appropriations, discretionary:			
1100 Appropriation	8	8	9
1930 Total budgetary resources available	8	8	9
Change in obligated balance:			
Unpaid obligations:			
3000 Unpaid obligations, brought forward, Oct 1	2	1	1
3010 New obligations, unexpired accounts	8	8	9
3020 Outlays (gross)	–9	–8	–9
3050 Unpaid obligations, end of year	1	1	1
Memorandum (non-add) entries:			
3100 Obligated balance, start of year	2	1	1
3200 Obligated balance, end of year	1	1	1
Budget authority and outlays, net:			
Discretionary:			
4000 Budget authority, gross	8	8	9
Outlays, gross:			
4010 Outlays from new discretionary authority	8	7	8
4011 Outlays from discretionary balances	1	1	1
4020 Outlays, gross (total)	9	8	9
4180 Budget authority, net (total)	8	8	9
4190 Outlays, net (total)	9	8	9

The National Capital Planning Commission (NCPC) is the central planning agency for the Federal Government in the National Capital Region. Through its planning initiatives, policy-making, and review of development proposals, NCPC helps guide Federal development while preserving the Capital City's unique resources. NCPC will continue to work with the District of Columbia and Federal and regional partners to develop comprehensive policies and planning initiatives that support the Federal interest and contribute to the best urban design, infrastructure, resource, and land-use outcomes for the Region. In addition, NCPC will continue to ensure that all Federal development in the Region meets the highest design standards and will review Federal plans for regional capital improvements.

Object Classification (in millions of dollars)

Identification code 394–2500–0–1–451	2021 actual	2022 est.	2023 est.
Direct obligations:			
11.1 Personnel compensation: Full-time permanent	4	4	5
12.1 Civilian personnel benefits	1	1	2
23.1 Rental payments to GSA		2	1
23.2 Rental payments to others	2		
25.3 Other goods and services from Federal sources	1	1	1
99.9 Total new obligations, unexpired accounts	8	8	9

Employment Summary

Identification code 394–2500–0–1–451	2021 actual	2022 est.	2023 est.
1001 Direct civilian full-time equivalent employment	33	35	35

NATIONAL COMMISSION ON MILITARY, NATIONAL, AND PUBLIC SERVICE

Federal Funds

NATIONAL COMMISSION ON MILITARY, NATIONAL, AND PUBLIC SERVICE

Program and Financing (in millions of dollars)

Identification code 236–2978–0–1–054	2021 actual	2022 est.	2023 est.
Budgetary resources:			
Unobligated balance:			
1000 Unobligated balance brought forward, Oct 1	1	1	1
1930 Total budgetary resources available	1	1	1
Memorandum (non-add) entries:			
1941 Unexpired unobligated balance, end of year	1	1	1
Change in obligated balance:			
Unpaid obligations:			
3000 Unpaid obligations, brought forward, Oct 1	9	9	4
3020 Outlays (gross)		–5	–4
3050 Unpaid obligations, end of year	9	4	
Memorandum (non-add) entries:			
3100 Obligated balance, start of year	9	9	4
3200 Obligated balance, end of year	9	4	
Budget authority and outlays, net:			
Discretionary:			
Outlays, gross:			
4011 Outlays from discretionary balances		5	4
4180 Budget authority, net (total)			
4190 Outlays, net (total)		5	4

NATIONAL COMMISSION ON MILITARY AVIATION SAFETY

Federal Funds

NATIONAL COMMISSION ON MILITARY AVIATION SAFETY

Program and Financing (in millions of dollars)

Identification code 246–2865–0–1–054	2021 actual	2022 est.	2023 est.
Obligations by program activity:			
0001 Direct program activity	2		
0900 Total new obligations, unexpired accounts (object class 25.3)	2		
Budgetary resources:			
Unobligated balance:			
1000 Unobligated balance brought forward, Oct 1	2		
1930 Total budgetary resources available	2		
Change in obligated balance:			
Unpaid obligations:			
3000 Unpaid obligations, brought forward, Oct 1	2	2	
3010 New obligations, unexpired accounts	2		
3020 Outlays (gross)	–2	–2	
3050 Unpaid obligations, end of year	2		
Memorandum (non-add) entries:			
3100 Obligated balance, start of year	2	2	
3200 Obligated balance, end of year	2		
Budget authority and outlays, net:			
Discretionary:			
Outlays, gross:			
4011 Outlays from discretionary balances	2	2	
4180 Budget authority, net (total)			
4190 Outlays, net (total)	2	2	

NATIONAL COUNCIL ON DISABILITY

Federal Funds

SALARIES AND EXPENSES

For expenses necessary for the National Council on Disability as authorized by title IV of the Rehabilitation Act of 1973, $3,850,000.

Note.—A full-year 2022 appropriation for this account was not enacted at the time the Budget was prepared; therefore, the Budget assumes this account is operating under the Continuing Appropriations Act, 2022 (Division A of Public Law 117–43, as amended). The amounts included for 2022 reflect the annualized level provided by the continuing resolution.

Program and Financing (in millions of dollars)

Identification code 413–3500–0–1–506	2021 actual	2022 est.	2023 est.
Obligations by program activity:			
0001 Salaries and expenses	3	3	3

OTHER INDEPENDENT AGENCIES

National Credit Union Administration
Federal Funds — 1289

		2021 actual	2022 est.	2023 est.
0002	Other services from non-Federal sources		1	1
0900	Total new obligations, unexpired accounts	3	4	4
	Budgetary resources:			
	Budget authority:			
	Appropriations, discretionary:			
1100	Appropriation	3	4	4
1930	Total budgetary resources available	3	4	4
	Change in obligated balance:			
	Unpaid obligations:			
3000	Unpaid obligations, brought forward, Oct 1	1	1	
3010	New obligations, unexpired accounts	3	4	4
3020	Outlays (gross)	−3	−5	−4
3050	Unpaid obligations, end of year	1		
	Memorandum (non-add) entries:			
3100	Obligated balance, start of year	1	1	
3200	Obligated balance, end of year	1		
	Budget authority and outlays, net:			
	Discretionary:			
4000	Budget authority, gross	3	4	4
	Outlays, gross:			
4010	Outlays from new discretionary authority	3	4	4
4011	Outlays from discretionary balances		1	
4020	Outlays, gross (total)	3	5	4
4180	Budget authority, net (total)	3	4	4
4190	Outlays, net (total)	3	5	4

The National Council on Disability (NCD), an independent Federal agency, is composed of nine members appointed by the President and the Congress. Established under the Rehabilitation Act of 1973, as amended by the Workforce Innovation and Opportunity Act, the NCD is responsible for reviewing the Federal Government's laws, programs, and policies which affect people with disabilities. The NCD also makes recommendations on issues affecting individuals with disabilities and their families to the President; the Congress; the Rehabilitation Services Administration; the National Institute on Disability, Independent Living, and Rehabilitation Research; and other Federal Departments and agencies.

Object Classification (in millions of dollars)

Identification code 413–3500–0–1–506	2021 actual	2022 est.	2023 est.
Direct obligations:			
11.1 Personnel compensation: Full-time permanent	1	1	1
25.2 Other services from non-Federal sources	1	2	2
99.0 Direct obligations	2	3	3
99.5 Adjustment for rounding	1	1	1
99.9 Total new obligations, unexpired accounts	3	4	4

Employment Summary

Identification code 413–3500–0–1–506	2021 actual	2022 est.	2023 est.
1001 Direct civilian full-time equivalent employment	12	12	12

NATIONAL CREDIT UNION ADMINISTRATION

Federal Funds

OPERATING FUND

Program and Financing (in millions of dollars)

Identification code 025–4056–0–3–373	2021 actual	2022 est.	2023 est.
Obligations by program activity:			
0801 Safety, Soundness, and Consumer Protection	200	221	252
0803 Improve Access to Equitable Financial Services	14	14	16
0804 Mission Support	91	94	105
0805 Office of Inspector General	3	4	4
0900 Total new obligations, unexpired accounts	308	333	377
Budgetary resources:			
Unobligated balance:			
1000 Unobligated balance brought forward, Oct 1	151	176	175
Budget authority:			
Spending authority from offsetting collections, mandatory:			
1800 Collected	320	332	365
1801 Change in uncollected payments, Federal sources	13		
1850 Spending auth from offsetting collections, mand (total)	333	332	365
1930 Total budgetary resources available	484	508	540
Memorandum (non-add) entries:			
1941 Unexpired unobligated balance, end of year	176	175	163
Change in obligated balance:			
Unpaid obligations:			
3000 Unpaid obligations, brought forward, Oct 1	63	61	21
3010 New obligations, unexpired accounts	308	333	377
3020 Outlays (gross)	−310	−373	−364
3050 Unpaid obligations, end of year	61	21	34
Uncollected payments:			
3060 Uncollected pymts, Fed sources, brought forward, Oct 1	−64	−77	−77
3070 Change in uncollected pymts, Fed sources, unexpired	−13		
3090 Uncollected pymts, Fed sources, end of year	−77	−77	−77
Memorandum (non-add) entries:			
3100 Obligated balance, start of year	−1	−16	−56
3200 Obligated balance, end of year	−16	−56	−43
Budget authority and outlays, net:			
Mandatory:			
4090 Budget authority, gross	333	332	365
Outlays, gross:			
4100 Outlays from new mandatory authority	197	315	347
4101 Outlays from mandatory balances	113	58	17
4110 Outlays, gross (total)	310	373	364
Offsets against gross budget authority and outlays:			
Offsetting collections (collected) from:			
4120 Federal sources	−195	−200	−221
4124 Offsetting governmental collections	−125	−132	−144
4130 Offsets against gross budget authority and outlays (total)	−320	−332	−365
Additional offsets against gross budget authority only:			
4140 Change in uncollected pymts, Fed sources, unexpired	−13		
4170 Outlays, net (mandatory)	−10	41	−1
4180 Budget authority, net (total)			
4190 Outlays, net (total)	−10	41	−1
Memorandum (non-add) entries:			
5000 Total investments, SOY: Federal securities: Par value	140	121	121
5001 Total investments, EOY: Federal securities: Par value	121	121	121

The mission of the National Credit Union Administration (NCUA) is to protect the system of cooperative credit and its member-owners through effective chartering, supervision, regulation, and insurance. Credit unions are member-owned, cooperative associations organized for the purpose of promoting thrift and creating a source of credit for members. As of September 30, 2021, there were 3,122 federally-chartered credit unions with total assets of more than $1 trillion.

NCUA, through its Operating Fund, conducts activities prescribed by the Federal Credit Union Act of 1934, which include: 1) chartering new Federal credit unions; 2) approving field of membership applications of Federal credit unions; 3) promulgating regulations and providing guidance; 4) performing regulatory compliance and safety and soundness examinations; 5) implementing and administering enforcement actions, such as prohibition orders, orders to cease and desist, orders of conservatorship and orders of liquidation; and 6) administering the National Credit Union Share Insurance Fund (SIF), which provides insurance to Federal credit unions (FCUs) and federally-insured state-chartered credit unions (FISCUs).

To better demonstrate how the NCUA's budget is used to achieve its strategic goals, the Operating Fund's obligations by program activity are presented in the same categories shown in the agency's 2022–2026 Strategic Plan. Amounts shown for "Safety and Soundness, and Consumer Protection" correspond to programs that contribute to the NCUA's goal to "Ensure a safe, sound and viable system of cooperative credit that protects consumers." Amounts shown for Improve Access to Equitable Financial Services" correspond to programs that contribute to the NCUA's goal to "Improve the

National Credit Union Administration—Continued
Federal Funds—Continued

OPERATING FUND—Continued

financial well-being of individuals and communities through access to affordable and equitable financial products and services," which encompasses the NCUA's ACCESS initiative and other agency efforts to increase financial inclusion." Amounts shown for "Mission Support" correspond to programs that contribute to the NCUA's goal to "Maximize organizational performance to enable mission success."

NCUA funds its activities through operating fees levied on all FCUs, and through reimbursements from the SIF, which is funded by FCUs and FISCUs.

Object Classification (in millions of dollars)

Identification code 025–4056–0–3–373		2021 actual	2022 est.	2023 est.
11.1	Reimbursable obligations: Personnel compensation: Full-time permanent	164	176	187
11.9	Total personnel compensation	164	176	187
12.1	Civilian personnel benefits	69	78	81
21.0	Travel and transportation of persons		18	24
23.2	Rental payments to others	5	1	1
23.3	Communications, utilities, and miscellaneous charges	6	4	5
25.2	Other services from non-Federal sources	45	37	67
25.3	Other goods and services from Federal sources	6	6	6
25.4	Operation and maintenance of facilities	3	3	3
26.0	Supplies and materials		1	1
31.0	Equipment	10	9	2
99.9	Total new obligations, unexpired accounts	308	333	377

Employment Summary

Identification code 025–4056–0–3–373		2021 actual	2022 est.	2023 est.
2001	Reimbursable civilian full-time equivalent employment	1,144	1,196	1,204

CREDIT UNION SHARE INSURANCE FUND

Program and Financing (in millions of dollars)

Identification code 025–4468–0–3–373		2021 actual	2022 est.	2023 est.
	Obligations by program activity:			
0801	Payments to the Operating Fund for services and facilities	208	200	221
0802	Other Administrative Expenses	6	6	5
0803	Working Capital	19	52	54
0804	Liquidation Expenses	218	261	271
0805	NCUA Guaranteed Notes program	1,306		211
0806	NGN Program closure final liquidation expenses	1,471		
0900	Total new obligations, unexpired accounts	3,228	519	762
	Budgetary resources:			
	Unobligated balance:			
1000	Unobligated balance brought forward, Oct 1	16,556	18,558	20,421
	Budget authority:			
	Spending authority from offsetting collections, mandatory:			
1800	Collected	5,217	2,382	1,367
1801	Change in uncollected payments, Federal sources	13		
1850	Spending auth from offsetting collections, mand (total)	5,230	2,382	1,367
1930	Total budgetary resources available	21,786	20,940	21,788
	Memorandum (non-add) entries:			
1941	Unexpired unobligated balance, end of year	18,558	20,421	21,026
	Change in obligated balance:			
	Unpaid obligations:			
3000	Unpaid obligations, brought forward, Oct 1	71	93	5
3010	New obligations, unexpired accounts	3,228	519	762
3020	Outlays (gross)	–3,206	–607	–762
3050	Unpaid obligations, end of year	93	5	5
	Uncollected payments:			
3060	Uncollected pymts, Fed sources, brought forward, Oct 1	–84	–97	–97
3070	Change in uncollected pymts, Fed sources, unexpired	–13		
3090	Uncollected pymts, Fed sources, end of year	–97	–97	–97
	Memorandum (non-add) entries:			
3100	Obligated balance, start of year	–13	–4	–92
3200	Obligated balance, end of year	–4	–92	–92
	Budget authority and outlays, net:			
	Mandatory:			
4090	Budget authority, gross	5,230	2,382	1,367
	Outlays, gross:			
4100	Outlays from new mandatory authority	1,836	519	762
4101	Outlays from mandatory balances	1,370	88	
4110	Outlays, gross (total)	3,206	607	762
	Offsets against gross budget authority and outlays:			
	Offsetting collections (collected) from:			
4120	Federal sources	–4		
4121	Interest on Federal securities	136	–278	–295
4123	Non-Federal sources	–2,923	–27	–53
4124	Offsetting governmental collections	–2,426	–2,077	–1,019
4130	Offsets against gross budget authority and outlays (total)	–5,217	–2,382	–1,367
	Additional offsets against gross budget authority only:			
4140	Change in uncollected pymts, Fed sources, unexpired	–13		
4170	Outlays, net (mandatory)	–2,011	–1,775	–605
4180	Budget authority, net (total)			
4190	Outlays, net (total)	–2,011	–1,775	–605
	Memorandum (non-add) entries:			
5000	Total investments, SOY: Federal securities: Par value	16,610	18,528	22,777
5001	Total investments, EOY: Federal securities: Par value	18,528	22,777	23,382

Status of Guaranteed Loans (in millions of dollars)

Identification code 025–4468–0–3–373		2021 actual	2022 est.	2023 est.
	Cumulative balance of guaranteed loans outstanding:			
2210	Outstanding, start of year	2,337		
2231	Disbursements of new guaranteed loans			
2251	Repayments and prepayments	–2,337		
2251	Repayments and prepayments			
2290	Outstanding, end of year			
	Memorandum:			
2299	Guaranteed amount of guaranteed loans outstanding, end of year			

The primary purpose of the National Credit Union Share Insurance Fund (SIF) is to provide insurance for deposits of member accounts (also known as insured member shares) for nearly 129 million members in federally-chartered credit unions and state-chartered credit unions that qualify for insurance under the Federal Credit Union Act. As of September 30, 2021, over 4,990 state and Federal credit unions and 11 corporate credit unions were insured by the SIF, with insured member shares of $1.6 trillion—an increase of $200 billion, or 14.3 percent, year-on-year.

Following a cost allocation method that distributes NCUA costs between its insurance and regulatory functions, the SIF reimburses the NCUA Operating Fund for its share of administrative costs. In calendar year 2021, the SIF paid reimbursements of approximately $208 million to the Operating Fund.

In 2017, the NCUA Board closed the Temporary Corporate Credit Union Stabilization Fund (TCCUSF) and distributed the TCCUSF's funds, property, and other assets to the SIF. Through the distribution, the SIF assumed the activities and obligations of the TCCUSF, including NCUA Guaranteed Notes (NGN). As of September 30, 2021, all of the NGNs have fully matured and the NCUA will have no further guarantee payments required under the program. The NCUA anticipates continuing the orderly liquidation of all remaining NGN assets in 2022.

The SIF's normal operating level, which is the Fund's equity level above which the Board would be expected to authorize distributions was lowered to 1.33 percent of insured shares in 2022.

For more information, please see the Credit and Insurance chapter in the *Analytical Perspectives* volume of the Budget.

Object Classification (in millions of dollars)

Identification code 025–4468–0–3–373		2021 actual	2022 est.	2023 est.
	Reimbursable obligations:			
11.1	Personnel compensation: Full-time permanent	1		
25.2	Other services from non-Federal sources	5	6	5

		2021 actual	2022 est.	2023 est.
25.3	Other goods and services from Federal sources	208	200	221
42.0	Working Capital	19	52	54
42.0	Liquidation Expenses	218	261	271
43.0	NGN Payments to Investors	1,306	....	....
43.0	NGN Program Closure Final Liquidation Expenses	1,471	....	211
99.9	Total new obligations, unexpired accounts	3,228	519	762

Employment Summary

Identification code 025–4468–0–3–373	2021 actual	2022 est.	2023 est.
1001 Direct civilian full-time equivalent employment	....	5	....

CENTRAL LIQUIDITY FACILITY

Program and Financing (in millions of dollars)

Identification code 025–4470–0–3–373	2021 actual	2022 est.	2023 est.
Obligations by program activity:			
0801 Administration	1	2	2
0802 Membership Activity	20	10	405
0809 Reimbursable program activities, subtotal	21	12	407
0900 Total new obligations, unexpired accounts	21	12	407
Budgetary resources:			
Unobligated balance:			
1000 Unobligated balance brought forward, Oct 1	1,032	1,147	1,169
Budget authority:			
Spending authority from offsetting collections, mandatory:			
1800 Offsetting Collections (Subscribed Stock, CCU Guarantee Program)	136	....	....
1800 Offsetting Collections (Subscribed Stock)	....	28	28
1800 Offsetting Collections (Interest)	....	6	6
1850 Spending auth from offsetting collections, mand (total)	136	34	34
1930 Total budgetary resources available	1,168	1,181	1,203
Memorandum (non-add) entries:			
1941 Unexpired unobligated balance, end of year	1,147	1,169	796
Change in obligated balance:			
Unpaid obligations:			
3010 New obligations, unexpired accounts	21	12	407
3020 Outlays (gross)	–21	–12	–407
Uncollected payments:			
3060 Uncollected pymts, Fed sources, brought forward, Oct 1	–1	–1	–1
3090 Uncollected pymts, Fed sources, end of year	–1	–1	–1
Memorandum (non-add) entries:			
3100 Obligated balance, start of year	–1	–1	–1
3200 Obligated balance, end of year	–1	–1	–1
Budget authority and outlays, net:			
Mandatory:			
4090 Budget authority, gross	136	34	34
Outlays, gross:			
4100 Outlays from new mandatory authority	20	2	2
4101 Outlays from mandatory balances	1	10	405
4110 Outlays, gross (total)	21	12	407
Offsets against gross budget authority and outlays:			
Offsetting collections (collected) from:			
4121 Interest on Federal securities	–5	–6	–6
4123 Non-Federal sources	–131	–28	–28
4130 Offsets against gross budget authority and outlays (total)	–136	–34	–34
4170 Outlays, net (mandatory)	–115	–22	373
4180 Budget authority, net (total)	....	....	....
4190 Outlays, net (total)	–115	–22	373
Memorandum (non-add) entries:			
5000 Total investments, SOY: Federal securities: Par value	1,033	1,148	1,169
5001 Total investments, EOY: Federal securities: Par value	1,148	1,169	796

The purpose of the Central Liquidity Facility (CLF), established under Title III of the Federal Credit Union (FCU) Act, is to improve the general financial stability of member credit unions by lending, subject to statutory limitations, to member credit unions experiencing unusual or unexpected liquidity shortfalls. The two primary sources of funds for the CLF are stock subscriptions from member credit unions and access to borrowing from the Federal Financing Bank.

As of September 30, 2021, the borrowing authority of the CLF was $36.1 billion.

Object Classification (in millions of dollars)

Identification code 025–4470–0–3–373	2021 actual	2022 est.	2023 est.
Reimbursable obligations:			
25.3 Other goods and services from Federal sources	1	2	2
44.0 Membership Activity	20	10	405
99.9 Total new obligations, unexpired accounts	21	12	407

Employment Summary

Identification code 025–4470–0–3–373	2021 actual	2022 est.	2023 est.
1001 Direct civilian full-time equivalent employment	....	5	5

COMMUNITY DEVELOPMENT REVOLVING LOAN FUND

For the Community Development Revolving Loan Fund program as authorized by 42 U.S.C. 9812, 9822, and 9910, $4,000,000 shall be available until September 30, 2024, for technical assistance to low-income designated credit unions: Provided, That credit unions designated solely as minority depository institutions shall be eligible to apply for and receive such technical assistance.

Note.—A full-year 2022 appropriation for this account was not enacted at the time the Budget was prepared; therefore, the Budget assumes this account is operating under the Continuing Appropriations Act, 2022 (Division A of Public Law 117–43, as amended). The amounts included for 2022 reflect the annualized level provided by the continuing resolution.

Program and Financing (in millions of dollars)

Identification code 025–4472–0–3–373	2021 actual	2022 est.	2023 est.
Obligations by program activity:			
0001 Technical assistance	2	2	4
0801 Loans	....	2	2
0900 Total new obligations, unexpired accounts	2	4	6
Budgetary resources:			
Unobligated balance:			
1000 Unobligated balance brought forward, Oct 1	8	10	10
Budget authority:			
Appropriations, discretionary:			
1100 Appropriation	2	2	4
Spending authority from offsetting collections, mandatory:			
1800 Collected	2	2	2
1900 Budget authority (total)	4	4	6
1930 Total budgetary resources available	12	14	16
Memorandum (non-add) entries:			
1941 Unexpired unobligated balance, end of year	10	10	10
Change in obligated balance:			
Unpaid obligations:			
3000 Unpaid obligations, brought forward, Oct 1	4	3	1
3010 New obligations, unexpired accounts	2	4	6
3020 Outlays (gross)	–3	–6	–7
3050 Unpaid obligations, end of year	3	1	....
Memorandum (non-add) entries:			
3100 Obligated balance, start of year	4	3	1
3200 Obligated balance, end of year	3	1	....
Budget authority and outlays, net:			
Discretionary:			
4000 Budget authority, gross	2	2	4
Outlays, gross:			
4010 Outlays from new discretionary authority	....	2	4
4011 Outlays from discretionary balances	2	....	....
4020 Outlays, gross (total)	2	2	4
Mandatory:			
4090 Budget authority, gross	2	2	2
Outlays, gross:			
4100 Outlays from new mandatory authority	1	2	2
4101 Outlays from mandatory balances	....	2	1
4110 Outlays, gross (total)	1	4	3

National Credit Union Administration—Continued
Federal Funds—Continued

COMMUNITY DEVELOPMENT REVOLVING LOAN FUND—Continued

Program and Financing—Continued

Identification code 025–4472–0–3–373	2021 actual	2022 est.	2023 est.
Offsets against gross budget authority and outlays:			
Offsetting collections (collected) from:			
4123 Non-Federal sources	–2	–2	–2
4180 Budget authority, net (total)	2	2	4
4190 Outlays, net (total)	1	4	5
Memorandum (non-add) entries:			
5000 Total investments, SOY: Federal securities: Par value	8	8	8
5001 Total investments, EOY: Federal securities: Par value	8	8	8

Status of Direct Loans (in millions of dollars)

Identification code 025–4472–0–3–373	2021 actual	2022 est.	2023 est.
Cumulative balance of direct loans outstanding:			
1210 Outstanding, start of year	7	5	5
1231 Disbursements: Direct loan disbursements		1	1
1251 Repayments: Repayments and prepayments	–2	–1	–3
1290 Outstanding, end of year	5	5	3

The Community Development Revolving Loan Fund (CDRLF) was established by Congress in 1979 with a $6 million appropriation to assist credit unions serving low-income communities to: 1) provide financial services to their communities; 2) stimulate economic activities in their communities, resulting in increased income and employment; and 3) operate more efficiently. CDRLF funds a revolving loan program and a technical assistance grant program.

For the revolving loan program, CDRLF had outstanding loans of $5.0 million (16 loans outstanding to 16 credit unions) as of September 30, 2021. For the 2021 round of technical assistance grants, which are administered on a calendar-year basis, NCUA awarded $1.5 million in technical assistance grants to help 105 low-income credit unions provide affordable financial services to their members and communities during the COVID-19 pandemic, and to establish professional mentoring relationships between staff at larger credit unions and those at smaller credit unions designated as minority depository institutions. The goals of the mentoring grants program include building staff capacity to develop new products and services that will benefit the community, strengthening staff skills to improve business and marketing plans, and promoting professional relationships.

Object Classification (in millions of dollars)

Identification code 025–4472–0–3–373	2021 actual	2022 est.	2023 est.
41.0 Direct obligations: Grants, subsidies, and contributions	2	2	4
33.0 Reimbursable obligations: Investments and loans		2	2
99.0 Reimbursable obligations		2	2
99.9 Total new obligations, unexpired accounts	2	4	6

NATIONAL ENDOWMENT FOR THE ARTS

Federal Funds

GRANTS AND ADMINISTRATION

For necessary expenses to carry out the National Foundation on the Arts and the Humanities Act of 1965, $203,550,000 shall be available to the National Endowment for the Arts for the support of projects and productions in the arts, including arts education and public outreach activities, through assistance to organizations and individuals pursuant to section 5 of the Act, for program support, and for administering the functions of the Act, to remain available until expended.

Note.—A full-year 2022 appropriation for this account was not enacted at the time the Budget was prepared; therefore, the Budget assumes this account is operating under the Continuing Appropriations Act, 2022 (Division A of Public Law 117–43, as amended). The amounts included for 2022 reflect the annualized level provided by the continuing resolution.

Program and Financing (in millions of dollars)

Identification code 417–0100–0–1–503	2021 actual	2022 est.	2023 est.
Obligations by program activity:			
0001 Promotion of the arts	186	221	161
0003 Program support	2	3	3
0004 Salaries and expenses	33	36	42
0799 Total direct obligations	221	260	206
0801 Reimbursable program activity	1	1	1
0900 Total new obligations, unexpired accounts	222	261	207
Budgetary resources:			
Unobligated balance:			
1000 Unobligated balance brought forward, Oct 1	8	92	2
1001 Discretionary unobligated balance brought fwd, Oct 1	8	9	
1021 Recoveries of prior year unpaid obligations	2	2	2
1070 Unobligated balance (total)	10	94	4
Budget authority:			
Appropriations, discretionary:			
1100 Appropriation	168	168	204
Appropriations, mandatory:			
1200 Appropriation	135		
Spending authority from offsetting collections, discretionary:			
1700 Collected	2	1	1
1701 Change in uncollected payments, Federal sources	–1		
1750 Spending auth from offsetting collections, disc (total)	1	1	1
1900 Budget authority (total)	304	169	205
1930 Total budgetary resources available	314	263	209
Memorandum (non-add) entries:			
1941 Unexpired unobligated balance, end of year	92	2	2
Change in obligated balance:			
Unpaid obligations:			
3000 Unpaid obligations, brought forward, Oct 1	211	243	228
3010 New obligations, unexpired accounts	222	261	207
3020 Outlays (gross)	–188	–274	–265
3040 Recoveries of prior year unpaid obligations, unexpired	–2	–2	–2
3050 Unpaid obligations, end of year	243	228	168
Uncollected payments:			
3060 Uncollected pymts, Fed sources, brought forward, Oct 1	–1		
3070 Change in uncollected pymts, Fed sources, unexpired	1		
Memorandum (non-add) entries:			
3100 Obligated balance, start of year	210	243	228
3200 Obligated balance, end of year	243	228	168
Budget authority and outlays, net:			
Discretionary:			
4000 Budget authority, gross	169	169	205
Outlays, gross:			
4010 Outlays from new discretionary authority	45	60	73
4011 Outlays from discretionary balances	139	146	129
4020 Outlays, gross (total)	184	206	202
Offsets against gross budget authority and outlays:			
Offsetting collections (collected) from:			
4030 Federal sources	–2	–1	–1
Additional offsets against gross budget authority only:			
4050 Change in uncollected pymts, Fed sources, unexpired	1		
4070 Budget authority, net (discretionary)	168	168	204
4080 Outlays, net (discretionary)	182	205	201
Mandatory:			
4090 Budget authority, gross	135		
Outlays, gross:			
4100 Outlays from new mandatory authority	4		
4101 Outlays from mandatory balances		68	63
4110 Outlays, gross (total)	4	68	63
4180 Budget authority, net (total)	303	168	204
4190 Outlays, net (total)	186	273	264

The NEA, established by Congress in 1965, is an independent Federal agency that is the largest funder of the arts and arts education in communities nationwide and a catalyst of public and private support for the arts. The Agency partners closely with the nation's state and regional arts organizations, as well as with private entities, leveraging resources to provide more arts funding and arts programs across the country. Through its grant awards, strategic partnerships, and honorific awards, the NEA supports learning in and about the arts, celebrating the nation's rich and diverse cultural heritage, and promoting equitable access to the arts in every community in the United States.

In 2023, the NEA will build on operations to further incorporate the principles of racial equity, civil rights, racial justice, and equal opportunity, as reflected in Executive Order 13985, by engaging proactively with underserved communities, including those in rural America, through grant programs and national initiatives. In 2023, support will continue for Creative Forces: NEA Military Healing Arts Network, a partnership with the Departments of Defense and Veterans Affairs and the state and local arts agencies that seeks to improve the health, wellness, and quality of life for military and veteran populations exposed to trauma, as well as their families and caregivers. In 2023, the NEA will continue to implement programming funded by the $135 million provided in the American Rescue Plan.

The National Foundation on the Arts and the Humanities Act of 1965, as amended, also authorizes the NEA to receive money and other donated property; such gifts may be used, sold, or otherwise disposed of to support arts projects and activities. This presentation includes the Arts and Artifacts Indemnity Fund, which the NEA administers on behalf of the Federal Council on the Arts and the Humanities.

Object Classification (in millions of dollars)

Identification code 417–0100–0–1–503		2021 actual	2022 est.	2023 est.
	Direct obligations:			
	Personnel compensation:			
11.1	Full-time permanent	15	16	19
11.3	Other than full-time permanent	2	2	2
11.5	Other personnel compensation	1	1	1
11.9	Total personnel compensation	18	19	22
12.1	Civilian personnel benefits	6	7	8
23.1	Rental payments to GSA	3	3	3
25.1	Advisory and assistance services	3	3	3
25.2	Other services from non-Federal sources	3	4	6
25.3	Other goods and services from Federal sources	2	2	2
31.0	Equipment	1	1	2
41.0	Grants, subsidies, and contributions	185	221	160
99.0	Direct obligations	221	260	206
99.0	Reimbursable obligations	1	1	1
99.9	Total new obligations, unexpired accounts	222	261	207

Employment Summary

Identification code 417–0100–0–1–503	2021 actual	2022 est.	2023 est.
1001 Direct civilian full-time equivalent employment	145	151	168

Trust Funds

GIFTS AND DONATIONS, NATIONAL ENDOWMENT FOR THE ARTS

Special and Trust Fund Receipts (in millions of dollars)

Identification code 417–8040–0–7–503		2021 actual	2022 est.	2023 est.
0100	Balance, start of year			
	Receipts:			
	Current law:			
1130	Gifts and Donations, National Endowment for the Arts	1	2	1
2000	Total: Balances and receipts	1	2	1
	Appropriations:			
	Current law:			
2101	Gifts and Donations, National Endowment for the Arts	–1	–2	–1
5099	Balance, end of year			

Program and Financing (in millions of dollars)

Identification code 417–8040–0–7–503		2021 actual	2022 est.	2023 est.
	Obligations by program activity:			
0102	Permanent authority		1	1
0900	Total new obligations, unexpired accounts (object class 41.0)		1	1

	Budgetary resources:			
	Unobligated balance:			
1000	Unobligated balance brought forward, Oct 1	3	4	5
	Budget authority:			
	Appropriations, mandatory:			
1201	Appropriation (special or trust fund)	1	2	1
1930	Total budgetary resources available	4	6	6
	Memorandum (non-add) entries:			
1941	Unexpired unobligated balance, end of year	4	5	5

	Change in obligated balance:			
	Unpaid obligations:			
3000	Unpaid obligations, brought forward, Oct 1			1
3010	New obligations, unexpired accounts		1	1
3050	Unpaid obligations, end of year		1	2
	Memorandum (non-add) entries:			
3100	Obligated balance, start of year			1
3200	Obligated balance, end of year		1	2

	Budget authority and outlays, net:			
	Mandatory:			
4090	Budget authority, gross	1	2	1
4180	Budget authority, net (total)	1	2	1
4190	Outlays, net (total)			

NATIONAL ENDOWMENT FOR THE HUMANITIES

Federal Funds

GRANTS AND ADMINISTRATION

For necessary expenses to carry out the National Foundation on the Arts and the Humanities Act of 1965, $200,680,000, to remain available until expended, of which $183,380,000 shall be available for support of activities in the humanities, pursuant to section 7(c) of the Act and for administering the functions of the Act; and $17,300,000 shall be available to carry out the matching grants program pursuant to section 10(a)(2) of the Act, including $15,300,000 for the purposes of section 7(h): Provided, That appropriations for carrying out section 10(a)(2) shall be available for obligation only in such amounts as may be equal to the total amounts of gifts, bequests, devises of money, and other property accepted by the chairman or by grantees of the National Endowment for the Humanities under the provisions of sections 11(a)(2)(B) and 11(a)(3)(B) during the current and preceding fiscal years for which equal amounts have not previously been appropriated.

Note.—A full-year 2022 appropriation for this account was not enacted at the time the Budget was prepared; therefore, the Budget assumes this account is operating under the Continuing Appropriations Act, 2022 (Division A of Public Law 117–43, as amended). The amounts included for 2022 reflect the annualized level provided by the continuing resolution.

Program and Financing (in millions of dollars)

Identification code 418–0200–0–1–503		2021 actual	2022 est.	2023 est.
	Obligations by program activity:			
0001	Promotion of the humanities	219	214	165
0004	Administration	31	32	36
0799	Total direct obligations	250	246	201
0801	Reimbursable program activity	1	1	1
0900	Total new obligations, unexpired accounts	251	247	202
	Budgetary resources:			
	Unobligated balance:			
1000	Unobligated balance brought forward, Oct 1	31	89	14
1001	Discretionary unobligated balance brought fwd, Oct 1	31	89	
1021	Recoveries of prior year unpaid obligations	5	3	2
1070	Unobligated balance (total)	36	92	16
	Budget authority:			
	Appropriations, discretionary:			
1100	Appropriation	168	168	201
	Appropriations, mandatory:			
1200	Appropriation	135		
	Spending authority from offsetting collections, discretionary:			
1700	Collected	1	1	
1900	Budget authority (total)	304	169	201
1930	Total budgetary resources available	340	261	217
	Memorandum (non-add) entries:			
1941	Unexpired unobligated balance, end of year	89	14	15

National Endowment for the Humanities—Continued
Federal Funds—Continued

GRANTS AND ADMINISTRATION—Continued

Program and Financing—Continued

Identification code 418–0200–0–1–503	2021 actual	2022 est.	2023 est.
Change in obligated balance:			
Unpaid obligations:			
3000 Unpaid obligations, brought forward, Oct 1	223	274	247
3010 New obligations, unexpired accounts	251	247	202
3020 Outlays (gross)	–195	–271	–201
3040 Recoveries of prior year unpaid obligations, unexpired	–5	–3	–2
3050 Unpaid obligations, end of year	274	247	246
Uncollected payments:			
3060 Uncollected pymts, Fed sources, brought forward, Oct 1	–1	–1	–1
3090 Uncollected pymts, Fed sources, end of year	–1	–1	–1
Memorandum (non-add) entries:			
3100 Obligated balance, start of year	222	273	246
3200 Obligated balance, end of year	273	246	245
Budget authority and outlays, net:			
Discretionary:			
4000 Budget authority, gross	169	169	201
Outlays, gross:			
4010 Outlays from new discretionary authority	60	84	100
4011 Outlays from discretionary balances	120	177	97
4020 Outlays, gross (total)	180	261	197
Offsets against gross budget authority and outlays:			
Offsetting collections (collected) from:			
4030 Federal sources	–1	–1	
4040 Offsets against gross budget authority and outlays (total)	–1	–1	
Mandatory:			
4090 Budget authority, gross	135		
Outlays, gross:			
4100 Outlays from new mandatory authority	15		
4101 Outlays from mandatory balances		10	4
4110 Outlays, gross (total)	15	10	4
4180 Budget authority, net (total)	303	168	201
4190 Outlays, net (total)	194	270	201

The National Endowment for the Humanities (NEH) serves and strengthens our republic by promoting excellence in the humanities and conveying the lessons of history to all Americans. In 2023, NEH will continue to support partnerships with state humanities councils; the strengthening of humanities teaching and learning in the nation's schools and institutions of higher education; basic research and original scholarship in the humanities; innovative use of digital information technology; efforts to preserve and increase access to books, U.S. newspapers, documents, and other reference materials; and museum exhibitions, documentary films, radio programming, and reading programs that reach millions of Americans. In 2023, NEH will bring fresh perspectives to its ongoing special initiative, "A More Perfect Union." The initiative is designed to demonstrate and enhance the critical role the humanities play in our nation, while also supporting projects that will help American commemorate the 250th anniversary of the Declaration of Independence in 2026. Support is provided through outright grants, matching grants, and a combination of the two. Eligible applicants include state humanities councils, educational institutions, libraries, archives, museums, historical organizations, and other scholarly and cultural institutions and organizations. Support is also provided to individuals for advanced research and scholarship in the humanities.

Gifts and Donations account: The National Foundation on the Arts and the Humanities Act of 1965, as amended, authorizes the Humanities Endowment to receive money and other donated property. Such gifts may be used, sold, or otherwise disposed of to support humanities projects and activities. Budget authority in this schedule reflects cash received each year by the Endowment.

Object Classification (in millions of dollars)

Identification code 418–0200–0–1–503	2021 actual	2022 est.	2023 est.
Direct obligations:			
11.1 Personnel compensation: Full-time permanent	17	17	21
12.1 Civilian personnel benefits	6	6	7
23.1 Rental payments to GSA	3	3	3
25.2 Other services from non-Federal sources	5	6	5
41.0 Grants, subsidies, and contributions	219	214	165
99.0 Direct obligations	250	246	201
99.0 Reimbursable obligations	1	1	1
99.9 Total new obligations, unexpired accounts	251	247	202

Employment Summary

Identification code 418–0200–0–1–503	2021 actual	2022 est.	2023 est.
1001 Direct civilian full-time equivalent employment	172	173	185

Trust Funds

GIFTS AND DONATIONS, NATIONAL ENDOWMENT FOR THE HUMANITIES

Special and Trust Fund Receipts (in millions of dollars)

Identification code 418–8050–0–7–503	2021 actual	2022 est.	2023 est.
0100 Balance, start of year			
Receipts:			
Current law:			
1130 Gifts and Donations, National Endowment for the Humanities		1	1
2000 Total: Balances and receipts		1	1
Appropriations:			
Current law:			
2101 Gifts and Donations, National Endowment for the Humanities		–1	–1
5099 Balance, end of year			

Program and Financing (in millions of dollars)

Identification code 418–8050–0–7–503	2021 actual	2022 est.	2023 est.
Obligations by program activity:			
0001 Promotion of the humanities	1	1	1
0900 Total new obligations, unexpired accounts (object class 41.0)	1	1	1
Budgetary resources:			
Unobligated balance:			
1000 Unobligated balance brought forward, Oct 1	1		
Budget authority:			
Appropriations, mandatory:			
1201 Appropriation (special or trust fund)		1	1
1930 Total budgetary resources available	1	1	1
Change in obligated balance:			
Unpaid obligations:			
3000 Unpaid obligations, brought forward, Oct 1		1	
3010 New obligations, unexpired accounts	1	1	1
3020 Outlays (gross)		–2	–1
3050 Unpaid obligations, end of year	1		
Memorandum (non-add) entries:			
3100 Obligated balance, start of year		1	
3200 Obligated balance, end of year	1		
Budget authority and outlays, net:			
Mandatory:			
4090 Budget authority, gross		1	1
Outlays, gross:			
4100 Outlays from new mandatory authority		1	1
4101 Outlays from mandatory balances		1	
4110 Outlays, gross (total)		2	1
4180 Budget authority, net (total)		1	1
4190 Outlays, net (total)		2	1

ADMINISTRATIVE PROVISIONS

None of the funds appropriated to the National Foundation on the Arts and the Humanities may be used to process any grant or contract documents which do not include the text of 18 U.S.C. 1913: *Provided*, That none of the funds appropriated to the National Foundation on the Arts and the Humanities may be used for official reception and representation expenses: *Provided further*, That funds from nonappropriated sources may be used as necessary for official reception and representation expenses: *Provided further*, That the Chairperson of the National Endowment for the Arts may approve grants of up to $10,000, if in the aggregate the amount of such grants does not exceed 5 percent of the sums appropriated for grantmaking purposes per year: *Provided further*, That such small grant actions are taken pursuant to the terms of an expressed and direct delegation of authority from the National Council on the Arts to the Chairperson.

NATIONAL LABOR RELATIONS BOARD

Federal Funds

SALARIES AND EXPENSES

For expenses necessary for the National Labor Relations Board to carry out the functions vested in it by the Labor-Management Relations Act, 1947, and other laws, $319,424,000, of which $45,200,000 shall remain available until September 30, 2024: Provided, That no part of this appropriation shall be available to organize or assist in organizing agricultural laborers or used in connection with investigations, hearings, directives, or orders concerning bargaining units composed of agricultural laborers as referred to in section 2(3) of the Act of July 5, 1935, and as amended by the Labor-Management Relations Act, 1947, and as defined in section 3(f) of the Act of June 25, 1938, and including in said definition employees engaged in the maintenance and operation of ditches, canals, reservoirs, and waterways when maintained or operated on a mutual, nonprofit basis and at least 95 percent of the water stored or supplied thereby is used for farming purposes.

Note.—A full-year 2022 appropriation for this account was not enacted at the time the Budget was prepared; therefore, the Budget assumes this account is operating under the Continuing Appropriations Act, 2022 (Division A of Public Law 117–43, as amended). The amounts included for 2022 reflect the annualized level provided by the continuing resolution.

Program and Financing (in millions of dollars)

Identification code 420–0100–0–1–505	2021 actual	2022 est.	2023 est.
Obligations by program activity:			
0001 Casehandling	152	160	177
0002 Administrative Law Judges	8	8	9
0003 Board Adjudication	20	21	23
0005 Mission Support	1	84	109
0006 Internal Review	92	1	1
0900 Total new obligations, unexpired accounts	273	274	319
Budgetary resources:			
Budget authority:			
Appropriations, discretionary:			
1100 Appropriation	274	274	319
1930 Total budgetary resources available	274	274	319
Memorandum (non-add) entries:			
1940 Unobligated balance expiring	–1		
Change in obligated balance:			
Unpaid obligations:			
3000 Unpaid obligations, brought forward, Oct 1	42	44	28
3010 New obligations, unexpired accounts	273	274	319
3011 Obligations ("upward adjustments"), expired accounts	1		
3020 Outlays (gross)	–271	–290	–315
3041 Recoveries of prior year unpaid obligations, expired	–1		
3050 Unpaid obligations, end of year	44	28	32
Memorandum (non-add) entries:			
3100 Obligated balance, start of year	42	44	28
3200 Obligated balance, end of year	44	28	32
Budget authority and outlays, net:			
Discretionary:			
4000 Budget authority, gross	274	274	319
Outlays, gross:			
4010 Outlays from new discretionary authority	237	252	293
4011 Outlays from discretionary balances	34	38	22
4020 Outlays, gross (total)	271	290	315
4180 Budget authority, net (total)	274	274	319
4190 Outlays, net (total)	271	290	315

The National Labor Relations Board resolves representation disputes in industry and also remedies and prevents specified unfair labor practices by employers or labor organizations. Case intake and additional program statistics appear in the table below.

	2021 actual	2022 est.	2023 est.
Case intake:			
Unfair labor practice cases	14,950	16,102	17,344
Representation cases	1,650	2,134	2,760
Administrative law judges:			
Hearings closed	135	140	160
Decisions issued	112	120	140
Board adjudication:			
Contested Board decisions issued	243	300	300
Regional director decisions	310	310	310
Board decisions requiring court enforcement	35	41	62

Casehandling (formerly Field investigations in 2015 and earlier).—Charges of unfair labor practices and petitions for elections to resolve representation disputes are investigated by regional office personnel. Approximately 90 percent of merit unfair labor practice cases are closed by settlement, dismissal, or withdrawal. The remainder are prepared for public hearing. About 85–90 percent of representation elections are held pursuant to agreement of the parties. The agency strives to maximize the voluntary settlement of all cases and to avoid litigation.

Administrative law judge hearing.—Administrative law judges conduct public hearings in unfair labor practice cases. Their findings and recommendations are set forth in their decisions.

Board adjudication.—In an unfair labor practice case, a judge's decision becomes a Board order if no exceptions are filed. About 30 percent of these decisions become automatic Board orders or are complied with voluntarily. The remainder, with exceptions filed, require a Board decision. In representation cases, regional directors initially decide the issues by Board delegation. The Board itself decides representation issues on referral from regional directors or by granting a request for review of a regional director's decision. The Board also rules on objection and challenge questions in election cases. Unlike other Federal agencies, Board orders are not self-enforcing in the absence of a timely petition to review. If the parties do not voluntarily comply with a Board order involving unfair labor practices, the Board must request that an appellate court enforce the decision.

Internal Review.—Office of the Inspector General.

Mission Support.—Previously spread across other program activities; includes administrative, personnel, and financial management functions conducted in the Headquarters office.

Object Classification (in millions of dollars)

Identification code 420–0100–0–1–505	2021 actual	2022 est.	2023 est.
Direct obligations:			
11.1 Personnel compensation: Full-time permanent	158	162	180
12.1 Civilian personnel benefits	54	58	65
21.0 Travel and transportation of persons			1
23.1 Rental payments to GSA	24	24	24
23.3 Communications, utilities, and miscellaneous charges	2	3	3
25.2 Other services from non-Federal sources	34	26	41
31.0 Equipment	1	1	5
99.9 Total new obligations, unexpired accounts	273	274	319

Employment Summary

Identification code 420–0100–0–1–505	2021 actual	2022 est.	2023 est.
1001 Direct civilian full-time equivalent employment	1,207	1,215	1,305

NATIONAL MEDIATION BOARD

Federal Funds

SALARIES AND EXPENSES

For expenses necessary to carry out the provisions of the Railway Labor Act, including emergency boards appointed by the President, $15,113,000.

National Mediation Board—Continued
Federal Funds—Continued

SALARIES AND EXPENSES—Continued

Note.—A full-year 2022 appropriation for this account was not enacted at the time the Budget was prepared; therefore, the Budget assumes this account is operating under the Continuing Appropriations Act, 2022 (Division A of Public Law 117–43, as amended). The amounts included for 2022 reflect the annualized level provided by the continuing resolution.

Program and Financing (in millions of dollars)

Identification code 421–2400–0–1–505	2021 actual	2022 est.	2023 est.
Obligations by program activity:			
0001 Mediatory services	8	8	8
0002 Representation services	3	3	3
0003 Arbitration services	3	3	3
0900 Total new obligations, unexpired accounts	14	14	14
Budgetary resources:			
Budget authority:			
Appropriations, discretionary:			
1100 Appropriation	14	14	15
1930 Total budgetary resources available	14	14	15
Memorandum (non-add) entries:			
1941 Unexpired unobligated balance, end of year			1
Change in obligated balance:			
Unpaid obligations:			
3000 Unpaid obligations, brought forward, Oct 1	4	4	1
3010 New obligations, unexpired accounts	14	14	14
3020 Outlays (gross)	–13	–17	–15
3041 Recoveries of prior year unpaid obligations, expired	–1		
3050 Unpaid obligations, end of year	4	1	
Memorandum (non-add) entries:			
3100 Obligated balance, start of year	4	4	1
3200 Obligated balance, end of year	4	1	
Budget authority and outlays, net:			
Discretionary:			
4000 Budget authority, gross	14	14	15
Outlays, gross:			
4010 Outlays from new discretionary authority	10	13	14
4011 Outlays from discretionary balances	3	4	1
4020 Outlays, gross (total)	13	17	15
4180 Budget authority, net (total)	14	14	15
4190 Outlays, net (total)	13	17	15

Mediatory and alternative dispute resolution (ADR) services.—The National Mediation Board mediates disputes over wages, hours, and working conditions for some 700 rail and air carriers and approximately 650,000 employees in the two industries.

The Board also provides technical assistance to enable labor and industry representatives to explore informally the relevant economic and noneconomic problems that condition collective bargaining in the railroad and airline industries. The Board's ADR program provides collective bargaining training, facilitation, and grievance mediation services to the labor-management community.

	2021 actual	2022 est.	2023 est.
Mediation & ADR cases:			
Pending, start of year	107	103	135
Received during year	46	72	55
Closed during year	50	40	47
Pending, end of year	103	135	143

Employee representation.—The Board investigates representation disputes involving the various crafts or classes of railroad and airline employees to determine their choice of representatives for the purpose of collective bargaining.

	2021 actual	2022 est.	2023 est.
Representation cases:			
Pending, start of year	10	14	9
Received during year	17	15	14
Closed during year	13	20	16
Pending, end of year	14	9	7
Freedom of Information Act (FOIA) requests received	20	17	17
Investigation cases closed	19	17	17

Emergency disputes.—When the parties fail to resolve their disputes through mediation, they are urged to submit their differences to arbitration. If neither mediation nor voluntary arbitration is successful, the President, when notified of disputes which substantially threaten to interrupt essential service, may appoint emergency boards to investigate and report on the dispute. Such reports usually serve as a basis for resolving the disputes.

	2021 actual	2022 est.	2023 est.
Board created:			
Emergency (sec. 160)	0	1	1
Emergency (sec. 159a)	0	1	1

Arbitration services.—Arbitration is governed by sections 3 and 7 of the Railway Labor Act. Railroad employee grievances resulting from disputes over the interpretation or application of collective bargaining contracts may be brought for settlement to the National Railroad Adjustment Board (NRAB). The divisions of the NRAB are composed of an equal number of carrier and union representatives compensated by the party or parties they represent. Public Law 89–456 provides for the adjustment of disputes involving grievances resulting from interpretation or application of bargaining agreements in the railroad industry and for disputes otherwise referable to the NRAB. In these disputes, the National Mediation Board compensates the neutral party selected to help resolve these grievances.

Administrative direction and support for the public law boards, special boards of adjustment, and the NRAB are provided by Federal employees who are compensated by the National Mediation Board.

	2021 actual	2022 est.	2023 est.
Arbitration cases:			
Pending, start of year	4,887	5,146	6,246
Received during year	4,462	4,800	4,900
Closed during year	4,203	3,700	3,500
Pending, end of year	5,146	6,246	7,646

Object Classification (in millions of dollars)

Identification code 421–2400–0–1–505	2021 actual	2022 est.	2023 est.
Direct obligations:			
Personnel compensation:			
11.1 Full-time permanent	7	7	7
11.8 Special personal services payments	2	2	2
11.9 Total personnel compensation	9	9	9
12.1 Civilian personnel benefits	2	2	2
23.1 Rental payments to GSA	1	1	1
25.2 Other services from non-Federal sources	2	2	2
99.0 Direct obligations	14	14	14
99.9 Total new obligations, unexpired accounts	14	14	14

Employment Summary

Identification code 421–2400–0–1–505	2021 actual	2022 est.	2023 est.
1001 Direct civilian full-time equivalent employment	52	52	52

NATIONAL RAILROAD PASSENGER CORPORATION OFFICE OF INSPECTOR GENERAL

Federal Funds

SALARIES AND EXPENSES

For necessary expenses of the Office of Inspector General for the National Railroad Passenger Corporation to carry out the provisions of the Inspector General Act of 1978 (5 U.S.C. App. 3), $27,720,000: Provided, That the Inspector General shall have all necessary authority, in carrying out the duties specified in such Act, to investigate allegations of fraud, including false statements to the Government under section 1001 of title 18, United States Code, by any person or entity that is subject to regulation by the National Railroad Passenger Corporation: Provided further, That the Inspector General may enter into contracts and other arrangements for audits, studies, analyses, and other services with public agencies and with private persons, subject to the applicable laws and regulations that govern the obtaining of such services within the National Railroad Passenger Corporation: Provided further, That the Inspector General may select, appoint, and employ such officers and employees as may be necessary for carrying out the functions, powers, and duties of the Office of Inspector General, subject to the applicable laws and regulations that govern such selections, appointments, and employment within the National Railroad Passenger Corporation: Provided further, That concurrent with the Pres-

ident's budget request for fiscal year 2024, the Inspector General shall submit to the House and Senate Committees on Appropriations a budget request for fiscal year 2024 in similar format and substance to budget requests submitted by executive agencies of the Federal Government.

Note.—A full-year 2022 appropriation for this account was not enacted at the time the Budget was prepared; therefore, the Budget assumes this account is operating under the Continuing Appropriations Act, 2022 (Division A of Public Law 117–43, as amended). The amounts included for 2022 reflect the annualized level provided by the continuing resolution.

Program and Financing (in millions of dollars)

Identification code 575–2996–0–1–401	2021 actual	2022 est.	2023 est.
Obligations by program activity:			
0001 Payment to Amtrak IG	24	26	28
0900 Total new obligations, unexpired accounts (object class 41.0)	24	26	28
Budgetary resources:			
Budget authority:			
Appropriations, discretionary:			
1100 Appropriation	25	26	28
1930 Total budgetary resources available	25	26	28
Memorandum (non-add) entries:			
1940 Unobligated balance expiring	–1		
Change in obligated balance:			
Unpaid obligations:			
3000 Unpaid obligations, brought forward, Oct 1	3	3	
3010 New obligations, unexpired accounts	24	26	28
3020 Outlays (gross)	–24	–29	–28
3050 Unpaid obligations, end of year	3		
Memorandum (non-add) entries:			
3100 Obligated balance, start of year	3	3	
3200 Obligated balance, end of year	3		
Budget authority and outlays, net:			
Discretionary:			
4000 Budget authority, gross	25	26	28
Outlays, gross:			
4010 Outlays from new discretionary authority	21	26	28
4011 Outlays from discretionary balances	3	3	
4020 Outlays, gross (total)	24	29	28
4180 Budget authority, net (total)	25	26	28
4190 Outlays, net (total)	24	29	28

The 2023 Budget proposes $27.720 million for activities for the National Railroad Passenger Corporation (Amtrak) Office of the Inspector General.

In addition to the appropriation amount above, Section 802 of Title VIII of Division J of The Infrastructure Investment and Jobs Act (Pub. L. No. 117–58, Division J, Title VIII, Sec. 802, 135 Stat. 429, 1437 (2021)) states that, "Amounts made available to the Secretary of Transportation or to the Federal Railroad Administration in this title in this Act for the costs of award, administration, and project management oversight of financial assistance under the programs that are administered by the Federal Railroad Administration may be transferred to a Financial Assistance Oversight and Technical Assistance account, to remain available until expended, for the necessary expenses to support the award, administration, project management oversight, and technical assistance of programs administered by the Federal Railroad Administration under this Act: Provided, That one-quarter of one percent of the amounts transferred pursuant to the authority in this section in each of 2022 through 2026 shall be transferred to the Office of Inspector General of the Department of Transportation for oversight of funding provided to the Department of Transportation in this title in this Act: Provided further, That one-quarter of one percent of the amounts transferred pursuant to the authority in this section in each of 2022 through 2026 shall be transferred to the National Railroad Passenger Corporation Office of Inspector General for oversight of funding provided to the National Railroad Passenger Corporation in this title in this Act." Based on the amounts made available to Amtrak pursuant to this Act and, in accordance with the calculation under this provision, the amount available to National Railroad Passenger Corporation Office of Inspector General under this provision equates to $495,000 for 2023.

NATIONAL SECURITY COMMISSION ON ARTIFICIAL INTELLIGENCE

Federal Funds

Expenses, National Security Commission on Artificial Intelligence

Program and Financing (in millions of dollars)

Identification code 245–2765–0–1–054	2021 actual	2022 est.	2023 est.
Change in obligated balance:			
Unpaid obligations:			
3000 Unpaid obligations, brought forward, Oct 1	5	2	
3020 Outlays (gross)	–3	–2	
3050 Unpaid obligations, end of year	2		
Memorandum (non-add) entries:			
3100 Obligated balance, start of year	5	2	
3200 Obligated balance, end of year	2		
Budget authority and outlays, net:			
Discretionary:			
Outlays, gross:			
4011 Outlays from discretionary balances	3	2	
4180 Budget authority, net (total)			
4190 Outlays, net (total)	3	2	

The National Security Commission on Artificial Intelligence (NSCAI), an independent Federal Agency, is composed of fifteen members appointed by select heads of key cabinet Departments along with key Congressional stakeholders. Established by section 1051 of P.L. 115–232, the NSCAI is responsible for assessing and recommending the competitiveness of the United States in artificial intelligence, machine learning, and other associated technologies, including matters related to national security, defense, public-private partnership and investments. The NSCAI also makes recommendations on the means and methods, international competitiveness, investments and risks, and the means and methods that the United States can leverage going forward to support this evolving technology.

NATIONAL TRANSPORTATION SAFETY BOARD

Federal Funds

Salaries and Expenses

For necessary expenses of the National Transportation Safety Board, including hire of passenger motor vehicles and aircraft; services as authorized by 5 U.S.C. 3109, but at rates for individuals not to exceed the per diem rate equivalent to the rate for a GS-15; uniforms, or allowances therefor, as authorized by law (5 U.S.C. 5901–5902), $129,300,000, of which not to exceed $2,000 may be used for official reception and representation expenses: Provided, That the amounts made available to the National Transportation Safety Board in this Act include amounts necessary to make lease payments on an obligation incurred in fiscal year 2001 for a capital lease.

Note.—A full-year 2022 appropriation for this account was not enacted at the time the Budget was prepared; therefore, the Budget assumes this account is operating under the Continuing Appropriations Act, 2022 (Division A of Public Law 117–43, as amended). The amounts included for 2022 reflect the annualized level provided by the continuing resolution.

Program and Financing (in millions of dollars)

Identification code 424–0310–0–1–407	2021 actual	2022 est.	2023 est.
Obligations by program activity:			
0001 Policy and Direction	17	17	19
0002 Communications	8	8	9
0003 Aviation Safety	33	34	36
0004 Information Technology and Services	10	10	11
0005 Research and Engineering	14	13	15
0006 NTSB Training Center	1	1	1
0007 Administrative Law Judges	2	2	3
0008 Highway Safety	9	9	9
0009 Marine Safety	6	6	6

National Transportation Safety Board—Continued
Federal Funds—Continued

SALARIES AND EXPENSES—Continued

Program and Financing—Continued

Identification code 424–0310–0–1–407	2021 actual	2022 est.	2023 est.
0010 Railroad, Pipeline, and Hazardous Materials Safety	9	9	10
0011 Administrative Support	8	9	10
0100 Sub-total, Direct obligations	117	118	129
0799 Total direct obligations	117	118	129
0900 Total new obligations, unexpired accounts	117	118	129
Budgetary resources:			
Unobligated balance:			
1000 Unobligated balance brought forward, Oct 1	10	11	12
Budget authority:			
Appropriations, discretionary:			
1100 Appropriation	118	118	129
Spending authority from offsetting collections, discretionary:			
1700 Collected	1	1	1
1900 Budget authority (total)	119	119	130
1930 Total budgetary resources available	129	130	142
Memorandum (non-add) entries:			
1940 Unobligated balance expiring	–1		
1941 Unexpired unobligated balance, end of year	11	12	13
Change in obligated balance:			
Unpaid obligations:			
3000 Unpaid obligations, brought forward, Oct 1	21	25	24
3010 New obligations, unexpired accounts	117	118	129
3020 Outlays (gross)	–112	–119	–130
3041 Recoveries of prior year unpaid obligations, expired	–1		
3050 Unpaid obligations, end of year	25	24	23
Memorandum (non-add) entries:			
3100 Obligated balance, start of year	21	25	24
3200 Obligated balance, end of year	25	24	23
Budget authority and outlays, net:			
Discretionary:			
4000 Budget authority, gross	119	119	130
Outlays, gross:			
4010 Outlays from new discretionary authority	97	95	104
4011 Outlays from discretionary balances	15	24	26
4020 Outlays, gross (total)	112	119	130
Offsets against gross budget authority and outlays:			
Offsetting collections (collected) from:			
4030 Federal sources		–1	–1
4033 Non-Federal sources	–1		
4040 Offsets against gross budget authority and outlays (total)	–1	–1	–1
4070 Budget authority, net (discretionary)	118	118	129
4080 Outlays, net (discretionary)	111	118	129
4180 Budget authority, net (total)	118	118	129
4190 Outlays, net (total)	111	118	129

The National Transportation Safety Board (NTSB) is an independent nonregulatory agency that promotes transportation safety by maintaining independence and objectivity; conducting objective, precise accident investigations and safety studies; performing fair and objective airman and mariner certification appeals; and advocating and promoting NTSB safety recommendations. The NTSB also provides assistance to victims of transportation accidents and their families.

In 2023, the Administration proposes a total funding level of $129.3 million for NTSB Salaries and Expenses to allow the NTSB to fulfill its role in improving safety on the Nation's transportation system.

Object Classification (in millions of dollars)

Identification code 424–0310–0–1–407	2021 actual	2022 est.	2023 est.
Direct obligations:			
Personnel compensation:			
11.1 Full-time permanent	55	58	62
11.3 Other than full-time permanent	2	2	3
11.5 Other personnel compensation	2	3	3
11.9 Total personnel compensation	59	63	68
12.1 Civilian personnel benefits	21	23	24
21.0 Travel and transportation of persons	1	2	4
23.1 Rental payments to GSA	10	10	10
23.2 Rental payments to others	3	3	2
23.3 Communications, utilities, and miscellaneous charges	1	1	1
25.2 Other services from non-Federal sources	17	15	17
26.0 Supplies and materials	1	1	1
31.0 Equipment	4		2
99.0 Direct obligations	117	118	129
99.9 Total new obligations, unexpired accounts	117	118	129

Employment Summary

Identification code 424–0310–0–1–407	2021 actual	2022 est.	2023 est.
1001 Direct civilian full-time equivalent employment	399	412	425

EMERGENCY FUND

Program and Financing (in millions of dollars)

Identification code 424–0311–0–1–407	2021 actual	2022 est.	2023 est.
Budgetary resources:			
Unobligated balance:			
1000 Unobligated balance brought forward, Oct 1	2	2	2
1930 Total budgetary resources available	2	2	2
Memorandum (non-add) entries:			
1941 Unexpired unobligated balance, end of year	2	2	2
4180 Budget authority, net (total)			
4190 Outlays, net (total)			

The National Transportation Safety Board is mandated by the Congress to investigate all catastrophic transportation accidents and, therefore, has no control over the frequency of costly accident investigations. The emergency fund provides a funding mechanism by which periodic accident investigation cost fluctuations can be met without delaying critical phases of the investigations. The current balance of $2 million is sufficient to cover unanticipated costs associated with an increased number of accidents, and thus the Administration does not propose new funding in 2023.

NEIGHBORHOOD REINVESTMENT CORPORATION

Federal Funds

PAYMENT TO THE NEIGHBORHOOD REINVESTMENT CORPORATION

For payment to the Neighborhood Reinvestment Corporation for use in neighborhood reinvestment activities, as authorized by the Neighborhood Reinvestment Corporation Act (42 U.S.C. 8101–8107), $170,000,000.

Note.—A full-year 2022 appropriation for this account was not enacted at the time the Budget was prepared; therefore, the Budget assumes this account is operating under the Continuing Appropriations Act, 2022 (Division A of Public Law 117–43, as amended). The amounts included for 2022 reflect the annualized level provided by the continuing resolution.

Program and Financing (in millions of dollars)

Identification code 082–1300–0–1–451	2021 actual	2022 est.	2023 est.
Obligations by program activity:			
0001 Payment for operations and grants	265	165	170
0900 Total new obligations, unexpired accounts (object class 41.0)	265	165	170
Budgetary resources:			
Budget authority:			
Appropriations, discretionary:			
1100 Appropriation	165	165	170
Appropriations, mandatory:			
1200 Appropriation	100		
1900 Budget authority (total)	265	165	170
1930 Total budgetary resources available	265	165	170
Change in obligated balance:			
Unpaid obligations:			
3010 New obligations, unexpired accounts	265	165	170
3020 Outlays (gross)	–265	–165	–170

OTHER INDEPENDENT AGENCIES

Nuclear Regulatory Commission
Federal Funds 1299

	Budget authority and outlays, net: Discretionary:			
4000	Budget authority, gross	165	165	170
	Outlays, gross:			
4010	Outlays from new discretionary authority	165	165	170
	Mandatory:			
4090	Budget authority, gross	100		
	Outlays, gross:			
4100	Outlays from new mandatory authority	100		
4180	Budget authority, net (total)	265	165	170
4190	Outlays, net (total)	265	165	170

The Neighborhood Reinvestment Corporation (NRC), doing business as "NeighborWorks America," was established by Federal charter in 1978 as a community/public/private partnership providing financial support (e.g. housing counseling, operating and capital grants), technical assistance, and training for affordable housing and community-based revitalization efforts nationwide. NRC receives both Federal and non-Federal funding to finance its program activities. The Budget requests $170 million for NRC for its core operations, along with support and grants to its 250 network member organizations, and other non-profit organizations and local governments.

NORTHERN BORDER REGIONAL COMMISSION

Federal Funds

NORTHERN BORDER REGIONAL COMMISSION

For expenses necessary for the Northern Border Regional Commission in carrying out activities authorized by subtitle V of title 40, United States Code, $36,000,000, to remain available until expended: Provided, That such amounts shall be available for administrative expenses, notwithstanding section 15751(b) of title 40, United States Code.

Note.—A full-year 2022 appropriation for this account was not enacted at the time the Budget was prepared; therefore, the Budget assumes this account is operating under the Continuing Appropriations Act, 2022 (Division A of Public Law 117–43, as amended). The amounts included for 2022 reflect the annualized level provided by the continuing resolution.

NORTHERN BORDER REGIONAL COMMISSION

[For an additional amount for "Northern Border Regional Commission", $150,000,000 to remain available until expended: *Provided*, That such amount is designated by the Congress as being for an emergency requirement pursuant to section 4112(a) of H. Con. Res. 71 (115th Congress), the concurrent resolution on the budget for fiscal year 2018, and to section 251(b) of the Balanced Budget and Emergency Deficit Control Act of 1985.] *(Infrastructure Investments and Jobs Appropriations Act.)*

Program and Financing (in millions of dollars)

Identification code 573–3742–0–1–452		2021 actual	2022 est.	2023 est.
	Obligations by program activity:			
0001	Northern Border Regional Commission	37	51	37
0002	Infrastructure Investment and Jobs Act Activities		2	25
0900	Total new obligations, unexpired accounts	37	53	62
	Budgetary resources:			
	Unobligated balance:			
1000	Unobligated balance brought forward, Oct 1	25	21	148
	Budget authority:			
	Appropriations, discretionary:			
1100	Appropriation	30	30	36
1100	Appropriation (IIJA)		150	
1160	Appropriation, discretionary (total)	30	180	36
	Spending authority from offsetting collections, discretionary:			
1700	Collected	4		
1701	Change in uncollected payments, Federal sources	–1		
1750	Spending auth from offsetting collections, disc (total)	3		
1900	Budget authority (total)	33	180	36
1930	Total budgetary resources available	58	201	184
	Memorandum (non-add) entries:			
1941	Unexpired unobligated balance, end of year	21	148	122
	Change in obligated balance:			
	Unpaid obligations:			
3000	Unpaid obligations, brought forward, Oct 1	40	65	87
3010	New obligations, unexpired accounts	37	53	62
3020	Outlays (gross)	–12	–31	–63
3050	Unpaid obligations, end of year	65	87	86
	Uncollected payments:			
3060	Uncollected pymts, Fed sources, brought forward, Oct 1	–1		
3070	Change in uncollected pymts, Fed sources, unexpired	1		
	Memorandum (non-add) entries:			
3100	Obligated balance, start of year	39	65	87
3200	Obligated balance, end of year	65	87	86
	Budget authority and outlays, net:			
	Discretionary:			
4000	Budget authority, gross	33	180	36
	Outlays, gross:			
4010	Outlays from new discretionary authority	3	10	9
4011	Outlays from discretionary balances	9	21	54
4020	Outlays, gross (total)	12	31	63
	Offsets against gross budget authority and outlays:			
	Offsetting collections (collected) from:			
4030	Federal sources	–4		
	Additional offsets against gross budget authority only:			
4050	Change in uncollected pymts, Fed sources, unexpired	1		
4070	Budget authority, net (discretionary)	30	180	36
4080	Outlays, net (discretionary)	8	31	63
4180	Budget authority, net (total)	30	180	36
4190	Outlays, net (total)	8	31	63

The Budget provides $36 million for the Northern Border Regional Commission (NBRC). NBRC, authorized by P.L. 110–234, was established as a Federal-State partnership to provide a comprehensive approach to addressing persistent economic distress in the northern border region. Covering portions of Maine, New Hampshire, New York, and Vermont, the NBRC helps coordinate Federal efforts to develop the basic building blocks for economic development, such as transportation and basic public infrastructure, workforce development, and business development.

Object Classification (in millions of dollars)

Identification code 573–3742–0–1–452		2021 actual	2022 est.	2023 est.
	Direct obligations:			
11.1	Personnel compensation: Full-time permanent	1	1	1
41.0	Grants, subsidies, and contributions	36	52	61
99.0	Direct obligations	37	53	62
99.9	Total new obligations, unexpired accounts	37	53	62

Employment Summary

Identification code 573–3742–0–1–452	2021 actual	2022 est.	2023 est.
1001 Direct civilian full-time equivalent employment	3	3	3

NUCLEAR REGULATORY COMMISSION

Federal Funds

SALARIES AND EXPENSES

For expenses necessary for the Commission in carrying out the purposes of the Energy Reorganization Act of 1974 and the Atomic Energy Act of 1954, $911,384,000, including official representation expenses not to exceed $25,000, to remain available until expended: Provided, That of the amount appropriated herein, not more than $9,500,000 may be made available for salaries, travel, and other support costs for the Office of the Commission, to remain available until September 30, 2024: Provided further, That revenues from licensing fees, inspection services, and other services and collections estimated at $777,498,000 in fiscal year 2023 shall be retained and used for necessary salaries and expenses in this account, notwithstanding 31 U.S.C. 3302, and shall remain available until expended: Provided further, That the sum herein appropriated shall be reduced by the amount of revenues received during fiscal year 2023 so as to result in a final fiscal year 2023 appropriation estimated at not more than $133,886,000.

Note.—A full-year 2022 appropriation for this account was not enacted at the time the Budget was prepared; therefore, the Budget assumes this account is operating under the Continuing Appropriations Act, 2022 (Division A of Public Law 117–43, as amended). The amounts included for 2022 reflect the annualized level provided by the continuing resolution.

Nuclear Regulatory Commission—Continued
Federal Funds—Continued

SALARIES AND EXPENSES—Continued

Special and Trust Fund Receipts (in millions of dollars)

Identification code 031–0200–0–1–276		2021 actual	2022 est.	2023 est.
0100	Balance, start of year	....	....	....
	Receipts:			
	Current law:			
1120	Nuclear Facility Fees, Nuclear Regulatory Commission	715	710	777
1120	Nuclear Facility Fees, Nuclear Regulatory Commission	....	11	15
1199	Total current law receipts	715	721	792
1999	Total receipts	715	721	792
2000	Total: Balances and receipts	715	721	792
	Appropriations:			
	Current law:			
2101	Salaries and Expenses	–703	–710	–777
2101	Office of Inspector General	–11	–11	–15
2199	Total current law appropriations	–714	–721	–792
2999	Total appropriations	–714	–721	–792
5098	Reconciliation adjustment	–1	....	....
5099	Balance, end of year	....	....	....

Program and Financing (in millions of dollars)

Identification code 031–0200–0–1–276		2021 actual	2022 est.	2023 est.
	Obligations by program activity:			
0001	Nuclear Reactor Safety	436	435	491
0005	Nuclear Materials and Waste Safety	100	102	112
0007	Decommissioning and Low-Level Waste	22	23	24
0010	Integrated University Program	19	....	....
0012	Corporate Support	287	271	285
0799	Total direct obligations	864	831	912
0801	Salaries and Expenses (Reimbursable)	5	6	6
0900	Total new obligations, unexpired accounts	869	837	918
	Budgetary resources:			
	Unobligated balance:			
1000	Unobligated balance brought forward, Oct 1	82	71	85
1021	Recoveries of prior year unpaid obligations	21	7	7
1033	Recoveries of prior year paid obligations	1	....	....
1070	Unobligated balance (total)	104	78	92
	Budget authority:			
	Appropriations, discretionary:			
1100	Appropriation (General Fund)	127	121	134
1101	Appropriation (NRC receipts)	703	710	777
1160	Appropriation, discretionary (total)	830	831	911
	Spending authority from offsetting collections, discretionary:			
1700	Collected	5	13	11
1701	Change in uncollected payments, Federal sources	1	....	....
1750	Spending auth from offsetting collections, disc (total)	6	13	11
1900	Budget authority (total)	836	844	922
1930	Total budgetary resources available	940	922	1,014
	Memorandum (non-add) entries:			
1941	Unexpired unobligated balance, end of year	71	85	96
	Change in obligated balance:			
	Unpaid obligations:			
3000	Unpaid obligations, brought forward, Oct 1	305	302	201
3010	New obligations, unexpired accounts	869	837	918
3020	Outlays (gross)	–851	–931	–902
3040	Recoveries of prior year unpaid obligations, unexpired	–21	–7	–7
3050	Unpaid obligations, end of year	302	201	210
	Uncollected payments:			
3060	Uncollected pymts, Fed sources, brought forward, Oct 1	–4	–5	–5
3070	Change in uncollected pymts, Fed sources, unexpired	–1	....	....
3090	Uncollected pymts, Fed sources, end of year	–5	–5	–5
	Memorandum (non-add) entries:			
3100	Obligated balance, start of year	301	297	196
3200	Obligated balance, end of year	297	196	205
	Budget authority and outlays, net:			
	Discretionary:			
4000	Budget authority, gross	836	844	922
	Outlays, gross:			
4010	Outlays from new discretionary authority	648	636	694
4011	Outlays from discretionary balances	203	295	208
4020	Outlays, gross (total)	851	931	902
	Offsets against gross budget authority and outlays:			
	Offsetting collections (collected) from:			
4030	Federal sources	–1	–6	–5
4033	Non-Federal sources	–5	–7	–6
4040	Offsets against gross budget authority and outlays (total)	–6	–13	–11
	Additional offsets against gross budget authority only:			
4050	Change in uncollected pymts, Fed sources, unexpired	–1	....	....
4053	Recoveries of prior year paid obligations, unexpired accounts	1	....	....
4070	Budget authority, net (discretionary)	830	831	911
4080	Outlays, net (discretionary)	845	918	891
4180	Budget authority, net (total)	830	831	911
4190	Outlays, net (total)	845	918	891

Nuclear Reactor Safety.—The Nuclear Regulatory Commission (NRC) Nuclear Reactor Safety Program encompasses licensing and overseeing civilian nuclear power reactors, research and test reactors, and other non-power production and utilization facilities (e.g., medical radioisotope facilities) in a manner that adequately protects public health and safety. This program also provides reasonable assurance of the security of facilities and protection against radiological sabotage. This program contributes to the NRC's safety and security strategic goals through the activities of the Operating Reactors and New Reactors Business Lines that regulate existing and new nuclear reactors to ensure they meet applicable requirements.

Nuclear Materials and Waste Safety.—The Nuclear Materials and Waste Safety Program encompasses the NRC's licensing and oversight of nuclear materials in a manner that adequately protects public health and safety. This program provides assurance of the physical security of the materials and waste and protection against radiological sabotage, theft, or diversion of nuclear materials. Through this program, the NRC regulates uranium processing and fuel facilities; research and pilot facilities; nuclear materials users (medical, industrial, research, and academic); spent fuel storage; spent fuel material transportation and packaging; decontamination and decommissioning of facilities; and low-level and high-level radioactive waste. The program contributes to the NRC's safety and security strategic goals through the activities of the Spent Fuel Storage and Transportation, Nuclear Materials Users, Decommissioning and Low-Level Waste, and Fuel Facilities Business Lines.

Corporate Support.—The NRC's Corporate Support Business Line involves centrally managed activities that are necessary for agency programs to accomplish the agency's mission. These activities include administrative services, financial management, human resource management, information technology (IT) and information management, outreach, policy support, training, and acquisitions.

Object Classification (in millions of dollars)

Identification code 031–0200–0–1–276		2021 actual	2022 est.	2023 est.
	Direct obligations:			
	Personnel compensation:			
11.1	Full-time permanent	381	389	433
11.3	Other than full-time permanent	4	4	4
11.5	Other personnel compensation	15	11	15
11.9	Total personnel compensation	400	404	452
12.1	Civilian personnel benefits	143	135	151
21.0	Travel and transportation of persons	6	10	15
22.0	Transportation of things	1	1	1
23.1	Rental payments to GSA	20	19	19
23.3	Communications, utilities, and miscellaneous charges	11	18	18
24.0	Printing and reproduction	2	1	2
25.1	Advisory and assistance services	34	32	32
25.2	Other services from non-Federal sources	97	64	84
25.3	Other goods and services from Federal sources	43	48	48
25.4	Operation and maintenance of facilities	....	3	3
25.5	Research and development contracts	2	2	2
25.7	Operation and maintenance of equipment	64	63	63
26.0	Supplies and materials	2	2	2
31.0	Equipment	11	13	11
32.0	Land and structures	9	12	9
41.0	Grants, subsidies, and contributions	19	4	....

		2021 actual	2022 est.	2023 est.
99.0	Direct obligations	864	831	912
99.0	Reimbursable obligations	5	6	6
99.9	Total new obligations, unexpired accounts	869	837	918

Employment Summary

Identification code 031–0200–0–1–276	2021 actual	2022 est.	2023 est.
1001 Direct civilian full-time equivalent employment	2,697	2,805	2,807
2001 Reimbursable civilian full-time equivalent employment	10	8	9

OFFICE OF INSPECTOR GENERAL

For expenses necessary for the Office of the Inspector General in carrying out the provisions of the Inspector General Act of 1978, $17,769,000, to remain available until September 30, 2024: Provided, That revenues from licensing fees, inspection services, and other services and collections estimated at $14,655,000 in fiscal year 2023 shall be retained and be available until September 30, 2024, for necessary salaries and expenses in this account, notwithstanding section 3302 of title 31, United States Code: Provided further, That the sum herein appropriated shall be reduced by the amount of revenues received during fiscal year 2023 so as to result in a final fiscal year 2023 appropriation estimated at not more than $3,114,000: Provided further, That of the amounts appropriated under this heading, $1,520,000 shall be for Inspector General services for the Defense Nuclear Facilities Safety Board.

Note.—A full-year 2022 appropriation for this account was not enacted at the time the Budget was prepared; therefore, the Budget assumes this account is operating under the Continuing Appropriations Act, 2022 (Division A of Public Law 117–43, as amended). The amounts included for 2022 reflect the annualized level provided by the continuing resolution.

Program and Financing (in millions of dollars)

Identification code 031–0300–0–1–276		2021 actual	2022 est.	2023 est.
	Obligations by program activity:			
0001	Inspector General	13	14	18
	Budgetary resources:			
	Unobligated balance:			
1000	Unobligated balance brought forward, Oct 1	3	2	1
	Budget authority:			
	Appropriations, discretionary:			
1100	Appropriation	2	2	3
1101	Appropriation (special or trust)	11	11	15
1160	Appropriation, discretionary (total)	13	13	18
1930	Total budgetary resources available	16	15	19
	Memorandum (non-add) entries:			
1940	Unobligated balance expiring	–1		
1941	Unexpired unobligated balance, end of year	2	1	1
	Change in obligated balance:			
	Unpaid obligations:			
3000	Unpaid obligations, brought forward, Oct 1	2	2	3
3010	New obligations, unexpired accounts	13	14	18
3020	Outlays (gross)	–13	–13	–17
3050	Unpaid obligations, end of year	2	3	4
	Memorandum (non-add) entries:			
3100	Obligated balance, start of year	2	2	3
3200	Obligated balance, end of year	2	3	4
	Budget authority and outlays, net:			
	Discretionary:			
4000	Budget authority, gross	13	13	18
	Outlays, gross:			
4010	Outlays from new discretionary authority	11	10	14
4011	Outlays from discretionary balances	2	3	3
4020	Outlays, gross (total)	13	13	17
4180	Budget authority, net (total)	13	13	18
4190	Outlays, net (total)	13	13	17

The NRC's Office of Inspector General (OIG) was established as a statutory entity on April 15, 1989, in accordance with the 1988 amendments to the Inspector General Act. Starting in 2014, the NRC's OIG has exercised the same authorities with respect to the Defense Nuclear Facilities Safety Board (DNFSB) per the Consolidated Appropriations Act, 2014. The OIG's mission is to provide independent, objective audit and investigative oversight of NRC and DNFSB operations to protect people and the environment.

Object Classification (in millions of dollars)

Identification code 031–0300–0–1–276		2021 actual	2022 est.	2023 est.
	Direct obligations:			
11.1	Personnel compensation: Full-time permanent	8	9	11
12.1	Civilian personnel benefits	3	3	4
25.1	Advisory and assistance services	1	1	2
25.2	Other services from non-Federal sources	1	1	1
99.9	Total new obligations, unexpired accounts	13	14	18

Employment Summary

Identification code 031–0300–0–1–276	2021 actual	2022 est.	2023 est.
1001 Direct civilian full-time equivalent employment	57	63	73

GENERAL PROVISIONS—INDEPENDENT AGENCIES

SEC. 401. (a) *The amounts made available by this title for the Nuclear Regulatory Commission may be reprogrammed for any program, project, or activity, and the Commission shall notify the Committees on Appropriations of both Houses of Congress at least 30 days prior to the use of any proposed reprogramming that would cause any program funding level to increase or decrease by more than $500,000 or 10 percent, whichever is less, during the time period covered by this Act.*

(b)

(1) The Nuclear Regulatory Commission may waive the notification requirement in subsection (a) if compliance with such requirement would pose a substantial risk to human health, the environment, welfare, or national security.

(2) The Nuclear Regulatory Commission shall notify the Committees on Appropriations of both Houses of Congress of any waiver under paragraph (1) as soon as practicable, but not later than 3 days after the date of the activity to which a requirement or restriction would otherwise have applied. Such notice shall include an explanation of the substantial risk under paragraph (1) that permitted such waiver and shall provide a detailed report to the Committees of such waiver and changes to funding levels to programs, projects, or activities.

(c) Except as provided in subsections (a), (b), and (d), the amounts made available by this title for "Nuclear Regulatory Commission—Salaries and Expenses" shall be expended as directed in the joint explanatory statement accompanying this Act.

(d) None of the funds provided for the Nuclear Regulatory Commission shall be available for obligation or expenditure through a reprogramming of funds that increases funds or personnel for any program, project, or activity for which funds are denied or restricted by this Act.

(e) The Commission shall provide a monthly report to the Committees on Appropriations of both Houses of Congress, which includes the following for each program, project, or activity, including any prior year appropriations—

(1) total budget authority;

(2) total unobligated balances; and

(3) total unliquidated obligations.

GENERAL FUND RECEIPT ACCOUNT

(in millions of dollars)

	2021 actual	2022 est.	2023 est.
Offsetting receipts from the public:			
031–322000 All Other General Fund Proprietary Receipts Including Budget Clearing Accounts			1
General Fund Offsetting receipts from the public			1

NUCLEAR WASTE TECHNICAL REVIEW BOARD

Federal Funds

SALARIES AND EXPENSES

For expenses necessary for the Nuclear Waste Technical Review Board, as authorized by Public Law 100–203, section 5051, $3,945,000, to be derived from the Nuclear Waste Fund, to remain available until September 30, 2024.

Note.—A full-year 2022 appropriation for this account was not enacted at the time the Budget was prepared; therefore, the Budget assumes this account is operating under the Continuing Appropriations Act, 2022 (Division A of Public Law 117–43, as amended). The amounts included for 2022 reflect the annualized level provided by the continuing resolution.

Program and Financing (in millions of dollars)

Identification code 431–0500–0–1–271		2021 actual	2022 est.	2023 est.
	Obligations by program activity:			
0001	Technical and scientific activities	4	4	4
0900	Total new obligations, unexpired accounts	4	4	4
	Budgetary resources:			
	Unobligated balance:			
1000	Unobligated balance brought forward, Oct 1	2	2	2
	Budget authority:			
	Appropriations, discretionary:			
1101	Appropriation (special or trust)	4	4	4
1930	Total budgetary resources available	6	6	6
	Memorandum (non-add) entries:			
1941	Unexpired unobligated balance, end of year	2	2	2
	Change in obligated balance:			
	Unpaid obligations:			
3010	New obligations, unexpired accounts	4	4	4
3020	Outlays (gross)	–4	–4	–4
	Budget authority and outlays, net:			
	Discretionary:			
4000	Budget authority, gross	4	4	4
	Outlays, gross:			
4010	Outlays from new discretionary authority	3	4	4
4011	Outlays from discretionary balances	1		
4020	Outlays, gross (total)	4	4	4
4180	Budget authority, net (total)	4	4	4
4190	Outlays, net (total)	4	4	4

As mandated by the Nuclear Waste Policy Amendments Act of 1987, the Nuclear Waste Technical Review Board (Board) evaluates the technical and scientific validity of activities undertaken by the Department of Energy (DOE) related to the management and disposition of spent nuclear fuel and high-level radioactive waste. The Board's purpose is to provide independent expert advice to DOE and Congress on technical issues and to review DOE's efforts to implement the relevant sections of the Nuclear Waste Policy Act. The Board must report its findings, conclusions, and recommendations to Congress and the Secretary of Energy.

Object Classification (in millions of dollars)

Identification code 431–0500–0–1–271		2021 actual	2022 est.	2023 est.
11.1	Direct obligations: Personnel compensation: Full-time permanent	2	2	2
99.5	Adjustment for rounding	2	2	2
99.9	Total new obligations, unexpired accounts	4	4	4

Employment Summary

Identification code 431–0500–0–1–271		2021 actual	2022 est.	2023 est.
1001	Direct civilian full-time equivalent employment	16	16	16

OCCUPATIONAL SAFETY AND HEALTH REVIEW COMMISSION

Federal Funds

SALARIES AND EXPENSES

For expenses necessary for the Occupational Safety and Health Review Commission, $15,449,000.

Note.—A full-year 2022 appropriation for this account was not enacted at the time the Budget was prepared; therefore, the Budget assumes this account is operating under the Continuing Appropriations Act, 2022 (Division A of Public Law 117–43, as amended). The amounts included for 2022 reflect the annualized level provided by the continuing resolution.

Program and Financing (in millions of dollars)

Identification code 432–2100–0–1–554		2021 actual	2022 est.	2023 est.
	Obligations by program activity:			
0001	Administrative Law Judge determinations	6	6	6
0002	Commission review	5	5	7
0003	Executive direction	2	2	2
0900	Total new obligations, unexpired accounts	13	13	15
	Budgetary resources:			
	Budget authority:			
	Appropriations, discretionary:			
1100	Appropriation	13	13	15
1930	Total budgetary resources available	13	13	15
	Change in obligated balance:			
	Unpaid obligations:			
3000	Unpaid obligations, brought forward, Oct 1	3	3	2
3010	New obligations, unexpired accounts	13	13	15
3020	Outlays (gross)	–13	–14	–14
3050	Unpaid obligations, end of year	3	2	3
	Memorandum (non-add) entries:			
3100	Obligated balance, start of year	3	3	2
3200	Obligated balance, end of year	3	2	3
	Budget authority and outlays, net:			
	Discretionary:			
4000	Budget authority, gross	13	13	15
	Outlays, gross:			
4010	Outlays from new discretionary authority	11	11	13
4011	Outlays from discretionary balances	2	3	1
4020	Outlays, gross (total)	13	14	14
4180	Budget authority, net (total)	13	13	15
4190	Outlays, net (total)	13	14	14

The Occupational Safety and Health Review Commission, established by the Occupational Safety and Health Act of 1970, adjudicates contested enforcement actions of the Secretary of Labor. The Commission holds fact-finding hearings and issues orders affirming, modifying, or vacating the Secretary's enforcement actions.

Object Classification (in millions of dollars)

Identification code 432–2100–0–1–554		2021 actual	2022 est.	2023 est.
	Direct obligations:			
11.1	Personnel compensation: Full-time permanent	7	7	8
12.1	Civilian personnel benefits	2	2	3
23.1	Rental payments to GSA	2	2	2
99.0	Direct obligations	11	11	13
99.5	Adjustment for rounding	2	2	2
99.9	Total new obligations, unexpired accounts	13	13	15

Employment Summary

Identification code 432–2100–0–1–554		2021 actual	2022 est.	2023 est.
1001	Direct civilian full-time equivalent employment	50	55	63

OFFICE OF GOVERNMENT ETHICS

Federal Funds

SALARIES AND EXPENSES

For necessary expenses to carry out functions of the Office of Government Ethics pursuant to the Ethics in Government Act of 1978, the Ethics Reform Act of 1989, and the Representative Louise McIntosh Slaughter Stop Trading on Congressional Knowledge Act, including services as authorized by 5 U.S.C. 3109, rental of conference rooms in the District of Columbia and elsewhere, hire of passenger motor vehicles, and not to exceed $1,500 for official reception and representation expenses, $22,400,000.

Note.—A full-year 2022 appropriation for this account was not enacted at the time the Budget was prepared; therefore, the Budget assumes this account is operating under the Continuing Appropriations Act, 2022 (Division A of Public Law 117–43, as amended). The amounts included for 2022 reflect the annualized level provided by the continuing resolution.

Program and Financing (in millions of dollars)

Identification code 434–1100–0–1–805		2021 actual	2022 est.	2023 est.
	Obligations by program activity:			
0001	Salaries and Expenses (Direct)	19	19	21
0801	Salaries and Expenses (Reimbursable)			1
0900	Total new obligations, unexpired accounts	19	19	22
	Budgetary resources:			
	Unobligated balance:			
1000	Unobligated balance brought forward, Oct 1			1
	Budget authority:			
	Appropriations, discretionary:			
1100	Appropriation	19	19	22
	Spending authority from offsetting collections, discretionary:			
1700	Collected		1	1
1900	Budget authority (total)	19	20	23
1930	Total budgetary resources available	19	20	24
	Memorandum (non-add) entries:			
1941	Unexpired unobligated balance, end of year		1	2
	Change in obligated balance:			
	Unpaid obligations:			
3000	Unpaid obligations, brought forward, Oct 1	3	4	3
3010	New obligations, unexpired accounts	19	19	22
3011	Obligations ("upward adjustments"), expired accounts	1		
3020	Outlays (gross)	–18	–20	–22
3041	Recoveries of prior year unpaid obligations, expired	–1		
3050	Unpaid obligations, end of year	4	3	3
	Memorandum (non-add) entries:			
3100	Obligated balance, start of year	3	4	3
3200	Obligated balance, end of year	4	3	3
	Budget authority and outlays, net:			
	Discretionary:			
4000	Budget authority, gross	19	20	23
	Outlays, gross:			
4010	Outlays from new discretionary authority	15	16	18
4011	Outlays from discretionary balances	3	4	4
4020	Outlays, gross (total)	18	20	22
	Offsets against gross budget authority and outlays:			
	Offsetting collections (collected) from:			
4030	Federal sources	–1		
4033	Non-Federal sources		–1	–1
4040	Offsets against gross budget authority and outlays (total)	–1	–1	–1
	Additional offsets against gross budget authority only:			
4052	Offsetting collections credited to expired accounts	1		
4070	Budget authority, net (discretionary)	19	19	22
4080	Outlays, net (discretionary)	17	19	21
4180	Budget authority, net (total)	19	19	22
4190	Outlays, net (total)	17	19	21

The U.S. Office of Government Ethics (OGE), established by the Ethics in Government Act of 1978, provides overall leadership and oversight of the Executive Branch ethics program designed to prevent and resolve conflicts of interest. OGE's mission is part of the very foundation of public service. The first principle in the Fourteen Principles of Ethical Conduct for Government Officers and Employees provides that, "[p]ublic service is a public trust, requiring employees to place loyalty to the Constitution, the laws and ethical principles above private gain." OGE undertakes this important prevention mission as part of a framework comprising Executive Branch agencies and entities whose work focuses on institutional integrity. Within this framework, the ethics program works to ensure that public servants carry out the governmental responsibilities entrusted to them with impartiality, and that they serve as good stewards of public resources.

To carry out its vital leadership and oversight responsibilities for the Executive Branch ethics program, OGE promulgates, maintains, and advises on enforceable standards of ethical conduct for more than 2.7 million employees in over 130 Executive Branch agencies, including the White House; offers education and training to the more than 5,000 ethics officials Executive Branch-wide; oversees a financial disclosure system that reaches more than 26,000 public and more than 380,000 confidential financial disclosure report filers; operates and maintains *Integrity*, a public financial disclosure management application required by the Representative Louise McIntosh Slaughter Stop Trading on Congressional Knowledge (STOCK) Act; monitors Executive Branch agency ethics programs and senior leaders' compliance with applicable ethics laws and regulations; prepares for presidential transitions and provides assistance to the President and Senate in the presidential appointments process; conducts outreach to the general public, the private sector, and non-governmental organizations; and makes ethics documents publicly available.

Object Classification (in millions of dollars)

Identification code 434–1100–0–1–805		2021 actual	2022 est.	2023 est.
	Direct obligations:			
11.1	Personnel compensation: Full-time permanent	10	10	11
12.1	Civilian personnel benefits	3	3	4
23.1	Rental payments to GSA	1	1	2
25.3	Other goods and services from Federal sources	4	4	4
99.0	Direct obligations	18	18	21
99.0	Reimbursable obligations			1
99.5	Adjustment for rounding	1	1	
99.9	Total new obligations, unexpired accounts	19	19	22

Employment Summary

Identification code 434–1100–0–1–805		2021 actual	2022 est.	2023 est.
1001	Direct civilian full-time equivalent employment	71	74	78

OFFICE OF NAVAJO AND HOPI INDIAN RELOCATION

Federal Funds

SALARIES AND EXPENSES

For necessary expenses of the Office of Navajo and Hopi Indian Relocation as authorized by Public Law 93–531, $4,000,000, to remain available until expended: *Provided*, That funds provided in this or any other appropriations Act are to be used to relocate eligible individuals and groups including evictees from District 6, Hopi-partitioned lands residents, those in significantly substandard housing, and all others certified as eligible and not included in the preceding categories: *Provided further*, That none of the funds contained in this or any other Act may be used by the Office of Navajo and Hopi Indian Relocation to evict any single Navajo or Navajo family who, as of November 30, 1985, was physically domiciled on the lands partitioned to the Hopi Tribe unless a new or replacement home is provided for such household: *Provided further*, That no relocatee will be provided with more than one new or replacement home: *Provided further*, That the Office shall relocate any certified eligible relocatees who have selected and received an approved homesite on the Navajo reservation or selected a replacement residence off the Navajo reservation or on the land acquired pursuant to section 11 of Public Law 93–531 (88 Stat. 1716).

Note.—A full-year 2022 appropriation for this account was not enacted at the time the Budget was prepared; therefore, the Budget assumes this account is operating under the Continuing Appropriations Act, 2022 (Division A of Public Law 117–43, as amended). The amounts included for 2022 reflect the annualized level provided by the continuing resolution.

Office of Navajo and Hopi Indian Relocation—Continued
Federal Funds—Continued

SALARIES AND EXPENSES—Continued

Program and Financing (in millions of dollars)

Identification code 435–1100–0–1–808		2021 actual	2022 est.	2023 est.
	Obligations by program activity:			
0001	Operation of relocation office	3	3	3
0003	Relocation payments (housing)	1	1	1
0900	Total new obligations, unexpired accounts	4	4	4
	Budgetary resources:			
	Unobligated balance:			
1000	Unobligated balance brought forward, Oct 1	21	21	21
	Budget authority:			
	Appropriations, discretionary:			
1100	Appropriation	4	4	4
1930	Total budgetary resources available	25	25	25
	Memorandum (non-add) entries:			
1941	Unexpired unobligated balance, end of year	21	21	21
	Change in obligated balance:			
	Unpaid obligations:			
3000	Unpaid obligations, brought forward, Oct 1	1	1	1
3010	New obligations, unexpired accounts	4	4	4
3020	Outlays (gross)	–4	–4	–3
3050	Unpaid obligations, end of year	1	1	2
	Memorandum (non-add) entries:			
3100	Obligated balance, start of year	1	1	1
3200	Obligated balance, end of year	1	1	2
	Budget authority and outlays, net:			
	Discretionary:			
4000	Budget authority, gross	4	4	4
	Outlays, gross:			
4010	Outlays from new discretionary authority		3	3
4011	Outlays from discretionary balances	4	1	
4020	Outlays, gross (total)	4	4	3
4180	Budget authority, net (total)	4	4	4
4190	Outlays, net (total)	4	4	3

The Office of Navajo and Hopi Indian Relocation was established by Public Law 93–531 to plan and conduct relocation activities associated with the settlement of a land dispute in northern Arizona between the two Tribes. Relocation of clients includes such activities as certification, housing acquisition and construction, and land acquisition. Discretionary funds will be used for activities which will facilitate and expedite the overall relocation effort, and to plan for the orderly closeout of the Office of Navajo and Hopi Indian Relocation.

Object Classification (in millions of dollars)

Identification code 435–1100–0–1–808		2021 actual	2022 est.	2023 est.
	Direct obligations:			
11.1	Personnel compensation: Full-time permanent	2	2	2
25.2	Other services from non-Federal sources	1	1	1
32.0	Land and structures	1	1	1
99.9	Total new obligations, unexpired accounts	4	4	4

Employment Summary

Identification code 435–1100–0–1–808	2021 actual	2022 est.	2023 est.
1001 Direct civilian full-time equivalent employment	18	18	17

OFFICE OF SPECIAL COUNSEL

Federal Funds

SALARIES AND EXPENSES

For necessary expenses to carry out functions of the Office of Special Counsel, including services as authorized by 5 U.S.C. 3109, payment of fees and expenses for witnesses, rental of conference rooms in the District of Columbia and elsewhere, and hire of passenger motor vehicles; $31,990,000, of which $1,599,500 shall remain available until September 30, 2024.

Note.—A full-year 2022 appropriation for this account was not enacted at the time the Budget was prepared; therefore, the Budget assumes this account is operating under the Continuing Appropriations Act, 2022 (Division A of Public Law 117–43, as amended). The amounts included for 2022 reflect the annualized level provided by the continuing resolution.

Program and Financing (in millions of dollars)

Identification code 062–0100–0–1–805		2021 actual	2022 est.	2023 est.
	Obligations by program activity:			
0001	Investigation and prosecution of reprisals for whistle blowing	29	30	32
	Budgetary resources:			
	Unobligated balance:			
1000	Unobligated balance brought forward, Oct 1		1	1
	Budget authority:			
	Appropriations, discretionary:			
1100	Appropriation	30	30	32
1930	Total budgetary resources available	30	31	33
	Memorandum (non-add) entries:			
1941	Unexpired unobligated balance, end of year	1	1	1
	Change in obligated balance:			
	Unpaid obligations:			
3000	Unpaid obligations, brought forward, Oct 1	4	4	3
3010	New obligations, unexpired accounts	29	30	32
3020	Outlays (gross)	–29	–31	–31
3050	Unpaid obligations, end of year	4	3	4
	Memorandum (non-add) entries:			
3100	Obligated balance, start of year	4	4	3
3200	Obligated balance, end of year	4	3	4
	Budget authority and outlays, net:			
	Discretionary:			
4000	Budget authority, gross	30	30	32
	Outlays, gross:			
4010	Outlays from new discretionary authority	26	27	29
4011	Outlays from discretionary balances	3	4	2
4020	Outlays, gross (total)	29	31	31
4180	Budget authority, net (total)	30	30	32
4190	Outlays, net (total)	29	31	31

The Office of Special Counsel (OSC): 1) investigates Federal employee and applicant allegations of prohibited personnel practices (including reprisal for whistleblowing), and other activities prohibited by civil service law and, when appropriate, prosecutes before the Merit Systems Protection Board; 2) provides a safe channel for whistleblowing by Federal employees and applicants; 3) investigates and enforces the Uniformed Services Employment and Reemployment Rights Act (USERRA); and, 4) advises on and enforces civil provisions of the Hatch Act. OSC may transmit whistleblower allegations to the agency head concerned and require an agency investigation. OSC submits the agency's investigative report to the President and the Congress when appropriate.

OSC received 3,518 new cases in 2021. While this is approximately 37 percent below the average caseload level received from 2016 to 2020, OSC attributes this decrease largely to the COVID-19 pandemic, and the resulting operational impact facing many federal agencies since March 2020. OSC expects a return to pre-pandemic caseload levels in future fiscal years, barring additional, unforeseen circumstances. Despite receiving fewer cases in 2021, OSC again achieved a significant amount of favorable outcomes across multiple programmatic units.

Specifically, OSC achieved 393 favorable actions on prohibited personnel practice cases, the second highest in agency history, and approximately 20 percent above the prior five-year average. OSC also resolved 375 Hatch Act cases, which is approximately 64 percent above the prior five-year average. In addition, OSC issued 62 warning letters and successfully obtained seven disciplinary actions against agency officials who committed Hatch Act violations. OSC also assisted 17 service members in asserting their employment and reemployment rights.

Of the 3,518 cases OSC received in 2021, 906 were new disclosures. While this number is more than 250 cases fewer than the number of disclosures received in 2020, primarily because of the pandemic, the five-year average of new disclosures is still over 1,350. Further, OSC expects caseloads to increase when government agency operations return to normal, once the pandemic subsides likely during 2022. OSC processed and closed 929 disclosures, and referred 65 disclosures of waste, fraud, and abuse to agency heads for investigation. During the last several years, OSC has received numerous whistleblower disclosures from employees at the Department of Veterans Affairs (VA). OSC's work with VA whistleblowers has been featured in the media, and has helped promote accountability and improvements within VA. OSC continues to receive a disproportionately large number of cases from VA employees and, to address this, has established a streamlined system of managing those cases which includes a monthly status call with the agency regarding pending investigations. Further, OSC continued to use enhanced methods to more efficiently resolve cases through its Alternative Dispute Resolution (ADR) program by completing 28 case mediations in 2021.

OSC conducts outreach and education activities on its programmatic areas to inform and train agencies to prevent prohibited personnel practices, whistleblower reprisals, and Hatch Act and USERRA violations, and encourage reporting of claims of waste, fraud, and abuse. In 2021, OSC conducted 178 outreach activities throughout the Federal Government.

Case Type:	Cases Received 2021	Cases Resolved 2021
Prohibited personnel practice complaints	2,304	2,390
Hatch Act complaints	289	375
Whistleblower Disclosures	906	929
USERRA cases	19	17
Totals	3,518	3,711

OSC projects intakes for whistleblower disclosures, Hatch Act, and prohibited personnel practice cases to return to recent trends, and stabilize at around 6,000 total new cases received in future, nonpandemic years, potentially beginning at some point in 2022. OSC's caseload will likely remain high in light of the increased media exposure whistleblowers in general are receiving.

Overall, the requested funding for 2023 will enable OSC to meet current demands for OSC's services, protect whistleblowers in the VA and other agencies, protect the employment rights of returning service members, and protect the Federal merit system from prohibited personnel and partisan political practices.

Object Classification (in millions of dollars)

Identification code 062–0100–0–1–805	2021 actual	2022 est.	2023 est.
Direct obligations:			
11.1 Personnel compensation: Full-time permanent	18	19	20
12.1 Civilian personnel benefits	6	7	7
23.1 Rental payments to GSA	2	2	2
25.2 Other services from non-Federal sources	3	2	3
99.9 Total new obligations, unexpired accounts	29	30	32

Employment Summary

Identification code 062–0100–0–1–805	2021 actual	2022 est.	2023 est.
1001 Direct civilian full-time equivalent employment	138	139	141

OTHER COMMISSIONS AND BOARDS

Federal Funds

COMMISSION FOR THE PRESERVATION OF AMERICA'S HERITAGE ABROAD

SALARIES AND EXPENSES

For necessary expenses for the Commission for the Preservation of America's Heritage Abroad, $655,000, as authorized by chapter 3123 of title 54, United States Code: Provided, That the Commission may procure temporary, intermittent, and other services notwithstanding paragraph (3) of section 312304(b) of such chapter: Provided further, That such authority shall terminate on October 1, 2023: Provided further, That the Commission shall notify the Committees on Appropriations prior to exercising such authority.

Note.—A full-year 2022 appropriation for this account was not enacted at the time the Budget was prepared; therefore, the Budget assumes this account is operating under the Continuing Appropriations Act, 2022 (Division A of Public Law 117–43, as amended). The amounts included for 2022 reflect the annualized level provided by the continuing resolution.

Program and Financing (in millions of dollars)

Identification code 095–9911–0–1–999	2021 actual	2022 est.	2023 est.
Obligations by program activity:			
0001 Other Commissions and Boards (Direct)	1	1	1
0900 Total new obligations, unexpired accounts (object class 99.5)	1	1	1
Budgetary resources:			
Budget authority:			
Appropriations, discretionary:			
1100 Appropriation	1	1	1
1930 Total budgetary resources available	1	1	1
Change in obligated balance:			
Unpaid obligations:			
3010 New obligations, unexpired accounts	1	1	1
3020 Outlays (gross)	–1	–1	–1
Budget authority and outlays, net:			
Discretionary:			
4000 Budget authority, gross	1	1	1
Outlays, gross:			
4010 Outlays from new discretionary authority	1	1	1
4180 Budget authority, net (total)	1	1	1
4190 Outlays, net (total)	1	1	1

This account presents data on small independent commissions and other entities on a consolidated basis. It includes the request for the Commission for the Preservation of America's Heritage Abroad, which helps preserve cultural sites associated with the foreign heritage of Americans from eastern and central Europe by identifying properties; negotiating U.S. agreements with foreign governments; and facilitating private restoration, preservation, and memorialization efforts. The request includes language needed to enable the Commission to meet its requirements for staff and professional assistance.

PATIENT-CENTERED OUTCOMES RESEARCH TRUST FUND

Federal Funds

PAYMENT TO THE PATIENT-CENTERED OUTCOMES RESEARCH TRUST FUND

Program and Financing (in millions of dollars)

Identification code 579–1299–0–1–552	2021 actual	2022 est.	2023 est.
Obligations by program activity:			
0001 General Fund Payment	285	294	312
0900 Total new obligations, unexpired accounts (object class 94.0)	285	294	312
Budgetary resources:			
Budget authority:			
Appropriations, mandatory:			
1200 Appropriation	285	294	312
1930 Total budgetary resources available	285	294	312
Change in obligated balance:			
Unpaid obligations:			
3010 New obligations, unexpired accounts	285	294	312
3020 Outlays (gross)	–285	–294	–312
Budget authority and outlays, net:			
Mandatory:			
4090 Budget authority, gross	285	294	312
Outlays, gross:			
4100 Outlays from new mandatory authority	285	294	312
4180 Budget authority, net (total)	285	294	312

PAYMENT TO THE PATIENT-CENTERED OUTCOMES RESEARCH TRUST FUND—Continued

Program and Financing—Continued

Identification code 579–1299–0–1–552	2021 actual	2022 est.	2023 est.
4190 Outlays, net (total)	285	294	312

This fund exists for issuance of general fund appropriations to the Patient-Centered Outcomes Research Trust Fund. In accordance with Public Law 116–94, annual appropriations will continue through 2029.

Trust Funds

PATIENT-CENTERED OUTCOMES RESEARCH TRUST FUND

Special and Trust Fund Receipts (in millions of dollars)

Identification code 579–8299–0–7–552	2021 actual	2022 est.	2023 est.
0100 Balance, start of year	45	82	85
Receipts:			
Current law:			
1110 Fees on Health Insurance and Self-insured Health Plans, PCORTF	327	367	387
1140 Payment from the General Fund, Patient-Centered Outcomes Research Trust Fund	285	294	312
1199 Total current law receipts	612	661	699
1999 Total receipts	612	661	699
2000 Total: Balances and receipts	657	743	784
Appropriations:			
Current law:			
2101 Patient-Centered Outcomes Research Trust Fund	–612	–661	–699
2103 Patient-Centered Outcomes Research Trust Fund	....	–35	–38
2132 Patient-Centered Outcomes Research Trust Fund	37	38	40
2199 Total current law appropriations	–575	–658	–697
2999 Total appropriations	–575	–658	–697
5099 Balance, end of year	82	85	87

Program and Financing (in millions of dollars)

Identification code 579–8299–0–7–552	2021 actual	2022 est.	2023 est.
Obligations by program activity:			
0001 Obligations to PCORI	479	526	558
0002 Obligations to HHS	119	132	139
0900 Total new obligations, unexpired accounts (object class 94.0)	598	658	697
Budgetary resources:			
Unobligated balance:			
1033 Recoveries of prior year paid obligations	23	....	....
Budget authority:			
Appropriations, mandatory:			
1201 Appropriation (special or trust fund)	612	661	699
1203 Appropriation (previously unavailable)(special or trust)	....	35	38
1232 Appropriations and/or unobligated balance of appropriations temporarily reduced	–37	–38	–40
1260 Appropriations, mandatory (total)	575	658	697
1900 Budget authority (total)	575	658	697
1930 Total budgetary resources available	598	658	697
Change in obligated balance:			
Unpaid obligations:			
3010 New obligations, unexpired accounts	598	658	697
3020 Outlays (gross)	–598	–658	–697
Budget authority and outlays, net:			
Mandatory:			
4090 Budget authority, gross	575	658	697
Outlays, gross:			
4100 Outlays from new mandatory authority	....	658	697
4101 Outlays from mandatory balances	598	....	....
4110 Outlays, gross (total)	598	658	697
Offsets against gross budget authority and outlays:			
Offsetting collections (collected) from:			
4123 Non-Federal sources	–23	....	....
Additional offsets against gross budget authority only:			
4143 Recoveries of prior year paid obligations, unexpired accounts	23	....	....
4160 Budget authority, net (mandatory)	575	658	697
4170 Outlays, net (mandatory)	575	658	697
4180 Budget authority, net (total)	575	658	697
4190 Outlays, net (total)	575	658	697
Memorandum (non-add) entries:			
5000 Total investments, SOY: Federal securities: Par value	....	36	38
5001 Total investments, EOY: Federal securities: Par value	36	38	40

Public Law 116–94 authorized the extension of the Patient-Centered Outcomes Research Trust Fund (PCORTF) to receive amounts from general fund appropriations, fees on health insurance and self-insured plans, and interest earned on investments. Amounts appropriated or credited to the PCORTF are available to the Patient-Centered Outcomes Research Institute and the Secretary of Health and Human Services for carrying out part D of Title XI of the Social Security Act and section 937 of the Public Health Service Act, respectively. The PCORTF terminates at the end of FY 2029

POSTAL SERVICE

Federal Funds

UNITED STATES POSTAL SERVICE

PAYMENT TO THE POSTAL SERVICE FUND

For payment to the Postal Service Fund for revenue forgone on free and reduced rate mail, pursuant to subsections (c) and (d) of section 2401 of title 39, United States Code, $50,253,000: Provided, That mail for overseas voting and mail for the blind shall continue to be free: Provided further, That 6-day delivery and rural delivery of mail shall continue at not less than the 1983 level: Provided further, That none of the funds made available to the Postal Service by this Act shall be used to implement any rule, regulation, or policy of charging any officer or employee of any State or local child support enforcement agency, or any individual participating in a State or local program of child support enforcement, a fee for information requested or provided concerning an address of a postal customer: Provided further, That none of the funds provided in this Act shall be used to consolidate or close small rural and other small post offices: Provided further, That the Postal Service may not destroy, and shall continue to offer for sale, any copies of the Multinational Species Conservation Funds Semipostal Stamp, as authorized under the Multinational Species Conservation Funds Semipostal Stamp Act of 2010 (Public Law 111–241).

Note.—A full-year 2022 appropriation for this account was not enacted at the time the Budget was prepared; therefore, the Budget assumes this account is operating under the Continuing Appropriations Act, 2022 (Division A of Public Law 117-43, as amended). The amounts included for 2022 reflect the annualized level provided by the continuing resolution.

Program and Financing (in millions of dollars)

Identification code 018–1001–0–1–372	2021 actual	2022 est.	2023 est.
Obligations by program activity:			
0001 Free Mail	55	55	50
0900 Total new obligations, unexpired accounts (object class 41.0)	55	55	50
Budgetary resources:			
Budget authority:			
Appropriations, discretionary:			
1100 Appropriation	55	55	50
1900 Budget authority (total)	55	55	50
1930 Total budgetary resources available	55	55	50
Change in obligated balance:			
Unpaid obligations:			
3010 New obligations, unexpired accounts	55	55	50
3020 Outlays (gross)	–55	–55	–50
Budget authority and outlays, net:			
Discretionary:			
4000 Budget authority, gross	55	55	50
Outlays, gross:			
4010 Outlays from new discretionary authority	55	55	50
4180 Budget authority, net (total)	55	55	50

4190 Outlays, net (total)	55	55	50

The Budget proposes $50,253,000 for the estimated 2023 costs of free mail service for the blind and overseas voting.

Pursuant to P.L. 93–328, the 2023 appropriation request of the U.S. Postal Service for Payment to the Postal Service Fund is $47,845,000. This amount includes $52,846,000 requested for the estimated 2023 costs of free mail service for the blind and overseas voting and a reduction of $5,001,000 as a reconciliation adjustment for 2020 actual mail volume of free mail service for the blind and overseas voting.

POSTAL SERVICE FUND

Program and Financing (in millions of dollars)

Identification code 018–4020–0–3–372	2021 actual	2022 est.	2023 est.
Obligations by program activity:			
0001 Direct program activity (Postal Service Fund)	10,000	....	....
0801 Postal field operations	44,615	55,856	56,026
0802 Transportation	9,653	9,615	9,431
0803 Building occupancy	3,504	3,787	3,899
0804 Supplies and services	2,981	3,292	3,252
0805 Research and development	15	16	16
0806 Administration and area operations	729	3,233	3,201
0807 Interest	151	139	123
0808 Servicewide expenses	113	186	189
0809 Reimbursable program activities, subtotal	61,761	76,124	76,137
0810 Capital Investment	2,367	8,129	3,412
0819 Reimbursable program activities, subtotal	2,367	8,129	3,412
0899 Total reimbursable obligations	64,128	84,253	79,549
0900 Total new obligations, unexpired accounts	74,128	84,253	79,549
Budgetary resources:			
Unobligated balance:			
1000 Unobligated balance brought forward, Oct 1	12,993	24,014	16,274
1023 Unobligated balances applied to repay debt	–3,000	–1,000	....
1070 Unobligated balance (total)	9,993	23,014	16,274
Budget authority:			
Borrowing authority, mandatory:			
1400 Borrowing authority - CARES Act (Repayment not required per PL 116–260)	10,000	....	....
Spending authority from offsetting collections, discretionary:			
1700 Collected	....	267	291
1710 Transferred to other accounts [018–0100]	....	–250	–271
1710 Transferred to other accounts [018–0200]	....	–17	–20
Spending authority from offsetting collections, mandatory:			
1800 Collected	78,419	77,516	78,526
1810 Spending authority from offsetting collections transferred to other accounts [018–0100]	–250		
1810 Spending authority from offsetting collections transferred to other accounts [018–0200]	–17	....	....
1810 Spending authority from offsetting collections transferred to other accounts [070–0530]	–3	–3	–5
1850 Spending auth from offsetting collections, mand (total)	78,149	77,513	78,521
1900 Budget authority (total)	88,149	77,513	78,521
1930 Total budgetary resources available	98,142	100,527	94,795
Memorandum (non-add) entries:			
1941 Unexpired unobligated balance, end of year	24,014	16,274	15,246
Change in obligated balance:			
Unpaid obligations:			
3000 Unpaid obligations, brought forward, Oct 1	4,327	3,037	4,987
3010 New obligations, unexpired accounts	74,128	84,253	79,549
3020 Outlays (gross)	–75,418	–82,303	–80,243
3050 Unpaid obligations, end of year	3,037	4,987	4,293
Memorandum (non-add) entries:			
3100 Obligated balance, start of year	4,327	3,037	4,987
3200 Obligated balance, end of year	3,037	4,987	4,293
Budget authority and outlays, net:			
Mandatory:			
4090 Budget authority, gross	88,149	77,513	78,521
Outlays, gross:			
4100 Outlays from new mandatory authority	74,125	69,085	69,884
4101 Outlays from mandatory balances	1,293	13,218	10,359
4110 Outlays, gross (total)	75,418	82,303	80,243
Offsets against gross budget authority and outlays:			
Offsetting collections (collected) from:			
4120 Federal sources	–1,268	–1,471	–1,469
4121 Interest on Federal securities	–9	–49	–49
4123 Non-Federal sources	–77,142	–75,993	–77,003
4130 Offsets against gross budget authority and outlays (total)	–78,419	–77,513	–78,521
4160 Budget authority, net (mandatory)	9,730	....	....
4170 Outlays, net (mandatory)	–3,001	4,790	1,722
4180 Budget authority, net (total)	9,730	....	....
4190 Outlays, net (total)	–3,001	4,790	1,722
Memorandum (non-add) entries:			
5000 Total investments, SOY: Federal securities: Par value	14,991	24,655	19,794
5001 Total investments, EOY: Federal securities: Par value	24,655	19,794	17,831

Summary of Budget Authority and Outlays (in millions of dollars)

	2021 actual	2022 est.	2023 est.
Enacted/requested:			
Budget Authority	9,730	....	....
Outlays	–3,001	4,790	1,722
Legislative proposal, subject to PAYGO:			
Budget Authority			500
Outlays			500
Total:			
Budget Authority	9,730	....	500
Outlays	–3,001	4,790	2,222

The Postal Reorganization Act of 1970, Public Law 91–375, converted the Post Office Department into the U.S. Postal Service, an independent establishment within the executive branch. This legislation reorganized the Postal Service to function in a businesslike manner, though Section 2401 authorized annual appropriations to reimburse the Postal Service for public service costs incurred and for revenue forgone when providing services for free or at reduced rates to groups such as the blind, non-profit organizations, local newspapers, military and overseas voters, and publishers of educational material. The Postal Service commenced operations July 1, 1971. The Agency is charged with providing patrons with reliable mail service at reasonable rates and fees.

The Postal Service is governed by an 11-member Board of Governors, including nine Governors appointed by the President, a Postmaster General who is selected by the Governors, and a Deputy Postmaster General who is selected by the Governors and the Postmaster General.

The activities of the Postal Service are financed from: 1) mail and services revenue; 2) reimbursements from Federal and non-Federal sources; 3) proceeds from borrowing; 4) interest from U.S. securities and other investments; and 5) appropriations by the Congress. All receipts and deposits are made to the Fund and are available without fiscal year limitation for payment of all expenses incurred, retirement of obligations, investment in capital assets, and investment in obligations and securities. Since 1971, there have been several reforms. Notably, the Omnibus Budget Reconciliation Act of 1989 moved the Postal Service "off-budget" so that, beginning in 1990, the receipts and disbursements of the Fund are not considered as part of the congressional and executive budget process. Annual appropriations to the Postal Service are recorded on-budget in the Payment to the Postal Service Fund.

The Revenue Forgone Reform Act of 1993 (Public Law 103–123) amended Section 2401 of the Postal Reorganization Act and replaced the indefinite authorization of appropriations to support reduced rates for non-profits with an authorization of annual appropriations of $29 million each year from 1994 through 2035. This amount was estimated to compensate for insufficient appropriations for fiscal years 1991 through 1993 and for revenue losses from mandated reductions to postage rates to non-profits through 1998. From 1994 to 2016, the Postal Service received $562 million in total appropriations under Public Law 103–123. No additional appropriations for this purpose have been enacted since that time. The Postal Service continues to receive annual appropriations to reimburse it for free postage

POSTAL SERVICE FUND—Continued

for the blind and overseas absentee balloting materials pursuant to Public Law 91–375.

The 2006 Postal Accountability and Enhancement Act (P.L. 109–435) made a number of changes affecting the operations and oversight of the Postal Service. The Act provided for separate accounting and reporting for market-dominant products such as First-Class Mail and competitive products such as package delivery. The Act also amended the process for determining rate increases for market-dominant products, in part by imposing a ten-year limit on rate increases linked to the Consumer Price Index for All Urban Consumers (CPI-U). In 2017, the Postal Regulatory Commission announced proposed changes to the rate structure including increases above the cap of the CPI-U. In November 2020, the Postal Regulatory Commission adopted final rules to give the Postal Service greater flexibility in establishing prices for Market Dominant mail products, and in August 2021, the first postage rates using this new market-dominant price flexibility took effect.

P.L. 109–435 also created the Postal Service Retiree Health Benefits Fund to place the Postal Service on a path that fully funds its substantial retiree (annuitant) health benefits liabilities. This Fund was to receive from the Postal Service: 1) the pension savings provided to the Postal Service by the Postal Civil Service Retirement System Funding Reform Act of 2003 (P.L. 108–18) that were held in escrow during 2006; 2) a 10-year stream of payments defined within P.L. 109–435 to begin the liquidation of the Postal Service's unfunded liability for post-retirement health benefits; 3) beginning in 2017, payments for the actuarial cost of Postal Service contributions for the post-retirement health benefits for its current employees; 4) beginning in 2017, a 40-year amortization payment to fund any remaining unfunded liabilities associated with post-retirement health benefits of Postal Service employees; and 5) the surplus resources of the Civil Service Retirement and Disability Fund that are not needed to finance future retirement benefits under the Civil Service Retirement System (CSRS) to current or former employees of the Postal Service that are attributable to civilian employment with the Postal Service. Since passage in 2006, the Postal Service has contributed $38 billion to the Fund but has failed to make required payments each year since FY 2012, thus steadily increasing the size of the unfunded liability.

Beginning in 2017, P.L. 109–435 also required the Postal Service to begin a 27-year amortization to retire its unfunded liability under the CSRS. However, the Postal Service has failed to make payments each year since that time. In total, as of September 30, 2021 the Postal Service reported $72 billion in past due obligations to the Office of Personnel Management (OPM) related to retiree health benefits, CSRS, and the Federal Employees Retirement System (FERS).

As amended by P.L. 109–435, the Postal Service has statutory borrowing from the Federal Financing Bank (FFB) authority capped at $15 billion with the annual increase in outstanding debt limited to $3 billion. As of September 30, 2021, the total debt outstanding to the FFB was $11.0 billion, including $3 billion in short-term debt that was repaid on April 2, 2021. Section 6001 of the Coronavirus Aid, Relief and Economic Security (CARES) Act of 2020, P.L. 116–136, provided an additional $10 billion in borrowing authority to be used exclusively for COVID-19 related operating expenses. Pursuant to Section 801 of the Consolidated Appropriations Act of 2021, P.L. 116–260, no repayment is required for amounts borrowed under the CARES Act.

Given the Postal Service's history of using defaults to continue operations despite losses, the Budget reflects defaults on required pension and retiree health amortization and normal cost payments to prevent the Postal Service from running unsustainable deficits. The Administration appreciates the bipartisan support in the Congress for the Postal Service Reform Act of 2022 (H.R. 3076), which will improve the Postal Services long-run financial outlook, without sacrificing quality, affordable health coverage for Postal employees and retirees. This legislation will allow the Postal Service and its dedicated employees to continue to provide an essential public service for the delivery of mail and packages to all Americans. The Administration looks forward to working with the Congress to ensure that the goals of this legislation are met in an efficient and equitable manner and to advance additional reforms and financial support to maintain and expand the public services that the Postal Service provides to the American people. See also the Budget Process section of *Analytical Perspectives*.

Object Classification (in millions of dollars)

Identification code 018–4020–0–3–372		2021 actual	2022 est.	2023 est.
	Direct obligations:			
	Personnel compensation:			
11.1	Full-time permanent	3,746		
11.3	Other than full-time permanent	687		
11.5	Other personnel compensation	1,085		
11.9	Total personnel compensation	5,518		
12.1	Civilian personnel benefits	1,630		
13.0	Benefits for former personnel	15		
21.0	Travel and transportation of persons	18		
22.0	Transportation of things	1,395		
23.1	Rental payments to GSA	4		
23.2	Rental payments to others	342		
23.3	Communications, utilities, and miscellaneous charges	118		
24.0	Printing and reproduction	7		
25.2	Other services from non-Federal sources	343		
26.0	Supplies and materials	251		
31.0	Equipment	228		
32.0	Land and structures	91		
42.0	Insurance claims and indemnities	20		
43.0	Interest and dividends	20		
99.0	Direct obligations	10,000		
	Reimbursable obligations:			
	Personnel compensation:			
11.1	Full-time permanent	24,022	27,695	27,702
11.3	Other than full-time permanent	4,405	5,964	5,951
11.5	Other personnel compensation	6,959	8,004	7,929
11.9	Total personnel compensation	35,386	41,663	41,582
12.1	Civilian personnel benefits	10,450	10,547	10,692
13.0	Benefits for former personnel	93	4,404	4,504
21.0	Travel and transportation of persons	113	146	150
22.0	Transportation of things	8,945	10,355	10,167
23.1	Rental payments to GSA	25	31	32
23.2	Rental payments to others	2,192	2,752	2,854
23.3	Communications, utilities, and miscellaneous charges	759	895	901
24.0	Printing and reproduction	43	119	107
25.2	Other services from non-Federal sources	2,197	3,132	3,120
26.0	Supplies and materials	1,608	1,773	1,733
31.0	Equipment	1,462	7,005	2,154
32.0	Land and structures	587	1,125	1,259
42.0	Insurance claims and indemnities	137	167	171
43.0	Interest and dividends	131	139	123
99.0	Reimbursable obligations	64,128	84,253	79,549
99.9	Total new obligations, unexpired accounts	74,128	84,253	79,549

Employment Summary

Identification code 018–4020–0–3–372		2021 actual	2022 est.	2023 est.
2001	Reimbursable civilian full-time equivalent employment	579,674	565,416	559,135

POSTAL SERVICE FUND

(Legislative proposal, subject to PAYGO)

Program and Financing (in millions of dollars)

Identification code 018–4020–4–3–372		2021 actual	2022 est.	2023 est.
	Obligations by program activity:			
0801	Postal field operations			500
0809	Reimbursable program activities, subtotal			500
0899	Total reimbursable obligations			500
0900	Total new obligations, unexpired accounts (object class 22.0)			500
	Budgetary resources:			
	Budget authority:			
	Appropriations, mandatory:			
1200	Appropriation			500

1900	Budget authority (total)			500
1930	Total budgetary resources available			500
	Change in obligated balance:			
	Unpaid obligations:			
3010	New obligations, unexpired accounts			500
3020	Outlays (gross)			–500
	Budget authority and outlays, net:			
	Mandatory:			
4090	Budget authority, gross			500
	Outlays, gross:			
4100	Outlays from new mandatory authority			500
4180	Budget authority, net (total)			500
4190	Outlays, net (total)			500

The Budget proposes legislation to strengthen services offered by the United States Postal Service to support secure, free and fair elections. This includes making official ballot materials free to mail and reducing the cost of other election-related mail for jurisdictions and voters, and enhancing the Postal Service's ability to securely and expeditiously deliver and receive mail in underserved areas. This proposal expands on the essential public services that the Postal Service provides to the American people and will also help to relieve budget strain on local election offices across the country. The Budget estimates associated costs of $5 billion over the 2023–2032 period.

SALARIES AND EXPENSES

(INCLUDING TRANSFER OF FUNDS)

For necessary expenses of the Office of Inspector General in carrying out the provisions of the Inspector General Act of 1978, $271,000,000, to be derived by transfer from the Postal Service Fund and expended as authorized by section 603(b)(3) of the Postal Accountability and Enhancement Act (Public Law 109–435).

Note.—A full-year 2022 appropriation for this account was not enacted at the time the Budget was prepared; therefore, the Budget assumes this account is operating under the Continuing Appropriations Act, 2022 (Division A of Public Law 117–43, as amended). The amounts included for 2022 reflect the annualized level provided by the continuing resolution.

Program and Financing (in millions of dollars)

Identification code 018–0100–0–1–372		2021 actual	2022 est.	2023 est.
	Obligations by program activity:			
0001	Audit	76	74	80
0002	Investigations	174	176	191
0799	Total direct obligations	250	250	271
0801	Office of Inspector General (Reimbursable)	2	2	2
0900	Total new obligations, unexpired accounts	252	252	273
	Budgetary resources:			
	Budget authority:			
	Spending authority from offsetting collections, discretionary:			
1700	Collected	2	2	2
1711	Transferred from other accounts [018–4020]	250	250	271
1750	Spending auth from offsetting collections, disc (total)	252	252	273
1930	Total budgetary resources available	252	252	273
	Change in obligated balance:			
	Unpaid obligations:			
3010	New obligations, unexpired accounts	252	252	273
3020	Outlays (gross)	–252	–252	–273
	Budget authority and outlays, net:			
	Discretionary:			
4000	Budget authority, gross	252	252	273
	Outlays, gross:			
4010	Outlays from new discretionary authority	252	252	273
	Offsets against gross budget authority and outlays:			
	Offsetting collections (collected) from:			
4030	Federal sources	–2	–2	–2
4180	Budget authority, net (total)	250	250	271
4190	Outlays, net (total)	250	250	271

The U.S. Postal Service Office of Inspector General (USPS OIG) is an independent organization charged with reporting to Congress on the overall efficiency, effectiveness, and economy of Postal Service programs and operations. The USPS OIG meets this responsibility by conducting audits, investigations, and other reviews. The USPS OIG focuses on the prevention, identification, and elimination of: 1) waste, fraud, and abuse; 2) violations of laws, rules, and regulations; and 3) inefficiencies in Postal Service programs and operations.

The Budget proposes $271,000,000 for the 2022 USPS OIG's operations. Pursuant to P.L. 109–435, the 2022 appropriation request of the USPS OIG is $290,312,000.

Section 603(b)(1) of P.L. 109–435 (Postal Accountability and Enhancement Act) authorizes appropriations for the USPS OIG out of the off-budget Postal Service Fund beginning in 2009. The authorization resulted in the reclassification of USPS OIG spending from off-budget mandatory to off-budget discretionary.

Object Classification (in millions of dollars)

Identification code 018–0100–0–1–372		2021 actual	2022 est.	2023 est.
	Direct obligations:			
	Personnel compensation:			
11.1	Full-time permanent	145	142	157
11.3	Other than full-time permanent	1	2	2
11.5	Other personnel compensation	1	1	1
11.9	Total personnel compensation	147	145	160
12.1	Civilian personnel benefits	64	63	69
21.0	Travel and transportation of persons	2	4	4
22.0	Transportation of things		1	1
23.2	Rental payments to others	5	6	6
23.3	Communications, utilities, and miscellaneous charges	2	2	2
25.1	Advisory and assistance services	14	15	15
25.3	Other goods and services from Federal sources	1	1	1
25.7	Operation and maintenance of equipment	8	8	8
26.0	Supplies and materials	1	1	1
31.0	Equipment	5	4	4
32.0	Land and structures	1		
99.0	Direct obligations	250	250	271
99.0	Reimbursable obligations	2	2	2
99.9	Total new obligations, unexpired accounts	252	252	273

Employment Summary

Identification code 018–0100–0–1–372		2021 actual	2022 est.	2023 est.
1001	Direct civilian full-time equivalent employment	988	939	1,000

POSTAL REGULATORY COMMISSION

SALARIES AND EXPENSES

(INCLUDING TRANSFER OF FUNDS)

For necessary expenses of the Postal Regulatory Commission in carrying out the provisions of the Postal Accountability and Enhancement Act (Public Law 109–435), $20,300,000, to be derived by transfer from the Postal Service Fund and expended as authorized by section 603(a) of such Act.

Note.—A full-year 2022 appropriation for this account was not enacted at the time the Budget was prepared; therefore, the Budget assumes this account is operating under the Continuing Appropriations Act, 2022 (Division A of Public Law 117–43, as amended). The amounts included for 2022 reflect the annualized level provided by the continuing resolution.

Program and Financing (in millions of dollars)

Identification code 018–0200–0–1–372		2021 actual	2022 est.	2023 est.
	Obligations by program activity:			
0001	Postal Service Accountability	9	9	11
0002	Public Access and Participation	4	4	4
0003	Integration and Support	3	3	4
0004	Office of Inspector General	1	1	1
0900	Total new obligations, unexpired accounts	17	17	20

POSTAL REGULATORY COMMISSION—Continued
Program and Financing—Continued

Identification code 018–0200–0–1–372		2021 actual	2022 est.	2023 est.
	Budgetary resources:			
	Budget authority:			
	Spending authority from offsetting collections, discretionary:			
1711	Transferred from other accounts [018–4020]	17	17	20
1930	Total budgetary resources available	17	17	20
	Change in obligated balance:			
	Unpaid obligations:			
3010	New obligations, unexpired accounts	17	17	20
3020	Outlays (gross)	–17	–17	–20
	Budget authority and outlays, net:			
	Discretionary:			
4000	Budget authority, gross	17	17	20
	Outlays, gross:			
4010	Outlays from new discretionary authority	17	17	20
4180	Budget authority, net (total)	17	17	20
4190	Outlays, net (total)	17	17	20

The Postal Regulatory Commission is an independent agency that oversees the U.S. Postal Service to ensure transparency and accountability of the Postal Service to Congress, stakeholders, and the public in order to foster a vital and efficient universal mail system. The Commission ensures the Postal Service complies with the applicable laws by conducting expert review and analysis of postal rates, product offerings, service quality, nationwide service changes, post office closing appeals, and complaints. The Commission also conducts data analysis in order to support accurate and objective regulatory decision-making, and provides transparency of postal data for policymakers and stakeholders.

Pursuant to P.L. 109–435, the 2023 appropriation request of the Commission is $20,300,000.00. Section 603(a) of PAEA authorizes appropriations for the Commission out of the off-budget Postal Service Fund beginning in 2009. The authorization resulted in the reclassification of the Commission's spending from off-budget mandatory to off-budget discretionary.

Object Classification (in millions of dollars)

Identification code 018–0200–0–1–372		2021 actual	2022 est.	2023 est.
	Direct obligations:			
11.1	Personnel compensation: Full-time permanent	11	11	12
12.1	Civilian personnel benefits	3	3	4
23.2	Rental payments to others	2	2	2
25.1	Advisory and assistance services	1	1	2
99.0	Direct obligations	17	17	20
99.9	Total new obligations, unexpired accounts	17	17	20

Employment Summary

Identification code 018–0200–0–1–372	2021 actual	2022 est.	2023 est.
1001 Direct civilian full-time equivalent employment	74	76	82

PRESIDIO TRUST

Federal Funds

PRESIDIO TRUST

The Presidio Trust is authorized to issue obligations to the Secretary of the Treasury pursuant to section 104(d)(2) of the Omnibus Parks and Public Lands Management Act of 1996 (Public Law 104–333), in an amount not to exceed $31,000,000.

Note.—A full-year 2022 appropriation for this account was not enacted at the time the Budget was prepared; therefore, the Budget assumes this account is operating under the Continuing Appropriations Act, 2022 (Division A of Public Law 117–43, as amended). The amounts included for 2022 reflect the annualized level provided by the continuing resolution.

Program and Financing (in millions of dollars)

Identification code 512–4331–0–3–303		2021 actual	2022 est.	2023 est.
	Obligations by program activity:			
0801	Presidio Trust (Reimbursable)	210	177	183
	Budgetary resources:			
	Unobligated balance:			
1000	Unobligated balance brought forward, Oct 1	185	127	134
	Budget authority:			
	Appropriations, discretionary:			
1100	Appropriation		20	31
	Borrowing authority, discretionary:			
1300	Borrowing authority	20		
	Spending authority from offsetting collections, discretionary:			
1700	Collected	172	179	185
1701	Change in uncollected payments, Federal sources	–37	–12	–12
1725	Spending authority from offsetting collections applied to repay debt	–3	–3	–3
1750	Spending auth from offsetting collections, disc (total)	132	164	170
1900	Budget authority (total)	152	184	201
1930	Total budgetary resources available	337	311	335
	Memorandum (non-add) entries:			
1941	Unexpired unobligated balance, end of year	127	134	152
	Change in obligated balance:			
	Unpaid obligations:			
3000	Unpaid obligations, brought forward, Oct 1	74	113	53
3010	New obligations, unexpired accounts	210	177	183
3020	Outlays (gross)	–171	–237	–197
3050	Unpaid obligations, end of year	113	53	39
	Uncollected payments:			
3060	Uncollected pymts, Fed sources, brought forward, Oct 1	–95	–58	–46
3070	Change in uncollected pymts, Fed sources, unexpired	37	12	12
3090	Uncollected pymts, Fed sources, end of year	–58	–46	–34
	Memorandum (non-add) entries:			
3100	Obligated balance, start of year	–21	55	7
3200	Obligated balance, end of year	55	7	5
	Budget authority and outlays, net:			
	Discretionary:			
4000	Budget authority, gross	152	184	201
	Outlays, gross:			
4010	Outlays from new discretionary authority	126	110	125
4011	Outlays from discretionary balances	45	127	72
4020	Outlays, gross (total)	171	237	197
	Offsets against gross budget authority and outlays:			
	Offsetting collections (collected) from:			
4030	Federal sources	–8	–2	–2
4031	Interest on Federal securities	–2	–2	–2
4033	Non-Federal sources	–162	–175	–181
4040	Offsets against gross budget authority and outlays (total)	–172	–179	–185
	Additional offsets against gross budget authority only:			
4050	Change in uncollected pymts, Fed sources, unexpired	37	12	12
4070	Budget authority, net (discretionary)	17	17	28
4080	Outlays, net (discretionary)	–1	58	12
4180	Budget authority, net (total)	17	17	28
4190	Outlays, net (total)	–1	58	12
	Memorandum (non-add) entries:			
5000	Total investments, SOY: Federal securities: Par value	153	153	150
5001	Total investments, EOY: Federal securities: Par value	153	150	150

The Presidio Trust (Trust) is a wholly-owned Government corporation established by the Omnibus Parks and Public Lands Management Act of 1996 (Public Law 104–333) to manage, improve, maintain and lease property in the Presidio of San Francisco and to operate the Presidio as a self-sustaining part of the national park system. The Trust has jurisdiction over 80% of the Presidio and has successfully converted the historic Army base into a thriving park community.

Object Classification (in millions of dollars)

Identification code 512–4331–0–3–303		2021 actual	2022 est.	2023 est.
	Reimbursable obligations:			
	Personnel compensation:			
11.1	Full-time permanent	31	34	36

OTHER INDEPENDENT AGENCIES

Public Buildings Reform Board
Federal Funds 1311

		2021 actual	2022 est.	2023 est.
11.5	Other personnel compensation	1	1	1
11.9	Total personnel compensation	32	35	37
12.1	Civilian personnel benefits	15	13	13
23.3	Communications, utilities, and miscellaneous charges	9	9	9
25.2	Other services from non-Federal sources	140	107	111
26.0	Supplies and materials	2	1	1
31.0	Equipment	4	4	4
32.0	Land and structures	8	8	8
99.9	Total new obligations, unexpired accounts	210	177	183

Employment Summary

Identification code 512–4331–0–3–303	2021 actual	2022 est.	2023 est.
2001 Reimbursable civilian full-time equivalent employment	284	314	310

PRIVACY AND CIVIL LIBERTIES OVERSIGHT BOARD

Federal Funds

SALARIES AND EXPENSES

For necessary expenses of the Privacy and Civil Liberties Oversight Board, as authorized by section 1061 of the Intelligence Reform and Terrorism Prevention Act of 2004 (42 U.S.C. 2000ee), $10,700,000, to remain available until September 30, 2024.

Note.—A full-year 2022 appropriation for this account was not enacted at the time the Budget was prepared; therefore, the Budget assumes this account is operating under the Continuing Appropriations Act, 2022 (Division A of Public Law 117–43, as amended). The amounts included for 2022 reflect the annualized level provided by the continuing resolution.

Program and Financing (in millions of dollars)

Identification code 535–2724–0–1–054		2021 actual	2022 est.	2023 est.
	Obligations by program activity:			
0001	Salaries and expenses	10	10	11
	Budgetary resources:			
	Unobligated balance:			
1000	Unobligated balance brought forward, Oct 1	3	2	2
	Budget authority:			
	Appropriations, discretionary:			
1100	Appropriation	9	10	11
1930	Total budgetary resources available	12	12	13
	Memorandum (non-add) entries:			
1941	Unexpired unobligated balance, end of year	2	2	2
	Change in obligated balance:			
	Unpaid obligations:			
3000	Unpaid obligations, brought forward, Oct 1	1	2	2
3010	New obligations, unexpired accounts	10	10	11
3020	Outlays (gross)	–9	–10	–11
3050	Unpaid obligations, end of year	2	2	2
	Memorandum (non-add) entries:			
3100	Obligated balance, start of year	1	2	2
3200	Obligated balance, end of year	2	2	2
	Budget authority and outlays, net:			
	Discretionary:			
4000	Budget authority, gross	9	10	11
	Outlays, gross:			
4010	Outlays from new discretionary authority	6	8	9
4011	Outlays from discretionary balances	3	2	2
4020	Outlays, gross (total)	9	10	11
4180	Budget authority, net (total)	9	10	11
4190	Outlays, net (total)	9	10	11

The Intelligence Reform and Terrorism Prevention Act of 2004 (IRTPA) created the Privacy and Civil Liberties Oversight Board (PCLOB). The IRTPA originally placed the Board within the Executive Office of the President. The Implementing Recommendations of the 9/11 Commission Act of 2007 reconstituted the Board as an independent oversight agency within the Executive Branch. All five members of the Board are nominated by the President and confirmed by the Senate for staggered six-year terms. The Board has two main responsibilities: 1) to analyze and review actions the executive branch takes to protect the United States from terrorism, ensuring that the need for such actions is balanced with the need to protect privacy and civil liberties; and 2) to ensure that liberty concerns are appropriately considered in the development and implementation of laws, regulations, and policies related to efforts to protect the Nation against terrorism. The Board is required to report semi-annually on its operations to the U.S. Congress, as well as inform the public of its activities, as appropriate.

Object Classification (in millions of dollars)

Identification code 535–2724–0–1–054		2021 actual	2022 est.	2023 est.
11.1	Direct obligations: Personnel compensation: Full-time permanent	5	5	6
11.9	Total personnel compensation	5	5	6
12.1	Civilian personnel benefits	1	1	1
23.1	Rental payments to GSA	1	1	1
23.3	Communications, utilities, and miscellaneous charges	1	1	1
25.1	Advisory and assistance services	1	1	1
25.3	Other goods and services from Federal sources	1	1	1
99.9	Total new obligations, unexpired accounts	10	10	11

Employment Summary

Identification code 535–2724–0–1–054	2021 actual	2022 est.	2023 est.
1001 Direct civilian full-time equivalent employment	29	37	37

PUBLIC BUILDINGS REFORM BOARD

Federal Funds

SALARIES AND EXPENSES

For salaries and expenses of the Public Buildings Reform Board in carrying out the Federal Assets Sale and Transfer Act of 2016 (Public Law 114–287), $4,000,000, to remain available until expended.

Note.—A full-year 2022 appropriation for this account was not enacted at the time the Budget was prepared; therefore, the Budget assumes this account is operating under the Continuing Appropriations Act, 2022 (Division A of Public Law 117–43, as amended). The amounts included for 2022 reflect the annualized level provided by the continuing resolution.

Program and Financing (in millions of dollars)

Identification code 290–2860–0–1–804		2021 actual	2022 est.	2023 est.
	Obligations by program activity:			
0001	Direct program activity	3	5	4
	Budgetary resources:			
	Unobligated balance:			
1000	Unobligated balance brought forward, Oct 1	2	3	3
	Budget authority:			
	Appropriations, discretionary:			
1100	Appropriation	4	5	4
1930	Total budgetary resources available	6	8	7
	Memorandum (non-add) entries:			
1941	Unexpired unobligated balance, end of year	3	3	3
	Change in obligated balance:			
	Unpaid obligations:			
3000	Unpaid obligations, brought forward, Oct 1	1	1	
3010	New obligations, unexpired accounts	3	5	4
3020	Outlays (gross)	–3	–6	–4
3050	Unpaid obligations, end of year	1		
	Memorandum (non-add) entries:			
3100	Obligated balance, start of year	1	1	
3200	Obligated balance, end of year	1		
	Budget authority and outlays, net:			
	Discretionary:			
4000	Budget authority, gross	4	5	4
	Outlays, gross:			
4010	Outlays from new discretionary authority	2	5	4
4011	Outlays from discretionary balances	1	1	
4020	Outlays, gross (total)	3	6	4
4180	Budget authority, net (total)	4	5	4

1312 **Public Buildings Reform Board**—Continued
Federal Funds—Continued

SALARIES AND EXPENSES—Continued

Program and Financing—Continued

Identification code 290–2860–0–1–804	2021 actual	2022 est.	2023 est.
4190 Outlays, net (total)	3	6	4

The Federal Assets Sale and Transfer Act of 2016 (Public Law 114–287), enacted in December 2016, authorizes the Public Buildings Reform Board. The role of the Board is to identify opportunities for the Government to significantly reduce its inventory of civilian real property and reduce cost to the Government, subject to approval by the Office of Management and Budget. By law, the Board sunsets in 2025.

Object Classification (in millions of dollars)

Identification code 290–2860–0–1–804	2021 actual	2022 est.	2023 est.
Direct obligations:			
11.1 Personnel compensation: Full-time permanent	1	1	1
25.1 Advisory and assistance services	2	4	3
99.9 Total new obligations, unexpired accounts	3	5	4

Employment Summary

Identification code 290–2860–0–1–804	2021 actual	2022 est.	2023 est.
1001 Direct civilian full-time equivalent employment	3	3	3

PUBLIC DEFENDER SERVICE FOR THE DISTRICT OF COLUMBIA

Federal Funds

FEDERAL PAYMENT TO THE DISTRICT OF COLUMBIA PUBLIC DEFENDER SERVICE

For salaries and expenses, including the transfer and hire of motor vehicles, of the District of Columbia Public Defender Service, as authorized by the National Capital Revitalization and Self-Government Improvement Act of 1997, $53,629,000: Provided, That notwithstanding any other provision of law, all amounts under this heading shall be apportioned quarterly by the Office of Management and Budget and obligated and expended in the same manner as funds appropriated for salaries and expenses of Federal agencies: Provided further, That the District of Columbia Public Defender Service may establish for employees of the District of Columbia Public Defender Service a program substantially similar to the program set forth in subchapter II of chapter 35 of title 5, United States Code, except that the maximum amount of the payment made under the program to any individual may not exceed the amount referred to in section 3523(b)(3)(B) of title 5, United States Code: Provided further, That for the purposes of engaging with, and receiving services from, Federal Franchise Fund Programs established in accordance with section 403 of the Government Management Reform Act of 1994, as amended, the District of Columbia Public Defender Service shall be considered an agency of the United States Government. Provided further, That the District of Columbia Public Defender Service may enter into contracts for the procurement of severable services and multiyear contracts for the acquisition of property and services to the same extent and under the same conditions as an executive agency under sections 3902 and 3903 of title 41, United States Code.

Note.—A full-year 2022 appropriation for this account was not enacted at the time the Budget was prepared; therefore, the Budget assumes this account is operating under the Continuing Appropriations Act, 2022 (Division A of Public Law 117–43, as amended). The amounts included for 2022 reflect the annualized level provided by the continuing resolution.

Program and Financing (in millions of dollars)

Identification code 511–1733–0–1–754	2021 actual	2022 est.	2023 est.
Obligations by program activity:			
0001 Public Defender Service	51	46	54
Budgetary resources:			
Unobligated balance:			
1000 Unobligated balance brought forward, Oct 1	6	1	1
Budget authority:			
Appropriations, discretionary:			
1100 Appropriation	46	46	54
1930 Total budgetary resources available	52	47	55
Memorandum (non-add) entries:			
1941 Unexpired unobligated balance, end of year	1	1	1
Change in obligated balance:			
Unpaid obligations:			
3000 Unpaid obligations, brought forward, Oct 1	6	12	7
3010 New obligations, unexpired accounts	51	46	54
3011 Obligations ("upward adjustments"), expired accounts	1	1	1
3020 Outlays (gross)	–44	–51	–55
3041 Recoveries of prior year unpaid obligations, expired	–2	–1	–1
3050 Unpaid obligations, end of year	12	7	6
Memorandum (non-add) entries:			
3100 Obligated balance, start of year	6	12	7
3200 Obligated balance, end of year	12	7	6
Budget authority and outlays, net:			
Discretionary:			
4000 Budget authority, gross	46	46	54
Outlays, gross:			
4010 Outlays from new discretionary authority	39	41	49
4011 Outlays from discretionary balances	5	10	6
4020 Outlays, gross (total)	44	51	55
4180 Budget authority, net (total)	46	46	54
4190 Outlays, net (total)	44	51	55

The Public Defender Service for the District of Columbia (PDS) is a federally funded, independent organization governed by an eleven-member Board of Trustees. PDS was created in 1970 by a Federal statute (P.L. 91–358; see also D.C. Code Sec. 2–1601, et seq.) to fulfill the constitutional mandate (under *Gideon v. Wainwright*) to provide criminal defense counsel for individuals who cannot afford to hire a lawyer. PDS's mission is to provide and promote quality legal representation for indigent adults and children facing a loss of liberty in the District of Columbia justice system and thereby protect society's interest in the fair administration of justice. PDS specializes in representation in the most complex and resource-intensive criminal and delinquency cases. PDS also represents individuals facing involuntary civil commitment in the District's mental health system and individuals facing parole revocation for D.C. Code offenses.

Object Classification (in millions of dollars)

Identification code 511–1733–0–1–754	2021 actual	2022 est.	2023 est.
Direct obligations:			
Personnel compensation:			
11.1 Full-time permanent	24	26	29
11.8 Special personal services payments	1	1	1
11.9 Total personnel compensation	25	27	30
12.1 Civilian personnel benefits	8	9	11
23.1 Rental payments to GSA	4	4	4
23.3 Communications, utilities, and miscellaneous charges	1	1	1
25.1 Advisory and assistance services	2	1	2
25.2 Other services from non-Federal sources	2	2	2
25.3 Other goods and services from Federal sources	7	1	2
25.7 Operation and maintenance of equipment	1	1	1
26.0 Supplies and materials	1		1
99.0 Direct obligations	51	46	54
99.9 Total new obligations, unexpired accounts	51	46	54

Employment Summary

Identification code 511–1733–0–1–754	2021 actual	2022 est.	2023 est.
1001 Direct civilian full-time equivalent employment	208	222	236

PAYMENT TO PUERTO RICO OVERSIGHT BOARD

Federal Funds

PAYMENT TO PUERTO RICO OVERSIGHT BOARD

Special and Trust Fund Receipts (in millions of dollars)

Identification code 328–5619–0–2–806	2021 actual	2022 est.	2023 est.
0100 Balance, start of year			
Receipts:			
Current law:			
1110 Payment from Puerto Rico, Puerto Rico Oversight Board	58	58	58
2000 Total: Balances and receipts	58	58	58
Appropriations:			
Current law:			
2101 Payment to Puerto Rico Oversight Board	–58	–58	–58
5099 Balance, end of year			

Program and Financing (in millions of dollars)

Identification code 328–5619–0–2–806	2021 actual	2022 est.	2023 est.
Obligations by program activity:			
0001 Payment to Oversight Board	58	58	58
0900 Total new obligations, unexpired accounts (object class 25.2)	58	58	58
Budgetary resources:			
Budget authority:			
Appropriations, mandatory:			
1201 Appropriation (special or trust fund)	58	58	58
1930 Total budgetary resources available	58	58	58
Change in obligated balance:			
Unpaid obligations:			
3010 New obligations, unexpired accounts	58	58	58
3020 Outlays (gross)	–58	–58	–58
Budget authority and outlays, net:			
Mandatory:			
4090 Budget authority, gross	58	58	58
Outlays, gross:			
4100 Outlays from new mandatory authority	58	58	58
4180 Budget authority, net (total)	58	58	58
4190 Outlays, net (total)	58	58	58

The Puerto Rico Oversight, Management, and Economic Stability Act (P.L. 114–187) created an oversight board that is not a department, agency, establishment, or instrumentality of the Federal Government but is an entity within the territorial government, which is not subject to the supervision or control of any Federal agency. See 42 U.S.C. 2121(c). Although the Board's financing is derived entirely from the territorial government, the flow of funds from the territory to the Board is mandated by Federal law. Because Federal law prescribes the flow of funds to the Board, the Budget reflects the allocation of resources by the territorial government to the new territorial entity with a net zero Federal deficit impact, consistent with long-standing budgetary concepts. Because the Board itself is not a Federal entity, its operations will not be included in the Federal Government's Budget. Data are presented here on a Puerto Rico fiscal year basis (July 1 to June 30).

RAILROAD RETIREMENT BOARD

Federal Funds

DUAL BENEFITS PAYMENTS ACCOUNT

For payment to the Dual Benefits Payments Account, authorized under section 15(d) of the Railroad Retirement Act of 1974, $9,000,000, which shall include amounts becoming available in fiscal year 2023 pursuant to section 224(c)(1)(B) of Public Law 98–76; and in addition, an amount, not to exceed 2 percent of the amount provided herein, shall be available proportional to the amount by which the product of recipients and the average benefit received exceeds the amount available for payment of vested dual benefits: Provided, That the total amount provided herein shall be credited in 12 approximately equal amounts on the first day of each month in the fiscal year.

Note.—A full-year 2022 appropriation for this account was not enacted at the time the Budget was prepared; therefore, the Budget assumes this account is operating under the Continuing Appropriations Act, 2022 (Division A of Public Law 117–43, as amended). The amounts included for 2022 reflect the annualized level provided by the continuing resolution.

Program and Financing (in millions of dollars)

Identification code 060–0111–0–1–601	2021 actual	2022 est.	2023 est.
Obligations by program activity:			
0001 Dual Benefits Payments Account (Direct)	11	13	9
0900 Total new obligations, unexpired accounts (object class 41.0)	11	13	9
Budgetary resources:			
Budget authority:			
Appropriations, discretionary:			
1100 Appropriation	12	12	8
Appropriations, mandatory:			
1200 Appropriation	1	1	1
1900 Budget authority (total)	13	13	9
1930 Total budgetary resources available	13	13	9
Memorandum (non-add) entries:			
1940 Unobligated balance expiring	–2		
Change in obligated balance:			
Unpaid obligations:			
3010 New obligations, unexpired accounts	11	13	9
3020 Outlays (gross)	–11	–13	–9
Budget authority and outlays, net:			
Discretionary:			
4000 Budget authority, gross	12	12	8
Outlays, gross:			
4010 Outlays from new discretionary authority	10	12	8
Mandatory:			
4090 Budget authority, gross	1	1	1
Outlays, gross:			
4100 Outlays from new mandatory authority	1	1	1
4180 Budget authority, net (total)	13	13	9
4190 Outlays, net (total)	11	13	9

This appropriation is a Federal subsidy to the rail industry pension for costs not financed by the railroad sector.

Established in conjunction with the Railroad Retirement Solvency Act of 1983, this account acts as a conduit for various financial transactions, such as interfund transfers and fund transfers from the Department of the Treasury.

FEDERAL PAYMENTS TO THE RAILROAD RETIREMENT ACCOUNTS

For payment to the accounts established in the Treasury for the payment of benefits under the Railroad Retirement Act for interest earned on unnegotiated checks, $150,000, to remain available through September 30, 2024, which shall be the maximum amount available for payment pursuant to section 417 of Public Law 98–76.

Note.—A full-year 2022 appropriation for this account was not enacted at the time the Budget was prepared; therefore, the Budget assumes this account is operating under the Continuing Appropriations Act, 2022 (Division A of Public Law 117–43, as amended). The amounts included for 2022 reflect the annualized level provided by the continuing resolution.

Program and Financing (in millions of dollars)

Identification code 060–0113–0–1–601	2021 actual	2022 est.	2023 est.
Obligations by program activity:			
0001 Federal Payments to Railroad Retirement Accounts (Direct)	1,337	814	790
0900 Total new obligations, unexpired accounts (object class 42.0)	1,337	814	790
Budgetary resources:			
Budget authority:			
Appropriations, mandatory:			
1200 Appropriation	1,337	814	790
1930 Total budgetary resources available	1,337	814	790

Railroad Retirement Board—Continued
Federal Funds—Continued

FEDERAL PAYMENTS TO THE RAILROAD RETIREMENT ACCOUNTS—Continued

Program and Financing—Continued

Identification code 060–0113–0–1–601	2021 actual	2022 est.	2023 est.
Change in obligated balance:			
Unpaid obligations:			
3010 New obligations, unexpired accounts	1,337	814	790
3020 Outlays (gross)	–1,337	–814	–790
Budget authority and outlays, net:			
Mandatory:			
4090 Budget authority, gross	1,337	814	790
Outlays, gross:			
4100 Outlays from new mandatory authority	1,337	814	790
4180 Budget authority, net (total)	1,337	814	790
4190 Outlays, net (total)	1,337	814	790

This account funds interest on uncashed checks and the transfer of income taxes on Tier I and Tier II railroad retirement benefits.

RAILROAD UNEMPLOYMENT INSURANCE EXTENDED BENEFIT PAYMENTS

Program and Financing (in millions of dollars)

Identification code 060–0117–0–1–603	2021 actual	2022 est.	2023 est.
Obligations by program activity:			
0001 Railroad Unemployment Extended Benefits	38		
0900 Total new obligations, unexpired accounts (object class 25.8)	38		
Budgetary resources:			
Unobligated balance:			
1000 Unobligated balance brought forward, Oct 1	119	83	83
Budget authority:			
Appropriations, mandatory:			
1200 Appropriation	2		
1930 Total budgetary resources available	121	83	83
Memorandum (non-add) entries:			
1941 Unexpired unobligated balance, end of year	83	83	83
Change in obligated balance:			
Unpaid obligations:			
3000 Unpaid obligations, brought forward, Oct 1	1	2	
3010 New obligations, unexpired accounts	38		
3020 Outlays (gross)	–37	–2	
3050 Unpaid obligations, end of year	2		
Memorandum (non-add) entries:			
3100 Obligated balance, start of year	1	2	
3200 Obligated balance, end of year	2		
Budget authority and outlays, net:			
Mandatory:			
4090 Budget authority, gross	2		
Outlays, gross:			
4101 Outlays from mandatory balances	37	2	
4180 Budget authority, net (total)	2		
4190 Outlays, net (total)	37	2	

This appropriation provides funding for extended unemployment benefits paid by the Railroad Retirement Board under the Worker, Homeownership, and Business Assistance Act of 2009 (P.L. 111–92), the Tax Relief, Unemployment Insurance Reauthorization, and Job Creation Act of 2010 (P.L. 111–312), the Temporary Payroll Tax Cut Continuation Act (P.L. 112–78), the Middle Class Tax Relief and Job Creation Act of 2012 (P.L. 112–96), the CARES Act (P.L. 116–136), the Consolidated Appropriations Act, 2021 (P.L. 116–260), and the American Rescue Plan Act of 2021 (P.L. 117–2).

RAILROAD UNEMPLOYMENT INSURANCE EXTENDED BENEFIT PAYMENTS, RECOVERY ACT

Program and Financing (in millions of dollars)

Identification code 060–0114–0–1–603	2021 actual	2022 est.	2023 est.
Budgetary resources:			
Unobligated balance:			
1000 Unobligated balance brought forward, Oct 1	9	9	9
1930 Total budgetary resources available	9	9	9
Memorandum (non-add) entries:			
1941 Unexpired unobligated balance, end of year	9	9	9
4180 Budget authority, net (total)			
4190 Outlays, net (total)			

This appropriation provides funding for extended unemployment benefits paid by the Railroad Retirement Board under the American Recovery and Reinvestment Act of 2009 (P.L. 111–5), the CARES Act (P.L. 116–136), the Consolidated Appropriations Act, 2021 (P.L. 116–260) and the American Rescue Plan Act of 2021 (P.L. 117–2).

RAILROAD UNEMPLOYMENT INSURANCE WAIVER OF 7 DAY PERIOD

Program and Financing (in millions of dollars)

Identification code 060–0123–0–1–603	2021 actual	2022 est.	2023 est.
Obligations by program activity:			
0003 Railroad Unemployment Insurance Waiver of 7 Day Period	7		
0900 Total new obligations, unexpired accounts (object class 25.8)	7		
Budgetary resources:			
Unobligated balance:			
1000 Unobligated balance brought forward, Oct 1	44		
1930 Total budgetary resources available	44		
Memorandum (non-add) entries:			
1940 Unobligated balance expiring	–37		
Change in obligated balance:			
Unpaid obligations:			
3000 Unpaid obligations, brought forward, Oct 1	1		
3010 New obligations, unexpired accounts	7		
3020 Outlays (gross)	–8		
Memorandum (non-add) entries:			
3100 Obligated balance, start of year	1		
Budget authority and outlays, net:			
Mandatory:			
Outlays, gross:			
4101 Outlays from mandatory balances	8		
4180 Budget authority, net (total)			
4190 Outlays, net (total)	8		

RAILROAD UNEMPLOYMENT INSURANCE ENHANCED BENEFIT PAYMENTS

Program and Financing (in millions of dollars)

Identification code 060–0122–0–1–603	2021 actual	2022 est.	2023 est.
Obligations by program activity:			
0003 Railroad Unemployment Insurance Enhanced Benefit Payments	67		
0900 Total new obligations, unexpired accounts (object class 25.8)	67		
Budgetary resources:			
Unobligated balance:			
1000 Unobligated balance brought forward, Oct 1	290	223	223
1930 Total budgetary resources available	290	223	223
Memorandum (non-add) entries:			
1941 Unexpired unobligated balance, end of year	223	223	223
Change in obligated balance:			
Unpaid obligations:			
3000 Unpaid obligations, brought forward, Oct 1		2	
3010 New obligations, unexpired accounts	67		

OTHER INDEPENDENT AGENCIES

Railroad Retirement Board—Continued
Trust Funds

1315

Identification code 060–0121–0–1–601		2021 actual	2022 est.	2023 est.
3020	Outlays (gross)	–65	–2	
3050	Unpaid obligations, end of year	2		
	Memorandum (non-add) entries:			
3100	Obligated balance, start of year		2	
3200	Obligated balance, end of year	2	2	
	Budget authority and outlays, net:			
	Mandatory:			
	Outlays, gross:			
4101	Outlays from mandatory balances	65	2	
4180	Budget authority, net (total)			
4190	Outlays, net (total)	65	2	

PAYMENT TO LIMITATION ON ADMINISTRATION

Program and Financing (in millions of dollars)

Identification code 060–0121–0–1–601		2021 actual	2022 est.	2023 est.
	Obligations by program activity:			
0001	Payment to Limitation on Administration	28		
0900	Total new obligations, unexpired accounts (object class 94.0)	28		
	Budgetary resources:			
	Budget authority:			
	Appropriations, mandatory:			
1200	Appropriation	28		
1900	Budget authority (total)	28		
1930	Total budgetary resources available	28		
	Change in obligated balance:			
	Unpaid obligations:			
3010	New obligations, unexpired accounts	28		
3020	Outlays (gross)	–28		
	Budget authority and outlays, net:			
	Mandatory:			
4090	Budget authority, gross	28		
	Outlays, gross:			
4100	Outlays from new mandatory authority	28		
4180	Budget authority, net (total)	28		
4190	Outlays, net (total)	28		

PAYMENT TO LIMITATION ON THE OFFICE OF INSPECTOR GENERAL, RAILROAD RETIREMENT BOARD

Program and Financing (in millions of dollars)

Identification code 060–0124–0–1–601		2021 actual	2022 est.	2023 est.
	Obligations by program activity:			
0001	Payment to Limitation on the Office of Inspector General	1		
0900	Total new obligations, unexpired accounts (object class 94.0)	1		
	Budgetary resources:			
	Budget authority:			
	Appropriations, mandatory:			
1200	Appropriation	1		
1900	Budget authority (total)	1		
1930	Total budgetary resources available	1		
	Change in obligated balance:			
	Unpaid obligations:			
3010	New obligations, unexpired accounts	1		
3020	Outlays (gross)	–1		
	Budget authority and outlays, net:			
	Mandatory:			
4090	Budget authority, gross	1		
	Outlays, gross:			
4100	Outlays from new mandatory authority	1		
4180	Budget authority, net (total)	1		
4190	Outlays, net (total)	1		

This no-year account includes funds from the American Rescue Plan Act of 2021 (P.L. 117–2) for audit, investigatory and review activities of the Railroad Retirement Board Office of Inspector General.

Trust Funds

RAILROAD UNEMPLOYMENT INSURANCE TRUST FUND

Program and Financing (in millions of dollars)

Identification code 060–8051–0–7–603		2021 actual	2022 est.	2023 est.
	Obligations by program activity:			
0001	Railroad Unemployment Insurance Trust Fund (Direct)	175	133	140
0801	Railroad Unemployment Insurance Trust Fund (Reimbursable)	16	15	15
0900	Total new obligations, unexpired accounts	191	148	155
	Budgetary resources:			
	Unobligated balance:			
1001	Discretionary unobligated balance brought fwd, Oct 1	6		
1033	Recoveries of prior year paid obligations	4		
	Budget authority:			
	Appropriations, discretionary:			
1101	Appropriation (special or trust)	20	20	20
1103	Appropriation (previously unavailable)(special or trust)	3		
1135	Appropriations precluded from obligation (special or trust)	–6		
1160	Appropriation, discretionary (total)	17	20	20
	Appropriations, mandatory:			
1201	Appropriation (special or trust fund)	100	255	294
1203	Appropriation (unavailable balances)	25	44	75
1220	Appropriations transferred to other acct [060–8011]		–107	
1221	Appropriations transferred from other acct [060–8011]	81		
1230	Appropriations and/or unobligated balance of appropriations permanently reduced		–7	
1235	Appropriations precluded from obligation (special or trust)	–50	–71	–248
1260	Appropriations, mandatory (total)	156	114	121
	Spending authority from offsetting collections, mandatory:			
1800	Collected	14	15	15
1823	New and/or unobligated balance of spending authority from offsetting collections temporarily reduced		–1	
1850	Spending auth from offsetting collections, mand (total)	14	14	15
1900	Budget authority (total)	187	148	156
1930	Total budgetary resources available	191	148	156
	Memorandum (non-add) entries:			
1941	Unexpired unobligated balance, end of year			1
	Change in obligated balance:			
	Unpaid obligations:			
3000	Unpaid obligations, brought forward, Oct 1	20	14	1
3010	New obligations, unexpired accounts	191	148	155
3020	Outlays (gross)	–197	–161	–149
3050	Unpaid obligations, end of year	14	1	7
	Memorandum (non-add) entries:			
3100	Obligated balance, start of year	20	14	1
3200	Obligated balance, end of year	14	1	7
	Budget authority and outlays, net:			
	Discretionary:			
4000	Budget authority, gross	17	20	20
	Outlays, gross:			
4010	Outlays from new discretionary authority	17	20	20
	Mandatory:			
4090	Budget authority, gross	170	128	136
	Outlays, gross:			
4100	Outlays from new mandatory authority	169	128	129
4101	Outlays from mandatory balances	11	13	
4110	Outlays, gross (total)	180	141	129
	Offsets against gross budget authority and outlays:			
	Offsetting collections (collected) from:			
4120	Federal sources	–1		
4123	Non-Federal sources	–17	–15	–15
4130	Offsets against gross budget authority and outlays (total)	–18	–15	–15
	Additional offsets against gross budget authority only:			
4143	Recoveries of prior year paid obligations, unexpired accounts	4		
4160	Budget authority, net (mandatory)	156	113	121

Railroad Retirement Board—Continued
Trust Funds—Continued

RAILROAD UNEMPLOYMENT INSURANCE TRUST FUND—Continued

Program and Financing—Continued

Identification code 060–8051–0–7–603	2021 actual	2022 est.	2023 est.
4170 Outlays, net (mandatory)	162	126	114
4180 Budget authority, net (total)	173	133	141
4190 Outlays, net (total)	179	146	134
Memorandum (non-add) entries:			
5080 Outstanding debt, SOY	–22	–22	–22
5081 Outstanding debt, EOY	–22		
5090 Unexpired unavailable balance, SOY: Offsetting collections	1	1	2
5092 Unexpired unavailable balance, EOY: Offsetting collections	1	2	2

The Board administers a separate fund for unemployment and sickness insurance payments. Administrative expenses are financed from employer unemployment taxes.

Object Classification (in millions of dollars)

Identification code 060–8051–0–7–603	2021 actual	2022 est.	2023 est.
Direct obligations:			
42.0 Benefit payments	175	113	122
94.0 Financial transfers		19	18
99.0 Direct obligations	175	132	140
99.0 Reimbursable obligations	16	16	15
99.9 Total new obligations, unexpired accounts	191	148	155

RAIL INDUSTRY PENSION FUND

Special and Trust Fund Receipts (in millions of dollars)

Identification code 060–8011–0–7–601	2021 actual	2022 est.	2023 est.
0100 Balance, start of year		524	386
Receipts:			
Current law:			
1110 Refunds, Rail Industry Pension Fund		–2	–2
1110 Taxes, Rail Industry Pension Fund	2,875	3,092	3,045
1140 Interest and Profits on Investments in Public Debt Securities, Rail Industry Pension Fund	14	16	15
1140 Payment from the National Railroad Retirement Investment Trust, Rail Industry Pension Fund	2,838	2,039	2,115
1140 Interest on Advances to Railroad Unemployment Insurance Account, Rail Industry Pension Fund		2	
1140 Federal Payments to Railroad Retirement Trust Funds, Rail Industry Pension Fund	499	426	428
1199 Total current law receipts	6,226	5,573	5,601
1999 Total receipts	6,226	5,573	5,601
2000 Total: Balances and receipts	6,226	6,097	5,987
Appropriations:			
Current law:			
2101 Rail Industry Pension Fund	–91	–92	–101
2101 Rail Industry Pension Fund	–6,134	–5,572	–5,601
2101 Limitation on the Office of Inspector General	–1		
2103 Rail Industry Pension Fund	–43	–896	–767
2135 Rail Industry Pension Fund	566	849	704
2199 Total current law appropriations	–5,703	–5,711	–5,765
2999 Total appropriations	–5,703	–5,711	–5,765
5098 Rounding adjustment	1		
5099 Balance, end of year	524	386	222

Program and Financing (in millions of dollars)

Identification code 060–8011–0–7–601	2021 actual	2022 est.	2023 est.
Obligations by program activity:			
0001 Rail Industry Pension Fund (Direct)	5,728	5,777	5,834
Budgetary resources:			
Unobligated balance:			
1000 Unobligated balance brought forward, Oct 1			11
1001 Discretionary unobligated balance brought fwd, Oct 1	–61		
1033 Recoveries of prior year paid obligations	4		
1070 Unobligated balance (total)	4		11
Budget authority:			
Appropriations, discretionary:			
1101 Appropriation (special or trust)	91	92	101
Appropriations, mandatory:			
1201 Appropriation (special or trust fund)	6,134	5,572	5,601
1203 Appropriation (unavailable balances)	43	896	767
1220 Appropriations transferred to other acct [060–8010]		–30	
1220 Appropriations transferred to other acct [060–8051]	–81		
1221 Appropriations transferred from other acct [060–8010]	103		76
1221 Appropriations transferred from other acct [060–8051]		107	
1235 Appropriations precluded from obligation (special or trust)	–566	–849	–704
1260 Appropriations, mandatory (total)	5,633	5,696	5,740
1900 Budget authority (total)	5,724	5,788	5,841
1930 Total budgetary resources available	5,728	5,788	5,852
Memorandum (non-add) entries:			
1941 Unexpired unobligated balance, end of year		11	18
Change in obligated balance:			
Unpaid obligations:			
3000 Unpaid obligations, brought forward, Oct 1	350	372	10
3010 New obligations, unexpired accounts	5,728	5,777	5,834
3020 Outlays (gross)	–5,706	–6,139	–5,833
3050 Unpaid obligations, end of year	372	10	11
Memorandum (non-add) entries:			
3100 Obligated balance, start of year	350	372	10
3200 Obligated balance, end of year	372	10	11
Budget authority and outlays, net:			
Discretionary:			
4000 Budget authority, gross	91	92	101
Outlays, gross:			
4010 Outlays from new discretionary authority	91	92	101
Mandatory:			
4090 Budget authority, gross	5,633	5,696	5,740
Outlays, gross:			
4100 Outlays from new mandatory authority	5,610	5,684	5,732
4101 Outlays from mandatory balances	5	363	
4110 Outlays, gross (total)	5,615	6,047	5,732
Offsets against gross budget authority and outlays:			
Offsetting collections (collected) from:			
4123 Non-Federal sources	–4		
Additional offsets against gross budget authority only:			
4143 Recoveries of prior year paid obligations, unexpired accounts	4		
4160 Budget authority, net (mandatory)	5,633	5,696	5,740
4170 Outlays, net (mandatory)	5,611	6,047	5,732
4180 Budget authority, net (total)	5,724	5,788	5,841
4190 Outlays, net (total)	5,702	6,139	5,833
Memorandum (non-add) entries:			
5000 Total investments, SOY: Federal securities: Par value	307	862	767
5001 Total investments, EOY: Federal securities: Par value	862	767	620

Railroad retirees generally receive the equivalent to a Social Security benefit and a rail industry pension collectively bargained like other private pension plans but embedded in Federal law. Approximately 5,500 individuals also receive a "windfall" benefit.

Status of Funds (in millions of dollars)

Identification code 060–8011–0–7–601	2021 actual	2022 est.	2023 est.
Unexpended balance, start of year:			
0100 Balance, start of year	358	906	413
0999 Total balance, start of year	358	906	413
Cash income during the year:			
Current law:			
Receipts:			
1110 Refunds, Rail Industry Pension Fund		–2	–2
1110 Taxes, Rail Industry Pension Fund	2,875	3,092	3,045
1130 Rail Industry Pension Fund	4		
1150 Interest and Profits on Investments in Public Debt Securities, Rail Industry Pension Fund	14	16	15
1160 Payment from the National Railroad Retirement Investment Trust, Rail Industry Pension Fund	2,838	2,039	2,115
1160 Interest on Advances to Railroad Unemployment Insurance Account, Rail Industry Pension Fund		2	

		2021 actual	2022 est.	2023 est.
1160	Federal Payments to Railroad Retirement Trust Funds, Rail Industry Pension Fund	499	426	428
1160	Limitation on the Office of Inspector General	13	13	15
1199	Income under present law	6,243	5,586	5,616
1999	Total cash income	6,243	5,586	5,616
	Cash outgo during year: Current law:			
2100	Rail Industry Pension Fund [Budget Acct]	−5,706	−6,139	−5,833
2100	Limitation on the Office of Inspector General [Budget Acct]	−12	−17	−15
2199	Outgo under current law	−5,718	−6,156	−5,848
2999	Total cash outgo (−)	−5,718	−6,156	−5,848
	Surplus or deficit:			
3110	Excluding interest	511	−586	−247
3120	Interest	14	16	15
3199	Subtotal, surplus or deficit	525	−570	−232
3230	Rail Industry Pension Fund		107	
3230	Rail Industry Pension Fund	−81		
3230	Rail Industry Pension Fund	103		76
3230	Rail Industry Pension Fund		−30	
3298	Reconciliation adjustment	1		
3299	Total adjustments	23	77	76
3999	Total change in fund balance	548	−493	−156
	Unexpended balance, end of year:			
4100	Uninvested balance (net), end of year	44	−354	−363
4200	Rail Industry Pension Fund	862	767	620
4999	Total balance, end of year	906	413	257

Object Classification (in millions of dollars)

Identification code 060–8011–0–7–601		2021 actual	2022 est.	2023 est.
	Direct obligations:			
42.0	Benefit payments	5,637	5,684	5,733
94.0	Financial transfers	91	93	101
99.9	Total new obligations, unexpired accounts	5,728	5,777	5,834

LIMITATION ON ADMINISTRATION

For necessary expenses for the Railroad Retirement Board ("Board") for administration of the Railroad Retirement Act and the Railroad Unemployment Insurance Act, $131,666,000, to be derived in such amounts as determined by the Board from the railroad retirement accounts and from moneys credited to the railroad unemployment insurance administration fund: Provided, That notwithstanding section 7(b)(9) of the Railroad Retirement Act this limitation may be used to hire attorneys only through the excepted service: Provided further, That the previous proviso shall not change the status under Federal employment laws of any attorney hired by the Railroad Retirement Board prior to January 1, 2013: Provided further, That notwithstanding section 7(b)(9) of the Railroad Retirement Act, this limitation may be used to hire students attending qualifying educational institutions or individuals who have recently completed qualifying educational programs using current excepted hiring authorities established by the Office of Personnel Management.

Note.—A full-year 2022 appropriation for this account was not enacted at the time the Budget was prepared; therefore, the Budget assumes this account is operating under the Continuing Appropriations Act, 2022 (Division A of Public Law 117–43, as amended). The amounts included for 2022 reflect the annualized level provided by the continuing resolution.

Special and Trust Fund Receipts (in millions of dollars)

Identification code 060–8237–0–7–601		2021 actual	2022 est.	2023 est.
0100	Balance, start of year			
	Receipts: Current law:			
1140	General Fund Payment, Limitation on Administration	28		
2000	Total: Balances and receipts	28		
	Appropriations: Current law:			
2101	Limitation on Administration	−28		
5099	Balance, end of year			

Program and Financing (in millions of dollars)

Identification code 060–8237–0–7–601		2021 actual	2022 est.	2023 est.
	Obligations by program activity:			
0001	Rail Industry Pension Fund	86	84	92
0002	Railroad Social Security Equivalent Benefit	25	22	22
0003	Railroad Unemployment Insurance Trust Fund	17	18	18
0005	American Rescue Plan 2021	7		
0100	Subtotal, direct program	135	124	132
0799	Total direct obligations	135	124	132
0801	Medicare and other reimbursements	33	40	31
0900	Total new obligations, unexpired accounts	168	164	163
	Budgetary resources: Unobligated balance:			
1000	Unobligated balance brought forward, Oct 1	20	37	37
1012	Unobligated balance transfers between expired and unexpired accounts	2		
1070	Unobligated balance (total)	22	37	37
	Budget authority: Appropriations, mandatory:			
1201	Appropriation (special or trust fund) P.L. 117–2	28		
	Spending authority from offsetting collections, discretionary:			
1700	Collected	157	164	163
1900	Budget authority (total)	185	164	163
1930	Total budgetary resources available	207	201	200
	Memorandum (non-add) entries:			
1940	Unobligated balance expiring	−2		
1941	Unexpired unobligated balance, end of year	37	37	37
	Special and non-revolving trust funds:			
1951	Unobligated balance expiring	2		
1952	Expired unobligated balance, start of year	6	7	7
1953	Expired unobligated balance, end of year	5	7	7
	Change in obligated balance: Unpaid obligations:			
3000	Unpaid obligations, brought forward, Oct 1	37	46	10
3010	New obligations, unexpired accounts	168	164	163
3011	Obligations ("upward adjustments"), expired accounts	2		
3020	Outlays (gross)	−159	−200	−171
3041	Recoveries of prior year unpaid obligations, expired	−2		
3050	Unpaid obligations, end of year	46	10	2
	Memorandum (non-add) entries:			
3100	Obligated balance, start of year	37	46	10
3200	Obligated balance, end of year	46	10	2
	Budget authority and outlays, net: Discretionary:			
4000	Budget authority, gross	157	164	163
	Outlays, gross:			
4010	Outlays from new discretionary authority	124	164	163
4011	Outlays from discretionary balances	33	23	
4020	Outlays, gross (total)	157	187	163
	Offsets against gross budget authority and outlays: Offsetting collections (collected) from:			
4030	Federal sources	−157	−164	−163
4033	Non-Federal sources	−1		
4040	Offsets against gross budget authority and outlays (total)	−158	−164	−163
	Additional offsets against gross budget authority only:			
4052	Offsetting collections credited to expired accounts	1		
4080	Outlays, net (discretionary)	−1	23	
	Mandatory:			
4090	Budget authority, gross	28		
	Outlays, gross:			
4100	Outlays from new mandatory authority	2		
4101	Outlays from mandatory balances		13	8
4110	Outlays, gross (total)	2	13	8
4180	Budget authority, net (total)	28		
4190	Outlays, net (total)	1	36	8

The table below shows anticipated workloads.

	2020 actual	2021 actual	2022 est.	2023 est.
Pending, start of year	10,039	9,450	8,012	8,197
New Railroad Retirement applications	26,540	25,520	28,000	27,000
New Social Security certifications	3,681	3,162	3,000	3,000
Total dispositions (excluding partial awards)	30,810	30,120	30,815	30,171
Pending, end of year	9,450	8,012	8,197	8,026

Railroad Retirement Board—Continued
Trust Funds—Continued

LIMITATION ON ADMINISTRATION—Continued

As shown below, the Board projects this workload will continue to decline as the number of beneficiaries declines.

	1980 act.	1990 act.	2010 act.	2020 act.	2021 act.	2022 est.
Total beneficiaries	1,009,500	894,196	549,154	502,553	491,611	484,500

In recognition of the continuing decline in virtually all its major workloads, the Board will explore and adopt new approaches to improve service to beneficiaries.

The President's Budget includes three (3) legislative proposals: the first legislative proposal is to amend the Railroad Retirement Act to allow the Railroad Retirement Board (RRB) to utilize various hiring authorities available to other Federal agencies. Section 7(b)(9) of the Railroad Retirement Act contains language requiring that all employees of the RRB, except for one assistant for each Board Member, must be hired under the competitive civil service. Elimination of this requirement would enable the RRB to use various hiring authorities offered by the Office of Personnel Management; the second legislative proposal is to amend the Railroad Retirement Act to allow the Railroad Retirement Board to utilize student and recent graduate hiring authority available to other Federal agencies; lastly the third legislative proposal is to amend the Railroad Retirement Act and the Railroad Unemployment Insurance Act to include a felony charge for individuals committing fraud against the Agency. Under this proposal, both the Railroad Retirement Act and the Railroad Unemployment Insurance Act would be amended to include a felony charge similar to violations under 42 U.S.C. 408, 18 U.S.C. 1001, or 18 U.S.C. 287.

Object Classification (in millions of dollars)

Identification code 060–8237–0–7–601		2021 actual	2022 est.	2023 est.
	Direct obligations:			
	Personnel compensation:			
11.1	Full-time permanent	64	62	66
11.3	Other than full-time permanent	1	1	1
11.5	Other personnel compensation	2	1	1
11.9	Total personnel compensation	67	64	68
12.1	Civilian personnel benefits	24	23	25
23.1	Rental payments to GSA	4	4	4
23.3	Communications, utilities, and miscellaneous charges	7	7	7
25.2	Other services from non-Federal sources	21	16	14
25.3	Other goods and services from Federal sources	3	4	5
25.4	Operation and maintenance of facilities	2	....	1
25.6	Medical care	1	1	1
25.7	Operation and maintenance of equipment	3	2	3
26.0	Supplies and materials	....	....	1
31.0	Equipment	1	....	2
99.0	Direct obligations	133	121	131
99.0	Reimbursable obligations	33	39	31
99.5	Adjustment for rounding	2	4	1
99.9	Total new obligations, unexpired accounts	168	164	163

Employment Summary

Identification code 060–8237–0–7–601	2021 actual	2022 est.	2023 est.
1001 Direct civilian full-time equivalent employment	673	657	648
2001 Reimbursable civilian full-time equivalent employment	104	99	95

NATIONAL RAILROAD RETIREMENT INVESTMENT TRUST

Special and Trust Fund Receipts (in millions of dollars)

Identification code 060–8118–0–7–601		2021 actual	2022 est.	2023 est.
0100	Balance, start of year	24,400	28,264	27,288
	Receipts:			
	Current law:			
1130	Gains and Losses on Non-Federal Securities, National Railroad Retirement Investment Trust	6,291	354	526
1130	Interest and Dividends on Non-Federal Securities, National Railroad Retirement Investment Trust	469	754	95
1140	Earnings on Investments in Federal Securities, National Railroad Retirement Investment Trust	11	34	13
1199	Total current law receipts	6,771	1,142	634
1999	Total receipts	6,771	1,142	634
2000	Total: Balances and receipts	31,171	29,406	27,922
	Appropriations:			
	Current law:			
2101	National Railroad Retirement Investment Trust	–2,906	–2,118	–2,193
5098	Reconciliation adjustment	–1	....	....
5099	Balance, end of year	28,264	27,288	25,729

Program and Financing (in millions of dollars)

Identification code 060–8118–0–7–601		2021 actual	2022 est.	2023 est.
	Obligations by program activity:			
0001	NRRIT expenses	2,906	2,118	2,193
	Budgetary resources:			
	Budget authority:			
	Appropriations, mandatory:			
1201	Appropriation (special or trust fund)	2,906	2,118	2,193
1930	Total budgetary resources available	2,906	2,118	2,193
	Change in obligated balance:			
	Unpaid obligations:			
3010	New obligations, unexpired accounts	2,906	2,118	2,193
3020	Outlays (gross)	–2,906	–2,118	–2,193
	Budget authority and outlays, net:			
	Mandatory:			
4090	Budget authority, gross	2,906	2,118	2,193
	Outlays, gross:			
4100	Outlays from new mandatory authority	2,906	2,118	2,193
4180	Budget authority, net (total)	2,906	2,118	2,193
4190	Outlays, net (total)	2,906	2,118	2,193
	Memorandum (non-add) entries:			
5000	Total investments, SOY: Federal securities: Par value	454	737	873
5001	Total investments, EOY: Federal securities: Par value	737	873	823
5010	Total investments, SOY: non-Fed securities: Market value	23,950	27,537	26,415
5011	Total investments, EOY: non-Fed securities: Market value	27,537	26,415	24,905

The Trust manages and invests the funds of the Railroad Retirement System in private securities and U.S. Treasury Securities.

Status of Funds (in millions of dollars)

Identification code 060–8118–0–7–601		2021 actual	2022 est.	2023 est.
	Unexpended balance, start of year:			
0100	Balance, start of year	24,400	28,265	27,289
0999	Total balance, start of year	24,400	28,265	–27,289
	Cash income during the year:			
	Current law:			
	Receipts:			
1150	Gains and Losses on Non-Federal Securities, National Railroad Retirement Investment Trust	6,291	354	526
1150	Earnings on Investments in Federal Securities, National Railroad Retirement Investment Trust	11	34	13
1150	Interest and Dividends on Non-Federal Securities, National Railroad Retirement Investment Trust	469	754	95
1199	Income under present law	6,771	1,142	634
1999	Total cash income	6,771	1,142	634
	Cash outgo during year:			
	Current law:			
2100	National Railroad Retirement Investment Trust [Budget Acct]	–2,906	–2,118	–2,193
2199	Outgo under current law	–2,906	–2,118	–2,193
2999	Total cash outgo (–)	–2,906	–2,118	–2,193
	Surplus or deficit:			
3110	Excluding interest	–2,906	–2,118	–2,193
3120	Interest	6,771	1,142	634
3199	Subtotal, surplus or deficit	3,865	–976	–1,559
3999	Total change in fund balance	3,865	–976	–1,559
	Unexpended balance, end of year:			
4100	Uninvested balance (net), end of year	27,528	26,416	24,907
4200	National Railroad Retirement Investment Trust	737	873	823

OTHER INDEPENDENT AGENCIES

Railroad Retirement Board—Continued
Trust Funds—Continued

1319

Identification code 060–8118–0–7–601		2021 actual	2022 est.	2023 est.
4999	Total balance, end of year	28,265	27,289	25,730

Object Classification (in millions of dollars)

Identification code 060–8118–0–7–601		2021 actual	2022 est.	2023 est.
	Direct obligations:			
25.2	Other services from non-Federal sources	68	79	78
94.0	Financial transfers	2,838	2,039	2,115
99.9	Total new obligations, unexpired accounts	2,906	2,118	2,193

LIMITATION ON THE OFFICE OF INSPECTOR GENERAL

For expenses necessary for the Office of Inspector General for audit, investigatory and review activities, as authorized by the Inspector General Act of 1978, not more than $13,269,000, to be derived from the railroad retirement accounts and railroad unemployment insurance account.

Note.—A full-year 2022 appropriation for this account was not enacted at the time the Budget was prepared; therefore, the Budget assumes this account is operating under the Continuing Appropriations Act, 2022 (Division A of Public Law 117–43, as amended). The amounts included for 2022 reflect the annualized level provided by the continuing resolution.

Program and Financing (in millions of dollars)

Identification code 060–8018–0–7–601		2021 actual	2022 est.	2023 est.
	Obligations by program activity:			
0001	Rail Industry Pension Fund	8	8	9
0002	Railroad Social Security Equivalent Benefit	2	2	2
0003	Railroad Unemployment Insurance Trust	2	1	2
0100	Subtotal, direct program	12	11	13
0799	Total direct obligations	12	11	13
0801	Medicare and other reimbursements	1	2	2
0900	Total new obligations, unexpired accounts	13	13	15
	Budgetary resources:			
	Budget authority:			
	Appropriations, mandatory:			
1201	Appropriation (special or trust fund)	1		
	Spending authority from offsetting collections, discretionary:			
1700	Collected	13	13	15
1900	Budget authority (total)	14	13	15
1930	Total budgetary resources available	14	13	15
	Memorandum (non-add) entries:			
1940	Unobligated balance expiring	–1		
	Special and non-revolving trust funds:			
1951	Unobligated balance expiring	1		
1952	Expired unobligated balance, start of year	5	6	6
1953	Expired unobligated balance, end of year	5	6	6
	Change in obligated balance:			
	Unpaid obligations:			
3000	Unpaid obligations, brought forward, Oct 1	3	4	
3010	New obligations, unexpired accounts	13	13	15
3020	Outlays (gross)	–12	–17	–15
3050	Unpaid obligations, end of year	4		
	Memorandum (non-add) entries:			
3100	Obligated balance, start of year	3	4	
3200	Obligated balance, end of year	4		
	Budget authority and outlays, net:			
	Discretionary:			
4000	Budget authority, gross	13	13	15
	Outlays, gross:			
4010	Outlays from new discretionary authority	10	13	15
4011	Outlays from discretionary balances	2	3	
4020	Outlays, gross (total)	12	16	15
	Offsets against gross budget authority and outlays:			
	Offsetting collections (collected) from:			
4030	Federal sources	–13	–13	–15
4040	Offsets against gross budget authority and outlays (total)	–13	–13	–15
	Mandatory:			
4090	Budget authority, gross	1		
	Outlays, gross:			
4101	Outlays from mandatory balances		1	
4180	Budget authority, net (total)	1		
4190	Outlays, net (total)	–1	4	

The Limitation on the Office of Inspector General receives an appropriation for audit, investigatory and review activities of the Railroad Retirement Board Office of Inspector General.

Object Classification (in millions of dollars)

Identification code 060–8018–0–7–601		2021 actual	2022 est.	2023 est.
	Direct obligations:			
11.1	Personnel compensation: Full-time permanent	5	6	7
12.1	Civilian personnel benefits	2	2	3
25.2	Other services from non-Federal sources	1		
25.3	Other goods and services from Federal sources	1		
99.0	Direct obligations	9	8	10
99.0	Reimbursable obligations	1	2	2
99.5	Adjustment for rounding	3	3	3
99.9	Total new obligations, unexpired accounts	13	13	15

Employment Summary

Identification code 060–8018–0–7–601		2021 actual	2022 est.	2023 est.
1001	Direct civilian full-time equivalent employment	40	46	48
2001	Reimbursable civilian full-time equivalent employment	7	8	8

RAILROAD SOCIAL SECURITY EQUIVALENT BENEFIT ACCOUNT

Special and Trust Fund Receipts (in millions of dollars)

Identification code 060–8010–0–7–601		2021 actual	2022 est.	2023 est.
0100	Balance, start of year	361	364	350
	Receipts:			
	Current law:			
1110	Refunds, Railroad Social Security Equivalent Benefit Account		–1	–1
1110	Railroad Social Security Equivalent Benefit Account, Taxes	2,394	2,850	2,788
1110	Railroad Social Security Equivalent Benefit Account, Receipts Transferred to Federal Hospital Insurance Trust Fund	–552	–527	–536
1140	Railroad Social Security Equivalent Benefit Account, Interest and Profits on Investments in Public Debt Securities	23	20	24
1140	General Fund Payment, Social Security Equivalent Benefit Account	551	33	
1140	Railroad Social Security Equivalent Benefit Account, Income Tax Credits	281	355	362
1140	Railroad Social Security Equivalent Benefit Account, Interest Transferred to Federal Hospital Insurance Trust Fund	–16	–10	–14
1140	Railroad Social Security Equivalent Benefit Account, Receipts from Federal Old-age Survivors Ins. Trust Fund	4,792	5,263	5,473
1140	Railroad Social Security Equivalent Benefit Account, Receipts from Federal Disability Insurance Trust Fund	107	94	91
1140	Advances from the General Fund for Financial Interchange Interest, Social Security Equivalent Benefit Account	6	6	6
1198	Rounding adjustment	1		
1199	Total current law receipts	7,587	8,083	8,193
1999	Total receipts	7,587	8,083	8,193
2000	Total: Balances and receipts	7,948	8,447	8,543
	Appropriations:			
	Current law:			
2101	Railroad Social Security Equivalent Benefit Account	–27	–24	–24
2101	Railroad Social Security Equivalent Benefit Account	–7,561	–8,082	–8,193
2103	Railroad Social Security Equivalent Benefit Account	–30	–979	–1,001
2135	Railroad Social Security Equivalent Benefit Account	33	988	1,073
2198	Rounding adjustment	1		
2199	Total current law appropriations	–7,584	–8,097	–8,145
2999	Total appropriations	–7,584	–8,097	–8,145
5099	Balance, end of year	364	350	398

RAILROAD SOCIAL SECURITY EQUIVALENT BENEFIT ACCOUNT—Continued

Program and Financing (in millions of dollars)

Identification code 060–8010–0–7–601		2021 actual	2022 est.	2023 est.
	Obligations by program activity:			
0001	Railroad Social Security Equivalent Benefit Account (Direct)	7,658	7,983	8,345
	Budgetary resources:			
	Unobligated balance:			
1000	Unobligated balance brought forward, Oct 1	....	1	....
1001	Discretionary unobligated balance brought fwd, Oct 1	–33	....	....
	Budget authority:			
	Appropriations, discretionary:			
1101	Appropriation (special or trust)	27	24	24
	Appropriations, mandatory:			
1201	Appropriation (special or trust fund)	7,561	8,082	8,193
1203	Appropriation (previously unavailable)(special or trust)	30	979	1,001
1220	Appropriations transferred to other accts [060–8011]	–103	....	–76
1221	Appropriations transferred from other acct [060–8011]	....	30	....
1235	Appropriations precluded from obligation (special or trust)	–33	–988	–1,073
1236	Appropriations applied to repay debt	–4,852	–4,994	–4,872
1260	Appropriations, mandatory (total)	2,603	3,109	3,173
	Borrowing authority, mandatory:			
1400	Borrowing authority	5,029	4,849	5,148
1900	Budget authority (total)	7,659	7,982	8,345
1930	Total budgetary resources available	7,659	7,983	8,345
	Memorandum (non-add) entries:			
1941	Unexpired unobligated balance, end of year	1	....	....
	Change in obligated balance:			
	Unpaid obligations:			
3000	Unpaid obligations, brought forward, Oct 1	607	604	37
3010	New obligations, unexpired accounts	7,658	7,983	8,345
3020	Outlays (gross)	–7,661	–8,550	–8,334
3050	Unpaid obligations, end of year	604	37	48
	Memorandum (non-add) entries:			
3100	Obligated balance, start of year	607	604	37
3200	Obligated balance, end of year	604	37	48
	Budget authority and outlays, net:			
	Discretionary:			
4000	Budget authority, gross	27	24	24
	Outlays, gross:			
4010	Outlays from new discretionary authority	25	24	24
	Mandatory:			
4090	Budget authority, gross	7,632	7,958	8,321
	Outlays, gross:			
4100	Outlays from new mandatory authority	7,618	7,922	8,310
4101	Outlays from mandatory balances	18	604	....
4110	Outlays, gross (total)	7,636	8,526	8,310
4180	Budget authority, net (total)	7,659	7,982	8,345
4190	Outlays, net (total)	7,661	8,550	8,334
	Memorandum (non-add) entries:			
5000	Total investments, SOY: Federal securities: Par value	944	955	1,001
5001	Total investments, EOY: Federal securities: Par value	955	1,001	1,060
5080	Outstanding debt, SOY	–4,384	–4,567	–4,422
5081	Outstanding debt, EOY	–4,567	–4,422	–4,698
5082	Borrowing	–5,035	–4,849	–5,148

All railroad retirees receive the equivalent of a Social Security benefit, and they may also receive other add-ons including rail industry pension payments, windfall payments, and supplemental annuities. Social Security benefits for former railroad employees are funded by the Social Security trust funds, and rail industry pension payments are the responsibility of the rail sector.

Under current law, a financial interchange occurs once each year between the Social Security trust funds and the Social Security Equivalent Benefit (SSEB) account. SSEB receives monthly advances from the general fund equal to an estimate of the transfer SSEB would have received for the previous month if the financial interchange transfers were on a monthly basis. Advances from the previous year are repaid annually to the general fund immediately after the financial interchange is received. In 2021, $5,035 million was advanced and $4,852 million was repaid.

Status of Funds (in millions of dollars)

Identification code 060–8010–0–7–601		2021 actual	2022 est.	2023 est.
	Unexpended balance, start of year:			
0100	Balance, start of year	–3,411	–3,588	–4,025
0999	Total balance, start of year	–3,411	–3,588	–4,025
	Cash income during the year:			
	Current law:			
	Receipts:			
1110	Refunds, Railroad Social Security Equivalent Benefit Account	....	–1	–1
1110	Railroad Social Security Equivalent Benefit Account, Taxes	2,394	2,850	2,788
1110	Railroad Social Security Equivalent Benefit Account, Receipts Transferred to Federal Hospital Insurance Trust Fund	–552	–527	–536
1150	Railroad Social Security Equivalent Benefit Account, Interest and Profits on Investments in Public Debt Securities	23	20	24
1150	Railroad Social Security Equivalent Benefit Account, Interest Transferred to Federal Hospital Insurance Trust Fund	–16	–10	–14
1160	General Fund Payment, Social Security Equivalent Benefit Account	551	33	....
1160	Railroad Social Security Equivalent Benefit Account, Income Tax Credits	281	355	362
1160	Railroad Social Security Equivalent Benefit Account, Receipts from Federal Old-age Survivors Ins. Trust Fund	4,792	5,263	5,473
1160	Railroad Social Security Equivalent Benefit Account, Receipts from Federal Disability Insurance Trust Fund	107	94	91
1160	Advances from the General Fund for Financial Interchange Interest, Social Security Equivalent Benefit Account	6	6	6
1199	Income under present law	7,586	8,083	8,193
1999	Total cash income	7,586	8,083	8,193
	Cash outgo during year:			
	Current law:			
2100	Railroad Social Security Equivalent Benefit Account [Budget Acct]	–7,661	–8,550	–8,334
2199	Outgo under current law	–7,661	–8,550	–8,334
2999	Total cash outgo (-)	–7,661	–8,550	–8,334
	Surplus or deficit:			
3110	Excluding interest	–82	–477	–151
3120	Interest	7	10	10
3199	Subtotal, surplus or deficit	–75	–467	–141
3230	Railroad Social Security Equivalent Benefit Account	....	30	....
3230	Railroad Social Security Equivalent Benefit Account	–103	....	–76
3298	Reconciliation adjustment	1	....	....
3299	Total adjustments	–102	30	–76
3999	Total change in fund balance	–177	–437	–217
	Unexpended balance, end of year:			
4100	Uninvested balance (net), end of year	–4,543	–5,026	–5,302
4200	Railroad Social Security Equivalent Benefit Account	955	1,001	1,060
4999	Total balance, end of year	–3,588	–4,025	–4,242

Object Classification (in millions of dollars)

Identification code 060–8010–0–7–601		2021 actual	2022 est.	2023 est.
	Direct obligations:			
42.0	Benefit payments	7,533	7,959	8,245
94.0	Financial transfers	99	....	76
94.0	Financial transfers	26	24	24
99.9	Total new obligations, unexpired accounts	7,658	7,983	8,345

SECURITIES AND EXCHANGE COMMISSION

Federal Funds

SALARIES AND EXPENSES

For necessary expenses for the Securities and Exchange Commission, including services as authorized by 5 U.S.C. 3109, the rental of space (to include multiple year leases) in the District of Columbia and elsewhere, and not to exceed $3,500 for official reception and representation expenses, $2,149,000,000, to remain available until expended; of which not less than $18,979,000 shall be for the Office of Inspector General; of which not to exceed $275,000 shall be available for a permanent secretariat for the International Organization of Securities Commissions; and of which not to exceed $100,000 shall be available for expenses for consultations and meetings hosted by the Commission with foreign governmental and other regulatory officials, members of their delegations and staffs to exchange views concerning securities matters, such expenses to include necessary logistic and administrative expenses and the expenses of Commission staff and foreign invitees in attendance including: (1) incidental expenses such as meals; (2) travel and transportation; and (3) related lodging or subsistence.

In addition to the foregoing appropriation, for move, replication, and related costs associated with a replacement lease for the Commission's District of Columbia headquarters facilities, not to exceed $57,405,000, to remain available until expended.

For purposes of calculating the fee rate under section 31(j) of the Securities Exchange Act of 1934 (15 U.S.C. 78ee(j)) for fiscal year 2023, all amounts appropriated under this heading shall be deemed to be the regular appropriation to the Commission for fiscal year 2023: Provided, That fees and charges authorized by section 31 of the Securities Exchange Act of 1934 (15 U.S.C. 78ee) shall be credited to this account as offsetting collections: Provided further, That not to exceed $2,149,000,000 of such offsetting collections shall be available until expended for necessary expenses of this account and not to exceed $57,405,000 of such offsetting collections shall be available until expended for move, replication, and related costs under this heading associated with a replacement lease for the Commission's District of Columbia headquarters facilities: Provided further, That the total amount appropriated under this heading from the general fund for fiscal year 2023 shall be reduced as such offsetting fees are received so as to result in a final total fiscal year 2023 appropriation from the general fund estimated at not more than $0: Provided further, That if any amount of the appropriation for move, replication, and related costs associated with a replacement lease for the Commission's District of Columbia headquarters facilities is subsequently de-obligated by the Commission, such amount that was derived from the general fund shall be returned to the general fund, and such amounts that were derived from fees or assessments collected for such purpose shall be paid to each national securities exchange and national securities association, respectively, in proportion to any fees or assessments paid by such national securities exchange or national securities association under section 31 of the Securities Exchange Act of 1934 (15 U.S.C. 78ee) in fiscal year 2023.

Note.—A full-year 2022 appropriation for this account was not enacted at the time the Budget was prepared; therefore, the Budget assumes this account is operating under the Continuing Appropriations Act, 2022 (Division A of Public Law 117–43, as amended). The amounts included for 2022 reflect the annualized level provided by the continuing resolution.

Program and Financing (in millions of dollars)

Identification code 050–0100–0–1–376		2021 actual	2022 est.	2023 est.
	Obligations by program activity:			
0001	Enforcement	628	613	681
0002	Compliance Inspections and Examinations	448	438	487
0003	Corporation Finance	173	166	191
0004	Trading and Markets	111	110	127
0005	Investment Management	85	85	96
0006	Economic and Risk Analysis	70	70	83
0007	General Counsel	61	60	69
0008	Other Program Offices	100	100	113
0009	Agency Direction and Administrative Support	258	265	302
0010	Inspector General	21	22	25
0011	Relocation Costs	253	22	57
0900	Total new obligations, unexpired accounts	2,208	1,951	2,231
	Budgetary resources:			
	Unobligated balance:			
1000	Unobligated balance brought forward, Oct 1	292	47	48
1021	Recoveries of prior year unpaid obligations	38	25	25
1070	Unobligated balance (total)	330	72	73
	Budget authority:			
	Appropriations, discretionary:			
1100	Appropriation	34		
	Spending authority from offsetting collections, discretionary:			
1700	Collected	1,862	1,896	2,149
1700	Collected [Relocation Costs]	31	31	57
1750	Spending auth from offsetting collections, disc (total)	1,893	1,927	2,206
1900	Budget authority (total)	1,927	1,927	2,206
1901	Adjustment for new budget authority used to liquidate deficiencies	–2		
1930	Total budgetary resources available	2,255	1,999	2,279

	Memorandum (non-add) entries:			
1941	Unexpired unobligated balance, end of year	47	48	48
	Change in obligated balance:			
	Unpaid obligations:			
3000	Unpaid obligations, brought forward, Oct 1	599	901	739
3010	New obligations, unexpired accounts	2,208	1,951	2,231
3020	Outlays (gross)	–1,868	–2,088	–2,360
3040	Recoveries of prior year unpaid obligations, unexpired	–38	–25	–25
3050	Unpaid obligations, end of year	901	739	585
	Memorandum (non-add) entries:			
3100	Obligated balance, start of year	599	901	739
3200	Obligated balance, end of year	901	739	585
	Budget authority and outlays, net:			
	Discretionary:			
4000	Budget authority, gross	1,927	1,927	2,206
	Outlays, gross:			
4010	Outlays from new discretionary authority	1,444	1,614	1,830
4011	Outlays from discretionary balances	424	474	530
4020	Outlays, gross (total)	1,868	2,088	2,360
	Offsets against gross budget authority and outlays:			
	Offsetting collections (collected) from:			
4033	Non-Federal sources		–1	
4034	Offsetting governmental collections	–1,862	–1,895	–2,149
4034	Offsetting governmental collections [Relocation Costs]	–31	–31	–57
4040	Offsets against gross budget authority and outlays (total)	–1,893	–1,927	–2,206
4070	Budget authority, net (discretionary)	34		
4080	Outlays, net (discretionary)	–25	161	154
4180	Budget authority, net (total)	34		
4190	Outlays, net (total)	–25	161	154
	Memorandum (non-add) entries:			
5090	Unexpired unavailable balance, SOY: Offsetting collections	7,175	7,175	7,175
5092	Unexpired unavailable balance, EOY: Offsetting collections	7,175	7,175	7,175
	Unfunded deficiencies:			
7000	Unfunded deficiency, start of year	–2		
	Change in deficiency during the year:			
7012	Budgetary resources used to liquidate deficiencies	2		

The mission of the Securities and Exchange Commission (SEC) is to: protect investors; maintain fair, orderly, and efficient markets; and facilitate capital formation. The SEC's six major programs include the following:

Enforcement.—The Division of Enforcement investigates and prosecutes civil violations of the Federal securities laws and works closely with the Department of Justice and other law enforcement partners to coordinate and assist in criminal prosecutions.

Examinations.—The Division of Examinations conducts the SEC's examination program to detect violations of the Federal securities laws and evaluate internal compliance controls at securities firms registered with the SEC.

Corporation Finance.—The Division of Corporation Finance selectively reviews company disclosures to ensure that investors have the information necessary to make informed investment decisions and to help deter fraud and misrepresentation in securities transactions.

Trading and Markets.—The Division of Trading and Markets' (TM) mission is to establish and maintain standards for fair, orderly, and efficient markets while fostering investor protection and confidence in the markets. TM oversees the activities of industry self-regulatory organizations, such as the Financial Industry Regulatory Authority, and directly regulates market participants where Commission rulemaking is more effective than self-regulation.

Investment Management.—The Division of Investment Management works to protect investors, promote informed investment decision making, and facilitate appropriate innovation in investment products and services through regulation of the asset management industry.

Economic and Risk Analysis.—The Division of Economic and Risk Analysis integrates financial economics and rigorous data analytics into the core mission of the SEC.

Additional program offices directly support the major programs: the Office of International Affairs, the Office of the Chief Accountant, the Office of

Securities and Exchange Commission—Continued
Federal Funds—Continued

SALARIES AND EXPENSES—Continued

Credit Ratings, the Office of Investor Education and Advocacy, the Office of the Investor Advocate, the Office of Administrative Law Judges, the Office of the Advocate for Small Business Capital Formation, the Office of Municipal Securities, and the Strategic Hub for Innovation and Financial Technology.

The SEC is funded through offsetting fees and assessments collected pursuant to section 31 of the Securities Exchange Act of 1934 (15 U.S.C. 78ee) at a rate intended to fully offset the SEC's appropriation.

In addition to amounts requested for operations, the Budget proposes an amount for move, replication, and related costs associated with a replacement lease for the Commission's District of Columbia headquarters facilities. This amount would not be used for the operations of the SEC, and the proposed appropriations language provides a mechanism whereby any unused portion of these funds could be refunded to fee payers (or returned to the general fund of the Treasury) as rapidly as practicable.

Object Classification (in millions of dollars)

Identification code 050–0100–0–1–376		2021 actual	2022 est.	2023 est.
	Direct obligations:			
	Personnel compensation:			
11.1	Full-time permanent	900	942	1,071
11.3	Other than full-time permanent	33	....	....
11.5	Other personnel compensation	6	12	18
11.8	Special personal services payments	4	3	3
11.9	Total personnel compensation	943	957	1,092
12.1	Civilian personnel benefits	344	351	410
13.0	Benefits for former personnel	3	....	....
21.0	Travel and transportation of persons	....	2	12
23.1	Rental payments to GSA	34	30	33
23.2	Rental payments to others	82	73	80
23.3	Communications, utilities, and miscellaneous charges	14	12	14
24.0	Printing and reproduction	8	3	9
25.1	Advisory and assistance services	60	54	58
25.2	Other services from non-Federal sources	75	69	70
25.3	Other goods and services from Federal sources	60	54	56
25.4	Operation and maintenance of facilities	10	9	23
25.7	Operation and maintenance of equipment	289	262	269
26.0	Supplies and materials	1	1	1
31.0	Equipment	40	60	82
32.0	Land and structures	245	13	21
42.0	Insurance claims and indemnities	....	1	1
99.9	Total new obligations, unexpired accounts	2,208	1,951	2,231

Employment Summary

Identification code 050–0100–0–1–376	2021 actual	2022 est.	2023 est.
1001 Direct civilian full-time equivalent employment	4,459	4,528	4,808

SECURITIES AND EXCHANGE COMMISSION RESERVE FUND

Special and Trust Fund Receipts (in millions of dollars)

Identification code 050–5566–0–2–376		2021 actual	2022 est.	2023 est.
0100	Balance, start of year	3	3	3
	Receipts:			
	Current law:			
1110	Registration Fees, Securities and Exchange Commission Reserve Fund	50	50	50
2000	Total: Balances and receipts	53	53	53
	Appropriations:			
	Current law:			
2101	Securities and Exchange Commission Reserve Fund	–50	–50	–50
2103	Securities and Exchange Commission Reserve Fund	–3	–3	–3
2132	Securities and Exchange Commission Reserve Fund	3	3	3
2199	Total current law appropriations	–50	–50	–50
2999	Total appropriations	–50	–50	–50
5099	Balance, end of year	3	3	3

Program and Financing (in millions of dollars)

Identification code 050–5566–0–2–376		2021 actual	2022 est.	2023 est.
	Obligations by program activity:			
0001	Enforcement	16	16	15
0002	Compliance Inspections and Examinations	12	12	12
0003	Corporation Finance	5	5	5
0004	Trading and Markets	3	3	3
0005	Investment Management	2	2	2
0006	Economic and Risk Analysis	2	2	2
0007	General Counsel	2	2	2
0008	Other Program Offices	3	3	3
0009	Agency Direction and Administrative Support	7	7	6
0010	Inspector General	1	....	....
0900	Total new obligations, unexpired accounts	53	52	50
	Budgetary resources:			
	Unobligated balance:			
1000	Unobligated balance brought forward, Oct 1	3	2	....
1021	Recoveries of prior year unpaid obligations	2	....	....
1070	Unobligated balance (total)	5	2	....
	Budget authority:			
	Appropriations, mandatory:			
1201	Appropriation (special or trust fund)	50	50	50
1203	Appropriation (previously unavailable)(special or trust)	3	3	3
1232	Appropriations and/or unobligated balance of appropriations temporarily reduced	–3	–3	–3
1260	Appropriations, mandatory (total)	50	50	50
1900	Budget authority (total)	50	50	50
1930	Total budgetary resources available	55	52	50
	Memorandum (non-add) entries:			
1941	Unexpired unobligated balance, end of year	2	....	....
	Change in obligated balance:			
	Unpaid obligations:			
3000	Unpaid obligations, brought forward, Oct 1	52	44	46
3010	New obligations, unexpired accounts	53	52	50
3020	Outlays (gross)	–59	–50	–50
3040	Recoveries of prior year unpaid obligations, unexpired	–2	....	....
3050	Unpaid obligations, end of year	44	46	46
	Memorandum (non-add) entries:			
3100	Obligated balance, start of year	52	44	46
3200	Obligated balance, end of year	44	46	46
	Budget authority and outlays, net:			
	Mandatory:			
4090	Budget authority, gross	50	50	50
	Outlays, gross:			
4100	Outlays from new mandatory authority	15	17	17
4101	Outlays from mandatory balances	44	33	33
4110	Outlays, gross (total)	59	50	50
4180	Budget authority, net (total)	50	50	50
4190	Outlays, net (total)	59	50	50

Section 991 of the Dodd-Frank Wall Street Reform and Consumer Protection Act (P.L. 111–203) (the Dodd-Frank Act) amended section 4 of the Securities Exchange Act of 1934 (15 U.S.C. 78d) to establish the Securities and Exchange Commission Reserve Fund. The Reserve Fund is a separate fund in the Treasury from which the Commission may obligate amounts determined necessary to carry out Commission functions. The Reserve Fund provisions took effect on October 1, 2011.

The Reserve Fund is funded by deposits from registration fees collected by the Commission under section 6(b) of the Securities Act of 1933 (15 U.S.C. 77f(b)) and section 24(f) of the Investment Company Act of 1940 (15 U.S.C. 80a–24(f)). In any one fiscal year, the amount deposited in the Reserve Fund may not exceed $50 million and obligations from the Reserve Fund may not exceed $100 million. The balance in the Reserve Fund may not exceed $100 million. Amounts in the Reserve Fund are available until expended. (The remainder of registration fee collections for each fiscal year are deposited in the general fund of the Treasury and are not available for obligation by the Commission.)

Amounts collected and deposited in the Reserve Fund are not subject to appropriation or apportionment. However, the Commission is required to notify the Congress of the amount and purpose of any obligations made utilizing amounts from the Reserve Fund within 10 days.

Object Classification (in millions of dollars)

Identification code 050–5566–0–2–376		2021 actual	2022 est.	2023 est.
	Direct obligations:			
25.1	Advisory and assistance services	4	4	4
25.7	Operation and maintenance of equipment	12	12	11
31.0	Equipment	37	36	35
99.9	Total new obligations, unexpired accounts	53	52	50

INVESTOR PROTECTION FUND

Special and Trust Fund Receipts (in millions of dollars)

Identification code 050–5567–0–2–376		2021 actual	2022 est.	2023 est.
0100	Balance, start of year	1	27	23
	Receipts:			
	Current law:			
1110	Monetary Sanctions, Investor Protection Fund	472	415	255
1140	Interest, Investor Protection Fund	3	4	4
1199	Total current law receipts	475	419	259
1999	Total receipts	475	419	259
2000	Total: Balances and receipts	476	446	282
	Appropriations:			
	Current law:			
2101	Investor Protection Fund	–475	–419	–258
2103	Investor Protection Fund	–1	–27	–23
2132	Investor Protection Fund	27	23	15
2199	Total current law appropriations	–449	–423	–266
2999	Total appropriations	–449	–423	–266
5099	Balance, end of year	27	23	16

Program and Financing (in millions of dollars)

Identification code 050–5567–0–2–376		2021 actual	2022 est.	2023 est.
	Obligations by program activity:			
0001	Enforcement	565	267	267
0900	Total new obligations, unexpired accounts (object class 11.8)	565	267	267
	Budgetary resources:			
	Unobligated balance:			
1000	Unobligated balance brought forward, Oct 1	260	144	300
	Budget authority:			
	Appropriations, mandatory:			
1201	Appropriation (special or trust fund)	475	419	258
1203	Appropriation (previously unavailable)(special or trust)	1	27	23
1232	Appropriations and/or unobligated balance of appropriations temporarily reduced	–27	–23	–15
1260	Appropriations, mandatory (total)	449	423	266
1930	Total budgetary resources available	709	567	566
	Memorandum (non-add) entries:			
1941	Unexpired unobligated balance, end of year	144	300	299
	Change in obligated balance:			
	Unpaid obligations:			
3000	Unpaid obligations, brought forward, Oct 1	95	194	246
3010	New obligations, unexpired accounts	565	267	267
3020	Outlays (gross)	–466	–215	–223
3050	Unpaid obligations, end of year	194	246	290
	Memorandum (non-add) entries:			
3100	Obligated balance, start of year	95	194	246
3200	Obligated balance, end of year	194	246	290
	Budget authority and outlays, net:			
	Mandatory:			
4090	Budget authority, gross	449	423	266
	Outlays, gross:			
4100	Outlays from new mandatory authority	109	79	174
4101	Outlays from mandatory balances	357	136	49
4110	Outlays, gross (total)	466	215	223
4180	Budget authority, net (total)	449	423	266
4190	Outlays, net (total)	466	215	223
	Memorandum (non-add) entries:			
5000	Total investments, SOY: Federal securities: Par value	309	258	258
5001	Total investments, EOY: Federal securities: Par value	258	258	258

As part of the Dodd-Frank Wall Street Reform and Consumer Protection Act (P.L. 111–203) (the Dodd-Frank Act), the Congress substantially expanded the Securities and Exchange Commission's (SEC or Commission) authority to pay whistleblower awards and enhanced the anti-retaliation protections available to whistleblowers. The intent is to incentivize submission of high-quality tips by motivating persons with knowledge of possible securities laws violations to assist the Federal Government in identifying and prosecuting individuals who violate the Federal securities laws.

To comply with direction provided in the Dodd-Frank Act, the SEC's Division of Enforcement established an Office of the Whistleblower to administer and enforce the whistleblower award program. The Investor Protection Fund (the Fund), established by the Dodd-Frank Act, provides resources for payments to whistleblowers and for the SEC's Office of the Inspector General Employee Suggestion Program. Deposits into the Fund are comprised of a portion of monetary sanctions collected by the SEC in judicial or administrative actions brought by the Commission under the Federal securities laws that are not added to a disgorgement fund or other fund under section 308 of the Sarbanes-Oxley Act of 2002 (P.L. 107–204), as well as amounts in such funds that will not be distributed to injured investors. No sanction collected by the Commission can be deposited into the Fund if the balance at the time the sanction is collected exceeds $300 million. No funds have been taken or withheld from harmed investors to pay whistleblower awards. The Commission is required to submit an annual report on the whistleblower award program to the Committee on Banking, Housing, and Urban Affairs of the Senate and the Committee on Financial Services of the House of Representatives.

The figures reported for 2022 and 2023 are based on assumptions regarding several variables inherent to litigation and to the Commission's whistleblower award process. Given the potential for significant variation in the payouts and their timing, it is possible that actual payouts will be either significantly higher or significantly lower than these estimates.

GENERAL FUND RECEIPT ACCOUNTS

(in millions of dollars)

	2021 actual	2022 est.	2023 est.
Offsetting receipts from the public:			
050–149200 Post-Judgment Interest	2	1	1
General Fund Offsetting receipts from the public	2	1	1

SMITHSONIAN INSTITUTION

Federal Funds

SALARIES AND EXPENSES

For necessary expenses of the Smithsonian Institution, as authorized by law, including research in the fields of art, science, and history; development, preservation, and documentation of the National Collections; presentation of public exhibits and performances; collection, preparation, dissemination, and exchange of information and publications; conduct of education, training, and museum assistance programs; maintenance, alteration, operation, lease agreements of no more than 30 years, and protection of buildings, facilities, and approaches; not to exceed $100,000 for services as authorized by 5 U.S.C. 3109; and purchase, rental, repair, and cleaning of uniforms for employees, $909,500,000, to remain available until September 30, 2024, except as otherwise provided herein; of which not to exceed $26,974,000 for the instrumentation program, collections acquisition, exhibition reinstallation, Smithsonian American Women's History Museum, National Museum of the American

Smithsonian Institution—Continued
Federal Funds—Continued

SALARIES AND EXPENSES—Continued

Latino, and the repatriation of skeletal remains program shall remain available until expended; and including such funds as may be necessary to support American overseas research centers: Provided, That funds appropriated herein are available for advance payments to independent contractors performing research services or participating in official Smithsonian presentations: Provided further, That the Smithsonian Institution may expend Federal appropriations designated in this Act for lease or rent payments, as rent payable to the Smithsonian Institution, and such rent payments may be deposited into the general trust funds of the Institution to be available as trust funds for expenses associated with the purchase of a portion of the building at 600 Maryland Avenue, SW, Washington, DC, to the extent that federally supported activities will be housed there: Provided further, That the use of such amounts in the general trust funds of the Institution for such purpose shall not be construed as Federal debt service for, a Federal guarantee of, a transfer of risk to, or an obligation of the Federal Government: Provided further, That no appropriated funds may be used directly to service debt which is incurred to finance the costs of acquiring a portion of the building at 600 Maryland Avenue, SW, Washington, DC, or of planning, designing, and constructing improvements to such building: Provided further, That any agreement entered into by the Smithsonian Institution for the sale of its ownership interest, or any portion thereof, in such building so acquired may not take effect until the expiration of a 30 day period which begins on the date on which the Secretary of the Smithsonian submits to the Committees on Appropriations of the House of Representatives and Senate, the Committees on House Administration and Transportation and Infrastructure of the House of Representatives, and the Committee on Rules and Administration of the Senate a report, as outlined in the explanatory statement described in section 4 of the Further Consolidated Appropriations Act, 2020 (Public Law 116–94; 133 Stat. 2536) on the intended sale.

Note.—A full-year 2022 appropriation for this account was not enacted at the time the Budget was prepared; therefore, the Budget assumes this account is operating under the Continuing Appropriations Act, 2022 (Division A of Public Law 117–43, as amended). The amounts included for 2022 reflect the annualized level provided by the continuing resolution.

Program and Financing (in millions of dollars)

Identification code 033–0100–0–1–503	2021 actual	2022 est.	2023 est.
Obligations by program activity:			
0001 Public programs	51	52	68
0002 Exhibitions	57	58	63
0003 Collections	78	80	87
0004 Research	97	101	113
0005 Facilities	263	271	284
0006 Security & safety	101	103	112
0007 Information technology	47	51	56
0008 Operations	97	99	108
0799 Total direct obligations	791	815	891
0821 Salaries and Expenses (Reimbursable)	10	9	9
0900 Total new obligations, unexpired accounts	801	824	900
Budgetary resources:			
Unobligated balance:			
1000 Unobligated balance brought forward, Oct 1	65	95	98
Budget authority:			
Appropriations, discretionary:			
1100 Appropriation	818	818	910
Spending authority from offsetting collections, discretionary:			
1700 Collected	7	9	9
1701 Change in uncollected payments, Federal sources	6		
1750 Spending auth from offsetting collections, disc (total)	13	9	9
1900 Budget authority (total)	831	827	919
1930 Total budgetary resources available	896	922	1,017
Memorandum (non-add) entries:			
1941 Unexpired unobligated balance, end of year	95	98	117
Change in obligated balance:			
Unpaid obligations:			
3000 Unpaid obligations, brought forward, Oct 1	154	177	138
3010 New obligations, unexpired accounts	801	824	900
3011 Obligations ("upward adjustments"), expired accounts	4		
3020 Outlays (gross)	–780	–863	–911
3041 Recoveries of prior year unpaid obligations, expired	–2		
3050 Unpaid obligations, end of year	177	138	127
Uncollected payments:			
3060 Uncollected pymts, Fed sources, brought forward, Oct 1	–6	–10	–10
3070 Change in uncollected pymts, Fed sources, unexpired	–6		
3071 Change in uncollected pymts, Fed sources, expired	2		
3090 Uncollected pymts, Fed sources, end of year	–10	–10	–10
Memorandum (non-add) entries:			
3100 Obligated balance, start of year	148	167	128
3200 Obligated balance, end of year	167	128	117
Budget authority and outlays, net:			
Discretionary:			
4000 Budget authority, gross	831	827	919
Outlays, gross:			
4010 Outlays from new discretionary authority	610	695	772
4011 Outlays from discretionary balances	170	168	139
4020 Outlays, gross (total)	780	863	911
Offsets against gross budget authority and outlays:			
Offsetting collections (collected) from:			
4030 Federal sources	–9	–9	–9
4040 Offsets against gross budget authority and outlays (total)	–9	–9	–9
Additional offsets against gross budget authority only:			
4050 Change in uncollected pymts, Fed sources, unexpired	–6		
4052 Offsetting collections credited to expired accounts	2		
4060 Additional offsets against budget authority only (total)	–4		
4070 Budget authority, net (discretionary)	818	818	910
4080 Outlays, net (discretionary)	771	854	902
4180 Budget authority, net (total)	818	818	910
4190 Outlays, net (total)	771	854	902

The Smithsonian Institution conducts research in natural and physical sciences, history and the history of cultures, technology and the arts. The Institution acquires and preserves more than 155 million items of scientific, cultural, and historic importance for reference and study purposes. These resources may be accessed by millions of visitors and researchers worldwide either in person, or increasingly online. Smithsonian's public exhibitions delve into subjects from aeronautics to zoology.

The Institution operates 19 museums and galleries, a zoological park and animal conservation and research center, research facilities, and supporting facilities. The Institution is in early planning stages for two additional museums established by Congress in December 2020.

Included in the presentation of the Salaries and Expenses account are data for the Canal Zone biological area fund. Donations, subscriptions, and fees are appropriated and used to defray part of the expenses of maintaining and operating the Canal Zone biological area (60 Stat. 1101; 20 U.S.C. 79, 79a).

Object Classification (in millions of dollars)

Identification code 033–0100–0–1–503	2021 actual	2022 est.	2023 est.
Direct obligations:			
Personnel compensation:			
11.1 Full-time permanent	334	344	372
11.3 Other than full-time permanent	3	3	4
11.5 Other personnel compensation	16	16	19
11.9 Total personnel compensation	353	363	395
12.1 Civilian personnel benefits	127	134	147
21.0 Travel and transportation of persons			4
22.0 Transportation of things	1	1	1
23.3 Rent, Communications, and Utilities	89	94	103
24.0 Printing and reproduction	1	1	1
25.2 Other services	180	181	190
26.0 Supplies and materials	17	17	21
31.0 Equipment	19	20	25
32.0 Land and structures	4	4	4
99.0 Direct obligations	791	815	891
99.0 Reimbursable obligations	10	9	9
99.9 Total new obligations, unexpired accounts	801	824	900

Employment Summary

Identification code 033–0100–0–1–503	2021 actual	2022 est.	2023 est.
1001 Direct civilian full-time equivalent employment	4,026	4,026	4,168

FACILITIES CAPITAL

For necessary expenses of repair, revitalization, and alteration of facilities owned or occupied by the Smithsonian Institution, by contract or otherwise, as authorized by section 2 of the Act of August 22, 1949 (63 Stat. 623), and for construction, including necessary personnel, $265,000,000, to remain available until expended, of which not to exceed $10,000 shall be for services as authorized by 5 U.S.C. 3109.

Note.—A full-year 2022 appropriation for this account was not enacted at the time the Budget was prepared; therefore, the Budget assumes this account is operating under the Continuing Appropriations Act, 2022 (Division A of Public Law 117–43, as amended). The amounts included for 2022 reflect the annualized level provided by the continuing resolution.

Program and Financing (in millions of dollars)

Identification code 033–0103–0–1–503		2021 actual	2022 est.	2023 est.
	Obligations by program activity:			
0010	Construction	3	1	35
0020	Revitalization	185	181	185
0030	Facilities planning and design	31	35	42
0900	Total new obligations, unexpired accounts	219	217	262
	Budgetary resources:			
	Unobligated balance:			
1000	Unobligated balance brought forward, Oct 1	29	26	24
	Budget authority:			
	Appropriations, discretionary:			
1100	Appropriation	215	215	265
	Spending authority from offsetting collections, discretionary:			
1700	Collected	1		
1900	Budget authority (total)	216	215	265
1930	Total budgetary resources available	245	241	289
	Memorandum (non-add) entries:			
1941	Unexpired unobligated balance, end of year	26	24	27
	Change in obligated balance:			
	Unpaid obligations:			
3000	Unpaid obligations, brought forward, Oct 1	467	470	303
3010	New obligations, unexpired accounts	219	217	262
3020	Outlays (gross)	−216	−384	−234
3050	Unpaid obligations, end of year	470	303	331
	Uncollected payments:			
3060	Uncollected pymts, Fed sources, brought forward, Oct 1	−1	−1	−1
3090	Uncollected pymts, Fed sources, end of year	−1	−1	−1
	Memorandum (non-add) entries:			
3100	Obligated balance, start of year	466	469	302
3200	Obligated balance, end of year	469	302	330
	Budget authority and outlays, net:			
	Discretionary:			
4000	Budget authority, gross	216	215	265
	Outlays, gross:			
4010	Outlays from new discretionary authority	20	54	64
4011	Outlays from discretionary balances	196	330	170
4020	Outlays, gross (total)	216	384	234
	Offsets against gross budget authority and outlays:			
	Offsetting collections (collected) from:			
4030	Federal sources	−1		
4180	Budget authority, net (total)	215	215	265
4190	Outlays, net (total)	215	384	234

This account provides funding for major new construction projects to support the Smithsonian's existing and future programs in research, collections management, public exhibitions, and education. This account also includes major repairs, revitalization, code compliance changes, minor construction, alterations and modifications, and building system renewals of Smithsonian museum buildings and facilities for storage and conservation of collections, research, and support. The Facilities Capital account also includes planning and design funding related to these activities and to plan new museums authorized by Congress. The President's Budget for Fiscal Year 2023 includes funds for critical infrastructure improvements at the National Museum of Natural History, the National Zoological Park, and the National Museum of American History. In addition, funds are included for improvements to the Smithsonian Tropical Research Institute and Astrophysical Observatory and other important revitalization projects throughout the Institution. Current long-term projects in this account include the Suitland Collections Facility and renovations at the National Air and Space Museum facilities, the Smithsonian Castle and Arts and Industries Building and the Hirshhorn Museum and Sculpture Garden, and planning for the American Women's History Museum and the National Museum of the American Latino.

Object Classification (in millions of dollars)

Identification code 033–0103–0–1–503		2021 actual	2022 est.	2023 est.
	Direct obligations:			
11.1	Personnel compensation: Full-time permanent	4	5	6
12.1	Civilian personnel benefits	2	2	3
23.3	Communications, utilities, and miscellaneous charges	1	1	1
25.2	Other services from non-Federal sources	1	1	1
26.0	Supplies and materials	1	1	1
31.0	Equipment	15	15	15
32.0	Land and structures	195	192	235
99.9	Total new obligations, unexpired accounts	219	217	262

Employment Summary

Identification code 033–0103–0–1–503	2021 actual	2022 est.	2023 est.
1001 Direct civilian full-time equivalent employment	48	48	53

JOHN F. KENNEDY CENTER FOR THE PERFORMING ARTS

OPERATIONS AND MAINTENANCE

For necessary expenses for the operation, maintenance, and security of the John F. Kennedy Center for the Performing Arts, $27,640,000, to remain available until September, 30, 2024.

Note.—A full-year 2022 appropriation for this account was not enacted at the time the Budget was prepared; therefore, the Budget assumes this account is operating under the Continuing Appropriations Act, 2022 (Division A of Public Law 117–43, as amended). The amounts included for 2022 reflect the annualized level provided by the continuing resolution.

Program and Financing (in millions of dollars)

Identification code 033–0302–0–1–503		2021 actual	2022 est.	2023 est.
	Obligations by program activity:			
0001	Operations and Maintenance, JFK Center for the Performing Arts (Direct)	25	25	28
	Budgetary resources:			
	Unobligated balance:			
1000	Unobligated balance brought forward, Oct 1	20	21	23
	Budget authority:			
	Appropriations, discretionary:			
1100	Appropriation	26	27	28
1900	Budget authority (total)	26	27	28
1930	Total budgetary resources available	46	48	51
	Memorandum (non-add) entries:			
1941	Unexpired unobligated balance, end of year	21	23	23
	Change in obligated balance:			
	Unpaid obligations:			
3000	Unpaid obligations, brought forward, Oct 1	13	9	3
3010	New obligations, unexpired accounts	25	25	28
3020	Outlays (gross)	−29	−31	−27
3050	Unpaid obligations, end of year	9	3	4
	Uncollected payments:			
3060	Uncollected pymts, Fed sources, brought forward, Oct 1	−20	−20	−20
3090	Uncollected pymts, Fed sources, end of year	−20	−20	−20
	Memorandum (non-add) entries:			
3100	Obligated balance, start of year	−7	−11	−17
3200	Obligated balance, end of year	−11	−17	−16
	Budget authority and outlays, net:			
	Discretionary:			
4000	Budget authority, gross	26	27	28
	Outlays, gross:			
4010	Outlays from new discretionary authority	18	22	22
4011	Outlays from discretionary balances	11	9	5
4020	Outlays, gross (total)	29	31	27
4180	Budget authority, net (total)	26	27	28

JOHN F. KENNEDY CENTER FOR THE PERFORMING ARTS—Continued
Program and Financing—Continued

Identification code 033–0302–0–1–503	2021 actual	2022 est.	2023 est.
4190 Outlays, net (total)	29	31	27

This appropriation provides for the operating and maintenance expenses of the John F. Kennedy Center for the Performing Arts, including maintenance, security, memorial interpretation, janitorial, short-term repair, and other services. In FY 2023, a two-year period of availability for appropriated funds is requested to enable efficient execution of these resources.

Object Classification (in millions of dollars)

Identification code 033–0302–0–1–503		2021 actual	2022 est.	2023 est.
	Direct obligations:			
11.1	Personnel compensation: Full-time permanent	6	6	6
23.3	Communications, utilities, and miscellaneous charges	5	5	5
25.2	Other services from non-Federal sources	14	14	17
99.9	Total new obligations, unexpired accounts	25	25	28

Employment Summary

Identification code 033–0302–0–1–503	2021 actual	2022 est.	2023 est.
1001 Direct civilian full-time equivalent employment	55	55	55

CAPITAL REPAIR AND RESTORATION

For necessary expenses for capital repair and restoration of the existing features of the building and site of the John F. Kennedy Center for the Performing Arts, $17,740,000, to remain available until expended.

Note.—A full-year 2022 appropriation for this account was not enacted at the time the Budget was prepared; therefore, the Budget assumes this account is operating under the Continuing Appropriations Act, 2022 (Division A of Public Law 117–43, as amended). The amounts included for 2022 reflect the annualized level provided by the continuing resolution.

Program and Financing (in millions of dollars)

Identification code 033–0303–0–1–503		2021 actual	2022 est.	2023 est.
	Obligations by program activity:			
0001	Capital Repair and Restoration	10	13	18
0900	Total new obligations, unexpired accounts (object class 25.2)	10	13	18
	Budgetary resources:			
	Unobligated balance:			
1000	Unobligated balance brought forward, Oct 1	38	42	42
	Budget authority:			
	Appropriations, discretionary:			
1100	Appropriation	14	13	18
1930	Total budgetary resources available	52	55	60
	Memorandum (non-add) entries:			
1941	Unexpired unobligated balance, end of year	42	42	42
	Change in obligated balance:			
	Unpaid obligations:			
3000	Unpaid obligations, brought forward, Oct 1	4	7	6
3010	New obligations, unexpired accounts	10	13	18
3020	Outlays (gross)	–7	–14	–16
3050	Unpaid obligations, end of year	7	6	8
	Memorandum (non-add) entries:			
3100	Obligated balance, start of year	4	7	6
3200	Obligated balance, end of year	7	6	8
	Budget authority and outlays, net:			
	Discretionary:			
4000	Budget authority, gross	14	13	18
	Outlays, gross:			
4010	Outlays from new discretionary authority	3	8	11
4011	Outlays from discretionary balances	4	6	5
4020	Outlays, gross (total)	7	14	16
4180	Budget authority, net (total)	14	13	18
4190	Outlays, net (total)	7	14	16

This appropriation provides for the repair, restoration and renovation of the Kennedy Center building, including safety improvements and major repair of interior spaces, including access for persons with disabilities.

NATIONAL GALLERY OF ART
SALARIES AND EXPENSES

For the upkeep and operations of the National Gallery of Art, the protection and care of the works of art therein, and administrative expenses incident thereto, as authorized by the Act of March 24, 1937 (50 Stat. 51), as amended by the public resolution of April 13, 1939 (Public Resolution 9, 76th Congress), including services as authorized by 5 U.S.C. 3109; payment in advance when authorized by the treasurer of the Gallery for membership in library, museum, and art associations or societies whose publications or services are available to members only, or to members at a price lower than to the general public; purchase, repair, and cleaning of uniforms for guards, and uniforms, or allowances therefor, for other employees as authorized by law (5 U.S.C. 5901–5902); purchase or rental of devices and services for protecting buildings and contents thereof, and maintenance, alteration, improvement, and repair of buildings, approaches, and grounds; and purchase of services for restoration and repair of works of art for the National Gallery of Art by contracts made, without advertising, with individuals, firms, or organizations at such rates or prices and under such terms and conditions as the Gallery may deem proper, $170,240,000, to remain available until September 30, 2024, of which not to exceed $3,875,000 for the special exhibition program shall remain available until expended.

Note.—A full-year 2022 appropriation for this account was not enacted at the time the Budget was prepared; therefore, the Budget assumes this account is operating under the Continuing Appropriations Act, 2022 (Division A of Public Law 117–43, as amended). The amounts included for 2022 reflect the annualized level provided by the continuing resolution.

Program and Financing (in millions of dollars)

Identification code 033–0200–0–1–503		2021 actual	2022 est.	2023 est.
	Obligations by program activity:			
0001	Salaries and expenses	152	153	170
	Budgetary resources:			
	Unobligated balance:			
1000	Unobligated balance brought forward, Oct 1	9	14	15
1021	Recoveries of prior year unpaid obligations	4	1	1
1070	Unobligated balance (total)	13	15	16
	Budget authority:			
	Appropriations, discretionary:			
1100	Appropriation	153	153	170
1930	Total budgetary resources available	166	168	186
	Memorandum (non-add) entries:			
1941	Unexpired unobligated balance, end of year	14	15	16
	Change in obligated balance:			
	Unpaid obligations:			
3000	Unpaid obligations, brought forward, Oct 1	38	43	43
3010	New obligations, unexpired accounts	152	153	170
3020	Outlays (gross)	–143	–152	–171
3040	Recoveries of prior year unpaid obligations, unexpired	–4	–1	–1
3050	Unpaid obligations, end of year	43	43	41
	Memorandum (non-add) entries:			
3100	Obligated balance, start of year	38	43	43
3200	Obligated balance, end of year	43	43	41
	Budget authority and outlays, net:			
	Discretionary:			
4000	Budget authority, gross	153	153	170
	Outlays, gross:			
4010	Outlays from new discretionary authority	113	129	143
4011	Outlays from discretionary balances	30	23	28
4020	Outlays, gross (total)	143	152	171
4180	Budget authority, net (total)	153	153	170
4190	Outlays, net (total)	143	152	171

The National Gallery of Art receives, holds, and administers works of art acquired for the Nation by the Gallery's board of trustees. It also maintains the Gallery buildings to give maximum care and protection to art treasures and to enable these works of art to be exhibited. This account

OTHER INDEPENDENT AGENCIES

supports upkeep and operations, protection and care of the works of art, and administrative expenses.

Object Classification (in millions of dollars)

Identification code 033–0200–0–1–503	2021 actual	2022 est.	2023 est.
Direct obligations:			
Personnel compensation:			
11.1 Full-time permanent	65	67	74
11.5 Other personnel compensation	5	5	5
11.9 Total personnel compensation	70	72	79
12.1 Civilian personnel benefits	25	25	30
22.0 Transportation of things	1	1	1
23.2 Rental payments to others	3	3	3
23.3 Communications, utilities, and miscellaneous charges	6	6	6
25.2 Other services	31	31	34
25.4 Operation and maintenance of facilities	5	5	5
26.0 Supplies and materials	2	2	3
31.0 Equipment	6	5	6
32.0 Land and structures	3	3	3
99.9 Total new obligations, unexpired accounts	152	153	170

Employment Summary

Identification code 033–0200–0–1–503	2021 actual	2022 est.	2023 est.
1001 Direct civilian full-time equivalent employment	767	786	791

REPAIR, RESTORATION AND RENOVATION OF BUILDINGS

For necessary expenses of repair, restoration, and renovation of buildings, grounds and facilities owned or occupied by the National Gallery of Art, by contract or otherwise, for operating lease agreements of no more than 10 years, with no extensions or renewals beyond the 10 years, that address space needs created by the ongoing renovations in the Master Facilities Plan, as authorized, $39,000,000, to remain available until expended: Provided, That of this amount, $27,208,000 shall be available for design and construction of an off-site art storage facility in partnership with the Smithsonian Institution and may be transferred to the Smithsonian Institution for such purposes: Provided further, That contracts awarded for environmental systems, protection systems, and exterior repair or renovation of buildings of the National Gallery of Art may be negotiated with selected contractors and awarded on the basis of contractor qualifications as well as price.

Note.—A full-year 2022 appropriation for this account was not enacted at the time the Budget was prepared; therefore, the Budget assumes this account is operating under the Continuing Appropriations Act, 2022 (Division A of Public Law 117–43, as amended). The amounts included for 2022 reflect the annualized level provided by the continuing resolution.

Program and Financing (in millions of dollars)

Identification code 033–0201–0–1–503	2021 actual	2022 est.	2023 est.
Obligations by program activity:			
0001 Repair, Restoration, and Renovation of Buildings	18	29	39
Budgetary resources:			
Unobligated balance:			
1000 Unobligated balance brought forward, Oct 1	8	13	7
Budget authority:			
Appropriations, discretionary:			
1100 Appropriation	23	23	39
1930 Total budgetary resources available	31	36	46
Memorandum (non-add) entries:			
1941 Unexpired unobligated balance, end of year	13	7	7
Change in obligated balance:			
Unpaid obligations:			
3000 Unpaid obligations, brought forward, Oct 1	57	41	36
3010 New obligations, unexpired accounts	18	29	39
3020 Outlays (gross)	–34	–34	–25
3050 Unpaid obligations, end of year	41	36	50
Memorandum (non-add) entries:			
3100 Obligated balance, start of year	57	41	36
3200 Obligated balance, end of year	41	36	50

Smithsonian Institution—Continued
Federal Funds—Continued

1327

		2021 actual	2022 est.	2023 est.
	Budget authority and outlays, net:			
	Discretionary:			
4000	Budget authority, gross	23	23	39
	Outlays, gross:			
4010	Outlays from new discretionary authority		2	4
4011	Outlays from discretionary balances	34	32	21
4020	Outlays, gross (total)	34	34	25
4180	Budget authority, net (total)	23	23	39
4190	Outlays, net (total)	34	34	25

This account encompasses repairs, alterations, and improvements; additions, renovations, and restorations of a long-term nature and utility; facilities planning and design, leases of space necessitated by such renovations, and the design and construction of an off-site art storage facility in partnership with the Smithsonian Institution. The funds are used to keep National Gallery of Art facilities in good repair and efficient operating condition.

Object Classification (in millions of dollars)

Identification code 033–0201–0–1–503	2021 actual	2022 est.	2023 est.
Direct obligations:			
23.2 Rental payments to others	5	7	7
25.2 Other services from non-Federal sources	2	2	2
32.0 Land and structures	11	20	30
99.9 Total new obligations, unexpired accounts	18	29	39

Employment Summary

Identification code 033–0201–0–1–503	2021 actual	2022 est.	2023 est.
1001 Direct civilian full-time equivalent employment	2	2	2

WOODROW WILSON INTERNATIONAL CENTER FOR SCHOLARS

SALARIES AND EXPENSES

For expenses necessary in carrying out the provisions of the Woodrow Wilson Memorial Act of 1968 (82 Stat. 1356) including hire of passenger vehicles and services as authorized by 5 U.S.C. 3109, $14,860,000, to remain available until September 30, 2024.

Note.—A full-year 2022 appropriation for this account was not enacted at the time the Budget was prepared; therefore, the Budget assumes this account is operating under the Continuing Appropriations Act, 2022 (Division A of Public Law 117–43, as amended). The amounts included for 2022 reflect the annualized level provided by the continuing resolution.

Program and Financing (in millions of dollars)

Identification code 033–0400–0–1–503	2021 actual	2022 est.	2023 est.
Obligations by program activity:			
0001 Salaries and expenses	15	14	15
Budgetary resources:			
Unobligated balance:			
1000 Unobligated balance brought forward, Oct 1	4	3	3
Budget authority:			
Appropriations, discretionary:			
1100 Appropriation	14	14	15
1930 Total budgetary resources available	18	17	18
Memorandum (non-add) entries:			
1941 Unexpired unobligated balance, end of year	3	3	3
Change in obligated balance:			
Unpaid obligations:			
3000 Unpaid obligations, brought forward, Oct 1	5	6	4
3010 New obligations, unexpired accounts	15	14	15
3020 Outlays (gross)	–14	–16	–15
3050 Unpaid obligations, end of year	6	4	4
Memorandum (non-add) entries:			
3100 Obligated balance, start of year	5	6	4
3200 Obligated balance, end of year	6	4	4
Budget authority and outlays, net:			
Discretionary:			
4000 Budget authority, gross	14	14	15

WOODROW WILSON INTERNATIONAL CENTER FOR SCHOLARS—Continued

Program and Financing—Continued

Identification code 033–0400–0–1–503	2021 actual	2022 est.	2023 est.
Outlays, gross:			
4010 Outlays from new discretionary authority	8	10	11
4011 Outlays from discretionary balances	6	6	4
4020 Outlays, gross (total)	14	16	15
4180 Budget authority, net (total)	14	14	15
4190 Outlays, net (total)	14	16	15

The Woodrow Wilson Center facilitates scholarship in the social sciences and humanities and communicates that scholarship to a wide audience within and beyond Washington, D.C. This is accomplished through fellowship awards, conferences, publications, and dialogue. The Budget provides $14.860 million in FY 2023.

Object Classification (in millions of dollars)

Identification code 033–0400–0–1–503	2021 actual	2022 est.	2023 est.
Direct obligations:			
11.1 Personnel compensation: Full-time permanent	5	6	7
12.1 Civilian personnel benefits	2	2	2
25.2 Other services from non-Federal sources	5	4	4
41.0 Grants, subsidies, and contributions	3	2	2
99.9 Total new obligations, unexpired accounts	15	14	15

Employment Summary

Identification code 033–0400–0–1–503	2021 actual	2022 est.	2023 est.
1001 Direct civilian full-time equivalent employment	40	47	54

SOUTHEAST CRESCENT REGIONAL COMMISSION

Federal Funds

SOUTHEAST CRESCENT REGIONAL COMMISSION

For expenses necessary for the Southeast Crescent Regional Commission in carrying out activities authorized by subtitle V of title 40, United States Code, $7,000,000, to remain available until expended.

Note.—A full-year 2022 appropriation for this account was not enacted at the time the Budget was prepared; therefore, the Budget assumes this account is operating under the Continuing Appropriations Act, 2022 (Division A of Public Law 117–43, as amended). The amounts included for 2022 reflect the annualized level provided by the continuing resolution.

SOUTHEAST CRESCENT REGIONAL COMMISSION

[For an additional amount for "Southeast Crescent Regional Commission", $5,000,000 to remain available until expended: *Provided*, That such amount is designated by the Congress as being for an emergency requirement pursuant to section 4112(a) of H. Con. Res. 71 (115th Congress), the concurrent resolution on the budget for fiscal year 2018, and to section 251(b) of the Balanced Budget and Emergency Deficit Control Act of 1985.] *(Infrastructure Investments and Jobs Appropriations Act.)*

Program and Financing (in millions of dollars)

Identification code 574–3744–0–1–452	2021 actual	2022 est.	2023 est.
Obligations by program activity:			
0001 Direct program activity		1	7
Budgetary resources:			
Unobligated balance:			
1000 Unobligated balance brought forward, Oct 1			9
1020 Adjustment of unobligated bal brought forward, Oct 1		4	
1070 Unobligated balance (total)		4	9
Budget authority:			
Appropriations, discretionary:			
1100 Appropriation		1	7
1100 Appropriation (IIJA)		5	
1160 Appropriation, discretionary (total)		6	7
1930 Total budgetary resources available		10	16
Memorandum (non-add) entries:			
1941 Unexpired unobligated balance, end of year		9	9
Change in obligated balance:			
Unpaid obligations:			
3000 Unpaid obligations, brought forward, Oct 1			1
3010 New obligations, unexpired accounts		1	7
3020 Outlays (gross)			–3
3050 Unpaid obligations, end of year		1	5
Memorandum (non-add) entries:			
3100 Obligated balance, start of year			1
3200 Obligated balance, end of year		1	5
Budget authority and outlays, net:			
Discretionary:			
4000 Budget authority, gross		6	7
Outlays, gross:			
4010 Outlays from new discretionary authority			2
4011 Outlays from discretionary balances			1
4020 Outlays, gross (total)			3
4180 Budget authority, net (total)		6	7
4190 Outlays, net (total)			3

The Budget provides $7 million for the Southeast Crescent Regional Commission (SCRC). Authorized by P.L. 110–234, SCRC is a Federal-State partnership created to provide a comprehensive approach to addressing persistent economic distress in seven states in the southeast region of the United States. SCRC covers portions of Alabama, Georgia, Mississippi, North Carolina, South Carolina, Virginia and the entire state of Florida. SCRC helps coordinate Federal efforts to develop building blocks for economic development, to include public infrastructure, transportation infrastructure, business development with an emphasis in entrepreneurship, job skills training and workforce development, as well as access to quality healthcare.

Object Classification (in millions of dollars)

Identification code 574–3744–0–1–452	2021 actual	2022 est.	2023 est.
Direct obligations:			
11.1 Personnel compensation: Full-time permanent			1
25.3 Other goods and services from Federal sources		1	
41.0 Grants, subsidies, and contributions			5
99.0 Direct obligations		1	6
99.5 Adjustment for rounding			1
99.9 Total new obligations, unexpired accounts		1	7

Employment Summary

Identification code 574–3744–0–1–452	2021 actual	2022 est.	2023 est.
1001 Direct civilian full-time equivalent employment		1	2

SOUTHWEST BORDER REGIONAL COMMISSION

Federal Funds

SOUTHWEST BORDER REGIONAL COMMISSION

For expenses necessary for the Southwest Border Regional Commission in carrying out activities authorized by subtitle V of title 40, United States Code, $2,500,000, to remain available until expended.

Note.—A full-year 2022 appropriation for this account was not enacted at the time the Budget was prepared; therefore, the Budget assumes this account is operating under the Continuing Appropriations Act, 2022 (Division A of Public Law 117–43, as amended). The amounts included for 2022 reflect the annualized level provided by the continuing resolution.

SOUTHWEST BORDER REGIONAL COMMISSION

[For an additional amount for "Southwest Border Regional Commission", $1,250,000 to remain available until expended: *Provided*, That such amount is designated by the Congress as being for an emergency requirement pursuant to section 4112(a) of H. Con. Res. 71 (115th Congress), the concurrent resolution on the budget for fiscal year 2018, and to section 251(b) of the Balanced Budget and Emergency

OTHER INDEPENDENT AGENCIES

Deficit Control Act of 1985.] *(Infrastructure Investments and Jobs Appropriations Act.)*

Program and Financing (in millions of dollars)

Identification code 569–1500–0–1–452	2021 actual	2022 est.	2023 est.
Obligations by program activity:			
0001 Direct program activity	....	....	1
0900 Total new obligations, unexpired accounts (object class 25.3)	....	....	1
Budgetary resources:			
Unobligated balance:			
1000 Unobligated balance brought forward, Oct 1	....	....	1
Budget authority:			
Appropriations, discretionary:			
1100 Appropriation	....	....	3
1100 Appropriation (IIJA)	....	1	....
1160 Appropriation, discretionary (total)	....	1	3
1930 Total budgetary resources available	....	1	4
Memorandum (non-add) entries:			
1941 Unexpired unobligated balance, end of year	....	1	3
Change in obligated balance:			
Unpaid obligations:			
3010 New obligations, unexpired accounts	....	....	1
3020 Outlays (gross)	....	....	–1
Budget authority and outlays, net:			
Discretionary:			
4000 Budget authority, gross	....	1	3
Outlays, gross:			
4010 Outlays from new discretionary authority	....	....	1
4180 Budget authority, net (total)	....	1	3
4190 Outlays, net (total)	....	....	1

The Budget provides $2.5 million for the Southwest Border Regional Commission (SBRC). SBRC, authorized by P.L. 110–234, was established as a Federal-State partnership to provide a comprehensive approach to addressing persistent economic distress in the southwest border region. SBRC covers parts of Arizona, California, New Mexico, and Texas.

STATE JUSTICE INSTITUTE

Federal Funds

SALARIES AND EXPENSES

For necessary expenses of the State Justice Institute, as authorized by the State Justice Institute Act of 1984 (42 U.S.C. 10701 et seq.) $7,640,000, of which $500,000 shall remain available until September 30, 2024: Provided, That not to exceed $2,250 shall be available for official reception and representation expenses: Provided further, That, for the purposes of section 504 of this Act, the State Justice Institute shall be considered an agency of the United States Government.

Note.—A full-year 2022 appropriation for this account was not enacted at the time the Budget was prepared; therefore, the Budget assumes this account is operating under the Continuing Appropriations Act, 2022 (Division A of Public Law 117–43, as amended). The amounts included for 2022 reflect the annualized level provided by the continuing resolution.

Program and Financing (in millions of dollars)

Identification code 453–0052–0–1–752	2021 actual	2022 est.	2023 est.
Obligations by program activity:			
0001 Salaries and Expenses (Direct)	7	7	8
0900 Total new obligations, unexpired accounts (object class 41.0)	7	7	8
Budgetary resources:			
Budget authority:			
Appropriations, discretionary:			
1100 Appropriation	7	7	8
1930 Total budgetary resources available	7	7	8
Change in obligated balance:			
Unpaid obligations:			
3000 Unpaid obligations, brought forward, Oct 1	11	10	5
3010 New obligations, unexpired accounts	7	7	8
3020 Outlays (gross)	–8	–12	–7
3050 Unpaid obligations, end of year	10	5	6
Memorandum (non-add) entries:			
3100 Obligated balance, start of year	11	10	5
3200 Obligated balance, end of year	10	5	6
Budget authority and outlays, net:			
Discretionary:			
4000 Budget authority, gross	7	7	8
Outlays, gross:			
4010 Outlays from new discretionary authority	2	1	1
4011 Outlays from discretionary balances	6	11	6
4020 Outlays, gross (total)	8	12	7
4180 Budget authority, net (total)	7	7	8
4190 Outlays, net (total)	8	12	7

The State Justice Institute (SJI) was established by Federal law (42 U.S.C. 10701 et seq.) as a non-profit corporation to award grants and undertake other activities to improve the quality of justice in State courts and foster innovative, efficient solutions to common issues faced by all courts. SJI has the authority to assist all State courts—criminal, civil, juvenile, family, and appellate—and the mandate to share the success of one State's innovations with every State court system and the Federal courts. The FY 2023 budget includes additional resources to address the unique challenges of the opioid epidemic, behavioral health issues, and technology in state courts.

SURFACE TRANSPORTATION BOARD

Federal Funds

SALARIES AND EXPENSES

For necessary expenses of the Surface Transportation Board, including services authorized by 5 U.S.C. 3109, United States Code, $41,429,000: Provided, That, notwithstanding any other provision of law, not to exceed $1,250,000 from fees established by the Surface Transportation Board shall be credited to this appropriation as offsetting collections and used for necessary and authorized expenses under this heading: Provided further, That the amounts made available under this heading from the general fund shall be reduced on a dollar-for-dollar basis as such offsetting collections are received during fiscal year 2023, to result in a final appropriation from the general fund estimated at not more than $40,179,000.

Note.—A full-year 2022 appropriation for this account was not enacted at the time the Budget was prepared; therefore, the Budget assumes this account is operating under the Continuing Appropriations Act, 2022 (Division A of Public Law 117–43, as amended). The amounts included for 2022 reflect the annualized level provided by the continuing resolution.

Program and Financing (in millions of dollars)

Identification code 472–0301–0–1–401	2021 actual	2022 est.	2023 est.
Obligations by program activity:			
0001 Direct program activity - Rail Carriers	37	37	40
0100 Direct program activities, subtotal	37	37	40
Budgetary resources:			
Unobligated balance:			
1000 Unobligated balance brought forward, Oct 1	....	....	1
Budget authority:			
Appropriations, discretionary:			
1100 Appropriation	36	37	40
Spending authority from offsetting collections, discretionary:			
1700 Collected	1	1	1
1900 Budget authority (total)	37	38	41
1930 Total budgetary resources available	37	38	42
Memorandum (non-add) entries:			
1941 Unexpired unobligated balance, end of year	....	1	2
Change in obligated balance:			
Unpaid obligations:			
3000 Unpaid obligations, brought forward, Oct 1	9	11	4
3010 New obligations, unexpired accounts	37	37	40
3020 Outlays (gross)	–35	–44	–41
3050 Unpaid obligations, end of year	11	4	3
Memorandum (non-add) entries:			
3100 Obligated balance, start of year	9	11	4

SALARIES AND EXPENSES—Continued
Program and Financing—Continued

Identification code 472–0301–0–1–401	2021 actual	2022 est.	2023 est.
3200 Obligated balance, end of year	11	4	3
Budget authority and outlays, net:			
Discretionary:			
4000 Budget authority, gross	37	38	41
Outlays, gross:			
4010 Outlays from new discretionary authority	29	34	37
4011 Outlays from discretionary balances	6	10	4
4020 Outlays, gross (total)	35	44	41
Offsets against gross budget authority and outlays:			
Offsetting collections (collected) from:			
4030 Federal sources	–1		
4033 Non-Federal sources	–1	–1	–1
4040 Offsets against gross budget authority and outlays (total)	–2	–1	–1
Additional offsets against gross budget authority only:			
4052 Offsetting collections credited to expired accounts	1		
4070 Budget authority, net (discretionary)	36	37	40
4080 Outlays, net (discretionary)	33	43	40
4180 Budget authority, net (total)	36	37	40
4190 Outlays, net (total)	33	43	40

The Surface Transportation Board (STB or Board) is primarily charged with the economic oversight of the nation's freight rail system. The economics of freight rail regulation impact the national transportation network and are important to our nation's economy. For this reason, Congress gave the STB sole jurisdiction over railroad rates, practices, and service. Congress also gave the STB sole jurisdiction over rail mergers and consolidations, abandonments of existing rail lines, and new rail line constructions, exempting STB-approved transactions from federal antitrust laws and state and municipal laws.[1] The bipartisan Board was established in 1996 as the successor agency to the Interstate Commerce Commission.[2] The Board was administratively aligned with the Department of Transportation until the enactment of the Surface Transportation Board Reauthorization Act of 2015.[3]

While a majority of the Board's work involves freight railroads, the STB's involvement with passenger rail matters has increased and will likely continue to expand. The STB also performs certain oversight of the intercity bus industry, non-energy pipelines, household goods carriers tariffs, and rate regulation of non-contiguous domestic water transportation (marine freight shipping involving the mainland United States, Hawaii, Alaska, Puerto Rico, and other U.S. territories and possessions).

2023 Program: The Board requests $41,429,000 to carry out its mission as directed under the law. This includes a request for $1,250,000 from offsetting collections of fees as a credit to the appropriation received, to the extent collected.

The STB's 2023 budget request would maintain current operational funding to meet its statutory responsibilities and continue meeting the needs of stakeholders and the public. The funding for personnel will support the Boards new passenger rail responsibilities by leveraging existing staff with diverse expertise to support the passenger rail unit and the equivalent of two fully dedicated staff assigned to it. The Board's non-personnel budget would continue to prioritize the agency's efforts toward information technology modernization and cybersecurity, and further the agencys efforts to strategically plan and organize evidence-building, data management, and data access functions in support of evidence-based decision making, management of its data, and the agencys mission in general. In addition, the agency would leverage the lessons learned during the coronavirus disease 2019 pandemic to help facilitate mission effectiveness in a hybrid work environment.

[1] 49 U.S.C. 10101–11908.

[2] ICC Termination Act of 1995, P.L. 101–88, 109 Stat. 803 (1995).

[3] Surface Transportation Board Reauthorization Act of 2015, P.L. 114–110, 129 Stat. 2228 (2015).

Object Classification (in millions of dollars)

Identification code 472–0301–0–1–401	2021 actual	2022 est.	2023 est.
Direct obligations:			
Personnel compensation:			
11.1 Full-time permanent	18	18	20
11.3 Other than full-time permanent	1	1	1
11.9 Total personnel compensation	19	19	21
12.1 Civilian personnel benefits	8	8	8
23.1 Rental payments to GSA	3	3	3
25.2 Other services from non-Federal sources	4	4	5
25.3 Other goods and services from Federal sources	3	3	3
99.9 Total new obligations, unexpired accounts	37	37	40

Employment Summary

Identification code 472–0301–0–1–401	2021 actual	2022 est.	2023 est.
1001 Direct civilian full-time equivalent employment	117	141	141
2001 Reimbursable civilian full-time equivalent employment	1	1	1

TENNESSEE VALLEY AUTHORITY

Federal Funds

TENNESSEE VALLEY AUTHORITY FUND

Program and Financing (in millions of dollars)

Identification code 455–4110–0–3–999	2021 actual	2022 est.	2023 est.
Obligations by program activity:			
0801 Power program: Operating expenses	7,657	8,475	8,622
0802 Power program: Capital expenditures	1,961	2,891	2,566
0803 Other Cash Items	17,055	19,077	23,147
0804 Non-Federal Investments	29,188	25,742	21,785
0809 Reimbursable program activities, subtotal	55,861	56,185	56,120
0900 Total new obligations, unexpired accounts	55,861	56,185	56,120
Budgetary resources:			
Unobligated balance:			
1000 Unobligated balance brought forward, Oct 1	8,680	9,857	11,365
1022 Capital transfer of unobligated balances to general fund	–4	–3	–4
1070 Unobligated balance (total)	8,676	9,854	11,361
Budget authority:			
Borrowing authority, mandatory:			
1400 Borrowing authority	945	1,802	1,456
Spending authority from offsetting collections, mandatory:			
1800 Collected	54,529	55,870	55,683
1801 Change in uncollected payments, Federal sources	1,566	24	–48
1802 Offsetting collections (previously unavailable)	26	26	26
1823 New and/or unobligated balance of spending authority from offsetting collections temporarily reduced	–24	–26	–26
1850 Spending auth from offsetting collections, mand (total)	56,097	55,894	55,635
1900 Budget authority (total)	57,042	57,696	57,091
1930 Total budgetary resources available	65,718	67,550	68,452
Memorandum (non-add) entries:			
1941 Unexpired unobligated balance, end of year	9,857	11,365	12,332
Change in obligated balance:			
Unpaid obligations:			
3000 Unpaid obligations, brought forward, Oct 1	4,007	6,222	6,134
3010 New obligations, unexpired accounts	55,861	56,185	56,120
3020 Outlays (gross)	–53,646	–56,273	–56,108
3050 Unpaid obligations, end of year	6,222	6,134	6,146
Uncollected payments:			
3060 Uncollected pymts, Fed sources, brought forward, Oct 1	–3,268	–4,834	–4,858
3070 Change in uncollected pymts, Fed sources, unexpired	–1,566	–24	48
3090 Uncollected pymts, Fed sources, end of year	–4,834	–4,858	–4,810
Memorandum (non-add) entries:			
3100 Obligated balance, start of year	739	1,388	1,276
3200 Obligated balance, end of year	1,388	1,276	1,336
Budget authority and outlays, net:			
Mandatory:			
4090 Budget authority, gross	57,042	57,696	57,091

	Outlays, gross:			
4100	Outlays from new mandatory authority	....	50,051	56,108
4101	Outlays from mandatory balances	53,646	6,222	....
4110	Outlays, gross (total)	53,646	56,273	56,108
	Offsets against gross budget authority and outlays:			
	Offsetting collections (collected) from:			
4120	Federal sources	–390	–2,000	–2,000
4123	Non-Federal sources	–54,139	–53,870	–53,683
4130	Offsets against gross budget authority and outlays (total)	–54,529	–55,870	–55,683
	Additional offsets against gross budget authority only:			
4140	Change in uncollected pymts, Fed sources, unexpired	–1,566	–24	48
4160	Budget authority, net (mandatory)	947	1,802	1,456
4170	Outlays, net (mandatory)	–883	403	425
4180	Budget authority, net (total)	947	1,802	1,456
4190	Outlays, net (total)	–883	403	425
	Memorandum (non-add) entries:			
5010	Total investments, SOY: non-Fed securities: Market value	470	469	270
5011	Total investments, EOY: non-Fed securities: Market value	469	270	270
5090	Unexpired unavailable balance, SOY: Offsetting collections	26	24	24
5092	Unexpired unavailable balance, EOY: Offsetting collections	24	24	24

Status of Direct Loans (in millions of dollars)

Identification code 455–4110–0–3–999		2021 actual	2022 est.	2023 est.
	Cumulative balance of direct loans outstanding:			
1210	Outstanding, start of year	42	39	55
1231	Disbursements: Direct loan disbursements	6	25	25
1251	Repayments: Repayments and prepayments	–9	–9	–10
1290	Outstanding, end of year	39	55	70

The Tennessee Valley Authority (TVA) was created in 1933 as a government-owned corporation charged with the mission to improve the quality of life in the Tennessee Valley through the integrated management of the regions resources. The TVA Act sets forth the agency's purpose: to address the Valley's most important issues in energy, environmental stewardship, and economic development. TVA is currently self-funded, financing its operations almost entirely from revenues and power system financings.

TVA's Power Program.—TVA supplies electric power to an area of 80,000 square miles covering parts of the seven Tennessee Valley states, Tennessee, Alabama, Mississippi, Kentucky, Georgia, North Carolina and Virginia. Estimated income from power operations, net of interest charges, depreciation, and other operating expenses, is expected to be $0.9 billion in 2023 on operating revenues of $10.7 billion. Power generating facilities are financed from power revenues and power system financings. TVA's power system financings consist primarily of the sale of debt securities and secondarily of alternative forms of financing, such as lease arrangements.

TVA's Non-Power Programs.—TVA operates a series of 49 dams and 47 reservoirs to reduce the risk of flooding, enable year-round navigation, supply affordable and reliable electricity, improve water quality and water supply, provide recreational opportunities, stimulate economic growth, and provide other public benefits. TVA is responsible for stewardship activities within the Tennessee Valley that include: water release regulation; maintenance of dam machinery and spillway gates; modifications on navigation locks and associated mooring facilities; improvement of water quality and supply; management of shoreline erosion; regulation of shoreline development along the Tennessee River and its tributaries; planning and management of 293,000 acres of public land; and operation of public recreation areas. These services are funded entirely by TVA's power revenues and its user fees.

Economic Development.—TVA is charged with providing the people of the Tennessee Valley region greater opportunities for prosperity. To that end, TVA works to foster capital investment and job growth in the Valley in collaboration with regional, state and local organizations. In fiscal year 2021, TVA worked in partnership with communities and the business sector to spur $8.8 billion in capital investment in the Tennessee Valley region and helped attract and retain more than 80,000 jobs.

Strategic Financial Plan.—In August 2019, the TVA Board approved an annual budget that reflects the first year of a new Strategic Financial Plan. This Strategic Financial Plan, which extends from FY 2020 through FY 2030, is flexible in aligning customer preferences and TVA's mission while at the same time establishing a long-term forecast of financial results. Key focus areas of the Strategic Financial Plan include (1) establishing alignment between the length of local power company (LPC) contracts and TVA's long-term commitments, (2) stabilizing debt, (3) maintaining flat rates, (4) driving efficiencies into the business, and (5) advancing the public power model. As TVA executes the plan, key assumptions and focus areas may change.

(1) Contract Alignment: Long-term power planning requires TVA to make long-term financial commitments. In order to better align customer contractual commitments with TVA's overall financial obligations, the TVA Board approved a long-term partnership proposal that was made available to all TVA-served LPCs in August 2019. Under this long-term partnership proposal, LPCs that agree to contractual changes, which include a rolling 20-year term and a termination notice period of 20 years, will receive a long-term partner credit. That credit is currently 3.1% of wholesale standard service demand, energy, and grid-access charges. TVA's effective wholesale rate and annual revenues will decline as LPCs commit to becoming long-term partners, and TVA's overall financial health will improve through better alignment of customer contract terms with TVA's overall financial obligations. As of December 31, 2021, 146 of the 153 LPCs served by TVA had signed the long-term partnership proposal, thus closing the gap between TVA's committed revenues and long-term obligations.

(2) Stabilizing Debt: TVA is focused on stabilizing debt in a range aligned to the balance between customer contractual commitments and total obligations. As TVA executes the plan, key assumptions and performance may change estimated debt and cash balances; however, TVA remains committed to keeping debt stable at or below $24 billion. Over the coming decade, debt may increase modestly as TVA makes continued investments in power system assets. TVA is comfortable with slightly higher debt levels (less than $24 billion), given the large number of local power companies that have committed to 20-year partnerships and long-term incentives with TVA.

(3) Maintain Flat Rates: As part of the updated Strategic Financial Plan, and to support our LPCs and communities, TVA implemented an aggressive objective that includes no planned base rate increases for 10 years. To this point, TVA has already foregone any rate increases through FY 2022 and continues to plan for no rate increases through FY 2030. Additionally, any LPC that commits to signing the long-term partner agreement is eligible to receive the aforementioned 3.1% partner credits on its monthly power invoices.

(4) Drive Efficiencies into the Business: Over the last decade, TVA was able to successfully reduce its annual non-fuel O&M expenses by $800 million compared to FY 2013 budget levels. Additionally, TVA's annual fuel and purchased power expenses were reduced by over $1 billion during the same timeframe. TVA remains committed to achieving operating efficiencies, while also maintaining the fuel cost benefits of a diverse portfolio. Also, as part of the organizations priority to drive efficiencies into the business, TVA currently maintains the objective to achieve top quartile performance with respect to its nuclear fleet by the end of 2022 and to lead the nation in nuclear fleet performance by the end of 2025.

(5) Advance the Public Power Model: Another focus area within the new financial plan is to continue to advance the public power model. This includes furthering strong, sustainable relationships with our customers. These long-term relationships help with regard to both long-term planning and creating an environment in which both TVA and LPCs share in the success of delivering low-cost, reliable power for everyone in the Tennessee Valley. In order to continue to achieve this objective, TVA plans to continue to deliver and develop differentiated

TENNESSEE VALLEY AUTHORITY FUND—Continued

products and solutions for our customers, including avenues for acquiring renewable energy to help our customers achieve their desired sustainability goals and our mutual carbon reduction aspirations. Additionally, this requires TVA to consider future risks as part of the decision-making process, while enabling future business development.

Financing.—Amounts estimated to become available for TVA programs in 2023 are to be derived from operating revenues of $10.7 billion. The outstanding balance of TVA's bonds, notes, and other evidences of indebtedness is limited by statute and cannot exceed $30 billion. TVA's outstanding debt and debt-like obligations were $20.5 billion at the beginning of 2022 and are estimated to be $21.4 billion by the end of 2023. At the beginning of 2022, TVA had $1.1 billion in debt-like obligations that was not counted against its statutory debt cap. In addition, TVA had an unfunded pension liability of $4.2 billion as of September 30, 2021.

Pension Funding.—As of September 30, 2021, the funding status of TVA employees' defined benefit pension plan (TVARS) was that of a 69% funding ratio and a $4.2 billion unfunded liability. This compares to a 58% funding ratio and $5.7 billion unfunded liability in 2020, and a 60% funding ratio and $5.3 billion unfunded liability in 2019. The increase in funding ratio and decrease in the unfunded liability in 2021 was driven by investment returns. TVA contributed $300 million to TVARS and incurred $287 million in actuarial costs in 2021. TVARS made $722 million in payments to beneficiaries and earned $1.6 billion, or a 20.3 percent rate of return, on the plan's investments in 2021. TVA is committed to meeting its obligations to current and future retirees and has worked with the TVARS Board in recent years to implement several significant changes to ensure the long-term health of the retirement system.

Operating Results and Financial Conditions.—Payments to the Treasury from power proceeds in 2023 are estimated at a $4 million return on the appropriation investment in the power program. Total capital spending for 2023 is estimated at $2.6 billion, which in addition to new generation capacity includes approximately $100 million for environmental projects and $1.1 billion to maintain TVA's existing generation assets. Total government equity at September 30, 2023, is estimated to be $0.9 billion more than that at September 30, 2022. This change includes the estimated net income from power operations and payments to the Treasury.

COVID-19 Response.—The COVID-19 pandemic has also created economic uncertainty for TVA's LPCs and the communities they serve. To support LPCs and strengthen the public power response to the COVID-19 pandemic, TVA created the following initiatives, among others, to support the people of the Tennessee Valley:

Community Care Fund: TVA is partnering with LPCs through the Community Care Fund by making available over $9 million in TVA matching funds to support local initiatives that address hardships created by the COVID-19 pandemic. As of September 30, 2021, over $4 million in matching funds had been provided by TVA, with nearly $2 million provided for the year ended September 30, 2021.

Pandemic Relief Credit: In August 2020, the TVA Board approved a Pandemic Relief Credit that was effective for FY 2021. The 2.5 percent monthly base rate credit, which totaled $221 million for FY 2021, applied to service provided to TVA's LPCs, their large commercial and industrial customers, and TVA directly served customers through September 2021. In August 2021, the TVA Board approved a 2.5 percent monthly base rate credit, the Pandemic Recovery Credit, which will be effective for FY 2022. The credit, expected to approximate $220 million, will also apply to service provided to TVA's LPCs, their large commercial and industrial customers, and TVA directly served customers. In November 2021, the TVA Board approved a 1.5 percent monthly base rate credit, which is an extension of the Pandemic Recovery Credit, to be effective for FY 2023. The FY 2023 credit is expected to approximate $133 million, and it will be administered in a manner similar to the Pandemic Recovery Credit.

These actions continue to show TVA's commitment to support both LPCs and the communities they serve across the Tennessee Valley during these challenging economic conditions caused by the COVID-19 pandemic. TVA is closely monitoring developments and will continue adjusting its response as necessary to ensure reliable service while protecting the safety of its workforce and supporting those in the Tennessee Valley.

Balance Sheet (in millions of dollars)

Identification code 455–4110–0–3–999		2020 actual	2021 actual
ASSETS:			
Federal assets:			
1101	Fund balances with Treasury	31	30
	Investments in U.S. securities:		
1106	Receivables, net	94	59
	Non-Federal assets:		
1201	Investments in non-Federal securities, net	3,203	4,053
1206	Receivables, net	1,435	1,507
1207	Advances and prepayments	85	288
1601	Direct loans, gross	182	169
1603	Allowance for estimated uncollectible loans and interest (-)	–1	–2
1604	Direct loans and interest receivable, net	181	167
1605	Accounts receivable from foreclosed property		
1699	Value of assets related to direct loans	181	167
	Other Federal assets:		
1801	Cash and other monetary assets	5,990	5,269
1802	Inventories and related properties	1,003	949
1803	Property, plant and equipment, net	35,573	36,441
1901	Regulatory assets due to pensions	4,447	3,668
1999	Total assets	52,042	52,431
LIABILITIES:			
2101	Federal liabilities: Accounts payable	180	150
	Non-Federal liabilities:		
2201	Accounts payable	1,981	2,274
2202	Interest payable	298	282
2203	Debt, Alternative Financing	1,313	1,074
2203	Debt, Notes/Bonds	19,800	19,266
2204	Liabilities for loan guarantees		
2206	Pension and post-retirement benefits	5,514	4,736
2207	Other	9,987	10,182
2999	Total liabilities	39,073	37,964
NET POSITION:			
3300	Cumulative results of operations	12,969	14,467
4999	Total liabilities and net position	52,042	52,431

Object Classification (in millions of dollars)

Identification code 455–4110–0–3–999		2021 actual	2022 est.	2023 est.
	Reimbursable obligations:			
	Personnel compensation:			
11.1	Full-time permanent	1,031	1,155	1,137
11.5	Other personnel compensation	206	226	213
11.9	Total personnel compensation	1,237	1,381	1,350
12.1	Civilian personnel benefits	801	591	593
21.0	Travel and transportation of persons	19	21	21
22.0	Transportation of things	13	5	5
23.2	Rental payments to others	77	63	64
24.0	Printing and reproduction	3	1	1
25.1	Advisory and assistance services	35	23	24
25.2	Other services from non-Federal sources	239	200	188
25.7	Operation and maintenance of equipment	2,090	2,469	2,035
26.0	Supplies and materials	1,529	1,633	1,690
31.0	Equipment	439	637	998
32.0	Land and structures	35	28	20
33.0	Investments and loans	49,308	49,089	49,087
41.0	Grants, subsidies, and contributions	34	43	43
42.0	Insurance claims and indemnities	2	1	1
99.9	Total new obligations, unexpired accounts	55,861	56,185	56,120

Employment Summary

Identification code 455–4110–0–3–999	2021 actual	2022 est.	2023 est.
2001 Reimbursable civilian full-time equivalent employment	10,192	10,600	10,600

U.S. AGENCY FOR GLOBAL MEDIA

Federal Funds

INTERNATIONAL BROADCASTING OPERATIONS

For necessary expenses to enable the United States Agency for Global Media (USAGM), as authorized, to carry out international communication activities, and to make and supervise grants for radio, Internet, and television broadcasting to the Middle East, $830,300,000, of which $41,515,000 shall remain available until September 30, 2024: Provided, That in addition to amounts otherwise available for such purposes, up to $40,708,000 of the amount appropriated under this heading may remain available until expended for satellite transmissions, rent, and Internet freedom programs, of which not less than $20,000,000 shall be for Internet freedom programs: Provided further, That of the total amount appropriated under this heading, not to exceed $35,000 may be used for representation expenses, of which $10,000 may be used for such expenses within the United States as authorized, and not to exceed $30,000 may be used for representation expenses of Radio Free Europe/Radio Liberty: Provided further, That funds appropriated under this heading shall be made available in accordance with the principles and standards set forth in section 303(a) and (b) of the United States International Broadcasting Act of 1994 (22 U.S.C. 6202) and section 305(b) of such Act (22 U.S.C. 6204): Provided further, That the USAGM Chief Executive Officer shall notify the Committees on Appropriations within 15 days of any determination by the USAGM that any of its broadcast entities, including its grantee organizations, provides an open platform for international terrorists or those who support international terrorism, or is in violation of the principles and standards set forth in section 303(a) and (b) of such Act or the entity's journalistic code of ethics: Provided further, That in addition to funds made available under this heading, and notwithstanding any other provision of law, up to $5,000,000 in receipts from advertising and revenue from business ventures, up to $500,000 in receipts from cooperating international organizations, and up to $1,000,000 in receipts from privatization efforts of the Voice of America and the International Broadcasting Bureau, shall remain available until expended for carrying out authorized purposes: Provided further, That significant modifications to USAGM broadcast hours previously justified to Congress, including changes to transmission platforms (shortwave, medium wave, satellite, Internet, and television), for all USAGM language services shall be subject to the regular notification procedures of the Committees on Appropriations: Provided further, That up to $7,000,000 from the USAGM Buying Power Maintenance account may be transferred to, and merged with, funds appropriated by this Act under the heading "International Broadcasting Operations", which shall remain available until expended: Provided further, That such transfer authority is in addition to any transfer authority otherwise available under any other provision of law and shall be subject to the regular notification procedures of the Committees on Appropriations: Provided further, That the USAGM may transfer to, and merge with, funds in the "United States International Broadcasting Surge Capacity Fund", authorized in section 316 of the United States International Broadcasting Act of 1994 (22 U.S.C. 6216), for obligation or expenditure by the USAGM for surge capacity, any of the following: (1) unobligated balances of expired funds appropriated under the heading "International Broadcasting Operations" for fiscal year 2023 at no later than the end of the fifth fiscal year after the last fiscal year for which such funds are available for their stated purposes; and (2) funds made available for surge capacity under this heading: Provided further, That section 3523(b)(3)(B) of title 5, United States Code, shall be applied with respect to funds made available under this heading by substituting "$40,000" for "$25,000".

Note.—A full-year 2022 appropriation for this account was not enacted at the time the Budget was prepared; therefore, the Budget assumes this account is operating under the Continuing Appropriations Act, 2022 (Division A of Public Law 117–43, as amended). The amounts included for 2022 reflect the annualized level provided by the continuing resolution.

Program and Financing (in millions of dollars)

Identification code 514–0206–0–1–154		2021 actual	2022 est.	2023 est.
	Obligations by program activity:			
0001	Broadcasting Board of Governors	827	794	824
0100	Subtotal, direct obligations	827	794	824
0801	International Broadcasting Operations (Reimbursable)	6	7	6
0900	Total new obligations, unexpired accounts	833	801	830
	Budgetary resources:			
	Unobligated balance:			
1000	Unobligated balance brought forward, Oct 1	25	5	1
1011	Unobligated balance transfer from other acct [514–1147]	7		
1021	Recoveries of prior year unpaid obligations	1		
1033	Recoveries of prior year paid obligations	8		
1070	Unobligated balance (total)	41	5	1
	Budget authority:			
	Appropriations, discretionary:			
1100	Appropriation	793	793	830
	Spending authority from offsetting collections, discretionary:			
1700	Collected	2	4	2
1701	Change in uncollected payments, Federal sources	3		
1750	Spending auth from offsetting collections, disc (total)	5	4	2
1900	Budget authority (total)	798	797	832
1930	Total budgetary resources available	839	802	833
	Memorandum (non-add) entries:			
1940	Unobligated balance expiring	–1		
1941	Unexpired unobligated balance, end of year	5	1	3
	Change in obligated balance:			
	Unpaid obligations:			
3000	Unpaid obligations, brought forward, Oct 1	156	174	162
3010	New obligations, unexpired accounts	833	801	830
3011	Obligations ("upward adjustments"), expired accounts	2	13	13
3020	Outlays (gross)	–804	–826	–827
3040	Recoveries of prior year unpaid obligations, unexpired	–1		
3041	Recoveries of prior year unpaid obligations, expired	–12		
3050	Unpaid obligations, end of year	174	162	178
	Uncollected payments:			
3060	Uncollected pymts, Fed sources, brought forward, Oct 1	–7	–6	–6
3070	Change in uncollected pymts, Fed sources, unexpired	–3		
3071	Change in uncollected pymts, Fed sources, expired	4		
3090	Uncollected pymts, Fed sources, end of year	–6	–6	–6
	Memorandum (non-add) entries:			
3100	Obligated balance, start of year	149	168	156
3200	Obligated balance, end of year	168	156	172
	Budget authority and outlays, net:			
	Discretionary:			
4000	Budget authority, gross	798	797	832
	Outlays, gross:			
4010	Outlays from new discretionary authority	677	669	699
4011	Outlays from discretionary balances	127	157	128
4020	Outlays, gross (total)	804	826	827
	Offsets against gross budget authority and outlays:			
	Offsetting collections (collected) from:			
4030	Federal sources	–5	–8	–7
4033	Non-Federal sources	–8		
4040	Offsets against gross budget authority and outlays (total)	–13	–8	–7
	Additional offsets against gross budget authority only:			
4050	Change in uncollected pymts, Fed sources, unexpired	–3		
4052	Offsetting collections credited to expired accounts	3	4	5
4053	Recoveries of prior year paid obligations, unexpired accounts	8		
4060	Additional offsets against budget authority only (total)	8	4	5
4070	Budget authority, net (discretionary)	793	793	830
4080	Outlays, net (discretionary)	791	818	820
4180	Budget authority, net (total)	793	793	830
4190	Outlays, net (total)	791	818	820

This appropriation provides operational funding for: United States non-military, international media programs including the Voice of America, the Office of Cuba Broadcasting; the necessary engineering and technical needs for all United States international media, administrative support activities, and grants to Radio Free Europe/Radio Liberty, Radio Free Asia, Middle East Broadcasting Networks, and the Open Technology Fund.

Object Classification (in millions of dollars)

Identification code 514–0206–0–1–154		2021 actual	2022 est.	2023 est.
	Direct obligations:			
	Personnel compensation:			
11.1	Full-time permanent	161	150	160
11.3	Other than full-time permanent	49	47	49
11.5	Other personnel compensation	11	11	11
11.9	Total personnel compensation	221	208	220
12.1	Civilian personnel benefits	65	60	65
13.0	Benefits for former personnel	1	1	1
21.0	Travel and transportation of persons	2	1	2
22.0	Transportation of things	1	1	1
23.1	Rental payments to GSA	31	30	31
23.2	Rental payments to others	1	1	1
23.3	Communications, utilities, and miscellaneous charges	53	50	53

U.S. Agency for Global Media—Continued
Federal Funds—Continued

INTERNATIONAL BROADCASTING OPERATIONS—Continued
Object Classification—Continued

Identification code 514–0206–0–1–154	2021 actual	2022 est.	2023 est.
25.1 Advisory and assistance services	4	4	4
25.2 Other services from non-Federal sources	95	90	95
25.4 Operation and maintenance of facilities	2	2	2
25.5 Research and development contracts	2	2	2
25.7 Operation and maintenance of equipment	1	1	1
26.0 Supplies and materials	7	7	7
31.0 Equipment	19	19	19
41.0 Grants, subsidies, and contributions	321	316	319
42.0 Insurance claims and indemnities	1	1	1
99.0 Direct obligations	827	794	824
99.0 Reimbursable obligations	6	7	6
99.9 Total new obligations, unexpired accounts	833	801	830

Employment Summary

Identification code 514–0206–0–1–154	2021 actual	2022 est.	2023 est.
1001 Direct civilian full-time equivalent employment	1,598	1,660	1,671

BROADCASTING CAPITAL IMPROVEMENTS

For the purchase, rent, construction, repair, preservation, and improvement of facilities for radio, television, and digital transmission and reception; the purchase, rent, and installation of necessary equipment for radio, television, and digital transmission and reception, including to Cuba, as authorized; and physical security worldwide, in addition to amounts otherwise available for such purposes, $9,700,000, to remain available until expended, as authorized.

Note.—A full-year 2022 appropriation for this account was not enacted at the time the Budget was prepared; therefore, the Budget assumes this account is operating under the Continuing Appropriations Act, 2022 (Division A of Public Law 117–43, as amended). The amounts included for 2022 reflect the annualized level provided by the continuing resolution.

Program and Financing (in millions of dollars)

Identification code 514–0204–0–1–154	2021 actual	2022 est.	2023 est.
Obligations by program activity:			
0002 Upgrade of existing relay station capabilities	3	10	10
0192 Total direct obligations	3	10	10
Budgetary resources:			
Unobligated balance:			
1000 Unobligated balance brought forward, Oct 1	16	23	23
Budget authority:			
Appropriations, discretionary:			
1100 Appropriation	10	10	10
1930 Total budgetary resources available	26	33	33
Memorandum (non-add) entries:			
1941 Unexpired unobligated balance, end of year	23	23	23
Change in obligated balance:			
Unpaid obligations:			
3000 Unpaid obligations, brought forward, Oct 1	16	13	11
3010 New obligations, unexpired accounts	3	10	10
3020 Outlays (gross)	–6	–12	–11
3050 Unpaid obligations, end of year	13	11	10
Memorandum (non-add) entries:			
3100 Obligated balance, start of year	16	13	11
3200 Obligated balance, end of year	13	11	10
Budget authority and outlays, net:			
Discretionary:			
4000 Budget authority, gross	10	10	10
Outlays, gross:			
4010 Outlays from new discretionary authority	1	3	3
4011 Outlays from discretionary balances	5	9	8
4020 Outlays, gross (total)	6	12	11
4180 Budget authority, net (total)	10	10	10
4190 Outlays, net (total)	6	12	11

This account provides funding for certain costs of capital projects for the agency, including large-scale capital projects, and the preservation, construction, purchase, and maintenance and improvement of the United States Agency for Global Media's worldwide technology infrastructure. This activity funds the upgrade and replacement of transmission facilities and equipment to improve transmission quality, and includes digital media management, the conversion of program production and operations to a digital domain, broadcast disaster recovery, and infrastructure projects. Further activities include the continuing repairs and improvements required to maintain the global transmission and communications network, assessing and maintaining building and physical security requirements, the construction and maintenance of the Satellite Interconnect System (SIS), Television Receive Only (TVRO) earth stations, advanced data networks, and upgrading global satellite distribution and operations.

Object Classification (in millions of dollars)

Identification code 514–0204–0–1–154	2021 actual	2022 est.	2023 est.
Direct obligations:			
23.2 Rental payments to others		10	2
25.2 Other services from non-Federal sources	2		5
25.4 Operation and maintenance of facilities	1		3
99.9 Total new obligations, unexpired accounts	3	10	10

BUYING POWER MAINTENANCE

Program and Financing (in millions of dollars)

Identification code 514–1147–0–1–154	2021 actual	2022 est.	2023 est.
Budgetary resources:			
Unobligated balance:			
1000 Unobligated balance brought forward, Oct 1	10	10	10
1010 Unobligated balance transfer to other accts [514–0206]	–7		
1012 Unobligated balance transfers between expired and unexpired accounts	7		
1070 Unobligated balance (total)	10	10	10
1930 Total budgetary resources available	10	10	10
Memorandum (non-add) entries:			
1941 Unexpired unobligated balance, end of year	10	10	10
4180 Budget authority, net (total)			
4190 Outlays, net (total)			

This account provides funding to offset losses due to exchange rate and overseas wage and price fluctuations unanticipated in the President's Budget. As authorized, gains due to fluctuations may be deposited into this account to be available to offset future losses.

Trust Funds

FOREIGN SERVICE NATIONAL SEPARATION LIABILITY TRUST FUND

Program and Financing (in millions of dollars)

Identification code 514–8285–0–7–602	2021 actual	2022 est.	2023 est.
Obligations by program activity:			
0001 Direct program activity	1		
0900 Total new obligations, unexpired accounts (object class 42.0)	1		
Budgetary resources:			
Unobligated balance:			
1000 Unobligated balance brought forward, Oct 1	6	5	5
1930 Total budgetary resources available	6	5	5
Memorandum (non-add) entries:			
1941 Unexpired unobligated balance, end of year	5	5	5
Change in obligated balance:			
Unpaid obligations:			
3000 Unpaid obligations, brought forward, Oct 1		1	1
3010 New obligations, unexpired accounts	1		

Line	Item	2021 actual	2022 est.	2023 est.
3050	Unpaid obligations, end of year	1	1	1
	Memorandum (non-add) entries:			
3100	Obligated balance, start of year		1	1
3200	Obligated balance, end of year	1	1	1
4180	Budget authority, net (total)			
4190	Outlays, net (total)			

This fund is maintained to pay separation costs for Foreign Service National employees of the United States Agency for Global Media in those countries in which such pay is legally authorized. The fund, as authorized by P.L. 102–138, and amended by Division G of P.L. 105–277, the Foreign Affairs Reform and Restructuring Act of 1998, is maintained by annual government contributions which are appropriated in the International Broadcasting Operations account.

UNITED STATES COURT OF APPEALS FOR VETERANS CLAIMS

Federal Funds

SALARIES AND EXPENSES

For necessary expenses for the operation of the United States Court of Appeals for Veterans Claims as authorized by sections 7251 through 7298 of title 38, United States Code, $46,900,000: Provided, That $3,385,000 shall be available for the purpose of providing financial assistance as described and in accordance with the process and reporting procedures set forth under this heading in Public Law 102–229.

Note.—A full-year 2022 appropriation for this account was not enacted at the time the Budget was prepared; therefore, the Budget assumes this account is operating under the Continuing Appropriations Act, 2022 (Division A of Public Law 117–43, as amended). The amounts included for 2022 reflect the annualized level provided by the continuing resolution.

Program and Financing (in millions of dollars)

Identification code 345–0300–0–1–705	2021 actual	2022 est.	2023 est.
Obligations by program activity:			
0001 Salaries and Expenses	37	37	47
Budgetary resources:			
Budget authority:			
Appropriations, discretionary:			
1100 Appropriation	37	37	47
1930 Total budgetary resources available	37	37	47
Change in obligated balance:			
Unpaid obligations:			
3000 Unpaid obligations, brought forward, Oct 1	3	3	6
3010 New obligations, unexpired accounts	37	37	47
3020 Outlays (gross)	–37	–34	–48
3050 Unpaid obligations, end of year	3	6	5
Memorandum (non-add) entries:			
3100 Obligated balance, start of year	3	3	6
3200 Obligated balance, end of year	3	6	5
Budget authority and outlays, net:			
Discretionary:			
4000 Budget authority, gross	37	37	47
Outlays, gross:			
4010 Outlays from new discretionary authority	35	33	42
4011 Outlays from discretionary balances	2	1	6
4020 Outlays, gross (total)	37	34	48
4180 Budget authority, net (total)	37	37	47
4190 Outlays, net (total)	37	34	48

The United States Court of Appeals for Veterans Claims (Court) is a national court of record established by the Veterans Judicial Review Act (Public Law 100–687), Division A (1988) (Act). The Act, as amended, is codified in part at 38 U.S.C. 7251–7299. The Court is located in Washington, D.C., but as a national court may sit anywhere in the United States.

The Court is part of the Federal judicial system and has a permanent authorization for seven judges, one of whom serves as chief judge. Per Public Law 114–315, the Congress temporarily authorized expansion of the Court to nine active judges. Judges are appointed by the President, and with the advice and consent of the Senate, for 15-year terms. The Court is currently staffed with nine active judges. Upon retirement, a judge may choose to be recall eligible, and thus willing to be recalled to service by the chief judge. Currently eight of the Court's ten retired judges are recall eligible and are recalled to service on a rotational basis. Recall-eligible judges may elect full retirement at any time.

The Court has exclusive jurisdiction to review decisions made by the Department of Veterans Affairs Board of Veterans' Appeals (Board) that adversely affect a person's entitlement to Department of Veterans Affairs benefits. This judicial review, although specialized in scope, is the same as that performed by all other United States Courts of Appeals. In cases before it, the Court has the authority to decide all relevant questions of law; to interpret constitutional, statutory, and regulatory provisions; and to determine the meaning or applicability of actions/decisions by the Secretary of Veterans Affairs. The Court may affirm, set aside, reverse, or remand those decisions as appropriate. Additionally, the Court has class action authority, has jurisdiction under 28 U.S.C. 1651 to issue all writs necessary or appropriate in aid of its jurisdiction, and may act on applications under 28 U.S.C. 2412(d), the Equal Access to Justice Act. Certain decisions by the Court are reviewable by the United States Court of Appeals for the Federal Circuit and, if *certiorari* is granted, by the Supreme Court of the United States. For management, administration, and expenditure of funds in areas beyond the bounds of Chapter 72 of Title 38, the Court may exercise the authorities provided for such purposes applicable to other courts as defined in Title 28, U.S. Code.

In 1992, the Congress authorized the Court to transfer funds from its appropriation that year to the Legal Services Corporation (LSC), for the purpose of providing, facilitating, and furnishing legal and other assistance, through grant or contract, to veterans and others seeking recourse in the Court. That program, often referred to as the pro bono representation program, has been ongoing since that time, with LSC responsible for oversight and grant distribution responsibilities. The Appropriations Subcommittees consider LSC's budget request separately from the Court's budget request, although both are submitted together.

Object Classification (in millions of dollars)

Identification code 345–0300–0–1–705	2021 actual	2022 est.	2023 est.
Direct obligations:			
11.3 Personnel compensation: Other than full-time permanent	16	17	20
12.1 Civilian personnel benefits	11	10	12
23.1 Rental payments to GSA	2	3	4
25.2 Other services from non-Federal sources	2	2	4
25.3 Other goods and services from Federal sources	1	1	1
31.0 Equipment	1	1	1
32.0 Land and structures	1		2
41.0 Grants, subsidies, and contributions	3	3	3
99.9 Total new obligations, unexpired accounts	37	37	47

Employment Summary

Identification code 345–0300–0–1–705	2021 actual	2022 est.	2023 est.
1001 Direct civilian full-time equivalent employment	128	139	156

Trust Funds

COURT OF APPEALS FOR VETERANS CLAIMS RETIREMENT FUND

Special and Trust Fund Receipts (in millions of dollars)

Identification code 345–8290–0–7–705	2021 actual	2022 est.	2023 est.
0100 Balance, start of year			1
Receipts:			
Current law:			
1140 Earnings on Investment, Court of Veterans Appeals Retirement Fund, LVE	1	1	3
1140 Employing Agency Contributions, Court of Appeals for Veterans Claims Retirement Fund	6	7	5

United States Court of Appeals for Veterans Claims—Continued
Trust Funds—Continued

COURT OF APPEALS FOR VETERANS CLAIMS RETIREMENT FUND—Continued

Special and Trust Fund Receipts—Continued

Identification code 345–8290–0–7–705	2021 actual	2022 est.	2023 est.
1199 Total current law receipts	7	8	8
1999 Total receipts	7	8	8
2000 Total: Balances and receipts	7	8	9
Appropriations:			
Current law:			
2101 Court of Appeals for Veterans Claims Retirement Fund	–7	–7	–5
5099 Balance, end of year		1	4

Program and Financing (in millions of dollars)

Identification code 345–8290–0–7–705	2021 actual	2022 est.	2023 est.
Obligations by program activity:			
0001 Court of Appeals for Veterans Claims Retirement Fund	3	3	5
0900 Total new obligations, unexpired accounts (object class 42.0)	3	3	5
Budgetary resources:			
Unobligated balance:			
1000 Unobligated balance brought forward, Oct 1	52	56	60
Budget authority:			
Appropriations, mandatory:			
1201 Appropriation (special or trust fund)	7	7	5
1930 Total budgetary resources available	59	63	65
Memorandum (non-add) entries:			
1941 Unexpired unobligated balance, end of year	56	60	60
Change in obligated balance:			
Unpaid obligations:			
3010 New obligations, unexpired accounts	3	3	5
3020 Outlays (gross)	–3	–3	–5
Budget authority and outlays, net:			
Mandatory:			
4090 Budget authority, gross	7	7	5
Outlays, gross:			
4100 Outlays from new mandatory authority	3	3	5
4180 Budget authority, net (total)	7	7	5
4190 Outlays, net (total)	3	3	5
Memorandum (non-add) entries:			
5000 Total investments, SOY: Federal securities: Par value	51	56	56
5001 Total investments, EOY: Federal securities: Par value	56	56	61

The United States Court of Appeals for Veterans Claims Retirement Fund (Retirement Fund or Fund), established under 38 U.S.C. 7298, is used for judges' retired pay and for annuities, refunds, and allowances provided to surviving spouses and dependent children. Participating judges pay 1-percent of their salaries to cover creditable service for retired pay purposes and 2.2-percent of their salaries for survivor annuity purposes. Additional funds needed to cover the unfunded liability may be transferred to the Retirement Fund from the Court's annual appropriation. The Court's contribution to the Fund is estimated annually by an actuarial firm retained by the Court. The Fund is invested solely in government securities.

UNITED STATES ENRICHMENT CORPORATION FUND

Federal Funds

UNITED STATES ENRICHMENT CORPORATION FUND

Program and Financing (in millions of dollars)

Identification code 486–4054–0–3–271	2021 actual	2022 est.	2023 est.
Budgetary resources:			
Budget authority:			
Spending authority from offsetting collections, discretionary:			
1702 Offsetting collections (previously unavailable)	291	1,449	609
1710 Spending authority from offsetting collections transferred to other accounts [089–5321]	–291	–841	–405
1710 Spending authority from offsetting collections transferred to other accounts [089–0315]			–123
1724 Spending authority from offsetting collections precluded from obligation (limitation on obligations)		–608	–81
Spending authority from offsetting collections, mandatory:			
1800 Collected	4	21	1
1824 Spending authority from offsetting collections precluded from obligation (limitation on obligations)	–4	–21	–1
Budget authority and outlays, net:			
Mandatory:			
Offsets against gross budget authority and outlays:			
Offsetting collections (collected) from:			
4121 Interest on Federal securities	–4	–21	–1
4180 Budget authority, net (total)	–4	–21	–1
4190 Outlays, net (total)	–4	–21	–1
Memorandum (non-add) entries:			
5000 Total investments, SOY: Federal securities: Par value	1,717	1,431	609
5001 Total investments, EOY: Federal securities: Par value	1,431	609	81
5090 Unexpired unavailable balance, SOY: Offsetting collections	1,717	1,430	610
5092 Unexpired unavailable balance, EOY: Offsetting collections	1,430	610	83

UNITED STATES HOLOCAUST MEMORIAL MUSEUM

Federal Funds

HOLOCAUST MEMORIAL MUSEUM

For expenses of the Holocaust Memorial Museum, as authorized by Public Law 106–292 (36 U.S.C. 2301–2310), $65,231,000, of which $1,000,000 shall remain available until September 30, 2025, for the Museum's equipment replacement program; and of which $4,000,000 for the Museum's repair and rehabilitation program and $1,264,000 for the Museum's outreach initiatives program shall remain available until expended.

Note.—A full-year 2022 appropriation for this account was not enacted at the time the Budget was prepared; therefore, the Budget assumes this account is operating under the Continuing Appropriations Act, 2022 (Division A of Public Law 117–43, as amended). The amounts included for 2022 reflect the annualized level provided by the continuing resolution.

Program and Financing (in millions of dollars)

Identification code 456–3300–0–1–503	2021 actual	2022 est.	2023 est.
Obligations by program activity:			
0001 Holocaust Memorial Museum	70	61	65
Budgetary resources:			
Unobligated balance:			
1000 Unobligated balance brought forward, Oct 1	18	16	16
1001 Discretionary unobligated balance brought fwd, Oct 1	17		
1021 Recoveries of prior year unpaid obligations	9		
1070 Unobligated balance (total)	27	16	16
Budget authority:			
Appropriations, discretionary:			
1100 Appropriation	61	61	65
1930 Total budgetary resources available	88	77	81
Memorandum (non-add) entries:			
1940 Unobligated balance expiring	–2		
1941 Unexpired unobligated balance, end of year	16	16	16
Change in obligated balance:			
Unpaid obligations:			
3000 Unpaid obligations, brought forward, Oct 1	23	25	23
3010 New obligations, unexpired accounts	70	61	65
3011 Obligations ("upward adjustments"), expired accounts	4		
3020 Outlays (gross)	–59	–63	–65
3040 Recoveries of prior year unpaid obligations, unexpired	–9		
3041 Recoveries of prior year unpaid obligations, expired	–4		
3050 Unpaid obligations, end of year	25	23	23
Memorandum (non-add) entries:			
3100 Obligated balance, start of year	23	25	23
3200 Obligated balance, end of year	25	23	23
Budget authority and outlays, net:			
Discretionary:			
4000 Budget authority, gross	61	61	65
Outlays, gross:			
4010 Outlays from new discretionary authority	43	46	49

OTHER INDEPENDENT AGENCIES

		2021 actual	2022 est.	2023 est.
4011	Outlays from discretionary balances	16	17	16
4020	Outlays, gross (total)	59	63	65
4180	Budget authority, net (total)	61	61	65
4190	Outlays, net (total)	59	63	65

A nonpartisan, Federal educational institution, the United States Holocaust Memorial Museum is America's national memorial to the victims of the Holocaust dedicated to ensuring the permanence of Holocaust memory, understanding, and relevance. Through the power of Holocaust history, the Museum challenges leaders and individuals worldwide to think critically about their role in society and to confront antisemitism and other forms of hate, prevent genocide, and promote human dignity.

Object Classification (in millions of dollars)

Identification code 456–3300–0–1–503		2021 actual	2022 est.	2023 est.
	Direct obligations:			
11.1	Personnel compensation: Full-time permanent	14	16	16
12.1	Civilian personnel benefits	5	7	7
21.0	Travel and transportation of persons	2		1
23.1	Rental payments to GSA	2	2	2
23.3	Communications, utilities, and miscellaneous charges	3	3	4
24.0	Printing and reproduction	9	1	1
25.2	Other services from non-Federal sources	9	10	10
25.4	Operation and maintenance of facilities	18	18	19
26.0	Supplies and materials	4	1	1
31.0	Equipment	4	3	4
99.9	Total new obligations, unexpired accounts	70	61	65

Employment Summary

Identification code 456–3300–0–1–503	2021 actual	2022 est.	2023 est.
1001 Direct civilian full-time equivalent employment	167	163	163

UNITED STATES INSTITUTE OF PEACE

Federal Funds

UNITED STATES INSTITUTE OF PEACE

For necessary expenses of the United States Institute of Peace, as authorized by the United States Institute of Peace Act (22 U.S.C. 4601 et seq.), $47,250,000, to remain available until September 30, 2024, which shall not be used for construction activities.

Note.—A full-year 2022 appropriation for this account was not enacted at the time the Budget was prepared; therefore, the Budget assumes this account is operating under the Continuing Appropriations Act, 2022 (Division A of Public Law 117–43, as amended). The amounts included for 2022 reflect the annualized level provided by the continuing resolution.

Program and Financing (in millions of dollars)

Identification code 458–1300–0–1–153		2021 actual	2022 est.	2023 est.
	Obligations by program activity:			
0001	Operating Expenses (Direct)	45	45	47
0801	Operating Expenses (Reimbursable)	29	29	29
0900	Total new obligations, unexpired accounts	74	74	76
	Budgetary resources:			
	Unobligated balance:			
1000	Unobligated balance brought forward, Oct 1	66	64	38
1021	Recoveries of prior year unpaid obligations	3	1	1
1070	Unobligated balance (total)	69	65	39
	Budget authority:			
	Appropriations, discretionary:			
1100	Appropriation	45	46	47
	Spending authority from offsetting collections, discretionary:			
1700	Collected	24	1	1
1900	Budget authority (total)	69	47	48
1930	Total budgetary resources available	138	112	87
	Memorandum (non-add) entries:			
1941	Unexpired unobligated balance, end of year	64	38	11

United States Interagency Council on Homelessness
Federal Funds 1337

	Change in obligated balance:			
	Unpaid obligations:			
3000	Unpaid obligations, brought forward, Oct 1	30	29	38
3010	New obligations, unexpired accounts	74	74	76
3011	Obligations ("upward adjustments"), expired accounts	3		
3020	Outlays (gross)	–70	–64	–48
3040	Recoveries of prior year unpaid obligations, unexpired	–3	–1	–1
3041	Recoveries of prior year unpaid obligations, expired	–5		
3050	Unpaid obligations, end of year	29	38	65
	Uncollected payments:			
3060	Uncollected pymts, Fed sources, brought forward, Oct 1	–74	–70	–70
3071	Change in uncollected pymts, Fed sources, expired	4		
3090	Uncollected pymts, Fed sources, end of year	–70	–70	–70
	Memorandum (non-add) entries:			
3100	Obligated balance, start of year	–44	–41	–32
3200	Obligated balance, end of year	–41	–32	–5
	Budget authority and outlays, net:			
	Discretionary:			
4000	Budget authority, gross	69	47	48
	Outlays, gross:			
4010	Outlays from new discretionary authority	45	38	39
4011	Outlays from discretionary balances	25	26	9
4020	Outlays, gross (total)	70	64	48
	Offsets against gross budget authority and outlays:			
	Offsetting collections (collected) from:			
4030	Federal sources	–26	–15	
4033	Non-Federal sources		–1	–1
4040	Offsets against gross budget authority and outlays (total)	–26	–16	–1
	Additional offsets against gross budget authority only:			
4052	Offsetting collections credited to expired accounts	2	15	
4060	Additional offsets against budget authority only (total)	2	15	
4070	Budget authority, net (discretionary)	45	46	47
4080	Outlays, net (discretionary)	44	48	47
4180	Budget authority, net (total)	45	46	47
4190	Outlays, net (total)	44	48	47

Created by Congress in 1984, the United States Institute of Peace (USIP) is an independent, nonpartisan institution charged with increasing the nation's capacity to prevent, mitigate, and help resolve international conflict without violence.

Object Classification (in millions of dollars)

Identification code 458–1300–0–1–153		2021 actual	2022 est.	2023 est.
	Direct obligations:			
11.8	Personnel compensation: Special personal services payments	12	12	13
12.1	Civilian personnel benefits	5	5	6
21.0	Travel and transportation of persons	3	3	3
25.2	Other services from non-Federal sources	22	22	22
41.0	Grants, subsidies, and contributions	3	3	3
99.0	Direct obligations	45	45	47
99.0	Reimbursable obligations	29	29	29
99.9	Total new obligations, unexpired accounts	74	74	76

UNITED STATES INTERAGENCY COUNCIL ON HOMELESSNESS

Federal Funds

OPERATING EXPENSES

For necessary expenses, including payment of salaries, authorized travel, hire of passenger motor vehicles, the rental of conference rooms, and the employment of experts and consultants under section 3109 of title 5, United States Code, of the United States Interagency Council on Homelessness in carrying out the functions pursuant to title II of the McKinney-Vento Homeless Assistance Act, as amended, $4,700,000.

Note.—A full-year 2022 appropriation for this account was not enacted at the time the Budget was prepared; therefore, the Budget assumes this account is operating under the Continuing Appropriations Act, 2022 (Division A of Public Law 117–43, as amended). The amounts included for 2022 reflect the annualized level provided by the continuing resolution.

1338   United States Interagency Council on Homelessness—Continued
Federal Funds—Continued
                                                     THE BUDGET FOR FISCAL YEAR 2023

OPERATING EXPENSES—Continued

Program and Financing (in millions of dollars)

Identification code 376–1300–0–1–808	2021 actual	2022 est.	2023 est.
Obligations by program activity:			
0101 Operations	3	4	5
Budgetary resources:			
Budget authority:			
Appropriations, discretionary:			
1100 Appropriation	4	4	5
1930 Total budgetary resources available	4	4	5
Memorandum (non-add) entries:			
1940 Unobligated balance expiring	–1		
Change in obligated balance:			
Unpaid obligations:			
3000 Unpaid obligations, brought forward, Oct 1		1	1
3010 New obligations, unexpired accounts	3	4	5
3020 Outlays (gross)	–3	–5	–5
3050 Unpaid obligations, end of year	1		
Memorandum (non-add) entries:			
3100 Obligated balance, start of year		1	1
3200 Obligated balance, end of year	1		
Budget authority and outlays, net:			
Discretionary:			
4000 Budget authority, gross	4	4	5
Outlays, gross:			
4010 Outlays from new discretionary authority	3	4	5
4011 Outlays from discretionary balances		1	
4020 Outlays, gross (total)	3	5	5
4180 Budget authority, net (total)	4	4	5
4190 Outlays, net (total)	3	5	5

The United States Interagency Council on Homelessness (USICH) is an independent Executive Branch agency whose mission is to coordinate the Federal response to homelessness and to create a national partnership at every level of government and with the private sector to prevent and end homelessness. The Budget proposes $4.7 million for USICH.

Object Classification (in millions of dollars)

Identification code 376–1300–0–1–808	2021 actual	2022 est.	2023 est.
Direct obligations:			
11.1 Personnel compensation: Full-time permanent	2	2	3
25.3 Other goods and services from Federal sources	1	1	1
99.0 Direct obligations	3	3	4
99.5 Adjustment for rounding		1	1
99.9 Total new obligations, unexpired accounts	3	4	5

Employment Summary

Identification code 376–1300–0–1–808	2021 actual	2022 est.	2023 est.
1001 Direct civilian full-time equivalent employment	18	18	22

VIETNAM EDUCATION FOUNDATION

Federal Funds

VIETNAM DEBT REPAYMENT FUND

Special and Trust Fund Receipts (in millions of dollars)

Identification code 519–5365–0–2–154	2021 actual	2022 est.	2023 est.
0100 Balance, start of year	6	6	6
2000 Total: Balances and receipts	6	6	6
5099 Balance, end of year	6	6	6

Program and Financing (in millions of dollars)

Identification code 519–5365–0–2–154	2021 actual	2022 est.	2023 est.
Budgetary resources:			
Unobligated balance:			
1000 Unobligated balance brought forward, Oct 1	10	10	10
1930 Total budgetary resources available	10	10	10
Memorandum (non-add) entries:			
1941 Unexpired unobligated balance, end of year	10	10	10
4180 Budget authority, net (total)			
4190 Outlays, net (total)			

The Vietnam Education Foundation Act of 2000 (Title II of Public Law 106–554) created the Vietnam Education Foundation (VEF) to administer an international fellowship program under which Vietnamese nationals can undertake graduate and post-graduate level studies in the United States in the sciences (natural, physical, and environmental), mathematics, medicine, and technology, and American citizens can teach in these fields in appropriate Vietnamese institutions of higher education. The Act also authorized the establishment of the Vietnam Debt Repayment Fund, in which all payments (including interest payments) made by the Socialist Republic of Vietnam under the United States-Vietnam debt agreement shall be deposited as offsetting receipts. Beginning in 2002, and in each subsequent year through 2018, $5 million of the amounts deposited into the fund from USDA and USAID shall be available to VEF for operations and fellowship programs. Beginning in 2015, and in each subsequent year through 2018, the remaining amounts deposited into the fund from USDA and USAID shall be available to support the establishment of an independent, not-for-profit academic institution in the Socialist Republic of Vietnam.

FEDERALLY CREATED NON-FEDERAL ENTITIES

The majority of budgetary accounts are associated with departments or other entities that are clearly Federal agencies. In other cases, budgetary accounts reflect a measure of Governmental activity in the economy, though the activity may have no direct relationship with the United States Treasury. Federally created non-Federal entities may be in the Budget because they were created by Federal law, they have some measure of regulatory or other authority conferred to them by law, or because they serve a public good directed by the Government. The following accounts are each deemed to be budgetary and fulfill the goal of presenting a Budget that is comprehensive of the full range of Federal activities.

AFFORDABLE HOUSING PROGRAM

Federal Funds

AFFORDABLE HOUSING PROGRAM

Special and Trust Fund Receipts (in millions of dollars)

Identification code 530–5528–0–2–604	2021 actual	2022 est.	2023 est.
0100 Balance, start of year			13
Receipts:			
Current law:			
1110 Contributions, Federal Home Loan Banks, Affordable Housing Program	224	224	224
2000 Total: Balances and receipts	224	224	237
Appropriations:			
Current law:			
2101 Affordable Housing Program	–224	–224	–224
2132 Affordable Housing Program		13	13
2199 Total current law appropriations	–224	–211	–211
2999 Total appropriations	–224	–211	–211
5099 Balance, end of year		13	26

OTHER INDEPENDENT AGENCIES

Electric Reliability Organization
Federal Funds   1339

Program and Financing (in millions of dollars)

Identification code 530–5528–0–2–604	2021 actual	2022 est.	2023 est.
Obligations by program activity:			
0001 Affordable Housing Program (Direct)	224	211	211
0900 Total new obligations, unexpired accounts (object class 41.0)	224	211	211
Budgetary resources:			
Budget authority:			
Appropriations, mandatory:			
1201 Appropriation (special or trust fund)	224	224	224
1232 Appropriations and/or unobligated balance of appropriations temporarily reduced	....	–13	–13
1260 Appropriations, mandatory (total)	224	211	211
1930 Total budgetary resources available	224	211	211
Change in obligated balance:			
Unpaid obligations:			
3010 New obligations, unexpired accounts	224	211	211
3020 Outlays (gross)	–224	–211	–211
Budget authority and outlays, net:			
Mandatory:			
4090 Budget authority, gross	224	211	211
Outlays, gross:			
4100 Outlays from new mandatory authority	224	211	211
4180 Budget authority, net (total)	224	211	211
4190 Outlays, net (total)	224	211	211

The Affordable Housing Program was created by the Financial Institutions Reform, Recovery, and Enforcement Act of 1989 (FIRREA). FIRREA requires each of the Federal Home Loan Banks to contribute 10-percent of its previous year's net earnings to an Affordable Housing Program (AHP) to be used to subsidize the cost of affordable homeownership and rental housing. The Federal Housing Finance Agency (FHFA) regulates the AHP and ensures that the AHP fulfills its mission.

CORPORATION FOR TRAVEL PROMOTION

Federal Funds

TRAVEL PROMOTION FUND

Special and Trust Fund Receipts (in millions of dollars)

Identification code 580–5585–0–2–376	2021 actual	2022 est.	2023 est.
0100 Balance, start of year	439	392	436
Receipts:			
Current law:			
1110 Fees, Travel Promotion Fund	13	60	150
2000 Total: Balances and receipts	452	452	586
Appropriations:			
Current law:			
2101 Travel Promotion Fund	–64	–13	–60
2103 Travel Promotion Fund	....	–4	–1
2132 Travel Promotion Fund	4	1	3
2199 Total current law appropriations	–60	–16	–58
2999 Total appropriations	–60	–16	–58
5099 Balance, end of year	392	436	528

Program and Financing (in millions of dollars)

Identification code 580–5585–0–2–376	2021 actual	2022 est.	2023 est.
Obligations by program activity:			
0001 Travel Promotion Fund	60	12	57
0900 Total new obligations, unexpired accounts (object class 41.0)	60	12	57
Budgetary resources:			
Unobligated balance:			
1000 Unobligated balance brought forward, Oct 1	....	....	4
Budget authority:			
Appropriations, mandatory:			
1201 Appropriation (special or trust fund)	64	13	60
1203 Appropriation (previously unavailable)(special or trust)	....	4	1
1232 Appropriations and/or unobligated balance of appropriations temporarily reduced	–4	–1	–3
1260 Appropriations, mandatory (total)	60	16	58
1930 Total budgetary resources available	60	16	62
Memorandum (non-add) entries:			
1941 Unexpired unobligated balance, end of year	....	4	5
Change in obligated balance:			
Unpaid obligations:			
3000 Unpaid obligations, brought forward, Oct 1	....	42	35
3010 New obligations, unexpired accounts	60	12	57
3020 Outlays (gross)	–18	–19	–36
3050 Unpaid obligations, end of year	42	35	56
Memorandum (non-add) entries:			
3100 Obligated balance, start of year	....	42	35
3200 Obligated balance, end of year	42	35	56
Budget authority and outlays, net:			
Mandatory:			
4090 Budget authority, gross	60	16	58
Outlays, gross:			
4100 Outlays from new mandatory authority	18	4	1
4101 Outlays from mandatory balances	....	15	35
4110 Outlays, gross (total)	18	19	36
4180 Budget authority, net (total)	60	16	58
4190 Outlays, net (total)	18	19	36

The Corporation for Travel Promotion (also known as Brand USA) was established by the Travel Promotion Act of 2009 to lead the nation's first global marketing effort to promote the United States as a premier travel destination and to communicate U.S. entry/exit policies and procedures. The public-private partnership, funded through a combination of private sector contributions and Federal matching funds, works closely with the travel industry to encourage increased travel and tourism in the United States.

A surcharge to the Electronic System for Travel Authorization (ESTA) fee that travelers from visa waiver countries pay before arriving in the United States provides Brand USA's Federal matching funds. Authorization to collect the surcharge under the Travel Promotion Act was set to expire September 30, 2020, but was extended to September 30, 2027, in the Brand USA Extension Act (part of the Further Consolidated Appropriations Act, 2020).

ELECTRIC RELIABILITY ORGANIZATION

Federal Funds

ELECTRIC RELIABILITY ORGANIZATION

Special and Trust Fund Receipts (in millions of dollars)

Identification code 531–5522–0–2–276	2021 actual	2022 est.	2023 est.
0100 Balance, start of year	7	7	15
Receipts:			
Current law:			
1110 Fees, Electric Reliability Organization	83	100	100
2000 Total: Balances and receipts	90	107	115
Appropriations:			
Current law:			
2101 Electric Reliability Organization	–83	–100	–100
2132 Electric Reliability Organization	....	8	8
2199 Total current law appropriations	–83	–92	–92
2999 Total appropriations	–83	–92	–92
5099 Balance, end of year	7	15	23

Program and Financing (in millions of dollars)

Identification code 531–5522–0–2–276	2021 actual	2022 est.	2023 est.
Obligations by program activity:			
0001 Electric Reliability Organization (Direct)	83	92	92

ELECTRIC RELIABILITY ORGANIZATION—Continued

Program and Financing—Continued

Identification code 531–5522–0–2–276	2021 actual	2022 est.	2023 est.
0900 Total new obligations, unexpired accounts (object class 25.2)	83	92	92
Budgetary resources:			
Budget authority:			
Appropriations, mandatory:			
1201 Appropriation (special or trust fund)	83	100	100
1232 Appropriations and/or unobligated balance of appropriations temporarily reduced	....	–8	–8
1260 Appropriations, mandatory (total)	83	92	92
1930 Total budgetary resources available	83	92	92
Change in obligated balance:			
Unpaid obligations:			
3010 New obligations, unexpired accounts	83	92	92
3020 Outlays (gross)	–83	–92	–92
Budget authority and outlays, net:			
Mandatory:			
4090 Budget authority, gross	83	92	92
Outlays, gross:			
4100 Outlays from new mandatory authority	83	92	92
4180 Budget authority, net (total)	83	92	92
4190 Outlays, net (total)	83	92	92

The Energy Policy Act of 2005 (P.L. 109–58) authorizes the Federal Energy Regulatory Commission (FERC) to certify an Electric Reliability Organization (ERO) to establish and enforce reliability standards for the electric bulk-power system. These standards include requirements for operating existing bulk-power system facilities, including cybersecurity protection, and design of planned additions or modifications to these facilities to provide for reliable operation, but does not include requirements to construct new transmission or generation capacity. On July 20, 2006, FERC certified the North American Electric Reliability Corporation as the ERO. ERO is funded by fees on end users of the bulk-power system. Since the ERO does not report budget data to Treasury, ERO funding is based on estimates.

FEDERAL RETIREMENT THRIFT INVESTMENT BOARD

Federal Funds

PROGRAM EXPENSES

Special and Trust Fund Receipts (in millions of dollars)

Identification code 026–5290–0–2–602	2021 actual	2022 est.	2023 est.
0100 Balance, start of year	....	....	....
Receipts:			
Current law:			
1130 Reimbursement for Program Expenses, Federal Retirement Thrift Investment Board	498	497	474
2000 Total: Balances and receipts	498	497	474
Appropriations:			
Current law:			
2101 Program Expenses	–498	–497	–474
5099 Balance, end of year	....	....	....

Program and Financing (in millions of dollars)

Identification code 026–5290–0–2–602	2021 actual	2022 est.	2023 est.
Obligations by program activity:			
0001 Administrative expenses	449	604	474
Budgetary resources:			
Unobligated balance:			
1000 Unobligated balance brought forward, Oct 1	58	107	....
Budget authority:			
Appropriations, mandatory:			
1201 Appropriation (special or trust fund)	498	497	474
1930 Total budgetary resources available	556	604	474
Memorandum (non-add) entries:			
1941 Unexpired unobligated balance, end of year	107	....	....
Change in obligated balance:			
Unpaid obligations:			
3000 Unpaid obligations, brought forward, Oct 1	....	....	107
3010 New obligations, unexpired accounts	449	604	474
3020 Outlays (gross)	–449	–497	–474
3050 Unpaid obligations, end of year	....	107	107
Memorandum (non-add) entries:			
3100 Obligated balance, start of year	....	....	107
3200 Obligated balance, end of year	....	107	107
Budget authority and outlays, net:			
Mandatory:			
4090 Budget authority, gross	498	497	474
Outlays, gross:			
4100 Outlays from new mandatory authority	442	497	474
4101 Outlays from mandatory balances	7	....	....
4110 Outlays, gross (total)	449	497	474
4180 Budget authority, net (total)	498	497	474
4190 Outlays, net (total)	449	497	474

The Federal Retirement Thrift Investment Board is responsible for managing the Thrift Savings Fund. Program administration for the Fund is financed from the Fund. Program expenses are funded first from forfeitures and loan fees and then from earnings on all participant and agency contributions to the Fund.

The Thrift Savings Fund is a special tax-deferred savings fund established by the Federal Employees' Retirement System Act of 1986. Due to the fiduciary nature of the Fund, it is not included in the totals of the Federal Budget. Information on the financial status and activities of the Fund follows this account.

Object Classification (in millions of dollars)

Identification code 026–5290–0–2–602	2021 actual	2022 est.	2023 est.
Direct obligations:			
11.1 Personnel compensation: Full-time permanent	38	41	41
12.1 Civilian personnel benefits	14	17	17
21.0 Travel and transportation of persons	....	1	1
23.2 Rental payments to others	12	13	13
23.3 Communications, utilities, and miscellaneous charges	27	26	22
24.0 Printing and reproduction	....	2	1
25.1 Advisory and assistance services	20	17	19
25.2 Other services from non-Federal sources	329	468	341
25.3 Other goods and services from Federal sources	1	12	12
31.0 Equipment	8	7	7
99.9 Total new obligations, unexpired accounts	449	604	474

Employment Summary

Identification code 026–5290–0–2–602	2021 actual	2022 est.	2023 est.
1001 Direct civilian full-time equivalent employment	285	294	294

INFORMATION SCHEDULES FOR THE THRIFT SAVINGS FUND

The Fund is composed of individual accounts maintained by the Federal Retirement Thrift Investment Board on behalf of the individual participants in the Fund. All Federal civilian employees and members of the uniformed services are eligible to contribute to the Fund. Civilian employees covered by the Federal Employees Retirement System (or equivalent retirement systems) receive an automatic agency 1 percent contribution and matching contributions in accordance with the formulas prescribed by law. Beginning in January 2018, all new members of the uniformed services, and those members of the uniformed services with less than 12 years of service who have made an affirmative election, receive an automatic agency one percent contribution and matching contributions in accordance with the formulas prescribed by law. Employees can invest in five investment funds: a U.S. Government securities investment fund; a fixed income index investment fund; a common stock index investment fund; a small capitalization stock index investment fund; an international stock index investment fund; or in ten lifecycle funds. These funds are composed of varying allocations of the five core investment funds. The allocations are based on the target maturity date of each fund.

The estimated status of the Fund is shown below:

STATUS OF THRIFT SAVINGS FUND

(in millions of dollars)

	2021 actual	2022 est.	2023 est.
Thrift Savings Fund investment balance, start of year	676,489	775,884	878,276
Receipts during the year:			
Employee contributions [1]		27,001	27,811	28,645
Contributions on behalf of employees [1]	11,680	12,030	12,391
Earnings and adjustments [2]	90,873	93,599	96,408
Total receipts	129,554	133,440	137,444
Outlays during the year:			
Withdrawals	29,891	30,788	31,711
Loans to employees, net of repayments	(230)	(237)	(244)
Administrative expenses	449	497	474
Total cash outlays	30,110	31,048	31,941
Thrift Savings Fund investment balance, end of year [3]	775,933	878,276	983,779

Notes:	2021 actual	2022 est.	2023 est.
[1] 2021 Employer contributions included:			
Automatic contributions for FERS employees:	2,598	2,676	2,756
Matching contributions for FERS employees:	9,082	9,354	9,635
	11,680	12,030	12,391
[2] 2021 Earnings included:			
Return on investment in Government Securities	3,575	3,682	3,793
Return on non-government instruments	87,132	89,746	92,438
Interest on loans to employees	157	162	167
Agency payments for lost earnings	9	9	10
[3] Investment Balances at 9/30/2021 were:			
U.S. Government Securities Investment Fund	273,097		
TSP F Fund - U.S. Debt Index Fund	37,638		
TSP C Fund - Equity Index Fund	293,772		
TSP S Fund - Extended Equity Index Fund	104,263		
TSP I Fund - EAFE Equity Index Fund	67,114		

Assumptions for growth:
FY 2022 and FY 2023: 3% estimated growth (except for 2022 Start of Year Balance). Administrative expenses for the new year and out year (FY 2022 and FY 2023) are the Board approved and estimated budget.

MEDICAL CENTER RESEARCH ORGANIZATIONS

Federal Funds

MEDICAL CENTER RESEARCH ORGANIZATIONS

Program and Financing (in millions of dollars)

Identification code 185–4026–0–3–703	2021 actual	2022 est.	2023 est.
Obligations by program activity:			
0801 Operating expenses	269	273	277
Budgetary resources:			
Budget authority:			
Spending authority from offsetting collections, mandatory:			
1800 Collected	269	273	277
1930 Total budgetary resources available	269	273	277
Change in obligated balance:			
Unpaid obligations:			
3000 Unpaid obligations, brought forward, Oct 1	....	....	205
3010 New obligations, unexpired accounts	269	273	277
3020 Outlays (gross)	–269	–68	–137
3050 Unpaid obligations, end of year	....	205	345
Memorandum (non-add) entries:			
3100 Obligated balance, start of year	....	....	205
3200 Obligated balance, end of year	....	205	345
Budget authority and outlays, net:			
Mandatory:			
4090 Budget authority, gross	269	273	277
Outlays, gross:			
4100 Outlays from new mandatory authority	269	68	69
4101 Outlays from mandatory balances	....	....	68
4110 Outlays, gross (total)	269	68	137
Offsets against gross budget authority and outlays:			
Offsetting collections (collected) from:			
4120 Federal sources	–269	–273	–277
4180 Budget authority, net (total)	....	....	....
4190 Outlays, net (total)	....	–205	–140

These nonprofit corporations provide a flexible funding mechanism for the conduct of approved research at Department of Veterans Affairs medical centers. These organizations will derive funds to operate various research activities from Federal and non-Federal sources. No appropriation is required to support these activities.

Object Classification (in millions of dollars)

Identification code 185–4026–0–3–703	2021 actual	2022 est.	2023 est.
Reimbursable obligations:			
21.0 Travel and transportation of persons	10	10	10
25.2 Other services from non-Federal sources	233	236	240
26.0 Supplies and materials	18	19	19
31.0 Equipment	8	8	8
99.9 Total new obligations, unexpired accounts	269	273	277

NATIONAL ASSOCIATION OF REGISTERED AGENTS AND BROKERS

Federal Funds

NATIONAL ASSOCIATION OF REGISTERED AGENTS AND BROKERS

Special and Trust Fund Receipts (in millions of dollars)

Identification code 543–5743–0–2–376	2021 actual	2022 est.	2023 est.
0100 Balance, start of year	....	....	....
Receipts:			
Current law:			
1110 Membership Fees, NARAB	....	2	2
2000 Total: Balances and receipts	....	2	2
Appropriations:			
Current law:			
2101 National Association of Registered Agents and Brokers	....	–2	–2
5099 Balance, end of year	....	....	....

Program and Financing (in millions of dollars)

Identification code 543–5743–0–2–376	2021 actual	2022 est.	2023 est.
Obligations by program activity:			
0001 Administrative support	....	1	1
0002 Advisory and assistant services	....	1	1
0900 Total new obligations, unexpired accounts	....	2	2
Budgetary resources:			
Budget authority:			
Appropriations, mandatory:			
1201 Appropriation (special or trust fund)	....	2	2
1930 Total budgetary resources available	....	2	2
Change in obligated balance:			
Unpaid obligations:			
3010 New obligations, unexpired accounts	....	2	2
3020 Outlays (gross)	....	–2	–2
Budget authority and outlays, net:			
Mandatory:			
4090 Budget authority, gross	....	2	2
Outlays, gross:			
4100 Outlays from new mandatory authority	....	2	2
4180 Budget authority, net (total)	....	2	2
4190 Outlays, net (total)	....	2	2

National Association of Registered Agents and Brokers—Continued
Federal Funds—Continued

NATIONAL ASSOCIATION OF REGISTERED AGENTS AND BROKERS—Continued

Object Classification (in millions of dollars)

Identification code 543–5743–0–2–376	2021 actual	2022 est.	2023 est.
Direct obligations:			
11.1 Personnel compensation: Full-time permanent	....	1	1
25.1 Advisory and assistance services	....	1	1
99.9 Total new obligations, unexpired accounts	....	2	2

Employment Summary

Identification code 543–5743–0–2–376	2021 actual	2022 est.	2023 est.
1001 Direct civilian full-time equivalent employment	....	7	7

NATIONAL OILHEAT RESEARCH ALLIANCE

Federal Funds

NATIONAL OILHEAT RESEARCH ALLIANCE

Special and Trust Fund Receipts (in millions of dollars)

Identification code 544–5643–0–2–276	2021 actual	2022 est.	2023 est.
0100 Balance, start of year	....	....	2
Receipts:			
Current law:			
1110 Fees, National Oilheat Research Alliance	7	9	8
2000 Total: Balances and receipts	7	9	10
Appropriations:			
Current law:			
2101 National Oilheat Research Alliance	–7	–7	–7
5099 Balance, end of year	....	2	3

Program and Financing (in millions of dollars)

Identification code 544–5643–0–2–276	2021 actual	2022 est.	2023 est.
Obligations by program activity:			
0001 Direct program activity	7	7	7
0900 Total new obligations, unexpired accounts (object class 25.2)	7	7	7
Budgetary resources:			
Budget authority:			
Appropriations, mandatory:			
1201 Appropriation (special or trust fund)	7	7	7
1930 Total budgetary resources available	7	7	7
Change in obligated balance:			
Unpaid obligations:			
3010 New obligations, unexpired accounts	7	7	7
3020 Outlays (gross)	–7	–7	–7
Budget authority and outlays, net:			
Mandatory:			
4090 Budget authority, gross	7	7	7
Outlays, gross:			
4100 Outlays from new mandatory authority	7	7	7
4180 Budget authority, net (total)	7	7	7
4190 Outlays, net (total)	7	7	7

The National Oilheat Research Alliance (NORA) was first authorized by The National Oilheat Research Alliance Act of 2000, as amended in 2014 (P.L. 113–79), and reauthorized by the Agriculture Improvement Act of 2018 (P.L. 115–334) to develop programs and projects and enter into contracts or other agreements to enhance consumer and employee safety and training; to provide for research, development, and demonstration of clean and efficient oilheat fuel utilization equipment; and to educate consumers. NORA is funded via statutorily-mandated fees of $0.002 on every gallon of heating oil sold, collected at the wholesale level. Since NORA does not report budget data to Treasury, NORA funding is based on estimates.

PUBLIC COMPANY ACCOUNTING OVERSIGHT BOARD

Federal Funds

PUBLIC COMPANY ACCOUNTING OVERSIGHT BOARD

Special and Trust Fund Receipts (in millions of dollars)

Identification code 526–5376–0–2–376	2021 actual	2022 est.	2023 est.
0100 Balance, start of year	20	19	21
Receipts:			
Current law:			
1110 Accounting Support Fees, Public Company Accounting Oversight Board	264	298	308
1120 Civil Monetary Penalties, Public Company Accounting Oversight Board	2	2	2
1130 Interest on Investments	....	1	2
1199 Total current law receipts	266	301	312
1999 Total receipts	266	301	312
2000 Total: Balances and receipts	286	320	333
Appropriations:			
Current law:			
2101 Public Company Accounting Oversight Board	–2	–2	–2
2101 Public Company Accounting Oversight Board	–264	–299	–310
2103 Public Company Accounting Oversight Board	–17	–16	–18
2132 Public Company Accounting Oversight Board	16	18	18
2199 Total current law appropriations	–267	–299	–312
2999 Total appropriations	–267	–299	–312
5099 Balance, end of year	19	21	21

Program and Financing (in millions of dollars)

Identification code 526–5376–0–2–376	2021 actual	2022 est.	2023 est.
Obligations by program activity:			
0001 Accounting Oversight	274	306	308
0002 Accounting Scholarship Program	1	1	....
0900 Total new obligations, unexpired accounts (object class 25.1)	275	307	308
Budgetary resources:			
Unobligated balance:			
1000 Unobligated balance brought forward, Oct 1	156	148	144
1020 Adjustment of unobligated bal brought forward, Oct 1 (Error in PY Gross Outlays)	....	4	....
1070 Unobligated balance (total)	156	152	144
Budget authority:			
Appropriations, discretionary:			
1101 Appropriation (special or trust) (Civil Money Penalties)	2	2	2
Appropriations, mandatory:			
1201 Appropriation (special or trust fund)	264	299	310
1203 Appropriation (previously unavailable)(special or trust)	17	16	18
1232 Appropriations and/or unobligated balance of appropriations temporarily reduced	–16	–18	–18
1260 Appropriations, mandatory (total)	265	297	310
1900 Budget authority (total)	267	299	312
1930 Total budgetary resources available	423	451	456
Memorandum (non-add) entries:			
1941 Unexpired unobligated balance, end of year	148	144	148
Change in obligated balance:			
Unpaid obligations:			
3000 Unpaid obligations, brought forward, Oct 1	....	....	8
3010 New obligations, unexpired accounts	275	307	308
3020 Outlays (gross)	–275	–299	–307
3050 Unpaid obligations, end of year	....	8	9
Memorandum (non-add) entries:			
3100 Obligated balance, start of year	....	....	8
3200 Obligated balance, end of year	....	8	9
Budget authority and outlays, net:			
Discretionary:			
4000 Budget authority, gross	2	2	2

OTHER INDEPENDENT AGENCIES

		2021 actual	2022 est.	2023 est.
	Outlays, gross:			
4010	Outlays from new discretionary authority	1	1	1
4011	Outlays from discretionary balances		1	1
4020	Outlays, gross (total)	1	2	2
	Mandatory:			
4090	Budget authority, gross	265	297	310
	Outlays, gross:			
4100	Outlays from new mandatory authority	265	297	305
4101	Outlays from mandatory balances	9		
4110	Outlays, gross (total)	274	297	305
4180	Budget authority, net (total)	267	299	312
4190	Outlays, net (total)	275	299	307
	Memorandum (non-add) entries:			
5000	Total investments, SOY: Federal securities: Par value	114	104	93
5001	Total investments, EOY: Federal securities: Par value	104	93	93

Note: Because the Public Company Accounting Oversight Board (PCAOB) does not report budgetary data to Treasury, amounts shown above were derived from the PCAOB's financial data, which is based on a calendar year.

The Sarbanes-Oxley Act of 2002 (the Act) (P.L. 107–204), as amended by the Dodd-Frank Wall Street Reform and Consumer Protection Act (P.L. 111–203), established the PCAOB to oversee the audits and auditors of both public companies that are subject to Federal securities laws and broker-dealers registered with the Securities and Exchange Commission (SEC) in order to protect the interests of investors and further the public interest in the preparation of informative, accurate, and independent audit reports.

Funding for the PCAOB comes from registration and annual fees paid by public accounting firms and accounting support fees paid by public companies and SEC-registered broker-dealers. The Act designated the Commission to oversee the PCAOB and specifies that the PCAOB's budget and the accounting support fee be subject to approval by the Commission.

SECURITIES INVESTOR PROTECTION CORPORATION

Federal Funds

SECURITIES INVESTOR PROTECTION CORPORATION

Special and Trust Fund Receipts (in millions of dollars)

Identification code 576–5600–0–2–376	2021 actual	2022 est.	2023 est.
0100 Balance, start of year	3,689	4,049	4,389
Receipts:			
Current law:			
1110 Assessments, SIPC	439	421	405
1130 Earnings on Investments, SIPC	72	83	89
1199 Total current law receipts	511	504	494
1999 Total receipts	511	504	494
2000 Total: Balances and receipts	4,200	4,553	4,883
Appropriations:			
Current law:			
2101 Securities Investor Protection Corporation	−152	−162	−174
2103 Securities Investor Protection Corporation	−10	−11	−9
2132 Securities Investor Protection Corporation	11	9	10
2199 Total current law appropriations	−151	−164	−173
2999 Total appropriations	−151	−164	−173
5099 Balance, end of year	4,049	4,389	4,710

Program and Financing (in millions of dollars)

Identification code 576–5600–0–2–376	2021 actual	2022 est.	2023 est.
Obligations by program activity:			
0001 Program Management	26	30	29
0002 Customer Claims	125	134	144
0900 Total new obligations, unexpired accounts (object class 25.1)	151	164	173
Budgetary resources:			
Budget authority:			
Appropriations, mandatory:			
1201 Appropriation (special or trust fund)	152	162	174
1203 Appropriation (previously unavailable)(special or trust)	10	11	9
1232 Appropriations and/or unobligated balance of appropriations temporarily reduced	−11	−9	−10
1260 Appropriations, mandatory (total)	151	164	173
1930 Total budgetary resources available	151	164	173
Change in obligated balance:			
Unpaid obligations:			
3010 New obligations, unexpired accounts	151	164	173
3020 Outlays (gross)	−151	−164	−173
Budget authority and outlays, net:			
Mandatory:			
4090 Budget authority, gross	151	164	173
Outlays, gross:			
4100 Outlays from new mandatory authority	151	164	173
4180 Budget authority, net (total)	151	164	173
4190 Outlays, net (total)	151	164	173
Memorandum (non-add) entries:			
5000 Total investments, SOY: Federal securities: Par value	3,667	4,030	4,377
5001 Total investments, EOY: Federal securities: Par value	4,030	4,377	4,702

Note: Because the Securities Investor Protection Corporation (SIPC) does not report budgetary data to Treasury, amounts shown above were derived from SIPC's financial data, which is based on a calendar year. Earnings on investments are presented for all three years using an unamortized cost rather than the market value, to comply with OMB Circular A-11 requirements.

SIPC was created by the Securities Investor Protection Act of 1970 (SIPA). Its purpose is to protect customers against loss resulting from broker-dealer failure and, thereby, promote investor confidence in the Nation's securities markets. SIPC is a non-profit membership corporation. Its members are, with some exceptions, all persons registered as brokers or dealers under section 15(b) of the Securities Exchange Act of 1934 and all persons who are members of a national securities exchange. SIPC's funding is derived entirely from assessments on its membership and from interest earned on its investments in U.S. Government securities.

SIPC may borrow up to $2.5 billion from the U.S. Department of the Treasury, through the Securities and Exchange Commission, in the event that the fund maintained by SIPC is insufficient to satisfy the claims of customers of brokerage firms in SIPA liquidation or for other purposes under the Act. SIPC has not accessed these loans to date and the Budget does not project that SIPC will require use of these loans over the next 10 years.

STANDARD SETTING BODY

Federal Funds

PAYMENT TO STANDARD SETTING BODY

Special and Trust Fund Receipts (in millions of dollars)

Identification code 527–5377–0–2–376	2021 actual	2022 est.	2023 est.
0100 Balance, start of year	2	2	2
Receipts:			
Current law:			
1110 Accounting Support Fees, Standard Setting Body	31	41	43
2000 Total: Balances and receipts	33	43	45
Appropriations:			
Current law:			
2101 Payment to Standard Setting Body	−31	−41	−43
2103 Payment to Standard Setting Body	−2	−2	−2
2132 Payment to Standard Setting Body	2	2	2
2199 Total current law appropriations	−31	−41	−43
2999 Total appropriations	−31	−41	−43
5099 Balance, end of year	2	2	2

Program and Financing (in millions of dollars)

Identification code 527–5377–0–2–376	2021 actual	2022 est.	2023 est.
Obligations by program activity:			
0001 Advisory and assistance services	31	41	43

PAYMENT TO STANDARD SETTING BODY—Continued

Program and Financing—Continued

Identification code 527–5377–0–2–376	2021 actual	2022 est.	2023 est.
0900 Total new obligations, unexpired accounts (object class 25.1)	31	41	43
Budgetary resources:			
Budget authority:			
Appropriations, mandatory:			
1201 Appropriation (special or trust fund)	31	41	43
1203 Appropriation (previously unavailable)(special or trust)	2	2	2
1232 Appropriations and/or unobligated balance of appropriations temporarily reduced	–2	–2	–2
1260 Appropriations, mandatory (total)	31	41	43
1930 Total budgetary resources available	31	41	43
Change in obligated balance:			
Unpaid obligations:			
3010 New obligations, unexpired accounts	31	41	43
3020 Outlays (gross)	–31	–41	–43
Budget authority and outlays, net:			
Mandatory:			
4090 Budget authority, gross	31	41	43
Outlays, gross:			
4100 Outlays from new mandatory authority	31	41	43
4180 Budget authority, net (total)	31	41	43
4190 Outlays, net (total)	31	41	43

Note: Because the standard setting body does not provide budgetary data to Treasury, amounts shown above were derived from the standard setting body's financial data, which is based on a calendar year.

The Financial Accounting Standards Board (FASB) is an independent, private-sector organization organized in 1973 within the Financial Accounting Foundation (FAF), which is an independent, private-sector, not-for-profit corporation. The FASB consists of a seven-member board, whose members are appointed by the FAF. The FASB was originally designated by the Securities and Exchange Commission (Commission) as the authoritative standard setter for purposes of the Federal securities laws in 1973. In April 2003, the Commission reaffirmed the status of the FASB as a designated private-sector standard setting body pursuant to the Sarbanes-Oxley Act of 2002 (the Act) (P.L. 107–204), stating that the FASB's financial accounting and reporting standards are recognized as "generally accepted" for purposes of the Federal securities laws.

The Act authorizes funding for the standard setting body to be derived from an accounting support fee assessed on public companies, although the FAF has, on a voluntary basis, partially offset the fees that could be assessed pursuant to the Act by payments derived from publication sales and licensing fees. Prior to the Act, the FASB was funded by voluntary contributions from public companies, public accounting firms, and other stakeholders. The standard setting body's accounting support fee is subject to review by the Commission.

UNITED MINE WORKERS OF AMERICA BENEFIT FUNDS

Trust Funds

UNITED MINE WORKERS OF AMERICA COMBINED BENEFIT FUND

Special and Trust Fund Receipts (in millions of dollars)

Identification code 476–8295–0–7–551	2021 actual	2022 est.	2023 est.
0100 Balance, start of year	52	52	52
Receipts:			
Current law:			
1110 Premiums, Combined Fund and 1992 Plan, UMWA	13	8	7
1140 Transfers from Abandoned Mine Reclamation Fund	29	19	82
1140 Federal Payment to United Mine Workers of America	322	381	381
1140 Federal Payment to United Mine Workers of America	388	331	340
1199 Total current law receipts	752	739	810
1999 Total receipts	752	739	810
2000 Total: Balances and receipts	804	791	862

	2021 actual	2022 est.	2023 est.
Appropriations:			
Current law:			
2101 United Mine Workers of America 1992 Benefit Plan	–76	–39	–69
2101 United Mine Workers of America Combined Benefit Fund	–49	–39	–47
2101 United Mine Workers of America 1993 Benefit Plan	–305	–280	–313
2101 United Mine Workers of America Pension Funds	–322	–381	–381
2199 Total current law appropriations	–752	–739	–810
2999 Total appropriations	–752	–739	–810
5099 Balance, end of year	52	52	52

Program and Financing (in millions of dollars)

Identification code 476–8295–0–7–551	2021 actual	2022 est.	2023 est.
Obligations by program activity:			
0001 United Mine Workers of America Combined Benefit Fund	49	39	47
0900 Total new obligations, unexpired accounts (object class 42.0)	49	39	47
Budgetary resources:			
Budget authority:			
Appropriations, mandatory:			
1201 Appropriation (special or trust fund)	49	39	47
1930 Total budgetary resources available	49	39	47
Change in obligated balance:			
Unpaid obligations:			
3010 New obligations, unexpired accounts	49	39	47
3020 Outlays (gross)	–49	–39	–47
Budget authority and outlays, net:			
Mandatory:			
4090 Budget authority, gross	49	39	47
Outlays, gross:			
4100 Outlays from new mandatory authority	49	39	47
4180 Budget authority, net (total)	49	39	47
4190 Outlays, net (total)	49	39	47

The Combined Benefit Fund was established by the Coal Industry Retiree Health Benefit Act of 1992 to take over paying for medical care of retired miners and their dependents who were eligible for health care from the private 1950 and 1974 United Mine Workers of America Benefit Plans. The Fund's trustees represent the United Mine Workers of America and coal companies. The Fund is financed by assessments on current and former signatories to labor agreements with the United Mine Workers; past transfers from the United Mine Workers pension fund; transfers from the Abandoned Mine Land Reclamation fund; and the General Fund of the Treasury.

UNITED MINE WORKERS OF AMERICA 1992 BENEFIT PLAN

Program and Financing (in millions of dollars)

Identification code 476–8260–0–7–551	2021 actual	2022 est.	2023 est.
Obligations by program activity:			
0001 United Mine Workers of America 1992 Benefit Plan	76	39	69
0900 Total new obligations, unexpired accounts (object class 42.0)	76	39	69
Budgetary resources:			
Budget authority:			
Appropriations, mandatory:			
1201 Appropriation (special or trust fund)	76	39	69
1930 Total budgetary resources available	76	39	69
Change in obligated balance:			
Unpaid obligations:			
3010 New obligations, unexpired accounts	76	39	69
3020 Outlays (gross)	–76	–39	–69
Budget authority and outlays, net:			
Mandatory:			
4090 Budget authority, gross	76	39	69
Outlays, gross:			
4100 Outlays from new mandatory authority	76	39	69
4180 Budget authority, net (total)	76	39	69

		2021 actual	2022 est.	2023 est.
4190	Outlays, net (total)	76	39	69

The 1992 Benefit Plan was established by the Coal Industry Retiree Health Benefit Act of 1992. It pays for health care for those miners who retired between July 21, 1992 and September 30, 1994, and their dependents, who are eligible for benefits under an employer plan and cease to be covered, usually because an employer is out of business. Plan trustees are appointed by the United Mine Workers of America and the Bituminous Coal Operators Association, a coal industry bargaining group. The Plan is supported by signers of the 1988 labor agreement with the United Mine Workers of America; transfers from the Abandoned Mine Land Reclamation fund; and the General Fund of the Treasury.

UNITED MINE WORKERS OF AMERICA 1993 BENEFIT PLAN

Program and Financing (in millions of dollars)

Identification code 476–8535–0–7–551		2021 actual	2022 est.	2023 est.
	Obligations by program activity:			
0001	United Mine Workers of America 1993 Benefit Plan	305	280	313
0900	Total new obligations, unexpired accounts (object class 42.0)	305	280	313
	Budgetary resources:			
	Budget authority:			
	Appropriations, mandatory:			
1201	Appropriation (special or trust fund)	305	280	313
1930	Total budgetary resources available	305	280	313
	Change in obligated balance:			
	Unpaid obligations:			
3010	New obligations, unexpired accounts	305	280	313
3020	Outlays (gross)	–305	–280	–313
	Budget authority and outlays, net:			
	Mandatory:			
4090	Budget authority, gross	305	280	313
	Outlays, gross:			
4100	Outlays from new mandatory authority	305	280	313
4180	Budget authority, net (total)	305	280	313
4190	Outlays, net (total)	305	280	313

The 1993 Benefit Plan provides health benefits to certain retired mine workers and disabled mine workers who are not eligible for benefits under the Coal Industry Retiree Health Benefit Act of 1992 and who are not receiving benefits from employers' benefit plans. The 1993 Benefit Plan was established through collective bargaining under the National Bituminous Coal Wage Agreement of 1993. Plan trustees are appointed by the United Mine Workers of America and the Bituminous Coal Operators Association, a coal industry bargaining group. The Plan is financed by signatories to the National Bituminous Coal Wage Agreement; transfers from the Abandoned Mine Land Reclamation fund; and the General Fund of the Treasury.

UNITED MINE WORKERS OF AMERICA PENSION FUNDS

Program and Financing (in millions of dollars)

Identification code 476–8553–0–7–601		2021 actual	2022 est.	2023 est.
	Obligations by program activity:			
0001	Direct program activity	322	381	381
0900	Total new obligations, unexpired accounts (object class 42.0)	322	381	381
	Budgetary resources:			
	Budget authority:			
	Appropriations, mandatory:			
1201	Appropriation (special or trust fund)	322	381	381
1930	Total budgetary resources available	322	381	381
	Change in obligated balance:			
	Unpaid obligations:			
3010	New obligations, unexpired accounts	322	381	381
3020	Outlays (gross)	–322	–381	–381
	Budget authority and outlays, net:			
	Mandatory:			
4090	Budget authority, gross	322	381	381
	Outlays, gross:			
4100	Outlays from new mandatory authority	322	381	381
4180	Budget authority, net (total)	322	381	381
4190	Outlays, net (total)	322	381	381

The 1974 United Mine Workers of America Pension Plan provides pensions to eligible mine workers who retire, to those who become totally disabled as a result of mine accidents, and to the eligible surviving spouses of mine workers. The Bipartisan Miners Act of 2019 (Division M of Public Law 116–94), authorizes mandatory Treasury payments to the 1974 United Mine Workers of America Pension Plan, subject to certain limitations, until the Plans funded percentage reaches 100 percent.

AMENDMENTS TO AND REVISIONS IN BUDGET AUTHORITY FOR 2022

STATEMENT ON CHANGES

(Between the Transmittal of the 2022 and 2023 Budgets)

A statement of all amendments to, or revisions in, budget authority requested between transmittal of the 2022 Budget and the 2023 Budget is presented below. This statement is included in the Budget in accordance with the Congressional Budget Act of 1974 (31 U.S.C. 1105(d)).

The modifications to proposals for 2022 budget authority that were made through the course of the past year took the form of Presidential amendments to the budget transmitted on May 28, 2021, and other requests.

These modifications were printed in the documents of the House of Representatives that are identified on the following listing.

Transmitted to the Congress on	Agencies affected	Printed as
July 20, 2021	Department of Agriculture	Not Available
	Department of Defense	
	Department of Education	
	Department of Health and Human Services	
	Department of Homeland Security	
	Department of Housing and Urban Development	
	Department of Justice	
	Department of Labor	
	Department of State	
	District of Columbia	
	United States Agency for International Development	
March 2, 2022	Department of Commerce	Not Available
	Department of Defense	
	Department of Energy	
	Department of Health and Human Services	
	Department of Justice	
	Department of State	
	Department of the Treasury	
	United States Agency for International Development	

ADVANCE APPROPRIATIONS

An advance appropriation is one made to become available one year or more beyond the year for which the appropriations act is passed. Advance appropriations in 2023 appropriations acts will become available for programs in 2024 or beyond. Since these appropriations are not available until after 2023, the amounts will not be included in the 2023 totals, but will be reflected in the totals for the year for which they are requested.

The Congressional Budget Act of 1974 (31 U.S.C. 1105(a)(17)) requires inclusion in the budget of "information on estimates of appropriations for the fiscal year following the fiscal year for which the budget is submitted for grants, contracts, and other payments under each program for which there is an authorization of appropriations for that following fiscal year when the appropriations are authorized to be included in an appropriation law for the fiscal year before the fiscal year in which the appropriation is to be available for obligation." In fulfillment of this requirement, the accompanying table lists those accounts that have either received discretionary or mandatory advance appropriations since 2021 or will request, in 2023, advance appropriations for 2024 and beyond and cites the applicable authorizing statute.

The Continuing Appropriations Act, 2022 (division A of Public Law 117–43, as amended), which was in place at the time the Budget was prepared, does not explicitly address advance appropriations for 2023. As a result, this Budget, as illustrated by the accompanying table, assumes that final full-year appropriations would include language to make 2023 advance appropriations available. This is in order to ensure comparability with annual funding provided under the Continuing Appropriations Act, 2022, and to depict accurately the 2023 discretionary request levels. In general, the Budget assumes that the 2023 level that would be enacted for discretionary appropriations is equal to the 2022 advance appropriations that were enacted in the 2021 appropriations Acts. However, for the Department of Veterans Affairs and the Corporation for Public Broadcasting (CPB), the 2023 level (and 2024 level for CPB) is instead consistent with the 2023 advance apppropriations (and 2024 for CPB) that were requested in the 2022 Budget.

For additional information on advance appropriations, please refer to the Budget Concepts chapter in the *Analytical Perspectives* volume.

Advance Appropriations by Agency in the 2023 Budget

(Budget authority in millions of dollars)

Agency/Program	Pre-cancellation, Pre-Transfer Enacted Levels 2021	2022	CR 2023	2024 Request
Discretionary One-year Advances:				
Department of Education (20 U.S.C. 1223):				
Education for the Disadvantaged	10,841	10,841	10,841	10,841
Special Education	9,283	9,283	9,283	9,283
Career, Technical, and Adult Education	791	791	791	791
School Improvement Programs	1,681	1,681	1,681	1,681
Department of Housing and Urban Development (42 U.S.C. 1437 et seq.):				
Tenant-Based Rental Assistance	4,000	4,000	4,000	4,000
Project-Based Rental Assistance	400	400	400	400
Department of Labor:				
Training and Employment Services (29 U.S.C. 2801 et seq.)	1,772	1,772	1,772	1,772
Department of Veterans Affairs (Public Law 111–81):				
Medical Services	56,158	58,897	70,323	74,004
Medical Community Care	17,131	20,148	24,157	33,000
Medical Support and Compliance	7,914	8,403	9,673	12,300
Medical Facilities	6,433	6,735	7,134	8,800
Discretionary Two-year Advances:				
Corporation for Public Broadcasting (47 U.S.C. 396)[1]	445	465	475	475
Subtotal, Discretionary Advance Appropriations	***116,849***	***123,416***	***140,530***	***157,347***
Mandatory:				
Department of Agriculture:				
Supplemental Nutrition Assistance Program (7 U.S.C. 2027)	......	......	......	27,795
Department of Health and Human Services:				
Grants to States for Medicaid (42 U.S.C. 1396–1)	139,903	148,732	165,722	197,580
Payments to States for Child Support Enforcement and Family Support (42 U.S.C. Ch. 7)	1,400	1,400	1,300	1,300
Payments for Foster Care and Permanency (Public Law 96–272)	3,000	3,000	3,200	3,200
Department of Labor:				
Special Benefits for Disabled Coal Miners (30 U.S.C. 921)	14	14	11	10
Department of Veterans Affairs (Public Law 113–235):				
Compensation and Pensions	118,247	130,228	152,017	146,778
Readjustment Benefits	12,579	14,947	8,907	8,453
Veterans Insurance and Indemnities	129	137	110	121
Social Security Administration:				
Supplemental Security Income Program (42 U.S.C. 1381)	19,900	19,600	15,600	15,800
Total, Advance Appropriations	***412,021***	***441,474***	***487,397***	***558,384***

[1] Historically, the Corporation for Public Broadcasting is provided a two-year advance appropriation. The 2023 request proposes a $565 million advance appropriation for the Corporation in 2025.

The Infrastructure Investments and Jobs Appropriations Act (division J of Public Law 117–58; IIJAA) was enacted in fiscal year 2022 and provided advance appropriations for several programs that become available in fiscal years 2023 through 2026. In accordance with the Congressional Budget Act requirement, the table below lists the programs that recieved advance appropriations in IIJAA.

Infrastructure Investments and Jobs Appropriations Act

(Budget authority in millions of dollars)

Agency/Program	Pre-transfer Enacted Levels 2023	2024	2025	2026
Department of Agriculture:				
Research and Education Activities	5	......	......	......
Capital Improvement and Maintenance	72	72	72	72
Forest and Rangeland Research	2	2	2	2
State and Private Forestry	305	305	305	305
National Forest System	530	530	530	530
Wildland Fire Management	36	36	36	36
Department of Commerce:				
Operations, Research, and Facilities	516	516	516	507
Pacific Coastal Salmon Recovery	34	34	34	34
Digital Equity	550	550	550	550
Department of Energy:				
Fossil Energy and Carbon Management	1,444	1,447	1,450	1,317
Electricity	1,610	1,610	1,610	1,610
Nuclear Energy	1,200	1,200	1,200	1,200
Energy Efficiency and Renewable Energy	2,222	1,945	1,945	1,945
Cybersecurity, Energy Security, and Emergency Response	100	100	100	100
Office of Clean Energy Demonstrations	4,426	4,476	4,526	2,900
Carbon Dioxide Transportation Infrastructure Finance and Innovation Program Account	2,097	......	......	......
Department of Health and Human Services:				
Indian Health Facilities	700	700	700	700
Low Income Home Energy Assistance	100	100	100	100
Department of Homeland Security:				
Cybersecurity Response and Recovery Fund	20	20	20	20
Federal Assistance, Federal Emergency Management Agency	500	400	200	100
Disaster Relief Fund	200	200	200	200
National Flood Insurance Fund	700	700	700	700
Department of the Interior:				
Water and Related Resources	1,660	1,660	1,660	1,660
Surveys, Investigations, and Research	69	69	69	64
Resource Management	91	91	91	91
Operation of Indian Programs	43	43	43	43
Construction, Bureau of Indian Affairs	50	50	50	50
Departmental Operations	142	142	142	142
Wildland Fire Management	263	263	263	263
Department of Transportation:				
National Infrastructure Investments	2,500	2,500	2,500	2,500
National Culvert Removal, Replacement, and Restoration Grants	200	200	200	200

ADVANCE APPROPRIATIONS—Continued
Infrastructure Investments and Jobs Appropriations Act—Continued

Agency/Program	Pre-transfer Enacted Levels			
	2023	2024	2025	2026
Strengthening Mobility and Revolutionizing Transportation Grant Program	100	100	100	100
Safe Streets and Roads for All	1,000	1,000	1,000	1,000
Facilities and Equipment	1,000	1,000	1,000	1,000
Airport Terminal Program	1,000	1,000	1,000	1,000
Airport Infrastructure Grants	3,000	3,000	3,000	3,000
Highway Infrastructure Programs	9,454	9,454	9,454	9,454
Motor Carrier Safety Grants	125	125	125	125
Motor Carrier Safety Operations and Programs	10	10	10	10
Vehicle Safety and Behavioral Research Programs	110	110	110	110
Crash Data	150	150	150	150
Supplemental Highway Traffic Safety Programs	62	62	62	62
Federal-State Partnership for Intercity Passenger Rail Grants	7,200	7,200	7,200	7,200
Railroad Crossing Elimination Program	600	600	600	600
Northeast Corridor Grants to the National Railroad Passenger Corporation	1,200	1,200	1,200	1,200
National Network Grants to the National Railroad Passenger Corporation	3,200	3,200	3,200	3,200
Consolidated Rail Infrastructure and Safety Improvements	1,000	1,000	1,000	1,000
Capital Investment Grants	1,600	1,600	1,600	1,600
Electric or Low-Emitting Ferry Program	50	50	50	50
All Stations Accessibility Program	350	350	350	350
Ferry Service for Rural Communities	200	200	200	200
Transit Infrastructure Grants	2,050	2,050	2,050	2,050
Natural Gas Distribution Infrastructure Safety and Modernization	200	200	200	200
Port Infrastructure Development Program	450	450	450	450
Corps of Engineers—Civil Works:				
Investigations	30	......	......	......
Construction	50	50	......	......
Operation and Maintenance	1,000	1,000	......	......
Environmental Protection Agency:				
State and Tribal Assistance Grants	10,819	11,221	11,621	11,621
Environmental Programs and Management	387	387	387	387
Appalachian Regional Commission:				
Appalachian Regional Commission	200	200	200	200
Federal Permitting Improvement Steering Council:				
Environmental Review Improvement Fund	1	1	1	......
Total, IIJAA Advance Appropriations	***68,985***	***66,931***	***66,134***	***64,260***

FINANCING VEHICLES AND THE BOARD OF GOVERNORS OF THE FEDERAL RESERVE

This chapter contains descriptions of, and data on, financing vehicles and the Board of Governors of the Federal Reserve System (Board). The Resolution Funding Corporation provided financing for the Resolution Trust Corporation (RTC) and is subject to the general oversight and direction of the Secretary of the Treasury.

The Board's transactions are not included in the Budget because of its unique status in the conduct of monetary policy. The Board provides data on its administrative budget, which is included here for information. Its budget is not subject to review by the President and is executed and presented here on a calendar-year basis. The previous year's data reflects the final budget, as approved by the Board.

The 2020 balance sheet for the Resolution Funding Corporation is as of December 31, 2020, and the 2021 balance sheet is as of September 30, 2021.

RESOLUTION FUNDING CORPORATION

The Resolution Funding Corporation (REFCORP) is a mixed-ownership Government corporation established by Title V of the Financial Institutions Reform, Recovery, and Enforcement Act of 1989 or FIRREA (P.L. 101–73). The sole purpose of REFCORP was to provide financing for the Resolution Trust Corporation (RTC). Pursuant to FIRREA, REFCORP was authorized to issue debentures, bonds, and other obligations, subject to limitations contained in the Act and regulations established by the Thrift Depositor Protection Oversight Board. The proceeds of the debt (less any discount, plus any premium, net of issuance cost) were used solely to purchase nonredeemable capital certificates of RTC or to refund any previously issued obligations.

Until October 29, 1998, REFCORP was subject to the general oversight and direction of the Thrift Depositor Protection Oversight Board. At that time, the Oversight Board was abolished and its authority and duties were transferred to the Secretary of the Treasury. The day-to-day operations of REFCORP are under the management of a three-member Directorate composed of the Chief Executive Officer of the Office of Finance of the Federal Home Loan Banks and two members selected from among the presidents of the 11 Federal Home Loan Banks (FHLBs). Members of the Directorate serve without compensation, and REFCORP is not permitted to have any paid employees.

FIRREA, as amended, and the regulations adopted by the Thrift Depositor Protection Oversight Board and the Secretary of the Treasury required that FHLBs contribute 20 percent of net earnings annually to assist in the payment of interest on bonds issued by REFCORP until such time as the total payments are equivalent to a $300 million annual annuity with a final maturity date of April 15, 2030. The FHLBs fulfilled this obligation on August 5, 2011. Since then, with the exception of funds derived from the sale of former RTC assets managed by the Federal Deposit Insurance Corporation's Federal Savings and Loan Insurance Corporation (FSLIC) Resolution Fund, only the U.S. Treasury has paid interest on REFCORP's long-term obligations. For details, please see the Payment to the Resolution Funding Corporation account in the Department of the Treasury section of the *Appendix* volume of the Budget.

Balance Sheet (in millions of dollars)

Identification code 920–4981–0–4–373		2020 actual	2021 actual
	ASSETS:		
	Federal assets:		
	Investments in U.S. securities:		
1102	Principal fund account investment, net	10,238	5,615
1206	Non-Federal assets: Assessments receivable for interest expense	504	322
1999	Total assets	10,742	5,937
	LIABILITIES:		
	Non-Federal liabilities:		
2202	Accrued interest payable on long-term obligations	504	322
2203	Debt	15,496	10,552
2999	Total liabilities	16,000	10,874
	NET POSITION:		
3100	Nonvoting capital stock issued to FHLBanks	2,513	2,513
3300	Cumulative results of operations	22,458	22,779
3300	RTC nonredeemable capital certificates	–31,286	–31,286
3300	Contributed capital - principal fund assessments	1,057	1,057
3999	Total net position	–5,258	–4,937
4999	Total liabilities and net position	10,742	5,937

BOARD OF GOVERNORS OF THE FEDERAL RESERVE SYSTEM

Program and Financing (in millions of dollars)

Identification code 920–4982–0–4–803		2020 actual	2021 est.	2022 est.
	Obligations by program activity:			
0801	Monetary policy	192	209	244
0802	Public programs	20	21	22
0803	Supervision and regulation	191	197	209
0804	Reserve Bank oversight	37	43	43
0805	Currency operating expenses (Board incurred)	48	66	71
0806	Support and overhead	371	414	448
0809	Reimbursable program activities, subtotal	859	950	1,037
0810	Office of Inspector General operating expenses	32	35	36
0900	Total new obligations, unexpired accounts	891	985	1,073
	Budgetary resources:			
	Financing authority:			
	Spending authority from offsetting collections, mandatory:			
1800	Collected	891	985	1,073
1930	Total budgetary resources available	891	985	1,073
	Change in obligated balance:			
	Unpaid obligations:			
3010	New obligations, unexpired accounts	891	985	1,073
3020	Outlays (gross)	–891	–985	–1,073
	Financing authority and disbursements, net:			
	Mandatory:			
4090	Budget authority, gross	891	985	1,073
4110	Outlays, gross (total)	891	985	1,073
	Offsets against gross financing authority and disbursements:			
	Offsetting collections (collected) from:			
4123	Non-Federal sources	–891	–985	–1,073
4180	Budget authority, net (total)			
4190	Outlays, net (total)			

The Federal Reserve System operates under the provisions of the Federal Reserve Act of 1913, as amended, and other acts of the Congress. To carry out its responsibilities under this Act, the Board of Governors (Board) determines general monetary, credit, and operating policies for the System as a whole and formulates the rules and regulations necessary to carry out the purposes of the Act. The Board's principal duties consist of exerting an influence over credit conditions and supervising the Federal Reserve banks and member banks.

Under the provisions of section 10 of the Federal Reserve Act, the Board levies upon the Federal Reserve banks, in proportion to their capital and surplus, an assessment sufficient to pay its estimated expenses. Also under the Act, the Board determines and prescribes the manner in which its obligations are incurred and its expenses paid. Funds derived from assessments are deposited in the Federal Reserve Bank of Richmond and the Act provides that such funds "not be construed to be Government funds or appropriated moneys." No Government appropriation is required to support operations of the Board.

The Board issues U.S. currency (Federal Reserve notes) and the Reserve Banks distribute currency through depository institutions. The Board incurs costs and assesses the Reserve Banks for these costs related to producing,

BOARD OF GOVERNORS OF THE FEDERAL RESERVE SYSTEM—Continued

issuing, and retiring Federal Reserve notes, as well as providing other services. The assessment is allocated based on each Reserve Bank's share of the number of notes comprising the System's net liability for Federal Reserve notes on December 31 of the prior year. The Board recognizes the assessment in the year in which the associated costs are incurred.

Since 2017, the Board has undertaken a greater role in the currency program, including in research and development and quality assurance. This expanded role is reflected in the reclassification of certain transactions compared to prior years. The information presented pertains to Board operations only, which includes these new programs; expenditures for the currency program costs specific to the work performed by Treasury, including production, issuance and retirement, are not included.

The Dodd-Frank Act (P.L. 111–203), enacted July 21, 2010, directed the Board to collect assessments, fees, or other charges equal to the total expenses the Board estimates are necessary or appropriate to carry out the supervisory and regulatory responsibilities of the Board for certain bank holding companies and savings and loan holding companies, as well as nonbank financial companies designated for Board supervision by the Financial Stability Oversight Council (FSOC). The Board does not recognize the supervision and regulation assessments as revenue nor does the Board use the collections to fund Board expenses; the funds are transferred to the Treasury. The Economic Growth, Regulatory Relief, and Consumer Protection Act (EGRRCPA, P.L. 115–174), enacted May 24, 2018, directed the Board to collect these assessments, fees, or other charges on such companies with total consolidated assets of $100 billion (from $50 billion in the Dodd-Frank Act), as well as to adjust amounts charged to reflect changes in supervisory and regulatory responsibilities resulting from EGRRCPA on firms with total consolidated assets less than $250 billion.

Object Classification (in millions of dollars)

Identification code 920–4982–0–4–803		2020 actual	2021 est.	2022 est.
	Reimbursable obligations:			
11.1	Personnel compensation: Full-time permanent	515	531	564
12.1	Civilian personnel benefits	103	108	114
13.0	Benefits for former personnel	22	30	36
21.0	Travel and transportation of persons	5	10	10
22.0	Transportation of things	25	34	37
23.2	Rental payments to others	37	38	38
23.3	Communications, utilities, and miscellaneous charges	10	10	9
24.0	Printing and reproduction	1	1	1
25.1	Advisory and assistance services	86	116	144
25.2	Other services from non-Federal sources	48	59	62
25.4	Operation and maintenance of facilities	4	5	5
25.7	Operation and maintenance of equipment	5	5	6
26.0	Supplies and materials	1	1	1
31.0	Equipment	29	37	46
99.9	Total new obligations, unexpired accounts	891	985	1,073

GOVERNMENT-SPONSORED ENTERPRISES

This chapter contains descriptions of the data on the Government-sponsored enterprises listed below. These enterprises were established and chartered by the Federal Government for public policy purposes. They are not included in the Federal Budget because they are private companies, and their securities are not backed by the full faith and credit of the Federal Government. However, because of their public purpose, statements of financial condition are presented, to the extent such information is available, on a basis that is as consistent as practicable with the basis for the budget data of Government agencies.

—The Federal National Mortgage Association and the Federal Home Loan Mortgage Corporation provide assistance to the secondary market for residential mortgages.

—The Federal Home Loan Banks assist thrift institutions, banks, insurance companies, and credit unions in providing financing for housing and community development.

—Institutions of the Farm Credit System, which include the Agricultural Credit Bank and Farm Credit Banks, provide financing to agriculture. They are regulated by the Farm Credit Administration.

—The Federal Agricultural Mortgage Corporation, also a Farm Credit System institution under the regulation of the Farm Credit Administration, provides a secondary market for agricultural real estate, rural housing loans, and certain rural utility loans, as well as for farm and business loans guaranteed by the U.S. Department of Agriculture.

FEDERAL NATIONAL MORTGAGE ASSOCIATION

PORTFOLIO PROGRAMS

Status of Direct Loans (in millions of dollars)

Identification code 915–4986–0–4–371		2021 actual	2022 est.	2023 est.
	Cumulative balance of direct loans outstanding:			
1210	Outstanding, start of year	172,108	110,910	110,910
1251	Repayments: Net repayments and prepayments	–61,198		
1290	Outstanding, end of year	110,910	110,910	110,910

The Federal National Mortgage Association (Fannie Mae) is a Government-sponsored enterprise (GSE) in the housing finance market. As a housing GSE, Fannie Mae is a federally chartered, shareholder-owned, private company with a public mission to provide stability in and increase the liquidity of the residential mortgage market and to help increase the availability of mortgage credit to low- and moderate-income families and in underserved areas. Fannie Mae engages primarily in two forms of business: guaranteeing residential mortgage securities and investing in portfolios of residential mortgages.

Fannie Mae was established in 1938 to assist private markets in providing a steady supply of funds for housing. Fannie Mae was originally a subsidiary of the Reconstruction Finance Corporation and was permitted to purchase only loans insured by the Federal Housing Administration (FHA). In 1954, Fannie Mae was restructured as a mixed ownership (part government, part private) corporation. Legislation directed the sale of the Government's remaining interest in Fannie Mae in 1968 and completed the transformation to private shareholder ownership in 1970.

The Housing and Economic Recovery Act of 2008 reformed housing GSE regulation by creating the Federal Housing Finance Agency (FHFA), a new independent regulator, and providing temporary authority for the U.S. Department of the Treasury to purchase obligations of the housing GSEs. On September 6, 2008, FHFA placed Fannie Mae under Federal conservatorship in response to the GSEs' declining capital adequacy and to support the safety and soundness of the GSEs. On the following day, the U.S. Department of the Treasury entered into a Senior Preferred Stock Purchase Agreement (PSPA) with Fannie Mae to make investments of up to $100 billion in senior preferred stock as required to maintain positive equity. In May 2009, Treasury increased the funding commitments for the PSPA to $200 billion and in December 2009, Treasury modified the funding commitments in the PSPA to the greater of $200 billion or $200 billion plus cumulative net worth deficits experienced during 2010–2012, less any surplus remaining as of December 31, 2012. Based on the financial results reported by Fannie Mae as of December 31, 2012, and under the terms of the PSPA, the cumulative funding commitment cap for Fannie Mae was set at $233.7 billion. As of December 31, 2021, Fannie Mae had received $119.8 billion under the PSPA, and had made a total of $181.4 billion in dividend payments to Treasury on the senior preferred stock. The Budget continues to reflect the GSEs as non-budgetary entities, though their status will continue to be reviewed. All of the current Federal assistance being provided to Fannie Mae, including the PSPA, is shown on-budget. For additional discussion of Fannie Mae, please see the *Analytical Perspectives* volume of the Budget documents.

Balance Sheet (in millions of dollars)

Identification code 915–4986–0–4–371		2020 actual	2021 actual
	ASSETS:		
	Federal assets:		
	Investments in U.S. securities:		
1102	Treasury securities, par	135,972	92,192
1201	Non-Federal assets: Investments in non-Federal securities, net	12,774	27,630
	Net value of assets related to direct loans receivable and acquired defaulted guaranteed loans receivable:		
1601	Mortgage Loans and Mortgage Related Securities	115,986	77,974
1601	Mortgage Loans and Mortgage Related Securities - Consolidated Trusts	3,439,678	3,831,578
1604	Direct loans and interest receivable, net	3,555,664	3,909,552
1606	Acquired Property, net	1,462	1,261
1699	Value of assets related to direct loans	3,557,126	3,910,813
	Other Federal assets:		
1801	Cash and other monetary assets	135,695	155,522
1901	Other assets	23,036	23,052
1999	Total assets	3,864,603	4,209,209
	LIABILITIES:		
	Non-Federal liabilities:		
2202	Interest payable	9,982	9,299
2203	Debt	289,423	234,843
2203	Debt - Consolidated Trusts	3,530,381	3,907,626
2207	Other	14,124	15,268
2999	Total liabilities	3,843,910	4,167,036
	NET POSITION:		
3300	Senior Preferred Stock	120,836	120,836
3300	Private Equity	–100,143	–78,663
3300	Noncontrolling Interest		
3999	Total net position	20,693	42,173
4999	Total liabilities and net position	3,864,603	4,209,209

MORTGAGE-BACKED SECURITIES

Status of Direct Loans (in millions of dollars)

Identification code 915–4987–0–4–371		2021 actual	2022 est.	2023 est.
	Cumulative balance of direct loans outstanding:			
1210	Outstanding, start of year	3,481,562	3,831,364	3,831,364
1231	Disbursements: Direct loan disbursements	1,595,052		
1251	Repayments: Repayments and prepayments	–1,245,250		
1290	Outstanding, end of year	3,831,364	3,831,364	3,831,364

Prior to January 1, 2010, the mortgages in the pools of loans supporting the mortgage-backed securities guaranteed by Fannie Mae were considered to be owned by the holders of these securities according to the accounting standards for private corporations. Consequently, on the books of Fannie Mae, these mortgages were not considered assets and the securities outstanding were not considered liabilities. New accounting standards imple-

1353

MORTGAGE-BACKED SECURITIES—Continued

mented on January 1, 2010, require consolidation of many, but not all, of these securities in Fannie Mae's financial statements. For the purposes of the Budget they are presented as direct loans for mortgage-backed securities. "Disbursements" and "Repayments" are budgetary terms. These items are reported by Fannie Mae as "Issuances" and "Liquidations," respectively.

FEDERAL HOME LOAN MORTGAGE CORPORATION

PORTFOLIO PROGRAMS

Status of Direct Loans (in millions of dollars)

Identification code 913–4988–0–4–371		2021 actual	2022 est.	2023 est.
	Cumulative balance of direct loans outstanding:			
1210	Outstanding, start of year	198,176	113,773	113,773
1251	Repayments: Repayments and prepayments	–84,403		
1290	Outstanding, end of year	113,773	113,773	113,773

The Federal Home Loan Mortgage Corporation (Freddie Mac) is a Government-sponsored enterprise (GSE) in the housing finance market. As a housing GSE, Freddie Mac is a federally chartered, shareholder-owned, private company with a public mission to provide stability in and increase the liquidity of the residential mortgage market, and to help increase the availability of mortgage credit to low- and moderate-income families and in underserved areas. Freddie Mac engages primarily in two forms of business: guaranteeing residential mortgage securities and investing in portfolios of residential mortgages.

Freddie Mac was established in 1970 under the Emergency Home Finance Act. The Congress chartered Freddie Mac to provide mortgage lenders with an organized national secondary market enabling them to manage their conventional mortgage portfolio more effectively and gain indirect access to a ready source of additional funds to meet new demands for mortgages. Freddie Mac serves as a conduit facilitating the flow of investment dollars from the capital markets to mortgage lenders, and ultimately, to homebuyers.

The Housing and Economic Recovery Act of 2008 reformed housing GSE regulation by creating the Federal Housing Finance Agency (FHFA), a new independent regulator, and provided temporary authority for the U.S. Department of the Treasury to purchase obligations of the housing GSEs. On September 6, 2008, FHFA placed Freddie Mac under Federal conservatorship in response to the GSEs' declining capital adequacy and to support the safety and soundness of the GSEs. On the following day, the U.S. Department of the Treasury entered into a Senior Preferred Stock Purchase Agreement (PSPA) with Freddie Mac to make investments of up to $100 billion in senior preferred stock as required to maintain positive equity. In May 2009, Treasury increased the funding commitments for the PSPA to $200 billion and in December 2009, Treasury modified the funding commitments in the PSPA to the greater of $200 billion or $200 billion plus cumulative net worth deficits experienced during 2010–2012, less any surplus remaining as of December 31, 2012. Based on the financial results reported by Freddie Mac as of December 31, 2012, and under the terms of the PSPA, the cumulative funding commitment cap for Freddie Mac was set at $211.8 billion. As of December 31, 2021, Freddie Mac had received $71.6 billion under the PSPA, and had made a total of $119.7 billion in dividend payments to Treasury on the senior preferred stock. The Budget continues to reflect the GSEs as non-budgetary entities, though their status will continue to be reviewed. All of the current federal assistance being provided to Freddie Mac, including the PSPA, is shown on-budget. For additional discussion of Freddie Mac, please see the *Analytical Perspectives* volume of the Budget documents.

Balance Sheet (in millions of dollars)

Identification code 913–4988–0–4–371		2020 actual	2021 actual
	ASSETS:		
	Federal assets:		
	Investments in U.S. securities:		
1102	Treasury securities, par	28,497	30,513
1201	Non-Federal assets: Investments in non-Federal securities, net	99,252	89,512
	Net value of assets related to direct loans receivable and acquired defaulted guaranteed loans receivable:		
1601	Mortgage Loans and Mortgage Related Securities	147,937	83,380
1601	Mortgage Loans and Mortgage Related Securities - Consolidated Trusts	2,115,509	2,671,954
1604	Direct loans and interest receivable, net	2,263,446	2,755,334
1606	Acquired property, net		
1699	Value of assets related to direct loans	2,263,446	2,755,334
	Other Federal assets:		
1801	Cash and other monetary assets	56,990	56,526
1901	Other assets	5,886	6,099
1999	Total assets	2,454,071	2,937,984
	LIABILITIES:		
	Non-Federal liabilities:		
2202	Interest payable	6,020	6,049
2203	Debt	284,896	193,896
2203	Debt - Consolidated Trusts	2,138,420	2,701,530
2207	Other	10,844	11,198
2999	Total liabilities	2,440,180	2,912,673
	NET POSITION:		
3300	Senior Preferred Stock	72,648	72,648
3300	Private Equity	–58,757	–47,337
3999	Total net position	13,891	25,311
4999	Total liabilities and net position	2,454,071	2,937,984

MORTGAGE-BACKED SECURITIES

Status of Direct Loans (in millions of dollars)

Identification code 914–4989–0–4–371		2021 actual	2022 est.	2023 est.
	Cumulative balance of direct loans outstanding:			
1210	Outstanding, start of year	2,459,232	3,025,320	3,025,320
1231	Disbursements: Direct loan disbursements	1,445,268		
1251	Repayments: Repayments and prepayments	–879,180		
1290	Outstanding, end of year	3,025,320	3,025,320	3,025,320

Prior to January 1, 2010, the mortgages in the pools of loans supporting the mortgage-backed securities guaranteed by Freddie Mac were considered to be owned by the holders of these securities according to the accounting standards for private corporations. Consequently, on the books of Freddie Mac, these mortgages were not considered assets and the securities outstanding were not considered liabilities. New accounting standards implemented on January 1, 2010, require consolidation of many, but not all, of these securities in Freddie Mac's financial statements. For the purposes of the Budget, they are presented as direct loans for mortgage-backed securities. "Disbursements" and "Repayments" are budgetary terms. These items are reported by Freddie Mac as "Issuances" and "Liquidations," respectively.

FEDERAL HOME LOAN BANK SYSTEM

FEDERAL HOME LOAN BANKS

Status of Direct Loans (in millions of dollars)

Identification code 913–4990–0–4–371		2021 actual	2022 est.	2023 est.
	Cumulative balance of direct loans outstanding:			
1210	Outstanding, start of year	547,118	406,234	406,234
1231	Disbursements: Direct loan disbursements	3,037,651		
1251	Repayments: Repayments and prepayments	–3,172,665		
1264	Other adjustments, net (+ or -)	–5,870		
1290	Outstanding, end of year	406,234	406,234	406,234

The Federal Home Loan Bank System is a Government-sponsored enterprise (GSE) in the housing finance market. The Federal Home Loan Banks (FHLBanks) were chartered by the Federal Home Loan Bank Board under the authority of the Federal Home Loan Bank Act of 1932 (Act). The 11 Federal Home Loan Banks are under the supervision of the Federal Housing Finance Agency (FHFA), established by the Congress in 2008. The common mission of FHLBanks is to facilitate the extension of credit through their members. To accomplish this mission, FHLBanks make loans, called "advances", and provide other credit products and services to their nearly 6,600 member commercial banks, savings associations, insurance companies, and credit unions. Advances and letters of credit must be fully secured by eligible collateral, and long-term advances may be made only for the purpose of providing funds for residential housing finance. However, "community financial institutions" may also use long-term advances to finance small businesses, small farms, and small agribusinesses. Specialized advance programs provide funds for community reinvestment and affordable housing programs. All regulated financial depositories, certified community development financial institutions, and insurance companies engaged in residential housing finance are eligible for membership, and must meet other requirements in the Act to obtain membership. Each FHLBank operates in a geographic district and together FHLBanks cover all of the United States, including the District of Columbia, Puerto Rico, the Virgin Islands, Guam, American Samoa, and the Northern Mariana Islands. The principal source of funds for the lending operation is the sale of consolidated obligations to the public. The consolidated obligations are not guaranteed by the U.S. Government as to principal or interest. Other sources of lendable funds include members' deposits and capital. Funds not immediately needed for advances to members are invested. The capital stock of the Federal Home Loan Banks is owned entirely by the members. Initially the U.S. Government purchased stock of the banks in the amount of $125 million. The banks had repurchased the Government's investment in full by mid–1951. The Act, as amended in 1989, requires each FHLBank to operate an Affordable Housing Program (AHP). Each FHLBank provides subsidies in the form of direct grants or below-market rate advances for members that use the funds for qualifying affordable housing projects. Each of the FHLBanks must set aside annually 10 percent of its previous year's net earnings, subject to an aggregate minimum of $100 million, for the AHP. For additional discussion of the FHLBanks, please see the *Analytical Perspectives* volume of the Budget.

Balance Sheet (in millions of dollars)

Identification code 913–4990–0–4–371		2020 actual	2021 actual
	ASSETS:		
	Federal assets:		
	Investments in U.S. securities:		
1102	Treasury securities, par	62,060	40,574
	Non-Federal assets:		
1201	Investments in non-Federal securities, net	270,730	254,233
1206	Accounts receivable	1,271	921
1401	Net value of assets related to direct loans receivable: Direct loans receivable, gross	547,070	406,211
	Other Federal assets:		
1801	Cash and other monetary assets	9,988	6,805
1803	Property, plant and equipment, net		
1901	Other assets	3,345	3,470
1999	Total assets	894,464	712,214
	LIABILITIES:		
2101	Federal liabilities: REFCORP and Affordable Housing Program	1,064	933
	Non-Federal liabilities:		
2202	Interest payable	928	776
2203	Debt	821,933	641,954
2207	Deposit funds and other borrowing	14,952	4,190
2207	Other	4,116	15,563
2999	Total liabilities	842,993	663,416
	NET POSITION:		
3100	Invested capital	51,471	48,798
4999	Total liabilities and net position	894,464	712,214

FARM CREDIT SYSTEM

The Farm Credit System (System) is a Government-sponsored enterprise that provides privately financed credit to agricultural and rural communities. The major functional entities of the System are: (1) the agricultural credit bank (ACB); (2) the farm credit banks (FCBs); and (3) the direct-lender associations. The Federal Agricultural Mortgage Corporation (Farmer Mac), which is also an institution of the System, is discussed separately below. The history and specific functions of the bank entities are discussed after the presentation of financial schedules for each bank.

System entities are regulated and examined by the Farm Credit Administration (FCA), an independent Federal agency. The administrative costs of FCA are financed by assessments on System institutions, including Farmer Mac.

System banks finance loans primarily from sales of bonds to the public and their own capital funds. The System bonds issued by the banks are not guaranteed by the U.S. Government as to either principal or interest. The bonds are backed by an insurance fund, administered by the Farm Credit System Insurance Corporation (FCSIC), an independent Federal Government-controlled corporation that collects insurance premiums from member banks to fund insurance reserves. All of FCSIC's operating expenses are also paid from the insurance premiums it receives from the System banks; as a result, the FCSIC does not require budgetary resources from the Federal Government.

AGRICULTURAL CREDIT BANK

Status of Direct Loans (in millions of dollars)

Identification code 912–4991–0–4–351		2021 actual	2022 est.	2023 est.
	Cumulative balance of direct loans outstanding:			
1210	Outstanding, start of year	111,985	119,056	126,405
1231	Disbursements: Direct loan disbursements	531,680	558,533	586,743
1251	Repayments: Repayments and prepayments	–524,613	–551,139	–580,315
1263	Write-offs for default: Direct loans		–45	–43
1264	Other adjustments, net (+ or -)	4		
1290	Outstanding, end of year	119,056	126,405	132,790

CoBank, Agricultural Credit Bank, which is headquartered near Denver, Colorado, provides funding to eligible cooperatives nationwide and agricultural credit associations (ACAs) in its chartered district. CoBank is the only ACB in the System. An ACB operates under statutory authority that combines the authorities of an FCB and a bank for cooperatives (BC). CoBank is the only System bank with the authorities of a BC. In exercising its FCB authority, CoBank's charter limits its lending to 20 ACAs located in the northeast, central, and western regions of the country. And, in exercising its BC authority, CoBank is chartered to provide credit and related services nationwide to eligible cooperatives primarily engaged in farm supply, grain, marketing, and processing (including sugar, dairy, and ethanol). CoBank also makes loans to rural utilities, including telecommunications companies, and it provides international loans for the financing of agricultural exports.

Statement of Changes in Net Worth (in thousands of dollars)

	2020 act.	2021 act.	2022 est.	2023 est.
Beginning balance of net worth	10,447,308	11,679,369	11,989,797	12,703,629
Capital stock and participations issued	121,516	203,577	750,000	35,000
Capital stock and participations retired	34,792	37,474	401,907	645,652
Net income	1,194,308	1,395,511	1,229,315	1,303,053
Cash/Dividends/Patronage Distributions	–607,179	–791,028	–735,817	–751,140
Other, net	558,208	–460,158	–127,759	–137,009
Ending balance of net worth	11,679,369	11,989,797	12,703,629	12,507,881

AGRICULTURAL CREDIT BANK—Continued

Financing Activities (in thousands of dollars)

	2020 act.	2021 act.	2022 est.	2023 est.
Beginning balance of outstanding system obligations	122,493,375	132,426,345	138,073,631	148,925,971
Consolidated systemwide and other bank bonds issued	78,143,926	70,689,889	74,260,203	78,010,842
Consolidated systemwide and other bank bonds retired	67,723,738	64,124,193	63,401,665	69,165,072
Consolidated systemwide notes, net	–471,800	–908,676	0	0
Other (Net)	–15,418	–9,734	–6,198	–4,437
Ending balance of outstanding system obligations	132,426,345	138,073,631	148,925,971	157,767,304

Balance Sheet (in millions of dollars)

Identification code 912–4991–0–4–351		2020 actual	2021 actual
	ASSETS:		
	Non-Federal assets:		
1201	Cash and investment securities	34,486	34,430
1206	Accrued interest receivable on loans	412	382
	Net value of assets related to direct loans receivable and acquired defaulted guaranteed loans receivable:		
1601	Direct loans, gross	111,984	119,055
1603	Allowance for estimated uncollectible loans and interest (-)	–631	–631
1699	Value of assets related to direct loans	111,353	118,424
1803	Other Federal assets: Property, plant and equipment, net	2,100	1,538
1999	Total assets	148,351	154,774
	LIABILITIES:		
2104	Federal liabilities: Resources payable to Treasury	2,179	2,401
	Non-Federal liabilities:		
2201	Consolidated systemwide and other bank bonds	132,426	138,074
2201	Notes payable and other interest-bearing liabilities	1,716	2,008
2202	Accrued interest payable	351	301
2999	Total liabilities	136,672	142,784
	NET POSITION:		
3300	Cumulative results of operations	11,679	11,990
4999	Total liabilities and net position	148,351	154,774

FARM CREDIT BANKS

Status of Direct Loans (in millions of dollars)

Identification code 912–4992–0–4–371		2021 actual	2022 est.	2023 est.
	Cumulative balance of direct loans outstanding:			
1210	Outstanding, start of year	153,942	168,327	180,806
1231	Disbursements: Direct loan disbursements	270,509	278,299	288,067
1251	Repayments: Repayments and prepayments	–256,124	–265,802	–276,051
1263	Write-offs for default: Direct loans		–18	–10
1290	Outstanding, end of year	168,327	180,806	192,812

The Agricultural Credit Act of 1987 (1987 Act) required the federal land banks (FLBs) and federal intermediate credit banks (FICBs) to merge into an FCB in each of the 12 Farm Credit districts. FCBs operate under statutory authority that combines the prior authorities of an FLB and of an FICB. Mergers and consolidations of FCBs across district lines, which began in 1992, have continued to date. As a result of this restructuring activity, three FCBs, headquartered in the following cities, remain as of October 1, 2021: AgFirst Farm Credit Bank, Columbia, South Carolina; AgriBank, FCB, St. Paul, Minnesota; and FCB of Texas, Austin, Texas.

FCBs serve as discount banks and, as of October 1, 2021, provided funds to one federal land credit association and 46 agricultural credit associations. These direct-lender associations, in turn, primarily make short- and intermediate-term production loans and long-term real estate loans to eligible farmers and ranchers, farm-related businesses, and rural homeowners. FCBs can also lend to other financing institutions, including commercial banks, as authorized by the Farm Credit Act of 1971, as amended (1971 Act).

All the capital stock of FICBs, from their organization in 1923 to December 31, 1956, was held by the U.S. Government. The Farm Credit Act of 1956 provided a long-range plan for the eventual ownership of the FICBs by the production credit associations and the gradual retirement of the Government's investment in the banks. This retirement was accomplished in full on December 31, 1968. The last of the Government capital that had been invested in FLBs was repaid in 1947.

Statement of Changes in Net Worth (in thousands of dollars)

	2020 act.	2021 act.	2022 est.	2023 est.
Beginning balance of net worth	10,559,072	11,405,805	11,843,457	12,286,453
Capital stock and participations issued	947,216	405,252	326,697	713,255
Capital stock and participations retired	446,022	69,968	16,751	305,935
Surplus Retired	118	2,254	1,460	0
Net income	1,347,161	1,449,394	1,347,538	1,302,829
Cash/Dividends/Patronage Distributions	–1,138,345	–1,315,316	–1,181,789	–1,103,034
Other, net	136,841	–29,456	–31,239	–216,894
Ending balance of net worth	11,405,805	11,843,457	12,286,453	12,676,675

Financing Activities (in thousands of dollars)

	2020 act.	2021 act.	2022 est.	2023 est.
Beginning balance of outstanding system obligations	160,146,949	176,239,909	190,764,160	202,962,898
Consolidated systemwide and other bank bonds issued	293,432,765	267,995,223	236,935,100	231,294,955
Consolidated systemwide and other bank bonds retired	277,598,044	253,607,721	224,749,651	219,647,768
Consolidated systemwide notes, net	0	0	0	0
Other (Net)	258,239	136,749	13,289	–54,809
Ending balance of outstanding system obligations	176,239,909	190,764,160	202,962,898	214,555,276

Balance Sheet (in millions of dollars)

Identification code 912–4992–0–4–371		2020 actual	2021 actual
	ASSETS:		
	Non-Federal assets:		
1201	Cash and investment securities	34,631	35,853
1206	Accrued Interest Receivable	686	669
	Net value of assets related to direct loans receivable and acquired defaulted guaranteed loans receivable:		
1601	Direct loans, gross	153,946	168,327
1603	Allowance for estimated uncollectible loans and interest (-)	–69	–71
1699	Value of assets related to direct loans	153,877	168,256
1803	Other Federal assets: Property, plant and equipment, net	1,040	965
1999	Total assets	190,234	205,743
	LIABILITIES:		
2104	Federal liabilities: Resources payable to Treasury	674	572
	Non-Federal liabilities:		
2201	Consolidated systemwide and other bank bonds	176,240	190,764
2201	Notes payable and other interest-bearing liabilities	1,545	2,230
2202	Accrued interest payable	369	334
2999	Total liabilities	178,828	193,900
	NET POSITION:		
3300	Cumulative results of operations	11,406	11,843
4999	Total liabilities and net position	190,234	205,743

FEDERAL AGRICULTURAL MORTGAGE CORPORATION

Status of Guaranteed Loans (in millions of dollars)

Identification code 912–4993–0–4–351		2021 actual	2022 est.	2023 est.
	Cumulative balance of guaranteed loans outstanding:			
2210	Outstanding, start of year	21,989	23,119	23,119
2231	Disbursements of new guaranteed loans	6,831		
2251	Repayments and prepayments	–5,701		
2290	Outstanding, end of year	23,119	23,119	23,119
	Memorandum:			
2299	Guaranteed amount of guaranteed loans outstanding, end of year	2,723		

FARMER MAC

Farmer Mac is authorized under the Farm Credit Act of 1971 (as amended by the 1987 Act) to create a secondary market for agricultural real estate and rural home mortgages. The Farmer Mac title of the 1971 Act was amended by the 1990 farm bill to authorize Farmer Mac to purchase, pool, and securitize the guaranteed portions of farmer program, rural business, and community development loans guaranteed by the U.S. Department of Agriculture (USDA). The Farmer Mac title was amended in 1991 to clarify Farmer Mac's authority to issue debt obligations, provide for the establishment of minimum capital standards, establish the Office of Secondary Market Oversight at the Farm Credit Administration (FCA), and expand the Agency's rulemaking authority. The Farm Credit System Reform Act of 1996 (1996 Act) amended the Farmer Mac title to allow Farmer Mac to purchase loans directly from lenders and to issue and guarantee mortgage-backed securities without requiring that a minimum cash reserve or subordinated (first loss) interest be maintained by poolers as had been required under its original authority. The 1996 Act expanded FCA's regulatory authority to include provisions for establishing a conservatorship or receivership, if necessary, and provided for increased core capital requirements at Farmer Mac phased in over three years. The 2008 Farm Bill, the Food, Conservation and Energy Act of 2008, amended the Farmer Mac title to authorize the financing of rural electric and telephone cooperatives. Most recently, the Agricultural Improvement Act of 2018, increased the acreage exception provided in section 8.8(c)(2) of the Farm Credit Act of 1971 from 1,000 acres to 2,000 acres. The change became effective on June 18, 2020.

Farmer Mac operates through several programs: the Farm & Ranch program involves mortgage loans secured by first liens on agricultural real estate or rural housing (qualified loans); the USDA Guarantees program involves the guaranteed portions of certain USDA-guaranteed loans; and the Rural Utilities program involves rural electric and telecommunications loans. Farmer Mac operates by: (1) purchasing, or committing to purchase, newly originated or existing qualified loans or guaranteed portions from lenders; (2) purchasing or guaranteeing AgVantage bonds backed by qualified loans; and (3) exchanging qualified loans, or guaranteed portions of qualified loans, for guaranteed securities. Loans purchased by Farmer Mac may be aggregated into pools that back Farmer Mac guaranteed securities, which are held by Farmer Mac or sold into the capital markets.

Farmer Mac is governed by a 15-member board of directors. Ten board members are elected by stockholders, including five by stockholders that are Farm Credit System (FCS) institutions and five by stockholders that are non-FCS financial services firms. Five are appointed by the President, subject to Senate confirmation.

Financing

Financial support and funding for Farmer Mac's operations come from several sources: sale of common and preferred stock, issuance of debt obligations, and income. Under procedures specified in the legislation, Farmer Mac may issue obligations to the U.S. Treasury in a cumulative amount not to exceed $1.5 billion to fulfill Farmer Mac's guarantee obligations.

Guarantees

Farmer Mac provides a guarantee of timely payment of principal and interest on securities backed by qualified loans or pools of qualified loans. These securities are not guaranteed by the United States and are not considered Government securities.

Farmer Mac is subject to reporting requirements under securities laws, and its guaranteed mortgage-backed securities are subject to registration with the Securities and Exchange Commission under the 1933 and 1934 Securities Acts.

Regulation

Farmer Mac is federally regulated by FCA through FCA's Office of Secondary Market Oversight. FCA is responsible for the supervision of, examination of, and rulemaking for Farmer Mac.

Balance Sheet (in millions of dollars)

Identification code 912–4993–0–4–351		2020 actual	2021 actual
	ASSETS:		
	Non-Federal assets:		
1201	Investment in securities	3,577	3,742
1206	Receivables, net	106	73
	Net value of assets related to direct loans receivable:		
1401	Direct loans receivable, gross	19,252	19,886
1402	Interest receivable	153	144
1499	Net present value of assets related to direct loans	19,405	20,030
1801	Other Federal assets: Cash and other monetary assets	911	899
1999	Total assets	23,999	24,744
	LIABILITIES:		
	Non-Federal liabilities:		
2201	Accounts payable	55	68
2202	Interest payable	93	83
2203	Debt	22,882	23,356
2204	Liabilities for loan guarantees	39	40
2999	Total liabilities	23,069	23,547
	NET POSITION:		
3300	Invested capital	930	1,197
4999	Total liabilities and net position	23,999	24,744

INDEX

	Page
10-Year Pediatric Research Initiative Fund	446
400 Years of African-American History Commission:	
9-11 Response and Biometric Exit Account	511

A

	Page
Abandoned Mine Reclamation Fund	630
Abandoned Seafarers Fund	522
Abandoned Well Remediation Fund	617
Access Board:	
Salaries and Expenses	1215
Acquisition Services Fund	1151
Acquisition Workforce Training Fund	1158
Administration for Children and Families	468
Administration for Community Living	478
Administration of Foreign Affairs	799
Administrative Conference of the United States:	
Salaries and Expenses	1216
Administrative Costs, The Medicare Improvements for Patients and Providers Act	1205
Administrative Expenses, Children's Health Insurance Program	1205
Administrative Expenses, Energy Employees Occupational Illness Compensation Fund	778
Administrative Expenses, Recovery Act	1208
Administrative Expenses	949
Administrative Office of the United States Courts	56
Administrative Services Franchise Fund	913
Administrative Support Offices	603
Advance Appropriations	1349
Advanced Research Projects Agency—Energy	377
Advanced Technology Vehicles Manufacturing Direct Loan Financing Account	401
Advanced Technology Vehicles Manufacturing Loan Program Account	401
Advances to the Unemployment Trust Fund and Other Funds	768
Advisory Council on Historic Preservation:	
Salaries and Expenses	1216
Aeronautics	1163
Affordable Connectivity Fund	1258
Affordable Housing Program:	
Affordable Insurance Exchange Grants	458
Afghanistan Security Forces Fund	262
African Development Foundation	867, 867
Agency for Healthcare Research and Quality	448
Agency for International Development	843
Agency for Toxic Substances and Disease Registry, Toxic Substances and Environmental Public Health	441
Agency Operations and Award Management	1175
Aging and Disability Services Programs	478
Aging Infrastructure Account	636
Agricultural Credit Bank	1355
Agricultural Credit Insurance Fund Direct Loan Financing Account	103
Agricultural Credit Insurance Fund Guaranteed Loan Financing Account	104
Agricultural Credit Insurance Fund Liquidating Account	105
Agricultural Credit Insurance Fund Program Account	101
Agricultural Disaster Relief Fund	114
Agricultural Marketing Service	88
Agricultural Research Service	74
Agriculture Buildings and Facilities and Rental Payments	70
Agriculture Wool Apparel Manufacturers Trust Fund	114
Agriculture, Department of:	
Agricultural Credit Insurance Fund Direct Loan Financing Account	103
Agricultural Credit Insurance Fund Guaranteed Loan Financing Account	104
Agricultural Credit Insurance Fund Liquidating Account	105
Agricultural Credit Insurance Fund Program Account	101
Agricultural Disaster Relief Fund	114

	Page
Agriculture, Department of—Continued	
Agricultural Marketing Service	88
Agricultural Research Service	74
Agriculture Buildings and Facilities and Rental Payments	70
Agriculture Wool Apparel Manufacturers Trust Fund	114
Alternative Agricultural Research and Commercialization Corporation Revolving Fund	147
Animal and Plant Health Inspection Service	83
Assistance for Socially Disadvantaged Farmers and Ranchers	105
Biomass Research and Development	79
Biorefinery Assistance Guaranteed Loan Financing Account	147
Biorefinery Assistance Program Account	146
Buildings and Facilities (Agricultural Research Service)	75
Buildings and Facilities (Animal and Plant Health Inspection Service)	85
Buildings and Facilities (National Institute of Food and Agriculture)	81
Buildings and Facilities	70
Capital Improvement and Maintenance	168
Child Nutrition Programs	165
Commodity Assistance Program	167
Commodity Credit Corporation Export Guarantee Financing Account	111
Commodity Credit Corporation Export Loans Program Account	110
Commodity Credit Corporation Fund	106
Commodity Credit Corporation Guaranteed Loans Liquidating Account	112
Communications Site Administration	178
Damage Assessment and Restoration Revolving Fund	123
Debt Reduction Financing Account	161
Discrimination Claims Settlement	100
Distance Learning, Telemedicine, and Broadband Direct Loan Financing Account	157
Distance Learning, Telemedicine, and Broadband Program	155
Economic Research Service	72
Emergency Boll Weevil Direct Loan Financing Account	113
Emergency Citrus Disease Research and Development Trust Fund	82
Emergency Conservation Program	100
Emergency Forest Restoration Program	101
Emergency Watershed Protection	121
Energy Assistance Payments	136
Executive Operations	67
Expenses and Refunds, Inspection and Grading of Farm Products	87
Expenses and Refunds, Inspection and Grading of Farm Products	93
Expenses, Public Law 480, Foreign Assistance Programs, Agriculture Liquidating Account	162
Extension Activities	81
Farm Production and Conservation Business Center	95
Farm Production and Conservation	95
Farm Security and Rural Investment Programs	117
Farm Service Agency	98
Farm Storage Facility Direct Loan Financing Account	113
Farm Storage Facility Loans Program Account	112
Federal Crop Insurance Corporation Fund	96
Fee Funded Inspection, Weighing, and Examination Services	90
Food and Nutrition Service	162
Food for Peace Title II Grants	160
Food Safety and Inspection Service	86
Food Supply Chain and Agriculture Pandemic Response Guaranteed Loans Financing Account	66
Food Supply Chain and Agriculture Pandemic Response Program Account	65
Foreign Agricultural Service	158
Foreign Service National Separation Liability Trust Fund	162

	Page
Agriculture, Department of—Continued	
Forest and Rangeland Research	169
Forest Service Operations	176
Forest Service Permanent Appropriations	181
Forest Service Trust Funds	184
Forest Service	168
Funds for Strengthening Markets, Income, and Supply (section 32)	92
General and Administrative Provisions	186
General Fund Receipt Accounts	186
Gifts and Bequests	67
Grassroots Source Water Protection Program	101
Healthy Foods Financing Initiative	137
Healthy Forests Reserve Program	122
High Energy Cost Grants	147
Integrated Activities	78
Intermediary Relending Program Fund Account	141
Land Acquisition	180
Management of National Forest Lands for Subsistence Uses	174
Marketing Services	88
McGovern-Dole International Food for Education and Child Nutrition Program	159
Milk Market Orders Assessment Fund	94
Miscellaneous Contributed Funds	76
Miscellaneous Contributed Funds	123
Miscellaneous Trust Funds	85
Multifamily Housing Revitalization Direct Loan Financing Account	127
Multifamily Housing Revitalization Program Account	126
Mutual and Self-help Housing Grants	128
National Agricultural Statistics Service	73
National Forest System	170
National Institute of Food and Agriculture	76
National Parks and Public Land Legacy Restoration Fund	179
Natural Resources Conservation Service	115
Nonrecurring Expenses Fund	69
Nutrition Programs Administration	162
Office of Inspector General (Office of Inspector General)	71
Office of Inspector General	71
Office of the Secretary	63
P.L. 480 Direct Credit Financing Account	161
Payments to States and Possessions	90
Perishable Agricultural Commodities Act Fund	91
Pima Agriculture Cotton Trust Fund	114
Private Lands Conservation Operations	115
Public Law 480 Title I Direct Credit and Food for Progress Program Account	160
Range Betterment Fund	178
Rental Assistance Program	125
Research and Education Activities	79
Risk Management Agency	96
RMA Salaries and Expenses	96
Rural Business and Industry Direct Loans Financing Account	140
Rural Business and Industry Guaranteed Loans Financing Account	140
Rural Business Investment Program Account	144
Rural Business Investment Program Guarantee Financing Account	144
Rural Business Program Account	139
Rural Business-Cooperative Service	136
Rural Community Facilities Program Account	128
Rural Community Facility Direct Loans Financing Account	130
Rural Community Facility Guaranteed Loans Financing Account	130
Rural Cooperative Development Grants	136
Rural Development Disaster Assistance Fund	125
Rural Development Insurance Fund Liquidating Account	157
Rural Development Loan Fund Direct Loan Financing Account	142
Rural Development Loan Fund Liquidating Account	142
Rural Development	124
Rural Economic Development Direct Loan Financing Account	143

	Page
Agriculture, Department of—Continued	
Rural Economic Development Grants	137
Rural Economic Development Loans Program Account	143
Rural Electrification and Telecommunications Direct Loan Financing Account	152
Rural Electrification and Telecommunications Guaranteed Loans Financing Account	153
Rural Electrification and Telecommunications Liquidating Account	153
Rural Electrification and Telecommunications Loans Program Account	151
Rural Energy for America Guaranteed Loan Financing Account	145
Rural Energy for America Program	145
Rural Housing Assistance Grants	125
Rural Housing Insurance Fund Direct Loan Financing Account	133
Rural Housing Insurance Fund Guaranteed Loan Financing Account	134
Rural Housing Insurance Fund Liquidating Account	135
Rural Housing Insurance Fund Program Account	131
Rural Housing Service	125
Rural Microenterprise Investment Direct Loan Financing Account	138
Rural Microentrepreneur Assistance Program	138
Rural Telephone Bank Direct Loan Financing Account	154
Rural Telephone Bank Program Account	154
Rural Utilities Service	147
Rural Water and Waste Disposal Direct Loans Financing Account	149
Rural Water and Waste Disposal Program Account	148
Rural Water and Waste Water Disposal Guaranteed Loans Financing Account	150
Salaries and Expenses (Agricultural Research Service)	74
Salaries and Expenses (Animal and Plant Health Inspection Service)	83
Salaries and Expenses (Farm Service Agency)	98
Salaries and Expenses (Food Safety and Inspection Service)	86
Salaries and Expenses (Foreign Agricultural Service)	158
Salaries and Expenses (Rural Development)	124
Special Supplemental Nutrition Program for Women, Infants, and Children (WIC)	166
State and Private Forestry	172
State Mediation Grants	99
Stewardship Contracting Product Sales	179
Supplemental Nutrition Assistance Program	163
Title VII—General Provisions	187
Tobacco Trust Fund	115
Urban Agriculture Program	122
USDA Supplemental Assistance	100
Water Bank Program	123
Watershed and Flood Prevention Operations	119
Watershed Rehabilitation Program	121
Wildfire Suppression Operations Reserve Fund	177
Wildland Fire Management	174
Working Capital Fund (Executive Operations)	69
Working Capital Fund (Forest Service)	183
Air and Marine Interdiction, Operations, Maintenance, and Procurement	508
Air Carrier Worker Support	988
Aircraft Procurement, Air Force	278
Aircraft Procurement, Army	268
Aircraft Procurement, Navy	273
Airport and Airway Trust Fund	914
Airport Infrastructure Grants	911
Airport Terminal Program	910
Alcohol and Tobacco Tax and Trade Bureau	1013
All Stations Accessibility Program	955
Allied Contributions and Cooperation Account	265
Allowances and Office Staff for Former Presidents	1156
Alteration of Bridges	520

INDEX

	Page
Alternative Agricultural Research and Commercialization Corporation Revolving Fund	147
Alyce Spotted Bear and Walter Soboleff Com. on Native Children	1217
Alyce Spotted Bear and Walter Soboleff Commission on Native Children: Alyce Spotted Bear and Walter Soboleff Com. on Native Children	1217
Amendments to and Revisions in Budget Authority	1347
American Battle Monuments Commission	1100
American Printing House for the Blind	337
American Sections, International Commissions	816
Analysis and Operations	502
Andean Counterdrug Programs	822
Animal and Plant Health Inspection Service	83
APEC Business Travel Card	511
Appalachian Development Highway System	919
Appalachian Regional Commission:	
Aquatic Resources Trust Fund	523
Architect of the Capitol	17
Armed Forces Retirement Home Trust Fund	1101
Armed Forces Retirement Home	1101
Assessment Funds	1032
Asset Concessions and Innovative Finance Assistance	894
Asset Infrastructure Review Commission	1069
Asset Proceeds and Space Management Fund	1149
Assets Forfeiture Fund	732
Assistance for Eastern Europe and the Baltic States	845
Assistance for Europe, Eurasia and Central Asia	844
Assistance for Socially Disadvantaged Farmers and Ranchers	105
Assistance for the Independent States of the Former Soviet Union	845
Assistance to American Samoa Direct Loan Financing Account	694
Assistance to Small Shipyards	966
Assistance to Territories	693
Automation Modernization, Customs and Border Protection	506
Automation Modernization, Immigration and Customs Enforcement	514
Aviation Insurance Revolving Fund	912
Aviation Manufacturing Jobs Protection Program	901
Aviation User Fees	912
Awards and Settlements Funds	16

B

	Page
Barry Goldwater Scholarship and Excellence in Education Foundation:	
Benefits Programs	1049
Biomass Research and Development	79
Biorefinery Assistance Guaranteed Loan Financing Account	147
Biorefinery Assistance Program Account	146
Black Lung Disability Trust Fund	780
Blackfeet Water Settlement Implementation Fund	637
Board of Governors of the Federal Reserve System	1351
Board of Veterans Appeals	1070
Boat Safety	524
Bonneville Power Administration Fund	414
Border Security Fencing, Infrastructure, and Technology	506
Botanic Garden	24, 24
Broadband Connectivity Fund	221
Broadband Equity, Access, and Deployment Program	223
Broadcasting Capital Improvements	1334
Brownfields Redevelopment	578
Build America Bond Payments, Recovery Act	1020
Buildings and Facilities	70
Buildings and Facilities:	
Agricultural Research Service, Department of Agriculture	75
Animal and Plant Health Inspection Service, Department of Agriculture	85
Centers for Disease Control and Prevention, Department of Health and Human Services	440
Environmental Protection Agency, Environmental Protection Agency	1113
Federal Prison System, Department of Justice	744
National Institute of Food and Agriculture, Department of Agriculture	81

	Page
Buildings Maintenance Fund	313
Bureau of Consumer Financial Protection:	
Bureau of Consumer Financial Protection Fund	1219
Consumer Financial Civil Penalty Fund	1219
Bureau of:	
Alcohol, Tobacco, Firearms, and Explosives	741
Census	196
Consumer Financial Protection Fund	1219
Consumer Financial Protection	1219
Economic Analysis	199
Engraving and Printing Fund	1014
Engraving and Printing	1014
Indian Affairs	670
Indian Education	682
Industry and Security	201
Labor Statistics	788
Land Management	615
Ocean Energy Management	625
Reclamation Direct Loan Financing Account	642
Reclamation Loan Liquidating Account	642
Reclamation Loan Program Account	642
Reclamation	632
Safety and Environmental Enforcement	627
Trust Funds Administration	684
Business Direct Loan Financing Account	1197
Business Guaranteed Loan Financing Account	1198
Business Loan Fund Liquidating Account	1199
Business Loans Program Account	1196
Business Systems Modernization	1020
Buying Power Maintenance	808, 1334

C

	Page
Cable Security Fleet	967
California Bay-Delta Restoration	635
Canteen Service Revolving Fund	1047
Capital and Debt Service Grants to the National Railroad Passenger Corporation	942
Capital Assistance for High Speed Rail Corridors and Intercity Passenger Rail Service	945
Capital Construction, Dwight D. Eisenhower Memorial Commission	41
Capital Improvement and Maintenance	168
Capital Investment Fund of the United States Agency for International Development	847
Capital Investment Fund	803
Capital Investment Grants	951
Capital Magnet Fund, Community Development Financial Institutions	1002
Capital Repair and Restoration, JFK Center for the Performing Arts	1326
Capitol Building	17
Capitol Construction and Operations	17
Capitol Grounds	18
Capitol Police Buildings, Grounds, and Security	21
Capitol Police	14
Capitol Power Plant	20
Capitol Visitor Center Revolving Fund	22
Capitol Visitor Center	22
Carbon Dioxide Transportation Infrastructure Finance and Innovation Program Account	404
Care of the Building and Grounds	49
Career, Technical and Adult Education	338
CDC-wide Activities and Program Support	437
Cemeterial Expenses	1103
Censuses and Survey Programs	197
Centennial Challenge	662
Center for Medicare and Medicaid Innovation	455
Center for Middle Eastern-Western Dialogue Trust Fund	826
Centers for Disease Control and Prevention	437
Centers for Medicare and Medicaid Services	449
Central America and Caribbean Emergency Disaster Recovery Fund	828
Central Hazardous Materials Fund	698

	Page
Central Intelligence Agency Retirement and Disability System Fund	1220
Central Intelligence Agency:	
Central Intelligence Agency Retirement and Disability System Fund	1220
Central Liquidity Facility	1291
Central Utah Project Completion Account	643
Central Utah Project	643
Central Valley Project Restoration Fund	638
Chapter 7 Trustee Fund	57
Check Forgery Insurance Fund	1010
Chemical Agents and Munitions Destruction, Defense	284
Chemical Demilitarization Construction, Defense-wide	298
Chemical Safety and Hazard Investigation Board:	
Salaries and Expenses	1220
Cheyenne River Sioux Tribe Terrestrial Wildlife Habitat Restoration Trust Fund	1011
Child and Dependent Care Tax Credit	1025
Child Care Entitlement to States	473
Child Enrollment Contingency Fund	456
Child Nutrition Programs	165
Child Survival and Health Programs	843
Children and Families Services Programs	475
Children's Health Insurance Fund	455
Children's Research and Technical Assistance	476
Choice Neighborhoods Initiative	564
Citizenship and Immigration Services	545
Civil Service Retirement and Disability Fund	1185
Civilian Board of Contract Appeals	1155
Claims, Judgments, and Relief Acts	1009
Clean Coal Technology	398
Clean Technology Fund Loans Financing Account	835
Clean Technology Fund Program Account	834
Coast Guard Housing Fund	522
Coastal Defense Augmentation	277
Coastal Impact Assistance	658
Coastal Wetlands Restoration Trust Fund	1094
Coastal Zone Management Fund	211
College Housing and Academic Facilities Loans Financing Account	342
College Housing and Academic Facilities Loans Liquidating Account	343
College Housing and Academic Facilities Loans Program Account	341
Colorado River Basins Power Marketing Fund, Western Area Power Administration	413
Colorado River Dam Fund, Boulder Canyon Project	639
Commerce, Department of:	
Broadband Connectivity Fund	221
Broadband Equity, Access, and Deployment Program	223
Bureau of Economic Analysis	199
Bureau of Industry and Security	201
Bureau of the Census	196
Census Working Capital Fund	199
Censuses and Survey Programs	197
Coastal Zone Management Fund	211
Concrete Masonry Products Board	194
Connecting Minority Communities Fund	221
Construction of Research Facilities (National Institute of Standards and Technology)	218
Damage Assessment and Restoration Revolving Fund	212
Departmental Management	191
Digital Equity	222
Digital Television Transition and Public Safety Fund	224
Economic Development Administration	195
Economic Development Assistance Programs	195
Environmental Improvement and Restoration Fund	211
Federal Ship Financing Fund Fishing Vessels Liquidating Account	214
First Responder Network Authority	225
Fisheries Disaster Assistance	210
Fisheries Enforcement Asset Forfeiture Fund	208
Fisheries Finance Direct Loan Financing Account	213

	Page
Commerce, Department of—Continued	
Fisheries Finance Program Account	212
Fishermen's Contingency Fund	210
General and Administrative Provisions	226
General Fund Receipt Accounts	226
General Provisions—Department of Commerce	226
Gifts and Bequests	194
Gulf Coast Ecosystem Restoration Science, Observation, Monitoring, and Technology	205
HCHB Renovation and Modernization	193
Industrial Technology Services	217
International Trade Administration	200
Limited Access System Administration Fund	207
Medicare-Eligible Retiree Health Fund Contribution, NOAA	208
Middle Mile Deployment	222
Minority Business Development Agency	202
Minority Business Development	202
National Institute of Standards and Technology	216
National Oceanic and Atmospheric Administration	203
National Technical Information Service	215
National Telecommunications and Information Administration	220
Network Construction Fund	224
Nonrecurring Expenses Fund	191
North Pacific Fishery Observer Fund	211
NTIS Revolving Fund	215
Office of the Inspector General (Departmental Management)	192
Operations and Administration	200
Operations and Administration	201
Operations, Research, and Facilities	203
Pacific Coastal Salmon Recovery	207
Patent and Trademark Fee Reserve Fund	215
Procurement, Acquisition and Construction	206
Promote and Develop Fishery Products and Research Pertaining to American Fisheries	209
Public Safety Communications Research Fund	219
Public Safety Trust Fund	226
Public Telecommunications Facilities, Planning and Construction	224
Salaries and Expenses (Bureau of Economic Analysis)	199
Salaries and Expenses (Departmental Management)	191
Salaries and Expenses (Economic Development Administration)	195
Salaries and Expenses (National Telecommunications and Information Administration)	220
Salaries and Expenses (U.S. Patent and Trademark Office)	214
Scientific and Technical Research and Services	216
State and Local Implementation Fund	224
Supplemental Surveys	196
U.S. Patent and Trademark Office	214
Working Capital Fund (Departmental Management)	193
Working Capital Fund (National Institute of Standards and Technology)	219
Commissary Funds, Federal Prisons (Trust Revolving Fund)	746
Commissary Stores Surcharge Program	317
Commission of Fine Arts:	
National Capital Arts and Cultural Affairs	1222
Salaries and Expenses	1221
Commission on Civil Rights:	
Salaries and Expenses	1222
Commission on Combating Synthetic Opioid Trafficking:	
Salaries and Expenses	1223
Committee for Purchase From People who are Blind or Severely Disabled, activities	1223
Committee for Purchase From People Who Are Blind Or Severely Disabled:	
Committee for Purchase From People who are Blind or Severely Disabled, activities	1223
Salaries and Expenses	1223
Committee on Foreign Investment in the United States Fund	981
Commodity Assistance Program	167
Commodity Credit Corporation Export Guarantee Financing Account	111

INDEX

Entry	Page
Commodity Credit Corporation Export Loans Program Account	110
Commodity Credit Corporation Fund	106
Commodity Credit Corporation Guaranteed Loans Liquidating Account	112
Commodity Futures Trading Commission:	
Customer Protection Fund	1226
Expenses, Customer Protection Fund	1225
Communications Site Administration	178
Community Development Financial Institutions Fund Direct Loan Financing Account	994
Community Development Financial Institutions Fund Program Account	992
Community Development Financial Institutions Fund Program, Emergency Support	995
Community Development Fund	571
Community Development Loan Guarantees Financing Account	573
Community Development Loan Guarantees Liquidating Account	574
Community Development Loan Guarantees Program Account	573
Community Development Revolving Loan Fund	1291
Community Financial Development Institutions Affordable Housing Supply Fund	996
Community Oriented Policing Services	751
Community Planning and Development	571, 605
Community Service Employment for Older Americans	764
Compact of Free Association	692
Compensation and Pensions	1049
Complex Crises Fund	821
Comptroller of the Currency	1032
Concrete Masonry Products Board	194
Concurrent Receipt Accrual Payments to the Military Retirement Fund	242
Conflict Stabilization Operations	803, 849
Congressional Budget Office	16
Congressional Publishing	32
Connecting Minority Communities Fund	221
Consolidated Rail Infrastructure and Safety Improvements	947
Construction:	
Bureau of Indian Affairs, Department of the Interior	673
Cemeterial Expenses, Other Defense—Civil Programs	1103
Corps of Engineers—Civil Works, Corps of Engineers—Civil Works	1080
Departmental Administration, Department of Veterans Affairs	1066, 1067
Drug Enforcement Administration, Department of Justice	740
Federal Bureau of Investigation, Department of Justice	738
International Commissions, Department of State	815
Legal Activities and U.S. Marshals, Department of Justice	726
National Aeronautics and Space Administration, National Aeronautics and Space Administration	1167
National Institute of Standards and Technology, Department of Commerce	218
National Park Service, Department of the Interior	664, 669
Power Marketing Administration, Department of Energy	410
United States Fish and Wildlife Service, Department of the Interior	650
Consular and Border Security Programs	801
Consumer Assistance to Recycle and Save Program	932
Consumer Financial Civil Penalty Fund	1219
Consumer Operated and Oriented Plan Financing Account	461
Consumer Operated and Oriented Plan Program Account	460
Consumer Operated and Oriented Plan Program Contingency Fund Financing Account	461
Consumer Operated and Oriented Plan Program Contingency Fund	460
Consumer Product Safety Commission:	
Salaries and Expenses	1227
Contingency Fund	468
Continued Dumping and Subsidy Offset	1010
Continuing Fund, Southeastern Power Administration	408
Continuing Fund, Southwestern Power Administration	409
Contract Support Costs	435, 672
Contributed Funds	647, 660
Contribution for Annuity Benefits, United States Secret Service	527
Contribution to Enterprise for the Americas Multilateral Investment Fund	840
Contribution to Multilateral Investment Guarantee Agency	838
Contribution to the African Development Bank	839
Contribution to the Asian Development Bank	838
Contribution to the European Bank for Reconstruction and Development	840
Contribution to the Green Climate Fund	835
Contribution to the Inter-American Development Bank	838
Contribution to the International Bank for Reconstruction and Development	836
Contribution to the International Development Association	837
Contribution to the North American Development Bank	840
Contributions for International Peacekeeping Activities	814
Contributions for Renewable Energy Impact Assessments and Mitigation, Defense	291
Contributions to IMF Facilities and Trust Funds Financing Account	870
Contributions to IMF Facilities and Trust Funds	869
Contributions to International Organizations	813
Contributions to the International Fund for Agricultural Development	840
Contributions	1101
Cooperative Acquisitions Program Revolving Fund	29
Cooperative Endangered Species Conservation Fund	655
Cooperative Threat Reduction Account	261
Coronavirus Relief Fund	989
Corporation for National and Community Service:	
General and Administrative Provisions	1232
General Fund Receipt Account	1232
National Service Trust	1230
Office of Inspector General	1229
Operating Expenses	1227
Payment to the National Service Trust Fund	1229
Salaries and Expenses	1229
VISTA Advance Payments Revolving Fund	1230
Corporation for Public Broadcasting:	
Corporation for Travel Promotion:	
Travel Promotion Fund	1339
Corps of Engineers—Civil Works:	
Coastal Wetlands Restoration Trust Fund	1094
Construction	1080
Expenses	1088
Flood Control and Coastal Emergencies	1085
Formerly Utilized Sites Remedial Action Program	1088
General and Administrative Provisions	1095
General Fund Receipt Accounts	1095
General Provisions—Corps of Engineers—Civil	1095
Harbor Maintenance Trust Fund	1092
Inland Waterways Trust Fund	1092
Interagency America the Beautiful Pass Revenues	1091
Investigations	1085
Mississippi River and Tributaries	1083
Office of the Assistant Secretary of the Army for Civil Works	1079
Operation and Maintenance	1082
Permanent Appropriations	1089
Regulatory Program	1087
Revolving Fund	1090
Rivers and Harbors Contributed Funds	1093
South Dakota Terrestrial Wildlife Habitat Restoration Trust Fund	1095
Special Recreation User Fee	1083
Special Use Permit Fees	1091
Washington Aqueduct	1089
Water Infrastructure Finance and Innovation Program Account	1079
Cost-sharing Reductions	458
Council of Economic Advisers	1133
Council of the Inspectors General on Integrity and Efficiency:	
Inspectors General Council Fund	1233
Pandemic Response Accountability Committee	1232

	Page
Council on Environmental Quality and Office of Environmental Quality	1134, 1134
Counter-Islamic State of Iraq and Syria Train and Equip Fund	262
Countering Weapons of Mass Destruction Office	552
Court of Appeals for Veterans Claims Retirement Fund	1335
Court Security	54
Court Services and Offender Supervision Agency for the District of Columbia:	
Federal Payment to the Court Services and Offender Supervision Agency for the District of Columbia	1233
Courts of Appeals, District Courts, and Other Judicial Services	51
Covered Countermeasure Process Fund	430
Crash Data	934
Credit Union Share Insurance Fund	1290
Credit:	
Direct loans:	
Advanced Technology Vehicles Manufacturing Direct Loan Financing Account	401
Agricultural Credit Insurance Fund Direct Loan Financing Account	103
Assistance to American Samoa Direct Loan Financing Account	694
Bureau of Reclamation Direct Loan Financing Account	642
Business Direct Loan Financing Account	1197
Clean Technology Fund Loans Financing Account	835
College Housing and Academic Facilities Loans Financing Account	342
Community Development Financial Institutions Fund Direct Loan Financing Account	994
Consumer Operated and Oriented Plan Financing Account	461
Consumer Operated and Oriented Plan Program Contingency Fund Financing Account	461
Contributions to IMF Facilities and Trust Funds Financing Account	870
Debt Reduction Financing Account	161
Defense Production Act, Direct Loan Financing Account	285
Disaster Assistance Direct Loan Financing Account	543
Disaster Direct Loan Financing Account	1201
Distance Learning, Telemedicine, and Broadband Direct Loan Financing Account	157
Economic Stabilization Direct Loan Financing Account	987
Emergency Boll Weevil Direct Loan Financing Account	113
Emergency Homeowners' Relief Financing Account	590
Export-Import Bank Direct Loan Financing Account	1251
Family Housing Improvement Direct Loan Financing Account	305
Farm Storage Facility Direct Loan Financing Account	113
Federal Direct Student Loan Program Financing Account	352
FHA-General and Special Risk Direct Loan Financing Account	592
Fisheries Finance Direct Loan Financing Account	213
Foreign Military Financing Direct Loan Financing Account	832
Green and Resilient Retrofit Program for Multifamily Housing, Financing Account	585
Green Retrofit Program for Multifamily Housing Financing Account	583
Historically Black College and University Capital Financing Direct Loan Financing Account	343
Housing Direct Loan Financing Account	1058
Indian Direct Loan Financing Account	679
Maritime Guaranteed Loan (Title XI) FFB Financing Account	970
Military Debt Reduction Financing Account	834
Multifamily Housing Revitalization Direct Loan Financing Account	127
Native American Direct Loan Financing Account	1061
P.L. 480 Direct Credit Financing Account	161
Railroad Rehabilitation and Improvement Direct Loan Financing Account	904
Repatriation Loans Financing Account	811

	Page
Credit—Continued	
Rural Business and Industry Direct Loans Financing Account	140
Rural Community Facility Direct Loans Financing Account	130
Rural Development Loan Fund Direct Loan Financing Account	142
Rural Economic Development Direct Loan Financing Account	143
Rural Electrification and Telecommunications Direct Loan Financing Account	152
Rural Housing Insurance Fund Direct Loan Financing Account	133
Rural Microenterprise Investment Direct Loan Financing Account	138
Rural Telephone Bank Direct Loan Financing Account	154
Rural Water and Waste Disposal Direct Loans Financing Account	149
Small Business Lending Fund Financing Account	1000
Spectrum Auction Direct Loan Financing Account	1258
State HFA Direct Loan Financing Account	1002
Student Loan Acquisition Account	356
TEACH Grant Financing Account	347
Temporary Student Loan Purchase Authority Conduit Financing Account	356
Temporary Student Loan Purchase Authority Financing Account	355
TIFIA General Fund Direct Loan Financing Account	898
TIFIA Highway Trust Fund Direct Loan Financing Account	896
Tiger TIFIA Direct Loan Financing Account, Recovery Act	891
Title 17 Innovative Technology Direct Loan Financing Account	404
Transitional Housing Direct Loan Financing Account	1062
Troubled Asset Relief Program Direct Loan Financing Account	997
Troubled Asset Relief Program Equity Purchase Financing Account	997
United States International Development Finance Corporation Direct Loan Financing Account	860
Vocational Rehabilitation Direct Loan Financing Account	1062
Water Infrastructure Finance and Innovation Direct Loan Financing Account	1119
Guaranteed loans:	
Agricultural Credit Insurance Fund Guaranteed Loan Financing Account	104
Biorefinery Assistance Guaranteed Loan Financing Account	147
Business Guaranteed Loan Financing Account	1198
Commodity Credit Corporation Export Guarantee Financing Account	111
Community Development Loan Guarantees Financing Account	573
Development Credit Authority Guaranteed Loan Financing Account	853
Export-Import Bank Guaranteed Loan Financing Account	1252
Family Housing Improvement Guaranteed Loan Financing Account	305
Federal Family Education Loan Program Financing Account	353
FHA-General and Special Risk Guaranteed Loan Financing Account	591
FHA-Loan Guarantee Recovery Fund Financing Account	594
FHA-Mutual Mortgage Insurance Guaranteed Loan Financing Account	587
Food Supply Chain and Agriculture Pandemic Response Guaranteed Loans Financing Account	66
Foreign Military Financing Guaranteed Loan Financing Account	833
Guarantees of Mortgage-backed Securities Financing Account	598
Health Center Guaranteed Loan Financing Account	432
Health Education Assistance Loans Financing Account	359
Home Ownership Preservation Equity Fund Financing Account	589

INDEX

Credit—Continued

- Housing Guaranteed Loan Financing Account 1059
- Indian Guaranteed Loan Financing Account 680
- Indian Housing Loan Guarantee Fund Financing Account 569
- Loan Guarantees to Israel Financing Account 851
- Maritime Guaranteed Loan (Title XI) Financing Account 972
- MENA Loan Guarantee Financing Account 852
- Microenterprise and Small Enterprise Development Guaranteed Loan Financing Account 862
- Native Hawaiian Housing Loan Guarantee Fund Financing Account 571
- Overseas Private Investment Corporation Guaranteed Loan Financing Account 855
- Rural Business and Industry Guaranteed Loans Financing Account 140
- Rural Business Investment Program Guarantee Financing Account 144
- Rural Community Facility Guaranteed Loans Financing Account 130
- Rural Electrification and Telecommunications Guaranteed Loans Financing Account 153
- Rural Energy for America Guaranteed Loan Financing Account 145
- Rural Housing Insurance Fund Guaranteed Loan Financing Account 134
- Rural Water and Waste Water Disposal Guaranteed Loans Financing Account 150
- Title 17 Innovative Technology Guaranteed Loan Financing Account 406
- Title VI Indian Federal Guarantees Financing Account 567
- Tribal Indian Energy Resource Development Loan Guarantee Financing Account 406
- Troubled Asset Relief Program, Housing Programs, Letter of Credit Financing Account 999
- U.S. International Development Finance Corporation Insurance of Debt Financing Account 861
- Ukraine Loan Guarantee Financing Account 872
- Ukraine Loan Guarantees Financing Account 850
- United States International Development Finance Corporation Guaranteed Loan Financing Account 859
- Urban and Environmental Credit Guaranteed Loan Financing Account 861

Liquidating accounts:
- Agricultural Credit Insurance Fund Liquidating Account 105
- Bureau of Reclamation Loan Liquidating Account 642
- Business Loan Fund Liquidating Account 1199
- Coastal Zone Management Fund 211
- College Housing and Academic Facilities Loans Liquidating Account 343
- Commodity Credit Corporation Guaranteed Loans Liquidating Account 112
- Community Development Loan Guarantees Liquidating Account 574
- Disaster Loan Fund Liquidating Account 1202
- Economic Assistance Loans Liquidating Account 853
- Expenses, Public Law 480, Foreign Assistance Programs, Agriculture Liquidating Account 162
- Export-Import Bank of the United States Liquidating Account 1253
- Federal Family Education Loan Liquidating Account 357
- Federal Ship Financing Fund Fishing Vessels Liquidating Account 214
- FHA-General and Special Risk Insurance Funds Liquidating Account 593
- FHA-Mutual Mortgage and Cooperative Housing Insurance Funds Liquidating Account 588
- Foreign Military Loan Liquidating Account 833
- Guarantees of Mortgage-backed Securities Liquidating Account 599
- Health Education Assistance Loans Liquidating Account 359
- Housing and Other Credit Guaranty Programs Liquidating Account 863

Credit—Continued

- Housing for the Elderly or Handicapped Fund Liquidating Account 594
- Housing Liquidating Account 1060
- Indian Loan Guaranty and Insurance Fund Liquidating Account 681
- Medical Facilities Guarantee and Loan Fund 432
- Revolving Fund (liquidating Programs) 578
- Revolving Fund for Loans Liquidating Account 679
- Rural Development Insurance Fund Liquidating Account 157
- Rural Development Loan Fund Liquidating Account 142
- Rural Electrification and Telecommunications Liquidating Account 153
- Rural Housing Insurance Fund Liquidating Account 135

Program accounts:
- Advanced Technology Vehicles Manufacturing Loan Program Account 401
- Agricultural Credit Insurance Fund Program Account 101
- Assistance to Territories 693
- Biorefinery Assistance Program Account 146
- Bureau of Reclamation Loan Program Account 642
- Business Loans Program Account 1196
- Carbon Dioxide Transportation Infrastructure Finance and Innovation Program Account 404
- Clean Technology Fund Program Account 834
- College Housing and Academic Facilities Loans Program Account 341
- Commodity Credit Corporation Export Loans Program Account 110
- Community Development Financial Institutions Fund Program Account 992
- Community Development Loan Guarantees Program Account 573
- Consumer Operated and Oriented Plan Program Account 460
- Consumer Operated and Oriented Plan Program Contingency Fund 460
- Contributions to IMF Facilities and Trust Funds 869
- Debt Restructuring 842
- Defense Production Act Program Account 284
- Department of Defense Family Housing Improvement Fund 304
- Development Credit Authority Program Account 853
- Disaster Assistance Direct Loan Program Account 542
- Disaster Loans Program Account 1200
- Distance Learning, Telemedicine, and Broadband Program 155
- Economic Development Assistance Programs 195
- Economic Stabilization Program Account 986
- Emergency Homeowners' Relief Fund 590
- Export-Import Bank Loans Program Account 1249
- Farm Storage Facility Loans Program Account 112
- Federal Direct Student Loan Program Account 349
- Federal Family Education Loan Program Account 353
- Federal-aid Highways 924
- FHA-General and Special Risk Program Account 590
- FHA-Mutual Mortgage Insurance Capital Reserve Account 588
- FHA-Mutual Mortgage Insurance Program Account 586
- Fisheries Finance Program Account 212
- Food Supply Chain and Agriculture Pandemic Response Program Account 65
- Foreign Military Financing Loan Program Account 832
- Green and Resilient Retrofit Program for Multifamily Housing 584
- Green Retrofit Program for Multifamily Housing, Recovery Act 583
- GSE Mortgage-backed Securities Purchase Program Account 1001
- Guarantees of Mortgage-backed Securities Loan Guarantee Program Account 597
- Health Education Assistance Loans Program Account 358
- Health Resources and Services 428
- Home Ownership Preservation Equity Fund Program Account 589
- Indian Guaranteed Loan Program Account 679

	Page
Credit—Continued	
Indian Housing Loan Guarantee Fund Program Account	568
Intermediary Relending Program Fund Account	141
Loan Guarantees to Israel Program Account	851
Maritime Guaranteed Loan (Title XI) Program Account	970
MENA Loan Guarantee Program Account	852
Microenterprise and Small Enterprise Development Program Account	862
Military Unaccompanied Housing Improvement Fund	306
Multifamily Housing Revitalization Program Account	126
Native American Programs	566
Native American Veteran Housing Loan Program Account	1061
Native Hawaiian Housing Loan Guarantee Fund Program Account	570
Overseas Private Investment Corporation Program Account	854
Procurement of Ammunition, Army	271
Public Law 480 Title I Direct Credit and Food for Progress Program Account	160
Railroad Rehabilitation and Improvement Program	903
Repatriation Loans Program Account	810
Rural Business Investment Program Account	144
Rural Business Program Account	139
Rural Community Facilities Program Account	128
Rural Economic Development Grants	137
Rural Economic Development Loans Program Account	143
Rural Electrification and Telecommunications Loans Program Account	151
Rural Energy for America Program	145
Rural Housing Insurance Fund Program Account	131
Rural Microentrepreneur Assistance Program	138
Rural Telephone Bank Program Account	154
Rural Water and Waste Disposal Program Account	148
Small Business Lending Fund Program Account	1000
Spectrum Auction Program Account	1257
TEACH Grant Program Account	347
TIFIA General Fund Program Account	898
TIFIA Highway Trust Fund Program Account	904
Title 17 Innovative Technology Loan Guarantee Program	402
Tribal Energy Loan Guarantee Program	405
Troubled Asset Relief Program Account	996
Troubled Asset Relief Program Equity Purchase Program	997
Troubled Asset Relief Program, Housing Programs	998
U.S. International Development Finance Corporation Insurance of Debt Program Account	856
Ukraine Loan Guarantee Program Account	872
Ukraine Loan Guarantees Program Account	849
United States International Development Finance Corporation Program Account	857
Urban and Environmental Credit Program Account	861
Veterans Housing Benefit Program Fund	1057
Water Infrastructure Finance and Innovation Program Account	1079
Crime Victims Fund	757
Customer Protection Fund	1226
Cyber Security Initiatives	899
Cybersecurity and Infrastructure Security Agency	530
Cybersecurity Enhancement Account	978
Cybersecurity Response and Recovery Fund	532
Cybersecurity, Energy Security, and Emergency Response	382

D

	Page
Damage Assessment and Restoration Revolving Fund	123, 212, 1123
Debt Collection Fund	489, 1005
Debt Reduction Financing Account	161, 862, 1251
Debt Restructuring	842
Deep Space Exploration Systems	1165
Defender Services	53
Defense Environmental Cleanup	370
Defense Health Program	257
Defense Nuclear Facilities Safety Board:	
Salaries and Expenses	1235
Defense Nuclear Nonproliferation	369
Defense Nuclear Waste Disposal	373

	Page
Defense Production Act Medical Supplies Enhancement	484
Defense Production Act Program Account	284
Defense Production Act Purchases	284
Defense Production Act, Direct Loan Financing Account	285
Defense—Military Programs, Department of:	
Administrative Provisions	318
Afghanistan Security Forces Fund	262
Aircraft Procurement, Air Force	278
Aircraft Procurement, Army	268
Aircraft Procurement, Navy	273
Allied Contributions and Cooperation Account	265
Buildings Maintenance Fund	313
Chemical Agents and Munitions Destruction, Defense	284
Chemical Demilitarization Construction, Defense-wide	298
Coastal Defense Augmentation	277
Commissary Stores Surcharge Program	317
Concurrent Receipt Accrual Payments to the Military Retirement Fund	242
Contributions for Renewable Energy Impact Assessments and Mitigation, Defense	291
Cooperative Threat Reduction Account	261
Counter-Islamic State of Iraq and Syria Train and Equip Fund	262
Defense Counterintelligence and Security Agency Working Capital Fund	314
Defense Health Program	257
Defense Production Act Program Account	284
Defense Production Act Purchases	284
Defense Production Act, Direct Loan Financing Account	285
Department of Defense Acquisition Workforce Development Account	263
Department of Defense Base Closure Account 1990	299
Department of Defense Base Closure Account 2005	299
Department of Defense Base Closure Account	298
Department of Defense Family Housing Improvement Fund	304
Department of Defense General Gift Fund	316
Department of Defense Rapid Prototyping Fund	290
Department of Defense Vietnam War Commemoration Fund	267
Department of Defense World War II Commemoration Fund	267
Disposal of Department of Defense Real Property	266
Drug Interdiction and Counter-Drug Activities, Defense	256
Emergency Response Fund	264
Emergency Response	264
Environmental Restoration, Formerly Used Defense Sites	259
Family Housing Construction, Air Force	302
Family Housing Construction, Army	299
Family Housing Construction, Navy and Marine Corps	301
Family Housing Improvement Direct Loan Financing Account	305
Family Housing Improvement Guaranteed Loan Financing Account	305
Family Housing Operation and Maintenance, Air Force	303
Family Housing Operation and Maintenance, Army	300
Family Housing Operation and Maintenance, Defense-wide	303
Family Housing Operation and Maintenance, Navy and Marine Corps	301
Family Housing	299
Foreign Currency Fluctuations, Construction	299
Foreign Currency Fluctuations	257
Foreign National Employees Separation Pay	317
General and Administrative Provisions	318
General Fund Receipt Accounts	318
Homeowners Assistance Fund	304
Host Nation Support Fund for Relocation	315
International Reconstruction and Other Assistance	268
Iraq Relief and Reconstruction Fund, Army	268
Iraq Train and Equip Fund	263
Joint Improvised-Threat Defeat Fund	273
Lease of Department of Defense Real Property	266
Medicare-Eligible Retiree Health Fund Contribution, Air Force	236
Medicare-Eligible Retiree Health Fund Contribution, Army	233

INDEX

	Page
Defense—Military Programs, Department of—Continued	
Medicare-Eligible Retiree Health Fund Contribution, Marine Corps	235
Medicare-Eligible Retiree Health Fund Contribution, National Guard Personnel, Air Force	242
Medicare-Eligible Retiree Health Fund Contribution, National Guard Personnel, Army	241
Medicare-Eligible Retiree Health Fund Contribution, Navy	234
Medicare-Eligible Retiree Health Fund Contribution, Reserve Personnel, Air Force	240
Medicare-Eligible Retiree Health Fund Contribution, Reserve Personnel, Army	237
Medicare-Eligible Retiree Health Fund Contribution, Reserve Personnel, Marine Corps	239
Medicare-Eligible Retiree Health Fund Contribution, Reserve Personnel, Navy	238
Medicare-Eligible Retiree Health Fund Contribution, Space Force	237
Military Construction, Air Force Reserve	297
Military Construction, Air Force	293
Military Construction, Air National Guard	296
Military Construction, Army National Guard	295
Military Construction, Army Reserve	296
Military Construction, Army	292
Military Construction, Defense-wide	294
Military Construction, Navy and Marine Corps	293
Military Construction, Navy Reserve	297
Military Construction	292
Military Personnel, Air Force	235
Military Personnel, Army	232
Military Personnel, Marine Corps	234
Military Personnel, Navy	233
Military Personnel, Space Force	236
Military Personnel	231
Military Unaccompanied Housing Improvement Fund	306
Miscellaneous Special Funds	265
Missile Procurement, Air Force	279
Missile Procurement, Army	269
Mutually Beneficial Activities	267
National Defense Sealift Fund	308
National Defense Stockpile Transaction Fund	306
National Guard and Reserve Equipment	283
National Guard Personnel, Air Force	241
National Guard Personnel, Army	240
National Sea-Based Deterrence Fund	276
National Security Education Trust Fund	317
North Atlantic Treaty Organization Security Investment Program	295
Office of the Inspector General (Operation and Maintenance)	249
Operation and Maintenance, Air Force Reserve	252
Operation and Maintenance, Air Force	246
Operation and Maintenance, Air National Guard	254
Operation and Maintenance, Army National Guard	253
Operation and Maintenance, Army Reserve	250
Operation and Maintenance, Army	242
Operation and Maintenance, Defense-wide	248
Operation and Maintenance, Marine Corps Reserve	252
Operation and Maintenance, Marine Corps	245
Operation and Maintenance, Navy Reserve	251
Operation and Maintenance, Navy	244
Operation and Maintenance, Space Force	247
Operation and Maintenance	242
Operational Test and Evaluation, Defense	291
Other DOD Trust Funds	316
Other Procurement, Air Force	281
Other Procurement, Army	272
Other Procurement, Navy	276
Overseas Contingency Operations Transfer Fund	255
Overseas Humanitarian, Disaster, and Civic Aid	260
Overseas Military Facility Investment Recovery	267
Pentagon Reservation Maintenance Revolving Fund	307
Procurement of Ammunition, Air Force	281

	Page
Defense—Military Programs, Department of—Continued	
Procurement of Ammunition, Army	271
Procurement of Ammunition, Navy and Marine Corps	274
Procurement of Weapons and Tracked Combat Vehicles, Army	270
Procurement, Defense-wide	282
Procurement, Marine Corps	277
Procurement, Space Force	280
Procurement	268
Red Hill Recovery Fund	255
Research, Development, Test and Evaluation, Air Force	288
Research, Development, Test and Evaluation, Army	286
Research, Development, Test and Evaluation, Defense-wide	289
Research, Development, Test and Evaluation, Navy	287
Research, Development, Test, and Evaluation, Space Force	289
Research, Development, Test, and Evaluation	286
Reserve Personnel, Air Force	239
Reserve Personnel, Army	237
Reserve Personnel, Marine Corps	239
Reserve Personnel, Navy	238
Revolving and Management Funds	306
Shipbuilding and Conversion, Navy	275
Space Procurement, Air Force	280
Support for International Sporting Competitions	257
Support of Athletic Programs	268
The Department of Defense Environmental Restoration Accounts	259
Title VIII—General Provisions	319
Trust Funds	314
United States Court of Appeals for the Armed Forces	255
Voluntary Separation Incentive Fund	314
Weapons Procurement, Navy	274
Working Capital Fund, Air Force (Revolving and Management Funds)	310
Working Capital Fund, Army (Revolving and Management Funds)	308
Working Capital Fund, Defense Commissary Agency (Revolving and Management Funds)	312
Working Capital Fund, Defense-wide (Revolving and Management Funds)	311
Working Capital Fund, Navy (Revolving and Management Funds)	309
Delta Regional Authority:	
Democracy Fund	822
Denali Commission Trust Fund	1237
Denali Commission:	
Denali Commission Trust Fund	1237
Gifts and Donations, Denali Commission	1237
Department of Defense Acquisition Workforce Development Account	263
Department of Defense Base Closure Account 1990	299
Department of Defense Base Closure Account 2005	299
Department of Defense Base Closure Account	298
Department of Defense Family Housing Improvement Fund	304
Department of Defense General Gift Fund	316
Department of Defense Medicare-Eligible Retiree Health Care Fund	1098
Department of Defense Rapid Prototyping Fund	290
Department of Defense Vietnam War Commemoration Fund	267
Department of Defense World War II Commemoration Fund	267
Department-Wide Programs	697
Department-Wide Systems and Capital Investments Programs	979
Departmental Administration:	
Departmental Administration, Department of Energy	416
Departmental Management	191, 361, 479, 789
Departmental Offices	687, 977
Deposit Insurance Fund	1260
Deposit Insurance	1260
Detailed Budget Estimates	3
Development Assistance Program	843
Development Credit Authority Guaranteed Loan Financing Account	853

	Page
Development Credit Authority Program Account	853
Development Fund for Africa	844
Digital Equity	222
Digital Television Transition and Public Safety Fund	224
Diplomatic Programs	799
Disaster Assistance Direct Loan Financing Account	543
Disaster Assistance Direct Loan Program Account	542
Disaster Direct Loan Financing Account	1201
Disaster Education Recovery	363, 363
Disaster Loan Fund Liquidating Account	1202
Disaster Loans Program Account	1200
Disaster Relief Fund	537
Discretionary Grants (Highway Trust Fund, Mass Transit Account)	956
Discrimination Claims Settlement	100
Disposal of Department of Defense Real Property	266
Disposal of Surplus Real and Related Personal Property	1149
Distance Learning, Telemedicine, and Broadband Direct Loan Financing Account	157
Distance Learning, Telemedicine, and Broadband Program	155
District of Columbia Courts	1237
District of Columbia Crime Victims Compensation Fund	1239
District of Columbia Federal Pension Fund	1242
District of Columbia General and Special Payments	1240
District of Columbia Judicial Retirement and Survivors Annuity Fund	1240
District of Columbia:	
District of Columbia Courts	1237
District of Columbia Crime Victims Compensation Fund	1239
District of Columbia Federal Pension Fund	1242
District of Columbia General and Special Payments	1240
District of Columbia Judicial Retirement and Survivors Annuity Fund	1240
Federal Payment for Defender Services in District of Columbia Courts	1238
Federal Payment for Emergency Planning and Security Costs in the District of Columbia	1242
Federal Payment for Resident Tuition Support	1240
Federal Payment for School Improvement	1241
Federal Payment for Water and Sewer Services	1243
Federal Payment to the District of Columbia Courts	1237
Federal Payment to the District of Columbia Judicial Retirement and Survivors Annuity Fund	1239
Federal Payment to the District of Columbia Pension Fund	1242
Federal Support for Economic Development and Management Reforms in the District	1241
General and Administrative Provisions	1244
General Fund Receipt Account	1244
Title VIII—General Provisions—District of Columbia	1244
Federal Payment to the District of Columbia Public Defender Service	1312
Public Defender Service for the District of Columbia	1312
Diversion Control Fee Account	740
DOD-VA Health Care Sharing Incentive Fund	1042
Domestic Trafficking Victims' Fund	758
Donations	1177
Drug Enforcement Administration	738
Drug Interdiction and Counter-Drug Activities, Defense	256
Dual Benefits Payments Account	1313
Duplication Services	29
Dwight D. Eisenhower Memorial Commission	41
Dwight D. Eisenhower Memorial Fund	42

E

	Page
Early Retiree Reinsurance Program	458
East-West Center	823
Economic Assistance Loans Liquidating Account	853, 864
Economic Development Administration	195
Economic Development Assistance Programs	195
Economic Research Service	72, 72
Economic Stabilization Direct Loan Financing Account	987
Economic Stabilization Program Account	986
Economic Support Fund	827

	Page
Education Benefits Fund	1099
Education Construction	683
Education for the Disadvantaged	327
Education Stabilization Fund	327
Education, Department of:	
American Printing House for the Blind	337
Career, Technical and Adult Education	338
College Housing and Academic Facilities Loans Financing Account	342
College Housing and Academic Facilities Loans Liquidating Account	343
College Housing and Academic Facilities Loans Program Account	341
Departmental Management	361
Disaster Education Recovery	363
Education for the Disadvantaged	327
Education Stabilization Fund	327
English Language Acquisition	334
Federal Direct Student Loan Program Account	349
Federal Direct Student Loan Program Financing Account	352
Federal Family Education Loan Liquidating Account	357
Federal Family Education Loan Program Account	353
Federal Family Education Loan Program Financing Account	353
Federal Student Loan Reserve Fund	349
Gallaudet University	338
General and Administrative Provisions	364
General Fund Receipt Accounts	364
General Provisions	364
Health Education Assistance Loans Financing Account	359
Health Education Assistance Loans Liquidating Account	359
Health Education Assistance Loans Program Account	358
Higher Education	339
Historically Black College and University Capital Financing Direct Loan Financing Account	343
Howard University	341
Impact Aid	328
Indian Education	331
Innovation and Improvement	332
Institute of Education Sciences	360
National Technical Institute for the Deaf	337
Office for Civil Rights	362
Office of Career, Technical, and Adult Education	338
Office of Elementary and Secondary Education	327
Office of English Language Acquisition	334
Office of Federal Student Aid	344
Office of Innovation and Improvement	332
Office of Inspector General (Departmental Management)	363
Office of Postsecondary Education	339
Office of Special Education and Rehabilitative Services	334
Program Administration	361
Rehabilitation Services	336
Safe Schools and Citizenship Education	331
School Improvement Programs	329
Special Education	334
Student Aid Administration	346
Student Financial Assistance Debt Collection	348
Student Financial Assistance	344
Student Loan Acquisition Account	356
TEACH Grant Financing Account	347
TEACH Grant Program Account	347
Temporary Student Loan Purchase Authority Conduit Financing Account	356
Temporary Student Loan Purchase Authority Financing Account	355
Educational and Cultural Exchange Programs	804
Educational Benefits	1099
EEOC Education, Technical Assistance, and Training Revolving Fund	1248
Election Assistance Commission:	
Election Data Collection Grants	1247
Election Security Grants	1246
Salaries and Expenses	1245

INDEX

	Page
Election Data Collection Grants	1247
Election Security Grants	1246
Electric or Low-Emitting Ferry Program	955
Electric Reliability Organization:	
Electric Vehicle Fleet	893
Electric Vehicles Fund	1157
Electricity	379
Electronic System for Travel Authorization	510
Electronic Visa Update System	510
Embassy Security, Construction, and Maintenance	805
Emergencies in the Diplomatic and Consular Service	807
Emergency Boll Weevil Direct Loan Financing Account	113
Emergency Capital Investment Fund	995
Emergency Citrus Disease Research and Development Trust Fund	82
Emergency Connectivity Fund for Educational Connections and Devices	1259
Emergency Conservation Program	100
Emergency Department of Veterans Affairs Employee Leave Fund	1048
Emergency EIDL Grants	1191
Emergency FAA Employee Leave Fund	908
Emergency Federal Employee Leave Fund	1185
Emergency Food and Shelter	542
Emergency Forest Restoration Program	101
Emergency Fund, Western Area Power Administration	412
Emergency Fund	1298
Emergency Homeowners' Relief Financing Account	590
Emergency Homeowners' Relief Fund	590
Emergency Preparedness Grants	962
Emergency Relief Program	918
Emergency Rental Assistance	990
Emergency Response Fund	264
Emergency Response	264
Emergency Watershed Protection	121
Employee Benefits Security Administration	772
Employees and Retired Employees Health Benefits Funds	1187
Employees Life Insurance Fund	1187
Employment and Training Administration	761
Energy Assistance Payments	136
Energy Community Revitalization Program	705
Energy Efficiency and Renewable Energy	383
Energy Employees Occupational Illness Compensation Fund	778
Energy Information Administration	396
Energy Programs	373
Energy Security and Infrastructure Modernization Fund	395
Energy Supply and Conservation	377
Energy, Department of:	
Advanced Research Projects Agency—Energy	377
Advanced Technology Vehicles Manufacturing Direct Loan Financing Account	401
Advanced Technology Vehicles Manufacturing Loan Program Account	401
Bonneville Power Administration Fund	414
Carbon Dioxide Transportation Infrastructure Finance and Innovation Program Account	404
Clean Coal Technology	398
Colorado River Basins Power Marketing Fund, Western Area Power Administration	413
Construction, Rehabilitation, Operation and Maintenance, Western Area Power Administration (Power Marketing Administration)	410
Continuing Fund, Southeastern Power Administration	408
Continuing Fund, Southwestern Power Administration	409
Cybersecurity, Energy Security, and Emergency Response	382
Defense Environmental Cleanup	370
Defense Nuclear Nonproliferation	369
Defense Nuclear Waste Disposal	373
Departmental Administration (Departmental Administration)	416
Departmental Administration	416
Electricity	379
Emergency Fund, Western Area Power Administration	412
Energy Efficiency and Renewable Energy	383

	Page
Energy, Department of—Continued	
Energy Information Administration	396
Energy Programs	373
Energy Security and Infrastructure Modernization Fund	395
Energy Supply and Conservation	377
Environmental and Other Defense Activities	370
Falcon and Amistad Operating and Maintenance Fund	412
Federal Energy Management Program	387
Federal Energy Regulatory Commission	397
Federal Salaries and Expenses	367
Fossil Energy and Carbon Management	392
General and Administrative Provisions	419
General Fund Receipt Accounts	419
General Provisions—Department of Energy	420
Global Clean Energy Manufacturing	388
Grid Deployment Office	381
Isotope Production and Distribution Program Fund	400
National Energy Technology Laboratory Research and Development	394
National Nuclear Security Administration	367
Naval Petroleum and Oil Shale Reserves	394
Naval Reactors	367
Non-defense Environmental Cleanup	391
Northeast Home Heating Oil Reserve	398
Nuclear Energy	377
Nuclear Waste Disposal	399
Office of Clean Energy Demonstrations	389
Office of Indian Energy Policy and Programs	390
Office of Manufacturing and Energy Supply Chains	386
Office of State and Community Energy Programs	387
Office of Technology Transitions	388
Office of the Inspector General (Departmental Administration)	418
Operation and Maintenance, Southeastern Power Administration	407
Operation and Maintenance, Southwestern Power Administration	408
Other Defense Activities	372
Payments to States under Federal Power Act	398
Power Marketing Administration	407
Science	373
SPR Petroleum Account	395
Strategic Petroleum Reserve	394
Title 17 Innovative Technology Direct Loan Financing Account	404
Title 17 Innovative Technology Guaranteed Loan Financing Account	406
Title 17 Innovative Technology Loan Guarantee Program	402
Transmission Facilitation Fund	381
Tribal Energy Loan Guarantee Program	405
Tribal Indian Energy Resource Development Loan Guarantee Financing Account	406
Ultra-deepwater and Unconventional Natural Gas and Other Petroleum Research Fund	398
Uranium Enrichment Decontamination and Decommissioning Fund	400
Weapons Activities	368
Western Area Power Administration, Borrowing Authority, Recovery Act	411
Working Capital Fund (Departmental Administration)	419
Enforcement	1017
English Language Acquisition	334
Enhanced Inspectional Services	508
Entrepreneurial Development Program	1194
Environmental and Other Defense Activities	370
Environmental Compliance and Restoration	519
Environmental Dispute Resolution Fund	1282
Environmental Improvement and Restoration Fund	211, 691
Environmental Programs and Management	1109
Environmental Protection Agency:	
Buildings and Facilities	1113
Damage Assessment and Restoration Revolving Fund	1123

	Page
Environmental Protection Agency—Continued	
Environmental Programs and Management	1109
Environmental Services	1120
General and Administrative Provisions	1130
General Provisions—Environmental Protection Agency	1130
Hazardous Substance Superfund	1124
Hazardous Waste Electronic Manifest System Fund	1123
Inland Oil Spill Programs	1128
Leaking Underground Storage Tank Trust Fund	1127
Office of Inspector General	1107
Payment to the Hazardous Substance Superfund	1120
Pesticide Registration Fund	1121
Reregistration and Expedited Processing Revolving Fund	1122
Science and Technology	1108
State and Tribal Assistance Grants	1113
TSCA Service Fee Fund	1121
Water Infrastructure Finance and Innovation Direct Loan Financing Account	1119
Water Infrastructure Finance and Innovation Program Account	1118
Working Capital Fund	1124
Environmental Restoration, Formerly Used Defense Sites	259
Environmental Review Improvement Fund	1158, 1271
Environmental Services	1120
Equal Employment Opportunity Commission:	
EEOC Education, Technical Assistance, and Training Revolving Fund	1248
Salaries and Expenses	1247
Essential Air Service and Rural Airport Improvement Fund	902
Exchange Stabilization Fund	986
Executive Office for Immigration Review	717
Executive Office of the President:	
Administrative Provisions—Executive Office of the President and Funds Appropriated to the President	1143
Council of Economic Advisers	1133
Council on Environmental Quality and Office of Environmental Quality	1134
Executive Residence at the White House	1131
General and Administrative Provisions	1143
General Fund Payment to the Trade Enforcement Trust Fund	1140
Information Technology Oversight and Reform	1142
Intellectual Property Enforcement Coordinator	1141
Management Fund, Office of Environmental Quality	1134
National Security Council and Homeland Security Council	1134
National Space Council	1139
Office of Administration	1136
Office of Management and Budget	1137
Office of National Drug Control Policy	1137
Office of Science and Technology Policy	1138
Office of the United States Trade Representative	1139
Office of theNational Cyber Director	1135
Operating Expenses (Executive Residence at the White House)	1131
Presidential Transition Administrative Support	1136
Salaries and Expenses (Council of Economic Advisers)	1133
Salaries and Expenses (National Security Council and Homeland Security Council)	1134
Salaries and Expenses (Office of Administration)	1136
Salaries and Expenses (Office of Management and Budget)	1137
Salaries and Expenses (Office of National Drug Control Policy)	1137
Salaries and Expenses (Office of the National Cyber Director)	1135
Salaries and Expenses (Office of the United States Trade Representative)	1139
Salaries and Expenses (Special Assistance to the President and the Official Residence)	1132
Salaries and Expenses (The White House)	1131
Special Assistance to the President and the Official Residence of the Vice President	1132
Spectrum Relocation Fund	1143

	Page
Executive Office of the President—Continued	
The White House	1131
Trade Enforcement Trust Fund	1140
Unanticipated Needs	1141
White House Repair and Restoration	1132
Executive Offices	602
Executive Operations	67, 67
Executive Residence at the White House	1131
Expenses and Refunds, Inspection and Grading of Farm Products	87, 93
Expenses of Transportation Audit Contracts and Contract Administration	1150
Expenses, Customer Protection Fund	1225
Expenses, National Security Commission on Artificial Intelligence	1297
Expenses, Presidential Transition	1157
Expenses, Public Law 480, Foreign Assistance Programs, Agriculture Liquidating Account	162
Expenses	1088
Export-Import Bank Direct Loan Financing Account	1251
Export-Import Bank Guaranteed Loan Financing Account	1252
Export-Import Bank Loans Program Account	1249
Export-Import Bank of the United States Liquidating Account	1253
Export-Import Bank of the United States:	
Debt Reduction Financing Account	1251
Export-Import Bank Direct Loan Financing Account	1251
Export-Import Bank Guaranteed Loan Financing Account	1252
Export-Import Bank Loans Program Account	1249
Export-Import Bank of the United States Liquidating Account	1253
General and Administrative Provisions	1254
General Fund Receipt Accounts	1254
Inspector General	1249
Extension Activities	81

F

	Page
Facilities and Equipment (Airport and Airway Trust Fund)	915
Facilities and Equipment	908
Facilities Capital	1324
Fair Housing Activities	600
Fair Housing and Equal Opportunity	600, 605
Falcon and Amistad Operating and Maintenance Fund	412
Family Housing Construction, Air Force	302
Family Housing Construction, Army	299
Family Housing Construction, Navy and Marine Corps	301
Family Housing Improvement Direct Loan Financing Account	305
Family Housing Improvement Guaranteed Loan Financing Account	305
Family Housing Operation and Maintenance, Air Force	303
Family Housing Operation and Maintenance, Army	300
Family Housing Operation and Maintenance, Defense-wide	303
Family Housing Operation and Maintenance, Navy and Marine Corps	301
Family Housing	299
Farm Credit Administration:	
Limitation on Administrative Expenses	1254
Farm Credit Banks	1356
Farm Credit System Insurance Corporation:	
Farm Credit System Insurance Fund	1255
Farm Credit System Insurance Fund	1255
Farm Credit System:	
Agricultural Credit Bank	1355
Farm Credit Banks	1356
Federal Agricultural Mortgage Corporation	1356
Farm Production and Conservation Business Center	95
Farm Production and Conservation	95
Farm Security and Rural Investment Programs	117
Farm Service Agency	98
Farm Storage Facility Direct Loan Financing Account	113
Farm Storage Facility Loans Program Account	112
FDA Innovation, Cures Act	427
FDIC—Office of Inspector General	1262

INDEX

	Page
Federal Additional Unemployment Compensation Program, Recovery	768
Federal Agricultural Mortgage Corporation	1356
Federal Aid in Wildlife Restoration	657
Federal Assistance	498, 533, 546, 554
Federal Aviation Administration	907
Federal Buildings Fund, Recovery Act	1148
Federal Buildings Fund	1145
Federal Bureau of Investigation	736
Federal Capital Revolving Fund	1148
Federal Citizen Services Fund	1158
Federal Communications Commission:	
Affordable Connectivity Fund	1258
Emergency Connectivity Fund for Educational Connections and Devices	1259
Salaries and Expenses	1255
Secure and Trusted Communications Networks Act Reimbursement Program	1258
Spectrum Auction Direct Loan Financing Account	1258
Spectrum Auction Program Account	1257
Telecommunications Relay Services Fund, Federal Communications Commission	1257
TV Broadcaster Relocation Fund	1259
Universal Service Fund	1256
Federal Crop Insurance Corporation Fund	96
Federal Deposit Insurance Corporation:	
Deposit Insurance Fund	1260
Deposit Insurance	1260
FDIC—Office of Inspector General	1262
FSLIC Resolution Fund	1261
FSLIC Resolution	1261
Office of the Inspector General (FDIC Office of Inspector General)	1262
Orderly Liquidation Fund	1261
Orderly Liquidation	1261
Federal Direct Student Loan Program Account	349
Federal Direct Student Loan Program Financing Account	352
Federal Disability Insurance Trust Fund	1210
Federal Drug Control Programs:	
High Intensity Drug Trafficking Areas Program	1262
Other Federal Drug Control Programs	1263
Federal Election Commission:	
Salaries and Expenses	1264
Federal Emergency Management Agency	533
Federal Energy Management Program	387
Federal Energy Regulatory Commission	397
Federal Family Education Loan Liquidating Account	357
Federal Family Education Loan Program Account	353
Federal Family Education Loan Program Financing Account	353
Federal Financial Institutions Examination Council Activities	1265
Federal Financial Institutions Examination Council Appraisal Subcommittee	1265
Federal Financial Institutions Examination Council:	
Federal Financial Institutions Examination Council Activities	1265
Federal Financial Institutions Examination Council Appraisal Subcommittee	1265
Registry Fees	1265
Federal Financing Bank	1012, 1012
Federal Highway Administration	918
Federal Home Loan Bank System:	
Federal Home Loan Banks	1354
Federal Home Loan Banks	1354
Federal Home Loan Mortgage Corporation:	
Mortgage-backed Securities	1354
Portfolio Programs	1354
Federal Hospital Insurance Trust Fund	462
Federal Housing Finance Agency, Administrative Expenses	1266
Federal Housing Finance Agency:	
Federal Housing Finance Agency, Administrative Expenses	1266
Office of Inspector General	1267
Federal Interest Liabilities to States	1008

	Page
Federal Judicial Center	57
Federal Labor Relations Authority:	
Salaries and Expenses	1268
Federal Law Enforcement Training Center	549
Federal Maritime Commission:	
Salaries and Expenses	1268
Federal Mediation and Conciliation Service:	
Salaries and Expenses	1269
Federal Mine Safety and Health Review Commission:	
Salaries and Expenses	1270
Federal Motor Carrier Safety Administration	928
Federal National Mortgage Association:	
Mortgage-backed Securities	1353
Portfolio Programs	1353
Federal Old-age and Survivors Insurance Trust Fund	1209
Federal Payment for Defender Services in District of Columbia Courts	1238
Federal Payment for Emergency Planning and Security Costs in the District of Columbia	1242
Federal Payment for Resident Tuition Support	1240
Federal Payment for School Improvement	1241
Federal Payment for Water and Sewer Services	1243
Federal Payment to Morris K. Udall and Stewart L. Udall Foundation Trust Fund	1282
Federal Payment to the Court Services and Offender Supervision Agency for the District of Columbia	1233
Federal Payment to the District of Columbia Courts	1237
Federal Payment to the District of Columbia Judicial Retirement and Survivors Annuity Fund	1239
Federal Payment to the District of Columbia Pension Fund	1242
Federal Payment to the District of Columbia Public Defender Service	1312
Federal Payments to the Railroad Retirement Accounts	1313
Federal Permitting Improvement Council	1271
Federal Permitting Improvement Steering Council:	
Environmental Review Improvement Fund	1271
Federal Permitting Improvement Council	1271
Federal Prison Industries, Incorporated	744
Federal Prison System	742
Federal Prisoner Detention	727
Federal Protective Service	500
Federal Railroad Administration	939
Federal Reserve Bank Reimbursement Fund	1007
Federal Retirement Thrift Investment Board:	
Program Expenses	1340
Federal Ship Financing Fund Fishing Vessels Liquidating Account	214
Federal Student Loan Reserve Fund	349
Federal Supplementary Medical Insurance Trust Fund	465
Federal Support for Economic Development and Management Reforms in the District	1241
Federal Tax Lien Revolving Fund	1031
Federal Trade Commission:	
Salaries and Expenses	1272
Federal Transit Administration	949
Federal Trust Programs	684
Federal Unemployment Benefits and Allowances	764
Federal-aid Highways	924
Federal-State Partnership for Intercity Passenger Rail Grants	946
Federally Created Non-Federal Entities	1338
Fedlink Program and Federal Research Program	30
Fee Funded Inspection, Weighing, and Examination Services	90
Fees and Expenses of Witnesses	728
Fees of Jurors and Commissioners	54
Ferry Service for Rural Communities	954
FHA-General and Special Risk Direct Loan Financing Account	592
FHA-General and Special Risk Guaranteed Loan Financing Account	591
FHA-General and Special Risk Insurance Funds Liquidating Account	593
FHA-General and Special Risk Program Account	590
FHA-Loan Guarantee Recovery Fund Financing Account	594

	Page
FHA-Mutual Mortgage and Cooperative Housing Insurance Funds Liquidating Account	588
FHA-Mutual Mortgage Insurance Capital Reserve Account	588
FHA-Mutual Mortgage Insurance Guaranteed Loan Financing Account	587
FHA-Mutual Mortgage Insurance Program Account	586
Filipino Veterans Equity Compensation Fund	1054
Financial Agent Services	1008
Financial Assistance Oversight and Technical Assistance	948
Financial Crimes Enforcement Network	1003
Financial Management Capital	899
Financial Research Fund	984
Financing Vehicles and the Board of Governors of the Federal Reserve:	
Board of Governors of the Federal Reserve System	1351
Resolution Funding Corporation	1351
First Responder Network Authority	225
Fiscal Service	1004
Fisheries Disaster Assistance	210
Fisheries Enforcement Asset Forfeiture Fund	208
Fisheries Finance Direct Loan Financing Account	213
Fisheries Finance Program Account	212
Fishermen's Contingency Fund	210
Fishermen's Guaranty Fund	825
Fishermen's Protective Fund	825
FLAME Wildfire Suppression Reserve Fund	702
Flexible Benefits Plan Reserve	1183
Flexible Subsidy Fund	583
Flood Control and Coastal Emergencies	1085
Flood Hazard Mapping and Risk Analysis Program	539
Food and Drug Administration	423
Food and Nutrition Service	162
Food for Peace Title II Grants	160
Food Safety and Inspection Service	86
Food Supply Chain and Agriculture Pandemic Response Guaranteed Loans Financing Account	66
Food Supply Chain and Agriculture Pandemic Response Program Account	65
Foreign Agricultural Service	158
Foreign Currency Fluctuations Account	1100
Foreign Currency Fluctuations, Construction	299
Foreign Currency Fluctuations	257, 865
Foreign Labor Certification Processing	770
Foreign Military Financing Direct Loan Financing Account	832
Foreign Military Financing Guaranteed Loan Financing Account	833
Foreign Military Financing Loan Program Account	832
Foreign Military Financing Program	828
Foreign Military Loan Liquidating Account	833
Foreign Military Sales Trust Fund	871
Foreign National Employees Separation Pay	317
Foreign Service National Defined Contributions Retirement Fund	809
Foreign Service National Separation Liability Trust Fund	162, 812, 853, 1334
Foreign Service Retirement and Disability Fund	811
Forest and Rangeland Research	169
Forest and Wildlife Conservation, Military Reservations	1104
Forest Service Operations	176
Forest Service Permanent Appropriations	181
Forest Service Trust Funds	184
Forest Service	168
Formerly Utilized Sites Remedial Action Program	1088
Formula Grants	950
Fossil Energy and Carbon Management	392
Franchise Fund	1074
FSLIC Resolution Fund	1261
FSLIC Resolution	1261
Funding for Indian Health Services	437
Funds for Strengthening Markets, Income, and Supply (section 32)	92

G

	Page
Gallaudet University	338

	Page
General Activities	1153
General Administration	715, 1068
General Departmental Management	479
General Expenses	14
General Fund Payment To National Surface Transportation and Innovative Finance Bureau Highway Trust Fund Account, Upward Reestimates	889
General Fund Payment to the Trade Enforcement Trust Fund	1140
General Fund Payment, Armed Forces Retirement Home	1101
General Gift Fund	525
General Operating Expenses, Veterans Benefits Administration	1054
General Post Fund, National Homes	1048
General Provisions Government-Wide	7
General Services Administration:	
Acquisition Services Fund	1151
Acquisition Workforce Training Fund	1158
Administrative Provisions—General Services Administration	1160
Allowances and Office Staff for Former Presidents	1156
Asset Proceeds and Space Management Fund	1149
Civilian Board of Contract Appeals	1155
Disposal of Surplus Real and Related Personal Property	1149
Electric Vehicles Fund	1157
Environmental Review Improvement Fund	1158
Expenses of Transportation Audit Contracts and Contract Administration	1150
Expenses, Presidential Transition	1157
Federal Buildings Fund, Recovery Act	1148
Federal Buildings Fund	1145
Federal Capital Revolving Fund	1148
Federal Citizen Services Fund	1158
General Activities	1153
General and Administrative Provisions	1160
General Fund Receipt Accounts	1160
Government-wide Policy	1153
Office of Inspector General (General Activities)	1155
Operating Expenses (General Activities)	1154
Pre-Election Presidential Transition	1157
Real Property Activities	1145
Real Property Relocation	1149
Supply and Technology Activities	1150
Technology Modernization Fund	1152
Working Capital Fund (General Activities)	1159
Geothermal Lease Revenues, Payment to Counties	690
Gift and Trust Fund Accounts	31
Gift Shop, Decimal Classification, Photo Duplication, and Related Services	30
Gifts and Bequests	67, 194, 1003
Gifts and Donations:	
African Development Foundation, International Assistance Programs	868
Botanic Garden, Legislative Branch	24
Bureau of Indian Affairs, Department of the Interior	682
Denali Commission, Denali Commission	1237
National Endowment for the Arts, National Endowment for the Arts	1293
National Endowment for the Humanities, National Endowment for the Humanities	1294
Office of the Secretary and Executive Management, Department of Homeland Security	498
Gifts to the United States for Reduction of the Public Debt	1029
Global Agriculture and Food Security Program	835
Global Clean Energy Manufacturing	388
Global Health Programs	817
Global HIV/AIDs Initiative	817
Global Security Contingency Fund	831
Government Accountability Office	35
Government National Mortgage Association	596
Government Payment for Annuitants, Employee Life Insurance	1182
Government Payment for Annuitants, Employees Health Benefits	1181

	Page
Government Publishing Office Business Operations Revolving Fund	34
Government Publishing Office	32
Government Sponsored Enterprises	1353
Government-Sponsored Enterprises:	
Government Sponsored Enterprises	1353
Government-wide Policy	1153
Grants and Administration	1292, 1293
Grants for Construction of State Extended Care Facilities	1067
Grants for Construction of Veterans Cemeteries	1068
Grants to States for Medicaid	449
Grants to the National Railroad Passenger Corporation	941
Grants-in-aid for Airports (Airport and Airway Trust Fund)	914
Grassroots Source Water Protection Program	101
Great Lakes St. Lawrence Seaway Development Corporation	958, 958
Green and Resilient Retrofit Program for Multifamily Housing, Financing Account	585
Green and Resilient Retrofit Program for Multifamily Housing	584
Green Retrofit Program for Multifamily Housing Financing Account	583
Green Retrofit Program for Multifamily Housing, Recovery Act	583
Grid Deployment Office	381
GSE Mortgage-backed Securities Purchase Program Account	1001
GSE Preferred Stock Purchase Agreements	1001
Guam World War II Claims Fund	1009
Guarantees of Mortgage-backed Securities Capital Reserve Account	596
Guarantees of Mortgage-backed Securities Financing Account	598
Guarantees of Mortgage-backed Securities Liquidating Account	599
Guarantees of Mortgage-backed Securities Loan Guarantee Program Account	597
Guarantees of Mortgage-Backed Securities Pass-Through Assistance	596
Gulf Coast Ecosystem Restoration Council:	
Gulf Coast Ecosystem Restoration Science, Observation, Monitoring, and Technology	205
Gulf Coast Restoration Trust Fund	1011
Gun Crime Prevention Strategic Fund	753

H

	Page
H&L Fraud Prevention and Detection Fee	799
H-1 B and L Fraud Prevention and Detection	783
H-1B and L Fraud Prevention and Detection Account	548
H-1B Nonimmigrant Petitioner Account	547
Harbor Maintenance Trust Fund	1092
Harry S Truman Memorial Scholarship Trust Fund	1274
Harry S Truman Scholarship Foundation:	
Harry S Truman Memorial Scholarship Trust Fund	1274
Payment to the Harry S Truman Scholarship Memorial Trust Fund	1274
Hazardous Materials Safety	959
Hazardous Substance Superfund	1124
Hazardous Waste Electronic Manifest System Fund	1123
HCHB Renovation and Modernization	193
Health Activities Funds	489
Health and Human Services, Department of:	
10-Year Pediatric Research Initiative Fund	446
Administration for Children and Families	468
Administration for Community Living	478
Affordable Insurance Exchange Grants	458
Agency for Healthcare Research and Quality	448
Agency for Toxic Substances and Disease Registry, Toxic Substances and Environmental Public Health	441
Aging and Disability Services Programs	478
Buildings and Facilities (Centers for Disease Control and Prevention)	440
CDC Working Capital Fund	440
CDC-wide Activities and Program Support	437
Center for Medicare and Medicaid Innovation	455
Centers for Disease Control and Prevention	437
Centers for Medicare and Medicaid Services	449
Child Care Entitlement to States	473

	Page
Health and Human Services, Department of—Continued	
Child Enrollment Contingency Fund	456
Children and Families Services Programs	475
Children's Health Insurance Fund	455
Children's Research and Technical Assistance	476
Consumer Operated and Oriented Plan Financing Account	461
Consumer Operated and Oriented Plan Program Account	460
Consumer Operated and Oriented Plan Program Contingency Fund Financing Account	461
Consumer Operated and Oriented Plan Program Contingency Fund	460
Contingency Fund	468
Contract Support Costs	435
Cost-sharing Reductions	458
Covered Countermeasure Process Fund	430
Debt Collection Fund	489
Defense Production Act Medical Supplies Enhancement	484
Departmental Management	479
Early Retiree Reinsurance Program	458
FDA Innovation, Cures Act	427
FDA Working Capital Fund	426
Federal Hospital Insurance Trust Fund	462
Federal Supplementary Medical Insurance Trust Fund	465
Food and Drug Administration	423
Funding for Indian Health Services	437
General and Administrative Provisions	492
General Departmental Management	479
General Fund Receipt Accounts	492
General Provisions	492
Grants to States for Medicaid	449
Health Activities Funds	489
Health Care Fraud and Abuse Control Account	464
Health Center Guaranteed Loan Financing Account	432
Health Insurance Reform Implementation Fund	486
Health Resources and Services Administration	428
Health Resources and Services	428
Healthcare Research and Quality	448
HHS Accrual Contribution to the Uniformed Services Retiree Health Care Fund	489
HHS Service and Supply Fund	489
Indian Health Facilities	436
Indian Health Service	433
Indian Health Services	433
Infectious Diseases Rapid Response Reserve Fund	441
Low Income Home Energy Assistance	469
Maternal, Infant, and Early Childhood Home Visiting Programs	431
Medical Facilities Guarantee and Loan Fund	432
Medicare Health Information Technology Incentive Payments, Recovery Act	457
Medicare Hearings and Appeals	482
Medicare Investments	462
Medicare Prescription Drug Account, Federal Supplementary Insurance Trust Fund	467
Mental Health Parity Enforcement Grants	462
Mental Health Transformation Fund	485
Miscellaneous Trust Funds	490
National Institutes of Health	443
NIH Innovation, Cures Act	446
No Surprises Implementation Fund	487
Nonrecurring Expenses Fund	486
Office for Civil Rights	481
Office of Inspector General (Office of the Inspector General)	491
Office of the Inspector General	491
Office of the National Coordinator for Health Information Technology	481
Payment to the FDA Innovation Account, CURES Act	426
Payment to the NIH Innovation Account, CURES Act	445
Payments for Foster Care and Permanency	477
Payments for Tribal Leases	435
Payments to Health Care Trust Funds	452

Health and Human Services, Department of—Continued

- Payments to States for Child Support Enforcement and Family Support Programs 468
- Payments to States for the Child Care and Development Block Grant 473
- Pre-Existing Condition Insurance Plan Program 457
- Pregnancy Assistance Fund 487
- PrEP for All to End the HIV Epidemic 485
- Prevention and Public Health Fund 487
- Program Management 453
- Program Support Center 488
- Promoting Safe and Stable Families 472
- Public Health and Social Services Emergency Fund 483
- Quality Improvement Organizations 452
- Rate Review Grants 457
- Refugee and Entrant Assistance 470
- Retirement Pay and Medical Benefits for Commissioned Officers 488
- Revolving Fund for Certification and Other Services 427
- Risk Adjustment Program Payments 459
- Salaries and Expenses (Food and Drug Administration) 423
- Section 241 Evaluation Transactions Account 488
- Social Services Block Grant 474
- State Grants and Demonstrations 451
- Substance Use And Mental Health Services Administration 446
- Temporary Assistance for Needy Families 468
- Transfers from the Patient-Centered Outcomes Research Trust Fund 485
- Transitional Reinsurance Program 459
- Vaccine Injury Compensation Program Trust Fund 433
- Vaccine Injury Compensation 430
- World Trade Center Health Program Fund 442

Health Care Fraud and Abuse Control Account 464
Health Center Guaranteed Loan Financing Account 432
Health Education Assistance Loans Financing Account 359
Health Education Assistance Loans Liquidating Account 359
Health Education Assistance Loans Program Account 358
Health Insurance Reform Implementation Fund 486
Health Resources and Services Administration 428
Health Resources and Services 428
Healthcare Research and Quality 448
Healthy Foods Financing Initiative 137
Healthy Forests Reserve Program 122
Helium Fund 623
HHS Accrual Contribution to the Uniformed Services Retiree Health Care Fund 489
HHS Service and Supply Fund 489
High Energy Cost Grants 147
High Intensity Drug Trafficking Areas Program 1262
High-Hazard Indian Dam Safety Deferred Maintenance Fund 674
Higher Education 339
Highway Infrastructure Programs 919
Highway Traffic Safety Grants 937
Highway Trust Fund 923
Historic Preservation Fund 667
Historically Black College and University Capital Financing Direct Loan Financing Account 343
Holocaust Memorial Museum 1336
Home Investment Partnership Program 574
Home Ownership Preservation Equity Fund Financing Account 589
Home Ownership Preservation Equity Fund Program Account 589

Homeland Security, Department of:
- 9-11 Response and Biometric Exit Account 511
- Abandoned Seafarers Fund 522
- Air and Marine Interdiction, Operations, Maintenance, and Procurement 508
- Alteration of Bridges 520
- Analysis and Operations 502
- APEC Business Travel Card 511
- Aquatic Resources Trust Fund 523
- Automation Modernization, Customs and Border Protection 506

Homeland Security, Department of—Continued

- Automation Modernization, Immigration and Customs Enforcement 514
- Boat Safety 524
- Border Security Fencing, Infrastructure, and Technology 506
- Citizenship and Immigration Services 545
- Coast Guard Housing Fund 522
- Contribution for Annuity Benefits, United States Secret Service 527
- Countering Weapons of Mass Destruction Office 552
- Cybersecurity and Infrastructure Security Agency 530
- Cybersecurity Response and Recovery Fund 532
- Disaster Assistance Direct Loan Financing Account 543
- Disaster Assistance Direct Loan Program Account 542
- Disaster Relief Fund 537
- Electronic System for Travel Authorization 510
- Electronic Visa Update System 510
- Emergency Food and Shelter 542
- Enhanced Inspectional Services 508
- Environmental Compliance and Restoration 519
- Federal Assistance 498
- Federal Assistance 533
- Federal Assistance 546
- Federal Assistance 554
- Federal Emergency Management Agency 533
- Federal Law Enforcement Training Center 549
- Federal Protective Service 500
- Flood Hazard Mapping and Risk Analysis Program 539
- General and Administrative Provisions 555
- General Fund Receipt Accounts 555
- General Gift Fund 525
- General Provisions 556
- Gifts and Donations (Office of the Secretary and Executive Management) 498
- H-1B and L Fraud Prevention and Detection Account 548
- H-1B Nonimmigrant Petitioner Account 547
- Immigration Examinations Fee 546
- Infrastructure Protection and Information Security 531
- Intelligence and Vetting 516
- International Registered Traveler 509
- Management Directorate 498
- Maritime Oil Spill Programs 526
- Medicare-Eligible Retiree Health Fund Contribution, Homeland Security 521
- National Flood Insurance Fund 539
- National Flood Insurance Reserve Fund 541
- National Pre-disaster Mitigation Fund 542
- Office of Biometric Identity Management 501
- Office of Health Affairs 533
- Office of the Inspector General 503
- Office of the Secretary and Executive Management 497
- Oil Spill Liability Trust Fund 525
- Operations and Support 497
- Operations and Support 498
- Operations and Support 502
- Operations and Support 503
- Operations and Support 504
- Operations and Support 512
- Operations and Support 515
- Operations and Support 518
- Operations and Support 526
- Operations and Support 530
- Operations and Support 533
- Operations and Support 536
- Operations and Support 545
- Operations and Support 549
- Operations and Support 550
- Operations and Support 552
- Payments to Wool Manufacturers 509
- Procurement, Construction and Improvements 554
- Procurement, Construction, and Improvements 499
- Procurement, Construction, and Improvements 507

INDEX

Homeland Security, Department of—Continued

Entry	Page
Procurement, Construction, and Improvements	514
Procurement, Construction, and Improvements	517
Procurement, Construction, and Improvements	519
Procurement, Construction, and Improvements	528
Procurement, Construction, and Improvements	531
Procurement, Construction, and Improvements	543
Procurement, Construction, and Improvements	545
Procurement, Construction, and Improvements	550
Procurement, Construction, and Improvements	551
Radiological Emergency Preparedness Program	537
Refunds, Transfers, and Expenses of Operation, Puerto Rico	508
Research and Development	518
Research and Development	521
Research and Development	528
Research and Development	532
Research and Development	552
Research and Development	553
Reserve Training	519
Retired Pay	522
Science and Technology	550
State and Local Programs	537
Supply Fund	523
Surface Transportation Security	516
Transportation Security Administration	515
Transportation Security Support	517
Trust Fund Share of Expenses	524
U.S. Customs and Border Protection	504
U.S. Customs Refunds, Transfers and Expenses, Unclaimed and Abandoned Goods	512
U.S. Immigration and Customs Enforcement	512
United States Coast Guard	518
United States Secret Service	526
Working Capital Fund (Management Directorate)	501
Yard Fund	523
Homeless Assistance Grants	575
Homeowner Assistance Fund	991
Homeowners Assistance Fund	304
Hope Reserve Fund	1007
Host Country Resident Contractors Separation Liability Fund	865
Host Nation Support Fund for Relocation	315
House Historic Buildings Revitalization Trust Fund	20
House of Representatives	12
House Office Buildings Fund	20
House Office Buildings	19
Housing and Other Credit Guaranty Programs Liquidating Account	863

Housing and Urban Development, Department of:

Entry	Page
Administrative Support Offices	603
Brownfields Redevelopment	578
Choice Neighborhoods Initiative	564
Community Development Fund	571
Community Development Loan Guarantees Financing Account	573
Community Development Loan Guarantees Liquidating Account	574
Community Development Loan Guarantees Program Account	573
Community Planning and Development	571
Community Planning and Development	605
Emergency Homeowners' Relief Financing Account	590
Emergency Homeowners' Relief Fund	590
Executive Offices	602
Fair Housing Activities	600
Fair Housing and Equal Opportunity	600
Fair Housing and Equal Opportunity	605
FHA-General and Special Risk Direct Loan Financing Account	592
FHA-General and Special Risk Guaranteed Loan Financing Account	591
FHA-General and Special Risk Insurance Funds Liquidating Account	593
FHA-General and Special Risk Program Account	590

Housing and Urban Development, Department of—Continued

Entry	Page
FHA-Loan Guarantee Recovery Fund Financing Account	594
FHA-Mutual Mortgage and Cooperative Housing Insurance Funds Liquidating Account	588
FHA-Mutual Mortgage Insurance Capital Reserve Account	588
FHA-Mutual Mortgage Insurance Guaranteed Loan Financing Account	587
FHA-Mutual Mortgage Insurance Program Account	586
Flexible Subsidy Fund	583
General and Administrative Provisions	608
General Fund Receipt Accounts	608
General Provisions—Department of Housing and Urban Development	608
Government National Mortgage Association	596
Green and Resilient Retrofit Program for Multifamily Housing, Financing Account	585
Green and Resilient Retrofit Program for Multifamily Housing	584
Green Retrofit Program for Multifamily Housing Financing Account	583
Green Retrofit Program for Multifamily Housing, Recovery Act	583
Guarantees of Mortgage-backed Securities Capital Reserve Account	596
Guarantees of Mortgage-backed Securities Financing Account	598
Guarantees of Mortgage-backed Securities Liquidating Account	599
Guarantees of Mortgage-backed Securities Loan Guarantee Program Account	597
Guarantees of Mortgage-Backed Securities Pass-Through Assistance	596
Home Investment Partnership Program	574
Home Ownership Preservation Equity Fund Financing Account	589
Home Ownership Preservation Equity Fund Program Account	589
Homeless Assistance Grants	575
Housing Certificate Fund	561
Housing Counseling Assistance	585
Housing for Persons with Disabilities	581
Housing for the Elderly or Handicapped Fund Liquidating Account	594
Housing for the Elderly	581
Housing Opportunities for Persons with AIDS	576
Housing Programs	579
Housing Supply Fund	596
Housing Supply	596
Housing Trust Fund	579
Housing	605
Indian Housing Loan Guarantee Fund Financing Account	569
Indian Housing Loan Guarantee Fund Program Account	568
Information Technology Fund	606
Lead Hazard Reduction	601
Management and Administration	602
Manufactured Housing Fees Trust Fund	595
Native American Programs	566
Native Hawaiian Housing Block Grant	568
Native Hawaiian Housing Loan Guarantee Fund Financing Account	571
Native Hawaiian Housing Loan Guarantee Fund Program Account	570
Neighborhood Stabilization Program	577
Office of Inspector General (Management and Administration)	606
Office of Lead Hazard Control and Healthy Homes	601
Other Assisted Housing Programs	582
Payment to Manufactured Housing Fees Trust Fund	595
Permanent Supportive Housing	578
Policy Development and Research	599
Program Offices	604
Project-based Rental Assistance	579
Public and Indian Housing Programs	559

	Page
Housing and Urban Development, Department of—Continued	
Public and Indian Housing	604
Public Housing Capital Fund	562
Public Housing Fund	563
Public Housing Operating Fund	562
Rental Housing Assistance Fund	582
Research and Technology	599
Revitalization of Severely Distressed Public Housing (HOPE VI)	565
Revolving Fund (liquidating Programs)	578
Rural Housing and Economic Development	578
Salaries and Expenses (Management and Administration)	605
Self-help and Assisted Homeownership Opportunity Program	577
Self-Sufficiency Programs	565
Tenant Based Rental Assistance	559
Title VI Indian Federal Guarantees Financing Account	567
Transformation Initiative	608
Working Capital Fund (Management and Administration)	607
Housing Certificate Fund	561
Housing Counseling Assistance	585
Housing Direct Loan Financing Account	1058
Housing for Persons with Disabilities	581
Housing for the Elderly or Handicapped Fund Liquidating Account	594
Housing for the Elderly	581
Housing Guaranteed Loan Financing Account	1059
Housing Liquidating Account	1060
Housing Opportunities for Persons with AIDS	576
Housing Programs	579
Housing Supply Fund	596
Housing Supply	596
Housing Trust Fund	579
Housing	605
Howard University	341

I

	Page
Immigration Examinations Fee	546
Impact Aid	328
Independent Counsel	729
Indian Direct Loan Financing Account	679
Indian Education Scholarship Holding Fund	686
Indian Education	331
Indian Guaranteed Loan Financing Account	680
Indian Guaranteed Loan Program Account	679
Indian Health Facilities	436
Indian Health Service	433
Indian Health Services	433
Indian Housing Loan Guarantee Fund Financing Account	569
Indian Housing Loan Guarantee Fund Program Account	568
Indian Irrigation Fund	675
Indian Land and Water Claim Settlements and Miscellaneous Payments to Indians	675
Indian Land Consolidation	677
Indian Loan Guaranty and Insurance Fund Liquidating Account	681
Indian Water Rights and Habitat Acquisition Program	677
Indian Water Rights Settlement Completion Fund	676
Industrial Technology Services	217
Infectious Diseases Rapid Response Reserve Fund	441
Informant Payments	1030
Information Technology Fund	606
Information Technology Oversight and Reform	1142
Information Technology Systems	1071
Infrastructure Protection and Information Security	531
Inland Oil Spill Programs	1128
Inland Waterways Trust Fund	1092
Innovation and Improvement	332
Inspector General	1249
Inspectors General Council Fund	1233
Institute of American Indian and Alaska Native Culture and Arts Development:	
Payment to the Institute	1275
Institute of Education Sciences	360, 360

	Page
Institute of Museum and Library Services:	
Office of Museum and Library Services: Grants and Administration	1275
Insular Affairs	692
Integrated Activities	78
Intellectual Property Enforcement Coordinator	1141
Intelligence and Vetting	516
Intelligence Community Management Account:	
Inter-American Foundation	866, 866
Interagency America the Beautiful Pass Revenues	1091
Interagency Law Enforcement	735
Intercity Passenger Rail Grant Program	944
Interest on the Public Debt	1033
Interest on Treasury Debt Securities (gross)	1033
Interest on Uninvested Funds	1008
Interest Paid to Credit Financing Accounts	1009
Interior Franchise Fund	704
Interior, Department of the:	
Abandoned Mine Reclamation Fund	630
Abandoned Well Remediation Fund	617
Aging Infrastructure Account	636
Assistance to American Samoa Direct Loan Financing Account	694
Assistance to Territories	693
Blackfeet Water Settlement Implementation Fund	637
Bureau of Indian Affairs	670
Bureau of Indian Education	682
Bureau of Land Management	615
Bureau of Ocean Energy Management	625
Bureau of Reclamation Direct Loan Financing Account	642
Bureau of Reclamation Loan Liquidating Account	642
Bureau of Reclamation Loan Program Account	642
Bureau of Reclamation	632
Bureau of Safety and Environmental Enforcement	627
Bureau of Trust Funds Administration	684
California Bay-Delta Restoration	635
Centennial Challenge	662
Central Hazardous Materials Fund	698
Central Utah Project Completion Account	643
Central Utah Project	643
Central Valley Project Restoration Fund	638
Coastal Impact Assistance	658
Colorado River Dam Fund, Boulder Canyon Project	639
Compact of Free Association	692
Construction (and Major Maintenance) (National Park Service)	664
Construction (trust Fund) (National Park Service)	669
Construction (Bureau of Indian Affairs)	673
Construction (United States Fish and Wildlife Service)	650
Contract Support Costs	672
Contributed Funds	647
Contributed Funds	660
Cooperative Endangered Species Conservation Fund	655
Department-Wide Programs	697
Departmental Offices	687
Education Construction	683
Energy Community Revitalization Program	705
Environmental Improvement and Restoration Fund	691
Federal Aid in Wildlife Restoration	657
Federal Trust Programs	684
FLAME Wildfire Suppression Reserve Fund	702
General and Administrative Provisions	707
General Fund Receipt Accounts	707
General Provisions	707
Geothermal Lease Revenues, Payment to Counties	690
Gifts and Donations, Bureau of Indian Affairs (Bureau of Indian Affairs)	682
Helium Fund	623
High-Hazard Indian Dam Safety Deferred Maintenance Fund	674
Historic Preservation Fund	667
Indian Direct Loan Financing Account	679
Indian Education Scholarship Holding Fund	686

INDEX

Interior, Department of the—Continued
- Indian Guaranteed Loan Financing Account 680
- Indian Guaranteed Loan Program Account 679
- Indian Irrigation Fund 675
- Indian Land and Water Claim Settlements and Miscellaneous Payments to Indians 675
- Indian Land Consolidation 677
- Indian Loan Guaranty and Insurance Fund Liquidating Account 681
- Indian Water Rights and Habitat Acquisition Program ... 677
- Indian Water Rights Settlement Completion Fund 676
- Insular Affairs 692
- Interior Franchise Fund 704
- Land Acquisition and State Assistance 665
- Land Acquisition 618
- Land Acquisition 652
- Land and Water Conservation Fund 691
- Landowner Incentive Program 653
- Leases of Lands Acquired for Flood Control, Navigation, and Allied Purposes 689
- Low-Hazard Indian Dam Safety Deferred Maintenance Fund 674
- Lower Colorado River Basin Development Fund 640
- Management of Lands and Resources 615
- Migratory Bird Conservation Account 653
- Mineral Leasing and Associated Payments 688
- Miscellaneous Permanent Appropriations 658
- Miscellaneous Permanent Appropriations 678
- Miscellaneous Permanent Payment Accounts 622
- Miscellaneous Trust Funds 624
- Miscellaneous Trust Funds 669
- Multinational Species Conservation Fund 651
- National Forests Fund, Payment to States 690
- National Indian Gaming Commission, Gaming Activity Fees 696
- National Indian Gaming Commission 696
- National Park Medical Services Fund 666
- National Park Service 661
- National Parks and Public Land Legacy Restoration Fund 705
- National Petroleum Reserve, Alaska 689
- National Recreation and Preservation 663
- National Wildlife Refuge Fund 656
- Natural Resource Damage Assessment Fund 699
- Neotropical Migratory Bird Conservation 652
- North American Wetlands Conservation Fund 654
- Ocean Energy Management 625
- Office of Inspector General 695
- Office of Natural Resources Revenue 697
- Office of Surface Mining Reclamation and Enforcement 629
- Office of the Solicitor 695
- Offshore Safety and Environmental Enforcement 627
- Oil Spill Research 628
- Operation and Maintenance of Quarters 677
- Operation of Indian Education Programs 682
- Operation of Indian Programs 670
- Operation of the National Park System 661
- Oregon and California Grant Lands 616
- Other Permanent Appropriations 668
- Payment to Alaska, Arctic National Wildlife Refuge 689
- Payments for Tribal Leases 673
- Payments in Lieu of Taxes 698
- Payments to States in Lieu of Coal Fee Receipts 631
- Payments to the United States Territories, Fiscal Assistance 693
- Permanent Operating Funds 620
- Policy and Administration 637
- Range Improvements 618
- Reclamation Fund 637
- Reclamation Trust Funds 643
- Reclamation Water Settlements Fund 636
- Recreation Enhancement Fee Program, FWS 656
- Recreation Fee Permanent Appropriations 666
- Regulation and Technology 629
- Resource Management 648
- Revolving Fund for Loans Liquidating Account 679

Interior, Department of the—Continued
- Salaries and Expenses (Departmental Offices) 687
- Salaries and Expenses (National Indian Gaming Commission) 696
- Salaries and Expenses (Office of Inspector General) 695
- Salaries and Expenses (Office of the Solicitor) 695
- San Joaquin Restoration Fund 639
- Selis-Qlispe Ksanka Settlement Trust Fund 681
- Service Charges, Deposits, and Forfeitures 619
- Sport Fish Restoration 659
- State Wildlife Grants 651
- States Share from Certain Gulf of Mexico Leases 691
- Supplemental Payments to UMWA Plans 632
- Surveys, Investigations, and Research 645
- Taos Settlement Fund 635
- Tribal Special Fund 685
- Tribal Trust Fund 686
- Trust Land Consolidation Fund 686
- Trust Territory of the Pacific Islands 692
- United States Fish and Wildlife Service 648
- United States Geological Survey 645
- Upper Colorado River Basin Fund 641
- Urban Park and Recreation Fund 664
- Utah Reclamation Mitigation and Conservation Account 644
- Visitor Experience Improvements Fund 662
- Water and Related Resources 632
- White Earth Settlement Fund 675
- Wildfire Suppression Operations Reserve Fund 702
- Wildland Fire Management 700
- Working Capital Fund (Bureau of Land Management) ... 624
- Working Capital Fund (Bureau of Reclamation) 641
- Working Capital Fund (Department-Wide Programs) 703
- Working Capital Fund (United States Geological Survey) 647

Intermediary Relending Program Fund Account 141
Internal Revenue Collections for Puerto Rico 1014
Internal Revenue Service 1016
International Affairs Technical Assistance Program 841

International Assistance Programs:
- African Development Foundation 867
- Agency for International Development 843
- Assistance for Eastern Europe and the Baltic States 845
- Assistance for Europe, Eurasia and Central Asia 844
- Assistance for the Independent States of the Former Soviet Union 845
- Capital Investment Fund of the United States Agency for International Development 847
- Central America and Caribbean Emergency Disaster Recovery Fund 828
- Child Survival and Health Programs 843
- Clean Technology Fund Loans Financing Account 835
- Clean Technology Fund Program Account 834
- Conflict Stabilization Operations 849
- Contribution to Enterprise for the Americas Multilateral Investment Fund 840
- Contribution to Multilateral Investment Guarantee Agency 838
- Contribution to the African Development Bank 839
- Contribution to the Asian Development Bank 838
- Contribution to the European Bank for Reconstruction and Development 840
- Contribution to the Green Climate Fund 835
- Contribution to the Inter-American Development Bank 838
- Contribution to the International Bank for Reconstruction and Development 836
- Contribution to the International Development Association 837
- Contribution to the North American Development Bank 840
- Contributions to IMF Facilities and Trust Funds Financing Account 870
- Contributions to IMF Facilities and Trust Funds 869
- Contributions to the International Fund for Agricultural Development 840
- Debt Reduction Financing Account 862
- Debt Restructuring 842

	Page
International Assistance Programs—Continued	
Development Assistance Program	843
Development Credit Authority Guaranteed Loan Financing Account	853
Development Credit Authority Program Account	853
Development Fund for Africa	844
Economic Assistance Loans Liquidating Account	853
Economic Assistance Loans Liquidating Account	864
Economic Support Fund	827
Foreign Currency Fluctuations	865
Foreign Military Financing Direct Loan Financing Account	832
Foreign Military Financing Guaranteed Loan Financing Account	833
Foreign Military Financing Loan Program Account	832
Foreign Military Financing Program	828
Foreign Military Loan Liquidating Account	833
Foreign Military Sales Trust Fund	871
Foreign Service National Separation Liability Trust Fund	853
General and Administrative Provisions	872
General Fund Receipt Accounts	872
General Provisions	872
Gifts and Donations, African Development Foundation (African Development Foundation)	868
Global Agriculture and Food Security Program	835
Global Security Contingency Fund	831
HIV/AIDS Working Capital Fund	844
Host Country Resident Contractors Separation Liability Fund	865
Housing and Other Credit Guaranty Programs Liquidating Account	863
Inter-American Foundation	866
International Affairs Technical Assistance Program	841
International Disaster Assistance	846
International Military Education and Training	829
International Monetary Programs	868
International Organizations and Programs	841
International Security Assistance	827
Loan Guarantees to Israel Financing Account	851
Loan Guarantees to Israel Program Account	851
Loans to International Monetary Fund	869
MENA Loan Guarantee Financing Account	852
MENA Loan Guarantee Program Account	852
Microenterprise and Small Enterprise Development Guaranteed Loan Financing Account	862
Microenterprise and Small Enterprise Development Program Account	862
Military Debt Reduction Financing Account	834
Military Sales Program	870
Millennium Challenge Corporation	826
Miscellaneous Trust Funds, AID	854
Multilateral Assistance	834
Nonproliferation, Antiterrorism, Demining, and Related Programs	830
Operating Expenses of the Agency for International Development (Agency for International Development)	846
Operating Expenses, Office of Inspector General (Agency for International Development)	849
Overseas Private Investment Corporation Guaranteed Loan Financing Account	855
Overseas Private Investment Corporation Noncredit Account	854
Overseas Private Investment Corporation Program Account	854
Overseas Private Investment Corporation	854
Pakistan Counterinsurgency Capability Fund	829
Peace Corps Miscellaneous Trust Fund	866
Peace Corps	864
Peacekeeping Operations	830
Property Management Fund	849
Special Defense Acquisition Fund	870
Trade and Development Agency	855
Transition Initiatives	848
U.S. International Development Finance Corporation Insurance of Debt Financing Account	861

	Page
International Assistance Programs—Continued	
U.S. International Development Finance Corporation Insurance of Debt Program Account	856
Ukraine Loan Guarantee Financing Account	872
Ukraine Loan Guarantee Program Account	872
Ukraine Loan Guarantees Financing Account	850
Ukraine Loan Guarantees Program Account	849
United States International Development Finance Corporation Corporate Capital Account	856
United States International Development Finance Corporation Direct Loan Financing Account	860
United States International Development Finance Corporation Guaranteed Loan Financing Account	859
United States International Development Finance Corporation Inspector General	858
United States International Development Finance Corporation Program Account	857
United States International Development Finance Corporation	856
United States Quota, International Monetary Fund	868
Urban and Environmental Credit Guaranteed Loan Financing Account	861
Urban and Environmental Credit Program Account	861
Working Capital Fund (Agency for International Development)	850
International Broadcasting Operations	1333
International Center, Washington, D.C.	824
International Commissions	814
International Disaster Assistance	846
International Fisheries Commissions	816
International Information Programs	802
International Litigation Fund	824
International Military Education and Training	829
International Monetary Programs	868
International Narcotics Control and Law Enforcement	821
International Organizations and Conferences	813
International Organizations and Programs	841
International Reconstruction and Other Assistance	268
International Registered Traveler	509
International Security Assistance	827
International Trade Administration	200
International Trade Commission:	
Salaries and Expenses	1277
Investigations	1085
Investor Protection Fund	1323
Iraq Relief and Reconstruction Fund, Army	268
Iraq Train and Equip Fund	263
IRS Miscellaneous Retained Fees	1029
Isotope Production and Distribution Program Fund	400
Israeli Arab and Eisenhower Exchange Fellowship Programs	825
IT Modernization	794

J

	Page
James Madison Memorial Fellowship Foundation:	
James Madison Memorial Fellowship Trust Fund	1278
James Madison Memorial Fellowship Trust Fund	1278
Japan-United States Friendship Commission:	
Japan-United States Friendship Trust Fund	1279
Japan-United States Friendship Trust Fund	1279
Job Access and Reverse Commute Grants	950
Job Corps	763
John C. Stennis Center for Public Service Training and Development	44
Joint Department of Defense-Department of Veterans Affairs Medical Facility Demonstration Fund	1045
Joint Improvised-Threat Defeat Fund	273
Joint Items	13
Judicial Branch:	
Administrative Office of the United States Courts	56
Administrative Provisions—the Judiciary	60
Care of the Building and Grounds	49
Chapter 7 Trustee Fund	57
Court Security	54

INDEX

	Page
Judicial Branch—Continued	
Courts of Appeals, District Courts, and Other Judicial Services	51
Defender Services	53
Federal Judicial Center	57
Fees of Jurors and Commissioners	54
General and Administrative Provisions	60
General Fund Receipt Accounts	60
Judicial Officers' Retirement Fund	58
Judicial Retirement Funds	58
Judicial Survivors' Annuities Fund	59
Judiciary Filing Fees	55
Judiciary Information Technology Fund	56
Payment to Judiciary Trust Funds	58
Registry Administration	55
Salaries and Expenses (Administrative Office of the United States Courts)	56
Salaries and Expenses (Courts of Appeals, District Courts, and Other Judicial Services)	51
Salaries and Expenses (Federal Judicial Center)	57
Salaries and Expenses (Supreme Court of the United States)	49
Salaries and Expenses (United States Court of Appeals for the Federal Circuit)	50
Salaries and Expenses (United States Court of International Trade)	51
Salaries and Expenses (United States Sentencing Commission)	60
Supreme Court of the United States	49
United States Court of Appeals for the Federal Circuit	50
United States Court of Federal Claims Judges' Retirement Fund	59
United States Court of International Trade	51
United States Sentencing Commission	60
Judicial Officers' Retirement Fund	58
Judicial Retirement Funds	58
Judicial Survivors' Annuities Fund	59
Judiciary Filing Fees	55
Judiciary Information Technology Fund	56
Judiciary Office Building Development and Operations Fund	23
Justice Information Sharing Technology	715
Justice Prisoner and Alien Transportation System Fund, U.S. Marshals	733
Justice, Department of:	
Assets Forfeiture Fund	732
Buildings and Facilities (Federal Prison System)	744
Bureau of Alcohol, Tobacco, Firearms, and Explosives	741
Commissary Funds, Federal Prisons (Trust Revolving Fund)	746
Community Oriented Policing Services	751
Construction (Drug Enforcement Administration)	740
Construction (Federal Bureau of Investigation)	738
Construction (Legal Activities and U.S. Marshals)	726
Crime Victims Fund	757
Diversion Control Fee Account	740
Domestic Trafficking Victims' Fund	758
Drug Enforcement Administration	738
Executive Office for Immigration Review	717
Federal Bureau of Investigation	736
Federal Prison Industries, Incorporated	744
Federal Prison System	742
Federal Prisoner Detention	727
Fees and Expenses of Witnesses	728
General Administration	715
General and Administrative Provisions	758
General Fund Receipt Accounts	758
General Provisions—Department of Justice	759
Gun Crime Prevention Strategic Fund	753
Independent Counsel	729
Interagency Law Enforcement	735
Justice Information Sharing Technology	715
Justice Prisoner and Alien Transportation System Fund, U.S. Marshals	733
Juvenile Justice Programs	755
Legal Activities and U.S. Marshals	721
National Security Division	734

	Page
Justice, Department of—Continued	
Office of Inspector General (General Administration)	718
Office of Justice Programs	746
Organized Crime and Drug Enforcement Task Forces	735
Payment to Radiation Exposure Compensation Trust Fund	735
Public Safety Officer Benefits	756
Radiation Exposure Compensation Trust Fund	735
Radiation Exposure Compensation	735
Research, Evaluation, and Statistics	746
Salaries and Expenses, Antitrust Division (Legal Activities and U.S. Marshals)	723
Salaries and Expenses, Community Relations Service (Legal Activities and U.S. Marshals)	729
Salaries and Expenses, Foreign Claims Settlement Commission (Legal Activities and U.S. Marshals)	725
Salaries and Expenses, General Legal Activities (Legal Activities and U.S. Marshals)	721
Salaries and Expenses, United States Attorneys (Legal Activities and U.S. Marshals)	724
Salaries and Expenses, United States Marshals Service (Legal Activities and U.S. Marshals)	725
Salaries and Expenses (Bureau of Alcohol, Tobacco, Firearms, and Explosives)	741
Salaries and Expenses (Drug Enforcement Administration)	738
Salaries and Expenses (Federal Bureau of Investigation)	736
Salaries and Expenses (Federal Prison System)	742
Salaries and Expenses (General Administration)	715
Salaries and Expenses (National Security Division)	734
Salaries and Expenses (United States Parole Commission)	720
State and Local Law Enforcement Assistance	747
Tactical Law Enforcement Wireless Communications	716
United States Parole Commission	720
United States Trustee System Fund	731
United States Victims of State Sponsored Terrorism Fund	730
Victims Compensation Fund	730
Violence against Women Prevention and Prosecution Programs	753
Working Capital Fund (General Administration)	719
Juvenile Justice Programs	755

L

	Page
Labor, Department of:	
Administrative Expenses, Energy Employees Occupational Illness Compensation Fund	778
Advances to the Unemployment Trust Fund and Other Funds	768
Black Lung Disability Trust Fund	780
Bureau of Labor Statistics	788
Community Service Employment for Older Americans	764
Departmental Management	789
Employee Benefits Security Administration	772
Employment and Training Administration	761
Energy Employees Occupational Illness Compensation Fund	778
Federal Additional Unemployment Compensation Program, Recovery	768
Federal Unemployment Benefits and Allowances	764
Foreign Labor Certification Processing	770
General and Administrative Provisions	796
General Fund Receipt Accounts	796
General Provisions	796
H-1 B and L Fraud Prevention and Detection	783
IT Modernization	794
Job Corps	763
Mine Safety and Health Administration	787
Occupational Safety and Health Administration	785
Office of Disability Employment Policy	791
Office of Federal Contract Compliance Programs	783
Office of Inspector General (Departmental Management)	792
Office of Labor Management Standards	784
Office of Workers' Compensation Programs	776
Panama Canal Commission Compensation Fund	779
Payments to the Unemployment Trust Fund	767
Pension Benefit Guaranty Corporation Fund	774
Pension Benefit Guaranty Corporation	774

	Page
Labor, Department of—Continued	
Program Administration	769
Salaries and Expenses (Bureau of Labor Statistics)	788
Salaries and Expenses (Departmental Management)	789
Salaries and Expenses (Employee Benefits Security Administration)	772
Salaries and Expenses (Mine Safety and Health Administration)	787
Salaries and Expenses (Occupational Safety and Health Administration)	785
Salaries and Expenses (Office of Federal Contract Compliance Programs)	783
Salaries and Expenses (Office of Labor Management Standards)	784
Salaries and Expenses (Office of Workers' Compensation Programs)	776
Salaries and Expenses (Wage and Hour Division)	782
Short Time Compensation Programs	767
Special Benefits for Disabled Coal Miners	779
Special Benefits	777
Special Workers' Compensation Expenses	781
State Unemployment Insurance and Employment Service Operations	765
Training and Employment Services	761
Unemployment Trust Fund	770
Veterans Employment and Training	792
Wage and Hour Division	782
Working Capital Fund (Departmental Management)	794
Land Acquisition and State Assistance	665
Land Acquisition	180, 618, 652
Land and Water Conservation Fund	691
Landowner Incentive Program	653
Lead Hazard Reduction	601
Leaking Underground Storage Tank Trust Fund	1127
Lease of Department of Defense Real Property	266
Leases of Lands Acquired for Flood Control, Navigation, and Allied Purposes	689
Legal Activities and U.S. Marshals	721
Legal Services Corporation:	
Payment to the Legal Services Corporation	1279
Legislative Branch Boards and Commissions	38
Legislative Branch:	
Architect of the Capitol	17
Awards and Settlements Funds	16
Botanic Garden	24
Capital Construction, Dwight D. Eisenhower Memorial Commission	41
Capitol Building	17
Capitol Construction and Operations	17
Capitol Grounds	18
Capitol Police Buildings, Grounds, and Security	21
Capitol Police	14
Capitol Power Plant	20
Capitol Visitor Center Revolving Fund	22
Capitol Visitor Center	22
Congressional Budget Office	16
Congressional Publishing	32
Congressional Research Service, Salaries and Expenses	27
Cooperative Acquisitions Program Revolving Fund	29
Copyright Office, Salaries and Expenses	26
Duplication Services	29
Dwight D. Eisenhower Memorial Commission	41
Dwight D. Eisenhower Memorial Fund	42
Fedlink Program and Federal Research Program	30
General and Administrative Provisions	45
General Expenses	14
General Fund Receipt Accounts	45
General Provisions	45
Gift and Trust Fund Accounts	31
Gift Shop, Decimal Classification, Photo Duplication, and Related Services	30
Gifts and Donations (Botanic Garden)	24

	Page
Legislative Branch—Continued	
Government Accountability Office	35
Government Publishing Office Business Operations Revolving Fund	34
Government Publishing Office	32
House Historic Buildings Revitalization Trust Fund	20
House of Representatives	12
House Office Buildings Fund	20
House Office Buildings	19
John C. Stennis Center for Public Service Training and Development	44
Joint Items	13
Judiciary Office Building Development and Operations Fund	23
Legislative Branch Boards and Commissions	38
Library Buildings and Grounds	21
Library of Congress National Collection Stewardship Fund	26
Library of Congress	24
Medicaid and CHIP Payment and Access Commission	38
Medicare Payment Advisory Commission	38
National Library Service For The Blind And Print Disabled	28
Office of Congressional Workplace Rights	15
Open World Leadership Center Trust Fund	42
Open World Leadership Center Trust Fund	44
Other Legislative Branch Boards and Commissions	43
Payments to Copyright Owners	29
Public Information Programs of the Superintendent of Documents, Salaries and Expenses	33
Recyclable Materials Revolving Fund	23
Salaries and Expenses, Library of Congress (Library of Congress)	24
Salaries and Expenses (Congressional Budget Office)	16
Salaries and Expenses (Government Accountability Office)	35
Salaries and Expenses (House of Representatives)	12
Salaries and Expenses (Office of Congressional Workplace Rights)	15
Salaries and Expenses (United States Tax Court)	36
Salaries	14
Security Enhancements	15
Senate Office Buildings	18
Senate	11
Tax Court Judges Survivors Annuity Fund	37
U. S. Tax Court Fees	37
U.S. Capitol Preservation Commission	44
United States Capitol Police Mutual Aid Reimbursements	15
United States Commission on International Religious Freedom	39
United States Semiquincentennial Commission	41
United States Tax Court	36
United States-China Economic and Security Review Commission	39
World War I Centennial Commission	40
Library Buildings and Grounds	21
Library of Congress National Collection Stewardship Fund	26
Library of Congress	24
Limitation on Administration	1317
Limitation on Administrative Expenses	1211, 1254
Limited Access System Administration Fund	207
Loan Guarantees to Israel Financing Account	851
Loan Guarantees to Israel Program Account	851
Loans to International Monetary Fund	869
Low Income Home Energy Assistance	469
Low-Hazard Indian Dam Safety Deferred Maintenance Fund	674
Lower Colorado River Basin Development Fund	640

M

	Page
Magnetic Levitation Technology Deployment Program	941
Major Research Equipment and Facilities Construction	1174
Management and Administration	602
Management Directorate	498
Management Fund, Office of Environmental Quality	1134
Management of Lands and Resources	615
Management of National Forest Lands for Subsistence Uses	174
Manufactured Housing Fees Trust Fund	595

INDEX

	Page
Marine Mammal Commission:	
Salaries and Expenses	1280
Maritime Administration	964
Maritime Guaranteed Loan (Title XI) FFB Financing Account	970
Maritime Guaranteed Loan (Title XI) Financing Account	972
Maritime Guaranteed Loan (Title XI) Program Account	970
Maritime Oil Spill Programs	526
Maritime Security Program	967
Marketing Services	88
Maternal, Infant, and Early Childhood Home Visiting Programs	431
McGovern-Dole International Food for Education and Child Nutrition Program	159
Medicaid and CHIP Payment and Access Commission	38
Medical and Prosthetic Research	1044
Medical Care Collections Fund	1046
Medical Center Research Organizations:	
Medical Community Care	1040
Medical Facilities Guarantee and Loan Fund	432
Medical Facilities	1042
Medical Services	1037
Medical Support and Compliance	1041
Medicare Health Information Technology Incentive Payments, Recovery Act	457
Medicare Hearings and Appeals	482
Medicare Investments	462
Medicare Payment Advisory Commission	38
Medicare Prescription Drug Account, Federal Supplementary Insurance Trust Fund	467
Medicare-Eligible Retiree Health Fund Contribution, Air Force	236
Medicare-Eligible Retiree Health Fund Contribution, Army	233
Medicare-Eligible Retiree Health Fund Contribution, Homeland Security	521
Medicare-Eligible Retiree Health Fund Contribution, Marine Corps	235
Medicare-Eligible Retiree Health Fund Contribution, National Guard Personnel, Air Force	242
Medicare-Eligible Retiree Health Fund Contribution, National Guard Personnel, Army	241
Medicare-Eligible Retiree Health Fund Contribution, Navy	234
Medicare-Eligible Retiree Health Fund Contribution, NOAA	208
Medicare-Eligible Retiree Health Fund Contribution, Reserve Personnel, Air Force	240
Medicare-Eligible Retiree Health Fund Contribution, Reserve Personnel, Army	237
Medicare-Eligible Retiree Health Fund Contribution, Reserve Personnel, Marine Corps	239
Medicare-Eligible Retiree Health Fund Contribution, Reserve Personnel, Navy	238
Medicare-Eligible Retiree Health Fund Contribution, Space Force	237
MENA Loan Guarantee Financing Account	852
MENA Loan Guarantee Program Account	852
Mental Health Parity Enforcement Grants	462
Mental Health Transformation Fund	485
Merit Systems Protection Board:	
Salaries and Expenses	1281
Microenterprise and Small Enterprise Development Guaranteed Loan Financing Account	862
Microenterprise and Small Enterprise Development Program Account	862
Middle Mile Deployment	222
Migration and Refugee Assistance	819
Migratory Bird Conservation Account	653
Military Compensation and Retirement Modernization Commission:	
Military Construction, Air Force Reserve	297
Military Construction, Air Force	293
Military Construction, Air National Guard	296
Military Construction, Army National Guard	295
Military Construction, Army Reserve	296
Military Construction, Army	292
Military Construction, Defense-wide	294
Military Construction, Navy and Marine Corps	293

	Page
Military Construction, Navy Reserve	297
Military Construction	292
Military Debt Reduction Financing Account	834
Military Personnel, Air Force	235
Military Personnel, Army	232
Military Personnel, Marine Corps	234
Military Personnel, Navy	233
Military Personnel, Space Force	236
Military Personnel	231
Military Retirement Fund	1097
Military Retirement	1097
Military Sales Program	870
Military Unaccompanied Housing Improvement Fund	306
Milk Market Orders Assessment Fund	94
Millennium Challenge Corporation	826, 826
Mine Safety and Health Administration	787
Mineral Leasing and Associated Payments	688
Minority Business Development Agency	202
Minority Business Development	202
Miscellaneous Appropriations	918
Miscellaneous Contributed Funds	76, 123
Miscellaneous Highway Trust Funds	926
Miscellaneous Permanent Appropriations	658, 678
Miscellaneous Permanent Payment Accounts	622
Miscellaneous Special Funds	265
Miscellaneous Trust Funds:	
Administration of Foreign Affairs, Department of State	813
Agency for International Development, International Assistance Programs	854
Animal and Plant Health Inspection Service, Department of Agriculture	85
Bureau of Land Management, Department of the Interior	624
Federal Highway Administration, Department of Transportation	926
Maritime Administration, Department of Transportation	973
National Park Service, Department of the Interior	669
Program Support Center, Department of Health and Human Services	490
Missile Procurement, Air Force	279
Missile Procurement, Army	269
Mississippi River and Tributaries	1083
Morris K. Udall and Stewart L. Udall Foundation:	
Environmental Dispute Resolution Fund	1282
Federal Payment to Morris K. Udall and Stewart L. Udall Foundation Trust Fund	1282
Mortgage-backed Securities	1353, 1354
Motor Carrier Safety Grants, General Fund	928
Motor Carrier Safety Grants	930
Motor Carrier Safety Operations and Programs, General Fund	929
Motor Carrier Safety Operations and Programs	931
Motor Carrier Safety	929
Multifamily Housing Revitalization Direct Loan Financing Account	127
Multifamily Housing Revitalization Program Account	126
Multilateral Assistance	834
Multinational Species Conservation Fund	651
Mutual and Self-help Housing Grants	128
Mutually Beneficial Activities	267

N

	Page
National Aeronautics and Space Administration:	
Aeronautics	1163
Construction and Environmental Compliance and Restoration	1167
Deep Space Exploration Systems	1165
General and Administrative Provisions	1172
General Fund Receipt Accounts	1172
Office of Inspector General	1169
Safety, Security and Mission Services	1166
Science, Space, and Technology Education Trust Fund	1171
Science, Technology, Engineering, and Mathematics Engagement	1166
Science	1163

	Page
National Aeronautics and Space Administration—Continued	
Space Operations	1168
Space Technology	1164
Working Capital Fund	1170
National Agricultural Statistics Service	73, 73
National Archives and Records Administration:	
National Archives Gift Fund	1286
National Archives Trust Fund	1287
National Historical Publications and Records Commission	1285
Office of the Inspector General—National Archives and Records Administration	1284
Operating Expenses	1283
Records Center Revolving Fund	1286
Repairs and Restoration	1285
National Archives Gift Fund	1286
National Archives Trust Fund	1287
National Association of Registered Agents and Brokers:	
National Capital Arts and Cultural Affairs	1222
National Capital Planning Commission:	
Salaries and Expenses	1287
National Cemetery Administration	1073
National Commission on Military Aviation Safety:	
National Commission on Military, National, and Public Service:	
National Council on Disability:	
Salaries and Expenses	1288
National Credit Union Administration:	
Central Liquidity Facility	1291
Community Development Revolving Loan Fund	1291
Credit Union Share Insurance Fund	1290
Operating Fund	1289
National Culvert Removal, Replacement, and Restoration Grant Program	895
National Defense Sealift Fund	308
National Defense Stockpile Transaction Fund	306
National Endowment for Democracy	823
National Endowment for the Arts:	
Gifts and Donations, National Endowment for the Arts	1293
Grants and Administration	1292
National Endowment for the Humanities:	
Gifts and Donations, National Endowment for the Humanities	1294
Grants and Administration	1293
National Energy Technology Laboratory Research and Development	394
National Flood Insurance Fund	539
National Flood Insurance Reserve Fund	541
National Forest System	170
National Forests Fund, Payment to States	690
National Guard and Reserve Equipment	283
National Guard Personnel, Air Force	241
National Guard Personnel, Army	240
National Highway Traffic Safety Administration	932
National Historical Publications and Records Commission	1285
National Indian Gaming Commission, Gaming Activity Fees	696
National Indian Gaming Commission	696
National Infrastructure Investments	892
National Institute of Food and Agriculture	76, 76
National Institute of Standards and Technology	216
National Institutes of Health	443, 443
National Labor Relations Board:	
Salaries and Expenses	1295
National Library Service For The Blind And Print Disabled	28
National Mediation Board:	
Salaries and Expenses	1295
National Military Cemeteries Concessions, Army	1104
National Motor Carrier Safety Program	929
National Network Grants to the National Railroad Passenger Corporation	942
National Nuclear Security Administration	367
National Oceanic and Atmospheric Administration	203
National Oilheat Research Alliance:	
National Park Medical Services Fund	666
National Park Service	661
National Parks and Public Land Legacy Restoration Fund	179, 705
National Petroleum Reserve, Alaska	689
National Pre-disaster Mitigation Fund	542
National Railroad Passenger Corporation Office of Inspector General:	
Salaries and Expenses	1296
National Railroad Retirement Investment Trust	1318
National Recreation and Preservation	663
National Science Foundation:	
Agency Operations and Award Management	1175
Donations	1177
General and Administrative Provisions	1178
General Fund Receipt Accounts	1178
Major Research Equipment and Facilities Construction	1174
Office of Inspector General	1176
Office of the National Science Board	1175
Research and Related Activities	1173
STEM Education	1176
National Sea-Based Deterrence Fund	276
National Security Commission on Artificial Intelligence:	
Expenses, National Security Commission on Artificial Intelligence	1297
National Security Council and Homeland Security Council	1134
National Security Division	734
National Security Education Trust Fund	317
National Service Life Insurance Fund	1063
National Service Trust	1230
National Space Council	1139, 1139
National Surface Transportation and Innovative Finance Bureau	890
National Technical Information Service	215
National Technical Institute for the Deaf	337
National Telecommunications and Information Administration	220
National Transportation Safety Board:	
Emergency Fund	1298
Salaries and Expenses	1297
National Wildlife Refuge Fund	656
Native American Direct Loan Financing Account	1061
Native American Programs	566
Native American Veteran Housing Loan Program Account	1061
Native Hawaiian Housing Block Grant	568
Native Hawaiian Housing Loan Guarantee Fund Financing Account	571
Native Hawaiian Housing Loan Guarantee Fund Program Account	570
Natural Gas Distribution Infrastructure Safety and Modernization Grant Program	960
Natural Resource Damage Assessment Fund	699
Natural Resources Conservation Service	115
Naval Petroleum and Oil Shale Reserves	394
Naval Reactors	367
Neighborhood Reinvestment Corporation:	
Payment to the Neighborhood Reinvestment Corporation	1298
Neighborhood Stabilization Program	577
Neotropical Migratory Bird Conservation	652
Network Construction Fund	224
Next Generation 911 Implementation Grants	934
Next Generation High-speed Rail	945
NIH Innovation, Cures Act	446
No Surprises Implementation Fund	487
Non-defense Environmental Cleanup	391
Nonproliferation, Antiterrorism, Demining, and Related Programs	830
Nonrecurring Expenses Fund	69, 191, 486
North American Wetlands Conservation Fund	654
North Atlantic Treaty Organization Security Investment Program	295
North Pacific Fishery Observer Fund	211
Northeast Corridor Grants to the National Railroad Passenger Corporation	943
Northeast Corridor Improvement Program	945
Northeast Home Heating Oil Reserve	398
Northern Border Regional Commission:	

INDEX

	Page
NTIS Revolving Fund	215
Nuclear Energy	377
Nuclear Regulatory Commission:	
General and Administrative Provisions	1301
General Fund Receipt Account	1301
Office of Inspector General	1301
Salaries and Expenses	1299
Nuclear Waste Disposal	399
Nuclear Waste Technical Review Board:	
Salaries and Expenses	1302
Nutrition Programs Administration	162

O

	Page
Occupational Safety and Health Administration	785
Occupational Safety and Health Review Commission:	
Salaries and Expenses	1302
Ocean Energy Management	625
Office for Civil Rights	362, 481
Office of Administration	1136
Office of Advocacy	1193
Office of Biometric Identity Management	501
Office of Career, Technical, and Adult Education	338
Office of Civil Rights	900
Office of Clean Energy Demonstrations	389
Office of Congressional Workplace Rights	15
Office of Disability Employment Policy	791
Office of Elementary and Secondary Education	327
Office of English Language Acquisition	334
Office of Federal Contract Compliance Programs	783
Office of Federal Student Aid	344
Office of Financial Stability	996
Office of Government Ethics:	
Salaries and Expenses	1303
Office of Health Affairs	533
Office of Indian Energy Policy and Programs	390
Office of Innovation and Improvement	332
Office of Inspector General	71, 695, 963
Office of Justice Programs	746
Office of Labor Management Standards	784
Office of Lead Hazard Control and Healthy Homes	601
Office of Management and Budget	1137
Office of Manufacturing and Energy Supply Chains	386
Office of Multimodal Freight Infrastructure and Policy	896
Office of Museum and Library Services: Grants and Administration	1275
Office of National Drug Control Policy	1137
Office of Natural Resources Revenue	697
Office of Navajo and Hopi Indian Relocation:	
Salaries and Expenses	1303
Office of Personnel Management:	
Civil Service Retirement and Disability Fund	1185
Emergency Federal Employee Leave Fund	1185
Employees and Retired Employees Health Benefits Funds	1187
Employees Life Insurance Fund	1187
Flexible Benefits Plan Reserve	1183
General and Administrative Provisions	1189
General Fund Receipt Account	1189
Government Payment for Annuitants, Employee Life Insurance	1182
Government Payment for Annuitants, Employees Health Benefits	1181
Office of Inspector General	1180
Payment to Civil Service Retirement and Disability Fund	1182
Postal Service Retiree Health Benefits Fund	1183
Revolving Fund	1184
Salaries and Expenses	1179
Office of Postsecondary Education	339
Office of Science and Technology Policy	1138, 1138
Office of Special Counsel:	
Salaries and Expenses	1304
Office of Special Education and Rehabilitative Services	334
Office of State and Community Energy Programs	387
Office of Surface Mining Reclamation and Enforcement	629
Office of Technology Transitions	388
Office of Terrorism and Financial Intelligence	978
Office of the Assistant Secretary of the Army for Civil Works	1079
Office of the Inspector General	491, 503
Office of the Inspector General:	
Administration of Foreign Affairs, Department of State	803
Agency for International Development, International Assistance Programs	849
Corporation for National and Community Service, Corporation for National and Community Service	1229
Departmental Administration, Department of Energy	418
Departmental Administration, Department of Veterans Affairs	1070
Departmental Management, Department of Commerce	192
Departmental Management, Department of Education	363
Departmental Management, Department of Labor	792
Departmental Offices, Department of the Treasury	980
Environmental Protection Agency, Environmental Protection Agency	1107
FDIC Office of Inspector General, Federal Deposit Insurance Corporation	1262
Federal Housing Finance Agency, Federal Housing Finance Agency	1267
General Activities, General Services Administration	1155
General Administration, Department of Justice	718
Management and Administration, Department of Housing and Urban Development	606
National Aeronautics and Space Administration, National Aeronautics and Space Administration	1169
National Archives and Records Administration, National Archives and Records Administration	1284
National Science Foundation, National Science Foundation	1176
Nuclear Regulatory Commission, Nuclear Regulatory Commission	1301
Office of Inspector General, Department of Agriculture	71
Office of Personnel Management, Office of Personnel Management	1180
Office of the Inspector General, Department of Health and Human Services	491
Operation and Maintenance, Department of Defense—Military Programs	249
Postal Service, Postal Service	1309
Railroad Retirement Board, Railroad Retirement Board	1315
Railroad Retirement Board, Railroad Retirement Board	1319
Small Business Administration, Small Business Administration	1193
Social Security Administration, Social Security Administration	1207
Office of the National Coordinator for Health Information Technology	481
Office of the National Science Board	1175
Office of the Secretary and Executive Management	497
Office of the Secretary	63, 63, 889
Office of the Solicitor	695
Office of the United States Trade Representative	1139
Office of theNational Cyber Director	1135
Office of Workers' Compensation Programs	776
Offshore Safety and Environmental Enforcement	627
Oil Spill Liability Trust Fund	525
Oil Spill Research	628
Open World Leadership Center Trust Fund	42, 44
Operating Expenses:	
Agency for International Development, International Assistance Programs	846
Corporation for National and Community Service, Corporation for National and Community Service	1227
Executive Residence at the White House, Executive Office of the President	1131
General Activities, General Services Administration	1154
National Archives and Records Administration, National Archives and Records Administration	1283

	Page
Operating Expenses—Continued	
United States Interagency Council on Homelessness, United States Interagency Council on Homelessness	1337
Operating Fund	1289
Operation and Maintenance of Quarters	677
Operation and Maintenance, Air Force Reserve	252
Operation and Maintenance, Air Force	246
Operation and Maintenance, Air National Guard	254
Operation and Maintenance, Army National Guard	253
Operation and Maintenance, Army Reserve	250
Operation and Maintenance, Army	242
Operation and Maintenance, Defense-wide	248
Operation and Maintenance, Marine Corps Reserve	252
Operation and Maintenance, Marine Corps	245
Operation and Maintenance, Navy Reserve	251
Operation and Maintenance, Navy	244
Operation and Maintenance, Southeastern Power Administration	407
Operation and Maintenance, Southwestern Power Administration	408
Operation and Maintenance, Space Force	247
Operation and Maintenance	242, 1082
Operation of Indian Education Programs	682
Operation of Indian Programs	670
Operation of the National Park System	661
Operational Expenses	959
Operational Test and Evaluation, Defense	291
Operations and Administration	200, 201
Operations and Maintenance, JFK Center for the Performing Arts	1325
Operations and Maintenance	958
Operations and Research (Highway Trust Fund)	936
Operations and Research	933
Operations and Support	497, 498, 502, 503, 504, 512, 515, 518, 526, 530, 533, 536, 545, 549, 550, 552
Operations and Training	964
Operations Support	1019
Operations, Research, and Facilities	203
Operations	907
Orderly Liquidation Fund	1261
Orderly Liquidation	1261
Oregon and California Grant Lands	616
Organized Crime and Drug Enforcement Task Forces	735
Other Assisted Housing Programs	582
Other Commissions and Boards:	
Other Defense Activities	372
Other Defense—Civil Programs:	
American Battle Monuments Commission	1100
Armed Forces Retirement Home Trust Fund	1101
Armed Forces Retirement Home	1101
Cemeterial Expenses	1103
Construction (Cemeterial Expenses)	1103
Contributions	1101
Department of Defense Medicare-Eligible Retiree Health Care Fund	1098
Education Benefits Fund	1099
Educational Benefits	1099
Foreign Currency Fluctuations Account	1100
Forest and Wildlife Conservation, Military Reservations	1104
General Fund Payment, Armed Forces Retirement Home	1101
Military Retirement Fund	1097
Military Retirement	1097
National Military Cemeteries Concessions, Army	1104
Payment to Department of Defense Medicare-Eligible Retiree Health Care Fund	1098
Payment to Military Retirement Fund	1097
Retiree Health Care	1098
Salaries and Expenses (American Battle Monuments Commission)	1100
Salaries and Expenses (Cemeterial Expenses)	1103
Salaries and Expenses (Selective Service System)	1105
Selective Service System	1105

	Page
Other Defense—Civil Programs—Continued	
Wildlife Conservation	1104
Other DOD Trust Funds	316
Other Federal Drug Control Programs	1263
Other Legislative Branch Boards and Commissions	43
Other Permanent Appropriations	668
Other Procurement, Air Force	281
Other Procurement, Army	272
Other Procurement, Navy	276
Other	817
Overseas Contingency Operations Transfer Fund	255
Overseas Humanitarian, Disaster, and Civic Aid	260
Overseas Military Facility Investment Recovery	267
Overseas Private Investment Corporation Guaranteed Loan Financing Account	855
Overseas Private Investment Corporation Noncredit Account	854
Overseas Private Investment Corporation Program Account	854
Overseas Private Investment Corporation	854

P

	Page
P.L. 480 Direct Credit Financing Account	161
Pacific Coastal Salmon Recovery	207
Pakistan Counterinsurgency Capability Fund	829
Panama Canal Commission Compensation Fund	779
Pandemic Response Accountability Committee	1232
Patent and Trademark Fee Reserve Fund	215
Patient-Centered Outcomes Research Trust Fund:	
Payment to the Patient-Centered Outcomes Research Trust Fund	1305
Payment of Government Losses in Shipment	1007
Payment to Alaska, Arctic National Wildlife Refuge	689
Payment to Civil Service Retirement and Disability Fund	1182
Payment to Department of Defense Medicare-Eligible Retiree Health Care Fund	1098
Payment to Foreign Service Retirement and Disability Fund	809
Payment to Grants-in-aid for Airports	909
Payment to Issuer of New Clean Renewable Energy Bonds	1026
Payment to Issuer of Qualified Energy Conservation Bonds	1026
Payment to Issuer of Qualified School Construction Bonds	1026
Payment to Issuer of Qualified Zone Academy Bonds	1027
Payment to Judiciary Trust Funds	58
Payment to Limitation on Administration	1315
Payment to Limitation on Administrative Expenses	1205
Payment to Manufactured Housing Fees Trust Fund	595
Payment to Military Retirement Fund	1097
Payment to Puerto Rico Oversight Board:	
Puerto Rico Oversight Board	1313
Payment to Radiation Exposure Compensation Trust Fund	735
Payment to Standard Setting Body	1343
Payment to the Airport and Airway Trust Fund	910
Payment to the American Institute in Taiwan	808
Payment to the Asia Foundation	823
Payment to the FDA Innovation Account, CURES Act	426
Payment to the Harry S Truman Scholarship Memorial Trust Fund	1274
Payment to the Hazardous Substance Superfund	1120
Payment to the Highway Trust Fund	919
Payment to the Institute	1275
Payment to the Legal Services Corporation	1279
Payment to the National Service Trust Fund	1229
Payment to the Neighborhood Reinvestment Corporation	1298
Payment to the NIH Innovation Account, CURES Act	445
Payment to the Patient-Centered Outcomes Research Trust Fund	1305
Payment to the Postal Service Fund	1306
Payment to the Resolution Funding Corporation	1007
Payment to United States Virgin Islands and Puerto Rico for Disaster Tax Relief	1027
Payment Where Adoption Credit Exceeds Liability for Tax	1031
Payment Where American Opportunity Credit Exceeds Liability for Tax	1025
Payment Where Certain Tax Credits Exceed Liability for Corporate Tax	1024

	Page
Payment Where Child Tax Credit Exceeds Liability for Tax	1022
Payment Where Earned Income Credit Exceeds Liability for Tax	1021
Payment Where Health Coverage Tax Credit Exceeds Liability for Tax	1023
Payment Where Small Business Health Insurance Tax Credit Exceeds Liability for Tax	1024
Payments for Foster Care and Permanency	477
Payments for Tribal Leases	435, 673
Payments in Lieu of Taxes	698
Payments to:	
Administration for Children and Families, Department of Health and Human Services	468
Administration for Children and Families, Department of Health and Human Services	473
Agricultural Marketing Service, Department of Agriculture	90
Centers for Medicare and Medicaid Services, Department of Health and Human Services	452
Employment and Training Administration, Department of Labor	767
Energy Programs, Department of Energy	398
Insular Affairs, Department of the Interior	693
Library of Congress, Legislative Branch	29
Office of Surface Mining Reclamation and Enforcement, Department of the Interior	631
Office of the Secretary, Department of Transportation	905
Social Security Administration, Social Security Administration	1205
U.S. Customs and Border Protection, Department of Homeland Security	509
Peace Corps Miscellaneous Trust Fund	866
Peace Corps	864, 864
Peacekeeping Operations	830
Pension Benefit Guaranty Corporation Fund	774
Pension Benefit Guaranty Corporation	774
Pentagon Reservation Maintenance Revolving Fund	307
Perishable Agricultural Commodities Act Fund	91
Permanent Appropriations	1089
Permanent Operating Funds	620
Permanent Supportive Housing	578
Pesticide Registration Fund	1121
Pima Agriculture Cotton Trust Fund	114
Pipeline and Hazardous Materials Safety Administration	959
Pipeline Safety	961
Policy and Administration	637
Policy Development and Research	599
Port Infrastructure Development Program	971
Port of Guam Improvement Enterprise Fund	969
Portfolio Programs	1353, 1354
Post-Vietnam Era Veterans Education Account	1063
Postal Service Fund	1307
Postal Service Retiree Health Benefits Fund	1183
Postal Service:	
Office of Inspector General	1309
Payment to the Postal Service Fund	1306
Postal Regulatory Commission, Salaries and Expenses	1309
Postal Service Fund	1307
Power Marketing Administration	407
Pre-Election Presidential Transition	1157
Pre-Existing Condition Insurance Plan Program	457
Pregnancy Assistance Fund	487
PrEP for All to End the HIV Epidemic	485
Presidential Election Campaign Fund	984
Presidential Transition Administrative Support	1136
Presidio Trust:	
Prevention and Public Health Fund	487
Privacy and Civil Liberties Oversight Board:	
Salaries and Expenses	1311
Private Collection Agent Program	1029
Private Lands Conservation Operations	115
Procurement of Ammunition, Air Force	281
Procurement of Ammunition, Army	271

	Page
Procurement of Ammunition, Navy and Marine Corps	274
Procurement of Weapons and Tracked Combat Vehicles, Army	270
Procurement, Acquisition and Construction	206
Procurement, Construction and Improvements	554
Procurement, Construction, and Improvements	499, 507, 514, 517, 519, 528, 531, 543, 545, 550, 551
Procurement, Defense-wide	282
Procurement, Marine Corps	277
Procurement, Space Force	280
Procurement	268
Program Administration	361, 769
Program Expenses	1340
Program Management	453
Program Offices	604
Program Support Center	488
Project-based Rental Assistance	579
Promote and Develop Fishery Products and Research Pertaining to American Fisheries	209
Promoting Safe and Stable Families	472
Property Management Fund	849
Protection of Foreign Missions and Officials	807
Public and Indian Housing Programs	559
Public and Indian Housing	604
Public Buildings Reform Board:	
Public Buildings Reform Board Salaries and Expenses	1311
Public Company Accounting Oversight Board:	
Public Defender Service for the District of Columbia:	
Federal Payment to the District of Columbia Public Defender Service	1312
Public Health and Social Services Emergency Fund	483
Public Housing Capital Fund	562
Public Housing Fund	563
Public Housing Operating Fund	562
Public Law 480 Title I Direct Credit and Food for Progress Program Account	160
Public Safety Communications Research Fund	219
Public Safety Officer Benefits	756
Public Safety Trust Fund	226
Public Telecommunications Facilities, Planning and Construction	224
Public Transportation Emergency Relief Program	952
Puerto Rico Oversight Board	1313

Q

Quality Improvement Organizations	452

R

Radiation Exposure Compensation Trust Fund	735
Radiation Exposure Compensation	735
Radiological Emergency Preparedness Program	537
Rail Industry Pension Fund	1316
Rail Line Relocation and Improvement Program	946
Rail Safety Technology Program	946
Railroad Crossing Elimination Program	948
Railroad Rehabilitation and Improvement Direct Loan Financing Account	904
Railroad Rehabilitation and Improvement Program	903
Railroad Research and Development	940
Railroad Retirement Board:	
Dual Benefits Payments Account	1313
Federal Payments to the Railroad Retirement Accounts	1313
Limitation on Administration	1317
Limitation on the Office of Inspector General	1319
National Railroad Retirement Investment Trust	1318
Payment to Limitation on Administration	1315
Payment to Limitation on the Office of Inspector General, Railroad Retirement Board	1315
Rail Industry Pension Fund	1316
Railroad Social Security Equivalent Benefit Account	1319
Railroad Unemployment Insurance Enhanced Benefit Payments	1314
Railroad Unemployment Insurance Extended Benefit Payments, Recovery Act	1314

	Page
Railroad Retirement Board—Continued	
Railroad Unemployment Insurance Extended Benefit Payments	1314
Railroad Unemployment Insurance Trust Fund	1315
Railroad Unemployment Insurance Waiver of 7 Day Period	1314
Railroad Safety Grants	940
Railroad Social Security Equivalent Benefit Account	1319
Railroad Unemployment Insurance Enhanced Benefit Payments	1314
Railroad Unemployment Insurance Extended Benefit Payments, Recovery Act	1314
Railroad Unemployment Insurance Extended Benefit Payments	1314
Railroad Unemployment Insurance Trust Fund	1315
Railroad Unemployment Insurance Waiver of 7 Day Period	1314
Range Betterment Fund	178
Range Improvements	618
Rate Review Grants	457
Readjustment Benefits	1050
Ready Reserve Force	968
Real Property Activities	1145
Real Property Relocation	1149
Reclamation Fund	637
Reclamation Trust Funds	643
Reclamation Water Settlements Fund	636
Records Center Revolving Fund	1286
Recreation Enhancement Fee Program, FWS	656
Recreation Fee Permanent Appropriations	666
Recurring Expenses Transformational Fund	1075
Recyclable Materials Revolving Fund	23
Red Hill Recovery Fund	255
Refugee and Entrant Assistance	470
Refundable Premium Tax Credit	1028
Refunding Internal Revenue Collections, Interest	1028
Refunds, Transfers, and Expenses of Operation, Puerto Rico	508
Registry Administration	55
Registry Fees	1265
Regulation and Technology	629
Regulatory Program	1087
Rehabilitation Services	336
Reimbursements to Federal Reserve Banks	1006
Relief for Airports	909
Rental Assistance Program	125
Rental Housing Assistance Fund	582
Repair, Restoration, and Renovation of Buildings, National Gallery of Art	1327
Repairs and Restoration	1285
Repatriation Loans Financing Account	811
Repatriation Loans Program Account	810
Representation Expenses	806
Reregistration and Expedited Processing Revolving Fund	1122
Research and Development	518, 521, 528, 532, 552, 553
Research and Education Activities	79
Research and Related Activities	1173
Research and Technology	599, 889
Research, Development, Test and Evaluation, Air Force	288
Research, Development, Test and Evaluation, Army	286
Research, Development, Test and Evaluation, Defense-wide	289
Research, Development, Test and Evaluation, Navy	287
Research, Development, Test, and Evaluation, Space Force	289
Research, Development, Test, and Evaluation	286
Research, Engineering and Development (Airport and Airway Trust Fund)	916
Research, Evaluation, and Statistics	746
Reserve Personnel, Air Force	239
Reserve Personnel, Army	237
Reserve Personnel, Marine Corps	239
Reserve Personnel, Navy	238
Reserve Training	519
Resolution Funding Corporation	1351
Resource Management	648
Restaurant Revitalization Fund	1195
Restitution of Forgone Interest	1009

	Page
Restoration and Enhancement Grants	941
Retired Pay	522
Retiree Health Care	1098
Retirement Pay and Medical Benefits for Commissioned Officers	488
Revitalization of Severely Distressed Public Housing (HOPE VI)	565
Revolving and Management Funds	306
Revolving Fund (liquidating Programs)	578
Revolving Fund for Certification and Other Services	427
Revolving Fund for Loans Liquidating Account	679
Revolving Fund	1090, 1184
Right-of-way Revolving Fund Liquidating Account	923
Risk Adjustment Program Payments	459
Risk Management Agency	96
Rivers and Harbors Contributed Funds	1093
Rural Business and Industry Direct Loans Financing Account	140
Rural Business and Industry Guaranteed Loans Financing Account	140
Rural Business Investment Program Account	144
Rural Business Investment Program Guarantee Financing Account	144
Rural Business Program Account	139
Rural Business-Cooperative Service	136
Rural Community Facilities Program Account	128
Rural Community Facility Direct Loans Financing Account	130
Rural Community Facility Guaranteed Loans Financing Account	130
Rural Cooperative Development Grants	136
Rural Development Disaster Assistance Fund	125
Rural Development Insurance Fund Liquidating Account	157
Rural Development Loan Fund Direct Loan Financing Account	142
Rural Development Loan Fund Liquidating Account	142
Rural Development	124
Rural Economic Development Direct Loan Financing Account	143
Rural Economic Development Grants	137
Rural Economic Development Loans Program Account	143
Rural Electrification and Telecommunications Direct Loan Financing Account	152
Rural Electrification and Telecommunications Guaranteed Loans Financing Account	153
Rural Electrification and Telecommunications Liquidating Account	153
Rural Electrification and Telecommunications Loans Program Account	151
Rural Energy for America Guaranteed Loan Financing Account	145
Rural Energy for America Program	145
Rural Housing and Economic Development	578
Rural Housing Assistance Grants	125
Rural Housing Insurance Fund Direct Loan Financing Account	133
Rural Housing Insurance Fund Guaranteed Loan Financing Account	134
Rural Housing Insurance Fund Liquidating Account	135
Rural Housing Insurance Fund Program Account	131
Rural Housing Service	125
Rural Microenterprise Investment Direct Loan Financing Account	138
Rural Microentrepreneur Assistance Program	138
Rural Telephone Bank Direct Loan Financing Account	154
Rural Telephone Bank Program Account	154
Rural Utilities Service	147
Rural Water and Waste Disposal Direct Loans Financing Account	149
Rural Water and Waste Disposal Program Account	148
Rural Water and Waste Water Disposal Guaranteed Loans Financing Account	150

S

	Page
Safe Schools and Citizenship Education	331
Safe Streets and Roads for All	894
Safety and Operations	939
Safety, Security and Mission Services	1166
Salaries and Expenses:	
Access Board, Access Board	1215
Administrative Conference of the United States, Administrative Conference of the United States	1216

INDEX

Salaries and Expenses—Continued

Entry	Page
Administrative Office of the United States Courts, Judicial Branch	56
Advisory Council on Historic Preservation, Advisory Council on Historic Preservation	1216
Agricultural Research Service, Department of Agriculture	74
Alcohol and Tobacco Tax and Trade Bureau, Department of the Treasury	1013
American Battle Monuments Commission, Other Defense—Civil Programs	1100
Animal and Plant Health Inspection Service, Department of Agriculture	83
Bureau of Alcohol, Tobacco, Firearms, and Explosives, Department of Justice	741
Bureau of Economic Analysis, Department of Commerce	199
Bureau of Labor Statistics, Department of Labor	788
Cemeterial Expenses, Other Defense—Civil Programs	1103
Chemical Safety and Hazard Investigation Board, Chemical Safety and Hazard Investigation Board	1220
Commission of Fine Arts, Commission of Fine Arts	1221
Commission on Civil Rights, Commission on Civil Rights	1222
Commission on Combating Synthetic Opioid Trafficking, Commission on Combating Synthetic Opioid Trafficking	1223
Committee for Purchase from People Who Are Blind or Severely Dis, Committee for Purchase From People Who Are Blind or Severely Disabled	1223
Congressional Budget Office, Legislative Branch	16
Consumer Product Safety Commission, Consumer Product Safety Commission	1227
Corporation for National and Community Service, Corporation for National and Community Service	1229
Council of Economic Advisers, Executive Office of the President	1133
Courts of Appeals, District Courts, and Other Judicial Services, Judicial Branch	51
Defense Nuclear Facilities Safety Board, Defense Nuclear Facilities Safety Board	1235
Departmental Management, Department of Commerce	191
Departmental Management, Department of Labor	789
Departmental Offices, Department of the Interior	687
Departmental Offices, Department of the Treasury	977
Drug Enforcement Administration, Department of Justice	738
Economic Development Administration, Department of Commerce	195
Election Assistance Commission, Election Assistance Commission	1245
Employee Benefits Security Administration, Department of Labor	772
Equal Employment Opportunity Commission, Equal Employment Opportunity Commission	1247
Farm Service Agency, Department of Agriculture	98
Federal Bureau of Investigation, Department of Justice	736
Federal Communications Commission, Federal Communications Commission	1255
Federal Election Commission, Federal Election Commission	1264
Federal Judicial Center, Judicial Branch	57
Federal Labor Relations Authority, Federal Labor Relations Authority	1268
Federal Maritime Commission, Federal Maritime Commission	1268
Federal Mediation and Conciliation Service, Federal Mediation and Conciliation Service	1269
Federal Mine Safety and Health Review Commission, Federal Mine Safety and Health Review Commission	1270
Federal Prison System, Department of Justice	742
Federal Trade Commission, Federal Trade Commission	1272
Financial Crimes Enforcement Network, Department of the Treasury	1003
Fiscal Service, Department of the Treasury	1004
Food and Drug Administration, Department of Health and Human Services	423
Food Safety and Inspection Service, Department of Agriculture	86

Salaries and Expenses—Continued

Entry	Page
Foreign Agricultural Service, Department of Agriculture	158
General Administration, Department of Justice	715
Government Accountability Office, Legislative Branch	35
Government Publishing Office, Legislative Branch	33
House of Representatives, Legislative Branch	12
International Commissions, Department of State	814
International Trade Commission, International Trade Commission	1277
Legal Activities and U.S. Marshals, Department of Justice	721
Legal Activities and U.S. Marshals, Department of Justice	723
Legal Activities and U.S. Marshals, Department of Justice	724
Legal Activities and U.S. Marshals, Department of Justice	725
Legal Activities and U.S. Marshals, Department of Justice	729
Library of Congress, Legislative Branch	24
Library of Congress, Legislative Branch	26
Library of Congress, Legislative Branch	27
Management and Administration, Department of Housing and Urban Development	605
Marine Mammal Commission, Marine Mammal Commission	1280
Merit Systems Protection Board, Merit Systems Protection Board	1281
Mine Safety and Health Administration, Department of Labor	787
National Capital Planning Commission, National Capital Planning Commission	1287
National Council on Disability, National Council on Disability	1288
National Indian Gaming Commission, Department of the Interior	696
National Labor Relations Board, National Labor Relations Board	1295
National Mediation Board, National Mediation Board	1295
National Nuclear Security Administration, Department of Energy	367
National Railroad Passenger Corporation Office of Inspector Gene, National Railroad Passenger Corporation Office of Inspector General	1296
National Security Council and Homeland Security Council, Executive Office of the President	1134
National Security Division, Department of Justice	734
National Telecommunications and Information Administration, Department of Commerce	220
National Transportation Safety Board, National Transportation Safety Board	1297
Nuclear Regulatory Commission, Nuclear Regulatory Commission	1299
Nuclear Waste Technical Review Board, Nuclear Waste Technical Review Board	1302
Occupational Safety and Health Administration, Department of Labor	785
Occupational Safety and Health Review Commission, Occupational Safety and Health Review Commission	1302
Office of Administration, Executive Office of the President	1136
Office of Congressional Workplace Rights, Legislative Branch	15
Office of Federal Contract Compliance Programs, Department of Labor	783
Office of Government Ethics, Office of Government Ethics	1303
Office of Inspector General, Department of the Interior	695
Office of Inspector General, Department of Transportation	963
Office of Labor Management Standards, Department of Labor	784
Office of Management and Budget, Executive Office of the President	1137
Office of National Drug Control Policy, Executive Office of the President	1137
Office of Navajo and Hopi Indian Relocation, Office of Navajo and Hopi Indian Relocation	1303
Office of Personnel Management, Office of Personnel Management	1179
Office of Special Counsel, Office of Special Counsel	1304
Office of the National Cyber Director, Executive Office of the President	1135

	Page
Salaries and Expenses—Continued	
Office of the Secretary, Department of Transportation	890
Office of the Solicitor, Department of the Interior	695
Office of the United States Trade Representative, Executive Office of the President	1139
Office of Workers' Compensation Programs, Department of Labor	776
Postal Service, Postal Service	1309
Privacy and Civil Liberties Oversight Board, Privacy and Civil Liberties Oversight Board	1311
Public Buildings Reform Board, Public Buildings Reform Board	1311
Risk Management Agency, Department of Agriculture	96
Rural Development, Department of Agriculture	124
Securities and Exchange Commission, Securities and Exchange Commission	1320
Selective Service System, Other Defense—Civil Programs	1105
Small Business Administration, Small Business Administration	1191
Smithsonian Institution, Smithsonian Institution	1323
Smithsonian Institution, Smithsonian Institution	1326
Smithsonian Institution, Smithsonian Institution	1327
Special Assistance to the President and the Official Residence, Executive Office of the President	1132
State Justice Institute, State Justice Institute	1329
Supreme Court of the United States, Judicial Branch	49
Surface Transportation Board, Surface Transportation Board	1329
The White House, Executive Office of the President	1131
U.S. Patent and Trademark Office, Department of Commerce	214
United States Court of Appeals for the Federal Circuit, Judicial Branch	50
United States Court of Appeals for Veterans Claims, United States Court of Appeals for Veterans Claims	1335
United States Court of International Trade, Judicial Branch	51
United States Parole Commission, Department of Justice	720
United States Sentencing Commission, Judicial Branch	60
United States Tax Court, Legislative Branch	36
Wage and Hour Division, Department of Labor	782
Salaries	14
San Joaquin Restoration Fund	639
School Improvement Programs	329
Science and Technology	550, 1108
Science, Space, and Technology Education Trust Fund	1171
Science, Technology, Engineering, and Mathematics Engagement	1166
Science	373, 1163
Scientific and Technical Research and Services	216
Section 241 Evaluation Transactions Account	488
Secure and Trusted Communications Networks Act Reimbursement Program	1258
Securities and Exchange Commission Reserve Fund	1322
Securities and Exchange Commission:	
General and Administrative Provisions	1323
General Fund Receipt Accounts	1323
Investor Protection Fund	1323
Salaries and Expenses	1320
Securities and Exchange Commission Reserve Fund	1322
Securities Investor Protection Corporation:	
Security Enhancements	15
Selective Service System	1105
Self-help and Assisted Homeownership Opportunity Program	577
Self-Sufficiency Programs	565
Selis-Qlispe Ksanka Settlement Trust Fund	681
Senate Office Buildings	18
Senate	11
Service Charges, Deposits, and Forfeitures	619
Service-disabled Veterans Insurance Fund	1055
Servicemembers' Group Life Insurance Fund	1056
Ship Disposal	966
Shipbuilding and Conversion, Navy	275
Short Time Compensation Programs	767

	Page
Shuttered Venue Operators	1195
Small and Disadvantaged Business Utilization and Outreach	900
Small Business Administration:	
Business Direct Loan Financing Account	1197
Business Guaranteed Loan Financing Account	1198
Business Loan Fund Liquidating Account	1199
Business Loans Program Account	1196
Disaster Direct Loan Financing Account	1201
Disaster Loan Fund Liquidating Account	1202
Disaster Loans Program Account	1200
Emergency EIDL Grants	1191
Entrepreneurial Development Program	1194
Information Technology System Modernization and Working Capital Fund	1195
Office of Advocacy	1193
Office of Inspector General	1193
Restaurant Revitalization Fund	1195
Salaries and Expenses	1191
Shuttered Venue Operators	1195
Surety Bond Guarantees Revolving Fund	1196
Small Business Lending Fund Financing Account	1000
Small Business Lending Fund Program Account	1000
Smithsonian Institution:	
Capital Repair and Restoration, JFK Center for the Performing Arts	1326
Facilities Capital	1324
Operations and Maintenance, JFK Center for the Performing Arts	1325
Repair, Restoration, and Renovation of Buildings, National Gallery of Art	1327
Salaries and Expenses, National Gallery of Art	1326
Salaries and Expenses, Woodrow Wilson International Center for Scholars	1327
Salaries and Expenses	1323
Social Impact Demonstration Projects	1001
Social Security Administration:	
Administrative Costs, The Medicare Improvements for Patients and Providers Act	1205
Administrative Expenses, Children's Health Insurance Program	1205
Administrative Expenses, Recovery Act	1208
Federal Disability Insurance Trust Fund	1210
Federal Old-age and Survivors Insurance Trust Fund	1209
General and Administrative Provisions	1213
General Fund Receipt Accounts	1213
Limitation on Administrative Expenses	1211
Office of Inspector General	1207
Payment to Limitation on Administrative Expenses	1205
Payments to Social Security Trust Funds	1205
Special Benefits for Certain World War II Veterans	1207
State Supplemental Fees	1208
Supplemental Security Income Program	1206
Social Services Block Grant	474
South Dakota Terrestrial Wildlife Habitat Restoration Trust Fund	1095
Southeast Crescent Regional Commission:	
Southwest Border Regional Commission:	
Space Operations	1168
Space Procurement, Air Force	280
Space Technology	1164
Special Assistance to the President and the Official Residence of the Vice President	1132
Special Benefits for Certain World War II Veterans	1207
Special Benefits for Disabled Coal Miners	779
Special Benefits	777
Special Defense Acquisition Fund	870
Special Education	334
Special Inspector General for Pandemic Recovery	992
Special Inspector General for the Troubled Asset Relief Program	999
Special Recreation User Fee	1083
Special Supplemental Nutrition Program for Women, Infants, and Children (WIC)	166

	Page
Special Use Permit Fees	1091
Special Workers' Compensation Expenses	781
Spectrum Auction Direct Loan Financing Account	1258
Spectrum Auction Program Account	1257
Spectrum Relocation Fund	1143
Sport Fish Restoration	659
SPR Petroleum Account	395
Standard Setting Body:	
Payment to Standard Setting Body	1343
State and Local Implementation Fund	224
State and Local Law Enforcement Assistance	747
State and Local Programs	537
State and Private Forestry	172
State and Tribal Assistance Grants	1113
State Grants and Demonstrations	451
State HFA Direct Loan Financing Account	1002
State Infrastructure Banks	919
State Justice Institute:	
Salaries and Expenses	1329
State Maritime Academy Operations	965
State Mediation Grants	99
State Small Business Credit Initiative	991
State Supplemental Fees	1208
State Unemployment Insurance and Employment Service Operations	765
State Wildlife Grants	651
State, Department of:	
Administration of Foreign Affairs	799
American Sections, International Commissions	816
Andean Counterdrug Programs	822
Buying Power Maintenance	808
Capital Investment Fund	803
Center for Middle Eastern-Western Dialogue Trust Fund	826
Complex Crises Fund	821
Conflict Stabilization Operations	803
Construction, IBWC (International Commissions)	815
Consular and Border Security Programs	801
Contributions for International Peacekeeping Activities	814
Contributions to International Organizations	813
Democracy Fund	822
Diplomatic Programs	799
East-West Center	823
Educational and Cultural Exchange Programs	804
Embassy Security, Construction, and Maintenance	805
Emergencies in the Diplomatic and Consular Service	807
Fishermen's Guaranty Fund	825
Fishermen's Protective Fund	825
Foreign Service National Defined Contributions Retirement Fund	809
Foreign Service National Separation Liability Trust Fund	812
Foreign Service Retirement and Disability Fund	811
General and Administrative Provisions	826
General Fund Receipt Accounts	826
Global Health Programs	817
Global HIV/AIDs Initiative	817
H&L Fraud Prevention and Detection Fee	799
International Center, Washington, D.C.	824
International Commissions	814
International Fisheries Commissions	816
International Information Programs	802
International Litigation Fund	824
International Narcotics Control and Law Enforcement	821
International Organizations and Conferences	813
Israeli Arab and Eisenhower Exchange Fellowship Programs	825
Migration and Refugee Assistance	819
Miscellaneous Trust Funds	813
National Endowment for Democracy	823
Office of Inspector General (Administration of Foreign Affairs)	803
Other	817
Payment to Foreign Service Retirement and Disability Fund	809
Payment to the American Institute in Taiwan	808

	Page
State, Department of—Continued	
Payment to the Asia Foundation	823
Protection of Foreign Missions and Officials	807
Repatriation Loans Financing Account	811
Repatriation Loans Program Account	810
Representation Expenses	806
Salaries and Expenses, IBWC (International Commissions)	814
Sudan Claims	802
United States Emergency Refugee and Migration Assistance Fund	820
Working Capital Fund (Administration of Foreign Affairs)	809
States Share from Certain Gulf of Mexico Leases	691
STEM Education	1176
Stewardship Contracting Product Sales	179
Strategic Petroleum Reserve	394
Strengthening Mobility and Revolutionizing Transportation Grant Program	895
Student Aid Administration	346
Student Financial Assistance Debt Collection	348
Student Financial Assistance	344
Student Loan Acquisition Account	356
Substance Use And Mental Health Services Administration	446, 4 4 6
Sudan Claims	802
Supplemental Highway Traffic Safety Programs	934
Supplemental Nutrition Assistance Program	163
Supplemental Payments to UMWA Plans	632
Supplemental Security Income Program	1206
Supplemental Surveys	196
Supply and Technology Activities	1150
Supply Fund	523, 1074
Support for International Sporting Competitions	257
Support of Athletic Programs	268
Supreme Court of the United States	49
Surety Bond Guarantees Revolving Fund	1196
Surface Transportation Board:	
Salaries and Expenses	1329
Surface Transportation Security	516
Surveys, Investigations, and Research	645

T

	Page
Tactical Law Enforcement Wireless Communications	716
Tanker Security Program	968
Taos Settlement Fund	635
Tax Court Judges Survivors Annuity Fund	37
Taxpayer Services	1016
TEACH Grant Financing Account	347
TEACH Grant Program Account	347
Technical Assistance and Training	952
Technology Modernization Fund	1152
Telecommunications Relay Services Fund, Federal Communications Commission	1257
Temporary Assistance for Needy Families	468
Temporary Student Loan Purchase Authority Conduit Financing Account	356
Temporary Student Loan Purchase Authority Financing Account	355
Tenant Based Rental Assistance	559
Tennessee Valley Authority Fund	1330
Tennessee Valley Authority:	
Tennessee Valley Authority Fund	1330
Terrorism Insurance Program	982
The Department of Defense Environmental Restoration Accounts	259
The White House	1131
Thriving Communities	892
TIFIA General Fund Direct Loan Financing Account	898
TIFIA General Fund Program Account	898
TIFIA Highway Trust Fund Direct Loan Financing Account	896
TIFIA Highway Trust Fund Program Account	904
Tiger TIFIA Direct Loan Financing Account, Recovery Act	891
Title 17 Innovative Technology Direct Loan Financing Account	404
Title 17 Innovative Technology Guaranteed Loan Financing Account	406
Title 17 Innovative Technology Loan Guarantee Program	402

	Page
Title VI Indian Federal Guarantees Financing Account	567
Tobacco Trust Fund	115
Trade and Development Agency	855, 855
Trade Enforcement Trust Fund	1140
Training and Employment Services	761
Transfers from the Patient-Centered Outcomes Research Trust Fund	485
Transformation Initiative	608
Transit Formula Grants	956
Transit Infrastructure Grants	953
Transit Research	951
Transition Initiatives	848
Transitional Housing Direct Loan Financing Account	1062
Transitional Reinsurance Program	459
Transmission Facilitation Fund	381
Transportation Demonstration Program	893
Transportation Planning, Research, and Development	901
Transportation Security Administration	515
Transportation Security Support	517
Transportation Services Economic Relief	989
Transportation, Department of:	
Administrative Expenses	949
Administrative Services Franchise Fund	913
Airport and Airway Trust Fund	914
Airport Infrastructure Grants	911
Airport Terminal Program	910
All Stations Accessibility Program	955
Appalachian Development Highway System	919
Asset Concessions and Innovative Finance Assistance	894
Assistance to Small Shipyards	966
Aviation Insurance Revolving Fund	912
Aviation Manufacturing Jobs Protection Program	901
Aviation User Fees	912
Cable Security Fleet	967
Capital and Debt Service Grants to the National Railroad Passenger Corporation	942
Capital Assistance for High Speed Rail Corridors and Intercity Passenger Rail Service	945
Capital Investment Grants	951
Consolidated Rail Infrastructure and Safety Improvements	947
Consumer Assistance to Recycle and Save Program	932
Crash Data	934
Cyber Security Initiatives	899
Discretionary Grants (Highway Trust Fund, Mass Transit Account)	956
Electric or Low-Emitting Ferry Program	955
Electric Vehicle Fleet	893
Emergency FAA Employee Leave Fund	908
Emergency Preparedness Grants	962
Emergency Relief Program	918
Essential Air Service and Rural Airport Improvement Fund	902
Facilities and Equipment (Airport and Airway Trust Fund)	915
Facilities and Equipment	908
Federal Aviation Administration	907
Federal Highway Administration	918
Federal Motor Carrier Safety Administration	928
Federal Railroad Administration	939
Federal Transit Administration	949
Federal-aid Highways	924
Federal-State Partnership for Intercity Passenger Rail Grants	946
Ferry Service for Rural Communities	954
Financial Assistance Oversight and Technical Assistance	948
Financial Management Capital	899
Formula Grants	950
General and Administrative Provisions	973
General Fund Payment To National Surface Transportation and Innovative Finance Bureau Highway Trust Fund Account, Upward Reestimates	889
General Fund Receipt Accounts	973
General Provisions—Department of Transportation	973
Grants to the National Railroad Passenger Corporation	941

	Page
Transportation, Department of—Continued	
Grants-in-aid for Airports (Airport and Airway Trust Fund)	914
Great Lakes St. Lawrence Seaway Development Corporation	958
Hazardous Materials Safety	959
Highway Infrastructure Programs	919
Highway Traffic Safety Grants	937
Highway Trust Fund	923
Intercity Passenger Rail Grant Program	944
Job Access and Reverse Commute Grants	950
Magnetic Levitation Technology Deployment Program	941
Maritime Administration	964
Maritime Guaranteed Loan (Title XI) FFB Financing Account	970
Maritime Guaranteed Loan (Title XI) Financing Account	972
Maritime Guaranteed Loan (Title XI) Program Account	970
Maritime Security Program	967
Miscellaneous Appropriations	918
Miscellaneous Highway Trust Funds	926
Miscellaneous Trust Funds, Maritime Administration	973
Miscellaneous Trust Funds	926
Motor Carrier Safety Grants, General Fund	928
Motor Carrier Safety Grants	930
Motor Carrier Safety Operations and Programs, General Fund	929
Motor Carrier Safety Operations and Programs	931
Motor Carrier Safety	929
National Culvert Removal, Replacement, and Restoration Grant Program	895
National Highway Traffic Safety Administration	932
National Infrastructure Investments	892
National Motor Carrier Safety Program	929
National Network Grants to the National Railroad Passenger Corporation	942
National Surface Transportation and Innovative Finance Bureau	890
Natural Gas Distribution Infrastructure Safety and Modernization Grant Program	960
Next Generation 911 Implementation Grants	934
Next Generation High-speed Rail	945
Northeast Corridor Grants to the National Railroad Passenger Corporation	943
Northeast Corridor Improvement Program	945
Office of Civil Rights	900
Office of Inspector General	963
Office of Multimodal Freight Infrastructure and Policy	896
Office of the Secretary	889
Operational Expenses	959
Operations and Maintenance	958
Operations and Research (Highway Trust Fund)	936
Operations and Research	933
Operations and Training	964
Operations	907
Payment to Grants-in-aid for Airports	909
Payment to the Airport and Airway Trust Fund	910
Payment to the Highway Trust Fund	919
Payments to Air Carriers	905
Pipeline and Hazardous Materials Safety Administration	959
Pipeline Safety	961
Port Infrastructure Development Program	971
Port of Guam Improvement Enterprise Fund	969
Public Transportation Emergency Relief Program	952
Rail Line Relocation and Improvement Program	946
Rail Safety Technology Program	946
Railroad Crossing Elimination Program	948
Railroad Rehabilitation and Improvement Direct Loan Financing Account	904
Railroad Rehabilitation and Improvement Program	903
Railroad Research and Development	940
Railroad Safety Grants	940
Ready Reserve Force	968
Relief for Airports	909
Research and Technology	889

INDEX

Transportation, Department of—Continued

	Page
Research, Engineering and Development (Airport and Airway Trust Fund)	916
Restoration and Enhancement Grants	941
Right-of-way Revolving Fund Liquidating Account	923
Safe Streets and Roads for All	894
Safety and Operations	939
Salaries and Expenses (Office of Inspector General)	963
Salaries and Expenses (Office of the Secretary)	890
Ship Disposal	966
Small and Disadvantaged Business Utilization and Outreach	900
State Infrastructure Banks	919
State Maritime Academy Operations	965
Strengthening Mobility and Revolutionizing Transportation Grant Program	895
Supplemental Highway Traffic Safety Programs	934
Tanker Security Program	968
Technical Assistance and Training	952
Thriving Communities	892
TIFIA General Fund Direct Loan Financing Account	898
TIFIA General Fund Program Account	898
TIFIA Highway Trust Fund Direct Loan Financing Account	896
TIFIA Highway Trust Fund Program Account	904
Tiger TIFIA Direct Loan Financing Account, Recovery Act	891
Transit Formula Grants	956
Transit Infrastructure Grants	953
Transit Research	951
Transportation Demonstration Program	893
Transportation Planning, Research, and Development	901
Trust Fund Share of FAA Activities (Airport and Airway Trust Fund)	917
Trust Fund Share of Pipeline Safety	963
Vehicle Safety and Behavioral Research Programs	935
Vessel Operations Revolving Fund	969
War Risk Insurance Revolving Fund	969
Washington Metropolitan Area Transit Authority	950
Working Capital Fund, Volpe National Transportation Systems Center (Office of the Secretary)	897
Working Capital Fund (Office of the Secretary)	902
Travel Promotion Fund	1339
Treasury Forfeiture Fund	983
Treasury Franchise Fund	985
Treasury Inspector General for Tax Administration	981

Treasury, Department of the:

	Page
Administrative Provisions—Department of the Treasury	1034
Air Carrier Worker Support	988
Alcohol and Tobacco Tax and Trade Bureau	1013
Assessment Funds	1032
Build America Bond Payments, Recovery Act	1020
Bureau of Engraving and Printing Fund	1014
Bureau of Engraving and Printing	1014
Business Systems Modernization	1020
Capital Magnet Fund, Community Development Financial Institutions	1002
Check Forgery Insurance Fund	1010
Cheyenne River Sioux Tribe Terrestrial Wildlife Habitat Restoration Trust Fund	1011
Child and Dependent Care Tax Credit	1025
Claims, Judgments, and Relief Acts	1009
Committee on Foreign Investment in the United States Fund	981
Community Development Financial Institutions Fund Direct Loan Financing Account	994
Community Development Financial Institutions Fund Program Account	992
Community Development Financial Institutions Fund Program, Emergency Support	995
Community Financial Development Institutions Affordable Housing Supply Fund	996
Comptroller of the Currency	1032
Continued Dumping and Subsidy Offset	1010
Coronavirus Relief Fund	989
Cybersecurity Enhancement Account	978

Treasury, Department of the—Continued

	Page
Debt Collection Fund	1005
Department-Wide Systems and Capital Investments Programs	979
Departmental Offices	977
Economic Stabilization Direct Loan Financing Account	987
Economic Stabilization Program Account	986
Emergency Capital Investment Fund	995
Emergency Rental Assistance	990
Enforcement	1017
Exchange Stabilization Fund	986
Federal Financing Bank	1012
Federal Interest Liabilities to States	1008
Federal Reserve Bank Reimbursement Fund	1007
Federal Tax Lien Revolving Fund	1031
Financial Agent Services	1008
Financial Crimes Enforcement Network	1003
Financial Research Fund	984
Fiscal Service	1004
General and Administrative Provisions	1033
General Fund Receipt Accounts	1033
Gifts and Bequests	1003
Gifts to the United States for Reduction of the Public Debt	1029
GSE Mortgage-backed Securities Purchase Program Account	1001
GSE Preferred Stock Purchase Agreements	1001
Guam World War II Claims Fund	1009
Gulf Coast Restoration Trust Fund	1011
Homeowner Assistance Fund	991
Hope Reserve Fund	1007
Informant Payments	1030
Interest on the Public Debt	1033
Interest on Treasury Debt Securities (gross)	1033
Interest on Uninvested Funds	1008
Interest Paid to Credit Financing Accounts	1009
Internal Revenue Collections for Puerto Rico	1014
Internal Revenue Service	1016
IRS Miscellaneous Retained Fees	1029
Office of Financial Stability	996
Office of Inspector General (Departmental Offices)	980
Office of Terrorism and Financial Intelligence	978
Operations Support	1019
Payment of Government Losses in Shipment	1007
Payment to Issuer of New Clean Renewable Energy Bonds	1026
Payment to Issuer of Qualified Energy Conservation Bonds	1026
Payment to Issuer of Qualified School Construction Bonds	1026
Payment to Issuer of Qualified Zone Academy Bonds	1027
Payment to the Resolution Funding Corporation	1007
Payment to United States Virgin Islands and Puerto Rico for Disaster Tax Relief	1027
Payment Where Adoption Credit Exceeds Liability for Tax	1031
Payment Where American Opportunity Credit Exceeds Liability for Tax	1025
Payment Where Certain Tax Credits Exceed Liability for Corporate Tax	1024
Payment Where Child Tax Credit Exceeds Liability for Tax	1022
Payment Where Earned Income Credit Exceeds Liability for Tax	1021
Payment Where Health Coverage Tax Credit Exceeds Liability for Tax	1023
Payment Where Small Business Health Insurance Tax Credit Exceeds Liability for Tax	1024
Presidential Election Campaign Fund	984
Private Collection Agent Program	1029
Refundable Premium Tax Credit	1028
Refunding Internal Revenue Collections, Interest	1028
Reimbursements to Federal Reserve Banks	1006
Restitution of Forgone Interest	1009
Salaries and Expenses (Alcohol and Tobacco Tax and Trade Bureau)	1013
Salaries and Expenses (Departmental Offices)	977
Salaries and Expenses (Financial Crimes Enforcement Network)	1003

	Page
Treasury, Department of the—Continued	
Salaries and Expenses (Fiscal Service)	1004
Small Business Lending Fund Financing Account	1000
Small Business Lending Fund Program Account	1000
Social Impact Demonstration Projects	1001
Special Inspector General for Pandemic Recovery	992
Special Inspector General for the Troubled Asset Relief Program	999
State HFA Direct Loan Financing Account	1002
State Small Business Credit Initiative	991
Taxpayer Services	1016
Terrorism Insurance Program	982
Title VI—General Provisions	1035
Transportation Services Economic Relief	989
Treasury Forfeiture Fund	983
Treasury Franchise Fund	985
Treasury Inspector General for Tax Administration	981
Troubled Asset Relief Program Account	996
Troubled Asset Relief Program Direct Loan Financing Account	997
Troubled Asset Relief Program Equity Purchase Financing Account	997
Troubled Asset Relief Program Equity Purchase Program	997
Troubled Asset Relief Program, Housing Programs, Letter of Credit Financing Account	999
Troubled Asset Relief Program, Housing Programs	998
U.S. Coronavirus Payments	1022
U.S. Coronavirus Refundable Credits	1023
United States Mint Public Enterprise Fund	1015
United States Mint	1015
Tribal Energy Loan Guarantee Program	405
Tribal Indian Energy Resource Development Loan Guarantee Financing Account	406
Tribal Special Fund	685
Tribal Trust Fund	686
Troubled Asset Relief Program Account	996
Troubled Asset Relief Program Direct Loan Financing Account	997
Troubled Asset Relief Program Equity Purchase Financing Account	997
Troubled Asset Relief Program Equity Purchase Program	997
Troubled Asset Relief Program, Housing Programs, Letter of Credit Financing Account	999
Troubled Asset Relief Program, Housing Programs	998
Trust Fund Share of Expenses	524
Trust Fund Share of FAA Activities (Airport and Airway Trust Fund)	917
Trust Fund Share of Pipeline Safety	963
Trust Funds	314
Trust Land Consolidation Fund	686
Trust Territory of the Pacific Islands	692
TSCA Service Fee Fund	1121
TV Broadcaster Relocation Fund	1259

U

	Page
U. S. Tax Court Fees	37
U.s. Agency for Global Media:	
Broadcasting Capital Improvements	1334
Buying Power Maintenance	1334
Foreign Service National Separation Liability Trust Fund	1334
International Broadcasting Operations	1333
U.S. Capitol Preservation Commission	44
U.S. Coronavirus Payments	1022
U.S. Coronavirus Refundable Credits	1023
U.S. Customs and Border Protection	504
U.S. Customs Refunds, Transfers and Expenses, Unclaimed and Abandoned Goods	512
U.S. Immigration and Customs Enforcement	512
U.S. International Development Finance Corporation Insurance of Debt Financing Account	861
U.S. International Development Finance Corporation Insurance of Debt Program Account	856
U.S. Patent and Trademark Office	214
Ukraine Loan Guarantee Financing Account	872

	Page
Ukraine Loan Guarantee Program Account	872
Ukraine Loan Guarantees Financing Account	850
Ukraine Loan Guarantees Program Account	849
Ultra-deepwater and Unconventional Natural Gas and Other Petroleum Research Fund	398
Unanticipated Needs	1141, 1141
Unemployment Trust Fund	770
United Mine Workers of America 1992 Benefit Plan	1344
United Mine Workers of America 1993 Benefit Plan	1345
United Mine Workers of America Benefit Funds:	
United Mine Workers of America 1992 Benefit Plan	1344
United Mine Workers of America 1993 Benefit Plan	1345
United Mine Workers of America Combined Benefit Fund	1344
United Mine Workers of America Pension Funds	1345
United Mine Workers of America Combined Benefit Fund	1344
United Mine Workers of America Pension Funds	1345
United States Capitol Police Mutual Aid Reimbursements	15
United States Coast Guard	518
United States Commission on International Religious Freedom	39
United States Court of Appeals for the Armed Forces	255
United States Court of Appeals for the Federal Circuit	50
United States Court of Appeals for Veterans Claims:	
Court of Appeals for Veterans Claims Retirement Fund	1335
Salaries and Expenses	1335
United States Court of Federal Claims Judges' Retirement Fund	59
United States Court of International Trade	51
United States Emergency Refugee and Migration Assistance Fund	820
United States Enrichment Corporation Fund:	
United States Fish and Wildlife Service	648
United States Geological Survey	645
United States Government Life Insurance Fund	1064
United States Holocaust Memorial Museum:	
Holocaust Memorial Museum	1336
United States Institute of Peace:	
United States Interagency Council on Homelessness:	
Operating Expenses	1337
United States International Development Finance Corporation Corporate Capital Account	856
United States International Development Finance Corporation Direct Loan Financing Account	860
United States International Development Finance Corporation Guaranteed Loan Financing Account	859
United States International Development Finance Corporation Inspector General	858
United States International Development Finance Corporation Program Account	857
United States International Development Finance Corporation	856
United States Mint Public Enterprise Fund	1015
United States Mint	1015
United States Parole Commission	720
United States Quota, International Monetary Fund	868
United States Secret Service	526
United States Semiquincentennial Commission	41
United States Sentencing Commission	60
United States Tax Court	36
United States Trustee System Fund	731
United States Victims of State Sponsored Terrorism Fund	730
United States-China Economic and Security Review Commission	39
Universal Service Fund	1256
Upper Colorado River Basin Fund	641
Uranium Enrichment Decontamination and Decommissioning Fund	400
Urban Agriculture Program	122
Urban and Environmental Credit Guaranteed Loan Financing Account	861
Urban and Environmental Credit Program Account	861
Urban Park and Recreation Fund	664
USDA Supplemental Assistance	100
Utah Reclamation Mitigation and Conservation Account	644

V

	Page
Vaccine Injury Compensation Program Trust Fund	433

	Page
Vaccine Injury Compensation	430
Vehicle Safety and Behavioral Research Programs	935
Vessel Operations Revolving Fund	969
Veterans Affairs Life Insurance	1057
Veterans Affairs, Department of:	
Asset Infrastructure Review Commission	1069
Benefits Programs	1049
Board of Veterans Appeals	1070
Canteen Service Revolving Fund	1047
Compensation and Pensions	1049
Construction, Major Projects (Departmental Administration)	1066
Construction, Minor Projects (Departmental Administration)	1067
Departmental Administration	1066
DOD-VA Health Care Sharing Incentive Fund	1042
Emergency Department of Veterans Affairs Employee Leave Fund	1048
Filipino Veterans Equity Compensation Fund	1054
Franchise Fund	1074
General Administration	1068
General and Administrative Provisions	1078
General Fund Receipt Accounts	1078
General Operating Expenses, Veterans Benefits Administration	1054
General Post Fund, National Homes	1048
General Provisions	1078
Grants for Construction of State Extended Care Facilities	1067
Grants for Construction of Veterans Cemeteries	1068
Housing Direct Loan Financing Account	1058
Housing Guaranteed Loan Financing Account	1059
Housing Liquidating Account	1060
Information Technology Systems	1071
Joint Department of Defense-Department of Veterans Affairs Medical Facility Demonstration Fund	1045
Medical and Prosthetic Research	1044
Medical Care Collections Fund	1046
Medical Community Care	1040
Medical Facilities	1042
Medical Services	1037
Medical Support and Compliance	1041
National Cemetery Administration	1073
National Service Life Insurance Fund	1063
Native American Direct Loan Financing Account	1061
Native American Veteran Housing Loan Program Account	1061
Office of Inspector General (Departmental Administration)	1070
Post-Vietnam Era Veterans Education Account	1063
Readjustment Benefits	1050
Recurring Expenses Transformational Fund	1075
Service-disabled Veterans Insurance Fund	1055
Servicemembers' Group Life Insurance Fund	1056
Supply Fund	1074
Transitional Housing Direct Loan Financing Account	1062
United States Government Life Insurance Fund	1064
Veterans Affairs Life Insurance	1057
Veterans Choice Fund	1047
Veterans Electronic Health Care Record	1072
Veterans Health Administration	1037
Veterans Housing Benefit Program Fund	1057
Veterans Insurance and Indemnities	1053
Veterans Medical Care and Health Fund	1044
Veterans Reopened Insurance Fund	1056
Veterans Special Life Insurance Fund	1065
Vocational Rehabilitation Direct Loan Financing Account	1062
Veterans Choice Fund	1047
Veterans Electronic Health Care Record	1072
Veterans Employment and Training	792
Veterans Health Administration	1037
Veterans Housing Benefit Program Fund	1057
Veterans Insurance and Indemnities	1053
Veterans Medical Care and Health Fund	1044
Veterans Reopened Insurance Fund	1056
Veterans Special Life Insurance Fund	1065
Victims Compensation Fund	730
Vietnam Debt Repayment Fund	1338
Vietnam Education Foundation:	
Vietnam Debt Repayment Fund	1338
Violence against Women Prevention and Prosecution Programs	753
Visitor Experience Improvements Fund	662
VISTA Advance Payments Revolving Fund	1230
Vocational Rehabilitation Direct Loan Financing Account	1062
Voluntary Separation Incentive Fund	314

W

	Page
Wage and Hour Division	782
War Risk Insurance Revolving Fund	969
Washington Aqueduct	1089
Washington Metropolitan Area Transit Authority	950
Water and Related Resources	632
Water Bank Program	123
Water Infrastructure Finance and Innovation Direct Loan Financing Account	1119
Water Infrastructure Finance and Innovation Program Account	1079, 1, 1, 1, 8
Watershed and Flood Prevention Operations	119
Watershed Rehabilitation Program	121
Weapons Activities	368
Weapons Procurement, Navy	274
Western Area Power Administration, Borrowing Authority, Recovery Act	411
White Earth Settlement Fund	675
White House Repair and Restoration	1132
Wildfire Suppression Operations Reserve Fund	177, 702
Wildland Fire Management	174, 700
Wildlife Conservation	1104
Working Capital Fund:	
Administration of Foreign Affairs, Department of State	809
Bureau of Land Management, Department of the Interior	624
Bureau of Reclamation, Department of the Interior	641
Bureau of the Census, Department of Commerce	199
Centers for Disease Control and Prevention, Department of Health and Human Services	440
Department-Wide Programs, Department of the Interior	703
Departmental Administration, Department of Energy	419
Departmental Management, Department of Commerce	193
Departmental Management, Department of Labor	794
Environmental Protection Agency, Environmental Protection Agency	1124
Executive Operations, Department of Agriculture	69
Food and Drug Administration, Department of Health and Human Services	426
Forest Service, Department of Agriculture	183
General Activities, General Services Administration	1159
General Administration, Department of Justice	719
Management and Administration, Department of Housing and Urban Development	607
Management Directorate, Department of Homeland Security	501
National Aeronautics and Space Administration, National Aeronautics and Space Administration	1170
National Institute of Standards and Technology, Department of Commerce	219
Office of the Secretary, Department of Transportation	897, 902
Small Business Administration, Small Business Administration	1195
United States Geological Survey, Department of the Interior	647
World Trade Center Health Program Fund	442
World War I Centennial Commission	40

Y

	Page
Yard Fund	523

NOTES

NOTES

NOTES

NOTES

NOTES

NOTES

NOTES

NOTES